2020 Higher Education Directory®

Published by

Higher Education Publications, Inc.

Edited by

Mary Pat Rodenhouse

Reston, Virginia

2020

2020 Edition

Higher Education Publications, Inc.
1801 Robert Fulton Drive, Suite 380
Reston, VA 20191-5499
(888) 349-7715
(571) 313-0478
FAX (571) 313-0526
Email: info@hepinc.com
Internet address: www.hepinc.com

Carnegie classification codes with permission from The Carnegie Foundation for the Advancement of Teaching.

Internet addresses (URL's) were originally drawn from lists maintained by Washington and Lee University and the University of North Carolina-Chapel Hill and through the annual survey sent out by Higher Education Publications, Inc.

Printed in the United States of America

ISBN-10: 0-914927-81-7; ISBN-13: 978-0-914927-81-5
ISSN 0736-0797
Library of Congress Catalogue Card Number: 83-641119
Library of Congress Cataloging-in Publication Data

HEP. . . Higher Education Directory®
Reston, VA; Higher Education Publications.
V.: 28cm
Annual
Began with issue for 1983.

A directory of accredited postsecondary, degree-granting institutions in the U.S., its possessions and territories accredited by regional, national, professional and specialized agencies recognized as accrediting bodies by the U.S. Secretary of Education and the Council for Higher Education Accreditation (CHEA) which honors recognition provided by the former Council on Postsecondary Accreditation (COPA)/Commission on Recognition of Postsecondary Accreditation (CORPA)
Description based on 2019.
Cover title: 2020 Higher Education Directory®
Spine title: 2020 Higher Education Directory® Thirty-eighth Edition

ISSN 0736-0797 = The Higher Education Directory®.

1. Education, Higher—United States—Directories.
2. Recognized accrediting agencies and associations—United States—Directories.
3. Acronyms, explanatory notes and symbols—United States—Directories.
4. Institution changes (additions, deletions, mergers and name changes)—United States—Directories.
5. Administrative officers, titles and title codes—United States—Directories.
6. United States Department of Education offices, statewide agencies for higher education and educational associations (and consortia)—United States—Directories.
7. Religious affiliation by denomination.
8. Carnegie classification codes.
9. Statistics.
10. Universities and colleges—United States—Directories.
11. College administrators alphabetical listing, phone numbers—United States—Directories.
12. Regional, national, professional and specialized accreditation alphabetical listing—United States—Directories.
13. Institutional FICE & Unit ID Number listing—United States—Directories.
14. Institutional alphabetical listing—United States—Directories.

I. Higher Education Publications, Inc.
II. Title: Higher Education Directory®.

L901.E34 378.73-dc19 83-641119 AACR 2 MARC-S

Table of Contents

Acknowledgments

Thirty-seven years ago, Higher Education Publications, Inc. was formed to produce a directory to succeed the Department of Education's *Education Directory: Colleges and Universities*.

When we undertook the *Higher Education Directory* project, we worked toward three main goals: To publish accurate data, to make the directory more usable, and to have the directory ready for distribution much earlier in the academic year.

We continue to meet these objectives and more, while keeping the changing landscape of reference publishing in mind. In 2014, we modified our definition of branch campuses to conform to the definition used by the United States Department of Education (34 CFR §600.2). As a result, we added or reclassified over 1,400 institutional listings. Due to space limitations in the printed directory, we list limited information on these additional branch campuses, but more detailed information is available online with HigherEd Direct.

Our thanks to the thousands of people who have supplied us the necessary data contained in the directory. Over this past year we have had a response/update rate of 97% from main campuses—truly outstanding! We are most appreciative of the many subscribers who have supported us in our efforts to bring you the most accurate and current information available. And, a special thanks to all of you who suggest improvements to our directory.

We continue to work on a tight schedule starting in mid-June to distribution in November—especially when you consider the complexity and increase in the size of the database.

The accuracy and completeness of the contents of the 2020 edition was assured by a group of editors, updating and proofing specialists including Mary Pat Rodenhouse, Jodi Mondragon, Emmy Brown, Jackie Hafner, Doris Jean, Ebony Neal, Bryan Callow and Fred Hafner. Barbara Herrman handled our typesetting. Mark Schreiber managed the HigherEd Direct update system and the database.

You may be familiar with our website, but if you have not yet visited it, I encourage you to go to www.hepinc.com. The site features the latest news on higher education, accreditations and administrative changes along with many helpful resources. Also, please visit our new LinkedIn and Facebook pages. We feel that our increased Internet and social media presence will help us to continue to meet the goals we established for ourselves thirty-seven years ago—to provide you with the most authoritative, timely and accurate information on the higher education community.

Frederick F. Hafner
Publisher

Reston, Virginia

Foreword

The 2020 edition of the *Higher Education Directory*® contains listings of accredited, degree-granting institutions of postsecondary education in the United States and its territories.

Criteria for Listing in this Directory

To be listed in this Directory, an institution must meet the following guidelines:

(1) They are degree-granting (legally authorized to offer and are offering a program of college-level studies leading toward a degree[1]);
(2) They have submitted the information required for listing; and
(3) They meet one of the following criteria for listing:
   A. The institution is accredited at the college level by an accrediting agency that is recognized by the U.S. Secretary of Education;
   B. The institution holds pre-accredited status with an accrediting agency recognized by the U.S. Secretary of Education whose recognition includes the pre-accreditation status;
   C. The institution is accredited at the college level by an accrediting agency recognized by the Council for Higher Education Accreditation (CHEA).

"College level" means a postsecondary associate, baccalaureate, post-baccalaureate, or rabbinical education program.

Verification of Accreditations

Verification of each accreditation for all institutions was done by comparing the accreditation against the current Directory (and updated lists) for each respective regional, national, professional and specialized association or agency, along with telephone calls to numerous accrediting associations whenever there was a question of accuracy. Over 20,000 accreditations were verified through September 2019.

The reader is reminded that many institutions have programs which may not be recognized by a professional or specialized association, but are considered fine programs. The institutions may or may not have sought such recognition.

General Organization of the Directory

Our approach to the organization of the material is to make the desired information readable and easy to find. There are four indexes which are cross-referenced to the main institutional listing.

A. Prologue
   1. Accrediting agencies with addresses. Regional accrediting commissions are listed alphabetically while national, professional and specialized bodies are listed alphabetically under headings showing their specialties.
   2. Acronyms used in the Directory for accrediting bodies are listed alphabetically.
   3. Explanatory notes and symbols.
   4. U.S. postal abbreviations of states.
   5. Institution changes.
   6. Administrative officers' description and job codes.
   7. U.S. Department of Education offices.
   8. Statewide agencies of higher education.
   9. Higher education associations.
   10. Consortia of institutions of higher education.
   11. Association name index.
   12. Religious affiliation by denomination.
   13. Carnegie classification codes.
   14. Statistical data.

B. College and university listings by state with institutional characteristics and administrative officers.
   1. Institution Name. If an * appears before the institution's name, it is a part of a system. A line between institutions separates two systems.
   2. Alpha Code. The first institution listed on a page is coded (A), the second (B), etc. The Administrators' index is also coded to enable the reader to locate the desired institution quickly.
   3. Address.
   4. County.
   5. FICE Identification. This was the Federal Interagency Commission on Education number originally assigned by the Department of Education. We continue to use the term FICE. However, the Department of Education in their Office of Student Financial Assistance uses OPEID, Office of Postsecondary Education Identification. OPEID consists of the first six digits of the FICE plus two more digits indicating branch campuses. Numbers beginning with 66 are for accredited institutions for which we cannot locate a FICE or OPEID number. These are identification numbers only.
   6. Telephone Number.
   7. Unit ID Number. A unique number developed by the National Center for Education Statistics (NCES) for the Education Department's IPEDS Reports.
   8. Carnegie Classification Code. (see page **xlix**)
   9. Main FAX Number.
   10. School Calendar.
   11. URL (Universal Resource Locator).
   12. Date Established.
   13. Annual Tuition & Fees for 2018-19 school year.
   14. Fall 2017 Enrollment. Head count (not FTE) in degree programs as reported on the latest IPEDS survey.
   15. Type of Student Body.
   16. Affiliation or Control.
   17. IRS Status.
   18. Highest Degree Offered.
   19. Accreditation (see page **vi**). **N.B. Institutional accreditation is in bold face.**
   20. Administrative and academic officers with job classification code (see page **xxvii** for descriptions).
   21. Non-system branch campuses. The names of these campuses are in italic type and their listings are shortened. Non-system branch campuses are listed if they are identified by the parent institutions' accrediting organization as a branch campus.

C. Index of administrators is an alphabetical listing of all the administrators with their most direct phone number and E-mail address. The page and reference letter indicate the page on which the administrator's institution listing begins.

D. Index of regional, national, professional and specialized accreditation alphabetically by state. This index standardizes and simplifies reviewing of the 138 accrediting classifications.

E. FICE number index. Numeric listing of FICE number and school.

F. Alphabetic index of institutions.

[1]The *Higher Education Directory*® lists degree-granting institutions approved by regional, national, professional or specialized accrediting agencies.

Accrediting Agencies

The following regional, national, professional and specialized accrediting agencies are recognized by the U.S. Secretary of Education or the Council for Higher Education Accreditation (CHEA). The U.S. Department of Education (USDE) dates specified are the date of initial listing as a U.S. Department of Education recognized agency, the date of the U.S. Secretary's most recent grant of renewed recognition based on the last full review of the agency by the National Advisory Committee on Institutional Quality and Integrity, and the date of the agency's next scheduled review for renewal of recognition.[1] The Council for Higher Education (CHEA) date reflects initial or continued recognition by CHEA.

Regional Accrediting Bodies

Delaware, District of Columbia, Maryland, New Jersey, New York, Pennsylvania, Puerto Rico, Virgin Islands

Middle States Commission on Higher Education M
USDE: 1952/2017/2023 CHEA: 2013
3624 Market Street, Second Floor West
Philadelphia, PA 19104
(267) 284-5000 Fax (215) 662-5501
Elizabeth H. Sibolski, President
E-mail: info@msche.org
URL: www.msche.org

Connecticut, Maine, Massachusetts, New Hampshire, Rhode Island, Vermont

New England Commission of Higher Education EH
USDE: 1952/2017/2023 CHEA: 2013
3 Burlington Woods Drive, Suite 100
Burlington, MA 01803-4514
(781) 425-7785 Fax (781) 425-1001
Barbara E. Brittingham, President
E-mail: info@neche.org
URL: http://neche.org

Arizona, Arkansas, Colorado, Illinois, Indiana, Iowa, Kansas, Michigan, Minnesota, Missouri, Nebraska, New Mexico, North Dakota, Ohio, Oklahoma, South Dakota, West Virginia, Wisconsin, Wyoming

Higher Learning Commission NH
USDE: 1952/2017/2023 CHEA: 2015
230 South LaSalle Street, Suite 7-500
Chicago, IL 60604-1411
(800) 621-7440 Fax (312) 263-7462
Barbara Gellman-Danley, President
E-mail: info@hlcommission.org
URL: www.hlcommission.org

Alaska, Idaho, Montana, Nevada, Oregon, Utah, Washington

Northwest Commission on Colleges and Universities NW
USDE: 1952/2018/2023 CHEA: 2019
8060 165th Avenue, NE, Suite 100
Redmond, WA 98052
(425) 558-4224 Fax (425) 376-0596
Sonny Ramaswamy, President
E-mail: sonny@nwccu.org
URL: www.nwccu.org

Alabama, Florida, Georgia, Kentucky, Louisiana, Mississippi, North Carolina, South Carolina, Tennessee, Texas, Virginia

Commission on Colleges
Southern Association of Colleges and Schools SC
USDE: 1952/2014/2019 CHEA: 2015
1866 Southern Lane
Decatur, GA 30033-4097
(404) 679-4500 Fax (404) 679-4558
Belle S. Wheelan, President
E-mail: questions@sacscoc.org
URL: www.sacscoc.org

California, Hawaii, American Samoa, Guam, Commonwealth of the Northern Marianas, Federated States of Micronesia, Republic of the Marshall Islands, Republic of Palau

Senior College and University Commission
Western Association of Schools and Colleges WC
USDE: 1952/2017/2023 CHEA: 2014
985 Atlantic Avenue, Suite 100
Alameda, CA 94501
(510) 748-9001 Fax (510) 748-9797
Jamienne Studley, President
E-mail: wasc@wscuc.org
URL: www.wscuc.org

Accrediting Commission for Community and Junior Colleges
Western Association of Schools and Colleges WJ
USDE: 1952/2015/2019 CHEA: 2016
10 Commercial Boulevard, Suite 204
Novato, CA 94949
(415) 506-0234 Fax (415) 506-0238
Richard Winn, President
E-mail: accjc@accjc.org
URL: www.accjc.org

[1] U.S. Department of Education, Nationally Recognized Accrediting Agencies, www2.ed.gov/admins/finaid/accred/accreditation.html.

National, Professional and Specialized Accrediting Bodies

Acupuncture

Accreditation Commission for Acupuncture and Oriental Medicine (ACAOM)
USDE: 1988/2016/2021
8941 Aztec Drive, Suite 2
Eden Praire, MN 55347
(952) 212-2434 Fax (952) 657-7068
Mark S. McKenzie, Executive Director
E-mail: info@acaom.org
URL: www.acaom.org

First-professional master's degree, professional master's level certificate and diploma programs and professional post-graduate doctoral programs in acupuncture and Oriental medicine, and free-standing institutions that offer such programs **ACUP**

Allied Health

Accrediting Bureau of Health Education Schools (ABHES)
USDE: 1969/2016/2021
7777 Leesburg Pike, Suite 314N
Falls Church, VA 22043
(703) 917-9503 Fax (703) 917-4109
India Y. Tips, Executive Director
E-mail: info@abhes.org
URL: www.abhes.org

Institutions specializing in allied health education **ABHES**
Specialized programs for
- Medical assistant **MAAB**
- Medical laboratory technician **MLTAB**
- Surgical technologist **SURTEC**

Commission on Accreditation of Allied Health Education Programs (CAAHEP)
CHEA: 2011
25400 US Hwy 19 N., Suite 158
Clearwater, FL 33756
(727) 210-2350 Fax (727) 210-2354
Kathleen Megivern, Executive Director
E-mail: mail@caahep.org
URL: www.caahep.org

The Commission on Accreditation of Allied Health Education Programs (CAAHEP) is recognized as an accrediting agency for accreditation of education for the allied health occupations. In carrying out its accreditation activities, CAAHEP cooperates with the Committees on Accreditation sponsored by various allied health and medical specialty organizations. CAAHEP is the coordinating agency for accreditation of education for the following allied health occupations:
- Anesthesia technologist **AT**
- Anesthesiologist assistant **AA**
- Blood bank technology **BBT**
- Cardiovascular technologist **CVT**
- Cytotechnologist **CYTO**
- Diagnostic medical sonographer **DMS**
- Emergency medical technician-paramedic **EMT**
- Exercise science **EXSC**
- Kinesiotherapy **KIN**
- Lactation consultant **LC**
- Medical assistant **MAC**
- Medical illustrator **MIL**
- Neurodiagnostic technologist **NDT**
- Orthotist/prosthetist **OPE**
- Perfusionist **PERF**
- Polysomnographic technologist **POLYT**
- Recreation therapist **CARTE**
- Surgical assistant **SURGA**
- Surgical technologist **SURGT**

Anesthesiologist Assistant

Commission on Accreditation of Allied Health Education Programs (see listing under Allied Health)
Accreditation Review Committee for the Anesthesiologist Assistant
(612) 836-3311
Jennifer Anderson Warwick, Executive Director
E-mail: arc-aa@arc-aa.org
URL: www.caahep.org/arc-aa

Post-baccalaureate programs for anesthesiologist assistant **AA**

Art

Commission on Accreditation
National Association of Schools of Art and Design (NASAD)
USDE: 1966/2017/2023
11250 Roger Bacon Drive, Suite 21
Reston, VA 20190
(703) 437-0700 Fax (703) 437-6312
Karen P. Moynahan, Executive Director
E-mail: info@arts-accredit.org
URL: nasad.arts-accredit.org

Institutions and departments within institutions offering degree and non-degree granting programs in art/design and art/design-related programs **ART**

Athletic Training

Commission on Accreditation of Athletic Training Education (CAATE)
CHEA: 2014
6850 Austin Center Boulevard, Suite 100
Austin, TX 78731-3184
(512) 733-9700
Danielle Duran Baron, Executive Director
E-mail: support@caate.net
URL: www.caate.net

Programs for athletic training **CAATE**

Audiology

Accreditation Commission for Audiology Education
CHEA: 2012
11480 Commerce Park Drive, Suite 220
Reston, VA 20191
(202) 986-9500 Fax (202) 986-9550
Andrew Stafford, Director of Professional Standards and Credentialing
E-mail: info@acaeaccred.org
URL: www.acaeaccred.org

Programs leading to the Doctor of Audiology degree **ACAE**

Council on Academic Accreditation in Audiology and Speech Language Pathology
American Speech-Language-Hearing Association (ASHA)
USDE: 1967/2015/2021 CHEA: 2003
2200 Research Boulevard
Rockville, MD 20850-3289
(301) 296-5700 Fax (301) 296-8580
Kimberlee Moore, Director of Accreditation
E-mail: accreditation@asha.org
URL: caa.asha.org

Doctoral degree programs in audiology **AUD**

Aviation

Aviation Accreditation Board International
CHEA: 2013
115 South 8th Street, Suite 102
Opelika, AL 36801
(334) 748-9359 Fax (334) 748-9360
Guy Smith, President
E-mail: ceci@aabi.aero
URL: www.aabi.aero

Non-engineering programs for aviation **AAB**

Bible College Education

Commission on Accreditation
Association for Biblical Higher Education (ABHE)
USDE: 1952/2017/2022 CHEA: 2011
5850 T. G. Lee Boulevard, Suite 130
Orlando, FL 32822
(407) 207-0808 Fax (407) 207-0840
Ron Kroll, Director, Commission on Accreditation
E-mail: coa@abhe.org
URL: www.abhe.org

Bible colleges and programs offering undergraduate and graduate programs **BI**

Blood Bank Technology

Commission on Accreditation of Allied Health Education Programs (see listing under Allied Health)
AABB
Committee on Accreditation of Specialists in Blood Bank Technology Schools
4550 Montgomery Avenue, Suite 700 North Tower
Bethesda, MD 20814
(301) 907-6977 Fax (301) 907-6895
Anne Chenoweth, Director of Accreditation and Quality
E-mail: accreditation@aabb.org
URL: www.aabb.org

Programs for blood bank technologist **BBT**

Business

Accrediting Council for Independent Colleges and Schools (ACICS)
USDE: 1956/2016/2021 CHEA: 2012
1350 Eye Street NW, Suite 560
Washington, DC 20005
(202) 336-6780 Fax (202) 842-2593
Michelle Edwards, President
E-mail: info@acics.org
URL: www.acics.org

Institutions offering certificates/diplomas, associate, baccalaureate and master's degree programs to educate students for professional, technical, or occupational careers **ACICS**

Accreditation Council for Business Schools and Programs (ACBSP)
CHEA: 2011
11520 West 119th Street
Overland Park, KS 66213
(913) 339-9356 Fax (913) 339-6226
Jeffrey Alderman, President/CEO
E-mail: info@acbsp.org
URL: www.acbsp.org

Business administration, management, accounting and related business fields **ACBSP**

International Accreditation Council for Business Education
CHEA: 2011
11374 Strang Line Rd
Lenexa, KS 66215
(913) 631-3009 Fax (913) 631-9154
Phyllis Okrepkie, President
E-mail: iacbe@iacbe.org
URL: www.iacbe.org

Undergraduate and graduate level business programs in institutions that grant associates, bachelor's and/or graduate degrees **IACBE**

Cardiovascular Technology

Commission on Accreditation of Allied Health Education Programs (see listing under Allied Health)
Joint Review Committee on Education in Cardiovascular Technology (JRC-CVT)

1449 Hill Street
Whitinsville, MA 01588-1032
(978) 456-5594 Fax (727) 210-2354
Jackie Long-Goding, Executive Director
E-mail: office@jrccvt.org
URL: www.jrccvt.org

Programs for cardiovascular technology **CVT**

Chiropractic

The Council on Chiropractic Education (CCE)
USDE: 1974/2016/2019 CHEA: 2005
8049 North 85th Way
Scottsdale, AZ 85258-4321
(480) 443-8877 Fax (480) 483-7333
Craig S. Little, President
E-mail: cce@cce-usa.org
URL: www.cce-usa.org

Programs leading to and institutions offering the Doctorate of Chiropractic (D.C.) degree **CHIRO**

Christian Studies Education

Accreditation Commission
Transnational Association of Christian Colleges and Schools (TRACS)
USDE: 1991/2018/2021 CHEA: 2011
15935 Forest Road
Forest, VA 24551
(434) 525-9539 Fax (434) 616-2638
Timothy Eaton, President
E-mail: info@tracs.org
URL: www.tracs.org

Christian liberal arts institutions which offer certificates/diplomas and associate, baccalaureate and graduate degrees **TRACS**

Clinical Laboratory Sciences

National Accrediting Agency for Clinical Laboratory Sciences (NAACLS)
CHEA: 2013
5600 North River Road, Suite 720
Rosemont, IL 60018
(773) 714-8880 Fax (773) 714-8886
Dianne M. Cearlock, Chief Executive Officer
E-mail: info@naacls.org
URL: www.naacls.org

Programs for:
- cytogenetic technologist **CGTECH**
- diagnostic molecular scientist **DMOLS**
- histologic technician/technologist **HT**
- medical laboratory technician **MLTAD**
- medical technologist/laboratory scientist **MT**
- pathologists' assistant **PA**

Clinical Pastoral Education

Accreditation Commission
Association for Clinical Pastoral Education, Inc. (ACPEI)
USDE: 1969/2017/2022
One West Court Square, Suite 325
Decatur, GA 30030
(404) 320-1472 Fax (404) 320-0849
Trace Haythorn, Executive Director/CEO
E-mail: acpe@acpe.edu
URL: www.acpe.edu

Basic, advanced and supervisory clinical pastoral education programs **PAST**

Construction Education

American Council for Construction Education (ACCE)
CHEA: 2011
300 Decker Drive
Irving, TX 75062
(972) 600-8800
Steve Nellis, President
E-mail: acce@acce-hq.org
URL: www.acce-hq.org

Associate, baccalaureate and master's degree programs **CONST**

Continuing Education

Accrediting Council for Continuing Education and Training (ACCET)
USDE: 1978/2013/2018
1722 N Street NW
Washington, DC 20036
(202) 955-1113 Fax (202) 955-1118
Judy Hendrickson, Interim Executive Director
E-mail: info@accet.org
URL: www.accet.org

Institutions offering noncollegiate continuing education and institutions offering occupational associate degree programs **CNCE**

Cosmetology

National Accrediting Commission of Career Arts and Sciences (NACCAS)
USDE: 1970/2015/2021
3015 Colvin Street
Alexandria, VA 22314
(703) 600-7600 Fax (703) 379-2200
Anthony Mirando, Executive Director
E-mail: naccas@naccas.org
URL: www.naccas.org

Postsecondary schools and departments of cosmetology arts and sciences and massage therapy **COSME**

Counseling and Related Educational Programs

Council for Accreditation of Counseling and Related Educational Programs (CACREP)
CHEA: 2002
1001 North Fairfax Street, Suite 510
Alexandria, VA 22314
(703) 535-5990 Fax (703) 739-6209
M. Sylvia Fernandez, President and CEO
E-mail: cacrep@cacrep.org
URL: www.cacrep.org

Programs in counseling and its specialties **CACREP**

Culinary Arts

Accrediting Commission
American Culinary Federation
CHEA: 2004
180 Center Place Way
St. Augustine, FL 32095
(904) 824-4468 Fax (904) 940-0741
Heidi Cramb, Executive Director
E-mail: acf@acfchefs.net
URL: www.acfchefs.org

Programs in culinary arts which award certificates, diplomas or associate degrees and bachelor degree programs in culinary management **ACFEI**

Cytotechnology

Commission on Accreditation of Allied Health Education Programs (see listing under Allied Health)
Cytotechnology Programs Review Committee
American Society of Cytopathology
100 West 10th Street, Suite 605
Wilmington, DE 19801
(302) 543-6583 Fax (302) 543-6597
Elizabeth Jenkins, Executive Director
E-mail: asc@cytopathology.org
URL: www.cytopathology.org

Programs for the cytotechnologist **CYTO**

Dance

Commission on Accreditation
National Association of Schools of Dance (NASD)
USDE: 1983/2015/2019
11250 Roger Bacon Drive, Suite 21
Reston, VA 20190
(703) 437-0700 Fax (703) 437-6312
Karen P. Moynahan, Executive Director
E-mail: info@arts-accredit.org
URL: nasd.arts-accredit.org

Institutions and departments within institutions offering degree and non-degree-granting programs in dance and dance-related disciplines **DANCE**

Dental and Dental Auxiliary Programs

Commission on Dental Accreditation
American Dental Association (ADA)
USDE: 1952/2017/2022
211 East Chicago Avenue, Suite 1900
Chicago, IL 60611
(800) 621-8099 Fax (312) 440-2915
Sherin Tooks, Director
E-mail: tookss@ada.org
URL: www.ada.org/coda

Programs leading to:
- D.D.S. or D.M.D. degree, advanced general dentistry and specialty programs **DENT**
- Dental hygiene **DH**
- Dental assisting **DA**
- Dental laboratory technology **DT**

Diagnostic Medical Sonography

Commission on Accreditation of Allied Health Education Programs (see listing under Allied Health)
Joint Review Committee on Education in Diagnostic Medical Sonography
6021 University Boulevard, Suite 500
Ellicot City, MD 21043-6090
(443) 973-3251 Fax (866) 738-3444
Gerry Magat, Executive Director
E-mail: mail@jrcdms.org
URL: www.jrcdms.org

Programs for the diagnostic medical sonographer **DMS**

Dietetics

Accreditation Council for Education in Nutrition and Dietetics
Academy of Nutrition and Dietetics
USDE: 1974/2017/2023
120 South Riverside Plaza, Suite 2190
Chicago, IL 60606-6995
(312) 899-0040 Fax (312) 899-4817
Rayane AbuSabha, Executive Director
E-mail: acend@eatright.org
URL: www.eatrightpro.org/acend

Coordinated programs in dietetics **DIETC**
Didactic programs **DIETD**
Post-baccalaureate internships **DIETI**
Dietetic technician programs **DIETT**

Distance Education and Training

Distance Education Accrediting Commission
USDE: 1959/2017/2022 CHEA: 2013
1101 17th Street NW, Suite 808
Washington, DC 20036
(202) 234-5100 Fax (202) 332-1386
Leah K. Matthews, Executive Director
E-mail: info@deac.org
URL: www.deac.org

Distance education institutions including associate, baccalaureate, master's, and doctoral degree-granting programs primarily through the distance learning method **DEAC** (formerly DETC)

Emergency Medical Services

Commission on Accreditation for Allied Health Programs (see listing under Allied Health)
Committee on Accreditation of Educational Programs for the Emergency Medical Services Professions
8301 Lakeview Parkway, Suite 111-312
Rowlett, TX 75088
(214) 703-8445 Fax (214) 703-8992
George Hatch Jr., Executive Director
E-mail: george@coaemsp.org
URL: www.coaemsp.org

Programs for the emergency medical technician-paramedic **EMT**

English Language

Commission on English Language Program Accreditation (CEA)
USDE: 2003/2016/2018
1001 North Fairfax Drive, Suite 630
Alexandria, VA 22314
(703) 665-3400 Fax (703) 519-2071
Mary Reeves, Executive Director
E-mail: info@cea-accredit.org
URL: www.cea-accredit.org

English language programs **CEA**

Exercise Sciences

Commission on Accreditation of Allied Health Education Programs (see listing under Allied Health)
Committee on Accreditation for the Exercise Sciences
401 W. Michigan Street
Indianapolis, IN 46202
(317) 777-1135 Fax (317) 634-7817
William Coale, Director
E-mail: wcoale@acsm.org
URL: www.coaes.org

Programs for exercise science and related departments **EXSC**

Family and Consumer Sciences

Council for Accreditation
American Association of Family and Consumer Sciences (AAFCS)
CHEA: 2001
400 North Columbus Street, Suite 202
Alexandria, VA 22314
(703) 706-4600 Fax (703) 706-4663
Carolyn W. Jackson, CEO
E-mail: accreditation@aafcs.org
URL: www.aafcs.org

Baccalaureate programs in family and consumer sciences **AAFCS**

Fire and Emergency

International Fire Service Accreditation Congress
CHEA: 2011
1723 West Tyler Avenue
Oklahoma State University
Stillwater, OK 74078
(405) 744-8303 Fax (405) 744-7377
Jillian Conaghan, Manager
E-mail: admin@ifsac.org
URL: www.ifsac.org

Fire and emergency related programs **IFSAC**

Forensic Science

Forensic Science Educational Program Accreditation Commission
American Academy of Forensic Sciences (AAFS)
CHEA: 2012
410 North 21st Street
Colorado Springs, CO 80904
(719) 636-1100 Fax (719) 636-1993
Nancy J. Jackson, Director of Development and Accreditation
Email: njackson@aafs.org
URL: www.aafs.org

Bachelor or master's degree programs in forensic science **FEPAC**

Funeral Service Education

Committee on Accreditation
American Board of Funeral Service Education (ABFSE)
USDE: 1972/2017/2021 CHEA: 2012
992 Mantua Pike, Suite 108
Woodbury Heights, NJ 08097
(816) 233-3747 Fax (856) 579-7354
Robert C. Smith III, Executive Director
E-mail: exdir@abfse.org
URL: www.abfse.org

Institutions and programs awarding diplomas, associate and bachelor's degrees in funeral service or mortuary science **FUSER**

Health Informatics and Information Management

Commission on Accreditation for Health Informatics and Information Management Education (CAHIIM)
CHEA: 2012
200 East Randolph Street, Suite 5100
Chicago, IL 60601
(312) 235-3255
Angela Kennedy, Chief Executive Officer
Email: info@cahiim.org
URL: www.cahiim.org

Associate and baccalaureate degree programs in health information management and master's degree programs in health informatics and health information management **CAHIIM**

Healthcare Management

Commission on Accreditation of Healthcare Management Education (CAHME)
CHEA: 2003
PO Box 911
Spring House, PA 19477
(301) 298-1820
Anthony Stanowski, President and CEO
E-mail: info@cahme.org
URL: www.cahme.org

Graduate programs in healthcare management **HSA**

Human Services

Council for Standards in Human Services Education (CSHSE)
CHEA: 2014
3337 Duke Street
Alexandria, VA 22314
(571) 257-3959
Elaine Green, President
E-mail: info@cshse.org
URL: www.cshse.org

Human services educational programs **CSHSE**

Industrial Technology

The Association of Technology, Management, and Applied Engineering
CHEA: 2013
3801 Lake Boone Trail, Suite 190
Raleigh, NC 27607
(919) 635-8335 Fax (919) 779-5642
Jim Thompson, Executive Director
E-mail: accreditation@atmae.org
URL: www.atmae.org

Technology, applied technology, engineering technology and technology-related programs at the associate, baccalaureate and master's degree level **NAIT**

Interior Design

Council for Interior Design Accreditation (CIDA)
CHEA: 2013
206 Grandville Avenue, Suite 350
Grand Rapids, MI 49503
(616) 458-0400 Fax (616) 458-0460
Holly Mattson, Executive Director
E-mail: info@accredit-id.org
URL: www.accredit-id.org

Professional degree level programs (master's and baccalaureate degrees) **CIDA**

Jewish Studies

Association of Institutions of Jewish Studies (AIJS)
USDE: 2015/2021
500 West Kennedy Boulevard
Lakewood, NJ 08701
(732) 363-7330 Fax (732) 415-8198
Doniel Ginsberg, President
E-mail: info@theaijs.com
URL: theaijs.com

Postsecondary institutions of Jewish studies **AIJS**

Journalism and Mass Communications

Accrediting Committee
Accrediting Council on Education in Journalism and Mass Communications (ACEJMC)
CHEA: 2002
University of Mississippi
201 Bishop Hall, PO Box 1848
University, MS 38677
(662) 915-5550
Patricia Thompson, Executive Director
E-mail: pthomps1@olemiss.edu
URL: www.acejmc.org

Units within institutions offering professional baccalaureate and master's degree programs in journalism and mass communications **JOUR**

Kinesiotherapy

Commission on Accreditation of Allied Health Education Programs (see listing under Allied Health)
Committee on Accreditation of Education Programs for Kinesiotherapy
118 College Drive #5142
Hattiesburg, MS 39406-0002
(601) 266-5371 Fax (601) 266-4445
Jerry W. Purvis, Coord COPSKT
E-mail: contact@coakt.org
URL: www.coakt.org

Kinesiotherapy programs **KIN**

Landscape Architecture

Landscape Architectural Accreditation Board
American Society of Landscape Architects (ASLA)
CHEA: 2003
636 Eye Street, NW
Washington, DC 20001-3736
(202) 898-2444 Fax (202) 898-1185
Kristopher Pritchard, Director Accreditation and Education
E-mail: info@asla.org
URL: www.asla.org

Baccalaureate and master's programs leading to the first professional degree **LSAR**

Law

Council of the Section of Legal Education and Admissions to the Bar
American Bar Association (ABA)
USDE: 1952/2018/2021
321 North Clark Street, 19th Floor
Chicago, IL 60654-7598
(312) 988-6738 Fax (312) 988-5681
Barry A. Currier, Managing Director of Accreditation and Legal Education
E-mail: legaled@americanbar.org
URL: www.americanbar.org/groups/legal_education.html

Programs in legal education; professional schools of law **LAW**

Library and Information Studies

Committee on Accreditation
American Library Association (ALA)
CHEA: 2013
50 East Huron Street
Chicago, IL 60611-2795
(312) 280-2432 Fax (312) 280-2433
Karen O'Brien, Director of Accreditation
E-mail: accred@ala.org
URL: www.ala.org/accreditation

Master's programs in library and information studies **LIB**

Marriage and Family Therapy

Commission on Accreditation for Marriage and Family Therapy Education
American Association for Marriage and Family Therapy (AAMFT)
CHEA: 2003
112 South Alfred Street
Alexandria, VA 22314-3061
(703) 253-0473 Fax (703) 253-0508
Tanya A. Tamarkin, Director of Accreditation
E-mail: coa@aamft.org
URL: www.coamfte.org

Clinical training programs at the master's, doctorate and post-graduate levels **MFCD**

Massage Therapy

Commission on Massage Therapy Accreditation
USDE: 2002/2015/2021
2101 Wilson Boulevard, Suite 302
Arlington, VA 22201
(202) 888-6790 Fax (202) 888-6787
Dawn Hogue, Executive Director
E-mail: info@comta.org
URL: www.comta.org

Institutions that award postsecondary certificates, diplomas, and associate degrees in the practice of massage therapy, bodywork, aesthetics/esthetics and skin care **COMTA**

Medical Assistant Education

(see listing under Allied Health)
Accrediting Bureau of Health Education Schools (ABHES)

Medical assistant programs **MAAB**

Commission on Accreditation of Allied Health Education Programs (see listing under Allied Health)
Medical Assisting Education Review Board
20 North Wacker Drive, Suite 1575
Chicago, IL 60606-2963
(800) 228-2262 Fax (312) 899-1259
Sarah R. Marino, Executive Director
E-mail: maerb@maerb.org
URL: www.maerb.org

One and two year medical assistant programs **MAC**

Medical Illustrator Education

Commission on Accreditation of Allied Health Education Programs (see listing under Allied Health)
Accreditation Review Committee for the Medical Illustrator
32531 Meadowlark Way
Pepper Pike, OH 44124
(216) 595-9363
Kathy Jung, Chair, ARC-MI
E-mail: info@ami.org
URL: www.ami.org

Programs for medical illustrator **MIL**

Medical Laboratory Technician Education

(see listing under Allied Health)
Accrediting Bureau of Health Education Schools (ABHES)

Schools and programs for the medical laboratory technician **MLTAB**

(see listing under Clinical Laboratory Sciences)
National Accrediting Agency for Clinical Laboratory Sciences (NAACLS)

Programs for medical laboratory technician **MLTAD**

Medical Physics

Commission on Accreditation of Medical Physics Education Programs, Inc.
CHEA: 2017
1631 Prince Street
Alexandria, VA 22314
(571) 298-1239 Fax (571) 298-1301
Edward Jackson, President
E-mail: campep_admin@campep.org
URL: www.campep.org

Medical physics programs **CAMPEP**

Medical Technology

(see listing under Clinical Laboratory Sciences)
National Accrediting Agency for Clinical Laboratory Sciences (NAACLS)

Programs for medical technologist/laboratory scientist **MT**

Medicine

Liaison Committee on Medical Education (LCME) of the Council on Medical Education of the American Medical Association and the Association of American Medical Colleges
USDE: 1952/2018/2023
The LCME is administered in odd-numbered years, beginning each July 1, by:
Council on Medical Education of the American Medical Association (AMA)
330 North Wabash Avenue, Suite 39300
Chicago, IL 60611
(312) 464-4933
Barbara Barzansky, LCME Co-Secretary
E-mail: barbara.barzansky@ama-assn.org
URL: www.ama-assn.org

The LCME is administered in even-numbered years, beginning each July 1, by:
Association of American Medical Colleges (AAMC)
655 K Street NW, Suite 100
Washington, DC 20001-2399
(202) 826-0596
Veronica Catanese, LCME Co-Secretary
E-mail: vcatanese@aamc.org
URL: www.aamc.org

Programs leading to the M.D. degree **MED**

Midwifery Education

Midwifery Education Accreditation Council (MEAC)
USDE: 2001/2015/2021
850 Mt. Pleasant Avenue
Ann Arbor, MI 48103
(360) 466-2080 Fax (480) 907-2936
Timberly Robinson, Executive Director
E-mail: info@meacschools.org
URL: www.meacschools.org

Accreditation of direct-entry midwifery educational institutions and programs conferring degrees and certificates **MEAC**

Montessori Teacher Education

Montessori Accreditation Council for Teacher Education (MACTE)
USDE: 1995/2017/2021
420 Park Street
Charlottesville, VA 22902
(434) 202-7793
Rebecca Pelton, President
E-mail: info@macte.org
URL: www.macte.org

Montessori teacher-education programs and institutions **MACTE**

Music

Commission on Accreditation
National Association of Schools of Music (NASM)
USDE: 1952/2015/2019
11250 Roger Bacon Drive, Suite 21
Reston, VA 20190
(703) 437-0700 Fax (703) 437-6312
Karen P. Moynahan, Executive Director
E-mail: info@arts-accredit.org
URL: nasm.arts-accredit.org

Institutions and departments within institutions offering degree and non-degree-granting programs in music and music-related disciplines **MUS**

Naturopathic Medical Education

Council on Naturopathic Medical Education (CNME)
USDE: 2003/2015/2021
PO Box 178
Great Barrington, MA 01230
(413) 528-8877
Daniel Seitz, Executive Director
E-mail: council@cnme.org
URL: www.cnme.org

Naturopathic doctoral education programs **NATUR**

Neurodiagnostic Technology

Commission on Accreditation of Allied Health Education Programs (see listing under Allied Health)
Committee on Accreditation for Education in Neurodiagnostic Technology

1449 Hill Street
Whitinsville, MA 01588
(978) 338-6300 Fax (978) 832-2638
Jackie Long-Goding, Executive Director
E-mail: office@coa-ndt.org
URL: http://coa-ndt.org

Programs for the electroneurodiagnostic technologist **NDT**

Nuclear Medicine Technology

Joint Review Committee on Educational Programs in Nuclear Medicine Technology
CHEA: 2013
820 West Danforth Road, #B1
Edmund, OK 73003
(405) 285-0546 Fax (405) 285-0579
Jan Winn, Executive Director
E-mail: mail@jrcnmt.org
URL: www.jrcnmt.org

Programs for the nuclear medicine technologist **NMT**

Nurse Anesthetists

Council on Accreditation of Nurse Anesthesia Educational Programs
USDE: 1955/2018/2023 CHEA: 2011
222 South Prospect Avenue, Suite 304
Park Ridge, IL 60068-4001
(847) 655-1160 Fax (847) 692-7137
Francis Gerbasi, Executive Director
E-mail: accreditation@coacrna.org
URL: www.coacrna.org

Nurse anesthesia educational institutions and programs at the post-master's certificate, master's and doctoral degree levels **ANEST**

Nurse-Midwifery

Accreditation Commission for Midwifery Education
USDE: 1982/2017/2023
8403 Colesville Road, Suite 1550
Silver Spring, MD 20910
(240) 485-1800 Fax (240) 485-1818
Heather Maurer, Executive Director
E-mail: hmaurer@acnm.org
URL: www.midwife.org/accreditation

Pre-certification, basic certificate and master's degree nurse-midwifery educational programs **MIDWF**

Nursing

Commission on Collegiate Nursing Education (CCNE)
USDE: 2000/2018/2023
655 K Street NW, Suite 750
Washington, DC 20001
(202) 887-6791 Fax (202) 887-8476
Jennifer Butlin, Executive Director
E-mail: jbutlin@ccneaccreditation.org
URL: www.aacnnursing.org/ccne

Baccalaureate and higher degree nursing education **NURSE**

Accreditation Commission for Education in Nursing
USDE: 1952/2017/2023 CHEA: 2011
3343 Peachtree Road NE, Suite 850
Atlanta, GA 30326
(404) 975-5000 Fax (404) 975-5020
Marsal P. Stoll, CEO
E-mail: info@acenursing.org
URL: www.acenursing.org

Programs in:
Practical nursing (certificate) **PNUR**
Diploma nurse education **DNUR**
Associate degree **ADNUR**
Baccalaureate and higher degree nurse education **NUR**

Occupational Education

Council on Occupational Education (COE)
USDE: 1969/2016/2021
7840 Roswell Road, Bldg 300, Suite 325
Atlanta, GA 30350
(770) 396-3898 Fax (770) 396-3790
Gary Puckett, Executive Director
E-mail: info@council.org
URL: www.council.org

Occupational/vocational institutions that grant certificates or diplomas and the applied associate degree in specific career and technical education **COE**

Occupational Therapy

Accreditation Council for Occupational Therapy Education
American Occupational Therapy Association
USDE: 1952/2017/2022 CHEA: 2013
4720 Montgomery Lane, Suite 200
Bethesda, MD 20814-3449
(301) 652-6611
Sabrina Salvant, Director of Accreditation
E-mail: accred@aota.org
URL: www.aota.org

Occupational therapy programs **OT**
Occupational therapy assistant programs **OTA**

Opticianry

Commission on Opticianry Accreditation
CHEA: 2010
PO Box 592
Canton, NY 13617
(703) 468-0566
Debra White, Director of Accreditation
E-mail: director@COAccreditation.com
URL: www.coaccreditation.com

Two-year opticianry degree programs **OPD**
One year programs for opthalmic laboratory technician **OPLT**

Optometry

Accreditation Council on Optometric Education
American Optometric Association (AOA)
USDE: 1952/2017/2023 CHEA: 2012
243 North Lindbergh Boulevard
St. Louis, MO 63141
(314) 991-4100 Fax (314) 991-4101
Joyce L. Urbeck, Administrative Director
E-mail: accredit@aoa.org
URL: www.theacoe.org

Programs in:
First professional **OPT**
Optometric residency **OPTR**
Optometric technology **OPTT**

Orthotic and Prosthetic Education

Commission on Accreditation of Allied Health Education Programs (see listing under Allied Health)
National Commission on Orthotic and Prosthetic Education (NCOPE)
330 John Carlyle Street, Suite 200
Alexandria, VA 22314
(703) 836-7114 Fax (703) 836-0838
Robin C. Seabrook, Executive Director
E-mail: info@ncope.org
URL: www.ncope.org

Programs for orthotic and prosthetic education **OPE**

Osteopathic Medicine

Commission on Osteopathic College Accreditation
American Osteopathic Association
USDE: 1952/2018/2021
Department of Education
142 East Ontario Street
Chicago, IL 60611-2864
(312) 202-8124 Fax (312) 202-8200
Josh Prober, Interim Secretary, COCA
E-mail: predoc@osteopathic.org
URL: www.osteopathic.org/accreditation

Programs leading to and institutions offering the D.O. (Doctor of Osteopathy/Osteopathic Medicine) degree **OSTEO**

Perfusion

Commission on Accreditation of Allied Health Education Programs (see listing under Allied Health)
Accreditation Committee - Perfusion Education (AC-PE)
552 West Jamison Place
Littleton, CO 80120
(303) 794-6283
Linda Cantu, Executive Director
E-mail: office@ac-pe.org
URL: www.ac-pe.org

Programs for the perfusionist **PERF**

Pharmacy

Accreditation Council for Pharmacy Education (ACPE)
USDE: 1952/2017/2022 CHEA: 2014
190 South LaSalle Street, Suite 2850
Chicago, IL 60603
(312) 664-3575 Fax (866) 228-2631
Janet P. Engle, Executive Director
E-mail: info@acpe-accredit.org
URL: www.acpe-accredit.org

Professional degree programs in pharmacy **PHAR**

Physical Therapy

Commission on Accreditation in Physical Therapy Education
American Physical Therapy Association (APTA)
USDE: 1977/2017/2023 CHEA: 2012
Trans Potomac Plaza
1111 North Fairfax Street
Alexandria, VA 22314
(703) 706-3245 Fax (703) 684-7343
Sandra Wise, Senior Director
E-mail: accreditation@apta.org
URL: www.capteonline.org

Professional programs for the physical therapist **PTA**
Programs for the physical therapist assistant **PTAA**

Physician Assistant

Accreditation Review Commission on Education for the Physician Assistant (ARC-PA)
CHEA: 2004
12000 Findley Road, Suite 275
John's Creek, GA 30097
(770) 476-1224 Fax (770) 476-1738
Sharon Luke, Executive Director
E-mail: arc-pa@arc-pa.org
URL: www.arc-pa.org

Programs for the physician assistant **ARCPA**

Planning (City and Regional)

Planning Accreditation Board
CHEA: 2013
2334 West Lawrence Avenue, Suite 209
Chicago, IL 60625
(773) 334-7200
Jesmarie Soto Johnson, Executive Director
E-mail: jjohnson@planningaccreditationboard.org
URL: www.planningaccreditationboard.org

Bachelor and master's level programs in planning **PLNG**

Podiatry

Council on Podiatric Medical Education
American Podiatric Medical Association (APMA)
USDE: 1952/2016/2022 CHEA: 2004
9312 Old Georgetown Road
Bethesda, MD 20814-1621
(301) 581-9200 Fax (301) 571-4903
Heather Stagliano, Director
E-mail: cpmestaff@cpme.org
URL: www.cpme.org

Colleges and programs of podiatric medicine, including first professional and doctorate degree programs **POD**

Polysomnographic Technology

Commission on Accreditation of Allied Health Education Programs (see listing under Allied Health)
Committee on Accreditation for Polysomnographic Technologist Education
1711 Frank Avenue
New Bern, NC 28560
(252) 626-3238
Karen Monarchy Rowe, Executive Director
E-mail: karenmonarchy@suddenlink.net
URL: www.coapsg.org

Programs for polysomnographic technology **POLYT**

Psychology

Psychological Clinical Science Accreditation System (PCSAS)
CHEA: 2012
1800 Massachusetts Avenue NW, Suite 402
Washington, DC 20036-1218
(301) 455-8046
Alan G. Kraut, Executive Director
Email: akraut@pcsas.org
URL: www.pcsas.org

Psychological clinical science doctoral training programs **PCSAS**

Commission on Accreditation
American Psychological Association (APA)
USDE: 1970/2018/2021 CHEA: 2013
750 First Street NE
Washington, DC 20002-4242
(202) 336-5979 Fax (202) 336-5978
Jacqueline Remondet Wall, Director Program Consultation and Accreditation
E-mail: apaaccred@apa.org
URL: www.apa.org/ed/accreditation

Doctoral programs in:
- Clinical psychology **CLPSY**
- Counseling psychology **COPSY**
- Combined professional-scientific psychology **PSPSY**
- School psychology **SCPSY**
- Doctoral internship program in health service psychology **IPSY**
- Post-doctoral residency in health service psychology **PDPSY**

Public Affairs and Administration

Commission on Peer Review and Accreditation
Network of Schools of Public Policy, Affairs and Administration (NASPAA)
CHEA: 2004
1029 Vermont Avenue, NW, Suite 1100
Washington, DC 20005
(202) 628-8965 Fax (202) 626-4978
Heather Hamilton, Chief Accreditation Officer
E-mail: hamilton@naspaa.org
URL: www.naspaa.org

Master's degree programs in public affairs, public policy and administration **SPAA**

Public Health

Council on Education for Public Health (CEPH)
USDE: 1974/2013/2019
1010 Wayne Avenue, Suite 220
Silver Spring, MD 20910-5600
(202) 789-1050
Laura Rasar King, Executive Director
E-mail: lking@ceph.org
URL: www.ceph.org

Baccalaureate and graduate level programs in schools of public health and public health programs outside of schools of public health **PH**

Rabbinical and Talmudic Education

Accreditation Commission
Association of Advanced Rabbinical and Talmudic Schools (AARTS)
USDE: 1974/2018/2023 CHEA: 2011
11 Broadway, Suite 405
New York, NY 10004
(212) 363-1991 Fax (212) 533-5335
Bernard Fryshman, Interim Executive Director
E-mail: office@aarts-schools.org

Advanced rabbinical and Talmudic schools **RABN**

Radiologic Technology

Joint Review Committee on Education in Radiologic Technology
USDE: 1957/2016/2022 CHEA: 2004
20 North Wacker Drive, Suite 2850
Chicago, IL 60606-3182
(312) 704-5300 Fax (312) 704-5304
Leslie F. Winter, Chief Executive Officer
E-mail: mail@jrcert.org
URL: www.jrcert.org

Programs for:
- Magnetic resonance **RADMAG**
- Medical dosimetry **RADDOS**
- Radiographer **RAD**
- Radiation therapist technologist **RTT**

Recreation, Park and Leisure Studies

Council on Accreditation of Parks, Recreation, Tourism and Related Professions
CHEA: 2003
1401 Marvin Road NE, Suite 307 #172
Lacey, WA 98516
(360) 205-2096 Fax (360) 453-7893
Larry Otos, COAPRT Operations Manager
E-mail: coaprt@accreditationcouncil.org
URL: www.accreditationcouncil.org

Baccalaureate degree programs in recreation, park resources and leisure studies **NRPA**

Recreation Therapy

Commission on Accreditation of Allied Health Education Programs (see listing under Allied Health)
Committee on Accreditation of Recreational Therapy Education (CARTE)
520 Wakara Way
Salt Lake City, UT 84108
(801) 213-6993
Rhonda Nelson, Chair
E-mail: rhonda.nelson@hsc.utah.edu
URL: www.atra-online.com/education

Recreational therapy education programs **CARTE**

Respiratory Care

Commission on Accreditation for Respiratory Care (CoARC)
CHEA: 2012
777 Cannon Drive, PO Box 54876
Hurst, TX 76054-4876
(817) 283-2835 Fax (817) 354-8519
Thomas Smalling, CEO
Email: tom@coarc.com
URL: www.coarc.com

Degree programs in respiratory care **COARC**
Certificate programs in polysomnography **COARCP**

Social Work

Commission on Accreditation
Council on Social Work Education (CSWE)
CHEA: 2003
1701 Duke Street, Suite 200
Alexandria, VA 22314-3457
(703) 683-8080 Fax (703) 683-8099
Jo Ann Regan, Vice President of Education
E-mail: info@cswe.org
URL: www.cswe.org

Baccalaureate and master's degree programs **SW**

Speech-Language Pathology

Council on Academic Accreditation in Audiology and Speech Language Pathology
American Speech-Language-Hearing Association (ASHA)
USDE: 1967/2015/2021 CHEA: 2003
2200 Research Boulevard
Rockville, MD 20850-3289
(301) 296-5700 Fax (301) 296-8580
Kimberlee Moore, Director of Accreditation
E-mail: accreditation@asha.org
URL: caa.asha.org

Master's in speech-language pathology **SP**

Sports Management

Commission on Sports Management Accreditation
CHEA: 2018
2236 Water Blossom Lane
Fort Collins, CO 80526
(202) 329-1189
Heather Alderman, Executive Director
Email: cosma@cosmaweb.com
URL: www.cosmaweb.com

Sports management degree programs **COSMA**

Surgical Assisting and Technology

(see listing under Allied Health)
Accrediting Bureau of Health Education Schools (ABHES)

Surgical technologist programs **SURTEC**

Commission on Accreditation of Allied Health Education Programs (see listing under Allied Health)
Accreditation Review Council on Education in Surgical Technology and Surgical Assisting
6 West Dry Creek Circle, Suite 110
Littleton, CO 80120
(303) 694-9262 Fax (303) 741-3655

Ron Kruzel, Executive Director
E-mail: info@arcstsa.org
URL: www.arcstsa.org

Programs for the surgical technologist **SURGT**
Programs for the surgical assistant **SURGA**

Teacher Education

Council for the Accreditation of Educator Preparation
CHEA: 2014
1140 19th Street NW, Suite 400
Washington, DC 20036
(202) 223-0077 Fax (202) 296-6620
Christopher Koch, President
Email: caep@caepnet.org
URL: caepnet.org

Educator preparation programs **CAEP**
NCATE Educator preparation program **CAEPN**
TEAC Education preparation program **CAEPT**

Theatre

Commission on Accreditation
National Association of Schools of Theatre (NAST)
USDE: 1982/2015/2019
11250 Roger Bacon Drive, Suite 21
Reston, VA 20190
(703) 437-0700 Fax (703) 437-6312
Karen P. Moynahan, Executive Director
E-mail: info@arts-accredit.org
URL: nast.arts-accredit.org

Institutions and departments within institutions offering degree granting and non-degree-granting programs in theatre and theatre-related disciplines **THEA**

Theology

The Commission on Accrediting
The Association of Theological Schools (ATS)
USDE: 1952/2016/2021 CHEA: 2012
10 Summit Park Drive
Pittsburgh, PA 15275-1110
(412) 788-6505 Fax (412) 788-6510
Frank Yamada, Executive Director
E-mail: commissioninformationservices@ats.edu
URL: www.ats.edu

Freestanding schools, as well as schools or programs affiliated with larger institutions, offering graduate professional education for ministry and graduate study of theology **THEOL**

Trade and Technical Education

Accrediting Commission of Career Schools and Colleges (ACCSC)
USDE: 1967/2016/2021
2101 Wilson Boulevard, Suite 302
Arlington, VA 22201
(703) 247-4212 Fax (703) 247-4533
Michale McComis, Executive Director
E-mail: info@accsc.org
URL: www.accsc.org

Private, postsecondary degree-granting and non-degree-granting institutions that are predominantly organized to educate students for trade, occupational or technical careers **ACCSC**

Veterinary Medicine

Council on Education
American Veterinary Medical Association (AVMA)
USDE: 1952/2016/2018 CHEA: 2012
1931 North Meacham Road, Suite 100
Schaumburg, IL 60173
(800) 248-2862 Fax (847) 285-5732
Karen Martens Brandt, Director Education and Research
E-mail: kbrandt@avma.org
URL: www.avma.org

Colleges of veterinary medicine offering programs leading to a D.V.M./D.M.V. professional degree **VET**

Other

New York State Board of Regents Commission of Education
USDE: 1952/2017/2023
State Education Department
The University of the State of New York
89 Washington Avenue, Room 1106B
Albany, NY 12234
(518) 474-5844 Fax (518) 473-4909
Beth Berlin, Acting Commissioner of Education
E-mail: commissioner@nysed.edu
URL: www.nysed.gov

Degree-granting institutions of higher education in New York that designate the agency as their sole or primary nationally recognized accrediting agency for purposes of establishing eligibility to participate in Higher Education Act programs **NY**

Accrediting Agencies Recognized for their Pre-accreditation Categories[1]

Under the terms of the Higher Education Act and other Federal legislation providing funding assistance to postsecondary education, an institution or program is eligible to apply for participation in certain Federal programs if, in addition to meeting other statutory requirements, it is accredited by a nationally recognized accrediting agency—or if it is an institution with respect to which the U.S. Secretary of Education has determined that there is satisfactory assurance the institution or program will meet the accreditation standards of such agency or association within a reasonable time. An institution or program may establish satisfactory assurance of accreditation by acquiring pre-accreditation status with a nationally recognized accrediting agency which has been recognized by the U.S. Secretary of Education for the award of such status. According to the Criteria for Nationally Recognized Accrediting Agencies, if an accrediting agency has developed a pre-accreditation status, it must demonstrate that it applies criteria and follows procedures that are appropriately related to those used to award accreditation status. The criteria for recognition also requires an agency's standards for pre-accreditation to permit an institution or program to hold pre-accreditation no more than five years.

The following is a list of accrediting agencies recognized by the U.S. Secretary of Education for their pre-accreditation categories and the categories which are recognized.

Regional Institution Accrediting Bodies

Middle States Commission on Higher Education:
Candidate for Accreditation

New England Commission of Higher Education:
Candidate for Accreditation

Higher Learning Commission: *Candidate for Accreditation*

Northwest Commission on Colleges and Universities:
Candidate for Accreditation

Southern Association of Colleges and Schools
Commission on Colleges: *Candidate for Accreditation*

Western Association of Schools and Colleges
Accrediting Commission for Community and Junior Colleges: *Candidate for Accreditation*

Western Association of Schools and Colleges
Senior College and University Commission: *Candidate for Accreditation*

National, Institutional and Specialized Accrediting Bodies

Academy of Nutrition and Dietetics
Accreditation Council for Education in Nutrition and Dietetics: *Pre-accreditation*

Accreditation Commission for Acupuncture and Oriental Medicine: *Pre-accreditation, Candidate for Accreditation*

Accreditation Commission for Midwifery Education: *Pre-accreditation*

Accreditation Council for Pharmacy Education: *Candidate, Pre-candidate*

American Optometric Association
Accreditation Council on Optometric Education: *Preliminary Approval* (for professional degree programs); *Candidacy Pending* (for optometric residency programs in Veterans Administration facilities)

American Osteopathic Association
Commission on Osteopathic College Accreditation: *Provisional Accreditation*

American Physical Therapy Association
Commission on Accreditation in Physical Therapy Education: *Candidate for Accreditation*

American Podiatric Medical Association
Council on Podiatric Medical Education: *Candidate for Accreditation*

American Psychological Association
Commission on Accreditation: *Preaccreditation (doctoral internship and postdoctoral residency programs only)*

American Speech-Language-Hearing Association
Council on Academic Accreditation in Audiology and Speech Language Pathology: *Candidate for Accreditation*

American Veterinary Medical Association
Council on Education: *Reasonable Assurance of Accreditation*

Association for Biblical Higher Education
Commission on Accreditation: *Candidate for Accreditation*

Association of Advanced Rabbinical and Talmudic Schools
Accreditation Commission: *Correspondent, Candidate for Accreditation*

The Association of Theological Schools
The Commission on Accrediting: *Candidate for Accredited Membership*

Council on Education for Public Health: *Pre-accreditation*

Council on Naturopathic Medical Education: *Pre-accreditation*

Council on Occupational Education: *Candidate for Accreditation*

Midwifery Education Accreditation Council: *Pre-accreditation*

Transnational Association of Christian Colleges and Schools
Accreditation Commission: *Candidate for Accreditation*

[1]U.S. Department of Education, Nationally Recognized Accrediting Agencies and Associations, www2.ed.gov/admins/finaid/accred/accreditation_pg8.html.

Abbreviations, Explanatory Notes and Symbols

Abbreviations

Listed below are the abbreviations used in this Directory for the recognized regional accrediting commissions and the recognized national, professional and specialized accrediting bodies. Addresses for these associations can be found under our listing of Accrediting Agencies beginning on page viii.

The recognized regional accrediting commissions are indicated throughout this Directory by the following abbreviations:

EH New England Commission of Higher Education

M Middle States Commission on Higher Education

NH Higher Learning Commission, North Central Association

NW Northwest Commission on Colleges and Universities

SC Southern Association of Colleges and Schools, Commission on Colleges

WC Western Association of Schools and Colleges, Senior College and University Commission

WJ Western Association of Schools and Colleges, The Accrediting Commission for Community and Junior Colleges

National, professional and specialized accrediting agencies and associations are listed below. Wherever possible, degree levels are shown by the following symbols: (C) diploma/certificate; (A) associate; (B) baccalaureate; (M) master's; (S) beyond master's but less than doctorate; (FP) first professional; (D) doctorate.

AA Commission on Accreditation of Allied Health Education Programs: anesthesiologist assistant (M)

AAB Aviation Accreditation Board International: aviation (A,B,M,D)

AAFCS American Association of Family and Consumer Sciences: family and consumer sciences (B)

ABHES Accrediting Bureau of Health Education Schools: allied health (C,A,B,M)

ACAE Accreditation Commission for Audiology Education: audiology (D)

ACBSP Accreditation Council for Business Schools and Programs: business administration, management, accounting and related business fields (A,B,M,D)

ACCSC Accrediting Commission of Career Schools and Colleges: occupational, trade and technical education (C,A,B,M)

ACFEI American Culinary Federation, Inc.: culinary arts and culinary management (C,A,B)

ACICS Accrediting Council for Independent Colleges and Schools: business and business-related programs (C,A,B,M)

ACUP Accreditation Commission for Acupuncture and Oriental Medicine: acupuncture (C,M,D)

ADNUR Accreditation Commission for Education in Nursing: nursing (A)

AIJS Association of Institutions of Jewish Studies: Jewish studies (C, A,B)

ANEST Council on Accreditation of Nurse Anesthesia Educational Programs: nurse anesthesia (C,M,D)

ARCPA Accreditation Review Commission on Education for the Physician Assistant: physician assisting programs (A,B,M)

ART National Association of Schools of Art and Design: art and design (C,A,B,M,D)

AT Commission on Accreditation of Allied Health Education Programs: anesthesia technologist (A)

AUD American Speech-Language-Hearing Association: audiology (D)

BBT Commission on Accreditation of Allied Health Education Programs: blood bank technology (C,M)

BI Association for Biblical Higher Education: bible college education (C,A,B,M,FP,D)

CAATE Commission on Accreditation of Athletic Training Education: athletic training (B,M)

CACREP Council for Accreditation of Counseling & Related Education programs: counseling and its specialties (M,D)

CAEP Council for the Accreditation of Educator Preparation: teacher education (B,M,D)

CAEPN Council for the Accreditation of Educator Preparation: teacher education (B,M,D)

CAEPT Council for the Accreditation of Educator Preparation: teacher education (B,M,D)

CAHIIM Commission on Accreditation for Health Informatics and Information Management Education: health information management and health informatics (A,B,M)

CAMPEP Commission on Accreditation of Medical Physics Education Programs, Inc.: medical physics (C,M,D)

CARTE Commission on Accreditation of Recreational Therapy Education: recreational therapy (B,M)

CEA Commission on English Language Program Accreditation: english language (C)

CGTECH National Accrediting Agency for Clinical Laboratory Sciences: cytogenetic technologist (B)

CHIRO Council on Chiropractic Education: chiropractic education (FP,D)

CIDA Council for Interior Design Accreditation: interior design (B,M)

CLPSY American Psychological Association: clinical psychology (D)

CNCE Accrediting Council for Continuing Education and Training: continuing education (C,A)

COARC Commission on Accreditation for Respiratory Care: respiratory care (A,B,M)

COARCP Commission on Accreditation for Respiratory Care: polysomnography (C)

COE Council on Occupational Education: occupational, trade, and technical education (C,A)

COMTA Commission on Massage Therapy Accreditation: massage therapy, bodywork, aesthetics/esthetics and skin care (C,A)

CONST American Council for Construction Education: construction education (A,B,M)

COPSY American Psychological Association: counseling psychology (D)

COSMA Commission on Sports Management: sports management (B, M,D)

COSME National Accrediting Commission of Career Arts and Sciences: cosmetology and massage therapy (C)

CSHSE Council for Standards in Human Services Education: human services (A,B,M)

CVT Commission on Accreditation of Allied Health Education Programs: cardiovascular technology (C,A,B)

CYTO Commission on Accreditation of Allied Health Education Programs: cytotechnology (C,B,M)

DA American Dental Association: dental assisting (C,A)

DANCE National Association of Schools of Dance: dance (C,A,B,M,D)

DEAC Distance Education and Accrediting Commission: home study schools (A,B,M,D)

DENT American Dental Association: dentistry (FP,D)

DH American Dental Association: dental hygiene (C,A,B,M)

DIETC Academy of Nutrition and Dietetics: coordinated dietetics programs (B,M)

DIETD Academy of Nutrition and Dietetics: didactic dietetics programs (B,M)

DIETI Academy of Nutrition and Dietetics: dietetic post-baccalaureate internships

DIETT Academy of Nutrition and Dietetics: dietetic technician (A)

DMOLS National Accrediting Agency for Clinical Laboratory Sciences: diagnostic molecular scientist (C,B,M)

DMS Commission on Accreditation of Allied Health Education Programs: diagnostic medical sonography (C,A,B,M)

DNUR Accreditation Commission for Education in Nursing: nursing (C)

DT American Dental Association: dental laboratory technology (C,A)

EMT Commission on Accreditation of Allied Health Education Programs: emergency medical technician-paramedic (C,A,B)

EXSC Commission on Accreditation of Allied Health Education Programs: exercise science (C,A,B,M)

FEPAC American Academy of Forensic Sciences: forensic science (B,M)

FUSER American Board of Funeral Service Education: funeral service education (C,A,B)

HSA Commission on Accreditation of Healthcare Management Education: healthcare management (M)

HT National Accrediting Agency for Clinical Laboratory Sciences: histologic technology (C,A,B)

IACBE International Accreditation Council for Business Education: business programs in institutions that grant bachelor/graduate degrees (A,B,M,D)

IFSAC International Fire Service Accreditation Congress Degree Assembly: fire and emergency related degree (A,B,M)

IPSY American Psychological Association: doctoral internships in health service psychology

JOUR Accrediting Council on Education for Journalism and Mass Communications: journalism and mass communications (B,M)

KIN Commission on Accreditation of Allied Health Education Programs: kinesiotherapy (B)

LAW American Bar Association: law (FP,D)

LC Commission on Accreditation of Allied Health Programs: lactation consultant (C,A,B,M)

LIB American Library Association: library and information studies (M)

LSAR American Society for Landscape Architects: landscape architecture (B,M)

MAAB Accrediting Bureau of Health Education Schools: medical assisting (C,A)

MAC Commission on Accreditation of Allied Health Education Programs: medical assisting (C,A)

MACTE Montessori Accreditation Council for Teacher Education: Montessori teacher education (C)

MEAC Midwifery Education Accreditation Council: midwifery education (C,A,B,M,D)

MED Liaison Committee on Medical Education: medicine (FP,D)

MFCD American Association for Marriage and Family Therapy: marriage and family therapy (M,D)

MIDWF Accreditation Commission for Midwifery Education: nurse midwifery (C,M,D)

MIL Commission on Accreditation of Allied Health Education Programs: medical illustrator (M)

MLTAB Accrediting Bureau of Health Education Schools: medical laboratory technician (C,A)

MLTAD National Accrediting Agency for Clinical Laboratory Sciences: medical laboratory technician (C,A)

MT National Accrediting Agency for Clinical Laboratory Sciences: medical technology/laboratory scientist (C,B)

MUS National Association of Schools of Music: music (C,A,B,M,D)

NAIT The Association of Technology, Management, and Applied Engineering: technology, applied technology, engineering technology and technology-related programs (A,B,M)

NATUR Council on Naturopathic Medical Education: naturopathic medical education (FP,D)

NDT Commission on Accreditation of Allied Health Education Programs: neurodiagnostic technology (C,A)

NMT Joint Review Committee on Educational Programs in Nuclear Medicine Technology: nuclear medicine technology (C,A,B,M)

NRPA Council on Accreditation of Parks, Recreation, Tourism and Related Professions: recreation, park resources, and leisure studies (B)

NUR Accreditation Commission for Education in Nursing: nursing (B, M,D)

NURSE Commission on Collegiate Nursing Education: nursing (B,M,D)

NY New York State Board of Regents:
Degree-granting institutions of higher education in New York that designate the agency as their sole or primary nationally recognized accrediting agency for purposes of establishing elibility to participate in Higher Education Act programs

OPD Commission on Opticianry Accreditation: opticianry (A)

OPE Commission on Accreditation of Allied Health Education Programs: orthotics and prosthetics (C,B,M)

OPLT Commission on Opticianry Accreditation: opthalmic laboratory technician (C)

OPT American Optometric Association: optometry (FP,D)

OPTR American Optometric Association: optometric residency programs

OPTT American Optometric Association: optometric technician (C,A)

OSTEO American Osteopathic Association, Office of Osteopathic Education: osteopathic medicine (FP,D)

OT American Occupational Therapy Association: occupational therapy (M,D)

OTA American Occupational Therapy Association: occupational therapy assistant (C,A)

PA National Accrediting Agency for Clinical Laboratory Sciences: pathologist's assistant (C,M)

PAST Association for Clinical Pastoral Education: clinical pastoral education

PCSAS Psychological Clinical Science Accreditation System: psychological clinical science (D)

PDPSY American Psychological Association: post-doctorate residency in health service psychology

PERF Commission on Accreditation of Allied Health Education Programs: perfusionist (C,B,M)

PH Council on Education for Public Health: public health (B,M,D)

PHAR Accreditation Council for Pharmacy Education: pharmacy (FP,D)

PLNG Planning Accreditation Board: certified planning (B,M)

PNUR Accreditation Commission for Education in Nursing: practical nursing (C)

POD American Podiatric Medical Association: podiatry (FP,D)

POLYT Commission on Accreditation of Allied Health Education Programs: polysomnographic technologist education (C,A)

PSPSY American Psychological Association: combined professional-scientific psychology (D)

PTA American Physical Therapy Association: physical therapy (D)

PTAA American Physical Therapy Association: physical therapy assistant (A)

RABN Association of Advanced Rabbinical and Talmudic Schools: rabbinical and Talmudic education (A,B,M,D)

RAD Joint Review Committee on Education in Radiologic Technology: radiography (C,A,B)

RADDOS Joint Review Committee on Education in Radiologic Technology: medical dosimetry (C,B,M)

RADMAG Joint Review Committee on Education in Radiologic Technology: magnetic resonance (C,A,B)

RTT Joint Review Committee on Education in Radiologic Technology: radiation therapist/technologist (C,A,B,M)

SCPSY American Psychological Association: school psychology (D)

SP American Speech-Language-Hearing Association: speech-language pathology (M)

SPAA Network of Schools of Public Policy, Affairs and Administration: public affairs and administration (M)

SURGA Commission on Accreditation of Allied Health Education Programs: surgical assistant (C,A)

SURGT Commission on Accreditation of Allied Health Education Programs: surgical technology (C,A)

SURTEC Accrediting Bureau of Health Education Schools: surgical technologist (C,A)

SW Council on Social Work Education: social work (B,M)

THEA National Association of Schools of Theatre: theatre (C,A,B,M,D)

THEOL Association of Theological Schools: theology (M,FP,D)

TRACS Transnational Association of Christian Colleges and Schools: christian studies education (C,A,B,M,D)

VET American Veterinary Medical Association: veterinary medicine (FP,D)

Explanatory Notes and Symbols

Associate degree: includes junior colleges, community colleges, technical institutes, and schools offering at least a two-year program of college-level studies, either leading to an associate degree wholly or principally creditable toward a baccalaureate degree.

Baccalaureate: includes those institutions offering programs of studies leading to the customary bachelor of arts or bachelor of science degrees.

First professional degree: includes those institutions that offer the academic requirements for selected professions based on programs that require at least two academic years of previous college work for entrance and a total of at least six years of college work for completion.

Master's: includes those institutions offering the customary first graduate degree, master of arts or master of science degree in the liberal arts and sciences, or the next degree in the same field after the first professional degree.

Beyond master's but less than doctorate: includes those institutions offering "postgraduate pre-doctoral degrees".

Graduate non-degree granting: includes institutions offering work beyond the bachelor's level but not conferring degrees. In some instances the degrees are conferred by cooperating institutions.

Doctorate: includes those institutions offering a Ph.D. or its equivalent in any field.

Postdoctoral research only: includes institutions operating solely for the purpose of research at the postdoctoral level.

First Talmudic degree: undergraduate degree granted by accredited Rabbinical schools. The schools in New York "using this designation do not imply that the 'First Talmudic Degree' is equivalent to any secular academic degree recognized by the Board of Regents".*

Second Talmudic degree: graduate degree granted by accredited Rabbinical schools. The schools in New York "using this designation do not imply that the 'Second Talmudic Degree' is equivalent to any secular academic degree recognized by the Board of Regents".*

---

*The University of the State of New York, The State Education Department, Albany, New York, letter August 17, 1983.

Symbols

* The institution is part of a system.

Used preceding any of the acronyms for the accrediting agencies the following symbols indicate that:

The accrediting agency has stated publicly that the institution or program is preliminary or provisionally accredited, accredited with some reservations, or approved on probation.

@ The institution or program has attained a pre-accredited status.

& The institution is covered under the regional accreditation of the parent institution.

U.S. Postal Abbreviation of States and Territories

Alabama .... AL
Alaska .... AK
American Samoa .... AS
Arizona .... AZ
Arkansas .... AR
California .... CA
Colorado .... CO
Connecticut .... CT
Delaware .... DE
District of Columbia .... DC
Florida .... FL
Georgia .... GA
Guam .... GU
Hawaii .... HI
Idaho .... ID
Illinois IL
Indiana .... IN
Iowa .... IA
Kansas .... KS
Kentucky .... KY
Louisiana .... LA
Maine .... ME
Maryland .... MD
Marshall Islands .... MH
Massachusetts .... MA
Michigan .... MI
Micronesia .... FM
Minnesota .... MN
Mississippi .... MS
Missouri .... MO
Montana .... MT
Nebraska .... NE
Nevada .... NV
New Hampshire .... NH
New Jersey .... NJ
New Mexico .... NM
New York .... NY
North Carolina .... NC
North Dakota .... ND
Northern Marianas .... MP
Ohio .... OH
Oklahoma .... OK
Oregon .... OR
Palau .... PW
Pennsylvania .... PA
Puerto Rico .... PR
Rhode Island .... RI
South Carolina .... SC
South Dakota .... SD
Tennessee .... TN
Texas .... TX
Utah .... UT
Vermont .... VT
Virgin Islands VI
Virginia .... VA
Washington .... WA
West Virginia .... WV
Wisconsin .... WI
Wyoming .... WY

Institution Changes

	FICE/ID Number

Institutions and Offices Added

Arizona

Cummings Gaduate Institute for Behavioral Health Studies	667376

California

Agape College of Business and Science	667362
Alder Graduate School of Education	667356
Calvary Chapel University	667372
Gnomon	040764
Hawthorn University	667358
Horizon University	667360
Los Angeles Pacific University	042788
PCI College	034793
Saint Photios Orthodox Theological Seminary	667366
Southern California State University	667374
Stanton University	667370
Viridis Graduate Institute	667375

Florida

Chi Institute of Traditional Chinese Veterinary Medicine	667354
Key College	023251
Marconi International University	667377
North Broward Technical Center	667357
NRI Institute of Health Sciences	042108

Georgia

Underwood University	667361

Minnesota

Hennepin Technical College	770299

Missouri

Graduate School of the Stowers Institute for Medical Research	667369

New Jersey

Jersey College	041341

New York

Albert Einstein College of Medicine	042797
New York Automotive and Diesel Institute	035373
Yeshiva Kollel Tifereth Elizer	667367
Yeshiva Shaar Ephraim	042590
Yeshiva Yesoda Hatorah Vetz Chaim	667368

North Carolina

Hosanna Bible College	667373

Rhode Island

College Unbound	667355

	FICE/ID Number

Tennessee

William Moore College of Technology	011553

Texas

Peloton College	041687
Southern Bible Institute and College	667365
Southern Reformed College and Seminary	667364
Texas Baptist Institute and Seminary	667363
The Bible Seminary	667371

Washington

Gather 4 Him Bible College	667359

Institutions and Offices Dropped

Alabama

Education Corporation of America *(Closed)*	666006
Virginia College *(Closed)*	030106
Virginia College *(Closed)*	666069
Virginia College *(Closed)*	666400
Virginia College *(Closed)*	666408

Arizona

Argosy University, Phoenix *(Closed)*	666790
Arizona Summit Law School *(Closed)*	041314
Golf Academy of America *(Closed)*	666023
The Art Institute of Phoenix *(Closed)*	040513
Western International University *(Closed)*	021715

Arkansas

Arkansas State University-Heber Springs *(No longer listed as branch by NH)*	770001
Arkansas State University-Searcy Campus *(No longer listed as branch by NH)*	770002
Remington College-Little Rock *(Closed)*	666286

California

Antioch University Los Angeles *(No longer listed as branch by NH)*	666236
Antioch University Santa Barbara *(No longer listed as branch by NH)*	666231
APT College *(No longer accredited by DEAC)*	666245
Argosy University, Los Angeles *(Closed)*	666011

Institution Changes

	FICE/ID Number
Argosy University, Orange County *(Closed)*	021799
Brightwood College *(Closed)*	023063
Brightwood College *(Closed)*	770559
Brightwood College *(Closed)*	020917
Brightwood College *(Closed)*	023519
Brightwood College *(Closed)*	770558
Brightwood College *(Closed)*	025391
Brightwood College *(Closed)*	025490
Brightwood College *(Closed)*	666291
Brightwood College *(Closed)*	770560
Concord Law School at Purdue University Global *(No longer listed as branch by NH)*	041259
DeVry University - Pomona Campus *(No longer listed as branch by NH)*	023329
Golden State University *(No longer accredited by ACUP)*	667261
Golf Academy of America *(Closed)*	015609
Mt. Sierra College *(Closed)*	031287
National Test Pilot School *(ABET is no longer a recognized accreditor)*	667009
Phillips Graduate University *(Withdrew accreditation from WC)*	022372
SBBCollege Ventura *(Closed)*	009989
Southern California University School of Oriental Medicine & Acupuncture *(No longer accredited by ACUP)*	041720
The Art Institute of California, A College of Argosy University - Hollywood *(Closed)*	031254
The Art Institute of California, A College of Argosy University - San Diego *(Closed)*	023276
University of Philosophical Research *(Closed)*	666373

Colorado

Academy of Natural Therapy *(No longer degree granting)*	040933
DeVry University - Westminster Campus *(No longer listed as branch by NH)*	666227
Ecotech Institute *(Closed)*	770840
Pueblo Community College Durango *(No longer listed as branch by NH)*	770043

Connecticut

Lincoln College of New England *(Closed)*	009407

Delaware

Irish American University *(Main Campus no longer in U.S.)*	667120

	FICE/ID Number

Florida

American College for Medical Careers *(Closed)*	770842
Argosy University, Tampa *(Closed)*	666082
Carlos Albizu University Miami Campus *(Now listed as an additional location, not a branch)*	666814
Cortiva Institute *(No longer degree granting)*	030086
DeVry University - Miramar Campus *(No longer listed as branch by NH)*	666196
DeVry University - Orlando Campus *(No longer listed as branch by NH)*	666112
Florida College of Health Science *(No longer accredited by ABHES)*	667265
Florida College of Natural Health *(No longer degree granting)*	666513
Florida College of Natural Health *(No longer degree granting)*	666514
Golf Academy of America *(Closed)*	666186
Med-Life Institute-Lauderdale Lakes *(No longer degree granting)*	667221
Medical Prep Institute *(No longer accredited by ABHES)*	667267
Orion College *(Closed)*	041359
Rasmussen College - Land O'Lakes *(No longer listed as branch by NH)*	770488
Rasmussen College - New Port Richey *(No longer listed as branch by NH)*	666425
Remington College Orlando *(Closed)*	770567
The Art Institute of Fort Lauderdale *(Closed)*	010195
Virginia College *(Closed)*	031005
Virginia College *(Closed)*	770839
WyoTech *(Closed)*	023462

Georgia

Argosy University, Atlanta *(Closed)*	666735
Central Georgia Technical College *(Closed)*	025086
DeVry University - Decatur Campus *(No longer listed as branch by NH)*	009224
Virginia College *(Closed)*	770833
Virginia College *(Closed)*	770834
Virginia College *(Closed)*	770835
Virginia College *(Closed)*	770836

Hawaii

Argosy University, Hawaii *(Closed)*	666787
Remington College-Honolulu Campus *(Closed)*	666028

Illinois

Argosy University, Chicago *(Closed)*	666736

	FICE/ID Number
Midstate College *(Closed)*	004568
Rasmussen College - Aurora *(No longer listed as branch by NH)*	667060
Rasmussen College - Mokena/Tinley Park *(No longer listed as branch by NH)*	667064
South Suburban College of Cook County University and College Center *(No longer listed as branch by NH)*	770094
Vatterott College-Fairview Heights *(Closed)*	770943
Vatterott College-Quincy *(Closed)*	020693

Indiana

Brightwood College *(Closed)*	022018
Crossroads Bible College *(No longer accredited by BI)*	034567
Harrison College - Anderson Campus *(Closed)*	666030
Harrison College - Columbus Indiana Campus *(Closed)*	666428
Harrison College - Evansville Campus *(Closed)*	666429
Harrison College - Fort Wayne Campus *(Closed)*	666029
Harrison College - Indianapolis Downtown Campus *(Closed)*	021584
Harrison College - Indianapolis East Campus *(Closed)*	666430
Harrison College - Indianapolis Northwest Campus *(Closed)*	666388
Harrison College - Lafayette Campus *(Closed)*	666431
Harrison College - Terre Haute Campus *(Closed)*	666433
Indiana Tech-Elkhart *(No longer listed as branch by NH)*	770102
Indiana Tech-Indianapolis *(No longer listed as branch by NH)*	770103

Iowa

Kirkwood Community College Iowa City *(No longer listed as branch by NH)*	770062
Purdue University Global-Cedar Falls *(Closed)*	770058
Purdue University Global-Cedar Rapids *(No longer listed as branch by NH)*	004220
Purdue University Global-Davenport *(Closed)*	770985
Purdue University Global-Des Moines *(No longer listed as branch by NH)*	666437
Purdue University Global-Mason City *(Closed)*	666438

Kansas

Cloud County Community College Geary County Campus *(No longer listed as branch by NH)*	770258
Rasmussen College Topeka *(No longer listed as branch by NH)*	770490

Kentucky

	FICE/ID Number
American National University *(Closed)*	666441
Indiana Tech-Louisville *(No longer listed as branch by NH)*	770104
University of Phoenix Louisville Campus *(Closed)*	770207

Louisiana

Cameron College *(Closed)*	022340
Southwest University *(No longer accredited by DEAC)*	666310
Virginia College *(Closed)*	770826
Virginia College *(Closed)*	770827

Maine

Purdue University Global-Augusta *(No longer listed as branch by NH)*	770060
Purdue University Global-Lewiston *(No longer listed as branch by NH)*	770061

Maryland

Brightwood College *(Closed)*	010410
Brightwood College *(Closed)*	020836
Purdue University Global-Hagerstown *(No longer listed as branch by NH)*	007946

Massachusetts

Andover Newton Theological School *(No longer offers degrees)*	002116
Newbury College *(Closed)*	007484
Salter College *(Closed)*	004666

Michigan

Baker College of Port Huron *(No longer listed as branch by NH)*	666943
Lake Michigan College Bertrand Crossing *(No longer listed as branch by NH)*	770277
Lake Michigan College South Haven *(No longer listed as branch by NH)*	770278
Marygrove College *(Closed)*	002284
University of Phoenix Detroit Main Campus *(Closed)*	770211
Walsh College Novi Campus *(No longer listed as branch by NH)*	770293

Minnesoota

Rasmussen College - Moorhead Park *(No longer listed as branch by NH)*	770487

Minnesota

Argosy University, Twin Cities *(Closed)*	007619
Rasmussen College - Blaine *(No longer listed as branch by NH)*	667061
Rasmussen College - Brooklyn Park *(No longer listed as branch by NH)*	666769

Institution Changes

	FICE/ID Number
Rasmussen College - Lake Elmo/Woodbury *(No longer listed as branch by NH)*	770486
Ridgewater College Hutchinson Campus *(No longer listed as branch by NH)*	770312

Mississippi

Virginia College *(Closed)*	666032
Virginia College *(Closed)*	666073

Missouri

DeVry University - Kansas City Campus *(No longer listed as branch by NH)*	002455
Vatterott College-Joplin *(Closed)*	666060
Vatterott College-Kansas City *(Closed)*	666519
Vatterott College-NorthPark *(Closed)*	025997
Vatterott College-Springfield *(Closed)*	666521
Vatterott College-St. Charles *(Closed)*	666584
Vatterott College-Sunset Hills *(Closed)*	666522

Nebraska

Nebraska Indian Community College-Santee *(No longer listed as branch by NH)*	770339
Nebraska Indian Community College-South Sioux City *(No longer listed as branch by NH)*	770340
Purdue University Global-Lincoln *(No longer listed as branch by NH)*	004721
Purdue University Global-Omaha *(Closed)*	008491

Nevada

Altierus Career College *(Closed)*	022375
Brightwood College *(Closed)*	030432

New Hampshire

Antioch University New England *(No longer listed as branch by NH)*	666992
St. Joseph School of Nursing *(Closed)*	021404

New Jersey

Bard High School Early College Newark *(No longer listed as branch by EH)*	770980
DeVry University - North Brunswick Campus *(No longer listed as branch by NH)*	009228

New York

	FICE/ID Number
AMDA College and Conservatory of the Performing Arts *(No longer offers degrees)*	007572
Beth Hatalmud Rabbinical College *(Resigned from AARTS)*	011922
Elmira Business Institute *(Main Campus in Elmira clsoed and Vestal became the main campus under FICE 9043)*	770745
Saint Joseph's College, New York - Suffolk Campus *(No longer listed as branch by M)*	029081
Suffolk County Community College Eastern Campus *(No longer listed as branch by M)*	004816
Suffolk County Community College Grant Campus *(No longer listed as branch by M)*	013204
The College of New Rochelle *(Closed)*	002704
Tri-State College of Acupuncture *(No longer accredited by ACUP)*	025460

North Carolina

King's College *(Closed)*	002937
The Chef's Academy *(Closed)*	770101
Virginia College *(Closed)*	770619

Ohio

AIC College of Design *(Closed)*	021286
American National University *(Closed)*	770697
Brightwood College *(Closed)*	020520
DeVry University - Columbus Campus *(No longer listed as branch by NH)*	003099
Harrison College-Columbus Ohio Campus *(Closed)*	770748
Herzing University Toledo Campus *(Closed)*	770434
Vatterott College-Cleveland *(Closed)*	666156

Oklahoma

Vatterott College-Tulsa *(Closed)*	666102

Oregon

Marylhurst University *(Closed)*	003199
Oregon College of Art and Craft *(Closed)*	030073
The Art Institute of Portland *(Closed)*	007819
University of Phoenix Oregon Campus *(Closed)*	770222

Pennsylvania

Art Institute of Philadelphia *(Closed)*	008350
Art Institute of Pittsburgh *(Closed)*	007470
Bradford School *(Closed)*	009721
Brightwood Career Institute *(Closed)*	004910
Brightwood Career Institute *(Closed)*	007436
Brightwood Career Institute *(Closed)*	022898
Brightwood Career Institute - Broomall Campus *(Closed)*	007781
Career Training Academy *(Closed)*	026095

	FICE/ID Number
Career Training Academy *(Closed)*	666100
Consolidated School of Business *(Closed)*	022896
DeVry University - Fort Washington Campus *(No longer listed as branch by NH)*	666218
Gwynedd Mercy University at East Norriton *(Closed)*	770155

South Carolina

Golf Academy of America *(Closed)*	666490
University of Phoenix Columbia SC Campus *(Closed)*	770223
Virginia College *(Closed)*	770829
Virginia College *(Closed)*	770830
Virginia College *(Closed)*	770831
Virginia College *(Closed)*	770832
Virginia College *(Closed)*	770838

Tennessee

Brightwood College *(Closed)*	023262
Fountainhead College of Technology *(Closed)*	007439
Hiwassee College *(Closed)*	003494
University of Phoenix Nashville Campus *(Closed)*	770225
Vatterott College-Memphis *(Closed)*	666308
Virginia College School of Business and Health *(Closed)*	666136
Virginia College School of Business and Health *(Closed)*	770828

Texas

Brightwood College *(Closed)*	009466
Brightwood College *(Closed)*	023122
Brightwood College *(Closed)*	025919
Brightwood College *(Closed)*	031158
Brightwood College *(Closed)*	032723
Brightwood College *(Closed)*	770544
Brightwood College *(Closed)*	770545
Brightwood College *(Closed)*	770546
Brightwood College *(Closed)*	770595
Brightwood College *(Closed)*	770596
Brightwood College *(Closed)*	770597
Brightwood College *(Closed)*	770598
Brightwood College-Friendswood *(Closed)*	667051

	FICE/ID Number
DeVry University - Irving Campus *(No longer listed as branch by NH)*	010139
Fortis College *(Closed)*	770937
Golf Academy of America *(Closed)*	770621
Northwood University *(No longer listed as branch by NH)*	770280
University of Phoenix El Paso Campus *(Closed)*	770228
Virginia College *(Closed)*	770547
Virginia College Austin *(Closed)*	666074

Utah

Broadview Entertainment Arts University *(Closed)*	770809
Ogden-Weber Applied Technical College *(No longer degree granting)*	023465
Uintah Basin Technical College *(No longer degree granting)*	011165

Vermont

College of St. Joseph *(Closed)*	003685
Green Mountain College *(Closed)*	003687
Southern Vermont College *(Closed)*	003693

Virginia

Argosy University, Washington DC *(Closed)*	666788
Arirang University *(Closed)*	667158
Baptist Theological Seminary at Richmond *(Closed)*	031169
DeVry University - Arlington Campus *(No longer listed as branch by NH)*	666220
Global Health College *(No longer ACICS accredited)*	041400
South Baylo University *(Closed)*	770912
Stratford University Glen Allen Campus *(Closed)*	770819
Stratford University Newport News Campus *(Closed)*	770818
Stratford University Virginia Beach Campus *(Closed)*	770857
Virginia College *(Closed)*	770837

Washington

Antioch University Seattle *(No longer listed as branch by NH)*	666812
The Art Institute of Seattle *(Closed)*	022913

Wisconsin

Madison Media Institute-College of Media Arts *(Closed)*	010913
Mid-State Technical College Marshfield Campus *(No longer listed as branch by NH)*	770441
Mid-State Technical College Stevens Point Campus *(No longer listed as branch by NH)*	770442

Institution Changes

	FICE/ID Number
Milwaukee Area Technical College *(No longer listed as branch by NH)*	770443
Milwaukee Area Technical College *(No longer listed as branch by NH)*	770444
Milwaukee Area Technical College *(No longer listed as branch by NH)*	770445
Rasmussen College - Wausau *(No longer listed as branch by NH)*	667068
University of Wisconsin Manitowoc *(No longer listed as branch by NH)*	770453
University of Wisconsin Marinette *(No longer listed as branch by NH)*	770454
University of Wisconsin Sheboygan *(No longer listed as branch by NH)*	770459

Wyoming

Carbon County Higher Education Center/Rawlins *(No longer listed as branch by NH)*	770481
Oyster Ridge BOCES/Kemmerer WWCC Outreach *(No longer listed as branch by NH)*	770479
Western Wyoming Community College Evanston Outreach *(No longer listed as branch by NH)*	770482
Western Wyoming Community College Outreach Afton/Star Valley *(No longer listed as branch by NH)*	770483

Merged Institutions

California

San Francisco Theological Seminary *into* 001279
University of Redlands 001322

Colorado

University of the Rockies *into* 035453
Ashford University 001881

Pennsylvania

Dean Institute of Technology *into* 009186
Rosedale Technical College 012050

Puerto Rico

Dominican Study Center of the Caribbean *into* 666337
Universidad Central de Bayamon 005022

Name Changes

Arizona

	FICE/ID Number
from: Coconino County Community College Flagstaff Fourth Street Campus *to:* Coconino County Community College Flagstaff Fourth Street Innovation Center	770005
from: Ottawa University *to:* Ottawa University Surprise	770982

Arkansas

from: Williams Baptist College *to:* Williams Baptist University	001106

California

from: Academy for Jewish Religion *to:* Academy for Jewish Religion, California	041555
from: Cedars-Sinai Medical Center Graduate Program in Biomedical Sciences *to:* Cedars-Sinai Graduate School of Biomedical Sciences	667071
from: International Sports Science Association *to:* College of Exercise Science, International Sports Sciences Association, LLC	042434
from: LACM, Los Angeles College of Music *to:* Los Angeles College of Music	038684
from: Life Pacific College *to:* Life Pacific University	022706

Colorado

from: Colorado Mountain College Buena Vista *to:* Colorado Mountain College Leadville	770036
from: Colorado State University-Global Campus *to:* Colorado State University Global	042087
from: Southwest Colorado Community College-West *to:* Pueblo Community College Southwest Campus	770044

District of Columbia

from: BAU International University *to:* Bay Atlantic University	667329

Florida

from: Advance Science College *to:* Advance Science International College	037573
from: Adventist University of Health Sciences *to:* AdventHealth University	031155
from: Ana G. Mendez University System Metro Orlando Campus *to:* Ana G. Mendez University Metro Orlando Campus	770921
from: Ana G. Mendez University System South Florida Campus *to:* Ana G. Mendez University South Florida Campus	770922
from: Ana G. Mendez University System Tampa Bay Campus *to:* Ana G. Mendez University Tampa Bay Campus	770923
from: Health Career Institute *to:* HCI College	667104
from: Medical Career Institute *to:* Braxton College	667266
from: Wolford College *to:* Keiser University	039393

Illinois

from: Flashpoint College *to:* Flashpoint Chicago, a Campus of Columbia College Hollywood	667083
from: John Marshall Law School *to:* UIC John Marshall Law School	001698
from: South Suburban College of Cook County *to:* South Suburban College	001769

Indiana

from: Bethel College *to:* Bethel University	001787

FICE/ID Number

Iowa

from: Dordt College — 001859
to: Dordt University

Kentucky

from: Thomas More College — 002001
to: Thomas More University

Louisiana

from: Northwest Louisiana Technical College Northwest Campus — 009975
to: Northwest Louisiana Technical Community College

Maryland

from: Ana G. Mendez University System Capital Area Campus — 770924
to: Ana G. Mendez University Capital Area Campus

from: University of Maryland University College — 011644
to: University of Maryland Global Campus

Massachusetts

from: Simmons College — 002208
to: Simmons University

Michigan

from: Calvin College — 002241
to: Calvin University

from: Michigan School of Professional Psychology — 021989
to: Michigan School of Psychology

from: Mid Michigan Community College — 006768
to: Mid Michigan College

from: Rochester College — 002288
to: Rochester University

Missouri

from: Southwest Baptist University Salem Center — 770327
to: Southwest Baptist University Salem

from: Southwest Baptist University Springfield Center — 770328
to: Southwest Baptist University Springfield

Montana

from: Montana Tech of The University of Montana — 002531
to: Montana Technological University

New Jersey

from: Brookdale Community College Western Monmouth Branch Campus — 770125
to: Brookdale Community College Freehold Campus

from: Cumberland County College — 002601
to: Rowan University of South Jersey Cumberland Campus

from: Rowan College at Gloucester County — 006901
to: Rowan College of South Jersey

New York

from: Corning Community College — 002863
to: SUNY Corning Community College

from: LIU Brentwood — 666076
to: Long Island University - LIU Brentwood

FICE/ID Number

from: LIU Brooklyn — 004779
to: Long Island University - LIU Brooklyn

from: LIU Hudson at Westchester — 666078
to: Long Island University - LIU Hudson

from: LIU Post — 002754
to: Long Island University - LIU Post

from: LIU Riverhead — 666174
to: Long Island University - LIU Riverhead

from: Memorial School of Nursing — 012203
to: Memorial College of Nursing

from: Mohawk Valley Community College — 770141
to: Mohawk Valley Community College Rome Campus

from: Suffolk County Community College Ammerman Campus — 002878
to: Suffolk County Community College

from: Touro Law School — 770148
to: Touro College, Jacob D. Fuchsberg Law Center

from: Weill Cornell Medical College — 004762
to: Weill Cornell Medicine

Ohio

from: Beckfield College — 666673
to: ATA College

Pennsylvania

from: La Roche College — 003987
to: La Roche University

Puerto Rico

from: Ponce School of Medicine & Health Sciences — 024824
to: Ponce Health Sciences University

from: Sistema Universitario Ana G. Mendez — 029078
to: Universidad Ana G. Mendez

from: Universidad Ana G. Mendez — 667292
to: Universidad Ana G. Mendez Online Campus

from: Universidad del Este — 003941
to: Universidad Ana G. Mendez Carolina Campus

from: Universidad Del Turabo — 011719
to: Universidad Ana G. Mendez Gurabo Campus

from: Universidad Metropolitana — 025875
to: Universidad Ana G. Mendez Cupey Campus

South Carolina

from: Coker College — 003427
to: Coker University

Texas

from: Ana G. Mendez University System-Dallas — 770947
to: Ana G. Mendez University Dallas Campus

from: Career Institute of Technology — 667323
to: College of Biomedical Equipment Technology

from: Graduate Institute of Applied Linguistics — 038513
to: Dallas International University

from: Laredo Community College — 003582
to: Laredo College

from: South Texas School of Christian Studies — 667345
to: Stark College & Seminary

from: South University — 770917
to: South University-Austin

from: University of Texas of the Permian Basin — 009930
to: University of Texas Permian Basin

	FICE/ID Number

Virginia

from: Danville Regional Medical Center School of Health Professions *to:* Sovah School of Health Professions	021116
from: Jefferson College of Health Sciences *to:* Radford University Carilion	006622

West Virginia

from: Wheeling Jesuit University *to:* Wheeling University	003831

Wisconsin

from: University of Wisconsin Baraboo/Sauk County *to:* University of Wisconsin-Platteville Baraboo Sauk County	770450
from: University of Wisconsin Barron County *to:* University of Wisconsin-Eau Claire - Barron County	770457
from: University of Wisconsin Marathon County *to:* University of Wisconsin-Stevens Point at Wausau	770461
from: University of Wisconsin Richland *to:* University of Wisconsin-Platteville Richland	770458

FICE/ID Number

Codes and Descriptions of Administrative Officers

We have modified the Manpower Codes used in the *Higher Education Directory* to better reflect the organizational structures of colleges and universities. Codes are now grouped by major organizational division—Executive, Academic, External Affairs, Fiscal Affairs, Institutional Affairs, Information Technology, and Student Affairs. Some codes have been redefined and several have been added. New and modified codes are marked by an asterisk (*).

Executive

(01) **Chief Executive Officer (President/Chancellor)** - Directs all affairs and operations of a higher education institution.

(02) **Chief Executive Officer Within a System (President/Chancellor)** - Directs all affairs and operations of a campus or an institution which is part of a university-wide system.

(03) **Executive Vice President** - Responsible for all or most functions and operations of an institution under the direction of the Chief Executive Officer.

(100) **Chief of Staff** - Senior non-secretarial staff assistant to the President/Chancellor. Manages administration and operations of The Office of the President.

(00)* **Chairman of the Board** - Directs the operations of the institution's Board of Directors.

(101) **Secretary of the Institution/Board of Governors** - Responsible for liaison between the Board and the institution. Maintains governance and official Board records.

(125)* **President/Chancellor Emeritus** - A past chief executive currently holding an advisory or honorary position at the institution.

(17) **Chief of Health Care Professions** - Senior administrator of academic health care programs, hospitals, clinic or affiliated health-care programs.

(12) **Director of Branch Campus** - Official who is in charge of a branch campus.

(04) **Administrative Assistant to the President** - Senior administrative assistant to the Chief Executive Officer.

(41) **Athletic Director** - Manages intramural and intercollegiate programs including employment, scheduling, promotion, maintenance and related functions.

Academic Affairs

(05) **Chief Academic Officer** - Directs the academic program of the institution. Typically includes academic planning, teaching, research, extensions and coordination of interdepartmental affairs. May include Provost.

(20) **Associate Academic Officer** - Responsible for many of the functions and operations under the direction of the Chief Academic Officer.

(08) **Chief Library Officer** - Directs the activities of all institutional libraries.

Dean or Director. Serves as the principal administrator for the institutional program indicated:

- (47) **Agriculture**
- (76) **Allied Health Sciences**
- (48) **Architecture/Interior Design**
- (49) **Art and Sciences**
- (50) **Business**
- (77) **Computer and Information Science**
- (51) **Continuing Education**
- (78) **Cooperative Education**
- (52) **Dentistry**
- (53) **Education**
- (54) **Engineering**
- (55) **Evening/Adult Programs**
- (56) **Extension**
- (59) **Family and Consumer Sciences**
- (57) **Fine Arts**
- (97) **General Studies**
- (80) **Government/Public Affairs**
- (58) **Graduate Programs**
- (92) **Honors Program**
- (79) **Humanities**
- (60) **Journalism/Communications**
- (61) **Law**
- (62) **Library Services**
- (81) **Mathematics/Sciences**
- (63) **Medicine**
- (64) **Music**
- (65) **Natural Resources**
- (66) **Nursing**
- (75) **Occupational Education**
- (106) **Online Education/E-learning**
- (67) **Pharmacy**
- (68) **Physical Education**
- (82) **Political Science/International Affairs**
- (107) **Professional Programs**
- (69) **Public Health**
- (83) **Social and Behavioral Sciences**
- (70) **Social Work**
- (87) **Summer Session/School**
- (72) **Technology**
- (73) **Theology**
- (74) **Veterinary Medicine**
- (94) **Women's Studies**

External Affairs

(111)* **Director of Institutional Advancement** - Responsible for the comprehensive plan to ensure ongoing growth in public awareness of an institution and its strategic goals.

(30) **Director of Development** - Organizes and directs programs connected with the fund raising activities of the institution. May include Advancement.

(110)* **Associate Advancement/Development Officer** - Assists and supports the Chief Advancement/Development Officer.

(29) **Director of Alumni Relations** - Coordinates alumni activities between the institution and the alumni.

(44) **Director Annual Giving** - Operates the annual giving from all supporters of the institutions.

(112)* **Director Planned Giving/Major Gifts** - Identifies, cultivates and solicits planned and major gifts for ongoing financial support.

(102) **Director of Foundation/Corporate Relations** - Directs institution's efforts in the area of soliciting grants and gifts from foundations and corporations.

(26) **Chief Public Relations/Marketing/Communications Officer** - Directs public relations program. May include alumni relations, publication, marketing and development.

(27) **Associate Public Relations/Marketing/Communications Officer** - Assists and reports to the Chief Public Relations/Marketing/Communications Officer.

(31) **Chief Community Relations Officer** - Directs the educational (usually non-credit), cultural and recreational services to the community.

(103) **Director of Workforce Development** - Directs the institution's efforts in course development and instruction for students and the community in skills necessary to gain employment.

Fiscal Affairs

(10) **Chief Financial/Business Officer** - Directs business and financial affairs including accounting, purchasing, investments, auxiliary enterprises and related business matters.

(21) **Associate Financial/Business Officer** - Assists and reports to the Chief Business Officer. May include Controller.

(45) **Chief Institutional Planning Officer** - Directs the long-range planning and the allocation of the institution's resources.

(115)* **Chief Investment Officer** - Responsible for the oversight of the endowment and other financial assets of the college.

(25) **Chief Contract and Grants Administrator** - Conducts administrative activities in connection with contracts and grants.

(109) **Chief Auxiliary Services Officer** - Responsible for management and operations of college support services including food service, bookstore, vending, student union, and printing.

(114)* **Chief Budget Administrator** - Responsible for preparation and management of institutional budgets.

(113)* **Bursar** - Responsible for the overall operations of student financial services including billing, receivables and cashiering functions.

(96) **Director of Purchasing** - Coordinates purchasing of goods and services.

(116)* **Audit Officer** - Responsible for independent assessment of the effectiveness of internal administrative accounting controls and helps ensure conformance with managerial policies.

(40) **Director of Bookstore** - Responsible for the operation of the bookstore including purchasing, advertising, sales, employment, inventory and related functions.

Institutional Affairs

(11) **Chief of Operations/Administration** - Responsible for administrative functions that are generally non-academic and non-financial.

(117)* **Chief Risk Management Officer** - Responsible for the oversight of the college's risk management programs including emergency and crisis response management, operational risk, technology and cyber risks, insurance and facility vulnerability, and threat assessment.

(15) **Chief Human Resources Officer** - Administers the institution's personnel policies and programs for staff or faculty and staff.

(16) **Associate Human Resources Officer** - Assists and reports to the Chief Human Resources Officer.

(118)* **Director Employee Benefits** - Manages the college's compensation and benefit programs, policies and procedures.

(09) **Director of Institutional Research** - Conducts research and studies on the institution including design of studies, data collection, analysis and reporting.

(46) **Chief Research Officer** - Initiates and directs research in using the facilities and personnel in new areas of academic and scientific exploration.

(108) **Director of Institutional Assessment** - Facilitates and directs institution-wide assessment activities for academic programs and non-academic departments.

(22) **Director of Affirmative Action/Equal Opportunity** - Responsible for the institution's program relating to affirmative action and equal opportunity.

(28) **Director of Diversity** - Responsible for the institution's diversity programs.

(43) **Director of Legal Services (General Counsel)** - Salaried staff person responsible for advising on legal rights, obligations and related matters.

(19) **Director of Security/Safety** - Manages campus police. Responsible for security programs, training, traffic and parking regulations.

(18) **Chief Facilities/Physical Plant Officer** - Responsible for the construction, rehabilitation and maintenance of buildings and grounds.

(86) **Director of Government Relations** - Coordinates institution's relations with local, state, and federal government.

Information Technology (IT)

(13) **Chief Information Technology Officer (CIO)** - Responsible for oversight of IT infrastructure and support, computation and communication infrastructure and services, and administrative information systems across the institution.

(14) **Associate Information Technology Officer** - Assists and reports to the Chief Information Officer.

(24) **Director of Educational Media** - Responsible for audio-visual services and multi-media learning devices.

(90) **Director of Academic Computing** - Responsible for operation and coordination of the institution's various academic computer facilities and labs.

(91) **Director of Administrative Computing** - Responsible for operation of the institution's administrative computing facility.

(105) **Director of Web Services** - Directs the development, operations and content of the institution's web sites.

(119)* **Director of IT Security** - Responsible for technology security in order to protect information and prevent unauthorized access.

(120)* **Director of Online/E-learning Platform** - Coordinates all aspects of institution's online learning platforms.

Student Affairs

(32) **Chief Student Affairs/Student Life Officer** - Responsible for the direction of student life programs including counseling and testing, housing, placement, student union, relationships with student organizations and related functions.

(35) **Associate Student Affairs/Student Life Officer** - Assists Chief Student Life Officer in the non-academic student life activities.

(84) **Director of Enrollment Management** - Plans, develops, and implements strategies to sustain enrollment. Supervises administration of all admissions and financial aid operations.

(07) **Director of Admissions** - Responsible for the recruitment, selection and admission of students.

(123)* **Director of Graduate Admissions** - Responsible for the recruitment, selection and admission of graduate students.

(06) **Registrar** - Responsible for student registration, scheduling of classes, examinations and classroom facilities, student records and related matters.

(37) **Director of Student Financial Aid** - Directs the administration of all forms of student aid.

(39) **Director Resident Life/Student Housing** - Manages student housing operations.

(36) **Director of Student Placement** - Directs the operation of the student placement office to provide career counseling and job placement services to undergraduates, graduates and alumni.

(38) **Director of Student Counseling** - Directs non-academic counseling and testing for students including referral to outside agencies.

(121)* **Director of Student Success/Academic Advising** - assists students in the development and ongoing achievement of their educational goals through academic support and planning.

(124)* **Director of Student Retention** - Develops and evaluates programs and initiatives to improve student retention, engagement and transition.

(89) **Director of First Year Experience** - Works with academic and students affairs to facilitate freshman engagement, learning, transition and integration into the college community.

(93) **Director of Minority Education/Students** - Develops and supports the overall success of students, particularly those from underrepresented minority groups.

(23) **Director of Health Services** - Directs the operation of clinics, medical staff and other programs which provide institutional health services.

(42) **Chaplain/Director Campus Ministry** - Plans, directs the pastoral ministry and religious activities.

(85) **Director of Foreign Students** - Directs student life activities solely concerned with foreign students.

(104) **Director of Study Abroad** - Coordinates and advises students and faculty on academic studies conducted internationally.

(33) **Dean of Men** - Directs student life activities solely concerned with male students.

(34) **Dean of Women** - Directs student life activities solely concerned with female students.

(122)* **Director of Greek Life** - Responsible for all aspects of fraternity and sorority life on campus.

Other

(88) Use this code for those titles that do not fit the above positions.

United States Department of Education Offices

Betsy DeVos (A)
Secretary of Education
United States Department of Education
400 Maryland Avenue, SW
Washington, DC 20202
(202) 401-3000
FAX: (202) 260-7867
URL: www.ed.gov

Ms. Diane Jones (B)
Acting Under Secretary of Education
United States Department of Education
400 Maryland Avenue, SW
Room 7E307
Washington, DC 20202
(202) 453-7333
URL: sites.ed.gov/ous/

Lynn Mahaffie (C)
Dpty Asst Secretary for Policy/Planning/Innovation
Office of Postsecondary Education
United States Department of Education
400 Maryland Avenue, SW
Room 293-01
Washington, DC 20202
(202) 453-7862
URL: www2.ed.gov/about/offices/list/ope/ppi.html

Jennifer Hong Ed.D. (D)
Executive Director
National Advisory Committee on Institutional Quality & Integrity
Office of Postsecondary Education
United States Department of Education
400 Maryland Avenue, SW
Room 271-03
Washington, DC 20202
(202) 453-7805
E-MAIL: jennifer.hong@ed.gov
URL: https://sites.ed.gov/naciqi

Herman Bounds Jr., Ed.S. (E)
Director
Accreditation Group
Office of Post Secondary Education
U.S. Department of Education
400 Maryland Avenue, SW
Room 270-12
Washington, DC 20202
(202) 453-7615
E-MAIL: herman.bounds@ed.gov
URL: www.ed.gov/accreditation?src=rn

Dr. James Woodworth (F)
Commissioner
National Center for Education Statistics
550 12th Street, SW
Room 4063
Washington, DC 20202
URL: www.nces.ed.gov

Jennifer Hong Ed.D. (G)
Executive Director
National Committee on Foreign Medical Education
and Accreditation (NCFMEA)
Office of Postsecondary Education
United States Department of Education
400 Maryland Avenue, SW
Room 6W250
Washington, DC 20202
(202) 453-7805
E-MAIL: jennifer.hong@ed.gov
URL: https://sites.ed.gov/ncfmea

Statewide Agencies of Higher Education

ALABAMA

Alabama Commission on Higher Education (H)
PO Box 302000
Montgomery, AL 36130-2000
(334) 242-2123
Dr. Jim Purcell
Executive Director
E-MAIL: jim.purcell@ache.edu
URL: www.ache.edu

Alabama Community College System (I)
PO Box 302130
Montgomery, AL 36130-2130
(334) 293-4524
FAX: (334) 293-4504
Jimmy H. Baker
Chancellor
E-MAIL: jimmy.baker@accs.edu
URL: www.accs.edu

ALASKA

Alaska Commission on Postsecondary Education (J)
PO Box 110505
Juneau, AK 99811-0505
(907) 465-6740
FAX: (907) 465-3293
Ms. Stephanie Butler
Executive Director
E-MAIL: eed.acpe-execdirector@alaska.gov
URL: www.acpe.alaska.gov

ARIZONA

Arizona Board of Regents (K)
2020 North Central Avenue
Suite 230
Phoenix, AZ 85004-4593
(602) 229-2507
Mr. John Arnold
Executive Director
E-MAIL: john.arnold@azregents.edu
URL: www.azregents.edu

Arizona Commission for Postsecondary Education (L)
2020 North Central Avenue
Suite 650
Phoenix, AZ 85004-4503
(602) 258-2435
FAX: (602) 258-2483
Dr. April L. Osborn
Executive Director
E-MAIL: acpe@azhighered.gov
URL: highered.az.gov

ARKANSAS

Arkansas Division of Higher Education (M)
423 Main Street
Suite 400
Little Rock, AR 72201
(501) 371-2030
FAX: (501) 371-2003
Dr. Maria Markham
Director
E-MAIL: maria.markham@adhe.edu
URL: www.adhe.edu

CALIFORNIA

California Community Colleges Chancellor's Office (N)
1102 Q Street
Suite 4400
Sacramento, CA 95811
(916) 322-4005
FAX: (916) 322-4783
Mr. Eloy Ortiz Oakley
Chancellor
E-MAIL: eoakley@cccco.edu
URL: www.cccco.edu

COLORADO

Colorado Department of Higher Education (O)
1600 Broadway
Suite 2200
Denver, CO 80202
(303) 862-3001
FAX: (303) 996-1329
Dr. Angie Paccione
Executive Director
URL: highered.colorado.gov

Colorado Community College System (P)
9101 East Lowry Boulevard
Denver, CO 80230-6011
(303) 595-1552
FAX: (303) 620-4043
Joseph Garcia
Chancellor
E-MAIL: chancellor@cccs.edu
URL: www.cccs.edu

CONNECTICUT

Board of Regents for Higher Education (Q)
Connecticut State Colleges & Universities
61 Woodland Street
Hartford, CT 06105
(860) 723-0011
FAX: (860) 723-0009
Mark Ojakian
President
E-MAIL: ojakianm@ct.edu
URL: www.ct.edu

Office of Higher Education (R)
450 Columbus Boulevard
Suite 707
Hartford, CT 06103
(860) 947-1801
Mr. Timothy D. Larson
Executive Director
E-MAIL: tlarson@ctohe.org
URL: www.ctohe.org

DELAWARE

Delaware Department of Education Higher Education Office (S)
Townsend Building
401 Federal Street
Dover, DE 19901
(302) 735-4120
FAX: (302) 739-5894
Shana Payne
Director
E-MAIL: dheo@doe.k12.de.us
URL: www.delawaregoestocollege.org

Delaware Technical Community College (T)
PO Box 897
Dover, DE 19903
(302) 857-1667
FAX: (302) 857-1647
Dr. Mark T. Brainard
President
E-MAIL: brainard@dtcc.edu
URL: www.dtcc.edu

DISTRICT OF COLUMBIA

Office of the State Superintendent of Education Government of the District of Columbia (U)
1050 First Street, NE
Washington, DC 20002
(202) 741-0471
FAX: (202) 727-2019
Antoinette S. Mitchell
Asst Superintendent, Postsecondary & Career Educ
E-MAIL: antoinette.mitchell@dc.gov
URL: www.osse.dc.gov

District of Columbia Higher Education Licensure Commission (V)
1050 1st Street, NE
5th Floor
Washington, DC 20002
(202) 481-3951
FAX: (202) 741-0229
Mrs. Angela Lee
Executive Director
E-MAIL: osse.elcmail@dc.gov
URL: helc.osse.dc.gov

FLORIDA

Board of Governors State University System of Florida (W)
325 West Gaines Street
Suite 1614
Tallahassee, FL 32399-0400
(850) 245-0466
FAX: (850) 245-9685
Mr. Marshall M. Criser III
Chancellor
E-MAIL: chancellor@flbog.edu
URL: www.flbog.edu

Florida Department of Education Division of Florida Colleges (X)
325 West Gaines Street
Suite 1244 Turlington Building
Tallahassee, FL 32399
(850) 245-0407
FAX: (850) 245-9525
Ms. Kathryn S. Hebda
Chancellor
E-MAIL: chancellorfcs@fldoe.org
URL: www.fldoe.org/schools/higher-ed/fl-college-system/

GEORGIA

Board of Regents of the University System of Georgia (Y)
270 Washington Street, SW
Atlanta, GA 30334
(404) 962-3000
Dr. Steve Wrigley
Chancellor
E-MAIL: chancellor@usg.edu
URL: www.usg.edu

HAWAII

University of Hawaii Board of Regents (Z)
2444 Dole Street
Bachman Hall, Room 209
Honolulu, HI 96822
(808) 956-8213
FAX: (808) 956-5156
Mr. Ben Kudo
Chair
E-MAIL: bor@hawaii.edu
URL: www.hawaii.edu/offices/bor/

IDAHO

Idaho State Board of Education (a)
PO Box 83720
Boise, ID 83720-0037
(208) 334-2270
FAX: (208) 334-2632
Mr. Matt Freeman
Executive Director
E-MAIL: matt.freeman@osbe.idaho.gov
URL: www.boardofed.idaho.gov

ILLINOIS

Illinois Board of Higher Education (A)
1 N. Old State Capitol Plaza
Suite 333
Springfield, IL 62701-1377
(217) 782-2551
FAX: (217) 782-8548
Mr. Nyle Robinson
Interim Executive Director
E-MAIL: deitsch@ibhe.org
URL: www.ibhe.org

Illinois Community College Board (B)
401 East Capitol Avenue
Springfield, IL 62701
(217) 785-0123
FAX: (217) 785-7495
Dr. Brian Durham
Executive Director
E-MAIL: brian.durham@illinois.gov
URL: www.iccb.org

INDIANA

Indiana Commission for Higher Education (C)
101 West Ohio Street
Suite 300
Indianapolis, IN 46204
(317) 464-4400
FAX: (317) 464-4410
Mrs. Teresa Lubbers
Commissioner for Higher Education
E-MAIL: tlubbers@che.in.gov
URL: www.che.in.gov

IOWA

Board of Regents, State of Iowa (D)
11260 Aurora Avenue
Urbandale, IA 50322-7905
(515) 281-3934
FAX: (515) 281-6420
Mr. Mark J. Braun
Executive Director
E-MAIL: mark.braun@iowaregents.edu
URL: www.iowaregents.edu

Iowa College Student Aid Commission (E)
475 SW 5th Street
Suite D
Des Moines, IA 50309
(515) 725-3410
FAX: (515) 725-3401
Ms. Karen Misjak
Executive Director
E-MAIL: karen.misjak@iowa.gov
URL: www.iowacollegeaid.gov

Iowa Department of Education Division of Community Colleges and Workforce Preparation (F)
400 East 14th Street
Des Moines, IA 50319-0146
(515) 281-8260
FAX: (515) 242-5988
Jeremy Varner
Administrator
E-MAIL: jeremy.varner@iowa.gov
URL: www.educateiowa.gov

KANSAS

Kansas Board of Regents (G)
1000 SW Jackson
Suite 520
Topeka, KS 66612-1368
(785) 430-4240
FAX: (785) 430-4233
Dr. Blake Flanders
President and CEO
E-MAIL: bflanders@ksbor.org
URL: www.kansasregents.org

Kansas Legislative Research Department (H)
Room 68 West, State Capitol Building
300 SW 10th Avenue
Topeka, KS 66612-1504
(785) 296-3181
FAX: (785) 296-3824
Mr. J. G. Scott
Acting Director
E-MAIL: kslegres@klrd.ks.gov
URL: www.kslegresearch.org

KENTUCKY

Kentucky Council on Postsecondary Education (I)
1024 Capital Center Drive
Suite 320
Frankfort, KY 40601
(502) 892-3001
Mr. Aaron Thompson
President
E-MAIL: aaron.thompson@ky.gov
URL: cpe.ky.gov

Kentucky Community & Technical College System (J)
300 North Main Street
Versailles, KY 40383
(859) 256-3132
FAX: (859) 256-3116
Dr. Jay K. Box
President
E-MAIL: president@kctcs.edu
URL: www.kctcs.edu

LOUISIANA

Louisiana Board of Regents (K)
PO Box 3677
Baton Rouge, LA 70821-3677
(225) 342-4253
FAX: (225) 342-9318
Dr. Kim Hunter Reed
Commissioner of Higher Education
E-MAIL: kim.reed@laregents.edu
URL: www.regents.la.gov

Louisiana Department of Education (L)
PO Box 94064
Baton Rouge, LA 70804-9064
(225) 342-3607
FAX: (225) 342-7316
Mr. John White
State Superintendent of Education
URL: www.louisianabelieves.com

MAINE

Maine Department of Education Higher Education and Educator Support Services (M)
23 State House Station
Augusta, ME 04333-0023
(207) 624-6600
FAX: (207) 624-6700
Ms. Pender Makin
Commissioner of Education
E-MAIL: commish.doe@maine.gov
URL: www.maine.gov/doe/

MARYLAND

Maryland Higher Education Commission (N)
6 North Liberty Street, 10th Floor
Baltimore, MD 21201
(410) 767-3300
FAX: (410) 332-0270
Dr. James D. Fielder
Secretary of Higher Education
E-MAIL: james.fielder@maryland.gov
URL: www.mhec.maryland.gov

MASSACHUSETTS

Massachusetts Department of Higher Education (O)
One Ashburton Place
Room 1401
Boston, MA 02108
(617) 994-6901
FAX: (617) 727-6656
Mr. Carlos Santiago
Commissioner
E-MAIL: commissioner@dhe.mass.edu
URL: www.mass.edu

MICHIGAN

Department of Licensing and Regulatory Affairs Corporations, Securities & Commercial Licensing Bureau Licensing Division (P)
PO Box 30018
Lansing, MI 48909-8214
(517) 241-9221
FAX: (517) 373-2162
Mrs. Linda Clegg
Director
E-MAIL: cleggl@michigan.gov
URL: www.michigan.gov/pss

Michigan Workforce Development Agency (Q)
201 North Washington Square
Victor Office Center, 3rd Floor
Lansing, MI 48913
(517) 335-5858
FAX: (517) 241-8217
URL: www.michigan.gov/wda

MINNESOTA

Minnesota Office of Higher Education (R)
1450 Energy Park Drive
Suite 350
St. Paul, MN 55108-5227
(651) 642-0567
FAX: (651) 642-0675
Mr. Dennis W. Olsen Jr.
Commissioner
E-MAIL: info.ohe@state.mn.us
URL: www.ohe.state.mn.us

Minnesota State Colleges and Universities (S)
30 7th Street East
Suite 350
St. Paul, MN 55101-7804
(651) 201-1696
FAX: (651) 297-7465
Dr. Devinder Malhotra
Chancellor
E-MAIL: chancellor@minnstate.edu
URL: www.minnstate.edu

MISSISSIPPI

Mississippi Board of Trustees of State Institutions of Higher Learning (T)
3825 Ridgewood Road
Jackson, MS 39211
(601) 432-6198
FAX: (601) 432-6972
Dr. Alfred Rankins Jr.
Commissioner of Higher Education
E-MAIL: commissioner@mississippi.edu
URL: www.mississippi.edu/ihl/

Mississippi Community College Board (U)
3825 Ridgewood Drive
Jackson, MS 39211
(601) 432-6684
FAX: (601) 432-6480
Dr. Andrea Mayfield
Executive Director
E-MAIL: info@sbcjc.cc.ms.us
URL: www.mccb.edu

MISSOURI

Coordinating Board for Higher Education Missouri Department of Higher Education (V)
PO Box 1469
Jefferson City, MO 65102-1469
(573) 751-2361
FAX: (573) 751-6635
Ms. Zora Mulligan
Commissioner of Higher Education
URL: https://.dhe.mo.gov/cbhe/

MONTANA

Office of the Commissioner of Higher Education (W)
PO Box 203201
Helena, MT 59620-3201
(406) 449-9125
FAX: (406) 449-9171
Mr. Clayton Christian
Commissioner
E-MAIL: cchristian@montana.edu
URL: www.mus.edu/che

NEBRASKA

Nebraska's Coordinating Commission for Postsecondary Education (X)
PO Box 95005
Lincoln, NE 68509-5005
(402) 471-2847
Dr. Michael Baumgartner
Executive Director
E-MAIL: mike.baumgartner@nebraska.gov
URL: ccpe.nebraska.gov

NEW HAMPSHIRE

New Hampshire Department of Education Division of Educator Support and Higher Education Higher Education Commission (Y)
101 Pleasant Street
Concord, NH 03301
(603) 271-0256
FAX: (603) 271-1953
Mr. Michael Seidel
Director
E-MAIL: patricia.edes@doe.nh.gov
URL: www.education.nh.gov/highered

Community College System of New Hampshire (Z)
26 College Drive
Concord, NH 03301
(603) 230-3501
FAX: (603) 271-2725
Dr. Ross Gittell
Chancellor
E-MAIL: rgittell@ccsnh.edu
URL: www.ccsnh.edu

NEW JERSEY

State of New Jersey Office of the Secretary of Higher Education (a)
1 John Fitch Plaza, 10th Floor
PO Box 542
Trenton, NJ 08625-0542
(609) 292-8052
FAX: (609) 292-7225
Zakiya Smith Ellis Ed.D.
Secretary of Higher Education
E-MAIL: lauren.banks@oshe.nj.gov
URL: www.state.nj.us/highereducation

NEW MEXICO

New Mexico Higher Education Department (b)
2044 Galisteo Street
Suite 4
Santa Fe, NM 87505
(505) 476-8400
FAX: (505) 476-8454
Dr. Kate O'Neill
Cabinet Secretary
E-MAIL: exec.admin@state.nm.us
URL: www.hed.state.nm.us

NEW YORK

New York State Education Department (c)
89 Washington Avenue
Education Building, Room 111
Albany, NY 12234
(518) 474-5844
FAX: (518) 473-4909
MaryEllen Elia
Commissioner
E-MAIL: commissioner@nysed.gov
URL: www.nysed.gov

Community Colleges and the Education Pipeline (d)
The State University of New York
SUNY Plaza, 353 Broadway, Room T9
Albany, NY 12246
(518) 320-1276
FAX: (518) 320-1570
Johanna Duncan-Poitier
Senior Vice Chancellor
E-MAIL: johanna.duncan-poitier@suny.edu
URL: www.suny.edu/powerofsuny/educationpipeline/

New York State Education Department Office of Higher Education (e)
Education Building Annex
Room 975
Albany, NY 12234
(518) 486-3633
Deputy Commissioner
URL: www.highered.nysed.gov

NORTH CAROLINA

The University of North Carolina System (f)
910 Raleigh Road
Chapel Hill, NC 27514
(919) 962-4622
Mr. William Roper
President
E-MAIL: president@northcarolina.edu
URL: www.northcarolina.edu

North Carolina Community Colleges (A)
200 West Jones Street
Raleigh, NC 27603
(919) 807-6950
Mr. Peter Hans
President
E-MAIL: hansp@nccommunitycolleges.edu
URL: www.nccommunitycolleges.edu

NORTH DAKOTA

North Dakota State Board of Higher Education (B)
600 East Boulevard Avenue, Dept 215
State Capitol, 10th Floor
Bismarck, ND 58505-0230
(701) 328-2960
FAX: (701) 328-2961
Mr. Nick Hacker
Board Chair
E-MAIL: nicholas.hacker@ndus.edu
URL: www.ndus.edu/board

OHIO

Ohio Department of Higher Education (C)
25 South Front Street
Columbus, OH 43215
(614) 466-6000
FAX: (614) 466-5866
Mr. Randy Gardner
Chancellor
E-MAIL: chancellor@highered.ohio.gov
URL: www.ohiohighered.org

OKLAHOMA

Oklahoma State Regents for Higher Education (D)
655 Research Parkway
Suite 200
Oklahoma City, OK 73104
(405) 225-9100
FAX: (405) 225-9235
Dr. Glen D. Johnson
Chancellor
E-MAIL: gjohnson@osrhe.edu
URL: www.okhighered.org

OREGON

Higher Education Coordinating Commission (E)
255 Capitol Street NE
Salem, OR 97310
(503) 378-5690
Ben Cannon
Executive Director
E-MAIL: info.HECC@state.or.us
URL: www.oregon.gov/HigherEd

Office of Community Colleges and Workforce Development (F)
255 Capitol Street, NE
3rd Floor
Salem, OR 97310
(503) 947-2414
Mr. Patrick Crane
Director
E-MAIL: patrick.crane@state.or.us
URL: www.oregon.gov/highered/about/pages/office-ccwd.aspx

PENNSYLVANIA

Pennsylvania Department of Education Office of Postsecondary and Higher Education (G)
333 Market Street
12th Floor
Harrisburg, PA 17126-0333
(717) 772-3737
FAX: (717) 772-3622
Noe Ortega
Deputy Secretary
E-MAIL: nortega@pa.gov
URL: www.education.pa.gov

Pennsylvania Department of Education Liaison to Postsecondary and Higher Education Institutions (H)
333 Market Street
12th Floor
Harrisburg, PA 17126-0333
(717) 783-8228
FAX: (717) 772-3622
Ms. Patricia Landis
Division Chief - Higher and Career Education
E-MAIL: plandis@pa.gov
URL: www.education.pa.gov

RHODE ISLAND

Rhode Island Office of the Postsecondary Commissioner (I)
560 Jefferson Boulevard
Suite 100
Warwick, RI 02886
(401) 736-1100
FAX: (401) 732-3541
Mr. Ron Cavallaro
Acting Commissioner of Postsecondary Education
URL: www.riopc.edu

Community College of Rhode Island (J)
400 East Avenue
Warwick, RI 02886
(401) 825-2188
FAX: (401) 825-2166
Dr. Meghan Hughes
President
E-MAIL: president@ccri.edu
URL: www.ccri.edu

SOUTH CAROLINA

South Carolina Commission on Higher Education (K)
1122 Lady Street
Suite 300
Columbia, SC 29201
(803) 737-2275
FAX: (803) 737-2297
Dr. Rusty L. Monhollon
President and Executive Director
E-MAIL: rmonhollon@che.sc.gov
URL: www.che.sc.gov

South Carolina State Board for Technical and Comprehensive Education (L)
111 Executive Center Drive
Columbia, SC 29210
(803) 896-5280
Dr. Tim Hardee
System President
URL: www.sctechsystem.edu

SOUTH DAKOTA

South Dakota Board of Regents (M)
306 East Capitol Avenue
Suite 200
Pierre, SD 57501
(605) 773-3455
FAX: (605) 773-5320
Dr. Paul Beran
Executive Director and Chief Executive Officer
E-MAIL: info@sdbor.edu
URL: www.sdbor.edu

South Dakota Department of Education (N)
Office of the Secretary
800 Governors Drive
Pierre, SD 57501-2291
(605) 773-5669
FAX: (605) 773-6139
Dr. Ben Jones
Secretary of Education
URL: www.doe.sd.gov

TENNESSEE

Tennessee Higher Education Commission (O)
404 James Robertson Parkway
Suite 1900
Nashville, TN 37243
(615) 741-7562
Mr. Mike Krause
Executive Director
URL: www.tn.gov/thec/

Tennessee Board of Regents (P)
1 Bridgestone Park
Nashville, TN 37214
(615) 365-1505
FAX: (615) 366-3903
Dr. Randy Schulte
Vice Chancellor for Academic Affairs
E-MAIL: randy.schulte@tbr.edu
URL: www.tbr.edu

University of Tennessee Board of Trustees (Q)
723 Andy Holt Tower
Knoxville, TN 37996-0170
(865) 974-3245
FAX: (865) 974-0100
Ms. Catherine S. Mizell
Secretary to the Board of Trustees
E-MAIL: cmizell@tennessee.edu
URL: trustees.tennessee.edu

TEXAS

Texas Higher Education Coordinating Board (R)
PO Box 12788
Austin, TX 78711
(512) 427-6101
FAX: (512) 427-6127
Dr. Raymund A. Paredes
Commissioner of Higher Education
E-MAIL: raymund.paredes@thecb.state.tx.us
URL: www.thecb.state.tx.us

Texas Higher Education Coordinating Board Division of College Readiness and Success (S)
PO Box 12788
Austin, TX 78711-2788
(512) 427-6247
FAX: (512) 427-6444
Jerel Booker J.D.
Assistant Commissioner
E-MAIL: jerel.booker@thecb.state.tx.us
URL: www.thecb.state.tx.us

UTAH

Utah System of Higher Education State Board of Regents (T)
60 South 400 West
Salt Lake City, UT 84101-1284
(801) 321-7101
FAX: (801) 321-7156
Mr. David Woolstenhulme
Interim Commissioner of Higher Education
E-MAIL: dwoolstenhulme@ushe.edu
URL: higheredutah.org

VERMONT

Vermont Agency of Education (U)
219 North Main Street
Suite 402
Barre, VT 05641
(802) 479-1043
Mr. Brad James
Education Finance Manager
E-MAIL: brad.james@vermont.gov
URL: www.education.vermont.gov

VIRGINIA

State Council of Higher Education for Virginia (V)
101 North 14th Street
James Monroe Building, 10th Floor
Richmond, VA 23219
(804) 225-2600
FAX: (804) 225-2604
Mr. Peter Blake
Director
E-MAIL: peterblake@schev.edu
URL: www.schev.edu

Virginia's Community Colleges (W)
300 Arboretum Place
Suite 200
Richmond, VA 23236
(804) 819-4903
Dr. Glenn DuBois
Chancellor
E-MAIL: gdubois@vccs.edu
URL: www.vccs.edu

WASHINGTON

Washington Student Achievement Council (X)
917 Lakeridge Way SW
Olympia, WA 98502
(360) 753-7800
Mr. Michael P. Meotti
Executive Director
E-MAIL: info@wsac.wa.gov
URL: www.wsac.wa.gov

Washington State Board for Community and Technical Colleges (Y)
PO Box 42495
Olympia, WA 98504-2495
(360) 704-4355
FAX: (360) 704-4415
Jan Yoshiwara
Executive Director
E-MAIL: jyoshiwara@sbctc.edu
URL: www.sbctc.edu

WEST VIRGINIA

West Virginia Higher Education Policy Commission (Z)
1018 Kanawha Boulevard, East
Suite 700
Charleston, WV 25301-2800
(304) 558-0699
FAX: (304) 558-1011
Dr. Sarah Armstrong Tucker
Interim Chancellor
E-MAIL: chancellor@wvhepc.edu
URL: www.wvhepc.edu

WISCONSIN

State of Wisconsin Higher Educational Aids Board (a)
PO Box 7885
Madison, WI 53707-7885
(608) 267-2206
FAX: (608) 267-2808
Dr. Connie Hutchison
Executive Secretary
E-MAIL: heabmail@wisconsin.gov
URL: heab.wi.gov

Wisconsin Technical College System (b)
PO Box 7874
Madison, WI 53707-7874
(608) 267-9066
FAX: (608) 266-1285
Dr. Morna K. Foy
President
E-MAIL: president@wtcsystem.edu
URL: www.wtcsystem.edu

WYOMING

Wyoming Community College Commission (c)
2300 Capitol Avenue
5th Floor, Suite B
Cheyenne, WY 82002
(307) 777-7763
Dr. Sandy Caldwell
Executive Director
E-MAIL: sandra.caldwell@wyo.gov
URL: communitycolleges.wy.edu

AMERICAN SAMOA

Board of Higher Education (American Samoa) American Samoa Community College (d)
PO Box 2609
Pago Pago, AS 96799
(684) 699-9155
E-MAIL: info@amsamoa.edu
URL: www.amsamoa.edu

FEDERATED STATES OF MICRONESIA

Board of Regents College of Micronesia-FSM (e)
PO Box 159
Kolonia Pohnpei, FM 96941
(691) 320-2480
FAX: (691) 320-2479
Dr. Tulensru Waguk
Chairman of the Board
E-MAIL: national@comfsm.fm
URL: www.comfsm.fm

PUERTO RICO

Puerto Rico Council on Education **(A)**
PO Box 19900
San Juan, PR 00910-1900
(787) 722-2121, ext. 388
FAX: (787) 641-2573
Ms. Maria L. Varas Garcia
Interim Executive Director
E-MAIL: mvaras@ce.pr.gov
URL: www.ce.pr.gov

Higher Education Associations

AACSB International (A)
777 South Harbour Island Boulevard
Suite 750
Tampa, FL 33602-5730
(813) 769-6500
Fax: (813) 769-6559
Mr. Thomas R. Robinson
President and Chief Executive Officer
E-mail: mediarelations@aacsb.edu
URL: www.aacsb.edu

AASA, The School Superintendents Association (B)
1615 Duke Street
Alexandria, VA 22314
(703) 528-0700
Fax: (703) 841-1543
Dr. Daniel A. Domenech
Executive Director
E-mail: ddomenech@aasa.org
URL: www.aasa.org

AAUW (C)
1310 L Street, NW
Suite 1000
Washington, DC 20005
(202) 785-7700
Fax: (202) 872-1425
Kimberly Churches
Chief Executive Officer
E-mail: connect@aauw.org
URL: www.aauw.org

ABET (D)
415 North Charles Street
Baltimore, MD 21201
(410) 347-7700
Fax: (443) 552-3644
Michael K. J. Milligan Ph.D., PE
Executive Director and CEO
E-mail: comms@abet.org
URL: www.abet.org

Academy of Legal Studies in Business (E)
Western Carolina University
College of Business
Forsyth Hall
Cullowhee, NC 28723
(513) 255-6950
Mr. Daniel Herron
Executive Secretary
E-mail: herron3653@gmail.com
URL: www.alsb.org

Academy of Nutrition and Dietetics Accreditation Council for Education in Nutrition and Dietetics (ACEND) (F)
120 South Riverside Plaza
Suite 2190
Chicago, IL 60606-6995
(312) 899-0040, ext. 5400
Fax: (312) 899-4817
Dr. Rayane AbuSabha
Executive Director
E-mail: acend@eatright.org
URL: www.eatrightpro.org/acend

Accreditation Commission for Acupuncture and Oriental Medicine (ACAOM) (G)
8941 Aztec Drive
Suite 2
Eden Prairie, MN 55347
(952) 212-2434
Mr. Mark McKenzie
Executive Director
E-mail: mark.mckenzie@acaom.org
URL: www.acaom.org

Accreditation Commission for Education in Nursing (ACEN) (H)
3343 Peachtree Road, NE
Suite 850
Atlanta, GA 30326
(404) 975-5000
Fax: (404) 975-5020
Dr. Marsal Stoll
CEO
E-mail: mstoll@acenursing.org
URL: www.acenursing.org

Accreditation Commission for Midwifery Education (ACME) (I)
8403 Colesville Road
Suite 1550
Silver Spring, MD 20910
(240) 485-1803
Fax: (240) 485-1818
Heather L. Maurer MA
Executive Director
E-mail: hmaurer@acnm.org
URL: www.midwife.org/Accreditation

Accreditation Committee - Perfusion Education (J)
552 W. Jamison Place
Littleton, CO 80120
(303) 794-6283
Ms. Theresa Sisneros
Executive Director
E-mail: office@ac-pe.org
URL: www.ac-pe.org

Accreditation Council for Business Schools and Programs (K)
11520 West 119th Street
Overland Park, KS 66213
(913) 339-9356
Fax: (913) 339-6226
Mr. Jeffrey Alderman
President & CEO
E-mail: info@acbsp.org
URL: www.acbsp.org

Accreditation Council for Pharmacy Education (L)
190 S. LaSalle Street
Suite 2850
Chicago, IL 60603
(312) 664-3575
Fax: (866) 228-2631
Janet P. Engle, PharmD PhD (Hon)
Executive Director
E-mail: pvlasses@acpe-accredit.org
URL: www.acpe-accredit.org

Accreditation Review Commission on Education for the Physician Assistant (ARC-PA) (M)
12000 Findley Road
Suite 275
Johns Creek, GA 30097
(770) 476-1224
Fax: (770) 476-1738
Ms. Sharon Luke
Executive Director
E-mail: sharonluke@arc-pa.org
URL: www.arc-pa.org

Accreditation Review Committee for the Anesthesiologist Assistant (N)
24500 US Highway 19 North
Suite 158
Clearwater, FL 33763
(612) 836-3311
Ms. Jennifer Anderson Warwick
Executive Director
E-mail: arc-aa@arc-aa.org
URL: www.caahep.org/arc-aa

Accreditation Review Committee for the Medical Illustrator (O)
32531 Meadowlark Way
Pepper Pike, OH 44124
(216) 595-9363
Kathleen Jung
ARC-MI Chair
E-mail: kijung@aol.com
URL: www.caahep.org/arc-mi

Accreditation Review Council on Education in Surgical Technology and Surgical Assisting (P)
6 West Dry Creek Circle
Suite 110
Littleton, CO 80120
(303) 694-9262
Fax: (303) 741-3655
Mr. Ron Kruzel
Executive Director
E-mail: info@arcstsa.org
URL: www.arcstsa.org

Accrediting Bureau of Health Education Schools (ABHES) (Q)
7777 Leesburg Pike
Suite 314 North
Falls Church, VA 22043
(703) 917-9503
Fax: (703) 917-4109
India Y. Tips
Executive Director
E-mail: itips@abhes.org
URL: www.abhes.org

Accrediting Commission for Community and Junior Colleges Western Association of Schools and Colleges (R)
10 Commercial Boulevard
Suite 204
Novato, CA 94949
(415) 506-0234
Fax: (415) 506-0238
Dr. Richard Winn
President
E-mail: accjc@accjc.org
URL: accjc.org

Accrediting Commission of Career Schools and Colleges (S)
2101 Wilson Boulevard
Suite 302
Arlington, VA 22201
(703) 247-4212
Fax: (703) 247-4533
Dr. Michale McComis
Executive Director
E-mail: mccomis@accsc.org
URL: www.accsc.org

Accrediting Council for Continuing Education & Training (ACCET) (T)
1722 N Street, NW
Washington, DC 20036
(202) 955-1113
Fax: (202) 955-1118
Mr. Bill Larkin
Executive Director
E-mail: info@accet.org
URL: www.accet.org

Accrediting Council for Independent Colleges and Schools (U)
1350 Eye Street, NW
Suite 560
Washington, DC 20005
(202) 336-6780
Fax: (202) 842-2593
Ms. Michelle Edwards
President
E-mail: medwards@acics.org
URL: www.acics.org

Accrediting Council on Education in Journalism and Mass Communications (V)
University of Mississippi
201 Bishop Hall
University, MS 38677
(662) 915-5500
Patricia Thompson
ACEJMC Executive Director
E-mail: pthomps1@olemiss.edu
URL: www.acejmc.org

ACPE: The Standard in Spiritual Care & Education (W)
One West Court Square
Suite 325
Decatur, GA 30030
(404) 320-1472
Fax: (404) 320-0849
RevDr. Trace Haythorn
Executive Director/CEO
E-mail: acpe@acpe.edu
URL: www.acpe.edu

ACT, Inc. (X)
500 ACT Drive
Box 168
Iowa City, IA 52243-0168
(319) 337-1079
Mr. Marten Roorda
CEO
E-mail: sandy.serbousek@act.org
URL: www.act.org

AEF: The Association of National Advertisers (ANA) Educational Foundation (Y)
10 Grand Central
155 E. 44th Street
3rd Floor
New York, NY 10017
(212) 986-8060
Fax: (212) 986-8061
Mr. Gordon McLean
President
E-mail: gm@aef.com
URL: www.aef.com

American Academy for Liberal Education (AALE) (Z)
Washington, DC 20016
(202) 389-6550
Mary Ann Powers
Executive Director
E-mail: aaleinfo@aale.org
URL: www.aale.org

American Anthropological Association (a)
2300 Clarendon Boulevard
Suite 1301
Arlington, VA 22201
(703) 528-1902
Fax: (703) 528-3546
Dr. Edward Liebow
Executive Director
E-mail: eliebow@americananthro.org
URL: www.americananthro.org

American Association for Adult and Continuing Education (AAACE) (b)
2900 Delk Road
Suite 700, PMB 321
Marietta, GA 30067
(678) 271-4319
Fax: (404) 393-9506
Dr. Larry Martin
President
E-mail: president@aaace.org
URL: www.aaace.org

American Association for Employment in Education (c)
PO Box 510
Sycamore, IL 60178
(614) 485-1111
Fax: (360) 244-7802
Mr. Tim Neubert
Executive Director
E-mail: execdir@aaee.org
URL: www.aaee.org

American Association for Marriage and Family Therapy Commission on Accreditation for Marriage and Family Therapy Education (d)
112 South Alfred Street
Alexandria, VA 22314-3061
(703) 253-0473
Fax: (703) 253-0508
Ms. Tanya A. Tamarkin
Director of Accreditation
E-mail: coa@aamft.org
URL: www.coamfte.org

American Association for Women in Community Colleges (AAWCC) (e)
PO Box 3098
Gaithersburg, MD 20855
Dr. Tyjaun Lee
President
E-mail: info@aawccnatl.org
URL: www.aawccnatl.org

American Association of Blood Banks Committee on Accreditation of Specialist in Blood Banking Technology Schools (f)
4550 Montgomery Avenue
Suite 700 North Tower
Bethesda, MD 20814-3304
(301) 215-6540
Fax: (301) 657-0957
Meredith Eller
Staff Liaison Accreditation and Quality
E-mail: meller@aabb.org
URL: www.aabb.org

American Association of Colleges for Teacher Education (g)
1307 New York Avenue, NW
Suite 300
Washington, DC 20005
(202) 293-2450
Fax: (202) 457-8095
Dr. Lynn M. Gangone
President & Chief Executive Officer
URL: www.aacte.org

American Association of Colleges of Nursing (h)
655 K Street, NW
Suite 750
Washington, DC 20001-2399
(202) 463-6930
Fax: (202) 785-8320
Dr. Deborah Trautman
President & Chief Executive Officer
E-mail: dtrautman@aacnnursing.org
URL: www.aacnnursing.org

Higher Education Associations

American Association of Colleges of Osteopathic Medicine (A)
7700 Old Georgetown Road
Suite 250
Bethesda, MD 20814
(301) 968-4100
FAX: (301) 968-4101
Dr. Robert Cain DO, MPH
President and CEO
E-MAIL: president@aacom.org
URL: www.aacom.org

American Association of Collegiate Registrars and Admissions Officers (AACRAO) (B)
1108 16th Street, NW
Suite 400
Washington, DC 20036
(202) 293-9161
FAX: (202) 872-8857
Mr. Michael Reilly
Executive Director
E-MAIL: reillym@aacrao.org
URL: www.aacrao.org

American Association of Community Colleges (C)
1 Dupont Circle, NW
Suite 700
Washington, DC 20036
(202) 728-0200, ext. 235
Dr. Walter G. Bumphus
President/CEO
E-MAIL: wbumphus@aacc.nche.edu
URL: www.aacc.nche.edu

American Association of Family and Consumer Sciences (AAFCS) (D)
400 North Columbus Street
Suite 202
Alexandria, VA 22314
(703) 706-4602
FAX: (703) 636-7648
Lori A. Myers PhD, CFCS
Sr Director, Credentialing, Education & Research
E-MAIL: lmyers@aafcs.org
URL: www.aafcs.org

American Association of Medical Assistants (E)
20 North Wacker Drive
Suite 1575
Chicago, IL 60606
(312) 899-1500
FAX: (312) 899-1259
Mr. Donald A. Balasa J.D., MBA
Chief Executive Officer
E-MAIL: dbalasa@aama-ntl.org
URL: www.aama-ntl.org

American Association of Physics Teachers (F)
One Physics Ellipse
College Park, MD 20740-3845
(301) 209-3311
FAX: (301) 209-0845
Dr. Beth A. Cunningham
Executive Officer
E-MAIL: eo@aapt.org
URL: www.aapt.org

American Association of Presidents of Independent Colleges and Universities (G)
PO Box 7070
Provo, UT 84602-7070
(801) 422-4722
Mr. Joshua Figueira
Executive Director
E-MAIL: joshua_figueira@byu.edu
URL: www.aapicu.org

American Association of State Colleges and Universities (H)
1307 New York Avenue, NW
5th Floor
Washington, DC 20005-4701
(202) 293-7070
FAX: (202) 296-5819
Dr. Mildred Garcia
President
E-MAIL: presg@aascu.org
URL: www.aascu.org

American Association of Teachers of Slavic and East European Languages (I)
University of Southern California
3501 Trousdale Parkway
THH 255L
Los Angeles, CA 90089-4353
(213) 740-2734
FAX: (213) 740-8550
Dr. Elizabeth Durst
Executive Director
E-MAIL: aatseel@usc.edu
URL: www.aatseel.org

American Association of University Professors (J)
1133 19th Street, NW
Suite 200
Washington, DC 20036
(202) 737-5900
FAX: (202) 737-5526
Dr. Julie Schmid
Executive Director
E-MAIL: aaup@aaup.org
URL: www.aaup.org

American Bar Association Section of Legal Education and Admissions to the Bar (K)
321 North Clark Street
19th Floor
Chicago, IL 60654
(312) 988-6746
Mr. Barry A. Currier
Managing Director Accreditation & Legal Education
E-MAIL: legaled@americanbar.org
URL: www.americanbar.org/groups/legal_education

American Board of Funeral Service Education Committee on Accreditation (L)
992 Mantua Pike
Suite 108
Woodbury Heights, NJ 08097
(816) 233-3747
FAX: (856) 579-7354
Robert C. Smith III
Executive Director
E-MAIL: exdir@abfse.org
URL: www.abfse.org

American Catholic Philosophical Association (M)
University of St. Thomas
3800 Montrose Boulevard
Houston, TX 77006
(713) 942-3483
FAX: (713) 525-6964
Dr. Stephen Striby
National Secretary
E-MAIL: acpa@stthom.edu
URL: www.acpaweb.org

American Chemical Society Committee on Professional Training (N)
1155 Sixteenth Street, NW
Washington, DC 20036
(202) 872-4589
FAX: (202) 872-6066
E-MAIL: cpt@acs.org
URL: www.acs.org/cpt

American College of Nurse-Midwives (O)
8403 Colesville Road
Suite 1550
Silver Spring, MD 20910
(240) 485-1800
FAX: (240) 485-1818
Dr. Sheri Sesay-Tuffour
Executive Director
E-MAIL: info@acnm.org
URL: www.midwife.org

American College Personnel Association (ACPA) (P)
1 Dupont Circle, NW
Suite 300
Washington, DC 20036-1188
(202) 835-2272
FAX: (202) 827-0601
Mr. Chris Moody
Executive Director
E-MAIL: info@acpa.nche.edu
URL: www.myacpa.org

American Collegiate Retailing Association (Q)
Texas Tech University
1301 Akron Avenue, HS, Room 601
Lubbock, TX 79415
(806) 742-3068
Dr. Robert P. Jones
President
E-MAIL: robert.p.jones@ttu.edu
URL: www.acraretail.org

American Conference of Academic Deans (ACAD) (R)
1818 R Street, NW
Washington, DC 20009
(202) 884-7419
FAX: (202) 265-9532
Ms. Laura A. Matthias
Executive Director
E-MAIL: info@acad.org
URL: www.acad.org

American Council for Construction Education (S)
300 Decker Drive
Suite 330
Irving, TX 75062
(972) 600-8800
Mr. Steve Nellis
President/CEO
E-MAIL: steve.nellis@acce-hq.org
URL: www.acce-hq.org

American Council of Trustees and Alumni (T)
1730 M Street, NW
Suite 600
Washington, DC 20036-4525
(202) 467-6787
FAX: (202) 467-6784
Dr. Michael B. Poliakoff
President
E-MAIL: info@goacta.org
URL: www.goacta.org

American Council on Education (U)
1 Dupont Circle, NW
Washington, DC 20036
(202) 939-9300
Ted Mitchell
President
E-MAIL: president@acenet.edu
URL: www.acenet.edu

American Counseling Association (V)
6101 Stevenson Avenue
Suite 600
Alexandria, VA 22304
(800) 347-6647, ext. 231
FAX: (800) 473-2329
Mr. Richard Yep CAE, FASAE
Chief Executive Officer
E-MAIL: ryep@counseling.org
URL: www.counseling.org

American Culinary Federation Education Foundation Accrediting Commission (W)
180 Center Place Way
St. Augustine, FL 32095
(904) 824-4468
FAX: (904) 940-0741
Director of Education & Programs
E-MAIL: acf@acfchefs.net
URL: www.acfchefs.org

American Educational Research Association (X)
1430 K Street, NW
Suite 1200
Washington, DC 20005
(202) 238-3200
FAX: (202) 238-3250
Dr. Felice J. Levine
Executive Director
E-MAIL: flevine@aera.net
URL: www.aera.net

American Forensic Association (Y)
PO Box 67021
Chestnut Hill, MA 02467-0001
(620) 341-5256
Dr. Heidi Hamilton
President
E-MAIL: hhamilto@emporia.edu

American Institute of Architecture Students (Z)
1735 New York Avenue, NW
Washington, DC 20006
(202) 808-0088
Ms. Karma Israelsen
Executive Director
E-MAIL: karmaisraelsen@aias.org
URL: www.aias.org

American Library Association Office for Accreditation (a)
50 East Huron Street
Chicago, IL 60611
(312) 280-2434
FAX: (312) 280-2433
Karen O'Brien
Director, Office for Accreditation
E-MAIL: kobrien@ala.org
URL: www.ala.org/accreditation

American Mathematical Association of Two Year Colleges (b)
Southwest Tennessee Community College
5983 Macon Cove
Memphis, TN 38134
(901) 333-5643
FAX: (901) 333-5651
Anne Dudley
Executive Director
E-MAIL: adudley@amatyc.org
URL: www.amatyc.org

American Occupational Therapy Association Accreditation Council for Occupational Therapy Education (ACOTE) (c)
4720 Montgomery Lane
Suite 200
Bethesda, MD 20814-3449
(301) 652-6611 Ext. 2042
FAX: (240) 762-5140
Dr. Sabrina Salvant
Director of Accreditation
E-MAIL: accred@aota.org
URL: www.aota.org

American Optometric Association Accreditation Council on Optometric Education (d)
243 North Lindbergh Boulevard
Floor 1
St. Louis, MO 63141
(314) 991-4100
FAX: (314) 991-4101
Ms. Joyce L. Urbeck
Director
E-MAIL: jlurbeck@aoa.org
URL: www.theacoe.org

American Osteopathic Association (e)
Commission on Osteopathic College Accreditation
142 East Ontario Street
Chicago, IL 60611-2864
(312) 202-8124
Mr. Josh Prober
Interim Secretary
E-MAIL: jprober@osteopathic.org
URL: osteopathic.org/accreditation

American Physical Therapy Association (f)
1111 North Fairfax Street
Alexandria, VA 22314
(703) 684-2782
Mr. Justin Moore
Chief Executive Officer
E-MAIL: dorisellmore@apta.org
URL: www.apta.org

American Political Science Association (g)
1527 New Hampshire Avenue, NW
Washington, DC 20036
(202) 483-2512
FAX: (202) 483-2657
Dr. Steven Rathgeb Smith
Executive Director
E-MAIL: apsa@apsanet.org
URL: www.apsanet.org

American Psychological Association Office of Program Consultation & Accreditation (h)
750 First Street, NE
Washington, DC 20002-4242
(202) 572-3037
FAX: (202) 336-5978
Dr. Jacqueline Remondet Wall
Director
E-MAIL: apaaccred@apa.org
URL: www.apa.org/ed/accreditation/

American Real Estate and Urban Economics Association (A)
c/o Travelink
404 BNA Drive, Suite 650
Nashville, TN 37217
(800) 242-0528
FAX: (615) 367-0012
Lindsay Buchanan CMP
Executive Director
E-MAIL: areuea@travelink.com
URL: www.areuea.org

American Society for Engineering Education (B)
1818 N Street, NW
Suite 600
Washington, DC 20036
(202) 331-3545
FAX: (202) 265-8504
Dr. Norman L. Fortenberry
Executive Director
E-MAIL: n.fortenberry@asee.org
URL: www.asee.org

American Society for Microbiology (C)
1752 N Street, NW
Washington, DC 20036
(202) 942-9264
Ms. Amy L. Chang
Director, Education Department
E-MAIL: education@asmusa.org
URL: www.asm.org

American Society for Microbiology Subcommittee on Postgraduate Educational Programs (D)
1752 N Street, NW
Washington, DC 20036-2804
(202) 942-9281
FAX: (202) 942-9353
Ms. Sue Williams
Program Coordinator
E-MAIL: certification@asmusa.org
URL: www.asm.org/cpep

American Society of Cytopathology Cytotechnology Programs Review Committee (CPRC) (E)
100 West 10th Street
Suite 605
Wilmington, DE 19801
(302) 543-6583
FAX: (302) 543-6597
Deborah M. Sheldon
Cytology Education Coordinator
E-MAIL: dmacintyre@cytopathology.org
URL: www.cytopathology.org

American Speech-Language-Hearing Association (ASHA) (F)
2200 Research Boulevard
Rockville, MD 20850
(301) 296-5700
Dr. Arlene A. Pietranton
Chief Executive Officer
E-MAIL: apietranton@asha.org
URL: www.asha.org

American Student Government Association (G)
412 NW 16th Avenue
Gainesville, FL 32601-4203
(352) 373-6907
FAX: (352) 373-8120
Mr. W. H. (Butch) Oxendine Jr.
Executive Director
E-MAIL: butch@asgaonline.com
URL: www.asgahome.org

American Veterinary Medical Association (H)
1931 North Meacham Road
Suite 100
Schaumburg, IL 60173
(800) 248-2862
FAX: (847) 925-1329
Dr. Karen Martens Brandt
Director Education and Research
E-MAIL: kbrandt@avma.org
URL: www.avma.org

APPA (I)
1643 Prince Street
Alexandria, VA 22314
(703) 684-1446
FAX: (703) 549-2772
E. Lander Medlin
Executive Vice President
E-MAIL: lander@appa.org
URL: www.appa.org

Association for Asian Studies (J)
825 Victors Way
Suite 310
Ann Arbor, MI 48108
(734) 665-2490
FAX: (734) 665-3801
Ms. Hilary Finchum-Sung
Executive Director
E-MAIL: hvfinchum@asian-studies.org
URL: www.asian-studies.org

Association for Biblical Higher Education Commission on Accreditation (K)
5850 T.G. Lee Boulevard
Suite 130
Orlando, FL 32822
(407) 207-0808
FAX: (407) 207-0840
Dr. Ronald C. Kroll
Director, Commission on Accreditation
E-MAIL: ron.kroll@abhe.org
URL: www.abhe.org

Association for Business Communication (L)
323 Shanks Hall (0112)
181 Turner Street, NW
Blacksburg, VA 24061
(540) 231-1939
Dr. Jim Dubinsky
Executive Director
E-MAIL: exec_director@businesscommunication.org
URL: www.businesscommunication.org

Association for Business Simulation and Experiential Learning (M)
University of South Carolina Aiken
School of Business Administration
471 University Parkway
Aiken, SC 29801
(803) 641-3340
Dr. Mick Fekula
VP/Executive Director
E-MAIL: mickf@usca.edu
URL: www.absel.org

The Association for Canadian Studies in the United States (ACSUS) (N)
Bridgewater State University
102 Tillinghast Hall
Bridgewater, MA 02325
(716) 645-8440
FAX: (716) 645-2166
Mr. James McHugh
President
E-MAIL: info@acsus.org
URL: www.acsus.org

Association for Collaborative Leadership (ACL) (O)
5329 Fayette Avenue
Madison, WI 53713
(608) 571-7096
E-MAIL: admin@national-acl.org
URL: www.national-acl.org

Association for Continuing Higher Education (P)
ETSU at Kingsport
1501 University Boulevard
Kingsport, TN 37660
(800) 807-2243
Dr. Rick Osborn
Interim Executive Vice President
E-MAIL: Osbornr@etsu.edu
URL: www.acheinc.org

Association for Education and Rehabilitation of the Blind and Visually Impaired AER Accreditation Program (Q)
5680 King Centre Drive
Suite 600
Alexandria, VA 22315
(703) 671-4500
FAX: (703) 671-6391
Ms. Janie Blome
Executive Director
E-MAIL: accreditation@aerbvi.org
URL: www.aerbvi.org

Association for Education in Journalism and Mass Communication (R)
234 Outlet Pointe Boulevard
Suite A
Columbia, SC 29210-5667
(803) 798-0271
FAX: (803) 772-3509
Ms. Jennifer H. McGill
Executive Director
E-MAIL: aejmchq@aol.com
URL: www.aejmc.org

Association for General and Liberal Studies (S)
428 5th Street
Columbus, IN 47201
(812) 376-7468
Ms. Joyce Lucke
Executive Director
E-MAIL: execdir@agls.org
URL: www.agls.org

Association for Information Systems (T)
PO Box 2712
Atlanta, GA 30301-2712
(404) 413-7445
Mr. Matthew Nelson
Associate Executive Director
E-MAIL: matt@aisnet.org
URL: aisnet.org

Association for Institutional Research (U)
1983 Centre Pointe Boulevard #101
Tallahassee, FL 32308
(850) 385-4155
FAX: (850) 385-5180
Dr. Christine M. Keller
Executive Director & CEO
E-MAIL: ckeller@airweb.org
URL: www.airweb.org

Association for Library and Information Science Education (ALISE) (V)
4 Lan Drive
Suite 310
Westford, MA 01886
(978) 674-6190
FAX: (978) 250-1117
Ms. Cambria Happ
Executive Director
E-MAIL: office@alise.org
URL: www.alise.org

Association for Prevention Teaching and Research (W)
1001 Connecticut Avenue, NW
Suite 610
Washington, DC 20036
(202) 463-0550
FAX: (202) 463-0555
Ms. Allison L. Lewis
Executive Director
E-MAIL: info@aptrweb.org
URL: www.aptrweb.org

Association for the Study of Higher Education (ASHE) (X)
UNLV
4505 South Maryland Parkway
Box 453068
Las Vegas, NV 89154-3068
(702) 895-2737
Dr. Jason P. Guilbeau
Executive Director
E-MAIL: ASHE@unlv.edu
URL: www.ashe.ws

Association for Theatre in Higher Education (ATHE) (Y)
PO Box 4369
Boulder, CO 80306-4369
(303) 530-3490
FAX: (855) 494-6777
Ms. Aimee Zygmonski
Executive Director
E-MAIL: aimee@athe.org
URL: www.athe.org

Association of Advanced Rabbinical and Talmudic Schools Accreditation Commission (Z)
11 Broadway
Suite 405
New York, NY 10004
(212) 363-1991
FAX: (212) 533-5335
Dr. Bernard Fryshman
Interim Executive Director
E-MAIL: office@aarts-schools.org

Association of American Colleges & Universities (a)
1818 R Street, NW
Washington, DC 20009
(202) 387-3760
Dr. Lynn Pasquerella
President
E-MAIL: commish@aacu.org
URL: www.aacu.org

Association of American Law Schools (b)
1614 20th Street, NW
Washington, DC 20009-1001
(202) 296-1526
FAX: (202) 296-8869
Ms. Judith Areen
Executive Director
E-MAIL: info@aals.org
URL: www.aals.org

Association of American Medical Colleges (c)
655 K Street, NW
Suite 100
Washington, DC 20001-2399
(202) 828-0460
FAX: (202) 862-6161
Dr. David J. Skorton
President/CEO
E-MAIL: aamcpresident@aamc.org
URL: www.aamc.org

Association of American Universities (d)
1200 New York Avenue, NW
Suite 550
Washington, DC 20005
(202) 408-7500
FAX: (202) 408-8184
Dr. Mary Sue Coleman
President
E-MAIL: leah.norton@aau.edu
URL: www.aau.edu

Association of Catholic Colleges and Universities (e)
1 Dupont Circle, NW
Suite 650
Washington, DC 20036
(202) 457-0650
FAX: (202) 728-0977
Rev. Dennis H. Holtschneider Ph.D.
President/CEO
E-MAIL: accu@accunet.org
URL: www.accunet.org

Association of College and University Housing Officers-International (f)
1445 Summit Street
Columbus, OH 43201-2105
(614) 292-0099
FAX: (614) 292-3205
Ms. Mary DeNiro
CEO/Executive Director
E-MAIL: office@acuho-i.org
URL: www.acuho-i.org

Association for College and University Religious Affairs (g)
Stanford University
Office for Religious Life
Memorial Church
Stanford, CA 94305-2090
(650) 725-0090
Rev.Dr. Joanne Sanders
President
E-MAIL: joanne.sanders@stanford.edu
URL: www.acurachaplains.org

Association of College Unions International (h)
One City Centre, Suite 200
120 West Seventh Street
Bloomington, IN 47404-3839
(812) 245-2284
Dr. John Taylor
Chief Executive Officer
E-MAIL: acui@acui.org
URL: www.acui.org

Association of Collegiate Conference and Events Directors-International (i)
2900 South College Avenue
Suite 3B
Fort Collins, CO 80525
(970) 449-4960, ext. 4
FAX: (970) 449-4965
Ms. Karen Nedbal
Executive Director
E-MAIL: karen@acced-i.org
URL: www.acced-i.org

Association of Collegiate Schools of Architecture (j)
1735 New York Avenue, NW
3rd Floor
Washington, DC 20006
(202) 785-2324
Michael Monti Ph.D.
Executive Director
E-MAIL: mmonti@acsa-arch.org
URL: www.acsa-arch.org

Higher Education Associations

Association of Collegiate Schools of Planning (A)
c/o Donna Dodd, Executive Director
2910 Kerry Forest Parkway, D4-206
Tallahassee, FL 32309
(850) 385-2054
Dr. Marlon Boarnet
President
E-MAIL: presidentsoffice@acsp.org
URL: www.acsp.org

Association of Community College Trustees (B)
1101 17th Street NW
Suite 300
Washington, DC 20036
(202) 775-4667
Mr. J. Noah Brown
President and CEO
E-MAIL: president@acct.org
URL: www.acct.org

Association of Departments of English (C)
85 Broad Street
Suite 500
New York, NY 10004-2434
(646) 576-5137
Dr. Douglas Steward
Director
E-MAIL: dsteward@mla.org
URL: ade.mla.org

Association of Departments of Foreign Languages (D)
85 Broad Street
Suite 500
New York, NY 10004-2434
(646) 576-5140
Dr. Dennis Looney
Director
E-MAIL: dlooney@mla.org
URL: www.adfl.org

Association of Governing Boards of Universities and Colleges (E)
1133 20th Street, NW
Suite 300
Washington, DC 20036
(202) 296-8400
FAX: (202) 223-7053
Mr. Henry V. Stoever
President and CEO
E-MAIL: hstoever@agb.org
URL: www.agb.org

Association of Graduate Liberal Studies Programs (F)
c/o Rice University
6100 Main Street, MS-550
Houston, TX 77005
(713) 348-6118
Mr. Michael Garval
President
E-MAIL: info@aglsp.org
URL: www.aglsp.org

Association of International Education Administrators-AIEA (G)
811 Ninth Street
Suite 215
Durham, NC 27705
(919) 893-4980
Dr. Darla K. Deardorff
Executive Director
E-MAIL: info@aieaworld.org
URL: www.aieaworld.org

Association of Jesuit Colleges and Universities (H)
1 Dupont Circle, NW
Suite 405
Washington, DC 20036
(202) 862-9893
FAX: (202) 862-8523
Rev. Michael J. Sheeran S.J.
President
E-MAIL: info@ajcunet.edu
URL: www.ajcunet.edu

Association of Military Colleges and Schools of the United States (I)
Fairfax, VA 22033
(703) 272-8406
Ray Rottman
Executive Director
E-MAIL: amcsus1@gmail.com
URL: www.amcsus.org

Association of Performing Arts Professionals (J)
919 18th Street, NW
Suite 650
Washington, DC 20006
(202) 833-2787
FAX: (202) 833-1543
Ms. Margaret Stevens
Director, Executive Affairs
E-MAIL: info@apap365.org
URL: www.apap365.org

Association of Practical Theology (K)
,
(214) 768-2349
Evelyn L. Parker PhD
President
E-MAIL: eparker@yale.edu
URL: www.practicaltheology.org

Association of Presbyterian Colleges and Universities (L)
c/o Agnes Scott College
Box 1102
141 E. College Avenue
Decatur, GA 30030
(470) 443-1948
Mr. Jeff Arnold
Executive Director
E-MAIL: jeff.arnold@presbyteriancolleges.org
URL: www.presbyteriancolleges.org

Association of Public and Land-Grant Universities (M)
1307 New York Avenue, NW
Suite 400
Washington, DC 20005-4722
(202) 478-6040
FAX: (202) 478-6046
M. Peter McPherson
President
E-MAIL: pmcpherson@aplu.org
URL: www.aplu.org

Association of Research Libraries (N)
21 Dupont Circle, NW
Suite 800
Washington, DC 20036
(202) 296-2296
FAX: (202) 872-0884
Mary Lee Kennedy
Executive Director
E-MAIL: mkennedy@arl.org
URL: www.arl.org

Association of Schools of Allied Health Professions (O)
122 C Street, NW
Suite 200
Washington, DC 20001-2151
(202) 237-6481
FAX: (202) 237-6485
Mr. John Colbert
Executive Director
E-MAIL: john@asahp.org
URL: www.asahp.org

Association of Specialized and Professional Accreditors (P)
3304 North Broadway Street
#214
Chicago, IL 60657
(773) 857-7900
Mr. Joseph Vibert
Executive Director
E-MAIL: aspa@aspa-usa.org
URL: www.aspa-usa.org

Association of Teacher Educators (Q)
PO Box 793
Manassas, VA 20113
(703) 659-1708
FAX: (703) 595-4792
Dr. David Ritchey
Executive Director
E-MAIL: dritchey@ate1.org
URL: www.ate1.org

The Association of Technology, Management, and Applied Engineering (ATMAE) (R)
3801 Lake Boone Trail
Suite 190
Raleigh, NC 27607
(919) 635-8335
FAX: (919) 779-5642
Mr. Jim Thompson IOM, CAE
Executive Director
E-MAIL: executive@atmae.org
URL: www.atmae.org

Association of Theological Schools in the United States and Canada The Commission on Accrediting (S)
10 Summit Park Drive
Pittsburgh, PA 15275-1110
(412) 788-6505
FAX: (412) 788-6510
Dr. Frank M. Yamada
Executive Director
E-MAIL: yamada@ats.edu
URL: www.ats.edu

Association of University Presses (T)
1412 Broadway
Suite 2135
New York, NY 10018
(212) 989-1010
FAX: (212) 989-0275
Peter M. Berkery Jr.
Executive Director
E-MAIL: pberkery@aupresses.org
URL: www.aupresses.org

Association of University Programs in Health Administration (U)
1730 M Street, NW
Suite 407
Washington, DC 20036
(202) 763-7283
Gerald L. Glandon Ph.D.
President & CEO
E-MAIL: gglandon@aupha.org
URL: www.aupha.org

Association of University Research Parks (V)
9070 South Rita Road
Suite 1750
Tucson, AZ 85747
(520) 529-2521
Mr. Brian Darmody
Chief Executive Officer
E-MAIL: info@aurp.net
URL: www.aurp.net

Aviation Accreditation Board International (W)
115 S. 8th Street
Suite 102
Opelika, AL 36801
(334) 749-9359
FAX: (334) 749-9360
Dr. Gary Northam
President
E-MAIL: bayenva@auburn.edu
URL: www.aabi.aero

Big Ten Academic Alliance (X)
1819 South Neil Street
Suite D
Champaign, IL 61820-7271
(217) 333-8475
FAX: (217) 244-7127
Mr. Keith Marshall
Executive Director
E-MAIL: info@btaa.org
URL: www.btaa.org

Broadcast Education Association (Y)
1771 N Street, NW
Washington, DC 20036-2891
(202) 602-0584
FAX: (202) 609-9940
Ms. Heather Birks
Executive Director
E-MAIL: heather@beaweb.org
URL: www.beaweb.org

Career Education Colleges & Universities (Z)
1530 Wilson Boulevard
Suite 1050
Arlington, VA 22209
(571) 970-3941
FAX: (571) 970-6753
Mr. Steve Gunderson
President and CEO
E-MAIL: president@career.org
URL: www.career.org

Carnegie Foundation for the Advancement of Teaching (a)
51 Vista Lane
Stanford, CA 94305
(650) 566-5100
FAX: (650) 326-0278
Dr. Anthony S. Bryk
President
URL: www.carnegiefoundation.org

CETE (Center on Education and Training for Employment) (b)
The Ohio State University
1900 Kenny Road
Columbus, OH 43210-1016
(614) 292-6869
FAX: (614) 292-3742
Ms. Traci Lepicki
Associate Director
E-MAIL: cete@osu.edu
URL: cete.osu.edu

College and University Professional Association for Human Resources (CUPA-HR) (c)
1811 Commons Point Drive
Knoxville, TN 37932
(877) 287-2474
FAX: (865) 637-7674
Mr. Andy Brantley
President & Chief Executive Officer
E-MAIL: memberservice@cupahr.org
URL: www.cupahr.org

College Art Association (d)
50 Broadway
21st Floor
New York, NY 10004
(212) 691-1051
FAX: (212) 627-2381
Mr. David Raizman
Interim Executive Director
E-MAIL: nyoffice@collegeart.org
URL: www.collegeart.org

The College Board (e)
250 Vesey Street
New York, NY 10281
(212) 713-8000
David Coleman
President and CEO
URL: www.collegeboard.org

College English Association (f)
1100 E. Fifth Street
Anderson, IN 46012
(765) 641-4424
Mr. Scott Borders
Executive Director
E-MAIL: cea.english@gmail.com
URL: cea-web.org

College Media Association (g)
355 Lexington Avenue
15th Floor
New York, NY 10017
(212) 297-2195
Meredith Taylor
Executive Director
E-MAIL: mltaylor@kellencompany.com
URL: www.collegemedia.org

Columbia Scholastic Press Association (h)
Columbia University
90 Morningside Drive
Suite B01
New York, NY 10027
(212) 854-9400
FAX: (212) 854-9401
Mr. Edmund J. Sullivan
Executive Director
E-MAIL: cspa@columbia.edu
URL: www.columbia.edu/cu/cspa

Commission on Accreditation for Health Informatics and Information Management Education (CAHIIM) (i)
200 E. Randolph Street
Suite 5100
Chicago, IL 60601
(312) 235-3255
Dr. Angela Kennedy
Chief Executive Director
E-MAIL: info@cahiim.org
URL: www.cahiim.org

Commission on Accreditation of Allied Health Education Programs (j)
25400 US Hwy 19 N
Suite 158
Clearwater, FL 33763
(727) 210-2350
FAX: (727) 210-2354
Dr. Kathleen Megivern J.D.
Executive Director
E-MAIL: megivern@caahep.org
URL: www.caahep.org

Commission on Accreditation of Healthcare Management Education (CAHME) (A)
PO Box 911
Spring House, PA 19477
(301) 298-1825
Dr. Anthony Stanowski
President & CEO
E-MAIL: astanowski@cahme.org
URL: www.cahme.org

Commission on Collegiate Nursing Education (CCNE) (B)
655 K Street NW
Suite 750
Washington, DC 20001
(202) 887-6791
FAX: (202) 887-8476
Dr. Jennifer Butlin
Executive Director
E-MAIL: jbutlin@ccneaccreditation.org
URL: www.ccneaccreditation.org

Commission on Dental Accreditation (C)
211 East Chicago Avenue
Suite 1900
Chicago, IL 60611
(312) 440-4653
FAX: (312) 587-5107
Dr. Sherin Tooks
Director
E-MAIL: tookss@ada.org
URL: www.ada.org/en/coda

Commission on English Language Program Accreditation (CEA) (D)
1001 North Fairfax Street
Suite 630
Alexandria, VA 22314
(703) 665-3400
Dr. Mary Reeves
Executive Director
E-MAIL: mhreeves@cea-accredit.org
URL: www.cea-accredit.org

The Commission on Independent Colleges and Universities (CICU) in New York (E)
17 Elk Street
Albany, NY 12207
(518) 436-4781
FAX: (518) 436-0417
Mrs. Mary Beth Labate
President
E-MAIL: info@cicu.org
URL: www.cicu.org

Commission on Massage Therapy Accreditation (F)
2101 Wilson Boulevard
Suite 302
Arlington, VA 22201
(202) 888-6790
FAX: (202) 888-6787
Ms. Dawn Hogue
Executive Director
E-MAIL: dhogue@comta.org
URL: www.comta.org

Commission on Opticianry Accreditation (G)
PO Box 592
Canton, NY 13617
(703) 468-0566
Mrs. Debra White
Director of Accreditation
E-MAIL: director@coaccreditation.com
URL: www.coaccreditation.com

Committee on Accreditation for Education in Neurodiagnostic Technology (H)
1449 Hill Street
Whitinsville, MA 01588
(978) 338-6300
FAX: (978) 832-2638
Dr. Jackie Long-Goding RRT-NPS
Executive Director
E-MAIL: office@coa-ndt.org
URL: www.coa-ndt.org

Committee on Accreditation for Education Programs for Kinesiotherapy (CoA-KT) (I)
University of Southern Mississippi
118 College Drive #5122
Hattiesburg, MS 39406-0002
(601) 266-5371
Jerry W. Purvis
E-MAIL: jerry.purvis@usm.edu
URL: www.coakt.org

Committee on Accreditation for the Exercise Sciences (J)
401 West Michigan Street
Indianapolis, IN 46202
(317) 777-1135
FAX: (317) 634-7817
Mr. William Coale
Director
E-MAIL: wcoale@coaes.org
URL: www.coaes.org

Committee on Accreditation for Polysomnographic Technologist Education (K)
1711 Frank Avenue
New Bern, NC 28560
(252) 626-3238
Ms. Karen Monarchy Rowe
Executive Director
E-MAIL: karenmonarchy@suddenlink.net
URL: caahep.org

Committee on Accreditation of Educational Programs for the Emergency Medical Services Professions (L)
8301 Lakeview Parkway
Suite 111-312
Rowlett, TX 75088
(214) 703-8445, ext. 112
FAX: (214) 703-8992
Dr. George W. Hatch Jr.
Executive Director
E-MAIL: george@coaemsp.org
URL: www.coaemsp.org

Conference on College Composition and Communication (M)
1111 West Kenyon Road
Urbana, IL 61801-1096
(877) 369-6283
FAX: (217) 328-0977
Dr. Jessie L. Moore
Secretary
E-MAIL: cccc@ncte.org
URL: cccc.ncte.org

Council for Accreditation of Counseling and Related Educational Programs (CACREP) (N)
1001 North Fairfax Street
Suite 510
Alexandria, VA 22314
(703) 535-5990
FAX: (703) 739-6209
Dr. M. Sylvia Fernandez
President and CEO
E-MAIL: cacrep@cacrep.org
URL: www.cacrep.org

Council for Adult and Experiential Learning (O)
55 East Monroe Street
Suite 2710
Chicago, IL 60603
(312) 499-2600
FAX: (312) 499-2601
Ms. Beth Doyle
Vice Presiden of Partner Services
E-MAIL: bdoyle@cael.org
URL: www.cael.org

Council for Advancement and Support of Education (P)
1307 New York Avenue, NW
Suite 1000
Washington, DC 20005-4701
(202) 328-2273
FAX: (202) 387-4973
Ms. Sue Cunningham
President and CEO
E-MAIL: president@case.org
URL: www.case.org

Council for Agricultural Science and Technology (CAST) (Q)
4420 West Lincoln Way
Ames, IA 50014-3447
(515) 292-2125
Mr. Kent G. Schescke
Executive Vice President
E-MAIL: cast@cast-science.org
URL: www.cast-science.org

Council for Aid to Education (R)
215 Lexington Avenue
16th Floor
New York, NY 10016-6023
(212) 661-5800
FAX: (212) 661-9766
Dr. Roger Benjamin
President & CEO
E-MAIL: roger@cae.org
URL: www.cae.org

Council for Christian Colleges & Universities (S)
321 8th Street, NE
Washington, DC 20002-6107
(202) 546-8713
FAX: (202) 546-8913
Shirley V. Hoogstra J.D.
President
E-MAIL: council@cccu.org
URL: www.cccu.org

Council for Economic Education (T)
122 East 42nd Street
Suite 2600
New York, NY 10168
(212) 730-7007
FAX: (212) 730-1793
Ms. Nan Morrison
President and CEO
E-MAIL: njmorrison@councilforeconed.org
URL: www.councilforeconed.org

Council for Higher Education Accreditation (U)
1 Dupont Circle, NW
Suite 510
Washington, DC 20036
(202) 955-6126
FAX: (202) 955-6129
Dr. Judith Eaton
President
E-MAIL: chea@chea.org
URL: www.chea.org

Council for Interior Design Accreditation (CIDA) (formerly FIDER) (V)
206 Grandville Avenue
Suite 350
Grand Rapids, MI 49503-4014
(616) 458-0400
FAX: (616) 458-0460
Ms. Holly Mattson
Executive Director
E-MAIL: info@accredit-id.org
URL: www.accredit-id.org

Council for Research in Music Education (W)
University of Illinois Press
1325 South Oak Street
Champaign, IL 61820
(217) 244-6310
FAX: (217) 244-9910
Dr. Janet R. Barrett
Editor
E-MAIL: janetbar@illinois.edu
URL: bcrme.press.illinois.edu

Council for the Accreditation of Educator Preparation (X)
1140 19th Street, NW
Suite 400
Washington, DC 20036
(202) 223-0077
Mr. Christopher Koch
President
E-MAIL: caep@caepnet.org
URL: www.caepnet.org

Council for the Advancement of Standards in Higher Education (Y)
PO Box 750
Cabot, AR 72023
(202) 862-1400
FAX: (202) 296-3286
Dr. Deborah Garrett
Interim Executive Director
E-MAIL: executive_director@cas.edu
URL: www.cas.edu

Council of Colleges of Acupuncture and Oriental Medicine (CCAOM) (Z)
1501 Sulgrave Avenue
Suite 301
Baltimore, MD 21209
(410) 464-6041
FAX: (410) 464-6042
Ms. Roberta Herman MBA, CAE
Executive Director
E-MAIL: rherman@ccaom.org
URL: www.ccaom.org

Council of Colleges of Arts & Sciences (a)
c/o The College of William and Mary
PO Box 8795
Williamsburg, VA 23187-8795
(757) 221-1784
FAX: (757) 221-1776
Amber Elaine Cox MSW
Executive Director
E-MAIL: ccas@wm.edu
URL: www.ccas.net

Council of Graduate Schools (b)
1 Dupont Circle, NW
Suite 230
Washington, DC 20036-1146
(202) 223-3791
Dr. Suzanne Ortega
President
E-MAIL: president@cgs.nche.edu
URL: www.cgsnet.org

Council of Independent Colleges (c)
1 Dupont Circle, NW
Suite 320
Washington, DC 20036-1142
(202) 466-7230
Dr. Richard Ekman
President
E-MAIL: cic@cic.nche.edu
URL: www.cic.edu

The Council of Writing Program Administrators (d)
University of Arkansas at Little Rock
College of Social Sciences and Communication
2801 S. University Avenue
Little Rock, AR 72204
(501) 569-8022
Ms. Sherry Rankins-Robertson
Secretary
E-MAIL: cwpasecretary@gmail.com
URL: www.wpacouncil.org

Council on Academic Accreditation in Audiology and Speech-Language Pathology American Speech-Language-Hearing Association (e)
2200 Research Boulevard #310
Rockville, MD 20850
(301) 296-5700
Ms. Kimberlee Moore
Director of Accreditation
E-MAIL: accreditation@asha.org
URL: caa.asha.org

Council on Accreditation of Nurse Anesthesia Educational Programs (COA) (f)
222 South Prospect Avenue
Park Ridge, IL 60068-4001
(847) 655-1160
Francis Gerbasi PhD, CRNA
Chief Executive Officer
E-MAIL: fgerbasi@coacrna.org
URL: www.coacrna.org

Council on Accreditation for Two-Year Colleges (g)
200 South 14th Street
Parsons, KS 67357
(620) 820-1223
FAX: (620) 421-0921
Dr. George Knox
Executive Director
E-MAIL: meganf@labette.edu
URL: www.catyc.com

Council on Accreditation of Parks, Recreation, Tourism and Related Professions (COAPRT) (h)
1401 Marvin Road NE
Suite 307, #172
Lacey, WA 98516
(360) 205-2096
FAX: (360) 453-7893
Mr. Larry Otos
Operations Manager
E-MAIL: COAPRT@accreditationcouncil.org
URL: https://accreditationcouncil.org

Council on Chiropractic Education (i)
8049 North 85th Way
Scottsdale, AZ 85258-4321
(480) 443-8877
FAX: (480) 483-7333
Craig S. Little D.C., M.Ed
President
E-MAIL: cce@cce-usa.org
URL: www.cce-usa.org

Council on Education for Public Health (j)
1010 Wayne Avenue
Suite 220
Silver Spring, MD 20910
(202) 789-1050
FAX: (202) 789-1895
Dr. Laura Rasar King
Executive Director
E-MAIL: lking@ceph.org
URL: www.ceph.org

Council on Governmental Relations (A)
1200 New York Avenue, NW
Suite 460
Washington, DC 20005
(202) 289-6655
Fax: (202) 289-6698
Ms. Wendy Streitz
President
E-mail: wstreitz@cogr.edu
URL: www.cogr.edu

Council on Higher Education Solutions for Adults (B)
104 Johnson Street
Marshall, TX 75670
(903) 472-2762
Dr. Tracy Andrus
President/CEO
E-mail: tandrus@chesa1.com
URL: www.chesa1.com

Council on Naturopathic Medical Education (C)
PO Box 178
Great Barrington, MA 01230
(413) 528-8877
Dr. Daniel Seitz J.D., Ed.D
Executive Director
E-mail: danseitz@cnme.org
URL: www.cnme.org

Council on Occupational Education (D)
7840 Roswell Road
Building 300, Suite 325
Atlanta, GA 30350
(800) 917-2081
Fax: (770) 396-3790
Dr. Gary Puckett
President/Executive Director
E-mail: gary.puckett@council.org
URL: www.council.org

Council on Podiatric Medical Education (E)
9312 Old Georgetown Road
Bethesda, MD 20814
(301) 581-9200
Fax: (301) 571-4903
Dr. Heather M. Stagliano
Director
E-mail: hmstagliano@cpme.org
URL: www.cpme.org

Council on Social Work Education (F)
1701 Duke Street
Suite 200
Alexandria, VA 22314-3457
(703) 519-2048
Fax: (703) 683-8099
Dr. Jo Ann Regan
VP of Education
E-mail: jregan@cswe.org
URL: www.cswe.org

Council on Undergraduate Research (G)
734 15th Street, NW
Suite 850
Washington, DC 20005
(202) 783-4810
Fax: (202) 783-4811
Mrs. Lindsay L. Currie
Executive Officer
E-mail: jdouglas@cur.org
URL: www.cur.org

CSAB, Inc. (H)
417 Terrace Way
Towson, MD 21204-3725
(410) 339-5456
Ms. Liz Glazer
Executive Director
E-mail: lglazer@csab.org
URL: www.csab.org

Cultural Vistas (I)
233 Broadway
Suite 2120
New York, NY 10279
(212) 497-3500
Fax: (212) 497-3535
Ms. Jennifer Clinton
President & CEO
E-mail: info@culturalvistas.org
URL: www.culturalvistas.org

Decision Sciences Institute (J)
University of Houston
C.T. Bauer College of Business
4750 Calhoun Road, Suite 325A
Houston, TX 77204-6021
(713) 743-4815
Ms. Vivian Landrum
Executive Director
E-mail: info@decisionsciences.org
URL: www.decisionsciences.org

Distance Education Accrediting Commission (K)
1101 17th Street, NW
Suite 808
Washington, DC 20036
(202) 234-5100
Dr. Leah K. Matthews
Executive Director
E-mail: info@deac.org
URL: www.deac.org

Education Commission of the States (L)
700 Broadway
Suite 810
Denver, CO 80203-3442
(303) 299-3600
Fax: (303) 296-8332
Mr. Jeremy Anderson
President
E-mail: ecs@ecs.org
URL: www.ecs.org

Education Development Center (M)
43 Foundry Avenue
Waltham, MA 02453-8313
(617) 969-7100
Fax: (617) 969-5979
Mr. David Offensend
President and CEO
E-mail: contact@edc.org
URL: www.edc.org

EDUCAUSE (N)
1150 18th Street, NW
Suite 900
Washington, DC 20036-3816
(202) 872-4200
Fax: (202) 872-4318
John O'Brien Ph.D.
President and CEO
E-mail: info@educause.edu
URL: www.educause.edu

FHI 360 (O)
359 Blackwell Street
Suite 200
Durham, NC 27701
(919) 544-7040
Fax: (919) 544-7261
Mr. Patrick C. Fine
Chief Executive Officer
URL: www.fhi360.org

Financial Management Association International (P)
University of South Florida
Muma College of Business
4202 East Fowler Avenue, BSN 3403
Tampa, FL 33620-5500
(813) 974-2084
Fax: (813) 974-3318
Ms. Michelle Lui
Executive Director
E-mail: fma@coba.usf.edu
URL: www.fma.org

Friends Association for Higher Education (Q)
1501 Cherry Street
Philadelphia, PA 19102
(215) 241-7116
Fax: (215) 241-7078
Ms. Kimberly Haas
Director
E-mail: fahe@quaker.org
URL: www.quakerfahe.com

The Gerontological Society of America (R)
1220 L Street, NW
Suite 901
Washington, DC 20005-4001
(202) 587-2821
Mr. James Appleby
CEO
E-mail: geron@geron.org
URL: www.geron.org

Graduate Record Examinations Board (S)
Educational Testing Service
660 Rosedale Road
Princeton, NJ 08541
(609) 683-2014
Fax: (609) 683-2040
Dr. David G. Payne
Vice President & COO of Global Education Division
E-mail: dpayne@ets.org
URL: www.ets.org/highered

H. Wiley Hitchcock Institute for Studies in American Music (T)
Brooklyn College, CUNY
2900 Bedford Avenue
Brooklyn, NY 11210-2889
(718) 951-5655
Dr. Jeffrey J. Taylor
Director
E-mail: isam@brooklyn.cuny.edu
URL: www.hisam.org

HEATH Resource Center at the National Youth Transitions Center The George Washington University Graduate School of Education & Human Development (U)
2134 G Street, NW
Suite 308
Washington, DC 20052-0001
E-mail: askheath@gwu.edu
URL: www.heath.gwu.edu

Higher Education Resource Services (HERS) (V)
University of Denver
1901 East Asbury Avenue
Suite 212
Denver, CO 80208
(303) 871-6866
Fax: (303) 871-6766
Dr. Verna Fitzsimmons
President/Executive Director
E-mail: vfitzsimmons@hersnetwork.org
URL: www.hersnetwork.org

Higher Learning Commission (W)
230 South LaSalle Street
Suite 7-500
Chicago, IL 60604-1411
(312) 263-0456 / (800) 621-7440
Fax: (312) 263-7462
Dr. Barbara Gellman-Danley
President
E-mail: info@hlcommission.org
URL: hlcommission.org

Hispanic Association of Colleges and Universities (X)
8415 Datapoint Drive
Suite 400
San Antonio, TX 78229
(210) 692-3805
Fax: (210) 692-0823
Dr. Antonio R. Flores
President and CEO
E-mail: hacu@hacu.net
URL: www.hacu.net

IACLEA (International Association of Campus Law Enforcement Administrators) (Y)
1110 Bonifant Street
Suite 330
Silver Spring, MD 20910
(855) 442-2532
Fax: (202) 618-8841
Ms. Sue Riseling
Executive Director
E-mail: sriseling@iaclea.org
URL: www.iaclea.org

The Institute for Higher Education Policy (Z)
1825 K Street, NW
Suite 720
Washington, DC 20006
(202) 861-8223
Fax: (202) 861-9307
Michelle A. Cooper Ph.D.
President
E-mail: institute@ihep.org
URL: www.ihep.org

Institute of International Education (a)
809 United Nations Plaza
New York, NY 10017-3580
(212) 883-8200
Fax: (212) 984-5452
E-mail: info@iie.org
URL: www.iie.org

Institute of International Education Council for International Exchange of Scholars (b)
1400 K Street, NW
Suite 700
Washington, DC 20005
(202) 686-4000
Fax: (202) 686-4029
E-mail: scholars@iie.org
URL: www.cies.org

Intercollegiate Broadcasting System, Inc. (c)
367 Windsor Highway
New Windsor, NY 12553-7900
(845) 565-0003
Mr. Fritz Kass
CEO
E-mail: ibs@ibsradio.org
URL: www.collegeradio.tv

International Accreditation Council for Business Education (d)
11374 Strang Line Road
Lenexa, KS 66215
(913) 631-3009
Fax: (913) 631-9154
Dr. Phyllis Okrepkie
President
E-mail: iacbe@iacbe.org
URL: www.iacbe.org

International Association of Baptist Colleges and Universities (e)
Samford University
800 Lakeshore Drive
Birmingham, AL 35229
(205) 726-2036
Mrs. Ashley Hill
Executive Secretary
E-mail: ashleyhill@baptistschools.org
URL: www.baptistschools.org

International Communication Association (f)
1500 21st Street, NW
Washington, DC 20036
(202) 955-1444
Fax: (202) 955-1448
Ms. Laura Sawyer
Executive Director
E-mail: lsawyer@icahdq.org
URL: www.icahdq.org

International Council on Education for Teaching (g)
5201 University Boulevard, KL-429A
Laredo, TX 78041
(956) 326-2420
Fax: (956) 326-2419
James O'Meara
President
E-mail: president@icet4u.org
URL: www.icet4u.org

International Fire Service Accreditation Congress (h)
1723 W. Tyler Avenue
Stillwater, OK 74078
(405) 744-8303
Fax: (405) 744-7377
Director
E-mail: admin@ifsac.org
URL: ifsac.org

Joint Review Committee on Education in Cardiovascular Technology (JRC-CVT) (i)
1449 Hill Street
Whitinsville, MA 01588-1032
(978) 456-5594
Fax: (727) 210-2354
Ms. Jackie Long-Goding
Executive Director
E-mail: office@jrccvt.org
URL: www.jrccvt.org

Joint Review Committee on Education in Diagnostic Medical Sonography (j)
6021 University Boulevard
Suite 500
Ellicott City, MD 21043
(443) 973-3251
Fax: (866) 738-3444
Mr. Gerry Magat MS
Executive Director
E-mail: mail@jrcdms.org
URL: www.jrcdms.org

Joint Review Committee on Education in Radiologic Technology (A)
20 North Wacker Drive
Suite 2850
Chicago, IL 60606-3182
(312) 704-5300
FAX: (312) 704-5304
Leslie F. Winter
Chief Executive Officer
E-MAIL: lwinter@jrcert.org
URL: www.jrcert.org

Joint Review Committee on Educational Programs in Nuclear Medicine Technology (B)
820 West Danforth Road
Suite B1
Edmond, OK 73003
(405) 285-0546
FAX: (405) 285-0579
Ms. Jan M. Winn
Executive Director
E-MAIL: mail@jrcnmt.org
URL: www.jrcnmt.org

Journalism Association of Community Colleges (C)
c/o CNPA Services, Inc.
2701 K Street
Sacramento, CA 95816-5131
(916) 288-6021
FAX: (916) 288-6002
Mr. Joe Wirt
Administrator
E-MAIL: joe@cnpa.com
URL: jacconline.org

Landscape Architectural Accreditation Board American Society of Landscape Architects (D)
636 Eye Street, NW
Washington, DC 20001-3736
(202) 216-2359
FAX: (202) 898-1185
Mr. Kristopher Pritchard
Accreditation & Education Director
E-MAIL: kpritchard@asla.org
URL: www.asla.org/laab

Laspau (E)
25 Mount Auburn Street
Suite 203
Cambridge, MA 02138-6095
(617) 495-5255
FAX: (617) 495-8990
Ms. Angelica Natera
Executive Director
E-MAIL: angelica_natera@harvard.edu
URL: www.laspau.harvard.edu

Law School Admission Council (F)
662 Penn Street
Newtown, PA 18940
(215) 968-1162
Ms. Kellye Testy
President and CEO
E-MAIL: fwilliams@lsac.org
URL: www.lsac.org

Liaison Committee on Medical Education (LCME) American Medical Association (G)
330 North Wabash
Suite 39300
Chicago, IL 60611-5885
(312) 464-4933
Barbara Barzansky Ph.D.,MHPE
LCME Co-Secretary
E-MAIL: barbara.barzansky@ama-assn.org
URL: www.lcme.org

Linguistic Society of America (H)
522 21st Street, NW
Suite 120
Washington, DC 20006-5012
(202) 835-1714
FAX: (202) 835-1717
Ms. Alyson Reed
Executive Director
E-MAIL: lsa@lsadc.org
URL: www.linguisticsociety.org

Literacy Research Association, Inc. (I)
PO Box 3105
LaGrange, GA 30241
(706) 443-1334
FAX: (706) 883-8215
Caitlin Hyatt
Executive Director
E-MAIL: chyatt@asginfo.net
URL: www.LiteracyResearchAssociation.org

Lutheran Educational Conference of North America (J)
PMB #377
2601 South Minnesota Avenue
Suite 105
Sioux Falls, SD 57105-4750
(605) 271-9894
FAX: (605) 271-9895
Ms. Wendy Hoyne
Director of Business Operations
E-MAIL: hoyne@lutherancolleges.org
URL: www.lutherancolleges.org

Marketing EDGE (K)
500 7th Avenue
8th Floor
New York, NY 10018
(212) 790-1512
Terri L. Bartlett
President
E-MAIL: admin@marketingedge.org
URL: www.marketingedge.org

Medical Assisting Education Review Board (L)
20 N. Wacker Drive
Suite 1575
Chicago, IL 60606-2963
(800) 228-2262
FAX: (312) 899-1259
Mr. Jim Hardman
Assistant Director of Accreditation
E-MAIL: jhardman@maerb.org
URL: www.maerb.org

Middle States Commission on Higher Education (M)
3624 Market Street
Second Floor West
Philadelphia, PA 19104-2680
(267) 284-5025
FAX: (215) 662-5501
Dr. Elizabeth H. Sibolski
President
E-MAIL: info@msche.org
URL: www.msche.org

Midwest Association of Colleges and Employers (N)
3601 East Joppa Road
Baltimore, MD 21234
(410) 931-8100
FAX: (410) 931-8111
E-MAIL: admin@mwace.org
URL: www.mwace.org

Midwestern Higher Education Compact (MHEC) (O)
105 Fifth Avenue South
Suite 450
Minneapolis, MN 55401
(612) 677-2777
FAX: (612) 767-3353
Ms. Susan G. Heegaard
President
E-MAIL: susanh@mhec.org
URL: www.mhec.org

Midwifery Education Accreditation Council (MEAC) (P)
850 Mt. Pleasant Avenue
Ann Arbor, MI 48103
(360) 466-2080, ext. 0
Ms. Beatrix Packmohr
Executive Director
E-MAIL: info@meacschools.org
URL: www.meacschools.org

Modern Language Association (Q)
85 Broad Street
Suite 500
New York, NY 10004-2434
(646) 576-5000
FAX: (646) 458-0030
Dr. Paula M. Krebs
Executive Director
E-MAIL: execdirector@mla.org
URL: www.mla.org

Montessori Accreditation Council for Teacher Education (MACTE) (R)
420 Park Street
Charlottesville, VA 22902
(434) 202-7793
Dr. Rebecca Pelton
President
E-MAIL: rebecca@macte.org
URL: www.macte.org

NACADA: The Global Community for Academic Advising (S)
Kansas State University
2323 Anderson Avenue
Suite 225
Manhattan, KS 66502-2912
(785) 532-5717
FAX: (785) 532-7732
Dr. Charlie L. Nutt
Executive Director
E-MAIL: nacada@ksu.edu
URL: www.nacada.ksu.edu

NACAS (T)
3 Boar's Head Lane
Suite B
Charlottesville, VA 22903-4610
(434) 245-8425
FAX: (434) 245-8453
Kelsey Finn
CEO
E-MAIL: info@nacas.org
URL: www.nacas.org

NASPA-Student Affairs Administrators in Higher Education (U)
111 K Street, NE
10th Floor
Washington, DC 20002-4409
(202) 265-7500
Dr. Kevin Kruger
President
E-MAIL: office@naspa.org
URL: www.naspa.org

The National Academy of Education (V)
500 5th Street, NW
Washington, DC 20001
(202) 334-2341
Mr. Gregory White
Executive Director
E-MAIL: info@naeducation.org
URL: www.naeducation.org

National Academy of Kinesiology (W)
2001 Juniper Drive
Mahomet, IL 61853
(217) 800-1156
FAX: (217) 590-0528
Ms. Kim Scott
Business Manager
E-MAIL: staff@nationalacademyofkinesiology.org
URL: www.nationalacademyofkinesiology.org

National Accrediting Agency for Clinical Laboratory Sciences (X)
5600 North River Road
Suite 720
Rosemont, IL 60018
(773) 714-8880
FAX: (773) 714-8886
Dianne M. Cearlock Ph.D.
CEO
E-MAIL: dcearlock@naacls.org
URL: www.naacls.org

National Accrediting Commission of Career Arts & Sciences (Y)
3015 Colvin Street
Alexandria, VA 22314
(703) 600-7600
FAX: (703) 379-2200
Tony Mirando M.S., D.C.
Executive Director
E-MAIL: amirando@naccas.org
URL: www.naccas.org

National Association for College Admission Counseling (Z)
1050 North Highland Street
Suite 400
Arlington, VA 22201
(703) 836-2222
FAX: (703) 243-9375
Ms. Joyce E. Smith
Chief Executive Officer
E-MAIL: jsmith@nacacnet.org
URL: www.nacacnet.org

National Association for Equal Opportunity in Higher Education (a)
110 Maryland Avenue, NE
Suite 509
Washington, DC 20002
(202) 552-3300
FAX: (202) 552-3330
Lezli Baskerville Esquire
President & CEO
E-MAIL: lbaskerville@nafeo.org
URL: www.nafeonation.org

National Association for the Legal Support of Alternative Schools (b)
18520 N.W. 67th Avenue #188
Miami, FL 33015
(800) 456-7784
FAX: (954) 538-8041
Mrs. Chau Trinh
Institutional Representative
E-MAIL: educate@nalsas.org
URL: www.nalsas.org

National Association for Practical Nurse Education and Service, Inc. (c)
2071 N. Bechtle Avenue
PMB 307
Springfield, OH 45504
(703) 933-1003
FAX: (703) 940-4089
Ann Bauer LPN
President
E-MAIL: president@napnes.org
URL: www.napnes.org

National Association of Agricultural Educators (d)
300 Garrigus Building
University of Kentucky
Lexington, KY 40546-0215
(859) 257-2224
FAX: (859) 323-3919
Dr. Wm. Jay Jackman
Executive Director
E-MAIL: jjackman.naae@uky.edu
URL: www.naae.org

National Association of College and University Attorneys (e)
1 Dupont Circle, NW
Suite 620
Washington, DC 20036
(202) 833-8390
FAX: (202) 296-8379
Ms. Kathleen Curry Santora Esq.
President & Chief Executive Officer
E-MAIL: ksantora@nacua.org
URL: www.nacua.org

National Association of College and University Business Officers (f)
1110 Vermont Avenue, NW
Suite 800
Washington, DC 20005
(202) 861-2500
FAX: (202) 861-2583
Ms. Susan W. Johnston
President
E-MAIL: susan.johnston@nacubo.org
URL: www.nacubo.org

The National Association of College & University Food Services (g)
1515 Turf Lane
Suite 100
East Lansing, MI 48823
(517) 332-2494
FAX: (517) 332-8144
Gretchen M. Couraud CAE, CFRE
Executive Director
E-MAIL: gcouraud@nacufs.org
URL: www.nacufs.org

National Association of College Stores (h)
500 East Lorain Street
Oberlin, OH 44074
(440) 775-7777
FAX: (440) 775-4769
Mr. Robert A. Walton
Chief Executive Officer
E-MAIL: info@nacs.org
URL: www.nacs.org

National Association of College Wind and Percussion Instructors (i)
University of Northern Iowa
School of Music
59 Russell Hall
Cedar Falls, IA 50614
(319) 273-2491
Ms. Heather Peyton
President
E-MAIL: heather.peyton@uni.edu
URL: www.nacwpi.org

Higher Education Associations

National Association of Colleges and Employers (A)
62 Highland Avenue
Bethlehem, PA 18017-9481
(610) 868-1421
FAX: (610) 868-0208
Dr. Marilyn Mackes
Executive Director
E-MAIL: mmackes@naceweb.org
URL: www.naceweb.org

National Association of Correctional Education Standards and Accreditation (NACESA) (B)
104 Johnson Street
Marshall, TX 75670
(903) 472-2762
Mr. Tracy L. Andrus Sr.
E-MAIL: tandrus26@gmail.com

National Association of Educational Procurement (C)
8840 Stanford Boulevard
Suite 2000
Columbia, MD 21045
(443) 281-9901
FAX: (443) 219-9687
Ms. Krista Ferrell
Executive Director
E-MAIL: kferrell@naepnet.org
URL: www.naepnet.org

National Association of Independent Colleges and Universities (D)
1025 Connecticut Avenue, NW
Suite 700
Washington, DC 20036-5405
(202) 785-8866
FAX: (202) 835-0003
Dr. Barbara Mistick
President
E-MAIL: geninfo@naicu.edu
URL: www.naicu.edu

National Association of Schools of Art and Design (E)
11250 Roger Bacon Drive
Suite 21
Reston, VA 20190
(703) 437-0700
FAX: (703) 437-6312
Karen P. Moynahan
Executive Director
E-MAIL: info@arts-accredit.org
URL: www.arts-accredit.org

National Association of Schools of Dance (F)
11250 Roger Bacon Drive
Suite 21
Reston, VA 20190
(703) 437-0700
FAX: (703) 437-6312
Karen P. Moynahan
Executive Director
E-MAIL: info@arts-accredit.org
URL: www.arts-accredit.org

National Association of Schools of Music (G)
11250 Roger Bacon Drive
Suite 21
Reston, VA 20190
(703) 437-0700
FAX: (703) 437-6312
Karen P. Moynahan
Executive Director
E-MAIL: info@arts-accredit.org
URL: www.arts-accredit.org

National Association of Schools of Theatre (H)
11250 Roger Bacon Drive
Suite 21
Reston, VA 20190
(703) 437-0700
FAX: (703) 437-6312
Karen P. Moynahan
Executive Director
E-MAIL: info@arts-accredit.org
URL: www.arts-accredit.org

National Association of State Directors of Teacher Education and Certification (I)
1629 K Street, NW
Suite 300
Washington, DC 20006
(202) 204-2208
Dr. Phillip S. Rogers
Executive Director
E-MAIL: philrogers@nasdtec.org
URL: www.nasdtec.net

National Association of Student Financial Aid Administrators (J)
1801 Pennsylvania Avenue, NW
Suite 850
Washington, DC 20006-3606
(202) 785-0453
FAX: (202) 785-1487
Mr. Justin Draeger
President & CEO
E-MAIL: info@nasfaa.org
URL: www.nasfaa.org

National Association of System Heads (K)
3300 Metzerott Road
Adelphi, MD 20783
(301) 445-2780
Rebecca Martin
Executive Director
E-MAIL: rebecca@nash-dc.org
URL: www.nashonline.org

National Catholic Educational Association (L)
1005 North Glebe Road
Suite 525
Arlington, VA 22201-5792
(571) 257-0010
FAX: (703) 243-0025
Dr. Thomas W. Burnford
President/CEO
E-MAIL: tburnford@ncea.org
URL: www.ncea.org

National Coalition for Campus Children's Centers (M)
188 Front Street
Suite 116-104
Franklin, TN 37064
(615) 614-3723
FAX: (615) 614-3723
Ms. Tonya Palla
Executive Director
E-MAIL: tonyap@campuschildren.org
URL: www.campuschildren.org

National Collegiate Athletic Association (N)
PO Box 6222
Indianapolis, IN 46206-6222
(317) 917-6222
FAX: (317) 917-6888
Mr. Todd Petr
Managing Director of Research
E-MAIL: tpetr@ncaa.org
URL: www.ncaa.org

National Commission on Orthotic and Prosthetic Education (NCOPE) (O)
330 John Carlyle Street
Suite 200
Alexandria, VA 22314
(703) 836-7114 x 225
FAX: (703) 836-0838
Ms. Robin Seabrook
Executive Director
E-MAIL: rseabrook@ncope.org
URL: www.ncope.org

National Communication Association (P)
1765 N Street, NW
Washington, DC 20036
(202) 464-4622
FAX: (202) 464-4600
Trevor Parry-Giles Ph.D.
Executive Director
E-MAIL: tparrygiles@natcom.org
URL: www.natcom.org

National Council for Continuing Education and Training (Q)
9526 Argyle Forest Boulevard
Suite B2-322
Jacksonville, FL 32222
(888) 771-0179
Mr. Ed Harper
Acting Executive Director
E-MAIL: nccet@nccet.org
URL: www.nccet.org

National Council of Instructional Administrators (NCIA) Dept of Educational Administration (R)
141 Teachers College Hall
PO Box 880360
University of Nebraska - Lincoln
Lincoln, NE 68588-0360
(402) 472-8958
FAX: (402) 472-4300
Katherine Wesley
Executive Director
E-MAIL: ncia@unl.edu
URL: ncia.unl.edu

National Council of University Research Administrators (S)
1015 18th Street, NW
Suite 901
Washington, DC 20036
(202) 466-3894
FAX: (202) 223-5573
Kathleen M. Larmett
Executive Director
E-MAIL: info@ncura.edu
URL: www.ncura.edu

National Education Association (T)
1201 16th Street, NW
Suite 810
Washington, DC 20036
(202) 833-4000
FAX: (202) 822-7974
Ms. Kim A. Anderson
Executive Director
E-MAIL: mboyd@nea.org
URL: www.nea.org/he

National Forensic Association (U)
Illinois State University
School of Communication
Campus Box 4480
Normal, IL 61790-4480
(309) 438-8447
FAX: (309) 438-3048
Prof. Megan Koch
National Secretary-Treasurer
E-MAIL: mkoch@ilstu.edu
URL: www.nationalforensics.org

National Institute for Learning Outcomes Assessment (V)
University of Illinois at Urbana-Champaign
360 Education Building
Champaign, IL 61820
(217) 244-2155
E-MAIL: niloa@education.illinois.edu
URL: www.learningoutcomeassessment.org

National League for Nursing (W)
The Watergate Building, 8th Floor
2600 Virginia Avenue, NW
Washington, DC 20037
(202) 909-2500
Dr. Beverly Malone
Chief Executive Officer
E-MAIL: oceo@nln.org
URL: www.nln.org

National Rural Education Association (X)
615 McCallie Avenue
Hunter Hall 212
Chattanooga, TN 37421
(423) 425-4539
Dr. Allen Pratt
Executive Director
E-MAIL: allen-pratt@utc.edu
URL: www.nrea.net

National Society for Experiential Education (Y)
c/o Talley Management Group, Inc.
19 Mantua Road
Mt. Royal, NJ 08061
(856) 423-3427
FAX: (856) 423-3420
Haley Brust
Executive Director
E-MAIL: nsee@talley.com
URL: www.nsee.org

National Writing Project (Z)
2120 University Avenue
University of California
Berkeley, CA 94704
(510) 679-2424
Elyse Eidman-Aadahl
Executive Director
E-MAIL: nwp@nwp.org
URL: www.nwp.org

Network of Schools of Public Policy, Affairs, and Administration (a)
1029 Vermont Avenue, NW
Suite 1100
Washington, DC 20005
(202) 628-8965
FAX: (202) 626-4978
Laurel McFarland
Executive Director
E-MAIL: naspaa@naspaa.org
URL: www.naspaa.org

New England Commission of Higher Education (NECHE) (b)
3 Burlington Woods Drive
Suite 100
Burlington, MA 01803-4514
(781) 425-7747
FAX: (781) 425-1001
Dr. Barbara E. Brittingham
President of the Commission
E-MAIL: info@neche.org
URL: www.neche.org

New England Board of Higher Education (c)
45 Temple Place
Boston, MA 02111
(617) 533-9519
FAX: (617) 338-1577
Dr. Michael K. Thomas
President and CEO
E-MAIL: mthomas@nebhe.org
URL: www.nebhe.org

North American Association of Summer Sessions (d)
North Carolina State University
2016 Harris Hall
Campus Box 7302
Raleigh, NC 27695-7302
(919) 515-2261
E-MAIL: naass@naass.org
URL: www.naass.org

Northwest Commission on Colleges and Universities (e)
8060 165th Avenue, NE
Suite 100
Redmond, WA 98052
(425) 558-4224
FAX: (425) 376-0596
Dr. Sonny Ramaswamy
President
E-MAIL: sonny@nwccu.org
URL: www.nwccu.org

Planning Accreditation Board (f)
2334 W. Lawrence Avenue
Suite 209
Chicago, IL 60625
(773) 334-7200
Ms. Jesmarie Soto Johnson
Executive Director
E-MAIL: jjohnson@planningaccreditationboard.org
URL: www.planningaccreditationboard.org

Quality Education for Minorities (QEM) Network (g)
1818 N Street, NW
Suite 350
Washington, DC 20036
(202) 659-1818
Dr. Ivory Toldson
President and CEO
E-MAIL: itoldson@qem.org
URL: www.qem.org

Society for College and University Planning (h)
1330 Eisenhower Place
Ann Arbor, MI 48108
(734) 669-3270
Mike Moss CAE
President
E-MAIL: info@scup.org
URL: www.scup.org

Society for Slovene Studies (i)
148 Russsell Street #3
Worcester, MA 01609
Ms. Kristina Helena Reardon
Secretary
E-MAIL: kristina.reardon@gmail.com
URL: www.slovenestudies.com

Society for Values in Higher Education (A)
c/o Western Kentucky University
1906 College Heights Boulevard
#8020
Bowling Green, KY 42101-1041
(270) 745-2907
FAX: (270) 745-5374
Dr. Eric Bain-Selbo
Executive Director
E-MAIL: society@svhe.org
URL: www.svhe.org

Society of American Foresters (B)
10100 Laureate Way
Bethesda, MD 20814-2198
(866) 897-8720
FAX: (301) 897-3690
Mr. Terry Baker
Chief Executive Officer
E-MAIL: membership@safnet.org
URL: www.eforester.org

Society of Professors of Education (C)
University of West Georgia
College of Education
Dept of LAI
1601 Maple Street
Carrollton, GA 30118-5160
(678) 839-6132
FAX: (678) 839-6097
Dr. Robert C. Morris
Secretary-Treasurer
E-MAIL: rmorris@westga.edu
URL: https://societyofprofessorsofeducation.wordpress.com

Southeastern Universities Research Association (D)
1201 New York Avenue, NW
Suite 430
Washington, DC 20005
(202) 408-7872
FAX: (202) 408-8250
Dr. Jerry Draayer
President & CEO
E-MAIL: draayer@sura.org
URL: www.sura.org

Southern Association for College Student Affairs (E)
Georgia Southern University-Armstrong
11935 Abercorn Street
Savannah, GA 31419
(912) 344-2510
Dr. Joe Buck
Executive Director
E-MAIL: jbuck@georgiasouthern.edu
URL: www.sacsa.org

Southern Association of Colleges and Schools Commission on Colleges (F)
1866 Southern Lane
Decatur, GA 30033-4097
(404) 679-4512
FAX: (404) 994-6592
Dr. Belle S. Wheelan
President
E-MAIL: bwheelan@sacscoc.org
URL: www.sacscoc.org

Southern States Communication Association (G)
University of Tennessee at Chattanooga
Dept. 5555, 102 Founders Hall
615 McCallie Avenue
Chattanooga, TN 37403
(423) 425-4633
FAX: (423) 756-5559
Dr. Jerold L. Hale
Executive Director
E-MAIL: director@ssca.net
URL: www.ssca.net

State Higher Education Executive Officers (H)
3035 Center Green Drive
Suite 100
Boulder, CO 80301-2205
(303) 541-1600
FAX: (303) 541-1639
Dr. Robert Anderson
President
E-MAIL: randerson@sheeo.org
URL: www.sheeo.org

Tennessee Independent Colleges and Universities Association (I)
555 Marriott Drive
Suite 315
Nashville, TN 37214
(615) 242-6400
Dr. Claude O. Pressnell Jr.
President
E-MAIL: pressnell@ticua.org
URL: www.ticua.org

Transnational Association of Christian Colleges and Schools (TRACS) (J)
15935 Forest Road
Forest, VA 24551
(434) 525-9539
Dr. Timothy W. Eaton
President
E-MAIL: info@tracs.org
URL: www.tracs.org

The Tuition Exchange (K)
3 Bethesda Metro Center
Suite 700
Bethesda, MD 20814
(301) 941-1827
FAX: (301) 657-9776
Mr. Robert D. Shorb
Executive Director/CEO
E-MAIL: rshorb@tuitionexchange.org
URL: www.tuitionexchange.org

UNCF (L)
1805 7th Street NW
Washington, DC 20001
(800) 331-2244
Dr. Michael Lomax
President & CEO
URL: www.uncf.org

University Aviation Association (M)
2787 N. 2nd Street
Memphis, TN 38127
(901) 563-0505
Ms. Dawn Vinson
Executive Director
E-MAIL: uaamail@uaa.aero
URL: www.uaa.aero

University Film and Video Association (N)
960 War Eagle Drive S
Colorado Springs, CO 80919
(646) 498-1182
Ms. Laura Vazquez
President
E-MAIL: ufvahome@gmail.com
URL: www.ufva.org

University Photographers' Association of America (O)
P.O. Box 433
Clalfon, NJ 07830-0433
(908) 335-0157
Mr. Glenn Carpenter
UPAA President
E-MAIL: carpenter@morainevalley.edu
URL: www.upaa.org

University Professional & Continuing Education Association (UPCEA) (P)
One Dupont Circle, NW
Suite 330
Washington, DC 20036
(202) 659-3130
FAX: (202) 785-0374
Dr. Robert Hansen
CEO
E-MAIL: rhansen@upcea.edu
URL: www.upcea.edu

University Risk Management and Insurance Association, Inc. (Q)
PO Box 1027
Bloomington, IN 47402
(812) 727-7130
FAX: (812) 727-7129
Ms. Jenny Whittington
Executive Director
E-MAIL: urmia@urmia.org
URL: www.urmia.org

Urban Affairs Association (R)
c/o Urban Studies Program
University of Wisconsin-Milwaukee
PO Box 413
Milwaukee, WI 53201-0413
(414) 229-3025
Dr. Margaret Wilder
UAA Executive Director
E-MAIL: info@uaamail.org
URL: www.urbanaffairsassociation.org

WASC Senior College and University Commission (S)
985 Atlantic Avenue
Suite 100
Alameda, CA 94501
(510) 748-9001
FAX: (510) 748-9797
Ms. Jamienne S. Studley
President
URL: www.wascsenior.org

Western Interstate Commission for Higher Education (T)
3035 Center Green Drive
Suite 200
Boulder, CO 80301-2204
(303) 541-0202
FAX: (303) 541-0245
Dr. Demaree K. Michelau
President
E-MAIL: dmichelau@wiche.edu
URL: www.wiche.edu

Consortia of Institutions of Higher Education

Alabama Association of Independent Colleges and Universities (A)
4266 Lomac Street
Montgomery, AL 36106
(334) 356-2220
FAX: (334) 356-2202
Paul M. Hankins
President
E-MAIL: hankinsp@knology.net
URL: www.aaicu.net

Arkansas' Independent Colleges and Universities (B)
PO Box 300
Little Rock, AR 72203
(501) 378-0843
FAX: (501) 374-1523
Mr. Andy Goodman
President
E-MAIL: agoodman@arkindcolleges.org
URL: www.arkindcolleges.org

Associated Colleges of the Midwest (C)
11 East Adams Street
Suite 800
Chicago, IL 60603
(312) 263-5000
FAX: (312) 263-5879
Ms. Sonya Malunda
President
E-MAIL: acm@acm.edu
URL: www.acm.edu

Association of Independent California Colleges and Universities (D)
1121 L Street
Suite 802
Sacramento, CA 95814
(916) 446-7626
FAX: (916) 446-7948
Ms. Kristen F. Soares
President
E-MAIL: aiccu@aiccu.edu
URL: www.aiccu.edu

Association of Independent Colleges and Universities in Massachusetts (E)
11 Beacon Street
Suite 1224
Boston, MA 02108-3093
(617) 742-5147
FAX: (617) 742-3089
Mr. Richard Doherty
President
E-MAIL: richard.doherty@aicum.org
URL: www.aicum.org

Association of Independent Colleges and Universities in New Jersey (F)
797 Springfield Avenue
Summit, NJ 07901-1107
(908) 277-3738
Louis T. Manzione Ph.D.
President and CEO
E-MAIL: manzione@njcolleges.org
URL: www.njcolleges.org

Association of Independent Colleges and Universities of Ohio (G)
41 South High Street
Suite 1690
Columbus, OH 43215
(614) 228-2196
FAX: (614) 228-8406
Mr. C. Todd Jones
President & General Counsel
E-MAIL: tjones@aicuo.edu
URL: www.aicuo.edu

Association of Independent Colleges and Universities of Pennsylvania (H)
101 North Front Street
Harrisburg, PA 17101-1405
(717) 232-8649
FAX: (717) 233-8574
Thomas P. Foley JD
President
E-MAIL: foley@aicup.org
URL: www.aicup.org

Association of Independent Colleges and Universities of Rhode Island (I)
50 Park Row West
Suite 100
Providence, RI 02903
(401) 272-8270
Mr. Daniel Egan
President
E-MAIL: degan@aicuri.org
URL: www.aicuri.org

Association of Independent Colleges of Art & Design (J)
236 Hope Street
Providence, RI 02906
(401) 270-5991
FAX: (401) 270-5993
Ms. Deborah Obalil
President & Executive Director
E-MAIL: deborah@aicad.org
URL: www.aicad.org

Association of Independent Kentucky Colleges and Universities (K)
484 Chenault Road
Frankfort, KY 40601
(502) 695-5007
FAX: (502) 695-5057
Dr. Gary S. Cox
President
E-MAIL: gary.cox@aikcu.org
URL: www.aikcu.org

Association of Vermont Independent Colleges (L)
PO Box 254
Montpelier, VT 05601
(802) 828-8826
Susan Stitely
President
E-MAIL: sstitely@vermont-icolleges.org
URL: www.vermont-icolleges.org

Atlanta Regional Council for Higher Education (M)
141 E. College Avenue
Box 1084
Decatur, GA 30030
(404) 471-6422
Ms. Tracey Brantley
Executive Director
E-MAIL: tbrantley@atlantahighered.org
URL: www.atlantahighered.org

Boston Theological Interreligious Consortium (N)
213 Bay State Road
Floor 2
Boston, MA 02215
(617) 353-7664
Dr. Ann McClenahan
Executive Director
E-MAIL: mcclenahan@bostontheological.org
URL: www.bostontheological.org

CCUMC (Consortium of College & University Media Centers) (O)
Indiana University
306 N. Union Street
Bloomington, IN 47405-3888
(812) 855-6049
Aileen Scales
Executive Director
E-MAIL: ccumc@ccumc.org
URL: www.ccumc.org

Central Pennsylvania Consortium (P)
c/o Franklin & Marshall College
PO Box 3003
Lancaster, PA 17604-3003
(717) 358-4282
FAX: (717) 358-4455
Ms. Kathryn Missildine
Executive Assistant
E-MAIL: kathy.missildine@fandm.edu
URL: www.centralpennsylvaniaconsortium.org

CHESLA, Connecticut Higher Education Supplemental Loan Authority (Q)
10 Columbus Boulevard
7th Floor
Hartford, CT 06106-1978
(860) 761-8453
Ms. Jeanette W. Weldon
Executive Director
E-MAIL: jweldon@chesla.org
URL: www.chesla.org

Christian College Consortium (R)
255 Grapevine Road
Wenham, MA 01984-1899
(978) 867-4802
FAX: (978) 867-4650
Dr. Stan D. Gaede
President
E-MAIL: stan.gaede@gordon.edu
URL: www.ccconsortium.org

Community College Futures Assembly (S)
Bellwether College Consortium
Alamo Colleges District
2222 N. Alamo Street
San Antonio, TX 78215
(210) 485-0019
Ms. Enedina Rodriguez-Cassity
E-MAIL: erodriguez40@alamo.edu
URL: www.bellwethercollegeconsortium.com

The Consortium for Graduate Study in Management (T)
229 Chesterfield Business Parkway
Chesterfield, MO 63005
(636) 681-5487
FAX: (636) 681-5497
Mr. Peter J. Aranda III
Executive Director and CEO
E-MAIL: recruiting@cgsm.org
URL: www.cgsm.org

Consortium of Universities of the Washington Metropolitan Area (U)
1020 19th Street, NW
Suite 500
Washington, DC 20036
(202) 331-8080
Dr. John Cavanaugh
President & CEO
E-MAIL: jcavanaugh@consortium.org
URL: www.consortium.org

Consortium on Financing Higher Education (V)
1 Main Street
Suite 1210
Cambridge, MA 02142
(617) 253-5030
Ms. Jane L. Rapelye
President
E-MAIL: cofhe-info@mit.edu
URL: www.mit.edu/cofhe/

Cooperating Raleigh Colleges (W)
Meredith College
Wainwright Hall 110
3800 Hillsborough Street
Raleigh, NC 27607-5298
(919) 760-8538
Ms. Jenny Spiker
Director
E-MAIL: spikerje@meredith.edu
URL: www.crcraleighcolleges.org

Council of Independent Colleges in Virginia (X)
PO Box 1005
Bedford, VA 24523
(540) 586-0606
FAX: (540) 586-2630
Mr. Robert B. Lambeth Jr.
President
E-MAIL: lambeth@cicv.org
URL: www.cicv.org

Council of Presidents (Y)
410 Eleventh Avenue, SE
Suite 101
Olympia, WA 98501
(360) 292-4100
FAX: (360) 292-4110
Mr. Paul Francis
Executive Director
E-MAIL: pfrancis@cop.wsu.edu
URL: www.councilofpresidents.org

Federation of Independent Illinois Colleges and Universities (Z)
1123 South Second Street
Springfield, IL 62704
(217) 789-1400
Mr. David W. Tretter
President
E-MAIL: davetretter@federationedu.org
URL: www.federationedu.org

Five College Consortium (a)
97 Spring Street
Amherst, MA 01002
(413) 542-4009
Dr. Sarah K. A. Pfatteicher
Executive Director
E-MAIL: fciexecdirector@fivecolleges.edu
URL: www.fivecolleges.edu

Georgia Independent College Association (b)
600 West Peachtree Street, NW
Suite 1710
Atlanta, GA 30308
(404) 233-5433, Ext. 21
Dr. Susanna Baxter
President
E-MAIL: sbaxter@georgiacolleges.org
URL: www.georgiacolleges.org

Graduate Theological Foundation (c)
116 E. Sheridan Avenue
Suite 207
Oklahoma City, OK 73104
(800) 423-5983
FAX: (405) 653-9435
Bethany Morgan MBA
Registrar
E-MAIL: studentservices@gtfeducation.org
URL: www.gtfeducation.org

Great Lakes Colleges Association (d)
535 West William
Suite 301
Ann Arbor, MI 48103
(734) 661-2350
FAX: (734) 661-2349
Dr. Michael (Mickey) McDonald
President
URL: www.glca.org

Greater Cincinnati Collegiate Connection (e)
Northern Kentucky University
241 Campbell Hall
Highland Heights, KY 41099
(859) 392-2428
Ms. Janet Piccirillo
Executive Director
E-MAIL: piccirillj1@nku.edu
URL: www.gccollegiateconnection.org

Hartford Consortium for Higher Education (f)
31 Pratt Street
5th Floor
Hartford, CT 06103
(860) 702-3800
FAX: (860) 241-1130
Dr. Martin Estey
Executive Director
E-MAIL: mestey@metrohartford.com
URL: www.hartfordconsortium.org

Higher Education Consortium for Urban Affairs, Inc. (HECUA) (g)
2233 University Avenue West
Suite 210
St. Paul, MN 55114
(651) 287-3300
FAX: (651) 659-9421
Ms. Ariella Tilsen
Interim Executive Director
E-MAIL: hecua@hecua.org
URL: www.hecua.org

Higher Education Consortium of Metropolitan St. Louis (h)
734 West Port Plaza
Suite 273
St. Louis, MO 63146
(314) 985-8833
FAX: (314) 985-8835
Ms. Cassandra M. Pinkston
Chief Executive Officer
URL: www.heccstl.com

Higher Education Data Sharing (HEDS) Consortium (i)
Wabash College
Trippet Hall
410 West Wabash Avenue
Crawfordsville, IN 47933
(765) 361-6331
Charles Blaich
Director
E-MAIL: skillruk@wabash.edu
URL: www.hedsconsortium.org

Independent Colleges and Universities of Missouri (j)
PO Box 1865
Jefferson City, MO 65102-1865
(573) 635-9160
FAX: (573) 635-6258
Mr. William A. Gamble
Executive Director
E-MAIL: bill@molobby.com
URL: www.icum.org

Independent Colleges and Universities of Texas, Inc. (A)
1303 San Antonio Street
Suite 820
Austin, TX 78701
(512) 472-9522
FAX: (512) 472-2371
Ray Martinez III
President
E-MAIL: sam.rauschenfels@icut.org
URL: www.icut.org

Independent Colleges of Indiana (B)
30 S. Meridian Street
Suite 800
Indianapolis, IN 46204
(317) 236-6090
Dr. David W. Wantz
President and CEO
E-MAIL: dwantz@icindiana.org
URL: www.icindiana.org

Independent Colleges of Washington (C)
600 Stewart Street
Suite 600
Seattle, WA 98101
(206) 623-4494
Terri Standish-Kuon Ph.D.
President & CEO
E-MAIL: info@icwashington.org
URL: www.icwashington.org

Inter-University Consortium for Political and Social Research (ICPSR) (D)
The University of Michigan
Institute for Social Research
PO Box 1248
Ann Arbor, MI 48106-1248
(734) 615-8400
Dr. Margaret Levenstein
Director
E-MAIL: maggiel@umich.edu
URL: www.icpsr.umich.edu

Inter-University Council of Ohio (IUC) (E)
10 West Broad Street
Suite 450
Columbus, OH 43215
(614) 464-1266
FAX: (614) 464-9281
Ms. Cindy McQuade
Vice President of Operations
E-MAIL: mcquade.2@osu.edu
URL: www.iuc-ohio.org

Iowa Association of Community College Trustees (F)
855 East Court Avenue
Des Moines, IA 50309
(515) 282-4692
FAX: (515) 282-3743
M. J. Dolan J.D.
Executive Director
E-MAIL: mjdolan@iacct.com
URL: www.iacct.com

Iowa Association of Independent Colleges and Universities (G)
505 Fifth Avenue
Suite 1030
Des Moines, IA 50309-2399
(515) 282-3175
FAX: (515) 282-8177
Mr. Gary W. Steinke
President
E-MAIL: president@iaicu.org
URL: www.iowaprivatecolleges.org

Kansas Independent College Association (H)
700 South Kansas Avenue
Suite 622
Topeka, KS 66603
(785) 235-9877
Mr. Matthew E. Lindsey
President
E-MAIL: matt@kscolleges.org
URL: www.kscolleges.org

Lehigh Valley Association of Independent Colleges (I)
1309 Main Street
Bethlehem, PA 18018
(610) 625-7888
Diane Dimitroff
Executive Director
E-MAIL: dimitroffd@lvaic.org
URL: www.lvaic.org

Louisiana Association of Independent Colleges and Universities (J)
PO Box 3332
Baton Rouge, LA 70821
(225) 389-9885
Dr. Kenya L. Messer
President
E-MAIL: kmesser@laicu.org
URL: www.laicu.org

Maryland Independent College and University Association (K)
140 South Street
Annapolis, MD 21401
(410) 269-0306
Ms. Tina M. Bjarekull
President
E-MAIL: tbjarekull@micua.org
URL: www.micua.org

Massachusetts Education & Career Opportunities Inc (L)
484 Main Street
Suite 500
Worcester, MA 01608
(508) 754-6829
FAX: (508) 797-0069
Mr. Mark Bilotta
CEO
E-MAIL: mbilotta@massedco.org
URL: www.massedco.org

Michigan Independent Colleges & Universities (M)
120 N. Washington Square
Suite 950
Lansing, MI 48933
(517) 372-9160
Robert LeFevre
President
E-MAIL: rlefevre@micolleges.org
URL: www.micolleges.org

Minnesota Private College Council, Inc. (N)
445 Minnesota Street
Suite 500
St. Paul, MN 55101-2903
(651) 228-9061
FAX: (651) 228-0379
E-MAIL: colleges@mnprivatecolleges.org
URL: www.mnprivatecolleges.org

National Student Exchange (O)
2613 Northridge Parkway
Suite 106
Ames, IA 50010
(515) 450-5529
Dr. Debra Sanborn
President
E-MAIL: info@nse.org
URL: www.nse.org

New England Faculty Development Consortium (P)
University of New England
Center for Excellence in Teaching and Learning
304 Hersey Hall
716 Stevens Avenue
Portland, ME 04103
(207) 602-2845
Marc Ebenfield Ph.D.
President
E-MAIL: mnebenfield@gmail.com
URL: www.nefdc.org

New Hampshire College & University Council (Q)
3 Barrell Court
Suite 100
Concord, NH 03301-8543
(603) 225-4199
FAX: (603) 225-8108
Dr. Debby Scire
Interim President and CEO
E-MAIL: scire@compactnh.org
URL: www.nhcuc.org

New Jersey Association of State Colleges and Universities (R)
150 West State Street
Trenton, NJ 08608
(609) 989-1100
Barbara Berreski JD, MS
Interim Executive Director/CEO
E-MAIL: bberreski@njascu.org
URL: www.njascu.org

New Jersey Council of County Colleges (S)
330 West State Street
Trenton, NJ 08618
(609) 392-3434
Dr. Aaron Fichtner
President
E-MAIL: afichtner@njccc.org
URL: www.njccc.org

New Orleans Educational Telecommunications Consortium (T)
2045 Lakeshore Drive
Suite 541
New Orleans, LA 70122
(504) 524-0350
E-MAIL: noetc@noetc.org
URL: www.noetc.org

North Carolina Independent Colleges and Universities (U)
530 North Blount Street
Raleigh, NC 27604
(919) 832-5817
FAX: (919) 833-0794
Dr. A. Hope Williams
President
E-MAIL: williams@ncicu.org
URL: www.ncicu.org

North Dakota Independent College Fund (V)
University of Mary
7500 University Drive
Bismarck, ND 58504
(701) 355-8329
FAX: (701) 255-7687
Mr. Jeff Beauchamp
Executive Director
E-MAIL: jrbeauchamp@umary.edu

Northeast Consortium of Colleges and Universities in Massachusetts (NECCUM) (W)
c/o Office of the President
Salem State University
352 Lafayette Street
Salem, MA 01970
(978) 542-7554
FAX: (978) 542-6126
Katie Sadowski
E-MAIL: ksadowski@salemstate.edu

Northeast Ohio Council on Higher Education (X)
1111 Superior Avenue
Suite 1600
Cleveland, OH 44114
(216) 302-3242
Ms. Holly J. Harris Bane
President
E-MAIL: hharrisbane@noche.org
URL: www.noche.org

Oak Ridge Associated Universities (Y)
MS-22
PO Box 117
Oak Ridge, TN 37831-0117
(865) 576-3300
FAX: (865) 576-3816
Mr. Andy Page
President and CEO
E-MAIL: andy.page@orau.org
URL: www.orau.org

Oklahoma Independent Colleges and Universities (Z)
PO Box 57148
Oklahoma City, OK 73157-7148
(405) 371-1780
Lesa Smaligo
Executive Director
E-MAIL: lesa@oicu.org
URL: www.oicu.org

Oregon Alliance of Independent Colleges & Universities (a)
15573 Bangy Road
Suite 320
Lake Oswego, OR 97035
(503) 342-0004
Mr. Jim Bauer
President
E-MAIL: jim@oaicu.org
URL: www.oaicu.org

Pennsylvania Association of Colleges and Universities (b)
950 Walnut Bottom Road
Suite 15-214
Carlisle, PA 17015
(800) 687-9010
FAX: (717) 240-0673
URL: www.pacu.org

Pennsylvania's State System of Higher Education Foundation, Inc. (c)
2986 North Second Street
Harrisburg, PA 17110
(717) 720-4056
Ms. Jennifer S. Hartman
President/CEO
E-MAIL: jhartman@thepafoundation.org
URL: www.thepafoundation.org

Pittsburgh Council on Higher Education (d)
201 Wood Street
Pittsburgh, PA 15222
(412) 657-8105
Ms. Karina Chavez
Executive Director
E-MAIL: kchavez@pointpark.edu
URL: www.pche-pa.org

Quad-Cities Graduate Study Center (e)
WIU - QC Campus
3300 River Drive
Moline, IL 61265
(309) 762-9481
Shirley Moore
E-MAIL: qc@gradcenter.org
URL: www.gradcenter.org

Second Nature (f)
18 Tremont Street
Suite 608
Boston, MA 02108
(617) 722-0036
FAX: (617) 259-1734
Dr. Timothy Carter
President
E-MAIL: president@secondnature.org
URL: www.secondnature.org

South Carolina Independent Colleges & Universities, Inc. (g)
PO Box 12007
Columbia, SC 29211
(803) 799-7122
FAX: (803) 254-7504
Dr. Jeffrey Perez
President & CEO
E-MAIL: jeff@scicu.org
URL: www.scicu.org

South Metropolitan Higher Education Consortium (h)
202 S. Halsted Street
Chicago Heights, IL 60411
(708) 709-3764
Ms. Allessandra Kummelehne
Executive Director
E-MAIL: akummelehne@prairiestate.edu
URL: southmetroed.org

Southern Regional Education Board (i)
592 Tenth Street, NW
Atlanta, GA 30318-5776
(404) 875-9211
FAX: (404) 872-1477
Dr. Stephen L. Pruitt
President
E-MAIL: stephen.pruitt@sreb.org
URL: www.sreb.org

Southwestern Ohio Council for Higher Education (SOCHE) (j)
3155 Research Boulevard
Suite 204
Dayton, OH 45420-4015
(937) 258-8890
FAX: (937) 258-8899
Ms. Cassie Barlow
President
E-MAIL: cassie.barlow@soche.org
URL: www.soche.org

Texas International Education Consortium (k)
1103 West 24th Street
Austin, TX 78705
(512) 477-9283
FAX: (512) 322-0592
Robin Lerner
President & CEO
E-MAIL: info@tiec.org
URL: www.tiec.org

Consortia of Institutions of Higher Education

Tuition Plan Consortium/Private College 529 Plan (A)
7425 Forsyth Boulevard
Suite 194
St. Louis, MO 63105
(314) 727-0900
Mr. Robert Cole
President & CEO
E-MAIL: robert@pc529.com
URL: www.privatecollege529.com

The Virginia College Fund (B)
1011 E. Main Street
Suite 205
Richmond, VA 23219-3537
(804) 355-3271
Mr. James K. Dill
President
E-MAIL: jkdill@thevcf.org
URL: www.thevcf.org

Virginia Tidewater Consortium for Higher Education (C)
4900 Powhatan Avenue
Norfolk, VA 23529-0293
(757) 683-3183
FAX: (757) 683-4515
Dr. Lawrence G. Dotolo
President
E-MAIL: lgdotolo@aol.com
URL: www.vtc.odu.edu

Washington Theological Consortium (D)
415 Michigan Avenue, NE
Suite 105
Washington, DC 20017
(202) 832-2675
Dr. Larry Golemon
Executive Director
E-MAIL: wtc@washtheocon.org
URL: washtheocon.org

West Virginia Independent Colleges & Universities (E)
900 Lee Street
Suite 910
Charleston, WV 25301
(304) 345-5622
Mr. Ben Beakes
Executive Director
E-MAIL: ben@3pswv.com
URL: www.wvicu.org

Wisconsin Association of Independent Colleges and Universities (F)
122 West Washington Avenue
Suite 700
Madison, WI 53703-2723
(608) 256-7761
FAX: (608) 256-7065
Dr. Rolf Wegenke
President
E-MAIL: mail@waicu.org
URL: www.waicu.org

The Work Colleges Consortium (G)
CPO 2163
Berea, KY 40404
(859) 985-3156
Ms. Cassie Barlow
Executive Director
E-MAIL: cassie.barlow@workcolleges.org
URL: www.workcolleges.org

NAME INDEX

US Department of Education Offices, Statewide Agencies of Higher Education, Higher Education Associations, Consortia of Institutions of Higher Education

Institutions By Religious Affiliation

African Methodist Episcopal
Allen University ... SC
Edward Waters College ... FL
Paul Quinn College ... TX
Payne Theological Seminary ... OH
Shorter College ... AR
Wilberforce University ... OH

African Methodist Episcopal Zion Church
Clinton College ... SC
Hood Theological Seminary ... NC
Livingstone College ... NC

Alabama Baptist State Convention
Judson College ... AL

American Baptist
Alderson Broaddus University ... WV
American Baptist Seminary of the West .. CA
Bacone College ... OK
Eastern University ... PA
Franklin College of Indiana ... IN
Judson University ... IL
Linfield College ... OR
Northern Seminary ... IL
Ottawa University ... KS
University of Sioux Falls ... SD

Assemblies Of God Church
Assemblies of God Theological Seminary MO
Bethel College ... VA
Evangel University ... MO
Global University ... MO
Native American Bible College ... NC
North Central University ... MN
Northpoint Bible College ... MA
Northwest University ... WA
Southeastern University ... FL
Southwestern Assemblies of God University ... TX
Trinity Bible College & Graduate School . ND
University of Valley Forge ... PA
Vanguard University of Southern California ... CA

Baptist
American Baptist College ... TN
Arkansas Baptist College ... AR
Arlington Baptist University ... TX
Baptist Bible College ... MO
Baptist Missionary Association Theological Seminary ... TX
Baptist University of the Americas ... TX
Baylor University ... TX
Bethel University ... MN
Bluefield College ... VA
Boston Baptist College ... MA
Brewton-Parker College ... GA
Campbell University ... NC
Campbellsville University ... KY
Cedarville University ... OH
Central Baptist College ... AR
Central Baptist Theological Seminary ... KS
Central Baptist Theological Seminary of Minneapolis ... MN
Chowan University ... NC
Clarks Summit University ... PA
Dallas Baptist University ... TX
East Texas Baptist University ... TX
Gardner-Webb University ... NC
Georgetown College ... KY
Hardin-Simmons University ... TX
Howard Payne University ... TX
Huntsville Bible College ... AL
International Baptist College and Seminary ... AZ
Jacksonville College ... TX
Maple Springs Baptist Bible College & Seminary ... MD
Missouri Baptist University ... MO
Morris College ... SC
Oakland City University ... IN
Selma University ... AL
Shaw University ... NC
Shorter University ... GA
Simmons College of Kentucky ... KY
Southeastern Baptist College ... MS
The Crown College of the Bible ... TN
The John Leland Center for Theological Studies ... VA
Trinity Baptist College ... FL
Truett McConnell University ... GA
University of the Cumberlands ... KY
Veritas Baptist College ... IN
Virginia Beach Theological Seminary ... VA
Virginia Union University ... VA
West Coast Baptist College ... CA

Brethren Church
Ashland University ... OH

Christian Church (Disciples Of Christ)
Barton College ... NC
Bethany College ... WV
Chapman University ... CA
Christian Theological Seminary ... IN
Columbia College ... MO
Culver-Stockton College ... MO
Eureka College ... IL
Jarvis Christian College ... TX
Lexington Theological Seminary ... KY
Midway University ... KY
Northwest Christian University ... OR
Phillips Theological Seminary ... OK
Texas Christian University ... TX
Transylvania University ... KY
University of Lynchburg ... VA
William Woods University ... MO

Christian Churches And Churches of Christ
Belmont University ... TN
Boise Bible College ... ID
Central Christian College of the Bible ... MO
Cincinnati Christian University ... OH
Dallas Christian College ... TX
Great Lakes Christian College ... MI
Johnson University ... TN
Kentucky Christian University ... KY
Lincoln Christian University ... IL
Manhattan Christian College ... KS
Point University ... GA

Christian Methodist Episcopal
Lane College ... TN
Miles College ... AL
Texas College ... TX

Christian Reformed Church
Calvin Theological Seminary ... MI
Calvin University ... MI
Dordt University ... IA

Church Of Christ
Pepperdine University ... CA

Church Of God
Anderson University ... IN
Lee University ... TN
Mid-America Christian University ... OK
Pentecostal Theological Seminary ... TN
The University of Findlay ... OH
Universidad Teologica Del Caribe ... PR
Warner Pacific College ... OR
Warner University ... FL

Church of New Jerusalem
Bryn Athyn College of the New Church ... PA

Church Of The Brethren
Bethany Theological Seminary ... IN
Bridgewater College ... VA
Elizabethtown College ... PA
Manchester University ... IN
McPherson College ... KS

Church Of The Nazarene
Eastern Nazarene College ... MA
MidAmerica Nazarene University ... KS
Mount Vernon Nazarene University ... OH
Nazarene Bible College ... CO
Nazarene Theological Seminary ... MO
Northwest Nazarene University ... ID
Olivet Nazarene University ... IL
Point Loma Nazarene University ... CA
Southern Nazarene University ... OK
Trevecca Nazarene University ... TN

Churches Of Christ
Abilene Christian University ... TX
Amridge University ... AL
Crowley's Ridge College ... AR
Faulkner University ... AL
Freed-Hardeman University ... TN
Harding University Main Campus ... AR
Heritage Christian University ... AL
Lipscomb University ... TN
Lubbock Christian University ... TX
Mid-Atlantic Christian University ... NC
Ohio Valley University ... WV
Southwestern Christian College ... TX
York College ... NE

Cumberland Presbyterian
Bethel University ... TN
Memphis Theological Seminary ... TN

Evangelical Congregational Church
Evangelical Theological Seminary ... PA

Evangelical Covenant Church Of America
North Park University ... IL

Evangelical Free Church Of America
Trinity International University ... IL

Evangelical Lutheran Church In America
Augsburg University ... MN
Augustana College ... IL
Augustana University ... SD
Bethany College ... KS
California Lutheran University ... CA
Capital University ... OH
Carthage College ... WI
Concordia College ... MN
Finlandia University ... MI
Gettysburg College ... PA
Grand View University ... IA
Gustavus Adolphus College ... MN
Lenoir-Rhyne University ... NC
Luther College ... IA
Luther Seminary ... MN
Lutheran School of Theology at Chicago IL
Midland University ... NE
Muhlenberg College ... PA
Newberry College ... SC
Pacific Lutheran University ... WA
Roanoke College ... VA
St. Olaf College ... MN
Susquehanna University ... PA
Texas Lutheran University ... TX
Thiel College ... PA
United Lutheran Seminary ... PA
Wartburg College ... IA
Wartburg Theological Seminary ... IA
Wittenberg University ... OH

Evangelical Lutheran Synod
Bethany Lutheran College ... MN

Fellowship Of Grace Brethren Churches
Grace College and Seminary ... IN

Free Methodist
Central Christian College of Kansas ... KS
Greenville University ... IL
Seattle Pacific University ... WA
Spring Arbor University ... MI

Free Will Baptist
California Christian College ... CA
Randall University ... OK
Southeastern Free Will Baptist College ... NC
Welch College ... TN

Friends
Earlham College and Earlham School of Religion ... IN
George Fox University ... OR
Guilford College ... NC
Malone University ... OH
William Penn University ... IA
Wilmington College ... OH

Greek Orthodox
Hellenic College-Holy Cross Greek Orthodox School of Theology ... MA

Interdenominational
Athens College of Ministry ... GA
Bethany Global University ... MN
California Graduate School of Theology .. CA
Christian Witness Theological Seminary . CA
Denver Seminary ... CO
Evangelical Seminary of Puerto Rico ... PR
Faith International University ... WA
God's Bible School and College ... OH
Interdenominational Theological Center .. GA
Kentucky Mountain Bible College ... KY
Messiah College ... PA
Oak Hills Christian College ... MN
Palm Beach Atlantic University ... FL
Phoenix Seminary ... AZ
Rocky Mountain College ... MT
South Florida Bible College ... FL
Union Bible College ... IN
Wesley Biblical Seminary ... MS
Yuin University ... CA

Jewish
Academy for Jewish Religion, California . CA
Bais Medrash Ateres Shlomo ... NY
Hebrew Union College-Jewish Institute of Religion ... NY
Mechon L'Hoyroa ... NY
New York Medical College ... NY
Reconstructionist Rabbinical College ... PA
Women's Institute of Torah Seminary ... MD

Latter-day Saints
Brigham Young University ... UT
Brigham Young University Hawaii ... HI
Brigham Young University-Idaho ... ID
LDS Business College ... UT

Lutheran
Valparaiso University ... IN

Lutheran Church - Missouri Synod
Concordia College ... NY
Concordia Seminary ... MO
Concordia Theological Seminary ... IN
Concordia University ... NE
Concordia University ... OR
Concordia University Chicago ... IL
Concordia University Irvine ... CA
Concordia University Texas ... TX
Concordia University Wisconsin ... WI
Concordia University, St. Paul ... MN

Mennonite Brethren Church
Fresno Pacific University ... CA
Tabor College ... KS

Mennonite Church
Anabaptist Mennonite Biblical Seminary .. IN
Bethel College ... KS
Bluffton University ... OH
Eastern Mennonite University ... VA
Goshen College ... IN
Hesston College ... KS
Rosedale Bible College ... OH

Missionary Church
Bethel University ... IN

Moravian Church
Moravian College ... PA
Salem College ... NC

Multiple Protestant Denominations
Huston-Tillotson University ... TX
LeMoyne-Owen College ... TN
Paine College ... GA

Non-denominational
Carolina College of Biblical Studies ... NC
Cedar Crest College ... PA
China Evangelical Seminary North America ... CA
Faith Theological Seminary ... MD
Grove City College ... PA
Heartland Christian College ... MO
Montreat College ... NC
North American University ... TX
Pacific Bible College ... OR
Providence Christian College ... CA
Southern Bible Institute and College ... TX
The Bible Seminary ... TX
University of Fort Lauderdale ... FL
Washington University of Virginia ... VA
Williamson College ... TN

North American Baptist
Sioux Falls Seminary ... SD

Original Free Will Baptist Church
University of Mount Olive ... NC

Other Protestant
Beulah Heights University ... GA
Grace College of Divinity ... NC
Ohio Christian University ... OH
Saint Louis Christian College ... MO
Urshan Graduate School of Theology ... MO

Pentecostal Church of God

Messenger College ... TX
Universidad Pentecostal Mizpa ... PR

Pentecostal Holiness Church

Emmanuel College ... GA
Southwestern Christian University ... OK

Presbyterian

Sterling College ... KS
Whitworth University ... WA

Presbyterian Church (U.S.A.)

Agnes Scott College ... GA
Austin College ... TX
Austin Presbyterian Theological Seminary ... TX
Belhaven University ... MS
Blackburn College ... IL
Bloomfield College ... NJ
Buena Vista University ... IA
Carroll University ... WI
Columbia Theological Seminary ... GA
Davis & Elkins College ... WV
Eckerd College ... FL
Grace Mission University ... CA
Hampden-Sydney College ... VA
Hanover College ... IN
Hastings College ... NE
King University ... TN
Lees-McRae College ... NC
Louisville Presbyterian Theological Seminary ... KY
Lyon College ... AR
Macalester College ... MN
Mary Baldwin University ... VA
McCormick Theological Seminary ... IL
Millikin University ... IL
Missouri Valley College ... MO
Monmouth College ... IL
Muskingum University ... OH
Pittsburgh Theological Seminary ... PA
Presbyterian College ... SC
Princeton Theological Seminary ... NJ
Queens University of Charlotte ... NC
Rhodes College ... TN
Schreiner University ... TX
Stillman College ... AL
Tusculum University ... TN
Union Presbyterian Seminary ... VA
University of Dubuque ... IA
University of Jamestown ... ND
University of Pikeville ... KY
University of the Ozarks ... AR
Warren Wilson College ... NC
Waynesburg University ... PA
Westminster College ... PA
William Peace University ... NC
Wilson College ... PA

Presbyterian Church In America

Covenant College ... GA
Covenant Theological Seminary ... MO
Presbyterian Theological Seminary in America ... CA
Reformed University ... GA
Virginia Christian University ... VA

Protestant Episcopal

Bexley Seabury ... IL
Church Divinity School of the Pacific ... CA
General Theological Seminary ... NY
Nashotah House ... WI
Protestant Episcopal Theological Seminary in Virginia ... VA
Saint Augustine's University ... NC
Seminary of the Southwest ... TX
Sewanee: The University of the South ... TN
Trinity Episcopal School for Ministry ... PA
Voorhees College ... SC

Reformed Church In America

Central College ... IA
Hope College ... MI
New Brunswick Theological Seminary ... NJ
Northwestern College ... IA
Western Theological Seminary ... MI

Reformed Episcopal Church

Reformed Episcopal Seminary ... PA

Reformed Presbyterian Church

Evangelia University ... CA
Geneva College ... PA
Reformed Presbyterian Theological Seminary ... PA

Roman Catholic

Alvernia University ... PA
Ancilla College ... IN
Anna Maria College ... MA
Aquinas College ... MI
Aquinas College ... TN
Aquinas Institute of Theology ... MO
Assumption College ... MA
Assumption College for Sisters ... NJ
Athenaeum of Ohio ... OH
Augustine Institute ... CO
Ave Maria School of Law ... FL
Avila University ... MO
Barry University ... FL
Belmont Abbey College ... NC
Benedictine College ... KS
Benedictine University ... IL
Boston College ... MA
Brescia University ... KY
Briar Cliff University ... IA
Cabrini University ... PA
Caldwell University ... NJ
Calumet College of Saint Joseph ... IN
Canisius College ... NY
Cardinal Stritch University ... WI
Carlow University ... PA
Carroll College ... MT
Catholic Theological Union ... IL
Chestnut Hill College ... PA
Christ the King Seminary ... NY
Christendom College ... VA
Christian Brothers University ... TN
Clarke University ... IA
College of Our Lady of the Elms ... MA
College of Saint Benedict ... MN
College of Saint Elizabeth ... NJ
College of Saint Mary ... NE
College of the Holy Cross ... MA
Conception Seminary College ... MO
Creighton University ... NE
DePaul University ... IL
DeSales University ... PA
Divine Word College ... IA
Dominican School of Philosophy and Theology ... CA
Dominican University ... IL
Donnelly College ... KS
Duquesne University ... PA
Edgewood College ... WI
Emmanuel College ... MA
Fairfield University ... CT
Felician University ... NJ
Fontbonne University ... MO
Franciscan Missionaries of Our Lady University ... LA
Franciscan University of Steubenville ... OH
Gannon University ... PA
Georgetown University ... DC
Georgian Court University ... NJ
Gonzaga University ... WA
Gwynedd Mercy University ... PA
Holy Apostles College and Seminary ... CT
Holy Cross College ... IN
Holy Family University ... PA
Immaculata University ... PA
John Carroll University ... OH
Kenrick-Glennon Seminary, Kenrick School of Theology ... MO
King's College ... PA
La Roche University ... PA
La Salle University ... PA
Laboure College ... MA
Lewis University ... IL
Loras College ... IA
Lourdes University ... OH
Loyola Marymount University ... CA
Loyola University Chicago ... IL
Loyola University Maryland ... MD
Loyola University New Orleans ... LA
Madonna University ... MI
Marian University ... IN
Marian University ... WI
Marquette University ... WI
Marymount California University ... CA
Marymount University ... VA
Marywood University ... PA
Mercy College of Health Sciences ... IA
Mercy College of Ohio ... OH
Mercyhurst University ... PA
Merrimack College ... MA
Misericordia University ... PA
Mount Angel Seminary ... OR
Mount Carmel College of Nursing ... OH
Mount Marty College ... SD
Mount Mary University ... WI
Mount Mercy University ... IA
Mount Saint Mary's University ... CA
Mount St. Joseph University ... OH
Mount St. Mary's University ... MD
Neumann University ... PA
Newman University ... KS
Northeast Catholic College ... NH
Notre Dame College ... OH
Notre Dame of Maryland University ... MD
Notre Dame Seminary, Graduate School of Theology ... LA
Oblate School of Theology ... TX
Ohio Dominican University ... OH
Our Lady of the Lake University ... TX
Pontifical College Josephinum ... OH
Pontifical Faculty of the Immaculate Conception at the Dominican House of Studies ... DC
Pontifical John Paul II Institute for Studies on Marriage and Family ... DC
Pope St. John XXIII National Seminary ... MA
Presentation College ... SD
Providence College ... RI
Quincy University ... IL
Regis University ... CO
Rivier University ... NH
Rockhurst University ... MO
Rosemont College ... PA
Sacred Heart Major Seminary ... MI
Sacred Heart Seminary and School of Theology ... WI
Saint Anselm College ... NH
Saint Anthony College of Nursing ... IL
Saint Bernard's School of Theology & Ministry ... NY
Saint Charles Borromeo Seminary ... PA
Saint Francis Medical Center College of Nursing ... IL
Saint Francis University ... PA
Saint Gregory the Great Seminary ... NE
Saint John's Seminary ... CA
Saint John's Seminary ... MA
Saint John's University ... MN
Saint Joseph Seminary College ... LA
Saint Joseph's College of Maine ... ME
Saint Joseph's Seminary ... NY
Saint Joseph's University ... PA
Saint Leo University ... FL
Saint Louis University ... MO
Saint Martin's University ... WA
Saint Mary Seminary and Graduate School of Theology ... OH
Saint Mary's College ... IN
Saint Mary's College of California ... CA
Saint Mary's Seminary and University ... MD
Saint Mary's University of Minnesota ... MN
Saint Mary-of-the-Woods College ... IN
Saint Meinrad School of Theology ... IN
Saint Michael's College ... VT
Saint Norbert College ... WI
Saint Patrick's Seminary & University ... CA
Saint Peter's University ... NJ
Saint Vincent College ... PA
Saint Vincent Seminary ... PA
Saint Xavier University ... IL
Salve Regina University ... RI
Seattle University ... WA
Seton Hall University ... NJ
Seton Hill University ... PA
Siena Heights University ... MI
Silver Lake College of the Holy Family ... WI
Spring Hill College ... AL
SS. Cyril and Methodius Seminary ... MI
St. Ambrose University ... IA
St. Bonaventure University ... NY
St. Catherine University ... MN
St. John Vianney College Seminary ... FL
St. John Vianney Theological Seminary ... CO
St. John's University ... NY
St. Mary's University ... TX
St. Thomas University ... FL
St. Vincent De Paul Regional Seminary ... FL
Stonehill College ... MA
The Catholic University of America ... DC
The College of Saint Scholastica ... MN
The Pontifical Catholic University of Puerto Rico ... PR
The University of Scranton ... PA
Thomas More University ... KY
Trinity Washington University ... DC
Universidad Central de Bayamon ... PR
University of Dallas ... TX
University of Dayton ... OH
University of Detroit Mercy ... MI
University of Holy Cross ... LA
University of Mary ... ND
University of Notre Dame ... IN
University of Providence ... MT
University of Saint Francis ... IN
University of Saint Joseph ... CT
University of Saint Mary ... KS
University of Saint Mary of the Lake-Mundelein Seminary ... IL
University of Saint Thomas ... MN
University of San Diego ... CA
University of San Francisco ... CA
University of St. Francis ... IL
University of St. Thomas ... TX
University of the Incarnate Word ... TX
University of the Sacred Heart ... PR
Ursuline College ... OH
Villanova University ... PA
Viterbo University ... WI
Walsh University ... OH
Wheeling University ... WV
Wyoming Catholic College ... WY
Xavier University ... OH
Xavier University of Louisiana ... LA

Russian Orthodox

Holy Trinity Orthodox Seminary ... NY

Seventh-day Adventist

AdventHealth University ... FL
Andrews University ... MI
Kettering College ... OH
La Sierra University ... CA
Loma Linda University ... CA
Oakwood University ... AL
Pacific Union College ... CA
Southern Adventist University ... TN
Southwestern Adventist University ... TX
Union College ... NE
Universidad Adventista de las Antillas ... PR
Walla Walla University ... WA
Washington Adventist University ... MD

Southern Baptist

B.H. Carroll Theological Institute ... TX
Blue Mountain College ... MS
California Baptist University ... CA
Carson-Newman University ... TN
Charleston Southern University ... SC
Clear Creek Baptist Bible College ... KY
Gateway Seminary ... CA
Hannibal-LaGrange University ... MO
Houston Baptist University ... TX
Louisiana College ... LA
Midwestern Baptist Theological Seminary MO
Mississippi College ... MS
New Orleans Baptist Theological Seminary ... LA
North Greenville University ... SC
Oklahoma Baptist University ... OK
Ouachita Baptist University ... AR
Samford University ... AL
Southeastern Baptist Theological Seminary ... NC
Southwest Baptist University ... MO
Southwestern Baptist Theological Seminary ... TX
The Baptist College of Florida ... FL
The Southern Baptist Theological Seminary ... KY
Union University ... TN
University of Mary Hardin-Baylor ... TX
University of Mobile ... AL
Wayland Baptist University ... TX
William Carey University ... MS
Williams Baptist University ... AR
Wingate University ... NC

The Christian And Missionary Alliance

Crown College ... MN
Nyack College ... NY
Simpson University ... CA
Toccoa Falls College ... GA

Unification Church

Unification Theological Seminary ... NY

Unitarian Universalist

Meadville Lombard Theological School ... IL
Starr King School for the Ministry ... CA

United Brethren Church

Huntington University ... IN

United Church Of Christ

Catawba College ... NC
Chicago Theological Seminary ... IL
Doane University ... NE
Eden Theological Seminary ... MO
Elmhurst College ... IL
Heidelberg University ... OH
Lakeland University ... WI
Lancaster Theological Seminary ... PA
Northland College ... WI
Piedmont College ... GA
The Defiance College ... OH
Tougaloo College ... MS
United Theological Seminary of the Twin Cities ... MN

United Methodist

Adrian College ... MI
Albion College ... MI
Albright College ... PA
Allegheny College ... PA
American University ... DC

Andrew College .... GA
Baker University .... KS
Bennett College .... NC
Bethune Cookman University .... FL
Birmingham-Southern College .... AL
Brevard College .... NC
Centenary College of Louisiana .... LA
Central Methodist University .... MO
Claflin University .... SC
Claremont School of Theology .... CA
Clark Atlanta University .... GA
Columbia College .... SC
Cornell College .... IA
Dakota Wesleyan University .... SD
DePauw University .... IN
Dillard University .... LA
Emory & Henry College .... VA
Emory University .... GA
Ferrum College .... VA
Florida Southern College .... FL
Garrett-Evangelical Theological Seminary IL
Greensboro College .... NC
Hamline University .... MN
Hendrix College .... AR
High Point University .... NC
Huntingdon College .... AL
Iliff School of Theology .... CO
Iowa Wesleyan University .... IA
Kansas Wesleyan University .... KS
Kentucky Wesleyan College .... KY
LaGrange College .... GA
Lebanon Valley College .... PA
Lindsey Wilson College .... KY
Louisburg College .... NC
Lycoming College .... PA
MacMurray College IL
Martin Methodist College .... TN
McKendree University IL
McMurry University .... TX
Methodist Theological School in Ohio ..... OH
Methodist University .... NC
Millsaps College .... MS
Morningside College .... IA
Nebraska Wesleyan University .... NE
North Carolina Wesleyan College .... NC
North Central College IL
Ohio Northern University .... OH
Ohio Wesleyan University .... OH
Oklahoma City University .... OK
Otterbein University .... OH
Pfeiffer University .... NC
Philander Smith College .... AR
Randolph College .... VA
Randolph-Macon College .... VA
Reinhardt University .... GA
Rust College .... MS
Saint Paul School of Theology .... KS
Shenandoah University .... VA
Simpson College .... IA
Southern Methodist University .... TX
Southwestern College .... KS
Southwestern University .... TX
Spartanburg Methodist College .... SC
Tennessee Wesleyan University .... TN
Texas Wesleyan University .... TX
Union College .... KY
United Theological Seminary .... OH
University of Evansville .... IN
University of Indianapolis .... IN
Virginia Wesleyan University .... VA
Wesley College .... DE
Wesley Theological Seminary .... DC
Wesleyan College .... GA
West Virginia Wesleyan College .... WV
Wiley College .... TX
Wofford College .... SC
Young Harris College .... GA

Wesleyan Church

Allegheny Wesleyan College .... OH
Houghton College .... NY
Indiana Wesleyan University .... IN
Oklahoma Wesleyan University .... OK
Southern Wesleyan University .... SC

Wisconsin Evangelical Lutheran Synod

Martin Luther College .... MN

Carnegie Classification Code Definitions*

The *Higher Education Directory*® lists the updated 2018 Carnegie Classifications. Due to space limitation, the *Higher Education Directory*® only lists the basic classification—which was substantially revised in 2018. These new codes are listed below:

Associate's Colleges: Institutions at which the highest level degree awarded is an associate's degree. The institutions are sorted into nine categories based on the intersection of two factors: disciplinary focus (transfer, career & technical or mixed) and dominant student type (traditional, nontraditional or mixed). Excludes Special Focus Institutions and Tribal Colleges.

Assoc/HT-High Trad: Associate's Colleges: High Transfer-High Traditional
Assoc/HT-Mix Trad/Non: Associate's Colleges: High Transfer-Mixed Traditional/Nontraditional
Assoc/HT-High Non: Associate's Colleges: High Transfer-High Nontraditional
Assoc/MT-VT-High Trad: Associate's Colleges: Mixed Transfer/Career & Technical-High Traditional
Assoc/MT-VT-Mix Trad/Non: Associate's Colleges: Mixed Transfer/Career & Technical-Mixed Traditional/Nontraditional
Assoc/MT-VT-High Non: Associate's Colleges: Mixed Transfer/Career & Technical-High Nontraditional
Assoc/HVT-High Trad: Associate's Colleges: High Career & Technical-High Traditional
Assoc/HVT-Mix Trad/Non: Associate's Colleges: High Career & Technical-Mixed Traditional/Nontraditional
Assoc/HVT-High Non: Associate's Colleges: High Career & Technical-High Nontraditional

Baccalaureate/Associate's Colleges. Includes four-year colleges (by virtue of having at least one baccalaureate degree program) that conferred more than 50 percent of degrees at the associate's level. Excludes Special Focus Institutions, Tribal Colleges, and institutions that have sufficient masterÕs or doctoral degrees to fall into those categories.

Bac/Assoc-Assoc Dom: Baccalaureate/Associate's Colleges: Associate's Dominant
Bac/Assoc-Mixed: Baccalaureate/Associate's Colleges: Mixed Baccalaureate/Associate's

Baccalaureate Colleges. Includes institutions where baccalaureate or higher degrees represent at least 50 percent of all degrees but where fewer than 50 master's degrees or 20 doctoral degrees were awarded during the update year. (Some institutions above the master's degree threshold are also included; see Methodology) Excludes Special Focus Institutions and Tribal Colleges.

Bac-A&S: Baccalaureate Colleges: Arts & Sciences Focus
Bac-Diverse: Baccalaureate Colleges: Diverse Fields

Master's Colleges and Universities. Generally includes institutions that awarded at least 50 master's degrees and fewer than 20 doctoral degrees during the update year (with occasional exceptions; see Methodology). Excludes Special Focus Institutions and Tribal Colleges.

Masters/L: Master's Colleges & Universities: Larger Programs
Masters/M: Master's Colleges & Universities: Medium Programs
Masters/S: Master's Colleges & Universities: Small Programs

Doctoral Universities. Includes institutions that awarded at least 20 research/scholarship doctoral degrees during the update year (this does not include professional practice doctoral-level degrees, such as the JD, MD, PharmD, DPT, etc.). Excludes Special Focus Institutions and Tribal Colleges.

DU-Highest: Doctoral Universities: Very High Research Activity
DU-Higher: Doctoral Universities: High Research Activity
DU-Mod: Doctoral/Professional Universities: Moderate Research Activity

Special Focus Institutions, Two-year. Institutions where a high concentration of degrees is in a single field or set of related fields. Excludes Tribal Colleges.

Spec 2-yr-Health: Special Focus Two-Year: Health Professions
Spec 2-yr-Tech: Special Focus Two-Year: Technical Professions
Spec 2-yr-A&S: Special Focus Two-Year: Arts & Design
Spec 2-yr-Other: Special Focus Two-Year: Other Fields

Special Focus Institutions, Four-year. Institutions where a high concentration of degrees is in a single field or set of related fields. Excludes Tribal Colleges.

Spec-4-yr-Faith: Special Focus Four-Year: Faith-Related Institutions
Spec-4-yr-Med: Special Focus Four-Year: Medical Schools & Centers
Spec-4-yr-Other Health: Special Focus Four-Year: Other Health Professions Schools
Spec-4-yr-Eng: Special Focus Four-Year: Engineering Schools
Spec-4-yr-Other Tech: Special Focus Four-Year: Other Technology-Related Schools
Spec-4-yr-Bus: Special Focus Four-Year: Business & Management Schools
Spec-4-yr-Arts: Special Focus Four-Year: Arts, Music & Design Schools
Spec-4-yr-Law: Special Focus Four-Year: Law Schools
Spec-4-yr-Other: Special Focus Four-Year: Other Special Focus Institutions

Tribal Colleges. Colleges and universities that are members of the American Indian Higher Education Consortium, as identified in IPEDS Institutional Characteristics.

Tribal: Tribal Colleges

*All data provided by Carnegie Classification of Institutions of Higher Education by Indiana University Center for Postsecondary Research. For more detailed information on the revised Carnegie Codes, please visit http://carnegieclassifications.iu.edu/. Basic Classification methodology can be found at http://carnegieclassifications.iu.edu/methodology/basic.php.

Statistics

Institutions of Higher Education by Control, Level and State

STATE	TWO YEAR		FOUR YEAR		TOTAL		SYSTEM	GRAND
	PRIVATE	PUBLIC	PRIVATE	PUBLIC	PRIVATE	PUBLIC	OFFICE	TOTAL
AL	0	24	20	15	20	39	2	61
AK	1	0	3	3	4	3	1	8
AZ	9	19	24	4	33	23	1	57
AR	3	22	14	12	17	34	2	53
CA	41	104	257	49	298	153	28	479
CO	13	7	23	22	36	29	2	67
CT	0	12	18	7	18	19	1	38
DE	1	0	3	3	4	3	0	7
DC	0	0	17	3	17	3	0	20
FL	36	1	73	41	109	42	1	152
GA	7	23	40	26	47	49	1	97
HI	2	6	6	4	8	10	2	20
ID	0	4	6	4	6	8	0	14
IL	11	47	83	12	94	59	6	159
IN	7	1	43	15	50	16	2	68
IA	0	18	37	3	37	21	3	61
KS	1	25	24	9	25	34	0	59
KY	1	16	31	8	32	24	1	57
LA	4	16	13	16	17	32	4	53
ME	2	7	13	7	15	14	2	31
MD	1	16	22	16	23	32	1	56
MA	2	16	74	14	76	30	2	108
MI	3	23	42	21	45	44	1	90
MN	5	30	41	11	46	41	3	90
MS	0	15	10	9	10	24	0	34
MO	10	17	59	13	69	30	3	102
MT	6	5	7	6	13	11	1	25
NE	6	7	16	7	22	14	2	38
NV	2	1	4	6	6	7	1	14
NH	0	7	10	4	10	11	2	23
NJ	4	18	37	13	41	31	0	72
NM	0	13	8	8	8	21	0	29
NY	24	36	188	44	212	80	5	297
NC	1	58	52	17	53	75	2	130
ND	1	4	7	7	8	11	1	20
OH	20	19	71	20	91	39	1	131
OK	4	12	14	15	18	27	0	45
OR	4	16	24	8	28	24	0	52
PA	37	16	111	20	148	36	1	185
RI	0	1	9	3	9	4	0	13
SC	1	18	24	15	25	33	0	58
SD	0	5	11	6	11	11	1	23
TN	10	13	48	9	58	22	2	82
TX	22	57	80	53	102	110	8	220
UT	2	1	13	7	15	8	1	24
VT	0	1	13	4	13	5	1	19
VA	13	24	55	17	68	41	1	110
WA	3	8	22	31	25	39	2	66
WV	6	8	12	11	18	19	2	39
WI	2	16	31	13	33	29	2	64
WY	1	7	1	1	2	8	0	10
AS	0	0	0	1	0	1	0	1
GU	0	1	1	1	1	2	0	3
MH	0	1	0	0	0	1	0	1
MP	0	0	0	1	0	1	0	1
PR	5	0	42	14	47	14	3	64
FM	0	1	0	0	0	1	0	1
PW	0	1	0	0	0	1	0	1
VI	0	0	0	1	0	1	0	1
Total	**334**	**844**	**1907**	**710**	**2241**	**1554**	**108**	**3903**

Figures do not include 782 additional branch campuses.

50 Largest Universities by Fall 2017 Enrollment

Institution	Enrollment
1. Western Governors University	98627
2. Southern New Hampshire University	90955
3. Grand Canyon University	83284
4. Liberty University	75044
5. Texas A & M University	67929
6. University of Central Florida	66059
7. The Ohio State University Main Campus	59837
8. University of Maryland Global Campus	59379
9. Florida International University	56718
10. University of Florida	52669
11. Brigham Young University-Idaho	51881
12. University of Minnesota	51848
13. University of Texas at Austin	51525
14. Arizona State University	51164
15. New York University	51123
16. Michigan State University	50019
17. Walden University	49680
18. Rutgers University - New Brunswick	49577
19. University of Illinois at Urbana-Champaign	48216
20. Penn State University Park	47119
21. The University of Texas at Arlington	46497
22. American Public University System	46420
23. University of Washington	46166
24. University of Michigan-Ann Arbor	46002
25. University of Southern California	45687
26. University of Houston	45364
27. University of California-Los Angeles	44027
28. University of Arizona	43751
29. Indiana University	43710
30. University of South Florida	43540
31. University of Wisconsin-Madison	42977
32. Purdue University Main Campus	42699
33. University of California-Berkeley	41891
34. Florida State University	41362
35. California State University-Northridge	41319
36. California State University-Fullerton	40905
37. University of Maryland College Park	40521
38. Temple University	39967
39. Texas State University	38666
40. The University of Alabama	38563
41. University of North Texas	38276
42. California State University-Long Beach	37622
43. University of Georgia	37606
44. University of California-Davis	37380
45. Utah Valley University	37282
46. University of Cincinnati Main Campus	37155
47. Texas Tech University	36996
48. Ashford University	36453
49. Capella University	36284
50. Iowa State University	36158

Institutions by Control and Tuition Range

Tuition	Public*	Private	Total
0 - 1,000	74	689	763
1,001 - 2,000	150	0	150
2,001 - 4,000	370	18	388
4,001 - 6,000	427	49	476
6,001 - 8,000	193	66	259
8,001 - 10,000	158	74	232
Over 10,000	182	1345	1527
Total	**1554**	**2241**	**3795**

* Figures for Public Institutions are In-State Tuitions

Universities, Colleges and Schools

by State*

*Includes the District of Columbia and, separately, U.S. Service Schools, American Samoa, Federated States of Micronesia, Guam, Marshall Islands, Northern Marianas, Palau, Puerto Rico, and Virgin Islands.

ALABAMA

Alabama Agricultural and Mechanical University (A)

4900 Meridian Street, Normal AL 35762-1357
County: Madison FICE Identification: 001002
Unit ID: 100654
Telephone: (256) 372-5230 Carnegie Class: Masters/L
FAX Number: (256) 372-5244 Calendar System: Semester
URL: www.aamu.edu
Established: 1875 Annual Undergrad Tuition & Fees (In-State): $9,744
Enrollment: 6,001 Coed
Affiliation or Control: State IRS Status: 501(c)3
Highest Offering: Doctorate
Accreditation: SC, AAFCS, CACREP, CAEP, DIETD, PLNG, SP, SW

01 President ... Dr. Andrew HUGINE, JR.
03 Executive VP/COO ... Vacant
05 Provost/VP Academic Affairs ... Dr. Daniel K. WIMS
10 Vice President Business & Finance ... Mr. Clayton GIBSON
111 VP Mktg/Comm/Advancement ... Dr. Archie TUCKER
32 Vice President Student Affairs ... Dr. Gary CROSBY
46 Interim VP Inst Rsrch/Spons Pgms ... Dr. James WALKE
88 Special Assistant to the President ... Dr. Malinda SWOOPE
114 AVP Budget & Planning ... Mr. Gregory JACKSON
84 AVP of Enrollment Mgmt/Dir Admiss ... Vacant
13 Interim Chief Information Officer ... Dr. Kylie NASH
21 AVP Finance/Comptroller ... Dr. Lynda BATISTE
15 Director Human Resources ... Dr. Jarrett WALTON
18 Dir Facilities and Admin Services ... Mr. Brian SHIPP
06 Registrar ... Ms. Brenda K. WILLIAMS
30 Director of Development ... Ms. Reba JASMIN
41 Director of Athletics ... Mr. Bryan HICKS
35 Director of Student Activities ... Ms. Diann ANDERSON
37 Director of Financial Aid ... Mr. Darryl JACKSON
23 Dir Student Health & Counseling ... Mr. Micah GRIFFIN
36 Dir Career Development Services ... Ms. Yvette CLAYTON
09 Dir Institutional Research ... Dr. James WALKE
26 Director Marketing & PR ... Mr. Jerome SAINTJONES
39 Dir of Residential Housing ... Ms. Karla MILLER
19 Chief of Police ... Mr. Nadis CARLISLE
08 Director Learning Resources Center ... Dr. Annie PAYTON
96 Director of Purchasing ... Mr. Timothy THORNTON
58 Dean Graduate School/AVP Acad Affs ... Dr. Derrek DUNN
47 Dean Col Agricultural/Life/Nat Sci ... Dr. Lloyd WALKER
53 Dean College of Education ... Dr. Lena WALTON
54 Dean College of Engineering ... Dr. Chance GLENN
50 Dean Col of Business/Pub Affs ... Dr. Del SMITH
49 Interim Dean University College ... Dr. Juarine STEWART
04 Executive Assistant to President ... Dr. Brittany A. HOLLOMAN
102 Dir Foundation/Corporate Relations ... Dr. Allen VITAL
29 Director Alumni Relations ... Mrs. Sandra STUBBS
43 Dir Legal Services/General Counsel ... Mrs. Angela DEBRO
45 Chief Institutional Planning ... Dr. Archie TUCKER
07 Director of Admissions ... Mr. Dwayne GREEN
86 Director Government Relations ... Ms. Roslyn CREWS

Alabama College of Osteopathic Medicine (B)

445 Health Sciences Boulevard, Dothan AL 36303
County: Houston Identification: 667138
Unit ID: 483975
Telephone: (334) 699-2266 Carnegie Class: Spec-4-yr-Med
FAX Number: N/A Calendar System: Semester
URL: www.acom.edu
Established: 2011 Annual Graduate Tuition & Fees: N/A
Enrollment: 608 Coed
Affiliation or Control: Independent Non-Profit IRS Status: 501(c)3
Highest Offering: First Professional Degree; No Undergraduates
Accreditation: OSTEO

01 President ... Rick SUTTON
05 Interim Dean ... James C. JONES
10 Chief Financial Officer ... Vacant
32 Assoc Dean Student Services ... Phillip REYNOLDS
84 Exec Dir Enrollment Management ... Bob WILLIS
06 Registrar ... Saimara SOTO
07 Dir of Admissions & Enrollment ... Linda GOODSON
26 Dir of Communications & Marketing ... Sarah SENN

*Alabama Community College System (C)

135 South Union Street, Montgomery AL 36104-4340
County: Montgomery Identification: 667303
Telephone: (334) 293-4500 Carnegie Class: N/A
FAX Number: (334) 293-4504
URL: www.accs.cc

01 Chancellor ... Mr. Jimmy H. BAKER
05 VC Teaching/Learning & Academics ... Ms. Tony HOLLAND
10 VC Admin/Financial Services ... Mr. Bryan HELMS
103 VC Workforce/Economic Development ... Mr. Jeff LYNN
32 VC Student Success ... Dr. Cynthia ANTHONY
100 Chief of Staff & VC SDSA ... Ms. Susan Y. PRICE
15 Director Human Resources ... Ms. Nikita T. PAYNE

*Bevill State Community College (D)

1411 Indiana Avenue, Jasper AL 35501
County: Walker FICE Identification: 005733
Unit ID: 102429
Telephone: (205) 387-0511 Carnegie Class: Assoc/HVT-Mix Trad/Non
FAX Number: (205) 387-5192 Calendar System: Semester
URL: www.bscc.edu
Established: 1965 Annual Undergrad Tuition & Fees (In-State): $5,086
Enrollment: 3,872 Coed
Affiliation or Control: State IRS Status: 501(c)3
Highest Offering: Associate Degree
Accreditation: SC, ADNUR, EMT, PNUR, SURGT

02 President ... Dr. Kim ENNIS
05 Vice President/Dean of Instruction ... Dr. Leslie HARTLEY
26 Director of Public Relations ... Ms. Tana COLLINS
10 Dean of Accounting & Finance ... Ms. Linda JONES
32 Dean of Students ... Ms. Melissa STOWE
15 Director of Human Resources ... Ms. Mary KINARD
18 Director of Facilities & Security ... Mr. Randy STULTS
121 Dean of Student Success ... Mr. Max WEAVER
76 Dean for Health Sciences ... Ms. Penne MOTT
103 Dean Workforce Solutions/Econ Dev ... Mr. Al MOORE
25 Director of Grants/Federal Programs ... Ms. Wanda JACKSON

*Bishop State Community College (E)

351 N Broad Street, Mobile AL 36603-5898
County: Mobile FICE Identification: 001030
Unit ID: 102030
Telephone: (251) 405-7000 Carnegie Class: Assoc/HVT-Mix Trad/Non
FAX Number: N/A Calendar System: Semester
URL: www.bishop.edu
Established: 1965 Annual Undergrad Tuition & Fees (In-State): $4,740
Enrollment: 3,233 Coed
Affiliation or Control: State IRS Status: 501(c)3
Highest Offering: Associate Degree
Accreditation: SC, ACBSP, ADNUR, CAHIIM, PNUR, PTAA

02 President ... Dr. Reginald SYKES
11 Vice President of Opers ... Mrs. Ann CLANTON
05 Dean of Instruction ... Vacant
12 Director of Carver Campus ... Mr. Wilber BRYANT
12 Dir Baker-Gaines Central Campus ... Mrs. Madeline STOKES
72 Dean of Tech Educ/Workforce Dev ... Vacant
32 Dean of Students ... Dr. Terry HAZZARD
10 Dean of Business/Finance ... Mr. LaKeith MILLER
20 Associate Academic Dean ... Mr. Theodore LABAY
06 Registrar ... Mr. Philip URBANEK
15 Director of Human Resources ... Mrs. Kenya PARISH-ONUKWULI
18 Director of Physical Plant ... Mr. Kenneth HOLDER
26 Director of Public Relations ... Ms. Courtney STEELE
45 Interim Dir of Inst Effectiveness ... Mr. Claude BUMPERS
37 Mgr Student Fin Aid/Veterans Svcs ... Vacant
13 Chief Info Technology Officer (CIO) ... Mrs. Mirian POWELL
19 Director Security/Safety ... Chief Lloyd WASHINGTON
41 Athletic Director ... Mr. Trenton EAGER

*Calhoun Community College (F)

PO Box 2216, Decatur AL 35609-2216
County: Limestone FICE Identification: 001013
Unit ID: 101514
Telephone: (256) 306-2500 Carnegie Class: Assoc/HT-Mix Trad/Non
FAX Number: (256) 306-2877 Calendar System: Semester
URL: www.calhoun.edu
Established: 1963 Annual Undergrad Tuition & Fees (In-State): $4,820
Enrollment: 9,861 Coed
Affiliation or Control: State IRS Status: 501(c)3
Highest Offering: Associate Degree
Accreditation: SC, ADNUR, DA, EMT, MLTAD, PNUR, PTAA, SURGT

02 Interim President ... Dr. Joe BURKE
05 VP Instruct/Student Success ... Dr. Alan STEPHENSON
32 Vice President of Student Services ... Dr. Patricia WILSON
10 Dean of Business & Finance ... Mr. Jason MORGAN
07 Acting Dir Admiss/Records/Registrar ... Ms. Alanna THOMPSON
08 Director of Library Services ... Mr. James LOYD
13 Director Information Systems ... Mr. Nathan TYLER
111 Acting Director of PR & CETV ... Mr. Wes TORAIN
12 Dean of Research Park Campus ... Mr. Mark BRANNON
18 Exec Director of Physical Plant ... Mr. Bruce CAUSEY
09 Dean Planning/Research & Grants ... Dr. Debra HENDERSHOT
103 Int Director Workforce Solutions ... Mr. Houston BLACKWOOD
76 Dean Health Sciences ... Mr. Bret MCGILL
81 Dean Math/Natural Sciences ... Mr. Rodney ALFORD
79 Dean Humanities & Social Sciences ... Dr. Donna ESTILL
15 Director Human Resources & Payroll ... Mrs. Kim GAINES
19 Director Public Safety ... Mr. Kevin DAVENPORT
36 Director of Career Services & Co-op ... Mrs. Kelli MORRIS
37 Director Student Financial Aid ... Mrs. Janett SPENCER
04 Secretary to President ... Ms. Belinda NOE
41 Athletic Director ... Dr. Nancy KEENUM
26 Acting Asst Dir of PR & CETV ... Ms. Sherika ATTIPOE
51 Director of Adult Education ... Ms. Dana WOLFE
72 Dean of Technologies ... Mr. John HOLLEY
50 Dean of Business and CIS ... Mr. James PAYNE

*Central Alabama Community College (G)

1675 Cherokee Road, Alexander City AL 35010
County: Tallapoosa FICE Identification: 001007
Unit ID: 100760
Telephone: (256) 234-6346 Carnegie Class: Assoc/HT-Mix Trad/Non
FAX Number: (256) 234-0384 Calendar System: Semester
URL: www.cacc.edu
Established: 1963 Annual Undergrad Tuition & Fees (In-State): $4,740
Enrollment: 1,835 Coed
Affiliation or Control: State IRS Status: 501(c)3
Highest Offering: Associate Degree
Accreditation: SC, ADNUR

02 President ... Dr. Susan BURROW
10 Dean of Financial Services ... Ms. Lisa SAWYER
05 Dean of Instruction ... Mr. Danny COLEMAN
32 Dean of Students ... Dr. Sherri TAYLOR
35 Associate Dean of Student Services ... Ms. Glenda BLAND
09 Assoc Dean of Inst Effect/Compl ... Ms. Cindy ENTREKIN
76 Associate Dean of Health Science ... Dr. Jennifer STEELE
08 Librarian ... Ms. Denita OLIVER
06 Records Manager ... Ms. Marian MARTIN
26 Public Relations Officer ... Mr. Brett PRITCHARD
13 Chief Information Officer ... Mr. Rickey CREEL
37 Director Student Financial Aid ... Mr. Jonathan MILES
04 Administrative Asst to President ... Ms. Linda WILLIAMS
15 Exec Director of Human Resources ... Ms. Tina SHAW

*Chattahoochee Valley Community College (H)

2602 College Drive, Phenix City AL 36869-7960
County: Russell FICE Identification: 012182
Unit ID: 101028
Telephone: (334) 291-4900 Carnegie Class: Assoc/HT-High Trad
FAX Number: (334) 291-4944 Calendar System: Semester
URL: www.cv.edu
Established: 1973 Annual Undergrad Tuition & Fees (In-State): $4,738
Enrollment: 1,424 Coed
Affiliation or Control: State IRS Status: 501(c)3
Highest Offering: Associate Degree
Accreditation: SC, ADNUR, MAAB, PNUR

02 President ... Ms. Jacqueline SCREWS
05 Vice President/Dean of the College ... Dr. David HODGE
103 Assoc Dean of Workforce Development . Dr. Shirley ARMSTRONG
50 Chair of Business/Comp Info Tech ... Dr. Beth MULLIN
81 Interim Chair of Science ... Ms. Merry CUERVO
79 Chair of English and Communication ... Ms. Samantha VANCE
76 Chair of Health Sciences ... Dr. Bridgett JACKSON
81 Chair of Mathematics ... Ms. Mary JOHNSON
88 Program Dir Public Safety Academy ... Mr. Kenneth HARRISON
08 Director Learning Resources Center ... Ms. Elizabeth BRADSHER
37 Director of Financial Aid ... Ms. Susan BRYANT
18 Director Facilities & Maintenance ... Mr. Johann WELLS
111 Dean of Advancement/Inst Effect ... Dr. Joree JONES
41 Director of Athletics ... Mr. Adam THOMAS
38 Testing and Student Services Coord ... Ms. Gloria CANTY
13 Director of Information Systems ... Mr. Jody NOLES
32 Assoc Dean of Student Development ... Mrs. Vickie WILLIAMS
51 Director of Adult Education ... Ms. Laodecea SEAY
15 Director of Human Resources ... Ms. Debbie BOONE
111 Coordinator of Inst Advancement ... Mr. David FLETCHER
10 Dean of Financial Affairs ... Mr. Dexter JACKSON
55 Evening Coordinator ... Mr. Reggie GORDY
07 Director of Admissions/Registrar ... Ms. Sanquita ALEXANDER
04 Administrative Asst to President ... Ms. Terrah LONG
19 Security/Safety ... Mr. Keith MANUEL
26 Marketing & Media Coordinator ... Ms. Myya ROBINSON

*Coastal Alabama Community College (I)

1900 Highway 31 S, Bay Minette AL 36507-2698
County: Baldwin FICE Identification: 001060
Unit ID: 101161
Telephone: (251) 580-2100 Carnegie Class: Assoc/MT-VT-Mix Trad/Non
FAX Number: (251) 580-2253 Calendar System: Semester
URL: www.coastalalabama.edu
Established: 1965 Annual Undergrad Tuition & Fees (In-State): $4,740
Enrollment: 4,968 Coed
Affiliation or Control: State IRS Status: 501(c)3
Highest Offering: Associate Degree
Accreditation: SC, ACFEI, ADNUR, DA, EMT, PNUR, SURGT

02 President ... Dr. Craig POUNCEY
111 EVP of Inst Advanc/Student Dev ... Dr. Brenda J. KENNEDY
15 VP Human Resources/Employee Rels ... Mrs. Laura BURKS
103 VP Instructnl/Workforce Development ... Vacant
32 Vice President of Student Svcs ... Mr. David JONES
05 Dean of Instruction ... Ms. Melinda BYRD-MURPHY
86 Dean of Federal Programs ... Mrs. Lena DEXTER
66 Dean Nursing & Allied Health ... Ms. Jean GRAHAM
11 Dean Administrative Services ... Vacant
35 Director Student Support Services ... Mr. Carl CUNNINGHAM
106 Director Distance Education ... Ms. Ann STRICKLAND
06 Registrar ... Ms. Beth BRYARS
08 Dir Learning Resource Center ... Ms. Rheena ELMORE

37 Financial Aid Director .... Dr. Jim THEEUWES
18 Director Maintenance/Facilities .... Mr. Richard LYNN
19 Chief College Police .... Mr. Chris JOHNSON
39 Residence Hall Director .... Ms. Danielle PITTS
36 Academic Career Advisor .... Ms. Theresa MCCLELLAND

*Enterprise State Community College (A)

PO Box 1300, Enterprise AL 36331-1300
County: Coffee FICE Identification: 001015
Unit ID: 101143
Telephone: (334) 347-2623 Carnegie Class: Assoc/MT-VT-Mix Trad/Non
FAX Number: (334) 393-6223 Calendar System: Semester
URL: www.escc.edu
Established: 1963 Annual Undergrad Tuition & Fees (In-State): $4,740
Enrollment: 1,778 Coed
Affiliation or Control: State IRS Status: 501(c)3
Highest Offering: Associate Degree
Accreditation: SC

02 President .... Mr. Matt RODGERS
05 Dean of Instruction .... Mr. Daniel LONG
32 Dean of Student Services .... Mr. Olivier CHARLES
10 Dir of Financial Affairs .... Ms. Paula HELMS
35 Assoc Dean of Students/Athletic Dir .... Mr. Kevin AMMONS
26 Dir Marketing & Media Relations .... Mr. Stephen SCHMIDT
37 Director Student Financial Aid .... Dr. Kevin AMMONS
55 Director Evening Division .... Mr. Carl HOLBROOK
04 Administrative Asst to President .... Ms. Jennifer ADAMS
07 Director of Admissions .... Mr. Joey HOLLEY
102 Dir Foundation/Community Relations .... Ms. Chellye STUMP
103 Dir Workforce Development .... Mr. Ian CAMPBELL
13 Chief Info Technology Officer (CIO) .... Mr. Jason TRULL
15 Director Personnel Services .... Ms. Jessica HERBSTER
18 Chief Facilities/Physical Plant .... Mr. Michael HELMS
38 Director Student Counseling .... Dr. Felisha FORD
105 Director Web Services .... Mr. Stephen SCHMIDT
106 Dir Online Education/E-learning .... Dr. Amy WISE
108 Director Inst Effectiveness & Plng .... Mr. Andrew DAVIS
19 Director Security/Safety .... Mr. Jeff SPENCE
50 Director of Business .... Mrs. Jennifer C. NELSON

*Gadsden State Community College (B)

1001 George Wallace Dr, PO Box 227,
Gadsden AL 35902-0227
County: Etowah FICE Identification: 001017
Unit ID: 101240
Telephone: (256) 549-8200 Carnegie Class: Assoc/HVT-High Trad
FAX Number: (256) 549-8288 Calendar System: Semester
URL: www.gadsdenstate.edu
Established: 1925 Annual Undergrad Tuition & Fees (In-State): $3,840
Enrollment: 4,979 Coed
Affiliation or Control: State IRS Status: 501(c)3
Highest Offering: Associate Degree
Accreditation: SC, ADNUR, COMTA, EMT, MLTAD, PNUR, RAD

02 President .... Dr. Martha G. LAVENDER
10 Dean Financial/Administrative Svcs .... Dr. Kevin MCFRY
84 Dean Enrollment & Retention .... Dr. Teresa C. RHEA
72 Dean Tech Educ/Workforce Develop .... Mr. Tim GREEN
76 Dean Health Sciences .... Dr. Deborah CURRY
05 Dean of Academic Programs/Services .Dr. Leslie WORTHINGTON
111 Assoc Dean Inst Advance/Cmty Svcs .... Ms. Pam JOHNSON
51 Assoc Dean Instruct Svcs/Adult Educ .. Dr. Karen BLYTHE-SMITH
26 Director Public Relations/Marketing .... Ms. Jackie EDMONDSON
19 Director Physical Plant .... Mr. Stewart DAVIS
21 Director of Financial Services .... Ms. Jacqueline CLARK
43 Director of Legal Affairs/Title IX .... Ms. Michele BRADFORD
15 Director Human Resources .... Ms. Kim S. COBB
41 Athletic Director .... Mr. Mike CANCILLA
124 Assoc Dean Enrollment & Retention .... Ms. Kelley H. PEARCE
37 Director of Financial Aid .... Ms. Kelly D'EATH
06 Registrar .... Ms. Cassie MORGAN
13 Chief Information Officer .... Mr. Tim SMITH

*George C. Wallace Community College - Dothan (C)

1141 Wallace Drive, Dothan AL 36303-9234
County: Dale FICE Identification: 001018
Unit ID: 101286
Telephone: (334) 983-3521 Carnegie Class: Assoc/HVT-High Trad
FAX Number: (334) 983-6066 Calendar System: Semester
URL: www.wallace.edu
Established: 1947 Annual Undergrad Tuition & Fees (In-State): $4,680
Enrollment: 4,645 Coed
Affiliation or Control: State IRS Status: 501(c)3
Highest Offering: Associate Degree
Accreditation: SC, ADNUR, COARC, EMT, MAC, PNUR, PTAA, RAD

02 President .... Dr. Linda C. YOUNG
30 VP/Dean Institutional Svcs/Cmty Dev .... Dr. Ashli WILKINS
32 Act Dean Student Affs/Sparks Campus .... Mr. Mickey BAKER
05 Dean of Instructional Affairs .... Ms. Leslie REEDER
10 Dean of Business Affairs .... Mr. Marc NICHOLAS
07 Director Enroll Svcs/Registrar .... Mr. Keith SAULSBERRY
08 Dir Learning Resources Ctrs System .... Mr. A. P. HOFFMAN
37 Director of Financial Aid .... Mr. Anthony JOUVENAS
13 AS-400 Program/System Admin .... Mr. Patrick ADKINSON
15 Director of Human Resources .... Ms. Brooke STRICKLAND
09 Dir Institutional Effectiveness .... Ms. Mandy LANIER
40 Bookstore Manager .... Mr. Jeremy JAMES
21 Director of Accounting & Finance .... Ms. Heather JOHNSON-WALKER
26 Dir Public Relations & Marketing .... Ms. Barbara THOMPSON
41 Athletic Director .... Mr. Mackey SASSER

*George Corley Wallace State Community College - Selma (D)

PO Box 2530, 3000 Earl Goodwin Pkwy,
Selma AL 36702-2530
County: Dallas FICE Identification: 005699
Unit ID: 101301
Telephone: (334) 876-9227 Carnegie Class: Assoc/MT-VT-Mix Trad/Non
FAX Number: (334) 876-9250 Calendar System: Semester
URL: www.wccs.edu
Established: 1963 Annual Undergrad Tuition & Fees (In-State): $4,440
Enrollment: 1,471 Coed
Affiliation or Control: State IRS Status: 501(c)3
Highest Offering: Associate Degree
Accreditation: SC, ACBSP, ADNUR, PNUR

02 President .... Dr. James M. MITCHELL
05 Dean of Instruction .... Dr. Tammie BRIGGS
20 Asst Dean of Instruction .... Mr. Raji GOURDINE
10 Dean of Business & Finance .... Dr. Rosa SPENCER
32 Dean of Students/Exec to President .... Dr. Donitha GRIFFIN
08 Librarian .... Ms. Minnie CARSTARPHEN
76 Director of Health Science .... Dr. Tracey SHANNON
37 Financial Aid Director .... Ms. Anessa KIDD
07 Director of Admissions/Counselor .... Mr. Lonzy CLIFTON
09 Asst Dean of Institutional Effect .... Mrs. Veronica BROWN
26 Director of Community Relations .... Mrs. Veronica CHESNUT
19 Public Safety Coordinator .... Mr. Charles DYSART
41 Athletic Director .... Mr. Marcus HANNAH
18 Director of Facilities & Safety .... Mr. Keith JACKSON
28 Director of Diversity .... Vacant
40 Bookstore Manager .... Ms. Marie JONES
15 Human Resource Director .... Vacant

*J.F. Drake State Community and Technical College (E)

3421 Meridian Street N, Huntsville AL 35811-1584
County: Madison FICE Identification: 005260
Unit ID: 101462
Telephone: (256) 539-8161 Carnegie Class: Assoc/HVT-High Trad
FAX Number: (256) 539-6439 Calendar System: Semester
URL: www.drakestate.edu
Established: 1961 Annual Undergrad Tuition & Fees (In-State): $4,710
Enrollment: 752 Coed
Affiliation or Control: State IRS Status: 501(c)3
Highest Offering: Associate Degree
Accreditation: SC

02 President .... Dr. Patricia SIMS
05 Dean of Instruction .... Dr. Carolyn HENDERSON
10 Director of Fiscal Affairs .... Mr. Akeem ALEXANDER
103 Director of Grants/Workforce Dev .... Vacant
15 Human Resource Specialist .... Mrs. Katie CHANCE
13 Director Computer Services .... Vacant
08 Director of Library Services .... Ms. Carla CLIFT
07 Director of Admissions/Registrar .... Dr. Pamela LITTLE
37 Director Student Financial Aid .... Ms. Jennifer O'LINGER
26 Director of Public Relations .... Mr. Kenya RUSSELL
36 College Counselor .... Vacant
108 Director of Institutional Effective .... Ms. Lesley SHOTTS
32 Acting Dean of Student Support Svc .... Dr. Pamela LITTLE
51 Director of Adult Education .... Vacant
18 Director of Operations .... Mr. Bruce BULLUCK
84 Enrollment Services Manager .... Ms. Tiffany GREEN

*J.F. Ingram State Technical College (F)

PO Box 220350, Deatsville AL 36022-0350
County: Elmore FICE Identification: 030025
Unit ID: 101471
Telephone: (334) 285-5177 Carnegie Class: Assoc/HVT-Mix Trad/Non
FAX Number: (334) 285-5328 Calendar System: Semester
URL: www.istc.edu
Established: 1965 Annual Undergrad Tuition & Fees (In-State): $5,328
Enrollment: 449 Coed
Affiliation or Control: State IRS Status: 501(c)3
Highest Offering: Associate Degree
Accreditation: COE

02 President .... Mrs. Annette FUNDERBURK
05 Dean of Instruction .... Mr. Bill GRISWOLD
11 Dean of Administration .... Dr. Brannon LENTZ
32 Dean of Students/Support Svcs .... Mrs. Rosie EDWARDS
20 Associate Dean of Instruction .... Dr. Julliana PROBST
35 Student Services Director .... Mrs. Tawanna THORNTON
15 Human Resources Coordinator .... Vacant
88 Re-Entry/Counseling Programs Coord .... Mr. Rick VEST
10 Business Office Director .... Mrs. Amelia FOX
04 Administrative Asst to President .... Mrs. Julie VARNER

*Jefferson State Community College (G)

2601 Carson Road, Birmingham AL 35215-3098
County: Jefferson FICE Identification: 001022
Unit ID: 101505
Telephone: (205) 853-1200 Carnegie Class: Assoc/HVT-Mix Trad/Non
FAX Number: (205) 853-8505 Calendar System: Semester
URL: www.jeffersonstate.edu
Established: 1963 Annual Undergrad Tuition & Fees (In-State): $4,800
Enrollment: 8,840 Coed
Affiliation or Control: State IRS Status: 501(c)3
Highest Offering: Associate Degree
Accreditation: SC, ACBSP, ACFEI, ADNUR, #COARC, CONST, EMT, FUSER, MLTAD, PTAA, RAD

02 President .... Mr. Keith A. BROWN
32 Vice President for Student Affairs .... Dr. Phillip M. HOBBS
05 Dean of Instruction .... Ms. Danielle COBURN
75 Dean Career & Technical Education .... Ms. Norma G. BELL
30 Dean Campus Development/Campus Svcs .... Vacant
10 Int Director Financial Services .... Mr. David MORRIS
97 Assoc Dean Transf Gen Stds Shelby .... Ms. Liesl W. HARRIS
97 Assoc Dean Transf Gen Stds Jeffrsn .... Dr. Aliakbar R. YAZDI
106 Associate Dean Distance Education .... Mr. Alan B. DAVIS
103 Dir Center for Workforce Education .... Ms. Kay C. POTTER
13 Chief Information Officer .... Mr. Stephen MOORE
37 Director Financial Aid .... Ms. Theresa MAYS
18 Director Maintenance .... Mr. Perry HARRIS
08 Director of Learning Resources .... Ms. Barbara GOSS
36 Director Career/Job Resource Center .... Dr. Tamara PAYNE
84 Associate Dean Enrollment Services .... Dr. Lillian OWENS
15 Director Human Resources .... Mr. Shain WILSON
26 Director Media Relations .... Mr. David BOBO
96 Purchasing Coordinator .... Ms. Ann CIMALORE
19 Director Safety & Security .... Mr. Mark BAILEY
09 Dean Institutional Effectiveness .... Ms. Amanda E. KIN
04 Administrative Asst to President .... Ms. Janie STARNES
25 Director Resource Development .... Ms. Kelli CREAMER
86 Director Community Outreach .... Mr. Guin ROBINSON
51 Director Adult Education .... Ms. Kassie MATHIS
88 Director of Articulation .... Mr. Adam GOODMAN

*Lawson State Community College (H)

3060 Wilson Road, SW, Birmingham AL 35221-1798
County: Jefferson FICE Identification: 001059
Unit ID: 101569
Telephone: (205) 925-2515 Carnegie Class: Assoc/MT-VT-High Trad
FAX Number: (205) 925-1390 Calendar System: Semester
URL: www.lawsonstate.edu
Established: 1949 Annual Undergrad Tuition & Fees (In-State): $4,740
Enrollment: 3,248 Coed
Affiliation or Control: State IRS Status: 501(c)3
Highest Offering: Associate Degree
Accreditation: SC, ACBSP, ADNUR, DA, PNUR

02 President .... Dr. Perry W. WARD
05 Vice Pres Instructional Services .... Dr. Bruce CRAWFORD
10 Vice President of Fiscal Services .... Mrs. Sharon CREWS
32 Executive VP & Dean of Students .... Dr. Cynthia ANTHONY
09 Coordinator of Data Management .... Mrs. Jamie GLASS
117 Dir Fin Services/Risk Assessment .... Dr. Craig D. LAWRENCE
20 Academic Dean .... Dr. Sherri DAVIS
21 Director of Accounting .... Ms. Monique SILAS
50 Assoc Dean Bus/Information Tech .... Dr. Alice MILTON
49 Assoc Dean Lib Arts/Coll Trans Pgms .... Dr. Karl PRUITT
76 Assoc Dean of Health Occupations .... Dr. Shelia MARABLE
75 Assoc Dean Career Tech Programs .... Mr. Donald SLEDGE
35 Acting Dean of Students .... Mr. Darren ALLEN
07 Director of Admissions .... Mr. Dorian WALUYN
08 Librarian .... Ms. Julie KENNEDY
37 Director Student Financial Aid .... Ms. Cassandra HOLLINS
15 Director of Personnel Services .... Mrs. Janice MCGEE
26 Chief Public Relations Officer .... Mrs. Geri ALBRIGHT
18 Chief Facilities/Physical Plant .... Mr. Chad YANCY
19 Director Safety/Security .... Mr. James BLANTON
13 Dir Computing and Information Mgmt ...Mr. James MANKOWICH
41 Athletic Director .... Mr. Carlton RICE
06 Registrar .... Ms. Lori CHISEM
38 Coordinator Student Counseling .... Dr. Renee HERNDON
106 Dir Online Education/E-learning .... Dr. Kesha JAMES
25 Chief Contracts/Grants Admin .... Dr. Myrtes D. GREEN
103 Asst Dean Workforce Development .... Mr. Tommy HOBBS

*Lurleen B. Wallace Community College (I)

PO Drawer 1418, 1000 Dannelly Blvd,
Andalusia AL 36420-1224
County: Covington FICE Identification: 008988
Unit ID: 101602
Telephone: (334) 222-6591 Carnegie Class: Assoc/MT-VT-Mix Trad/Non
FAX Number: (334) 881-2300 Calendar System: Semester
URL: www.lbwcc.edu
Established: 1969 Annual Undergrad Tuition & Fees (In-State): $4,740
Enrollment: 1,838 Coed
Affiliation or Control: State IRS Status: 501(c)3
Highest Offering: Associate Degree
Accreditation: SC, ADNUR, DMS, EMT, SURGT

02 President .... Dr. Herbert RIEDEL
04 Administrative Asst to President .... Ms. Cindy GREEN
10 CFO and Senior Personnel Officer .... Ms. Lisa CARNLEY
05 Dean of Instruction .... Ms. Peggy LINTON
32 Dean of Student Affairs .... Mr. Jason JESSIE
12 Dean of the Greenville Campus .... Ms. Peige JOSEY
103 Assoc Dean Adult Ed/Wkforce/Cont Ed .... Ms. Jennifer HALL
13 Assoc Dean Instr/Info Technology .... Mr. Greg APLIN
111 Assoc Dean of Inst Advancement .... Dr. Arlene DAVIS
09 Assoc Dean Inst Effect & Quality .... Dr. Shannon LEVITZKE
21 Director of Business Services .... Ms. Debra MOODY
15 Human Resources Coordinator .... Ms. Ashley WILLIAMSON
18 Dir College Facilities/Maintenance .... Mr. Tim JONES
07 Director Admissions & Records .... Ms. Jan RILEY
41 Athletic Director .... Mr. Steve HELMS
08 Director of Learning Resources .... Mr. Hugh CARTER
121 Director Student Support Services .... Dr. Patricia POWELL
37 Director of Financial Aid .... Ms. Donna BASS
26 Public Info Officer/Dir Mktg .... Ms. Renee LEMAIRE

*Marion Military Institute (A)

1101 Washington Street, Marion AL 36756-3213
County: Perry   FICE Identification: 001026
Unit ID: 101648
Telephone: (800) 664-1842   Carnegie Class: Assoc/HT-High Trad
FAX Number: (334) 683-2380   Calendar System: Semester
URL: www.marionmilitary.edu
Established: 1842   Annual Undergrad Tuition & Fees (In-State): $9,418
Enrollment: 446   Coed
Affiliation or Control: State   IRS Status: 501(c)3
Highest Offering: Associate Degree
Accreditation: SC

02 President .... Col. David J. MOLLAHAN
03 Executive Vice President/CAO .... Dr. Susan G. STEVENSON
10 VP for Finance & Business Affs .... Mr. Brian HARRISON
05 Chief Instructional Officer .... Mr. David IVEY
32 Actg VP Student Affairs/Commandant .... Col. Ed PASSMORE
111 VP for Institutional Advancement .... Mrs. Suzanne MCKEE
41 Director of Athletics .... Dr. Michelle IVEY
84 Director of Enrollment Management .... Mrs. Brittany CRAWFORD
29 Director of Alumni and Comm Affairs .... Mrs. O'Neal C. HOLMES
88 ROTC Professor of Military Science .... LTC. Cory ARMSTEAD
09 Director of Institutional Research .... Mrs. Donna LEEMON
06 Registrar .... 1Lt. Caleb LOGAN
15 Dir Human Resources/Compliance .... Ms. Carmon P. FIELDS
37 Director of Financial Aid .... Ms. Jacqueline WILSON
08 Director Service Academy Program .... LTC. Thomas BOWEN
18 Director of Facilities .... SCPO. Robert D. SUMLIN
17 Director of Health Services .... Mrs. Rene SUMLIN

*Northeast Alabama Community College (B)

PO Box 159, 138 Alabama Highway 35,
Rainsville AL 35986-0159
County: DeKalb/Jackson   FICE Identification: 001031
Unit ID: 101897
Telephone: (256) 638-4418   Carnegie Class: Assoc/MT-VT-Mix Trad/Non
FAX Number: (256) 638-3052   Calendar System: Semester
URL: www.nacc.edu
Established: 1963   Annual Undergrad Tuition & Fees (In-State): $4,740
Enrollment: 2,736   Coed
Affiliation or Control: State   IRS Status: 501(c)3
Highest Offering: Associate Degree
Accreditation: SC, ADNUR, EMT, PNUR

02 President .... Dr. J. David CAMPBELL
05 Vice Pres/Dean of Instruction .... Mr. Chad GORHAM
56 Director Extended Day/Distance Educ .... Mr. Chad GORHAM
32 Dean of Student Services .... Ms. Sherie GRACE
11 Dean of Admin Services .... Mr. Rodney BONE
37 Director of Financial Aid .... Mr. Nixon WILLMON
103 Dir Workforce Devel/Skills Training .... Mr. Mike KENNAMER
26 Director of Promotions & Marketing .... Mrs. Debra A. BARRENTINE
45 Dir Inst Planning & Assessment .... Mr. Brad DUDLEY
18 Chief Facilities/Physical Plant .... Mr. Kent JONES
06 Registrar/Chief Bus Ofcr/Dir Purchg .... Mr. Rodney BONE
30 Development Director .... Ms. Heather RICE
19 Director of Police/Security .... Mr. Norman SMITH
04 Administrative Asst to President .... Ms. Brenda STRINGER
08 Dir Learning Resource Ctr/Library .... Mrs. Julia EVERETT
15 Human Resources Director .... Mrs. Lynde MANN
29 Event Planning/Alumni Relations .... Ms. Chasley BELLOMY
72 Director of Educational Technology .... Ms. Patricia COMBS

*Northwest - Shoals Community College (C)

800 George Wallace Boulevard,
Muscle Shoals AL 35661-3205
County: Colbert   FICE Identification: 005697
Unit ID: 101736
Telephone: (256) 331-5200   Carnegie Class: Assoc/MT-VT-Mix Trad/Non
FAX Number: (256) 331-5222   Calendar System: Semester
URL: www.nwscc.edu
Established: 1963   Annual Undergrad Tuition & Fees (In-State): $4,711
Enrollment: 3,440   Coed
Affiliation or Control: State   IRS Status: 501(c)3
Highest Offering: Associate Degree
Accreditation: SC, ADNUR, EMT, MAC

02 President .... Dr. Glenda COLAGROSS
09 Assoc Dean Inst Effect/Dist Ed/Dev .... Mr. John MCINTOSH
05 Assoc Dean Instructional Programs .... Dr. Timmy JAMES
37 Director of Financial Aid .... Ms. Lisa LILLEY
32 Assistant Dean of Student Success .... Dr. Crystal REED
07 Asst Dean Recruit/Adm/FA .... Mr. Tom CARTER
15 Human Resources Coordinator .... Ms. Tia STONE
88 Talent Search Director .... Ms. Cindy STEWART
13 Director of Management Info Systems .... Mr. Alan MITCHELL
06 Registrar/Coordinator of Admissions .... Ms. Tracy RABY
103 Assoc Dean of Workforce Develop .... Ms. Rose JONES
88 Director of Adult Educ and RTW .... Ms. Tara BRANSCOME
04 Administrative Asst to President .... Ms. Teresa HARRISON
26 Public Information Officer .... Mr. Trent RANDOLPH
124 Director of Student Support Svcs .... Ms. Brittany JONES
25 Grants Admin .... Ms. Leslie TOMLINSON
10 Dean of Finance .... Ms. Dawnelle ROBINSON
09 Director of Institutional Research .... Ms. Angie STONE

*Reid State Technical College (D)

PO Box 588, 100 Hwy 83, Evergreen AL 36401-0588
County: Conecuh   FICE Identification: 005692
Unit ID: 101994
Telephone: (251) 578-1313   Carnegie Class: Assoc/HVT-Mix Trad/Non
FAX Number: (251) 578-5355   Calendar System: Semester
URL: www.rstc.edu
Established: 1966   Annual Undergrad Tuition & Fees (In-State): $4,800
Enrollment: 392   Coed
Affiliation or Control: State   IRS Status: 501(c)3
Highest Offering: Associate Degree
Accreditation: COE

02 Acting President/Business Manager .... Mr. David J. RHODES
05 Dean Students/Instructional Svcs .... Dr. Tangela PURIFOY
103 Assoc Dean Workforce Development .... Dr. Alesia K. STUART
09 Asst Dean for Institutional Effect .... Ms. Coretta BOYKIN
37 Director Financial Aid .... Ms. Christy GOODWIN
15 Director of Human Resources .... Ms. Brenda JACKSON
07 Asst Dir Admissions & Records .... Ms. Mandy GODWIN
10 Office Administration .... Ms. Lois ROBINSON
06 Registrar .... Ms. Vickie NICHOLSON
38 Director of Counseling/ADA Coord .... Vacant
19 Chief of Campus Security .... Ms. Brenda RILEY

*Shelton State Community College (E)

9500 Old Greensboro Road, Tuscaloosa AL 35405-8522
County: Tuscaloosa   FICE Identification: 005691
Unit ID: 102067
Telephone: (205) 391-2211   Carnegie Class: Assoc/HVT-High Trad
FAX Number: (205) 391-2426   Calendar System: Semester
URL: www.sheltonstate.edu
Established: 1953   Annual Undergrad Tuition & Fees (In-State): $4,467
Enrollment: 4,607   Coed
Affiliation or Control: State   IRS Status: 501(c)3
Highest Offering: Associate Degree
Accreditation: SC, ADNUR, COARC, PNUR

02 President .... Dr. William J. ASHLEY
10 Comptroller Business Services .... Mrs. Ann BRACKNELL
32 Dean of Student Services .... Mrs. Amanda HARBISON
13 Assoc Dean of Technology .... Mr. Grant COCKRELL
12 Dean Fredd Campus/Title III .... Mr. Ronald RANGE
88 Dean for Corporate Programs .... Mr. Jason MOORE
32 Assoc Dean of Student Services .... Dr. Byron ABSTON
76 Allied Health Assistant Dean .... Ms. Gladys HILL
37 Director of Financial Aid .... Ms. Rhonda SMITH
04 Executive Asst to the President .... Ms. Channing H. MARLOWE
07 Director of Admissions/Registrar .... Mrs. Fannie BATES-REESE
08 Director Library Services .... Mr. Don BELL
103 Dean of Instruction & Workforce Dev .... Ms. Joye JONES
88 Director Adult Education .... Mr. Phillip JOHNSON
15 Director of Human Resources .... Mr. Kevin DAVIS
14 Assoc Dean of Technical Services .... Mr. Claude LAKE
109 Dean of Auxiliary Services .... Dr. Thomas TAYLOR
04 Administrative Asst to President .... Mrs. Ann H. TINSLEY
09 Dir Institutional Effective/Rsrch .... Dr. Louis SHEDD
106 Instructional Tech and eLearning .... Mr. John ALEXANDER
106 Instructional Tech and eLearning .... Mr. Robert PRESSLEY
18 Chief of Facilities .... Mr. Tim HINTON
26 Asst Dir of Media Communication .... Ms. Lisa WALDROP
105 Assoc Dean of Info/Tech Services .... Mr. Claude LAKE
102 Foundation .... Ms. Kimberly CHAMBLESS
25 Director of Grants .... Mr. Jonathan KOH
41 Athletic Director .... Ms. Cara CROSSLIN
21 Dean of Business Services .... Mr. Rodney J. LANDRUM
88 Director of Educational Planning .... Ms. Sophia EVERETT

*Snead State Community College (F)

PO Box 734, Boaz AL 35957-0734
County: Marshall   FICE Identification: 001038
Unit ID: 102076
Telephone: (256) 593-5120   Carnegie Class: Assoc/HT-Mix Trad/Non
FAX Number: N/A   Calendar System: Semester
URL: www.snead.edu
Established: 1898   Annual Undergrad Tuition & Fees (In-State): $4,800
Enrollment: 2,220   Coed
Affiliation or Control: State   IRS Status: Exempt
Highest Offering: Associate Degree
Accreditation: SC, ADNUR

02 President .... Dr. Robert EXLEY
32 Vice President for Student Services .... Mr. Jason CANNON
10 VP for Finance & Administration .... Mr. Joe WHITMORE
13 Acting Chief IT Officer .... Mr. Don RODEN
26 Director of Marketing/PR .... Ms. Shelley SMITH
88 Coordinator of Testing/Secondary Ed .... Ms. Tonya SHIELDS
05 Vice President for Academic Affairs .... Dr. Annette CEDERHOLM
106 Assoc Dean Online Lrng/Career Tech .... Mr. Michael GIBSON
81 Science Division Director .... Ms. Deborah RHODEN
79 English/Languages Division Director .... Dr. Cynthia DENHAM
83 Soc Sci/Human Svcs/PS Div Director .... Dr. Karen WATTS
81 Mathematics Division Director .... Mr. Blake LEETH
50 Business Division Director .... Mr. Vann SCOTT
57 Art/Humanites/Commun/Design Div Dir .... Dr. Jonathan WATTS
103 Director Workforce Development .... Ms. Teresa WALKER
76 Director Health Sciences .... Dr. Delores MCCLELLAN
41 Athletic Director .... Mr. Mark RICHARD
08 Head Librarian .... Mr. John MILLER
15 Director of Human Resources .... Ms. Amanda GUNNELS
18 Director of Physical Plant .... Mr. Steve WILLIAMS
07 Director of Admissions/Recruitment .... Ms. Tristin CALLAHAN
19 Director Security/Safety .... Mr. Paul GORE
29 Director Alumni Relations .... Ms. Shelley SMITH
30 Development Coordinator .... Ms. Kelli CONLEY
37 Director of Financial Aid .... Ms. Amanda CHILDRESS
04 Executive Asst to President .... Ms. Kelli CONLEY

*Southern Union State Community College (G)

PO Box 1000, Wadley AL 36276-1000
County: Randolph   FICE Identification: 001040
Unit ID: 251260
Telephone: (256) 395-2211   Carnegie Class: Assoc/MT-VT-High Trad
FAX Number: (256) 395-2215   Calendar System: Semester
URL: www.suscc.edu
Established: 1922   Annual Undergrad Tuition & Fees (In-State): $4,440
Enrollment: 4,828   Coed
Affiliation or Control: State   IRS Status: 501(c)3
Highest Offering: Associate Degree
Accreditation: SC, ADNUR, EMT, RAD, SURGT

02 President .... Mr. Todd SHACKETT
05 Dean of Academics .... Dr. Linda NORTH
32 Dean Student Development .... Mr. Gary BRANCH
35 Dean of Students .... Ms. Tiffany SANDERS
20 Assoc Dean of Instruction .... Mr. Steve SPRATLIN
72 Dean of Technical Educ/Wrkfce Dev .... Dr. Darin BALDWIN
41 Athletic Director .... Mr. Ron RADFORD
06 Registrar .... Ms. Catherine STRINGFELLOW
10 Chief Financial/Business Office .... Mr. Ben JORDAN
04 Admin Assistant to the President .... Ms. Alison OSBORN
09 Assoc Dean of Inst Research .... Mr. Eddie PIGG
13 Director of MIS .... Ms. Cheryl JORDAN
15 Director of Human Resources .... Ms. Sandra HUGHLEY
31 Director of Media Relations .... Ms. Shondae BROWN
37 Director Student Financial Aid .... Ms. Melissa TODD
45 Assoc Dean of Inst Effectiveness .... Ms. Robin BROWN
19 Chief of Campus Police .... Mr. Jimmy HOLMES

*Trenholm State Technical College (H)

PO Box 10048, Montgomery AL 36108
County: Montgomery   FICE Identification: 005734
Unit ID: 102313
Telephone: (334) 420-4200   Carnegie Class: Assoc/HVT-High Trad
FAX Number: (334) 420-4206   Calendar System: Semester
URL: www.trenholmstate.edu
Established: 1963   Annual Undergrad Tuition & Fees (In-State): $4,650
Enrollment: 1,845   Coed
Affiliation or Control: State   IRS Status: 501(c)3
Highest Offering: Associate Degree
Accreditation: SC, ACFEI, #COARC, DA, DMS, EMT, MAC, PNUR, #RAD

02 President .... Mr. Sam MUNNERLYN
10 Dean of Finance/Admin Svcs .... Ms. Sharon MAHAFFEY
05 Exec VP of Instructional Services .... Dr. Kemba CHAMBERS
30 Dean of Development .... Dr. Suresh C. KAUSHIK
32 Dean of Students .... Vacant
20 Dean of Instruction .... Dr. Nakia ROBINSON
103 Dean of Workforce Development .... Mr. Danny PERRY
76 Associate Dean of Health Svcs .... Dr. Tracie CARTER
13 Director of IT .... Mr. Robert ROLLINS
09 Dir of Institutional Effectiveness .... Dr. Mimi JOHNSON
18 Director Physical Plant .... Mr. Robert ALLEN
37 Director Student Financial Aid .... Ms. Betty EDWARDS
06 Registrar .... Dr. Tennie S. MCBRYDE
84 Director of Enrollment Management .... Ms. Valerie ALLEN-PORTERFIELD
08 Head Librarian .... Mr. Paul BLACKMON
26 Public Information Officer .... Ms. Angela HURST
15 Director of Human Resources .... Dr. Pam ROLLINS
51 Dir Title III/Marketing/Cont Educ .... Ms. Arlinda KNIGHT
36 Coordinator Job Placement .... Ms. Maria RICHARDSON
04 Administrative Asst to President .... Ms. Angela W. CONE

*Wallace State Community College - Hanceville (A)

PO Box 2000, 801 Main Street, NW,
Hanceville AL 35077-2000

County: Cullman | FICE Identification: 007871 | Unit ID: 101295
Telephone: (256) 352-8000 | Carnegie Class: Assoc/HVT-High Trad
FAX Number: (256) 352-8228 | Calendar System: Semester
URL: www.wallacestate.edu
Established: 1966 | Annual Undergrad Tuition & Fees (In-State): $4,740
Enrollment: 5,301 | Coed
Affiliation or Control: State | IRS Status: 501(c)3
Highest Offering: Associate Degree
Accreditation: SC, ACBSP, ACFEI, ADNUR, CAHIIM, COARC, DA, DH, DMS, EMT, MAC, MLTAD, OTA, PNUR, POLYT, PTAA, RAD

Code	Title	Name
02	President	Dr. Vicki KAROLEWICS
45	College Dean	Dr. Johnny MCMOY
10	Dean of Finance & Admin Svcs	Vacant
05	Dean of Academic Affairs	Dr. Beth BOWNES-JOHNSON
20	Dean of Applied Technologies	Jimmy HODGES
76	Dean of Health Sciences	Lisa GERMAN
32	Dean of Students	Dr. Ryan SMITH
84	Asst Dean Enrollment Management	Jennifer HILL
121	Director of Advising	Vacant
109	Auxiliary Director	Mark BOLIN
08	Head Librarian	Lisa HULLETT
37	Director of Financial Aid	Becky GRAVES
55	Extended Day Program Director	Wayne MANORD
15	Director of Human Resources	Alyce FLANIGAN
111	Director of Advancement	Suzanne HARBIN
18	Director of Physical Plant	Billy ROSE
26	Director Communications/Marketing	Kristen HOLMES
06	Registrar	Jennifer TWITTY
36	Job Placement Coordinator	Jamie BLACKMON
09	Coordinator of Inst Research	Mattie HUDSON

Alabama State University (B)

915 S Jackson Street, Montgomery AL 36101-0271

County: Montgomery | FICE Identification: 001005 | Unit ID: 100724
Telephone: (334) 229-4100 | Carnegie Class: Masters/M
FAX Number: (334) 834-6861 | Calendar System: Semester
URL: www.alasu.edu
Established: 1867 | Annual Undergrad Tuition & Fees (In-State): $11,068
Enrollment: 4,760 | Coed
Affiliation or Control: State | IRS Status: 501(c)3
Highest Offering: Doctorate
Accreditation: SC, ACBSP, ART, CACREP, CAEPN, CAHIIM, MUS, OPE, OT, #PTA, SW, THEA

Code	Title	Name
01	President	Dr. Quinton T. ROSS, JR.
05	Int Provost/Vice Pres Academic Affs	Dr. Carl PETTIS
10	Int Vice Pres Business & Finance	Mr. William HOPPER
13	Director Technology Services	Mr. Larry COBB
111	Int Vice Pres Institutional Advance	Ms. Lois RUSSELL
15	Director Human Resources	Mr. Derrick CARR
20	Int Asst Provost Academic Affairs	Dr. Tanjula PETTY
32	Vice Pres Student Affairs	Dr. Davida HAYWOOD
18	Vice Pres Facilities Mgt/Operations	Mr. Donald DOTSON
45	Assoc Vice Pres Inst Effectiveness	Dr. Christine THOMAS
35	Asst Vice Pres Student Affairs	Dr. Rolundus RICE
21	Int Comptroller/AVP Business & Fin	Mrs. Alondrea J. PRITCHETT
108	Dir Acad Planning & Evaluation	Vacant
09	Director Institutional Research	Dr. Bryn BAKOYEMA
88	Coord Quality Enhancement Planning	Mr. Keonn NETTLES
08	Dean Libraries/Learning Resource	Dr. Janice FRANKLIN
07	Director Admissions/Recruitment	Mr. Freddie WILLIAMS
37	Financial Aid Director	Ms. Tallya REAUX
36	Dir Placement Svcs/Cooperative Educ	Mr. Jeremy HODGE
50	Dean College Business Admin	Dr. Kamal HINGORANI
89	Dean University College	Dr. Evelyn HODGE
53	Dean College of Education	Dr. Aletha HAMPTON
64	Dean Visual & Performing Arts	Dr. Tommie T. STEWART
58	Dean Graduate Studies	Vacant
81	Dean College of Sci Math & Tech	Dr. Kennedy WEKESA
49	Dean Liberal Arts/Social Sci	Dr. Anthony T. ADAMS
76	Dean College Health Sciences	Dr. Charlene PORTEE
51	Director Continuing Education	Mr. Olan L. WESLEY
29	Director Alumni Relations	Mr. Cromwell HANDY
23	Director Student Health Services	Ms. Gwendolyn MANN
19	Depty Director of Public Safety	Mr. James GRABOYS
38	Dir Counseling & Development Svcs	Mr. Chris JOHNS
39	Dir Housing/Residential Life	Ms. Rakesia HINES
41	Int Director of Athletics	Ms. Jennifer WILLIAMS
25	Director Research & Sponsored Pgms	Dr. Ella TEMPLE
96	Director of Purchasing	Ms. Arlene THOMPSON
101	Board Liaison	Mrs. Danielle KENNEDY-JONES
106	Dir Online Education/E-learning	Vacant
43	General Counsel	Mr. Kenneth THOMAS
06	Registrar	Ms. Marie MCNEAR
26	Chief Public Relations/Marketing	Mr. Kenneth MULLINAX
28	Dir of Diversity/International Affs	Mr. Linwood WHITTEN

Amridge University (C)

1200 Taylor Road, Montgomery AL 36117-3553

County: Montgomery | FICE Identification: 025034 | Unit ID: 100690
Telephone: (800) 351-4040 | Carnegie Class: Masters/S
FAX Number: (334) 387-3878 | Calendar System: Semester
URL: www.amridgeuniversity.edu
Established: 1967 | Annual Undergrad Tuition & Fees: $6,900
Enrollment: 675 | Coed
Affiliation or Control: Churches Of Christ | IRS Status: 501(c)3
Highest Offering: Doctorate
Accreditation: SC

Code	Title	Name
01	President	Dr. Michael C. TURNER
05	Academic Vice President/Dean	Dr. Lee TAYLOR
32	VP of Student Affairs & Technology	Mrs. Laina T. COSTANZA
06	Registrar	Mrs. Elaine P. TARENCE
08	Director Learning Resources	Ms. Kay S. NEWMAN
10	Chief Business Officer	Mrs. B. P. TURNER
21	Controller	Dr. Anita L. CROSBY
37	Financial Aid Director	Ms. Starr FAIN
42	Advancement/Spiritual Leadership	Vacant
29	Director of Alumni Relations	Vacant
13	System Admin Network Operations	Mr. Jack TEMPLE
18	Maintenance	Mr. Robert SHIRLEY
24	Coordinator of Network Opers	Mr. Thomas PATTERSON
38	Director of Student Counseling	Vacant
26	Chief Public Relations Officer	Vacant
73	Chair School of Theology	Dr. Rodney CLOUD
50	Chair Col of Business & Ldrshp	Dr. Kenyetta MCCURTY
97	Dean of College of General Studies	Vacant
15	Human Resources Coordinator	Mrs. Patsy MORETZ
08	Head Librarian	Mr. Terence SHERIDAN
84	Enrollment Coordinator	Mr. Brooks HOUSLEY

Athens State University (D)

300 N Beaty Street, Athens AL 35611-1902

County: Limestone | FICE Identification: 001008 | Unit ID: 100812
Telephone: (256) 233-8100 | Carnegie Class: Bac-Diverse
FAX Number: (256) 216-3324 | Calendar System: Semester
URL: www.athens.edu
Established: 1822 | Annual Undergrad Tuition & Fees (In-State): N/A
Enrollment: 3,114 | Coed
Affiliation or Control: State | IRS Status: 501(c)3
Highest Offering: Master's
Accreditation: SC, ACBSP, CAEPN

Code	Title	Name
01	President	Dr. Philip K. WAY
05	Provost & VP for Academic Affs	Dr. Joe DELAP
20	Associate VP for Academic Affairs	Dr. Jackie SMITH
20	Asst VP for Academic Affairs	Dr. Ronald MERRITT
84	Vice Pres for Enroll & Student Supp	Ms. Sarah MCABEE
32	Asst VP for Enrollment & Stdnt Svcs	Ms. Crystal CREEKMORE
10	Vice President Financial Affairs	Mr. Mike MCCOY
21	Business Manager/Asst VP Finance	Mr. Jonathan CRAFT
111	Vice Pres for University Advance	Dr. Keith FERGUSON
08	Director of Libraries	Dr. Katherine QUINNELL
50	Dean College of Business	Dr. Kimberly LAFEVOR
53	Dean College of Education	Dr. Rosemary HODGES
49	Dean College of Arts & Sciences	Dr. Stephen SPENCER
36	Dir of Career Development Center	Dr. Michael RADDEN
37	Dir of Student Financial Services	Mr. Mitchell BAZZEL
06	Registrar	Dr. Greg HOLLIDAY
07	Chief of Records	Ms. Teresa SUIT
29	Director of Alumni Affairs/Ann Giv	Ms. Rachel O'SULLIVAN
30	Dir of Institutional Development	Mr. David BROWN
26	Director of Printing & Public Rels	Mr. Chris LATHAM
09	Director of Institutional Research	Mr. Jeffrey GUENTHER
18	Director of Physical Plant	Mr. Kerry WARREN
15	Director of Human Resources	Ms. Suzanne SIMS
51	Director of Ctr for Lifelong Lrng	Dr. Kimberly BELL
121	Director of Student Success Ctr	Mr. Derrek SMITH
28	Coordinator Student Inclusion	Mr. Richard COLLIE
04	Administrative Asst to President	Mrs. Carol E. RACHAL
101	Secretary of the Institution/Board	Mrs. Jackie GOOCH
13	Chief InfoTechnology Officer (CIO)	Ms. Belinda KRIGEL
19	Chief of Security/Safety	Mr. Jerry CRABTREE

Auburn University (E)

Auburn AL 36849

County: Lee | FICE Identification: 001009 | Unit ID: 100858
Telephone: (334) 844-4000 | Carnegie Class: DU-Highest
FAX Number: N/A | Calendar System: Semester
URL: www.auburn.edu
Established: 1856 | Annual Undergrad Tuition & Fees (In-State): $11,276
Enrollment: 29,776 | Coed
Affiliation or Control: State | IRS Status: 501(c)3
Highest Offering: Doctorate
Accreditation: SC, AAB, ART, AUD, CACREP, CAEPN, CIDA, CLPSY, CONST, COPSY, DIETD, @DIETI, IPSY, #JOUR, LSAR, MFCD, MUS, NURSE, PHAR, SP, SPAA, SW, THEA, VET

Code	Title	Name
01	Interim President	Dr. Jay GOGUE
100	Chief of Staff/VP Economic Dev	Mr. Steve PELHAM
05	Provost/Senior VP Academic Affairs	Dr. Bill C. HARDGRAVE
29	VP Alumni Affairs	Ms. Gretchen R. VANVALKENBURG
10	VP Business & Finance & CFO	Ms. Kelli D. SHOMAKER
30	VP Development	Ms. Jane DIFOLCO PARKER
32	Senior VP Student Affairs	Dr. Bobby R. WOODARD
84	Vice Pres Enrollment Services	Ms. Joffery GAYMON
46	Vice Pres Research	Dr. James WEYHENMEYER
101	Secretary to Board of Trustees	Mr. Jon G. WAGGONER
43	General Counsel	Ms. Jaime S. HAMMER
13	VP & Chief Information Officer	Mr. James O'CONNOR
11	Chief Operating Officer	Lt Gen. Ronald L. BURGESS
56	Dir AL Cooperative Extension Sys	Dr. Gary D. LEMME
41	Director of Athletics	Mr. C. Allen GREENE
86	Exec Director Governmental Affairs	Mr. Charles J. HINCY
11	Director Public Affairs	Mr. Brian C. KEETER
116	AVP Internal Audit/Compl & Privacy	Mr. M. Kevin ROBINSON
117	Exec Director Risk Mgmt & Safety	Mr. Chris O'GWYNN
26	Assistant VP Univ Comm & Mktg	Mr. Mike CLARDY, JR.
88	Univ Ombudsperson	Mr. Kevin COONROD
20	Associate Provost & Professor	Dr. Emmett WINN
28	Assoc Prov/VP Inclus & Diversity	Dr. Taffye BENSON-CLAYTON
25	Assistant VP Research	Ms. Martha M. TAYLOR
35	Assistant VP Student Engagement	Ms. Lady D. COX
88	Assistant VP Student Development	Ms. Haven L. HART
56	VP University Outreach	Dr. Royrickers COOK
85	Asst Provost Intl Programs	Dr. Andrew R. GILLESPIE
18	Associate VP Facilities	Mr. Daniel P. KING
15	Associate VP Human Resources	Ms. Karla S. MCCORMICK
21	Assoc VP Financial Svcs/Controller	Ms. Amy K. DOUGLAS
96	Exec Dir Business Svcs	Ms. Melissa M. MORRIS
37	Exec Dir Student Financial Svcs	Mr. Michael C. REYNOLDS
22	Director Affirmative Action/EEO	Ms. Kelley G. TAYLOR
108	Director Academic Assessment	Dr. Megan R. GOOD
09	Director Institutional Research	Dr. James A. CLARK
88	Director University Writing	Dr. Margaret J. MARSHALL
88	Director Teaching & Learning Center	Vacant
88	Exec Dir Performing Arts Center	Mr. Christopher J. HEACOX
39	Dir Univ Housing/Residence Life	Dr. Kevin J. HOULT
36	Director Career Center	Mr. Mike P. MCCAY
38	Director Student Counseling Svcs	Dr. Doug HANKES
14	Exec Dir Office of Info Tech	Mr. Bliss N. BAILEY
40	Director University Bookstore	Ms. Catherine LEE
06	Interim University Registrar	Dr. George W. CRANDELL
47	Dean Agriculture & Dir AAES	Dr. Paul M. PATTERSON
48	Dean Architecture/Design/Construct	Dr. Vini NATHAN
50	Dean Business	Dr. Annette L. RANFT
53	Dean Education	Dr. Betty Lou WHITFORD
54	Dean Engineering	Dr. Christopher B. ROBERTS
65	Dean Forestry/Wildlife Sci	Dr. Janaki R. ALAVALAPATI
59	Dean Human Sciences	Dr. Susan G. HUBBARD
49	Dean Liberal Arts	Dr. Joseph AISTRUP
66	Dean Nursing	Dr. Gregg NEWSCHWANDER
67	Dean Pharmacy	Dr. Richard A. HANSEN
81	Dean Sciences & Mathematics	Dr. Nicholas J. GIORDANO
74	Dean Veterinary Medicine	Dr. Calvin M. JOHNSON
58	Dean Graduate School	Dr. George FLOWERS
08	Dean University Libraries	Dr. Shali L. ZHANG
04	Administrative Asst to President	Ms. Janie A. BOLES

Auburn University at Montgomery (F)

PO Box 244024, Montgomery AL 36124-4023

County: Montgomery | FICE Identification: 008310 | Unit ID: 100830
Telephone: (334) 244-3000 | Carnegie Class: Masters/L
FAX Number: (334) 244-3762 | Calendar System: Semester
URL: www.aum.edu
Established: 1967 | Annual Undergrad Tuition & Fees (In-State): $8,404
Enrollment: 4,894 | Coed
Affiliation or Control: State | IRS Status: 501(c)3
Highest Offering: Doctorate
Accreditation: SC, CACREP, CAEPN, MT, NURSE, SPAA

Code	Title	Name
01	Chancellor	Dr. Carl A. STOCKTON
05	Provost/Sr Vice Chancellor	Dr. Mrinal VARMA
111	Vice Chancellor of Advancement	Ms. Carolyn GOLDEN
32	Vice Chancellor of Student Affairs	Vacant
10	Vice Chanc Financial & Admin Svcs	Mr. Scott PARSONS
58	Assoc Provost Grad Studies/Faculty	Dr. Matthew RAGLAND
20	Assoc Provost Undergraduate Studies	Dr. Joy CLARK
84	Assoc Provost Enrollment	Dr. Sameer PANDE
09	Asst Provost IE & Accreditation	Dr. Cara Mia BRASWELL
41	Athletic Director	Ms. Jessie ROSA
85	Director of Global Initiatives	Mr. Ayush TANEJA
15	Interim Chief HR Officer	Ms. Twyla WILLIAMS
08	Dean of Library	Mr. Phill JOHNSON
07	Director of Admissions/Recruiting	Mr. Ronnie MCKINNEY
37	Sr Director of Financial Aid	Mr. Anthony RICHEY
109	Chief Campus Services Officer	Mr. Daryl MORRIS
39	Dir Housing & Residence Life	Mr. Iyisha HAMPTON
13	Chief Information Officer	Mr. Tobias MENSE
28	Asst Vice Chanc Diversity/Inclus	Dr. Chaundra THOMPSON
19	Director of Police Operations	Ms. Brenda MITCHELL
06	Registrar	Ms. Holly BENSON
36	Director Career Development	Mr. Bradley ROBBINS
26	Director of Communications	Mr. Troy JOHNSON
25	Director of Sponsored Programs	Ms. Fariba S. DERAVI
88	Intl Enrollment Manager	Vacant
50	Dean of College of Business	Dr. Wanda Rhea INGRAM
53	Dean of College of Education	Dr. Sheila AUSTIN
83	Dean Col Liberal Arts/Social Sci	Dr. Andrew MCMICHAEL
66	Dean of Nursing/Health Sci	Dr. Jean LEUNER
88	Associate Director of Clinical Svcs	Ms. Greta CHAMBLESS
81	Dean College of Sciences	Dr. Robert GRANGER
04	Executive Admin Asst to Chancellor	Ms. Robin FORESTER
88	Special Asst/Collab Part/Dist Educ	Dr. Shanta VARMA
106	Dir Online/Digital Learning	Ms. Carolyn RAWL
29	Alumni Program Manager	Ms. Valerie RANKIN
22	Manager Disability Services	Ms. Tamara MASSEY-GARRETT
96	Dir of Procurement & Payment Svcs	Vacant

Birmingham-Southern College (A)

900 Arkadelphia Road, Birmingham AL 35254-0001
County: Jefferson FICE Identification: 001012
Unit ID: 100937
Telephone: (205) 226-4600 Carnegie Class: Bac-A&S
FAX Number: (205) 226-4627 Calendar System: 4/1/4
URL: www.bsc.edu
Established: 1856 Annual Undergrad Tuition & Fees: $17,650
Enrollment: 1,283 Coed
Affiliation or Control: United Methodist IRS Status: 501(c)3
Highest Offering: Baccalaureate
Accreditation: SC, MUS

01 President .... Mr. Daniel COLEMAN
05 VP Academic Affairs/Provost .... Dr. Brad CASKEY
10 VP Business and Finance/CFO .... Mr. Eli PHILLIPS
100 VP Cmty Initiatives/Chief of Staff .... Mr. Lane ESTES
111 VP Advancement and Communications ..... Ms. Virginia G. LOFTIN
13 VP Information Technology .... Mr. Anthony HAMBEY
32 VP Student Development .... Dr. David EBERHARDT
84 VP Enrollment Management .... Mr. Trent GILBERT
88 Asst to the President Emeriti .... Mrs. Terri HICKS
20 VP Academic Affairs/Assoc Provost .... Dr. Tim SMITH
20 Assistant Provost .... Ms. Martha Ann STEVENSON
06 Registrar .... Mr. Keith KARRIKER
42 Chaplain .... Rev. Julie HOLLY
29 Director Alumni Engagement .... Ms. Jennifer WATERS
23 Director of Health Services .... Ms. Yvette SPENCER
04 Asst to the President .... Mr. Chuck EVANS
26 Director of Communications .... Ms. Amy BICKERS
08 Director of the Library .... Vacant
18 Director of Facilities & Events .... Mr. Travis PRINCE
15 Assoc VP/Director Human Resources .... Ms. Susan KINNEY
38 Director of Counseling .... Ms. Cara BLAKES
41 Athletic Director .... Ms. Kyndall WATERS
19 Chief of Campus Police .... Mr. Jeff HARRIS
36 Director of Career Services .... Mr. Michael LEBEAU
111 Director Advancement Services .... Ms. Kimberly BURNETT
28 Dir Student Diversity & Inclusion .... Dr. Kristie WILLIAMS
68 Dir Physical Fitness & Recreation .... Mr. Mike ROBINSON
88 Director of Leadership Studies .... Dr. Kent ANDERSEN
88 Director of Service Learning .... Ms. Kristin HARPER
104 Assoc Dir of International Programs .... Ms. Anne LEDVINA
40 Bookstore Manager .... Mr. William ALEXANDER
96 Purchasing Manager .... Mr. Tim WILDING
30 Director Development .... Ms. Allison HEDGE
30 Director Development .... Ms. Meredith ALSABROOK
44 Director Development-Annual Giving .... Ms. Sarah-Kate ROBERTS
112 Director Donor Relations .... Ms. Daphne POWELL
09 Dir Inst Rsrch and Effectiveness .... Ms. Debbie DAILEY
25 Director Grants & Special Projects .... Dr. Joe CHANDLER
39 Associate Dean of Students .... Mr. David MILLER

Columbia Southern University (B)

21982 University Lane, Orange Beach AL 36561-3845
County: Baldwin FICE Identification: 041215
Unit ID: 450933
Telephone: (251) 981-3771 Carnegie Class: DU-Mod
FAX Number: (251) 981-3815 Calendar System: Other
URL: www.columbiasouthern.edu
Established: 1993 Annual Undergrad Tuition & Fees: $5,535
Enrollment: 20,818 Coed
Affiliation or Control: Proprietary IRS Status: Proprietary
Highest Offering: Doctorate
Accreditation: DEAC

01 President .... Mr. Ken STYRON
05 Provost and Chief Academic Officer .... Dr. Barry GOLDSTEIN
100 Chief of Staff .... Mrs. Chelsea HOFFMAN
26 Chief Marketing Officer .... Mr. Eric MCHANEY
13 Chief Information Officer .... Mr. Scott OSWALD
10 Chief Financial Officer .... Mr. Pat TROUP
88 VP Business Development/Mil Init .... Mr. Rick COOPER
15 VP of Human Resources/Train & Dev .... Mrs. Sue BUTTS
20 Vice Provost Acad & Student Affairs .... Mrs. Janell GIBSON
49 Dean Col Arts & Sciences/Asst Prov .... Dr. Sonya ROGERS
88 Dean Col Safety/Emerg Svc/Asst Prov .... Dr. Misti KILL
50 Dean College of Business/Asst Prov .... Dr. Elwin JONES
88 Assistant Provost Special Programs .... Dr. Joe MANJONE
108 Asst Prov Inst Effect/Accreditation .... Mrs. Khalilah BURTON
14 Assoc VP of Business Intelligence .... Mr. Ed WITHERINGTON
31 Associate VP University Relations .... Mrs. Caroline WALTERS
32 Dean & Asst Prov for Stdnt Affairs .... Dr. Lee BARNETT
20 Dean Faculty Development Svcs & Sup .... Dr. John WILLEY
24 Director of Instructional Design .... Mrs. Dayna FULLER
27 Director of Marketing Research .... Mr. Beau VIGNES
29 Dir of Community & Alumni Relations .... Mrs. Vicki BARNES
40 Director of Bookstore Operations .... Mr. David BARNES
09 Director of Institutional Research .... Mrs. Cherea SCHELLHASE
06 Registrar .... Mrs. Rachel FARRIS
37 Director of Financial Aid .... Mrs. Marie WILLIAMS
08 Dean of Library .... Ms. Jennifer STEINFORD
88 Director of State Auth & TIX Coord .... Mrs. Alexis HARRIS
07 Director of Admissions .... Ms. Cassandra TAGGE
121 Dir of Success Center .... Mrs. Wendy TROUP
121 Dir Academic Adv & Student Support .... Mrs. Jennifer SCHROEDER
21 Assistant VP of Finance .... Mr. Craig TAYLOR
16 Director of Human Resources .... Mrs. Danielle BURGE
108 Dir Acad Assessment & Data Analysis .... Dr. John HOPE
88 Director of Curriculum Planning .... Ms. Sonya KOPP
102 Director of Corporate Outreach .... Ms. Sherri TWITTY
51 Director of Continuing Education .... Ms. Nickie COOPER
113 Director of Student Accounts .... Mr. Aaron COLLINS
114 Dir of Administrative Operations .... Mr. Jason LONGCRIER
36 Director of Career Services .... Mr. Keith CULLEN
19 Manager Security and Reception .... Mr. Mike JOHNS

Edward Via College of Osteopathic Medicine-Auburn Campus (C)

910 S. Donahue Drive, Auburn AL 36832
Telephone: (334) 442-4000 Identification: 770965
Accreditation: &OSTEO

† Branch campus of Edward Via College of Osteopathic Medicine, Blacksburg, VA

Faulkner University (D)

5345 Atlanta Highway, Montgomery AL 36109-3398
County: Montgomery FICE Identification: 001003
Unit ID: 101189
Telephone: (334) 272-5820 Carnegie Class: Masters/M
FAX Number: (334) 386-7107 Calendar System: Semester
URL: www.faulkner.edu
Established: 1942 Annual Undergrad Tuition & Fees: $21,690
Enrollment: 3,350 Coed
Affiliation or Control: Churches Of Christ IRS Status: 501(c)3
Highest Offering: Doctorate
Accreditation: SC, CAEPN, IACBE, LAW, @SP, THEOL

01 President .... Dr. Michael D. WILLIAMS
00 Chancellor .... Dr. Billy D. HILYER
05 Vice President Academic Affairs .... Dr. Dave RAMPERSAD
10 Vice President Financial Services .... Mr. Joseph VICKERY
32 Vice President Student Services .... Dr. Jean-Noel THOMPSON
84 Vice President Enrollment Mgmt .... Mr. Mark HUNT
15 Vice President Human Resources .... Ms. Renee DAVIS
111 Vice President Advancement .... Dr. John TYSON
43 General Counsel .... Dr. Gerald JONES
61 Interim Dean Jones School of Law .... Dr. Charles CAMPBELL
49 Dean College Arts & Sciences .... Dr. Jeffrey ARRINGTON
50 Dean College Business/Exec Educ .... Dr. Dave KHADANGA
73 Dean College of Biblical Studies .... Dr. Scott GLEAVES
53 Dean College of Education .... Dr. Leslie COWELL
21 Associate Vice President of Finance .... Mr. Jamie HORN
30 Assoc Vice President Development .... Mr. Billy CAMP
61 Assoc Dean Academics Jones Law .... Dr. Layne KEELE
06 Registrar .... Mr. Don REYNOLDS
37 Director Student Financial Aid .... Mr. Buddy JACKSON
12 Director Mobile Center .... Mrs. Diane NEWELL
12 Director Birmingham Center .... Mrs. Karen BRUCE
12 Director Huntsville Center .... Mr. Bryan COLLINS
41 Athletic Director .... Mr. Hal WYNN
08 Director of Libraries .... Mrs. Barbara KELLY
104 Director of Study Abroad .... Dr. Terry EDWARDS
26 Director of University Marketing .... Mr. Patrick GREGORY
07 Director of Admissions .... Mr. Neil SCOTT
121 Director Student Success .... Mrs. Michelle OTWELL
92 Director of Honors Program .... Dr. Andrew JACOBS
35 Dean of Students .... Ms. Candace CAIN
36 Director Career Services .... Mrs. Marie OTTINGER
38 Director Counseling Center .... Mrs. Michelle BOND
04 Exec Assistant to the President .... Mrs. Beverly TOLLIVER
19 Director Security/Safety .... Mr. Phillip CALVERT
39 Director Student Housing .... Mrs. Keri ALFORD
106 Director Faulkner University Online .... Mrs. Tiffany CANTRELL

Fortis Institute (E)

100 London Parkway Suite 150, Birmingham AL 35211
Telephone: (205) 940-7800 Identification: 666683
Accreditation: ACICS, DH, MLTAD

† Branch campus of Fortis Institute, Erie, PA.

Heritage Christian University (F)

PO Box HCU, Florence AL 35630-0050
County: Lauderdale FICE Identification: 021997
Unit ID: 101453
Telephone: (256) 766-6610 Carnegie Class: Spec-4-yr-Faith
FAX Number: N/A Calendar System: Semester
URL: www.hcu.edu
Established: 1968 Annual Undergrad Tuition & Fees: $11,232
Enrollment: 89 Coed
Affiliation or Control: Churches Of Christ IRS Status: 501(c)3
Highest Offering: Master's
Accreditation: BI

01 President .... Dr. Kirk BROTHERS
05 Vice President of Academic Affairs .... Dr. Bill BAGENTS
11 Vice Pres Administration .... Mr. Freddie P. MOON
111 Vice President of Advancement .... Mr. Philip GOAD
20 Assoc VP Academic Affairs .... Dr. Michael JACKSON
32 Dean of Students .... Mr. Travis HARMON
33 Dean of Men .... Dr. Ed GALLAGHER
34 Dean of Women .... Dr. Rosemary SNODGRASS
58 Director of Graduate Programs .... Dr. Jeremy BARRIER
06 Registrar .... Mrs. Alana MARKS
08 Librarian .... Miss Jamie S. COX
42 Director of Christian Service .... Mr. Brad MCKINNON
84 Dir Enrollment Svcs/Stdnt Fin Aid .... Mr. Jim COLLINS
106 Dir Online Education/E-learning .... Mr. Travis HARMON
09 Dir of Institutional Effectiveness .... Dr. Michael JACKSON
13 Web Communications and Tech Manager .. Mr. Justin CONNOLLY

Herzing University (G)

280 W Valley Avenue, Birmingham AL 35209-4816
Telephone: (205) 916-2800 FICE Identification: 010193
Accreditation: &NH, EMT

† Regional accreditation is carried under the parent institution in Madison, WI.

Huntingdon College (H)

1500 East Fairview Avenue, Montgomery AL 36106-2148
County: Montgomery FICE Identification: 001019
Unit ID: 101435
Telephone: (334) 833-4497 Carnegie Class: Bac-Diverse
FAX Number: (334) 833-4347 Calendar System: Semester
URL: www.huntingdon.edu
Established: 1854 Annual Undergrad Tuition & Fees: $27,400
Enrollment: 1,102 Coed
Affiliation or Control: United Methodist IRS Status: 501(c)3
Highest Offering: Baccalaureate
Accreditation: SC, MUS

01 President .... Rev. J. Cameron WEST
10 Treasurer & SVP for IE/Plng & Admin .... Mr. Jay A. DORMAN
30 SVP for Student & Inst Development .... Mr. Anthony J. LEIGH
05 Provost & Dean of the College .... Dr. Anna MCEWAN
84 VP for Enrollment Management .... Ms. Leanne M. CARROLL
09 VP Inst Research & Accreditation .... Dr. Sidney J. STUBBS
26 VP Communications & Marketing .... Ms. Suellen S. OFE
32 VP Stdnt Affairs/Dean of Students .... Ms. Francis H. TAYLOR
20 Associate Provost .... Dr. Tom PERRIN
04 Exec Asst to President/Corp Secy .... Ms. Sandra B. KELSER
21 Comptroller .... Ms. Jo-Ann M. HOLSTON
19 Chief of Security .... Mr. Michael S. WARD
06 Registrar .... Mr. Kevin THORNTHWAITE
16 Assoc VP Hum Res & Risk Mgmt .... Dr. Christopher CLARK
21 Assoc VP Fin Svcs & Reporting .... Ms. Belinda G. DUETT
41 Director of Athletics .... Mr. Eric LEVANDA
08 Director Houghton Memorial Library .... Mr. Eric A. KIDWELL
121 Dir Staton Ctr for Lrng Enrichment .... Ms. Maryann M. BECK
13 Vice President for Technology .... Dr. Anneliese H. SPAETH
18 Director of Facilities and Grounds .... Mr. T. Michael DUNN
37 Director of Financial Aid .... Ms. Brittany DAVIS
36 Dir of Center for Career & Vocation .... Ms. Sherry Leigh LACEY
38 Director of Counseling Services .... Vacant
35 Director of Student Activities .... Ms. Kathleen PENNEY
88 Dir Huntingdon Leadership Academy .... Mr. Macon ARMISTEAD
07 Assoc Dir of Admission .... Ms. Stephanie HICKS
42 Chaplain .... Rev. Rhett BUTLER
40 Bookstore Manager .... Ms. Nancy JACKSON

Huntsville Bible College (I)

906 Oakwood Avenue NW, Huntsville AL 35811-1632
County: Madison FICE Identification: 038943
Unit ID: 449348
Telephone: (256) 469-7536 Carnegie Class: Spec-4-yr-Faith
FAX Number: (256) 469-7549 Calendar System: Semester
URL: www.hbc1.edu
Established: 1986 Annual Undergrad Tuition & Fees: $4,560
Enrollment: 141 Coed
Affiliation or Control: Baptist IRS Status: 501(c)3
Highest Offering: Doctorate
Accreditation: BI

01 President .... Dr. John L. CLAY
05 Dean of Academics/Instruction .... Rev. David L. FAYLOR
07 Admissions Officer .... Ms. Vernita CHANDLER
10 Chief Financial Officer .... Ms. Jacqueline ROBINSON
111 Advancement Officer .... Ms. Eloise MCNEALEY
58 Dean of Graduate Studies .... Dr. Mitchell WALKER
08 Director of Library Media .... Ms. Victoria RICHARDSON

Jacksonville State University (J)

700 Pelham Road N, Jacksonville AL 36265-1602
County: Calhoun FICE Identification: 001020
Unit ID: 101480
Telephone: (256) 782-5781 Carnegie Class: Masters/L
FAX Number: (256) 782-5291 Calendar System: Semester
URL: www.jsu.edu
Established: 1883 Annual Undergrad Tuition & Fees (In-State): $8,760
Enrollment: 8,567 Coed
Affiliation or Control: State IRS Status: 501(c)3
Highest Offering: Doctorate
Accreditation: SC, AAFCS, ART, CACREP, CAEPN, #COARC, DIETD, JOUR, MUS, NAIT, NURSE, SPAA, SW, THEA

01 President .... Dr. John M. BEEHLER
05 Provost/VP Academic Affairs .... Dr. Christi SHELTON
10 VP Finance & Administration .... Mr. Jim BRIGHAM
111 VP University Advancement .... Dr. Charles R. LEWIS
32 VP Student Affairs .... Dr. Tim KING
116 Chief Internal Auditor .... Mr. Nelson CLARK
15 Chief Human Res/Diversity Officer .... Vacant
13 Chief Information Officer .... Mr. Vinson HOUSTON

43 Legal Counsel ... Mr. Sam MONK
41 Director Athletics ... Mr. Greg SEITZ
86 Chief Govt Rels/Cmty Engagement ... Dr. Don KILLINGSWORTH
20 Vice Provost ... Dr. Joe WALSH
57 Dean School of Arts & Hum ... Dr. Staci L. STONE
81 Dean School of Science ... Dr. Timothy LINDBLOM
76 Dean School Health Prof & Wellness ... Dr. Christie SHELTON
53 Dean School of Education ... Dr. Tommy TURNER
50 Dean School of Business & Industry ... Dr. William FIELDING
83 Dean School Human Svc & Soc Science ... Dr. Maureen NEWTON
08 Dean Library Services ... Mr. John-Bauer GRAHAM
32 Dean of Students Office ... Mr. Terry CASEY
88 Associate Vice Provost ... Ms. Lisa M. WILLIAMS
06 Registrar ... Ms. Emily WHITE
84 Assoc VP of Enrollment Management ... Dr. Emily W. MESSER
21 University Controller ... Vacant
109 Exec Dir Business Svcs ... Mr. Jim BRIGHAM
30 Director University Development ... Mr. Earl WARREN
39 Director Residence Life ... Ms. Rochelle SMITH
39 Dir Univ Housing Operations ... Ms. Brooke LYON
88 Dir International Programs ... Ms. Chandni KHADKA
09 Dir Inst Research & Effectiveness ... Ms. Kim PRESSON
29 Director of Alumni Relations ... Ms. Kaci OGLE
37 Dir Student Financial Svcs ... Ms. Jessica WIGGINS
18 Dir Capital Planning/Facilities ... Mr. David THOMPSON
36 Director Career Placement Services ... Ms. Rebecca E. TURNER
38 Dir Counseling/Disability Sppt Svcs ... Ms. Julie NIX
96 Procurement/Fixed Assets ... Ms. Denise HUNT
26 Chief Marketing/Comm Officer ... Mr. Tim GARNER
19 Director Security/Safety ... Mr. Rob SCHAFFER
22 Coordinator Title IX ... Ms. Jennifer ARGO
28 Director of Diversity & Inclusion ... Ms. Kandace HAMILTON

Judson College (A)

302 Bibb Street, Marion AL 36756-2504
County: Perry
FICE Identification: 001023
Unit ID: 101541
Telephone: (334) 683-5100
Carnegie Class: Bac-A&S
FAX Number: (334) 683-5147
Calendar System: Semester
URL: www.judson.edu
Established: 1838
Annual Undergrad Tuition & Fees: $18,510
Enrollment: 315
Female
Affiliation or Control: Alabama Baptist State Convention
IRS Status: 501(c)3
Highest Offering: Baccalaureate
Accreditation: SC, MUS, SW

01 President ... Dr. Mark TEW
05 Interim Academic Dean ... Dr. Stacey G. PARHAM
32 VP & Dean of Students ... Ms. Susan JONES
84 VP for Enrollment & Communications ... Mr. Kevin KIRK
111 VP for Institutional Advancement ... Dr. Terry MORGAN
10 VP for Business Affairs ... Ms. Betty A. MIDDLEBROOKS
13 Assoc VP for Data Mgmt & IT ... Mrs. Traci L. FOSTER
26 Assoc VP Marketing & Communications ... Ms. Mary A. TAYLOR
06 Registrar ... Mrs. Alyssa SNYDER
106 Dir of Distance Learning ... Dr. Michael BERGMAN
37 Dir Student Financial Aid ... Mr. James GIBSON

Miles College (B)

5500 Myron Massey Boulevard, Fairfield AL 35064-2621
County: Jefferson
FICE Identification: 001028
Unit ID: 101675
Telephone: (205) 929-1000
Carnegie Class: Bac-Diverse
FAX Number: (205) 929-1453
Calendar System: Semester
URL: www.miles.edu
Established: 1898
Annual Undergrad Tuition & Fees: $12,132
Enrollment: 1,650
Coed
Affiliation or Control: Christian Methodist Episcopal
IRS Status: 501(c)3
Highest Offering: Baccalaureate
Accreditation: SC, ACBSP, CAEPN, SW

01 Interim President ... Ms. Bobbie KNIGHT
05 Dean & VP Academic Affairs ... Mr. Charles GIBBS
10 Sr VP Finance/Business Admin ... Ms. Diana KNIGHTON
09 VP Institutional Advancement ... Mr. Arthur J. BRIGATI
42 VP/Dean Student Engagement/Chapel ... Rev. Larry BATIE
100 Special Asst/Chief of Staff ... Mr. Kenneth COACHMAN
07 Assoc Dir of Operations Admissions ... Ms. Courtney PARKS SANKEY
32 VP of Student Success ... Mr. Michael A. JOHNSON
20 Assoc Dean of Academic Affairs ... Dr. Joyce DUGAN-WOOD
88 VP Strategic Initiatives ... Ms. Ba-Shen T. WELCH
37 Director Financial Aid ... Mr. Percy LANIER
18 Director Building Operations ... Mr. Richard WILLIS
38 Dir Counseling/Advising/Testing ... Ms. Keisha LEWIS
15 Director Human Resources ... Mrs. Verlanda TATE

Oakwood University (C)

7000 Adventist Boulevard, NW, Huntsville AL 35896-0003
County: Madison
FICE Identification: 001033
Unit ID: 101912
Telephone: (256) 726-7000
Carnegie Class: Bac-Diverse
FAX Number: (256) 726-8334
Calendar System: Semester
URL: www.oakwood.edu
Established: 1896
Annual Undergrad Tuition & Fees: $19,732
Enrollment: 1,711
Coed
Affiliation or Control: Seventh-day Adventist
IRS Status: 501(c)3
Highest Offering: Master's
Accreditation: SC, ACBSP, CAEPN, DIETD, DIETI, NUR, SW

01 President/CEO ... Dr. Leslie POLLARD
05 Provost & Sr Vice President ... Dr. Colwick WILSON
10 Vice President Financial Admin ... Ms. Sabrina COTTON
32 Vice President Student Services ... Mr. David KNIGHT
46 VP Research & Faculty Development ... Dr. Prudence L. POLLARD
84 VP Mission/Enroll Svcs/Retention ... Dr. David RICHARDSON
111 Exec Dir Advancement/Development ... Mrs. Cheri WILSON
20 Asst VP Academic Administration ... Vacant
21 Asst VP Financial Admin/Controller ... Mrs. Gail CALDWELL
35 Asst Vice Pres Student Services ... Ms. Adrienne MATTHEWS
13 Chief Info Technology Officer (CIO) ... Mr. Kirk NUGENT
15 Exec Dir of Employee Srvs/Human Res ... Ms. Pamela HOLIDA
25 Contracts ... Ms. Cheryl SULLIVAN
26 Director Public Relations ... Dr. Maquisha FORD MULLINS
84 Director Enrollment Management ... Mr. James KELLY
37 Director Financial Aid ... Vacant
06 Registrar ... Ms. Traci MOORE
39 Residence Life Coordinator-Men ... Mr. Woodrow VAUGHN
88 Resident Life Coordinator-Women ... Ms. Linda ANDERSON
08 Director Library Services ... Dr. Ruth SWAN
18 Director Physical Plant ... Mr. Henry HAWKINS
19 Director Security ... Mr. Melvin HARRIS
38 Dir Counseling & Health Services ... Vacant
51 Dir Adult & Continuing Education ... Mrs. Ellengold GOODRIDGE
88 Dean for Student Success ... Dr. Brandon GAMBLE
50 Dean Business & Info Systems ... Dr. Theodore BROWN
53 Dean Education ... Dr. James MBYIRUKIRA
76 Dean Allied Health ... Dr. Earl HENRY
60 Dean English & Foreign Languages ... Dr. Ramona HYMAN
64 Dean Music ... Dr. Jason FERDINAND
65 Dean Biological Sciences ... Dr. Elaine VANTERPOOL
65 Dean Chemistry ... Dr. Kenneth LAI HING
66 Dean Nursing ... Dr. Karen ANDERSON
68 Dean Health & Exercise Sciences ... Dr. Andrew YOUNG
70 Dean Social Work ... Dr. Octavio RAMIREZ
73 Dean Religion & Theology ... Dr. Agniel SAMSON
81 Dean Math & Computer Science ... Dr. Lisa JAMES
82 Dean History ... Dr. Samuel LONDON
83 Dean Psychology ... Dr. Martin HODNETT
60 Dean Communication ... Dr. Rennae ELLIOTT

Remington College, Mobile Campus (D)

828 Downtowner Loop W, Mobile AL 36609-5404
County: Mobile
FICE Identification: 026055
Unit ID: 366535
Telephone: (251) 343-8200
Carnegie Class: Spec-4-yr-Other Tech
FAX Number: (251) 343-0577
Calendar System: Quarter
URL: www.remingtoncollege.edu
Established: 1986
Annual Undergrad Tuition & Fees: $15,700
Enrollment: 373
Coed
Affiliation or Control: Independent Non-Profit
IRS Status: 501(c)3
Highest Offering: Baccalaureate
Accreditation: ACCSC

01 Director of Campus Administration ... Jesse KLENK

Samford University (E)

800 Lakeshore Drive, Birmingham AL 35229-0001
County: Jefferson
FICE Identification: 001036
Unit ID: 102049
Telephone: (205) 726-2011
Carnegie Class: DU-Mod
FAX Number: (205) 726-2171
Calendar System: 4/1/4
URL: www.samford.edu
Established: 1841
Annual Undergrad Tuition & Fees: $31,650
Enrollment: 5,509
Coed
Affiliation or Control: Southern Baptist
IRS Status: 501(c)3
Highest Offering: Doctorate
Accreditation: SC, ANEST, #ARCPA, @AUD, CAATE, CAEPN, CIDA, #COARC, DIETD, DIETI, LAW, MUS, NURSE, PHAR, PTA, SP, SW, THEA, THEOL

01 President ... Dr. T. Andrew WESTMORELAND
05 Provost ... Dr. Michael HARDIN
32 Vice President for Student Affairs ... Dr. Phil KIMREY
111 Vice President of Advancement ... Mr. W. Randall PITTMAN
10 Exec VP Business/Financial Affairs ... Mr. Harry B. BROCK, III
26 VP for Marketing and Communication ... Dr. Betsy B. HOLLOWAY
20 Senior Assoc Provost ... Dr. Howard FINCH
45 Chief Strategy Officer ... Mr. Colin M. COYNE
04 Assistant to the President ... Dr. Michael D. MORGAN
21 Controller ... Mr. Mike DARWIN
27 Executive Dir Broadcast Media ... Mr. Brad RADICE
13 Chief Information Officer ... Mr. Doug RIGNEY
43 General Counsel ... Mr. W. Clark WATSON
11 Associate Provost Administration ... Dr. Nancy BIGGIO
108 Associate Provost Assess & Accred ... Dr. Katrina H. MINTZ
41 Athletic Director ... Mr. Martin NEWTON
88 Director Parent Programs ... Ms. Susan DOYLE
88 Director of Business Services ... Mr. Wade WALKER
88 Dir Event Management ... Ms. Allison BRYMER
18 Director of Facilities Management ... Mr. Mark FULLER
37 Dir of Student Financial Services ... Mr. Lane M. SMITH
21 Sr AVP Business & Financial Affairs ... Ms. Lisa IMBRAGULIO
88 Assoc VP Operations ... Dr. Kimberly BROWN
08 Dean of University Library ... Dr. Kimmetha D. HERNDON
15 Asst VP & Dir of Human Resources ... Mr. Joel WINDHAM
30 Asst VP Univ Adv & Exec Dir Devel ... Mr. Douglas WILSON
19 Int Dir Public Safety/Emergency Mgt ... Mr. Scott LEIGH
39 Asst VP Campus & Residential Life ... Ms. Lauren M. TAYLOR
117 Dir of Risk Management & Insurance ... Mr. James A. CLEMENT
114 Dir of Budget & Financial Planning ... Mr. Matt DEFORE
102 Dir Development & Legacy League ... Ms. Sharon SMITH
07 Dean of Admissions ... Mr. Jason BLACK
35 Asst VP for Student Development ... Ms. April ROBINSON
35 Asst VP Stdnt Affs/Title IX Coord ... Mr. Garry L. ATKINS
88 Director of University Fellows ... Mr. Bryan M. JOHNSON
53 Dean OB Beason School of Education ... Vacant
49 Dean Howard College Arts/Sciences ... Mr. Tim HALL
17 Vice Provost College Health Science ... Dr. Nena F. SANDERS
76 Dean of Health Professions ... Dr. Alan JUNG
69 Dean of Public Health ... Dr. Keith ELDER
67 Dean School of Pharmacy ... Dr. Michael A. CROUCH
73 Dean Beeson School of Divinity ... Dr. Douglas A. SWEENEY
50 Int Dean Brock School of Business ... Dr. Chad M. CARSON
61 Dean Cumberland School of Law ... Mr. Henry C. STRICKLAND
57 Dean School of the Arts ... Dr. Joseph HOPKINS
06 Registrar ... Mr. Jay FLYNN
110 Director of Stewardship ... Ms. Kimberly CRIPPS
112 Director Gift and Estate Planning ... Mr. Gene HOWARD
28 Assistant Provost Diversity ... Dr. Denise GREGORY
104 Director Global Engagement ... Ms. Lauren DOSS
105 Exec Dir Web/Digital Marketing ... Mr. Todd COTTON
88 Dir of Congregational Resources ... Mr. Michael WILSON
88 Dir Strat & Appl Analysis ... Dr. Randolph HORN
88 Director QEP & CTLS ... Dr. Eric FOURNIER
88 Creative Dir Marketing & Comm ... Ms. Laine WILLIAMS
09 Director of Institutional Research ... Mr. Toner EVANS
25 Chief Contract/Grants Administrator ... Ms. Linnea MINNEMA
29 Director Alumni Affairs ... Ms. Casey RAMEY
36 Director Student Placement ... Ms. Dora DITCHFIELD
38 Director Student Counseling ... Mr. Richard YOAKUM
44 Director Annual Giving ... Ms. Karen TEMPLETON

Selma University (F)

1501 Lapsley Street, Selma AL 36701-5232
County: Dallas
FICE Identification: 001037
Unit ID: 102058
Telephone: (334) 872-2533
Carnegie Class: Spec-4-yr-Faith
FAX Number: (334) 872-7746
Calendar System: Semester
URL: www.selmauniversity.edu
Established: 1878
Annual Undergrad Tuition & Fees: $7,410
Enrollment: 324
Coed
Affiliation or Control: Baptist
IRS Status: 501(c)3
Highest Offering: Master's
Accreditation: BI

01 President ... Dr. Alvin A. CLEVELAND, SR.
05 Vice President Academic Affairs ... Dr. Stanford ANGION
32 Vice Pres Student Affairs ... Rev. Frankie HUTCHINS
06 Registrar ... Mr. Terrence JACKSON
37 Director of Financial Aid ... Ms. Yolanda GORDON-JACKSON
07 Director of Admissions ... Vacant
10 Chief Financial/Business Officer ... Mrs. Robin THOMAS

South University (G)

5355 Vaughn Road, Montgomery AL 36116-1120
Telephone: (334) 395-8800
FICE Identification: 004463
Accreditation: &SC, ACBSP, MAC, NURSE, PTAA

† Regional accreditation is carried under the parent institution in Savannah, GA.

Spring Hill College (H)

4000 Dauphin Street, Mobile AL 36608-1791
County: Mobile
FICE Identification: 001041
Unit ID: 102234
Telephone: (251) 380-4000
Carnegie Class: Bac-A&S
FAX Number: (251) 460-2182
Calendar System: Semester
URL: www.shc.edu
Established: 1830
Annual Undergrad Tuition & Fees: $39,464
Enrollment: 1,485
Coed
Affiliation or Control: Roman Catholic
IRS Status: 501(c)3
Highest Offering: Master's
Accreditation: SC, NURSE

01 President ... Dr. Joseph LEE
05 Provost/Vice Pres Academic Affairs ... Dr. Marc MANGANARO
10 Vice President Finance/Accounting ... Ms. Rhonda SHIRAZI
30 Vice Pres Alumni Relations/Devel ... Mrs. Mary MCDONALD
32 Vice Pres Student Affairs ... Mr. Kevin ABEL
84 Vice Pres Enrollment Svcs ... Mr. Gary BRACKEN
13 Chief Information Officer ... Vacant
20 Associate Provost ... Ms. Jennifer GOOD
35 Dean of Students ... Vacant
21 Controller ... Ms. Marianne WILKINS
37 Director of Financial Aid ... Mrs. Melinda MCCALL
06 Registrar ... Ms. Linnea BATTLES
88 Director Student Advising Services ... Ms. Ashley DUNKLIN
29 Director of Alumni Programs ... Vacant
15 Director of Personnel ... Ms. Patricia A. DAVIS
07 Director of Admissions ... Mr. Patrick SPRAGUE
19 Director of Public Safety/Security ... Mr. Kevin ANDERSON
23 Director of Health Services ... Mrs. Melissa MELTON
42 Director of Campus Ministry ... Ms. Colleen LEE
41 Director Athletics & Recreation ... Mr. Joe NILAND
31 Dir Foley Community Service Center ... Dr. Erik GOLDSCHMIDT
26 Dir Communications/Instl Marketing ... Mrs. Cathy HELEAN
27 Communications Officer ... Mr. Fletcher DEVERY

36 Director of Career Services ....Mr. Jeremy MOORE
40 Bookstore Manager ....Mr. Jason MEIER

Stillman College (A)

3601 Stillman Boulevard, Tuscaloosa AL 35401
County: Tuscaloosa FICE Identification: 001044
Unit ID: 102270
Telephone: (205) 366-8817 Carnegie Class: Bac-A&S
FAX Number: N/A Calendar System: Semester
URL: www.stillman.edu
Established: 1876 Annual Undergrad Tuition & Fees: $11,092
Enrollment: 677 Coed
Affiliation or Control: Presbyterian Church (U.S.A.) IRS Status: 501(c)3
Highest Offering: Baccalaureate
Accreditation: SC, CAEPN, IACBE

01 President ....Dr. Cynthia WARRICK
05 Provost/VP Academic Affairs ....Dr. Mark MCCORMICK
10 Chief Financial Officer ....Mr. Melvin WAITS
108 VP Institutional Effectiveness ....Dr. Mary J. KROTZER
111 VP Institutional Advancement ....Ms. Luanne BAKER
32 Vice President for Students Affairs ....Rev. Tyshawn GARDNER
31 Director Community Relations ....Mr. Mason BONNER
13 Director of Info Tech ....Ms. Tamara MARSHALL
26 VP Strategic Initiatives ....Dr. Lamin DRAMMEH
29 Director Alumni Affairs ....Ms. Jean WILSON-SYKES
18 Senior Director Campus Services ....Vacant
53 Dean of Education ....Dr. Alicia CURRY
49 Dean of Arts & Sciences ....Dr. Josiah SAMPSON
50 Dean School of Business ....Mr. Isaac MCCOY
08 Dean of Library ....Mr. Robert HEATH
37 Interim Director of Financial Aid ....Mr. Kenneth WILLIAMS
23 Dir Student Development/Health Svcs ....Vacant
13 Director of Info Technology ....Mr. Michael HUBBARD
85 Director of Intl Student Affairs ....Mr. Kyris BROWN
19 Chief of Campus Police ....Ms. Cassandra COOPER
41 Athletic Director ....Mr. Kenyon ALSTON
15 Director Human Resources ....Ms. LaKeya GOINS
42 College Chaplain ....Dr. Joseph SCRIVNER
101 Board Liaison ....Ms. RaSheda WORKMAN
04 Executive Asst to President ....Ms. Larcia WARTHAW
35 Dean of Student Life ....Mr. Marcus KENNEDY
06 Registrar ....Dr. Victoria BOMAN

Talladega College (B)

627 W. Battle Street, Talladega AL 35160-2354
County: Talladega FICE Identification: 001046
Unit ID: 102298
Telephone: (256) 761-6100 Carnegie Class: Bac-A&S
FAX Number: (256) 761-9206 Calendar System: Semester
URL: www.talladega.edu
Established: 1867 Annual Undergrad Tuition & Fees: $13,571
Enrollment: 782 Coed
Affiliation or Control: Independent Non-Profit IRS Status: 501(c)3
Highest Offering: Master's
Accreditation: SC, SW

01 President ....Dr. Billy C. HAWKINS
05 Provost/VP for Academic Affairs ....Dr. Lisa LONG
10 Vice Pres Finance & Administration ....Mr. Sama MONDEH
32 President Student Affairs ....Dr. Jeffrey BURGIN
111 VP of Institutional Advancement ....Mr. Seddrick HILL
18 Director Facilities Management ....Mr. Geno MCGRUE
37 Director Financial Aid ....Mrs. Amanda HEADEN
07 Director of Admissions ....Mr. John W. BELL
09 Int Director Institutional Research ....Dr. Syed RAZA
35 Dean/Director of Student Activities ....Ms. Cara GUILBEAU
41 Athletic Director ....Mr. Kevin HEROD
08 Librarian ....Ms. Caitlin COX
13 Information Technology Consultant ....Mr. Laurie HARPER, III
36 Director of Career Placement ....Ms. Sherissa GAITOR
19 Chief Campus Police ....Mr. Ronald DYE
50 Dean Div Administration & Business ....Dr. Jonathan ELIMIMIAN
79 Dean Div Humanities/Fine Arts ....Dr. Ernestene SHEROW
81 Dean Div of Natural Sci/Math ....Dr. Alison BROWN
83 Dean Div EWJ Social Sciences/Educ ....Dr. Rebecca MCKAY
21 Senior Associate Vice President ....Mr. Bruce SMITH
23 Health Services on Campus ....Ms. Stacy FINCHER
25 Title III Coor/Grants Administrator ....Ms. Abina BILLUPS
29 Director Alumni Relations ....Vacant
06 Registrar ....Ms. Barbra SMITH
38 Director Office of Counseling/ADA ....Mr. Michael BROWN
04 Office Assistant President's Office ....Dr. Monique AKASSI
104 Director Study Abroad ....Vacant
22 Dir Affirmative Action/EEO ....Mrs. Brenda RHODEN
15 Human Resources Manager ....Mrs. Brenda RHODEN
26 Director of Public Relations ....Mrs. Mary SOOD
39 Director of Housing and Residence ....Mr. LeMarques MCCLIDE
124 Director of Special Events/Protocol ....Mr. Anthony JONES

Troy University (C)

University Avenue, Troy AL 36082-0001
County: Pike FICE Identification: 001047
Unit ID: 102368
Telephone: (334) 670-3100 Carnegie Class: Masters/L
FAX Number: (334) 670-3774 Calendar System: Semester
URL: www.troy.edu
Established: 1887 Annual Undergrad Tuition & Fees (In-State): $8,908
Enrollment: 17,521 Coed
Affiliation or Control: State IRS Status: 501(c)3
Highest Offering: Doctorate
Accreditation: SC, ACBSP, ADNUR, CAATE, CACREP, CAEP, COSMA, MUS, NUR, SW

01 Chancellor ....Dr. Jack HAWKINS, JR.
05 Sr Vice Chanc for Academic Affairs ....Dr. Earl INGRAM
32 Sr Vice Chanc Student Svcs/Admin ....Dr. John SCHMIDT
111 Sr Vice Chanc Advance/External Affs ....Gen. Walter GIVHAN
10 Sr VC for Fin Affs & Online Educ ....Dr. James BOOKOUT
15 Assoc VC for Human Resources ....MS. Ashley ENGLISH
12 Vice Chancellor Troy Dothan ....Dr. Don JEFFREY
12 Vice Chancellor Troy Phenix City ....Dr. David WHITE
35 Assoc Dean of Student Svcs Dothan ....Ms. Sandra HENRY
49 Asst Dean Col Arts/Sci Troy Dothan ....Dr. Robert SAUNDERS
20 Asst Dean of Academics ....Dr. Carmen LEWIS
53 Assoc Dean Col of Education ....Dr. Kerry PALMER
12 Vice Chanc Troy Montgomery ....Mr. Ray WHITE
11 Asst Dean of Administration ....Dr. Siegfried HARDEN
30 Assoc Vice Chanc for Development ....Ms. Rebecca WATSON
37 Director of Financial Aid ....Ms. Angela JOHNSON
20 Associate Provost for Academics ....Dr. Lee VARDAMAN
26 Assoc VC for Mktg/Communication ....Ms. Donna SCHUBERT
06 Registrar ....Ms. Vickie MILES
84 Assoc VC for Enrollment Management ....Mr. Buddy STARLING
08 Dean Library Services ....Dr. Chris SHAFFER
13 Chief Technology Officer ....Dr. Greg PRICE
27 Director University Relations ....Mr. Matthew CLOWER
29 Director Alumni Affairs ....Ms. Faith W. WARD
36 Coordinator Career Services ....Ms. Lauren COLE
18 Director Facilities/Physical Plant ....Mr. Mark SALMON
60 Director of Journalism ....Dr. Jefferson SPURLOCK
04 Exec Assistant to the Chancellor ....Mr. Tom DAVIS
38 Coordinator of Student Counseling ....Ms. Fran SCHEEL
123 Director of Graduate Admissions ....Ms. Haley MCKINNON
88 Dir Not for Profit/Assoc Controller ....Vacant
106 Senior Dir/Dean for TROY-Online ....Mr. Ronnie CREEL
86 Director of Governmental Relations ....Mr. Marcus PARAMORE
44 Director of Annual Giving ....Vacant
25 Director Sponsored Programs ....Ms. Judy FULMER
08 Int Dir of Library Svcs Troy Dothan ....Mr. Martin OLLIFF
08 Dir of Lib Svcs Troy Montgomery ....Mr. Jeff SIMPSON
20 Dean Undergrad Pgms/Assoc Provost ....Dr. Hal FULMER
35 Dean of Student Svcs Troy Campus ....Mr. Herbert REEVES
49 Dean Arts & Sciences ....Dr. Steven TAYLOR
49 Assoc Dean Col Arts/Sci ....Dr. Bill GRANTHAM
50 Dean Business ....Dr. Judson EDWARDS
53 Dean Education ....Dr. Dionne ROSSER-MIMS
58 Assoc Provost/Dean Graduate Pgms ....Dr. Mary TEMPLETON
76 Dean Health/Human Services ....Dr. Denise GREEN
57 Dean Communication/Fine Arts ....Dr. Larry BLOCHER
35 Assoc Dean Student Svcs Troy Mont ....Dr. James SMITH
09 Director of Institutional Research ....Ms. Kimberly B. JONES
39 Director Student Housing ....Mr. Herbert REEVES
41 Director of Athletics ....Mr. Brent JONES
85 Assoc Dean Intl Student Services ....Ms. Maria FRIGGE
105 Director Web Services ....Mr. John LESTER
108 Director Institutional Assessment ....Ms. Wendy BROYLES
19 Police Chief ....Mr. John MCCALL
104 Study Abroad Coordinator ....Ms. Sarah MCKENZIE
96 Director of Procurement & Asset Mgt ....Ms. April JOHNSON

Tuskegee University (D)

1200 W. Montgomery Road, Tuskegee Inst. AL 36088
County: Macon FICE Identification: 001050
Unit ID: 102377
Telephone: (334) 727-8011 Carnegie Class: Masters/M
FAX Number: (334) 727-5276 Calendar System: Semester
URL: www.tuskegee.edu
Established: 1881 Annual Undergrad Tuition & Fees: $22,170
Enrollment: 3,289 Coed
Affiliation or Control: Independent Non-Profit IRS Status: 501(c)3
Highest Offering: Doctorate
Accreditation: SC, CAEPN, DIETD, MT, NUR, OT, SW, VET

01 President ....Dr. Lily D. MCNAIR
05 Int Provost/VP Academic Affairs ....Dr. Roberta TROY
10 Vice President Finance/CFO ....Dr. Sharron T. BURNETT
46 Vice Pres Research/Dean Grad Stdnts ....Dr. Shaik JEELANI
18 Vice Pres Facilities/Construction ....Mr. Harold (Kippy) TATE
84 VP Student Affairs/Enrollment Mgmt ....Vacant
15 VP Human Resources/Admin ....Vacant
43 VP External Affairs/General Counsel ....Mr. Charles S. JOHNSON
26 Sr Dir Comm/Public Rels/Mktg ....Mr. Michael TULLIER
101 Exec Asst to Pres/Secy to the Board ....Mrs. Chandra CHAMBLISS
13 Int Chief Information Officer ....Ms. Jamie REYNOLDS
114 Asst Vice Pres Budget & Planning ....Vacant
20 Asst Provost ....Dr. Tamara FLOYD-SMITH
47 Dean of CAENS ....Dr. Walter A. HILL
09 AVP Institutional Research ....Dr. Kellei BISHOP -SAMUELS
53 Dean School of Education ....Dr. Carlton E. MORRIS
50 Dean Col Business/Info Sciences ....Dr. Kia KOONG
54 Dean College of Engineering ....Dr. Heshmat AGLAN
66 Dean Sch Nursing/Allied Health ....Dr. Constance HENDRICKS
32 Dean of Students ....Ms. Tameka ANGOLA HARPER
42 Dean of the Chapel ....Dr. Gregory S. GRAY
08 Director of Library Services ....Mrs. Juanita ROBERTS
30 Director of Development ....Ms. Krystal FLOYD
29 Alumni Affairs Director ....Ms. Kimberly HOLLAND
102 Dir Corp/Foundation Relations ....Vacant
51 Int Assoc Prov Cont Educ/Extension ....Dr. Ntam BAHARANYI
36 Asst Career Development/Placement ....Ms. Chantel BOYD
113 Asst Bursar ....Ms. Stacie HENDERSON
37 Director of Financial Aid ....Mr. Advergus D. JAMES, JR.
18 Project Mgr Sodexho/Physical Plant ....Mr. Tony WARD
91 Director of Applications Support ....Ms. Jamie REYNOLDS
06 Registrar ....Dr. Elaine BROMFIELD
96 Director of Purchasing ....Ms. Cassandra PARKER
48 Dean School of Architecture ....Dr. Carla BELL
74 Dean College of Veterinary Medicine ....Dr. Rubye PERRY
49 Dean College of Arts and Sciences ..Dr. Channapatana PRAKASH
88 Dean National Center Bioethics ....Dr. Reuben WARREN
07 Director of Admissions ....Mr. Donovan COLEY
100 Chief of Staff ....Dr. Shirley FRIAR
104 Director Study Abroad ....Dr. Rhonda COLLIER
11 Chief of Operations ....Dr. Charles SMITH
19 Director Security/Safety ....Chief Patrick MARDIS
38 Coordinator Student Counseling ....Mrs. Ardelia M. LUNN
39 Director Housing & Residence Life ....Mr. William SAMUEL, SR.
41 Athletic Director ....Mr. Willie SLATER

United States Sports Academy (E)

One Academy Drive, Daphne AL 36526-7055
County: Baldwin FICE Identification: 021706
Unit ID: 102395
Telephone: (251) 626-3303 Carnegie Class: Spec-4-yr-Other
FAX Number: (251) 621-2527 Calendar System: Semester
URL: www.ussa.edu
Established: 1972 Annual Undergrad Tuition & Fees: N/A
Enrollment: 242 Coed
Affiliation or Control: Independent Non-Profit IRS Status: 501(c)3
Highest Offering: Doctorate
Accreditation: SC

01 President & CEO ....Dr. Thomas J. ROSANDICH
05 Vice President of Academic Affairs ....Dr. Tomi WAHLSTROM
10 Director of Admin & Finance ....Ms. Gayla JACKSON
26 Director of Communications ....Mr. Eric MANN
88 Chair of Sports Management ....Dr. Brandon SPRADLEY
58 Director of Doctoral Studies ....Dr. Fred CROMARTIE
88 Chair of Sports Coaching ....Dr. Roch KING
88 Director Rec Mgmt & Sports Studies ....Dr. Sandra GERINGER
88 Chair of Sports Exercise Science ....Dr. Brian WALLACE
107 Exec Director Professional Studies ....Dr. Carlos AQUINO
32 Director of Student Affairs ....Dr. Lou RIGGANS
06 Registrar ....Mr. Cullen CAREY
08 Director of Library/Archivist ....Dr. Vandy PACETTI-DONELSON
18 Building and Grounds ....Mr. Ed SWANN

*University of Alabama System Office (F)

500 University Boulevard East, Tuscaloosa AL 35401
County: Tuscaloosa FICE Identification: 008004
Unit ID: 100733
Telephone: (205) 348-5861 Carnegie Class: N/A
FAX Number: (205) 348-9788
URL: www.uasystem.ua.edu

01 Chancellor ....Mr. Finis E. ST. JOHN, IV
101 General Counsel/Secretary BOT ....Mr. Sid J. TRANT
05 Vice Chanc Academic/Student Affairs ....Dr. Charles R. NASH
10 Vice Chanc Finance/Administration ....Dr. Dana S. KEITH
26 Vice Chanc Communications/Cmty Rels ....Mrs. Kellee C. REINHART
86 VC Govt Affs/Econ & Workforce Dev ....Mr. Clay M. RYAN
43 Dir of Risk/Compliance/Sys Counsel ....Ms. Katie OSBORNE

*The University of Alabama (G)

Box 870100, Tuscaloosa AL 35487
County: Tuscaloosa FICE Identification: 001051
Unit ID: 100751
Telephone: (205) 348-5100 Carnegie Class: DU-Highest
FAX Number: N/A Calendar System: Semester
URL: www.ua.edu
Established: 1831 Annual Undergrad Tuition & Fees (In-State): $10,780
Enrollment: 38,563 Coed
Affiliation or Control: State IRS Status: 501(c)3
Highest Offering: Doctorate
Accreditation: SC, ART, CAATE, CACREP, CAEPN, CEA, CIDA, CLPSY, DANCE, DIETC, DIETD, JOUR, LAW, LIB, MUS, NURSE, SP, SPAA, SW, THEA

02 President ....Dr. Stuart R. BELL
05 Executive Vice President & Provost ....Dr. Kevin WHITAKER
28 VP for Diversity/Equity & Inclusion ....Dr. G. Christine TAYLOR
10 Vice Pres for Financial Affairs ....Mr. Matt FAJACK
111 Vice Pres for Advancement ....Mr. Robert 'Bob' PIERCE
32 Vice Pres for Student Life ....Dr. David L. GRADY
88 Vice Pres for Community Affairs ....Dr. Samory T. PRUITT
26 Vice President Communications ....Ms. Linda BONNIN
46 Vice President for Research ....Dr. Russell J. MUMPER
13 Vice Provost/Chief Information Ofcr ....Dr. John MCGOWAN
18 Assistant VP University Facilities ....COL. Duane LAMB
18 Assoc VP Facilities/Construction ....Mr. Tim LEOPARD
19 VP Public Safety ....Dr. Ralph CLAYTON
21 Assoc Prov Financial/Business Affs ....Ms. Lisa RHINEY
20 Assoc Provost Academic Affairs ....Dr. Luoheng HAN
20 Assoc Provost Academic Affairs ....Dr. Patty SOBECKY
11 Assoc Provost for Administration ....Vacant
15 Assoc VP Human Resources ....Ms. Nancy H. WHITTAKER
21 Assoc Vice President for Finance ....Ms. Julie SHELTON
21 Asst Vice Pres Financial Affairs ....Ms. Cheryl MOWDY
27 Assoc VP Communications ....Ms. Monica WATTS
88 Assoc VP Marketing & Brand Strategy ....Mr. Ryan BRADLEY
29 Director of Alumni Affairs ....Mr. Calvin BROWN

85 Assoc Provost Internatl Educ ... Dr. Teresa WISE
06 University Registrar ... Dr. Kenneth H. FOSHEE
09 Director Inst Research/Assessment ... Dr. Lorne KUFFEL
36 Exec Director of Career Center ... Ms. Melinda KING
84 Int Assoc VP Enrollment Mgmt ... Mr. Landon WAID
22 University Compliance Officer/Direc ... Ms. Gwendolyn D. HOOD
37 Director of Student Financial Aid ... Ms. Helen ALLEN
88 Director Enrollment Management ... Mr. Landon WAID
39 Director Dept of Housing/Res Cmty ... Mr. Matthew KERCH
40 Asst VP Enterprise Operations ... Ms. Teresa SHREVE
41 Athletic Director ... Mr. Greg BYRNE
43 Chief University Counsel ... Mr. Mike SPEARING
08 Dean of University Libraries ... Dr. Donald GILSTRAP
49 Dean of Arts & Sciences ... Dr. Robert F. OLIN
50 Dean Culverhouse Col of Business ... Dr. Kay M. PALAN
51 Dean Col of Cont Studies ... Dr. Jonathon HALBESLEBEN
53 Dean College of Education ... Dr. Peter HLEBOWITSH
54 Dean College of Engineering ... Dr. Charles L. KARR
58 Assoc Provost/Dean Graduate School ... Dr. Susan CARVALHO
59 Dean Human Environmental Sciences ... Dr. Stuart USDAN
60 Dean Col of Communication/Info Sci ... Dr. Mark NELSON
61 Dean School of Law ... Dr. Mark E. BRANDON
62 Dir Sch of Library/Info Studies ... Dr. James ELMBORG
38 Manager Stdnt Support Svcs-Trio Pgm ... Ms. Wendy L. COGBURN
96 Purchasing Manager ... Mr. Lane COX
76 Dean Cmty Health Sciences ... Dr. Ricky FRIEND
66 Dean Capstone College of Nursing ... Dr. Suzanne S. PREVOST
70 Int Dean School of Social Work ... Dr. Lesley REID
92 Int Dean of Honors College ... Dr. Kenneth FRIDLEY
94 Dir Women & Gender Resource Ctr ... Ms. Lamea SHAABAN-MAGANA
100 Chief Administrative Officer ... Mr. Chad TINDOL

*University of Alabama at Birmingham (A)

1720 2nd Avenue South, Birmingham AL 35294-0001
County: Jefferson FICE Identification: 001052
Unit ID: 100663
Telephone: (205) 934-4011 Carnegie Class: DU-Highest
FAX Number: N/A Calendar System: Semester
URL: www.uab.edu
Established: 1969 Annual Undergrad Tuition & Fees (In-State): $8,568
Enrollment: 20,902 Coed
Affiliation or Control: State IRS Status: 501(c)3
Highest Offering: Doctorate
Accreditation: SC, ANEST, ARCPA, ART, CACREP, CAEPN, CAHIIM, CEA, CLPSY, DENT, @DIETC, DIETI, FEPAC, HSA, IPSY, MED, MT, MUS, NMT, NURSE, OPT, OPTR, OT, PAST, PH, PTA, SPAA, SW, THEA

02 President ... Dr. Ray L. WATTS
05 Provost ... Dr. Pam BENOIT
10 Sr VP Financial Affairs/Admin ... Mr. G. Allen BOLTON, JR.
17 CEO UAB Health System ... Dr. Will FERNIANY
30 VP Development ... Mr. Thomas I. BRANNAN
13 Vice Pres Info Technology/CIO ... Dr. Curtis A. CARVER, JR.
28 Vice Pres for Equity and Diversity ... Dr. Paulette P. DILWORTH
46 Vice Pres for Research ... Dr. Chris BROWN
63 Sr VP/Dean School of Medicine ... Dr. Selwyn M. VICKERS
20 Sr VProv Student/Faculty Success ... Dr. Suzanne E. AUSTIN
32 Vice Pres Student Affairs ... Dr. John R. JONES, III
43 University Counsel ... Mr. W. John DANIEL
49 Dean College of Arts & Sciences ... Dr. Robert PALAZZO
50 Dean School of Business ... Dr. Eric JACK
52 Dean School of Dentistry ... Dr. Russell TAICHMAN
53 Dean School of Education ... Dr. Autumn TOOMS CYPRES
54 Dean School of Engineering ... Dr. Iwan ALEXANDER
76 Dean Sch of Health Professions ... Dr. Andrew J. BUTLER
66 Dean School of Nursing ... Dr. Doreen C. HARPER
88 Dean School of Optometry ... Dr. Kelly NICHOLS
69 Dean School of Public Health ... Dr. Paul ERWIN
58 Dean Graduate School ... Dr. Lori L. MCMAHON
18 Assoc Vice President Facilities ... Mr. Greg PARSONS
29 Executive Director Alumni ... Dr. Jennifer R. BRELAND
110 Assoc Vice Pres Development ... Ms. Rebecca J. GORDON
26 Assoc VP Communications ... Ms. Anne BUCKLEY
26 Interim Assoc VP Dig Strat & Mktg ... Ms. Rosie O'BEIRNE
84 Assoc Provost Enrollment Management ... Dr. Bradley BARNES
21 Assoc VP Financial Affairs ... Ms. Stephanie B. MULLINS
08 Dean of Libraries ... Mr. John M. MEADOR
08 Director Lister Hill Library ... Vacant
41 Director of Athletics ... Mr. Mark T. INGRAM
15 Chief Human Resources Officer ... Ms. Alesia M. JONES
09 Vice Provost Instl Effectiveness ... Ms. Eva LEWIS
19 Assistant VP & Chief of Police ... Mr. Anthony B. PURCELL
07 Director Undergraduate Admissions ... Mr. Tyler M. PETERSON
37 Director of Financial Aid ... Ms. Helen M. MCINTYRE
06 University Registrar ... Ms. Cynthia TERRY
39 Director Student Housing ... Mr. Marc BOOKER
36 Exec Dir Career Services ... Mr. Brandon WRIGHT
38 Asst VP Student Dev/Health & Well ... Dr. Rebecca KENNEDY
04 Executive Asst to President ... Ms. Jane K. LUCAS
106 Exec Dir E-Learning & Prof Studies ... Dr. Pamela E. PAUSTIAN
96 Director of Purchasing ... Mr. Ron COLLINS
101 Board Liaison ... Ms. Kirsten N. BURDICK

*University of Alabama in Huntsville (B)

301 Sparkman Drive, Huntsville AL 35899-1911
County: Madison FICE Identification: 001055
Unit ID: 100706
Telephone: (256) 824-1000 Carnegie Class: DU-Higher
FAX Number: (256) 824-6073 Calendar System: Semester
URL: www.uah.edu
Established: 1950 Annual Undergrad Tuition & Fees (In-State): $10,714
Enrollment: 9,101 Coed
Affiliation or Control: State IRS Status: 501(c)3
Highest Offering: Doctorate
Accreditation: SC, ART, CAEPN, MUS, NURSE

02 President ... Dr. Darren DAWSON
05 Provost & Exec VP Academic Affairs ... Dr. Christine CURTIS
10 VP Finance & Administration ... Vacant
41 Director Intercollegiate Athletics ... Dr. William E. BROPHY, JR.
43 Chief University Counsel ... Mr. John CATES
32 VP of Student Affairs ... Dr. Kristi MOTTER
100 Chief of Staff/Dir Community Rels ... Mr. Ray GARNER
35 Assoc VP for Student Affairs ... Mr. John MAXON
46 Assoc VP Research ... Dr. Thomas M. KOSHUT
46 Associate VP for Research ... Dr. Robert LINDQUIST
11 Assoc VP Finance & Business Svcs ... Mr. Robert LEONARD
13 Interim CIO ... Mr. Malcolm RICE
20 Assoc Prov UG Studies/Inst Effect ... Dr. Brent M. WREN
114 Associate VP Budgets & Fin Planning ... Mr. Chih LOO
26 Assoc VP of Marketing and Comm ... Mr. Joel C. LONERGAN
15 Assoc VP Human Resources ... Ms. Laurel LONG
116 Director Internal Audit ... Ms. Tharanee M. RAVINDRAN
85 Dir International Engagement ... Dr. David BERKOWITZ
25 Director Sponsored Programs ... Ms. Gloria GREENE
88 Director Institute for Science Educ ... Dr. James A. MILLER
08 Director Library ... Dr. David P. MOORE
79 Dean Arts/Humanities/Soc Science ... Dr. Mitch BERBRIER
81 Dean College of Science ... Dr. Sundar CHRISTOPHER
50 Dean College Business Admin ... Dr. Jason GREENE
51 Dean Prof & Cont Studies ... Dr. Karen CLANTON
54 Dean College of Engineering ... Dr. Shankar MAHALINGAM
58 Dean Graduate Studies ... Dr. David BERKOWITZ
66 Dean College of Nursing ... Dr. Marsha ADAMS
53 Dean Education ... Dr. Beth QUICK
88 Dir of Cybersecurity Research & Edu ... Mr. Tommy MORRIS
37 Director Financial Aid ... Mr. Patrick JAMES
23 Dir Faculty & Staff Clinic ... Ms. Louise O'KEEFE
19 Director Public Safety ... Mr. Michael R. SNELLGROVE
06 Registrar ... Ms. Janet WALLER
07 Director Admissions ... Ms. Peggy MASTERS
29 Director Alumni Relations ... Ms. Mallie HALE
110 Director Advancement Services ... Ms. Marcie T. EPPLING
23 Director Student Health Services ... Ms. Kathleen S. RHODES
88 Director ITSC ... Dr. Sara J. GRAVES
88 Dir Small Business Develop Center ... Mr. Foster PERRY
102 Asst Dir Corp & Foundation Gifts ... Ms. Katie S. THURSTON
96 Director of Procurement ... Mr. Terence HALEY
88 Director Library Computer Systems ... Mr. Jack DROST
90 Manager Academic Technology ... Mr. John THYGERSON
88 Director Research Institute ... Dr. Steven MESSERVY
88 Director CMSA ... Dr. Sara GRAVES
88 Director SMAP Center ... Dr. Gary MADDUX
88 Director Ctr for Applied Optics ... Dr. Robert LINDQUIST
88 Dir Ctr Mgmt & Econ Research ... Mr. Nic LOYD
88 Director Propulsion Research Center ... Dr. Robert FREDERICK
88 Dir Center Space Plsm & Aeron Res ... Dr. Gary ZANK
88 Director Earth Systems Science Ctr ... Dr. John R. CHRISTY
88 Dir University Ctr & Charger Union ... Mr. William M. HALL
91 Director Enterprise Apps & IAM ... Mr. Malcolm RICE
104 Director Global Studies Program ... Dr. David JOHNSON
92 Dean of the Honors College ... Dr. William WILKERSON

University of Mobile (C)

5735 College Parkway, Mobile AL 36613-2842
County: Mobile FICE Identification: 001029
Unit ID: 101693
Telephone: (251) 675-5990 Carnegie Class: Bac-Diverse
FAX Number: N/A Calendar System: Semester
URL: www.umobile.edu
Established: 1961 Annual Undergrad Tuition & Fees: $23,230
Enrollment: 1,604 Coed
Affiliation or Control: Southern Baptist IRS Status: 501(c)3
Highest Offering: Doctorate
Accreditation: SC, ACBSP, #CAATE, MUS, NURSE

00 Chairman of the Board of Trustees ... Mr. Fred WILSON
01 Interim President ... Dr. Lonnie BURNETT
05 Provost/VP for Academic Affairs ... Dr. Chris MCCAGHREN
10 Chief Financial Officer ... Mr. Joseph WIEGAND
111 VP for Advancement ... Ms. Tonya GOLLOTTE
84 VP Enrollment/Student Life ... Mrs. Charity WITTNER
26 VP for Marketing/Public Relations ... Mrs. Lesa MOORE
32 VP for Student Life ... Mrs. Charity WITTNER
21 Associate VP for Business Affairs ... Ms. Carol CAMP
37 Assoc VP for Financial Aid ... Ms. Marie BATSON
108 Assistant VP for Accreditation ... Dr. Debra H. CHANCEY
27 Asst VP for Campus Communications ... Mrs. Kathy L. DEAN
41 Athletic Director ... Mr. Mike JACOBS
07 Director for Admissions/Enrollment ... Mrs. Hali GIVENS
09 Senior Dir for Inst Research ... Mrs. Kim LEOUSIS
08 Director for Library Services ... Mr. Jeffrey D. CALAMETTI
15 Director for Human Resources ... Mrs. Diane BLACK
50 Dean School of Business ... Dr. Todd GREER
53 Dean School of Education ... Dr. Carolyn CORLISS
66 Interim Dean School of Nursing ... Dr. Sarah WITHERSPOON
57 Dean AL School of the Arts ... Dr. Al MILLER
88 Dean Office for Global Engagement ... Dr. Doug WILSON
107 Dean Sch of Prof/Cont Studies ... Dr. Bruce EARNEST
49 Assoc Dean College of Arts/Sciences ... Dr. Ted MASHBURN
29 Sr Dir for Alumni/Annual Giving ... Mrs. Lauren MCCAGHREN

121 Director for Student Success ... Mrs. Shirley SUTTERFIELD
06 Registrar ... Ms. Eileen GARDNER
13 Director of Information Technology ... Ms. Larkisha WINBUSH
88 Director for Transfers ... Mr. Danny CHANCEY
89 Asst Dir for 1st Year Experience ... Mrs. Brenda DAVIS

University of Montevallo (D)

Station 6001, Montevallo AL 35115-6001
County: Shelby FICE Identification: 001004
Unit ID: 101709
Telephone: (205) 665-6000 Carnegie Class: Masters/M
FAX Number: N/A Calendar System: Semester
URL: www.montevallo.edu
Established: 1896 Annual Undergrad Tuition & Fees (In-State): $12,760
Enrollment: 2,717 Coed
Affiliation or Control: State IRS Status: 501(c)3
Highest Offering: Beyond Master's But Less Than Doctorate
Accreditation: SC, AAFCS, ART, CACREP, CAEPN, DIETC, MUS, SP, SW

01 President ... Dr. John W. STEWART, III
05 Provost and VP Academic Affairs ... Dr. Mary Beth ARMSTRONG
32 Dean of Students ... Dr. Tammi DAHLE
10 VP Business Affairs & Treasurer ... Ms. Mary Ellen HEUTON
18 Director Physical Plant ... Mr. Cody JONES
35 Director Student Life ... Ms. Jenny BELL
06 Registrar ... Ms. Amanda FOX
08 Director Libraries ... Dr. Charlotte FORD
07 Director Admissions ... Ms. Audrey CRAWFORD
13 Chief Information Officer ... Mr. Craig GRAY
37 Dir of Student Financial Services ... Ms. Nikki BRADBURY
38 Director Counseling Services ... Mr. Joshua MILLER
19 Chief of Police ... Mr. Tim ALEXANDER
39 Dir Housing & Residence Life ... Mr. John DENSON
41 Director Athletics ... Mr. Mark RICHARD
15 Director of HR and Risk Management ... Ms. Barbara FORREST
51 Dir of Regional Inservice Center ... Mr. Dwight JINRIGHT
49 Dean College Arts & Sciences ... Dr. Mary Beth ARMSTRONG
50 Dean College of Business ... Dr. Stephen CRAFT
53 Dean College of Education ... Dr. Courtney BENTLEY
57 Dean College of Fine Arts ... Dr. Steven PETERS
09 Director of Institutional Research ... Ms. Kris MASCETTI

University of North Alabama (E)

One Harrison Plaza, Florence AL 35632-0001
County: Lauderdale FICE Identification: 001016
Unit ID: 101879
Telephone: (256) 765-4100 Carnegie Class: Masters/L
FAX Number: (256) 765-4644 Calendar System: Semester
URL: www.una.edu
Established: 1830 Annual Undergrad Tuition & Fees (In-State): $10,142
Enrollment: 7,204 Coed
Affiliation or Control: State IRS Status: 501(c)3
Highest Offering: Beyond Master's But Less Than Doctorate
Accreditation: SC, ACBSP, ART, CACREP, CAEPN, CIDA, JOUR, MUS, NURSE, SW

01 President ... Dr. Kenneth KITTS
05 Vice Pres Acad Affairs & Provost ... Dr. Ross ALEXANDER
85 Senior Vice Provost Intl Affairs ... Dr. Chunsheng ZHANG
10 VP Business/Financial Affs ... Mr. Evan THORNTON
32 Interim VP Student Affairs ... Dr. Kimberly GREENWAY
111 Vice President Advancement ... Mr. Kevin R. HASLAM
21 Assoc VP Business/Financial Affs ... Ms. Cindy H. CONLON
84 Chief Enrollment Officer ... Mr. Ron PATTERSON
49 Dean College of Arts & Sciences ... Dr. Carmen L. BURKHALTER
50 Dean College of Business ... Dr. Gregory A. CARNES
53 Dean Col Education/Human Sciences ... Dr. Katie KINNEY
66 Dean Anderson College of Nursing ... Dr. Vicki G. PIERCE
88 Director University Events ... Dr. Kevin JACQUES
41 Director of Athletics ... Mr. Mark LINDER
43 General Counsel ... Ms. Amber FITE-MORGAN
21 Controller ... Mr. Mike NELSON
37 Director Student Financial Svcs ... Ms. Shauna JAMES
15 Asst VP for Human Resources ... Ms. Catherine D. WHITE
13 Exec Dir Info Technology Services ... Mr. Ethan HUMPHRES
26 Assoc Dir Univ Communications ... Ms. Michelle EUBANKS
18 Asst VP for Facilities ... Mr. Michael B. GAUTNEY
19 Chief of University Police ... Mr. Kevin L. GILLLILAN
23 Director University Health Services ... Ms. Teresa U. DAWSON
07 Director of Admissions ... Ms. Julie Y. TAYLOR
09 Director of Institutional Research ... Dr. Molly VAUGHN
29 Director Alumni Relations ... Mr. Bishop ALEXANDER
28 Dir Diversity/Institutional Equity ... Ms. Joan J. WILLIAMS
36 Dir Career Planning & Development ... Ms. Melissa T. MEDLIN
06 Registrar ... Ms. Leana WILSON
38 Director Student Counseling Svcs ... Ms. Lynne MARTIN
40 Manager University Bookstore ... Mr. Griffin HITE
04 Administrative Asst to President ... Ms. Regina B. SHERRILL
89 Dir First Yr Experience & Acad Supp ... Ms. Tammy RHODES
25 Dir Grants/Sponsored Programs ... Mr. Nathan WILLINGHAM

University of South Alabama (F)

307 University Boulevard, N, Mobile AL 36688-0002
County: Mobile FICE Identification: 001057
Unit ID: 102094
Telephone: (251) 460-6111 Carnegie Class: DU-Higher
FAX Number: (251) 461-1537 Calendar System: Semester
URL: www.southalabama.edu
Established: 1963 Annual Undergrad Tuition & Fees (In-State): $8,396
Enrollment: 15,569 Coed
Affiliation or Control: State IRS Status: 501(c)3

Highest Offering: Doctorate
Accreditation: SC, ARCPA, AUD, CACREP, CAEPN, COARC, EMT, MED, MUS, NURSE, OT, PSPSY, PTA, RAD, RTT, SP, SW

01 President .... Dr. Tony G. WALDROP
03 Executive Vice President .... Dr. John SMITH
05 Provost & Sr VP Academic Affairs .... Dr. G. David JOHNSON
23 Vice Pres Med Affairs/Dean COM .... Dr. John MARYMONT
10 VP Financial Affairs & Admin .... Mr. Scott WELDON
30 Vice Pres Developmental/Alumni Rels .... Ms. Margaret SULLIVAN
46 VP for Research & Economic Devel .... Dr. Lynne CHRONISTER
43 Sr University Attorney .... Ms. Jean TUCKER
58 Assc VP Acad Affs/Dean Grad Sch .... Dr. J. Harold PARDUE
20 Assc VP Acad Success/SVP Acad Affs .... Dr. Nicole T. CARR
84 Director Enrollment Services .... Mr. Christopher LYNCH
13 Asst Vice Pres of Information Tech .... Mr. Chris CANNON
20 Sr Vice Provost Academic Affairs .... Dr. Charles GUEST
15 Asst Vice President Human Resources .... Mr. Harold GATTIS
63 Dean College of Medicine .... Dr. John MARYMONT
86 Exec Director Government Relations .... Mr. Nicholas LAWKIS
32 VP Student Affairs/Dean of Students .... Dr. Michael MITCHELL
88 Dir Assessment/Sr VP Acad Affairs .... Ms. Cecelia MARTIN
26 Asst VP Marketing/Communication .... Mr. Michael HASKINS
41 Director of Athletics .... Dr. Joel ERDMANN
07 Director of Admissions .... Ms. Norma J. TANNER
85 Dir International Student Services .... Ms. Regina GEORGE
07 Director New Student Recruitment .... Mr. Christopher LYNCH
09 Dir Inst Research/Plng & Analysis .... Dr. Gordon E. MILLS, JR.
06 Registrar .... Ms. Kelly OSTERBIND
29 Director Alumni Relations .... Ms. Karen EDWARDS
19 Chief of Police .... Mr. Zeke AULL, JR.
37 Director of Financial Aid .... Ms. Marla SKOPLAN
36 Director Career Services .... Ms. Bevley W. GREEN
12 Director USA Baldwin County .... Ms. Cynthia WILSON
18 Director Facilities Management .... Mr. Randy MOON
38 Int Dir Student Counseling/Testing .... Dr. Darlene DEMPSTER
28 Director Multicultural Student Affs .... Ms. Jamora VALRIE
96 Purchasing Agent .... Mr. Robert M. BROWN
54 Dean College of Engineering .... Dr. John USHER
51 Assc VP of Global USA .... Dr. Richard CARTER
49 Dean of Arts and Sciences .... Dr. Andrzej WIERZBICKI
08 Exec Dir of University Libraries .... Ms. Lorene FLANDERS
50 Dean Mitchell College of Business .... Dr. Bob WOOD
53 Dean College of Educ & Prof Studies .... Dr. Andrea KENT
66 Dean of College of Nursing .... Dr. Debra C. DAVIS
76 Dean of Allied Health Professions .... Dr. Gregory FRAZER
77 Dean Computer & Information Science .... Dr. Alec YASINSAC
39 Asst VP Auxiliary Svcs/Univ Housing .... Dr. Mary Christine VINET
04 Executive Asst to President .... Ms. Suzanne GOINS
101 Executive Asst Board Affairs .... Ms. Monica EZELL
104 Director Study Abroad .... Ms. Holly HUDSON
105 Director Web Services .... Mr. Ian HARBAUGH
108 Director Institutional Assessment .... Ms. Angela COLEMAN
22 Director Affirmative Action/Equal O .... Ms. Paula BUERGER
25 Chief Contract/Grants Administrator .... Ms. Tammy SILCOX
44 Director Annual Giving .... Ms. Tracy COLEMAN
45 Chief Institutional Planning Office .... Mr. Gordon MILLS

The University of West Alabama (A)

205 N Washington Street, Livingston AL 35470-2099
County: Sumter FICE Identification: 001024
Unit ID: 101587
Telephone: (205) 652-3400 Carnegie Class: Masters/L
FAX Number: (205) 652-3718 Calendar System: Semester
URL: www.uwa.edu
Established: 1835 Annual Undergrad Tuition & Fees (In-State): $10,040
Enrollment: 4,646 Coed
Affiliation or Control: State IRS Status: 501(c)3
Highest Offering: Doctorate
Accreditation: SC, ACBSP, ADNUR, CAATE, CAEPN

01 President .... Dr. Ken TUCKER
05 Provost .... Dr. Tim EDWARDS
10 Vice Pres Financial Affairs .... Mr. Lawson EDMONDS
111 Vice Pres Institutional Advancement .... Mr. Chris THOMASON
32 Vice President for Student Affairs .... Mr. Richard HESTER
49 Dean of Liberal Arts .... Dr. Mark DAVIS
50 Inter Dean of Business & Technology .... Dr. Aliquippa ALLEN
53 Dean College of Education .... Dr. Jan MILLER
81 Dean of Natural Science/Math .... Dr. John MCCALL
58 Dean of Graduate Studies .... Dr. B.J KIMBROUGH
51 Dean Continuing Education .... Dr. Tina N. JONES
106 Dean Online Programs .... Dr. Jan MILLER
66 Chairperson of Nursing .... Dr. Mary HANKS
08 Director of Library .... Dr. Neil SNIDER
09 Dir Institutional Effectiveness .... Mrs. Angel JOWERS
41 Athletic Director .... Mr. Bobby WALLACE
35 Director of Student Life .... Mr. Byron THETFORD
06 Registrar .... Mrs. Susan SPARKMAN
37 Director Student Financial Aid .... Mr. Steve SMITH
13 Director Information Systems .... Mr. Michael PRATT
18 Director of Physical Plant .... Mr. Bobby TRUELOVE
109 Director of Auxiliary Services .... Ms. Willie JONES
36 Director Career Services/Placement .... Ms. Tammy S. WHITE
29 Director Alumni Relations .... Ms. Danielle BUCKALEW
86 Director Government Relations .... Mr. Tom TARTT
07 Int Dir of Undergraduate Recruiting .... Mrs. Libba BAKER
96 Director of Purchasing .... Mr. Lawson C. EDMONDS
89 Director Freshmen Studies .... Dr. James GENTSCH
92 Director Honors Program .... Dr. Lesa SHAUL
15 Director Personnel Services .... Mrs. Brenda KILLOUGH
30 Director of Development .... Mr. Chris THOMASON
20 Associate Academic Officer .... Mrs. Angel JOWERS
26 Chief Public Relations Officer .... Ms. Betsy COMPTON
19 Director of Security/Safety .... Mr. Jeff MANUEL
103 Director Economic Development .... Mrs. Allison BRANTLEY
105 Director of Web Services .... Mrs. Christi GEORGE
101 Secretary Board of Trustees .... Mrs. Katie BEARD
28 Director of Diversity .... Dr. B. J KIMBROUGH
85 Director of Foreign Students .... Dr. Mark DAVIS

ALASKA

Alaska Bible College (B)

248 East Elmwood Avenue, Palmer AK 99645
County: Matanuska-Susitna FICE Identification: 008843
Unit ID: 102580
Telephone: (907) 745-3201 Carnegie Class: Spec-4-yr-Faith
FAX Number: (907) 745-3210 Calendar System: Semester
URL: www.akbible.edu
Established: 1966 Annual Undergrad Tuition & Fees: $9,600
Enrollment: 42 Coed
Affiliation or Control: Independent Non-Profit IRS Status: 501(c)3
Highest Offering: Baccalaureate
Accreditation: BI

01 President .... Mr. David LEY
05 Vice Pres Academic Affairs .... Mr. Ben OLSON
32 Vice Pres Student Development .... Mr. Jonathan GARLAND
10 Vice Pres Business Admin .... Mr. Matthew COTE
111 Vice Pres Institutional Advancement .... Mr. Raymond ROSE
06 Registrar .... Mr. Ben OLSON
08 Library Director .... Ms. Noel MAXWELL
07 Director of Admissions .... Mr. Justin ARCHULETTA
37 Director Financial Aid .... Ms. Christy COTE
26 Director of Communications .... Mr. Brandon EVANS
35 Dean of Students .... Mr. Brandon EVANS

Alaska Career College (C)

1415 E. Tudor Road, Anchorage AK 99507-1033
County: Anchorage FICE Identification: 025410
Unit ID: 103501
Telephone: (907) 563-7575 Carnegie Class: Spec 2-yr-Other
FAX Number: (907) 563-8330 Calendar System: Other
URL: www.alaskacareercollege.edu
Established: 1985 Annual Undergrad Tuition & Fees: N/A
Enrollment: 430 Coed
Affiliation or Control: Proprietary IRS Status: Proprietary
Highest Offering: Associate Degree
Accreditation: ACCSC

01 Director .... Ms. Linda STURE
07 Director of Admissions .... Vacant
10 Chief Financial/Business Officer .... Ms. Jennifer DEITZ
18 Chief Facilities/Physical Plant Ofc .... Ms. Donna BLEVINS
37 Director Student Financial Aid .... Mr. Chaz ALEXANDER
54 Dean or Director Engineering .... Ms. LaraNoelle MADDEN

Alaska Pacific University (D)

4101 University Drive, Anchorage AK 99508-4672
County: Anchorage FICE Identification: 001061
Unit ID: 102669
Telephone: (907) 561-1266 Carnegie Class: Masters/S
FAX Number: (907) 562-4276 Calendar System: Semester
URL: www.alaskapacific.edu
Established: 1957 Annual Undergrad Tuition & Fees: $20,760
Enrollment: 509 Coed
Affiliation or Control: Independent Non-Profit IRS Status: 501(c)3
Highest Offering: Doctorate
Accreditation: NW, CAEPN, IACBE

01 President .... Dr. Robert ONDERS
04 Executive Assistant to President .... Ms. Debbie J. ROLL
05 Provost .... Dr. Hilton HALLOCK
10 Chief Financial Officer .... Mr. Mark REGOORD
32 Dean of Students .... Mr. Ben HAHN
06 Registrar .... Ms. Michelle WHEELER
07 Director of Admissions .... Ms. Kate HILLENBRAND
88 Asst Director of Admissions .... Mr. Brian MCDERMOTT
37 Director of Financial Aid .... Mr. Scott GRAVES
18 Director Facilities Management .... Ms. Kathy MINCKS
13 Director Information Technology .... Mr. Kristofer GILLS
111 Chief Advancement Officer .... Ms. Clarice DICKESS
42 Chaplain .... Mr. Brian ANDERSON
15 Director Human Resources .... Ms. Kathleen WYRICK
40 Campus Store Manager .... Ms. Lydia JOHNSON
29 Alumni Relations Coordinator .... Mr. Barry PISER
117 Compliance & Risk Officer .... Ms. Stephanie HARROD
38 Dir of Career/Counseling & Disabil .... Vacant
39 Director Student Housing .... Ms. Manda HILL
26 Director of Marketing/Communication .... Mr. Elias ROJAS

Charter College (E)

2221 E Northern Lights Blvd, #120,
Anchorage AK 99508-4157
Telephone: (907) 277-1000 Identification: 770822
Accreditation: ABHES, ADNUR

† Branch campus of Charter College, Vancouver, WA

Ilisagvik College (F)

PO Box 749, Barrow AK 99723
County: North Slope Borough FICE Identification: 034613
Unit ID: 434584
Telephone: (907) 852-3333 Carnegie Class: Tribal
FAX Number: (907) 852-3003 Calendar System: Semester
URL: www.ilisagvik.edu
Established: 1996 Annual Undergrad Tuition & Fees: $4,300
Enrollment: 111 Coed
Affiliation or Control: Independent Non-Profit IRS Status: 501(c)3
Highest Offering: Baccalaureate
Accreditation: NW

01 President .... Dr. Pearl K. BROWER
11 Vice President/Chief of Operations .... Mr. Brian PLESSINGER
06 Registrar .... Mrs. Meghan GALLIGAN
05 Dean of Academic Affairs .... Mrs. Birgit MEANY
15 Director Human Resources .... Mrs. Linda STANFORD
18 Chief Facilities/Physical Plant .... Mr. Tom CARAWAY
26 Chief Public Relations Officer .... Vacant
111 Dean of Institutional Advancement .... Mrs. Justina WILHELM
32 Dean of Students .... Ms. Amanda SIALOFI
37 Director Student Financial Aid .... Mrs. Nancy GRANT
08 Chief Library Officer .... Ms. Christie BURKE
10 Chief Financial/Business Officer .... Mr. Kent PENDLETON
101 Secretary of the Institution/Board .... Mr. Malcolm X. NOBLE
13 Chief Information Tech Officer .... Mr. Phillip GAIDA
04 Admin Assistant to the President .... Mr. Malcolm NOBLE

*University of Alaska System (G)

2025 Yukon Drive, Suite 202, Fairbanks AK 99775-5000
County: Fairbanks FICE Identification: 008005
Unit ID: 103529
Telephone: (907) 450-8000 Carnegie Class: N/A
FAX Number: (907) 450-8002
URL: www.alaska.edu

01 President .... Dr. James R. JOHNSEN
26 Vice President for Univ Relations .... Ms. Michelle RIZK
05 VP for Academic & Student Affairs .... Dr. Paul LAYER
10 Chief Finance Officer/Controller .... Mr. Myron DOSCH
46 Chief Strategy/Planning/Budget Ofcr .... Ms. Michelle RIZK
09 AVP Institutional Rsrch & Analysis .... Ms. Gwendolyn GRUENIG
84 Assoc VP Student/Enrollment Strat .... Mr. Saichi T. OBA
86 Assoc VP Public Affairs .... Ms. Robbie GRAHAM
43 General Counsel .... Mr. Michael HOSTINA
15 Chief HR Officer .... Ms. Keli H. MCGEE
13 Chief Information Technology Ofcr .... Mr. Mark KONDRAK
16 Director Labor & Employee Relations .... Mr. Geoff BACON
117 Chief Risk Officer .... Mr. Timothy EDWARDS

*University of Alaska Anchorage (H)

3211 Providence Drive, Anchorage AK 99508-8000
County: Anchorage FICE Identification: 011462
Unit ID: 102553
Telephone: (907) 786-1800 Carnegie Class: Masters/L
FAX Number: (907) 786-4888 Calendar System: Semester
URL: www.uaa.alaska.edu
Established: 1954 Annual Undergrad Tuition & Fees (In-State): $8,580
Enrollment: 15,733 Coed
Affiliation or Control: State IRS Status: 501(c)3
Highest Offering: Doctorate
Accreditation: NW, ACFEI, ADNUR, ART, CAEPN, CLPSY, CONST, CSHSE, DA, DH, DIETD, DIETI, EMT, MAC, MLTAD, MT, MUS, NUR, NURSE, PH, PTAA, SW

02 Chancellor .... Cathy SANDEEN
05 Interim Provost .... John STALVEY
10 Vice Chanc Admin Services .... Beverly SHUFORD
09 Sr Vice Provost Inst Effectiveness .... Renee CARTER-CHAPMAN
84 Int Assoc Vice Chanc Enroll Svcs .... Lora VOLDEN
111 Vice Chanc University Advancement .... Megan OLSON
32 Vice Chancellor Student Affairs .... Bruce SCHULTZ
26 Director of Philanthropy .... Brian IBSEN
13 CIO/Assoc Vice Chanc ITS .... Adam PAULICK
09 Assoc Vice Provost Inst Research .... Erin HOLMES
18 Int Assoc VC Facilities/Campus Svcs .... Kim MAHONEY
29 Asst Vice Chanc Alumni Relations .... Tanya PONT
88 Exec Dir Acad & Multicul Success .... Theresa LYONS
35 Dean of Students .... Ben MORTON
37 Interim Financial Aid Director .... Shauna GRANT
85 Director Multicultural Center .... E. Andre THORN
35 Director Student Life & Leadership .... Kimberly MORTON
07 Director of Admissions .... Cassandra KEEFER
41 Director Athletics .... Greg MYFORD
06 University Registrar .... Lindsey CHADWELL
15 Director Human Resources .... Ron KAMAHELE
08 Dean Consortium Library .... Stephen ROLLINS
63 Director WWAMI Biomedical Program .... Jane SHELBY
88 Director Native Student Services .... Vacant
38 Director Student Health & Counsel .... Vacant
50 Dean Col Business & Public Policy .... Karen MARKEL
51 Dean Community & Technical College .... Denise RUNGE
76 Dean College of Health .... Jeffrey JESSEE
54 Int Dean College of Engineering .... Kenrick MOCK
49 Int Dean College Arts & Sciences .... John PETRAITIS
92 Dean Honors College .... John MOURACADE
106 Director Academic Innov E-learning .... Dave DANNENBERG
20 Vice Provost Undergrad Acad Affairs .... Susan KALINA
58 Vice Prov Research & Grad School .... Vacant

39 Director Univ Housing Dining & Conf David WEAVER
25 Director Grants & Contracts Heather PAULSEN
45 Dir Facility Planning & Construct Chris MCCONNELL

*University of Alaska Fairbanks (A)

505 South Chandlar Drive, Fairbanks AK 99775
County: Fairbanks North Star Borough FICE Identification: 001063
Unit ID: 102614
Telephone: (907) 474-7500 Carnegie Class: DU-Higher
FAX Number: (907) 474-5379 Calendar System: Semester
URL: www.uaf.edu
Established: 1917 Annual Undergrad Tuition & Fees (In-State): $6,657
Enrollment: 7,664 Coed
Affiliation or Control: State IRS Status: 501(c)3
Highest Offering: Doctorate
Accreditation: NW, CACREP, CAEP, CAEPN, EMT, MAC, SW

02 Chancellor Dr. Daniel M. WHITE
05 Provost Dr. Anupma PRAKASH
11 Vice Chancellor Administrative Svcs Ms. Julie QUEEN
18 Assoc Vice Chancellor Facilities Ms. Jenny CAMPBELL
32 Vice Chancellor Student Affairs Dr. Keith CHAMPAGNE
46 Vice Chancellor Research Dr. Larry HINZMAN
10 AVC for Financial Services Mrs. Julie QUEEN
30 Director of Development Ms. Kate RIPLEY
58 Interim Dean Graduate School Dr. Michael CASTELLINI
81 Dean Col of Natural Science/Math Dr. Leah BERMAN
35 Assoc Vice Chanc for Student Life Mr. Alexis KNABE
31 VC Rural/Cmty & Native Educ Mr. Evon PETER
12 Dean UAF Comm & Tech College Ms. Michele STALDER
88 Dean Col Fisheries & Ocean Sciences Mr. Bradley MORAN
50 Dean School of Management Dr. Mark HERRMANN
54 Dean Col of Engineering & Mines Dr. William SCHNABEL
88 Dir Intl Arctic Research Center Dr. Hajo EICKEN
88 Dir Institute of Arctic Biology Dr. Brian M. BARNES
54 Int Dir Inst Northern Engineering Dr. David BARNES
15 Director Human Resources Ms. Keli MCGEE
19 Chief of Police Mr. Stephen GOETZ
37 Director Financial Aid Ms. Deanna L. DIERINGER
41 Director Athletics Dr. Keith CHAMPAGNE
35 Dean of Students Ms. Laura L. MCCOLLOUGH
56 Vice Provost for Extension/Outreach Dr. Milan SHIPKA
109 Director of Aux/Recharge/Cntrct Ops Vacant
85 Director International Programs Ms. Donna ANGER
88 Fire Chief Mr. Doug SCHRAGE
88 Dir Institute of Marine Science Dr. Terry WHITLEDGE
49 Dean College of Liberal Arts Mr. Todd SHERMAN
53 Dean School of Education Dr. Steve ATWATER
12 Director Bristol Bay Campus Ms. Sarah ANDREW
12 Dir Chukchi Campus Ms. Stacey GLASER
12 Dir Interior Alaska Campus Mr. Bryan UHER
12 Director Kuskokwim Campus Ms. Linda KURDA
12 Director Northwest Campus Ms. Barbara AMAROK
28 Director of Diversity & EO Ms. Margo GRIFFITH
23 Director Health and Counseling Dr. BJ ALDRICH
29 Exec Director Alumni Association Ms. Theresa BAKKER
06 Registrar Mr. Mike EARNEST
88 Director Geophysical Institute Dr. Robert MCCOY
21 Director Business Operations Ms. Amanda WALL
36 Director Career Services Ms. Patti PICHA
121 Director Academic Advising Center Ms. Linda M. HAPSMITH
92 Director Honors Program Dr. Alex HIRSCH
94 Coordinator Women's Studies Dr. Sine ANAHITA
09 Dir Planning/Analysis/Inst Research Mr. Adam WATSON
26 Director University Relations Ms. Michelle RENFREW
08 Director of Libraries Ms. Karen JENSEN
88 Dir UA Museum of the North Dr. Patrick DRUCKENMILLER
13 Chief Info Technology Officer Ms. Martha MASON
22 Director for Disability Services Ms. Amber CAGWIN
96 Dir of Procurement & Contract Svcs Mr. John HEBARD
88 Director Wood Center Student Union Mr. Mark OLDMIXON
97 Vice Provost/Dean Gen Studies Dr. Alex FITTS
04 Assistant to the Chancellor Ms. Jeannie PHILLIPS
106 Executive Director for E-learning Dr. Owen GUTHRIE

*University of Alaska Southeast (B)

11066 Auke Lake Way, Juneau AK 99801
County: Juneau FICE Identification: 001065
Unit ID: 102632
Telephone: (907) 796-6100 Carnegie Class: Masters/M
FAX Number: N/A Calendar System: Semester
URL: www.uas.alaska.edu
Established: 1956 Annual Undergrad Tuition & Fees (In-State): $7,092
Enrollment: 2,342 Coed
Affiliation or Control: State IRS Status: 501(c)3
Highest Offering: Master's
Accreditation: NW, CAEPN, CAHIIM, MAC

02 Chancellor Dr. Richard CAULFIELD
05 Provost & Dean of Graduate Studies Dr. Karen CAREY
84 VC Enrollment Mgmt & Stdnt Affs Ms. Lori KLEIN
75 Exec Dean of Career/Tech Educ Mr. Pete TRAXLER
46 Vice Provost for Research Dr. Tom THORTON
11 Vice Chanc Administration Mr. Michael CIRI
12 Sitka Campus Director Ms. Leslie GORDON
12 Ketchikan Campus Director Dr. Priscilla SCHULTE
49 Dean of Arts & Sciences Dr. Tom THORTON
53 Exec Dean College of Education Dr. Steve ATWATER
37 Acting Financial Aid Director Mr. Michael CIRI
26 Exec Asst to Chanc Public Relations Ms. Keni CAMPBELL
06 Registrar Ms. Trisha LEE

09 Dir Institutional Effectiveness Ms. Kristen HANDLEY
10 Dir Business Operations Mr. Jon LASINSKI
15 Director Human Resources Dr. Gail CHENEY
18 Director Facilities Services Mr. Nathan LEIGH
08 Dean Library Services Ms. Elise TOMLINSON
13 Director Information/Technology Mr. Michael CIRI
30 Dir Development/Alumni Relations Ms. Lynne JOHNSON
21 Chief Budget Officer Ms. Julie VIGIL
88 Director Learning Center Vacant
16 Title IX Coordinator/HR Training Mr. Chase PARKEY
32 Dean Students & Campus Life Mr. Eric SCOTT
88 Dir of PITAAS/AVC AK Native Pgms Ms. Ronalda CADIENTE-BROWN
88 Director of AK Coastal Rainforest Ms. Allison BIDLACK
07 Actg Dir of Admissions/Recruitment Ms. Lori KLEIN
104 Coordinator Study Abroad Ms. Marsha SQUIRES
105 Web Coordinator Mr. Colin OSTERHOUT
96 Procurement Services Manager Mr. Richard HITCHCOCK

*Prince William Sound Community College (C)

PO Box 97, 303 Lowe Street, Valdez AK 99686-0097
Telephone: (907) 834-1600 Identification: 666659
Accreditation: &NW

† Branch campus of University of Alaska Anchorage, Anchorage, AK

ARIZONA

Acacia University (D)

7665 South Research Drive, Tempe AZ 85284-1812
County: Maricopa Identification: 667017
Telephone: (480) 428-6034 Carnegie Class: Not Classified
FAX Number: (480) 428-6033 Calendar System: Other
URL: www.acacia.edu
Established: 2003 Annual Undergrad Tuition & Fees: N/A
Enrollment: N/A Coed
Affiliation or Control: Proprietary IRS Status: Proprietary
Highest Offering: Doctorate
Accreditation: DEAC

01 President Mr. Tim MOMAN
05 Provost/Executive Vice President Dr. Marilynn D. HENLEY
13 CIO Mr. Michael TURICO

Arizona Christian University (E)

1 W. Firestorm Way, Glendale AZ 85306
County: Maricopa FICE Identification: 007113
Unit ID: 105899
Telephone: (602) 489-5300 Carnegie Class: Bac-Diverse
FAX Number: (602) 404-2159 Calendar System: Semester
URL: www.arizonachristian.edu
Established: 1960 Annual Undergrad Tuition & Fees: $26,796
Enrollment: 786 Coed
Affiliation or Control: Independent Non-Profit IRS Status: 501(c)3
Highest Offering: Baccalaureate
Accreditation: NH

01 President Mr. Len MUNSIL
05 Provost and Chief Operating Officer Dr. Steve ADAMSON
10 Chief Financial Officer Mr. Timothy FISCHER
20 Dean of Academic Affairs Dr. Edward CLAVELL
06 Registrar/Dir Institutional Rsrch Mr. Lambert CRUZ
07 Director of Admissions Mr. Jeff RUTTER
106 Director of Online Students Mrs. Tiffany THOMAS
111 VP of University Engagement Mr. James GRIFFITHS
32 Dean of Students Dr. Jared BLACK
41 Athletic Director Dr. Peter DRYER
18 Sr Director of Campus Operations Mr. Jon CLINE
21 Controller Mrs. Kelly BULLOCK
37 Director Financial Aid Mrs. Kelsey HJERPE
13 Director of Information Technology Mr. Bill REED
08 Head Librarian Mr. Robert OLIVERIO
19 Director of Campus Security Mr. John HOEBEE
39 Director of Resident Life Mr. Donlan PAGE
04 Asst to President & Provost/COO Mrs. Julie ROSEN
84 Director of Enrollment Management Mr. Steven VALDEZ
38 Director of Counseling Services Mrs. Andra PERRYMAN
121 Director of Academic Services Mrs. Brenda SPEAR

Arizona College (F)

4425 W Olive Avenue, Suite 300,
Glendale AZ 85302-3851
County: Maricopa FICE Identification: 031150
Unit ID: 421708
Telephone: (602) 222-9300 Carnegie Class: Spec 2-yr-Health
FAX Number: (602) 200-8726 Calendar System: Other
URL: www.arizonacollege.edu
Established: 1991 Annual Undergrad Tuition & Fees: $15,685
Enrollment: 535 Coed
Affiliation or Control: Proprietary IRS Status: Proprietary
Highest Offering: Associate Degree
Accreditation: ABHES

01 President Mr. Nick MANSOUR

Arizona College-Mesa (G)

163 N. Dobson Road, Mesa AZ 85201
Telephone: (855) 706-8382 Identification: 770514
Accreditation: ABHES, NURSE

Arizona School of Acupuncture and Oriental Medicine (H)

2856 E Fort Lowell Rd., Tucson AZ 85716
County: Pima FICE Identification: 036955
Unit ID: 446039
Telephone: (520) 795-0787 Carnegie Class: Spec-4-yr-Other Health
FAX Number: (877) 222-4606 Calendar System: Quarter
URL: www.asaom.edu
Established: 1996 Annual Graduate Tuition & Fees: N/A
Enrollment: 30 Coed
Affiliation or Control: Proprietary IRS Status: Proprietary
Highest Offering: Master's; No Undergraduates
Accreditation: ACUP

00 Owner Mr. Jonathan HU
01 President Mr. Joshua HANNUM
05 Academic Dean Dr. Julian CHANG
37 Financial Aid Advisor Ms. Susan WAGNER
07 Admissions Director Miss Charlotte AUDET
06 Registrar Ms. Carol MCCLUER

Arizona State University (I)

300 E. University Drive, Tempe AZ 85281
County: Maricopa FICE Identification: 001081
Unit ID: 104151
Telephone: (855) 278-5080 Carnegie Class: DU-Highest
FAX Number: N/A Calendar System: Semester
URL: www.asu.edu
Established: 1885 Annual Undergrad Tuition & Fees (In-State): $10,822
Enrollment: 51,164 Coed
Affiliation or Control: State IRS Status: 501(c)3
Highest Offering: Doctorate
Accreditation: NH, AAB, ART, AUD, CIDA, CLPSY, CONST, COPSY, DIETD, DIETI, IPSY, JOUR, LAW, LSAR, MT, MUS, NRPA, NURSE, PCSAS, PLNG, SP, SPAA, SW

01 President Dr. Michael M. CROW
05 Exec VP & University Provost Dr. Mark S. SEARLE
10 Exec Vice President/Treasurer & CFO Dr. Morgan R. OLSEN
101 Sr Vice Pres/Sec of the University Dr. Christine K. WILKINSON
102 CEO ASU Foundation Ms. Gretchen E. BUHLIG
43 Sr Vice President & General Counsel Mr. Jose A. CARDENAS
32 Sr VP Educ Outreach & Student Svcs Dr. James A. RUND
84 VP Enrollment Svcs/Admissions Mr. Kent HOPKINS
41 Vice President University Athletics Mr. Ray ANDERSON
13 Chief Information Officer Mr. Lev GONICK
15 VP & Chief Human Resources Ofc Mr. Kevin J. SALCIDO
100 Sr VP Univ Affairs/Chief of Staff Mr. Jim O'BRIEN
106 Dean Ed Initiatives/CEO EdPlus Dr. Philip R. REGIER
49 VP/Dean of Liberal Arts & Sciences Dr. Patrick KENNEY
50 Dean WP Carey School of Business Dr. Amy HILLMAN
54 Dean Fulton School of Engineering Dr. Kyle SQUIRES
53 Dean Mary Lou Fulton Teachers Col Dr. Carole BASILE
92 Dean of Barrett Honors College Dr. Mark JACOBS
12 Dean New College of Int Arts & Sci Dr. Todd SANDRIN
57 Dean Herberger Inst for Design/Arts Dr. Steven J. TEPPER
60 Dean Cronkite Sch Journal/Mass Comm Mr. Christopher CALLAHAN
61 Dean College of Law Mr. Douglas SYLVESTER
66 Dean Coll Nursing/Health Innovation Dr. Judy KARSHMER
47 Dean School of Sustainability Dr. Christopher G. BOONE
20 Vice Provost Undergrad Education Dr. Frederick C. COREY
76 Dean Health Solutions Dr. Deborah HELITZER
88 Dean Edson Col of Public Svc/Comm Dr. Jonathan KOPPELL
08 University Librarian Dr. James O'DONNELL
107 Dn/Dir Thunderbird Sch Global Mgmt Dr. Sanjeev KHAGRAM
97 Dean Col Letters & Sci/Univ College Dr. Duane ROEN

Arizona Western College (J)

2020 South Avenue 8E, Yuma AZ 85365
County: Yuma FICE Identification: 001071
Unit ID: 104160
Telephone: (928) 317-6000 Carnegie Class: Assoc/HT-High Trad
FAX Number: N/A Calendar System: Semester
URL: www.azwestern.edu
Established: 1963 Annual Undergrad Tuition & Fees (In-District): $2,720
Enrollment: 7,557 Coed
Affiliation or Control: State/Local IRS Status: Exempt
Highest Offering: Associate Degree
Accreditation: NH, ADNUR, EMT, RAD

01 President Dr. Daniel P. CORR
05 Vice President Learning Services Dr. Linda ELLIOTT-NELSON
10 Vice Pres Finance/Administration Mr. Shahrooz ROOHPARVAR
111 Vice President of Advancement Ms. Lori STOFFT
25 Director of Grants Ms. Rainier DISCHINGER
51 Assoc Dean of Continuing Educ Mrs. Maria AGUIRRE
32 Vice President for Student Services Mr. Bryan E. DOAK
75 Dean of Career & Tech Educ Ms. Reetika DHAWAN
110 Director Institutional Advancement Mrs. Renee L. SMITH
84 Associate Dean of Enrollment Svcs Mrs. Nicole D. HARRAL
21 Dir Financial Services/Controller Mrs. Michelle LANDIS

15 Chief Human Resources Officer .... Vacant
96 Dir Purchasing & Auxiliary Services .... Ms. Margaret HAYES
18 Director of District Operations .... Mr. Steve ECKERT
13 Chief Information Officer .... Vacant
08 Director of Library Services .... Ms. Angie CREEL
41 Director of Athletics .... Mr. Jerry SMITH
19 Chief of Police .... Mr. John EDMUNDSON
35 Associate Dean of Campus Life .... Ms. Nikki HAGE
12 Associate Dean La Paz County Svcs .... Ms. Kathy OCAMPO
12 Assoc Dean for South Yuma County .... Ms. Susanna ZAMBRANO
37 Director of Financial Aid .... Ms. Ana ENGLISH
85 Coord of International Student .... Ms. Aybuke KEEHN
106 Associate Dean for Distance Educ .... Mrs. Jana MOORE
88 Director of Testing Services .... Mrs. Leticia MARTINEZ
105 Webmaster II .... Mr. Damien BATES
04 Executive Assistant to President .... Mrs. Ashley HERRINGTON
36 Director Career/Advisement Services ... Mr. James R. HUTCHISON
101 Executive Assistant to the District .... Mrs. Ashley HERRINGTON

Benedictine University Mesa (A)

51 E Main Street, Suite 105, Mesa AZ 85201
Telephone: (602) 888-5000 Identification: 770068
Accreditation: &NH

† Branch campus of Benedictine University, Lisle, IL

Brighton College (B)

8777 E. Via de Ventura, Scottsdale AZ 85258
County: Maricopa Identification: 666710
Telephone: (602) 212-0501 Carnegie Class: Not Classified
FAX Number: (602) 212-0502 Calendar System: Other
URL: www.brightoncollege.edu
Established: 1961 Annual Undergrad Tuition & Fees: N/A
Enrollment: N/A Coed
Affiliation or Control: Proprietary IRS Status: Proprietary
Highest Offering: Associate Degree
Accreditation: DEAC

01 President .... Paul ZAGNONI
03 Executive Vice President .... Sam FERNENDEZ
05 Vice Pres Academic Affairs .... Gilda RADA
10 Director of Financial Operations .... Patricia MCCOY
32 Director of Student Services .... Sean DIXON

Brookline College (C)

2445 West Dunlap Avenue, Suite 100, Phoenix AZ 85021
County: Maricopa FICE Identification: 022188
Unit ID: 104090
Telephone: (602) 242-6265 Carnegie Class: Spec-4-yr-Other Health
FAX Number: (602) 973-2572 Calendar System: Other
URL: www.brooklinecollege.edu
Established: 1979 Annual Undergrad Tuition & Fees: N/A
Enrollment: 1,148 Coed
Affiliation or Control: Proprietary IRS Status: Proprietary
Highest Offering: Baccalaureate
Accreditation: ABHES, MLTAD, MT, NURSE, PTAA

01 Campus Director .... Mr. Glen THARP

Brookline College (D)

1140 South Priest Drive, Tempe AZ 85281
Telephone: (480) 545-8755 Identification: 666403
Accreditation: ABHES, SURTEC

† Branch campus of Brookline College, Phoenix, AZ.

Brookline College (E)

5441 E 22nd Street, Suite 125, Tucson AZ 85711-5444
Telephone: (520) 748-9799 Identification: 666402
Accreditation: ABHES

† Branch campus of Brookline College, Phoeniz, AZ.

Bryan University (F)

350 West Washington Street, Ste 100, Tempe AZ 85281
County: Maricopa FICE Identification: 007164
Unit ID: 110219
Telephone: (602) 384-2555 Carnegie Class: Spec-4-yr-Other Health
FAX Number: (602) 759-8742 Calendar System: Quarter
URL: www.bryanuniversity.edu
Established: 1940 Annual Undergrad Tuition & Fees: $11,025
Enrollment: 1,249 Coed
Affiliation or Control: Proprietary IRS Status: Proprietary
Highest Offering: Master's
Accreditation: ACCSC, CAHIIM

01 President/COO .... Mr. Eric EVANS
00 Chief Executive Officer/COB .... Mr. Chad EVANS
12 President Los Angeles Campus .... Mr. John KOLACINSKI
05 Vice Pres Academic Affairs .... Dr. Jennifer BROCK
10 Chief Financial Officer .... Mr. Dave ROGERS
07 Dean of Admissions .... Mr. Larry KARCHER
06 Registrar .... Ms. Hope BEJARANO
37 Regional Director of Financial Aid .... Ms. Roxane ROMERO
32 Dean of Students .... Ms. Mary MULES
08 Head Librarian .... Ms. Margot CASSIDY

26 Chief Public Relations/Marketing .... Mr. Mark EVANS
36 Director Career Services .... Ms. Betty NAVARETTE

Carrington College - Mesa (G)

1001 W Southern Avenue, Suite 130, Mesa AZ 85210
Telephone: (480) 212-1600 FICE Identification: 023352
Accreditation: &WJ, DH, MAAB, PTAA

† Regional accreditation is carried under the parent institution in Sacramento, CA.

Carrington College - Phoenix East (H)

2149 W Dunlap Avenue, Phoenix AZ 85021
Telephone: (602) 427-0660 Identification: 666248
Accreditation: &WJ, COARC

† Regional accreditation is carried under the parent institution in Sacramento, CA.

Carrington College - Phoenix North (I)

8503 N 27th Avenue, Phoenix AZ 85051
Telephone: (602) 393-5900 FICE Identification: 021006
Accreditation: &WJ, ADNUR, MAAB

† Regional accreditation is carried under the parent institution in Sacramento, CA.

Carrington College - Tucson (J)

201 N. Bonita Avenue, Suite 101, Tucson AZ 85745
Telephone: (520) 888-5885 FICE Identification: 030898
Accreditation: &WJ, MAAB

† Regional accreditation is carried under the parent institution in Sacramento, CA.

Central Arizona College (K)

8470 N Overfield Road, Coolidge AZ 85128-9779
County: Pinal FICE Identification: 007283
Unit ID: 104346
Telephone: (520) 494-5444 Carnegie Class: Assoc/HT-Mix Trad/Non
FAX Number: (520) 494-5008 Calendar System: Semester
URL: www.centralaz.edu
Established: 1961 Annual Undergrad Tuition & Fees (In-District): $2,580
Enrollment: 5,405 Coed
Affiliation or Control: Local IRS Status: 501(c)3
Highest Offering: Associate Degree
Accreditation: NH, ADNUR, CAHIIM, DIETT, EMT, IFSAC, MAC, RAD

01 President .... Dr. Jacquelyn ELLIOTT
05 VP Academic Affairs .... Dr. Mary K. GILLILAND
32 VP Student Services .... Dr. Jenni CARDENAS
107 Academic Dean .... Dr. Tina BERRY
49 Academic Dean .... Dr. Terri ACKLAND
103 Academic Dean .... Dr. Jani ATTEBERY
81 Academic Dean .... Mr. Jeff BUNKELMANN
10 VP/CFO Business Affairs .... Mr. Chris WODKA
15 VP Talent Development/Legal Affairs .... Ms. Brandi BAIN
08 Director Library Services .... Ms. Adriana SAAVEDRA
37 Director of Financial Aid .... Ms. Elisa JUAREZ
41 Athletic Director .... Mr. Chuck SCHNOOR
39 Director of Residence Life .... Ms. Rosemary RAMIREZ
18 Exec Director of Facilities .... Mr. Ernesto VALENZUELA
96 Director of Purchasing .... Mr. Mark SALAZ
06 Registrar/Int Dean of Enrollment .... Ms. Veronica DURAN
07 Director of Admissions/Recruitment .... Dr. Luis SANCHEZ
21 Exec Dir Accounting Svc/Comptroller .... Ms. Luisa OTT
30 Director Institutional Development .... Ms. Margaret DOOLEY
35 Dean of Student Life .... Dr. Tramaine RAUSAW
04 Exec Asst to President & Gov Board . Ms. Mary Lou HERNANDEZ
13 Chief Info Technology Officer (CIO) .... Vacant
19 Chief of Police .... Mr. Gregory L. ROBERTS
26 Exec Dir PR & Marketing .... Ms. Angela ASKEY
09 Exec Dir Inst Effectiveness .... Mr. Dustin MARONEY
25 Director Resource Development .... Mr. Hugo STEINCAMP
38 Director of Advising .... Mr. Derek SHANK

Chamberlain University-Phoenix (L)

2149 West Dunlap Avenue, Phoenix AZ 85021
Telephone: (602) 331-2720 Identification: 770502
Accreditation: &NH, NURSE

† Branch campus of Chamberlain University-Addison, Addison, IL

Cochise College (M)

901 N Colombo Avenue, Sierra Vista AZ 85635-2317
County: Cochise FICE Identification: 001072
Unit ID: 104425
Telephone: (800) 966-7943 Carnegie Class: Assoc/HVT-High Non
FAX Number: (520) 417-4006 Calendar System: Semester
URL: www.cochise.edu
Established: 1964 Annual Undergrad Tuition & Fees (In-District): $2,040
Enrollment: 3,907 Coed
Affiliation or Control: State/Local IRS Status: 170(c)1
Highest Offering: Associate Degree
Accreditation: NH

01 Chief Executive Officer (President) ..... Dr. James D. ROTTWEILER
04 Executive Asst to President .... Ms. Crystal WHEELER
05 Executive VP/Provost .... Dr. Verlyn FICK
15 VP Administration/Human Resources .... Dr. Wendy DAVIS
13 Chief Technology Officer .... Mr. David LUNA
20 Executive Dean of Academics .... Dr. Alan BIEL
102 Exec Dir Foundation & Ext Relations .... Ms. Denise HOYOS
18 Exec Dir Facilities & Maintenance .... Mr. Frank DYKSTRA
07 Registrar/Director of Admissions .... Ms. Debra QUICK
06 Assistant Registrar .... Ms. Heather AUGENSTEIN
49 Dean Liberal Arts .... Mr. Eric BROOKS
81 Dean Math and Sciences .... Ms. Angela GARCIA
76 Dean Nursing/Allied Health .... Ms. Jennifer LAKOSIL
50 Dean Business and Technology .... Mr. Rod FLANIGAN
32 Dean Student Services/Athl Director .... Dr. James HALL
121 Dean Student Success .... Mr. Mark BOGGIE
08 Director Library Services .... Dr. John WALSH
96 Director Procurement Services .... Mr. Jeff MOUNTJOY
39 Director Student Housing .... Ms. Jennifer TAGABAN
88 Director Occ Health Safety .... Mr. Randy DENNEY
37 Director Student Financial Aid .... Ms. Karen EMMER
38 Director Counseling and Advising .... Ms. Nanette ROMO
88 Dir TRIO Student Support Services .... Ms. Gabriela AMAVIZCA
22 Director Disability Support Service .... Ms. Carla BOYD
84 Asst Dean Enroll Mgmt & Marketing .... Ms. Robyn MARTIN
88 Dir Fac Support & Acad Improvement .... Ms. Karen DALE
66 Director Nursing .... Ms. Beth HILL
88 Director Aviation Programs .... Mr. James "Mike" KEHOE
88 Director Adult Education .... Ms. Susan MORSS
88 Director Small Business Dev Center .... Mr. Mark SCHMITT
51 Director Ctr for Lifelong Learning .... Mr. Gabriel GALINDO
12 Director Fort Huachuca .... Mr. John SOMERS
56 Assistant Dean Outreach .... Ms. Barbara RICHARDSON

Cochise College (N)

4190 W. Highway 80, Douglas AZ 85607-6190
Telephone: (800) 966-7943 Identification: 770004
Accreditation: &NH, ADNUR, EMT

Coconino Community College (O)

2800 S Lone Tree Road, Flagstaff AZ 86005
County: Coconino FICE Identification: 031004
Unit ID: 404426
Telephone: (928) 527-1222 Carnegie Class: Assoc/HT-High Non
FAX Number: (928) 226-4105 Calendar System: Semester
URL: www.coconino.edu
Established: 1991 Annual Undergrad Tuition & Fees (In-State): $3,480
Enrollment: 3,515 Coed
Affiliation or Control: State IRS Status: 501(c)3
Highest Offering: Associate Degree
Accreditation: NH

01 President .... Dr. Colleen A. SMITH
26 Chief External Affairs Officer .... Mr. Steve PERU
05 Provost .... Dr. J. Nathaniel SOUTHERLAND
03 Executive Vice President .... Ms. Jami VAN ESS
32 Dean of Student Affairs .... Vacant
49 Dean of Learning Services CTE .... Mr. Jeff JONES
75 Dean Learning Svcs/Arts & Sciences .... Dr. Kimberly BATTY-HERBERT
15 Exec Director for Human Resources .... Mr. Dietrich SAUER
09 Dir Institutional Research/Assess .... Mr. Michael MERICA
37 Director for Financial Aid/Veterans .... Mr. Robert VOYTEK
06 Registrar/Dir Enrollment Services .... Ms. Kimmi GRULKE
04 Assistant to the President .... Ms. April SANDOVAL

Coconino County Community College Flagstaff Fourth Street Innovation Center (P)

3000 N Fourth Street, Flagstaff AZ 86004
Telephone: (928) 526-7600 Identification: 770005
Accreditation: &NH

CollegeAmerica-Flagstaff (Q)

399 S. Malpais, 2nd Floor, Flagstaff AZ 86001
County: Coconino FICE Identification: 031203
Unit ID: 103945
Telephone: (928) 213-6060 Carnegie Class: Spec-4-yr-Other Health
FAX Number: (928) 526-3468 Calendar System: Other
URL: www.collegeamerica.edu
Established: 2001 Annual Undergrad Tuition & Fees: $16,972
Enrollment: 78 Coed
Affiliation or Control: Independent Non-Profit IRS Status: 501(c)3
Highest Offering: Baccalaureate
Accreditation: ACCSC

01 Campus Director/Dean of Education .... Mr. Tresban RIVERA
07 Director of Admissions .... Ms. Jennifer CURTIS

CollegeAmerica-Phoenix (R)

9801 N. Metro Parkway East, Phoenix AZ 85051
Telephone: (602) 257-7522 Identification: 666017
Accreditation: ACCSC

† Branch campus of CollegeAmerica-Flagstaff, Flagstaff, AZ

Cummings Gaduate Institute for Behavioral Health Studies (A)
16515 40th Street Ste 140, Phoenix AZ 85048
County: Maricopa Identification: 667376
Telephone: (480) 285-1761 Carnegie Class: Not Classified
FAX Number: N/A Calendar System: Quarter
URL: www.cummingsinstitute.com
Established: 2015 Annual Graduate Tuition & Fees: N/A
Enrollment: N/A Coed
Affiliation or Control: Independent Non-Profit IRS Status: 501(c)3
Highest Offering: Doctorate; No Undergraduates
Accreditation: DEAC

01 President .... Dr. Cara ENGLISH

DeVry University - Phoenix Campus (B)
2149 W Dunlap Avenue, Phoenix AZ 85021
Telephone: (602) 749-7301 FICE Identification: 008322
Accreditation: &NH, ACBSP, MT

† Regional accreditation is carried under the parent institution in Downers Grove, IL.

Diné College (C)
One Circle Drive, Tsaile AZ 86556-9998
County: Apache FICE Identification: 008246
Unit ID: 105297
Telephone: (928) 724-6671 Carnegie Class: Tribal
FAX Number: (928) 724-3327 Calendar System: Semester
URL: www.dinecollege.edu
Established: 1968 Annual Undergrad Tuition & Fees (In-District): $1,410
Enrollment: 1,465 Coed
Affiliation or Control: Local IRS Status: 501(c)3
Highest Offering: Baccalaureate
Accreditation: NH

01 President .... Dr. Charles ROESSEL
10 Vice Pres Finance/Administration .... Ms. Bo LEWIS
32 Vice Pres of Student Affairs .... Ms. Glennita HASKEY
05 Provost .... Dr. Geraldine GARRITY
86 Vice Pres Government Affairs/PR .... Ms. Marie R. NEZ
06 Registrar .... Ms. Louise LITZIN
37 Financial Aid Officer .... Mr. Nolan S. BEGAYE
15 Dir Department of Human Resources .... Mr. Meryl DAYZIE
18 Supt Maintenance Operations .... Mr. Delbert PAQUIN
21 Controller .... Ms. Raychelle LEONARD
46 Dir Inst Grants/Sponsored Projects .... Ms. Amanda MCNEILL

Dunlap-Stone University (D)
19820 North 7th Street, Suite 100, Phoenix AZ 85024
County: Maricopa Identification: 666315
Telephone: (602) 648-5750 Carnegie Class: Not Classified
FAX Number: (602) 648-5755 Calendar System: Other
URL: www.dunlap-stone.edu
Established: 1995 Annual Undergrad Tuition & Fees: N/A
Enrollment: N/A Coed
Affiliation or Control: Proprietary IRS Status: Proprietary
Highest Offering: Master's
Accreditation: DEAC

01 President .... Dr. Donald N. BURTON
05 Chief Academic Officer .... Mrs. Caulyne BARRON

Eastern Arizona College (E)
615 N Stadium Avenue, Thatcher AZ 85552-0769
County: Graham FICE Identification: 001073
Unit ID: 104577
Telephone: (928) 428-8233 Carnegie Class: Assoc/MT-VT-High Non
FAX Number: (928) 428-2578 Calendar System: Semester
URL: www.eac.edu
Established: 1888 Annual Undergrad Tuition & Fees (In-District): $2,700
Enrollment: 6,365 Coed
Affiliation or Control: State/Local IRS Status: 501(c)3
Highest Offering: Associate Degree
Accreditation: NH, ADNUR, EMT

01 President .... Mr. Todd HAYNIE
10 Vice President of Finance .... Mr. Timothy CURTIS
05 Vice President of Academics .... Mrs. Jeanne BRYCE
11 Vice President of Operations .... Mr. Heston WELKER
13 Chief Information Officer .... Mr. Thomas THOMPSON
20 Dean of Instruction .... Mr. Michael CROCKETT
20 Dean of Instruction .... Dr. Phil MCBRIDE
20 Dean of Curriculum and Instruction .... Dr. Janice LAWHORN
32 Dean of Students .... Dr. Gary SORENSEN
06 Associate Dean/Registrar .... Dr. Randall SKINNER
38 Assistant Dean of Counseling .... Mr. Kenny SMITH
12 Director of Discovery Park Campus .... Mr. Paul ANGER
21 Director Fiscal Control/Controller .... Mr. Wayne LAYTON
37 Director of Financial Aid .... Ms. Exsa SMITH
88 Director of Accreditation .... Mrs. Shannon SEBALLOW
08 Director of Library Services .... Ms. Kristen BECKER
26 Dir of Marketing & Public Relations .... Mr. Kris MCBRIDE
18 Director of Physical Resources .... Mr. Jeremy HUGHES
102 Executive Director EAC Foundation .... Mr. David UDALL
35 Director of Student Life .... Mr. Danny BATTRAW
41 Athletic Director .... Mr. James BAGNALL
15 Director Admin Support/HR .... Ms. Lauri AVILA
04 Exec Asst to the President and DGB .... Mrs. Laurie PENNINGTON
86 Special Asst Government Relations .... Mr. Keith ALEXANDER

Eastern Arizona College Gila Pueblo Campus (F)
8274 Six Shooter Canyon,PO Box 2656, Globe AZ 85502
Telephone: (928) 425-8481 Identification: 770008
Accreditation: &NH

Eastern Arizona College Payson Campus (G)
201 North Mud Springs Rd,PO Box 359, Payson AZ 85547
Telephone: (928) 468-8039 Identification: 770009
Accreditation: &NH

Embry-Riddle Aeronautical University-Prescott (H)
3700 Willow Creek Road, Prescott AZ 86301-3270
Telephone: (800) 888-3728 FICE Identification: 021047
Accreditation: AAB, ACBSP

† Regional accreditation is carried under the parent institution in Daytona Beach, FL.

Fortis College, Phoenix (I)
555 N 18th Street, Suite 110, Phoenix AZ 85006
Telephone: (602) 254-3099 Identification: 666761
Accreditation: ACCSC, DH

† Branch campus of Fortis College, Centerville, OH. Tuition varies by degree program.

Grand Canyon University (J)
3300 W Camelback Road, Phoenix AZ 85017-3030
County: Maricopa FICE Identification: 001074
Unit ID: 104717
Telephone: (602) 639-7500 Carnegie Class: DU-Mod
FAX Number: N/A Calendar System: Semester
URL: www.gcu.edu
Established: 1949 Annual Undergrad Tuition & Fees: $17,050
Enrollment: 83,284 Coed
Affiliation or Control: Independent Non-Profit IRS Status: 501(c)3
Highest Offering: Doctorate
Accreditation: NH, ACBSP, CAATE, NURSE, THEOL

01 President/Chief Executive Officer .... Mr. Brian MUELLER
05 Provost .... Dr. Hank RADDA
10 Chief Financial Officer .... Mr. Dan BACHUS
11 Chief Operating Officer .... Dr. Stan MEYER
13 Chief Information Officer .... Mr. Joseph MILDENHALL
43 General Counsel .... Mr. Brian ROBERTS
20 Sr VP Academic Affs/Univ Registrar .... Dr. Jennifer LECH
108 Vice Pres Inst Effectiveness .... Dr. Antoinette FARMER-THOMPSON
41 Vice President of Athletics .... Mr. Mike VAUGHT
32 VP Student Svcs/Dean of Students .... Pastor Tim GRIFFIN
50 Dean Colangelo College Business .... Dr. Randy GIBB
53 Dean College of Education .... Dr. Kimberly LAPRADE
66 Dean College Nursing/Hlth Care Prof .... Dr. Lisa SMITH
49 Dean College Sci/Engineering/Tech .... Dr. K. Mark WOODEN
58 Dean College Doctoral Studies .... Dr. Michael BERGER
57 Dean of Fine Arts and Production .... Mr. Claude PENSIS
73 Dean College of Theology .... Dr. Jason HILES
79 Dean College Human/Social Science .... Dr. Sherman ELLIOTT

Han University of Traditional Medicine (K)
2856 E. Fort Lowell Road, Tucson AZ 85716
County: Pima FICE Identification: 041193
Telephone: (520) 322-6330 Carnegie Class: Not Classified
FAX Number: (520) 322-5661 Calendar System: Quarter
URL: www.hanuniversity.edu
Established: 2000 Annual Undergrad Tuition & Fees: N/A
Enrollment: N/A Coed
Affiliation or Control: Proprietary IRS Status: Proprietary
Highest Offering: Master's
Accreditation: ACUP

01 President .... Mr. Alex HOLLAND
05 Academic Dean .... Mr. Chiu-An CHANG
07 Admissions Director .... Mr. Gary BONHARD
06 Registrar .... Mr. Alex HOLLAND

Harrison Middleton University (L)
1105 East Broadway Road, Tempe AZ 85282-1505
County: Maricopa Identification: 666169
Telephone: (877) 248-6724 Carnegie Class: Not Classified
FAX Number: (800) 762-1622 Calendar System: Other
URL: www.hmu.edu
Established: 1998 Annual Undergrad Tuition & Fees: N/A
Enrollment: N/A Coed
Affiliation or Control: Proprietary IRS Status: Proprietary
Highest Offering: Doctorate
Accreditation: DEAC

01 President .... Dr. Joseph COULSON
05 Vice Pres of Education/CEO .... Mr. Michael CURD
51 VP/Dean Continuing Education .... Ms. Rebecca FISHER
09 Vice Pres of Accreditation .... Ms. Lauren GUTHRIE
06 Registrar .... Ms. Lauren GUTHRIE

Indian Bible College (M)
2237 E. Cedar Avenue, Flagstaff AZ 86004
County: Coconino Identification: 667317
Telephone: (928) 774-3890 Carnegie Class: Not Classified
FAX Number: (928) 774-2655 Calendar System: Semester
URL: www.indianbible.org
Established: 1958 Annual Undergrad Tuition & Fees: N/A
Enrollment: N/A Coed
Affiliation or Control: Independent Non-Profit IRS Status: 501(c)3
Highest Offering: Baccalaureate
Accreditation: @BI

01 President .... Dr. Jason KOPPEN
03 Executive Vice President .... Mr. Clint ROSS
05 Academic Dean .... Dr. Kevin NEWMAN
30 Director Development .... Dr. Doug HANSON
07 Director Admissions .... Mr. Daniel ESPLIN

International Baptist College and Seminary (N)
2211 W Germann Road, Chandler AZ 85286
County: Maricopa FICE Identification: 033473
Unit ID: 436614
Telephone: (480) 245-7903 Carnegie Class: Spec-4-yr-Faith
FAX Number: (480) 245-7909 Calendar System: 4/1/4
URL: www.ibcs.edu
Established: 1980 Annual Undergrad Tuition & Fees: $11,250
Enrollment: 81 Coed
Affiliation or Control: Baptist IRS Status: 501(c)3
Highest Offering: Doctorate
Accreditation: TRACS

00 Chancellor .... Dr. Jerry C. TETREAU
01 President .... Pastor Nathan M. MESTLER
32 Dean of Students .... Dr. Emmanuel MALONE
05 Chief Academic Officer .... Dr. Jerry C. TETREAU
10 Chief Financial Officer .... Mr. Matt EBERLE
20 Seminary Dean .... Dr. David SHUMATE
30 Chief Development/Advancement .... Dr. Jerry C. TETREAU
07 Director of Admissions .... Pastor Dan OLSON
09 Director of Inst Effectiveness .... Mrs. Lauren BRADY
88 Teaching Site Liaison .... Dr. Keith HUHTA
08 Media Center Director .... Mr. Lee WILL
34 Dean of Women .... Mrs. Marcia L. GAMMON
06 Registrar .... Mrs. Rebecca M. STERTZBACH
37 Financial Aid Administrator .... Mrs. Jane L. BUSHEY
04 Exec Asst to President/Office Mgr .... Mrs. Rebecca M. STERTZBACH

*Maricopa County Community College District Office (O)
2411 W 14th Street, Tempe AZ 85281-6941
County: Maricopa FICE Identification: 001075
Unit ID: 105136
Telephone: (480) 731-8000 Carnegie Class: N/A
FAX Number: (480) 731-8850
URL: www.maricopa.edu

01 Chancellor .... Dr. Maria HARPER-MARINICK
11 Chief Operating Officer .... Mr. James HIBBS
05 Vice Chancellor and Provost .... Dr. Karla FISHER
102 Interim President/CEO Foundation .... Mr. Brian SPICKER
15 Chief Human Resources Officer .... Ms. Georgetta KELLY
13 Chief Information Officer .... Dr. Mark KOAN
103 Int Assoc VC Workforce Development .... Mr. Daniel BARAJAS
30 Exec Director Resource Development .... Ms. Mary O'CONNOR
09 Assoc VC Inst Strategy/Rsrch/Effect .... Mr. Matthew ASHCRAFT
18 Assoc VC Capital Plng/Spec Proj .... Mr. Arlen SOLOCHEK

*Chandler-Gilbert Community College (P)
2626 E Pecos Road, Chandler AZ 85225-2499
County: Maricopa FICE Identification: 030722
Unit ID: 364025
Telephone: (480) 732-7000 Carnegie Class: Assoc/HT-High Non
FAX Number: (480) 732-7090 Calendar System: Semester
URL: www.cgc.maricopa.edu
Established: 1992 Annual Undergrad Tuition & Fees (In-District): $2,070
Enrollment: 14,906 Coed
Affiliation or Control: State/Local IRS Status: 501(c)3
Highest Offering: Associate Degree
Accreditation: NH, ADNUR, DIETT

02 College President .... Dr. Gregory PETERSON
04 Administrative Asst to President .... Ms. Susan D. AROZ
05 Vice President Academic Affairs .... Dr. William GUERRIERO
32 VP Student Affairs .... Ms. Veronica HIPOLITO
11 VP Administrative Services .... Mr. Bradley S. KENDREX

49 Dean of Arts and Sciences ..... Mr. Chris SCHNICK
20 Dean of Instruction ..... Ms. Gabriela ROSU
31 Assoc VP of Community Affairs ..... Ms. Jenna KAHL
10 Assoc VP of Business Operations ..... Ms. Bernadette LA MAZZA
84 Dean of Enrollment Services ..... Dr. Felicia RAMIREZ-PEREZ
07 Director Admissions ..... Ms. Linda SHAW
13 VP of IT & Media Svcs ..... Dr. Charles NWANKWO
09 Director Planning & Research ..... Ms. Theresa WONG
36 Dir Career/Education Planning Svcs ..... Vacant
85 Director International Educ Program ..... Ms. Annie A. JIMENEZ
88 Dir Disability Resources & Svcs ..... Ms. Dawn GRUICHICH
18 Director Col Facil Plng & Develop ..... Vacant
32 Director Student Life & Leadership ..... Mr. Michael GREENE
41 Athletic Director ..... Mr. Edward YEAGER
19 College Police Commander ..... Mr. Charles MOUNT
37 Director Financial Aid ..... Mr. Timothy WOLSEY
88 Director Learning Center ..... Ms. Eva R. FALLETTA
88 Director Early Outreach Programs ..... Mr. Lambert YAZZIE
88 Director Instr Tech & Course Prod ..... Mr. Jeremy TUTTY
66 Division Chair Nursing ..... Ms. Karen FLANIGAN
14 Int Dir Computer Labs/Instr Svcs ..... Ms. Sonya BRIESKE
113 Manager College Cashiers Office ..... Ms. Julie WRIGHT
15 Senior Human Resource Manager ..... Vacant

*Estrella Mountain Community College (A)

3000 N Dysart Road, Avondale AZ 85392

County: Maricopa FICE Identification: 031563
Unit ID: 384333

Telephone: (623) 935-8000 Carnegie Class: Assoc/HT-Mix Trad/Non
FAX Number: (623) 935-8008 Calendar System: Semester
URL: www.estrellamountain.edu
Established: 1990 Annual Undergrad Tuition & Fees (In-District): $2,070
Enrollment: 9,788 Coed
Affiliation or Control: State/Local IRS Status: 501(c)3
Highest Offering: Associate Degree
Accreditation: NH, ADNUR

02 President ..... Dr. Rey RIVERA
11 Vice President Admin Services ..... Dr. Heather WEBER
32 Vice President Student Affairs ..... Dr. Patricia CARDENAS-ADAME
05 Vice President of Learning ..... Vacant
20 Dean of Academic Affairs ..... Dr. Sylvia ORR
35 Dean of Student Services ..... Ms. Laura DULGAR
09 Dean Planning/Rsrch/Effectiveness ..... Dr. Rene G. WILLEKENS
08 Division Chair Information Resource ..... Mr. Terry MEYER
18 Director Facilities Planning/Devel ..... Mr. Randy L. NAUGHTON
13 Associate Vice President IT ..... Mr. Chad GALLIGAN
35 Student Services Director ..... Mr. Ralph CAMPBELL
10 Fiscal Director ..... Ms. Leda JOHNSON
102 Dir Corp Foundation Rels/Dev Ops ..... Mr. Jonathan ROBLES
37 Director Student Financial Aid ..... Ms. Rosanna SHORT
114 Fiscal Director Budget ..... Ms. Maggie CASTILLO

*Gateway Community College (B)

108 N 40th Street, Phoenix AZ 85034-1795

County: Maricopa FICE Identification: 008303
Unit ID: 105145

Telephone: (602) 286-8000 Carnegie Class: Assoc/HVT-Mix Trad/Non
FAX Number: (602) 286-8072 Calendar System: Semester
URL: www.gatewaycc.edu/
Established: 1968 Annual Undergrad Tuition & Fees (In-District): $2,070
Enrollment: 5,087 Coed
Affiliation or Control: State/Local IRS Status: 501(c)3
Highest Offering: Associate Degree
Accreditation: NH, ADNUR, COARC, DMS, MAC, NDT, NMT, POLYT, PTAA, RAD, SURGT

02 President ..... Dr. Steven GONZALEZ
05 Int Vice President Academic Affairs ..... Dr. Amy DIAZ
32 Vice President Student Affairs ..... Dr. Maria WISE
11 Vice President Administrative Svcs ..... Mr. Tony ASTI
07 Director Enrollment Services ..... Ms. Kristie FOK
09 Dir Research Planning & Development ..... Ms. Cathy HERNANDEZ
114 College Budget Analyst ..... Ms. Janet BOSE
10 Manager College Fiscal Services ..... Ms. Cecilia SOTO
18 Chief Facilities/Physical Plant ..... Vacant
26 Director Marketing/Public Relations ..... Ms. Christine LAMBRAKIS
30 Asst Director of Development ..... Ms. Kristin GUBSER
37 Director Student Financial Aid ..... Ms. Suzanne RINGLE
15 Manager College Employee Services ..... Ms. Jessica BELL
06 Registrar ..... Ms. Kristie FOK

*Glendale Community College (C)

6000 W Olive Avenue, Glendale AZ 85302-3006

County: Maricopa FICE Identification: 001076
Unit ID: 104708

Telephone: (623) 845-3000 Carnegie Class: Assoc/HT-Mix Trad/Non
FAX Number: (623) 845-3329 Calendar System: Semester
URL: www.gccaz.edu
Established: 1965 Annual Undergrad Tuition & Fees (In-District): $2,070
Enrollment: 19,033 Coed
Affiliation or Control: State/Local IRS Status: 170(c)1
Highest Offering: Associate Degree
Accreditation: NH, ADNUR, EMT

02 President ..... Dr. Teresa LEYBA RUIZ
05 VP Academic Affairs ..... Mr. Scott SCHULZ
32 Int VP Student Affairs ..... Ms. Monica CASTAÑEDA
11 Int VP Admin Services & CIO ..... Ms. Augustine ERPELDING
108 Assoc VP Instl Effectiveness ..... Dr. Alka ARORA SINGH
20 Dean of Academic Affairs ..... Dr. Fernando CAMOU
20 Interim Dean of Academic Affairs ..... Dr. Susan CAMPBELL
20 Dean of Academic Affairs ..... Mr. Charles JEFFERY
20 Interim Dean of Academic Affairs ..... Dr. Lorelei CARVAJAL
84 Dean Enrollment Services ..... Ms. Yolanda ESPIZONA
35 Interim Dean Student Life ..... Mr. Miguel LUCAS
12 Dean GCC North ..... Mr. Charles JEFFERY
37 Director Financial Aid ..... Ms. Annette LINDERS
18 Director Facilities ..... Mr. Al GONZALES
10 Director College Business Services ..... Ms. Kim GOLIS
26 Dir Sales Mktg & Public Rels ..... Mr. John HECKENLAIBLE
45 Dir Institutional Effectiveness ..... Mr. Kerry MITCHELL
15 Dir College Employee Svcs ..... Ms. June S. FESSENDEN
30 Director of Development ..... Ms. Frances MATEO
13 Director College Technology Svcs ..... Mr. Isaiah WASHINGTON
38 Dept Chair Counseling ..... Mr. Paul ROMO
08 Dept Chair Library ..... Mr. Frank TORRES
19 Police Commander ..... Ms. Debra PALOK
04 Admin Coordinator to College Pres ..... Ms. Esmeralda M. ACOSTA
41 Athletic Director ..... Mr. Peter OLISZCZAK
79 Dept Chair Art & Humanities ..... Mr. Brendan REGAN
81 Dept Chair Biology ..... Ms. Karen CONZELMAN
50 Dept Chair Business & Info Tech ..... Ms. Rachelle HALL
81 Dept Chair Chemistry ..... Ms. Debbie LEEDY
79 Dept Chair Comm & World Languages ..... Dr. Pam JORAANSTAD
60 Dept Chair Eng/Reading/Journalism ..... Mr. David MILLER
88 Dept Chair Fitness & Wellness ..... Ms. Lisa LEWIS
77 Dept Chair Math/Computer Science ..... Mr. Chris MILLER
66 Dept Chair Nursing ..... Dr. Susan MAYER
57 Dept Chair Performing Arts ..... Mr. Donald SMITH
88 Dept Chair Philosophy/Religious Std ..... Mr. Peter LUPU
81 Dept Chair Physical Sciences ..... Mr. David RAFFAELLE
83 Dept Chair Psychology ..... Dr. Julie MORRISON
88 Dept Chair Public Safety Sciences ..... Mr. Chris COUGHLIN
83 Dept Chair Social Sciences ..... Mr. Dean WHEELER
72 Dept Chair Tech & Consumer Sciences ..... Ms. Angela JORDAN
88 Dept Chair Automotives ..... Mr. Jay COVEY

*Mesa Community College (D)

1833 W Southern Avenue, Mesa AZ 85202-4866

County: Maricopa FICE Identification: 001077
Unit ID: 105154

Telephone: (480) 461-7000 Carnegie Class: Assoc/HT-Mix Trad/Non
FAX Number: N/A Calendar System: Semester
URL: www.mesacc.edu/
Established: 1965 Annual Undergrad Tuition & Fees (In-District): $2,070
Enrollment: 20,424 Coed
Affiliation or Control: State/Local IRS Status: 501(c)3
Highest Offering: Associate Degree
Accreditation: NH, ADNUR, DH, EMT

02 President ..... Dr. Rich HANEY
32 EVP Academic & Student Affairs ..... Dr. Lori BERQUAM
05 Interim Vice Pres Academic Affairs ..... Dr. Rodney HOLMES
10 Vice Pres Admin Services ..... Vacant
13 Interim VP Information Technology ..... Dr. Tony BRYSON
09 Int Dean of Inst Plng & Analysis ..... Mr. Dennis MITCHELL
20 Dean Academic Affairs ..... Mr. Michael VOSS
20 Interim Dean Instruction ..... Dr. Jeffrey ANDELORA
20 Dean Instruction ..... Ms. Carol ACHS
12 Vice Provost MCC Red Mountain ..... Dr. Nora REYES
84 Dean Enrollment Services ..... Dr. Carmen NEWLAND
111 Director of Institutional Advance ..... Vacant
30 Interim Director of Development ..... Mr. Christos CHRONIS
37 Dir Financial Aid/Scholarships ..... Ms. Patricia PEPPIN
19 Director Security/Safety ..... Mr. Steve LIEBER
25 Chief Contracts/Grants Admin ..... Mr. Kenichi MARUYAMA
29 Director Alumni Relations ..... Ms. Marcy SNITZER
41 Athletic Director ..... Mr. John MULHERN
18 Interim Director Facilities ..... Mr. Steve AZEVEDO
04 Administrative Asst to President ..... Ms. Kacie TAKATA
07 Supv Admiss/Registration/Records ..... Vacant
06 Registrar ..... Mr. Jeffrey RHOADS
22 Dir Affirm Action/Equal Opportunity ..... Mr. Garrett SMITH

*Paradise Valley Community College (E)

18401 N 32nd Street, Phoenix AZ 85032-1210

County: Maricopa FICE Identification: 026236
Unit ID: 364016

Telephone: (602) 787-6500 Carnegie Class: Assoc/HT-Mix Trad/Non
FAX Number: (602) 787-6625 Calendar System: Semester
URL: www.paradisevalley.edu
Established: 1985 Annual Undergrad Tuition & Fees (In-District): $2,070
Enrollment: 8,447 Coed
Affiliation or Control: State/Local IRS Status: 501(c)3
Highest Offering: Associate Degree
Accreditation: NH, ADNUR, DIETT, EMT

02 President ..... Dr. Paul DALE
05 Vice President of Academic Affairs ..... Dr. Eric LESHINSKIE
11 VP Administrative Services ..... Mr. Herman GONZALEZ
32 Vice President of Student Affairs ..... Dr. Jana SCHWARTZ
20 Dean of Academic Affairs ..... Dr. Doug BERRY
35 Dean of Students ..... Dr. Anne SUZUKI
84 Dean Admin Affs/Enrollment Services ..... Vacant
15 Director Personnel Services ..... Ms. Lori LINDSETH
18 Chief Facilities/Physical Plant ..... Mr. Robert METEVIER
37 Director Student Financial Aid ..... Ms. Katharine JOHNSON
38 Director Student Counseling ..... Dr. James RUBIN
06 Registrar ..... Mr. Frank AMPARO
36 Director Student Placement ..... Ms. Norma CHANDLER
26 Dir of Marketing/Public Relations ..... Ms. Tina MILLER
09 Dir Institutional Research/Effect ..... Mr. John SNELLING
19 Director Security/Safety ..... Mr. Scott MEEK
41 Athletic Director ..... Ms. Christina HUNDLEY
30 Director of Development ..... Ms. Jessi WRIGHT

*Phoenix College (F)

1202 W Thomas Road, Phoenix AZ 85013-4234

County: Maricopa FICE Identification: 001078
Unit ID: 105428

Telephone: (602) 285-7777 Carnegie Class: Assoc/MT-VT-Mix Trad/Non
FAX Number: (602) 285-7700 Calendar System: Semester
URL: www.pc.maricopa.edu
Established: 1920 Annual Undergrad Tuition & Fees (In-District): $2,070
Enrollment: 11,428 Coed
Affiliation or Control: State/Local IRS Status: 501(c)3
Highest Offering: Associate Degree
Accreditation: NH, ADNUR, CAHIIM, DA, DH, EMT, HT, MLTAD

02 President ..... Dr. Larry JOHNSON, JR.
05 VP of Academic Affairs ..... Dr. Doug BERRY
11 VP Administrative Services ..... Mr. Paul DEROSE
32 Vice Pres of Student Affairs ..... Dr. Heather KRUSE
10 Assoc VP Business/Finance ..... Ms. Angela GENNA
35 Dean of Student Affairs ..... Ms. Julie VOLLER
20 Dean of Academic Affairs ..... Mr. Wilbert NELSON
88 Int Dean Industry/Public Service ..... Ms. Julie STIAK
13 Chief Information Ofcr/AVP IT ..... Vacant
08 Department Chair Library ..... Ms. Christine MOORE
38 Department Chair Counseling ..... Mr. Robert VILLEGAS GOLD
06 Dir Admissions/Registration/Records ..... Ms. Brenda STARCK
07 Director of Enrollment Services ..... Vacant
41 Athletic Director ..... Mr. Jonathan BERZINS
37 Director Financial Aid ..... Ms. Cynthia RAMOS
88 Int Director Student Leadership ..... Ms. Diana MARTINEZ
84 Director Advisement Enrollment ..... Ms. Felicia RAMIREZ-PEREZ
09 Dir Instl Plng/Rsrch/Effectiveness ..... Vacant
19 Director of College Safety ..... Mr. Doug SPARKS
30 Director Institutional Advancement ..... Ms. Michelle KLINGER
18 Director of Facilities ..... Mr. Douglas MCCARTHY
30 Development Director ..... Ms. Deborah SPOTTS
04 Assistant to the President ..... Ms. Briana JORDAN

*Rio Salado College (G)

2323 W 14th Street, Tempe AZ 85281-6950

County: Maricopa FICE Identification: 021775
Unit ID: 105668

Telephone: (480) 517-8000 Carnegie Class: Assoc/HVT-High Non
FAX Number: (480) 377-4719 Calendar System: Semester
URL: www.riosalado.edu
Established: 1978 Annual Undergrad Tuition & Fees (In-District): $2,070
Enrollment: 17,635 Coed
Affiliation or Control: State/Local IRS Status: 501(c)3
Highest Offering: Associate Degree
Accreditation: NH, DH

02 Interim President ..... Ms. Kate SMITH
05 Vice President Academic Affairs ..... Ms. Kate SMITH
10 Vice Pres Business & Employee Svcs ..... Mr. Todd SIMMONS
32 Vice Pres Student Affairs ..... Mr. Greg PEREIRA
12 Int Vice Pres Maricopa Corp College ..... Ms. Patricia O'BRIEN
13 Vice President Information Services ..... Mr. David O'SHEA
20 Dean of Instruction ..... Mr. Rick KEMP
15 Dean Administrative and Empl Svcs ..... Ms. Maria BELLINO
20 Interim Dean Instr Tech & Support ..... Vacant
20 Dean of Instruction ..... Ms. Karol SCHMIDT
84 Dean Stdnt Affs/Enrollment Mgmt ..... Ms. Rachelle CLARKE
88 Assoc Dean Instruction and Support ..... Ms. Earnestine HARRISON
31 Interim Dean Instruction & Cmty Dev ..... Ms. Barbara KHALSA
88 Assoc Dean Judicial Affairs ..... Vacant
21 Assoc Dean Business Service ..... Mr. Anthony DISCALA
37 Associate Dean of Financial Aid ..... Ms. Nanci REGEHR
09 Assoc Dean Institutional Research ..... Mr. Dustin MARONEY
06 Dir Registration/Records/Admission ..... Ms. Laurel REDMAN
18 Director of Facilities ..... Mr. Richard OROS
19 Public Safety Commander ..... Mr. John PORVAZNIK
16 Senior Manager Employee Services ..... Ms. Anna FLORES
08 Library Faculty Chair ..... Ms. Hazel DAVIS
04 Admin Coordinator to President ..... Ms. Kevyn MILLER

*Scottsdale Community College (H)

9000 E Chaparral, Scottsdale AZ 85256-2626

County: Maricopa FICE Identification: 008304
Unit ID: 105747

Telephone: (480) 423-6000 Carnegie Class: Assoc/HT-High Non
FAX Number: (480) 423-6200 Calendar System: Semester
URL: www.scottsdalecc.edu
Established: 1970 Annual Undergrad Tuition & Fees (In-District): $2,070
Enrollment: 9,458 Coed
Affiliation or Control: State/Local IRS Status: 501(c)3
Highest Offering: Associate Degree
Accreditation: NH, ACFEI, ADNUR

02 President ..... Ms. Chris M. HAINES

32 Vice Pres Student Affairs .... Dr. Donna YOUNG
05 Vice Pres Academic Affairs .... Dr. Stephanie FUJII
11 Vice Pres Administrative Services .... Ms. Colleen O'NEILL
13 Dir ITS/College CTO .... Mr. Vargha MOHEBBI
20 Dean of Instruction .... Dr. Kathleen IUDICELLO
35 Dean of Student Affairs .... Ms. Larissa TRAIN
84 Dean of Student Enrollment .... Ms. Gia TAYLOR
07 Director of Admissions .... Ms. Laura KRUEGER
09 Director of Institutional Research .... Dr. Laurie COHEN
08 Director of Library Services .... Ms. Danielle CARLOCK
37 Director Financial Aid/Placement .... Ms. Stacie BECK
18 Director Buildings/Grounds .... Mr. Tony MIELE
19 Director of College Safety .... Mr. Arlyn WALZ
41 Athletic Director .... Mr. Michael MCNALLY
38 Director Student Advisement .... Mr. Michael CORNELIUS
04 Administrative Asst to President .... Ms. Donna COLE
10 Chief Business Officer .... Ms. Mirna ROSAS
15 Director Personnel Services .... Vacant

*South Mountain Community College (A)

7050 S 24th Street, Phoenix AZ 85042-5806

County: Maricopa FICE Identification: 021466
Unit ID: 105792
Telephone: (602) 243-8000 Carnegie Class: Assoc/HT-Mix Trad/Non
FAX Number: (602) 243-8329 Calendar System: Semester
URL: www.southmountaincc.edu
Established: 1979 Annual Undergrad Tuition & Fees (In-District): $2,070
Enrollment: 4,120 Coed
Affiliation or Control: State/Local IRS Status: 501(c)3
Highest Offering: Associate Degree
Accreditation: NH

02 President .... Dr. Shari L. OLSON
05 Vice Pres of Learning .... Dr. Clyne NAMUO
11 Vice Pres Administrative Svcs .... Dr. Janet ORTEGA
32 Vice Pres Student Affairs .... Dr. Osaro IGHODARO
09 Dean Research/Plng & Development .... Ms. Damita KALOOSTIAN
20 Interim Dean Academic Affairs .... Ms. Christianne NIEUWSMA
84 Dean Enrollment Services .... Mr. Guy GOODMAN
37 Director Financial Aid .... Ms. Inez MORENO-WEINERT
07 Director of Admission & Records .... Ms. Jean WATERMOLEN
10 Director College Business Services .... Mr. Mark MCCAIN
18 Interim Director of Facilities .... Mr. David BANNENBERG
21 Manager Fiscal Services .... Vacant
15 Coordinator Human Resources .... Ms. Judy BELSHER
07 Coordinator Recruitment .... Mr. Christopher ERRAN
36 Coordinator Job Placement .... Ms. Suzanne HIPPS
41 Athletic Director .... Mr. Todd EASTIN

*Chandler-Gilbert Community College-Williams Campus (B)

7360 E Tahoe Avenue, Mesa AZ 85212-0908
Telephone: (480) 988-8000 Identification: 770178
Accreditation: &NH, FUSER

*Glendale Community College North (C)

5727 W Happy Valley Road, Phoenix AZ 85310
Telephone: (623) 845-4000 Identification: 770179
Accreditation: &NH

*Mesa Community College at Red Mountain (D)

7110 East McKellips Road, Mesa AZ 85207
Telephone: (480) 654-7200 Identification: 770180
Accreditation: &NH

Midwestern University (E)

19555 N 59th Avenue, Glendale AZ 85308
Telephone: (623) 572-3400 Identification: 666001
Accreditation: &NH, ANEST, ARCPA, CLPSY, DENT, OPT, OPTR, OSTEO, OT, PERF, PHAR, POD, PTA, @SP, VET

† Regional accreditation is carried under the parent institution in Downers Grove, IL.

Mohave Community College (F)

1971 E. Jagerson Avenue, Kingman AZ 86409-1238
County: Mohave FICE Identification: 011864
Unit ID: 105206
Telephone: (866) 664-2832 Carnegie Class: Assoc/MT-VT-Mix Trad/Non
FAX Number: (928) 757-0836 Calendar System: Semester
URL: www.mohave.edu
Established: 1971 Annual Undergrad Tuition & Fees (In-District): $2,112
Enrollment: 4,312 Coed
Affiliation or Control: State/Local IRS Status: 501(c)3
Highest Offering: Associate Degree
Accreditation: NH, ADNUR, DH, EMT, PTAA, RAD, SURGT

05 Chief Academic Officer .... Mr. Stephen EATON
32 Chief Student Services Officer .... Ms. Ana MASTERSON
10 Chief Financial Officer .... Ms. Sonni MARBURY
111 Director College Advancement .... Ms. Carrie KELLY
13 Chief Information Officer .... Mr. Mark VANPELT
26 Chief Public Relations Officer .... Mr. James JARMAN
15 Chief Human Resources Officer .... Ms. Jenny DIXON
12 Campus Dean Bullhead City .... Mr. Shawn BRISTLE
12 Campus Dean Lake Havasu .... Ms. Jann WOODS
12 Campus Dean Neal Kingman .... Dr. Fred GILBERT
12 Campus Dean North Mohave .... Ms. Carolyn HAMBLIN
37 Financial Aid Director .... Ms. Heather PATENAUDE
09 Dir of Institutional Research .... Mr. Bob FAUBERT
84 Enrollment Services Manager .... Ms. Sharon HANKS
06 Registrar .... Ms. Michelle BREHMEYER
04 Administrative Asst to President .... Ms. Amy CURLEY

National Paralegal College (G)

717 East Maryland Avenue, Phoenix AZ 85014-1561
County: Maricopa FICE Identification: 041574
Unit ID: 461023
Telephone: (800) 371-6105 Carnegie Class: Spec-4-yr-Other
FAX Number: (866) 347-2744 Calendar System: Other
URL: nationalparalegal.edu
Established: 2003 Annual Undergrad Tuition & Fees: $7,995
Enrollment: 854 Coed
Affiliation or Control: Proprietary IRS Status: Proprietary
Highest Offering: Master's
Accreditation: DEAC

01 President .... Avi KATZ
05 Dean/Director .... Stephen HAAS
88 Technical Director .... David COHEN
07 Director of Admissions .... Dana WASSERSTROM
37 Director Student Financial Aid .... Lisa PIMBER

Northern Arizona University (H)

South San Francisco Street, Flagstaff AZ 86011-0001
County: Coconino FICE Identification: 001082
Unit ID: 105330
Telephone: (928) 523-9011 Carnegie Class: DU-Higher
FAX Number: (928) 523-1848 Calendar System: Semester
URL: www.nau.edu
Established: 1899 Annual Undergrad Tuition & Fees (In-State): $11,564
Enrollment: 31,051 Coed
Affiliation or Control: State IRS Status: 501(c)3
Highest Offering: Doctorate
Accreditation: NH, ACBSP, ARCPA, CAATE, CACREP, CAEP, CIDA, CONST, DH, EXSC, MUS, NRPA, NURSE, OT, PSPSY, PTA, SP, SW

01 President .... Dr. Rita H. CHENG
03 Executive VP and Chief of Staff .... Ms. Joanne KEENE
05 Provost .... Dr. Daniel KAIN
09 VP Finance Inst Plng & Analysis .... Mr. Bjorn FLUGSTAD
10 VP Capital Planning & Campus Ops .... Dr. Daniel T. OKOLI
46 Vice President Research .... Dr. David R. SCHULTZ
86 VP Govt Affairs/Bus Partnerships .... Ms. Christy FARLEY
41 VP Intercollegiate Athletics .... Ms. Mike MARLOW
88 VP of Native American Initiatives .... Dr. Chad S. HAMILL
88 Ex Dir Inst for Tribal Env Prof .... Dr. AnnMarie CHISCHILLY
88 Exec Dir Native Amer Cultural Ctr .... Dr. Ora MAREK-MARTINEZ
43 General Counsel .... Ms. Michelle G. PARKER
88 Vice Provost Academic Personnel .... Dr. Roger G. BOUNDS
13 Chief Information Officer .... Dr. Steven C. BURRELL
32 Associate VP Student Affairs .... Ms. Erin GRISHAM
12 Assoc VP/Campus Exec Officer - Yuma .... Dr. Michael J. SABATH
15 Int Chief Human Resources Officer .... Ms. Cindy CHILCOAT
21 Associate VP Comptrollers Office .... Ms. Wendy A. SWARTZ
85 Int Exec Dir International Educ .... Mr. Daniel PALM
108 Chief Institutional Data Officer .... Ms. Laura A. JONES
110 Assoc VP Devel & Alumni Engagement .... Ms. Bonnie BAKER
29 Director Alumni Engagement .... Ms. Stephanie SMITH
08 Dean/University Librarian .... Dr. Cynthia A. CHILDREY
53 Dean College of Education .... Dr. Ramona N. MELLOTT
54 Dean College Eng/Forestry/Nat Sci .... Dr. Paul W. JAGODZINSKI
50 Dean WA Franke College of Business .... Dr. Dan J. GOEBEL
83 Dean Col Social/Behavioral Sciences .... Dr. Karen L. PUGLIESI
88 Dean Col of Health/Human Svcs .... Dr. Lynda B. RANSDELL
06 University Registrar .... Ms. Pamela L. ANASTASSIOU
19 Chief of Police .... Ms. Kelli J. SMITH
22 Assistant VP Equity and Access .... Ms. Priscilla L. MILLS
23 Exec Dir Campus Health Svcs .... Ms. Julie A. RYAN
39 Exec Dir Housing/Residence Life .... Mr. Rich PAYNE
36 Dir Gateway Student Success Center .... Ms. Monica S. BAI
07 Interim Director of Admissions .... Mr. Chad A. EICKHOFF
96 Executive Director of Purchasing .... Ms. Becky E. MCGAUGH
88 Assistant to the President ECMR .... Ms. Kim A. OTT
104 Director Study Abroad .... Dr. Eric N. DESCHAMPS
37 Director Student Financial Aid .... Ms. Nydia C. NITTMANN
16 Director Human Resource Programs .... Ms. Cynthia A. CHILCOAT
64 Director School of Music .... Vacant
94 Director Women and Gender Studies .... Ms. Sheila NAIR
58 Dean Graduate College .... Dr. Maribeth WATWOOD
106 Director E-Learning Center .... Mr. Don CARTER
121 Exec Dir Academic Advising .... Ms. Terri L. HAYES
88 VProvost Tchg/Lrng/Design & Assmt .... Dr. Laurie DICKSON
88 Associate VP Research .... Dr. Diane M. STEARNS
88 Assoc VP NAU Online .... Ms. Gina K. VANCE
88 Assoc VP for Government Affairs .... Ms. Katy YANEZ
88 Assoc VP Educational Partnerships .... Ms. Kathrine H. YEAGER
88 Assoc VP Sponsored Projects .... Dr. Michael L. NICHOLS
88 Asst VP Regulatory Compliance .... Dr. David M. FAGUY

Northern Arizona University Yuma Branch Campus (I)

2020 S Avenue 8E, Yuma AZ 85365
Telephone: (928) 317-6450 Identification: 770011
Accreditation: &NH, SW

Northland Pioneer College (J)

PO Box 610, Holbrook AZ 86025-0610
County: Navajo FICE Identification: 011862
Unit ID: 105349
Telephone: (928) 524-7311 Carnegie Class: Not Classified
FAX Number: (928) 524-7312 Calendar System: Semester
URL: www.npc.edu
Established: 1973 Annual Undergrad Tuition & Fees (In-State): N/A
Enrollment: N/A Coed
Affiliation or Control: State IRS Status: 501(c)3
Highest Offering: Associate Degree
Accreditation: NH, ADNUR, EMT

01 College President .... Mr. Mark H. VEST
101 Secretary of the Institution/Board .... Mr. John Paul HEMPSEY
05 VP Learning & Student Services .... Mr. Rickey JACKSON
10 VP for Administrative Services .... Ms. Maderia ELLISON
13 Director Information Services (CIO) .... Vacant
49 Int Dean of Arts & Sciences .... Dr. Wei MA
103 Dean of Career/Technical Education .... Ms. Peggy BELKNAP
66 Dean of Nursing and Allied Health .... Dr. Debra MCGINTY
53 Dean of Education/College/Career Pr .... Ms. Gail CAMPBELL
15 Human Resources Director .... Ms. Chris ROEDIGER
84 Director of Enrollment Services .... Mr. Jeremy RAISOR
06 Assistant Registrar .... Ms. Deena GILLESPIE
32 Director of Student Services .... Mr. Josh ROGERS
18 Director of Facilities and Vehicles .... Mr. David HUISH
26 Dir of Marketing/Public Relations .... Ms. Ann HESS
09 Director of Institutional Effective .... Dr. Judy YIP-REYES
88 Director Small Business Development .... Ms. Tracy HOLT-MANCUSO
19 Director of Public Safety Education .... Mr. Jon WISNER
102 Pgm Director NPC Friends & Family .... Ms. Betsyann WILSON
37 Manager of Financial Aid Operations .... Ms. Marletha BALOO
21 Controller .... Ms. Amber HILL
08 Head Librarian .... Mr. Stan PIROG
96 Procurement Manager .... Mr. Robert JOHNSON
07 Coordinator of High School Programs .... Ms. Karen ZIMMERMAN
25 Grant Accountant .... Ms. Donna SOSEMAN

Northland Pioneer College Little Colorado Campus (K)

1400 E. Third Street, Winslow AZ 86047
Telephone: (928) 289-6511 Identification: 770015
Accreditation: &NH

Northland Pioneer College Painted Desert Campus (L)

2251 E Navajo Boulevard, Holbrook AZ 86025
Telephone: (928) 524-7311 Identification: 770012
Accreditation: &NH

Northland Pioneer College Silver Creek Campus (M)

1611 S Main Street, Snowflake AZ 85937
Telephone: (928) 536-6211 Identification: 770014
Accreditation: &NH

Northland Pioneer College White Mountain Campus (N)

1001 W Deuce of Clubs, Show Low AZ 85901
Telephone: (928) 532-6111 Identification: 770013
Accreditation: &NH

Ottawa University Arizona (O)

9414 North 25th Avenue, Phoenix AZ 85021
Telephone: (602) 371-1188 Identification: 666066
Accreditation: &NH

† Regional accreditation is carried under the parent institution in Ottawa, KS.

Ottawa University Surprise (P)

15950 N. Civic Center Plaza, Surprise AZ 85374
Telephone: (855) 546-1342 Identification: 770982
Accreditation: &NH

† Regional accreditation is carried under the parent institution in Ottawa, KS.

The Paralegal Institute at Brighton College (Q)

8777 E. Via de Ventura, Suite 300, Scottsdale AZ 85258
County: Maricopa FICE Identification: 030737
Telephone: (602) 212-0501 Carnegie Class: Not Classified
FAX Number: (602) 212-0502 Calendar System: Other
URL: www.theparalegalinstitute.edu
Established: 1974 Annual Undergrad Tuition & Fees: N/A
Enrollment: N/A Coed
Affiliation or Control: Proprietary IRS Status: Proprietary
Highest Offering: Associate Degree

Accreditation: DEAC

00 Corporate President .... Paul ZAGNONI
01 Campus President .... Kathleen MIRABILE
03 Vice President .... Sam FERNANDEZ
05 Vice President Academic Affairs .... Gilda RADA
32 Director of Student Services .... Sean DIXON

Penn Foster College (A)

14300 N Northsight Blvd, Suite 125,
Scottsdale AZ 85260-3673
County: Maricopa FICE Identification: 004049
Unit ID: 211486
Telephone: (480) 947-6644 Carnegie Class: Not Classified
FAX Number: N/A Calendar System: Other
URL: www.pennfoster.edu
Established: 1974 Annual Undergrad Tuition & Fees: N/A
Enrollment: N/A Coed
Affiliation or Control: Proprietary IRS Status: Proprietary
Highest Offering: Baccalaureate
Accreditation: DEAC

01 Chief Executive Officer .... Mr. Frank BRITT
05 Chief Certification/Licensing Ofcr .... Ms. Connie DEMPSEY
10 Chief Financial Officer .... Mr. Thomas BLESSO
11 Chief Operating Officer .... Ms. Dara WARN
26 Vice Pres Marketing .... Ms. Kate MOSTELLER
07 Vice Pres Admissions .... Mr. Pat GAFFEY
13 VP Info Technology/Data Services .... Mr. Matthew BENNER

Phoenix Institute of Herbal Medicine and Acupuncture (B)

301 E Bethany Home Road, Ste A-100,
Phoenix AZ 85012-1275
County: Maricopa FICE Identification: 036175
Unit ID: 447698
Telephone: (602) 274-1885 Carnegie Class: Spec-4-yr-Other Health
FAX Number: (602) 274-1895 Calendar System: Semester
URL: www.pihma.edu
Established: 1996 Annual Graduate Tuition & Fees: N/A
Enrollment: 81 Coed
Affiliation or Control: Proprietary IRS Status: Proprietary
Highest Offering: Master's; No Undergraduates
Accreditation: ACUP

01 President .... Ms. Catherine NIEMIEC
05 Dean for Academic Affairs .... Mr. David MYRICK
07 Admissions .... Ms. Lisa DUNN
06 Registrar .... Ms. Judy DRAYER
30 Regulatory/Inst Development Ofcr .... Mr. Jonathan LINDSEY

Phoenix Seminary (C)

7901 E. Shea Boulevard, Scottsdale AZ 85260-5510
County: Maricopa FICE Identification: 034784
Unit ID: 381459
Telephone: (602) 850-8000 Carnegie Class: Spec-4-yr-Faith
FAX Number: (602) 850-8080 Calendar System: Semester
URL: www.ps.edu
Established: 1988 Annual Graduate Tuition & Fees: N/A
Enrollment: 217 Coed
Affiliation or Control: Interdenominational IRS Status: 501(c)3
Highest Offering: Doctorate; No Undergraduates
Accreditation: NH, THEOL

01 President .... Dr. Darryl L. DELHOUSAYE
05 Exec VP/Chief Academic Officer .... Dr. W. Bingham HUNTER
32 Vice President Student Development .... Vacant
20 Asst Dean Academic Services .... Ms. Roma ROYER
06 Registrar .... Mrs. Merry STENSON
84 Dir Enrollment & Student Services .... Mrs. Carrie STEPHENS
10 Comptroller .... Mrs. Deborah ARNITZ
08 Director of Library Services .... Mr. Doug OLBERT
35 Dean of Students .... Dr. Joshua ANDERSON

Pima Community College (D)

4905 East Broadway Boulevard, Tucson AZ 85709-1005
County: Pima FICE Identification: 007266
Unit ID: 105525
Telephone: (520) 206-4500 Carnegie Class: Assoc/HT-High Trad
FAX Number: (520) 206-4535 Calendar System: Semester
URL: www.pima.edu
Established: 1966 Annual Undergrad Tuition & Fees (In-District): $2,142
Enrollment: 24,347 Coed
Affiliation or Control: State/Local IRS Status: 501(c)3
Highest Offering: Associate Degree
Accreditation: NH, ADNUR, COARC, DA, DH, DT, EMT, MAC, MLTAD, RAD

01 Chancellor .... Mr. Lee D. LAMBERT
05 Provost/Chief Academic Ofcr .... Dr. Dolores DURAN-CERDA
10 Exec Vice Chanc for Finance & Admin .... Dr. David BEA
15 Acting Chief HR Officer .... Mr. Jeffrey LANUEZ
26 Vice Chancellor External Relations .... Ms. Lisa BROSKY
18 Vice Chancellor Facilities .... Mr. Bill WARD
12 Pres NW/Downtown & Cmty Campuses .... Dr. David DORE
12 Pres East/West & Desert Vista Camp .... Dr. Morgan PHILLIPS
43 College General Counsel .... Mr. Jeffrey SILVYN
13 Asst Vice Chanc Information Tech .... Dr. Raj MURTHY
20 Associate Provost .... Dr. Bruce MOSES
09 AVC Planning & Inst Research .... Dr. Nicola RICHMOND
32 VP Student Affairs .... Dr. Irene ROBLES-LOPEZ
21 Asst Vice Chanc Finance .... Mr. Daniel SOZA
86 Exec Dir Media & Govt Rels .... Ms. Elizabeth HOWELL
19 Exec Dir College Police .... Mr. Christopher ALBERS
37 Exec Director of Financial Aid .... Ms. Norma NAVARRO-CASTELLANOS
28 Ex Dir Diversity/Equity & Inclusion .... Ms. Hilda LADNER
76 Dean of Allied Health Programs .... Mr. James CRAIG
96 Director of Procurement .... Mr. Terryl ROBINSON
07 Director Admissions & Registrar .... Mr. Michael TULINO
103 VP Workforce Development .... Dr. Ian ROARK
41 Actg Athletic Director .... Mr. Jim MONACO

Pima Community College Community Campus (E)

401 North Bonita Avenue, Tucson AZ 85709
Telephone: (520) 206-3933 Identification: 770016
Accreditation: &NH

Pima Community College Desert Vista Campus (F)

5901 South Calle Santa Cruz, Tucson AZ 85709
Telephone: (520) 206-5000 Identification: 770017
Accreditation: &NH, SURGT

Pima Community College Downtown Campus (G)

1255 North Stone Avenue, Tucson AZ 85709-3000
Telephone: (520) 206-7171 Identification: 770018
Accreditation: &NH

Pima Community College East Campus (H)

8181 East Irvington Road, Tucson AZ 85709
Telephone: (520) 206-7000 Identification: 770019
Accreditation: &NH

Pima Community College Northwest Campus (I)

7600 North Shannon Road, Tucson AZ 85709-7200
Telephone: (520) 206-2200 Identification: 770020
Accreditation: &NH

Pima Community College West Campus (J)

2202 West Anklam Road, Tucson AZ 85709-0001
Telephone: (520) 206-6600 Identification: 770021
Accreditation: &NH

Pima Medical Institute-East Valley (K)

2160 S Power Road, Mesa AZ 85209
Telephone: (480) 898-9898 Identification: 770515
Accreditation: ABHES

Pima Medical Institute-Mesa (L)

957 S Dobson Road, Mesa AZ 85202-2903
Telephone: (480) 644-0267 FICE Identification: 011570
Accreditation: ABHES, COARC, EMT, OTA, PTAA, RAD

Pima Medical Institute-Tucson (M)

2121 N Craycroft Road, Bldg 1, Tucson AZ 85712
County: Pima FICE Identification: 022171
Unit ID: 105534
Telephone: (520) 326-1600 Carnegie Class: Spec-4-yr-Other Health
FAX Number: (520) 326-4125 Calendar System: Other
URL: www.pmi.edu
Established: 1972 Annual Undergrad Tuition & Fees: N/A
Enrollment: 2,300 Coed
Affiliation or Control: Proprietary IRS Status: Proprietary
Highest Offering: Baccalaureate
Accreditation: ABHES, COARC, NURSE, OTA, PTAA, RAD

01 Director .... Mr. Dale BERG

Prescott College (N)

220 Grove Avenue, Prescott AZ 86301-2912
County: Yavapai FICE Identification: 020653
Unit ID: 105589
Telephone: (928) 350-2100 Carnegie Class: Masters/S
FAX Number: (928) 776-5137 Calendar System: Semester
URL: www.prescott.edu
Established: 1966 Annual Undergrad Tuition & Fees: $31,485
Enrollment: 711 Coed
Affiliation or Control: Independent Non-Profit IRS Status: 501(c)3
Highest Offering: Doctorate
Accreditation: NH

01 President .... Mr. John FLICKER
05 Executive Vice President & Provost .... Dr. Paul BURKHARDT
10 Chief Financial Officer .... Ms. Andrea JAECKEL
84 Chief Enrollment Management .... Dr. Stephanie KRUSEMARK
111 Chief Advancement Officer .... Mr. Sturgis ROBINSON
32 Chief Student Affairs Officer .... Ms. Kristine PREZIOSI
124 Director of Student Retention .... Ms. Jerri BROWN
06 Registrar .... Ms. Aimee WALKER
07 Director of Admissions .... Mr. David WHITE
09 Director of Institutional Research .... Vacant
15 Director of Human Resources .... Ms. Susan KRAUSE
39 Housing Director .... Ms. Megan LETCHWORTH
18 Director of Facilities .... Mr. Brad SINN
08 Dir of Library/Learning Commons .... Ms. Alexis WEISS
13 Dir Information Technology Services .... Vacant
29 Director of Alumni Relations .... Ms. Marie SMITH
20 Associate Dean for Instruction .... Ms. Erin LOTZ

The Refrigeration School (O)

4210 E Washington Street, Phoenix AZ 85034-1816
County: Maricopa FICE Identification: 011689
Unit ID: 105659
Telephone: (602) 275-7133 Carnegie Class: Spec 2-yr-Tech
FAX Number: (602) 267-4805 Calendar System: Other
URL: www.refrigerationschool.com
Established: 1965 Annual Undergrad Tuition & Fees: N/A
Enrollment: 732 Coed
Affiliation or Control: Proprietary IRS Status: Proprietary
Highest Offering: Associate Degree
Accreditation: ACCSC

01 Campus President .... Mr. Stephen M. MALUTICH
37 Director of Financial Aid .... Ms. Melanie ZUVERINK
07 Director of Admissions .... Mr. John PALUMBO
05 Director of Education .... Mr. Greg HARRIS
10 Director of Accounting .... Mr. David FULFORD
06 Registrar .... Ms. Tara BOURLOTOS

The School of Architecture at Taliesin (P)

12621 N Frank Lloyd Wright Blvd, Scottsdale AZ 85259
County: Maricopa FICE Identification: 025332
Unit ID: 104665
Telephone: (480) 627-5345 Carnegie Class: Spec-4-yr-Arts
FAX Number: (480) 860-8472 Calendar System: Other
URL: www.taliesin.edu
Established: 1932 Annual Undergrad Tuition & Fees: N/A
Enrollment: 17 Coed
Affiliation or Control: Independent Non-Profit IRS Status: 501(c)3
Highest Offering: Master's
Accreditation: NH

01 President .... Mr. Aaron BETSKY
05 Dean .... Dr. Chris LASCH
08 Director of Libraries .... Ms. Elizabeth AL-HAZZAM DAWASARI
07 Dir Admissions/Student Services .... Ms. Sandra L. PIERRE
10 Chief Financial Officer .... Ms. Nicole HOLLENBECK
30 Director of Development .... Ms. Alexandra MOQUAY
39 Residence Academic Manager .... Vacant
06 Registrar .... Ms. Sandra L. PIERRE

Sessions College for Professional Design (Q)

51 W. Third Street, Suite E-301, Tempe AZ 85281
County: Maricopa FICE Identification: 042176
Unit ID: 475839
Telephone: (480) 212-1704 Carnegie Class: Spec 2-yr-A&S
FAX Number: (480) 212-1705 Calendar System: Semester
URL: www.sessions.edu
Established: 1997 Annual Undergrad Tuition & Fees: $8,700
Enrollment: 131 Coed
Affiliation or Control: Proprietary IRS Status: Proprietary
Highest Offering: Associate Degree
Accreditation: DEAC

00 CEO .... Ms. Doris GRANATOWSKI
01 President .... Mr. Gordon DRUMMOND
03 Executive Vice President .... Mr. Louis J. SCHILT
11 Chief Operating Officer .... Vacant
10 Chief Financial Officer/Bursar .... Ms. Carole Anne BAILO
32 Dir Student Services/Acad Pgms .... Mr. Tyler DRAKE

Sonoran Desert Institute (R)

1555 W University Drive, Suite 103, Tempe AZ 85281
County: Maricopa Identification: 667057
Unit ID: 488077
Telephone: (480) 314-2102 Carnegie Class: Spec 2-yr-Tech
FAX Number: (480) 314-2138 Calendar System: Semester
URL: www.sdi.edu
Established: 2000 Annual Undergrad Tuition & Fees: $9,440
Enrollment: 1,980 Coed
Affiliation or Control: Proprietary IRS Status: Proprietary
Highest Offering: Associate Degree
Accreditation: DEAC

01 President .... Traci LEE
03 Sr Vice President .... Wes LEMAY
05 Vice Pres Academic Affairs .... Mike OLSON

Southwest College of Naturopathic Medicine & Health Sciences (A)

2140 E Broadway Road, Tempe AZ 85282-1751

County: Maricopa | FICE Identification: 031070 | Unit ID: 420246
Telephone: (480) 858-9100 | Carnegie Class: Spec-4-yr-Other Health
FAX Number: (480) 858-9116 | Calendar System: Quarter
URL: www.scnm.edu
Established: 1993 | Annual Graduate Tuition & Fees: N/A
Enrollment: 360 | Coed
Affiliation or Control: Independent Non-Profit | IRS Status: 501(c)3
Highest Offering: First Professional Degree; No Undergraduates
Accreditation: NH, NATUR

- 01 President/Chief Executive Officer ... Paul A. MITTMAN
- 05 Dean of Academic Affairs ... Garrett THOMPSON
- 10 Vice Pres Finance & Administration ... David NEAL
- 32 Vice President Student Affairs ... Melissa WINQUIST
- 13 Chief Information Officer ... Vacant
- 04 Executive Asst to President ... Tracy LINDBERGH
- 06 Registrar ... Brian MCCARTHY
- 07 Director of Admissions ... Eve ADAMS
- 08 Head Librarian ... Sally HARVEY
- 103 Dir Workforce/Career Development ... Joanna HAGAN
- 108 Director Institutional Assessment ... Tammy ARAGON

Southwest Institute of Healing Arts (B)

1538 E. Southern Ave, Tempe AZ 85282

County: Maricopa | FICE Identification: 035933 | Unit ID: 442879
Telephone: (480) 994-9244 | Carnegie Class: Spec 2-yr-Health
FAX Number: (480) 994-3228 | Calendar System: Other
URL: www.swiha.edu
Established: 1992 | Annual Undergrad Tuition & Fees: N/A
Enrollment: 988 | Coed
Affiliation or Control: Proprietary | IRS Status: Proprietary
Highest Offering: Associate Degree
Accreditation: CNCE

- 01 President/Owner ... Mrs. K. C. MILLER
- 11 Chief Exec Director SWIHA ... Ms. Mary RITTER
- 05 Dean of Education ... Mr. Tom SHELLEY
- 32 Dean of Student Services ... Dr. Bradley BOUTE
- 10 Dir Finance & Human Res/Controller ... Ms. Salisha TAMANDL
- 35 Associate Dean of Student Services ... Mrs. Angelica DIAZ
- 106 Associate Dean Online Student Svcs ... Ms. Bernadett BILACH
- 37 Director of Financial Aid ... Ms. Amber IMES
- 06 Registrar ... Ms. Frannie WALSH

Southwest University of Visual Arts (C)

2525 N Country Club Road, Tucson AZ 85716-2505

County: Pima | FICE Identification: 024915 | Unit ID: 104188
Telephone: (520) 325-0123 | Carnegie Class: Spec-4-yr-Arts
FAX Number: (520) 325-5535 | Calendar System: Semester
URL: www.suva.edu
Established: 1983 | Annual Undergrad Tuition & Fees: $23,069
Enrollment: 129 | Coed
Affiliation or Control: Independent Non-Profit | IRS Status: 501(c)3
Highest Offering: Master's
Accreditation: NH

- 01 President/CEO ... Mrs. Sharmon WOODS
- 05 Chief Academic Officer ... Marvin WOODS
- 84 Dir Enrol Mgmt/Admiss/Stdnt Svcs ... Mr. Rob MAIRS
- 10 Chief Business Officer ... Ms. Julie MAIRS
- 06 Registrar ... Ms. Crystal ROCHE

Tohono O'odham Community College (D)

PO Box 3129, Sells AZ 85634-3129

County: Pima | FICE Identification: 037844 | Unit ID: 442781
Telephone: (520) 383-8401 | Carnegie Class: Tribal
FAX Number: (520) 383-0029 | Calendar System: Semester
URL: www.tocc.edu
Established: 1998 | Annual Undergrad Tuition & Fees: $932
Enrollment: 400 | Coed
Affiliation or Control: Tribal Control | IRS Status: 501(c)3
Highest Offering: Associate Degree
Accreditation: NH

- 01 President ... Dr. Paul ROBERTSON
- 05 Academic Dean ... Mr. Mario MONTES-HELU
- 10 Int Vice Pres of Finance ... Ms. Joann MIGUEL
- 32 Dean of Student Services ... Ms. Naomi TOM
- 75 Acad Chair Occupational Pgms ... Mr. George MIGUEL
- 97 Acad Chair for General Education ... Dr. Mario MONTES-HELU
- 07 Director of Admissions/Records ... Mr. Leslie LUNA
- 08 College Librarian ... Ms. Elaine CUBBINS
- 37 Financial Aid Officer ... Ms. Novia JAMES
- 88 Director Project NATIVE ... Ms. Camille MARTINEZ-YADEN
- 88 Director Project NATIVE ... Dr. Sandra LUCAS
- 30 Director of Fundraising ... Ms. Andrea AHMED
- 15 Director Human Resources ... Ms. Stacy OWSLEY
- 09 Institutional Effectiveness Dir ... Mr. Blaine ANTONE

Universal Technical Institute (E)

10695 W Pierce Street, Avondale AZ 85323-7946

County: Maricopa | FICE Identification: 008221 | Unit ID: 106041
Telephone: (623) 245-4600 | Carnegie Class: Spec 2-yr-Tech
FAX Number: (623) 245-4601 | Calendar System: Other
URL: www.uti.edu
Established: 1965 | Annual Undergrad Tuition & Fees: N/A
Enrollment: 1,860 | Coed
Affiliation or Control: Proprietary | IRS Status: Proprietary
Highest Offering: Associate Degree
Accreditation: ACCSC

- 01 Campus President ... Mr. Adrian CORDOVA
- 05 Director of Education ... Mr. Patrick BENNETT
- 32 Director of Student Services ... Ms. Lindsay KINGSLEY
- 10 Director of Campus Accounting ... Mrs. Gayle PARSONS
- 07 Admissions Director ... Mr. Adam HELLER
- 36 Director of Graduate Employment ... Ms. Cheryl RADKE
- 37 Director of Financial Aid ... Ms. Terri MEIXSEL-CORDERO
- 18 Maintenance Director ... Mr. George MICKENS

University of Advancing Technology (F)

2625 W Baseline Road, Tempe AZ 85283-1056

County: Maricopa | FICE Identification: 025590 | Unit ID: 363934
Telephone: (602) 383-8228 | Carnegie Class: Spec-4-yr-Other Tech
FAX Number: (602) 383-8250 | Calendar System: Other
URL: www.uat.edu
Established: 1983 | Annual Undergrad Tuition & Fees: $16,598
Enrollment: 789 | Coed
Affiliation or Control: Proprietary | IRS Status: Proprietary
Highest Offering: Master's
Accreditation: NH

- 01 President ... Mr. Jason PISTILLO
- 05 Provost and Dean ... Mr. Dave BOLMAN
- 100 Chief of Staff ... Ms. Valerie CIMAROSSA
- 11 Chief of Operations ... Mrs. Karla ARAGON-JOYCE
- 32 Director of Student Services ... Ms. Brandi BEALS
- 07 Director of Admissions ... Ms. Megan BENSON
- 10 Senior Controller ... Ms. Jodi ROBINSON
- 113 Bursar ... Ms. Renee GRAUBERGER
- 06 Registrar ... Mr. Tyler WALLING
- 04 Executive Asst to the President ... Ms. Taylor NAKAKIHARA
- 37 Director Student Financial Aid ... Ms. Elizabeth HENRY
- 88 Administrative Assistant ... Ms. Eva FROHNA

University of Arizona (G)

1200 E University Boulevard, Tucson AZ 85721-0001

County: Pima | FICE Identification: 001083 | Unit ID: 104179
Telephone: (520) 621-2211 | Carnegie Class: DU-Highest
FAX Number: (520) 621-9323 | Calendar System: Semester
URL: www.arizona.edu
Established: 1885 | Annual Undergrad Tuition & Fees (In-State): $12,467
Enrollment: 43,751 | Coed
Affiliation or Control: State | IRS Status: 501(c)3
Highest Offering: Doctorate
Accreditation: NH, ANEST, ART, AUD, CACREP, CAMPEP, CEA, CLPSY, DANCE, DIETD, IPSY, JOUR, LAW, LIB, LSAR, MED, MUS, NURSE, PCSAS, PERF, PH, PHAR, PLNG, SCPSY, SP, SPAA, THEA

- 01 President ... Dr. Robert C. ROBBINS
- 05 Actg SVP for Acad Affairs & Provost ... Dr. Jeffrey B. GOLDBERG
- 10 Sr VP Business Affairs & CFO ... Ms. Lisa RULNEY
- 17 Sr VP Health Sciences ... Dr. Michael DAKE
- 32 VP Stdnt Affs/Enr Mgmt/Dean Admiss ... Dr. Kasandra K. URQUIDEZ
- 88 VP Strategic Initiatives ... Dr. Jane HUNTER
- 43 SVP Legal Affairs/General Counsel ... Dr. Laura T. JOHNSON
- 88 VP Global Initiatives ... Dr. Brent WHITE
- 46 VP Innovation & Strategy ... Dr. Joaquin RUIZ
- 21 VP University Planning/Design/Ops ... Mr. Robert R. SMITH
- 29 VP Alumni Relations ... Ms. Melinda W. BURKE
- 15 VP Business Affairs/Human Resources ... Dr. Allison M. VAILLANCOURT
- 88 VP Digital Learning/Student Engmnt ... Vacant
- 27 VP Communications ... Mr. Chris W. SIGURDSON
- 47 VP/Dean Agri/Life & Veterinary Sci ... Dr. Shane C. BURGESS
- 20 Sr Vice Provost Academic Affairs ... Dr. Gail D. BURD
- 86 Sr AVP Legistration/Cmty Relations ... Vacant
- 101 SVP/Sr Assoc to the Pres/Sec Univ ... Dr. Jon DUDAS
- 88 Assoc VP for Research ... Ms. Caroline M. GARCIA
- 88 Director Bio5 Institute ... Dr. Jennifer K. BARTON
- 76 AVP Health Sci/Community Engagement ... Dr. Sally J. REEL
- 88 Assoc VP Precision Health Sciences ... Vacant
- 23 Assoc VP Clinical Affairs ... Dr. Ann MATHIAS
- 09 Assoc VP Institutional Analysis ... Mr. James S. FLORIAN
- 88 Assoc VP Tech Parks Arizona ... Ms. Carol A. STEWART
- 108 Assoc Vice Prov Instruct/Assessment ... Dr. Lisa K. ELFRING
- 88 Exec Dir Population Health Sciences ... Ms. Elizabeth CALHOUN
- 88 Assoc VP Research ... Mr. Neal R. ARMSTRONG
- 88 Interim Assoc VP Financial Services ... Mr. Duc D. MA
- 13 CIO/Director UITS ... Mr. Barry BRUMMUND
- 21 Sr Asst VP Finance Administration ... Ms. Marilyn TAYLOR
- 35 Asst VP Student Affs/Enroll Mgmt ... Mr. Joel S. HAUFF
- 18 Asst VP Plng/Design & Construction ... Mr. Peter DOURLEIN
- 88 Asst VP Tribal Relations ... Ms. Karen F. BEGAY
- 88 Asst VP Health Sciences/Pub Affairs ... Mr. George D. HUMPHREY
- 114 Sr Assoc VP/Chief Budget Officer ... Ms. Kathryn E. WHISMAN
- 18 Asst VP Facilities Management ... Mr. Christopher M. KOPACH
- 19 Asst VP Risk Management/Safety ... Mr. Steven C. HOLLAND
- 88 Asst VP Govt Affairs ... Mr. Ethan R. ORR
- 83 Dean Social/Behavioral Science ... Dr. John P. JONES
- 35 Vice Prov Campus Life/Dean Students ... Ms. Kendal H. WASHINGTON WHITE
- 92 Dean Honors College ... Dr. Terry L. HUNT
- 48 Dean Col Arch/Plng/Landscape Arch ... Dr. Shane C. BURGESS
- 53 Dean Education ... Dr. Bruce JOHNSON
- 58 Dean Graduate College ... Dr. Andrew H. CARNIE
- 61 Dean James E Rogers College of Law ... Dr. Marc L. MILLER
- 66 Interim Dean College of Nursing ... Dr. Ida M. MOORE
- 12 Interim Dean UA South ... Dr. Melody J. BUCKNER
- 79 Dean College of Humanities ... Dr. Alain-Philippe DURAND
- 57 Dean Fine Arts ... Dr. Andrew SCHULZ
- 54 Dean College of Engineering ... Dr. David HAHN
- 50 Dean Eller College of Management ... Dr. Paulo GOES
- 69 Dean Public Health ... Dr. Iman A. HAKIM
- 63 Dean College of Med-Phoenix Campus ... Dr. Guy L. REED
- 81 Dean College of Optical Sciences ... Dr. Thomas L. KOCH
- 67 Dean Pharmacy ... Dr. Rick SCHNELLMAN
- 22 Dir Office of Institutional Equity ... Ms. Kris KLOTZ
- 40 Int AVP Business Affs/Auxillary Svc ... Ms. Debby L. SHIVELY
- 88 Co-Int Exec Director Campus Health ... Dr. David B. SALAFSKY
- 88 Co-Int Exec Director Campus Health ... Dr. Michael STILSON
- 88 Int Exec Dir Analytics/Inst Rsrch ... Mr. Ravneet CHADHA
- 96 Dir Procurement & Contract Services ... Mr. Edward D. NASSER
- 25 Director Sponsored Proj/Services ... Mr. Paul SANDOVAL

University of Arizona Phoenix Biomedical Campus (H)

550 E Van Buren Street, Phoenix AZ 85004

Telephone: (602) 827-2002 | Identification: 770023
Accreditation: &NH, MED, PHAR

University of Arizona South (I)

1140 N Colombo Avenue, Sierra Vista AZ 85635

Telephone: (520) 458-8278 | Identification: 770024
Accreditation: &NH

University of Phoenix (J)

4025 S Riverpoint Pkwy, Phoenix AZ 85040

County: Maricopa | FICE Identification: 020988 | Unit ID: 484613
Telephone: (480) 557-2000 | Carnegie Class: DU-Mod
FAX Number: N/A | Calendar System: Other
URL: www.phoenix.edu
Established: 1976 | Annual Undergrad Tuition & Fees: $9,552
Enrollment: 103,975 | Coed
Affiliation or Control: Proprietary | IRS Status: Proprietary
Highest Offering: Doctorate
Accreditation: NH, ACBSP, CACREP, NURSE, @SW

- 01 President University of Phoenix ... Mr. Peter COHEN
- 04 Assistant to the President ... Ms. Cindy WHIPPO
- 05 Chief Academic Officer/Provost ... Dr. John WOODS
- 10 Chief Financial Officer ... Mr. Chris LYNNE
- 45 Chief Strategy & Customer Officer ... Ms. Ruth VELORIA
- 11 Chief Operating Officer ... Mr. Raghu KRISHNAIAH
- 26 SVP/Chief Marketing Officer ... Ms. Joan BLACKWOOD
- 13 Chief Information Officer ... Mr. Jamie SMITH
- 15 Chief Human Resources ... Ms. Cheryl NAUMANN
- 108 Vice Provost Inst Effectiveness ... Dr. Kathleen SCHNIER
- 20 Vice Provost Sch of Advanced Stds ... Dr. Hinrich EYLERS
- 20 Vice Provost Colleges ... Ms. Doris SAVRON
- 84 SVP Enrollment Services ... Mr. Brett ROMNEY
- 21 VP Financial Services ... Mr. Bronson LEDBETTER
- 43 SVP & General Counsel ... Mr. Dan LITTERAL
- 06 Registrar ... Ms. Audra MCQUARIE
- 19 Director Security/Safety ... Mr. Steve LINDSEY

University of Phoenix Southern Arizona Campus (K)

300 S Craycroft Road, Tucson AZ 85711-4574

Telephone: (520) 881-6512 | Identification: 770236
Accreditation: &NH, ACBSP

† No longer accepting campus-based students.

West Coast Ultrasound Institute (L)

4250 E Camelback Road, Bld K - 190, Phoenix AZ 85018

Telephone: (602) 954-3834 | Identification: 770550
Accreditation: ACCSC

† Branch campus of West Coast Ultrasound Institute, Beverly Hills, CA

Yavapai College (M)

1100 E Sheldon Street, Prescott AZ 86301-3297

County: Yavapai | FICE Identification: 001079 | Unit ID: 106148

Telephone: (928) 445-7300 Carnegie Class: Assoc/MT-VT-High Non
FAX Number: (928) 777-3154 Calendar System: Semester
URL: www.yc.edu
Established: 1966 Annual Undergrad Tuition & Fees (In-District): $2,360
Enrollment: 7,370 Coed
Affiliation or Control: Local IRS Status: 501(c)3
Highest Offering: Associate Degree
Accreditation: NH, ADNUR, EMT, IFSAC, RAD

01 President Dr. Lisa RHINE
05 VP Instruction/Stdnt Dev Dr. Ron LISS
10 Vice Pres Finance/Admin Svcs Dr. Clint EWELL
26 VP Community Relations Mr. Rodney JENKINS
20 Dean for Comp Tech & Instr Support Ms. Stacey HILTON
12 Exec Dean Verde Valley Campus Dr. James PEREY
75 Dean Career Technical Education Mr. John MORGAN
66 Dean Sci/Health/Public Safety Mr. Scott FARNSWORTH
79 Dir of Performing Arts Center Dr. Craig RALSTON
32 Assoc VP for Student Development Ms. Tania SHELDAHL
27 Director of Marketing/Public Info Mr. Tyler RUMSEY
35 Assoc Dean Student Devel Ms. Diana DOWLING
09 Dir Inst Effectiveness & Research Mr. Tom HUGHES
15 Director for Human Resources Ms. Emily WEINACKER
19 Chief of Police Mr. Jerald MONAHAN
21 Dir of Business Svcs & Controller Mr. Frank D'ANGELO
18 Director for Facilities Mr. David LAURENCE
13 Chief Information Officer Mr. Patrick BURNS
06 Registrar Ms. Sheila JARRELL
96 Director of Purchasing Mr. Ryan BOUWHUIS
04 Administrative Asst to President Vacant
07 Director of Admissions/Enr Mgmt Ms. Heather MULCAIRE
29 Director of Alumni Affairs Ms. Kammie KOBYELSKI
30 Chief Development Officer Mr. Paul KIRCHGRABER
37 Director Student Financial Aid Mr. Raymond CEO

Yavapai College Verde Valley Campus (A)

601 Black Hills Drive, Clarkdale AZ 86324
Telephone: (928) 634-7501 Identification: 770029
Accreditation: &NH

ARKANSAS

Arkansas Baptist College (B)

1600 Dr. Martin Luther King Drive,
Little Rock AR 72202-6099
County: Pulaski FICE Identification: 001087
Unit ID: 106306
Telephone: (501) 420-1200 Carnegie Class: Bac/Assoc-Mixed
FAX Number: (501) 414-0861 Calendar System: Semester
URL: www.arkansasbaptist.edu
Established: 1884 Annual Undergrad Tuition & Fees: $8,760
Enrollment: 593 Coed
Affiliation or Control: Baptist IRS Status: 501(c)3
Highest Offering: Baccalaureate
Accreditation: #NH

01 Interim President Ms. Regina FAVORS
05 Vice President of Academic Affairs Dr. Tracey MOORE
32 VP Student Affs & Enrollment Mgmt Mr. Brian MILLER
04 President's Executive Assistant Ms. Patsy BIGGS
10 Chief Finance Officer Ms. Rachel KREMER
11 Executive Director of Operations Vacant
37 VP Div of Student Financial Aid Dr. Carlos CLARK
100 Chief of Staff Vacant
09 Dir of IR/Internal Audit Control Dr. Jerelyn L. DUNCAN
88 Ombudsman Dr. Vicki WILLIAMS
08 Director of Library/Media Services Ms. Jacqueline ELDRIDGE
26 Marketing Coord & Webmaster Mr. Kristofer ANDERSON
19 Interim Chief of Campus Safety Ms. Shae SMITH
18 Director Maintenance Vacant
06 Registrar Ms. Delores VOLIBER
13 Director of Information Technology Mr. Trey WHITE
15 Human Resources Director Mrs. Pamela BRIMLEY
30 Director of Development Vacant
39 Director Resident Life/Housing Mr. Marlow ROCKWELL

Arkansas College of Osteopathic Medicine (C)

7000 Chad Colley Boulevard, Fort Smith AR 72916
County: Sebastion FICE Identification: 042568
Unit ID: 488527
Telephone: (479) 308-2200 Carnegie Class: Not Classified
FAX Number: (479) 308-2766 Calendar System: Semester
URL: arcomed.org
Established: 2017 Annual Graduate Tuition & Fees: N/A
Enrollment: 162 Coed
Affiliation or Control: Independent Non-Profit IRS Status: 501(c)3
Highest Offering: Doctorate; No Undergraduates
Accreditation: @OSTEO

01 CEO Kyle D. PARKER
02 President Brian G. KIM
05 Provost & Exec VP AA Dr. Ray E. STOWERS
20 Associate VP and Provost Dr. Elizabeth MCCLAIN
100 Senior Executive Assistant Dr. Benny L. GOODEN
10 VP & CFO Dennis BAUER
45 VP & COO Thomas H. WEBB, JR.
13 VP & CTO Jonathan W. HATAWAY
63 Dean DO Program Dr. Rance MCCLAIN
63 Associate Dean Clinical Medicine Vacant
63 Assoc Dean Biomedicine Dr. Ross LONGLEY
63 Asst Dean Academic Affairs Dr. Melissa EFURD
32 Assistant Dean Student Affairs Laurel MCINTOSH
58 Dean Physical Therapy Dr. Clayton HOLMES
58 Dean Occupational Therapy Dr. Jennifer MOORE
58 Dean Physicians Assistant Dr. Henry LEMKE
58 Program Dir MSB Dr. Kenneth HENSLEY
108 Director of Data Analytics Dr. Ashley GERHARDSON
08 Director of Library Services Elizabeth WRIGHT
38 Director of Mental Wellness Vacant
30 Director of Development Jackie KRUTSCH
19 Chief of Police Levi RISLEY
18 Director of Building & Grounds Eric BURNS
35 Director of Student Services Amanda EVENSON
06 Registrar Shawna MASON
37 Director of Financial Aid Glenna GILLIAM
07 Director of Admissions Kelly DEWITT
121 Director of Academic Support Debbie FINDLAY
15 Director of Human Resources Barbara JETTON
16 Human Resources Manager Sheila BENTLEY
26 Executive Director of Communication Susan DEVERO
96 Director of Procurement Diana JORDAN

Arkansas Northeastern College (D)

2501 S Division Street, Blytheville AR 72315-5111
County: Mississippi FICE Identification: 012860
Unit ID: 107327
Telephone: (870) 762-1020 Carnegie Class: Assoc/HVT-High Non
FAX Number: (870) 763-3704 Calendar System: Semester
URL: www.anc.edu
Established: 1974 Annual Undergrad Tuition & Fees (In-District): $2,318
Enrollment: 1,474 Coed
Affiliation or Control: State/Local IRS Status: 501(c)3
Highest Offering: Associate Degree
Accreditation: NH, DA, EMT

01 President Dr. James SHEMWELL
05 Executive Vice President/CAO Mrs. June WALTERS
10 Vice President for Administration Mr. Don RAY
88 Vice Pres for College Readiness Mrs. Sherri BENNETT
13 Vice President Student Affairs/IT Mr. James W. MCCLAIN
30 Assoc VP for Dev/College Relations Ms. Rachel GIFFORD
09 Dean Effectiveness/Assess/Planning Mrs. Robin SINGLETON
88 Assoc VP for Economic Development Mr. Gene BENNETT
26 Assoc VP Community Relations Dr. Blanchie HUNT
21 Assoc Vice President for Finance Ms. Pacey BOWENS
66 Dean Nursing/Allied Hlth/PE/Rec Mrs. Brenda HOLIFIELD
49 Dean for Arts and Sciences Mrs. Deanita HICKS
32 Director for Student Services Mrs. Courtney FISHER
31 Community Education Specialist Ms. Mary Ann GARREN
08 Director of College Library/AV Ms. Karen ELLIS
36 Director ACE Advising Center Dr. Bridget SHEMWELL
37 Director Financial Aid Mrs. Melinda WALKER
72 Associate Dean MITS Mrs. Ruby MEADOR
21 Controller Ms. Kim MARSHALL
15 Human Resources & ADA Coordinator Mrs. Tabatha HAMPTON
90 Director Academic Tech Services Mr. James ODOM
18 Director Physical Plant and Grounds Mr. Scott CREECY
88 Director Talent Search/Educ Opp Ctr Mrs. Tonya HARRIS
35 Director Student Support Services Ms. Lisa MCGHEE
04 Assistant to Board/President Mrs. Marlene BANKS
06 Registrar Mrs. Rosemary LOWE
27 Media Director Mr. James HARTLEY

*Arkansas State University System (E)

501 Woodlane Drive, Suite 600, Little Rock AR 72201
County: Pulaski Identification: 666187
Telephone: (501) 660-1000 Carnegie Class: N/A
FAX Number: (501) 660-1010
URL: www.asusystem.edu

01 President Dr. Charles L. WELCH
04 Exec Assistant to the President Ms. Pam KAIL
10 Executive Vice President Ms. Julie BATES
86 Vice Pres Governmental Relations Mr. Shane BROADWAY
45 Vice Pres Strategic Comm/Econ Dev Mr. Jeff HANKINS
43 Legal Counsel Mr. Brad PHELPS
09 VP for Strategic Research Mr. Eric ATCHISON
102 President ASU System Foundation Mr. Philip JACKSON
116 Internal Auditor Ms. Jo LUNBECK

*Arkansas State University-Beebe (F)

PO Box 1000, Beebe AR 72012-1000
County: White FICE Identification: 001091
Unit ID: 106449
Telephone: (501) 882-3600 Carnegie Class: Assoc/MT-VT-Mix Trad/Non
FAX Number: (501) 882-8970 Calendar System: Semester
URL: www.asub.edu
Established: 1927 Annual Undergrad Tuition & Fees (In-State): $2,880
Enrollment: 3,739 Coed
Affiliation or Control: State IRS Status: 501(c)3
Highest Offering: Associate Degree
Accreditation: NH, EMT, MLTAD, NAIT

02 Chancellor Dr. Jennifer METHVIN
100 Executive Assistant to Chancellor Ms. Pam JONES
05 Vice Chanc of Academics/CAO Dr. Jason GOODNER
12 Campus Ops Mgr ASU-Heber Springs Mr. Cody MCMICHAEL
12 Campus Operations Mgr ASU-Searcy Ms. LaShanda OWENS
10 Vice Chanc Finance/Admin/CFO Dr. Roger MOORE
13 VC Information Technology Services Mr. Leon LEWIS, JR.
32 Assoc Vice Chanc Student Services Dr. Arch JONES
111 Assoc VC Advancement Ms. Rose Mary JACKSON
15 Assoc VC Human Resources Ms. Susan A. COLLIE
14 Assoc VP ITS and Assessment Ms. Janet LILES
35 Assoc VC/Dean Student Affairs Dr. David M. MAYES
26 Exec Director of Marketing/PR Mr. Keith MOORE
06 University Registrar Mr. Tyler BITTLE
08 Library Director Ms. Tracy D. SMITH
19 Police Commander Mr. James J. MARTIN
18 Director of Physical Plant Mr. Jerry L. THOMPSON
37 Director Student Financial Aid Ms. Rachel HALL
09 Director of Institutional Research Ms. Bonnie SMYTH-MCGAHA
21 Controller Ms. Sharon A. BEEN
72 Director Advanced Tech/Allied Hlth Mr. Michael TROOP
106 Director of Distance Learning Ms. Rhonda DURHAM
96 Executive Director Procurement Ms. Robin LANCASTER
12 Dir ASU-Beebe Degree Ctr at LRAFB Vacant
07 Director of Admissions Vacant
35 Manager of Campus Relations Mr. Andy ISOM
105 Webmaster Mr. Rikky L. FREE
88 Coord Concurrent Enrollment Ms. Kristine PENIX
24 Learning Center Coordinator Ms. Kayla DEAN

*Arkansas State University-Jonesboro (G)

PO Box 600, State University AR 72467
County: Craighead FICE Identification: 001090
Unit ID: 106458
Telephone: (870) 972-2100 Carnegie Class: DU-Higher
FAX Number: (870) 972-3465 Calendar System: Semester
URL: www.astate.edu
Established: 1909 Annual Undergrad Tuition & Fees (In-State): $8,607
Enrollment: 13,930 Coed
Affiliation or Control: State IRS Status: 501(c)3
Highest Offering: Doctorate
Accreditation: NH, ADNUR, ANEST, ART, CACREP, CAEP, CAEPN, CEA, COSMA, #DIETC, DMS, JOUR, MLTAD, MT, MUS, NUR, OT, OTA, PTA, PTAA, RAD, RADMAG, RTT, SP, SPAA, SW, THEA

02 Chancellor Dr. Kelly DAMPHOUSSE
05 Provost & Exec VC Acad Affairs Dr. Alan UTTER
10 Exec VC Finance & Administration Dr. Len T. FREY
84 Vice Chancellor Enrollment Mgmt Dr. Bryan TERRY
111 Vice Chancellor Univ Advancement Dr. Jason PENRY
28 VC for Diversity and Community Dr. Maurice GIPSON
41 VC of Intercollegiate Athletics Mr. Terry MOHAJIR
20 Sr Assoc Vice Chancellor AAR Dr. Karen WHEELER
21 Assoc Vice Chancellor Finance Dr. Russ HANNAH
114 Asst Vice Chanc Budget Ms. Donna MCMILLIN
15 Asst VC Human Resources Ms. Lori WINN
88 Special Asst to the Chancellor Dr. Lonnie R. WILLIAMS
46 Vice Provost for Research & Tech Dr. Thomas RISCH
32 Asst Vice Chanc Student Affairs Dr. Craig JOHNSON
13 Asst Vice Chanc/CIO Mr. Henry TORRES
18 Asst Vice Chancellor Facilities Mr. David HANDWORK
84 Asst Vice Chanc Enrollment Services Mr. Terry FINNEY
108 Asst VC Institutional Effectiveness Vacant
85 Exec Dir Global Engage/Outreach Dr. Thilla SIVAKUMARAN
06 Dir Admissions/Records/Registration Ms. Tracy FINCH
07 Admissions/Records/Registration Vacant
39 Director of Residence Life Vacant
35 Dean of Students Ms. Martha SPACK
19 Chief University Police Mr. Randy MARTIN
22 Director of Disability Services Dr. Jenifer RICE-MASON
36 Director Career Services Ms. Tiffany JOHNSON
38 Director Counseling Center Dr. Phil HESTAND
23 Director Student Health Center Ms. Victoria WILLIAMS
29 Exec Dir Alumni Relations Ms. Lindsay BURNETT
26 Assoc VC University Marketing/Comm Dr. Bill SMITH
27 Director of Media Relations/Comm Mr. Tom MOORE
88 Dir of Digital Creative Services Mr. Todd CLARK
96 Dir Procurement & Travel Svcs Ms. Carol BARNHILL
04 Admin Assistant to the Chancellor Ms. Julie WYATT
08 Dir Library Mr. Jeff BAILEY
47 Interim Dean College Agri/Tech Dr. Donald KENNEDY
81 Dean College Sciences & Math Dr. Lynn BOYD
50 Interim Dean College of Business Dr. Jim WASHAM
53 Dean Col of Educ & Behavioral Sci Dr. Mary Jane BRADLEY
60 Dean Liberal Arts & Communication Dr. Carl CATES
66 Dean College of Nursing Health Prof Dr. Susan N. HANRAHAN
88 Assoc VC Undergraduate Studies Dr. Jill SIMONS
57 Dean Fine Arts Vacant
92 Director of The Honors College Ms. Rebecca OLIVER
54 Dean College of Engineering Dr. Abhijit BHATTACHARYYA

*Arkansas State University Mid-South (H)

2000 W Broadway Avenue,
West Memphis AR 72301-3829
County: Crittenden FICE Identification: 023482
Unit ID: 107318
Telephone: (870) 733-6722 Carnegie Class: Assoc/HT-High Non
FAX Number: (870) 733-6799 Calendar System: Semester
URL: www.asumidsouth.edu
Established: 1992 Annual Undergrad Tuition & Fees (In-District): $2,674
Enrollment: 1,561 Coed

Affiliation or Control: State/Local IRS Status: 501(c)3
Highest Offering: Associate Degree
Accreditation: NH, #COARC

02 Chancellor ..... Dr. Debra WEST
05 Vice Chanc Learning/Instruction ..... Dr. Debbie THOMAS
10 Vice Chanc Finance & Administration ..... Ms. JaNan ABERNATHY
111 Vice Chanc Inst Advancement ..... Ms. Diane HAMPTON
32 Vice Chanc Student Affairs ..... Mr. Jeremy REECE
103 Interim AVC Workforce Education ..... Dr. Callie DUNAVIN
21 AVC Finance ..... Ms. Karyn WEAVER
20 AVC Learning/Instruction ..... Ms. Roshell COLEMAN
37 Interim Director of Financial Aid ..... Ms. Crystal BURGER
08 Director of Library/Media Center ..... Ms. Rene JONES
06 Registrar ..... Ms. Leslie ANDERSON
15 Director of Human Resources ..... Ms. Jackie LEECH
18 Director Facilities/Physical Plant ..... Mr. Ed COOK
84 AVC Enrollment Management ..... Mr. John EASLEY
13 AVC for Information Systems Tech ..... Mr. Ernesto MUNIZ
09 AVC Institutional Research ..... Dr. Michael LEJMAN
121 Dir of Learning Success Center ..... Mr. Brice JAMES-BATTELLE
04 Administrative Asst to Chancellor ..... Ms. Emilee SIDES
19 Director Public Safety ..... Mr. Ross PROCTOR
25 Chief Contracts/Grants Admin ..... Ms. Sherri REID
41 Athletic Director ..... Mr. Chris PARKER
30 Director of Development ..... Ms. Debbie YEN
96 Business Manager ..... Ms. Wendy CRAWFORD

*Arkansas State University-Mountain Home (A)

1600 S College Street, Mountain Home AR 72653-5326
County: Baxter Identification: 666311
Unit ID: 420538
Telephone: (870) 508-6100 Carnegie Class: Assoc/MT-VT-Mix Trad/Non
FAX Number: (870) 508-6287 Calendar System: Semester
URL: www.asumh.edu
Established: 1995 Annual Undergrad Tuition & Fees (In-District): $2,856
Enrollment: 1,410 Coed
Affiliation or Control: State/Local IRS Status: 501(c)3
Highest Offering: Associate Degree
Accreditation: NH, EMT, #FUSER, PTAA

02 Chancellor ..... Dr. Robin MYERS
05 Provost/Vice Chanc Academic Affairs ..... Vacant
10 Vice Chanc Administrative Affairs ..... Ms. Laura YARBROUGH
18 Chief Facilities/Physical Plant ..... Mr. Nickey L. ROBBINS
26 Director Comm & Inst Advancement ..... Mrs. Christy C. KEIRN
32 Director Student Affairs ..... Mr. William KIMBRIEL
37 Director Student Financial Aid ..... Mr. Clay BERRY
08 Director of Library ..... Ms. Tina BRADLEY
09 Dir of Inst Research/Effectiveness ..... Mr. David CULLIPHER
07 Admissions Coordinator ..... Mr. Christopher CONSTANTINE

*Arkansas State University-Newport (B)

7648 Victory Boulevard, Newport AR 72112-8912
County: Jackson Identification: 666153
Unit ID: 440402
Telephone: (870) 512-7800 Carnegie Class: Assoc/MT-VT-High Non
FAX Number: (870) 512-7807 Calendar System: Semester
URL: www.asun.edu
Established: 2001 Annual Undergrad Tuition & Fees (In-State): $2,760
Enrollment: 2,512 Coed
Affiliation or Control: State IRS Status: Exempt
Highest Offering: Associate Degree
Accreditation: NH, SURGT

02 Chancellor ..... Dr. Sandra MASSEY
04 Exec Assistant to the Chancellor ..... Ms. Kristen SMITH
05 Vice Chancellor Academic Affairs ..... Dr. Holly SMITH
10 Vice Chancellor Finance & Admin ..... Mr. Adam ADAIR
32 Vice Chancellor Student Affairs ..... Dr. Ashley BUCHMAN
103 Vice Chancellor Econ/Workforce Dev ..... Mr. Jeff BOOKOUT
30 Dean for Community Engagement ..... Mr. Ike WHEELER
121 Dean of Student Success/Registrar ..... Dr. Allen MOONEYHAN
72 Dean for Applied Science ..... Mr. Robert BURGESS
97 Dean for General Education ..... Mr. Joseph CAMPBELL
84 Dean of Enrollment Services ..... Ms. Candace GROSS
124 Dean of Student Development ..... Ms. Veronica MANNING
13 Director of IT Services ..... Ms. Tamya STALLINGS
15 Director Human Resources ..... Ms. Sara MOSS
06 Assistant Registrar ..... Ms. Phyllis WORTHINGTON
18 Director of Physical Plant ..... Mr. Brian PETTIE
21 Controller ..... Ms. Monika PHILLIPS
37 Director Financial Aid ..... Ms. Stacey DUNLAP
88 Dean of Compliance/Accountability ..... Ms. Kimberly LONG
08 Director of Library Services ..... Vacant
09 Director of Institutional Research ..... Ms. Christy MANN
19 Chief of Police ..... Mr. Johnathan TUBBS
96 Director of Procurement ..... Ms. Lee WEBB
66 Dean of Nursing/Allied Health ..... Vacant
36 Director of Career Pathways ..... Ms. Cheryl CROSS
75 Director of Adult Education ..... Vacant
26 Director Marketing & Communications ..... Mr. Jeremy SHIRLEY
111 Advancement Officer ..... Ms. Teriann TURNER

Arkansas Tech University (C)

1509 North Boulder Avenue, Russellville AR 72801-2222
County: Pope FICE Identification: 001089
Unit ID: 106467
Telephone: (479) 968-0389 Carnegie Class: Masters/L
FAX Number: (479) 964-0522 Calendar System: Semester
URL: www.atu.edu
Established: 1909 Annual Undergrad Tuition & Fees (In-State): $7,254
Enrollment: 11,830 Coed
Affiliation or Control: State IRS Status: 501(c)3
Highest Offering: Doctorate
Accreditation: NH, ART, CAEPN, CAHIIM, CEA, MAC, MUS, NRPA, NUR, PTAA

01 President ..... Dr. Robin E. BOWEN
10 Vice Pres Administration/Finance ..... Ms. Bernadette HINKLE
05 Vice Pres Academic Affairs ..... Dr. Barbara J. JOHNSON
32 VP Student Affairs ..... Dr. Keegan NICHOLS
111 Interim Vice President Advancement ..... Mr. Bryan FISHER
84 Vice Pres Enrollment Management ..... Dr. C. Blake BEDSOLE
12 Chancellor Ozark Campus ..... Mr. Bruce SIKES
43 Associate VP & Counsel to President . Mr. Thomas PENNINGTON
20 Assoc Vice Pres Academic Affairs ..... Vacant
88 Assoc VP University Initiatives ..... Vacant
110 Associate VP for Development ..... Mr. Bryan FISHER
121 Assistant VP for Student Success ..... Vacant
35 Assoc VP Student Affairs/Title IX ..... Ms. Amy PENNINGTON
35 Chief Student Officer Ozark Campus ..... Mr. Richard HARRIS
05 Chief Academic Officer Ozark Campus ..... Ms. Sheila JACOBS
100 Chief of Staff ..... Dr. Mary GUNTER
06 Registrar ..... Ms. Tammy WEAVER
21 Controller ..... Ms. Suzanne MCCALL
08 Director of Library ..... Mr. Brent ETZEL
86 Director Government Relations ..... Ms. Ashley GOLLEHER
114 Director of Budget ..... Ms. Sandra CHEFFER
09 Director of Institutional Research ..... Mr. Wyatt WATSON
13 Director Information Systems ..... Mr. Ken WESTER
37 Director of Student Accounts ..... Ms. Angela CROW
15 Director of Human Resources ..... Mr. Robert FREEMAN
37 Director Student Financial Aid ..... Ms. Niki SCHWARTZ
29 Director Alumni Relations ..... Mr. Kelly DAVIS
85 Assoc Dean International Students ..... Mr. Yasushi ONODERA
18 Director of Physical Plant Services ..... Mr. Brian LASEY
96 Director of Purchasing ..... Ms. Jessica HOLLOWAY
92 Director of Honors Program ..... Dr. Jan JENKINS
22 Director of Affirmative Action ..... Mr. Robert FREEMAN
108 Dir Assessment/Inst Effectiveness ..... Dr. Christine AUSTIN
105 Director Web Strategies/Operations ..... Mr. Michael STOKER
19 Director Public Safety ..... Mr. Josh MCMILLIAN
26 Director of University Relations ..... Mr. Sam STRASNER
36 Director of Career Services ..... Ms. Amanda JOHNSON
44 Director Annual Giving Programs ..... Ms. Caroline VINING
07 Director of Admissions ..... Ms. Jessica BROCK
41 Athletic Director ..... Mr. Steve MULLINS
88 Director of Prospect Research ..... Ms. Pam COOPER
112 Director of Gift Planning ..... Ms. Peggy MITCHELL-FERRIS
53 Dean College of Education ..... Dr. Linda BEAN
49 Int Dean Col Arts & Humanities ..... Dr. Wayne POWELL
50 Dean of College of Business ..... Dr. Lisa TOMS
54 Dn Col Engineering & Applied Sci ..... Dr. Judy CEZEAUX
81 Dean College of Natural & Health Sc ..... Dr. Jeff ROBERTSON
106 Interim Dean College of eTech ..... Dr. Jeff AULGUR
58 Interim Dean of Graduate College ..... Dr. Jeff ROBERTSON
28 Asst Dean Diversity & Inclusion ..... Dr. NaQuindra BROOKS
38 Assoc Dean Student Student Wellness ..... Ms. Kristy DAVIS
39 Associate Dean Residence Life ..... Mr. Delton GORDON
04 Admin Assistant to the President ..... Ms. Jennifer FLEMING

Arkansas Tech University-Ozark Campus (D)

1700 Helberg Lane, Ozark AR 72949
Telephone: (479) 667-2117 Identification: 770003
Accreditation: &NH, CAHIIM, CSHSE, CVT, EMT, OTA

Baptist Health College Little Rock (E)

11900 Colonel Glenn Rd, Ste 1000, Little Rock AR 72210
County: Pulaski FICE Identification: 031052
Unit ID: 106546
Telephone: (501) 202-6200 Carnegie Class: Spec 2-yr-Health
FAX Number: N/A Calendar System: Semester
URL: www.bhclr.edu
Established: 1921 Annual Undergrad Tuition & Fees: $10,439
Enrollment: 676 Coed
Affiliation or Control: Independent Non-Profit IRS Status: 501(c)3
Highest Offering: Associate Degree
Accreditation: ABHES, ADNUR, HT, MT, NMT, OTA, PNUR, POLYT, RAD, SURGT, SURTEC

01 Chancellor ..... Dr. Judy INGRAM PILE
11 Vice President & Administrator ..... Greg CRAIN
06 Registrar ..... Kristin WADDELL
08 Head Librarian ..... Rita REED
66 Dean of Nursing ..... Laura HAMILTON

Black River Technical College (F)

PO Box 468/1410 Hwy 304 East,
Pocahontas AR 72455-0468
County: Randolph FICE Identification: 020522
Unit ID: 106625
Telephone: (870) 248-4000 Carnegie Class: Assoc/MT-VT-High Trad
FAX Number: (870) 248-4100 Calendar System: Semester
URL: www.blackrivertech.org
Established: 1991 Annual Undergrad Tuition & Fees (In-State): $3,168
Enrollment: 1,530 Coed
Affiliation or Control: State IRS Status: 501(c)3
Highest Offering: Associate Degree
Accreditation: NH, COARC, EMT

01 President ..... Dr. Martin EGGENSPERGER
05 Interim VP for Academics ..... Mrs. Sissy GRAY
84 VP for Enrollment Management ..... Mr. Jason SMITH
111 VP for Institutional Advancement ..... Mrs. Karen LIEBHABER
10 VP for Finance and Administration ..... Mrs. Rhonda STONE
37 Director of Financial Aid ..... Mrs. Brandi CHESTER
06 Registrar ..... Mrs. Kimberly BIGGER
04 Administrative Asst to President ..... Mrs. Vickie FRENCH
106 Dir Online Education/E-learning ..... Mrs. Regina MOORE
15 Director Personnel Services ..... Mrs. Julie EDINGTON
19 Director Security/Safety ..... Mr. Tony SAYLORS
26 Chief Public Relations/Marketing ..... Ms. Ann SAVAGE
96 Director of Purchasing ..... Mrs. Janice HARVEY
13 Chief Info Technology Officer (CIO) ..... Mr. Mike GREENE
18 Chief Facilities/Physical Plant ..... Mr. Trent INGRAM
09 Director of Institutional Research ..... Mrs. Shana AKERS
07 Director of Admissions ..... Mrs. Angie FRENCH
50 Dean or Director Business ..... Mr. Phillip DICKSON
53 Dean or Director Education ..... Mrs. Donna STATLER
08 Library Director ..... Ms. Pat CAGLE
32 Dean of Students ..... Mr. Neal HARWELL

Bryan University (G)

3704 West Walnut Street, Rogers AR 72756-1825
Telephone: (479) 899-6644 Identification: 666252
Accreditation: ACICS

† Branch campus of Bryan University, Springfield, MO.

Central Baptist College (H)

1501 College Avenue, Conway AR 72034-6470
County: Faulkner FICE Identification: 001093
Unit ID: 106713
Telephone: (501) 329-6872 Carnegie Class: Bac-Diverse
FAX Number: (501) 329-2941 Calendar System: Semester
URL: www.cbc.edu
Established: 1952 Annual Undergrad Tuition & Fees: $16,200
Enrollment: 745 Coed
Affiliation or Control: Baptist IRS Status: 501(c)3
Highest Offering: Baccalaureate
Accreditation: NH, CAEP

01 President ..... Mr. Terry KIMBROW
04 Admin Asst to President ..... Mrs. Peggy PILLOW
05 VP for Academic Affairs ..... Dr. Gary MCALLISTER
10 VP for Finance ..... Mr. Paul CHERRY
111 VP for Advancement ..... Mrs. Sancy FAULK
84 VP for Enrollment Mgmt ..... Mr. Ryan JOHNSON
32 Assoc VP for Student Services ..... Vacant
06 Registrar ..... Mr. Brooks WALTHALL
07 Director of Admissions ..... Mr. Justin MOORE
88 Director Nontraditional Enrollment ..... Mr. Brooks WALTHALL
106 Director of Online Studies ..... Mr. Steve ELDER
19 Dean of Students/Campus Security ..... Mr. Chris MITCHELL
08 Library Director ..... Mrs. Rachel WHITTINGHAM
26 Director of Public Relations ..... Vacant
37 Director of Financial Aid ..... Mrs. Tonya HAMMONTREE
09 Institutional Research Analyst ..... Ms. Lauren WALLER
41 Athletic Director ..... Mr. Lyle MIDDLETON
15 Director of Human Resources ..... Mrs. Britni ELDER
29 Director of Alumni Engagement ..... Mrs. Jessica FAULKNER
88 Director of Military Relations ..... Ms. Pam SIMS
18 Director of Physical Plant ..... Vacant

Champion Christian College (I)

600 Garland Ave, Hot Springs AR 71913
County: Garland Identification: 667324
Telephone: (501) 623-2272 Carnegie Class: Not Classified
FAX Number: (501) 623-4262 Calendar System: Semester
URL: championchristiancollege.com
Established: 2005 Annual Undergrad Tuition & Fees: N/A
Enrollment: N/A Coed
Affiliation or Control: Independent Non-Profit IRS Status: 501(c)3
Highest Offering: Baccalaureate
Accreditation: @TRACS

01 President ..... Mr. Eric CAPACI
03 Executive Vice President ..... Dr. Jeremy HORTON
05 Vice Pres Academic Affairs ..... Mrs. Claudia KEMP
32 Vice President Student Affairs ..... Mr. Stephen SELLERS
06 Registrar ..... Mrs. Digna WILKIE
10 Director of Finance ..... Mrs. Marcia THOMAS

College of the Ouachitas (J)

One College Circle, Malvern AR 72104-0816
County: Hot Spring FICE Identification: 009976
Unit ID: 107521
Telephone: (501) 337-5000 Carnegie Class: Assoc/HVT-High Non
FAX Number: (501) 332-4100 Calendar System: Semester
URL: www.coto.edu
Established: 1969 Annual Undergrad Tuition & Fees (In-State): $3,890
Enrollment: 1,272 Coed
Affiliation or Control: State IRS Status: 501(c)3
Highest Offering: Associate Degree
Accreditation: NH

01 President Dr. Steve ROOK
04 Executive Asst to President Ms. Mitzi OVERTURF
05 Vice President for Academic Affairs Mr. Pat SIMMS
32 Vice President of Student Affairs Dr. Kim ARMSTRONG
10 VP of Admin & Operations Mr. David SEE
111 Exec Dir College Advancement Ms. Amber CHILDERS
108 Exec Dir Planning & Assessment Ms. Carla CRUTCHFIELD
20 Dean of Learning Ms. Tricia BAAR
76 Dean of Health Sciences Ms. Melinda SANDERS
51 Director Adult Education Ms. Casson BROCK
08 Director Learning Resources Ms. Allison MALONE
75 Director Career & Technical Studies Ms. Kim ROBERSON
92 Director Honors College Ms. Tricia BAAR
88 Director Concurrent Enrollment Ms. Tara BRATTON
37 Director of Financial Aid Ms. Angela BOBUS
36 Director Career Pathways Ms. Johnnie MITCHELL
88 Dir TRIO Student Support Services Ms. Vergina SMITH
121 Director Student Success Ms. Janet HUNT
84 Director of Enrollment Management Ms. Keesha JOHNSON
21 Controller Ms. Anita MARTIN
15 Dir Human Resources Ms. Kori CLAYTON
103 Director Workforce Development Mr. Mason ROBINSON
18 Maintenance Supervisor Mr. Danny COTTRELL

Crowley's Ridge College (A)

100 College Drive, Paragould AR 72450-9775
County: Greene FICE Identification: 001095
Unit ID: 106810
Telephone: (870) 236-6901 Carnegie Class: Bac-Diverse
FAX Number: (870) 236-7748 Calendar System: Semester
URL: www.crc.edu
Established: 1964 Annual Undergrad Tuition & Fees: $13,600
Enrollment: 214 Coed
Affiliation or Control: Churches Of Christ IRS Status: 501(c)3
Highest Offering: Baccalaureate
Accreditation: NH, CAEP

01 President Mr. Ken HOPPE
05 Vice President for Academic Affairs Dr. Bruce BRYANT
32 Vice President for Student Affairs Mr. Art SMITH
111 Vice President for Advancement Mr. Richard JOHNSON
06 Registrar Treka CLARK
37 Director Student Financial Services Mr. David W. GOFF
26 Director Public Information Mrs. Andrea JOHNSON
07 Director Admissions Mr. Chris HUGHES
41 Athletic Director/Campus Minister Mr. Paul MCFADDEN
08 Director Learning Center Mr. Mark WARNICK
10 Business Office Manager Mrs. Sonia JOHNSON
13 Director of Information Services Mr. Larry JOHNSON

East Arkansas Community College (B)

1700 Newcastle Road, Forrest City AR 72335-2204
County: Saint Francis FICE Identification: 012260
Unit ID: 106883
Telephone: (870) 633-4480 Carnegie Class: Assoc/HT-High Non
FAX Number: (870) 633-7222 Calendar System: Semester
URL: www.eacc.edu
Established: 1974 Annual Undergrad Tuition & Fees (In-District): $2,880
Enrollment: 1,045 Coed
Affiliation or Control: State/Local IRS Status: Exempt
Highest Offering: Associate Degree
Accreditation: NH, EMT

01 President Dr. Cathie CLINE
88 Vice President for Transfer Educ Mrs. Michelle WILSON
10 Vice President Finance & Admin Mr. Richard STIPE
75 Vice President Vocational Education Mr. Robert P. SUMMERS
32 Assoc VP for Student Success Mr. Chris HEIGLE
37 Director Student Financial Aid Mr. Kevin JUMPER
08 Director Library Services Mrs. Paige LAWS
84 Director Enrollment Management Mrs. Sharon COLLIER
26 Director of PR/Community Programs Mrs. Lindsay MIDKIFF
15 Director of Human Resources Mr. Ike SANDERS
18 Director Physical Plant Mr. Glenn FORD
96 Purchasing Specialist Mrs. Lisa SILER
51 Director of Continuing Education Mrs. Logan BRASFIELD
121 Director of Advising & Counseling Mr. Errin JAMES
88 Dean of Transfer Education Mrs. Samantha SHARP
88 Dean of Vocational Education Mr. Chris NELSON
09 Coord of Institutional Research Mrs. Roni HORTON

Ecclesia College (C)

9653 Nations Drive, Springdale AR 72762-8159
County: Benton FICE Identification: 038553
Unit ID: 446233
Telephone: (479) 248-7236 Carnegie Class: Spec-4-yr-Faith
FAX Number: (479) 248-1455 Calendar System: Semester
URL: www.ecollege.edu
Established: 1975 Annual Undergrad Tuition & Fees: $15,140
Enrollment: 232 Coed
Affiliation or Control: Independent Non-Profit IRS Status: 501(c)3
Highest Offering: Master's
Accreditation: BI

01 President Dr. Randall E. BELL
05 Academic Dean Dr. Robert HEADRICK
10 Business Office Manager Ms. Melissa K. RICKS
32 Dean of Students Mr. Jesse E. WADKINS
106 Distance Education Academic Dean Mr. Larry MCULLOUGH
30 Director of Financial Development Mr. Mike A. NOVAK
26 Director of Communications Ms. Angie P. SNYDER
37 Director Student Financial Aid Mr. Don PRESTON
41 Athletic Director Mr. Pat BRILEY
06 Registrar Mrs. Donna P. BROWN
08 Head Librarian Mrs. Joanne CAMPBELL
103 Director Work/Learning/Service Pgms Mr. Jesse E. WADKINS
07 Director of Admissions Mr. Chad E. HOWARD
04 Administrative Asst to President Mrs. Elizabeth NEWLUN
18 Chief Facilities/Physical Plant Mr. Dennis HAGGARD
39 Director Student Housing Ms. Kathrynn FINK

Harding University Main Campus (D)

915 E. Market Avenue, Searcy AR 72149-5615
County: White FICE Identification: 001097
Unit ID: 107044
Telephone: (501) 279-4000 Carnegie Class: DU-Mod
FAX Number: (501) 279-4600 Calendar System: Semester
URL: www.harding.edu
Established: 1924 Annual Undergrad Tuition & Fees: $19,845
Enrollment: 5,541 Coed
Affiliation or Control: Churches Of Christ IRS Status: 501(c)3
Highest Offering: Doctorate
Accreditation: NH, ACBSP, ARCPA, CAATE, CACREP, CAEP, CIDA, DIETD, MUS, NURSE, PHAR, PTA, SP, SW

01 President Dr. Bruce D. MCLARTY
03 Executive Vice President Dr. David COLLINS
05 Provost Dr. Marty SPEARS
10 Vice President Finance Mrs. Tammy HALL
30 Vice President Advancement Dr. Bryan BURKS
42 Vice President of Church Relations Dr. Dan WILLIAMS
13 VP Information Systems & Technology Mr. Keith CRONK
41 Athletic Director Mr. Jeff MORGAN
29 VP of Alumni Relations Mrs. Liz HOWELL
20 VP Accred/Inst Effect/Vice Provost Dr. Julie HIXSON-WALLACE
88 Dean College of Bible & Ministry Dr. Monte COX
92 Dean of Honors College Dr. Mike JAMES
50 Dean College of Business Dr. Al FRAZIER
53 Dean College of Education Dr. Donny LEE
66 Dean College of Nursing Dr. Susan KEHL
79 Dean College of Arts & Humanities Dr. Warren CASEY
81 Dean College of Sciences Dr. Zane GASTINEAU
76 Dean College of Allied Health Dr. Mike MCGALLIARD
104 Exec Dir of International Programs Dr. Audra PLEASANT
84 Asst VP Enrollment Management Mr. Scott HANNIGAN
21 Senior Finance Officer Mr. Tim JONES
32 Asst VP Student Life/Dean Students Mr. Zach NEAL
88 Asst VP of IS&T Mr. Mike CHALENBURG
06 Registrar Mr. Tod MARTIN
38 Director of Counseling Dr. Lew MOORE
19 Director Security/Safety Mr. Craig RUSSELL
26 VP of Communication/Enrollment Mrs. Jana RUCKER
37 Director Student Financial Aid Dr. Jonathan ROBERTS
58 Director of Graduate Studies Vacant
08 Librarian Mrs. Jean WALDROP
18 Chief Facilities/Physical Plant Mr. Danny DERAMUS
15 Asst Vice Pres Human Resources Mr. David ROSS
36 Director Student Placement Mr. Butch GARDNER
09 Director of Institutional Research Mr. Dustin HOWELL
96 Purchasing Coordinator Mrs. Shelly MATHEWS
35 Assistant Dean of Students Mr. Marcus THOMAS
35 Assistant Dean of Students Mrs. Kara ABSTON
35 Assistant Dean of Students Mrs. Ranan HESTER
35 Assistant Dean of Students Mr. Chad JOICE
28 Director of Diversity Mr. Alex JAMERISON
39 Director Student Housing Mrs. Kathy ALLEN
07 Director of Admissions Mr. Scott HANNIGAN

Henderson State University (E)

1100 Henderson Street, Arkadelphia AR 71999-0001
County: Clark FICE Identification: 001098
Unit ID: 107071
Telephone: (870) 230-5000 Carnegie Class: Masters/M
FAX Number: (870) 230-5144 Calendar System: Semester
URL: www.hsu.edu
Established: 1890 Annual Undergrad Tuition & Fees (In-State): $8,530
Enrollment: 3,334 Coed
Affiliation or Control: State IRS Status: 501(c)3
Highest Offering: Beyond Master's But Less Than Doctorate
Accreditation: NH, #CAATE, CACREP, CAEP, DIETD, MUS, NURSE

01 Acting President Ms. Elaine KNEEBONE
05 Provost/VPAA Dr. Steve ADKISON
10 Interim VP Finance & Administration Ms. Lecia FRANKLIN
32 VP Student Affs & Student Success Dr. Brad PATTERSON
111 VP Advancement Ms. Jennifer BOYETT
43 General Counsel Ms. Elaine KNEEBONE
35 Asst VP Student Engagement Dr. Veronikha SALAZAR
39 Asst VP Housing/Community Standard Dr. Nicole LAIRD
13 AVP Computer/Comm Svcs & CIO Dr. Al VALBUENA
30 Assoc VP Development & Alumni Rels Dr. Gary BOUSE
41 Director Athletics Mr. Shawn JONES
26 Exec Director of Marketing/Comm Ms. Tina HALL
49 Dean Ellis Col Arts/Sciences Dr. Angela BOSWELL
50 Dean of School of Business Dr. Marc MILLER
53 Dean Teachers College Henderson Dr. Celya TAYLOR
58 Vice Provost/Dean of Grad School Dr. Kenneth TAYLOR
06 Assoc Provost/Registrar Dr. Elwyn MARTIN
08 Director Huie Library Ms. Lea Ann ALEXANDER
15 Director of Human Resources Ms. Mickey QUATTLEBAUM
19 Director of University Police Mr. Jonathan CAMPBELL
38 Dir Student Health/Counseling Ctr Ms. Deborah COLLINS
07 Assoc Provost Univ Rels/Admissions Dr. Brandie BENTON
37 Director of Financial Aid Ms. Christina JONES
92 Director of Honors College Dr. David T. THOMSON
88 Director of Student Research Dr. David BATEMAN
96 Director of Purchasing Mr. Tim JONES
72 Dir Academic Tech & Help Desk Ms. Jennifer HOLBROOK

Hendrix College (F)

1600 Washington Avenue, Conway AR 72032-3080
County: Faulkner FICE Identification: 001099
Unit ID: 107080
Telephone: (501) 329-6811 Carnegie Class: Bac-A&S
FAX Number: (501) 450-1200 Calendar System: Semester
URL: www.hendrix.edu
Established: 1876 Annual Undergrad Tuition & Fees: $45,790
Enrollment: 1,249 Coed
Affiliation or Control: United Methodist IRS Status: 501(c)3
Highest Offering: Master's
Accreditation: NH

01 President Dr. William M. TSUTSUI
04 Executive Assistant to President Ms. Donna PLEMMONS
100 VP for Strategic Initiatives/Chief Ms. Courtney Lee CORWIN
111 Sr Exec Vice Pres/Dean Inst Advance Mr. W. Ellis ARNOLD, III
05 Provost Dr. Terri BONEBRIGHT
26 Vice Pres Marketing Communications Mr. Rob O'CONNOR
10 Executive Vice President and CFO Mr. Tom SIEBENMORGEN
84 Vice Pres for Enrollment Mr. Sam NICHOLS
15 Vice Pres for Human Resources Ms. Vicki LYNN
18 VP Operations/Facilities Mr. Skip HARTSELL
32 Exec VP Student Affs/Dean of Stdnts Mr. Jim WILTGEN, JR.
27 Assoc VP Marketing Communications Ms. Amy FORBUS
06 Registrar Ms. Brenda ADAMS
08 Director of Libraries Ms. Britt Anne MURPHY
13 VP Technology/Chief Info Officer Mr. Sam NICHOLS
29 Director Alumni Relations Ms. Pamela OWEN
37 Director of Financial Aid Ms. Kristina BURFORD
40 Bookstore Manager Ms. Suzannne TOLLETT
79 Area Head/Humanities Dr. Rod MILLER
81 Area Head/Natural Sciences Dr. Ann WRIGHT
83 Area Head/Social Sciences Dr. Todd BERRYMAN
42 Chaplain Rev. J.J WHITNEY
07 Director of Admission Mr. Sam NICHOLS
20 Associate Academic Officer Dr. David SUTHERLAND
21 Associate Business Officer Mr. Shawn MATHIS
36 Director Career Services Ms. Leigh LASSITER-COUNTS
38 Director Student Counseling Ms. Mary Anne SIEBERT
09 Director of Institutional Research Mr. Randy PETERSON
28 Int VP for Diversity & Inclusion Ms. Kesha BAOUA

Jefferson Regional Medical Center School of Nursing (G)

1600 W. 40th Avenue, Pine Bluff AR 71603
County: Jefferson FICE Identification: 023308
Unit ID: 107123
Telephone: (870) 541-7858 Carnegie Class: Not Classified
FAX Number: (870) 541-7807 Calendar System: Semester
URL: www.jrmc.org
Established: 1981 Annual Undergrad Tuition & Fees: N/A
Enrollment: 65 Coed
Affiliation or Control: Independent Non-Profit IRS Status: 501(c)3
Highest Offering: Associate Degree
Accreditation: ABHES, PAST

01 Director Ms. Michelle NEWTON
06 Registrar/School Secretary Ms. Lucy MULLIKIN

John Brown University (H)

2000 W University Street, Siloam Springs AR 72761-2121
County: Benton FICE Identification: 001100
Unit ID: 107141
Telephone: (479) 524-9500 Carnegie Class: Masters/M
FAX Number: (479) 524-7278 Calendar System: Semester
URL: www.jbu.edu
Established: 1919 Annual Undergrad Tuition & Fees: $26,928
Enrollment: 2,613 Coed
Affiliation or Control: Independent Non-Profit IRS Status: 501(c)3
Highest Offering: Master's
Accreditation: NH, ACBSP, CAEP, CONST, NURSE

01 President Dr. Charles POLLARD
10 Vice Pres Finance & Administration Dr. Kim HADLEY
84 Vice Pres Enrollment Management Mr. Donald W. CRANDALL
111 Vice Pres of University Advancement Dr. Jim KRALL
32 Vice Pres for Student Development Dr. Stephen T. BEERS
05 VP Academic Affairs/Dean of Faculty Dr. Ed ERICSON, III
42 Campus Pastor/Assoc Dean of Stdnts Vacant
06 Registrar Dr. Rebecca WEIMER
21 Controller Mr. Tom PERRY
13 Chief Information Systems Ofcr Mr. Paul NAST
18 Director of Facilities Services Mr. Steve BRANKLE
112 Director of Planned Giving Mr. Eric GREENHAW
08 Director of Library Mr. Brent SWEARINGEN
85 Director International Programs Mr. Bill STEVENSON
29 Director of Alumni/Parent Relations Mr. Brad EDWARDS

37 Director of Financial Aid ... Mr. David BURNEY
07 JBU Online Recruiting ... Mr. Kent SHAFFER
41 Athletic Director ... Ms. Robyn DAUGHERTY
04 Administrative Asst to President ... Ms. Kory J. DALE
09 Director of Institutional Research ... Mrs. Lynette DUNCAN
106 Dean Online Education/E-learning ... Dr. Stacey DUKE
15 Chief Human Resources Officer ... Mrs. Amy FISHER
19 Director Security/Safety ... Mr. Scott WANZER
26 Director University Communications ... Ms. Julie GUMM
39 Director Residence Life ... Dr. Andre BROQUARD
108 Director Institutional Assessment ... Dr. Robert NORWOOD

Lyon College (A)

PO Box 2317, Batesville AR 72503-2317
County: Independence FICE Identification: 001088
Unit ID: 106342
Telephone: (870) 307-7000 Carnegie Class: Bac-A&S
FAX Number: (870) 307-7001 Calendar System: Semester
URL: https://www.lyon.edu/
Established: 1872 Annual Undergrad Tuition & Fees: $28,790
Enrollment: 672 Coed
Affiliation or Control: Presbyterian Church (U.S.A.) IRS Status: 501(c)3
Highest Offering: Baccalaureate
Accreditation: NH, CAEP

01 President ... Dr. W. Joseph KING
05 Provost ... Dr. Melissa P. TAVERNER
10 Vice President Business & Finance ... Mr. Richard GAUMER
32 Vice President Student Life ... Dr. Patrick MULICK
07 VP Enrollment Services ... Mr. Matthew CRISMAN
08 Director Library ... Dr. Robert KRAPOHL
26 Dir of Marketing & Communication ... Mrs. Keli JACOBI
111 Executive Dir of Advancement ... Mrs. Gina GARRETT
100 Chief of Staff/VP Administration ... Mrs. Clarinda L. FOOTE
37 Director of Financial Assistance ... Mr. Tommy TUCKER
36 Director Career Development ... Mrs. Annette CASTLEBERRY
13 Director Information Services ... Vacant
41 Director of Athletics ... Mr. Kevin JENKINS
42 Chaplain ... Rev. Margaret ALSUP
53 Director of Teacher Education ... Dr. Kim CROSBY
38 Director Student Counseling ... Ms. Diane ELLIS
18 Director Security ... Vacant
40 Director Bookstore ... Mrs. Donna GLASCOCK
08 Head Librarian ... Vacant
23 Director of Health Services ... Mrs. Haley HAILE
18 Chief Facilities/Physical Plant ... Vacant
20 Associate Academic Officer ... Dr. Anthony GRAFTON
06 Registrar ... Mrs. Tami HALL
44 Director Annual Giving ... Mrs. Jill MOBLEY
09 Director of Institutional Research ... Mr. Andrew ENGLISH
15 Director of Human Resources ... Mr. Donald TAYLOR
21 Associate Business Officer ... Mrs. Karen MOORE
28 Director of Diversity ... Mr. Lai-Monte HUNTER
29 Director of Alumni Affairs ... Mrs. Cindy BARBER
35 Associate Student Affairs Officer ... Mr. Lai-Monte HUNTER

National Park College (B)

101 College Drive,
Hot Springs National Park AR 71913-9174
County: Garland FICE Identification: 012105
Unit ID: 106980
Telephone: (501) 760-4222 Carnegie Class: Assoc/HVT-High Trad
FAX Number: (501) 760-4100 Calendar System: Semester
URL: www.np.edu
Established: 1973 Annual Undergrad Tuition & Fees (In-District): $3,750
Enrollment: 2,768 Coed
Affiliation or Control: State/Local IRS Status: 501(c)3
Highest Offering: Associate Degree
Accreditation: NH, ACBSP, ADNUR, CAHIIM, COARC, EMT, MLTAD, RAD

01 President ... Dr. John HOGAN
05 Vice Pres Academic Affairs ... Dr. Wade DERDEN
10 Vice Pres Finance & Admin ... Mr. Steve TRUSTY
32 VP Student Affairs/Enrollment Mgmt ... Dr. Jerry THOMAS
26 Vice Pres External Relations ... Ms. Darla THURBER
13 Chief Info Technology Officer ... Mr. Blake BUTLER
103 VP Workforce/Strategic Initiatives ... Ms. Kelli EMBRY
21 Dean Business & Technology ... Vacant
15 Assoc Vice Pres Human Resources ... Ms. Janet BREWER
35 Dean of Students ... Mr. John TUCKER
07 Dean of Enrollment Services ... Mr. Jason HUDNELL
09 Director Institutional Research ... Mr. Chris COBLE
08 Director of Library Services ... Ms. Lynn VALETUTTI
37 Director of Financial Aid ... Ms. Lisa HOPPER
102 Executive Director of Foundation ... Ms. Nicole HERNDON
06 Registrar ... Vacant
04 Exec Assistant to the President ... Ms. Jill HOULIHAN
18 Director Physical Plant ... Mr. Brad HOPPER

North Arkansas College (C)

1515 Pioneer Drive, Harrison AR 72601-5599
County: Boone FICE Identification: 012261
Unit ID: 107460
Telephone: (870) 743-3000 Carnegie Class: Assoc/MT-VT-High Trad
FAX Number: (870) 391-3250 Calendar System: Semester
URL: www.northark.edu
Established: 1974 Annual Undergrad Tuition & Fees (In-District): $2,280
Enrollment: 1,821 Coed
Affiliation or Control: State/Local IRS Status: 501(c)3
Highest Offering: Associate Degree
Accreditation: NH, ACBSP, ADNUR, EMT, MLTAD, RAD, SURGT

01 President ... Dr. Randy ESTERS
05 Vice President of Academic Affairs ... Dr. Rick MASSENGALE
10 Vice Pres Finance & Administration ... Mr. Donald SUGG
111 Vice Pres Institutional Advancement ... Dr. Rodney ARNOLD
04 Executive Assistant to President ... Mrs. Amanda KILBOURN
49 Dean Arts & Science/Business & IT ... Dr. Laura BERRY
66 Dean Nursing/Allied Hlth/Tech Pgms ... Mrs. Cindy MAYO
103 Dean of Outreach & Workforce Dev ... Mrs. Nell BONDS
08 Student Resource Coordinator ... Mrs. Sharla HELLEN
108 Dir Institutional Effectiveness ... Mrs. Katherine VAUGHN
121 Dean of Student Success ... Mrs. Tavonda BROWN
41 Athletic Director ... Mr. Bobby HOWARD
15 Director Human Resources ... Mrs. Kris GREENING
18 Chief Facilities/Physical Plant ... Mr. Kevin SOMERS
96 Director of Purchasing ... Mrs. Shari HOLT
37 Director Student Financial Aid ... Mrs. Jennifer HADDOCK
06 Registrar ... Mrs. Charla JENNINGS
07 Director of Admissions ... Mrs. Charla JENNINGS
26 Director of Public Relations ... Mrs. Micki SOMERS
13 Director of IT Services ... Mr. Rick WILLIAMS
31 Asst Dir of Community Education ... Ms. Sarah BING

NorthWest Arkansas Community College (D)

1 College Drive, Bentonville AR 72712-5091
County: Benton FICE Identification: 030633
Unit ID: 367459
Telephone: (479) 986-4000 Carnegie Class: Assoc/HT-Mix Trad/Non
FAX Number: (479) 619-4118 Calendar System: Semester
URL: www.nwacc.edu
Established: 1989 Annual Undergrad Tuition & Fees (In-District): $3,238
Enrollment: 7,715 Coed
Affiliation or Control: State/Local IRS Status: 501(c)3
Highest Offering: Associate Degree
Accreditation: NH, ACBSP, ACFEI, ADNUR, CAHIIM, COARC, EMT, IFSAC, PTAA

01 President ... Dr. Evelyn E. JORGENSON
10 Int VP Finance & Administration ... Ms. Gulizar BAGGSON
05 Vice Pres for Learning/CAO ... Dr. Ricky TOMPKINS
32 VP of Student Services ... Dr. Todd KITCHEN
36 VP of Career & Workforce Education ... Mr. Tim CORNELIUS
103 Dean of Workforce Education ... Dr. Megan BOLINDER
13 AVP IT/Chief Information Officer ... Mr. Jason DEGN
56 AVP of Washington Co Programs ... Ms. Brenda GREEN
88 Dir Retail & Supplier Education ... Ms. Teresa WARREN
11 Executive Director of Operations ... Mr. Jack THOMPSON
51 Dean of Adult Education ... Mr. Ben ALDAMA
35 Dean of Students ... Ms. Dale MONTGOMERY
30 Executive Director of Development ... Ms. Annetta TIREY
20 Assoc VP Learning ... Dr. Diana JOHNSON
108 Exec Dir Planning Effectiveness/PR ... Dr. Lisa ANDERSON
26 Exec Dir Community/Government Rels ... Mr. Jim HALL
21 Controller ... Ms. Rai STARR
15 Int Exec Director Human Resources ... Ms. Beverly HILL
106 Assoc Dean of Distance Learning ... Dr. Kate BURKES
88 Coordinator of Building Sciences ... Mr. Mike DEWBERRY
88 Director of Learning Resources ... Ms. Gwen DOBBS
84 Dir Enrollment Services ... Ms. Beverly GRAU
37 Director Student Financial Aid ... Ms. Michelle CORDELL
121 Exec Director of Student Success ... Mr. Eric VEST
88 Policy & Staff Enhancement Director ... Ms. Brenda MEYER
109 Dir Food Services/Event Management ... Ms. Diane BOSS
09 Director of Institutional Research ... Ms. Kim PURDY
18 Director of Physical Plant ... Mr. Jim NELSON
77 Dean for Bus/Computer Information ... Dr. Christine DAVIS
76 Dean of Health Professions ... Mr. Mark WALLENMEYER
04 Exec Asst to President & BOT ... Ms. Lindsey WHITE
22 Exec Dir Policy/Risk & Comp ... Ms. Teresa TAYLOR
84 Exec Director Enrollment Management ... Mr. Justin WHITE
19 Director of Public Safety ... Mr. Steve TOSH
104 Director Global Intl Programs ... Mr. Jeremy YOUMANS

Ouachita Baptist University (E)

410 Ouachita Street, Arkadelphia AR 71998-0001
County: Clark FICE Identification: 001102
Unit ID: 107512
Telephone: (870) 245-5000 Carnegie Class: Bac-Diverse
FAX Number: (870) 245-5500 Calendar System: Semester
URL: www.obu.edu
Established: 1886 Annual Undergrad Tuition & Fees: $26,790
Enrollment: 1,545 Coed
Affiliation or Control: Southern Baptist IRS Status: 501(c)3
Highest Offering: Baccalaureate
Accreditation: NH, CAEP, DIETD, MUS

01 President ... Dr. Ben R. SELLS
111 Vice Pres Institutional Advancement ... Dr. Keldon HENLEY
100 Chief of Staff ... Dr. Keldon HENLEY
05 Vice President Academic Affairs ... Dr. Stan POOLE
10 Chief Financial Officer ... Mr. Jason TOLBERT
32 Vice Pres for Student Development ... Dr. Wesley KLUCK
30 Vice President for Development ... Mrs. Terry G. PEEPLES
26 Asst to Pres for Comm/Mktg ... Mrs. Brooke ZIMNY
07 Director of Admissions Counseling ... Mrs. Lori MOTL
09 Director of Institutional Research ... Dr. Deborah ROOT
15 Director of Human Resources ... Mrs. Sherri PHELPS
18 Chief Facilities/Physical Plant ... Mr. John HARDMAN
29 Director of Alumni Relations ... Mr. Jon MERRYMAN
35 Dean of Students ... Mr. Rickey ROGERS
20 Assoc Vice Pres Academic Affairs ... Dr. Doug REED
36 Director of Career Services ... Mrs. Rachel ROBERTS
38 University Counselor ... Mr. Dan JARBOE
08 Librarian ... Dr. Ray GRANADE
06 Registrar/Director of Admissions ... Mrs. Susan ATKINSON
37 Assoc Vice Pres Student Fin Svcs ... Mrs. Susan HURST
92 Director Honors Program ... Dr. Barbara PEMBERTON
13 Asst to Pres for Info Tech Svcs ... Mr. Bill PHELPS
39 Director of Housing ... Ms. Caitlin HETZEL
41 Athletic Director ... Mr. David SHARP
43 General Counsel ... Mr. Bryan MCKINNEY
21 Director of Financial Services ... Mr. Jason TOLBERT
40 Bookstore Manager ... Ms. Jennifer FORTHMAN
57 Dean of School of Fine Arts ... Dr. Gary GERBER
50 Dean of the School of Business ... Mr. Bryan MCKINNEY
53 Dean Sch of Interdisciplinary Stds ... Dr. Stan POOLE
73 Dean School of Christian Studies ... Dr. Danny HAYS
79 Dean School of Humanities & Educ ... Dr. Jeff ROOT
81 Dean School of Natural Sciences ... Dr. Tim KNIGHT
83 Dean School of Social Sciences ... Dr. Randall WIGHT
101 Secretary of the Institution/Board ... Mrs. Tracey KNIGHT
108 Director Institutional Assessment ... Dr. Deborah ROOT
19 Director Security/Safety ... Mr. Jeff CROW
04 Executive Asst to the President ... Mrs. Tracey KNIGHT
104 VP for Community/Intl Engagement ... Mr. Ian COSH
106 Asst to Pres for Grad/Prof Studies ... Dr. Monica HARDIN

Ozarka College (F)

PO Box 10, Melbourne AR 72556-0010
County: Izard FICE Identification: 020870
Unit ID: 107549
Telephone: (870) 368-7371 Carnegie Class: Assoc/HVT-Mix Trad/Non
FAX Number: (870) 368-2091 Calendar System: Semester
URL: www.ozarka.edu
Established: 1991 Annual Undergrad Tuition & Fees (In-State): $3,004
Enrollment: 1,186 Coed
Affiliation or Control: State IRS Status: 501(c)3
Highest Offering: Associate Degree
Accreditation: NH, ACFEI

01 President ... Dr. Richard L. DAWE
05 Vice President for Academic Affairs ... Dr. Chris LORCH
10 Vice President of Finance ... Mrs. Tina WHEELIS
11 Vice President of Administration ... Mr. Jason LAWRENCE
32 Vice President of Student Services ... Dr. Joshua WILSON
45 Vice President of Planning/IR ... Dr. Deltha SHARP
13 Chief Information Officer ... Mr. Scott PINKSTON
04 Executive Asst to the President ... Mrs. Candace D. KILLIAN
30 Director of College Advancement ... Mrs. Suellen DAVIDSON
29 Development Officer/Dir Alumni Rels ... Vacant
37 Director of Financial Aid ... Ms. Laura LAWRENCE
07 Director of Admissions ... Ms. Erika CAMPBELL
06 Registrar ... Mrs. Zeda WILKERSON
26 Dir Public Relations/Marketing ... Ms. Kendra COLLIER
21 Business Manager ... Mrs. Amber RUSH

Philander Smith College (G)

900 W. Daisy L. Gatson Bates Drive,
Little Rock AR 72202-3799
County: Pulaski FICE Identification: 001103
Unit ID: 107600
Telephone: (501) 375-9845 Carnegie Class: Bac-Diverse
FAX Number: (501) 370-5277 Calendar System: Semester
URL: www.philander.edu
Established: 1877 Annual Undergrad Tuition & Fees: $13,014
Enrollment: 891 Coed
Affiliation or Control: United Methodist IRS Status: 501(c)3
Highest Offering: Baccalaureate
Accreditation: NH, ACBSP, CAEPN, SW

01 President ... Dr. Roderick L. SMOTHERS, SR.
04 Senior Exec Assistant to President ... Mrs. Anita L. HATLEY
05 VP of Academic Affairs ... Dr. Zollie STEVENSON, JR.
32 VP of Student Affs/Enrollment Mgmt ... Dr. Dakota DOMAN
111 VP Institutional Advancement ... Mr. Charles KING
10 Interim VP of Fiscal Affairs ... Mrs. LaTonya HAYES
108 Assoc VP of Inst Effectiveness ... Vacant
06 Registrar ... Ms. Bertha OWENS
42 Chaplain/Dean of Religious Life ... Rev. Ronnie MILLER-YOW
35 Dean of Students ... Ms. Rhonda LOVELACE
15 Exec Director of Human Resources ... Ms. Yolanda COLEMAN
37 Director of Financial Aid ... Mr. Kevin BARNES
18 Director of Physical Plant ... Mr. Robert YOUNG
26 Director Marketing/Public Relations ... Mrs. Jenelle PRIMM
88 Executive Director of WISE -P3 ... Mr. Glenn SERGEANT, SR.
07 Interim Director of Admissions ... Mr. Yohannis JOB
08 Director of the Library ... Mrs. Kathy ANDERSON
29 Director of Alumni Relations ... Mrs. Brenda HATTON-FICKLIN
41 Interim Athletic Director ... Mr. Brandon GREENWOOD
13 Chief Information Officer ... Mr. Brian CLAY
09 Director of Institutional Research ... Ms. Beverly RICHARDSON
19 Chief of Security ... Mr. Arthur WILLIAMS
51 Dir of Continuing Education (PSMI) ... Mr. Bruce JAMES
88 Kendall Mission Center Director ... Dr. Cynthia BURROUGHS
40 Bookstore Manager ... Mr. Alvin HARRIS
17 Campus Nurse ... Ms. Regina STEWARD
88 Dean of Campus Culture ... Mr. Ronnie MILLER-YOW
49 Div Chair Natural/Physical Sciences ... Dr. Samar SWAID

50 Div Chair of Business/Economics .... Vacant
53 Div Chair of Education .... Dr. Charity SMITH
79 Div Chair Humanities .... Dr. Lia STEELE-MARCELL
83 Div Chair Social Sciences .... Dr. Daniel EGBE
38 Director of Counseling Services .... Mrs. LaTisha JACKSON
39 Director of Housing and Res Life .... Ms. Brittany JACKSON

Shorter College (A)

604 Locust Street, North Little Rock AR 72114
County: Pulaski FICE Identification: 001105
Unit ID: 107840
Telephone: (501) 374-6305 Carnegie Class: Assoc/HT-Mix Trad/Non
FAX Number: (501) 374-9333 Calendar System: Semester
URL: www.shortercollege.edu
Established: 1886 Annual Undergrad Tuition & Fees: $5,500
Enrollment: 521 Coed
Affiliation or Control: African Methodist Episcopal IRS Status: 501(c)3
Highest Offering: Associate Degree
Accreditation: TRACS

01 President .... Dr. O. Jerome GREEN
05 Dean of Academic Affairs .... Dr. George HERTS
10 Chief Financial Officer .... Mr. George MACKEY
32 Student Services Coordinator .... Ms. Margaret BOYD-OWENS
06 Registrar .... Ms. Cindy CONLEY
07 Director of Admissions .... Ms. Arnella HAYES-CARTER
15 Chief Human Resources Officer .... Ms. Cordelia MITCHELL
18 Chief Facilities/Physical Plant Off .... Mr. Nathan ALEXANDER
20 Associate Academic Officer .... Mr. Demetrius GILBERT
29 Director Alumni Affairs .... Ms. Paula PUMPHREY
36 Director Student Placement .... Ms. Daven MCCOY
37 Director Student Financial Aid .... Ms. Janice IVORY
84 Director Enrollment Management .... Ms. Janice IVORY

South Arkansas Community College (B)

300 S West Avenue, PO Box 7010,
El Dorado AR 71731-7010
County: Union FICE Identification: 020746
Unit ID: 107974
Telephone: (870) 862-8131 Carnegie Class: Assoc/MT-VT-Mix Trad/Non
FAX Number: (870) 864-7190 Calendar System: Semester
URL: www.southark.edu
Established: 1992 Annual Undergrad Tuition & Fees (In-State): $2,700
Enrollment: 1,481 Coed
Affiliation or Control: State IRS Status: 501(c)3
Highest Offering: Associate Degree
Accreditation: NH, EMT, OTA, PTAA, RAD, SURGT

01 President .... Dr. Barbara JONES
05 VP for Academic Affairs .... Mr. Michael MURDERS
32 Vice Pres for Student Services .... Dr. Derek MOORE
11 VP for Finance & Administration .... Mr. Carey TUCKER
13 Chief Information Officer .... Dr. Tim KIRK
26 Public Information Officer .... Mr. Heath WALDROP
84 Dean of Enrollment Services .... Mr. Dean INMAN
08 Director Library Media Center .... Mr. Philip SHACKELFORD
37 Director of Financial Aid .... Ms. Veronda TATUM
04 Executive Asst to the President .... Ms. Susan JORDAN
15 Human Resources Director .... Mr. Bill FOWLER
18 Director of Physical Plant .... Vacant
30 Dir of Foundation/External Funding .... Ms. Cynthia REYNA
09 CIEAO .... Dr. Stephanie TULLY-DARTEZ
96 Director of Procurement/Budget .... Ms. Ann SOUTHALL
31 Dean Workforce & Continuing Educ .... Ms. Sherry HOWARD
49 Assoc VP Arts/Sci/Academic Support .... Dr. James YATES
76 Dean Health Sciences .... Ms. Caroline HAMMOND

Southeast Arkansas College (C)

1900 Hazel Street, Pine Bluff AR 71603-3900
County: Jefferson FICE Identification: 005707
Unit ID: 107637
Telephone: (870) 543-5900 Carnegie Class: Assoc/HT-High Trad
FAX Number: (870) 850-8636 Calendar System: Semester
URL: www.seark.edu
Established: 1991 Annual Undergrad Tuition & Fees (In-State): $3,855
Enrollment: 1,304 Coed
Affiliation or Control: State IRS Status: 501(c)3
Highest Offering: Associate Degree
Accreditation: NH, ADNUR, COARC, EMT, RAD, SURGT

01 President .... Dr. Stephen BLOOMBERG
05 Vice President Academic Affairs .... Ms. Gina TEEL
32 Vice President Student Affairs .... Mr. Scott KUTTENKULER
10 Vice President Fiscal Affairs .... Ms. Debbie WALLACE
21 Controller .... Mr. Steve BALLARD
13 Director of Technology Services .... Ms. JoAnn DUPRA
06 Registrar .... Ms. Lozanne CALHOUN
07 Director of Admissions .... Ms. Lozanne CALHOUN
15 Human Resources .... Ms. Rebecca MONK
18 Chief Facilities/Physical Plant .... Mr. Jerry MONK
37 Director Student Financial Aid .... Ms. Donna COX
04 Administrative Asst to President .... Ms. Karen BOGARD
08 Director of Library .... Ms. Kim WILLIAMS
105 Webmaster .... Mr. Terry CLAUSEN
97 Dean General Studies .... Dr. Mark SHANLEY
66 Dean Nursing & Allied Health .... Ms. Joyce SCOTT
103 Dean Technical Studies/Wkforce Dev .... Ms. Lyric SEYMORE

09 Director of Institutional Research .... Ms. Phylesia DAVIS
25 Compliance Officer .... Prof. Tracy HARRELL
26 Chief PR/Marketing/Comm Ofcr .... Mr. Cordell JORDAN
30 Director of Development .... Ms. Barbara DUNN
36 Dir Workforce/Career Development .... Mr. Jeff PULLIAM
121 Director of Advising & Retention .... Mr. Gene WHITE

Southern Arkansas University (D)

100 E University Street, Magnolia AR 71753-5000
County: Columbia FICE Identification: 001107
Unit ID: 107983
Telephone: (870) 235-4000 Carnegie Class: Masters/L
FAX Number: (870) 235-5005 Calendar System: Semester
URL: www.saumag.edu
Established: 1909 Annual Undergrad Tuition & Fees (In-State): $8,756
Enrollment: 4,643 Coed
Affiliation or Control: State IRS Status: 501(c)3
Highest Offering: Master's
Accreditation: NH, CAATE, CAEP, NUR, SW

01 President .... Dr. Trey BERRY
05 Provost/Vice Pres Academic Affairs .... Dr. David LANOUE
11 VP Administration/General Counsel .... Mr. Roger W. GILES
32 Vice President Student Affairs .... Dr. Donna Y. ALLEN
18 Director of Facilities .... Mr. Robert NASH
10 Vice President for Finance .... Ms. Shawana REED
30 Asst Vice President for Development .... Mr. Josh KEE
49 Dean Col Liberal/Perform Arts .... Dr. Helmut LANGERBEIN
50 Dean College of Business .... Dr. Robin SRONCE
53 Dean College of Education .... Dr. Kim BLOSS
81 Int Dean College of Sci & Eng .... Dr. Abdel BACHRI
58 Dean School of Graduate Studies .... Dr. Kim K. BLOSS
06 Registrar .... Mrs. Sandra WALKER
84 Dean Enrollment Services .... Ms. Sarah E. JENNINGS
35 Associate Dean of Students .... Mr. Carey BAKER
08 Director of Library .... Mr. Del G. DUKE
13 Director Info Technology Services .... Mr. Mike A. ARGO
38 Director Counsel/Testing Center .... Ms. Paula WASHINGTON-WOODS
39 Dean of Housing .... Ms. Sandra E. MARTIN
29 Director of Alumni Affairs .... Ms. Megan MCCURDY
110 Director of Development .... Ms. Macy BRASWELL
37 Director of Financial Aid .... Ms. Marcela C. MCRAE-BRUNSON
51 Director of Continuing Education .... Ms. Caroline WALLER
41 Director of Athletics .... Mr. Steve BROWNING
121 Director Student Support Services .... Ms. Eunice E. WALKER
36 Director of Placement Services .... Vacant
28 Assoc Dean Multicultural Affairs .... Mr. Cledis D. STUART
27 Assoc Dir Communications Center .... Ms. Caleigh MOYER
04 Asst to President .... Ms. LaTricia DAVIS
09 Director of Institutional Research .... Ms. Christine PACHECO
86 Director Government Relations .... Mrs. Sheryl EDWARDS
102 Director Foundation .... Ms. Macy BRASWELL

Southern Arkansas University Tech (E)

P.O. Box 3499, 6415 Spellman Road, Camden AR 71711
County: Calhoun FICE Identification: 007738
Unit ID: 107992
Telephone: (870) 574-4500 Carnegie Class: Assoc/HVT-High Non
FAX Number: (870) 574-4520 Calendar System: Semester
URL: www.sautech.edu
Established: 1967 Annual Undergrad Tuition & Fees (In-State): $4,977
Enrollment: 1,010 Coed
Affiliation or Control: State IRS Status: 501(c)3
Highest Offering: Associate Degree
Accreditation: NH

01 Chancellor .... Dr. Jason MORRISON
10 VC for Finance & Administration .... Mrs. Gaye MANNING
05 VC for Academics & Planning .... Dr. Valerie WILSON
32 VC for Student Services .... Mr. David MCLEANE
26 Dir Communications/Public Relations .... Mrs. Kim COKER
09 Dir Inst Effectiveness & Research .... Mr. Lee SANDERS
84 Dean of Enrollment Services .... Mrs. Jenny SANDERS
103 Director of Career Pathways .... Ms. LaTonya REED
88 Director of Career Academy .... Dr. Juanita MITCHELL
107 Director AETA & Workforce Education .... Mr. Randy HARPER
88 Director of AFTA .... Mrs. Rachel NIX
13 Dir Info Tech & Telephone Services .... Mrs. Laura JOHNSON
37 Director of Financial Aid .... Mrs. Connie RILEY
18 Director of Physical Plant .... Mr. Mike LARKINS
35 Director of Student Life .... Mr. Courtney HAYGOOD
06 Registrar .... Mr. Wayne BANKS
08 Director Rocket Success Ctr/Library .... Ms. Kyra JERRY
04 Assistant to the Chancellor .... Mrs. Tammy LARKINS
15 Director Human Resources .... Mrs. Olivia CLACK
21 Controller .... Mr. Dale TOMMEY
96 Buyer .... Mrs. Angela FRY
51 Director of Adult Education .... Mrs. Barbara HAMILTON
19 Director Security/Safety .... Mr. Jud MITCHELL
41 Athletic Director .... Mr. David MCLEANE
07 Director of Admissions .... Mrs. Jenny SANDERS
108 Director Institutional Assessment .... Mrs. Rita GIVENS

*University of Arkansas System Office (F)

2404 N University Avenue, Little Rock AR 72207-3608
County: Pulaski FICE Identification: 008008
Unit ID: 108056
Telephone: (501) 686-2500 Carnegie Class: N/A
FAX Number: (501) 686-2507
URL: www.uasys.edu

01 President .... Dr. Donald R. BOBBITT
04 Assistant to the President .... Ms. Angela HUDSON
05 Vice President Academic Affairs .... Dr. Michael K. MOORE
26 Vice President University Relations .... Ms. Melissa RUST
47 Vice President Agriculture .... Dr. Mark J. COCHRAN
10 Chief Financial Officer .... Ms. Gina TERRY
43 General Counsel .... Mrs. JoAnn MAXEY
116 Chief Audit Executive .... Mr. Jacob W. FLOURNOY
27 Director of Communications .... Mr. Nate HINKEL

*University of Arkansas Main Campus (G)

1125 W. Maple St., Fayetteville AR 72701-1201
County: Washington FICE Identification: 001108
Unit ID: 106397
Telephone: (479) 575-4140 Carnegie Class: DU-Highest
FAX Number: (479) 575-2361 Calendar System: Semester
URL: www.uark.edu
Established: 1871 Annual Undergrad Tuition & Fees (In-State): $9,130
Enrollment: 27,558 Coed
Affiliation or Control: State IRS Status: 501(c)3
Highest Offering: Doctorate
Accreditation: NH, ART, CAATE, CACREP, CAEPN, CIDA, CLPSY, DIETD, JOUR, LAW, LSAR, MUS, NURSE, SP, SW, THEA

02 Chancellor .... Dr. Joseph E. STEINMETZ
04 Executive Asst to the Chancellor .... Ms. Sally Ann ADAMS
05 Provost & EVC Academic Affs .... Dr. James COLEMAN
10 Vice Chanc Finance & Admin .... Mr. Tim O'DONNELL
111 Vice Chanc for Advancement .... Mr. Mark POWER
86 Vice Chanc Governmental Relations .... Mr. Randy MASSANELLI
45 Vice Provost Planning .... Vacant
46 Int Vice Provost Research/Econ Dev .... Dr. Kim NEEDY
32 Vice Chanc Student Affairs .... Mr. Charles ROBINSON
84 Vice Prov Enrol Mgt/Dean Admissions .... Dr. Suzanne MCCRAY
100 Assoc Vice Chanc and Chief of Staff .... Ms. Laura JACOBS
25 AVP Research & Sponsored Pgms .... Ms. Jennifer TAYLOR
15 Assoc Vice Chanc Human Resources .... Ms. Debbie MCLOUD
18 Assoc Vice Chanc Facilities Mgmt .... Mr. Mike JOHNSON
21 Assoc Vice Chanc Business Affairs .... Ms. Colleen M. BRINEY
35 Sr Assoc VC & Dean of Students .... Ms. Melissa HARDWOOD-ROM
26 Asst Vice Chanc University Rels .... Mr. Mark RUSHING
08 Dean of Libraries .... Ms. Carolyn H. ALLEN
49 Dean of Arts & Sciences .... Dr. Todd G. SHIELDS
50 Dean Sam Walton College of Business .... Dr. Matthew WALLER
47 Dean of Agriculture .... Dr. Deacue FIELDS
53 Dean Education/Health Professions .... Dr. Michael T. MILLER
48 Dean of Architecture .... Mr. Peter MACKEITH
58 Dean of Graduate School .... Dr. Kim NEEDY
54 Dean of Engineering .... Dr. John ENGLISH
92 Dean Honors College .... Dr. Lynda COON
61 Dean of the Law School .... Ms. Margaret MCCABE
29 Assoc Vice Chanc for Alumni .... Ms. Brandy A. COX
22 Director of Equal Opportunity .... Ms. Danielle L. WOOD-WILLIAMS
07 Assoc Vice Provost for Enroll .... Ms. Wendy D. STOUFFER
38 Dir of Counseling/Psych Services .... Dr. Josette CLINE
19 Director University Police .... Mr. Steve GAHAGANS
36 Exec Dir of Career Develop Center .... Ms. Angela S. WILLIAMS
13 Assoc VC for Info Technology .... Dr. Chris MCCOY
06 Registrar .... Mr. Dave DAWSON
96 Director of Purchasing .... Ms. Linda FAST
123 Director Graduate & Intl Admissions .... Ms. Lynn MOSESSO
37 Director of Financial Aid .... Mr. Phillip Andrew BLEVINS
09 Dir Institutional Research & Assess .... Mr. Gary GUNDERMAN
102 Sr Dir Ofc Corporate & Found Rels .... Ms. Cherie RACHEL
104 Director Study Abroad .... Ms. Sarah L. MALLOY
41 Athletic Director .... Mr. Hunter YURACHEK
44 Director Annual Giving .... Ms. Lizzie JOHNSON

*University of Arkansas at Fort Smith (H)

PO Box 3649, Fort Smith AR 72913-3649
County: Sebastian FICE Identification: 001110
Unit ID: 108092
Telephone: (479) 788-7000 Carnegie Class: Bac-Diverse
FAX Number: (479) 788-7003 Calendar System: Semester
URL: www.uafs.edu
Established: 1928 Annual Undergrad Tuition & Fees (In-District): $5,593
Enrollment: 6,638 Coed
Affiliation or Control: State/Local IRS Status: 501(c)3
Highest Offering: Master's
Accreditation: NH, ART, CAEP, DH, DMS, MUS, NAIT, NURSE, RAD, SURGT, @SW

02 Chancellor .... Dr. Terisa C. RILEY
05 Provost/Vice Chanc Academic Affairs .... Dr. Georgia HALE
111 Vice Chancellor Univ Advancement .... Mr. Blake RICKMAN
10 Vice Chanc Finance & Administration .... Dr. Brad SHERIFF
32 Vice Chancellor Student Affairs .... Dr. Lee KREHBIEL
58 Assoc Provost/Dir of Grad Studies .... Dr. Margaret TANNER
31 Assoc VC Campus/Cmty Events .... Mr. Stacey JONES
86 Director Govt & Univ Relations .... Mr. Jordan HALE
20 Asst to Provost/Dir Dev Educ .... Ms. Diana ROWDEN
100 Chief of Staff & Vice Chanc .... Vacant

76 Int Dean College Health Sciences .... Dr. Ron DARBEAU
50 Dean College of Business .... Dr. Ashok SUBRAMANIAN
72 Dean Col Applied Science/Tech .... Dr. Ken WARDEN
72 Dean Col Sci/Tech/Engineering/Math .... Dr. Ron DARBEAU
60 Dean Col of Comm/Lang/Arts & Soc .... Dr. Paul HANKINS
15 Dir Human Resources/EEO Officer .... Ms. Bev MCCLENDON
12 Interim Dir Western AR Tech Ctr .... Dr. Andrea SLATON
88 Dir of Student Professional Dev Ctr .... Mr. Ron ORICK
45 Asst Provost Inst Effectiveness .... Dr. John JONES
88 Director of Instructional Support .... Dr. Tara MISHRA
08 Director of Library Services .... Ms. Anne LIEBST
39 Director of Student Housing .... Ms. Beth EPPINGER
37 Director of Financial Aid .... Mr. David SEWARD
07 Dean of Admissions .... Mr. Steve ERVIN
121 Director of Advisement .... Ms. Julie MOSLEY
06 Registrar .... Mr. Wayne WOMACK
88 Exec Dir of International Relations .... Mr. Nicolas PATTILLO
26 Dir Marketing/Communications .... Mr. Chris KELLY
41 Director of Athletics .... Mr. Curtis JANZ
96 Director of Procurement Services .... Ms. Rhonda CATON
27 Interim Dir of Public Information .... Ms. Rachel PUTMAN
18 Director of Plant Operations .... Mr. Bill PIERCE
103 Dir CBPD/Family Enterprise Ctr .... Mr. Dave ROBERTSON
13 Director Technology Services .... Mr. Terry MEADOWS
19 Dir Chief of University Police .... Mr. Ray OTTMAN
29 Director of Alumni Affairs .... Mr. Rick GOINS
112 Director of Planned Giving .... Ms. Anne THOMAS
36 Asst Director Career Services .... Mr. Jeff ADAMS
53 Int Executive Director Education .... Dr. Monica RILEY

*University of Arkansas Hope-Texarkana (A)

PO Box 140, 2500 S Main Street, Hope AR 71802-0140

County: Hempstead | FICE Identification: 005732 | Unit ID: 107725
Telephone: (870) 777-5722 | Carnegie Class: Assoc/MT-VT-High Trad
FAX Number: (870) 777-5957 | Calendar System: Semester
URL: www.uacch.edu
Established: 1991 | Annual Undergrad Tuition & Fees (In-State): $2,830
Enrollment: 1,536 | Coed
Affiliation or Control: State | IRS Status: 501(c)3
Highest Offering: Associate Degree
Accreditation: NH, EMT, FUSER

02 Chancellor .... Mr. Chris THOMASON
10 Exec Vice Chanc Stdnt Svc & Finance .... Mr. Brian BERRY
05 Vice Chancellor for Academics .... Ms. Laura CLARK
32 Dean of Students .... Mr. Christopher SMITH
108 Dean of Institutional Effectiveness .... Mr. John HOLLIS
88 Director of Hempstead Hall .... Ms. Amanda LANCE
111 Dir of Institutional Advancement .... Ms. Anna POWELL
13 Chief Info Technology Officer (CIO) .... Mr. Chuck JORDAN

*University of Arkansas at Little Rock (B)

2801 S University Avenue, Little Rock AR 72204-1099

County: Pulaski | FICE Identification: 001101 | Unit ID: 106245
Telephone: (501) 569-3000 | Carnegie Class: DU-Higher
FAX Number: (501) 569-8915 | Calendar System: Semester
URL: www.ualr.edu
Established: 1927 | Annual Undergrad Tuition & Fees (In-State): $9,544
Enrollment: 11,624 | Coed
Affiliation or Control: State | IRS Status: 501(c)3
Highest Offering: Doctorate
Accreditation: NH, ADNUR, ART, CACREP, CAEP, CONST, DENT, LAW, MUS, NUR, SPAA, SW, THEA

02 Chancellor .... Dr. Andrew ROGERSON
05 Executive Vice Chancellor & Provost .... Dr. Christina S. DRALE
32 Vice Chancellor for Student Affairs .... Dr. Mark A. POISEL
10 Vice Chanc Finance & Administration .. Mr. Steve J. MCCLELLAN
111 Vice Chancellor Advancement .... Mr. Christian O'NEAL
41 Vice Chancellor & Dir of Athletics .... Mr. Chasse S. CONQUE
86 Vice Chancellor University Affairs .... Ms. Joni C. LEE
13 Associate Vice Chancellor & CIO .... Dr. Thomas BUNTON
06 Registrar .... Ms. Malissa MATHIS
15 Director of Human Resources .... Dr. Ignatius C. AZEBEOKHAI
26 Associate VC of Communications Mktg ... Ms. Judy G. WILLIAMS
09 Assoc Provost & Chief Data Officer .... Dr. William C. DECKER
37 Director Financial Aid .... Ms. Carlia G. SMITH
07 Director of Admissions .... Ms. Chelsea B. WARD
88 Assoc Prov for UALR Collect and Arc .... Dr. Deborah J. BALDWIN
19 Chief of Police .... Ms. Regina W. CARTER
25 Director Research & Sponsored Pgm .... Ms. Tammie L. CASH

*University of Arkansas for Medical Sciences (C)

4301 W Markham, Little Rock AR 72205-7199

County: Pulaski | FICE Identification: 001109 | Unit ID: 106263
Telephone: (501) 686-7000 | Carnegie Class: Spec-4-yr-Med
FAX Number: (501) 686-5905 | Calendar System: Semester
URL: www.uams.edu
Established: 1879 | Annual Undergrad Tuition & Fees (In-State): N/A
Enrollment: 2,836 | Coed
Affiliation or Control: State | IRS Status: 501(c)3
Highest Offering: Doctorate
Accreditation: NH, ARCPA, AUD, CAHIIM, COARC, CYTO, DH, DIETI, DMS, HSA, IPSY, MED, MT, NMT, NURSE, PH, PHAR, PTA, RAD, SP, SURGT

02 Chancellor .... Dr. Cam PATTERSON
05 Provost and CAO .... Dr. Stephanie F. GARDNER
10 Vice Chancellor Finance & CFO .... Ms. Amanda GEORGE
26 Vice Chanc Communications/Marketing ..... Ms. Leslie W. TAYLOR
111 VC Institutional Advancement .... Ms. Angela WIMMER
11 Assoc Vice Chanc Campus Operations .... Mr. Brian COTTEN
28 VC Diversity/Equity & Inclusion .... Dr. Brian E. GITTENS
13 Assoc VC IT/CIO .... Mr. Michael D. GREER
08 Assoc Provost Library/Stdnt Svcs .... Dr. Jan HART
15 Int Assoc Vice Chancellor for HR .... Ms. Becky HARWELL
20 Asst Provost Teaching Lrng Support .... Dr. Steve E. BOONE
32 Assoc Provost Students & Admin .... Dr. Kristen STERBA
37 Director Financial Services .... Ms. Gloria KEMP
63 Dean College of Medicine .... Dr. Christopher T. WESTFALL
76 Dean College of Health Professions .... Dr. Susan LONG
66 Dean College of Nursing .... Dr. Patricia COWAN
67 Dean College of Pharmacy .... Dr. Cindy STOWE
58 Dean of the Graduate School .... Dr. Robert E. MCGEHEE, JR.
88 Dean College of Public Health .... Dr. Mark WILLIAMS
06 Dir Enrollment Svcs/Chief Registrar ..... Mr. Clinton D. EVERHART
39 Dir Campus Life/Stdnt Support Svcs .... Ms. Cheri D. GOFORTH
100 Chief of Staff .... Ms. Amy WENGER

† Tuition figure is for Medical School. Other school's tuitions vary widely.

*University of Arkansas at Monticello (D)

346 University Drive, Monticello AR 71656-3596

County: Drew | FICE Identification: 001085 | Unit ID: 106485
Telephone: (870) 367-1020 | Carnegie Class: Masters/M
FAX Number: (870) 460-1321 | Calendar System: Semester
URL: www.uamont.edu
Established: 1909 | Annual Undergrad Tuition & Fees (In-State): $7,462
Enrollment: 3,700 | Coed
Affiliation or Control: State | IRS Status: 501(c)3
Highest Offering: Master's
Accreditation: NH, CAEPN, EMT, MUS, SW

02 Chancellor .... Dr. Karla HUGHES
05 VC for Academic Affairs .... Dr. Peggy DOSS
111 VC for Advancement .... Mr. Jeff WEAVER
32 VC for Student Engagement .... Dr. Moses GOLDMON
10 VC for Finance and Administration .... Mr. Alex BECKER
12 VC for UAM College of Tech-Crossett .... Ms. Linda RUSHING
12 VC for UAM College of Tech-McGehee .... Mr. Bob WARE
04 Assistant to the Chancellor .... Ms. Christy PACE
21 Assoc VC for Finance and Admin .... Ms. Debbie GASAWAY
13 Chief Information Officer .... Ms. Anissa ROSS
86 Director of Government Relations .... Dr. John DAVIS
35 Dean of Students .... Vacant
84 Exec Dir of Admission/Enroll Mgmt .... Ms. Tawana GREENE
19 Director of University Police .... Mr. John KIDWELL
22 Dir Affirmative Action/EEO .... Ms. Sage LOYD
41 Director of Athletics .... Mr. Padraic MCMEEL
38 Director of Counseling/Testing .... Ms. Roberta THOMAS
37 Director of Financial Aid .... Ms. Becky HAMMETT
09 Director of Institutional Research .... Ms. Lisa CATER
08 Director of Library .... Mr. Daniel BOICE
26 Director of Marketing/Public Rels .... Ms. Ember DAVIS
18 Director of Physical Plant .... Mr. Rusty RIPPEE
96 Director of Purchasing .... Ms. Gay PACE
06 Registrar .... Ms. Sylvia MILLER
39 Director of Housing .... Ms. Rachel COOPER

*University of Arkansas at Pine Bluff (E)

1200 N University Drive, Pine Bluff AR 71601-2799

County: Jefferson | FICE Identification: 001086 | Unit ID: 106412
Telephone: (870) 575-8000 | Carnegie Class: Bac-Diverse
FAX Number: (870) 543-8009 | Calendar System: Semester
URL: www.uapb.edu
Established: 1873 | Annual Undergrad Tuition & Fees (In-State): $8,038
Enrollment: 2,612 | Coed
Affiliation or Control: State | IRS Status: 501(c)3
Highest Offering: Doctorate
Accreditation: NH, AAFCS, ACBSP, ART, CAEPN, MUS, NAIT, NURSE, SW

02 Chancellor .... Dr. Laurence B. ALEXANDER
05 Vice Chanc Academic Affairs .... Dr. Robert CARR
10 Vice Chanc Finance & Admin .... Dr. Carla M. MARTIN
32 Vice Chancellor Student Affairs .... Mr. Elbert BENNETT
45 Vice Chanc Research/Innovation .... Dr. Mansour MORTAZAVI
84 Vice Chanc Enrollment Management .... Dr. Linda OKIROR
100 Chief of Staff .... Mrs. Janet BROILES
41 Athletics Director .... Mr. Melvin HINES, JR.
15 Director of Human Resources .... Mrs. Gladys BENFORD
13 Director of Technical Services .... Mrs. Willette TOTTEN
09 Director of Institutional Research .... Mrs. Margaret TAYLOR
06 Registrar .... Mrs. Erica FULTON
29 Director of Alumni Affairs .... Mr. John KUYKENDALL
08 Head Librarian .... Mr. Edward FONTENETTE
103 Dir Workforce/Career Development .... Mrs. Shirley CHERRY
108 Director Institutional Assessment .... Dr. Steve LOCHMANN
37 Director Student Financial Aid .... Mrs. Janice KEARNEY
22 Dir Affirmative Action/EEO .... Vacant
88 Director of Recruitment .... Mr. Chris ROBINSON
07 Director of Admissions .... Ms. Philomena OWASOYO
18 Director Facilities/Physical Plant .... Vacant
19 Director Security/Safety .... Chief Maxcie THOMAS
30 VC Development/Advancement .... Mr. George COTTON
44 Director Annual or Planned Giving ... Dr. Margaret MARTIN-HALL
50 Dean Sch of Business & Management ... Mr. Lawrence AWOPETU
53 Dean School of Education .... Dr. Pamela RUSS
96 Director of Purchasing .... Mrs. Wauntia TROTTER
104 Director Study Abroad .... Dr. Pamela MOORE
38 Director Student Counseling .... Ms. Joyce VAUGHN
39 Int Assoc Dean Residential Services .... Mr. Ralph OWENS
86 Director Government Relations .... Mr. John KUYKENDALL

*University of Arkansas System eVersity (F)

2402 N. University Avenue, Little Rock AR 72207

County: Pulaski | Identification: 667336
Telephone: (844) 837-7489 | Carnegie Class: Not Classified
FAX Number: N/A | Calendar System: Other
URL: eversity.edu
Established: 2014 | Annual Undergrad Tuition & Fees (In-State): N/A
Enrollment: N/A | Coed
Affiliation or Control: State | IRS Status: 501(c)3
Highest Offering: Baccalaureate
Accreditation: DEAC

05 Chief Academic & Operating Officer .... Dr. Michael K. MOORE

*Cossatot Community College of the University of Arkansas (G)

183 College Drive, De Queen AR 71832

County: Sevier | FICE Identification: 022209 | Unit ID: 106795
Telephone: (870) 584-4471 | Carnegie Class: Assoc/MT-VT-High Non
FAX Number: N/A | Calendar System: Semester
URL: www.cccua.edu
Established: 1991 | Annual Undergrad Tuition & Fees (In-District): $3,450
Enrollment: 1,506 | Coed
Affiliation or Control: State/Local | IRS Status: 501(c)3
Highest Offering: Associate Degree
Accreditation: NH, ACBSP, OTA, @PTAA

02 Chancellor .... Dr. Steve COLE
05 Vice Chancellor of Academics .... Mrs. Ashley AYLETT
45 VC of Planning and Facilities .... Mr. Mike KINKADE
10 Vice Chancellor Business/Finance .... Mrs. Charlotte JOHNSON
32 Director of Student Services .... Mrs. Suzanne WARD
37 Director Student Financial Aid .... Mrs. Denise HAMMOND
06 Registrar/Institutional Reporting .... Mrs. Brenda MORRIS
103 Dir of Public Svc/Workforce Dev .... Mrs. Tammy COLEMAN
12 Director of Ashdown Campus .... Mr. Barrett REED
15 Director of Human Resources .... Ms. Kelly PLUNK
13 Director of Technology .... Mr. Tony HARGROVE
102 Coordinator of Foundation .... Mr. Dustin ROBERTS
04 Executive Assistant to Chancellor .... Ms. Wendy GARCIA

*Phillips Community College of the University of Arkansas (H)

PO Box 785, Helena AR 72342-0785

County: Phillips | FICE Identification: 001104 | Unit ID: 107619
Telephone: (870) 338-6474 | Carnegie Class: Assoc/MT-VT-High Non
FAX Number: (870) 338-7542 | Calendar System: Semester
URL: www.pccua.edu
Established: 1965 | Annual Undergrad Tuition & Fees (In-District): $2,930
Enrollment: 1,636 | Coed
Affiliation or Control: State/Local | IRS Status: 501(c)3
Highest Offering: Associate Degree
Accreditation: NH, ACBSP, ADNUR, MLTAD

02 Chancellor .... Dr. G. Keith PINCHBACK
05 Vice Chancellor for Instruction .... Dr. Deborah KING
10 Vice Chanc Finance & Administration .... Mr. Stan SULLIVANT
32 Vice Chanc Student Svcs/Registrar .... Mr. Scott POST
30 Vice Chanc Col Advancement/Res Dev .... Mrs. Rhonda ST. COLUMBIA
12 Vice Chancellor Stuttgart Campus .... Mrs. Kim KIRBY
12 Vice Chancellor DeWitt Campus .... Mrs. Carolyn TURNER
84 Director Enrollment Management .... Mr. Von DANIELS
13 Director IT .... Mr. Jason JACO
37 Director Financial Aid .... Ms. Barbra STEVENSON

*University of Arkansas Community College at Batesville (I)

2005 White Drive, PO Box 3350, Batesville AR 72503-3350

County: Independence | FICE Identification: 020735 | Unit ID: 106999
Telephone: (870) 612-2000 | Carnegie Class: Assoc/HVT-High Trad
FAX Number: (870) 793-4988 | Calendar System: Semester
URL: www.uaccb.edu
Established: 1975 | Annual Undergrad Tuition & Fees (In-District): $2,482
Enrollment: 1,246 | Coed
Affiliation or Control: State/Local | IRS Status: 501(c)3
Highest Offering: Associate Degree

Accreditation: NH, ADNUR, EMT

02 Chancellor .... Ms. Deborah J. FRAZIER
04 Assistant to the Chancellor .... Ms. Jodie HIGHTOWER
05 Vice Chancellor for Academics .... Dr. Brian SHONK
32 Vice Chanc Student Affairs .... Mr. Greg THORNBURG
10 Vice Chancellor Finance and Admin .... Mr. Gayle COOPER
09 VC Research/Planning/Assessment .... Dr. Anne AUSTIN
49 Chair Div of Arts & Humanities .... Ms. Susan TRIPP
50 Chair Div Business/Tech/Public Svc .... Dr. Tamara GRIFFIN
76 Chair Div Nursing/Allied Health .... Ms. Marietta CANDLER
81 Chair Div of Math and Science .... Mr. Douglas MUSE
75 Dir of Career and Tech Educ .... Mr. Zachery HARBER
09 Dir of Institutional Research .... Mr. Rob MONTGOMERY
07 Director of Admissions .... Ms. Amy FOREE
13 Director Information Services .... Mr. Steve COLLINS
06 Dir Student Information/Registrar .... Ms. Casey BROMLEY
37 Director of Financial Aid .... Ms. Kristen CROSS
111 Director of Advancement .... Ms. Kim WHITTEN
18 Director of Maintenance .... Mr. Heath WOOLDRIDGE
36 Director Student Development .... Ms. Louise HUGHES
103 Dir of Workforce and Career Svcs .... Ms. Becky WARREN
08 Director Library .... Mr. Jay STRICKLAND
21 Controller .... Ms. Waynna DOCKINS
15 Human Resources Specialist .... Ms. Julie JOHNSON
96 Purchasing Agent .... Ms. Peggy JACKSON
40 Bookstore Manager .... Ms. Luanne BARBER

*University of Arkansas Community College at Morrilton (A)

1537 University Boulevard, Morrilton AR 72110-9601
County: Conway FICE Identification: 005245
Unit ID: 107585
Telephone: (501) 354-2465 Carnegie Class: Assoc/MT-VT-High Trad
FAX Number: (501) 977-2044 Calendar System: Semester
URL: www.uaccm.edu
Established: 1961 Annual Undergrad Tuition & Fees (In-State): $3,140
Enrollment: 1,921 Coed
Affiliation or Control: State IRS Status: 501(c)3
Highest Offering: Associate Degree
Accreditation: NH

02 Chancellor .... Vacant
05 Vice Chancellor Academic Services .... Ms. Diana ARN
10 Vice Chancellor for Finance .... Ms. Lisa WILLENBERG
32 Vice Chancellor Student Services .... Mr. Darren JONES
09 Director of Institutional Research .... Ms. Beth HAWKINS
08 Librarian .... Ms. Kristen COOKE
06 Registrar .... Ms. Linda HOLLAND
37 Financial Aid Director .... Ms. Jennifer WILLIAMS
26 Dir Marketing & Public Relations .... Ms. Mary CLARK
13 Director of Information Tech .... Mr. Steve WALLACE
18 Director of the Physical Plant .... Mr. C. Allen HOLLOWAY
07 Director of Admissions .... Ms. Rachel MULLINS
103 Coord Workforce Develop/Cmty Educ .... Ms. Jessica ROHLMAN
15 Director Personnel Services .... Ms. Judy SANDERS
30 Chief Development .... Ms. Anne CADLE
38 Director Student Counseling .... Mr. Cody DAVIS
96 Director of Purchasing .... Ms. Anna HALBROOK

*University of Arkansas - Pulaski Technical College (B)

3000 W Scenic Drive, North Little Rock AR 72118-3399
County: Pulaski FICE Identification: 020753
Unit ID: 107664
Telephone: (501) 812-2200 Carnegie Class: Assoc/HT-High Trad
FAX Number: (501) 771-2844 Calendar System: Semester
URL: www.uaptc.edu
Established: 1991 Annual Undergrad Tuition & Fees (In-State): $5,252
Enrollment: 6,038 Coed
Affiliation or Control: State IRS Status: 501(c)3
Highest Offering: Associate Degree
Accreditation: NH, ACFEI, COARC, DA, EMT, OTA

02 Chancellor .... Dr. Margaret ELLIBEE
05 Provost .... Dr. Marla STRECKER
10 Vice Chancellor for Finance .... Ms. Charlette MOORE
111 Vice Chancellor for Advancement .... Ms. Shannon BOSHEARS
103 Director of Workforce/Comm Educ .... Ms. Sharon CANTRELL
32 Dean of Student Affairs .... Mr. Mason CAMPBELL
07 Dean of Admissions/Financial Aid .... Dr. John LEWIS
84 Director Enrollment Svcs .... Mr. Zachary PERRINE
07 Director of Admissions .... Ms. Kyanna BEARD
08 Library Director .... Ms. Wendy DAVIS
18 Director of Physical Plant .... Mr. Bryan RUSHER
09 Director of Institutional Research .... Ms. Jasmine RAY
96 Director of Purchasing .... Ms. Emily FISHER
13 Director of Information Services .... Mr. David GLOVER
15 Director of Human Resources .... Ms. Britni ELDER
04 Assistant to the President .... Ms. Tena CARRIGAN
37 Director of Financial Aid .... Ms. Lori TAYLOR
26 Director Public Relations/Marketing .... Mr. Tim JONES
72 Dean Technical/Professional Studies .... Dr. Bentley WALLACE
81 Dean Science/Math/Allied Health .... Dr. Marcio BRYANT HOWE
57 Dean Fine Arts/Humanities/Social Sc .... Dr. Christy OBERSTE
06 Registrar .... Ms. Ana HUNT
19 Director Security/Safety .... Mr. Mark STAFFORD

*University of Arkansas Rich Mountain (C)

1100 College Drive, Mena AR 71953-2500
County: Polk FICE Identification: 021111
Unit ID: 107743
Telephone: (479) 394-7622 Carnegie Class: Assoc/MT-VT-High Non
FAX Number: (479) 394-7295 Calendar System: Semester
URL: www.uarichmountain.edu
Established: 1983 Annual Undergrad Tuition & Fees (In-District): $2,880
Enrollment: 938 Coed
Affiliation or Control: State/Local IRS Status: 501(c)3
Highest Offering: Associate Degree
Accreditation: NH

02 Chancellor .... Dr. Phillip WILSON
05 Vice Chancellor Academic Affairs .... Dr. Krystal THRAILKILL
32 VC Student Affairs/Registrar .... Mr. Chad FIELDS
10 Vice Chancellor Administration/CFO .... Mr. Morris BOYDSTUN
13 Chief Information Officer .... Mr. Chris MASTERS
08 Director Library Services .... Ms. Brenda MINER
37 Financial Aid Director .... Ms. Mary STANDERFER
30 Director Business Outreach .... Ms. LeAnn DILBECK
18 Associate Director Physical Plant .... Mr. Mike BECK
97 Director Adult Basic Education .... Mr. Joel BUSH
15 Director of Human Resources .... Ms. Amy LUDWIG
07 Director of Admissions .... Ms. Wendy MCDANIEL
21 Controller .... Ms. Patricia HALL
26 Dir Marketing/Community Relations .... Ms. LeAnn DILBECK
04 Executive Asst to Chancellor .... Ms. Yanel RIOS
88 Student Union Manager .... Mr. Jason WOOD
09 Coordinator Institutional Research .... Ms. Tammy ODOM
21 Budget Analysis Coordinator .... Ms. Amy LUDWIG
18 Constructions/Grounds Supervisor .... Mr. David DILBECK

*Phillips Community College of the University of Arkansas-DeWitt (D)

1210 Rice Belt Avenue, DeWitt AR 72042
Telephone: (870) 946-3506 Identification: 770174
Accreditation: &NH

*Phillips Community College of the University of Arkansas-Stuttgart (E)

2807 Hwy 165 South, Stuttgart AR 72160-2408
Telephone: (870) 673-4201 Identification: 770175
Accreditation: &NH

*University of Arkansas at Monticello College of Technology-Crossett (F)

1326 Highway 52 W, Crossett AR 71635
Telephone: (870) 364-6414 Identification: 770176
Accreditation: &NH

*University of Arkansas at Monticello College of Technology-McGehee (G)

PO Box 747, McGehee AR 71654
Telephone: (870) 222-5360 Identification: 770177
Accreditation: &NH

University of Central Arkansas (H)

201 Donaghey Avenue, Conway AR 72035-0001
County: Faulkner FICE Identification: 001092
Unit ID: 106704
Telephone: (501) 450-5000 Carnegie Class: DU-Mod
FAX Number: (501) 450-5003 Calendar System: Semester
URL: uca.edu
Established: 1907 Annual Undergrad Tuition & Fees (In-State): $8,752
Enrollment: 11,343 Coed
Affiliation or Control: State IRS Status: 501(c)3
Highest Offering: Doctorate
Accreditation: NH, ART, CAATE, CIDA, COPSY, DIETD, DIETI, MUS, NURSE, OT, PTA, SCPSY, SP, THEA

01 President .... Dr. Houston D. DAVIS
05 Provost/Exec VP Academic Affairs .... Dr. Patricia S. POULTER
10 VP Finance/Administration .... Ms. Diane D. NEWTON
32 VP Student Services/Inst Diversity .... Mr. Ronnie D. WILLIAMS
43 General Counsel .... Mr. Warren READNOUR
22 Asc Gen Counsel/Compliance Officer .... Ms. Mindy PIPKIN
26 Director of Media Relations .... Ms. Amanda HOELZEMAN
111 VP for University Advancement .... Dr. T. Kale GOBER
41 Athletic Director .... Dr. Brad TEAGUE
15 AVP for Human Resources .... Dr. Graham GILLIS
85 AVP Intl Education/Engagement .... Dr. Phillip BAILEY
100 Chief of Staff .... Ms. Amy WHITEHEAD
21 Controller .... Mr. Jeremy BRUNER
108 Assoc Provost Inst Effectiveness .... Dr. Jonathan A. GLENN
20 Associate Provost Academic Success .... Dr. Kurt A. BONIECKI
58 Dean of Graduate School .... Dr. Angela BARLOW
50 Dean College of Business .... Dr. Michael HARGIS
53 Dean College of Education .... Dr. Victoria GROVES-SCOTT
76 Dean Col Health/Behavioral Science .... Dr. Jimmy ISHEE
49 Dean Col of Liberal Arts .... Dr. Thomas WILLIAMS
81 Dean Col Natural Sci/Math .... Dr. Steve ADDISON
57 Dean Fine Arts & Communication .... Mr. Terry WRIGHT

35 Dean of Students .... Ms. Kelly OWENS
92 Dean of Honors College .... Dr. Patricia SMITH
07 Director of Admissions .... Ms. Courtney BRYANT
08 Library Director .... Mr. R. Dean COVINGTON
06 Registrar .... Ms. Becky D. RASNICK
09 Director Institutional Research .... Ms. Amber L. HALL
13 Chief Information Officer .... Mr. Michael LLOYD
37 Director Student Financial Aid .... Ms. Cheryl C. LYONS
36 Dir Career Svcs/Cooperative Educ .... Dr. Kathy RICE-CLAYBORN
19 Chief University Police .... Mr. John MERGUIE
38 Director Counseling Center .... Dr. Susan SOBEL
39 Director Housing & Residence Life .... Dr. Stephanie H. MCBRAYER
29 Director of Alumni Services .... Mr. Jesse THILL
116 Director Internal Audits .... Ms. Pamela L. MASSEY
18 Director Physical Plant .... Mr. Larry D. LAWRENCE
96 Director of Purchasing .... Ms. Cassandra MCCUIEN-SMITH
113 Director Student Accounts .... Mr. Chad HEARNE

University of the Ozarks (I)

415 College Avenue, Clarksville AR 72830-2880
County: Johnson FICE Identification: 001094
Unit ID: 107558
Telephone: (479) 979-1000 Carnegie Class: Bac-Diverse
FAX Number: (479) 979-1355 Calendar System: Semester
URL: www.ozarks.edu
Established: 1834 Annual Undergrad Tuition & Fees: $24,230
Enrollment: 755 Coed
Affiliation or Control: Presbyterian Church (U.S.A.) IRS Status: 501(c)3
Highest Offering: Baccalaureate
Accreditation: NH, CAEP

01 President .... Mr. Richard L. DUNSWORTH
05 Provost .... Dr. Alyson A. GILL
10 VP for Finance & Administration .... Vacant
84 VP for Enrollment Management .... Mr. Reggie HILL
07 Assistant Director of Admission .... Mr. Joseph HUGHES
42 Chaplain .... Rev. Jeremy WILHEMI
06 Registrar .... Ms. Monica FRIZZELL
08 Librarian .... Mr. Stuart P. STELZER
36 Director of Career Services .... Ms. Ruth WALTON
29 Director Alumni Affairs .... Vacant
41 Athletic Director .... Mr. Jimmy CLARK
26 Dir University/Public Relations .... Mr. Larry A. ISCH
111 VP of Advancement .... Ms. Lori A. MCBEE
88 Director Jones Learning Center .... Ms. Dody PELTS
09 Director of Institutional Research .... Ms. Cara FLINN
13 Director of Information Technology .... Ms. Vickie ALSTON
32 Dean of Students .... Mr. Lucas MORRILL
81 Dean Div of Mathematics & Sciences .... Dr. Sean COLEMAN
79 Dean Div Humanities & Fine Arts .... Dr. David DAILY
15 Human Resources Manager .... Ms. Karen SCHLUTERMAN
19 Director Security/Safety .... Mr. Larry GRAHAM
21 Controller .... Mr. Albert LEDING
18 Chief Facilities/Physical Plant .... Mr. Joey ETHERIDGE
37 Dir of Student Financial Services .... Ms. Kim MADDOX
30 Director of Development .... Ms. Cara GRAHAM
04 Admin Assistant to the President .... Ms. Connie BOOTY
83 Dean Div of Social Sciences .... Mr. Joel ROSSMAIER
38 Director Student Counseling .... Mr. Matthew EUBANKS

Williams Baptist University (J)

60 W. Fulbright Avenue, Walnut Ridge AR 72476
County: Lawrence FICE Identification: 001106
Unit ID: 107877
Telephone: (870) 886-6741 Carnegie Class: Bac-A&S
FAX Number: (870) 886-3924 Calendar System: Semester
URL: www.williamsbu.edu
Established: 1941 Annual Undergrad Tuition & Fees: $17,320
Enrollment: 501 Coed
Affiliation or Control: Southern Baptist IRS Status: 501(c)3
Highest Offering: Master's
Accreditation: NH, CAEPN

01 President .... Dr. Stan NORMAN
05 VP Academic Affairs & Campus Life .... Dr. Brad BAINE
111 VP for University Advancement/COO .... Dr. Doug WALKER
13 VP Creative Services & Technology .... Dr. Brett COOPER
84 VP for Enrollment Management .... Mrs. Angela FLIPPO
32 Dean of Students .... Mr. Amber N. GRADY
06 Registrar .... Mrs. Tonya D. BOLTON
04 Administrative Asst to President .... Mrs. Jo C. PHILLIPS
08 Director Library Services .... Mrs. Pamela MERIDITH
37 Director Student Financial Aid .... Dr. Andrew WATSON
38 Director of Counseling .... Ms. Aneita COOPER
42 Campus Minister .... Ms. Shannon LANE
18 Director Physical Plant .... Mr. Tony CONLEY
113 Bursar .... Mr. Aaron ANDREWS
14 Director Information Technologies .... Mr. Blake MCGINNIS
41 Athletic Director .... Mr. Jeff RIDER

CALIFORNIA

Abraham Lincoln University (K)

100 W Broadway, Suite 600, Glendale CA 91210
County: Los Angeles Identification: 667049
Unit ID: 488031
Telephone: (213) 252-5100 Carnegie Class: Spec-4-yr-Law
FAX Number: N/A Calendar System: Other
URL: www.alu.edu
Established: 1996 Annual Undergrad Tuition & Fees: N/A

Enrollment: 197 Coed
Affiliation or Control: Proprietary IRS Status: Proprietary
Highest Offering: First Professional Degree
Accreditation: DEAC

01 President & CEO .... Mr. Hyung J. PARK
61 Vice President/Dean School of Law .... Ms. Jessica K. PARK
05 Chief Academic Officer .... Mr. Robert ABEL, JR.
20 Academic Program Coordinator .... Mr. Andrew CHO
06 Registrar/Student Svcs Coord .... Ms. Lidby LOPEZ
07 Director of Admissions .... Mr. Daniel JUNG
10 Chief Financial Officer .... Mr. Joshua SUNG
37 Director of Financial Aid .... Dr. Robin BAILEY-CHEN
13 Director of Technology .... Mr. Michael YAP
50 Program Director Business Admin .... Dr. Greg HERBERT
108 Assoc Dean Accreditation/ Compliance .... Ms. Bernadette M. AGATON

Academy for Jewish Religion, California (A)

574 Hilgard Avenue, Los Angeles CA 90024-3234
County: Los Angeles FICE Identification: 041555
Unit ID: 457271
Telephone: (213) 884-4133 Carnegie Class: Spec-4-yr-Faith
FAX Number: N/A Calendar System: Semester
URL: www.ajrca.edu
Established: 2001 Annual Graduate Tuition & Fees: N/A
Enrollment: 53 Coed
Affiliation or Control: Jewish IRS Status: 501(c)3
Highest Offering: Master's; No Undergraduates
Accreditation: WC

01 President .... Rabbi Mel GOTTLIEB
73 VP/Dean of Chaplaincy School .... Rabbi Rochelle ROBINS
88 Dean of Cantorial School .... Cantor Hazzan Nathan LAM
88 Associate Dean Cantorial School .... Cantor Perryne ANKER
73 Interim Dean of Rabbinical School .... Rabbi Mel GOTTLIEB
58 Dean of MJS Program .... Cantor Jonathan FRIEDMANN
11 Director of Administration .... Ms. Lauren GOLDNER
10 Chief Financial Officer .... Dr. Alvin MARTIN
07 Director of Admissions/Recruitment .... Ms. Robin FEDERMAN
06 Registrar/Operations Coordinator .... Ms. Elea FRIEDMAN
36 Director of Internships/Placement .... Rabbi Faith TESSLER
09 Director of Institutional Research .... Cantor Jonathan FRIEDMANN
37 Director Student Financial Aid .... Ms. Lauren GOLDNER

Academy of Art University (B)

79 New Montgomery Street, San Francisco CA 94105-3410
County: San Francisco FICE Identification: 007531
Unit ID: 108232
Telephone: (415) 274-2200 Carnegie Class: Masters/L
FAX Number: (415) 274-8665 Calendar System: Semester
URL: www.academyart.edu
Established: 1929 Annual Undergrad Tuition & Fees: $22,308
Enrollment: 11,672 Coed
Affiliation or Control: Proprietary IRS Status: Proprietary
Highest Offering: Master's
Accreditation: WC, ART, CIDA

01 President .... Dr. Elisa STEPHENS

Academy of Chinese Culture and Health Sciences (C)

1600 Broadway Street, Suite 200, Oakland CA 94612
County: Alameda FICE Identification: 032883
Unit ID: 108269
Telephone: (510) 763-7787 Carnegie Class: Spec-4-yr-Other Health
FAX Number: (510) 834-8646 Calendar System: Other
URL: www.acchs.edu
Established: 1982 Annual Undergrad Tuition & Fees: N/A
Enrollment: 99 Coed
Affiliation or Control: Independent Non-Profit IRS Status: 501(c)3
Highest Offering: Master's; No Lower Division
Accreditation: ACUP

01 Acting President .... Mr. Yen Wei CHOONG
03 Exec Vice President .... Mr. Andres BELLA
11 Vice President of Administration .... Ms. Julie WANG

Acupuncture and Integrative Medicine College-Berkeley (D)

2550 Shattuck Avenue, Berkeley CA 94704-2724
County: Alameda FICE Identification: 033274
Unit ID: 384306
Telephone: (510) 666-8248 Carnegie Class: Spec-4-yr-Other Health
FAX Number: (510) 666-0111 Calendar System: Trimester
URL: www.aimc.edu
Established: 1990 Annual Undergrad Tuition & Fees: N/A
Enrollment: 81 Coed
Affiliation or Control: Independent Non-Profit IRS Status: 501(c)3
Highest Offering: Master's; No Lower Division
Accreditation: ACUP

01 President .... Mr. Yasuo TANAKA

05 DAIM Director .... Dr. Thomas SIEMANN
17 Clinic Dean .... Dr. Ken MORRIS
07 Director of Admissions .... Ms. Chelsea BROIDO
06 Registrar .... Vacant
20 Director of Academic Administration .... Ms. Annie CHI-WEI YU
08 Head Librarian .... Ms. Patricia WARD
37 Director Student Financial Aid .... Ms. Victoria LABRADOR
15 Admin Support Specialist .... Ms. Stacy WATERS
32 Director of Student Services .... Ms. Robbyn KAWAGUCHI
28 Director of Diversity .... Ms. Katrina HANSON

Advanced College (E)

13180 Paramount Boulevard, South Gate CA 90280-7956
County: Los Angeles FICE Identification: 037863
Unit ID: 444343
Telephone: (562) 408-6969 Carnegie Class: Spec 2-yr-Health
FAX Number: (562) 408-0471 Calendar System: Other
URL: www.advancedcollege.edu
Established: 1999 Annual Undergrad Tuition & Fees: N/A
Enrollment: 44 Coed
Affiliation or Control: Proprietary IRS Status: Proprietary
Highest Offering: Associate Degree
Accreditation: COE

01 Chief Executive Officer .... Mr. Amin VOHRA
66 Director Vocational Nursing .... Ms. Cathy CALVIN
37 Director Financial Aid .... Mr. Roberto QUINONES
05 Chief Academic Officer .... Mr. Ghazanfar MAHMOOD
11 Chief Operating Officer .... Mr. Bharpur SINGH
108 Compliance Officer .... Mrs. Rumaana R. KHAN

Advanced Training Associates (F)

1810 Gillespie Way, Suite 104, El Cajon CA 92020-1234
County: San Diego FICE Identification: 035324
Unit ID: 444361
Telephone: (619) 596-2766 Carnegie Class: Spec 2-yr-Tech
FAX Number: (619) 596-4526 Calendar System: Other
URL: www.advancedtraining.edu
Established: 2000 Annual Undergrad Tuition & Fees: N/A
Enrollment: 101 Coed
Affiliation or Control: Proprietary IRS Status: Proprietary
Highest Offering: Associate Degree
Accreditation: COE

01 President/CEO .... Henry MARENTES
11 Vice President of Operations .... Valerie PHILLIPS
88 Director of Compliance .... Nick FLEETWOOD
07 Director of Admissions .... Steven HOWARD
05 Director of Education .... James R. KYLE
06 Registrar/Financial Aid Officer .... Dionne SIMPSON

Agape College of Business and Science (G)

1313 P Street, Fresno CA 93721
County: Fresno Identification: 667362
Telephone: (559) 486-1166 Carnegie Class: Not Classified
FAX Number: N/A Calendar System: Quarter
URL: www.acbscollege.org
Established: 2006 Annual Undergrad Tuition & Fees: N/A
Enrollment: N/A Coed
Affiliation or Control: Independent Non-Profit IRS Status: 501(c)3
Highest Offering: Associate Degree
Accreditation: ACICS

01 CEO .... Dr. Linda SCOTT
05 Chief Academic Officer .... Dr. Jeffrey HUNT
20 Dean of Schools .... Ms. Diana PADILLA

Alder Graduate School of Education (H)

2946 Broadway St., Ste B, Redwood City CA 94062
County: San Mateo Identification: 667356
Telephone: (650) 362-3997 Carnegie Class: Not Classified
FAX Number: N/A Calendar System: Semester
URL: aldergse.org
Established: 2010 Annual Graduate Tuition & Fees: N/A
Enrollment: N/A Coed
Affiliation or Control: Independent Non-Profit IRS Status: 501(c)3
Highest Offering: Master's; No Undergraduates
Accreditation: WC

01 CEO/President .... Heather KIRKPATRICK
10 Chief Financial/Operating Officer .... Monica BONNY
05 Dean .... Nathanield MONLEY
09 Senior Inst Research Officer .... Vacant

Alhambra Medical University (I)

2215 West Mission Road, Suite 280, Alhambra CA 91803
County: Los Angeles Identification: 667052
Unit ID: 487995
Telephone: (626) 289-7719 Carnegie Class: Spec-4-yr-Other Health
FAX Number: (626) 289-8641 Calendar System: Quarter
URL: www.amuedu.com
Established: 2005 Annual Graduate Tuition & Fees: N/A
Enrollment: 146 Coed
Affiliation or Control: Proprietary IRS Status: Proprietary
Highest Offering: Master's; No Undergraduates
Accreditation: ACUP

01 President .... Dr. Jonathan WU
05 Academic Dean .... Dr. David LEE
23 Director of University Clinic .... Elizabeth JIN
07 Director of Admissions .... Qing MA
06 Registrar .... Xiao Ting DING

Allan Hancock College (J)

800 S College Drive, Santa Maria CA 93454-6399
County: Santa Barbara FICE Identification: 001111
Unit ID: 108807
Telephone: (805) 922-6966 Carnegie Class: Assoc/HT-Mix Trad/Non
FAX Number: (805) 347-9896 Calendar System: Semester
URL: www.hancockcollege.edu
Established: 1920 Annual Undergrad Tuition & Fees (In-District): $1,352
Enrollment: 11,739 Coed
Affiliation or Control: State/Local IRS Status: 501(c)3
Highest Offering: Associate Degree
Accreditation: WJ

01 Superintendent/President .... Dr. Kevin G. WALTHERS
04 Executive Asst to President .... Ms. Carmen S. CAMACHO
10 Assoc Supt/VP Finance/Admin .... Mr. Eric D. SMITH
05 Assoc Supt/VP Academic Affairs .... Dr. Robert CURRY
32 Assoc Supt/VP Student Services .... Ms. Nohemy ORNELAS
108 Vice Pres Inst Effectiveness .... Dr. Paul MURPHY
15 Director Human Resources .... Mr. Ruben RAMIREZ
35 Dean Student Services .... Ms. Mary DOMINGUEZ
38 Dean Counseling & Matriculation .... Ms. Yvonne TENIENTE
20 Dean Academic Affairs .... Dr. Richard MAHON
20 Dean Academic Affairs .... Dr. Sofia RAMIREZ-GELPI
20 Dean Academic Affairs .... Ms. Margaret LAU
20 Dean Academic Affairs .... Mr. Rick RANTZ
20 Dean Academic Affairs .... Dr. Mary PATRICK
41 Assoc Dean Kines/Rec/Athletics .... Ms. Kim ENSING
88 Assoc Dean Law Enforcement .... Mr. Mitch MCCANN
111 Exec Director College Advancement .... Mr. Jon HOOTEN
88 Artistic Director PCPA .... Mr. Mark BOOHER
13 Interim Dir Information Technology .... Mr. Andy SPECHT
21 Interim Director Business Services .... Ms. Keli SEYFERT
07 Director Admissions & Records .... Ms. Marian QUAID-MALTAGLIATI
37 Director Student Financial Aid .... Ms. Mary DOMINGUEZ
26 Dir Public Affairs/Publications .... Ms. Lauren MILBOURNE
78 Dir Cooperative Work Experience .... Mr. Thomas LAMICA
88 Director EOPS & Special Outreach .... Mr. Gustavo ENRIQUEZ-FERNANDEZ
18 Interim Director Plant Services .... Mr. Jim HARVEY
19 Dir Public Safety/Chief of Police .... Ms. Catherine FARLEY
88 Director Cal-SOAP .... Ms. Diana PEREZ
88 Director College Achievement Now .... Ms. Petra GOMEZ
25 Director Institutional Grants .... Ms. LeeAnne MCNULTY
88 Counselor/Coordinator MESA .... Ms. Christine REED
88 Managing Director PCPA .... Ms. Jennifer SCHWARTZ
88 Dir Environmental Training Center .... Ms. Holly NOLAN-CHAVEZ
88 Dir Special Projects .... Ms. Marina WASHBURN

*Alliant International University President's Office (K)

One Beach Street, Suite 100, San Francisco CA 94133-1221
County: San Francisco Identification: 666132
Telephone: (415) 955-2100 Carnegie Class: N/A
FAX Number: (414) 955-2062
URL: www.alliant.edu

01 President .... Mr. Andy VAUGHN
05 Provost/SVP Academic Affairs .... Dr. Tracy HELLER
30 Sr Vice Pres Development/Inclusion .... Dr. Mary OLING-SISAY
11 Sr Vice President of Operations .... Ms. Amy KWIATKOWSKI
10 Interim Chief Financial Officer .... Mr. Christoph WINTER
06 Registrar .... Mr. Paul WELCH
15 Human Resources/Employee Rels Dir .... Ms. Victoria DAVIDSON
13 VP/Int Chief Information Officer .... Mr. John JENNINGS
32 Vice President of Student Services .... Ms. Amber ECKERT

*Alliant International University-San Diego (L)

10455 Pomerado Road, San Diego CA 92131-1799
County: San Diego FICE Identification: 011117
Unit ID: 110468
Telephone: (858) 635-4772 Carnegie Class: DU-Mod
FAX Number: (858) 693-8562 Calendar System: Semester
URL: www.alliant.edu
Established: 1952 Annual Undergrad Tuition & Fees: $14,600
Enrollment: 3,780 Coed
Affiliation or Control: Independent Non-Profit IRS Status: 501(c)3
Highest Offering: Doctorate
Accreditation: WC, ACBSP, CLPSY, MFCD

12 Campus Director .... Ms. Michelle JACKSON
05 Provost/Vice Pres Academic Affairs .... Dr. Tracy HELLER
32 VP Student Services .... Ms. Amber ECKERT

* *Alliant International University-Fresno* (A)

5130 E Clinton Way, Fresno CA 93727-2014
Telephone: (559) 456-2777 FICE Identification: 001158
Accreditation: &WC, CLPSY, MFCD

* *Alliant International University-Irvine* (B)

2855 Michelle Drive, Suite 300, Irvine CA 92606
Telephone: (949) 812-7440 Identification: 666157
Accreditation: &WC, MFCD

* *Alliant International University-Los Angeles* (C)

1000 S Fremont Avenue, Unit 5,
Alhambra CA 91803-1360
Telephone: (626) 284-2777 FICE Identification: 010013
Accreditation: &WC, CLPSY, MFCD

* *Alliant International University-San Francisco* (D)

One Beach Street, San Francisco CA 94133-1221
Telephone: (415) 955-2100 FICE Identification: 011881
Accreditation: &WC, CLPSY, IPSY, MFCD

AMDA College and Conservatory of the Performing Arts (E)

6305 Yucca Street, Los Angeles CA 90028
County: Los Angeles Identification: 666721
Telephone: (323) 469-3300 Carnegie Class: Not Classified
FAX Number: (323) 469-1448 Calendar System: Semester
URL: www.amda.edu
Established: 1964 Annual Undergrad Tuition & Fees: N/A
Enrollment: N/A Coed
Affiliation or Control: Independent Non-Profit IRS Status: 501(c)3
Highest Offering: Baccalaureate
Accreditation: THEA

01 President/Artistic Director .... David MARTIN
05 Executive Director/Vice President .... Jan RUGGAR MARTIN
07 Director Admissions .... Joseph SIRIANO
37 Associate Director of Financial Aid .... Jillian DOYLE
20 Director Education Services .... Cynthia MOJ
32 Director Student Affairs .... Debra WALSH

American Academy of Dramatic Arts, Los Angeles Campus (F)

1336 N La Brea Avenue, Hollywood CA 90028-7504
Telephone: (323) 464-2777 FICE Identification: 021069
Accreditation: &M, THEA

† Regional accreditation is carried under the parent institution in New York, NY.

American Baptist Seminary of the West (G)

2606 Dwight Way, Berkeley CA 94704-3097
County: Alameda FICE Identification: 001120
Unit ID: 108861
Telephone: (510) 841-1905 Carnegie Class: Spec-4-yr-Faith
FAX Number: (510) 841-2446 Calendar System: Semester
URL: www.absw.edu
Established: 1871 Annual Graduate Tuition & Fees: N/A
Enrollment: 52 Coed
Affiliation or Control: American Baptist IRS Status: 501(c)3
Highest Offering: Doctorate; No Undergraduates
Accreditation: THEOL

01 President .... Dr. James E. BRENNEMAN
05 VP of Academics/Dean of Faculty .... Dr. LeAnn SNOW FLESHER
10 Vice Pres/Chief Financial Officer .... Ms. Yvonne WATSON
111 Vice Pres Institutional Advancement .... Ms. Lori D. SPEARS
07 Director of Admissions .... Megan WOOD
06 Registrar & Dir of Student Services .... Ms. Kat A. CROSWELL
04 Executive Asst to President .... Rev. Carolyn E. MATTHEWS

American Career College-Los Angeles (H)

4021 Rosewood Avenue, Los Angeles CA 90004
County: Los Angeles FICE Identification: 022418
Unit ID: 109040
Telephone: (323) 668-7555 Carnegie Class: Spec 2-yr-Health
FAX Number: (322) 953-3654 Calendar System: Other
URL: www.americancareercollege.edu
Established: 1978 Annual Undergrad Tuition & Fees: N/A
Enrollment: 1,237 Coed
Affiliation or Control: Proprietary IRS Status: Proprietary
Highest Offering: Associate Degree
Accreditation: ABHES, SURTEC

01 Executive Director .... Ms. Lani TOWNSEND

American Career College-Ontario (I)

3130 East Sedona Court, Ontario CA 91764
County: San Bernardino FICE Identification: 039713
Unit ID: 447768
Telephone: (909) 218-3253 Carnegie Class: Spec 2-yr-Health
FAX Number: (909) 218-3340 Calendar System: Other
URL: www.americancareercollege.edu
Established: 2006 Annual Undergrad Tuition & Fees: N/A
Enrollment: 1,275 Coed
Affiliation or Control: Proprietary IRS Status: Proprietary
Highest Offering: Associate Degree
Accreditation: ABHES, COARC

01 Executive Director .... Ms. Rita TOTTEN
05 Director of Education .... Mr. Tom BUSTAMANTE

American Career College (J)

4021 Rosewood Avenue, Los Angeles CA 90004
Telephone: (323) 668-7555 Identification: 667073
Accreditation: ABHES, COARC, OTA, PTAA, SURTEC

American Conservatory Theater (K)

30 Grant Avenue, 6th floor, San Francisco CA 94108-5800
County: San Francisco FICE Identification: 020992
Unit ID: 109086
Telephone: (415) 439-2350 Carnegie Class: Spec-4-yr-Arts
FAX Number: (415) 834-3210 Calendar System: Semester
URL: www.act-sf.org
Established: 1969 Annual Graduate Tuition & Fees: $29,560
Enrollment: 49 Coed
Affiliation or Control: Independent Non-Profit IRS Status: 501(c)3
Highest Offering: Master's; No Undergraduates
Accreditation: WC

01 Executive Director .... Jennifer BIELSTEIN
64 Conservatory Director .... Melissa SMITH
88 Artistic Director .... Pam MACKINNON
05 Director of Academic Affairs .... Jack SHARRAR
10 Finance Director .... Robert FORE
30 Director Development .... Caitlin QUINN
37 Director of Financial Aid .... Jerry LOPEZ
26 Acting Marketing Director .... Randy TARADASH
15 Chief Human Resources Officer .... Amanda WILLIAMS

America Evangelical University (L)

1818 S. Western Avenue #409, Los Angeles CA 90006
County: Los Angeles Identification: 667090
Unit ID: 490081
Telephone: (323) 643-0301 Carnegie Class: Spec-4-yr-Faith
FAX Number: (323) 643-0302 Calendar System: Semester
URL: www.aeu.edu
Established: 2001 Annual Undergrad Tuition & Fees: $5,500
Enrollment: 47 Coed
Affiliation or Control: Independent Non-Profit IRS Status: 501(c)3
Highest Offering: Doctorate
Accreditation: BI

01 President/CEO .... Dr. Sanghhoon LEE
05 Int Vice President for Academics .... Dr. Sanghoon LEE
32 Dean of Stdnts/Spiritual Formation .... Young WOON LEE
10 CFO .... Rev. Sung CHO
30 Chief Development Officer .... Vacant
08 Director of Library .... Dr. Duk YOUNG WON
06 Registrar/Dir Financial Aid .... Isaac JEON
07 Director of Admissions .... Vacant

American Film Institute Conservatory (M)

2021 N Western Avenue, Los Angeles CA 90027-1657
County: Los Angeles FICE Identification: 022220
Unit ID: 108870
Telephone: (323) 856-7600 Carnegie Class: Spec-4-yr-Arts
FAX Number: (323) 467-4578 Calendar System: Semester
URL: www.afi.com
Established: 1969 Annual Graduate Tuition & Fees: N/A
Enrollment: 341 Coed
Affiliation or Control: Independent Non-Profit IRS Status: 501(c)3
Highest Offering: Master's; No Undergraduates
Accreditation: WC

01 Director American Film Institute .... Mr. Bob GAZZALE
05 Dean AFI Conservatory/EVP .... Ms. Susan RUSKIN
10 Chief Financial Officer .... Mr. Lang FREDRICKSON
111 Chief Advancement Officer .... Mr. Tom WEST
88 Vice Dean of Administration .... Mr. Michael CHUNG
20 Vice Dean of Academic Affairs .... Mr. Tom ENGFER
88 Director Thesis Production .... Ms. Patty WEST
88 Assoc Dean Productions Svcs .... Ms. Betsy POLLOCK
32 Director Fellow Affairs .... Mr. Jonathan S. LEOS
57 Artistic Director .... Mr. James L. BROOKS
06 Registrar .... Ms. Carmela CHANEY
15 Director Human Resources .... Ms. Roschoune FRANKLIN
37 Financial Aid Director .... Ms. Trina RODLER
08 Librarian .... Mr. Robert VAUGHN
13 Director Information Technology .... Mr. Scott BLY
113 Bursar .... Ms. Jasmin CARROLL

American Graduate University (N)

733 N Dodsworth Avenue, Covina CA 91724-2408
County: Los Angeles Identification: 666982
Telephone: (626) 966-4576 Carnegie Class: Not Classified
FAX Number: (626) 915-1709 Calendar System: Other
URL: www.agu.edu
Established: 1969 Annual Graduate Tuition & Fees: N/A
Enrollment: N/A Coed
Affiliation or Control: Proprietary IRS Status: Proprietary
Highest Offering: Master's; No Undergraduates
Accreditation: DEAC

01 President .... Mr. Paul R. MCDONALD
06 Vice President/Registrar .... Ms. Debbie MCDONALD
05 Director Academic Affairs .... Mr. Paul R. MCDONALD
07 Dir Admissions/Student Achievement .... Ms. Laurie MEJIA
32 Dir Student Svcs/Student Support .... Ms. Rachel RUIZ
26 Director of Marketing .... Mr. Neil GRIFFIN

American Jewish University (O)

15600 Mulholland Drive, Los Angeles CA 90077-1599
County: Los Angeles FICE Identification: 002741
Unit ID: 116846
Telephone: (310) 476-9777 Carnegie Class: Bac-A&S
FAX Number: (310) 471-1278 Calendar System: Semester
URL: www.aju.edu
Established: 1947 Annual Undergrad Tuition & Fees: $31,946
Enrollment: 153 Coed
Affiliation or Control: Independent Non-Profit IRS Status: 501(c)3
Highest Offering: Master's
Accreditation: WC

01 President .... Dr. Jeffrey HERBST
05 Int Chief Academic Officer .... Dr. Robbie TOTTEN
10 Vice Pres Finance/Administration .... Mr. Adrian BREITFELD
11 Vice Pres Advancement/Chf Dev Ofcr .. Ms. Catherine SCHNEIDER

American Medical Sciences Center (P)

225 West Broadway, Ste 115, Glendale CA 91204
County: Los Angeles FICE Identification: 041597
Unit ID: 461263
Telephone: (818) 240-6900 Carnegie Class: Not Classified
FAX Number: (818) 240-6902 Calendar System: Semester
URL: www.amscedu.com
Established: 1996 Annual Undergrad Tuition & Fees: N/A
Enrollment: 105 Coed
Affiliation or Control: Proprietary IRS Status: Proprietary
Highest Offering: Associate Degree
Accreditation: ABHES

01 President .... Mr. Vardan KARAGEZIAN

American University of Armenia (Q)

1000 Broadway, Suite 280, Oakland CA 94607
County: Alameda Identification: 666013
Telephone: (510) 925-4282 Carnegie Class: Not Classified
FAX Number: (510) 925-4283 Calendar System: Semester
URL: www.aua.am
Established: 1991 Annual Undergrad Tuition & Fees: N/A
Enrollment: N/A Coed
Affiliation or Control: Independent Non-Profit IRS Status: 501(c)3
Highest Offering: Master's
Accreditation: WC

01 President .... Dr. Karin MARKIDES
05 Provost .... Dr. Randall RHODES
11 Vice President Operations .... Ashot GHAZARYAN
10 Vice President of Finance .... Gevorg GOYUNYAN
30 VP Development/External Relations .... Paul YEGHIAYAN
06 Associate Registrar .... Chaghig ARZROUNI-CHAHINIAN
26 Public Relations Coordinator .... Diana MANUKYAN
07 Dir Admissions/Recruit/Intl Stdnts .... Arina ZOHRABIAN
09 Institutional Research Manager .... Vacant
08 Head Librarian .... Satenik AVAKIAN
101 Secretary of the Institution/Board .... Caren MEGHREBLIAN
15 Director Personnel Services .... Arina BEKCHIAN
29 Director Alumni Relations .... Narine PETROSYAN
13 Dir Information/Communications Tech .... Berj GATRJYAN
50 Dean of Business and Economics .... Eric VAN GENDEREN
69 Dean of Public Health .... Varduhi PETROSYAN

American University of Health Sciences (R)

1600 E Hill Street, Building #1, Signal Hill CA 90755
County: Los Angeles FICE Identification: 032253
Unit ID: 433004
Telephone: (562) 988-2278 Carnegie Class: Spec-4-yr-Other Health
FAX Number: (562) 988-1791 Calendar System: Quarter
URL: www.auhs.edu
Established: 1994 Annual Undergrad Tuition & Fees: $22,570
Enrollment: 249 Coed
Affiliation or Control: Proprietary IRS Status: Proprietary
Highest Offering: Doctorate
Accreditation: WC, NURSE, @PHAR, TRACS

01 President .... Dr. Caroll RYAN
11 Chief Operating Officer .... Dr. Marilyn UVERO
05 Provost .... Dr. John MINCHIN
06 Registrar .... Alma PINEDA
07 Sr Director of Admissions .... Claudia ROSSMAN
09 Director of Institutional Research .... Dr. David TURBOW
10 Chief Financial/Business Officer .... Sandy SARGE
13 Chief Information Technology Office .... Rex AGLIBOT
32 Chief Student Affairs/Student Life .... Ivy JAVALUYAS

Anaheim University (A)

1240 S State College Blvd, Ste 110,
Anaheim CA 92806-5152
County: Orange — Identification: 666651
Telephone: (714) 772-3330 — Carnegie Class: Not Classified
FAX Number: (714) 772-3331 — Calendar System: Other
URL: www.anaheim.edu
Established: 1996 — Annual Graduate Tuition & Fees: N/A
Enrollment: N/A — Coed
Affiliation or Control: Proprietary — IRS Status: Proprietary
Highest Offering: Doctorate; No Undergraduates
Accreditation: DEAC

01 President .... Dr. Andrew E. HONEYCUTT
05 Vice President Academic Affairs .... Dr. Rod ELLIS
11 Vice President of Admin Affairs .... Ms. Kate STRAUSS
30 Chief Development/Advancement .... Mr. David BRACEY

Angeles College (B)

3440 Wilshire Boulevard, Suite 310,
Los Angeles CA 90010
County: Los Angeles — FICE Identification: 041604
Unit ID: 457299
Telephone: (213) 487-2211 — Carnegie Class: Spec-4-yr-Other Health
FAX Number: (213) 487-2299 — Calendar System: Semester
URL: www.angelescollege.edu
Established: 2004 — Annual Undergrad Tuition & Fees: N/A
Enrollment: 156 — Coed
Affiliation or Control: Proprietary — IRS Status: Proprietary
Highest Offering: Baccalaureate
Accreditation: ABHES, NURSE

01 CEO/School Director .... Ms. Teresa KRAUSE

Angeles College-City of Industry (C)

17595 Almahurst Street, Suite 101-3,
City of Industry CA 91748
Telephone: (626) 965-5566 — Identification: 770518
Accreditation: ABHES

Antelope Valley College (D)

3041 W Avenue K, Lancaster CA 93536-5426
County: Los Angeles — FICE Identification: 001113
Unit ID: 109350
Telephone: (661) 722-6300 — Carnegie Class: Bac/Assoc-Assoc Dom
FAX Number: (661) 722-6333 — Calendar System: Semester
URL: www.avc.edu
Established: 1929 — Annual Undergrad Tuition & Fees (In-District): $1,124
Enrollment: 14,125 — Coed
Affiliation or Control: State/Local — IRS Status: 501(c)3
Highest Offering: Baccalaureate
Accreditation: WJ, COARC, RAD

01 President/Superintendent .... Mr. Edward T. KNUDSON
05 VP Academic Affairs .... Dr. Les UHAZY
32 VP Student Services .... Dr. Erin E. VINES
15 Vice President Human Resources .... Vacant
84 Dean Enrollment Services .... Ms. LaDonna TRIMBLE
35 Dean of Student Life .... Dr. Jill ZIMMERMAN
22 Dir Ofc Students with Disabilities .... Dr. Louis LUCERO
26 Exec Director Marketing/Public Info .... Vacant
18 Exec Director Facilities Services .... Mr. Doug JENSEN
13 Director Information Technology .... Mr. Rick SHAW
30 Dir Inst Advancement & Foundation .... Ms. Dianne KNIPPEL
09 Director Inst Research & Planning .... Dr. Meeta GOEL
37 Director Financial Aid .... Ms. Nichelle WILLIAMS
76 Dean Health & Safety Science .... Mr. Gregory BORMANN
79 Dean Arts & Humanities .... Dr. Duane RUMSEY
83 Dean Soc & Beh Sci/Bus/Comp Stds .... Dr. Irit GAT
38 Dean Counseling & Matriculation .... Mr. Gary ROGGENSTEIN
72 Dean Career Technical Education .... Dr. Laureano FLORES
81 Dean of Math/Science & Engineering .... Dr. Les UHAZY

Art Center College of Design (E)

1700 Lida Street, Pasadena CA 91103-1999
County: Los Angeles — FICE Identification: 001116
Unit ID: 109651
Telephone: (626) 396-2200 — Carnegie Class: Spec-4-yr-Arts
FAX Number: N/A — Calendar System: Semester
URL: www.artcenter.edu
Established: 1930 — Annual Undergrad Tuition & Fees: $43,416
Enrollment: 2,251 — Coed
Affiliation or Control: Independent Non-Profit — IRS Status: 501(c)3
Highest Offering: Master's
Accreditation: WC, ART

01 President .... Dr. Lorne M. BUCHMAN
10 Chief Financial & Admin Officer .... Mr. Rich HALUSCHAK
05 Provost .... Ms. Karen HOFMANN
30 Sr Vice Pres Development .... Ms. Emily LASKIN
07 SVP Admissions/Enrollment Mgmt .... Ms. Kit BARON
88 VP Exhibitions/Dir Gallery .... Mr. Steve NOWLIN
13 VP Information Technology .... Ms. Theresa ZIX
26 VP Marketing & Communication .... Mr. Jered GOLD
15 Vice Pres Human Resources .... Ms. Lisa M. SANCHEZ
28 Vice President & Diversity Officer .... Dr. Aaron BRUCE
18 Assoc VP Facilities/Campus Planning .... Mr. Rollin HOMER
88 VP Professional Dev/Industry Engage .... Ms. Kristine BOWNE
32 Associate Provost Student Affairs .... Mr. Ray QUIROLGICO
08 College Librarian & Managing Dir .... Mr. Mario ASCENCIO
21 Controller .... Ms. Diane WITTENBERG
37 Managing Director Financial Aid .... Ms. Cheryl GILLIES
06 Registrar/Director of Enrollment .... Mr. Greg YAMAMOTO
09 Director of Institutional Research .... Ms. Esmeralda NAVA
20 Director Academic Affairs .... Ms. Leslie JOHNSON
102 Sr Dir Foundation/Govt Relations .... Mr. Darryl MORI
36 Director of Career Development .... Ms. Amanda RAJOTTE
96 Director of Purchasing .... Ms. Monica MATSUO
19 Director Security .... Mr. Jim FINCH
29 Director Alumni Affairs .... Ms. Keiko DOI

Asher College (F)

1215 Howe Street, Suite 101, Sacramento CA 95825
County: Sacramento — FICE Identification: 040573
Unit ID: 447777
Telephone: (916) 649-9600 — Carnegie Class: Assoc/HVT-High Trad
FAX Number: (916) 649-9700 — Calendar System: Other
URL: www.asher.edu
Established: 1998 — Annual Undergrad Tuition & Fees: N/A
Enrollment: 587 — Coed
Affiliation or Control: Proprietary — IRS Status: Proprietary
Highest Offering: Associate Degree
Accreditation: CNCE

01 President .... David VICE
12 Campus Director Sacramento .... Linda FREEMAN
12 Campus Director Las Vegas .... Anne BUZAK
12 Campus Director Dallas .... Josh PAULSEN
88 Director of Compliance .... Kathryn JOHNSON
26 Director of Marketing .... Kim GASPER
37 Director Student Financial Aid .... Elona OWENS

Ashford University (G)

8620 Spectrum Center Blvd, San Diego CA 92123
County: San Diego — FICE Identification: 001881
Unit ID: 154022
Telephone: (866) 711-1700 — Carnegie Class: Masters/L
FAX Number: (866) 685-4091 — Calendar System: Semester
URL: www.ashford.edu
Established: 1918 — Annual Undergrad Tuition & Fees: $12,160
Enrollment: 36,453 — Coed
Affiliation or Control: Proprietary — IRS Status: Proprietary
Highest Offering: Master's
Accreditation: WC, CAHIIM, IACBE, NURSE

01 University President/CEO .... Dr. Craig SWENSON
05 SVP Academic Affairs/CAO .... Dr. Laura PALMER-NOONE
10 SVP Finance/Chief Finance Officer .... Mr. Jim SMITH
11 SVP University Svcs & Strat Plng .... Ms. Sheri JONES
15 VP Human Resources .... Ms. Anna ALLEN
06 VP University Registrar .... Ms. Katie SCHEIE
21 VP Accounting Controller .... Ms. Heather WEINMANN
35 AVP Student Affairs .... Ms. Poppy FITCH
88 AVP Center for Teaching/Learning .... Ms. Morgan JOHNSON
12 President Clinton Campus .... Dr. Charlie MINNICK
49 Dean College of Liberal Arts .... Dr. Adam SELHORST
69 Dean College of Health/Human Svcs .... Dr. Laura SLIWINSKI
88 Dean Doctoral Studies .... Dr. Iris LAFFERTY
97 Dean Division of General Education .... Dr. Justin HARRISON
50 Dean Forbes School of Business .... Mr. Bob DAUGHERTY
53 Dean College of Education .... Dr. Tony FARRELL
37 Dir Financial Aid & Policy .... Ms. Stephanie COWSERT
09 Director of Institutional Research .... Dr. Stephen NETTLES
101 Secretary of the Institution/Board .... Ms. Patricia OGDEN
29 Director Alumni Affairs .... Ms. Graciela WILLIAMSON
22 Title IX Coordinator .... Dr. Poppy FITCH
04 Executive Administrative Manager .... Ms. Thuy LIEN

Azusa Pacific University (H)

901 E Alosta Avenue, Azusa CA 91702-7000
County: Los Angeles — FICE Identification: 001117
Unit ID: 109785
Telephone: (626) 969-3434 — Carnegie Class: DU-Higher
FAX Number: (626) 969-7180 — Calendar System: Semester
URL: www.apu.edu
Established: 1899 — Annual Undergrad Tuition & Fees: $38,880
Enrollment: 9,926 — Coed
Affiliation or Control: Independent Non-Profit — IRS Status: 501(c)3
Highest Offering: Doctorate
Accreditation: WC, ART, CAATE, CAEPN, CLPSY, IACBE, MUS, NURSE, PTA, SW, THEOL

01 President .... Dr. Paul W. FERGUSON
05 Provost .... Dr. Mark STANTON
26 Exec Vice Pres External Affairs .... Mr. David E. BIXBY
97 Chancellor University College .... Dr. John C. REYNOLDS
32 Senior Vice Pres for Student Life .... Dr. Shino SIMONS
10 Vice President Finance/Business/CFO .... Mr. Ross ALLEN
03 Senior Vice President/Gen Counsel .... Dr. Mark DICKERSON
43 General Counsel .... Mr. Chris JENNINGS
13 Vice President Admin/CIO .... Dr. Don DAVIS
84 VP Enrollment Management .... Dr. Heather PETRIDIS
58 Vice Provost Graduate Programs .... Dr. Diane GUIDO
20 Vice Provost Undergraduate Programs .... Dr. Vicky BOWDEN
35 AVP Student Life/Chief Judicial Ofc .... Mr. Willie HAMLETT
88 Assoc VP University Services .... Mr. Roger HODSDON
27 VP University Relations .... Dr. David PECK
49 Dean College Liberal Arts/Sci .... Dr. Jennifer WALSH
83 Dean School Behav/Applied Sciences .... Dr. Robert WELSH
50 Dean School of Business Mgmt .... Dr. Robert ROLLER
53 Dean School of Education .... Dr. Anita HENCK
73 Dean Haggard School of Theology .... Dr. Robert DUKE
64 Dean College of Music and the Arts .... Dr. Stephen JOHNSON
66 Dean School of Nursing .... Dr. Aja LESH
92 Dean Honors College .... Dr. David WEEKS
35 Assoc Dean Students/Dir Student Act .... Vacant
15 Exec Director Human Resources .... Mr. John BAUGUS
111 VP University Advancement .... Mr. Corbin HOORNBEEK
21 Executive Director Finance .... Ms. Cynthia SOUZA
42 Campus Pastor .... Dr. Woody MOORWOOD
37 Dir Graduate Student Financial Svcs .... Mr. Jon KRIMMEL
06 Registrar-Graduate .... Mrs. Michelle JOHNSON
06 Associate Registrar-Undergraduate .... Ms. Mona MIKHAIL
29 Director Alumni Relations .... Mr. Phil BRAZELL
09 Director Acad Info Mgmt Analysis .... Vacant
41 Director Athletics .... Mr. Gary PINE
38 Director Counseling Center .... Dr. Bill FIALA
37 AVP for UG Academic Financial Svcs .... Mr. Jon KRIMMEL
18 Associate VP Facilities Management .... Mr. Donato POWELL
07 Director Undergraduate Admissions .... Mr. Samuel KIM
36 Director Career Services .... Mr. Phil BRAZELL
28 Exec Dir Ctr Div/Equity/Inclusive .... Mr. Richard MARTINEZ

Barstow Community College District (I)

2700 Barstow Road, Barstow CA 92311-6699
County: San Bernardino — FICE Identification: 001119
Unit ID: 109907
Telephone: (760) 252-2411 — Carnegie Class: Assoc/HVT-High Trad
FAX Number: (760) 252-1875 — Calendar System: Semester
URL: www.barstow.edu
Established: 1959 — Annual Undergrad Tuition & Fees (In-District): $1,104
Enrollment: 3,077 — Coed
Affiliation or Control: State/Local — IRS Status: 170(c)1
Highest Offering: Associate Degree
Accreditation: WJ

01 Superintendent/President .... Dr. Eva BAGG
04 Exec Assistant to the President .... Ms. Michelle HENDERSON
10 Vice President Admin Services .... Mr. Dave CLAUSEN
05 Interim VP Academic Affairs .... Dr. Karen KANE
32 Interim VP Student Services .... Dr. Karen KANE
15 Vice President of HR .... Mr. Lyle ENGELDINGER
20 Dean of Instruction OL & LSS .... Mr. Tim BOTENGAN
103 Dean Workforce & Econ Dev .... Ms. Sandi THOMAS
09 Dir Research Dev & Planning .... Ms. Lisa HOLMES
41 Athletic Director .... Mr. Mynor MENDOZA
26 Dir of Public Rels/Comm & Marketing .... Ms. Amanda SIMPSON
18 Director Maintenance & Operations .... Mr. Richard HERNANDEZ
21 Director Fiscal Services .... Ms. Pattie GRANADOS
91 Director of Information Technology .... Mr. Bryce PRUTSOS
84 Dean Enrollment Management & Svcs .... Ms. Heather MINEHART
35 Director Student Life & Dev .... Ms. Joann GARCIA
25 Director CTE Grants .... Mr. James LEE
88 Director Military Programs .... Mr. Robbie EVANS
88 Director Special Pgms & Svcs .... Ms. Christina CALDERON
16 Dir HR Org Dev & Process Imp .... Ms. Kim YOUNG
88 Civic Center & Event Manager .... Mr. Ed WILL
90 Dir Guided Path/Equity & Achvmt .... Ms. Melissa MEADOWS
13 Dir Inst Tech & OL Svcs .... Ms. Nancy OLSON
91 Dir Learning Support Svcs .... Mr. Bryan ASDEL
88 Dir Adult Educ Consortium .... Ms. Elean RIVERA
51 Dir Adult Educ & Basic Skill .... Mr. Elias VALENCIA
114 Budget Analyst .... Ms. Terri WALKER

Bergin College of Canine Studies (J)

10201 Old Redwood Highway, Penngrove CA 94951
County: Sonoma — FICE Identification: 041763
Unit ID: 461643
Telephone: (707) 545-3647 — Carnegie Class: Spec-4-yr-Other
FAX Number: (707) 545-0800 — Calendar System: Semester
URL: www.berginu.edu
Established: 1991 — Annual Undergrad Tuition & Fees: N/A
Enrollment: 80 — Coed
Affiliation or Control: Independent Non-Profit — IRS Status: 501(c)3
Highest Offering: Master's
Accreditation: ACICS

01 President & Director of Education .... Dr. Bonita M. BERGIN
05 Chief Academic Officer .... Rebecca RICHARDSON
06 Registrar & Chief Operating Officer .... Denise GREGERSEN
07 Director of Admissions Services .... Connie VAN GUILDER

Bethesda University of California (A)

730 N Euclid Street, Anaheim CA 92801-4115
County: Orange FICE Identification: 032663
Unit ID: 110060
Telephone: (714) 517-1945 Carnegie Class: Spec-4-yr-Faith
FAX Number: (714) 683-1440 Calendar System: Semester
URL: www.buc.edu
Established: 1976 Annual Undergrad Tuition & Fees: $8,095
Enrollment: 375 Coed
Affiliation or Control: Independent Non-Profit IRS Status: 501(c)3
Highest Offering: Doctorate
Accreditation: BI, TRACS

01 President ....Dr. Seung Je Jeremiah CHO
10 Vice President/Chief Financial Ofcr ....Dr. Esther CHO
05 Chief Academic Officer ....Dr. Hyo In KIM
06 Registrar/Academic Officer ....Mr. Daniel WOO
08 Librarian ....Ms. Ho Kyung WOO
07 Admissions Officer ....Ms. Jane CHIANG
37 Financial Aid Officer ....Ms. Yae Oee SHIN

Beverly Hills Design Institute (B)

8484 Wilshire Boulevard, Suite 730,
Beverly Hills CA 90211-3235
County: Los Angeles FICE Identification: 041855
Unit ID: 475635
Telephone: (310) 360-8888 Carnegie Class: Spec-4-yr-Arts
FAX Number: (310) 857-6974 Calendar System: Quarter
URL: www.bhdi.edu
Established: 2005 Annual Undergrad Tuition & Fees: $23,220
Enrollment: 18 Coed
Affiliation or Control: Proprietary IRS Status: Proprietary
Highest Offering: Baccalaureate
Accreditation: ACICS

01 CEO ....Sonia ETE
05 Chief Academic Officer ....Douglas SPESERT
10 CFO/COO/Dir HR ....Thierry ETE
07 Director of Admissions/Career Svcs ....Brittany WISE

Biola University (C)

13800 Biola Avenue, La Mirada CA 90639-0001
County: Los Angeles FICE Identification: 001122
Unit ID: 110097
Telephone: (562) 903-6000 Carnegie Class: DU-Mod
FAX Number: (562) 903-4748 Calendar System: Semester
URL: www.biola.edu
Established: 1908 Annual Undergrad Tuition & Fees: $40,488
Enrollment: 6,172 Coed
Affiliation or Control: Independent Non-Profit IRS Status: 501(c)3
Highest Offering: Doctorate
Accreditation: WC, ACBSP, ART, CLPSY, IPSY, MUS, NURSE, @SP, THEOL

01 President ....Dr. Barry H. COREY
05 Provost/Sr Vice President ....Dr. Deborah TAYLOR
10 Vice Pres Univ Operations & Finance ....Mr. Michael PIERCE
111 VP Advancement & Strategic Planning ....Dr. Adam MORRIS
26 VP Enrollment/Marketing & Comms ....Mr. Lee WILHITE
32 VP Student Development ....Mr. Andre STEPHENS
20 Vice Provost/Academic Admin ....Dr. Patricia PIKE
07 Assoc VP University Admissions ....Ms. Amanda SLAUGHTER
73 Dean Talbot School Theology ....Dr. Clinton E. ARNOLD
83 Dean Rosemead School Psychology ....Dr. Tamara ANDERSON
88 Dean Cook Sch Intercultural Studies ....Dr. Bulus GALADIMA
53 Dean School of Education ....Dr. June HETZEL
50 Dean Crowell School of Business ....Dr. Gary LINDBLAD
81 Dean of Science/Tech & Health ....Dr. Paul FERGUSON
57 Dean of Fine Arts & Comm ....Dr. Todd GUY
79 Dean of Humanities/Social Sciences ....Dr. Melissa SCHUBERT
08 Dean of the Library ....Dr. Gregg GEARY
42 Dean of Spiritual Development ....Dr. Todd PICKETT
06 Dean Acad Records & Univ Registrar ....Dr. Ken GILSON
15 Sr Director Human Resources ....Vacant
109 Sr Dir Auxiliary Services ....Ms. Sandie WEAVER
110 Senior Director of Advancement ....Dr. Richard BEE
37 Sr Director Financial Aid ....Mr. Geoff MARSH
21 Sr Dir Financial Mgmt/Reporting ....Mr. David KOONTZ
19 Chief Campus Safety ....Mr. John O. OJEISEKHOBA
13 Sr Director Information Technology ....Mr. Steven R. EARLE
36 Dir Career Development & Success ....Ms. Tiffany LEE
41 Sr Director of Athletics ....Dr. Bethany MILLER
40 Manager Bookstore ....Ms. Melissa CASTELLANO
18 Sr Director Facilities Management ....Mr. Brian PHILLIPS
38 Director Counseling Center ....Dr. Melanie TAYLOR
96 Purchasing Manager ....Mrs. Breanna KLETT
106 Chief Education Technology Officer ....Mrs. Susan ISHII
108 Director of University Assessment ....Vacant
43 University Legal Counsel ....Ms. Paula T. VICTOR
09 Director of Institutional Research ....Mr. Gary WYTCHERLEY
28 Chief Diversity Officer ....Ms. Tamra MALONE
29 Sr Director Alumni ....Ms. Lily TSAU
100 Chief of Staff ....Mr. Brian J. SHOOK

Brandman University (D)

16355 Laguna Canyon Road, Irvine CA 92618
County: Orange FICE Identification: 041618
Unit ID: 262086
Telephone: (949) 753-4774 Carnegie Class: DU-Mod
FAX Number: (714) 753-7875 Calendar System: Other
URL: www.brandman.edu
Established: 1958 Annual Undergrad Tuition & Fees: $12,380
Enrollment: 7,812 Coed
Affiliation or Control: Independent Non-Profit IRS Status: 501(c)3
Highest Offering: Doctorate
Accreditation: WC, CAEPN, NURSE, SW

01 Chancellor ....Dr. Gary BRAHM
12 Campus Director ....Ms. Tara PULLEE
05 Associate Dean School of Education . Ms. Patricia CLARK-WHITE
10 Finance Director ....Ms. Kathy BLACKLOCK

† A member of the Chapman University System.

The Broad Center for the Management of School Systems (E)

2121 Avenue of the Stars, Ste 3000,
Los Angeles CA 90067
County: Los Angeles Identification: 667228
Telephone: (310) 954-5080 Carnegie Class: Not Classified
FAX Number: N/A Calendar System: Other
URL: www.broadcenter.org
Established: Annual Graduate Tuition & Fees: N/A
Enrollment: N/A Coed
Affiliation or Control: Independent Non-Profit IRS Status: 501(c)3
Highest Offering: Master's; No Undergraduates
Accreditation: WC

01 Executive Director ....Becca BRACY KNIGHT
13 Asst Director Information Systems ....Eulogio GALLO
26 Senior Director Communications ....Stephanie GERMERAAD
07 Senior Director Recruitment ....Erin KELLER

Butte College (F)

3536 Butte Campus Drive, Oroville CA 95965-8399
County: Butte FICE Identification: 008073
Unit ID: 110246
Telephone: (530) 895-2511 Carnegie Class: Assoc/HVT-High Trad
FAX Number: (530) 895-2345 Calendar System: Semester
URL: www.butte.edu
Established: 1966 Annual Undergrad Tuition & Fees (In-District): $1,368
Enrollment: 11,386 Coed
Affiliation or Control: State/Local IRS Status: 501(c)3
Highest Offering: Associate Degree
Accreditation: WJ, COARC, EMT

01 Superintendent/President ....Dr. Samia YAQUB
05 Vice Pres Instruction ....Ms. Virginia GULEFF
10 VP Administrative Service/CBO ....Mr. Andrew SULESKI
45 VP Institutional Effectiveness ....Mr. Gregory STOUP
32 Vice President Student Services ....Mr. Allen RENVILLE
20 Dean for Instruction ....Ms. Kam BULL
20 Dean for Instruction ....Dr. Carrie MONLUX
20 Dean for Instruction ....Ms. Denise ADAMS
20 Dean for Instruction ....Ms. Teresa DOYLE
37 Director Financial Aid/Vet Svcs ....Ms. Tammera SHINAR
35 Dean Student Services ....Mr. Clinton SLAUGHTER
35 Dean Student Services ....Mr. Brad ZUNIGA
15 Director Human Resources ....Mr. Chris LITTLE
18 Dir Facilities Planning/Management ....Ms. Kim JONES
09 Director of Institutional Research ....Mr. Brian MURPHY
07 Director Admissions/Records ....Ms. Monica BOYES
103 Exec Dir Econ Workforce Development ....Ms. Linda ZORN
111 Director Institutional Advancement ....Ms. Lisa DELABY
41 Director Athletics/Kinesiology ....Mr. Craig RIGSBEE
13 Chief Technology Officer ....Ms. Andrea MOX
21 Director Business Services ....Mr. Jim NICHOLAS
38 Coordinator of Counseling ....Ms. Debbie REYNOLDS
109 Director Auxiliary Services ....Mr. Steve DEMAGGIO
22 Director Student Equity ....Ms. Monica BROWN
100 Exec Asst to President & Board ....Ms. Shannon M. MCCOLLUM
108 Director Assessment ....Mr. Eric HOILAND
19 Chief of Police ....Mr. Casey CARLSON

Cabrillo College (G)

6500 Soquel Drive, Aptos CA 95003-3194
County: Santa Cruz FICE Identification: 001124
Unit ID: 110334
Telephone: (831) 479-6100 Carnegie Class: Assoc/HT-High Trad
FAX Number: (831) 479-6425 Calendar System: Semester
URL: www.cabrillo.edu
Established: 1959 Annual Undergrad Tuition & Fees (In-District): $1,270
Enrollment: 11,836 Coed
Affiliation or Control: State/Local IRS Status: 501(c)3
Highest Offering: Associate Degree
Accreditation: WJ, DH, MAC, RAD

01 Superintendent/President ....Dr. Matthew WETSTEIN
04 Confidential Executive Assistant ....Ms. Ronnette CHANDLER
05 Asst Supt/Vice Pres Instruction ....Dr. Kathleen WELCH
11 Asst Supt/VP Administrative Svcs ....Mr. Bradley OLIN
32 Asst Supt/Vice Pres Student Svcs ....Ms. Suzanne GOCHIS
15 Director of HR and Labor Relations ....Ms. Angela HOYT
13 Director Information Technology ....Ms. Spring ANDREWS
07 Director of Admissions/Records ....Mr. Kip NEAD
96 Dir Purchasing/Contracts/Risk Mgmt ....Mr. Michael ROBINS
26 Director Marketing & Communications ....Ms. Kristin FABOS
10 Director Business Services ....Vacant
31 Dir Community and Contract Ed ....Mr. Scott JOHNSON
18 Dir Planning & Facilities ....Mr. Jon SALISBURY
25 Dir Grants Development ....Ms. Carrie MULCAIRE
22 Dir Student Equity and Success ....Mr. Keith JOHNSON
88 Dir Student Resource and Support ....Ms. Karen REYES
08 Director Library ....Mr. Georg ROMERO
88 Dir Small Business Development Ctr ....Mr. Brandon NAPOLI
09 Dean Research/Planning/Inst Effect ....Mr. Terrence WILLETT
35 Dean Student Services ....Ms. Michelle DONOHUE
38 Dean Counseling/Educ Support ....Mrs. Amy LEHMAN
102 Exec Dir Cabrillo Col Foundation ....Ms. Eileen HILL
40 Bookstore Manager ....Ms. Linda CULLENS
37 Director Financial Aid ....Ms. Tootie TZIMBAL
103 Dean CTE & Workforce Development ....Ms. Gerlinde BRADY
106 Dean Online Education/E-learning ....Mrs. Rachel MAYO

Cal Northern School of Law (H)

1395 Ridgewood Drive, Ste 100, Chico CA 95973
County: Butte Identification: 667331
Telephone: (530) 891-6900 Carnegie Class: Not Classified
FAX Number: (530) 891-3429 Calendar System: Semester
URL: www.calnorthern.edu
Established: 1992 Annual Undergrad Tuition & Fees: N/A
Enrollment: N/A Coed
Affiliation or Control: Proprietary IRS Status: Proprietary
Highest Offering: First Professional Degree
Accreditation: @WC

01 Dean and President ....Sandra BOOKS
10 CFO ....Vacant
09 Director of Institutional Research ....Martha WILSON

California Arts University (I)

4100 W. Commonwealth Ave #101, Fullerton CA 92833
County: Orange Identification: 667348
Telephone: (714) 222-1110 Carnegie Class: Not Classified
FAX Number: (714) 907-1511 Calendar System: Semester
URL: cau-edu.us
Established: Annual Graduate Tuition & Fees: N/A
Enrollment: N/A Coed
Affiliation or Control: Independent Non-Profit IRS Status: 501(c)3
Highest Offering: Master's; No Undergraduates
Accreditation: TRACS

01 President ....Dr. Sae KWANG CHUNG
05 Academic Dean ....Dr. Tae YEON LIM

California Baptist University (J)

8432 Magnolia Avenue, Riverside CA 92504-3297
County: Riverside FICE Identification: 001125
Unit ID: 110361
Telephone: (951) 689-5771 Carnegie Class: Masters/L
FAX Number: N/A Calendar System: Semester
URL: www.calbaptist.edu
Established: 1950 Annual Undergrad Tuition & Fees: $33,478
Enrollment: 9,941 Coed
Affiliation or Control: Southern Baptist IRS Status: 501(c)3
Highest Offering: Doctorate
Accreditation: WC, ACBSP, #ARCPA, CAATE, CONST, MUS, NURSE, PH, @PTAA, RAD, @SP, SW

01 President ....Dr. Ronald L. ELLIS
04 Admin Asst to the President ....Ms. Janie ARMENTROUT
10 VP for Finance & Administration ....Mr. Mark HOWE
05 VP for Academic Affairs/Provost ....Dr. Charles SANDS
84 VP Enrollment & Student Services ....Mr. Kent DACUS
111 VP for University Advancement ....Mr. Paul J. ELDRIDGE
26 VP for Marketing & Communication ....Dr. Mark A. WYATT
43 VP and General Counsel ....Mr. Adam BURTON
106 VP for Online & Prof Studies ....Ms. Pamela DALY
88 VP for Global Initiatives ....Dr. Larry LINAMEN
15 Director of Human Resources ....Ms. Julie FRESQUEZ
18 Director Facilities/Planning Svcs ....Mr. Steve SMITH
21 Director of Financial Services ....Mr. Calvin SPARKMAN
21 Director of Accounting ....Ms. Jackie STILWELL
37 Director of Financial Aid ....Mr. Joshua MOREY
40 Director of University Campus Store ....Ms. Carol BRACEY
88 Director of Conferences & Events ....Mr. Coreylon POLK
27 Director of Marketing ....Mr. Jacob M. ROBERTSON
27 Director of Communications ....Mr. Isaiah AGUIRRE
105 Sr Web Services Manager ....Mr. Daniel AKERS
32 Dean of Students ....Mr. Anthony LAMMONS
07 Dean of Admissions ....Mr. Taylor NEECE
41 Director of Athletics ....Dr. Micah PARKER
42 Dean Spiritual Life/Campus Minister ....Mr. John MONTGOMERY
19 Director of Safety Services ....Mr. Leon PHILLIPS
39 Dir Residence Life & Housing ....Mr. Daron HUBBERT
36 Sr Director Career Services ....Mr. Mike BISHOP
111 Assoc VP University Advancement ....Mr. Dan WESTERMANN
44 Coordinator of Donor Stewardship ....Ms. Michelle BAHU
102 Grants Administrator ....Vacant
29 Director of Alumni & Parent Relations ....Mr. Joshua MOSS
88 Assoc Dir of Intl Admissions ....Mr. Ryan FALSETTI
85 Dean of International Programs ....Mr. Bryan DAVIS
13 Assoc VP of Technology ....Dr. Tran HONG
106 Assoc VP Academics Online/Prof Stds ....Dr. Dirk DAVIS
88 Assoc Provost/Administration ....Dr. Tracy WARD
20 Director Faculty Development ....Dr. Ted MURCRAY
108 Assoc Provost/Accred & Assessment ....Dr. Elizabeth MORRIS

06 University Registrar ..... Ms. Shawnn KONING
08 Director of Library ..... Dr. Steve EMERSON
90 Dir of Instructional Technology ..... Mr. Keith CASTILLO
121 Dean of Student Success ..... Dr. Jeffrey BARNES
09 Director of Institutional Research ..... Dr. Brian NIEMEIER
48 Dean College of Architecture ..... Mr. Mark A. ROBERSON
49 Dean College of Arts & Sciences ..... Dr. Lisa HERNANDEZ
50 Dean School of Business ..... Dr. Andrea SCOTT
53 Dean School of Education ..... Dr. Robin DUNCAN
54 Dean College of Engineering ..... Dr. Anthony DONALDSON
64 Dean School of Music ..... Dr. Joseph BOLIN
66 Dean College of Nursing ..... Dr. Karen BRADLEY
73 Dean School of Christian Ministries ..... Dr. Chris MORGAN
83 Dean Col Behavioral & Social Sci ..... Dr. Jacqueline GUSTAFSON
76 Dean College of Health Science ..... Dr. David PEARSON
124 Director of Academic Engagements ..... Mr. Garrett ENGLISH

California Career College (A)

7003 Owensmouth Avenue, Canoga Park CA 91303

County: Los Angeles | FICE Identification: 039745 | Unit ID: 447713
Telephone: (818) 710-1310 | Carnegie Class: Spec 2-yr-Health
FAX Number: (818) 710-1329 | Calendar System: Semester
URL: www.californiacareercollege.edu
Established: 2001 | Annual Undergrad Tuition & Fees: N/A
Enrollment: 69 | Coed
Affiliation or Control: Proprietary | IRS Status: Proprietary
Highest Offering: Associate Degree
Accreditation: ABHES

01 President ..... Haleh NAIMI
05 ADN Director ..... Susan NAIMI
07 Admissions Coordinator ..... Armenohy TELIME

California Christian College (B)

5364 E. Belmont Avenue, Fresno CA 93727

County: Fresno | FICE Identification: 008844 | Unit ID: 110918
Telephone: (559) 251-4215 | Carnegie Class: Spec-4-yr-Faith
FAX Number: (559) 385-2329 | Calendar System: Semester
URL: www.calchristiancollege.edu
Established: 1955 | Annual Undergrad Tuition & Fees: $9,570
Enrollment: 16 | Coed
Affiliation or Control: Free Will Baptist | IRS Status: 501(c)3
Highest Offering: Baccalaureate
Accreditation: TRACS

01 President ..... Dr. Timothy M. POWELL
05 Vice Pres of Academic Affairs ..... Mrs. Joanna FELTS
06 Registrar ..... Mrs. Makenzie ZUERCHER
10 Business Officer/Bookkeeper ..... Mrs. Pam DELL'OLIO
09 Dir Institutional Effectiveness ..... Ms. Jennifer WALLEY
08 Head Librarian ..... Mrs. Nanne SINGH
37 Coordinator Financial Aid ..... Ms. Melinda SCROGGINS
07 Director of Admissions/Recruitment . Mr. Brendan BLANKENSHIP
39 Housing Coordinator ..... Ms. Jennifer WALLEY

California Coast University (C)

925 N. Spurgeon Street, Santa Ana CA 92701-3515

County: Orange | FICE Identification: 041276
Telephone: (714) 547-9625 | Carnegie Class: Not Classified
FAX Number: (714) 547-5777 | Calendar System: Other
URL: www.calcoast.edu
Established: 1973 | Annual Undergrad Tuition & Fees: N/A
Enrollment: N/A | Coed
Affiliation or Control: Proprietary | IRS Status: Proprietary
Highest Offering: Doctorate
Accreditation: DEAC

01 President ..... Dr. Thomas M. NEAL
03 Executive Vice President ..... Ms. Shelly MARQUARDT
32 Vice Pres of Student Affairs/CAO ..... Dr. Murl TUCKER
05 Director of Academic Affairs ..... Mr. Douglas PETRIKAT
06 Registrar ..... Ms. Angela CENINA
13 Dir Management Information Systems ..... Ms. Jojo SOBERANO

California College of the Arts (D)

1111 Eighth Street, San Francisco CA 94107-2247

County: San Francisco | FICE Identification: 001127 | Unit ID: 110370
Telephone: (415) 703-9500 | Carnegie Class: Spec-4-yr-Arts
FAX Number: (510) 655-3541 | Calendar System: Semester
URL: www.cca.edu
Established: 1907 | Annual Undergrad Tuition & Fees: $49,138
Enrollment: 1,927 | Coed
Affiliation or Control: Independent Non-Profit | IRS Status: 501(c)3
Highest Offering: Master's
Accreditation: WC, ART

01 President ..... Mr. Stephen BEAL
05 Provost ..... Ms. Tammy Rae CARLAND
10 CFO/Sr VP Finance & Administration ..... Vacant
111 Sr Vice President of Advancement ..... Ms. Susan AVILA
45 VP of Institutional Planning ..... Vacant
84 Vice Pres of Enrollment Svcs ..... Mr. Scott CLINE
26 Vice Pres Marketing/Comm Strategy ..... Ms. Ann WIENS
32 Vice President Student Affairs ..... Mr. George SEDANO
15 Vice President Human Resources ..... Ms. Leslie GRAY
21 Assoc Vice Pres Financial Services ..... Mr. Ken TANZER
20 Associate Provost ..... Ms. Julianne KIRGIS
36 Director Career Development ..... Dr. Diana CHAVEZ
06 Registrar ..... Vacant
37 Director Financial Aid ..... Mr. Dewayne BARNES
29 Sr Mgr Alumni/Parent Engagement ..... Ms. Lisa JONAS
13 CIO/Sr VP Operations ..... Ms. Mara HANCOCK
07 Director Undergrad Admissions ..... Ms. Shiraz CHAVAN
38 Director Student Counseling ..... Vacant
88 Director Campus Planning ..... Mr. David MECKEL
18 Assoc VP for Operations ..... Ms. Noel KNILLE
123 Director Graduate Admissions ..... Mr. David MURRAY
09 Director of Institutional Research ..... Ms. Jennifer JURAS
96 Manager of Purchasing ..... Ms. Jackie CRADDOCK
04 Exec Assistant to the President ..... Ms. Gail DAVIES
08 Assoc VP of Libraries ..... Ms. Annemarie HAAR
104 Dir International Programs ..... Ms. Jessica MCMILLAN
19 Director Public Safety ..... Mr. Abe LEAL
28 Coordinator for Diversity ..... Ms. Jane SON
39 Director Residential Life ..... Ms. Monique BUTLER
44 Director of Annual Giving ..... Ms. Jennifer JANSEN
101 Special Asst & Board Liaison ..... Ms. Adriana LOBOVITS
102 Director Leadership Giving ..... Ms. Carleigh MCDONALD
105 Director Digital Content ..... Ms. Sarah BAILEY HOGARTY
108 Assoc Provost Accreditation & Curr ..... Ms. Dominick TRACY
86 Sr Dir of Inst Partnerships ..... Ms. Karen WEBER
90 Assoc Dir Academic Computing ..... Mr. Matthew GORDON
91 Sr Dir Web & Infrastructure ..... Mr. Eli COCHRAN
41 Athletic Director ..... Vacant

California College San Diego (E)

6602 Convoy Court, Suite 100, San Diego CA 92111

County: San Diego | FICE Identification: 021108 | Unit ID: 485263
Telephone: (619) 680-4430 | Carnegie Class: Spec-4-yr-Other Health
FAX Number: (619) 295-5985 | Calendar System: Other
URL: www.cc-sd.edu
Established: 1978 | Annual Undergrad Tuition & Fees: $16,972
Enrollment: 875 | Coed
Affiliation or Control: Independent Non-Profit | IRS Status: 501(c)3
Highest Offering: Baccalaureate
Accreditation: ACCSC, COARC

01 President ..... Mr. Eric JUHLIN
11 Executive Director ..... Dr. Ken WEBB
05 Dean of Education/CAO ..... Dr. Jason KART
06 Registrar ..... Ms. Ariana GONZALEZ
07 Director of Admissions ..... Ms. Denise NGUYEN
08 Head Librarian ..... Ms. Patricia BERMEL
36 Director Student Placement ..... Mr. Gary ROTHY

California College San Diego (F)

277 Rancheros Drive, Suite 200, San Marcos CA 92069

Telephone: (760) 621-4333 | Identification: 770551
Accreditation: ACCSC

California Graduate School of Theology (G)

11277 Garden Grove Blvd, 2nd Floor,
Garden Grove CA 92843

County: Orange | Identification: 667307
Telephone: (714) 636-1722 | Carnegie Class: Not Classified
FAX Number: (714) 636-1725 | Calendar System: Semester
URL: cgsot.edu
Established: 1969 | Annual Undergrad Tuition & Fees: N/A
Enrollment: N/A | Coed
Affiliation or Control: Interdenominational | IRS Status: 501(c)3
Highest Offering: Doctorate
Accreditation: TRACS

01 President/CEO ..... Mr. Kang WON LEE
10 VP/Dean Admin & Business Affairs ..... Vacant
05 Dean of Academic Affairs ..... Dr. Seong HEE LEE

California Health Sciences University (H)

120 N. Clovis Ave, Clovis CA 93612

County: Fresno | Identification: 667218 | Unit ID: 488572
Telephone: (559) 325-3600 | Carnegie Class: Not Classified
FAX Number: (559) 473-1487 | Calendar System: Semester
URL: www.chsu.edu
Established: 2012 | Annual Graduate Tuition & Fees: N/A
Enrollment: 259 | Coed
Affiliation or Control: Proprietary | IRS Status: Proprietary
Highest Offering: Doctorate; No Undergraduates
Accreditation: WC, @OSTEO, @PHAR

01 President ..... Florence DUNN
04 Administrative Asst to President ..... Kathleen HAEBERLE
05 SVP Academic Affairs/Provost/Dean ..... Wendy DUNCAN
09 Dir Inst Effectiveness & Research ..... Stephanie WRAGG
11 VP Operations ..... Jimmy DUNN
10 Controller ..... Tanya BOHORQUEZ
13 Exec Dir of Info Technology ..... John BRIAR
32 Asst Dean of Student Affairs ..... Jeremy HUGHES
06 Registrar ..... Jonathan VELEZ
07 Director of Admissions ..... Leslie WILLIAMS
26 VP Marketing/Communications ..... Richele KLEISER
20 Asst Dean of Education ..... Will OFSTAD
08 Librarian ..... Anna YANG
37 Director Student Financial Aid ..... Kevin HOOVER

California Institute for Human Science (I)

701 Garden View Court, Encinitas CA 92024

County: San Diego | Identification: 667342
Telephone: (760) 634-1771 | Carnegie Class: Not Classified
FAX Number: N/A | Calendar System: Quarter
URL: www.cihs.edu
Established: 1992 | Annual Undergrad Tuition & Fees: N/A
Enrollment: N/A | Coed
Affiliation or Control: Independent Non-Profit | IRS Status: 501(c)3
Highest Offering: Doctorate
Accreditation: @WC

01 President ..... Dr. Thomas BROPHY

California Institute of Advanced Management (J)

1000 S. Fremont Avenue, #45, A10, Alhambra CA 91803

County: Los Angeles | FICE Identification: 042506 | Unit ID: 487649
Telephone: (626) 350-1500 | Carnegie Class: Spec-4-yr-Bus
FAX Number: (626) 350-1515 | Calendar System: Other
URL: www.ciam.edu
Established: | Annual Graduate Tuition & Fees: N/A
Enrollment: 33 | Coed
Affiliation or Control: Independent Non-Profit | IRS Status: 501(c)3
Highest Offering: Master's; No Undergraduates
Accreditation: WC, DEAC

01 President ..... Ms. Jennie TA
05 Vice Pres/Chief Academic Officer ..... Dr. Eric MCLAUGHLIN
10 Chief Financial Officer ..... Mr. Kien TIET
20 Associate VP ..... Dr. Harish AMAR

California Institute of the Arts (K)

24700 McBean Parkway, Valencia CA 91355-2397

County: Los Angeles | FICE Identification: 001132 | Unit ID: 111081
Telephone: (661) 255-1050 | Carnegie Class: Spec-4-yr-Arts
FAX Number: (661) 254-8352 | Calendar System: Semester
URL: www.calarts.edu
Established: 1961 | Annual Undergrad Tuition & Fees: $49,276
Enrollment: 1,498 | Coed
Affiliation or Control: Independent Non-Profit | IRS Status: 501(c)3
Highest Offering: Doctorate
Accreditation: WC, ART, DANCE

01 President ..... Ravi S. RAJAN
05 Provost/SVP Academic Affairs ..... Tracie COSTANTINO
10 Senior VP Finance & Opers/CFO ..... Maeesha MERCHANT
111 Senior VP Advancement ..... Terry MORELLO
21 Assoc Vice President and Controller ..... Karla TALAVERA
15 Assoc Vice Pres Human Resources ..... Charmagne SHEARRILL
11 Assoc VP/Chief Operating Officer ..... Jesse SMITH
32 VP Student Experience ..... Brian HARLAN
84 VP Enrollment Management ..... Robert BORDEN
30 Vice President for Development ..... Meredith ROBBINS
28 Institute Diversity Officer ..... Eva GRAHAM
20 Assoc Provost Academic Affairs ..... Bree HOWARD
08 Dean Div of Library & Info Resource ..... Vacant
57 Dean School of Art ..... Thomas LAWSON
64 Dean Herb Alpert School of Music ..... David ROSENBOOM
88 Dean School of Critical Studies ..... Amanda BEECH
88 Dean Sharon D Lund School of Dance ..... Dimitri CHAMBLAS
88 Dean School Film & Video ..... Vacant
88 Dean School of Theater ..... Travis PRESTON
88 Assistant VP Enrollment ..... Anna JABLONSKI
26 Executive Director Marketing ..... James WOLKEN
07 Exec Director Admissions ..... Steve CASTLES
37 Director of Financial Aid ..... Lisa SEALS
29 Director Alumni & Family Engagement ..... Vacant
88 Director Community Arts Partnership ..... Veronica ALVAREZ
39 Assoc Director of Residence Life ..... Dionne SIMMONS
87 Director of Summer Session ..... Hilary DARLING
19 Campus Safety Supervisor ..... Mark FARLEY
88 Director of Leadership Gifts ..... Sally BICKERTON
112 Director of Development/Major Gift ..... Aaron CAMPBELL
23 Director Health Services ..... Vacant
88 Director Advancement Services ..... Korey JANSE
88 Director Prospect Strategy ..... Natalie LARMON
13 Director Information Technology ..... Christopher CUTTRISS
102 Director Corp/Foundation/Govt ..... Sarah NELSON
44 Director Development/Indiv Giving ..... Aiza KEESEY
88 Director Special Events ..... Lindsey SCHIFF-ABRAMS
36 Director Career Services ..... Vacant
18 Director Facilities Management ..... John THOMAS
04 Sr Administrative Asst to President ..... Vacant
85 Director Intl Students and Programs ..... Fumiyo ARAKI
105 Director Web Communications ..... Christine ZIEMBA
88 Director of Creative Services ..... Stuart SMITH

88 Director of Project Development .... Lisa BARR
114 Director Academic Contracts/Budget .... Trish PATRYLA
09 Assoc Dir of Institutional Research .... Zachary MORGAN
101 Board Liaison & Special Projects .... Heather SURAN
43 Director of Legal Affairs .... Nikhil PILLAI
06 Registrar .... Erin COLLINS
100 Chief of Staff .... Chebon MARSHALL

California Institute of Arts & Technology (A)

2820 Camino Del Rio South, Ste 100,
San Diego CA 92108
County: San Diego | Identification: 667289
Unit ID: 490285
Telephone: (877) 559-3621 | Carnegie Class: Not Classified
FAX Number: N/A | Calendar System: Other
URL: www.ciat.edu
Established: 2008 | Annual Undergrad Tuition & Fees: $14,040
Enrollment: 804 | Coed
Affiliation or Control: Proprietary | IRS Status: Proprietary
Highest Offering: Associate Degree
Accreditation: CNCE

01 President .... Jamie DOYLE
05 Director of Education .... Pete LIMON
11 Vice President for Compliance .... Claire PARK
06 Registrar .... Ed BRANCHEAU
07 Director of Admissions .... Joe RAMIREZ
13 Director of IT .... Rob SUMABAT

California Institute of Integral Studies (B)

1453 Mission Street, 4th Floor,
San Francisco CA 94103-2557
County: San Francisco | FICE Identification: 012154
Unit ID: 110316
Telephone: (415) 575-6100 | Carnegie Class: DU-Mod
FAX Number: (415) 575-1264 | Calendar System: Semester
URL: www.ciis.edu
Established: 1968 | Annual Undergrad Tuition & Fees: N/A
Enrollment: 1,417 | Coed
Affiliation or Control: Independent Non-Profit | IRS Status: 501(c)3
Highest Offering: Doctorate
Accreditation: WC, ACUP

01 President .... Dr. Judie G. WEXLER
05 Provost .... Dr. Liz BEAVEN
10 Controller/VP of Finance .... Ms. Gail BERGUNDE
111 Vice President of Advancement .... Ms. Jillian ELLIOT
88 VP China Projects/Exec Dir ACTCM .... Ms. Lixin HUANG
32 Dean of Students .... Ms. Yunny YIP
29 Dean of Alumni/Dir of Travel Pgms .... Dr. Richard BUGGS
20 Associate Provost .... Mr. Chip B. GOLDSTEIN
07 Director of Admissions .... Ms. Ellen DURST
06 Registrar .... Mr. Dan GURLER
26 Director of Communications .... Ms. Lisa DENENMARK
37 Director of Financial Aid .... Mr. Larry BLAIR
18 Associate Director of Operations .... Ms. Monica MUNJAL
85 International Student Advisor .... Ms. Jody O'CONNOR
04 Administrative Asst to President .... Ms. Christine FILIMONOVA
09 Director of Institutional Research .... Mr. Peter JONES
28 Director of Diversity .... Ms. Rachel BRYANT

California Institute of Technology (C)

1200 E California Boulevard, Pasadena CA 91125-0001
County: Los Angeles | FICE Identification: 001131
Unit ID: 110404
Telephone: (626) 395-6811 | Carnegie Class: DU-Highest
FAX Number: (626) 795-1547 | Calendar System: Trimester
URL: www.caltech.edu
Established: 1891 | Annual Undergrad Tuition & Fees: $52,362
Enrollment: 2,238 | Coed
Affiliation or Control: Independent Non-Profit | IRS Status: 501(c)3
Highest Offering: Doctorate
Accreditation: WC

01 President .... Dr. Thomas F. ROSENBAUM
101 Secretary to the BOT .... Mrs. Mary L. WEBSTER
05 Provost .... Dr. David A. TIRRELL
88 Vice President/Director JPL .... Dr. Michael WATKINS
10 VP of Admin/Chief Financial Officer .... Ms. Margo STEURBAUT
21 AVP for Finance & Treasurer .... Ms. Sharon E. PATTERSON
111 VP for Advancement & Alumni Rels .... Mr. Dexter F. BAILEY, JR.
45 VP for Strategy Implementation .... Dr. Diana JERGOVIC
32 Vice President Student Affairs .... Dr. Joseph E. SHEPHERD
43 General Counsel .... Ms. Victoria D. STRATMAN
04 Exec Asst to the Pres/Asst Sec BOT .... Ms. Carol SCHUIL
20 Vice Provost .... Dr. Cindy A. WEINSTEIN
20 Vice Provost .... Dr. Kaushik BHATTACHARYA
15 Assoc Vice Pres Human Resources .... Ms. Julia M. MCCALLIN
110 Assoc Vice President Development .... Ms. Valerie A. OTTEN
112 AVP for Campaigns .... Ms. Diane M. BINNEY
44 Asst VP Engagement & Annual Program .... Ms. Theresa A. DAVIS
86 Director Government Relations .... Mr. Ken HARGREAVES
35 Senior Director Student Activities .... Mr. Tom N. MANNION
26 Chief Strat Communications Officer .... Ms. Shayna CHABNER
81 Chair Biology & Biological Engr Div .... Dr. Stephen L. MAYO
81 Chair Chemistry & Chemical Engr Div .... Dr. Dennis A. DOUGHERTY
54 Chair Engr & Applied Science Div .... Dr. Guruswami RAVICHANDRAN
65 Chair Geology/Planet Science Div .... Dr. John P. GROTZINGER
79 Chair Humanities/Social Science Div .... Dr. Jean-Laurent ROSENTHAL
81 Chair Physics/Math/Astro Division .... Dr. Fiona HARRISON
06 Registrar .... Ms. Christy SALINAS
07 Exec Director of Admissions .... Mr. Jarrid WHITNEY
08 University Librarian .... Ms. Kara M. WHATLEY
13 Chief Information Officer .... Mr. Jin CHANG
18 Assoc Vice Pres for Facilities .... Mr. James W. COWELL, JR.
18 Interim Sr Dir Facilities Mgmt .... Mr. Christopher MCALARY
19 Chief of Campus Sec & Parking .... Mr. Victor A. CLAY
16 Exec Director of Human Resources .... Ms. Tara KRUCKEBERG
23 Director Health Services .... Dr. John Y. TSAI
25 Assoc VP of Research Admin .... Dr. Richard P. SELIGMAN
117 Assoc VP Audit Svcs & Inst Comp .... Ms. Pamela D. KOYZIS
29 Int Exec Dir Alumni Association .... Ms. Emily FISCHER
37 Director Financial Aid .... Mr. Don CREWELL
109 AVP for Student Affairs Operations .... Mr. Dimitris SAKELLARIOU
36 Director Career Development .... Ms. Lauren B. STOLPER
40 Manager Bookstore .... Ms. Karyn SEIXAS
41 Dir Athletics & Physical Education .... Ms. Betsy MITCHELL
58 Dean of Graduate Studies .... Dr. Doug C. REES
35 Dean of Students .... Dr. Kevin M. GILMARTIN
85 Assoc Dir International Student Pgm .... Ms. Laura FLOWER KIM
96 Dir Purchasing & Payment Services .... Ms. Tina LOWENTHAL
102 Director Foundation Relations .... Ms. Nelly KHIDEKEL
104 Dir Fellowshp Advising/Study Abroad .... Ms. Lauren B. STOLPER
38 Director Counseling Center .... Ms. Jennifer HOWES
09 Sr Institutional Research Analyst .... Dr. Lindsey E. MALCOM-PIQUEUX
39 Director Student Housing .... Ms. Maria A. KATSAS

California Institute of Management and Technology (D)

2361 Campus Drive, Suite 180, Irvine CA 92612
County: Orange | Identification: 667286
Telephone: (949) 872-2224 | Carnegie Class: Not Classified
FAX Number: (949) 872-2229 | Calendar System: Other
URL: www.calimt.edu
Established: 2010 | Annual Graduate Tuition & Fees: N/A
Enrollment: N/A | Coed
Affiliation or Control: Proprietary | IRS Status: Proprietary
Highest Offering: Master's; No Undergraduates
Accreditation: DEAC

05 Provost .... Dr. H. Clarissa CHAIY
11 Director of Operations .... Tey LY
06 Registrar .... Elaine LINDMARK

California Intercontinental University (E)

17310 Red Hill Ave, Ste 200, Irvine CA 92614
County: Orange | Identification: 666670
Unit ID: 485546
Telephone: (866) 687-2258 | Carnegie Class: Spec-4-yr-Bus
FAX Number: (949) 861-9431 | Calendar System: Other
URL: www.caluniversity.edu
Established: 2003 | Annual Undergrad Tuition & Fees: $10,565
Enrollment: 543 | Coed
Affiliation or Control: Proprietary | IRS Status: Proprietary
Highest Offering: Doctorate
Accreditation: DEAC

01 Chief Executive Officer/President .... Dr. Leslie GARGIULO
11 Director of Operations .... Mr. Donald GARGIULO
06 Registrar .... Mr. Mark WILLS
37 Director Student Financial Aid .... Mr. Richard MADRIGAL
05 Chief Academic Officer .... Dr. Nichole KARPEL
58 Dean of Faculty & Graduate Studies .... Dr. Brian STARK

California International Business University (F)

550 West B Street, San Diego CA 92101
County: San Diego | Identification: 666711
Unit ID: 483586
Telephone: (619) 702-9400 | Carnegie Class: Not Classified
FAX Number: (619) 702-9476 | Calendar System: Semester
URL: www.cibu.edu
Established: 1994 | Annual Undergrad Tuition & Fees: N/A
Enrollment: N/A | Coed
Affiliation or Control: Independent Non-Profit | IRS Status: 501(c)3
Highest Offering: Master's
Accreditation: ACICS

01 Acting President .... Mr. Brian HAWKINS
32 Dean Stdnt Affs/Special Pgms/MBA .... Mr. Brian HAWKINS
10 Chief Financial Officer .... Mr. Dan ERSHADI
58 Dean Graduate Pgms/Compliance Ofcr .... Dr. Marcus BENNIEFIELD
06 Registrar/Admin Ofcr .... Ms. Susi HAUGH

California Jazz Conservatory (G)

2087 Addison Street, Berkeley CA 94704
County: Alameda | Identification: 667217
Unit ID: 486488
Telephone: (510) 845-5373 | Carnegie Class: Spec-4-yr-Arts
FAX Number: (510) 841-5373 | Calendar System: Semester
URL: www.cjc.edu
Established: 2009 | Annual Undergrad Tuition & Fees: $19,100
Enrollment: 61 | Coed
Affiliation or Control: Independent Non-Profit | IRS Status: 501(c)3
Highest Offering: Baccalaureate
Accreditation: MUS

01 President .... Susan MUSCARELLA
05 Dean of Instruction .... Jeff DENSON
11 Director Jazz School at CJC .... Rob EWING
08 Head Librarian .... Jayn PETTINGILL

California Lutheran University (H)

60 W Olsen Road, Thousand Oaks CA 91360-2787
County: Ventura | FICE Identification: 001133
Unit ID: 110413
Telephone: (805) 492-2411 | Carnegie Class: Masters/L
FAX Number: (805) 493-3513 | Calendar System: Semester
URL: www.callutheran.edu
Established: 1959 | Annual Undergrad Tuition & Fees: $42,692
Enrollment: 4,236 | Coed
Affiliation or Control: Evangelical Lutheran Church In America
IRS Status: 501(c)3
Highest Offering: Doctorate
Accreditation: WC, CLPSY, THEOL

01 President .... Dr. Christopher KIMBALL
05 Provost/Vice Pres Academic Affairs .... Dr. Leanne NEILSON
111 Vice Pres University Advancement .... Dr. Regina BIDDINGS-MURO
10 Vice Pres Admin/Finance/Treasurer .... Ms. Karen DAVIS
32 Vice Pres Stdnt Life/Dean of Stdnts .... Ms. Melinda ROPER
84 VP Enrollment Mgmt & Marketing .... Dr. Matthew WARD
13 Chief Information Officer .... Mr. Zareh MARSELIAN
18 Assoc Vice Pres Facilities .... Mr. Ryan VAN OMMEREN
26 Assoc VP University Relations .... Ms. Lynda FULFORD
49 Dean College Arts & Sciences .... Dr. Jessica LAVARIEGA MONFORTI
53 Dean of School of Education .... Dr. Michael HILLIS
50 Dean of School of Management .... Dr. Gerhard APFELTHALER
83 Dean Grad School of Psychology .... Dr. Rick HOLIGROCKI
15 Asst VP for Human Resources .... Ms. Patricia PARHAM
06 Assoc Prov Academic Svcs/Registrar .... Ms. Maria KOHNKE
42 University Pastor .... Rev. Scott MAXWELL-DOHERTY
42 Vice President Mission and Identity .... Rev. Melissa MAXWELL-DOHERTY
112 Director Major Planned Giving .... Mr. Richard HOLMES, IV
41 Director Athletics .... Dr. Daniel KUNTZ
107 Director Professionals .... Dr. Lisa BUONO
36 Director of Career Services .... Ms. Cindy LEWIS
85 Sr Dir Multicultural/Intl Std Svc .... Dr. Juanita HALL
114 Dir of Budget/Management Analysis .... Vacant
29 Dir Alumni and Family Relations .... Ms. Rachel RONNING LINDGREN
38 Director Counseling Services .... Dr. Virginia MARIL
19 Director Security/Safety .... Mr. David HILKE
07 Dean of Undergrad Admissions .... Mr. Michael ELGARICO
09 Director of Institutional Research .... Dr. Rodney REYNOLDS
37 Director of Financial Aid .... Mr. Jerry MCKEEN
104 Director of Study Abroad .... Vacant
39 Asst Dean of Stdnts/Dir of Res Life .... Dr. Christine PAUL
23 Director of Health Services .... Ms. Kerri LAUCHNER
101 Secretary of the Institution/Board .... Ms. Rian CURLEY
04 Executive Asst to the President .... Ms. Nancy TRUBE

California Miramar University (I)

3550 Camino Del Rio N. Suite 208, San Diego CA 92108
County: San Diego | Identification: 666713
Unit ID: 480781
Telephone: (858) 653-3000 | Carnegie Class: Spec-4-yr-Bus
FAX Number: (858) 653-6786 | Calendar System: Other
URL: www.calmu.edu
Established: 2005 | Annual Undergrad Tuition & Fees: $8,977
Enrollment: 267 | Coed
Affiliation or Control: Proprietary | IRS Status: Proprietary
Highest Offering: Master's
Accreditation: ACICS, DEAC

01 President/CEO .... Ali GOOYABADI
05 Dean Academic Affs/Comp Info System .... John MCCREADY
10 Chief Financial Officer .... Jack THRIFT
07 International Admissions Director .... Carol KULIS
06 Registrar .... Kristen HABEN
37 Director Student Financial Aid .... Dune TRINN
41 Athletic Director .... Chris SHADE

California Northstate University (J)

9700 West Taron Dr, Elk Grove CA 95757
County: Sacramento | Identification: 667020
Telephone: (916) 686-7400 | Carnegie Class: Not Classified
FAX Number: (916) 686-8143 | Calendar System: Semester
URL: www.cnsu.edu
Established: 2008 | Annual Undergrad Tuition & Fees: N/A
Enrollment: N/A | Coed
Affiliation or Control: Independent Non-Profit | IRS Status: 501(c)3
Highest Offering: Doctorate
Accreditation: WC, #MED, PHAR

01 President ... Dr. Alvin CHEUNG
05 VP Academic Affairs ... Dr. Katherine YANG
63 VP Med Affs/Dean Col of Medicine ... Dr. Joseph SILVA
10 VP of Finance/CFO ... Ms. Shoua XIONG
11 VP of University Operations ... Dr. Mike LEE
108 VP of Inst Rsrch/Quality/Assessment ... Dr. Karen MCCLENDON
32 VP for Admissions & Student Service ... Dr. Xiaodong FENG
43 Legal Counsel ... Mr. Paul WAGSTAFFE
67 Dean of Pharmacy ... Dr. Hieu TRAN
08 Director of Library Resources ... Mr. Scott MINOR
06 Registrar ... Ms. Janine DRAGNA
07 Asst Dean Admissions/Student Affs ... Dr. Tiffany-Jade KREYS
76 Dean of Health Sciences ... Dr. Heather BROWN

California Southern University (A)

3330 Harbor Boulevard, Costa Mesa CA 92626
County: Orange — Identification: 666770
Telephone: (800) 477-2254 — Carnegie Class: Not Classified
FAX Number: (714) 480-0834 — Calendar System: Semester
URL: www.calsouthern.edu
Established: 1978 — Annual Undergrad Tuition & Fees: N/A
Enrollment: N/A — Coed
Affiliation or Control: Proprietary — IRS Status: Proprietary
Highest Offering: Doctorate
Accreditation: WC, ACBSP, NURSE

01 President ... Dr. Gwen FINESTONE
05 Provost ... Dr. LaSharnda BECKWITH
03 VP Organizational Effectiveness ... Brett O'ROURKE
10 VP Administration ... Amanda STEED
04 Exec Assistant to the President ... Linda GINEX
32 Chief Officer Student Affairs ... Maria DILLON-OWENS

*The California State University System Office (B)

401 Golden Shore, Long Beach CA 90802-4210
County: Los Angeles — FICE Identification: 001136
Unit ID: 110501
Telephone: (562) 951-4000 — Carnegie Class: N/A
FAX Number: (562) 951-4986
URL: www.calstate.edu

01 Chancellor ... Dr. Timothy P. WHITE
05 Exec Vice Chanc Acad/Stdnt Affairs ... Dr. Loren J. BLANCHARD
10 Executive Vice Chancellor & CFO ... Mr. Steve RELYEA
15 Vice Chancellor Human Resources ... Ms. Evelyn NAZARIO
111 Vice Chanc Univ Rels/Advancement ... Mr. Garrett P. ASHLEY
43 Exec Vice Chanc/General Counsel ... Mr. Andrew JONES
116 Vice Chancellor/Chief Audit Officer ... Mr. Larry MANDEL
100 Chief of Staff ... Dr. Karen NAKAI

*California Polytechnic State University-San Luis Obispo (C)

1 Grand Avenue, San Luis Obispo CA 93407-9000
County: San Luis Obispo — FICE Identification: 001143
Unit ID: 110422
Telephone: (805) 756-1111 — Carnegie Class: Masters/L
FAX Number: (805) 756-5400 — Calendar System: Quarter
URL: www.calpoly.edu
Established: 1901 — Annual Undergrad Tuition & Fees (In-State): $9,816
Enrollment: 22,370 — Coed
Affiliation or Control: State — IRS Status: 501(c)3
Highest Offering: Master's
Accreditation: WC, ART, CONST, DIETD, DIETI, LSAR, MUS, NAIT, NRPA, PLNG

02 President ... Dr. Jeffrey D. ARMSTRONG
100 AVP & Chief of Staff ... Ms. Jessica DARIN
05 Interim Provost ... Dr. Mary PEDERSEN
32 Vice President Student Affairs ... Dr. Keith HUMPHREY
30 COO University Development ... Mr. David DOBIS
10 Senior Vice Pres Admin & Finance ... Ms. Cynthia VILLA
58 Vice Provost Intl/Grad & Ext Educ ... Dr. Brian TIETJE
41 Athletic Director ... Mr. Don OBERHELMAN
13 Vice President ITS & CIO ... Mr. Bill BRITTON
20 Assoc Vice Provost Acad Affairs ... Dr. Bruno GIBERTI
88 Assoc VP Comm Svc/Exec Dir CPC ... Ms. Lorlie LEETHAM
46 Int VP Research & Economic Dev ... Mr. Bradford ANDERSON
21 Associate Vice Pres Admin & Finance ... Mr. Victor BRANCART
26 Chief Communications Officer ... Mr. Chris MURPHY
18 Associate VP Facil Mgmt & Dev ... Ms. Juanita HOLLER
39 AVP Stdnt Affs/Exec Dir of UH ... Dr. Jo CAMPBELL
15 Vice Prov Acad Aff & Personnel ... Dr. Al LIDDICOAT
84 VP Enr Dev & Chief Market Officer ... Mr. James L. MARAVIGLIA
88 Dir Ctr Teaching/Learning & Tech ... Mr. Patrick O'SULLIVAN
29 Assoc VP Alumni Outreach ... Ms. Ellen COHUNE
19 University Police Department ... Chief George HUGHES
06 University Registrar ... Mr. Cem SUNATA
28 VP & CDO Diversity & Inclusion ... Dr. Jozi DELEON
22 Director Equal Opp/Title IX Coord ... Ms. Maren HUFTON
43 University Counsel ... Mr. Kyle ROWEN
23 AVP Health & Well Being ... Dr. Tina HADAWAY-MELLIS
38 Director of Counseling Services ... Dr. Geneva ABIKO
35 ASI Executive Director ... Ms. Marcy MALONEY
14 Deputy Chief Information Officer ... Mr. Ryan MATTESON
40 Operations Manager University Store ... Vacant
35 Assoc VP Student Affairs & DOS ... Dr. Kathleen MCMAHON
88 Director Econ Dev & Tech Transfr ... Mr. Jim DUNNING
47 Dean Agriculture/Food & Env Sci ... Dr. Andrew THULIN
48 Dean Architect/Environmental Design ... Ms. Christine THEODOROPOULOS
50 Dean College of Business ... Mr. Scott DAWSON
54 Dean College of Engineering ... Dr. Amy FLEISCHER
49 Int Dean College of Liberal Arts ... Dr. Kathryn RUMMELL
81 Dean Science & Mathematics ... Dr. Dean WENDT
53 Director School of Education ... Dr. J. Kevin TAYLOR
16 Assoc VP Human Resources ... Ms. Beth E. GALLAGHER
96 Asst VP Strat Business Sup Svcs ... Mr. Dru ZACHMEYER
37 Exec Director Fin Aid/Scholarship ... Ms. Gerrie HATTEN
36 Exec Director Career Services ... Ms. Eileen C. BUECHER
09 Exec Director Inst Research ... Mr. Mauricio SAAVEDRA
104 Director International Center ... Ms. Caroline VANDERKAR
92 Director Honors Program ... Dr. Gregg FIEGEL
04 Executive Asst to President ... Ms. Monica MOLINA
07 Director of Admissions ... Mr. Terrance HARRIS
08 Dean of Library Services ... Ms. Adriana POPESCU
25 Director Grants Dev & Sponsored Pgm ... Ms. Amy VELASCO
86 Dir Govt & Community Relations ... Mr. Justin WELLNER
108 Director Academic Assessment ... Dr. Michael NGUYEN
44 Director Cmp Engage & Annual Giving ... Mr. Chris MCBRIDE

*California State Polytechnic University-Pomona (D)

3801 W Temple Avenue, Pomona CA 91768-2557
County: Los Angeles — FICE Identification: 001144
Unit ID: 110529
Telephone: (909) 869-7659 — Carnegie Class: Masters/L
FAX Number: (909) 869-4535 — Calendar System: Semester
URL: www.cpp.edu
Established: 1938 — Annual Undergrad Tuition & Fees (In-State): $7,353
Enrollment: 26,053 — Coed
Affiliation or Control: State — IRS Status: 501(c)3
Highest Offering: Master's
Accreditation: WC, ART, CEA, CIDA, DIETD, DIETI, LSAR, MUS, PLNG, SPAA

02 President ... Dr. Soraya M. COLEY
05 Provost/VP Academic Affairs ... Dr. Sylvia A. ALVA
32 Interim VP Student Affairs ... Dr. Eileen SULLIVAN
10 VP Administrative Affairs/CFO ... Ms. Danielle MANNING
111 VP University Advancement ... Mr. Daniel MONTPLAISIR
102 Int Exec Dir CPP Foundation Inc ... Ms. Danielle MANNING
20 Assoc Provost Academic Affairs ... Dr. Sepehr ESKANDARI
18 Int AVP Facilities Planning & Mgmt ... Mr. Daniel C. JOHNSON
35 Interim AVP & Dean of Students ... Dr. Benardo DARGAN
84 Sr AVP Enrollment Services ... Ms. Jessica M. WAGONER
88 Exec Asst to the Provost ... Ms. Diane R. GONZALEZ
46 AVP Research/Innovation/Econ Dev ... Dr. Sadiq SHAH
26 Assoc Vice Pres for Univ Relations ... Mr. Tim LYNCH
21 Assoc VP Finance/Admin Svcs ... Mr. Joseph SIMONESCHI
35 AVP/Chief of Opers/Student Affairs ... Dr. Kevin T. COLANER
35 Int Pres Assoc Stdnt Affs Prtnrshp ... Dr. Reginald S. BLAYLOCK
13 Vice President & CIO ... Mr. John W. MCGUTHRY
09 AVP Inst Rsrch/Planning & Analytics ... Dr. Heather BROWN
15 AVP for Human Resources ... Ms. Sharon L. REITER
100 Chief of Staff ... Ms. Nicole A. HAWKES
04 Director of Administration ... Ms. Francine M. RAMIREZ
47 Interim Dean College of Agriculture ... Dr. Lisa KESSLER
49 Dean Col Letters/Arts/Soc Sci ... Dr. Iris S. LEVINE
50 Dean Col of Business Admin ... Dr. Erik ROLLAND
54 Dean College of Engineering ... Dr. Joseph J. RENCIS
48 Int Dean Col Environmental Design ... Dr. Lauren W. BRICKER
88 Dean Collins College of Hosp Mgmt ... Dr. Lea R. DOPSON
81 Dean College of Science ... Dr. Alison BASKI
53 Dean Col Education/Integrat Studies ... Dr. Jeff PASSE
30 Assoc VP for Development ... Mr. Douglas NELSON
08 Interim Dean University Library ... Ms. Emma C. GIBSON
41 Director of Athletics ... Mr. Brian R. SWANSON
86 Asst VP for Govt & External Affairs ... Ms. Frances TEVES
19 Chief of Police ... Mr. Dario ROBINSON
88 Exec Dir Acad Rsrch & Acad Resource ... Ms. Lisa M. ROTUNNI
37 Int Dir Financial Aid/Scholarships ... Mr. Gary BYERS
06 Registrar ... Mr. Daniel A. PARKS
96 Director of Procurement ... Vacant
07 Exec Dir Admissions & Outreach ... Ms. Deborah L. BRANDON
106 Int Dean College of Extended Univ ... Dr. Cheryl WYRICK
28 Int Dir Employee Diver/Inclusion ... Ms. Nicole L. BUTTS
29 Exec Dir Alumni/External Affairs ... Ms. Melissa RIORDAN
39 Exec Director University Housing ... Ms. Megan STANG

*California State University-Bakersfield (E)

9001 Stockdale Highway, Bakersfield CA 93311-1022
County: Kern — FICE Identification: 007993
Unit ID: 110486
Telephone: (661) 654-2782 — Carnegie Class: Masters/L
FAX Number: (661) 654-3194 — Calendar System: Semester
URL: www.csub.edu
Established: 1965 — Annual Undergrad Tuition & Fees (In-State): $7,309
Enrollment: 10,131 — Coed
Affiliation or Control: State — IRS Status: 501(c)3
Highest Offering: Doctorate
Accreditation: WC, CAEPN, NURSE, SPAA, SW

02 President ... Dr. Lynnette ZELEZNY
100 Chief of Staff to the President ... Mr. Michael LUKENS
04 Admin Asst to the President ... Ms. Valerie STROM
05 Interim Provost/VP Academic Affairs ... Dr. Vernon HARPER
10 Vice Pres Business/Admin Services ... Mr. Thom DAVIS
32 Vice President Student Affairs ... Dr. Thomas WALLACE
111 VP University Advancement ... Mr. Victor MARTIN
20 VP Academic Affairs ... Dr. David SCHECTER
84 Assoc VP Enrollment Mgmt ... Dr. Dwayne CANTRELL
20 Assoc VP for Academic Programs ... Dr. Vernon HARPER
85 Director of International Students ... Ms. Sonia SILVA
15 AVP Human Res/Administrative Svcs ... Ms. Kellie GARCIA
13 AVP & Chief Information Officer ... Mr. Faust GORHAM
88 Spec Asst to Provost Academic Aff ... Ms. Leslie WILLIAMS
21 Controller ... Ms. Queen KING
114 Univ Budget Director ... Ms. Michelle MILLS
18 Interim Asst VP Facilities Mgmt/Dev ... Mr. Hasit PANCHAL
09 Asst VP Inst Rsrch/Planning/Assess ... Dr. Kris KRISNAN
25 Assoc Vice Pres Grants/Resources ... Dr. Imeh EBONG
124 Assoc VP Student Success ... Dr. Vikash LAKHANI
12 Dean CSUB Antelope Valley ... Dr. Randy SCHULTZ
50 Dean Business/Public Admin ... Dr. Angappa GUNASEKARAN
53 Dean Social Sciences/Education ... Dr. Tanya BOONE-HOLLADAY
79 Dean Arts & Humanities ... Dr. Robert FRAKES
81 Dean Natural Sciences/Math/Eng ... Dr. Kathleen MADDEN
56 Dean Extended Educ/Global Outreach ... Dr. Mark NOVAK
88 Dir of Acad Opers & Support ... Ms. Lisa ZUZARTE
08 Dean University Library ... Dr. Curt ASHER
06 Interim Registrar ... Ms. Jennifer MCCUNE
07 Director Admissions & Records ... Mr. Ben PERLADO
29 Director Alumni Relations ... Ms. Sarah HENDRICK
41 Director Athletics ... Mr. Kenneth (Ziggy) SIEGFRIED
36 Dir for Cmty Engagement/Career Edu ... Dr. Markel QUARLES
88 Director Children's Center ... Ms. Gladys GARCIA
96 Dir Contract Services/Procurement ... Mr. Michael CHAVEZ
38 Admin Supervisor Counseling Center ... Dr. Janet MILLAR
106 Director E-Learning Services ... Vacant
37 Director Financial Aid ... Mr. Chad MORRIS
92 Int Director CSUB Honors Program ... Dr. Jacquelyn KEGLEY
39 Director Housing & Residential Life ... Ms. Crystal BECKS
117 Director Safety & Risk Management ... Mr. Tim RIDLEY
22 Dir Svcs Students w/Disabilities ... Ms. Janice CLAUSEN
17 Director Student Health Services ... Dr. Oscar RICO
30 Co-Director of Development ... Ms. Martha LEON
30 Co-Director of Development ... Mr. Heath NIEMEYER
88 Director Outreach Services ... Mr. Darius RIGGINS
19 Chief University Police ... Chief Marty WILLIAMSON
109 Director of Food Services ... Mr. Owen SMITH
18 Manager Facilities Operations ... Mr. Tom VELASQUEZ
40 Bookstore Manager ... Mr. Richard SALCEDO
26 Director of Public Affairs & Comm ... Ms. Jennifer SELF
28 Chief Diversity Ofcr & Pres Asst ... Ms. Claudia CATOTA
44 Interim Director Annual Giving ... Mr. Daniel RODELA
04 Asst to the President ... Ms. Ana SANTOS
22 Dir Equity/Inclusion/Compliance ... Mr. Marcus BROWN
102 Dir Corporate & Foundation Rels ... Ms. Lourdes NILON
108 Director Institutional Assessment ... Dr. Kris KRISHNAN
43 University Counsel ... Mr. Andrew MAIORANO

*California State University Channel Islands (F)

One University Drive, Camarillo CA 93012-8599
County: Ventura — FICE Identification: 039803
Unit ID: 441937
Telephone: (805) 437-8400 — Carnegie Class: Masters/M
FAX Number: (805) 437-8414 — Calendar System: Semester
URL: www.csuci.edu
Established: 2002 — Annual Undergrad Tuition & Fees (In-District): $6,817
Enrollment: 7,455 — Coed
Affiliation or Control: State/Local — IRS Status: 501(c)3
Highest Offering: Master's
Accreditation: WC, ACBSP, NURSE

02 President ... Dr. Erika D. BECK
05 Interim Provost ... Dr. Elizabeth Anne SAY
10 VP Business & Financial Affairs ... Ms. Ysabel TRINIDAD
32 VP Student Affairs ... Dr. Richard D. YAO
111 VP University Advancement ... Ms. Nichole IPACH
100 Chief of Staff ... Dr. Genevieve M. EVANS-TAYLOR
56 Associate VP & Dean Extended Univ ... Vacant
49 Dean of Arts & Sciences ... Dr. Vandana KOHLI
50 Int Dean MVS School of Bus & Econ ... Dr. Susan ANDRZEJEWSKI
84 Associate VP Enrollment Management ... Mr. Hung D. DANG
53 Dean of School of Education ... Dr. Brian SEVIER
25 Director Sponsored Programs ... Mr. Scott PEREZ
08 Interim Dean of University Library ... Dr. Stephen E. STRATTON
35 Associate VP & Dean of Students ... Ms. Toni DEBONI
15 Senior Director Human Resources ... Ms. Laurie NICHOLS
86 Sr Dir Community & Govt Relations ... Ms. Celina ZACARIAS
110 Dir Advancement Operations ... Mr. Christopher ABE
88 Dir Major Gifts ... Mr. Carrick DEHART
29 Dir Development/Alumni Engagement ... Dr. Amanda CARPENTER
112 Director Planned & Major Gifts ... Ms. Grace G. ROBINSON
44 Dir Annual Giving & Special Gifts ... Ms. Eva C. GOMEZ
19 Chief of Police ... Mr. Michael MORRIS
39 AVP Housing/Residential Educ & ASI ... Ms. Cindy DERRICO
06 Associate Registrar ... Ms. Colleen FOREST
07 AVP/Dir of Admissions & Records ... Ms. Ginger REYES
108 Assoc VP for SA/ROISS ... Dr. Charles E. OSIRIS
104 Dir Intl Pgms/AD Ctr Intl Affairs ... Dr. Osman OZTURGUT
26 Dir Communication & Marketing ... Ms. Nancy GILL
37 Dir Financial Aid & Scholarships ... Ms. Sunshine GARCIA
88 Dir Special Projects for F&A ... Ms. Caroline DOLL
04 Presidential Aide ... Ms. Alanna TREJO
18 Senior Director Facilities Svcs ... Mr. Wes COOPER

*California State University-Chico (A)

400 W First Street, Chico CA 95929-0001

County: Butte FICE Identification: 001146
Unit ID: 110538
Telephone: (530) 898-6116 Carnegie Class: Masters/L
FAX Number: (530) 898-6824 Calendar System: Semester
URL: www.csuchico.edu
Established: 1887 Annual Undergrad Tuition & Fees (In-State): $7,608
Enrollment: 17,875 Coed
Affiliation or Control: State IRS Status: 501(c)3
Highest Offering: Master's
Accreditation: WC, ART, CONST, DIETD, DIETI, JOUR, MUS, NAIT, NRPA, NURSE, SP, SPAA, SW, THEA

02 President ... Dr. Gayle E. HUTCHINSON
100 Chief of Staff ... Dr. Brooke F. BANKS
05 Provost/Vice Pres Academic Affairs ... Dr. Debra S. LARSON
10 Assoc Vice Pres Budget/Operations ... Ms. Jeni KITCHELL
32 Acting Assoc VP Student Affairs ... Ms. Sandy PARSONS-ELLIS
111 Vice Pres University Advancement ... Mr. Ahmad BOURA
45 Vice Prov Planning/Res Allocation ... Vacant
46 Assoc Vice Pres Research ... Vacant
84 Assoc Vice Pres Enroll Management ... Ms. Barbara FORTIN
13 Vice Prov Information Resources/CIO ... Mr. Michael SCHILLING
21 Assoc VP Financial Svcs/Univ Budget ... Ms. Stacie CORONA
15 Assoc Vice Pres Human Resources ... Ms. Sheryl WOODWARD
16 Int Assoc Vice Pres OAPL ... Ms. Evanne O'DONNELL
47 Dean College of Agriculture ... Dr. John A. UNRUH
51 Int Dean Continuing Education ... Ms. Clare ROBY
72 Dean Col Engr/Comp Sci/Const Mgmt ... Ms. Melody STAPLETON
83 Dean Col Behavior & Social Sci ... Dr. Eddie VELA
50 Dean College of Business ... Mr. Terence LAU
79 Int Dean College Humanities ... Ms. Tracy BUTTS
81 Dean College Natural Sciences ... Dr. David M. HASSENZAHL
60 Dean Coll Communication & Educ ... Dr. Angela TRETHEWEY
20 Int Dean Undergraduate Education ... Ms. Kate MCCARTHY
58 Interim Dean Graduate Studies ... Dr. Sharon A. BARRIOS
08 Dean Library ... Dr. Patrick A. NEWELL
26 Director Univ Public Engagement ... Mr. Stephen B. CUMMINS
29 Director Alumni Relations ... Mr. Jay R. FRIEDMAN
09 Interim Director Inst Research ... Mr. Thomas C. ROSENOW
06 University Registrar ... Mr. Michael C. ALLEN
07 Director of Admissions ... Ms. Kimberly GUANZON
36 Director Career Center ... Ms. Megan ODOM
37 Director Financial Aid/Scholarships ... Mr. Dan REED
18 Assoc VP Facilities Mgmt Svcs ... Mr. Michael A. GUZZI
96 Director of Procurement ... Ms. Sara RUMIANO
92 Director Univ Honors Program ... Mr. John MAHONEY
35 Int Dir Stdnt Conduct/Rights/Respon ... Ms. Emily N. PEART
28 Director of Diversity and Inclusion ... Mr. Tray ROBINSON
04 Executive Asst to President ... Mr. Michael JOHNSTON
104 Int Assoc VP International Educ ... Ms. Sara TRECHTER
25 Int CEO Research Foundation ... Mr. David M. HASSENZAHL
109 Exec Director Associated Students ... Mr. David BUCKLEY
23 Director Student Health Center ... Ms. Juanita D. MOTTLEY
38 Assoc Director Counseling ... Dr. Juni BANERJEE-STEVENS
39 Director University Housing ... Ms. Connie HUYCK
41 Athletic Director ... Ms. Anita S. BARKER
53 Director School of Education ... Ms. Rebecca JUSTESON
19 Chief of Police ... Mr. John REID
22 Director of Labor Relations ... Mr. Dylan SAAKE
30 Director of Development ... Ms. Daria BOOTH
43 University Counsel ... Ms. Sasha DANNA
44 Asst Director Annual Giving ... Mr. Allen K. LUNDE

*California State University-Dominguez Hills (B)

1000 E Victoria Street, Carson CA 90747-0005

County: Los Angeles FICE Identification: 001141
Unit ID: 110547
Telephone: (310) 243-3696 Carnegie Class: Masters/L
FAX Number: N/A Calendar System: Semester
URL: www.csudh.edu
Established: 1960 Annual Undergrad Tuition & Fees (In-State): $6,942
Enrollment: 16,219 Coed
Affiliation or Control: State IRS Status: 501(c)3
Highest Offering: Master's
Accreditation: WC, MT, MUS, NURSE, OPE, OT, SPAA, SW, THEA

02 President ... Dr. Thomas A. PARHAM
05 Provost/VP Academic Affairs ... Dr. Michael SPAGNA
10 Interim VP Administration/Finance ... Mr. Ron COLEY
32 Vice President Student Affairs ... Dr. William FRANKLIN
111 VP Univ Advancement ... Ms. Carrie E. STEWART
13 VP/Chief Information Officer ... Mr. Chris MANRIQUEZ
11 Interim AVP Administration/Finance ... Mr. Wayne NISHIOKA
30 Assoc Vice President Development ... Mr. Jeff POLTORAK
35 Int AVP Stdnt Life/Dean of Stdnts ... Mr. Matthew SMITH
84 Interim AVP Enrollment Management ... Ms. Christina RIOS
100 Chief of Staff ... Ms. Deborah ROBERSON-SIMMS
07 Director of Admissions ... Ms. Michelle TAYLOR
09 Assoc Director Institutional Rsrch ... Mr. Pete VAN HAMERSVELD
37 Director of Financial Aid ... Ms. Delores LEE
06 University Registrar ... Dr. Tara HARDEE
28 Chief Diversity/Equity & Incl Ofcr ... Mr. Dwight HAMILTON
04 Senior Exec Asst to the President ... Mr. Tony LITTLE

*California State University-East Bay (C)

25800 Carlos Bee Boulevard, Hayward CA 94542-3001

County: Alameda FICE Identification: 001138
Unit ID: 110574
Telephone: (510) 885-3000 Carnegie Class: Masters/L
FAX Number: N/A Calendar System: Semester
URL: www.csueastbay.edu
Established: 1957 Annual Undergrad Tuition & Fees (In-State): $6,983
Enrollment: 16,538 Coed
Affiliation or Control: State IRS Status: 501(c)3
Highest Offering: Doctorate
Accreditation: WC, MUS, NURSE, SP, SW

02 President ... Dr. Leroy M. MORISHITA
05 Provost/VP Academic Affairs ... Dr. Edward INCH
10 Vice Pres Admin & Finance ... Ms. Debbie CHAW
111 Vice President Univ Advancement ... Mr. William JOHNSON
32 Vice Pres Student Affs ... Dr. Suzanne ESPINOZA
28 University Diversity Officer ... Ms. Kimberly BAKER-FLOWERS
100 Chief of Staff ... Mr. Derek AITKEN
49 Dean Col of Ltrs/Arts/Soc Sci ... Dr. Kathleen ROUNTREE
50 Dean Col of Business/Econ ... Dr. George LOW
53 Dean Col of Educ/Allied Studies ... Dr. Carolyn NELSON
81 Dean College of Science ... Dr. Jason SINGLEY
08 Dean of Libraries ... Dr. John WENZLER
13 CIO ... Dr. Jake HORNSBY
06 Exec Dir Admiss & Registrar ... Ms. Angela SCHNEIDER

*California State University-Fresno (D)

5200 N. Barton Avenue, Fresno CA 93740-8027

County: Fresno FICE Identification: 001147
Unit ID: 110556
Telephone: (559) 278-4240 Carnegie Class: DU-Mod
FAX Number: (559) 278-4715 Calendar System: Semester
URL: www.csufresno.edu
Established: 1911 Annual Undergrad Tuition & Fees (In-State): $6,587
Enrollment: 25,325 Coed
Affiliation or Control: State IRS Status: 501(c)3
Highest Offering: Doctorate
Accreditation: WC, #CAATE, CACREP, CAEPN, CIDA, CONST, DIETD, DIETI, MUS, NAIT, NRPA, NURSE, PH, PTA, SP, SPAA, SW, THEA

02 President ... Dr. Joseph I. CASTRO
05 Provost/VP Academic Affairs ... Dr. Saul JIMENEZ-SANDOVAL
10 VP Administration/CFO ... Dr. Deborah ADISHIAN-ASTONE
111 Vice Pres University Advancement ... Ms. Paula CASTADIO
32 Vice Pres Student Affs/Enroll Mgmt ... Dr. Frank LAMAS
100 Chief of Staff ... Ms. Diana RALLS
43 General Counsel ... Mr. Darryl HAMM
26 Dir of University Communications ... Ms. Patti WAID
20 Vice Provost Academic Affairs ... Dr. Dennis L. NEF
09 AVP Institutional Effectiveness ... Dr. Rudy SANCHEZ
15 AVP for Human Resources ... Ms. Marylou MENDOZA-MILLER
30 Assoc VP University Development ... Ms. Caty PEREZ
18 Associate Vice President Facilities ... Ms. Tinnah MEDINA
84 Assoc Vice Pres Enrollment Mgmt ... Ms. Malisa LEE
13 Chief Information Officer ... Mr. Orlando LEON
51 Dean/AVP Continuing/Global Educ ... Dr. Scott MOORE
47 Int Dean Agricultural Science/Tech ... Dr. Dennis L. NEF
79 Int Dean of Arts & Humanities ... Dr. Honora CHAPMAN
50 Int Dean Craig School of Business ... Dr. Donald STENGEL
53 Dean of Kremen School of Education ... Dr. Laura ALAMILLO
54 Dean of Engineering ... Dr. Ramakrishna NUNNA
76 Dean of Health/Human Services ... Dr. Jody HIRONAKA-JUTEAU
83 Dean of Social Sciences ... Dr. Michelle DENBESTE
81 Dean of Science & Mathematics ... Dr. Christopher G. MEYER
08 Dean of Library Services ... Ms. Delritta HORNBUCKLE
58 Dean Research/Graduate Studies ... Dr. James MARSHALL
86 Exec Dir Governmental Relations ... Mr. Larry SALINAS
23 AVP of Student Health ... Dr. Janell MORILLO
19 Dir of Public Safety/Chief Police ... Mr. David HUERTA
41 Director of Athletics ... Mr. Terrance TUMEY
37 Director of Financial Aid ... Ms. Kelly RUSSELL
29 Executive Director Alumni Relations ... Ms. Jacquelyn GLASENER
36 Dir of Career Development Center ... Ms. Debbie YOUNG
39 Director Univ Courtyard (Housing) ... Ms. Erin BOELE
96 Dir Procurement & Support Services ... Mr. Brian COTHAM
07 Director of Admissions/Recruitment ... Mr. Phong YANG
35 Assoc Dean Student Involvement ... Mr. Colin STEWART
40 Bookstore Director ... Mr. Curt PARKINSON
06 Registrar ... Ms. Laura YAGER
44 Director Annual Giving ... Ms. Patricia O'CONNOR
90 Director Academic Computing ... Dr. Brent AUERNHEIMER

*California State University-Fullerton (E)

PO Box 34080, 800 N State Col Blvd,
Fullerton CA 92831-3547

County: Orange FICE Identification: 001137
Unit ID: 110565
Telephone: (657) 278-2011 Carnegie Class: Masters/L
FAX Number: (657) 278-2649 Calendar System: Semester
URL: www.fullerton.edu
Established: 1957 Annual Undergrad Tuition & Fees (In-State): $6,886
Enrollment: 40,905 Coed
Affiliation or Control: State IRS Status: 501(c)3
Highest Offering: Doctorate
Accreditation: WC, ANEST, ART, CAATE, CACREP, CAEPN, CSHSE, DANCE, IPSY, JOUR, MIDWF, MUS, NURSE, PH, SP, SPAA, SW, THEA

02 President ... Mr. Framroze (Fram) VIRJEE
100 Chief of Staff ... Ms. Danielle GARCIA
05 Provost & VP Academic Affairs ... Dr. Pamella OLIVER
10 VP Admin & Finance/CFO ... Mr. Danny C. KIM
32 Vice President of Student Affairs ... Dr. Berenecea J. EANES
111 VP University Advancement ... Mr. Greg SAKS
13 VP Info Tech/Chief Info Ofcr ... Mr. Amir DABIRIAN
15 VP of HR/Diversity & Inclusion ... Dr. David FORGUES
88 VP of Budget for Student Affairs ... Mr. Robert SCIALDONE
16 COO HR/Diversity & Inclusion ... Ms. Tara GARCIA
43 University Counsel ... Ms. Gaelle GRALNEK
110 Assoc VP University Advancement ... Mr. Todd FRANDSEN
35 AVP Student Affairs ... Dr. Tonantzin OSEGUERA
35 AVP Student Affairs ... Dr. Clint-Michael RENEAU
58 AVP Academic Programs ... Dr. Mark FILOWITZ
26 AVP Strategic Communications ... Ms. Ellen TREANOR
20 AVP Academic Operations ... Dr. Karyn SCISSUM GUNN
28 AVP Diversity/Inclusion/Equity Pgms ... Mrs. Bobbie PORTER
88 AVP Research and Sponsored Projects ... Dr. Chris LIU
88 Int AVP South County Ops & Init ... Dr. Steve WALK
86 Assc VP Public Affs/Government Rels ... Mrs. Tami BUI
16 AVP Human Resource Services ... Ms. Phenicia MCCULLOUGH
45 Asst VP for Resource Planning ... Ms. Laleh GRAYLEE
88 Int Chief of Operations Stdnt Affs ... Dr. Deanna LEONE
11 Chief of Operations ... Ms. May WONG
18 AVP Capital Planning/Fac Mgt ... Dr. Ali IZADIAN
84 Asst Vice Pres Enrollment Services ... Ms. Nancy DORITY
29 Exec Director Alumni Relations ... Ms. Dianna L. FISHER
109 Exec Dir/CEO Auxiliary Svcs Corp ... Mr. Chuck KISSEL
08 Dean of the Library ... Dr. Emily BONNEY
07 Int Director of Admissions ... Mr. Larry MARTIN
36 Director Career Center ... Dr. Elizabeth ZAVALA-ACEVEZ
40 Director Titan Shops ... Ms. Kimberly BALL
23 Interim Director Health Center ... Mr. Richard BOUCHER
19 Chief University Police ... Mr. Raymund AGUIRRE
37 Int Director Financial Aid ... Ms. Jessica BARCO
41 Director of Athletics ... Mr. James DONOVAN
96 Sr Director Contracts & Procurement ... Mr. Nelson NAGAI
35 Dean of Students ... Ms. Hallie HUNT
94 Director Women's Center/Re-Entry ... Dr. Alisa FLOWERS
88 Dir Educational Partnerships ... Ms. Melba CASTRO
39 Director Housing ... Mr. Larry MARTIN
89 Dir Univ Outreach/New Stdnt Pgm ... Ms. Sharnette UNDERDUE
88 Dir Athletic Academic Services ... Ms. Meredith BASIL
88 Dir Center for Internship/Com Eng ... Ms. Dawn MACY
88 Dir Student Academic Services ... Dr. Rochelle WOODS
88 Dir Veteran Student Services ... Mr. Cameron COOK
38 Int Dir Counseling/Psych Svcs ... Mrs. Jaime SHEEHAN
14 AVP IT/Infrastructure Services ... Mr. Berhanu TADESSE
90 Int AVP IT/Academic Technology Svcs ... Mr. Willie PENG
51 Dean Extend Educ/AVP Intl Pgm ... Vacant
79 Dean Humanities/Social Sciences ... Dr. Sheryl FONTAINE
81 Dean Natural Sciences & Math ... Dr. Marie JOHNSON
50 Dean Mihaylo Col Business/Econ ... Dr. Morteza RAHMATIAN
83 Dean Health/Human Development ... Dr. Laurie ROADES
57 Dean College of the Arts ... Mr. Dale MERRILL
53 Dean College of Education ... Dr. Lisa KIRTMAN
54 Dean Col Engineering & Comp Sci ... Dr. Susamma BARUA
60 Dean College of Communications ... Dr. Bey-Ling SHA
88 Title IX Coordinator ... Ms. Mary BECERRA
88 ASI Executive Director ... Dr. Dave EDWARDS
117 Executive Director Risk Mgmt ... Dr. John BEISNER
88 Exec Dir Labor/Employee Relations ... Ms. Michelle TAPPER
88 University Controller ... Mr. Steven YIM
114 Dir of Acct Services & Fin Report ... Ms. Lynn GANAC
88 Director of Accounts Payable ... Ms. Mary Ann TORRES
113 Dir of Student Financial Services ... Ms. Pearl BOELTER
88 Director of Physical Plant ... Mr. Tuan NGUYEN
88 Director of Construction ... Mr. Sarabdayal SINGH
88 Director of Planning and Design ... Mr. Emil ZORDILLA
88 Dir of Parking and Transportation ... Ms. Kristen JASKO
116 Dir of Audit Svcs & Coordination ... Ms. Cindy MERIDA
88 AVP Institutional Effectiveness ... Dr. Su SWARAT
88 Int AVP Extension & Int Programs ... Dr. Christopher SWARAT
20 COO Academic Affairs ... Ms. Erinn BANKS
88 Exec Dir Academic Fin & Space Mgmt ... Ms. Alyssa ADAMSON
88 AVP Faculty Support Services ... Dr. Kristin STANG
04 Presidential Assistant ... Mrs. Sandra QUINTERO

*California State University-Long Beach (F)

1250 Bellflower Boulevard, Long Beach CA 90840

County: Los Angeles FICE Identification: 001139
Unit ID: 110583
Telephone: (562) 985-4111 Carnegie Class: Masters/L
FAX Number: (562) 985-5419 Calendar System: Semester
URL: www.csulb.edu
Established: 1949 Annual Undergrad Tuition & Fees (In-State): $6,798
Enrollment: 37,622 Coed
Affiliation or Control: State IRS Status: 501(c)3
Highest Offering: Doctorate
Accreditation: WC, AAFCS, ART, CAATE, CAEPN, CEA, CONST, DANCE, DIETD, DIETI, HSA, IPSY, JOUR, MUS, NRPA, NURSE, PH, PTA, SP, SPAA, SW, THEA

02 President ... Dr. Jane C. CONOLEY
05 Provost/Sr Vice Pres Academic Affs ... Dr. Brian JERSKY
11 Vice Pres Administration/Finance ... Mr. Scott APEL
13 VP/Chief Information Officer ... Dr. Min YAO

32 Interim VP Student Affairs ... Dr. Mary Ann TAKEMOTO
30 Vice Pres Univ Rels/Development ... Ms. Michele CESCA
100 Chief of Staff ... Dr. Neal SCHNOOR
10 Assoc VP Financial Management ... Ms. Tracey RICHARDSON
20 Assoc VP Undergraduate Studies ... Dr. Kerry JOHNSON
35 Assoc Vice Pres Student Affairs ... Vacant
82 AVP/Dean College Prof & Intl Educ ... Dr. Jeet JOSHEE
18 AVP Physical Plng/Facilities Mgt ... Mr. Tony MALAGRINO
58 Vice Provost/Dean Grad Studies ... Dr. Jody CORMACK
20 Vice Provost Academic Planning ... Dr. Dhushy SATHIANATHAN
46 Assoc Vice Pres University Research ... Dr. Simon KIM
15 AVP Human Resource Mgmt ... Ms. Nancy TORRES
91 Assoc VP Academic Technology ... Dr. Shawna DARK
29 Assoc VP Alumni and Univ Relations ... Ms. Janice HATANAKA
09 Director Institutional Research ... Dr. Mahmoud ALBAWANEH
84 Asst VP Enrollment Services ... Ms. Susan LEIGH
14 Assoc VP Information Technology ... Ms. Janet FOSTER
76 Dean College Health/Human Svcs ... Dr. Monica LOUNSBERY
50 Dean College of Business ... Dr. Michael SOLT
53 Dean College of Education ... Dr. Shireen PAVRI
54 Dean College of Engineering ... Dr. Forouzan GOLSHANI
57 Dean College of the Arts ... Ms. Cyrus PARKER-JEANNETTE
81 Dean College Natural Sciences/Math ... Dr. Curtis BENNETT
49 Dean College of Liberal Arts ... Dr. David WALLACE
51 Dean College Continuing/Prof Ed ... Dr. Jeet JOSHEE
08 Dean Library ... Mr. Roman KOCHAN
06 University Registrar ... Ms. Donna GREEN
39 Executive Dir Housing & Res Life ... Mr. Corry COLONNA
16 Dir Staff Human Resources ... Mr. Neil IACONO
41 Director Athletics ... Mr. Andy FEE
07 Director of Admissions ... Mr. Andrew WRIGHT
36 Interim Dir Career Development Ctr ... Ms. Erin BOOTH-CARO
23 Co-Director Health Services ... Ms. Angela GIRARD
23 Co-Director Health Services ... Dr. Kimberly FODRAN
19 Chief University Police ... Mr. Fernando SOLORZANO
38 Director Counseling/Psych Svcs ... Dr. Bong JOO
37 Director Financial Aid ... Mr. Nicolas VALDIVIA
25 Senior Director Sponsored Programs ... Ms. Maria REYES
102 Chief Op Ofcr/Rsrch Foundation ... Dr. Brian NOWLIN
28 Director of Equity & Diversity ... Ms. Larisa HAMADA
96 Director Procurement & Contracts ... Ms. Malia KINIMAKA
109 General Manager/49'er Shops ... Mr. Donald PENROD
104 Director Education Abroad ... Ms. Sharon OLSON
44 Director Leadership Giving ... Ms. Sireth TORRES
26 AVP of University Relations ... Mr. Christopher REESE
114 Assoc VP Budget & Univ Svcs ... Mr. Ted KADOWAKI
88 Asst VP Administrative Services ... Ms. Mishelle LAWS
20 Assoc VP Faculty Affairs ... Dr. Kirsty FLEMING
04 Deputy Chief of Staff ... Ms. Coleen FOLLOWELL
108 Director Program Review/Assessment ... Dr. Sharlene SAYEGH
22 Dir Affirmative Action/EEO ... Ms. Larisa HAMADA
26 AVP Strategic Communications ... Mr. Jeff COOK
116 Audit Liaison ... Mr. Gene WOHLGEZOGEN

*California State University-Los Angeles (A)

5151 State University Drive, Los Angeles CA 90032-8530
County: Los Angeles — FICE Identification: 001140
Unit ID: 110592
Telephone: (323) 343-3000 — Carnegie Class: Masters/L
FAX Number: (323) 343-2670 — Calendar System: Semester
URL: www.calstatela.edu
Established: 1947 — Annual Undergrad Tuition & Fees (In-State): $6,749
Enrollment: 28,531 — Coed
Affiliation or Control: State — IRS Status: 501(c)3
Highest Offering: Doctorate
Accreditation: WC, ART, CACREP, DIETC, DIETD, MT, MUS, NAIT, NURSE, SP, SPAA, SW

02 President ... Dr. William A. COVINO
11 Exec VP and Chief Operating Officer ... Dr. Jose A. GOMEZ
05 Int Provost/Vice Pres Academic Affs ... Dr. Jose A. GOMEZ
10 VP Administration & CFO ... Ms. Lisa M. CHAVEZ
32 Vice President Student Life ... Dr. Nancy WADA-MCKEE
13 AVP for Information Technology ... Ms. Tosha PHAM
44 Vice Pres University Advancement ... Dr. Janet S. DIAL
84 Vice Provost for Enrollment Svcs ... Mr. Tom ENDERS
28 VP Equity/Diversity/Inclusion ... Dr. Octavio VILLALPANDO
21 Assoc VP Financial Services ... Dr. Joyce WILLIAMS
35 Dean of Students ... Dr. Jennifer MILLER
111 Assoc VP University Advancement ... Dr. Mario PEREZ
20 AVP Research ... Dr. Jeffrey UNDERWOOD
29 Exec Director Alumni Relations ... Ms. Maria UBAGO
26 Exec Dir Comm/Public Affairs ... Mr. Robert LOPEZ
41 Exec Dir Intercollegiate Athletics ... Dr. Daryl J. GROSS
83 Dean Natural & Social Sciences ... Dr. Pamela SCOTT-JOHNSON
88 Assoc Dean Natural/Social Sciences ... Dr. Nancy MCQUEEN
08 Dean of the University Library ... Mr. Carlos RODRIGUEZ
88 Assoc Dean of the Univ Library ... Ms. Marla PEPPERS
06 University Registrar ... Mr. Christopher COBB
58 Dean Graduate Studies ... Dr. Karin A. ELLIOT BROWN
09 Asst VP Institutional Research ... Dr. Sunny MOON
36 Director Career Placement & Plng ... Vacant
37 Director Student Financial Services ... Ms. Tamie NGUYEN
23 Director Health Center ... Dr. Monica JAZZABI
39 Director Housing Svc/Residence Life ... Ms. Rebecca PALMER
22 Director Equal Opportunity Pgm ... Mr. Lui AMADOR
18 AVP Fac/Plng/Design & Construct ... Ms. Barbara QUEEN
19 Chief of Police ... Mr. Rick WALL
15 AVP Human Resources Management ... Ms. Susie VARELA
85 Director Intl Programs & Services ... Vacant
43 University Counsel ... Mr. Victor I. KING

07 Director Admissions & Recruitment ... Mr. Vince LOPEZ
96 Director Procurement & Contracts ... Mr. Thomas JOHNSON
28 Dir HR Equity/Div/Pol/Procedures ... Ms. Aundreia M. CAMERON
40 General Manager Bookstore ... Ms. Elaine REED
88 Assoc Dean Undergrad Studies ... Dr. Margaret GARCIA
49 Dean Arts & Letters ... Dr. Linda ESSIG
88 Int Associate Dean Arts/Letters ... Dr. Kevin BAASKE
54 Dean Engr/Computer Science/Tech ... Dr. Emily ALLEN
88 Assoc Dean Engr/Comp Sci/Tech ... Dr. Jianyu (Jane) DONG
107 Dean Col of Profess/Global Studies ... Dr. Eric A. BULLARD
88 Assoc Dean of Administration/PaGE ... Dr. Harkmore LEE
76 Dean Health & Human Services ... Dr. Ronald VOGEL
88 Assoc Dean Health & Human Svcs ... Dr. Evaon WONG-KIM
53 Dean Charter Col of Education ... Dr. Cheryl L. NEY
88 Assoc Dean Charter Col of Education ... Dr. Diane FAZZI
88 Assoc Dean of Pgms/Acad Innovation ... Ms. Regina CASH
50 Int Dean Business & Economics ... Dr. Tyrone JACKSON
88 Associate Dean Business & Economics ... Dr. Angela YOUNG
97 Dean Undergraduate Studies ... Dr. Michelle HAWLEY
92 Interim Director Honors College ... Dr. Rennie SCHOEPFLIN

† Grants Joint Doctoral degree in cooperation with the University of California-Los Angeles.

*CSU Maritime Academy (B)

200 Maritime Academy Drive, Vallejo CA 94590-0644
County: Solano — FICE Identification: 001134
Unit ID: 111188
Telephone: (707) 654-1000 — Carnegie Class: Bac-Diverse
FAX Number: (707) 654-1001 — Calendar System: Semester
URL: www.csum.edu
Established: 1929 — Annual Undergrad Tuition & Fees (In-State): $7,056
Enrollment: 1,090 — Coed
Affiliation or Control: State — IRS Status: 501(c)3
Highest Offering: Master's
Accreditation: WC, IACBE

02 President ... RADM. Thomas A. CROPPER, USMS
05 Provost/VP Academic Affairs ... Dr. Susan OPP
10 VP of Administration/Finance ... Mr. Franz LOZANO
32 VP of Student Affairs ... Mr. Stan HEBERT
111 VP of University Advancement ... Mr. Robert ARP
15 Sr AVP of Human Resources/Diversity ... Dr. Ingrid WILLIAMS
13 Chief Information Officer ... Ms. Juliann TOLSON
100 Chief of Staff ... Mr. Brigham TIMPSON
88 Master of Training Ship ... Capt. Harry BOLTON
20 Associate Vice President ... Dr. Graham BENTON
112 Senior Development Officer ... Ms. Melissa COHEA
06 Registrar ... Ms. Julia L. ODOM
08 Dean of Library ... Ms. Michele VAN HOECK
07 Director of Admissions ... Mr. Marc MCGEE
37 Director of Financial Aid ... Ms. Priscilla MUHA
109 Associate Vice President ... Mr. Mark GOODRICH
88 Director of SEAS ... Ms. Vineeta DHILLON
35 Dean of Students ... Mr. James DALSKE
18 AVP Facilities Management ... Mr. Audun AABERG
19 Chief of Police Services ... Chief Donny GORDON
21 University Controller ... Mr. Rabi JOSEPH
41 Director of Athletics ... Mr. Marv CHRISTOPHER
26 Director of Public Relations ... Mr. Robert KING
40 Bookstore Manager ... Mr. Andre JIMENEZ
96 Director of Purchasing ... Ms. Lorrie DINEEN-THACKERAY
09 Director of Institutional Research ... Mr. Gary MOSER
29 Director of Alumni Relations ... Mr. Eric COOPER
101 Asst Director University Affairs ... Ms. Jennifer HEMBREE
114 Budget Director ... Mr. Andrew SOM
11 Associate Vice President ... Mr. Kevin BERTELSEN
117 Director of Risk Management ... Ms. Marianne SPOTORNO
39 Director Residential Life ... Ms. Kate KIMBLE-TUSZYNSKI
36 Director Career Services ... Ms. Wendy HIGGINS
23 Chief Medical Officer ... Mr. Bruce WILBUR

*California State University-Monterey Bay (C)

100 Campus Center, Seaside CA 93955-8000
County: Monterey — FICE Identification: 032603
Unit ID: 409698
Telephone: (831) 582-3000 — Carnegie Class: Masters/M
FAX Number: (831) 582-3783 — Calendar System: Semester
URL: www.csumb.edu
Established: 1994 — Annual Undergrad Tuition & Fees (In-State): $7,143
Enrollment: 7,584 — Coed
Affiliation or Control: State — IRS Status: 501(c)3
Highest Offering: Master's
Accreditation: WC, #ARCPA, NURSE, SW

02 President ... Dr. Eduardo M. OCHOA
05 Interim Provost ... Dr. Fran HORVATH
10 Vice Pres Admin & Finance/CFO ... Mr. Kevin SAUNDERS
30 Vice Pres University Development ... Ms. Barbara ZAPPAS
32 VP Student Affairs & Enroll Service ... Dr. Ronnie HIGGS
26 Assoc VP for University Affairs ... Mr. Andre LEWIS
35 Dean of Students/AVP Student Affs ... Dr. Leslie WILLIAMS
21 Assoc Vice President for Finance ... Mr. Stephen MACKEY
28 AVP for Inclusive Excellence ... Dr. Brian CORPENING
108 Int AVP Institutional Effectiveness ... Dr. Daniel SHAPIRO
06 Registrar ... Ms. Sheila HERNANDEZ
13 Chief Information Officer ... Dr. Chip LENNO
88 Director Employee & Labor Relations ... Ms. Melanie CHAVEZ
37 Director Financial Aid ... Ms. Angeles FUENTES

15 Assoc VP for Human Resources ... Ms. Natalie KING
19 Chief of Police ... Chief Earl LAWSON
18 AVP Facilities Services & Operation ... Mr. Marcel FORTE
07 Director of Admissions ... Ms. Paula CARTER
29 Director Alumni Relations ... Ms. Annie WARR
41 Athletic Director ... Mr. Kirby GARRY
96 Director of Purchasing ... Mr. Art EVJEN
100 Chief of Staff ... Dr. Lawrence SAMUELS

*California State University-Northridge (D)

18111 Nordhoff Street, Northridge CA 91330-0001
County: Los Angeles — FICE Identification: 001153
Unit ID: 110608
Telephone: (818) 677-1200 — Carnegie Class: Masters/L
FAX Number: N/A — Calendar System: Semester
URL: www.csun.edu
Established: 1958 — Annual Undergrad Tuition & Fees (In-State): $6,893
Enrollment: 41,319 — Coed
Affiliation or Control: State — IRS Status: 501(c)3
Highest Offering: Doctorate
Accreditation: WC, AAFCS, ART, CAATE, #CIDA, CONST, DIETD, DIETI, HSA, IPSY, JOUR, MFCD, MUS, NRPA, NURSE, PH, PTA, RAD, SP, SW, THEA

02 President ... Dr. Dianne F. HARRISON
05 Provost/Vice Pres Academic Affairs ... Vacant
10 Vice President Admin Finance/CFO ... Mr. Colin DONAHUE
32 VP Student Affairs/Dean of Students ... Dr. William WATKINS
111 VP Univ Advan/Foundation President ... Dr. Robert GUNSALUS
13 Vice President IT/CIO ... Ms. Hilary BAKER
88 Exec Director University Corp ... Mr. Rick EVANS
20 Vice Provost Academic Affairs ... Dr. Stella THEODOULOU
100 Chief of Staff ... Ms. Jill SMITH
18 Assoc VP Facilities Dev/Operations ... Mr. Ken ROSENTHAL
58 Assoc VP Grad Studies/Intl Pgms ... Vacant
21 Associate VP Financial Services ... Ms. Deborah WALLACE
15 Assoc VP of Human Resources ... Ms. Kristina DE LA VEGA
29 Asst Vice Pres Alumni Relations ... Ms. Shellie HADVINA
26 Assoc VP of Mktg/Comm ... Mr. Jeffrey NOBLITT
20 Assoc VP for Student Success ... Dr. Elizabeth T. ADAMS
91 Assoc VP of Acad Resources/Planning ... Ms. Diane S. STEPHENS
07 Director of Admissions and Records ... Mr. David R. DUFAULT-HUNTER
08 Dean University Library ... Dr. Mark STOVER
51 Dean College of Extended Learning ... Dr. Joyce A. FEUCHT-HAVIAR
79 Int Dean College of Humanities ... Dr. Jackie E. STALLCUP
50 Int Dean College Business/Economics ... Dr. Deborah A. COURS
53 Interim Dean College of Education ... Dr. Shari A. TARVER-BEHRING
57 Dean College Arts/Media/Comm ... Mr. Dan HOSKEN
83 Dean Col Social/Behavioral Sci ... Dr. Yan Dominic SEARCY
76 Dean Col Health/Human Development ... Dr. Farrell WEBB
81 Dean College Science & Math ... Dr. Jerry STINNER
54 Int Dean College Engr/Computer Sci ... Dr. Hamid JOHARI
09 Dir Institutional Research ... Dr. Janet S. OH
37 Director Financial Aid/Scholarships ... Ms. Linda M. BRIGNONI
38 Director Univ Counseling Services ... Dr. Julie L. PEARCE
36 Director Career Center ... Ms. Ann N. MOREY
25 Dir Research/Graduate Studies ... Ms. Hedy L. CARPENTER
18 Senior Dir Physical Plant Mgmt ... Mr. Jason WANG
19 Director of Police Services ... Chief Gregory MURPHY
28 Director of Equity/Diversity ... Ms. Susan HUA
86 Dir Government/Community Relations ... Ms. Francesca VEGA
23 Director Student Health Center ... Dr. Linda REID-CHASSIAKOS
39 Int Co-Dir Stdnt Housing/Conf Svcs ... Ms. Claire DAVIS
39 Int Co-Dir Stdnt Housing/Conf Svcs ... Ms. Melissa GILES
40 Director Matador Bookstore ... Ms. Amy C. BERGER
41 Dir of Intercollegiate Athletics ... Vacant
88 Director Student Involvement & Dev ... Mr. Patrick BAILEY
92 Dir General Education Honors Pgm ... Dr. Beth A. WIGHTMAN
96 Manager Purchasing ... Ms. Deborah FLUGUM
06 Registrar ... Mr. Todd WOLFE
28 Chief Div Ofcr/Title IX Coordinator ... Ms. Natalie L. MASON-KINSEY
04 Int Exec Assistant to the President ... Ms. Elbi MAGANA
11 Dir of Administrative Operations ... Mr. Randy REYMALDO

*California State University-Sacramento (E)

6000 J Street, Sacramento CA 95819-2694
County: Sacramento — FICE Identification: 001150
Unit ID: 110617
Telephone: (916) 278-6011 — Carnegie Class: Masters/L
FAX Number: (916) 278-6664 — Calendar System: Semester
URL: www.csus.edu
Established: 1947 — Annual Undergrad Tuition & Fees (In-State): $7,310
Enrollment: 31,255 — Coed
Affiliation or Control: State — IRS Status: 501(c)3
Highest Offering: Doctorate
Accreditation: WC, ART, CAATE, CACREP, CONST, DIETD, DIETI, EMT, MUS, NRPA, NURSE, PTA, SP, SW, THEA

02 President ... Dr. Robert S. NELSEN
05 Int Provost/VP Academic Affairs ... Dr. Steve PEREZ
111 VP Univ Advancement ... Dr. Lisa CARDOZA
32 VP Student Affairs ... Dr. Edward MILLS
13 VP & Chief Information Officer ... Dr. Christine E. DIVINE
10 VP Admin & CFO ... Mr. Jonathan BOWMAN

15 Sr AVP Human Resources Management ..... Ms. Machelle MARTIN
26 Vice Pres Public Affairs/Advocacy .... Dr. Phil GARCIA
46 AVP Research Innovation & Econ Dev .... Dr. Yvonne HARRIS
20 Interim Vice Provost ....Dr. Christine M. MILLER
30 AVP University Development .... Ms. Tracy LATINO-NEWMAN
18 Assoc Vice Pres Facilities Mgmt ....Dr. Justin REGINATO
84 AVP Enrollment & Student Svcs ....Vacant
27 Senior Assoc VP Univ Communications ....Ms. Jeannie WONG
35 AVP Student Engagement & Support ....Dr. Beth LESEN
21 Assoc VP Financial Svcs ....Ms. Gina CURRY
07 Dir Outreach & Admissions ....Mr. Brian HENLEY
08 Library Dean .... Ms. Amy KAUTZMAN
29 Assoc VP Alumni Relations ....Ms. Jennifer BARBER
19 Chief of Police .... Mr. Mark IWASA
39 Exec Dir Univ Housing Services .... Mr. Michael SPEROS
41 Director of Athletics ....Dr. Mark ORR
37 Director Financial Aid ....Ms. Anita KERMES
22 Director of Equal Opportunity ....Mr. William BISHOP
40 Bookstore Director .... Ms. Pam PARSONS
100 Interim Chief of Staff ....Ms. Cely SMART
06 University Registrar ....Ms. Danielle AMBROSE
85 AVP for International Affairs ....Dr. Paul HOFMANN
23 AVP Student Health & Counseling Svc ....Dr. Joy STEWART-JAMES
96 Mgr Procurement/Contract Services ....Mr. John GUION
88 Dean Undergrad Studies .... Dr. James GERMAN
49 Dean College of Arts & Letters ....Dr. Sheree MEYER
50 Dean College of Business Admin ....Dr. William CORDEIRO
53 Dean College of Education ....Dr. Alexander SIDORKIN
54 Dean College of Engr/Computer Sci ....Dr. Lorenzo SMITH
76 Int Dean College Health/Human Svcs ....Dr. Robin CARTER
81 Int Dean Col of Natural Sci/Math .... Dr. Lisa HAMMERSLEY
51 Dean College Continuing Educ .... Dr. Jenni MURPHY
83 Dean Col Soc Sci/Interdisc Stds .... Dr. Dianne HYSON
58 Dean Graduate Studies .... Dr. Chevelle NEWSOME
28 VP for Inclusive Excellence .... Dr. Diana VERMEIRE
113 University Bursar ....Ms. Elena LARSON
112 Director of Planned Giving .... Ms. Lisa WOODARD-MINK
44 Exec Dir Annual Giving .... Ms. Sharon TAKEDA
88 Exec Dir Ctr Innov/Entrepreneurship ....Vacant
14 Assoc Chief Info Officer .... Dr. Jennifer SCHWEDLER
119 Info Security Officer ....Mr. Mark HENDRICKS

*California State University-San Bernardino (A)

5500 University Parkway, San Bernardino CA 92407-2393
County: San Bernardino FICE Identification: 001142
Unit ID: 110510
Telephone: (909) 537-5000 Carnegie Class: Masters/L
FAX Number: N/A Calendar System: Quarter
URL: www.csusb.edu
Established: 1960 Annual Undergrad Tuition & Fees (In-State): $6,922
Enrollment: 20,692 Coed
Affiliation or Control: State IRS Status: 501(c)3
Highest Offering: Doctorate
Accreditation: WC, ART, CACREP, DIETD, MUS, NURSE, PH, SPAA, SW, THEA

02 President ....Dr. Tomas MORALES
05 Provost/VP Academic Affairs .... Dr. Shari MCMAHAN
10 Vice Pres Administration/Finance .... Dr. Doug FREER
111 Vice Pres University Advancement ....Mr. Robert NAVA
13 Vice Pres ITS/CIO ....Dr. Samuel SUDHAKAR
28 Co-Chief Diversity Officer ....Mr. Alex NAJERA
28 Co-Chief Diversity Officer .... Dr. Jacqueline HUGHES
29 AVP Alumni/Govt & Comm Relations ..... Ms. Pamela LANGFORD
20 Dep/Assoc Provost Academic Programs ....Dr. Clare WEBER
46 Assoc Provost Research ....Dr. Dorota HUIZINGA
20 Assoc VP & Dean Undergrad Studies ....Dr. Craig R. SEAL
21 Assoc VP Finance .... Mr. M. Monir AHMED
15 Assoc VP Human Resources ....Mr. Alex NAJERA
121 Assoc VP Stdnt Success/Educ Equity .... Ms. Olivia ROSAS
35 Assoc VP and Dean of Students ....Vacant
14 Assoc VP ITS .... Mr. Gerard AU
26 Assoc VP Strategic Communications ....Mr. Bob TENCZAR
88 Assoc Provost Faculty Affairs & Dev ....Dr. Seval YILDIRIM
22 Director Title IX & Gender Equity .... Ms. Cristina ALVAREZ
06 Int Director University Registrar .... Ms. Amy BRACEROS
07 Dir Enrollment Management & Admiss .... Ms. Tiffany BONNER
23 Director Health Center ....Dr. Grace CASTILLO JOHNSON
08 University Librarian ....Mr. Cesar CABALLERO
37 Director Financial Aid .... Mr. Stephen FAHEY
39 Director Housing & Residential Life ....Vacant
18 Director Facilities Management .... Ms. Jennifer SORENSON
41 Director Athletics ....Mr. Shawn FARRELL
94 Director Gender & Sexuality Studies ....Dr. Todd JENNINGS
92 Director University Honors Program ....Dr. David MARSHALL
56 Dean Col of Extended Learning .... Dr. Tatiana KARMANOVA
83 Dean Col Social/Behavioral Sciences ....Dr. Rafik MOHAMED
53 Dean College of Education ....Dr. Chinaka DOMNWACHUKWU
50 Dean College of Business ....Dr. Lawrence D. ROSE
58 Dean Graduate Studies .... Dr. Dorota HUIZINGA
12 Dean CSUSB Palm Desert ....Dr. Jake ZHU
100 Chief of Staff ....Ms. Julie M. LAPPIN
102 Sr Dir Foundation/Corp Rels ....Mr. Robert NAVA
44 Operations Manager Annual Giving .... Ms. Carolina VAN ZEE
104 Study Abroad Coordinator ....Ms. Amy CHIEN
104 Study Abroad Coordinator ....Mr. Emilio RODRIGUEZ
09 AVP Institutional Effectiveness ....Ms. Muriel LOPEZ-WAGNER
29 Director Alumni Affairs ....Ms. Crystal WYMER-LUCERO

*California State University-San Marcos (B)

333 S Twin Oaks Valley Road,
San Marcos CA 92096-0001
County: San Diego FICE Identification: 030113
Unit ID: 366711
Telephone: (760) 750-4000 Carnegie Class: Masters/L
FAX Number: (760) 750-4030 Calendar System: Semester
URL: www.csusm.edu
Established: 1989 Annual Undergrad Tuition & Fees (In-State): $7,713
Enrollment: 15,755 Coed
Affiliation or Control: State IRS Status: 501(c)3
Highest Offering: Doctorate
Accreditation: WC, IPSY, NURSE, SP, SW

02 President ....Dr. Karen S. HAYNES
04 Presidential Aide ....Ms. Viviana GARCIA
10 Vice President Finance/Admin Svcs ....Mr. Neal HOSS
05 Interim Provost/VP Academic Affairs ....Dr. Kamel HADDAD
32 Vice President of Student Affairs .... Dr. Lorena CHECA
111 Vice Pres University Advancement ....Mrs. Cathy BAUR
20 Dean Academic Programs ....Dr. Regina EISENBACH
45 Int Vice Prov Plng/Acad Resources ....Dr. Suzanne MOINEAU
84 Assoc Vice Pres Enrollment Mgmt .... Mr. Scott HAGG
15 Assoc VP Human Resource/Equal Oppty ...... Mr. Travis GREGORY
49 Int Dn Col Hum Arts/Behav & Soc Sci . Dr. Elizabeth MATTHEWS
50 Dean Col Business Administration .... Dr. Jim HAMERLY
53 Dean Col Educ/Health & Human Svcs ....Dr. Emiliano AYALA
08 Dean of Library Services .... Dr. Jennifer FABBI
81 Dean Col of Science & Mathematics .... Dr. Katherine KANTARDJIEFF
56 Dean of Extended Studies .... Mr. Michael SCHRODER
13 Dean Instructional/Info Technology ......Mr. Kevin MORNINGSTAR
06 Registrar ....Ms. Lisa MEDINA
07 Dir Admissions & Student Outreach ....Ms. Carol MCALLISTER
100 Chief of Staff ....Ms. Jennifer WILLIAMS
21 AVP Business and Fin Svcs ....Mr. Clint ROBERTS
29 Director Alumni/Parent Relations .... Ms. Lori BROCKETT
96 Assoc VP Procurement/Support Svcs ....Ms. Bella NEWBERG
121 Director Undergraduate Advising ....Mr. David MCMARTIN
09 Dir Inst Planning & Analysis ....Mr. Jeffrey MARKS
104 Executive Director Global Education ....Mr. Robert CAROLIN
18 AVP Facilities Dev & Mgmt ....Mr. Mark NORITA
19 Interim Chief UPD .... Mr. Lamine SECKA
22 AVP Inclusive Excellence .... Dr. Joe-Joe MCMANUS
26 AVP Communications .... Ms. Margaret CHANTUNG
39 Director Student Housing ....Mr. Malik ISMAIL
41 Athletic Director .... Ms. Jennifer MILO
88 AVP Faculty Affairs ....Ms. Michelle HUNT
44 Director Annual Programs ....Mr. Sean BRINER
86 Director Government Relations .... Mr. Sean BRADBURY

† Grants Joint Doctoral degree in cooperation with the University of California-San Diego.

*California State University-Stanislaus (C)

1 University Circle, Turlock CA 95382-0299
County: Stanislaus FICE Identification: 001157
Unit ID: 110495
Telephone: (209) 667-3122 Carnegie Class: Masters/L
FAX Number: N/A Calendar System: Semester
URL: www.csustan.edu
Established: 1957 Annual Undergrad Tuition & Fees (In-State): $7,072
Enrollment: 10,327 Coed
Affiliation or Control: State IRS Status: 170(c)1
Highest Offering: Doctorate
Accreditation: WC, ART, MUS, NURSE, SPAA, SW, THEA

02 President ....Dr. Ellen JUNN
05 Provost/VP Academic Affairs ....Dr. Kimberly GREER
10 VP Business/Finance/CFO .... Mr. Darrell HAYDON
32 VP Student Affairs .... Dr. Christine ERICKSON
111 VP University Advancement ....Dr. Michele LAHTI
84 VP Strategic Plng/Enroll Mgmt/Innov ....Dr. Gitanjali KAUL
15 Sr AVP HR/EO/Compliance ....Ms. Julie JOHNSON
100 Dir Presidential Initiatives ....Ms. Neisha RHODES
79 Dean College Arts/Humanities & SS .... Dr. James A. TUEDIO
50 Dean College of Business Admin ....Dr. Thomas GOMEZ-ARIAS
53 Dean College of Education ....Dr. Oddmund R. MYHRE
81 Dean College of Science .... Dr. David EVANS
08 Dean Library Services ....Mr. Ron RODRIGUEZ
106 Dean Stockton Center .... Dr. Faimous HARRISON
51 Dean Extended Education ....Dr. Helene CAUDILL
20 AVP Academic Affairs .... Dr. Shawna YOUNG
41 Director Athletics .... Mr. Terry DONOVAN
07 Dir Admissions & Fin Aid ....Ms. Noelia GONZALEZ
35 AVP Student Affs/Dean of Students .... Mr. Matthew LOPEZ-PHILLIPS
21 Assoc VP Financial Services .... Ms. Regan LINDERMAN
13 Interim Chief Information Officer ....Mr. Matt COLLINS
18 Assoc VP Facilities Services .... Ms. Melody MAFFEI
26 Sr AVP Comm & Public Affairs .... Dr. Rosalee RUSH
19 Chief of Police .... Mr. Clint STRODE
06 Registrar .... Ms. Lisa M. BERNARDO
09 Director of Institutional Research ....Vacant
103 Director Career Development ....Ms. Julie SEDLEMEYER
28 Director of Diversity Center .... Ms. Carolina ALFARO
38 Director Student Counseling .... Dr. Dan BERKOW
39 Dir Resident Life/Student Housing .... Ms. Jennifer HUMPHREY

*Humboldt State University (D)

1 Harpst Street, Arcata CA 95521-8222
County: Humboldt FICE Identification: 001149
Unit ID: 115755
Telephone: (707) 826-3011 Carnegie Class: Masters/M
FAX Number: (707) 826-5555 Calendar System: Semester
URL: www.humboldt.edu
Established: 1913 Annual Undergrad Tuition & Fees (In-State): $7,675
Enrollment: 8,525 Coed
Affiliation or Control: State IRS Status: 501(c)3
Highest Offering: Master's
Accreditation: WC, ART, IACBE, MUS, SW

02 President ....Dr. Tom JACKSON, JR.
100 Chief of Staff ....Vacant
05 Provost .... Dr. Alex ENYEDI
20 Vice Prov Acad Pgms/Undergrad Stds ....Dr. Rock BRAITHWAITE
32 VP Student Affairs .... Dr. Wayne BRUMFIELD
10 Vice Pres Admin & Finance .... Mr. Douglas DAWES
111 Int Vice President of Advancement ....Mr. Frank WHITLATCH
15 AVP Human Resources ....Mr. David MONTOYA, III
88 AVP Philanthropy ....Ms. Deborah RICE
26 Assoc VP for Mktg & Communications .... Mr. Frank WHITLATCH
18 Assoc Vice President Facilities ....Ms. Jeanne RYNNE
09 Assc VP Institutional Effectiveness ....Dr. Lisa CASTELLINO
84 AVP Enrollment Management ....Dr. Randy HYMAN
114 Director University Budget Office ....Ms. Amber BLAKESLEE
88 Director of Academic Resources ....Ms. Holly MARTEL
06 Registrar .... Mr. Clint REBIK
07 Director of Admissions .... Mr. Pedro MARTINEZ
08 Dean of Library ....Dr. Cyril OBERLANDER
44 Director of Annual Giving .... Mr. Travis WILLIAMS
19 Chief of University Police ....Chief Donn PETERSON
41 Athletic Director .... Mr. Duncan ROBINS
39 Director of Housing .... Mr. Stephen ST. ONGE
13 Chief Information Officer .... Ms. Bethany RIZZARDI
36 Director Career Devel Center ....Ms. Kathy THORNHILL
28 Executive Director ODEI .... Dr. Cheryl JOHNSON
46 Executive Director Sponsored Pgms ....Ms. Kacie FLYNN
104 Study Abroad Coordinator .... Ms. Emily KIRSCH
35 Dean Student Affairs ....Vacant
37 Director Student Financial Aid ....Ms. Peggy METZGER
96 Director of Contracts & Procurement ....Ms. Tawny FLEMING
90 Director ITS User Support ....Ms. Jeanne WIELGUS
23 Dir Health/Counseling/Psych Svcs ....Dr. Brian MISTLER
38 Director Counseling & Psy Svc .... Dr. Jennifer SANFORD
56 Dean of eLearning & Ext Education ....Mr. Carl F. HANSEN
79 Dean Col Arts/Humanities/Soc Sci ....Dr. Lisa BOND-MAUPIN
107 Dean College Professional Studies ....Dr. Shawna YOUNG
65 Dean Col Natural Resources/Science ....Dr. Dale OLIVER
21 Controller ....Ms. Lynne SANDSTROM
06 Registrar eLearning & Ext Educ .... Mr. Christian GUILLEN
105 Web Manager .... Mr. Matt HODGSON
29 Alumni Relations Outreach .... Ms. Stephanie LANE
04 Administrative Asst to President ....Ms. Kay LIBOLT
117 Dir of Risk Management & Safety .... Ms. Kimberly COMET
16 AVP Faculty Affairs .... Dr. Laura HAHN

*San Diego State University (E)

5500 Campanile Drive, San Diego CA 92182-8000
County: San Diego FICE Identification: 001151
Unit ID: 122409
Telephone: (619) 594-5200 Carnegie Class: DU-Higher
FAX Number: (619) 594-8894 Calendar System: Semester
URL: www.sdsu.edu
Established: 1897 Annual Undergrad Tuition & Fees (In-State): $7,488
Enrollment: 35,158 Coed
Affiliation or Control: State IRS Status: 501(c)3
Highest Offering: Doctorate
Accreditation: WC, ART, AUD, CAATE, CACREP, CAMPEP, CIDA, CLPSY, DIETD, HSA, JOUR, MFCD, NURSE, PH, PTA, SP, SPAA, SW, THEA

02 President ....Dr. Adela DE LA TORRE
05 Interim Provost .... Dr. Hector OCHOA
10 Vice President/CFO Business Affairs .... Ms. Agnes WONG NICKERSON
32 Int Vice Pres for Student Affairs ....Ms. Christy SAMARKOS
30 Int VP Univ Rel & Development ....Ms. Adrienne VARGAS
46 VP for Research & Graduate Dean ....Dr. Stephen WELTER
20 Assoc Vice Pres Academic Affairs ....Dr. Radmila PRISLIN
88 Assoc VP Real Estate Planning & Dev ....Mr. Robert SCHULZ
21 Int Assoc VP Financial Operations .... Ms. Crystal LITTLE
15 Associate VP Administration .... Ms. Jessica RENTTO
85 Int Dir International Programs ....Dr. Stuart HENRY
26 Interim AVP/Chief Comm Officer .... Dr. La Monica EVERETT-HAYNES
35 Assoc VP for Student Affairs ....Mr. Tony CHUNG
35 Assoc VP for Student Affairs .... Dr. Andrea DOOLEY
35 Assoc VP for Student Affairs .... Dr. Antionette MARBRAY
35 Assoc VP for Student Affairs ....Dr. Randy TIMM
88 Asst VP Special Projects ....Mr. James S. HERRICK
100 Chief of Staff President's Office .....Ms. Brittany SANTOS-DERIEG
84 Int Assoc VP Enrollment Management .... Ms. Sandra TEMORES
38 Director Counseling/Psych Services ....Dr. Jennifer RIKARD
08 Int Dean Library/Information Access ....Mr. Patrick MCCARTHY
110 Int Associate VP for Development .... Ms. Mary DARLING
88 AVP & Exec Director Rsrch Found ....Ms. Michele GOETZ
51 Dean College of Extended Studies ....Dr. Radhika SESHAN
58 Assoc Dean Graduate & Rsrch Affairs ....Dr. Edmund BALSDON
49 Assoc VP AA/Student Achievement .... Dr. Norah SHULTZ
79 Dean of College Arts & Letters ....Dr. Norma BOUCHARD

81 Dean of College of Sciences Dr. Jeffrey ROBERTS
54 Interim Dean College of Engineering Dr. Eugene OLEVSKY
50 Int Dean Fowler College of Business Dr. Bruce REINIG
76 Dean College Health/Human Svcs Dr. Steven P. HOOKER
53 Dean of College of Education Dr. Y. Barry CHUNG
12 Dean of Imperial Valley Campus Dr. Gregorio PONCE
57 Interim Dean Prof Studies/Fine Arts Ms. Donna M. CONATY
84 Sr Director Enrollment Services Ms. Sandra TEMORES-VALDEZ
117 Director of Emergency Services Mr. Lamine SECKA
28 CDO/AVP Faculty Diversity & Incl Dr. J. Luke WOOD
06 Registrar Ms. Rayanne WILLIAMS
07 Director of Admissions Ms. Sabrina CORTELL
36 Executive Director Career Services Dr. James TARBOX
39 Director Office of Housing Admin Ms. Cynthia CERVANTES
40 Assoc VP & CEO Aztec Shops Mr. Todd SUMMER
41 Director Intercollegiate Athletics Mr. John David WICKER
85 Dir International Student Center Mr. Noah HANSEN
88 Director Environ Health & Safety Mr. Terry GEE
13 Chief Tech Officer/Interim CIO Mr. Rick NORNHOLM
09 Dir Analytic Studies/Inst Research Ms. Jeanne STRONACH
86 Dir Govt & Comm Relations Ms. Rachel GREGG
96 Mgr Contract/Procurement Mgmt Mr. Bruce PETROZZA
21 University Controller Ms. Beth WARREM
18 Director of Facilities Services Mr. John FERRIS
22 Dir Educational Opportunity Program Ms. Miriam CASTANON
37 Dir Financial Aid & Scholarships Ms. Rose PASENELLI
88 Ombudsman Ms. Julie LOGAN
39 Director of Residential Education Dr. Kara BAUER
121 Dir Student Ability Success Ctr Dr. Pamela STARR
88 Sr Director Enterprise Tech Svcs Mr. Rick NORNHOLM
29 Asst VP Alumni Engagement Mr. Dan MONTOYA
04 Admin Assistant to the President Mr. Luis MURILLO

*San Francisco State University (A)

1600 Holloway Avenue, San Francisco CA 94132-1740

County: San Francisco FICE Identification: 001154
Unit ID: 122597
Telephone: (415) 338-1111 Carnegie Class: Masters/L
FAX Number: (415) 338-2514 Calendar System: Semester
URL: www.sfsu.edu
Established: 1899 Annual Undergrad Tuition & Fees (In-State): $7,260
Enrollment: 29,758 Coed
Affiliation or Control: State IRS Status: 501(c)3
Highest Offering: Doctorate
Accreditation: WC, AAFCS, ART, CACREP, DIETD, DIETI, JOUR, MT, MUS, NRPA, NURSE, PH, PTA, SP, SPAA, SW, THEA

02 President Dr. Lynn MAHONEY
05 Provost & VP Academic Affairs Dr. Jennifer SUMMIT
111 Vice Pres University Advancement Ms. Venesia THOMPSON RAMSAY
32 VP Student Affairs/Enroll Mgmt Dr. Luoluo HONG
20 Assoc VP Academic Resources Dr. Alan JUNG
46 Assoc VP Research Sponsored Pgms Mr. Michael SCOTT
20 Assoc VP Academic Affairs Operation Dr. Brian BEATTY
85 Assoc VP International Education Dr. Yenbo WU
13 Interim AVP Info Tech Services Mr. Nish MALIK
84 Senior AVP Enrollment Management Dr. Maria MARTINEZ
15 Sr Assoc VP Human Resources Ms. Ann M. SHERMAN
35 Assoc VP Student Affairs Mr. Gene CHELBERG
100 Chief of Staff Ms. Alison SANDERS
53 Dean College Education Dr. Cynthia GRUTZIK
88 Dean College Ethnic Studies Dr. Amy SUEYOSHI
51 Interim AVP/Dean of CELIA Dr. Guido KRICKX
69 Dean Col Health & Soc Science Dr. Alvin ALVAREZ
79 Dean Col Lib Sci & Creative Arts Dr. Andrew HARRIS
88 Dean Faculty Affairs & Prof Dev Dr. Sacha BUNGE
58 Dean Graduate Studies Dr. Sophie CLAVIER
97 Dean Undergraduate Education Dr. Lori Beth WAY
102 Int President SF State Foundation Ms. Venesia THOMPSON-RAMSAY
08 University Librarian Ms. Deborah C. MASTERS
90 Director Academic Technology Dr. Maggie BEERS
117 Risk Manager Mr. Michael BEATTY
39 Director Resident Life Mr. David ROURKE
88 Director Student Outreach Services Mr. Rodolfo T. SANTOS
07 Director Undergrad Admissions Mr. Edward CARRIGAN
114 Director Univ Budget Planning Mr. Jay ORENDORFF
38 Director Counseling & Psych Svcs Dr. Stephen CHEN
22 Dir Education Opportunity Program Mr. Oscar M. GARDEA
19 Int Chief Police/Dir Public Safety Chief Reginald PARSON
110 Chief of Operations Advancement Ms. Venesia THOMPSON
88 Exec Dir Budget Adm & Oper Mr. Jay ORENDORFF
88 Dir Environmental Health & Safety Mr. Marc MAJEWSKI
109 AVP Facilities & Service Enter Mr. Frank FASANO
04 Deputy Chief of Staff Ms. Leshia CLAUDIO
06 Registrar Mr. Rogelio A. MANAOIS
37 Director Student Financial Aid Ms. Tracie HUNTER
41 Athletic Director Ms. Stephanie E. SHRIEVE-HAWKINS
86 Director Government Relations Ms. Dominique CANO-STOCCO

† Grants additional Doctoral degrees in cooperation with the UC-Berkeley and UC-San Francisco.

*San Jose State University (B)

One Washington Square, San Jose CA 95192-0001

County: Santa Clara FICE Identification: 001155
Unit ID: 122755
Telephone: (408) 924-1000 Carnegie Class: Masters/L
FAX Number: (408) 924-1018 Calendar System: Semester
URL: www.sjsu.edu
Established: 1857 Annual Undergrad Tuition & Fees (In-State): $7,796
Enrollment: 35,835 Coed
Affiliation or Control: State IRS Status: 501(c)3
Highest Offering: Doctorate
Accreditation: WC, ART, CAATE, CEA, DANCE, DIETD, DIETI, IPSY, JOUR, LIB, MT, MUS, NAIT, NRPA, NURSE, OT, PH, PLNG, SP, SPAA, SW, THEA

02 President Dr. Mary PAPAZIAN
05 Provost/Sr Vice Pres Acad Affs Dr. Vincent DEL CASINO
10 Vice Pres Administration & Finance Mr. Charles FAAS
32 Vice President Student Affairs Mr. Patrick K. DAY
13 Deputy CIO Ms. Terry VAHEY
100 VP Org Development/Chief of Staff Ms. Jaye BAILEY
09 Assoc VP Research Dr. Pamela STACKS
20 Assoc VP Grad/Undergrad Programs Dr. Thalia ANAGNOS
21 Assoc VP Finance Ms. Marna GENES
18 Assoc VP for Facilities/Operations Vacant
15 Senior AVP University Personnel Ms. Joanne WRIGHT
26 AVP Strategic Comm/Public Affairs Vacant
29 AVP Alumni Engagement and Giving Mr. Brian BATES
22 Chief Diversity Officer Dr. Kathleen WONG (LAU)
51 Dean Col of Intnl/Extended Studies Dr. Ruth HUARD
84 Int AVP Admin/Enrollment Services Ms. Coleetta MCELROY
08 Dean University Library Dr. Tracy ELLIOTT
28 Sr Dir Equal Opport/Employee Rels Ms. Julie PAISANT
06 University Registrar Ms. Marian YAO
41 Director Intercollegiate Athletics Ms. Marie TUITE
07 Dir Undergrad Admissions/Outreach Ms. Deanna GONZALES
40 B&N Asst Dir Spartan Bookstore Ms. Lisa TOWNS
36 Director Career Center Ms. Catherine VOSS PLAXTON
38 Dir Counseling/Psychological Svcs Mr. Kell FUJIMOTO
37 Int Dir Financial Aid/Scholarships Ms. Carolyn GUEL
39 Dir University Housing Services Mr. Kevin KINNEY
50 Dean Lucas Col/Grad Sch of Business Dr. Dan MOSHAVI
53 Dean Connie L Lurie Col of Educ Dr. Heather LATTIMER
54 Dean Charles W Davidson Col of Eng Dr. Sheryl EHRMAN
79 Dean Col of Humanities and the Arts Dr. Shannon MILLER
81 Dean College of Science Dr. Michael KAUFMAN
83 Dean College Social Sciences Dr. Walt JACOBS
04 Presidential Aide Ms. Zaynna TELLO

*Sonoma State University (C)

1801 E Cotati Avenue, Rohnert Park CA 94928-3609

County: Sonoma FICE Identification: 001156
Unit ID: 123572
Telephone: (707) 664-2880 Carnegie Class: Masters/L
FAX Number: (707) 664-2505 Calendar System: Semester
URL: www.sonoma.edu
Established: 1960 Annual Undergrad Tuition & Fees (In-State): $7,798
Enrollment: 9,481 Coed
Affiliation or Control: State IRS Status: 501(c)3
Highest Offering: Master's
Accreditation: WC, ART, CACREP, MUS, NUR

02 President Dr. Judy SAKAKI
05 Provost/Exec VP Academic Affs/CAO Dr. Lisa VOLLENDORF
10 VP Administration/Finance/CFO Ms. Joyce LOPES
111 Vice President for Advancement Mr. Gordon MCDOUGALL
32 Vice President for Student Affairs Mr. Wm. Gregory SAWYER
20 Assoc VP for Faculty Affairs Dr. Deborah ROBERTS
13 Assoc VP Academic Affairs/CIO Ms. Lee KRICHMAR
18 Assoc VP Facilities Services/CPDC Mr. Christopher DINNO
100 Chief of Staff/AVP Strat Initiative Ms. Jerlena GRIFFIN-DESTA
88 Assoc VP Entrepreneurial Services Mr. Neil MARKLEY
08 Dean of Library Ms. Karen SCHNEIDER
79 Dean School of Arts & Humanities Dr. Hollis ROBBINS
50 Int Dean Sch of Business/Economic Dr. Daniel PETREE
81 Dean School Science & Technology Dr. Lynn STAUFFER
83 Dean of Social Sciences Dr. John D. WINGARD
53 Dean School of Education/Intl Educ Dr. Robert EYLER
09 Sr Dir Records/Report & Analytics Mr. Sean JOHNSON
38 Dir of Counseling/Psych Services Dr. Laura WILLIAMS
37 Director of Financial Aid Mrs. Susan GUTIERREZ
41 Director Athletics Vacant
19 Chief Police Services Mr. David DOUGHERTY
21 Director Seawolf Services Ms. Elizabeth O'BRIEN
06 Registrar Ms. Lisa NOTO
07 Director of Admissions Ms. Natalie KALOGIANNIS
84 Director of Enrollment Management Mr. Gustavo FLORES
29 Dir Alumni Relations/Annual Giving Ms. Laurie OGG
15 Sr Director Human Resources Vacant
96 Managing Dir for Purchasing Ms. Jenifer BARNETT

California University of Management and Sciences (D)

721 North Euclid Street, Anaheim CA 92801

County: Orange FICE Identification: 041331
Unit ID: 460075
Telephone: (714) 533-3946 Carnegie Class: Masters/M
FAX Number: (714) 533-7778 Calendar System: Quarter
URL: www.calums.edu
Established: 1998 Annual Undergrad Tuition & Fees: $6,540
Enrollment: 223 Coed
Affiliation or Control: Independent Non-Profit IRS Status: 501(c)3
Highest Offering: Master's
Accreditation: ACICS

01 President Jong S. YOON
10 Finance Director Fred J. KIM
05 Academic Dean Rasool MASOOMIAN
20 Associate Academic Dean Sasha SAFARZADEH
11 Dean of Administration/HR Yukari NISHIOKA
07 Admissions Director Vacant
84 Enrollment Director Vacant
32 Acting Student Services Advisor Cindy SZETO
08 Librarian Vanga ANDERSON
06 Registrar Hongjun AHN
85 International Student Advisor Cindy SZETO
101 Board Secretary Jong S. YOON
37 Financial Aid Officer Yukari NISHIOKA

California University of Science and Medicine (E)

217 East Club Center Drive, Ste A,
San Bernardino CA 92408

County: San Bernardino Identification: 667343
Telephone: (909) 580-9661 Carnegie Class: Not Classified
FAX Number: (909) 424-0345 Calendar System: Semester
URL: www.calmedu.org
Established: 2015 Annual Graduate Tuition & Fees: N/A
Enrollment: N/A Coed
Affiliation or Control: Independent Non-Profit IRS Status: 501(c)3
Highest Offering: Doctorate; No Undergraduates
Accreditation: WC, #MED

01 President/Dean Dr. Paul LYONS
05 Vice Pres of Medical Affairs Dr. Robert SUSKIND
11 Chief Operating Officer Mr. Moe ABOUFARES
13 Chief Information Officer Mr. Nasser SALOMON
10 Chief Financial Officer Mr. Mike HEATHER
63 Sr Assoc Dean Medical Education Dr. Alfred TENORE

California Western School of Law (F)

225 Cedar Street, San Diego CA 92101-3046

County: San Diego FICE Identification: 013103
Unit ID: 111391
Telephone: (619) 239-0391 Carnegie Class: Spec-4-yr-Law
FAX Number: (619) 525-7092 Calendar System: Trimester
URL: www.cwsl.edu
Established: 1924 Annual Graduate Tuition & Fees: N/A
Enrollment: 761 Coed
Affiliation or Control: Independent Non-Profit IRS Status: 501(c)3
Highest Offering: First Professional Degree; No Undergraduates
Accreditation: @WC, LAW

01 President & Dean Dean Neils SCHAUMANN
05 Vice Dean Academic Affairs Prof. Don SMYTHE
46 Associate Dean Research & Fac Devel Prof. Daniel YEAGER
88 Assoc Dean of Exper Learning Prof. Floralynn EINESMAN
32 Associate Dean of Student Life Ms. Wendy BASHANT
35 Asst Dean Students/Diversity Svcs Ms. Susan GARRETT FINSTER
36 Assistant Dean Career Services Ms. Courtney MIKLUSAK
88 Asst Dean Mission Development Mr. James M. COOPER
37 Exec Director Financial Aid Mr. William KAHLER
13 Exec Director of Enterprise System Ms. Jane COURCY
18 Exec Dir Facilities Management Ms. Jolie L. CARTIER
88 Ex Dir Inst for Criminal Def Advoc Prof. Justin P. BROOKS
88 Dir Inst of Health Law Studies Prof. Joanna SAX
08 Assoc Dean Law Library/Info Res Prof. Philip T. GRAGG
10 Chief Financial Officer Ms. Pamela A. DUFFY
07 Assistant Dean Admissions Mr. Christopher E. BAIDOO
06 Registrar Ms. Sandra E. MOREAU
88 Director MCL/LLM Program Prof. Lisa BLACK
31 Dir of Community Relations Ms. Marilyn JORDAN
29 Director Alumni Relations Ms. Lori BOYLE
15 VP Human Resources Mr. Dave BLAKE
21 Controller & Dir Business Office Ms. Tolly DEWEY
04 Exec Asst to the President & Dean Ms. Margaret O'DONNELL
43 Dir Organizational & Legal Compl Ms. Lisa JORDAN
30 Major Gift Officer Mr. Brian DALY
111 VP Institutional Advancement Mr. Bruce MACDONALD

Calvary Chapel University (G)

8344 Clairemont Mesa Blvd, Ste 100,
San Diego CA 92111

County: San Diego Identification: 667372
Telephone: (954) 453-9228 Carnegie Class: Not Classified
FAX Number: N/A Calendar System: Other
URL: calvarychapeluniversity.com
Established: 2005 Annual Undergrad Tuition & Fees: N/A
Enrollment: N/A Coed
Affiliation or Control: Independent Non-Profit IRS Status: 501(c)3
Highest Offering: Master's
Accreditation: @TRACS

01 President Dr. F. Chapin MARSH, III
05 Chief Academic Officer Dr. Kathy MORALES

Cambridge Junior College (H)

990-A Klamath Lane, Yuba City CA 95993-8978

County: Sutter FICE Identification: 038743
Unit ID: 446093
Telephone: (530) 674-9199 Carnegie Class: Spec 2-yr-Other
FAX Number: (530) 671-7319 Calendar System: Other
URL: www.cambridge.edu
Established: 2010 Annual Undergrad Tuition & Fees: N/A
Enrollment: 132 Coed
Affiliation or Control: Proprietary IRS Status: Proprietary
Highest Offering: Associate Degree

Accreditation: ACCSC

05 CEO and Founder ... Mr. Dan FLORES

Carnegie Mellon University Silicon Valley Campus (A)

PO Box 98, Moffett Field CA 94035
Telephone: (650) 335-2810 Identification: 770149
Accreditation: &M

† Branch campus of Carnegie Mellon University, Pittsburgh, PA

*Carrington College - Administrative Office (B)

7801 Folsom Boulevard, Sacramento CA 95826
County: Sacramento Identification: 666086
Telephone: (916) 388-2800 Carnegie Class: N/A
FAX Number: (916) 381-1809
URL: www.carrington.edu

01 President Carrington Colleges ... Dr. Donna LORAINE
10 VP Accred & Profession ... Dr. Danika BOWEN
11 Chief Operating Officer ... Vacant
12 Vice President Operation ... Mr. Jim MURPHY
07 VP Student Services ... Mr. Mitch CHARLES
32 Sr Dir Student Affairs/Ombudsman ... Dr. Scott SAND
10 Dir Finance & Infrastructure ... Mr. Joshua OLMSTED

*Carrington College - Sacramento (C)

8909 Folsom Boulevard, Sacramento CA 95826
County: Sacramento FICE Identification: 009748
Unit ID: 125532
Telephone: (916) 361-1660 Carnegie Class: Spec 2-yr-Health
FAX Number: (916) 361-6666 Calendar System: Other
URL: www.carrington.edu
Established: 1983 Annual Undergrad Tuition & Fees: N/A
Enrollment: 1,124 Coed
Affiliation or Control: Proprietary IRS Status: Proprietary
Highest Offering: Associate Degree
Accreditation: WJ, DH, MAC

02 Regional Director of Operations ... Tara MICELI
121 Student Success Center Manager ... Becky CARDWELL

* *Carrington College - Citrus Heights* (D)

7301 Greenback Lane, Suite A, Citrus Heights CA 95621
Telephone: (916) 722-8200 Identification: 667042
Accreditation: &WJ, MAC

† Regional accreditation is carried under the parent institution in Sacramento, CA.

* *Carrington College - Pleasant Hill* (E)

380 Civic Drive, Suite 300, Pleasant Hill CA 94523
Telephone: (925) 609-6650 Identification: 666043
Accreditation: &WJ, COARC, MAC, PTAA

† Regional accreditation is carried under the parent institution in Sacramento, CA.

* *Carrington College - Pomona* (F)

901 Corporate Center Drive, #300, Pomona CA 91768
Telephone: (909) 868-5834 Identification: 770506
Accreditation: &WJ

† Regional accreditation is carried under the parent institution in Sacramento, CA.

* *Carrington College - San Jose* (G)

5883 Rue Ferrari, Suite 125, San Jose CA 95138
Telephone: (408) 960-0161 Identification: 666042
Accreditation: &WJ, DH, MAC, SURGT

† Regional accreditation is carried under the parent institution in Sacramento, CA.

* *Carrington College - San Leandro* (H)

15555 E 14th Street, Suite 500, San Leandro CA 94578
Telephone: (510) 276-3888 Identification: 666751
Accreditation: &WJ, MAC

† Regional accreditation is carried under the parent institution in Sacramento, CA.

* *Carrington College - Stockton* (I)

1313 W Robinhood Drive, Suite B, Stockton CA 95207
Telephone: (209) 956-1240 Identification: 666140
Accreditation: &WJ, MAC

† Regional accreditation is carried under the parent institution in Sacramento, CA.

Casa Loma College-Van Nuys (J)

6725 Kester Avenue, Van Nuys CA 91405
County: Los Angeles FICE Identification: 006731
Unit ID: 111638
Telephone: (818) 785-2726 Carnegie Class: Spec 2-yr-Health
FAX Number: (818) 785-2191 Calendar System: Other
URL: www.casalomacollege.edu
Established: 1966 Annual Undergrad Tuition & Fees: N/A
Enrollment: 215 Coed
Affiliation or Control: Independent Non-Profit IRS Status: 501(c)3
Highest Offering: Associate Degree
Accreditation: ABHES, PTAA

01 Campus Director/Controller ... Ms. Veronica PANTOJA
05 Dean of Education ... Dr. Stephanie SHELBURNE
06 Registrar ... Ms. Kimberly DUNCAN
07 Director of Admissions ... Mr. Nicholas WALSH-DAVIS
86 Director of Compliance ... Vacant
37 Director Student Financial Aid ... Mr. George MCPHATTER
08 Head Librarian ... Ms. Jennifer MEYER
106 Dir Online Education/E-learning ... Ms. Stephanie SHELBURNE
13 Chief Info Technology Officer ... Mr. Cyrill REISER
18 Chief Facilities/Physical Plant ... Ms. Veronica PANTOJA
36 Director Student Placement ... Vacant

CBD College (K)

3699 Wilshire Boulevard, 4th Floor,
Los Angeles CA 90010
County: Los Angeles FICE Identification: 032503
Unit ID: 439367
Telephone: (213) 427-2200 Carnegie Class: Spec 2-yr-Health
FAX Number: (213) 427-9278 Calendar System: Other
URL: www.cbd.edu
Established: 1982 Annual Undergrad Tuition & Fees: N/A
Enrollment: 500 Coed
Affiliation or Control: Independent Non-Profit IRS Status: 501(c)3
Highest Offering: Associate Degree
Accreditation: ABHES, DMS, OTA, PTAA, SURTEC

01 President ... Mr. Alan HESHEL

Cedars-Sinai Graduate School of Biomedical Sciences (L)

8700 Beverly Boulevard, Los Angeles CA 90048
County: Los Angeles Identification: 667071
Telephone: (310) 423-8294 Carnegie Class: Not Classified
FAX Number: N/A Calendar System: Trimester
URL: www.cedars-sinai.org/education/graduate-school.html
Established: 1902 Annual Graduate Tuition & Fees: N/A
Enrollment: N/A Coed
Affiliation or Control: Independent Non-Profit IRS Status: 501(c)3
Highest Offering: Doctorate; No Undergraduates
Accreditation: WC

01 President/CEO ... Mr. Thomas PRISELAC
03 Executive Vice President ... Dr. John JENRETTE
05 Exec Vice Pres Academic Affairs ... Dr. Shlomo MELMED
10 Exec Vice Pres Finance/CFO ... Mr. Edward PRUNCHUNAS

Cerritos College (M)

11110 Alondra Boulevard, Norwalk CA 90650-6298
County: Los Angeles FICE Identification: 001161
Unit ID: 111887
Telephone: (562) 860-2451 Carnegie Class: Assoc/MT-VT-High Trad
FAX Number: (562) 467-5005 Calendar System: Semester
URL: www.cerritos.edu
Established: 1955 Annual Undergrad Tuition & Fees (In-District): $1,346
Enrollment: 17,218 Coed
Affiliation or Control: State/Local IRS Status: 501(c)3
Highest Offering: Associate Degree
Accreditation: WJ, ADNUR, DA, DH, PTAA

01 President ... Dr. Jose L. FIERRO
04 Executive Assistant ... Ms. Andrea WITTIG
05 Vice President Academic Affairs ... Mr. Edmund (Rick) MIRANDA
10 Vice President Business Services ... Mr. Felipe LOPEZ
32 Vice President Student Services ... Dr. Dilcie D. PEREZ
15 Vice President Human Resources .. Dr. Adriana FLORES-CHURCH
20 Dean of Academic Affairs ... Vacant
07 Dean of Admissions/Records & Svcs ... Ms. Stephanie MURGUIA
38 Interim Dean of Counseling Services .. Dr. Stephanie RODRIGUEZ
86 Dir College/Govt Rels & Pub Affs ... Ms. Miya WALKER
22 Acting Dean of DSPS ... Dr. Steven LA VIGNE
121 Acting Dean Student Support Svcs ... Ms. Jaime QUIROS
50 Dean Business/Humanities/SS ... Ms. Rachel MASON
57 Dean Fine Arts/Communications ... Dr. Gary PRITCHARD
76 Dean Health Occupations ... Ms. Sandra MARKS
83 Dean Academic Success ... Ms. Shawna BASKETTE
49 Dean Liberal Arts ... Dr. Frank MIXSON
68 Dean Health/PE/Dance/Athl ... Dr. Rory NATIVIDAD
54 Dean Sci/Engineering/Math ... Mr. Andrew VINES
72 Dean Technology ... Dr. Yannick REAL
13 Director Information Technology ... Mr. Patrick O'DONNELL
21 Director of Fiscal Services ... Mr. Noorali DELAWALLA
35 Dean of Student Services ... Dr. Elizabeth MILLER
36 Dir of Career/Assessment Services ... Ms. Theresa LOPEZ
18 Director Physical Plant & Const Svc ... Vacant
102 Exec Dir Foundation/Inst Advance ... Ms. Carol KRUMBACH
88 Director Community Advancement ... Ms. Bellegran GOMEZ
96 Dir Purchasing/Contract Admin ... Mr. Mark LOGAN
16 Director Human Resources/Risk Mgmt ... Ms. Nancy BUVINGER
19 Chief of Campus Police ... Mr. Thomas GALLIVAN
88 Assoc Dn Adult Educ/Diversity Pgms ... Ms. Graciela VASQUEZ
31 Director Community Education ... Dr. Patricia ROBBINS SMITH
88 Director Child Development Center ... Ms. Debra WARD
88 Operations Manager ... Mr. Carlos SERNA
88 Payroll Manager ... Ms. Deanna HART
114 Budget Manager ... Mr. Conrad SELORIO
14 Manager Information Technology ... Mr. Javier BANUELOS
23 Assoc Dean Student Health Wellness ... Dr. Hillary MENNELLA
88 Director of Student Program Svcs ... Ms. Norma RODRIGUEZ
09 Dir Inst Effect/Research & Planning ... Dr. Kristi BLACKBURN
88 Director Adv Trans Tech Projects ... Ms. Jannet MALIG
28 Dir Diver/Compliance/Title IX Coord ... Dr. Valencia RAPHAEL
88 EOPS Assistant Director ... Ms. Yvette TAFOYA
19 Dir Educational Partnerships ... Ms. Colleen MCKINLEY
88 Dual Enrollment Manager ... Ms. Carla YORKE
88 Accounting Manager ... Ms. Kathy BURGOS
88 Facilities Manager ... Mr. Shannon KAVENEY
29 Director Alumni Affairs ... Mr. Matthew HARMS
30 Chief Development Officer ... Ms. Monica Lee COPELAND
37 Acting Asst Director Financial Aid ... Mr. Juan MERCADO

*Chabot-Las Positas Community College District (N)

7600 Dublin Blvd., 3rd Flr., Dublin CA 94568
County: Alameda Identification: 666925
Telephone: (925) 485-5208 Carnegie Class: N/A
FAX Number: (925) 485-5256
URL: www.clpccd.org

01 Interim Chancellor ... Mr. Ronald GERHARD
10 Acting Vice Chanc Business Svcs ... Mr. Douglas ROBERTS
05 Vice Chanc Educational Svcs ... Ms. Theresa FLEISCHER ROWLAND
15 Vice Chanc Human Resource Svcs ... Mr. Wyman FONG
18 Vice Chanc Facilities/Bond Program ... Mr. Owen LETCHER
13 Chief Technology Officer ... Mr. Bruce GRIFFIN

*Chabot College (O)

25555 Hesperian Boulevard, Hayward CA 94545-2400
County: Alameda FICE Identification: 001162
Unit ID: 111920
Telephone: (510) 723-6600 Carnegie Class: Assoc/HT-High Trad
FAX Number: (510) 782-9315 Calendar System: Semester
URL: www.chabotcollege.edu
Established: 1961 Annual Undergrad Tuition & Fees (In-District): $1,142
Enrollment: 13,670 Coed
Affiliation or Control: State/Local IRS Status: 501(c)3
Highest Offering: Associate Degree
Accreditation: WJ, ART, DH, MAC, MUS

02 President ... Dr. Susan S. SPERLING
05 VP Academic Services ... Ms. Stacy THOMPSON
32 Vice President Student Services ... Dr. Matthew KRITSCHER
11 Vice Pres Administrative Services ... Mr. Dale WAGONER
10 Actg Chief Financial Officer ... Mr. Dale WAGONER
04 Exec Asst to the College President ... Ms. Kirti REDDY
08 Librarian ... Ms. Kim MORRISON
38 Dean Counseling ... Ms. Debra TRIGG
41 Dean Health/PE/Athletics ... Mr. Kevin KRAMER
07 Dir Admissions & Records/Registrar ... Mrs. Paulette LINO
37 Director of Financial Aid ... Ms. Kathryn LINZMEYER
19 Director Safety & Security ... Sgt. Brandon WILSON
09 Int Dir Institutional Effectiveness ... Ms. Samantha KESSLER
15 Director Human Resources ... Dr. Wyman FONG
18 Chief Facilities/Physical Plant ... Mr. Walter BELVINS
111 Exec Director Inst Advancement ... Ms. Yvonne WU CRAIG
35 Dir Student Life/Student Services ... Mr. Arnold PAGUIO
96 Manager Purchasing/Warehouse Svcs ... Ms. Marie HAMPTON

*Las Positas College (P)

3000 Campus Hill Drive, Livermore CA 94551-7623
County: Alameda FICE Identification: 030357
Unit ID: 366401
Telephone: (925) 424-1000 Carnegie Class: Assoc/HT-High Trad
FAX Number: (925) 443-0742 Calendar System: Semester
URL: www.laspositascollege.edu
Established: 1975 Annual Undergrad Tuition & Fees (In-District): $1,134
Enrollment: 8,989 Coed
Affiliation or Control: State/Local IRS Status: 501(c)3
Highest Offering: Associate Degree
Accreditation: WJ, EMT

02 Interim President ... Ms. Roanna V. BENNIE
05 Vice Pres Academic Svcs ... Dr. Kristina WHALEN
32 Vice President Student Svcs ... Mr. William L. GARCIA
11 Vice Pres Administrative Services ... Ms. Diane BRADY
04 Exec Assistant to the President ... Vacant
35 Dean of Student Services ... Ms. Elizabeth DAVID
49 Interim Dean Arts & Humanities ... Dr. Stuart MCELDERRY
81 Dean Math/Science/Eng/Public Safety ... Dr. Nan HO
50 Dean Bus/Health/Athletics/Work Exp ... Dr. Amir LAW
77 Dn Computing/Applied Tech/Soc Svcs ... Mr. Don CARLSON
84 Dean of Enrollment Services ... Ms. Tamica WARD

45 Director of Research & Planning ... Mr. Rajinder SAMRA
37 Financial Aid/Veterans Assistance ... Ms. Andi SCHREIBMAN
19 Campus Safety Supervisor ... Mr. Sean PRATHER
08 Head Librarian ... Dr. Tina INZERILLA
102 Executive Director LPC Foundation ... Mr. Kenneth COOPER
41 Athletic Director ... Vacant
10 Associate Business Officer ... Ms. Natasha LANG
18 Project Planner/Manager Facilities ... Ms. Ann KROLL
06 Registrar ... Vacant
88 Project Manager CTE ... Ms. Vicki SHIPMAN
88 Director Child Development Center ... Ms. Angea LOPEZ

Chaffey College (A)

5885 Haven Avenue, Rancho Cucamonga CA 91737-3002
County: San Bernardino — FICE Identification: 001163
Unit ID: 111939
Telephone: (909) 652-6000 — Carnegie Class: Assoc/HT-High Trad
FAX Number: (909) 652-6006 — Calendar System: Semester
URL: www.chaffey.edu
Established: 1883 — Annual Undergrad Tuition & Fees (In-State): $1,172
Enrollment: 22,508 — Coed
Affiliation or Control: State — IRS Status: 501(c)3
Highest Offering: Associate Degree
Accreditation: WJ, ADNUR, DA, RAD

01 Superintendent/President ... Dr. Henry D. SHANNON
11 Assoc Supt Administrative Affairs ... Ms. Melanie SIDDIQI
10 Assoc Supt Bus Svcs/Econ Dev ... Ms. Lisa BAILEY
05 Assoc Supt Instruction/Inst Effect ... Ms. Laura HOPE
32 Assoc Supt Student Svcs/Legis Engag ... Dr. Eric BISHOP
09 Dean Inst Research/Research Dev ... Mr. Jim FILLPOT
29 Director Alumni Relations ... Ms. Janeth RODRIGUEZ
85 Director International Students ... Vacant
35 Dean Student Life ... Mr. Christopher BRUNELLE
07 Admin Admissions/Records ... Ms. Kathy LUCERO
21 Exec Director Business Services ... Ms. Kim ERICKSON
88 Director Technical Services ... Mr. Michael FINK
88 Director Childrens Center ... Ms. Birgit MONKS
23 Director Student Health Services ... Ms. Katherine PEEK
37 Director Financial Aid ... Ms. Patricia BOPKO
109 Director Auxiliary Services ... Vacant
26 Director Marketing/Public Relations ... Ms. Alisha ROSAS
114 Exec Dir Budgeting & Fiscal Svc ... Ms. Anita UNDERCOFFER
88 Director Museum Gallery ... Ms. Rebecca TRAWICK
18 Manager Facilities Development ... Ms. Sarah RILEY
12 Dean Chino Campus ... Dr. Teresa HULL
88 Dean Visual Performing Arts ... Dr. Jason CHEVALIER
50 Dean Business & Applied Tech ... Ms. Joy HAERENS
81 Dean Mathematics & Science ... Mr. Theodore YOUNGLOVE
83 Dean Social & Behav Sci ... Dr. Corene SCHWARTZ
88 Dean Language Arts ... Mr. Anthony DISALVO
38 Dean Counseling & Matriculation ... Ms. Amy NEVAREZ
12 Dean Fontana Campus ... Dr. Yolanda FRIDAY
76 Dean Health Sciences ... Ms. Sherrie LOEWEN
04 Exec Assistant Supt/Pres Office ... Ms. Julie SANCHEZ
41 Interim Director Athletics ... Mr. Jeff KLEIN
86 Manager Government Relations ... Ms. Lorena CORONA
15 Director Human Resources ... Ms. Susan HARDIE
102 Executive Director Foundation ... Ms. Lisa NASHUA

Chamberlain University-Sacramento (B)

10971 Sun Center Drive, Rancho Cordova CA 95670
Telephone: (916) 330-3410 — Identification: 770978
Accreditation: &NH, NURSE

† Branch campus of Chamberlain University-Addison, Addison, IL

Chapman University (C)

One University Drive, Orange CA 92866-1099
County: Orange — FICE Identification: 001164
Unit ID: 111948
Telephone: (714) 997-6815 — Carnegie Class: DU-Higher
FAX Number: (714) 997-6713 — Calendar System: 4/1/4
URL: www.chapman.edu
Established: 1861 — Annual Undergrad Tuition & Fees: $52,724
Enrollment: 9,392 — Coed
Affiliation or Control: Christian Church (Disciples Of Christ)
IRS Status: 501(c)3
Highest Offering: Doctorate
Accreditation: WC, #ARCPA, CAEPT, DANCE, LAW, MFCD, MUS, PHAR, PTA, SP, THEA

01 President ... Dr. Daniele C. STRUPPA
05 Provost & Exec VP Academic Affairs ... Dr. Glenn PFEIFFER
03 Executive Vice President & COO ... Mr. Harold W. HEWITT, JR.
111 Exec VP University Advancement ... Ms. Sheryl BOURGEOIS
32 VP & Dean of Students ... Dr. Jerry PRICE
84 VP/Dean Enrollment Management ... Mr. Michael PELLY
20 Assoc Provost of Academic Admin ... Dr. Lawrence BROWN
09 Vice Provost Inst Eff & Fac Affairs ... Mr. Joseph SLOWENSKY
49 Dean Wilkinson Col Hum/Soc Sci ... Dr. Jennifer KEENE
61 Dean School of Law ... Dr. Matthew J. PARLOW
50 Dean School Business/Economics ... Dr. Thomas TURK
67 Dean School of Pharmacy ... Dr. Ronald JORDAN
121 Director of Academic Advising ... Mr. Roberto CORONEL
53 Dean College of Educational Studies ... Dr. Margaret GROGAN
88 Int Dean College of Film/Media Arts ... Mr. Michael KOWALSKI
57 Dean College of Performing Arts ... Dr. Guilio ONGARO
83 Dean Col Health/Behavioral Sciences ... Dr. Janeen M. HILL
81 Int Dean College of Science/Tech ... Dr. Jason K. KELLER
54 Dean School of Engineering ... Dr. L. Andrew LYON
57 Dean/Artistic Dir Center for Arts ... Dr. William HALL
88 Director Ctr for Global Education ... Ms. Kristin BEAVERS
97 Vice Provost Undergrad Education ... Dr. Nina LENOIR
45 Interim VP Campus Planning ... Mr. Rick TURNER
15 Vice President/CHRO ... Mr. Brian POWELL
43 Assoc Vice Pres of Legal Affairs ... Ms. Janine DUMONTELLE
10 Assoc Vice President & Controller ... Mr. Behzad BINESH
07 Asst VP of Undergrad Admissions ... Ms. Marcela MEJIA MARTINEZ
20 Assistant Provost ... Ms. Iris GERBASI
26 VP of Strategic Marketing ... Ms. Jamie CEMAN
18 Assoc VP Facilities ... Mr. Rick TURNER
27 Director Public Relations ... Ms. Lara WYSS
08 Dean of Library ... Ms. Charlene BALDWIN
29 Asst VP Strategic Engagement/Dev ... Ms. Delite TRAVIS
13 VP/Chief Information Officer ... Ms. Helen NORRIS
88 VP of Community Relations ... Mr. Jack RAUBOLT
09 Director of Institutional Research ... Dr. Marisol ARREDONDO
06 Registrar ... Ms. Jan MCCUEN
46 VP Research & Sponsored Pgms Admin ... Dr. Thomas PIECHOTA
28 Director of Diversity and Inclusion ... Ms. Erin PULLIN
37 Director Undergrad Financial Aid ... Mr. David CARNEVALE
85 Director Intl Student Services ... Ms. Susan SAMS
19 Chief of Public Safety ... Mr. Randy BURBA
39 Director Residence Life ... Mr. David SUNDBY
41 Athletic Director ... Mr. Terry BOESEL
42 Dean of the Chapel ... Dr. Gail STEARNS
04 Associate to the President ... Dr. Christina MARSHALL
88 Exec Assistant to the Provost ... Ms. Shehani REEDER
23 Director Student Health Services ... Ms. Jacqueline DEATS
35 Asst Dean of Student Engagement ... Dr. Chris HUTCHISON
36 Asst Dir Career Education ... Ms. Susan I. CHANG
38 Assoc Dean/Dir Student Psych Couns ... Dr. Jeannie WALKER
96 Purchasing Coordinator ... Ms. Elizabeth ROSERO
04 Executive Asst to the President ... Ms. Erika CURIEL
58 Vice Provost for Graduate Educ ... Dr. Roxanne MILLER
102 Dir Corporate/Foundation Relations ... Mr. Mike STRINGER
44 Dir Legacy Planning ... Mr. David MOORE
90 Dir Educational Tech Services ... Dr. Jana REMY
104 Assoc Director Ctr for Global Educ ... Ms. Kristy BEAVERS
105 Webmaster ... Ms. Mandy THOMAS

Charles R. Drew University of Medicine & Science (D)

1731 E 120th Street, Los Angeles CA 90059-3025
County: Los Angeles — FICE Identification: 010365
Unit ID: 111966
Telephone: (323) 563-4800 — Carnegie Class: Spec-4-yr-Other Health
FAX Number: (323) 563-5987 — Calendar System: Semester
URL: www.cdrewu.edu
Established: 1966 — Annual Undergrad Tuition & Fees: $13,972
Enrollment: 543 — Coed
Affiliation or Control: Independent Non-Profit — IRS Status: 501(c)3
Highest Offering: Master's
Accreditation: WC, #ARCPA, NURSE, PH, RAD

01 President & CEO ... Dr. David M. CARLISLE
05 EVP Academic Affairs/Provost ... Dr. Steve O. MICHAEL
100 Chief of Staff ... Vacant
45 VP Research & Health Affairs ... Dr. Jadutt VADGAMA
111 VP for Strategic Advancement ... Ms. Angela L. MINNIEFIELD
10 VP Finance/Chief Business Officer ... Mr. Carl MCLANEY
15 Director of Human Resources ... Ms. Nicola MARTIN
63 Dean College of Medicine ... Dr. Deborah PROTHROW-STITH
66 Dean School of Nursing ... Dr. Diane BRECKENRIDGE
76 Dean College of Science & Health ... Dr. Hector BALCAZAR
20 Asst Provost Faculty Affairs ... Dr. William SHAY
32 Dean Student Affairs ... Vacant
20 Sr Assoc Dean Academic Affairs ... Dr. Ronald A. EDELSTEIN
09 Dir Inst Research & Effectiveness ... Mr. Richard W. LINDSTROM
21 Chief Financial Officer ... Ms. Elizabeth BASKERVILLE
08 Director Health Sciences Library ... Ms. Darlene PARKER-KELLY
06 Registrar ... Ms. Raquel MUNOZ
07 Director of Enrollment Management ... Ms. Karen JACKSON
13 Chief Information Officer ... Mr. Aaron WEATHERSBY

Charter College-Oxnard (E)

2000 Outlet Center Drive, Suite 150, Oxnard CA 93036
Telephone: (805) 973-1240 — Identification: 666675
Accreditation: ABHES

† Branch campus of Charter College, Vancouver, WA

Chicago School of Professional Psychology Los Angeles Campus (F)

707 Wilshire Blvd. Suite 600, Los Angeles CA 90017
County: Los Angeles — FICE Identification: 021553
Unit ID: 455664
Telephone: (213) 615-2700 — Carnegie Class: Spec-4-yr-Other Health
FAX Number: (213) 615-7274 — Calendar System: Semester
URL: www.thechicagoschool.edu
Established: 2008 — Annual Undergrad Tuition & Fees: $14,738
Enrollment: 2,442 — Coed
Affiliation or Control: Independent Non-Profit — IRS Status: 501(c)3
Highest Offering: Doctorate
Accreditation: WC, CLPSY

01 President ... Dr. Michele NEALON
05 Vice Pres AA/Chief Academic Officer ... Dr. Ted SCHOLZ
10 Sr Director of Business Operations ... Mr. Chris JACKSON
32 Dean for Student Success ... Ms. Jennifer STRIPE PORTILLO
15 Vice Pres Human Resources ... Dr. David IWANE
11 Chief Operating Officer ... Dr. Michael FALOTICO
111 Director Inst Advancement ... Dr. Nicole FLOWERS
26 Director of Communications ... Mr. Victor ABALOS
04 Administrative Asst to President ... Ms. Adriana KLEIMAN
06 National Registrar ... Ms. Connie KUANG
08 Campus Librarian ... Ms. Kim WOBICK
100 Chief of Staff ... Ms. Shari MIKOS
101 Secretary of the Institution/Board ... Ms. Patti TYRA
19 Director of Facilities ... Mr. Brian LA BELLE
37 Regional Assoc Director of Fin Aid ... Mr. Seph RODRIGUEZ
09 Director of Institutional Research ... Ms. Ericka KILBURN
108 Dir Institutional Effectiveness ... Ms. Virginia QUINONEZ
07 Director of Admissions ... Mr. John MACFIE

Chicago School of Professional Psychology-Irvine Campus (G)

4199 Campus Drive, Suite 400, Irvine CA 92612
Telephone: (949) 769-7700 — Identification: 770492
Accreditation: &WC

China Evangelical Seminary North America (H)

1520 W. Cameron Avenue Ste 275,
West Covina CA 91790
County: Los Angeles — Identification: 667256
Telephone: (626) 917-9482 — Carnegie Class: Not Classified
FAX Number: (626) 851-1371 — Calendar System: Quarter
URL: www.cesna.edu
Established: 2007 — Annual Graduate Tuition & Fees: N/A
Enrollment: N/A — Coed
Affiliation or Control: Non-denominational — IRS Status: 501(c)3
Highest Offering: Doctorate; No Undergraduates
Accreditation: THEOL

01 President ... Dr. Katheryn LEUNG
05 Academic Dean ... Dr. Raymond HSU
11 Chief of Administration ... Rev. Hokeung C. CHAN
30 Chief Development/Advancement ... Dr. Agnes CHIU
37 Director Student Financial Aid ... Rev. Chun K. LEE
08 Chief Library Officer ... Vacant
13 Chief Info Technology Ofcr (CIO) ... Dr. Frank LIU

Christian Witness Theological Seminary (I)

1975 Concourse Drive, San Jose CA 95131
County: Santa Clara — Identification: 667255
Telephone: (408) 433-2280 — Carnegie Class: Not Classified
FAX Number: (408) 433-9855 — Calendar System: Other
URL: www.cwts.edu
Established: 1978 — Annual Graduate Tuition & Fees: N/A
Enrollment: N/A — Coed
Affiliation or Control: Interdenominational — IRS Status: 501(c)3
Highest Offering: Doctorate; No Undergraduates
Accreditation: THEOL

01 President ... Rev. Jeffrey LU
11 Vice President Administration ... Rev. James IP
05 Academic Dean ... RevDr. Kenny LAI
07 Admissions Dir/Dean Student Affairs ... Dr. Peter TIE

Church Divinity School of the Pacific (J)

2451 Ridge Road, Berkeley CA 94709-1217
County: Alameda — FICE Identification: 001165
Unit ID: 112127
Telephone: (510) 204-0700 — Carnegie Class: Spec-4-yr-Faith
FAX Number: N/A — Calendar System: Semester
URL: www.cdsp.edu
Established: 1893 — Annual Graduate Tuition & Fees: N/A
Enrollment: 86 — Coed
Affiliation or Control: Protestant Episcopal — IRS Status: 501(c)3
Highest Offering: Doctorate; No Undergraduates
Accreditation: THEOL

01 President & Dean ... Dr. W. Mark RICHARDSON
11 Vice President & COO ... Rev. John DWYER
05 Dean Academic Affairs ... Dr. Ruth MEYERS
32 Dean of Students ... Rev. Andrew HYBL
06 Registrar ... Ms. Mary MCCHESNEY-YOUNG
123 Director of Recruitment ... Rev. Spencer HATCHER
10 Operations Manager ... Mr. Melville HAYES-MARTIN
88 Program Manager ... Ms. Alissa FENCSIK
37 Director of Financial Aid ... Ms. Mary MCCHESNEY-YOUNG
04 Executive Assistant ... Mr. Jamie NELSON

Citrus College (K)

1000 W Foothill Boulevard, Glendora CA 91741-1899
County: Los Angeles — FICE Identification: 001166
Unit ID: 112172
Telephone: (626) 963-0323 — Carnegie Class: Assoc/HT-High Trad
FAX Number: (626) 914-8618 — Calendar System: Semester

URL: www.citruscollege.edu
Established: 1915 Annual Undergrad Tuition & Fees (In-District): $1,190
Enrollment: 13,263 Coed
Affiliation or Control: State/Local IRS Status: 501(c)3
Highest Offering: Associate Degree
Accreditation: WJ, DA

01 Superintendent/President ....Dr. Geraldine M. PERRI
05 Vice President Academic Affairs ....Dr. Arvid SPOR
32 Vice President Student Services ....Dr. Martha A. MCDONALD
10 Vice Pres Finance/Admin Services ....Ms. Claudette E. DAIN
07 Dean Enrollment Services ....Dr. Gerald SEQUEIRA
51 Dean Career/Tech & Cont Educ ....Vacant
38 Dean of Counseling ....Vacant
15 Director Human Resources ....Dr. Robert L. SAMMIS
102 Director Foundation ....Ms. Christina M. GARCIA
35 Dean of Students ....Dr. Maryann TOLANO-LEVEQUE
18 Director Facilities & Construction ....Mr. Fred DIAMOND
09 Director of Institutional Research ....Dr. Lan HAO
06 Registrar ....Mr. Brian DEAN
37 Director Financial Aid ....Ms. Carol THOMAS
21 Director of Fiscal Services ....Ms. Rosalinda BUCHWALD
28 Manager HR/Staff Diversity ....Ms. Brenda FINK
13 Chief Information Services Officer ....Mr. Robert HUGHES
19 Director of Campus Safety ....Mr. Benjamin MACIAS
83 Dean Social/Behavioral Sciences/DE ....Dr. Dana HESTER
41 Dean Kinesiology/Athletics/Health ....Mr. Junior DOMINGO
79 Dean Language Arts & Library ....Dr. Gina HOGAN
65 Dean Natural/Physical Sci & Health ....Dr. Eric RABITOY
57 Dean Visual & Performing Arts ....Mr. John VAUGHAN
81 Dean Math & Business ....Mr. Michael WANGLER
88 Director EOPS CARE CalWORKS ....Ms. Sarah GONZALES-TAPIA
25 Dir Grants/Development Oversight ....Dr. Marianne SMITH
101 Secretary of the Institution/Board ....Ms. Christine A. LINK
88 Director of Business Services ....Mr. Shawn JONES
26 Exec Dir of Cmty & External Rels ....Ms. Melissa UTSUKI
88 Director Haugh Performing Arts Ctr ....Ms. Tiina MITTLER
76 Director Health Sciences ....Ms. Salima ALLAHBACHAYO
121 Director Student Support Svcs ....Ms. Jessica LOPEZ-JIMINEZ
40 Enterprise Services Manager ....Mr. Eric MAGALLON

City College of San Francisco (A)

50 Frida Kahlo Way, Smith Hall Room,
San Francisco CA 94103-1292
County: San Francisco FICE Identification: 001167
Unit ID: 112190
Telephone: (415) 239-3000 Carnegie Class: Assoc/MT-VT-Mix Trad/Non
FAX Number: (415) 239-3919 Calendar System: Semester
URL: www.ccsf.edu
Established: 1935 Annual Undergrad Tuition & Fees (In-District): $1,696
Enrollment: 26,299 Coed
Affiliation or Control: State/Local IRS Status: 501(c)3
Highest Offering: Associate Degree
Accreditation: WJ, ACFEI, CAHIIM, DA, EMT, MAC, RAD

01 Chancellor ....Dr. Mark ROCHA
11 Sr Vice Chanc Admin/Stdnt Affs ....Ms. Dianna GONZALES
05 Sr Vice Chancellor Academic Affairs ....Mr. Thomas BOEGEL
108 Dean of Institutional Effectiveness ....Dr. Pam MERY
12 Dean Civic Center Campus ....Dr. Geisce LY
12 Dean Southeast Campus ....Mr. Torrance BYNUM
12 Int Dean Mission Campus ....Ms. Gregoria CAHILL
12 Dean Downtown/Business School ....Dr. Geisce LY
32 Assoc Vice Chanc of Student Affairs ....Dr. Elizabeth CORIA
37 Dean Financial Aid/Student Success ....Mr. Guillermo VILLANUEVA
07 Dean Admissions & Records ....Ms. Marylou LEYBA-FRANK
20 Assoc Vice Chanc of Instruction ....Vacant
103 Int Dean Workforce Development ....Mr. John HALPIN
15 Assoc Vice Chanc Human Resources ....Ms. Clara STARR
38 Dean Matriculation & Counseling ....Ms. Lidia JENKINS
88 Assoc Dean Student Equity ....Ms. Tessa HENDERSON-BROWN
12 Dean Chinatown/Contract & Cont Ed ....Ms. Kit DAI
88 Dean Sch of Visual/Performing Arts ....Vacant
83 Int Dean Behavioral/Social Sci ....Ms. Jill YEE
81 Dean Science/Math/Technology/Engr ....Mr. David YEE
68 Dean J Adams Campus/Sch Hlth Educ ....Ms. Edith KAEUPER
30 Assoc Vice Chanc Institutional Dev ....Ms. Kristin CHARLES
13 Technical Operations Manager ....Mr. Tim RYAN
16 Int Director Employee Relations ....Ms. Cassandra LAWSON
18 Director Buildings/Grounds ....Mr. Jimmy KIRK
96 Dean of Purchasing ....Mr. Garth KWIECIEN
19 Chief of Police/Public Safety ....Ms. Coleen FATOOH
88 ADA Compliance Officer ....Dr. Leilani BATTISTE
21 Assoc Vice Chanc/CFO ....Dr. Abdul NASSER
25 Int Dean Grants & Resource Dev ....Ms. Ilona MCGRIFF
06 Assoc Dean Admission & Records ....Ms. Monika LIU
88 Dean Faculty Support Svcs ....Dr. Minh-Hoa TA
101 Liaison to the Board of Trustees ....Ms. Linda SHAW
41 Athletic Director ....Mr. Harold BROWN
43 Dir Legal Services/General Counsel ....Mr. Steve BRUCKMAN
26 Director of External Affairs ....Vacant
04 Assistant to the Chancellor ....Ms. Angela WU
08 Chief Library Officer ....Dr. Donna REED
100 Chief of Staff ....Ms. Leslie MILLOY
106 Dir Online Education/E-learning ....Ms. Cynthia DEWAR

City of Hope (B)

1500 East Duarte Road, Duarte CA 91010-3000
County: Los Angeles FICE Identification: 035924
Unit ID: 441238
Telephone: (626) 256-4673 Carnegie Class: Spec-4-yr-Other Health
FAX Number: (626) 301-8105 Calendar System: Semester
URL: www.cityofhope.org
Established: 1994 Annual Graduate Tuition & Fees: N/A
Enrollment: 95 Coed
Affiliation or Control: Independent Non-Profit IRS Status: 501(c)3
Highest Offering: Doctorate; No Undergraduates
Accreditation: WC, RTT

01 President/CEO ....Robert STONE
05 Provost/Chief Scientific Officer ....Dr. Steven T. ROSEN
11 Chief Operating Officer ....Jeff WALKER
10 Chief Financial Officer ....Jennifer PARKHURST
26 Sr VP & Chief Marketing/Comm Ofcr ....John WESTON
43 General Counsel/Secretary ....Gregory SCHETINA
15 Chief of Human Resources ....Kety DURON
58 Dean of Graduate School ....Dr. John J. ROSSI
06 Registrar ....Tracy KURZY
07 Director of Admissions ....Stephanie PATTERSON
08 Head Librarian ....Andrea LYNCH

*The Claremont College Services (C)

101 South Mills Avenue, Claremont CA 91711-5053
County: Los Angeles Identification: 666003
Telephone: (909) 621-8026 Carnegie Class: N/A
FAX Number: (909) 621-8517
URL: https://services.claremont.edu

01 Chief Executive Officer ....Mr. Stig LANESSKOG
10 Vice President of Financial Affairs ....Mr. Steven HOLLEY
32 Vice President of Student Affairs ....Ms. Janet SMITH DICKERSON
10 AVP Financial Services/Controller ....Ms. Mia ALONZO
26 Director of Communications ....Vacant
19 Asst Vice Pres Campus Safety ....Mr. Stan SKIPWORTH
13 Chief Information Officer ....Mr. Chuck THOMPSON
101 Sec to Board/AVP Comm Relations ....Mr. Colin TUDOR
08 Dean TCC Library ....Ms. Janet BISHOP
15 Director Human Resources ....Ms. Stephanie DORNES

*Claremont Graduate University (D)

150 E 10th Street, Claremont CA 91711-5909
County: Los Angeles FICE Identification: 001169
Unit ID: 112251
Telephone: (909) 621-8000 Carnegie Class: DU-Higher
FAX Number: (909) 621-8390 Calendar System: Semester
URL: www.cgu.edu
Established: 1925 Annual Graduate Tuition & Fees: N/A
Enrollment: 1,913 Coed
Affiliation or Control: Independent Non-Profit IRS Status: 501(c)3
Highest Offering: Doctorate; No Undergraduates
Accreditation: WC, PH

02 President ....Dr. Len JESSUP
04 Exec Asst to the President ....Ms. Donna STANDLEA
05 Exec Vice President and Provost ....Dr. Patricia EASTON
10 VP for Finance and Admin/Treasurer ....Ms. Leslie NEGRITTO
111 Vice Pres of Advancement ....Ms. Kristen ANDERSEN-DALEY
84 VP for Enrollment Services ....Ms. Christine BELL
46 Vice Provost/Research ....Dr. Andrew CONWAY
108 AVP Institutional Effectiveness ....Dr. Teresa SHAW
15 Assoc VP for Human Resources ....Ms. Brenda LESWICK
47 Botany Center ....Dr. Lucinda MCDADE
50 Drucker-Ito Grad School of Mgt ....Dr. Jenny DARROCH
83 Behavioral & Organizational Sci ....Dr. Michelle BLIGH
69 Community & Global Health ....Dr. Alan STACY
53 Educational Studies ....Dr. DeLacy GANLEY
77 Center for Information Science ....Dr. Lorne OLFMAN
81 Mathematical Sciences Institute ....Dr. Henry SCHELLHORN
82 Politics & Economics ....Dr. Michelle BLIGH
73 Arts and Humanities ....Vacant
09 Institutional Research Officer ....Vacant
08 Interim Head Librarian ....Dr. Bonnie CLEMENS
19 Director of Campus Safety ....Mr. Stan SKIPWORTH
21 Assoc VP Finance/Admin ....Vacant
29 Assoc Director of Alumni Engagement ....Ms. Rachel JIMENEZ
32 Asst VP for Student Services ....Vacant
35 Dean of Students ....Ms. Quamina CARTER
36 Director of Career Development ....Dr. Christine KELLY
37 Director Student Financial Aid ....Ms. Kristal GAMMA
85 Director of International Students ....Dr. Ariel CARPENTER
07 Dean of Admissions ....Mr. Timothy COUNCIL
06 Registrar ....Ms. Lindsay STADLER
18 Director of Facilities ....Mr. Michael VILLEGAS
90 AVP/Tech & Info Systems ....Mr. Manoj CHITRE
91 Dir of Enterprise Infrastructure ....Mr. Robert FORD
101 Secretary to the Board ....Ms. Cindy BIERMAN

*Claremont McKenna College (E)

500 E 9th Street, Claremont CA 91711-6400
County: Los Angeles FICE Identification: 001170
Unit ID: 112260
Telephone: (909) 621-8111 Carnegie Class: Bac-A&S
FAX Number: (909) 621-8790 Calendar System: Semester
URL: www.claremontmckenna.edu
Established: 1946 Annual Undergrad Tuition & Fees: $54,405
Enrollment: 1,345 Coed
Affiliation or Control: Independent Non-Profit IRS Status: 501(c)3
Highest Offering: Master's
Accreditation: WC

02 President and CEO ....Hiram E. CHODOSH
05 VP Academic Affs/Dean Faculty ....Peter UVIN
36 VP Advance/Dean Stdnt Opportunities ....Michelle CHAMBERLAIN
10 Vice Pres of Business and COO ....Coreen RODGERS
11 VP for Planning and Administration ....Matthew G. BIBBENS
32 VP Student Affairs/Dean of Students ....Sharon BASSO
115 Pres/CEO Claremont Invest Mgmt Co ....James J. FLOYD
13 VP/Chief Information Officer ....James J. FLOYD
29 Asst Vice Pres Alumni/Parent Rels ....Evan RUTTER
07 AVP & Dean Admission/Financial Aid ....Vacant
26 Assoc VP Public Affs/Communications ....Peter HONG
14 Assoc VP/Chief Technology Officer ....Cynthia HUMES
88 Dean of Robert Day Scholars Program ....Michelle CHAMBERLAIN
06 Registrar/Dir Institutional Rsrch ....Elizabeth MORGAN
15 Director of Human Resources ....Andrea GALE
104 Director of Off-Campus Study ....Kristen MALLORY
41 Director of Athletics ....Erica PERKINS JASPER
04 Special Assistant to the President ....Cheryl M. AGUILAR

*Claremont School of Theology (F)

1325 N College Avenue, Claremont CA 91711-3199
County: Los Angeles FICE Identification: 001288
Unit ID: 124283
Telephone: (909) 447-2500 Carnegie Class: Spec-4-yr-Faith
FAX Number: (909) 626-7062 Calendar System: Semester
URL: www.cst.edu
Established: 1885 Annual Graduate Tuition & Fees: N/A
Enrollment: 393 Coed
Affiliation or Control: United Methodist IRS Status: 501(c)3
Highest Offering: Doctorate; No Undergraduates
Accreditation: WC, THEOL

02 President ....Dr. Jeffrey KUAN
04 Exec Assistant to the President ....Ms. Maria Lise IANNUZZI
10 Vice Pres for Business Affairs/CFO ....Mr. Gamward QUAN
05 Vice Pres Academic Affairs & Dean ....Dr. Sheryl KUJAWA-HOLBROOK
88 Vice President for Intl Relations ....Dr. JongOh LEE
20 Assoc Dean/VP Curriculum/ Assessment ....Rev. Belva Brown JORDAN
08 Dean of Library & Info Services ....Dr. Tom PHILLIPS
32 Assoc Dean Student & Community Life ....Ms. Lea APPLETON
111 VP Advancement & Communications ....Ms. Sharalyn HAMILTON
26 Director of Communications ....Ms. Kendra FREDRICKSON-LAOUINI
29 Director of Alumni/ae Relations ....Rev. Les LENGREN
21 Controller ....Vacant
07 Dir Admissions/Enrollment Svcs ....Mr. Nathan ARAUJO
37 Sr Dir Fin Aid & Enrollment Service ....Ms. Brenda NIEVES
06 Registrar ....Ms. Sansu WOODMANCY
42 Director of Field Education ....Ms. Alma JOHNSON-HAWKINS
28 Campus Diversity Officer ....Ms. Christine WHANG

*Keck Graduate Institute (G)

535 Watson Drive, Claremont CA 91711-4817
County: Los Angeles FICE Identification: 038533
Unit ID: 440031
Telephone: (909) 607-7855 Carnegie Class: Masters/S
FAX Number: (909) 607-8086 Calendar System: Semester
URL: www.kgi.edu
Established: 1997 Annual Graduate Tuition & Fees: N/A
Enrollment: 591 Coed
Affiliation or Control: Independent Non-Profit IRS Status: 501(c)3
Highest Offering: Doctorate; No Undergraduates
Accreditation: WC, PHAR

00 Board Chair ....James WIDERGREN
02 President/CEO ....Dr. Sheldon M. SCHUSTER
04 Exec Asst to Pres & Secy BOT ....Patricia ROBIDOUX
05 Chief Academic Officer ....Vacant
30 VP Inst Development & Partnerships ....Kelly ESPERIAS
10 VP for Finance & Operations ....Michael JONES
06 Registrar ....Melissa S. BROWN
32 Dean of Students ....Dr. Cynthia MARTINEZ
76 Dean School of Applied Life Science ....Steven CASPER
67 Dean School of Pharmacy & Health ....Gail ORUM
46 Dean of Research ....Larry GRILL
123 Dean of Admissions/Financial Aid ....Sofia TORO
35 Assistant Dir Student Affairs ....Andrea MOZQUEDA
21 Asst VP Finance & Business Svcs ....David CARTER
15 Director Human Resources ....Cheryl MERRITT
16 Manager Human Resources ....Michelle VEGA
18 Director of Facilities ....Mark BENNETT
37 Director Financial Aid ....Maryville TUZON
09 Director of Institutional Research ....Royal DAWSON
88 Chief Dev Ofcr School of Medicine ....Molly CHESTNUT
110 Sr Director Inst Development ....Juliet NUSBAUM
102 Dir Corporate & Found Philanthropy ....Mary GEISSLER
29 External Relations & Giving Officer ....Sandi MERO
25 Dir Sponsored Research Services ....Kirsten TORGUSON
26 Sr Dir Marketing & Communications ....Ivan ALBER
120 Dir Instructional Design & Dev ....George BRADFORD
13 Director IT ....William ROBERTS

Claremont Lincoln University (H)

250 West First Street Ste 330, Claremont CA 91711
County: Los Angeles Identification: 667215
Unit ID: 488387
Telephone: (909) 667-4400 Carnegie Class: Spec-4-yr-Bus
FAX Number: (909) 399-3443 Calendar System: Quarter
URL: claremontlincoln.edu
Established: 2011 Annual Graduate Tuition & Fees: N/A

Enrollment: 107 Coed
Affiliation or Control: Independent Non-Profit IRS Status: 501(c)3
Highest Offering: Master's; No Undergraduates
Accreditation: WC

01 Interim CEO .... Mr. Tony DIGIOVANNI
05 VP for Academic Affairs .... Dr. David CARTER
32 Dean of Student Affairs .... Dr. Diana ASAAD
111 VP for University Advancement .... Ms. Melissa PULS
10 Chief Financial Officer .... Ms. Linda RABITOY
35 Director of Student Relations .... Ms. Clair BACA
04 Executive Asst to President .... Ms. Judy MORAVITZ
30 Director of Development .... Ms. Sara GERTLER
15 Director of Administrative Services .... Ms. Nancy BARNES
37 Director Student Financial Aid .... Mr. Cesar PEREZ
06 Registrar .... Ms. Clair BACA
11 Chief Operating Officer .... Mr. Joseph SALLUSTIO

CNI College (A)

610 East St. Andrew Place, Ste 200, Santa Ana CA 92702
County: Orange FICE Identification: 032423
Unit ID: 433013
Telephone: (714) 437-9697 Carnegie Class: Spec-4-yr-Other Health
FAX Number: (714) 437-9356 Calendar System: Other
URL: www.cnicollege.edu
Established: 1994 Annual Undergrad Tuition & Fees: N/A
Enrollment: 403 Coed
Affiliation or Control: Proprietary IRS Status: Proprietary
Highest Offering: Baccalaureate
Accreditation: ABHES, NURSE, SURTEC

01 President .... Mr. James BUFFINGTON

*Coast Community College District Administration Offices (B)

1370 Adams Avenue, Costa Mesa CA 92626-5429
County: Orange FICE Identification: 008711
Unit ID: 112376
Telephone: (714) 438-4600 Carnegie Class: N/A
FAX Number: (714) 438-4882
URL: www.cccd.edu

01 Chancellor .... Dr. John WEISPFENNING
10 Vice Chancellor Finance & Adm Svcs .... Dr. Andrew DUNN
05 Vice Chanc Educ Svcs & Technology .... Dr. Andreea SERBAN
15 Vice Chanc Human Resources .... Dr. Marco BAEZA
26 Dir Public Affairs/Mktg/Govt .... Ms. Letitia CLARK
96 Director of Purchasing .... Mr. John ERIKSEN

*Coastline Community College (C)

11460 Warner Avenue, Fountain Valley CA 92708-2597
County: Orange FICE Identification: 020635
Unit ID: 112385
Telephone: (714) 546-7600 Carnegie Class: Assoc/HT-Mix Trad/Non
FAX Number: (714) 241-6277 Calendar System: Semester
URL: www.coastline.edu
Established: 1976 Annual Undergrad Tuition & Fees (In-District): $1,150
Enrollment: 11,172 Coed
Affiliation or Control: State/Local IRS Status: 501(c)3
Highest Offering: Associate Degree
Accreditation: WJ

02 President .... Dr. Loretta P. ADRIAN
05 Vice Pres of Instruction .... Mr. Vince RODRIGUEZ
10 VP of Administrative Services .... Ms. Christine NGUYEN
32 Vice Pres Student Services .... Dr. Kate MUELLER
38 Dean Counseling/Matriculation .... Dr. Bruce KEELER
106 Assoc Dean of Distance Learning .... Mr. Bob NASH
12 Dean of Instruction Newport Beach .... Dr. Tom NEAL
12 Dean Instruct Tech Ed Garden Grove .... Dr. Nancy JONES
79 Dean Instruction Hum/Basic Skills .... Dr. Dana EMERSON
20 Dean Innovative Learning .... Dr. Shelly BLAIR
56 Exec Dean Extended Learning .... Ms. Joycelyn GROOT
26 Director Public Relations/Marketing .... Ms. Dawn WILLSON
07 Director of Admissions/Records .... Ms. Jennifer MCDONALD
37 Interim Director of Financial Aid .... Mr. David LEVY
18 Director Maintenance & Operations .... Mr. Mark THISSELL
21 Director Business Services .... Mr. Derek BUI
102 Exec Director College Foundation .... Ms. Mariam KHOSRAVANI
09 Dir Research/Planning/Development .... Dr. Aeron ZENTNER
24 Director of Electronic Media .... Ms. Judy GARVEY
15 Director of Personnel Services .... Ms. Renate AKINS
35 Director Student Life .... Mr. Nathan BRAIS
13 Director of Information Technology .... Mr. Dave THOMPSON
04 Admin Assistant to the President .... Ms. Laila MERTZ
19 Director Security/Safety .... Mr. Mike COLVER

*Golden West College (D)

15744 Golden West Street,
Huntington Beach CA 92647-2748
County: Orange FICE Identification: 001206
Unit ID: 115126
Telephone: (714) 892-7711 Carnegie Class: Assoc/HT-High Trad
FAX Number: (714) 895-8243 Calendar System: Semester
URL: www.goldenwestcollege.edu
Established: 1966 Annual Undergrad Tuition & Fees (In-District): $1,178
Enrollment: 11,610 Coed
Affiliation or Control: State/Local IRS Status: Exempt
Highest Offering: Associate Degree
Accreditation: WJ, ADNUR

02 President .... Mr. Tim MCGRATH
05 Acting VP Instruction .... Mr. Albert GASPARIAN
32 Vice Pres Student Services .... Dr. Claudia LEE
11 Vice Pres Admin Services .... Ms. Janet M. HOULIHAN
38 Dean Counseling .... Dr. Robyn BRAMMER
50 Executive Dean Business & Career Ed .... Mr. Christopher WHITESIDE
81 Interim Dean Math & Science .... Mr. Rick HICKS
49 Dean Arts & Letters .... Dr. David D. HUDSON
66 Dir School of Nursing .... Vacant
23 Director Student Health Svcs .... Dr. Judy CHENG
09 Dean Research/Plng/Inst Effect .... Dr. Kay NGUYEN
61 Dean Criminal Justice .... Mr. Ron LOWENBERG
35 Dean of Students and Library .... Ms. Carla MARTINEZ
84 Dean Enrollment Services .... Ms. Christina RYAN RODRIGUEZ
83 Dean Social Sci/Kines/Lrng Res .... Dr. Alex MIRANDA
15 Director Human Resources .... Ms. Danielle HEINBUCH
10 Director Fiscal Services .... Mr. Paul WISNER
102 Director Foundation .... Mr. Bruce BERMAN
88 Coord Scholarships & Spec Events .... Ms. Valerie A. VENEGAS
07 Director of Enrollment Services .... Ms. Jennifer L. ORTBERG
37 Director of Financial Aid .... Ms. Adrienne BURTON
18 Director Maintenance & Operations .... Mr. Joseph B. DOWLING
68 Acting Athletic Director .... Mr. Danny JOHNSON
04 Admin Asst to the President .... Ms. Diana RETES
19 Dir Public Safety/Emerg Prep .... Mr. Jon ARNOLD
35 Dir Student Life & Leadership Dev .... Mr. Frank CIRIONI
26 Dir Marketing & Public Relations .... Ms. Pam BRASHEAR
104 Dir of Global & Cultural Programs .... Ms. Melissa LYON
90 Dir Academic & User Support Svcs .... Mr. Kevin HARRISON
106 Dir Online Instruction .... Mr. Jorge ASCENCIO
31 Dir Community Educ & Swapmeet .... Ms. Candy LUNDELL
88 Dir Guided Pathways/Dual Enroll .... Mr. Matt VALERIUS
88 Dir EOP&S .... Ms. Natalie TIMPSON
22 Dir DSPS .... Dr. Chad BOWMAN

*Orange Coast College (E)

2701 Fairview Road, POB 5005,
Costa Mesa CA 92628-5005
County: Orange FICE Identification: 001250
Unit ID: 120342
Telephone: (714) 432-0202 Carnegie Class: Assoc/HT-High Trad
FAX Number: (714) 432-5609 Calendar System: Semester
URL: www.orangecoastcollege.edu
Established: 1947 Annual Undergrad Tuition & Fees (In-District): $1,186
Enrollment: 22,156 Coed
Affiliation or Control: State/Local IRS Status: 501(c)3
Highest Offering: Associate Degree
Accreditation: WJ, ACFEI, COARC, CVT, DA, DIETT, DMS, NDT, POLYT, RAD

02 President .... Ms. Angelica SUAREZ
05 Vice President Instruction .... Mr. Kevin BALLINGER
32 Vice President Student Services .... Dr. Madjid NIROUMAND
10 Director of Fiscal Services .... Ms. Rachel KUBIK
11 Vice President Admin Services .... Dr. Richard PAGEL
84 Dean Enrollment Services .... Ms. Rozanne CAPOCCIA-WHITE
38 Dean of Counseling .... Dr. Renee DE LONG
32 Dean of Students .... Dr. Derek VERGARA
88 Associate Dean Title IX .... Ms. Shannon QUIHUIZ
35 Director Student Life .... Mr. Michael MORVICE
26 Director Marketing & PR .... Mr. Juan GUTIERREZ
111 Exec Dir Institutional Advancement .... Mr. Douglas BENNETT
09 Admin Dir Research/Planning/IE .... Ms. Sheri STERNER
07 Director Admiss/Records/Enroll Tech .... Mr. Efren GALVAN
15 Director HR & Staff Develop .... Ms. Rebecca MORGAN
06 Manager Enrollment Services .... Ms. Richelle PENALBA
18 Director Maintenance & Operations .... Mr. Jose RECINOS
37 Director Financial Aid .... Ms. Tanisha BRADFIELD
13 Director Information Technology .... Ms. Sandy WHITESIDE
23 Director Student Health Services .... Ms. Kelly DALY
88 Director Children's Center .... Ms. Patricia MENDOZA
41 Dean Kinesiology & Athletics .... Dr. Michael SUTLIFF
88 Dean Consumer Health & Sciences .... Dr. Jane MCLAUGHLIN
72 Dean of Technology .... Dr. Daniel SHRADER
50 Dean of Business & Computer Science .... Dr. Ronald JOHNSON
83 Dean of Social & Behavioral Science .... Dr. Kevin HENSON
88 Dean of Literature & Languages .... Dr. Michael MANDELKERN
81 Dean of Math & Sciences .... Dr. Tara GIBLIN
57 Dean of Visual & Performing Arts .... Ms. Larissa NAZARENKO
25 Director CTE/Grants .... Ms. Lisa KNUPPEL
19 Interim Director Campus Security .... Mr. James RUDY
40 Manager Bookstore .... Mr. Todd MURPHY
85 Assoc Dean Global Engagement Ctr .... Mr. Nathan JENSEN
121 Dean Student Success & Student Svcs .. Mr. Stephen TAMANAHA
04 Executive Asst to President .... Ms. Thuy NGUYEN
08 Dean Library & Learning Support .... Mr. John TAYLOR
88 Director Marine Programs .... Mr. Brad AVERY
88 Director Disabled Student Services .... Ms. Vanessa DOMINGUEZ

Cogswell Polytechnical College (F)

191 Baypointe Parkway, San Jose CA 95134-1697
County: Santa Clara FICE Identification: 001177
Unit ID: 112394
Telephone: (408) 498-5100 Carnegie Class: Bac-Diverse
FAX Number: (408) 877-7373 Calendar System: Trimester
URL: www.cogswell.edu
Established: 1887 Annual Undergrad Tuition & Fees: $20,056
Enrollment: 608 Coed
Affiliation or Control: Proprietary IRS Status: Proprietary
Highest Offering: Baccalaureate
Accreditation: WC

01 CEO .... Mr. Charles RESTIVO
05 Dean of Education .... Mr. Jerome SOLOMON
10 Chief Financial Officer .... Ms. Ilona KREYNIS
26 VP of Marketing .... Mr. Eric RAJASALU
13 VP Info Technology/Campus Svcs .... Dr. Audrey FEDIN
09 Vice Pres Inst Research & QA .... Ms. Milla ZLATANOV
07 VP of Admissions .... Ms. Sheri STEIN
88 VP of Compliance .... Dr. Reba SMITH
32 Dean of Students .... Vacant
06 Registrar .... Ms. Angela ACUNA
04 Executive Assistant to President .... Ms. Monique TAYLOR
02 Provost and CAO .... Dr. Brian SHEPARD
36 Dir Career Services .... Ms. Rosa TADEO
08 Librarian & Resource Center Manager . Ms. Louise PASTERNACK
37 Director of Financial Aid .... Ms. Janett CABANERO

The Colburn School (G)

200 S Grand Avenue, Los Angeles CA 90012-3007
County: Los Angeles Identification: 666233
Telephone: (213) 621-2200 Carnegie Class: Not Classified
FAX Number: (213) 621-2110 Calendar System: Semester
URL: www.colburnschool.edu
Established: 2003 Annual Undergrad Tuition & Fees: N/A
Enrollment: N/A Coed
Affiliation or Control: Independent Non-Profit IRS Status: 501(c)3
Highest Offering: Master's
Accreditation: MUS

01 President & CEO .... Mr. Sel KARDAN
05 Provost .... Dr. Adrian DALY
03 Senior Vice President .... Mr. Ed HORNER
26 Vice President Communications .... Ms. Jennifer KALLEND
111 Vice President Advancement .... Ms. Annie WICKERT
15 Vice Pres Human Resources .... Ms. Linda CORMIER
10 Chief Financial Officer .... Mr. Seth WEINTRAUB

† Full room, board, and tuition are provided to accepted students through the school's endowment.

College of the Canyons (H)

26455 Rockwell Canyon Road,
Santa Clarita CA 91355-1899
County: Los Angeles FICE Identification: 008903
Unit ID: 111461
Telephone: (661) 259-7800 Carnegie Class: Assoc/HT-Mix Trad/Non
FAX Number: (661) 259-8302 Calendar System: Semester
URL: www.canyons.edu
Established: 1967 Annual Undergrad Tuition & Fees (In-District): $1,156
Enrollment: 20,008 Coed
Affiliation or Control: State/Local IRS Status: 501(c)3
Highest Offering: Associate Degree
Accreditation: WJ, MLTAD

01 Chancellor SCCCD & President COC ... Dr. Dianne G. VAN HOOK
03 Deputy Chancellor .... Dr. Barry GRIBBONS
05 Int Asst Supt/Vice Pres Instruction .... Mr. Joseph GERDA
10 Asst Supt/VP Business Services .... Ms. Sharlene COLEAL
15 Asst Supt/Vice Pres Human Resources .... Dr. Diane FIERO
18 Asst Supt/VP Facil Plng Op/Const .... Mr. Jim SCHRAGE
32 Asst Superintendent/VP Student Svcs .... Dr. Michael WILDING
103 VP Econ & Workforce Development .... Mr. Jeffrey FORREST
26 VP Public Info/Advoc/Ext Relations .... Mr. Eric HARNISH
13 Vice President Technology .... Dr. James TEMPLE
12 VP Canyon Country Campus and Grants .... Dr. Ryan THEULE
21 Assoc VP Business Services .... Mr. Jason HINKLE
35 Assoc VP Student Services .... Mr. Michael JOSLIN
46 Assoc VP Inst Research & Planning .... Dr. Daylene MEUSCHKE
84 Assoc VP Enrollment Services .... Dr. Jasmine RUYS
20 Int Assoc VP Academic Affairs .... Mr. Omar TORRES
88 Int Assoc VP Educ Pathways .... Mr. Paul WICKLINE
50 Int Dean Sch of Business & AppTech .... Mr. Donald CARLSON
36 Dean Career Svcs and Special Pgms .... Ms. Gina BOGNA
85 Dean Intl Affairs/Global Engagement .... Dr. Jia-Yi CHENG-LEVINE
57 Int Dean Visual & Perf Arts .... Mr. Floyd MOOS
106 Dean Educ Tech/Lrng Res/Dist Educ .... Mr. James GLAPA-GROSSKLAG
75 Dean Career and Technical Educ .... Ms. Harriet HAPPEL
41 Dean PE/Kinesiology and Athl .... Mr. Charles LYON
51 Dean Continuing & Community Educ .... Mr. John MAKEVICH
79 Dean Schs of Human/Social/Beh Sci .... Mr. Andy MCCUTCHEON
88 Dean Campus Services & Ops (CCC) .... Mr. Anthony MICHAELIDES
83 Int Dean Social/Behavioral Science .... Ms. Isabelle SABER
76 Dean Health Prof & Public Safety .... Dr. Micah YOUNG
30 Chief Devel Officer COC Foundation .... Mr. Murray WOOD
102 COO COC Foundation/Int Dir UC .... Ms. Cathy RITZ
88 Sector Navigator Health .... Mr. John CORDOVA
88 Deputy Sector Navigator Adv Manuf .... Mr. Michael BASTINE
88 Exec Director Employee Training .... Mr. John MILBURN
88 Int Deputy Sector Nav/Health .... Ms. Irene ORNELAS
88 Deputy Sector Navigator ICT/DM .... Ms. Paula HODGE
113 Director Student Business Office .... Ms. Kathleen BENZ
37 Director Financial Aid .... Mr. Tom BILBRUCK
88 Director Professional Development .... Ms. Leslie CARR
19 Director Campus Safety .... Ms. Tamela CASTOR
88 Director Fiscal Services .... Ms. Balbir CHANDI
88 Dir Student Dev & Campus Activity .... Ms. Kelly DAPP
105 Director Enterprise Systems .... Mr. Michael DIOQUINO
07 Director Admissions/Records & Onl .... Mr. Steve ERWIN

88 MESA Program Director .... Ms. Amy FOOTE
31 Director of Community Relations .... Ms. Jasmine FOSTER
88 Managing Director SC Perf Arts Ctr .... Ms. Lindsay GAMBINI
90 Director Mgmt Info Systems .... Mr. Mark GARCIA
96 Director Contracts Proc & Risk Mgmt .... Ms. April GRAHAM
27 Managing Dir District Communication .... Mr. John GREEN
88 Director Small Bus Devel Ctr .... Ms. Catherine GROOMS
85 Director Intl Services and Programs .... Mr. Tim HONADEL
14 Director Technology Services .... Mr. Hsiawen HULL
88 Dir Volunteer & Stdnt Employment .... Mr. Yasser ISSA
88 Director Facilities Projects .... Mr. William KARRAT
110 Director of Development Foundation .... Mr. James KNEBLIK
88 Director Art Galleries .... Ms. Pamela LEWIS
23 Director Student Health & Wellness .... Ms. Mary MANUEL
16 Director Human Resource Programs .... Ms. Maria MARTINEZ
28 Director Diversity and Inclusion .... Mr. Flavio MEDINA-MARTIN
16 Dir HR Recruit & Employee Services .... Dr. Rian MEDLIN
88 Director Facilities .... Mr. Jason MUNOZ
88 Director Public Relations & Sports .... Mr. Jesse MUNOZ
31 Director Noncredit Enrollment Svcs .... Ms. Lisa PAVIK
88 Int Dir Educ Futures Grant .... Ms. Gina PETERSON
25 Dir Grant/Categorical Accounting .... Ms. Carolyn SHAW
88 Dir Outreach & School Relations .... Ms. Kari SOFFA
88 Director Veterans Resource Ctr .... Mr. Renard THOMAS
88 Dir Advertising/Social Media .... Ms. Wendy TRUJILLO
88 Director Educational Partnerships .... Mr. Justin WALLACE
120 Director Distance/Accel Learning .... Mr. Brian WESTON
88 Director Civic Center .... Mr. Robin WILLIAMS
88 Director Grants Development .... Ms. Theresa ZUZEVICH
04 Special Assistant to the Chancellor .... Ms. Claudia DUNN
88 Dean Ctr for Applied Technologies .... Dr. Devin DAUGHERTY

College of the Desert (A)

43-500 Monterey Avenue, Palm Desert CA 92260-9399
County: Riverside FICE Identification: 001182
Unit ID: 113573
Telephone: (760) 346-8041 Carnegie Class: Assoc/HT-High Trad
FAX Number: (760) 341-8678 Calendar System: Semester
URL: www.collegeofthedesert.edu
Established: 1958 Annual Undergrad Tuition & Fees (In-District): $1,335
Enrollment: 11,146 Coed
Affiliation or Control: State/Local IRS Status: 501(c)3
Highest Offering: Associate Degree
Accreditation: WJ

01 Superintendent/President .... Dr. Joel L. KINNAMON
05 Vice President Instruction .... Dr. Annebelle NERY
32 VP Student Services .... Mr. Jeff BAKER
10 Vice President Admin Services .... Mr. John RAMONT
15 Acting VP Human Resources .... Dr. Mark ZACOVIC
111 Exec Dir Institutional Advancement .... Ms. Pam HUNTER
102 Exec Dir of Foundation .... Dr. John MOSSER
13 Exec Dir Educational Technology .... Ms. Sherilyn WILLIS
18 Director of Maintenance/Operations .... Mr. Brandon TOEPFER
29 Director Alumni Relations .... Ms. Betsy YOUNG
37 Director Financial Aid .... Ms. Kristen MILLIGAN
21 Interim Director Fiscal Services .... Ms. Virginia ORTEGA
06 Director Admissions and Records .... Mr. Curt LUTTRELL
103 Dir Workforce Solutions/Career Ctr .... Mr. Robert ST JULIANA, II
36 Dir Career/Col Access Pathways .... Ms. Michelle BLEZA
09 Director Institutional Research .... Dr. Daniel MARTINEZ
12 Director Education Centers East .... Ms. Jessica ENDERS
12 Director Education Centers West .... Mr. Scott ADKINS
19 Dir Pub Safety Dept/Emergency Prep .... Mr. Tim NAKAMURA
16 Director Human Resources .... Ms. Andrea STAEHLE
83 Dean of Social Science and Arts .... Ms. Kelly HALL
04 Exec Admin Assistant to President .... Ms. Julia BREYER
08 Dir of Library & Learning Resources .... Mr. Gary GINTHER
79 Dean of Communication & Humanities .... Mr. Dean PAPAS
88 Exec Director Bond & Facilities .... Mr. John WHITE
25 Director Institutional Grants .... Ms. Caroline MALONEY
35 Director Student Life .... Mr. Carlos MALDONADO
38 Dean Counseling Services .... Ms. Amanda PHILLIPS
41 Director of Kinesiology & Athletics .... Mr. Gary PLUNKETT
44 Director Annual Giving .... Mr. Christopher ALVAREZ
50 Dean Applied Sciences and Business .... Ms. Zerryl BECKER
53 Dean Health Sciences and Education .... Ms. Leslie YOUNG
84 Dean Enrollment Services .... Dr. Oscar ESPINOZA-PARRA
81 Dean of Math and Science .... Ms. Karen TABOR

College of Exercise Science, International Sports Sciences Association, LLC (B)

1015 Mark Avenue, Carpinteria CA 93013-2912
County: Santa Barbara FICE Identification: 042434
Unit ID: 485519
Telephone: (800) 650-4772 Carnegie Class: Spec 2-yr-Other
FAX Number: N/A Calendar System: Quarter
URL: https://college.issaonline.edu
Established: 1988 Annual Undergrad Tuition & Fees: N/A
Enrollment: 321 Coed
Affiliation or Control: Proprietary IRS Status: Proprietary
Highest Offering: Baccalaureate
Accreditation: DEAC

01 President & CEO .... Sal A. ARRIA
05 Academic Dean .... Alex HOFFMAN

College of Marin (C)

835 College Avenue, Kentfield CA 94904-2590
County: Marin FICE Identification: 001178
Unit ID: 118347
Telephone: (415) 457-8811 Carnegie Class: Assoc/MT-VT-Mix Trad/Non
FAX Number: (415) 456-6017 Calendar System: Semester
URL: www.marin.edu
Established: 1926 Annual Undergrad Tuition & Fees (In-District): $1,492
Enrollment: 5,749 Coed
Affiliation or Control: State/Local IRS Status: 501(c)3
Highest Offering: Associate Degree
Accreditation: WJ, DA

01 Superintendent/President .... Dr. David W. COON
32 VP Student Svcs & Success .... Mr. Jonathan ELDRIDGE
10 Vice President Finance & Oper .... Mr. Greg NELSON
05 Asst VP Instructional Support .... Ms. Cari TORRES
15 Exec Dir Human Res/Labor Relations .... Ms. Kristina A. COMBS
84 Dean Enrollment Services .... Mr. Jon HORINEK
49 Dean Arts & Humanities .... Dr. David SNYDER
103 Dean Career & Tech Education .... Ms. Elizabeth PRATT
81 Dean Math/Sciences .... Dr. Carol HERNANDEZ
21 Director Fiscal Services .... Ms. Peggy ISOZAKI
09 Exec Dir Plng/Research/Inst Plng .... Dr. Christina LEIMER
37 Asst Dean Enroll/Financial Aid .... Vacant
18 Dir Facil Planning & M&O .... Mr. Klaus CHRISTIANSEN
13 CIO & Director of IT .... Mr. Patrick EKOUE-TOTOU
35 Dir Student Activities/Advocacy .... Ms. Sadika SULAIMAN HARA
19 Chief of Police .... Mr. Jeff MAROZICK
68 Dir Kinesiolgy/Athletics .... Mr. Ryan BYRNE
76 Dean Health Sciences .... Dr. Marshall ALAMEIDA
51 Dir Cmty/Lifelong/Intl Education .... Ms. Carol HILDEBRAND
30 Exec Director of Development .... Dr. Linda FRANK
08 Director of Library Services .... Vacant
04 Exec Asst to Pres/Board .... Ms. Micol A. BENET
43 General Counsel .... Ms. Mia ROBERTSHAW

College of the Redwoods Community College District (D)

7351 Tompkins Hill Road, Eureka CA 95501-9300
County: Humboldt FICE Identification: 001185
Unit ID: 121707
Telephone: (707) 476-4100 Carnegie Class: Assoc/HVT-High Trad
FAX Number: (707) 476-4400 Calendar System: Semester
URL: www.redwoods.edu
Established: 1964 Annual Undergrad Tuition & Fees (In-District): $1,182
Enrollment: 4,399 Coed
Affiliation or Control: State/Local IRS Status: 501(c)3
Highest Offering: Associate Degree
Accreditation: WJ, DA, EMT, NAIT

01 President/Superintendent .... Dr. Keith FLAMER
05 Vice President of Instruction .... Dr. Angela HILL
04 Exec Assistant to the President .... Ms. Cynthia PETRUSHA
10 VP Administrative Services .... Ms. Julia MORRISON
32 Vice Pres of Student Development .... Mr. Joseph HASH
103 Director Workforce & Community Educ .... Ms. Pru RATLIFF
15 Director Human Resources/EEO .... Ms. Wendy BATES
12 Director Del Norte Campus .... Mr. Rory JOHNSON
84 Dean of Enrollment Services .... Ms. Rianne CONNOR
88 Director of Special Programs .... Dr. Kinte JOHNSON
22 Director Disabled Student Pgm Svcs .... Ms. Patricia BLAIR
18 Director Maintenance & Operations .... Mr. Steve MCKENZIE
102 Exec Director of the Foundation .... Mr. Marty COELHO
08 Director Library Svcs/Acad Support .... Ms. Cathy COX
19 Director of Public Safety .... Vacant
88 Director Administration of Justice .... Mr. Ron WATERS
41 Director of PE & Athletics .... Mr. Bob BROWN
09 Director Institutional Research .... Mr. Paul CHOWN
26 Career Outreach & Marketing Manager ... Ms. Molly BLAKEMORE

College of the Sequoias (E)

915 S Mooney Boulevard, Visalia CA 93277-2234
County: Tulare FICE Identification: 001186
Unit ID: 123217
Telephone: (559) 730-3700 Carnegie Class: Assoc/HT-High Trad
FAX Number: (559) 730-3894 Calendar System: Semester
URL: www.cos.edu
Established: 1925 Annual Undergrad Tuition & Fees (In-District): $1,390
Enrollment: 12,277 Coed
Affiliation or Control: State/Local IRS Status: 501(c)3
Highest Offering: Associate Degree
Accreditation: WJ, PTAA

01 Superintendent/President .... Mr. Brent CALVIN
05 Vice President Academic Services ..Dr. Jennifer VEGA-LA SERNA
11 Vice President Administrative Svcs .... Mr. Ron BALLASTEROS-PEREZ
114 Dir Budgets & Categorical Accts .... Ms. Leangela MILLER-HERNANDEZ
32 Vice President Student Services .... Ms. Jessica MORRISON
35 Dean Student Services .... Mr. Juan VAZQUEZ
35 Dean Student Services .... Ms. Michele BROCK
35 Dean Student Services .... Ms. Jenny SAE CHAO
12 Provost Tulare Center .... Dr. Louann WALDNER
12 Provost Hanford Center .... Dr. Kristin ROBINSON
81 Dean Science/Math/Eng .... Mr. Francisco BANUELOS
76 Assoc Dean Allied Health .... Dr. Jonna SCHENGEL

49 Dean Arts & Letters .... Mr. Richard LUBBEN
15 Dean Human Resources/Legal Affairs .... Mr. John BRATSCH
18 Dean Facilities .... Mr. Byron WOODS
102 Director Foundation .... Mr. Tim FOSTER
66 Dir Nursing/Allied Health .... Ms. Belen KERSTEN
08 Dir Library/Instructional Tech .... Ms. Mary-Catherine OXFORD
09 Dean of Research .... Dr. Dali OZTURK
06 Registrar/Admissions Coordinator .... Ms. Velia RODRIGUEZ
41 Associate Dean/Athletic Director .... Mr. Brent DAVIS
19 Chief District Police .... Mr. Kevin MIZNER
40 Bookstore Manager .... Mr. Charles SLAGHT
23 Director Health Center .... Ms. Joan DANIELS
35 Dir Student Activities/Affairs .... Ms. Debbie DOUGLASS
103 Dean CTE/Voc Ed .... Mr. Thad RUSSELL
88 Coord Welcome/Transfer Center .... Ms. Catherine MCGUIRE
26 Manager Marketing & PR .... Ms. Lauren FISHBACK
04 Executive Asst to President .... Ms. Meghan TIERCE
13 Dean Info Technology .... Mr. Glen PROFETA
10 Chief Accounting Officer .... Ms. Linda MCCAULEY
106 Coord Distance Education .... Dr. Deborah NOLAN

College of the Siskiyous (F)

800 College Avenue, Weed CA 96094-2899
County: Siskiyou FICE Identification: 001187
Unit ID: 123484
Telephone: (530) 938-5555 Carnegie Class: Assoc/HVT-High Non
FAX Number: (530) 938-5506 Calendar System: Semester
URL: www.siskiyous.edu
Established: 1957 Annual Undergrad Tuition & Fees (In-District): $1,156
Enrollment: 2,111 Coed
Affiliation or Control: State/Local IRS Status: 501(c)3
Highest Offering: Associate Degree
Accreditation: WJ, EMT

01 Superintendent/President .... Dr. Stephen SCHOONMAKER
10 Vice President Administrative Svcs .... Ms. Darlene MELBY
05 Vice President Instruction .... Vacant
32 Vice President Student Services .... Ms. Melissa GREEN
09 Int Dean Research & Evaluation .... Mr. Nathan REXFORD
41 Assoc Dean Instruction/Dir Athletic .... Mr. Dennis ROBERTS
75 Dean Career & Technical Education .... Vacant
07 Director Admissions & Records .... Ms. Meghan WITHERELL
15 Assoc Vice Pres Human Resources .... Ms. Theresa RICHMOND
37 Director Financial Aid .... Ms. Janette HARRIS
18 Director Facilities .... Mr. Eric RULOFSON
111 Dir of Institutional Advancement .... Vacant
28 Director of Diversity .... Ms. Theresa RICHMOND
39 Director Student Housing .... Dr. Doug HAUGEN
26 Dir Comm Relations/Foundation .... Ms. Dawnie SLABAUGH
13 Director of Information Technology .... Mr. Wayne KELLER
103 Director of Workforce Development .... Mr. Mark KLEVER
35 Director of Student Life .... Dr. Doug HAUGEN
36 Assoc Dean Student Success Programs .... Ms. Valerie ROBERTS

Columbia College Hollywood (G)

18618 Oxnard Street, Tarzana CA 91356-1411
County: Los Angeles FICE Identification: 021102
Unit ID: 112570
Telephone: (800) 785-0585 Carnegie Class: Spec-4-yr-Arts
FAX Number: (818) 345-9053 Calendar System: Quarter
URL: www.columbiacollege.edu
Established: 1952 Annual Undergrad Tuition & Fees: $24,495
Enrollment: 453 Coed
Affiliation or Control: Independent Non-Profit IRS Status: 501(c)3
Highest Offering: Baccalaureate
Accreditation: WC

01 President/CEO .... Mr. Bill SMITH
10 Chief Financial Officer .... Mr. Richard CROWE
26 Chief Marketing Officer .... Ms. Kelly STACK
07 Vice President of Admissions .... Ms. Wendi FRANCZYK
05 Interim Dean of Academic Affairs .... Mr. Peter GEND
37 VP Financial Aid .... Mr. Adrian GONZALEZ
11 VP Operations .... Mr. Patrick OLMSTEAD
32 VP Student Affairs .... Ms. Kelly PARKER
108 VP Institutional Effectiveness .... Ms. Lex SANDERSON
06 Registrar .... Ms. Tina OLVERA
36 Sr Dir Career Dev & Alumni Affairs .... Ms. Kelley LEWIS
13 Director of IT and Production Svcs .... Mr. Ronald REEVES
121 Director of Student Success .... Ms. Jessica JOHNSON-MILLS
15 Director of Human Resources .... Ms. Rena WRIGHT
84 Senior Director Admissions .... Ms. Carmen MUNOZ

Community Christian College (H)

1849 N. Wabash Avenue, Redlands CA 92374
County: San Bernardino FICE Identification: 038744
Unit ID: 446163
Telephone: (909) 794-1084 Carnegie Class: Assoc/HT-High Trad
FAX Number: (909) 794-1093 Calendar System: Quarter
URL: www.cccollege.edu
Established: 1995 Annual Undergrad Tuition & Fees: $8,175
Enrollment: 47 Coed
Affiliation or Control: Independent Non-Profit IRS Status: 501(c)3
Highest Offering: Associate Degree
Accreditation: TRACS

01 President .... Mr. Brian CARROLL
05 Vice Pres of Academic Affairs .... Dr. Robert GEE
10 Vice Pres Finance/Operations .... Mr. Richard DURANT

Compton College (A)

1111 E Artesia Boulevard, Compton CA 90221-5393
County: Los Angeles FICE Identification: 001188
Unit ID: 112686
Telephone: (310) 900-1600 Carnegie Class: Assoc/MT-VT-Mix Trad/Non
FAX Number: (310) 605-1458 Calendar System: Semester
URL: www.compton.edu
Established: 1927 Annual Undergrad Tuition & Fees (In-State): $1,142
Enrollment: 7,422 Coed
Affiliation or Control: State IRS Status: 501(c)3
Highest Offering: Associate Degree
Accreditation: WJ

01 President/CEO Compton Cmty Col Dist ....Dr. Keith CURRY
03 Vice President Compton College .... Ms. Barbara PEREZ
32 Vice President Student Services .... Ms. Elizabeth MARTINEZ
10 Vice Pres Finance/Admin Svcs .... Mr. Steven HAIGLER
15 Vice President Human Resources .... Mrs. Rachelle SASSER
05 Dean Academic Affairs .... Vacant
76 Dean Health/Human Services .... Ms. Wanda MORRIS
41 Dir Student Development/Athletics .... Mr. Junior DOMINGO
08 Director Learning Resources .... Mr. Rodney MURRAY
88 Director CalWORKs & DSPS .... Ms. Patricia BONACIC
22 Director EOP & S/CARE .... Ms. Christine ALDRICH
09 Director Institutional Research .... Vacant
37 Director Financial Aid .... Dr. Mytha PASCUAL
84 Int Dir Enrollment Management .... Ms. Nelly ALVARADO
21 Director Fiscal Affairs .... Mr. Ruben JAMES
18 Dir Facilities Plng/Operations .... Ms. Linda OWENS
13 Dir Information Technology Services .... Mr. Andrei YERMAKOV
07 Director Admissions & Records .... Ms. Richette BELL

† Regional accreditation is carried under the parent institution in Torrance, CA.

Concorde Career College (B)

12951 S. Euclid Street, Suite 101,
Garden Grove CA 92840-1451
County: Orange FICE Identification: 008071
Unit ID: 123679
Telephone: (714) 703-1900 Carnegie Class: Spec 2-yr-Health
FAX Number: (714) 530-8421 Calendar System: Semester
URL: www.concorde.edu
Established: 1960 Annual Undergrad Tuition & Fees: N/A
Enrollment: 577 Coed
Affiliation or Control: Proprietary IRS Status: Proprietary
Highest Offering: Associate Degree
Accreditation: ACCSC, COARC, DH, PTAA

01 Campus President .... Ms. Lisa RHODES

Concorde Career College (C)

12412 Victory Boulevard, North Hollywood CA 91606-3134
County: Los Angeles FICE Identification: 007607
Unit ID: 124937
Telephone: (818) 766-8151 Carnegie Class: Spec 2-yr-Health
FAX Number: (818) 766-1587 Calendar System: Quarter
URL: www.concorde.edu
Established: 1955 Annual Undergrad Tuition & Fees: N/A
Enrollment: 671 Coed
Affiliation or Control: Proprietary IRS Status: Proprietary
Highest Offering: Associate Degree
Accreditation: ACCSC, COARC, PTAA

01 Campus President .... Carmen BOWEN
05 Academic Dean .... Michelle ARMAS
07 Director of Admissions .... Allan GUECO
37 Director Student Financial Aid .... Cynthia STEIN

Concorde Career College (D)

201 E Airport Drive, San Bernadino CA 92408
County: San Bernardino FICE Identification: 008537
Unit ID: 124706
Telephone: (909) 884-8891 Carnegie Class: Spec 2-yr-Health
FAX Number: (909) 884-1831 Calendar System: Semester
URL: www.concorde.edu
Established: 1970 Annual Undergrad Tuition & Fees: N/A
Enrollment: 617 Coed
Affiliation or Control: Proprietary IRS Status: Proprietary
Highest Offering: Associate Degree
Accreditation: ACCSC, COARC, DH, NDT, POLYT

01 Campus President .... Nick EWELL

Concorde Career College (E)

4393 Imperial Avenue, Suite 100,
San Diego CA 92113-1962
County: San Diego FICE Identification: 007930
Unit ID: 120661
Telephone: (619) 688-0800 Carnegie Class: Spec 2-yr-Health
FAX Number: (619) 220-4177 Calendar System: Other
URL: www.concorde.edu
Established: 1966 Annual Undergrad Tuition & Fees: N/A
Enrollment: 581 Coed
Affiliation or Control: Proprietary IRS Status: Proprietary
Highest Offering: Associate Degree
Accreditation: ACCSC, DH, PTAA, SURGT

01 Campus President .... Ms. Rachel SAFFEL
06 Registrar .... Ms. Amy KRUEGER
07 Director of Admissions .... Ms. Kelly ACKERSON

Concordia University Irvine (F)

1530 Concordia West, Irvine CA 92612-3299
County: Orange FICE Identification: 020705
Unit ID: 112075
Telephone: (949) 854-8002 Carnegie Class: Masters/L
FAX Number: (949) 214-3520 Calendar System: Semester
URL: www.cui.edu
Established: 1972 Annual Undergrad Tuition & Fees: $35,400
Enrollment: 4,249 Coed
Affiliation or Control: Lutheran Church - Missouri Synod
IRS Status: 501(c)3
Highest Offering: Doctorate
Accreditation: WC, #CAATE, CACREP, IACBE, MUS, NURSE

01 President .... Dr. Kurt J. KRUEGER
05 Exec Vice Pres Acad Affairs/Provost .... Dr. Peter SENKBEIL
11 Exec VP/COO .... Dr. Gary R. MCDANIEL
111 Exec VP Advancement .... Mr. Timothy J. JAEGER
10 Exec VP/Chief Financial Officer .... Mr. Kevin TILDEN
20 Assoc Provost .... RevDr. Scott ASHMON
49 Dean School of Arts & Sciences .... Dr. Terry OLSON
50 Dean of Business .... Mr. George WRIGHT
107 Dean School of Professional Studies .... Mr. Mike SHURANCE
53 Dean School of Education .... Dr. Deborah MERCIER
73 Dean Christ College .... RevDr. Steven P. MUELLER
06 Registrar .... Ms. Dessa SOPER
09 Director of Institutional Research .... Mrs. Deborah LEE
32 Dean of Students .... Dr. Gilbert FUGITT
07 Director of Undergrad Admissions .... Ms. Susan PARK
123 Sr Director of Graduate Admissions .... Mr. Justin MOSCHINA
37 Director of Financial Aid .... Ms. Lori MCDONALD
113 Bursar .... Mr. Edgar LOPEZ
43 AVP & General Counsel .... Mr. Ronald VAN BLARCOM
15 Interim Dir of Human Resources .... Mrs. Melinda MARTINEZ
08 Director of Library Services .... Ms. Laura GUZMAN
41 Athletic Director .... Mr. Mo ROBERSON
35 Assoc Dean of Students .... Ms. Kristy FOWLER
19 Director Security/Safety .... Mr. Steven RODRIGUEZ
29 Exec Director of Alumni Relations .... Mr. Michael BERGLER
24 Senior Director of Faculty Training .... Prof. John RANDALL
36 Director of Career Services .... Mrs. Victoria JAFFEE
13 Director of IT Services .... Mr. Chris HARRIS
28 Director of Inclusion/Diversity .... Dr. Terilyn WALKER
106 Exec Dir Innov Instruction & eLrng .... Dr. Jason NEBEN

*Contra Costa Community College District Office (G)

500 Court Street, Martinez CA 94553-1278
County: Contra Costa FICE Identification: 001189
Unit ID: 112817
Telephone: (925) 229-1000 Carnegie Class: N/A
FAX Number: (925) 370-2019
URL: www.4cd.edu

01 Chancellor .... Dr. Fred E. WOOD
05 Exec VC Education & Technology ...... Ms. Mojdeh MEHDIZADEH
11 Exec VC Administrative Services .... Mr. Eugene C. HUFF
20 Assoc Vice Chanc Education Svcs .... Ms. Kelly SCHELIN
18 VC Facilities Plng/Construction .... Ms. Ines ZILDZIC
10 Assoc Vice Chanc/CFO .... Mr. Johah NICHOLAS
15 Assoc Vice Chanc Human Resources .... Mr. Dio SHIPP

*Contra Costa College (H)

2600 Mission Bell Drive, San Pablo CA 94806-3195
County: Contra Costa FICE Identification: 001190
Unit ID: 112826
Telephone: (510) 235-7800 Carnegie Class: Assoc/MT-VT-Mix Trad/Non
FAX Number: (510) 236-6768 Calendar System: Semester
URL: www.contracosta.edu
Established: 1948 Annual Undergrad Tuition & Fees (In-District): $1,312
Enrollment: 6,727 Coed
Affiliation or Control: State/Local IRS Status: 501(c)3
Highest Offering: Associate Degree
Accreditation: WJ

02 Acting President .... Mojdheh MEHDIZADEH
03 Vice President of Academic Affairs .... Vacant
10 Director of Business Services .... Ms. Mariles MAGALONG
108 Dean Inst Effectiveness & Equity .... Dr. Mayra PADILLA
26 Director of Marketing/Media Design .... Ms. Brandy HOWARD
30 Foundation/Development Officer .... Ms. Sara MARCELLINO
05 Senior Dean of Instruction .... Dr. Tish YOUNG
49 Dean Liberal Arts .... Jason BERNER
76 Interim Dean LAVA .... Sandra MOORE
83 Interim Dean of NSAS .... Ameer THOMPSON
32 Dean of Student Services .... Mr. Dennis FRANCO
84 Dean of Enrollment Services .... Mr. Rod SANTOS
103 Dean Workforce & Econ Development .... Vacant
07 Director Admissions & Records .... Ms. Catherine FROST
41 Athletics Director .... Mr. John WADE
09 Director of Institutional Research .... Vacant
18 Manager Buildings & Grounds .... Mr. Bruce KING
37 Financial Aid Supervisor .... Ms. Monica RODRIGUEZ
04 Senior Exec Asst to the President .... Ms. Joy BRUCELAS

*Diablo Valley College (I)

321 Golf Club Road, Pleasant Hill CA 94523-1544
County: Contra Costa FICE Identification: 001191
Unit ID: 113634
Telephone: (925) 685-1230 Carnegie Class: Assoc/HT-High Trad
FAX Number: (925) 685-1551 Calendar System: Semester
URL: www.dvc.edu
Established: 1949 Annual Undergrad Tuition & Fees (In-District): $1,312
Enrollment: 19,775 Coed
Affiliation or Control: State/Local IRS Status: 501(c)3
Highest Offering: Associate Degree
Accreditation: WJ, ACFEI, DA, DH

02 President .... Ms. Susan LAMB
05 Vice President Instruction .... Ms. Mary GUTIERREZ
32 Vice President Student Services .... Dr. Newin ORANTE
10 Vice Pres Business & Admin Svcs .... Vacant
20 Senior Dean of Curriculum & Instr .... Ms. Kimberely SCHENK
84 Dean Outreach/Enroll Mgt/ Matric .... Ms. Elizabeth HAUSCARRIAGUE
12 Dean San Ramon Campus .... Mr. Mike HOLZCLAW
41 Dean of PE/Athl/Dance/Athletic Dir .... Ms. Christine WORSLEY
62 Dean Library/Ed Tech & Learn Sup .... Mr. Rick ROBISON
26 Dir of Marketing & Communications .... Ms. Chrisanne KNOX
57 Dean Applied & Fine Arts .... Ms. Toni FANNIN
81 Dean Phys Sci/Bio Sci .... Mr. Joe GORGA
83 Dean English & Social Science .... Mr. Obed VAZQUEZ
50 Dean Business Ed/Math/Comp Sci ...... Ms. Despina PRAPAVESSI
06 Registrar/Admissions .... Ms. Stephanie ALVES
35 Dean Student Support Services .... Ms. Emily STONE

*Los Medanos College (J)

2700 E Leland Road, Pittsburg CA 94565-5197
County: Contra Costa FICE Identification: 010340
Unit ID: 117894
Telephone: (925) 439-2181 Carnegie Class: Assoc/HT-High Trad
FAX Number: (925) 427-1599 Calendar System: Semester
URL: www.losmedanos.edu
Established: 1973 Annual Undergrad Tuition & Fees (In-District): $1,312
Enrollment: 9,048 Coed
Affiliation or Control: State/Local IRS Status: 501(c)3
Highest Offering: Associate Degree
Accreditation: WJ

02 President .... Dr. Bob KRATOCHVIL
04 Senior Executive Assistant .... Ms. Jennifer ADAMS
05 VP Instruction .... Dr. Sally MONTEMAYOR LENZ
10 VP Business & Admin Services .... Dr. Carlos MONTOYA
32 VP of Student Services .... Dr. Tanisha MAXWELL
45 Sr Dean Plng & Inst Effectiveness .... Dr. Chialin HSIEH
28 Dean of Equity & Inclusion .... Dr. Sabrina T. KWIST
75 Dean Career Tech Educ & Social Sci ..... Ms. Nicolette MOULTRIE
79 Dean of Liberal Arts .... Ms. Nancy YBARRA
81 Dean of Math & Sciences .... Mr. Ryan PEDERSEN
103 Dean Workforce & Econ Development .... Ms. Natalie HANNUM
38 Dean Counseling & Student Support .... Mr. Jeffrey BENFORD
121 Dean of Student Success .... Mr. David BELMAN
124 Dir Student Success/Retention Pgrms .... Ms. Carla ROSAS
36 Director Transfer & Career Services .... Ms. Rachel ANICETTI
88 Dir Student Life & Intl Student Pgm .... Ms. Teresea ARCHAGA
88 Director Early Childhood Lab School .... Vacant
88 Asst Dir EOPS/CARE .... Mr. Steven FREEMAN, JR.
88 Outreach/Assessment Svcs Mgr .... Mr. Jorge CEA
40 Bookstore Manager .... Mr. Robert ESTRADA
88 Manager Disability Support Services .... Ms. Virginia RICHARDS
88 Pgm Mgr Workforce & Econ Dev .... Vacant
18 Buildings & Grounds Manager .... Mr. Russ HOLT
88 Custodial Manager .... Mr. Frank ICHIGAYA
21 Business Office Supervisor .... Mr. Dave VIGO
37 Financial Aid Supervisor .... Ms. Jennifer MA
88 Office of Instruction Supervisor .... Ms. Eileen VALENZUELA
30 Foundation Development Officer .... Dr. Trinh NGUYEN
41 Athletic Director .... Mr. Richard VILLEGAS
19 Police Services .... Lt. Chad WEHRMEISTER

Copper Mountain College (K)

6162 Rotary Way, Box 1398, Joshua Tree CA 92252-6102
County: San Bernardino FICE Identification: 035424
Unit ID: 395362
Telephone: (760) 366-3791 Carnegie Class: Assoc/MT-VT-High Trad
FAX Number: (760) 366-5255 Calendar System: Semester
URL: www.cmccd.edu
Established: 1999 Annual Undergrad Tuition & Fees (In-District): $1,112
Enrollment: 1,844 Coed
Affiliation or Control: State/Local IRS Status: 170(c)1
Highest Offering: Associate Degree
Accreditation: WJ

01 Superintendent/President .... Mr. Daren OTTEN
05 Exec Dean of Academic Affairs/CIO .... Mr. Tony DISALVO
20 Dean of Instruction .... Ms. Melynie SCHIEL
32 Exec Dean of Student Services/CSSO .... Ms. Jane ABELL
15 Chief Human Resources Ofcr .... Ms. Bonnie BILGER
18 Director of Facilities & Operations .... Mr. Kevin COLE
102 Executive Director of Foundation .... Ms. Sandy SMITH
10 Chief Business Officer .... Ms. Meredith PLUMMER
35 Interim Dean of Student Services .... Ms. Jennifer SPARLING
108 Dean of Institutional Effectiveness .... Mr. Jacob KEVARI
66 Coordinator for Nursing Programs .... Ms. Dawn PAGE

13 Director of Information Systems ... Mr. Steve KEMP
26 Public Relations & Event Specialist ... Ms. Jolie ALPIN
04 Executive Asst to the President ... Ms. Crisandra KAUFFMANN
07 Admissions & Records Specialist ... Ms. Lynda BURNS
08 Library Coordinator ... Mr. Derek MONYPENY
41 Athletic Director ... Mr. Ken SIMONDS

Cuesta College (A)

PO Box 8106, San Luis Obispo CA 93403-8106
County: San Luis Obispo FICE Identification: 001192
Unit ID: 113193
Telephone: (805) 546-3100 Carnegie Class: Assoc/HT-Mix Trad/Non
FAX Number: N/A Calendar System: Semester
URL: www.cuesta.edu
Established: 1963 Annual Undergrad Tuition & Fees (In-District): $1,338
Enrollment: 10,836 Coed
Affiliation or Control: State/Local IRS Status: 501(c)3
Highest Offering: Associate Degree
Accreditation: WJ, EMT

01 Superintendent/President ... Dr. Jill STEARNS
05 VP/Asst Supt Academic Affairs ... Dr. Deborah WULFF
10 VP/Asst Supt Administrative Svcs ... Mr. Dan TROY
32 VP/Asst Supt Student Svcs Col Ctrs ... Dr. Mark SANCHEZ
12 Dean North Co Campus/S Co Ctr ... Dr. Maria ESCOBEDO
111 Exec Dir Found/Inst Advancement ... Ms. Shannon HILL
08 Dean Library/Lrng Resources ... Dr. Ryan CARTNAL
88 Coordinator Student Life/Leadership ... Dr. Anthony GUTIERREZ
13 Exec Director Info Sys and Tech ... Mr. Keith STEARNS
66 Director of Nursing ... Ms. Marcia SCOTT
15 Vice Pres Human Resource/Labor Rels . Ms. Melissa RICHERSON
19 Chief of Police/College Safety ... Mr. Bryan MILLARD
40 Director of Bookstore ... Vacant
41 Director of Athletics ... Mr. Robert MARIUCCI
18 Dir Facilities Svcs/Plng/Cap Proj ... Mr. Terry REECE
38 Director Outreach/Enrollment Svcs ... Mr. Jeffery ALEXANDER
103 Dir Workforce Econ Devel Cmty Pgm ... Dr. Matthew GREEN
23 Coordinator of Health Services ... Vacant
81 Dean Acad Affs Sciences & Math ... Dr. Jason CURTIS
79 Dean Acad Affs Arts/Human/Soc Sci ... Ms. Madeline MEDEIROS
103 Dean Acad Affs Workforce Econ Dev ... Dr. John CASCAMO
21 Director Fiscal Services ... Mr. Chris GREEN
102 Director Foundation Programs ... Ms. Karen TACKET
88 Director Foundation Fiscal Services ... Mr. Richard CAMARILLO
25 Director of Grant Development ... Ms. Janet SHEPHARD
04 Executive Asst to President ... Mr. Todd FREDERICK

The Culinary Institute of America at Greystone (B)

2555 Main Street, Saint Helena CA 94574-9504
Telephone: (707) 967-1100 Identification: 666260
Accreditation: &M

† Regional accreditation is carried under the parent institution in Hyde Park, NY.

Deep Springs College (C)

HC 72 Box 45001, Via Dyer, NV 89010-9803
County: Inyo FICE Identification: 001194
Telephone: (760) 872-2000 Carnegie Class: Not Classified
FAX Number: (760) 874-7077 Calendar System: Other
URL: www.deepsprings.edu
Established: 1917 Annual Undergrad Tuition & Fees: $0
Enrollment: N/A Male
Affiliation or Control: Independent Non-Profit IRS Status: 501(c)3
Highest Offering: Associate Degree
Accreditation: WJ

01 President ... Mr. David NEIDORF
05 Academic Dean ... Ms. Sarah STICKNEY
88 Ranch Manager ... Mr. Tim GIPSON
10 Director of Operations ... Mr. Padraic MACLEISH
30 Development Director ... Mr. John DEWIS
06 Registrar/Librarian ... Ms. Gwen VON KLAN
21 Office Manager ... Ms. Niki FRISHMAN
88 Chef/BH Manager ... Ms. Martha CLARK
88 Farm Manager ... Mr. Gabriel DELGADO

† A scholarship covers the costs of tuition, room, and board for every student.

Dell'Arte International School of Physical Theatre (D)

P.O. Box 816, 131 H Street, Blue Lake CA 95525
County: Humboldt FICE Identification: 030256
Unit ID: 113537
Telephone: (707) 668-5663 Carnegie Class: Spec-4-yr-Arts
FAX Number: (707) 668-5665 Calendar System: Other
URL: www.dellarte.com
Established: 1975 Annual Graduate Tuition & Fees: $13,350
Enrollment: 47 Coed
Affiliation or Control: Independent Non-Profit IRS Status: 501(c)3
Highest Offering: Master's; No Undergraduates
Accreditation: THEA

01 Executive Director ... Ms. Fran BEATTY
57 Producing Artistic Director ... Mr. Michael FIELDS
05 School Director ... Ms. Lauren WILSON

10 Finance Director ... Ms. Kathy BAUN
06 Exec School Administrator/PDSO ... Ms. Alyssa HUGHLETT
07 Director of Admissions ... Mr. Matt CHAPMAN
11 School Administrator ... Ms. Rebecca FINNEY

Design Institute of San Diego (E)

8555 Commerce Avenue, San Diego CA 92121-2685
County: San Diego FICE Identification: 022980
Unit ID: 113582
Telephone: (858) 566-1200 Carnegie Class: Spec-4-yr-Arts
FAX Number: (858) 566-2711 Calendar System: Semester
URL: www.disd.edu
Established: 1977 Annual Undergrad Tuition & Fees: $23,860
Enrollment: 126 Coed
Affiliation or Control: Proprietary IRS Status: Proprietary
Highest Offering: Baccalaureate
Accreditation: WC, CIDA

01 CEO ... Ms. Margot DOUCETTE
11 Director of Operations ... Ms. Jessyca ANDREWS
10 Chief Financial Officer ... Mr. Dennis DOUCETTE
05 Program Director ... Ms. Natalia WORDEN
07 Admissions ... Ms. Liz BARRY
37 Director Financial Aid ... Ms. Jackie GLORIA
32 Director of Student Services ... Ms. Tena MOIOLA
08 Library Director ... Ms. Lisa SCHATTMAN
06 Registrar ... Ms. Tracy GULINO
36 Career Advisor ... Mr. Richard HESS

Dharma Realm Buddhist University (F)

4951 Bodhi Way, Ukiah CA 95482
County: Sacramento Identification: 667334
Telephone: (707) 621-7000 Carnegie Class: Not Classified
FAX Number: N/A Calendar System: Semester
URL: www.drbu.org
Established: 1976 Annual Undergrad Tuition & Fees: N/A
Enrollment: N/A Coed
Affiliation or Control: Independent Non-Profit IRS Status: 501(c)3
Highest Offering: Master's
Accreditation: WC

01 President ... Susan ROUNDS
10 VP Finance & Admin/Provost ... Douglas POWERS
05 Dean of Academics ... Martin VERHOEVEN
32 Dean of Students ... Heng LIANG

Dominican School of Philosophy and Theology (G)

2301 Vine Street, Berkeley CA 94708-1816
County: Alameda FICE Identification: 001296
Unit ID: 113704
Telephone: (510) 849-2030 Carnegie Class: Spec-4-yr-Faith
FAX Number: (510) 849-1372 Calendar System: Semester
URL: www.dspt.edu
Established: 1932 Annual Undergrad Tuition & Fees: N/A
Enrollment: 61 Coed
Affiliation or Control: Roman Catholic IRS Status: 501(c)3
Highest Offering: Master's
Accreditation: WC, THEOL

01 President ... Fr. Peter ROGERS
05 Academic Dean ... Rev. Christopher M. RENZ
10 Vice Pres Finance/Administration ... Mr. Ian BROOKS
07 Director of Admissions/Recruitment ... Mr. Aaron ANDERSON
06 Registrar/Student Services ... Ms. Leslie BORQUEZ
26 Director of Communications ... Ms. Heidi MCKENNA
30 Director of Development ... Mr. Marc ROVETTI

Dominican University of California (H)

50 Acacia Avenue, San Rafael CA 94901-2298
County: Marin FICE Identification: 001196
Unit ID: 113698
Telephone: (415) 457-4440 Carnegie Class: Masters/M
FAX Number: (415) 485-3214 Calendar System: Semester
URL: www.dominican.edu
Established: 1890 Annual Undergrad Tuition & Fees: $45,850
Enrollment: 1,744 Coed
Affiliation or Control: Independent Non-Profit IRS Status: 501(c)3
Highest Offering: Master's
Accreditation: WC, #ARCPA, ART, NURSE, OT

01 President ... Dr. Mary B. MARCY
05 Vice President Academic Affairs ... Dr. Nicola PITCHFORD
10 VP Finance and Administration ... Mr. Anthony DECOCINIS
32 Dean of Student Affairs ... Dr. Paul RACCANELLO
84 Vice Pres Enrollment and Marketing ... Ms. Vickie ALLEMAN
111 VP for Advancement ... Ms. Marly NORRIS
97 Dean of General Studies ... Dr. Mojgan BEHMAND
26 Senior Director of Marketing ... Ms. Sierra ALVIS ROBINSON
27 Sr Director Comm & Media Relations ... Ms. Sarah GARDNER
04 Exec Assistant to the President ... Ms. Sandy PEARSON
101 Special Asst to Pres/Board Sec ... Ms. Jennifer KRENGEL
49 Dean Sch Liberal Arts & Education ... Dr. Laura STIVERS
81 Dean Sch Health/Natural Science ... Dr. Ruth RAMSEY
18 Exec Dir Facilities/Auxiliary Svcs ... Mr. John HASHIZUME
08 University Librarian ... Mr. Gary GORKA
09 Director Institutional Research ... Mr. Christopher ANTONS

37 Director Financial Aid ... Ms. Zelotes SMITH
07 Director Undergrad Admissions ... Ms. Maria GENTILE
15 Director Human Resources ... Ms. Wendy LEE
121 Director of Academic Advising ... Ms. Naomi ELVOVE
28 Dean Diversity and Equity ... Dr. Suresh APPAVOO
92 Director Honors Program ... Ms. Lynn SONDAG
38 Director Counseling Center ... Dr. Diane SUFFRIDGE
85 Director of GEO ... Dr. Kati BELL
41 Director of Athletics ... Ms. Amy HENKELMAN
102 Dir Foundation/Corp/Govt Relations ... Ms. Cyndi WEINGARD
108 Director of Assessment ... Vacant

Dongguk University Los Angeles (I)

440 Shatto Place, 2nd floor, Los Angeles CA 90020
County: Los Angeles FICE Identification: 031095
Unit ID: 122117
Telephone: (213) 487-0110 Carnegie Class: Spec-4-yr-Other Health
FAX Number: (213) 487-0527 Calendar System: Quarter
URL: www.dula.edu
Established: 1979 Annual Undergrad Tuition & Fees: N/A
Enrollment: 162 Coed
Affiliation or Control: Independent Non-Profit IRS Status: 501(c)3
Highest Offering: Doctorate; No Lower Division
Accreditation: ACUP

01 President ... Dr. Seung Deok LEE
05 Dean of Academic Affairs ... Dr. Yae CHANG
11 Chief Operating Officer ... Mr. John JEON
37 Director Financial Aid ... Ms. Andreas CHOI
21 Accounting Manager ... Ms. Kelly KIM
04 Office Manager ... Ms. Min PARK
06 Registrar/Program Director ... Mr. Stephen SEO
18 Facilities Manager ... Mr. Emilio LOPEZ

Eagle Rock College (J)

3450 Wilshire Boulevard, Suite 600, Los Angeles CA 90010
County: Los Angeles FICE Identification: 041192
Unit ID: 451005
Telephone: (323) 254-2203 Carnegie Class: Not Classified
FAX Number: (323) 254-2254 Calendar System: Semester
URL: eaglerockcollege.edu
Established: 2001 Annual Undergrad Tuition & Fees: N/A
Enrollment: N/A Coed
Affiliation or Control: Proprietary IRS Status: Proprietary
Highest Offering: Associate Degree
Accreditation: CNCE

01 President & CEO ... Al MOAYERI
32 Exec Vice Pres Student Services ... Ellie MIRAFTABI
26 Exec Vice Pres Marketing/Admissions ... Shah RAZA
37 Sr Financial Aid Officer ... Xiomara GARCIA
06 Registrar ... Rosette MARIANO

East San Gabriel Valley Regional Occupational Program and Technical Center (K)

1501 W. Del Norte Street, West Covina CA 91790
County: Los Angeles FICE Identification: 031166
Unit ID: 413802
Telephone: (626) 472-5121 Carnegie Class: Assoc/HVT-High Non
FAX Number: (626) 472-5125 Calendar System: Semester
URL: www.esgvrop.org
Established: Annual Undergrad Tuition & Fees (In-District): N/A
Enrollment: 118 Coed
Affiliation or Control: State/Local IRS Status: 501(c)3
Highest Offering: Associate Degree
Accreditation: COE, MAC

01 Superintendent ... Dr. Sherry CARTER
10 Chief Financial Officer ... Ms. Leticia COVARRUBIAS

El Camino College (L)

16007 Crenshaw Boulevard, Torrance CA 90506-0002
County: Los Angeles FICE Identification: 001197
Unit ID: 113980
Telephone: (310) 660-3670 Carnegie Class: Assoc/HT-High Trad
FAX Number: (310) 660-7798 Calendar System: Semester
URL: www.elcamino.edu
Established: 1947 Annual Undergrad Tuition & Fees (In-District): $1,144
Enrollment: 24,349 Coed
Affiliation or Control: State/Local IRS Status: 501(c)3
Highest Offering: Associate Degree
Accreditation: WJ, COARC, RAD

01 President ... Dr. Dena P. MALONEY
05 Vice President Academic Affairs ... Dr. Jean SHANKWEILER
10 Vice Pres Administrative Services ... Ms. Iris INGRAM
32 Vice Pres Student Services ... Mr. Ross MIYASHIRO
15 Vice Pres of Human Resources ... Ms. Jane MIYASHIRO
111 Dean Community Advancement ... Mr. Jose ANAYA
72 Dean Industry & Technology ... Mr. David GONZALES
81 Dean Math ... Ms. Jacquelyn SIMS
50 Dean of Business ... Dr. Virginia RAPP
83 Dean Behavioral & Social Science ... Dr. Chris GOLD
68 Int Dean Health Science & Athletics ... Mr. Russel SERR

57 Dean Fine Arts .... Dr. Berkeley PRICE
76 Dean Natural Sciences .... Dr. Amy GRANT
79 Dean Humanities .... Ms. Debra BRECKHEIMER
08 Director Learning Resources .... Ms. Crystle MARTIN
121 Dean Counseling & Student Success .... Dr. Dipte PALEL
121 Dean of Student Support Services .... Ms. Idania REYES
84 Dean of Enrollment Services .... Mr. Robin DREIZLER
88 Director Special Resource Center .... Mr. Gary GRECO
13 Chief Technology Officer .... Dr. Art LEIBLE
26 Exec Dir Marketing/Communications .... Ms. Ann O'BRIEN
106 Coordinator Distance Education .... Dr. Moses WOLFENSTEIN
88 Director Public Safety .... Chief Jeffrey BAUMUNK
66 Director of Nursing .... Dr. Wanda MORRIS
86 Public Info & Government Relations .... Mr. Marc STEVENS
102 Executive Director Foundation .... Ms. Andrea SALA
96 Dir Purchasing & Risk Management .... Mr. Michael PASCUAL
40 Director of Bookstore .... Ms. Julie BOURLIER
19 Chief of Campus Police .... Mr. Michael TREVIS
18 Exec Dir Facilities Planning/Svcs .... Mr. Jorge GUTIERREZ
35 Director of Student Development .... Dr. Gregory TOYA
37 Director Student Financial Aid .... Ms. Melissa GUESS
06 Registrar .... Ms. Lillian JUSTICE
09 Dir Institutional Research/Planning .... Ms. Viviana UNDA
28 Director of Diversity .... Dr. Jayne ISHIKAWA
21 Business Manager .... Mr. Jeffrey HINSHAW
103 Director Career Education .... Ms. Adriana ESTRADA
25 Grants Development & Management .... Ms. Roberta BECKA
41 Athletic Director .... Mr. Colin PRESTON
04 Executive Asst to President .... Ms. Rose MAHOWALD

Emperor's College of Traditional Oriental Medicine (A)

1807-B Wilshire Boulevard, Santa Monica CA 90403-5678
County: Los Angeles FICE Identification: 026090
Unit ID: 114114
Telephone: (310) 453-8300 Carnegie Class: Spec-4-yr-Other Health
FAX Number: (310) 829-3838 Calendar System: Quarter
URL: www.emperors.edu
Established: 1983 Annual Undergrad Tuition & Fees: N/A
Enrollment: 189 Coed
Affiliation or Control: Proprietary IRS Status: Proprietary
Highest Offering: Doctorate
Accreditation: ACUP

01 Chief Executive Officer/President .... Yun KIM
05 Academic Dean .... Jacques MORAMARCO
63 Dean of Clinical Education .... Robert NEWMAN
11 Chief Operations Officer .... George PARK

Empire College (B)

3035 Cleveland Avenue, Santa Rosa CA 95403-2100
County: Sonoma FICE Identification: 009032
Unit ID: 114123
Telephone: (707) 546-4000 Carnegie Class: Bac/Assoc-Mixed
FAX Number: (707) 546-4058 Calendar System: Other
URL: www.empcol.edu
Established: 1961 Annual Undergrad Tuition & Fees: N/A
Enrollment: 433 Coed
Affiliation or Control: Proprietary IRS Status: Proprietary
Highest Offering: Master's
Accreditation: ACICS

01 President .... Mr. Roy HURD
26 Vice Pres Marketing/Administration .... Mrs. Sherie HURD

Epic Bible College & Graduate School (C)

4330 Auburn Boulevard, Sacramento CA 95841
County: Sacramento FICE Identification: 034033
Unit ID: 124487
Telephone: (916) 348-4689 Carnegie Class: Spec-4-yr-Faith
FAX Number: (916) 468-0866 Calendar System: Trimester
URL: www.EPIC.edu
Established: 1974 Annual Undergrad Tuition & Fees: $9,689
Enrollment: 172 Coed
Affiliation or Control: Independent Non-Profit IRS Status: 501(c)3
Highest Offering: Doctorate
Accreditation: TRACS

01 President/CEO .... Dr. Ronald W. HARDEN
05 Vice President of Academics .... Dr. Greg L. HARTLEY
58 Director Graduate Studies .... Dr. Ed FUNK
73 Chair of Worship Arts .... Dr. David YODER
08 Director Learning Resource .... Rev. Dale SOLBERG
37 Director of Financial Services .... Mr. David PINESCHI
06 Director of Records/Office Manager .... Ms. Kathy CLARKE
106 Director of Online Program .... Rev. John GALLEGOS
26 Director Enrollment/Marketing .... Rev. Daniel HARDEN

Eternity Bible College (D)

2136 Winifred Street, Simi Valley CA 93063
County: Ventura Identification: 667045
Telephone: (805) 581-1233 Carnegie Class: Not Classified
FAX Number: (805) 581-1245 Calendar System: Semester
URL: www.eternitybiblecollege.com
Established: 2004 Annual Undergrad Tuition & Fees: N/A
Enrollment: N/A Coed
Affiliation or Control: Independent Non-Profit IRS Status: 501(c)3
Highest Offering: Baccalaureate
Accreditation: BI

01 President .... Spencer MACCUISH
05 Academic Dean .... Joshua WALKER
32 Dean of Students .... Chris KOTTRE
07 Director of Admissions .... Mary Beth DRAGOUN
06 Registrar/Finance Manager .... Ryan MCGLADDERY
35 Dir Student Life/Exec Asst .... Nicole MCGLADDERY

Evangelia University (E)

2660 West Woodland Drive, Suite 200,
Anaheim CA 92801-2650
County: Orange Identification: 666640
Telephone: (714) 527-0691 Carnegie Class: Not Classified
FAX Number: (714) 527-0693 Calendar System: Other
URL: www.evangelia.edu
Established: 1999 Annual Undergrad Tuition & Fees: N/A
Enrollment: N/A Coed
Affiliation or Control: Reformed Presbyterian Church IRS Status: 501(c)3
Highest Offering: Doctorate
Accreditation: TRACS

01 President .... Dr. David H. SHIN
03 Vice President .... Dr. Sung Soo KIM
05 Dean of Academic Affairs .... Dr. Soonhae KANG
11 Dean Admin/Chief Operating Officer .... Ki Won HAN
32 Dean of Student Affairs .... Ki Won HAN
10 Chief Financial Officer .... Chang Ho SON
06 Registrar/Foreign Student Advisor .... Charley LEE
57 Chair Masters of Arts Program .... Cha Hi WON
106 Director of Distance Education .... Soonhae KANG

Ezra University (F)

2064 Marengo Street, Suite 200, Los Angeles CA 90033
County: Los Angeles Identification: 667316
Telephone: (323) 221-1024 Carnegie Class: Not Classified
FAX Number: (323) 221-1025 Calendar System: Quarter
URL: www.ezrauniversity.org
Established: 1997 Annual Undergrad Tuition & Fees: N/A
Enrollment: N/A Coed
Affiliation or Control: Independent Non-Profit IRS Status: 501(c)3
Highest Offering: Master's
Accreditation: @BI

01 President .... Dr. John PYEON
05 Dean of Academics .... Dr. L. Arik GREENBERG
10 Director Business & Admin Affairs .... Mr. James PARK
06 Registrar .... Mr. Peter SONG

Fashion Institute of Design and Merchandising-Orange County (G)

17590 Gillette Avenue, Irvine CA 92614-5610
Telephone: (888) 974-3436 Identification: 666004
Accreditation: &WC, ART

† Regional accreditation is carried under the parent institution in Los Angeles, CA.

Feather River College (H)

570 Golden Eagle Avenue, Quincy CA 95971-9124
County: Plumas FICE Identification: 008597
Unit ID: 114433
Telephone: (530) 283-0202 Carnegie Class: Bac/Assoc-Assoc Dom
FAX Number: (530) 283-3757 Calendar System: Semester
URL: www.frc.edu
Established: 1968 Annual Undergrad Tuition & Fees (In-District): $1,461
Enrollment: 2,151 Coed
Affiliation or Control: State/Local IRS Status: 501(c)3
Highest Offering: Baccalaureate
Accreditation: WJ

01 Superintendent/President .... Dr. Kevin TRUTNA
10 Chief Financial Officer .... Mr. Jim SCOUBES
05 Dean of Instruction/CIO .... Dr. Derek LERCH
20 Assistant Dean of Instruction .... Dr. Kim BEATON
32 Chief Student Services Officer .... Ms. Carlie MCCARTHY
15 Director Human Resources/EEO .... Mr. David BURRIS
18 Director of Facilities/CTO .... Mr. Nick BOYD
07 Registrar/Dir of Admissions .... Ms. Gretchen BAUMGARTNER
37 Director Student Financial Aid .... Mr. Andre VAN DER VELDEN
96 Purchasing Agent .... Ms. Tamara CLINE
04 Administrative Asst to President .... Ms. Cynthia HALL
09 Director of Institutional Research .... Dr. Agnes KOOS

FIDM/Fashion Institute of Design and Merchandising-Los Angeles (I)

919 S Grand Avenue, Los Angeles CA 90015-1421
County: Los Angeles FICE Identification: 011112
Unit ID: 114354
Telephone: (213) 624-1200 Carnegie Class: Spec-4-yr-Arts
FAX Number: (213) 624-9354 Calendar System: Quarter
URL: www.fidm.edu
Established: 1969 Annual Undergrad Tuition & Fees: $32,293
Enrollment: 2,384 Coed
Affiliation or Control: Proprietary IRS Status: Proprietary
Highest Offering: Master's
Accreditation: WC, ART

01 President .... Ms. Tonian HOHBERG
10 Vice President/Treasurer .... Ms. Tess STOLZER
45 Vice President Planning .... Ms. Vivien LOWY
05 Vice President Education .... Ms. Barbara BUNDY
108 Dean of Accreditation .... Ms. Lisa SCHOENING
08 Director Library .... Ms. Kathy BAILON
06 Registrar .... Mr. Michael GILBERT
37 Director Financial Aid .... Mr. Chris JENNINGS
26 Director Public Rels/Publicity .... Ms. Shirley WILSON
38 Personal Counselor .... Ms. Jessica CATTANI
96 Director College Services .... Ms. Ella VAN NORT
07 Exec Director of Admissions .... Ms. Susan ARONSON
13 Chief Info Technology Officer (CIO) .... Ms. Suzanna GRUESER
15 Exec Director Human Resources .... Ms. Julie Ann OTTESON
04 Executive Asst to President .... Ms. Megan NOWAK
104 Director International Affairs .... Ms. Sarah REPETTO
105 Director Web Mktg Ops/Publications .... Mr. Michael KAMINSKI
18 Director of FIDM Facilities .... Mr. John (Buddy) BOLOGNONE
19 Director of Security .... Mr. Todd J. ANDERSON
22 Title IX Coordinator .... Ms. Julie Ann OTTESON
29 Director Alumni Relations .... Ms. Carrie SHAY
32 Director of Student Activities .... Ms. Caitlin MADDEN
53 Dean of Education .... Ms. Sheryl RABINOVICH
86 Director Government Relations .... Ms. Norine FULLER
90 Director Academic Computing .... Ms. Cheryl BENSMILLER

FIDM/Fashion Institute of Design & Merchandising-San Diego (J)

350 10th Avenue, 3rd Floor, San Diego CA 92101
Telephone: (619) 235-2049 Identification: 666005
Accreditation: &WC, ART

† Regional accreditation is carried under the parent institution in Los Angeles, CA.

FIDM/Fashion Institute of Design and Merchandising-San Francisco (K)

55 Stockton Street, San Francisco CA 94108-5829
Telephone: (415) 675-5200 FICE Identification: 013041
Accreditation: &WC, ART

† Regional accreditation is carried under the parent institution in Los Angeles, CA.

Fielding Graduate University (L)

2020 De La Vina Street, Santa Barbara CA 93105-3538
County: Santa Barbara FICE Identification: 020961
Unit ID: 114549
Telephone: (800) 340-1099 Carnegie Class: DU-Mod
FAX Number: (805) 687-9793 Calendar System: Trimester
URL: www.fielding.edu
Established: 1974 Annual Graduate Tuition & Fees: N/A
Enrollment: 957 Coed
Affiliation or Control: Independent Non-Profit IRS Status: 501(c)3
Highest Offering: Doctorate; No Undergraduates
Accreditation: WC, CLPSY

01 President .... Dr. Katrina ROGERS
04 Exec Asst to President .... Mr. Bryan LOPES
09 VP Strategic Initiative/Research .... Dr. Orlando TAYLOR
10 VP and Chief Financial Officer .... Ms. Prema WINDOKUN
05 Provost & Senior VP .... Dr. Monique L. SNOWDEN
15 Director of Human Resources .... Mr. Dino FERRARE
06 Registrar/Dir of Curriculum Svcs .... Ms. Bridget BRADY
21 Int Dir of Academic Business Svcs .... Ms. Andrea MCKENNA
28 Chief Diversity Officer .... Mr. Tomas LEAL

Five Branches University, Graduate School of Traditional Chinese Medicine (M)

1885 Lundy Avenue, Suite 108, San Jose CA 95131
County: Santa Clara Identification: 667008
Telephone: (408) 260-0208 Carnegie Class: Not Classified
FAX Number: (408) 261-3166 Calendar System: Trimester
URL: www.fivebranches.edu
Established: 2005 Annual Undergrad Tuition & Fees: N/A
Enrollment: N/A Coed
Affiliation or Control: Proprietary IRS Status: Proprietary
Highest Offering: Doctorate; No Lower Division
Accreditation: ACUP

01 President/CEO .... Ron ZAIDMAN
05 VP Academic Affairs .... Joanna ZHAO
10 VP Finance .... Liana CHEN
13 VP Operations .... Gina HUANG
06 Registrar .... Ling ZHANG
58 Director of Doctoral Program .... Robyn GRIEVE
26 Director of Marketing .... Sean ZAIDMAN
37 Director of Financial Aid .... Daryl CULLEN
58 Associate Director Doctoral Program .... Vacant
84 Director of Enrollment .... Alex HU
56 Extension Program Admin .... Lykos YANG
23 Clinic Manager .... Joyce HE
08 Library & Facility Manager .... Songsong GAO

Five Branches University, Graduate School of Traditional Chinese Medicine (A)

200 7th Avenue, Santa Cruz CA 95062-4669

County: Santa Cruz FICE Identification: 031313
Unit ID: 114585
Telephone: (831) 476-9424 Carnegie Class: Spec-4-yr-Other Health
FAX Number: (831) 476-8928 Calendar System: Trimester
URL: www.fivebranches.edu
Established: 1984 Annual Undergrad Tuition & Fees: N/A
Enrollment: 305 Coed
Affiliation or Control: Proprietary IRS Status: Proprietary
Highest Offering: Doctorate; No Lower Division
Accreditation: ACUP

01 President & CEO .... Ron ZAIDMAN
05 Vice President & Dean .... Joanna ZHAO
11 Vice President Operations .... Gina HUANG
10 Vice President Finance & Accounting .... Liana CHEN
26 Dir of Marketing & Communications .... Sean ZAIDMAN
08 Librarian .... Jim EMDY
06 Registrar San Jose .... Ling ZHANG
32 Director Student Services .... Kim PFISTER
07 Admissions Director .... Eleonor MENDELSON
37 Director Student Financial Aid .... Daryl CULLEN
56 Director Extension Programs .... Fay DENNIS

*Foothill-De Anza Community College District System Office (B)

12345 El Monte Road, Los Altos Hills CA 94022-4597

County: Santa Clara FICE Identification: 009020
Unit ID: 114831
Telephone: (650) 949-6100 Carnegie Class: N/A
FAX Number: (650) 941-6289
URL: www.fhda.edu

01 Chancellor .... Dr. Judy C. MINER
10 Vice Chancellor Business Services .... Ms. Susan CHEU
15 Vice Chancellor Human Resources .... Ms. Dorene NOVOTNY
13 Vice Chancellor Technology .... Mr. Joseph MOREAU
09 Exec Dir of Inst Research/Planning .... Mr. David ULATE
19 Chief of Police .... Mr. Daniel ACOSTA
26 Coordinator District Communication .... Ms. Becky BARTINDALE
102 Exec Dir Foundation .... Mr. Dennis CIMA
96 Director of Purchasing .... Ms. Maria CONTRERAS-TANORI

*De Anza College (C)

21250 Stevens Creek Boulevard, Cupertino CA 95014-5793

County: Santa Clara FICE Identification: 004480
Unit ID: 113333
Telephone: (408) 864-5678 Carnegie Class: Assoc/HVT-High Trad
FAX Number: (408) 864-8238 Calendar System: Quarter
URL: www.deanza.edu
Established: 1967 Annual Undergrad Tuition & Fees (In-District): $1,561
Enrollment: 20,674 Coed
Affiliation or Control: State/Local IRS Status: 501(c)3
Highest Offering: Associate Degree
Accreditation: WJ, MLTAD

02 Interim President .... Ms. Christina G. ESPINOSA-PIEB
05 Acting Vice Pres of Instruction .... Ms. Lorrie RANCK
32 VP of Student Services .... Dr. Rob MIESO
10 Acting VP Administrative Services .... Ms. Pam GREY
20 Assoc Vice Pres Instruction .... Vacant
35 Dean Student Development/EOPS ... Ms. Michele LEBLEU BURNS
38 Dean Counseling & Matriculation .... Ms. Laureen BALDUCCI
07 Dean Admissions & Records .... Ms. Nazy GALOYAN
37 Director Student Financial Aid .... Ms. Lisa MANDY
21 Director Fiscal Services .... Mr. Martin VALERA
18 Assoc Vice Pres College Operations .... Ms. Pam GREY
26 AVP Communications & External Rel ...... Ms. Marisa SPATAFORE
102 Exec Director Foundation .... Mr. Dennis CIMA
28 Dean Equity & Engagement .... Ms. Alicia CORTEZ
96 Dir Purchasing/Contracts/Risk Mgmt .... Ms. Maria CONTRERAS-TANORI
36 Supervisor Student Placement .... Ms. Casie WHEAT
09 Institutional Researcher .... Dr. Mallory NEWELL
06 Supervisor Admissions and Records .... Mr. Barry JOHNSON
04 Executive Assistant to President .... Ms. Pippa GIBSON
08 Head Librarian .... Mr. Tom DOLEN
13 Chief Info Technology Officer (CIO) .... Mr. Joe MOREAU
41 Athletic Director .... Mr. Kulwant SINGH
50 Dean Business/Comp Sys/Applied Tech .... Mr. Moaty FAYEK

*Foothill College (D)

12345 El Monte Road, Los Altos Hills CA 94022-4599

County: Santa Clara FICE Identification: 001199
Unit ID: 114716
Telephone: (650) 949-7777 Carnegie Class: Bac/Assoc-Assoc Dom
FAX Number: (650) 949-7375 Calendar System: Quarter
URL: www.foothill.edu
Established: 1957 Annual Undergrad Tuition & Fees (In-District): $1,563
Enrollment: 15,697 Coed
Affiliation or Control: State/Local IRS Status: 501(c)3
Highest Offering: Baccalaureate
Accreditation: WJ, COARC, DA, DH, DMS, EMT, RAD

02 President .... Ms. Thuy NGUYEN
04 Assistant to the President ...... Ms. Veronica CASAS HERNANDEZ
10 VP Finance & Admin Services .... Mr. Bret WATSON
05 Exec VP Instruction & Inst Research .... Dr. Kristy LISLE
20 Int Associate VP Instruction .... Mr. Paul STARER
32 Associate VP Student Services .... Dr. Laurie SCOLARI
21 Associate VP Finance & Admin Svcs .... Mr. Elias REGALADO
35 Dean Student Affairs & Activities .... Vacant
38 Dean Counseling & Special Programs .... Ms. Lan TRUONG
12 Dean Sunnyvale Center .... Vacant
88 Dean Disabled Stdnt Svcs/Vet Pgms .... Ms. Neelam AGARWAL
40 Director Bookstore .... Mr. Romeo PAULE
84 Dean Enroll Svcs & Intl Stdnt Pgm .... Vacant
37 Director Financial Aid .... Mr. Kevin HARRAL
22 Dean of Equity Programs .... Dr. Melissa CERVANTES
23 Director Health Services .... Vacant
76 Dean Biology & Health Sciences .... Mr. Ram SUBRAMANIAM
50 Dean Business & Social Sciences .... Mr. Kurt HUEG
106 Dean Foothill Online Learning .... Vacant
57 Dean Fine Arts & Communications .... Vacant
79 Dean Language Arts & LRC .... Ms. Valerie FONG
81 Dean Physical Sci/Math & Engr .... Mr. Ram SUBRAMANIAM
09 Supervisor Institutional Research .... Ms. Lisa LY
41 Athletic Director .... Mr. Mike TEIJEIRO
103 Associate VP Workforce .... Ms. Teresa ONG

Franciscan School of Theology (E)

5998 Alcal Park, San Diego CA 92110

County: San Diego FICE Identification: 011792
Unit ID: 114734
Telephone: (619) 574-1800 Carnegie Class: Spec-4-yr-Faith
FAX Number: (619) 849-8431 Calendar System: Semester
URL: www.fst.edu
Established: 1968 Annual Graduate Tuition & Fees: N/A
Enrollment: 44 Coed
Affiliation or Control: Independent Non-Profit IRS Status: 501(c)3
Highest Offering: Master's; No Undergraduates
Accreditation: WC, THEOL

01 President .... Fr. Michael J. HIGGINS, TOR
03 Executive Vice President and Rector .... Fr. Garrett GALVIN, OFM
10 VP Finance/Business Operations .... Ms. Kimberly RENNA
06 Registrar .... Fr. Garrett GALVIN
07 Assoc Dir Admissions/Recruitment .... Ms. Christine AVELLA
30 Director of Development .... Mr. Alan ANDRADE
26 Marketing/Recruitment Coord .... Ms. Gigi BETANCOURT

Fremont College (F)

18000 Studebaker Road, Suite 900A, Cerritos CA 90703

County: Los Angeles FICE Identification: 030399
Unit ID: 372073
Telephone: (562) 809-5100 Carnegie Class: Bac/Assoc-Mixed
FAX Number: (562) 809-7100 Calendar System: Other
URL: https://fremont.edu
Established: 1985 Annual Undergrad Tuition & Fees: N/A
Enrollment: 182 Coed
Affiliation or Control: Proprietary IRS Status: Proprietary
Highest Offering: Baccalaureate
Accreditation: ACCSC

01 Chancellor/CEO .... Dr. Sabrina KAY
05 Chief Academic Officer .... Jonathan DAITCH
11 Director of Operations .... Tony WONG
36 Director of Student Placement .... Tasha SKIPPS
37 Director of Financial Aid .... Israel RODRIGUEZ
06 Registrar .... Leivera FONOTI
15 Director Human Resources/Comm .... Brian KIM

Fresno Pacific University (G)

1717 S Chestnut Avenue, Fresno CA 93702-4798

County: Fresno FICE Identification: 001253
Unit ID: 114813
Telephone: (559) 453-2000 Carnegie Class: Masters/L
FAX Number: (559) 453-2007 Calendar System: Semester
URL: www.fresno.edu
Established: 1944 Annual Undergrad Tuition & Fees: $32,458
Enrollment: 4,105 Coed
Affiliation or Control: Mennonite Brethren Church IRS Status: 501(c)3
Highest Offering: Master's
Accreditation: WC, NURSE, SW, THEOL

01 President .... Dr. Joseph JONES
05 Provost/Senior VP Academic Affairs .... Dr. D. Gayle COPELAND
10 Vice President Finance .... Mr. Robert LIPPERT
26 Assoc VP University Communications .... Mrs. Jillian FREEMAN
11 Vice Pres of Operations .... Vacant
84 Vice Pres Enrollment Mgmt .... Mr. Jon ENDICOTT
111 VP for Advancement/Exec Dir Found .... Mr. Donald GRIFFITH
32 Vice President Student Life .... Mr. Dale SCULLY
50 Dean School of Business .... Dr. Katie FLEENER
79 Dean Sch of Human/Rel/Soc Sci .... Dr. Ron HERMS
53 Dean School of Education .... Dr. Gary GRAMENZ
78 Dean School of Natural Sciences .... Dr. Karen CIANCI
42 Dean of Spiritual Formation/CDO .... Rev. Angulus WILSON
08 Director of Library .... Mr. Kevin ENNS-REMPEL
36 Director of Career Resource Center .... Ms. Rose WINN
15 Human Resources Director .... Mr. Jordan SHARP
27 Publications Director .... Mr. Wayne STEFFEN
29 Director Alumni Development .... Ms. Ali SENA
37 Dir Student Financial Services .... Mr. David RICHARDS
41 Athletic Director .... Mr. Aaron HENDERSON
19 Chief of Campus Safety .... Mr. Javier CAMPOS
26 Chief Public Relations Officer .... Mr. Wayne STEFFENS
104 Dir International Pgms/Svcs Ofc .... Ms. Angela CHAPA
07 Director of Admissions .... Mrs. Krista BROOKS
18 Facilities Manager .... Mr. Gary METCALF
04 Executive Asst to President .... Ms. Gwenevera E. BURKS
73 VP and Dean of the Seminary .... Dr. Valerie REMPEL
102 Dir Foundation/Corporate Relations .... Mr. Mark DEFFENBACHER
112 Dir of Leadership Gifts/Corp Rels .... Mr. Robert JENSEN
09 Director of Institutional Research .... Ms. Maribel VIVEROS
13 Exec Director ITS .... Mr. Dave RICHERT
105 Director Web Services .... Mr. Justin GABLE
39 Asst Dean Student Dev/Resident Life .... Ms. Pam SCHOCK
106 Director Center for Online Learning .... Dr. Henrietta SIEMENS
25 Grants Administrator .... Ms. Allison ENS
86 Director Government Relations .... Mr. Jon ENDICOTT

Fuller Theological Seminary (H)

135 N Oakland, Pasadena CA 91182-1780

County: Los Angeles FICE Identification: 001200
Unit ID: 114840
Telephone: (626) 584-5200 Carnegie Class: Spec-4-yr-Faith
FAX Number: (626) 795-8767 Calendar System: Quarter
URL: www.fuller.edu
Established: 1947 Annual Graduate Tuition & Fees: N/A
Enrollment: 2,463 Coed
Affiliation or Control: Independent Non-Profit IRS Status: 501(c)3
Highest Offering: Doctorate; No Undergraduates
Accreditation: WC, CLPSY, THEOL

01 President .... Dr. Mark A. LABBERTON
05 Provost .... Dr. Mari L. CLEMENTS
88 Senior Advisor .... Mr. Bill CLARK
10 Chief Financial Officer .... Mr. Dan COOPER
30 Vice President Development .... Ms. Kimberly THOMPSON
26 Vice President Communications .... Ms. Lauralee FARRER
88 Vice President/Chief of Leadership .... Dr. Tod BOLSINGER
73 Dean School of Theology .... Dr. Amos YONG
83 Dean School of Psychology .... Dr. Ted COSSE
88 Dean School Intercultural Studies .... Dr. Amos YONG
88 Assoc Dean Doctor of Ministry Pgm .... Dr. Kurt FREDRICKSON
15 Exec Director of HR & Org Dev .... Ms. Bernadette (BJ) BARBER
35 Exec Dir Student Engagement/Success .... Mr. Sam BANG
07 Exec Director Admissions .... Mr. Max WEDEL
106 Exec Dir Teaching and Learning .... Mr. Tommy LISTER
43 General Counsel .... Mr. Brent S. KAMPE
19 Chief of Campus Safety .... Mr. Gary L. MEJIA
108 Accreditation Liaison Officer .... Dr. Mari L. CLEMENTS
09 Director of Institutional Research .... Dr. Dave SCOTT
06 Registrar .... Mr. Stephen RONETTI
11 Director of Finance and Operations .... Mr. Al SEJCEK
39 Manager of Housing Services .... Ms. Cynthia TUPAS
04 Assistant to President .... Mr. Mandy MACINTOSH
18 Facilities Director .... Mr. Nathan MERRITT
109 Director of Auxiliary Services .... Mrs. Jeanne HANDOJO
85 Dir Student Affs/International Svcs .... Mr. Sam BANG
37 Actg Dir Student Financial Svcs .... Ms. Shannon LEWIS
08 Director of the DAH Library .... Ms. Daniell WHITTINGTON
29 Director Alumni Engagement .... Ms. Bert JACKLITCH

Gateway Seminary (I)

3210 E. Guasti Rd, Ontario CA 91761-8642

County: San Bernadino FICE Identification: 001204
Telephone: (909) 687-1800 Carnegie Class: Not Classified
FAX Number: N/A Calendar System: Semester
URL: www.gs.edu
Established: 1944 Annual Graduate Tuition & Fees: N/A
Enrollment: N/A Coed
Affiliation or Control: Southern Baptist IRS Status: 501(c)3
Highest Offering: Doctorate; No Undergraduates
Accreditation: WC, THEOL

01 President .... Dr. Jeff IORG
111 Vice Pres Advancement .... Dr. Jeff JONES
05 Vice President Academic Affairs .... Dr. D. Michael MARTIN
32 VP Enroll/Student Svcs/Dean Stdnts .... Dr. Adam GROZA
10 VP Business Services .... Mr. Tom HIXSON
21 Controller .... Mr. Harry WEAVER
06 Registrar .... Ms. Deena CARTER
08 Director of Library Services .... Dr. Bob PHILLIPS
12 Director PNW Campus .... Dr. Mark BRADLEY
12 Director Arizona Campus .... Dr. Dallas BIVINS
12 Director Rocky Mountain Campus .... Dr. Steve VETETO
13 Director Information Technology .... Mr. Steve POLCYN
15 Director Personnel Services .... Ms. Jennifer PALMER
18 Chief Facilities/Physical Plant .... Mr. Robert DVORAK
30 Director of Development .... Mr. Jay BADRY
84 Director Enrollment Management .... Mr. Cameron SCHWEITZER
32 Director of Student Life .... Mr. Shane TANIGAWA

Gavilan College (J)

5055 Santa Teresa Boulevard, Gilroy CA 95020-9599

County: Santa Clara FICE Identification: 001202
Unit ID: 114938
Telephone: (408) 848-4800 Carnegie Class: Assoc/MT-VT-High Trad
FAX Number: (408) 848-4801 Calendar System: Semester
URL: www.gavilan.edu
Established: 1919 Annual Undergrad Tuition & Fees (In-District): $1,166
Enrollment: 5,995 Coed

Affiliation or Control: State/Local IRS Status: 501(c)3
Highest Offering: Associate Degree
Accreditation: WJ

01 Superintendent/President ... Dr. Kathleen A. ROSE
05 Vice Pres Academic Affairs ... Ms. Denee PESCARMONA
11 Vice Pres Administrative Services ... Mr. Michael RENZI
32 Vice President Student Services ... Ms. Denee PESCARMONA
10 Assoc VP Business Svcs & Security ... Mr. Wade ELLIS
07 Director of Admissions and Records ... Ms. Candice WHITNEY
29 Dir Alumni Affs/Foundation Coord ... Ms. Jan BERNSTEIN CHARGIN
08 Head Librarian ... Dr. Douglas ACHTERMAN
84 Interim Dean Enrollment Services ... Ms. Veronica MARTINEZ
88 Interim Dean Foundational Skills ... Dr. Randy BROWN
15 Assoc VP Human Resources/Labor Rels ... Dr. Eric RAMONES
18 Director of Facilities and Maint ... Mr. Jeff GOPP
13 Director Information Technology ... Mr. Kyle BILLUPS
26 Director Public Information ... Ms. Jan BERNSTEIN-CHARGIN
23 Student Health Nurse ... Vacant
88 Dean Health and Wellness ... Mr. Ron HANNON
40 Manager Bookstore ... Ms. Laura JIMINEZ
49 Int Dean Arts/Humanities/Social Sci ... Dr. Eduardo CERVANTES
75 Dean Career Education ... Ms. Sherrean CARR
96 Purchasing Specialist ... Ms. Jeanne ALAMADARI
04 Admin Assistant to the President ... Ms. Debra BRITT-PETTY

Glendale Career College (A)

240 N. Brand Blvd, Lower Level, Glendale CA 91203
County: Los Angeles FICE Identification: 023385
Unit ID: 115010
Telephone: (818) 243-1131 Carnegie Class: Spec 2-yr-Health
FAX Number: (818) 243-6028 Calendar System: Semester
URL: www.glendalecareer.com
Established: 1946 Annual Undergrad Tuition & Fees: N/A
Enrollment: 507 Coed
Affiliation or Control: Proprietary IRS Status: Proprietary
Highest Offering: Associate Degree
Accreditation: ABHES, SURGT, SURTEC

01 Campus Director ... Mr. Rick HOKE

Glendale Community College (B)

1500 N Verdugo Road, Glendale CA 91208-2894
County: Los Angeles FICE Identification: 001203
Unit ID: 115001
Telephone: (818) 240-1000 Carnegie Class: Assoc/MT-VT-High Trad
FAX Number: (818) 549-9436 Calendar System: Semester
URL: www.glendale.edu
Established: 1927 Annual Undergrad Tuition & Fees (In-District): $1,175
Enrollment: 14,598 Coed
Affiliation or Control: State/Local IRS Status: 501(c)3
Highest Offering: Associate Degree
Accreditation: WJ

01 Superintendent/President ... Dr. David VIAR
11 Exec Vice Pres Administrative Svcs ... Dr. Anthony CULPEPPER
05 Vice Pres Instructional Services ... Dr. Michael RITTERBROWN
32 Vice President Student Services ... Dr. Paul SCHLOSSMAN
51 Admin Dean Continuing/Cmty Educ ... Dr. Alfred RAMIREZ
15 VP Human Resources ... Ms. Victoria SIMMONS
45 Dean Research/Planning/Grants ... Dr. Edward KARPP
07 Director Admissions & Records ... Ms. Michelle MORA
20 Dean Instructional Services ... Ms. Agnes EGUARAS
103 Dean Workforce Development ... Ms. Jan SWINTON
32 Dean Student Affairs ... Ms. Tzoler OUKAYAN
35 Dean of Student Services ... Dr. Robert HILL
37 Assoc Dean Stdnt Financial Aid Svcs . Dr. Christina TANGALAKIS
10 Director Business Services ... Ms. Susan COURTEY
102 Exec Director College Foundation ... Ms. Lisa BROOKS
41 Int Assoc Dean Athletics ... Mr. Chris CICUTO
103 Int Assoc Dn Career Educ/Wkfrc Dev ... Mr. Federico SAUCEDO
31 Assoc Dean Cont/Community Education ... Dr. Ramona BARRIO-SOTILLO

Gnomon (C)

1015 N. Cahuenga Blvd, Los Angeles CA 90038
County: Los Angeles FICE Identification: 040764
Unit ID: 449384
Telephone: (323) 466-6663 Carnegie Class: Not Classified
FAX Number: (323) 466-6710 Calendar System: Quarter
URL: www.gnomon.edu
Established: 1997 Annual Undergrad Tuition & Fees: $29,067
Enrollment: N/A Coed
Affiliation or Control: Proprietary IRS Status: Proprietary
Highest Offering: Baccalaureate
Accreditation: ACCSC

01 President ... Alex ALVAREZ

Golden Gate University (D)

536 Mission Street, San Francisco CA 94105-2968
County: San Francisco FICE Identification: 001205
Unit ID: 115083
Telephone: (415) 442-7000 Carnegie Class: Masters/L
FAX Number: N/A Calendar System: Trimester
URL: www.ggu.edu
Established: 1901 Annual Undergrad Tuition & Fees: N/A
Enrollment: 2,592 Coed
Affiliation or Control: Independent Non-Profit IRS Status: 501(c)3
Highest Offering: Doctorate
Accreditation: WC, LAW

01 President ... Dr. David J. FIKE
05 VP of Academic Affairs ... Ms. Barbara H. KARLIN
10 VP of Business Affairs & CFO ... Vacant
30 VP of Development/Alumni Relations .. Ms. Mary Ellen MCGILLAN
84 VP Enrollment Strategy & Services ... Mr. John REED
26 VP of Strategic Communications ... Ms. Natalie MAZANOWSKI
61 Dean School of Law ... Mr. Anthony NIEDWIECKI
50 Dean School of Business ... Dr. Gordon SWARTZ
88 Dean School Taxation ... Ms. Amy MCLELLAN
106 Director E-Learning ... Mr. Doug GEIER
32 Dean of Students & Student Affairs ... Ms. Kayla KRUPNICK-WALSH
08 Director University Library ... Mr. James KRUSLING
08 Associate Dean Law Library ... Mr. Michael DAW
06 University Registrar ... Mr. Steven LIND
13 Director Information Technology ... Mr. Daniel FORTSON
27 Director of Marketing ... Mr. Ryan BADOWSKI
09 Dir Financial Planning/Analysis ... Mr. Sathyapal MENON
18 Director Business Svcs/Facilities ... Mr. Mike KOPERSKI
21 Controller ... Ms. Grace LEE
37 Director Student Financial Aid ... Ms. Gabriela DE LA VEGA
108 Director Institutional Assessment ... Ms. Lisa KRAMER
15 Head Human Resources ... Ms. S. Jamila BUCKNER
97 Dean School of Undergrad Studies ... Mr. Marc SINGER

Grace Mission University (E)

1645 West Valencia Drive, Fullerton CA 92833-3860
County: Orange Identification: 666642
Unit ID: 481058
Telephone: (714) 525-0088 Carnegie Class: Spec-4-yr-Faith
FAX Number: (714) 525-0089 Calendar System: Semester
URL: www.gm.edu
Established: 1995 Annual Undergrad Tuition & Fees: $2,840
Enrollment: 202 Coed
Affiliation or Control: Presbyterian Church (U.S.A.) IRS Status: 501(c)3
Highest Offering: Doctorate
Accreditation: BI, THEOL, TRACS

01 President & CEO ... Dr. Kyunam CHOI
05 Academic Dean ... Dr. Hyunwan KIM
10 Chief Financial Officer ... Dr. Changsoo LEE
32 Dean of Students ... Dr. Dong Hyun HUH
11 Dir Administration/Financial Aid ... Mr. Jahyuk KOO
06 Registrar ... Ms. Min LEE
08 Librarian ... Ms. Eun Ja SEO
07 Director of Admissions ... Ms. Won Ja KIM
111 Chief Development/Advancement ... Mrs. Souk RHIE

Graduate Theological Union (F)

2400 Ridge Road, Berkeley CA 94709-1212
County: Alameda FICE Identification: 001207
Unit ID: 115214
Telephone: (510) 649-2400 Carnegie Class: Spec-4-yr-Faith
FAX Number: (510) 649-1417 Calendar System: Semester
URL: www.gtu.edu
Established: 1962 Annual Graduate Tuition & Fees: N/A
Enrollment: 192 Coed
Affiliation or Control: Independent Non-Profit IRS Status: 501(c)3
Highest Offering: Doctorate; No Undergraduates
Accreditation: WC, THEOL

01 President ... Rabbi Daniel LEHMANN
05 Dean/Vice Pres Academic Affairs ... Dr. Uriah Y. KIM
10 Chief Financial Officer ... Ms. Ellen PETERSON
11 Chief Operating Officer ... Mr. Jeff PACE
111 Vice President for Advancement ... Ms. Alison MUNDY
32 VP Student Affairs/Dean Students ... Dr. Kathleen KOOK
07 Director of Admissions ... Dr. Andrea SHEAFFER
08 Library Director ... Mr. Clay-Edward DIXON
06 Consortial Registrar ... Mr. John SEAL
13 Chief Information Officer ... Mr. Jeffrey DIGREORIO
18 Building & Grounds Engineer ... Mr. Curtis OSBORNE
15 Director Human Resources ... Ms. Deborah WALKER
37 Director of Financial Aid ... Ms. Denise MORITA
04 Executive Assistant to President ... Ms. Teresa JOYE

*Grossmont-Cuyamaca Community College District (G)

8800 Grossmont College Drive, El Cajon CA 92020-1799
County: San Diego FICE Identification: 007006
Unit ID: 115287
Telephone: (619) 644-7010 Carnegie Class: N/A
FAX Number: (619) 644-7936
URL: www.gcccd.edu

01 Chancellor ... Dr. Cindy MILES
10 Vice Chanc Business Services ... Ms. Sue REARIC
15 Vice Chanc Human Resources ... Mr. Tim CORCORAN

*Cuyamaca College (H)

900 Rancho San Diego Parkway, El Cajon CA 92019-4304
County: San Diego FICE Identification: 021113
Unit ID: 113218
Telephone: (619) 660-4000 Carnegie Class: Assoc/HT-Mix Trad/Non
FAX Number: (619) 660-4399 Calendar System: Semester
URL: www.cuyamaca.edu
Established: 1978 Annual Undergrad Tuition & Fees (In-District): $1,386
Enrollment: 9,424 Coed
Affiliation or Control: State/Local IRS Status: 501(c)3
Highest Offering: Associate Degree
Accreditation: WJ

02 President ... Dr. Julianna BARNES
05 Vice President Instruction ... Mr. Pat SETZER
32 Vice Pres Student Services ... Ms. Jessica ROBINSON
11 Vice Pres Admin Services ... Ms. Sahar ABUSHABAN
81 Dean of Math/Sci/Engineering ... Dr. Pam KERSEY
79 Dean of Arts/Human/Social Sci ... Ms. Alicia MUNOZ
72 Dean of Career Technical Education ... Mr. Larry MCLEMORE
08 Dean Learning/Technology Resources ... Ms. Kerry KILBER REBMAN
41 Dean Athl/Kines/Health Ed ... Mr. Terry DAVIS
35 Dean Student Affairs ... Dr. Lauren VAKNIN
38 Dean Counseling Services ... Ms. Nicole JONES
37 Director of Financial Aid ... Mr. Ray REYES
07 Director Admissions & Records ... Mr. Gregory VEGA
18 Director Facilities ... Mr. Francisco GONZALEZ
04 Executive Asst to President ... Ms. Valeri WILSON
09 Sr Dean Inst Effectiv/Succ/Equity ... Ms. Brianna HAYS
26 Director College & Cmty Relations ... Ms. Christianne PENUNURI

*Grossmont College (I)

8800 Grossmont College Drive, El Cajon CA 92020-1799
County: San Diego FICE Identification: 001208
Unit ID: 115296
Telephone: (619) 644-7000 Carnegie Class: Assoc/HT-High Trad
FAX Number: (619) 644-7922 Calendar System: Semester
URL: www.grossmont.edu
Established: 1961 Annual Undergrad Tuition & Fees (In-District): $1,386
Enrollment: 18,288 Coed
Affiliation or Control: State/Local IRS Status: 501(c)3
Highest Offering: Associate Degree
Accreditation: WJ, ADNUR, CEA, COARC, CVT, OTA

02 President ... Dr. Nabil ABU-GHAZALEH
05 Int Vice Pres of Academic Affairs ... Dr. Michael REESE
32 Sr Dean CPIE/Student Services ... Dr. Catherine WEBB
07 Dean Admissions/Records/Fin Aid ... Mr. Aaron STARCK
38 Dean Counseling Svcs ... Ms. Martha CLAVELLE
72 Dean Career & Technical Workforce ... Mr. Javier AYALA
81 Int Dean Math/Natural Sci/Phys Educ ... Dr. Cary WILLARD
60 Dean Arts/Languages/Comm ... Dr. Joan AHRENS
79 Dean English/Social & Behav Sci ... Mr. Agustin ALBARRAN
08 Int Dean of Learning Resources ... Mr. Matt CALFIN
35 Dean Student Affairs ... Ms. Sara VARGHESE
09 Assoc Vice Chanc Inst Research ... Mr. Christopher TARMAN
10 Chief Business Officer ... Mr. Bill MCGREEVY
18 Chief Facilities/Physical Plant ... Mr. Loren HOLMQUIST
26 Chief Public Relations Officer ... Ms. Lorena RUGGERO
36 Director Student Placement ... Ms. Renee NASORI
37 Director Student Financial Aid ... Mr. Michael COPENHAVER
96 Director of Purchasing ... Ms. Linda BERTOLUCCI
04 Executive Assistant to President ... Ms. Bernadette BLACK

Gurnick Academy of Medical Arts (J)

2121 S. El Camino Real Bldg C200, San Mateo CA 94403
County: San Mateo FICE Identification: 041698
Unit ID: 459213
Telephone: (650) 685-6616 Carnegie Class: Spec-4-yr-Other Health
FAX Number: (650) 685-6640 Calendar System: Other
URL: www.gurnick.edu
Established: 2004 Annual Undergrad Tuition & Fees: N/A
Enrollment: 1,395 Coed
Affiliation or Control: Proprietary IRS Status: Proprietary
Highest Offering: Associate Degree
Accreditation: ABHES, PTAA, RAD

01 CEO ... Konstantin GOURJI
12 Campus Director ... Fred FARIDIAN
11 Chief Operating Officer ... Burke MALIN
05 Chief Academic Officer ... Larisa REVZINA

Hartnell College (K)

411 Central Avenue, Salinas CA 93901-1697
County: Monterey FICE Identification: 001209
Unit ID: 115393
Telephone: (831) 755-6700 Carnegie Class: Assoc/HT-High Trad
FAX Number: (831) 755-6751 Calendar System: Semester
URL: www.hartnell.edu
Established: 1920 Annual Undergrad Tuition & Fees (In-District): $1,420
Enrollment: 12,072 Coed
Affiliation or Control: State/Local IRS Status: 501(c)3
Highest Offering: Associate Degree
Accreditation: WJ, ADNUR, #COARC, PNUR

01 Superintendent/President ... Dr. Willard LEWALLEN
32 VP Student Affairs ... Dr. Romero JALOMO
10 VP Administrative Services ... Vacant
13 VP Information & Tech Systems ... Mr. David PHILLIPS
05 VP Academic Affairs ... Dr. Sonja LOLLAND
111 VP Advancement/Development ... Ms. Jackie CRUZ
15 Assoc VP Human Resources/EEO ... Ms. Terri PYER
21 Controller ... Ms. Ramona PAYNE
18 Exec Dir Constr/Facilities Mgmt ... Mr. Joseph REYES

20 Dean Academic Aff Programs/Support .. Ms. Kathy MENDELSOHN
81 Dean Academic Affs Math/Science ..... Ms. Shannon BLISS
35 Director of Student Life ..... Mr. Augustine NEVAREZ
26 Director of Communications ..... Mr. Scott FAUST
22 Dir of Student Affairs/EOPS ..... Mr. Paul CASEY
66 Dean Academic Affairs/Nursing ..... Ms. Debra KACZMAR
83 Dean Acad Affs Soc/Fine Lang Arts ..... Dr. Celine PINET
88 Dean South County Educ Programs ..... Mr. Mostafa GHOUS
04 Senior Executive Assistant ..... Ms. Lucille SERRANO
07 Dean of Student Affairs/Enrol Svcs ..... Vacant
09 Director of Institutional Research ..... Dr. Matthew TRENGOVE
101 Secretary of the Institution/Board ..... Ms. Lucille SERRANO
35 Dean of Student Affairs ..... Ms. Carla JOHNSON
41 Director Athletics ..... Mr. Daniel TERESA
45 Dean Inst Planning and Effective ..... Dr. Brian LOFMAN
103 Dir Workforce/Career Development ..... Ms. Sharon ALBERT
19 Dir Public Safety/Emergency Mgmt ..... Mr. Kenneth LAIRD

Harvey Mudd College (A)

301 Platt Boulevard, Claremont CA 91711-5990

County: Los Angeles
FICE Identification: 001171
Unit ID: 115409
Telephone: (909) 621-8000
Carnegie Class: Bac-A&S
FAX Number: (909) 621-8360
Calendar System: Semester
URL: www.hmc.edu
Established: 1955
Annual Undergrad Tuition & Fees: $56,620
Enrollment: 861
Coed
Affiliation or Control: Independent Non-Profit
IRS Status: 501(c)3
Highest Offering: Baccalaureate
Accreditation: WC

01 President ..... Dr. Maria M. KLAWE
111 Vice President Advancement ..... Mr. Hieu NGUYEN
10 Vice President Admin/Fin/Treasurer .... Mr. Andrew R. DORANTES
05 VP Acad Affairs/Dean of the Faculty ..... Dr. Lisa SULLIVAN
07 Vice Pres Admissions/Financial Aid ..... Ms. Thyra BRIGGS
32 VP Student Affairs/Dean of Students ..... Dr. Anna GONZALEZ
13 VP/CIO ..... Mr. Joseph VAUGHAN
15 Senior Director for Human Resources ..... Ms. Dana NAGENGAST
18 AVP Facilities/Physical Plant ..... Mr. Joel PETERSON
28 Assoc Dean Institutional Diversity ..... Dr. Jennifer ALANIS
06 Registrar ..... Mr. Mark ASHLEY
26 Director of College Relations ..... Ms. Stephanie GRAHAM
29 Director of Alumni Relations ..... Ms. Jennifer GREEN
37 Director of Student Financial Aid ..... Ms. Gilma LOPEZ
101 Director of Pres Ofc/Secy to Board ..... Ms. Karen ANGEMI
100 Chief of Staff ..... Ms. Karen ANGEMI
09 Director of Institutional Research ..... Dr. Laura PALUCKI BLAKE

Hawthorn University (B)

475 Hungry Gulch Rd, Ste C, Whitethorn CA 95589

County: Humboldt
Identification: 667358
Telephone: (707) 986-4153
Carnegie Class: Not Classified
FAX Number: N/A
Calendar System: Quarter
URL: www.hawthornuniversity.org
Established: 2002
Annual Graduate Tuition & Fees: N/A
Enrollment: N/A
Coed
Affiliation or Control: Independent Non-Profit
IRS Status: 501(c)3
Highest Offering: Doctorate; No Undergraduates
Accreditation: DEAC

01 President ..... Dr. Dorothy GERMANO

High Tech High Graduate School of Education (C)

2861 Womble Road, San Diego CA 92106-6025

County: San Diego
Identification: 667118
Unit ID: 485403
Telephone: (619) 398-4902
Carnegie Class: Spec-4-yr-Other
FAX Number: (619) 758-1960
Calendar System: Other
URL: https://hthgse.edu
Established: 2007
Annual Graduate Tuition & Fees: N/A
Enrollment: 26
Coed
Affiliation or Control: Independent Non-Profit
IRS Status: 501(c)3
Highest Offering: Master's; No Undergraduates
Accreditation: WC

01 President ..... Ben DAELY
05 Dean ..... Kelly WILSON
11 Chief Admin Officer/General Counsel ..... Maria HEREDIA
10 Chief Financial Officer ..... Vacant
32 Director Student Affairs ..... Hayley MURUGESAN

Holy Names University (D)

3500 Mountain Boulevard, Oakland CA 94619-1699

County: Alameda
FICE Identification: 001183
Unit ID: 115728
Telephone: (510) 436-1000
Carnegie Class: Masters/M
FAX Number: (510) 436-1199
Calendar System: Semester
URL: www.hnu.edu
Established: 1868
Annual Undergrad Tuition & Fees: $39,316
Enrollment: 884
Coed
Affiliation or Control: Independent Non-Profit
IRS Status: 501(c)3
Highest Offering: Master's
Accreditation: WC, NURSE

01 President ..... Mr. Michael GROENER
05 Provost/VP Academic Affairs ..... Dr. Sheila SMITH MCKOY
10 Vice President for Finance/Admin ..... Mr. Rob KINNARD
32 Vice President for Student Affairs ..... Ms. Laura LYNDON
84 VP Strategic Enrollment Mgmt ..... Mr. Alan LIEBRECHT
06 Registrar ..... Mr. Stephen STICKA
08 Director of Library Services ..... Ms. Sonia ROBLES
37 Dir Student Financial Assistance ..... Ms. Tam LEE-OPERARIO
31 Director Campus Services ..... Mr. Luis GUERRA
42 Co-Director of Campus Ministry ..... Ms. Jenny GIRARD-MALLEY
42 Co-Director of Campus Ministry ..... Fr. Sal RAGUSA
41 Director of Athletics ..... Ms. Debbie SNELL
26 University Communications Manager ..... Ms. Stephanie SILVA
29 Director of Alumni Relations ..... Vacant
13 Director Information Technology ..... Mr. Jay CASTILLO
15 Director Human Resources ..... Ms. Patricia BARTON
04 Executive Asst to President ..... Ms. Vicki TOM
09 Director of Institutional Research ..... Mr. Francisco HERRERA
18 Chief Facilities/Physical Plant ..... Mr. Luis GUERRA
53 Dean Education ..... Ms. Kimberly MAYFIELD
39 Dir Resident Life/Student Housing ..... Mr. Justin VACCA
44 Director Annual Giving ..... Ms. Kelsey LINDQUIST
100 Chief of Staff ..... Mr. Kevin GIN
102 Dir Foundation/Corporate Relations ..... Mr. Stefan AMRINE
101 Secretary of the Institution/Board ..... Sr. Carol SELLMAN, SNJM
19 Director Security/Safety ..... Mr. Antonio ROSAS
30 Director of Development ..... Mr. William TORREY

Homestead Schools (E)

23800 Hawthorne Blvd, Suite 200, Torrance CA 90505

County: Los Angeles
FICE Identification: 041497
Unit ID: 457086
Telephone: (310) 791-9975
Carnegie Class: Spec-4-yr-Other Health
FAX Number: (310) 791-0135
Calendar System: Other
URL: homesteadschools.net
Established: 2007
Annual Undergrad Tuition & Fees: N/A
Enrollment: 150
Coed
Affiliation or Control: Independent Non-Profit
IRS Status: 501(c)3
Highest Offering: Baccalaureate
Accreditation: ABHES, NURSE

01 President/CEO ..... Mr. Vijay FADIA
10 Chief Financial Officer ..... Ms. Christy MAGLES
05 Chief Academic Officer ..... Mr. Rafael TOLENTINO
07 Director of Admissions ..... Mr. George DAYRIT

Hope International University (F)

2500 E Nutwood Avenue, Fullerton CA 92831-3104

County: Orange
FICE Identification: 001252
Unit ID: 120537
Telephone: (714) 879-3901
Carnegie Class: Masters/M
FAX Number: (714) 681-7451
Calendar System: 4/1/4
URL: www.hiu.edu
Established: 1928
Annual Undergrad Tuition & Fees: $33,400
Enrollment: 1,373
Coed
Affiliation or Control: Independent Non-Profit
IRS Status: 501(c)3
Highest Offering: Master's
Accreditation: WC, BI, IACBE, MFCD

01 President ..... Dr. John L. DERRY
04 Exec Asst to the President ..... Mrs. Sharon L. CARTER
05 Vice President for Academic Affairs ..... Dr. Paul H. ALEXANDER
12 Dean Nebraska Christian College ..... Dr. Mark KRAUSE
49 Dean College of Arts and Sciences ..... Dr. Steve EDGINGTON
50 Dean College of Business & Mgmt ..... Dr. Jim WOEST
53 Dean College of Education ..... Dr. Douglas S. DOMENE
88 Dean Col of Ministry & Bible Stds ..... Dr. Joe GRANA
83 Dean College of Psych & Counseling ..... Dr. Laura L. STEELE
09 Director of Institutional Research ..... Dr. Hector GALANO
08 Librarian ..... Mrs. Robin HARTMAN
06 Registrar ..... Mr. Ron ARCHER
10 Vice President for Business/Finance ..... Mr. Tom MCGLINCHEY
37 Director Student Financial Services ..... Mrs. Shannon O'SHIELDS
15 Director of Human Resources ..... Ms. Ellen NIALIS
13 Director of Information Technology ..... Mr. Darrell C. JONES
18 Director of Campus Facilities ..... Mr. Steve MULLINS
111 Vice Pres Institutional Advancement ..... Mr. Michael MULRYAN
26 Chief Public Relations Officer ..... Mr. Michael MULRYAN
32 Vice President for Student Affairs ..... Dr. Mark COMEAUX
41 Athletic Director ..... Mr. John G. TUREK
42 Chaplain/Director Campus Ministry ..... Mr. Bryan A. SANDS
85 Director of International Students ..... Mrs. Judy E. KIM
38 Director Student Counseling ..... Dr. Laura L. STEELE
36 Dir Student Career Services ..... Mrs. Kirsten M. MCCORMICK
84 Vice Pres for Enrollment Management ..... Mrs. Teresa L. SMITH
07 Director Undergraduate Admissions ..... Mrs. Barbara MOORE
106 Dir Learning Technology ..... Ms. Micah N. ALSTON

Horizon University (G)

2040 S. Brea Canyon Rd, Ste 100, Diamond Bar CA 91765

County: Los Angeles
Identification: 667360
Telephone: (909) 895-7138
Carnegie Class: Not Classified
FAX Number: (909) 895-7143
Calendar System: Quarter
URL: horizonuniversity.org
Established:
Annual Undergrad Tuition & Fees: N/A
Enrollment: N/A
Coed
Affiliation or Control: Independent Non-Profit
IRS Status: 501(c)3
Highest Offering: Master's
Accreditation: @TRACS

01 President ..... Henry KHOR
05 Chief Academic Officer (Provost) ..... Abraham OH

Humphreys University (H)

6650 Inglewood Street, Stockton CA 95207-3896

County: San Joaquin
FICE Identification: 001212
Unit ID: 115773
Telephone: (209) 478-0800
Carnegie Class: Bac-Diverse
FAX Number: (209) 478-8721
Calendar System: Quarter
URL: www.humphreys.edu
Established: 1896
Annual Undergrad Tuition & Fees: $14,292
Enrollment: 421
Coed
Affiliation or Control: Independent Non-Profit
IRS Status: 501(c)3
Highest Offering: First Professional Degree
Accreditation: WC

01 President ..... Dr. Robert G. HUMPHREYS, JR.
05 Dn Instruction/Dir Arts & Sciences ..... Ms. Cynthia BECERRA
11 Director of Administrative Services ..... Ms. Carrie CASTILLON
58 Dean of Graduate Studies ..... Dr. Jess BONDS
61 Dean Law School ..... Mr. Patrick L. PIGGOTT
09 Dean of Institutional Research ..... Dr. Lisa KOOREN
06 Registrar ..... Ms. Maria GARCIA-MILLER
07 Director of Admissions ..... Ms. Santa E. LOPEZ
26 Chief Public Relations Officer ..... Vacant
88 Director Court Reporting Program ..... Mrs. Kay REINDL
10 Chief Business Officer ..... Ms. Carol KRAMLICH
37 Director Student Financial Aid ..... Ms. Rita FRANCO

Imperial Valley College (I)

380 E Aten Road, Imperial CA 92251-0158

County: Imperial
FICE Identification: 001214
Unit ID: 115861
Telephone: (760) 352-8320
Carnegie Class: Assoc/MT-VT-High Trad
FAX Number: (760) 355-2663
Calendar System: Semester
URL: www.imperial.edu
Established: 1922
Annual Undergrad Tuition & Fees (In-District): $1,125
Enrollment: 8,449
Coed
Affiliation or Control: Local
IRS Status: 501(c)3
Highest Offering: Associate Degree
Accreditation: WJ, EMT

01 Superintendent/President ..... Dr. Martha O. GARCIA
05 Vice President Academic Services ..... Dr. Christina TAFOYA
32 VP for Student Services and Equity ..... Dr. Lennor JOHNSON
10 VP Administrative Services ..... Ms. Josanna GARCIA
15 Chief Human Resources Officer ..... Mr. Clint C. DOUGHERTY
103 Dean Economic & Workforce Develop ..... Mr. Efrain SILVA
76 Dean of Health & Public Safety ..... Dr. Robert PRICE
49 Act Dean Arts/Letters/Learning Svcs ..... Dr. Robert PRICE
84 Dean Student Affairs/Enroll Svcs ..... Mr. Victor C. TORRES
35 Dean Student Svcs/Special Proj ..... Dr. Henry COVARRUBIAS
07 Director of Admissions and Records ..... Mrs. Vikki CARR
37 Director of Financial Aid ..... Ms. Lisa SEALS
09 Dir Institutional Research ..... Mr. Jose CARRILLO
59 Dir Child/Family/Consumer Sciences ..... Ms. Rebecca GREEN
26 Chief Public Relations Officer ..... Vacant
13 Chief Technology Officer ..... Mr. Jeff ENZ
81 Dean of Math and Sciences ..... Mr. David DRURY

Institute for Business and Technology (J)

2400 Walsh Avenue, Santa Clara CA 95051

County: Santa Clara
FICE Identification: 021283
Unit ID: 115931
Telephone: (408) 727-1060
Carnegie Class: Spec 2-yr-Health
FAX Number: N/A
Calendar System: Semester
URL: www.ibttech.com
Established: 1965
Annual Undergrad Tuition & Fees: N/A
Enrollment: 587
Coed
Affiliation or Control: Proprietary
IRS Status: Proprietary
Highest Offering: Associate Degree
Accreditation: ACCSC

01 President/CEO ..... Peter MIKHAIL
05 Director of Education ..... Fred WIEHE

Institute of Buddhist Studies (K)

2140 Durant Avenue, Berkeley CA 94704

County: Alameda
Identification: 667312
Telephone: (510) 809-1444
Carnegie Class: Not Classified
FAX Number: N/A
Calendar System: Semester
URL: www.shin-ibs.edu
Established: 1949
Annual Graduate Tuition & Fees: N/A
Enrollment: N/A
Coed
Affiliation or Control: Independent Non-Profit
IRS Status: 501(c)3
Highest Offering: Master's; No Undergraduates
Accreditation: @WC

00 Chancellor ..... Rev. Kodo UMEZU
01 President & Vice Pres Academic Affs .... Rev. David MATSUMOTO
30 Vice Pres Development ..... Rev.Dr. Seiger YAMAOKA
32 Dean of Students ..... Mr. Scott MITCHELL
10 Director of Finance ..... Ms. Linda SHIOZAKI
06 Registrar ..... Ms. Helen TAGAWA

Institute of Technology (A)

564 West Herndon Avenue, Clovis CA 93612
County: Fresno FICE Identification: 030675
Unit ID: 431141
Telephone: (559) 297-4500 Carnegie Class: Assoc/HVT-High Trad
FAX Number: (559) 297-5822 Calendar System: Semester
URL: www.iot.edu
Established: Annual Undergrad Tuition & Fees: N/A
Enrollment: 1,189 Coed
Affiliation or Control: Proprietary IRS Status: Proprietary
Highest Offering: Associate Degree
Accreditation: ACCSC, ACFEI, PTAA

01 President .... Ron GARDNER
05 Director of Education .... Carol SMITH
66 Director of Nursing .... Paula RICHARDS
32 Director of Student Services .... Melinda WOOD
07 Director of Admissions .... Marissa MARZAN
06 Registrar .... Anita RAMOS
37 Director of Financial Aid .... Sandi PUGH
36 Director of Career Services .... Tim KEARN
08 Librarian .... Laura HABERSTICH
18 Facilities Coordinator .... Tony LEON

Institute of Technology (B)

5601 Stoddard Road, Modesto CA 95356
Telephone: (209) 572-7800 Identification: 770554
Accreditation: ACCSC, ACFEI

Intercoast College (C)

388 West Cerritos Avenue, Bldg 7, Anaheim CA 92805
County: Orange FICE Identification: 025594
Unit ID: 366289
Telephone: (714) 712-7900 Carnegie Class: Spec 2-yr-Health
FAX Number: (714) 937-1983 Calendar System: Other
URL: www.intercoast.edu
Established: 1985 Annual Undergrad Tuition & Fees: N/A
Enrollment: 285 Coed
Affiliation or Control: Proprietary IRS Status: Proprietary
Highest Offering: Associate Degree
Accreditation: CNCE

01 President .... Geeta A. BROWN
12 Campus President .... Christine SANCHEZ

Interior Designers Institute (D)

1061 Camelback Road, Newport Beach CA 92660-3228
County: Orange FICE Identification: 025203
Unit ID: 116226
Telephone: (949) 675-4451 Carnegie Class: Spec-4-yr-Arts
FAX Number: (949) 759-0667 Calendar System: Quarter
URL: www.idi.edu
Established: 1984 Annual Undergrad Tuition & Fees: $18,250
Enrollment: 208 Coed
Affiliation or Control: Proprietary IRS Status: Proprietary
Highest Offering: Master's
Accreditation: ACCSC, CIDA

01 Executive Director .... Ms. Judy DEATON
37 Financial Aid Director .... Ms. Shanen FOYE
07 Director of Admissions .... Ms. Carrie BACHMAYER

International Reformed University and Seminary (E)

125 S. Vermont Avenue, Los Angeles CA 90004
County: Los Angeles Identification: 667132
Telephone: (213) 381-0081 Carnegie Class: Not Classified
FAX Number: (213) 381-0010 Calendar System: Semester
URL: www.irus.edu
Established: 1977 Annual Undergrad Tuition & Fees: N/A
Enrollment: N/A Coed
Affiliation or Control: Independent Non-Profit IRS Status: 501(c)3
Highest Offering: Doctorate
Accreditation: BI

01 President .... Dr. Hun Sung PARK
05 Academic Dean .... Dr. Kwang Hoon LEE
32 Dean of Students .... Dr. John KIM
11 Dean of Administrative Services .... Dr. Joha OH
108 Director of Assessment & Planning .... Dr. Yumee RAH
08 Librarian .... Ms. Hannah LEE
20 Director of Teaching & Learning Tec .... Ms. Hala SUN
88 Secretary .... Ms. Hyang LEE

International Technological University (F)

2711 N. First Street, San Jose CA 95134
County: Santa Clara Identification: 667070
Unit ID: 443128
Telephone: (888) 488-4968 Carnegie Class: Masters/L
FAX Number: (408) 331-1026 Calendar System: Trimester
URL: www.itu.edu
Established: 1994 Annual Graduate Tuition & Fees: N/A
Enrollment: 827 Coed
Affiliation or Control: Independent Non-Profit IRS Status: 501(c)3
Highest Offering: Doctorate; No Undergraduates
Accreditation: WC, ACBSP

01 President and CEO .... Dr. Gregory O'BRIEN
05 Provost .... Dr. Eric TAO
46 VP Technology & Research .... Karl WANG
10 Chief Financial Officer .... Edward LAM
13 Chief Technology Officer .... Kranthi LAMMATHA
32 Director Student Affairs .... Joe MAZARES
06 University Registrar .... Marcos CARMELO CRUZ-ALVARADO
08 Head Librarian .... Marion HAYES
101 Dir University Affs/Board Liaison .... Angie LO
26 Exec Dir Marketing/Enrollment Mgmt .... Micah THOMAS
15 Director Human Resources .... Leslie ANDERSON
85 Dir International Student Office .... Amy CHAUNG

International Theological Seminary (G)

540 E Vine Avenue, West Covina CA 91790
County: Los Angeles Identification: 666360
Unit ID: 396985
Telephone: (626) 448-0023 Carnegie Class: Not Classified
FAX Number: (626) 350-6343 Calendar System: Quarter
URL: www.itsla.edu
Established: 1982 Annual Undergrad Tuition & Fees: N/A
Enrollment: N/A Coed
Affiliation or Control: Independent Non-Profit IRS Status: 501(c)3
Highest Offering: Doctorate
Accreditation: THEOL

01 President .... Dr. James S. LEE
05 Vice Pres for Academic Affairs .... Dr. Priscilla ADOYO
11 Vice President for Administration .... Rev. Paul Zhaohui YANG
32 Dean of Students .... Dr. Premkumar DHARMARAJ
06 Interim Registrar .... Ms. Letty CHEN
08 Librarian .... Ms. Susan LIU
26 Communication Director/Asst to Pres .... Ms. Ei MEREN ACIERTO

John F. Kennedy University (H)

100 Ellinwood Way, Pleasant Hill CA 94523-4817
County: Contra Costa FICE Identification: 004484
Unit ID: 116712
Telephone: (925) 969-3300 Carnegie Class: DU-Mod
FAX Number: (925) 969-3399 Calendar System: Quarter
URL: www.jfku.edu
Established: 1964 Annual Undergrad Tuition & Fees: $8,500
Enrollment: 815 Coed
Affiliation or Control: Independent Non-Profit IRS Status: 501(c)3
Highest Offering: Doctorate
Accreditation: WC, CLPSY, IACBE

01 President .... Dr. Tom STEWART
10 Chief Financial Officer .... James MIRR
13 Assoc VP Technology/Education Svcs .... Matthew BRUCE
32 Assoc VP Student Experience .... Dr. Judy CASTRO
26 Assoc VP Marketing/Communication .... Michael DAVIDSON
04 Administrative Asst to President .... Marie PAVONE
06 Registrar .... Diane CVETIC
84 Director of Enrollment .... Catherine REED
09 Director of Institutional Research .... Dr. Mark KURAI
100 Chief of Staff .... Dr. Jack PADUNTIN
102 Dir Foundation/Corporate Relations .... Rhea JOHNSON
15 Director Human Resources .... Dr. Robert JAKO
18 Director Facilities/Physical Plant .... David SADLER
37 Director Student Financial Aid .... Mindy BERGERON
38 Exec Dir Community Counseling Ctrs .... Gail KINSLEY-DAME

John Paul the Great Catholic University (I)

220 West Grand Avenue, Escondido CA 92025
County: San Diego FICE Identification: 041937
Unit ID: 462354
Telephone: (858) 653-6740 Carnegie Class: Bac-Diverse
FAX Number: (858) 653-3791 Calendar System: Quarter
URL: www.jpcatholic.com
Established: 2003 Annual Undergrad Tuition & Fees: $26,100
Enrollment: 329 Coed
Affiliation or Control: Independent Non-Profit IRS Status: 501(c)3
Highest Offering: Master's
Accreditation: WC

01 President .... Dr. Derry CONNOLLY
05 Chief Academic Officer .... Vacant
10 Chief Finance Officer .... Kevin MAZIERE
11 VP for Administration .... Lidy CONNOLLY
07 VP of Admissions .... Martin HAROLD
13 VP for Technology & Real Estate .... Kevin MEZIERE
32 Dean of Students .... Jonathan SPERLING
37 Director of Financial Aid .... Lisa WILLIAMS
06 Registrar .... Nick HEYE
42 Director Campus Ministry .... Austin SCHNEIDER
09 Director Institutional Research .... Fran WISE
39 Dir of Admissions & Marketing .... Joe HOUDE

Kaiser Permanente School of Allied Health Sciences (J)

938 Marina Way South, Richmond CA 94804
County: Contra Costa Identification: 667152
Telephone: (510) 231-5000 Carnegie Class: Not Classified
FAX Number: (510) 231-5001 Calendar System: Quarter
URL: www.kpsahs.edu
Established: 1989 Annual Undergrad Tuition & Fees: N/A
Enrollment: N/A Coed
Affiliation or Control: Proprietary IRS Status: Proprietary
Highest Offering: Baccalaureate
Accreditation: WC, DMS, NMT, RAD

01 Medical Director .... Dr. C. Darryl JONES
10 Assoc Director of Finance/CFO .... Pamela PRESSLEY
11 Regional School Administrator/CEO .... James FITZGIBBON
09 Dir Assessment/Inst Research .... Bert CHRISTENSEN
04 Admin Assistant to the President .... Diana K. JACKSON

*Kern Community College District (K)

2100 Chester Avenue, Bakersfield CA 93301-4099
County: Kern FICE Identification: 006994
Unit ID: 436313
Telephone: (661) 336-5100 Carnegie Class: N/A
FAX Number: (661) 336-5134
URL: www.kccd.edu

01 Chancellor .... Mr. Thomas J. BURKE
05 Vice Chanc Educational Services .... Mr. John MEANS
15 Vice Chanc Human Resources .... Ms. Tonya DAVIS
10 Chief Financial Officer .... Ms. Deborah MARTIN
13 Chief Technology Officer .... Mr. Gary MOSER
43 General Counsel .... Mr. Christopher HINE

*Bakersfield College (L)

1801 Panorama Drive, Bakersfield CA 93305-1299
County: Kern FICE Identification: 001118
Unit ID: 109819
Telephone: (661) 395-4011 Carnegie Class: Bac/Assoc-Assoc Dom
FAX Number: (661) 395-4241 Calendar System: Semester
URL: www.bakersfieldcollege.edu
Established: 1913 Annual Undergrad Tuition & Fees (In-District): $1,325
Enrollment: 23,195 Coed
Affiliation or Control: State/Local IRS Status: 501(c)3
Highest Offering: Baccalaureate
Accreditation: WJ, EMT, RAD

02 President .... Dr. Sonya CHRISTIAN
05 Vice President Instruction .... Ms. Billie Jo RICE
10 VP Finance & Administrative Svcs .... Mr. Mike GIACOMINI
32 Vice Pres Student Affairs .... Dr. Zavareh DADABHOY
09 Dean Institutional Effectiveness .... Mr. Craig HAYWARD
20 Dean of Instruction .... Dr. Rich MCCROW
66 Dean of Instruction .... Ms. Andrea THORSON
20 Dean of Instruction .... Dr. Stephen WALLER
20 Dean of Instruction .... Dr. Emmanuel MOURTZANOS
30 Director Foundation & Development .... Mr. Tom GELDER
18 Dir Facilities/Maintenance/Ops .... Mr. Bill POTTER
12 Director Delano Center .... Mr. Rich MCCROW
37 Director Financial Aid .... Ms. Jennifer ACHAN
84 Director Enrollment Services .... Ms. Michelle PENA
26 Dir Communication/Cmty Relations .... Ms. Norma ROJAS-MORA
04 Admin Assistant to the President .... Ms. Jennifer MARDEN
13 Director Information Technology .... Mr. Todd COSTON
41 Director of Athletics .... Ms. Sandi TAYLOR

*Cerro Coso Community College (M)

3000 College Heights Boulevard,
Ridgecrest CA 93555-7777
County: Kern FICE Identification: 010111
Unit ID: 111896
Telephone: (760) 384-6100 Carnegie Class: Assoc/HT-Mix Trad/Non
FAX Number: (760) 375-4776 Calendar System: Semester
URL: www.cerrocoso.edu
Established: 1973 Annual Undergrad Tuition & Fees (In-District): $1,290
Enrollment: 5,725 Coed
Affiliation or Control: State/Local IRS Status: 501(c)3
Highest Offering: Associate Degree
Accreditation: WJ

02 President .... Ms. A. Jill BOARD
05 Vice President Instruction .... Dr. Corey MARVIN
10 Vice Pres Finance/Admin Services .... Ms. Lisa COUCH
32 Vice President of Student Services .... Ms. Heather OSTASH
20 Dean of Instruction .... Mr. Chad HOUCH
12 Dir Eastern Sierra College Center .... Ms. Deanna CAMPBELL
12 Dir of East Kern/Kern River Valley .... Ms. Lisa STEPHENS
75 Dean Career Technical Education .... Ms. Maura MURABITO
38 Dir of Counseling Svcs/SSSP .... Ms. Christine SMALL
07 Dir Admiss/Records/VA/Fin Aid .... Mr. William BLOOM
15 Manager Human Resources .... Ms. Resa HESS
88 Program Mgr Child Development Ctr .... Ms. Jessica KRALL
26 Dir Public Relations/Instl Advance .... Ms. Natalie DORRELL
13 Director Information Technology .... Mr. Michael CAMPBELL
35 Director Outreach Services .... Ms. Katie BACHMAN
106 Director Distance Education .... Ms. Rebecca PANG
04 Administrative Asst to President .... Ms. Jennifer CURTIS

41 Athletic Director .... Mr. John MCHENRY
18 Dir Maintenance/Operations .... Mr. John DALY

*Porterville College (A)

100 E College Avenue, Porterville CA 93257-6058
County: Tulare FICE Identification: 001268
Unit ID: 121363
Telephone: (559) 791-2200 Carnegie Class: Assoc/HVT-High Trad
FAX Number: (559) 784-4779 Calendar System: Semester
URL: www.portervillecollege.edu
Established: 1927 Annual Undergrad Tuition & Fees (In-District): $1,322
Enrollment: 4,054 Coed
Affiliation or Control: State/Local IRS Status: 501(c)3
Highest Offering: Associate Degree
Accreditation: WJ

02 President .... Dr. Claudia HABIB
04 Administrative Asst to President .... Mrs. Felisa HANNAH
05 Int Vice President Instruction .... Dr. Gregory SOUTH
10 Vice Pres Finance & Admin Services .... Dr. Arlitha WILLIAMS-HARMON
32 Vice President Student Services .... Ms. Primavera ARVIZU
20 Dean Instruction .... Ms. Kailani KNUTSON
37 Assistant Director Financial Aid .... Ms. Tiffany HAYNES
76 Assoc Dean Health Careers .... Ms. Kim BEHRENS
18 Director Maintenance & Operations .... Mr. John WORD
102 Exec Director PC Foundation .... Ms. Ramona CHIAPA
84 Director Enrollment Services .... Ms. Erin CRUZ
09 Institutional Researcher .... Mr. Michael CARLEY
13 Director Information Technology .... Mr. Jay NAVARRETTE
35 Director Student Services .... Ms. Diane THOMPSON
08 Librarian .... Mr. Chris EBERT
41 Athletic Director .... Mr. Joseph CASCIO
88 Program Manager Child Dev Center .... Ms. Karen BALL
21 Accounting Manager .... Ms. Sonia HUCKABAY
26 Manager Communications & Marketing .... Mr. Roger PEREZ
105 Web Content Editor .... Ms. Samantha SOUSA
15 Human Resources Manager .... Ms. Anne VANDERHORST

Kernel University (B)

905 S. Euclid Street #213, Fullerton CA 92833
County: Orange Identification: 667308
Telephone: (714) 995-9988 Carnegie Class: Not Classified
FAX Number: (714) 995-9989 Calendar System: Semester
URL: www.kernel.edu
Established: 1995 Annual Undergrad Tuition & Fees: N/A
Enrollment: N/A Coed
Affiliation or Control: Independent Non-Profit IRS Status: 501(c)3
Highest Offering: Master's
Accreditation: TRACS

01 President .... Matthew D. WOO
05 Academic Dean .... Ihn Chae CHUNG
10 Chief Financial Officer .... Joanne C. LEE
08 Head Librarian .... David CHUNG

La Sierra University (C)

4500 Riverwalk Parkway, Riverside CA 92515-8247
County: Riverside FICE Identification: 001215
Unit ID: 117627
Telephone: (951) 785-2000 Carnegie Class: Masters/M
FAX Number: (951) 785-2901 Calendar System: Quarter
URL: www.lasierra.edu
Established: 1922 Annual Undergrad Tuition & Fees: $32,778
Enrollment: 2,449 Coed
Affiliation or Control: Seventh-day Adventist IRS Status: 501(c)3
Highest Offering: Doctorate
Accreditation: WC, MUS, SW, THEOL

01 President .... Dr. Randal R. WISBEY
05 Acting Provost .... Ms. Cindy PARKHURST
10 Vice President for Finance .... Mr. David GERIGUIS
32 Vice President for Student Life .... Ms. Yamilet BAZAN
111 Vice Pres Advancement/Univ Rels .... Mr. Norman YERGEN
84 Vice Pres Enrollment Services .... Mr. David R. LOFTHOUSE
26 VP Communication/Integrated Mktg .... Dr. Marilyn THOMSEN
21 Associate Vice President Finance .... Ms. Pamela CHRISPENS
20 Associate Provost .... Ms. Cindy PARKHURST
49 Dean College Arts/Sciences .... Dr. April SUMMITT
50 Dean School of Business .... Dr. John THOMAS
53 Dean School of Education .... Dr. Ginger KETTING-WELLER
73 Dean School of Divinity .... Dr. Friedbert NINOW
35 Dean of Student Life .... Ms. Marjorie ROBINSON
102 Exec Director University Foundation .... Mr. Larry GERATY
55 Director Adult Evening Program .... Ms. Nancy DITTEMORE
29 Alumni Director .... Ms. Julie NARDUCCI
15 Director Human Resources .... Ms. Dell Jean VAN FOSSEN
08 Director Library .... Ms. Kitty SIMMONS
37 Director Student Financial Services .... Ms. Esther KINZER
42 Director Campus Ministries .... Mr. Samuel E. LEONOR, JR.
13 Director Information Technology .... Mr. Geoff INGRAM
09 Director of Institutional Research .... Ms. Jan LONG
18 Director Physical Plant .... Mr. Al VALDEZ
38 Director Counseling Center .... Ms. Debra WRIGHT
92 Director Honors Program .... Dr. Douglas R. CLARK
07 Director of Admissions/Registrar .... Mr. Issmael NZAMUTUNA
36 Career Advisor .... Mr. William PENICK
41 Athletic Director .... Mr. Javier KRUMM

Laguna College of Art & Design (D)

2222 Laguna Canyon Road,
Laguna Beach CA 92651-1136
County: Orange FICE Identification: 023305
Unit ID: 117168
Telephone: (949) 376-6000 Carnegie Class: Spec-4-yr-Arts
FAX Number: (949) 376-6009 Calendar System: Semester
URL: www.lcad.edu
Established: 1961 Annual Undergrad Tuition & Fees: $30,700
Enrollment: 688 Coed
Affiliation or Control: Independent Non-Profit IRS Status: 501(c)3
Highest Offering: Master's
Accreditation: WC, ART

01 President .... Dr. Jonathan BURKE
05 Provost .... Dr. Helene GARRISON
111 Vice Pres of College Advancement .... Mr. Dominic MUMOLO
10 Chief Financial Officer .... Mr. Jim GODEK
07 Dean of Admissions .... Mr. Christopher BROWN
32 Asst Dean of Students .... Mr. Julian VELARDE
06 Registrar .... Ms. Laura PATRICK
08 Library Director .... Ms. Viet VU
04 Assistant to the President .... Ms. Jeni RICHARDS
37 Director Financial Aid .... Mr. Christopher BROWN
09 Director of Institutional Research .... Ms. Laura PATRICK
15 Director Human Resources .... Ms. Caroline CARLSON
13 Director of IT .... Mr. Matt MORTON
18 Director Facilities/Physical Plant .... Mr. Mark DAY
26 Communications Manager .... Mr. Mike STICE

Lake Tahoe Community College (E)

1 College Drive, South Lake Tahoe CA 96150-4524
County: El Dorado FICE Identification: 012907
Unit ID: 117195
Telephone: (530) 541-4660 Carnegie Class: Assoc/MT-VT-High Non
FAX Number: (530) 541-7852 Calendar System: Quarter
URL: www.ltcc.edu
Established: 1975 Annual Undergrad Tuition & Fees (In-District): $1,224
Enrollment: 2,108 Coed
Affiliation or Control: State/Local IRS Status: 501(c)3
Highest Offering: Associate Degree
Accreditation: WJ

01 Superintendent/President .... Mr. Jeff DEFRANCO
04 Executive Assistant to President .... Ms. Lisa SHAFER
05 VP Academic Affairs .... Dr. Michelle RISDON
10 Vice Pres Administrative Svcs .... Ms. Russi EGAN
103 Dean of Workforce Development/Inst .... Mr. Brad DEEDS
32 VP Student Services .... Mr. Jonathan KING
20 Dean of Instruction .... Ms. Ali BISSONNETTE
08 Director of Library .... Ms. Melanie CHU
13 Director Tech & Education Svcs .... Mr. Dave BURBA
84 Director Enrollment Services .... Ms. Steve BERRY
21 Director of Fiscal Services .... Ms. Andrea SALAZAR
15 Director of Human Resources .... Ms. Shelley HANSEN
18 Director of Facilities .... Vacant
88 Dir Child Development Programs .... Ms. Leslie AMATO
37 Director Financial Aid .... Vacant
09 Director of Institutional Research .... Ms. Donna SOHAN
26 Public Information Officer .... Ms. Diane LEWIS
102 Foundation Director .... Ms. Nancy HARRISON
40 Bookstore Manager .... Mr. Trevor OSTENDORF
96 Purchasing Agent .... Ms. Heather CADE
41 Athletic Director .... Mr. Steve BERRY
28 Director of Equity .... Ms. Laura SALINAS

Lassen Community College (F)

PO Box 3000, 478-200 Highway 139,
Susanville CA 96130-3000
County: Lassen FICE Identification: 001217
Unit ID: 117274
Telephone: (530) 257-6181 Carnegie Class: Assoc/HT-Mix Trad/Non
FAX Number: (530) 251-8872 Calendar System: Semester
URL: www.lassencollege.edu
Established: 1925 Annual Undergrad Tuition & Fees (In-District): $1,127
Enrollment: 2,484 Coed
Affiliation or Control: State/Local IRS Status: 501(c)3
Highest Offering: Associate Degree
Accreditation: WJ

01 District Superintendent/President .... Dr. Marlon R. HALL
04 Assistant to President .... Ms. Julie L. JOHNSTON
05 VP Academic Services .... Vacant
20 Dean of Instruction .... Dr. Trevor ALBERTSON
20 Dean of Instruction .... Ms. Karissa MOREHOUSE
11 Interim VP Administrative Services .... Ms. Terry BARTLEY
32 Dean of Student Services .... Vacant
121 Assoc Dean Student Success/Equity .... Ms. Brady REED
08 Librarian .... Ms. Shar MURPHY
09 Assoc Dean Inst Effectiveness/Rsrch .... Dr. Randall JOSLIN
37 Director Financial Aid .... Mr. Davis MURPHY
35 Director Student Life .... Mr. Francis BEAUJON
41 Athletic Director .... Mr. Glen YONAN
18 Interim Assoc VP Fac/Operations .... Mr. Gregory COLLINS
15 Director Human Resources .... Ms. Vickie RAMSEY
13 Director of Information Technology .... Mr. David CORLEY

Latin American Bible Institute (G)

14209 E. Lomitas Avenue, La Puente CA 91746
County: Los Angeles Identification: 667319
Telephone: (626) 968-1328 Carnegie Class: Not Classified
FAX Number: (626) 961-7253 Calendar System: Semester
URL: www.labi.edu
Established: 1926 Annual Undergrad Tuition & Fees: N/A
Enrollment: N/A Coed
Affiliation or Control: Independent Non-Profit IRS Status: 501(c)3
Highest Offering: Associate Degree
Accreditation: @BI

01 President .... Dr. Marty HARRIS
05 Provost/Dean of Academic Affairs .... Mr. Nehemias ROMERO
10 Chief Financial Officer .... Ms. Gabriela MORA-ALVAREZ
32 Dean of Students .... Ms. Yvette ROBLES
100 Chief of Staff .... Vacant

Laurus College (H)

81 Higuera Street, Ste 110, San Luis Obispo CA 93401
County: San Luis Obispo FICE Identification: 041414
Unit ID: 454786
Telephone: (805) 267-1690 Carnegie Class: Assoc/HVT-High Trad
FAX Number: (805) 352-1307 Calendar System: Quarter
URL: www.lauruscollege.edu
Established: 2006 Annual Undergrad Tuition & Fees: N/A
Enrollment: 1,117 Coed
Affiliation or Control: Proprietary IRS Status: Proprietary
Highest Offering: Baccalaureate
Accreditation: ACICS, DEAC

00 President/CEO .... Dr. Wayne NEALE
01 School Chancellor .... Mr. Jeff REDMOND
32 Vice Pres Student Programs .... Ms. Cecilia MORTELA
37 Director Financial Aid .... Mr. Tim REDMOND
06 Registrar .... Mr. Brendan COYLE

Learnet Academy (I)

3251 W. 6th Street, 2nd Floor, Los Angeles CA 90020
County: Los Angeles Identification: 667223
Unit ID: 483221
Telephone: (213) 387-4242 Carnegie Class: Spec 2-yr-Other
FAX Number: (213) 387-5365 Calendar System: Other
URL: www.learnet.edu
Established: 1993 Annual Undergrad Tuition & Fees: N/A
Enrollment: 131 Coed
Affiliation or Control: Proprietary IRS Status: Proprietary
Highest Offering: Associate Degree
Accreditation: ACCSC

01 Executive Director .... Ms. Tia SHIN

Life Chiropractic College West (J)

25001 Industrial Boulevard, Hayward CA 94545-2801
County: Alameda FICE Identification: 022285
Unit ID: 117520
Telephone: (510) 780-4500 Carnegie Class: Spec-4-yr-Other Health
FAX Number: (510) 780-4525 Calendar System: Quarter
URL: www.lifewest.edu
Established: 1976 Annual Undergrad Tuition & Fees: N/A
Enrollment: 620 Coed
Affiliation or Control: Independent Non-Profit IRS Status: 501(c)3
Highest Offering: First Professional Degree; No Lower Division
Accreditation: WC, CHIRO

01 President .... Dr. Ron OBERSTEIN
03 Executive Vice President .... Dr. Anatole BOGATSKI
17 Vice President Clinical Operations .... Dr. Scott DONALDSON
05 Vice President of Academic Affairs .... Dr. Pardeep KULLAR
111 VP Institutional Advancement .... Dr. Mark ZIEGLER
09 Director of Institutional Research .... Vacant
10 Controller .... Angelito TOLENTINO
46 Director of Research .... Dr. Monica SMITH
51 Director of Continuing Education .... Dr. Laurie ISENBERG
08 Library Director .... Vacant
29 Director Alumni Relations .... Dr. Palmer PEET
37 Director Financial Aid .... Brenda JOHNSON
06 Registrar .... Maria LOPEZ
15 Director Human Resources .... Sunita RANADIVE
32 Student Life Manager .... Danielle LORTA
105 Webmaster .... Vacant
40 Bookstore Manager .... Michael BALDWIN
41 Athletic Director .... Adriaan FERRIS
84 Dean of Enrollment .... Dr. Mary LUCUS-FLANNERY
30 Director of Development .... Thomas HYLAND
108 Director of Assessment & Education .... Dr. Scott KERLIN
04 Executive Assistant to President .... Sharon SETO
07 Director of Admissions .... Marc MARTIN
18 Chf Facilities/Physical Plant Ofcr .... Michael BALDWIN
26 Director of Marketing .... Alana HOPE
121 Academic Counselor .... Lori PINO

Life Pacific University (K)

1100 W. Covina Boulevard, San Dimas CA 91773-3298
County: Los Angeles FICE Identification: 022706
Unit ID: 117104
Telephone: (909) 599-5433 Carnegie Class: Bac-Diverse
FAX Number: (909) 599-6690 Calendar System: Semester

URL: www.lifepacific.edu
Established: 1923 Annual Undergrad Tuition & Fees: $15,654
Enrollment: 581 Coed
Affiliation or Control: Other IRS Status: 501(c)3
Highest Offering: Master's
Accreditation: WC, BI

01 President .... Dr. Jim J. ADAMS
04 Exec Assistant to the President .... Mrs. Karli ALBANESE
05 Vice President Academic Affairs .... Dr. Terry SAMPLES
84 Vice President Enrollment Mgt .... Rev. Angie RICHEY
32 Assoc VP of Student Development .... Mr. George BOSTANIC
10 CFO .... Mr. Todd ESKES
08 Librarian .... Mr. Gary MERRIMAN
06 Registrar .... Mrs. Amber BURNETT
18 Director of Facilities .... Mr. Rick MEYER
37 Director of Financial Aid .... Mrs. Luci PEREZ
09 Dean Institutional Effectiveness .... Mr. Brian TOMHAVE
15 Human Resources Director .... Ms. Heidi BONADIE
39 Director Residence Life .... Mrs. Kristen ZIMMERMAN
41 Athletic Director .... Mr. Tim COOK
13 IT Administrator (CIO) .... Mr. Marlon ESTELLA
111 Chief Development/Advancement .... Mr. Mike MEYER

Lincoln University (A)

401 15th Street, Oakland CA 94612-2801
County: Alameda FICE Identification: 006975
Unit ID: 117557
Telephone: (510) 628-8010 Carnegie Class: Spec-4-yr-Bus
FAX Number: (510) 628-8012 Calendar System: Semester
URL: www.lincolnuca.edu
Established: 1919 Annual Undergrad Tuition & Fees: $11,110
Enrollment: 659 Coed
Affiliation or Control: Independent Non-Profit IRS Status: 501(c)3
Highest Offering: Doctorate
Accreditation: @WC, ACICS, IACBE

01 President .... Dr. Mikhail BRODSKY
11 Administrative Vice President .... Dr. Michael GUERRA
32 Dean of Students .... Mr. William HESS
07 Director of Admissions & Records .... Ms. Peggy AU
05 Provost .... Dr. Marshall J. BURAK
08 Head Librarian .... Ms. Nicole Y. MARSH
35 Director of Student Services .... Ms. Ana Maria GOWER
13 Director of Computer Laboratory .... Mr. Shakil SHRESTHA
06 Registrar .... Ms. Maggie HUA
10 CFO .... Ms. Sherry LIANG
108 Dir of Accreditation/Compliance .... Dr. Harpal DHILLON
09 Institutional Research Coordinator .... Dr. Igor HIMELFARB
37 Director Student Financial Aid .... Ms. Wendy VASQUEZ

Logos Evangelical Seminary (B)

9358 Telstar Avenue, El Monte CA 91731-2816
County: Los Angeles FICE Identification: 039454
Unit ID: 397553
Telephone: (626) 571-5115 Carnegie Class: Not Classified
FAX Number: N/A Calendar System: Semester
URL: www.logos-seminary.edu
Established: 1989 Annual Graduate Tuition & Fees: N/A
Enrollment: N/A Coed
Affiliation or Control: Other IRS Status: 501(c)3
Highest Offering: Doctorate; No Undergraduates
Accreditation: WC, THEOL

01 President .... Dr. Kuo-Liang LIN
05 Academic Dean .... Dr. Ekron CHEN
111 Director of Advancement .... Rev. Mark SHEN
10 Director Finance/Administration .... Mr. Steven WU
32 Dean of Students .... Rev. Samuel LIU
12 Director Logos Training Institute .... Ms. Sandra SUN
04 Executive Asst to President .... Ms. Kathleen LIN
08 Head Librarian .... Ms. Shelley SII
09 Institutional Research Specialist .... Ms. Teresa KAO
13 Chief Info Technology Officer (CIO) .... Mr. Alex HUNG

Loma Linda University (C)

11139 Anderson Street, Loma Linda CA 92350
County: San Bernardino FICE Identification: 001218
Unit ID: 117636
Telephone: (909) 558-1000 Carnegie Class: Spec-4-yr-Med
FAX Number: (909) 558-0242 Calendar System: Quarter
URL: www.llu.edu
Established: 1905 Annual Undergrad Tuition & Fees: N/A
Enrollment: 4,417 Coed
Affiliation or Control: Seventh-day Adventist IRS Status: 501(c)3
Highest Offering: Doctorate
Accreditation: WC, ANEST, ARCPA, CAHIIM, CAMPEP, CLPSY, COARC, CVT, CYTO, DENT, DH, DIETC, DMS, IPSY, MED, MFCD, MT, NMT, NURSE, OPE, OT, PA, PAST, PH, PHAR, PTA, PTAA, RAD, RADDOS, RTT, SP, SW

01 President .... Dr. Richard H. HART
05 Provost .... Dr. Ronald L. CARTER
10 Sr Vice President Financial Affairs .... Mr. Rodney NEAL
30 Sr Vice President Advancement .... Mrs. Rachelle BUSSELL
13 Vice President Information Systems .... Dr. David P. HARRIS
84 VP Enrollment Mgmt/Student Services .... Vacant
46 VP for Research Affairs .... Dr. Michael SAMARDZIJA
15 VP Human Resource Management .... Ms. Lizette NORTON
63 Dean of Medicine .... Dr. Tamara THOMAS
52 Dean of Dentistry .... Dr. Robert HANDYSIDES
69 Dean of Public Health .... Dr. Helen Hopp MARSHAK
66 Dean of Nursing .... Dr. Elizabeth (Becky) BOSSERT
76 Dean of Allied Health Professions .... Dr. Craig R. JACKSON
67 Dean School of Pharmacy .... Dr. Michael D. HOGUE
83 Dean School of Behavioral Health .... Dr. Beverly J. BUCKLES
73 Interim Dean School of Religion .... Dr. Leo RANZOLIN
58 Int Exec Dir Faculty Grad Studies .... Dr. Ronald L. CARTER
06 Director of Records .... Ms. Erin SEHEULT
08 Acting Dir University Libraries .... Ms. Shanalee TAMARES
38 Director of Counseling .... Dr. William G. MURDOCH
43 General Legal Counsel .... Mr. Kent A. HANSEN
33 Dean of Men .... Mr. John NAFIE
34 Dean of Women .... Ms. Lynette BATES
37 Director Student Financial Aid .... Ms. Verdell SCHAEFER
09 Dir Educational Effectiveness .... Dr. Marilyn EGGERS
18 Director Campus Engineering .... Mr. Randy STEVENS
96 Director of Purchasing .... Mr. Tim HICKMAN
40 Campus Bookstore Manager .... Ms. Arlene ALVAREZ
42 Campus Chaplain .... Pastor Terry SWENSON

Long Beach City College (D)

4901 E Carson Street, Long Beach CA 90808-1780
County: Los Angeles FICE Identification: 001219
Unit ID: 117645
Telephone: (562) 938-4111 Carnegie Class: Assoc/MT-VT-High Trad
FAX Number: (562) 938-4118 Calendar System: Other
URL: www.lbcc.edu
Established: 1927 Annual Undergrad Tuition & Fees (In-District): $1,174
Enrollment: 24,658 Coed
Affiliation or Control: State/Local IRS Status: 501(c)3
Highest Offering: Associate Degree
Accreditation: WJ, ADNUR

01 Superintendent-President .... Dr. Reagan ROMALI
05 Vice Pres Academic Affairs .... Dr. Kathy SCOTT
11 Vice Pres Business Services .... Marlene DUNN
32 Vice Pres Student Supp Svcs .... Dr. Mike MUÑOZ
15 Interim Vice Pres Human Resources .... Gene DURAND
13 Chief Information Systems Officer .... Sylvia LYNCH
16 Interim Assoc VP Human Resources .... Kristin OLSON
07 Exec Dean Enrollment Services .... Corey RODGERS
121 Senior Exec Dir College Adv & Econ .... Sheneui WEBER
75 Dean Career & Technical Education .... Gene CARBONARO
20 Dean Academic Services .... Michelle GRIMES-HILLMAN
38 Dean Counseling/Stdnt Supp Svcs .... Nohel CORRAL
79 Dean of Language Arts .... Lee DOUGLAS
35 Dean Student Affairs .... Ramon KNOX
76 Dean School Health & Science .... Paul CREASON
09 Dean Inst Effectiveness .... Heather Van VOLKINBURG
83 Interim Dean Social Sciences & Arts .... Elisabeth ORR
62 Interim Assoc Dean Library .... Jennifer RODDEN
102 Exec Director Foundation .... Elizabeth MCCANN
26 Exec Dir Public Affairs & Marketing .... Joshua CASTELLANOS
100 Director of the President's Office .... Jeff WOOD
96 Int Director Business Support Svcs .... Bob RAPOZA
18 Interim Dir Facilities/Maint/Oper .... Medhanie EPHREM
21 Director Fiscal Services & Payroll .... John THOMPSON
37 Dep Dir Enrollment Svcs/Fin Aid .... Juan MENJIVAR
41 Athletic Director .... Randy TOTORP
103 Director Workforce Development .... Melissa INFUSINO

Los Angeles Academy of Figurative Art (E)

16926 Saticoy Street, Van Nuys CA 91406
County: Los Angeles Identification: 667231
Unit ID: 490124
Telephone: (818) 708-9232 Carnegie Class: Spec-4-yr-Arts
FAX Number: (818) 474-8679 Calendar System: Quarter
URL: www.laafa.edu
Established: 2002 Annual Undergrad Tuition & Fees: $32,093
Enrollment: 14 Coed
Affiliation or Control: Proprietary IRS Status: Proprietary
Highest Offering: Baccalaureate
Accreditation: ART

01 President .... Maryam STORM

Los Angeles College of Music (F)

300 South Fair Oaks Avenue, Pasadena CA 91105
County: Los Angeles FICE Identification: 038684
Unit ID: 446385
Telephone: (626) 568-8850 Carnegie Class: Spec-4-yr-Arts
FAX Number: (626) 568-8854 Calendar System: Quarter
URL: www.lacm.edu
Established: 1996 Annual Undergrad Tuition & Fees: $24,304
Enrollment: 235 Coed
Affiliation or Control: Proprietary IRS Status: Proprietary
Highest Offering: Baccalaureate
Accreditation: MUS

01 President .... Charles T. AYLESBURY
03 Executive Vice President .... Erin WORKMAN
06 Registrar .... Jorge OJEDA
05 Dean of Academics .... Vacant
37 Director of Financial Aid .... Jennifer OLEVSON
07 Director of Admissions .... Emilio RODRIGUEZ
10 Controller .... Kristin BARRIOS

*Los Angeles Community College District Office (G)

770 Wilshire Boulevard, Los Angeles CA 90017
County: Los Angeles FICE Identification: 001221
Unit ID: 117681
Telephone: (213) 891-2000 Carnegie Class: N/A
FAX Number: N/A
URL: www.laccd.edu

01 Chancellor .... Dr. Francisco C. RODRIGUEZ
05 VC Educ Pgms/Inst Effective .... Dr. Ryan M. CORNNER
43 General Counsel .... Mr. Jeffrey M. PRIETO
10 VC Finance and Resource Development .... Dr. Robert B. MILLER
15 VC Human Resources .... Dr. Albert J. ROMAN
18 Interim Chief Facilities Executive .... Mr. Thomas HALL
20 Deputy Chancellor .... Dr. Adriana D. BARRERA

*East Los Angeles College (H)

1301 Avenida Cesar Chavez,
Monterey Park CA 91754-6001
County: Los Angeles FICE Identification: 022260
Unit ID: 113856
Telephone: (323) 265-8650 Carnegie Class: Assoc/MT-VT-Mix Trad/Non
FAX Number: (323) 265-8763 Calendar System: Semester
URL: www.elac.edu
Established: 1945 Annual Undergrad Tuition & Fees (In-District): $1,220
Enrollment: 34,578 Coed
Affiliation or Control: State/Local IRS Status: 501(c)3
Highest Offering: Associate Degree
Accreditation: WJ, CAHIIM, COARC

02 Interim President .... Dr. Raul RODRIGUEZ
05 Interim VP Academic Affairs .... Mr. Ruben ARENAS
11 VP Administrative Services .... Ms. Myeshia ARMSTRONG
32 VP Student Services .... Ms. Julie BENAVIDES
51 VP Continuing Educ/Workforce Dev .... Dr. Armida ORNELAS
81 Assoc Dean STEM .... Dr. Djuradj BABIC
35 Dean Student Services .... Dr. Laura CANTU
35 Dean Student Services .... Ms. Danelle FALLERT
35 Dean Student Services .... Ms. Sonia LOPEZ
121 Dean Student Services/Success .... Ms. Paulina PALOMINO
103 Dean Cont Ed/Wkfce Dev at SGEC .... Dr. Michelle CHEANG
20 Assoc Dean Academic Affairs .... Ms. Gina CHELSTROM
102 Dean Resource Development .... Mr. Paul DE LA CERDA
88 Assoc Dean Student Services .... Mr. Miguel DUENAS
88 Assoc Dean Student Services .... Dr. Vanessa OCHOA
88 Assoc Dean Student Services .... Ms. Grace HERNANDEZ
49 Dean Academic Affairs .... Mr. James KENNY
57 Dean Academic Affairs .... Ms. Ming-huei LAM
83 Dean Academic Affairs .... Ms. Kerrin MCMAHAN
11 Assoc Vice President Admin Svcs .... Mr. Nghi NGHIEM
51 Dean Cont Educ & Workforce Dev .... Mr. Alfonso RIOS
51 Dean Cont Educ & Workforce Dev .... Ms. Angelica TOLEDO
51 Dean Cont Educ & Workforce Dev .... Dr. Juan URDIALES
18 Director Facilities .... Mr. Abel RODRIGUEZ
88 Director Vincent Price Art Museum . Ms. Pilar TOMPKINS RIVAS
09 Acting Dean Inst Effectiveness .... Mr. Bryan VENTURA
21 College Financial Administrator .... Mr. Hao XIE
26 Public Information Officer .... Mr. Kevin JIMENEZ
40 Bookstore Supervisor .... Mr. Miguel PEREZ
41 Athletics Co-Director .... Mr. Bobby GODINEZ
41 Athletics Co-Director .... Mr. James HINES
08 Library Dept Chair .... Ms. Unjoo LEE
88 Director Child Development Center .... Ms. Marcia CAGIGAS
04 Admin Assistant to the President .... Ms. Kristen M. VAN HALA
06 Registrar .... Ms. Anna SALAZAR

*Los Angeles City College (I)

855 N Vermont Avenue, Los Angeles CA 90029-9990
County: Los Angeles FICE Identification: 001223
Unit ID: 117788
Telephone: (323) 953-4000 Carnegie Class: Assoc/HT-Mix Trad/Non
FAX Number: (323) 953-4013 Calendar System: Semester
URL: www.lacitycollege.edu
Established: 1929 Annual Undergrad Tuition & Fees (In-District): $1,220
Enrollment: 13,827 Coed
Affiliation or Control: Local IRS Status: 501(c)3
Highest Offering: Associate Degree
Accreditation: WJ, DT, RAD

02 President .... Dr. Mary GALLAGHER
05 Vice President Academic Affairs .... Dr. James LANCASTER
10 Vice President Administrative Svcs .... Mr. James REEVES
32 Vice President of Student Services .... Dr. Regina SMITH
21 Asst Vice Pres Administrative Svcs .... Mr. Anil JAIN
20 Dean of Academic Affairs .... Dr. Thelma DAY
103 Dean of Workforce Development .... Dr. Armando RIVERA-FIGUEROA
09 Dean of Institutional Effectiveness .... Dr. Anna BADALYAN
124 Dean of EOPS .... Dr. Saadia PORCHE
37 Dean Financial Aid .... Dr. Jeremy VILLAR
35 Dean Office of Student Life .... Mr. Alen ANDRIASSIAN
40 Bookstore Manager .... Ms. Christi O'CONNOR
85 Director International Students .... Vacant
15 Human Resources Manager .... Vacant
66 Nursing Department Chair .... Dr. Christiana BASKARAN
38 Counseling Chairperson .... Ms. Luisa CORTEZ
18 Facilities Director .... Mr. Kahlil HARRINGTON
04 Executive Assistant to President .... Ms. Lillian T. JOHNSON

*Los Angeles Harbor College (A)

1111 Figueroa Place, Wilmington CA 90744-2397
County: Los Angeles FICE Identification: 001224
Unit ID: 117690
Telephone: (310) 233-4000 Carnegie Class: Assoc/HT-Mix Trad/Non
FAX Number: (310) 233-4223 Calendar System: Semester
URL: www.lahc.edu
Established: 1949 Annual Undergrad Tuition & Fees (In-District): $1,220
Enrollment: 8,861 Coed
Affiliation or Control: State/Local IRS Status: 501(c)3
Highest Offering: Associate Degree
Accreditation: WJ, ADNUR

02 President .... Dr. Otto LEE
04 Executive Assistant to President .... Ms. Sylvia FILES
05 Vice Pres Academic Affairs .... Dr. Bobbi VILLALOBOS
10 Vice Pres Administrative Services .... Mr. Robert E. SUPPELSA
32 Vice Pres Student Services .... Mr. Luis DORADO
21 Assoc Vice Pres Administrative Svcs .... Vacant
09 Dean of Institutional Effectiveness .... Dr. Edward PAI
20 Dean of Academic Affairs .... Ms. Sandra SANCHEZ
07 Dean Enrollment/Eve Ops .... Mr. Tiffany SERGIO
22 Dean Student Services & Equity .... Ms. Mercy YANEZ
35 Dean of Student Services .... Mrs. Dawn REID
25 Assoc Dean Grants Mgmt/ED .... Ms. Priscilla LOPEZ
103 Dean of Economic/Workforce Devel .... Ms. Erica MAYORGA
83 Div Chair Behavioral/Social Sci .... Mr. Son NGUYEN
50 Division Chairperson Business .... Mr. Stanley C. SANDELL
60 Div Chairperson Communications .... Ms. Ann WARREN
57 Div Chair Humanities/Fine Arts .... Mr. Juan BAEZ
81 Div Chairperson Math/Phys Science .... Ms. Farah SADDIGH
76 Div Chairperson Health Sciences .... Mrs. Lynn YAMAKAWA
68 Div Chairperson Physical Education .... Mr. Nabeel M. BARAKAT
59 Div Chair Sci/Family Consumer Stds .... Dr. Basil IBE
08 Division Chairperson Library .... Mr. Jonathan LEE
38 Division Chairperson Counseling .... Ms. Joy FISHER
41 Athletic Director .... Mr. Dean DOWTY
37 Director Student Financial Aid .... Ms. Peggy LOEWY-WELLISCH
18 Facilities Manager .... Mr. Alex NELSON
13 Manager Information Technology .... Mr. Ivan CLARKE
31 Community Services Manager .... Ms. Priscilla LOPEZ
85 International Student Program .... Ms. Jessica CRUZ
15 Payroll & Personnel Supervisor .... Ms. Hsin (Gina) PENG
88 Assoc Dean of STEM Pathways .... Ms. Nelly RODRIGUEZ
102 Foundation Development Officer .... Mr. Peter BOSTIC

*Los Angeles Mission College (B)

13356 Eldridge Avenue, Sylmar CA 91342-3244
County: Los Angeles FICE Identification: 012550
Unit ID: 117867
Telephone: (818) 364-7600 Carnegie Class: Assoc/HT-High Trad
FAX Number: (818) 364-7826 Calendar System: Semester
URL: www.lamission.edu
Established: 1975 Annual Undergrad Tuition & Fees (In-District): $1,220
Enrollment: 9,765 Coed
Affiliation or Control: State/Local IRS Status: 501(c)3
Highest Offering: Associate Degree
Accreditation: WJ

02 President .... Dr. Monte E. PEREZ
05 Vice President Academic Affairs .... Dr. Nicole M. ALBO-LOPEZ
11 Vice President Administrative Svcs .... Mr. Daniel G. VILLANUEVA
32 Vice President of Student Services .... Dr. Larry L. RESENDEZ
20 Dean of Academic Affairs .... Ms. Darlene MONTES
35 Dean of Student Services .... Ms. Ludi VILLEGAS-VIDAL
88 Dean of CTE .... Ms. Maria ULIANA
35 Dean of Student Services .... Mr. Carlos R. GONZALEZ
09 Dean of Institutional Effectiveness .... Dr. Sarah L. MASTER
20 Dean of Academic Affairs .... Ms. Madelline HERNANDEZ
20 Dean DSP & S .... Dr. Larry RESENDEZ
26 Chief Public Relations Officer .... Mr. Alejandro GUZMAN
88 Director Child Development Center .... Ms. Diane STEIN
41 Athletic Director .... Mr. Steve RUYS
08 Head Librarian .... Ms. Donna AYERS
38 Counseling Chairperson .... Ms. Michong PARK
37 Financial Aid Manager .... Mr. Dennis J. SCHROEDER
31 Community Services Manager .... Mr. Dennis SOLARES
18 Facilities/Physical Plant Manager .... Mr. Andrew GOOD
88 EOP & S/Care Director .... Ms. Ludi VILLEGAS-VIDAL
04 Executive Asst to President .... Ms. Oliva AYALA
10 Chief Business Officer .... Mr. Jerry HUANG
102 Dir Foundation/Corporate Relations .... Mr. Daryl SMITH
15 Personnel Services Assistant .... Mr. Pio CASTILLO
07 Director of Admissions/Records .... Ms. Rosalie TORRES
36 Director Student Placement .... Ms. Wendy RIVERA
84 Director Enrollment Management .... Dr. Nicole ALBO-LOPEZ
96 Director of Purchasing .... Ms. Isabel RUIZ-MORENO
13 Chief Info Technology Officer (CIO) .... Mr. Rod G. AUSTRIA

*Los Angeles Pierce College (C)

6201 Winnetka Avenue, Woodland Hills CA 91371-0001
County: Los Angeles FICE Identification: 001226
Unit ID: 117706
Telephone: (818) 710-4100 Carnegie Class: Assoc/HT-High Trad
FAX Number: N/A Calendar System: Semester
URL: www.piercecollege.edu
Established: 1947 Annual Undergrad Tuition & Fees (In-District): $1,220
Enrollment: 17,655 Coed
Affiliation or Control: State/Local IRS Status: 501(c)3
Highest Offering: Associate Degree
Accreditation: WJ

02 President .... Dr. Alexis MONTEVIRGEN
05 Vice President Academic Affairs .... Ms. Sheri BERGER
11 Vice President Administrative Svcs .... Mr. Rolf SCHLEICHER
32 Vice President Student Services .... Dr. Earic DIXON-PETERS
10 Assoc Vice President Admin Services .... Mr. Bruce ROSKY
08 Chair Library .... Ms. Lauren SASLOW
38 Chair Counseling .... Ms. Alyce MILLER
20 Dean of Academic Affairs .... Dr. Donna-Mae VILLANUEVA
20 Dean of Academic Affairs .... Ms. Mary Anne GAVARRA-OH
20 Dean of Academic Affairs .... Ms. Susan RHI-KLEINERT
20 Dean of Academic Affairs .... Ms. Sharon DALMAGE
37 Director of Financial Aid .... Ms. Anafe ROBINSON
108 Dean Institutional Effectiveness .... Mr. Amari WILLIAMS
26 Public Information Officer .... Ms. Doreen CLAY
18 Director of College Facilities .... Mr. Paul NIEMAN
106 Dir Online Education/E-learning .... Ms. Wendy BASS KEER
121 Dean of Student Success .... Dr. Kalynda WEBBER MCLEAN
35 Dean Student Services .... Mr. William MARMOLEJO
06 Registrar .... Ms. Lorena LOPEZ
35 Dean of Student Services & Equity .... Dr. Genice SARCEDO-MAGRUDER
124 Dean of Student Engagement .... Mr. Juan Carlos ASTORGA

*Los Angeles Southwest College (D)

1600 W Imperial Highway, Los Angeles CA 90047-4899
County: Los Angeles FICE Identification: 007047
Unit ID: 117715
Telephone: (323) 241-5225 Carnegie Class: Assoc/HT-Mix Trad/Non
FAX Number: (323) 241-5220 Calendar System: Semester
URL: www.lasc.edu
Established: 1967 Annual Undergrad Tuition & Fees (In-District): $1,220
Enrollment: 5,848 Coed
Affiliation or Control: State/Local IRS Status: 501(c)3
Highest Offering: Associate Degree
Accreditation: WJ

02 President .... Dr. Seher AWAN
05 Vice President Academic Affairs .... Dr. Lawrence BRADFORD
32 Vice President Student Services .... Dr. Howard IRVIN
10 Vice President Admin Services .... Mr. Daniel B. HALL
111 Dean Institutional Advancement .... Mr. Jose Alfred GALLEGOS
103 Dean Career/Technical Education .... Mr. Rick HODGE
20 Dean Academic Affairs .... Dr. Tangelia ALFRED
20 Dean Academic Affairs .... Dr. Kristi BLACKBURN
35 Dean Student Services .... Dr. Ralph DAVIS
88 Dean Special Programs & Services .... Ms. Jeanette MAGEE
88 Dean Adult Non-credit .... Ms. Laura PEREZ
38 Chairperson Counseling .... Dr. Lisa FORD
08 Chairperson Library .... Ms. Parissa SAMAIE
06 Registrar .... Ms. Kimberly CARPENTER
18 Director of Facilities .... Mr. Preston MORTLEY
13 Manager College Information System .... Mr. Jorge MATA
37 Manager Student Financial Aid .... Ms. Muniece BRUTON
26 Chief Public Relations Officer .... Mr. Ben DEMERS
04 Executive Assistant/Confidential .... Ms. Chauncine` R. STEWART

*Los Angeles Trade-Technical College (E)

400 W Washington Boulevard,
Los Angeles CA 90015-4108
County: Los Angeles FICE Identification: 001227
Unit ID: 117724
Telephone: (213) 763-7000 Carnegie Class: Assoc/HVT-Mix Trad/Non
FAX Number: (213) 763-5393 Calendar System: Semester
URL: www.lattc.edu
Established: 1925 Annual Undergrad Tuition & Fees (In-District): $1,220
Enrollment: 12,984 Coed
Affiliation or Control: State/Local IRS Status: 501(c)3
Highest Offering: Associate Degree
Accreditation: WJ, ACFEI

02 Interim President .... Dr. Andrew JONES
11 Int VP Administrative Services .... Dr. Ann TOMLINSON
05 Vice President Instruction .... Dr. Abraham FARKAS
32 Actg VP Pathways/Student Affairs .... Dr. Henan JOOF
21 Assoc Vice Pres Administrative Svcs .... Vacant
20 Dean Academic Affairs & Workforce .... Mr. Vincent JACKSON
20 Dean Academic Affairs & Workforce .... Ms. Cynthia MORLEY-MOWER
20 Dean Academic Affairs & Workforce .... Mr. Benjamin GOLDSTEIN
20 Dean Academic Affairs & Workforce .... Ms. Nicole ALBO-LOPEZ
37 Supervisor Financial Aid .... Ms. Ruth BLEDSOE
09 Int VP Inst Effectiveness .... Dr. Kristi BLACKBURN
35 Dean Student Services .... Ms. Dorothy SMITH
35 Dean Student Services .... Dr. Henan JOOF
10 Chief Business Officer .... Vacant
38 Chair Student Counseling .... Mr. Tom DAWKINS
102 Director Foundation/Corporate Rels .... Vacant
26 Public Relations Manager .... Mr. David YSAIS
13 Mgr College Information System .... Mr. Sang BAIK

*Los Angeles Valley College (F)

5800 Fulton Avenue, Valley Glen CA 91401-4096
County: Los Angeles FICE Identification: 001228
Unit ID: 117733
Telephone: (818) 947-2600 Carnegie Class: Assoc/HT-High Trad
FAX Number: N/A Calendar System: Semester
URL: www.lavc.edu
Established: 1949 Annual Undergrad Tuition & Fees (In-District): $1,220
Enrollment: 15,648 Coed
Affiliation or Control: State/Local IRS Status: 501(c)3
Highest Offering: Associate Degree
Accreditation: WJ, ADNUR, COARC

02 President .... Dr. Barry C. GRIBBONS
05 Vice President Academic Affairs .... Ms. Karen DAAR
10 Vice President Admin Services .... Mr. Mike C. LEE
32 Vice President Student Services .... Mr. Florentino MANZANO
11 Associate VP Administrative Svcs .... Ms. Sarah SONG
20 Dean Academic Affairs .... Dr. Douglas MARRIOTT
20 Dean Academic Affairs .... Dr. Laurie NALEPA
20 Dean Academic Affairs .... Dr. Deborah A. DICESARE
20 Dean Academic Affairs .... Mr. Matthew JORDAN
20 Dean Academic Affairs .... Mr. Jermain PIPKINS
09 Dean Institutional Effectiveness .... Ms. Michelle R. FOWLES
35 Dean Student Life .... Dr. Elizabeth NEGRETE
88 Dean of Special Programs .... Dr. Sherri RODRIGUEZ
121 Dean Student Success & Support Svcs .... Dr. Sorangel HERNANDEZ
88 Associate Dean SSP .... Mr. David M. GREEN
35 Associate Dean Student Services .... Ms. Annie G. REED
35 Associate Dean Student Services .... Dr. Llanet MARTIN
102 Executive Director LAVC Foundation .... Mr. Raul V. CASTILLO
41 Athletic Director .... Mr. Jim FENWICK
18 Director College Facilities .... Mr. Tom LOPEZ
40 College Store Manager .... Ms. Mary JOHN
26 Public Relations Manager .... Ms. Jennifer C. BORUCKI
31 Community Services Manager .... Mr. Michael B. ATKIN
13 Manager College Info Services .... Ms. Hanh TRAN
37 Financial Aid Manager .... Mr. Vernon D. BRIDGES
21 College Fiscal Administrator .... Mr. Robert MEDINA
06 Registrar .... Ms. Ashley DUNN

*West Los Angeles College (G)

9000 Overland Avenue, Culver City CA 90230-5002
County: Los Angeles FICE Identification: 008596
Unit ID: 125471
Telephone: (310) 287-4200 Carnegie Class: Bac/Assoc-Assoc Dom
FAX Number: (310) 841-0396 Calendar System: Semester
URL: www.wlac.edu
Established: 1969 Annual Undergrad Tuition & Fees (In-District): $1,220
Enrollment: 10,477 Coed
Affiliation or Control: State/Local IRS Status: 501(c)3
Highest Offering: Baccalaureate
Accreditation: WJ, DH

02 President .... Dr. James M. LIMBAUGH
05 VP Academic Affairs .... Ms. Aracely AGUIAR
11 Vice President Administrative Svcs .... Vacant
32 VP Student Services .... Dr. Roberto O. GONZALEZ
97 Dean General Education & Transfer .... Dr. Walter JONES
75 Dean Academic Affairs/CTE .... Dr. Kimberly MANNER
51 Dean Adult & Cont Education .... Dr. Allison TOM-MIURA
76 Dean of Health Sciences .... Ms. Carmen DONES
106 Dean Distance Learning/Inst Tech .... Mr. Eric ICHON
20 Dean Teaching & Learning .... Dr. Mary-Jo APIGO
09 Dean Institutional Effectiveness .... Dr. Patricia QUINONES
22 Dean Student Services/Equity .... Mr. Angel VIRAMONTES
84 Dean Student Svcs/Enrollment .... Mr. Michael GOLTERMANN
35 Dean Student Svcs .... Ms. Angeles ABRAHAM
35 Dean Student Svcs .... Mr. Christopher SWEETEN
35 Assoc Dean Student Services . Dr. Celena ALCALA-BURKHARDT
41 Athletic Director .... Mr. Ricardo HOOPER
40 College Enterprise Manager .... Vacant
10 Chief Financial Administrator .... Ms. Rasel MENENDEZ
18 Facilities Manager .... Mr. Joachim MORERA
37 Financial Aid Manager .... Mr. Glenn SCHENK
13 Manager Info System .... Mr. Tak FUJII
88 Operations Manager .... Mr. Bruce HICKS
19 Sheriff/Deputy .... Mr. Melvin YOUNG
88 Academic Senate President .... Ms. Holly BAILEY-HOFMANN
26 Dir Advtg/Marketing/Public Rels .... Ms. Michelle LONG-COFFEE
102 Executive Director WLAC Foundation .Ms. Etelvina DE LA TORRE
08 Library Chair .... Ms. Susan TRUJILLO

Los Angeles County College of Nursing and Allied Health (H)

1237 N Mission Road, Los Angeles CA 90033-1083
County: Los Angeles FICE Identification: 006165
Unit ID: 117803
Telephone: (323) 409-5911 Carnegie Class: Spec 2-yr-Health
FAX Number: (323) 226-6343 Calendar System: Semester
URL: dhs.lacounty.gov/wps/portal/dhs/conah/
Established: 1895 Annual Undergrad Tuition & Fees (In-District): N/A
Enrollment: 208 Coed
Affiliation or Control: Local IRS Status: 501(c)3
Highest Offering: Associate Degree
Accreditation: WJ

11 Provost/Administrator .... Ms. Vivian BRANCHICK
66 Interim Dean of Nursing Programs .... Ms. Mildred GONZALES
32 Dean College Operations/Student Svc .... Ms. Sarah C. GRANGER
108 Dean Institutional Effectiveness .... Ms. Herminia HONDA
05 Dean Education/Consulting Services .... Dr. Tammy BLASS
37 Director of Financial Aid .... Ms. Sarah GRANGER
38 Director Advisement/Counseling .... Ms. Maria CABALLERO
13 College Information Officer .... Mr. Visna KIENG

Los Angeles Film School (A)

6363 Sunset Boulevard, Hollywood CA 90028
County: Los Angeles FICE Identification: 040373
Unit ID: 436429
Telephone: (323) 860-0789 Carnegie Class: Spec-4-yr-Arts
FAX Number: (323) 646-0770 Calendar System: Other
URL: www.lafilm.edu
Established: 1999 Annual Undergrad Tuition & Fees: N/A
Enrollment: 3,653 Coed
Affiliation or Control: Proprietary IRS Status: Proprietary
Highest Offering: Baccalaureate
Accreditation: ACCSC

01 President ... Ms. Tammy ELLIOTT
05 Chief Academic Officer ... Ms. Jenna LANGER
06 Registrar ... Ms. Andrea NOTO
07 Director of Admissions ... Ms. Ernesta MENSAH
08 Chief Library Officer ... Ms. Georgina GARCIA-CAMPOS
10 Chief Financial/Business Officer ... Ms. Pamela PAYAWAL
13 Chief Information Technology Office ... Mr. Iyob ARIA
15 Chief Human Resources Officer ... Vacant
18 Chief Facilities/Physical Plant Ofc ... Mr. Brian MITCHELL
29 Director Alumni Affairs ... Mr. Joseph BYRON
36 Director Student Placement ... Ms. Angelia BIBB-SANDERS
37 Director Student Financial Aid ... Mr. Dustin WEIR

Los Angeles ORT College (B)

6435 Wilshire Boulevard, Los Angeles CA 90048
County: Los Angeles FICE Identification: 025703
Unit ID: 368780
Telephone: (323) 966-5444 Carnegie Class: Assoc/HVT-Mix Trad/Non
FAX Number: (323) 966-5455 Calendar System: Other
URL: www.laort.edu
Established: 1985 Annual Undergrad Tuition & Fees: N/A
Enrollment: 164 Coed
Affiliation or Control: Independent Non-Profit IRS Status: 501(c)3
Highest Offering: Associate Degree
Accreditation: CNCE

01 Director ... Vacant

Los Angeles Pacific College (C)

3325 Wilshire Boulevard, Ste 550,
Los Angeles CA 90010-1758
County: Los Angeles Identification: 667143
Telephone: (213) 384-2318 Carnegie Class: Not Classified
FAX Number: (213) 384-0419 Calendar System: Semester
URL: www.lapacific.net
Established: 1989 Annual Undergrad Tuition & Fees: N/A
Enrollment: N/A Coed
Affiliation or Control: Proprietary IRS Status: Proprietary
Highest Offering: Associate Degree
Accreditation: #COE, CEA

01 President ... Ms. Mary YOON
10 Controller ... Mr. Ho Sung YOON

Los Angeles Pacific University (D)

300 N. Lone Hill Ave #200, San Dimas CA 91773
County: Los Angeles FICE Identification: 042788
Unit ID: 474863
Telephone: (858) 527-2768 Carnegie Class: Not Classified
FAX Number: (626) 276-7034 Calendar System: Semester
URL: www.lapu.edu
Established: 2014 Annual Undergrad Tuition & Fees: $10,200
Enrollment: N/A Coed
Affiliation or Control: Independent Non-Profit IRS Status: 501(c)3
Highest Offering: Master's
Accreditation: WC

01 President ... Dr. John REYNOLDS
11 Executive Vice Pres/COO ... Frank ROJAS
05 Vice Pres/Chief Academic Officer ... Dr. Wayne HERMAN

† Affiliated with Azusa Pacific University.

*Los Rios Community College District Office (E)

1919 Spanos Court, Sacramento CA 95825-3981
County: Sacramento FICE Identification: 001231
Unit ID: 117900
Telephone: (916) 568-3021 Carnegie Class: N/A
FAX Number: (916) 561-0574
URL: www.losrios.edu

01 Chancellor ... Dr. Brian KING
04 Chancellor's Executive Officer ... Ms. Jennifer DELUCCHI
10 Vice Chancellor Finance/Admin ... Ms. Theresa MATISTA
05 Vice Chancellor Education/Tech ... Dr. Jamey NYE
30 Assoc Vice Chanc Resource Dev ... Ms. Paula ALLISON
26 Assoc Vice Chanc Comm/Media Rels ... Mr. Gabe ROSS
18 Assoc Vice Chanc Facilities Mgmt ... Mr. Pablo MANZO
15 Assoc Vice Chanc Human Resources ... Mr. Ryan COX
21 Assoc Vice Chanc of Finance ... Mr. Mario RODRIGUEZ
13 Chief Information Officer ... Ms. Tamara ARMSTRONG
20 Assoc Vice Chanc Instruction ... Ms. Tammy MONTGOMERY
32 Assoc Vice Chanc Ed Svcs/Stdnt Succ ... Ms. Melanie DIXON
43 General Counsel ... Mr. J.P SHERRY
37 Director Financial Aid ... Mr. Roy BECKHORN
96 Director General Services ... Ms. Anita SINGH
09 Director Institutional Research ... Ms. Betty GLYER-CULVER

*American River College (F)

4700 College Oak Drive, Sacramento CA 95841-4286
County: Sacramento FICE Identification: 001232
Unit ID: 109208
Telephone: (916) 484-8011 Carnegie Class: Assoc/MT-VT-High Trad
FAX Number: (916) 484-8674 Calendar System: Semester
URL: www.arc.losrios.edu
Established: 1955 Annual Undergrad Tuition & Fees (In-District): $1,104
Enrollment: 31,858 Coed
Affiliation or Control: State/Local IRS Status: 501(c)3
Highest Offering: Associate Degree
Accreditation: WJ, COARC, EMT, FUSER

02 President ... Dr. Thomas G. GREENE
10 Vice President Admin Services ... Ms. Kuldeep KAUR
05 Vice President Instruction ... Dr. Lisa LAWRENSON
32 Vice President Student Services ... Dr. Jeff STEPHENSON
20 Assoc VP Instruction ... Dr. Kate JAQUES
62 Assoc VP Instruction/Lrng Res ... Dr. Kale BRADEN
32 Assoc VP Student Services ... Mr. Chad FUNK
103 Assoc VP Workforce Development ... Dr. Frank KOBAYASHI
57 Dean Fine & Applied Arts ... Ms. Angela MILANO
07 Dean Enrollment Services ... Mr. Parrish GEARY
83 Dean Behavioral & Social Science ... Mr. Steven BOYD
88 Dean English ... Mr. Doug HERNDON
79 Dean Humanities ... Ms. Diana HICKS
68 Dean Kinesiology/Athletics ... Dr. Derrick BOOTH
81 Dean Mathematics ... Mr. Adam WINDHAM
56 Dean McClellan Center ... Mr. Steve SEGURA
35 Dean Student Services ... Ms. Kolleen OSTGAARD
09 Dean Planning/Research/Technology ... Dr. Adam KARP
66 Dean Health & Education ... Ms. Jan DELAPP
81 Dean Science/Engineering ... Dr. Rina ROY
56 Dean Natomas Center ... Mr. Roger DAVIDSON
88 Dean Equity Programs & Pathways ... Dr. Joshua MOON JOHNSON
50 Dean Business/Computer Science ... Ms. Kirsten CORBIN
72 Dean Technical Education ... Dr. Trish CALDWELL
04 Administrative Asst to President ... Ms. Sue MCCOY
11 Director Administrative Services ... Ms. Cheryl SEARS
30 Director Donor Relations ... Ms. Kirsten DUBRAY
26 Public Information Officer ... Mr. Scott CROW
37 Financial Aid Supervisor ... Ms. Robin GALLOWGLAS
88 Dean DE/Virtual Ed Center ... Ms. Marsha RESKE
75 Dean Career Ed & Workforce Dev ... Ms. Raquel ARATA
38 Dean Counseling ... Ms. Sonia ORTIZ-MERCADO

*Cosumnes River College (G)

8401 Center Parkway, Sacramento CA 95823-5799
County: Sacramento FICE Identification: 007536
Unit ID: 113096
Telephone: (916) 691-7344 Carnegie Class: Assoc/HT-High Trad
FAX Number: (916) 691-7375 Calendar System: Semester
URL: www.crc.losrios.edu
Established: 1970 Annual Undergrad Tuition & Fees (In-District): $1,104
Enrollment: 14,120 Coed
Affiliation or Control: State/Local IRS Status: 501(c)3
Highest Offering: Associate Degree
Accreditation: WJ, CAHIIM, DMS, MAC

02 President ... Dr. Edward C. BUSH
05 VP Instruction & Student Learning ... Dr. Robert MONTANEZ
11 VP Admin Svcs & Student Support ... Vacant
32 VP Student Svcs/Enrollment Mgmt ... Dr. Kimberly MCDANIEL
84 Dean Student Svcs/Enrollment ... Mr. Chad FUNK
20 Assoc VP Instruction/Student Lrng ... Mr. Torence POWELL
08 Dean Library and Technology Service ... Mr. Stephen MCGLOUGHLIN
38 Dean Counseling & Student Services ... Dr. Shannon COOPER
50 Dean Business & Family Science ... Mr. Joel POWELL
79 Dean Humanities & Social Science ... Dr. LaTonya WILLIAMS
68 Dean Kinesiology & Athletics ... Mr. Collin PREGLIASCO
81 Dean Science/Math/Engineering ... Dr. Kathryn SORENSEN
72 Dean Careers & Technology ... Dr. Kimberly HARRELL
60 Dean Comm/Visual/Performing Arts ... Dr. Colette HARRIS-MATHEWS
45 Dean of Institutional Effectiveness ... Dr. Heather TILSON
06 Registrar/Admissions & Records ... Mr. Richard ANDREWS
18 Chief Facilities/Physical Plant ... Mr. Augustine CHAVEZ
26 Communications/Public Info Officer ... Ms. Kristie WEST
30 Chief Development/Advancement ... Vacant
121 Dean of Student Services and Equity ... Mr. Tadael EMIRU
40 Bookstore Manager ... Ms. Maria HYDE

*Folsom Lake College (H)

10 College Parkway, Folsom CA 95630-6798
County: Sacramento FICE Identification: 038713
Unit ID: 444219
Telephone: (916) 608-6500 Carnegie Class: Assoc/HT-High Trad
FAX Number: N/A Calendar System: Semester
URL: www.flc.losrios.edu
Established: 2004 Annual Undergrad Tuition & Fees (In-District): $1,104
Enrollment: 8,682 Coed
Affiliation or Control: State/Local IRS Status: 501(c)3
Highest Offering: Associate Degree
Accreditation: WJ, MLTAD

02 President ... Whitney YAMAMURA
11 Vice Pres Administration ... Augustine CHAVEZ
05 Vice President Instruction ... Dr. Monica PACTOL
32 Vice President Student Services ... Christine THOMAS
12 Dean of Instruction RCC ... Brian ROBINSON
12 Dean of Instruction EDC ... John ALEXANDER
81 Dean Instruction BLIT/MSE ... Greg MCCORMAC
57 Dean of Instruction VAPA/LALI ... Dr. Robert (BJ) SNOWDEN
68 Dean of Instruction KHAN ... Matthew WRIGHT
72 Dean of Instruction CTE ... Victoria MARYATT
09 Dean Planning & Research ... Dr. Molly SENECAL
35 Dean of Student Success ... Dr. Davin BROWN
18 Director of Administrative Services ... Melissa WILLIAMS
10 Business Services Supervisor ... Joany HARMAN
26 Public Information Officer ... Kristy HART
30 Director Donor Relations ... Sally BUCHANAN
37 Financial Aid Supervisor ... Ali PADASH
07 Admissions & Records Supervisor ... Christine WURZER
88 Executive Director Harris Center ... David PIER
40 College Store Manager ... Rob MULLIGAN
04 Assistant to the President ... Lindsey CAMPBELL

*Sacramento City College (I)

3835 Freeport Boulevard, Sacramento CA 95822-1386
County: Sacramento FICE Identification: 001233
Unit ID: 122180
Telephone: (916) 558-2111 Carnegie Class: Assoc/MT-VT-High Trad
FAX Number: (916) 558-2449 Calendar System: Semester
URL: www.scc.losrios.edu
Established: 1916 Annual Undergrad Tuition & Fees (In-State): $1,104
Enrollment: 21,323 Coed
Affiliation or Control: State Related IRS Status: 501(c)3
Highest Offering: Associate Degree
Accreditation: WJ, DA, DH, OTA, PTAA

02 President ... Mr. Michael GUTIERREZ
05 Vice Pres of Instruction ... Dr. Albert GARCIA
10 Vice Pres Administrative Services ... Ms. Carrie BRAY
32 Int Vice Pres Student Services ... Dr. Davin BROWN
20 Associate Vice Pres Instruction ... Ms. Gabriel MEEHAN
20 Interim Assoc VP Instruction ... Ms. Ginny MCREYNOLDS
84 AVP Enrollment/Student Services ... Vacant
13 Dean Information Technology ... Mr. Kirk SOSA
37 Dean Financial Aid/Student Svcs ... Dr. Miguel MOLINA
46 Dean Planning/Research/Development ... Dr. Marybeth BUECHNER
08 Dean Learning Resources ... Mr. Kevin FLASH
36 Dean Counseling/Student Success ... Dr. Andre COLEMAN
22 Dean Student Equity/Success ... Ms. Molly SPRINGER
40 Director College Store ... Ms. Maria HYDE
66 Director Nursing ... Ms. Carel MOUNTAIN
18 Director College Operations ... Ms. Margaret LEDNICKY
30 Director of Donor Relations ... Mr. Dan MCCARTY
26 Comm & Public Information Officer ... Ms. Kaitlyn MACGREGOR
76 Dean Science & Allied Health ... Mr. James COLLINS
50 Dean Business ... Dr. Deborah SAKS
79 Dean Humanities/Fine Arts ... Mr. Chris IWATA
79 Interim Dean Languages/Literature ... Ms. Robin IKEGAMI
72 Dean Advanced Technology ... Ms. Donnetta WEBB
68 Dean PE/Health/Athletics ... Mr. Mitchell L. CAMPBELL
81 Dean Statistics/Math/Engineering ... Dr. Daniel STYER
83 Dean Behavioral/Social Science ... Ms. Kasey GARDNER
56 Dean Davis Center ... Vacant
56 Int Dean West Sacramento Ctr ... Dr. Ashu MISHRA
06 Records & Admissions Officer ... Ms. Kim GOFF
04 Administrative Asst to President ... Ms. Pamela MORRISON
88 Director HSI-SAGE ... Vacant

Loyola Marymount University (J)

1 LMU Drive, Los Angeles CA 90045-2659
County: Los Angeles FICE Identification: 011649
Unit ID: 117946
Telephone: (310) 338-2700 Carnegie Class: DU-Higher
FAX Number: N/A Calendar System: Semester
URL: www.lmu.edu
Established: 1911 Annual Undergrad Tuition & Fees: $48,522
Enrollment: 9,618 Coed
Affiliation or Control: Roman Catholic IRS Status: 501(c)3
Highest Offering: Doctorate
Accreditation: WC, ART, CAEPN, DANCE, LAW, MUS, THEA, THEOL

01 President ... Dr. Timothy L. SNYDER
00 Chancellor ... Fr. Robert WALSH, SJ
05 Exec Vice President & Provost ... Dr. Thomas POON
42 VP for Mission & Ministry ... Dr. John SEBASTIAN
20 Vice Provost for Academic Affairs ... Dr. David A. SAPP
84 Vice Provost Enrollment Management ... Dr. Maureen WEATHERALL
88 Vice Prov Global-Local Initiatives ... Dr. Roberta ESPINOZA
10 Sr Vice Pres/Chief Financial Ofcr ... Mr. Thomas O. FLEMING
111 Interim SVP University Advancement ... Ms. Kristi WADE
32 Sr Vice Pres for Student Affairs ... Dr. Elena M. BOVE
11 EVP & Chief Administrative Officer ... Ms. Lynne B. SCARBORO
13 VP for Information Technology Svcs ... Mr. Patrick FRONTIERA
35 VP Student Affairs/Dean Students ... Dr. Terri MANGIONE
15 Vice President for Human Resources ... Ms. Rebecca CHANDLER
18 VP for Construction and Planning ... Mr. Timothy HAWORTH
11 Vice President of Campus Operations ... Mr. Michael WONG
26 Vice Pres Marketing/Communications ... Mr. John KIRALLA
28 Interim VP Intercultural Affairs ... Dr. Jennifer ABE

36 Assoc Provost Career & Professional ..... Mr. Branden GRIMMETT
20 Assoc Provost Undergraduate Educ .... Fr. José BADENES
88 Assoc Prov Rsrch/Professional Dev .... Dr. Kathleen WEAVER
109 Assoc VP Auxiliary Mgmt & Business .... Mr. Andrew O'REILLY
100 Special Assistant to the President .... Dr. John M. PARRISH
08 Dean University Library .... Ms. Kristine BRANCOLINI
06 University Registrar .... Dr. Jennifer SILVERMAN
61 Dean Loyola Law School .... Mr. Michael WATERSTONE
49 Dean College Liberal Arts .... Dr. Robbin D. CRABTREE
53 Interim Dean Sch of Education .... Dr. Mary MCCULLOUGH
50 Dean College of Business Admin .... Dr. Dayle SMITH
57 Dean Communication & Fine Arts .... Dr. Bryant K. ALEXANDER
54 Dean College of Science & Engineer .... Dr. Tina CHOE
88 Dean School of Film/Television .... Ms. Peggy RAJSKI
30 Sr Dir Development/Gift Planning .... Vacant
07 Asst Vice Prov Undergrad Admissions .... Mr. Matthew X. FISSINGER
37 Associate Director of Financial Aid .... Ms. Darlene WILSON
41 Athletics Director .... Mr. Craig PINTENS
27 Social Media Manager .... Ms. Shelbey GALLIHER
09 Sr Dir Inst Rsrch/Decision Support .... Ms. Christine CHAVEZ
108 Sr Dir Educ Effectivenss/Assessmnt .... Dr. Rebecca HONG
29 Executive Director of Alumni Rels .... Ms. Lisa FARLAND
23 Director of Student Health Services .... Ms. Katherine ARCE
104 Director Study Abroad .... Dr. Lisa LOBERG
25 Dir Research & Sponsored Projects .... Vacant
90 Director of Educational Technology .... Ms. Crista COPP
04 Executive Asst to President .... Ms. Debbie CAVANAGH
04 Admin Specialist to Ofc of the Pres .... Ms. Rosa CALDERON
102 Exec Dir Corp/Foundation Relations .... Ms. Michelle PLASSE
19 Chief of Public Safety .... Mr. Danny MARTINEZ
22 EEO Officer and Title IX Coord .... Ms. Sara TRIVEDI
39 Director Student Housing .... Mr. Steven NYGAARD
43 General Counsel .... Mr. Harold A. BRIDGES
04 Admin Specialist to Ofc of the Pres .Ms. Sheila WEISENBERGER
38 Dir Student Psychological Services .... Ms. Kristin LINDEN

Marshall B. Ketchum University (A)

2575 Yorba Linda Boulevard, Fullerton CA 92831-1699
County: Orange FICE Identification: 001230
Unit ID: 123943
Telephone: (714) 870-7226 Carnegie Class: Spec-4-yr-Other Health
FAX Number: (714) 879-9834 Calendar System: Quarter
URL: www.ketchum.edu
Established: 1904 Annual Graduate Tuition & Fees: N/A
Enrollment: 618 Coed
Affiliation or Control: Independent Non-Profit IRS Status: 501(c)3
Highest Offering: Doctorate; No Undergraduates
Accreditation: WC, ARCPA, OPT, OPTR, @PHAR

01 President .... Dr. Kevin L. ALEXANDER
111 Vice Pres University Advancement .... Ms. Joan RUBIO
100 Sr Vice President & Chief of Staff .... Dr. Julie A. SCHORNACK
32 Vice President for Student Affairs ..... Dr. Carmen N. BARNHARDT
15 Vice Pres Human Resources .... Ms. Gail S. DEUTSCH
10 Senior Vice Pres Admin & Finance .... Mr. Frank SCOTTI
05 VP Educational Effectiveness .... Dr. Judy ORTIZ
46 Associate Dean Research SCCO .... Dr. Jerry PAUGH
18 Director Campus Operations .... Mr. Gregory SMITH
51 Director Continuing Education .... Ms. Bonnie DELLATORRE
13 Director of Information Technology .... Mr. Samuel YOUNG
37 Director Financial Aid .... Ms. Barbara BREFFLE
08 Director of Library Services .... Mr. Scott JOHNSON
23 Dir Special Clinic Programs .... Ms. Michele WHITECAVAGE
26 Dir Marketing/Communications .... Ms. Katie SANTOS-COY
88 Interim Dean for Optometry .... Dr. Eric BORSTING
67 Dean for Pharmacy .... Dr. Edward FISHER
88 Director PA Program .... Ms. Allison MOLLET
108 Dir Institutional Effectiveness .... Dr. Ajoy KOOMER
04 Executive Asst to the President .... Ms. Carole JOLLY
23 Assoc Dean Clinics .... Dr. Mark E. NAKANO
24 Director Multi-Media Services .... Mr. Matt BRENEMAN
00 Chairman of the Board .... Ms. Carol NAJERA
29 Asst Director Alumni/Donor Relation .... Vacant
31 Director of Community Relations .... Mr. Wayne HEIDLE
109 Auxiliary Services Manager .... Ms. Debra WOODS
06 Registrar .... Ms. Lisa CASSIDY
19 Director Campus Safety/Security .... Mr. Craig COOPER
38 Director Univ Student Counseling .... Ms. Alyse KIRSCHEN

Marymount California University (B)

30800 Palos Verdes Drive E,
Rancho Palos Verdes CA 90275-6299
County: Los Angeles FICE Identification: 010474
Unit ID: 118541
Telephone: (310) 377-5501 Carnegie Class: Bac-A&S
FAX Number: (310) 377-6223 Calendar System: Semester
URL: www.marymountcalifornia.edu
Established: 1932 Annual Undergrad Tuition & Fees: $36,134
Enrollment: 967 Coed
Affiliation or Control: Roman Catholic IRS Status: 501(c)3
Highest Offering: Master's
Accreditation: WC

01 President .... Dr. Brian MARCOTTE
03 Executive Vice President .... Dr. Ariane SCHAUER
10 Interim Chief Financial Officer .... Ms. Debora YAVAS
05 Provost/Dean of Faculty .... Dr. Ariane SCHAUER
30 Dean Institutional Development .... Mr. Ruben BARAJAS
84 Vice President Enrollment Mgmt .... Ms. Robyn JONES
32 Dean of Students .... Mr. Ryan ALCANTARA
20 Associate Academic Officer .... Ms. Susie MARTIN
08 Librarian .... Mr. Jose RICON
37 Assoc Director Financial Aid .... Ms. Nataly DE LA PENA
15 Dir Human Res & Risk Mgmt/Title IX .. Ms. Karen THORDARSON
18 Chief Facilities/Physical Plant .... Mr. Robert ROOKER
26 Chief Public Relations Officer .... Vacant
29 Director Alumni Relations .... Vacant
36 Director Student Placement .... Mr. Maury HILLSTROM
38 Director Student Counseling .... Ms. Osmara REYES-OSARIO
96 Director of Purchasing .... Mr. Monte SCHMEISER
06 Registrar .... Ms. Paula AVERY
35 Dir Student Life & Engagement .... Vacant
09 Director of Institutional Research .... Mr. Michael SEMENOFF
21 Associate Business Officer .... Ms. Debra YAVAS
04 Administrative Asst to President .... Ms. Kimberly RAMSEY
19 Director Security/Safety .... Ms. Naja JAMES
39 Director Student Housing .... Mr. Chad FEHR
41 Athletic Director .... Ms. Courtney THOMSEN
104 Director Study Abroad .... Mr. Ryan O'CONNELL
105 Director Web Services .... Mr. Maury HILLSTROM
13 Chief Info Technology Officer .... Mr. Monte SCHMEISER
101 Secretary of the Institution/Board .... Ms. Kimberly RAMSAY
07 Interim Director of Admissions .... Mr. Ryan O'CONNELL

The Master's University (C)

21726 Placerita Canyon Road,
Santa Clarita CA 91321-1200
County: Los Angeles FICE Identification: 001220
Unit ID: 117751
Telephone: (661) 259-3540 Carnegie Class: Masters/M
FAX Number: N/A Calendar System: Semester
URL: www.masters.edu
Established: 1927 Annual Undergrad Tuition & Fees: $25,390
Enrollment: 1,946 Coed
Affiliation or Control: Independent Non-Profit IRS Status: 501(c)3
Highest Offering: Doctorate
Accreditation: #WC, MUS

01 President .... Dr. John STEAD
05 Interim Provost .... Dr. Mitchell HOPEWELL
32 Dean of Student Life .... Mr. Adam ASHOFF
58 Vice President Graduate School .... Mr. Rich GREGORY
11 Vice President of Operations/COO .... Mr. Todd KOSTJUK
30 Vice President of Development .... Mr. Luke CHERRY
09 Director of Institutional Research .... Mr. John MILTON
26 Director of Communications .... Mr. Brian HARR
42 Campus Pastor .... Rev. Harry WALLS
06 Registrar .... Mr. Don GILMORE
08 Director Library Services .... Mr. John STONE
07 Director of Admissions .... Mr. Dariu DUMITRU
33 Dean of Men .... Mr. David HULET
41 Athletic Director .... Mr. Kelvin STARR
37 Director Financial Aid .... Mr. Kenneth PIESTER
34 Dean of Women .... Ms. Kim WILSON
29 Director Alumni Affairs .... Mr. AJ WORK
85 International Students Advisor .... Mr. Josh ENGLISH
04 Administrative Asst to President .... Ms. Allison PARI
13 Chief Information Officer .... Mr. Paul SEDY
15 Director Personnel Services .... Ms. Kim WILSON
19 Director Security/Safety .... Mr. Chris POWELL
50 Dean Business .... Mr. Dwight HAM
53 Dean Education .... Dr. Jordan MORTON

† The Master's Seminary is located at 13248 Roscoe Boulevard, Sun Valley, CA 91352.

Mayfield College (D)

35-325 Date Palm Drive, Suite 101,
Cathedral City CA 92234
County: Riverside FICE Identification: 041156
Unit ID: 454698
Telephone: (760) 328-5554 Carnegie Class: Spec 2-yr-Tech
FAX Number: (760) 328-5357 Calendar System: Semester
URL: www.mayfieldcollege.org
Established: 1997 Annual Undergrad Tuition & Fees: N/A
Enrollment: 403 Coed
Affiliation or Control: Proprietary IRS Status: Proprietary
Highest Offering: Associate Degree
Accreditation: COE

01 Campus President .... Kevin HA

Mendocino College (E)

1000 Hensley Creek Road, Ukiah CA 95482-7821
County: Mendocino FICE Identification: 011672
Unit ID: 118684
Telephone: (707) 468-3000 Carnegie Class: Assoc/MT-VT-Mix Trad/Non
FAX Number: (707) 468-3120 Calendar System: Semester
URL: www.mendocino.edu
Established: 1973 Annual Undergrad Tuition & Fees (In-District): $1,423
Enrollment: 3,870 Coed
Affiliation or Control: State/Local IRS Status: 501(c)3
Highest Offering: Associate Degree
Accreditation: WJ

01 Superintendent/President .... Vacant
05 Vice Pres Academic Affairs .... Ms. Debra POLAK
10 Asst Superintendent/VP Admin Svcs .... Ms. Eileen CICHOCKI
32 Vice Pres Student Services .... Mr. Ulises VELASCO
08 Head Librarian .... Vacant
20 Dean of Instruction .... Ms. Rebecca MONTES
75 Dean Applied Academics .... Mr. Dennis ASELTYNE
38 Dean of Counseling/Student Programs .... Mr. Antonio LOPEZ
15 Director Human Resources .... Ms. Nicole MARIN
18 Director of Facilities .... Mr. MacAdam LOJOWSKY
26 Director Communications & Cmty Rels .... Ms. Janelle BIRD
41 Director of Athletics .... Mr. Matthew GORDON
21 Director Fiscal Services .... Mr. Joe ATHERTON
13 Director Information Technology .... Vacant
09 Director of Institutional Research .... Ms. Minerva FLORES
07 Director Admissions/Registrar ...... Ms. Anastasia SIMPSON-LOGG
37 Director of Financial Aid .... Ms. Yuliana SANDOVAL
04 Administrative Asst to President .... Ms. Mary LAMB
12 Director of Lake Center .... Ms. Judith KANAVLE
102 Exec Dir Mendocino Col Foundation .... Ms. Katie FAIRBAIRN
88 MESA/Stem Success Director .... Mr. Eric HOEFLER
12 Dean of Centers .... Dr. Amanda XU

Menlo College (F)

1000 El Camino Real, Atherton CA 94027-4301
County: San Mateo FICE Identification: 001236
Unit ID: 118693
Telephone: (800) 556-3656 Carnegie Class: Spec-4-yr-Bus
FAX Number: (650) 543-4085 Calendar System: Semester
URL: www.menlo.edu
Established: 1927 Annual Undergrad Tuition & Fees: $42,800
Enrollment: 744 Coed
Affiliation or Control: Independent Non-Profit IRS Status: 501(c)3
Highest Offering: Baccalaureate
Accreditation: WC

01 President .... Mr. Steven A. WEINER
05 Provost .... Mr. Grande H. LUM
10 VP Finance & Admin/CFO .... Mr. Frank WASILEWSKI
41 VP Enrollment & Athletics .... Mr. Keith SPATARO
121 VP Student Success .... Dr. Angela SCHMIEDE
21 Dir Finance & Business Affairs .... Ms. Rita YON
13 Director Information Technology .... Mr. Minh HUYNH
84 Dean of Enrollment Mgmt .... Ms. Priscila DESOUZA
08 Dean Library Services .... Ms. Valeria MOLTENI
32 Dean of Student Affairs .... Dr. Andrea PEETERS
108 Director IR & Assessment .... Dr. Kristina POWERS
29 Exec Dir Alumni Engagement & Dev .... Ms. Laura KOO
15 Director of Human Resources .... Mr. Jay NAIDU
18 Director Facilities & Operations .... Mr. Robert TALBOTT
36 Director Internship Program .... Mr. Zach OSBORNE
26 Director of Communications .... Vacant
06 Registrar .... Ms. Cristine RABAGO
11 Director of Operations .... Ms. Linda TEUTSCHEL

Merced College (G)

3600 M Street, Merced CA 95348-2898
County: Merced FICE Identification: 001237
Unit ID: 118718
Telephone: (209) 384-6000 Carnegie Class: Assoc/MT-VT-High Trad
FAX Number: (209) 384-6043 Calendar System: Semester
URL: www.mccd.edu
Established: 1962 Annual Undergrad Tuition & Fees (In-District): $1,150
Enrollment: 10,912 Coed
Affiliation or Control: State/Local IRS Status: 501(c)3
Highest Offering: Associate Degree
Accreditation: WJ, DMS, RAD

01 President .... Mr. Chris VITELLI
04 Executive Assistant to President .... Ms. Stacey HICKS
05 Vice President Instruction .... Ms. Kelly FOWLER
32 Vice Pres Student Services .... Mr. Michael MCCANDLESS
10 Vice Pres Administrative Services .... Mr. Joseph ALLISON
12 Dean Los Banos Campus .... Dr. Lonita CORDOVA
45 Dean Institutional Effectiveness .... Vacant
81 Dean Science/Math/Engineering .... Dr. Douglas KAIN
79 Dean English & Humanities .... Dr. Candace TAYLOR
75 Dean Career Technical Education .... Vacant
50 Dean Business/Allied Health/Safety .... Dr. Bobby ANDERSON
83 Dean Social Sci/Fine & Perf Arts .... Mr. John ALBANO
35 Dean of Student Services .... Vacant
22 Dean of Student Equity & Success .... Vacant
26 Chief Public Relations Officer .... Ms. Jill CUNNINGHAM
13 Chief Information Officer .... Mr. Arlis BORTNER
06 Registrar & Dir Financial Aid .... Mrs. Traci VEYL
15 Associate VP of Human Resources .... Ms. Kelly UNDERWOOD
07 Dir Admissions & Records .... Ms. Sherry ELMS
41 Athletic Director .... Mr. Steve CASSADY
96 Director of Purchasing .... Mr. Charles HERGENRAEDER

Meridian University (H)

47 Sixth Street, Petaluma CA 94952
County: Sonoma Identification: 667300
Telephone: (707) 765-1836 Carnegie Class: Not Classified
FAX Number: (707) 765-2351 Calendar System: Other
URL: www.meridianuniversity.edu
Established: 1993 Annual Graduate Tuition & Fees: N/A
Enrollment: N/A Coed
Affiliation or Control: Proprietary IRS Status: Proprietary
Highest Offering: Doctorate; No Undergraduates
Accreditation: WC

00 Chancellor .... Dr. Jean HOUSTON
01 CEO .... Dr. Aftab OMER
05 Vice President Academic Affairs .... Dr. Melissa SCHWARTZ
10 Chief Financial Officer .... Mr. Rob GALL
108 Dir Assessment/Student Development .... Ms. Courtney LUBELL

Merit University (A)

3699 Wilshire Blvd., Ste 970, Los Angeles CA 90010
County: Los Angeles Identification: 667293
Telephone: (213) 325-2760 Carnegie Class: Not Classified
FAX Number: (213) 325-2761 Calendar System: Quarter
URL: www.meritu.edu
Established: Annual Graduate Tuition & Fees: N/A
Enrollment: N/A Coed
Affiliation or Control: Proprietary IRS Status: Proprietary
Highest Offering: Master's; No Undergraduates
Accreditation: ACICS

01 President .... Dr. Jae D. KIM
05 Chief Academic Officer (Provost) .... Dr. Min KIM
06 Registrar .... Namy CHAH

Methodist Theological Seminary in America (B)

1325 N College Avenue, #106, Claremont CA 91711
County: Orange Identification: 667133
Telephone: (213) 386-0080 Carnegie Class: Not Classified
FAX Number: (213) 386-5229 Calendar System: Semester
URL: mtsamerica.edu/
Established: 1880 Annual Undergrad Tuition & Fees: N/A
Enrollment: N/A Coed
Affiliation or Control: Independent Non-Profit IRS Status: 501(c)3
Highest Offering: Master's
Accreditation: BI

Middlebury Institute of International Studies at Monterey (C)

460 Pierce Street, Monterey CA 93940-2691
Telephone: (831) 647-4100 FICE Identification: 001241
Accreditation: &EH, CEA

† Regional accrediation is carried under parent institution Middlebury College, VT.

Mills College (D)

5000 MacArthur Boulevard, Oakland CA 94613-1301
County: Alameda FICE Identification: 001238
Unit ID: 118888
Telephone: (510) 430-2255 Carnegie Class: Masters/M
FAX Number: (510) 430-2256 Calendar System: Semester
URL: www.mills.edu
Established: 1852 Annual Undergrad Tuition & Fees: $30,257
Enrollment: 1,310 Female
Affiliation or Control: Independent Non-Profit IRS Status: 501(c)3
Highest Offering: Doctorate
Accreditation: WC

01 President .... Ms. Elizabeth L. HILLMAN
05 Provost & Dean of Faculty .... Dr. Chinyere OPARAH
10 VP Finance & Administration .... Ms. Maria CAMMARATA
88 VP Strategic Partnerships .... Ms. Renee JADUSHLEVER
111 VP for Inst Advancement .... Dr. Jeffrey JACKANICZ
84 VP for Enrollment Marketing .... Dr. Audrey TANNER
20 Associate Provost .... Dr. Maggie HUNTER
08 Director of Library .... Ms. Janice E. BRAUN
32 VP Student Life/Dean of Students .... Dr. Chicora MARTIN
07 Director of Undergraduate Admission .... Ms. Robynne LOFTON
09 Dir Acad Assess/Inst Research/Plng .... Vacant
18 Associate VP for Operations .... Ms. Linda ZITZNER
38 Asst Dir Counsel/Psych Svcs .... Ms. Shenaaz JANMOHAMMAD
41 Director of Athletics/PE/Recreation .... Ms. Allie LITTLEFOX
04 Senior Exec Asst to the Pres .... Ms. Carrie M. HALL
06 Registrar .... Mr. Cole MOYER
102 Dir Corporate & Foundation Rels .... Ms. Dyana CURRERI-ERMATINGER
13 Chief Technology Officer (CIO) .... Mr. Reza YAZDI
15 Chief Human Resources Officer .... Ms. Kamala GREEN
19 Director of Public Safety .... Ms. Yolanda HARRIS
37 Director Student Financial Aid .... Ms. Angie HARRIS

MiraCosta College (E)

One Barnard Drive, Oceanside CA 92056-3899
County: San Diego FICE Identification: 001239
Unit ID: 118912
Telephone: (760) 757-2121 Carnegie Class: Bac/Assoc-Assoc Dom
FAX Number: (760) 795-6609 Calendar System: Semester
URL: www.miracosta.edu
Established: 1934 Annual Undergrad Tuition & Fees (In-District): $1,336
Enrollment: 14,617 Coed
Affiliation or Control: State/Local IRS Status: 501(c)3
Highest Offering: Baccalaureate
Accreditation: WJ, SURGT

01 Superintendent/President .... Dr. Sunita COOKE
04 Exec Assistant to Supt/President .... Ms. Julie BOLLERUD
04 Exec Assistant to Supt/President .... Ms. Jeanne KOSCHWANEZ
05 Vice President Instructional Svcs .... Dr. Diane DIECKMEYER
32 Vice President Student Svcs .... Dr. Alketa WOJCIK
11 Vice President Administrative Svcs .... Mr. Tim FLOOD
15 Vice President Human Resources .... Mr. Charles NG
12 Dean San Elijo Campus-Letters/Comm .... Ms. Dana SMITH
20 Dean Academic Information Svcs .... Dr. Mario VALENTE
38 Dean Counseling/Student Devel .... Dr. Wendy STEWART
07 Dean Admissions/Student Support .... Mr. Freddy RAMIREZ
51 Interim Dean Community Education .... Dr. Kate ALDER
49 Dean Arts/Intl Languages .... Mr. Jonathan FOHRMAN
81 Dean Math/Sciences .... Mr. Mike FINO
75 Dean Career/Technical Education .... Dr. Al TACCONE
88 Director Small Business Dev Ctr .... Mr. Sudershan SHAUNAK
31 Director Community Services .... Ms. Linda KUROKAWA
06 Registrar .... Ms. Jane SPARKS
09 Dean Institutional Research .... Dr. Chris HILL
26 Director Marketing/Communications .... Dr. Kristen HUYCK
102 AVP Foundation/Fund Development .... Ms. Cynthia RICE-CARROLL
18 Director Facilities .... Mr. Tom MACIAS
37 Director Financial Aid .... Mr. Michael DEAR
117 District Risk Management Officer .... Mr. Joseph MAZZA
88 Director Cashiering Services .... Ms. Jo FERRIS
16 Director Human Resources .... Ms. Lori SHONLEY
36 Director Career Center .... Ms. Donna DAVIS
88 Director Transfer Center .... Ms. Lise FLOCKEN
96 Int Dir Purchasing/Material Mgmt .... Ms. Peggy STROIKA
124 Director Retention Services .... Dr. Edward POEHLERT
21 Director Fiscal Services .... Ms. Katie WHITE
19 Director Campus Police .... Chief Robert NORCROSS
106 Director Online Education .... Dr. James JULIUS

Monterey Peninsula College (F)

980 Fremont Street, Monterey CA 93940-4799
County: Monterey FICE Identification: 001242
Unit ID: 119067
Telephone: (831) 646-4000 Carnegie Class: Assoc/HT-Mix Trad/Non
FAX Number: (831) 655-2627 Calendar System: Semester
URL: www.mpc.edu
Established: 1947 Annual Undergrad Tuition & Fees (In-District): $1,176
Enrollment: 7,816 Coed
Affiliation or Control: State/Local IRS Status: 501(c)3
Highest Offering: Associate Degree
Accreditation: WJ, ADNUR

01 Interim Superintendent/President .... Mr. David MARTIN
05 Acting VP of Academic Affairs .... Dr. Jon KNOLLE
11 Vice Pres Administrative Services .... Vacant
32 VP of Student Services .... Mr. Laurence WALKER
20 Dean of Instruction .... Dr. Vincent VAN JOOLEN
20 Dean of Instruction .... Dr. Jon KNOLLE
20 Dean of Instruction .... Ms. Judith CUTTING
20 Dean of Instruction .... Dr. Cathryn WILKINSON
35 Interim Dean of Student Services .... Mr. Lyndon SCHUTZLER
45 Dean of PRIE .... Dr. Robert PACHECO
15 Director Human Resources .... Vacant
09 Director of Institutional Research .... Dr. Rosaleen RYAN
07 Director of Admissions & Records .... Ms. Nicole DUNNE
08 Director of Library .... Mr. Jeffery SUNDQUIST
37 Student Financial Services Director .... Mr. Francisco TOSTADO
41 Athletic Director .... Mr. Lyndon SCHUTZLER
18 Facilities Operations Supervisor .... Mr. Pete OLSEN
96 Purchasing Agent .... Ms. Mary WEBER
19 Director of Security .... Ms. Jo Anna BUTRON
04 Admin Assistant to the President .... Ms. Shawn ANDERSON
101 Secretary of the Institution/Board .... Ms. JoRene FINNELL
102 Dir Foundation/Corporate Relations .... Ms. Rebecca MICHAEL
13 Director Information Systems .... Mr. Michael MIDKIFF
26 Dir Marketing & Communications .... Ms. Kristin DARKEN

Mount Saint Mary's University (G)

12001 Chalon Road, Los Angeles CA 90049-1599
County: Los Angeles FICE Identification: 001243
Unit ID: 119173
Telephone: (310) 954-4000 Carnegie Class: Masters/L
FAX Number: (310) 954-4379 Calendar System: Semester
URL: www.msmu.edu
Established: 1925 Annual Undergrad Tuition & Fees: $41,170
Enrollment: 3,226 Female
Affiliation or Control: Roman Catholic IRS Status: 501(c)3
Highest Offering: Doctorate
Accreditation: WC, ACBSP, NURSE, PTA

01 President .... Dr. Ann MCELANEY-JOHNSON
05 Provost .... Dr. Robert J. PERRINS
111 Vice Pres Institutional Advancement .... Dr. Stephanie CUBBA
10 Vice Pres Administration & Finance .... Ms. Debra MARTIN
13 VP Strategic Initiatives .... Mr. Larry SMITH
32 Vice President Student Affairs .... Dr. Jane LINGUA
84 VP Enrollment Management .... Mr. Brian O'ROURKE
20 Associate Provost & ALO .... Dr. Michele STARKEY
09 Interim Dir Inst Planning/Research .... Ms. Maria NARVAEZ
58 Graduate Dean .... Dr. Robert J. PERRINS
55 Dean of Weekend College .... Ms. Suzanne WILLIAMS
88 Asst VP Enrollment Management .... Mr. Dean KILGOUR
06 Registrar .... Ms. Rocio DELEON
26 Director Communications/Marketing .... Ms. Debbie REAM
15 Director of Human Resources .... Ms. Dana LOPEZ
18 Director of Facilities Mgmt .... Mr. Rick TORKELSON
37 Director of Student Financing .... Ms. La Royce HOUSLEY
08 Director of MSMU Libraries .... Ms. Danielle SALOMON
28 Assoc VP Diversity and Inclusion .... Ms. Bernadette ROBERT
29 Director Alumni Relations .... Ms. Elizabeth ROBLES JIMENEZ
38 Director Student Counseling .... Dr. Susan SALEM
07 Director of Admissions .... Ms. Erika YAMASAKI
36 Director Career Services .... Ms. Kimberly TERRILL
04 Administrative Asst to President .... Ms. Lucille VILLEGAS
19 Director Security/Safety .... Mr. Michael MCFATRIDGE
35 Dean of Student Life .... Ms. Jessica CUEVAS
44 Director Individual Giving .... Ms. Maria SOLANO
104 Study Away Coordinator .... Ms. Jaime WOOD
105 Web Manager .... Mr. Brian FREEMAN
106 Int Dir Online Education/E-learning .... Mr. Edgar CHABOLLA
39 Director of Residence Life .... Ms. Michelle SALDANA
102 Director Foundation/Corporate Rels .... Mr. Matthew MEYER
30 Director of Development .... Ms. Megan SHOCKRO
41 Athletic Director .... Ms. Autumn JOHNSON
50 Dept Chair Business Administration .... Mr. Mark ALHANATI
53 Dept Chair Education .... Dr. Carol JOHNSTON

Mt. San Antonio College (H)

1100 N Grand, Walnut CA 91789-1399
County: Los Angeles FICE Identification: 001245
Unit ID: 119164
Telephone: (909) 274-7500 Carnegie Class: Assoc/MT-VT-High Trad
FAX Number: N/A Calendar System: Semester
URL: www.mtsac.edu
Established: 1946 Annual Undergrad Tuition & Fees (In-District): $1,350
Enrollment: 29,960 Coed
Affiliation or Control: State/Local IRS Status: 501(c)3
Highest Offering: Associate Degree
Accreditation: WJ, COARC, EMT, HT, RAD

01 President/CEO .... Dr. William T. SCROGGINS
05 Vice President Instruction .... Dr. Richard MAHON
10 Vice President Administrative Svcs .... Mr. Michael D. GREGORYK
32 Vice President Student Services .... Dr. Audrey YAMAGATA-NOJI
15 Vice President Human Resources .... Mr. Abe ALI
20 Assoc Vice Pres Instruction .... Dr. Joumana MCGOWAN
35 Dean Student Services .... Dr. Koji UESUGI
08 Dean Library/Learning Resources .... Dr. Meghan CHEN
38 AVP Student Svcs/Dn of Counseling .... Mr. Tom MAUCH
13 Chief Technology Officer/Info Tech .... Mr. Dale VICKERS
84 Dean Enrollment Management .... Dr. George BRADSHAW
21 Assoc Vice Pres Fiscal Services .... Mr. Doug JENSEN
102 Executive Director of Foundation .... Mr. Bill LAMBERT
37 Director Financial Aid .... Ms. Chau DAO
117 Director Risk Management .... Ms. Duetta LANGEVIN
46 Director Grants .... Ms. Adrienne PRICE
26 Director Marketing/Communications .... Ms. Uyen MAI
09 Dir Research & Inst Effectiveness .... Ms. Barbara MCNEICE-STALLARD
18 Director Facilities Planning & Mgmt .... Mr. Gary NELLESEN
35 Director Student Life .... Ms. Andrea SIMS
96 Purchasing Manager .... Ms. Teresa PATTERSON
50 Dean Business .... Ms. Jennifer GALBRAITH
68 Dean Kinesiology/Athletics/Dance .... Mr. Joe JENNUM
79 Dean Humanities & Social Science .... Dr. Karelyn HOOVER
72 Dean Tech/Health Science .... Mr. Sam AGDASI
65 Assoc Dean Natural Sciences .... Mr. Matthew JUDD
57 Dean Arts .... Dr. Susan LONG
51 Dean School of Continuing Education .... Dr. Madelyn ARBALLO
04 Exec Asst to President & BOT .... Ms. Carol NELSON

Mt. San Jacinto College (I)

1499 N State Street, San Jacinto CA 92583-2399
County: Riverside FICE Identification: 001246
Unit ID: 119216
Telephone: (951) 487-6752 Carnegie Class: Assoc/MT-VT-High Trad
FAX Number: (951) 654-9712 Calendar System: Semester
URL: www.msjc.edu
Established: 1962 Annual Undergrad Tuition & Fees (In-District): $1,386
Enrollment: 15,718 Coed
Affiliation or Control: State/Local IRS Status: 501(c)3
Highest Offering: Associate Degree
Accreditation: WJ, DMS

01 Superintendent/President .... Dr. Roger W. SCHULTZ
04 Executive Assistant to President .... Ms. Kristen GRIMES
05 Int Vice Pres of Instruction .... Dr. Jeremy BROWN
32 Vice President Student Services .... Dr. John COLSON
10 Vice President Business Svcs .... Ms. Beth GOMEZ
15 Chief Human Resources Officer .... Ms. Jeannine STOKES
84 Vice Pres Inst Effect/Enroll Mgmt .... Mr. Brandon MOORE
20 Executive Dean of Instruction .... Ms. Joyce JOHNSON
20 Int Dean of Academic Programs .... Ms. Rickianne RYCRAFT
20 Int Dean of Academic Programs - SJC .... Dr. Alma RAMIREZ
72 Dean Instruct Acad Success/Tech .... Mr. Micah ORLOFF
103 Dean Career Education-MVC .... Dr. Marilyn HARVEY
103 Dean Career Education-SJC .... Mr. Von LAWSON
20 Dean of Academic Programs - MVC .... Mr. Marc DONNHAUSER
21 Dean of Admin Services/Controller .... Ms. Gail JENSEN
13 Dean Information Tech .... Mr. Brian ORLAUSKI
18 Int Dn Facilities Plng/Cap Constr .... Vacant
35 Dean Student Services .... Ms. Susan LOOMIS
41 Dean of Athletics .... Mr. Patrick SPRINGER
45 Dean Institutional Planning .... Ms. Rebecca TEAGUE
108 Dean Institutional Effectiveness .... Dr. Carlos TOVARES
26 Public Information Officer .... Ms. Karin MARRIOTT
37 Dean of Student Svcs/Financial Aid .... Ms. Dolores SMITH
66 Assoc Dean of Nursing/Allied Health .... Dr. Crystal NASIO

88 Int Assoc Dn Instructional Support .... Ms. Cheri NAISH
18 Director Maint & Operations ....Mr. Brian TWITTY
09 Director of Research ....Mr. Nikilos 'Nik' MESARIS
07 Int Director Enrollment Services .... Ms. Elizabeth MASCARO
19 Director Campus Safety .... Mr. David PASEMAN
96 Director Procurement & Gen Svcs ......Ms. Tamara CUNNINGHAM

MTI College (A)

5221 Madison Avenue, Sacramento CA 95841-3037
County: Sacramento FICE Identification: 012912
Unit ID: 118198
Telephone: (916) 339-1500 Carnegie Class: Assoc/HVT-High Trad
FAX Number: (916) 339-0305 Calendar System: Quarter
URL: mticollege.edu
Established: 1965 Annual Undergrad Tuition & Fees: N/A
Enrollment: 781 Coed
Affiliation or Control: Proprietary IRS Status: Proprietary
Highest Offering: Associate Degree
Accreditation: WJ

01 President .... Mr. Michael A. ZIMMERMAN
10 Vice Pres/Chief Financial Officer .... Mr. David W. ALLEN
12 Campus Director .... Mr. Donald BLACK

Musicians Institute (B)

6752 Hollywood Boulevard, Hollywood CA 90028
County: Los Angeles FICE Identification: 021618
Unit ID: 119270
Telephone: (323) 462-1384 Carnegie Class: Spec-4-yr-Arts
FAX Number: (323) 462-1575 Calendar System: Quarter
URL: www.mi.edu
Established: 1977 Annual Undergrad Tuition & Fees: $24,030
Enrollment: 990 Coed
Affiliation or Control: Proprietary IRS Status: Proprietary
Highest Offering: Baccalaureate
Accreditation: MUS

01 President ....Mr. Todd BERHORST
05 Chief Academic Officer ....Dr. Rachel YOON
108 Director of Compliance ....Mrs. Danielle SASSMAN
06 Registrar ....Mr. Shaun VIETEN
13 Director of Information Technology ....Mr. Tim METZ
37 Director Student Financial Aid ....Mr. Michael HONG
07 Director of Admissions .... Mr. Vin CHHABRA
10 Chief Financial/Business Officer ....Mr. Kengo KIDO

Napa Valley College (C)

2277 Napa-Vallejo Highway, Napa CA 94558-6236
County: Napa FICE Identification: 001247
Unit ID: 119331
Telephone: (707) 256-7000 Carnegie Class: Assoc/MT-VT-High Trad
FAX Number: (707) 253-3015 Calendar System: Semester
URL: www.napavalley.edu
Established: 1942 Annual Undergrad Tuition & Fees (In-District): $1,142
Enrollment: 6,076 Coed
Affiliation or Control: State/Local IRS Status: 501(c)3
Highest Offering: Associate Degree
Accreditation: WJ, COARC, EMT

01 Superintendent/President ....Dr. Ronald D. KRAFT
05 Int Vice President Instruction .... Ms. Faye SMYLE
10 Vice Pres Admin Svcs/Asst Supt .... Mr. Robert PARKER
32 Vice Pres Student Svcs/Asst Supt ....Mr. Oscar DE HARO
38 Dean Counseling Svcs/Stdnt Success ....Mr. Howard WILLIS
20 Dean of Instruction .... Ms. Maria VILLAGOMEZ
37 Dean Fin Aid/EOPS/Pre-Col TRIO Pgms .....Ms. Patricia MORGAN
103 Dean Career Tech Educ/Workforce Dev ....Ms. Miraglia GREGORY
13 Dean Institutional Technology .... Mr. Eric MOUCK
09 Dean Research Plng/Instl Effect ....Dr. Robyn WORNALL
36 Dean Counselor/WA III .... Mr. Howard WILLIS
12 Int Director Upper Valley Campus ....Ms. Melissa GIBBS
07 Assoc Dean Admissions/Records ....Ms. Jessica ERICKSON
15 Exec Director Human Resources .... Ms. Charo ALBARRAN
26 Public Relations Officer .... Mr. Doug ERNST
18 Director Facilities .... Mr. Matt CHRISTENSEN
111 Exec Dir Institutional Advancement ....Ms. Anne BRANCH
19 Director College Police .... Mr. Kenneth L. ARNOLD
84 Enrollment Management .... Mr. Erik SHEARER
88 Coordinator Trans Center ....Ms. Marci SANCHEZ
28 Director of Equity & Inclusivity ....Dr. Craig ALIMO
04 Exec Asst to the President ....Ms. Carolee CATTOLICA
96 Business Services Asst/Purchasing ....Ms. Solange KADAD
23 Director Student Health Services ....Ms. Nancy TAMARISK

National Career College (D)

14355 Roscoe Boulevard, Panorama City CA 91402
County: Los Angeles FICE Identification: 041460
Unit ID: 455868
Telephone: (818) 988-2300 Carnegie Class: Spec 2-yr-Health
FAX Number: (818) 988-9944 Calendar System: Semester
URL: www.nccusa.edu
Established: 2005 Annual Undergrad Tuition & Fees: N/A
Enrollment: 270 Coed
Affiliation or Control: Proprietary IRS Status: Proprietary
Highest Offering: Associate Degree
Accreditation: ABHES

01 President .... Gayane KHANOYAN
37 Director Student Financial Aid .... Anna TOVMASYAN

National Polytechnic College (E)

4105 South Street, Lakewood CA 90712
County: Los Angeles FICE Identification: 039104
Unit ID: 447759
Telephone: (888) 243-2493 Carnegie Class: Not Classified
FAX Number: (888) 640-7732 Calendar System: Semester
URL: www.npcollege.edu
Established: 1996 Annual Undergrad Tuition & Fees: N/A
Enrollment: 144 Coed
Affiliation or Control: Proprietary IRS Status: Proprietary
Highest Offering: Associate Degree
Accreditation: ACCSC, CEA

01 CEO and President ....Dariush (David) MADDAHI

National University (F)

11255 N Torrey Pines Road, La Jolla CA 92037-1011
County: San Diego FICE Identification: 011460
Unit ID: 119605
Telephone: (858) 642-8000 Carnegie Class: Masters/L
FAX Number: (858) 642-8714 Calendar System: Other
URL: www.nu.edu
Established: 1971 Annual Undergrad Tuition & Fees: $13,320
Enrollment: 17,097 Coed
Affiliation or Control: Independent Non-Profit IRS Status: 501(c)3
Highest Offering: Doctorate
Accreditation: WC, ANEST, CAEPN, IACBE, NURSE, #PH, RTT

00 Chancellor .... Dr. Michael R. CUNNINGHAM
01 University President .... Dr. David ANDREWS
05 Provost .... Dr. Gangaram SINGH

New York Film Academy, Los Angeles (G)

3300 Riverside Drive, Burbank CA 91505
County: Burbank FICE Identification: 041188
Unit ID: 461148
Telephone: (818) 333-3558 Carnegie Class: Spec-4-yr-Arts
FAX Number: (818) 333-3557 Calendar System: Semester
URL: www.nyfa.edu
Established: 2006 Annual Undergrad Tuition & Fees: $31,438
Enrollment: 1,487 Coed
Affiliation or Control: Proprietary IRS Status: Proprietary
Highest Offering: Master's
Accreditation: WC, ART

01 Dean of the College .... Mr. Dan MACKLER
05 Dean of Faculty .... Mr. Nunzio DEFILIPPIS
32 Dean of Students .... Dr. Susan ASHE
10 Chief Financial Officer .... Mr. Kirk LENGA
06 Registrar .... Mr. Vince VOSKANIAN
07 Director of Admissions .... Mr. Michael KELLER
08 Head Librarian ....Mr. Josh MOORMON
39 Housing Coordinator ....Ms. Aerial SEGARD-GOMEZ

NewSchool of Architecture and Design (H)

1249 F Street, San Diego CA 92101-6634
County: San Diego FICE Identification: 030439
Unit ID: 119775
Telephone: (619) 684-8800 Carnegie Class: Spec-4-yr-Arts
FAX Number: (619) 684-8880 Calendar System: Quarter
URL: www.newschoolarch.edu
Established: 1980 Annual Undergrad Tuition & Fees: $27,501
Enrollment: 554 Coed
Affiliation or Control: Proprietary IRS Status: Proprietary
Highest Offering: Master's
Accreditation: WC

01 President ....Mr. Marvin MALECHA
05 Chief Academic Officer ....Mr. Marvin MALECHA
32 Dean Division of Student Affairs .... Dr. Sheila SULLIVAN
88 Dean School of Design .... Dr. Elena PACENTI
48 Head of Architecture .... Mr. Len ZEGARSKI

Nobel University (I)

505 Shatto Place #300, Los Angeles CA 90020
County: Los Angeles Identification: 667274
Telephone: (213) 382-1136 Carnegie Class: Not Classified
FAX Number: (213) 382-1187 Calendar System: Semester
URL: nobeluniversity.edu
Established: 2000 Annual Undergrad Tuition & Fees: N/A
Enrollment: N/A Coed
Affiliation or Control: Proprietary IRS Status: Proprietary
Highest Offering: Master's
Accreditation: ACICS

01 President ....Chong S. KIM
05 Chief Academic Officer (Provost) .... Michael KAHLER

*North Orange County Community College District (J)

1830 W Romneya Drive, Anaheim CA 92801-1819
County: Orange FICE Identification: 009742
Unit ID: 120023
Telephone: (714) 808-4500 Carnegie Class: N/A
FAX Number: (714) 808-4791
URL: www.nocccd.edu

01 Chancellor ....Dr. Cheryl A. MARSHALL
10 Vice Chanc Finance/Facilities ....Mr. Fred WILLIAMS
15 Vice Chancellor Human Resources .... Ms. Irma RAMOS
05 Vice Chanc Educational Svcs/Tech .... Dr. Cherry LI-BUGG
26 Director Public/Government Affairs .....Ms. Kai STEARNS MOORE
04 Exec Admin Aide to Chancellor ....Ms. Alba RECINOS
22 Dist Director Diversity/Compliance ....Mr. Arturo OCAMPO

*Cypress College (K)

9200 Valley View, Cypress CA 90630-5897
County: Orange FICE Identification: 001193
Unit ID: 113236
Telephone: (714) 484-7000 Carnegie Class: Bac/Assoc-Assoc Dom
FAX Number: (714) 527-8238 Calendar System: Semester
URL: www.cypresscollege.edu
Established: 1966 Annual Undergrad Tuition & Fees (In-District): $1,142
Enrollment: 15,673 Coed
Affiliation or Control: State/Local IRS Status: 501(c)3
Highest Offering: Baccalaureate
Accreditation: WJ, ADNUR, CAHIIM, DA, DH, DMS, FUSER, RAD

02 President ....Dr. JoAnna SCHILLING
05 Vice Pres Instruction .... Dr. Carmen DOMINGUEZ
32 Vice President Student Services .... Dr. Paul DE DIOS
10 Vice Pres Administrative Services .... Mr. Alex PORTER
08 Dean Library/Learning Resource Ctr ....Dr. Treisa CASSENS
88 Dean Language Arts ....Mr. Eldon YOUNG
121 Int Dean Counseling/Student Dev .... Dr. Flor HUERTA
06 Registrar .... Mr. David BOOZE
26 Director Campus Communications .... Mr. Marc POSNER
102 Exec Dir Foundation/Community Rels ....Mr. Howard KUMMERMAN
32 Dean Student Support Services .... Dr. Richard RAMS
22 Director Disabled Student Services .... Ms. Celeste PHELPS
90 Manager Systems Technology Svcs .... Mr. Peter MAHARAJ
37 Director Financial Aid ....Mr. Korey LINDLEY
09 Dir Institutional Research/Planning ....Mr. Philip DYKSTRA
18 Director Physical Plant/Facilities ....Mr. Philip FLEMING
19 Director Campus Safety ....Mr. Ralph WEBB
04 Int Exec Assistant to President ....Mrs. Christina MIX
68 Dean Physical Education/Kinesiology .... Dr. Richard RAMS
57 Dean Fine Arts ....Dr. Katy REALISTA
50 Dean Business/CIS ....Mr. Henry HUA
83 Interim Dean Social Sciences ....Ms. Lisa GAETJE
53 Dean Science Engineering & Math .... Dr. Richard FEE
76 Dean Health Sciences .... Ms. Rebecca GOMEZ
75 Int Dean Career Technical Education .... Ms. Kathleen REILAND
113 Bursar .... Ms. Dao DO
22 Director EOPS .... Ms. AnnMarie RUELAS
88 Asst Proj Manager Campus Cap Proj ....Vacant
88 Proj Manager Campus Cap Proj .... Mr. Ryan LIPPMANN

*Fullerton College (L)

321 E Chapman Avenue, Fullerton CA 92832-2095
County: Orange FICE Identification: 001201
Unit ID: 114859
Telephone: (714) 992-7000 Carnegie Class: Assoc/HT-High Trad
FAX Number: (714) 992-9930 Calendar System: Semester
URL: www.fullcoll.edu
Established: 1913 Annual Undergrad Tuition & Fees (In-District): $1,138
Enrollment: 24,124 Coed
Affiliation or Control: State/Local IRS Status: 501(c)3
Highest Offering: Associate Degree
Accreditation: WJ

02 President .... Dr. Greg SCHULZ
05 Vice President Instruction .... Dr. Jose Ramon NUNEZ
32 Vice Pres Student Services .... Dr. Gilbert CONTRERAS
11 Vice Pres Administrative Svcs .... Mr. Rodrigo GARCIA
50 Interim Dean Business & CIS .... Mr. Carlos AYON
57 Dean Fine Arts .... Mr. John TEBAY
79 Dean Humanities .... Mr. Dan WILLOUGHBY
81 Dean Math/Computer Science .... Mr. Mark GREENHALGH
88 Dean Natural Sciences ....Dr. Richard HARTMANN
68 Dean Physical Education ....Dr. David GROSSMAN
83 Dean Social Sciences ....Mr. Jorge GAMBOA
72 Dean Technology & Engr ....Mr. Kenneth STARKMAN
37 Director of Financial Aid ....Mr. Greg RYAN
23 Interim Director Health Services .... Mr. Dana TIMMERMANS
18 Dir Facilities/Physical Plant ....Mr. Larry LARA
40 Director of Bookstore ....Mr. Nick KARVIA
35 Director Student Activities ....Ms. Naomi ABESAMIS
06 Registrar ....Ms. Rena MARTINEZ STLUKA
19 Director Campus Safety .... Mr. Steve SELBY
38 Dean Counseling/Student Development ...Ms. Jennifer LABOUNTY
08 Dean Library (LLR & ISPS) ....Ms. Dani WILSON
07 Dean Admissions & Records ....Mr. Albert ABUTIN
90 Academic Computing Technologies ....Mr. Co HO
09 Director Inst Research & Planning ....Vacant
88 Director Cadena Transfer Center .... Ms. Cecilia ARRIAZA

26 Director Campus Communications .... Ms. Lisa MCPHERON
04 Exec Assistant to the President .... Ms. Jean FOSTER
88 Dean Student Support Services ....Dr. Elaine LIPIZ GONZALEZ

Northcentral University (A)

2488 Historic Decatur Rd, Suite 100, San Diego CA 92106

County: San Diego FICE Identification: 038133
Unit ID: 444130
Telephone: (866) 776-0331 Carnegie Class: DU-Mod
FAX Number: (844) 851-5889 Calendar System: Other
URL: www.ncu.edu
Established: 1996 Annual Undergrad Tuition & Fees: N/A
Enrollment: 10,788 Coed
Affiliation or Control: Independent Non-Profit IRS Status: 501(c)3
Highest Offering: Doctorate
Accreditation: WC, ACBSP, MFCD

01 President .... Dr. David HARPOOL
05 Provost/Chief Academic Officer .... Dr. John LANEAR
20 Vice Pres Academic Affairs .... Vacant
37 VP Student and Financial Services .... Dr. Ian COOPER
07 VP Enrollment .... Mr. Ken BOUTELLE
15 VP Human Resources .... Ms. Angie WALKER
13 Chief Technology Learning Officer .... Dr. Colin MARLAIRE
26 Chief Marketing Officer .... Vacant
43 General Counsel .... Dr. David HARPOOL
50 Dean School of Business .... Dr. Kelley WALTERS
53 Dean School of Education .... Dr. Andy RIGGLE
76 Dean School of Health Sciences ....Dr. Laurie SHANDERSON
83 Dean Sch of Social/Behavioral Sci .... Dr. James BILLINGS
72 Dean School of Technology .... Dr. Robert SAPP
09 Director Institutional Research .... Vacant
108 Director Institutional Assessment .... Dr. Heather HUSSEY
06 University Registrar .... Ms. Jennifer RACER
08 Director of Library Services .... Ms. Amanda ZIEGLER

Northern California Bible College (B)

4439 Stonebridge Dr, Ste 210, Pleasanton CA 94588

County: Alameda Identification: 667349
Telephone: (925) 846-6464 Carnegie Class: Not Classified
FAX Number: N/A Calendar System: Quarter
URL: www.ncbc.net
Established: 1971 Annual Undergrad Tuition & Fees: N/A
Enrollment: N/A Coed
Affiliation or Control: Independent Non-Profit IRS Status: 501(c)3
Highest Offering: Baccalaureate
Accreditation: @TRACS

01 President .... David G. SELL

Northwestern Polytechnic University (C)

47671 Westinghouse Drive, Fremont CA 94539-7474

County: Alameda Identification: 666759
Telephone: (510) 592-9688 Carnegie Class: Not Classified
FAX Number: (510) 657-8975 Calendar System: Trimester
URL: www.npu.edu
Established: 1984 Annual Undergrad Tuition & Fees: N/A
Enrollment: N/A Coed
Affiliation or Control: Independent Non-Profit IRS Status: 501(c)3
Highest Offering: Master's
Accreditation: @WC, ACICS

01 President .... Mr. Peter HSIEH
03 Executive Vice President .... Mr. Paul CHOI
05 Chief Academic Officer .... Ms. Nelly MANGAROVA
10 Chief Financial Officer .... Ms. Anne SUTARDJI
43 General Transactions & Corp Counsel ....Mr. Mark SCHULTZ
07 Dir of Admissions/Special Projects ....Ms. Monica SINHA
84 Dir of Student Outreach/Enrollment ....Mr. David LINNEVERS
54 Dean of School of Engineering ....Dr. Thawi IWAGOSHI
50 Dean of School of Business ....Mr. James CONNOR

Notre Dame de Namur University (D)

1500 Ralston Avenue, Belmont CA 94002-1908

County: San Mateo FICE Identification: 001179
Unit ID: 120184
Telephone: (650) 508-3500 Carnegie Class: Masters/M
FAX Number: (650) 508-3477 Calendar System: Semester
URL: www.ndnu.edu
Established: 1851 Annual Undergrad Tuition & Fees: $35,350
Enrollment: 1,605 Coed
Affiliation or Control: Independent Non-Profit IRS Status: 501(c)3
Highest Offering: Doctorate
Accreditation: WC, ACBSP

01 President .... Dr. Judith M. GREIG
05 Provost .... Dr. Hernan BUCHELI
10 Vice Pres Finance & Administration .... Mr. Henry ROTH
32 Chief Student Success Officer ....Dr. Diana HERNANDEZ
111 Int Vice Pres for Advancement .... Ms. Barbara ALVAREZ
53 Dean Education/Psychology ....Dr. Caryl HODGES
06 Registrar .... Mr. J. T BROWN
36 Director Career Development ....Ms. Carrie MCKNIGHT
37 Director Financial Aid .... Mr. Charles WALZ
38 Director Student Counseling ....Ms. Karin SPONHOLZ
41 Athletic Director .... Mr. Josh DOODY
42 Director Spirituality ....Ms. Diana ENRIQUEZ FIELD
19 Director of Public Safety ....Mr. William PALMINI, JR.
29 Director Alumni Relations ....Ms. Elizabeth VALENTE
26 Exec Dir Marketing/Communication .... Ms. Karen SCHORNSTEIN
15 Executive Director Human Resources .... Ms. Mary HAESLOOP
08 Director Library Services .... Ms. Mary WEGMANN
13 Director Office of Information Tech .... Mr. Merle MASON
18 Director Facilities .... Mr. Chris KORNAHRENS
20 Associate Provost .... Mr. Greg WHITE
21 Controller .... Ms. Emiko YAMADA
09 Director of Institutional Research .... Mr. John HOFMANN
04 Exec Assistant to the President .... Ms. Deirdre SARGENT
106 Asst Provost Online Programs .... Mr. Brad WASHINGTON
44 Director Annual Giving .... Ms. Barbara ALVAREZ

Occidental College (E)

1600 Campus Road, Los Angeles CA 90041-3314

County: Los Angeles FICE Identification: 001249
Unit ID: 120254
Telephone: (323) 259-2500 Carnegie Class: Bac-A&S
FAX Number: (323) 259-2958 Calendar System: Semester
URL: www.oxy.edu
Established: 1887 Annual Undergrad Tuition & Fees: $54,686
Enrollment: 1,972 Coed
Affiliation or Control: Independent Non-Profit IRS Status: 501(c)3
Highest Offering: Master's
Accreditation: WC

01 President .... Dr. Jonathan VEITCH
05 VP Academic Affairs/Dean of College ..Dr. Wendy F. STERNBERG
10 Vice Pres/Chief Operating Officer .... Mr. Amos HIMMELSTEIN
07 VP Admissions/Financial Aid ....Mr. Vincent CUSEO
111 Vice Pres Inst Advancement ....Mr. Charlie CARDILLO
32 VP Student Affairs/Dean of Students ....Mr. Rob FLOT
43 General Counsel .... Mr. Jon MCNUTT
100 Chief of Staff .... Ms. Kimberly URIBE
41 Athletic Dir/VP Student Affairs .... Ms. Shanda NESS
18 Assoc VP for Facilities Management .... Mr. Thomas POLANSKY
26 VP Marketing/Communications .... Mr. Marty SHARKEY
13 AVP ITS/Chief Technology Officer .... Mr. James UHRICH
36 AVP/Exec Director Career Services .... Ms. Cherena JAMES WALKER
04 Exec Assistant to President .... Ms. Marlene LOZANO
08 Interim Library Director ....Ms. Marsha SCHNIRRING
29 Director Alumni/Parent Engagement ....Ms. Monika MOORE
37 Director of Financial Aid ....Ms. Gina BECERRIL
15 Director of Human Resources .... Ms. Danita MAXWELL
27 Director of Communications ....Mr. Jim TRANQUADA
09 Director of Institutional Research ....Ms. Teresa KALDOR
19 Chief of Campus Safety ....Mr. Rick TANKSLEY
101 Secretary of the Institution/Board ....Ms. Marsha SCHNIRRING

Ohlone College (F)

43600 Mission Boulevard, Fremont CA 94539-0390

County: Alameda FICE Identification: 004481
Unit ID: 120290
Telephone: (510) 659-6000 Carnegie Class: Assoc/HVT-Mix Trad/Non
FAX Number: N/A Calendar System: Semester
URL: www.ohlone.edu
Established: 1966 Annual Undergrad Tuition & Fees (In-District): $1,164
Enrollment: 9,273 Coed
Affiliation or Control: State/Local IRS Status: 501(c)3
Highest Offering: Associate Degree
Accreditation: WJ, ADNUR, COARC, PTAA

01 President/Superintendent ....Dr. Gari BROWNING
05 Int Vice President Academic Affairs ....Dr. Andrew LAMANQUE
10 Int Vice Pres Administrative Svcs ....Dr. Chris DELA ROSA
32 Int Vice President Student Services .... Mr. Binh NGUYEN
13 Assoc Vice Pres Information Tech ....Dr. Chris DELA ROSA
15 Vice Pres Human Resources .... Ms. Shairon ZINGSHEIM
08 Dean Business & Career Tech Educ .... Ms. Lesley BUEHLER
38 Dean Counseling .... Dr. Eva Margarita MUNGUIA
09 Exec Dean Institutional Research ....Mr. Michael BOWMAN
83 Dean Social Science .... Dr. Ghada AL-MASRI
76 Dean Health Sciences .... Mr. Robert GABRIEL
83 Dean Language/Comm/Academic Success ....Mr. Mark LIEU
81 Dean Science/Engineering/Math .... Ms. Lori SILVERMAN
88 Dean Deaf Studies .... Ms. Darline GUNSAULS
102 Executive Director Foundation ....Mr. Binh NGUYEN
35 Int Director EOPS/Student Services .. Ms. Nancy NAVARRO-LECA
21 Exec Director Business Services .... Mr. Farhad SABIT
30 Director College Advancement .... Ms. Tina VOSSUGH
19 Chief Safety & Security .... Mr. John WORLEY
18 Director of Facilities ....Mr. Oscar GUILLEN
37 Director Financial Aid .... Vacant
96 Director of Purchasing .... Mr. Alex LEBEDEFF
104 Director International Programs .... Vacant
88 Director Curriculum & Scheduling .... Ms. Kimberly ROBBIE
04 Administrative Asst to President .... Ms. Shelby FOSTER
07 Int Dean Enrollment Services .... Mr. Michael LEIB
68 Dean Kinesiology/Athl/Brdcstg/Arts ....Mr. Chris WARDEN

Oikos University (G)

7901 Oakport St, Ste 3000, Oakland CA 94621

County: Alameda Identification: 667212
Telephone: (510) 639-7879 Carnegie Class: Not Classified
FAX Number: (510) 639-7810 Calendar System: Semester
URL: www.oikos.edu
Established: 2004 Annual Undergrad Tuition & Fees: N/A
Enrollment: N/A Coed
Affiliation or Control: Independent Non-Profit IRS Status: 501(c)3
Highest Offering: Doctorate
Accreditation: TRACS

01 President .... Dr. Jongin KIM
05 Director of Academic Affairs ....Dr. Ki Wook MIN
11 Director Administration ....Dr. Dongjin LEE
10 Chief Financial Officer .... Ms. Myungsoon YOON

Olivet University (H)

36401 Tripp Flats Road, Anza CA 92539

County: San Francisco Identification: 666176
Telephone: (951) 763-0500 Carnegie Class: Not Classified
FAX Number: (415) 371-0003 Calendar System: Quarter
URL: www.olivetuniversity.edu
Established: 1992 Annual Undergrad Tuition & Fees: N/A
Enrollment: N/A Coed
Affiliation or Control: Independent Non-Profit IRS Status: 501(c)3
Highest Offering: Doctorate
Accreditation: BI

01 University President ....Dr. Tracy DAVIS
03 Vice President ....Dr. Nathanael TRAN
05 Academic Dean .... Dr. Christy TRAN
11 Chief Operating Officer ....Dr. Walker TZENG
10 Chief Financial Officer .... Mr. Barnabas JUNG

Otis College of Art and Design (I)

9045 Lincoln Boulevard, Los Angeles CA 90045-3550

County: Los Angeles FICE Identification: 001251
Unit ID: 120403
Telephone: (310) 665-6800 Carnegie Class: Spec-4-yr-Arts
FAX Number: (310) 665-6805 Calendar System: Semester
URL: www.otis.edu
Established: 1918 Annual Undergrad Tuition & Fees: $46,860
Enrollment: 1,115 Coed
Affiliation or Control: Independent Non-Profit IRS Status: 501(c)3
Highest Offering: Master's
Accreditation: WC, ART

00 Chair Board of Trustees .... Ms. Mei-Lee NEY
01 Interim President .... Mr. Randall LAVENDER
05 Interim Provost .... Ms. Kim RUSSO
13 VP of IT and Operations .... Mr. Ankush MAHINDRA
10 Interim VP of Financial Services ....Ms. Vivien ROTHWELL
32 VP of Campus Life .... Dr. Laura KIRALLA
15 VP of Human Resources/Risk Mgmt .... Ms. Karen HILL
26 VP of Communications and Marketing .... Mr. Jeffrey PERKINS
111 VP of Institutional Advancement ....Mr. Patrick MAHANY
35 Dean of Student Affairs .... Dr. Nick NEGRETE
56 Dean of Extension .... Mr. Mark MANROSE
84 Dean of Enrollment Mgmt .... Mr. Matthew GALLAGHER
06 Registrar .... Ms. Anna MANZANO
08 Sr Director Library & Library Ctrs .... Vacant
90 Sr Director End-User Computing .... Mr. Felipe GUTIERREZ
18 Chief Facilities/Operation Officer .... Mr. Claude NICA
37 Director Student Fin Services ....Ms. Natasha KOBRINSKY
09 Dir Inst Research & Effectiveness .... Dr. Angila ROMIOUS
14 Director Technology Infrastructure .... Mr. Matthew BALLARD
108 Assoc Provost Assessment & Accred ....Ms. Debra BALLARD
20 Interim Asst Provost .... Ms. Joanne MITCHELL
28 Asst Dean of Stdnt Affs/Title IX .... Dr. Carol BRANCH
88 Exec Director College Initiatives .... Ms. Mahtem SHIFERRAW
112 Director of Strategic Partnerships .... Vacant
19 Chief Safety and Security Officer .... Mr. Rick GONZALEZ
101 Board Relations Mgr ....Ms. Doniell PETERS
04 Exec Asst to President ....Ms. April KULLIS
07 Assoc Dean of Admissions .... Ms. Yoi GAYLER
23 Director Student Health & Wellness ....Dr. Julie SPENCER
39 Director Housing & Res Life ....Ms. Morgan BROWN
96 Director of Purchasing ....Ms. Barbara TECLE
29 Director Alumni Relations ....Ms. Hazel MANDUJANO

Pacific College (J)

3160 Redhill Avenue, Costa Mesa CA 92626-3402

County: Orange FICE Identification: 032993
Unit ID: 422695
Telephone: (800) 867-2243 Carnegie Class: Spec-4-yr-Other Health
FAX Number: (714) 662-1702 Calendar System: Semester
URL: www.pacific-college.edu
Established: 1993 Annual Undergrad Tuition & Fees: N/A
Enrollment: 350 Coed
Affiliation or Control: Proprietary IRS Status: Proprietary
Highest Offering: Master's
Accreditation: WC, NURSE

01 President .... Mr. William L. NELSON
03 Vice President .... Ms. Donna WOO
11 Sr Vice Pres Operations .... Mr. Marcus TROMP

Pacific College of Oriental Medicine (K)

7445 Mission Valley Road, #104,
San Diego CA 92108-4408

County: San Diego FICE Identification: 030277
Unit ID: 378576
Telephone: (619) 574-6909 Carnegie Class: Spec-4-yr-Other Health
FAX Number: (619) 574-6641 Calendar System: Trimester
URL: www.pacificcollege.edu

Established: 1986 Annual Undergrad Tuition & Fees: $9,791
Enrollment: 941 Coed
Affiliation or Control: Proprietary IRS Status: Proprietary
Highest Offering: Doctorate
Accreditation: WC, ACUP

01 President .... Mr. Jack MILLER
05 Vice Pres of Academic Affairs .... Ms. Stacy GOMES
10 Chief Operating Officer .... Mr. Malcolm YOUNGREN
37 Vice Pres of Financial Aid .... Ms. Beatrice SMITH
26 Vice President Marketing .... Ms. Nathalie TUROTTE
12 Director NY Campus .... Mr. Malcolm YOUNGREN
12 Director CH Campus .... Mr. Dave FRECH
07 Vice President Admissions .... Ms. April PANIAGUA
12 Director SD Campus .... Ms. Teri POWERS
06 Registrar .... Mr. Nayeli CORONA
23 Director of Clinical Services .... Ms. Leng TANG-RITCHIE
08 Head Librarian .... Ms. Patricia BENEFIEL
13 Information Technology Director .... Mr. Greg RUSSO
88 Pacific Symposium .... Ms. Candace UNGER
29 Director Alumni Affairs .... Ms. Cynthia NEIPRIS

Pacific Oaks College (A)

55 Eureka Street, Pasadena CA 91103
County: Los Angeles FICE Identification: 001255
Unit ID: 120768
Telephone: (626) 529-8500 Carnegie Class: Spec-4-yr-Other
FAX Number: N/A Calendar System: Semester
URL: www.pacificoaks.edu
Established: 1945 Annual Undergrad Tuition & Fees: $13,688
Enrollment: 1,100 Coed
Affiliation or Control: Independent Non-Profit IRS Status: 501(c)3
Highest Offering: Master's
Accreditation: WC

01 President .... Dr. Patricia A. BREEN
05 Dean Academic Affairs .... Dr. Terry RATCLIFF
11 Chief Operating Officer .... Ms. Melanie SAUER
32 Assoc Vice Pres Student Services .... Mr. Frank FRIAS
88 Exec Director Children's School .... Mr. Robert BOYMAN
15 Assoc VP Human Resources .... Ms. Carolyn MATHIS
10 AVP Financial/Admin Operations .... Ms. Yug Fon CHIQUITO
08 Campus Librarian .... Ms. Kelsey VUKIC
35 Dir Ctr Stdnt Achievmt/Res/Enrich .... Ms. Pat MEDA
07 Assoc Vice President Admissions .... Mr. Michael PATTON
13 IT Director .... Mr. Carlos BONILLA
04 Exec Asst to Pres/Sec to Cabinet .... Ms. Carrie ZALKIND
12 Campus Dean San Jose .... Dr. Marcia BANKIRER
88 Assoc Dean School of CFP .... Dr. Bree COOK
88 Assoc Dean School of HD .... Dr. Donald GRANT
30 Dir Advancement/External Affairs .... Ms. Johanna ATIENZA
26 Director Communications/Marketing .... Mr. Larry RENICK

Pacific School of Religion (B)

1798 Scenic Avenue, Berkeley CA 94709-1323
County: Alameda FICE Identification: 001256
Unit ID: 120795
Telephone: (510) 849-8200 Carnegie Class: Spec-4-yr-Faith
FAX Number: (510) 845-8948 Calendar System: Semester
URL: www.psr.edu
Established: 1866 Annual Graduate Tuition & Fees: N/A
Enrollment: 110 Coed
Affiliation or Control: Independent Non-Profit IRS Status: 501(c)3
Highest Offering: Doctorate; No Undergraduates
Accreditation: WC, THEOL

01 President .... Rev. David VASQUEZ-LEVY
05 Vice Pres Academic Affairs/Dean .... Dr. Susan ABRAHAM
10 Chief Business Officer .... Mr. Patrick O'LEARY
30 Chief Advancement Officer .... Ms. Wanda SCOTT
06 Asst Dean Academic Pgms/Registrar .... Ms. Lyndsey REED
07 Admissions/Financial Aid Officer .... Mr. Ruben CORTEZ
15 Human Resource Director .... Ms. Deborah WALKER
04 Executive Asst to President .... Ms. Jen GALL
26 Marketing/Communications Manager .... Ms. Erin BURNS

Pacific States University (C)

3424 Wilshire Boulevard, 12th Floor,
Los Angeles CA 90010
County: Los Angeles FICE Identification: 031633
Unit ID: 120838
Telephone: (323) 731-2383 Carnegie Class: Spec-4-yr-Bus
FAX Number: (323) 731-7276 Calendar System: Quarter
URL: www.psuca.edu
Established: 1928 Annual Undergrad Tuition & Fees: $16,065
Enrollment: 56 Coed
Affiliation or Control: Independent Non-Profit IRS Status: 501(c)3
Highest Offering: Master's
Accreditation: ACCSC, ACICS

01 President .... Mr. Hee Young AHN
05 Dean Academic Affairs .... Dr. Heidi CROCKER
88 Asst Dean General Affairs .... Miss Rosy LIM
37 Financial Aid .... Mr. Moonsik KIM
26 Asst Dean Public Rels/Intl Affs .... Ms. Sarah MIN
13 Dir General & Technology Services .... Mr. Kuang Kai LU
08 University Librarian .... Vacant
06 Registrar .... Mr. Kuang Kai LU

Pacific Union College (D)

One Angwin Avenue, Angwin CA 94508-9797
County: Napa FICE Identification: 001258
Unit ID: 120865
Telephone: (707) 965-6311 Carnegie Class: Bac-Diverse
FAX Number: (707) 965-6390 Calendar System: Quarter
URL: www.puc.edu
Established: 1882 Annual Undergrad Tuition & Fees: $30,060
Enrollment: 1,229 Coed
Affiliation or Control: Seventh-day Adventist IRS Status: 501(c)3
Highest Offering: Master's
Accreditation: WC, ADNUR, IACBE, MUS, NUR, SW

01 President .... Dr. Robert A. CUSHMAN, JR.
05 Academic Dean/VP Academic Admin .... Mr. Milbert MARIANO
10 VP Financial Administration/CFO .... Mr. Brandon C. PARKER
32 Vice President Student Services .... Mrs. Jennifer TYNER
84 Vice Pres Enrollment Mgmt/Marketing .... Ms. Haley WESLEY
111 Assoc Vice President Advancement .... Mrs. Kellie LIND
33 Dean of Men .... Mr. Hernan GRANADOS
34 Dean of Women .... Mrs. Gena PHILPOTT
08 Director Library Services .... Mr. Patrick BENNER
37 Director Student Financial Services .... Mr. Frederick WHITESIDE
13 Director Information Technology .... Mr. David RAI
06 Registrar .... Mr. Jonathan BRADLEY
15 Director Human Resources .... Mr. Stacy NELSON
114 Director Budgets & Fiscal Services .... Mrs. Sharon MAPES
38 Director Counseling Center .... Mr. Michael JEFFERSON
18 Chief Facilities/Facil Management .... Mr. Dale WITHERS
20 Associate Academic Officer .... Dr. Marlo WATERS
07 Admissions Counselor .... Mr. Chris ROMERO
09 Director of Institutional Research .... Mr. Serhii KALYNOVSKYI

Pacifica Graduate Institute (E)

249 Lambert Road, Carpinteria CA 93013-3019
County: Carpinteria FICE Identification: 031268
Unit ID: 115746
Telephone: (805) 969-3626 Carnegie Class: Spec-4-yr-Other Health
FAX Number: (805) 565-1932 Calendar System: Quarter
URL: www.pacifica.edu
Established: 1974 Annual Graduate Tuition & Fees: N/A
Enrollment: 852 Coed
Affiliation or Control: Proprietary IRS Status: Proprietary
Highest Offering: Doctorate; No Undergraduates
Accreditation: WC

00 Chancellor/Founding President .... Dr. Stephen AIZENSTAT
01 President/CEO .... Dr. Joseph CAMBRAY
10 Int Chief Financial Officer .... Ms. Catherine PAULETTO
43 General Counsel .... Mr. Frank MICHAELSON
07 Dir of Enrollment/Inst Advancement .... Mr. Randall RADCLIFF
13 Senior Director of IT/Library .... Mr. Alain DUSSERT
37 Director of Financial Aid .... Ms. Tracie TEAGUE
20 Director of Academic Affairs .... Ms. Lauren LASTRA
06 Registrar .... Ms. Francine MATAS
15 Director of Human Resources .... Ms. Norma MESA
39 Director of Guest Services .... Ms. Heather SLADE
29 Director of Alumni Relations .... Ms. Dianne TRAVIS-TEAGUE

Palmer College of Chiropractic, West Campus (F)

90 E Tasman Drive, San Jose CA 95134-1617
Telephone: (408) 944-6000 FICE Identification: 021849
Accreditation: &NH, &CHIRO

† Regional accreditation is carried under the parent institution in Davenport, IA.

Palo Alto University (G)

1791 Arastradero Road, Palo Alto CA 94304
County: San Mateo FICE Identification: 021383
Unit ID: 120698
Telephone: (800) 818-6136 Carnegie Class: Spec-4-yr-Other Health
FAX Number: (650) 433-3888 Calendar System: Quarter
URL: www.paloaltou.edu
Established: 1975 Annual Undergrad Tuition & Fees: N/A
Enrollment: 1,074 Coed
Affiliation or Control: Independent Non-Profit IRS Status: 501(c)3
Highest Offering: Doctorate
Accreditation: WC, CACREP, CLPSY

01 President .... Dr. Maureen O'CONNOR
108 VP for Institutional Effectiveness .... Dr. James BRECKENRIDGE
05 Interim VP for Academic Affairs .... Dr. Risa DICKSON
10 VP for Business Affairs & CFO .... Dr. June KLEIN
107 VP for Continuing & Prof Studies .... Dr. Patricia ZAPF
07 Asst VP for Admissions .... Ms. Alaina DUNN
32 Director of Student Services .... Mr. Thom SHEPARD
26 Director of External Affairs .... Ms. Rebecca LEVY
04 Executive Assistant to President .... Ms. Melanie MORRISON
15 Sr Human Resource Manager .... Ms. Holly LINDLEY
13 Chief Information Officer .... Mr. David LEAVITT
21 Controller .... Mr. Howard SMALLS
37 Director of Financial Aid .... Ms. Jessica AYRES
30 Director of Development .... Vacant
06 Director of Registration .... Ms. Nora MARQUEZ
17 Director of Gronowski Center .... Dr. Sandra MACIAS
09 Director of Institutional Research .... Vacant

08 Librarian & Dir Academic Tech .... Mr. Scott HINES
113 Billing Supervisor .... Ms. Anna LITSITSA
83 Dept Chair Counseling .... Dr. William SNOW
83 Dept Chair Psychology .... Dr. Kimberly BALSAM

Palo Verde College (H)

One College Drive, Blythe CA 92225-9561
County: Riverside FICE Identification: 001259
Unit ID: 120953
Telephone: (760) 921-5500 Carnegie Class: Assoc/HT-Mix Trad/Non
FAX Number: (760) 921-5590 Calendar System: Semester
URL: www.paloverde.edu
Established: 1947 Annual Undergrad Tuition & Fees (In-District): $1,288
Enrollment: 4,041 Coed
Affiliation or Control: State/Local IRS Status: 501(c)3
Highest Offering: Associate Degree
Accreditation: WJ

01 Superintendent/President .... Dr. Donald WALLACE
05 Vice Pres Instructional/Stdnt Svcs .... Dr. Scott BAUER
15 Assoc Vice Pres Human Resources/EEO .... Ms. Cecilia GARCIA
04 Executive Asst to Supt/President .... Ms. Denise HUNT
66 Assoc Dean Nursing & Allied Health .... Dr. Theresa CICCI
08 Librarian .... Ms. June TURNER
07 Director of Admissions and Records .... Ms. Shelley HAMILTON
88 Site Supervisor of Child Dev Center .... Ms. Dana RETHWISCH
09 Director of Institutional Research .... Mr. Adam HOUSTON
18 Director Facilities and Operations .... Mr. Shad LEE
13 Director of Information Technology .... Mr. Eric EGAN
35 Mgr of Student Life/Development .... Ms. Staci LEE
10 Vice Pres Administrative Svcs .... Ms. Stephanie SLAGAN
20 Manager of Instructional Services .... Ms. Maria KEHL
37 Director of Financial Aid .... Ms. Diana MENDEZ
101 Exec Asst to Supt/President/Board .... Ms. Carrie MULLION
102 Executive Director Foundation .... Ms. Stephanie SLAGAN

Palomar College (I)

1140 W Mission Road, San Marcos CA 92069-1487
County: San Diego FICE Identification: 001260
Unit ID: 120971
Telephone: (760) 744-1150 Carnegie Class: Assoc/MT-VT-High Trad
FAX Number: (760) 744-8123 Calendar System: Semester
URL: www.palomar.edu
Established: 1946 Annual Undergrad Tuition & Fees (In-District): $1,338
Enrollment: 23,848 Coed
Affiliation or Control: State/Local IRS Status: 501(c)3
Highest Offering: Associate Degree
Accreditation: WJ, ADNUR, DA, EMT

01 Superintendent/President .... Dr. Joi Lin BLAKE
05 Int Asst Supt/Vice Pres Instruction .... Dr. Jack KAHN
32 Asst Supt/VP Student Services .... Dr. Star RIVERA-LACEY
10 Actg Asst Supt/VP Finance/Admn Svcs .... Mr. Stephen GARCIA
15 Asst Supt/VP Human Resources .... Dr. Lisa NORMAN
04 Exec Assistant to the President .... Ms. Cheryl ASHOUR
79 Dean Languages & Literature .... Vacant
81 Int Dean Math/Science & Engineering .... Vacant
38 Int Dean Counseling Services .... Ms. Olga DIAZ
75 Dean Career/Tech/Extended Educ .... Ms. Margie FRITCH
50 Dean Arts/Media/Bus & Comp Sci .... Mr. Justin SMILEY
83 Dean Social/Behavioral Sciences .... Ms. Pearl LY
13 Director Info Systems & Services .... Ms. Connie MOISE
84 Director Enrollment Svcs/Admissions .... Mr. Kendyl MAGNUSON
09 Sr Director Institutional Research .... Ms. Michelle BARTON
18 Director of Facilities .... Mr. Chris MILLER
35 Director Student Affairs .... Ms. Sherry TITUS
37 Director Student Financial Aid .... Ms. Adriana LEE
26 Int Dir Comm/Mktg/Public Affairs .... Ms. Julie LANTHIER-BANDY
102 Executive Director for Foundation .... Ms. Stacy RUNGAITIS
19 Chief of Police .... Mr. Chris MOORE
23 Director Health Services .... Ms. Judy HARRIS
41 Director Athletics .... Vacant

Pardee RAND Graduate School of Policy Studies (J)

1776 Main Street, Santa Monica CA 90407-2138
County: Los Angeles FICE Identification: 010441
Unit ID: 121628
Telephone: (310) 393-0411 Carnegie Class: Spec-4-yr-Other
FAX Number: (310) 451-6978 Calendar System: Quarter
URL: www.prgs.edu
Established: 1970 Annual Graduate Tuition & Fees: N/A
Enrollment: 104 Coed
Affiliation or Control: Independent Non-Profit IRS Status: 501(c)3
Highest Offering: Doctorate; No Undergraduates
Accreditation: WC

01 Dean/RAND VP Innovation .... Dr. Susan MARQUIS
05 Associate Dean .... Ms. Rachel SWANGER
06 Registrar .... Ms. Mary PARKER
07 Asst Dean Admissions .... Ms. Stefanie HOWARD
20 Asst Dean for Academic Affairs .... Dr. Gery RYAN

Pasadena City College (K)

1570 E Colorado Boulevard, Pasadena CA 91106-2041
County: Los Angeles FICE Identification: 001261
Unit ID: 121044
Telephone: (626) 585-7123 Carnegie Class: Assoc/HT-High Trad
FAX Number: (626) 585-7910 Calendar System: Semester

URL: www.pasadena.edu
Established: 1924 Annual Undergrad Tuition & Fees (In-District): $1,166
Enrollment: 27,324 Coed
Affiliation or Control: State/Local IRS Status: 501(c)3
Highest Offering: Associate Degree
Accreditation: WJ, DA, DH, DT, MAC, RAD

01 Superintendent-President .... Dr. Erika A. ENDRIJONAS
12 Senior VP Non-credit & Offsite Camp .... Dr. Robert H. BELL
05 VP Instruction .... Dr. Terry GIUGNI
10 VP Business & Administrative Svcs ....Dr. Michael BUSH
32 Vice President Student Services .... Dr. Cynthia OLIVO
15 Vice President Human Resources .... Mr. Bob BLIZINSKI
09 Exec Dir Inst Research/Planning .... Ms. Crystal KOLLROSS
56 Director Extension .... Ms. Elaine CHAPMAN
38 Dean Counseling .... Mr. Armando DURAN
88 Dean Special Services .... Ms. Ketmani KOUANCHAO
84 Dir Admissions/Records/Enrollment ....Ms. Arlene REED
37 Director Financial Aid ....Mr. Manuel CERDA
13 Exec Director/Chief Tech Officer ....Ms. Candace JONES
26 Exec Dir Strategic Comm/Marketing .... Mr. Alex BOEKELHEIDE
18 Int Exec Dir Facilities Services ....Dr. Todd HAMPTON
04 Exec Asst to President ....Ms. Armine GALUKYAN
19 Chief Police & Safety Services ....Mr. Steven MATCHAN
35 Dean Student Life .... Ms. Rebecca COBB
96 Director of Purchasing & Contracts .... Mr. George CHIDIAC
101 Secretary of the Institution/Board ....Ms. Mary THOMPSON
102 Executive Director Foundation ....Ms. Bobbi ABRAM
103 Exec Director Workforce Development .... Ms. Salvatrice CUMMO
28 Director of Equity ....Dr. Michaela MARES
21 Exec Director Fiscal Services .... Ms. Chedva WEINGART

Patten University (A)

2100 Franklin Street, Suite 350, Oakland CA 94612
County: Alameda FICE Identification: 004490
Telephone: (415) 494-8240 Carnegie Class: Not Classified
FAX Number: N/A Calendar System: Semester
URL: www.patten.edu
Established: 1944 Annual Undergrad Tuition & Fees: N/A
Enrollment: N/A Coed
Affiliation or Control: Proprietary IRS Status: Proprietary
Highest Offering: Master's
Accreditation: WC

01 President .... Dr. Thomas STEWART
05 Vice Pres Academic Affairs .... Dr. Marc PORTER
10 VP Finance/Operations .... Mr. Ramon DOURADO
06 Registrar .... Mr. Aaron HIATT

† In Teach-Out Mode

PCI College (B)

17215 Studebaker Rd Ste 310, Cerritos CA 90703
County: Los Angeles FICE Identification: 034793
Unit ID: 439871
Telephone: (562) 916-5055 Carnegie Class: Not Classified
FAX Number: (562) 916-5057 Calendar System: Semester
URL: www.pci-ed.com
Established: 1996 Annual Undergrad Tuition & Fees: N/A
Enrollment: N/A Coed
Affiliation or Control: Proprietary IRS Status: Proprietary
Highest Offering: Baccalaureate
Accreditation: ACCSC

Pepperdine University (C)

24255 Pacific Coast Highway, Malibu CA 90263-0001
County: Los Angeles FICE Identification: 010149
Unit ID: 121150
Telephone: (310) 506-4000 Carnegie Class: DU-Mod
FAX Number: (310) 506-4861 Calendar System: Semester
URL: www.pepperdine.edu
Established: 1937 Annual Undergrad Tuition & Fees: $53,932
Enrollment: 7,710 Coed
Affiliation or Control: Church Of Christ IRS Status: 501(c)3
Highest Offering: Doctorate
Accreditation: WC, CLPSY, DIETD, LAW, MUS

01 President ....Mr. James A. GASH
100 Chief of Staff .... Mr. Daniel DEWALT
03 Executive Vice President ....Mr. Gary A. HANSON
04 Exec Assistant to the President ....Mrs. Cynthia PAVELL
05 Provost .... Dr. Rick MARRS
10 Chief Financial Officer ....Dr. Joan SINGLETON
111 Sr VP Advancement & Public Affairs .... Mr. Keith HINKLE
115 Senior Vice President Investments ....Mr. Jeff PIPPIN
43 General Counsel ....Mr. Marc P. GOODMAN
11 VP of Administration .... Mr. Phil E. PHILLIPS
21 Chief Business Officer .... Ms. Nicolle TAYLOR
13 Chief Information Officer ....Mr. Jonathan SEE
26 Chief Marketing Officer ....Mr. Rick GIBSON
06 Assoc VP & University Registrar .... Mr. Hung V. LE
104 Dean of International Programs ....Ms. Beth LAUX
84 Dean of Admission/Enrollment Mgmt .... Dr. Kristy COLLINS
32 VP of Student Affairs ....Dr. Connie HORTON
08 Dean of Libraries ....Mr. Mark S. ROOSA
61 Dean of the School of Law ....Mr. Paul CARON
50 Dean Graziadio Sch Business & Mgmt ....Dr. Deryck VAN RENSBURG
53 Dean of Graduate School Educ/Psych ...... Dr. Helen E. WILLIAMS
49 Dean of Seaver College ....Dr. Michael E. FELTNER
80 Dean of School of Public Policy .... Mr. Pete PETERSON
42 University Chaplain .... Ms. Sara BARTON
46 Vice Provost for Research and Strat ....Dr. Lee KATS
108 Assoc Provost Inst Effectiveness .... Dr. Lisa BORTMAN
29 Exec Director for Alumni Affairs .... Mr. Bob CLARK
15 Chief Human Resources Officer ....Mrs. Lauren COSENTINO
88 Director of Ministry Outreach ....Mr. Michael COPE
46 Director Research & Sponsored Pgm ....Vacant
39 Assoc Dean of Students/Housing ....Vacant
88 Managing Dir Center for the Arts ....Ms. Rebecca CARSON
88 Director of Special Programs ....Ms. Holly MOYE
85 Dir Intl Student Services ....Ms. Brooke CUTLER
27 Assoc VP IM Communications .... Mr. Matthew MIDURA
23 Director of Student Health Services ....Vacant
36 Assoc Dean of Students/Career Ctr ....Mr. Brad D. DUDLEY
41 Director of Athletics ....Dr. Steven POTTS
19 Assoc VP & Dir of Public Safety .... Mr. Lance BRIDGESMITH
18 Director Facilities Services .... Ms. Carly MISCHKE
86 Assoc VP Govt & Regulatory Affairs ....Ms. Rhiannon BAILARD
37 Dir of Seaver Financial Assistance ....Mrs. Janet LOCKHART
38 Assoc VP & Dir Student Counseling ....Dr. Connie HORTON
09 Director of Institutional Research .... Ms. Jazmine ZANE
112 Exec Dir Estate and Gift Planning .... Mr. Curt PORTZEL
22 Director Disability Services .... Ms. Sandra HARRISON
116 Director of Auditing Services .... Ms. Norma IADEVAIA
102 Dir Corporate/Foundation Relations ....Ms. Sheila D. KING
28 Title IX Coordinator for Students .... Ms. LaShonda COLEMAN
44 Director Pepperdine Fund .... Ms. Cynthia WARE
07 Director of Admission ....Mr. Falone SERNA

*Peralta Community Colleges District Office (D)

333 E Eighth Street, Oakland CA 94606-2889
County: Alameda FICE Identification: 001265
Unit ID: 121178
Telephone: (510) 466-7200 Carnegie Class: N/A
FAX Number: (510) 835-4078
URL: www.peralta.edu

01 Acting Chancellor ....Dr. Frances L. WHITE
10 VC Finance & Administration ....Mr. Romaneir JOHNSON
13 VC Information Technology .... Mr. Jason COLE
26 Int Exec Dir Public Info/Comm/Media .... Mr. Spencer MOORE

*Berkeley City College (E)

2050 Center Street, Berkeley CA 94704-1183
County: Alameda FICE Identification: 022427
Unit ID: 125170
Telephone: (510) 981-2800 Carnegie Class: Assoc/HT-Mix Trad/Non
FAX Number: (510) 841-7333 Calendar System: Semester
URL: www.berkeleycitycollege.edu
Established: 1974 Annual Undergrad Tuition & Fees (In-District): $1,254
Enrollment: 6,356 Coed
Affiliation or Control: State/Local IRS Status: 501(c)3
Highest Offering: Associate Degree
Accreditation: WJ

02 President .... Dr. Rowena M. TOMANENG
05 Vice President Instruction ....Ms. Kuniko HAY
32 Vice President Student Services .... Dr. Stacey SHEARS
50 Dean Business/Science/App Tech .... Dr. Francisco GAMEZ
49 Dean Lib Arts/Soc Sciences/Math .... Ms. Lisa R. COOK
35 Dean Student Support Services .... Ms. Brenda JOHNSON
10 Director Business Services & Admin ......Ms. Shirley SLAUGHTER
121 Assoc Dean Educational Success .... Mr. Martin DE MUCHA FLORES
27 Public Information Officer .... Dr. Felicia L. BRIDGES
15 Int Vice Chancellor HR .... Ms. Chanelle WHITTAKER
18 Int Vice Chancellor Gen Services ....Mr. Leigh SATA
21 Supervisor Business Services ....Mr. John PANG
09 Research Analyst ....Dr. Phoumy SAYAVONG
04 Executive Assistant to President ....Ms. Cynthia REESE
84 Coordinator Enrollment Services ....Ms. Gail PENDLETON
37 Supervisor Student Financial Aid ....Ms. Loan NGUYEN

*College of Alameda (F)

555 Ralph Appezzato Memorial Pkwy, Alameda CA 94501-2109
County: Alameda FICE Identification: 006720
Unit ID: 108667
Telephone: (510) 522-7221 Carnegie Class: Assoc/HT-Mix Trad/Non
FAX Number: (510) 337-0619 Calendar System: Semester
URL: www.alameda.peralta.edu
Established: 1968 Annual Undergrad Tuition & Fees (In-District): $1,254
Enrollment: 5,760 Coed
Affiliation or Control: State/Local IRS Status: 501(c)3
Highest Offering: Associate Degree
Accreditation: WJ, DA

02 President ....Dr. Tim KARAS
05 Vice President of Instruction ....Dr. Don MILLER
32 Vice President of Student Svcs ....Ms. Tina VASCONCELLOS
26 Chief Public Relations Officer ....Vacant
20 Dean of STEAM ....Ms. Ana MCCLANAHAN
88 Dean Special Programs .... Mr. William BRUCE
84 Dean Enrollment Services .... Dr. Amy LEE
49 Dean Liberal Studies/Language Arts ....Ms. Lilia CELHAY
103 Dean Career/Workforce Education ....Ms. Eva JENNINGS
10 Dir Business & Administrative Svcs .... Ms. Chungwai CHUM
07 Admissions & Records Specialist ....Ms. Marcean BRYANT
35 Director of Campus Life ....Ms. Aja BUTLER
121 Assoc Dean of Educational Success ....Ms. Paula ARMSTEAD

*Laney College (G)

900 Fallon Street, Oakland CA 94607-4893
County: Alameda FICE Identification: 001266
Unit ID: 117247
Telephone: (510) 834-5740 Carnegie Class: Assoc/MT-VT-Mix Trad/Non
FAX Number: (510) 464-3528 Calendar System: Semester
URL: laney.edu
Established: 1953 Annual Undergrad Tuition & Fees (In-District): $1,254
Enrollment: 10,891 Coed
Affiliation or Control: State/Local IRS Status: 501(c)3
Highest Offering: Associate Degree
Accreditation: WJ

02 President ....Dr. Tammeil Y. GILKERSON
05 Vice President of Instruction ....Dr. Rudolph BESIKOF
32 Vice Pres Student Services .... Ms. Vicki FERGUSON
10 Vice Pres Administrative Services .... Dr. Derek PINTO
75 Dean Career & Technical Educ .... Mr. Peter CRABTREE
84 Dean Enrollment Services ....Dr. Mildred LEWIS
79 Dean Humanities/Social Science ....Mr. Mark FIELDS
49 Dean Liberal Arts ....Dr. Chuen CHAN
81 Dean Mathematics and Science .... Ms. Denise RICHARDSON
35 Dean Student Services ....Mr. Jean Paul (JP) SCHUMACHER
121 Assoc Dean Educational Success ....Ms. Diane T. CHANG
04 Executive Assistant to President ....Ms. Maisha JAMESON
18 Director of Facilities & Operations .... Ms. Amy MARSHALL
35 Dir Student Activities/Campus Life .... Mr. Gary ALBURY
13 Director IT .... Mr. Rupinder BHATIA
88 Director Gateway to College Pgm .... Mr. Shawn TAYLOR
88 Director of AANAPISI .... Mr. David LEE
88 Director of BEST Center ....Ms. Pamela WALLACE
41 Director Athletics ....Mr. John BEAM
88 Food Services Manager ....Mr. Neil BURMENKO
08 Head Librarian ....Ms. Evelyn LORD
37 Financial Aid Supervisor ....Dr. Joseph KOROMA

*Merritt College (H)

12500 Campus Drive, Oakland CA 94619-3196
County: Alameda FICE Identification: 001267
Unit ID: 118772
Telephone: (510) 531-4911 Carnegie Class: Assoc/HVT-Mix Trad/Non
FAX Number: (510) 436-2405 Calendar System: Semester
URL: www.merritt.edu
Established: 1953 Annual Undergrad Tuition & Fees (In-District): $1,254
Enrollment: 6,952 Coed
Affiliation or Control: State/Local IRS Status: 501(c)3
Highest Offering: Associate Degree
Accreditation: WJ, DIETT, HT, RAD

02 President .... Dr. Marie-Elaine BURNS
00 Chancellor .... Dr. Jowel LAGUERRE
05 Vice President of Instruction .... Dr. David JOHNSON
32 Vice President of Student Services ..... Ms. Christine HERNANDEZ
32 Vice Pres Student Services ....Mr. Arnulfo CEDILLO
96 Vice Chancellor of General Services .... Dr. Sadiq IKHARO
15 Vice Chancellor for Human Resources .... Ms. Trudy LARGENT
20 Vice Chanc Educational Services .... Dr. Michael ORKIN
13 Assoc VC of Information Technology .... Mr. Calvin MADLOCK
25 Dean Special Programs & Grants .... Dr. Lilia CHAVEZ
26 Exec Dir Marketing/Public Rels/Comm .... Mr. Jeffrey HEYMAN
08 Head Librarian .... Mr. Timothy HACKETT
06 Registrar ....Ms. Susana DE LA TORRE
10 Director of Business/Admin Services ....Ms. Victoria MENZIES
35 Dir Student Activities/Campus Life ....Dr. Herbert KITCHEN
09 Director of Institutional Research .... Mr. Nathan PELLEGRIN
101 Board Clerk ....Ms. Brenda MARTINEZ
102 Interim Exec Dir Foundation .... Ms. Kaia BURKETT
18 Facilities Director/Physical Plant .... Mr. Kevin BERTELSEN
37 Financial Aid Supervisor ....Mr. Ernesto NERY

Pima Medical Institute-Chula Vista (I)

780 Bay Boulevard, Chula Vista CA 91910-5261
Telephone: (619) 425-3200 Identification: 666272
Accreditation: ABHES, COARC, RAD

† Branch campus of Pima Medical Institute, Tucson, AZ.

Pitzer College (J)

1050 N Mills Avenue, Claremont CA 91711-6110
County: Los Angeles FICE Identification: 001172
Unit ID: 121257
Telephone: (909) 621-8198 Carnegie Class: Bac-A&S
FAX Number: N/A Calendar System: Semester
URL: www.pitzer.edu
Established: 1963 Annual Undergrad Tuition & Fees: $54,056
Enrollment: 1,074 Coed
Affiliation or Control: Independent Non-Profit IRS Status: 501(c)3
Highest Offering: Baccalaureate
Accreditation: WC

01 President ....Dr. Melvin L. OLIVER
05 Vice Pres Acad Affs/Dean of Faculty ....Dr. Allen OMOTO
100 Chief of Staff ....Dr. James D. JORGENSEN

10 VP Finance/Administration/Treas ....Ms. Laura TROENDLE
111 VP College Advancement ....Mr. Neil MACREADY
07 VP Admissions/Financial Aid ....Ms. Yvonne BERUMEN
32 Vice Pres Student Affairs ....Mr. Mike SEGAWA
26 VP Comm/Marketing/Public Relations ....Mr. Mark BAILEY
30 Assoc VP of Development ....Ms. Pam JONES-TINTLE
20 Associate Dean of Faculty .... Ms. Melinda HERROLD-MENZIES
20 Associate Dean of Faculty ....Ms. Kathleen YEP
06 Registrar ....Ms. Eva PETERS
37 Director Financial Aid ....Ms. Kara MOORE
09 Director of Institutional Research ....Mr. Marco Antonio CRUZ
15 AVP Human Resources and Payroll .... Ms. Deanna CABALLERO
18 Asst VP Facilities ....Ms. Patrice LANGEVIN
21 AVP Finance ....Ms. Pamela MADER
36 Director Career Services ....Mr. Brad THARPE
29 Director Alumni/Parent Relations ....Vacant
101 Sr Exec Asst/Secretary to the Board ....Ms. Melanie LACY SORENSON

Platt College (A)

1000 S Fremont Avenue, Bldg A10 S, Alhambra CA 91803-8845

County: Los Angeles FICE Identification: 030627
Unit ID: 260789

Telephone: (626) 300-5444 Carnegie Class: Spec-4-yr-Other Health
FAX Number: (626) 457-8295 Calendar System: Other
URL: www.plattcollege.edu
Established: 1987 Annual Undergrad Tuition & Fees: $13,794
Enrollment: 587 Coed
Affiliation or Control: Proprietary IRS Status: Proprietary
Highest Offering: Baccalaureate
Accreditation: ACCSC, COARC

01 President ....Mr. Mike GIACOMINI
06 Registrar ....Ms. Cathy WOLFE
07 Director of Admissions ....Mr. Steven BROYLES

Platt College (B)

3700 Inland Empire Blvd, Ste 400, Ontario CA 91764-4906

Telephone: (909) 941-9410 Identification: 666056
Accreditation: ACCSC, COARC

† Branch campus of Platt College, Ahambra, CA.

Platt College (C)

6465 Sycamore Canyon Blvd, Ste 100, Riverside CA 95207

Telephone: (951) 572-4300 Identification: 770561
Accreditation: ACCSC

Platt College (D)

6250 El Cajon Boulevard, San Diego CA 92115-3919

County: San Diego FICE Identification: 023043
Unit ID: 121275

Telephone: (619) 265-0107 Carnegie Class: Spec-4-yr-Arts
FAX Number: (619) 265-8655 Calendar System: Other
URL: www.platt.edu
Established: 1980 Annual Undergrad Tuition & Fees: $17,235
Enrollment: 178 Coed
Affiliation or Control: Proprietary IRS Status: Proprietary
Highest Offering: Baccalaureate
Accreditation: ACCSC

00 Chairman ....Mr. Robert D. LEIKER
01 President ....Mrs. Meg LEIKER
03 Vice President ....Mr. Alfred MEDRO
10 Chief Business Officer ....Ms. Marianne TAXTER
05 Director of Education ....Mr. Julio FRIZZA-POMPA
06 Registrar ....Ms. Raquel AVINION

Point Loma Nazarene University (E)

3900 Lomaland Drive, San Diego CA 92106-2899

County: San Diego FICE Identification: 001262
Unit ID: 121309

Telephone: (619) 849-2200 Carnegie Class: Masters/L
FAX Number: (619) 849-2579 Calendar System: Semester
URL: www.pointloma.edu
Established: 1902 Annual Undergrad Tuition & Fees: $35,700
Enrollment: 4,417 Coed
Affiliation or Control: Church Of The Nazarene IRS Status: 501(c)3
Highest Offering: Doctorate
Accreditation: WC, ACBSP, CAATE, CAEPN, DIETD, EMT, MUS, NURSE, SW

01 President ....Dr. Bob BROWER
03 Executive Vice President ....Vacant
05 Provost/Chief Academic Officer ....Dr. Kerry FULCHER
10 VP Finance/Administrative Svcs ....Mr. George LATTER
32 VP Student Dev & Chief Title IX Ofc ....Dr. Caye SMITH
88 Vice Pres Spiritual Development ....Dr. Mary PAUL
111 Vice President Univ Advancement ....Ms. Kelly SMITH
13 Vice President University Services ....Dr. Jeff BOLSTER
15 Assoc VP for Human Resources ....Mr. Jeffrey HERMAN
58 Assoc VP for Grad and Prof Services .... Mrs. Cindy CHAPPELL
35 Assc VP Stdnt Dev/Chf Diversity Ofc ....Dr. Jeffrey CARR
114 Assoc VP for Budget/Accounting ....Ms. Janet CAPRARIO
84 Assoc VP Enrollment & Retention ....Dr. Scott SHOEMAKER
20 Vice Prov Academic Administration ....Dr. Holly IRWIN
108 Vice Prov Accred & IE ....Dr. Karen LEE
35 Dean of Students ....Dr. Jake GILBERTSON
13 Chief Information Officer ....Mr. Corey FLING
09 Dir Institutional Research ....Mr. Brent GOODMAN
12 Interim Director of Wesleyan Center ....Dr. Sam POWELL
18 Director of Campus Facilities ....Mr. Dan TORO
36 Executive Dir Strengths & Vocation ....Ms. Rebecca SMITH
88 Exec Dir of Enrollment Mgmt ....Ms. Jeanne COCHRAN
86 Dir Public Affairs ....Ms. Jill MONROE
88 Director Center Pastoral Leadership ....Dr. John CALHOUN
42 Ld Con for Mission Res & Pst Rel ....Dr. Ron BENEFIEL
88 Director of Community Ministries ....Ms. Dana HOJSACK
88 Director of Worship Arts ....Mr. George WILLIAMSON
49 Dean of the Colleges ....Dr. Jim DAICHENDT
83 Dean College of Social Sciences ....Vacant
07 Director Undergraduate Admissions ....Ms. Shannon HUTCHISON-CARAVEO
08 Director of Ryan Library ....Dr. Denise NELSON
56 Dean Extended Learning ....Dr. Dave PHILLIPS
06 Dir Records/Institutional Research .... Ms. Cheryl GAUGHAN
26 Assoc Vice Pres for Marketing ....Vacant
88 Assoc Dean Stdnt Success/Wellness .... Dr. Kim BOGAN
19 Director of Public Safety ....Mr. Mark RYAN
29 Director of Alumni Relations ....Ms. Kendall LUCAS
40 Bookstore Manager ....Mr. Brian SIMO
85 Dir Multicultural/Intl Stdnt Svcs ....Mr. Sam KWAPONG
41 Athletic Director ....Mr. Ethan HAMILTON
88 Director of Nicholson Commons ....Mr. Milton KARAHADIAN
94 Dir Stevenson Ctr for Women's Stds ....Dr. Linda BEAIL
104 Director Study Abroad Program ....Ms. Sandy SOOHOO-REFAEI
88 Dir of Programs & Operations ....Mr. Nick WOLF
04 Exec Asst to President ....Ms. Hillary BEAVER
106 Dir Online Education/E-learning ....Dr. Dave PHILLIPS
39 Asst Dir Student Housing ....Ms. Molly PETERSEN
110 Exec Dir Advancement Operations ....Ms. Christina GARDNER
50 Dean of Business ....Mr. Dan BOTHE
53 Dean of Education ....Ms. Deb ERICKSON
101 Secretary of the Institution/Board ....Dr. Joe WATKINS
28 Chief Diversity Officer ....Dr. Jeffrey CARR
44 Director Annual or Planned Giving ....Mr. William BURFITT
37 Director Student Financial Services ....Ms. Molly PORTER
43 General Counsel ....Mr. Kevin CAHILL

Pomona College (F)

550 N College Avenue, #206, Claremont CA 91711-6301

County: Los Angeles FICE Identification: 001173
Unit ID: 121345

Telephone: (909) 621-8000 Carnegie Class: Bac-A&S
FAX Number: (909) 621-8403 Calendar System: Semester
URL: www.pomona.edu
Established: 1887 Annual Undergrad Tuition & Fees: $52,780
Enrollment: 1,599 Coed
Affiliation or Control: Independent Non-Profit IRS Status: 501(c)3
Highest Offering: Baccalaureate
Accreditation: WC

01 President ....Dr. G. Gabrielle STARR
05 Int Vice President/Dean of College ....Dr. Robert GAINES
13 Vice President Information ....Mr. William MORSE
10 Vice President/Treasurer ....Dr. Karen SISSON
111 Int VP Institutional Advancement ....Ms. Robin TROZPEK
32 Vice President/Dean of Students ....Ms. Avis HINKSON
07 VP of Admissions & Financial Aid ....Mr. Seth ALLEN
26 Sr Director News/Strategic Content ....Mr. Mark KENDALL
100 Chief of Staff ....Ms. Christine CIAMBRIELLO
06 Registrar ....Ms. Elisa C. ALBAN
27 Director Public Relations ....Mr. Mark WOOD
29 Assistant VP Alumni & Parent Engage ....Mr. Craig ARTEAGA-JOHNSON
37 Director Financial Aid ....Ms. Robin THOMPSON
36 Sr Assoc Dir Career Development Ofc ....Ms. Wanda GIBSON
15 Director Human Resources ....Ms. Brenda RUSHFORTH
41 Interim Athletic Director ....Ms. Jennifer SCANLON
44 Director Annual Giving ....Mr. Michael SPICER
21 Assoc Treasurer/Controller ....Ms. Mary Lou WOODS
09 Director of Institutional Research .... Dr. Jennifer RACHFORD
18 Chief Facilities/Physical Plant ....Mr. Robert ROBINSON
115 Chief Investment Officer ....Mr. David WALLACE

Presbyterian Theological Seminary in America (G)

15605 Carmenita Road, Santa Fe Springs CA 90670

County: Los Angeles FICE Identification: 041228
Unit ID: 490045

Telephone: (562) 926-1023 Carnegie Class: Spec-4-yr-Faith
FAX Number: (562) 926-1025 Calendar System: Semester
URL: www.ptsa.edu
Established: 1977 Annual Undergrad Tuition & Fees: $6,860
Enrollment: 160 Coed
Affiliation or Control: Presbyterian Church In America IRS Status: 501(c)3
Highest Offering: First Professional Degree
Accreditation: BI, THEOL

01 President ....Dr. Sang Meyng LEE
05 Dean of Academic Affairs/CAO ....Rev. Kyung Mo KOO
10 Chief Financial Officer ....Mr. Sun Kyu LEE
32 Dean of Students/Student Ministry ....Rev. Choong Gi PARK
85 Dean/Dir of Intl Students/Fin Aid ....Mrs. Karen CHOI
08 Librarian ....Ms. Dou Ho IM

21 Managing Treasurer/Accountant ....Mrs. Mihyun PARK
06 Registrar ....Mrs. Michelle YOON
106 Dir Online Education/E-learning ....Mr. Dong Sik PARK
13 IT Director ....Mr. Eliot LEE

Presidio Graduate School (H)

1202 Ralston Avenue, #300, San Francisco CA 94129

County: San Francisco Identification: 667150
Unit ID: 486433

Telephone: (415) 561-6555 Carnegie Class: Masters/S
FAX Number: (415) 561-6483 Calendar System: Semester
URL: www.presidio.edu
Established: 2003 Annual Graduate Tuition & Fees: N/A
Enrollment: 100 Coed
Affiliation or Control: Independent Non-Profit IRS Status: 501(c)3
Highest Offering: Master's; No Undergraduates
Accreditation: WC

01 President ....Suzanne FARVER
05 Provost ....Dr. Dariush RAFINEJAD
11 Vice President of Operations ....Eric CETNARSKI
07 Director of Admissions ....Kari DORTH

Professional Golfers Career College (I)

26109 Ynez Road, Temecula CA 92591-6013

County: Riverside FICE Identification: 033673
Unit ID: 437750

Telephone: (951) 719-2994 Carnegie Class: Spec 2-yr-Other
FAX Number: (951) 719-1643 Calendar System: Semester
URL: www.golfcollege.edu
Established: 1990 Annual Undergrad Tuition & Fees: $18,512
Enrollment: 78 Coed
Affiliation or Control: Proprietary IRS Status: Proprietary
Highest Offering: Associate Degree
Accreditation: CNCE

01 President .... Dr. Tim SOMERVILLE

Providence Christian College (J)

1539 E. Howard Street, Pasadena CA 91104

County: Los Angeles FICE Identification: 041539
Unit ID: 455770

Telephone: (866) 323-0233 Carnegie Class: Bac-A&S
FAX Number: (626) 696-4040 Calendar System: Semester
URL: www.providencecc.edu
Established: 2002 Annual Undergrad Tuition & Fees: $30,370
Enrollment: 167 Coed
Affiliation or Control: Non-denominational IRS Status: 501(c)3
Highest Offering: Baccalaureate
Accreditation: WC

01 President ....Dr. Jim BELCHER
05 Interim Chief Academic Officer ....Ann HAMILTON
10 VP Finance & Operations ....Dawn DIRKSEN
111 VP Advancement ....Michael KILEDJIAN
06 Registrar ....Patty TSAI
07 Director Admissions/Marketing ....Larissa KAMPS
32 Int Director Student Life ....Geoff SHAW

*Rancho Santiago Community College District (K)

2323 N. Broadway, Santa Ana CA 92706-1640

County: Orange FICE Identification: 006991
Unit ID: 438665

Telephone: (714) 480-7300 Carnegie Class: N/A
FAX Number: (714) 796-3915
URL: www.rsccd.edu

01 Chancellor ....Mr. Marvin MARTINEZ
10 Vice Chanc Business & Fiscal Svcs ....Mr. Peter HARDASH
05 Vice Chanc Educational Svcs ....Mr. Enrique PEREZ
15 Vice Chanc Human Resources ....Ms. Tracie GREEN
13 Asst Vice Chanc Info Tech Svcs ....Mr. Jesse GONZALEZ
19 Chief District Safety & Security ....Mr. Michael TOLEDO
04 Exec Asst to the Chancellor ....Ms. Debra GERARD

*Santa Ana College (L)

1530 W 17th Street, Santa Ana CA 92706-3398

County: Orange FICE Identification: 001284
Unit ID: 121619

Telephone: (714) 564-6000 Carnegie Class: Bac/Assoc-Assoc Dom
FAX Number: (714) 564-6379 Calendar System: Semester
URL: www.sac.edu
Established: 1915 Annual Undergrad Tuition & Fees (In-District): $1,160
Enrollment: 28,083 Coed
Affiliation or Control: State/Local IRS Status: 501(c)3
Highest Offering: Baccalaureate
Accreditation: WJ, ADNUR, OTA

02 President ....Dr. Linda D. ROSE
05 Vice President Academic Affairs ....Dr. Jeffrey N. LAMB
10 Vice Chanc Bus Ops/Fiscal Svcs .... Mr. Peter HARDASH
51 Vice President Continuing Educ ....Dr. James KENNEDY
32 Dean Student Affairs ....Alicia KRUIZENGA

11 Int Vice Pres Administrative Svcs .... Dr. Bart HOFFMAN
07 Dean Enrollment Services .... Mark LIANG
06 Registrar .... Chris TRUONG
50 Dean Business Division .... Madeline GRANT
35 Assoc Dean Student Development .... Jennifer DE LA ROSA
38 Interim Dean Counseling .... Dr. Maria DELA CRUZ
37 Director of Financial Aid .... Robert MANSON
41 Dean Kinesiology & Athletics .... Dr. R. Douglas MANNING
57 Int Dean Fine & Performing Arts .... Dr. Brian KEHLENBACH
111 Exec Director College Advancement .... Christina ROMERO
18 Director Physical Plant/Facilities .... Mario GASPAR
79 Dean Humanities & Social Sciences .... Shelly JAFFRAY
81 Dean Science/Math/Health Sci .... Dr. Michelle PRIEST
103 Dean Career Educ/Workforce Develop .... Bart HOFFMAN
56 Associate Dean EOPS .... Christine LEON
88 Associate Dean DSPS .... Dr. Veronica OFORLEA
04 Assistant to the President .... Kennethia J. VEGA
26 Public Information Officer .... Melissa UTSUKI
09 Director of College Research .... Janice LOVE
35 Assistant Dean Student Services .... Teresa MERCADO-COTA

*Santiago Canyon College (A)

8045 E Chapman Avenue, Orange CA 92869-4512
County: Orange FICE Identification: 036957
Unit ID: 399212
Telephone: (714) 628-4900 Carnegie Class: Assoc/HT-High Trad
FAX Number: (714) 628-4723 Calendar System: Semester
URL: www.sccollege.edu
Established: 1997 Annual Undergrad Tuition & Fees (In-District): $1,154
Enrollment: 12,307 Coed
Affiliation or Control: State/Local IRS Status: 501(c)3
Highest Offering: Associate Degree
Accreditation: WJ

02 President .... Dr. John HERNANDEZ
04 Assistant to the President .... Ms. Esther ODEGARD
32 Vice President Student Services .... Mr. Syed RIZVI
05 Vice President Academic Affairs .... Dr. Marilyn FLORES
51 Vice President Continuing Educ .... Mr. Jose VARGAS
11 Vice Pres Administrative Services .... Dr. Arleen SATELE
38 Dean Counseling .... Ms. Ruth BABESHOFF
41 Dean Math & Sciences/Athletic Dir .... Mr. Martin STRINGER
79 Dean Arts/Humanities/Social Science .... Mr. Dave VAKIL
50 Int Dean Business/Career Educ .... Ms. Elizabeth ARTEAGA
108 Dean Institutional Effectiveness .... Mr. Aaron VOELCKER
20 Dean Instruction/Student Services .... Ms. Lori FASBINDER
84 Int Dean Enrollment Support Svcs .... Dr. Jennifer COTO
20 Assistant Dean DSPS .... Ms. Starr AVEDESIAN
07 Asst Dean of Admissions & Records .... Mr. Tuyen NGUYEN
37 Asst Dean Fin Aid/Scholarships .... Ms. Sheena TRAN
18 Facilities Manager .... Mr. Chuck WALES

Reach Institute for School Leadership (B)

1221 Preservation Park Way, Ste 100, Oakland CA 94612
County: Alameda Identification: 667313
Telephone: (510) 501-5075 Carnegie Class: Not Classified
FAX Number: (510) 868-2215 Calendar System: Semester
URL: www.reachinst.org
Established: 2007 Annual Graduate Tuition & Fees: N/A
Enrollment: N/A Coed
Affiliation or Control: Independent Non-Profit IRS Status: 501(c)3
Highest Offering: Master's; No Undergraduates
Accreditation: WC

01 Executive Director .... Ben SANDERS
11 Associate Director .... Jonna JUSTINIANO
05 Chief Academic Officer .... Liz BAHAN

Regan Career Institute (C)

11350 Valley Blvd, El Monte CA 91731
County: Los Angeles FICE Identification: 042554
Unit ID: 490197
Telephone: (626) 455-0312 Carnegie Class: Not Classified
FAX Number: (626) 455-0316 Calendar System: Other
URL: www.rci.edu
Established: 2004 Annual Undergrad Tuition & Fees: N/A
Enrollment: 19 Coed
Affiliation or Control: Proprietary IRS Status: Proprietary
Highest Offering: Baccalaureate
Accreditation: ABHES

01 President & CEO .... Julian C. LEE

Reiss-Davis Graduate Center (D)

3200 Motor Avenue, Los Angeles CA 90034
County: Los Angeles Identification: 667332
Telephone: (310) 204-1666 Carnegie Class: Not Classified
FAX Number: N/A Calendar System: Other
URL: www.reissdavis.org
Established: 1976 Annual Graduate Tuition & Fees: N/A
Enrollment: N/A Coed
Affiliation or Control: Independent Non-Profit IRS Status: 501(c)3
Highest Offering: Doctorate; No Undergraduates
Accreditation: @WC

01 President .... Nancy TALLERINO

11 COO .... Don MCLELLAN
05 Provost .... James INCORVAIN
09 Director of Institutional Research .... Brian STERN

Rio Hondo College (E)

3600 Workman Mill Road, Whittier CA 90601-1699
County: Los Angeles FICE Identification: 001269
Unit ID: 121886
Telephone: (562) 692-0921 Carnegie Class: Bac/Assoc-Assoc Dom
FAX Number: (562) 699-7386 Calendar System: Semester
URL: www.riohondo.edu
Established: 1960 Annual Undergrad Tuition & Fees (In-District): $1,360
Enrollment: 19,948 Coed
Affiliation or Control: State/Local IRS Status: 501(c)3
Highest Offering: Baccalaureate
Accreditation: WJ, NAIT

01 Superintendent/President .... Dr. Arturo REYES
05 Vice President Academic Svcs .... Dr. Laura RAMIREZ
10 Vice President Finance/Business .... Mr. Yulian LIGIOSO
32 Vice President Student Services .... Mr. Henry GEE
86 Dir Govt & Community Relations .... Mr. Russell CASTANEDA-CALLEROS
15 Executive Director Human Resources .... Mr. Shawn SMITH
26 Dir Marketing & Communications .... Ms. Ruthie RETANA
35 Dir Student Life & Leadership .... Ms. Shaina PHILLIPS
06 Dir Admin & Records/Registrar .... Ms. Leigh UNGER
38 Int Dean Counseling .... Ms. Lisa CHAVEZ
102 Acting Exec Dir RHC Foundation .... Mr. Henry GEE
37 Int Dir Fin Aid & Veteran Services .... Mr. David LEVY
18 Director of Facilities .... Vacant
96 Director of Purchasing .... Mr. Felix G. SARAO
04 Admin Assistant to President .... Ms. Renee D. GALLEGOS
09 Dean Inst Research & Plng .... Dr. Caroline DURDELLA
88 Dean Educational Centers .... Ms. Yolanda EMERSON
41 Athletic Director .... Mr. Steve HEBERT
50 Dean Business .... Ms. Gita RUNKLE

*Riverside Community College District (F)

3801 Market Street, Riverside CA 92501
County: Riverside Identification: 667039
Telephone: (951) 222-8000 Carnegie Class: N/A
FAX Number: (951) 682-5339
URL: www.rccd.edu

01 Chancellor .... Dr. Wolde-Ab ISAAC
05 VC Educ Svcs/Strategic Planning .... Dr. Susan MILLS
10 VC Business & Financial Svcs .... Mr. Aaron BROWN
15 VC Div & Human Resources .... Dr. Terri HAMPTON
100 Chief of Staff & Facilities Devel .... Vacant
12 President Moreno Valley College .... Dr. Robin STEINBACK
12 Interim President Norco College .... Vacant
12 President Riverside City College .... Dr. Gregory ANDERSON

*Moreno Valley College (G)

16130 Lasselle Street, Moreno Valley CA 92551
County: Riverside FICE Identification: 041735
Unit ID: 460394
Telephone: (951) 571-6100 Carnegie Class: Assoc/HT-Mix Trad/Non
FAX Number: N/A Calendar System: Semester
URL: www.mvc.edu
Established: 2010 Annual Undergrad Tuition & Fees (In-District): $1,420
Enrollment: 9,914 Coed
Affiliation or Control: State/Local IRS Status: 501(c)3
Highest Offering: Associate Degree
Accreditation: WJ, DA, DH, EMT

02 President .... Dr. Robin L. STEINBACK
05 Vice Pres Academic Affairs .... Mr. Carlos LOPEZ
10 Vice Pres Business Services .... Dr. Nathaniel JONES
32 Vice Pres of Student Services .... Dr. Dyrell FOSTER
20 Dean of Instruction .... Mrs. Anna Marie AMEZQUITA
121 Associate Dean Academic Support .... Vacant
84 Director Enrollment Services .... Ms. Jamie CLIFTON
37 Director Student Financial Services .... Ms. Sandra MARTINEZ
18 Director Facilities .... Mr. Robert BEEBE
35 Dean Student Services .... Mrs. Eugenia VINCENT
38 Dean Student Svcs & Counseling .... Dr. Michael Paul WONG
22 Dean Grants/Stdnt Equity Initiative .... Dr. Andrew SANCHEZ
89 Director First Year Experience .... Mr. Ed ALVAREZ
13 Manager Tech Support Services .... Mr. Julio CUZ
23 Director Health Services .... Ms. Susan TARCON
25 Dean Grants & Business Services .... Mrs. Mary Ann DOHERTY
88 Dean Public Safety Educ & Trng .... Mr. Arthur TURNIER
75 Dean CTE .... Mrs. Melody GRAVEEN
81 Director STEM Innovation .... Mr. Donnell LAYNE
88 Director TRIO Programs .... Mrs. Micki GRAYSON
04 Executive Admin Asst to the Pres .... Ms. Eden ANDOM

*Norco College (H)

2001 Third Street, Norco CA 92860
County: Riverside FICE Identification: 041761
Unit ID: 460464
Telephone: (951) 372-7000 Carnegie Class: Assoc/HT-Mix Trad/Non
FAX Number: N/A Calendar System: Semester
URL: www.norcocollege.edu
Established: 2010 Annual Undergrad Tuition & Fees (In-District): $1,420
Enrollment: 10,277 Coed

Affiliation or Control: State/Local IRS Status: 501(c)3
Highest Offering: Associate Degree
Accreditation: WJ

02 Interim President .... Dr. Monica GREEN
05 Vice Pres Academic Affairs .... Dr. Samuel LEE
32 Interim Vice Pres Student Services .... Dr. Kaneesha TARRANT
04 Executive Asst to President .... Ms. Denise TERRAZAS
07 Dean Admissions & Records .... Mr. Mark DEASIS
09 Dean Institutional Effectiveness .... Dr. Greg AYCOCK
10 Vice Pres Business Services .... Dr. Michael COLLINS
13 Dean Technology/Learning Resources .... Mr. Damon NANCE
18 Director Facilities .... Mr. Steven MARSHALL
25 Dean Grants/Stdnt Equity Initiative .... Dr. Gustavo OCEGUERA
37 Director Student Financial Services .... Dr. Maria GONZALEZ
20 Dean Instruction .... Dr. Jason PARKS
20 Dean Instruction .... Dr. Marshall FULBRIGHT
75 Int VP Strategic Development .... Dr. Kevin FLEMING

*Riverside City College (I)

4800 Magnolia Avenue, Riverside CA 92506
County: Riverside FICE Identification: 001270
Unit ID: 121901
Telephone: (951) 222-8000 Carnegie Class: Assoc/HT-High Trad
FAX Number: (951) 222-8036 Calendar System: Semester
URL: www.rcc.edu
Established: 1916 Annual Undergrad Tuition & Fees (In-District): $1,420
Enrollment: 20,863 Coed
Affiliation or Control: State/Local IRS Status: 501(c)3
Highest Offering: Associate Degree
Accreditation: WJ, ADNUR

02 President .... Dr. Gregory ANDERSON
05 Vice Pres Academic Affairs .... Dr. Carol FARRAR
10 Vice Pres Business Services .... Dr. Raymond WEST, III
45 Vice Pres Planning & Development .... Dr. Monica GREEN
32 Vice President Student Services .... Dr. FeRita CARTER
20 Int Dean Instruc/Special Assignment .... Dr. Arun GOYAL
66 Dean School of Nursing .... Dr. Sandy BAKER
83 Dean Instruction Hum/Soc Sci .... Dr. Kristi WOODS
88 Special Asst to the President .... Dr. Scott BAUER
75 Dean of Career/Tech Educ .... Ms. Kristine DIMEMMO
121 Dean Student Success & Support .... Ms. Allison DOUGLAS-CHICOYE
84 Dean Enrollment Services .... Ms. Kyla O'CONNOR
35 Dean Student Services .... Ms. Cecilia ALVARADO
41 Director Athletics .... Mr. James WOOLDRIDGE
23 Director Health Services .... Ms. Renee MARTIN-THORNTON
19 Sergeant Safety & Police .... Mr. Robert KLEVENO

Sacramento Ultrasound Institute (J)

2233 Watt Avenue #150, Sacramento CA 95825
County: Sacramento Identification: 667264
Unit ID: 490160
Telephone: (916) 877-7977 Carnegie Class: Not Classified
FAX Number: (916) 481-4032 Calendar System: Other
URL: www.sui.edu
Established: 2002 Annual Undergrad Tuition & Fees: N/A
Enrollment: 80 Coed
Affiliation or Control: Proprietary IRS Status: Proprietary
Highest Offering: Associate Degree
Accreditation: ABHES

01 President/CEO .... Mrs. Sima DERMISHYAN
11 Chief Operating Officer .... Mr. Samuel YARMAGYAN
07 Admissions Director .... Mr. Armine KOCHARYAN
06 Registrar .... Ms. Pamela WLADON

SAE Expression College (K)

6601 Shellmound Street, Emeryville CA 94608-1021
County: Alameda FICE Identification: 039733
Unit ID: 447458
Telephone: (510) 654-2934 Carnegie Class: Spec-4-yr-Arts
FAX Number: (510) 658-3414 Calendar System: Semester
URL: www.sae.edu
Established: 1999 Annual Undergrad Tuition & Fees: $26,079
Enrollment: 345 Coed
Affiliation or Control: Proprietary IRS Status: Proprietary
Highest Offering: Baccalaureate
Accreditation: ACCSC

01 Campus Director .... Ms. Valerie CURRY
05 Director of Education .... Mr. Chris COLATOS

Saint John's Seminary (L)

5012 Seminary Road, Camarillo CA 93012-2500
County: Ventura FICE Identification: 001299
Unit ID: 123855
Telephone: (805) 482-2755 Carnegie Class: Spec-4-yr-Faith
FAX Number: (805) 482-3470 Calendar System: Semester
URL: www.stjohnsem.edu
Established: 1939 Annual Graduate Tuition & Fees: N/A
Enrollment: 118 Male
Affiliation or Control: Roman Catholic IRS Status: 501(c)3
Highest Offering: Master's; No Undergraduates
Accreditation: WC, THEOL

01 Rector/President .... Rev. Marco A. DURAZO
03 Executive Vice President .... Rev. Slawomir SZKREDKA
05 Academic Dean .... Rev. John O'BRIEN
07 Director of Admissions .... Rev. Thinh PHAM
06 Registrar .... Mr. Kevin GODFREY
04 Administrative Asst to President .... Ms. Maria GAETA
10 Director of Finance .... Mr. Michael COLLINS
15 Director Personnel Services .... Ms. Mary BISSINGER
18 Chief Facilities/Physical Plant .... Mr. Greg JULIUS
30 Chief Development/Advancement .... Ms. Julia SCALISE
32 Chief Student Affairs/Student Life .... Rev. Raymond MARQUEZ
96 Director of Purchasing .... Ms. Delia GALICIA
08 Chief Library Officer .... Dr. Victoria BRENNAN

St. Luke University (A)

1460 E. Holt Ave., Suite 72, Pomona CA 91767
County: Los Angeles — Identification: 667299
Telephone: (909) 623-0302 — Carnegie Class: Not Classified
FAX Number: (909) 623-0480 — Calendar System: Semester
URL: www.sluedu.us
Established: 2004 — Annual Undergrad Tuition & Fees: N/A
Enrollment: N/A — Coed
Affiliation or Control: Independent Non-Profit — IRS Status: 501(c)3
Highest Offering: Master's
Accreditation: TRACS

01 Founder/President .... Rev. Young D. KIM
05 Chief Academic Officer .... Dr. Sungyi CHOI
10 Director Administration/Finance .... Jung Ae KIM
32 Director Student Affairs .... Rev. Seongeun JEONG
06 Registrar .... Jaewon LEE
08 Librarian .... Ricky STROBEL

Saint Mary's College of California (B)

1928 Saint Mary's Road, Moraga CA 94556-2744
County: Contra Costa — FICE Identification: 001302
Unit ID: 123554
Telephone: (925) 631-4000 — Carnegie Class: Masters/L
FAX Number: (925) 376-8497 — Calendar System: 4/1/4
URL: www.stmarys-ca.edu
Established: 1863 — Annual Undergrad Tuition & Fees: $47,280
Enrollment: 3,913 — Coed
Affiliation or Control: Roman Catholic — IRS Status: 501(c)3
Highest Offering: Doctorate
Accreditation: WC, MACTE

01 President .... Dr. James A. DONAHUE
05 Provost/Vice President Acad Affairs .... Dr. Margaret KASIMATIS
32 Vice Provost Student Life .... Dr. Jane CAMARILLO
10 VP for Finance & Administration .... Ms. Susan H. COLLINS
111 Vice President for Advancement .... Ms. Lisa MOORE
26 Asst VP College Communication .... Vacant
88 Vice President for Mission .... Dr. Frances SWEENEY
84 Vice Prov Enrollment/Communications .... Dr. William MULLEN
20 Associate Prov Acad Affairs/CDO .... Dr. Kathy LITTLES
43 General Counsel .... Mr. Larry NUTI
53 Dean School of Education .... Dr. Carol Ann GITTENS
50 Int Dean School Econ & Bus Admin .... Dr. Yung Jae LEE
81 Dean School of Science .... Dr. Roy WENSLEY
49 Dean School Liberal Arts .... Dr. Sheila HUGHES
35 Dean of Students .... Dr. Evette CASTILLO CLARK
08 Dean Library & Academic Resources ... Ms. Lauren MACDONALD
42 Director Mission & Ministry .... Ms. Karin MCCLELLAND
07 Dean of Admissions .... Ms. Angelica MOORE
15 Associate VP Human Resources .... Ms. Laurie PANIAN
29 Assistant VP of Alumni Engagement .... Ms. Mary POPPINGO
110 Assistant VP of Development ...... Ms. Carolyn OTIS CATANZARO
58 Assoc Dean Grad & Global Pgms .... Dr. Yung Jae LEE
06 Registrar .... Vacant
35 Associate Dean of Students .... Mr. Jim SCIUTO
37 Associate Director of Financial Aid .... Ms. Linda JUDGE
88 Director of Kinesiology .... Dr. Claire WILLIAMS
57 Director MFA in Creative Writing .... Dr. Matthew ZAPRUDER
102 Dir Corporate & Foundation Rels .... Mr. William OLDS
14 Deputy CTO .... Mr. Lance HOURANY
13 Interim Chief Technology Officer .... Mr. Lance HOURANY
19 Director of Public Safety .... Vacant
38 Director of Counseling Center .... Ms. Dai L. TO
41 Director of Athletics .... Mr. Michael MATOSO
88 Museum Administrator .... Mr. John SCHNEIDER
88 Director of January Term Program .... Dr. Aaron SACHOWITZ
18 Director of Facilities .... Mr. Michael VIOLA
88 Director of Office of Research .... Ms. Elizabeth GALLAGHER
36 Dir of Career Devel Center .... Ms. Beverly MCLEAN
23 Medical Director Health & Wellness .... Vacant
27 Director Media Relations .... Mr. Michael MCALPIN
86 Director Community & Govt Relations .... Vacant
94 Director Women's Resource Ctr .... Ms. Sharon SOBOTTA
88 Director of CILSA .... Dr. Jennifer PIGZA
88 Assistant Director of CILSA .... Mr. Ryan LAMBERTON
21 Controller .... Ms. Jeanne DEMATTEO
104 Director Ctr International Programs . Ms. M. Susan MILLER-REID
88 Director Meetings/Events/Conf Svcs .... Vacant
121 Dir Student Engage & Academic Svcs ... Mr. Michael HOFFSHIRE
28 Dir of Delphine Intercultural Ctr .... Ms. Desiree ANDERSON
09 Director of Institutional Research .... Mr. Gregg THOMSON
88 Dir New Student/Family Programs .... Ms. Jennifer HERZOG
96 Purchasing/Buyer .... Mr. Joe ROSA
39 Director Student Housing .... Mr. Marcus WEEMES
04 Executive Asst to President .... Dr. David FORD

Saint Patrick's Seminary & University (C)

320 Middlefield Road, Menlo Park CA 94025-3596
County: San Mateo — FICE Identification: 010074
Telephone: (650) 325-5621 — Carnegie Class: Not Classified
FAX Number: (650) 323-5447 — Calendar System: Semester
URL: www.stpsu.edu
Established: 1898 — Annual Undergrad Tuition & Fees: N/A
Enrollment: N/A — Male
Affiliation or Control: Roman Catholic — IRS Status: 501(c)3
Highest Offering: Master's
Accreditation: WC, THEOL

01 President-Rector/Vice Chancellor .. Bishop Robert CHRISTIAN, OP
03 Vice Rector .... Rev. Daniel DONOHOO
05 Academic Dean .... Dr. Anthony LILLES
10 Director of Operations .... Mr. Richard DIZON
08 Library Director .... Mr. David KRIEGH
06 Registrar .... Mr. Manvinder (Vinay) SHAHI
07 Director of Admissions .... Ms. Grace LAXAMANA

Saint Photios Orthodox Theological Seminary (D)

510 Collier Way, PO Box 797, Etna CA 96027
County: Siskiyou — Identification: 667366
Telephone: (530) 467-3544 — Carnegie Class: Not Classified
FAX Number: N/A — Calendar System: Semester
URL: www.spots.school
Established: — Annual Undergrad Tuition & Fees: N/A
Enrollment: N/A — Coed
Affiliation or Control: Independent Non-Profit — IRS Status: 501(c)3
Highest Offering: Master's
Accreditation: @BI

The Salvation Army College for Officer Training at Crestmont (E)

30840 Hawthorne Boulevard,
Rancho Palos Verdes CA 90275-5301
County: Los Angeles — FICE Identification: 036954
Telephone: (310) 377-0481 — Carnegie Class: Not Classified
FAX Number: (310) 541-1697 — Calendar System: Quarter
URL: www.crestmont.edu
Established: 1878 — Annual Undergrad Tuition & Fees: N/A
Enrollment: N/A — Coed
Affiliation or Control: Other — IRS Status: 501(c)3
Highest Offering: Associate Degree
Accreditation: WJ

01 Training Principal .... Major Brian SAUNDERS
03 Assistant Training Principal .... Major Nigel CROSS
05 Director of Education .... Major Stacy CROSS
10 Director of Business Administration .... Capt. Jared ARNOLD
32 Director of Cadet Services .... Major Catherine BOYD
04 Exec Secretary to Trng Principal .... Ms. Celeste SKINNER
09 Director of Institutional Research .... Dr. Duncan SUTTON

Samuel Merritt University (F)

3100 Telegraph Avenue, Oakland CA 94609
County: Alameda — FICE Identification: 007012
Unit ID: 122296
Telephone: (510) 869-6511 — Carnegie Class: Spec-4-yr-Other Health
FAX Number: (510) 869-6525 — Calendar System: Semester
URL: www.samuelmerritt.edu
Established: 1909 — Annual Undergrad Tuition & Fees: N/A
Enrollment: 2,141 — Coed
Affiliation or Control: Independent Non-Profit — IRS Status: 501(c)3
Highest Offering: Doctorate
Accreditation: WC, ANEST, ARCPA, NURSE, OT, POD, PTA

01 President .... Dr. Ching-Hua WANG
05 Academic Vice President/Provost .... Dr. Fred BALDINI
10 Vice Pres Finance/Admin/CFO .... Mr. Gregory GINGRAS
84 Vice President Enrollment Services .... Dr. Terrence NORDSTROM
111 Vice Pres Institutional Advancement .... Mr. Al FRISONE
20 Asst Academic Vice President .... Dr. Celeste VILLANUEVA
20 Asst Academic Vice President .... Dr. Michael NEGRETE
04 Assistant to the President .... Ms. Margrette PETERSON
66 Int Dean & Professor of Nursing .... Dr. Celeste VILLANUEVA
88 Chair Dept Physical Therapy .... Dr. Nicole CHRISTENSEN
88 Chair Dept Occupational Therapy .... Dr. Kate HAYNER
88 Chair ABSN Program .... Ms. Rene ENGELHART
88 Chair Physician Assistant Pgm .... Dr. Michael DEROSA
07 Dean Admission .... Mr. Timothy CRANFORD
15 Exec Director Human Resources .... Ms. Elaine LEMAY
45 Exec Dir Planning/Business Dev .... Ms. Cynthia ULMAN
26 Exec Dir Communications/Ext Rels .... Vacant
28 Chief Diversity Officer .... Ms. Shirley STRONG
09 Director Institutional Research .... Ms. Nandini DASGUPTA
06 Registrar .... Ms. Anne SCHER
08 Library Director .... Ms. Hai-Thom SOTA
37 Director Financial Aid .... Mr. Tyler PRUETT
88 Dir Family Nurse Practitioner Pgm .... Ms. Rhonda RAMIREZ
29 Director of Alumni Relations .... Ms. Susan VALENCIA
18 Director Facilities Management .... Ms. Lillian HARVIN
32 Asst Director Student Services .... Ms. Kathryn WARD
12 Site Manager Sacramento .... Ms. Rene ENGELHART
13 Dir of Information Technology Svcs .... Mr. Blair SIMMONS

*San Bernardino Community College District (G)

114 S. Del Rosa Drive, San Bernardino CA 92401
County: San Bernardino — Identification: 667040
Telephone: (909) 382-4091 — Carnegie Class: N/A
FAX Number: (909) 382-0153
URL: www.sbccd.edu

01 Chancellor .... Bruce BARON
10 Vice Chanc Business/Fiscal Services .... Jose TORRES
15 Vice Chanc Human Resources .... Jose TORRES
72 Assoc VC Technology/Educ Sppt Svcs .... Dr. Glen KUCK
111 Assoc VC Economic Development .... Richard GALOPE

*Crafton Hills College (H)

11711 Sand Canyon Road, Yucaipa CA 92399-1799
County: San Bernardino — FICE Identification: 009272
Unit ID: 113111
Telephone: (909) 794-2161 — Carnegie Class: Assoc/MT-VT-High Trad
FAX Number: (909) 794-0423 — Calendar System: Semester
URL: www.craftonhills.edu
Established: 1972 — Annual Undergrad Tuition & Fees (In-District): $1,144
Enrollment: 6,251 — Coed
Affiliation or Control: State/Local — IRS Status: 501(c)3
Highest Offering: Associate Degree
Accreditation: WJ, COARC, EMT

02 President .... Dr. Kevin HORAN
05 Vice Pres of Instruction .... Dr. Keith WURTZ
11 Vice President Administrative Svcs .... Mr. Mike STRONG
32 Vice President Student Services .... Vacant
35 Dean Stdnt Svcs/Stdnt Development .... Mr. Joe CABRALES
83 Dean Social/Info/Natural Science .... Dr. Van MUSE
49 Interim Dean Letters/Arts/Math .... Ms. June YAMAMOTO
36 Dean Career Educ & Human Devel .... Mr. Daniel WORD
38 Dean Student Services/Counseling .... Ms. Kirsten S. COLVEY
09 Dean Inst Effect/Research/Planning .... Mr. Giovanni SOSA
30 Director Resource Development .... Ms. Michelle RIGGS
88 Director EOPS/CARE .... Dr. Rejoice CHAVIRA
37 Director Financial Aid .... Mr. John W. MUSKAVITCH
35 Director Student Life .... Dr. Ericka PADDOCK
18 Director Facilities .... Mr. Larry COOK
13 Director Technology Services .... Ms. Melissa OSHMAN
26 Director Marketing/Public Relations .... Ms. Donna HOFFMANN
07 Director Admissions & Records .... Mr. Larry AYCOCK
04 Executive Asst to President .... Mrs. Cyndie ST. JEAN

*San Bernardino Valley College (I)

701 S Mt. Vernon Avenue,
San Bernardino CA 92410-2798
County: San Bernardino — FICE Identification: 001272
Unit ID: 123527
Telephone: (909) 384-4400 — Carnegie Class: Assoc/MT-VT-High Trad
FAX Number: N/A — Calendar System: Semester
URL: www.valleycollege.edu
Established: 1926 — Annual Undergrad Tuition & Fees (In-District): $1,238
Enrollment: 13,892 — Coed
Affiliation or Control: State/Local — IRS Status: 501(c)3
Highest Offering: Associate Degree
Accreditation: WJ, ADNUR

02 President .... Ms. Diana RODRIGUEZ
05 Vice President Instruction .... Ms. Dina HUMBLE
11 VP Administrative Services .... Mr. Scott STARK
32 VP Student Services .... Dr. Scott THAYER
121 Dean Acad Success & Learning .... Ms. Patricia QUACH
72 Dean AT/TRANS/CULA .... Mr. Albert MANIAOL
79 Dean Arts & Humanities .... Dr. Kay WEISS
38 Dean Counseling/Matriculation .... Mr. Marco COTA
50 Dean Math/Bus/Computer Tech .... Dr. Stephanie LEWIS
09 Dean Research/Planning/Inst Effect .... Dr. James SMITH
81 Interim Dean Science .... Ms. Lorrie BURNHAM
83 Dean SS/Human Development & PE .... Dr. Wallace JOHNSON
22 Dean Student Equity & Success .... Ms. Carmen RODRIGUEZ
07 Director Admissions/Records .... Ms. April DALE-CARTER
88 Director Child Development Ctr .... Mr. Mark MERJIL
30 Int Dir Devel & Community Relations .... Mr. Nick NAZARIAN
88 Director EOP&S/CARE .... Ms. Joanne HINOJOSA
37 Director Financial Aid .... Mr. Ernesto NERY
89 Director First Year Experience .... Ms. Sharaf WILLIAMS
25 Int Dir Grant Develop/Management .... Ms. Joanna OXENDINE
08 Dir Library/Learning Support Svcs .... Mr. Ron HASTINGS
26 Director Marketing/PR .... Mr. Paul BRATULIN
35 Director Student Life .... Mr. Raymond CARLOS
13 Director Technology Services .... Mr. Rick HRDLICKA
88 Mgr Cafeteria & Snack Bar .... Mr. Erik MORDEN
103 Mgr CalWORKS/Workforce Dev .... Ms. Shalita TILLMAN
66 Assoc Dean & Nursing Director .... Ms. Carol WELLS
68 Director Athletics .... Mr. Dave RUBIO
88 Director Police Academies .... Mr. Paul DENNIS
18 Dir Facilities M&O .... Mr. Robert JENKINS
88 Director DSP&S .... Mr. Marty MILLIGAN
88 AEBG Administrator .... Ms. Emma DIAZ

San Diego Christian College (A)

200 Riverview Parkway, Santee CA 92071
County: San Diego FICE Identification: 012031
Unit ID: 112084
Telephone: (619) 201-8700 Carnegie Class: Bac-Diverse
FAX Number: (619) 201-8749 Calendar System: Semester
URL: www.sdcc.edu
Established: 1970 Annual Undergrad Tuition & Fees: $31,404
Enrollment: 680 Coed
Affiliation or Control: Independent Non-Profit IRS Status: 501(c)3
Highest Offering: Master's
Accreditation: #WC

01 President ..... Dr. Paul E. AGUE
04 Exec Assistant to the President ..... Mrs. Kelly BUCHANAN
10 Chief Financial Officer ..... Mr. Allen GARRETT
05 VP for Academic Affairs ..... Dr. Elizabeth STANTON
32 Dean of Students ..... Vacant
84 Dean of Enrollment Management ..... Ms. Rina CAMPBELL
35 Director of Student Life ..... Mr. Ricardo RAMOS
06 Registrar ..... Mrs. Tammy DALLY
37 Dir Student Financial Services ..... Mr. James MCHUGH
07 Director of Admissions ..... Ms. Rina CAMPBELL
42 Director of Spiritual Life ..... Mr. Steve JENKINS
111 Director of Advancement ..... Mr. Jim BODOR
15 Human Resources Specialist ..... Ms. Kendra CHAMBERLAIN
08 Director of Library Services ..... Ms. Ruth MARTIN
29 Manager of Alumni/Donor Relations ..... Vacant
09 Dean of Assessment and Planning ..... Mrs. Lundie CARSTENSEN
41 Asst Athletic Director ..... Mr. Nick FORTINI
23 Director of Health Services ..... Mrs. Malia JENKINS
28 Director of Diversity ..... Mr. Fred BLACKBURN

*San Diego Community College District Administrative Offices (B)

3375 Camino Del Rio South, San Diego CA 92108-3883
County: San Diego FICE Identification: 008895
Unit ID: 122320
Telephone: (619) 388-6500 Carnegie Class: N/A
FAX Number: (619) 388-6913
URL: www.sdccd.edu

01 Chancellor ..... Dr. Constance M. CARROLL
10 Exec Vice Chanc Business Tech Svcs ..... Dr. Bonnie Ann DOWD
32 Vice Chancellor Student Services ..... Dr. Lynn C. NEAULT
15 Vice Chancellor Human Resources ..... Mr. Will SURBROOK
18 Vice Chanc Facilities Management ..... Mr. Christopher MANIS
05 Vice Chanc Instructional Svcs ..... Dr. Stepahnie BULGER
26 Director Comm & Public Relations ..... Mr. Jack BERESFORD
04 Exec Assistant to the Chancellor ..... Ms. Margaret LAMB
13 Chief Info Technology Officer ..... Vacant
19 Chief of Police ..... Mr. Joseph RAMOS
101 Board Recording Secretary ..... Ms. Amanda FICKEN-DAVIS
106 Dean Online & Distributed Education ..... Dr. Kats GUSTAFSON
30 Development Coordinator ..... Ms. Lisa COLE-JONES
45 Chief Institutional Planning Office ..... Ms. Natalia CORDOBA-VELASQUEZ

*San Diego City College (C)

1313 Park Boulevard, San Diego CA 92101-4787
County: San Diego FICE Identification: 001273
Unit ID: 122339
Telephone: (619) 388-3400 Carnegie Class: Assoc/HT-Mix Trad/Non
FAX Number: (619) 388-3063 Calendar System: Semester
URL: www.sdcity.edu
Established: 1914 Annual Undergrad Tuition & Fees (In-District): $1,144
Enrollment: 15,569 Coed
Affiliation or Control: State/Local IRS Status: 501(c)3
Highest Offering: Associate Degree
Accreditation: WJ, ADNUR

02 President ..... Dr. Ricky SHABAZZ
04 Executive Asst to President ..... Ms. Erin FLANAGAN
11 Acting VP of Admin Services ..... Ms. Roxann AUBREY
05 VP of Instruction ..... Ms. Matilda CHAVEZ
68 Dean Health/Exercise Sci/Athletics ..... Mr. Randy BARNES
83 Dean Behav & Soc Sci/Consumer Stds ..... Ms. Lori ERRECA
08 Dean Information/Learning Tech ..... Mr. Robbi EWELL
79 Acting Dean Sch of Arts/Humanities ..... Ms. Jeanie TYLER
50 Dean Sch Business/Info Tech ..... Ms. Rose LAMURAGLIA
124 Dean Student Dev/Matriculation ..... Dr. Nesha SAVAGE
32 Dean of Student Affairs ..... Mr. Marciano PEREZ
54 Dean Engr & Tech/Math/Sci/Nursing ..... Dr. Lisa WILL
28 Dean of Student Equity ..... Mr. Roberto VALADEZ
22 Affirmative Action Officer ..... Mr. Edwin HIEL
40 Bookstore Supervisor ..... Ms. DeeDee PORTER
26 Public Information Officer ..... Mr. Cesar GUMAPAS
88 Pgm Mgr Disabled Student Services ..... Ms. Brianne KENNEDY
37 Financial Aid Supervisor ..... Mr. Gregory SANCHEZ
88 Director EOPS ..... Ms. Lillian GARCIA
56 Director Off-Campus Programs ..... Ms. Catherine SCHAFER
92 Director Honors Program ..... Vacant
18 Chief Facilities/Physical Plant ..... Mr. Derrall CHANDLER
07 Admissions & Records Supervisor ..... Ms. Megan SOTO

*San Diego Mesa College (D)

7250 Mesa College Drive, San Diego CA 92111-4998
County: San Diego FICE Identification: 001275
Unit ID: 122375
Telephone: (619) 388-2721 Carnegie Class: Bac/Assoc-Assoc Dom
FAX Number: (619) 388-2929 Calendar System: Semester
URL: www.sdmesa.edu
Established: 1962 Annual Undergrad Tuition & Fees (In-District): $1,144
Enrollment: 23,532 Coed
Affiliation or Control: State/Local IRS Status: 501(c)3
Highest Offering: Baccalaureate
Accreditation: WJ, CAHIIM, DA, PTAA, RAD

02 President ..... Dr. Pamela T. LUSTER
05 Vice President Instruction ..... Dr. Isabel O'CONNOR
32 Vice Pres Student Services ..... Dr. Ashanti HANDS
11 Vice Pres Administrative Services ..... Mr. Lorenze LEGASPI
88 Dean Student Development ..... Ms. Aileen CRAKES
79 Dean Arts & Languages ..... Ms. Leslie SHIMAZAKI
76 Dean Health Sciences/Public Svc ..... Dr. Tina RECALDE
81 Dean School Math/Natural Sciences ..... Dr. Susan TOPHAM
50 Dean Sch Business Technology ..... Dr. Danene BROWN
08 Dean Lrng Res/Academic Support ..... Dr. Andrew MACNEILL
68 Dean PE/Health Educ/Athletics Dir ..... Dr. Ryan SHUMAKER
79 Dean of Humanities ..... Ms. Linda HENSLEY
83 Dean Social/Behav Sci/Mult Stds ..... Dr. Charles ZAPPIA
35 Dean Student Affairs ..... Ms. Victoria MILLER
93 Dean of Student Success/Equity ..... Mr. Larry MAXEY
09 Acting Dean Inst Effectiveness ..... Dr. Bridget HERRIN
26 Public Information Officer ..... Ms. Jennifer KEARNS
37 Financial Aid Officer ..... Ms. Gilda MALDONADO
07 Student Svcs Supervisor Admission ..... Ms. Ivonne ALVAREZ
04 Exec Asst to the President ..... Ms. Sara Beth CAIN

*San Diego Miramar College (E)

10440 Black Mountain Road, San Diego CA 92126-2999
County: San Diego FICE Identification: 011820
Unit ID: 122384
Telephone: (619) 388-7800 Carnegie Class: Assoc/MT-VT-Mix Trad/Non
FAX Number: (619) 388-7901 Calendar System: Semester
URL: www.sdmiramar.edu
Established: 1969 Annual Undergrad Tuition & Fees (In-District): $1,144
Enrollment: 15,692 Coed
Affiliation or Control: State/Local IRS Status: 501(c)3
Highest Offering: Associate Degree
Accreditation: WJ, MLTAD

02 President ..... Dr. Patricia HSIEH
05 Vice President Instruction ..... Dr. Paulette HOPKINS
32 Vice President Student Services ..... Mr. Adrian GONZALES
10 Vice President Admin Services ..... Mr. Brett BELL
49 Dean Liberal Arts ..... Dr. Lou ASCIONE
50 Dean Business/Tech/Workforce Init ..... Mr. Jesse LOPEZ
81 Dean Math/Bio/Exer/Phys Sci ..... Dr. Linda WOODS
19 Dean Public Safety ..... Ms. Gail WARNER
108 Dean PRIE/Library & Technology ..... Dr. Daniel MIRAMONTEZ
35 Dean Student Affairs ..... Dr. Cheryl BARNARD
124 Dean Matriculation & Student Dev ..... Dr. Tonia TERESH
103 Associate Dean Strong Workforce ..... Mr. Benjamin GAMBOA
35 Associate Dean Outreach/School Rel ..... Mr. Truongson (Sonny) NGUYEN
04 Executive Assistant to President ..... Ms. Malia KUNST
26 Public Information Officer ..... Mr. Steve QUIS
37 Financial Aid Officer ..... Mr. Vincent NGO
07 Admissions & Records Officer ..... Ms. Dana STACK

San Diego Global Knowledge University (F)

1095 K Street Suite B, San Diego CA 92101
County: San Diego Identification: 667294
Telephone: (619) 934-0797 Carnegie Class: Not Classified
FAX Number: N/A Calendar System: Semester
URL: www.sdgku.edu
Established: Annual Undergrad Tuition & Fees: N/A
Enrollment: N/A Coed
Affiliation or Control: Proprietary IRS Status: Proprietary
Highest Offering: Master's
Accreditation: ACICS

01 President ..... Dr. Miguel A. CARDENAS
05 Chief Academic Officer ..... Dr. Miguel A. CARDENAS, JR.
07 Dir of Admissions & Registrar ..... Devahn PARKER
32 Director of Student Services ..... Beatriz ESCOBEDO
11 Director of Administration ..... Ilian ROSALES

San Francisco Art Institute (G)

800 Chestnut Street, San Francisco CA 94133-2206
County: San Francisco FICE Identification: 003948
Unit ID: 122454
Telephone: (415) 771-7020 Carnegie Class: Spec-4-yr-Arts
FAX Number: (415) 749-4590 Calendar System: Semester
URL: www.sfai.edu
Established: 1871 Annual Undergrad Tuition & Fees: $46,534
Enrollment: 433 Coed
Affiliation or Control: Independent Non-Profit IRS Status: 501(c)3
Highest Offering: Master's
Accreditation: WC, ART

01 President ..... Gordon KNOX
00 Chair of the Board ..... Pam RORKE LEVY
05 VP & Dean of Academic Affairs ..... Jennifer RISSLER
111 VP Institutional Advancement ..... Ann DABOVICH
84 VP Enrollment & Marketing ..... Elizabeth O'BRIEN
11 VP of Operations & Facilities ..... Heather HICKMAN HOLLAND
32 VP & Dean of Student Affairs ..... Yasmin LAMBIE-SIMPSON
06 Dir Inst Research & Registrar ..... Jose DE LOS REYES
07 Director of Admissions ..... Vacant
08 Librarian ..... Jeff GUNDERSON
13 Senior Network Administrator ..... Patrick MAGEE
14 Technical Architect ..... Andrew SIMAS
15 Human Resources Manager ..... Catherine GUTHRIE
18 Director of Operations & Facilities ..... John SEDEN
10 Director of Finance ..... Annette BROWN
28 Dir Equity/Access & Inclusion ..... Vacant
44 Director Annual Giving ..... Angela LEGG
29 Alumni & Donor Relations Manager ..... Brianna HYNEMAN
35 Assistant Dean of Student Affairs ..... Galen CRAWFORD
37 Director of Financial Aid ..... Annita ALLDREDGE
38 Director of Counseling Services ..... Mira ELWELL
39 Dir Housing Res Life & Conduct ..... Vacant
88 Public Education Coordinator ..... Ileana TEJADA
58 Director of MFA Programs ..... Tony LABAT
58 Director of MA Programs ..... Claire DAIGLE
20 Assistant Dean of Academic Affairs ..... Zeina BARAKEH
85 International Student Advisor ..... Ana SUEK
06 Enrollment Records & Data Manager ..... Jeremy SIMMONS
88 Director of BFA Studios ..... Vacant
90 Academic Technology Manager ..... Mark HELLAR
100 Chief of Staff ..... Vacant

San Francisco Conservatory of Music (H)

50 Oak Street, San Francisco CA 94102-6011
County: San Francisco FICE Identification: 001278
Unit ID: 122506
Telephone: (415) 864-7326 Carnegie Class: Spec-4-yr-Arts
FAX Number: (415) 503-6299 Calendar System: Semester
URL: www.sfcm.edu
Established: 1917 Annual Undergrad Tuition & Fees: $46,210
Enrollment: 414 Coed
Affiliation or Control: Independent Non-Profit IRS Status: 501(c)3
Highest Offering: Beyond Master's But Less Than Doctorate
Accreditation: WC

01 President ..... David STULL
05 Provost and Dean ..... Jonas WRIGHT
10 Vice Pres Finance & Administration ..... Kathryn WITTENMYER
45 Vice Pres of Strategic Initiatives ..... Susan MCCONKEY
111 Vice Pres Advancement ..... Kathleen NICELY
20 Assoc Dean of Academic Affairs ..... Ryan BROWN
32 Associate Dean of Student Life ..... Jason SMITH
64 Asc Dean for New Media & Music Tech ..... MaryClare BRZYTWA
15 Human Resources Manager ..... Michael PATTERSON
07 Director of Admission ..... Lisa NICKELS
37 Director of Financial Aid ..... Doris HOWARD
56 Director PreCollege/Extension ..... Michael ROEST
26 Director of Communications ..... Margot FREY
06 Registrar & VA Certifying Official ..... Karen SIVERSON
31 Director of Community Engagement ..... Rachael SMITH
18 Chief Facilities Engineer ..... David MITCHELL
35 Asst Director of Student Affairs ..... Susannah WHITE
20 Assistant to the Dean ..... Sam NEDEL
29 Alumni Relations Officer ..... Maria SHAW
04 Administrative Asst to President ..... Marina KENNEDY
102 Institutional Gifts Manager ..... Rhiannon LEWIS
19 Director Security/Safety ..... Stephanie MENDOZA
30 Chief Development/Advancement ..... Kathleen NICELY
44 Director of Legacy Giving ..... Nic MEREDITH

San Joaquin College of Law (I)

901 Fifth Street, Clovis CA 93612-1312
County: Fresno FICE Identification: 025000
Unit ID: 122649
Telephone: (559) 323-2100 Carnegie Class: Spec-4-yr-Law
FAX Number: (559) 323-5566 Calendar System: Semester
URL: www.sjcl.edu
Established: 1969 Annual Graduate Tuition & Fees: N/A
Enrollment: 170 Coed
Affiliation or Control: Independent Non-Profit IRS Status: 501(c)3
Highest Offering: Doctorate; No Undergraduates
Accreditation: WC

01 Dean ..... Janice L. PEARSON
05 Academic Dean ..... Justin ATKINSON
18 Facilities Manager ..... Richard RODRIGUEZ
10 Chief Financial Officer ..... Jill A. RANDLES
32 Director of Student Services ..... Joyce K. MORODOMI
37 Financial Aid Administrator ..... Melisa NILMEIER
08 Library Director ..... Mark MASTERS
26 Public Relations Director ..... Missy M. CARTIER
15 Chief of Personnel ..... Beth PITCOCK
30 Chief Development ..... Janice L. PEARSON
84 Director Enrollment Management ..... Diane M. STEEL
61 Law Program Coordinator ..... Pat A. SMITH
20 Associate Academic Dean ..... Vacant

San Joaquin Delta College (J)

5151 Pacific Avenue, Stockton CA 95207-6370
County: San Joaquin FICE Identification: 001280
Unit ID: 122658
Telephone: (209) 954-5151 Carnegie Class: Assoc/MT-VT-High Trad
FAX Number: (209) 954-7001 Calendar System: Semester
URL: www.deltacollege.edu

Established: 1935 Annual Undergrad Tuition & Fees (In-District): $1,288
Enrollment: 17,849 Coed
Affiliation or Control: State/Local IRS Status: 501(c)3
Highest Offering: Associate Degree
Accreditation: WJ, ADNUR

01 Superintendent/President .... Dr. Kathleen HART
05 Asst Supt/VP of Instruction .... Mr. Salvador VARGAS
32 Asst Supt/VP of Student Svc .... Dr. Lisa COOPER
10 Vice Pres of Administrative Svcs .... Vacant
15 Vice Pres of Human Resources .... Ms. DeAnna SOLINA
11 Vice Pres of Operations .... Mr. Gerardo CALDERON
38 Dean Counseling & Special Svcs .... Mrs. Delecia NUNNALLY
09 Director Inst Effectiveness .... Ms. Tina MERLINO
103 Dean Workforce/Economic Development .... Ms. Julie KAY
108 Dean Student Learning & Assessment .... Dr. Ginger HOLDEN
07 Dean Enrollment Services .... Ms. Angela TOS
08 Div Dean Library/Learning Res/Lang .... Ms. Sheli AYERS
12 Associate Dean of Tracy Center ..... Dr. Jessie GARZA-RODERICK
26 Director of Marketing/Stdnt Outrch .... Ms. Shelly VALENTON
18 Director Facilities Management .... Mr. Paul ACOSTA
07 Director of Admissions & Records .... Ms. Amy COURTRIGHT
37 Director of Financial Aid/Vet Svcs .... Ms. Tina LENT
06 Registrar .... Ms. Karen SEA
04 Exec Assistant to the President .... Ms. Robin SADBERRY
19 District Police Chief .... Mr. Robert DI PIERO

San Joaquin Valley College, Inc. - Visalia (A)

8344 West Mineral King Avenue, Visalia CA 93291-9283
County: Tulare FICE Identification: 021207
Unit ID: 122685
Telephone: (559) 651-2500 Carnegie Class: Bac/Assoc-Assoc Dom
FAX Number: (559) 651-0574 Calendar System: Other
URL: www.sjvc.edu/campuses/central-california/visalia
Established: 1977 Annual Undergrad Tuition & Fees: N/A
Enrollment: 5,239 Coed
Affiliation or Control: Proprietary IRS Status: Proprietary
Highest Offering: Associate Degree
Accreditation: WJ, COARC, DH

01 Campus President .... Mr. Ben ALMAGUER

San Joaquin Valley College-Antelope Valley (Lancaster) (B)

42135 10th Street West, Ste 147, Lancaster CA 93534
Telephone: (661) 974-8282 Identification: 770968
Accreditation: &WJ

San Joaquin Valley College-Bakersfield (C)

201 New Stine Road, Bakersfield CA 93309-2668
Telephone: (661) 834-0126 FICE Identification: 023135
Accreditation: &WJ, COARC, SURGT

† Regional accreditation is carried under the parent institution in Visalia, CA.

San Joaquin Valley College-Fresno (D)

295 East Sierra Avenue, Fresno CA 93710-3616
Telephone: (559) 448-8282 Identification: 666008
Accreditation: &WJ, SURGT

† Regional accreditation is carried under the parent institution in Visalia, CA.

San Joaquin Valley College-Fresno Aviation Campus (E)

4985 East Andersen Avenue, Fresno CA 93727
Telephone: (559) 453-0123 Identification: 666009
Accreditation: &WJ

† Regional accreditation is carried under the parent institution in Visalia, CA.

San Joaquin Valley College-Modesto (F)

5380 Pirrone Road, Salida CA 95368-9090
Telephone: (209) 543-8800 Identification: 666128
Accreditation: &WJ

† Regional accreditation is carried under the parent institution in Visalia, CA.

San Joaquin Valley College-Ontario (G)

4580 Ontario Mills Parkway, Ontario CA 91764
Telephone: (909) 948-7582 Identification: 666096
Accreditation: &WJ, COARC

† Regional accreditation is carried under the parent institution in Visalia, CA.

San Joaquin Valley College-Rancho Cordova (H)

11050 Olson Drive, Suite 210,
Rancho Cordova CA 95670-5600
Telephone: (916) 638-7582 Identification: 666133
Accreditation: &WJ, COARC

† Regional accreditation is carried under the parent institution in Visalia, CA.

San Joaquin Valley College-Temecula (I)

27270 Madison Avenue, Suite 103, Temecula CA 92590
Telephone: (951) 296-6015 Identification: 770507
Accreditation: &WJ, COARC

San Joaquin Valley College-Victor Valley (Hesperia) (J)

9331 Mariposa Road, Hesperia CA 92344-8000
Telephone: (760) 948-1947 Identification: 667044
Accreditation: &WJ

† Regional accreditation is carried under the parent institution in Visalia, CA.

*San Jose/Evergreen Community College District (K)

40 South Market Street, San Jose CA 95113-2367
County: Santa Clara FICE Identification: 029042
Unit ID: 122737
Telephone: (408) 274-6700 Carnegie Class: N/A
FAX Number: (408) 531-8722
URL: www.sjeccd.edu

01 Chancellor .... Dr. Byron D. CLIFT BRELAND
11 Vice Chanc Administrative Services .... Mr. Jorge L. ESCOBAR
15 Vice Chanc Human Resources .... Ms. Beatriz S. CHAIDEZ
13 Vice Chanc Information Tech Svcs .... Dr. Ben SEABERRY
103 Interim Exec Dir of Workforce Inst .... Mr. William WATSON
09 Exec Dir Inst Effect/Stdnt Success .... Ms. Ann MACHAMER
86 Exec Dir Government/External Affs .... Ms. Rosalie LEDESMA
18 AVC PPDO .... Vacant
10 Int Exec Dir of Fiscal Services .... Ms. Linda WILCZEWSKI
26 Dir Communications/Community Rels .... Mr. Sam HO
27 Marketing & Public Info Officer .... Mr. Ryan BROWN

*Evergreen Valley College (L)

3095 Yerba Buena Road, San Jose CA 95135-1598
County: Santa Clara FICE Identification: 012452
Unit ID: 114266
Telephone: (408) 274-7900 Carnegie Class: Assoc/MT-VT-Mix Trad/Non
FAX Number: (408) 238-3179 Calendar System: Semester
URL: www.evc.edu
Established: 1975 Annual Undergrad Tuition & Fees (In-District): $1,358
Enrollment: 9,575 Coed
Affiliation or Control: State/Local IRS Status: 501(c)3
Highest Offering: Associate Degree
Accreditation: WJ, ADNUR

02 President .... Mr. Keith AYTCH
05 Interim VP Academic Affairs .... Mr. Mark GONZALES
32 VP Student Services .... Ms. Adela SWINSON
10 VP Administrative Services .... Ms. Andrea ALEXANDER
50 Dean Business & Workforce .... Dr. Maniphone DICKERSON
66 Dean Nursing & Allied Health .... Ms. Lynette APEN
81 Dean Math/Science/Engineering .... Dr. Antoinette HERRERA
83 Int Dean Soc Sci/PE/Arts/Humanities .... Dr. Brad CAROTHERS
84 Dean Enrollment Services .... Mr. Octavio CRUZ
79 Dean Language Arts/Library/Lrng Res .... Dr. Merryl KRAVITZ
121 Dean Student Success/Counseling .... Dr. Victor GARZA, JR.
09 Dean Research/Plng/Inst Effective .... Ms. Jacqueline HONDA
88 Associate Dean Noncredit Education .... Vacant
93 Int Assoc Dean Student Svcs/EOPS .... Mr. Michael OSORIO
37 Director Financial Aid .... Vacant
35 Director Student Life .... Ms. Raniyah JOHNSON
88 Director CalWorks/WIN .... Ms. Elizabeth TYRRELL
20 Supervisor Academic Services .... Ms. Tina NGUYEN
13 Supervisor Campus Tech Svcs .... Mr. Eugenio CANOY
88 Student Success Supervisor .... Mr. Song-Ho TRAN
26 Public Information Officer .... Mr. Josh RUSSELL

*San Jose City College (M)

2100 Moorpark Avenue, San Jose CA 95128-2799
County: Santa Clara FICE Identification: 001282
Unit ID: 122746
Telephone: (408) 298-2181 Carnegie Class: Assoc/MT-VT-Mix Trad/Non
FAX Number: (408) 298-1935 Calendar System: Semester
URL: www.sjcc.edu
Established: 1921 Annual Undergrad Tuition & Fees (In-District): $1,358
Enrollment: 9,336 Coed
Affiliation or Control: State/Local IRS Status: 501(c)3
Highest Offering: Associate Degree
Accreditation: WJ, DA

02 Acting President .... Mr. Roland MONTEMAYOR
05 Vice President Academic Affairs .... Dr. Elizabeth PRATT
11 Interim VP Administrative Svcs .... Ms. Marilyn MORIKANG
32 Acting VP Student Affairs .... Dr. Lucha ORTEGA
88 Vice President Strategic Partners .... Dr. Lena TRAN
10 Chief Financial/Business Officer .... Ms. Marilyn MORIKANG
88 Director Support Programs .... Vacant
37 Financial Aid Director .... Mr. Takeo KUBO
41 Dean of Athletics & Kinesiology .... Mr. Lamel HARRIS
04 Assistant to the President .... Ms. Maria GAETA
50 Dean Buisness/Workforce Devel .... Dr. Hoa Minh TA
79 Dean Humanities/Social Science .... Mr. Ilder BETANCOURT
38 Dean Counseling/Matriculation .... Dr. Eliazer AYALA-AUSTIN
49 Dean Language Arts .... Dr. Celia CRUZ-JOHNSON
81 Dean Mathematics/Sciences Division .... Mr. Robert GUTIERREZ
09 Director of Institutional Research .... Dr. Joyce LUI
07 Director of Admissions .... Ms. Teresa PAIZ
26 Dir Marketing & Public Rels .... Mr. Daniel GARZA

*San Mateo County Community College District Office (N)

3401 CSM Drive, San Mateo CA 94402-3651
County: San Mateo FICE Identification: 004697
Unit ID: 122782
Telephone: (650) 574-6500 Carnegie Class: N/A
FAX Number: (650) 574-6566
URL: www.smccd.edu

01 Acting Chancellor .... Mr. Michael CLAIRE
15 Director of Human Resources .... Mr. David FEUNE
05 Vice Chanc Educ Svcs/Plng .... Dr. Aaron MCVEAN
18 Vice Chanc Facil Plng/Maint/Oper .... Mr. Jose NUNEZ
109 Vice Chanc Auxiliary Services .... Mr. Tom BAUER
100 Chief of Staff .... Mr. Mitchell A. BAILEY
104 Provost International Education .... Dr. Jing LUAN
10 Chief Financial Officer .... Ms. Bernata SLATER
13 Chief Information Officer .... Daman GREWAL

*Cañada College (O)

4200 Farm Hill Boulevard, Redwood City CA 94061-1099
County: San Mateo FICE Identification: 006973
Unit ID: 111434
Telephone: (650) 306-3100 Carnegie Class: Assoc/HT-Mix Trad/Non
FAX Number: (650) 306-3457 Calendar System: Semester
URL: www.canadacollege.edu
Established: 1968 Annual Undergrad Tuition & Fees (In-District): $1,360
Enrollment: 6,152 Coed
Affiliation or Control: State/Local IRS Status: 501(c)3
Highest Offering: Associate Degree
Accreditation: WJ, RAD

02 President .... Dr. Jamillah MOORE
05 VP Instruction .... Dr. Tammy ROBINSON
32 VP Student Services .... Dr. Manuel Alejandro PEREZ
11 VP Administrative Services .... Mr. Graciano MENDOZA
10 College Business Officer .... Ms. Mary Chries CONCHA THIA
38 Dean Counseling .... Mr. C. Max HARTMAN
06 Registrar .... Ms. Ruth MILLER
26 Director Comm Rel & Mktg .... Ms. Megan RODRIGUEZ ANTONE
45 Dean PRIE .... Dr. Karen ENGEL
37 Director Financial Aid Services .... Ms. Margie CARRINGTON
18 Facilities Manager .... Ms. Karen PINKHAM
103 Dean Business/Design & Workforce .... Ms. Leonor CABRERA
79 Dean Humanities & Soc Sci .... Mr. James CARRANZA
81 Dean Science & Tech .... Mr. Adam WINDHAM
88 Dean Acad Support & Learning Tech .... Mr. David REED

*College of San Mateo (P)

1700 W Hillsdale Boulevard, San Mateo CA 94402-3795
County: San Mateo FICE Identification: 001181
Unit ID: 122791
Telephone: (650) 574-6161 Carnegie Class: Assoc/HT-Mix Trad/Non
FAX Number: (650) 574-6680 Calendar System: Semester
URL: www.collegeofsanmateo.edu
Established: 1922 Annual Undergrad Tuition & Fees (In-District): $1,344
Enrollment: 9,263 Coed
Affiliation or Control: State/Local IRS Status: 501(c)3
Highest Offering: Associate Degree
Accreditation: WJ, DA

02 President .... Mr. Michael CLAIRE
05 Vice President Instruction .... Dr. Sandra Stefani COMERFORD
10 Vice Pres Administrative Services .... Ms. Jan ROECKS
32 Vice President Student Services .... Ms. Kim LOPEZ
84 Dean Enrollment Svcs/Support Pgms .... Ms. Lizette BRICKER
38 Dean Counsel/Advis/Matriculation .... Ms. Krystal DUNCAN
09 Int Dean Plng/Research/Inst Effect .... Dr. Hilary GOODKIND
20 Dean Academic Support/Learning Tech .... Ms. Tarana CHAPPIE
35 Dean Student Services/Counseling .... Ms. Marsha RAMEZANE
79 Int Dean Language Arts Division .... Dr. Kristi RIDGEWAY
68 Dean Kinesiology/Athletics Division .... Mr. Andreas WOLF
81 Dean Math/Science Division .... Dr. Charlene FRONTIERA
83 Dean Creative Arts/Social Sci Div .... Dr. Laura DEMSETZ
50 Dean Business & Technology Division .... Ms. Heidi DIAMOND
06 Registrar .... Ms. Niruba SRINIVASAN
37 Director Financial Aid Services .... Ms. Claudia I. MENJIVAR
26 Dir Marketing/Comm/Public Relations .... Mr. Richard ROJO
18 Facilities Manager .... Ms. Michelle RUDOVSKY

*Skyline College (Q)

3300 College Drive, San Bruno CA 94066-1698
County: San Mateo FICE Identification: 007713
Unit ID: 123509
Telephone: (650) 738-4100 Carnegie Class: Bac/Assoc-Assoc Dom
FAX Number: (650) 738-4338 Calendar System: Semester
URL: www.skylinecollege.edu
Established: 1969 Annual Undergrad Tuition & Fees (In-District): $1,461

Enrollment: 9,235 Coed
Affiliation or Control: State/Local IRS Status: 501(c)3
Highest Offering: Baccalaureate
Accreditation: WJ, ACBSP, COARC, SURGT

02 President Dr. Jannett JACKSON
05 Vice President Instruction Dr. Jennifer TAYLOR-MENDOZA
32 Vice President Student Services Dr. Angelica GARCIA
84 Dean Enrollment Svcs/Financial Aid Mr. William MINNICH
09 Dean Plng/Research/Inst Effective Ms. Ingrid VARGAS
10 Vice President Business Service Ms. Eloisa M. BRIONES
83 Int Dean Soc Sci/Creative Arts Ms. Danni REDDING LAPUZ
50 Dean Business/Educ/Prof Pgm Mr. Michael KANE
60 Dean Language Arts/Learning Res Mr. Christopher GIBSON
68 Dean Kinesiology/Athletics/Dance Mr. Joseph MORELLO, JR.
81 Dean Science/Math/Technology Mr. Raymond HERNANDEZ
38 Dean Counsel/Advis/Matric Dr. Luis ESCOBAR
103 Director SparkPoint at Skyline Col Mr. Chad THOMPSON
26 Chief Marketing Officer Ms. Cherie COLIN
08 Director Learning Commons Gabriela NOCITO
103 Dean Strat Partnerships/WF Devel Ms. Andrea VIZENOR
85 Int Dean Global Learning Programs Mr. Russell WALDON
121 Dean Acad Support & Learning Tech Dr. Sha-Shonda PORTER
22 Exec Dir of the Equity Institute Mr. Lasana HOTEP
06 Registrar Ms. Susan LORENZO
04 Executive Asst to President Ms. Theresa TENTES
104 Director Study Abroad Mr. Zaid GHORI
18 Facilities Manager Mr. John DOCTOR
19 Chief Public Safety Officer Mr. Jim VANGELE
37 Director Student Financial Aid Ms. Regina MORRISON
21 Finance and Operations Manager Mr. Paul CASSIDY

Sanford Burnham Prebys Medical Discovery Institute (A)

10901 North Torrey Pines Road, La Jolla CA 92037
County: San Diego Identification: 667069
Unit ID: 481535
Telephone: (858) 646-3100 Carnegie Class: Spec-4-yr-Other Health
FAX Number: (858) 646-3199 Calendar System: Quarter
URL: www.sbpdiscovery.org
Established: 2005 Annual Graduate Tuition & Fees: N/A
Enrollment: 31 Coed
Affiliation or Control: Independent Non-Profit IRS Status: 501(c)3
Highest Offering: Doctorate; No Undergraduates
Accreditation: WC

01 President Dr. Kristiina VUORI
10 Chief Financial Officer Mr. Louie COFFMAN
05 Dean Grad Sch Biomedical Sciences Dr. Guy SALVESEN
15 Vice Pres Human Resources Ms. Teddi REILLY
88 Sr Vice Pres Drug Discovery/Devel Dr. Michael JACKSON
30 Vice Pres Business Development Dr. Lee BLUMENFELD
100 Vice Pres/Chief of Staff Ms. Tara MARATHE
26 Vice Pres Communications Vacant
58 Director Office of Education Dr. Diane KLOTZ

The Santa Barbara and Ventura Colleges of Law (B)

4475 Market Street, Ventura CA 93003
County: Ventura Identification: 667229
Unit ID: 125037
Telephone: (805) 765-9300 Carnegie Class: Spec-4-yr-Law
FAX Number: (805) 658-0529 Calendar System: Semester
URL: www.collegesoflaw.edu
Established: 1969 Annual Graduate Tuition & Fees: N/A
Enrollment: 109 Coed
Affiliation or Control: Independent Non-Profit IRS Status: 501(c)3
Highest Offering: Doctorate; No Undergraduates
Accreditation: WC

01 Executive Director Dr. Matthew NEHMER
05 Dean Ms. Jackie GARDINA
07 Director of Admissions Mr. Shawn TAYLOR
06 Asst Dean & Registrar Ms. Barbara DOYLE
32 Student Services Coordinator Ms. Jennifer MACKIE
04 Administrative Asst to Executive Ms. Alexis BURDICK
26 Public Affairs Director Mr. Kryztofr KAINE
106 Fac Dir Hybrid & Online Programs Ms. Andrea FUNK

Santa Barbara City College (C)

721 Cliff Drive, Santa Barbara CA 93109-2394
County: Santa Barbara FICE Identification: 001285
Unit ID: 122889
Telephone: (805) 965-0581 Carnegie Class: Assoc/HT-Mix Trad/Non
FAX Number: (805) 963-7222 Calendar System: Semester
URL: www.sbcc.edu
Established: 1909 Annual Undergrad Tuition & Fees (In-District): $1,374
Enrollment: 16,385 Coed
Affiliation or Control: State/Local IRS Status: 501(c)3
Highest Offering: Associate Degree
Accreditation: WJ, ADNUR, CAHIIM, DMS, RAD

01 Interim Superintendent/President Dr. Helen BENJAMIN
05 Exec Vice Pres Educ Pgms Dr. Pamela RALSTON
10 VP Business Services Ms. Lyndsay MAAS
15 Interim VP Human Resources Ms. Marcia WADE
13 VP Information Technology Dr. Paul BISHOP
56 VP Sch of Extended Learning Dr. Melissa MORENO
72 Dean Educational Programs Mr. Arturo RODRIGUEZ
76 Dean Educational Programs Dr. Alan PRICE
81 Dean Educational Programs Dr. Jens-Uwe KUHN
57 Dean Educational Programs Dr. Priscilla MORA
72 Dean Educational Programs Mr. Kenley NEUFELD
50 Dean Educational Programs Ms. Carola SMITH
07 Associate Dean Admissions Mr. Christopher JOHNSON
08 Librarian Ms. Elizabeth BOWMAN
102 Exec Dir Foundation for SBCC Mr. Geoff GREEN
09 Dir Institutional Research & Plng Dr. Z. REISZ
26 Exec Dir Public Affairs Ms. Luz REYES-MARTIN
37 Director of Student Financial Aid Ms. Maureen GOLDBERG
18 Director of Facilities Mr. Robert MORALES
85 Director International Students Ms. Carola SMITH
06 Director of Records Mr. Michael MEDEL
96 Manager of Purchasing Mr. Robert MORALES
04 Executive Asst to President Ms. Angie ESQUEDA
19 Director Security/Safety Mr. Erik FRICKE
41 Athletic Director Mr. Rocco CONSTANTINO
84 Coordinator for Enrollment Services Ms. Vanessa PELTON
28 Director of Diversity Mr. Luis GIRALDO

Santa Clara University (D)

500 El Camino Real, Santa Clara CA 95053-0001
County: Santa Clara FICE Identification: 001326
Unit ID: 122931
Telephone: (408) 554-4000 Carnegie Class: DU-Mod
FAX Number: (408) 554-2700 Calendar System: Quarter
URL: www.scu.edu
Established: 1851 Annual Undergrad Tuition & Fees: $51,711
Enrollment: 8,629 Coed
Affiliation or Control: Independent Non-Profit IRS Status: 501(c)3
Highest Offering: Doctorate
Accreditation: WC, IPSY, LAW, THEOL

01 President Rev. Kevin F. O'BRIEN, SJ
05 Interim Provost Ms. Lisa KLOPPENBERG
10 Vice President Finance/Admin Mr. Michael CROWLEY
43 General Counsel Mr. John OTTOBONI
111 Vice President University Relations Mr. James LYONS
100 Chief of Staff to the President Ms. Molly MCDONALD
49 Interim Dean of Arts & Sciences Dr. Terri PERETTI
50 Dean of Business Ms. Caryn BECK-DUDLEY
53 Dean Educ & Counseling Psych Dr. Sabrina ZIRKEL
54 Dean of Engineering Dr. Elaine SCOTT
61 Interim Dean of Law Ms. Anna HAN
73 Interim Dean of JST Dr. Alison BENDERS
121 Dean Academic Support Services Ms. Kathryn PALMIERI
20 Vice Provost Academic Affairs Ms. Elsa Y. CHEN
32 Vice Provost and Dean Student Life Ms. Jeanne ROSENBERGER
84 Vice President for Enrollment Mgmt Mr. Mike B. SEXTON
45 Vice Prov Inst Effectiveness Dr. Ed RYAN
13 CIO/Vice Provost Info Services Dr. Robert OWEN
20 Assoc Vice Prov Undergrad Studies Dr. Philip R. KESTEN
20 Assoc Provost Undergraduate Studies Mr. Jim BENNETT
88 Sr Assoc Provost Rsrch Faculty Affs Dr. Amy M. SHACHTER
88 Assoc Vice Provost Faculty Devel Dr. Eileen R. ELROD
07 Dean Undergraduate Admission Ms. Eva BLANCO MASIAS
37 Dean University Financial Aid Svcs Ms. Nan MERZ
21 Assoc Vice President Finance Ms. Jessica MATSUMORI
15 Associate VP Human Resources Mr. Charlie AMBELANG
30 Assoc Vice President Development Mr. Mike J. WALLACE
109 Asst Vice Pres Auxiliary Services Ms. Robin REYNOLDS
35 Assoc Dean for Student Life Mr. Matthew DUNCAN
06 University Registrar Mr. Duane VOIGT
29 Asst Vice President Alumni Rels Ms. Kathy KALE
41 Director Athletics and Recreation Dr. Renee BAUMGARTNER
08 University Librarian Ms. Jennifer NUTEFALL
90 Deputy CIO Academic Technology Ms. Nancy CUTLER
36 Director Career Center Ms. Rose NAKAMOTO
09 Director Institutional Research Ms. Barbara A. STEWART
25 Director Sponsored Projects Ms. Mary-Ellen FORTINI
38 Director Health & Counseling Svcs Dr. Jill ROVARIS
85 Assoc Provost International Pgm Ms. Susan POPKO
115 Chief Investment Officer Mr. John E. KERRIGAN
21 Controller Ms. Ramona SAUTER
18 Director of Facilities Mr. Jeffrey R. CHARLES
96 Director University Support Service Mr. Ed MERRYMAN
19 Director Campus Safety Services Mr. Philip BELTRAN
40 General Manager Bookstore Vacant
42 Director of Campus Ministry Rev. Dennis SMOLARSKI, SJ
22 EEO & Title IX Coordinator Ms. Belinda GUTHRIE
88 Director de Saisset Museum Ms. Rebecca M. SCHAPP
88 Exec Dir Ignatian Ctr Jesuit Educ Rev. Dorian LLYWELYN, SJ
88 Exec Dir Miller Ctr Soc Entrepren Dr. Thane KREINER
88 Exec Dir Markkula Ctr Applied Ethic Mr. Don HEIDER
110 Assoc Vice President Development Ms. Nancy T. CALDERON
28 Assoc Provost Diversity & Inclusion Ms. Margaret RUSSELL
44 Asst Vice President Advance Svcs Mr. Jeff BEACHY
92 Director University Honors Program Dr. Leilani M. MILLER
94 Director Womens & Gender Studies Dr. Linda GARBER
93 Director Ethnic Studies Dr. Anna C. SAMPAIO
04 Exec Assistant to the President Mrs. Bonnie SHEIKH
102 Exec Dir Corp & Found Relations Mr. Ali HASSAN
104 Director Study Abroad Vacant
105 Webmaster Mr. Brian WASHBURN
26 AVP Marketing & Communications Ms. Celine SCHMIDEK
39 Director of Residence Life Ms. Heather DUMAS-DYER

Santa Monica College (E)

1900 Pico Boulevard, Santa Monica CA 90405-1628
County: Los Angeles FICE Identification: 001286
Unit ID: 122977
Telephone: (310) 434-4000 Carnegie Class: Bac/Assoc-Assoc Dom
FAX Number: (310) 434-4386 Calendar System: Semester
URL: www.smc.edu
Established: 1929 Annual Undergrad Tuition & Fees (In-District): $1,142
Enrollment: 29,760 Coed
Affiliation or Control: State/Local IRS Status: 501(c)3
Highest Offering: Associate Degree
Accreditation: WJ, ADNUR

01 Superintendent/President Dr. Kathryn E. JEFFERY
03 Executive Vice President Ms. Elaine POLACHEK
10 Vice President Business/Admin Mr. Christopher BONVENUTO
15 Vice President Human Resources Ms. Sherri LEE-LEWIS
05 Vice President Academic Affairs Dr. Jennifer MERLIC
84 Vice Pres Enrollment Development Dr. Teresita RODRIGUEZ
32 Vice President Student Affairs Mr. Michael TUITASI
20 Dean Academic Affairs Ms. Erica LEBLANC
16 Interim Dean Human Resources Ms. Tre'Shawn HALL-BAKER
08 Dean Learning Resources Ms. Patricia BURSON
85 Dean International Education Ms. Denise KINSELLA
56 Dean Noncredit/External Programs Ms. Dione CARTER
124 Dean Counseling/Retention Ms. Brenda BENSON
13 Chief Director Info Technology Mr. Marc DRESCHER
88 Dean Education Enterprise Mr. Mitch HESKEL
43 Campus Counsel Mr. Robert MYERS
106 Int Assoc Dean Online Svcs/Support Ms. Tammara WHITAKER
88 Associate Dean Emeritus Mr. Scott SILVERMAN
35 Associate Dean of Students Vacant
17 Associate Dean of Health Sciences Dr. Eve ADLER
26 Public Information Officer Ms. Grace SMITH
31 Dean Community & Academic Relations Ms. Kiersten ELLIOTT
86 Sr Director Government Relations Mr. Don GIRARD
07 Dean of Admissions Dr. Esau TOVAR
37 Assoc Dean Financial Aid/Scholarshp Vacant
18 Director Facilities Mgmt/Operations Mr. Devin STARNES
114 Budget Manager Ms. Veronica DIAZ
09 Dean Institutional Research Ms. Hannah LAWLER
104 Assoc Dean International Education Ms. Catherine WEIR
41 Asst Director Athletics Mr. Reggie ELLIS
102 Associate Dean Grants Ms. Laurel MCQUAY-PENINGER
88 Director of Classified Personnel Ms. Carol LONG
88 Director Network Services Vacant
25 Director of Contracts Mr. Charlie YEN
96 Director of Purchasing Ms. Cynthia MOORE
19 Chief of Campus Police Mr. Johnnie ADAMS
04 Admin Asst to the President Ms. Letty KILIAN
14 Director Management Info Systems Vacant
40 Bookstore Manager Mr. David DEVER
103 Dean Workforce Development Dr. Patricia RAMOS
101 Coordinator Board of Trustees Ms. Lisa ROSE
88 Director Radio Station (KCRW) Ms. Jennifer FERRO
88 Director Facilities Programming Ms. Linda SULLIVAN
89 Dean First Year Programs Dr. Delores RAVELING
88 Dir Sustainability Coordination Mr. Ferris KAWAR
75 Dir Career & Contract Education Ms. Michelle KING
88 Assoc Dir Dual Enroll/Instr Svcs Ms. Maral HYELER
88 Dir Supplemental Instruct/Tutoring Ms. Wendi DEMORST
88 Director Student Equity & STEM Pgm Ms. Melanie BOCANEGRA
88 Director Business Development Ms. Sasha KING
36 Interim Dean Career Education Mr. Frank DAWSON
29 Dir Student and Alumni Rels Ms. Deirdre WEAVER
105 Web/Social Media Manager Ms. Regina IP
102 Dean Foundation/Inst Advancement Ms. Lizzy MOORE

Santa Rosa Junior College (F)

1501 Mendocino Avenue, Santa Rosa CA 95401-4395
County: Sonoma FICE Identification: 001287
Unit ID: 123013
Telephone: (707) 527-4011 Carnegie Class: Assoc/HVT-High Trad
FAX Number: (707) 527-4816 Calendar System: Semester
URL: www.santarosa.edu
Established: 1918 Annual Undergrad Tuition & Fees (In-District): $1,328
Enrollment: 20,671 Coed
Affiliation or Control: State/Local IRS Status: 501(c)3
Highest Offering: Associate Degree
Accreditation: WJ, DH, DIETT, EMT, RAD

01 Superintendent/President Dr. Frank CHONG
05 Int VP Academic Affairs Dr. Jane SALDANA-TALLEY
12 Vice President Petaluma Vacant
10 VP Business Services Ms. Kate JOLLEY
32 VP Student Svcs/Asst Superintendent Mr. Pedro AVILA
15 VP Human Resources Ms. Karen FURUKAWA
88 Sr Director Capital Projects Mr. Leigh SATA
75 Dean Career/Tech Ed/Economic Dev Mr. Jerry MILLER
18 Director Facilities Operations Vacant
88 Dean Curriculum/Education Support Mr. Josh ADAMS
49 Dean Liberal Arts & Sciences Vacant
08 Dean Learning Res/Educ Tech Ms. Phyllis USINA
88 Dean Public Safety Ms. April CHAPMAN
81 Dean Sci/Tech/Engr/Math Mr. Victor TAM
17 Dean Health Sciences Ms. Deborah CHIGAZOLA
50 Dean Business/Professional Studies Mr. Joshua ADAMS
79 Dean Arts & Humanities Mr. Kerry LOEWEN
88 Dean Language Arts/Acad Foundation Mr. Robert HOLCOMB
41 Dean Kinesiology/Dance/Athletic Dir Mr. Matthew MARKOVITCH
22 Dean Disabled Students Pgm & Svcs Ms. Kim STARKE
88 Dean Instr & Enrollment Svcs Pet Ms. Catherine WILLIAMS
35 Dean Student Services Petaluma Mr. Matthew LONG
88 Mgr Child Development Services Ms. Maleese WARNER
121 Sr Dean Counseling & Stdnt Success Ms. Li COLLIER
47 Dean Agriculture/Natural Resources Mr. Benjamin GOLDSTEIN

19 Chief of Police ... Mr. Robert BROWNLEE
13 Sr Director Information Technology ... Mr. Scott CONRAD
103 Dean Workforce Development ... Mr. Brad DAVIS
21 Director of Fiscal Services ... Ms. Kate JOLLEY
37 Director Student Financial Services ... Ms. Jana COX
23 Director Student Health Services ... Ms. Susan QUINN
09 Director Institutional Research ... Dr. KC GREANEY
35 Sr Dean of Students ... Mr. Robert ETHINGTON
96 Director Purchasing & Graphics ... Vacant
40 Director Bookstore ... Vacant
102 Executive Director Foundation ... Ms. Kate MCCLINTOCK
66 Associate Degree Nursing Program ... Ms. Anna VALDEZ
06 Dean Acad Records/Intl Admissions ... Ms. Freyja PEREIRA
07 Director Admissions/Enrollment Svcs ... Ms. Vayta SMITH
31 Director Community Education ... Mr. Jeffrey RHOADES
16 Director Human Resources ... Ms. Sarah HOPKINS
26 Director District & Comm Relations ... Ms. Erin BRICKER
90 Manager Instructional Computing ... Mr. Michael ROTH
24 Manager Media Services Petaluma ... Mr. Matt PEARSON
04 Admin Assistant to the President ... Ms. Zehra SONKAYNAR

Saybrook University (A)

475 14th Street, Oakland CA 94612
County: Alameda — FICE Identification: 021206
Unit ID: 123095
Telephone: (510) 593-2900 — Carnegie Class: Spec-4-yr-Other
FAX Number: (510) 455-7046 — Calendar System: Semester
URL: www.saybrook.edu
Established: 1971 — Annual Graduate Tuition & Fees: N/A
Enrollment: 685 — Coed
Affiliation or Control: Independent Non-Profit — IRS Status: 501(c)3
Highest Offering: Doctorate; No Undergraduates
Accreditation: WC, CACREP

01 President ... Dr. Nathan LONG
05 VP Academics/Student Affs (CAO) ... Dr. Carol R. HUMPHREYS
84 VP Enrollment Mgmt/Chief Enroll Ofc ... Vacant
06 Registrar ... Mr. Thomas CHAMPION
08 Librarian ... Mr. Noah LOWENSTEIN
04 Executive Assistant ... Ms. LaTanya O. HICKS
26 Dir Cmty Engagement/Strateg Partner ... Mr. Anthony MOLINAR
15 Director Business Operations ... Ms. Jolene PRUITT
13 IT Manager ... Mr. Alex SALTZBERG
32 Dean of Students/Chf Stdnt Affs ... Ms. Alexis LEWIS
29 Director Alumni Affairs ... Mr. Anthony MOLINAR

SBBCollege Bakersfield (B)

5300 California Ave, Bakersfield CA 93309-2139
County: Kern — FICE Identification: 025779
Unit ID: 122834
Telephone: (661) 835-1100 — Carnegie Class: Bac/Assoc-Mixed
FAX Number: (661) 835-0242 — Calendar System: Other
URL: www.sbbcollege.edu
Established: 1982 — Annual Undergrad Tuition & Fees: $11,658
Enrollment: 332 — Coed
Affiliation or Control: Proprietary — IRS Status: Proprietary
Highest Offering: Master's
Accreditation: ACICS

01 President ... Matthew JOHNSTON
26 Director of Marketing ... Monica RAYMOND

SBBCollege Rancho Mirage (C)

34275 Monterey Ave, Rancho Mirage CA 92270
Telephone: (760) 341-7602 — Identification: 666582
Accreditation: ACCSC

SBBCollege Santa Maria (D)

303 E Plaza Drive, Santa Maria CA 93454
County: Santa Barbara — FICE Identification: 025780
Unit ID: 122852
Telephone: (805) 922-8256 — Carnegie Class: Bac/Assoc-Mixed
FAX Number: (805) 346-1857 — Calendar System: Other
URL: www.sbbcollege.edu
Established: 1980 — Annual Undergrad Tuition & Fees: $11,658
Enrollment: 78 — Coed
Affiliation or Control: Proprietary — IRS Status: Proprietary
Highest Offering: Baccalaureate
Accreditation: ACICS

01 President ... Matthew JOHNSTON
26 Director of Marketing ... Monica RAYMOND

Scripps College (E)

1030 Columbia, Claremont CA 91711-3948
County: Los Angeles — FICE Identification: 001174
Unit ID: 123165
Telephone: (909) 621-8000 — Carnegie Class: Bac-A&S
FAX Number: (909) 621-8323 — Calendar System: Semester
URL: www.scrippscollege.edu
Established: 1926 — Annual Undergrad Tuition & Fees: $55,024
Enrollment: 1,083 — Female
Affiliation or Control: Independent Non-Profit — IRS Status: 501(c)3
Highest Offering: Baccalaureate
Accreditation: WC

01 President ... Dr. Lara TIEDENS
05 VP Academic Affairs/Dean of Faculty ... Ms. Amy MARCUS-NEWHALL
111 VP for External Rels/Advancement ... Ms. Binti HARVEY
10 VP for Business Affairs/Treasurer ... Mr. Dean CALVO
32 Vice President of Student Affairs ... Ms. Charlotte JOHNSON
07 Vice President for Enrollment ... Ms. Victoria ROMERO
101 VP/Secretary of Board of Trustees ... Ms. Denise NELSON NASH
04 Executive Asst to the President ... Ms. Damaris ROBERTSON LOWE
20 Associate Dean of Faculty ... Ms. Jennifer ARMSTRONG
15 Director of Human Resources ... Ms. Jennifer L. BERKLAS
09 Dir of Assessment/Inst Research ... Ms. Junelyn PEEPLES
08 Librarian ... Ms. Judy B. HARVEY-SAHAK
06 Registrar ... Ms. Kelly HOGENCAMP
37 Director of Financial Aid ... Mr. Patrick MOORE
36 Director of Career Planning ... Ms. Vicki P. KLOPSCH
13 Director of Information Technology ... Mr. Jeff SESSLER
18 Director of Facilities ... Mr. Josh REEDER
104 Director of Off-Campus Study ... Ms. Neva BARKER

The Scripps Research Institute (F)

10550 N Torrey Pines Road, TPC19, La Jolla CA 92037-1000
County: San Diego — FICE Identification: 033213
Unit ID: 435338
Telephone: (858) 784-8469 — Carnegie Class: Not Classified
FAX Number: (858) 784-2802 — Calendar System: Quarter
URL: www.scripps.edu
Established: 1989 — Annual Graduate Tuition & Fees: N/A
Enrollment: N/A — Coed
Affiliation or Control: Independent Non-Profit — IRS Status: 501(c)3
Highest Offering: Doctorate; No Undergraduates
Accreditation: WC

01 President/CEO ... Dr. Peter G. SCHULTZ
03 Exec Vice Pres/Secretary ... Mr. Douglas A. BINGHAM
05 VP Acad Affs/Dean Graduate Studies ... Dr. James R. WILLIAMSON
11 Chief Operating Officer ... Dr. Matthew TREMBLAY
10 Chief Financial Officer/Treasurer ... Mr. Jared MACHADO

Shasta Bible College and Graduate School (G)

2951 Goodwater Avenue, Redding CA 96002-1544
County: Shasta — FICE Identification: 023593
Unit ID: 123280
Telephone: (530) 221-4275 — Carnegie Class: Spec-4-yr-Faith
FAX Number: (530) 221-6929 — Calendar System: Semester
URL: www.shasta.edu
Established: 1972 — Annual Undergrad Tuition & Fees: $12,060
Enrollment: 55 — Coed
Affiliation or Control: Independent Non-Profit — IRS Status: 501(c)3
Highest Offering: Master's
Accreditation: TRACS

01 President/CEO ... Dr. David R. NICHOLAS
04 Exec Assistant to the President ... Ms. Jane DEANGELO
05 Vice President of Academics ... Dr. Stephen G. BROWN
32 Vice President of Student Services ... Mr. George A. GUNN
10 Chief Finance Officer ... Mr. Eric BROWN
49 Dean Undergraduate Studies ... Mrs. Faith MCCARTHY
34 Dean of Women ... Mrs. Donna R. NICHOLAS
18 Director Maintenance ... Mr. Ted RIVERS
06 Registrar ... Mrs. Faith MCCARTHY
37 Director of Financial Aid ... Ms. Linda ILES
08 Head Librarian ... Mrs. Virginia M. WILLIAMS

Shasta College (H)

PO Box 496006, 11555 Old Oregon Tr, Redding CA 96049-6006
County: Shasta — FICE Identification: 001289
Unit ID: 123299
Telephone: (530) 242-7500 — Carnegie Class: Bac/Assoc-Assoc Dom
FAX Number: (530) 225-4990 — Calendar System: Semester
URL: www.shastacollege.edu
Established: 1950 — Annual Undergrad Tuition & Fees (In-District): $1,185
Enrollment: 9,160 — Coed
Affiliation or Control: State/Local — IRS Status: Exempt
Highest Offering: Baccalaureate
Accreditation: WJ, CAHIIM, DH

01 Superintendent/President ... Dr. Joe WYSE
04 Asst to Superintendent/President ... Ms. Andree BLANCHIER
102 Executive Director SC Foundation ... Ms. Eva JIMENEZ
10 Asst Supt/VP of Admin Services ... Mr. Morris RODRIGUE
05 Asst Supt/VP of Instruction ... Dr. Frank NIGRO
32 Asst Supt/VP of Student Services ... Dr. Kevin O'RORKE
103 AVP Economic/Workforce Development ... Ms. Eva JIMENEZ
15 AVP of Human Resources ... Mr. Gregory SMITH
16 Director of Human Resources ... Ms. Amy WESTLUND
84 AVP of SS/Dean Enrollment Services ... Dr. Timothy JOHNSTON
35 Dean Student Services ... Ms. Sandra HAMILTON SLANE
35 Interim Dean of Student Services ... Dr. Zhanjing (John) YU
57 Dean Arts/Communication/Soc Science ... Ms. Stacey BARTLETT
50 Dean Business/Ag/Ind/Tech/Safety ... Mr. Zachary ZWEIGLE
56 Dean Extended Education ... Dr. Andy FIELDS
76 Dean Health Sciences ... Ms. Ioanna IATRIDIS
76 Director Allied Health Programs ... Ms. Carie PALMER
88 Dir Hlth Sci Path/Outrch/Retention ... Vacant
76 Dir Hlth Sci Info Tech & Info Mgmt ... Ms. Janet JANUS
52 Director of Dental Health Programs ... Vacant
62 Dean Library Services/Educ Tech ... Mr. William BREITBACH
51 Dean of Pathways & Learning Support ... Ms. Jennifer MCCANDLESS
68 Dean Phys Education and Athletics ... Mr. Mike MARI
81 Dean Science/Language Arts/Math ... Mr. Carlos REYES
09 Dean Institutional Effectiveness ... Dr. Kate MAHAR
28 Assoc Dean Student Services ... Dr. Sharon BRISOLARA
37 Assoc Dean Student Services ... Ms. Becky MCCALL
21 Comptroller ... Ms. Jill AULT
19 Director of Campus Safety ... Mr. Lonnie SEAY
88 Director of Center of Excellence ... Ms. Sara PHILLIPS
109 Director of Food Services ... Ms. Denise AXTELL
25 Director of Grant Development ... Ms. Amy WEBB
13 Director of Information Technology ... Mr. James CRANDALL
88 Dir of Innovation & Spec Projects ... Ms. Buffy TANNER
26 Director of Marketing and Outreach ... Mr. Peter GRIGGS
18 Director of Physical Plant ... Mr. George ESTRADA
39 Director Residence Life ... Mr. Nick WEBB
32 Dir of Student Life & Title IX Inv ... Ms. Tina DUENAS
88 Director of TRIO ... Ms. Sue HUIZINGA

Sierra College (I)

5100 Sierra College Blvd., Rocklin CA 95677
County: Placer — FICE Identification: 001290
Unit ID: 123341
Telephone: (916) 624-3333 — Carnegie Class: Assoc/MT-VT-High Trad
FAX Number: N/A — Calendar System: Semester
URL: www.sierracollege.edu
Established: 1914 — Annual Undergrad Tuition & Fees (In-District): $1,144
Enrollment: 18,221 — Coed
Affiliation or Control: State/Local — IRS Status: 501(c)3
Highest Offering: Associate Degree
Accreditation: WJ

01 Superintendent/President ... Mr. William H. DUNCAN
05 Supt/Vice President Instruction ... Dr. Rebecca BOCCHICCHIO
10 Vice Pres Administrative Services ... Mr. Erik SKINNER
32 Vice Pres Student Services ... Ms. Mandy DAVIES
04 Exec Assistant Presidents Office ... Ms. Jeannette BISCHOFF
08 Dean Library/Learning Resource Ctr ... Ms. Sabrina PAPE
50 Assoc Dean Business & Technology ... Ms. Darlene JACKSON
81 Dean Science & Mathematics ... Dr. Randy LEHR
49 Dean Liberal Arts ... Dr. Anne FLEISCHMANN
41 Interim Dean Phys Ed/Athletics Dir ... Ms. Rachel JOHNSON
09 Dean Planning/Research/Res Devel ... Mr. Erik COOPER
66 Dean Nursing ... Ms. Nancy JAMES
13 Chief Information Officer ... Mr. Tom BENTON
21 Director of Finance ... Ms. Linda FISHER
15 Director Human Resources ... Mr. Cameron ABBOTT
18 Dir of Facilities & Construction ... Ms. Laura DOTY
37 Director Financial Aid ... Dr. Linda WILLIAMS
31 Community Education Pgm Manager ... Ms. Jill ALCORN
22 EEO Program Manager ... Ms. LaToya JACKSON
26 Manager Marketing/Public Relations ... Vacant
39 Residence Life Supervisor ... Ms. Cortney MAGORIAN
07 Director of Admissions & Records ... Ms. Gail MODDER

Sierra States University (J)

1818 S. Western Ave #304, Los Angeles CA 90006
County: Los Angeles — Identification: 667325
Telephone: (323) 641-7009 — Carnegie Class: Not Classified
FAX Number: (323) 641-7035 — Calendar System: Quarter
URL: sierrastates.edu
Established: 2002 — Annual Undergrad Tuition & Fees: N/A
Enrollment: N/A — Coed
Affiliation or Control: Independent Non-Profit — IRS Status: 501(c)3
Highest Offering: Doctorate
Accreditation: TRACS

01 President ... Dr. P. KWON

Simpson University (K)

2211 College View Drive, Redding CA 96003-8606
County: Shasta — FICE Identification: 001291
Unit ID: 123457
Telephone: (530) 224-5600 — Carnegie Class: Masters/S
FAX Number: (530) 226-4860 — Calendar System: Semester
URL: www.simpsonu.edu
Established: 1921 — Annual Undergrad Tuition & Fees: $30,200
Enrollment: 903 — Coed
Affiliation or Control: The Christian And Missionary Alliance — IRS Status: 501(c)3
Highest Offering: Master's
Accreditation: WC, NURSE

01 President ... Dr. Norman D. HALL
11 Acting Chief Operating Officer ... Mr. Walter QUIRK
05 Provost ... Dr. Dale SIMMONS
10 Chief Financial Officer ... Mr. Tim DIETZ
88 Faculty President ... Dr. Dan S. PINKSTON
84 Dean of Admissions ... Mr. Randy COMFORT
88 Director of Admissions Data & Comm ... Vacant
73 Dean AW Tozer Seminary ... Dr. Patrick A. BLEWETT
53 Dean School of Education ... Ms. Irene LOPEZ
66 Dean School of Nursing ... Mrs. Kristie D. STEPHENS

107 Dean of Adult & Graduate Prof Stds ... Ms. Wendy SMITH
88 Director of Veterans Success Center ... Mr. Justin R. SPEARS
13 Director of IT ... Vacant
41 Director of Athletics ... Mr. Thomas J. GALBRAITH
32 Dean of Students/Title IX Coord ... Mr. Mark C. ENDRASKE
38 Director of Wellness Center ... Ms. Beverly G. KLAIBER
15 Director of Human Resources ... Ms. Holly CLARK
109 Director of Campus Operations ... Mr. Paul R. DAVIS
121 Director of Academic Success Center ... Mr. Louis E. BURKWHAT
35 Director of Student Engagement ... Ms. Isis C. MARTIN
08 Interim Director of Library Service ... Mr. Eric WHEELER
21 Controller ... Mr. Jared GRECO
06 Registrar ... Ms. Addie JACKSON
04 Exec Assistant to the President ... Mrs. Regina ERICKSON
19 Campus Safety Operations Coord ... Mr. Dennis SMITH
40 Bookstore Manager ... Vacant

Sofia University (A)

1069 E Meadow Circle, Palo Alto CA 94303-4231
County: Santa Clara FICE Identification: 022676
Unit ID: 110778
Telephone: (888) 820-1484 Carnegie Class: Spec-4-yr-Other Health
FAX Number: (650) 493-6835 Calendar System: Quarter
URL: www.sofia.edu
Established: 1975 Annual Undergrad Tuition & Fees: N/A
Enrollment: 345 Coed
Affiliation or Control: Proprietary IRS Status: Proprietary
Highest Offering: Doctorate
Accreditation: WC

01 President & CEO ... Dr. Barry T. RYAN
05 Provost & CAO ... Dr. Stuart SIGMAN
10 Interim CFO ... Mr. Bill CHEN
88 VP of International ... Mrs. Arti Patel MARTINEZ
26 VP Marketing and Enrollment ... Ms. Lillian GONZALEZ
32 Dean Student Services ... Ms. Rosalie COOK
15 Human Resources Director ... Ms. Aida SMAILAGIC
37 Director of Compliance & Finance ... Mr. Brandon HUINER
04 Executive Assistant to President ... Mrs. Renate KROGDAHL

† Formerly Institute of Transpersonal Psychology.

Soka University of America (B)

1 University Drive, Aliso Viejo CA 92656-8081
County: Orange FICE Identification: 038144
Unit ID: 399911
Telephone: (949) 480-4000 Carnegie Class: Bac-A&S
FAX Number: (949) 480-4001 Calendar System: Semester
URL: www.soka.edu
Established: 2001 Annual Undergrad Tuition & Fees: $33,146
Enrollment: 427 Coed
Affiliation or Control: Independent Non-Profit IRS Status: 501(c)3
Highest Offering: Master's
Accreditation: WC

01 President/Professor of Economics ... Dr. Daniel Y. HABUKI
101 Exec Asst to President/Board Sec ... Mr. Hiro SAKAI
05 Vice Pres Academic Affairs/CAO ... Dr. Edward M. FEASEL
10 Vice President Finance & Admin/CFO ... Mr. Archibald E. ASAWA
09 VP Inst Rsch/Dean of Graduate Sch ... Dr. Tomoko TAKAHASHI
15 Vice Pres of Human Resources ... Ms. Katherine KING
20 Dean of Faculty/CAO ... Dr. Bryan E. PENPRASE
84 Dean of Enrollment Services ... Mr. Andrew WOOLSEY
32 Dean of Students ... Dr. Hyon J. MOON
11 Chief of Operations ... Mr. Tom HARKENRIDER
19 Director Safety/Security ... Mr. Craig LEE
31 Director of Community Relations ... Ms. Wendy WETZEL HARDER
41 Director of Athletics & Recreation ... Mr. Mike MOORE
35 Director of Student Services ... Mr. Brian DURICK
39 Dir Stdnt Activities/Resident Life ... Ms. Michelle HOBBY-MEARS
30 Director of Philanthropy ... Ms. Linda KENNEDY
13 Director Information Technology ... Mr. John MIN
44 Dir of International Development ... Ms. Toshiko SATO
104 Dir Study Abroad & Intl Internships ... Mr. Alex H. OKUDA
06 Registrar ... Ms. Nancy YOSHIMURA
08 Director of Library ... Mr. Hiroko TONONO

Solano Community College (C)

4000 Suisun Valley Road, Fairfield CA 94534-3197
County: Solano FICE Identification: 001292
Unit ID: 123563
Telephone: (707) 864-7000 Carnegie Class: Bac/Assoc-Assoc Dom
FAX Number: (707) 864-0361 Calendar System: Semester
URL: www.solano.edu
Established: 1945 Annual Undergrad Tuition & Fees (In-District): $1,140
Enrollment: 9,625 Coed
Affiliation or Control: State/Local IRS Status: 501(c)3
Highest Offering: Associate Degree
Accreditation: WJ

01 Superintendent/President ... Dr. Celia ESPOSITO-NOY
05 VP Academic Affairs ... Dr. David WILLIAMS
10 Vice President Finance & Admin ... Mr. Robert DIAMOND
13 Interim Chief Technology Officer ... Mr. James (Kimo) CALILAN
32 Vice President Student Services ... Vacant
38 Dean Counseling/Special Services ... Dr. Kristin CONNER
37 Director Financial Aid ... Vacant
09 Dean Research and Planning ... Vacant
15 Human Resources Manager ... Mr. Salavatore ABBATE
18 Director Facilities ... Vacant
88 Director Children's Programs ... Ms. Christie SPECK
103 Assoc Dean Workforce Development ... Vacant
26 Outreach/Public Relations Manager ... Vacant
96 Purchasing Tech/Buyer ... Ms. Laura SCOTT
36 Career & Job Placement Coordinator ... Ms. Patricia YOUNG
49 Dean School of Liberal Arts ... Mr. Neil GLINES
83 Dean Sch of Social/Behav Science ... Dr. Sandy LAMBA
81 Dean School Math/Science ... Mr. Joseph RYAN
76 Dn Sch Career Tech Ed/Bus/Vcvl/TAFB ... Mrs. Maire MORINEC
12 Center Dean Vallejo ... Dr. Shirley LEWIS
76 Interim Dean Health Sciences ... Dr. Dan BRIDGES
41 Director of Athletics ... Mr. Erik VISSER

South Baylo University (D)

1126 N Brookhurst Street, Anaheim CA 92801-1702
County: Orange FICE Identification: 025973
Unit ID: 123633
Telephone: (714) 533-1495 Carnegie Class: Spec-4-yr-Other Health
FAX Number: (714) 533-6040 Calendar System: Quarter
URL: www.southbaylo.edu
Established: 1977 Annual Undergrad Tuition & Fees: N/A
Enrollment: 522 Coed
Affiliation or Control: Independent Non-Profit IRS Status: 501(c)3
Highest Offering: Doctorate
Accreditation: ACUP

01 President ... Dr. Edwin FOLLICK
03 Vice President ... Dr. Jennifer PARK
05 Academic Dean ... Dr. Pia MELEN
07 Director of Admission ... Ms. Seon KIM
06 Registrar ... Dr. Woo Jin HAN
10 Director of Finance ... Ms. Michelle JANG
15 Personnel Director ... Ms. Yukari NISHIOKA
36 Program Student Advisor ... Dr. Henry CHOI
08 University Librarian ... Dr. Vanja ANDERSON
13 Dir Computer Information System ... Mr. James KIM
88 Director of Clinics ... Dr. Sandjaya TRI
37 Financial Aid Officer ... Ms. Mimi PARK
32 Student/Alumni Coordinator ... Ms. Alyona CARRICO
85 International Student Advisor ... Dr. Woo Jin HAN
88 Doctoral Clerkship Coordinator ... Dr. Anne AHN
88 Doctoral Program Director ... Dr. Soo KIM
88 Master Program Director ... Dr. Hyo Jeong KANG
18 Chief Facilities/Physical Plant ... Mr. Yong Hee PARK
38 CCE Coordinator ... Dr. Sung Hoon YOON
88 Compliance Officer ... Dr. Rhiannon KRONE

*South Orange County Community College District (E)

28000 Marguerite Parkway, Mission Viejo CA 92692-3697
County: Orange FICE Identification: 033433
Unit ID: 432144
Telephone: (949) 582-4850 Carnegie Class: N/A
FAX Number: (949) 364-2726
URL: www.socccd.edu

01 Chancellor ... Dr. Kathleen F. BURKE
05 Vice Chanc Technology/Learning Svcs ... Dr. Robert S. BRAMUCCI
15 Vice Chancellor Human Resources ... Ms. Cindy VYSKOCIL
10 Vice Chancellor Business Svcs ... Ms. Ann-Marie GABEL
26 Dir Public Affairs/Govt Relations ... Ms. Letitia CLARK
12 President Saddleback College ... Dr. Elliot STERN
12 President Irvine Valley College ... Dr. Glenn ROQUEMORE

*Irvine Valley College (F)

5500 Irvine Center Drive, Irvine CA 92618-4399
County: Orange FICE Identification: 025395
Unit ID: 116439
Telephone: (949) 451-5100 Carnegie Class: Assoc/HT-Mix Trad/Non
FAX Number: (949) 451-5270 Calendar System: Semester
URL: www.ivc.edu
Established: 1979 Annual Undergrad Tuition & Fees (In-District): $1,142
Enrollment: 13,395 Coed
Affiliation or Control: State/Local IRS Status: 501(c)3
Highest Offering: Associate Degree
Accreditation: WJ

02 President ... Dr. Glenn R. ROQUEMORE
100 Manager Office of the President ... Ms. Sandy JEFFRIES
05 Vice President Instruction ... Dr. Christopher MCDONALD
32 Vice President Student Services ... Dr. Linda FONTANILLA
11 Vice President Admin Services ... Mr. Davit KHACHATRYAN
26 Exec Dir Marketing/Creative Svcs ... Ms. Diane G. OAKS
102 Exec Director College Foundation ... Ms. Elissa ORANSKY
41 Dean Kinesiology/Health/Athletics ... Mr. Keith SHACKLEFORD
83 Dean Social & Behavioral Sciences ... Ms. Traci FAHIMI
38 Dean Counseling Services ... Dr. Elizabeth CIPRES
09 Dir Research/Planning/Accreditation ... Dr. Loris FAGIOLI
19 Chief of Police ... Mr. John MEYER
79 Interim Dean Liberal Arts ... Dr. Brooke CHOO
103 Int Dean Econ/Workforce Dev ... Ms. Debbie VANSCHOELANDT
81 Dean Math/Sciences and Engr ... Dr. Lianna ZHAO
57 Dean The Arts ... Mr. Joseph POSHEK
84 Dean of Enrollment Services ... Mr. Corey RODGERS
23 Asst Dean Health/Wellness/Vet Svcs ... Ms. Nancy MONTGOMERY
37 Asst Dean Financial Aid/Student Sup ... Mr. Ken LIRA
85 Dir International Student Programs ... Ms. Christina DELGADO
18 Director IVC Facilities ... Mr. Jeffrey HURLBUT
44 Director Annual Giving/Devel Svcs ... Ms. Karen ORLANDO
35 Director Student Life & Equity ... Ms. Anissa HEARD
121 Director Student Success/Support ... Mr. Deejay SANTIAGO
13 Director Technology Services ... Mr. Bruce HAGAN
06 Registrar/Admissions/Records ... Mr. Ruben GUZMAN
88 Director Arts Production Management ... Mr. Patric TAYLOR

*Saddleback College (G)

28000 Marguerite Parkway, Mission Viejo CA 92692-3635
County: Orange FICE Identification: 008918
Unit ID: 122205
Telephone: (949) 582-4500 Carnegie Class: Assoc/HT-Mix Trad/Non
FAX Number: (949) 347-0438 Calendar System: Semester
URL: www.saddleback.edu
Established: 1968 Annual Undergrad Tuition & Fees (In-District): $1,328
Enrollment: 19,783 Coed
Affiliation or Control: State/Local IRS Status: 501(c)3
Highest Offering: Associate Degree
Accreditation: WJ, ADNUR, CAHIIM, EMT

02 President ... Dr. Elliot STERN
05 Vice President of Instruction ... Ms. Tram VO-KUMAMOTO
10 Vice Pres Administrative Svcs ... Mr. Cory WATHEN
32 Vice President of Student Services ... Dr. Juan AVALOS
100 Manager Office of the President ... Mr. Ryan BROOK
45 Director Planning/Research/Accred ... Ms. Jennifer KLEIN
06 Registrar ... Dr. James M. FEIGERT
84 Dean of Enrollment Services ... Mr. Christian ALVARADO
19 Chief Of Police ... Mr. Pat HIGA
26 Dir Marketing/Communications ... Ms. Jennie MCCUE
124 Director Outreach and Recruitment ... Ms. Lesley HUMPHREY
102 Exec Dir College Foundation ... Ms. Elizabeth MCCANN
35 Director Student Life ... Mr. Christopher HARGRAVES
20 Asst VP Cmty Ed/Emeritus & K-12 ... Dr. Karima FELDHUS
88 Assistant Dean Emeritus Institute ... Mr. Dan PREDOEHL
44 Director Annual/Planned Giving ... Ms. Erin MCHENRY
66 Director of Nursing ... Ms. Dee OLIVERI
15 Vice Chancellor of Human Resources ... Ms. Cindy VYSKOCIL
18 Dir Facilities/Maint/Operation ... Mr. James ROGERS
23 Director Student Health Center ... Dr. Jeanne HARRIS-CALDWELL
13 Director Technology Services ... Dr. Anthony MACIEL
37 Director Financial Assistance ... Ms. Amber GALLAGHER
96 Director of Purchasing ... Ms. Brandye D'LENA
85 Director of Intl Student Program ... Ms. Angela YANG
92 Honors Program ... Ms. Alannah ROSENBERG
38 Dean Counseling Svcs/Special Pgms ... Ms. Penny SKAFF
57 Dean Fine Arts ... Dr. Cadence WYNTER
50 Dean Bus Science/Econ/Workforce Dev ... Dr. John JARAMILLO
76 Dean Health Sciences/Human Svcs ... Dr. Diane PESTOLESI
81 Dean Math/Science & Engineering ... Dr. Akira NITTA
79 Dean Liberal Arts/Learning Res ... Dr. Kevin O'CONNOR
106 Dean Online Education/Learning Res ... Dr. Marina AMINY
72 Dean Advanced Tech Appl Science ... Dr. Anthony TENG
68 Dean Kinesiology/Athletic Director ... Mr. Daniel CLAUSS
83 Int Dean Social/Behavioral Sciences ... Dr. Christina HINKLE
121 Director Learning Assistance ... Dr. Kim D'ARCY
22 Dean Student Equity & Spec Programs ... Dr. Georgina GUY
103 Dir Economic/Workforce Development ... Mr. Israel DOMINGUEZ
25 Director Fiscal Contract Services ... Ms. Roxanne METZ

Southern California Institute of Architecture (H)

960 E 3rd Street, Los Angeles CA 90013-1822
County: Los Angeles FICE Identification: 020758
Unit ID: 123952
Telephone: (213) 613-2200 Carnegie Class: Spec-4-yr-Arts
FAX Number: (213) 613-2260 Calendar System: Semester
URL: www.sciarc.edu
Established: 1972 Annual Undergrad Tuition & Fees: $44,960
Enrollment: 514 Coed
Affiliation or Control: Independent Non-Profit IRS Status: 501(c)3
Highest Offering: Master's
Accreditation: WC

01 Director ... Mr. Herman DIAZ ALONSO
05 Vice Director/Chief Academic Ofcr ... Mr. John ENRIGHT
10 Chief Financial Officer ... Ms. Sue GOSNEY
11 Chief Administration Officer ... Mr. Paul HOLLIDAY
13 Chief Information Officer ... Mr. Vic JABRASSIAN
111 Chief Advancement Officer ... Ms. Kate O'NEAL
30 Assoc Director Development ... Vacant
58 Graduate Program Chair ... Ms. Elena MANFERDINI
88 Undergraduate Program Chair ... Mr. Tom WISCOMBE
04 Executive Assistant to Director ... Ms. Yasil NAVARRO
07 Admissions Director ... Mr. Angel MONTES
06 Registrar/International Advisor ... Ms. Lisa RUSSO
37 Financial Aid Manager ... Ms. Marisela DE LA TORRE
08 Library Manager ... Mr. Kevin MCMAHON
88 Wood & Metal Shop Manager ... Mr. Rodney ROJAS
18 Facilities Director ... Mr. Peter ZYCHOWSKI
20 Academic Affairs Coordinator ... Ms. Andrea YOUNG
19 Security Manager ... Mr. Reginald BENSON

Southern California Institute of Technology (I)

525 North Muller Street, Anaheim CA 92801-5454
County: Orange FICE Identification: 031136
Unit ID: 399869
Telephone: (714) 300-0300 Carnegie Class: Spec-4-yr-Eng
FAX Number: (714) 300-0311 Calendar System: Quarter

URL: www.scitech.edu
Established: 1987 Annual Undergrad Tuition & Fees: $18,390
Enrollment: 583 Coed
Affiliation or Control: Proprietary IRS Status: Proprietary
Highest Offering: Baccalaureate
Accreditation: ACCSC

01 President .... Dr. Parviz SHAMS
03 Vice President .... Mrs. Nazila SHAMS
11 Director of Operations .... Mr. Arian SHAMS

Southern California Seminary (A)

2075 E Madison Avenue, El Cajon CA 92019-1108
County: San Diego FICE Identification: 033323
Unit ID: 117575
Telephone: (619) 201-8999 Carnegie Class: Spec-4-yr-Faith
FAX Number: (619) 201-8975 Calendar System: Trimester
URL: www.socalsem.edu
Established: 1946 Annual Undergrad Tuition & Fees: $17,540
Enrollment: 206 Coed
Affiliation or Control: Independent Non-Profit IRS Status: 501(c)3
Highest Offering: Doctorate
Accreditation: TRACS

00 Chancellor .... Dr. David JEREMIAH
01 President .... Dr. Gary F. COOMBS
05 Provost & Chief Academic Officer .... Dr. Gino PASQUARIELLO
83 Dean Grad Sch Behavioral Science .... Dr. Elizabeth ELENWO
73 Dean of Biblical Studies/Theology .... Mr. James I. FAZIO
06 Registrar .... Mr. Brian BARGA
32 Director of Student Services .... Mrs. Jillian HINES
37 Director of Financial Aid .... Mrs. Yuli MARTINEZ
08 Library Director .... Miss Jennifer EWING
07 Dean of Admissions Services .... Dr. Bob FREIBERG
06 Dean of Online Learning .... Dr. Joseph R. MILLER

Southern California State University (B)

3470 Wilshire Blvd, Ste 380, Los Angeles CA 90010
County: Los Angeles Identification: 667374
Telephone: (213) 382-5300 Carnegie Class: Not Classified
FAX Number: (213) 403-5636 Calendar System: Quarter
URL: www.scus.us
Established: 2012 Annual Undergrad Tuition & Fees: N/A
Enrollment: N/A Coed
Affiliation or Control: Independent Non-Profit IRS Status: 501(c)3
Highest Offering: Master's
Accreditation: @TRACS

Southern California University of Health Sciences (C)

16200 E Amber Valley Drive, Whittier CA 90604-4051
County: Los Angeles FICE Identification: 001229
Unit ID: 117672
Telephone: (562) 947-8755 Carnegie Class: Spec-4-yr-Other Health
FAX Number: (562) 947-5724 Calendar System: Trimester
URL: www.scuhs.edu
Established: 1911 Annual Undergrad Tuition & Fees: $7,000
Enrollment: 1,096 Coed
Affiliation or Control: Independent Non-Profit IRS Status: 501(c)3
Highest Offering: First Professional Degree
Accreditation: WC, ACUP, #ARCPA, CHIRO

01 President .... Dr. John SCARINGE
100 Chief of Staff/VP Operations .... Mr. Chuck SWEET
10 VP Finance/CFO .... Mr. Thomas K. ARENDT
17 VP SCU Health Sys/Chief Clin Ofcr .... Dr. Melissa NAGARE
05 Provost/Chief Academic Officer .... Dr. Tamara ROZHON
13 Chief Information Officer/VP IT .... Mr. Brendan MAAS
107 Asst VP School of Prof Studies .... Vacant
37 Director of Financial Aid .... Mrs. Nina MARTINEZ
06 Registrar .... Ms. Kate MCCUNE
88 Dean LA College of Chiropractic .... Dr. Jonathon EGAN
88 Dean College of Eastern Med .... Dr. Jenny YU
09 Dean Office Inst Effectiveness .... Dr. Taiwo ANDE
21 Asst VP for Accounting .... Mrs. Kelly GALLO
109 Asst VP Auxiliary Services .... Mr. Joseph EGGLESTON
08 Exec Dir of Seabury Learning Center .... Ms. Kathleen E. SMITH
15 Human Resources/Payroll Specialist .... Mrs. Cindy SCHEIBEL
29 Director Alumni Relations .... Mrs. Elizabeth ROBLEDO
18 Director of Physical Plant .... Mr. Bob HARRISON
88 Assistant Controller .... Mrs. Christine HUYNH
04 Exec Asst to President/BOR .... Mrs. Regina TORRES-ELLIS
121 Director Academic Support Office .... Ms. Samaneh SADRI
26 Executive Director Marketing .... Mr. Jim BRENNER

Southern States University (D)

2855 Michelle Drive, Irvine CA 92606
Telephone: (949) 833-8868 Identification: 770629
Accreditation: ACICS

Southern States University (E)

1094 Cudahy Place, Suite 120, San Diego CA 92110
County: San Diego Identification: 667108
Unit ID: 490063
Telephone: (619) 298-1829 Carnegie Class: Spec-4-yr-Bus
FAX Number: (619) 704-0175 Calendar System: Quarter

URL: www.ssu.edu
Established: 1985 Annual Undergrad Tuition & Fees: $5,409
Enrollment: 137 Coed
Affiliation or Control: Proprietary IRS Status: Proprietary
Highest Offering: Master's
Accreditation: ACICS

01 Chancellor .... John D. TUCKER
05 Chief Academic Officer .... Charlotte HISLOP
06 Univ Registrar/Compliance Officer .... Wendy DU
08 University Librarian .... Cheryl CYR
37 Financial Aid/Human Resources Mgr .... Denise MASTRO

Southwestern College (F)

900 Otay Lakes Road, Chula Vista CA 91910-7299
County: San Diego FICE Identification: 001294
Unit ID: 123800
Telephone: (619) 421-6700 Carnegie Class: Assoc/HT-High Trad
FAX Number: (619) 482-6413 Calendar System: Semester
URL: www.swccd.edu
Established: 1961 Annual Undergrad Tuition & Fees (In-District): $1,338
Enrollment: 18,413 Coed
Affiliation or Control: State/Local IRS Status: 501(c)3
Highest Offering: Associate Degree
Accreditation: WJ, ADNUR, DH, EMT, MLTAD, SURGT

01 Superintendent/President .... Dr. Kindred MURILLO
05 Interim VP Academic Affairs .... Dr. Renee KILMER
10 VP Business & Financial Affairs .... Mr. Tim FLOOD
32 VP Student Affairs .... Dr. Angelica SUAREZ
12 Dn High Ed Ctr Otay Mesa/San Ysidro .... Ms. Silvia CORNEJO
12 Dn High Ed Ctr Natl City/Crown Cove .... Ms. Christine PERRI
79 Dean Language & Literature .... Dr. Joel LEVINE
81 Dean Math/Science Engineering .... Dr. Michael ODU
68 Dean Wellness/Ex Sci/Athletics .... Mr. James SPILLERS
50 Dean Business & Technology .... Dr. Mink STAVENGA
57 Dean School of Arts/Comm and SS .... Dr. Cynthia MCGREGOR
108 Dean Inst Effect/Dir of Foundation .... Ms. Linda GILSTRAP
08 Dean Inst Support Services/Library .... Ms. Mia C. MCCLELLAN
38 Dean Couns/Student Support Pgms .... Dr. Jonathan KING
26 Chief Public Info/Govt Relations .... Ms. Lillian LEOPOLD
15 Acting VP for Human Resources .... Dr. Robert UNGER
88 Director Payroll Services .... Ms. Janet TAYLOR
88 Dir Center Ops San Ysidro .... Ms. Cynthia K. NAGURA
88 Director Crown Cove Aq Ctr .... Ms. Patrice MILKOVICH
37 Director Financial Aid/Veterans .... Ms. Patti LARKIN
07 Director Admissions/Records .... Mr. Nicholas MONTEZ
35 Dean Student Services .... Dr. Malia FLOOD
88 Director EOPS .... Mr. Omar ORIHUELA
88 Director Child Development Center .... Ms. Patricia BARTOW
04 Exec Asst to Superintendent .... Ms. Mary GANIO
19 Acting Police Chief .... Mr. Davis NIGHSWONGER
13 Chief Info Technology Officer (CIO) .... Mr. Daniel BORGES
28 Director Equity/Inclusion/Diversi .... Dr. Guadalupe CORONA
102 Director Foundation .... Ms. Zaneta ENCARNACION
88 Director Student Development .... Mr. Brett ROBERTSON
88 Director of Police Academy .... Mr. David ESPIRITU
103 Dean Workforce Development .... Ms. Jennifer LEWIS
88 Director EMT & Fire Science .... Mr. Devin PRICE
52 Director Dental Hygiene .... Ms. Jean HONNY
66 Director Nursing & Health Occup .... Dr. Geoffrey SCHRODER
88 Director MEDOPS .... Ms. Deanna REINACHER
88 Director Title V .... Ms. Martha GARCIA
16 Acting Director for Human Resources .... Cynthia CARRENO
51 Acting Director Cont Education .... Ms. Myesha JACKSON
88 Director DSS .... Ms. Patricia FLORES CHARTER
88 Regional Director SD SBDC Network .... Ms. Marquise JACKSON

Southwestern Law School (G)

3050 Wilshire Boulevard, Los Angeles CA 90010-1106
County: Los Angeles FICE Identification: 001295
Unit ID: 123970
Telephone: (213) 738-6700 Carnegie Class: Spec-4-yr-Law
FAX Number: (213) 383-1688 Calendar System: Semester
URL: www.swlaw.edu
Established: 1911 Annual Graduate Tuition & Fees: N/A
Enrollment: 784 Coed
Affiliation or Control: Independent Non-Profit IRS Status: 501(c)3
Highest Offering: Master's; No Undergraduates
Accreditation: LAW

01 Chief Executive Officer .... Ms. Susan WESTERBERG PRAGER
05 EVP & Chief Academic Officer .... Mr. Michael CARTER
10 Chief Financial Officer .... Ms. Linda ROSS
13 Chief Information Officer .... Mr. Sean MURPHY
26 Chief Comm & Marketing Officer .... Ms. Hillary KANE
20 Vice Dean .... Mr. Dov WAISMAN
04 Executive Assistant to the Dean .... Ms. Janis K. YOKOYAMA
20 Sr Assoc Dean for Academic Admin .... Ms. Doreen E. HEYER
32 Assoc Dean of Student Affairs .... Dr. Robert MENA
28 Assoc Dean of Students .... Ms. Nydia DUEÑEZ
111 Assoc Dean for Institutional Advanc .... Ms. Debra L. LEATHERS
36 Assoc Dean of Career Services .... Ms. Shahrzad POORMOSLEH
08 Assoc Dean of Library Services .... Ms. Linda WHISMAN
11 Assoc Dean of Operations & Risk .... Ms. Marcie CANAL
09 Assoc Dean for Research .... Ms. Hila KEREN
88 Assoc Dean for SCALE .... Ms. Harriet M. ROLNICK
46 Assoc Dean Strategic Initiatives .... Mr. Byron G. STIER
88 Assoc Dean Experiential Learning .... Ms. Julie K. WATERSTONE
61 Asst Dean of Bar Preparation .... Ms. Mary BASICK
121 Asst Dean of Academic Success .... Ms. Natalie RODRIGUEZ
07 Asst Dean of Admissions .... Ms. Lisa L. GEAR
37 Director of Financial Aid .... Ms. Lina BORJORQUEZ
88 Director of Externship Program .... Ms. Anahid GHARAKANIAN
88 Director of Immigration Law Clinic .... Ms. Andrea RAMOS
88 Director of Bar Preparation .... Ms. Tina SCHINDLER
88 Director of Legal Analysis/Writing .... Ms. Tracy TURNER
88 Director Biederman Ent & Media Law .... Ms. Orly RAVID
92 Co-Director of Moot Court Honors .... Ms. Catherine CARPENTER
92 Co-Director of Moot Court Honors .... Ms. Alexandra D'ITALIA
92 Co-Director of Trial Ad Honors .... Mr. Joseph P. ESPOSITO
92 Co-Director of Trial Ad Honors .... Mr. Bill H. SEKI
92 Co-Director of Negotiation Honors .... Ms. Cristina C. KNOLTON
06 Interim Director of Registration .... Ms. Alma PAZ
39 Property Manager of Residences .... Ms. Michelle TAFOYA

Spartan College of Aeronautics and Technology (H)

8911 Aviation Blvd, Inglewood CA 90301
County: Los Angeles FICE Identification: 025964
Unit ID: 413680
Telephone: (310) 879-0554 Carnegie Class: Spec 2-yr-Tech
FAX Number: N/A Calendar System: Other
URL: www.spartan.edu
Established: 2014 Annual Undergrad Tuition & Fees: N/A
Enrollment: 471 Coed
Affiliation or Control: Proprietary IRS Status: Proprietary
Highest Offering: Associate Degree
Accreditation: COE

01 President .... Mr. Rick MENDOZA

Stanbridge University (I)

2041 Business Center Dr., Suite 107, Irvine CA 92612
County: Orange FICE Identification: 038893
Unit ID: 446561
Telephone: (949) 794-9090 Carnegie Class: Spec-4-yr-Other Health
FAX Number: (949) 794-9098 Calendar System: Other
URL: www.stanbridge.edu
Established: 1996 Annual Undergrad Tuition & Fees: N/A
Enrollment: 1,331 Coed
Affiliation or Control: Proprietary IRS Status: Proprietary
Highest Offering: Master's
Accreditation: ACCSC, NURSE, OT, OTA, PTAA

01 Chief Executive Officer .... Mr. Yasith WEERASURIYA
10 Chief Financial Officer .... Ms. Nazi MASOUM
05 Vice Pres of Instruction .... Dr. Kelly HAMILTON
105 Exec VP Internet & Media Technology .... Mr. Monir BOKTOR
66 Director of VN Program .... Ms. Renee HYPOLITE
66 Director of RN Program .... Ms. Tracy FRYE
66 Director of BSN & MSN Program .... Dr. Margaret SANTANDREA
76 Director of OTA Program .... Mr. Satch PURCELL
76 Interim Director of OT Program .... Dr. Mark PETERSEN
76 Director of PTA Program .... Dr. Christie KARLE
32 Dean of Students .... Ms. Elizabeth PEYTON
37 Director of Financial Aid .... Mr. Brian SILVANO
07 Director of Admissions .... Mr. Greg LOW
74 Int Director of ASVT .... Ms. Emma CUSACK
88 Asst Program Director ASVT .... Ms. Kristin ILARDI
08 Librarian .... Dr. David BROWN
36 Director of Career Services .... Mr. John ANDREWS

Stanford University (J)

450 Serra Mall, Stanford CA 94305-2004
County: Santa Clara FICE Identification: 001305
Unit ID: 243744
Telephone: (650) 723-2300 Carnegie Class: DU-Highest
FAX Number: (650) 725-6847 Calendar System: Quarter
URL: www.stanford.edu
Established: 1885 Annual Undergrad Tuition & Fees: $51,354
Enrollment: 17,534 Coed
Affiliation or Control: Independent Non-Profit IRS Status: 501(c)3
Highest Offering: Doctorate
Accreditation: WC, ARCPA, IPSY, LAW, MED, PDPSY

01 President .... Dr. Marc TESSIER-LAVIGNE
43 Vice President & General Counsel .... Ms. Debra L. ZUMWALT
05 Provost .... Dr. Persis DRELL
26 VP/Chief External Relations Ofcr .... Mr. Martin SHELL
10 Vice President Business Affairs/CFO .... Mr. Randy LIVINGSTON
30 Vice Pres for Development .... Mr. Jon DENNEY
86 Int Vice Pres for Public Affairs .... Mr. Martin SHELL
88 Vice Pres SLAC Natl Accel Lab .... Dr. William J. MADIA
15 Vice President for Human Resources .... Ms. Elizabeth ZACHARIAS
27 Vice President for Communications .... Ms. Farnaz KHADEM
29 President of Alumni Association .... Mr. Howard E. WOLF
46 Vice Provost/Dean of Research .... Dr. Kathryn A. MOLER
20 Vice Provost for Academic Affairs .... Dr. Stephanie KALFAYAN
88 Vice Provost Faculty Development .... Ms. Karen COOK
20 Senior Vice Provost for Education .... Mr. Harry J. ELAM
18 Vice President for Land & Buildings .... Mr. Robert C. REIDY
114 Vice Provost Budget & Auxiliaries .... Mr. Timothy R. WARNER
32 Vice Provost Student Affairs .... Ms. Susie BRUBAKER-COLE
100 Chief of Staff .... Ms. Megan PIERSON
106 Int Vice Prov Teaching & Learning .... Mr. Michael KELLER
63 Dean School of Medicine .... Dr. Lloyd MINOR
50 Dean Graduate School Business .... Dr. Jonathan LEVIN

65 Dean School of Earth Sciences ... Dr. Stephen GRAHAM
53 Dean School of Education ... Dr. Daniel SCHWARTZ
54 Dean School of Engineering ... Dr. Jennifer WIDOM
49 Dean School Humanities & Sciences ... Dr. Debra SATZ
61 Dean School of Law ... Ms. Jenny S. MARTINEZ
87 Dean Summer Session/Cont Stds ... Dr. Charles L. JUNKERMAN
42 Dean for Religious Life ... Vacant
88 Director Hoover Institution ... Dr. Thomas GILLIGAN
88 Director Stanford Lin Accelerator ... Mr. Chi-Chang KAO
13 Executive Director IT Services ... Mr. Bill CLEBSCH
08 University Librarian ... Mr. Michael A. KELLER
41 Athletic Director ... Mr. Bernard MUIR
07 Dean of Admission and Financial Aid ... Mr. Richard SHAW
88 CEO Stanford Management Company ... Mr. Robert WALLACE
118 Director of Compensation ... Ms. Linda S. LEE
21 AVP of Business Development ... Ms. Susan L. WEINSTEIN
06 Registrar ... Mr. Thomas BLACK
36 Director Career Development Center ... Mr. Farouk DEY
09 Dir Inst Research/Assessment ... Ms. Corrie POTTER
37 Director of Student Financial Aid ... Ms. Karen S. COOPER
27 Sr Director Stanford News Service ... Ms. Donna LOVELL
19 Director Public Safety ... Ms. Laura L. WILSON
96 Chief Procurement Officer ... Mr. Ben MORENO
35 Director of Student Activities ... Ms. Nanci HOWE
38 Director Student Counseling ... Dr. Ronald ALBURCHER
101 Secretary of the Board of Trustees ... Mr. Phil TAUBMAN
102 Dir Foundation/Corporate Relations ... Ms. Kathy VEIT
104 Director Study Abroad ... Ms. Irene KENNEDY
39 Director Student Housing ... Mr. Roger WHITNEY
88 Director Knight-Hennessy Scholars ... Dr. John L. HENNESSY

Stanton University (A)

9618 Garden Grove Blvd., Ste 201,
Garden Grove CA 92844

County: Orange — Identification: 667370
Telephone: (714) 539-6561 — Carnegie Class: Not Classified
FAX Number: (714) 539-6542 — Calendar System: Quarter
URL: www.stantonuniversity.com
Established: 1996 — Annual Undergrad Tuition & Fees: N/A
Enrollment: N/A — Coed
Affiliation or Control: Independent Non-Profit — IRS Status: 501(c)3
Highest Offering: Master's
Accreditation: @WC

01 President ... Dr. David KIM

Starr King School for the Ministry (B)

2441 Le Conte Avenue, Berkeley CA 94709-1299

County: Alameda — FICE Identification: 004080
Unit ID: 123916
Telephone: (510) 845-6232 — Carnegie Class: Spec-4-yr-Faith
FAX Number: (510) 845-6273 — Calendar System: Semester
URL: www.sksm.edu
Established: 1904 — Annual Graduate Tuition & Fees: N/A
Enrollment: 87 — Coed
Affiliation or Control: Unitarian Universalist — IRS Status: 501(c)3
Highest Offering: Master's; No Undergraduates
Accreditation: THEOL

01 President ... Rev. Rosemary Bray MCNATT
111 Vice President Advancement ... Ms. Jessica CLOUD
10 VP for Finance & Admin ... Mr. Kelly GIBBS
32 Vice Pres Student Services ... Ms. Rain JORDAN
05 Dean of the Faculty ... Dr. Gabriella LETTINI
35 Dean of Students ... Dr. Chris SCHELIN
06 Registrar ... Blyth BARNOW
07 Admissions/Recruitment Coordinator ... Mr. Matthew WATERMAN
20 Coordinator of Academic Programs ... Ms. Shannon EIZENGA
106 Director Online Education ... Dr. Hugo CORDOVA QUERO
26 Communications Officer ... Mr. Xander HUFFMAN

*State Center Community College District (C)

1171 Fulton Street, Fresno CA 93721

County: Fresno — FICE Identification: 001306
Unit ID: 123925
Telephone: (559) 243-7100 — Carnegie Class: N/A
FAX Number: N/A
URL: www.scccd.edu

01 Chancellor ... Dr. Paul PARNELL
10 Vice Chancellor Finance & Admin ... Ms. Cheryl SULLIVAN
05 VC Educ Svcs/Inst Effectiveness ... Mr. Jerome COUNTEE
15 Vice Chanc Human Resources ... Ms. Julianna MOSIER
11 Vice Chancellor Operations & IS ... Ms. Christine MIKTARIAN
26 Exec Dir Pub/Legislative Rels ... Ms. Lucy RUIZ
102 Executive Director Foundation ... Mr. Rico GUERRERO
43 General Counsel ... Mr. Matthew BESMER
25 Dir Grants/External Funding ... Ms. Cherylyn CRILL-HORNSBY
16 Director Human Resources ... Ms. Samerah CAMPBELL
96 Director of Purchasing ... Mr. Randy VOGT
21 Director of Finance ... Mr. William SCHOFIELD
13 Director of Information Systems ... Vacant
88 Director of Classified Personnel ... Ms. Elba GOMEZ

*Clovis Community College (D)

10309 N. Willow Avenue, Fresno CA 93730

County: Fresno — Identification: 667125
Unit ID: 489201
Telephone: (559) 325-5200 — Carnegie Class: Assoc/HT-High Trad
FAX Number: (559) 499-6065 — Calendar System: Semester
URL: www.cloviscollege.edu
Established: 2007 — Annual Undergrad Tuition & Fees (In-District): $1,304
Enrollment: 7,420 — Coed
Affiliation or Control: State/Local — IRS Status: 501(c)3
Highest Offering: Associate Degree
Accreditation: WJ

02 President ... Dr. Lori BENNETT
05 VP Instruction ... Ms. Monica CHAHAL
10 VP Administrative Services ... Ms. Lorrie HOPPER
32 VP Student Services ... Mr. Marco J. DE LA GARZA
79 Dean of Instruction ... Dr. James ORTEZ
75 Dean of Instruction CTE ... Ms. Roberta KUNKEL
20 Dean of Instruction ... Dr. John FORBES
35 Dean of Students ... Ms. Kira TIPPINS
13 Director of Technology ... Dr. John FORBES
26 Director of Marketing ... Ms. Stephanie BABB
35 Dean of Student Services ... Ms. Gurdeep HEBERT
09 Director of Institutional Research ... Mr. Alex ADAMS
41 Athletic Director ... Ms. Susan YATES
37 Director of Financial Aid ... Mr. Matt LEVINE
07 Admissions & Records Manager ... Ms. Reynani HAWKINS
04 Assistant to the President ... Ms. Emilie GERETY
18 Chief Facilities/Physical Plant Ofc ... Mr. Sergio SALINAS

*Fresno City College (E)

1101 E University Avenue, Fresno CA 93741-0002

County: Fresno — FICE Identification: 001307
Unit ID: 114789
Telephone: (559) 442-4600 — Carnegie Class: Assoc/MT-VT-Mix Trad/Non
FAX Number: (559) 499-6045 — Calendar System: Semester
URL: www.fresnocitycollege.edu
Established: 1910 — Annual Undergrad Tuition & Fees (In-District): $1,304
Enrollment: 22,771 — Coed
Affiliation or Control: State/Local — IRS Status: 501(c)3
Highest Offering: Associate Degree
Accreditation: WJ, CAHIIM, COARC, DH, RAD

02 President ... Dr. Carole GOLDSMITH
05 Vice President of Instruction ... Mr. Don LOPEZ
32 VP of Student Services ... Dr. Lataria HALL
10 Vice Pres Administrative Services ... Mr. Omar GUTIERREZ
108 VP of Educ Svcs/Inst Effectiveness ... Dr. Robert PIMENTEL
07 District Dean Admissions & Records ... Ms. Mirna DUARTE
121 Dean Student Success/Learning ... Dr. Donna COOPER
50 Dean Business Division ... Dr. Tim WOODS
57 Dean Fine/Performing/Comm Arts ... Mr. Neil VANDERPOOL
79 Dean Humanities Division ... Ms. Tabitha VILLALBA
54 Dean Math/Science/Engineering Div ... Ms. Shirley MCMANUS
83 Dean Social Sciences Division ... Dr. Margaret E. MERICLE
76 Dean Health Sciences Division ... Ms. Lorraine SMITH
72 Dean Applied Technology Division ... Dr. Becky BARABE
38 Dean Counseling/Guidance ... Ms. Monica CUEVAS
35 Dean of Student Services ... Mr. Sean HENDERSON
75 Dean Educ Svcs/Pathway Effective ... Mr. Gurminder SANGHA
22 Dir Disabled Stdnt Pgms & Svcs ... Ms. Susan ARRIOLA
09 Int Dir Institutional Research ... Ms. Carol RAINS-HEISDORF
88 Director Police Academy ... Mr. Gary FIEF
35 Director of Student Activities ... Dr. Ernie MARTINEZ
26 Director Marketing/Communications ... Ms. Cris M. BREMER
37 Director Financial Aid ... Ms. Mikki JOHNSON
27 Public Information Officer ... Ms. Kathleen BONILLA
41 Athletic Director ... Ms. Pammella ZIERFUSS-HUBBARD
106 Dir Distance Education/Inst Tech ... Dr. Jodie STEELEY
72 Director of Technology ... Vacant
88 Dir College Relations & Outreach ... Ms. Emilee SLATER
66 Director of Nursing ... Dr. Stephanie R. ROBINSON
88 Director CalWORKs Program ... Ms. Mary Beth MOSSETTE
06 Director Admissions & Records ... Dr. Andy HERNANDEZ
88 Director TRIO Programs ... Dr. Bernardo REYNOSO
88 Director EOPS/CARE ... Mr. Thomas GAXIOLA
103 Int Dir Workforce Development ... Ms. Julie LYNES

*Reedley College (F)

995 N Reed Avenue, Reedley CA 93654-2099

County: Fresno — FICE Identification: 001308
Unit ID: 117052
Telephone: (559) 638-0300 — Carnegie Class: Assoc/HT-Mix Trad/Non
FAX Number: N/A — Calendar System: Semester
URL: www.reedleycollege.edu
Established: 1926 — Annual Undergrad Tuition & Fees (In-District): $1,304
Enrollment: 10,562 — Coed
Affiliation or Control: State/Local — IRS Status: 501(c)3
Highest Offering: Associate Degree
Accreditation: WJ

02 College President ... Dr. Jerry L. BUCKLEY
05 Vice President of Instruction ... Mr. Dale VAN DAM
11 Vice Pres Administrative Svcs ... Ms. Donna BERRY
32 Vice Pres of Student Services ... Ms. Renee CRAIG-MARIUS
35 Dean of Student Services ... Ms. Shannon SOLIS
47 Dean of Instruction/Agri/Nat Res ... Mr. David CLARK
79 Dean of Instruction/Humanities ... Dr. G. Todd DAVIS
81 Dean Instruct/Math/Sci/Tech/PE/Hlth ... Ms. Marie BYRD-HARRIS
88 MO Dean of Inst CTE & STEM ... Dr. Ganesan SRINIVASAN
49 MO Dean of Inst LASS ... Dr. Shelly CONNER
35 MO Dean of Student Services ... Ms. Leticia CANALES
09 Dir IR/Effectiveness & Planning ... Ms. Janice OFFENBACH
26 Dir Marketing/Communications ... Mr. George TAKATA
22 Director DSP&S ... Dr. Samuel MORGAN
22 Director EOPS ... Mr. Mario GONZALES
13 Provost/Director of Technology ... Mr. Teng HER
37 Financial Aid Manager ... Ms. Chris CORTES
07 Admissions & Records Mgr/Registrar ... Ms. Veronica JURY
08 Librarian ... Ms. Shivon HESS
41 Director of Athletics ... Dr. David SANTESTEBAN
12 MCCC Campus President ... Ms. Angel REYNA
20 VP Instruction Madera/Oakhurst Ctrs ... Dr. Claudia HABIB
04 Exec Assistant to the President ... Ms. Kendelynn MENDOZA

Stockton Christian Life College (G)

9023 West Lane, Stockton CA 95210

County: San Joaquin — Identification: 667333
Telephone: (209) 476-7840 — Carnegie Class: Not Classified
FAX Number: (209) 476-7868 — Calendar System: Semester
URL: www.clc.edu
Established: 1949 — Annual Undergrad Tuition & Fees: N/A
Enrollment: N/A — Coed
Affiliation or Control: Independent Non-Profit — IRS Status: 501(c)3
Highest Offering: Baccalaureate
Accreditation: WC

01 President & CEO ... Eli LOPEZ
11 COO ... Laird G. SILLIMON
05 CAO ... Rev. Micah JOHNSON
10 CFO ... Dr. William RIDDELL
113 Student Financial Services Asst ... Joshua ABREGO
04 Special Asst to the CEO ... Andrew PUENTES
06 Registrar ... Jennifer C. LLAMAS
124 Recruitment & Retention ... Joanne GRESHAM
08 Director of Learning Center ... Regina LOPEZ
09 Director of Institutional Research ... Kenneth FITZPATRICK
105 Web/Media Services ... Josh RIVAS
108 Office of Assessment ... Israel RODRIGUEZ
13 Director of Information Technology ... Timothy MILLER
15 Director of Human Resources ... James LANGSTON
26 Dir of Marketing ... Josh RIVAS
29 Alumni Affairs ... Ralph GRESHAM
32 Dean of Students ... Richard BISHOP
35 Student Affairs Coordinator ... Mychail HANEY
53 General Education Chair ... Tamara FITZPATRICK
73 Bible & Theology Chair ... Micah JOHNSON
84 Enrollment Management ... Laird G. SILLIMON
96 Purchasing ... Connie SMITH

Studio School (H)

1201 West 5th St., Ste F10, Los Angeles CA 90017

Telephone: (800) 762-1993 — Identification: 770969
Accreditation: ACCSC

† Branch campus of Hussian School of Art, Philadelphia, PA

SUM Bible College and Theological Seminary (I)

1107 Investment Blvd, Suite 290, Eldorado Hills CA 95762

County: El Dorado — FICE Identification: 037524
Unit ID: 447953
Telephone: (916) 306-1628 — Carnegie Class: Spec-4-yr-Faith
FAX Number: (510) 568-1024 — Calendar System: Trimester
URL: www.sum.edu
Established: 1999 — Annual Undergrad Tuition & Fees: $9,964
Enrollment: 638 — Coed
Affiliation or Control: Independent Non-Profit — IRS Status: 501(c)3
Highest Offering: Master's
Accreditation: WC, BI

01 President/Chancellor ... Rev. George NEAU
05 Chief Academic Officer ... Dr. Gary MUNSON
20 Vice President Cohort Development ... Rev. Melanie FRANCIS
10 Chief Financial Officer ... Mr. Robert HORNICK
11 Chief Operating Officer ... Vacant
84 Director of Enrollment Management ... Ms. Sara HUSON
09 Director Institutional Research ... Dr. Andrew ANANE-ASANE
08 Director of the Library ... Vacant
32 Director Student Life/Ministries ... Ms. Crystal GONZALES
20 Assoc Academic Officer ... Dr. Bill OLIVERO
06 Registrar ... Mr. Tyler HUSON
07 Director of Admissions ... Mr. Daniel MULLEN
21 Business Office Coordinator ... Ms. Maritza GONZALEZ

† Affiliated with School of Urban Missions-New Orleans, Gretna, LA.

Taft College (J)

29 Cougar Court, Taft CA 93268-2329

County: Kern — FICE Identification: 001309
Unit ID: 124113
Telephone: (661) 763-7700 — Carnegie Class: Assoc/MT-VT-High Non
FAX Number: (661) 763-7703 — Calendar System: Semester
URL: www.taftcollege.edu
Established: 1922 — Annual Undergrad Tuition & Fees (In-District): $1,410
Enrollment: 6,260 — Coed
Affiliation or Control: State/Local — IRS Status: 501(c)3
Highest Offering: Associate Degree
Accreditation: WJ, DH

01 Superintendent/President ... Dr. Debra DANIELS

10 Exec Vice Pres/Administrative Svcs .... Mr. Brock MCMURRAY
05 Vice President of Instruction .... Dr. Leslie MINOR
32 Vice Pres of Student Services .... Mr. Severo BALASON, JR.
04 Assistant to the President .... Ms. Sarah CRISS
30 Director Foundation & Development .... Ms. Sheri HORN BUNK
13 Director Information Services .... Mr. Andrew PRESTAGE
08 Research and Instruction Librarian .... Ms. Terri SMITH
09 Director Inst Research/Assessment .... Ms. Xiaohong LI
41 Director Athletics .... Ms. Kanoe BANDY
15 Director of Human Resources .... Ms. Heather DEL ROSARIO
21 Director of Fiscal Services .... Ms. Amanda BAUER
07 Director of Admissions & Records .... Mr. Harold RUSSELL
18 Supervisor Facilities and Planning .... Mr. Richard TREECE
37 Director Student Financial Aid .... Ms. Barbara AMERIO
121 Dean of Student Success .... Dr. Windy MARTINEZ

Taft Law School (A)

3700 South Susan Street, Office 200,
Santa Ana CA 92704-6954
County: Orange — Identification: 666398
Telephone: (714) 850-4800 — Carnegie Class: Not Classified
FAX Number: (714) 708-2082 — Calendar System: Other
URL: www.taftu.edu
Established: 1976 — Annual Undergrad Tuition & Fees: N/A
Enrollment: N/A — Coed
Affiliation or Control: Proprietary — IRS Status: Proprietary
Highest Offering: Doctorate
Accreditation: DEAC

01 Chancellor .... Mr. David L. BOYD
05 Dean .... Mr. Robert K. STROUSE
86 VP of Governmental Relations .... Ms. Joan L. SLAVIN
20 Associate Dean .... Ms. Melody JOLLY
37 Director of Financial Aid .... Ms. Lucy CORDOVA

Teachers College of San Joaquin (B)

2857 Transworld Dr, Stockton CA 95206
County: San Joaquin — Identification: 667087
Unit ID: 488800
Telephone: (209) 468-4926 — Carnegie Class: Spec-4-yr-Other
FAX Number: (209) 468-9124 — Calendar System: Semester
URL: teacherscollegesj.edu
Established: 2009 — Annual Graduate Tuition & Fees: N/A
Enrollment: 846 — Coed
Affiliation or Control: State — IRS Status: 501(c)3
Highest Offering: Master's; No Undergraduates
Accreditation: WC

01 President .... Dr. Diane CARNAHAN
06 Registrar/Admissions .... Vacant
58 Director Graduate Studies .... Dr. Sylvia TURNER
04 Senior Admin Asst to President .... Ms. Victoria L. DE PRATER
10 Chief Business Officer .... Mr. Scott ANDERSON
88 Director of Credential Programs .... Ms. Michele BADOVINAC
09 Director of Institutional Research .... Dr. Sylvia TURNER

Theatre of Arts (C)

6767 Sunset Boulevard, Suite 210, Los Angeles CA 90028
County: Los Angeles — Identification: 667098
Unit ID: 486123
Telephone: (323) 463-2500 — Carnegie Class: Spec 2-yr-A&S
FAX Number: (323) 463-2500 — Calendar System: Trimester
URL: www.toa.edu
Established: 1927 — Annual Undergrad Tuition & Fees: $19,800
Enrollment: 53 — Coed
Affiliation or Control: Proprietary — IRS Status: Proprietary
Highest Offering: Associate Degree
Accreditation: THEA

00 President .... Todd BERHORST
01 Executive Director .... Jason WEISS
07 Manager Admissions .... Michael JURY
11 Chief of Administration .... Elizabeth INIGUEZ
37 Dir Student Financial Services .... Michael HONG

Thomas Aquinas College (D)

10,000 Ojai Road, Santa Paula CA 93060-9621
County: Ventura — FICE Identification: 023580
Unit ID: 124292
Telephone: (805) 525-4417 — Carnegie Class: Bac-A&S
FAX Number: (805) 525-9342 — Calendar System: Semester
URL: www.thomasaquinas.edu
Established: 1971 — Annual Undergrad Tuition & Fees: $25,000
Enrollment: 369 — Coed
Affiliation or Control: Independent Non-Profit — IRS Status: 501(c)3
Highest Offering: Baccalaureate
Accreditation: WC

01 President .... Dr. Michael F. MCLEAN
04 Secretary to the President .... Miss Jordan S. BRITTAIN
26 Asst to Pres/Dir College Relations .... Mrs. Anne S. FORSYTH
30 Vice President for Development .... Dr. Paul J. O'REILLY
43 General Counsel .... Mr. John Q. MASTELLER
10 Vice President for Admn & Finance .... Mr. Dennis K. MCCARTHY
05 Academic Dean .... Dr. John GOYETTE
112 Director of Gift Planning .... Mr. Thomas J. SUSANKA
44 Director of the Annual Fund .... Mr. Paul LAZENBY

88 Associate Director of Gift Planning .... Mr. Robert A. BAGDAZIAN
07 Director of Admissions .... Mr. Jonathan P. DALY
21 Supervisor Business/Finance .... Mrs. Yolanda RIVERA
37 Director of Financial Aid .... Mr. Gregory J. BECHER
32 Asst Dean for Student Affairs .... Dr. Jared KUEBLER
11 Director of Operations .... Mr. Mark KRETSCHMER
08 Librarian .... Ms. Richena CURPHEY
42 Chaplain .... Fr. Paul RAFTERY, OP
27 Communications Manager .... Mr. Christopher WEINKOPF
88 Development Database Manager .... Mr. Aaron DUNKEL
102 Dir Foundation/Corporate Relations .... Mrs. Sharon REISER
13 Chief Information Technology Office .... Mr. Pat NICHOLS
18 Chief Facilities/Physical Plant Ofc .... Mr. Clark TULBERG
29 Director Alumni Affairs .... Mr. Aaron DUNKEL

Thomas Jefferson School of Law (E)

701 B Street, Ste. 110, San Diego CA 92101
County: San Diego — FICE Identification: 010854
Unit ID: 126049
Telephone: (619) 297-9700 — Carnegie Class: Spec-4-yr-Law
FAX Number: (619) 961-4370 — Calendar System: Semester
URL: www.tjsl.edu
Established: 1969 — Annual Graduate Tuition & Fees: N/A
Enrollment: 569 — Coed
Affiliation or Control: Independent Non-Profit — IRS Status: 501(c)3
Highest Offering: Doctorate; No Undergraduates
Accreditation: @WC, #LAW

01 Interim Dean and Professor of Law .... Dean Linda KELLER
05 Assoc Dean Acad Affairs & Professor .... Dean Anders KAYE
43 Interim President & General Counsel .... Karin K. SHERR
04 Exec Asst to the President/Dean .... Jan DAUSS
10 VP and Chief Financial Officer .... Nancy VU
32 Assistant Dean for Student Affairs .... Lisa FERREIRA
84 Asst Dean of Enrollment Mgmt .. Michelle SLAUGHTER ALLISON
88 Non-JD Enrol Mgr & Instruc Designer .... Mary PUSZYKOWSKI
08 Library Director .... Leigh INMAN
36 Director of Career Services .... Jeffrey CHINN
20 Director of Academic Administration .... Natasha DABNEY
37 Director of Financial Assistance .... Marc BERMAN
06 Registrar .... Carrie KAZYAKA
21 Financial Operations Specialist .... Anh PHAN
88 Externship Director/Pro Bono .... Judybeth TROPP
15 Director of Human Resources .... Lisa CHIGOS
13 Director of IT .... Gil SUSANA

Touro University California (F)

1310 Club Drive, Vallejo CA 94592
County: Solano — FICE Identification: 041426
Unit ID: 459736
Telephone: (707) 638-5200 — Carnegie Class: Spec-4-yr-Med
FAX Number: (707) 638-5255 — Calendar System: Trimester
URL: www.tu.edu
Established: 1997 — Annual Undergrad Tuition & Fees: N/A
Enrollment: 1,478 — Coed
Affiliation or Control: Independent Non-Profit — IRS Status: 501(c)3
Highest Offering: Doctorate
Accreditation: WC, ARCPA, NURSE, OSTEO, PH, PHAR

01 President & CEO Univ System .... Dr. Alan KADISH
12 Sr Provost/CEO Touro Western Div .... Hon. Shelley BERKLEY
05 Provost & Chief Academic Officer .... Dr. Sarah SWEITZER
32 Dean of Student Affairs .... Dr. Steven JACOBSEN
35 Associate Dean of Students .... Dr. James BINKERD
07 Director of Admissions .... Mr. Steven DAVIS
09 AVP Institutional Effectiveness .... Dr. Meiling TANG
10 Dir of Fiscal Affairs & Accounting .... Ms. Amber SHOMO
15 Director Human Resources .... Mr. Bob FICKEN
11 Associate VP of Administration .... Vacant
08 Director University Library .... Ms. Tamara TRUJILLO
63 Dean College of Osteopathic Med .... Dr. Michael CLEARFIELD
67 Dean College of Pharmacy .... Dr. Rae MATSUMOTO
53 Dean Col of Education & Health Sci .... Dr. Lisa NORTON
13 Director of Information Technology .... Vacant
111 AVP Univ Advancement .... Ms. Andrea GARCIA
37 Financial Aid Director .... Ms. Kim KANE
35 Director of Campus Life .... Rabbi Elchonon TENENBAUM
23 Director of Student Health Center .... Ms. Judith CORTE
06 Registrar .... Mr. Ron TRAVENICK

Touro University Worldwide (G)

10601 Calle Lee Ste 179, Los Alamitos CA 90720
County: Orange — FICE Identification: 041425
Unit ID: 459727
Telephone: (818) 575-6800 — Carnegie Class: Masters/S
FAX Number: (818) 707-0316 — Calendar System: Semester
URL: www.tuw.edu
Established: 2005 — Annual Undergrad Tuition & Fees: N/A
Enrollment: 1,355 — Coed
Affiliation or Control: Independent Non-Profit — IRS Status: 501(c)3
Highest Offering: Doctorate
Accreditation: WC

01 Chancellor & CEO .... Dr. Yoram NEUMANN
05 Provost & Chief Academic Officer .... Dr. Sheila LEWIS
10 Chief Financial Officer (CFO) .... Mr. Jayson CAPUNO
11 Chief Operating Officer (COO) .... Mr. Roy FINALY
15 Chief Human Resources Officer .... Mrs. Melody ERBES

Touro College Los Angeles (H)

1317 N Crescent Heights Blvd, West Hollywood CA 90046
Telephone: (323) 822-9700 — Identification: 770944
Accreditation: WC

† Branch campus of Touro University Worldwide, Los Alamitos, CA.

Trident University International (I)

5757 Plaza Drive, Suite 100, Cypress CA 90630
County: Orange — FICE Identification: 041279
Unit ID: 450979
Telephone: (714) 816-0366 — Carnegie Class: DU-Mod
FAX Number: (714) 816-0367 — Calendar System: Semester
URL: www.trident.edu
Established: 1998 — Annual Undergrad Tuition & Fees: $9,240
Enrollment: 6,982 — Coed
Affiliation or Control: Proprietary — IRS Status: Proprietary
Highest Offering: Doctorate
Accreditation: WC

01 President/CEO .... Mr. Travis J. ALLEN
05 Provost/Chief Academic Officer .... Dr. Mihaela TANASESCU
10 Chief Financial Officer .... Mr. David BARRETT
13 Chief Information Officer .... Mr. Vahid SHARIAT
88 SVP/Chief Compliance Officer .... Dr. Afshin AFROOKHTEH
07 Vice President of Admissions .... Ms. Christina HOANG
53 Dean College of Education .... Dr. Heidi SMITH
50 Dean GJ Col Business/Info Systems .... Dr. Debra LOUIS
76 Dean Educ/Health Sciences .... Dr. Mickey SHACHAR
04 Executive Assistant .... Ms. Patricia PARKS
06 Registrar .... Ms. Abby DOLAN
37 Student Finance Manager .... Ms. Brittney DRAKE
09 Director of Institutional Research .... Dr. Heidi SATO
08 Librarian .... Ms. Leslie ANDERSEN
21 Director of Financial Operation .... Vacant
18 Facilities Manager .... Mr. Fred WILSON
101 Board of Trustees Secretary .... Mr. Brian VAN KLOMPENBERG

Trinity Law School (J)

2200 N Grand Avenue, Santa Ana CA 92705
Telephone: (714) 836-7500 — Identification: 770098
Accreditation: &NH

† Branch campus of Trinity International University, Deerfield, IL

Trinity School of Health and Allied Sciences (K)

1149 W. 190th St., Ste 2000, Gardena CA 90248
County: Los Angeles — FICE Identification: 041601
Unit ID: 459161
Telephone: (310) 834-3065 — Carnegie Class: Spec-4-yr-Other Health
FAX Number: (310) 834-6236 — Calendar System: Semester
URL: www.tshas.edu
Established: 2002 — Annual Undergrad Tuition & Fees: N/A
Enrollment: 113 — Coed
Affiliation or Control: Proprietary — IRS Status: Proprietary
Highest Offering: Baccalaureate
Accreditation: ABHES

01 President/CEO .... Dr. Estrella AGUINALDO
11 School Administrator .... Alice THOMPSON
05 Academic Dean .... Alice THOMPSON
06 Registrar .... Kulwant SINGH
37 Financial Aid Officer .... Odessa MATHIS

Union University of California (L)

14200 Goldenwest Street, Westminster CA 92683
County: Orange — Identification: 667269
Telephone: (714) 903-2762 — Carnegie Class: Not Classified
FAX Number: N/A — Calendar System: Semester
URL: www.uuc.edu
Established: 1986 — Annual Graduate Tuition & Fees: N/A
Enrollment: N/A — Coed
Affiliation or Control: Independent Non-Profit — IRS Status: 501(c)3
Highest Offering: Doctorate; No Undergraduates
Accreditation: DEAC

01 President/CEO .... Dr. Linh DOAN
03 Senior Vice President .... Dr. Son Xuan NGUYEN
05 Vice President Academic Affairs .... Dr. Margaret SCOTT
32 Vice Pres Student Affairs .... Dr. Kim-Lien THI NGO
13 Chief Information Officer .... Mr. Thai-Hoa NGUYEN
07 Director Admissions/Registrar .... Dr. Kim-Lien THI NGO

United States University (M)

7675 Mission Valley Road, San Diego CA 92108
County: San Diego — FICE Identification: 040053
Unit ID: 447050
Telephone: (619) 876-4250 — Carnegie Class: Masters/M
FAX Number: N/A — Calendar System: Semester
URL: www.usuniversity.edu
Established: 1997 — Annual Undergrad Tuition & Fees: $10,800
Enrollment: 429 — Coed
Affiliation or Control: Proprietary — IRS Status: Proprietary
Highest Offering: Master's

Accreditation: WC, NURSE

01 President and CEO ... Dr. Steven A. STARGARDTER
05 Provost/Chief Academic Officer ... Dr. Jennifer NEWMANN
07 VP of Enroll Mgmt/Stdnt Svcs/Mktg ... Vacant
10 Chief Financial Officer ... William TITERA
20 Assoc Provost Accred/Curriculum ... Dr. Elizabeth ARCHER
66 Int Dean College of Nursing ... Dr. Ann MCNAMARA
06 Registrar ... David NORIEGA
29 Director Alumni Relations ... Vacant
37 Director Student Financial Aid ... Natalie ROBINSON
08 Director of the Library ... Catalina LOPEZ
88 International Student Advisor ... Tina RICAFRENTE

Unitek College (A)

4670 Auto Mall Parkway, Fremont CA 94538
County: Alameda
FICE Identification: 041697
Unit ID: 459204
Telephone: (888) 775-1514
Carnegie Class: Spec-4-yr-Other Health
FAX Number: (510) 249-9125
Calendar System: Other
URL: www.unitekcollege.edu
Established: 1992
Annual Undergrad Tuition & Fees: $33,559
Enrollment: 2,715
Coed
Affiliation or Control: Proprietary
IRS Status: Proprietary
Highest Offering: Baccalaureate
Accreditation: ACCSC, NURSE

01 Director ... Mr. Benjamin ELIAS

University of Antelope Valley (B)

44055 Sierra Hwy, Lancaster CA 93534
County: Los Angeles
FICE Identification: 034275
Unit ID: 442930
Telephone: (661) 726-1911
Carnegie Class: Bac-Diverse
FAX Number: (661) 726-5158
Calendar System: Other
URL: www.uav.edu
Established: 1997
Annual Undergrad Tuition & Fees: N/A
Enrollment: 714
Coed
Affiliation or Control: Proprietary
IRS Status: Proprietary
Highest Offering: Master's
Accreditation: WC, EMT

01 President ... Mr. Marco JOHNSON
10 Vice President/CFO ... Ms. Sandra JOHNSON
05 Assoc Dean of Academic Affairs ... Ms. Chonnea HARRIS
32 Dean of Student Affairs ... Mr. Ronald FELTS
37 Financial Aid Director ... Ms. Araceli JIMENEZ
09 Dir Institutional Effectiveness ... Ms. Crystal STEPHENS
13 Director Information Technology ... Mr. Noel SANCHEZ
36 Director Career Services ... Ms. Karyn FRAHM
07 Director of Admissions ... Ms. Mirna TURCIOS

*University of California Office of the President (C)

1111 Franklin Street, 12th Floor, Oakland CA 94607-5200
County: Alameda
FICE Identification: 001311
Unit ID: 124557
Telephone: (510) 987-0700
Carnegie Class: N/A
FAX Number: (510) 987-0328
URL: www.ucop.edu

01 President ... Janet NAPOLITANO
05 Provost/EVP Academic Affairs ... Michael BROWN
10 EVP/Chief Financial Officer ... Nathan E. BROSTROM
11 EVP/Chief Operating Officer ... Rachael NAVA
17 Exec Vice Pres UC Health ... John D. STOBO
26 SVP External Rels/Communications ... Claire HOLMES
86 Int AVP Government Relations ... Chris HARRINGTON
108 SVP Compliance/Audit Services ... Alexander BUSTAMANTE
47 VP Agriculture/Natural Resources ... Barbara H. ALLEN-DIAZ
45 VP Budget & Capital Resources ... Patrick J. LENZ
115 Vice President of Investments ... Jagdeep S. BACHHER
09 Vice Pres Inst Rsrch/Acad Planning ... Pamela BROWN
88 VP Office of National Laboratories ... Craig LEASURE
15 Vice Pres Human Resources ... Dwaine B. DUCKETT
43 General Counsel/VP Legal Affairs ... Charles F. ROBINSON
32 Vice President Student Affairs ... Yvette GULLATT
46 Interim VP Innovation Alliance Svcs ... William TUCKER
13 CIO Information Technology Svcs ... Tom ANDRIOLA
20 Vice Provost/Chief Outreach Officer ... Yvette GULLATT
20 Vice Provost Academic Personnel ... Susan CARLSON
21 Int Assoc VP Budget Analysis/Plng ... David ALCOCER
111 AVP Institutional Advancement ... Geoff O'NEILL
04 Admin Assistant to the President ... Sutton BENNETT

*University of California-Berkeley (D)

Berkeley CA 94720-0001
County: Alameda
FICE Identification: 001312
Unit ID: 110635
Telephone: (510) 642-6000
Carnegie Class: DU-Highest
FAX Number: (510) 643-5499
Calendar System: Semester
URL: www.berkeley.edu
Established: 1868
Annual Undergrad Tuition & Fees (In-State): $14,184
Enrollment: 41,891
Coed
Affiliation or Control: State
IRS Status: 501(c)3
Highest Offering: Doctorate
Accreditation: WC, CLPSY, DIETD, IPSY, LAW, LSAR, OPT, OPTR, PCSAS, PH, PLNG, SCPSY, SW

02 Chancellor ... Carol CHRIST
05 Exec Vice Chancellor/Provost ... Paul ALIVISATOS
11 Vice Chancellor Administration ... Marc FISHER
10 Vice Chancellor Finance/CFO ... Rosemarie RAE
46 Vice Chancellor for Research ... Randy KATZ
32 Vice Chancellor Student Affairs ... Steve SUTTON
26 Vice Chanc Univ Dev/Alumni Rels ... Julie HOOPER
53 Vice Chanc Undergrad Education ... Cathy KOSHLAND
22 Vice Chanc Equity & Inclusion ... Oscar DUBON
43 Chief Campus Counsel ... David ROBINSON
100 Assoc Chancellor/Chief of Staff ... Khira ADAMS GRISCAVAGE
25 Asst VC Research Admin & Compliance ... Patrick SCHLESINGER
13 Asst Vice Chanc Info Technology ... Lyle NEVELS
84 Int AVC Admission/Enrollment ... Amy JARICH
87 AVC/Dean Summer Session/Stdy Abroad ... Richard RUSSO
27 AVP Communications/Public Affairs ... Diana HARVEY
21 Asst Vice Chanc Finance/Controller ... Delphine REGALIA
07 Asst VC & Dir Undergrad Admissions ... Olufemi OGUNDELE
35 Assc Vice Chanc/Dean of Students ... Joseph D. GREENWELL
37 Asst VC/Dir Fin Aid & Scholarship ... Rachelle FELDMAN
08 University Librarian ... Jeffrey MACKIE-MASON
06 Registrar ... Walter WONG
38 Dir Counseling & Psychological Svcs ... Vacant
36 Director Career Center ... Thomas C. DEVLIN
41 Director of Athletics ... James KNOWLTON
58 Dean of the Graduate Division ... Fiona M. DOYLE
61 Dean Boalt School of Law ... Erwin CHEMERINSKY
88 Dean School of Optometry ... John FLANAGAN
54 Dean College of Engineering ... Tsu-Jae KING LIU
88 Dean of Environmental Design ... Jennifer WOLCH
65 Dean College of Natural Resources ... David D. ACKERLY
50 Dean Haas School of Business ... Richard K. LYONS
70 Dean School of Social Welfare ... Jeffrey EDELSON
72 Dean School of Information ... AnnaLee SAXENIAN
69 Dean School of Public Health ... Michael C. LU
53 Dean Graduate School of Education ... Prudence CARTER
60 Dean Graduate School of Journalism ... Ed WASSERMAN
81 Dean College of Chemistry ... Douglas S. CLARK
80 Dean Goldman School Public Policy ... Henry E. BRADY
79 Dean of Arts and Humanities ... Anthony CASCARDI
88 Dean of Biological Sciences ... Michael R. BOTCHAN
81 Dean Mathematical/Physical Sciences ... Frances HELLMAN
49 Dean College of Letters & Sciences ... Carla HESSE
97 Dean of the Undergrad Division ... Bob JACOBSON
56 Dean of University Extension ... Diana WU

*University of California-Davis (E)

One Shields Avenue, Davis CA 95616-5270
County: Yolo
FICE Identification: 001313
Unit ID: 110644
Telephone: (530) 752-1011
Carnegie Class: DU-Highest
FAX Number: N/A
Calendar System: Quarter
URL: www.ucdavis.edu
Established: 1905
Annual Undergrad Tuition & Fees (In-State): $14,402
Enrollment: 37,380
Coed
Affiliation or Control: State
IRS Status: 501(c)3
Highest Offering: Doctorate
Accreditation: WC, ARCPA, DIETD, DIETI, IPSY, LAW, LSAR, MED, NURSE, PAST, PH, VET

02 Chancellor ... Dr. Gary S. MAY
05 Provost & Exec Vice Chancellor ... Dr. Ralph J. HEXTER
100 Associate Chancellor/Chief of Staff ... Mr. Karl M. ENGELBACH
26 Chief Marketing & Comm Officer ... Ms. Dana TOPOUSIS
46 Vice Chancellor Research ... Dr. Prasant MOHAPATRA
30 Vice Chanc Dev/Alumni Relations ... Dr. Shaun B. KEISTER
32 Int Vice Chancellor Student Affairs ... Dr. Emily GALINDO
10 VC Finance/Operation & Admin ... Ms. Kelly RATLIFF
28 Int Lead Diversity/Eqty/Inclusion ... Mr. Rahim REED
17 VC Human Hlth Sci/CEO UC Davis Hlth ... Dr. David A. LUBARSKY
66 Assoc VC/Dean Sch of Nursing ... Dr. Heather M. YOUNG
31 Assoc Exec VC Campus Cmty Relations ... Mr. Rahim REED
21 Asst VC Office of the COO ... Mr. Blair STEPHENSON
88 Exec Assoc VC Research ... Dr. Cindy M. KIEL
88 Assoc Vice Provost Global Affairs ... Dr. Ermias KEBREAB
88 Assoc Vice Provost Global Affairs ... Dr. Fadi FATHALLAH
88 Assoc VC Research ... Dr. Paul DODD
88 Assoc VC Research ... Dr. Dushyant PATHAK
15 Chief Human Resources Officer ... Ms. Christine LOVELY
88 Assoc VC Development ... Mr. Jason L. WOHLMAN
88 Assoc VC Development ... Mr. Paul PROKOP
88 Assoc VC Development Health Sci ... Ms. Chong U. PORTER
39 Int Assoc VC Student Affs/Aux Svcs ... Mr. Mike SHEEHAN
35 Assoc VC Student Affairs/Stdnt Life ... Dr. Sheri ATKINSON
84 Int Assoc VC Enrollment Management ... Mr. Steve WEISLER
88 Assoc VC Safety Services ... Mr. Eric KVIGNE
88 Assoc VC Design & Construct ... Mr. Jim CARROLL
18 Assoc VC Facilities Management ... Mr. Allen TOLLEFSON
45 AVC Campus Plng/Env Stewardship ... Mr. Robert B. SEGAR
88 Asst VC Student Affairs Div Svcs ... Mr. Cory N. VU
86 Int Lead Govt & Cmty Relations ... Ms. Mabel SALON
88 Asst VC & Campus Controller ... Mr. Matt OKAMOTO
88 Asst Exec Vice Chanc Provost Ofc ... Mr. Karl MOHR
114 Asst VC Budget ... Ms. Sarah MANGUM
88 Asst VC Capital Plng & Real Estate ... Mr. Grant ROCKWELL
88 Asst VC Development Outreach ... Ms. Angela JOENS
88 Asst VC Development ... Ms. Beth BRENNER
112 Asst VC Planned Giving ... Mr. Brian CASEY
102 Asst VC Foundation & Corp Giving ... Vacant
88 Asst VC Student Affs & Chf of Staff ... Ms. Emily PRIETO-TSEREGOUNIS
29 AVC/Exec Director Alumni Relations ... Mr. Richard R. ENGEL
13 CIO & VP Info/Educ Tech ... Ms. Viji MURALI
88 VP & Dean Undergraduate Educ ... Dr. Carolyn THOMAS
58 Interim VP Grad Educ/Dean Grad Stds ... Dr. Jean-Pierre DELPLANQUE
20 Vice Provost Academic Affairs ... Dr. Phil KASS
104 VP & Assoc Chanc Global Affairs ... Dr. Joanna REGULSKA
47 Dean Agricultural/Environ Sci ... Dr. Helene DILLARD
88 Dean Biological Sciences ... Dr. Mark WINEY
54 Dean Engineering ... Dr. Jennifer SINCLAIR CURTIS
49 Dean College of Letters and Science ... Dr. Elizabeth SPILLER
61 Dean School of Law ... Dr. Kevin R. JOHNSON
50 Dean Grad School of Management ... Dr. H. Rao UNNAVA
74 Dean Veterinary Medicine ... Dr. Michael D. LAIRMORE
53 Dean School of Education ... Dr. Lauren LINDSTROM
51 Int Lead Div of Cont/Prof Education ... Dr. Susan D. CATRON
63 Interim Dean School of Medicine ... Dr. Lars BERGLUND
88 Exec Director Mondavi Center ... Dr. Don F. ROTH
109 Exec Dir Campus Rec/Unions ... Mr. Jason LORGAN
36 Exec Dir Internship & Career Center ... Ms. Marcie KIRK-HOLLAND
23 Exec Student Health Services ... Dr. Margaret WALTER
37 Director Financial Aid ... Ms. Deborah G. AGEE
88 Director Medical ... Dr. Cindy M. SCHORZMAN
38 Director Student Health Counseling ... Dr. Sarah HAHN
41 Dir Intercollegiate Athletics ... Mr. Kevin BLUE
116 Dir Audit & Mgmt Advisory Services ... Ms. Leslyn KRAUS
88 Int Director Student Health Admin ... Ms. Julienne DEGEYTER
19 Chief of Police ... Chief Joseph FARROW
43 Chief Campus Counsel ... Mr. Michael SWEENEY
06 University Registrar ... Ms. Erin K. MORGAN
08 University Librarian ... Ms. MacKenzie SMITH

*University of California-Hastings College of the Law (F)

200 McAllister Street, San Francisco CA 94102-4978
County: San Francisco
FICE Identification: 003947
Unit ID: 110398
Telephone: (415) 565-4600
Carnegie Class: Spec-4-yr-Law
FAX Number: (415) 565-4865
Calendar System: Semester
URL: www.uchastings.edu
Established: 1878
Annual Graduate Tuition & Fees: N/A
Enrollment: 1,028
Coed
Affiliation or Control: State
IRS Status: 501(c)3
Highest Offering: First Professional Degree; No Undergraduates
Accreditation: WC, LAW

02 Chancellor and Dean ... Dean David L. FAIGMAN
05 Academic Dean ... Dr. Morris RATNER
43 General Counsel ... Mr. John DIPAOLO
10 Chief Financial Officer ... Mr. David SEWARD
11 Executive Director of Operations ... Ms. Rhiannon BAILARD
13 Chief Information Officer ... Ms. Camilla TUBBS
30 Chief Development Officer ... Mr. Eric DUMBLETON
20 Associate Academic Dean ... Ms. Grace HUM
84 Sr Asst Dean Enrollment Management ... Ms. June SAKAMOTO
15 Human Resources Director ... Mr. Andrew SCOTT
32 Director of Student Services ... Ms. Emily HAAN
06 Registrar ... Ms. Sarah REED
07 Director of Admissions ... Mr. Bryan ZERBE
36 Asst Dean Career & Professional Dev ... Ms. Sari ZIMMERMAN
26 Dir Communications/Public Affairs ... Mr. Alex A G. SHAPIRO
09 Dir of Accreditation & Assessment ... Ms. Andrea BING
22 Director LEOP ... Ms. Elizabeth MCGRIFF
23 Student Health Manager/Admin Nurse ... Ms. Laurie BROOKNER
21 Controller ... Ms. Sandra PLENSKI
37 Director Financial Aid ... Mr. Victor HO
18 Property Manager ... Mr. Jarda BRYCH
96 Director of Purchasing ... Mr. Darryl SWEET

*University of California-Irvine (G)

Campus Drive, Irvine CA 92697-0001
County: Orange
FICE Identification: 001314
Unit ID: 110653
Telephone: (949) 824-5011
Carnegie Class: DU-Highest
FAX Number: N/A
Calendar System: Quarter
URL: www.uci.edu
Established: 1965
Annual Undergrad Tuition & Fees (In-State): $13,700
Enrollment: 35,242
Coed
Affiliation or Control: State
IRS Status: 501(c)3
Highest Offering: Doctorate
Accreditation: WC, CEA, IPSY, LAW, MACTE, MED, MT, NURSE, PH, PLNG, RADDOS

02 Chancellor ... Howard A. GILLMAN
05 Provost & Exec Vice Chancellor ... Enrique J. LAVERNIA
10 Vice Chanc Admin/Finance & CFO ... Ronald CORTEZ
46 Vice Chancellor for Research ... Pramod KHARGONEKAR
32 Vice Chanc Student Affairs ... Willie L. BANKS
111 Vice Chanc Univ Advancement ... Brian T. HERVEY
17 Vice Chancellor Health Affairs ... Steve GOLDSTEIN
20 Vice Provost for Academic Planning ... Judith STEPAN-NORRIS
88 Vice Provost for Academic Personnel ... Diane K. O'DOWD
28 Vice Provost for AED & Inclusion ... Douglas M. HAYNES
100 Associate Chancellor/Chief of Staff ... Lars T. WALTON
20 Assoc Prov & Exec Vice Chancellor ... Jeff LEFKOFF
22 Assoc Chancellor ED & Inclusion ... Kirsten K. QUANBECK
88 Assoc Chancellor Sustainability ... Wendell BRASE
15 Assoc Chancellor & Chief HR Exec ... Ramona AGRELA
26 Assoc Chanc Comms & Public Affairs ... Ria M. CARLSON
35 Asst VC Stdnt Affs/Chief of Staff ... Edgar J. DORMITORIO

35 Asst Vice Chanc/Dean of Students ... Rameen A. TALESH
23 Assoc VC/Chief of Staff Health Affs ... Rebecca BRUSUELAS-JAMES
13 Interim Chief Information Officer ... Kian COLESTOCK
84 Asst Vice Chanc Enrollment Services ... Patricia MORALES
21 Assoc Vice Chanc Admin/Business Svc ... Richard COULON
06 University Registrar ... Elizabeth C. BENNETT
43 Chief Campus Counsel ... Andrea GUNN EATON
51 Dean Continuing Educ/Summer Session ... Gary W. MATKIN
08 University Librarian ... Lorelei A. TANJI
36 Assoc Vice Prov Div Career Pathway ... Suzanne C. HELBIG
37 Director Financial Aid ... Rebecca SANCHEZ
41 Director Intercollegiate Athletics ... Paula Y. SMITH
09 Asst Vice Chanc Inst Research ... Ryan M. CHERLAND
20 Dean Undergrad Education & VP ... Michael DENNIN
58 Dean Graduate Division & VP ... Frances M. LESLIE
49 Dean Arts ... Stephen BARKER
50 Dean Paul Merage School of Business ... Eric SPANGENBERG
53 Dean School of Education ... Richard ARUM
81 Dean Biological Sciences ... Frank LAFERLA
54 Dean School of Engineering ... Gregory WASHINGTON
79 Dean Humanities ... Tyrus MILLER
77 Dean Bren Sch of Info & Comp Sci ... Marios PAPAEFTHYMIOU
61 Dean of Law School ... L. Song RICHARDSON
63 Dean School of Medicine ... Michael STAMOS
81 Dean Physical Sciences ... James BULLOCK
83 Dean Social Ecology ... Nancy GUERRA
83 Dean School of Social Sciences ... William M. MAURER
66 Dean School of Nursing ... Dr. Adey NYAMATHI
88 Chair Academic Senate ... Linda COHEN

*University of California-Los Angeles (A)

405 Hilgard Avenue, Los Angeles CA 90095-1405

County: Los Angeles — FICE Identification: 001315
Unit ID: 110662
Telephone: (310) 825-4321 — Carnegie Class: DU-Highest
FAX Number: N/A — Calendar System: Quarter
URL: www.ucla.edu
Established: 1919 — Annual Undergrad Tuition & Fees (In-State): $13,226
Enrollment: 44,027 — Coed
Affiliation or Control: State — IRS Status: 501(c)3
Highest Offering: Doctorate
Accreditation: WC, CAMPEP, CLPSY, CYTO, DENT, DIETI, EMT, IPSY, LAW, LIB, MED, NURSE, PAST, PCSAS, PH, PLNG, RAD, SW, THEA

02 Chancellor ... Gene D. BLOCK
05 Exec Vice Chancellor and Provost ... Scott WAUGH
11 Administrative Vice Chancellor ... Michael J. BECK
10 Vice Chancellor/CFO ... Gregg GOLDMAN
15 Vice Chancellor Academic Personnel ... Michael LEVINE
28 VChanc Equity Diversity & Inclusion ... Jerry KANG
26 Vice Chancellor External Affairs ... Rhea TURTELTAUB
23 Vice Chancellor Health Sciences ... John MAZZIOTTA
43 Vice Chancellor Legal Affairs ... Louise C. NELSON
46 Vice Chancellor Research ... Roger WAKIMOTO
32 Vice Chancellor Student Affairs ... Monroe GORDEN, JR.
58 Vice Provost & Dean Graduate Educ ... Robin L. GARRELL
20 Vice Provost & Dean Undergrad Educ ... Patricia A. TURNER
13 Vice Provost Information Technology ... James DAVIS
88 Vice Prov Inst of American Cultures ... David K. YOO
88 VProv Interdiscip/Cross-Campus Affs ... Timothy BREWER
104 Vice Prov Intl Studies/Global Engmt ... C. Cindy FAN
17 President UCLA Health ... Johnese Maria SPISSO
79 Dean of Humanities ... David SCHABERG
88 Dean of Life Sciences ... Victoria SORK
81 Dean of Physical Sciences ... Miguel GARCIA-GARIBAY
83 Dean of Social Sciences ... Darnell HUNT
52 Dean School of Dentistry ... Paul KREBSBACH
48 Dean Sch of the Arts & Arch ... Brett STEELE
53 Dean Grad Sch Educ & Info Studies ... Marcelo M. SUAREZ-OROZCO
54 Dean Sch of Eng & App Sci ... Jayathi Y. MURTHY
61 Dean School of Law ... Jennifer L. MNOOKIN
50 Int Dean Grad Sch of Mgmt ... Alfred E. OSBORNE, JR.
63 Dean School of Medicine ... Kelsey C. MARTIN
64 Dean School of Music ... Judith L. SMITH
66 Dean School of Nursing ... Linda SARNA
80 Dean School of Public Affairs ... Gary SEGURA
69 Dean Sch of Public Health ... Jody HEYMANN
88 Dean School of Theater Film & TV ... Teri SCHWARTZ
51 Dean Continuing Ed and Extension ... Vacant
88 Assoc VC Academic Planning & Budget ... Jeff ROTH
29 Assoc VC Alumni Affairs/Advancemnt ... Julie SINA
16 Assoc VC Campus Human Resources ... Lubbe LEVIN
21 Assoc Vice Chancellor/Controller ... Allison BAIRD-JAMES
30 Assoc VC Development ... Laura PARKER
84 Vice Provost Enrollment Management ... Youlonda COPELAND-MORGAN
35 Asst VC of Student Development ... Suzanne SEPLOW
35 Asst VC of Campus Life ... Mick DELUCA
27 Assoc VC UCLA Comm/Public Outreach ... Kathryn KRANHOLD
20 Assistant Provost ... Laurie K. SUMMERS
20 Assistant Provost ... Margaret LEAL-SOTELO
18 Asst VC Facilities Management ... Kelly J. SCHMADER
86 Assoc VC Govt/Community Relations ... Jennifer POULAKIDAS
39 Asst VC Housing & Hospitality Svcs ... Peter ANGELIS
25 Asst VC Research/Compliance ... Ann M. POLLACK
04 Executive Asst to the Chancellor ... Vacant
88 Executive Director ASUCLA ... Pouria ABBASSI
09 Executive Director Inst Research ... Adam SUGANO
88 Director Volunteer Center ... Ashley LOVE-SMITH
96 Dir Campus Purchasing & Payables ... William S. PROPST
36 Int Director Career Center ... Christine WILSON
85 Int Director Ctr for Intl Students ... Sam NAHIDI
37 Director Financial Aid Office ... Ronald W. JOHNSON
41 Director Intercollegiate Athletics ... Daniel G. GUERRERO
90 Chief Technologist ... Scott FRIEDMAN
38 Exec Dir Couns & Psych Svcs ... Nicole GREEN
07 Director Undergraduate Admission ... Gary A. CLARK
06 Registrar ... Frank Y. WADA
08 University Librarian ... Virginia STEEL
19 Chief of Police ... Tony LEE

*University of California-Merced (B)

5200 North Lake Road, Merced CA 95343

County: Merced — FICE Identification: 041271
Unit ID: 445188
Telephone: (209) 228-4400 — Carnegie Class: DU-Higher
FAX Number: (209) 228-4424 — Calendar System: Semester
URL: www.ucmerced.edu
Established: 2005 — Annual Undergrad Tuition & Fees (In-District): $13,538
Enrollment: 7,967 — Coed
Affiliation or Control: State/Local — IRS Status: 501(c)3
Highest Offering: Doctorate
Accreditation: WC

02 Interim Chancellor ... Nathan BROSTROM
88 Assoc Chancellor & Senior Advisor ... Luanna PUTNEY
05 Provost/Exec Vice Chancellor ... Dr. Gregg CAMFIELD
10 Interim VC & Chief Fin/Admin Ofcr ... Mike RILEY
30 Vice Chancellor Develop/Alumni Rels ... Ed KLOTZBIER
32 Vice Chancellor Student Affairs ... Dr. Charles NIES
114 Vice Chancellor Budget/Planning ... Mike RILEY
46 Vice Chancellor Research ... Dr. Samuel TRAINA
84 Assoc Vice Chanc Enrollment Mgmt ... Jill ORCUTT
26 Asst Vice Chanc Univ Communications ... Ed KLOTZBIER
58 Vice Provost/Dean of Graduate Educ ... Marjorie ZATZ
20 Vice Provost UG Education ... Elizabeth WHITT
86 Exec Director of Govt Relations ... Cori LUCERO
04 Exec Assistant to the Chancellor ... Molly ELAZIER
13 AVC Information Technology ... Ann KOVALCHICK
65 Dean Natural Sciences ... Dr. Betsy DUMONT
79 Interim Dean School of SSHA ... Jeffrey GILGER
54 Dean Engineering ... Dr. Mark MATSUMOTO
07 Director of Admissions ... Vacant
06 University Registrar ... Erin WEBB
37 Director of Financial Aid ... Ron RADNEY
41 Director of Campus Athletics & Rec ... David DUNHAM
23 Assoc Vice Chanc Health & Wellness ... Vacant
85 Director of International Affairs ... Garett GIETZEN
08 University Librarian ... Haipeng LI
39 Director of Housing and Residence ... Martin REED
43 Campus Counsel ... Elisabeth GUNTHER
100 Associate Chancellor/Chief of Staff ... Luanna PUTNEY
19 Chief of Police ... Chou HER
09 Director of Inclusive Research ... Andres HERNANDEZ
15 Chief Human Resources Officer ... Nicole POLLACK
18 Chief Facilities/Physical Plant Ofc ... Michael MCLEOD
21 Associate Business Officer ... Connie MCBRIDE
28 Director of Diversity ... Dania MATOS
29 Director Alumni Affairs ... Chris ABRESCY
35 Associate Student Affairs Officer ... Charles NIES
36 Director Student Placement ... Brian O'BRUBA
38 Director Student Counseling ... Myrla SEIBOLD
96 Director of Purchasing ... Stephanie ZUNIGA

*University of California-Riverside (C)

900 University Avenue, Riverside CA 92521

County: Riverside — FICE Identification: 001316
Unit ID: 110671
Telephone: (951) 827-1012 — Carnegie Class: DU-Highest
FAX Number: N/A — Calendar System: Quarter
URL: www.ucr.edu
Established: 1954 — Annual Undergrad Tuition & Fees (In-State): $13,827
Enrollment: 23,279 — Coed
Affiliation or Control: State — IRS Status: 501(c)3
Highest Offering: Doctorate
Accreditation: WC, IPSY, MED, SCPSY

02 Chancellor ... Dr. Kim A. WILCOX
100 Associate Chancellor ... Dr. Christine VICTORINO
05 Interim Provost/EVC ... Dr. Thomas M. SMITH
45 CFO & Vice Chanc Planning & Budget ... Mr. Gerry BOMOTTI
32 Vice Chancellor Student Affairs ... Dr. Brian HAYNES
111 Vice Chanc University Advancement ... Mr. Peter A. HAYASHIDA
46 Interim Vice Chancellor Research ... Dr. Gillian WILSON
63 Dean School of Med/CEO Clin Affs ... Dr. Deborah DEAS
20 Vice Provost Academic Personnel ... Dr. Ameae WALKER
18 Exec Dir Facilities Services ... Ms. Susan MARSHBURN
84 Assoc Vice Chanc Enrollment ... Ms. LaRae LUNDGREN
30 Assoc Vice Chanc Development ... Mr. Hieu NGUYEN
09 Asst Vice Chanc For Research ... Mr. Charles GREER
28 Director Equal Emp/Affirm Action ... Vacant
58 Dean Graduate Division ... Dr. Shaun BOWLER
50 Dean School of Business Admin ... Dr. Yungzeng WANG
53 Dean Grad School of Educ ... Dr. Thomas SMITH
54 Dean Bourns College of Engineering ... Dr. Christoher LYNCH
79 Dean College of Humanities Arts SS ... Dr. Milagros PENA
81 Dean Col of Nat and Agr Sciences ... Dr. Kathryn UHRICH
06 Registrar ... Ms. Bracken J. DAILEY
80 Dean School of Public Policy ... Dr. Anil DEOLALIKAR
36 Director Career Center ... Mr. Sean GIL
37 Director Financial Aid ... Mr. Jose A. AGUILAR
38 Director Counseling Center ... Dr. Elizabeth MONDRAGON
07 Director of Admissions ... Ms. Emily D. ENGELSCHALL
96 Director Procurement/BC/AP/Trav ... Mr. Ellery TRICHE
08 Head Librarian ... Mr. Steve MANDEVILLE-GAMBLE
04 Executive Asst to the Chancellor ... Ms. Suzette M. LYONS
41 Athletics Director ... Ms. Tamica SMITH JONES
13 AVC Info Tech Services ... Ms. Danna GIANFORTE
15 Assoc Vice Chanc Human Resources ... Ms. Jadie LEE
26 Asst VC & Chief Communications Ofcr ... Mr. Johnny CRUZ
43 Chief Campus Counsel ... Mr. David BERGQUIST
86 AVC Govt/Community Relations ... Ms. Elizabeth ROMERO
102 Exec Dir Foundation Development ... Mr. Bryan CARLSON
104 Director of Education Abroad ... Dr. Karolyn ANDREWS
108 Asst VC Institutional Research ... Mr. Scott HEIL
109 Assoc Vice Chanc Auxiliary Svcs ... Mr. Andy PLUMLEY
44 Director Gift Administration ... Ms. Lisa M. WILSON

*University of California-San Diego (D)

9500 Gilman Drive, La Jolla CA 92093-0014

County: San Diego — FICE Identification: 001317
Unit ID: 110680
Telephone: (858) 534-2230 — Carnegie Class: DU-Highest
FAX Number: (858) 534-6523 — Calendar System: Quarter
URL: www.ucsd.edu
Established: 1960 — Annual Undergrad Tuition & Fees (In-State): $14,167
Enrollment: 35,772 — Coed
Affiliation or Control: State — IRS Status: 501(c)3
Highest Offering: Doctorate
Accreditation: WC, AUD, CEA, CLPSY, DIETI, DMS, IPSY, LC, MED, PDPSY, PHAR

02 Chancellor ... Dr. Pradeep K. KHOSLA
05 EVC Academic Affairs ... Dr. Elizabeth H. SIMMONS
10 VC and Chief Financial Officer ... Mr. Pierre-Yves OUILLET
32 VC Student Affairs ... Dr. Alysson SATTERLUND
11 Vice Chanc Resource Mgmt/Planning ... Mr. Gary C. MATTHEWS
65 Vice Chancellor Marine Sciences ... Dr. Margaret LEINEN
63 VC Health Science/Dean Sch Med ... Dr. David A. BRENNER
46 Vice Chancellor Research ... Dr. Sandra BROWN
28 VC for Equity/Diversity & Inclusion ... Dr. Becky R. PETITT
111 Vice Chancellor Advancement ... Vacant
100 Assistant Chancellor/Chief of Staff ... Mr. Jeffrey P. GATTAS
22 Chief Ethics and Compliance Officer ... Ms. Judith BRUNER
56 Assoc VC Public Pgms/Dean Univ Ext ... Dr. Mary L. WALSHOK
43 Chief Campus Counsel ... Mr. Daniel W. PARK
13 Chief Information Officer ... Mr. Vince KELLEN
21 AVC Business Fin Svcs/Controller ... Ms. Cheryl ROSS
08 University Librarian ... Dr. Erik T. MITCHELL
88 Assistant Chancellor ... Ms. Suzi M. STERNER
88 Director Policy Admin ... Ms. Paula J. JOHNSON, CRM
23 Exec Dir Student Health/Wellness ... Ms. Karen J. CALFAS
26 University Communications ... Vacant
20 Sr Assoc VC Academic Planning ... Dr. William S. HODGKISS
20 AVC Academic Affairs ... Dr. Barbara SAWREY
15 Asst VC Human Resources ... Ms. Catherine M. LEDFORD
46 Associate Vice Chancellor Research ... Dr. Miroslav KRSTIC
88 AVC Innovation & Commercialization ... Mr. Paul W. ROBEN
84 Assoc Vice Chanc Enrollment Mgmt ... Ms. Adele C. BRUMFIELD
06 University Registrar ... Vacant
23 CEO UCSD Medical Center ... Ms. Patty MAYSENT
35 Asst VC Student Life ... Ms. Sharon VAN BRUGGEN
96 Assoc Controller/Chief Procurement ... Mr. Ted JOHNSON
54 Dean Jacobs Sch of Engineering ... Dr. Albert P. PISANO
49 Dean Arts & Humanities ... Dr. Cristina DELLA COLETTA
81 Dean Div of Biological Sciences ... Dr. William MCGINNIS
83 Dean of Social Sciences ... Dr. Carol A. PADDEN
50 Dean Rady School of Management ... Mr. Robert S. SULLIVAN
81 Dean Div of Physical Science ... Dr. Steven E. BOGGS
82 Dean Global Policy and Strategy ... Dr. Peter COWHEY
58 Dean Graduate Studies ... Dr. Kit POGLIANO
12 Provost John Muir College ... Dr. K. Wayne YANG
12 Prov Thurgood Marshall Coll ... Dr. Leslie CARVER
88 Dean of Undergraduate Education ... Dr. John C. MOORE
12 Provost Earl Warren College ... Dr. Emily ROXWORTHY
12 Provost Revelle College ... Dr. Paul K. YU
12 Provost Eleanor Roosevelt College ... Dr. Ivan EVANS
12 Provost Sixth College ... Dr. Lakshmi CHILUKURI
38 Director Stdt Psych/Counseling Svcs ... Dr. Reina JUAREZ
18 AVC EH&S and Facilities Management ... Vacant
41 Intercollegiate Athletics Director ... Mr. Earl W. EDWARDS
19 Police Chief Community Safety ... Mr. David S. ROSE

*University of California-San Francisco (E)

513 Parnassus Avenue, Box 0402,
San Francisco CA 94143

County: San Francisco — FICE Identification: 001319
Unit ID: 110699
Telephone: (415) 476-1000 — Carnegie Class: Spec-4-yr-Med
FAX Number: N/A — Calendar System: Quarter
URL: www.ucsf.edu
Established: 1864 — Annual Graduate Tuition & Fees: N/A
Enrollment: 3,107 — Coed
Affiliation or Control: State — IRS Status: 501(c)3
Highest Offering: Doctorate; No Undergraduates
Accreditation: WC, DENT, DIETI, IPSY, MED, MIDWF, NURSE, PAST, PHAR, PTA

02 Chancellor ... Dr. Sam HAWGOOD

03 Executive Vice Chancellor & Provost ... Dr. Daniel H. LOWENSTEIN
100 Associate Chancellor ... Dr. Theresa O'BRIEN
10 Senior VC Finance & Administration ... Mr. Paul JENNY
21 Interim Chief Financial Officer ... Mr. Michael CLUNE
05 Vice Provost Academic Affairs ... Dr. Brian ALLDREDGE
32 Vice Chanc Student Academic Affairs ... Dr. Elizabeth WATKINS
30 VC Univ Development/Alumni Rels ... Ms. Jennifer ARNETT
26 Vice Chanc Communications ... Mr. Won HA
86 VC Community & Govt Relations ... Ms. Francesca VEGA
28 VC Diversity & Outreach ... Dr. Renee NAVARRO
13 Assoc VC & Chief Info Officer ... Mr. Joseph BENGFORT
109 Assoc VC Campus Life Services ... Ms. Clare SHINNERL
15 Chief Human Resources Officer ... Mr. Corey JACKSON
18 Assoc VC Cap Pgms/Campus Architect ... Mr. Michael BADE
20 Vice Dean Academic Affairs ... Dr. Elena FUENTES-AFFLICK
37 Director Student Financial Aid ... Mr. Jerry LOPEZ
43 Chief Campus Counsel ... Ms. Greta SCHNETZLER
08 University Librarian/Asst VC ... Mr. Chris SHAFFER
63 Dean School of Medicine/VC Med Affs ... Dr. Talmadge E. KING, JR.
19 Chief of Police ... Mr. Michael DENSON
66 Dean School of Nursing ... Dr. Catherine GILLISS
52 Dean School of Dentistry ... Dr. Michael REDDY
67 Dean School of Pharmacy ... Dr. B. Joseph GUGLIELMO
58 Dean Graduate Division ... Dr. Elizabeth WATKINS
96 Assoc VC/Chief Procurement Officer ... Mr. James HINE
06 Registrar/Asst VC Student Info ... Mr. Douglas CARLSON
88 Associate Registrar ... Ms. Jina SHAMIM
36 Asst VC Career Advancement ... Mr. William LINDSTAEDT
23 Asst VC Student Health & Counseling ... Dr. Chaitali MUKHERJEE
09 Director Institutional Research ... Dr. Ning WANG

*University of California-Santa Barbara (A)

552 University Road, Santa Barbara CA 93106-0001

County: Santa Barbara | FICE Identification: 001320 | Unit ID: 110705
Telephone: (805) 893-8000 | Carnegie Class: DU-Highest
FAX Number: N/A | Calendar System: Quarter
URL: www.ucsb.edu
Established: 1909 | Annual Undergrad Tuition & Fees (In-State): $14,391
Enrollment: 25,057 | Coed
Affiliation or Control: State | IRS Status: 501(c)3
Highest Offering: Doctorate
Accreditation: WC, IPSY, PSPSY

02 Chancellor ... Dr. Henry T. YANG
04 Exec Assistant to the Chancellor ... Ms. Diane O'BRIEN
05 Executive Vice Chancellor ... Dr. David B. MARSHALL
46 Vice Chancellor Research ... Dr. Joe INCANDELA
11 Vice Chancellor Admin Services ... Mr. Garry MAC PHERSON
32 Vice Chancellor Student Affairs ... Ms. Margaret KLAWUNN
10 Exec Dir/Controller Bus & Fin Svc ... Mr. Jim R. CORKILL
15 Assoc Vice Chanc Acad Personnel ... Dr. Alison BUTLER
28 AVC Diversity/Equity/Acad Policy ... Dr. Maria HERRERA-SOBEK
20 AVC/Dean Undergraduate Education ... Dr. Jeffrey STOPPLE
30 Assoc Vice Chancellor Development ... Ms. Beverly COLGATE
26 AVC Public Affairs & Communications ... Mr. John LONGBRAKE
84 AVC Enrollment Services ... Mr. Mike MILLER
88 Acting AVC Student Acad Support Svc ... Ms. Lupe GARCIA
114 Asst Chanc Fin & Resource Mgmt ... Mr. Chuck HAINES
29 Asst Vice Chanc Alumni Affairs ... Mr. George THURLOW, III
88 Interim Dean Col Creative Studies ... Dr. Kathy FOLTZ
54 Dean College of Engineering ... Dr. Rod ALFERNESS
58 Dean Graduate Division ... Dr. Carol GENETTI
53 Dean Gevirtz Grad Sch Educ ... Dr. Jeffrey MILEM
65 Dean Bren School of Env Sci & Mgmt ... Dr. Steven D. GAINES
51 Dean Professional and Cont Educ ... Dr. Robert YORK
35 Dean of Student Life ... Ms. Katya ARMISTEAD
49 Exec Dean College Letters & Sci ... Dr. Pierre WILTZIUS
79 Dean Humanities & Fine Arts ... Dr. John MAJEWSKI
87 Director Summer Sessions ... Dr. James FORD
83 Dean Social Sciences ... Dr. Charles R. HALE
85 Dir International Students/Scholars ... Dr. Simran SINGH
06 Registrar ... Ms. Leesa BECK
16 Director Human Resources ... Ms. Cynthia SENERIZ
37 Director Financial Aid ... Dr. Michael MILLER
116 Acting Dir Audit & Advisory Service ... Ms. Jessie MASEK
07 Director Admissions ... Ms. Lisa PRZEKOP
09 Director Institutional Research ... Dr. Steven C. VELASCO
23 Exec Director Student Health Svcs ... Dr. Mary FERRIS
39 AVC Housing/Dining & Aux Enterpris ... Mr. Wilfred E. BROWN
40 Director of UCSB Bookstore ... Mr. Mark BEISECKER
19 Chief of Police ... Mr. Dustin OLSON
41 Director Intercollegiate Athletics ... Mr. John MCCUTCHEON
86 Dir Governmental Relations ... Ms. Kirsten DESHLER
21 Director Finance/Administration ... Vacant
08 University Librarian ... Ms. Kristin ANTELMAN
89 Director Orientation Programs ... Ms. Tricia RASCON
88 Acting Director Capital Development ... Mr. Mark NOCCIOLO
88 Director Campus Planning & Design ... Ms. Alissa HUMMER
88 Executive Director Arts & Lectures ... Ms. Celesta BILLECI
22 Director Disabled Students Pgm ... Mr. Gary R. WHITE
104 Dir Campus Education Abroad Program ... Dr. Juan E. CAMPO
88 Director Env Health & Safety ... Mr. John STERRITT
88 Director MultiCultural Center ... Ms. Zaveeni KHAN-MARCUS
38 Assoc Dir Counseling & Psych Svcs ... Dr. Brian OLOWUDE
94 Director Women's Center ... Ms. Kim EQUINOA
88 Campus Ombuds ... Ms. Caroline ADAMS
88 Exec Dir Instructional Devel ... Mr. George H. MICHAELS
36 Director Career Services ... Mr. Ignacio GALLARDO
13 AVC IT & Chief Information Officer ... Mr. Matthew HALL
43 Chief Campus Counsel ... Ms. Nancy G. HAMILL
22 Dir Equal Op & Discrim Prevention ... Mr. Ricardo ALCAINO
88 Dir Design & Construction ... Mr. Julie HENDRICKS
88 Dir Univ Center/Events Center ... Mr. Gary LAWRENCE
88 Director of Recreation ... Mr. Jeff HUSKEY
92 Honors Program Analyst ... Ms. Summer HOWATT-NAB
108 Institutional Assessment Coord ... Dr. Amanda BREY
44 Director Annual Giving ... Mr. Brandon FRIESEN

*University of California-Santa Cruz (B)

1156 High Street, Santa Cruz CA 95064-1077

County: Santa Cruz | FICE Identification: 001321 | Unit ID: 110714
Telephone: (831) 459-0111 | Carnegie Class: DU-Highest
FAX Number: (831) 459-0146 | Calendar System: Quarter
URL: www.ucsc.edu
Established: 1965 | Annual Undergrad Tuition & Fees (In-State): $13,960
Enrollment: 19,457 | Coed
Affiliation or Control: State | IRS Status: 501(c)3
Highest Offering: Doctorate
Accreditation: WC, IPSY

02 Chancellor ... Dr. Cynthia LARIVE
05 Campus Provost/Exec Vice Chancellor ... Dr. Lori KLETZER
10 Vice Chanc Business/Admin Services ... Dr. Sarah LATHAM
45 Vice Chancellor Planning/Budget ... Dr. Peggy DELANEY
46 Vice Chancellor Research ... Dr. Scott BRANDT
30 Int Vice Chanc University Relations ... Mr. Jeff SHILLING
13 Vice Chanc Information Technology ... Dr. Van WILLIAMS
20 Vice Prov/Dean Undergrad Educ ... Dr. Richard HUGHEY
20 Vice Provost Academic Affairs ... Dr. Herbert LEE
84 Assoc VC Enrollment Mgmt ... Ms. Michelle L. WHITTINGHAM
16 Asst VC Academic Personnel ... Ms. Grace MCCLINTOCK
18 Campus Architect ... Mr. Felix ANG
15 Assoc VC Staff Human Resources ... Mr. Steve STEIN
32 AVC Campus Life/Dn of Students ... Mr. Garrett NAIMAN
08 University Librarian ... Ms. Elizabeth COWELL
79 Dean of Humanities ... Dr. Tyler STOVALL
81 Dean Physical & Biological Sci ... Dr. Paul KOCH
49 Interim Dean of the Arts ... Dr. Ted WARBURTON
83 Dean of Social Sciences ... Dr. Katharyne MITCHELL
54 Dean of Engineering ... Dr. Alexander WOLF
58 Int Vice Prov/Dean of Grad Studies ... Dr. Quentin WILLIAMS
65 Director Institute Marine Sciences ... Dr. Daniel COSTA
81 Director Institute Particle Physics ... Dr. Steven RITZ
88 Director UCO/Lick Observatory ... Dr. Claire MAX
12 Provost Stevenson College ... Dr. Alice YANG
12 Provost Cowell College ... Dr. Alan CHRISTY
12 Provost Crown College ... Dr. Manel CAMPS
12 Provost Merrill College ... Dr. Elizabeth ABRAMS
12 Provost Porter College ... Dr. Sean KEILEN
12 Provost Kresge College ... Dr. Ben LEEDS CARSON
12 Provost Rachel Carson College ... Dr. Sue CARTER
12 Provost College Nine & Ten ... Dr. Flora LU
12 Interim Provost Oakes College ... Dr. Marcia OCHOA
06 Registrar ... Mr. Tchad SANGER
09 Director Institutional Research ... Dr. Julian L. FERNALD
37 Director Financial Aid/Operations ... Mr. Patrick REGISTER
22 Assoc Dir EEO/Affirmative Action ... Ms. Sonje DAYRIES
29 Director of Alumni Relations ... Ms. Shayna KENT
26 Dir Marketing/Communications ... Ms. Lisa NIELSEN
86 Director Government Relations ... Ms. Melissa WHATLEY
38 Director Student Counseling ... Dr. Gary DUNN
07 Director of Admissions ... Ms. Blia YANG
41 Athletic Director ... Ms. Susan WITTMANN HARRIMAN
108 Asst Director for Assessment ... Dr. Anna SHER
102 Dir Foundation/Corporate Relations ... Ms. Lynne STOOPS

University of East-West Medicine (C)

595 Lawrence Expressway, Sunnyvale CA 94085

County: Santa Clara | FICE Identification: 039953 | Unit ID: 447801
Telephone: (408) 733-1878 | Carnegie Class: Spec-4-yr-Other Health
FAX Number: (408) 636-7705 | Calendar System: Trimester
URL: www.uewm.edu
Established: 1997 | Annual Undergrad Tuition & Fees: N/A
Enrollment: 30 | Coed
Affiliation or Control: Proprietary | IRS Status: Proprietary
Highest Offering: Master's
Accreditation: ACUP

01 President ... Dr. Eric TAO
05 VP Academic Leadership ... Dr. Bei LIU
07 Director of Admissions/Admin ... Dr. Sharon ZHOU
37 Director of Financial Aid/Govt Rels ... Ms. Pei Chi CHEN

† Granted candidacy at the Doctorate level.

University of La Verne (D)

1950 Third Street, La Verne CA 91750-4443

County: Los Angeles | FICE Identification: 001216 | Unit ID: 117140
Telephone: (909) 593-3511 | Carnegie Class: DU-Mod
FAX Number: (909) 593-0965 | Calendar System: Semester
URL: www.laverne.edu
Established: 1891 | Annual Undergrad Tuition & Fees: $43,050
Enrollment: 8,159 | Coed
Affiliation or Control: Independent Non-Profit | IRS Status: 501(c)3
Highest Offering: Doctorate
Accreditation: WC, #ARCPA, CAATE, CAEPN, CLPSY, LAW, SPAA

01 President ... Dr. Devorah A. LIEBERMAN
05 Provost & Vice President ... Dr. Jonathan REED
10 Chief Financial Officer ... Mr. Avedis (Avo) KECHICHIAN
111 Vice President Univ Advancement ... Mrs. Sherri MYLOTT
84 Vice Pres Strategic Enrollment Mgmt ... Mrs. Mary AGUAYO
50 Dean College Business/Public Mgmt ... Dr. Ibrahim (Abe) HELOU
53 Dean College Educ/Org Ldrship ... Dr. Kimberly WHITE-SMITH
61 Dean College of Law ... Mr. Kevin MARSHALL
32 Chief Student Affairs Officer ... Dr. Loretta RAHMANI
12 Dean Regional & Online Programs ... Ms. Nelly KAZMAN
07 Interim Dean of Admissions ... Mr. Todd ECKEL
121 Assoc VP Academic Sppt/Retent Svcs ... Ms. Adeline CARDENAS-CLAGUE
21 Associate Vice President of Finance ... Ms. Lori K. GORDIEN CASE
15 Associate VP/Chief HR Officer ... Ms. Mia BASIC
18 Vice President of Facilities/Tech ... Vacant
35 Deputy Chief Student Affairs Office ... Mrs. Ruby S. MONTANO-CORDOVA
88 Asst Dean Grad Acad Supp/Ret Svcs ... Ms. Jo Nell BAKER
88 Asst VP & Adv & Recruit Mktg ... Mr. Fred A. CHYR
85 Director International Services ... Mr. Pressian NICOLOV
18 Sr Dir Physical Plant Ops & Svcs ... Mr. Garth JONES
11 Director Administration and Opers ... Mr. Jason NEAL
27 Exec Director of Strategic Comm ... Mr. Rod LEVEQUE
29 Sr Dir Advancement Oper & Services ... Ms. Bianca ROMERO
38 Dir Counseling & Psych Services ... Dr. Elleni R. KOULOS
113 Director Student Accounts ... Ms. Xochitl E. MARTINEZ
96 Director Purchasing & Procurement ... Mrs. Deborah S. DEACY
28 Director Multicultural Affairs ... Dr. Daniel L. LOERA
23 Dir Health Svcs/Svcs for Stds-Disab ... Ms. Cynthia K. DENNE
39 Assoc Dean Stdnts/Dir Stdnt Housing ... Mr. Juan REGALADO
36 Asst Dean Student Career Support ... Ms. Mindy BAGGISH
88 Dir Center for Adv/Teaching & Lrng ... Dr. Sammy ELZARKA
88 Director Graduate Success Center ... Dr. Linda DE LONG
41 Athletic Director ... Mr. Scott WINTERBURN
06 Registrar ... Ms. Marilyn S. DAVIES
08 University Librarian ... Dr. Vinaya L. TRIPURANENI
28 Chief Diversity Officer ... Vacant
09 Director of Institutional Research ... Dr. Leeshawn MOORE
42 Chaplain/Dir of Campus Ministry ... Dr. Zandra L. WAGONER
90 Sr Dir Admission Oper/Tech Svcs ... Mrs. Loreto D'MONTE
88 Director High Desert & Inland Empir ... Ms. Juli ROBERTS
88 Director Kern County ... Dr. Nora DOMINGUEZ
88 Director Orange County ... Ms. Alison RODRIGUEZ-BALLES
88 Int Director San Fernando Valley ... Ms. Susan LOMELI
88 Senior Executive Director Regional ... Ms. Kitt VINCENT
88 Asst Director Oxnard Campus ... Mr. Samuel LANG
88 Director International Admission ... Mr. Adam WU
20 Vice Provost ... Vacant
88 Asst Director of Civic Engagement ... Ms. Julissa ESPINOZA
04 Dir President Office/Board Affairs ... Dr. Shannon CAPALDI
19 Director Security/Safety ... Mr. Ruben IBARRA
26 Exec Dir Ofc of Strategic Comm ... Mr. Rod LEVEQUE
37 Director Student Financial Aid ... Mr. Nicholas NOVELLO

University of the Pacific (E)

3601 Pacific Avenue, Stockton CA 95211-0197

County: San Joaquin | FICE Identification: 001329 | Unit ID: 120883
Telephone: (209) 946-2011 | Carnegie Class: DU-Mod
FAX Number: (209) 946-2845 | Calendar System: Semester
URL: www.pacific.edu
Established: 1851 | Annual Undergrad Tuition & Fees: $48,164
Enrollment: 6,255 | Coed
Affiliation or Control: Independent Non-Profit | IRS Status: 501(c)3
Highest Offering: Doctorate
Accreditation: WC, ACAE, #ARCPA, @AUD, CAATE, DENT, DH, IPSY, LAW, MUS, PHAR, PTA, SP

01 Interim President ... Dr. Maria G. PALLAVICINI
05 Interim Provost ... Michael H. SCHWARTZ
10 VP Business & Finance ... Ken MULLEN
32 VP Student Life ... Dr. Carrie L. PETR
30 VP Development & Alumni Relations ... G. Burnham 'Burnie' ATTERBURY
13 VP Technology/CIO ... Art SPRECHER
21 Assoc VP Business & Finance ... Ron ELLISON
84 VP Enrollment Management ... Roberta KASKEL
26 Assoc VP Marketing & Communication ... Marge GREY
119 Interim Assoc VP Info Security/CISO ... Ken KERRICK
115 Asst VP Treasury/Chf Invest Ofcr ... Jol MANILAY
49 Dean College of the Pacific ... Rena FRADEN
50 Dean Eberhardt School of Business ... Tim CARROLL
52 Dean Dugoni School of Dentistry ... Nader NADERSHAHI
53 Dean Benerd School of Education ... Patricia CAMPBELL
54 Dean School of Eng/Comp Sci ... Steven HOWELL
61 Dean McGeorge School of Law ... Michael SCHWARTZ
64 Dean Conservatory of Music ... Peter WITTE
67 Dean Long School Pharm/Hlth Sci ... Phillip R. OPPENHEIMER
36 Assoc VP/Exec Dir Career Dev ... Tom VECCHIONE
08 Dean University Library ... Mary SOMERVILLE
58 Dean Graduate School ... Thomas NAEHR
51 Dean University College ... Patricia CAMPBELL
25 Sponsored Pgms Administrator ... Vacant
29 Asst VP Alumni Relations ... Kelli PAGE
37 Exec Director Financial Aid ... Aquila GALGON
07 Interim Exec Director Admissions ... Jonathan LATTA
06 University Registrar ... Margo LANDY
09 Assoc Prov Inst Research ... Mike ROGERS
35 Exec Director Campus Life ... Marc FALKENSTEIN
96 Director Purchasing ... Ronda MARR

92 Director Honors Program .... Balint SZATARAY
93 Dir Intercultural Student Success .... Ines RUIZ-HUSTON
94 Director Gender Studies .... Traci ROBERTS-CAMPS
38 Director Counseling Services .... Stacie TURKS
39 Exec Director Residential Life .... Joe BERTHIAUME
41 Director of Athletics .... Janet LUCAS
42 Director Religious & Spiritual Life .... Laura STEED
15 Asst VP Human Resources .... Linda JEFFERS
40 Director Bookstore .... Nicole CASTILLO
19 Exec Director Public Safety .... Grant BEDFORD
18 Director Physical Plant .... Steve GREENWOD
82 Director School Intl Studies .... Dr. William HERRIN
110 Sr Assoc VP Development .... Scott BIEDERMANN
88 Asst VP Development .... Judy NAGAI
100 Chief of Staff to the President .... Vacant
104 Dir International Programs Services .... Ryan GRIFFITH
43 General Counsel .... Kevin MILLS
12 Director Sacramento Campus .... Dr. Patrick FAVERTY
04 Exec Asst to the President .... Shim LACY
88 Asst Dean Admissions .... Tracy SIMMONS
117 Director Enterprise Risk Mgmt .... Roberta MARTOZA
116 Director Internal Audit .... Randy SCHWANTES
114 Director University Budget .... Jonallie PARRA
105 Director Web Services .... Vacant
108 Vice Prov Strategy/Educ Effective .... Cyd JENEFSKY
11 Asst Dean Operations .... Kyle HARKNESS
22 Director Affirmative Action/EEO .... Deborah FREEMAN
44 Exec Director Annual Giving .... Michael RICHMOND
90 Asst VP Tech Customer Experience .... Peggy KAY
91 Asst Dir Integrated Services .... Raoul VILLALPANDO
88 Asst VP Development .... Molly BYRNE

University of the People (A)

225 S. Lake Avenue, Suite 300, Pasadena CA 91101
County: Los Angeles Identification: 667160
Unit ID: 488846
Telephone: (626) 264-8880 Carnegie Class: Bac/Assoc-Mixed
FAX Number: N/A Calendar System: Other
URL: www.uopeople.edu
Established: 2009 Annual Undergrad Tuition & Fees: $1,000
Enrollment: 2,138 Coed
Affiliation or Control: Independent Non-Profit IRS Status: 501(c)3
Highest Offering: Master's
Accreditation: DEAC

01 President & Founder .... Mr. Shai RESHEF
05 Provost .... Dr. David HARRIS COHEN
11 Sr Vice Pres Operations .... Mr. Rami ISH-HURVITZ
45 VP for Strategy & Planning .... Mr. Yoav VENTURA
84 Sr Vice President Enrollment .... Mr. Asaf WOLFF
13 Vice Pres Technology .... Ms. Hadass ADMON
10 Chief Financial Officer .... Mr. Paul AFFUSO

University of Phoenix Bay Area Campus (B)

3590 N First Street, San Jose CA 95134-1805
Telephone: (800) 266-2107 Identification: 770193
Accreditation: &NH, ACBSP

† Branch campus of University of Phoenix, Tempe, AZ. No longer accepting campus-based students.

University of Phoenix Central Valley Campus (C)

45 River Park Place West, Suite 201,
Fresno CA 93720-1552
Telephone: (559) 312-1133 Identification: 770190
Accreditation: &NH, ACBSP

† Branch campus of University of Phoenix, Tempe, AZ

University of Phoenix Sacramento Valley Campus (D)

2860 Gateway Oaks Drive, Sacramento CA 95833-4334
Telephone: (800) 266-2107 Identification: 770191
Accreditation: &NH, ACBSP

† Branch campus of University of Phoenix, Tempe, AZ

University of Phoenix San Diego Campus (E)

9645 Granite Ridge Dr, Suite 200,
San Diego CA 92123-2658
Telephone: (800) 473-4346 Identification: 770192
Accreditation: &NH, ACBSP

† Branch campus of University of Phoenix, Tempe, AZ

University of Phoenix Southern California Campus (F)

3110 E. Guasti Rd, Ontario CA 91761
Telephone: (800) 888-1968 Identification: 770189
Accreditation: &NH, ACBSP

† Branch campus of University of Phoenix, Tempe, AZ.

University of Redlands (G)

PO Box 3080, Redlands CA 92373-0999
County: San Bernardino FICE Identification: 001322
Unit ID: 121691
Telephone: (909) 793-2121 Carnegie Class: Masters/L
FAX Number: (909) 793-2029 Calendar System: Semester
URL: www.redlands.edu
Established: 1907 Annual Undergrad Tuition & Fees: $49,504
Enrollment: 4,898 Coed
Affiliation or Control: Independent Non-Profit IRS Status: 501(c)3
Highest Offering: Doctorate
Accreditation: WC, ACBSP, MUS, PAST, SP, THEOL

01 President .... Dr. Ralph W. KUNCL
05 Provost/Chief Academic Officer .... Dr. Kathy OGREN
10 Sr Vice Pres Finance/Administration .... Mr. Cory NOMURA
32 University Dean of Student Affairs .... Dr. Donna EDDLEMAN
84 Vice President for Enrollment .... Mr. Kevin M. DYERLY
111 Vice Pres for Advancement .... Ms. Tamara M. JOSSERAND
26 Chief Communications Officer .... Ms. Wendy SHATTUCK
43 General Counsel .... Mr. Brent G. GERATY
100 Chief of Staff .... Ms. Michelle ROGERS
53 Dean School of Education .... Dr. Andrew WALL
50 Dean School of Business .... Dr. Thomas HORAN
49 Dean Arts & Sciences .... Dr. Kendrick BROWN
64 Interim Dean School of Music .... Dr. Joseph MODICA
30 Assoc Vice Pres Development .... Mr. Ray WATTS
21 Director Financial Ops & Controller .... Ms. Patricia M. CAUDLE
28 Asc Dean Campus Diversity/Inclusion .... Vacant
42 Chaplain .... Rev. John T. WALSH
06 Registrar .... Ms. Maria JOHNSON
104 Director Study Abroad .... Mr. Leo ROWLAND
37 Director of Financial Aid .... Ms. Emily BAKER
08 Int Director of Library Services .... Ms. Shana HIGGINS
15 Director of Human Resources .... Mr. Jeremy HAMMOND
09 Asst Provost Institutional Research .... Dr. Yan XIE
19 Chief of Public Safety .... Mr. Jeffrey TALBOTT
88 Director Administrative Services .... Mr. Brett TELFORD
18 Director of Facilities Management .... Mr. Roger CELLINI
29 Director of Alumni Relations .... Ms. Shelli STOCKTON
20 Asst Dean of Academic/Student Life .... Ms. Amy WILMS
38 Director Student Counseling Ctr .... Dr. Matt GRAGG
41 Director of PE & Athletics .... Mr. Jeffrey MARTINEZ
36 Director Student Employment .... Ms. Kathryn WOOD
07 Director of Admissions .... Ms. Belinda SANDOVAL
13 Exec Dir Information Tech Svcs .... Mr. Steve GARCIA
04 Executive Assistant to President .... Ms. Lauri GRIER
39 Director of Student Housing .... Ms. Cassandra MORTON
88 Dir Military & Veteran Services .... Ms. Monique POPE
44 Director Annual Giving .... Ms. Molly WIDDICOMBE
88 Dir Community Service Learning .... Mr. Tony MUELLER
103 Dir Professional Development .... Mr. Erik LARSEN

University of St. Augustine for Health Sciences (H)

700 Windy Point Drive, San Marcos CA 92069
County: San Diego FICE Identification: 031713
Unit ID: 367954
Telephone: (904) 826-0084 Carnegie Class: Spec-4-yr-Other Health
FAX Number: N/A Calendar System: Trimester
URL: www.usa.edu
Established: 1979 Annual Graduate Tuition & Fees: N/A
Enrollment: 2,992 Coed
Affiliation or Control: Proprietary IRS Status: Proprietary
Highest Offering: Doctorate; No Undergraduates
Accreditation: WC, NURSE, OT, PTA

01 CEO .... Ms. Vivian SANCHEZ
02 President/Chief Academic Officer .... Dr. Divina GROSSMAN
10 Executive Director of Finance .... Mr. Jeff LAGASSE
05 Sr VP Educational Effectiveness .... Dr. Karen GERSTEN
15 Exec Director Human Resources .... Ms. Susan WAUGH
13 Exec Director IT .... Mr. Matt MOLINE
107 Dean of Post-Professional Studies .... Dr. Cindy MATHENA
09 Director of Institutional Research .... Ms. Nga PHAN
37 Director Student Financial Aid .... Ms. Rhonda JAMES
84 Director Enrollment Management .... Ms. Julie GONICK
06 Registrar .... Ms. Diane RONDINELLI
88 Chair of the Occupational Therapy .... Dr. Anne HULL
88 Chair of the Institute of PT .... Dr. Jodi LIPHART

University of Saint Katherine (I)

1637 Capalina Road, San Marcos CA 92069
County: San Diego Identification: 667263
Telephone: (760) 471-1316 Carnegie Class: Not Classified
FAX Number: (760) 704-1314 Calendar System: Semester
URL: www.usk.edu
Established: Annual Undergrad Tuition & Fees: N/A
Enrollment: N/A Coed
Affiliation or Control: Independent Non-Profit IRS Status: 501(c)3
Highest Offering: Baccalaureate
Accreditation: WC

01 President & Founder .... Dr. Frank PAPATHEOFANIS
05 Dean of College/Chief Academic Ofcr .Dr. Fernando ARZOLA, JR.
10 Chief Financial Officer .... Ryan WEST
09 Dir of Inst Research/Effectiveness .... Christos KORGAN
07 Dean of Admissions/Registrar .... Marina KARAVOKIRIS

32 Dean of Students .... Bre WILLIAMS
08 Librarian .... Mike ANDERS HARRISON

University of San Diego (J)

5998 Alcala Park, San Diego CA 92110-2492
County: San Diego FICE Identification: 010395
Unit ID: 122436
Telephone: (619) 260-4600 Carnegie Class: DU-Higher
FAX Number: (619) 260-6833 Calendar System: 4/1/4
URL: www.sandiego.edu
Established: 1949 Annual Undergrad Tuition & Fees: $49,358
Enrollment: 8,905 Coed
Affiliation or Control: Roman Catholic IRS Status: 501(c)3
Highest Offering: Doctorate
Accreditation: WC, CACREP, CAEPN, CEA, IPSY, LAW, MFCD, NURSE

01 President .... Dr. James T. HARRIS
04 Special Assistant to the President .... Ms. Elaine ATENCIO
05 Vice President & Provost .... Dr. Gail F. BAKER
10 VP Finance/Chief Financial Officer .... Vacant
45 VP Inst Effectiveness & Strategic .... Dr. Andrew ALLEN
42 Vice President Mission & Ministry .... Msgr. Daniel J. DILLABOUGH
32 Vice President Student Affairs .... Ms. Carmen M. VAZQUEZ
111 Vice President Univ Advancement .... Mr. Richard P. VIRGIN
11 Vice President of Operations .... Mr. Ky L. SNYDER
49 Dean College of Arts & Sciences .... Dr. Noelle NORTON
50 Interim Dean School of Business .... Dr. Barbara LOUGEE
54 Dean Shiley-Marcos School of Engr .... Dr. Chell ROBERTS
61 Dean School of Law .... Mr. Stephen C. FERRUOLO
53 Dean Sch Leadership/Educ Sciences .... Dr. Nicholas LADANY
66 Dean Sch Nursing/Health Sci .... Dr. Jane GEORGES
88 Dean School of Peace Studies .... Dr. Patricia MARQUEZ
08 Dean University Library .... Dr. Theresa BYRD
43 General Counsel .... Ms. Kelly C. DOUGLAS
20 Vice Provost Academic Affairs .... Dr. Thomas R. HERRINTON
13 Interim Chief Information Officer .... Dr. Elazar HAREL
06 University Registrar .... Ms. Elizabeth SILVA
46 Associate Provost Research & Dev .... Dr. Jennifer ZWOLINSKI
28 Assoc Provost for Incl & Diversity .... Dr. Esteban DEL RIO
20 Assoc Provost International Affairs .... Dr. Denise DIMON
21 Assoc VP Reporting & Compliance .... Ms. Katy ROIG
41 Assoc VP & Exec Dir of Athletics .... Mr. Bill MCGILLIS
84 Asst VP Enrollment Management .... Mr. Stephen F. PULTZ
15 AVP & Chief Human Resources Officer .... Dr. Karen BRIGGS
18 Asst VP Facilities Management .... Mr. Andre HUTCHINSON
26 Assoc Vice Pres Univ Communications .... Mr. Peter MARLOW
27 Asst Vice President Media Comm .... Ms. Pamela GRAY PAYTON
19 Asst VP & Chief Public Safety .... Mr. James MIYASHIRO
35 Asst VP & Dean of Students .... Dr. Donald R. GODWIN
109 Asst VP Auxiliary Services .... Mr. Andre MALLIE
07 Director of Admissions .... Ms. Minh-Ha HOANG
09 Dir Inst Research & Planning .... Dr. Paula S. KRIST
90 Sr Director Customer Support .... Ms. Shahra MESHKATY
91 Senior Director ERP Technologies .... Ms. Stephanie HOIE
102 Sr Director Foundation Relations .... Ms. Annette KETNER
86 Dir Community/Govt Relations .... Vacant
112 Director Planned Giving .... Ms. Erin JONES
29 Senior Director Alumni Relations .... Mr. Charles BASS
44 Senior Director Annual Giving .... Mr. Philip GARLAND
36 Senior Director Career Dev Center .... Ms. Robin DARMON
38 Director Counseling Center .... Vacant
37 Director Financial Aid Services .... Ms. Kellie NEHRING
92 Director Honors Program .... Dr. Susannah STERN
39 Director Residential Life Admin .... Mr. Luke LACROIX
85 Dir International Students/Scholars .... Ms. Chia-Yen LIN
104 Dir International Studies Abroad .... Dr. Kira A. ESPIRITU
93 Director Multicultural Center .... Dr. Mayte PEREZ-FRANCO
88 Sr Director Media Relations .... Ms. Elizabeth HARMAN
96 Director Procurement Services .... Ms. Theresa L. ROBINSON HARRIS
25 Director Sponsored Programs .... Ms. Traci MERRILL
23 Director Student Health Center .... Ms. Pamela J. SIKES
106 Dir Online Education .... Ms. Roxanne MORRISON
22 Dir Title IX/EEO .... Dr. Nicole SCHUESSLER

University of San Francisco (K)

2130 Fulton Street, San Francisco CA 94117-1080
County: San Francisco FICE Identification: 001325
Unit ID: 122612
Telephone: (415) 422-5555 Carnegie Class: DU-Mod
FAX Number: (415) 422-2303 Calendar System: 4/1/4
URL: www.usfca.edu
Established: 1855 Annual Undergrad Tuition & Fees: $48,066
Enrollment: 11,063 Coed
Affiliation or Control: Roman Catholic IRS Status: 501(c)3
Highest Offering: Doctorate
Accreditation: WC, CLPSY, IPSY, LAW, NURSE, PH, SPAA

01 President .... Rev. Paul J. FITZGERALD, SJ
05 Provost & Vice Pres Acad Affairs .... Dr. Donald HELLER
10 Vice President Business & Finance .... Mr. Charles E. CROSS
26 Vice Pres Marketing/Communications .... Ms. Ellen RYDER
30 Vice President Development .... Mr. Peter J. WILCH
43 General Counsel .... Ms. Donna J. DAVIS
13 Vice President IT & CIO .... Mr. Opinder BAWA
20 Senior Vice Provost Acad Affairs .... Dr. Shirley MCGUIRE
32 Vice Provost Student Life .... Ms. Julie J. ORIO
28 Vice Prov Diversity & Community .... Dr. Mary J. WARDELL-GHIRARDUZZI
114 Vice Prov Inst Budget/Plng/Analytic .... Dr. Jeff HAMRICK

84 Vice Provost Strategic Enroll Mgmt .... Mr. Michael BESEDA
61 Dean School of Law .... Ms. Susan FREIWALD
49 Dean College Arts & Sciences .... Dr. Marcelo F. CAMPERI
08 Dean of University Library .... Dr. Tyrone H. CANNON
53 Dean School of Education .... Dr. Shabnam KOIRALA-AZAD
66 Dean School of Nursing/Health Prof .... Dr. Margaret W. BAKER
50 Interim Dean School of Management .... Dr. Charles MOSES
18 Assoc Vice Pres Facilities Mgmt .... Mr. Michael E. LONDON
21 Assoc Vice Pres Finance & Treasury .... Ms. Stacy LEWIS
15 Assoc Vice Pres Human Resources .... Ms. Diane NELSON
114 AVP Accounting & Business Svcs .... Ms. Neva NGUYEN
88 Rector of Jesuit Community .... Rev. Timothy S. GODFREY, SJ
42 Director University Ministry .... Dr. Julia A. DOWD
88 Asst Vice Prov Digital Strat/Online .... Mr. John DEVOY
37 Asst Vice Prov Student Fin Svcs .... Ms. Mary L. BOOKER
04 Exec Asst to President/Sec BOT .... Ms. Jaci E. NEESAM
27 Media Relations Specialist .... Ms. Kellie SAMSON
45 Assoc Vice Prov Planning and Budget .... Mr. Michael J. HARRINGTON
110 Sr Assoc VP Development .... Mr. Preston S. WALTON
06 Assoc Dean University Registrar .... Mr. Robert L. BROMFIELD
96 Dir Purchasing & Ancillary Svc .... Ms. Janet L. TEYMOURTASH
38 Senior Dir Counseling & Psych Svcs .... Dr. Barbara J. THOMAS
36 Senior Director Career Svcs .... Mr. Alex HOCHMAN
19 Senior Director of Public Safety .... Dr. Daniel L. LAWSON
88 Asst Vice Prov Graduate Enrollment .... Mr. Michael HUGHES
88 Asst Vice Prov Integ Enrollment Mgt .... Mr. Patrick KAO
104 Director Ctr for Global Education .... Ms. Sharon F. LI
07 Asst Vice Prov Undergrad Admissions .... Ms. April CRABTREE
85 Director Intl Student/Scholar Svcs .... Ms. Marcella PITCHER DEPROTO
41 Director of Athletics .... Ms. Joan MCDERMOTT
29 Assoc VP for Development .... Ms. Leslie WETZEL
44 Assoc VP Giving & Devel Svc & PR&M .... Vacant
102 Dir Corp/Foundation Relations .... Vacant
29 Director University Initiatives .... Mr. Bill CARTWRIGHT
16 Dir of Employee Relations .... Ms. Liliana ROJAS
09 Dir Inst Research and Analytics .... Mr. Theodore M. LYDON, JR.
39 Sr Dir Student Housing/Resident Ed .... Mr. Torry BROUILLARD-BRUCE
24 Dir Ctr Learning Instruct & Tech .... Dr. John BANSAVICH
105 Sr Dir Web & Digital Communication .... Ms. Marlene K. TOM
108 AVP Educ Effectiveness/Assessment .... Ms. Deborah PANTER
25 Director Contracts/Grants Admin .... Mr. Donald CAMPBELL
22 Asst Dean/Director Disability Svcs .... Mr. Tom MERRELL
14 AVP & Dir Educ Technology Services .... Mr. David KIRMSE
88 Asst Vice Prov Enroll Communication ... Ms. Katherine EDWARDS
116 AVP Tax Compliance & Internal Audit .... Mr. Dominic DAHER
88 Director of Inst Analytics .... Mr. Joseph HENSON
101 Secretary of the Board .... Ms. Jaci NEESAM

University of South Los Angeles (A)

555 W Redondo Beach Blvd, Gardena CA 90248

County: Los Angeles — Identification: 667326
Telephone: (310) 756-0001 — Carnegie Class: Not Classified
FAX Number: (310) 756-0004 — Calendar System: Quarter
URL: www.uosla.org
Established: 1993 — Annual Undergrad Tuition & Fees: N/A
Enrollment: N/A — Coed
Affiliation or Control: Proprietary — IRS Status: Proprietary
Highest Offering: Doctorate
Accreditation: @TRACS

01 Chancellor .... Dr. Paul LEE
11 Vice Chanc Admin & Student Affs .... Dr. Richard KANG
10 CFO & Director of Admin .... Jackie JUNG
05 Chief Academic Officer .... Dr. Guy LANGVARDT
32 Dean of Student Affairs .... Dr. Tania MAYNE
07 Dir of Admiss & Records/Registrar .... Joseph ROH

University of Southern California (B)

University Park, Los Angeles CA 90089-0012

County: Los Angeles — FICE Identification: 001328
Unit ID: 123961
Telephone: (213) 740-2311 — Carnegie Class: DU-Highest
FAX Number: (213) 740-8502 — Calendar System: Semester
URL: www.usc.edu
Established: 1880 — Annual Undergrad Tuition & Fees: $56,225
Enrollment: 45,687 — Coed
Affiliation or Control: Independent Non-Profit — IRS Status: 501(c)3
Highest Offering: Doctorate
Accreditation: WC, ANEST, ARCPA, CAEPN, CLPSY, DENT, DH, DIETC, DIETI, HSA, IPSY, JOUR, LAW, LIB, LSAR, MED, NURSE, OT, PCSAS, PDPSY, PH, PHAR, PLNG, PTA, SPAA, SW

01 President .... Dr. Carol L. FOLT
05 Provost & SVP Academic Affairs .... Dr. Charles F. ZUKOSKI
26 Interim SVP University Relations .... Mr. David BROWN
111 Sr VP University Advancement .... Mr. Albert R. CHECCIO
23 Sr VP & CEO for USC Health .... Mr. Thomas E. JACKIEWICZ
115 Chief Investment Officer .... Ms. Lisa MAZZOCCO
27 SVP/Chief Communication Officer .... Glenn OSAKI
10 Sr VP Finance & CFO .... Mr. James STATEN
41 Interim Athletic Director .... Mr. Dave ROBERTS
15 Sr VP Human Resources .... Ms. Felicia WASHINGTON
11 Sr VP Administration .... Mr. David W. WRIGHT
43 Interim Head of Legal Affairs .... Mr. Mark MERRITT
32 VP for Student Affairs .... Mr. Winston B. CRISP
07 VP Admissions and Planning .... Dr. L. Katharine HARRINGTON
46 VP for Research .... Dr. Randolph W. HALL
88 VP for Athletic Compliance .... Mr. Michael BLANTON
18 VP Capital Construction/Facilities .... Mr. Lloyd SILBERSTEIN
88 VP Health Sciences Advancement .... Ms. Kathryn CARRICO
27 VP Public Relations & Marketing .... Ms. Brenda K. MACEO
88 VP Ofc of Professionalism/Ethics .... Mr. Michael BLANTON
100 Chief of Staff .... Ms. Rene K. PAK
60 Dean Annenberg School Communication .... Dr. Willow C. BAY
48 Dean School of Architecture .... Mr. Milton S. CURRY
50 Dean Marshall School of Business .... Mr. James G. ELLIS
88 Dean School of Cinematic Arts .... Dr. Elizabeth M. DALEY
66 Dean Kaufman School of Dance .... Dr. Robert A. CUTIETTA
52 Dean Ostrow School of Dentistry .... Dr. Avishai SADAN
53 Dean Rossier School of Education .... Dr. Karen S. GALLAGHER
54 Dean Viterbi School of Engineering .... Dr. Yannis C. YORTSOS
57 Dean Roski School of Fine Arts .... Dr. Erica MUHL
88 Dean Davis School of Gerontology .... Dr. Pinchas COHEN
61 Dean Gould School of Law .... Dr. Andrew GUZMAN
63 Dean Keck School of Medicine .... Dr. Rohit VARMA
64 Dean Thornton School of Music .... Dr. Robert A. CUTIETTA
67 Dean School of Pharmacy .... Dr. Vassilios PAPADOPOULOS
70 Interim Dean School of Social Work .... Dr. John CLAPP
88 Dean School of Dramatic Arts .... Mr. David BRIDEL
88 Dean Price School of Public Policy .... Dr. Jack H. KNOTT
49 Dean Dornsife Col Ltrs/Arts & Sci .... Dr. Amber D. MILLER
42 Dean Religious Life .... Dr. Varun SONI
06 Registrar .... Dr. Frank CHANG
08 Dean University Libraries .... Ms. Catherine QUINLAN
07 Dean of Admission .... Mr. Timothy BRUNOLD
37 Dean of Financial Aid .... Mr. Thomas MCWHORTER
29 Assoc Sr VP and Campaign Director .... Mr. Sam M. LOPEZ
28 Exec Dir of Equity/Diversity .. Ms. Gretchen DAHLINGER MEANS
38 Dir Counseling & Psychological Svcs .... Dr. Ilene ROSENSTEIN
88 Vice Provost and Senior Advisor .... Dr. Martin L. LEVINE
58 Vice Prov for Graduate Programs .... Dr. Sally PRATT
20 Vice Prov for Undergraduate Program .... Dr. Andrea HODGE
13 Chief Information Officer .... Dr. Douglas SHOOK
88 Vice Prov Academic Ops .... Dr. Mark TODD
88 Exec Dir USC Stevens Ctr for Innov .... Ms. Jennifer DYER
88 VP of Global Initiatives .... Dr. Anthony BAILEY
20 Vice Prov for Acad/Faculty Affairs .... Dr. Elizabeth GRADDY

University of the West (C)

1409 Walnut Grove Avenue, Rosemead CA 91770-3709

County: Los Angeles — FICE Identification: 036963
Unit ID: 449870
Telephone: (626) 571-8811 — Carnegie Class: Bac-A&S
FAX Number: (626) 571-1413 — Calendar System: Semester
URL: www.uwest.edu
Established: 1991 — Annual Undergrad Tuition & Fees: $12,592
Enrollment: 354 — Coed
Affiliation or Control: Independent Non-Profit — IRS Status: 501(c)3
Highest Offering: Doctorate
Accreditation: WC

01 President .... Dr. Otto CHANG
05 Chief Academic Officer .... Dr. Peter M. ROJCEWICZ
32 Dean of Student Affairs .... Ms. Vanessa KARAM
84 Dean of Enrollment .... Dr. Maria AYON
114 Chief Budget Officer .... Mr. Michael OERTEL
08 Director of Library .... Ms. Ling Ling KUO
06 Registrar .... Ms. Jeanette ANDERSON
35 Student Life Director .... Mr. Eddie ESCALANTE
73 Chair of Religious Studies .... Dr. Jane IWAMURA
50 Chair of Business Admin .... Dr. Bill CHEN
97 Chair of General Education .... Dr. Kanae OMURA
83 Chair of Psychology .... Dr. Hiroshi SASASKI
88 Director of English .... Ms. Jennifer AVILA
04 Admin Assistant to the President .... Ms. Grace HSIAO
37 Director Financial Aid .... Ms. Lezli FANG
39 Director Housing/Resident Life .... Mr. Juan TINOCO

University of West Los Angeles (D)

9800 La Cienga Blvd., 12th Floor, Inglewood CA 90301-4423

County: Los Angeles — Identification: 667301
Unit ID: 484862
Telephone: (310) 342-5200 — Carnegie Class: Not Classified
FAX Number: N/A — Calendar System: Semester
URL: www.uwla.edu
Established: 1966 — Annual Undergrad Tuition & Fees: N/A
Enrollment: N/A — Coed
Affiliation or Control: Proprietary — IRS Status: Proprietary
Highest Offering: First Professional Degree
Accreditation: WC

01 President .... Robert BROWN
10 Chief Financial Officer .... Richard MIYAKE
84 VP/Director Recruitment .... Troy BROWN
43 VP/General Counsel .... Tiffany CLINTON
11 VP/Director Business Office .... Johnetta HEGWOOD
61 Dean School of Law .... Jay FRYKBERG
09 Director Institutional Research .... Jesse ALDAVA

Valley College of Medical Careers (E)

8399 Topanga Canyon Blvd Ste 200, West Hills CA 91304

County: Los Angeles — FICE Identification: 041145
Unit ID: 449445
Telephone: (818) 883-9002 — Carnegie Class: Not Classified
FAX Number: (818) 883-9003 — Calendar System: Semester
URL: www.vcmc.edu
Established: — Annual Undergrad Tuition & Fees: N/A
Enrollment: 85 — Coed
Affiliation or Control: Proprietary — IRS Status: Proprietary
Highest Offering: Associate Degree
Accreditation: ABHES, SURTEC

01 President .... Mr. Ronny SUSSMAN

Vanguard University of Southern California (F)

55 Fair Drive, Costa Mesa CA 92626-6597

County: Orange — FICE Identification: 001293
Unit ID: 123651
Telephone: (714) 556-3610 — Carnegie Class: Masters/S
FAX Number: (714) 957-9317 — Calendar System: Semester
URL: www.vanguard.edu
Established: 1920 — Annual Undergrad Tuition & Fees: $33,720
Enrollment: 2,116 — Coed
Affiliation or Control: Assemblies Of God Church — IRS Status: 501(c)3
Highest Offering: Master's
Accreditation: WC, MUS, NURSE, THEA

01 President .... Dr. Michael J. BEALS
100 Dir Oper Strategic Plng/Spec Proj .... Ms. Shree CARTER
04 Exec Assistant to the President .... Mrs. Alexis SCHNOOR
05 Provost/Vice President Acad Affairs .... Dr. Pete MENJARES
49 Assoc Provost/Dean Col Arts & Sci .... Dr. Michael D. WILSON
107 Dean Professional Studies .... Vacant
73 Co-Director of Graduate Religion .... Dr. Roger HEUSER
73 Co-Director of Graduate Religion .... Dr. Doug PETERSEN
58 Director for Graduate Education .... Dr. Sylvia KANE
83 Director for Graduate Psychology .... Vacant
06 Registrar .... Vacant
104 Director Global Outreach/Educ .... Ms. Kayli HILLEBRAND
09 Assoc Dir of Institutional Research .... Mr. John KIM
08 Head Librarian .... Ms. Pamela CRENSHAW
41 Athletic Director .... Mr. Jeff BUSSELL
10 Vice President Finance .... Mr. Jeremy MOSER
21 Controller .... Ms. Jill ROBINSON
96 Director of Fiscal Management .... Ms. Katy MCINTOSH
19 Dir of Campus Safety Services .... Mr. Kenton FERRIN
13 Director Informational Technology .... Mr. Sean MCCLEAN
15 Senior Director of Human Resources .... Mr. Joe BAFFA
18 Director of Facility Operations .... Vacant
40 Bookstore Manager .... Ms. Stephanie BUNT
101 Board Professional .... Ms. Shree CARTER
42 Associate University Pastor .... Rev. Michael WHITFORD
32 Vice President of Student Affairs .... Dr. Tim YOUNG
39 Student Housing Coordinator .... Ms. Megan SISK
121 Dir Stdnt Success/Acad Res/Fam Rels .... Ms. Amanda LEBRECHT
38 Director of Counseling Services .... Dr. Doug HUTCHINSON
36 Career Planning Coordinator .... Vacant
28 Chief Diversity Officer .... Dr. April HARRIS
84 VP for Enrollment Management .... Ms. Kim JOHNSON
07 Director of Admissions Recruitment .... Ms. Karen BENITEZ
123 Dir of Grad/Prof Studies Admissions .... Vacant
37 Director of Student Financial Aid .... Ms. Crystal MADAULE
111 VP University Advancement .... Mr. Justin MCINTEE
44 Director of Annual Fund .... Vacant
29 Director of Alumni Engagement .... Mrs. Laura CAPO
26 Chief Communications Officer .... Vacant
86 Director of Veteran/Government Rels .... Ms. Shree CARTER
102 Director of External Relations .... Mr. David VAZQUEZ
108 Director Institutional Assessment .... Ms. Ludmilla PRASLOVA
106 Dean of Teaching and Learning .... Ms. Bonni STACHOWIAK

*Ventura County Community College District (G)

761 East Daily Drive, Suite 200, Camarillo CA 93010

County: Ventura — FICE Identification: 006863
Unit ID: 125019
Telephone: (805) 652-5500 — Carnegie Class: N/A
FAX Number: N/A
URL: www.vcccd.edu

01 Chancellor .... Dr. Greg GILLESPIE
101 Admin Officer to Chancellor/Board .... Ms. Patti BLAIR
10 Vice Chanc Business Svcs/Fin Mgmt .... Dr. David EL FATTAL
15 Vice Chanc of Human Resources .... Vacant
108 Vice Chancellor Inst Effectiveness .... Dr. Larry BUCKLEY
13 Assoc Vice Chanc of IT .... Mr. Dan WATKINS
12 Moorpark College President .... Dr. Julius SOKENU
12 Oxnard College President .... Mr. Luis SANCHEZ
12 Ventura College President .... Dr. Kimberly HOFFMANS

*Moorpark College (H)

7075 Campus Road, Moorpark CA 93021-1695

County: Ventura — FICE Identification: 007115
Unit ID: 119137
Telephone: (805) 378-1400 — Carnegie Class: Assoc/HT-High Trad
FAX Number: (805) 378-1499 — Calendar System: Semester
URL: www.moorparkcollege.edu
Established: 1967 — Annual Undergrad Tuition & Fees (In-State): $1,388
Enrollment: 14,343 — Coed
Affiliation or Control: State — IRS Status: 501(c)3
Highest Offering: Associate Degree
Accreditation: WJ, ADNUR, RAD

02 President .... Dr. Julius SOKENU

05 Vice President Academic Affairs .... Ms. Mary REES
10 Vice President Business Services .... Ms. Silvia BARAJAS
32 Vice President Student Support .... Dr. Amanuel GEBRU
04 Executive Assistant to President .... Ms. Linda RESENDIZ
20 Dean of Student Learning .... Mr. Howard DAVIS
20 Dean of Student Learning .... Ms. Monica GARCIA
20 Dean of Student Learning .... Mr. Samuel LINGROSSO
20 Dean of Student Learning .... Mr. David GATEWOOD
20 Dean of Student Learning .... Mr. Matthew CALFIN
20 Dean of Student Learning .... Ms. Khushnur DADABHOY
109 College Fiscal Services Supervisor .... Ms. Michele PERRY
18 Director Maintainence/Operations .... Mr. John SINUTKO
13 Director Information Technology .... Mr. Dan MCMICHAEL
113 Bursar .... Ms. Lindy CHAU
23 Director Student Health Services .... Ms. Sharon MANAKAS
41 Athletic Director .... Mr. Vance MANAKAS
121 Supervisor Student Success Services .... Ms. Claudia SITLINGTON
06 Registrar .... Mr. David ANTER
37 Student Financial Aid Officer .... Ms. Kim KORINKE
111 Director of Inst Advancement .... Mr. James SCHUELKE
35 Student Activities Specialist .... Ms. Kristen ROBINSON
85 Director Outreach & International .... Ms. Claudia WILROY

*Oxnard College (A)

4000 S Rose Avenue, Oxnard CA 93033-6699
County: Ventura FICE Identification: 012842
Unit ID: 120421
Telephone: (805) 678-5800 Carnegie Class: Assoc/HT-High Trad
FAX Number: (805) 678-5806 Calendar System: Semester
URL: www.oxnardcollege.edu
Established: 1975 Annual Undergrad Tuition & Fees (In-District): $1,388
Enrollment: 7,451 Coed
Affiliation or Control: State/Local IRS Status: 501(c)3
Highest Offering: Associate Degree
Accreditation: WJ, DH, IFSAC

02 Interim President .... Mr. Luis P. SANCHEZ
05 Vice Pres Academic Affairs .... Vacant
10 Acting Vice Pres Business Services .... Mr. Christopher RENBARGER
32 Vice Pres Student Development .... Dr. Oscar COBIAN
79 Dean Liberal Studies .... Mr. Art SANDFORD
75 Dean Career & Technical Education .... Mr. Robert CABRAL
81 Dean Math Science/Health .... Dr. Carolyn INOUYE
09 Dean Institutional Effectiveness .... Dr. Cynthia HERRERA
18 Director Maintenance/Operations .... Mr. Bob SUBE
41 Director of Athletics .... Mr. Jonas CRAWFORD
06 Registrar .... Mr. Joel DIAZ
88 Director STEM .... Dr. Marcella KLEIN-WILLIAMS
37 Financial Aid Officer .... Ms. Linda FAASUA
109 College Services Supervisor .... Ms. Darlene INDA

*Ventura College (B)

4667 Telegraph Road, Ventura CA 93003-3899
County: Ventura FICE Identification: 001334
Unit ID: 125028
Telephone: (805) 289-6000 Carnegie Class: Assoc/HT-High Trad
FAX Number: (805) 289-6466 Calendar System: Semester
URL: www.venturacollege.edu
Established: 1925 Annual Undergrad Tuition & Fees (In-District): $1,388
Enrollment: 13,174 Coed
Affiliation or Control: State/Local IRS Status: 501(c)3
Highest Offering: Associate Degree
Accreditation: WJ, ADNUR, EMT

02 President .... Dr. Kim HOFFMANS
05 Vice President Academic Affairs .... Dr. Jennifer KALFSBEEK-GOETZ
32 Vice Pres Student Affairs .... Dr. Damien A. PENA
10 Vice Pres Business/Admin Services .... Ms. Cathy BOJORQUEZ
04 Exec Assistant to the President .... Ms. Andrea RAMBO
108 Dean Institutional Effectiveness .... Mr. Phillip BRIGGS
81 Dean Sciences .... Mr. Dan KUMPF
88 Dean Health/Kines/Ath/Perf Ar .... Mr. Tim HARRISON
83 Dean Behav & Social Sci/Lang .... Ms. Lisa PUTNAM
103 Dean Career Education .... Ms. Debbie NEWCOMB
103 Dean Career Education .... Ms. Felicia DUENAS
81 Dean Eng/Math/Lrng Resources .... Ms. Lynn WRIGHT
35 Dean Student Services .... Mr. Marcelo VAZQUEZ
102 Executive Director Foundation .... Ms. Anne KING
06 Registrar .... Vacant
18 Director Maintenance/Operations .... Vacant
35 Coordinator Student Activities .... Ms. Libby FATTA
37 Financial Aid Officer .... Ms. Alma RODRIGUEZ
09 Institutional Research .... Mr. Michael CALLAHAN
85 International Students .... Ms. Ellie YOO
23 Director Student Health Center .... Ms. Mary JONES
19 Campus Police .... Lt. Mike PALLOTO
26 Marketing Specialist .... Ms. Cindy JONES
41 Athletic Director .... Mr. Jimmy WALKER

Veritas International University (C)

3000 W. MacArthur Blvd, Suite 207, Santa Ana CA 92704
County: Orange Identification: 667103
Telephone: (714) 966-8500 Carnegie Class: Not Classified
FAX Number: (714) 966-8510 Calendar System: Semester
URL: www.ves.edu
Established: 2008 Annual Graduate Tuition & Fees: N/A
Enrollment: N/A Coed
Affiliation or Control: Independent Non-Profit IRS Status: 501(c)3
Highest Offering: Doctorate; No Undergraduates
Accreditation: TRACS

00 Chancellor .... Norman L. GEISLER
01 President .... Joseph M. HOLDEN
06 Registrar/Dir of Admissions .... Vanessa ACOSTA
05 Chief Academic Officer .... Miguel A. ENDARA
08 Library Director .... Joe MCELROY
10 Chief Business Officer .... Deborah DELARGY
09 Dir Inst Effectiveness/Assessment .... Frank CORREA
32 Director Student/Alumni Affairs .... Deborah DELARGY

Victor Valley College (D)

18422 Bear Valley Road, Victorville CA 92395-5850
County: San Bernardino FICE Identification: 001335
Unit ID: 125091
Telephone: (760) 245-4271 Carnegie Class: Assoc/HVT-Mix Trad/Non
FAX Number: (760) 245-9019 Calendar System: Semester
URL: www.vvc.edu
Established: 1961 Annual Undergrad Tuition & Fees (In-District): $1,126
Enrollment: 11,971 Coed
Affiliation or Control: State/Local IRS Status: 501(c)3
Highest Offering: Associate Degree
Accreditation: WJ, COARC, EMT

01 Superintendent/President .... Dr. Daniel W. WALDEN
05 Exec VP Instruction .... Dr. Peter MAPHUMULO
10 Deputy Supt/Exec VP Admin Svcs .... Mr. John NAHLEN
32 Vice President Student Services .... Dr. Karen ENGELSEN
15 Vice President Human Resources .... Ms. Monica MARTINEZ
76 Dean Health Science & Public Safety .... Dr. Todd SCOTT
79 Dean Acad Pgms Humanities/Soc Sci .... Ms. Jackie AUGUSTINE-CARREIRA
21 Director Fiscal Services .... Ms. Shawntee MILTON
07 Director of Admissions .... Mrs. Greta MOON
26 Director Public Info/Marketing .... Mr. Robert SEWELL
41 Director Athletics/Athletic Trainer .... Mrs. Jaye TASHIMA
18 Exec Dir Facilities/Operations .... Mr. Stephen R. GARCIA
37 Director Financial Aid .... Mr. Jason JUDKINS
109 Director Auxiliary Services/ASB Adv .... Mrs. Deanna SANABRIA
35 Dean Student Services .... Mr. Arthur LOPEZ
18 Director Facilities Construction .... Vacant
19 Chief Campus Police .... Mr. Leonard KNIGHT
13 Chief Information Officer .... Mr. Kevin LEAHY
88 Dir EOPS/CARE/CALWORKS .... Mr. Carl SMITH
09 Exec Dean Inst Effectiveness .... Ms. Virginia MORAN
04 Executive Asst to President .... Mrs. Michelle PAINTER
08 Head Librarian .... Ms. Leslie HUINER
102 Exec Dir Foundation .... Mrs. Catherine ABBOTT
104 Facilitator Study Abroad .... Vacant

Viridis Graduate Institute (E)

417 Bryant Street, Ojai CA 93023
County: Ventura Identification: 667375
Telephone: (805) 889-0169 Carnegie Class: Not Classified
FAX Number: N/A Calendar System: Trimester
URL: www.viridisinstitute.org
Established: 2011 Annual Undergrad Tuition & Fees: N/A
Enrollment: N/A Coed
Affiliation or Control: Independent Non-Profit IRS Status: 501(c)3
Highest Offering: Doctorate
Accreditation: DEAC

01 President .... Dr. Lori PYE

Weimar Institute (F)

20602 W. Paoli Lane, Weimar CA 95736
County: Placer Identification: 667302
Telephone: (530) 422-7927 Carnegie Class: Not Classified
FAX Number: N/A Calendar System: Semester
URL: www.weimar.edu
Established: 1978 Annual Undergrad Tuition & Fees: N/A
Enrollment: N/A Coed
Affiliation or Control: Independent Non-Profit IRS Status: 501(c)3
Highest Offering: Baccalaureate
Accreditation: WC

01 President .... Neil NEDLEY
05 Vice President Academic Affairs .... Verlyn BENSON
10 Chief Financial Officer .... Dale NORTHROP
09 Director of Institutional Research .... Christina HARRIS
32 Director Student Services .... Rodolfo RAMIREZ
84 Director of Enrollment Management .... Wanda SWENSEN
06 Registrar .... Ashley STEFFENS

West Coast Baptist College (G)

4010 E. Lancaster Boulevard, Lancaster CA 93535
County: Los Angeles Identification: 667268
Telephone: (661) 946-2274 Carnegie Class: Not Classified
FAX Number: (661) 946-4510 Calendar System: Semester
URL: www.wcbc.edu
Established: 1995 Annual Undergrad Tuition & Fees: N/A
Enrollment: N/A Coed
Affiliation or Control: Baptist IRS Status: 501(c)3
Highest Offering: Master's
Accreditation: TRACS

01 Founder & President .... Dr. Paul CHAPPELL
03 Exec Vice Pres/Chief Operating Ofcr .... Dr. John GOETSCH
05 Chief Academic Officer .... Dr. Thomas SHEPHERD
11 Dean of Administrative Affairs .... Dr. Jerry GODDARD
32 Dean of Students .... Dr. Toby WEAVER

West Coast Ultrasound Institute (H)

3580 Wilshire Boulevard, 4th Floor, Los Angeles CA 90010
County: Los Angeles FICE Identification: 036393
Unit ID: 441229
Telephone: (310) 289-5123 Carnegie Class: Spec 2-yr-Health
FAX Number: (310) 289-5136 Calendar System: Quarter
URL: www.wcui.edu
Established: 1998 Annual Undergrad Tuition & Fees: $18,600
Enrollment: 822 Coed
Affiliation or Control: Proprietary IRS Status: Proprietary
Highest Offering: Baccalaureate
Accreditation: ACCSC

01 Campus Director .... Ms. Myra CHASON
06 Registrar .... Ms. Erika BRIZUELA
07 Director of Admissions .... Ms. Leslie SANTANA
10 Chief Financial/Business Officer .... Ms. Mieke WIBOWO
11 Chief of Operations/Administration .... Mr. Andrew HIGH
36 Director Student Placement .... Mr. Anthony SHARP
37 Director Student Financial Aid .... Ms. Dora RUIZ

West Coast Ultrasound Institute (I)

3700 E. Inland Empire Blvd, Ste 235, Ontario CA 91764
Telephone: (909) 483-3808 Identification: 770942
Accreditation: ACCSC

† Main campus is West Coast Ultrasound Institute in Los Angeles, CA.

West Coast University (J)

151 Innovation Dr., Irvine CA 92617
Telephone: (949) 783-4800 Identification: 770480
Accreditation: &WC, DH

West Coast University (K)

12215 Victory Boulevard, North Hollywood CA 91606-3206
County: Los Angeles FICE Identification: 036983
Unit ID: 443331
Telephone: (818) 299-5500 Carnegie Class: Spec-4-yr-Other Health
FAX Number: (818) 299-5545 Calendar System: Semester
URL: www.westcoastuniversity.edu
Established: 1909 Annual Undergrad Tuition & Fees: $34,835
Enrollment: 1,660 Coed
Affiliation or Control: Proprietary IRS Status: Proprietary
Highest Offering: Doctorate
Accreditation: WC, NURSE, OT, PHAR, PTA

01 Co-President .... Dr. Jeb EGBERT
01 Co-President .... Ms. Sandra PHAM
03 Executive Director .... Mr. Deb THIBODEAUX
05 Provost .... Mr. Arte LIBUNAO
10 Business Ops/Chief Financial Ofcr .... Ms. Sandra PHAM
66 Dean of Nursing Los Angeles Campus .... Dr. Robyn NELSON
20 Academic Dean .... Dr. Miriam KAHAN
07 Director of Admissions .... Ms. Julie WONG
37 Director of Financial Aid .... Ms. Tracy CABUCO
32 Director of Student Affairs .... Mr. Anthony STEIN
08 Librarian .... Ms. Angelica LYONS
06 Registrar .... Ms. Felicia LOCKHART

West Coast University (L)

2855 E Guasti Road, Suite 100, Ontario CA 91761
Telephone: (909) 467-6100 Identification: 770484
Accreditation: &WC

*West Hills Community College District (M)

9900 Cody Street, Coalinga CA 93210
County: Fresno Identification: 667041
Telephone: (559) 934-2180 Carnegie Class: N/A
FAX Number: (559) 934-2810
URL: www.westhillscollege.com

01 Chancellor .... Dr. Stuart VAN HORN
10 Deputy Chancellor .... Dr. Richard STORTI
05 Vice Chanc Education & Technology .... Dr. Kelly COOPER
13 Assoc VC Educ Svcs/Info Technology .... Ms. Michelle KOZLOWSKI
102 Exec Director WHCC Foundation .... Mr. Alex PEREZ
15 Director of Human Resources .... Ms. Becky CAZARES
21 Director of Fiscal Services .... Vacant
26 Dir of Marketing/Comm/Public Info .... Ms. Amber MYRICK
25 Director of Grants .... Mr. Brian BOOMER
14 Dir of Info Technology Systems .... Mr. Shaun VETTER
88 Dir of Child Development Centers .... Ms. Conne CLEVELAND
103 Director of Special Grant Programs .... Mr. Cecilio MORA
103 Director of Special Grant Programs .... Mr. David CASTILLO
09 Dir of Accred/Research/Inst Eff .... Mr. Kyle CRIDER
04 Executive Assistant to Chancellor .... Ms. Donna ISAAC

*West Hills College Coalinga (A)

300 Cherry Lane, Coalinga CA 93210-1399
County: Fresno FICE Identification: 001176
Unit ID: 125462
Telephone: (559) 934-2000 Carnegie Class: Assoc/HT-Mix Trad/Non
FAX Number: N/A Calendar System: Semester
URL: www.westhillscollege.com/coalinga
Established: 1932 Annual Undergrad Tuition & Fees (In-District): $1,380
Enrollment: 3,550 Coed
Affiliation or Control: State/Local IRS Status: Exempt
Highest Offering: Associate Degree
Accreditation: WJ

02 President ... Ms. Brenda THAMES
03 Vice Pres of Educational Services ... Mr. Samasoni AUNAI
32 Dean of Student Services ... Mr. Javier CAZARES
41 Associate Dean of Athletics ... Vacant
47 Director of Farm of the Future ... Mr. Terry BRASE
85 Dir of International Student Svcs ... Mr. Daniel TAMAYO
88 Director of Title IV Projects ... Ms. Amy LONG
88 Assoc Dean of North District Center ... Dr. Bertha FELIX-MATA
37 Director of Financial Aid ... Ms. Malinali FLOOD
04 Administrative Asst to President ... Ms. Lorna DAVIS
08 Head Librarian ... Mr. Matthew MAGNUSON
18 Dir of Maintenance & Operations ... Mr. Shaun BAILEY
39 Director of Residential Living ... Mr. Alex VILLALOBOS
72 Dean of Career & Technical Educ ... Vacant
88 Director of MESA ... Mr. Zack SOTO
06 Director of Adm & Records/Registrar ... Ms. Bethany MATOS

*West Hills College Lemoore (B)

555 College Avenue, Lemoore CA 93245-9248
County: Kings FICE Identification: 041113
Unit ID: 448594
Telephone: (559) 925-3000 Carnegie Class: Assoc/MT-VT-High Trad
FAX Number: (559) 924-1243 Calendar System: Semester
URL: www.westhillscollege.com/lemoore
Established: 2002 Annual Undergrad Tuition & Fees (In-District): $1,380
Enrollment: 4,202 Coed
Affiliation or Control: State/Local IRS Status: Exempt
Highest Offering: Associate Degree
Accreditation: WJ, EMT

02 President ... Dr. Kristin CLARK
05 Vice President of Educational Svcs ... Mr. James PRESTON
32 Vice President of Student Services ... Mr. Valentin GARCIA
20 Dean of Educational Services ... Ms. Sue WARNER
35 Dean of Student Services ... Mr. Elmer AGUILAR
75 Dean of Career & Technical Educ ... Ms. Kris COSTA
37 Director of Financial Aid ... Ms. Deborah SORIA
41 Associate Dean of Athletics ... Mr. Christopher HAWKEN
08 Head Librarian ... Mr. Ron OXFORD
18 Dir of Maintenance & Operations ... Mr. Patrick SWEENEY
88 Director of Upward Bound ... Mr. Oscar VILLARREAL
04 Administrative Asst to President ... Ms. Amber AVITIA
66 Director of Nursing ... Ms. Kathryn DEFEDE
25 Dir of Special Grant Programs ... Ms. Giselle SIMON
06 Director of Adm & Records/Registrar ... Mr. Nestor LOMELI

*West Valley-Mission Community College District (C)

14000 Fruitvale Avenue, Saratoga CA 95070-5698
County: Santa Clara FICE Identification: 029139
Unit ID: 125222
Telephone: (408) 741-2011 Carnegie Class: N/A
FAX Number: (408) 867-8273
URL: www.wvm.edu

01 Chancellor ... Mr. Bradley J. DAVIS
04 Exec Assistant to Chancellor ... Ms. Brenda ROGERS
11 Vice Chanc Administrative Services ... Mr. Ed MADULI
15 Vice Chanc Human Resources ... Mr. Albert MOORE
13 Director Information Systems ... Vacant
18 Director of Facilities ... Mr. Javier CASTRUITA
19 Chief of Police ... Mr. Dalton Chris ROLEN

*Mission College (D)

3000 Mission College Boulevard, Santa Clara CA 95054-1897
County: Santa Clara FICE Identification: 021191
Unit ID: 118930
Telephone: (408) 988-2200 Carnegie Class: Assoc/HT-Mix Trad/Non
FAX Number: (408) 496-0462 Calendar System: Semester
URL: www.missioncollege.org
Established: 1976 Annual Undergrad Tuition & Fees (In-District): $1,192
Enrollment: 7,420 Coed
Affiliation or Control: State/Local IRS Status: 501(c)3
Highest Offering: Associate Degree
Accreditation: WJ

02 President ... Mr. Daniel A. PECK
05 Vice President of Instruction ... Dr. Leandra MARTIN
32 Vice President Student Services ... Dr. Omar MURILLO
11 Vice Pres Administrative Services ... Dr. Danny NGUYEN
35 Dean of Student Support Services ... Mr. Richard ALFARO
20 Dean of Instruction ... Ms. Valerie JENSEN
26 Director of Marketing ... Mr. Niall ADLER
50 Dean Business/Tech & Kinesiology ... Mr. Jeff PALLIN
19 Chief of Police ... Lt. Kenneth TANAKA
18 Manager of Facilities ... Mr. Don HOUSTON
07 Director of Admissions ... Mr. Asmare TADESSE
09 Director of Institutional Research ... Ms. Inge BOND
37 Dir Student Enroll & Financial Aid ... Ms. Maria ESCOBAR
04 Exec Assistant to the President ... Ms. Milani ZEPEDA
76 Dean of Health Occupations ... Ms. Carol Ann FRIEDMAN
81 Dean of Math/Science & Engineering ... Mr. Clement LAM
83 Dean Humanities/Social Sci & Art ... Mr. Brian MILLER
75 Dean of Career Education ... Ms. Jackie ESCAJEDA

*West Valley College (E)

14000 Fruitvale Avenue, Saratoga CA 95070-5698
County: Santa Clara FICE Identification: 001338
Unit ID: 125499
Telephone: (408) 867-2200 Carnegie Class: Assoc/HT-Mix Trad/Non
FAX Number: (408) 867-5033 Calendar System: Semester
URL: www.westvalley.edu
Established: 1963 Annual Undergrad Tuition & Fees (In-District): $1,463
Enrollment: 7,779 Coed
Affiliation or Control: State/Local IRS Status: 501(c)3
Highest Offering: Associate Degree
Accreditation: WJ

02 President ... Mr. Bradley DAVIS
05 VP Instruction ... Mr. Jamie ALONZO
32 VP Student Services ... Ms. Stephanie KASHIMA
11 VP Administrative Services ... Mr. Patrick FENTON
20 Interim Dean Instruction ... Mr. Chris DYER
30 Dean Advancement ... Mr. Paul MCNAMARA
36 Dean Career Pgm/Wrkforce Dev ... Mr. Bradley WEISBERG
26 Director Marketing/Communications ... Mr. Scott LUDWIG
35 Dean of Student Services ... Dr. Matais POUNCIL
100 Assoc Vice Chanc Human Resources ... Mr. Albert MOORE
57 Dean School of Art & Design ... Mr. Andrew CHANDLER
22 Director Student Equity & Success ... Ms. Debra GRIFFITH
18 Chief Facilities/Physical Plant ... Mr. Bill TAYLOR
37 Dir Student Financial Aid/Admiss ... Ms. Maritza CANTARERO
09 Research Analyst ... Mr. Miqueas DIAL
29 Director Alumni Relations ... Vacant
106 Coord Instruct Tech/Distance Lrng ... Vacant
04 Sr Executive Assistant to the Pres ... Ms. Gloria GUTIERREZ
41 Athletic Director ... Mr. John VLAHOS

Westcliff University (F)

4199 Campus Drive #650, Irvine CA 92612
County: Orange Identification: 667203
Unit ID: 490133
Telephone: (888) 491-8686 Carnegie Class: Spec-4-yr-Bus
FAX Number: (888) 409-7306 Calendar System: Trimester
URL: www.westcliff.edu
Established: 1993 Annual Undergrad Tuition & Fees: $8,220
Enrollment: 1,301 Coed
Affiliation or Control: Proprietary IRS Status: Proprietary
Highest Offering: Doctorate
Accreditation: WC, DEAC

01 CEO/President ... Dr. Anthony LEE
05 CAO/Provost ... Dr. David C. MCKINNEY
10 Chief Financial Officer ... Mr. Sean MURRAY
06 Registrar ... Ms. Rebeca IARATE-CERVANTES

Western Covenant University (G)

680 Wilshire Place, Ste 310, Los Angeles CA 90005
County: Los Angeles Identification: 667350
Telephone: (213) 293-1771 Carnegie Class: Not Classified
FAX Number: (213) 896-7265 Calendar System: Quarter
URL: www.wcuniversity.com
Established: 2014 Annual Graduate Tuition & Fees: N/A
Enrollment: N/A Coed
Affiliation or Control: Independent Non-Profit IRS Status: 501(c)3
Highest Offering: Master's; No Undergraduates
Accreditation: @TRACS

01 Western Covenant University ... David K. OH

Western State University College of Law (H)

1 Banting, Irvine CA 92618-3601
Telephone: (714) 459-1101 FICE Identification: 010832
Accreditation: &WC, LAW

Western University of Health Sciences (I)

309 E 2nd Street, Pomona CA 91766-1854
County: Los Angeles FICE Identification: 024827
Unit ID: 112525
Telephone: (909) 623-6116 Carnegie Class: Spec-4-yr-Med
FAX Number: N/A Calendar System: Semester
URL: www.westernu.edu
Established: 1977 Annual Graduate Tuition & Fees: N/A
Enrollment: 3,847 Coed
Affiliation or Control: Independent Non-Profit IRS Status: 501(c)3
Highest Offering: Doctorate; No Undergraduates
Accreditation: WC, ARCPA, DENT, NURSE, OPT, OSTEO, PHAR, POD, PTA, VET

01 President ... Dr. Daniel R. WILSON
05 Sr VP & Provost ... Dr. David BARON
10 Sr VP & Chief Financial Officer ... Mr. Kevin SHAW
11 Sr VP & COO ... Dr. Clive HOUSTON-BROWN
46 Sr VP Research ... Dr. Devendra AGRAWAL
32 SVP Univ Student Affs/Enroll Mgmt . Dr. Beverly SANKS GUIDRY
111 Sr VP University Advancement ... Dr. Diane ABRAHAM
15 VP Human Resources Admin ... Ms. Linda EMILIO
25 Asst VP Spons Pgms/Contract Mgmt ... Mr. Matthew KATZ
20 Vice Provost for Academic Dev ... Dr. Elizabeth REGA
106 Asst Provost Online Learning ... Mr. Jonathan DAITCH
88 Asst Provost Ventures ... Dr. Dean SMYLIE
18 Exec Dir Facilities/Physical Plant ... Mr. Todd CLARK
86 Chief of Community & Gov Affairs ... Mr. Jeffery KEATING
07 Interim Director Admiss COP/CGN ... Ms. Daniell MENDOZA
07 Director Admissions COMP/MSHS ... Ms. Susan HANSON
07 Director Admissions CO/CPM/CDM ... Ms. Marie ANDERSON
07 Director Admissions CVM/PT/PA ... Ms. Karen HUTTON-LOPEZ
17 Exec Dir for Patient Ctr Clinic ... Dr. Robert WARREN
08 Dir University Library ... Ms. Karoline ALMANZAR
37 Co-Director of Financial Aid ... Ms. Theresa POULLARD
37 Co-Director of Financial Aid ... Ms. Linda FRENZA
88 Dir Ctr Disability Issues/Hlth Prof ... Ms. Brenda PREMO
13 Exec Director Information Tech ... Ms. Denise WILCOX
96 Director of Procurement Services ... Mr. Michael BUTLER
26 Chief Communications Officer ... Vacant
121 Chief of Mission Integration ... Dr. Stephanie BOWLIN
09 Director of Institutional Research ... Dr. Juan RAMIREZ
40 Bookstore Director ... Ms. Elizabeth GUERRA
63 Dean College of Osteopathic Med ... Dr. Paula CRONE
52 Dean College of Dental Medicine .. Dr. Steven W. FRIEDRICHSEN
67 Dean College of Pharmacy ... Dr. Daniel C. ROBINSON
88 Founding Dean College of Optometry ... Dr. Elizabeth HOPPE
88 Dean College of Podiatry ... Dr. Kathleen SATTERFIELD
76 Interim Dean Col of Health Sciences ... Dr. Dee SCHILLING
66 Dean Col of Graduate Nursing ... Dr. Mary LOPEZ
58 Int Dean Grad Col Biomedical Sci ... Dr. Guru BETAGERI
74 Dean College of Veterinary Medicine ... Dr. Phil NELSON
63 Chr Dept Osteopath Manipulative Med ... Dr. Rebecca GIUSTI
88 Chair Dept of Physical Therapy ... Dr. Dayle ARMSTRONG
76 Chair Dept of Health Sciences ... Dr. Gail EVANS
88 Chair Physician Assistant Program ... Mr. Roy GUIZADO
63 Chair Department Family Medicine ... Dr. Alan CUNDARI
06 Registrar ... Mr. Ivan NOE
19 Director Security/Safety ... Vacant
29 Director Alumni Relations ... Ms. Susan TERRAZAS
04 Administrative Asst to President ... Ms. Liz PAWELL
102 Dir Foundation/Corporate Relations ... Mr. Bill BURROWS
44 Director of Annual Giving ... Ms. Susan TERRAZAS
16 Exec Director Human Resources ... Ms. Cynthia FERRINI
88 Director Center for Innovation ... Mr. Miary ANDRIAMIARISOA
43 General Counsel ... Ms. Simone MILLER

Westminster Theological Seminary in California (J)

1725 Bear Valley Parkway, Escondido CA 92027-4128
County: San Diego FICE Identification: 022768
Unit ID: 125718
Telephone: (760) 480-8474 Carnegie Class: Spec-4-yr-Faith
FAX Number: (760) 480-0252 Calendar System: Semester
URL: www.wscal.edu
Established: 1979 Annual Graduate Tuition & Fees: N/A
Enrollment: 113 Coed
Affiliation or Control: Independent Non-Profit IRS Status: 501(c)3
Highest Offering: Master's; No Undergraduates
Accreditation: WC, THEOL

01 President ... Rev. Joel E. KIM
11 Vice President for Administration ... Dr. Marcus MCARTHUR
05 Academic Dean ... Dr. John FESKO
30 Vice President for Advancement ... Ms. Dawn DOORN
84 VP for Enrollment Management ... Mr. Mark MACVEY
10 Chief Financial Officer ... Ms. Phyllis PIZZUTO
32 Dean of Students ... Dr. Julius KIM
08 Library Director ... Mr. James LUND
06 Registrar ... Mr. Danny MARRIOTT

Westmont College (K)

955 La Paz Road, Santa Barbara CA 93108-1089
County: Santa Barbara FICE Identification: 001341
Unit ID: 125727
Telephone: (805) 565-6000 Carnegie Class: Bac-A&S
FAX Number: (805) 565-7006 Calendar System: Semester
URL: www.westmont.edu
Established: 1937 Annual Undergrad Tuition & Fees: $45,304
Enrollment: 1,300 Coed
Affiliation or Control: Independent Non-Profit IRS Status: 501(c)3
Highest Offering: Baccalaureate
Accreditation: WC, MUS

01 President ... Dr. Gayle D. BEEBE
05 Provost/Dean of Faculty ... Dr. Mark L. SARGENT
10 Vice President Finance ... Mr. Douglas W. JONES
32 VP Student Life/Dean of Students ... Dr. Edee SCHULZE
111 Vice President for Advancement ... Dr. Reed L. SHEARD
13 VP Information Technology & CIO ... Dr. Reed SHEARD
84 VP Enrollment/Mktg/Communications ... Mrs. Irene NELLER

121 Dean of Student Success ... Dr. Angela D'AMOUR
88 Dean of Students for Res Life ... Dr. Stu CLEEK
06 Registrar ... Mrs. Michelle M. HARDLEY
09 Assoc Provost/Dir of Inst Research ... Dr. Patti HUNTER
15 Director of Human Resources ... Ms. Beth CAUWELS
18 Director of Physical Plant ... Mr. Thomas BEVERIDGE
21 Controller ... Mr. Paul V. LARSON
23 Director of Student Health Services ... Dr. David HERNANDEZ
19 Chief of Public Safety ... Mr. William BOYD
26 Director of Public Events ... Mrs. Mary Pat WHITNEY
36 Director of Career/Development ... Mr. Paul BRADFORD
88 Director of Internships/Practica ... Mrs. Jennifer TAYLOR
37 Director of Financial Aid ... Mr. Sean SMITH
38 Director Counseling Services ... Dr. Eric NELSON
39 Director of Housing/Parking ... Mr. David W. KING
40 Asst Director Bookstore ... Mrs. Joanne GISH
41 Athletic Director ... Mr. David ODELL
42 Campus Pastor ... Mr. Scott LISEA
45 Director of Campus Planning ... Mr. Randy JONES
96 Assc Dir Procurement/Auxiliary Svcs ... Mr. Bill GROENEVELD
28 Director of Intercultural Programs ... Mr. Jason CHA
20 Associate Academic Officer ... Dr. Tatiana NAZARENKO

Whittier College (A)

13406 E Philadelphia St, PO Box 634,
Whittier CA 90608-4413
County: Los Angeles FICE Identification: 001342
Unit ID: 125763
Telephone: (562) 907-4200 Carnegie Class: Bac-A&S
FAX Number: (562) 907-4242 Calendar System: 4/1/4
URL: www.whittier.edu
Established: 1887 Annual Undergrad Tuition & Fees: $48,086
Enrollment: 1,987 Coed
Affiliation or Control: Independent Non-Profit IRS Status: 501(c)3
Highest Offering: Doctorate
Accreditation: WC, LAW, SW

01 President ... Dr. Linda OUBRÉ
10 Vice Pres Finance & Administration ... Mr. James DUNKELMAN
05 Int VP Acad Affs/Dean of Faculty ... Dr. Sal JOHNSTON
61 Dean of Whittier Law School ... Mr. Rudy HASL
111 VP for Advancement ... Mr. Timothy ANDERSON
32 VP & Dean of Students ... Dr. Bruce SMITH
37 Director of Student Financial Aid ... Ms. Julie ALDAMA
08 Library Director ... Mr. David MCCASLIN
20 Dir Whtr Scholar Pgm/Assc Acad Dean ... Ms. Andrea REHN
26 Assoc VP Marketing & Communication ... Ms. Ana Lilia BARRAZA
13 Director of Computing Services ... Mr. Troy GREENUP
09 Dir of Institutional Research ... Mr. Gary WHISENAND
41 Director of Athletics ... Mr. Rock CARTER
62 Dir Lib Educ Pgm/Assoc Acad Dean ... Dr. Fritz SMITH
15 Assoc VP HR & Org Development ... Ms. Cynthia JOSEPH
19 Director of Campus Safety ... Mr. Jose PADILLA
06 Registrar ... Mr. John T. HILL

William Jessup University (B)

2121 University Avenue, Rocklin CA 95765-3707
County: Placer FICE Identification: 001281
Unit ID: 122728
Telephone: (916) 577-2200 Carnegie Class: Bac-Diverse
FAX Number: (916) 577-2203 Calendar System: Semester
URL: www.jessup.edu
Established: 1939 Annual Undergrad Tuition & Fees: $33,550
Enrollment: 1,504 Coed
Affiliation or Control: Independent Non-Profit IRS Status: 501(c)3
Highest Offering: Master's
Accreditation: WC, BI

01 President ... Dr. John JACKSON
05 Provost/Chief Academic Officer ... Dr. Dennis JAMESON
10 Chief Financial Officer ... Mr. David PUNT
30 Chief Development Officer ... Mr. Tom SASSER
13 Chief Operating Officer ... Mrs. Judy RENTZ
88 Accreditation Liaison Officer ... Dr. Kay LLOVIO
32 Chief Student Life Ofcr/Assoc Prov ... Dr. Kay LLOVIO
15 Human Resources Manager ... Ms. Linda GIUSTI
21 Controller ... Ms. Diane AHN
08 University Librarian ... Mr. Kevin PISCHKE
88 Director of Church Relations ... Mr. Jim JESSUP
35 Dean of Students ... Mr. Dave HEITMAN
06 Registrar ... Mrs. Tina PETERSEN
84 Director of Enrollment Management ... Mr. Steve JIN
09 Institutional Research Director ... Mrs. Karen LAMBRECHTSEN
42 Campus Pastor ... Mr. Thomas FITZPATRICK
41 Athletic Director ... Mr. Lance VON VOGT
18 Facilities Director ... Vacant
12 Academic Director Bay Area Center ... Dr. Daniel ALBRECHT
04 Executive Asst to President ... Mrs. Janice NEWMAN
19 Director of Campus Safety ... Mr. Paul YBARRA
36 Director Student Placement ... Ms. Christy JEWELL
106 Dir Online Education/E-learning ... Vacant
37 Director Student Financial Aid ... Mr. John SWAN

Woodbury University (C)

7500 North Glenoaks Boulevard, Burbank CA 91504-7520
County: Los Angeles FICE Identification: 001343
Unit ID: 125897
Telephone: (818) 767-0888 Carnegie Class: Masters/M
FAX Number: (818) 767-3470 Calendar System: Semester
URL: www.woodbury.edu
Established: 1884 Annual Undergrad Tuition & Fees: $39,790
Enrollment: 1,160 Coed
Affiliation or Control: Independent Non-Profit IRS Status: 501(c)3
Highest Offering: Master's
Accreditation: WC, ACBSP, ART, CIDA

01 President ... David M. STEELE-FIGUEREDO
101 Secretary of the Institution/Board ... Seta JAVOR
05 Senior Vice Pres Academic Affairs ... Randy STAUFFER
10 VP Finance & Accounting ... Vacant
11 VP Administration & Human Resources ... Natalie AVALOS
84 Assoc VP Admissions ... Sabrina TAYLOR
30 VP Development & Marketing ... Vacant
13 VP Information Technology ... Eric WANG
32 Dean of Students ... Tracci JOHNSON
50 Dean School of Business ... Joan MARQUES
48 Dean School of Architecture ... Ingalill WAHLROOS-RITTER
07 Director of Admissions ... Ani BONIADI
20 Dean of Faculty ... Christoph KORNER
49 Int Dean College of Liberal Arts ... Reuben ELLIS
09 Director of Institutional Research ... Christie RAINEY
82 Dean of International Affairs ... Mauro DIAZ
08 University Librarian ... Nedra PETERSON

World Mission University (D)

500 Shatto Place, Suite 600, Los Angeles CA 90020-1789
County: Los Angeles FICE Identification: 038683
Unit ID: 401223
Telephone: (213) 385-2322 Carnegie Class: Spec-4-yr-Faith
FAX Number: (213) 385-2332 Calendar System: Semester
URL: www.wmu.edu
Established: 1989 Annual Undergrad Tuition & Fees: $6,200
Enrollment: 373 Coed
Affiliation or Control: Independent Non-Profit IRS Status: 501(c)3
Highest Offering: First Professional Degree
Accreditation: BI, THEOL

01 President ... Dr. Paul S. LIM
05 Vice President/Chief Acad Officer ... Dr. Seonmook P. SHIN
32 Dean of Student Affairs ... Dr. Uncheol SONG
10 Chief Financial Officer ... Ms. Jong Ho LIM
06 Registrar ... Mrs. Hayoung JEONG
37 Dir Financial Aid/Admissions Coord ... Ms. KyungHae KIM

The Wright Institute (E)

2728 Durant Avenue, Berkeley CA 94704-1796
County: Alameda FICE Identification: 008846
Unit ID: 126012
Telephone: (510) 841-9230 Carnegie Class: Spec-4-yr-Other Health
FAX Number: (510) 841-0167 Calendar System: Trimester
URL: www.wi.edu
Established: 1969 Annual Graduate Tuition & Fees: N/A
Enrollment: 506 Coed
Affiliation or Control: Independent Non-Profit IRS Status: 501(c)3
Highest Offering: Doctorate; No Undergraduates
Accreditation: WC, CLPSY, IPSY

01 President ... Mr. Peter DYBWAD
05 Dean/Director Clinical Training ... Dr. Gilbert NEWMAN
10 VP of Finance & Administrative Affs ... Ms. Tricia O'REILLY
32 Dean of Students/Registrar ... Ms. Ginny MORGAN
07 Dir of Admissions/Student Services ... Mr. John PITTS
08 Library Director ... Mr. Jason STRAUSS
37 Director of Financial Aid ... Ms. Julia KALYAYEVA

Yeshiva Ohr Elchonon Chabad/ West Coast Talmudical Seminary (F)

7215 Waring Avenue, Los Angeles CA 90046-7660
County: Los Angeles FICE Identification: 022624
Unit ID: 126076
Telephone: (323) 937-3763 Carnegie Class: Spec-4-yr-Faith
FAX Number: (323) 937-9456 Calendar System: Semester
URL: www.yoec.edu
Established: 1953 Annual Undergrad Tuition & Fees: $14,700
Enrollment: 143 Male
Affiliation or Control: Independent Non-Profit IRS Status: 501(c)3
Highest Offering: Baccalaureate
Accreditation: RABN

01 Chief Executive Officer ... Rabbi Ezra B. SCHOCHET
03 Executive Vice President ... Rabbi Mendel SPALTER
05 Curriculum Suprv/Education Counsel ... Rabbi Shimon RAICHIK
37 Director Student Financial Aid ... Mrs. Hendy TAUBER
06 Registrar ... Rabbi Chaim CITRON
38 Director Student Counseling ... Rabbi Mendel SCHAPIRO
08 Head Librarian ... Rabbi Ben Zion OSTER

Yo San University of Traditional Chinese Medicine (G)

13315 W Washington Boulevard, Los Angeles CA 90066
County: Los Angeles FICE Identification: 030982
Unit ID: 401250
Telephone: (310) 577-3000 Carnegie Class: Spec-4-yr-Other Health
FAX Number: (310) 577-3033 Calendar System: Trimester
URL: www.yosan.edu
Established: 1989 Annual Undergrad Tuition & Fees: N/A
Enrollment: 131 Coed
Affiliation or Control: Independent Non-Profit IRS Status: 501(c)3
Highest Offering: Doctorate; No Lower Division
Accreditation: ACUP

01 President/CEO ... Dr. Lawrence LAU
10 Chief Financial Officer ... Tracy WANG
06 Director Operations & Registrar ... Tora FLINT
63 Dean MATCM Program ... Dr. Brady CHIN
63 Dean DAOM Program ... Dr. Robert HOFFMAN
63 Dean Clinical Education ... Dr. John FANG
84 Director Enrollment Management ... Daouia AMRIR
37 Financial Aid Coordinator ... Edgar TROVADA
32 Alumni & Student Affairs Officer ... Sean GATES

*Yosemite Community College District (H)

PO Box 4065, Modesto CA 95352-4065
County: Stanislaus FICE Identification: 009146
Unit ID: 126100
Telephone: (209) 575-6509 Carnegie Class: N/A
FAX Number: (209) 575-6565
URL: www.yosemite.edu

01 Chancellor ... Mr. Henry YONG
10 Vice Chancellor Fiscal Service ... Dr. Susan YEAGER
15 Vice Chancellor Human Resources ... Vacant
13 Vice Chancellor Info Tech ... Vacant
04 Executive Assistant to Chancellor ... Ms. Graciela MOLINA
26 District Director Public Affairs ... Ms. Coni CHAVEZ
16 Director Human Resources ... Ms. Kathren PRITCHARD
09 Dir District Research & Planning ... Ms. Shawna DEAN
19 Dir District Security/Comp & EP ... Vacant
117 Dir Risk Management/Purch & Rec ... Ms. Dorothy PIMENTEL

*Columbia College (I)

11600 Columbia College Drive, Sonora CA 95370-8580
County: Tuolumne FICE Identification: 007707
Unit ID: 112561
Telephone: (209) 588-5100 Carnegie Class: Assoc/HT-High Trad
FAX Number: (209) 588-5104 Calendar System: Semester
URL: www.gocolumbia.edu
Established: 1968 Annual Undergrad Tuition & Fees (In-District): $1,166
Enrollment: 2,545 Coed
Affiliation or Control: State/Local IRS Status: 501(c)3
Highest Offering: Associate Degree
Accreditation: WJ, ACFEI

02 President ... Dr. Santanu BANDYOPADHYAY
05 Vice Pres Instruction ... Dr. Brian SANDERS
11 VP College & Administrative Svcs ... Trevor STEWART
72 Dean Instruct Svcs/Career Tech Educ ... Dr. Brandon PRICE
49 Dean of Instruction/Arts & Sciences ... Raelene JUAREZ
41 Athletic Director ... Mr. Nate RIEN
37 Financial Aid Manager ... Ms. Marnie SHIVELY
30 Director of Development ... Ms. Amy NILSON
06 Registrar ... Ms. Lesley MICHTAVY
09 Dir of Institutional Rsrch & Plng ... Vacant
40 Bookstore Manager ... Mr. Jeff WHALEN
18 Manager Facilities/Operations ... Mr. Jake RADETICH

*Modesto Junior College (J)

435 College Avenue, Modesto CA 95350-9977
County: Stanislaus FICE Identification: 001240
Unit ID: 118976
Telephone: (209) 575-6498 Carnegie Class: Bac/Assoc-Assoc Dom
FAX Number: (209) 575-6630 Calendar System: Semester
URL: www.mjc.edu
Established: 1921 Annual Undergrad Tuition & Fees (In-District): $1,166
Enrollment: 17,880 Coed
Affiliation or Control: State/Local IRS Status: 501(c)3
Highest Offering: Baccalaureate
Accreditation: WJ, COARC, MAC

02 President ... Dr. James HOUPIS
05 Vice President for Instruction ... Dr. Jennifer ZELLET
32 Vice Pres for Student Services ... Ms. Flerida ARIAS
11 VP College & Administrative Svcs ... Vacant
57 Div Dean Arts/Humanites/Comm ... Mr. Mike SUNDQUIST
83 Div Dean Business/Behav/Social Sci ... Dr. Nancy SILL
76 Div Dean Inst/All Hlth/Fam/Con Sci ... Ms. Martha ROBLES
79 Div Dean Literature/Language Arts ... Ms. Jillian DALY
54 Div Dean Science/Math/Engineering ... Dr. Laura MAKI
47 Dean Agri/Envir Science/Tech Ed ... Dr. Donald BORGES
88 Dean Public Safety/Tech Ed/Cmty Ed ... Mr. Pedro MENDEZ
09 Dean Institutional Effectiveness ... Ms. Jenni ABBOTT
07 Director Admissions & Records ... Ms. Angelica GUZMAN
37 Director Student Financial Aid ... Ms. Peggy FIKSE
26 Marketing/Public Information Ofcr ... Ms. Linda HOILE

The Young Americans College of Performing Arts (K)

1132 Olympic Dr, Corona CA 92881
County: Riverside Identification: 667330
Telephone: (951) 493-6753 Carnegie Class: Not Classified
FAX Number: (951) 493-6793 Calendar System: Semester
URL: yacollege.edu
Established: 2002 Annual Undergrad Tuition & Fees: N/A
Enrollment: N/A Coed
Affiliation or Control: Independent Non-Profit IRS Status: 501(c)3
Highest Offering: Associate Degree

Accreditation: WJ

01 President .... Katiina DULL

*Yuba Community College District (A)

2088 North Beale Road, Marysville CA 95901
County: Yuba Identification: 666478
Telephone: (530) 741-6700 Carnegie Class: N/A
FAX Number: N/A
URL: www.yccd.edu

01 Chancellor .... Dr. Douglas B. HOUSTON
05 VC Educ Planning & Services .... Dr. Sandra MAYO
11 VC Administrative Services .... Ms. Mazie BREWINGTON
13 Chief Technology Officer .... Mr. Devin CROSBY
102 Grants/Research/Development Officer .... Ms. Tonya MACK
15 Chief Human Resources Officer .... Mr. Jacques WHITFIELD
10 Chief Business Officer .... Mrs. Kuldeep KAUR

*Woodland Community College (B)

2300 East Gibson Road, Woodland CA 95776-5156
County: Yolo FICE Identification: 041438
Unit ID: 455512
Telephone: (530) 661-5700 Carnegie Class: Assoc/HVT-Mix Trad/Non
FAX Number: (530) 666-9028 Calendar System: Semester
URL: www.yccd.edu/woodland/
Established: 2008 Annual Undergrad Tuition & Fees (In-District): $1,124
Enrollment: 3,332 Coed
Affiliation or Control: State/Local IRS Status: 501(c)3
Highest Offering: Associate Degree
Accreditation: WJ

02 President .... Dr. Art PIMENTEL
05 Vice Pres Academic/Student Svcs .... Vacant
04 Executive Asst to President .... Mr. Edwin ORTEGA BELTRAN
04 Executive Asst to Vice President .... Ms. Carid SERVIN
75 Dean Career Technical Education .... Ms. Ioanna IATRIDIS
49 Dean Arts and Sciences .... Vacant
09 Dean Student Succes/Inst Effective .... Dr. Siria MARTINEZ
32 Dean Student Services .... Dr. Genevieve SIWABESSY
37 Director Student Financial Aid .... Ms. Kimberly REED
06 District Registrar .... Ms. Sonya HORN
07 Director of Matriculation .... Ms. Mariella GUZMAN-AGUILAR

*Yuba College (C)

2088 N Beale Road, Marysville CA 95901-7699
County: Yuba FICE Identification: 001344
Unit ID: 126119
Telephone: (530) 741-6700 Carnegie Class: Assoc/HVT-High Trad
FAX Number: (530) 741-3541 Calendar System: Semester
URL: https://yc.yccd.edu/
Established: 1927 Annual Undergrad Tuition & Fees (In-District): $1,124
Enrollment: 5,529 Coed
Affiliation or Control: State/Local IRS Status: 501(c)3
Highest Offering: Associate Degree
Accreditation: WJ, RAD

02 President .... Dr. G. H JAVAHERIPOUR
05 VP Academic/Student Services .... Dr. Carla TWEED
32 Dean Student Services .... Dr. Delmy SPENCER
50 Dean Applied Academics .... Dr. Pete VILLARREAL
09 Dean Inst Research/Student Success .... Mr. Jeremy BROWN
38 Director Counseling .... Ms. Amandeep KANDOLA
88 Dir Child Dev Center/Foster Care .... Ms. Karen STANIS
66 Director Nursing/Allied Health .... Mr. Clark SMITH
19 Director Public Safety .... Dr. Pete VILLARREAL
79 Dean of Humanities & Education .... Vacant
37 Director Financial Aid .... Mr. Martin GUTIERREZ
68 Director Athletics/Health/PE .... Mr. Erick BURNS
81 Dean STEM & Outreach Centers .... Dr. Michael BAGLEY
88 Director Academic Excellence .... Ms. Kristina VANNUCCI

Yuin University (D)

2007 E. Compton Blvd, Compton CA 90221
County: Los Angeles Identification: 667351
Telephone: (310) 609-2704 Carnegie Class: Not Classified
FAX Number: (310) 609-1415 Calendar System: Semester
URL: www.yuin.edu
Established: 1977 Annual Undergrad Tuition & Fees: N/A
Enrollment: N/A Coed
Affiliation or Control: Interdenominational IRS Status: 501(c)3
Highest Offering: Doctorate
Accreditation: TRACS

01 President/CEO .... Christopher DENT

Zaytuna College (E)

2401 Le Conte Avenue, Berkeley CA 94709
County: Alameda Identification: 667230
Unit ID: 458575
Telephone: (510) 356-4760 Carnegie Class: Not Classified
FAX Number: (510) 327-2688 Calendar System: Semester
URL: www.zaytuna.edu
Established: 2009 Annual Undergrad Tuition & Fees: $19,350
Enrollment: N/A Coed
Affiliation or Control: Independent Non-Profit IRS Status: 501(c)3
Highest Offering: Master's
Accreditation: WC

01 President .... Hamza YUSUF
05 Provost .... Dr. Hatem BAZIAN
20 Dean of Faculty .... Dr. Mark Damien DELP
10 Head of Operations .... Cathrine HAMZE
108 Dir of Assessment & Accreditation .... Sumaira AKHATAR

COLORADO

Adams State University (F)

208 Edgemont Boulevard, Alamosa CO 81101-2320
County: Alamosa FICE Identification: 001345
Unit ID: 126182
Telephone: (719) 587-7011 Carnegie Class: Masters/L
FAX Number: (719) 587-7522 Calendar System: Semester
URL: www.adams.edu
Established: 1921 Annual Undergrad Tuition & Fees (In-State): $9,440
Enrollment: 3,314 Coed
Affiliation or Control: State IRS Status: 501(c)3
Highest Offering: Doctorate
Accreditation: NH, CACREP, MUS, NURSE

01 President .... Dr. Cheryl D. LOVELL
05 Interim VP for Academic Affairs .... Dr. Margaret DOELL
84 Director Enrollment Management .... Ms. Karla HARDESTY
26 Dir Public Relations & Marketing .... Mr. Chris LOPEZ
18 Director of Facilities Services .... Mr. Wade SMITH
10 Chief Financial Officer .... Ms. Heather HEERSINK
20 Associate VP for Academic Affairs .... Ms. Margaret DOELL
32 VP for Student Services .... Mr. Kenneth L. MARQUEZ
09 Senior Research Analyst .... Ms. Sarah RHETT
08 Director Library .... Mr. Jeffrey BULLINGTON
37 Director Student Financial Aid .... Vacant
06 Registrar .... Ms. Belen MAESTAS
13 Chief Information Officer .... Mr. Kevin S. DANIEL
41 Athletic Director .... Mr. Larry MORTENSEN
109 Director of Auxiliary Services .... Mr. Bruce DEL TONDO
38 Int Director Counseling/Career Svcs .... Ms. Carol COTTER
15 Director Human Resources .... Ms. Tracy ROGERS
102 Executive Director ASU Foundation .... Ms. Tammy L. LOPEZ
29 Director Alumni and Donor Relations .... Ms. Lori L. LASKE
96 Director of Purchasing .... Ms. Renee VIGIL
19 Dir Adams State Univ Police Dept .... Ms. Erika DEROUIN
40 Director Bookstore .... Ms. Amy GOODWIN
57 Chair English/Theatre/Communication .... Dr. Aaron ABEYTA
50 Chair Business & Economics .... Dr. Patrica ROBBINS
53 Chair Education .... Dr. Rich LOOSBROCK
77 Chair Chemistry/Computer Sci/Math .... Dr. Christina MILLER
81 Chair Biology/Earth Science .... Dr. Benita BRINK

Aims Community College (G)

Box 69, Greeley CO 80632-0069
County: Weld FICE Identification: 007582
Unit ID: 126207
Telephone: (970) 330-8008 Carnegie Class: Assoc/HT-High Non
FAX Number: N/A Calendar System: Semester
URL: www.aims.edu
Established: 1967 Annual Undergrad Tuition & Fees (In-District): $1,835
Enrollment: 5,982 Coed
Affiliation or Control: Local IRS Status: 501(c)3
Highest Offering: Associate Degree
Accreditation: NH, ADNUR, EMT, IFSAC, SURGT

01 President .... Dr. Leah L. BORNSTEIN
03 Executive Vice President .... Dr. Russ ROTHAMER
10 VP Admin Services .... Mr. Chuck JENSEN
05 Vice President Academic Affairs .... Ms. Deborah KISH
32 Vice President Student Affairs .... Dr. Sarah WYSCAVER
26 Vice President Cmty & College Rels .... Mr. Timothy ULLMANN
49 Dean Arts & Sciences .... Mr. Scott REICHEL
50 Dean Business & Technology .... Mr. Jeff SMITH
88 Dean Public Svcs & Transportation .... Mr. Robert ABERNATHY
35 Dean of Students .... Ms. Shannon MCCASLAND
102 Executive Director Foundation .... Ms. Kelly JACKSON
15 Exec Director Human Resources .... Ms. Dee SHULTZ
09 Exec Dir Inst Research/Assessment .... Vacant
114 Budget Director/Asst Controller .... Ms. Kailey BLOCK
18 Exec Director Facilities/Operations .... Mr. Michael MILLSAPPS
37 Executive Director Financial Aid .... Ms. Nancy GRAY
06 Registrar .... Ms. Kelley CHRISTMAN
13 Exec Director IT Admin Services .... Ms. Andria ROGERS
21 Assistant VP/Controller .... Ms. Kara BERG
31 Exec Dir Comm/Public Info Ofcr .... Mr. Zachary MCFARLANE
35 Exec Dir Student Leadership & Dev .... Dr. Patrick CALL
12 Exec Campus Dir Loveland .... Ms. Heather LELCHOOK
12 Exec Campus Dir Windsor .... Ms. Mary GABRIEL
12 Exec Campus Dir Fort Lupton .... Ms. Julie LUEKENGA

American Sentinel University (H)

2260 South Xanadu Way, Ste 310, Aurora CO 80014
County: Arapahoe FICE Identification: 041277
Unit ID: 460738
Telephone: (303) 991-1575 Carnegie Class: Spec-4-yr-Other Health
FAX Number: (303) 991-1577 Calendar System: Other
URL: www.americansentinel.edu
Established: 2000 Annual Undergrad Tuition & Fees: $10,140
Enrollment: 2,637 Coed
Affiliation or Control: Proprietary IRS Status: Proprietary
Highest Offering: Doctorate
Accreditation: @NH, DEAC, NUR, NURSE

01 President .... Ms. Mary A. ADAMS
05 Chief Academic Ofcr/SVP Strategy .... Dr. William TAMMONE
66 Dean of Nursing .... Dr. Elaine FOSTER
06 Registrar .... Mr. Thomas SMITH
07 VP Admissions Services .... Ms. Loren ELLISON

Arapahoe Community College (I)

5900 S Santa Fe Drive, PO Box 9002,
Littleton CO 80160-9002
County: Arapahoe FICE Identification: 001346
Unit ID: 126289
Telephone: (303) 797-4222 Carnegie Class: Assoc/MT-VT-High Non
FAX Number: (303) 797-5935 Calendar System: Semester
URL: www.arapahoe.edu
Established: 1965 Annual Undergrad Tuition & Fees (In-State): $3,918
Enrollment: 12,421 Coed
Affiliation or Control: State IRS Status: 501(c)3
Highest Offering: Baccalaureate
Accreditation: NH, ADNUR, CAHIIM, EMT, FUSER, MLTAD, PTAA

01 President .... Dr. Diana M. DOYLE
05 VP for Instruction & Provost .... Ms. Rebecca WOULFE
32 Vice President of Student Affairs .... Dr. Lisa MATYE EDWARDS
11 VP of Finance & Admin Svcs .... Dr. Belinda AARON
103 AVP/Dean Comm/Workforce Partnershp .... Dr. Eric DUNKER
20 Assoc Vice Pres for Instruction .... Dr. Joise MILLER
35 Dean of Students .... Mr. Javon BRAME
124 Exec Dir of Advising & Retention .... Mr. Mark NELSON
07 Assoc Dean of Enrollment Services .... Dr. Darcy BRIGGS
37 Dir of Student Financial Services .... Ms. Gail MCKINNEY
79 Dean Comm/Hum/Arts and Design .... Dr. Vanessa ANDERSON
81 Dean Mathematics & Sciences .... Dr. Samuel DEVRIES
69 Dean of Health and Public Services .... Dr. Darius NAVRAN
102 Executive Director Foundation .... Ms. Courtney LOEHFELM
13 Director Information Technology .... Mr. Jeff NESHEIM
21 Controller/Dir Financial Operations .... Ms. Jill BECKER-LUTZ
19 Chief of Police .... Mr. Joseph MORRIS
09 Director Institutional Research .... Mr. Yared BELETE
08 Director Learning Resource Center .... Ms. Lisa CHESTNUT
26 Dir of Marketing/Public Relations .... Ms. Tina GRIESHEIMER
35 Assoc Dean of Judicial Affairs .... Ms. Jennifer HUSUM
96 Purchasing Manager .... Mr. Daniel HOHN
18 Facilities Director .... Mr. David CRAWFORD
15 Director Personnel Services .... Ms. Angela JOHNSON
04 Executive Assistant .... Ms. Carol PATTERSON
108 Director Institutional Assessment .... Dr. Terry BARMANN
06 Registrar .... Dr. Darcy BRIGGS
106 Director E-learning .... Ms. Lee C. CHRISTOPHER

Aspen University (J)

1660 S. Albion Street Suite 525, Denver CO 80222
County: Denver FICE Identification: 040803
Unit ID: 454829
Telephone: (303) 333-4224 Carnegie Class: Masters/L
FAX Number: (303) 200-7428 Calendar System: Other
URL: www.aspen.edu
Established: 1987 Annual Undergrad Tuition & Fees: $3,920
Enrollment: 4,973 Coed
Affiliation or Control: Proprietary IRS Status: Proprietary
Highest Offering: Doctorate
Accreditation: DEAC, NURSE

01 Chairman & CEO .... Mr. Michael MATHEWS
05 Chief Academic Officer .... Dr. Cheri ST. ARNAULD
11 Chief Operating Officer .... Mr. Gerard WENDOLOWSKI
10 Chief Financial Officer .... Vacant
06 Registrar .... Ms. Katie BROWN

Auguste Escoffier School of Culinary Arts (K)

637 South Broadway, Ste H, Boulder CO 80305
County: Boulder FICE Identification: 037763
Unit ID: 454810
Telephone: (303) 494-7988 Carnegie Class: Not Classified
FAX Number: N/A Calendar System: Quarter
URL: www.escoffier.edu
Established: Annual Undergrad Tuition & Fees: N/A
Enrollment: 1,064 Coed
Affiliation or Control: Proprietary IRS Status: Proprietary
Highest Offering: Associate Degree
Accreditation: CNCE, ACFEI

01 President .... Kimberly JENSEN
07 Director of Admissions .... Matt VEARIL
37 Director of Financial Aid .... Pamela TRANDAHL
36 Director of Career Services .... Kate SWEASY
06 Registrar and Compliance Manager .... MaryKate HOWLAND

Augustine Institute (L)

6160 S. Syracuse Way #310,
Greenwood Village CO 80111
County: Arapahoe Identification: 667219
Telephone: (303) 937-4420 Carnegie Class: Not Classified
FAX Number: (303) 468-2933 Calendar System: Semester
URL: augustineinstitute.org
Established: 2005 Annual Graduate Tuition & Fees: N/A
Enrollment: N/A Coed

Affiliation or Control: Roman Catholic   IRS Status: 501(c)3
Highest Offering: Master's; No Undergraduates
Accreditation: **THEOL**

01 President .... Mr. Tim GRAY
05 Academic Dean .... Dr. Christopher BLUM
11 Chief Operating Officer .... Mr. Darren WALSH
07 Director of Admissions .... Ms. Kathryn GILLETE

Bel-Rea Institute of Animal Technology (A)

1681 S Dayton Street, Denver CO 80247-3048
County: Arapahoe   FICE Identification: 012670
Unit ID: 126359
Telephone: (303) 751-8700   Carnegie Class: Spec 2-yr-Health
FAX Number: (303) 751-9969   Calendar System: Quarter
URL: www.belrea.edu
Established: 1971   Annual Undergrad Tuition & Fees: $12,338
Enrollment: 321   Coed
Affiliation or Control: Proprietary   IRS Status: Proprietary
Highest Offering: Associate Degree
Accreditation: **ACCSC**

01 President/Dean of Education .... Nolan RUCKER
11 Chief Operating & Compliance Ofcr .... Tracy PETERSON
04 Administrative Assistant .... Mimi PFAFF
32 Director Student Services .... Rebecca BROWN
10 Director of Business and Financial .... Stacey SLOAN
18 Facilities Director .... Walter FRANKEWICZ
35 Student Affairs Assistant .... Brittany HANDLER
07 Admissions Manager .... Johanna HEGEL
37 Financial Aid Manager .... Stasi BOTTINELLI
06 Registrar .... Jennifer HILLGROVE

College for Financial Planning (B)

9000 E. Nichols Avenue #200, Centennial CO 80112
County: Denver   Identification: 666809
Telephone: (303) 220-1200   Carnegie Class: Not Classified
FAX Number: (303) 220-4940   Calendar System: Other
URL: www.cffp.edu
Established: 1972   Annual Graduate Tuition & Fees: N/A
Enrollment: N/A   Coed
Affiliation or Control: Proprietary   IRS Status: Proprietary
Highest Offering: Master's; No Undergraduates
Accreditation: **NH**

01 President .... Mr. Dirk PANTONE
05 Vice President Academic Affairs .... Dr. Amy RELL
84 Director of Enrollment .... Ms. Alicia CHRISTIENSEN
06 Registrar .... Vacant
32 Director Student Service Center .... Mr. Spencer CAMERON
26 Director of Marketing .... Mr. Christopher ALLEN

CollegeAmerica Colorado Springs (C)

2020 N Academy Boulevard, Ste 100,
Colorado Springs CO 80909
Telephone: (719) 227-0170   Identification: 666293
Accreditation: **ACCSC**

† Branch campus of CollegeAmerica Denver, Denver, CO.

CollegeAmerica Denver (D)

1385 S Colorado Blvd, 5th Floor, Denver CO 80222
County: Denver   FICE Identification: 025943
Unit ID: 126872
Telephone: (303) 300-8740   Carnegie Class: Spec 2-yr-Health
FAX Number: (303) 692-9156   Calendar System: Other
URL: www.collegeamerica.edu
Established: 1964   Annual Undergrad Tuition & Fees: $16,972
Enrollment: 139   Coed
Affiliation or Control: Independent Non-Profit   IRS Status: 501(c)3
Highest Offering: Baccalaureate
Accreditation: **ACCSC**

01 Executive Director .... Ms. Suzanne SCALES
05 Dean of Education .... Ms. Ruby ROWE
37 Vice President of Financial Aid .... Mr. Scott SCHULER
03 Associate Director .... Ms. Mary GORDY
06 Registrar .... Ms. Alexandra COOPER

CollegeAmerica Fort Collins (E)

4601 S Mason, Fort Collins CO 80525-3740
Telephone: (970) 225-4860   Identification: 666362
Accreditation: **ACCSC**

† Branch campus of CollegeAmerica Denver, Denver, CO.

Colorado Academy of Veterinary Technology (F)

2766 Janitell Road, Colorado Springs CO 80906
County: El Paso   FICE Identification: 041850
Unit ID: 461953
Telephone: (719) 219-9636   Carnegie Class: Spec 2-yr-Health
FAX Number: (719) 302-5577   Calendar System: Quarter
URL: www.cavt.edu
Established: 2007   Annual Undergrad Tuition & Fees: $11,435
Enrollment: 109   Coed
Affiliation or Control: Proprietary   IRS Status: Proprietary
Highest Offering: Associate Degree
Accreditation: **COE**

01 CEO/Admissions Officer/Registrar .... Dr. Steve RUBIN
05 Program Director .... Ms. Lindsey WILLIAMS
38 Dir Student Counseling/Fin Aid .... Mrs. Traci THOMPSON

Colorado Christian University (G)

8787 W Alameda Avenue, Lakewood CO 80226-7499
County: Jefferson   FICE Identification: 009401
Unit ID: 126669
Telephone: (303) 963-3000   Carnegie Class: Masters/M
FAX Number: (303) 963-3001   Calendar System: Semester
URL: www.ccu.edu
Established: 1914   Annual Undergrad Tuition & Fees: $31,866
Enrollment: 7,398   Coed
Affiliation or Control: Independent Non-Profit   IRS Status: 501(c)3
Highest Offering: Doctorate
Accreditation: **NH**, CACREP, MUS, NURSE

01 President .... Dr. Donald W. SWEETING
10 VP of Business Affairs & CFO .... Mr. Daniel L. COHRS
05 VP of Academic Affairs CUS .... Dr. Kyle B. USREY
111 VP of University Advancement .... Mr. Eric HOGUE
18 VP of Campus Development .... Mr. Shannon DREYFUSS
32 VP of Enrollment & Student Life .... Mr. Jim S. MCCORMICK
20 VP of Academic Affairs CAGS .... Dr. Sarah SCHERLING
35 Asst VP Stdnt Pgm/Dean of Students .... Ms. Sharon M. FELKER
84 VP of Enrollment CAGS .... Ms. Allison SIEVERS
121 VP of Student Success .... Mr. Roger CHANDLER
50 Dean School of Business/Leadership .... Dr. Gary EWEN
72 Dean School of Business/Technology .... Dr. Mellani J. DAY
53 Dean School of Education .... Dr. Debora SCHEFFEL
83 Dean of Social Science & Humanities .... Dr. Ryan HARTWIG
53 Dean School of Education Prof .... Dr. Wendy WENDOVER
79 Dean Sch Humanities & Sciences .... Dr. William R. SAXBY
64 Dean School of Music .... Mr. Steven T. TAYLOR
73 Dean School of Theology .... Dr. David KOTTER
66 Dean of Nursing & Sciences .... Dr. Barbara WHITE
73 Dean of Biblical Studies & Theology .... Dr. Earl WAGGONER
07 Director of Admissions .... Ms. Jo Leda MARTIN
43 University Counsel .... Mr. Thomas SCHEFFEL
21 Asst VP and Controller .... Ms. Karen FARRAND
06 Registrar .... Ms. Linda K. PERCIANTE
41 Athletic Director .... Mr. Brian WALL
38 Director of Counseling Services .... Ms. Alisa SHANKS
88 Director of Centennial Institute .... Mr. Jeff HUNT
30 Senior Director of Development .... Ms. Kathy PETTIT
18 Director of Facilities .... Mr. Mathew J. GOTHARD
37 Asst VP of Financial Aid .... Mr. Steve M. WOODBURN
23 Director of Health Services .... Ms. Anita LIEBSCH
15 Director of Human Resources .... Mr. Rick GARRIS
13 Asst VP of Information Systems .... Ms. Renee MARTIN
08 Library Director .... Ms. Gayle C. GUNDERSON
36 Director of Life Directions Center .... Ms. Leah SMITH
39 Director of Residence Life .... Mr. Neal ANDERSON
19 Director of Security .... Mr. John MAXFIELD
26 Dir of University Communications .... Mr. Lance OVERSOLE
29 Director Alumni Relations .... Ms. Kara JOHNSTON
105 Asst VP of Creative Services .... Ms. Chris FRANZ
106 Asst VP of Technical Support .... Mr. Jordan HEERSINK
04 Executive Assistant to President .... Ms. Kerry BLEIKAMP

Colorado College (H)

14 E Cache La Poudre St.,
Colorado Springs CO 80903-3294
County: El Paso   FICE Identification: 001347
Unit ID: 126678
Telephone: (719) 389-6000   Carnegie Class: Bac-A&S
FAX Number: (719) 634-4180   Calendar System: Other
URL: www.coloradocollege.edu
Established: 1874   Annual Undergrad Tuition & Fees: $55,470
Enrollment: 2,118   Coed
Affiliation or Control: Independent Non-Profit   IRS Status: 501(c)3
Highest Offering: Master's
Accreditation: **NH**

01 President .... Dr. Jill TIEFENTHALER
05 Dean of College & Faculty .... Dr. Claire GARCIA
03 Provost .... Dr. Alan TOWNSEND
10 Sr VP/Finance & Administration .... Mr. Robert G. MOORE
111 Vice Pres for Advancement .... Mr. Mark HILLE
100 Chief of Staff/Special Asst of BOT .... Dr. Kim WALDRON
84 Vice Pres Enrollment Management .... Mr. Mark HATCH
32 VP Student Life/Dean of Students .... Mr. Mike EDMONDS
13 VP for Information Management/CTO .... Mr. Brian YOUNG
45 Asst VP for Inst Planning & Eff .... Ms. Lyrae WILLIAMS
20 Assoc Dean of Academic Programs .... Dr. Emily CHAN
110 Asst VP Advancement Operations .... Ms. Molly BODNAR
35 Sr Assc VP for Student Life .... Mr. John LAUER
35 Sr Associate Dean of Students .... Ms. Rochelle MASON
37 Director of Financial Aid .... Ms. Shannon AMUNDSON
06 Registrar .... Mr. Phillip C. APODACA
26 Vice President for Communications .... Ms. Jane TURNIS
41 Vice Pres/Director of Athletics .... Mrs. Lesley IRVINE
104 Director International Programs .... Mr. Allen BERTSCHE
15 Director Human Resource .... Mrs. Heather KISSACK
07 Director of Admissions .... Vacant
18 Assoc VP of Facilities .... Mr. Chris COULTER
19 Director Campus Safety .... Ms. Maggie SANTOS
08 Library Director .... Ms. JoAnn JACOBY
36 Director Career Center .... Ms. Megan NICKLAUS
28 Asst VP/Director of Butler Ctr .... Mr. Paul BUCKLEY
29 Director Alumni Relations .... Mrs. Tiffany KELLY
09 Dir Assessment/Program Review .... Ms. Amanda UDIS-KESSLER
21 Assoc VP of Finance/Controller .... Mrs. Lori SEAGER
14 Asst VP for Information Technology .... Vacant
105 Director Web & Digital .... Ms. Karen TO
114 Senior Budget Analyst .... Ms. Enid RUIZ-MATTEI
38 Director of Counseling Center .... Mr. Bill DOVE
22 Director of Accessibility Resources .... Ms. Jan EDWARDS
27 Director of News & Media Relations .... Ms. Leslie WEDDELL
90 Director Educational Solutions .... Vacant
88 Dir Collab Cmty Engagement .... Ms. Jordan RADKE
42 Chaplain .... Dr. Alex HERNANDEZ-SIEGEL
04 Executive Asst to the President .... Ms. Lori HAMACHER
39 Assoc Dir Ofc of Housing & Conf .... Vacant

Colorado Mesa University (I)

1100 North Avenue, Grand Junction CO 81501-3122
County: Mesa   FICE Identification: 001358
Unit ID: 127556
Telephone: (970) 248-1020   Carnegie Class: Masters/S
FAX Number: (970) 248-1076   Calendar System: Semester
URL: www.coloradomesa.edu
Established: 1925   Annual Undergrad Tuition & Fees (In-State): $8,627
Enrollment: 9,591   Coed
Affiliation or Control: State   IRS Status: 501(c)3
Highest Offering: Doctorate
Accreditation: **NH**, #ARCPA, MLTAD, MUS, NURSE, PNUR, RAD, SURGT, SW

01 President .... Mr. Tim FOSTER
05 Vice Pres Academic Affairs .... Dr. Kurt HAAS
10 Vice President Financial/Admin Svcs .... Ms. Laura GLATT
12 Actg Vice Pres Community College .... Ms. Brigitte SUNDERMANN
109 Asst Vice Pres Auxiliary Services .... Mr. Andy RODRIGUEZ
32 Vice Pres Student Services .... Mr. John MARSHALL
13 VP of Information Technology/Comm .... Mr. Jeremy BROWN
20 Provost .... Dr. Carol FUTHEY
08 Library Director .... Ms. Sylvia RAEL
30 Director of Development .... Ms. Liz MEYER
37 Director Financial Aid .... Mr. Curt MARTIN
26 Director of Media Relations .... Mr. David LUDLAM
06 Registrar .... Ms. Holly TEAL
07 Director of Admissions .... Ms. Sharaya SELSOR-COWAN
09 Dir of Inst Research/Assessment .... Ms. Heather MCKIM
18 Actg Dir Facilities/Physical Plant .... Mr. David DETWILER
29 Director Alumni Relations .... Mr. Jared MEIER
07 Director of Admissions .... Ms. Sharaya COWAN
15 Director of Human Resources .... Ms. Jill KNUCKLES
28 Director of Diversity .... Mr. Bob LANG
41 Co-Athletic Director .... Ms. Kristin MORT
41 Co-Athletic Director .... Mr. Bryan ROOKS
96 Purchasing Manager .... Ms. Suzanne ELLINWOOD

Colorado Mesa University-Montrose Campus (J)

245 South Cascade Avenue, Montrose CO 81401
Telephone: (970) 249-7009   Identification: 770031
Accreditation: **&NH**

Colorado Mountain College (K)

802 Grand Avenue, Glenwood Springs CO 81602-3961
County: Garfield   FICE Identification: 004506
Unit ID: 126711
Telephone: (970) 945-8691   Carnegie Class: Bac/Assoc-Mixed
FAX Number: (970) 947-8385   Calendar System: Semester
URL: www.coloradomtn.edu
Established: 1965   Annual Undergrad Tuition & Fees (In-District): $2,220
Enrollment: 5,934   Coed
Affiliation or Control: Local   IRS Status: 501(c)3
Highest Offering: Baccalaureate
Accreditation: **NH**, ADNUR, EMT, NUR, NURSE

01 President .... Dr. Carrie BESNETTE HAUSER
05 VP Academic Affairs .... Ms. Kathryn REGJO
10 CFO .... Ms. Mary BOYD
32 VP Student Affairs .... Mr. Shane LARSON
15 Vice President of Human Resources .... Vacant
26 Public Relations Officer .... Ms. Debbie CRAWFORD
13 Chief Information Officer .... Vacant
07 Dir Pre-Enrollment Svcs/Registrar .... Mr. Shane LARSON
37 Director of Financial Aid .... Mr. Thomas VALLER
18 Director of College Facilities .... Mr. Sean NESBITT
27 Director of Marketing/Publications .... Mr. Brian BARKER
96 Director of Purchasing .... Ms. Julie HANSON
88 Dean Sch of Transitional Education .... Ms. A. Yvette MYRICK
04 Administrative Asst to President .... Ms. Debbie NOVAK
100 Chief of Staff .... Mr. Matt GIANNESCHI
43 Dir Legal Services/General Counsel .... Mr. Richard GONZALES
06 Registrar .... Ms. Natalie TORRES

Colorado Mountain College Alpine Campus (L)

1275 Crawford Avenue, Steamboat Springs CO 80487
Telephone: (970) 870-4444   Identification: 770038
Accreditation: **&NH**

Colorado Mountain College Aspen (A)

0255 Sage Way, Aspen CO 81611
Telephone: (970) 925-7740 Identification: 770032
Accreditation: &NH

Colorado Mountain College Leadville (B)

901 South Hwy 24, Leadville CO 80461
Telephone: (719) 486-2105 Identification: 770036
Accreditation: &NH

Colorado Mountain College Rifle (C)

3695 Airport Road, Rifle CO 81650
Telephone: (970) 625-1871 Identification: 770037
Accreditation: &NH

Colorado Mountain College Roaring Fork Campus-Spring Valley (D)

690 Colorado Avenue, Carbondale CO 81623
Telephone: (970) 963-2172 Identification: 770035
Accreditation: &NH

Colorado Mountain College Summit Campus-Breckinridge Center (E)

PO Box 2208, Breckinridge CO 80424
Telephone: (970) 453-6757 Identification: 770033
Accreditation: &NH

Colorado Mountain College Vail Valley Campus at Edwards (F)

150 Miller Ranch Road, Edwards CO 81632
Telephone: (970) 569-2900 Identification: 770034
Accreditation: &NH, MAC

Colorado Northwestern Community College (G)

500 Kennedy Drive, Rangely CO 81648-3598
County: Rio Blanco FICE Identification: 001359
Unit ID: 126748
Telephone: (970) 675-2261 Carnegie Class: Assoc/MT-VT-High Non
FAX Number: (970) 675-5046 Calendar System: Semester
URL: www.cncc.edu
Established: 1962 Annual Undergrad Tuition & Fees (In-District): $4,018
Enrollment: 1,201 Coed
Affiliation or Control: State/Local IRS Status: 170(c)1
Highest Offering: Associate Degree
Accreditation: NH, ADNUR, DH

01 President .... Mr. Ron GRANGER
32 Vice Pres Student Services .... Mr. John ANDERSON
05 Vice Pres Instruction .... Mr. Keith PETERSON
10 Vice Pres Business/Administration .... Mr. James CALDWELL
13 Director of Information Technology .... Mr. Fred BYERS
06 Registrar .... Ms. Grace STEWART
08 Library Director .... Ms. Leana COX
26 Director of Marketing .... Mr. Reuben TALBOT
15 Human Resource Director .... Ms. Angie MILLER
102 CNCC Foundation Director .... Ms. Sue SAMANIEGO
18 Facilities Director .... Ms. Lindsey BLAKE
09 Director of Institutional Research .... Ms. Kelly SCOTT
121 Director of Student Support .... Ms. Caitlan MOORE
37 Financial Aid Director .... Ms. Merrie BYERS
49 Dean of Arts & Science .... Mr. Todd WARD
75 Dean of CTE Craig .... Ms. Martha POWELL-CASE
75 Dean of CTE Rangely .... Ms. Meghan DAVIS
41 Athletics Director .... Ms. Candra ROBIE
113 Bursar .... Ms. Janet MACKAY
19 Safe Campus Coordinator .... Mr. Trevor SPERRY
51 Director of Community Education .... Ms. Sasha NELSON
39 Director of Campus Life .... Ms. Amy BLAKE
96 Purchasing Coordinator .... Ms. Kathy KOTTENSTETTE
04 Admin Assistant to the President .... Ms. Keely WINGER

Colorado Northwestern Community College Craig (H)

2801 W 9th Street, Craig CO 81625
Telephone: (970) 824-1101 Identification: 770039
Accreditation: &NH

Colorado School of Mines (I)

1500 Illinois Street, Golden CO 80401-1843
County: Jefferson FICE Identification: 001348
Unit ID: 126775
Telephone: (303) 273-3000 Carnegie Class: DU-Higher
FAX Number: (303) 273-3278 Calendar System: Semester
URL: www.mines.edu
Established: 1874 Annual Undergrad Tuition & Fees (In-State): $18,964
Enrollment: 6,209 Coed
Affiliation or Control: State IRS Status: 501(c)3
Highest Offering: Doctorate
Accreditation: NH

01 President .... Dr. Paul C. JOHNSON
05 Provost .... Dr. Richard HOLZ
11 Executive Vice Pres Admin & Ops .... Ms. Kirsten VOLPI
100 Chief of Staff .... Mr. Peter HAN
32 Vice Pres Student Life .... Dr. Dan FOX
88 Sr VP Research & Tech Transfer .... Dr. Stefanie TOMPKINS
111 Pres for Institutional Advancement .... Mr. Brian WINKELBAUER
65 Dean Earth Resources & Environ Pgms .... Dr. John BRADFORD
92 Dean Honors/Integrative Programs .... Dr. Kevin MOORE
88 Dean Energy & Materials Pgm .... Dr. Michael KAUFMAN
43 Vice Prov Legal Svcs/Gen Counsel .... Ms. Anne WALKER
84 Assoc Prov Enrollment Management .... Ms. Lori KESTER
20 Associate Provost .... Dr. Wendy ZHOU
10 Assoc Prov Finance & Admin .... Ms. Victoria NICHOL
20 Assoc Provost .... Dr. Thomas BOYD
35 AVP Student Service & Admin .... Ms. Rebecca FLINTOFT
15 AVP HR & Title IX .... Ms. Camille TORRES
11 AVP Infrastructure & Operations .... Mr. Gary BOWERSOCK
15 AVP Organizational Strategy .... Vacant
13 Chief Information Officer .... Mr. Michael ERICKSON
26 Chief Marketing Officer .... Mr. Jason HUGHES
35 Dean of Students .... Dr. Derek MORGAN
35 Assoc Dean of Students .... Mr. Colin TERRY
88 Exec Dir for Strategic Development .... Ms. Deb LASICH
04 Executive Asst to the President .... Ms. Tammy STRANGE
04 President's Office Executive Asst .... Ms. Jennifer BAICHI
41 Athletic Director .... Mr. David HANSBURG
08 University Librarian .... Ms. Carol SMITH
88 Dir of Trefny Innov & Instruction .... Dr. Sam SPIEGEL
37 Director of Financial Aid .... Ms. Jill ROBERTSON
88 Director of WISEM .... Ms. Annette PILKINGTON
09 Director of Institutional Research .... Ms. Tricia DOUTHIT
92 Director Honors Program .... Dr. Tonya LEFTON
06 Registrar .... Mr. Paul MYSKIW
93 Dir Multicultural Engineering Pgm .... Ms. Andrea MORGAN
29 Director Alumni Relations .... Mr. Damian FRIEND
91 Director Enterprise Systems .... Mr. David LEE
104 Director of International Programs .... Ms. Kay GODEL-GENGENBACH
108 Sr Assessment Associate .... Ms. Megan SANDERS
44 Senior Director Annual Giving .... Ms. Sara POND
102 Dir Foundation/Corporate Relations .... Ms. Emily KELTON
38 Dir of Counseling Center .... Ms. Sandra SIMS
96 Director of Procurement/Contracting .... Mr. Ryan MCGUIRK
27 Director Communication Center .... Ms. Allyce HORAN
21 Controller .... Ms. Noelle SANCHEZ
115 Associate Treasurer .... Mr. Kevin GRAVINA
25 Director Research Admin .... Ms. Johanna EAGAN
109 Dir Student Life Business Admin .... Ms. Lisa GOBERIS
114 Director Budget .... Ms. Laura LOWRY
113 Bursar .... Vacant
16 Assoc Dir Human Resources .... Ms. Veronica GRAVES
118 Benefits Manager .... Ms. Ann HIX
28 Director of Diversity .... Dr. Amy LANDIS
19 Director Public Safety .... Mr. Dustin OLSON
18 Director Fac Mgmt .... Mr. Samuel CRISPIN
14 Deputy Chief Info Officer .... Ms. Monique SENDZE
119 Chief Information Security Officer .... Mr. Phillip ROMIG
07 Director of Admissions .... Ms. Kimberly MEDINA
123 Director of Graduate Admissions .... Ms. Megan STEELMAN
39 Director Housing/Residence Life .... Ms. Mary ELLIOTT
121 Dir of Acad Services and Advising .... Ms. Jennifer DRUMM
85 Asst Provost International Affairs .... Mr. David WRIGHT
117 Exec Dir of Bus Ops/Risk Mgmt .... Ms. Natalie VEGA
88 Manager Classroom Technology .... Ms. Sara SCHWARZ
89 Dir New Student/Trans Services .... Ms. Jessica KEEFER
88 Dir of Financial & HR Systems .... Vacant
88 Dir of Title IX Programs .... Ms. Katryn SCHMALZEL
88 Dir Office Design & Construction .... Mr. Mike BOWKER
88 Dir of Research Compliance .... Mr. Ralph BROWN
88 Dir Infrastructure Solutions .... Mr. Jorge RICARDINO CSAPO
88 Director Business Services .... Ms. Anna WELSCOTT
88 Dir Entrepreneurship/Innovator .... Mr. Werner KUHR
88 Dir Intramural & Club Sports .... Mr. John HOWARD
88 Dir Acad Affairs Operations .... Ms. Jennie KENNEY
88 Dir of Campus Events .... Ms. Brandy BURGESS
88 Dir of Fitness .... Ms. Heather HAMILTON
88 Dir Intramurals .... Mr. Adam HICKLE
88 Dir Administrative Processing Svcs .... Ms. Janice LANDER
88 Dir of Student Activities .... Ms. Kelsi STREICH
88 Dir of Wellness Programs .... Ms. Emma GRIFFIS
88 Dir Outdoor Recreation .... Mr. Nathanael BONDI
88 Dir Research & Technology Transfer .... Mr. William VAUGHAN
88 Dir Research Development .... Ms. Lisa KINZEL
88 Dir Facilities/Aquatics .... Mr. Bradford AVENIA
88 Dir Student Disability Services .... Ms. Marla DRAPER
88 Manager Application Systems .... Mr. Bryan SIEBUHR
88 Exec Dir Envir Health & Safety .... Ms. Barbara O'KANE
88 Exec Dir of Oper Excellence .... Ms. Tressa CONSTANTINEAU RIES
88 Museum Curator .... Ms. Renata LAFLER

Colorado School of Trades (J)

1575 Hoyt Street, Lakewood CO 80215-2996
County: Jefferson FICE Identification: 011572
Unit ID: 126784
Telephone: (303) 233-4697 Carnegie Class: Spec 2-yr-Tech
FAX Number: (303) 233-4723 Calendar System: Other
URL: www.schooloftrades.edu
Established: 1947 Annual Undergrad Tuition & Fees: N/A
Enrollment: 156 Coed
Affiliation or Control: Proprietary IRS Status: Proprietary
Highest Offering: Associate Degree
Accreditation: ACCSC

01 President .... Mr. Robert E. MARTIN

Colorado School of Traditional Chinese Medicine (K)

1441 York Street, Suite 202, Denver CO 80206-2127
County: Denver FICE Identification: 036863
Unit ID: 381352
Telephone: (303) 329-6355 Carnegie Class: Spec-4-yr-Other Health
FAX Number: (303) 388-8165 Calendar System: Trimester
URL: www.cstcm.edu
Established: 1989 Annual Undergrad Tuition & Fees: N/A
Enrollment: 100 Coed
Affiliation or Control: Proprietary IRS Status: Proprietary
Highest Offering: Master's
Accreditation: ACUP

01 Administrative Director .... William WALLIN
05 Dean of Faculty .... Parago JONES
20 Assistant Academic Dean .... Christopher SHIFLETT
88 Clinic Director .... Zack GUTMAN
88 Assistant Clinic Director .... Anthony MCCLOSKEY
37 Financial Aid Administrator .... Joel SPENCER
06 Registrar .... Vacant
07 Recruiting Director .... Chris DUXBURY-EDWARDS
88 Administrator for the Dean .... Kirsten WEEKS

*Colorado State University System Office (L)

475 17th Street, Suite 1550, Denver CO 80202
County: Denver FICE Identification: 033437
Telephone: (303) 534-6290 Carnegie Class: N/A
FAX Number: (303) 534-6298
URL: www.csusystem.edu

01 Chancellor .... Dr. Tony FRANK
03 Executive Vice Chancellor .... Ms. Amy PARSONS
05 Chief Academic Officer .... Dr. Rick MIRANDA
43 General Counsel .... Mr. Jason JOHNSON
10 Chief Financial Officer .... Mr. Henry SOBANET
26 Director of Public Relations .... Mr. Mike HOOKER
04 Executive Asst to Chancellor .... Ms. Melanie GEARY

*Colorado State University (M)

200 W. Lake Street, Fort Collins CO 80523-0015
County: Larimer FICE Identification: 001350
Unit ID: 126818
Telephone: (970) 491-1101 Carnegie Class: DU-Highest
FAX Number: (970) 491-0501 Calendar System: Semester
URL: www.colostate.edu
Established: 1870 Annual Undergrad Tuition & Fees (In-State): $11,707
Enrollment: 33,083 Coed
Affiliation or Control: State IRS Status: 501(c)3
Highest Offering: Doctorate
Accreditation: NH, CACREP, CAEPT, CEA, CIDA, CONST, COPSY, DIETC, DIETD, IPSY, JOUR, LSAR, MFCD, MUS, OT, PH, SW, VET

02 President .... Ms. Joyce E. MCCONNELL
05 Senior Executive VP/Provost .... Dr. Rick MIRANDA
46 Vice President for Research .... Dr. Alan S. RUDOLPH
32 Vice Pres Student Affairs .... Dr. Blanche M. HUGHES
11 VP for University Operations .... Ms. Lynn JOHNSON
111 VP Advancement/Strategic Initiative .... Ms. Kim TOBIN
84 Vice Pres for Enrollment/Access .... Ms. Leslie TAYLOR
26 Interim VP for External Relations .... Mr. Pam JACKSON
56 VP Engagement/Dir CO State Univ Ext .... Dr. Louis SWANSON
20 Vice Prov for Undergraduate Affairs .... Dr. Kelly LONG
58 Vice Provost Graduate Affairs .... Dr. Mary STOMBERGER
91 Director of Acad Comp/Network Svc .... Mr. Scott BAILY
15 Dir Human Resource Svcs .... Ms. Diana PRIETO
36 Director Career Services .... Mr. Jon CLEVELAND
28 VP for Diversity .... Ms. Mary R. ONTIVEROS
29 Exec Director Alumni Relations .... Ms. Kristi BOHLENDER
41 Athletic Director .... Mr. Joe PARKER
35 Dean of Students .... Dr. Jody DONOVAN
43 Deputy General Counsel .... Ms. Jannine R. MOHR
47 Interim Dean Agriculture Sciences .... Dr. James PRITCHETT
88 Dean Applied Human Sciences .... Dr. Jeff MCCUBBIN
50 Dean of Business .... Dr. Beth WALKER
54 Dean of Engineering .... Dr. David MCLEAN
49 Dean of Liberal Arts .... Dr. Ben WITHERS
62 VP for IT/Dean of Libraries .... Dr. Patrick BURNS
65 Dean of Natural Resources .... Dr. John HAYES
81 Dean of Natural Sciences .... Dr. Janice L. NERGER
74 Dean of Veterinary Med & Biomed Sci .... Dr. Mark STETTER
06 Registrar .... Mr. Chris SENG
18 Chief Facilities/Physical Plant .... Mr. Tom SATTERLY
22 Dir of Equal Opportunity .... Ms. Diana PRIETO
37 Director of Student Financial Aid .... Mr. Joe DONLAY
39 Exec Dir Housing & Dining Services .... Dr. Mari STROMBOM
40 Director of Bookstore .... Mr. John PARRY
96 Director of Procurement Services .... Ms. Linda MESERVE
92 Director University Honors Program .... Dr. Donald MYKLES
94 Director Center for Women's Studies .... Dr. Caridad SOUZA
09 Vice Provost Institutional Research .... Dr. Laura JENSEN
100 Chief of Staff Office of the Pres .... Mr. Mark GILL

*Colorado State University Global (N)

585 Salida Way, Aurora CO 80011
County: Arapahoe FICE Identification: 042087
Unit ID: 476975
Telephone: (800) 462-7845 Carnegie Class: Masters/L

FAX Number: N/A Calendar System: Trimester
URL: https://csuglobal.edu
Established: 2008 Annual Undergrad Tuition & Fees (In-State): N/A
Enrollment: 12,381 Coed
Affiliation or Control: State IRS Status: 170(c)1
Highest Offering: Master's
Accreditation: NH, ACBSP

02 President & CEO .... Dr. Becky TAKEDA-TINKER
11 Senior VP of Operations .... Pamela TONEY
05 Provost/VP Strategic Development .... Dr. Karen FERGUSON
10 AVP of Finance and Compliance .... Jason WARR
26 AVP of Marketing .... Andrew DIXON

*Colorado State University-Pueblo (A)

2200 Bonforte Boulevard, Pueblo CO 81001-4901
County: Pueblo FICE Identification: 001365
Unit ID: 128106
Telephone: (719) 549-2100 Carnegie Class: Masters/S
FAX Number: (719) 549-2650 Calendar System: Semester
URL: www.csupueblo.edu
Established: 1933 Annual Undergrad Tuition & Fees (In-State): $10,408
Enrollment: 6,639 Coed
Affiliation or Control: State IRS Status: 501(c)3
Highest Offering: Master's
Accreditation: NH, #CAATE, MUS, NUR, SW

02 President .... Dr. Timothy MOTTET
05 Provost/EVP for Academic Affs .... Dr. Mohamed ABDELRAHMAN
10 VP Finance & Administration .... Mr. Karl SPIECKER
84 VP Enrollment Mgmt/Student Affairs .... Ms. Chrissy HOLLIDAY
18 Asst VP Facilities Management .... Mr. Craig CASON
20 Asst Provost Assess/Student Lrng .... Dr. Helen CAPRIOGLIO
13 Executive Director of IT .... Mr. Chris MILLIKEN
08 Dean Library Services .... Ms. Rhonda GONZALES
50 Dean Hasan School of Business .... Dr. Bruce RAYMOND
79 Dean Col of Humanities/Soc Sci .... Dr. William FOLKESTAD
54 Dean Col Engr/Educ/Prof Studies .... Dr. Sylvester KALEVELA
81 Dean Col Science/Math .... Dr. David LEHMPUHL
102 Executive Director Foundation .... Mr. Todd KELLY
26 Exec Director Marketing .... Mr. Greg HOYE
09 Dir Institutional Research/Analysis .... Ms. Maureen O'KEEFE
21 Director of BFS/Controller .... Ms. Juanita PENA
37 Director Student Financial Services .... Ms. Angela MOORE
06 Registrar .... Ms. Tanya BAIRD
36 Director Career Center .... Mrs. Michelle B. GJERDE
41 Director Athletics .... Mr. Paul PLINSKE
15 Director Human Resources .... Ms. Kat ABERNATHY
39 Dir Residence Life & Housing .... Ms. Gwendolyn YOUNG
109 Director Auxiliary Services .... Mr. Chris FENDRICH
23 Dir Student Health/Counseling .... Ms. Carolyn DAUGHERTY
29 Director Alumni Relations .... Ms. Tracy SAMORA
88 Director Center for Acad Enrichment .... Dr. John SANDOVAL
07 Director of Admissions .... Ms. Tiffany KINGREY
32 Dean of Student Affairs .... Dr. Marie HUMPHREY
100 Chief of Staff .... Ms. Niki WHITAKER
19 Manager Parking and Safety .... Ms. Laurie KILPATRICK
22 Dir Affirm Action/Equal Opportunity .... Mr. Josh ERNST
38 Director of Counseling .... Ms. Cori CAMERON
43 Deputy General Counsel .... Ms. Johnna DOYLE
96 Director of Purchasing .... Ms. Geraldine TRUJILLO-MARTINEZ

Colorado Technical University (B)

3151 South Vaughn Way, Suite 150, Aurora CO 80014
Telephone: (303) 632-2300 Identification: 666732
Accreditation: &NH, ACBSP

† Regional accreditation is carried under the parent institution in Colorado Springs, CO.

Colorado Technical University (C)

4435 N Chestnut Street, Colorado Springs CO 80907-3896
County: El Paso FICE Identification: 010148
Unit ID: 126827
Telephone: (719) 598-0200 Carnegie Class: DU-Mod
FAX Number: (719) 598-3740 Calendar System: Quarter
URL: www.coloradotech.edu
Established: 1965 Annual Undergrad Tuition & Fees: $11,960
Enrollment: 25,517 Coed
Affiliation or Control: Proprietary IRS Status: Proprietary
Highest Offering: Doctorate
Accreditation: NH, ACBSP, NURSE

01 Campus President .... Mr. Andrew HURST
05 Chief Academic Officer/Provost .... Dr. Connie JOHNSON
10 Vice President Finance .... Ms. Erin KRAFT
07 Vice President of Admissions .... Mr. Keith ARMSTRONG
11 VP Univ Strategy/Operations .... Ms. Elise BASKEL
20 Vice Provost .... Dr. Douglas STEIN
20 Vice Provost .... Dr. Susan MALEKPOUR
13 Manager of Information Systems .... Mr. Thomas LEIGH

Community College of Aurora (D)

16000 E Centre Tech Parkway, Aurora CO 80011-9036
County: Arapahoe FICE Identification: 022769
Unit ID: 126863
Telephone: (303) 360-4700 Carnegie Class: Assoc/HT-High Non
FAX Number: (303) 360-4761 Calendar System: Semester
URL: www.ccaurora.edu
Established: 1983 Annual Undergrad Tuition & Fees (In-State): $3,826
Enrollment: 8,026 Coed
Affiliation or Control: State IRS Status: 501(c)3
Highest Offering: Associate Degree
Accreditation: NH, EMT

01 President .... Dr. Elizabeth OUDENHOVEN
05 Vice President of Academic Affairs .... Dr. Tricia JOHNSON
32 Vice President of Student Affairs .... Dr. Paulette DALPES
45 VP of Institutional Effectiveness .... Dr. Chris WARD
15 Director of Human Resources .... Ms. Cindy HESSE
10 VP of Administrative Services .... Mr. George NOE
21 Controller .... Ms. Xochil HERRERA
35 Dean of Students .... Dr. Reyna ANAYA
20 Dean Academic Affairs .... Dr. Bobby PACE
20 Dean Academic Affairs .... Mr. Chris TOMBARI
19 Director of Security .... Mr. Travis HOGAN
36 Director of Advising .... Ms. LeeDel COHENOUR
13 Director Information Technology .... Mr. Sam THOMAS
18 Facilities Director .... Mr. John BOTTELBERGHE
26 Director Marketing/Communications .... Mr. Alex SCHULTZ
37 Director Financial Aid .... Mr. John YOUNG
06 Director Admissions & Registrar .... Ms. Kristen CUSACK
08 Director Library Services .... Mr. Dan LAWRENCE
09 Director of Institutional Research .... Dr. HyeKyung LEE
102 Exec Dir CCA Foundation .... Mr. John WOLFKILL
28 Director of Diversity .... Ms. Quill PHILLIPS

Community College of Denver (E)

Campus Box 250, PO Box 173363,
Denver CO 80217-3363
County: Denver FICE Identification: 009542
Unit ID: 126942
Telephone: (303) 556-2400 Carnegie Class: Bac/Assoc-Assoc Dom
FAX Number: (303) 556-8555 Calendar System: Semester
URL: www.ccd.edu
Established: 1967 Annual Undergrad Tuition & Fees (In-State): $4,750
Enrollment: 8,556 Coed
Affiliation or Control: State IRS Status: 501(c)3
Highest Offering: Associate Degree
Accreditation: NH, CSHSE, DH, RAD, SURGT

01 President .... Dr. Everette FREEMAN
05 Provost/Chief Academic Officer .... Ms. Ruthanne ORIHUELA
10 Vice Pres Finance & Admin/CFO .... Ms. Kathryn KAOUDIS
32 Vice Pres Student Affairs .... Dr. Kevin WILLIAMS
83 Dean Perf Arts/Humanities & Soc Sci .... Dr. Robert STUDINGER
81 Dean Health & Natural Sciences .... Ms. Stephanie HARRISON
89 Dean First Year Experience .... Mr. Peter LINDSTROM
75 Dean Career/Technical Education .... Mr. James KYNOR
20 Dean of Instruction .... Dr. Kaylah ZELIG
124 Dean Student Development/Retention .... Mrs. Tina GARCIA
84 Dean of Enrollment Services .... Dr. Tami SELBY
35 Director of Student Life .... Ms. Kathryn MAHONEY
37 Director Financial Aid .... Ms. Theresa CLAPHAM LAVIN
07 Dir Admissions/Recruit/Outreach .... Mr. Andrew GARCIA
15 Director Human Resources .... Ms. Patty DAVIES
13 Director IT Services .... Mr. Chris ARCARESE
09 Director Institutional Research .... Vacant
06 Registrar .... Ms. Nu TRAN
18 Facilities Director .... Mr. Kevin SEILER
102 Foundation Director .... Ms. Leah GOSS

Concorde Career College (F)

111 N Havana Street, Aurora CO 80010-4314
County: Arapahoe FICE Identification: 008871
Unit ID: 126687
Telephone: (303) 861-1151 Carnegie Class: Spec 2-yr-Health
FAX Number: (303) 839-5478 Calendar System: Other
URL: www.concorde.edu
Established: 1969 Annual Undergrad Tuition & Fees: N/A
Enrollment: 676 Coed
Affiliation or Control: Proprietary IRS Status: Proprietary
Highest Offering: Associate Degree
Accreditation: ACCSC, COARC, DH, PTAA, RAD, SURGT

01 Campus President .... Mr. Thomas WICKE
05 Academic Dean .... Ms. Sue KUHL
37 Director of Financial Aid .... Ms. Kimberly MARTINEZ
07 Director of Admissions .... Mr. Nick HRUBY

Denver College of Nursing (G)

1401 19th Street, Denver CO 80202
County: Denver FICE Identification: 041483
Unit ID: 454856
Telephone: (303) 292-0015 Carnegie Class: Spec-4-yr-Other Health
FAX Number: (720) 974-0290 Calendar System: Quarter
URL: www.denvercollegeofnursing.edu
Established: 2003 Annual Undergrad Tuition & Fees: N/A
Enrollment: 796 Coed
Affiliation or Control: Proprietary IRS Status: Proprietary
Highest Offering: Master's
Accreditation: NH, ADNUR, NUR, NURSE

01 President .... Dr. Cathy MAXWELL
10 Director of Business Operations .... Mr. Tim HEINTZ
32 Director of Student Services .... Mr. Michael RUSCHIVAL
05 Dean/Dir of Nursing Education Pgms .... Dr. Z. JoAnna HILL
37 Director of Financial Aid .... Ms. Geri REICHMUTH
07 Director of Admissions .... Mr. Jeff JOHNSON
06 Registrar .... Ms. April GONZALES

Denver Seminary (H)

6399 S Santa Fe Drive, Littleton CO 80120-2912
County: Arapahoe FICE Identification: 001352
Unit ID: 126979
Telephone: (303) 761-2482 Carnegie Class: Spec-4-yr-Faith
FAX Number: (303) 761-8060 Calendar System: Semester
URL: www.denverseminary.edu
Established: 1950 Annual Graduate Tuition & Fees: N/A
Enrollment: 908 Coed
Affiliation or Control: Interdenominational IRS Status: 501(c)3
Highest Offering: Doctorate; No Undergraduates
Accreditation: NH, CACREP, PAST, THEOL

01 President .... Dr. Mark S. YOUNG
05 Provost/Dean .... Dr. Lynn H. COHICK
10 Vice President of Finance .... Ms. Deborah KELLAR
111 Vice President of Advancement .... Mr. Chris JOHNSON
32 VP Student Life/Enrollment Mgmt .... Mr. Dusty DI SANTO
06 Registrar .... Mrs. Katie PEDERSON
35 Dean of Students .... Mr. Rob FOLEY
07 Director of Admissions .... Ms. Amy CARR
109 Director of Auxiliary Services .... Mr. Jay STIMSON
13 Director of Information Systems .... Vacant
26 Sr Director of Communications .... Mrs. Andrea WEYAND
09 Director of Inst Effectiveness .... Mrs. Janet RANDERSON
18 Director of Facilities .... Mr. Rob BACHMAN
37 Director of Financial Aid .... Mrs. Gina KELBERT
08 Director of Library Services .... Mrs. Nadine GINKEL
73 Director of DMin Program .... Dr. Marshall SHELLEY
21 Controller/Dir Financial Services .... Ms. Diana SMITH
15 Director of Human Resources .... Mrs. Wendi GOWING
28 Assoc Dean for Ethnic Communities .... Mr. Wilmer RAMIREZ
56 Assoc Dean Innovation/Extension Ed .... Mr. Tim KOLLER
04 Executive Asst to the President .... Mrs. Ty HECKELMANN
106 Associate Dean of Educational Tech .... Mr. Aaron JOHNSON

Fort Lewis College (I)

1000 Rim Drive, Durango CO 81301-3999
County: La Plata FICE Identification: 001353
Unit ID: 127185
Telephone: (970) 247-7010 Carnegie Class: Bac-A&S
FAX Number: (970) 247-7175 Calendar System: Semester
URL: www.fortlewis.edu
Established: 1911 Annual Undergrad Tuition & Fees (In-State): $9,040
Enrollment: 3,332 Coed
Affiliation or Control: State IRS Status: 170(c)1
Highest Offering: Master's
Accreditation: NH, CAEPT, MUS

01 President .... Dr. Tom STRITIKUS
05 Provost/Vice Pres Academic Affairs .... Dr. Cheryl NIXON
10 Vice Pres Finance & Administration .... Mr. Steven J. SCHWARTZ
111 Vice President for Advancement .... Mr. Mark A. JASTORFF
32 Vice President Student Affairs .... Vacant
21 Assoc Vice Pres Finance & Admin .... Ms. Michele PETERSON
06 Registrar .... Ms. Theresa E. RODRIGUEZ
21 Controller .... Ms. Cheryl WIESCAMP
25 Int Dir of Grants Management .... Ms. Shannon MALONE
37 Director Financial Aid .... Ms. Tracey PICCOLI
07 Director of Admission .... Ms. Jess SAVAGE
38 Dir Counseling Center .... Ms. Amie BRYANT
08 Director of the Library .... Ms. Astrid OLIVER
15 Dir Human Res/Equal Opportunity .... Mr. Greg MCCLURG
41 Athletic Director .... Mr. Brandon LEIMBACH
13 Director Computing & Telecomm .... Mr. Matt MCGLAMERY
29 Director Alumni Engagement .... Ms. Krista KNOTT
96 Director of Purchasing .... Mr. Wayne J. HERMES
26 Public Relations Officer .... Ms. Lauren SAVAGE
35 Associate VP Student Affairs .... Ms. Julie N. LOVE
35 Assoc VP Student Affairs .... Mr. Jeff DUPONT
49 Dean Arts and Science .... Dr. Jesse PETERS
50 Dean Sch of Business Admin .... Dr. Steven M. ELIAS
20 Assoc VP Academic Affairs .... Ms. Anne E. MCCARTHY
53 Dean of Teacher Education .... Dr. Richard FULTON
04 Admin Assistant to the President .... Ms. Esther M. RYSER
09 Director of Institutional Research .... Ms. Orien S. MCGLAMERY

Front Range Community College (J)

3645 W 112th Avenue, Westminster CO 80031-2105
County: Adams FICE Identification: 007933
Unit ID: 127200
Telephone: (303) 404-5000 Carnegie Class: Assoc/HT-Mix Trad/Non
FAX Number: (303) 466-1623 Calendar System: Semester
URL: www.frontrange.edu
Established: 1968 Annual Undergrad Tuition & Fees (In-State): $3,986
Enrollment: 19,259 Coed
Affiliation or Control: State IRS Status: 501(c)3
Highest Offering: Baccalaureate
Accreditation: NH, ADNUR, CAHIIM, DA, MAC, SURGT

01 President .... Mr. Andrew R. DORSEY
04 Asst to the President .... Ms. Denise BUCHER
05 Vice Pres Academic/Student Affairs .... Dr. Gillian MCKNIGHT-TUTEIN
10 Int VP Finance/Administration .... Ms. Patti ARROYO
12 VP Westminster Campus/Brighton Ctr .... Ms. Cathy PELLISH
12 Vice Pres Larimer Campus .... Dr. Jean RUNYON
12 Vice Pres Boulder County Campus .... Dr. Elena SANDOVAL-LUCERO

84 Assoc VP Enroll Mgmt & Student Svcs ....Ms. Tamara WHITE
18 Assoc VP Facilities Planning/Mgmt .... Mr. Derek BROWN
20 Dean of Instruction Larimer .... Dr. Shashi UNNITHAN
106 Dean of Online Learning .... Ms. Tammy VERCAUTEREN
20 Dean of Instruction Larimer ....Ms. Darcy OROZCO
20 Dean of Instruction Boulder County ....Mr. Matt JAMISON
20 Dean of Instruction Westminster .... Ms. Andrea DECOSMO
32 Dean of Student Svcs Boulder County .... Ms. Carla STEIN
32 Dean of Student Svcs Westminster .... Mr. Aaron PRESTWICH
15 Exec Director of Human Resources ....Ms. JoAnne WILKINSON
09 Director of Institutional Research .... Ms. Kim WALLACE
114 Director of Budget & Auxiliary Svcs .... Ms. Karen STEINER
06 Registrar .... Ms. Sonia GONZALES
07 Director of Admissions ....Ms. Cynthia FARMER
37 Dir of Financial Aid Larimer ....Ms. Carolee GOLDSMITH
08 Librarian .... Vacant
18 Director of Facilities Westminster ....Mr. Patrick O'NEILL
18 Director of Facilities Larimer .... Mr. Dennis DEREMER
35 Director Student Life Westminster ....Ms. Mindy KINNAMAN
35 Director Student Life Larimer ......Ms. Mary BRANTON-HOUSLEY
35 Dir Student Life Boulder County ....Ms. Amanda CLANCY
102 Exec Director of Foundation .... Mr. Ryan MCCOY
26 Lead Dir Marketing/Communications .... Ms. Marian MAHARAS
27 Public Information Officer ....Ms. Jessica PETERSON
13 Dir of Information Technology Svcs . Ms. Malinda MASCARENAS
19 Dir Campus Security/Preparedness .... Mr. Gordon GOLDSMITH

Front Range Community College-Boulder County Campus (A)

2190 Miller Drive, Longmont CO 80501
Telephone: (303) 678-3722 Identification: 770041
Accreditation: &NH

Front Range Community College Larimer Campus (B)

4616 S Shields Street, Fort Collins CO 80526
Telephone: (970) 226-2500 Identification: 770040
Accreditation: &NH, ADNUR

Holmes Institute of Consciousness Studies (C)

573 Park Point Drive, Golden CO 80401
County: Jefferson Identification: 666255
Telephone: (720) 496-1370 Carnegie Class: Not Classified
FAX Number: (303) 526-0913 Calendar System: Quarter
URL: www.holmesinstitute.edu
Established: 1972 Annual Graduate Tuition & Fees: N/A
Enrollment: N/A Coed
Affiliation or Control: Other IRS Status: 501(c)3
Highest Offering: Master's; No Undergraduates
Accreditation: DEAC

01 President ....Rev Dr. Kim KAISER
06 Registrar ....Ms. Maureen THURSTON
56 Dean of Distance Education .... Rev Dr. Christina TILLOTSON

IBMC College (D)

3842 South Mason Street, Fort Collins CO 80526
County: Larimer FICE Identification: 030063
Unit ID: 372329
Telephone: (970) 223-2669 Carnegie Class: Assoc/HVT-High Non
FAX Number: (970) 223-2796 Calendar System: Quarter
URL: www.ibmc.edu
Established: 1987 Annual Undergrad Tuition & Fees: $12,960
Enrollment: 359 Coed
Affiliation or Control: Proprietary IRS Status: Proprietary
Highest Offering: Associate Degree
Accreditation: ACCSC

00 CEO ....Mr. Steven STEELE
06 Registrar .... Ms. Jami ZENNER

IBMC College (E)

2863 35th Avenue, Greeley CO 80634-9421
Telephone: (970) 356-4733 Identification: 770631
Accreditation: ACCSC

Iliff School of Theology (F)

2323 E. Iliff Ave, Denver CO 80210-4798
County: Denver FICE Identification: 001354
Unit ID: 127273
Telephone: (303) 744-1287 Carnegie Class: Spec-4-yr-Faith
FAX Number: (303) 765-1141 Calendar System: Quarter
URL: www.iliff.edu
Established: 1892 Annual Graduate Tuition & Fees: N/A
Enrollment: 286 Coed
Affiliation or Control: United Methodist IRS Status: 501(c)3
Highest Offering: Doctorate; No Undergraduates
Accreditation: NH, THEOL

01 President and CEO ....Dr. Thomas V. WOLFE
05 Vice Pres/Dean Academic Affairs ....Dr. Boyung LEE
10 Interim VP for Business Affairs ....Mr. Bob WAGNER
111 VP Inst Advancement/Enrollment ....Mr. David WORLEY
110 Asst VP of Inst Advancement .... Ms. Kelsey COCHRANE
26 Director of Communications .... Dr. Soon Beng YEAP
06 Registrar .... Ms. Carmen E. BACA-DOSTER
13 Dir of Academic and Info Technology ... Mr. Michael HEMENWAY
04 Executive Asst to President ....Mrs. Alisha ENO
18 Dir of Facilities Mgmt ....Mr. Andy RIEDER
15 Director of Human Resources ....Ms. Caran WARE JOSEPH
08 Head Librarian ....Dr. Micah SAXTON
19 Campus Safety Coordinator ....Mr. Kyle MONROE
37 Director Student Financial Aid ....Ms. Goldie ECTOR

Institute of Business and Medical Careers (G)

2315 North Main Street, Longmont CO 80501
Telephone: (303) 651-6819 Identification: 770630
Accreditation: ACCSC

Institute of Taoist Education and Acupuncture (H)

317 West South Boulder Road, Ste 5, Louisville CO 80027
County: Boulder FICE Identification: 041212
Unit ID: 454838
Telephone: (720) 890-8922 Carnegie Class: Spec-4-yr-Other Health
FAX Number: (720) 890-7719 Calendar System: Other
URL: www.itea.edu
Established: 1996 Annual Graduate Tuition & Fees: N/A
Enrollment: 34 Coed
Affiliation or Control: Independent Non-Profit IRS Status: 501(c)3
Highest Offering: Master's; No Undergraduates
Accreditation: ACUP

01 President .... Sandra LILLIE
05 Director ....Hilary SKELLON
06 Registrar ....Suzanne WILLIAMSON
10 Financial Administrator .... Kathy KNAUS
11 Director of Operations .... Claudia O'NEILL

IntelliTec College (I)

2315 E Pikes Peak Avenue,
Colorado Springs CO 80909-6096
County: El Paso FICE Identification: 022537
Unit ID: 128179
Telephone: (719) 632-7626 Carnegie Class: Assoc/HVT-High Trad
FAX Number: (719) 632-7451 Calendar System: Quarter
URL: www.intellitec.edu
Established: 1965 Annual Undergrad Tuition & Fees: N/A
Enrollment: 635 Coed
Affiliation or Control: Proprietary IRS Status: Proprietary
Highest Offering: Associate Degree
Accreditation: ACCSC

01 Vice President of Operations ....Wayne ZELLNER
02 Campus Director ....David SCOTT
07 Director of Academics ....Catherine LECKMAN

Johnson & Wales University - Denver Campus (J)

7150 Montview Boulevard, Denver CO 80220-1866
Telephone: (303) 256-9300 Identification: 666411
Accreditation: &EH, DIETD

† Regional accreditation is carried under the parent institution in Providence, RI.

Lamar Community College (K)

2401 S Main, Lamar CO 81052-3999
County: Prowers FICE Identification: 001355
Unit ID: 127389
Telephone: (719) 336-2248 Carnegie Class: Assoc/MT-VT-Mix Trad/Non
FAX Number: (719) 336-2448 Calendar System: Semester
URL: www.lamarcc.edu
Established: 1937 Annual Undergrad Tuition & Fees (In-State): $3,950
Enrollment: 811 Coed
Affiliation or Control: State IRS Status: 501(c)3
Highest Offering: Associate Degree
Accreditation: NH, ADNUR

01 President ....Dr. Linda LUJAN
05 VP Academic Services/Student Svcs .... Dr. Lisa SCHLOTTERHAUSEN
11 VP Admin Svcs/Inst Effectiveness ....Mr. Chad DE BONO
20 Dean of Academic Services ....Dr. Annessa STAGNER
10 VP Administrative Services ....Mr. Chad DEBONO
26 Director of Communication .... Vacant
06 Registrar .... Ms. Amber THOMPSON
08 Library Tech ....Vacant
18 Director of Facilities ....Mr. Sean LIRLEY
15 Director Personnel Services .... Ms. Shelly TOMBLESON
39 Director Student Housing .... Mr. Pat CHRISTENSEN
27 Director of Marketing ....Vacant
38 Director Student Counseling ....Vacant
96 Director of Purchasing ....Ms. Ava BAIR
41 Athletic Director .... Mr. Scott CRAMPTON
37 Director Financial Aid ....Ms. Teresa TURNER
07 Director of Admissions ....Ms. Jenna DAVIS
21 Controller ....Mrs. Aubrie CLEAVINGER
111 Dir Inst Advancement/Foundation Dir .... Mrs. Anne-Marie CRAMPTON
09 Coordinator Institutional Research .... Ms. Kim WALLACE
84 Coord for Concurrent Enrollment .... Mr. Del CHASE

Lincoln College of Technology (L)

11194 East 45th Avenue, Denver CO 80239
County: Denver FICE Identification: 007547
Unit ID: 126951
Telephone: (303) 722-5724 Carnegie Class: Spec 2-yr-Tech
FAX Number: (303) 778-8264 Calendar System: Semester
URL: www.lincolnedu.com
Established: 1963 Annual Undergrad Tuition & Fees: N/A
Enrollment: 916 Coed
Affiliation or Control: Proprietary IRS Status: Proprietary
Highest Offering: Associate Degree
Accreditation: ACCSC

01 Campus President ....Dr. Kelly THUMM MOORE
07 Sr Director of Admissions ....Ms. Jennifer HASH
05 Academic Dean ....Mr. Dwayne ISBELL
20 Director of Education ....Mr. Ivan SMITH
04 Administrative Asst to President .... Ms. Beverly SOTELO
06 Registrar .... Ms. Stacy SWINBURN
36 Director of Career Services .... Ms. Jennifer CONDREAY
11 Director of Admin Services .... Ms. Christine GRAY
37 Director of Financial Aid .... Ms. Loriann WEISS
13 IT Administrator ....Mr. Travis HANSEL
26 Events/Marketing Coordinator .... Ms. Theresa SIMMONS

McKinley College (M)

2001 Lowe Street, Fort Collins CO 80525-3474
County: Larimer Identification: 666237
Telephone: (970) 207-4550 Carnegie Class: Not Classified
FAX Number: (877) 599-5863 Calendar System: Other
URL: www.mckinleycollege.edu
Established: 2004 Annual Undergrad Tuition & Fees: N/A
Enrollment: N/A Coed
Affiliation or Control: Proprietary IRS Status: Proprietary
Highest Offering: Associate Degree
Accreditation: DEAC

01 President ....Ann ROHR
05 Vice Pres Academics/Compliance ....Janet PERRY
32 Vice President of Student Affairs .... Joyce LINDQUIST
20 Dean of Faculty .... Jill BEAR
106 Dir Online Education/E-learning ....Leslie BALLENTINE
91 Applications Development Director ....Scott LYNCH
15 Human Resources Manager ....Joy DAVIS
26 Marketing Director ....Holly COOK
36 Graduate Services Supervisor .... Karen THOMPSON
37 Financial Aid Supervisor ....Jennifer BRIGGLE
07 Admissions Manager .... Jennifer MANNS

Metropolitan State University of Denver (N)

PO Box 173362, Denver CO 80217-3362
County: Denver FICE Identification: 001360
Unit ID: 127565
Telephone: (303) 556-5740 Carnegie Class: Masters/L
FAX Number: (303) 556-3912 Calendar System: Semester
URL: www.msudenver.edu
Established: 1963 Annual Undergrad Tuition & Fees (In-State): $7,666
Enrollment: 20,304 Coed
Affiliation or Control: State IRS Status: 501(c)3
Highest Offering: Master's
Accreditation: NH, ART, CAATE, COSMA, CSHSE, DIETD, EXSC, MT, MUS, NRPA, NUR, SW, THEA

01 President ....Dr. Janine A. DAVIDSON
05 Provost/VP Academic Affairs .... Dr. Vicki L. GOLICH
10 Vice Pres Admin/Finance/Facilities ....Mr. Larry SAMPLER
111 VP Advancement/Exec Dir Foundation ....Ms. Christine MARQUEZ-HUDSON
100 Chief of Staff/VP Strategy ....Ms. Catherine LUCAS
43 General Counsel/Secretary to Board ....Mr. David FINE
13 AVP Info Technology Services/CIO .... Mr. Kevin TAYLOR
84 Assoc VP Enrollment Services .... Mr. Thad SPAULDING
32 AVP Stdnt Engage & Well/Dean Stdnts ....Ms. Braelin PANTEL
45 Asst VP Strategic Engagement ....Ms. Jamie HURST
50 Dean School Business ....Dr. Ann B. MURPHY
107 Dean Sch Professional Studies ....Dr. Jennifer CAPPS
15 AVP Human Resources .... Ms. Stacy M. DVERGSDAL
06 Registrar .... Ms. Connie SANDERS
37 Interim Director Financial Aid ....Mr. Michael NGUYEN
41 Athletic Director ....Dr. G. Anthony GRANT
35 Assoc Director Student Activities .... Ms. Gretta MINCER
36 Director Career Services .... Ms. Bridgette COBLE
28 Assoc to Pres Inst Diversity ....Vacant
07 Director of Admissions ....Mr. Vaughn TOLAND
09 Director of Institutional Research ....Ms. Ellen BOSWELL
04 Admin Assistant to the President ....Ms. Summer VALDEZ
106 Director Online Learning ....Dr. Matt GRISWOLD
108 Director Institutional Assessment .... Ms. Kim BARRON
25 Chief Contract/Grants Administrator .... Ms. Betsy JINKS
53 Dean School of Education ....Dr. Liz HINDE

Morgan Community College (A)

920 Barlow Road, Fort Morgan CO 80701-4399
County: Morgan FICE Identification: 009981
Unit ID: 127617
Telephone: (970) 542-3100 Carnegie Class: Assoc/MT-VT-High Non
FAX Number: (970) 542-3115 Calendar System: Semester
URL: www.morgancc.edu
Established: 1967 Annual Undergrad Tuition & Fees (In-State): $3,765
Enrollment: 1,383 Coed
Affiliation or Control: State IRS Status: Exempt
Highest Offering: Baccalaureate
Accreditation: NH, ADNUR, PTAA

01 President Dr. Curt FREED
10 Vice Pres Finance/Admin Services Ms. Susan CLOUGH
05 Vice President of Instruction Ms. Kathy FRISBIE
32 Vice President of Student Services Vacant
04 Assistant to the President Ms. Jane FRIES
20 Dean of Gen Ed & Health Sciences Dr. Marc THOMAS
88 Dean of Concurrent Enrollment Ms. Kim MAXWELL
103 Dean of Workforce Development Ms. Andrea L'HEUREUX
26 Dir of Comm/Mktg & Recruitment Ms. Ariella GONZALES
30 Director of Development Ms. Kari LINKER
37 Director of Financial Aid Ms. Sally SHAWCROFT
15 Director of Human Resources Ms. Julie BEYDLER
07 Director of Admissions Ms. Maria CARDENAS
08 Director of Learning Resources Ms. April AMACK
09 Dir of Institutional Effectiveness Mr. Derek GRUBB
88 Director of Access/Enrollment Mr. Ivan DIAZ
96 Director of Purchasing Ms. Chloe HIRSCHFELD
13 Director Information Technology Mr. Mark FRASCO
109 Director of Auxiliary Operations Ms. Kellie OVERTURF
18 Director of Physical Facilities Mr. Gene KIND
40 Coordinator of College Store Ms. Debbie CASTENEDA

Naropa University (B)

2130 Arapahoe Avenue, Boulder CO 80302-6697
County: Boulder FICE Identification: 021175
Unit ID: 127653
Telephone: (303) 444-0202 Carnegie Class: Masters/M
FAX Number: (303) 444-0410 Calendar System: Semester
URL: www.naropa.edu
Established: 1974 Annual Undergrad Tuition & Fees: $31,790
Enrollment: 966 Coed
Affiliation or Control: Independent Non-Profit IRS Status: 501(c)3
Highest Offering: Master's
Accreditation: NH

01 President Mr. Charles G. LIEF
04 Assistant to the President Ms. Rachel SOLUM
10 Vice President of Operations Mr. Tyler KELSCH
26 Director of Marketing Ms. Kelly WATT
30 Director of Development Ms. Angela MADURA
88 Sr Advisor for Inst Effectiveness Ms. Cheryl BARBOUR
13 Director of IT Mr. David EDMINSTER
97 Dean Naropa College Ms. Carole CLEMENTS
28 Dir Office for Inclusive Comm Ms. Regina SMITH
38 Director Counseling Center Ms. Jo-Lynne PARKS
06 Registrar Ms. Keely PRESTON
08 Library Director Ms. Amanda RYBIN KOOB
18 Director of Safety/Facilities & Ops Mr. Aaron COOK
37 Dir Student Financial Services Ms. Jessica BREJC
15 Director of Human Resources Mr. Kert HUBIN
106 Director of Online Education Mr. Jirka HLADIS

Nazarene Bible College (C)

1111 Academy Park Loop, Colorado Springs CO 80910
County: El Paso FICE Identification: 013007
Unit ID: 127714
Telephone: (719) 884-5000 Carnegie Class: Spec-4-yr-Faith
FAX Number: (719) 884-5199 Calendar System: Trimester
URL: www.nbc.edu
Established: 1964 Annual Undergrad Tuition & Fees: $11,760
Enrollment: 743 Coed
Affiliation or Control: Church Of The Nazarene IRS Status: 501(c)3
Highest Offering: Baccalaureate
Accreditation: NH, BI

01 President Dr. Harold B. GRAVES
05 Vice President for Academic Affairs Dr. Alan D. LYKE
10 Vice President for Finance Mrs. Shirley A. CADLE
84 VP for Enrollment Management Dr. David M. CHURCH
37 Financial Aid Officer Mrs. Jan EDWARDS
06 Registrar Rev. Duane A. MATHIAS
13 Chief Information Officer Mr. Fred R. PHILLIPS
04 Executive Asst to President Rev. Susan P. MCKEITHEN
09 Institutional Research Mrs. Jan EDWARDS
15 Director Personnel Services Mrs. Carol CRIPPEN
29 Director Alumni Relations Rev. Susan P. MCKEITHEN
90 Director Academic Computing Dr. David HERRON
07 Director of Enrollment Management Rev. Will MACKEY
88 Exec Asst to VP Academic Affairs Ms. Karen COLSTON
88 Exec Asst to VP Enroll Mgt/Finance Ms. Avery SUNNARBORG
08 Librarian Mr. Addison LUCCHI
88 Recruiting Representative Dr. Gary HAINES
88 Alliance Director Mrs. Cheryl GRAVES
88 Admissions Counselor Mr. Quinn NORTH
88 Admissions Counselor Mr. Stephen EDWARDS
121 Academic Advisor Mr. Gabe HAYSE

Northeastern Junior College (D)

100 College Avenue, Sterling CO 80751-2399
County: Logan FICE Identification: 001361
Unit ID: 127732
Telephone: (970) 521-6600 Carnegie Class: Assoc/MT-VT-Mix Trad/Non
FAX Number: (970) 522-4945 Calendar System: Semester
URL: www.njc.edu
Established: 1941 Annual Undergrad Tuition & Fees (In-State): $5,072
Enrollment: 1,547 Coed
Affiliation or Control: State IRS Status: 501(c)3
Highest Offering: Associate Degree
Accreditation: NH, ADNUR

01 President Mr. Jay LEE
05 Vice President Instruction Mr. Danen JOBE
10 Vice Pres Finance & Administration Ms. Lisa LEFEVRE
32 Vice President Student Services Mr. Steven SMITH
29 Alumni Director Mr. Jack ANNAN
102 Executive Director NJC Foundation Ms. Kathleen REINHARDT
06 Director Records/Admission Process Ms. Lisa SCHAEFER
37 Director of Financial Aid Ms. Alice WEINGARDT
39 Dir Resident Life & Student Activit Mr. Timothy STAHLEY
18 Physical Plant Director Mr. Tracey KNOX
15 Human Resources Director Ms. Jeri ESTRADA
41 Athletic Director Ms. Marci HENRY
96 Director of Purchasing Ms. Martha GAREIS
09 Dir of Inst Research/Plng/Devel Ms. Leslie WEINSHEIM
26 Director of Communications Mr. David WEBB
21 Controller Ms. Judy MCFADDEN
13 Director Information Technology Ms. Cherie BRUNGARDT
40 Bookstore Director Ms. Heather BRUNGARDT
04 Executive Asst to President Ms. Shawn ROSE
07 Director of Admissions Mr. Adam KUNKEL
106 Dir Online Education/E-learning Vacant
108 Director Institutional Assessment Ms. Maret FELZIEN
25 Chief Contracts/Grants Admin Ms. Rebecca ROMERO

Otero Junior College (E)

1802 Colorado Avenue, La Junta CO 81050-3346
County: Otero FICE Identification: 001362
Unit ID: 127778
Telephone: (719) 384-6800 Carnegie Class: Assoc/HT-Mix Trad/Non
FAX Number: (719) 384-6933 Calendar System: Semester
URL: www.ojc.edu
Established: 1941 Annual Undergrad Tuition & Fees (In-State): $3,975
Enrollment: 1,330 Coed
Affiliation or Control: State IRS Status: 501(c)3
Highest Offering: Associate Degree
Accreditation: NH, ADNUR, MLTAD

01 President Dr. Timothy ALVAREZ
11 Vice Pres Administrative Services Mr. Pat MALOTT
05 Vice Pres Instructional Services Ms. Kim GRIMSLEY
32 Vice President Student Services Dr. Sara MATA
84 Assoc VP Enrollment Management Mrs. Almabeth KAESS
20 Assoc VP Instructional Services Mr. Ryan TROSPER
08 Director Learning Resources Ms. Chelsea HERASINGH
41 Athletic Director Mr. Gary ADDINGTON
15 Director of Human Resources Ms. Carol NOLL
18 Director of Physical Plant Mr. David GIRARD
40 Bookstore Coordinator Ms. Tanisha HERASINGH
37 Director of Financial Aid Mrs. Kelsey BARBEE
109 Director of Auxiliary Services Mr. Dillon MARTIN
26 Dir of Communications/Development Mrs. Almabeth KAESS
13 Director of Computer Services Mr. Mark ALLEN
09 Director of Institutional Research Vacant

Pikes Peak Community College (F)

5675 S Academy Boulevard,
Colorado Springs CO 80906-5498
County: El Paso FICE Identification: 008896
Unit ID: 127820
Telephone: (719) 502-2000 Carnegie Class: Assoc/HT-Mix Trad/Non
FAX Number: (719) 502-2201 Calendar System: Semester
URL: www.ppcc.edu
Established: 1968 Annual Undergrad Tuition & Fees (In-State): $3,840
Enrollment: 13,275 Coed
Affiliation or Control: State IRS Status: 501(c)3
Highest Offering: Baccalaureate
Accreditation: NH, ACFEI, ADNUR, DA, EMT

01 President Dr. Lance BOLTON
04 Exec Assistant to the President Ms. Misha JAMES
05 Vice Pres of Instruction Dr. Josh BAKER
32 Vice President Student Services Mr. Homer WESLEY
10 Vice Pres Administrative Services Mr. Duane RISSE
103 Vice Pres of Workforce Development Vacant
35 Assoc Vice Pres of Student Services Ms. Dawna HAYNES
20 Director of Instructional Support Ms. Julie HAZEL
37 Director of Financial Aid Mr. Ronald SWARTWOOD
08 Director of Libraries Ms. Carole OLDS
15 Exec Dir of Human Resource Services Mr. Carlton BROOKS
26 Exec Dir Marketing/Communications Mr. Warren EPSTEIN
22 Exec Director of Diversity/Equity Mr. Keith BARNES
21 Director of Business Svcs Mr. Hugh BRADFORD
06 Registrar/Coordinator of Records Ms. Twila HUMPHREY
07 Director of Admissions Mr. Kevin HUDGENS
102 Exec Director of Foundation Ms. Lisa JAMES
18 Dir Facilities and Operations Mr. Clint GARCIA

13 Chief Technology Officer Mr. Cyrille PARENT
19 Dir Public Safety/Emergency Mgmt Mr. Jim BARRENTINE
09 Exec Dir of Inst Effectiveness Dr. Patrica DIWARA
36 Director of Advising & Testing Mr. Lincoln WULF
96 Director of Purchasing Ms. Rockie HURRELL
38 Director Counseling Center Ms. Yolanda HARRIS
109 Director Auxiliary Services Ms. Lorelle DAVIES
09 Director of Institutional Research Dr. Li-Ling HSU
88 Project Dir of Stdnt Support Svcs Mr. Michael COUILLARD
76 Dean Health and Science Ms. Kristen JOHNSON
81 Dean Mathematics & English Mr. Joe SOUTHCOTT
50 Dean Business/Public Service/SS Mr. Rob HUDSON
60 Dean Comm/Humanities/Tech Studies Ms. Fran HETRICK
88 Dean of High School Programs Ms. Chelsy HARRIS
56 Dean of Academic Resources .. Ms. Jacquelyn GAITERS-JORDAN

Pima Medical Institute (G)

13750 E. Mississippi Avenue, Aurora CO 80012
County: Arapahoe FICE Identification: 041771
Unit ID: 461689
Telephone: (303) 368-7462 Carnegie Class: Spec 2-yr-Health
FAX Number: N/A Calendar System: Other
URL: pmi.edu
Established: 2012 Annual Undergrad Tuition & Fees: N/A
Enrollment: 257 Coed
Affiliation or Control: Proprietary IRS Status: Proprietary
Highest Offering: Associate Degree
Accreditation: ABHES

01 Campus Director Ms. Terri SPENCER

Pima Medical Institute-Colorado Springs (H)

5725 Mark Dabling Blvd, Suite 150,
Colorado Springs CO 80919
Telephone: (719) 482-7462 Identification: 770516
Accreditation: ABHES

† Branch campus of Pima Medical Institute-Tucson, Tucson, AZ

Pima Medical Institute-Denver (I)

7475 Dakin Street, Denver CO 80221
Telephone: (303) 426-1800 Identification: 666171
Accreditation: ABHES, COARC, OTA, PTAA, RAD

† Branch campus of Pima Medical Institute, Tucson, AZ.

Platt College (J)

3100 S Parker Road, Suite 200, Aurora CO 80014-3141
County: Arapahoe FICE Identification: 030149
Unit ID: 260813
Telephone: (303) 369-5151 Carnegie Class: Spec-4-yr-Other Health
FAX Number: (303) 745-1433 Calendar System: Quarter
URL: www.plattcolorado.edu
Established: 1986 Annual Undergrad Tuition & Fees: $19,286
Enrollment: 236 Coed
Affiliation or Control: Proprietary IRS Status: Proprietary
Highest Offering: Baccalaureate
Accreditation: ACCSC, NUR

01 President/CEO Mr. Jerald B. SIRBU
05 Vice President of Academic Affairs Dr. Julie BASLER
10 Director of Financial Services Mr. Robert CRAVER
37 Director of Financial Aid Mr. Michael J. VIGIL
08 Head Librarian Ms. Laura CULLERTON
66 Dean College of Nursing Ms. Jama GOERS
06 Registrar Ms. Katie DAHL
07 Admissions Representative Ms. Kylie IZIENICKI
13 Coordinator of IT Services Mr. Mark FINKEN

Pueblo Community College (K)

900 W Orman Avenue, Pueblo CO 81004-1499
County: Pueblo FICE Identification: 021163
Unit ID: 127884
Telephone: (719) 549-3200 Carnegie Class: Bac/Assoc-Assoc Dom
FAX Number: (719) 544-1179 Calendar System: Semester
URL: www.pueblocc.edu
Established: 1933 Annual Undergrad Tuition & Fees (In-State): $5,179
Enrollment: 5,991 Coed
Affiliation or Control: State IRS Status: 501(c)3
Highest Offering: Baccalaureate
Accreditation: NH, ACFEI, ADNUR, COARC, DH, EMT, OTA, PTAA, SURGT

01 President Dr. Patricia ERJAVEC
10 Chief Business Officer Vacant
05 Chief Academic Officer Dr. Todd ECKLUND
32 Chief of Student Services Dr. Heather SPEED
12 Exec Dean SWCCC Campus Ms. Tonya NELSON
12 Dean Fremont Campus Dr. Lana CARTER
76 Dean Health & Public Safety Ms. Mary CHAVEZ
49 Dean of Arts & Science Dr. Jeff ALEXANDER
50 Dean Business/Advance Technology Dr. Jennifer SHERMAN
88 Exec Dir Pueblo Corporate College Ms. Amanda CORUM
102 Director of PCC Foundation Ms. Martha SIMMONS
07 Dir Admissions & Records/Registrar Ms. Barbara BENEDICT
21 Controller Ms. Emma ALCALA
37 Director Financial Aid Ms. Monica HARDWICK
15 Director Human Resources Mr. Ken NUFER

13 Director Information Technology .... Mr. Bryan CRAWFORD
18 Director Facility Svcs/Capital Plng .... Mr. Joe WANEKA
88 Director Learning Center .... Mr. Ross BARNHART
08 Director Library Services .... Ms. Chris MCGRATH
26 Director Marketing/Communications .... Ms. Erin WHITE
35 Dir Student & Judicial Affairs .... Mr. Dennis JOHNSON
09 Dir Institutional Effectiveness .... Mr. Kevin J. MILDER
96 Director of Purchasing .... Mr. Edmond INIGUEZ
121 Director of Academic Advising .... Mr. Gage MICHAEL
04 Administrative Asst to President .... Ms. Julie JIMENEZ
106 Multimedia Tech Specialist .... Mr. Robin LEACH

Pueblo Community College Fremont Campus (A)

51320 W Highway 50, Canon City CO 81212
Telephone: (719) 296-6100 Identification: 770042
Accreditation: &NH

Pueblo Community College Southwest Campus (B)

33057 Highway 160, Mancos CO 81328
Telephone: (970) 564-6200 Identification: 770044
Accreditation: &NH

Red Rocks Community College (C)

13300 W Sixth Avenue, Lakewood CO 80228-1255
County: Jefferson FICE Identification: 009543
Unit ID: 127909
Telephone: (303) 914-6600 Carnegie Class: Bac/Assoc-Assoc Dom
FAX Number: (303) 914-6666 Calendar System: Semester
URL: www.rrcc.edu
Established: 1969 Annual Undergrad Tuition & Fees (In-State): $4,158
Enrollment: 7,355 Coed
Affiliation or Control: State IRS Status: 501(c)3
Highest Offering: Master's
Accreditation: NH, ARCPA, MAC, RAD

01 President .... Dr. Michele HANEY
04 Exec Assistant to the President .... Ms. Kathy SCHISSLER
10 Vice Pres Administrative Services .... Mr. Bryan BRYANT
05 Vice President Instruction .... Ms. Linda COMEAUX
32 Vice Pres Stdnt Svc/Enrollment Mgt .... Vacant
35 Vice Pres Student Success .... Dr. Lisa FOWLER
103 Vice Pres Workforce/Community Devel .... Mr. Ron SLINGER
20 Dean Academic Services .... Ms. Kelly CIRCLE
20 Dean Instructional Services .... Ms. Nicole LACROIX
20 Dean Instructional Services .... Mr. Mike COSTE
13 Dean Technology CTE .... Ms. Dorothy WELTY
88 Dean of Instruct/Exec Dir RMEC-OSHA .... Ms. Joan SMITH
85 Director International Education .... Ms. Linda YAZDANI
07 Dir Student Recruit/Advising/Admiss .... Dr. Cynthia SHIELDS
21 Controller .... Ms. Holly WREN
37 Director Financial Aid .... Ms. Shannon WEBBER
06 Dean Enrollment Services .... Dr. Seidel MOSES
18 Director Facilities .... Mr. Mark BANA
15 Interim Director Human Resources .... Mr. Arnie OUDENHOVEN
102 Assoc VP of Inst Advancement .... Mr. Ron SLINGER
26 Director Marketing/Communications .... Mr. David BARNES
35 Director Campus Life .... Dr. Steven ZEEH
88 Dir Childhood Ed & Support Svcs .... Ms. Janiece KNEPPE
09 Director Institutional Research .... Mr. Charles DUELL
28 Director of Diversity & Inclusion .... Ms. Jennifer MACKEN
96 Coordinator Purchasing .... Ms. Renee ARCHULETA
36 Director Student Outreach .... Vacant
46 Exec Dir Planning/Rsrch/Inst Effect .... Dr. Tim GRIFFIN

Red Rocks Community College Arvada Campus (D)

10280 W. 55th Avenue, Arvada CO 80002
Telephone: (303) 914-6010 Identification: 770045
Accreditation: &NH

Regis University (E)

3333 Regis Boulevard, #B-4, Denver CO 80221-1099
County: Denver FICE Identification: 001363
Unit ID: 127918
Telephone: (303) 458-4100 Carnegie Class: DU-Mod
FAX Number: (303) 964-5449 Calendar System: Semester
URL: www.regis.edu
Established: 1877 Annual Undergrad Tuition & Fees: $36,810
Enrollment: 8,341 Coed
Affiliation or Control: Roman Catholic IRS Status: 501(c)3
Highest Offering: Doctorate
Accreditation: NH, CACREP, CAHIIM, MFCD, NURSE, PHAR, PTA

01 President .... Rev. John P. FITZGIBBONS, SJ
43 VP/General Counsel .... Ms. Erika M. HOLLIS
05 Provost .... Dr. Janet HOUSER
10 Sr Vice President/CFO .... Dr. Salvador D. ACEVES
111 Vice President Advancement .... Ms. Myrna HALL
100 Chief of Staff .... Ms. Terri CAMPBELL
88 Vice President Mission .... Dr. Kevin F. BURKE
84 VP Enrollment Management .... Mr. Robert BLUST
32 Vice President Student Affairs .... Dr. Barbara WILCOTS
50 Interim Dean of Business .... Dr. Thomas BOWIE
109 Assoc VP Auxiliary & Business Svcs .... Ms. Susan LAYTON
15 Assoc VP Human Resources .... Vacant
18 Assoc VP Physical Plant .... Mr. Michael J. REDMOND
26 Assoc VP Marketing/Communication .... Mr. Todd COHEN
20 Asst Provost/Chief of Staff Provost .... Ms. Kristi GONSALVES-MCCABE
110 Asst VP University Advancement .... Ms. Mary BROZOVICH
29 Int Asst VP Alumni Engagement Pgms .... Ms. Margaret LINN-ADDISON
13 Chief Information Officer .... Mr. Jaganmohan GUDUR
107 Senior Director Adult Outreach .... Dr. Elisa ROBYN
77 Dean Computer & Info Sciences .... Dr. Shari PLANTZ-MASTERS
76 Dean Health Professions .... Dr. Linda OSTERLUND
88 Assoc Dean Health Professions .... Dr. Tristen AMADOR
49 Dean of Regis College .... Dr. Thomas BOWIE
66 Dean School of Nursing .... Dr. Catherine WITT
55 Dean Col of Contemporary Lib Arts .... Dr. Bryan HALL
08 Dean of Libraries .... Vacant
35 Dean of Students .... Mr. Patrick ROMERO-ALDAZ
07 Dean of Admissions .... Ms. Kim FRISCH
37 Director Financial Aid .... Ms. Cindy HEJL
06 Director Registration .... Ms. Cathy GORRELL
06 Director Academic Records .... Ms. Terry GAURMER
38 Int Dir Counseling/Personal Dev .... Ms. Melissa AURINGER
19 Director of Campus Safety .... Mr. Lance JONES
88 Director of Advancement Services .... Ms. Alicia GOULD
42 Int Director of University Ministry .... Mr. Kyle TURNER
36 Director Career & Prof Development .... Mr. Brent VOGEL
41 Assistant VP Athletics .... Mr. David SPAFFORD
04 Assistant to the President .... Ms. Christi GREBENC
39 Assoc Dir Resident Life/Housing .... Mr. Eric BARNES
112 Director Estate/Gift Planning .... Ms. Karen WIBREW
28 Director of Diversity .... Dr. Nicki GONZALES
44 Assistant Director Annual Giving .... Mr. Alec THORNTON

Rocky Mountain College of Art & Design (F)

1600 Pierce Street, Lakewood CO 80214-1433
County: Denver FICE Identification: 007649
Unit ID: 127945
Telephone: (303) 753-6046 Carnegie Class: Spec-4-yr-Arts
FAX Number: (303) 759-4970 Calendar System: Semester
URL: www.rmcad.edu
Established: 1963 Annual Undergrad Tuition & Fees: $19,020
Enrollment: 869 Coed
Affiliation or Control: Proprietary IRS Status: Proprietary
Highest Offering: Master's
Accreditation: NH, ART, CIDA

01 President .... Mr. Chris SPOHN
05 Senior Vice Pres Academic Affairs .... Ms. Neely PATTON
26 Senior Vice Pres of Marketing .... Mr. Daron RODRIGUEZ
07 Vice President of Admissions .... Mr. Marc ABRAHAM
32 Dean of Students .... Mr. Robert FLADRY
88 Director Accreditation/Compliance .... Dr. Terence BRENNAN

Rocky Vista University (G)

8401 South Chambers Road, Parker CO 80134
County: Douglas Identification: 667002
Unit ID: 480790
Telephone: (303) 373-2008 Carnegie Class: Spec-4-yr-Med
FAX Number: N/A Calendar System: Other
URL: www.rvu.edu
Established: 2006 Annual Graduate Tuition & Fees: N/A
Enrollment: 779 Coed
Affiliation or Control: Proprietary IRS Status: Proprietary
Highest Offering: Doctorate; No Undergraduates
Accreditation: NH, #ARCPA, OSTEO

01 President .... Dr. Clint ADAMS
04 Executive Administrative Assistant .... Ms. Michele SOBCZYK
09 VP for Institutional Effectiveness .... Dr. Jennifer WILLIAMS
88 Compliance Coordinator .... Ms. Laura DEMENT
05 VP Academic Affairs/CAO .... Dr. Thomas TOLD
10 Chief Operating Officer/CFO .... Mr. Peter FREYTAG
37 Dir Student Financial Svc .... Ms. Fran LATA
84 VP Enroll Mgmt/Mktg/Ext Rels .... Ms. Julie ROSENTHAL
32 Assoc Dean Student Affairs .... Ms. Amy SCHLUETER
06 Registrar .... Mr. David PALTZA
08 Director of Library Services .... Dr. Brian SCHWARTZ
19 Manager Security/Safety .... Mr. Andrew STEVENS
15 VP of Human Resources .... Mr. Jerry ARMSTRONG
101 Secretary of the Institution/Board .... Ms. Michele SOBCZYK
38 Director Student Counseling .... Mr. Kade RUCKER
39 Director Resident Life/Student Hous .... Ms. Vielane VAN NOY
88 Dean RVUCOM .... Dr. Tom TOLD
88 Dean RVUCOM-SU .... Dr. David PARK
13 Manager Information Services .... Mr. Brad ELLIS

St. John Vianney Theological Seminary (H)

1300 S Steele Street, Denver CO 80210-2526
County: Denver Identification: 666127
Telephone: (303) 282-3427 Carnegie Class: Not Classified
FAX Number: (303) 282-3453 Calendar System: Semester
URL: www.sjvdenver.edu
Established: 1999 Annual Graduate Tuition & Fees: N/A
Enrollment: N/A Male
Affiliation or Control: Roman Catholic IRS Status: 501(c)3
Highest Offering: Master's; No Undergraduates
Accreditation: THEOL

01 Rector .... Rev. Daniel LEONARD
03 Vice Rector .... Rev. Jason WALLACE
05 Academic Dean .... Dr. Joel BARSTAD
10 Director of Finance .... Mr. Paul VILLAMARIA
08 Library Director .... Mr. Stephen SWEENEY
06 Registrar .... Ms. Denise SEERY
04 Administrative Asst to President .... Ms. Val CAREY

Southwest Acupuncture College (I)

6630 Gunpark Drive Suite 200, Boulder CO 80301-3339
Telephone: (303) 581-9955 Identification: 666618
Accreditation: ACUP

† Branch campus of Southwest Acupuncture College, Santa Fe, NM.

Spartan College (J)

10851 W 120th Avenue, Broomfield CO 80021-3401
County: Broomfield FICE Identification: 007297
Unit ID: 126605
Telephone: (303) 466-1714 Carnegie Class: Spec 2-yr-Tech
FAX Number: (303) 496-0211 Calendar System: Other
URL: www.spartan.edu
Established: 1965 Annual Undergrad Tuition & Fees: $15,190
Enrollment: 319 Coed
Affiliation or Control: Proprietary IRS Status: Proprietary
Highest Offering: Associate Degree
Accreditation: ACCSC

01 Campus President .... Mr. Nicholas BROWN
05 Dean of Academic Affairs .... Mr. Tim GUERRERO
07 Director of Admissions .... Mr. Andrew MARMO
32 Dean of Student Affairs .... Mr. Corey O'BRIEN
06 Registrar .... Ms. Vicki MIDDEKER

Trinidad State Junior College (K)

600 Prospect, Trinidad CO 81082-2396
County: Las Animas FICE Identification: 001368
Unit ID: 128258
Telephone: (719) 846-5011 Carnegie Class: Assoc/MT-VT-High Non
FAX Number: (719) 846-5667 Calendar System: Semester
URL: www.trinidadstate.edu
Established: 1925 Annual Undergrad Tuition & Fees (In-State): $5,160
Enrollment: 1,663 Coed
Affiliation or Control: State IRS Status: 501(c)3
Highest Offering: Baccalaureate
Accreditation: NH, ADNUR

01 President .... Dr. Rhonda EPPER
05 Vice President of Academic Affairs .... Ms. Lynette BATES
32 VP Student Services .... Ms. Kerry GABRIELSON
10 VP of Business & Finance .... Ms. Lorrie VELASQUEZ
11 Vice Pres Administrative Services .... Ms. Lorrie VELASQUEZ
20 Dean of Instruction .... Dr. Evert BROWN
20 Dean of Instruction .... Mr. Keith GIPSON
20 Dean of Instruction .... Mr. Jack WILEY
37 Director Financial Aid .... Ms. Wilma ATENCIO
06 Registrar .... Ms. Christy HOLDEN
18 Facilities Director .... Mr. Al MALESPINI
21 Budget Director .... Ms. Shannon SHIVELEY
106 Dir Online Educ/Dir of Technology .... Mr. Doug BAK
04 Admin Asst to President .... Ms. Linda PERRY
26 Director of Marketing .... Mr. Greg BOYCE
41 Athletic Director .... Mr. Mike SALBATO

Trinidad State Junior College San Luis Valley Campus (L)

1011 Main Street, Alamosa CO 81101
Telephone: (719) 589-7000 Identification: 770047
Accreditation: &NH

UCH Memorial Hospital School Of Radiologic Technology (M)

2420 E. Pikes Peak Avenue, Colorado Springs CO 80910
County: El Paso Identification: 667097
Telephone: (719) 365-8291 Carnegie Class: Not Classified
FAX Number: (719) 365-5374 Calendar System: Semester
URL: www.uchealth.org/radschool
Established: 1969 Annual Undergrad Tuition & Fees: N/A
Enrollment: N/A Coed
Affiliation or Control: Independent Non-Profit IRS Status: 501(c)3
Highest Offering: Associate Degree
Accreditation: RAD

01 Director .... Elaine R. IVAN
05 Dean of Education .... Jarad MUASAU
06 Registrar/Clinical Coordinator .... Karen GEORGE
07 Director of Admissions .... Elaine R. IVAN
08 Head Librarian .... Char LONGWELL

*University of Colorado System Office (N)

1800 Grant Street, Suite 800, Denver CO 80203
County: Denver FICE Identification: 007996
Unit ID: 128300

Telephone: (303) 860-5600 Carnegie Class: N/A
FAX Number: (303) 860-5610
URL: www.cu.edu

01	President	Mr. Mark R. KENNEDY
05	Vice Pres Academic Affairs	Dr. Michael LIGHTNER
100	Senior VP & Chief of Staff	Mr. Leonard DINEGAR
10	VP & Chief Financial Officer	Mr. Todd SALIMAN
43	VP University Counsel/Secy Board	Mr. Pat O'ROURKE
111	VP for Advancement	Mr. Johnnie RAY
15	Sr AVP/Chief Human Resource Ofcr	Ms. Kathy NESBITT
86	VP Government Relations	Ms. Tanya KELLY-BOWRY
26	Assoc VP University Relations	Mr. Ken MCCONNELLOGUE
21	Asst VP & University Controller	Mr. Robert KUEHLER
13	Asst VP & Chief Information Ofcr	Mr. Scott MUNSON
27	Sr Asst VP for University Relations	Ms. Elizabeth COLLINS
88	Asst VP External Rels & Advocacy	Ms. Michele MCKINNEY
45	Asst VP Strategic Initiatives	Ms. Angelique FOSTER

*University of Colorado Boulder (A)

Regent Drive At Broadway, Boulder CO 80309-0001
County: Boulder FICE Identification: 001370
Unit ID: 126614
Telephone: (303) 492-1411 Carnegie Class: DU-Highest
FAX Number: N/A Calendar System: Semester
URL: www.colorado.edu
Established: 1876 Annual Undergrad Tuition & Fees (In-State): $12,532
Enrollment: 35,338 Coed
Affiliation or Control: State IRS Status: 501(c)3
Highest Offering: Doctorate
Accreditation: NH, AUD, CEA, CLPSY, IPSY, JOUR, LAW, MUS, SP

02	Chancellor	Dr. Phillip P. DISTEFANO
05	Provost & Exec VC for Acad Affairs	Dr. Russell MOORE
10	Sr Vice Chanc/Chief Financial Ofcr	Ms. Kelly L. FOX
46	Vice Chancellor for Research	Dr. Terri FIEZ
11	VC Infrastructure/Sustainability	Mr. David KANG
32	Vice Chanc for Student Affairs	Ms. Christina GONZALES
28	Vice Chanc for Diversity/Equity	Dr. Robert BOSWELL
26	Vice Chanc for Strategic Relations	Ms. Frances DRAPER
111	Vice Chanc for Advancement	Ms. Deb COFFIN
20	Exec VC for Academic Affairs	Dr. William H. KAEMPFER
20	Sr Vice Prov Academic Resource Mgmt	Dr. Ann SCHMIESING
20	Assoc Vice Chanc Faculty Affairs	Dr. Jeffrey N. COX
13	Assoc VC for IT/Chief Info Officer	Dr. Lawrence M. LEVINE
35	Assoc Vice Chanc Student Affairs	Dr. Akirah BRADLEY
29	Asst Vice Chanc Alumni Relations	Mr. Ryan CHREIST
18	Asst VC Facilities Operations/Svcs	Mr. Brian LINDOERFER
100	Chief of Staff	Ms. Catherine SHEA
58	Dean of the Graduate School	Dr. E. Scott ADLER
61	Dean of the Law	Dr. James ANAYA
49	Dean of Arts & Sciences	Dr. James WHITE
54	Dean of Engineering	Dr. Robert D. BRAUN
50	Dean of Business	Dr. Sharon MATUSIK
53	Dean of Education	Dr. Katherine SCHULTZ
64	Dean of Music	Dr. Robert S. SHAY
60	Dean of Media/Communications/Info	Dr. Lori BERGEN
51	Dean of Division of Continuing Educ	Dr. Sara THOMPSON
08	Dean of Libraries	Mr. Robert H. MCDONALD
35	Dean of Students	Dr. Sandy JONES
37	Director of Financial Aid	Ms. Ofelia A. MORALES
07	Interim Exec Director of Admissions	Mr. Kevin MACLENNAN
06	Registrar	Dr. Kristi WOLD-MCCORMICK
22	Exec Director Title IX Programs	Ms. Valerie SIMONS
09	Dir of Institutional Research	Mr. Robert STUBBS
25	Dir of Contracts and Grants	Ms. Denitta D. WARD
15	Chief Human Resources Officer	Ms. Charlotte Katherine ERWIN
41	Athletic Director	Mr. Rick GEORGE
19	Chief of Police	Ms. Doreen JOKERST
23	Exec Dir Student Health Ctr	Ms. Melissa LOWE
36	Director of Career Services	Dr. Lisa SEVERY
39	Exec Dir Housing & Dining Services	Ms. Amy D. BECKSTROM
88	Director of Museum	Dr. Patrick KOCIOLEK
104	Director of Education Abroad	Ms. Mary DANDO
43	Managing Assoc Univ Counsel	Ms. Elvira U. STREHLE-HENSON
38	Dir Counseling & Psychiatric Svcs	Dr. Monica NG

*University of Colorado Colorado Springs (B)

1420 Austin Bluffs Parkway, Colorado Springs CO 80918
County: El Paso FICE Identification: 004509
Unit ID: 126580
Telephone: (719) 255-8227 Carnegie Class: DU-Higher
FAX Number: (719) 255-3362 Calendar System: Semester
URL: www.uccs.edu
Established: 1965 Annual Undergrad Tuition & Fees (In-State): $8,523
Enrollment: 12,932 Coed
Affiliation or Control: State IRS Status: 501(c)3
Highest Offering: Doctorate
Accreditation: NH, CACREP, CAEP, CLPSY, DIETD, NURSE, SPAA

02	Chancellor	Dr. Venkat REDDY
05	Provost	Dr. Tom CHRISTENSEN
10	Vice Chanc Admin & Finance	Charles LITCHFIELD
32	Vice Chanc Student Success	Dr. Sentwali BAKARI
111	Vice Chanc Univ Advancement	Martin WOOD
20	Interim Assoc VC Academic Affairs	Dr. Susan TAYLOR
18	Chief Facilities/Physical Plant	Kent MARSH
11	Assoc VC Admin & Finance	Carlos GARCIA
43	Legal Counsel	Jennifer GEORGE
13	AVC Info Technology/CIO	Harper JOHNSON
46	Assoc Vice Chanc Research	Dr. Jessi L. SMITH
25	Director of Sponsored Programs	Gwen GENNARO
09	Director of Institutional Research	Dr. Robyn MARSCHKE
15	Director of Human Resources	Vacant
19	Director Public Safety	Marc PINO
37	Director Financial Aid	Jevita ROGERS
26	Director University Communications	Jared VERNER
38	Director Student Counseling	Dr. Benek ALTAYLI
41	Director of Athletics	Nathan GIBSON
29	Director Alumni Relations	Joanna BEAN
35	Dean of Students	Steve LINHART
49	Int Dean of Letters/Arts/Science	Dr. Robert (Rex) WELSHON
50	Dean of Business	Vacant
53	Dean of Education	Dr. Valerie CONLEY
54	Interim Dean of Engineering	Dr. Charles ZHOU
80	Dean of Public Affairs	Dr. George REED
66	Dean Nursing/Health Sciences	Dr. Kevin LAUDNER
58	Dean of Graduate School	Dr. Kelli KLEBE
08	Dean of Library	Dr. Martin GARNAR
39	Director Campus Housing	Ralph GIESE
06	Registrar	Tracy BARBER
07	Dir of Admissions/Recruitment	Chris BEISWANGER
04	Executive Asst to the Chancellor	Brenda BONN
105	Director Web Services	Craig DECKER
40	Director of Bookstore	Paul DENISTON
104	Director Study Abroad	Dr. Mandy HANSEN
106	Director of Extended Studies	Vacant
30	Director of Development	Melinda HAGEMANN
100	Chief of Staff	Andrea CORDOVA
28	Associate Vice Chancellor Diversity	Andrea HERRERA

*University of Colorado Denver | Anschutz Medical Campus (C)

P.O. Box 173364, Denver CO 80217
County: Denver FICE Identification: 004508
Unit ID: 126562
Telephone: (303) 556-2400 Carnegie Class: DU-Highest
FAX Number: N/A Calendar System: Semester
URL: www.ucdenver.edu
Established: 1912 Annual Undergrad Tuition & Fees (In-State): $9,283
Enrollment: 24,839 Coed
Affiliation or Control: State IRS Status: 501(c)3
Highest Offering: Doctorate
Accreditation: NH, AA, ARCPA, CACREP, CLPSY, DENT, DMS, HSA, IPSY, LSAR, MED, MIDWF, NURSE, PAST, PH, PHAR, PLNG, PTA, SCPSY, SPAA

02	Chancellor	Dr. Jeremy HAEFNER
03	VP Health Affairs/Exec VC AMC	Ms. Lilly MARKS
46	Vice Chancellor for Research	Dr. Richard TRAYSTMAN
10	Sr Vice Chanc Admin/Finance	Ms. Terri C. CARROTHERS
17	VC Health Affairs/Dean of Medicine	Dr. John REILLY
26	Vice Chanc of Univ Communications	Ms. Leanna CLARK
05	Provost & VC Academic/Student Affs	Dr. Roderick NAIRN
30	Vice Chanc of Development Anschutz	Mr. Scott ARTHUR
30	Vice Chanc of Development Denver	Mr. Matthew WASSERMAN
52	Dean School of Dental Medicine	Dr. Denise KASSEBAUM
66	Dean College of Nursing	Dr. Elias PROVENCIO-VASQUEZ
67	Dean School of Pharmacy	Dr. Ralph ALTIERE
69	Dean CO School of Public Health	Dr. David GOFF
58	Interim Dean Graduate School	Dr. Terry POTTER
64	Dean College of Arts/Media	Dr. Laurence KAPTAIN
80	Dean School of Public Affairs	Dr. Paul TESKE
49	Dean College Liberal Arts & Sci	Dr. Pamela JANSMA
48	Dean College of Arch/Planning	Mr. Mark GELERNTER
50	Dean Business School	Ms. Sueann AMBRON
53	Dean School of Education	Dr. Rebecca KANTOR
54	Dean College of Engineering	Dr. Marc INGBER
46	Assoc Vice Chancellor for Research	Dr. Robert DAMRAUER
20	Assoc VC Academic Affairs	Dr. Laura GOODWIN
32	Assoc VC Student Affairs	Dr. Raul CARDENAS
28	Assoc VC Diversity/Inclusion	Dr. Brenda ALLEN
21	Assoc VC Finance/Controller	Ms. E. Kim HUBER
18	Assoc VC Facilities Management	Mr. David C. TURNQUIST
88	Assoc VC of Academic Planning	Dr. Terry POTTER
15	Assoc VC Human Resources	Ms. Carolyn BROWNAWELL
13	Asst VC Information Technology Svcs	Mr. Russell POOLE
88	Asst VC Academic Tech/Extd Learning	Mr. Robert TOLSMA
84	Asst VC UG Admissions/K-12 Outreach	Mr. Chris DOWEN
09	Asst VC Institutional Research	Dr. Christine STROUP-BENHAM
88	Asst VC Student Success	Ms. Peggy LORE
88	Interim Asst VC University Life	Mr. Sam KIM
06	Registrar	Ms. Ingrid ESCHHOLZ
08	Director Auraria Library	Dr. Mary SOMERVILLE
08	Interim Dir Health Sciences Library	Ms. Melissa DESANTIS
27	Director PR/Media Relations	Vacant
37	Director Financial Aid Svcs	Mr. Justin JARAMILLO
19	Chief of Police	Mr. Doug ABRAHAM
29	Director Alumni Relations	Ms. Joy FRENCH
43	Assistant University Counsel	Mr. Christopher PUCKETT
35	Interim Dean of Students	Dr. Kristin KUSHMIDER
104	Director International Education	Mr. John SUNNYGARD
45	Chief Institutional Planning	Mr. Michale DEL GIUDICE

University of Denver (D)

2199 S. University Blvd., Denver CO 80208-0001
County: Denver FICE Identification: 001371
Unit ID: 127060
Telephone: (303) 871-2000 Carnegie Class: DU-Higher
FAX Number: (303) 871-3301 Calendar System: Quarter
URL: www.du.edu
Established: 1864 Annual Undergrad Tuition & Fees: $50,556
Enrollment: 11,434 Coed
Affiliation or Control: Independent Non-Profit IRS Status: 501(c)3
Highest Offering: Doctorate
Accreditation: NH, ART, CAEP, CEA, CLPSY, COPSY, IPSY, LAW, LIB, MUS, SW

01	Chancellor	Dr. Jeremy HAEFNER
05	Provost & Exec Vice Chancellor	Dr. Corinne LENGSFELD
43	Vice Chanc Legal Affs/Gen Counsel	Mr. Paul H. CHAN
32	Vice Chanc Campus Life/Inclus Excel	Dr. Liliana RODRIGUEZ
10	Vice Chanc Business/Financial Affs	Ms. Leslie BRUNELLI
41	Vice Chanc Athletics and Recreation	Mr. Karlton CREECH
111	Vice Chanc University Advancement	Mr. Brandon BUZBEE
26	Vice Chancellor Communications	Ms. Renea MORRIS
13	Vice Chancellor/Chief Info Officer	Mr. Donald HARRIS
84	Vice Chancellor for Enrollment	Mr. Todd RINEHART
100	Chief of Staff/Vice Chancellor	Dr. Nancy NICELY
37	Assoc Vice Chanc Financial Aid	Mr. John E. GUDVANGEN
04	Exec Assistant to the Chancellor	Ms. Allison RIOLA
20	Vice Provost Academic Program	Dr. Jennifer KARAS
07	AVC Enroll/Dir Undergrad Admissions	Ms. Allana FORTE
88	Assoc Vice Chancellor IE	Dr. Niki LATINO
28	Sr Advisor to Chancellor/Provost	Dr. Art JONES
58	Int Assoc Provost Graduate Studies	Dr. Corinne LENGSFELD
08	Dean/Dir University Libraries	Mr. Michael LEVINE-CLARK
34	Dean CO Women's College	Dr. Ann AYERS
20	Senior Assoc Provost Academic Admin	Dr. Linda KOSTEN
88	Assoc Vice Chanc Global Networks	Mr. Brandon BUZBEE
30	Asst Vice Chanc Development	Ms. Lissy GARRISON
06	Registrar	Mr. Dennis M. BECKER
21	Controller	Mr. Andrew CULLEN
29	Dir Alumni/Career/Prof Development	Ms. Cindy HYMAN
22	Title IX Coordinator	Mr. Jeremy ENLOE
18	Assoc Vice Chancellor Facilities	Mr. James ROSNER
09	Asst Provost Institutional Research	Mr. Mike FURNO
15	Vice Chanc Human Resources	Ms. Laura MARESCA
19	Director Campus Safety	Mr. Donald ENLOE
113	Dir Student Financial Services	Ms. Janet BURKHARDT
88	Asst Vice Chanc Enterprise Services	Ms. Susan LUTZ
38	Dir of Counseling Services	Dr. Jacaranda PALMATEER
54	Dean Engr/Computer Science	Mr. J.B HOLSTON
79	Dean Arts/Humanities/Social Science	Dr. Daniel MCINTOSH
81	Dean Natural Science/Math	Dr. Andrei KUTATELADZE
50	Dean College of Business	Mr. Vivek CHOUDHURY
61	Dean College of Law	Dr. Bruce SMITH
82	Dean Graduate Sch of Intl Studies	Mr. Fritz MAYER
70	Dean Graduate School of Social Work	Dr. Amanda MCBRIDE
55	Dean University College	Mr. Michael MCGUIRE
53	Dean College of Education	Dr. Karen RILEY
64	Exec Dir Newman Center	Ms. Kendra INGRAM
88	Exec Dir Conference Event Services	Ms. Amanda FUDALA
57	Director School of Art/Art History	Dr. Sarah GJERTSON
35	Exec Director of Campus Life	Vacant
101	Secretary of the Institution/Board	Ms. Nancy NICELY
105	Senior Digital Design and Architect	Mr. Matt ESCHENBAUM
88	Director University Teaching	Ms. Virgina PITTS
108	Director of Assessment	Dr. Christina PAGUYO

University of Northern Colorado (E)

501 20th Street, Greeley CO 80639-6900
County: Weld FICE Identification: 001349
Unit ID: 127741
Telephone: (970) 351-1890 Carnegie Class: DU-Mod
FAX Number: (970) 351-1880 Calendar System: Semester
URL: www.unco.edu
Established: 1889 Annual Undergrad Tuition & Fees (In-State): $9,918
Enrollment: 13,399 Coed
Affiliation or Control: State IRS Status: 501(c)3
Highest Offering: Doctorate
Accreditation: NH, ART, AUD, CAATE, CACREP, CEA, COPSY, DIETD, DIETI, IPSY, MUS, NURSE, PH, SCPSY, SP, THEA

01	President	Mr. Andrew FEINSTEIN
05	Provost/Vice Pres Academic Affairs	Dr. Theo KALIKOW
11	Sr Vice President Administration	Ms. Michelle QUINN
43	Vice President & University Counsel	Mr. Dan SATRIANA
26	VP External & University Relations	Mr. Dan WEAVER
30	Vice Pres Development/Alumni Rels	Ms. Allie STEG HASKETT
28	VP for Campus Community & Climate	Dr. Katrina RODRIGUEZ
58	Dean Grad School	Ms. Linda BLACK
20	Ast VP Undergrad Stds/Dean Univ Col	Vacant
114	Asst Vice Pres Budgets/Analysis	Ms. Susan SIMMERS
13	Asst Vice President Info Technology	Mr. Bret NABER
110	Asst VP for Development	Mr. Ben BARNHART
84	Asst Vice Pres for Enrollment Mgmt	Mr. Tobias GUZMAN
26	AVP Marketing	Mr. Jason HUGHES
88	AVP for Equity and Inclusion	Ms. Fleurette KING
79	Dean Humanities/Social Sciences	Dr. Laura CONNOLLY
50	Dean Business	Dr. Paul BOBROWSKI
53	Dean Education/Behavioral Sciences	Dr. Eugene SHEEHAN
76	Dean Natural & Health Sciences	Dr. Englert BURKHARD
57	Dean Performing Visual Arts	Dr. Leo WELCH
08	Dean University Libraries	Ms. Helen REED
32	Dean of Students	Dr. Gardiner TUCKER
102	President University Foundation	Mr. Rod ESCH
06	Registrar	Mr. Charlie COUCH
07	Director of Admissions	Dr. Sean M. BROGHAMMER
25	AVP Sponsored Pgms/Research	Dr. Robert HOUSER
37	Dir Student Financial Resources	Mr. Marty SOMERO
36	Director of Career Services	Ms. Renee WELCH
15	Director of Human Resources	Mr. Marshall PARKS
29	Asst VP Alumni Relations	Ms. Lyndsey CRUM

18 Director Facilities Management .... Mr. Kirk LEICHLITER
41 Director of NCAA Athletics ....Mr. Darren DUNN
39 Director of Residential Education .... Mr. Montez BUTTS
38 Director Student Counseling .... Ms. Kim WILCOX
19 Chief of University Police .... Mr. Dennis PUMPHREY
44 Director of Annual Giving ....Vacant
27 Dir News & Public Relations ....Mr. Nate HAAS
96 Director of Purchasing .... Ms. Cristal SWAIN
85 Director Ctr for International Educ .... Ms. Maureen ULEVICH
104 Director Study Abroad ....Ms. Teneisha ELLIS
108 Director Institutional Assessment .... Ms. Kim BLACK
04 Administrative Asst to President ....Ms. Elaine QUAM
100 Chief of Staff .... Ms. Gloria REYNOLDS
101 Secretary of the Institution/Board .... Ms. Victoria NICCUM
105 Director Web Services ....Mr. Jesse CLARK
106 Dir Online Education/E-learning ....Ms. Nancy RUBIN
22 Dir Affirmative Action/EEO ....Mr. Larry LOFTEN

University of Phoenix Colorado Main Campus (A)

1000H Park Meadows Drive, Lone Tree CO 80124-5453
Telephone: (303) 755-9090 Identification: 770195
Accreditation: &NH, ACBSP

† No longer accepting campus-based students.

U.S. Career Institute (B)

2001 Lowe Street, Fort Collins CO 80525
County: Larimer Identification: 666776
Telephone: (970) 207-4500 Carnegie Class: Not Classified
FAX Number: (970) 223-1678 Calendar System: Other
URL: www.uscareerinstitute.edu
Established: 1981 Annual Undergrad Tuition & Fees: N/A
Enrollment: N/A Coed
Affiliation or Control: Proprietary IRS Status: Proprietary
Highest Offering: Associate Degree
Accreditation: DEAC

01 President .... Ms. Ann ROHR
32 Vice President Student Affairs .... Ms. Joyce LINDQUIST
26 Vice Pres Student Rels/Marketing ....Ms. Holly COOK
05 Vice Pres of Academics/Compliance ....Ms. Janet PERRY
106 Dean of Curriculum .... Ms. Leslie BALLENTINE

Western Colorado Community College-Tilman M. Bishop Campus (C)

2508 Blichmann Avenue, Grand Junction CO 81505
Telephone: (970) 255-2600 Identification: 770030
Accreditation: &NH

Western State Colorado University (D)

1 Western Way, Gunnison CO 81231-0001
County: Gunnison FICE Identification: 001372
Unit ID: 128391
Telephone: (970) 943-0120 Carnegie Class: Masters/S
FAX Number: (970) 943-7069 Calendar System: Semester
URL: www.western.edu
Established: 1901 Annual Undergrad Tuition & Fees (In-State): $10,114
Enrollment: 2,814 Coed
Affiliation or Control: State IRS Status: 501(c)3
Highest Offering: Master's
Accreditation: NH, MUS

01 President .... Dr. Greg SALSBURY
11 Exec Vice Pres and COO ....Mr. Brad BACA
05 Vice Pres for Academic Affairs ....Dr. Bill NIEMI
111 Vice Pres Advancement .... Mr. Mike LAPLANTE
10 Chief Financial Officer ....Ms. Julie BACA
32 VP Student Affairs/Dean of Students ....Mr. Gary PIERSON
84 Vice Pres Mktg/Enrollment .... Ms. Sarah HIGGINS
20 Assoc Vice Pres Academic Affairs .... Dr. Kevin ALEXANDER
35 Assoc Vice Pres for Student Affairs .... Mr. Chris LUEKENGA
06 Registrar ....Ms. Laurel BECKER
37 Director of Financial Aid .... Ms. Carrie SHAW
104 Dir Intl Student Pgms/Study Abroad ....Ms. Katie WHEATON
41 Athletic Director ....Mr. Miles VAN HEE
15 Director of Human Resources ....Ms. Kim GAILEY
40 Director Retail Operations ....Ms. Teri HAUS
13 Chief Information Ofcr/IT Director ....Mr. Chad ROBINSON
08 Director Library Services .... Mr. Dustin FIFE
51 Director Extended Studies ....Ms. Kirky LOKIE
39 Director of Residence Life .... Ms. Shelley JANSEN
36 Career Services Coordinator ....Mr. Craig BEEBE
26 Director of Public Relations .... Ms. Sarah HIGGINS
29 Director of Alumni Relations .... Ms. Ann JOHNSTON
44 Director Annual & Special Gifts .... Mr. Tom BURGRAFF
09 Director Institutional Research .... Mr. Doug DRIVER
28 Director of Multicultural Center ....Ms. Sally ROMERO
07 Dir Recruitment/Admissions ....Ms. Lauren SHONDECK
96 Business Services Manager .... Ms. Sherry FORD
04 Admin Assistant to the President ....Ms. Joy KEAN
105 Director Web Services ....Mr. RJ TONEY
18 Chief Facilities/Physical Plant Ofc .... Mr. Bryce HANNA
19 Director Security/Safety .... Mr. Nathan KUBES
25 Chief Contract Grants Admin .... Ms. Janice WELBORN
50 Dean School of Business ....Mr. Peter SHERMAN

William Howard Taft University (E)

3333 South Wadsworth Blvd, Ste D228,
Lakewood CO 80227
County: Jefferson FICE Identification: 041004
Unit ID: 454689
Telephone: (303) 867-1155 Carnegie Class: Spec-4-yr-Other
FAX Number: (303) 867-1156 Calendar System: Semester
URL: www.taft.edu
Established: 1976 Annual Undergrad Tuition & Fees: N/A
Enrollment: 751 Coed
Affiliation or Control: Proprietary IRS Status: Proprietary
Highest Offering: Doctorate
Accreditation: DEAC

01 President ....Dr. Neil A. JOHNSON
03 Chief Operating Officer ....Mr. Robert K. STROUSE
11 Director of Administration ....Ms. Christine A. BALDWIN
50 Dean School of Business ....Dr. Laura POGUE
53 Dean School of Education ....Dr. Barry RESNICK
05 Chief Academic Officer ....Mr. Neil A. JOHNSON
07 Director of Admissions ....Ms. Ni PHAM

† Tuition varies by degree program.

CONNECTICUT

Albertus Magnus College (F)

700 Prospect Street, New Haven CT 06511-1189
County: New Haven FICE Identification: 001374
Unit ID: 128498
Telephone: (203) 773-8550 Carnegie Class: Masters/M
FAX Number: (203) 773-9539 Calendar System: Semester
URL: www.albertus.edu
Established: 1925 Annual Undergrad Tuition & Fees: $32,060
Enrollment: 1,464 Coed
Affiliation or Control: Independent Non-Profit IRS Status: 501(c)3
Highest Offering: Master's
Accreditation: EH, IACBE

01 President ....Dr. Marc M. CAMILLE
05 Vice Pres Academic Affairs ....Dr. Sean O'CONNELL
10 Vice President Finance/Treasurer .... Mr. William B. HAWKINS
13 VP Information Technology Services .... Dr. Steven GSTALDER
30 VP Development/Alumni Relations ....Ms. Carolyn A. BEHAN KRAUS
32 Vice President for Student Services ....Mr. Andrew FOSTER
26 VP Communications/Marketing .... Ms. Andrea KOVACS
84 VP Enrollment Management ....Vacant
35 Asst Dean Campus Activities/Orien ....Ms. Erin MORRELL
06 Registrar ....Mrs. Melissa DELUCIA
08 Director Library/Information Svcs ....Ms. Anne LEENEY-PANAGROSSI
09 Dir Inst Research & Assessment ....Ms. Viola SIMPSON
37 Director Financial Aid .... Mrs. Michelle COCHRAN
41 Director of Athletics .... Mr. James ABROMAITIS
58 Director MALS Program ....Vacant
121 Director of Academic Advising .... Ms. Heather WOTTON
92 Director of Honors Program ....Dr. Christine ATKINS
11 Asst VP Operations .... Mr. James A. SCHAFRICK
15 Director Human Resources .... Ms. Renee SULLIVAN
27 Dir Communications/Community Rels ....Vacant
36 Director Career Services .... Mr. Patrick CLIFFORD
42 Coord of Dominican Ministries .... Sr. Joan SCANLON
18 Supervisor of Facilities Services ....Mr. Dan SECOR
04 Administrative Asst to President .... Ms. Lynne M. HENNESSY
07 Director of Admissions ....Mr. Ben AMARONE
107 Dean Prof & Graduate Studies ....Ms. Annette BOSLEY-BOYCE
29 Director Alumni & Parent Engagement ....Mr. Antonio ALVES
39 Director Resident Life & Community ....Ms. Shannon LEE
44 Director Annual & Individual Giving ....Ms. Siobhan LIDINGTON

Charter Oak State College (G)

55 Paul Manafort Drive, New Britain CT 06053-2142
County: Hartford FICE Identification: 029171
Unit ID: 128780
Telephone: (860) 515-3800 Carnegie Class: Bac-A&S
FAX Number: (860) 606-9615 Calendar System: Other
URL: www.charteroak.edu
Established: 1973 Annual Undergrad Tuition & Fees (In-State): $8,301
Enrollment: 1,500 Coed
Affiliation or Control: State IRS Status: 501(c)3
Highest Offering: Master's
Accreditation: EH, CAHIIM

01 President .... Mr. Edward KLONOSKI
05 Provost .... Dr. Shirley M. ADAMS
10 Chief Financial/Administrative Ofcr ...... Mr. Michael J. MORIARTY
13 Chief Information Officer .... Vacant
09 Dir Institutional Effectiveness .... Mr. Michael BRODERICK
06 Registrar .... Ms. Jennifer WASHINGTON
37 Dir Financial Aid/Veterans Benefits ....Mr. Ralph BRASURE, III
20 Director Academic Services .... Ms. Wanda WARSHAUER
07 Director Admissions .... Ms. Lori GAGNE PENDLETON
88 Dir Prior Learning Assessment Pgm ....Ms. Linda WILDER
26 Director Marketing/Public Relations .... Ms. Carolyn HEBERT
04 Administrative Asst to President .... Ms. Carol HALL
30 Assoc Director Development .... Ms. Carol HALL
105 Web Developer ....Mr. Jon ELLIS
15 Director Personnel Services ....Ms. Rowena MCGOLDRICK
29 Director Alumni Relations .... Ms. Carol HALL

*Connecticut Board of Regents for Higher Education (H)

61 Woodland Street, Hartford CT 06105-2345
County: Hartford Identification: 666656
Telephone: (860) 723-0000 Carnegie Class: N/A
FAX Number: (860) 723-0009
URL: www.ct.edu

01 President CTCU .... Mr. Mark E. OJAKIAN
05 Provost/SVP Acad & Student Affairs ....Dr. Jane McBride GATES
88 VP for CT State Universities ....Dr. Elsa NUNEZ
88 VP for Cmty Colleges at CT BOR ....Dr. David LEVINSON
15 VP for Human Resources .... Mr. Steve WEINBERGER
18 VP Facilities/RE/Infrastruct Plng .... Mr. Keith EPSTEIN
10 Chief Financial Officer ....Mr. Benjamin BARNES
13 Chief Information Officer ....Mr. Joseph TOLISANO
101 Assoc Director Board Affairs .... Ms. Erin FITZGERALD
04 Admin Assistant to the President ....Ms. Victoria LEE-THOMAS
100 Chief of Staff .... Dr. Alice PRITCHARD
26 Director Public Relations/Marketing ......Mr. Michael KOZLOWSKI
09 Director of Institutional Research ....Dr. William GAMMELL
43 Dir Legal Services/General Counsel ....Ms. Ernestine WEAVER
27 Director of Communications ....Ms. Leigh APPLEBY

*Central Connecticut State University (I)

1615 Stanley Street, New Britain CT 06050-4010
County: Hartford FICE Identification: 001378
Unit ID: 128771
Telephone: (860) 832-3000 Carnegie Class: Masters/L
FAX Number: N/A Calendar System: Semester
URL: www.ccsu.edu
Established: 1849 Annual Undergrad Tuition & Fees (In-State): $10,616
Enrollment: 11,880 Coed
Affiliation or Control: State IRS Status: 501(c)3
Highest Offering: Doctorate
Accreditation: EH, ANEST, CAATE, CACREP, CAEPN, CONST, EXSC, MFCD, MUS, NAIT, NURSE, SW

02 President ....Dr. Zulma R. TORO
04 Exec Assistant to the President .... Ms. Susan MATTERAZZO
05 Provost/VP Academic Affairs .... Dr. David DAUWALDER
111 Vice Pres Institutional Advancement .... Dr. Chris GALLIGAN
32 Vice President Student Affairs .... Dr. Michael JASEK
35 Associate Dean Student Affairs .... Mr. Ramon HERNANDEZ
20 Associate VP Academic Affairs ....Dr. Joseph P. PAIGE
58 Associate VP Graduate Studies ....Vacant
43 University Counsel .... Ms. Carolyn MAGNAN
11 Chief Administrative Officer ....Vacant
10 Chief Financial Officer ....Mrs. Charlene CASAMENTO
15 Chief Human Resources Officer . Mrs. Anna SUSKI-LENCZEWSKI
28 Chief Diversity Officer ....Vacant
49 Dean Liberal Arts/Soc Sciences ....Dr. Robert WOLFF
50 Int Dean School of Business ....Dr. Joseph FARHAT
53 Dean School Educ & Prof Studies .... Dr. Kimberly KOSTELIS
54 Int Dean School Engr/Science/Tech ....Dr. Zdzislaw KREMENS
104 Dir Center International Education .... Dr. Momar NDIAYE
51 Dir Continuing Educ/Cmty Engagement .... Ms. Christa STERLING
07 Director Admissions & Recruitment .... Mr. Lawrence HALL
41 Director Athletics ....Mr. Brian BARRIO
39 Director Residence Life .... Ms. Jean ALICANDRO
19 Director Public Safety ....Mr. Gregory SNEED
37 Director Student Financial Aid ....Mr. Richard BISHOP
29 Director Alumni/Development ....Ms. Lisa BIGELOW
26 Director Public Relations .... Ms. Janice PALMER
08 Director Library Services .... Mr. Carl ANTONUCCI
36 Int Dir Career Success Center .... Mr. Paul ROSSITTO
23 Dir Student Wellness Svcs ....Vacant
06 Registrar .... Mr. Patrick TUCKER
38 Coordinator Office Wellness Educ ....Mr. Jonathan POHL
18 Asst Chief Admin Ofcr/Dir Facil Mgt .... Mr. Salvatore CINTORINO
21 University Controller ....Ms. Julie DEFALCO
96 Purchasing Manager .... Mr. Thomas BRODEUR
09 Dir Inst Research/Assessment .... Ms. Yvonne KIRBY
13 Chief Info Technology Officer (CIO) .... Dr. George CLAFFEY
84 Assoc VP Enrollment Management .... Ms. Karissa PECKHAM

*Eastern Connecticut State University (J)

83 Windham Street, Willimantic CT 06226-2295
County: Windham FICE Identification: 001425
Unit ID: 129215
Telephone: (860) 465-5000 Carnegie Class: Masters/S
FAX Number: (860) 465-4690 Calendar System: Semester
URL: www.easternct.edu
Established: 1889 Annual Undergrad Tuition & Fees (In-State): $11,356
Enrollment: 5,282 Coed
Affiliation or Control: State IRS Status: 501(c)3
Highest Offering: Master's
Accreditation: EH, CAEPN, SW

02 President .... Dr. Elsa M. NUNEZ
05 Interim Provost ....Dr. William SALKA
10 VP Finance/Administration ....Mr. James R. HOWARTH
32 Vice Pres Student Affairs .... Mr. Walter DIAZ

111 Vice Pres Institutional Advance ... Mr. Kenneth J. DELISA
28 Assoc Provost/VP Equity & Diversity ... Dr. Stacey CLOSE
35 Dean of Students ... Ms. Michelle DELANY
13 Chief Information Officer ... Mr. Gary BOZYLINSKY
09 Asst Dir of Institutional Research ... Vacant
41 Director of Athletics ... Ms. Lori RUNKSMEIER
08 Director of Library Services ... Ms. Janice WILSON
84 Dir of Enrollment Mgmt/Fin Aid ... Dr. Jennifer HORNER
36 Director of Career Services ... Mr. Clifford MARRETT
29 Director of Alumni Affairs ... Mr. Michael STENKO
06 Registrar ... Ms. Jennifer HUOPPI
19 Director of Public Safety ... Mr. Jeffrey A. GAREWSKI
39 Director Housing/Residence Life ... Mr. LaMar COLEMAN
40 Director of Bookstore ... Ms. Allyson HALL
42 Director of Campus Ministry ... Rev. Laurence LAPOINTE
18 Dir of Facilities Mgmt/Planning ... Ms. Renee KEECH
26 Director University Relations ... Mr. Edward H. OSBORN
49 Dean of Arts & Sciences ... Dr. Carmen R. CID
51 Assoc Dean Continuing Education ... Dr. Indira PETOSKEY
58 Dean Educ/Prof Studies/Grad Pgm ... Dr. Elizabeth SCOTT
96 Assoc Dir Fiscal Affs/Acquisition ... Ms. Terry O'BRIEN
38 Interim Dir Counseling/Psych Svcs ... Dr. Bryce CRAPSER
07 Director of Admissions ... Mr. Christopher DORSEY
21 University Controller ... Ms. Shirley AUDET
14 Director IT ... Mr. Steve NELSON
110 Director Institutional Advancement ... Mr. Joesph MCGANN
88 Director Energy Institute ... Ms. Lynn STODDARD

*Southern Connecticut State University (A)

501 Crescent Street, New Haven CT 06515-0901
County: New Haven | FICE Identification: 001406
Unit ID: 130493
Telephone: (203) 392-7278 | Carnegie Class: Masters/L
FAX Number: N/A | Calendar System: Semester
URL: www.southernct.edu
Established: 1893 | Annual Undergrad Tuition & Fees (In-State): $10,954
Enrollment: 10,202 | Coed
Affiliation or Control: State | IRS Status: 501(c)3
Highest Offering: Doctorate
Accreditation: EH, CAATE, CACREP, CAEPN, EXSC, MFCD, NURSE, PH, SP, SW

02 President ... Dr. Joe BERTOLINO
04 Admin Assistant to the President ... Ms. Charmaine R. LLOYD
05 Provost/Vice Pres Acad Affairs ... Dr. Robert PREVANT
10 EVP for Finance & Administration ... Mr. Mark ROZEWSKI
32 Vice Pres Student Affairs ... Dr. Tracy TYREE
30 Vice President Inst Advancement ... Dr. Michael KINGAN
84 Assoc VP for Enrollment Management ... Vacant
15 Chief Human Resources Officer ... Ms. Diane MAZZA
18 Assoc VP Capital Budgeting/Fac Ops ... Mr. Robert G. SHEELEY
13 Chief Info Tech Officer ... Dr. Dennis REIMAN
49 Dean School Arts & Sciences ... Dr. Bruce KALK
50 Dean School of Business ... Dr. Ellen DURNIN
53 Dean School Education ... Dr. Stephen HEGEDUS
58 Dean School Graduate Studies ... Dr. Manohar SINGH
70 Int Dean School Health/Human Svcs ... Dr. Sandra BULMER
41 Director of Athletics ... Mr. Jay MORAN
26 Director of Public Affairs ... Mr. Patrick DILGER
29 Director Alumni Affairs ... Mr. Gregory BERNARD
07 Director Admissions ... Dr. Tony PACE
06 Registrar ... Ms. Alicia CARROLL
08 Director of Library Services ... Vacant
19 Director of Public Safety ... Mr. Joseph M. DOOLEY
25 Director of Sponsored Research ... Ms. Amy TAYLOR
37 Director of Financial Aid ... Ms. Gloria LEE
23 Director of Health Services ... Dr. Diane S. MORGENTHALER
35 Dean of Student Affairs ... Dr. Jules TETREAULT
88 Assoc VP for Strategic Initiatives ... Dr. Colleen Q. BIELITZ
38 Director of Counseling Services ... Dr. Nick PINKERTON
21 University Controller ... Ms. Loren LOOMIS HUBBELL
92 Director of Honors Program ... Dr. Terese GEMME
94 Director of Women's Studies ... Dr. Yi-Chun Tricia LIN
88 Dir of Academic & Career Advising ... Mr. Harry TWYMAN
39 Director of Residence Life ... Mr. Robert C. DEMEZZO

*Western Connecticut State University (B)

181 White Street, Danbury CT 06810-6885
County: Fairfield | FICE Identification: 001380
Unit ID: 130776
Telephone: (203) 837-8200 | Carnegie Class: Masters/M
FAX Number: (203) 837-8276 | Calendar System: Semester
URL: www.wcsu.edu
Established: 1903 | Annual Undergrad Tuition & Fees (In-State): $10,859
Enrollment: 5,664 | Coed
Affiliation or Control: State | IRS Status: 501(c)3
Highest Offering: Doctorate
Accreditation: EH, ART, CACREP, CAEPN, MUS, NURSE, PH, SW, THEA

02 President ... Dr. John B. CLARK
05 Provost/Vice Pres Academic Affairs ... Dr. Missy ALEXANDER
10 Assoc VP Finance & Administration ... Mr. Sean LOUGHRAN
32 VP Student Affairs ... Dr. Keith BETTS
88 Dean of Visual/Performing Arts ... Mr. Brian VERNON
35 Dean of Student Affairs ... Dr. Walter CRAMER
49 Dean Macricostas Sch Arts & Sci ... Dr. Michelle L. BROWN
50 Dean of Ancell Sch of Business ... Dr. David MARTIN
107 Int Dean of Sch of Prof Studies ... Dr. Joan PALLADINO
15 Chief Human Resources Officer ... Mr. Frederic W. CRATTY
13 Director of Info Systems ... Mr. John DEROSA
21 Director Fiscal Affairs/Controller ... Mr. Peter ROSA
111 Int VP of Inst Advancement ... Ms. Lynne LEBARRON
28 Chief Diversity Officer ... Ms. Jesenia MINIER-DELGADO
06 Registrar ... Mr. Keith R. GAUVIN
08 Director of Library Services ... Ms. Veronica KENAUSIS
09 Director Inst Research/Assessment ... Dr. Jerome WILCOX
25 Director of Grant/Programs ... Ms. Gabrielle E. JAZWIECKI
38 Director of Counseling Svcs ... Dr. Rée GUNTER
37 Director of Financial Aid ... Ms. Melissa STEPHENS
36 Director Career Development Center ... Ms. Kathleen LINDENMAYER
26 Director Univ & Cmty Relations ... Mr. Paul STEINMETZ
39 Director Housing & Residence Life ... Mr. Ron MASON
35 Director Student Life ... Dr. Paul M. SIMON
41 Director of Athletics ... Ms. Lori MAZZA
29 Director of Alumni Relations ... Mr. Thomas CRUCITTI
07 Director of Admissions ... Mr. Luis SANTIAGO
88 Dir of Facilities Plng & Engr ... Mr. Peter VISENTIN
11 Director of Administrative Services ... Mr. Mark R. CASE
18 Assoc VP Facilities ... Mr. Luigi MARCONE
88 Dir Facil Utilization & Promotion ... Mr. John MURPHY
114 Director of Fin Planning & Budgets ... Ms. Mary Ann DEASE
27 Assoc Dir of Public Relations ... Ms. Sherri HILL
19 Chief of Police ... Mr. Roger CONNOR
14 Dir Info Tech & Media Svcs ... Ms. Rebecca WOODWARD
04 Exec Asst to President ... Ms. Janet MCKAY
84 Assoc VP Enrollment Services ... Mr. Jay MURRAY

*Asnuntuck Community College (C)

170 Elm Street, Enfield CT 06082-3800
County: Hartford | FICE Identification: 011150
Unit ID: 128577
Telephone: (860) 253-3000 | Carnegie Class: Assoc/HVT-High Trad
FAX Number: (860) 253-3014 | Calendar System: Semester
URL: www.asnuntuck.edu
Established: 1972 | Annual Undergrad Tuition & Fees (In-State): $4,464
Enrollment: 1,870 | Coed
Affiliation or Control: State | IRS Status: 501(c)3
Highest Offering: Associate Degree
Accreditation: EH

00 Chief Executive Officer ... Mrs. Michelle COACH
02 Regional President ... Dr. James P. LOMBELLA
05 Dean of Academic Affairs ... Ms. Teresa FOLEY
10 Interim Dean of Administration ... Mr. Gennaro DEANGELIS
32 Interim Dean of Student Services ... Mr. Tim ST. JAMES
15 Interim Director of HR ... Ms. Cheryl A. CYR
84 Director of Enrollment Management ... Vacant
06 Registrar ... Ms. Diane CLOKEY
37 Interim Director of Financial Aid ... Ms. Beth-Anne EGAN
09 Director of Institutional Research ... Ms. Qing L. MACK
111 Director Institutional Advancement ... Mr. Keith MADORE
103 Dean Workforce Dev/Cont Educ ... Ms. Eileen PELTIER
18 Bldg Superintendent II/Phys Plant ... Mr. Joseph MULLER
26 Coord of Mktg/Business/Industry ... Mr. Gary CARRA
04 Exec Asst to Regional President ... Ms. Margaret G. VAN COTT
07 Interim Director of Admissions ... Ms. Jennifer ANILOWSKI
13 Director of Information Technology ... Mr. Jeff D. CLARK
121 Dir Ctr for Advising/Stdnt Achvmt ... Ms. Jill RUSHBROOK

*Capital Community College (D)

950 Main Street, Hartford CT 06103-1207
County: Hartford | FICE Identification: 007635
Unit ID: 129367
Telephone: (860) 906-5000 | Carnegie Class: Assoc/MT-VT-High Trad
FAX Number: (860) 520-7906 | Calendar System: Semester
URL: www.capitalcc.edu
Established: 1967 | Annual Undergrad Tuition & Fees (In-State): $4,464
Enrollment: 3,282 | Coed
Affiliation or Control: State | IRS Status: 501(c)3
Highest Offering: Associate Degree
Accreditation: EH, ADNUR, EMT, MAC, RAD

02 Chief Executive Officer ... Dr. G. Duncan HARRIS
05 Dean of Academic & Student Affairs ... Dr. Miah LAPIERRE DREGER
32 Associate Dean of Student Affairs ... Mr. Jason SCAPPATICCI
11 Associate Dean of Campus Operations ... Mr. Eduardo MIRANDA
51 Dean Cont Educ/Workforce Dev ... Dr. Linda GUZZO
09 Director of Institutional Research ... Ms. Jenny WANG
10 Director Finance/Administration ... Mr. Ted HALE
06 Registrar ... Mr. Argelio MARRERO
08 Director of Library Services ... Ms. Eileen RHODES
84 Interim Director of Enrollment Mgmt ... Mr. Gregg GORNEAULT
37 Director of Financial Aid ... Ms. Margaret MALASPINA
13 Interim Asst Director of IMT ... Ms. Stephanie CALHOUN-WARD
66 Dir Cont Educ Nurse/Allied Health ... Dr. Ruth KREMS
26 Director of Information/Marketing ... Ms. Jane BRONFMAN
15 Director of Human Resources ... Ms. Josephine AGNELLO-VELEY
88 Asst to the Academic Dean ... Mr. Ryan PIERSON
111 Director Institutional Advancement ... Mr. John MCNAMARA
04 Executive Assistant/Staff Liaison ... Ms. Jessica BENIASH

*Gateway Community College (E)

20 Church St., New Haven CT 06510-5970
County: New Haven | FICE Identification: 008037
Unit ID: 130396
Telephone: (203) 285-2000 | Carnegie Class: Assoc/MT-VT-High Trad
FAX Number: (203) 285-2018 | Calendar System: Semester
URL: www.gatewayct.edu
Established: 1968 | Annual Undergrad Tuition & Fees (In-State): $4,424
Enrollment: 7,015 | Coed
Affiliation or Control: State | IRS Status: 501(c)3
Highest Offering: Associate Degree
Accreditation: EH, ADNUR, #DIETT, DMS, NMT, RAD, RTT

02 President ... Dr. Paul BROADIE, II
30 Dean of Devel/Community Partnership ... Ms. Mary Ellen CODY
05 Dean of Academics ... Dr. Mark KOSINSKI
51 Dean of Cont Educ/Workforce Develop ... Vacant
15 Interim Director of Human Resources ... Ms. Theresa EISENBACH
04 Executive Assistant to President ... Ms. Tanya R. GIBBS
09 Director Institutional Research ... Dr. Vincent P. TONG
26 Director Public Info & Marketing ... Ms. Evelyn GARD
10 Director Finance & Admin Svcs ... Ms. Jill MCDOWELL
08 Director Library ... Ms. Clara OGBAA
84 Director of Enrollment Management ... Mr. Joseph CARBERRY
36 Director Career Services ... Vacant
37 Director Financial Aid ... Mr. Raymond ZEEK
38 Director Student Counseling ... Ms. Kathleen AHERN
32 Interim Dir of Student Activities ... Ms. Leigh ROBERTS
24 Director of Educational Technology ... Mr. Alfonzo LEWIS
25 Grants Facilitator ... Vacant
13 Director Computer Services ... Mr. Lawrence SALAY
88 Director Early Learning Center ... Ms. Sarah CHAMBERS
121 Coord Center for Education Svcs ... Ms. Clara MENA
50 Chair Business Department ... Mr. Richard REES
79 Chair Humanities Department ... Mr. Chester H. SCHNEPF
83 Chair Social Sciences Department ... Mr. Jonah COHEN
88 Coord Early Childhood Education ... Ms. Carmelita E. VALENCIA-DAYE
88 Coord Drug/Alcohol Rehab Counseling ... Vacant
67 Coordinator Pharmacy Tech Program ... Ms. Louise A. PETROKA
81 Chair Math/Natural Sci Department ... Mr. Rocky TREMBLAY
50 Director Business & Industry Svcs ... Ms. Marilee BAKER-ROUSSAT
88 Director Dietetic Technician Pgm ... Ms. Marcia DORAN
76 Director Allied Health ... Ms. Sheila SOLERNOU
54 Dir Engineering/Applied Technology ... Mr. Eric F. FLYNN
18 Chief Facilities/Physical Plant ... Mr. Lucian SIMONE
06 Registrar ... Ms. Maribel LOPEZ

*Housatonic Community College (F)

900 Lafayette Boulevard, Bridgeport CT 06604-4704
County: Fairfield | FICE Identification: 004513
Unit ID: 129543
Telephone: (203) 332-5000 | Carnegie Class: Assoc/MT-VT-High Trad
FAX Number: (203) 332-5123 | Calendar System: Semester
URL: www.housatonic.edu
Established: 1967 | Annual Undergrad Tuition & Fees (In-State): $4,404
Enrollment: 5,138 | Coed
Affiliation or Control: State | IRS Status: 501(c)3
Highest Offering: Associate Degree
Accreditation: EH, SURGT

02 President ... Dr. Paul BROADIE, II
05 Dean of Academic Affairs ... Ms. Robin AVANT
11 Int Dean Administrative Affairs ... Ms. Adell BROWN
32 Dean of Student Services ... Dr. Kim M. MCGINNIS
20 Associate Dean Student Success ... Ms. Alese MULVHILL
06 Registrar & Director of Enrollment ... Mr. James CONNOLLY
07 Director of Admissions ... Mr. Earl GRAHAM
08 Librarian ... Ms. Shelly STROHM
37 Director of Financial Aid ... Mr. Omar LIVINGSTON
26 Associate Dean Comm & Marketing ... Ms. Evelyn GARD
19 Director of Security ... Mr. Christopher GOUGH
09 Director Institutional Research ... Mr. Vincent TONG
13 Director of Computer Services ... Mr. Anthony VITOLA
15 Director of Human Resources ... Ms. Theresa EISENBACH
30 Director of Community Campus Rels ... Mr. Richard DUPONT
35 Director of Student Life ... Dr. Kelly HOPE
10 Director of Finance/Admin Svcs ... Ms. Teresa ORAVETZ
18 Coordinator of Facilities ... Vacant
04 Executive Asst to President ... Ms. Camilla COSTANTINI
38 Director Counseling/Wellness ... Ms. Lisa SLADE
102 Exec Director of HCC Foundation ... Ms. Fiona HODGSON
121 Director of Academic Support Ctr ... Ms. Marianne TECUN

*Manchester Community College (G)

PO Box 1046, Great Path, Manchester CT 06045-1046
County: Hartford | FICE Identification: 001392
Unit ID: 129695
Telephone: (860) 512-3000 | Carnegie Class: Assoc/MT-VT-High Trad
FAX Number: (860) 512-3631 | Calendar System: Semester
URL: www.manchestercc.edu
Established: 1963 | Annual Undergrad Tuition & Fees (In-State): $4,464
Enrollment: 6,321 | Coed
Affiliation or Control: State | IRS Status: 501(c)3
Highest Offering: Associate Degree
Accreditation: EH, ACFEI, COARC, DA, MUS, OTA, RAD, RTT, SURGT

02 Interim CEO ... Dr. Tanya MILLNER-HARLEE
05 Interim Academic Dean ... Dr. Tuesday COOPER
32 Interim Dean of Student Affairs ... Mr. Peter HARRIS
11 Dean of Administrative Affairs ... Mr. James MCDOWELL
102 Int Executive Dir MCC Foundation ... Ms. Susan ALSTON
51 Dean of Continuing Education ... Vacant
20 Associate Dean of Academic Affairs ... Dr. Pamela MITCHELL
10 Dir Finance & Admin Services ... Ms. Regina FERRANTE

07 Int Assoc Director of Admissions .... Mr. Elijah OLIVER
06 Registrar .... Ms. Anita SPARROW
08 Dir Library Svcs/Educational Tech .... Ms. Deborah HERMAN
13 Director of Information Technology .... Mr. Barry GRANT
09 Dir Plng/Research & Assessment .... Mr. David NIELSEN
15 Director of Human Resources .... Ms. Patricia LINDO
18 Dir Facilities Management/ Planning .... Ms. Darlene MANCINI-BROWN
26 Dir Marketing and Public Relations .... Ms. Charlene TAPPAN
37 Director of Financial Aid .... Ms. Anna TORRES
79 Director of Liberal & Creative Arts .... Ms. Samantha GONZALEZ
35 Director of Student Activities .... Mr. Trent J. BARBER
30 Dir of Development & Alumni Affairs .... Ms. Diana REID
38 Dir Counseling and Career Svcs .... Ms. Julie GREENE
84 Dir of Enrollment Management .... Ms. Sara VINCENT
04 Interim Executive Assistant .... Ms. Karyn CASE
103 Director of Business & Industry .... Mr. Miguel PIGOTT
90 Director of Academic Support Ctr .... Mr. Brian CLEARY
28 Chief Diversity Officer .... Ms. Debra FREUND
96 Assoc Director of Purchasing .... Mr. Paul MOUNDS

*Middlesex Community College (A)

100 Training Hill Road, Middletown CT 06457-4889
County: Middlesex FICE Identification: 008038
Unit ID: 129756
Telephone: (860) 343-5800 Carnegie Class: Assoc/MT-VT-Mix Trad/Non
FAX Number: (860) 344-7488 Calendar System: Semester
URL: www.mxcc.edu
Established: 1966 Annual Undergrad Tuition & Fees (In-State): $4,384
Enrollment: 2,682 Coed
Affiliation or Control: State IRS Status: 501(c)3
Highest Offering: Associate Degree
Accreditation: EH, CAHIIM, OPD, RAD

02 Campus CEO .... Dr. Steven MINKLER
05 Dean of Academic & Student Affairs .... Dr. Sharale MATHIS
11 Dean of Administration .... Ms. Kimberly HOGAN
20 Associate Dean of Academic Affairs .... Dr. Wesley FOX
04 Executive Assistant to the CEO .... Ms. Corey MARTELL
08 Director of the Learning Commons .... Ms. Melissa BEHNEY
09 Director of Institutional Research .... Dr. Paul CARMICHAEL
13 Director Information Technology .... Ms. Annie SCOTT
84 Director of Enrollment Management .... Dr. Sara HANSON
15 Director Personnel Services .... Ms. Anastasia PYCH
37 Director Financial Aid .... Ms. Irene MARTIN
124 Retention Specialist .... Ms. Judy MAZGULSKI
88 Disability Services Coordinator .... Ms. Hilary PHELPS
06 Associate Registrar .... Ms. Joanne FAUST
18 Chief Facilities/Physical Plant .... Mr. Steven CHESTER

*Naugatuck Valley Community College (B)

750 Chase Parkway, Waterbury CT 06708-3089
County: New Haven FICE Identification: 006982
Unit ID: 129729
Telephone: (203) 575-8044 Carnegie Class: Assoc/MT-VT-High Trad
FAX Number: (203) 575-8096 Calendar System: Semester
URL: www.nv.edu
Established: 1964 Annual Undergrad Tuition & Fees (In-State): $4,424
Enrollment: 6,373 Coed
Affiliation or Control: State IRS Status: 501(c)3
Highest Offering: Associate Degree
Accreditation: EH, ADNUR, COARC, PTAA, RAD

02 President .... Dr. Daisy Cocco DE FILIPPIS
11 Dean of Administration .... Ms. Dana ELM
05 Dean of Academic Affairs .... Dr. Lisa DRESDNER
30 Associate Dean of Development .... Ms. Angela CHAPMAN
32 Dean of Student Services .... Ms. Sarah GAGER
88 Dean of Community Engagement .... Mr. Waldemar KOSTRZEWA
13 Assoc Dean Information Technology .... Mr. Conal LARKIN
06 Registrar .... Ms. Lourdes CRUZ
37 Director of Financial Aid .... Ms. Catherine HARDY
84 Assoc Dean of Enrollment Management .... Ms. Noel ROSAMILIO
22 Affirmative Action Officer .... Mr. Ron CLYMER
08 Director Learning Resource Ctr .... Ms. Jaime HAMMOND
10 Director of Finance/Admin Services .... Ms. Lisa PALEN
35 Director of Student Activities .... Ms. Karen BLAKE
18 Chief Facilities/Physical Plant .... Mr. Robert DIVJAK
09 Int Dir of Institutional Research .... Dr. Lisa RODRIGUES-DOOLABH
121 Dir of Student Development Services .... Ms. Bonnie GOULET
15 Director of Human Resources .... Ms. Kimberly CAROLINA
26 Director of Marketing .... Ms. Sydney VOGHEL-OCHS
27 Public Relations Associate .... Ms. Claudia WARD-DE LEON

*Northwestern Connecticut Community-Technical College (C)

Park Place E, Winsted CT 06098-1798
County: Litchfield FICE Identification: 001398
Unit ID: 130040
Telephone: (860) 738-6300 Carnegie Class: Assoc/MT-VT-Mix Trad/Non
FAX Number: (860) 738-6488 Calendar System: Semester
URL: www.nwcc.commnet.edu/
Established: 1965 Annual Undergrad Tuition & Fees (In-State): $4,414
Enrollment: 1,295 Coed
Affiliation or Control: State IRS Status: 501(c)3
Highest Offering: Associate Degree
Accreditation: EH, ADNUR

02 President .... Dr. Michael ROOKE
05 Dean of Academic & Student Affairs .... Dr. David FERREIRA
07 Associate Dean of Enrollment .... Ms. Kalia KELLOGG
11 Associate Dean of Campus Operations .. Mr. Joseph DANAJOVITS
08 Director of Library Services .... Mr. James PATTERSON
06 Registrar .... Ms. Debra ZAVATKAY
15 Director of Human Resources .... Ms. Wendy BOVIA
32 Dir of Student Development .... Ms. Ruth GONZALEZ
09 Director of Institutional Research ... Ms. Caitlin BOGER-HAWKINS
26 Director Marketing/Public Relations .... Mr. Grantley ADAMS
10 Director Financial/Admin Services .... Ms. Kimberly DRAGAN

*Norwalk Community College (D)

188 Richards Avenue, Norwalk CT 06854-1655
County: Fairfield FICE Identification: 001399
Unit ID: 130004
Telephone: (203) 857-7000 Carnegie Class: Assoc/MT-VT-Mix Trad/Non
FAX Number: (203) 857-7287 Calendar System: Semester
URL: www.norwalk.edu
Established: 1961 Annual Undergrad Tuition & Fees (In-State): $4,414
Enrollment: 5,836 Coed
Affiliation or Control: State IRS Status: 501(c)3
Highest Offering: Associate Degree
Accreditation: EH, ADNUR, COARC, MAC, PTAA

02 Chief Executive Officer .... Ms. Cheryl DEVONISH
32 Dean of Students .... Dr. Kellie BYRD DANSO
05 Interim Dean of Academics .... Dr. Michael BUTCARIS
30 Executive Director of Development .... Ms. Carrie BERNIER
103 Assoc Dean Ext Stds/Workforce Dev . Dr. Kristina TESTA-BUZZEE
08 Director of Library Services .... Ms. Linda LERMAN
37 Director Financial Aid .... Mr. Luis GUAMAN
66 Int Director of Nursing Education .... Ms. Angela CHLEBOWSKI
06 Registrar .... Mr. Steve MENDES
15 Assoc Director Human Resources .... Ms. Louisa JONES
26 Director of Public Relations .... Ms. Madeline K. BARILLO
38 Director Student Counseling .... Ms. Catherine MILLER
07 Director of Admissions .... Mr. William CHAGNON
10 Director Finance/Administration .... Ms. Carrie MCGEE-YUROF
18 Chief Facilities/Physical Plant .... Mr. Craig CARLSON
04 Executive Asst to CEO .... Mrs. Thomasina L. CALISE

*Quinebaug Valley Community College (E)

742 Upper Maple Street, Danielson CT 06239-1440
County: Windham FICE Identification: 010530
Unit ID: 130217
Telephone: (860) 932-4000 Carnegie Class: Assoc/HT-High Trad
FAX Number: (860) 932-4306 Calendar System: Semester
URL: www.qvcc.edu
Established: 1971 Annual Undergrad Tuition & Fees (In-State): $4,414
Enrollment: 1,524 Coed
Affiliation or Control: State IRS Status: 501(c)3
Highest Offering: Associate Degree
Accreditation: EH, MAC

02 Interim Chief Executive Officer .... Dr. Rose ELLIS
05 Dean Academic Affs & Student Svcs .... Mr. John LEWIS
11 Dean of Administrative Services .... Mr. Paul MARTLAND
08 Director of Library Services .... Vacant
37 Director of Student Financial Aid .... Ms. Kim RICH
09 Director of Institutional Research .... Vacant
10 Dir Finance/Administrative Svcs .... Ms. Alessandra LUNDBERG
18 Chief Facilities/Physical Plant .... Mr. Martin CHARETTE
26 Chief Public Relations Officer .... Ms. Susan BREAULT
111 Dir of Institutional Advancement .... Ms. Monique WOLANIN
32 Dir of Student Services/Registrar .... Mr. Matt SOUCY
27 Coordinator of Marketing .... Ms. Paige CARITO
07 Associate Director of Admissions .... Ms. Sarah HENDRICK
04 Administrative Asst to President .... Ms. Jennifer GREEN
13 Chief Info Technology Officer (CIO) .... Mr. Jarrod BOREK
15 Director Personnel Services .... Ms. Karla DESJARDINS
29 Director Alumni Relations .... Ms. Elle GOSLIN

*Three Rivers Community College (F)

574 New London Turnpike, Norwich CT 06360
County: New London FICE Identification: 009765
Unit ID: 129808
Telephone: (860) 215-9000 Carnegie Class: Assoc/MT-VT-High Trad
FAX Number: (860) 215-9901 Calendar System: Semester
URL: www.threerivers.edu
Established: 1963 Annual Undergrad Tuition & Fees (In-State): $4,464
Enrollment: 4,187 Coed
Affiliation or Control: State IRS Status: 501(c)3
Highest Offering: Associate Degree
Accreditation: EH, ADNUR

02 President .... Dr. Mary Ellen JUKOSKI
05 Academic Dean .... Mr. Robert FARINELLI
11 Dean of Administration/HR and IT .... Mr. Stephen H. GOETCHIUS
13 Dir of Information Technology .... Mr. Larry DAVENPORT
111 Dir Institutional Advancement .... Ms. Betty BAILLARGEON
06 Registrar .... Mr. Kevin KELLY
10 Dir of Finance/Admin Svcs .... Ms. Gayle O'NEILL
08 Director Library Services .... Ms. Pamela WILLIAMS
37 Actg Dir Student Financial Aid .... Mr. Kenneth BRIGGS
18 Director of Facilities .... Mr. Arnie DELAROSSA
09 Office of Institutional Research .... Mr. Kem BARFIELD
26 Dir of Marketing/Public Relations .... Ms. Kathryn GAFFNEY
14 Dir of Educational Technology .... Mr. Kem BARFIELD
121 Dir of Student Success .... Ms. Christine LANGUTH
04 Exec Assistant to President .... Ms. April HODSON
07 Director of Admissions .... Ms. Peg STROUP
35 Director of Student Programs .... Ms. Alycia ZIEGLER
103 Assoc Dean Workforce Dev .... Ms. Marjorie VALENTIN

*Tunxis Community College (G)

271 Scott Swamp Road, Farmington CT 06032-3187
County: Hartford FICE Identification: 009764
Unit ID: 130606
Telephone: (860) 773-1300 Carnegie Class: Assoc/MT-VT-High Trad
FAX Number: N/A Calendar System: Semester
URL: www.tunxis.edu/
Established: 1969 Annual Undergrad Tuition & Fees (In-State): $4,464
Enrollment: 3,857 Coed
Affiliation or Control: State IRS Status: 501(c)3
Highest Offering: Associate Degree
Accreditation: EH, ACBSP, DA, DH

02 Regional President .... Dr. James P. LOMBELLA
05 Interim Dean of Academic Affairs .... Ms. Amy FEEST
08 Director Library Services .... Dr. Lisa LAVOIE
09 Director of Institutional Research .... Dr. Qing Lin MACK
10 Dir Finance/Administrative Services .... Ms. Nancy ESCHENBRENNER
11 Interim Dean of Administration .... Mr. Gennaro DEANGELIS
32 Dean of Student Affairs .... Dr. Kirk PETERS
13 Interim Director of Info Technology .... Mr. Peter HAFFNER
15 Interim Director Human Resources .... Mr. Charles CLEARY
18 Director of Facilities .... Mr. John LODOVICO
26 Interim Director Marketing & PR .... Ms. Melissa LAMAR
06 Registrar .... Ms. Susan WINN
12 Director Tunxis@Bristol .... Mr. Victor MITCHELL
35 Director of Student Activities .... Mr. Christopher LAPORTE
88 Interim Director Early Childhood .... Ms. Francine CASALINO
102 Executive Director TXCC Foundation .... Mr. Ketih MADORE
90 Director of Education Technology .... Ms. Adrianne MARKHAM
88 Director of College Trans Outreach .... Mr. Peter MCCLUSKEY
103 Dean of Workforce Development .... Ms. Eileen PELTIER
84 Interim Assoc Dean of Enrollment .... Ms. Jean MAIN
07 Associate Director of Admissions .... Ms. Ashkhen STRACK
07 Associate Director of Admissions .... Ms. Alison MCCARTHY
37 Director Financial Aid Services .... Ms. Sandy VITALE

Connecticut College (H)

270 Mohegan Avenue, New London CT 06320-4125
County: New London FICE Identification: 001379
Unit ID: 128902
Telephone: (860) 447-1911 Carnegie Class: Bac-A&S
FAX Number: (860) 439-2700 Calendar System: Semester
URL: www.conncoll.edu
Established: 1911 Annual Undergrad Tuition & Fees: $54,820
Enrollment: 1,817 Coed
Affiliation or Control: Independent Non-Profit IRS Status: 501(c)3
Highest Offering: Master's
Accreditation: EH

01 President .... Dr. Katherine BERGERON
05 Dean of the Faculty .... Dr. Jeffrey COLE
10 Vice Pres Finance and Admin .... Mr. Richard MADONNA
111 Vice President College Advancement . Ms. Kimberly VERSTANDIG
08 Vice Pres of Info Svcs/Librarian .... Dr. W. Lee HISLE
26 Vice President Communications .... Ms. Pamela DUMAS SERFES
07 VP of Admission & Financial Aid .... Mr. Andrew STRICKLER
15 Asst VP HR/Professional Development .... Ms. Cheryl L. MILLER
20 Dean of the College .... Dr. Jefferson SINGER
32 Dean of Student Life .... Dr. Victor J. ARCELUS
28 Dean of Institution Equity and Incl .... Dr. John MCKNIGHT
20 Associate Dean of Faculty .... Dr. Anne BERNHARD
06 Registrar .... Ms. Elisabeth S. LABRIOLA
09 Director of Institutional Research .... Dr. John D. NUGENT
21 Controller .... Ms. Amanda B. MAYFIELD
37 Director of Financial Aid .... Mr. Sean MARTIN
41 Director of Athletics .... Mr. Francis SHIELDS
29 Director of Alumni Relations .... Ms. Tori MCKENNA
38 Director Student Counseling Service .... Dr. Janet D. SPOLTORE
96 Director of Purchasing .... Mr. Christopher RUST
88 Secretary of the College .... Ms. Bonnie WELLS
04 Executive Asst to the President .... Ms. Lauren MIDDLETON
102 Dir Foundation/Corporate Relations .... Ms. Naima GHERBI
13 Asst VP Enterprise/Tech Systems .... Ms. Jean KILBRIDE
19 Director Security/Safety .... Ms. Mary SAVAGE
22 Dir Affirmative Action/EEO .... Dr. John MCKNIGHT
36 Director Student Placement .... Ms. Persephone HALL
39 Director Student Housing .... Dr. Sara ROTHENBERGER
44 Director Annual or Planned Giving .... Ms. Kristin ZUMMO
104 Director Study Abroad .... Ms. Shirley PARSON
18 Chf Facilities/Physical Plant Ofcr .... Ms. Trina LEARNED
101 Secretary of the Institution/Board .... Ms. Bonnie WELLS
11 Chief of Operations/Administration .... Mr. Richard MADONNA

Fairfield University (I)

1073 N Benson Road, Fairfield CT 06824-5195
County: Fairfield FICE Identification: 001385
Unit ID: 129242
Telephone: (203) 254-4000 Carnegie Class: Masters/L
FAX Number: (203) 254-4101 Calendar System: Semester
URL: www.fairfield.edu

Established: 1942 Annual Undergrad Tuition & Fees: $48,350
Enrollment: 5,192 Coed
Affiliation or Control: Roman Catholic IRS Status: 501(c)3
Highest Offering: Doctorate
Accreditation: EH, ANEST, CACREP, CAEPN, MFCD, @MIDWF, NURSE

01 University President ..... Dr. Mark R. NEMEC
42 Univ Chaplain/Special Asst to Pres ..... Rev. Charles H. ALLEN, SJ
11 Exec VP & Chief Operating Officer ..... Mr. Kevin P. LAWLOR
05 Provost ..... Dr. Christine SIEGEL
10 VP Finance/CFO and Treasurer ..... Mr. Michael TRAFECANTE
111 Vice Pres Univ Advancement ..... Mr. Wally HALAS
15 Vice President of Human Resources ..... Mr. Scott ESPOSITO
88 Vice Pres for Mission and Identity ..... Rev. Gerry BLASZCZAK, SJ
26 VP Marketing and Communications ..... Ms. Jennifer ANDERSON
84 VP Strategic Enrollment Management ..... Mr. Corry D. UNIS
32 Vice President for Student Life ..... Ms. Karen A. DONOGHUE
88 Vice Provost Undergrad Excellence ..... Dr. Mark LIGAS
58 Vice Prov Grad/Cont & Prof Stds ..... Dr. Walter RANKIN
18 Vice President Facilities Mgmt ..... Mr. David W. FRASSINELLI
38 Asst Vice Pres/Dir Counseling Svcs ..... Dr. Susan N. BIRGE
109 Asst Vice Pres Auxiliary Services ..... Mr. James D. FITZPATRICK
88 AVProv Scholar/Creativ/Cmty Engage ..... Dr. Jocelyn BORYCZKA
09 Dir Institutional Research/Plng ..... Ms. Amy BOCZER
123 Dir Grad & Cont Stds Admission ..... Ms. Marianne L. GUMPPER
06 University Registrar ..... Ms. Lynn M. KOHRN
13 Chief Information Officer ..... Mr. Jonathan CARROLL
37 Director of Financial Aid ..... Ms. Diana M. DRAPER
36 Dir Career/Leadership & Prof Dev ..... Ms. Cathleen M. BORGMAN
29 Asst Vice Pres of Alumni Relations ..... Ms. Janet A. CANEPA
42 Director of Campus Ministry ..... Rev. Mark SCALESE
19 Director of Public Safety ..... Mr. Todd A. PELAZZA
41 Director of Athletics ..... Mr. Paul SCHLICKMANN
49 Dean College Arts & Science ..... Dr. Richard GREENWALD
50 Dean Dolan Sch of Business ..... Dr. Zhan LI
54 Interim Dean School of Engineering ..... Dr. Richard H. HEIST
66 Dean School of Nursing/Health Stds ..... Dr. Meredith W. KAZER
53 Dean Grad Sch Educ/Allied Prof ..... Dr. Robert HANNAFIN
88 Asst VP Ofc of Conference & Events ..... Mr. Matthew A. DINNAN
35 Dean of Students ..... Mr. William H. JOHNSON
39 Assoc Dean/Dir Res Life & Diversity ..... Dr. Ophelie ROWE-ALLEN
104 Assoc Vice Provost Global Strategy ..... Ms. Jennifer EWALD
92 Co-Director of Honors Program ..... Dr. Laura NASH
92 Co-Director of Honors Program ..... Dr. Giovanni RUFFINI
08 Interim Dean of Libraries ..... Ms. Christina MCGOWAN
23 Director of Student Health Center ..... Ms. Julia A. DUFFY
16 Director Human Resources ..... Mr. Mark J. GUGLIELMONI
96 Director of Purchasing ..... Mr. Peter PEREZ

Goodwin College (A)

One Riverside Drive, East Hartford CT 06118-2777
County: Hartford FICE Identification: 022449
Unit ID: 129154
Telephone: (860) 528-4111 Carnegie Class: Spec-4-yr-Other Health
FAX Number: (860) 291-9550 Calendar System: Semester
URL: www.goodwin.edu
Established: 1999 Annual Undergrad Tuition & Fees: $20,898
Enrollment: 3,410 Coed
Affiliation or Control: Independent Non-Profit IRS Status: 501(c)3
Highest Offering: Master's
Accreditation: EH, ADNUR, COARC, DH, FUSER, HT, MAC, NURSE, OPD, OTA, @SW

01 President ..... Mr. Mark E. SCHEINBERG
03 Exec Vice Pres/Provost Emerita ..... Ms. Ann B. CLARK
05 VP Academic Affs/Dean Faculty ..... Dr. Danielle WILKEN
10 Vice President for Finance/CFO ..... Mr. Eddie MEYER
30 Vice Pres Economic/Strategic Dev ..... Mr. Todd J. ANDREWS
18 Vice Pres Facilities/Technology ..... Mr. Bryant L. HARRELL
84 Vice Pres Enrollment/Mrktg/Comm ..... Mr. Daniel NOONAN
111 Vice President for Advancement ..... Vacant
15 VP Human Resources ..... Ms. Jean MCGILL
32 VP Stdnt Affs/Dean of Students ..... Mr. Tyrone BLACK
88 Asst VP Strategy/Business Devel ..... Dr. Clifford THERMER
84 Asst VP Enrollment Services ..... Mr. Nicholas LENTINO
08 Director of Library Services ..... Ms. Susan HANSEN
56 Dean of Magnet Schools ..... Vacant
36 Director of Career Services ..... Ms. Patricia SHAW
26 Dir Marketing/Communications ..... Mr. Phil MOORE
21 Director of Finance/Controller ..... Mr. Bryan SOLTIS
13 Director Information Technology ..... Mr. John RUGGIRELLO
37 Director of Financial Aid ..... Ms. Bonnie SOLTZ-KNOWLTON
07 Director of Admissions ..... Mr. Dan WILLIAMSON
09 Sr Dir Inst Research/Educ Assessment ..... Dr. Melissa QUINLAN
106 Director of Online Learning ..... Dr. Lisa MANLEY
06 Registrar ..... Ms. Allison MISKY
29 Alumni Relations Coordinator ..... Ms. Vanessa PERGOLIZZI
04 Executive Assistant to President ..... Ms. Ann ZAJCHOWSKI
66 Dept Chair/Director Nursing ..... Ms. Janice WATTS
19 Dir of Campus Safety & Security ..... Mr. Richard VIBBERTS

Hartford Seminary (B)

77 Sherman Street, Hartford CT 06105-2260
County: Hartford FICE Identification: 001387
Unit ID: 129491
Telephone: (860) 509-9500 Carnegie Class: Spec-4-yr-Faith
FAX Number: (860) 509-9509 Calendar System: Semester
URL: www.hartsem.edu
Established: 1834 Annual Graduate Tuition & Fees: N/A
Enrollment: 123 Coed
Affiliation or Control: Independent Non-Profit IRS Status: 501(c)3
Highest Offering: Doctorate; No Undergraduates
Accreditation: EH, THEOL

01 President ..... Dr. Joel LOHR
05 Academic Dean ..... Dr. David GRAFTON
11 Director of Admin and Facilities ..... Ms. Roseann LEZAK JANOW
30 Director of Philanthropy ..... Ms. Kaaren VAN DYKE
07 Director of Recruitment/Admissions ..... Ms. Tina DEMO
08 Director Library Services ..... Ms. Ann CRAWFORD
10 Chief Business Officer ..... Mr. Michael SANDNER
06 Registrar/Financial Aid Coord ..... Ms. Danielle LAVINE
04 Exec Assistant to the President ..... Ms. Lorraine BROWNE
26 Director of Communications ..... Ms. Susan SCHOENBERGER
15 Acting Director Human Resources ..... Mr. Michael SANDNER

Holy Apostles College and Seminary (C)

33 Prospect Hill Road, Cromwell CT 06416-2027
County: Middlesex FICE Identification: 001389
Unit ID: 129534
Telephone: (860) 632-3010 Carnegie Class: Spec-4-yr-Faith
FAX Number: (860) 632-3030 Calendar System: Semester
URL: www.holyapostles.edu
Established: 1956 Annual Undergrad Tuition & Fees: $7,870
Enrollment: 525 Coed
Affiliation or Control: Roman Catholic IRS Status: 501(c)3
Highest Offering: Beyond Master's But Less Than Doctorate
Accreditation: EH, THEOL

01 Interim President & Rector ..... Rev. Peter Samuel KUCER
11 Vice Rector ..... Rev. Anthony MCLAUGHLIN
30 VP External Affs/Govt Compliance ..... Dr. Sebastian MAHFOOD
05 Academic Dean/Chief Academic Ofcr ..... Dr. Cynthia TOOLIN-WILSON
29 Dir Alumni/Student Services ..... Mrs. Karen ROCHE
10 Chief Financial Officer ..... Mr. William RUSSELL
08 Director of Library Services ..... Ms. Clare ADAMO
07 Director Graduate Admissions ..... Dr. Elizabeth REX
07 Director Undergraduate Admissions ..... Mrs. Taylor RISO

Mitchell College (D)

437 Pequot Avenue, New London CT 06320-4498
County: New London FICE Identification: 001393
Unit ID: 129774
Telephone: (860) 701-5000 Carnegie Class: Bac-Diverse
FAX Number: (860) 701-5090 Calendar System: Semester
URL: www.mitchell.edu
Established: 1938 Annual Undergrad Tuition & Fees: $33,200
Enrollment: 707 Coed
Affiliation or Control: Independent Non-Profit IRS Status: 501(c)3
Highest Offering: Baccalaureate
Accreditation: EH

01 Interim Co-President ..... Ms. Mary Jane MCLAUGHLIN
01 Interim Co-President ..... Dr. Catherine WRIGHT
84 VP for Enrollment Management ..... Mr. Jamie ROMEO
37 Director of Financial Aid ..... Mr. David RENSKI
07 Director of Admission ..... Mr. Kelby CHAPELLE
41 Director of Athletics ..... Vacant
110 Advancement Director ..... Ms. Audrey NATHANSON
06 Registrar ..... Ms. Amy VAN OOT
88 Director of Thames @ Mitchell ..... Ms. Beverly SCULLY
13 Chief Information Officer ..... Ms. Joanne KOSSUTH
10 Chief Financial/Business Officer ..... Vacant
90 Director of Academic Technologies ..... Mr. Rich WALL
37 Assoc Dir Strategic EM ..... Mr. Dan BREWER
05 Assoc Dn Acad Affs/First Year Exp ..... Ms. Jennifer R. WELSH
18 Director of Facilities ..... Mr. Joseph PARDEE
113 Bursar ..... Ms. Leah BRENNAN
04 Office Administrator to President ..... Ms. Kristen TRAINI
32 Director of Campus Life ..... Mr. Curtis CLARK
121 Director of Advising ..... Ms. Christina HODGE
38 Director Health & Wellness ..... Ms. Stacey TORPEY
19 Director Security/Safety ..... Mr. Erik COSTA
26 Director of Marketing ..... Ms. Lisa STINSON
36 Director Career Services ..... Mr. Paul DUNN
15 Human Resource Manager ..... Ms. Aruna IYER
39 Director of Residence Life ..... Ms. Katrina FEYERHERM

Paier College of Art (E)

20 Gorham Avenue, Hamden CT 06514-3902
County: New Haven FICE Identification: 007459
Unit ID: 130110
Telephone: (203) 287-3031 Carnegie Class: Spec-4-yr-Arts
FAX Number: (203) 287-3021 Calendar System: Semester
URL: www.paiercollegeofart.edu
Established: 1946 Annual Undergrad Tuition & Fees: $17,570
Enrollment: 79 Coed
Affiliation or Control: Proprietary IRS Status: Proprietary
Highest Offering: Baccalaureate
Accreditation: ACCSC

01 President ..... Mr. Jonathan E. PAIER
03 Vice President ..... Mrs. Maureen E. PAIER
05 Dean of the College ..... Ms. Tammy VAZ
10 Director Finance ..... Mrs. Maureen E. PAIER
57 Director Design/Graphics ..... Mr. Peter MISERENDINO
102 Director Foundation/Arts ..... Mr. Robert E. ZAPPALORTI
20 Director of Academics ..... Mr. Francis COOLEY
08 Librarian ..... Ms. Beth HARRIS
37 Director Student Financial Aid ..... Mr. John DE ROSE
32 Director of Student Services ..... Mrs. Angela DEROSE
20 Assistant to the Dean ..... Ms. Angela DEROSE
88 Director Interior Design ..... Mr. Pierre STRAUCH
88 Director Photography ..... Mr. Peter BENSON
07 Admissions Secretary ..... Ms. Lynn PASCALE

Post University (F)

800 Country Club Road, Waterbury CT 06723-2540
County: New Haven FICE Identification: 001401
Unit ID: 130183
Telephone: (203) 596-4500 Carnegie Class: Masters/L
FAX Number: (203) 841-1163 Calendar System: Semester
URL: www.post.edu
Established: 1890 Annual Undergrad Tuition & Fees: $16,610
Enrollment: 8,540 Coed
Affiliation or Control: Proprietary IRS Status: Proprietary
Highest Offering: Master's
Accreditation: EH, ACBSP, NURSE

01 Chief Executive Officer & President ..... Mr. John L. HOPKINS
03 Vice President ..... Mr. Mark CHESNEY
05 Provost ..... Dr. Elizabeth JOHNSON
11 Chief Operations Officer ..... Mr. Bobby REESE
10 Chief Financial Officer ..... Mr. Scott T. ALLEN
26 Chief Marketing Officer ..... Mr. Richard SCHECHTER
13 Chief Information Officer ..... Mr. Greg THEISEN
88 VP Operations Analysis ..... Mr. Shane LIVELY
15 Chief Assoc Experience Officer ..... Ms. Vicki WHISENHANT
86 Chief Regulatory Officer ..... Ms. Elaine NEELY
84 Vice President for Enrollment ..... Mr. Jeff OLSEN
32 Dean of Students ..... Ms. Erica PERYGA
07 Director Admissions Main Campus ..... Mr. Joseph CHABOT
123 Director Grad Admiss-ADP ..... Ms. Gina WELLMAN
07 Director Admissions-ADP ..... Ms. Jeanna SINN
41 Director of Athletics ..... Mr. Ronnie PALMER
124 Dir of Acad Success & Retention ..... Ms. Megan LUCIA
50 Acting Dean of School of Business . Mr. Christopher SZPRYNGEL
80 Dean John P Burke Sch Pub Svcs & Ed ..... Dr. James WHITLEY
49 Dean of School of Arts & Sciences ..... Dr. Jeremi BAUER
37 Director Financial Aid ..... Mr. Michael GREER
06 Registrar ..... Mr. Mitch HECHT
88 Director of Compliance ..... Ms. Jillian DIAZ
113 Director of Student Accounts ..... Ms. Michelle ORBE
88 Dir of Military Field Enrollment ..... Mr. Charles YOUNG
04 Executive Asst to the CEO ..... Ms. Melissah KOCHERA
88 Executive Asst to the Vice Pres ..... Ms. Patricia JENNINGS
38 Director Student Counseling ..... Ms. Lisa ANTEL
08 Library Director ..... Ms. Tracy RALSTON
16 Human Resources Director ..... Ms. Madelaine KELSEY
18 Facilities Manager ..... Mr. Bill DAVIS
19 Director of Campus Safety ..... Vacant
36 Director Career Services ..... Vacant
09 Dir Inst Rsrch/Assess/Effectiveness ..... Dr. Zvi GOLDMAN
88 Director of Corporate Partnerships ..... Mr. Shawn WHISENHANT
88 Director of Strategic Partnerships ..... Ms. Christina AGVENT
27 Director of Univ Communications ..... Ms. Joan HUWILER
88 Director of Accreditation ..... Mr. Thomas BRYANT

Quinnipiac University (G)

275 Mount Carmel Avenue, Hamden CT 06518-1908
County: New Haven FICE Identification: 001402
Unit ID: 130226
Telephone: (203) 582-8200 Carnegie Class: DU-Mod
FAX Number: (203) 582-4703 Calendar System: Semester
URL: www.quinnipiac.edu
Established: 1929 Annual Undergrad Tuition & Fees: $47,960
Enrollment: 10,200 Coed
Affiliation or Control: Independent Non-Profit IRS Status: 501(c)3
Highest Offering: First Professional Degree
Accreditation: EH, AA, ANEST, ARCPA, CAATE, CAEPN, LAW, MED, NURSE, OT, PA, PERF, PTA, RAD, SW

01 President ..... Dr. Judy D. OLIAN
05 Interim Exec VP/Provost ..... Ms. Jennifer G. BROWN
100 Vice President/Chief of Staff ..... Ms. Bethany C. ZEMBA
10 VP Finance/Chief Financial Ofcr ..... Mr. Mark VARHOLAK
26 Vice President for Public Affairs ..... Vacant
18 Vice Pres Facilities & Capital Plng ..... Mr. Salvatore FILARDI
15 AVP for Human Resources ..... Ms. Anna M. SPRAGG
84 Int VP for Enrollment Management ..... Mr. Adam BARRETT
114 Assoc VP Budget & Fin Planning ..... Mr. Sandip PATEL
30 Vice Pres Devel & Alumni Affairs ..... Mr. Donald J. WEINBACH
32 Vice President & Dean of Students ..... Dr. Monique DRUCKER
13 VP/Chief Info & Tech Officer ..... Mr. Fred E. TARCA
20 VP for Acad Innovation & Effective ..... Dr. Annalisa ZINN
27 AVP Integrated Mktg Communications ..... Mr. James P. RYAN
27 Assoc VP for Public Relations ..... Mr. John MORGAN
06 Registrar ..... Mr. Joshua BERRY
106 Interim Asst VP for QU Online ..... Mr. Joseph CARMEN
28 AVP Acad Aff & Chief Diversity Ofcr ..... Mr. Donald C. SAWYER
35 Assoc Dean Student Affairs ..... Ms. Lynn Nicole HENDRICKS
39 Director of Resident Life ..... Mr. Mark DEVILBISS
23 Dir of Student Health Services ..... Ms. Christy CHASE
38 Director of Health & Wellness ..... Ms. Kerry PATTON
19 AVP & Chief of Public Safety ..... Mr. Edgar RODRIGUEZ
08 Director of Arnold Bernhard Library ..... Mr. Robert JOVEN
41 Director of Athletics & Recreation ..... Mr. Greg AMODIO
40 Campus Store Manager ..... Ms. Cheryl CARTIER
104 Director for Global Education ..... Ms. Andrea HOGAN

21 Assoc VP for Finance/Controller ..... Mr. Stephen A. ALLEGRETTO
96 Manager of Strategic Sourcing .... Ms. Daniella VIZZIELLO
109 Assoc VP for Auxiliary Services .... Mr. John MERIANO
29 Sr Dir Parent/Family Development .... Ms. Melinda FORMICA
37 AVP/Director of Financial Aid .... Vacant
108 Dir Academic Assessment/Research .... Ms. Sungah KIM
90 Director of Academic Technology .... Ms. Lauren ERARDI
66 Dean School of Nursing .... Dr. Lisa G. O'CONNOR
50 Dean School of Business .... Dr. Matthew L. O'CONNOR
49 Dean College of Arts & Sciences .... Dr. Robert SMART
76 Dean School of Health Sciences .... Vacant
61 Interim Dean School of Law .... Mr. Brad SAXTON
61 Associate Dean School of Law .... Mr. Robert FARRELL
60 Dean School of Communications .... Mr. Chris G. ROUSH
53 Dean School of Education .... Dr. Anne M. DICHELE
63 Dean School of Medicine .... Dr. Bruce KOEPPEN
54 Dean School of Engineering .... Dr. Justin KILE
94 Director of Women's Studies .... Dr. Jennifer SACCO

Rensselaer at Hartford (A)

275 Windsor Street, Hartford CT 06120-2991
Telephone: (860) 548-2400 FICE Identification: 002804
Accreditation: &M

† Regional accreditation is carried under the parent institution, Rensselaer Polytechnic Institute, NY.

Sacred Heart University (B)

5151 Park Avenue, Fairfield CT 06825-1000
County: Fairfield FICE Identification: 001403
Unit ID: 130253
Telephone: (203) 371-7999 Carnegie Class: DU-Mod
FAX Number: (203) 365-7652 Calendar System: Semester
URL: www.sacredheart.edu
Established: 1963 Annual Undergrad Tuition & Fees: $41,420
Enrollment: 8,543 Coed
Affiliation or Control: Independent Non-Profit IRS Status: 501(c)3
Highest Offering: Doctorate
Accreditation: EH, ADNUR, #ARCPA, CAATE, CAEP, CEA, NURSE, OT, PTA, RAD, SP, SW

01 President & CEO .... Dr. John J. PETILLO
10 Sr VP Finance .... Mr. Michael J. KINNEY
05 Provost/VP Academic Affairs .... Dr. Rupendra PALIWAL
32 Sr VP Student Affairs & Athletics .... Mr. James M. BARQUINERO
11 Sr VP Administration & Planning .... Dr. David COPPOLA
15 VP Human Resources .... Mr. Robert M. HARDY
26 VP Marketing & Communication .... Mr. Michael L. IANNAZZI
88 VP Mission/Catholic Identity .... Fr. Anthony CIORRA
10 VP Finance .... Mr. Philip J. MCCABE
13 VP Information Technology .... Ms. Shirely CANAAN
111 VP University Advancement .... Mr. William REIDY
43 University General Counsel .... Mr. Michael D. LAROBINA
49 Dean College of Arts & Sciences .... Mrs. Robin CAUTIN
50 Dean College of Business .... Dr. Martha J. CRAWFORD
76 Interim Dean Col Health Professions .... Dr. Jody BORTONE
53 Dean College of Education .... Dr. Michael ALFANO
66 Dean College of Nursing .... Ms. Mary Alice DONIUS
58 Dean of Graduate Studies .... Dr. Brian V. CAROLAN
12 Dean St. Vincent's College .... Ms. Maryanne DAVIDSON
108 President University Acad Assembly .... Dr. Donna BOWERS
07 Exec Director Undergrad Admissions .... Mr. Kevin O'SULLIVAN
06 Registrar .... Ms. Dona PERRONE

Trinity College (C)

300 Summit Street, Hartford CT 06106-3100
County: Hartford FICE Identification: 001414
Unit ID: 130590
Telephone: (860) 297-2000 Carnegie Class: Bac-A&S
FAX Number: (860) 297-5359 Calendar System: Semester
URL: www.trincoll.edu
Established: 1823 Annual Undergrad Tuition & Fees: $56,910
Enrollment: 2,282 Coed
Affiliation or Control: Independent Non-Profit IRS Status: 501(c)3
Highest Offering: Master's
Accreditation: EH

01 President .... Dr. Joanne BERGER-SWEENEY
10 Vice Pres Finance/CFO .... Mr. Dan HITCHELL
13 Vice Pres Information Svcs/CIO .... Ms. Suzanne ABER
111 Vice Pres College Advancement .... Mr. Michael CASEY
32 Vice Pres Stdnt Affs/Dean Stdnts .... Mr. Joseph DICHRISTINA
84 Vice Pres Enrollment/Stdnt Success .... Dr. Angel B. PEREZ
26 VP of Marketing/Communications .... Ms. Angela SCHAEFFER
05 Int Dean of Faculty/VP Acad Affairs .... Dr. Sonia CARDENA
43 General Counsel & Secretary .... Mr. Dickens MATHIEU
37 Director of Financial Aid .... Ms. Ashley DUTTON
100 Chief of Staff .... Mr. Jason ROJAS
07 Director of Admissions .... Mr. Anthony T. BERRY
28 VP Diversity/Equity and Inclusion .... Ms. Anita DAVIS
27 Director of Media Relations .... Vacant
06 Registrar .... Ms. Alexis YUSOV
21 Director of Business Operations .... Mr. Michael ELLIOTT
114 Budget Director .... Ms. Marcia PHELAN JOHNSON
19 Director of Campus Safety .... Mr. Brian HEAVREN
30 Director of Development .... Mr. Christopher FRENCH
21 Comptroller .... Mr. Guy DRAPEAU
41 Director of Athletics .... Mr. Drew GALBRAITH
09 Dir Analytics/Strategic Initiatives .... Mr. David ANDRES
39 Director of Residential Life .... Ms. Susan SALISBURY

42 College Chaplain .... Rev. Allison READ
38 Director Student Counseling .... Dr. Randolph LEE
96 Director of Purchasing .... Mr. Michael S. ELLIOTT
88 Dean of Urban and Global Studies .... Dr. Xiangming CHEN
29 Director of Alumni Relations .... Mr. Steve DONOVAN
08 Head Librarian .... Ms. Janine S. KINEL
04 Executive Asst to President .... Ms. Patrice A. LEMOINE

University of Bridgeport (D)

126 Park Avenue, Bridgeport CT 06604-5620
County: Fairfield FICE Identification: 001416
Unit ID: 128744
Telephone: (203) 576-4000 Carnegie Class: DU-Mod
FAX Number: (203) 576-4653 Calendar System: Semester
URL: www.bridgeport.edu
Established: 1927 Annual Undergrad Tuition & Fees: $33,055
Enrollment: 5,434 Coed
Affiliation or Control: Independent Non-Profit IRS Status: 501(c)3
Highest Offering: Doctorate
Accreditation: EH, ACBSP, ACUP, ARCPA, ART, CAEP, CHIRO, DH, MT, NATUR, NURSE

01 President .... Dr. Laura SKANDERA TROMBLEY
04 Executive Assistant to President .... Ms. Rashida MITCHELL
05 Provost & VP for Academic Affairs .... Dr. Stephen E. HEALEY
10 VP Administration & Finance .... Mr. Yuet LEE
111 VP for Advancement .... Ms. Marie MUHVIC
18 VP of Facilities .... Mr. George ESTRADA
84 VP for Enrollment Mgmt & Athletics .... Mr. Louis IZZI
26 VP Marketing & Communications .... Ms. Susan ANDREWS
108 VP Univ System Effect/Planning .... Dr. Jason E. RIVERA
32 Dean of Students .... Mr. Craig LENNON
08 University Librarian .... Ms. Deborah L. DULEPSKI
15 Dir Human Resources/Affirm Act Ofcr .. Dr. Melitha R. PRZYGODA
21 Controller .... Mr. Malhar SHARMA
37 Director Student Financial Services . Ms. Christine E. FALZERANO
90 Director of Academic Computing . Mr. Abdelshakour A. ABUZNEID
19 Exec Director of Campus Security .... Ms. April J. VOURNELIS
38 Director of Counseling Services .... Ms. Amy L. SCEERY
06 University Registrar .... Ms. Carmen ROSA
85 Director of Intl Student Affairs .... Ms. Yumin WANG
76 Dean College of Health Sciences .... Dr. Carol PAPP
39 Exec Dir Res Life/Comm Standards .... Mr. Jon CONLOGUE
96 Director of Purchasing .... Ms. Jacqueline A. REEVES
35 Dir Campus Activity .... Ms. Kelli A. MEYER
12 Director of Waterbury Center .... Ms. Karen K. RINGWOOD
29 Director Alumni Relations .... Ms. Kathleen O'LEARY
43 University Counsel .... Ms. Carolyn R. LINSEY
107 Dir School of Professional Studies .... Mr. Timothy RAYNOR
23 Director of Health Center .... Vacant
88 Director of Acupuncture Institute .... Dr. Jennifer BRETT
40 Manager of the Bookstore .... Mr. Richard HEBERT
36 Director of Career Services .... Vacant
54 Dean Engr/Business/Education .... Dr. Tarek M. SOBH
49 Dean Arts & Sciences .... Dr. Manyul IM
53 Dir School of Education .... Dr. Allen P. COOK
88 Dir School of Chiropractic .... Dr. Michael A. CIOLFI
88 Dir College Naturopathic Medicine ..... Dr. Marcia A. PRENGUBER
50 Dir School of Business .... Ms. Elena CAHILL
121 Director Academic Resource Center .... Ms. Roxie L. RAY
52 Dir School of Dental Hygiene .... Dr. Marcia H. LORENTZEN
106 Deputy Provost .... Dr. Aaron PERKUS
57 Dir School of Design .... Mr. Richard YELLE
88 Dir Physician Assistant Institute .... Dr. Monica LOCKWOOD
44 Director Annual Giving .... Mr. Ryan ZAPOLSKI
100 Chief of Staff .... Ms. Ashley M. PERZYNA
91 Dir Acad & Campus Tech Services .... Mr. Walter SCHWARZ

University of Connecticut (E)

352 Mansfield Road, Storrs CT 06269-1048
County: Tolland FICE Identification: 001417
Unit ID: 129020
Telephone: (860) 486-2337 Carnegie Class: DU-Highest
FAX Number: (860) 486-2627 Calendar System: Semester
URL: www.uconn.edu
Established: 1881 Annual Undergrad Tuition & Fees (In-State): $15,730
Enrollment: 27,578 Coed
Affiliation or Control: State IRS Status: 501(c)3
Highest Offering: Doctorate
Accreditation: EH, ART, AUD, CAATE, CACREP, CAEPN, CEA, CGTECH, CLPSY, DIETC, DIETD, DIETI, DMOLS, IPSY, JOUR, LAW, LSAR, MT, MUS, NURSE, PHAR, PTA, SCPSY, SP, SPAA, SW

01 President .... Thomas KATSOULEAS
100 Chief of Staff .... Rachel RUBIN
05 Int Provost/Exec VP Academic Affs .... John ELLIOTT
17 Exec VP for Health Affairs .... Andrew AGWUNOBI
10 Exec VP for Admin and CFO .... Scott JORDAN
32 Vice President for Student Affairs .... Michael GILBERT
46 Vice President for Research .... Radenka MARIC
101 Executive Secretary to the Board .... Rachel RUBIN
26 Vice Pres for Communications .... P. Tysen KENDIG
41 Director of Athletics .... David BENEDICT
43 VP and General Counsel .... Nicole GELSTON
13 Vice President & Chief Info Officer .... Michael MUNDRANE
114 Int Assoc VP for Budget & Planning .... Lloyd BLANCHARD
19 Assoc VP for Public Safety .... Hans RHYNHART
28 Interim AVP/Chief Diversity Officer .... Dana WILDER
88 Assoc VP for Institutional Equity .... Elizabeth CONKLIN
09 Assoc VProv for Inst Rsrch & Effect .... Lloyd BLANCHARD

102 Pres & CEO Univ of CT Foundation .... Scott ROBERTS
20 Vice Provost for Academic Affairs .... John VOLIN
20 Vice Provost Academic Operations .... Deborah SHELBY
84 VP Enrollment Planning & Mgmt .... Nathan FUERST
08 Dean of Univ Library .... Anne LANGLEY
12 Director Stamford Campus .... Terrence CHENG
12 Director Avery Point Campus .... Annemarie SEIFERT
12 Director Waterbury Campus .... William J. PIZZUTO
12 Director Hartford Campus .... Mark OVERMYER-VELAZQUEZ
92 AVProv Enrich Pgms/Dir Honors Pgms .... Jennifer LEASE BUTTS
25 AVP Research/Sponsored Pgm Svcs .... Michael GLASGOW
86 Sr Director Government Relations .... Joann LOMBARDO
86 Dir Govt Relations/Health Affairs .... Andrea KEILTY
06 Registrar .... Gregory BOUQUOT
07 Director Undergrad Admissions .... Vern GRANGER
37 Director Student Financial Aid .... Suzanne PETERS
29 Asst Vice Pres Alumni Relations .... Montique COTTON KELLY
23 Exec Director Student Health Svcs .... Suzanne ONORATO
15 Director of Human Resources .... Aliza WILDER
96 Dir Procurement/Logistical Svcs .... Matthew LARSON
47 Dean Col of Agric/Natural Resources .... Indrajeet CHAUBEY
50 Interim Dean School of Business .... David SOUDER
53 Dean Neag School of Education .... Gladis KERSAINT
54 Dean of Engineering .... Kazem KAZEROUNIAN
88 Assoc Vice Prov Excell Teach/Lrng .... Peter DIPLOCK
57 Dean of Fine Arts .... Anne D'ALLEVA
58 Vice Prov Grad Ed/Dean Grad Sch .... Kent HOLSINGER
61 Dean School of Law .... Timothy FISHER
49 Dean Col of Lib Arts/Sciences .... Juli WADE
66 Dean School of Nursing .... Deborah A. CHYUN
67 Interim Dean School of Pharmacy .... Philip HRITCKO
70 Dean School of Social Work .... Nina ROVINELLI HELLER
52 Dean of Dental Medicine .... Sharon GORDON
63 Dean School of Medicine .... Liang BRUCE
38 Dir Student Counslg/Mental Hlth Svc .... Elizabeth CRACCO
39 Executive Director Residential Life .... Pamela SCHIPANI
88 Deputy Chief of Staff .... Michael KIRK
88 Master Planner/Chief Architect .... Laura CRUICKSHANK
88 Vice Provost for Global Affairs .... Daniel WEINER
36 Asst VProv/Exec Dir Career Services .... James R. LOWE
121 Asst VProvost for Student Success .... Maria D. MARTINEZ
27 Director Marketing Communications .... Patricia FAZIO
88 Ombuds .... James WOHL
88 Dir Institute for Materials Science .... Steven L. SUIB
04 Executive Asst to President .... Debra MERRITT
104 Director Education Abroad .... Matthew YATES
18 Assoc VP Facilities Ops & Bldg Svcs .... P. Michael JEDNAK
30 Vice President for Development .... Brian OTIS
112 Director of Gift Planning .... Greg KNOTT
106 Dir Online Education/E-learning .... Peter DIPLOCK
88 Dir Vet Affs & Military Programs .... Alyssa KELLEHER

University of Connecticut Health Center (F)

263 Farmington Avenue, Farmington CT 06030-1827
Telephone: (860) 679-2000 FICE Identification: 009867
Accreditation: &EH, DENT, MED, PH

† Regional accreditation is carried under the parent institution in Storrs, CT.

University of Connecticut School of Law (G)

55 Elizabeth Street, Hartford CT 06105-2290
Telephone: (860) 570-5000 Identification: 770108
Accreditation: &EH, LAW

University of Hartford (H)

200 Bloomfield Avenue, West Hartford CT 06117-1599
County: Hartford FICE Identification: 001422
Unit ID: 129525
Telephone: (860) 768-4100 Carnegie Class: DU-Mod
FAX Number: (860) 768-4070 Calendar System: Semester
URL: www.hartford.edu
Established: 1877 Annual Undergrad Tuition & Fees: $40,694
Enrollment: 6,561 Coed
Affiliation or Control: Independent Non-Profit IRS Status: 501(c)3
Highest Offering: Doctorate
Accreditation: EH, ART, CAEPN, CLPSY, COARC, DANCE, MUS, NURSE, OPE, PTA, RAD, THEA

01 President .... Dr. Gregory S. WOODWARD
05 Provost .... Dr. H. Frederick SWEITZER
10 Vice Pres Finance & Administration .... Ms. Laura WHITNEY
111 Vice Pres Institutional Advance .... Ms. Kate PENDERGAST
32 Vice Pres Student Affs/Dean Stdnts .... Dr. Aaron ISAACS
26 Vice Pres for Mktg & Communications .... Ms. Molly POLK
21 Controller .... Mr. Darryl LONGLEY
04 Senior Advisor to the President .... Ms. Susan FITZGERALD
35 Assoc Vice Pres for Student Life .... Dr. Jessica NICKLIN
21 Assoc Vice Pres/Treasurer .... Mr. Brett CARROLL
43 Vice Pres/Gen Counsel & Secretary .... Ms. Maria FEELEY
84 Sr Assoc Provost/Dean Enroll Mgmt .... Vacant
58 Int Assoc Prov/Dean of Grad Studies .... Dr. Clark SAUNDERS
07 Dean of Admission .... Mr. Richard A. ZEISER
04 Exec Assistant to the President .... Ms. Ilena ROSENSTEIN
15 Exec Dir Human Resources & Devel .... Ms. Jamie HARLOW
08 Director University Libraries .... Ms. Randi L. ASHTON-PRITTING
37 Dean Enroll Mgt & Dir Financial Aid .... Ms. Victoria HAMPTON
06 Registrar .... Ms. Natalie DURANT
38 Dir Counsel & Personal Development .... Dr. Jeffrey BURDA
36 Exec Director of Career Services .... Ms. Brooke PENDERS

13 Chief Information Officer Vacant
19 Director Public Safety Mr. Michael KASELOUSKAS
23 Director Health Services Ms. Amy WISNIEWSKI
24 Director User Services Mr. Sebastian SORRENTINO
25 Dir Inst Prtnrshp/Sponsored Rsrch Mr. Christopher STANDISH
29 Director Alumni Relations Ms. Heather CORBETT
18 Assoc Vice Pres for Facilities/Mgmt Mr. Norman YOUNG
41 Director Athletics Ms. Mary Ellen GILLESPIE
104 Director International Studies Ms. Nicole KURKER-STEWART
108 Dir Institutional Effectiveness Ms. Kathleen NEAL
94 Director of Women's Center Ms. Kenna GRANT
88 Director of Student Conduct & Admin Mr. David STENDER
96 Director of Purchasing Ms. Lisa CONDON
92 Director of University Honors Dr. Donald JONES
106 Asst Prov Online Lrng/Dean Univ Pgm Dr. R. J. MCGIVNEY
57 Dean Hartford Art School Dr. Nancy M. STUART
72 Dean College Engineer/Tech/Arch Dr. Hisham ALNAJJAR
49 Dean College Arts & Science Dr. Katherine BLACK
50 Dean Barney School of Business Dr. Amy ZENG
53 Int Dean Col of Educ/Nurs/Hlth Prof Dr. Cesarina THOMPSON
64 Dean Hartt School Dr. Larry Alan SMITH
12 Dean Hillyer College Dr. David H. GOLDENBERG
39 Asst Vice Pres for Residential Life Mr. Michael MALONE
27 Dir of Marketing/Communications Mr. Jonathan EASTERBROOK
102 Dir Foundation/Corporate Relations Ms. Lynn BARONAS
103 Dir Workforce/Career Development Ms. Linda SCHULTZ
112 Director Planned Giving Ms. Lauren PARDA
28 Asst to Pres Diversity/Comm Engage Ms. Christine GRANT

University of New Haven (A)

300 Boston Post Road, West Haven CT 06516-1916
County: New Haven | FICE Identification: 001397 | Unit ID: 129941
Telephone: (203) 932-7000 | Carnegie Class: Masters/L
FAX Number: (203) 931-6060 | Calendar System: 4/1/4
URL: www.newhaven.edu
Established: 1920 | Annual Undergrad Tuition & Fees: $39,270
Enrollment: 6,984 | Coed
Affiliation or Control: Independent Non-Profit | IRS Status: 501(c)3
Highest Offering: Doctorate
Accreditation: EH, ART, DH, DIETD, @DIETI, HSA

01 President Dr. Steven H. KAPLAN
05 Interim Provost/SVP of Acad Affairs Dr. Mario GABOURY
10 VP of Finance & Administration Mr. George S. SYNODI
111 VP of Advancement Mr. Stephen J. MORIN
84 VP of Enrollment Management Mr. Walter F. CAFFEY
15 VP of Human Resources Ms. Caroline KOZIATEK
32 VP Student Affairs/Dean of Students Ms. Rebecca D. JOHNSON
26 VP of Marketing & Communication Ms. Lyn CHAMBERLIN
100 Chief of Staff Ms. Jean HUSTED
20 VP for Academic Affairs Dr. Daniel MAY
49 Interim Dean of Arts & Sciences Dr. Elizabeth BEAULIEU
50 Dean College Business Dr. Brian KENCH
54 Dean Tagliatela Col Engineering Dr. Ronald HARICHANDRAN
76 Dean School of Health Sciences Dr. Summer J. MCGEE
83 Actg Dean Crim Justice/Forensic Sci Dr. David SCHROEDER
07 Sr Assoc VP Enrollment Management Mr. Kevin J. PHILLIPS
18 Associate VP for Facilities Mr. Louis ANNINO
21 Associate VP for Finance Mr. Patrick TORRE
110 Assoc VP for Advancement Operations Ms. Lisa HONAN
110 Associate VP for Development Ms. Roslyn REABACK
113 Assoc VP Financial/Registrar Svcs Mr. Marc MANIATIS
13 Assoc VP for Information Technology Mr. Vincent P. MANGIACAPRA
19 Assoc VP for Public Safety/Admin Mr. Ronald QUAGLIANI
20 Assoc Provost Strategic Initiatives Dr. Stuart SIDLE
20 Assoc Provost UG Studies/Accred Dr. Gordon SIMERSON
20 Assoc Provost External Partnerships Dr. William NORTON
06 University Registrar Ms. Elizabeth REZENDES
16 Exec Director of Human Resources Ms. Iris CALOVINE
85 Exec Dir of International Programs Ms. Kathy KAUTZ
09 Director Institutional Research Ms. Susan TURNER
37 Director of Financial Aid Mr. Erin CHIARO
08 University Librarian Ms. Hanko H. DOBI
35 Exec Dir of Student Activities Mr. Gregory OVEREND
41 Director of Athletics & Recreation Vacant
29 Director of Alumni Relations Ms. Jennifer PJATAK
19 Chief of University Police Chief James T. GILMAN
91 Dir Enterprise Applications Mr. Todd MCINERNEY
96 Director of Procurement Services Mr. Robert STEVENS
108 Director of Academic Assessment Dr. Kristy HUNTLEY
103 Exec Director of Career Development Mr. Matthew CAPORALE
39 Associate Dean of Residential Life Ms. Nicole MCGRATH
104 Director Study Abroad Ms. Michelle MASON
04 President's Office Coordinator Ms. Jennifer FAZEKAS
28 Director of Myatt Ctr for Diversity Mr. Juan HERNANDEZ

University of Saint Joseph (B)

1678 Asylum Avenue, West Hartford CT 06117-2791
County: Hartford | FICE Identification: 001409 | Unit ID: 130314
Telephone: (860) 232-4571 | Carnegie Class: DU-Mod
FAX Number: (860) 232-6927 | Calendar System: Semester
URL: www.usj.edu
Established: 1932 | Annual Undergrad Tuition & Fees: $38,173
Enrollment: 2,405 | Coed
Affiliation or Control: Roman Catholic | IRS Status: 501(c)3
Highest Offering: Doctorate
Accreditation: EH, #ARCPA, CACREP, CAEP, CAEPN, DIETD, DIETI, MFCD, NURSE, PHAR, SW

01 President Dr. Rhona C. FREE
05 Provost Dr. Michelle KALIS
10 Sr VP Finance and Strategy Mr. Shawn M. HARRINGTON
111 VP Inst Advancement Ms. Maggie PINNEY
84 VP Enrollment Management Ms. Kimberly CRONE
32 VP Student Affairs Mr. Ken BEDINI
21 Assoc VP Finance/Controller Ms. Lucy LUCKER
26 AVP Marketing & Public Affairs Ms. Diana SOUSA
67 Dean Sch Pharmacy/PA Studies Dr. Joseph OFOSU
49 Dean Sch Arts/Sci/Business/Ed Dr. Raouf BOULES
76 Dean Sch Interdisc Health & Science Dr. Elizabeth FRANCIS-CONNOLLY
08 Librarian Vacant
06 Registrar Ms. Angela ANDERSON
41 Director of Athletics Ms. Amanda DEVITT
15 Director of Human Resources Ms. Deborah SPENCER
13 Director of Info Tech (CIO) Mr. Jason LAWRENCE
18 Director of Facilities Mr. Andrew LEVESQUE
19 Director of Public Safety Mr. Derrick MCBRIDE
07 Director of Admissions Ms. Molly DEVER
37 Director of Student Financial Svcs Ms. Ashley DUTTON
36 Dir Career Dev/Women's Ldrship Ctr Ms. Melanie SINCHE
35 Director of Student Affairs Ms. Kristy SANTOS
28 Director of Diversity/Title IX Ms. Rayna DYTON-WHITE
23 Director of Health Services Ms. Elizabeth COCOLA
38 Director of Counseling & Wellness Dr. Meredith YUHAS
29 Dir of Alumni Rels/Annual Giving Ms. Katie DASILVA BURKE
09 Interim Dir Institutional Research Dr. Lauren H. FRIEDMAN
04 Exec Asst to President Ms. Ruth FOXMAN

Wesleyan University (C)

45 Wyllys Avenue, Middletown CT 06459
County: Middlesex | FICE Identification: 001424 | Unit ID: 130697
Telephone: (860) 685-2000 | Carnegie Class: Bac-A&S
FAX Number: (860) 685-2001 | Calendar System: Semester
URL: www.wesleyan.edu
Established: 1831 | Annual Undergrad Tuition & Fees: $54,944
Enrollment: 3,213 | Coed
Affiliation or Control: Independent Non-Profit | IRS Status: 501(c)3
Highest Offering: Doctorate
Accreditation: EH

01 President Dr. Michael S. ROTH
05 Provost/Vice Pres Academic Affairs Dr. Joyce JACOBSEN
10 SVP/Chief Admin Ofcr/Treasurer Mr. Andrew Y. TANAKA
100 Vice Pres/Chief of Staff Mr. David CHEARO
26 Vice President University Relations Mr. Frantz WILLIAMS, JR.
28 Int VP Equity/Inclusion/Title IX Ms. Debbie COLUCCI
32 Vice Pres of Student Affairs Mr. Michael J. WHALEY
13 VP Information Technology/CIO Dr. David BAIRD
27 Assoc VP University Relations Ms. Gemma F. EBSTEIN
30 Senior Development Officer Mr. Stephen KIRSCHE
20 Associate Provost Academic Affairs Dr. Mark HOVEY
18 Asst Vice President for Facilities Ms. Joyce TOPSHE
35 Asst Vice Pres/Dean of Students Mr. Richard CULLITON
58 Dir Cont Stds/Graduate Liberal Stds Ms. Jennifer CURRAN
06 Registrar Ms. Anna VAN DER BURG
08 University Librarian Mr. Andrew WHITE
09 Director of Institutional Research Mr. Michael E. WHITCOMB
37 Director Financial Aid Mr. Robert D. COUGHLIN
36 Director Career Development Ms. Sharon CASTONGUAY
15 Chief Human Resources Officer Vacant
19 Director Public Safety Mr. Scott ROHDE
41 Director of Athletics Mr. Michael WHALEN

Yale University (D)

3 Prospect Street, New Haven CT 06520
County: New Haven | FICE Identification: 001426 | Unit ID: 130794
Telephone: (203) 432-2550 | Carnegie Class: DU-Highest
FAX Number: (203) 432-7105 | Calendar System: Semester
URL: www.yale.edu
Established: 1701 | Annual Undergrad Tuition & Fees: $53,430
Enrollment: 12,974 | Coed
Affiliation or Control: Independent Non-Profit | IRS Status: 501(c)3
Highest Offering: Doctorate
Accreditation: EH, ARCPA, CLPSY, IPSY, LAW, MED, MIDWF, NURSE, PAST, PH, THEOL

01 President Peter SALOVEY
05 Provost Benjamin POLAK
03 Senior Vice President Jack F. CALLAHAN, JR.
32 Secretary & VP Student Affairs Kimberly GOFF-CREWS
10 Vice Pres Finance & CFO Stephen MURPHY
30 Vice President Development Joan E. O'NEILL
43 Vice President & General Counsel Alexander DREIER
15 Vice Pres/Chief HR Officer Janet LINDNER
46 Vice Provost of Research Peter SCHIFFER
88 Vice President Global Strategy Pericles LEWIS
20 Deputy Prov Health Affairs and Acad Stephanie SPANGLER
20 Deputy Provost Academic Resources J. Lloyd SUTTLE
18 VP Facilities & Campus Development John H. BOLLIER
20 Deputy Provost Emily P. BAKEMEIER
26 Vice President for Communications Nathaniel NICKERSON
102 Assoc VP/Dir Corp & Found Rels Patricia E. PEDERSEN
08 Univ Librarian & Deputy Provost Susan GIBBONS
09 Asst VP for Strategy & Analysis Tim PAVLIS
13 Assoc VP & Chief Information Ofcr John BARDEN
96 Assoc VP Administration Operations John A. MAYES
19 Dir Public Safety/Chief Univ Police Ronnell A. HIGGINS
06 University Registrar Emily SHANDLEY
07 Dean Undergraduate Admissions Jeremiah QUINLAN
29 Exec Director Assoc of Yale Alumni Weili CHENG
35 Sr Assoc Dean & Dean Student Affs Mark SCHENKER
22 Dir Ofc Equal Opportunities Valarie J. STANLEY
23 Director University Health Services Dr. Paul GENECIN
25 Exec Dir Sponsored Projects Lisa MOSLEY
36 Assoc Dean/Director Career Services Jeanine DAMES
37 University Director Financial Aid Caesar T. STORLAZZI
112 Univ Director Planned Giving Marybeth CONGDON
39 Dir Grad & Prof Student Housing George E. LONGYEAR, JR.
41 Director Athletics Victoria CHUN
42 University Chaplain Sharon KUGLER
48 Dean of the School of Architecture Deborah BERKE
49 Dean of Yale College Marvin CHUN
50 Dean School of Management Kerwin CHARLES
85 Director Intl Students & Scholars Ann KUHLMAN
54 Acting Dean School of Engineering Mitchell SMOOKE
57 Dean of the School of Art Marta KUZMA
58 Dean of Grad Sch Arts & Science Lynn COOLEY
57 Dean of the School of Drama James A. BUNDY
61 Dean of the Law School Heather GERKEN
64 Dean of the School of Music Robert L. BLOCKER
65 Dean Sch of Forestry & Environ Stds Indy BURKE
73 Dean of the Divinity School Gregory E. STERLING
88 Director Inst of Sacred Music Martin D. JEAN
63 Dean of School of Medicine Dr. Robert J. ALPERN
66 Dean of the School of Nursing Ann KURTH
69 Dean of Public Health Sten VERMUND
28 Chief Diversity Officer Deborah STANLEY-MCAULAY
104 Dean Intl & Professional Experience Jane EDWARDS
88 Assoc VP New Haven Aff & Univ Prop Lauren ZUCKER
100 Chief of Staff April Joy MCGRATH

DELAWARE

Delaware College of Art and Design (E)

600 N Market Street, Wilmington DE 19801-3007
County: New Castle | FICE Identification: 041398 | Unit ID: 432524
Telephone: (302) 622-8000 | Carnegie Class: Spec 2-yr-A&S
FAX Number: (302) 622-8870 | Calendar System: Semester
URL: www.dcad.edu
Established: 1997 | Annual Undergrad Tuition & Fees: $25,710
Enrollment: 143 | Coed
Affiliation or Control: Independent Non-Profit | IRS Status: 501(c)3
Highest Offering: Associate Degree
Accreditation: M, ART

01 President Ms. Jean DAHLGREN
05 Dean Ms. Katy RO
20 Assistant Dean Ms. Krista ROTHWELL
10 Chief Financial Officer Mr. Eric SAUL
08 Library Director Ms. Megan JOHNSON
13 Information Technology Coordinator Mr. Bates CARTER
30 Director of Development Ms. Renee GARNICK
37 Director Student Financial Aid Ms. Sharna PATTERSON
32 Director of Student Services Ms. Sarah GARNER
26 Director of Communications Ms. Susan COULBY
07 Director of Admissions Ms. Jane CAMPBELL
06 Registrar Ms. Hailey MCCRACKEN

Delaware State University (F)

1200 N DuPont Highway, Dover DE 19901-2275
County: Kent | FICE Identification: 001428 | Unit ID: 130934
Telephone: (302) 857-6000 | Carnegie Class: DU-Higher
FAX Number: (302) 857-6069 | Calendar System: Semester
URL: www.desu.edu
Established: 1891 | Annual Undergrad Tuition & Fees (In-State): $7,868
Enrollment: 4,352 | Coed
Affiliation or Control: State | IRS Status: 501(c)3
Highest Offering: Doctorate
Accreditation: M, CAEPN, @DIETC, NUR, SW

01 President Dr. Wilma MISHOE
05 Provost/Exec Vice President Dr. Tony ALLEN
10 Vice President Finance Mr. Robert SCHROF
111 Vice Pres Inst Advancement Dr. Vita C. PICKRUM
32 Vice Pres Student Affairs Dr. Stacy L. DOWNING
84 Vice Pres Strategic Enrollment Mr. Antonio BOYLE
46 Vice President for Research Vacant
13 CIO Mr. Darrell MCMILLON
09 AVP Inst Research/Planning/Analysis Dr. Kimberly R. SUDLER
15 Vice Pres Human Resources Ms. Irene HAWKINS
20 Vice Provost Dr. Saundra DELAUDER
43 General Counsel Mr. Cleon CAULEY
18 AVP of Facilities Vacant
06 Registrar/AVP Mr. Terrell HOLMES
07 Exec Director of Admissions Mr. Kareem MCLEMORE
08 Dean University Libraries Ms. Rebecca BATSON
37 Exec Director of Financial Aid Mr. Al DORSETT
29 Executive Director Alumni Relations Dr. Marcia TAYLOR
36 Interim Director Career Services Ms. Jasmine BUXTON
19 Director of Public Safety Mr. Harry W. DOWNES
38 Director of Student Counseling Mr. Ralph ROBINSON
27 Director News Services Mr. Carlos HOLMES

41 Director of Athletics ... Dr. D. Scott GINES
44 Director Annual Giving ... Mrs. Charity SHOCKLEY
86 Director Government Relations ... Mrs. Jackie GRIFFITH
100 Chief of Staff ... Ms. Tamara L. STONER
104 Director Study Abroad ... Dr. Fengshan LIU
105 Director Web Services ... Mr. Stuart GROOBY
58 Dean Grad & Extended Studies ... Dr. Patrice GILLIAM JOHNSON
26 Exec Director of Marketing ... Ms. Dawn MOSLEY
39 Director of Housing ... Mr. Phillip HOLMES
50 Dean Business ... Mrs. Francine EDWARDS
47 Dean Agricult/Science & Technology ... Dr. Dyremple MARSH

Delaware Technical Community College, Orlando J. George Campus (A)

300 N. Orange Street, Wilmington DE 19801
Telephone: (302) 571-5300 Identification: 770855
Accreditation: &M, CAHIIM, COARC, DH, DMS, MAC, OTA, PTAA

Delaware Technical Community College, Owens Campus (B)

21179 College Drive, Georgetown DE 19947-0610
Telephone: (302) 259-6000 FICE Identification: 007053
Accreditation: &M, ADNUR, COARC, CSHSE, DMS, MLTAD, OTA, PNUR, PTAA, RAD

Delaware Technical Community College, Stanton Campus (C)

400 Stanton-Christiana Road, Newark DE 19713-2197
Telephone: (302) 454-3900 FICE Identification: 021449
Accreditation: &M, ACFEI, ADNUR, CSHSE, HT, NMT, RAD

Delaware Technical Community College, Terry Campus (D)

100 Campus Drive, Dover DE 19904-1383
County: Kent FICE Identification: 011727
Unit ID: 130907
Telephone: (302) 857-1000 Carnegie Class: Bac/Assoc-Assoc Dom
FAX Number: (302) 857-1096 Calendar System: Semester
URL: www.dtcc.edu/terry
Established: 1972 Annual Undergrad Tuition & Fees (In-State): $4,904
Enrollment: 14,195 Coed
Affiliation or Control: State IRS Status: 501(c)3
Highest Offering: Baccalaureate
Accreditation: M, ACFEI, ADNUR, CSHSE, EMT, NUR, PNUR, SURGT

01 Vice President & Campus Director ... Ms. Cornelia JOHNSON
05 Dean Instruction ... Mr. John M. BUCKLEY
32 Dean Student Affairs ... Ms. Jennifer P. PIRES
26 Director Communication and Planning ... Dr. Lisa STRUSOWSKI
103 Director Workforce Development ... Ms. Kristen YENCER
15 Director of Human Resources ... Ms. Janis BEACH
18 Director of Facilities ... Mr. Ray PARSONS
10 Director Business Services ... Ms. Noelle SUGALSKI
88 Asst Director of Facilities ... Mr. Allan NELSON
20 Assistant Dean of Instruction ... Mr. Bill J. MORROW

Goldey-Beacom College (E)

4701 Limestone Road, Wilmington DE 19808-0551
County: New Castle FICE Identification: 001429
Unit ID: 130989
Telephone: (302) 998-8814 Carnegie Class: Spec-4-yr-Bus
FAX Number: (302) 998-8631 Calendar System: Semester
URL: www.gbc.edu
Established: 1886 Annual Undergrad Tuition & Fees: $24,300
Enrollment: 1,823 Coed
Affiliation or Control: Independent Non-Profit IRS Status: 501(c)3
Highest Offering: Doctorate
Accreditation: M, ACBSP

01 President ... Dr. Colleen PERRY KEITH
03 Executive Vice President ... Ms. Kristine M. SANTOMAURO
05 Vice President for Academic Affairs ... Ms. Alison Boord WHITE
10 Exec Dir of Finance/HR ... Ms. Susan M. MANNERING
32 Dean of Students ... Mr. Charles A. HAMMOND
84 Dean Enrollment Mgmt/Registrar ... Ms. Jane H. LYSLE
13 Dean of Information Technology/ACC ... Ms. Emily S. JACKSON
07 Director of Admissions ... Mr. Larry EBY
51 Director of the DBA Program ... Dr. William D. YOUNG
39 Director of Residence/Student Life ... Vacant
41 Director of Athletics ... Dr. Thomas M. BRENNAN
30 Director of External Affairs ... Ms. Janine SORBELLO
18 Director of Facilities/Operations ... Mr. Meezie FOSTER
08 Director of Library/Learning Center ... Mr. Russell MICHALAK
72 Director of Information Technology ... Mr. Peter RYSAVY
09 Dir Institutional Research/Training ... Dr. Monica RYSAVY
36 Career Services Coordinator ... Ms. Elizabeth KIRKER

University of Delaware (F)

104 Hullihen Hall, Newark DE 19716
County: New Castle FICE Identification: 001431
Unit ID: 130943
Telephone: (302) 831-2000 Carnegie Class: DU-Highest
FAX Number: (302) 831-8000 Calendar System: 4/1/4
URL: www.udel.edu
Established: 1743 Annual Undergrad Tuition & Fees (In-State): $13,680
Enrollment: 23,774 Coed
Affiliation or Control: State Related IRS Status: 501(c)3
Highest Offering: Doctorate
Accreditation: M, CAATE, CAEPN, CEA, CLPSY, CSHSE, DIETD, DIETI, IPSY, MT, MUS, NURSE, PCSAS, PTA, @SP, SPAA

01 President ... Dr. Dennis ASSANIS
05 Provost ... Dr. Robin W. MORGAN
03 Exec VP & Chief Operating Officer ... Mr. John LONG
26 VP Comm & Marketing ... Mr. Glenn CARTER
08 Vice Prov Libraries & Museums ... Mr. Trevor A. DAWES
30 VP Development & Alumni Relations ... Mr. James DICKER
58 Interim Vice Prov Grad/Prof Educ ... Dr. Douglas DOREN
43 Vice Pres and General Counsel ... Ms. Laure ERGIN
101 Vice Pres & Univ Secretary ... Mr. Jeffrey W. GARLAND
15 Vice President Human Resources ... Mr. Wayne GUTHRIE
28 Vice Provost for Diversity ... Dr. Carol HENDERSON
88 Vice Provost for Faculty Affairs ... Dr. Matt KINSERVIK
18 VP Facilities/Real Est/Aux Svcs ... Mr. Peter KRAWCHYK
84 Vice Pres Enrollment Management ... Vacant
20 Deputy Provost Academic Affairs ... Dr. Lynn OKAGAKI
10 Vice Pres Finance/Dept Treasurer ... Mr. Gregory S. OLER
13 VP Information Technologies ... Ms. Sharon PITT
41 Dir Intercol Athletics & Rec Svcs ... Ms. Christine RAWAK
45 VP Strategic Planning & Analysis ... Ms. Mary M. REMMLER
32 Vice President for Student Life ... Dr. José-Luis RIERA
46 VP Research/Scholarship/Innovation ... Dr. Charles RIORDAN
47 Dean Agric & Natural Resources ... Dr. Mark RIEGER
49 Interim Dean Arts & Sciences ... Dr. John PELESKO
50 Dean Lerner Col Business & Econ ... Dr. Bruce WEBER
65 Dean Earth Ocean & Environment ... Dr. Estella ATEKWANA
53 Dean Educ & Human Development ... Dr. Carol VUKELICH
54 Dean Engineering ... Dr. Levi T. THOMPSON
76 Dean Health Sciences ... Dr. Kathleen MATT
51 Int AVP Professional/Cont Studies ... Dr. George IRVINE
09 AVP Inst Research & Effectiveness ... Mr. Richard J. REEVES
09 Director Institutional Research ... Dr. Heather A. KELLY
108 Dir Ctr Teach/Assessment/Lrng ... Dr. Matthew TREVETT-SMITH
29 AVP Alumni Engagement/Annual Giving ... Ms. Lauren E. SIMIONE
104 Director Inst for Global Studies ... Dr. Trevor NELSON
37 Exec Dir Student Financial Svcs ... Ms. Melissa STONE
36 Director Career Services ... Mr. Nathan ELTON
19 Exec Dir Campus & Public Safety ... Mr. Albert J. HOMIAK, JR.
92 Director Univ Honors Program ... Dr. Michael J. CHAJES
07 Exec Director Undergrad Admissions ... Dr. William D. ZANDER
123 Director of Graduate Admissions ... Mr. Michael ALEXO
16 Assoc VP HR Strategic Operations ... Ms. Darcell GRIFFITH
96 Manager Purchasing Services ... Mr. George WALUEFF
06 University Registrar ... Mr. Jeff PALMER
114 Chief Budget Officer ... Ms. Mandy MINNER
22 Interim Title IX Coordinator ... Ms. Danica A. MYERS
35 Dean of Students ... Mr. Adam D. CANTLEY
38 Dir Ctr for Counseling/Student Dev ... Dr. Brad WOLGAST
39 Assoc VP Student Life ... Dr. Kathleen G. KERR
85 Exec Dir Intl Students & Scholars ... Mr. Ravi AMMIGAN
23 Director Student Health Services ... Dr. Timothy F. DOWLING
04 Exec Assistant to the President ... Ms. Susan L. WILLIAMS

Wesley College (G)

120 N State Street, Dover DE 19901-3876
County: Kent FICE Identification: 001433
Unit ID: 131098
Telephone: (302) 736-2300 Carnegie Class: Bac-Diverse
FAX Number: (302) 736-2301 Calendar System: Semester
URL: www.wesley.edu
Established: 1873 Annual Undergrad Tuition & Fees: $26,406
Enrollment: 1,561 Coed
Affiliation or Control: United Methodist IRS Status: 501(c)3
Highest Offering: Master's
Accreditation: M, NUR, OT

01 President ... Mr. Robert E. CLARK, II
05 Provost & VP for Academic Affairs ... Dr. Jeffrey GIBSON
10 VP Finance/COO/CFO ... Mr. Dennis STARK
111 Vice Pres Institutional Advancement ... Vacant
84 VP of Enrollment Management ... Mr. David BUCKINGHAM
32 Dean of Students ... Dr. Wanda ANDERSON
42 Dir Spiritual Life and Comm Involv ... Pastor Bonnie MULLEN
21 CPA/Controller ... Ms. Sasha LEE
43 General Counsel ... Vacant
06 Registrar/Dir Student Acad Records ... Ms. Patricia SEUNARINE
12 Admin Coord DAFB ... Ms. Tracey LUNDBLAD
08 Director of Parker Library ... Ms. Katherine GOFF
07 Dir of Admissions Operations ... Ms. Sue HOUSER
88 Dir of Admissions Communication ... Vacant
121 Ex Dir Student Success/Retention ... Ms. Christine MCDERMOTT
26 Dir Communications & Marketing ... Ms. Naomi WAKIAGA
09 Director of Institutional Research ... Vacant
46 Data & Strat Res Specialist ... Mr. Abdul HAMEED
07 Assoc Director of Admissions ... Mr. Christopher JESTER
41 Exec Dir of Sports & Recreation ... Ms. Tracey SHORT
18 Director of the Physical Plant ... Mr. Tom IDNURM
40 Director of the Bookstore ... Ms. Tiara WHITE
19 Director of Safety/Security ... Mr. Garrick CORNISH
23 Director Student Health Services ... Ms. Jiggy PATEL
30 Dir of Advancement Services ... Vacant
39 Asst Dean of Students/Dir Res Life ... Mr. Christopher WILLIS
35 Director of Campus Life ... Mr. Mark BERRY
37 Dir of Student Financial Planning ... Mr. Michael HALL
38 Director of Counseling Service ... Ms. Liz HORSEY
85 Director of International Programs ... Ms. Rebecca MILLER
29 Director Alumni Affairs ... Ms. Laura MAYSE
04 Assistant to the President ... Ms. Ellen COLEMAN

88 Supervisor Business Operations ... Ms. Adele FLAMM
103 Dir for Career Development ... Vacant
13 Chief Info Technology Officer (CIO) ... Mr. Paul COPELAND
15 Human Resources Director ... Ms. Heather SCHALK
104 Director Study Abroad ... Ms. Rebecca SCHRODER

Widener University Delaware Law School (H)

PO Box 7474, Wilmington DE 19803-0474
Telephone: (302) 477-2100 FICE Identification: 012962
Accreditation: &M, LAW

† Branch campus of Widener University in Pennsylvania. This listing reflects the administrators for the school of law for the Harrisburg (PA) and Delaware campuses.

Wilmington University (I)

320 N Dupont Highway, New Castle DE 19720-6491
County: New Castle FICE Identification: 007948
Unit ID: 131113
Telephone: (302) 356-4636 Carnegie Class: DU-Mod
FAX Number: (302) 328-5902 Calendar System: Trimester
URL: www.wilmu.edu
Established: 1967 Annual Undergrad Tuition & Fees: $11,210
Enrollment: 14,170 Coed
Affiliation or Control: Independent Non-Profit IRS Status: 501(c)3
Highest Offering: Doctorate
Accreditation: M, CACREP, CAEPN, IACBE, NURSE

00 Chairman of the Board ... Hon. Joseph J. FARNAN, JR.
01 President ... Dr. LaVerne T. HARMON
100 Executive Director ... Ms. Donna M. QUINN
11 Senior Vice President/COO ... Dr. Erin DIMARCO
10 Senior VP/CFO Financial Affairs ... Ms. Heather A. O'CONNELL
12 University Vice President ... Ms. Carole D. PITCHER
86 VP External Affairs ... Dr. Peter A. BAILEY
05 VP Academic Affairs ... Dr. James D. WILSON, JR.
11 VP Admin & Legal Affairs ... Dr. Christian A. TROWBRIDGE
84 VP Enrollment Management ... Dr. Eileen G. DONNELLY
32 VP Student Affairs/Alumni Rel ... Dr. Tina M. BARKSDALE
111 VP Institutional Advancement ... Dr. Jacque R. VARSALONA
35 AVP Student Affairs ... Dr. Regina C. ALLEN-SHARPE
19 AVP Admin & Legal Affairs ... Dr. Jack L. CUNNINGHAM
43 AVP Admin & Legal Affairs ... Mr. P. Donald HAGERMANN
88 AVP Student Services ... Dr. Bonnie L. KIRKPATRICK
21 Asst Vice President/Controller ... Mr. David R. LEWIS
88 AVP Admin Affs & Dean of Location ... Mr. Robert P. MILLER
88 AVP Academic Support Services ... Ms. Peg P. MITCHELL
88 AVP External Affairs ... Mr. Christopher G. PITCHER
106 AVP Admin Affs/Dean Online ... Dr. Sallie A. REISSMAN
20 AVP Academic Affairs ... Dr. Robert W. RESCIGNO
15 Asst Vice President/CHRO ... Dr. Nicole ROMANO
20 AVP Academic Affairs ... Dr. Sheila M. SHARBAUGH
108 Assistant Vice President ... Dr. Angela C. SUCHANIC
26 AVP University Relations ... Mr. Bill F. SWAIN
13 Asst Vice President/CIO ... Mr. Peter E. LUTUS
101 Liaison to the Board of Trustees ... Ms. Ashley R. MUNDY
125 President Emeritus ... Dr. Jack P. VARSALONA
88 Exec Director Admin & Legal Affairs ... Ms. Linda M. ANDRZJEWSKI
41 Athletics Director ... Dr. Stefanie A. WHITBY
06 Registrar ... Ms. Misty B. WILLIAMS
88 Senior Dir External Affairs ... Ms. Melanie C. BALDWIN
105 Sr Dir of Web/System Communications ... Mr. Kevin G. BARRY
14 Senior Dir Information Technology ... Mr. Brian C. BEARD
120 Sr Dir Online Learning Ed Tech ... Dr. Matthew H. DAVIS
113 Sr Dir Student Financial Services ... Ms. Trudy E. HITE
88 Sr Dir Academic Support Services ... Dr. Elizabeth P. JORDAN
07 Sr Director of Admissions ... Ms. Laura M. MORRIS
18 Sr Director Buildings/Maintenance ... Mr. William P. QUINN
09 Sr Dir of Institutional Research ... Dr. Dana S. SANTORO
53 Dean College of Education ... Dr. John C. GRAY
83 Dean College of Soc & Beh ... Dr. Edward L. GUTHRIE
50 Dean College of Business ... Dr. Kathy S. KENNEDY-RATAJACK
49 Dean College of Arts and Sciences ... Dr. Mary Ann K. WESTERFIELD
76 Dean College of Health Professions ... Dr. Denise Z. WESTBROOK
72 Dean College of Technology ... Dr. Antony J. CARCILLO
88 Dir Center for Teaching Excellence ... Dr. Adrienne M. BEY
85 Director International Affairs ... Ms. Angelina L. BURNS
78 Director Cooperative Learning ... Dr. David C. CAFFO
86 Director Government Relations ... Ms. Simone M. GEORGE
29 Director Alumni Relations ... Mr. Stuart J. HANF
121 Dir Student Success Center ... Ms. Sally J. HEALY
08 Director Library ... Mr. James M. MCCLOSKEY
37 Director Financial Aid ... Ms. Nicole L. MCDANIEL-SMITH
30 Director of Development ... Ms. Felicia K. QUINN
16 Dir Human Resources ... Ms. Karen A. SHEATS
40 Bookstore Manager ... Ms. Carmen L. CASANOVA
96 Purchasing Specialist ... Mr. Mark S. PARIS
89 Chair First Year Experience ... Dr. Matthew J. WILSON
118 Benefits Coordinator ... Ms. Jennifer L. WORKMAN

DISTRICT OF COLUMBIA

American University (J)

4400 Massachusetts Avenue, NW, Washington DC 20016
FICE Identification: 001434
Unit ID: 131159
Telephone: (202) 885-1000 Carnegie Class: DU-Higher
FAX Number: N/A Calendar System: Semester
URL: www.american.edu

Established: 1893 Annual Undergrad Tuition & Fees: $48,459
Enrollment: 13,858 Coed
Affiliation or Control: United Methodist IRS Status: 501(c)3
Highest Offering: Doctorate
Accreditation: M, CAEPN, CLPSY, IPSY, JOUR, LAW, MUS, SPAA

01 President .... Ms. Sylvia M. BURWELL
05 Provost/Chief Academic Officer .... Dr. Daniel J. MYERS
30 Vice President Development & Alumni .... Ms. Courtney SURLS
10 Vice President Finance & Treasurer .... Mr. Douglas KUDRAVETZ
32 VP Campus Life/Inclusive Excellence .... Dr. Fanta AW
43 Vice President & General Counsel .... Ms. Traevena BYRD
11 Vice Provost for Academic Admin .... Ms. Violeta ETTLE
18 Asst VP Facilities Management .... Mr. Vincent HARKINS
35 Dean of Students .... Mr. Jeffery BROWN
108 Asst Provost Inst Rsrch/ Assessment .... Ms. Karen L. FROSLID JONES
29 Asst Vice Pres of Alumni Relations .... Ms. Raina LENNEY
21 Asst Vice President of Treasury .... Ms. Laura MCANDREW
28 Asst VP Diversity/Equity/Inclusiv .... Dr. Amanda TAYLOR
84 Vice Provost Undergrad Enrollment .... Dr. Sharon ALSTON
13 Vice President and CIO .... Mr. David L. SWARTZ
100 Chief of Staff President's Office .... Mr. Seth GROSSMAN
20 Deputy Provost and Dean of Faculty .... Dr. Mary CLARK
20 Assoc Vice Provost Academic Affairs .... Dr. Stephen SILVIA
58 Interim Dean Graduate Studies .... Dr. Wendy BOLAND
20 Dean UG Ed & VP Acad Student Svcs .... Dr. Jessica WATERS
49 Dean College Arts & Sciences .... Dr. Peter STARR
60 Interim Dean Sch of Communication .... Dr. Laura DENARDIS
50 Dean Kogod Sch of Business .... Dr. John T. DELANEY
61 Dean Washington College of Law .... Dr. Camille A. NELSON
82 Dean School of Intl Service .... Dr. Christine CHIN
107 Interim Dean Sch of Prof & Ext Stds .... Ms. Jill KLEIN
80 Dean School of Public Affairs .... Dr. Vicky WILKINS
15 Asst VP of Human Resources .... Ms. Beth MUHA
36 Exec Director Career Center .... Mr. Gihan FERNANDO
88 Assoc Vice Provost/Acad Admin .... Ms. Prita PATEL
26 Vice President of Communication .... Mr. Matthew BENNETT
06 Interim University Registrar .... Dr. Michael GIESE
08 University Librarian .... Ms. Nancy DAVENPORT
21 Controller .... Ms. Nicole BRESNAHAN
88 Dir Student Account Operations .... Mr. Darrell COOK
114 Asst VP Budget & Finance Res Ctr .... Ms. Nana AN
42 University Chaplain .... Rev. Mark SCHAEFER
19 AVP Risk/Safety/Transportation .... Mr. Daniel NICHOLS
37 Asst Vice Provost Financial Aid .... Mr. Brian LEE SANG
38 Exec Director Counseling Center .... Dr. Jeff VOLKMANN
96 Sr Dir Procurement and Contracts .... Mr. Brian BLAIR
07 Asst Vice Provost UG Adm .... Dr. Andrea FELDER
85 Director Intl Student/Scholar Svcs .... Ms. Senem BAKAR
92 Dir Univ Honors Program .... Dr. Patrick T. JACKSON
41 Director Athletics & Recreation .... Dr. William (Billy) WALKER
28 Sr Dir Ctr Diversity & Inclusion .... Ms. Tiffany SPEAKS
104 Director AU Abroad .... Ms. Sara E. DUMONT
46 Asst VP Planning/Project Mgmt .... Mr. David DOWER
88 Asst VP Univ Programs/Development .... Ms. Lee HOLSOPPLE
07 Asst Vice Provost Ops/Enrollment .... Mr. Robert LINSON
04 Senior Assistant to the President .... Ms. Stephanie LEIGH
22 Sr Dir Employee Relations/Recruit .... Ms. Deadre JOHNSON
14 Assoc Chief Information Officer .... Ms. Kamalika SANDELL
25 Director Sponsored Programs .... Dr. Ashley ALEXANDER
09 Asst Provost Inst Res & Assessment .... Ms. Karen L. FROSLID JONES
103 Interim Dir Talent Development .... Ms. Michelle FREDERICK
53 Dean School of Education .... Dr. Cheryl HOLCOMB-MCCOY
86 Asst VP Community & Govt Relations .... Mr. Ed FISHER
91 Director Network Operations .... Mr. Hassan MARVI
101 Asst Secretary to the Board .... Ms. Leslis WONG
88 Deputy Chief of Staff .... Mr. Brian CHIGLINSKY
46 Interim Dean Office of Research .... Dr. Sarah IRVINE BELSON
31 Dir Cmty Rels President's Office .... Ms. Maria BARRY
45 Exec Dir Strategic Implementation .... Ms. Geralynn FRANCESCHINI

Bay Atlantic University (A)

1510 H Street NW, Washington DC 20005
Identification: 667329
Telephone: (202) 644-7210 Carnegie Class: Not Classified
FAX Number: N/A Calendar System: Semester
URL: www.bau.edu
Established: 2014 Annual Undergrad Tuition & Fees: N/A
Enrollment: N/A Coed
Affiliation or Control: Independent Non-Profit IRS Status: 501(c)3
Highest Offering: Master's
Accreditation: ACICS

01 President .... Dr. Sinem VATANARTIRAN
11 CFO .... Ms. Melek EDIB
06 Registrar .... Ms. Izel UGUR
08 Chief Library Officer .... Ms. Amy BILLERBECK
108 Director Institutional Assessment .... Mr. James MOSES
28 Director of Diversity .... Mr. Tyler CARGILL

The Catholic University of America (B)

620 Michigan Avenue, NE, Washington DC 20064-0002
FICE Identification: 001437
Unit ID: 131283
Telephone: (202) 319-5100 Carnegie Class: DU-Higher
FAX Number: (202) 319-4441 Calendar System: Semester
URL: www.cua.edu
Established: 1887 Annual Undergrad Tuition & Fees: $45,804
Enrollment: 6,023 Coed
Affiliation or Control: Roman Catholic IRS Status: 501(c)3
Highest Offering: Doctorate
Accreditation: M, CAEPN, CLPSY, IPSY, LAW, LIB, MUS, NURSE, SW, THEOL

01 President .... Mr. John H. GARVEY
100 Chief of Staff/Counselor to Pres .... Mr. Lawrence J. MORRIS
05 Provost .... Dr. Aaron DOMINGUEZ
10 Vice Pres Finance & Treasurer .... Mr. Robert M. SPECTER
32 Int Vice President Student Affairs .... Mr. Jonathan SAWYER
84 Vice Pres Enroll Mgmt/Marketing .... Mr. Christopher P. LYDON
108 Vice Provost/Dean of Assessment .... Dr. Duilia DE MELLO
11 Vice Provost for Administration .... Vacant
35 Assoc VP Student Life/Dean Students .... Mr. Jonathan C. SAWYER
43 General Counsel .... Ms. Nancy M. O'CONNOR
15 Assoc VP/Chief Human Resources .... Vacant
18 Assoc VP Facilities Operations .... Ms. Debra NAUTA-RODRIGUEZ
41 Assoc VP & Director Athletics .... Mr. Sean M. SULLIVAN
88 Executive Director for Housing .... Mr. Timothy CARNEY
111 Vice Pres for Univ Advancement .... Mr. Scott REMBOLD
44 Assoc VP Univ Advancement .... Ms. Deborah BROWN
44 Assoc VP University Advancement .... Mr. William WARREN
25 Assoc Prov Sponsored Research .... Mr. Ralph ALBANO
26 Assoc VP Marketing/Communications .... Mr. Kevin BURKE
106 Assoc Vice Prov Online Education .... Dr. James MONAGHAN
58 Dean Graduate Studies .... Dr. J. Steven BROWN
48 Dean of Architecture .... Mr. Randall OTT
49 Acting Dean of Arts & Sciences .... Dr. David WALSH
50 Dean School of Business .... Dr. Andrew V. ABELA
54 Dean of Engineering .... Dr. John JUDGE
61 Dean of Law .... Mr. Stephen C. PAYNE
64 Dean of Music .... Dr. Jacqueline LEAVY-WARSAW
70 Act Dean Natl Cath Sch Social Svcs .... Dr. Marie RABER
66 Dean of Nursing .... Dr. Patricia MCMULLEN
73 Dean Theology/Religious Studies .... VRev. Mark MOROZOWICH
107 Dean Metro Sch Professional Studies .... Dr. Vincent KIERNAN
79 Dean of Philosophy .... Dr. John C. MCCARTHY
88 Dean of Canon Law .... Msgr. Ronny JENKINS
07 Dean of Undergrad Admissions .... Mr. James DEWEY-ROSENFELD
13 Chief Information Officer .... Mr. Matthew MCNALLY
27 Exec Dir Strategic Communications .... Ms. Karna LOZOYA
08 Director of Libraries .... Mr. Stephen CONNAGHAN
06 Registrar .... Ms. Julie ISHA
36 Director of Career Services .... Mr. Anthony CHIAPPETTA
19 Assoc VP Public Safety & Emergency .... Ms. Thomasine JOHNSON
38 Director of Counseling Center .... Dr. T. Monroe RAYBURN
23 Medical Director of Health Center .... Dr. Loretta STAUDT
37 Dir Student Financial Assistance .... Ms. Mindy SCHAEFFER
39 Assoc Dean of Students .... Ms. Heidi E. ZEICH
44 Director of Regional Engagement .... Mr. Patrick DAVEY
42 Director University Campus Ministry .... Rev. Jude DEANGELO, OFM CONV
09 Assoc VP Fin Plng/Inst Res/Assess .... Mr. Brian A. JOHNSTON
88 Vice Provost & Assoc Dean Undergrad .... Dr. Lynn MAYER
96 Assoc VP for Strategic Sourcing .... Mr. Dick BLACKWELL
22 Title IX Coordinator/EOO .... Mr. Frank VINIK
88 Compliance and Ethics Officer .... Mr. Vincent A. LACOVARA
40 Manager Bookstore .... Mr. Brett MCMICHAEL

Chicago School of Professional Psychology-Washington DC (C)

901 15th Street NW, Washington DC 20005
Telephone: (202) 706-5000 Identification: 770493
Accreditation: &WC, CACREP, CLPSY

† Branch campus of Chicago School of Professional Psychology Los Angeles Campus, Los Angeles, CA

Daniel Morgan Academy (D)

1620 L Street NW, 7th Floor, Washington DC 20036
Identification: 667304
Telephone: (202) 759-4988 Carnegie Class: Not Classified
FAX Number: N/A Calendar System: Semester
URL: www.dmgs.org
Established: 2014 Annual Graduate Tuition & Fees: N/A
Enrollment: N/A Coed
Affiliation or Control: Independent Non-Profit IRS Status: 501(c)3
Highest Offering: Master's; No Undergraduates
Accreditation: M

01 Acting President & CEO .... Mr. Eric R. EATON
05 Dean of Graduate Studies .... Dr. Steven MEYER
10 Chief Financial Officer .... Mr. Eric R. EATON
06 Registrar .... Ms. Cassandra CREEK
32 Director Student Services .... Ms. Tisia SAFFOLD
07 Director of Admissions .... Ms. Jacqueline M. LINDE
15 Chief Human Resources Officer .... Mr. Luke MCCABE

Gallaudet University (E)

800 Florida Avenue, NE, Washington DC 20002-3695
FICE Identification: 001443
Unit ID: 131450
Telephone: (202) 651-5000 Carnegie Class: DU-Higher
FAX Number: (202) 651-5508 Calendar System: Semester
URL: www.gallaudet.edu
Established: 1864 Annual Undergrad Tuition & Fees: $17,038
Enrollment: 1,578 Coed
Affiliation or Control: Independent Non-Profit IRS Status: 501(c)3
Highest Offering: Doctorate
Accreditation: M, ACBSP, AUD, CACREP, CAEPN, CEA, CLPSY, SP, SW

01 President .... Ms. Roberta (Bobbi) CORDANO
05 Provost .... Dr. Carol J. ERTING
10 Int Vice Pres Admin & Finance .... Ms. Lisa CLARKE
30 Vice Pres Dev & Alumni Relations .... Mr. Paul JULIN
28 VP for Diversity/Equity/Inclusion .... Dr. Elavie NDURA
12 Chief Admin Ofcr LClerc Natl Ctr .... Ms. Nicole SUTCLIFFE
20 CAO Laurent Clerc Natl Ctr .... Ms. Marianne BELSKY
101 Spec Asst to Pres/Board Liaison .... Ms. Rita JENOURE
100 Chief of Staff President .... Ms. Heather HARKER
09 Exec Dir Strategic Planning .... Ms. Susan JACOBY
53 Dean Sch Educ/Bus/Human Svcs .... Dr. Khadijat RASHID
58 Dean Graduate School .... Dr. Guarav MATHUR
32 Int Dean Student Affs/Acad Support .... Mr. Travis IMEL
49 Dean College Arts & Sciences .... Dr. Genie GERTZ
121 Assoc Prov Stdnt Succ/Acad Quality .... Dr. Thomas HOREJES
96 Exec Dir Business Support Services .... Mr. Gary ALLER
18 Director Facilities .... Mr. Amon BROWN
112 Dir Major Gifts .... Mr. David REEKERS
26 Dir Communications .... Ms. Kaitlin LUNA
09 Director Institutional Research .... Ms. Lindsay BUCHKO
29 Exec Director Alumni Relations .... Mr. Samuel SONNENSTRAHL
15 Director Human Resources Svcs .... Ms. Christina SHEN-AUSTIN
13 Exec Director Technology Services .... Mr. Earl PARKS
14 Dir Enterprise Info Systems .... Mr. Daryl FRELICH
88 University Ombuds .... Ms. Elizabeth STONE
08 Dir Library Deaf Collection/Archive .... Mr. Michael OLSON
22 Director Equal Opportunity Programs .... Ms. Sharrell MCCASKILL
06 Registrar .... Ms. Elice PATTERSON
07 Director of Admissions .... Mr. Young Hae PARK

George Washington University (F)

2121 I Street, NW, Washington DC 20052-0002
FICE Identification: 001444
Unit ID: 131469
Telephone: (202) 994-1000 Carnegie Class: DU-Highest
FAX Number: (202) 994-0458 Calendar System: Semester
URL: www.gwu.edu
Established: 1821 Annual Undergrad Tuition & Fees: $55,230
Enrollment: 27,973 Coed
Affiliation or Control: Independent Non-Profit IRS Status: 501(c)3
Highest Offering: Doctorate
Accreditation: M, ARCPA, ART, CACREP, CAEPN, CIDA, CLPSY, FEPAC, HSA, IPSY, LAW, MED, MT, NURSE, PH, PLNG, PTA, SP, SPAA

01 President .... Dr. Thomas J. LEBLANC
100 Chief of Staff President's Office .... Mr. Aristide J. COLLINS
05 Provost & Exec VP Academic Affairs .... Dr. Forrest MALTZMAN
84 Interim Sr Vice Provost Enroll Mgmt .... Mr. Ed GILLIS
30 Vice Pres for Dev/Alumni Relations .... Ms. Donna ARBIDE
10 Exec Vice President & Treasurer .... Mr. Mark DIAZ
43 Senior Vice Pres & General Counsel .... Ms. Beth NOLAN
26 Vice President External Relations .... Ms. Lorraine A. VOLES
20 Deputy Provost Academic Affairs .... Dr. Teresa MURPHY
45 VP Financial Planning & Ops .... Mr. Jared ABRAMSON
114 Vice Provost of Budget and Finance .... Vacant
28 Vice Provost Diversity & Inclusion .... Ms. Caroline LAGUERRE-BROWN
15 Int Chief Human Resources Officer .... Mr. Dale A. MCLEOD
13 Chief Information Officer .... Ms. Loretta EARLY
20 Vice Provost Faculty Affairs .... Dr. Christopher A. BRACEY
11 Senior Assoc VP of Operations .... Ms. Alicia M. O'NEIL KNIGHT
32 Dean of Student Experience .... Dr. Marcia L. PETTY
88 Assoc Provost Diversity & Inclusion .... Ms. Helen CANNADAY SAULNY
90 Deputy Chief Academic Tech Officer .... Mr. Jared W. JOHNSON
108 Assoc VP of Acad Plng & Assessment .... Dr. Cheryl BEIL
46 Vice President for Research .... Dr. Robert H. MILLER
88 AVP Budget & Financial Analysis .... Ms. Cynthia VILLAVERDE
21 University Controller .... Ms. Sharon HEINLE
09 Director Inst Research & Planning .... Mr. Joachim W. KNOP
86 Asst VP Government Relations .... Ms. Renee MCPHATTER
104 Associate VP for International Pgms .... Dr. Donna SCARBORO
08 University Librarian .... Ms. Geneva HENRY
27 Asst VP for Communications .... Ms. Sarah GEGENHEIMER BALDASSARO
27 Interim Exec Dir of Media Relations .... Ms. Lindsay C. HAMILTON
29 Sr Associate VP Development .... Mr. David B. ANDERSON
06 Registrar .... Ms. Elizabeth A. AMUNDSON
07 Dean of Undergrad Admissions .... Dr. Costas SOLOMOU
38 Director Counseling Center .... Vacant
37 Interim Director Financial Aid .... Ms. Michelle C. ARCIERI
36 Asst Provost Career Center .... Ms. Rachel A. BROWN
85 Director International Services .... Ms. Jennifer H. DONAGHUE
19 Sr Assoc VP Safety & Security .... Ms. Kathleen FOX
22 Dir EEO & Affirmative Action .... Ms. Vickie FAIR
23 Director Student Health Services .... Dr. Isabel GOLDENBERG
40 Director GW Bookstore .... Ms. Janet F. UZZELL
107 Int Dean Col Professional Studies .... Dr. Christopher J. DEERING
49 Int Dean Columbian Col Arts/Sci .... Dr. Paul J. WAHLBECK
63 Dean Medicine & Health Sciences .... Dr. Jeffrey S. AKMAN
69 Dean School of Public Health .... Dr. Lynn R. GOLDMAN
61 Interim Dean Law School .... Dr. Christopher A. BRACEY
54 Dean Engineering/Applied Science .... Dr. John LACH
53 Dean Education/Human Development .... Dr. Michael J. FEUER
50 Dean School of Business .... Dr. Anuj MEHROTRA
82 Dean Elliott School Intl Affairs .... Dr. Reuben E. BRIGETY
66 Dean School of Nursing .... Dr. Pamela R. JEFFRIES
12 Dean GW Virginia Sci/Tech Campus .... Dr. Ali ESKANDARIAN
41 Director Athletics/Recreation .... Ms. Tanya VOGEL
92 Director University Honors Program .... Vacant
93 Director Multicultural Student Svc .... Mr. Michael R. TAPSCOTT
39 Director Student Housing .... Mr. Seth D. WEINSHEL

Georgetown University (A)

37th & O Streets, NW, Washington DC 20057-1947
FICE Identification: 001445
Unit ID: 131496
Telephone: (202) 687-0100 Carnegie Class: DU-Highest
FAX Number: N/A Calendar System: Semester
URL: www.georgetown.edu
Established: 1789 Annual Undergrad Tuition & Fees: $54,104
Enrollment: 19,005 Coed
Affiliation or Control: Roman Catholic IRS Status: 501(c)3
Highest Offering: Doctorate
Accreditation: M, ANEST, CEA, HSA, LAW, MED, MIDWF, NURSE, PAST

01 President .... Dr. John (Jack) J. DEGIOIA
46 SVP Research/Chief Technology Ofcr .... Dr. Spiros DIMOLITSAS
05 Provost .... Dr. Robert M. GROVES
17 Exec Vice Pres Health Sciences .... Dr. Edward B. HEALTON
61 Exec Vice Pres/Dean of Law School .... Dr. William M. TREANOR
111 Vice Pres for Advancement .... Mr. R. Bartley MOORE
42 Vice Pres for Mission and Ministry .... Rev. Mark BOSCO, SJ
13 Interim Vice Pres/CIO .... Mr. Judd NICHOLSON
26 VP Public Affairs & Strategic Dev .... Mr. Erik SMULSON
32 VP Student Affairs .... Dr. Todd OLSON
28 VP for Inst Diversity & Equity .... Ms. Rosemary KILKENNY
19 Chief of Police Dept Public Safety .... Mr. Jay GRUBER
43 VP & General Counsel .... Ms. Lisa M. BROWN
85 VP for Global Engagement .... Dr. Thomas BANCHOFF
11 VP & COO Main Campus .... Mr. Darryl E. CHRISTMON
109 Assoc VP for Auxiliary Services .... Ms. Joelle D. WIESE
118 AVP Benefits/Chief Benefits Officer .... Mr. Charles E. DESANTIS
20 Vice Provost Education .... Dr. Randall BASS
88 Vice Provost Research .... Dr. Janet MANN
20 Vice Provost Faculty .... Dr. Reena AGGARWAL
21 Assoc Vice President for Operations .... Ms. Christina ROBERTS
114 Asst VP Finance Planning & Budget .... Mr. Matthew C. GREAVES
06 Assoc VP & University Registrar .... Ms. Annamarie BIANCO
35 Assoc VP Student Affairs .... Dr. Jeanne F. LORD
23 Asst VP for Student Health .... Dr. Vince C. WINKLERPRINS
08 University Librarian .... Ms. Artemis G. KIRK
88 Ex Dir Ctr New Designs Lrng/Schlrs .... Dr. Edward J. MALONEY
25 Senior Research Compliance Officer .... Ms. Mary E. SCHMIEDEL
49 Dean Georgetown College .... Dr. Christopher CELENZA
82 Dean School Foreign Service .... Dr. Joel HELLMAN
50 Dean School of Business .... Dr. Paul A. ALMEIDA
63 Dean Medical School .... Dr. Edward B. HEALTON
66 Dean Sch of Nursing/Health Stds .... Dr. Patricia CLOONAN
51 Dean Continuing Studies .... Dr. Kelly OTTER
58 Dean of Grad School .... Dr. Norberto M. GRZYWACZ
80 Dean McCourt School Public Policy .... Dr. Michael A. BAILEY
31 Dir Partnerships & Cmty Engagement .... Ms. Brenda ATKINSON-WILLOUGHBY
96 Asst VP Procurement .... Mr. O.T WELLS
85 Director of Global Services .... Ms. Vanessa MEYERS
104 Director of Global Education .... Mr. Craig RINKER
22 Director Affirmative Action Pgm .... Mr. Michael W. SMITH
24 Exec Dir Classroom Educ/Tech Svcs .... Mr. Mark J. COHEN
38 Director Counseling Center .... Dr. Philip W. MEILMAN
39 Director of Residence Life .... Ms. Stephanie J. LYNCH
108 Asst Dir CNDLS/Assessment .... Ms. Mindy MCWILLIAMS
112 Exec Director Gift Planning .... Mr. Stephen LINK

Howard University (B)

2400 Sixth Street, NW, Washington DC 20059-0001
FICE Identification: 001448
Unit ID: 131520
Telephone: (202) 806-6100 Carnegie Class: DU-Higher
FAX Number: (202) 806-5934 Calendar System: Semester
URL: www.howard.edu
Established: 1867 Annual Undergrad Tuition & Fees: $26,756
Enrollment: 9,392 Coed
Affiliation or Control: Independent Non-Profit IRS Status: 501(c)3
Highest Offering: Doctorate
Accreditation: M, ART, CAEP, CLPSY, COPSY, DENT, DH, DIETC, IPSY, JOUR, LAW, MED, MT, MUS, NURSE, OT, PHAR, PTA, RTT, #SP, SW, THEA, THEOL

01 President .... Dr. Wayne FREDERICK
05 Provost/Chief Academic Officer .... Dr. Anthony K. WUTOH
101 Vice President & Secretary .... Ms. Florence PRIOLEAU
43 General Counsel .... Ms. Florence PRIOLEAU
10 Chief Financial Officer & Treasurer .... Mr. Michael MASCH
26 Vice President for External Affairs .... Ms. Gracia HILLMAN
15 Int VP/Chief Human Resources Ofcr .... Ms. Ariana Wright ARNOLD
30 VP Development & Alumni Relations .... Mr. David P. BENNETT
17 CEO University Hospital .... Mr. James DIEGEL
46 Assoc Provost Research/Grad Studies .... Dr. Gary L. HARRIS
20 Associate Provost .... Dr. Joseph P. REIDY
20 Assoc Provost Undergraduate Studies .... Dr. Melanie CARTER
32 Vice President Student Affairs .... Mr. Kenneth M. HOLMES
88 AVP Regulatory/Research Compliance .... Dr. Thomas O. OBISESAN
88 AVP for Research and Faculty .... Dr. Kristy F. WOODS
13 Chief Information Officer .... Dr. Kevin DAWSON
100 Chief of Staff .... Mr. D. Paul MONTEIRO, JR.
58 Interim Dean Graduate School .... Dr. Dana WILLIAMS
49 Int Dean College Arts/Sciences .... Dr. Edna MEDFORD
50 Dean School of Business .... Dr. Barron H. HARVEY
61 Dean School of Law .... Ms. Danielle R. HOLLEY-WALKER
63 Dean Medicine/VP Clinical Affairs .... Dr. Hugh E. MIGHTY
52 Dean College of Dentistry .... Dr. Dexter A. WOODS
54 Dean Col Engineering/Architecture .... Dr. Achille MESSAC
53 Dean School of Education .... Dr. Dawn WILLIAMS
60 Dean School of Communications .... Dr. Gracie LAWSON-BORDERS
66 Int Dean Nursing/Allied Hlth Sc .... Dr. Mary HILL
70 Dean School of Social Work .... Dr. Sandra CREWE
73 Dean School of Divinity .... Dr. Yolanda PIERCE
67 Dean School of Pharmacy .... Dr. Toyin TOFADE
48 Director School of Architecture .... Prof. Hazel EDWARDS
76 Assoc Dean/Div Allied Health Sci .... Dr. Shirley J. JACKSON
66 Assoc Dean/Div of Nursing .... Ms. Tammi L. DAMAS
57 Assoc Dean/Division of Fine Arts .... Dr. Gwendolyn H. EVERETT
81 Assoc Dean/Div Natural Sciences .... Dr. Robert CATCHINGS
83 Interim Assoc Dean/Social Sciences .... Dr. Terri ADAMS
79 Associate Dean Humanities .... Dr. James J. DAVIS
06 Registrar/Director of Admissions .... Ms. Latrice BYAM
37 Director Financial Aid .... Vacant
42 Dean Andrew Rankin Chapel .... Dr. Bernard L. RICHARDSON
35 Dean Student Life & Activities .... Vacant
39 Int Dir Residence Life/Univ Housing .... Mr. Joe UTER
36 Director Career Services Office .... Dr. Joan M. BROWNE
08 Executive Director Libraries .... Ms. Rhea BALLARD-THROWER
88 Interim Director Law Library .... Ms. Eileen SANTOS
24 Dir Teaching Learning & Assmnt Ctr .... Dr. Helen BOND
16 Senior Director Human Resources .... Mr. Michael MCFADDEN
22 Dir Equal Employment Opportunity .... Mr. Antwan LOFTON
29 Director Alumni Relations .... Ms. Sharon STRANGE LEWIS
44 Principal Gift Officer .... Mr. Ken ASHWORTH
27 AVP of External Affairs .... Ms. Cynthia BROCK-SMITH
18 AVP Facilities .... Vacant
19 Chief of Campus Police .... Mr. Alonzo F. JOY
31 Director HU Community Association .... Ms. Maybelle T. BENNETT
109 Director Auxiliary Enterprises .... Mr. Antwan D. CLINTON
41 Athletics Director .... Mr. Kery DAVIS
23 Exec Director Student Health Center .... Dr. Michelle R. CARTER
40 Gen Manager Barnes & Noble at HU .... Mr. Alex BAMFO
94 Director of Women's Studies .... Vacant
18 Director Physical Facilities .... Mr. Victor MCNAUGHTON
108 Director Institutional Assessment .... Dr. Gerunda B. HUGHES
88 Director Events & Protocol .... Mr. Andrew RIVERS

The Institute of World Politics (C)

1521 16th Street, NW, Washington DC 20036-1464
FICE Identification: 041144
Unit ID: 455804
Telephone: (202) 462-2101 Carnegie Class: Spec-4-yr-Other
FAX Number: (202) 464-0335 Calendar System: Semester
URL: www.iwp.edu
Established: 1990 Annual Graduate Tuition & Fees: N/A
Enrollment: 145 Coed
Affiliation or Control: Independent Non-Profit IRS Status: 501(c)3
Highest Offering: Doctorate; No Undergraduates
Accreditation: M

01 President .... Dr. John LENCZOWSKI
03 Executive Vice President .... Lawrence COSGRIFF
05 Academic Dean .... Dr. Francis (Frank) MARLO
10 Chief Financial Officer .... Matt RYAN
120 SVP Cyber Intelligence Init .... Dean LANE
88 SVP Professional Affiliations .... CAPT. Chris GLASS
111 VP Institutional Advancement .... John BERGHOLZ
32 VP Student Affairs and Admissions .... Jason JOHNSRUD
06 Registrar & Institutional Research .... Hasanna BENSON-TYUS
84 Director Student Recruitment .... Tim STEBBINS
29 Alumni/Communications Officer .... Katie BRIDGES
36 Director Career Services .... Derrick DORTCH
37 Director Financial Aid .... Thelbert SNOWDEN
26 Director Marketing and Comm .... MaryAnne GARNER
08 Library Manager .... Dmitry KULIK

Inter-American Defense College (D)

210 B Street SW, Bldg 52, Ft McNair,
Washington DC 20319-5008
County: USA Identification: 667275
Telephone: (202) 646-1337 Carnegie Class: Spec-4-yr-Other
FAX Number: N/A Calendar System: Semester
URL: www.iadc.edu
Established: 1962 Annual Graduate Tuition & Fees: N/A
Enrollment: N/A Coed
Affiliation or Control: Independent Non-Profit IRS Status: 501(c)3
Highest Offering: Master's; No Undergraduates
Accreditation: @M, ACICS

01 Director .... MGen. James E. TAYLOR
05 Chief of Studies .... BGen. Ruben Dario DIAZ ESPARZA
03 Vice Director .... RAdm. Silvio LUIS
06 Registrar .... Mr. Elias CROMWELL
08 Chief Library Officer .... Mr. Conor BIGLEY

Pontifical Faculty of the Immaculate Conception at the Dominican House of Studies (E)

487 Michigan Avenue, NE, Washington DC 20017-1585
FICE Identification: 012803
Unit ID: 131405
Telephone: (202) 495-3820 Carnegie Class: Spec-4-yr-Faith
FAX Number: (202) 495-3873 Calendar System: Semester
URL: www.dhs.edu
Established: 1902 Annual Graduate Tuition & Fees: N/A
Enrollment: 102 Coed
Affiliation or Control: Roman Catholic IRS Status: 501(c)3
Highest Offering: Master's; No Undergraduates
Accreditation: M, THEOL

01 President .... Fr. John LANGLOIS, OP
05 Vice President/Academic Dean .... Fr. Thomas PETRI, OP
20 Secretary of Studies .... Fr. Brian CHRZASTEK, OP
08 Librarian .... Fr. John Martin RUIZ, OP
18 Director of Facilities .... Ms. Shauna ROYE
42 Chaplain to Commuter Students .... Fr. James BRENT, OP
06 Registrar .... Mrs. Garrya DUNSTON
10 Treasurer/Director of Financial Aid .... Ms. Shauna ROYE
111 Assistant Director of Advancement .... Mr. George CERVANTES
13 IT Director .... Mr. Carlos MOLINA
04 Executive Assistant .... Mrs. Patricia WORK
88 Administrative Secretary .... Ms. Daniela TALAMANTE

Pontifical John Paul II Institute for Studies on Marriage and Family (F)

620 Michigan Ave, NE, McGivney Hall,
Washington DC 20064
FICE Identification: 041427
Unit ID: 455813
Telephone: (202) 526-3799 Carnegie Class: Spec-4-yr-Faith
FAX Number: (202) 269-6090 Calendar System: Other
URL: www.johnpaulii.edu
Established: 1988 Annual Graduate Tuition & Fees: N/A
Enrollment: 68 Coed
Affiliation or Control: Roman Catholic IRS Status: 501(c)3
Highest Offering: Doctorate; No Undergraduates
Accreditation: M

01 President .... RevMsg. Pierangelo SEQUERI
03 Vice President .... Carl A. ANDERSON
05 Provost/Dean .... Fr. Antonio LOPEZ
20 Associate Dean for Academic Affairs .... David S. CRAWFORD
11 Assoc Dean Programs/Administration .... Nick J. BAGILEO
07 Director of Admissions .... Sara L. TRUDEAU

† Affiliated with The Catholic University of America, DC.

Strayer University (G)

1133 15th Street, NW, Suite 200,
Washington DC 20005-2710
FICE Identification: 001459
Unit ID: 131803
Telephone: (202) 379-7808 Carnegie Class: Masters/M
FAX Number: (202) 419-1423 Calendar System: Quarter
URL: www.strayer.edu
Established: 1892 Annual Undergrad Tuition & Fees: $13,380
Enrollment: 959 Coed
Affiliation or Control: Proprietary IRS Status: Proprietary
Highest Offering: Master's
Accreditation: M, ACBSP, CAEPT, NURSE

01 President .... Mr. Brian W. JONES
05 Provost/Chief Academic Ofcr .... Mr. Cale HOLMAN
20 Vice Provost of Academics .... Ms. Jennifer NEWELL
32 Senior Vice Provost Student Affairs .... Vacant
08 University Librarian .... Ms. Mary SNYDER
06 University Registrar .... Ms. Alison MORRISON
106 Global Online Campus Dean .... Vacant
20 Chamblee PA Campus Dean .... Ms. Tonya MOORE
12 Chamblee PA Campus Director .... Mr. Richard WYLIE
20 Chesterfield VA Campus Dean .... Dr. Carol WILLIAMS
12 Chesterfield VA Campus Director .... Mr. Thomas BERNHARDT
20 San Antonio TX Campus Dean .... Mr. Kendall JOHNSON
12 San Antonio TX Campus Director .... Mr. Coner GILL
20 Stafford TX Campus Dean .... Dr. Samuel GOODING
12 Stafford TX Campus Director .... Ms. Tracey MARTIN
20 Teays Valley WV Campus Dean .... Dr. Joel GOLDSTEIN
12 Lower Bucks PA Campus Director .... Ms. Lauren PLINER
12 Teays Valley WV Campus Director .... Ms. Christine VITO
20 Cobb County GA Campus Dean .... Vacant
12 Cobb County GA Campus Director .... Ms. Miriam SANCHEZ
12 Virginia Beach VA Campus Director .... Ms. Collette REID
20 Columbia SC Campus Dean .... Ms. Piper LORICK
12 Columbia SC Campus Director .... Mr. Ryan BUCKSON
12 Newport News VA Campus Director .... Ms. Colette REID
20 Delaware County PA Campus Dean .... Ms. Cornelia ZAVADSKY
12 Delaware County PA Campus Director .... Ms. Amy CESTONE
20 Fredericksburg VA Campus Dean .... Ms. Jenelle THORMAN
12 Fredericksburg VA Campus Director .... Mr. Duan BUTLER
20 North Charlotte NC Campus Dean .... Ms. Shawna MAGBIE-CARR
20 Greensboro NC Campus Dean .... Ms. Melissa REID ALSTON
12 Greensboro NC Campus Director .... Mr. Patrick DIXON
12 Maitland FL Campus Director .... Mr. Jason MARTINE
20 Greenville SC Campus Dean .... Dr. William DUERR
12 Greenville SC Campus Director .... Ms. Jeanne POINDEXTER
20 Loudoun VA Campus Dean .... Dr. Richelle RESTO
12 Loudoun VA Campus Director .... Mr. Carl FREDERICK
20 Manassas VA Campus Dean .... Ms. Leila STEGLICH
12 White Marsh MD Campus Director .... Mr. Leator KNUCKLES
12 Manassas VA Campus Director .... Mr. Debra SANFORD
20 North Raleigh NC Campus Dean .... Mr. Jason HARRIS
12 North Raleigh NC Campus Director .... Mr. Jared ELLISON
20 Morrow GA Campus Dean .... Dr. Shadrack KOROS
12 Takoma Park DC Campus Director .... Mr. Cristen JONES
12 Morrow GA Campus Director .... Ms. Allisha OUSLEY
12 North Charlotte NC Campus Director .... Ms. Stephanie JOHNSON
20 Nashville TN Campus Dean .... Dr. Dasie SCHULZ
12 Nashville TN Campus Director .... Dr. Kimberly MALONE-HADDOX

20 Owings Mills MD Campus Dean ... Ms. LaToya HALE
12 Owings Mills MD Campus Director ... Ms. Shawne SCOTT
20 Arlington VA Campus Dean ... Dr. Isaac MOONZWE
20 Shelby TN Campus Dean ... Dr. Clinton MILLER
20 Takoma Park DC Campus Dean ... Mr. Vishnu DZIDZIENYO
12 Shelby TN Campus Director ... Mr. Sam THOMAS
20 Maitland FL Campus Dean ... Ms. April HUDSON
20 Prince Georges MD Campus Dean ... Dr. Camilla CRAIG
12 Prince Georges MD Campus Director ... Ms. Candy COLLINS
20 Research Triangle Park NC Campus Dn ... Dr. Donna LEVESQUE
12 Research Triangle Pk NC Campus Dir ... Mr. Patrick DIXON
20 Rockville MD Int Assoc Campus Dean ... Dr. Isaac MOONSWE
12 Arlington VA Campus Director ... Ms. Patrice JONES
12 Rockville MD Campus Director ... Ms. Patrice JONES
20 South Charlotte NC Campus Dean ... Dr. Jeffrey ROMANCZUK
20 Tampa FL East Campus Dean ... Ms. DeNeen ATTORD
12 South Charlotte NC Campus Director ... Ms. Christina VITO
20 Virginia Beach VA Campus Dean ... Ms. Ashley CASTLE
12 Tampa FL East Campus Director ... Mr. Jeffrey KEITH
20 Alexandria VA Campus Dean ... Dr. Peter DEDOMINICI
20 Woodbridge VA Campus Dean ... Dr. Ras ACOLASTE
20 Lithonia GA Campus Dean ... Ms. Tariva SMITH
12 Woodbridge VA Campus Director ... Ms. Toni THORTON
12 Thousand Oaks TN Campus Director ... Ms. Mara JEFFERSON
20 Thousand Oaks TN Campus Dean ... Mr. Stanley WOOTEN
20 Miramar FL Campus Dean ... Dr. Joann RAPHAEL
20 Washington DC Campus Dean ... Ms. Timera WILLIAMS
12 Washington DC Campus Director ... Ms. Ashley COLLINS
20 White Marsh MD Campus Dean ... Ms. Tafadzwa NHIRA
12 Alexandria VA Campus Director ... Ms. Natalie THOMAS
20 Macon GA Assoc Campus Dean ... Mr. Akinola DARE
12 Macon GA Campus Director ... Ms. Clairesse QUADIR
12 Lithonia GA Campus Director ... Mr. Travis NORRIS
20 Center City PA Campus Dean ... Ms. Saadia OULAMINE
12 Center City PA Campus Director ... Mr. Isaac WALTERS
12 Miramar FL Campus Director ... Ms. Trish ADIA
20 Anne Arundel MD Campus Dean ... Ms. Aerin GILBERT
12 Anne Arundel MD Campus Director ... Ms. Cherone VALLEY
20 South Raleigh NC Campus Dean ... Ms. Kimberly WILLIAMS
12 Birmingham AL Campus Director ... Ms. Irina ROGERS
20 Birmingham AL Campus Dean ... Mr. Keith JOHNSON
20 Chesapeake VA Campus Dean ... Ms. Amber EAKIN
12 Chesapeake VA Campus Director ... Ms. Sarah UEBELHOER
20 Savannah GA Campus Dean ... Dr. Denise OGDEN
20 Huntsville AL Campus Dean ... Mr. Dustin VICK
12 Huntsville AL Campus Director ... Ms. Julie PRYOR
20 Little Rock AR Campus Dean ... Dr. Stephanie COX
12 Little Rock AR Campus Director ... Mr. Sean HOFER
20 Orlando FL East Campus Dean ... Ms. April HUDSON
20 Baymeadows FL Campus Dean ... Ms. Sarah FRADEN
12 South Raleigh NC Campus Director ... Mr. Matthew KOCH
12 Baymeadows FL Campus Director ... Ms. Kristina HILLIARD
12 Orlando FL East Campus Director ... Mr. Jason MARTINE
20 Palm Beach Gardens FL Campus Dean ... Dr. Joann RAPHAEL
12 Savannah GA Campus Director ... Ms. Dora JENKINS
12 Palm Beach Gardens FL Campus Dir ... Ms. Trish ADIA
20 Fort Lauderdale FL Campus Dean ... Dr. Joann RAPHAEL
12 Fort Lauderdale FL Campus Director ... Mr. Geoffrey RAMGOLAM
20 Sand Lake FL Assoc Campus Dean ... Ms. April HUDSON
12 Sand Lake FL Campus Director ... Mr. Jason MARINE
20 Augusta GA Campus Dean ... Ms. Cathy VU
12 Augusta GA Campus Director ... Mr. Louis DAVIS
20 Allentown PA Campus Dean ... Ms. Holli QUINN
20 Columbus GA Campus Dean ... Dr. Kanidrus PRATHER
12 Columbus GA Campus Director ... Mr. Jonathan MURRAY
20 Douglasville GA Campus Dean ... Dr. A. Fitzgerald JONES
12 Douglasville GA Campus Director ... Ms. Monica POINTER
20 Jackson MS Campus Dean ... Dr. Dana EVANS
12 Allentown PA Campus Director ... Ms. Lauren PLINER
12 Jackson MS Campus Director ... Ms. Angela MILLER
20 Cherry Hill NJ Campus Dean ... Dr. R. Renee THOMPSON
12 Cherry Hill NJ Campus Director ... Ms. Allegra GLIEM
20 Henrico VA Campus Dean ... Mr. Marcus RALPH
20 Piscataway NJ Campus Dean ... Ms. R. Renee THOMPSON
12 Piscataway NJ Campus Director ... Mr. Khioverny DUARTE
12 Warrendale PA Campus Director ... Ms. Molly MAZZARINI
20 Warrendale PA Campus Dean ... Mr. Timothy GRIFFIN
20 Willingboro NJ Campus Dean ... Dr. A. Renee THOMPSON
12 Willingboro NJ Campus Director ... Ms. Allegra GLIEM
20 Knoxville TN Campus Dean ... Dr. Chelsie SWEPSON
20 Huntersville NC Campus Dean ... Dr. Jonita HENRY POWELL
12 Huntersville NC Campus Director ... Ms. Krystal MOREHEAD
12 Henrico VA Campus Director ... Ms. Sarah UEBELHOER
12 Knoxville TN Campus Director ... Mr. Jason ADKINS
20 Cedar Hill TX Campus Dean ... Mr. Jay CULLINS
12 Cedar Hill TX Campus Director ... Ms. Marisol GREENWOOD
20 Charleston SC Campus Dean ... Mr. Elliot DILLIHAY
20 Newport News VA Campus Dean ... Mr. Terrell MASON
20 North Austin TX Campus Dean ... Mr. Kendall JOHNSON
12 North Austin TX Campus Director ... Mr. Coner GILL
20 North Dallas TX Campus Dean ... Dr. T.A ESSEX
20 Lower Bucks PA Campus Dean ... Dr. Byron WESS
12 North Dallas TX Campus Director ... Ms. Kedecia RITCHIE-MITCHELL
20 Northwest Houston TX Campus Dean ... Dr. Samuel GOODING
12 Northwest Houston TX Campus Dir ... Ms. Tracey MARTIN
12 Charleston SC Campus Director ... Mr. Scott ANDERSON

TEACH-NOW Graduate School of Education (A)

1701 K Street NW, Ste 250, Washington DC 20036

Identification: 667305

Telephone: (844) 283-2246 Carnegie Class: Not Classified
FAX Number: N/A Calendar System: Other
URL: teach-now.com
Established: 2012 Annual Graduate Tuition & Fees: N/A
Enrollment: N/A Coed
Affiliation or Control: Proprietary IRS Status: Proprietary
Highest Offering: Master's; No Undergraduates
Accreditation: DEAC, CAEP

01 President/CEO ... Dr. Emily FEISTRITZER
05 Chief Academic Officer ... Dr. Donna A. GOLLNICK
10 Chief Financial Officer ... Mr. Richard FEISTRITZER
26 Vice Pres Marketing ... Mr. Brandon FINLEN
11 Director of Operations ... Mr. Greg GARRISON
07 Admissions Officer ... Mr. Andre BARNES

Trinity Washington University (B)

125 Michigan Avenue, NE, Washington DC 20017-1090

FICE Identification: 001460
Unit ID: 131876

Telephone: (202) 884-9000 Carnegie Class: Masters/M
FAX Number: (202) 884-9229 Calendar System: Semester
URL: www.trinitydc.edu
Established: 1897 Annual Undergrad Tuition & Fees: $24,150
Enrollment: 1,964 Female
Affiliation or Control: Roman Catholic IRS Status: 501(c)3
Highest Offering: Master's
Accreditation: M, CACREP, NURSE, OT, #OTA

01 President ... Ms. Patricia A. MCGUIRE
05 Provost ... Dr. Carlota OCAMPO
111 Vice Pres Institutional Advancement ... Ms. Ann PAULEY
32 Vice President for Student Affairs ... Dr. Karen GERLACH
13 Chief Info Technology Officer (CIO) ... Mr. Michael BURBACK
49 Dean College of Arts & Science ... Dr. Sita RAMAMURTI
53 Dean School of Education ... Dr. Nicole STRANGE-MARTIN
107 Dean School of Professional Studies ... Dr. Peggy LEWIS
66 Dean Sch Nursing/Health Professions ... Dr. Mary ROMANELLO
35 Dean of Student Services ... Ms. Michelle BOWIE
15 Director for Human Resources ... Ms. Tracey PRINCE ROSS
41 Athletic Director ... Ms. Monique MCLEAN
42 Director of Campus Ministry ... Sr. Ann HOWARD
18 Director Facilities Services ... Mr. Matthew LAPOINTE
29 Director Alumnae Affairs ... Ms. Stephanie MELVIN
07 Executive Director of Admissions ... Ms. Iris ESCARRAMAN
08 University Librarian ... Ms. Trisha SMITH
10 Controller/Business Officer ... Mr. Jared BASCO
51 Director Continuing Education ... Ms. Katie OMENITSCH

University of the District of Columbia (C)

4200 Connecticut Avenue, NW,
Washington DC 20008-1174

FICE Identification: 001441
Unit ID: 131399

Telephone: (202) 274-5000 Carnegie Class: Masters/M
FAX Number: (202) 274-5304 Calendar System: Semester
URL: www.udc.edu
Established: 1976 Annual Undergrad Tuition & Fees (In-District): $5,888
Enrollment: 4,247 Coed
Affiliation or Control: Local IRS Status: 501(c)3
Highest Offering: First Professional Degree
Accreditation: M, ACBSP, CACREP, CAEP, COARC, DIETD, LAW, NUR, SP, SW

01 President ... Mr. Ronald MASON, JR.
05 Chief Academic Officer ... Dr. Lawrence POTTER
12 Chief Community College Officer ... Dr. Tony SUMMERS
32 Chief Student Devel & Success Ofcr ... Dr. William LATHAM
11 Chief Operating Officer ... Mr. Troy LEMAILE-STOVALL
43 Acting General Counsel ... Ms. Avis RUSSELL
100 Chief of Staff ... Ms. Evola BATES
15 Vice President Talent Management ... Ms. Patricia JOHNSON
18 VP Real Estate & Facility Mgmt ... Mr. Erik THOMPSON
111 Vice President for Advancement ... Mr. Rodney TRAPP
10 Chief Financial Officer ... Mr. Munetsi MUSARA
49 Dean Arts & Sciences ... Dr. April MASSEY
50 Dean Sch Business & Public Admin ... Dr. Mohamad SEPEHRI
61 Dean School of Law ... Ms. Renee MCDONALD HUTCHINS
54 Dean Engineering/Applied Scis ... Dr. Devdas SHETTY
56 Dean Agric/Urban Sustainability ... Dr. Sabine O'HARA
46 VP Research & Sponsored Programs ... Dr. Victor MCCRARY
06 University Registrar ... Ms. Tiffany COOPER
37 Director Student Financial Aid ... Ms. Nailah WILLIAMS
26 Director of Communications ... Mr. John GORDON
08 Director of Learning Resources ... Ms. Melba BROOME
25 Capital Program Officer ... Ms. Cassandra PARKER
41 Athletic Director ... Ms. Patricia A. THOMAS
88 General Manager UDC Cable TV ... Mr. Edward JONES, JR.
88 Dir of Operations and Maintenance ... Vacant
09 Dir of Institutional Effectiveness ... Mrs. Maria BYRD
38 Director Student Counseling ... Ms. Serena BUTLER-JOHNSON
88 Dean Student Achievement ... Ms. Hermina P. PETERS
103 Dean Workforce Development ... Vacant
19 Dir Public Safety/Chief of Police ... Mr. Marieo FOSTER
36 Exec Director Career Services ... Mr. Jared E. MOFFETT
86 Director State & Local Affairs ... Mr. Thomas E. REDMOND
21 Deputy Chief Operating Ofcr/Dir Fin ... Mr. David FRANKLIN
88 Director STEM ... Ms. Barbara J. HOLMES
29 Director Alumni Affairs ... Ms. Alexandria WASHINGTON
97 Assistant Director of General Educ ... Ms. Kimberly CREWS
102 Director Sponsored Programs ... Ms. Laura-Lee DAVIDSON
13 Dir Information Technology ... Mr. Michael ROGERS
07 Director Admissions/TRIO Programs ... Ms. Saundra CARTER
101 Exec Secretary Office the Board ... Ms. Beverly FRANKLIN
16 Director of Labor & Employee Rels ... Ms. Jennifer MATTHEWS
35 Asst Director of Student Success ... Ms. Latosha BALDWIN

University of the Potomac (D)

1401 H Street NW, Suite 100, Washington DC 20005

FICE Identification: 032183
Unit ID: 384412

Telephone: (202) 274-2303 Carnegie Class: Spec-4-yr-Bus
FAX Number: N/A Calendar System: Semester
URL: www.potomac.edu
Established: 1991 Annual Undergrad Tuition & Fees: $15,984
Enrollment: 90 Coed
Affiliation or Control: Proprietary IRS Status: Proprietary
Highest Offering: Doctorate
Accreditation: M

01 President/Chief Executive Officer ... Dr. Rick MURPHREE
05 Dean of Academics ... Dr. Sergei ANDRONIKOV
10 Chief Financial Officer ... John MCGOVERN
11 Chief Operating Officer ... Andrea FORD
08 Director of Learning Resource Ctr ... Edward ROBINSON
07 Director of Admissions ... Gina RICE-HOLLAND
26 Director of Marketing ... April HOCKSTALL

Wesley Theological Seminary (E)

4500 Massachusetts Avenue, NW,
Washington DC 20016-5690

FICE Identification: 001464
Unit ID: 131973

Telephone: (202) 885-8600 Carnegie Class: Spec-4-yr-Faith
FAX Number: (202) 885-8605 Calendar System: Semester
URL: www.wesleyseminary.edu
Established: 1882 Annual Graduate Tuition & Fees: N/A
Enrollment: 570 Coed
Affiliation or Control: United Methodist IRS Status: 501(c)3
Highest Offering: Doctorate; No Undergraduates
Accreditation: M, THEOL

01 President ... Dr. David MCALLISTER-WILSON
04 Executive Assistant to President ... Ms. Tonya MILES
10 Vice Pres Finance/CFO ... Mr. Jeffrey STRAITS
05 Dean ... Dr. Philip WINGEIER-RAYO
20 Associate Dean Academic Affairs ... Dr. Michael KOPPEL
07 Associate Dean of Admissions ... Rev. William D. ALDRIDGE
32 Assoc Dean for Campus Life ... Dr. Asa LEE
88 Vice President of Intl Relations ... Dr. Kyunglim SHIN LEE
45 Vice Pres of Strategic Initiatives ... Rev. Beth LUDLUM
30 Vice Pres Development ... Vacant
21 Controller ... Mr. William WALKER
06 Registrar ... Mr. Joseph E. ARNOLD
88 Dir Luce Ctr for Arts & Religion ... Dr. Aaron ROSEN
31 Director Community Engagement Inst ... Dr. Lorena PARRISH
88 Director Ctr for Public Theology ... Mr. Michael MCCURRY
88 Faculty Dir Ctr Public Theology ... Mr. Rick ELGENDY
26 Director Communications/Marketing ... Ms. Sheila GEORGE
88 Director Doctor of Ministry Program ... Dr. Douglas TZAN
24 Director of Educational Technology ... Ms. Berkeley COLLINS
88 Director of Enrollment ... Ms. JaNice PARKS
88 Director Heal the Sick Initiative ... Thomas PRUSKI
15 Director Human Resources ... Dr. Josie HOOVER
39 Director of Housing ... Ms. Monica PETTY
85 Dir International Student Services ... Ms. Karen SANTIAGO
88 Dir Lewis Ctr Church Leadership ... Dr. F. Douglas POWE
08 Director of Library ... Dr. James ESTES
88 Dir Practice Ministry in Mission ... Dr. Joseph BUSH
37 Director Student Financial Aid ... Mr. Dane SMITH
88 Director Writing Center ... Ms. Raedorah STEWART
18 Chief Facilities/Physical Plant ... Mr. Randall ADAMS
28 Diversity Officer ... Mr. Matt LYONS

FLORIDA

Academy for Five Element Acupuncture (F)

305 SE Second Avenue, Gainesville FL 32601-6811

County: Alachua FICE Identification: 035243
Unit ID: 451079

Telephone: (352) 335-2332 Carnegie Class: Spec-4-yr-Other Health
FAX Number: (352) 337-2535 Calendar System: Trimester
URL: www.acupuncturist.edu
Established: 1998 Annual Graduate Tuition & Fees: N/A
Enrollment: 48 Coed
Affiliation or Control: Independent Non-Profit IRS Status: 501(c)3
Highest Offering: Master's; No Undergraduates
Accreditation: ACUP

01 President ... Ms. Misti OXFORD-PICKERAL
11 Vice President Administration ... Ms. Joanne EPSTEIN
05 Academic Dean ... Ms. Valerie RAZUTIS
10 Finance Director ... Ms. Odalis CRUZ
37 Financial Aid Officer ... Ms. Sue STEININGER
06 Registrar ... Ms. Jessica BABAPOUR
07 Admissions Counselor ... Ms. Isabelle WINZELER

Academy for Nursing and Health Occupations (A)

5154 Okeechobee Blvd #201, West Palm Beach FL 33417
County: Palm Beach FICE Identification: 033463
Unit ID: 412173
Telephone: (561) 683-1400 Carnegie Class: Spec 2-yr-Health
FAX Number: (561) 683-6773 Calendar System: Other
URL: www.anho.edu
Established: 1978 Annual Undergrad Tuition & Fees: N/A
Enrollment: 408 Coed
Affiliation or Control: Independent Non-Profit IRS Status: 501(c)3
Highest Offering: Associate Degree
Accreditation: COE, ADNUR

01 President .... Dr. Lois M. GACKENHEIMER
05 Assistant Director/Dean .... Renee WERNER
06 Registrar .... Elizabeth RODRIGUEZ
07 Admissions Specialist .... Angela STILES

Acupuncture & Massage College (B)

10506 N Kendall Drive, Miami FL 33176-1509
County: Miami-Dade FICE Identification: 034145
Unit ID: 439969
Telephone: (305) 595-9500 Carnegie Class: Spec-4-yr-Other Health
FAX Number: (305) 595-2622 Calendar System: Semester
URL: www.amcollege.edu
Established: 1983 Annual Undergrad Tuition & Fees: $10,866
Enrollment: 151 Coed
Affiliation or Control: Proprietary IRS Status: Proprietary
Highest Offering: Master's
Accreditation: ACCSC, ACUP

01 President .... Ms. Christy WOOD
05 Academic Dean .... Dr. Yaly FLORES-SOTO
17 Clinic Director .... Dr. Jean Pierre CHACON
37 Financial Aid Director .... Mr. Guy JACKMAN
07 Admissions Director .... Mr. Joe CALARESO
06 Registrar/Student Services .... Ms. Maria GARCIA

Advance Science International College (C)

5190 North West 167 Street, Ste 200,
Miami Lakes FL 33014
County: Miami-Dade FICE Identification: 037573
Unit ID: 444334
Telephone: (305) 626-6007 Carnegie Class: Not Classified
FAX Number: N/A Calendar System: Semester
URL: asicollege.edu
Established: 1998 Annual Undergrad Tuition & Fees: N/A
Enrollment: 69 Coed
Affiliation or Control: Proprietary IRS Status: Proprietary
Highest Offering: Associate Degree
Accreditation: ACCSC

01 President/Director of School .... Pablo PEREZ

AdventHealth University (D)

671 Winyah Drive, Orlando FL 32803-1204
County: Orange FICE Identification: 031155
Unit ID: 133872
Telephone: (407) 303-9798 Carnegie Class: Spec-4-yr-Other Health
FAX Number: (407) 303-5671 Calendar System: Trimester
URL: www.ahu.edu
Established: 1992 Annual Undergrad Tuition & Fees: $12,240
Enrollment: 1,809 Coed
Affiliation or Control: Seventh-day Adventist IRS Status: 501(c)3
Highest Offering: Doctorate
Accreditation: SC, ANEST, #ARCPA, DMS, NMT, NURSE, OT, OTA, PTA, RAD

01 President .... Dr. Edwin I. HERNANDEZ
05 Provost .... Dr. Sandra DUNBAR
10 Sr VP for Finance/CFO .... Mr. Ruben O. MARTINEZ
32 Sr VP for Student Services .... Dr. Stephen H. ROCHE
26 VP Marketing & Public Relations .... Mr. Lonnie MIXON
106 VP Educational Tech/Distance Educ .... Dr. Dan LIM
20 VP for Academic Administration .... Dr. Len ARCHER
09 Dir of Inst Effectiveness/Accred .... Mr. Joe HAWKINS
37 Director of Financial Aid .... Ms. Daisy TABACHOW
06 Registrar .... Dr. Janet CALDERON
88 Dir Ctr for Academic Achievement .... Dr. Ndala BOOKER
08 Library Director .... Ms. Deanna L. FLORES
07 Director of Enrollment Services .... Ms. Lillian GARRIDO
21 Chief Accountant .... Mr. Grayson GOODMAN
39 Director of Residence Hall .... Ms. Cassandra PHILOGENE
30 Director of Philanthropy .... Dr. Carol BRADFIELD
15 Director of Human Resources .... Ms. Angela MARTINEZ
13 Director of Information Technology .... Mr. Travis WOOLEY
04 Executive Asst to the President .... Ms. Viviana CALANDRA
88 Chief Compliance Officer .... Ms. Starr S. BENDER
88 COO for Online Education .... Dr. Deena SLOCKETT
29 Director Alumni Relations .... Ms. Dawn H. CREFT

American Medical Academy (E)

12215 SW 112th Street, Miami FL 33186
County: Miami-Dade FICE Identification: 041921
Unit ID: 475714
Telephone: (305) 271-6555 Carnegie Class: Spec 2-yr-Health
FAX Number: (305) 271-6556 Calendar System: Semester
URL: www.ama.edu
Established: 2006 Annual Undergrad Tuition & Fees: N/A
Enrollment: 371 Coed
Affiliation or Control: Proprietary IRS Status: Proprietary
Highest Offering: Associate Degree
Accreditation: ABHES

01 Chief Executive Officer .... Mr. Eduardo GUTIERREZ

Ana G. Mendez University Metro Orlando Campus (F)

5601 S Semoran Boulevard, #55, Orlando FL 32822
Telephone: (407) 207-3363 Identification: 770921
Accreditation: &M

† Branch campus of Universidad Ana G. Mendez, Rio Piedras, PR

Ana G. Mendez University South Florida Campus (G)

15201 NW 79th Court, Miami Lakes FL 33016
Telephone: (954) 885-5595 Identification: 770922
Accreditation: &M

† Branch campus of Universidad Ana G. Mendez, Rio Piedras, PR

Ana G. Mendez University Tampa Bay Campus (H)

3655 West Waters Avenue, Tampa FL 33614
Telephone: (813) 932-7500 Identification: 770923
Accreditation: &M

† Branch campus of Universidad Ana G. Mendez, Rio Piedras, PR

Antigua College International (I)

14505 Commerce Way, Suite 522,
Miami Lakes FL 33016-1573
County: Miami-Dade Identification: 667344
Telephone: (786) 391-1167 Carnegie Class: Not Classified
FAX Number: (786) 452-9265 Calendar System: Semester
URL: www.antigua.edu
Established: 2012 Annual Undergrad Tuition & Fees: N/A
Enrollment: N/A Coed
Affiliation or Control: Proprietary IRS Status: Proprietary
Highest Offering: Baccalaureate
Accreditation: ABHES

00 CEO .... Diony ANTIGUA
01 President .... Jose ANTIGUA
10 CFO .... Justin GARCIA
11 Vice Pres Operations .... Taima GONZALEZ

The Art Institute of Tampa, a branch of Miami International University of Art & Design (J)

4401 North Himes Avenue, Suite 150, Tampa FL 33614
Telephone: (813) 393-5321 Identification: 770935
Accreditation: &SC, ACFEI

† Branch campus of Miami International University of Art & Design, Miami, FL.

ATA Career Education-Spring Hill (K)

7351 Spring Hill Drive, Suite 11, Spring Hill FL 34606
Telephone: (866) 438-2432 Identification: 770521
Accreditation: ABHES

† Branch campus of ATA College, Louisville, KY

Atlantic Institute of Oriental Medicine (L)

100 E Broward Boulevard, Suite 100,
Fort Lauderdale FL 33301-3510
County: Broward FICE Identification: 034296
Unit ID: 439446
Telephone: (954) 763-9840 Carnegie Class: Spec-4-yr-Other Health
FAX Number: (954) 763-9844 Calendar System: Trimester
URL: www.atom.edu
Established: 1994 Annual Graduate Tuition & Fees: N/A
Enrollment: 150 Coed
Affiliation or Control: Independent Non-Profit IRS Status: 501(c)3
Highest Offering: Doctorate; No Undergraduates
Accreditation: ACUP

01 President .... Johanna C. YEN
03 Executive Vice President .... Di FU
05 Academic Dean .... Yan CHENG
11 Executive Director .... Dort BIGG
10 Financial Officer .... Celia MUNOZ
06 Registrar .... Milagros FERREIRA
08 Head Librarian .... Jeanne THOMAS

† Granted candidacy at the Doctorate level.

Atlantis University (M)

1442 Biscayne Boulevard, Miami FL 33132
County: Miami-Dade FICE Identification: 042339
Unit ID: 485768
Telephone: (305) 377-8817 Carnegie Class: Bac-Diverse
FAX Number: (305) 377-9557 Calendar System: Semester
URL: www.atlantisuniversity.edu
Established: 1975 Annual Undergrad Tuition & Fees: $5,400
Enrollment: 367 Coed
Affiliation or Control: Proprietary IRS Status: Proprietary
Highest Offering: Master's
Accreditation: ACCSC, CEA

01 Executive Director .... Ms. Carol PALACIOS

Ave Maria School of Law (N)

1025 Commons Circle, Naples FL 34119
County: Collier FICE Identification: 036914
Unit ID: 442295
Telephone: (239) 687-5300 Carnegie Class: Spec-4-yr-Law
FAX Number: (239) 353-3173 Calendar System: Semester
URL: www.avemarialaw.edu
Established: 2000 Annual Graduate Tuition & Fees: N/A
Enrollment: 241 Coed
Affiliation or Control: Roman Catholic IRS Status: 501(c)3
Highest Offering: First Professional Degree; No Undergraduates
Accreditation: LAW

01 President and Dean .... Mr. Kevin CIEPLY
04 Executive Assistant to the Dean .... Ms. Pamela KRAMER
05 Assoc Dean Academic Affairs .... Ms. Maureen MILLIRON
08 Director of the Law Library .... Mr. Ulysses JAEN
42 Chaplain .... Msgr. Frank MCGRATH
06 Registrar .... Mr. Anthony COLE
37 Director of Financial Aid .... Mr. Kevin MCGOWAN
111 Chief Advancement Officer .... Ms. Donna HEISER
07 Director of Admissions .... Ms. Claire O'KEEFE
36 Director of Career Services .... Ms. Jennifer LUCAS-ROSS
10 Assoc Dean Finance/Student Admin .... Ms. Kaye CASTRO
13 Chief Information Officer .... Ms. Monica RENGIFO
15 Director of Human Resources .... Ms. Kathleen SHELMERDINE

Ave Maria University (O)

5050 Ave Maria Boulevard, Ave Maria FL 34142-9505
County: Collier FICE Identification: 039413
Unit ID: 446048
Telephone: (239) 280-2500 Carnegie Class: Bac-A&S
FAX Number: (239) 352-2392 Calendar System: Semester
URL: www.avemaria.edu
Established: 2003 Annual Undergrad Tuition & Fees: $20,850
Enrollment: 1,113 Coed
Affiliation or Control: Independent Non-Profit IRS Status: 501(c)3
Highest Offering: Doctorate
Accreditation: SC

00 Chancellor .... Mr. Thomas S. MONAGHAN
01 President/CEO .... Mr. James TOWEY
03 Executive Vice President .... Mr. Dennis GRACE
05 VP Academic Affairs .... Dr. Roger NUTT
10 VP Finance/Administration .... Mr. Eugene MUNIN
30 VP Institutional Advancement .... Vacant
32 VP Student Affairs .... Ms. Kimberly KING
26 VP Marketing/Communications .... Mr. Mark MCCORMICK
13 Chief Information Officer .... Mr. Eddie DEJTHAI
07 Director of Admissions .... Vacant
06 Registrar .... Ms. Angela LLANOS
41 Athletic Director .... Mr. John LAMANNA
42 Director of Campus Ministry .... Fr. Rick MARTIGNETTI
44 Sr Director of Principal Gifts .... Mr. Patrick O'CONNELL
35 Director of Student Life .... Vacant
88 Director of Mission/Outreach .... Mr. Michael O'DONNELL
08 Director of Library Services .... Ms. Jennifer NODES
15 Director of Human Resources .... Ms. Kathy PHELPS
18 Director Physical Plant .... Mr. Jason SYLVESTER
38 Director Counseling Services .... Ms. AnaMaria LI-ROSI
39 Director Resident Life .... Mrs. Vivian CROCKETT
19 Director Security/Safety .... Mr. Michael MILLER
37 Financial Aid Coordinator .... Ms. Sandy SHIMP
04 Admin Assistant to the President .... Ms. Cristine BUZZANCA
29 Program Manager Alumni Relations .... Ms. Paula SHUTE

Aviator College of Aeronautical Science & Technology (P)

3800 St. Lucie Boulevard, Fort Pierce FL 34946
County: Saint Lucie FICE Identification: 039863
Unit ID: 447847
Telephone: (772) 466-4822 Carnegie Class: Spec 2-yr-Tech
FAX Number: (772) 462-4886 Calendar System: Semester
URL: www.aviator.edu
Established: 1984 Annual Undergrad Tuition & Fees: $74,514
Enrollment: 259 Coed
Affiliation or Control: Proprietary IRS Status: Proprietary
Highest Offering: Associate Degree
Accreditation: ACCSC, CEA

01 President .... Mr. Michael E. COHEN
10 Sr Vice Pres/Chief Financial Ofcr .... Ms. T.J METE

05 Vice Pres Academic Affairs ..... Mr. Pierre LAVIAL
06 Registrar/Director Student Services ..... Ms. Lisa KREAMER
37 Financial Aid Officer ..... Ms. Amy ROTH
43 Legal Counsel/Compliance ..... Mr. Kendall PHILLIPS

Azure College (A)

3201 W Commercial Blvd, Suite 127,
Fort Lauderdale FL 33309

County: Highlands | Identification: 667116
Unit ID: 483762
Telephone: (954) 500-2987 | Carnegie Class: Spec 2-yr-Health
FAX Number: N/A | Calendar System: Quarter
URL: www.azure.edu
Established: 2004 | Annual Undergrad Tuition & Fees: N/A
Enrollment: N/A | Coed
Affiliation or Control: Proprietary | IRS Status: Proprietary
Highest Offering: Baccalaureate
Accreditation: ABHES

01 Campus Director ..... Mr. Jose NAPOLEON

The Baptist College of Florida (B)

5400 College Drive, Graceville FL 32440-3306

County: Jackson | FICE Identification: 021596
Unit ID: 132408
Telephone: (850) 263-3261 | Carnegie Class: Spec-4-yr-Faith
FAX Number: (850) 263-9026 | Calendar System: Semester
URL: www.baptistcollege.edu
Established: 1943 | Annual Undergrad Tuition & Fees: $11,400
Enrollment: 426 | Coed
Affiliation or Control: Southern Baptist | IRS Status: 501(c)3
Highest Offering: Master's
Accreditation: SC, MUS

01 President ..... Dr. Thomas A. KINCHEN
30 Vice President for Development ..... Dr. Charles R. PARKER
05 Academic Dean ..... Dr. G. Robin JUMPER
06 Registrar ..... Ms. Stephanie W. ORR
32 Director of Student Life/Marketing ..... Mrs. Sandra K. RICHARDS
09 Director of Institutional Research ..... Dr. Ed SCOTT
37 Director of Financial Aid & VA ..... Mrs. Stephanie E. POWELL
18 Maintenance Director ..... Mr. Huie G. WILSON
10 Associate Business Officer ..... Ms. Polly K. FLOYD
04 Administrative Asst to President ..... Ms. Laura L. TICE
08 Head Librarian ..... Mr. John E. SHAFFETT
39 Housing Manager ..... Mrs. Rose A. STRICKLAND
41 Athletic Coordinator ..... Mr. Neal POTTER
19 Director of Campus Safety ..... Mr. Olan C. STRICKLAND

Barry University (C)

11300 NE Second Avenue, Miami Shores FL 33161-6695

County: Dade | FICE Identification: 001466
Unit ID: 132471
Telephone: (305) 899-3000 | Carnegie Class: DU-Mod
FAX Number: (305) 899-3054 | Calendar System: Semester
URL: www.barry.edu
Established: 1940 | Annual Undergrad Tuition & Fees: $30,014
Enrollment: 7,358 | Coed
Affiliation or Control: Roman Catholic | IRS Status: 501(c)3
Highest Offering: Doctorate
Accreditation: SC, ANEST, ARCPA, CAATE, CACREP, EXSC, HT, LAW, MACTE, MT, NURSE, OT, PERF, POD, SW, THEOL

01 President ..... Dr. Michael ALLEN
04 Executive Assist to the President ..... Ms. Mary Ellen LETSCHE
00 President Emerita ..... Sr. Linda BEVILACQUA
05 Provost ..... Dr. John D. MURRAY
10 Vice Pres Business & Finance ..... Mrs. Susan ROSENTHAL
15 VP Admin Services & Org Development ..... Mrs. Jennifer N. BOYD-PUGH
20 Vice Provost & Interim Dean PACE .... Dr. Christopher STARRATT
32 VP Mission & Student Engagement ..... Dr. Scott F. SMITH
13 VP Enroll & Digital Strategies/CIO ..... Ms. Yvette KOOTTUNGAL
43 General Counsel ..... Mr. David DUDGEON
49 Dean College of Arts/Sciences ..... Dr. Karen A. CALLAGHAN
50 Dean School of Business ..... Dr. Joan M. PHILLIPS
53 Dean School of Education ..... Dr. Jill FARRELL
76 Dean College of Health Sciences ..... Dr. John MCFADDEN
61 Dean School of Law ..... Dr. Leticia M. DIAZ
63 Dean School of Pod Med ..... Dr. Bryan CALDWELL
20 Associate Vice Provost ..... Dr. Victor ROMANO
70 Dean School of Social Work ..... Dr. Phyllis SCOTT
35 Associate VP & Dean of Students ..... Dr. Maria L. ALVAREZ
35 Assoc VP Mission & Stdnt Engagement ..... Dr. Eileen MCDONOUGH
29 Assoc VP Alum Rels & Annual Giving ..... Mr. Matthew BLAIR
84 Assoc Vice Pres Recruit & Admission ..... Ms. Roxanna CRUZ
105 Assistant VP Web Marketing ..... Mr. Michel SILY
19 Director Public Safety & Emerg Mgt ..... Mr. John BUHRMASTER
08 Director Library Services ..... Dr. Jan FIGA
42 Chaplain ..... Fr. Cristobal TORRES
06 University Registrar ..... Ms. Cynthia A. CHRUSZCZYK
39 Director Housing and Residence Life .. Mr. Matthew R. CAMERON
36 Director Career Services ..... Mr. John MORIARTY
37 Director Financial Aid ..... Mrs. Aida CLARO
92 Director Honors Program ..... Dr. Pawena SIRIMANGKALA
38 Director Student Counseling Center ..... Vacant
26 Assoc VP Brand Mkt & Communications ..... Vacant
123 Director of Graduate Admission ..... Ms. Betsy THOMAS

09 Director Institutional Research ..... Ms. Shaunette GRANT
14 AVP & Chief Technology Officer ..... Mr. Hernan LONDONO
41 Director of Athletics ..... Mr. Michael COVONE
102 Dir Foundation Rels & Major Gifts ..... Mr. Frank SAAVEDRA
88 Director Mkt for Prod Dev & Design ..... Mr. Miguel RAMIREZ
109 Dir Student Union & Food Services ..... Mr. Mickie VOUTSINAS
25 Director Grant & Sponsored Programs .Mrs. Sandra L. MANCUSO
40 Manager Bookstore ..... Vacant
96 Dir Procurement & Accounts Payable ..... Ms. Monica SOTO

Beacon College (D)

105 E Main Street, Leesburg FL 34748-5162

County: Lake | FICE Identification: 033733
Unit ID: 384254
Telephone: (352) 787-7660 | Carnegie Class: Bac-Diverse
FAX Number: (352) 787-0721 | Calendar System: Semester
URL: www.beaconcollege.edu
Established: 1989 | Annual Undergrad Tuition & Fees: $39,016
Enrollment: 348 | Coed
Affiliation or Control: Independent Non-Profit | IRS Status: 501(c)3
Highest Offering: Baccalaureate
Accreditation: SC

01 President ..... Dr. George J. HAGERTY
05 Provost ..... Dr. Shelly CHANDLER
32 Dean of Student Affairs ..... Dr. Kerry GREENSTEIN
30 VP of Institutional Development ..... Mr. Stephen MULLER
10 VP of Finance & Administration ..... Mr. Otis VANCE
06 Registrar ..... Mr. David BROWN
18 Director of Facilities ..... Mr. Ken RAMELLA
37 Director of Financial Aid ..... Ms. Dale HEROLD
08 Director of Library Resources ..... Ms. Tiffany REITZ
13 Director of Information Technology ..... Mr. Tim PAIGE
04 Exec Assistant to the President ..... Ms. Tamara SYNDER
15 Director of Human Resources ..... Mr. Tom BROWN
07 Dean of Admissions Enrollment Mgmt ..... Ms. Dale HEROLD
101 Admin Asst to the Board ..... Ms. Tamara SNYDER
103 Dir Workforce/Career Development ..... Ms. Theresa ELLIOTT
29 Director Alumni Relations ..... Ms. Chelsea EUBANK
23 Executive Director Student Health ..... Ms. Monika RANKIN
19 Chief of Campus Security ..... Mr. Elyas MALIK
39 Director Student Housing ..... Ms. Sara BAILEY
38 Director Student Counseling ..... Ms. Dana MANZO
44 Director Annual Giving ..... Ms. Keri Jo PHILLIPS

Bethesda College of Health Sciences (E)

3800 S Congress Avenue, Suite 9,
Boynton Beach FL 33426

County: Palm Beach | Identification: 667258
Telephone: (561) 364-3064 | Carnegie Class: Not Classified
FAX Number: (561) 364-3059 | Calendar System: Semester
URL: www.BethesdaCollege.net
Established: 2011 | Annual Undergrad Tuition & Fees: N/A
Enrollment: N/A | Coed
Affiliation or Control: Independent Non-Profit | IRS Status: 501(c)3
Highest Offering: Associate Degree
Accreditation: ACICS, RAD

01 Dean ..... Amanda MURPHY

Bethune Cookman University (F)

640 Dr. Mary McLeod Bethune Blvd,
Daytona Beach FL 32114-3099

County: Volusia | FICE Identification: 001467
Unit ID: 132602
Telephone: (386) 481-2000 | Carnegie Class: Bac-A&S
FAX Number: (386) 481-2010 | Calendar System: Semester
URL: www.cookman.edu
Established: 1904 | Annual Undergrad Tuition & Fees: $14,814
Enrollment: 4,143 | Coed
Affiliation or Control: United Methodist | IRS Status: 501(c)3
Highest Offering: Master's
Accreditation: #SC, ACBSP, CAATE, CAEP, MUS, NUR, PH

01 President ..... Dr. E. LaBrent CHRITE
00 Chair Board of Trustees ..... Mr. Belvin PERRY
125 President Emerita ..... Dr. Trudie KIBBE REED
03 Sr Advisor to the President for IE ..... Dr. Narendra H. PATEL
10 CFO/VP for Fiscal Affairs ..... Mr. John PITTMAN
05 VP for Academic Affairs/ Provost ..... Dr. Helena MARIELLA-WALROND
32 VP for Student Affairs ..... Vacant
84 VP for Enrollment Management ..... Mr. Warren HEUSNER
111 VP for Institutional Advancement ..... Dr. Clifford PORTER
13 CIO/VP for Information Technology ... Dr. Franklin E. PATTERSON
41 VP for Intercollegiate Athletics ..... Mr. Lynn W. THOMPSON
43 VP for Legal Affairs ..... Vacant
21 AVP for Fiscal Affairs ..... Vacant
20 Assoc Prov/Chief Research Officer ..... Vacant
20 Associate Provost for Faculty ..... Dr. Herbert THOMPSON
25 AVP Title III & Spons Research ..... Ms. Chelsea WASHINGTON
35 AVP/Dean of Students ..... Vacant
39 Assoc Dean Res Life & Housing ..... Dr. Janice WADE
102 AVP Foundations & Corp Relations ..... Ms. Chipella JORDAN
23 Asst VP for Health & Wellness ..... Mrs. Nadine HEUSNER
50 Dean College of Business ..... Mrs. Ida WRIGHT
53 Dean College of Education ..... Dr. Stephanie PASLEY-HENRY

58 Dean School of Graduate Studies ..... Dr. Deanna WATHINGTON
76 Exec Dean College of Health Sci ..... Dr. Deanna WATHINGTON
88 Dean Hospitality Management .... Dr. Deanne WILLIAMS-BRYANT
49 Dean College of Liberal Arts ..... Dr. Janice ALLEN-KELSEY
66 Dean School of Nursing ..... Dr. Sandra TUCKER
104 Dean Global Online ..... Dr. Arletha MCSWAIN
60 Dean Perf Arts & Communication ..... Dr. Hiram POWELL
73 Dean School of Religion ..... Dr. Randolph BRACY, JR.
81 Dean Science/Engineering and Math ..... Dr. Herbert THOMPSON
08 Dean of the Library/Chief Librarian ..... Dr. Tasha LUCAS-YOUMANS
19 Exec Director Campus Safety ..... Mr. Gary PRICE
07 Director of Admissions ..... Vacant
04 Executive Asst to the President ..... Vacant
37 Director of Financial Aid ..... Ms. Salina HAMILTON
91 Director of Administrative Systems ..... Ms. Anna HEIN
06 Acting Registrar ..... Mr. Hubert L. JAMES, II
15 Director of Human Resources ..... Ms. Valencia STUBBS
42 Chaplain ..... Rev. Kenya LOVELL
101 Board Liaison ..... Vacant
36 Director of Career Development ..... Ms. Davita BONNER
26 Director of Communications ..... Ms. Joy JONES
30 Director of Development ..... Mrs. Ashley STOEKEL
88 Director of Testing ..... Ms. Annette YEARBY
105 Director Web Services ..... Mr. Julian WALKER
29 Director Alumni Affairs ..... Ms. Marah BELTZ
88 Director Male Develop Initiatives ..... Mr. Jermaine MCKINNEY
121 Director New Student Services ..... Ms. LaToya SHANNON
113 Director Student Accounts ..... Ms. Sandra BROWN
108 Assessment Coordinator ..... Mrs. Jennifer DASH

Braxton College (G)

27975 Old 41 Road, Suite 201, Bonita Springs FL 34135

County: Lee | Identification: 667266
Telephone: (239) 992-4624 | Carnegie Class: Not Classified
FAX Number: (239) 405-8024 | Calendar System: Semester
URL: www.braxton.edu
Established: 2008 | Annual Undergrad Tuition & Fees: N/A
Enrollment: N/A | Coed
Affiliation or Control: Proprietary | IRS Status: Proprietary
Highest Offering: Associate Degree
Accreditation: ABHES

01 Medical Director/Founder ..... Dr. Antonio GANDIA
05 Vice President of Academics ..... Mr. Bill MCGRATH
07 VP Admissions & Compliance ..... Mr. Richard GONZALEZ
13 Director of Information Technology ..... Mr. Freddie BATISTA

Broward College (H)

111 E Las Olas Boulevard,
Fort Lauderdale FL 33301-2298

County: Broward | FICE Identification: 001500
Unit ID: 132709
Telephone: (954) 201-7350 | Carnegie Class: Bac/Assoc-Assoc Dom
FAX Number: (954) 201-7576 | Calendar System: Trimester
URL: www.broward.edu
Established: 1959 | Annual Undergrad Tuition & Fees (In-State): $2,830
Enrollment: 40,754 | Coed
Affiliation or Control: State | IRS Status: 501(c)3
Highest Offering: Baccalaureate
Accreditation: SC, ADNUR, ART, CAHIIM, COARC, DA, DH, DMS, EMT, MAC, MUS, NMT, NURSE, OPD, PTAA, RAD, RTT, THEA

01 President ..... Mr. Gregory Adam HAILE
05 Int Provost/Sr VP Academic Affairs ..... Dr. Marielena DESANCTIS
10 Sr Vice Pres Finance/Administration ..... Mr. Thomas OLLIFF
84 Vice Pres Enrollment Mgmt ..... Dr. Marielena DESANCTIS
32 Vice Pres Student Services ..... Ms. Janice STUBBS
26 VP Public Affairs and Marketing ..... Mr. Don COOK
11 Vice President of Operations ..... Mr. John DUNNUCK
111 VP Advanc/Exec Dir BC Foundation ..... Ms. Nancy O'DONNELL-WILSON
13 Vice President Info Technology ..... Ms. Patti BARNEY
86 VP Govt Policy/Regulatory Affairs ..... Vacant
103 Executive Director Workforce Educ ..... Ms. Mildred COYNE
100 Chief of Staff ..... Ms. Adriana FAZZANO FICANO
12 Campus President BC Online ..... Dr. David SHULMAN
12 Int Campus President Central Campus ..... Dr. Sunem BEATON-GARCIA
12 Campus President North Campus ..... Dr. Avis PROCTOR
12 Campus President South Campus ..... Dr. Rolando GARCIA
21 Chief Financial Officer ..... Mr. Jayson IROFF
18 Chief Facilities/Physical Plant ..... Mr. Sean DEVANEY
09 Dean Institutional Research ..... Vacant
45 Dean Inst Planning/Effectiveness ..... Dr. Deborah POSNER
08 Dean of Libraries/Learning Res ..... Ms. Sarah WIGGINS
37 AVP Student Financial Aid ..... Ms. Theresa COWAN
15 Exec Director Human Res & Equity ..... Dr. Denese EDSALL
06 Registrar ..... Ms. Karen LEE MURPHY
29 Director Alumni Relations ..... Ms. Mary WORKMAN
04 Sr Exec Asst to the President ..... Mrs. Avis M. MCCOY
19 Director Security/Safety ..... Mr. Peter AGNESI
25 Chief Contracts/Grants Admin ..... Ms. Kareen TORRES
96 Director of Purchasing ..... Dr. Judy SCHMELZER

Cambridge College (I)

5150 Linton Boulevard, Suite 340, Delray Beach FL 33484

County: Palm Beach | FICE Identification: 040834
Unit ID: 454865
Telephone: (561) 381-4990 | Carnegie Class: Spec 2-yr-Health
FAX Number: (561) 381-4992 | Calendar System: Other

URL: www.cambridgehealth.edu
Established: Annual Undergrad Tuition & Fees: $15,190
Enrollment: 164 Coed
Affiliation or Control: Proprietary IRS Status: Proprietary
Highest Offering: Associate Degree
Accreditation: ABHES, DMS

01 Chancellor and CEO .... Dr. Terrence LAPIER

Cambridge Institute of Allied Health & Technology-Altamonte Springs (A)

460 E. Altamonte Drive, Third Floor, Altamonte Springs FL 32701
County: Seminole FICE Identification: 038425
Unit ID: 446109
Telephone: (407) 265-8383 Carnegie Class: Not Classified
FAX Number: (407) 265-8384 Calendar System: Other
URL: www.cambridgehealth.edu
Established: Annual Undergrad Tuition & Fees: $14,837
Enrollment: 61 Coed
Affiliation or Control: Proprietary IRS Status: Proprietary
Highest Offering: Baccalaureate
Accreditation: ABHES

01 President .... Dr. Terrance LAPIER
12 Campus Director .... Michael ZUCCHERI
07 Director of Admissions .... Sheree FORD
06 Registrar .... Kristie MCCARTHY
08 Librarian .... Barbara LUNDI
37 Financial Aid Manager .... Monica ROBLES
36 Careers Services Director .... Theresa MANTOVANI

Center of Cinematography, Art & Television (B)

1637 NW 27th Avenue, Miami FL 33125
Telephone: (305) 634-0550 Identification: 770562
Accreditation: ACCSC

† Branch campus of Colegio de Cinematografia, Artes y Television, Bayamon, PR

Chamberlain University-Jacksonville (C)

5200 Belfort Road, Suite 100, Jacksonville FL 32256
Telephone: (904) 251-8100 Identification: 770501
Accreditation: &NH, NURSE

† Branch campus of Chamberlain University-Addison, Addison, IL

Chamberlain University-Miramar (D)

2300 SW 145th Avenue, Miramar FL 33027
Telephone: (954) 885-3510 Identification: 770498
Accreditation: &NH, NURSE

† Branch campus of Chamberlain University-Addison, Addison, IL

Chi Institute of Traditional Chinese Veterinary Medicine (E)

9650 West Highway 318, Reddick FL 32686
County: Marion Identification: 667354
Telephone: (352) 591-5385 Carnegie Class: Not Classified
FAX Number: (800) 860-1543 Calendar System: Other
URL: www.tcvm.com
Established: 1998 Annual Graduate Tuition & Fees: N/A
Enrollment: N/A Coed
Affiliation or Control: Proprietary IRS Status: Proprietary
Highest Offering: Master's; No Undergraduates
Accreditation: DEAC

01 Campus Director .... Mr. Zhen ZHAO

Chipola College (F)

3094 Indian Circle, Marianna FL 32446-3065
County: Jackson FICE Identification: 001472
Unit ID: 133021
Telephone: (850) 526-2761 Carnegie Class: Bac/Assoc-Mixed
FAX Number: (850) 718-2388 Calendar System: Semester
URL: www.chipola.edu
Established: 1947 Annual Undergrad Tuition & Fees (In-District): $3,120
Enrollment: 2,092 Coed
Affiliation or Control: State/Local IRS Status: 501(c)3
Highest Offering: Baccalaureate
Accreditation: SC, ADNUR, EMT, NUR

01 President .... Dr. Sarah CLEMMONS
05 VP of Instructional Affairs .... Dr. Pam RENTZ
10 Vice Pres of Admin & Business Svcs .... Mr. Steve YOUNG
15 Assoc VP of HR & Equity .... Mrs. Wendy PIPPEN
13 Associate VP Information Systems .... Mr. Dennis F. EVERETT
108 Dean Assessment/Compliance & Grant .... Dr. Matthew HUGHES
18 Dir Facilities & Campus Operations .... Mr. Dennis KOSCIW
26 Director Public Relations .... Dr. Bryan C. CRAVEN
07 Dir of Enrollment Services .... Mr. Shannon MERCER
37 Director of Financial Aid .... Ms. Beverly HAMBRIGHT
41 Director of Athletics .... Mr. Jeffrey JOHNSON
06 Registrar .... Ms. Melynda HOWELL
04 Administrative Asst to President .... Ms. Jan CUMMINGS
103 Dir Workforce/Career Development .... Mr. Darwin GILMORE
08 Dir of Learning Resources .... Ms. Vikki MILTON
102 Dir Found/Corporate Relations .... Ms. Julie FUQUA

City College (G)

177 Montgomery Road, Altamonte Springs FL 32714
County: Seminole FICE Identification: 030799
Unit ID: 417327
Telephone: (407) 831-9816 Carnegie Class: Assoc/HVT-High Trad
FAX Number: (407) 831-1147 Calendar System: Quarter
URL: www.citycollegeorlando.edu
Established: 1997 Annual Undergrad Tuition & Fees: $14,539
Enrollment: 189 Coed
Affiliation or Control: Independent Non-Profit IRS Status: 501(c)3
Highest Offering: Associate Degree
Accreditation: ABHES, ADNUR, EMT, SURTEC

01 President .... Mrs. Esther FIKE-CURRY
05 Executive Director .... Mrs. Heidi K. POLLPETER
07 Director Admissions .... Mr. Richard CZENSZAK

City College (H)

2000 W Commercial Boulevard, Fort Lauderdale FL 33309-1916
County: Broward FICE Identification: 025154
Unit ID: 244233
Telephone: (954) 492-5353 Carnegie Class: Bac/Assoc-Mixed
FAX Number: (954) 958-9257 Calendar System: Quarter
URL: www.citycollege.edu
Established: 1983 Annual Undergrad Tuition & Fees: $14,539
Enrollment: 401 Coed
Affiliation or Control: Independent Non-Profit IRS Status: 501(c)3
Highest Offering: Baccalaureate
Accreditation: ABHES, EMT, SURTEC

01 President .... Esther FIKE-CURRY
05 Director of Education .... Dr. Anie BONILLA
36 Director of Career Development .... Carl BRUNSWICK
07 Director of Admissions .... Stacey KRAHE
13 Director Information Technology .... Alan BUSHKIN
08 Director of Library .... Vacant
06 Registrar .... Jennifer TOSUM
15 Director Human Resources .... Natasga GROYSMAN
37 Asst Director Student Financial Aid .... Patty PATTERSON
106 Dir Online Education/E-learning .... Dr. Suzanne MORRISON-WILLAIMS
108 Dir Institutional Effectiveness .... Heather PAYNE
18 Director of Facilities .... Donna VARELA

City College (I)

7001 NW Fourth Boulevard, Gainesville FL 32607
Telephone: (352) 415-4497 Identification: 666413
Accreditation: ABHES, EMT

† Branch campus of City College, Fort Lauderdale, FL.

City College (J)

6565 Taft Street, Hollywood FL 33024
Telephone: (954) 744-1777 Identification: 770674
Accreditation: ABHES

City College (K)

9300 S Dadeland Blvd, Suite 200, Miami FL 33156
Telephone: (305) 666-9242 Identification: 666414
Accreditation: ABHES, EMT, SURTEC

† Branch campus of City College, Fort Lauderdale, FL.

College of Business and Technology (L)

8700 W. Flagler Street, Suite 420, Miami FL 33174
County: Miami-Dade FICE Identification: 030716
Unit ID: 417318
Telephone: (305) 273-4499 Carnegie Class: Bac/Assoc-Mixed
FAX Number: (305) 270-0779 Calendar System: Semester
URL: www.cbt.edu
Established: 1988 Annual Undergrad Tuition & Fees: $13,052
Enrollment: 5 Coed
Affiliation or Control: Proprietary IRS Status: Proprietary
Highest Offering: Associate Degree
Accreditation: ACICS

01 CEO/President .... Ms. Monica LLERENA
10 Finance Director .... Ms. Maricel SPEZZACATENA
12 Campus Director .... Mr. Peter BASTIONY
20 Director of Academic Operations .... Mr. Kibrab ASEFAW
37 Financial Aid Director .... Mrs. Yazmin PALMA
07 Director of Admissions .... Ms. Jenny HERNANDEZ
36 Career Services Director .... Ms. Danaweise JEAN-JOSEPH
30 Director Business Development .... Mr. Luis LLERENA
08 Head Librarian .... Ms. Jennifer ROMAN
15 HR Manager .... Ms. Odalys DIPP
88 Compliance Manager .... Mr. Hector DUENAS

College of Business and Technology - Cutler Bay (M)

19151 South Dixie Highway, Cutler Bay FL 33157
Telephone: (305) 273-4499 Identification: 770677
Accreditation: ACICS, CAHIIM

College of Business and Technology - Hialeah Campus (N)

935 West 49th Street, Hialeah FL 33012
Telephone: (305) 273-4499 Identification: 770675
Accreditation: ACICS

College of Central Florida (O)

3001 S.W. College Road, Ocala FL 34474
County: Marion FICE Identification: 001471
Unit ID: 132851
Telephone: (352) 237-2111 Carnegie Class: Bac/Assoc-Mixed
FAX Number: (352) 291-4450 Calendar System: Semester
URL: www.cf.edu
Established: 1957 Annual Undergrad Tuition & Fees (In-District): $2,570
Enrollment: 7,151 Coed
Affiliation or Control: Local IRS Status: 501(c)3
Highest Offering: Baccalaureate
Accreditation: SC, ADNUR, CAHIIM, DA, EMT, NUR, PTAA, RAD, SURGT

01 President .... Dr. James D. HENNINGSEN
10 Vice Pres Administration & Finance .... Mr. Francis J. MAZUR, III
05 Vice President Academic Affairs .... Dr. Mark PAUGH
32 Vice President Student Affairs .... Dr. Saul REYES
12 Vice President Regional Campuses .... Dr. Vernon LAWTER, JR.
86 Manager Government Relations .... Ms. Jessica KUMMERLE
09 VP Inst Effectiveness/College Rels .... Dr. Jillian RAMSAMMY
26 Director Marketing/Public Relations .... Ms. Lois BRAUCKMULLER
102 Executive Director Foundation .... Mr. Christopher KNIFE
21 Assistant VP for Finance .... Mr. Steven ASH
12 Provost Jack Wilkinson Levy Campus . Ms. Holland MCGLASHAN
88 Dean Public Service/Criminal Just .... Mr. Charles MCINTOSH
75 Dean Bus Tech Careers & Tech Educ .... Dr. Rob WOLF
35 Dean Student Services .... Dr. Henri BENLOLO
49 Associate Vice Pres Arts & Sciences .... Dr. Allan DANUFF
35 Dean Student Success .... Vacant
103 Assoc Vice Pres Career & Prof Pgms .... Dr. Jennifer FRYNS
84 Dean Enrollment Management .... Ms. Maureen ANDERSON
76 Dean Health Sciences .... Dr. Stephanie CORTES
106 Dean E-learning & Learning Resource .... Dr. Tamara VIVIANO-BRODERICK
37 Director Financial Aid .... Mr. Patrick HOFFMAN
09 Dir Inst Research & Effectiveness .... Ms. Judy MENADIER
07 Dir Admissions/Stdnt Recruitment .... Dr. Raphel ROBINSON
18 Director Facilities .... Mr. Tommy MORELOCK
15 Director Human Resources .... Ms. Jennifer KLEPFER
35 Director Student Life .... Ms. Marjorie MCGEE
88 Director Student Support Services .... Ms. Lisa SMITH
41 Director Athletics/Wellness .... Mr. Bob ZELINSKI
88 Director Access and Counsel Service .... Ms. Victoria COLLELI
121 Dir Stdnt Success & Educ Outreach .... Dr. Leonard EVERETT
88 Director Appleton Museum of Art .... Vacant
25 Director of Resource Dev/Accred .... Mr. Matt MATTHEWS
96 Dir Purchasing & Risk Mgmt .... Mr. Stewart TRAUTMAN
08 Library Director .... Ms. Teresa FAUST
19 Manager Public Safety .... Mr. Lewis PREVATT
109 Manager Printing & Postal Service .... Mr. Andrew LOWREY
109 Manager Conference & Food Service .... Ms. Cheryl CROSBY
13 Associate VP Information Technology .... Mr. Henry GLASPIE
06 Director Enroll Services/Registrar .... Dr. Alton AUSTIN
30 Director of Development .... Ms. Traci MASON

Concorde Career Institute (P)

7259 Salisbury Road, Jacksonville FL 32256
County: Duval FICE Identification: 020896
Unit ID: 133845
Telephone: (904) 725-0525 Carnegie Class: Spec 2-yr-Health
FAX Number: (904) 721-9944 Calendar System: Semester
URL: www.concorde.edu
Established: 1988 Annual Undergrad Tuition & Fees: N/A
Enrollment: 621 Coed
Affiliation or Control: Proprietary IRS Status: Proprietary
Highest Offering: Associate Degree
Accreditation: ACCSC, COARC, PTAA, SURGT

01 Campus President .... Melissa RYAN

Concorde Career Institute (Q)

10933 Marks Way, Miramar FL 33025
County: Broward FICE Identification: 022751
Unit ID: 133854
Telephone: (954) 731-8880 Carnegie Class: Spec 2-yr-Health
FAX Number: (954) 484-2961 Calendar System: Other
URL: www.concorde.edu
Established: 1989 Annual Undergrad Tuition & Fees: N/A
Enrollment: 528 Coed
Affiliation or Control: Proprietary IRS Status: Proprietary
Highest Offering: Associate Degree
Accreditation: ACCSC, COARC, OTA, PTAA, SURGT

01 Campus President .... Matthew DIACONT

Concorde Career Institute (A)

3444 McCrory Place, Orlando FL 32803
Telephone: (407) 812-3060 Identification: 770563
Accreditation: ACCSC

Concorde Career Institute (B)

4202 West Spruce Street, Tampa FL 33607-4127
County: Hillsborough FICE Identification: 021727
Unit ID: 133863
Telephone: (813) 874-0094 Carnegie Class: Spec 2-yr-Health
FAX Number: (813) 872-6884 Calendar System: Other
URL: www.concorde.edu
Established: 1978 Annual Undergrad Tuition & Fees: N/A
Enrollment: 511 Coed
Affiliation or Control: Proprietary IRS Status: Proprietary
Highest Offering: Associate Degree
Accreditation: ACCSC, COARC, SURGT

01 Campus President ... Ms. Debra WENINGER

Daytona College (C)

425 South Nova Road, Ormond Beach FL 32174-8449
County: Volusia FICE Identification: 039396
Unit ID: 447014
Telephone: (386) 267-0565 Carnegie Class: Spec 2-yr-Health
FAX Number: (386) 267-0567 Calendar System: Semester
URL: www.daytonacollege.edu
Established: 1996 Annual Undergrad Tuition & Fees: N/A
Enrollment: 270 Coed
Affiliation or Control: Proprietary IRS Status: Proprietary
Highest Offering: Associate Degree
Accreditation: ACCSC, ADNUR

01 President ... Mr. Roger BRADLEY
05 Director ... Mr. Justin BERKOWITZ

Daytona State College (D)

PO Box 2811, Daytona Beach FL 32120-2811
County: Volusia FICE Identification: 001475
Unit ID: 133386
Telephone: (386) 506-3000 Carnegie Class: Bac/Assoc-Mixed
FAX Number: N/A Calendar System: Semester
URL: www.DaytonaState.edu
Established: 1957 Annual Undergrad Tuition & Fees (In-District): $3,104
Enrollment: 13,970 Coed
Affiliation or Control: State/Local IRS Status: 501(c)3
Highest Offering: Baccalaureate
Accreditation: SC, ADNUR, CAHIIM, COARC, DA, DH, EMT, MAC, NUR, OTA, PTAA, SURGT

01 President ... Dr. Thomas LOBASSO
03 Executive Vice President ... Mr. Brian T. BABB
05 Provost ... Dr. Amy LOCKLEAR
10 Chief Business Officer ... Ms. Isalene MONTGOMERY
13 VP Information Technology ... Mr. Roberto LOMBARDO
15 AVP Human Resources ... Ms. Robin BARR
84 VP Enrollment Services ... Dr. Erik D'AQUINO
103 AVP Workforce & Cont Educ ... Dr. Sherryl WEEMS
08 Head Librarian ... Ms. Mercedes CLEMENT
49 AVP Arts & Science ... Dr. Alycia EHLERT
69 AVP College of Health ... Dr. Colin CHESLEY
106 Director Instructional Resources ... Mr. Hector VALLE
32 VP Student Development ... Mr. Keith KENNEDY
18 AVP Facilities Planning ... Mr. Christopher WAINWRIGHT
09 Dir Institutional Research ... Dr. Andrea GIBSON
37 Director Financial Aid ... Ms. Heidi PINNEY
88 Dean School of Health & Wellness ... Mr. Will DUNNE
19 Director Campus Safety ... Mr. Louie MERCER
12 Dean DeLand & Deltona Campuses ... Mr. Neil CLEMONS
12 Dean New Smryna Beach Campus ... Mr. Clarence MCCLOUD
43 College Counsel ... Mr. Brian BABB
51 Director Ctr for Business/Industry ... Mr. Frank MERCER
35 Asst Dean Student Life ... Mr. Bruce COOK
121 Director Academic Advising ... Ms. Michelle GOLDYS
07 Director Admissions/Recruitment ... Ms. Karen SANDERS
22 Director of Equity & Inclusion ... Mr. Lonnie THOMPSON
21 AVP Accounting ... Ms. Tina MYERS
06 Director Student Accounts ... Ms. Cerese RAMOS
26 Director of Marketing ... Mr. Chris THOMES
09 Dean Institutional Effectiveness ... Dr. Karla MOORE
102 Executive Director Foundation ... Mr. Timothy NORTON
29 Director Alumni Relations ... Ms. Suzette CAMERON
96 Director of Purchasing ... Ms. Elaine THIEL
50 AVP Business/Engr & Tech ... Mr. Dante LEON

Dolphin Research Center Training Institute (E)

58901 Overseas Hwy, Grassy Key FL 33050
County: Monroe Identification: 667338
Telephone: (305) 289-1121 Carnegie Class: Not Classified
FAX Number: N/A Calendar System: Other
URL: www.DolphinInstitute.edu
Established: 2012 Annual Undergrad Tuition & Fees: N/A
Enrollment: N/A Coed
Affiliation or Control: Independent Non-Profit IRS Status: 501(c)3
Highest Offering: Associate Degree
Accreditation: ACCSC

01 President & CEO ... Rita IRWIN
05 Director ... Linda ERB
06 Registrar ... Maria COVELLI

Doral College (F)

11100 NW 27th St, Bldg C-109, Doral FL 33172
County: Miami-Dade Identification: 667335
Telephone: (305) 463-7210 Carnegie Class: Not Classified
FAX Number: (305) 477-3525 Calendar System: Semester
URL: www.doralcollege.edu
Established: 2011 Annual Undergrad Tuition & Fees: N/A
Enrollment: N/A Coed
Affiliation or Control: Independent Non-Profit IRS Status: 501(c)3
Highest Offering: Associate Degree
Accreditation: DEAC

01 President ... Douglas RODRIGUEZ

Dragon Rises College of Oriental Medicine (G)

1000 NE 16th Ave., Building F, Gainesville FL 32601-4557
County: Alachua FICE Identification: 038883
Unit ID: 449481
Telephone: (352) 371-2833 Carnegie Class: Spec-4-yr-Other Health
FAX Number: (352) 244-0003 Calendar System: Semester
URL: www.dragonrises.edu
Established: 2001 Annual Undergrad Tuition & Fees: N/A
Enrollment: 49 Coed
Affiliation or Control: Independent Non-Profit IRS Status: 501(c)3
Highest Offering: Master's
Accreditation: ACUP

01 Director/CEO ... Dr. George VALCOURT
05 Academic Dean ... Dr. George VALCOURT
23 Clinic Director ... Mr. Jerrod FLETCHER
32 Dir of Admissions/Student Services ... Mr. Victor WYATT
37 Director of Financial Aid ... Ms. Karen MARTIN-BROWN

East West College of Natural Medicine (H)

3808 N Tamiami Trail, Sarasota FL 34234-5362
County: Sarasota FICE Identification: 034297
Unit ID: 439394
Telephone: (941) 355-9080 Carnegie Class: Spec-4-yr-Other Health
FAX Number: (941) 355-3243 Calendar System: Trimester
URL: www.ewcollege.edu
Established: 1994 Annual Undergrad Tuition & Fees: N/A
Enrollment: 111 Coed
Affiliation or Control: Proprietary IRS Status: Proprietary
Highest Offering: Master's
Accreditation: ACCSC, ACUP

01 President/CEO ... Mr. Russell BATTIATA
05 Academic Dean ... Mr. Yoseph FELEKE
07 Director of Admissions ... Mr. Russell BATTIATA

Eastern Florida State College (I)

3865 N. Wickham Road, Melbourne FL 32935
County: Brevard FICE Identification: 001470
Unit ID: 132693
Telephone: (321) 632-1111 Carnegie Class: Bac/Assoc-Assoc Dom
FAX Number: (321) 633-4565 Calendar System: Semester
URL: www.easternflorida.edu
Established: 1960 Annual Undergrad Tuition & Fees (In-District): $2,496
Enrollment: 15,769 Coed
Affiliation or Control: Local IRS Status: 501(c)3
Highest Offering: Baccalaureate
Accreditation: SC, ADNUR, #COARC, DA, DH, DMS, EMT, MLTAD, PTAA, RAD, SURGT

01 President ... Dr. James H. RICHEY
10 Chief Financial Officer ... Mr. Mark CHERRY
11 VP Operations ... Mr. Richard LAIRD
32 VP Academic & Student Affairs/CLO ... Dr. Linda L. MIEDEMA
41 Assoc Vice Pres of Athletics ... Mr. Jeffrey CARR
18 AVP Facilities & Special Projects ... Mr. Stockton WHITTEN
15 AVP Human Resources ... Ms. Darla FERGUSON
05 AVP Academic Affairs/Provost ... Dr. Sandy HANDFIELD
86 VP External Affairs ... Mr. Jack PARKER
26 AVP Communications ... Mr. John GLISCH
12 Provost Palm Bay Campus ... Dr. Wayne STEIN
12 Provost Cocoa Campus ... Dr. Dedra SIBLEY
12 Provost Titusville Campus/eLearning ... Dr. Philip SIMPSON
103 Executive Director Workforce Pgms ... Mr. Stephen TAYLOR
37 Director Collegewide Financial Aid ... Ms. Eileen BRZOZOWSKI
07 Dir Collegewide Admissions ... Ms. Michelle LOUFEK
04 Executive Asst to the President ... Ms. Gina TAYLOR
06 Registrar ... Ms. Stephanie BURNETTE
09 Exe Dir Plng/Assessment/CIRO ... Dr. Mark QUATHAMER
102 Director EFSC Foundation ... Ms. Jennie KRIETE
36 Exec Dir Career Plng/Development ... Dr. Cathy CADY

Eckerd College (J)

4200 54th Avenue S, Saint Petersburg FL 33711-4700
County: Pinellas FICE Identification: 001487
Unit ID: 133492
Telephone: (727) 867-1166 Carnegie Class: Bac-A&S
FAX Number: (727) 864-1877 Calendar System: 4/1/4
URL: www.eckerd.edu
Established: 1958 Annual Undergrad Tuition & Fees: $44,540
Enrollment: 2,037 Coed
Affiliation or Control: Presbyterian Church (U.S.A.) IRS Status: 501(c)3
Highest Offering: Baccalaureate
Accreditation: SC

01 President ... Dr. Donald R. EASTMAN, III
05 VP/Dean of Faculty ... Dr. Suzan HARRISON
10 VP Business and Finance ... Mr. Christopher P. BRENNAN
03 VP and Secretary of the College ... Dr. Lisa A. METS
111 Vice President Advancement ... Mr. Matthew S. BISSET
107 VP/Dean for Executive Education ... Mr. Kelly KIRSCHNER
32 VP/Dean for Student Life ... Dr. James J. ANNARELLI
84 VP Enrollment Management ... Mr. John SULLIVAN
20 Assoc Dean Faculty Development ... Dr. Kathryn J. WATSON
26 VP Marketing and Communications ... Ms. Valerie GLIEM
15 Director Human Resources ... Ms. Liana HEMINGWAY
09 Exec Director Inst Effectiveness ... Ms. Jacqueline MACNEIL
21 Controller ... Ms. Robin SMALLEY
20 Associate Dean ... Dr. Marjorie SANFILIPPO
110 Assoc VP Advancement ... Mr. Tom SCHNEIDER
11 Assistant VP Operations ... Mr. Adam COLBY
105 Dir Web/Marketing/Communication ... Mr. Michel FOUGERES
88 Director of ASPEC ... Mr. Ken WOLFE
104 Director of International Education ... Ms. Diane L. FERRIS
85 Dir International Student Programs ... Mr. Olivier DEBURE
13 Director of Information Technology ... Mr. Ashley BURT
06 Registrar ... Ms. Laura RAYMOND
08 Director of Library ... Ms. Lisa JOHNSTON
38 Exec Director Counseling & Outreach ... Ms. Linda ABBOTT
29 Director Alumni Relations ... Vacant
19 Director Campus Safety ... Ms. Tonya WOMACK
37 Director Financial Aid ... Dr. Pat E. WATKINS
41 Acting Athletic Director ... Mr. Tom RYAN
07 Director of Admission ... Mr. Jacob BROWNE
42 Chaplain ... Rev. Doug MCMAHON
25 Director of Grant Development ... Ms. Anna RUTH
124 Asst Dean Students for Engagement ... Mr. Fred SABOTA
51 Associate Dean Cont Education ... Ms. Amy APICERNO
04 Administrative Asst to President ... Ms. JoAnn TOWNSEND

ECPI University College of Nursing (K)

660 Century Point, Ste 1050, Lake Mary FL 32746
Telephone: (407) 562-9100 Identification: 770566
Accreditation: &SC, NURSE

† Branch campus of ECPI University, Virginia Beach, VA

Edward Waters College (L)

1658 Kings Road, Jacksonville FL 32209-6199
County: Duval FICE Identification: 001478
Unit ID: 133526
Telephone: (904) 470-8000 Carnegie Class: Bac-Diverse
FAX Number: (904) 470-8039 Calendar System: Semester
URL: www.ewc.edu
Established: 1866 Annual Undergrad Tuition & Fees: $13,525
Enrollment: 3,443 Coed
Affiliation or Control: African Methodist Episcopal IRS Status: 501(c)3
Highest Offering: Baccalaureate
Accreditation: SC, IACBE

01 President ... Dr. A. Zachary FAISON, JR.
11 Executive Vice President/COO ... Dr. Donna H. OLIVER
88 Special Assistant to the President ... Vacant
05 Provost/Sr VP Academic Affairs ... Dr. Donna H. OLIVER
10 VP Business & Finance ... Mr. Randolph MITCHELL
09 VP Inst Research/Plng/ Effectiveness ... Dr. Rigo RINCONES-GOMEZ
111 VP Inst Advance/Dev/Mktg/Comm ... Dr. DeShanna K. BROWN
84 VP Enroll Mgt/Strat Matriculant Svc ... Dr. Thomas J. CALHOUN, JR.
121 VP Student Success/Engagement ... Mr. Mandrake MILLER
21 Assoc VP Business and Finance ... Vacant
15 Director Human Resources ... Ms. Carla GRAVES
25 Dir Title III & Sponsored Pgms ... Vacant
06 Coord of Records/Registration ... Dr. Andrew GORDON
20 Assoc Provost Acad Stdnt Success/RI ... Dr. Stephanie CAMPBELL
37 Director Financial Aid ... Ms. Janice NOWAK
88 Director Upward Bound ... Dr. Delacy SANFORD
36 Career Services Director ... Mr. Antonio STARKE
11 Director Administrative Services ... Vacant
30 Director Development ... Vacant
07 Director of Admissions ... Mr. Joel WALKER
88 Int Director of Support Services ... Ms. Andrea M. CUMMINGS
31 Dir Community Resource Center ... Ms. Marie HEATH
88 Director of CTL ... Vacant
88 Director of FAME ... Ms. Trina WILEY
13 Director IT ... Mr. David SIMFUKWE
08 Library Director ... Ms. Brenda HARRELL
101 Secy of the College/Clerk of Board ... Ms. Jessica RUSSO
26 Marketing/Communication Manager ... Vacant
29 Director of Alumni Affairs ... Vacant
38 Director Counseling Center ... Ms. Ragan SUMMERS

35 Dean of Students .... Vacant
96 Purchasing Clerk .... Ms. Shalliah MCMILLIAN

Embry-Riddle Aeronautical University-Daytona Beach (A)

1 Aerospace Boulevard, Daytona Beach FL 32114-3900
County: Volusia FICE Identification: 001479
Unit ID: 133553
Telephone: (386) 226-6000 Carnegie Class: Masters/M
FAX Number: N/A Calendar System: Semester
URL: www.erau.edu
Established: 1926 Annual Undergrad Tuition & Fees: $35,814
Enrollment: 6,338 Coed
Affiliation or Control: Independent Non-Profit IRS Status: 501(c)3
Highest Offering: Doctorate
Accreditation: SC, AAB, ACBSP, CEA, IFSAC

01 President .... Dr. Barry BUTLER
05 SVP Academic Affairs & Provost .... Mr. Lon D. MOELLER
10 SVP for Finance and CFO .... Dr. Randy B. HOWARD
30 SVP Philanthropy/Alumni Engagement .... Mr. Marc ARCHAMBAULT
15 VP/Chief Human Resources Officer .... Mr. Brandon L. YOUNG
43 Vice President & General Counsel .... Mr. Charlie W. SEVASTOS
26 VP Marketing & Communications .... Ms. Anne BRODERICK BOTTERI
13 Chief Information Officer .... Ms. Becky L. VASQUEZ
09 Exec Dir of Institutional Research .... Ms. Maria FRANCO
29 Exec Director of Alumni Relations .... Mr. William G. THOMPSON
39 Dir of Housing & Res Life .... Mr. Edward j. WALICKI
41 Director of Athletics .... Mr. John M. PHILLIPS
04 Senior Executive Asst to President .... Ms. Chantal C. CRISWELL
84 Dean of Enrollment Management .... Mr. Robert J. ADAMS
104 Dir Office of Global Engagement .... Mrs. Sue A. MACCHIARELLA
108 Exec Dir of Academic Assessment .... Ms. Tiffany D. PHAGAN
32 Assoc Provost and Dean of Students .... Ms. Lisa S. KOLLAR
36 Executive Director of Career Svcs .... Ms. Alicia SMYTH
37 Director Student Financial Aid .... Ms. Barbara DRYDEN
49 Dean College of Arts & Sciences .... Dr. Karen GAINES
88 Dean College of Aviation .... Dr. Alan STOLZER
50 Dean O'Maley College of Business .... Dr. Michael J. WILLIAMS
54 Dean College of Engineering .... Dr. Maj MIRMIRANI
08 Hunt Library Director .... Ms. Anne M. CASEY

Embry-Riddle Aeronautical University-Worldwide (B)

1 Aerospace Boulevard, Daytona Beach FL 32114-3900
Telephone: (800) 522-6787 Identification: 666089
Accreditation: &SC, AAB, ACBSP

† Regional accreditation is carried under the parent institution in Daytona Beach, FL.

Emergency Educational Institute (C)

3111 N. University Dr., Ste 300, Coral Springs FL 33065
County: Broward Identification: 667310
Telephone: (954) 753-6869 Carnegie Class: Not Classified
FAX Number: (954) 755-9050 Calendar System: Other
URL: www.eei.edu
Established: 2002 Annual Undergrad Tuition & Fees: N/A
Enrollment: N/A Coed
Affiliation or Control: Proprietary IRS Status: Proprietary
Highest Offering: Associate Degree
Accreditation: ABHES

01 CEO .... Michelle UGALDE
66 Director of Nursing .... Michelle UGALDE
07 Admissions/Registrar .... Toni Ann LABRIOLA

Everglades University (D)

5002 T-Rex Avenue, Suite 100,
Boca Raton FL 33431-4493
County: Palm Beach FICE Identification: 031085
Unit ID: 385619
Telephone: (888) 772-6077 Carnegie Class: Masters/M
FAX Number: (561) 912-1191 Calendar System: Semester
URL: www.evergladesuniversity.edu
Established: 1990 Annual Undergrad Tuition & Fees: $17,600
Enrollment: 2,444 Coed
Affiliation or Control: Independent Non-Profit IRS Status: 501(c)3
Highest Offering: Master's
Accreditation: SC

01 President/CEO .... Ms. Kristi L. MOLLIS
05 Vice President of Academic Affairs .... Dr. Jared BEZET
37 Regional Director of Financial Aid .... Mrs. Seeta SINGH MOONILALL
10 Chief Financial Officer .... Mr. Joseph BERARDINELLI
26 Director of Marketing .... Ms. Christina OAKLEY
09 Director Inst Effectiveness .... Chee PIOG
88 Program Dir of Aviation .... Ms. Vickie RAMOS
84 Regional Dir Enrollment Management .... Ms. Marci TULLT

Flagler College (E)

74 King Street, Saint Augustine FL 32084-4342
County: Saint Johns FICE Identification: 007893
Unit ID: 133711
Telephone: (904) 829-6200 Carnegie Class: Bac-Diverse
FAX Number: (904) 824-6017 Calendar System: Semester
URL: www.flagler.edu
Established: 1968 Annual Undergrad Tuition & Fees: $18,950
Enrollment: 2,689 Coed
Affiliation or Control: Independent Non-Profit IRS Status: 501(c)3
Highest Offering: Master's
Accreditation: SC

01 President .... Dr. Joseph G. JOYNER
00 Chancellor .... Dr. William L. PROCTOR
10 Vice President Business Services .... Mr. David L. CARSON
111 VP of Institutional Advancement .... Ms. Kristina MYERS
05 Vice President Academic Affairs .... Dr. Alan WOOLFOLK
26 Vice Pres Marketing/Communications .... Ms. Carol BRANSON
09 Dir Inst Research & Effectiveness .... Ms. Jessica STOWELL
27 Director of News and Information .... Mr. Brian L. THOMPSON
84 Vice Pres for Enrollment Mgmt .... Ms. Deborah L. THOMPSON
32 Vice President of Student Affairs .... Dr. Sandra MILES
20 Dean of Academic Life .... Dr. Art VANDEN HOUTEN
35 Dean of Student Affairs .... Dr. Dirk HIBLER
38 Director of Counseling .... Dr. Kathy O. PAYNE
06 Registrar .... Mrs. Miriam C. ROBERSON
37 Director of Financial Aid .... Ms. Sheia I. PLEASANT-DOINE
124 Sr Director of Student Engagement .... Ms. Tara STEVENSON
08 Director of Library Services .... Mr. Brian NESSELRODE
41 Director Intercollegiate Athletics .... Mr. Jud DAMON
19 Director of Safety & Security .... Mr. Creig DOYLE
40 Bookstore Manager .... Mr. Trevor SMITH
24 Director Educational Media Services .... Mr. Chris F. CHAYA
13 Chief Information Officer .... Ms. Gwen PECHAN
39 Director of Residence Life .... Ms. Michelle HOLLAND
35 Director of Student Activities .... Ms. Kristina LOMBARDO
12 Dean Flagler College - Tallahassee .... Dr. Wayne RIGGS
22 Dir of Disability Services .... Mr. Phillip POWNALL
18 Superintendent of Plant & Grounds .... Mr. Victor CHENEY
04 Assistant to the President .... Ms. Laura STEVENSON DUMAS
21 Director of Business Services .... Mr. Larry D. WEEKS
29 Sr Dir Alumni & College Relations .... Ms. Margo THOMAS
30 Sr Director of Development .... Mr. Jeffrey DAVITT
15 Chief Human Resources Officer .... Mr. Jim SPRINGFIELD
88 Senior Woman Admin Athletic Dept .... Ms. Karen HUDGINS
07 Dean of Admissions .... Ms. Rachel U. BRANCH
104 Director Study Abroad .... Ms. Lisa FIALA
105 Director Web Services .... Ms. Holly L. HILL
106 Dir Online Education & Inst Design .... Ms. Amy COOK
50 Dean Sch Business/Educ/Math .... Dr. Allison ROBERTS
86 Director Government Relations .... Ms. Beth SWEENY
96 Director of Purchasing .... Ms. Sarah PRODROMOU

Florida Career College (F)

1743 N Congress Avenue, Boynton Beach FL 33426
Telephone: (561) 810-1810 Identification: 770678
Accreditation: ACICS, COE

Florida Career College (G)

3750 West 18th Avenue, Hialeah FL 33012-7028
Telephone: (786) 534-0940 Identification: 666624
Accreditation: ACICS, COE

Florida Career College (H)

6600-10 Youngerman Circle, Jacksonville FL 32244
Telephone: (904) 990-8500 Identification: 770679
Accreditation: ACICS, COE

Florida Career College (I)

3383 North State Road 7,
Lauderdale Lakes FL 33319-5617
Telephone: (954) 908-4700 Identification: 666622
Accreditation: ACICS, COE

Florida Career College - Margate Campus (J)

3271 North State Road 7, Margate FL 33063
Telephone: (954) 935-7921 Identification: 770681
Accreditation: ACICS, COE

Florida Career College (K)

1321 SW 107th Avenue, Suite 201B,
Miami FL 33174-2521
County: Miami-Dade FICE Identification: 023058
Unit ID: 133997
Telephone: (786) 534-0500 Carnegie Class: Assoc/HVT-Mix Trad/Non
FAX Number: (786) 534-0558 Calendar System: Quarter
URL: www.floridacareercollege.edu
Established: 1982 Annual Undergrad Tuition & Fees: N/A
Enrollment: 502 Coed
Affiliation or Control: Proprietary IRS Status: Proprietary
Highest Offering: Associate Degree
Accreditation: ACICS, COE

01 President/CEO .... Mr. Derek KOEBEL
06 Registrar .... Ms. Cheyla DAVILA

Florida Career College (L)

989 N Semoran Boulevard, Orlando FL 32807
Telephone: (321) 430-8300 Identification: 770613
Accreditation: ACICS, COE

Florida Career College (M)

7891 Pines Boulevard, Pembroke Pines FL 33024-6916
Telephone: (954) 399-4801 Identification: 666025
Accreditation: ACICS, COE

Florida Career College (N)

9950 Princess Palm Ave, Suite 100, Tampa FL 33619
Telephone: (813) 906-5900 Identification: 770682
Accreditation: ACICS, COE

Florida Career College (O)

6058 Okeechobee Boulevard, West Palm Beach FL 33417
Telephone: (561) 408-9910 Identification: 770683
Accreditation: ACICS, COE

Florida Coastal School of Law (P)

8787 Baypine, Jacksonville FL 32256-8528
County: Duval FICE Identification: 033743
Unit ID: 434715
Telephone: (904) 680-7700 Carnegie Class: Spec-4-yr-Law
FAX Number: N/A Calendar System: Semester
URL: www.fcsl.edu
Established: 1995 Annual Graduate Tuition & Fees: N/A
Enrollment: 383 Coed
Affiliation or Control: Proprietary IRS Status: Proprietary
Highest Offering: First Professional Degree; No Undergraduates
Accreditation: LAW

01 Dean .... Mr. Scott DEVITO
07 Director of Admissions .... Ms. Megan SCHADE
32 Assistant Dean of Student Affairs .... Mr. James ARTLEY
05 Dean of Academics .... Ms. Jennifer REIBER
88 Director of Experiential Learning .... Ms. Ericka CURRAN
09 Mgr of Institutional Effectiveness .... Ms. Karen EUBANKS
88 Process Partner .... Ms. Lisa VERVYNCK
10 Comptroller .... Mr. Ron BAMBACUS

Florida College (Q)

119 N Glen Arven Avenue,
Temple Terrace FL 33617-5578
County: Hillsborough FICE Identification: 001482
Unit ID: 133809
Telephone: (813) 988-5131 Carnegie Class: Bac/Assoc-Mixed
FAX Number: (813) 899-6772 Calendar System: Semester
URL: www.floridacollege.edu
Established: 1944 Annual Undergrad Tuition & Fees: $17,142
Enrollment: 508 Coed
Affiliation or Control: Independent Non-Profit IRS Status: 501(c)3
Highest Offering: Baccalaureate
Accreditation: SC, MUS

01 President .... Dr. Harry E. PAYNE, JR.
05 Vice President & Academic Dean .... Dr. Daniel W. PETTY
32 Dean of Student Services .... Dr. Jason S. LONGSTRETH
10 Chief Business Officer .... Mr. Jamie LEWIS
37 Director Student Financial Aid .... Miss Erin MCALLISTER
07 Dir of Admissions & Retention Svcs .... Miss Virginia MANESS
09 Director of Institutional Research .... Dr. M. Thaxter DICKEY
88 Director of Advising .... Dr. Brian L. CRISPELL
06 Registrar .... Ms. Beth A. GRANT
08 Director of Library .... Mrs. Wanda DICKEY
91 Director of Information Technology .... Mr. Jon RAE
30 Director of Development .... Mr. Adam OLSON
29 Director of Alumni Relations .... Mr. Adam J. OLSON
40 Manager of Bookstore .... Mr. Stephen BLAYLOCK
88 Events Coordinator .... Mrs. Sharon L. CLARK
41 Athletic Director .... Mr. Pat TODD

Florida College of Integrative Medicine (R)

7100 Lake Ellenor Drive, Orlando FL 32809-5721
County: Orange FICE Identification: 032383
Unit ID: 434441
Telephone: (407) 888-8689 Carnegie Class: Spec-4-yr-Other Health
FAX Number: (407) 888-8211 Calendar System: Semester
URL: www.fcim.edu
Established: 1990 Annual Undergrad Tuition & Fees: N/A
Enrollment: 90 Coed
Affiliation or Control: Proprietary IRS Status: Proprietary
Highest Offering: Master's; No Lower Division
Accreditation: ACUP

01 President .... Mr. Lincoln Z. ZHAO
03 Vice President .... Ms. Jenjen HAN
108 Vice Pres/Chief Quality Officer .... Ms. Yuan-Yuan HAN
05 Dean of Academic Affairs .... Dr. Lin CHAI
10 Director of Finance .... Ms. Susan HOEH
07 Admissions Representative .... Ms. Michelle COLON
37 Director of Financial Aid .... Ms. Mary SIMMONS

Florida Gateway College (A)

149 SE College Place, Lake City FL 32025-2007
County: Columbia FICE Identification: 001501
Unit ID: 135160
Telephone: (386) 752-1822 Carnegie Class: Bac/Assoc-Assoc Dom
FAX Number: (386) 755-1521 Calendar System: Semester
URL: www.fgc.edu
Established: 1947 Annual Undergrad Tuition & Fees (In-State): $3,100
Enrollment: 3,292 Coed
Affiliation or Control: State IRS Status: 501(c)3
Highest Offering: Baccalaureate
Accreditation: SC, ADNUR, CAHIIM, EMT, NURSE, PTAA

01 President .... Dr. Lawrence BARRETT
10 Vice President Business Services .... Ms. Michelle HOLLOWAY
04 Assistant to the President .... Ms. Karyn CONGRESSI
05 Vice President for Academic Affairs .... Dr. Brian DOPSON
84 VP Enroll Mgmt & Student Affairs .... Dr. Jennifer PRICE
20 Dean of Academic Pgm & Bacc Liaison .... Dr. Paula GAVIN
13 Exec Dir Info Technology/CIO .... Mr. Mark STEINGART
72 Exec Dir of Tech Pgm & Public Svcs .... Mr. John JEWETT
15 Executive Director Human Resources .... Ms. Sharon BEST
53 Exec Dir Teacher Prep Programs .... Ms. Pamela CARSWELL
30 Exec Director Resource Development .... Mr. Lee PINCHOUCK
26 Exec Dir Media & Community Info .... Mr. Mike MCKEE
37 Director Financial Aid .... Mrs. Becky WESTBERRY
26 Dir Recruitment & Communication .... Ms. Kacey SCHRADER
06 Registrar & Dir of Enrollment Svcs .... Ms. Gayle HUNTER
21 Director Business Services .... Mr. Joseph HOLMES
25 Director of Grants & Grant Mgmt .... Ms. Sandra JOHNSTON
09 Director of Inst Effect & Assess .... Ms. Rebecca VANHOEK
66 Exec Director Nursing .... Dr. Shane NEELY-SMITH
18 Director Facilities .... Mr. Lance JONES
96 Director Procurement & Contracts .... Ms. Misty TAYLOR
121 Director Student Engagement .... Ms. Michele CUADRAS
36 Director of Career Services .... Vacant
88 Director Public Service Trng Pgms .... Mr. Jay SWISHER
08 Director Library .... Ms. Christine BOATRIGHT
32 Director of Student Life .... Dr. Mary Ann BEGLEY

Florida Institute of Technology (B)

150 W University Boulevard, Melbourne FL 32901-6975
County: Brevard FICE Identification: 001469
Unit ID: 133881
Telephone: (321) 674-8000 Carnegie Class: DU-Higher
FAX Number: (321) 984-8461 Calendar System: Semester
URL: www.fit.edu
Established: 1958 Annual Undergrad Tuition & Fees: $41,850
Enrollment: 6,402 Coed
Affiliation or Control: Independent Non-Profit IRS Status: 501(c)3
Highest Offering: Doctorate
Accreditation: SC, AAB, CLPSY, IACBE

01 President .... Dr. T. Dwayne MCCAY
04 Exec Asst to Pres .... Ms. Rebecca CROOK
05 Sr VP Academic Administration .... Dr. Monica BALOGA
10 Sr Vice Pres Financial Affairs/CFO .... Ms. Marsha BEWERSDORF
11 Sr Vice Pres Operations .... Mr. Eric KLEDZIK
46 Sr Vice Pres Strategic Initiatives .... Dr. Gisele BENNETT
88 Sr Advisor to the President .... Capt. Winston SCOTT
100 Chief of Staff/Govt Relations .... Mr. Frank KINNEY
88 Dean College of Aeronautics .... Dr. Korhan OYMAN
50 Dean College of Business .... Dr. Theodore RICHARDSON
54 Dean College of Engr & Science .... Dr. Marco CARVALHO
83 Dean College of Psych/Lib Arts .... Dr. Lisa STEELMAN
08 Dean of Libraries .... Dr. Holly MILLER
43 General Counsel .... Mr. Patrick HEALY
29 Sr VP Student Life/Alumni Affairs .... Mr. Albino P. CAMPANINI
30 Vice President Development .... Mr. Gary GRANT
84 Interim Vice Pres Enrollment Mgmt .... Mr. Brian EHRLICH
13 VP Information Technology .... Mr. Daniel FLORES
18 Vice Pres Facilities Operations .... Mr. Chad SHOULTZ
26 Vice Pres Marketing & Communication ... Dr. Wesley D. SUMNER
106 Int VP Online Learning/Off Campus .... Ms. Julie SHANKLE
102 Vice Pres Corporation Relations .... Ms. Gretchen SAUERMAN
110 Assoc Vice Pres Development Service .... Dr. Ali FAISAL
37 AVP Enrollment Mgmt/Financial Aid .... Mr. Jay LALLY
86 Assoc VP Federal & Govt Relations .... Dr. Tristan FIEDLER
21 Controller .... Ms. Susan DENYER
15 Assoc Vice Pres Human Resources .... Ms. Dondi KUENNEN
09 Assoc VP Inst Research & Effect .... Ms. Jessica ICKES
88 Assoc Vice Pres Operations .... Ms. Mischka MAXWELL
25 Int VP Research Administration .... Dr. Donn MILLER-KERMANI
35 AVP Student Affs/Dean of Students .... Mr. Rodney BOWERS
109 Asst VP Business & Ret Operation .... Mr. Greg GRAHAM
06 Registrar .... Ms. Caroline JOHNSTON
88 Director Academic Support Services .... Mr. Rodd NEWCOMBE
41 Director Athletics .... Mr. William K. JURGENS
19 Director Campus Security .... Mr. Frank IANNONE
36 Director Career Services .... Ms. Dona E. GAYNOR
38 Dir Counseling/Psychological Svcs .... Dr. Robyn TAPLEY
88 Director Creative Services .... Ms. Christena CALLAHAN
88 Dir Environ/Regulatory Compliance .... Mr. Selvin MCLEAN
18 Director Facilities Operations .... Mr. John M. MILBOURNE
123 Director Graduate Admissions .... Ms. Cheryl-Ann BROWN
58 Director Graduate Programs .... Dr. Rosemary LAYNE
09 Director Institutional Research .... Ms. Leslie L. SAVOIE
85 Director Intl Students/Scholar Svcs .... Ms. Jackie LINGNER
123 Dir Admissions Online/Off-Campus .... Ms. Carolyn P. FARRIOR
39 Dir Resident Life/Student Housing .... Mr. Gregory CONNELL
104 Director Study Abroad .... Ms. Heather WAUTLET
07 Director Undergraduate Admission .... Mr. Michael PERRY
88 Director University Museums .... Ms. Carla FUNK
90 Executive Director Ellucian .... Ms. Rebecca ARCHER
28 Title IX Coordinator .... Ms. Linda JANCHESON
96 Director of Purchasing .... Ms. Lee KARNBACH

Florida Keys Community College (C)

5901 College Road, Key West FL 33040-4397
County: Monroe FICE Identification: 001485
Unit ID: 133960
Telephone: (305) 296-9081 Carnegie Class: Bac/Assoc-Assoc Dom
FAX Number: (305) 292-5155 Calendar System: Trimester
URL: www.fkcc.edu
Established: 1963 Annual Undergrad Tuition & Fees (In-District): $3,276
Enrollment: 1,030 Coed
Affiliation or Control: State/Local IRS Status: 501(c)3
Highest Offering: Baccalaureate
Accreditation: SC, ADNUR

01 President .... Dr. Jonathan GUEVERRA
05 Vice President Academic Affairs .... Mrs. Brittany SYNDER
10 Vice Pres Business & Admin Svcs .... Mrs. Jean MAUK
111 Vice President Advancement .... Dr. Frank WOOD
84 Int Assoc Dean Enrollment Mgmt .... Mrs. Kathleen CLARK
88 Dir Institute for Public Safety .... Mrs. Cathy TORRES
04 Director President's Office .... Ms. Rachel OROPEZA
26 Dir Marketing and Public Relations .... Mrs. Amber ERNST-LEONARD
06 Registrar .... Mrs. Kathleen CLARK
08 Director Learning Resources .... Ms. Kristina NEIHOUSE
37 Director Financial Aid .... Ms. Victoria SARACENO
18 Dir Purchasing & Plant Operations .... Mr. Paul SHAMP
13 Director of IT .... Mrs. Michelle ADAM
15 Director Human Resources .... Ms. Kathleen DANIEL
21 Controller .... Ms. Heather GARCIA
09 Director Institutional Research .... Vacant
81 Dean of Science & Nursing .... Mr. Mark ROBY
50 Dean Business and Marine Science .... Mr. Jack SUEBERT
49 Dean Arts & Sciences .... Mr. Michael MCPHERSON

Florida Memorial University (D)

15800 NW 42nd Avenue, Miami Gardens FL 33054-6199
County: Miami-Dade FICE Identification: 001486
Unit ID: 133979
Telephone: (305) 626-3600 Carnegie Class: Bac-Diverse
FAX Number: (305) 626-3769 Calendar System: Semester
URL: www.fmuniv.edu
Established: 1879 Annual Undergrad Tuition & Fees: $15,536
Enrollment: 1,250 Coed
Affiliation or Control: Independent Non-Profit IRS Status: 501(c)3
Highest Offering: Master's
Accreditation: SC, AAB, ACBSP, MUS, SW

01 President .... Dr. Jaffus HARDRICK
05 Executive VP and Provost .... Dr. Adrienne COOPER
32 VP Student Affairs/Dean of Students .... Mr. Kareem CONEY
20 Associate Provost .... Dr. Denise CALLWOOD-BRATHWAITE
04 Assistant to President .... Ms. Rachel TURNER
49 Interim Dean of Arts and Sciences .... Dr. William E. HOPPER
10 Exec VP Finance/Administration .... Ms. Cynthia CURRY
07 Director of Admissions .... Mr. Wilkins AUGUSTE
111 Vice Pres University Advancement .... Mr. Cory WITHERSPOON
45 Assc VP Institutional Effectiveness ... Dr. William E. HOPPER, JR.
88 Chair Aviation and Safety .... Mrs. Vena SYMONETTE-JOHNSON
50 Dean School of Business .... Dr. Abbass ENTESSARI
53 Dean School of Education .... Dr. Idriss ABDOULAYE
81 Chair Health and Natural Sciences .... Dr. Rose Mary STIFFIN
83 Interim Chair Social Sciences .... Dr. Kim FINCH-KAREEM
64 Chair Visual/Perf Arts .... Vacant
77 Chair Comp Science/Math & Tech .... Dr. Ben WONGSAROJ
79 Chair Humanities .... Dr. William HOBBS, III
124 Dir Ctrs Acad Support & Reten .... Ms. Carla KING-CROCKETT
08 Interim Director Library Services .... Ms. Cheryl WILCHER
37 Director Financial Aid .... Ms. Faye RODNEY
06 Registrar .... Ms. Lelia EFFORD
09 Director of Institutional Research .... Dr. Carlos CANAS
15 Dir Human Resources Management .... Ms. Phyllis TYNES
41 Director Intercollegiate Athletics .... Vacant
36 Director Career Development .... Vacant
39 Director Residential Life .... Vacant
19 Chief of Campus Safety .... Chief Margo WRIGHT
18 Dir Facility Mgmt/Plant Operations .... Mr. David JACCARINO
42 Dean of Campus Ministry .... Dr. Jeffrey D. SWAIN
29 Director Alumni Affairs .... Vacant
35 Director Student Activities .... Ms. Sharhonda FORD
85 International Student Advisor .... Mr. Trevor LEWIS
13 Associate CIO .... Mr. Christopher BROMFIELD
108 Director Institutional Assessment .... Dr. Richard YAKLICH
07 Assistant Director of Admissions .... Mr. Maurice VAUGHEN
105 Web Master/Tech Support Engineer .... Mr. Cesar DOMINGUEZ
26 VP Public Relations/Marketing .... Vacant
38 Director Student Development .... Dr. Angela BRINSON-BROWN

Florida National University Hialeah Campus (E)

4425 W. Jose Regueiro (20th) Ave,
Hialeah FL 33012-4108
County: Dade FICE Identification: 025476
Unit ID: 408844
Telephone: (305) 821-3333 Carnegie Class: Bac/Assoc-Mixed
FAX Number: (305) 362-0595 Calendar System: Semester
URL: www.fnu.edu
Established: 1982 Annual Undergrad Tuition & Fees: $13,688
Enrollment: 4,169 Coed
Affiliation or Control: Proprietary IRS Status: Proprietary
Highest Offering: Master's
Accreditation: SC, COARC, NURSE, PTAA

01 President/CEO .... Dr. Maria C. REGUEIRO
09 VP of Assessment & Research/FA Dir .... Mr. Omar SANCHEZ
11 Vice President of Operations .... Mr. Frank ANDREU
05 Vice President of Academic Affairs ..... Dr. Barbara J. RODRIGUEZ
10 Controller .... Dr. Lourdes ANDREU
88 Accreditation Liaison .... Dr. Barbara J. RODRIGUEZ
07 Director of Admissions On Campus .... Mr. Robert LOPEZ
07 Director of Online Admissions .... Mr. Giancarlo LIGNAROLO
06 University Registrar .... Mr. Jose L. VALDES
106 Director of Distance Learning .... Dr. Emry SOMNARAIN
12 Campus Dean .... Dr. Jorge ALFONSO
32 Director of Student Services .... Mr. John FERRARI
50 Business & Economics Division Head .... Dr. James BULLEN
76 Allied Health Division Head .... Dr. Loreto ALMONTE
79 Humanities and Fine Arts Division .... Dr. Barbara RODRIGUEZ
88 ESL Division Head .... Mr. Oscar PEREZ
66 RN Program Director .... Mrs. Maida BURGOS
66 BSN Program Director .... Mr. Yunieski FARRADAS
66 MSN Program Director .... Dr. Lydie JANVIER
15 Human Resources Generalist .... Mrs. Andrea WYBRANSKI
32 Student Services Officer .... Ms. Seilyn SANTOS
41 Athletic Director/Head Men's Soccer . Mr. Fernando VALENZUELA
88 Military Admissions Advisor .... Mrs. Yolanda NAVARRO
31 Director Community Relations .... Mrs. Rachel TOURGEMAN
36 Job Placement Officer .... Mrs. Ariadne LOPEZ
88 Social Media Coordinator .... Mr. Anthony GUIVAS
26 Digital Marketing Coordinator .... Mrs. Maria ZEGARRA
108 Director Assessment & Research .... Mr. Rodrigo LOAIZA
08 Library Director .... Mrs. Ida TOMSHINSKY
88 Academic Advisor .... Dr. Rosa HERNANDEZ
13 Systems Administrator .... Mr. Michael ANDREU
15 Human Resources Generalist .... Mrs. Isel CASALES

Florida National University South Campus (F)

11865 SW 26th Street Unit H-3, Miami FL 33175
Telephone: (305) 226-9999 Identification: 666691
Accreditation: &SC

† Regional accreditation is carried under the parent institution Florida National College, Hialeah, FL.

Florida National University Training Center (G)

4206 West 12th Avenue, Hialeah FL 33012
Telephone: (305) 231-3326 Identification: 666690
Accreditation: &SC

† Regional accreditation is carried under the parent institution Florida National College, Hialeah, FL.

Florida Southern College (H)

111 Lake Hollingsworth Drive, Lakeland FL 33801-5698
County: Polk FICE Identification: 001488
Unit ID: 134079
Telephone: (863) 680-4111 Carnegie Class: Masters/M
FAX Number: (863) 680-4112 Calendar System: Semester
URL: www.flsouthern.edu
Established: 1883 Annual Undergrad Tuition & Fees: $36,348
Enrollment: 3,055 Coed
Affiliation or Control: United Methodist IRS Status: 501(c)3
Highest Offering: Doctorate
Accreditation: SC, MUS, NURSE, @PTA

01 President .... Dr. Anne B. KERR
05 Provost .... Dr. Brad HOLLINGSHEAD
111 Vice President Advancement .... Dr. Robert H. TATE
10 Vice President Finance & Admin .... Mr. Terry DENNIS
84 VP Enrollment Management .... Mr. John GRUNDIG
20 Assoc Provost Experiential Educ .... Dr. Mary L. CROWE
30 VP Development .... Ms. Heather PHARRIS
32 VP of Student Life .... Dr. Susan FREEMAN
102 Asst VP Foundation/Corp Relations .... Ms. Kathy ELLIS
15 AVP Operations/HR Director .... Ms. Katherine PAWLAK
42 Chaplain Director Campus Ministry .... Rev. Timothy S. WRIGHT
13 Chief Information Officer .... Mr. John L. THOMAS
21 Controller .... Ms. Judy ROBINSON
104 Coordinator Student Travel .... Ms. Bridgette MCARTHUR
49 Interim Dean Art and Sciences .... Dr. Sarah HARDING
50 Dean Business and Free Enterprise .... Dr. James FENTON
53 Dean Education .... Dr. Tracey D. TEDDER
66 Dean Nursing and Health Science .... Dr. Linda S. COMER
121 Dean of Student Success .... Ms. Shari SZABO
35 Asst Dean of Student Development .... Mr. Mike CRAWFORD
07 Director of Admissions .... Ms. Arden MITCHELL
123 Director of Adult & Graduate Admiss .... Ms. Kristen PINNER
44 Director Annual Giving .... Ms. Melaina CHROMY
41 Director of Athletics .... Mr. Drew HOWARD
36 Director of Career Development .... Ms. Melissa KULP
39 Director of Community Living .... Ms. Laura RYCHALSKY
23 Director of Health Services .... Ms. Katherine PAWLAK
112 Director of Major Gifts .... Ms. Sara OLSON
92 Director of Honors Program .... Dr. Brian HAMILTON
09 Dir Inst Research/Effectiveness .... Ms. Jazmine ESPARZA

119 Director of IT Services ... Ms. Francine NEILING
108 Director of the Library ... Mr. Randall M. MACDONALD
28 Director Life and Cultural Center ... Ms. Brenda LEWIS
26 Director of Marketing and Comm ... Ms. Rebecca PAUL
18 Director of Operations ... Mr. Jon P. CAMP
06 Registrar ... Ms. Sally L. THISSEN
19 Director of Security/Safety ... Mr. Eric RAUCH
38 Director of Student Counseling ... Dr. Carol BALLARD
37 Director of Student Financial Aid ... Mr. William L. HEALY
105 Director of Web Services ... Mr. James JARRETT
106 Director Teaching/Learning Ctr ... Ms. Autumn GRUBB
29 Coordinator of Alumni Relations ... Ms. Tara JOHNSON
04 Executive Asst to President ... Ms. Joan HILLHOUSE
40 Manager Bookstore ... Mr. James BAUER

Florida SouthWestern State College (A)

8099 College Parkway, SW, Fort Myers FL 33919-5566
County: Lee FICE Identification: 001477
Unit ID: 133508
Telephone: (239) 489-9300 Carnegie Class: Bac/Assoc-Mixed
FAX Number: (239) 489-9103 Calendar System: Semester
URL: www.fsw.edu
Established: 1961 Annual Undergrad Tuition & Fees (In-State): $3,401
Enrollment: 15,731 Coed
Affiliation or Control: State IRS Status: 501(c)3
Highest Offering: Baccalaureate
Accreditation: SC, ADNUR, CAHIIM, COARC, CVT, DH, EMT, NUR, RAD

01 President ... Dr. Jeffery ALLBRITTEN
100 Chief of Staff ... Dr. Henry PEEL
05 Provost ... Dr. Eileen DELUCA
32 Vice Provost Student Affairs ... Dr. Christine DAVIS
11 VP Administrative Services ... Dr. Gina DOEBLE
26 VP Economic Dev/External Affairs ... Dr. Robert JONES
43 General Counsel ... Mr. Mark LUPE
50 Dean Business & Technology ... Dr. Debbie PSIHOUNTAS
76 Dean Health Professions ... Dr. Paula TROPELLO
53 Dean Education and Charter Schools ... Vacant
79 Dean Arts/Hum & Social Sci ... Dr. Deborah TEED
81 Dean Pure & Applied Sci ... Dr. Martin MCCLINTON
41 Director Intercollegiate Athletics ... Mr. George SANDERS
45 Asst VP Office of Planning ... Mr. Tobias DISCENZA
84 Asst VP Enrollment/Student Success ... Dr. Christy GILFERT
12 Campus Director ... Ms. Gail MURPHY
32 Dean of Students ... Mr. Mark BUKOWSKI
06 Registrar ... Mrs. Brenda KNIGHT
13 Chief Information Officer ... Mr. Jason DUDLEY
08 Library Coordinator/Head Librarian ... Mr. William SHULUK
110 Asst VP Institutional Advancement ... Ms. Susan DESANTIS
27 Exec Director Marketing & Media ... Mr. Greg TURCHETTA
108 AVP Inst Research/Assessment ... Dr. Joseph VAN GAALEN
09 Dir Inst Reporting & Analysis ... Ms. Kelli DUNLAP
12 Director Hendry/Glades Center ... Ms. Amanda LEHRIAN
113 Bursar ... Ms. Amber REDFERN
19 Director Public Safety ... Vacant
109 Director Auxiliary Services ... Vacant
37 Director Student Financial Aid ... Mr. Matthew SANCHEZ
15 Chief HR & Organizational Dev Ofc ... Ms. Susan BRONSTEIN
07 Director Admissions ... Ms. Amber MCCOWN
18 Dir Facilities Plng & Space Mgmt ... Mr. JR SHERMAN
88 Director Academic Support Programs ... Ms. Monica MOORE
39 Dir Housing & Res Life ... Mr. Justin LONG
88 Director Adaptive Services ... Ms. Angela HARTSELL
36 Director Advising ... Vacant
96 Director of Procurement Services ... Ms. Lisa TUDOR
88 Director Testing Services ... Ms. Denise SWAFFORD
22 Title IX Coord Equity Officer ... Ms. Jana SABO
10 Director Finance and Accounting ... Ms. Kathleen PORTER
88 Director Corporate Sponsorships ... Mr. Kevin ANDERSON
88 Director Teaching and Learning Ctr ... Vacant
30 Senior Director Development ... Mr. Joseph KRAMP
88 Director Exhibitions & Collections ... Mr. Jade DELLINGER
88 Director Strategic Initiatives ... Ms. Whitney RHYNE
88 Director Corp Training & Services ... Mr. Adrian KERR
88 Director Simulation Education ... Ms. Lynne CRANDALL

Florida State College at Jacksonville (B)

501 W State Street, Jacksonville FL 32202-4097
County: Duval FICE Identification: 001484
Unit ID: 133702
Telephone: (904) 646-2300 Carnegie Class: Bac/Assoc-Mixed
FAX Number: N/A Calendar System: Semester
URL: www.fscj.edu
Established: 1965 Annual Undergrad Tuition & Fees (In-District): $2,878
Enrollment: 21,092 Coed
Affiliation or Control: Local IRS Status: Exempt
Highest Offering: Baccalaureate
Accreditation: SC, ACBSP, ACFEI, ADNUR, CAHIIM, COARC, CVT, DA, DH, EMT, FUSER, HT, MLTAD, NUR, OTA, PTAA, SURGT

01 College President ... Dr. John AVENDANO
05 Provost/Vice President Academics ... Dr. John WALL
10 Vice Pres of Business Services ... Mr. Albert LITTLE
43 College General Counsel ... Vacant
32 Vice President Student Services ... Dr. Linda HERLOCKER
12 Campus President North ... Vacant
108 VP Institutional Effectiveness ... Dr. Marie F. GNAGE
106 VP Online/Workforce Education ... Ms. Jana KOOI
103 AVP Workforce Development ... Dr. Cedrick GIBSON
18 Assoc Vice Pres Facilities ... Mr. Jamey A. HUSER
88 Exec Director Academic Operations ... Dr. Rich TURNER
49 Assoc Provost Liberal Arts/Sciences ... Dr. Ian NEUHARD
56 Assoc Provost Outreach & Extension ... Dr. Nancy K. WEBSTER
20 Assoc Prov Curriculum/Instruction ... Dr. Kathleen CIEZ-VOLZ
21 AVP Finance ... Ms. Anita KOVACS
121 AVP Student Success ... Dr. Erin RICHMAN
45 AVP Institutional Effectiveness ... Dr. Jerrett DUMOUCHEL
103 AVP Workforce Educ/Econ Development ... Ms. Linda WOODARD
15 Chief Human Resource Officer ... Mr. Mark LACEY
21 Chief Business Affairs Officer ... Mr. Laurence I. SNELL
13 Chief Information Tech Officer ... Mr. Ronald SMITH
22 Exec Dir Employee Rels/Equity ... Ms. Lisa J. MOORE
88 Exec Director Artist Series ... Dr. Milton A. RUSSOS
88 Executive Director College Data Rep ... Ms. Theresa LOTT
88 Exec Director Talent Acquisition ... Ms. Barbara HUNTER
88 Executive Director Enterprise App ... Mr. Chris MARTIN
08 Executive Dean of Library Services ... Dr. Tom MESSNER
14 Exec Dir Computer Infrastructure ... Mr. Ron SMITH
19 Executive Director Public Safety ... Mr. James W. STEVENSON
12 Executive Director of Nassau Center ... Ms. Donna MARTIN
102 Executive Director Foundation ... Mr. Cleve WARREN
12 Executive Director Cecil Center ... Mr. Paul MCNAMARA
96 Executive Director Purchasing ... Ms. Randi BROKVIST
86 Dir Government/Cmty Engagement ... Ms. Jennifer SILVA
88 Director of Student Onboarding ... Dr. Roland BULLARD
19 Director of Security ... Mr. Gordon BASS
37 Director Financial Aid ... Ms. Christine HUBBARD
41 Director of Athletics ... Ms. Ginny ALEXANDER
25 Director of Resource Development ... Ms. Jennifer PETERSON
06 Registrar ... Ms. Jacqueline SCHMIDT
09 Director Student Analytics/Research ... Mr. Gregory MICHALSKI
26 Director Marketing/Communications ... Ms. Jill K. JOHNSON

Florida Technical College (C)

1199 S Woodland Boulevard, Deland FL 32720-7415
Telephone: (386) 734-3303 Identification: 666419
Accreditation: &M

Florida Technical College (D)

3831 West Vine Street, Kissimmee FL 34741
Telephone: (844) 402-3337 Identification: 770684
Accreditation: &M, ACFEI

Florida Technical College (E)

4715 South Florida Avenue, Suite 4, Lakeland FL 33813-2101
Telephone: (866) 967-8822 FICE Identification: 025981
Accreditation: &M

Florida Technical College (F)

12900 Challenger Parkway, Orlando FL 32826
Telephone: (407) 447-7300 FICE Identification: 022187
Accreditation: &M

Florida Technical College (G)

12520 Pines Boulevard, Pembroke Pines FL 33027
Telephone: (844) 332-3409 Identification: 770685
Accreditation: &M

Fortis College (H)

19600 South Dixie Highway, Ste B, Cutler Bay FL 33157
Telephone: (786) 345-5300 Identification: 770565
Accreditation: ACCSC, ADNUR

† Branch campus of Fortis College, Centerville, OH.

Fortis College (I)

700 Blanding Boulevard, Suite 16, Orange Park FL 32065
County: Clay FICE Identification: 034343
Unit ID: 439792
Telephone: (904) 269-7086 Carnegie Class: Spec 2-yr-Health
FAX Number: (904) 269-6664 Calendar System: Semester
URL: www.fortis.edu
Established: 1985 Annual Undergrad Tuition & Fees: $15,254
Enrollment: 398 Coed
Affiliation or Control: Proprietary IRS Status: Proprietary
Highest Offering: Associate Degree
Accreditation: ACCSC, ADNUR, SURGT

01 Campus President ... Mr. Wyman DICKEY

Fortis Institute-Port St. Lucie (J)

9022 South Federal Highway/US-1, Port St. Lucie FL 34952
Telephone: (772) 221-9799 Identification: 770527
Accreditation: ABHES, ADNUR

† Branch campus of Fortis Institute, Baton Rouge, LA.

Full Sail University (K)

3300 University Boulevard, Winter Park FL 32792
County: Orange FICE Identification: 023621
Unit ID: 134237
Telephone: (407) 679-0100 Carnegie Class: Masters/L
FAX Number: (407) 679-9685 Calendar System: Other
URL: www.fullsail.edu
Established: 1979 Annual Undergrad Tuition & Fees: $24,109
Enrollment: 18,605 Coed
Affiliation or Control: Proprietary IRS Status: Proprietary
Highest Offering: Master's
Accreditation: ACCSC, CEA

01 President ... Mr. Garry JONES
07 Sr Vice President of Admissions ... Mr. Matt PENGRA

Galen College of Nursing (L)

10200 Dr Martin Luther King Jr St N, St. Petersburg FL 33716
Telephone: (727) 577-1497 Identification: 770539
Accreditation: &SC, ADNUR, NURSE

† Branch campus of Galen College of Nursing, Louisville, KY

Gordon-Conwell Theological Seminary-Jacksonville (M)

7235 Bonneval Road, Jacksonville FL 32256
Telephone: (904) 354-4800 Identification: 770111
Accreditation: &EH, THEOL

† Branch campus of Gordon-Conwell Theological Seminary, South Hamilton, MA

Gulf Coast State College (N)

5230 W Highway 98, Panama City FL 32401-1058
County: Bay FICE Identification: 001490
Unit ID: 134343
Telephone: (850) 769-1551 Carnegie Class: Bac/Assoc-Assoc Dom
FAX Number: (850) 913-3319 Calendar System: Semester
URL: www.gulfcoast.edu
Established: 1957 Annual Undergrad Tuition & Fees (In-State): $2,370
Enrollment: 5,379 Coed
Affiliation or Control: State Related IRS Status: 501(c)3
Highest Offering: Baccalaureate
Accreditation: SC, ACFEI, ADNUR, COARC, DA, DH, EMT, NURSE, PTAA, RAD, SURGA, SURGT

01 President ... Dr. John R. HOLDNAK
10 Vice Pres Administration & Finance ... Mr. John D. MERCER
05 VP Academic Affairs ... Dr. Holly KUEHNER
32 VP Student Affairs ... Dr. Melissa LAVENDER
45 VP Institutional Effect/Stratg Plng ... Dr. Cheryl L. FLAX-HYMAN
13 Chief Information Officer ... Ms. Rhonda BARKER
08 Director of Library ... Ms. Lori DRISCOLL
84 Dean of Enrollment Services ... Ms. Sharon O. TODD
15 Exec Director of Human Resources ... Vacant
26 Exec Director Marketing & Comm ... Mr. Christopher P. THOMES
103 Dean Workforce Education ... Mr. Al MCCAMBRY
96 Director Procurement ... Ms. Tonia LAWSON
37 Exec Director Student Financial Svc ... Mr. Christopher J. WESTLAKE
09 Institutional Research Analyst ... Ms. Amber COKER
04 Executive Asst to President ... Ms. Dottie TERRYN
19 Director Security/Safety ... Mr. David THOMASEE
41 Athletic Director ... Mr. Mike KANDLER

HCI College (O)

1764 North Congress Avenue, West Palm Beach FL 33409
County: Palm Beach Identification: 667104
Unit ID: 490054
Telephone: (561) 586-0121 Carnegie Class: Spec 2-yr-Health
FAX Number: (561) 471-4010 Calendar System: Semester
URL: www.hci.edu
Established: 1993 Annual Undergrad Tuition & Fees: $21,420
Enrollment: 433 Coed
Affiliation or Control: Proprietary IRS Status: Proprietary
Highest Offering: Associate Degree
Accreditation: ACCSC

01 President/COO ... Robert BONDS
12 Campus Director Fort Lauderdale ... Zac GELOW
88 Vice President Regulatory Affairs ... Dr. Arlette PETERSSON
07 Director of Admissions ... David SHELPMAN

Herzing University (P)

1865 SR 436, Winter Park FL 32792
Telephone: (407) 641-5227 Identification: 666422
Accreditation: &NH, ADNUR, NURSE, PTAA

† Regional accreditation is carried under the parent institution in Madison, WI.

Hillsborough Community College (A)

39 Columbia Drive, Tampa FL 33606
County: Hillsborough　FICE Identification: 007870
Unit ID: 134495
Telephone: (813) 253-7000　Carnegie Class: Assoc/HT-High Trad
FAX Number: N/A　Calendar System: Semester
URL: www.hccfl.edu
Established: 1968　Annual Undergrad Tuition & Fees (In-State): $2,506
Enrollment: 27,626　Coed
Affiliation or Control: State　IRS Status: 501(c)3
Highest Offering: Associate Degree
Accreditation: SC, ACFEI, ADNUR, COARC, CSHSE, DA, DH, DIETT, DMS, EMT, MT, MUS, NMT, OPD, RAD, RTT

01 President .... Dr. Ken ATWATER
10 VP Administration/CFO .... Mr. Al ERDMAN
05 Interim VP for Academic Affairs .... Mr. Richard SENKER
13 VP IT/Chief Information Officer .... Mr. Daya PENDHARKAR
32 VP Student Services/Enrollment Mgt .... Dr. Ken RAY
12 Campus President Dale Mabry .... Dr. Allen WITT
12 Campus President Ybor City Campus .... Dr. Ginger CLARK
12 Campus President Plant City Campus .... Dr. Martyn CLAY
12 Interim Campus Pres Brandon .... Dr. Alex ANZALONE
12 Campus President South Shore Campus .... Dr. Jennifer CHINA
28 CDO for Equity & Diversity .... Ms. Cheryl GONZALEZ
26 Exec Dir Marketing/Public Relations .... Ms. Ashley CARL
09 Spc Asst to Pres Strat Plng & Analy .... Dr. Paul NAGY
102 Exec Director HCC Foundation .... Mr. Stephen SHEAR
43 College Attorney .... Ms. Martha Kaye KOEHLER
15 Exec Dir Human Resources .... Ms. Kristin SMUDER
21 Controller .... Ms. Kimberly MCMILLON
75 Director Technical Programs .... Dr. Brian MANN
88 Director Assoc in Arts Programs .... Dr. Karen GRIFFIN
90 Director of Academic Technology .... Mr. Mark LEWIS
20 Dean of Academic Affairs .... Dr. Keith BERRY
88 Dean of Acad Affairs - Plant City .... Dr. Anthony BORRELL
88 Dean of AA Programs - Brandon .... Ms. Debarati GHOSH
88 Dean of AS Programs - Brandon .... Dr. Alessandro ANZALONE
88 Dean of Arts & Sciences-Dale Mabry .... Dr. Dustin LEMKE
88 Dean of AS Programs - Dale Mabry .... Dr. Barry HUBBARD
81 Dean AA Math/Science - Dale Mabry .... Dr. James WYSONG
76 Dean of Health Sciences .... Mr. Leif PENROSE
37 Financial Aid Director .... Ms. Tierra SMITH
06 Registrar .... Ms. Nevaler DAVIS
18 Director Facilities/Physical Plant .... Mr. Ben MARSHALL
96 Director of Purchasing .... Ms. Vonda MELCHIOR
31 Dir of Community & Govt Relations .... Mr. Eric JOHNSON
19 Director Security/Safety .... Mr. John "Sam" COX
04 Admin Assistant to the President .... Ms. Suzy HOLLEY
29 Director Alumni Affairs .... Ms. Ann MENCHEN
30 Director of Development .... Ms. Lee LOWRY

Hobe Sound Bible College (B)

11298 SE Gomez Avenue, Hobe Sound FL 33455
County: Martin　FICE Identification: 021889
Unit ID: 134510
Telephone: (772) 545-1400　Carnegie Class: Spec-4-yr-Faith
FAX Number: (772) 545-1422　Calendar System: Semester
URL: www.hsbc.edu
Established: 1960　Annual Undergrad Tuition & Fees: $6,595
Enrollment: 233　Coed
Affiliation or Control: Independent Non-Profit　IRS Status: 501(c)3
Highest Offering: Baccalaureate
Accreditation: BI

01 President .... Dr. P. Daniel STETLER
05 Academic Dean .... Dr. Clifford W. CHURCHILL
10 Director of Finances .... Mr. Rick HUFF
11 Director of Administrative Services .... Mr. Wesley HOLDEN
32 Dean of Students .... Mr. John S. JONES
33 Dean of Men .... Mr. Jonathan STRATTON
08 Librarian .... Mr. Phil JONES
26 Public Relations Director .... Mr. Paul STETLER
06 Registrar .... Mr. Lucas RYDER
07 Admissions Director .... Ms. Pam DAVIS
51 Dean of External Studies .... Mr. Dalbert N. WALKER
111 Dir Institutional Advancement .... Mr. Patrick DAVIS
42 Director of Christian Services .... Mr. David BUBB
37 Director of Financial Aid .... Mr. Fred WINGHAM

Hodges University (C)

2647 Professional Circle, Naples FL 34119
County: Collier　FICE Identification: 030375
Unit ID: 367884
Telephone: (239) 513-1122　Carnegie Class: Masters/S
FAX Number: (239) 598-6251　Calendar System: Trimester
URL: www.hodges.edu
Established: 1990　Annual Undergrad Tuition & Fees: $14,180
Enrollment: 1,313　Coed
Affiliation or Control: Independent Non-Profit　IRS Status: 501(c)3
Highest Offering: Master's
Accreditation: SC, CACREP, IACBE, MAC, PTAA

01 President .... Dr. John D. MEYER
10 Exec Vice Pres Admin Operations/CFO .... Ms. Erica VOGT
05 Sr Vice Pres Academic Affairs .... Dr. Marie A. COLLINS
26 Asst Vice Pres of Marketing .... Ms. Teresa M. ARAQUE
84 Asst Vice Pres Enrollment Mgmt .... Mr. Branislav LUJIC
37 Asst VP Student Financial Svcs .... Mr. Noah B. LAMB
28 Chief Diversity Officer .... Ms. Gail B. WILLIAMS
50 Dean Johnson School of Business .... Dr. Dolores A. BATIATO
107 Dean Nichols School of Prof Studies .... Dr. Mary NUOSCE
97 Dean School of Liberal Studies .... Dr. Elsa P. ROGERS
72 Assoc Dean Fisher School of Tech .... Ms. Tracey M. LANHAM
76 Dir School of Health Sciences .... Dr. Diana C. SCHULTZ
108 Director Institutional Assessment .... Dr. Thelma M. WOODARD
06 Dir Student Records and Registrar .... Mr. Joshua R. CARCOPA
08 Director of the Library .... Ms. Gayle HARING
13 Director of Information Technology .... Vacant
15 Director of Human Resources .... Ms. Kim M. UPTON
18 Dir Facilities Mgmt/Campus Security .... Mr. Skip L. CAMP
121 Director of Student Experience .... Dr. Laura R. STANFORD
07 Director or Admissions .... Mr. Erlis ABAZI
04 Executive Asst to President .... Ms. Marian K. WOOD

Hope College of Arts & Sciences (D)

1200 SW 3rd Street, Pompano Beach FL 33069
County: Broward　FICE Identification: 042517
Unit ID: 488332
Telephone: (954) 532-9614　Carnegie Class: Spec-4-yr-Other Health
FAX Number: N/A　Calendar System: Other
URL: www.hcas.edu
Established: 2011　Annual Undergrad Tuition & Fees: N/A
Enrollment: 120　Coed
Affiliation or Control: Proprietary　IRS Status: Proprietary
Highest Offering: Associate Degree
Accreditation: ACICS

05 Dean of Nursing .... Ms. Andre DERBY
11 Chief Operating Officer .... Mr. Kris GEORGE
13 Distance Learning/IT Director .... Mr. Felipe LOPEZ
37 Director of Financial Aid .... Ms. Carmen TIRADO
07 Director of Admissions .... Ms. Judith HERNANDEZ
06 Registrar/Student Services .... Mr. James DORNEVIL

Indian River State College (E)

3209 Virginia Avenue, Fort Pierce FL 34981-5596
County: Saint Lucie　FICE Identification: 001493
Unit ID: 134608
Telephone: (772) 462-4772　Carnegie Class: Bac/Assoc-Mixed
FAX Number: (772) 462-4796　Calendar System: Semester
URL: www.irsc.edu
Established: 1960　Annual Undergrad Tuition & Fees (In-District): $2,764
Enrollment: 17,598　Coed
Affiliation or Control: Local　IRS Status: 501(c)3
Highest Offering: Baccalaureate
Accreditation: SC, ADNUR, CAHIIM, COARC, DA, DH, EMT, MAC, MLTAD, NUR, PTAA, RAD, SURGT

01 President .... Dr. Edwin MASSEY
84 Vice President Enrollment Services .... Dr. Christina HART
72 Vice Pres Applied Science & Tech .... Dr. Pamela WELMON
45 VP Institutional Effectiveness .... Dr. Angela BROWNING
05 Vice President Academic Affairs .... Dr. Heather BELMONT
10 Vice President Financial Services .... Mr. Barry KEIM
32 Vice President Student Affairs .... Mr. Frank WATKINS
13 Vice President Institutional Tech .... Mr. Paul O'BRIEN
17 Dean Health Science .... Dr. Ann HUBBARD
12 Dean Northwest Center .... Vacant
08 Dean Learning Resources .... Dr. Akos DELNEKY
75 Dean Industrial Education .... Ms. Donna RIVETT
12 Provost Pt St Lucie/St Lucie W .... Dr. Harvey ARNOLD
12 Provost Okeechobee County .... Mr. Russ BROWN
12 Provost Martin County .... Ms. Elizabeth GASKIN
12 Provost Indian River County .... Mr. Casey LUNCEFORD
102 Executive Director Foundation .... Ms. Ann DECKER
83 Dean Communication & Social Science .... Dr. Scott STEIN
66 Dean Nursing .... Dr. Patricia GAGLIANO
80 Dean Public Service Education .... Mr. Evan BERRY
50 Dean Business Technology .... Dr. Prashanth PILLY
72 Dean Advanced Technology .... Mr. Kevin COOPER
53 Dean School of Education .... Dr. Kelly AMATUCCI
15 Dean Human Resources .... Mrs. Melissa WHIGHAM
18 Dean Facilities & Sustainability .... Mr. Sean DONAHUE
07 Dean Enrollment & Student Services .... Ms. Eileen STORCK
49 Dean Arts & Sciences .... Dr. Anthony DRIBBEN
21 Dean Finance .... Ms. Edith PACACHA
14 Dean Enterprise Systems .... Dr. Meredith COUGHLIN
41 Director Athletics .... Mr. Scott KIMMELMAN
106 Director Virtual Campus .... Ms. Kendall ST. HILAIRE
93 Director Minority Affairs .... Mrs. Adriene JEFFERSON
26 Director Executive Communications .... Mr. Andrew TREADWELL
111 Director Institutional Advancement .... Ms. Suzanne SELDES
88 Director Enrollment Management .... Dr. Michael GRANT
121 Director Instructional Advising .... Ms. Dale HAYES
36 Director Career & Transfer Services .... Ms. Flossie JACKSON
37 Director Financial Aid .... Ms. Mary LEWIS
35 Director Student Affairs .... Ms. Rochelle POPP-FINCH
22 Equity Officer .... Ms. Adriene JEFFERSON
96 Purchasing Agent .... Mr. Don WINDHAM
19 Director Safety/Security .... Mr. Alan MONTGOMERY

International College of Health Sciences (F)

2300 S. Congress Avenue #105, Boynton Beach FL 33426
County: Palm Beach　Identification: 667238
Telephone: (561) 202-6333　Carnegie Class: Not Classified
FAX Number: (561) 296-9647　Calendar System: Semester
URL: www.ihep.edu
Established:　Annual Undergrad Tuition & Fees: N/A
Enrollment: N/A　Coed
Affiliation or Control: Proprietary　IRS Status: Proprietary
Highest Offering: Baccalaureate
Accreditation: ACCSC, ADNUR, CVT, NUR

01 Campus President .... Karyn J. VIDAL

Jacksonville University (G)

2800 University Boulevard N, Jacksonville FL 32211-3394
County: Duval　FICE Identification: 001495
Unit ID: 134945
Telephone: (904) 256-8000　Carnegie Class: Masters/L
FAX Number: N/A　Calendar System: Semester
URL: www.ju.edu
Established: 1934　Annual Undergrad Tuition & Fees: $36,670
Enrollment: 4,222　Coed
Affiliation or Control: Independent Non-Profit　IRS Status: 501(c)3
Highest Offering: Doctorate
Accreditation: SC, AAB, CACREP, DANCE, DENT, MUS, NURSE, SP

01 President .... Mr. Timothy P. COST
05 Interim Provost/SVPAA .... Dr. Christine SAPIENZA
10 SVP CFO .... Mr. Randal FREEBOURN
84 SVP Enrollment Management .... Mr. Robert STEWART
32 SVP/Dean of Students .... Dr. Kristie GOVER
111 SVP University Advancement .... Ms. Kimberly JONES
84 SVP EDEE .... Ms. Margaret DEES
13 Director/CIO .... Mr. Dominic VENETO
04 Exec Assistant to the President .... Ms. Ellita BLACK
06 Asst Vice President/Registrar .... Mr. Robert BERWICK
09 Coord of Research & Assessment .... Vacant
08 Director of the Library .... Ms. Jessica COLLOGAN
35 Associate Dean of Students .... Ms. DaVina HAMILTON
36 Director of Career Resource Center .... Ms. Toni HIGGS
37 Director of Financial Aid .... Mr. Charles MOORE
21 Assoc VP for Financial Management .... Vacant
88 Director of Insurance and RM .... Ms. Ellen PAIGE
109 Exec Director of Campus Services .... Mr. Michael BOBBIN
40 Director of the Bookstore .... Mr. Patrick JONES
42 Campus Minister .... Mr. Lance BEAUCHAMP
15 Director of Human Resources .... Mr. James V. WILLIAMS, JR.
57 Dean of Fine Arts .... Dr. Timothy SNYDER
49 Dean College of Arts & Sciences .... Dr. Matthew CORRIGAN
50 Interim Dean College of Business .... Dr. William CROSBY
76 Interim Dean BRCHS .... Dr. Cheryl BERGMAN
64 Chairman Division of Music .... Dr. Timothy SNYDER
79 Chair Division of Humanities .... Dr. Scott KIMBROUGH
81 Chair Division of Science & Math .... Dr. Nisse GOLDBERG
38 Director Counseling Center .... Dr. Kristin ALBERTS
83 Chair Division of Social Science .... Dr. Jesse HINGSON
88 Chair Division of Naval Science .... Capt. Neil KARNES
57 Division Chair Dance & Theatre .... Mr. Brian PALMER
57 Chair Division Visual Arts .... Mr. Dana TUPA
18 Sr Director of Facilities Services .... Vacant
19 Director of Campus Security .... Mr. Kevin BENNETT
102 Dir Corporate/Foundation Relations .... Vacant
29 Sr Dir of Engage/Annual Philanth .... Ms. Lauren GRIFFITH
39 Director of Residential Life .... Mr. Lucas MULLIN
112 Director Major Gifts/Planned Giving .... Ms. Maria PELLEGRINO-YOKITIS
25 Dir Research & Sponsored Pgms .... Ms. Renee ROSSI

Johnson & Wales University (H)

1701 NE 127th Street, North Miami FL 33181-2518
Telephone: (305) 892-7000　Identification: 666423
Accreditation: &EH

† Regional accreditation is carried under the parent institution in Providence, RI.

Johnson University Florida (I)

1011 Bill Beck Boulevard, Kissimmee FL 34744-5301
Telephone: (407) 847-8966　FICE Identification: 021567
Accreditation: &SC, &BI

† Branch campus of Johnson University, Knoxville, TN

Jose Maria Vargas University (J)

10131 Pines Boulevard, Pembroke Pines FL 33026
County: Broward　FICE Identification: 041620
Unit ID: 461281
Telephone: (954) 322-4460　Carnegie Class: Spec-4-yr-Other
FAX Number: (954) 322-4131　Calendar System: Semester
URL: www.jmvu.edu
Established: 2003　Annual Undergrad Tuition & Fees: $10,480
Enrollment: 313　Coed
Affiliation or Control: Proprietary　IRS Status: Proprietary
Highest Offering: Master's
Accreditation: ACICS

01 President .... Dr. Alicia F. PARRA
06 Registrar .... Ms. Lelis ORTIZ PARRA

Keiser University (K)

1800 Business Park Blvd, Daytona Beach FL 32114
Telephone: (386) 274-5060　Identification: 770900
Accreditation: &SC, ACBSP, DMS, MAC, OTA, RAD

Keiser University (A)

1900 West Commercial Blvd, Fort Lauderdale FL 33309
County: Broward FICE Identification: 021519
Unit ID: 135081
Telephone: (954) 776-4479 Carnegie Class: DU-Mod
FAX Number: N/A Calendar System: Semester
URL: www.keiseruniversity.edu
Established: 1977 Annual Undergrad Tuition & Fees: $20,208
Enrollment: 18,335 Coed
Affiliation or Control: Independent Non-Profit IRS Status: 501(c)3
Highest Offering: Doctorate
Accreditation: SC, ACBSP, ADNUR, #ARCPA, CAHIIM, COARC, @DIETI, DMS, MLTAD, NURSE, OT, OTA, PTAA, RAD

01 Chancellor/CEO ... Dr. Arthur KEISER
11 Executive Vice Chancellor/COO ... Mr. Peter CROCITTO
05 Vice Chancellor of Academic Affairs ... Dr. John SITES
31 Vice Chancellor of Community Rels ... Mrs. Belinda KEISER
84 Vice Chancellor of Enrollment Mgmt ... Ms. Teri DEL VECCHIO
10 Sr Vice Chancellor of Finance ... Mr. Joseph BERARDINELLI
85 Vice Chancellor International Affs ... Mr. Xun LI
26 Reg Dir Media & Public Relations ... Ms. Lauren RAINIER
06 Registrar ... Ms. Jazmine FERNANDEZ
09 Asst Vice Chanc Institutional Rsrch ... Dr. Syeda QADRI
29 Director Alumni Relations ... Ms. Kerri PERCY
32 AVP Student Affairs/Student Life ... Ms. Jacqueline BONERI

Keiser University (B)

9100 Forum Corporate Pkwy, Fort Myers FL 33905
Telephone: (239) 277-1336 Identification: 770901
Accreditation: &SC, ACBSP, DMS, OTA

Keiser University-Jacksonville Campus (C)

6430 Southpoint Pkwy, Jacksonville FL 33216
Telephone: (904) 296-3440 Identification: 770902
Accreditation: &SC, ACBSP, ADNUR, OTA, PTAA, RAD

Keiser University (D)

2400 Interstate Drive, Lakeland FL 33805
Telephone: (863) 682-6020 Identification: 770903
Accreditation: &SC, ACBSP, ADNUR, DIETC, NMT, PTAA, RAD

Keiser University (E)

900 South Babcock Street, Melbourne FL 32901
Telephone: (321) 409-4800 Identification: 770904
Accreditation: &SC, ACBSP, ACFEI, ADNUR, @DIETC, DMS, OTA, PTAA, RAD

Keiser University (F)

2101 NW 117th Avenue, Miami FL 33172
Telephone: (305) 596-2226 Identification: 770905
Accreditation: &SC, ACBSP, ADNUR, OTA, PTAA, RAD

Keiser University (G)

1336 Creekside Boulevard, Suite 2,
Naples FL 34108-1931
Telephone: (239) 513-1135 FICE Identification: 039393
Accreditation: &SC, ANEST

Keiser University (H)

6014 US Hwy 19 North, Ste 250,
New Port Richey FL 34652
Telephone: (727) 484-3110 Identification: 770854
Accreditation: &SC, DMS

Keiser University (I)

5600 Lake Underhill Road, Orlando FL 32807
Telephone: (407) 273-5800 Identification: 770906
Accreditation: &SC, ACBSP, ADNUR, HT, MLTAD, OTA

Keiser University (J)

1640 SW 145th Avenue, Pembroke Pines FL 33027
Telephone: (954) 431-4300 Identification: 770907
Accreditation: &SC, ACBSP, DIETC, OTA

Keiser University (K)

9400 Discovery Way, Port Saint Lucie FL 34987
Telephone: (772) 398-9990 Identification: 666289
Accreditation: &SC, ACBSP, ADNUR, DIETC

† Regional accreditation is carried under the parent institution Keiser University, Fort Lauderdale, FL.

Keiser University (L)

6151 Lake Osprey Drive, Sarasota FL 34240
Telephone: (941) 907-3900 Identification: 770908
Accreditation: &SC, ACBSP, ACFEI, ADNUR, PTAA, RAD

Keiser University (M)

1700 Halstead Blvd, Bldg 2, Tallahassee FL 32309
Telephone: (850) 906-9494 Identification: 770909
Accreditation: &SC, ACBSP, ACFEI, ADNUR, OTA

Keiser University (N)

5002 West Waters Ave, Tampa FL 33634
Telephone: (813) 885-4900 Identification: 770910
Accreditation: &SC, ACBSP, ADNUR, OTA

Keiser University (O)

2085 Vista Parkway, West Palm Beach FL 33411-2719
Telephone: (561) 471-6000 Identification: 667032
Accreditation: &SC, ACBSP, ADNUR, CHIRO, OTA, PTAA

† Regional accreditation is carried under the parent institution Keiser University, Fort Lauderdale, FL.

Keiser University at Clearwater (P)

16120 US Hwy 19 N, Clearwater FL 33764
Telephone: (727) 373-1380 Identification: 666758
Accreditation: &SC, SURGT

Key College (Q)

1040 Bayview Drive, Suite 200, Fort Lauderdale FL 33304
County: Broward FICE Identification: 023251
Unit ID: 134422
Telephone: (754) 312-2898 Carnegie Class: Spec-4-yr-Law
FAX Number: (954) 900-3446 Calendar System: Quarter
URL: www.keycollege.edu
Established: 1982 Annual Undergrad Tuition & Fees: N/A
Enrollment: N/A Coed
Affiliation or Control: Proprietary IRS Status: Proprietary
Highest Offering: Associate Degree
Accreditation: ACCSC

01 President ... Mr. Ronald H. DOOLEY
05 EVP/Director of Academic Affairs ... Ms. Marella DOOLEY
07 Director of Admissions ... Mr. Ron DOOLEY
37 Director of Financial Services ... Ms. Traci ANDREWS
06 Registrar ... Mr. Guy ETIENNE
08 Librarian ... Ms. Barbara HIJEK
20 Academic Coordinator ... Ms. Ursala CLARKE
106 Information Technology Technician ... Mr. Mark ROSE

Knox Theological Seminary (R)

5555 N Federal Highway, Fort Lauderdale FL 33308-3209
County: Broward FICE Identification: 039923
Unit ID: 484288
Telephone: (954) 771-0376 Carnegie Class: Spec-4-yr-Faith
FAX Number: (954) 351-3343 Calendar System: Semester
URL: www.knoxseminary.edu
Established: 1989 Annual Undergrad Tuition & Fees: N/A
Enrollment: N/A Coed
Affiliation or Control: Independent Non-Profit IRS Status: 501(c)3
Highest Offering: Doctorate
Accreditation: THEOL

01 President & CEO ... Dr. Scott MANOR
11 Vice President of Administration ... Dr. Timothy SANSBURY
05 Dean of Faculty/Dean of Students ... Vacant
106 Director of Distance Education ... Dr. Tim FOX
30 Director of Development ... Ms. Janet COPLAND
06 Registrar ... Ms. Lori GOTTSHALL
08 Head Librarian ... Mr. Alan WIBBELS
04 Administrative Asst to President ... Ms. Laura KASTENSMIDT
07 Dir of Admissions & Communications ... Ms. Stephany GALLO

Lake Erie College of Osteopathic Medicine Bradenton (S)

5000 Lakewood Rance Boulevard, Bradenton FL 34211
Telephone: (941) 756-0690 Identification: 770160
Accreditation: &M, DENT, OSTEO, PHAR

† Branch campus of Lake Erie College of Osteopathic Medicine, Erie, PA

Lake-Sumter State College (T)

9501 US Highway 441, Leesburg FL 34788-8751
County: Lake FICE Identification: 001502
Unit ID: 135188
Telephone: (352) 787-3747 Carnegie Class: Bac/Assoc-Assoc Dom
FAX Number: (352) 365-3548 Calendar System: Semester
URL: www.lssc.edu
Established: 1962 Annual Undergrad Tuition & Fees (In-District): $3,172
Enrollment: 4,881 Coed
Affiliation or Control: State/Local IRS Status: 501(c)3
Highest Offering: Baccalaureate
Accreditation: SC, ADNUR, CAHIIM

01 President ... Dr. Stanley SIDOR
10 VP Admin/Business Services ... Dr. Heather BIGARD
05 VP Academic Affairs ... Dr. Douglas A. WYMER
84 VP Enrollment & Student Affairs ... Dr. Claire BRADY
21 Assoc VP for Business Affairs ... Ms. Melinda BARBER
97 Assoc VP General Studies ... Mr. Thom KIEFT
15 Exec Director Human Resources ... Ms. Pam FLETCHER
13 Chief Information Officer ... Mr. Douglas GUILER
111 AVP Inst Advancement/Foundation ... Dr. Laura BYRD
18 Director Facilities ... Mr. Andrew BICANOVSKY
08 Director Libraries ... Ms. Katie SACCO
32 Dean of Students ... Ms. Carolyn SCOTT
81 Dean Math & Science ... Ms. Karen HOGANS
66 Director Nursing ... Dr. Barbara LANGE
08 Interim Director Learning Center ... Vacant
26 Dir Marketing/College Relations ... Mr. Kevin YURASEK
37 Director Financial Aid ... Ms. Katrina BENNETT
06 Registrar ... Ms. Caitlin MOORE
41 Athletic Director ... Mr. Michael K. MATULIA
106 Director Distance Learning ... Mr. Mike NATHANSON
07 Director Enrollment Mgmt ... Ms. Jenni KOTOWSKI
28 Equity/Diversity Officer ... Vacant
96 Purchasing and Accounts Payable Mgr ... Ms. Tammy SPENCER
04 Executive Asst to the President ... Ms. Claudia MORRIS
103 Dean Workforce Programs ... Vacant

Larkin University (U)

18301 North Miami Avenue, Suite 1, Miami FL 33169
County: Miami-Dade Identification: 667288
Telephone: (305) 760-7500 Carnegie Class: Not Classified
FAX Number: N/A Calendar System: Semester
URL: ularkin.org
Established: Annual Graduate Tuition & Fees: N/A
Enrollment: N/A Coed
Affiliation or Control: Independent Non-Profit IRS Status: 501(c)3
Highest Offering: Doctorate; No Undergraduates
Accreditation: @PHAR

01 Chief Executive Officer/President ... Dr. Rudi ETTRICH
67 Vice President/Dean of Pharmacy ... Dr. Gary M. LEVIN
88 Vice Pres/Dean Biomedical Sci ... Ms. Marti ECHOLS
13 Director of Technology ... Dr. Jorge E. MACHADO
08 Director of the Library ... Dr. Sharon ARGOV

Lynn University (V)

3601 N Military Trail, Boca Raton FL 33431-5598
County: Palm Beach FICE Identification: 001505
Unit ID: 132657
Telephone: (561) 237-7000 Carnegie Class: Masters/L
FAX Number: (561) 237-7100 Calendar System: Semester
URL: www.lynn.edu
Established: 1962 Annual Undergrad Tuition & Fees: $38,210
Enrollment: 3,010 Coed
Affiliation or Control: Independent Non-Profit IRS Status: 501(c)3
Highest Offering: Doctorate
Accreditation: SC, CACREP, IACBE, MUS

01 President ... Dr. Kevin M. ROSS
00 President Emeritus ... Dr. Donald E. ROSS
11 Sr Vice President Administration ... Mr. Gregory J. MALFITANO
05 Vice President Academic Affairs ... Dr. Katrina CARTER-TELLISON
84 Vice Pres Enrollment Management ... Dr. Gareth FOWLES
10 Vice President Business & Finance ... Ms. Laurie LEVINE
32 Vice President for Student Life ... Dr. Anthony ALTIERI
30 Vice Pres Development/Alumni Affs ... Mr. Gregory J. MALFITANO
13 Chief Strategy & Technology Officer ... Mr. Chris G. BONIFORTI
26 Chief Marketing Officer ... Mrs. Sherrie WELDON
18 Dir Construction/Sustainability ... Mr. Thomas J. HEFFERNAN
35 Dean of Students ... Mr. Gary MARTIN
43 General Counsel ... Mr. Michael ANTONELLO
20 Academic Dean ... Mr. Mike PETROSKI
113 Exec Dir Stdnt Administrative Svcs ... Ms. Evelyn C. NELSON
39 Director Housing & Residence Life ... Ms. Meagan ELSBERRY
36 Executive Director Career Develop ... Ms. Barbara CAMBIA
41 Director of Athletics ... Mr. Devin CROSBY
109 Director Auxiliary Services ... Mr. Matthew P. CHALOUX
23 Director Health Center ... Ms. Rita ALBERT
27 Director of Marketing and Comm ... Ms. Stephanie BROWN
112 Director of Major Gifts ... Ms. Ashleigh FOWLES
07 Dir Undergraduate Admissions ... Mr. Stefano PAPALEO
37 Dir of Financial Aid ... Mr. John CHAMBERS
38 Director of the Counseling Center ... Ms. Nicole R. OVEDIA
96 Director of Purchasing ... Ms. Maria BIMONTE
06 Registrar ... Ms. Jenifer SCHOLL
21 Director of Accounting ... Mr. Michael C. BOLDUC
123 Dir Graduate & Online Admission ... Mr. Steven PRUITT
09 Director of Institutional Research ... Mrs. Lara MARTIN
15 Director of Employee Services ... Mr. Aaron GREENBERG
40 Campus Store Manager ... Ms. Rita D. LOUREIRO
50 Dean College Business & Management ... Mr. RT GOOD
49 Dean College of Arts & Sciences ... Dr. Gary VILLA
88 Dean College of Aeronautics ... Dr. Jeffrey C. JOHNSON
53 Dean Ross College of Education ... Dr. Kathleen WEIGEL
60 Dean College Comm and Design ... Dr. David L. JAFFE
64 Dean Conservatory of Music ... Dr. Jon H. ROBERTSON
88 Exe Dir Inst Achievement Learning ... Mr. Shaun EXSTEEN
08 Director of the Library ... Ms. Amy FILIATREAU
104 Director of International Programs ... Mrs. Erin GARCIA
19 Campus Safety Chief ... Mr. Larry RICKARD
44 Director Annual Programs ... Ms. Lisa MILLER

Marconi International University (W)

141 NE 3rd Ave., 7th Floor, Miami FL 33132
County: Miami-Dade Identification: 667377
Telephone: (305) 266-7678 Carnegie Class: Not Classified

FAX Number: (786) 866-2106
Calendar System: Semester
URL: www.miuniversity.edu
Established: 2018
Annual Undergrad Tuition & Fees: N/A
Enrollment: N/A
Coed
Affiliation or Control: Proprietary
IRS Status: Proprietary
Highest Offering: Master's
Accreditation: ACICS

01 President/CEO .... Laura RICCI

Med-Life Institute-Naples (A)

4995 Tamiami Trail E, Naples FL 34113
County: Collier
Identification: 667220
Unit ID: 487834
Telephone: (239) 732-1300
Carnegie Class: Spec 2-yr-Health
FAX Number: (239) 417-5110
Calendar System: Semester
URL: www.medlifeinstitute.com
Established: 2003
Annual Undergrad Tuition & Fees: N/A
Enrollment: 128
Coed
Affiliation or Control: Proprietary
IRS Status: Proprietary
Highest Offering: Associate Degree
Accreditation: #ABHES

01 President .... Mr. Cleophat TANIS

Mercy Hospital College of Nursing (B)

3663 South Miami Ave Ste 1500, Miami FL 33133
County: Miami-Dade
Identification: 667222
Unit ID: 419217
Telephone: (305) 285-2777
Carnegie Class: Not Classified
FAX Number: (305) 285-2671
Calendar System: Semester
URL: www.mercymiami.com/professionals/college-of-nursing
Established: 2008
Annual Undergrad Tuition & Fees: N/A
Enrollment: 90
Coed
Affiliation or Control: Proprietary
IRS Status: Proprietary
Highest Offering: Associate Degree
Accreditation: ABHES, ADNUR, PNUR

66 Dean .... Ms. Elizabeth HERNANDEZ

Meridian College (C)

7020 Professional Pkwy E, Sarasota FL 34240
County: Sarasota
FICE Identification: 023268
Unit ID: 244279
Telephone: (941) 377-4880
Carnegie Class: Spec 2-yr-Health
FAX Number: (941) 378-2842
Calendar System: Other
URL: www.meridian.edu
Established: 1982
Annual Undergrad Tuition & Fees: N/A
Enrollment: 227
Coed
Affiliation or Control: Proprietary
IRS Status: Proprietary
Highest Offering: Associate Degree
Accreditation: ACCSC

01 Campus Director .... Mr. Patrick MCDERMOTT
05 Director of Education .... Mr. Andre DODSON
07 Director of Admissions .... Ms. Kim MILES
36 Director Career Services .... Ms. Tracy FORDHAM

Miami Dade College (D)

300 NE Second Avenue, Miami FL 33132-2204
County: Miami-Dade County
FICE Identification: 001506
Unit ID: 135717
Telephone: (305) 237-8888
Carnegie Class: Bac/Assoc-Mixed
FAX Number: (305) 237-7913
Calendar System: Semester
URL: www.mdc.edu
Established: 1960
Annual Undergrad Tuition & Fees (In-State): $2,838
Enrollment: 56,001
Coed
Affiliation or Control: State
IRS Status: 501(c)3
Highest Offering: Baccalaureate
Accreditation: SC, ADNUR, ARCPA, ART, CAHIIM, COARC, DANCE, DH, DMS, EMT, FUSER, HT, MLTAD, MUS, NMT, NUR, NURSE, OPD, PTAA, RAD, THEA

01 College President .... Dr. Eduardo J. PADRON
05 Executive Vice President & Provost .... Dr. Lenore RODICIO
10 Sr Vice Provost/CFO .... Mr. Jayson IROFF
11 Vice Provost Business Affairs .... Mr. Christopher STARLING
13 Vice Provost Information Technology .... Dr. Wendy CHANG
18 Vice Provost Facilities .... Mr. Leobardo BOBADILLA
15 Vice Provost Human Resources .... Ms. Iliana CASTILLO-FRICK
09 Vice Provost Inst Effectiveness .... Dr. Joaquin MARTINEZ
12 Campus President Hialeah .... Dr. Anthony CRUZ
12 Campus President Wolfson .... Ms. Beatriz GONZALEZ
12 Campus President Kendall .... Dr. Pascale CHARLOT
12 Campus President Medical .... Dr. Bryan STEWART
12 Campus President North/EJP .... Dr. Malou HARRISON
12 Campus President Homestead/West .... Dr. Jeanne JACOBS
21 Assoc Vice Prov Business Affs .... Ms. Delilah ALMEDA
32 Vice Provost Student Services .... Dr. Kathy MAALOUF
102 Executive Dir MDC Foundation .... Mr. Mark COLE
37 Assoc VP Student Financial Services .... Ms. Mercedes AMAYA
06 Collegewide Registrar .... Ms. Elisabet VIZOSO
26 Chief Public Rels Officer/Dir Comm .... Mr. Juan MENDIETA
29 Director Alumni Relations .... Mr. Adlar GARCIA
35 Director Student Life .... Ms. Shamona MCFADDEN
88 Dir Testing Admin/Pgm Evaluation .... Mr. Silvio RODRIGUEZ
22 Dir Equal Opportunity Pgm/ADA Coord .... Dr. Joy C. RUFF
121 Director Student Advisement .... Mr. Jacob SHILTS
84 Director Enrollment Management .... Mr. Harry LINENBERG
96 Director of Purchasing .... Mr. Roman MARTINEZ
41 Director Athletics & Student Life .... Mr. Anthony FIORENZA
09 Director of Institutional Research .... Ms. Diana BARBU
43 Legal Counsel .... Mr. Javier LEY-SOTO
86 Director Governmental Affairs .... Ms. Victoria HERNANDEZ
100 Chief of Staff .... Mr. George ANDREWS
103 Vice Provost Academic Schools .... Dr. John WENSVEEN
104 Director Global Student Pgm .... Ms. Carol REYES
105 College Webmaster .... Mr. Andrew SEAGA
08 Head Librarian/Dir Lrng Resources .... Mr. Erick DOMINICIS
85 Dir International Student Services .... Dr. Zoraya CUESTA

Miami International University of Art & Design (E)

1501 Biscayne Boulevard, Suite 100,
Miami FL 33132-1418
County: Miami-Dade
FICE Identification: 008878
Unit ID: 134811
Telephone: (305) 428-5700
Carnegie Class: Spec-4-yr-Arts
FAX Number: (305) 374-7946
Calendar System: Quarter
URL: www.artinstitutes.edu/miami
Established: 1965
Annual Undergrad Tuition & Fees: $17,604
Enrollment: 1,461
Coed
Affiliation or Control: Independent Non-Profit
IRS Status: 501(c)3
Highest Offering: Master's
Accreditation: SC, CIDA

01 President .... Ms. Erika FLEMING
05 Dean of Academic Affairs .... Dr. Chance APES
10 Dir Admin & Financial Services .... Ms. Leslie THEROULDE
32 Dean of Student Affairs .... Mr. John OSBORNE
07 Senior Director of Admissions .... Mr. Kevin RYAN
08 Librarian .... Vacant

Miami Regional University (F)

700 S. Royal Poinciana Blvd #100,
Miami Springs FL 33166
County: Miami-Dade
FICE Identification: 041284
Unit ID: 451103
Telephone: (305) 442-9223
Carnegie Class: Spec-4-yr-Other Health
FAX Number: (305) 442-8723
Calendar System: Other
URL: www.mru.edu
Established: 1996
Annual Undergrad Tuition & Fees: N/A
Enrollment: 976
Coed
Affiliation or Control: Proprietary
IRS Status: Proprietary
Highest Offering: Master's
Accreditation: ACCSC, NUR

01 President & CEO .... Ophelia SANCHEZ
03 Executive Vice President .... Richard GRILLO
05 Assoc Vice Pres Academic Affairs .... Dr. Santarvis BROWN
32 Senior Director Student Services .... Mirizza MENENDEZ
07 Assoc VP Enroll Services .... Fernando MACHADO
08 Librarian .... Katia NUNEZ
10 VP Finance .... Henry BABANI
15 VP Employment Affairs .... Mirizza MENENDEZ
36 Lead Career Services Rep .... Mirizza MENENDEZ
37 Assoc VP Student Financial Aid .... Marcie SILVA

Millennia Atlantic University (G)

3801 NW 97th Avenue, Doral FL 33178
County: Miami-Dade
FICE Identification: 041825
Unit ID: 461883
Telephone: (786) 331-1000
Carnegie Class: Spec-4-yr-Bus
FAX Number: (305) 503-9680
Calendar System: Semester
URL: www.maufl.edu
Established:
Annual Undergrad Tuition & Fees: $11,156
Enrollment: 172
Coed
Affiliation or Control: Proprietary
IRS Status: Proprietary
Highest Offering: Master's
Accreditation: ACCSC, ACICS

01 President .... Dr. Aristides MAZA-DUERTO
00 Chancellor .... Mr. Luis E. MARTINEZ
10 CFO .... Mrs. Orianna M. MOSS
05 Vice Director of Academic Programs .... Mrs. Teresa FITZGERALD
06 Registrar .... Ms. Natasha ALEONG
37 Financial Aid Manager .... Ms. Maria VELAR
26 Coord of Marketing & Public Rels .... Mr. Sergio CUBILLOS
36 Student Services and Placement Mgr .... Ms. Jakelin MIRANDA
07 Director of Admissions .... Mr. Juan Carlos RODRIGUEZ
08 Librarian .... Dr. Otis ALEXANDER
113 Bursar .... Mrs. Jenice MAZA-DUERTO

Naaleh College (H)

16375 NE 18th Avenue Ste 304,
North Miami Beach FL 33162
County: Miami-Dade
Identification: 667347
Telephone: (305) 944-0035
Carnegie Class: Not Classified
FAX Number: (305) 944-0335
Calendar System: Semester
URL: www.naalehcollege.edu
Established: 2011
Annual Undergrad Tuition & Fees: N/A
Enrollment: N/A
Coed
Affiliation or Control: Independent Non-Profit
IRS Status: 501(c)3
Highest Offering: Baccalaureate
Accreditation: DEAC

New York Film Academy, South Beach (I)

420 Lincoln Rd #200, Miami Beach FL 33139
Telephone: (305) 534-6009
Identification: 770984
Accreditation: &WC, ART

† Regional accreditation is carried under the parent institution in Burbank, CA.

North Broward Technical Center (J)

1871 West Hillsboro Blvd, Deerfield Beach FL 33442
County: Broward
Identification: 667357
Telephone: (954) 427-8830
Carnegie Class: Not Classified
FAX Number: (954) 427-8836
Calendar System: Other
URL: www.nbtechcenter.com
Established:
Annual Undergrad Tuition & Fees: N/A
Enrollment: N/A
Coed
Affiliation or Control: Proprietary
IRS Status: Proprietary
Highest Offering: Associate Degree
Accreditation: ABHES

North Florida Community College (K)

325 NW Turner Davis Drive, Madison FL 32340-1610
County: Madison
FICE Identification: 001508
Unit ID: 136145
Telephone: (850) 973-2288
Carnegie Class: Bac/Assoc-Assoc Dom
FAX Number: (850) 973-1696
Calendar System: Semester
URL: www.nfcc.edu
Established: 1958
Annual Undergrad Tuition & Fees (In-State): $3,054
Enrollment: 1,367
Coed
Affiliation or Control: State
IRS Status: 501(c)3
Highest Offering: Baccalaureate
Accreditation: SC, ADNUR, EMT, NUR

01 President .... Mr. John GROSSKOPF
05 Dean of Academic Affairs/CAO .... Ms. Jennifer PAGE
10 Dean Administrative Svcs & CBO .... Mr. Andrew BARNES
84 Dean of Enrollment/Student Services .... Ms. Kay HOGAN
09 Manager of Networking Systems .... Mr. Nick SKIPPER
15 Director of Personnel Services .... Mr. Bill HUNTER
08 Head Librarian .... Ms. Lynn WYCHE
88 SSS and Disability Coordinator .... Ms. Sheila NOBLES
88 Director of Public Safety Academy .... Mr. Rick DAVIS
06 Registrar .... Ms. Lori PLEASANT
18 Chief Facilities/Physical Plant .... Mr. Glenn STRICKLAND
26 Public Information Officer .... Ms. Kim SCARBORO
102 Dir Foundation/Alumni Relations .... Dr. Cheryl JAMES
37 Director Student Financial Aid .... Ms. Karen SURLES
28 Director of Diversity .... Ms. Denise BELL
96 Director of Purchasing .... Ms. Sarah NEWSOME
04 Executive Asst to President .... Ms. Cindy M. GAYLARD
103 Dir Workforce/Career Development .... Mr. David DUNKLE
19 Director Security/Safety .... Mr. Skip JAMES

Northwest Florida State College (L)

100 College Boulevard, Niceville FL 32578-1295
County: Okaloosa
FICE Identification: 001510
Unit ID: 136233
Telephone: (850) 678-5111
Carnegie Class: Bac/Assoc-Mixed
FAX Number: (850) 729-5215
Calendar System: Semester
URL: www.nwfsc.edu
Established: 1963
Annual Undergrad Tuition & Fees (In-State): $3,133
Enrollment: 5,727
Coed
Affiliation or Control: State
IRS Status: 501(c)3
Highest Offering: Baccalaureate
Accreditation: SC, ADNUR, DA, EMT, NURSE, RAD

01 President .... Dr. Devin STEPHENSON
05 Vice Pres of Teaching and Learning .... Dr. Deborah KISH
11 Vice Pres of Business Operations .... Mr. Randy WHITE
111 Vice Pres College Advancement .... Mrs. Cristie KEDROSKI
13 Chief Information Officer .... Mr. Cole ALLEN
113 Student Accounts & Billing .... Mrs. Tamara ADAMS
09 Dean of Institutional Research .... Ms. Pauline ANDERSON
15 Director Human Resources/Diversity .... Ms. Roberta MACKEY
121 Exec Dir Student Success Navigation .... Mr. Carter CAYWOOD
30 Director of Development .... Ms. Carla REINLIE
41 Athletic Director .... Mr. Ramsey ROSS
37 Exec Dir Fin Planning/Scholarships .... Dr. Aimee WATTS
18 Facilities Director .... Mr. Sam JONES
08 Director Learning Resources Center .... Ms. Janice HENDERSON
26 Director Strategic Communications .... Mrs. Laura COALE
121 Vice President Student Success .... Dr. Nate SLATON
04 Executive Assistant to President .... Ms. Julie SCHRODT
06 Exec Dir Acad Records/Enrollment .... Ms. Stephanie LINARD
106 Director of Online Learning .... Dr. Diedre PRICE
75 Dean of Career & Technical Educ .... Vacant
97 Dean of General Education .... Dr. Anne SOUTHARD
32 Dir Student Dev/Campus Engagement .... Ms. LaTosha PINCKEY
43 General Counsel .... Mr. Jack CAPRA
19 Director of College Safety/Security .... Mr. Aaron MURRAY
25 Exec Dir of Grant Development .... Mr. Sam RENFROE
96 Director of Purchasing .... Ms. Dedria LUNDERMAN

Nova Southeastern University (M)

3301 College Avenue, Fort Lauderdale FL 33314-7796
County: Broward
FICE Identification: 001509
Unit ID: 136215
Telephone: (800) 541-6682
Carnegie Class: DU-Higher

FAX Number: (954) 262-3800 Calendar System: Trimester
URL: www.nova.edu
Established: 1964 Annual Undergrad Tuition & Fees: $30,900
Enrollment: 20,793 Coed
Affiliation or Control: Independent Non-Profit IRS Status: 501(c)3
Highest Offering: Doctorate
Accreditation: SC, AA, ACAE, ARCPA, AUD, CAATE, CAEP, CLPSY, #COARC, CVT, DENT, DMS, IACBE, IPSY, LAW, #MED, MFCD, NURSE, OPT, OPTR, OSTEO, OT, PH, PHAR, PTA, SCPSY, SP, SPAA

01 President & CEO .... Dr. George L. HANBURY, II
05 Int Provost & EVP Academic Affairs .... Dr. Ronald J. CHENAIL
10 VP Finance/CFO .... Ms. Alyson SILVA
00 Chancellor Nova Southeastern Univ .... Mr. Ray FERRERO, JR.
17 Chancellor Health Professions Div .... Dr. Fred LIPPMAN
11 Vice President for Operations/HPD .... Dr. Irving ROSENBAUM
88 Special Assistant to the President .... Dr. H. Thomas TEMPLE
08 Interim VP Info Svcs/Univ Librarian .... Mr. James HUTCHENS
43 VP Legal Affairs .... Mr. Joel BERMAN
46 VP Research Tech Transfer .... Dr. Gary S. MARGULES
32 VP Student Affairs/Dean UG Studies .... Dr. Brad WILLIAMS
111 VP Inst Advancement .... Dr. Jennifer O'FLANNERY ANDERSON
13 VP Info Tech/Chief Info Ofcr .... Mr. Tom WEST
15 VP Human Resources .... Mr. Robert J. PIETRYKOWSKI
84 VP Enrollment and Stdnt Svcs .... Dr. Stephanie BROWN
21 VP Business Services .... Mr. Marc CROCQUET
106 VP Reg Campus & Online Educ .... Mr. Ricardo BELMAR
18 VP Facilities Mgmt .... Mr. Daniel ALFONSO
23 Vice Pres Clinical Operations .... Mr. Leonard POUNDS
26 Exec Director Univ Relations .... Mr. Brandon HENSLER
19 Director Public Safety .... Mr. James EWING
09 VP Institutional Effectiveness .... Dr. Donald J. RUDAWSKY
88 Dir Accreditation/Acad Pgm Rev .... Mr. Adam ROSENTHAL
24 Exec Dir Ed Tech/Digital Media Prod .... Ms. Diane LIPPE
25 Director Sponsored Programs .... Ms. Cathy HARLAN
86 Exec Dir Licensure/State Relations .... Dr. Greg F. STIBER
12 Headmaster University School .... Mr. William KOPAS
27 Director University Publications .... Mr. Ron RYAN
36 Director of Career Development .... Ms. Shari SAPERSTEIN
29 Exec Dir Alumni Relations/Advance .... Ms. Barbara SAGEMAN
06 Dir University Registrar's Office .... Ms. G. Elaine N. POFF
41 Director Athletics .... Mr. Michael MOMINEY
88 Director Campus Recreation .... Mr. Tom VITUCCI
116 Executive Dir Internal Auditing .... Mr. Ron MIDEI
88 VP Compliance/Chief Integrity Ofcr .... Ms. Robin SUPLER
88 Dir Museum of Art .... Ms. Bonnie CLEARWATER
63 Dean College Osteopathic Medicine .... Ms. Elaine WALLACE
67 Int Dean College Pharmacy .... Dr. Michelle CLARK
88 Dean College Optometry .... Dr. David LOSHIN
76 Dean College of Hlth Care Sciences .... Dr. Stanley WILSON
54 Int Dean College Engineering/Comp .... Dr. Meline KEVORKIAN
61 Dean Shepard Broad Law Center .... Mr. Jon GARON
65 College of Natural Sci/Oceanography .... Dr. Richard DODGE
66 Dean College of Nursing .... Dr. Marcella M. RUTHERFORD
50 Int Dean Huizenga Col of Bus/Entr .... Dr. James T. SIMPSON
92 Dean Farquhar Honors College .... Dr. Donald ROSENBLUM
88 Dean College of Psychology .... Dr. Karen GROSBY
83 Dean College Arts/Humani/Social Sci .... Dr. Honggang YANG
88 Dean Mailman Ctr for Human Devel .... Dr. Roni LEIDERMAN
63 Dean College of Medical Sciences .... Dr. Irving ROSENBAUM
52 Interim Dean of Dental Medicine .... Dr. Steven KALTMAN
53 Dean Fischler College of Education .... Dr. Kimberly DURHAM
88 Dean College Allopathic Med .... Dr. Johannes VIEWEG

NRI Institute of Health Sciences (A)

503 Royal Palm Blvd, Royal Palm Beach FL 33411
County: Palm Beach FICE Identification: 042108
Unit ID: 481252
Telephone: (561) 688-5112 Carnegie Class: Not Classified
FAX Number: (561) 688-5113 Calendar System: Semester
URL: www.nriinstitute.edu
Established: 2015 Annual Undergrad Tuition & Fees: N/A
Enrollment: N/A Coed
Affiliation or Control: Proprietary IRS Status: Proprietary
Highest Offering: Associate Degree
Accreditation: COE

01 President & Director .... Elizabeth STOLKOWSKI

Orlando Medical Institute (B)

6220 S. Orange Blossom Tr, Ste 420, Orlando FL 32809
County: Orange Identification: 667127
Telephone: (407) 251-0007 Carnegie Class: Not Classified
FAX Number: (407) 251-0352 Calendar System: Semester
URL: www.omi.edu
Established: 2004 Annual Undergrad Tuition & Fees: N/A
Enrollment: N/A Coed
Affiliation or Control: Proprietary IRS Status: Proprietary
Highest Offering: Associate Degree
Accreditation: ABHES

01 President .... Felix J. MARQUEZ, JR.
11 Vice Pres/Director Operations .... Abigail MARQUEZ

Palm Beach Atlantic University (C)

901 S. Flagler Drive, West Palm Beach FL 33401
County: Palm Beach FICE Identification: 008849
Unit ID: 136330
Telephone: (561) 803-2000 Carnegie Class: DU-Mod
FAX Number: (561) 803-2186 Calendar System: Semester
URL: www.pba.edu
Established: 1968 Annual Undergrad Tuition & Fees: $31,450
Enrollment: 3,839 Coed
Affiliation or Control: Interdenominational IRS Status: 501(c)3
Highest Offering: Doctorate
Accreditation: SC, CAATE, IACBE, MUS, NURSE, PHAR, @THEOL

01 President .... Mr. William M. FLEMING
05 Provost/CAO .... Dr. E. Randolph RICHARDS
10 Sr VP for Finance/Admin & CFO .... Mr. John KAUTZ, III
30 Vice President Development .... Mrs. Vicki PUGH
07 Vice President for Admissions .... Mr. Tim WORLEY
09 Asst Provost Rsrch/Effectiveness .... Mrs. Carolanne BROWN
13 Assoc VP Campus Information Svcs .... Mr. Phillip MAJOR
26 Assoc VP Univ Relations & Marketing .... Mrs. Rebecca PEELING
51 Dean MacArthur School of Leadership .... Dr. Craig DOMECK
49 Dean School of Arts & Sciences .... Dr. Robert LLOYD
50 Dean School of Business .... Dr. Leslie TURNER
53 Dean School of Education .... Dr. Gene SALE
57 Dean School of Music/Fine Arts .... Dr. Lloyd MIMS
66 Dean School of Nursing .... Dr. Joanne MASELLA
67 Dean Gregory School of Pharmacy .... Dr. Jeff LEWIS
60 Dean School Communication/Media .... Dr. J. Duane MEEKS
73 Dean School of Ministry .... Dr. Jonathan GRENZ
06 Registrar .... Ms. Kathy MAJZNER
08 Dean of the Library .... Mr. Steven BAKER
20 Associate Provost for Instruction .... Dr. Nathan LANE
15 Assoc VP of Human Resources .... Ms. Mona L. HICKS
32 Dean of Students .... Mr. Bob LUTZ
18 Director of Physical Plant .... Mr. Matt STEVENS
21 Controller .... Mrs. Carla CROW
29 AVP Alumni Relations/Annual Fund .... Mrs. Delesa MORRIS
31 Dir of Campus and Community Events .... Mrs. Mary WARD
35 Assistant Dean of Students .... Mr. Bob LUTZ
37 Director of Financial Aid .... Ms. Darly ADAMS
40 Director of Campus Store .... Mrs. Abbie ROSEMEYER
41 Director of Athletics .... Vacant
42 Director of Campus Ministries .... Mr. Mark KAPRIVE
92 Director of Supper Honors Program .... Dr. Tom ST. ANTOINE
19 Director Security/Safety .... Mr. Wayne BUCHANAN

Palm Beach State College (D)

4200 Congress Avenue, Lake Worth FL 33461-4796
County: Palm Beach FICE Identification: 001512
Unit ID: 136358
Telephone: (561) 967-7222 Carnegie Class: Bac/Assoc-Assoc Dom
FAX Number: (561) 868-3504 Calendar System: Semester
URL: www.palmbeachstate.edu
Established: 1933 Annual Undergrad Tuition & Fees (In-State): $2,444
Enrollment: 30,052 Coed
Affiliation or Control: State IRS Status: 501(c)3
Highest Offering: Baccalaureate
Accreditation: SC, ACBSP, ADNUR, CAHIIM, COARC, DA, DH, DMS, EMT, MAC, NUR, RAD, SURGT

01 President .... Ms. Ava L. PARKER
05 Vice President Academic Affairs .... Dr. Roger YOHE
10 VP Administration/Business Services .... Mr. Robbi STIVERS
32 Vice President Student Services .... Dr. Peter BARBATIS
13 Vice President Information Svcs .... Dr. Ginger L. PEDERSEN
31 Exec Director Community Engagement .... Ms. Rachael E. BONLARRON
43 General Counsel .... Mr. Kevin A. FERNANDER
111 Vice President Advancement .... Mr. David RUTHERFORD
45 Vice Pres Growth Expan Prov .... Dr. Maria M. VALLEJO
106 Vice Pres E-Lrn Inst Tech Prov .... Dr. Bernadette MENDONEZ RUSSELL
20 Int Assoc VP Academic Affairs .... Dr. Holly L. BENNETT
103 Vice Pres Workforce Dev Prov .... Dr. Jean WIHBEY
75 Dean Bus/Trade & Indus & Pub Safety .... Ms. Patricia V. RICHIE
20 Dean Academic Affairs Loxahatchee .... Mr. Ed W. WILLEY
20 Dean Academic Affairs Lake Worth .... Dr. Irving BERKOWITZ
20 Dean Academic Affairs Boca Raton .... Dr. Roy M. VARGAS
20 Provost & Dean Palm Beach Gardens .... Dr. Tunjarnika L. COLEMAN-FERRELL
97 Dean Bachelor Degree Programs .... Dr. Anita S. KAPLAN
20 Dean Curriculum .... Dr. Velmarie ALBERTINI
35 Dean Student Services Boca Raton .... Dr. Sheri E. GOLDSTEIN
88 Executive Dean Center .... Ms. Latanya L. MCNEAL
84 Dean Enrollment Management .... Mr. Chuck H. ZETTLER
37 Director Financial Aid .... Mr. Eddie VIERA
41 Athletics Director .... Mr. Thomas SEITZ
09 Exec Dir Inst Rsrch/Effectiveness .... Mr. David WEBER
18 Facilities Director .... Mr. John T. WASUKANIS
15 Exec Director Human Resources .... Mr. Michael PUSTIZZI
26 Dir College Relations & Mktg .... Mr. Diego MEEROFF
21 Controller .... Mr. James E. DUFFIE
06 College Registrar .... Mr. Peter BIEGEL
96 Procurement Director .... Mr. David CHOJNACKI
13 Chief Information Officer .... Mr. Ken LIBUTTI
25 Dir Resource & Grant Development .... Ms. Maureen CAPP
106 E-Learning Director .... Mr. Sidney BEITLER
108 Assessment Director .... Dr. Karen D. PAIN
19 Security & Risk Management Director .... Ms. Delsa BUSH
76 Dean Health Services .... Mr. Al BALDWIN
35 Dean Student Services .... Mr. Van P. WILLAIMS

Palmer College of Chiropractic, Florida Campus (E)

4777 City Center Parkway, Port Orange FL 32129-4153
Telephone: (386) 763-2709 Identification: 666330
Accreditation: &NH, &CHIRO

† Regional accreditation is carried under the parent institution in Davenport, IA.

Pasco-Hernando State College (F)

10230 Ridge Road, New Port Richey FL 34654-5112
County: Pasco FICE Identification: 010652
Unit ID: 136400
Telephone: (727) 847-2727 Carnegie Class: Bac/Assoc-Assoc Dom
FAX Number: (727) 816-1815 Calendar System: Semester
URL: www.phsc.edu
Established: 1972 Annual Undergrad Tuition & Fees (In-District): $3,155
Enrollment: 11,947 Coed
Affiliation or Control: State/Local IRS Status: 501(c)3
Highest Offering: Baccalaureate
Accreditation: SC, ADNUR, DH, EMT, NURSE, SURGT

01 President .... Dr. Timothy L. BEARD
05 VP Acad Affs & Fac Dev/Col Provost .... Dr. Stanley M. GIANNET
32 VP Stdnt Affairs/Enrollment Mgmt .... Dr. Robert E. BADE
10 VP Finance & Auxiliary Services .... Mr. Brian S. HORN
12 Provost of the East Campus .... Dr. Edwin G. GOOLSBY
12 Provost North Campus .... Dr. Donna R. BURDZINSKI
12 Provost Spring Hill Campus .... Dr. Amy E. ANDERSON
12 Provost Porter Campus at Wiregrass .... Dr. Kevin F. O'FARRELL
103 Dean of Workforce Development .... Dr. Marcia M. AUSTIN
120 VP of Technology & Distance Educ .... Dr. Melissa L. HARTS
84 Dean Stdnt Dev & Enroll Mgmt .... Ms. Chiquita A. HENDERSON
20 Dean of Acad Aff & Inst Accr .... Ms. Sonia B. THORN
49 Dean Arts and Sciences .... Dr. Gerene M. THOMPSON
18 Asst VP Facilities Mgmt .... Mr. Tony A. RIVAS
09 Assoc Dean Inst Effectiveness .... Ms. Carla M. ROSSITER-SMITH
13 Assoc Dean of Enterprise Systems .... Ms. Janice L. SCOTT
111 AVP Alumni & Col Rel/Exec Dir Fdn .... Dr. Lisa A. RICHARDSON
66 Associate Dean of Nursing .... Ms. Michele R. GODWIN
07 Assoc Dean of Admiss & Enroll Mgmt .... Mr. Chris J. BIBBO
37 Dean Financial Aid .... Ms. Rebecca SHANAFELT
43 Asst VP of Policy/General Counsel .... Vacant
08 Director of Libraries .... Mr. Raymond J. CALVERT
26 Assoc Dean Marketing Media Rels .... Ms. Melanie WAXLER
18 Director of Facilities .... Mr. Keith V. BRAUN
15 Exec Director of Human Resources .... Mr. Darrell L. CLARK
109 Auxiliary Services Manager .... Mr. John D. COLLINS
22 Dir of Global & Multi Aware & Spec .... Mr. Imani D. ASUKILE
96 Purchasing Agent .... Ms. Christy L. AULICINO
04 Executive Asst to President & DBOT .... Ms. Rhonda M. DODGE
29 Director Alumni & Donor Relations .... Ms. Michelle L. BULLWINKEL
41 Athletics Director .... Mr. Stephen A. WINTERLING

Pensacola Christian College (G)

250 Brent Lane, Pensacola FL 32503
County: Escambia Identification: 667101
Telephone: (850) 478-8496 Carnegie Class: Not Classified
FAX Number: (850) 479-6552 Calendar System: Semester
URL: www.pcci.edu
Established: 1974 Annual Undergrad Tuition & Fees: N/A
Enrollment: N/A Coed
Affiliation or Control: Independent Non-Profit IRS Status: 501(c)3
Highest Offering: Doctorate
Accreditation: TRACS, NURSE

01 President .... Dr. Troy SHOEMAKER
05 Academic Vice President .... Dr. Raylene COCHRAN
32 Vice President for Student Life .... Mr. Tim MCLAUGHLIN
10 Chief Financial Officer .... Mr. Jim THOMPSON
06 Registrar .... Mrs. Linda TROUTMAN
09 Dir Institutional Effectiveness .... Dr. Mark SMITH
41 Athletic Director .... Mr. Mark GOETSCH
08 Chief Librarian .... Mr. Kelly GRANDSTAFF
07 Director of Admissions .... Mrs. Amy ABBOTT
106 Director of Online Learning .... Mr. Steve MARTIN
19 Chief of Safety and Security .... Mr. Shawn ROSS

Pensacola State College (H)

1000 College Boulevard, Pensacola FL 32504-8998
County: Escambia FICE Identification: 001513
Unit ID: 136473
Telephone: (850) 484-1000 Carnegie Class: Bac/Assoc-Assoc Dom
FAX Number: (850) 484-1826 Calendar System: Semester
URL: www.pensacolastate.edu
Established: 1948 Annual Undergrad Tuition & Fees (In-District): $2,704
Enrollment: 9,655 Coed
Affiliation or Control: Local IRS Status: 501(c)3
Highest Offering: Baccalaureate
Accreditation: SC, ACFEI, ADNUR, CAHIIM, DH, EMT, MAC, NUR, NURSE, PNUR, PTAA, RAD, SURGT

01 President .... Dr. Ed MEADOWS
05 VP Academic and Student Affairs .... Dr. Erin SPICER
11 VP Administrative Services .... Mr. Tom GILLIAM
10 VP Business Affairs .... Mrs. Gean Ann EMOND
20 Dean Bacc Studies/Academic Sup .... Dr. Kirk BRADLEY
20 Senior Dean Academic Affairs .... Dr. Brenda KELLY
12 Dean Milton Campus .... Dr. Anthea AMOS
76 Dean Health Sciences .... Dr. Dusti SLUDER
102 Exec Director College Foundation .... Ms. Andrea KRIEGER
13 Exec Director ITS .... Mr. Bert MERRITT
86 Associate VP Govt Relations .... Ms. Sandy RAY
26 Exec Dir Marketing/College Info .... Ms. Sheila NICHOLS
105 Coordinator Internet Systems .... Mr. Jason KING
28 Ex Dir Inst Diversity/Stdnt Conduct .... Ms. Lynsey LISTAU
06 Registrar .... Ms. Susan DESBROW

25 Dean Grants and Federal Programs .... Dr. Debbie DOUMA
18 Director Facilities and Planning .... Ms. Diane BRACKEN
14 Director Technology Support .... Ms. Liz GOMEZ
15 Director Human Resources .... Ms. Tammy HENDERSON
37 Dir Fin Aid/Veterans/Scholarships .... Ms. Joanne ROZBORSKI
75 Director Career & Technical Educ .... Ms. Deborah HOOKS
38 Director Student Support Services .... Ms. Rachelle BURNS
19 Director Public Safety .... Mr. Sean FAGAN
43 General Counsel .... Mr. Thomas J. GILLIAM
08 District Dept Head Libraries .... Ms. LisaMarie BARTUSIK
96 Director Purchasing .... Ms. Ted YOUNG
91 Director MIS Support .... Mr. Beau MCHENRY
21 Comptroller .... Ms. Nan JACKSON
29 Exec Director Alumni Affairs .... Ms. Patrice WHITTEN
07 Director Admissions .... Ms. Samantha HILL
36 Dean Advising & Career Svcs .... Dr. Monique COLLINS
41 Director Athletics .... Mr. Bill HAMILTON
32 Dean Student Affairs .... Ms. Kathy DUTREMBLE
12 Director South Santa Rosa Center .... Ms. Karen MCCABE
12 Director Century Center .... Ms. Paula BYRD
51 Coordinator Continuing Education . Ms. Deven WALTHER-THEAD
04 Exec Assistant to the President .... Ms. Patricia S. CREWS
106 Director Distributed Learning .... Dr. Bill WATERS
09 Exec Dir Institutional Research .... Mr. Michael JOHNSTON

Polk State College (A)

999 Avenue H, NE, Winter Haven FL 33881-4299

County: Polk — FICE Identification: 001514
Unit ID: 136516
Telephone: (863) 297-1000 — Carnegie Class: Bac/Assoc-Mixed
FAX Number: (863) 297-1065 — Calendar System: Semester
URL: www.polk.edu
Established: 1964 — Annual Undergrad Tuition & Fees (In-District): $3,366
Enrollment: 10,659 — Coed
Affiliation or Control: Local — IRS Status: 501(c)3
Highest Offering: Baccalaureate
Accreditation: **SC**, ADNUR, COARC, CVT, DMS, EMT, NUR, OTA, PTAA, RAD

01 President .... Dr. Angela FALCONETTI
10 Vice Pres Administrative Svcs/CFO .... Mr. Peter ELLIOTT
05 Provost/VP Academic Affairs .... Mr. Stephen HULL
32 Vice Pres Student Services .... Mr. Reginal WEBB
111 Vice Pres Inst Advanc/Exec Dir PSCF .... Ms. Tracy PORTER
09 VP Inst Effectiveness/Accred/Rsrch .... Dr. Mary CLARK
13 Chief Information Officer .... Mr. Robert STACK
26 AVP Communications & Public Affs .... Ms. Tamara SAKAGAWA
103 District Dean Wkfc Educ/Econ Dev .... Dr. Orathai NORTHERN
15 Director Human Resources .... Ms. Jill HALL
35 Dean Student Services-WH .... Mr. Lawrence PAKOWSKI
35 Dean Student Services-LK .... Mr. Sylvester LITTLE
20 Dean Academic Affairs-WH .... Ms. April ROBINSON
20 Dean of Academic Success .... Mr. Donald PAINTER
21 Controller .... Ms. Teresa VOROUS
84 Director Stdnt Enrollment/Registrar .... Ms. Kathy BUCKLEW
37 Director Student Financial Svcs .... Ms. Ronshetta HOWELL
66 Director Nursing .... Dr. Annette HUTCHERSON
102 Director Financial Affs/PSC Found .... Mr. Lynn WILSON
18 Director Facilities .... Mr. George URBANO
22 Director Equity/Diversity/Inclusion .... Ms. Valparisa BAKER
103 Director Corporate College .... Mr. Howard DRAKE
88 Principal Chain of Lakes CHS .... Mr. Keith BONNEY
88 Principal Lakeland Col HS .... Mr. Rick JEFFRIES
88 Center Director JDA .... Mr. Andy OGUNTOLA
41 Athletic Director .... Vacant
96 Director Purchasing .... Mr. Mark LILLQUIST
04 Administrative Asst to President .... Mrs. Christine LEE
104 Director Study Abroad .... Ms. Kim SIMPSON
106 Dir Instructional Tech/e-learning .... Mr. Christopher AMATO
19 Director Security/Safety .... Ms. Denise ANDREU
25 Chief Contracts/Grants Admin .... Ms. Jennifer FIORENZA
29 Director Alumni Relations .... Mrs. Marianne GEORGE
38 Dir Disability/Counseling Services .... Ms. Kim PEARSALL
43 Dir Legal Services/General Counsel .... Mr. Don WILSON
50 Program Director Business .... Ms. Maria LOHOCZKY
53 Program Director Education .... Dr. Patty LINDER
54 Program Director Engineering Tech .... Dr. Mori TOOSI

Polytechnic University of Puerto Rico (B)

8180 NW 36th Street, Suite 401, Miami FL 33166-6674

Telephone: (305) 418-8000 — Identification: 666238
Accreditation: **&M**

† Regional accreditation is carried under the parent institution, Universidad Politecnica de Puerto Rico, San Juan, PR.

Polytechnic University of Puerto Rico-Orlando Campus (C)

550 N Econlockhatchee Trail, Orlando FL 32825

Telephone: (407) 677-7000 — Identification: 770172
Accreditation: **&M**

† Branch campus of Universidad Politecnica De Puerto Rico, San Juan, PR

The Praxis Institute (D)

1850 SW 8th Street, 4th Floor, Miami FL 33135

County: Miami-Dade — FICE Identification: 031147
Unit ID: 430582
Telephone: (305) 642-4104 — Carnegie Class: Not Classified
FAX Number: N/A — Calendar System: Semester
URL: www.praxis.edu
Established: 1988 — Annual Undergrad Tuition & Fees: N/A
Enrollment: 404 — Coed
Affiliation or Control: Proprietary — IRS Status: Proprietary
Highest Offering: Associate Degree
Accreditation: **COE**, OTA, PTAA

01 Executive Director .... Rebeca ALFIE
06 Campus Registrar .... Zoila ESPINOSA

Premiere International College (E)

2055 Central Avenue, Fort Myers FL 33901

County: Palm Beach — Identification: 667295
Telephone: (239) 454-5000 — Carnegie Class: Not Classified
FAX Number: (239) 454-0456 — Calendar System: Quarter
URL: www.premierecollege.com
Established: 2009 — Annual Undergrad Tuition & Fees: N/A
Enrollment: N/A — Coed
Affiliation or Control: Proprietary — IRS Status: Proprietary
Highest Offering: Associate Degree
Accreditation: **ACICS**

01 President .... Cynthia RUE

Professional Hands Institute (F)

3383 NW 7th Street, Suite 200, Miami FL 33125

County: Miami-Dade — FICE Identification: 041431
Unit ID: 454908
Telephone: (305) 442-6011 — Carnegie Class: Spec 2-yr-Health
FAX Number: (305) 442-6013 — Calendar System: Semester
URL: www.prohands.edu
Established: 2004 — Annual Undergrad Tuition & Fees: N/A
Enrollment: 105 — Coed
Affiliation or Control: Proprietary — IRS Status: Proprietary
Highest Offering: Associate Degree
Accreditation: **COE**

12 Campus Director .... Ms. Caridad TRIANA

Rasmussen College - Fort Myers (G)

9160 Forum Corporate Parkway, Fort Myers FL 33905

Telephone: (239) 477-2100 — Identification: 667062
Accreditation: **&NH**, ADNUR, MAAB

† Regional accreditation is carried under the parent institution in Saint Cloud, MN. The tuition figure is an average, actual tuition may vary.

Rasmussen College - Ocala (H)

4755 SW 46th Court, Ocala FL 34474

Telephone: (352) 629-1941 — FICE Identification: 008501
Accreditation: **&NH**, ADNUR, MAAB

† Regional accreditation carried under the parent institution in Saint Cloud, MN. The tuition figure is an average, actual tuition may vary.

Rasmussen College - Tampa/Brandon (I)

4042 Park Oaks Boulevard, Tampa FL 33610

Telephone: (813) 246-7600 — Identification: 667067
Accreditation: **&NH**, ADNUR, MAAB

† Regional accreditation is carried under the parent institution in Saint Cloud, MN. The tuition figure is an average, actual tuition may vary.

Reformed Theological Seminary (J)

1231 Reformation Drive, Oviedo FL 32765-7197

Telephone: (407) 366-9493 — Identification: 666628
Accreditation: **&SC**, THEOL

† Regional accreditation is carried under the parent institution in Jackson, MS.

Ringling College of Art and Design (K)

2700 N Tamiami Trail, Sarasota FL 34234-5895

County: Sarasota — FICE Identification: 012574
Unit ID: 136774
Telephone: (941) 351-5100 — Carnegie Class: Spec-4-yr-Arts
FAX Number: (941) 359-7517 — Calendar System: Semester
URL: www.ringling.edu
Established: 1931 — Annual Undergrad Tuition & Fees: $46,420
Enrollment: 1,456 — Coed
Affiliation or Control: Independent Non-Profit — IRS Status: 501(c)3
Highest Offering: Baccalaureate
Accreditation: **SC**, ART, CIDA

01 President .... Dr. Larry R. THOMPSON
04 Executive Assistant to the Pres .... Ms. Kerry SCHAFFER
100 Special Assistant to the Pres .... Ms. Raelyn LINCOLN
05 VP for Academic Affairs .... Dr. Peter MCALLISTER
20 Assoc VP for AA/Dean of Faculty .... Mr. David H. JACKSON
20 Assoc VP for AA/Dean of UG Studies .... Mr. Jeff SCHWARTZ
51 Asst VP/Dir Cont Stds/Special Pgms .... Dr. Mona CALLIES
06 Registrar .... Mr. Justin SELPH
36 Director Career Services .... Mr. Charles KOVACS
08 Dir of Library Services .... Dr. Kristina KEOGH
26 Int Dir Marketin/Digital Strategies .... Ms. Lisa MOODY
27 Editorial & PR Manager .... Ms. Stephanie LEDERER
108 Director of Assessment .... Ms. Kelly BEACHLER
111 VP for Advancement .... Ms. Stacey CORLEY
110 Asst VP for Constituent Engagement .... Ms. Lisa INTAGLIATA
112 Asst VP for Strategic Philanthropy .... Ms. Lora WEY
29 Dir Alumni Relations/Annual Giving .... Ms. Susan BOROZAN
10 VP for Finance & Administration .... Dr. Tracy A. WAGNER
21 Asst VP for Fin & Admn/Controller .... Ms. Monica K. WAID
18 Asst VP/Dir Facilities Operations .... Mr. Viron LYNCH
19 Director of Public Safety .... Mr. Don STROM
37 Dir of Financial Aid .... Mr. Lee HARRELL
15 VP for Human/Organizational Dev .... Ms. Christine C. DEGEORGE
09 Asst VP for Planning & IE .... Dr. Pat MIZAK
16 Dir of Human Resources .... Mr. Darren MATHEWS
32 VP for Student Life/Dean Stdnts .... Dr. Tammy S. WALSH
39 Assoc Dean of Students/Res Life .... Mr. Chris SHAFFER
35 Assoc Dean of Students/Student Dev .... Mr. Jekeyma ROBINSON
23 Dir Student Health Services .... Dr. Erin ROBINSON
07 Dean of Admissions .... Mr. James H. DEAN
07 Director of Admissions .... Mr. Gregg PRIGERSON
13 Dir of Institutional Technology .... Ms. Mahmoud PEGAH
90 Dir of Academic Computing .... Ms. Karissa MILLER
91 Dir of Administrative Computing .... Ms. Kris PEGAH

The Robert E. Webber Institute for Worship Studies (L)

4001 Hendricks Ave, Jacksonville FL 32207

County: Duval — Identification: 666616
Telephone: (904) 264-2172 — Carnegie Class: Not Classified
FAX Number: (904) 379-5534 — Calendar System: Semester
URL: www.iws.edu
Established: 1998 — Annual Graduate Tuition & Fees: N/A
Enrollment: N/A — Coed
Affiliation or Control: Independent Non-Profit — IRS Status: 501(c)3
Highest Offering: Doctorate; No Undergraduates
Accreditation: **BI**

01 Chief Executive Officer/President .... Dr. James R. HART
05 Academic Dean .... Dr. Dinelle FRANKLAND
10 Chief Financial Officer/Controller .... Ms. Christi G. MATTESON
42 VP of Spiritual Life .... Dr. Darrell A. HARRIS
84 Director Enrollment Management .... Mr. Mark J. MURRAY
08 Library Director .... Ms. Susan A. MASSEY
29 Director Alumni Relations .... Dr. Kent L. WALTERS
24 Dir of Technical Services .... Mr. Samuel L. HOROWITZ
04 Asst to the President .... Vacant
32 Dir Student Services/Office Admin .... Ms. Sandy E. DINKINS
45 Director Assessment/Planning .... Dr. Steve E. HUNTLEY
13 Information Technology Coordinator .... Dr. James Kenneth RUSHING
26 Dir of Missional Relations .... Dr. Frank FORTUNATO
30 Development Coordinator .... Ms. Carol HART

Rollins College (M)

1000 Holt Avenue, Winter Park FL 32789-4499

County: Orange — FICE Identification: 001515
Unit ID: 136950
Telephone: (407) 646-2000 — Carnegie Class: Masters/L
FAX Number: (407) 646-2600 — Calendar System: Semester
URL: www.rollins.edu
Established: 1885 — Annual Undergrad Tuition & Fees: $49,760
Enrollment: 3,278 — Coed
Affiliation or Control: Independent Non-Profit — IRS Status: 501(c)3
Highest Offering: Doctorate
Accreditation: **SC**, CACREP, MUS

01 President .... Dr. Grant H. CORNWELL
05 VP Acad Affairs/Provost .... Dr. Susan R. SINGER
32 Vice President Student Affairs .... Dr. Mamta M. ACCAPADI
10 Vice President Business/Finance .... Mr. Ed KANIA
13 Chief Information Officer .... Mr. Troy THOMASON
20 Dean of the Faculty .... Dr. Jennifer CAVENAUGH
35 Asst VP Stdnt Affs & Dean of Stdnts .... Dr. Meghan HARTE WEYANT
84 VP of Enrollment Mgmt and Marketing .... Dr. Faye F. TYDLASKA
50 Dean Crummer Grad Sch of Business .... Dr. Deborah F. CROWN
55 Dean Holt School .... Dr. Robert SANDERS
42 Dean of Religious Life .... Rev. Katrina JENKINS
21 Assoc VP Finance/Asst Treasurer .... Mr. William SHORT
26 VP Communications & External Rels .... Mr. Sam STARK
15 Assoc VP Human Res/Risk Management .... Mr. Matt HAWKS
108 Asst Provost Inst Effectiveness .... Dr. Toni STROLLO HOLBROOK
41 Athletic Director .... Ms. Pennie PARKER
37 Director of Financial Aid .... Mr. Steve BOOKER
09 Director of Institutional Research .... Mr. Udeth LUGO
104 Director of International Programs .... Ms. Giselda BEAUDIN
07 Dean of Admission .... Ms. Zaire MCCOY
39 Assoc Dean of Students .... Mr. Leon HAYNER
36 Asst VP of Career & Life Planning .... Dr. Lisa JOHNSON
18 AVP of Facilities Management .... Mr. Scott BITIKOFER
19 Assistant VP Public Safety .... Mr. Ken MILLER
29 Sr Director Alumni Engagement .... Ms. Katherine PAPPAS
111 VP for Institutional Advancement .... Ms. Laurie HOUCK
102 Director of Foundation Relations .... Mr. Joseph MONTI
06 Registrar .... Ms. Stephanie HENNING
40 Manager of Bookstore .... Ms. Mary VITELLI
04 Exec Assistant to the President .... Ms. Jillian SCHUMM
23 Director of Wellness .... Ms. Connie BRISCOE
25 Director Contracts/Grants Admin .... Ms. Devon MASSOT
35 Asst VP Student Affairs/Community .... Ms. Michele MEYER
08 Director of Olin Library .... Dr. Deborah PROSSER

88 Director of Institutional Analytics ... Mr. Meghal PARIKH
113 Director of Student Accounts/Bursar ... Mr. Cory BADEN

Saber College (A)

3990 West Flagler Street, Ste 103, Miami FL 33134
County: Miami-Dade FICE Identification: 036964
Unit ID: 449506
Telephone: (305) 443-9170 Carnegie Class: Spec 2-yr-Health
FAX Number: (305) 443-8441 Calendar System: Other
URL: www.sabercollege.edu
Established: 1972 Annual Undergrad Tuition & Fees: N/A
Enrollment: 342 Coed
Affiliation or Control: Independent Non-Profit IRS Status: 501(c)3
Highest Offering: Associate Degree
Accreditation: COE, PTAA

01 Director Nursing Program ... Ms. Anita GOINS
05 Dean of Academic Affairs ... Ms. Amarilis SOMOZA

St. John Vianney College Seminary (B)

2900 SW 87th Avenue, Miami FL 33165-3244
County: Miami-Dade FICE Identification: 008075
Unit ID: 137272
Telephone: (305) 223-4561 Carnegie Class: Spec-4-yr-Faith
FAX Number: (305) 223-0650 Calendar System: Semester
URL: www.sjvcs.edu
Established: 1959 Annual Undergrad Tuition & Fees: $21,000
Enrollment: 70 Male
Affiliation or Control: Roman Catholic IRS Status: 501(c)3
Highest Offering: Master's
Accreditation: SC

01 Rector & President ... Rev. Ferdinand R. SANTOS
32 Vice Rector/Dean of Students ... Rev. Matías A. HUALPA
42 Head Spiritual Director ... Rev. Joseph KOTTAYIL

St. Johns River State College (C)

5001 St. Johns Avenue, Palatka FL 32177-3897
County: Putnam FICE Identification: 001523
Unit ID: 137281
Telephone: (386) 312-4200 Carnegie Class: Bac/Assoc-Assoc Dom
FAX Number: (386) 312-4229 Calendar System: Semester
URL: www.sjrstate.edu
Established: 1958 Annual Undergrad Tuition & Fees (In-District): $2,830
Enrollment: 7,249 Coed
Affiliation or Control: State/Local IRS Status: 501(c)3
Highest Offering: Baccalaureate
Accreditation: SC, ADNUR, ART, CAHIIM, COARC, EMT, NUR, RAD

01 President ... Mr. Joe PICKENS
43 Senior VP/General Counsel ... Dr. Melissa C. MILLER
32 Vice President Student Affairs ... Dr. Gilbert L. EVANS, JR.
05 VP & CAO/Exec Dir St Augustine ... Dr. Melanie A. BROWN
10 Vice President Finance & Admin/CFO ... Dr. Lynn POWERS
30 Vice Pres Develop/External Affairs ... Mrs. Caroline D. TINGLE
108 VP Assessment/Research & Tech ... Dr. Rosalind M. HUMERICK
103 VP Workforce/Exec Dir Orange Park ... Vacant
20 Associate VP Academic Affairs ... Dr. Edward K. JORDAN
15 Associate VP Human Resources ... Mrs. Ginger C. STOKES
09 Assistant VP Ass/Research & Grants ... Dr. Ellen BURNS
13 Chief Information Officer ... Mr. Richard C. ANDERSON
49 Dean of Arts & Sciences ... Mr. Mike KELLER
19 Dean of Crim Justice/Public Safety ... Dr. Jeffrey C. LEE
57 Dean of Florida School of the Arts ... Mr. Alain R. HENTSCHEL
08 Dean of Library Services ... Dr. Christina WILL
66 Dean of Nursing ... Dr. Diane P. PAGANO
55 Dean of Adult Education ... Dr. Melissa PERRY
53 Dean of Teacher Education ... Dr. Myrna L. ALLEN
75 Dean of Workforce & Technical Ed ... Dr. John W. PATERSON
76 Dean of Allied Health ... Dr. Holly COULLIETTE
88 Exec Dir TH Center for the Arts ... Ms. Anna ZIRBEL
50 Director of Business Education ... Mr. Joel C. ABO
77 Director of Computer Education ... Dr. John ETIENNE
51 Dir of Dual Enroll & College Access ... Mrs. Meghan DEPUTY
26 Director of Public Relations ... Mrs. Susan B. KESSLER
121 Director of Academic Advising ... Ms. Karen THOMAS
88 Director of Testing & Stdnt Support ... Mr. Todd DIXON
06 Registrar ... Mrs. Susanne B. LINEBERGER
21 Controller ... Mr. Randall PETERSON
37 Director of Financial Aid ... Ms. Suzanne M. EVANS
106 Director of eLearning ... Mr. Jack C. HALL

Saint Leo University (D)

33701 State Road 52 W, Saint Leo FL 33574-6665
County: Pasco FICE Identification: 001526
Unit ID: 137032
Telephone: (352) 588-8200 Carnegie Class: Masters/L
FAX Number: (352) 588-8654 Calendar System: Semester
URL: www.saintleo.edu
Established: 1889 Annual Undergrad Tuition & Fees: $23,020
Enrollment: 13,099 Coed
Affiliation or Control: Roman Catholic IRS Status: 501(c)3
Highest Offering: Doctorate
Accreditation: SC, ACBSP, CEA, COSMA, SW

01 President ... Dr. Jeffrey SENESE
05 VP Academic Affairs ... Dr. Mary SPOTO
84 VP Enrollment ... Mr. Matthew MILLS
10 VP Business Affairs/CFO ... Mr. John NISBET
111 VP University Advancement ... Mr. Denny MOLLER
03 Senior Vice President ... Ms. Melanie STORMS
04 Assistant to the President ... Vacant
13 Chief Information Officer ... Mr. Thomas HULL
88 Associate VP Regional Accreditation ... Dr. Diane BALL
43 Associate VP/General Counsel ... Ms. Kelly HILL
15 AVP Human Resources ... Mr. David TOMANIO
42 Chaplain for University Ministries ... Fr. Kyle SMITH
32 Associate VP Student Affairs ... Mr. Kenneth POSNER
32 Associate VP Worldwide Stdnt Svcs ... Mr. Shadel HAMILTON
38 Director Counseling Services ... Mr. Lawson JOLLY
49 Dean School of Arts & Sciences ... Vacant
53 Dean School of Educ/Social Svcs ... Dr. Susan KINSELLA
50 Interim Dean School of Business ... Dr. Charles HALE
58 Dir Grad Studies Criminal Justice ... Dr. Robert DIEMER
58 Dir Grad Studies in Education ... Dr. Fern AEFSKY
70 Dir Grad Studies in Social Work ... Dr. Cindy LEE
73 Dir Graduate Studies in Theology ... Dr. Randall WOODARD
88 Director Graduate Creative Writing ... Dr. Steven KISTULENTZ
06 Registrar ... Mrs. Karen HATFIELD
08 Interim Director Library Services ... Dr. Doris VAN KAMPEN-BREIT
07 Assoc VP of Enrollment/Support Svcs ... Mr. Jeffrey WALSH
88 Asst VP of Learning Design ... Dr. Karen HAHN
88 Director Student Learning ... Ms. Erica HICKS
39 Dir Residence Life & Leadership ... Mr. Sean VANGUILDER
88 Exec Dir Academic Administration ... Mr. Joseph TADEO
41 Director Intercollegiate Athletics ... Mr. Francis REIDY
18 AVP Facilities Management ... Mr. Jose CABAN
19 Director Campus Security & Safety ... Mr. Vincent D'AMBROSIO
22 Director Accessibility Services ... Mr. Michael BAILEY
29 Director Alumni Engagement ... Ms. Elizabeth BARR
110 Director Advancement Services ... Mr. Stephen KUBASEK
85 Exec Director PDSO Global Affairs ... Ms. Paige RAMSEY-HAMACHER
16 Executive Director Human Resources ... Ms. Susan MARTIN
21 Senior Assoc VP Finance ... Mr. James DETUCCIO
96 Mgr Accts Payable/Sponsor Billing ... Ms. Laura SOLBERG
114 Director of Budgets ... Mr. Mark WILLIAMS
116 Director Internal Audit Services ... Ms. Monica MOYER
12 Asst VP Military Center Operations ... Mr. Tyler UPSHAW
12 Asst VP Central Region ... Ms. Candis WHITFIELD
12 Asst VP Tampa Region ... Mr. Tyler UPSHAW
12 Asst VP Florida Region ... Ms. Katie DEGNER
103 Learning & Development Manager ... Ms. Shannon MOORE
109 Director Dining Services ... Mr. Justin BUSH
88 Executive Officer ... Ms. Marcia MALIA
37 Associate VP of Financial Aid ... Ms. Melinda CLARK
27 Director University Communications ... Ms. Marie THORNSBERRY
88 VP UC Adm/Center Global Engagement ... Dr. Senthil KUMAR
108 Dir of Institutional Effectiveness ... Dr. Ellen BOYLAN
88 Asst Vice President Enrollment ... Mr. Mark RUSSUM
89 Director First Year Experience ... Ms. Dawn MCELVEEN
119 Director Information Security ... Mr. Darius LEWIS
121 Director Student Advising ... Ms. Zaheda HERMAN

St. Petersburg College (E)

PO Box 13489, Saint Petersburg FL 33733-3489
County: Pinellas FICE Identification: 001528
Unit ID: 137078
Telephone: (727) 341-4772 Carnegie Class: Bac/Assoc-Mixed
FAX Number: (727) 341-3318 Calendar System: Semester
URL: www.spcollege.edu
Established: 1927 Annual Undergrad Tuition & Fees (In-District): $2,682
Enrollment: 29,548 Coed
Affiliation or Control: Local IRS Status: 501(c)3
Highest Offering: Baccalaureate
Accreditation: SC, ADNUR, CAHIIM, CEA, COARC, DH, EMT, FUSER, NURSE, PTAA, RAD

01 President ... Dr. Tonjua L. WILLIAMS
05 VP Instruction/Academic Pgm ... Vacant
32 VP Student Affairs ... Dr. Jamelle CONNER
10 VP Admin/Bus Svcs & Info Tech ... Brian MILES
18 Acting Assoc VP Facilities/Inst ... Diana WRIGHT
15 Associate VP Human Resources ... Carol SUMTER
111 VP Inst Advance/Exec Dir Foundation ... Jesse TURTLE
114 Assoc VP Budget and Compliance ... Janette HUNT
84 Assoc VP Enrollment Services ... Dr. Pat RINARD
37 Assoc VP Financial Asst Svcs ... Michael J. BENNETT
20 Assoc VP Academic Affs/Partnership ... Catherine C. KENNEDY
103 Career Connections Director ... Dr. Jason KRUPP
43 General Counsel ... Suzanne GARDNER
12 Provost Clearwater Campus ... Dr. Stanley VITTETOE
12 Provost/Health Ed Ctr and Allstate ... Dr. Eric CARVER
12 Provost St Petersburg Campus ... Vacant
12 Provost Seminole Campus/eCampus ... Mark STRICKLAND
12 Provost Tarpon Springs Campus ... Dr. Rodrigo DAVIS
12 Provost Downtown/Midtown ... Dr. Tashika GRIFFITH
22 Dir Equal Access/Equal Opp/Title IX ... Pam SMITH
96 Dir Procurement & Asset Mgmt ... Vacant
38 Student Support Manager ... Joe DVORACSEK
88 Dean College of Public Safety Admin ... Dr. Brian FRANK
88 Dean Col of Policy Ethics/Leg Stds ... Dr. Susan S. DEMERS
83 Dean Social & Behavioral Sciences ... Dr. Joseph SMILEY
88 Associate VP Collegiate High School ... Starla METZ
88 President Faculty Senate ... Dr. Jeffrey BRIGGS
50 Acting Dean College of Business ... Marta PRZYBOROWSKI
81 Dean Mathematics ... Jimmy CHANG
65 Dean Natural Science ... Dr. Natavia MIDDLETON
79 Acting Dean Humanities/Fine Arts ... Dr. Barbara HUBBARD
53 Dean College of Education ... Dr. Kimberly HARTMAN
60 Dean Communications ... Joseph LEOPOLD
76 Dean College of Health Sciences ... Dr. Deanna STENTIFORD
74 Assoc Dean Veterinary Technology ... Dr. Cynthia GREY
72 Dean College of Comp & Info Tech ... Dr. James STEWART
66 Dean College of Nursing ... Dr. Louisana LOUIS
08 Exec Director Learning Resources ... Matthew BODIE
04 Administrative Coordinator ... Rebecca TURNER
07 Director of Admissions and Records ... Eva CHRISTENSEN
09 Director of Institutional Research ... Djuan FOX
100 Chief of Staff ... Jackie SKRYD
104 Director International Programs ... Vacant
106 Associate VP Online Learning/Svcs ... Vacant
108 Dir Institutional Effectiveness ... Magaly TYMMS
13 Chief Information Officer ... Zoran STANISIC
19 Director College Security Services ... Daniel BARTO
25 Exec Dir of Grants Development ... Katie SHULTZ
86 Director Government Relations ... Eired EDDY
41 Athletic Director ... Davie GILL

St. Thomas University (F)

16401 NW 37th Avenue, Miami Gardens FL 33054-6498
County: Miami-Dade FICE Identification: 001468
Unit ID: 137476
Telephone: (305) 625-6000 Carnegie Class: Masters/L
FAX Number: (305) 628-6510 Calendar System: Semester
URL: www.stu.edu
Established: 1961 Annual Undergrad Tuition & Fees: $31,830
Enrollment: 4,538 Coed
Affiliation or Control: Roman Catholic IRS Status: 501(c)3
Highest Offering: Doctorate
Accreditation: SC, LAW, NURSE, @THEOL

01 President ... Mr. David A. ARMSTRONG
05 Provost/Chief Academic Officer ... Dr. Jeremy L. MORELAND
10 VP Admin/Chief Financial Officer ... Ms. Linda WAGNER
111 VP Philanthropy/Communications ... Ms. Janine LAUDISIO
106 Vice Provost Online/Adult Education ... Dr. Theodore BLASHAK
26 Director University Marketing ... Ms. Erin AYRIM
06 Registrar ... Mrs. Maria ABDEL
37 Director Financial Aid ... Ms. Yamirka RIAL
08 Associate Library Director ... Ms. Jessica OROZCO
21 Controller ... Mrs. Maribel SMITH
18 Assoc VP Facilities/Physical Plant ... Mr. Eric WILKYMACKY
15 Associate VP Human Resources ... Ms. Nadine LEWIS-SEVILLA
09 Associate Vice Provost IR ... Dr. Diana BARBU
117 Assoc Dir Risk Mgmt/Compliance ... Ms. Monique BRIJBASI
41 Director of Athletics ... Mrs. Laura J. COURTLEY-TODD
32 Dean of Students ... Mr. Richard MCNAB
20 Dean of Academic Programs ... Dr. Luis C. FERNANDEZ-TORRES
16 Assoc Director Human Resources ... Ms. Lenore M. PRADO
44 Director of Annual Giving ... Ms. DeAnna ARANA
88 SACSCOC Liaison ... Dr. Pamela CINGEL
29 Director Alumni Relations ... Ms. Lorena HIDALGO
07 Assistant Director of Admissions ... Mr. Otis MILLER
07 Assistant Director of Admissions ... Mr. Yasdanee VALDES
04 Admin Assistant to the President ... Ms. Marina UGALDE
100 Chief of Staff ... Ms. Jameka A. WINDHAM

St. Vincent De Paul Regional Seminary (G)

10701 S Military Trail, Boynton Beach FL 33436-4899
County: Palm Beach FICE Identification: 008223
Unit ID: 136701
Telephone: (561) 732-4424 Carnegie Class: Spec-4-yr-Faith
FAX Number: (561) 737-2205 Calendar System: Semester
URL: www.svdp.edu
Established: 1963 Annual Graduate Tuition & Fees: N/A
Enrollment: 146 Coed
Affiliation or Control: Roman Catholic IRS Status: 501(c)3
Highest Offering: Master's; No Undergraduates
Accreditation: THEOL

01 Rector/President ... Rev. David L. TOUPS
05 Vice Rector/Dean Acad Formation ... Rev. Alfredo HERNANDEZ
10 Treasurer ... Mr. Keith PARKER
08 Director of the Library ... Mr. Arthur QUINN
04 Administrative Asst to President ... Mrs. Herminia C. GARCIA
09 Dir Inst Research/Assessment ... Dr. Mary FROEHLE
111 Chief Development/Advancement ... Ms. Daniella COY
06 Registrar ... Mrs. Alicia RUEFF

San Ignacio University (H)

3905 NW 107th Ave, Suite 301, Doral FL 33178
County: Miami-Dade Identification: 667130
Unit ID: 486239
Telephone: (305) 629-2929 Carnegie Class: Spec-4-yr-Bus
FAX Number: N/A Calendar System: Semester
URL: www.sanignaciouniversity.edu
Established: 2007 Annual Undergrad Tuition & Fees: $10,400
Enrollment: 275 Coed
Affiliation or Control: Proprietary IRS Status: Proprietary
Highest Offering: Master's
Accreditation: ACICS

01 President ... Luis LAUREDO

05 Vice President Academic Affairs ... Marisol SALCEDO
08 Head Librarian ... Silvia LOPEZ
15 Human Resources Senior Coordinator ... Ivette BAJANDAS
37 Financial Aid Coordinator ... Fabiola LAGARDERE
10 Director of Administration/Finance ... Carmen RODRIGUEZ

Santa Fe College (A)

3000 NW 83rd Street, Gainesville FL 32606-6200
County: Alachua | FICE Identification: 001519 | Unit ID: 137096
Telephone: (352) 395-5000 | Carnegie Class: Bac/Assoc-Assoc Dom
FAX Number: (352) 395-5581 | Calendar System: Semester
URL: www.sfcollege.edu
Established: 1965 | Annual Undergrad Tuition & Fees (In-District): $2,563
Enrollment: 14,588 | Coed
Affiliation or Control: Local | IRS Status: 501(c)3
Highest Offering: Baccalaureate
Accreditation: SC, ADNUR, CAHIIM, COARC, CONST, CVT, DA, DH, DMS, EMT, MT, NMT, NURSE, POLYT, PTAA, RAD, SURGT

01 President ... Dr. Jackson N. SASSER
05 Provost/Vice Pres Academic Affairs ... Dr. Edward BONAHUE
10 Chief Financial Ofcr/VP Admin Affs ... Ms. Ginger GIBSON
32 Vice President Student Affairs ... Dr. Naima BROWN
111 Vice President Ofc for Advancement ... Mr. Chuck CLEMONS
108 VP Assessment/Research/Technology ... Dr. Lisa ARMOUR
04 Assistant to the President ... Ms. Cathy KEEN
20 Assoc Vice Pres Academic Affairs ... Dr. Jodi LONG
20 Assoc Vice Pres Academic Affairs ... Dr. Stefanie WASCHULL
104 Asst VP Academic Affairs ... Dr. Vilma FUENTES
13 Assoc VP Information Tech Services ... Mr. Bill PENNEY
18 Assoc VP Facilities Services ... Mr. Gary COTHREN
35 Assoc VP Student Affairs ... Dr. Dan RODKIN
22 Dean Access and Inclusion ... Dr. Cheryl CALHOUN
25 Director Grants/Projects ... Ms. Kathryn LEHMAN
35 Asst Vice Pres Student Affairs ... Dr. Beatrice AWONIYI
43 Legal Counsel ... Ms. Patti P. LOCASCIO
06 College Registrar ... Mr. Mike HUTLEY
88 Dir High Sch Dual Enrollment Pgm ... Ms. Jennifer HOMARD
121 Int Dir Advising & Career Resources ... Ms. Andrea LEE
41 Athletic Director ... Mr. Jim KEITES
08 Director Library Service ... Ms. Pat PROFETA
19 Director Institute of Public Safety ... Mr. Tom ACKERMAN
35 Director of Student Life ... Dr. Tracey REEVES
96 Director of Purchasing ... Mr. David SHLAFER
28 Coordinator Col Achievement Pgm ... Ms. Dana LINDSEY
37 Director Student Financial Aid ... Ms. Kamia MWANGO
15 Director Human Resources ... Ms. Lela FRYE
09 Director of Institutional Research ... Mr. Gary HARTGE
07 Coordinator for Admissions ... Ms. Carolyn DAS
26 Chief Public Relations/Marketing ... Ms. Teri MCCLELLAN
110 Assoc VP Advancement ... Mr. Mike CURRY
106 Asst VP Academic Technologies ... Vacant
86 Asst to President Govt Relations ... Mr. Liam MCCLAY

Sarasota University (B)

6371 Business Blvd, Ste 200, Sarasota FL 34240
County: Sarasota | Identification: 667337
Telephone: (866) 582-8448 | Carnegie Class: Not Classified
FAX Number: N/A | Calendar System: Trimester
URL: www.sarasotauniversity.org
Established: 2013 | Annual Graduate Tuition & Fees: N/A
Enrollment: N/A | Coed
Affiliation or Control: Independent Non-Profit | IRS Status: 501(c)3
Highest Offering: Master's; No Undergraduates
Accreditation: DEAC

01 Founder & President ... Dr. Ronald OGRODNIK
05 Vice Pres Academic Affairs ... Dr. Chuck MLYNARCZYK

Schiller International University (C)

8560 Ulmerton Road, Largo FL 33771
County: Pinellas | FICE Identification: 023141 | Unit ID: 404338
Telephone: (727) 736-5082 | Carnegie Class: Spec-4-yr-Bus
FAX Number: (727) 738-8405 | Calendar System: Semester
URL: www.schiller.edu
Established: 1964 | Annual Undergrad Tuition & Fees: $14,360
Enrollment: 408 | Coed
Affiliation or Control: Proprietary | IRS Status: Proprietary
Highest Offering: Master's
Accreditation: ACICS

01 Campus Director ... Ms. Jeanette ESPINAL
05 Provost ... Dr. Craig MCCLELLAN

Seminole State College of Florida (D)

100 Weldon Boulevard, Sanford FL 32773-6199
County: Seminole | FICE Identification: 001520 | Unit ID: 137209
Telephone: (407) 708-4722 | Carnegie Class: Bac/Assoc-Assoc Dom
FAX Number: (407) 708-2139 | Calendar System: Semester
URL: www.seminolestate.edu
Established: 1965 | Annual Undergrad Tuition & Fees (In-District): $3,131
Enrollment: 17,550 | Coed
Affiliation or Control: Local | IRS Status: 501(c)3
Highest Offering: Baccalaureate
Accreditation: SC, ADNUR, CAHIIM, CIDA, COARC, EMT, PTAA

01 President ... Dr. Georgia LORENZ
10 Executive VP/CFO ... Mr. Richard COLLINS
05 VP Academic Affairs/CAO ... Dr. Laura ROSS
32 VP Student Affairs ... Dr. Johnny CRAIG
13 VP Information Resources/CIO ... Dr. Dick HAMANN
30 VP Resource Develop & Economic Dev ... Dr. John GYLLIN
21 AVP Finance & Budget ... Ms. Judi COOPER
35 AVP Student Development ... Dr. Jan LLOYD
12 Dean of Students Altamonte Springs ... Ms. Lynn GARRETT
12 Dean of Students Oviedo Campus ... Mr. Jeffery GIBBS
08 Dean Learning Resources ... Ms. Barbara HILDERBRAND
36 AVP School of Career and Profession ... Dr. Cheryl CICOTTI
54 AVP Engineering and Design ... Mr. Michael STALEY
88 AVP School of Academic Foundations ... Mr. Frank BONJIONE
26 Dir College & Community Relations ... Ms. Deborah RICHARD
91 Director Networks ... Mr. Julio VALENTIN
38 Director Counseling and Advising ... Ms. Deborah LYNCH
20 Director Curriculum ... Ms. Carlene MCNEIL
15 AVP Human Resources ... Ms. Mae ASHBY
07 Dir Enrollment Svcs/Registrar . Ms. Barbara RODRIQUEZ LAMAS
37 Director Student Financial Aid ... Ms. Roseann AMATO
09 AVP Institutional Effectiveness ... Dr. Mark MORGAN
41 Director Intercollegiate Athletics ... Mr. Kurt ESSER
84 AVP Student Recruitment ... Mrs. Pamela MENNECHEY
36 Director Career Development ... Ms. Heather ENGELKING
14 AVP Information Technology ... Ms. Pilar ACOSTA
106 Dir Online Education/E-learning ... Ms. Michelle FRANZ
28 Director of Diversity ... Ms. Janet BALANOFF
102 Dir Foundation Finance & Operations ... Ms. Christina BEHRENS
110 Assistant Director of Development ... Ms. Amber COX
04 Admin Assistant to the President ... Ms. Cheryl R. DALEY
19 Director Security/Safety ... Ms. Maxine OLIVER
43 Director Legal Svcs/General Counsel ... Mr. J. Paul CARLAND

South Florida Bible College (E)

2200 SW 10th Street, Deerfield Beach FL 33442
County: Broward | FICE Identification: 032643 | Unit ID: 366003
Telephone: (954) 637-2268 | Carnegie Class: Spec-4-yr-Faith
FAX Number: (954) 719-3780 | Calendar System: Semester
URL: www.sfbc.edu
Established: 1985 | Annual Undergrad Tuition & Fees: $6,900
Enrollment: 382 | Coed
Affiliation or Control: Interdenominational | IRS Status: 501(c)3
Highest Offering: Master's
Accreditation: BI

01 President ... Dr. Mary A. DRABIK
03 Vice President ... Josiah STEPHAN
05 Chief Academic Officer ... Dr. Jodyann REID
10 Chief Financial Officer ... Zil WENCESLAU
06 Registrar ... Dr. Michael RACKLEY
08 Librarian ... Paula STEVENSON
20 Dean of Faculty ... Dr. Esa AUTERO
32 Dean of Students ... Vacant
29 Director Alumni Relations ... Casey PALACIOUS
84 Director Enrollment Management ... Lara FERREIRA
13 Chief Info Technology Officer (CIO) ... Joshua DRABIK
111 Chief Development/Advancement ... Vacant
04 Administrative Asst to President ... Neeta PRAKASH
09 Director of Institutional Research ... Davi BAKTHAKUMAR
15 Chief Human Resources Officer ... Crystal BERTLING
19 Director Security/Safety ... Hector PEREZ
37 Director Student Financial Aid ... Dr. Thomas DRABIK
07 Director of Admissions ... Lara FERRIERA

South Florida State College (F)

600 W College Drive, Avon Park FL 33825-9399
County: Highlands | FICE Identification: 001522 | Unit ID: 137315
Telephone: (863) 453-6661 | Carnegie Class: Bac/Assoc-Assoc Dom
FAX Number: (863) 453-0165 | Calendar System: Trimester
URL: www.southflorida.edu
Established: 1965 | Annual Undergrad Tuition & Fees (In-District): $3,165
Enrollment: 2,860 | Coed
Affiliation or Control: Local | IRS Status: 501(c)3
Highest Offering: Baccalaureate
Accreditation: SC, ADNUR, DA, DH, EMT, NUR, RAD

01 President ... Dr. Thomas C. LEITZEL
05 Vice Pres Educational/Stdnt Svcs ... Dr. Sidney VALENTINE
10 Controller ... Ms. Melissa LEE
11 Vice Pres Administrative Services ... Mr. Glenn W. LITTLE
75 Dean Applied Science & Tech ... Mr. Erik CHRISTENSEN
49 Int Dean Arts & Sciences ... Dr. James HAWKER
88 Director Cultural Programs ... Ms. Cynthia GARREN
111 Exec Dir Institutional Advancement ... Mrs. Jamie BATEMAN
32 Dean Student Services ... Dr. Timothy WISE
12 Director DeSoto Campus ... Mrs. Asena MOTT
12 Director Hardee Campus ... Ms. Teresa CRAWFORD
12 Director Lake Placid Center ... Mr. Randall K. PAEPLOW
26 Director Community Relations ... Mrs. Melissa KUEHNLE
106 Director eLearning ... Vacant
15 Director Human Res/EA-EO & ADA Ofcr ... Mr. Donald KESTERSON
18 Dir Remodeling/Reno & Maint ... Dr. Robert E. FLORES
06 Registrar ... Mr. Jonathan STERN
41 Athletic Director ... Mr. Richard J. HITT
36 Director Career Development Center ... Mrs. Colleen RAFATTI
37 Director Financial Aid ... Mrs. Heidi MARKEY
13 Chief Information Officer ... Dr. Christopher VAN DER KAAY

38 Chair Counseling ... Mrs. Charla ELLERKER
08 Library Services ... Ms. Lena PHELPS
96 Coordinator Purchasing ... Mrs. Deborah OLSON
07 Director of Admissions ... Vacant
76 Dean Division of Health Services ... Dr. Michele HESTON

South University (G)

9801 Belevedere Road, Royal Palm Beach FL 33411
Telephone: (561) 273-6500 | Identification: 666117
Accreditation: &SC, ACBSP, CACREP, NURSE, #OTA, PTAA

† Regional accreditation is carried under the parent institution in Savannah, GA.

South University (H)

4401 North Himes Ave Ste 175, Tampa FL 33614-7095
Telephone: (813) 393-3800 | Identification: 770913
Accreditation: &SC, ACBSP, ARCPA, NURSE, OTA, PTAA

† Branch campus of South University, Savannah, GA

Southeastern College (I)

17395 NW 59th Avenue, Miami Lakes FL 33015-5111
Telephone: (305) 820-5003 | Identification: 666290
Accreditation: ACCSC, ADNUR, DMS, SURGT

† Branch campus of Southeastern College, West Palm Beach, FL.

Southeastern College (J)

1756 North Congress Avenue,
West Palm Beach FL 33409
County: Palm Beach | FICE Identification: 031239 | Unit ID: 428170
Telephone: (561) 433-2330 | Carnegie Class: Spec 2-yr-Health
FAX Number: (561) 433-9025 | Calendar System: Other
URL: www.sec.edu
Established: 1988 | Annual Undergrad Tuition & Fees: $19,819
Enrollment: 499 | Coed
Affiliation or Control: Proprietary | IRS Status: Proprietary
Highest Offering: Associate Degree
Accreditation: ACCSC, MAAB, SURGT

01 Vice President ... Ms. Dana HUPPON
06 Registrar ... Ms. Cindy GALT

Southeastern University (K)

1000 Longfellow Boulevard, Lakeland FL 33801-6099
County: Polk | FICE Identification: 001521 | Unit ID: 137564
Telephone: (863) 667-5000 | Carnegie Class: Masters/M
FAX Number: (863) 667-5200 | Calendar System: Semester
URL: www.seu.edu
Established: 1935 | Annual Undergrad Tuition & Fees: $25,870
Enrollment: 7,163 | Coed
Affiliation or Control: Assemblies Of God Church | IRS Status: 501(c)3
Highest Offering: Doctorate
Accreditation: SC, ACBSP, NURSE, SW

01 President ... Dr. Kent INGLE
03 Executive Vice President ... Dr. James (Chris) OWEN
05 Provost ... Dr. William C. HACKET, JR.
32 VP for Student Development ... Mrs. Bethany THOMAS
84 VP for Enrollment Management ... Mr. Roy ROWLAND, IV
09 VP Inst Research/Effectiveness ... Dr. Andrew H. PERMENTER
10 VP for Finance ... Mr. Jeff SPEAR
88 VP for Unrestricted Education ... Mr. Nicholas WALLSTEADT
08 Director of Library Services ... Mrs. Amy BEATTY
06 Registrar ... Mrs. Melissa MAISENBACHER
37 Exec Dir Student Financial Services ... Mr. Michael YOHE
88 Director of Hispanic Learning Ctr ... Ms. Betania TORRES
07 Director of Admissions ... Mrs. Sarah E. CLARK
15 Director Human Resources ... Ms. Betty KELLEY
29 Director Alumni Relations ... Mr. Joel JOHNSON
18 Exec Dir Facilities/Physical Plant ... Mr. Norman (Mike) M. ALDERMAN
20 Director Academic Auxiliary Svcs ... Mrs. Laura C. BROWN
36 Dir Center for Calling & Career ... Mrs. Emilee HILL
10 Senior Director Finance & Treasury ... Mr. Mark BIDDINGER
84 Director Enrollment Marketing ... Mrs. Kendra KRAMER
38 Dir Counseling/Health & Wellness ... Mrs. Paula WHITAKER
56 Assoc Provost Sch Unrestricted Educ ... Mrs. Meghan GRIFFIN
13 Chief Info Technology Officer (CIO) ... Mr. Jerry RAINS
19 Director Security/Safety ... Mr. David BRIGHT
20 Associate Provost ... Mrs. Amy BRATTEN
28 Director of Student Conduct ... Mrs. Estefania S. FLEMING

Southern Technical College (L)

1685 Medical Lane, Fort Myers FL 33907-1158
County: Lee | FICE Identification: 022788 | Unit ID: 366553
Telephone: (239) 939-4766 | Carnegie Class: Bac/Assoc-Mixed
FAX Number: (239) 790-2118 | Calendar System: Quarter
URL: www.southerntech.edu
Established: 1974 | Annual Undergrad Tuition & Fees: $12,924
Enrollment: 887 | Coed
Affiliation or Control: Proprietary | IRS Status: Proprietary
Highest Offering: Baccalaureate

Accreditation: ACICS, SURTEC

01 Executive Director .... Mr. Alex RODRIGUEZ
05 Director Education .... Mr. Esmail DARIAROW

Southern Technical College-Auburndale (A)

450 Havendale Boulevard, Auburndale FL 33823
Telephone: (863) 551-1112 Identification: 770705
Accreditation: ACCSC

Southern Technical College-Brandon (B)

608 E Bloomingdale Avenue, Brandon FL 33511
Telephone: (813) 820-0200 Identification: 770707
Accreditation: ACCSC

Southern Technical College (C)

1485 Florida Mall Avenue, Orlando FL 32809
County: Orange FICE Identification: 039035
Unit ID: 446552
Telephone: (407) 438-6000 Carnegie Class: Assoc/HVT-High Trad
FAX Number: (407) 438-6005 Calendar System: Quarter
URL: www.southerntech.edu
Established: Annual Undergrad Tuition & Fees: N/A
Enrollment: 1,321 Coed
Affiliation or Control: Proprietary IRS Status: Proprietary
Highest Offering: Associate Degree
Accreditation: ACCSC

Southern Technical College-Port Charlotte (D)

950 Tamiami Trail, Unit 109, Port Charlotte FL 33953
Telephone: (941) 391-8888 Identification: 770709
Accreditation: ACICS, SURTEC

Southern Technical College-Sanford (E)

2910 South Orlando Drive, Sanford FL 32773
Telephone: (407) 917-7658 Identification: 770704
Accreditation: ACCSC

Southern Technical College-Tampa (F)

3910 Riga Boulevard, Tampa FL 33619-1269
Telephone: (813) 630-4401 Identification: 770708
Accreditation: ACICS, DMS, SURTEC

State College of Florida, Manatee-Sarasota (G)

PO Box 1849, Bradenton FL 34206-7046
County: Manatee FICE Identification: 001504
Unit ID: 135391
Telephone: (941) 752-5000 Carnegie Class: Bac/Assoc-Mixed
FAX Number: (941) 727-6230 Calendar System: Semester
URL: www.scf.edu
Established: 1957 Annual Undergrad Tuition & Fees (In-District): $3,074
Enrollment: 10,886 Coed
Affiliation or Control: Local IRS Status: 501(c)3
Highest Offering: Baccalaureate
Accreditation: SC, ADNUR, DH, NUR, OTA, PTAA, RAD

01 President .... Dr. Carol F. PROBSTFELD
04 Exec Assistant to President .... Ms. Susan MARROCCO
10 VP Finance/Admin Services .... Ms. Julie JAKWAY
05 VP Academic Affairs .... Vacant
84 VP Strategic Enrollment .... Dr. Richard BARNHOUSE
32 Dean Student Services .... Ms. Jaquelyn MCNEIL
12 Dean Venice .... Mr. Ryan HALE
06 College Registrar .... Mr. Billy C. BENTON
12 Dean Bradenton .... Mr. Mike KIEFER
102 Executive Director SCF Foundation .... Ms. Cassandra HOLMES
12 Dean Lakewood Ranch .... Ms. Daisy VULOVICH
18 Director Facilities Manager .... Mr. Chris WELLMAN
103 Director Workforce Services .... Ms. Lee KOTWICKI
21 Director Business Services .... Mr. Josef RILL
08 Director Library Services .... Ms. Margaret E. HAWKINS
09 Director Institutional Research .... Ms. Su-hua MEN
13 Director IT Operations .... Ms. Karla LAUER
07 Director of Admissions .... Ms. Stacey SHARPLES
41 Director Athletics .... Mr. Matt ENNIS
43 General Counsel .... Mr. Steve PROUTY
88 Head of SCF Collegiate School .... Ms. Kelly MONOD
106 Director Online Learning .... Mr. Gary BAKER
26 Director Communications & Marketing .... Ms. Jamie M. SMITH
19 Manager Public Safety .... Mr. Shawn PATTEN
15 Director Human Resources .... Mr. Jennifer LAHURD

*State University System of Florida, Board of Governors (H)

325 W Gaines Street, Suite 1614,
Tallahassee FL 32399-0400
County: Leon FICE Identification: 008068
Unit ID: 137449
Telephone: (850) 245-0466 Carnegie Class: N/A
FAX Number: (850) 245-9685
URL: www.flbog.edu

01 Chancellor .... Mr. Marshall M. CRISER, III
05 Vice Chanc Academic/Student Affairs .... Dr. Christy ENGLAND
10 Vice Chanc Budget & Finance .... Mr. Tim JONES
43 General Counsel .... Mrs. Vikki SHIRLEY
22 Inspector General & Compliance .... Mrs. Julie LEFTHERIS
101 Corporate Secretary .... Mrs. Vikki SHIRLEY
86 Assoc Vice Chanc Govt Relations .... Mrs. Kristin WHITAKER
04 Assistant to the Chancellor .... Mrs. Shannon M. TRUE
26 Director of Communications .... Mrs. Brittany WISE
13 Chief Info Technology Officer (CIO) .... Mr. Gene KOVACS
15 Director Personnel Services .... Mrs. Abigail MARTIN
18 Chief Facilities/Physical Plant .... Mr. Chris KINSLEY
09 Chief Data Officer .... Mr. Jason JONES
106 Assoc VC Innovation & Online Educ .... Dr. Nancy C. MCKEE

*Florida Agricultural and Mechanical University (I)

1601 S. Martin Luther King Jr. Blvd, Tallahassee FL 32307
County: Leon FICE Identification: 001480
Unit ID: 133650
Telephone: (850) 599-3000 Carnegie Class: DU-Higher
FAX Number: (850) 599-3952 Calendar System: Semester
URL: www.famu.edu
Established: 1887 Annual Undergrad Tuition & Fees (In-State): $5,785
Enrollment: 9,913 Coed
Affiliation or Control: State IRS Status: 501(c)3
Highest Offering: Doctorate
Accreditation: SC, ACBSP, CAEPN, CAHIIM, COARC, #JOUR, LAW, NUR, OT, PH, PHAR, PTA, SW

00 Chair Board of Trustees .... Mr. Kelvin LAWSON
02 President .... Dr. Larry ROBINSON
05 Provost/VP Academic Affairs .... Dr. Maurice EDINGTON
10 Interim VP Finance & Administration .... Ms. Joyce INGRAM
32 Vice President Student Affairs .... Dr. William HUDSON, JR.
25 Interim VP Research .... Dr. Charles WEATHERFORD
111 VP Univ Advancement/Exec Dir Fndn .... Dr. Shawnta FRIDAY-STROUD
116 VP Audit .... Mr. Joseph MALESZEWSKI
45 VP Strategic Planning/Analysis/IE .... Ms. Beverly BARRINGTON
43 VP Legal Affairs/Gen Counsel .... Ms. Denise WALLACE
100 Chief of Staff/BOT Liaison .... Ms. Linda BARGE-MILES
41 Director Athletics .... Dr. John EASON
26 Exec Assoc Director Communications .... Ms. Kathy TIMES
86 Director Governmental Relations .... Ms. Barbara PIPPIN
04 Executive Asst to the President .... Ms. Cynthia HENRY
117 Chief Ethics and Compliance Officer .... Ms. Rica CALHOUN
53 Dean Education .... Dr. Allyson WATSON
67 Dean Pharmacy .... Dr. Johnnie EARLY
72 Dean Science & Technology .... Dr. Richard ALO
47 Dean Agriculture & Food Sciences .... Dr. Robert TAYLOR
83 Dean Social Sci/Arts & Humanities .... Dr. Valencia E. MATTHEWS
54 Dean FAMU-FSU Engineering .... Dr. J. Murray GIBSON
61 Interim Dean College of Law .... Ms. Nicola BOOTHE PERRY
48 Dean Architecture & Engr Tech .... Mr. Rodner WRIGHT
76 Dean Allied Health Sciences .... Dr. Cynthia HUGHES HARRIS
50 Dean Business and Industry .... Dr. Shawnta FRIDAY-STROUD
60 Dean Journalism/Graphic Comm .... Dr. Michelle FERRIER
65 Dean School of the Environment .... Dr. Victor IBEANUSI
66 Dean Nursing .... Dr. Henry TALLEY
58 Assoc Provost & Dean Grad Studies .... Dr. David JACKSON, JR.
08 Dean University Libraries .... Ms. Faye WATKINS
20 Assoc Provost for Undergrad Educ .... Dr. Lewis JOHNSON
20 Assoc Provost for Student Services .... Dr. Carl GOODMAN
20 Assoc Provost Faculty Affairs & Dev .... Dr. Genyne BOSTON
06 University Registrar .... Dr. Agatha ONWUNLI
37 Director Financial Aid .... Ms. Lisa STEWART
07 Interim Director Admissions .... Mr. Chester HOOD
19 Chief of Police/Dir Public Safety .... Mr. Terence CALLOWAY
35 Interim Assoc VP Student Affairs .... Ms. Antoneia ROE
88 University Ombuds & Student Life .... Mr. Bryan F. SMITH
84 Assoc VP Student Affairs .... Mr. Nigel EDWARDS
13 Associate VP/CIO Info Tech Svcs .... Mr. Ronald HENRY
18 Assoc VP Facilities/Construction .... Mr. Sameer KAPILESHWAR
15 Associate VP Human Resources .... Ms. Joyce INGRAM
88 Assoc VP Research .... Dr. Charles WEATHERFORD
102 Assoc VP University Advancement .... Vacant
88 Assoc VP Admin & Financial Services .... Mr. Archie BOUIE, II
09 Interim Dir Institutional Research .... Dr. Katherine SCHEUCH
21 Interim Asst VP/Univ Controller .... Mr. Archie BOUIE
104 Asst VP International Educ & Dev .... Dr. William HYNDMAN, III
88 Interim Exec Dir Title III Programs .... Dr. Charles WEATHERFORD
105 Director ITS Services & Telcomm .... Mr. Ronald HENRY
36 Director Career Center .... Ms. Shereada HARRELL
88 Director Technology Transfer .... Mr. Reis ALSBERRY
88 Director Sponsored Programs .... Ms. Glory BROWN
25 Director Contracts & Grants .... Ms. Pamela BLOUNT
39 Director Student Housing .... Dr. Jennifer WILDER
38 Director Counseling Services .... Ms. Anika FIELDS
96 Director Procurement Services .... Ms. Mattie HOOD
23 Director Student Health Services .... Ms. Tanya TATUM
108 Director University Assessment .... Dr. Melanie WICINSKI
112 Asst VP Major/Principal Gifts .... Ms. Kimberly HANKERSON
30 Business Manager Univ Development .... Ms. Juanita JOHNSON
29 Executive Director Alumni Affairs .... Ms. Carmen CUMMINGS
22 Director EEO .... Ms. Carrie GAVIN
51 Director Continuing Education .... Ms. Phyllis WATSON
120 Director Instr Tech & Distance Ed .... Ms. Franzetta FITZ
109 Asst VP Administrative Services .... Ms. Rebecca BROWN
109 Director Business & Auxiliary Svc .... Mr. Michael SMITH
88 Director Veteran and Military Affs .... Mr. Louis DILBERT
119 Chief Information Security Officer .... Mr. Clifford STOKES
88 Director Center for Disability .... Mr. Jovany FELIX
121 Dir Student Success/Dev Stds .... Dr. Jamie DAVIS
114 Interim Director University Budgets .... Mr. Archie BOUIE

*Florida Atlantic University (J)

PO Box 3091, 777 Glades Road,
Boca Raton FL 33431-0991
County: Palm Beach FICE Identification: 001481
Unit ID: 133669
Telephone: (561) 297-3000 Carnegie Class: DU-Higher
FAX Number: (561) 297-3942 Calendar System: Semester
URL: www.fau.edu
Established: 1961 Annual Undergrad Tuition & Fees (In-State): $4,831
Enrollment: 30,208 Coed
Affiliation or Control: State IRS Status: 501(c)3
Highest Offering: Doctorate
Accreditation: SC, CACREP, CAEP, CAMPEP, IPSY, MED, MUS, NURSE, PLNG, SP, SPAA, SW

02 President .... Dr. John KELLY
05 Provost/VP Academic Affairs .... Dr. Gary W. PERRY
32 VP Student Affairs/Enrollment .... Dr. Corey KING
46 Vice President Research .... Dr. Daniel FLYNN
11 Vice Pres Administrative Affairs .... Ms. Stacy VOLNICK
13 Assoc Provost IT/CIO .... Mr. Jason BALL
35 Assoc VP Student Affairs/Dean .... Dr. Larry FAERMAN
43 General Counsel .... Mr. David KIAN
22 Exec Dir Equity/Inclusion/Compl .... Vacant
37 Asst VP Financial Aid/New Student .... Ms. Tracy BOULUKOS
20 Vice Provost Academic Affairs .... Dr. Michele HAWKINS
80 Dean of Design/Social Inquiry .... Dr. Wesley E. HAWKINS
49 Dean of Arts & Letters .... Dr. Michael HORSWELL
50 Dean of Business .... Dr. Daniel GROPPER
53 Dean of Education .... Dr. Valerie BRISTOR
66 Dean of Nursing .... Dr. Marlaine SMITH
20 Dean Undergraduate Studies .... Dr. Edward E. PRATT
58 Interim Dean of Graduate Studies .... Dr. Khaled SOBHAN
88 Asst Dean/PK-12 Sch/Educational Pgm .... Mr. Joel HERBST
90 Director Enterprise Computing Svcs .... Mr. Mehran BASIRATMAND
15 Asst Vice Pres Human Resources .... Mr. David TOMANIO
85 Exec Dir Center Global Engagement .... Dr. Mihaela METIANU

*Florida Gulf Coast University (K)

10501 FGCU Boulevard S, Fort Myers FL 33965-6565
County: Lee FICE Identification: 032553
Unit ID: 433660
Telephone: (239) 590-1000 Carnegie Class: Masters/L
FAX Number: (239) 590-1166 Calendar System: Semester
URL: www.fgcu.edu
Established: 1991 Annual Undergrad Tuition & Fees (In-State): $6,118
Enrollment: 14,965 Coed
Affiliation or Control: State IRS Status: 501(c)3
Highest Offering: Doctorate
Accreditation: SC, ANEST, #ARCPA, CAATE, CACREP, CAEPN, IPSY, MT, MUS, NURSE, OT, PTA, SPAA, SW

02 President .... Dr. Michael V. MARTIN
05 Provost & VP Academic Affairs .... Dr. James LLORENS
10 Vice Pres Admin Services/Finance .... Mr. Steve L. MAGIERA
111 VP Univ Advance/Exec Dir Foundation .... Ms. Katherine GREEN
88 Sr VP Strategy & Program Innovation .... Dr. J. Michael ROLLO
100 Vice President & Chief of Staff .... Ms. Susan EVANS
43 Vice President & General Counsel .... Ms. Vee LEONARD
84 Vice Pres Stdnt Success/Enrol Mgmt .... Dr. Mitch CORDOVA
20 Assoc VP Academic/Curriculum Sppt .... Dr. Cathy DUFF
45 Sr Asc Prov/Asc VP Plng & Inst Perf .... Dr. Paul SNYDER
58 Assoc VP Research/Dean Grad Studies .... Dr. T. C YIH
26 AVP Communications & Marketing .... Ms. Deborah WILTROUT
18 Asst VP Physical Plant .... Mr. Jim HEHL
04 Asst to Pres/University Ombudsman .... Ms. Monique MCKAY
21 Assoc VP Admin Svcs & Finance .... Mr. Joseph MCDONALD
13 Asst VP Business Technology Svcs .... Ms. Mary BANKS
15 Asst Vice Pres Human Resources .... Ms. Pamela BOWMAN
20 Assoc Provost/VP Academic Affs .... Dr. Tony BARRINGER
21 Controller .... Ms. June GUTKNECHT
32 Asst VP/Dean of Students .... Dr. Michele YOVANOVICH
49 Int Dean College Arts & Sciences .... Dr. Chuck LINDSEY
20 Dean of Undergraduate Studies .... Dr. Dawn LATTA KIRBY
50 Int Dean Lutgert Col of Business .... Dr. Chris WESTLEY
53 Dean College of Education .... Dr. Eunsook HYUN
76 Dean Col of Health/Human Svcs .... Dr. Ann CARY
54 Dean U.A. Whitaker Col Engineering .... Dr. Richard A. BEHR
62 Dean Library Services .... Dr. Kathleen MILLER
38 Sr Dir Counselng/Wellness Svcs .... Dr. Jon L. BRUNNER
35 Asst Dean Student Affairs .... Mr. Chad TRISLER
07 Director of Admissions .... Vacant
96 Director of Procurement Services .... Ms. Maryan EGAN
19 Director Campus Police & Safety .... Chief Steven C. MOORE
18 Director Facilities Planning .... Mr. Tom MAYO
37 Asst VP Student Enroll & Fin Svc .... Mr. Jorge LOPEZ-ROSADO
06 University Registrar .... Ms. Susan BYARS
23 Medical Director .... Dr. Brian BOZZA
41 Director of Athletics .... Mr. Kenneth KAVANAGH
28 Dir EEC & Title IX Coord .... Ms. Precious GUNTER
85 Director International Services .... Dr. Elaine HOZDIK
106 Director Instructional Technology .... Mr. David JAEGER
13 Director Technology Services .... Ms. Pat O'CONNOR-BENSON
36 Director Career Development Svcs .... Mr. Reid LENNERTZ
29 Director Alumni Relations .... Ms. Kimberly WALLACE
92 Director Honors Program .... Dr. Clay MOTLEY

09 Director Inst Research/Analysis .... Dr. Robert VINES
114 Asst VP University Budgets .... Mr. David VAZQUEZ
39 Assoc VP Student Engagement .... Dr. Brian FISHER
86 Director Government Relations .... Ms. Jennifer GOEN
88 Dir Environmental Health/Safety .... Ms. Rhonda HOLTZCLAW
51 Exec Dir Cont Educ/Off-Campus Pgms .... Dr. Paul THORNTON
88 General Manager/WGCU .... Mr. Rick JOHNSON
40 Manager The University Store .... Mr. Rodney ROLLER
121 Int Dir Ctr Academic Achievement .... Ms. Lindsey SINGH
04 Exec Asst to the President .... Ms. Beverly D. BROWN

*Florida International University (A)

University Park, 11200 SW 8 Street, Miami FL 33199-0001
County: Miami-Dade FICE Identification: 009635
Unit ID: 133951
Telephone: (305) 348-2000 Carnegie Class: DU-Highest
FAX Number: N/A Calendar System: Semester
URL: www.fiu.edu
Established: 1965 Annual Undergrad Tuition & Fees (In-State): $6,556
Enrollment: 56,718 Coed
Affiliation or Control: State IRS Status: 501(c)3
Highest Offering: Doctorate
Accreditation: SC, ANEST, ARCPA, ART, CAATE, CACREP, CAEP, CAEPN, CAHIIM, CIDA, CLPSY, CONST, DIETD, @DIETI, FEPAC, HSA, IPSY, JOUR, LAW, LSAR, MED, MUS, NURSE, OPE, OT, PH, PTA, SP, SPAA, SW, THEA

02 President .... Dr. Mark ROSENBERG
100 Chief of Staff .... Mr. Javier MARQUES
11 Executive VP & COO .... Dr. Kenneth FURTON
05 SVP Academic/Student Affairs .... Dr. Elizabeth BEJAR
17 Sr Vice President Health Affairs .... Dr. Robert SACKSTEIN
88 VP for Engagement .... Mr. Saif ISHOOF
10 CFO & Sr VP for Administration .... Dr. Kenneth JESSELL
111 Vice President for Advancement .... Mr. Howard LIPMAN
09 AVP Analysis/Info Mgmt .... Dr. Hiselgis PEREZ
46 Vice President of Research .... Dr. Andres GIL
13 Vice President/CIO .... Mr. Robert GRILLO
12 Vice Prov Biscayne Bay Campus .... Mr. Stephen MOLL
84 Int VP Enrollment Mgmt .... Dr. Kevin COUGHLIN
88 Interim Ombudsman .... Dr. Sofia TRELLES
15 Vice President Human Resources .... Ms. El Pagnier HUDSON
18 Assoc VP Facilities Operations .... Mr. John CAL
07 Dir Undergraduate Admissions .... Ms. Jody GLASSMAN
49 Dean Col Arts/Sciences/Educ .... Dr. Michael HEITHAUS
50 Dean College Business Admin .... Dr. Joanne LI
54 Dean Col Engineering/Computing .... Dr. John VOLAKIS
53 Director College of Education .... Dr. Laura DINEHART
88 Int Dean Sch Hospitality Mgmt .... Dr. Michael CHENG
82 Dean School Intl/Pub Affairs .... Dr. John STACK
66 Dean Col Nursing/Health Science .... Dr. Ora STRICKLAND
69 Dean College of Public Health .... Dr. Tomas GUILARTE
61 Dean College of Law .... Dr. Antony PAGE
63 Dean College of Medicine .... Dr. Robert SACKSTEIN
92 Dean Honors College .... Dr. Juan Carlos ESPINOSA
48 Dean Col Comm/Architecture/Arts .... Dr. Brian SCHRINER
77 Dir Sch Computing/Info Sciences .... Dr. Sundararaj IYENGAR
23 Dir Stdnt Hlth & Counseling .... Dr. Todd LENGNICK
22 Director Equal Opportunity Program .... Ms. Shirlyon J. MCWHORTER
88 Director School Accounting .... Dr. Clark WHEATLEY
88 Dir Multicultural Programs Admin .... Dr. Dorret SAWYERS
62 Dean of Libraries .... Dr. Anne PRESTAMO
41 Athletics Director .... Mr. Pete GARCIA
86 VP for Government Relations .... Ms. Michelle PALACIO
06 University Registrar .... Ms. Dulce BELTRAN
26 Sr AVP Public Affairs .... Ms. Dania ADAMS
37 Director Student Financial Aid .... Mr. Francisco VALINES
36 Director Career Services .... Ms. Ivette DUARTE
23 Medical Director Stdnt Hlth Svcs .... Dr. Saara SCHWARTZ
39 Dir of Housing/Residential Life .... Mr. Joe PAULICK
22 Director Disability Student Svcs .... Dr. Amanda NIGUIDULA
116 Chief Audit Executive .... Mr. Trevor WILLIAMS
24 Dir University IT/Media Support .... Mr. Matthew HAGOOD
21 Associate VP and Univ Controller .... Ms. Katharine BROPHY
88 Dir Environmental Health/Safety .... Ms. Tamece KNOWLES
19 Chief of Police .... Chief Alexander CASAS
26 Asst VP Media Relations .... Ms. Maydel SANTANA-BRAVO
43 General Counsel .... Mr. Carlos CASTILLO
85 Sr Dir International Stdnt Svcs .... Ms. Alejandra PARRA
25 Assistant VP for Research .... Mr. Roberto GUTIERREZ
04 Assistant Chief of Staff .... Ms. Claudia GONZALEZ
44 Exec Dir Dev/Foundation Relations .... Ms. Jamie DIPTEE-BAY
102 Sr Dir Corporate/Found Relations .... Ms. Karla HERNANDEZ
29 AVP Alumni Relations .... Mr. Duane WILES

*Florida Polytechnic University (B)

4700 Research Way, Lakeland FL 33805-8531
County: Polk Identification: 667279
Unit ID: 482936
Telephone: (863) 583-9050 Carnegie Class: Bac-Diverse
FAX Number: N/A Calendar System: Semester
URL: www.floridapoly.edu
Established: 2012 Annual Undergrad Tuition & Fees (In-State): $4,940
Enrollment: 1,456 Coed
Affiliation or Control: State IRS Status: 501(c)3
Highest Offering: Master's
Accreditation: SC

02 President .... Dr. Randy K. AVENT
05 Provost .... Dr. Terry PARKER
43 Vice President & General Counsel .... Miss Gina DEIULIO
111 Vice President Advancement .... Ms. Kathy BOWMAN
10 Vice President/CFO .... Mr. Mark MROCZKOWSKI

*Florida State University (C)

222 S. Copeland Street, Tallahassee FL 32306
County: Leon FICE Identification: 001489
Unit ID: 134097
Telephone: (850) 644-2525 Carnegie Class: DU-Highest
FAX Number: (850) 644-9936 Calendar System: Semester
URL: www.fsu.edu
Established: 1851 Annual Undergrad Tuition & Fees (In-State): $5,656
Enrollment: 41,362 Coed
Affiliation or Control: State IRS Status: 501(c)3
Highest Offering: Doctorate
Accreditation: SC, ANEST, #ARCPA, ART, CACREP, CEA, CIDA, CLPSY, DANCE, DIETD, DIETI, IPSY, LAW, LIB, MED, MFCD, MUS, NURSE, PH, PLNG, PSPSY, SP, SPAA, SW, THEA

02 President .... Mr. John E. THRASHER
05 Prov/Exec VP Academic Affairs .... Dr. Sally E. MCRORIE
10 Vice Pres Finance & Admin .... Mr. Kyle CLARK
32 Vice President Student Affairs .... Dr. Amy HECHT
46 Vice President Research .... Dr. Gary K. OSTRANDER
26 Assoc VP University Relations .... Ms. Kathleen DALY
45 VP Planning and Programs .... Vacant
111 VP University Advancement .... Mr. Thomas W. JENNINGS
102 Exec VP FSU Foundation .... Mr. Andy A. JHANJI
20 Vice Pres Faculty Development .... Dr. Janet KISTNER
100 Chief of Staff to President .... Ms. Liz HIRST
88 Assoc Vice President for Research .... Dr. Laurel FULKERSON
18 Associate VP for Facilities .... Mr. Dennis A. BAILEY
21 Assoc VP Finance & Admin .... Mr. Michael WILLIAMS
13 AVP Info Tech Svcs/CIO .... Ms. Jane LIVINGSTON
20 Asst VP for Academic Affairs .... Mr. Paul HARLACHER
15 Assoc Vice Pres for Human Resources .... Ms. Renisha L. GIBBS
11 Asst VP for Administrative Services .... Mr. Steven CONNER
84 Asst VP Enrollment Mgmt .... Mr. John BARNHILL
27 Asst VP of University Communication .... Ms. Browning BROOKS
88 Dir Academic Pgm Professional Svcs .... Mr. Bill LINDNER
49 Dean Arts & Sciences .... Dr. Sam HUCKABA
50 Dean Business .... Dr. Michael HARTLINE
53 Dean Education .... Dr. Damon ANDREW
59 Dean Human Sciences .... Dr. Michael DELP
88 Dean Communication & Information .... Dr. Larry DENNIS
66 Dean Nursing .... Dr. Laurie GRUBBS
88 Dean Criminology .... Dr. Thomas BLOMBERG
61 Dean Law .... Dr. Erin O'HARA O'CONNOR
83 Dean Social Sciences .... Dr. Timothy CHAPIN
70 Dean Social Work .... Dr. James J. CLARK
88 Dean Motion Picture Arts .... Mr. Reb BRADDOCK
64 Dean Music .... Dr. Patricia J. FLOWERS
57 Dean Fine Arts .... Mr. James FRAZIER
54 Dean Engineering .... Dr. Murray GIBSON
63 Dean Medicine .... Dr. John FOGARTY
58 Dean Graduate School .... Dr. Mark RILEY
88 Dean Undergraduate Studies .... Dr. Karen L. LAUGHLIN
35 Dean of Students .... Dr. Victoria DOBIYANSKI
12 Dean Panama City Branch Campus .... Dr. Randy HANNA
06 University Registrar .... Dr. Kimberly BARBER
07 Director Admissions .... Ms. Hege FERGUSON
92 Dir University Honors Program .... Ms. Annette SCHWABE
37 Director Student Financial Aid .... Mr. Somnath CHATTERJEE
08 Director Libraries .... Ms. Gale ETSCHMAIER
90 Sr Director Enterprise Applications .... Mr. Byron MENCHION
43 General Counsel .... Ms. Carolyn EGAN
104 Director International Programs .... Dr. James E. PITTS
88 Chief Budget Officer .... Mr. Michael P. LAKE
09 Director Institutional Research .... Dr. James HUNT
86 Director Governmental Relations .... Ms. Kathy MEARS
41 Athletic Director .... Dr. David COBURN
38 Director Student Counseling .... Dr. Carlos J. GOMEZ
19 Director Public Safety .... Mr. David L. PERRY
23 Director University Health Services .... Dr. Amy MAGNUSON
36 Director Career Center .... Ms. Myrna HOOVER
116 Chief Audit Officer .... Dr. Sam MCCALL
28 Dir Diversity/Equal Opportunity .... Ms. Michelle DOUGLAS
39 Director Student Housing .... Ms. Shannon STATEN
88 Director Business Services .... Mr. Charles FRIEDRICH, II
25 Director Sponsored Research .... Ms. Pamela RAY
14 Director Information Technology .... Mr. Kenneth JOHNSON

*New College of Florida (D)

5800 Bay Shore Road, Sarasota FL 34243-2109
County: Sarasota FICE Identification: 001507
Unit ID: 262129
Telephone: (941) 487-4100 Carnegie Class: Bac-A&S
FAX Number: (941) 487-4101 Calendar System: 4/1/4
URL: www.ncf.edu
Established: 1960 Annual Undergrad Tuition & Fees (In-State): $6,916
Enrollment: 859 Coed
Affiliation or Control: State IRS Status: 501(c)3
Highest Offering: Master's
Accreditation: SC

02 President .... Dr. Donal E. O'SHEA
05 Provost .... Dr. Barbara FELDMAN
10 Vice Pres Finance & Administration .... Mr. John U. MARTIN
79 Chair of Humanities .... Dr. Miriam WALLACE
81 Chair of Natural Sciences .... Dr. Katherine WALSTROM
83 Chair of Social Sciences .... Dr. David HARVEY
08 Dean Cook Library .... Dr. Brian DOHERTY
84 Dean of Enrollment & Info Tech .... Dr. K. Joy HAMM
32 Acting Dean of Students .... Dr. Mark STIER
28 Exec Dir Outreach/Engage/Inclusion .... Dr. William WOODSON
07 Associate Dean of Admissions .... Ms. Sonia WU
20 Associate Academic Officer .... Dr. Suzanne SHERMAN
21 Associate Business Officer .... Ms. Kimberly BENDICKSON
13 Dir of Information Technology .... Mr. Ben FOSS
14 Director of Technology Support .... Mr. Jeff SMITH
29 Asst Director Alumnae/i Association .... Ms. Kathleen MCCOY
06 Registrar .... Mr. Brian SCHOLTEN
26 Director Public Affairs .... Ms. Ann COMER-WOODS
38 Director Counseling .... Dr. Anne E. FISHER
09 Director of Institutional Research .... Ms. Hui-Men WEN
100 Chief of Staff President's Office .... Dr. Bradley THIESSEN
15 Director Personnel Services .... Ms. Loretta SHIELDS
18 Chief Facilities/Physical Plant .... Mr. Alan BURR
96 Director of Purchasing .... Ms. Jean HARRIS
37 Director Student Financial Aid .... Ms. Tara KARAS
43 General Counsel .... Mr. David FUGETT
25 Contract Administrator .... Ms. Michelle GOODING
30 Chief Development .... Ms. MaryAnne YOUNG
19 Chief of Police .... Sgt. Michael KESSIE
39 Director Student Housing .... Dr. Mark STIER
41 Athletic Director .... Mr. Colin JORDAN
04 Administrative Asst to President .... Ms. Shelley WILBUR
104 Director Study Abroad .... Ms. Florence ZAMSKY
36 Director Student Placement .... Vacant

*University of Central Florida (E)

PO Box 160000, Orlando FL 32816-0001
County: Orange FICE Identification: 003954
Unit ID: 132903
Telephone: (407) 823-2000 Carnegie Class: DU-Highest
FAX Number: N/A Calendar System: Semester
URL: www.ucf.edu
Established: 1963 Annual Undergrad Tuition & Fees (In-State): $6,368
Enrollment: 66,059 Coed
Affiliation or Control: State IRS Status: 501(c)3
Highest Offering: Doctorate
Accreditation: SC, CAATE, CACREP, CAHIIM, CEA, CLPSY, FEPAC, HSA, IPSY, MED, MT, MUS, NURSE, PLNG, PTA, SP, SPAA, SW, THEA

02 Interim President .... Mr. Thad SEYMOUR
05 Provost .... Dr. Elizabeth DOOLEY
100 Vice President and Chief of Staff .... Dr. John SCHELL
11 Interim COO Admin & Finance .... Ms. Misty SHEPHERD
10 Interim Chief Financial Officer .... Ms. Kathy MITCHELL
43 Vice President/General Counsel .... Mr. W. Scott COLE
32 VP Student Dev/Enrollment Svcs .... Dr. Maribeth EHASZ
30 VP Dev/Alum Rels/Foundation CEO .... Mr. Michael J. MORSBERGER
31 Vice President Emerita Comm Rels .... Ms. Helen DONEGAN
63 VP Medical Affairs/Dean Med College .... Dr. Deborah GERMAN
41 Vice Pres & Dir of Athletics .... Mr. Danny WHITE
49 Dean College of Arts & Humanities .... Mr. Jeffrey MOORE
50 Dean College of Business Admin .... Dr. Paul JARLEY
53 Dean Col of Comm Innovation & Educ ... Dr. Pamela S. CARROLL
54 Dean College of Engr/Comp Sci .. Dr. Michael GEORGIOPOULOS
76 Interim Dean Col Health Prof Sci .... Dr. Jeffrey STOUT
88 Dean Rosen College Hospitality Mgt .... Dr. Youcheng WANG
66 Dean College of Nursing .... Dr. Mary L. SOLE
88 Dean/Dir Col of Optics & Photonics .... Dr. Bahaa SALEH
81 Dean College of Sciences .... Dr. Michael D. JOHNSON
92 Dean Burnett Honors Col .... Dr. Sheila PINERES
13 Vice Provost & CIO Info Tech/Res .... Dr. Joel L. HARTMAN
12 Vice Provost UCF Connect & Global .... Dr. Jeff JONES
12 Vice Provost UCF Downtown .... Mr. Thad SEYMOUR
46 Assoc VP Research Administration .... Ms. Dorothy YATES
58 Vice Pres Res/Dean Grad Studies .... Dr. Elizabeth KLONOFF
97 Int VP/Dean Undergrad Studies .... Dr. Melody BOWDON
82 VP Fac Exc/Intl Affs/Global Strat .... Dr. Jana JASINSKI
09 Assoc Prov APQ and Assoc VP IKM .... Dr. M. Paige BORDEN
18 Assoc VP Facilities and Safety .... Ms. Lee KERNEK
29 Sr Assoc Vice Pres Alumni Relations .... Ms. Julie C. STROH
86 Sr Assoc VP University Relations .... Mr. Fred KITTINGER
111 AVP of Col/Univ Advancement .... Mr. Jeff COATES
46 Assoc VP Rsrch & Commercialization .... Dr. Thomas O'NEAL
20 Assoc Prov/Chief Staff Acad Affairs .... Dr. Ronnie KOROSEC
84 Assoc VP Enrollment Services .... Dr. Gordon CHAVIS
26 VP Communications & Marketing .... Mr. Grant HESTON
37 Dir Student Financial Asst .... Ms. Alicia KEATON
06 University Registrar .... Mr. Brian BOYD
08 Director Libraries .... Mr. Barry BAKER
15 Assoc VP HR/Chief HR Officer .... Ms. Maureen BINDER
19 Assoc VP Safety & Chief of Police .... Mr. Carl METZGER
93 Dir Multicultural Acad Support Svcs .... Mr. Wayne JACKSON
14 AVP/COO UCF IT .... Mr. Michael SINK
38 Director Counseling Center .... Dr. Karen HOFMANN
22 Dir Office of Institutional Equity .... Ms. Nancy MYERS
23 Assoc VP Student Health Services .... Dr. Michael G. DEICHEN
39 Exec Dir Housing and Residence Life .... Dr. April HICKS KONVALINKA
28 Chief Diversity Officer .... Ms. Karen MORRISON
96 Asst Vice President Procurement .... Mr. Gregory ROBINSON
36 Exec Director Career Services .... Ms. Lynn HANSEN

*University of Florida (F)

235 Tigert Hall, Gainesville FL 32611-9500
County: Alachua FICE Identification: 001535
Unit ID: 134130
Telephone: (352) 392-3261 Carnegie Class: DU-Highest

FAX Number: (352) 392-8735 Calendar System: Semester
URL: www.ufl.edu
Established: 1853 Annual Undergrad Tuition & Fees (In-State): $6,381
Enrollment: 52,669 Coed
Affiliation or Control: State IRS Status: 501(c)3
Highest Offering: Doctorate
Accreditation: SC, ARCPA, ART, AUD, CAATE, CACREP, CAEP, CAMPEP, CEA, CIDA, CLPSY, CONST, COPSY, DANCE, DENT, DIETD, DIETI, HSA, IFSAC, IPSY, JOUR, LAW, LSAR, MED, MUS, NURSE, OT, PH, PHAR, PLNG, PTA, SCPSY, SP, THEA, VET

02 President .... Dr. W. Kent FUCHS
05 Provost & Senior Vice President .... Dr. Joseph GLOVER
47 Sr Vice Pres Agric/Natural Res .... Dr. Jack M. PAYNE
17 Sr Vice Pres Health Affairs .... Dr. David NELSON
10 VP/Chief Financial Ofcr .... Mr. Michael MCKEE
11 Sr Vice Pres/Chief Operating Ofcr .... Dr. Charles E. LANE
111 Vice President Advancement .... Mr. Thomas J. MITCHELL
21 Vice President Business Affairs .... Mr. Curtis REYNOLDS
32 Int Vice President Student Affairs .... Dr. Winfred M. PHILLIPS
26 Vice President Govt & Cmty Relation .... Mr. Mark KAPLAN
15 Vice Pres Human Resource Services .... Ms. Jodi D. GENTRY
46 Vice President Research .... Dr. David P. NORTON
43 Vice President and General Counsel .... Ms. Amy M. HASS
13 Vice President & CIO .... Mr. Elias G. ELDAYRIE
84 Vice Pres Enroll Mgmt/Assoc Provost .... Dr. Zina EVANS
100 Exec Chief of Staff .... Dr. Winfred PHILLIPS
28 Chf Diversity Ofcr/Spc Asst to Pres .... Dr. Antonio FARIAS
86 Assoc VP Government Relations .... Vacant
88 Associate Provost Teaching & Tech .... Dr. William A. MCCOLLOUGH
27 Asst Vice Pres Marketing .... Vacant
27 Senior Director Media Relations .... Mr. Stephen F. ORLANDO
21 AVP Business Affs/Finance/Admin .... Mr. Craig R. HILL
18 Asst VP/Fac/Plng/Construction .... Mr. Carlos DOUGNAC
20 Associate Provost Academic Affairs .... Dr. Chris J. HASS
20 Assoc Provost Undergrad Affairs .... Dr. Angela LINDNER
09 Asst Provost/Dir Inst Research/Plng .... Dr. Cathy LEBO
35 Assoc Vice Pres/Dean of Students .... Ms. Heather WHITE
08 Dean University Libraries .... Ms. Judith RUSSELL
50 Dean of Business Administration .... Dr. John KRAFT
49 Dean of Liberal Arts & Science .... Mr. David E. RICHARDSON
68 Dean of Health/Human Performance .... Dr. Michael B. REID
61 Dean of Law .... Ms. Laura A. ROSENBURY
66 Dean of Nursing .... Dr. Anna M. MCDANIEL
67 Dean of Pharmacy .... Dr. Julie A. JOHNSON
54 Dean of Engineering .... Dr. Cammy ABERNATHY
47 Dean Agricultural/Life Sciences .... Dr. R. Elaine TURNER
60 Dean of Journalism/Communications .... Ms. Diane H. MCFARLIN
76 Dean Pub Health/Health Professions .... Dr. Michael PERRI
53 Dean of Education .... Dr. Glenn GOOD
47 Dean IFAS Extension .... Dr. Nick T. PLACE
74 Interim Dean of Veterinary Medicine .... Dr. Tom VICKROY
57 Dean of the Arts .... Dr. Onye OZUZU
48 Dean Design Construction Planning .... Dr. Chimay ANUMBA
63 Interim Dean of Medicine .... Dr. Adrian TYNDALL
46 Dean of IFAS Research .... Dr. Robert GILBERT
52 Dean of Dentistry .... Dr. Isabel GARCIA
58 Dean Graduate School .... Dr. Henry T. FRIERSON
65 Dir School Natural Res/Envir .... Dr. Thomas K. FRAZER
06 University Registrar .... Mr. Stephen J. PRITZ
23 Director of Student Health .... Dr. Guy NICOLETTE
38 Assoc Dir of Counseling & Well Ctr .... Dr. Alvin LAWRENCE
37 Director Student Financial Aid .... Ms. Donna KOLB
36 Sr Dir of Career Connections Ctr .... Ms. Ja'Net GLOVER
14 Director of Computer Center .... Mr. Timothy J. FITZPATRICK
19 Director of University Police .... Ms. Linda J. STUMP
24 Director of Academic Technology .... Dr. Mark MCCALLISTER
65 Director of Forestry .... Dr. Timothy L. WHITE
39 Director of Housing .... Ms. Tina KUHLENGEL HORVATH
41 Athletic Director .... Mr. Scott STRICKLIN
29 Exec Director Alumni Affairs .... Ms. Danita NIAS
96 Director of Purchasing .... Ms. Lisa DEAL
07 Director of Admissions .... Mr. Rick BRYANT
04 Executive Asst to President .... Ms. Beth BOONE
106 Dir Online Education/E-learning .... Ms. Evangeline CUMMINGS
108 Director Institutional Assessment .... Dr. Timothy S. BROPHY
101 Secretary of the Institution/Board .... Mr. Mark KAPLAN

*University of North Florida (A)

1 UNF Drive, Jacksonville FL 32224-7699
County: Duval FICE Identification: 009841
Unit ID: 136172
Telephone: (904) 620-1000 Carnegie Class: DU-Mod
FAX Number: (904) 620-2414 Calendar System: Semester
URL: www.unf.edu
Established: 1965 Annual Undergrad Tuition & Fees (In-State): $6,394
Enrollment: 16,309 Coed
Affiliation or Control: State IRS Status: 501(c)3
Highest Offering: Doctorate
Accreditation: SC, ANEST, ART, CAATE, CACREP, CAEPN, CONST, COSMA, DIETD, DIETI, EXSC, HSA, IPSY, JOUR, MUS, NURSE, PH, PTA, SPAA, SW

02 President .... Dr. David SZYMANKSI
05 Interim Provost .... Dr. Pamela S. CHALLY
20 Int Associate Provost .... Dr. Daniel C. MOON
86 VP Governmental Affairs .... Ms. Heather DUNCAN
43 VP/General Counsel .... Ms. Karen J. STONE
10 VP Administration/Finance .... Ms. Shari A. SHUMAN
30 VP Development/Alumni Affairs .... Mr. Joshua D. MERCHANT
88 VP Data Analytics .... Dr. Bob J. COLEMAN
07 Interim Director of Admissions .... Ms. Tayrin R. EVANS
88 Assoc VP/Compliance Officer .... Dr. Joann N. CAMPBELL
21 Assoc VP Admin & Finance .... Mr. Scott BENNETT
35 Assoc VP Student Affairs .... Mr. Everett J. MALCOLM, III
45 Asst VP Research .... Dr. John KANTNER
110 Asst VP Development .... Ms. Ann S. MCCULLEN
35 Asst VP Student Affairs .... Dr. Lucy S. CROFT
58 Dean of the Graduate School .... Dr. John KANTNER
08 Interim Dean of the Library .... Ms. Lisandra CARMICHAEL
97 Dean of Undergraduate Studies .... Dr. Karen B. PATTERSON
50 Dean Coggin College of Business .... Dr. Mark DAWKINS
53 Dean College of Education .... Dr. Diane YENDOL-HOPPEY
76 Dean Brooks College of Health .... Dr. Curt LOX
77 Int Dean Computing/Engr/Constr .... Dr. William KLOSTERMEYER
22 Dir Equal Opportunity Programs .... Ms. Marlynn JONES
88 Dir Professional Dev Training .... Ms. Kelly G. HARRISON
114 Chief Budget Officer .... Mrs. Devany GROVES
21 Controller .... Ms. Valerie O. STEVENSON
88 Dir of Compliance .... Ms. Donna R. KIRK
88 Dir Environment Health/Safety .... Mr. Daniel D. ENDICOTT
22 Dir ADA Compliance .... Ms. Rocelia T. GONZALEZ
14 Dir IT Networking .... Mr. Jeffrey A. DURFEE
21 Treasurer .... Mr. Michael S. NEGLIA
18 Dir Campus Planning .... Mr. Paul STEWART
88 Dir University Center .... Mr. George ANDROUIN
19 Dir Safety Security .... Mr. Francis J. MACKESY
36 Dir Career Development Services .... Mr. Rick ROBERTS
88 Dir Child Development Ctr .... Ms. Mahreen N. MIAN
23 Chief Medical Officer .... Dr. Lisa DYNAN-DOBBERTIEN
38 Dir Univ Counseling Center .... Dr. Andrew B. KING
39 Dir Housing Residence Life .... Mr. Robert J. BOYLE
41 Athletic Director .... Mr. Lee L. MOON
88 Dir Faculty Enhancement .... Dr. Dan RICHARD
108 Director of Assessment .... Ms. Amanda KULP
37 Dir Student Financial Aid .... Mrs. Anissa AGNE
06 Registrar .... Mrs. Megan R. KUEHNER
09 Dir Institutional Research .... Ms. Abby WILLCOX
88 Exec Dir FL Inst of Education .... Dr. Cheryl A. FOUNTAIN
88 Dir Small Business Dev Ctr .... Ms. Janice W. DONALDSON
96 Dir Purchasing .... Ms. Shawn ASMUTH
51 Int Dean Continuing Education .... Mr. Abdullah E. EDYTHE
106 Asst VP Center for Instr & Res Tech .... Ms. Deb MILLER
90 Director Academic Technology .... Dr. Gordon F. RAKITA

*University of South Florida (B)

4202 E Fowler Avenue, Tampa FL 33620-6100
County: Hillsborough FICE Identification: 001537
Unit ID: 137351
Telephone: (813) 974-2011 Carnegie Class: DU-Highest
FAX Number: N/A Calendar System: Semester
URL: www.usf.edu
Established: 1956 Annual Undergrad Tuition & Fees (In-State): $6,410
Enrollment: 43,540 Coed
Affiliation or Control: State IRS Status: 501(c)3
Highest Offering: Doctorate
Accreditation: SC, ANEST, #ARCPA, ART, AUD, CAATE, CACREP, CAEPN, CAMPEP, CEA, CLPSY, DANCE, @DIETI, HSA, IPSY, LIB, MED, MUS, NURSE, PCSAS, PH, PHAR, PTA, SCPSY, SP, SPAA, SW, THEA

02 President .... Dr. Steven C. CURRALL
45 Sr VP Business/Financial Strategy .... Mr. David LECHNER
100 Chief of Staff President's Office .... Dr. Cynthia S. VISOT
43 General Counsel .... Mr. Gerard SOLIS
05 Prov/Exec Vice Pres Academic Affs .... Dr. Ralph WILCOX
15 Vice Provost for HR and Space Plng .... Dr. James GAREY
20 Vice Provost for Plng/Perf & Acct .... Dr. Theresa H. CHISOLM
20 Vice Provost and VP USF World .... Dr. Roger BRINDLEY
104 Director Education Abroad .... Dr. Amanda C. MAURER
46 Sr Vice Pres Research & Innovation .... Dr. Paul SANBERG
17 Sr Vice Pres USF Health .... Dr. Charles LOCKWOOD
58 Sr Vice Provost/Dean Grad School .... Dr. Dwayne SMITH
10 Vice Pres Business & Finance .... Mr. Nick TRIVUNOVICH
88 Assistant Treasurer .... Ms. Dawn M. RODRIGUEZ
11 Vice Pres Administrative Services .... Mr. Calvin WILLIAMS
18 Asst VP Physical Plant .... Mr. Chris DUFFY
102 CEO USF Foundation Inc .... Mr. Joel MOMBERG
32 Asst VP and Dean of Students .... Ms. Danielle MCDONALD
13 Vice Pres Information Technology .... Mr. Sidney FERNANDES
14 AVP Information Technology .... Ms. Jenny PAULSEN
14 AVP Information Technology .... Mr. Swapna CHACKRAVARTHY
105 Director Information Technology .... Mr. Christopher L. AKIN
29 Assoc Vice Pres Alumni Affairs .... Mr. Bill MCCAUSLAND
22 Chief Diversity Officer .... Dr. Haywood BROWN
121 Vice Provost for Student Success .... Dr. Paul J. DOSAL
16 Assoc Vice Pres Human Resources .... Ms. Donna KEENER
86 Asst Vice Pres Government Rels .... Mr. Mark WALSH
88 University Ombudsman .... Mr. Steven D. PREVAUX
39 Asst VP Housing/Residential Educ .... Ms. Ana HERNANDEZ
83 Dean Behavioral/Community Sci .... Dr. Julianne SEROVICH
50 Dean Business Administration .... Dr. Moez LIMAYEM
53 Dean College of Education .... Dr. Robert C. KNOEPPEL
54 Dean Engineering .... Dr. Robert H. BISHOP
57 Dean College of the Arts .... Dr. James S. MOY
67 Dean College of Pharmacy .... Dr. Kevin B. SNEED
49 Dean Arts & Sciences .... Dr. Eric EISENBERG
92 Dean Honors College .... Dr. Charles H. ADAMS
88 Dean Marine Science .... Dr. Jacqueline DIXON
69 Dean Public Health .... Dr. Donna PETERSEN
88 Int Dean Global Sustainability .... Dr. Govindan PARAYIL
89 Dean Undergraduate Studies .... Dr. Paul ATCHLEY
106 Asst Vice Provost Innovative Educ .... Dr. Cynthia A. DELUCA
48 Dir Sch of Architecture/Cmty Design .... Mr. Robert MACLEOD
12 Regional Chanc Sarasota-Manatee .... Dr. Karen HOLBROOK
12 Reg Chanc USF St Petersburg .... Dr. Martin TADLOCK
21 Controller .... Ms. Jennifer CONDON
26 Director of Media Relations .... Mr. Adam FREEMAN
06 Registrar .... Ms. Lois PALMER
114 University Budget Officer .... Ms. Nell PETERSON
84 Assoc VP Enrollment Management .... Ms. Billie Jo HAMILTON
38 Director Counseling Center .... Dr. Scott STRADER
36 Asst Vice President Career Services .... Ms. Ruth Ann ATCHLEY
19 Chief of Police .... Mr. Chris DANIEL
08 USF Libraries Dean .... Dr. Todd CHAVEZ
41 Director of Athletics .... Mr. Michael KELLY
28 Director of Diversity & Inclusion .... Ms. Patsy FELICIANO
96 Int Director Purchasing & Property .... Mr. George COTTER
09 Asst VP Office of Decision Support .... Dr. Valeria GARCIA

*University of South Florida St. Petersburg (C)

140 7th Avenue S, Saint Petersburg FL 33701-5016
County: Pinellas FICE Identification: 009016
Unit ID: 448840
Telephone: (727) 873-4873 Carnegie Class: Masters/L
FAX Number: (727) 873-4131 Calendar System: Semester
URL: www.usfsp.edu
Established: 1956 Annual Undergrad Tuition & Fees (In-District): $5,821
Enrollment: 4,895 Coed
Affiliation or Control: State/Local IRS Status: 501(c)3
Highest Offering: Master's
Accreditation: SC, CAEPN, JOUR

02 Regional Chancellor .... Dr. Martin TADLOCK
05 Regional Vice Chancellor .... Vacant
10 Interim Reg VC Admin/Financial Svcs .... Mr. Nicholas SETTEDUCATO
86 Reg Vice Chanc Government Relations .... Dr. Helen LEVINE
32 Reg Vice Chanc Student Affs .... Dr. Patricia HELTON
111 Reg Vice Chanc Advancement .... Ms. Deborah READ
53 Associate Dean College of Education .... Dr. Brenda WALKER
50 Dean College of Business .... Dr. Sridhar SUNDARAM
49 Dean College of Arts & Sciences .... Dr. Magali MICHAEL
08 Dean of the Library .... Ms. Catherine CARDWELL
19 Chief of Police .... Dr. David HENDRY
13 Assoc Director of Campus Computing .... Ms. Rea BURLESON
15 Director Human Resources .... Ms. Denelta ADDERLEY HENRY
37 Associate Director of Financial Aid .... Ms. Erin DUNN
06 Assoc Dir Records & Registration .... Ms. Lynn LYNCH
18 Dir Facil Plng/Construction Svcs .... Mr. James WAECHTER
96 Purchasing Manager .... Ms. Patricia SHOVAN-MORRIS
21 Regional Assoc Vice Chancellor .... Mr. David EVERINGHAM
26 Communications & Mktg Officer .... Mr. Matthew CIMITILE
30 Asst Director Development .... Ms. Alexis SEARFOSS
105 Webmaster .... Ms. Kathleen HOLDEN
28 Campus Diversity Officer .... Dr. Michelle MADDEN
07 Director of Admissions .... Mr. Serge DESIR, JR.
104 Associate Director Study Abroad .... Ms. Wendy BAKER
108 Director Institutional Assessment .... Dr. Michelle MADDEN
38 Director Student Counseling .... Dr. Anita SAHGAL
84 Reg Asst Vice Chanc for Enrollment .... Ms. Shari SCHWARTZ

*University of South Florida Sarasota-Manatee (D)

8350 Tamiami Trail, Sarasota FL 34243-2049
County: Manatee Identification: 667058
Unit ID: 451671
Telephone: (941) 359-4200 Carnegie Class: Masters/S
FAX Number: N/A Calendar System: Semester
URL: www.usfsm.edu
Established: 1956 Annual Undergrad Tuition & Fees (In-State): $5,587
Enrollment: 2,117 Coed
Affiliation or Control: State IRS Status: 501(c)3
Highest Offering: Master's; No Lower Division
Accreditation: SC, CAEPN

02 Regional Chancellor .... Dr. Karen HOLBROOK
10 Vice Chancellor Business & Finance .... Mr. Edwin BEAUCHAMP
05 Vice Chanc Academic & Student Affs .... Dr. Brett KEMKER
111 Vice Chancellor Advancement .... Ms. Lee WILLIAMS
09 AVP Institutional Research .... Dr. Bonnie J. JONES
20 Asst Vice Chancellor Acad Affairs .... Dr. Phil WAGNER
49 Dean College of Lib Arts & Soc Sci .... Dr. Jane ROSE
50 Dean College of Business .... Vacant
81 Dean College of Science & Math .... Dr. Paul KIRCHMAN
88 Dean College of Hosp & Tourism Mgmt .... Dr. Patrick MOREO
09 Director of Institutional Research .... Ms. Laura HOFFMAN
13 Chief Info Technology Officer (CIO) .... Mr. Bryan MUDD
07 Interim Director of Admissions .... Mr. Brandon AVERY
96 Director of Purchasing .... Ms. Michelle KRUEGER
32 Director Student Engagement .... Ms. Kimberly MONES
04 Administrative Asst to President .... Ms. Lisa BARKER
08 Head Librarian .... Ms. Diane FULKERSON
106 Dir Online Education/E-learning .... Ms. Timi HAGER
15 Assoc Dir Admin Services .... Ms. Carolyn DYSON
26 Director Information Services .... Mr. Shawn AHEARN
104 Director Global Engagement .... Ms. Amela MALKIC
19 Asst Director Security/Safety .... Mr. David BJELKE
37 Asst Director Student Financial Aid .... Ms. Gabriela VEGA

*University of West Florida (E)

11000 University Parkway, Pensacola FL 32514-5750
County: Escambia FICE Identification: 003955
Unit ID: 138354

Telephone: (850) 474-2000 Carnegie Class: Masters/L
FAX Number: (850) 474-3131 Calendar System: Semester
URL: uwf.edu
Established: 1963 Annual Undergrad Tuition & Fees (In-State): $6,360
Enrollment: 13,040 Coed
Affiliation or Control: State IRS Status: 501(c)3
Highest Offering: Doctorate
Accreditation: SC, CAATE, CAEPN, EXSC, MT, MUS, NURSE, PH, SW

02 President ... Dr. Martha D. SAUNDERS
04 Executive Assistant ... Ms. Anamarie MIXSON
05 Provost and Senior Vice President ... Dr. George B. ELLENBERG
10 VP Finance & Administration ... Ms. Betsy BOWERS
84 Int VP Enrollment & Student Affs ... Dr. Kim LEDUFF
111 Vice Pres for Univ Advancement ... Dr. Howard J. REDDY
20 Vice Provost ... Dr. Kimberly MCCORKLE
49 Dean Arts/Social Sci/Humanities ... Dr. Steven BROWN
50 Dean of Business ... Dr. Timothy O'KEEFE
107 Dean Education & Prof Studies ... Dr. William CRAWLEY
81 Int Dean Science/Engineering/Health ... Dr. Jaromy KUHL
08 Dean University Libraries ... Ms. Stephanie CLARK
58 Interim Dean Graduate Programs ... Dr. Kuiyuan LI
13 Exec Dir/Chief Tech Officer ITS ... Mrs. Melanie J. HAVEARD
76 Dean College of Health ... Dr. Denise SEABERT
12 Dir Branch Campus ... Dr. Melinda BOWERS
09 Dir Institutional Research ... Mr. Keith KING
108 Dir Institutional Effectiveness ... Dr. Angela BRYAN
43 General Counsel ... Ms. Pamela LANGHAM
21 Asst VP Financial Services ... Ms. Colleen M. ASMUS
96 Director Procurement & Contracts ... Ms. Angela JONES
109 Director Business/Auxiliary Svcs ... Ms. Ellen TILL
19 Chief of University Police ... Mr. Marc COSSICH
32 Sr Assoc Vice Pres Student Affairs ... Dr. James R. HURD
35 Associate VP/Dean of Students ... Dr. Brandon FRYE
35 Associate Dean of Students ... Dr. Ben STUBBS
07 Executive Director of Admissions ... Ms. Katherine CONDON
38 Exec Dir Counseling Services ... Ms. Michele MANASSAH
37 Director of Financial Aid ... Ms. Shana GORE
06 Registrar ... Ms. Kelley BRUNDAGE
39 Director of Housing/Residence Life ... Mr. Neil MCMILLION
20 Vice President Academic Engagement ... Dr. Kimberly LEDUFF
22 Exec Dir Equity & Diversity ... Ms. Karen RENTZ
92 Int Dir of Kugelman Honors Pgm ... Dr. Gregory TOMSO
104 Director of International Programs ... Mr. William VITTETOE
09 VP Research & Strategic Innovation ... Dr. Pamela NORTHRUP
15 Assoc VP Human Resources ... Ms. Jamie SPRAGUE
116 AVP Internal Audit/Mgmt Consulting ... Mr. Vito HITE
26 Exec Dir Institutional Comm ... Ms. Megan GONZALEZ
29 Director of Alumni Relations ... Mrs. Melissa H. GRACE
110 AVP of Advancement ... Mr. Daniel LUCAS
30 AVP for Development ... Vacant
31 AVP of External Affairs ... Ms. Janice GILLEY
41 Athletic Director ... Mr. David SCOTT
86 Sr Exec Spc Governmental Relations ... Mr. Andrew ROMER
101 Assistant Corporate Secretary ... Ms. Becky LUNTSFORD

Stetson University (A)

421 N Woodland Boulevard, DeLand FL 32723-0001
County: Volusia FICE Identification: 001531
Unit ID: 137546
Telephone: (386) 822-7000 Carnegie Class: Masters/L
FAX Number: (386) 822-8832 Calendar System: Semester
URL: www.stetson.edu
Established: 1883 Annual Undergrad Tuition & Fees: $46,030
Enrollment: 4,252 Coed
Affiliation or Control: Independent Non-Profit IRS Status: 501(c)3
Highest Offering: Doctorate
Accreditation: SC, CACREP, CAEP, LAW, MUS

01 President ... Dr. Wendy B. LIBBY
05 Exec VP & Provost ... Dr. Noel PAINTER
10 Exec Vice Pres & CFO ... Mr. F. Robert HUTH
111 VP for Devel & Alumni Engagement ... Mr. Jeffrey ULMER
84 VP Enrollment Management ... Mr. Joel BAUMAN
26 VP for University Marketing ... Mr. Bruce CHONG
32 Vice Pres for Student Affairs ... Dr. Lua HANCOCK
61 Dean College of Law ... Ms. Michele ALEXANDRE
49 Dean Col Arts & Sciences ... Dr. Elizabeth SKOMP
50 Dean of School of Business Admin ... Dr. Neal P. MERO
64 Dean of School of Music ... Dr. Timothy PETER
08 Dean of duPont-Ball Library ... Ms. Susan RYAN
20 Assoc Provost for Faculty Develop ... Dr. Rosalie RICHARDS
06 Interim Registrar ... Ms. Terri RICHARDS
41 Director of Athletics ... Mr. Jeffrey P. ALTIER
13 Assoc VP & CIO ... Dr. Jose BERNIER
15 Assoc VP for Human Resources ... Ms. Drew MACAN
18 Assoc Vice Pres Facilities Mgmt ... Ms. Bonita DUKES
21 Assoc Vice Pres for Finance ... Mr. Jeffrey MARGHEIM
114 Assoc VP Budget ... Ms. Melissa PETERS
35 Dean of Students ... Ms. Lynn SCHOENBERG
36 Exec Dir Career Dev & Advising ... Mr. Timothy STILES
09 Dir Institutional Research ... Dr. Resche HINES
104 Director of International Learning ... Ms. Paula HENTZ
30 Asst VP Development ... Ms. Katheryn P. PEARCE
112 Asst VP for Devel/Alumni Engagement ... Ms. Rina ARROYO
30 Assoc VP Dev & Communications ... Ms. Amy GIPSON
29 Asst VP Alumni/Parent Engagement ... Mr. Woody O'CAIN
07 Director of Admissions ... Ms. Dana DOLBOW
37 Dir Student Financial Aid ... Ms. Beth Anne CONSOLAZIO
39 Dir of Res Educ & Housing ... Dr. Larry CORRELL-HUGHES
16 Director Human Resources ... Ms. Betty WHITEMAN
96 Director of Purchasing ... Ms. Valinda WIMER
19 Chief Public Safety ... Mr. Francisco ORTIZ
04 Executive Asst to President ... Ms. Joan BEASLEY
102 Dir Ofc of Grants/Sponsored Rsrch ... Ms. Carol BUCKELS
38 Director Counseling Ctr ... Dr. Leigh BAKER
105 Director Web Services ... Mr. Gary SIPE
44 Director Donor Relations ... Mr. Don BURRHUS

Suncoast College of Health (B)

6513 14th Street West #103, Bradenton FL 34207
County: Manatee Identification: 667296
Telephone: (941) 727-2273 Carnegie Class: Not Classified
FAX Number: (941) 727-2274 Calendar System: Quarter
URL: www.suncoastcollege.edu
Established: Annual Undergrad Tuition & Fees: N/A
Enrollment: N/A Coed
Affiliation or Control: Proprietary IRS Status: Proprietary
Highest Offering: Baccalaureate
Accreditation: ACICS

01 President ... Lori BARNES

Tallahassee Community College (C)

444 Appleyard Drive, Tallahassee FL 32304-2895
County: Leon FICE Identification: 001533
Unit ID: 137759
Telephone: (850) 201-6200 Carnegie Class: Bac/Assoc-Assoc Dom
FAX Number: (850) 201-8682 Calendar System: Semester
URL: www.tcc.fl.edu
Established: 1966 Annual Undergrad Tuition & Fees (In-District): $2,026
Enrollment: 11,782 Coed
Affiliation or Control: Local IRS Status: 501(c)3
Highest Offering: Baccalaureate
Accreditation: SC, ADNUR, COARC, DA, DH, EMT, NUR, SURGT

01 President ... Dr. Jim MURDAUGH
05 Executive Vice President/Provost ... Ms. Madeline PUMARIEGA
10 Vice Pres Administrative Svcs/CFO ... Dr. Barbara WILLS
13 VP Information Technology ... Mr. Bret INGERMAN
32 Vice President for Student Affs ... Dr. Sheri ROWLAND
103 Vice Pres Workforce Development ... Ms. Kimberly MOORE
26 VP Communications and Marketing ... Mr. Al MORAN
108 Assoc VP Inst Effectiveness ... Dr. Lei WANG
12 Exec Dir Florida Public Safety Inst ... Mr. E. E. EUNICE
12 Exec Dir Wakulla Environmental Inst ... Mr. Bob BALLARD
12 Exec Dir Center for Innovation ... Dr. Scott BALOG
100 Chief of Staff ... Ms. Candice GRAUSE
22 Equity Officer ... Ms. Renae TOLSON
21 Asst Vice President Admin Services ... Mr. Bobby JONES
81 Dean of Science & Mathematics ... Dr. Anthony JONES
79 Dean Communications & Humanities ... Dr. Tracy WOODARD-MEYERS
83 Dean Behavioral/Social Science/Educ ... Dr. Richard MURGO
50 Dean Business Industry & Technology .. Mr. Stephen DUNNIVANT
75 Business & Industry Svc Ctr Dir ... Dr. Catrenia MCLENDON
97 Dean Transitional Studies ... Ms. Sharisse TURNER
08 Director of Library Services ... Mr. Stephen BANISTER
76 Dean Health Care Professions ... Ms. Stephanie SOLOMON
37 Director of Financial Aid ... Mr. William SPIERS
06 Registrar ... Ms. Brenda KNIGHT
124 Dir of Advising/New Stdnt Retention ... Mr. Mark SLIK
35 Dean of Student Services ... Dr. Gerald JONES
15 Director of Human Resources ... Ms. Nyla DAVIS
102 Director of TCC Foundation ... Ms. Heather MITCHELL
41 Director of Athletics ... Mr. Rob CHANEY
18 Dir Facilities/Construction/Plng ... Mr. Don HERR
21 Controller ... Ms. Patricia MANNING
88 Director of Educational Research ... Dr. Barbara J. GILL
09 Director of Institutional Research ... Ms. Margaret WINGATE
106 Dir Center for Distance Learning ... Dr. Lemond HALL
88 Dir Ctr for Teach/Learn/Ldrshp ... Ms. Summer DUSEK
85 Coordinator Intl Student Services ... Ms. Emily MAUER
14 Director of User Services ... Mr. Chip SINGLETARY
14 Director of Enterprise Systems ... Mr. Mike ROBECK
14 Director of IT Infrastructure ... Mr. Jason FOWLER
45 Director of Financial Planning ... Ms. Amy BRADBURY
25 Director Grants & Special Projects ... Mr. Steven SOLOMON
96 Purchasing Manager ... Mr. Bobby HINSON
19 Chief of Police ... Mr. Gregory GIBSON
20 Dean of Curriculum and Instruction ... Mrs. Calandra STRINGER
36 Director of Career Services ... Ms. Catie GOODMAN
43 Dir Legal Services/General Counsel ... Mr. Craig KNOX
27 Director of Comm & Public Info ... Ms. Alice MAXWELL
27 Director of Integrated Marketing ... Mr. Travis JORDAN
04 Administrative Asst to President ... Ms. Lenda KLING

Talmudic College of Florida (D)

4000 Alton Road, Miami Beach FL 33140
County: Dade FICE Identification: 025089
Unit ID: 137777
Telephone: (305) 534-7050 Carnegie Class: Spec-4-yr-Faith
FAX Number: (305) 534-8444 Calendar System: Semester
URL: www.talmudicu.edu
Established: 1974 Annual Undergrad Tuition & Fees: $13,250
Enrollment: 32 Male
Affiliation or Control: Independent Non-Profit IRS Status: 501(c)3
Highest Offering: Master's
Accreditation: RABN

01 President ... Rabbi Yitzchak ZWEIG
05 Dean/Vice President ... Rabbi Yochanan ZWEIG
06 Registrar ... Rabbi Yitzchak WINKLER
37 Director Student Financial Aid ... Ms. Sharon BRECHER
20 Director Educational Programs ... Rabbi Akiva ZWEIG
07 Director of Admissions ... Rabbi Yaakov BURSTYN

Taylor College (E)

5190 SE 125th Street, Belleview FL 34420
County: Marion FICE Identification: 041166
Unit ID: 449524
Telephone: (352) 245-4119 Carnegie Class: Spec 2-yr-Health
FAX Number: (352) 245-0276 Calendar System: Other
URL: www.taylorcollege.edu
Established: 1999 Annual Undergrad Tuition & Fees: $11,272
Enrollment: 166 Coed
Affiliation or Control: Proprietary IRS Status: Proprietary
Highest Offering: Associate Degree
Accreditation: ABHES, ADNUR, PNUR, PTAA

01 President ... Rebecca JONES
04 Admin Assistant to the President ... Glee KARLOFF
10 Controller ... Amy DINELLA
66 Director Nursing ... Shelby HAVENS
66 Assistant Director Nursing ... Sherilyn BAL
76 Director Physical Therapy ... Lisa JORANLIEN
53 Director General Education ... Elizabeth THOMPSON
37 Director Financial Aid ... Brandy BARNETT
88 Director Compliance ... Ingrid ZEKAN
06 Registrar ... Susie BRADLEY

Trinity Baptist College (F)

800 Hammond Boulevard, Jacksonville FL 32221-1398
County: Duval FICE Identification: 031019
Unit ID: 137953
Telephone: (904) 596-2400 Carnegie Class: Bac-Diverse
FAX Number: (904) 596-2532 Calendar System: Semester
URL: www.tbc.edu
Established: 1974 Annual Undergrad Tuition & Fees: $12,140
Enrollment: 366 Coed
Affiliation or Control: Baptist IRS Status: 501(c)3
Highest Offering: Master's
Accreditation: TRACS

00 Chancellor ... Dr. Thomas C. MESSER
01 President/CEO ... Mr. Mac HEAVENER
05 Senior Vice President ... Dr. Matthew BEEMER
32 Vice President of Student Affairs ... Mr. Jeremiah STANLEY
84 VP Enrollment Mgmt & Development ... Mr. Matthew HEAVENER
37 Director of Financial Aid ... Mr. Mark ELKINS
04 Administrative Asst to President ... Mrs. Michelle MARSHALL
06 Registrar ... Dr. John CASH
08 Head Librarian ... Dr. John LUCY
10 Chief Business Officer ... Mr. Mike AKINS
41 Athletic Director ... Mr. John JONES
18 Chief Facilities/Physical Plant ... Mr. Dennis RIFFLE
19 Director Security/Safety ... Mr. John CASH, JR.
29 Director Alumni Relations ... Vacant
07 Director of Admissions ... Mrs. Jenny STANLEY
106 Dean or Director Online Education/E ... Mrs. Teresa DUSTMAN
30 Director of Development ... Mr. Michael HEAVENER

Trinity College of Florida (G)

2430 Welbilt Boulevard, Trinity FL 34655-4401
County: Pasco FICE Identification: 030282
Unit ID: 137962
Telephone: (727) 376-6911 Carnegie Class: Spec-4-yr-Faith
FAX Number: (727) 376-0781 Calendar System: Semester
URL: www.trinitycollege.edu
Established: 1932 Annual Undergrad Tuition & Fees: $16,340
Enrollment: 189 Coed
Affiliation or Control: Independent Non-Profit IRS Status: 501(c)3
Highest Offering: Baccalaureate
Accreditation: BI

01 President ... Dr. Mark T. O'FARRELL
32 Vice President Student Development ... Rev. Al DEPOUTOT
05 Vice President Academic Affairs ... Dr. Dennis COX
111 Vice President for Advancement ... Dr. Charlie MARTIN
10 Vice Pres for Business & Finance ... Mr. Greg MITCHELL
06 Registrar ... Mrs. Sheila M. JOHNSON
26 Asst VP Marketing/Communications ... Vacant
07 Director of Admissions ... Mrs. Rachel NOBLE
04 Administrative Asst to President ... Mrs. Billie O'FARRELL
08 Head Librarian ... Mrs. Cindy T. HYER
13 Chief Info Technology Ofcr/CIO ... Mr. Charles PAYNTER
84 Director Enrollment Management ... Mr. Anthony ABELL

Ultimate Medical Academy-Clearwater (H)

1255 Cleveland Street, Clearwater FL 33756
County: Pinellas FICE Identification: 035493
Unit ID: 441371
Telephone: (727) 298-8685 Carnegie Class: Spec 2-yr-Health
FAX Number: (727) 446-2489 Calendar System: Semester
URL: www.ultimatemedical.edu
Established: 1998 Annual Undergrad Tuition & Fees: N/A
Enrollment: 18,563 Coed
Affiliation or Control: Proprietary IRS Status: Proprietary

Highest Offering: Associate Degree
Accreditation: ABHES

01 Campus Director ....Ms. Rebecca SARLO

Ultimate Medical Academy Online-Tampa (A)

3101 W Dr. Martin Luther King Blvd, Tampa FL 33607
Telephone: (888) 205-2456 Identification: 770528
Accreditation: ABHES, CAHIIM

Unilatina International College (B)

3130 Commerce Pkwy, Miramar FL 33025
County: Broward Identification: 667155
Unit ID: 486354
Telephone: (954) 607-4344 Carnegie Class: Spec-4-yr-Bus
FAX Number: (954) 357-1766 Calendar System: Quarter
URL: www.unilatina.edu
Established: 2001 Annual Undergrad Tuition & Fees: $8,907
Enrollment: 76 Coed
Affiliation or Control: Proprietary IRS Status: Proprietary
Highest Offering: Baccalaureate
Accreditation: ACICS

01 President ....Lydia B. BAUTISTA MOLLER
05 Academic Director ....Angelica MOYANO

Universal Career School (C)

10720 W. Flagler Street Ste 21, Sweetwater FL 33174
County: Miami-Dade FICE Identification: 038563
Unit ID: 446589
Telephone: (305) 485-7700 Carnegie Class: Not Classified
FAX Number: (305) 485-8515 Calendar System: Semester
URL: www.ucs.edu
Established: Annual Undergrad Tuition & Fees: N/A
Enrollment: 231 Coed
Affiliation or Control: Proprietary IRS Status: Proprietary
Highest Offering: Associate Degree
Accreditation: COE

01 Director ....Blanca BURGOS
06 Registrar ....Hermes VEGA

University of Fort Lauderdale (D)

4131 NW 16th Street, Lauderhill FL 33313
County: Broward FICE Identification: 041563
Unit ID: 457402
Telephone: (954) 486-7728 Carnegie Class: Spec-4-yr-Other
FAX Number: (954) 486-7667 Calendar System: Other
URL: www.uftl.edu
Established: 1995 Annual Undergrad Tuition & Fees: $7,410
Enrollment: 77 Coed
Affiliation or Control: Non-denominational IRS Status: 501(c)3
Highest Offering: Doctorate
Accreditation: TRACS

00 Chancellor ....Dr. Henry B. FERNANDEZ
01 President ....Ms. Ilona M. HOLMES
10 Chief Financial Officer ....Mr. Brian HANKERSON
06 Registrar ....Ms. Lenice BARNETT
07 Director Admissions/Student Svcs ....Dr. Debra WHITE
37 Director Financial Aid ....Ms. Rossana LEWIS
21 Comptroller ....Ms. Daneida BENJAMIN
100 Executive Assistant to President ....Ms. Tiffany BACON
41 Athletic Director ....Mr. Isaac BRUCE

University of Miami (E)

1252 Memorial Drive, Coral Gables FL 33124
County: Miami-Dade FICE Identification: 001536
Unit ID: 135726
Telephone: (305) 284-2211 Carnegie Class: DU-Highest
FAX Number: N/A Calendar System: Semester
URL: www.miami.edu
Established: 1925 Annual Undergrad Tuition & Fees: $50,226
Enrollment: 17,003 Coed
Affiliation or Control: Independent Non-Profit IRS Status: 501(c)3
Highest Offering: Doctorate
Accreditation: SC, ANEST, CAATE, CAMPEP, CEA, CLPSY, COPSY, DENT, HSA, IPSY, LAW, MED, MUS, NURSE, PH, PTA

01 President ....Dr. Julio FRENK
05 Executive Vice President & Provost ....Dr. Jeffrey DUERK
10 Exec VP Business/Finance & COO ....Dr. Jacqueline TRAVISANO
21 Vice President & CFO ....Mr. Brandon GILLILAND
17 Exec VP Health Affairs/CEO UHealth ....Dr. Edward ABRAHAM
111 SVP Development & Alumni Relations ....Mr. Joshua FRIEDMAN
84 VP Enrollment Management ....Mr. John G. HALLER
115 AVP Treasury ....Mr. Charmel MAYNARD
18 VP Facilities Operations & Planning ....Ms. Jessica BRUMLEY
26 VP University Communications ....Ms. Jacqueline R. MENENDEZ
15 VP Human Resources ....Mrs. Mary HARPER HAGAN
43 VP/General Counsel ....Ms. Aileen M. UGALDE
32 VP Student Affairs ....Dr. Patricia A. WHITELY
00 Chairman Board of Trustees ....Ms. Hilarie BASS
100 President's Chief of Staff ....Mr. Rodolfo J. FERNANDEZ
20 Sr Vice Provost/Dean Undergrad Educ ....Dr. William S. GREEN
46 Vice Provost Research ....Dr. John L. BIXBY
20 Vice Provost Faculty Affairs ....Dr. David J. BIRNBACH
41 Director Athletics ....Mr. Blake JAMES
31 AVP Community Relations ....Ms. Sarah N. ARTECONA
16 Assoc Vice Pres Med Human Resources ....Ms. Dorinda CAROLINA
27 Executive Director Comm & PR ....Ms. Megan M. ONDRIZEK
19 Chief of Police ....Major David A. RIVERO
63 Dean School of Medicine ....Dr. Henri FORD
49 Dean College of Arts & Sciences ....Dr. Leonidas G. BACHAS
48 Dean School of Architecture ....Dr. Rodolphe EL-KHOURY
50 Dean Miami Business School ....Dr. John A. QUELCH
60 Dean School Communication ....Dr. Karin J. WILKINS
53 Dean Education/Human Development ....Dr. Laura KOHN-WOOD
54 Int Dean College of Engineering ....Dr. Daniel BERG
61 Dean School of Law ....Mr. Anthony VARONA
64 Dean School of Music ....Dr. Shelton G. BERG
65 Dean Marine & Atmospheric Science ....Dr. Roni AVISSAR
66 Dean Nursing & Health Studies ....Dr. Cindy L. MUNRO
58 Dean Graduate School ....Dr. Guillermo PRADO
35 AVP Stdnt Affs & Dean of Students ....Dr. Ryan C. HOLMES
07 Asst VP Undergraduate Admissions ....Mr. Nate CROZIER
38 Director Student Counseling ....Dr. Rene MONTEAGUDO
85 Director Intl Services ....Ms. Teresa S. DE LA GUARDIA
39 Exec Director Student Housing ....Mr. James G. SMART
96 Executive Director Purchasing ....Ms. Susan R. MONTES
88 AVP Enterprise Business Solutions ....Mr. Anurag SARIN
119 Assoc VP and CISO ....Mr. Thomas MURPHY
90 AVP Chief Academic Tech Officer ....Mr. Allan GYORKE
14 Assoc VP Information Technology ....Mr. Brad ROHRER
109 Executive Director Auxiliary Svcs ....Ms. Ana ALVAREZ
51 Dean Continuing Education ....Dr. Rebecca MACMILLAN FOX
40 Director Bookstore ....Ms. Wendy SMITH
06 Registrar ....Ms. Karen J. BECKETT
08 Dean Libraries ....Dr. Charles ECKMAN
101 University Secretary ....Ms. Leslie DELLINGER ACEITUNO
102 Exec Director Foundation Relations ....Ms. Joanna DE VELASCO
36 Assoc Dean Career Services ....Mr. Christian GARCIA
104 Director Study Abroad ....Ms. Devika M. MILNER
22 AVP Workplace Equity ....Ms. Beverly PRUITT
25 AVP Business Services ....Mr. Humberto M. SPEZIANI
37 Exec Director Financial Assistance ....Ms. Carrie GLASS
13 VP Information Technology & CIO ....Mr. Ernie FERNANDEZ
44 Executive Director Annual Giving ....Ms. Erica ARROYO
114 AVP Financial Planning & Analysis ....Ms. Aintzane CELAYA
04 Administrative Manager to President ....Ms. Alicia BLATCHFORD
86 Sr VP for Pub Affairs & Comm ....Mr. Rodolfo J. FERNANDEZ
116 AVP Chief Audit/Compliance Officer ....Ms. Blanca MALAGON
117 Executive Director Risk Management ....Mr. Craig MCALLISTER
09 Assc Provost Institutional Research ....Dr. Dave BECHER
106 Exec Director Online Education ....Mr. Chris KOELSCH

University of Phoenix Central Florida Main Campus (F)

8325 South Park Circle Ste 100, Orlando FL 32819
Telephone: (407) 345-8868 Identification: 770932
Accreditation: &NH, ACBSP

† No longer accepting campus-based students.

University of Phoenix North Florida Campus (G)

4500 Salisbury Road, Jacksonville FL 32216-0959
Telephone: (904) 636-6645 Identification: 770197
Accreditation: &NH, ACBSP

† No longer accepting campus-based students.

University of Phoenix South Florida Main Campus (H)

2400 SW 145th Avenue, Suite 150,
Miramar FL 33027-4145
Telephone: (954) 628-1605 Identification: 770237
Accreditation: &NH

† No longer accepting campus-based students.

University of St. Augustine for Health Sciences (I)

One University Boulevard, St. Augustine FL 32086
Telephone: (904) 826-0084 Identification: 770939
Accreditation: &WC, OT, PTA

† Branch campus of University of St. Augustine for Health Sciences, San Marcos, CA.

University of Tampa (J)

401 W Kennedy Boulevard, Tampa FL 33606-1490
County: Hillsborough FICE Identification: 001538
Unit ID: 137847
Telephone: (813) 253-3333 Carnegie Class: Masters/L
FAX Number: (813) 258-7207 Calendar System: Other
URL: www.ut.edu
Established: 1931 Annual Undergrad Tuition & Fees: $29,208
Enrollment: 8,895 Coed
Affiliation or Control: Independent Non-Profit IRS Status: 501(c)3
Highest Offering: Doctorate
Accreditation: SC, #ARCPA, CAATE, COSMA, FEPAC, MUS, NURSE

01 President ....Dr. Ronald L. VAUGHN
05 Provost/Vice Pres Academic Affairs ....Dr. David STERN
10 Vice Pres Administration/Finance ....Mr. Kevin LAFFERTY
84 Vice President Enrollment ....Mr. Dennis L. NOSTRAND
111 Vice Pres Development/Univ Rels ....Mr. L. Keith TODD
45 Vice Pres Operations & Planning ....Dr. Linda W. DEVINE
13 Chief Information Security Officer ....Ms. Tammy L. CLARK
32 Dean of Students ....Ms. Stephanie R. KREBS
20 Assoc Provost & Dean of Acad Svcs ....Vacant
06 Registrar ....Ms. Michelle PELAEZ
08 Director of the Library ....Ms. Marlyn PETHE-COOK
29 Director of Alumni Relations ....Mr. James HARDWICK
37 Director of Financial Aid ....Ms. Jacqueline LATORELLA
26 Director of Public Information ....Mr. Eric D. CARDENAS
18 Director of Facilities Management ....Ms. Jennifer ISENBECK
15 Exec Director of Human Resources ....Ms. Donna B. POPOVICH
07 Dir Enrollment Mgmt/Admissions ....Mr. Brent W. BENNER
41 Athletic Director ....Mr. Larry J. MARFISE
40 Manager Campus Store ....Mr. Nick FAGNONI
39 Director of Residence Life ....Vacant
22 Affirmative Action Officer ....Ms. Donna B. POPOVICH
19 Director Safety & Security ....Mr. Kevin A. HOWELL
23 Dir Health Center/Stdnt Counseling ....Ms. Sharon P. SCHAEFER
38 Director Student Counseling ....Ms. Sharon P. SCHAEFER
96 Director of Procurement ....Ms. Cyn D. EZELL
09 Dir Institutional Effectiveness ....Dr. Jeanne M. ROBERTS
92 Director of Honors Program ....Dr. Gary S. LUTER
50 Dean College of Business ....Dr. F. Frank GHANNADIAN
83 Dean Social Science/Math Education ....Dr. Jack M. GELLER
81 Dean College Natural/Health Sci ....Dr. Paul GREENWOOD
57 Dean College of Arts/Letters ....Dr. David GUDELUNAS
51 Assoc Dean Graduate/Continuing Stds ....Dr. Donald D. MORRILL
89 Dir First Year/Baccalaureate Exp ....Ms. Edesa SCARBOROUGH
36 Assoc Dean Career Dev & Engagement ....Mr. Timothy HARDING
104 Assoc Dean International Programs ....Dr. Marca BEAR
04 Executive Asst to President ....Ms. Madelyn CASTRO

Valencia College (K)

PO Box 3028, Orlando FL 32802-3028
County: Orange FICE Identification: 006750
Unit ID: 138187
Telephone: (407) 299-5000 Carnegie Class: Bac/Assoc-Assoc Dom
FAX Number: (407) 426-8970 Calendar System: Semester
URL: www.valenciacollege.edu
Established: 1967 Annual Undergrad Tuition & Fees (In-State): $2,474
Enrollment: 44,834 Coed
Affiliation or Control: State IRS Status: 501(c)3
Highest Offering: Baccalaureate
Accreditation: SC, ADNUR, CAHIIM, CEA, COARC, CVT, DH, DMS, EMT, RAD

01 President ....Dr. Sandy C. SHUGART
03 Executive Vice President/Provost ....Dr. Kathleen A. PLINSKE
45 VP Analytics & Planning ....Dr. Brandon MCKELVEY
05 VP Academic Affairs ....Dr. Isis ARTZE VEGA
10 VP Business Ops & Finance ....Mr. Loren J. BENDER
107 VP Global/Prof & Cont Education ....Mr. Joe N. BATTISTA
15 VP Org Dev & Human Resources ....Dr. Amy N. BOSLEY
43 VP Policy & General Counsel ....Dr. Bill J. MULLOWNEY
26 VP Public Affairs & Marketing ....Mr. Jay R. GALBRAITH, II
32 VP Student Affairs ....Dr. Joe C. RICHARDSON
84 Associate VP Enrollment Management ....Dr. Sonya F. JOSEPH
88 Assoc General Counsel ....Dr. Leslie B. GOLDEN
07 Int AVP Admissions & Records ....Mr. Edwin SANCHEZ VELEZ
13 Chief Information Officer ....Ms. Patti T. SMITH
114 Asst VP Budgets & Analysis ....Mr. Oscar J. CRISTANCHO MERCADO
103 Asst VP Career & Workforce Educ ....Dr. Nasser HEDAYAT
90 Managing Dir Campus Tech Svcs ....Dr. Jamie D. ROST
88 Asst VP College Transition ....Dr. Amy E. KLEEMAN
18 Asst VP Fac Plng/Real Est Dev ....Mr. Jose A. FERNANDEZ
37 Asst VP Fin Aid/Vet Affairs ....Mr. Daniel T. BARKOWITZ
88 Asst VP Analytics & Reporting ....Mr. Daryl J. DAVIS
21 Asst VP Financial Services ....Ms. Jackie D. LASCH
51 Asst VP Global & Cont Educ ....Ms. Lisa G. ELI
27 Asst VP Marketing ....Ms. Traci A. BJELLA
19 Asst VP Operations ....Mr. Paul ROONEY
16 Asst VP Org Dev & Incl ....Mr. Ryan D. KANE
88 Asst VP Prof & Continuing Education ....Dr. Carolyn R. MCMORRAN
25 Asst VP Resource Development ....Ms. Kristeen R. CHRISTIAN
35 Asst VP Student Affairs ....Vacant
88 Asst VP Education Partnership ....Ms. Eda DAVIS-LOWE
16 Asst VP Talent Acq/Total Rew ....Ms. Mary Beth CLIFTON
88 Asst VP Teaching & Learning ....Dr. Wendi M. DEW
12 Campus President East/Winter Park ....Dr. Stacey R. JOHNSON
12 Campus President Osceola/LNC/PNC ....Vacant
12 Campus President West/Downtown ....Dr. Falecia D. WILLIAMS
88 Executive Dean Downtown ....Mr. Eugene G. JONES, II
88 Executive Dean Lake Nona ....Dr. Mike BOSLEY
88 Interim Executive Dean Osceola ....Dr. Melissa D. PEDONE
88 Executive Dean Poinciana ....Dr. Jennifer ROBERTSON
88 Executive Dean School Public Safety ....Dr. Jeff W. GOLTZ
88 Executive Dean Winter Park ....Dr. Terri G. DANIELS
88 Dean School of Arts/Entertain ....Ms. Wendy L. GIVOGLU
102 Foundation President and CEO ....Dr. Geraldine M P. GALLAGHER
20 Dean Academic Affairs East ....Ms. Michelle R. FOSTER
20 Dean Academic Affairs Osc ....Vacant
20 Dean Academic Affairs West ....Dr. Molly MCINTIRE
102 Foundation VP & COO ....Ms. Michelle D. MATIS
97 Campus Dean Learning Support East ....Dr. Leonard C. BASS
97 Campus Dean Learning Supprt Osceola ....Dr. Landon P. SHEPHARD
97 Campus Dean Learning Support West ....Dr. Karen L. REILLY
35 Dean of Students East/WP ....Mr. Joe M. SARRUBBO, JR.

35 Dean of Students Osceola .... Dr. Jill M. SZENTMIKLOSI
35 Dean of Students West ....Dr. Ben C. LION
35 Dean of Students DTC ....Dr. Edna D. JONES MILLER
76 Dean Allied Health ....Ms. Marie E. VASQUEZ-BROOKS
49 Dean Arts & Humanities West . Ms. Ana J. CALDERO FIGUEROA
83 Interim Dean Behav/Soc Science West ....Ms. Adrienne L. MATHEWS
50 Dean Business & Hospitality ....Dr. Terry L. ALLCORN
50 Dean Bus/Info Tech/Pub Svc East ....Dr. Carin M. GORDON
75 Dean Career & Technical Programs .....Dr. James R. MCDONALD
60 Dean Communications East .... Ms. Linda R. NEAL
60 Dean Comm/Languages Osceola .... Ms. Jenni L. CAMPBELL
60 Dean Communications West ....Vacant
54 Dean Engr/Computer Pgm & Tech ....Dr. Paul J. WILDER
79 Dean Humanities/Foreign Lang East ....Mr. David O. SUTTON
79 Dean Humanities/Social Science ....Dr. Scott F. CREAMER
81 Dean Math East ....Ms. Keri S. SILER
81 Dean Math Osceola ....Dr. Nichole A. SEGARRA
81 Dean Math West ....Dr. Paul D. BLANKENSHIP
66 Dean School of Nursing ....Dr. Barb L. AKE
49 Dean Science East ....Dr. Jennifer L. SNYDER
81 Dean Science Osceola ....Dr. Anitza M. SAN MIGUEL
49 Dean Science West ....Dr. Bob F. GESSNER
83 Dean Social Science East ....Dr. Mark G. COLLINS
88 Dean School of Hospitality/Culinary ....Mr. Alex ERDMANN
08 Campus Director Library W ....Ms. Ruth S. SMITH
29 Director Alum Engage/Annual Giving ....Ms. Erin C. OHLSEN
40 Director Aux Svcs Campus Store ....Ms. Lisa M. ELVERS
96 Director Auxiliary Svcs Contracts ....Mr. Jeffrey D. FILKO
116 Director Compliance & Audit .. Ms. Cynthia SANTIAGO-GUZMAN
88 Director Corporate Partnerships ....Mr. Brian B. HENTIES
88 Director Curriculum Initiatives ....Ms. Robyn M. BRIGHTON
84 Director Enrollment Services ....Vacant
88 Director HR Policy & Compliance ....Ms. Michelle T. SEVER
22 Director Eq Op & Emp Relations ....Ms. Lauren E. KELLY
92 Director Honors Program ....Dr. Cheryl ROBINSON
119 Managing Dir Network & Security ....Mr. John E. KNIGHTS
108 Director Institutional Evaluation ....Dr. Laura N. BLASI
88 Director Institution Effectiveness ....Mr. Darren A. SMITH
120 Director Online Teach/Learning ....Ms. Page A. JERZAK
18 Managing Director Plant Operations ....Mr. Shaun D. ANDREWS
19 Managing Director Safety & Security .... Mr. Mike D. FAVORIT
96 Managing Director Procurement ....Ms. Yaremis P. FULLANA
44 Chief Philanthropy Officer ....Ms. Angela J. MENDOLARO
04 Executive Assistant Senior ....Ms. Barbara E. HALSTEAD

Warner University (A)

13895 Highway 27, Lake Wales FL 33859-2549
County: Polk FICE Identification: 008848
Unit ID: 138275
Telephone: (863) 638-1426 Carnegie Class: Bac-Diverse
FAX Number: (863) 638-1472 Calendar System: Semester
URL: www.warner.edu
Established: 1968 Annual Undergrad Tuition & Fees: $21,694
Enrollment: 1,212 Coed
Affiliation or Control: Church Of God IRS Status: 501(c)3
Highest Offering: Master's
Accreditation: SC, SW

01 President ....Dr. David A. HOAG
88 Sr Dir of Non-Traditional Education ....Dr. James G. MOYER
10 Vice Pres for Finance & Business ....Mr. Mike PICHA
111 Vice President for Advancement ....Mrs. Andrea THIES
84 VP for Enrollment Mgmt & Marketing .... Mr. Derry EBERT
32 VP of Student Life ....Rev. Dawn MEADOWS
06 Registrar ....Mrs. Sara F. KANE
37 Director Student Financial Aid ....Ms. Elease COX
21 Asst VP for Business & Finance ....Mr. Dean MEADOWS
29 Alumni & Annual Fund Coord ....Ms. Abby CRAWFORD
18 Chief Facilities/Physical Plant ....Mr. Mark THOMAS
97 Director of General Studies ....Mrs. Kelly MILLS
20 Dean of Faculty ....Dr. Michael SANDERS
13 Director of Institutional Tech ....Mr. Mark THOMAS
19 Director Campus Security ....Mr. James MOYER
88 Director Academic Skills Ctr ....Mrs. Kelly MORGAN
106 Director Online Services ....Mr. Shawn TAYLOR
107 Dean Adult Prof Div & Grad Studies ....Dr. James MOYER
04 Executive Asst to President ....Mrs. Jera LAUREL
15 Director of Human Resources .... Mrs. Janet CRAIGMILES

Webber International University (B)

1201 Scenic Highway N/P.O. Box 96,
Babson Park FL 33827-0096
County: Polk FICE Identification: 001540
Unit ID: 138293
Telephone: (863) 638-1431 Carnegie Class: Bac-Diverse
FAX Number: (863) 638-2823 Calendar System: Semester
URL: www.webber.edu
Established: 1927 Annual Undergrad Tuition & Fees: $26,116
Enrollment: 682 Coed
Affiliation or Control: Independent Non-Profit IRS Status: 501(c)3
Highest Offering: Master's
Accreditation: SC

01 President ....Dr. H. Keith WADE
05 Academic Dean ....Dr. Charles SHIEH
10 Vice President Finance ....Ms. Christina JORDON
09 VP of Inst Effectiveness/Research ....Dr. Nelson MARQUEZ
32 Campus VP of Student Life ....Mr. Jay CULVER
06 Vice Pres of Student Record Svcs ....Mrs. Kathy A. WILSON

36 Dir Career Service & Cmty Outreach .... Mrs. Devyn MONTALVO
08 Director Library Services ....Ms. Sue DUNNING
41 Athletic Director ....Mr. Darren RICHIE
13 Director Information Technology ....Mr. Davius ROSIUS
18 Director of Campus Svcs/Maintenance ....Mr. Matt YENTES
40 Director of Bookstore .... Mr. Matt SALIBA
07 Director of Admissions ....Ms. Bobbi ANDREWS
50 Chair of Business Education ....Dr. Jeanette EBERLE
53 Chair of General Education Division .... Dr. Charles WUNKER
04 Executive Asst to President ....Ms. Gerlinde DANCY
19 Director Security/Safety ....Mr. Michael RITTER
29 Dir Annual Fund/Alumni Relations .... Ms. Rebecca KLEPACKI

West Coast University - Miami (C)

9250 NW 36th Street, Doral FL 33178
Telephone: (786) 501-7070 Identification: 770936
Accreditation: &WC

† Branch campus of West Coast University, North Hollywood, CA.

WMU - Cooley Law School Tampa Bay Campus (D)

9445 Camden Field Parkway, Riverview FL 33578
Telephone: (813) 419-5100 Identification: 770290
Accreditation: &NH

† Branch campus of Western Michigan University Cooley Law School, Lansing, MI

Yeshiva Gedolah Rabbinical College (E)

1140 Alton Road, Miami Beach FL 33139-4708
County: Dade FICE Identification: 032563
Unit ID: 363712
Telephone: (305) 653-8770 Carnegie Class: Spec-4-yr-Faith
FAX Number: (305) 653-6790 Calendar System: Semester
URL: www.lecfl.com
Established: 1973 Annual Undergrad Tuition & Fees: $8,300
Enrollment: 24 Male
Affiliation or Control: Independent Non-Profit IRS Status: 501(c)3
Highest Offering: Master's
Accreditation: RABN

01 Executive Vice President ....Rabbi Benzion KORF
05 Dean ....Rabbi Abraham KORF
06 Registrar .... Ayelet BORTUNK
07 Director of Admissions ....Rabbi Chaim STERN

GEORGIA

Abraham Baldwin Agricultural College (F)

ABAC 1 - 2802 Moore Highway, Tifton GA 31793-2601
County: Tift FICE Identification: 001541
Unit ID: 138558
Telephone: (229) 391-5001 Carnegie Class: Bac/Assoc-Mixed
FAX Number: (229) 391-5002 Calendar System: Semester
URL: www.abac.edu
Established: 1908 Annual Undergrad Tuition & Fees (In-State): $3,503
Enrollment: 3,394 Coed
Affiliation or Control: State IRS Status: 501(c)3
Highest Offering: Baccalaureate
Accreditation: SC, ADNUR, NUR

01 President ....Dr. David BRIDGES
05 Provost and VP for Academic Affairs .... Dr. Jerry BAKER
10 EVP for Finance and Administration ....Mr. Paul WILLIS
111 Int VP External Affairs/Advancement ....Mr. Paul WILLIAMS
12 Exec Dir ABAC at Bainbridge ....Dr. Michael KIRKLAND
08 Director of Library Services ....Dr. Laura K. CLARK
32 Dean of Students ....Ms. Bernice HUGHES
41 Athletic Director .... Dr. Alan KRAMER
06 Registrar .... Dr. Amy WILLIS
38 Director of Student Development ....Dr. Maggie MARTIN
37 Director of Student Financial Svcs ....Mr. Michael WRIGHT
15 Director of Human Resources ....Mr. Richard SPANCAKE
26 Director of Public Relations .... Ms. Lindsey ROBERTS
108 Director of Assessment ....Vacant
84 Director Enrollment Management ....Ms. Donna WEBB
96 Director of Procurement ....Ms. Teri MATHIS
19 Chief of Police ....Mr. Frank STRICKLAND
04 Admin Associate to President ....Ms. Jordan BEARD
39 Director of Student Housing ....Dr. Chris S. KINSEY
13 VP of Technology and CIO ....Mr. Robert GERHART
07 Director of Admissions ....Ms. Donna WEBB
30 Chief Development Officer ....Ms. Deidre MARTIN

† Part of the University System of Georgia.

Agnes Scott College (G)

141 E. College Avenue, Decatur GA 30030-3770
County: DeKalb FICE Identification: 001542
Unit ID: 138600
Telephone: (404) 471-6000 Carnegie Class: Bac-A&S
FAX Number: (404) 471-6067 Calendar System: Semester
URL: www.agnesscott.edu
Established: 1889 Annual Undergrad Tuition & Fees: $41,160
Enrollment: 921 Female
Affiliation or Control: Presbyterian Church (U.S.A.) IRS Status: 501(c)3
Highest Offering: Master's
Accreditation: SC

01 President ....Ms. Leocadia (Lee) I. ZAK
05 Interim VP for Academic Affairs ....Dr. Christine COZZENS
32 VP for Student Life ....Dr. Karen GOFF
10 VP Business & Finance ....Dr. Kenneth W. ENGLAND
111 VP for College Advancement ....Dr. Robiaun R. CHARLES
84 VP for Enrollment/Dean of Admission ....Ms. Alexa GAETA
26 VP Communications/Marketing ....Ms. Danita KNIGHT
101 Associate VP & Board Secretary ....Ms. Lea Ann HUDSON
13 Assoc VP Technology ....Ms. LaNeta COUNTS
15 Associate VP for Human Resources .... Ms. Karen GILBERT
06 Registrar ....Ms. Gail N. MEIS
08 Director of Library Services ....Ms. Elizabeth BAGLEY
29 Senior Director Alumnae Relations ....Vacant
18 Director of Facilities ....Mr. Dave MARDER
42 Chaplain ....Vacant
37 Director of Financial Aid ....Mr. Patrick BONONES
09 Director of Institutional Research ....Dr. Corey DUNN
07 Director of Admissions ....Ms. Aimee S. KAHN-FOSS
23 Wellness Center Director ....Dr. Michelle HAMM
19 Director of Public Safety ....Mr. Henry HOPE
36 Director of Career Development .... Ms. Dawn KILLENBERG

Albany State University (H)

504 College Drive, Albany GA 31705-2796
County: Dougherty FICE Identification: 001544
Unit ID: 138716
Telephone: (229) 500-2000 Carnegie Class: Masters/M
FAX Number: N/A Calendar System: Semester
URL: https://www.asurams.edu
Established: 1903 Annual Undergrad Tuition & Fees (In-State): $5,735
Enrollment: 6,615 Coed
Affiliation or Control: State IRS Status: 501(c)3
Highest Offering: Beyond Master's But Less Than Doctorate
Accreditation: SC, ACBSP, ADNUR, CACREP, CAEPN, CAHIIM, COARC, DH, DMS, EMT, FEPAC, HT, MLTAD, NUR, OTA, PTAA, RAD, SPAA, SW

01 President ....Ms. Marion FEDRICK
100 Chief of Staff/VP Univ Relations ....Dr. Wendy WILSON
05 Interim Provost/VP Academic Affairs .... Dr. Rajeev PARIKH
10 VP Admin & Fiscal Affairs ....Mr. Shawn MCGEE
13 VP Information Technology Svcs ....Mr. William MOORE
111 VP Institutional Advancement ....Mr. Arkeem FLEMING
32 Acting VP Student Affairs & Enroll ....Mrs. Kenyatta JOHNSON
108 VP Inst Effectiveness/Dir Title II ....Dr. Kimberly HOLMES
116 Exec Dir Internal Audits ....Ms. Katherine KIKIVARAKIS
88 Exec Dir Cordele Ctr ....Mrs. Wendy WILSON
46 Assoc Prov Sponsored Pgms ....Dr. Louise WRENSFORD
58 Graduate School Dean ....Dr. Louise WRENSFORD
84 Asst VP Enrollment Management ....Mrs. Stephanie LAWRENCE
06 Registrar ....Ms. Frances CARR
19 Police Chief ....Mr. John FIELDS
21 Controller ....Mr. Jeffrey HALL
83 Dean Arts & Humanities ....Dr. Rani GEORGE
50 Dean College of Business ....Dr. Alicia JACKSON
53 Interim Dean College of Education ....Dr. Rhonda PORTER
88 Dean Sciences & Health Professions ....Dr. Seyed ROOSTA
41 Director of Athletics ....Ms. Sherie GORDON
114 Chief Budget Officer ....Mrs. Marion RYANT
109 Bursar ....Ms. Jan ROGERS
18 Dir Facilities Management ....Mr. Oren HOWELL
15 Director Human Resources ....Ms. Laurie JONES
16 Asst Director Human Resources Mgmt .... Ms. Cassandra ALEXANDER
91 Director Application Services ....Mr. Sekar PONNAR
106 Exec Dir Distance Learning ....Mrs. Renita LUCK
92 Director Honors Program ....Dr. Florence LYONS
104 Director International Programs ....Dr. Nneka-Nora OSAKWE
26 Director Univ Marketing/Communicati ....Ms. Denise WARD
29 Director Alumni Affairs ....Mrs. Sue POLITE-WILLIAMS
36 Director Career Services ....Ms. Tracy S. WILLIAMS
35 Interim Dean of Students ....Dr. Michara DELANEY
38 Director Counseling/Disability Svcs .... Dr. Stephanie HARRIS-JOLLY
23 Director Student Health Services ....Dr. Vicki PHILLIPS
88 Director MALES Mentors ....Mr. Antonio LEROY
07 Interim Director of Admissions .... Ms. Michele APPLING
37 Director Financial Aid ....Mr. Thomas VO
124 Dir New Student Success ....Dr. Maria LUMPKIN
88 Director Undergrad Research Ctr .... Dr. Zephyrinus OKONKWO
08 Director Library Services ....Dr. LaVerne MCLAUGHLIN
88 Director Learning Ctrs ....Mrs. Flo HILL
88 Director Water Policy Center .... Dr. Mark MASTERS
09 Director Institutional Research ....Vacant
30 Director of Development ....Mr. Andrew FLOYD
40 Director Bookstore ....Ms. Tara JOHNSON
88 Interim Dir Auxiliary Svcs ....Mrs. Martha SNOW
88 Director of Testing Ctr ....Ms. Deborah BEATY
121 Interim Dir Advisng/Retention Ctr ....Mr. Jeremiah PITTS
88 Dir Military & Adult Educ .... Mrs. Stefane RAULERSON
39 Dir Resident Life/Student Housing ..... Ms. Daphne WASHINGTON

† Part of the University System of Georgia.

Albany Technical College (I)

1704 S Slappey Boulevard, Albany GA 31701-3587
County: Dougherty FICE Identification: 005601
Unit ID: 138682
Telephone: (229) 430-3500 Carnegie Class: Assoc/HVT-Mix Trad/Non

FAX Number: (229) 430-3594 Calendar System: Semester
URL: www.albanytech.edu
Established: 1961 Annual Undergrad Tuition & Fees (In-State): $2,712
Enrollment: 3,167 Coed
Affiliation or Control: State IRS Status: 501(c)3
Highest Offering: Associate Degree
Accreditation: SC, ADNUR, DA, EMT, MAC, RAD, SURGT

01 President .... Dr. Anthony O. PARKER
100 Special Assistant to the President .... Mrs. Lorraine ALEXANDER
05 Vice Pres Academic Affairs .... Dr. Emmett GRISWOLD
10 Vice Pres Administrative Services .... Mrs. Kathy SKATES
26 Dir Public Relations/Marketing .... Mr. Bobby ELLIS
32 VP Student Affairs/Enrollment Mgmt .... Mrs. Barbara BROWN
36 Assoc Vice Pres of Career Svcs .... Mrs. Judy JIMMERSON
09 Vice Pres of Inst Effectiveness .... Dr. Kimberly LEE
46 Vice President Economic Development .... Mr. Matt TRICE
55 Vice Pres of Adult Education .... Mrs. Linda COSTON
15 Executive Director Human Resources .... Mrs. Lola EDWARDS
88 Academic Dean Economic Dev .... Dr. Steve EIDSON
51 Dean of Cont Educ & Off-Campus Pgm ...... Mrs. Tracy WALLACE
55 Dean of Evening Administration .... Mr. Don LAYE
37 Director of Financial Aid .... Mrs. Helen CATT
20 Dean of Academic Affairs .... Mr. Matt DENNIS
20 Dean of Academic Affairs .... Ms. Tomekia COOPER
20 Dean of Academic Affairs .... Mrs. Lisa HARRELL
88 Assoc Dean Early Childhood .... Mrs. Angela ROBINSON
56 Academic Dean Instructional Tech .... Mrs. Troycia WEBB
18 Director of Facilities .... Mr. Lavon ACKLEY
07 Director of Admissions .... Vacant
21 Director of Accounting Services .... Ms. Janet HAYES
06 Registrar .... Ms. Kennosha HAWKINS
35 Director Student Activities .... Dr. Mary RICHARDSON
13 Director of Computer/Info Systems .... Mr. Bruce HOPKINS
04 Executive Asst to the President .... Mrs. Natasha PRICE
08 Chief Library Officer .... Mr. Roy CALHOUN

American InterContinental University - Atlanta (A)

6600 Peachtree Dunwoody Road, Atlanta GA 30328
Telephone: (404) 965-6500 Identification: 666723
Accreditation: &NH, ACBSP

† Regional accreditation is carried under the parent institution in Schaumburg, IL.

Andrew College (B)

501 College Street, Cuthbert GA 39840-5550
County: Randolph FICE Identification: 001545
Unit ID: 138761
Telephone: (229) 732-2171 Carnegie Class: Bac/Assoc-Assoc Dom
FAX Number: (229) 732-2176 Calendar System: Semester
URL: www.andrewcollege.edu
Established: 1854 Annual Undergrad Tuition & Fees: $17,388
Enrollment: 285 Coed
Affiliation or Control: United Methodist IRS Status: 501(c)3
Highest Offering: Baccalaureate
Accreditation: SC, #COARC

01 President .... Dr. Linda R. BUCHANAN
05 Dean of Academic Affairs .... Mrs. Karan B. PITTMAN
10 Vice President for Finance .... Mrs. Julie CADLE
111 Vice President for Advancement .... Mr. Spencer SEALY
84 Vice President for Enrollment .... Mr. Andy GEETER
21 Controller .... Ms. Beth STRICKLAND
32 Dean of Student Affairs .... Mr. James MCCOY
41 Athletic Director .... Mr. Blake WILLIAMS
42 Chaplain .... Ms. Ivelisse QUINONES
08 Director of Library Services .... Ms. Mckenzie RAGAN
40 Director of Bookstore .... Ms. Allyson KING
26 Dir of Communications & Marketing .... Ms. Sheri MICHAELS
06 Registrar .... Ms. Tekesha JACKSON
18 Director of Maintenance .... Mr. Andrew LOWERY
19 Chief of Police .... Mr. Freddie JENKINS
39 Director of Residence Life .... Vacant
105 Web Services .... Mr. Brice HERRIN
88 FOCUS Director .... Mrs. Bennie MATTOX
09 Director of Student Success Ctr/IR .... Ms. Julia WILLIAMS
37 Director of Financial Aid .... Ms. Daphne HARDEN
15 Director of Human Resources .... Mrs. Jennifer MITCHELL

The Art Institute of Atlanta (C)

6600 Peachtree Dunwoody Road, Atlanta GA 30328-1635
County: Fulton FICE Identification: 009270
Unit ID: 138813
Telephone: (770) 394-8300 Carnegie Class: Spec-4-yr-Arts
FAX Number: (770) 394-0008 Calendar System: Quarter
URL: www.artinstitutes.edu/atlanta/
Established: 1949 Annual Undergrad Tuition & Fees: $17,496
Enrollment: 1,582 Coed
Affiliation or Control: Independent Non-Profit IRS Status: 501(c)3
Highest Offering: Baccalaureate
Accreditation: SC, ACFEI, CIDA

01 President .... Mr. Newton MYVETT
05 Provost/Dean of Academic Affairs .... Dr. Linda WOOD
10 Director of Financial Services .... Ms. Audry SANDIMANIE
07 Senior Director of Admissions .... Ms. Phyllis HORTON-MACK
32 Dean of Student Affairs .... Mr. Nadraqua DAWES
37 Director of Student Financial Svcs . Ms. Precious PRENDERGAST
09 Dir of Inst Effectiveness/Research .... Vacant
08 Librarian .... Mr. Robert SARWARK
06 Registrar .... Ms. Sheldon WOODS
36 Director of Career Services .... Mr. Enrique (Leo) ORTIZ
26 Director of Campus Relations .... Ms. Vivian LETT
18 Director of Facilities .... Ms. Stacey CARMICHAEL
04 Exec Assistant to the President .... Ms. Sophia PITTMAN
15 Human Resources Manager .... Ms. Mary HARRIEL

Ashworth College (D)

6625 The Corners Parkway, Suite 500, Norcross GA 30092-3406
County: Gwinnett Identification: 666106
Telephone: (770) 729-8400 Carnegie Class: Not Classified
FAX Number: (770) 729-9296 Calendar System: Semester
URL: www.ashworthcollege.edu
Established: 2000 Annual Undergrad Tuition & Fees: N/A
Enrollment: N/A Coed
Affiliation or Control: Proprietary IRS Status: Proprietary
Highest Offering: Master's
Accreditation: DEAC, NURSE

01 President .... Mr. Robert KLAPPER
05 Chief Academic Officer .... Mr. William KAKISH

Athens College of Ministry (E)

PO Box 7593, Athens GA 30604
County: Clarke Identification: 667306
Telephone: (706) 769-1472 Carnegie Class: Not Classified
FAX Number: (706) 769-1479 Calendar System: Semester
URL: www.acmin.org
Established: 2012 Annual Undergrad Tuition & Fees: N/A
Enrollment: N/A Coed
Affiliation or Control: Interdenominational IRS Status: 501(c)3
Highest Offering: Master's
Accreditation: @TRACS

01 President .... Dr. Marcia WILBUR
05 Chief Academic Officer .... Dr. Raymond MORRIS
32 Director of Student Affairs .... Mr. Paul COOKE
42 Chairman Christian Ministry Program ...... Ms. Deborah HUCKABY

Athens Technical College (F)

800 US Highway 29 N, Athens GA 30601-1500
County: Clarke FICE Identification: 005600
Unit ID: 246813
Telephone: (706) 355-5000 Carnegie Class: Assoc/HVT-High Trad
FAX Number: (706) 369-5753 Calendar System: Semester
URL: www.athenstech.edu
Established: 1958 Annual Undergrad Tuition & Fees (In-State): $2,798
Enrollment: 4,493 Coed
Affiliation or Control: State IRS Status: 501(c)3
Highest Offering: Associate Degree
Accreditation: SC, ACBSP, ADNUR, CAHIIM, DA, DH, EMT, PTAA, RAD, SURGT

01 President .... Dr. Andrea D. DANIEL
05 Vice President Academic Affairs .... Dr. Keli FEWOX
32 Vice President Student Affairs .... Ms. Jennifer BENSON
10 Vice Pres Administrative Services .... Mrs. Kathryn S. THOMAS
36 Vice President Career Academies .... Mr. James PRICE
45 Vice President Economic Development .... Mr. Al MCCALL
13 Vice Pres Information Technology .... Mr. Dennis ASHWORTH
88 Vice President Adult Education .... Mrs. Stephanie G. BENSON
106 Dean General Ed and Online Learning .... Dr. Jennifer PALMER
72 Dean Technology/Engineering/Manufac .... Mr. Alvie COES
76 Dean Life Sciences/Public Safety .... Mr. Glenn HENRY
50 Dean Business and Education .... Mr. Nick CHAPMAN
37 Exec Director Fin Aid & Info Tech .... Mr. Dustin MCDANIEL
88 Exec Director Economic Development .... Mr. Andrew PALMER
12 Exec Dir Greene & Walton Co Campus .... Mr. Lenzy REID, III
18 Executive Director Facilities .... Mr. Jim WALTER
26 Executive Director PR/Foundation .... Mr. Antoine BOYNTON
19 Chief of Police .... Mr. John GAISSERT
06 Director Registration & Records .... Vacant
108 Director Inst Effectiveness .... Ms. Amelia MILLS
07 Director Admissions .... Ms. Justin MCCALLA
08 Director Library Services .... Ms. Carol STANLEY
35 Director Student Activities .... Mr. James SAUCEDA
121 Director Student Support .... Ms. Jessica FELTS
15 Director Human Resources .... Ms. Becky BURTON
111 Director Institutional Advancement .... Vacant
21 Director of Accounting .... Mr. Ryan STANLEY

Atlanta Metropolitan State College (G)

1630 Metropolitan Parkway, SW, Atlanta GA 30310-4498
County: Fulton FICE Identification: 012165
Unit ID: 138901
Telephone: (404) 756-4000 Carnegie Class: Bac/Assoc-Mixed
FAX Number: (404) 756-4460 Calendar System: Semester
URL: www.atlm.edu
Established: 1974 Annual Undergrad Tuition & Fees (In-State): $3,416
Enrollment: 2,501 Coed
Affiliation or Control: State IRS Status: 501(c)3
Highest Offering: Baccalaureate
Accreditation: SC, ACBSP

01 President .... Dr. Gary A. MCGAHA, SR.
05 Vice President Academic Affairs .... Dr. Michael HEARD
10 Vice President Fiscal Affairs .... Mr. Kwabena BOAKYE
32 Vice President Student Affairs .. Dr. Kimberly GRIMES-SOLOMON
111 Vice Pres Strategic Marketing & Adv .... Ms. Lauretta HANNON
21 Director of Business Services .... Ms. Dakiesha PICKETT
50 Dean Div Business/Information Tech .... Dr. Vincent MANGUM
79 Int Dean Div Humanities/Fine Arts .... Ms. Lisa MALLORY
81 Dean Div of Sci/Math/Health Profess .... Dr. Bryan MITCHELL
83 Dean Div of Social Sciences .... Dr. Vance GRAY
06 Registrar/Dir Enrollment Svcs .... Ms. Candace PERRY
15 Chief Human Resources Officer .... Mrs. Mitzi WILLIAMS
08 Director of the Library .... Mr. Robert QUARLES
35 Dir of Student Life and Leadership .... Ms. Iris SHANKLIN
37 Director of Financial Aid .... Dr. Michelle CHAPMAN
38 Dir of Counseling/Disability Svcs .... Dr. Dorothy WILLIAMS
13 Chief Information/Tech Officer .... Mr. Antonio TRAVIS
108 VP Institutional Effectiveness .... Dr. Mark CUNNINGHAM
19 Interim Director of Public Safety .... Capt. Vicinda CRAWFORD
35 Dir of Student Outreach & Access .... Mr. Stephen WOODALL
18 Dir Plant Operations/Facilities .... Mr. Keith WILLIAMS
40 Bookstore Manager .... Ms. Gloria MCCLAIN
26 Director of Communications .... Ms. Sonja ROBERTS
41 Athletic Director .... Vacant

† Part of the University System of Georgia.

Atlanta Technical College (H)

1560 Metropolitan Parkway, SW, Atlanta GA 30310-4446
County: Fulton FICE Identification: 008543
Unit ID: 138840
Telephone: (404) 225-4400 Carnegie Class: Assoc/HVT-High Trad
FAX Number: (404) 225-4445 Calendar System: Semester
URL: www.atlantatech.edu
Established: 1967 Annual Undergrad Tuition & Fees (In-State): $2,820
Enrollment: 4,098 Coed
Affiliation or Control: State IRS Status: 501(c)3
Highest Offering: Associate Degree
Accreditation: SC, ACFEI, CAHIIM, DA, DH, EMT, MAC, PTAA, #RAD, SURGT

01 President .... Dr. Victoria SEALS
05 Exec VP Academic & Student Affairs .... Ms. Caroline ANGELO
11 Vice Pres Administrative Services .... Ms. Teresa BROWN
30 Vice President Economic Development .... Ms. Yulonda DARDEN-BEAUFORD
04 Assistant to the President .... Dr. Joni WILLIAMS
26 Director Communications & Marketing .... Mr. Adam SWEAT
37 Director of Financial Aid .... Mr. LaMario PRIMAS
84 Dean Enrollment Services .... Ms. Niya EADY
88 Dean Industrial and Transportation .... Dr. Ian TOPPIN
51 Director of Continuing Education .... Mr. Curtis HALTON
36 Director Career Placement .... Mr. Michael BURNSIDE
50 Dean Business and Public Services .... Mr. Britt PITRE
88 Dean Health and Public Safety .... Dr. Katrina WALKER
06 Registrar .... Ms. Niya EADY
15 Director Human Resources .... Mr. Travis SALLEY
18 VP Operations and IT .... Ms. Gail EDWARDS
09 Director of Institutional Research .... Dr. Bobbi JOHNSTONE
49 Dean Arts and Sciences .... Ms. Sonya MCCOY-WILSON
08 Director of Library Services .... Ms. Tosha BUSSEY
106 Dean of Students .... Dr. Shawn ADAMS
13 Director of Information Technology .... Vacant
25 Director of Sponsored Programs .... Mr. Lance WISE
96 Procurement Officer .... Ms. Meinya LESLIE
102 Dir Foundation/Corporate Relations .... Dr. Jamar JEFFERS

Atlanta's John Marshall Law School (I)

1422 West Peachtree Street NW, Atlanta GA 30309
County: Fulton FICE Identification: 031733
Unit ID: 138929
Telephone: (678) 916-2600 Carnegie Class: Spec-4-yr-Law
FAX Number: (404) 873-3802 Calendar System: Semester
URL: www.johnmarshall.edu
Established: 1933 Annual Graduate Tuition & Fees: N/A
Enrollment: 463 Coed
Affiliation or Control: Proprietary IRS Status: Proprietary
Highest Offering: First Professional Degree; No Undergraduates
Accreditation: #LAW

01 Dean/CEO .... Mr. Malcolm L. MORRIS
32 Assoc Dean of Students .... Ms. Sheryl E. HARRISON-MERCER
10 Exec Dir of Business Affairs .... Mr. Duane WRIGHT
06 Registrar .... Ms. Cheryl FEREBEE
26 Asst Dir Marketing & Communications .... Ms. Hilary WALDO
07 Director of Admissions .... Mrs. Rebecca MILTER
37 Director of Financial Aid .... Ms. Michelle JACKSON
29 Alumni Director .... Mrs. Erika S. MURRAY
36 Exec Dir of Career Development .... Mr. Nicholas JONES
05 Assoc Dean for Academic Program .... Mr. Jace GATEWOOD
20 Assoc Dean of Academic Admin .... Ms. Judith BARGER
08 Director of Law Library .... Mr. Michael LYNCH
58 Assoc Dean of Graduate Programs .... Mr. Jace GATEWOOD
04 Executive Assistant to the Dean/CEO .... Mrs. Erika S. MURRAY

Augusta Technical College (J)

3200 Augusta Tech Drive, Augusta GA 30906-3399
County: Richmond FICE Identification: 005599
Unit ID: 138956
Telephone: (706) 771-4000 Carnegie Class: Assoc/HVT-High Trad
FAX Number: (706) 771-4016 Calendar System: Semester

URL: www.augustatech.edu
Established: 1961 Annual Undergrad Tuition & Fees (In-District): $2,794
Enrollment: 4,595 Coed
Affiliation or Control: State/Local IRS Status: 501(c)3
Highest Offering: Associate Degree
Accreditation: SC, COARC, CVT, DA, MAC, OTA, PNUR, RAD, SURGT

01 President .... Mr. Terry D. ELAM
05 Exec Vice President Academic Affs .. Dr. Melissa FRANK-ALSTON
10 Vice Pres Administrative Services .... Ms. Sheila M. HILL
32 Vice Pres Student Affairs .... Dr. Nichole SPENCER
88 Vice President Economic Development .... Dr. Lisa PALMER
12 Dean of Operations Off Site Campus .... Ms. Julie LANGHAM
108 VP Institutional Effective/Research ... Dr. Melissa FRANK-ALSTON
12 Dean/Director Waynesboro Campus .... Mr. Greg COURSEY
13 Chief Info Technology Officer (CIO) .... Mr. Pete WILKINSON
37 Director Financial Aid .... Ms. Beverly SMYRE HINES
84 Director Enrollment Services .... Ms. Christine BALL
111 Director Institutional Advancement .... Ms. Beverly PELTIER
06 Registrar .... Mr. Justin OTTO
21 Director Accounting .... Ms. Sherrick L. JOHNSON
26 Dir Cmty Engagements/Public Rels .... Ms. Kimberly HOLDEN
15 Director Human Resources .... Ms. Shannon PATTERSON
36 Director Career Services .... Ms. Donna WENDT
08 Head Librarian .... Vacant
18 Facilities Director .... Mr. Garry STEPHENS
19 Director Security/Safety .... Mr. Mike ANCHOR
04 Administrative Asst to President .... Mrs. Charlene LEWIS
12 Coordinator Thomson Campus .... Ms. Jeanette LOWE
88 High School Coordinator .... Mrs. Jan BLACKBURN
76 Dean Allied Health Science .... Dr. Gwen TAYLOR
50 Dean Business/Public Safety .... Ms. Elizabeth A. JULIAN
49 Dean Arts/Science/Learning Support .... Mr. John RICHARDSON
54 Dean Industrial & Engineering Tech .... Mr. Quentin COOKS
106 Dean of Info Tech/Dist Educ/Lib .... Mrs. Tammy O'BRIEN

Augusta University (A)

1120 Fifteenth Street, Augusta GA 30912-0004
County: Richmond FICE Identification: 001579
Unit ID: 482149
Telephone: (706) 721-0211 Carnegie Class: DU-Mod
FAX Number: N/A Calendar System: Semester
URL: www.augusta.edu
Established: 1828 Annual Undergrad Tuition & Fees (In-State): $8,604
Enrollment: 8,220 Coed
Affiliation or Control: State IRS Status: 501(c)3
Highest Offering: Doctorate
Accreditation: SC, ANEST, ARCPA, ART, CACREP, CAHIIM, #CAMPEP, COARC, DENT, DH, DIETI, EMT, IPSY, MED, MIL, MT, MUS, NMT, NURSE, OT, PH, PTA, RTT, SPAA, SW

01 President .... Dr. Brooks A. KEEL
05 Exec VP for Acad Affairs/Provost .... Dr. Gretchen CAUGHMAN
10 Int EVP & CFO for Finance .... Ms. Yvonne TURNER
26 EVP Operations .... Ms. Karla LEEPER
31 Exec VP External Rel/Chief of Staff .... Mr. Russell KEEN
43 General Counsel/VP Legal Affairs .... Mr. Chris MELCHER
17 EVP Medical Affairs/Dean Medicine .... Dr. David HESS
86 EVP Strategic Partnerships/Econ Dev .... Mr. W. Michael SHAFFER
46 Senior Vice President for Research .... Dr. Michael DIAMOND
30 VP of Development .... Ms. Debra VAUGHN
15 Enterprise VP Human Resources .... Ms. Susan A. NORTON
20 VP Academic & Faculty Affairs .... Dr. Kathy BROWDER
32 VP Enrollment/Student Affairs .... Dr. Susan B. DAVIES
09 VP Institutional Effectiveness .... Mrs. Beth P. BRIGDON
18 VP Facilities Service .... Mr. Ronald BOOTH
27 VP Communications & Marketing .... Mr. Jack EVANS
20 VP Instruction & Innovation .... Dr. Zach KELEHEAR
21 Vice Pres for Finance .... Mr. Lee FRUITTICHER
88 VP & CMO for Medical Center .... Dr. Phillip L. COULE
58 Dean The Graduate School .... Dr. Mitchell WATSKY
76 Dean College of Allied Health .... Dr. Lester PRETLOW
52 Dean College of Dental Med .... Dr. Carol LEFEBVRE
66 Dean College of Nursing .... Dr. Lucy N. MARION
77 Dean Sch of Computer/Cyber Science .... Dr. Alex SCHWARZMANN
50 Dean Hull College of Business .... Dr. Richard M. FRANZA
49 Dean College of Arts/Hum/Soc Sci .... Dr. Elna C. GREEN
53 Interim Dean College of Education .... Dr. Judi WILSON
81 Dean College of Science & Math .... Dr. John SUTHERLAND
88 Chief Audit Officer .... Mr. Clay SPROUSE
88 Chief Integrity Officer .... Mr. James RUSH, JR.
13 VP Information Technology/CIO .... Dr. Michael CASDORPH
88 Interim Director Cancer Center .... Dr. John K. COWELL
06 Registrar .... Ms. Heather B. METRESS
113 Bursar .... Ms. Beth WELSH
41 Director of Athletics .... Mr. Clint BRYANT
19 Assistant VP Public Safety & Police .... Chief James LYON
08 Director of Libraries .... Dr. Brenda SEAGO
96 Director Supply Management .... Mr. Greg WOODLIEF
109 Asst Chief Aux Services Officer .... Mr. Karl MUNSCHY
37 Director of Financial Aid .... Ms. Debra TURNER
07 Director of Admissions .... Ms. Maura FLASCHNER
04 Exec Admin Asst to President .... Mrs. Jacqueline B. STEPHENS
104 Director Study Abroad .... Ms. Maria DARLEY
22 Director Employment Equity .... Mr. Glenn POWELL
29 Director Alumni Affairs .... Ms. Kim KOSS
36 Director Career Services .... Ms. Julie GOLEY
38 Int Director Student Counseling .... Ms. Elena PETROVA
39 Director Student Housing .... Dr. Heather SCHNELLER
84 Assoc VP Enrollment Services .... Mr. David BARRON

† Part of the University System of Georgia.

Berry College (B)

2277 Martha Berry Highway, NW, Mount Berry GA 30149
County: Floyd FICE Identification: 001554
Unit ID: 139144
Telephone: (706) 232-5374 Carnegie Class: Masters/S
FAX Number: (706) 236-2238 Calendar System: Semester
URL: www.berry.edu
Established: 1902 Annual Undergrad Tuition & Fees: $36,556
Enrollment: 2,110 Coed
Affiliation or Control: Independent Non-Profit IRS Status: 501(c)3
Highest Offering: Beyond Master's But Less Than Doctorate
Accreditation: SC, MUS, NURSE

01 President .... Dr. Stephen R. BRIGGS
05 Provost .... Dr. Mary K. BOYD
10 Vice President Finance .... Mr. Brian I. ERB
32 VP Student Affairs/Dean of Students .... Ms. Lindsey TAYLOR
111 Vice Pres Institutional Advancement .... Ms. Cynthia COURT
84 VP of Enrollment Management .... Dr. Andrew BRESSETTE
26 VP Marketing & Communications .... Ms. Nancy REWIS
100 Chief of Staff .... Ms. Debbie HEIDA
42 Chaplain .... Rev. Jonathan HUGGINS
19 Asst VP Campus Police/Emergency Mgt .... Mr. Gary WILL
50 Dean Campbell School of Business .... Dr. Joyce HEAMES
53 Dean Charter School of Education .... Dr. Jackie MCDOWELL
79 Dean School Humanities/Arts/Soc Sci .... Dr. Thomas D. KENNEDY
66 Director of Nursing .... Dr. Pam DUNAGAN
81 Dean School of Math/Nat Sci .... Dr. Gary BRETON
78 Dean of Student Work .... Vacant
20 Associate Provost .... Dr. David SLADE
39 Assoc Dean Students/Residence Life .... Mrs. Lindsay NORMAN
07 Director of Admissions .... Mrs. Adrienne ODDI
30 Asst VP Campaign/Leadership Giving ...... Mr. Scott BREITHAUPT
08 Director of the Library .... Ms. Sherre Lee HARRINGTON
29 Director of Alumni Affairs .... Ms. Jennifer SCHAKNOWSKI
13 Chief Information Officer .... Ms. Penny EVANS-PLANTS
38 Director of Counseling Center .... Dr. J. Marshall JENKINS
37 Director Financial Aid .... Ms. Noemi SARRION-CORTES
36 Director of Career Center .... Mrs. Sue TARPLEY
09 Dir Institutional Research .... Dr. Bryce DURBIN
46 Dir Research & Sponsored Programs .... Mrs. Donna DAVIN
18 Director Physical Plant .... Mr. Mark HOPKINS
89 Director First Year Experience .... Mrs. Katherine POWELL
92 Co-Director Honors Program .... Dr. Todd TIMBERLAKE
92 Co-Director Honors Program .... Dr. Lauren HELLER
94 Director Women's Studies .... Dr. Susan CONRADSEN
96 Director Purchasing .... Mr. Brad BARRIS
85 Director International Programs .... Mr. Christopher BORDA
15 Director Human Resources .... Mr. Wayne PHIPPS
43 Director of Legal Services .... Mr. Danny PRICE
06 Registrar .... Dr. Bryce DURBIN
41 Director of Athletics .... Ms. Angel MASON
121 Director of Academic Success Center .... Ms. Anna SHARPE
44 Dir of Annual Giv & Specialty Pgms .... Ms. Sharman TURNER
35 Director Student Activities .... Ms. Cecily CROW
23 Director Health & Wellness Center .... Ms. Emma CORDLE

Beulah Heights University (C)

892 Berne Street, SE, PO Box 18145,
Atlanta GA 30316-1873
County: Fulton FICE Identification: 030763
Unit ID: 139153
Telephone: (404) 627-2681 Carnegie Class: Spec-4-yr-Faith
FAX Number: (404) 627-0702 Calendar System: Semester
URL: www.beulah.edu
Established: 1918 Annual Undergrad Tuition & Fees: $10,150
Enrollment: 390 Coed
Affiliation or Control: Other Protestant IRS Status: 501(c)3
Highest Offering: Doctorate
Accreditation: BI, TRACS

01 President .... Dr. Benson M. KARANJA
04 Administrative Asst to President .... Ms. Kimberly WIGLEY
11 Vice Pres Operations .... Mr. Peter KARANJA
05 Vice Pres/Dean Academic Affairs .... Dr. James KEILLER
88 Vice Pres Asian Affairs .... Dr. Kyung Soo JHO
32 Vice Pres Student Life .... Dr. Wes WILSON
106 Dean of Distance Education .... Dr. Mark HARDGROVE
42 Dean of Chapel .... Rev. Billy JOHNSON
06 University Registrar .... Ms. Georgia SKINNER
10 Director of Finance/Comptroller .... Mr. Julian IVEY
37 Assoc Director of Financial Aid .... Ms. Ukemah D. CODY
07 Director of Admissions .... Ms. Jasmine DOUGLAS
73 Chair Religious Studies .... Dr. Walter TURNER
08 Director of Library Services .... Mr. Pradeep K. DAS
15 Director Personnel Services (HR) .... Ms. Trish STATON
26 Director of Marketing .... Mr. Junior KIAKU
09 Director of Institutional Research .... Dr. Josiane CAROLINO
19 Director Security/Safety .... Mr. Michael C. JOHNSON
39 Dir Resident Life/Student Housing .... Dr. Wes C. WILSON

Brenau University (D)

500 Washington Street, SE, Gainesville GA 30501-3668
County: Hall FICE Identification: 001556
Unit ID: 139199
Telephone: (770) 534-6299 Carnegie Class: Masters/L
FAX Number: (770) 534-6114 Calendar System: Semester
URL: www.brenau.edu
Established: 1878 Annual Undergrad Tuition & Fees: $29,050
Enrollment: 2,932 Coed
Affiliation or Control: Independent Non-Profit IRS Status: 501(c)3
Highest Offering: Doctorate
Accreditation: SC, ACBSP, CIDA, NURSE, OT, PTA

01 President .... Dr. Anne A. SKLEDER
03 Executive VP/CFO .... Dr. David L. BARNETT
05 Provost & VP For Academic Affairs .... Dr. Jim ECK
100 Chief of Staff .... Ms. Jody Y. WALL
10 Vice President Financial Services .... Mr. Toby R. HINTON
84 Vice Pres Enrollment Management .... Mr. Ray TATUM
111 Vice Pres External Relations .... Mr. J. Matthew THOMAS
13 Vice Pres Information Technology .... Mr. Chip L. ANDREWS
26 VP Communications/Publications .... Mr. Ben MCDADE
32 VP for Student Services .... Dr. Amanda LAMMERS
09 Director of Research & Planning .... Ms. Claudia GEORGE
37 Assoc VP & Dir Financial Aid .... Ms. Pam J. BARRETT
21 Asst VP Financial Svcs/Controller .... Ms. Holly REYNOLDS
15 Asst VP Director of Human Resources ...... Ms. Kelley L. MADDOX
36 Director of Career Services .... Mr. George BAGEL
121 Director of Learning Center .... Ms. Jennifer WILSON-LOGGINS
41 Athletic Director .... Mr. Mike LOCHSTAMPFOR
53 Dean College of Education .... Dr. Eugene WILLIAMS
76 Dean College of Health Sciences .... Dr. Gale H. STARICH
50 Dean College Business & Comm .... Dr. Suzanne ERICKSON
79 Dean College of Fine Arts & Human .... Dr. Andrea C. BIRCH
08 Dean of Library Services .... Ms. Linda KERN
07 Executive Director for Admissions .... Mr. Nathan R. GOSS
06 Registrar & Dir of Student Records .... Ms. Barbara WILSON
29 Exec Director Alumni .... Ms. Ashley CARTER
19 Director Campus Safety & Security .... Ms. Paula DAMPIER
104 Director Study Abroad .... Ms. Jordan ANDERSON

Brewton-Parker College (E)

201 David-Eliza Fountain Circle,
Mount Vernon GA 30445-0197
County: Montgomery FICE Identification: 001557
Unit ID: 139205
Telephone: (912) 583-2241 Carnegie Class: Bac-A&S
FAX Number: (912) 583-4498 Calendar System: Semester
URL: www.bpc.edu
Established: 1904 Annual Undergrad Tuition & Fees: $18,240
Enrollment: 783 Coed
Affiliation or Control: Baptist IRS Status: 501(c)3
Highest Offering: Baccalaureate
Accreditation: SC

01 President .... Dr. Steven F. ECHOLS
04 Executive Asst to President .... Ms. Laura HAY
43 General Counsel .... Mr. Thomas EVERETT
10 Chief Financial Officer .... Dr. Nicole SHEPARD
05 Provost .... Dr. Robert M. BRIAN
121 Assoc Provost Student Engagement .... Dr. Beverly ROBINSON
41 VP Athletics & Student Development .... Mr. Daniel PREVETT
07 VP of Enrollment Services .... Mr. Chris DOOLEY
11 Director of Operations .... Mr. Ted TOWNS
15 Director Human Resources .... Ms. Keri NESTER
37 Director of Financial Aid .... Ms. Loretta WATSON
07 Director of Admissions .... Ms. Michelle HARTER
38 Dir Counseling Services .... Mr. Thadeus HOLLOWAY
08 Librarian .... Mr. Daryl FLETCHER
06 Registrar .... Ms. Elizabeth ADAMS
09 Dir of Inst Effectiveness/Research .... Ms. Toni BANKS
26 Dir Public Relations and Marketing .... Mr. Chad RITCHIE
88 Textbook Coordinator .... Ms. Lynn ADDISON
111 Director of Advancement .... Mr. Chad RITCHIE
22 Dir Affirmative Action/EEO .... Mr. Forrest RICH
50 Chair Business .... Dr. Sherida HABERSHAM
53 Chair Education/Behavioral Sci .... Dr. Justin RUSSELL
79 Chair Christian Studies Humanities .... Dr. Grant LILFORD
81 Chair Math and Natural Sci .... Dr. Helene PETERS
42 Campus Pastor .... Mr. Steve EDWARDS
88 Director of Baptist Col Ministry .... Mr. Madison HERRIN
13 Chief Information Technology Office .... Vacant

Brown College of Court Reporting (F)

1100 Spring Street NW, Suite 101, Atlanta GA 30309
County: Fulton FICE Identification: 020609
Unit ID: 139214
Telephone: (404) 876-1227 Carnegie Class: Spec 2-yr-Other
FAX Number: (404) 876-4415 Calendar System: Quarter
URL: www.bccr.edu
Established: 1972 Annual Undergrad Tuition & Fees: $12,945
Enrollment: 198 Coed
Affiliation or Control: Proprietary IRS Status: Proprietary
Highest Offering: Associate Degree
Accreditation: COE

01 President .... Russell FREEMAN
03 Director .... Marita CAREY
07 Director of Admissions .... Carlette JENNINGS
05 Director of Education .... Julie MORRIS
06 Registrar .... Lisa LOWE
10 Chief Financial/Business Officer .... Greg ROBERTSON
29 Director Alumni Affairs .... Ciarra ODUKA
37 Director Student Financial Aid .... Felicia CHESS-GLORE

Cambridge Institute of Allied Health & Technology (G)

5669 Peachtree Dunwoody Rd, Ste 100, Atlanta GA 30342
Telephone: (404) 255-4500 Identification: 770938
Accreditation: ABHES, DMS

† Branch campus of Cambridge Institute of Allied Health and Technology, Delray Beach, FL.

Central Georgia Technical College (A)

80 Cohen Walker Drive, Warner Robins GA 31088
County: Houston FICE Identification: 005763
Unit ID: 483045
Telephone: (478) 988-6800 Carnegie Class: Not Classified
FAX Number: (478) 757-3454 Calendar System: Semester
URL: www.centralgatech.edu
Established: 1966 Annual Undergrad Tuition & Fees (In-State): $2,778
Enrollment: N/A Coed
Affiliation or Control: State IRS Status: 501(c)3
Highest Offering: Associate Degree
Accreditation: SC, CVT, DH, EMT, MLTAD, POLYT, @PTAA, RAD, SURGT

01 President Dr. Ivan ALLEN
03 Executive Vice President Mr. Jeff SCRUGGS
05 Vice President Academic Affairs Dr. Amy HOLLOWAY
10 Vice President Admin/Fin Svcs Dr. Michelle SINIARD
32 Vice President Student Affairs Mr. Craig JACKSON
31 Vice President Economic Development Ms. Andrea GRINER
11 AVP Facilities/Ancillary Svcs Mr. Jimmy FAIRCLOTH
13 Chief Information Officer Mr. Brian SNELGROVE
12 VP for Satellite Operations Ms. Dana DAVIS
06 Registrar Ms. Sonja JENKINS
111 Asst VP for Advancement Ms. Tonya MCCLURE
08 Director Library & Media Services Ms. Allison REPZYNSKI
15 Executive Director Human Resources Ms. Carol DOMINY
18 Facilities Director Mr. Robert DOMINY
51 Director of Continuing Education Mr. Clay TEAGUE
04 Admin Assistant to the President Ms. Danielle STEELE
09 Director of Institutional Research Ms. Bonnie QUINN
104 Director Study Abroad Mr. Rick HUTTO
22 Dir Affirmative Action/Equal Opp Ms. Cathy JOHNSON
26 Dir Marketing & Public Relations Dr. Janet KELLY
38 Exec Dir for Counseling Svcs Ms. Tonja SIMMONS
84 Director Enrollment Management Ms. Brandi MITCHEM

Chamberlain University-Atlanta (B)

5775 Peachtree-Dunwoody Rd NE,A100,
Atlanta GA 30342
Telephone: (404) 250-8500 Identification: 770504
Accreditation: &NH, NURSE

† Branch campus of Chamberlain University-Addison, Addison, IL

Chattahoochee Technical College (C)

980 South Cobb Drive, Marietta GA 30060
County: Cobb FICE Identification: 030290
Unit ID: 140331
Telephone: (770) 528-4545 Carnegie Class: Assoc/HVT-Mix Trad/Non
FAX Number: (770) 975-4126 Calendar System: Quarter
URL: www.chattahoocheetech.edu
Established: 1981 Annual Undergrad Tuition & Fees (In-State): $2,816
Enrollment: 10,201 Coed
Affiliation or Control: State IRS Status: 501(c)3
Highest Offering: Associate Degree
Accreditation: SC, ACFEI, ADNUR, EMT, MAC, MLTAD, OTA, PTAA, RAD, SURGT

01 President Dr. Ron NEWCOMB
04 Administrative Asst to President Ms. Tammy COLLUM
05 Vice President for Academics Dr. Jason TANNER
11 Vice Pres for Administrative Svcs Ms. Catrice HUFSTETLER
13 VP Student Affairs/Technology Ms. Jennifer NELSON
32 VP Student Affairs/External Affairs Ms. Jennifer NELSON
18 Vice President for Facilities Mr. David SIMMONS
15 Vice President Human Resources Mr. Ron PRICE
26 Exec Dir External Affs/Brd Liaison Ms. Jennifer NELSON

Clark Atlanta University (D)

223 James P. Brawley Drive, SW, Atlanta GA 30314-4391
County: Fulton FICE Identification: 001559
Unit ID: 138947
Telephone: (404) 880-8000 Carnegie Class: DU-Higher
FAX Number: N/A Calendar System: Semester
URL: www.cau.edu
Established: 1988 Annual Undergrad Tuition & Fees: $22,186
Enrollment: 3,992 Coed
Affiliation or Control: United Methodist IRS Status: 501(c)3
Highest Offering: Doctorate
Accreditation: SC, CACREP, CAEPN, SPAA, SW

01 Interim President Ms. Lucille MAUGE
05 Int Provost/VP for Acad Affairs Dr. Dorcas BOWLES
111 VP for Inst Advance/Univ Rels Mr. Sam BURSTON
10 CFO & Sr VP Business/Fin Svcs Dr. Lanze THOMPSON
07 Assoc VP & Dean UG Admissions Ms. Lorri SADDLER-RICE
46 Asst VP Research & Sponsored Pgms Ms. De Lisa WILSON
20 Assoc Provost Dr. Calvin BROWN
13 Assoc VP/Chief Info Ofcr Mr. Charles COOPER
21 Assoc VP/Controller Mr. Donal CHRISTIAN
09 AVP Planning Assess/Inst Rsrch Dr. Lauren LOPEZ
43 General Counsel Mr. Lance DUNNINGS
06 University Registrar Ms. Susan GIBSON
26 AVP Strategic Comm/Univ Relations Vacant
29 Director Alumni Relations Ms. Gay-linn JASHO
15 AVP/Chief People Officer Ms. Debra HOYT
07 Dir Recruitment & Admissions Vacant
38 Director University Counseling Ctr Dr. Vicki JESTER
32 Dean of Student Svcs/Campus Life Dr. Omar TORRES
37 Director Student Financial Aid Mr. James STOTTS
96 Director of Purchasing Ms. Donna BYRD
41 Director of Athletics Mr. J. Lin DAWSON
49 Dean Arts & Sciences Dr. Danille K. TAYLOR
50 Dean School of Business Dr. Silvanus UDOKA
53 Dean School of Education Dr. J. Fidel TURNER
70 Dean School of Social Work Dr. Jenny L. JONES
19 Chief of Public Safety Chief Debra A. WILLIAMS
23 Director Health Services Ms. Caroline B. RICHARDS
25 Director Grants & Contracts/Account Ms. Rotesha HARRIS
39 Director of Residence Life Dr. Lamar WHITE
88 Director Instructional Media Mr. Frank EDWARDS
101 Coordinator for Board Relations Ms. Natalie BAKER
104 Coordinator Multicultural Affairs Ms. Gwen WADE
22 University Compliance Officer Mr. Robert CLARK
18 Director of Facilities Mr. William BROOME
108 Exec Dir Institutional Assessment Dr. Lauren LOPEZ
04 Executive Asst to President Ms. Toni FANNIN
100 Exec Advisor to President Ms. Marilyn DAVIS
102 Asst VP IAUR Ms. Quisa FOSTER

Clayton State University (E)

2000 Clayton State Boulevard, Morrow GA 30260-0285
County: Clayton FICE Identification: 008976
Unit ID: 139311
Telephone: (678) 466-4000 Carnegie Class: Masters/M
FAX Number: (770) 961-3700 Calendar System: Semester
URL: www.clayton.edu
Established: 1969 Annual Undergrad Tuition & Fees (In-State): $5,419
Enrollment: 7,003 Coed
Affiliation or Control: State IRS Status: 501(c)3
Highest Offering: Master's
Accreditation: SC, DH, EXSC, MUS, NURSE

01 President Dr. Tim HYNES
05 Provost/Vice Pres Academic Affairs Dr. Kevin DEMMITT
10 VP for Operations/Planning/Budget Ms. Corlis CUMMINGS
32 Vice President for Student Affairs Dr. Shakeer ABDULLAH
111 Vice President Univ Advancement Mr. Chase MOORE
13 Vice Pres Information Tech & Svcs Mr. Bill GRUSZKA
20 Associate Provost Dr. Jill L. LANE
35 Assistant Vice Pres Student Affairs Dr. Allen WARD
84 VP for Enrollment Management Dr. Stephen SCHULTHEIS
41 Director of Athletics Mr. Ryan ERLACHER
88 Executive Director of Spivey Hall Mr. Samuel DIXON
15 Director Human Resources & Services Mr. Rodney BYRD
49 Dean of Arts & Sciences Dr. Nasser MOMAYEZI
50 Dean of Business Dr. Jacob CHACKO
76 Dean of Health Sciences Dr. Lisa EICHELBERGER
81 Dean Information/Mathematical Sci Dr. Lila ROBERTS
08 Dean of Library Services Dr. Sonya GAITHER
124 Director Advising & Retention Mr. Eric TACK
88 Dir Center for Instructional Dev Mr. Justin MAYS
51 Exec Director Continuing Education Mr. Reginald TURNER
06 University Registrar Ms. Rebecca GMEINER
07 Director of Admissions Dr. Stephen JENKINS
109 Sr Director of Auxiliary Services Ms. Julie COILE
26 Asst VP Marketing/Communications Ms. Asia HAUTER
18 AVP of Facilities Management Mr. Harun BISWAS
19 Director of Public Safety Chief Antonio LONG
09 Director of Institutional Research Dr. Narem REDDY
24 Director Media Services Mr. Todd BIRCHFIELD
38 Director of Counseling Services Dr. Christine SMITH
37 Director Student Financial Aid Ms. Lakisha SANDERS
96 Director of Purchasing Ms. Marcia JONES
29 Director of Alumni Engagement Mr. Michael LITTLE
21 AVP Budget & Finance/Comptroller Ms. Akwai AGOONS
36 Director of Career Services Ms. Bridgette MCDONALD
121 Dir Center for Academic Success Dr. Mari Ann BANKS
04 Exec Assistant to the President Ms. Brenda CARR
104 Director of International Programs Mr. Ryan PACKARD
39 Dir Resident Life/Student Housing Mr. Robert MORTON

† Part of the University System of Georgia.

Coastal Pines Technical College (F)

1701 Carswell Avenue, Waycross GA 31503-4016
County: Ware FICE Identification: 005511
Unit ID: 485458
Telephone: (912) 287-6584 Carnegie Class: Assoc/HVT-High Non
FAX Number: N/A Calendar System: Semester
URL: www.coastalpines.edu
Established: 1965 Annual Undergrad Tuition & Fees (In-State): $2,748
Enrollment: 3,053 Coed
Affiliation or Control: State IRS Status: 501(c)3
Highest Offering: Associate Degree
Accreditation: SC, COARC, EMT, MAC, RAD, SURGT

01 President Dr. Glenn DEIBERT
03 Provost Mr. Lonnie ROBERTS
05 Vice Pres for Academic Affairs Ms. Amanda MORRIS
11 VP of Administrative Services Ms. Melissa LAMB
46 Vice Pres for Economic Development Dr. Pete SNELL
32 Vice President for Student Affairs Ms. Karla EUBANKS
06 Registrar Ms. Tara EICHFIELD
111 Director Institutional Advancement Ms. Stephanie ROBERTS
18 Facilities Director Mr. Chad BOYETT
36 Career Placement & Develop Coord Mr. Buck THIGPEN
37 Director Student Financial Aid Ms. Tina MANNING
108 VP for Institutional Effectiveness Mr. Vince E. JACKSON
07 Director of Admissions Mr. Chris JEANCAKE
15 Human Resources Coordinator Ms. Cynthia LINDER
04 Administrative Asst to President Ms. Natasha KING
08 Director of Library Services Ms. Cassie CLEMONS
13 Chief Info Technology Officer (CIO) Mr. Derrell HARRIS
38 Director Student Counseling Ms. Cathy MONTGOMERY

College of Coastal Georgia (G)

One College Drive, Brunswick GA 31520-3632
County: Glynn FICE Identification: 001558
Unit ID: 139250
Telephone: (912) 279-5700 Carnegie Class: Bac/Assoc-Mixed
FAX Number: (912) 262-3072 Calendar System: Semester
URL: www.ccga.edu
Established: 1961 Annual Undergrad Tuition & Fees (In-State): $4,696
Enrollment: 3,663 Coed
Affiliation or Control: State IRS Status: 501(c)3
Highest Offering: Baccalaureate
Accreditation: SC, ACFEI, ADNUR, CAEPN, NUR, RAD

01 President Dr. Michelle JOHNSTON
05 Provost/VPAA Dr. Johnny EVANS
111 VP Advancement Mr. James BESSETTE
10 Vice President Business Affairs Ms. Michelle HAM
32 VP Student Affairs & Enrollment Dr. Jason W. UMFRESS
20 Asst VP Academic Affairs Dr. German VARGAS
20 Asst VP Academic Affairs Dr. Laura LYNCH
21 Fiscal Dir Budgets and Foundation Ms. Lorraine MOYER
84 Asst VP Recruitment & Admissions Dr. Amy CLINES
13 Chief Information Officer Mr. Alan OURS
19 Chief of Police Mr. Bryan SIPE
08 Dean of Library Services Ms. Debra HOLMES
35 Dean of Students Dr. Michael BUTCHER
49 Dean Sch of Arts & Sciences Dr. Andrea WALLACE
50 Dean Sch of Business & Public Mgmt Dr. William MOUNTS
66 Dean Sch of Nursing & Health Sci Dr. Lydia WATKINS
41 Director of Athletics Dr. William CARLTON
12 Director of the Camden Center Mr. Joseph LODMELL
106 Director of E-Learning Dr. Lisa MCNEAL
09 Dir Institutional Effectiveness Dr. James LYNCH
104 Int Dir International Initiatives Dr. James LYNCH
15 AVP Human Resources & Auxiliary Svc Ms. Phyllis BROADWELL
18 Director of Facilities and Plant Op Mr. Gary STRICKLAND
26 Director of Marketing & Public Rels Ms. Christy Lynn WILSON
37 Director Student Financial Aid Ms. Terral HARRIS
06 Registrar Ms. Lisa LESSEIG
07 Asst Dir of Admissions Operations Ms. Kimberly BURGESS
04 Executive Asst President's Office Ms. Judy JOHNSTON
88 Faculty Affairs Specialist Ms. Connie HIOTT
96 Purchasing Officer Ms. Deborah MILES
36 Director Career Development Mr. Brian WEESE
38 Dir Counseling & Disability Svcs Ms. Jennifer ZAK
108 Assessment Specialist Dr. Yi HUA
29 Dir of Development & Alumni Rel Ms. Linda SACKETT
39 Assoc Dir Residence Life/Housing Ms. Lacey KONDRACKI

† Part of the University System of Georgia.

Columbia Theological Seminary (H)

P.O. Box 520, 701 S Columbia Drive,
Decatur GA 30031-0520
County: DeKalb FICE Identification: 001560
Unit ID: 139348
Telephone: (404) 378-8821 Carnegie Class: Spec-4-yr-Faith
FAX Number: (404) 377-9696 Calendar System: 4/1/4
URL: www.ctsnet.edu
Established: 1828 Annual Graduate Tuition & Fees: N/A
Enrollment: 187 Coed
Affiliation or Control: Presbyterian Church (U.S.A.) IRS Status: 501(c)3
Highest Offering: Doctorate; No Undergraduates
Accreditation: SC, THEOL

01 President Dr. Leanne VAN DYK
05 VP Academic Affairs Dr. Love L. SECHREST
10 VP Business and Finance Mr. Martin SADLER
32 Dean of Students Rev. Brandon MAXWELL
111 VP Institutional Advancement Mr. Steven P. MILLER
20 Academic Administrator Dr. Ann Clay ADAMS
13 Assoc Dean Info Svcs/Dir of Library Dr. Kelly D. CAMPBELL
107 Assoc Dean Advanced Prof Studies Dr. Jeffery TRIBBLE
06 Registrar Mr. Mike MEDFORD
84 Chief Enrollment Management Officer Rev. Ruth-Aimee BELONNI-ROSARIO
26 Director of Communications Mr. Michael THOMPSON
04 Executive Assistant to President Ms. Cindy SEMMES
29 Director Alumni Affairs Rev. Julie BAILEY

Columbus State University (I)

4225 University Avenue, Columbus GA 31907-5645
County: Muscogee FICE Identification: 001561
Unit ID: 139366
Telephone: (706) 507-8800 Carnegie Class: Masters/L
FAX Number: (706) 568-2123 Calendar System: Semester
URL: www.columbusstate.edu
Established: 1958 Annual Undergrad Tuition & Fees (In-State): $6,134
Enrollment: 8,453 Coed
Affiliation or Control: State IRS Status: 501(c)3
Highest Offering: Doctorate
Accreditation: SC, ART, CACREP, CAEPN, MUS, NURSE, THEA

01 President Dr. Chris MARKWOOD
05 Provost/VP Academic Affairs Dr. Deborah BORDELON
10 Vice President Business & Finance Mr. Jeffery DAVIS
32 VP Student Affairs & Enrollment Mgt Dr. Gina SHEEKS
111 VP University Advancement Dr. Rocky KETTERING
13 Chief Information Officer Vacant
20 Assoc Provost Undergrad Education Vacant
84 Asst VP for Enrollment Mgmt Vacant
100 Chief of Staff Dr. Ed HELTON
50 Dean College of Business & Comp Sci Dr. Linda HADLEY
08 Dean of Libraries Vacant
15 Director Human Resources Mrs. Carole CLERIE
09 Director Institutional Research Dr. Sri SITHARAMAN
41 Athletic Director Mr. Todd REESER
07 Director of Admissions Ms. Viola ALEXANDER

† Part of the University System of Georgia.

Columbus Technical College (A)

928 Manchester Expressway, Columbus GA 31904-6572
County: Muscogee FICE Identification: 005624
Unit ID: 139357
Telephone: (706) 649-1800 Carnegie Class: Assoc/HVT-High Trad
FAX Number: (706) 649-1885 Calendar System: Semester
URL: www.columbustech.edu
Established: 1961 Annual Undergrad Tuition & Fees (In-State): $2,778
Enrollment: 3,097 Coed
Affiliation or Control: State IRS Status: Exempt
Highest Offering: Associate Degree
Accreditation: SC, ADNUR, COARC, DA, DH, DMS, MAC, RAD, SURGT

01 Interim President Ms. Martha Ann TODD
11 VP Administrative Services Ms. Karen THOMAS
05 Vice President Academic Affairs Vacant
32 Vice President Student Affairs Dr. Tara ASKEW
18 Vice President Operations Mr. Tommy WILSON
45 Dir Institutional Effectiveness Mr. Kevin PEOPLES
88 Vice President Economic Development Mr. James LOYD
51 Director of Adult Education Ms. April HOPSON
15 Exec Dir of Human Resources Ms. Madelyn BROWN
26 Exec Dir Community/College Rels Ms. Cheryl MYERS
37 Associate VP of Financial Aid Ms. Debbie HENSHAW
13 Director Information Technology Mr. Jonathan NORRED
111 Director Institutional Advancement Ms. Susan SEALY

Covenant College (B)

14049 Scenic Highway, Lookout Mountain TN 30750-4164
County: Dade FICE Identification: 003484
Unit ID: 139393
Telephone: (706) 820-1560 Carnegie Class: Bac-A&S
FAX Number: (706) 820-2165 Calendar System: Semester
URL: www.covenant.edu
Established: 1955 Annual Undergrad Tuition & Fees: $34,330
Enrollment: 1,068 Coed
Affiliation or Control: Presbyterian Church In America IRS Status: 501(c)3
Highest Offering: Master's
Accreditation: SC

01 President Dr. J. Derek HALVORSON
05 Vice Pres of Academic Affairs Dr. Jeffrey B. HALL
10 Vice Pres of Finance & Operations Mr. Fred VERWOERD
30 Vice President of Development Mr. Marc ERICKSON
32 Vice Pres of Student Development Mr. Brad VOYLES
84 Asst VP of Enrollment Management Mr. Brad TOMAS
09 AVP for Institutional Effectiveness Dr. Karen NELSON
08 Director of Library Services Mr. John HOLBERG
06 Dean of Records and Registrar Mr. Rodney E. MILLER
42 Chaplain Mr. Grant LOWE
58 Dean of Master of Education Pgm Dr. Jim DREXLER
21 Controller Mr. Jamie GROSS
88 Campus Architect Mr. David NORTHCUTT
37 Director of Financial Aid Mr. Matthew BAZZEL
15 Director of Human Resources Ms. Rebekah MCNAIR
41 Director of Athletics Mr. Tim SCEGGEL
13 Director of Technology Services Ms. Marjorie CROCKER
29 Director of Alumni Relations Vacant
23 Director of Health Services Ms. Tina HOLT
26 Dir of Marketing & Communications Vacant
121 Coordinator of Student Success Ms. Becca MOORE
36 Dir of Center for Calling & Career Mr. John PLATING
04 Admin Asst to Office of President Mrs. Cassandra JONES
19 Director of Safety & Security Mr. Keith MCCLEARN
109 Director of Business Operations Mr. Tom SCHREINER
104 Coordinator of Global Education Ms. Lindsay SAUNDS

Dalton State College (C)

650 College Drive, Dalton GA 30720-3797
County: Whitfield FICE Identification: 003956
Unit ID: 139463
Telephone: (706) 272-4436 Carnegie Class: Bac-Diverse
FAX Number: (706) 272-4588 Calendar System: Semester
URL: www.daltonstate.edu
Established: 1963 Annual Undergrad Tuition & Fees (In-State): $4,246
Enrollment: 5,164 Coed
Affiliation or Control: State IRS Status: 501(c)3
Highest Offering: Baccalaureate
Accreditation: SC, ADNUR, COARC, MLTAD, NUR, RAD, SW

01 President Dr. Margaret VENABLE
05 VP for Academic Affairs Dr. Pat CHUTE
10 Vice President Fiscal Affairs Mr. Nick HENRY
84 VP Student Affairs & Enroll Mgmt Dr. Jodi JOHNSON
37 Director of Financial Aid/Vet Svcs Ms. Carol JONES
08 Director Library Services Ms. Melissa WHITESELL
18 Director Plant Opers Mr. George BREWER
26 Director of Marketing Mr. Philip SCHLESINGER
102 Director Foundation Mr. David ELROD
32 Dean of Students Dr. Jami HALL
15 Director Human Resources Ms. Lori MCCARTY
96 Purchasing Coordinator Ms. Penny CORDELL
13 Director Computing & Info Services Mr. Terry BAILEY
19 Director Public Safety Mr. Michael MASTERS
29 Director Alumni Relations Mr. Josh WILSON
39 Director Student Housing Mr. Tim REILLY
50 Dean School of Business Dr. Marilyn HELMS
53 Dean School of Education Dr. Sharon HIXON
49 Dean School of Liberal Arts Dr. Mary NIELSEN
81 Dean School of Science/Tech/Math Dr. Randall GRIFFUS
76 Dean Health Professions Dr. Gina KERTULIS-TARTAR
06 Registrar Mr. Rob WINGFIELD
04 Administrative Asst to President Mrs. Mary Ellen GURLEY
07 Director of Admissions Mrs. Katherine LOGAN
41 Interim Athletic Director Mr. Saif ALSAFEER
88 Director Hispanic/Latino Outreach Mr. Quincy JENKINS
104 Director Study Abroad Dr. Fernando GARCIA
36 Director Student Placement Ms. Mallory SAFLEY
38 Director Student Counseling Ms. Robin ROE
100 Interim Chief of Staff Mr. Jon JAUDON
86 Director Government Relations Ms. Vallarie PRATT
108 Director Institutional Assessment Dr. Henry CODJOE

† Part of the University System of Georgia.

East Georgia State College (D)

131 College Circle, Swainsboro GA 30401-3643
County: Emanuel FICE Identification: 010997
Unit ID: 139621
Telephone: (478) 289-2000 Carnegie Class: Bac/Assoc-Assoc Dom
FAX Number: (478) 289-2038 Calendar System: Semester
URL: www.ega.edu
Established: 1973 Annual Undergrad Tuition & Fees (In-State): $3,110
Enrollment: 3,003 Coed
Affiliation or Control: State IRS Status: 501(c)3
Highest Offering: Baccalaureate
Accreditation: SC, NUR

01 President Dr. Robert G. BOEHMER
05 VP for Academic & Student Affairs Dr. Deborah L. VESS
10 Vice President for Business Affairs Mr. Cliff GAY
13 Vice Pres Information Technology Mr. Mike ROUNTREE
100 Chief of Staff/Legal Counsel Mrs. Mary C. SMITH
04 Executive Assistant to President Vacant
08 Librarian Ms. Cynthia E. JONES
06 Registrar Ms. Lynette M. SAULSBERRY
09 Dir of Institutional Effectiveness Mr. David GRIBBIN
84 Assoc Vice Pres Enrollment Mgmt Mrs. Karen S. JONES
15 Director of Human Resources Mrs. Tracy WOODS
111 Vice Pres Institutional Advancement Ms. Elizabeth GILMER
11 Director of Business Operations Mrs. Michelle GOFF
110 Assoc VP Institutional Advancement Ms. Norma KENNEDY
12 Assoc VP External Campuses Mr. Nick KELCH
19 Dir Public Safety/Chief of Police Mr. Deryl M. SECKINGER
35 Director of Student Life Ms. Stacey GRANT
07 Director of Admissions Ms. Georgia MATHEWS
38 Dir Counseling/Disability Services Ms. Lori BURNS
39 Director of Housing Ms. Angela STORCK
41 Director of Athletics Mr. Chuck WIMBERLY
88 Dir Sudie A Fulford Cmty Lrng Ctr Mrs. Jean D. SCHWABE
18 Director of Plant Operations Mr. David STEPTOE
21 Director of Accounting Services Vacant
12 Director of EGSC Statesboro Ms. Jessica WILLIAMSON
106 Assoc Dean of eLearning Vacant
121 Dir of Academic Support Services Ms. Deborah KITTRELL-MIKELL
88 Dir of the Learning Commons Ms. Karen MURPHREE
109 Director of Dining Operations Ms. Ruth UNDERWOOD
88 Director of Student Conduct Ms. Sherrie HELMS
81 Dean of Mathematics & Sciences Dr. Jim WEDINCAMP
83 Dean Humanities & Social Sciences Dr. Carlos CUNHA
81 Chair of Biology Department Dr. David CHEVALIER
88 Dir of FESA Ms. Beverley WALKER
66 Director of Nursing Dr. Linda UPCHURCH
88 Coord of MRC & Athletic Advisement Ms. Denise DANIELS
88 Director Financial Accounting Ms. Sheila D. WENTZ

† Part of the University System of Georgia.

Emmanuel College (E)

181 Springs Street, Franklin Springs GA 30639
County: Franklin FICE Identification: 001563
Unit ID: 139630
Telephone: (706) 245-7226 Carnegie Class: Bac-Diverse
FAX Number: (706) 245-4424 Calendar System: Semester
URL: www.ec.edu
Established: 1919 Annual Undergrad Tuition & Fees: $20,292
Enrollment: 953 Coed
Affiliation or Control: Pentecostal Holiness Church IRS Status: 501(c)3
Highest Offering: Baccalaureate
Accreditation: SC

01 President Dr. Ronald WHITE
32 Vice President for Student Life Dr. Tracy REYNOLDS
05 Vice President for Academic Affairs Dr. John R. HENZEL, JR.
10 Vice President for Finance Mr. Greg K. HEARN
30 Vice President for Development Mr. W. Brian JAMES
84 Vice Pres Enrollment Mgmt/Marketing Ms. Donna QUICK
08 Director of Library Services Ms. Deborah MILLIER
06 Registrar Mrs. Debra F. GRIZZLE
37 Director of Financial Aid Mrs. Niki STINSON
13 Director of Information Technology Mr. Glenn TONEY
11 Assoc VP of Campus Operations Mr. Matt MCREE
41 Athletics Director Mr. Nate MOORMAN
42 Dir Spiritual Life/Campus Pastor Mr. Chris MAXWELL
15 Director of Human Resources Mrs. Joann HARPER
26 Chief Public Relations Officer Mrs. Ashley WESTBROOK
96 Director of Accounting Services Mrs. Anita RAY
18 Physical Plant Director Mr. Wayne CRIDER
09 Director of Institutional Research Ms. Sharon SYNAN
29 Director Alumni Relations Mr. Harrell W. QUEEN
36 Dir Career Svcs/Student Counseling Mr. Jason CROY
04 Administrative Asst to President Mrs. Mary BEADLES
19 Director Security/Safety Mr. Joel SWAILS
39 Director Student Housing Mrs. Sherri CAREY
07 Director of Admissions Ms. Kelley CHAPPA
106 Dir Online Education/E-learning Ms. Sharon SYNAN

Emory University (F)

201 Dowman Drive, Atlanta GA 30322-0001
County: DeKalb FICE Identification: 001564
Unit ID: 139658
Telephone: (404) 727-6123 Carnegie Class: DU-Highest
FAX Number: (404) 727-5997 Calendar System: Semester
URL: www.emory.edu
Established: 1836 Annual Undergrad Tuition & Fees: $51,306
Enrollment: 14,263 Coed
Affiliation or Control: United Methodist IRS Status: 501(c)3
Highest Offering: Doctorate
Accreditation: SC, AA, ANEST, ARCPA, CAMPEP, CLPSY, DENT, IPSY, LAW, MED, MIDWF, NURSE, PAST, PCSAS, PH, PTA, RAD, THEOL

01 President Dr. Claire E. STERK
05 Provost/Exec VP Academic Affairs Dr. Dwight A. MCBRIDE
10 Exec VP for Business/Admin Mr. Christopher AUGOSTINI
17 Exec Vice Pres Health Affairs Dr. Jonathan S. LEWIN
101 VP/Secretary of the University Ms. Allison K. DYKES
84 VP Enr Mgmt/Interim VP Campus Life Dr. Paul P. MARTHERS
100 VP and Chief of Staff Mr. Daniel L. GORDON
26 Sr VP Comm and Public Affairs Mr. David B. SANDOR
46 Sr Vice Pres for Research Dr. Deborah W. BRUNER
111 SVP Advancement/Alumni Engagement Mr. Joshua NEWTON
88 Senior Advisor to the Pres Dr. Robert M. FRANKLIN, JR.
43 Sr Vice Pres & General Counsel Mr. Stephen D. SENCER
114 Deputy Prov Admin/Plng Mr. Michael ANDRECHAK
20 Deputy Provost for Academic Affairs Dr. Christa D. ACAMPORA
08 Enterprise CIO/Sr VP Lib Svcs Mr. Richard A. MENDOLA
15 VP Human Resources Ms. Theresa MILAZZO
15 VP Human Resources Mr. Del KING
20 Vice Prov Academic Planning Dr. Nancy BLIWISE
28 Vice Provost Equity/Inclusion Ms. Lynell CADRAY
18 Vice President Campus Services Mr. Matthew EARLY
10 Vice President for Finance/CFO Vacant
88 VP Strategic Research Initiatives Dr. Lanny S. LIEBESKIND
20 VP Faculty Affairs Mr. Tim HOLBROOK
20 Vice Prov Undergrad Education Dr. Pamela SCULLY
86 VP Governmental Affairs Ms. Cameron P. TAYLOR
58 Vice Provost/Dean Graduate Sch Dr. Lisa A. TEDESCO
88 Vice Provost International Affairs Dr. Philip WAINWRIGHT
21 VP Financial Plng/Analytics Dr. Qiang XU
11 VP Business Operations Ms. Debby MOREY
45 VP Planning/Chief Plng Ofcr Mr. Robin MOREY
115 VP Investments Mr. Srinivas PULAVARTI
100 Vice Prov/Chief of Staff Dr. Jennifer E. HOBBS
29 Sr AVP Alumni Engagement Ms. Sarah COOK
21 Assoc VP Finance & Controller Ms. Allison S. BERG
25 Assoc Vice President Research Dr. Todd SHERER
07 AVP Undergrad Enroll/Dean of Admiss Dr. John LATTING
88 Assoc Vice Prov Undergrad Education Ms. Heather MUGG
88 Chief Compliance Officer Ms. Kristin WEST
20 Asc Vice Prov Acad Innovation Dr. Paul WELTY
06 Asst Vice Prov/University Registrar Ms. JoAnn MCKENZIE
19 Assistant VP Public Safety Mr. Craig T. WATSON
20 Asst Vice Prov Faculty Affairs Dr. Carol A. FLOWERS
37 Asst Vice Prov/Dir Student Fin Aid Mr. John LEACH
38 Assistant VP Counseling/Psych Svcs Dr. Wanda COLLINS
108 Asst VProv Academic Pgm/Plng Dr. David M. JORDAN
49 Dean of Emory College Dr. Michael A. ELLIOTT
12 Dean & CEO Oxford College Dr. Douglas A. HICKS
63 Dean of Medicine Dr. Vikas P. SUKHATME
66 Dean of Nursing Dr. Linda MCCAULEY
73 Dean of Theology Dr. Jan LOVE
61 Interim Dean of Law Mr. James B. HUGHES, JR.
50 Dean of Business School Ms. Erika JAMES
69 Dean of Public Health Dr. James W. CURRAN
42 Dean of the Chapel & Spiritual Life Rev. Bridgette YOUNG ROSS
80 Pres & CEO of the Carter Center Ms. Mary Ann PETERS
36 Exec Director Career Service Mr. Paul FOWLER
44 Executive Director of Annual Giving Ms. Kimberly JULIAN BOWDEN
39 Sr Director Residence Life Dr. Scott K. RAUSCH
39 Sr Director Housing Operations Ms. Elaine TURNER
40 Director Bookstore Mr. Bruce COVEY

88 Dir Communications/Outreach ..... Ms. Caroline DRIEBE
96 Director Contract Admin/Compliance ..... Mr. Rex HARDAWAY
12 Director Yerkes Research Ctrs ..... Dr. Paul JOHNSON
88 University Historian ..... Dr. Gary S. HAUK
85 Dir Intl Student Scholar Program ..... Ms. Shinsaeng KO
09 Dir Inst Research and Dec Support ..... Dr. Justin SHEPHERD
88 Director M C Carlos Museum ..... Ms. Bonnie SPEED
41 Director Athletics/Recreation ..... Dr. Michael VIENNA
08 University Librarian ..... Ms. Yolanda COOPER

Fort Valley State University (A)

1005 State University Drive, Fort Valley GA 31030-4313
County: Peach FICE Identification: 001566
Unit ID: 139719
Telephone: (478) 825-6211 Carnegie Class: Masters/M
FAX Number: (478) 825-6394 Calendar System: Semester
URL: www.fvsu.edu
Established: 1895 Annual Undergrad Tuition & Fees (In-State): $6,658
Enrollment: 2,752 Coed
Affiliation or Control: State IRS Status: 501(c)3
Highest Offering: Beyond Master's But Less Than Doctorate
Accreditation: SC, AAFCS, CACREP, SW

01 President ..... Dr. Paul JONES
05 Provost/VP for Academic Affairs ..... Dr. Ramon STUART
10 CBO/VP for Business & Finance ..... Mr. Dexter ODOM
111 VP for Advancement ..... Mr. Anthony HOLLOMAN
84 VP Student Affairs and Enrollment ..... Mr. Jesse KANE
09 AVP Academic Affairs/Dir of OIRPE ..... Dr. Frank ARCHER, III
56 Extension Administrator ..... Dr. Mark LATTIMORE
32 Dean of Students ..... Mr. Wallace KEESE
49 Dean Arts & Sciences ..... Dr. Gregory FORD
21 Assistant Vice President/Controller ..... Mr. Allen SALTER
06 Registrar ..... Ms. Sharee LAWRENCE
43 Legal Affairs ..... Ms. Emma WILLIAMS
13 Director for Information Technology ..... Mr. Charlie WEAVER
08 Director Hunt Memorial Library ..... Mr. Frank MAHITAB
07 Executive Director Admissions ..... Mr. George NORTON
37 Director Financial Aid ..... Ms. Kimberly MORRIS
29 Director Alumni Affairs ..... Mr. Ed BOSTON
15 Interim Director of Human Resources ..... Ms. Patrice TERRELL
19 Director Campus Safety ..... Ms. Anita ALLEN
47 Dean Agriculture ..... Dr. Ralph NOBLE
23 Dir Student Health & Behav Coun ..... Ms. Jacqueline CASKEY-JAMES
18 Director of Facilities Management ..... Mr. Edwidge DUFRESNE
36 Director of Career Development ..... Vacant
26 Chief Communications Officer ..... Mr. Cedric MOBLEY
41 Interim Director of Athletics ..... Mr. Anthony HOLLOMAN
124 Dean of University College ..... Vacant
53 Dean College of Education ..... Dr. Rebecca MCMULLEN
22 Dir Affirmative Act/EEO/Diversity ..... Ms. Patrice TERRELL
25 Director of Sponsored Programs ..... Ms. Joyce Y. JOHNSON
39 Director Student Housing ..... Mr. Shawn MODENA
96 Director of Purchasing ..... Ms. Becky HORTON
88 Dir Title III Administration ..... Ms. Danyell BARRY
04 Admin Assistant to the President ..... Mr. RJ MATHIS
100 Interim Chief of Staff ..... Dr. Olufunke FONTENOT
106 Director Online Learning Office ..... Dr. Darryl HANCOCK
30 Director of Development ..... Ms. Nadia RAHAMAN
86 Director Government Relations ..... Dr. Govind KANNAN

† Part of the University System of Georgia.

Georgia Central University (B)

6789 Peachtree Industrial Boulevard, Atlanta GA 30360
County: DeKalb FICE Identification: 041565
Unit ID: 461236
Telephone: (770) 279-0507 Carnegie Class: Bac-Diverse
FAX Number: (770) 279-0308 Calendar System: Semester
URL: www.gcuniv.edu
Established: 1993 Annual Undergrad Tuition & Fees: N/A
Enrollment: 55 Coed
Affiliation or Control: Independent Non-Profit IRS Status: 501(c)3
Highest Offering: Doctorate
Accreditation: THEOL, CEA

01 President ..... Dr. Paul C. KIM
03 Vice President ..... Dr. Hee Sook SONG
07 Director of Admissions ..... Ms. Young Sil HWANG
20 Associate Dir of Academic Affairs ..... Dr. Mia KANG
45 Director of Planning ..... Mr. Alain GALLIE
10 Chief Financial Officer ..... Ms. Eunice KIM
12 Dir of New Jersey Extension Site ..... Dr. Samuel S. HEO
12 Dir of S California Extension Site ..... Dr. Byonghark KIM
13 Senior Director of IT ..... Dr. Byungchil KIM
106 Director of Distance Education ..... Dr. Kyueil KWAK
24 Director Literature & Information ..... Dr. Hyun Sung CHO
18 Chief Facilities/Physical Plant ..... Rev. Min Soo KIM
19 Director Security/Safety ..... Mr. Samuel KIM
21 Director of Business Affairs ..... Mr. Jonguk KIM
108 Dir of Institutional Effectiveness ..... Dr. Yong Hwan KIM
88 Director of ESOL ..... Mr. Alain GALLIE
29 President of Alumni Relations ..... Dr. Eunjo LEE
26 Chief Public Relations Officer ..... Vacant
06 Registrar ..... Ms. Sara KIM
37 Director Student Financial Aid ..... Dr. Hee Sook SONG
50 Dean School of Business ..... Dr. William STAUFF
73 Dean School of Christianity ..... Dr. Hyun Sung CHO
73 Dean School of Divinity ..... Dr. Jin Ki HWANG
64 Dean School of Music ..... Ms. Kyung Mi YANG
88 Director of Doctoral Programs ..... Dr. Eun Moo LEE
88 International Student Advisor ..... Mr. Rafael MIGUEL
42 Chaplain ..... Dr. Hyun Sung CHO
08 Director of the Library ..... Mr. Jarian R. JONES
32 Director of Student Affairs ..... Vacant

Georgia College & State University (C)

231 West Hancock Street, Milledgeville GA 31061-0490
County: Baldwin FICE Identification: 001602
Unit ID: 139861
Telephone: (478) 445-5004 Carnegie Class: Masters/L
FAX Number: (478) 445-1191 Calendar System: Semester
URL: www.gcsu.edu
Established: 1889 Annual Undergrad Tuition & Fees (In-State): $9,346
Enrollment: 6,952 Coed
Affiliation or Control: State IRS Status: 501(c)3
Highest Offering: Doctorate
Accreditation: SC, CAATE, CAEPN, MUS, NURSE, SPAA

01 President ..... Dr. Steve M. DORMAN
04 Special Assistant to the President ..... Ms. Monica STARLEY
05 Interim Provost/VP for Acad Affairs ..... Dr. Costas SPIROU
10 VP Finance/Administration ..... Ms. Susan ALLEN
32 Vice President for Student Affairs ..... Dr. Shawn BROOKS
111 VP for University Advancement ..... Ms. Monica DELISA
88 Dir of Econ Dev/External Relations ..... Mr. Johnny GRANT
20 Interim Assoc Provost ..... Dr. Sandra GANGSTEAD
121 Assoc Provost for Student Success ..... Dr. Carolyn DENARD
45 Assoc VP for Strategic Initiatives ..... Dr. Mark PELTON
26 Assoc VP Strategic Communications ..... Mr. Omar ODEH
84 Assoc VP for Enrollment Management ..... Ms. Suzanne PITTMAN
109 Asst VP for Auxiliary Services ..... Mr. Kyle CULLARS
114 Sr Dir for Budget Planning & Admin ..... Mr. Russ WILLIAMS
49 Dean College of Arts & Sciences ..... Dr. Eric TENBUS
50 Dean College of Business ..... Dr. Dale YOUNG
53 Dean College of Education ..... Dr. Joseph PETERS
76 Dean College of Health Sciences ..... Dr. Sheri NOVIELLO
39 Exec Director of University Housing ..... Mr. Larry CHRISTENSON
88 Univ Architect/Dir Facilities Plng ..... Mr. Michael RICKENBAKER
18 Asst VP of Facilities Operations ..... Mr. Mark DUCLOS
19 Dir Public Safety & Chief of Police ..... Mr. Brett STANELLE
09 Assoc VP of Institutional Research ..... Dr. Chris FERLAND
13 Interim Chief Information Officer ..... Mr. Charlie WEAVER
08 Interim Director of Libraries ..... Dr. Shaundra WALKER
36 Director Career Center ..... Ms. Mary ROBERTS
15 Chief Human Resources Officer ..... Ms. Carol WARD
28 Chief Diversity Officer ..... Dr. Veronica WOMACK
07 Sr Assoc Director of Admissions ..... Mr. Will BROWN
06 Registrar ..... Ms. Kay ANDERSON
41 Director of Athletics ..... Mr. Wendell STATON
29 Asst Dir of Alumni Engagement ..... Ms. Mimi PATEL
43 General Counsel ..... Ms. Qiana WILSON
38 Director of Counseling Services ..... Dr. Stephen WILSON
37 Director of Financial Aid ..... Ms. Shannon SIMMONS
88 Sr Dir Materials Mgmt/Central Svcs ..... Mr. Mark MEEKS
116 Dir of Internal Audit ..... Ms. Stacy MULVANEY
35 Asst Dean of Students ..... Mr. Tom MILES
104 Asst VP for International Educ ..... Dr. James CALLAGHAN

Georgia Gwinnett College (D)

1000 University Center Lane, Lawrenceville GA 30043
County: Gwinnett FICE Identification: 041429
Unit ID: 447689
Telephone: (678) 407-5000 Carnegie Class: Bac-Diverse
FAX Number: N/A Calendar System: Semester
URL: www.ggc.edu
Established: 2005 Annual Undergrad Tuition & Fees (In-District): $5,634
Enrollment: 12,287 Coed
Affiliation or Control: State/Local IRS Status: 501(c)3
Highest Offering: Baccalaureate
Accreditation: SC, CAEPN, NURSE

01 President ..... Dr. Jann L. JOSEPH
05 SVP Academic/Stdnt Affairs/Provost ..... Dr. T.J ARANT
111 Vice Pres Advancement ..... Ms. Lori BUCKHEISTER
10 VP of Business & Finance/CFO ..... Ms. Laura MAXWELL
84 Vice Pres Enrollment Management ..... Mr. Michael POLL
100 Chief of Staff ..... Mr. Dan NOLAN
04 Executive Asst to President ..... Mrs. Luann CAUSLAND
50 Dean School of Business ..... Dr. Tyler YU
53 Dean School of Education ..... Dr. Cathy D. MOORE
49 Dean School of Liberal Arts ..... Vacant
81 Dean School Science and Technology ..... Dr. Thomas MUNDIE
66 Dean School of Health Sciences ..... Dr. Diane WHITE
121 Dean School of Transitional Studies ..... Dr. Justin JERNIGAN

Georgia Highlands College (E)

3175 Cedartown Highway, Rome GA 30161-3897
County: Floyd FICE Identification: 009507
Unit ID: 139700
Telephone: (706) 802-5000 Carnegie Class: Bac/Assoc-Assoc Dom
FAX Number: (706) 295-6341 Calendar System: Semester
URL: www.highlands.edu
Established: 1970 Annual Undergrad Tuition & Fees (In-State): $3,288
Enrollment: 6,013 Coed
Affiliation or Control: State IRS Status: 501(c)3
Highest Offering: Baccalaureate
Accreditation: SC, ADNUR, DH, NUR

01 President ..... Dr. Donald J. GREEN
05 Vice President Academic Affairs ..... Dr. Dana J. NICHOLS
10 Vice Pres Finance/Administration ..... Mr. Jeff DAVIS
32 Vice President Student Affairs ..... Dr. Todd G. JONES
15 Vice President Human Resources ..... Ms. Ginni SILER
111 VP Advanc/Exec Dir GHC Foundation ..... Ms. Mary TRANSUE
13 VP Information Technology/CIO ..... Mr. Jeff PATTY
37 Director Financial Aid ..... Ms. Donna CHILDRES
08 Dean Libraries/College Testing ..... Mr. Julius FLESCHNER
12 Dean Floyd ..... Dr. Todd G. JONES
12 Dean Cartersville ..... Ms. Leslie JOHNSON
12 Dean Marietta ..... Mr. Ken REAVES
12 Director Paulding ..... Vacant
12 Director Douglasville ..... Ms. Julia AREH
04 Executive Asst to the President ..... Ms. Stephanie STAPLETON
41 Director of Athletics ..... Mr. Phillip GAFFNEY
18 Director Plant Operations ..... Mr. Phillip KIMSEY
06 Registrar ..... Mr. Edward ROSSER
09 Dean Research/Plng & Accreditation ..... Dr. Jesse BISHOP
19 Police Chief/Dir of Campus Safety ..... Mr. David HORACE
26 Sr Dir Marketing & Communications ..... Ms. Sheila JONES
28 Director of Diversity ..... Dr. Sean CALLAHAN
38 Dir Student Support & Counseling ..... Ms. Angela WHEELUS
96 Purchasing Manager ..... Ms. Cynthia PARKER
07 Director of Admissions ..... Ms. Maggie SCHUYLER
104 Director Study Abroad ..... Dr. Bronson LONG

† Part of the University System of Georgia.

Georgia Institute of Technology (F)

225 North Avenue, NW, Atlanta GA 30332-0002
County: Fulton FICE Identification: 001569
Unit ID: 139755
Telephone: (404) 894-2000 Carnegie Class: DU-Highest
FAX Number: (404) 894-1277 Calendar System: Semester
URL: www.gatech.edu
Established: 1885 Annual Undergrad Tuition & Fees (In-State): $12,424
Enrollment: 29,376 Coed
Affiliation or Control: State IRS Status: 501(c)3
Highest Offering: Doctorate
Accreditation: SC, ART, CAMPEP, CEA, IPSY, OPE, PLNG

01 President ..... Dr. G. P. (Bud) PETERSON
05 Provost/Exec VP Academic Affairs ..... Dr. Rafael BRAS
10 Int Exec VP Administration/Finance ..... Mr. James FORTNER
46 Executive Vice President Research ..... Dr. Chaouki ABDALLAH
100 Associate Vice Pres/Chief of Staff ..... Ms. Lynn DURHAM
30 Vice President Development ..... Mr. Barrett H. CARSON
26 Vice Pres Communications/Marketing ..... Ms. Renee KOPKOWSKI
32 VP Student Life & Dean of Students ..... Mr. John STEIN
88 Interim SVP GA Tech Res Inst ..... Dr. Lora WEISS
46 Vice President Research ..... Ms. Jilda GARTON
86 Vice Pres Government/Cmty Relations ..... Mr. Dene SHEHEANE
88 VP Enterprise Innovation Inst ..... Mr. Chris DOWNING
29 Interim President GT Alumni Assoc ..... Mr. William TODD
58 Vice Prov Grad Educ/Faculty Affairs ..... Dr. Bonnie FERRI
84 Vice Prov Enrollment Services ..... Dr. Paul KOHN
20 Vice Prov Undergraduate Education ..... Dr. Colin POTTS
43 VP Ethics/Compliance/Legal Affairs ..... Ms. Ling-Ling NIE
28 Vice President Institute Diversity ..... Dr. Archie ERVIN
15 Assoc VP Human Resources ..... Dr. Kim HARRINGTON
18 Vice President Facilities ..... Mr. Charles G. RHODE
11 Associate Vice Pres Campus Services ..... Ms. Kasey HELTON
13 VP Information Tech/CIO ..... Vacant
41 Director of Athletics ..... Mr. Todd STANSBURY
22 Exec Dir Staff Diversity/Inclusion ..... Ms. Pearl ALEXANDER
12 Dean Ivan Allen Col Liberal Arts ..... Dr. Jacqueline J. ROYSTER
48 Dean College of Design ..... Dr. Steve FRENCH
77 Dean College of Computing ..... Dr. Zvi GALIL
54 Dean College of Engineering ..... Dr. Steven MCLAUGHLIN
08 Dean Libraries ..... Ms. Catherine MURRAY-RUST
82 Dean Scheller College of Business ..... Dr. Maryam ALAVI
81 Interim Dean College of Sciences ..... Dr. David COLLARD
06 Registrar ..... Ms. Reta PIKOWSKY
40 Director Georgia Tech Bookstore ..... Ms. Reshma PATEL
19 Director of Security & Police ..... Mr. Robert CONNOLLY
107 Dean Professional Education ..... Dr. Nelson BAKER
36 Int Exec Dir Career Development ..... Dr. Steven GIRARDOT
37 Director Student Financial Aid ..... Ms. Marie MONS
23 Sr Director Student Health Svcs ..... Dr. Benjamin HOLTON
39 Asst VP Housing ..... Vacant
09 Asst VP Institutional Res/EDM ..... Ms. Sandra J. BRAMBLETT
85 Vice Prov International Initiatives ..... Dr. Yves BERTHELOT
104 Exec Dir International Education ..... Ms. Amy HENRY
38 Director Counseling Center ..... Dr. Carla BRADLEY
109 Senior Director Auxiliary Services ..... Ms. Carolina AMERO
07 Director Undergraduate Admission ..... Mr. Richard CLARK
96 Director of Procurement Services ..... Mr. Frans BARENDS
114 Exec Dir Inst Budget Plng & Admin ..... Ms. Jamie FERNANDES
88 Int Dir Capital Planning/Space Mgmt ..... Ms. Jennifer HUBERT
88 Exec Director Strategic Consulting ..... Dr. Sonia ALVAREZ-ROBINSON
113 Bursar ..... Mr. Terry FAIR
88 Interim AVP Inst Plng/Resource Mgt ..... Ms. Jennifer HUBERT
88 Interim SVP Administration ..... Mr. Mark DEMYANEK

† Part of the University System of Georgia.

Georgia Military College (G)

201 E Greene Street, Milledgeville GA 31061-3398
County: Baldwin FICE Identification: 001571
Unit ID: 485111
Telephone: (478) 387-4900 Carnegie Class: Bac/Assoc-Assoc Dom
FAX Number: N/A Calendar System: Quarter

URL: www.gmc.edu
Established: 1879 Annual Undergrad Tuition & Fees: $6,480
Enrollment: 8,595 Coed
Affiliation or Control: Independent Non-Profit IRS Status: 501(c)3
Highest Offering: Baccalaureate
Accreditation: SC

01 President ... LtGen. William B. CALDWELL, IV
11 Executive Vice President/COO ... BGen. Curt RAUHUT
05 Chief Academic Ofcr/Dn of Faculty ... Dr. Phillip M. HOLMES
10 Chief Financial Officer ... COL. James WATKINS
13 VP Info Technology/Online Campus ... Mr. Jody YEARWOOD
15 VP Human Resources ... Ms. Jill ROBBINS
21 Assoc Vice Pres Resource Management ... Ms. Susan MEEKS
06 Associate VP Academic Records ... Mr. David FULMER
32 Dean of Students ... COL. Steve PITT
30 Chief College Relations Officer ... Mr. Mark STROM
09 Director Institutional Research ... Dr. Susan ISAAC
41 Athletic Director ... Mr. Bert WILLIAMS
18 Director Facilities/Engineer ... Mr. Jeff GRAY
08 Director of Library Services ... Ms. Erin NEWTON
19 Chief Security/Safety/Campus Police ... Mr. James HODNETT
26 Dir Communication/Public Relations ... Mr. Jay BENTLEY
20 Academic Dean ... Ms. Laura BOOTH
84 Director of Enrollment Management ... Mr. Jody YEARWOOD
04 Administrative Asst to President ... Ms. Joelle TRUMBO
37 Director Student Financial Aid ... Ms. Alisa STEPHENS
100 Director of Staff ... Ms. Jeannie ZIPPERER

Georgia Northwestern Technical College (A)

One Maurice Culberson Drive, Rome GA 30161
County: Floyd FICE Identification: 005257
Unit ID: 139384
Telephone: (706) 295-6963 Carnegie Class: Assoc/HVT-Mix Trad/Non
FAX Number: (706) 295-6944 Calendar System: Semester
URL: www.gntc.edu
Established: 1966 Annual Undergrad Tuition & Fees (In-State): $2,798
Enrollment: 5,643 Coed
Affiliation or Control: State IRS Status: 501(c)3
Highest Offering: Associate Degree
Accreditation: SC, ADNUR, CAHIIM, COARC, DA, DMS, EMT, LC, MAC, RAD, SURGT

01 President ... Dr. Heidi POPHAM
05 Vice President Academic Affairs ... Dr. Elizabeth ANDERSON
11 Vice Pres Administrative Services ... Ms. Kelly BARNES
30 Vice Pres Econ Development ... Ms. Stephanie SCEARCE
09 Exec Vice Pres Inst Effectiveness ... Vacant
51 Vice President Adult Education ... Vacant
32 Vice Pres Student Affairs ... Mr. Stuart PHILLIPS
06 Registrar ... Ms. Selena MAGNUSSON
08 Director of Library Services ... Mr. John LASSITER
19 Director Safety & Security ... Mr. Chad CARDIN
37 Exec Director of Financial Aid ... Mr. Stephen ANDERSEN
18 Director Facilities Management ... Mr. Jeffrey AGAN
26 Dir Marketing/Public Relations ... Ms. Amber JORDAN
15 Director of Human Resources ... Ms. Peggy CORDELL

Georgia Piedmont Technical College (B)

495 N Indian Creek Drive, Clarkston GA 30021-2397
County: DeKalb FICE Identification: 005622
Unit ID: 244446
Telephone: (404) 297-9522 Carnegie Class: Assoc/HVT-Mix Trad/Non
FAX Number: (404) 297-4234 Calendar System: Semester
URL: www.gptc.edu
Established: 1961 Annual Undergrad Tuition & Fees (In-State): $2,924
Enrollment: 4,115 Coed
Affiliation or Control: State IRS Status: 501(c)3
Highest Offering: Associate Degree
Accreditation: SC, EMT, MAC, MLTAD

01 President ... Dr. Tavarez HOLSTON
04 Exec Dir & Spec Asst to President ... Vacant
05 EVP Academic/Student Affairs ... Vacant
10 Vice Pres Business/Financial Svcs ... Vacant
31 VP Economic Devel/Cmty Engagement ... Vacant
30 VP Institutional Advancement ... Vacant
20 Assoc Vice Pres Academic Affairs ... Vacant
37 Assistant VP of Financial Aid ... Ms. Lakisha SANDERS
32 Dean of Student Affairs ... Dr. Candice JONES
20 Dean of Academic Affairs ... Vacant
108 Dean of Quality Initiatives ... Vacant
15 Director of Human Resources ... Ms. Lolita MORRISON
26 Exec Dir Marketing/Public Relations ... Mr. Cory THOMPSON
06 Registrar ... Ms. Joana BLANKSON
07 Director Admissions/Recruiting ... Mr. Corey PARKER
55 Dean of Adult Education ... Dr. Meghan MCBRIDE
18 Director Facilities/Auxiliary Svcs ... Vacant
36 Dir Adv/Career & Retention Svcs ... Ms. Angela CUMMINGS
13 Director of Information Technology ... Mr. Keith PERRY

Georgia Southern University (C)

PO Box 8033, Statesboro GA 30460-8033
County: Bulloch FICE Identification: 001572
Unit ID: 139931
Telephone: (912) 478-4636 Carnegie Class: DU-Higher
FAX Number: N/A Calendar System: Semester
URL: www.georgiasouthern.edu
Established: 1906 Annual Undergrad Tuition & Fees (In-State): $6,356
Enrollment: 20,418 Coed
Affiliation or Control: State IRS Status: 501(c)3
Highest Offering: Doctorate
Accreditation: SC, ART, CAATE, CACREP, CIDA, CLPSY, COARC, CONST, CVT, DIETD, DIETI, DMS, HSA, IPSY, MT, MUS, NMT, NRPA, NURSE, PH, PTA, RAD, RTT, SP, SPAA, THEA

01 President ... Dr. Kyle MARRERO
05 Provost/VPAA ... Dr. Carl REIBER
10 VP Business & Finance ... Mr. Rob WHITAKER
84 VP Enrollment Management ... Dr. Scot LINGRELL
32 Interim VP Student Affairs ... Dr. Melanie MILLER
111 VP Univ Advancement ... Mr. Trip ADDISON
12 VP Armstrong/Liberty Campus Op ... Dr. Chris CURTIS
13 Chief Information Officer ... Mr. Ron STALNAKER
09 Assoc VP/Dir Institutional Research ... Ms. Laura MILLS
20 Vice Provost ... Dr. Diana CONE
35 Interim AVP & Dean of Student Svcs ... Dr. Mark WHITESEL
35 Assoc VP Student Engagement ... Dr. Ken GASSIOT
43 Executive Counsel ... Ms. Maura COPELAND
110 Assoc VP University Advancement ... Mr. William KELSO
04 Exec Associate to the President ... Ms. Leigh PRICE
07 Acting Director of Admissions ... Ms. Amy SMITH
58 Dir College of Graduate Studies ... Dr. Ashley WALKER
50 Dean Parker College of Business ... Dr. Allen AMASON
53 Dean College of Education ... Dr. Thomas KOBALLA
76 Dean Waters College of Health Prof ... Dr. Barry JOYNER
49 Dean Col of Behavioral/Social Sci ... Dr. John KRAFT
49 Dean College Arts/Humanities ... Dr. Curtis RICKER
81 Dean College Science & Mathematics ... Dr. Delana NIVENS
54 Dean AEP College of Engineering ... Dr. Mohammad DAVOUD
51 Exec Director Continuing Educ ... Dr. Belkis CAPELES
69 Dean JPH College of Public Health ... Dr. R. Gregory EVANS
62 Dean University Library ... Dr. Bede MITCHELL
88 Dir NCAA Compliance ... Mr. Keith ROUGHTON
116 Chief Auditor ... Ms. Jana BRILEY
26 Interim VP Communications & Mktg ... Dr. John LESTER
121 Director Academic Success Center ... Dr. Cathy ROBERTS-COOPER
37 Director Financial Aid ... Ms. Tracey MINGO
06 Interim Registrar ... Mr. Wallace BROWN
109 Assoc VP Auxiliary Services ... Mr. Edward D. MILLS
21 Assoc VP Finance ... Mr. Justin JANNEY
15 Assoc VP Human Resources ... Ms. Rebecca CARROLL
41 Athletic Director ... Mr. Tom KLEINLEIN
18 Assoc VP Facilities ... Ms. Katie TWINING
19 Director Public Safety ... Ms. Laura MCCULLOUGH
36 Director Career Services ... Mr. Glenn GIBNEY
38 Director Counseling Services ... Dr. Jodi K. CALDWELL
23 Director Health Services ... Ms. Elissa NORRIS
39 Exec Director University Housing ... Mr. Peter BLUTREICH
28 Dir Multicultural Student Center ... Ms. Takeshia BROWN
88 Dir Leadership/Outreach ... Ms. Jodi KENNEDY
88 Director Advancement IT ... Ms. Jill GERIG
29 Director Alumni Relations ... Mr. Wendell TOMPKINS, JR.
88 Director Botanic Garden ... Ms. Carolyn ALTMAN
14 Director Technical Services ... Mr. Joey REEVES
90 Director Learning Tech Support ... Ms. Pam CULBERSON
88 Director Museum ... Dr. Brent THARP
88 Director Wildlife Educ/Raptor Ctr ... Mr. Steven M. HEIN
96 Director of Procurement & Contract ... Vacant
22 Interim Dir Equal Opp/Title IX ... Ms. Amber CULPEPPER
89 Director First-Year Experience ... Dr. Chris CAPLINGER
92 Director Univ Honors Program ... Dr. Steven ENGEL
119 Chief Information Tech Security Ofc ... Vacant
88 Director Centers for Teaching & Tec ... Dr. Nancy REMLER
22 Dir Stdnt Affs/Disability Res Ctr ... Vacant
102 Director Foundation Acct ... Ms. Tina ADAMS
100 Chief of Staff & External Affairs ... Ms. Annalee ASHLEY
104 Director IPS/Study Abroad ... Dr. Dorothee MERTZ-WEIGEL
108 Director Institutional Assessment ... Dr. Teresa FLATEBY
25 Dir Research Svcs/Sponsored Program ... Ms. Bruxanne HEIN
44 Director Annual Giving ... Ms. Gloria GOOSBY
86 Director Government Relations ... Ms. Annalee ASHLEY

† Part of the University System of Georgia.

Georgia Southwestern State University (D)

800 GA Southwestern State Univ Dr,
Americus GA 31709-4693
County: Sumter FICE Identification: 001573
Unit ID: 139764
Telephone: (877) 871-4594 Carnegie Class: Masters/M
FAX Number: N/A Calendar System: Semester
URL: www.gsw.edu
Established: 1906 Annual Undergrad Tuition & Fees (In-State): $5,381
Enrollment: 3,052 Coed
Affiliation or Control: State IRS Status: 501(c)3
Highest Offering: Beyond Master's But Less Than Doctorate
Accreditation: SC, CAEPN, NURSE

01 President ... Dr. Neal R. WEAVER
05 Vice President Academic Affairs ... Dr. Suzanne R. SMITH
10 Vice Pres Business & Finance ... Mr. W. Cody KING
32 VP for Student Engagement & Success ... Dr. Laura D. BOREN
84 Asst VP Enroll Mgmt/Dir Admiss ... Dr. Gaye HAYES
09 Director Institutional Research ... Dr. Lisa A. COOPER
08 Dean Library Services ... Ms. Ru STORY-HUFFMAN
13 Dir Information Technology/CIO ... Mr. Royce HACKETT
102 Asst VP for Univ Advance/GSW Found ... Mr. Stephen SNYDER
06 Registrar ... Ms. Krista SMITH
36 Director Career Services Center ... Ms. Sandra FOWLER
37 Director Student Financial Aid ... Dr. Angela V. BRYANT
26 Director Marketing & Communications ... Ms. Chelsea COLLINS
88 Dir Student Rights/Responsibility ... Dr. Darcy BRAGG
41 Athletic Director ... Mr. Mike LEEDER
44 Annual Giving Specialist ... Ms. Kimberly COMER
15 Director of Human Resources ... Ms. Gena WILSON
19 Director of Public Safety ... Mr. Michael TRACY
20 Interim AVP of Academic Affairs ... Dr. Bryan P. DAVIS
38 Asst Director of Counseling ... Ms. Alma G. KEITA
96 Director of Purchasing ... Ms. Michelle W. UNDERWOOD
04 Exec Assistant to the President ... Ms. Terry THORPE

† Part of the University System of Georgia.

Georgia State University (E)

PO Box 3999, Atlanta GA 30302-3999
County: Fulton FICE Identification: 001574
Unit ID: 139940
Telephone: (404) 413-2000 Carnegie Class: DU-Highest
FAX Number: (404) 413-1380 Calendar System: Semester
URL: www.gsu.edu
Established: 1913 Annual Undergrad Tuition & Fees (In-State): $9,112
Enrollment: 32,816 Coed
Affiliation or Control: State IRS Status: 501(c)3
Highest Offering: Doctorate
Accreditation: SC, ADNUR, ART, CACREP, CEA, CLPSY, COARC, COPSY, DH, DIETC, EXSC, HSA, IPSY, LAW, MUS, NURSE, OT, PH, PTA, SCPSY, SP, SPAA, SW

01 President ... Dr. Mark P. BECKER
05 Sr VP Academic Affairs & Provost ... Dr. Wendy F. HENSEL
10 Sr VP Finance & Administration ... Dr. Jerry J. RACKLIFFE
84 Sr VP Enroll Mgmt & Student Success ... Dr. Timothy M. RENICK
12 Dean Perimeter College ... Dr. Nancy P. KROPF
46 Int VP Research/Economic Dev ... Dr. Michael P. ERIKSEN
32 VP Student Engagement & Programs ... Dr. Allison CALHOUN-BROWN
30 Vice President Development ... Mr. Walter T. MASSEY
26 VP PR & Mktg Communications ... Mr. Don HALE
43 University Attorney ... Dr. Kerry L. HEYWARD
49 Dean Arts & Sciences ... Dr. Sara ROSEN
50 Dean Business ... Dr. Richard D. PHILLIPS
53 Dean Education & Human Development ... Dr. Paul A. ALBERTO
66 Int Dean Nursing/Health Professions ... Dr. Huanbiao MO
69 Interim Dean Public Health ... Dr. Rodney LYN
61 Interim Dean Law ... Dr. Leslie WOLF
80 Dean Policy Studies ... Dr. Sally WALLACE
92 Dean Honors College ... Dr. Larry S. BERMAN
08 Dean Libraries ... Mr. Jeff STEELY
58 Assoc Provost Grad Programs ... Dr. Lisa P. ARMISTEAD
09 Assoc Provost Inst Effectiveness ... Dr. Michael GALCHINSKY
82 Assc Prov International Initiatives ... Dr. Wolfgang SCHLOER
20 Assoc Provost Faculty Affairs ... Dr. Kavita PANDIT
88 Assistant Provost Admin Operations ... Mr. Christopher D. HILL
45 Assoc VP Research Integrity ... Dr. Brenda J. CHAPMAN
13 Chief Innovation Officer for IT ... Mr. Phil VENTIMIGLIA
18 Assoc VP Facilities ... Mr. Ramesh VAKAMUDI
21 Assoc Vice President Finance ... Ms. Elizabeth R. JONES
21 Assoc VP Finance & Comptroller ... Mr. Bruce R. SPRATT
88 Assoc VP Central Development ... Ms. Tabatha MICHEL
110 Assoc VP Constituent Programs Dev ... Vacant
102 Assoc VP GSU Foundation ... Mr. Dale J. PALMER
35 Interim Dean of Students ... Ms. Lanette BROWN
27 Assoc VP Public Relations ... Ms. Andrea JONES
07 Asst VP Undergraduate Admissions ... Mr. Scott M. BURKE
124 Asst VP Student Retention ... Dr. Allison CALHOUN-BROWN
29 Asst VP Alumni Relations ... Ms. Christina C. MILLION
15 Asst VP Human Resources ... Ms. Linda J. NELSON
22 Asst VP Opp Dev/Diversity Educ ... Ms. Linda J. NELSON
19 Asst VP/Chief University Police ... Mr. Joseph SPILLANE
06 Registrar ... Ms. Tarrah N. MIRUS
85 Dir Intl Students/Scholars Svcs ... Ms. Heather L. HOUSLEY
39 Interim Director University Housing ... Ms. Shannon COREY
38 Director Psychological & Health Svc ... Dr. Jill LEE-BARBER
28 Director Diversity Programs ... Mr. John R. DAY
88 Director Application Engineering ... Mr. John M. BANDY, JR.
14 Director Technology Engineering ... Mr. Keith E. CAMPBELL
36 Director University Career Svcs ... Ms. Catherine NEINER
37 Director Financial Aid ... Vacant
96 Director of Business Services ... Mr. Michael E. DAVIDSON
116 Dir Univ Auditing & Advisory Svcs ... Ms. Wanda L. RILEY
88 Director Emergency Management ... Mr. Keith P. SUMAS
31 Director Govt & Community Affairs ... Ms. Julia M. KERLIN
41 Athletic Director ... Mr. Charles G. COBB
04 Assistant to the President ... Ms. Ethel B. WRIGHT

† Part of the University System of Georgia.

Gordon State College (F)

419 College Dr., Barnesville GA 30204-1746
County: Lamar FICE Identification: 001575
Unit ID: 139968
Telephone: (678) 359-5555 Carnegie Class: Bac/Assoc-Mixed
FAX Number: (678) 359-5080 Calendar System: Semester
URL: www.gordonstate.edu
Established: 1852 Annual Undergrad Tuition & Fees (In-State): $3,828
Enrollment: 3,986 Coed
Affiliation or Control: State IRS Status: 501(c)3
Highest Offering: Baccalaureate
Accreditation: SC, ADNUR, NUR

01 President .... Dr. Kirk NOOKS
05 Provost & VP Academic Affairs .... Dr. Jeffery KNIGHTON
10 VP Finance and Administration .... Ms. Megan DAVIDSON
32 VP Enrollment Mgmt/Student Affairs .... Dr. John HEAD
111 VP Institutional Advancement .... Ms. Montrese ADGER FULLER
20 Asst VP Innovative Education and SI .... Dr. Ric CALHOUN
08 Library Director .... Vacant
09 Director of Institutional Research .... Mr. Britt LIFSEY
49 Dean School of Arts & Sciences .... Dr. Barry KICKLIGHTER
53 Dean School of Education .... Dr. Joseph JONES
66 Dean School of Nursing .... Dr. Victor VILCHIZ
121 Assistant VP Academic Excellence .... Mr. Peter J. HIGGINS
21 Controller .... Mrs. April MASON
15 Director of Human Resources .... Ms. Wendy BYRD
113 Bursar .... Mr. Kenneth HUTTO
114 Dir of Budgets & Aux Operations .... Vacant
18 Director of Facilities .... Mr. Richard VEREEN
37 Senior Director of Financial Aid .... Mrs. Jody DEFORE
13 Director of Information Technology .... Vacant
19 Director of Public Safety .... Chief Jeff MASON
41 Athletic Director .... Mr. Gary SHARPE
38 Director of Counseling Services .... Ms. Alicia DORTON
39 Director of Residence Life .... Ms. Tonya R. COLEMAN
35 Int Director of Student Activities .... Mr. Jeremy MONROE
06 Registrar .... Mrs. Kristi HAYES
30 Development Officer .... Mr. Steve ARGO
26 Chief Public Information Officer .... Mrs. Tamara BOATWRIGHT
40 Bookstore Manager .... Mrs. Connie H. WADE
04 Special Assistant to the President .... Ms. LaSha SANDERS
07 Assistant Director of Admissions .... Mr. Justin MATHIS
103 Director of Career Services .... Dr. Tonya MOORE
29 Alumni & Annual Fund Administrator .... Mr. Austin SHIPPAM

† Part of the University System of Georgia.

Gupton Jones College of Funeral Service (A)

5141 Snapfinger Woods Drive, Decatur GA 30035-4022
County: DeKalb FICE Identification: 010771
Unit ID: 139995
Telephone: (770) 593-2257 Carnegie Class: Spec 2-yr-A&S
FAX Number: (770) 593-1891 Calendar System: Quarter
URL: www.gupton-jones.edu
Established: 1920 Annual Undergrad Tuition & Fees: $11,700
Enrollment: 249 Coed
Affiliation or Control: Independent Non-Profit IRS Status: 501(c)3
Highest Offering: Associate Degree
Accreditation: FUSER

01 President .... Ms. Hope INGLEHART
05 Campus Dean .... Mr. Mark PALUMBO
06 Registrar .... Ms. Lisa STAPLES

Gwinnett College (B)

4230 Highway 29, Suite 11, Lilburn GA 30047-3447
County: Gwinnett FICE Identification: 025830
Unit ID: 140003
Telephone: (770) 381-7200 Carnegie Class: Assoc/HVT-Mix Trad/Non
FAX Number: (770) 381-0454 Calendar System: Other
URL: www.gwinnettcollege.com
Established: 1976 Annual Undergrad Tuition & Fees: $9,925
Enrollment: 252 Coed
Affiliation or Control: Proprietary IRS Status: Proprietary
Highest Offering: Associate Degree
Accreditation: ACICS

01 President .... Mr. Michael DAVIS
05 Director of Education .... Ms. Lisa MCLARIO

Gwinnett College-Sandy Springs (C)

6690 Roswell Rd, NE, Ste 2200, Sandy Springs GA 30328
County: Fulton FICE Identification: 034183
Unit ID: 425250
Telephone: (770) 457-2021 Carnegie Class: Spec 2-yr-Health
FAX Number: (404) 574-2234 Calendar System: Other
URL: www.risingspirit.edu
Established: 1994 Annual Undergrad Tuition & Fees: N/A
Enrollment: 114 Coed
Affiliation or Control: Proprietary IRS Status: Proprietary
Highest Offering: Associate Degree
Accreditation: ACCSC

01 President .... Mr. Michael DAVIS
04 Assistant to President .... Mr. Ty DAVIS

Gwinnett College-Marietta (D)

1130 North Chase Parkway, Suite 100, Marietta GA 30067
County: Cobb FICE Identification: 038044
Unit ID: 444714
Telephone: (770) 859-9779 Carnegie Class: Spec 2-yr-Health
FAX Number: (770) 859-9778 Calendar System: Quarter
URL: www.medtech.edu
Established: Annual Undergrad Tuition & Fees: N/A
Enrollment: 115 Coed
Affiliation or Control: Proprietary IRS Status: Proprietary
Highest Offering: Associate Degree
Accreditation: COE

01 Campus President .... Mr. Michael DAVIS

Gwinnett Technical College (E)

5150 Sugarloaf Parkway, Lawrenceville GA 30043-5702
County: Gwinnett FICE Identification: 022884
Unit ID: 140012
Telephone: (770) 962-7580 Carnegie Class: Assoc/HVT-Mix Trad/Non
FAX Number: (770) 962-7985 Calendar System: Semester
URL: www.gwinnetttech.edu
Established: 1984 Annual Undergrad Tuition & Fees (In-State): $2,972
Enrollment: 8,321 Coed
Affiliation or Control: State IRS Status: 501(c)3
Highest Offering: Associate Degree
Accreditation: SC, ACFEI, ADNUR, CAHIIM, COARC, CVT, DA, DMS, EMT, MAC, RAD, SURGT

01 President .... Dr. D. Glen CANNON
05 VP of Academic Affairs .... Ms. Rebecca ALEXANDER
111 VP of Inst Advancement .... Mr. Charles MCKINNON
32 VP of Student Affairs .... Dr. Julie POST
103 VP Economic Development .... Mr. Melvin EVERSON
13 VP Technology & Operations .... Mr. Galen MARTIN
15 VP of Human Resources .... Ms. LaShanta' COX
53 VP of Adult Education .... Ms. Stephanie ROOKS
11 VP Administrative Services .... Ms. Sonya MCDANIEL
19 Chief of Campus Police & Security .... Mr. Mike BLOUIN
84 Exec Dir Enrollment Processing .... Ms. Betsy HARRIS-BRACKETT
07 Exec Dir Enrollment Support .... Ms. Janelle PIERCE
08 Director of Library Services .... Ms. Deborah GEORGE
09 Dir Inst Research & Effectiveness .... Dr. Carla MORELON
36 Director of Career Services .... Ms. Ave MILLER
37 Director of Financial Aid .... Ms. Andra PETERSON
06 Registrar .... Mr. Brad THOMAS
04 Exec Assistant to the President .... Ms. Melissa FLANAGAN

Helms College (F)

5171 Eisenhower Pkwy, Macon GA 31206-5309
County: Bibb FICE Identification: 042064
Unit ID: 481155
Telephone: (478) 471-4394 Carnegie Class: Spec 2-yr-A&S
FAX Number: N/A Calendar System: Quarter
URL: helms.edu
Established: 2007 Annual Undergrad Tuition & Fees: $13,460
Enrollment: 256 Coed
Affiliation or Control: Independent Non-Profit IRS Status: 501(c)3
Highest Offering: Associate Degree
Accreditation: CNCE

01 President .... Mr. James STIFF
32 SVP Student Svcs/Fin Aid/Admission .... Dr. Gary MARKOWITZ
05 Provost/Vice Pres Academic Affairs .... Dr. Paul BAO
84 AVP Enrollment Management .... Mr. Andrew ROBINSON
36 Vice Pres Career Services .... Vacant
07 Director of Admissions .... Vacant

Herzing University (G)

50 Hurt Plaza SE, Suite 400, Atlanta GA 30303
Telephone: (404) 816-4533 FICE Identification: 020897
Accreditation: &NH, NURSE

† Regional accreditation is carried under the parent institution in Madison, WI.

Interactive College of Technology (H)

5303 New Peachtree Road, Chamblee GA 30341-2818
County: DeKalb FICE Identification: 022843
Unit ID: 138655
Telephone: (770) 216-2960 Carnegie Class: Spec 2-yr-Other
FAX Number: (678) 287-3474 Calendar System: Semester
URL: www.ict.edu
Established: 1986 Annual Undergrad Tuition & Fees: $9,890
Enrollment: 536 Coed
Affiliation or Control: Proprietary IRS Status: Proprietary
Highest Offering: Associate Degree
Accreditation: COE

00 Chief Executive Officer .... Mr. Elmer R. SMITH
01 President .... Mr. Thomas A. BLAIR
03 Executive Vice President/CFO .... Mr. Michael K. POWER
12 Campus Director Pasadena Texas .... Mr. Keith CRAVENS
12 Campus Dir SW Houston Texas .... Ms. Cynthia BRYSON
12 Campus Dir North Houston Texas .... Mr. Valory HEMPHILL
12 Campus Director Newport KY .... Mr. William K. MCGUIRE
12 Campus Director Morrow GA .... Mr. Greg KOCH
12 Campus Administrator Gainesville GA .... Ms. Doug COLE
12 Vice-President/Campus Director .... Ms. Jo Ann KOCH
88 Senior Administrative Assistant .... Ms. Liesa PEAVY
26 Vice President/Marketing .... Mr. Jim C. HARRIS
36 Director Student Placement .... Mr. Andre GIPSON
04 Administrative Asst to President .... Ms. Karen A. MILLER
06 Registrar .... Ms. Rosalind HOLT
07 Director of Admissions .... Ms. Larisa I. NAYDENOVA
37 Director Student Financial Aid .... Ms. Nataliya CHORNIY

Interactive College of Technology (I)

2323-C Browns Bridge Road, Gainesville GA 30504
Telephone: (678) 456-0550 Identification: 770533
Accreditation: COE

Interactive College of Technology (J)

1580 Southdale Parkway, Morrow GA 30260
Telephone: (770) 960-1298 Identification: 770534
Accreditation: COE

Interdenominational Theological Center (K)

700 Martin L. King, Jr. Drive, SW, Atlanta GA 30314-4143
County: Fulton FICE Identification: 001568
Unit ID: 140146
Telephone: (404) 527-7700 Carnegie Class: Spec-4-yr-Faith
FAX Number: (404) 527-0901 Calendar System: Semester
URL: www.itc.edu
Established: 1958 Annual Graduate Tuition & Fees: N/A
Enrollment: 295 Coed
Affiliation or Control: Interdenominational IRS Status: 501(c)3
Highest Offering: Doctorate; No Undergraduates
Accreditation: SC, THEOL

01 President .... Dr. Edward LORENZA WHEELER
05 VP for Academic Services/Provost .... Dr. Maisha HANDY
10 Int Vice Pres Financial Services .... Mr. Thomas POITIER
111 Int VP Institutional Advancement .... Ms. Staphea CAMPBELL
06 Registrar .... Ms. Arlene V. CLARKE
32 AVP Student Affairs .... Dr. Catherine BINUYA
37 Financial Aid Director .... Mr. Johnny NIMES
15 Chief Human Resources Officer .... Ms. Idell HENDERSON
07 Director of Admissions/Recruitment .... Ms. Natasha JORDAN
42 Chaplain .... Dr. Willie F. GOODMAN
108 Director Institutional Assessment .... Dr. Itihari TOURE

Kennesaw State University (L)

585 Cobb Avenue NW, MD #0101,
Kennesaw GA 30144-5563
County: Cobb FICE Identification: 001577
Unit ID: 486840
Telephone: (470) 578-6033 Carnegie Class: DU-Higher
FAX Number: (470) 578-9117 Calendar System: Semester
URL: www.kennesaw.edu
Established: 1963 Annual Undergrad Tuition & Fees (In-State): $6,347
Enrollment: 35,846 Coed
Affiliation or Control: State IRS Status: 501(c)3
Highest Offering: Doctorate
Accreditation: SC, ART, CAEPN, CGTECH, CONST, CSHSE, MUS, NURSE, SPAA, SW, THEA

01 President .... Dr. Pamela WHITTEN
10 Chief Business Officer .... Ms. Julie PETERSON
108 Interim VP Inst Effectiveness .... Ms. Danielle BUEHRER
05 Provost/VP Academic Affairs .... Dr. Kathy S. SCHWAIG
111 VP Advancement/CEO Univ Foundation .... Mr. Lance BURCHETT
32 Vice Pres Student Affairs .... Dr. Kathleen C. WHITE
09 VP for Research .... Dr. Tricia CHASTAIN
26 VP for External Affairs and COS .... Mr. Alex MCGEE
27 AVP Marketing/Communications .... Ms. Alice WHEELWRIGHT
88 VP Economic Dev/Cmty Engagement .... Vacant
20 Senior Vice Provost Academic Affs .... Vacant
43 VP/Chief Legal Affairs Officer .... Ms. Nwakaego NKUMEH
20 Assoc Vice Pres for Curriculum .... Dr. Pamela COLE
97 Dean University College .... Dr. Lynn DISBROW
15 AVP Human Resources .... Ms. Karen MCDONNELL
13 Chief Information Officer .... Mr. Jeff DELANEY
84 Vice Pres Enrollment Svcs .... Ms. Brenda STOPHER
106 AVP Technology Enhanced Learning .... Vacant
88 AVP Strategic Comm/Issues Mgmt .... Ms. Tammy DEMEL
88 Asst VP University Comm .... Mr. James COOPER
08 Asst Vice Pres for Library Services .... Dr. J. David EVANS
18 Asst Vice Pres Facilities Services .... Mr. Michael GEBEKE
09 Asst VP Institutional Research .... Dr. Phaedra CORSO
79 Dean Humanities/Social Science .... Dr. Shawn LONG
81 Int Dean Science & Mathematics .... Dr. Don MCGAREY
53 Dean Bagwell College of Education .... Dr. Cynthia REED
50 Int Dean Coles College of Business .... Dr. Robin CHERAMIE LATIN
76 Dean WellStar Col Health/Human Svcs .... Dr. Mark TILLMAN
57 Dean College of the Arts .... Dr. Ivan PULINKALA
48 Dean Architecture/Construction Mgmt .... Dr. Khalid SIDDIQI
77 Dean Col Computing/Software Eng .... Dr. Jon PRESTON
58 Dean Graduate College .... Dr. Mike DISHMAN
92 Dean Honors College .... Dr. Rita BAILEY
51 Int Dean Continuing/Prof Educ .... Dr. Timothy BLUMENTRITT
54 Int Dean of Engineering/Eng Tech .... Dr. Renee BUTLER
80 Dir Sch Government/Intl Affairs .... Dr. Kerwin SWINT
35 Assoc VP Student Affairs .... Dr. Michael L. SANSEVIRO
121 Assoc VP/Dir Student Success Svcs .... Dr. Bob J. MATTOX
28 Chief Diversity Officer .... Ms. Sylvia CAREY-BUTLER
06 Registrar .... Ms. Ana EDWARDS
91 Exec Dir Enterprise Systems & Svcs .... Vacant
37 Director Student Financial Aid .... Mr. Rondall H. DAY
07 Exec Dir Undergraduate Programs .... Vacant
25 Director Procurement & Contracting .... Vacant
88 Exec Dir Internships & Coops .... Ms. Ana BAIDA
41 Director of Athletics .... Mr. Milton OVERTON
29 Int Director Alumni Relations .... Mr. Steve RUTHSATZ
19 AVP Public Safety/Chief of Police .... Mr. Edward STEPHENS
100 Exec Admin to Pres/Chf of Protocol .... Mr. James TAYLOR
104 Education Abroad Program Coord .... Ms. Nicole MEANOR
105 Dir Web Services/Mobile Development .... Mr. Chris WARD
39 Director University Housing .... Mr. Christopher BRUNO

86 Assoc VP of Government Relations ......Ms. Julia AYERS
116 Chief Internal Auditor ......Vacant
88 Director of Financial Compliance ......Mr. Robert BRIDGES

† Part of the University System of Georgia.

LaGrange College (A)

601 Broad Street, La Grange GA 30240-2999
County: Troup FICE Identification: 001578
Unit ID: 140234
Telephone: (706) 880-8000 Carnegie Class: Bac-Diverse
FAX Number: (706) 880-8358 Calendar System: 4/1/4
URL: www.lagrange.edu
Established: 1831 Annual Undergrad Tuition & Fees: $30,500
Enrollment: 1,049 Coed
Affiliation or Control: United Methodist IRS Status: 501(c)3
Highest Offering: Master's
Accreditation: SC, ACBSP, NUR

01 President ......Dr. Dan MCALEXANDER
04 Executive Assistant to President ......Mrs. Carla RHODES
41 VP of Athletics ......Mrs. Jennifer D. CLAYBROOK
05 VP Academic Affairs ......Dr. Karen AUBREY
32 VP of Student Engagement ......Dr. Brian A. CARLISLE
06 Registrar ......Mr. Todd K. PRATER
08 Director of Library Services ......Ms. Kelly ANSLEY
09 Director Inst Effectiveness ......Dr. Carol YIN
36 Director Career Development Center ......Dr. Karen PRUETT
38 Director Counseling Center ......Mrs. Pamela TREMBLAY
20 Associate Provost ......Dr. Maranah SAUTER
39 Director Res Educ & Housing ......Vacant
30 VP of External Relations ......Mrs. Rebecca ROTH NICKS
26 Sr Director Communications/Mktg ......Mr. Dean A. HARTMAN
37 Director Student Financial Aid ......Mrs. Michelle REEVES
110 Director of Development ......Mr. Mark E. DAVIS
29 Director Alumni & Cmty Relations ......Mrs. Martha W. PIRKLE
84 VP of Enrollment ......Mr. Joseph C. MILLER
112 Major Gift Officer ......Vacant
07 Director of Admission ......Vacant
105 Asst Director Communications & Mktg ......Vacant
10 VP of Finance & Operations ......Ms. Deborah P. HALL
21 Director of Finance ......Mrs. Patti D. HOXSIE
15 VP of Human Resources ......Mrs. Dawn C. COKER
18 Manager Facilities/Physical Plant ......Mr. Michael CONIGLIO
19 Director of Security ......Mr. Michael A. THOMAS
13 Sr Director Information Technology ......Mr. James BLACKWOOD
42 Director Spiritual Life & Chaplain ......Dr. Adam ROBERTS
106 Director Online Instruction ......Dr. Jon ERNSTBERGER
91 Database Administrator ......Vacant
88 Events Coordinator ......Ms. Tammy ROGERS

Lanier Technical College (B)

2990 Landrum Education Drive, Oakwood GA 30566-3405
County: Hall FICE Identification: 005254
Unit ID: 140243
Telephone: (770) 533-7000 Carnegie Class: Assoc/HVT-High Trad
FAX Number: (678) 989-3107 Calendar System: Semester
URL: www.laniertech.edu
Established: 1964 Annual Undergrad Tuition & Fees (In-State): $3,336
Enrollment: 3,681 Coed
Affiliation or Control: State IRS Status: 501(c)3
Highest Offering: Associate Degree
Accreditation: SC, DA, DH, EMT, MAC, PTAA, RAD, SURGT

01 President ......Dr. Ray PERREN
03 Executive Vice President ......Mr. Tim MCDONALD
103 Vice President Economic Development ......Mr. Carl ROGERS
05 Vice President Academic Affairs ......Mrs. Donna BRINSON
45 Vice President IE ......Dr. Joanne P. TOLLESON
32 Vice President Student Affairs ......Ms. Nancy BEAVER
10 Vice Pres Administrative Services ......Mr. Les SALTER
13 Vice Pres Information Technology ......Mr. Anthony HARDY
04 Executive Assistant to President ......Ms. Karen MINOR
75 Dean Business/Public Safety/Profess ......Ms. Beth HEFNER
54 Dean Advanced Tech/Engr ......Dr. John DUNBAR
72 Dean of Applied Technology ......Mr. Christian TETZLAFF
97 Dean of General Education ......Ms. Kathy ALDEN
76 Dean of Allied Health ......Dr. Deanne COLLINS
12 Dean of Barrow Campus ......Mr. Chip REYNOLDS
12 Dean of Dawson Campus ......Mr. Troy LINSEY
12 Dean of Jackson Campus ......Dr. Howard LEDFORD
09 Dir of Institutional Effectiveness ......Mr. Brad GADBERRY
111 Vice Pres Institutional Advancement ......Ms. Lauren ARMOUR
26 Director of Marketing ......Mr. Dave PARRISH
07 Director of Admissions ......Ms. Holly BATES
06 Registrar ......Ms. Mandy ORR
37 Director Student Financial Aid ......Ms. Angela TATE
21 Director Administrative Services ......Ms. Mary FOWLER
15 Director of Human Resources ......Ms. Jill CANTRELL
18 Director of Facilities ......Mr. Mike SCHMIDT
36 Career Services Specialist ......Ms. Sarah JOLLY
22 Disability Services Coordinator ......Ms. Allison HAYNES
08 Library Services Director ......Ms. Kathryn S. THOMPSON
19 College Police Chief ......Mr. Jeff STRICKLAND
96 Purchasing Agent ......Ms. Kathy PHAGAN

Life University (C)

1269 Barclay Circle, Marietta GA 30060-2996
County: Cobb FICE Identification: 020748
Unit ID: 140252
Telephone: (770) 426-2600 Carnegie Class: Spec-4-yr-Other Health
FAX Number: (770) 429-4819 Calendar System: Quarter
URL: www.life.edu
Established: 1974 Annual Undergrad Tuition & Fees: $12,696
Enrollment: 2,619 Coed
Affiliation or Control: Independent Non-Profit IRS Status: 501(c)3
Highest Offering: Doctorate
Accreditation: SC, #CAATE, CHIRO, DIETD, DIETI

01 President ......Dr. Rob SCOTT
00 Chancellor ......Dr. Guy F. RIEKEMAN
05 VP Academic Affairs ......Dr. Tim GROSS
10 Exec VP of Finance ......Mr. William JARR
41 Director of Athletics ......Ms. Jayme PENDERGAST
13 Chief Information Officer ......Mr. John ALTIKULAC
15 Interim Dir Human Resources ......Mr. James BASKETT
88 Dean College of Chiropractic ......Dr. Leslie KING
20 Dean College of Grad and Undergrad ......Dr. Jana W. HOLWICK
104 VP Global Initiatives ......Dr. John DOWNES
14 Director Information Technology ......Mr. Thorton MUIR
58 Assoc Dean Grad & Undergrad Studies ......Dr. Michael D. SMITH
88 Assoc Dean College of Chiropractic ......Dr. Michael CLUSSERATH
32 Dean of Students ......Dr. Janna BREDESON
106 Dean Online Education ......Dr. Richard BELCASTRO
23 Associate Dean of Clinics ......Dr. Bernadette LAVENDER
97 Assistant Dean CGUS ......Mr. Raj PRADHAN
59 Assistant Dean CGUS ......Dr. Denise PICKETT-BERNARD
82 Assistant Dean CGUS ......Dr. Cory VIEHL
88 Associate Dean ......Dr. Mary Catherine FAUST
81 Chair Basic Sciences ......Dr. Mamie WARE
21 Controller ......Ms. Jo Ann MILLER
101 Board Secretary ......Ms. Nita LOONEY
114 Budget Director ......Ms. Amy MCILVANE
84 Executive Director Enrollment ......Ms. Robyn STANLEY
35 Exec Dir of Student Services ......Ms. Jennifer VALTOS
18 Director Facilities/Physical Plant ......Mr. Larry RIDDLE
07 Regional Director Outreach ......Dr. Dawn CADWALLADER
27 Director of Marketing ......Ms. Shelly BATCHER
88 Dir of Student Administrative Svcs ......Ms. Melissa WATERS
08 Director of Library ......Ms. Karen PRESTON
88 Exec Director Neurolife Institute ......Dr. Micheal HALL
88 Executive Director Level III Clinic ......Dr. Mark MARKHAM
37 Director Student Financial Aid ......Ms. Jessica MAGAZU
44 Director of Advancement Services ......Ms. Lauren NIELSON
108 Director of Inst Effectiveness ......Dr. Vince ERARIO
09 Director of Institutional Research ......Dr. Howard WRIGHT
46 Director of Sponsored Research ......Dr. Olivia SCRIVEN
06 Registrar ......Ms. Heather HOFFMAN
29 Director of Alumni Relations ......Ms. Mary Ellen LEFFARD
121 Director of University Advising ......Ms. Tameka GLASS
68 Director Sports Science Institute ......Dr. Mark KOVACS
121 Director Student Success ......Dr. Lisa RUBIN
88 Director CCHOP ......Dr. Susan SHARKEY
88 Director Chiropractic Research ......Dr. Stephanie SULLIVAN
30 Director of Development ......Ms. Erin DANCER
111 VP of University Advancement ......Ms. Kristen BARBARICS
07 Director of Admissions Operations ......Ms. Detrenyona CHESTER
88 Director Academic Support ......Dr. Nicoly MYLES
88 Director of Clinic Services ......Dr. Mark MAIYER
88 Director Community Outreach Clinics ......Dr. Steven MIRTSCHINK
88 Director CETL ......Mr. William WATSON
88 Director of the Harris Center ......Dr. Krista BOLINE
89 Assistant Dean Student Engagement ......Ms. Jennifer STROBLE
88 Director Enrollment Events ......Ms. Nakita SWANIGAN
88 Director CHOP ......Dr. Mark FERDARKO
36 Director of Career Services ......Ms. Susan DUDT
32 VP for Student Services ......Dr. Marc SCHNEIDER
88 Director Wellness Center ......Ms. Patti BANKS
88 Director Professional Relations ......Dr. Cierra HOFFMAN
113 Director Student Accounts ......Ms. Phyllis SHROPSHIRE
16 Employee Relations Officer ......Ms. Monica WARD
96 Director of Purchasing ......Mr. Mel BURTON
88 Asst Dean Community Living ......Mr. Andre CLANTON
88 Director Special Events ......Ms. Brenda BOONE
22 Director Disability Services ......Dr. Genelle HANEY
88 Director Sports Information ......Mr. William HUDSPETH
11 VP of Operations ......Mr. John MCGEE
88 Director Clinical Education ......Dr. Melissa LOSCHIAVO
07 Director Recruitment ......Ms. Erica MICHEALS
88 Director Clinical Ops Costa Rica ......Dr. Ziola STEWART
84 VP of Enrollment & Mktg ......Dr. Cynthia BOYD
26 VP of Professional Relations ......Dr. Gilles LAMARCHE
88 Presidential Liaison for Ext Rels ......Dr. Gerald CLUM
88 Chair Chiropractic Sciences ......Dr. Lydia DEVER
88 Chair Clinical Sciences ......Dr. Timothy GOODING
88 Director of Post Graduate Educ ......Ms. Kathleen BANNISTER

Luther Rice College and Seminary (D)

3038 Evans Mill Road, Lithonia GA 30038-2454
County: DeKalb FICE Identification: 031009
Unit ID: 135364
Telephone: (770) 484-1204 Carnegie Class: Spec-4-yr-Faith
FAX Number: (770) 484-1155 Calendar System: Semester
URL: www.lutherrice.edu
Established: 1962 Annual Undergrad Tuition & Fees: $7,616
Enrollment: 1,022 Coed
Affiliation or Control: Independent Non-Profit IRS Status: 501(c)3
Highest Offering: Doctorate
Accreditation: BI, TRACS

01 President ......Dr. James L. FLANAGAN
10 Vice President Financial Affairs ......Mr. Louis B. HARDCASTLE
05 Vice President for Academic Affairs ......Dr. Evan POSEY
58 Director Doctor of Ministry Program ......Dr. Ron K. COBB

11 Executive Vice President ......Mr. Steven STEINHILBER
13 Chief Info Technology Officer (CIO) ......Mr. Ken STOKES

Mercer University (E)

1501 Mercer University Drive, Macon GA 31207-0003
County: Bibb FICE Identification: 001580
Unit ID: 140447
Telephone: (478) 301-2700 Carnegie Class: DU-Higher
FAX Number: (478) 301-2108 Calendar System: Semester
URL: www.mercer.edu
Established: 1833 Annual Undergrad Tuition & Fees: $36,894
Enrollment: 8,653 Coed
Affiliation or Control: Independent Non-Profit IRS Status: 501(c)3
Highest Offering: Doctorate
Accreditation: SC, ARCPA, CACREP, CLPSY, LAW, MED, MFCD, MUS, NURSE, PH, PHAR, PTA, THEOL

01 President and CEO ......Mr. William D. UNDERWOOD
125 Chancellor ......Dr. R. Kirby GODSEY
10 Executive VP for Admin & Finance ......Dr. James S. NETHERTON
100 Sr VP Mktg Comm & Chief of Staff ......Mr. Larry D. BRUMLEY
05 Provost ......Dr. D. Scott DAVIS
88 VP for Strategic Initiatives ......Ms. Kellie APPEL
111 Sr VP for University Advancement ......Mr. John A. PATTERSON
111 Senior AVP for Advancement ......Mr. Allen S. LONDON
84 Sr Vice Pres Enrollment Management ......Dr. Penny L. ELKINS
43 Vice President and General Counsel ......Mr. William G. SOLOMON
13 Assoc VP & Chief Technology Officer ......Mr. Michael R. BELOTE
41 Athletic Director ......Mr. Jim COLE
46 Sr VProv Rsrch/Dn Savannah Camp Med ......Dr. Wayne C. GLASGOW
09 Vice Provost for Inst Effectiveness ......Dr. Susan C. MALONE
21 Assoc VP Finance & Treasurer ......Ms. Julia T. DAVIS
18 Assoc Vice President for Facilities ......Mr. Russell VULLO
15 Assoc Vice Pres for Human Resources ......Ms. Rhonda W. LIDSTONE
26 Sr Asst VP Marketing Communications ......Mr. Richard L. CAMERON
37 Assoc VP Student Financial Planning ......Ms. Maria A. HAMMETT
32 VP Stdnt Affairs & Dean of Students ......Dr. Doug R. PEARSON
35 Assoc Dean of Student Services ......Dr. Stephen R. BROWN
39 Director of Residence Life ......Mr. Jeff TAKAC
49 Dean College of Liberal Arts ......Dr. Anita O. GUSTAFSON
61 Dean School of Law ......Ms. Cathy COX
67 Dean of Pharmacy ......Dr. Brian CRABTREE
63 Dean School of Medicine ......Dr. Jean R. SUMNER
54 Dean School of Engineering ......Dr. Laura W. LACKEY
50 Int Dean Sch of Business/Economics ......Dr. Julie PETHERBRIDGE
73 Int Dean School of Theology/Dev Dir ......Dr. C. Gregory DELOACH
53 Dean College of Education ......Dr. Thomas R. KOBALLA, JR.
66 Dean College of Nursing ......Dr. Linda A. STREIT
51 Dean Penfield College ......Dr. Priscilla R. DANHEISER
64 Dean School of Music ......Dr. C. David KEITH
76 Dean Col of Health Professions ......Dr. Lisa M. LUNDQUIST
08 Dean of University Libraries ......Dr. Jeffrey A. WALDROP
42 Univ Minister/Dean of Chapel ......Dr. Craig T. MCMAHAN
06 Registrar ......Ms. Alba RODRIGUEZ
19 Chief Police Department ......Mr. Gary COLLINS
09 Director of Institutional Research ......Ms. Sarah E. MAY
36 Director Student Placement ......Ms. Maureen SWEATMAN
38 Dir Counseling & Psychological Svcs ......Dr. Emily PIASSICK
96 Director of Purchasing ......Ms. Debra G. CANADA
04 Administrative Asst to President ......Ms. Vonne SHEFFIELD
29 AVP & Exec Dir Alumni Assn ......Ms. Jill H. KINSELLA
86 VP for Government Relations ......Mr. Hugh D. SOSEBEE, JR.
07 AVP for Enrollment Management ......Dr. Kelly L. HOLLOWAY
25 Chief Contract/Grants Administrator ......Ms. DeLaine SAMPLES

Middle Georgia State University (F)

100 University Parkway, Macon GA 31206-5145
County: Bibb FICE Identification: 007728
Unit ID: 482158
Telephone: (478) 471-2700 Carnegie Class: Bac-Diverse
FAX Number: (478) 471-2846 Calendar System: Semester
URL: www.mga.edu
Established: 1884 Annual Undergrad Tuition & Fees (In-State): $3,924
Enrollment: 7,341 Coed
Affiliation or Control: State IRS Status: 501(c)3
Highest Offering: Master's
Accreditation: SC, ADNUR, COARC, NUR, OTA

01 President ......Dr. Christopher BLAKE
05 Provost/Vice Pres Academic Affairs ......Dr. Jon ANDERSON
10 Exec VP Finance & Operations ......Ms. Nancy STROUD
32 VP Student Affairs ......Dr. Jennifer BRANNON
111 VP Univ Advancement/Exec Dir Fdn ......Mr. Ken FINCHER
20 Associate Provost ......Dr. Debra MATTHEWS
20 Associate Provost ......Dr. Deepa ARORA
79 Dean School of Arts and Letters ......Dr. Mary WEARN
100 Chief of Staff/Govt Relations Ofcr ......Ms. Ember BISHOP BENTLEY
13 Chief Information Officer ......Mr. Roger DIXON
43 Dir Legal Services/General Counsel ......Mr. Josh WATERS
26 VP Recruit/Mktg & Chief Mktg Ofcr ......Ms. Cheryl CARTY
15 Exec Dir Human Resources ......Ms. Vicky SMITH
112 Exec Dir Major and Planning Giving ......Ms. Julie DAVIS
35 Asst VP Student Affairs ......Dr. Michael STEWART
18 Asst VP Facilities ......Mr. David SIMS
19 Asst VP Risk Mgmt and Police Svcs ......Mr. Shane ROLAND
21 Controller ......Mr. Brian STANLEY
06 Registrar ......Ms. Dian MITCHELL

07 Director of Admissions .... Ms. Margo WOODHAM
29 Director Alumni Relations .... Ms. Natalie RISCHBIETER
41 Director Athletics/Rec/Wellness .... Mr. Chip SMITH
109 Director Auxiliary Services .... Mr. Ryan GREENE
40 Director Campus Stores .... Ms. Jessica HALL
38 Director Counseling .... Ms. Predita HOWARD
37 Director Financial Aid .... Ms. LeeAnn KIRKLAND
25 Director Grants and Contracts .... Ms. Barbara RATZLAFF
09 Exec Dir Institutional Research .... Dr. Michael GIBBONS
08 Director Library Services .... Ms. Tamatha LAMBERT
96 Director Purchasing .... Ms. Barbara BURNS
39 Director of Residence Life .... Mr. Brian HARRELL
12 Director Cochran/Eastman Campuses .... Mr. Henry WHITFIELD
20 Associate Provost .... Dr. Kevin CANTWELL
88 Dean Aviation .... Mr. Adon CLARK
50 Dean of Business .... Dr. Stephen MORSE
53 Dean of Education & Behavioral Sci .... Dr. David BIEK
81 Dean Health & Natural Sciences .... Dr. Tara UNDERWOOD
72 Dean Computing .... Dr. Alex KOOHANG

† Part of the University System of Georgia.

Miller-Motte Technical College (A)

621 Frontage Road NW, Augusta GA 30907

Telephone: (706) 619-2090 Identification: 770710
Accreditation: ACCSC

† Branch campus of Platt College, Tulsa, OK.

Miller-Motte Technical College (B)

1800 Box Road, Columbus GA 31907

Telephone: (706) 225-5637 Identification: 770711
Accreditation: ACCSC

† Branch campus of Platt College, Tulsa, OK.

Miller-Motte Technical College (C)

175 Tom Hill Sr Boulevard, Macon GA 31210

Telephone: (478) 257-3912 Identification: 770844
Accreditation: ACCSC

† Branch campus of Platt College, Tulsa, OK.

Morehouse College (D)

830 Westview Drive SW, Atlanta GA 30314-3773

County: Fulton FICE Identification: 001582
Unit ID: 140553
Telephone: (404) 639-0999 Carnegie Class: Bac-A&S
FAX Number: (404) 681-2650 Calendar System: Semester
URL: www.morehouse.edu
Established: 1867 Annual Undergrad Tuition & Fees: $27,576
Enrollment: 2,202 Male
Affiliation or Control: Independent Non-Profit IRS Status: 501(c)3
Highest Offering: Baccalaureate
Accreditation: SC, MUS

01 President .... Dr. David A. THOMAS
04 Sr Exec Assistant to the President .... Mrs. Samantha STEWART-ELMORE
04 Executive Asst to the President .... Ms. Nakia WASHINGTON
116 Chief Audit Officer .... Ms. Undria STALLING
05 SVP & Provost .... Dr. Michael HODGE
10 VP/Chief Financial Officer .... Mr. Gerald HECTOR
111 VP for Institutional Advancement .... Ms. Monique DOZIER
13 VP of Information Technology & CIO .... Mrs. Kimberley MARSHALL
26 VP Strategic Comm/Chief Mktg Ofcr .... Mr. Jose MALLABO
29 VP Ext Relations/Alumni Engagement .... Mr. Henry GOODGAME
43 VP Legal Affs/GC/Chief Compl Ofcr .... Mrs. Joy WHITE
19 Chief of Campus Police .... Chief Valerie DALTON
15 AVP for HR/Chief Compliance Officer .... Mrs. Cassandra TARVER-ROSS
84 AVP of Enrollment Management .... Mr. Terrance DIXON
35 AVP Student Svcs/Dean of College .... Mr. Maurice WASHINGTON
21 AVP & Controller .... Mr. Haskell RUFF
42 Dean Martin Luther King Jr Chapel .... Dr. Lawrence E. CARTER
06 Dean/Registrar .... Ms. Marie BROWN
35 Assoc Dean for Student Life .... Mr. Kevin BOOKER
07 Director Admissions & Recruitment .... Mr. Darryl ISOM
37 Director of Financial Aid .... Vacant
09 Director of Institutional Research .... Ms. Sharmyne EVANS
41 Athletic Director .... Vacant
85 Interim Director Andrew Young Ctr .... Dr. Jan ADAMS
38 Director for Student Counseling .... Mr. Steven ALLWOOD
105 Director Web Services .... Ms. Kara WALKER
22 Title IX Coordinator .... Ms. Sophia BRELVI
39 Sr Assoc Dean Residential Educ .... Mr. DeMarcus CREWS

Morehouse School of Medicine (E)

720 Westview Drive, SW, Atlanta GA 30310-1495

County: Fulton FICE Identification: 024821
Unit ID: 140562
Telephone: (404) 752-1500 Carnegie Class: Spec-4-yr-Med
FAX Number: (404) 752-1027 Calendar System: Semester
URL: www.msm.edu
Established: 1975 Annual Graduate Tuition & Fees: N/A
Enrollment: 520 Coed
Affiliation or Control: Independent Non-Profit IRS Status: 501(c)3
Highest Offering: Doctorate; No Undergraduates
Accreditation: SC, #ARCPA, MED, PH

01 President .... Dr. Valerie MONTGOMERY RICE
05 Dean .... Dr. Valerie MONTGOMERY RICE
10 Sr Vice Pres Finance/CFO .... Dr. John CASE
43 Sr Vice President/General Counsel .... Mr. Michael RAMBERT
111 Sr Vice Pres of Inst Advancement .... Dr. Bennie L. HARRIS
100 Chief of Staff/VP Strategic Plng .... Dr. Taya SCOTT
26 VP of Marketing & Communications .... Vacant
46 VP/Ex Vice Dean Research/Acad Admin .... Ms. Sandra HARRIS-HOOKER
15 Associate VP of Human Resources .... Ms. Denise BRITT
102 Assoc VP Development/Advance .... Mr. John WHITE
20 Sr Assoc Dean Educational Affairs .... Dr. Martha ELKS
88 Sr Assoc Director Clinical Research .... Vacant
20 Assoc Dean Faculty Affairs .... Dr. Erika BROWN
86 Exec Director of Government Affairs .... Mr. Daniel DAWES
37 Director Student Fiscal Affairs .... Ms. Cynthia H. HANDY
08 Library Manager .... Mr. Joe SWANSON, JR.
25 Exec Director of Grants & Contracts .... Vacant
29 Dir Alumni Constituent Engagement .... Ms. Samra COOTE
07 Assoc Dn Admissions/Student Affairs .... Dr. Ngozi F. ANACHEBE
96 Director Purchasing .... Mr. Philmon THOMAS
22 Chief Compliance Officer .... Mr. Keith HENDERSON
13 Chief Information Officer .... Mr. Reginald BRINSON
06 Registrar .... Ms. Angela FREEMAN
19 Chief of Police .... Mr. Joseph CHEVALIER, JR.

North Georgia Technical College (F)

PO Box 65, Clarkesville GA 30523-0065

County: Habersham FICE Identification: 005619
Unit ID: 140678
Telephone: (706) 754-7700 Carnegie Class: Assoc/HVT-High Trad
FAX Number: (706) 754-7777 Calendar System: Semester
URL: www.northgatech.edu
Established: 1943 Annual Undergrad Tuition & Fees (In-State): $2,738
Enrollment: 2,698 Coed
Affiliation or Control: State IRS Status: 501(c)3
Highest Offering: Associate Degree
Accreditation: SC, ACFEI, EMT, MAC, MLTAD

01 President .... Dr. Mark IVESTER
05 Vice President for Academic Affairs .... Mindy GLANDER
32 Vice President for Student Affairs .... Dr. Michael KING
11 VP for Administrative Services .... Carol CARSON
30 VP of Economic Development .... Keith POWELL
26 VP College & Community Relations .... Amy HULSEY
15 Human Resources Coordinator .... Lorna CHAPMAN
18 Chief Facilities/Physical Plant .... Michael BOYD
19 Chief of Campus Police .... Mark PULLIAM
29 Director Alumni Relations .... Cynthia BROWN
35 Campus Life Director .... Sherry SEAL
36 Director for Job Placement .... Patrick LEDFORD
07 Director of Admissions .... Kallan WILLIAMS
37 Financial Aid Director .... Audra JIMENEZ
20 Dean for Academic Affairs .... Michelle LIKINS
108 Institutional Effectiveness Dir .... Janet LOVELL
20 Dean for Academic Affairs .... Leslie MCFARLIN
20 Dean for Academic Affairs .... Christy BIVINS
106 Distance Education Specialist .... Dr. Renee DEIBERT
06 Registrar .... Kelsey MCINTIRE
13 Information Technology Director .... Savonda TURNER
96 Procurement Officer .... Rebekah FRANKLIN

Oconee Fall Line Technical College-North Campus (G)

1189 Deepstep Road, Sandersville GA 31082-9337

County: Washington FICE Identification: 031555
Unit ID: 420431
Telephone: (478) 553-2050 Carnegie Class: Assoc/HVT-Mix Trad/Non
FAX Number: (478) 553-2118 Calendar System: Semester
URL: www.oftc.edu
Established: 1996 Annual Undergrad Tuition & Fees (In-State): $2,678
Enrollment: 1,452 Coed
Affiliation or Control: State IRS Status: 501(c)3
Highest Offering: Associate Degree
Accreditation: SC

01 President .... Dr. Lloyd HORADAN
05 Vice Pres Academic/Student Affs .... Ms. Erica HARDEN
10 Vice Pres Administrative Services .... Ms. Rosemary SELBY
30 Vice Pres Economic Development .... Ms. Kim DAVID
49 Dean Arts & Sciences/Business Svcs .... Ms. Michele STRICKLAND
06 Registrar .... Ms. Geri CLEMENTS
07 Director of Admissions .... Ms. Raydor CONEWAY
15 Director Human Resources .... Ms. Sharon O'NEAL
21 Director of Administrative Services .... Ms. Penny KITCHENS
18 Director Facilities/Physical Plant .... Mr. Jim HARRISON
37 Financial Aid Director .... Ms. Betty YOUNG
28 Dir of Spec Populations/Stdnt Life .... Ms. Susan HAMMOCK

Oconee Fall Line Technical College-South Campus (H)

560 Pinehill Road, Dublin GA 31021-1599

County: Laurens FICE Identification: 022795
Telephone: (478) 275-6589 Carnegie Class: Not Classified
FAX Number: (478) 275-6642 Calendar System: Semester
URL: www.oftc.edu
Established: 1984 Annual Undergrad Tuition & Fees (In-State): N/A
Enrollment: N/A Coed
Affiliation or Control: State IRS Status: 501(c)3
Highest Offering: Associate Degree
Accreditation: SC, COARC, MAC, RAD

01 President .... Dr. Lloyd HORADAN
09 Vice Pres Inst Effectiveness .... Dr. Katie DAVIS
32 Dean Student Affairs .... Mr. Jay MULLIS
18 Director Facilities .... Mr. Ragan GREEN
30 Exec Dir Institutional Advancement .... Mrs. Jenny SHUMAN
19 Chief Security & Facilities .... Mr. Mark ROGERS
76 Dean Allied Health/Prof Svcs .... Ms. Tammy BAYTO
37 Asst Director Financial Aid .... Ms. Teresa CRAFTON
08 Director Library Services .... Ms. Wendi MORRIS
07 Director of Admissions .... Mr. Raydor CONEWAY
36 Coord Career Services .... Ms. Saketta BROWN

Ogeechee Technical College (I)

One Joseph E. Kennedy Boulevard, Statesboro GA 30458-8049

County: Bulloch FICE Identification: 030300
Unit ID: 366465
Telephone: (912) 681-5500 Carnegie Class: Assoc/HVT-Mix Trad/Non
FAX Number: (912) 486-7704 Calendar System: Semester
URL: www.ogeecheetech.edu
Established: 1986 Annual Undergrad Tuition & Fees (In-State): $2,876
Enrollment: 1,984 Coed
Affiliation or Control: State IRS Status: 170(c)1
Highest Offering: Associate Degree
Accreditation: SC, CAHIIM, DA, DMS, FUSER, MAC, OPD, RAD, SURGT

01 President .... Ms. Lori S. DURDEN
04 Exec Assistant to the President .... Ms. Karen MOBLEY
05 Exec VP Academic & Student Affairs .... Dr. Ryan FOLEY
88 Vice President Economic Development .... Ms. Jan MOORE
108 VP Institutional Effectiveness .... Ms. Brandy TAYLOR
10 Vice President for Administration .... Ms. Eyvonne HART
13 VP Technology & Institutional Supp .... Mr. Jeff DAVIS
111 VP for College Advancement .... Mrs. Michelle DAVIS
09 Director for Inst Research & Plng .... Vacant
08 Director for Library Services .... Ms. Lisa LANIER
51 Dir Continuing Educ & Ind Training .... Ms. Kathleen KOSMOSKI
07 Director for Admissions .... Ms. Molly BICKERTON
06 Registrar .... Ms. Michelle STUBBS
37 Director for Financial Aid .... Ms. Kristie SANDERS
15 Director for Human Resources .... Mr. Steve MILLER
109 Exec Director Auxiliary Services .... Mr. J.J ALTMAN
18 Director for Plant Operations .... Mr. Charlie COLLINS
19 Director Campus Safety & Security .... Vacant
20 Dean for Academic Affairs .... Ms. Leanne ROBINSON
97 Senior Academic Dean .... Ms. Jennifer WITHERINGTON
20 Dean for Academic Affairs .... Mr. Neal OWENS
21 Asst VP for Administration .... Ms. Tonya VICKERS
88 Dean of Adult Education .... Ms. Samantha SMITH
35 Assistant VP for Student Affairs .... Mrs. Christy RIKARD
36 Career Placement/Stdnt Supp Svc Dir .... Ms. Cindy PHILLIPS

Oglethorpe University (J)

4484 Peachtree Road, NE, Atlanta GA 30319-2797

County: DeKalb FICE Identification: 001586
Unit ID: 140696
Telephone: (404) 261-1441 Carnegie Class: Bac-A&S
FAX Number: N/A Calendar System: Semester
URL: www.oglethorpe.edu
Established: 1835 Annual Undergrad Tuition & Fees: $38,100
Enrollment: 1,250 Coed
Affiliation or Control: Independent Non-Profit IRS Status: 501(c)3
Highest Offering: Baccalaureate
Accreditation: SC

01 President .... Dr. Lawrence M. SCHALL
05 Provost/VP Academic Affairs .... Dr. Glenn SHARFMAN
10 Vice Pres for Business & Finance .... Vacant
30 Vice Pres Devel & Alumni Relations .... Ms. Robyn FURNESS-FALLIN
84 VP Enrollment/FinancialAid .... Ms. Lucy LEUSCH
26 VP Marketing/Communications .... Mr. Todd BENNETT
32 Dean of Students/VP Campus Life .... Ms. Michelle HALL
20 Assistant Provost .... Mr. Brian COLDREN
04 Exec Assistant to the President .... Ms. Colleen DONALDSON
08 Int Univ Librarian/Library Director .... Mr. Eli ARNOLD
06 Registrar .... Mr. Brian COLDREN
09 Director of Institutional Research .... Ms. Carolyn MATA
41 Athletic Director .... Mr. Todd BROOKS
37 Director of Financial Aid .... Mr. Chris SUMMERS
39 Director of Residence Life .... Dr. Amy PALDER
21 Director of Finance/Controller .... Mr. Mark BERGER
13 Chief Information Officer .... Mr. Mike JACOBS
27 Dir University Communications .... Ms. Renee VARY KEELE
29 Director of Alumni/Donor Relations .... Ms. Mary RINALDI WINN
36 Director of Career Development .... Ms. Erin SHERRILL
44 Director of Donor Relations .... Ms. Barb HENRY
15 Director Human Resources .... Ms. Sandy BUTLER
31 Director A_LAB for Civic Engagement .... Ms. Beth CONCEPCION
18 Director Facilities/Physical Plant .... Mr. Lance KNIGHT
07 Associate Director of Admissions .... Ms. Whitney LEWIS
40 Bookstore Manager .... Ms. Kathleen GUY

Paine College (K)

1235 Fifteenth Street, Augusta GA 30901-3182

County: Richmond FICE Identification: 001587
Unit ID: 140720

Telephone: (706) 821-8200 Carnegie Class: Bac-Diverse
FAX Number: (706) 821-8373 Calendar System: Semester
URL: www.paine.edu
Established: 1882 Annual Undergrad Tuition & Fees: $16,096
Enrollment: 426 Coed
Affiliation or Control: Multiple Protestant Denominations IRS Status: 501(c)3
Highest Offering: Baccalaureate
Accreditation: #SC, ACBSP, CAEPN, @TRACS

01 Acting President .... Dr. Cheryl EVANS JONES
04 Office Manager/President's Office .... Mrs. Juanita HARPS
05 Provost/VP Academic Affairs .... Dr. Cheryl EVANS JONES
10 VP Administrative & Fiscal Affairs .... Dr. Dwayne CREW
30 Asst VP Institutional Development .... Ms. Helene CARTER
42 Campus Pastor .... Dr. Luther FELDER
41 Director of Athletics .... Mrs. Selina KOHN
88 Exec Asst to Provost/VP AA .... Ms. Frances WIMBERLY
50 Chair Business Dept .... Dr. Okoroafor NZEH
53 Chair Education Dept .... Dr. Gloria BENNETT
79 Interim Chair Humanities Dept .... Dr. Daniel BRONSTEIN
81 Chair Math Sci Tech Dept .... Dr. Raul PETERS
60 Chair Media Studies Dept .... Ms. Teri BURNETTE
83 Interim Chair Social Sciences Dept .... Dr. Elias E. ETINGE
09 Dir Inst Research/Qual Enhance Plan .... Mrs. Alice M. SIMPKINS
08 Director Library/LRC .... Mrs. Alana LEWIS
06 Registrar .... Mrs. Symphoni WIGGINS
36 Director Career Services .... Mrs. April EWING
38 Int Dir Counseling & Wellness Ctr .... Ms. Jenease HORSTEAD
39 Residence Life Coordinator .... Mrs. Shelia PAIGE
19 Chief of Police .... Chief Leroy MORGAN, JR.
13 Interim Dir Information Technology .... Mr. Jeffrey OWENS
37 Director of Financial Aid .... Ms. Consuelo QUINN
15 Coordinator Human Resources .... Mrs. Cathy WILSON
29 Director Alumni Relations .... Vacant
26 Dir Communications & Marketing .... Vacant
25 Dir Sponsored Prog/Title III .... Mr. Chester WHEELER
108 Director of Assessment & Eval .... Vacant
24 Info Tech Mgr Learning Resources .... Mrs. Rosa L. MARTIN
07 Admissions Coordinator .... Mrs. Felicia FENNER
88 Sr Women's Athletics Administrator .... Ms. Kisha LUCETTE
21 Chief Fiscal Officer .... Mr. Kevin HOWARD

Philadelphia College of Osteopathic Medicine Georgia Campus (A)

625 Old Peachtree Road NW, Suwanee GA 30024
Telephone: (678) 225-7500 Identification: 770165
Accreditation: &M, OSTEO, PHAR, PTA

† Branch campus of Philadelphia College of Osteopathic Medicine, Philadelphia, PA

Piedmont College (B)

PO Box 10, Demorest GA 30535-0010
County: Habersham FICE Identification: 001588
Unit ID: 140818
Telephone: (706) 778-3000 Carnegie Class: Masters/L
FAX Number: (706) 776-0701 Calendar System: Semester
URL: www.piedmont.edu
Established: 1897 Annual Undergrad Tuition & Fees: $25,920
Enrollment: 2,361 Coed
Affiliation or Control: United Church Of Christ IRS Status: 501(c)3
Highest Offering: Doctorate
Accreditation: SC, ACBSP, CAATE, CVT, NUR

01 President .... Dr. James F. MELLICHAMP
05 Vice Pres Academic Affairs .... Dr. Daniel SILBER
10 Vice Pres Administration & Finance .... Mr. Brant WRIGHT
84 Vice Pres Enrollment Management .... Dr. Perry RETTIG
111 Vice President for Advancement .... Mr. Craig ROGERS
13 AVP of Information Technology .... Dr. Shahryar HEYDARI
04 Assistant to the President .... Ms. Beth STEED
32 Dean of Student Engagement .... Ms. Emily PETTIT
07 Dean of Admiss/Undergrad Enrol Mgmt .... Ms. Cynthia L. PETERSON
08 Dean of Libraries/College Librarian .... Mr. Robert GLASS, JR.
06 Registrar .... Ms. Courtney THOMAS
09 Director of Institutional Research .... Mr. Jody ANDERSON
84 Director Graduate Enrollment Mgmt .... Ms. Kathleen CARTER
07 Director Undergraduate Admissions .... Mrs. Brenda BOONSTRA
37 Director of Financial Aid .... Mr. David MCMILLION
42 Campus Minister .... Rev. Timothy GARVIN-LEIGHTON
15 Director Human Resources .... Ms. Rose Mariee ALLISON
26 Director Marketing/Communications .... Mr. John ROBERTS
41 Dir of Intercollegiate Athletics .... Mr. Jim PEEPLES
21 Compliance & Treasury Officer .... Ms. Leesa P. ANDERSON
19 Director Security/Campus Police .... Ms. Marie G. TAYLOR
66 Dean School of Nursing/Health Sci .... Dr. Julie BEHR
50 Dean School of Business Admin .... Dr. Edward TAYLOR
49 Dean School of Arts & Sciences .... Dr. Steven NIMMO
53 Dean School of Education .... Dr. Donald GNECCO

Point University (C)

507 West 10th St, West Point GA 31833
County: Troup FICE Identification: 001547
Unit ID: 138868
Telephone: (706) 385-1000 Carnegie Class: Bac-Diverse
FAX Number: (706) 645-9473 Calendar System: Semester
URL: www.point.edu
Established: 1937 Annual Undergrad Tuition & Fees: $20,600
Enrollment: 1,952 Coed
Affiliation or Control: Christian Churches And Churches of Christ IRS Status: 501(c)3
Highest Offering: Master's
Accreditation: SC

01 President .... Mr. Dean C. COLLINS
05 Chief Academic Officer .... Dr. W. Darryl HARRISON
11 Chief Operations Officer .... Vacant
108 Vice Pres for Inst Effectiveness .... Dr. Dennis GLENN
10 Chief Financial Officer .... Arthur B. DANA
58 Vice Pres Graduate & Prof Studies .... Chris DAVIS
107 Asst Vice Pres Prof Studies .... Leon REESE
84 Vice Pres for Enrollment Management .... Tiffany WOOD
07 Executive Director of Enrollment .... Rusty HASSELL
26 Director of Communications .... Kara JOHNSON
06 Registrar .... Obie KILLCREAS
106 Dir OL Learning and Instruc Design .... Valarie WILLIAMS
113 Director of Student Accounts .... John LANIER
37 Interim Director of Financial Aid .... Mike LAGE
32 Dean of Students .... Laura SCHAAF
41 Athletic Director .... Alan WILSON
19 Chief of Security .... Eric FLOURNOY
18 Dir of Facilities and Maintenance .... Phil JOHNSON
15 Director of Human Resources .... Margaret HODGE
42 Vice Pres for Spiritual Formation .... Wye HUXFORD
08 Library Director .... Michael BAIN
13 Vice Pres for Info Technology .... Bill DORMINY
111 Vice President of Advancement .... Dr. Stacy BARTLETT
100 Chief of Staff to the President .... Phil SHOMO
09 Institutional Research Manager .... Amanda YANCEY

† Formerly Atlanta Christian College

Reformed University (D)

1724 Atkinson Road, Lawrenceville GA 30043
County: Gwinnett Identification: 667247
Unit ID: 490230
Telephone: (770) 232-2717 Carnegie Class: Not Classified
FAX Number: N/A Calendar System: Semester
URL: www.runiv.edu
Established: 1992 Annual Undergrad Tuition & Fees: $5,360
Enrollment: 139 Coed
Affiliation or Control: Presbyterian Church In America IRS Status: Exempt
Highest Offering: Master's
Accreditation: TRACS

01 President .... Dr. Jae-sig PARK
03 Executive Vice President .... Dr. Won W. MOON
05 Director of Academic Affairs .... Dr. Hee-duck YOO
07 Director of Admissions .... Dr. Charlie KIM
08 Chief Library Officer .... Ms. Dianne MURRAY
10 Chief Financial/Business Officer .... Vacant
104 Director Study Abroad .... Dr. Hyang-joo KIM
106 Dean of Distance Education .... Dr. Dennis C. MALONE
108 Director Institutional Assessment .... Dr. Heung-sung NHO

Reinhardt University (E)

7300 Reinhardt Circle, Waleska GA 30183-2981
County: Cherokee FICE Identification: 001589
Unit ID: 140872
Telephone: (770) 720-5600 Carnegie Class: Masters/S
FAX Number: (770) 720-5602 Calendar System: Semester
URL: www.reinhardt.edu
Established: 1883 Annual Undergrad Tuition & Fees: $23,300
Enrollment: 1,508 Coed
Affiliation or Control: United Methodist IRS Status: 501(c)3
Highest Offering: Master's
Accreditation: SC, MUS

01 President .... Dr. Kina S. MALLARD
04 Executive Assistant to President .... Mrs. Bonnie H. DEBORD
05 Provost .... Dr. Mark A. ROBERTS
10 Chief Financial Officer .... Mrs. Stephanie R. OWENS
111 VP for Advancement .... Vacant
32 Dean of Students .... Dr. Walter P. MAY
84 VP for Enrollment Mgmt .... Mrs. Julie C. FLEMING
41 VP for Athletics & Athletic Dir .... Mr. William C. POPP
20 Assoc Provost of Academics .... Dr. Jacob P. HARNEY
101 Asst Secretary Board of Trustees .... Mrs. Bonnie H. DEBORD
18 Director of Facilities Management .... Mr. Jeffrey DALE
26 Dir of Marketing & Communications .... Mrs. Erika B. NELDNER
13 Director of IT .... Mr. Jonathan HARDEMAN
88 Director of Funk Heritage Ctr .... Mr. Jeff BISHOP
07 Director of Admissions .... Ms. Lacey L. SATTERFIELD
06 Registrar .... Ms. Janet M. RODNING
09 Dir Inst Research/Effectiveness .... Mr. Justin A. MITCHELL
08 Director of Library Services .... Mr. Joel C. LANGFORD
19 Director of Public Safety .... Mr. Jay R. DUNCAN
42 Campus Pastor .... Rev. Jamie HUDGINS
21 Controller .... Ms. Deborah WALKER
37 Director Student Financial Aid .... Vacant
15 Director Human Resources .... Ms. Kristy L. STARLING
39 Director of Residence Life .... Ms. Jeanne SEVIGNY
23 University Nurse .... Mrs. Kristy M. HOUGH
35 Asst Dean of Students .... Mrs. Jamie M. JOHNSTON
38 Director of Counseling Svcs .... Mr. Adam C. POWELL
121 Dir Center for Student Success .... Dr. Catherine B. EMANUEL
36 Dir Vocation & Career Services .... Mrs. Karen W. MATHEWS
40 Bookstore Manager .... Mrs. Janet SWEENEY
49 Dean School of Arts & Humanities .... Dr. Arthur W. GLOWKA
81 Dean School of Maths & Sciences .... Dr. Jake P. HARNEY
50 Dean McCamish Sch Bus & Sport Stdy .... Dr. Stephen C. MORSE
53 Dean Price School of Education .... Dr. Nancy J. MARSH
64 Dean School of Performing Arts .... Dr. Fredrick A. TARRANT
107 Int Dean Sch Professional Studies .... Mr. Lester W. DRAWDY
66 Dean School Nursing/Health Sciences .. Dr. Glynis D. BLACKARD

SAE Institute Atlanta (F)

215 Peachtree Street NE, Suite 300, Atlanta GA 30303-1739
Telephone: (404) 526-9366 FICE Identification: 042066
Accreditation: ACCSC

Savannah College of Art and Design (G)

342 Bull Street, PO Box 3146, Savannah GA 31402-6263
County: Chatham FICE Identification: 021415
Unit ID: 140951
Telephone: (912) 525-5000 Carnegie Class: Spec-4-yr-Arts
FAX Number: (912) 525-6263 Calendar System: Quarter
URL: www.scad.edu
Established: 1978 Annual Undergrad Tuition & Fees: $37,130
Enrollment: 13,163 Coed
Affiliation or Control: Independent Non-Profit IRS Status: 501(c)3
Highest Offering: Master's
Accreditation: SC, CIDA

01 President .... Mrs. Paula WALLACE
11 Chief Operating Officer .... Mr. Glenn WALLACE
10 Chief Financial Officer .... Mr. J.J WALLER
113 VP for Student Financial Services .... Mr. Scott LINZEY
05 Chief Academic Officer .... Dr. Gokhan OZAYSIN
43 VP International & Legal Services .... Ms. Hannah FLOWER
12 VP SCAD Atlanta .... Ms. Audra PRICE PITTMAN
12 VP SCAD Hong Kong .... Mr. Khoi VO
84 Sr VP Admission/Student Success .... Dr. Philip ALLETTO
13 VP for Information Technology .... Mr. Brad GRANT
106 VP for SCAD Savannah .... Mr. John BUCKOVICH
15 VP for Human Resources .... Ms. Lesley HANAK
09 VP for Institutional Effectiveness .... Ms. Erin O'LEARY
07 VP for Admission .... Mr. Steve MINEO
20 Dean of Academic Svcs Atlanta .... Mr. Dale CLIFFORD
26 Director of Univ Communications .... Ms. Ally HUGHES
18 Exec Dir of Physical Resources .... Ms. Helen MORGAN
08 Senior Director of Library Services .... Mr. Darrell NAYLOR-JOHNSON
37 Director of Financial Aid .... Ms. Kim BEVERIDGE
07 Exec Dir Adm Recruitment .... Ms. Jenny JAQUILLARD
19 VP for University Safety .... Mr. John BUCKOVICH
41 Athletics Director .... Mr. Doug WOLLENBURG
38 Dir Counseling/Student Support Svc .... Mr. Christopher CORBETT
06 Sr Dir of Registrar Services .... Ms. Sarah MCCARN
88 Dean of School of Building Arts .... Dr. Geoffrey TAYLOR
88 Dean of School Communication Arts .... Mr. Anthony FISHER
88 Dean of School of Design .... Mr. Victor ERMOLI
88 Dean of School of Digital Media .... Ms. Marilynn ALMY
57 Dean of School of Fine Arts .... Ms. Maureen GARVIN
49 Dean of School of Liberal Arts .... Ms. Kate NEWELL
88 Dean School of Fashion .... Mr. Michael FINK
88 Dean School of Foundation Studies .... Ms. Maureen GARVIN
88 Dean of Entertainment Arts .... Mr. Andra REEVE-RABB
36 Exec Dir of Career & Alumni Success .... Ms. Kimberly LOPEZ
44 Exec Director of Giving .... Ms. Tish CAMPBELL
20 AVP of Academic Services .... Mr. Jesus ROJAS
35 Dean of Students Atlanta .... Mr. Lucas BUCKOVICH
35 Dean of Students Savannah .... Mr. David BLAKE
104 Director SCAD Study Abroad .... Ms. Stephanie JACKSON
39 Assoc Dean/Dir of Residence Life .... Mr. Jason RIGSBEE

Savannah State University (H)

3219 College Street, Savannah GA 31404-5308
County: Chatham FICE Identification: 001590
Unit ID: 140960
Telephone: (912) 358-3004 Carnegie Class: Masters/S
FAX Number: N/A Calendar System: Semester
URL: www.savannahstate.edu
Established: 1890 Annual Undergrad Tuition & Fees (In-State): $5,743
Enrollment: 4,429 Coed
Affiliation or Control: State IRS Status: 501(c)3
Highest Offering: Master's
Accreditation: SC, JOUR, SPAA, SW

01 Interim University President .... Dr. Kimberly BALLARD-WASHINGTON
05 Executive VP Academic Affairs .... Dr. Linda NOBLE
10 Interim VP Business & Finance .... Ms. Elaine CAMPBELL
32 Vice President Student Affairs .... Dr. Carl WALTON
111 VP Advancement/Exec Dir SSU Found .... Mr. Phillip D. ADAMS
13 Chief Information Officer .... Vacant
50 Interim Dean College Business Admin .... Dr. Reginald LESEANE
81 Dean Col Science & Tech .... Dr. Mohamad MUSTAFA
49 Int Dean Col Liberal Arts/Soc Sci .... Dr. Emmanuel NANIUZEYI
53 Dean College of Education .... Dr. Mary KROPIEWNICKI
07 Director of Admissions for Recruit .... Mr. Brian DAWSEY
26 Asst VP Marketing/Communications .... Ms. Loretta HEYWARD
15 Chief Human Resources Officer .... Ms. Jacqueline STEPHERSON
08 Interim Librarian .... Mrs. Louise WYCHE
19 Interim Chief of Police .... Mr. Ulyssess BRYANT
18 Director Facilities/Physical Plant .... Mr. Randall LOWERY
43 Dir Legal Services/General Counsel .... Ms. Flora DEVINE

09 AVP Inst Rsrch/Plng/Assess ... Dr. Bernard MOSES
29 Director Alumni Relations ... Ms. Barbara S. MYERS
37 Director Financial Aid ... Mr. Kenneth WILSON
41 Director Athletics ... Mr. Opio MASHARIKI
35 Director of Student Development ... Ms. Jacqueline AWE
06 Registrar ... Ms. Kathleen PLATT
04 Exec Asst to President ... Ms. Lisa SCIPIO
39 Director Student Housing ... Dr. Priscilla WILLIAMS
100 Chief of Staff ... Ms. Cynthia HOKE
106 Dir Online Education/E-learning ... Vacant
104 Director International Education ... Dr. Emmanuel NANIUZEYI, SR.
84 Asst VP Enrollment Management ... Dr. Dedra ANDREWS
38 Director Student Counseling ... Dr. Shawntell PHOENIX-MARTIN
96 Director of Purchasing ... Ms. Alicia WILLIAMS
30 Director of Development ... Mr. Phil COLE

† Part of the University System of Georgia.

Savannah Technical College (A)

5717 White Bluff Road, Savannah GA 31405-5521

County: Chatham FICE Identification: 005618
Unit ID: 140942
Telephone: (912) 443-5700 Carnegie Class: Assoc/HVT-Mix Trad/Non
FAX Number: (912) 443-5705 Calendar System: Semester
URL: www.savannahtech.edu
Established: 1967 Annual Undergrad Tuition & Fees (In-State): $2,744
Enrollment: 3,935 Coed
Affiliation or Control: State IRS Status: 501(c)3
Highest Offering: Associate Degree
Accreditation: SC, ACFEI, DA, DH, EMT, MAC, SURGT

01 President ... Dr. Kathy S. LOVE
05 Vice President for Academic Affairs ... Dr. Al CUNNINGHAM
11 Vice Pres Administrative Services ... Ms. Connie CLARK
32 Vice President for Student Affairs ... Mr. Pete HOFFMAN
45 Vice Pres Economic Development ... Dr. Brent STUBBS
108 VP Institutional Effectiveness ... Dr. Vic BURKE
111 Exec Director Inst Advance & Comm ... Ms. Gail EUBANKS
13 Exec Director Information Tech ... Mr. Jamie DAVIS
07 Director of Admissions ... Ms. Tiffany DONALD
37 Director Financial Aid ... Ms. Faith ANDERSON
06 Registrar ... Ms. Regina THOMAS-WILLIAMS
18 Director Facilities ... Mr. Gary STRICKLAND
15 Director Human Resources ... Ms. Melissa BANKS
08 Library Services Director ... Mr. Jim BURCH
26 Director of Communications ... Ms. Amy SHAFFER
12 Campus Dean Liberty Campus ... Ms. Terrie SELLERS
12 Campus Dean Effingham Campus ... Ms. Patricia BOYLES
92 Purchasing Manager ... Mr. Kevin CHIEVES
76 Dean Health Science ... Ms. Kathleen BOMBERY
50 Dean Business and Professional Svcs ... Dr. Ashley MORRIS
97 Dean General Studies ... Dr. Lonnie GRIFFIN
88 Dean Industrial Technology ... Mr. Joseph POWELL
88 Dean Aviation ... Mr. Tal LOOS
56 Adult Education Coordinator ... Dr. Brent STUBBS
88 Military Outreach Coordinator ... Mr. Steven CISNEROS
88 Dir of Enterprise Tech Specialist ... Ms. Tammy BRANNEN
19 Chief of Police ... Mr. Wayne WILLCOX
36 Coordinator of Career Services ... Ms. Sylvia PERRY
88 Student Navigator ... Ms. Kelley RIFFE
88 High School Initiatives Coordinator ... Ms. Shatealy JOHNSON
22 Special Population Disability Svcs ... Ms. Melanie WILDER

Shorter University (B)

315 Shorter Avenue, Rome GA 30165-4298

County: Floyd FICE Identification: 001591
Unit ID: 140988
Telephone: (706) 291-2121 Carnegie Class: Masters/S
FAX Number: (706) 236-1515 Calendar System: Semester
URL: www.shorter.edu
Established: 1873 Annual Undergrad Tuition & Fees: $22,370
Enrollment: 1,520 Coed
Affiliation or Control: Baptist IRS Status: 501(c)3
Highest Offering: Master's
Accreditation: SC, MUS, NURSE

01 President ... Dr. Donald V. DOWLESS
05 Executive Vice President & Provost ... Dr. Donald L. MARTIN
11 VP for Administrative Affairs ... Vacant
10 VP for Finance & CFO ... Ms. Susan ZEIRD
84 Vice Pres Enrollment Management ... Mr. Karl HATTON
30 Vice President for Advancement ... Dr. Ben BRUCE
32 VP Student Affairs/Dean of Students ... Mr. Ken WHITLOW
26 Assoc VP University Communications ... Dr. Dawn C. TOLBERT
104 Asst Vice Pres International Pgms ... Mrs. Linda PALUMBO-OLSZANSKI
06 Registrar ... Mrs. Gina FLOYD
35 Director of Student Life & Conduct ... Mr. Anthony CHATMAN
08 Director of Libraries ... Mr. John SHAFFETT
09 Director of Inst Planning/Research ... Dr. Earl KELLETT
37 Director of Financial Aid ... Ms. Colleen LASSITER
15 Director Human Resources ... Mrs. Stacy HARDY
56 Director Special Programs ... Vacant
13 Director of Information Technology ... Mr. Jeff BRAMLETTE
18 Director of Facilities Management ... Mr. Bob BAGLEY
38 Director of Student Support Svcs ... Dr. Chris WHEELUS
23 Director of Health Services ... Mrs. Allison STARTUP
41 Athletic Director ... Mr. Tony LUNDY
44 Director of Annual Giving ... Vacant
07 Director of Admissions ... Mr. Patrick MCELHANEY
39 Director Residence Life ... Mr. Anthony CHATMON

40 Bookstore Manager ... Ms. Julie BINKLEY
57 Dean School of the Arts ... Dr. John REAMS
50 Dean College of Business ... Dr. Heath HOOPER
53 Dean School of Education ... Dr. Dana KING
66 Dean School of Nursing ... Dr. Roxanne JOHNSTON
81 Dean Col of Natural Sci/Mathematics ... Dr. Clint HELMS
79 Dean Col of Humanities/Soc Sciences ... Dr. Cory BARNES
73 Chair Dept of Christian Studies ... Dr. Brent BASKIN
77 Chair Dept of Mathematics ... Dr. Diana SWANAGAN
60 Chair Dept of Communication Arts ... Dr. Bill MULLEN
83 Chair Dept of Social Sciences ... Dr. Jared LINEBACH
42 Campus Minister ... Rev. David E. ROLAND

South Georgia State College (C)

100 W College Park Drive, Douglas GA 31533-5098

County: Coffee FICE Identification: 001592
Unit ID: 482699
Telephone: (912) 260-4394 Carnegie Class: Bac/Assoc-Mixed
FAX Number: (912) 260-4454 Calendar System: Semester
URL: www.sgsc.edu
Established: 1906 Annual Undergrad Tuition & Fees (In-State): $3,254
Enrollment: 2,540 Coed
Affiliation or Control: State IRS Status: 501(c)3
Highest Offering: Baccalaureate
Accreditation: SC, ADNUR, NUR

01 President ... Dr. Ingrid THOMPSON-SELLERS
05 Vice Pres Academic/Student Affs ... Dr. Robert PAGE
84 Exec Dir Enrollment Mgmt ... Dr. Donald AVERY
10 Interim Vice Pres Fiscal Affairs ... Ms. Diane OWENS
13 Chief Info Technology Officer ... Mr. Jimmy HARPER
08 Director of Libraries ... Ms. Lynn KELLY
06 Registrar ... Ms. Ame WILKERSON
37 Director of Financial Aid ... Mr. Doug TANNER
15 Interim Director of Human Resources ... Ms. Maria STUCKEY
07 Interim Director of Admissions ... Ms. Jamica COATES
88 Dir of Entry Programs and Planning ... Ms. Valerie WEBSTER
40 Bookstore Manager ... Ms. Daphne FRENCH
32 Interim Dean of Students ... Ms. Sandra ADAMS
09 Dir of Inst Effectiveness & Rsrch ... Ms. Dani SUTLIFF
19 Campus Police Chief ... Ms. Sonja MCCULLOCH
26 Marketing Coordinator ... Ms. Barbara OBRENTZ

† Part of the University System of Georgia.

South Georgia Technical College (D)

900 South Georgia Tech Parkway,
Americus GA 31709-8167

County: Sumter FICE Identification: 005617
Unit ID: 141006
Telephone: (229) 931-2394 Carnegie Class: Assoc/HVT-Mix Trad/Non
FAX Number: (229) 931-2924 Calendar System: Semester
URL: www.southgatech.edu
Established: 1948 Annual Undergrad Tuition & Fees (In-State): $2,798
Enrollment: 1,850 Coed
Affiliation or Control: State IRS Status: 501(c)3
Highest Offering: Associate Degree
Accreditation: SC

01 President ... Dr. John WATFORD
11 Vice Pres Administrative Services ... Lea COE
10 Vice Pres Business & Industry Svcs ... Wally SUMMERS
05 Vice President for Academic Affairs ... David KUIPERS
09 Vice Pres of Institutional Support ... Karen J. WERLING
04 Special Assistant to the President ... Don SMITH
20 Dean of Academic Affairs ... Raymond HOLT
20 Dean of Academic Affairs ... Vanessa WALL
20 Dean of Academic Affairs ... Dr. Andrea OATES
20 Dean of Academic Affairs ... Dr. David FINLEY
111 Vice Pres Institutional Advancement ... Su Ann BIRD
13 Technology Director ... Dianne TRUEBLOOD
37 Director of Financial Aid ... Carrie WILDER
15 Director Personnel Services ... Sandy LARSON
32 Director of Campus Life ... Cynthia CARTER
21 Director of Accounting ... Robin BELL
88 Director of Administrative Services ... Mark BROOKS
06 Registrar ... Eulish KINCHENS
08 Librarian ... Jerry STOVALL
07 Director of Admissions ... Whitney CRISP
41 Athletic Director ... James FREY
29 Director Alumni Relations ... SuAnn BIRD
38 Director Student Counseling ... LaKenya JOHNSON
84 Dean Enrollment Management ... Julie PARTAIN
18 Chief Facilities/Physical Plant ... Don SMITH
96 Purchasing Agent ... Gail CLARY
19 Director Security/Safety ... Sammy STONE

South University (E)

709 Mall Boulevard, Savannah GA 31406-4881

County: Chatham FICE Identification: 013039
Unit ID: 139579
Telephone: (912) 201-8000 Carnegie Class: Spec-4-yr-Other Health
FAX Number: (912) 201-8070 Calendar System: Quarter
URL: www.southuniversity.edu
Established: 1899 Annual Undergrad Tuition & Fees: $17,014
Enrollment: 1,228 Coed
Affiliation or Control: Independent Non-Profit IRS Status: 501(c)3
Highest Offering: Doctorate
Accreditation: SC, AA, ACBSP, ARCPA, CACREP, MAC, NURSE, PHAR, PTAA

01 Chancellor ... Dr. Steven YOHO
12 President Montgomery Campus ... Mr. Victor K. BIEBIGHAUSER
12 President West Palm Beach Campus ... Mr. David D. MCGUIRE
12 President Columbia Campus ... Mr. Karl STERNER
12 President Richmond Campus ... Mr. Troy RALSTON
12 President Tampa Campus ... Mr. James F. MCCOY, JR.
12 President Virginia Beach Campus ... Mr. Scot HAYNES
12 President Austin Campus ... Mr. Brian SILVER
12 President Cleveland Campus ... Mr. Scott BEHMER
12 President High Point Campus ... Vacant
12 President Savannah Campus ... Dr. Tim BLACKSTON
14 Regional Director of Technology ... Mr. Dustin BARRETT
10 Vice Chancellor for Finance ... Mr. John PAPP
05 Vice Chancellor Academic Affairs ... Dr. Jay STUBBLEFIELD
20 Assoc Vice Chanc Academic Affairs ... Dr. Theodore RICHARDSON
20 Assoc Vice Chan Academic Affairs ... Dr. Frances W. OBLANDER
20 Assoc Vice Chanc Academic Affairs ... Dr. Devin BYRD
08 Asst Vice Chanc Univ Library ... Ms. Nancy SPEISSER
06 University Registrar ... Ms. Anita MACIAS
86 Director of State Licensing ... Ms. Misty BLACKSTON
09 Sr Director Inst Effectiveness ... Vacant
108 Director for Academic Assessment ... Ms. Elizabeth DEVITA
49 Int Dean College of Arts & Sciences ... Dr. April TAYLOR
50 Dean College of Business ... Dr. Cheryl NOLL
76 Dean College of Health Professions ... Ms. Gina SCARBORO
66 Dean College of Nursing & PH ... Dr. Mable H. SMITH
67 Dean School of Pharmacy ... Dr. Curtis JONES
84 Regional Director of Admissions ... Ms. Ashley WEEKS
15 Assoc Chancellor of Human Resources ... Ms. Lynne HAINES
16 Human Resources Generalist ... Ms. Cathy GIRARDEAU
16 Human Resources Generalist ... Ms. Ashley MIRACLE
32 Asst Chancellor for Student Affairs ... Ms. Alisa KROUSE
26 Vice Chancellor for Marketing ... Mr. Jefff BEAMON
27 Digital Marketing Director ... Ms. Kalani ROBINSON
27 Marketing Director SU Online ... Mr. John MAAS

Southeastern Technical College (F)

3001 E First Street, Vidalia GA 30474-8817

County: Toombs FICE Identification: 030665
Unit ID: 368911
Telephone: (912) 538-3100 Carnegie Class: Assoc/HVT-Mix Trad/Non
FAX Number: (912) 538-3156 Calendar System: Semester
URL: www.southeasterntech.edu
Established: 1989 Annual Undergrad Tuition & Fees (In-State): $2,863
Enrollment: 1,713 Coed
Affiliation or Control: State IRS Status: 501(c)3
Highest Offering: Associate Degree
Accreditation: SC, DH, EMT, MAC, MLTAD, RAD

01 President ... Mr. Larry CALHOUN
05 Vice Pres Academic Affairs ... Ms. Teresa COLEMAN
11 Vice Pres Administrative Services ... Ms. Denise POWELL
10 Vice President Fiscal Affairs ... Vacant
32 Vice President Student Affairs ... Dr. Barry DOTSON
84 Director Enrollment Services ... Mr. Brad HART
06 Registrar ... Ms. Amanda LIVELY
37 Director Financial Aid ... Mr. Mitchell FAGLER
36 Director Job Placement ... Mr. Lance HELMS
103 Special Populations Coordinator ... Ms. Helen THOMAS
40 Bookstore Manager ... Ms. Stacy FREEMAN
26 Dir Marketing & Public Relations ... Ms. Natalie OSBORNE
08 Head Librarian ... Mrs. Leah DASHER
19 Director Security/Safety ... Mr. Travis AKRIDGE

Southern Crescent Technical College (G)

501 Varsity Road, Griffin GA 30223-2042

County: Spalding FICE Identification: 005621
Unit ID: 139986
Telephone: (770) 228-7348 Carnegie Class: Assoc/HVT-High Trad
FAX Number: (770) 229-3227 Calendar System: Semester
URL: www.sctech.edu
Established: 1963 Annual Undergrad Tuition & Fees (In-State): $2,842
Enrollment: 4,756 Coed
Affiliation or Control: State IRS Status: 501(c)3
Highest Offering: Associate Degree
Accreditation: SC, ACFEI, COARC, DA, EMT, MAC, SURGT

01 President ... Dr. Alvetta P. THOMAS
03 Executive Vice President ... Dr. Mark ANDREWS
05 Vice Pres for Academic Affairs ... Dr. Steve PEARCE
04 Exec Admin Asst to President ... Ms. Kim SANTERRE
32 Vice Pres for Student Affairs ... Dr. Xenia JOHNS
10 Vice Pres Administrative Services ... Ms. Miriam CASLIN
111 Vice President Advancement ... Ms. Barbara Jo COOK
46 Vice Pres Inst Effectiveness ... Dr. Chris DANIEL
18 Assoc VP Facilities & Opers ... Dr. Alan STANFIELD
06 Registrar ... Ms. Kathlyn STROZIER
26 Dir Marketing & Public Relations ... Ms. Anna TAYLOR
37 Director of Financial Aid ... Dr. Michelle BEDFORD
49 Dean Arts & Sciences ... Dr. Sean BRUMFIELD
76 Dean Allied Health & ParaMedicine ... Ms. Kimberly REGISTER
75 Dean Film/Public Safety/Ind Tech ... Mr. Lemuel MERCADO
50 Dean Business/CIS/Prof Services ... Dr. Roslyn MCCURRY
84 Director of Enrollment Management ... Dr. Jasper FOUST
15 Director of Human Resources ... Ms. Sharon HILL
35 Director of Student Affairs ... Ms. Cherryl BURKS
21 Director of Administrative Services ... Ms. Stacy ACEY
36 Director of Career Placement & Acad ... Ms. Susan MURRAY
19 Campus Police Chief ... Mr. Kenneth TROISI
13 Chief Information Officer ... Mr. Michael SHIVER

Southern Regional Technical College (A)

15689 US Highway 19 N, Thomasville GA 31792-2622
County: Thomas — FICE Identification: 005615
Unit ID: 487162
Telephone: (229) 225-4096 — Carnegie Class: Assoc/HVT-High Non
FAX Number: (229) 225-4330 — Calendar System: Semester
URL: www.southernregional.edu
Established: 2015 — Annual Undergrad Tuition & Fees (In-State): $2,728
Enrollment: 3,884 — Coed
Affiliation or Control: State — IRS Status: 501(c)3
Highest Offering: Associate Degree
Accreditation: SC, ADNUR, #COARC, EMT, MAC, MLTAD, RAD, SURGT

01 President .... Mr. Jim GLASS
11 Vice Pres Administrative Services .... Mr. Ross COX
05 Vice Pres Academic Affairs .... Dr. Ron O'MEARA
32 Exec Vice President Student Affairs .... Ms. Leigh WALLACE
30 Vice President Economic Development .... Mr. Dennis LEE
09 VP Institutional Effectiveness .... Dr. Ron O'MEARA
76 Dean School of Health Sciences .... Ms. Carla BARROW
50 Dean School of Bus/Industrial Tech .... Ms. Abby CARTER
107 Dean School of Professional Svcs .... Ms. Tina STRICKLAND
49 Dean School of Art and Sciences .... Ms. Kathryn KENT
37 Executive Director Financial Aid .... Ms. Judi LOVVORN
26 VP Marketing/Inst Devel/Pub Rels .... Dr. Amy MAISON
88 Director Adult Education .... Ms. Melissa BURTLE
07 Director of Admissions .... Ms. Wanda HANCOCK
35 Director Student Affairs .... Ms. Lisa GRIFFIN
06 Registrar .... Dr. Wendi TOSTENSON
08 Executive Director Library Services .... Ms. Udella SPICER
36 Dir Career Services & Counseling .... Dr. Jeanine LONG
15 Director Human Resources .... Mr. Michael HEARD
18 VP Operations .... Mr. David EVANS

Spelman College (B)

350 Spelman Lane, SW, Atlanta GA 30314-4399
County: Fulton — FICE Identification: 001594
Unit ID: 141060
Telephone: (404) 681-3643 — Carnegie Class: Bac-A&S
FAX Number: N/A — Calendar System: Semester
URL: www.spelman.edu
Established: 1881 — Annual Undergrad Tuition & Fees: $29,064
Enrollment: 2,137 — Female
Affiliation or Control: Independent Non-Profit — IRS Status: 501(c)3
Highest Offering: Baccalaureate
Accreditation: SC, CAEPN, MUS

01 President .... Dr. Mary SCHMIDT CAMPBELL
100 Chief of Staff/Govt Relations Dir .... Ms. Helga GREENFIELD
05 Provost & VP Academic Affairs .... Prof. Sharon DAVIES
10 VP Business/Financial Affairs/Treas .... Mr. Robert D. FLANIGAN, JR.
32 Vice President for Student Affairs .... Dr. Darryl HOLLOMAN
31 Vice President College Relations .... Dr. Jane SMITH
84 Vice Pres Enrollment Management .... Ms. Ingrid HAYES
111 VP of Institutional Advancement .... Mr. Jessie BROOKS
45 VP of IR/Planning & Effectiveness .... Dr. Myra BURNETT
101 VP/Secretary of College .... Dr. Terri REED
13 Interim VP & Chief Info Officer .... Ms. Chandra MCCRARY
114 Director of Budgets & Contracts .... Ms. Asella BRAXTON
21 Controller .... Ms. April AUSTIN
27 Director Marketing & Communications .... Ms. Joyce E. DAVIS
04 Special Assistant .... Ms. Jarvis RIDGES
88 Dir Office of Civic Engagement .... Ms. Jilo TISDALE
20 Dean of Undergraduate Studies .... Dr. Desiree PEDESCLEAUX
42 Dean of Sisters Chapel .... Dr. Neichelle GUIDRY
06 Registrar .... Mr. John BROWN
07 Director of Admissions .... Ms. Tiffany NELSON
29 Director of Alumnae Engagement .... Ms. Sharon OWENS
37 Director of Financial Aid .... Ms. Lenora JACKSON
36 Director Career Planning/Devel .... Mr. Harold BELL
78 Director of Cooperative Education .... Mr. Keith WEBB
15 Director Human Resources .... Ms. Bernadette COHEN
38 Director Counseling Services .... Dr. Ave MARSHALL
09 Director Institutional Research .... Mr. James SANDERS
88 Director Women's Resource Center .... Dr. Beverly GUY-SHEFTAL
18 Director Facilities Mgmt & Svcs .... Mr. Arthur E. FRAZIER, III
19 Director of Public Safety .... Mr. Steve BOWSER
24 Technology Services Coordinator .... Ms. Belinda GRIFFITH
88 Dir Corporate Rels/Partnerships .... Ms. Cassandra JOSEPH
102 Director Foundation Relations .... Ms. Eda GARCIA
88 Director of Special Events .... Ms. Heather HAWES
39 Director Housing & Residence Life .... Ms. Alison CUMMINGS
28 Coord Diversity & Inclusion Pgms .... Ms. Letitia J. DENARD
08 Library Director/CEO .... Ms. Loretta PARHAM
23 Director Health Services .... Dr. Brenda DALTON
46 Assoc Provost of Research .... Dr. Tasha INNISS
35 Dean of Students .... Dr. Fran'Cee BROWN MCCLURE
40 Bookstore Manager .... Ms. Tiffani HODGE
96 Dir Administrative Support Svcs .... Ms. Jacqueline JAMES
21 AVP Business & Financial Affairs .... Ms. Dawn ALSTON

Thomas University (C)

1501 Millpond Road, Thomasville GA 31792-7499
County: Thomas — FICE Identification: 001555
Unit ID: 141167
Telephone: (229) 226-1621 — Carnegie Class: Masters/M
FAX Number: (229) 226-1653 — Calendar System: Semester
URL: www.thomasu.edu
Established: 1950 — Annual Undergrad Tuition & Fees: $16,940
Enrollment: 1,601 — Coed
Affiliation or Control: Independent Non-Profit — IRS Status: 501(c)3
Highest Offering: Master's
Accreditation: SC, CACREP, MT, NUR, SW

01 President .... Dr. Andy SHEPPARD
05 Vice President of Academic Affairs .... Dr. John MEIS
111 Vice Pres Institutional Advancement .... Mr. Kurt STRINGFELLOW
32 Vice President Student Life .... Dr. Robert BOHMAN
84 VP Enrollment Management .... Dr. Susan BACKOFEN
08 Director of Library Services .... Ms. Tara HAGAN
06 Registrar .... Mrs. Michelle WENDEL
09 Director of Institutional Research .... Dr. Daňáe JOHNSON
37 Director of Financial Aid .... Mr. Clifton MITCHELL
41 Director of Athletics .... Mr. Michael D. LEE
10 Controller .... Ms. Sue STONE
44 Director of Annual Fund .... Vacant
26 Director of Communications .... Mrs. Cindy MONTGOMERY
04 Assistant to the President .... Mrs. Linda M. HERNDON

Toccoa Falls College (D)

107 Kincaid Drive, Toccoa Falls GA 30598-0068
County: Stephens — FICE Identification: 001596
Unit ID: 141185
Telephone: (706) 886-6831 — Carnegie Class: Bac-Diverse
FAX Number: (706) 282-6005 — Calendar System: Semester
URL: www.tfc.edu
Established: 1907 — Annual Undergrad Tuition & Fees: $22,744
Enrollment: 1,411 — Coed
Affiliation or Control: The Christian And Missionary Alliance
IRS Status: 501(c)3
Highest Offering: Baccalaureate
Accreditation: SC, MUS, NURSE

01 President .... Dr. Robert M. MYERS
04 Sr Exec Administrative Assistant .... Mrs. Paula S. ELKINS
32 VP Student Affairs .... Miss Abigail H. DAVIS
111 VP for Advancement .... Vacant
10 Vice President for Finance .... Dr. Dewanna MOONEY
05 Provost/VP for Academic Affairs .... Dr. W. Brian SHELTON
84 VP for Enrollment Services .... Mrs. Emily C. KERR
42 Director Spiritual Formation .... Mr. Chris STRATTON
09 Director Institutional Research .... Dr. Kieran CLEMENTS
106 Dean of Online & Dual Enrollment Ed .... Mr. Andrew THORNE
39 Director Residence/Community Life .... Mrs. Katie THORNE
29 Director Alumni Assoc/Col Relations .... Mrs. Deborah WILKES
38 Dir Counseling/Career Svcs .... Mrs. Amy MARSHALL
37 Director Student Financial Aid .... Mrs. Wanda PICKENS
07 Asst Director of Admissions .... Miss Lauren BANKS
06 Registrar .... Mr. Kelly G. VICKERS
41 Athletic Director .... Mr. Kevin HALL
18 Chief Facilities/Physical Plant .... Mr. Merlin SCHENCK
19 Director of Security/Safety .... Mr. Stephen JOHANNES
15 Director Human Resources .... Ms. Mary Kaye RITCHEY
21 Director of Business Services .... Mrs. Allison HOTALEN
66 Dean of Nursing .... Mrs. Deborah ALVATER
11 Assistant VP of Operations .... Mr. Merlin SCHENCK
88 Assistant VP Enrollment .... Mr. Ronnie STEWART
08 Head Librarian .... Mr. Armand TERNAK
108 Dir Institutional Effectiveness .... Ms. Allison BRADY
13 Information Technology Director .... Mr. Zachary HIGHTOWER
26 Public Rels/Mktg/Communication Ofcr .... Mrs. Tracy WIEGMAN
30 Development Officer .... Mr. Joseph MURREY

Truett McConnell University (E)

100 Alumni Drive, Cleveland GA 30528-1264
County: White — FICE Identification: 001597
Unit ID: 141237
Telephone: (706) 865-2134 — Carnegie Class: Bac-Diverse
FAX Number: (706) 243-4968 — Calendar System: Semester
URL: www.truett.edu
Established: 1946 — Annual Undergrad Tuition & Fees: $20,230
Enrollment: 2,622 — Coed
Affiliation or Control: Baptist — IRS Status: 501(c)3
Highest Offering: Master's
Accreditation: SC, MUS, NURSE

01 President .... Dr. Emir CANER
05 Vice Pres Academic Services .... Dr. Brad REYNOLDS
32 Vice President of Student Services .... Mr. Chris EPPLING
10 VP Finance/Operations/CFO .... Dr. Jason GRAFFAGNINO
21 Assoc Vice President of Finance .... Mr. Paul WILLARD
88 Assoc VP Enterprise Data Mgmt .... Mr. Truitt FRANKLIN
04 Executive Assistant to President .... Ms. Cindy ERBELE
41 Athletic Director .... Mrs. Jenni SHEPARD
06 Registrar .... Mrs. Kamille GAUNTT
37 Director of Financial Aid .... Mrs. Karli GREENFIELD
08 Director of Library Resources .... Mrs. Teresa HAYMORE
86 Director of Public Policy .... Dr. John YARBROUGH
07 Director of Admissions .... Mr. Bryan WISDOM
42 Director of Alumni/Church Relations .... Dr. David DRAKE
40 Campus Store Director .... Mr. Eddie O'BRIEN
18 Director of Facilities .... Mr. Justin COALLEY
09 Director Institutional Research .... Mrs. Melissa FORTNER
121 Director of Student Success .... Mr. Andrew GAILEY
19 Director of Campus Safety .... Mr. Kerry SEABOLT
120 Director of Online Learning .... Mrs. Amy HAYES

Underwood University (F)

2855 Rolling Pin Lane, Suite 200, Suwanee GA 30024
County: Gwinnett — Identification: 667361
Telephone: (770) 831-9500 — Carnegie Class: Not Classified
FAX Number: (770) 831-8858 — Calendar System: Semester
URL: underwooduniversity.com
Established: 2011 — Annual Undergrad Tuition & Fees: N/A
Enrollment: N/A — Coed
Affiliation or Control: Independent Non-Profit — IRS Status: 501(c)3
Highest Offering: Master's
Accreditation: @TRACS

01 President .... Richard S. YOON

University of Georgia (G)

Athens GA 30602-0001
County: Clarke — FICE Identification: 001598
Unit ID: 139959
Telephone: (706) 542-3000 — Carnegie Class: DU-Highest
FAX Number: N/A — Calendar System: Semester
URL: www.uga.edu
Established: 1785 — Annual Undergrad Tuition & Fees (In-State): $11,830
Enrollment: 37,606 — Coed
Affiliation or Control: State — IRS Status: 501(c)3
Highest Offering: Doctorate
Accreditation: SC, AAFCS, ART, CAATE, CACREP, CEA, CIDA, CLPSY, COPSY, DANCE, DIETD, DIETI, JOUR, LAW, LSAR, MFCD, MUS, PCSAS, PH, PHAR, PLNG, SCPSY, SP, SPAA, SW, THEA, VET

01 President .... Mr. Jere W. MOREHEAD
100 Chief of Staff & Assoc VP .... Dr. Kathy R. PHARR
04 Assistant to the President .... Dr. Kyle TSCHEPIKOW
04 Assistant to the President .... Ms. Sheila J. DAVIS
04 Assistant to the President .... Mr. Alton M. STANDIFER
05 Sr VP Academic Affs/Provost .... Dr. Jack HU
10 Sr Assoc VP Finance & Admin .... Mr. James SHORE
20 Vice Provost Academic Affairs .... Dr. Marisa A. PAGNATTARO
11 Vice Pres for Finance & Admin .... Mr. Ryan A. NESBIT
30 Vice Pres for Devel & Alumni Rels .... Mr. Kelly K. KERNER
20 Vice President for Instruction .... Dr. Rahul SHRIVASTAV
46 Vice President for Research .... Dr. David C. LEE
88 Vice Pres Public Svc/Outreach .... Dr. Jennifer L. FRUM
32 Vice President Student Affairs .... Dr. Victor K. WILSON
86 Vice President for Govt Relations .... Mr. Tobin R. CARR
26 Vice President for Marketing & Comm .... Ms. Karri HOBSON-PAPE
13 VP for Information Technology .... Dr. Timothy M. CHESTER
92 Assoc Prov/Dir of Honors Program .... Dr. David S. WILLIAMS
104 Int Assoc Prov International Educ .... Dr. Noel FALLOWS
28 Vice Prov Diversity & Inclusion .... Dr. Michelle G. COOK
20 Assoc Provost Academic Programs .... Dr. Margaret AMSTUTZ
08 Assoc Provost/University Librarian .... Dr. Toby GRAHAM
88 Assoc Provost Faculty Affairs .... Ms. Sarah COVERT
07 Assoc VP Admissions/Enroll Mgmt .... Mr. Patrick WINTER
21 Assoc VP Univ Business & Acct Svcs .... Ms. Holley W. SCHRAMSKI
18 Assoc VP Facilities Management .... Mr. Ralph F. JOHNSON
15 Associate VP Human Resources .... Mr. Juan JARRETT
43 Executive Director Legal Affairs .... Mr. Michael RAEBER
49 Dean of Arts & Sciences .... Dr. Alan T. DORSEY
47 Dean of Agricultural & Environ Sci .... Dr. Samuel PARDUE
61 Dean of Law .... Mr. Peter RUTLEDGE
67 Dean of Pharmacy .... Dr. Kelly M. SMITH
65 Dean Forestry & Natural Resources .... Dr. Dale GREENE
53 Dean of Education .... Dr. Denise SPANGLER
58 Dean of the Graduate School .... Dr. Suzanne BARBOUR
50 Dean of Business .... Dr. Benjamin C. AYERS
60 Dean Journalism & Mass Comm .... Dr. Charles N. DAVIS
59 Dean of Family & Consumer Sci .... Dr. Linda K. FOX
74 Dean of Veterinary Medicine .... Dr. Lisa K. NOLAN
70 Dean of Social Work .... Dr. Anna M. SCHEYETT
48 Dean of Environment & Design .... Dr. Sonia A. HIRT
80 Dean Public/International Affs .... Dr. Matthew R. AUER
69 Dean of Public Health .... Dr. Marsha DAVIS
88 Dean School of Ecology .... Dr. John L. GITTLEMAN
88 Dean GRU/UGA Medical .... Dr. Shelley NUSS
54 Dean of Engineering .... Dr. Donald LEO
41 Athletic Director .... Mr. William G. MCGARITY
22 Director of Equal Opportunity .... Ms. E. Janyce DAWKINS
06 Registrar .... Ms. Fiona B. LIKEN
19 Chief of Police .... Chief Dan SILK
37 Director of Student Financial Aid .... Mr. Anthony P. JONES
36 Director of Career Services Center .... Mr. Scott T. WILLIAMS
39 Executive Director of Housing .... Ms. Linda KASPER
23 Exec Director of Health Services .... Dr. Garth S. RUSSO
35 Dean of Students .... Dr. William M. MCDONALD
38 Dir Counseling/Psychological Svcs .... Dr. Ash THOMPSON
88 Director Georgia Center .... Dr. Dawn H. CARTEE
29 Exec Dir of Alumni Relations .... Ms. Meredith G. JOHNSON
110 Sr Assoc VP for Dev & Alumni Rel .... Mr. Jay STROMAN
09 Director of Institutional Research .... Mr. Paul KLUTE
121 Director of Academic Enhancement .... Dr. Thomas HAGOOD
94 Director Inst of Women's Studies .... Dr. Juanita JOHNSON-BAILEY
96 Director of Purchasing .... Ms. Annette EVANS
106 Dir Online Education/E-learning .... Dr. Stephen P. BALFOUR
88 Sr Director for Accreditation .... Mr. Allan AYCOCK
44 Exec Dir Annual or Planned Giving .... Mr. David JONES
88 Director Office of Economic Dev .... Mr. Sean MCMILLAN

† Part of the University System of Georgia.

University of North Georgia (A)

82 College Circle, Dahlonega GA 30597-1001

County: Lumpkin FICE Identification: 001585
Unit ID: 482680
Telephone: (706) 864-1800 Carnegie Class: Masters/M
FAX Number: (706) 864-1478 Calendar System: Semester
URL: ung.edu
Established: 1873 Annual Undergrad Tuition & Fees (In-State): $4,692
Enrollment: 18,782 Coed
Affiliation or Control: State IRS Status: 501(c)3
Highest Offering: Doctorate
Accreditation: SC, ART, CAATE, CACREP, CAEPN, CSHSE, NUR, PTA

01 President ... Dr. Bonita JACOBS
05 Int Provost & Sr VP Acad Affairs ... Dr. Chaudron GILLE
10 Sr VP Business & Finance ... Dr. Frank J. MCCONNELL
88 Sr VP Leadership & Global Engage ... Dr. Billy WELLS
32 VP Student Affairs ... Dr. James CONNEELY
12 VP of Gainesville Campus ... Dr. Richard OATES
111 VP of University Advancement ... Mr. Jeff TARNOWSKI
20 Int Assoc Provost ... Dr. Steve LLOYD
108 Assoc Provost Inst Effectiveness ... Dr. Holly VERHASSELT
46 Assoc Prov & Chief Research Officer ... Dr. Andy NOVOBILSKI
20 Assoc VP & Dean Univ College ... Dr. Carol ADAMS
58 Assoc VP Graduate Studies ... Dr. Bill GASH
21 AVP Financial Svcs & Comptroller ... Ms. Donna CALDWELL
109 Assoc VP Aux Services & Real Estate ... Mr. Gerald SULLIVAN
13 Int Chief Technology Officer ... Mr. Steve MCLEOD
84 Assoc VP Enrollment Management ... Dr. Brett E. MORRIS
35 Asst VP Stdnt Affs & Dean of Stdnts ... Dr. Michelle BROWN
35 Assoc VPSA & Dean of Students ... Dr. Alyson PAUL
29 Director Alumni Relations & Annual ... Ms. Wendy HUGULEY ROTHIER
106 Dir Distance Educ/Tech Integration ... Dr. Irene KOKKALA
07 Director of Undergrad Admissions ... Ms. Molly POTTS
07 Director of Cadet Admissions ... Mr. Mike IVY
92 Dean of Honors Program ... Dr. Tanya BENNETT
41 Director of Athletics ... Ms. Lindsay REEVES
116 Director of Internal Audit ... Ms. Jill HOLMAN
06 University Registrar ... Mr. Steve STUBBS
25 Director of Grants & Contracts ... Dr. Yolanda CARR
37 Director of Financial Aid ... Ms. Jill RAYNER
09 Director Institutional Research ... Ms. Linda ROWLAND
08 Int Dean of Libraries ... Dr. Joy BOLT
49 Dean College of Arts & Letters ... Dr. Christopher JESPERSEN
50 Dean M C College of Business ... Dr. Mary A. GOWAN
53 Dean of College of Education ... Dr. Sheri HARDEE
81 Int Dean College of Science & Math ... Dr. John LEYBA
76 Dean College of Health Sciences ... Dr. Teresa CONNER-KERR
104 Assoc VP International Programs ... Ms. Sheila SCHULTE
15 Assoc VP Human Resources ... Ms. Beth ARBUTHNOT
18 Asst VP of Facilities ... Mr. Ken CROWE
19 Director of Public Safety ... Mr. Justin GAINES
14 CIO ... Dr. Steve MCLEOD
100 Chief of Staff ... Ms. Kate MAINE
35 Commandant Corp of Cadets ... Col. Joseph MATTHEWS
36 Director of Career Services ... Ms. Diane FARRELL
38 Director Counseling Services ... Dr. Simon CORDERY
39 Director of Residence Life ... Ms. Treva SMITH
23 Director of Student Health Services ... Ms. Karen TOMLINSON
12 Exec Dir Cumming Campus ... Mr. Jason PRUITT
12 Exec Director Oconee Campus ... Dr. Cyndee MOORE
108 Dir Accreditation & Assessment ... Ms. Betsy CANTRELL
51 Director Continuing Education ... Dr. Wendy ESTES
86 Exec Director External Relations ... Dr. Edward MIENIE
43 General Counsel & Dir Gov Relations ... Ms. Jenna COLVIN
96 Director Purchasing ... Ms. Beverly LONG
85 Dir Multicultural Student Affairs ... Dr. Robert ROBINSON
04 Admin Asst to the President ... Ms. Linda SMITH
28 Director of Diversity & Inclusion ... Dr. Pablo MENDOZA
105 Director Web Services ... Ms. Joanie CHEMBARS
91 Asst CIO ... Mr. Rick CRAIN
26 Exec Director for Communications ... Ms. Sylvia CARSON

† Part of the University System of Georgia.

University of Phoenix Atlanta Campus (B)

859 Mount Vernon Hwy NE, Atlanta GA 30328

Telephone: (678) 731-0555 Identification: 770200
Accreditation: &NH, ACBSP

† No longer accepting campus-based students.

University of Phoenix Augusta Campus (C)

3150 Perimeter Parkway, Augusta GA 30909-4583

Telephone: (706) 868-2000 Identification: 770198
Accreditation: &NH, ACBSP

† No longer accepting campus-based students.

University of Phoenix Columbus GA Campus (D)

7200 North Lake Drive, Columbus GA 31909

Telephone: (706) 317-3924 Identification: 770199
Accreditation: &NH, ACBSP

† No longer accepting campus-based students.

University of West Georgia (E)

1601 Maple Street, Carrollton GA 30118-0001

County: Carroll FICE Identification: 001601
Unit ID: 141334
Telephone: (678) 839-5000 Carnegie Class: DU-Mod
FAX Number: N/A Calendar System: Semester
URL: www.westga.edu
Established: 1906 Annual Undergrad Tuition & Fees (In-State): $6,288
Enrollment: 13,520 Coed
Affiliation or Control: State IRS Status: 501(c)3
Highest Offering: Doctorate
Accreditation: SC, ART, CACREP, CAEPN, MUS, NURSE, SP, SPAA, THEA

01 Interim President ... Dr. Michael CRAFTON
05 Int Provost & VP for Acad Affairs ... Dr. David JENKS
10 Exec VP for Business & Finance ... Mr. Jim SUTHERLAND
32 Int VP Student Affairs & Enroll Mgt ... Dr. Xavier WHITAKER
111 VP for University Advancement ... Mr. Dave FRABONI
13 VP Info Tech Services/CIO ... Ms. Annemarie EADES
30 Exec Dir of Development ... Ms. Nichole FANNIN
84 AVP for Enrollment Management ... Dr. Jennifer JORDAN
20 Assoc VP for Academic Affairs ... Dr. Jill DRAKE
20 Assoc VP for Academic Affairs ... Dr. David JENKS
20 Assoc VP & Int Dean Univ College ... Dr. David NEWTON
21 Assoc VP Finance/Univ Controller ... Mr. Richard SEARS
14 Assoc VP for Info Tech Services ... Ms. Kathy KRAL
88 Assoc VP for IT Strategic Planning ... Mr. Dale DRIVER
83 Interim Dean Social Sciences ... Dr. Amber SMALLWOOD
50 Dean Richards College of Business ... Dr. Faye S. MCINTYRE
53 Dean Education ... Dr. Dianne HOFF
79 Dean Arts & Humanities ... Dr. Pauline GAGNON
81 Dean Science & Mathematics ... Vacant
92 Dean Honors College ... Dr. Janet DONOHOE
06 Registrar ... Ms. Donna HALEY
07 Director Admissions ... Mr. Justin BARLOW
08 Dean of Libraries ... Dr. Beth SHEPPARD
37 Director Financial Aid ... Ms. Leigh Ann HUSSEY
36 Director Career Services ... Ms. Jymmyca WYATT
51 Director Continuing Education ... Mr. Marty DAVIS
15 Asst VP for Human Resources ... Ms. Christina BROGDON
18 Asst VP Campus Planning/Facilities ... Mr. Brendan BOWEN
19 Director of Public Safety ... Mr. Tom SACCENTI
23 Interim Dir of Health Services ... Dr. Michael POSS
39 Director Housing & Residence Life ... Mr. Stephen WHITLOCK
41 Director of Athletics ... Mr. Daryl DICKEY
38 Director Counseling Center ... Dr. Lisa ADAMS SOMERLOT
109 Assoc VP Auxiliary Services ... Mr. Mark REEVES
108 AVP Inst Effectiveness & Assessment ... Dr. Catherine JENKS
29 Exec Dir of Alumni Relations ... Ms. Alison ROSBOROUGH
26 Assoc VP Communication & Marketing ... Ms. Jami BOWER
58 Assoc VP & Dean of Graduate School ... Dr. Denise OVERFIELD
106 Dean USG eCore ... Dr. Melanie N. CLAY
43 University General Counsel ... Ms. Jane SIMPSON
102 Dir of Advancement Services ... Mr. Bart GILLESPIE
66 Dean Tanner School of Nursing ... Dr. Jennifer SCHUESSLER
96 Director of Purchasing ... Ms. Lisa ELLIOTT LITTLE
22 Social Equity Officer/Title IX Coor ... Ms. Claudia LYERLY
86 Spec Asst Pres Govt & External Rels . Mr. Russell CRUTCHFIELD
12 Chief Admin Ofcr Off-Campus Pgms ... Dr. Robert HEABERLIN
105 Manager Web Innovations ... Mr. Denny CHASTEEN
40 Bookstore Manager ... Ms. Wanda WALKER
85 Dir International Services & Pgms ... Mr. Brett REICHERT
28 Senior Diversity Officer ... Ms. Yves-Rose PORCENA
44 Director Annual Giving ... Ms. Allyson BRETCH
04 Admin Assistant to the President ... Ms. Tina BENNETT

† Part of the University System of Georgia.

*University System of Georgia Office (F)

270 Washington Street, SW, Atlanta GA 30334-9007

County: Fulton FICE Identification: 008290
Telephone: (404) 962-3000 Carnegie Class: N/A
FAX Number: (404) 962-3013
URL: www.usg.edu

01 Chancellor ... Dr. Steve WRIGLEY
04 Executive Assistant to Chancellor ... Ms. Shelia ELDER
11 Exec Vice Chanc Administration ... Ms. Teresa MACCARTNEY
05 Exec Vice Chanc/Chief Academic Ofcr ... Dr. Tristan DENLEY
45 Exec VC Strategy/Fiscal Affairs ... Ms. Tracey COOK
116 Interim Chief Audit Officer ... Ms. Claire ARNOLD
20 Vice Chancellor Academic Affairs ... Dr. Martha VENN
18 Vice Chancellor Facilities ... Mr. Jim JAMES
43 Vice Chancellor Legal Affairs ... Mr. Edward TATE
26 Vice Chancellor for Communications ... Ms. Jen RYAN
13 Vice Chanc/Chief Information Ofcr ... Dr. Robert LAURINE
10 Vice Chancellor for Fiscal Affairs ... Ms. Diane HICKEY
32 Vice Chancellor for Student Affairs ... Dr. Joyce JONES
30 Vice Chancellor for Development ... Ms. Karen MCCAULEY
88 Vice Chancellor Org Effectiveness ... Mr. John FUCHKO
15 Vice Chancellor for Human Resources ... Dr. Juanita HICKS
09 Vice Chanc of Research & Policy ... Dr. Angela BELL
100 Vice Chancellor for Leadership ... Dr. Stuart RAYFIELD
86 COS/Director Government Relations ... Ms. Ashley JONES

Valdosta State University (G)

1500 N Patterson Street, Valdosta GA 31698-0010

County: Lowndes FICE Identification: 001599
Unit ID: 141264
Telephone: (229) 333-5800 Carnegie Class: DU-Mod
FAX Number: (229) 333-7400 Calendar System: Semester
URL: www.valdosta.edu
Established: 1906 Annual Undergrad Tuition & Fees (In-State): $6,410
Enrollment: 11,341 Coed
Affiliation or Control: State IRS Status: 501(c)3
Highest Offering: Doctorate
Accreditation: SC, ART, CAATE, CACREP, CAEP, EXSC, LIB, MFCD, MUS, NURSE, SP, SPAA, SW, THEA

01 President ... Dr. Richard CARVAJAL
05 Provost & VPAA ... Dr. Robert T. SMITH
10 Vice President for Finance & Admin ... Ms. Traycee F. MARTIN
111 Vice President for Advancement ... Mr. John D. CRAWFORD
32 VP for Student Affairs ... Dr. Vince MILLER
58 Assoc Prov Grad Studies & Research ... Dr. Becky DACRUZ
20 Assoc Provost Academic Affairs ... Dr. Sharon L. GRAVETT
20 Dean Undergrad Studies AA ... Dr. Lai K. ORENDUFF
30 Assoc VP for Devel & Alum Rel ... Ms. Hilary H. GIBBS
79 Dean Col of Humanities & Social Sci ... Dr. James T. LAPLANT
81 Dean College of Sci & Math ... Dr. Keith WALTERS
50 Dean College of Business Admin ... Dr. Wayne L. PLUMLY
57 Dean College of the Arts ... Mr. Arthur B. PEARCE
53 Dean College of Educ & Hum Svc ... Dr. Bernie OLIVER
66 Dean College of Nursing & Hlth Sci ... Dr. Sheri R. NOVIELLO
92 Dean of Honors College ... Dr. Michael P. SAVOIE
08 Univ Librarian & Dean of Faculty ... Dr. Alan BERNSTEIN
06 Registrar ... Mr. Stanley JONES
106 Int Dir of Ofc of Extended Learning ... Mr. Jarrod K. MURRAY
13 Chief Information Officer ... Mr. Brian HAUGABROOK
14 Chief Technology Officer ... Mr. Joseph A. NEWTON
124 VP Div of Student Success ... Dr. Rodney CARR
39 Dir Housing & Residence Life ... Dr. Zduy CHU
41 Director of Athletics ... Mr. Herb REINHARD
37 Director of Financial Aid ... Mr. Douglas R. TANNER
36 Director of Career Opportunities ... Dr. Gerald WILLIAMS
29 Assoc Dir Alumni Rels/Annual Giving ... Ms. Merritt WALL
15 Director of Human Resources ... Ms. Jeanine BODDIE-LAVAN
88 Director Division Aerospace Studies ... LtCol. Daniel WALLS
22 Director of Social Equity ... Dr. Maggie J. VIVERETTE
43 University Attorney ... Mr. Lee DAVIS
18 Dir Phys Plant & Facilities Plng ... Mr. Ray SABLE
26 Ex Dir of Communications & Mktg ... Mr. Keith WARBURG
38 Director of Counseling Center ... Dr. Tricia A. HALE
121 Exec Director of Advising ... Mr. Rob FREIDHOFF
40 Manager of Bookstore ... Ms. Lee Ann JOHNSON
23 Director of Student Health Services ... Dr. Richard RICKMAN
19 Dir Public Safety/Police Chief ... Mr. Alan ROWE
108 Director of Inst Effectiveness ... Dr. Michael M. BLACK
88 Dir of Info Tech Svcs for Adv Svcs ... Ms. Amelia REAMS
04 Special Assistant to the President ... Ms. Melinda CUTCHENS
96 Dir of Procurement & Accounting ... Ms. Antolina PILGRIM
09 Director Inst Research ... Mr. Barrie D. FITZGERALD
07 Director of Admissions ... Mr. Ryan HOGAN
104 Director of Intl Programs ... Dr. Ivan NIKOLOV
105 Director of Creative Services ... Mr. Jeff GRANT
28 Dir of Diversity & Inclusion ... Ms. Sandra JONES
84 Assoc VP of Enrollment Services ... Mr. Tee MITCHELL
25 Dir Spons Pgm & Rsrch Admin ... Ms. Elizabeth OLPHIE
86 Director Government Affairs ... Mr. Zachary LOUIS

† Part of the University System of Georgia.

Wesleyan College (H)

4760 Forsyth Road, Macon GA 31210-4462

County: Bibb FICE Identification: 001600
Unit ID: 141325
Telephone: (478) 477-1110 Carnegie Class: Bac-A&S
FAX Number: (478) 757-4030 Calendar System: Semester
URL: www.wesleyancollege.edu
Established: 1836 Annual Undergrad Tuition & Fees: $23,000
Enrollment: 603 Female
Affiliation or Control: United Methodist IRS Status: 501(c)3
Highest Offering: Master's
Accreditation: SC, MUS, NURSE

01 President ... Dr. Vivia L. FOWLER
05 Provost/VP for Academic Affairs ... Dr. Melody A. BLAKE
111 VP Institutional Advancement ... Ms. Andrea G. WILLIFORD
10 Vice Pres Finance/Treasurer ... Mr. Robert L. MOYE
32 Dean of Students ... Ms. Christy S. HENRY
84 VP for Strategic Enrollment ... Mr. Clinton G. HOBBS
06 Assistant Dean/Registrar ... Ms. Angie WRIGHT
04 Assistant to the President ... Mrs. Denise W. HOLLOWAY
04 Assistant to the President ... Mrs. Ashley C. MILLER
08 Library Director ... Ms. Kristi PEAVY
13 Director of Information Services ... Mr. Kevin L. ULSHAFER
29 Director of Alumnae Affairs ... Ms. Cathy C. SNOW
26 Director of Communications ... Ms. Mary Ann HOWARD
44 Director of Annual Fund ... Ms. Whitney DAVIS
37 Director of Financial Aid ... Mr. Clinton G. HOBBS
39 Director of Residence Life ... Ms. Dionne GEORGE
18 Director of Physical Plant ... Mr. James FLEENOR
41 Athletic Director ... Ms. Penny SIQUEIROS
42 Chaplain ... Rev. Tyler SCHWALLER
19 Director Security/Safety ... Mr. Emory KENDRICK
15 Director Human Resources ... Ms. Meagon DAVIS
07 Director of Admissions ... Mr. Clinton G. HOBBS
09 Director of Institutional Research ... Ms. Glenda FERGUSON
35 Chief Student Life Officer ... Ms. Alexandra LYON
36 Director Career Development ... Ms. Stephanie BAUGH
38 Director Student Counseling ... Ms. Jamie THAMES
96 Director of Purchasing ... Ms. Hannah DOAN
20 Associate Academic Officer ... Vacant

21 Associate Business Officer .... Ms. Quintress HOLLIS
40 Bookstore Manager .... Ms. Barbara MONTGOMERY
22 Director of Disability and Advocacy .... Ms. Jill AMOS
28 Director of Diversity & Inclusion .... Ms. LaTonya PARKER
30 Chief Development Officer .... Mrs. Susan B. ALLEN

West Georgia Technical College (A)

176 Murphy Campus Boulevard, Waco GA 30182-2407
County: Haralson　FICE Identification: 010487
Unit ID: 139278
Telephone: (770) 537-6000　Carnegie Class: Assoc/HVT-Mix Trad/Non
FAX Number: (770) 537-7976　Calendar System: Semester
URL: www.westgatech.edu
Established: 1968　Annual Undergrad Tuition & Fees (In-State): $2,838
Enrollment: 6,682　Coed
Affiliation or Control: State　IRS Status: 501(c)3
Highest Offering: Associate Degree
Accreditation: SC, ACBSP, ADNUR, CAHIIM, DH, MAC, MLTAD, RAD, SURGT

01 President .... Dr. Scott RULE
11 VP Admin Services .... Ms. Carol REID
05 Vice President Academic Affairs .... Dr. Kristen DOUGLAS
32 Vice President Student Affairs .... Dr. Tonya F. WHITLOCK
09 VP Institutional Effectiveness .... Mr. John PARTON
103 VP Economic Development .... Ms. Angela BERCH
51 VP of Adult Education .... Mrs. Kerri HOSMER
08 Exec Director Library Services .... Mr. Chris CAROL
06 Registrar .... Mrs. Laura THORNTON
13 Exec Dir Information Technology .... Mr. Sam JENKINS
07 Director of Admissions .... Mrs. Mary ADERHOLD
18 Director Facilities .... Mr. Michael JILES
04 Executive Asst to President .... Mrs. Julia WATSON
36 Manager Career Services .... Ms. Dawne WHITE
37 Director Student Financial Aid .... Mrs. Kim KELLEY
15 Exec Director of Human Resources .... Mr. Rodd RUSSOW
19 Chief of Police .... Mr. James PERRY
50 Dean Sch of Business & Public Svcs .... Ms. Babs RUSSELL
53 Dean Sch of Arts & Sciences .... Mr. Brian BARKLEY
54 Dean Sch of Trade & Technology .... Ms. Linda SULLIVAN
106 Director Online Learning .... Mr. Jeremy EASON
108 Director Institutional Assessment .... Mr. AJ THOMAS
26 Dir of Public Relations & Info .... Mr. Ben CHAMBERS
111 Exec Dir of Institutional Advance .... Ms. Kelsey JONES

Wiregrass Georgia Technical College (B)

4089 Val Tech Road, Valdosta GA 31602
County: Lowndes　FICE Identification: 005256
Unit ID: 141255
Telephone: (229) 333-2100　Carnegie Class: Assoc/HVT-High Non
FAX Number: (229) 333-2129　Calendar System: Semester
URL: www.wiregrass.edu
Established: 1963　Annual Undergrad Tuition & Fees (In-State): $2,794
Enrollment: 3,936　Coed
Affiliation or Control: State　IRS Status: 501(c)3
Highest Offering: Associate Degree
Accreditation: SC, ADNUR, CAHIIM, DA, DH, EMT, MAC, RAD, SURGT

01 President .... Dr. Tina K. ANDERSON
05 Exec Vice Pres Academic Affairs .... Dr. Shawn UTLEY
18 Vice President Facilities .... Ms. Lidell GREENWAY
09 Assoc VP Institutional Research .... Dr. Bonnie KELLY
11 VP for Administrative Services .... Ms. Keren WYNN
84 VP for Enrollment Management .... Ms. Angela HOBBY
108 Assoc VP for Inst Effectiveness .... Mrs. April MCDUFFIE
88 VP Community Affs/Minority Recruit .... Vacant
88 Assoc VP Economic Development .... Ms. Brandy WILKES
13 Chief Info Technology Officer (CIO) .... Mr. Jarrod BROGDON
88 Exec Dir Administrative Services .... Dr. Penelope SCHMIDT
32 Dean of Student Affairs .... Ms. Shannon MCCONICO
26 Dir for Cmty/College Relations .... Ms. Lydia HUBERT
07 Executive Dir High School Services .... Ms. Brooke JARAMILLO
04 Administrative Asst to President .... Ms. Cheryl ACREE
06 Assistant Registrar .... Ms. Julie DREXLER
08 Head Librarian .... Ms. Kathryn TOMLINSON
105 Director Web Services .... Ms. Mary Ann GARNER
106 Exec Director Online Education .... Ms. Sabrina COX
15 Assoc VP of Human Resources .... Ms. Shalonda SANDERS
19 Chief of Police .... Mr. Tim ALLMOND
37 Financial Aid Coordinator .... Ms. Paula HERRING
96 Director of Purchasing .... Mr. Jim RAGO
50 Dean of Business/Education .... Ms. Holly GREENE
49 Dean of Arts and Science .... Mr. Michael WILLIAMS
76 Dean of Allied Health .... Ms. Jackie SPRIGGS

Young Harris College (C)

1 College Street, Young Harris GA 30582-0098
County: Towns　FICE Identification: 001604
Unit ID: 141361
Telephone: (706) 379-3111　Carnegie Class: Bac-A&S
FAX Number: (706) 379-4319　Calendar System: Semester
URL: www.yhc.edu
Established: 1886　Annual Undergrad Tuition & Fees: $29,067
Enrollment: 1,202　Coed
Affiliation or Control: United Methodist　IRS Status: 501(c)3
Highest Offering: Master's
Accreditation: SC, MUS

01 President .... Dr. Drew L. VAN HORN
05 Provost .... Dr. Jason PIERCE
10 CFO .... Mr. Wade M. BENSON
32 Vice Pres of Student Development .... Dr. Laura WHITAKER-LEA
84 Vice Pres for Enrollment Management .... Mr. Clayton DANIELS
111 Vice President of Advancement .... Mr. Mark DOTSON
45 VP for Planning/Special Projects .... Ms. Rosemary R. ROYSTON
13 Vice President of Campus Technology .... Mr. Ken FANEUFF
29 Director of Alumni Relations .... Ms. Dana ENSLEY
20 Assoc VP for Academic Services .... Dr. Keith DEFOOR
08 Dean of Library Services .... Ms. Debra MARCH
38 Dir Counseling/Psychological Svcs .... Ms. Lynne GRADY
06 Registrar .... Ms. Tammy GIBSON
37 Director of Financial Aid .... Ms. Michelle BERNARD
15 Human Resources Director .... Mr. Vince ROBELOTTO
26 Dir of Communication & Marketing .... Vacant
18 Facilities General Manager .... Mr. Mark WILLIAMS
19 Director of Safety & Compliance .... Vacant
41 Director of Athletics .... Ms. Jennifer RUSHTON
42 Chaplain & Dean of the Chapel .... Vacant
04 Administrative Asst to President .... Ms. Teresa KELLEY
07 Director of Admissions .... Ms. Karen FULL
44 Director Annual Giving .... Ms. Mackenzie HARKINS

HAWAII

Babel University Professional School of Translation (D)

1833 Kalakaua Avenue, #208, Honolulu HI 96815
County: Honolulu　Identification: 666350
Telephone: (808) 946-3773　Carnegie Class: Not Classified
FAX Number: (808) 946-3993　Calendar System: Other
URL: www.babel.edu
Established: 2000　Annual Graduate Tuition & Fees: N/A
Enrollment: N/A　Coed
Affiliation or Control: Proprietary　IRS Status: Proprietary
Highest Offering: Master's; No Undergraduates
Accreditation: DEAC

01 Chancellor .... Dr. Miyoko YUASA
03 Vice Chancellor/Educational Dir .... Mr. Tomoki HOTTA
43 General Counsel .... Mr. Yoshiharu ISHIDA
05 Head of Deans .... Mr. Yoshiharu ISHIDA
11 Director of Administration .... Dr. Miyoko YUASA
32 Student Services Manager .... Ms. Yuji TATENO

Brigham Young University Hawaii (E)

55-220 Kulanui Street, Laie Oahu HI 96762-1294
County: Honolulu　FICE Identification: 001606
Unit ID: 230047
Telephone: (808) 675-3211　Carnegie Class: Bac-Diverse
FAX Number: (808) 675-3329　Calendar System: Semester
URL: www.byuh.edu
Established: 1955　Annual Undergrad Tuition & Fees: $5,560
Enrollment: 3,143　Coed
Affiliation or Control: Latter-day Saints　IRS Status: 501(c)3
Highest Offering: Baccalaureate
Accreditation: WC, CAEPT, SW

01 President .... Dr. John S. TANNER
05 Vice President for Academics .... Dr. John D. BELL
11 VP of Administration .... Mr. Steve W. TUELLER
32 VP for Student Development & Svcs .... Dr. Debbie HIPPOLITE WRIGHT
04 Admin Assistant to the President .... Ms. Sydney WILLIAMS
108 Assoc Acad VP Curriculum/Assessment .... Dr. Rosalind RAM
20 Assoc Academic VP for Faculty .... Dr. David BYBEE
81 Dean Faculty of Sciences .... Dr. Mark B. CANNON
77 Dean Faculty of Math/Computing .... Dr. James D. LEE
83 Dean Faculty of Religious Education .... Dr. Jennifer LANE
79 Dean Fac of Culture/Lang/Perf Arts .... Dr. Tevita KAILI
49 Dean Faculty of Arts & Letters .... Dr. Yifen BEUS
50 Dean Faculty of Business/Government .... Dr. Brian HOUGHTON
53 Dean Faculty of Educ & Social Work .... Dr. Karen LATHAM
13 University Technology Officer .... Mr. Kevin SCHLAG
07 Director Admissions .... Mr. James FAUSTINO
41 Mgr of Seasider Sports/Student Act .... Mr. Brandyn AKANA
08 Director Library & Academic Success .... Mr. Michael ALDRICH
21 Managing Director of Budget .... Mr. Michael TEJADA
96 Dir of Purchasing/Retail Services .... Mr. Robert OWAN
19 Director Campus Safety/Security .... Mr. Michael KUEHN
15 Director of Human Resources .... Mr. Reid MILLERBERG
18 Director Facilities Management .... Mr. Randy SHARP
10 Dir Financial Services/Controller .... Mr. Eric MARLER
23 Director of Health Services .... Mrs. Laurie ABREGANO
116 Dir Compliance & Internal Audit .... Mr. Christopher BEARD
36 Director Alumni & Career Services .... Mr. Mark MACDONALD
38 Dir Counseling/Disability Services .... Mrs. Debbie HIPPOLITE WRIGHT
35 Dir Student Leadership/Services .... Ms. Alison WHITING
109 Director Food Services .... Mr. David KEALA
26 Director Communications/Marketing .... Mrs. Laura TEVAGA
88 Manager of Univ Testing/Evaluation .... Mr. Christopher WRIGHT
06 Registrar .... Mrs. Daryl WHITFORD
39 Director Housing Administration .... Mr. Edwin ROGERS
51 Manager of Educational Outreach .... Ms. Diedra ULII
40 Manager Bookstore .... Mr. David FONOIMOANA
85 Dir Recruiting/Intl Student Svcs .... Mr. Arapata MEHA
37 Sr Mgr Financial Aid/Scholarships .... Mr. Mamoe SANERIVI

† Affiliated with Brigham Young University, Provo, UT.

Chaminade University of Honolulu (F)

3140 Waialae Avenue, Honolulu HI 96816-1578
County: Honolulu　FICE Identification: 001605
Unit ID: 141486
Telephone: (808) 735-4711　Carnegie Class: Masters/L
FAX Number: (808) 735-4870　Calendar System: Semester
URL: www.chaminade.edu
Established: 1955　Annual Undergrad Tuition & Fees: $25,374
Enrollment: 2,389　Coed
Affiliation or Control: Independent Non-Profit　IRS Status: 501(c)3
Highest Offering: Doctorate
Accreditation: WC, CAEPT, CIDA, IACBE, MACTE, NURSE

01 President .... Dr. Lynn BABINGTON
05 Provost .... Dr. Lance ASKILDSON
111 VP for Institutional Advancement .... Ms. Diane PETERS-NGUYEN
10 Vice President Finance/Facilities .... Ms. Aulani KAANOI
13 Dean of Info Technologies & Support .... Mr. Kyle JOHNSON
84 VP of Enrollment Management .... Vacant
32 Dean of Students .... Ms. Allison JEROME
15 Exec Dir Compliance/Human Resources .... Ms. Christine DENTON
90 Director Network/Desktop Services .... Mr. Eddie PANG
51 Dir Professional & Continuing Educ .... Vacant
29 Director of Alumni Relations .... Ms. Geraldine ALLEN
41 Director of Athletics .... Mr. William VILLA
42 Director of Campus Ministry .... Bro. Allen PACQUING
36 Dir Career Devel/Job Placement .... Ms. Danielle MASUDA
18 Director Facilities Operations .... Mr. Michael HAISEN
21 Director of Finance .... Mr. Choong LIM
08 Director of Library .... Ms. Sharon LEPAGE
19 Director of Security .... Mr. Milton OLMOS
38 Director of Student Counseling .... Vacant
06 Registrar .... Mr. John MORRIS
37 Director of Financial Aid .... Ms. Amy TAKIGUCHI
09 Dir of Institutional Research .... Mr. Hieu NGUYEN
26 Senior Dir of Univ Communications .... Ms. Lisa FURUTA
07 Director of Admissions .... Vacant

Hawaii Medical Institute Inc. DBA Hawaii Medical College (G)

1221 Kapiolani Blvd Suite 644, Honolulu HI 96814
County: Honolulu　FICE Identification: 041822
Unit ID: 460756
Telephone: (808) 237-5140　Carnegie Class: Spec 2-yr-Health
FAX Number: (808) 237-5805　Calendar System: Other
URL: www.hmi.edu
Established: 2007　Annual Undergrad Tuition & Fees: $21,704
Enrollment: 622　Coed
Affiliation or Control: Proprietary　IRS Status: Proprietary
Highest Offering: Associate Degree
Accreditation: CNCE

01 Executive Director .... Ashton CUDJOE
05 Director of Education .... Charis MATSUWAKI
06 Registrar .... Mandy MORIMOTO
07 Director of Admissions .... Bernard NUNEZ
10 Accounting Manager .... Renz BELTRAN
106 Dean Online Education/E-learning .... Rodney A. WEST
13 Chief Information Technology Office .... Kevin BORRAS
15 Human Resources Administrator .... Josephine BUSANO
18 Chief Facilities/Physical Plant Off .... Vacant
36 Director Career Services .... Jared NAMUMNART
37 Director Student Financial Aid .... Bradley TAGUINOD
38 Director Student Counseling .... Cheryl CHAR

Hawaii Pacific University (H)

1164 Bishop Street, Suite 800, Honolulu HI 96813-2882
County: Honolulu　FICE Identification: 007279
Unit ID: 141644
Telephone: (808) 544-0200　Carnegie Class: Masters/L
FAX Number: (808) 544-1136　Calendar System: Semester
URL: www.hpu.edu
Established: 1965　Annual Undergrad Tuition & Fees: $25,980
Enrollment: 4,146　Coed
Affiliation or Control: Independent Non-Profit　IRS Status: 501(c)3
Highest Offering: Doctorate
Accreditation: WC, CAEPT, NURSE, SW

01 President .... Mr. John GOTANDA
00 President Emeritus .... Mr. Chatt G. WRIGHT
05 Sr VP and Provost .... Dr. Jennifer WALSH
11 Sr Vice Pres Admin/Gen Counsel .... Ms. Janet BOIVIN
10 Sr VP/Chief Financial Officer .... Mr. David KOSTECKI
84 Vice Pres Enrollment Management .... Mr. Greg GRAUMAN
26 VP University Relations/Govt Affs .... Mr. Sam MOKU
20 VP of Advancement .... Ms. Brooke CARROLL
15 Int AVP of Human Resources .... Ms. Diana NILES-HANSEN
13 Assoc VP/Chief Information Officer .... Mr. Cody DOWN
21 Associate VP/Controller .... Mr. James BRESE
50 Dean College Business .... Dr. William RHEY
76 Dean College Health Society .... Dr. Halaevalu VAKALAHI
81 Dean Col Natural/Computational Sci .... Dr. Brenda JENSEN
49 Dean College of Liberal Arts .... Dr. Allison GOUGH
35 AVP/Dean of Students .... Ms. Marites MCKEE
56 Dean College of Prof Studies .... Mr. Mani SEHGAL
07 Assoc Dir International Admissions .... Mr. Jimmi HEMMENBACH
97 Asst Dean College of Prof Studies .... Dr. Valentina ABORDONADO
07 Director of Admissions .... Ms. Marissa BRATTON

104 Director Intl Exchange/Study Abroad ... Ms. Melissa MATSUBARA
36 VP of Communications and Marketing ... Mr. Stephen WARD
06 AVP of Enrollment Management ... Ms. Sara SATO
37 Assoc Director Financial Aid ... Ms. Alyson MACHADO
41 Exe Dir of Athletics & Comm Rel ... Mr. Sam MOKU
08 Dean Libraries and Learning Commons ... Ms. Pam LOUGH
18 AVP of Facilities Safety/Security ... Mr. Kevin G. MATSUKADO
29 Sr Dir Development/Alumni Relations ... Ms. Tara K. WILSON

Hawaii Tokai International College (A)

91-971 Farrington Hwy, Kapolei HI 96707

County: Honolulu — FICE Identification: 037603
Telephone: (808) 983-4000 — Carnegie Class: Not Classified
FAX Number: (808) 983-4107 — Calendar System: Quarter
URL: www.htic.edu
Established: 1992 — Annual Undergrad Tuition & Fees: N/A
Enrollment: N/A — Coed
Affiliation or Control: Independent Non-Profit — IRS Status: 501(c)3
Highest Offering: Associate Degree
Accreditation: WJ

01 Chancellor ... Dr. Gene AWAKUNI
11 Vice Chanc Administrative Affairs ... Mr. Zack (Yuzo) OIDA
05 Dean of Instruction ... Dr. Sandra WU-BOTT
07 Director of Admissions ... Mr. Darrell KICKER
32 Director of Student Affairs ... Dr. Nathan PIERCE

Institute of Clinical Acupuncture and Oriental Medicine (B)

100 N Beretania Street, Suite 203 B,
Honolulu HI 96817-4709

County: Honolulu — FICE Identification: 037353
Unit ID: 444699
Telephone: (808) 521-2288 — Carnegie Class: Spec-4-yr-Other Health
FAX Number: (808) 521-2271 — Calendar System: Semester
URL: www.orientalmedicine.edu
Established: 1996 — Annual Graduate Tuition & Fees: N/A
Enrollment: 50 — Coed
Affiliation or Control: Proprietary — IRS Status: Proprietary
Highest Offering: Master's; No Undergraduates
Accreditation: ACUP

01 President ... Dr. Wai Hoa LOW
05 Chancellor Academic Affairs ... Dr. Edmund BERNAUER
32 Director of Student Affairs ... Dr. Craig TWENTYMAN
10 Director of Finance ... Dr. Catherine Yu-Ling LOW
06 Registrar ... Ms. Jeanne BERNAUER

Pacific Rim Christian University (C)

290 Sand Island Access Road, Honolulu HI 96819

County: Honolulu — Identification: 667010
Unit ID: 457484
Telephone: (808) 853-1040 — Carnegie Class: Bac-A&S
FAX Number: (808) 853-1042 — Calendar System: Semester
URL: www.pacrim.edu
Established: 1998 — Annual Undergrad Tuition & Fees: $10,460
Enrollment: 158 — Coed
Affiliation or Control: Independent Non-Profit — IRS Status: 501(c)3
Highest Offering: Master's
Accreditation: BI

00 Founder ... Dr. Wayne CORDEIRO
01 President ... Dr. Kent KEITH
58 Dean Grad Sch/Pres Emeritus ... Dr. Randall FURUSHIMA
05 Vice Pres Academic Affairs ... Dr. Steve HOSTETTER
32 Vice Pres Student Services ... Craig PANKOW
07 Director of Admissions ... Jade RANESES
08 Library Director ... Karen CLARKE
37 Director of Financial Aid ... Eli JENNINGS
13 Director IT & Facilities ... James MCELMURRY
06 Registrar ... Melodie ALVAREZ

*University of Hawaii System (D)

2444 Dole Street, Honolulu HI 96822

County: Honolulu — FICE Identification: 007885
Unit ID: 141963
Telephone: (808) 956-8207 — Carnegie Class: N/A
FAX Number: (808) 956-5286
URL: www.hawaii.edu

01 President ... Dr. David K. LASSNER
05 VP for Academic Planning & Policy ... Mr. Donald O. STRANEY
46 VP for Research and Innovation ... Dr. Vassilis L. SYRMOS
43 VP for Legal Affs/Univ Gen Counsel ... Ms. Carrie K. OKINAGA
10 VP for Budget and Finance/CFO ... Mr. Kalbert K. YOUNG
88 Interim VP for Community Colleges ... Dr. Erika LACRO
11 VP for Administration ... Ms. Jan N. GOUVEIA
13 VP for Information Tech/CIO ... Mr. Garret T. YOSHIMI
111 VP for Advancement ... Mr. Tim DOLAN
32 Assoc VP Student Affairs ... Ms. Hae K. OKIMOTO
102 President & CEO UH Foundation ... Mr. Tim DOLAN
21 Director of Budget ... Mr. Michael M. NG
15 Interim Sys Dir Human Resources ... Ms. Donna F. KIYOSAKI
14 Director Management Info Systems ... Ms. Susan K. INOUYE
45 Interim Dir Ofc of Research Svcs ... Ms. Darcie S. YOSHINAGA
21 Dir Fin Mgmt & Controller ... Ms. Susan X. LIN
09 Director Data Govt & Operations ... Ms. Sandra K. FURUTO
22 Director EEO/AA ... Mr. Mark G. AU
26 Director of Communications ... Mr. Dan T. MEISENZAHL
101 Exec Administrator/Sec to the BOR ... Ms. Kendra OISHI
86 Director Government Relations ... Ms. Stephanie C. KIM
100 Executive Asst to President ... Ms. Lynne K. MONACO
100 Executive Asst to President ... Ms. Amy M. LUKE
04 Administrative Asst to President ... Ms. Courtney N. DOMINGO

*University of Hawaii at Hilo (E)

200 W Kawili Street, Hilo HI 96720-4091

County: Hawaii — FICE Identification: 001611
Unit ID: 141565
Telephone: (808) 932-7348 — Carnegie Class: DU-Mod
FAX Number: (808) 932-7338 — Calendar System: Semester
URL: www.hilo.hawaii.edu
Established: 1947 — Annual Undergrad Tuition & Fees (In-State): $7,720
Enrollment: 3,539 — Coed
Affiliation or Control: State — IRS Status: 501(c)3
Highest Offering: Doctorate
Accreditation: WC, CAEPT, CEA, NUR, NURSE, PHAR

02 Chancellor ... Dr. Bonnie D. IRWIN
05 Int Vice Chanc Academic Affairs ... Dr. Ken HON
10 Int Vice Chanc Admin Affairs ... Mr. Kalei RAPOZA
46 Vice Chancellor for Research ... Vacant
32 Vice Chancellor Student Affairs ... Ms. Farrah-Marie GOMES
35 Int Asst VC for Student Affairs ... Ms. Kainoa ARIOLA-SUKISAKI
114 Exec Budget Director & Business Mgt ... Ms. Lois M. FUJIYOSHI
88 Director University Disability Svcs ... Ms. Susan SHIRACHI
15 Acting Director Human Resources ... Ms. Annette SUGIMOTO
18 Director Facilities Planning ... Mr. Jerry WATANABE
26 Int Director University Relations ... Ms. Alyson KAKUGAWA-LEONG
08 University Librarian ... Mr. Joseph SANCHEZ
24 Director Media Relations ... Ms. Alyson Y. KAKUGAWA-LEONG
07 Director Admissions ... Mr. Zach STREET
38 Clinical Team Leader ... Mr. Andrew POLLOI
39 Director of Housing ... Ms. Sherri AKAU
35 Acting Director of Campus Center ... Ms. Lai Sha BUGADO
37 Director Financial Aid ... Ms. Sherrie PADILLA
06 University Registrar ... Ms. Chelsea KAY-WONG
49 Int Dean College of Arts & Sciences ... Dr. Michael BITTER
50 Int Dean Col of Business/Economics ... Dr. Emmeline DE PILLIS
67 Dean College of Pharmacy ... Dr. Carolyn MA
47 Dean Col Agri/For/Nat Res Mgmt ... Dr. Bruce MATHEWS
51 Actg Dir Ctr for Community Engage ... Dr. Julie MOWRER
41 Director of Athletics ... Mr. Patrick J. GUILLEN
40 Bookstore Manager ... Ms. Margaret STANLEY
85 Exec Dir Intl Student Services ... Mr. James P. MELLON
36 Exec Director Career Services ... Vacant
22 Director EEO/AA ... Dr. Jennifer STOTTER
09 Institutional Research Analyst ... Ms. Kelli OKUMURA
27 Dir Marketing Imiloa Astronomy Ctr ... Ms. Yu Yok PEARRING
30 Regional Director of Development ... Ms. Andrea FURULI
94 Interim Director Women's Center ... Ms. Karishma KAMATH
23 Director Medical Services ... Ms. Heather HIRATA
88 Dir College of Hawaiian Language ... Ms. Keiki KAWAI`AE`A
19 Director Security/Safety ... Mr. Richard MURRAY

*University of Hawaii at Manoa (F)

2500 Campus Road, Honolulu HI 96822-2217

County: Honolulu — FICE Identification: 001610
Unit ID: 141574
Telephone: (808) 956-8111 — Carnegie Class: DU-Highest
FAX Number: N/A — Calendar System: Semester
URL: www.manoa.hawaii.edu
Established: 1907 — Annual Undergrad Tuition & Fees (In-State): $11,970
Enrollment: 17,612 — Coed
Affiliation or Control: State — IRS Status: 501(c)3
Highest Offering: Doctorate
Accreditation: WC, CAATE, CACREP, CEA, CLPSY, DH, DIETD, IPSY, LAW, LIB, MED, MT, MUS, NURSE, PH, PLNG, SP, SPAA, SW

00 Chair Board of Regents ... Dr. Lee PUTNAM
02 President ... Dr. David LASSNER
22 Dir & Title IX Coord ... Dr. Dee UWONO
88 Native Hawaiian Affairs Pgm Officer ... Dr. Kaiwipuni LIPE
10 Vice Chanc Admin/Finance/Operations ... Ms. Kathleen D. CUTSHAW
109 Director Campus Services ... Ms. Deborah HUEBLER
113 Bursar ... Mr. Wendall K. HO
114 Director Manoa Budget ... Mr. Robert NAGAO
92 Asst VC Undergrad Edu ... Dr. Ronald CAMBRA
96 Dir Procure/Real Prop Mgmt UH Sys ... Mr. Duff ZWALD
116 Director Internal Audit ... Mr. Glenn Y. SHIZUMURA
21 Dir Finance & Accounting ... Ms. Alexandra FRENCH
05 Provost ... Dr. Michael BRUNO
20 Interim Assoc VC Academic Affairs ... Dr. Laura LYONS
46 Interim VC Research ... Dr. Velma KAMEOKA
15 Asst VC Academic Personnel ... Dr. Beverly MCCREARY
32 Int Vice Chanc Students ... Dr. Lori IDETA
13 VP Info Technology/CIO UH System ... Mr. Garret YOSHIMI
06 University Registrar ... Mr. Stuart LAU
08 Interim University Librarian ... Dr. Monica GHOSH
37 Director Financial Aid Services ... Ms. Jodie M. KUBA
38 Dir Counselling/Student Devel Ctr ... Dr. Allyson M. TANOUYE
23 Director University Health Center ... Dr. Andrew W. NICHOLS
39 Int Dir Student Affairs/Housing ... Ms. Laurie FURUTANI
40 Director University Bookstore ... Ms. Tricia R. EJIMA
41 Athletics Director ... Mr. David MATLIN
86 Director of Cmty/Govt Affairs ... Mr. Elmer KAAI
28 Dir Student Affs/Equity/Excl/Div ... Dr. Christine QUEMUEL
36 Interim Dir Manoa Career Center ... Ms. Wendy SORA
15 Interim Director Human Resources ... Ms. Donna KIYOSAKI
88 Director Cancer Center ... Dr. Randall HOLCOMBE
88 Interim Dir Institute for Astronomy ... Dr. Robert MCLAREN
88 Director Waikiki Aquarium ... Dr. Andrew ROSSITER
88 Dir Pacific Bioscience Research Ctr ... Dr. Margaret MCFALL-NGAI
51 Int Dean Outreach College ... Dr. William G. CHISMAR
50 Dean Shidler College of Business ... Dr. V. Vance ROLEY
58 Dean Graduate Education ... Dr. Krystyna AUNE
88 Int Dean Sch of Travel Industry Mgt ... Mr. Tom BINGHAM
53 Dean College of Education ... Dr. Nathan MURATA
54 Dean College of Engineering ... Dr. Brennon MORIOKA
47 Dean Col Trop Agric & Human Res ... Dr. Nicholas COMERFORD
63 Dean John A Burns Sch of Med ... Dr. Jerris R. HEDGES
66 Dean Sch Nursing & Dental Hygiene ... Dr. Mary G. BOLAND
70 Dean M P Thompson Sch of Soc Work ... Dr. Noreen K. MOKUAU
61 Dean Wm S Richardson Sch of Law ... Mr. Aviam SOIFER
48 Interim Dean School of Architecture ... Dr. William CHAPMAN
49 Dean College Arts & Humanities ... Dr. Peter ARNADE
81 Dean College Natural Sciences ... Dr. Aloysius HELMINCK
83 Dean College Social Sciences ... Dr. Denise E. KONAN
88 Dean Sch Ocean & Earth Sci & Tech ... Dr. Brian TAYLOR
88 Dean Pacific and Asian Studies ... Dr. R. Anderson SUTTON
88 Dean Sch of Hawaiian Knowledge ... Dr. Jonhathan OSORIO
09 Director Institutional Research ... Dr. Yang ZHANG
04 Executive Assistant to President ... Ms. Debra ISHII
04 Executive Assistant to President ... Ms. Amy LUKE
07 Assoc Director of Admissions ... Mr. Ryan YAMAGUCHI
101 Exec Administrator & Secy to BOR ... Ms. Kendra OISHI
104 Director Study Abroad ... Dr. Sarita RAI
11 VP Administration UH System ... Ms. Jan GOUVEIA
19 Chief Public Safety ... Mr. Andrew BLACK
22 Dir Affirm Action/Equal Opp UH Sys ... Mr. Mark AU
25 Director Research Services UH Sys ... Mr. Leonard R. GOUVEIA, JR.
26 Director Communications UH System ... Mr. Dan MEISENZAHL
43 VP Legal Affairs UH System ... Ms. Carrie OKINAGA
84 Asst VC Enroll Mgmt & Dir of Admiss ... Ms. Roxie SHABAZZ
90 Asc VP Stdnt Aff/Dir Acad Tech UHS ... Ms. Hae OKIMOTO
102 VP Advance & CEO UH Foundation ... Mr. Tim DOLAN

*University of Hawaii - West Oahu (G)

91-1001 Farrington Highway, Kapolei HI 96707

County: Honolulu — FICE Identification: 021078
Unit ID: 141981
Telephone: (808) 689-2770 — Carnegie Class: Bac-Diverse
FAX Number: (808) 689-2771 — Calendar System: Semester
URL: www.uhwo.hawaii.edu
Established: 1976 — Annual Undergrad Tuition & Fees (In-State): $7,512
Enrollment: 3,082 — Coed
Affiliation or Control: State — IRS Status: 501(c)3
Highest Offering: Baccalaureate
Accreditation: WC, ACBSP, CAEPN

02 Chancellor ... Dr. Maenette BENHAM
05 Vice Chanc Academic Affairs ... Dr. Jeffrey MONIZ
32 Vice Chanc for Student Affairs ... Dr. Judy OLIVEIRA
11 Vice Chanc for Administration ... Mr. Kevin ISHIDA
84 Director for Enrollment Services ... Mr. Jim CROMWELL
09 Director of Institutional Research ... Mr. John STANLEY
26 Director of Communications ... Ms. Leila SHIMOKAWA
08 Library Director ... Ms. Michiko JOSEPH
06 Registrar ... Ms. Robyn OSHIRO
37 Financial Aid Officer ... Vacant
15 Director of Human Resources ... Ms. Nancy K. NAKASONE
10 Director of Budget ... Ms. Sheri CHING

*University of Hawaii Community Colleges (H)

2444 Dole Street, Honolulu HI 96822-2411

County: Honolulu — FICE Identification: 006751
Unit ID: 420592
Telephone: (808) 956-7038 — Carnegie Class: N/A
FAX Number: (808) 956-9219
URL: www.hawaii.edu

01 Vice Pres for Community Colleges ... Dr. Erika L. LACRO
05 Assoc Vice Pres Academic Affairs ... Dr. Peter QUIGLEY
11 Assoc Vice Pres Admin/Cmty Col Oper ... Mr. Michael T. UNEBASAMI
04 Executive Assistant to the VP & Dir ... Ms. Deborah NAKAGAWA
10 Director Budget & Planning ... Mr. Lance YAMAMOTO
15 Director Human Resources ... Ms. Sandra UYENO
18 Director Facilities/Physical Plant ... Ms. Denise YOSHIMORI-YAMAMOTO
22 Director Affirmative Action/EEO ... Ms. Mary PERREIRA
26 Director Marketing & Communications ... Ms. Susan LEE

*Kapiolani Community College (I)

4303 Diamond Head Road, Honolulu HI 96816-4221

County: Honolulu — FICE Identification: 001613
Unit ID: 141796
Telephone: (808) 734-9000 — Carnegie Class: Assoc/MT-VT-Mix Trad/Non
FAX Number: N/A — Calendar System: Semester
URL: www.kapiolani.hawaii.edu
Established: 1957 — Annual Undergrad Tuition & Fees (In-State): $3,144
Enrollment: 7,095 — Coed
Affiliation or Control: State — IRS Status: 501(c)3

Highest Offering: Associate Degree
Accreditation: WJ, ACBSP, ACFEI, ADNUR, COARC, DA, EMT, MAC, MLTAD, OTA, PTAA, RAD, SURGT

02 Chancellor .... Dr. Louise PAGOTTO
05 Interim VC Academic Affairs .... Dr. Maria BAUTISTA
10 Vice Chancellor for Admin Services .... Mr. Brian FURUTO
32 Interim VC Student Affairs .... Mr. Thomas KEOPUHIWA
49 Dean Arts and Sciences .... Mr. Nawa?a NAPOLEON
50 Dean Hospitality/Business/Legal .... Mr. John RICHARDS
76 Interim Dean Health Programs .... Ms. Karen BOYER
51 Dir Continuing Educ & Training .... Vacant
04 Exec Asst to the Chancellor .... Ms. Joanne WHITAKER
88 Dir Culinary Inst of the Pacific .... Vacant
09 Dir Institutional Effectiveness .... Dr. Robert FRANCO
08 Interim Head Librarian .... Ms. Annie THOMAS
06 Registrar .... Ms. Jerilyn ENOKAWA
37 Financial Aid Officer .... Ms. Jennifer BRADLEY
109 Auxiliary Services Officer .... Vacant
26 Dean College & Community Relations .... Dr. Carol HOSHIKO
30 Development Officer .... Ms. Linh HOANG POE
15 Director Personnel Office .... Ms. Kelli BRANDVOLD
21 Fiscal Officer .... Mr. Justin KASHIWAEDA

*University of Hawaii Hawaii Community College (A)

1175 Manono Street, Hilo HI 96720-5096
County: Hawaii | FICE Identification: 005258
Unit ID: 383190
Telephone: (808) 934-2500 | Carnegie Class: Assoc/MT-VT-High Trad
FAX Number: (808) 934-2501 | Calendar System: Semester
URL: www.hawaii.hawaii.edu
Established: 1941 | Annual Undergrad Tuition & Fees (In-State): $3,144
Enrollment: 2,819 | Coed
Affiliation or Control: State | IRS Status: 501(c)3
Highest Offering: Associate Degree
Accreditation: WJ, ACFEI, ADNUR

02 Chancellor .... Dr. Rachel H. SOLEMSAAS
05 Vice Chanc Academic Affairs .... Ms. Joni Y. ONISHI
10 Interim Vice Chanc Admin Affairs ... Mr. Kenneth K. KALEIWAHEA
32 Vice Chanc Student Affairs .... Ms. Dorinna CORTEZ
51 Director Continuing Educ/Training .... Ms. Jessica YAMAMOTO
37 Financial Aid Manager .... Vacant
12 Interim Director Palamanui .. Ms. Raynette Kalei HALEAMAU-KAM
15 Human Resource Manager .... Ms. Mari CHANG
07 Interim Registrar/A&R Mgr .... Ms. Sherise TIOGANGCO
114 Budget Analyst .... Ms. Jodi MINE
04 Private Secretary to the Chancellor .... Ms. Luane K. ISHII
19 Campus Safety and Security Chief .... Vacant
49 Dean for Liberal Arts & Public Svcs .... Dr. Melanie WILSON

*University of Hawaii Honolulu Community College (B)

874 Dillingham Boulevard, Honolulu HI 96817-4598
County: Honolulu | FICE Identification: 001612
Unit ID: 141680
Telephone: (808) 845-9211 | Carnegie Class: Assoc/HVT-Mix Trad/Non
FAX Number: (808) 845-9173 | Calendar System: Semester
URL: www.honolulu.hawaii.edu
Established: 1920 | Annual Undergrad Tuition & Fees (In-State): $3,114
Enrollment: 3,563 | Coed
Affiliation or Control: State | IRS Status: 501(c)3
Highest Offering: Associate Degree
Accreditation: WJ

02 Interim Chancellor .... Ms. Karen LEE
11 Vice Chancellor of Admin Svcs .... Mr. Derek INAFUKU
05 Int Vice Chancellor of Acad Affairs .... Ms. Susan KAZAMA
88 Director PCATT .... Mr. Steven AUERBACH
88 Int Dean Transport & Trades .... Ms. Fumiko TAKASUGI
27 Dean Communications & Services .... Mr. Kasey "Keala" CHOCK
08 Librarian in Charge .... Ms. Stefanie SASAKI
37 Financial Aid Officer .... Ms. Heather FLORENDO
15 Human Resources Mgr/EEO/AA Coord ... Ms. Monique TINGKANG
32 Director Student Affairs .... Ms. Emily Ann KUKULIES
06 Registrar .... Ms. Josephine STENBERG
09 Director Management Info & Research .... Mr. Steven SHIGEMOTO
36 Dir Student Placement/Counselor .... Ms. Silvan CHUNG
20 Int Dean University College .... Ms. Jennifer HIGA-KING
10 Chief Business Officer .... Ms. Myrna PATTERSON
26 Chief Public Relations Officer .... Vacant
88 Dean of Academic Support .... Mr. Wayne SUNAHARA
96 Acting Director of Purchasing .... Ms. Myrna PATTERSON
88 Director Secondary Education Pgms .... Ms. Lara SUGIMOTO
13 Chief Info Technology Officer (CIO) .... Mr. Michael MEYER
35 Dean of Student Services .... Ms. Lara SUGIMOTO

*University of Hawaii Kauai Community College (C)

3-1901 Kaumualii Highway, Lihue HI 96766-9500
County: Kauai | FICE Identification: 001614
Unit ID: 141802
Telephone: (808) 245-8311 | Carnegie Class: Assoc/HVT-High Trad
FAX Number: (808) 245-8220 | Calendar System: Semester
URL: kauai.hawaii.edu/
Established: 1964 | Annual Undergrad Tuition & Fees (In-State): $3,192
Enrollment: 1,346 | Coed
Affiliation or Control: State | IRS Status: 501(c)3
Highest Offering: Associate Degree
Accreditation: WJ, ACFEI, ADNUR, MAC

02 Chancellor .... Dr. Helen COX
05 Vice Chanc Academic Affairs .... Dr. Frankie HARRISS
32 Vice Chanc Student Affairs .... Ms. Margaret SANCHEZ
11 Vice Chanc Administrative Services .... Ms. Amy FLAHERTY
10 Chief Financial Officer .... Ms. Deanne KOSHI
51 Director Continuing Educ/Training .... Mr. Calvin SHIRAI
08 Head Librarian .... Mr. Robert KAJIWARA
37 Financial Aid Officer .... Mr. Jeff ANDERSON
15 Human Resource Manager .... Ms. JoRae BAPTISTE
35 Counselor/Student Life Coordinator .... Mr. John CONSTANTINO
09 Dir Institutional Effect/Univ Ctr .... Ms. Valerie BARKO

*University of Hawaii - Leeward Community College (D)

96-045 Ala Ike, Pearl City HI 96782-3393
County: Honolulu | FICE Identification: 004549
Unit ID: 141811
Telephone: (808) 455-0011 | Carnegie Class: Assoc/HT-Mix Trad/Non
FAX Number: (808) 455-0471 | Calendar System: Semester
URL: www.leeward.hawaii.edu
Established: 1968 | Annual Undergrad Tuition & Fees (In-State): $3,144
Enrollment: 6,805 | Coed
Affiliation or Control: State | IRS Status: 501(c)3
Highest Offering: Associate Degree
Accreditation: WJ, ACFEI, CAEPT, CAHIIM

02 Chancellor .... Dr. Carlos PEÑALOZA
05 Vice Chanc Academic Affairs .... Ms. Della TERAOKA
11 Vice Chancellor Admin Services .... Mr. Mark LANE
10 Fiscal Manager .... Ms. Cecilia LUCAS
49 Dean Arts & Sciences .... Mr. James GOODMAN
72 Dean Career & Tech Education .... Mr. Ron UMEHIRA
32 Interim Dean Student Services .... Ms. Kami KATO
20 Interim Dean of Academic Services .... Ms. Kay ONO
08 Librarian .... Mr. Wayde OSHIRO
06 Registrar .... Mr. Grant HELGESON
37 Financial Aid Officer .... Mr. Gregg YOSHIMURA
18 Aux & Facilities Services Mgr .... Mr. Grant OKAMURA
09 Policy/Planning/Assessment Coord .... Ms. Shuqi WU
26 Marketing Director .... Ms. Kathleen CABRAL
15 Human Resources Mgr/EEO/AA Coord .... Ms. Lori Lei HAYASHI
13 Information Technology Coord .... Mr. Byron WATANABE
12 Int Coord Waianae Education Center .... Mr. Danny WYATT
24 Media Coordinator .... Ms. Leanne RISELEY
35 Student Activities Coordinator .... Ms. Lexer CHOU

*University of Hawaii Maui College (E)

310 Kaahumanu Avenue, Kahului HI 96732-1644
County: Maui | FICE Identification: 001615
Unit ID: 141839
Telephone: (808) 984-3500 | Carnegie Class: Bac/Assoc-Assoc Dom
FAX Number: (808) 984-3546 | Calendar System: Semester
URL: maui.hawaii.edu
Established: 1931 | Annual Undergrad Tuition & Fees (In-State): $3,218
Enrollment: 3,302 | Coed
Affiliation or Control: State | IRS Status: 501(c)3
Highest Offering: Baccalaureate
Accreditation: WC, ACFEI, ADNUR, DH

02 Chancellor .... Dr. Lui HOKOANA
05 Vice Chanc Academic Affairs .... Dr. Jonathon MCKEE
32 Vice Chancellor of Student Affs .... Ms. Debra NAKAMA
10 Vice Chanc of Administrative Affs .... Mr. David TAMANAHA
20 Int Assistant Dean of Instruction .... Mr. David GROOMS
51 Director Continuing Educ/Training .... Ms. Karen HANADA
08 Librarian .... Ms. Ellen PETERSON
12 Director University Center Maui .... Ms. Tamone Karen HANADA
07 Director of Admissions/Registrar .... Ms. Flora MORA
09 Director of Institutional Research .... Dr. Jeannie PEZZOLI
15 Director Human Resources .... Ms. Susan TOKUNAGA
18 Chief Facilities/Physical Plant .... Mr. Robert BURTON
21 Associate Fiscal Officer .... Ms. Cindy YAMAMOTO
30 Chief Development .... Ms. Jocelyn Romero DEMIRBAG
36 Director Student Placement .... Ms. Debra NAKAMA
37 Interim Financial Aid Officer .... Ms. Davileigh NAE`OLE
38 Director Student Counseling .... Ms. Kulamanu ISHIHARA

*University of Hawaii Windward Community College (F)

45-720 Keaahala Road, Kaneohe HI 96744-3598
County: Honolulu | FICE Identification: 011220
Unit ID: 141990
Telephone: (808) 235-7400 | Carnegie Class: Assoc/HT-High Non
FAX Number: (808) 247-5362 | Calendar System: Semester
URL: www.windward.hawaii.edu
Established: 1972 | Annual Undergrad Tuition & Fees (In-State): $3,124
Enrollment: 2,511 | Coed
Affiliation or Control: State | IRS Status: 501(c)3
Highest Offering: Associate Degree
Accreditation: WJ

02 Chancellor .... Dr. Ardis ESCHENBERG
05 Int Vice Chancellor Academic Affs .... Mr. Charles S. SASAKI
32 Int Vice Chancellor Student Affairs .... Ms. Heipua KAOPUA
11 Vice Chanc Administrative Services .... Mr. Brian PACTOL
20 Dean of Academic Affairs Div I .... Ms. Colette HIGGINS
20 Int Dean of Academic Affairs Div II .... Dr. David KRUPP
75 Dir Vocational/Cmty Education .... Vacant
08 Head Librarian .... Ms. Sarah Gilman SUR
06 Registrar .... Ms. Geri IMAI
09 Director of Institutional Research .... Mr. Jeffrey HUNT
37 Director Student Financial Aid .... Ms. Dayna ISA
15 Personnel Officer .... Ms. Karen CHO
26 Marketing/Public Relations Dir .... Ms. Bonnie BEATSON

University of Phoenix Hawaii Campus (G)

949 Kamokila Blvd. Suite 101, Kapolei HI 96707
Telephone: (808) 536-2686 | Identification: 770202
Accreditation: &NH, ACBSP, CAEPN

IDAHO

Boise Bible College (H)

8695 W Marigold Street, Boise ID 83714-1220
County: Ada | FICE Identification: 022345
Unit ID: 142090
Telephone: (208) 376-7731 | Carnegie Class: Spec-4-yr-Faith
FAX Number: (208) 376-7743 | Calendar System: Semester
URL: www.boisebible.edu
Established: 1945 | Annual Undergrad Tuition & Fees: $12,520
Enrollment: 130 | Coed
Affiliation or Control: Christian Churches And Churches of Christ
IRS Status: 501(c)3
Highest Offering: Baccalaureate
Accreditation: BI

01 President .... Dr. Derek VOORHEES
05 Academic Dean .... Mr. Charles FABER
32 Dean of Students .... Dr. Cody CHRISTENSEN
10 Business Officer .... Mr. Mark STEVENS
30 Director of Development .... Mr. David DAVOLT
06 Registrar .... Mr. Ross KNUDSEN
07 Director of Admissions .... Mr. Russell GROVE
08 Librarian .... Mrs. Amber GROVE
37 Financial Aid Director .... Mr. Ben BISHOP
18 Director of Physical Plant .... Mr. Mike MORRIS
04 Executive Assistant .... Mrs. Rhonda HETHERINGTON

Boise State University (I)

1910 University Drive, Boise ID 83725-1000
County: Ada | FICE Identification: 001616
Unit ID: 142115
Telephone: (208) 426-1000 | Carnegie Class: DU-Higher
FAX Number: (208) 426-3765 | Calendar System: Semester
URL: www.boisestate.edu
Established: 1932 | Annual Undergrad Tuition & Fees (In-State): $7,694
Enrollment: 24,121 | Coed
Affiliation or Control: State | IRS Status: 501(c)3
Highest Offering: Doctorate
Accreditation: NW, ART, CAATE, CACREP, CAEP, COARC, CONST, DMS, MUS, NURSE, RAD, SPAA, SW, THEA

01 President .... Dr. Marlene TROMP
05 Interim Provost .... Dr. Tony ROARK
10 VP/Chief Financial Officer .... Mr. Mark HEIL
32 VP Student Affairs/Enrollment Mgmt .... Dr. Leslie WEBB
111 Interim VP Univ Advancement .... Mr. Rick FRISCH
11 VP Campus Operations & COO .... Ms. Randi MCDERMOTT
20 Vice Provost Academic Planning .... Dr. Zeynep HANSEN
20 Int Vice Provost Undergrad Students .... Dr. Andrew FINSTUEN
21 Assoc VP Finance & Administration .... Ms. Jo Ellen DINUCCI
35 Assoc VP for Student Affairs .... Dr. Jeremiah SHINN
46 Int VP Research & Economic Dev .... Dr. Harold BLACKMAN
13 Assoc VP/Chief Info Tech .... Mr. Max DAVIS-JOHNSON
08 Dean of University Library .... Dr. Tracy BICKNELL-HOLMES
35 Dean of Students .... Dr. Chris WUTHRICH
84 Interim Assoc VP Enrollment Service .... Ms. Kris COLLINS
15 Assoc VP Human Resources .... Mr. Shawn MILLER
29 Executive Director Alumni Relations .... Ms. Lisa GARDNER
17 Director of Clinical Operations .... Dr. Julia BEARD
06 Interim Registrar .... Ms. Mandy NELSON
19 Assoc VP Public Safety .... Mr. John KAPLAN
09 Director Institutional Research .... Dr. Shari ELLERTSON
07 Director of Admissions .... Dr. Kelly TALBERT
26 AVP Communications/Marketing .... Mr. Greg HAHN
41 Exec Director Athletics .... Mr. Curt APSEY
22 Director of Compliance .... Mr. John MCDONALD
38 Director Counseling Services .... Dr. Matthew NIECE
37 Interim Asst Dir of Financial Aid .... Ms. Kimberly BRANDT
96 Director of Purchasing .... Ms. Terri SPINAZZA
51 Dean Extended Studies .... Mr. Mark WHEELER
49 Interim Dean of Arts & Sciences .... Dr. Leslie DURHAM
50 Interim Dean Business & Economics .... Dr. Mark BANNISTER
53 Dean of Education .... Dr. Richard OSGUTHORPE
58 Dean of the Graduate College .... Dr. Tammi VACHA-HAASE
76 Dean of Health Sciences .... Dr. Tim DUNNAGAN
54 Dean of Engineering .... Dr. JoAnn LIGHTY
88 Dean of Innovation & Design .... Mr. Gordon JONES
104 Asst Prov for Global Educ .... Dr. Gonzalo BRUCE
88 Dean School of Public Service .... Dr. Corey COOK
104 Dir Center for Global Education .... Ms. Corrine HENKE
39 Exec Dir Housing/VP Asst .... Dr. Luke JONES
88 Director of Wellness .... Dr. Michelle IHMELS

36 Director Career Center .... Ms. Debbie KAYLOR
106 Exec Director e-Campus Center .... Ms. Christine BAUER
28 Dir of Student Diversity/Inclusion .... Mr. Francisco SALINAS
102 Dir of Corp & Foundation Rels .... Ms. Virginia PELLEGRINI
30 Senior Development Director .... Ms. Gerti ARNOLD
100 Chief of Staff & CC Officer .... Ms. Alicia ESTEY

Brigham Young University-Idaho (A)

525 South Center Street, Rexburg ID 83460
County: Madison FICE Identification: 001625
Unit ID: 142522
Telephone: (208) 496-1411 Carnegie Class: Bac-Diverse
FAX Number: (208) 496-1103 Calendar System: Semester
URL: www.byui.edu
Established: 1888 Annual Undergrad Tuition & Fees: $4,118
Enrollment: 51,881 Coed
Affiliation or Control: Latter-day Saints IRS Status: 501(c)3
Highest Offering: Baccalaureate
Accreditation: NW, MUS, NURSE, PTAA, SW

01 President .... Dr. Henry J. EYRING
05 Academic Vice President .... Mr. Kelly T. BURGENER
11 University Resources Vice President .... Mr. Jeffrey R. MORRIN
32 Student Life Vice President .... Mrs. Amy R. LABAUGH
106 Online Vice President .... Dr. Jon F. LINFORD
45 VP for Exec Strategy & Planning .... Mr. Rob J. GARRETT
20 Assoc Academic VP Instruction .... Mr. Rob I. EATON
20 Assoc Acad VP Curriculum .... Dr. Van D. CHRISTMAN
121 Assoc Acad VP Student Success .... Dr. Scott W. GALER
35 Dean of Students .... Mr. Wynn N. HILL
88 Student Well-Being Mng Director .... Ms. Kristie LORDS
13 Chief Information Officer .... Mr. Joe TAYLOR
09 Inst Research Managing Director .... Dr. Ben FRYAR
45 Institutional Planning Managing Dir .... Mr. Aaron SANNS
06 Student Records & Registration .... Mrs. Lauri D. ARENSMEYER
37 Int Stdnt Fin Aid/Scholarship Dir .... Mr. Ken L. JACKSON
08 University Librarian .... Mrs. Laurie S. FRANCIS
10 Univ Operations Managing Director .... Mr. Wayne N. CLARK
15 Human Resources Director .... Mr. Kevin L. PRICE
23 Student Health Services Director .... Mr. Shaun ORR
38 Student Counseling Center Director .... Mr. Reed J. STODDARD
19 University Public Safety Dir .... Mr. Stephen P. BUNNELL
07 Admissions Director .... Mr. Tyler R. WILLIAMS
29 Alumni Director .... Mr. Steven J. DAVIS
88 Student Activities Mng Director .... Mr. Derek R. FAY
26 University Relations Mng Director .... Mr. Merv R. BROWN
30 LDS Philanthropies Director .... Mr. Kelly REEVES
39 Housing & Student Living Director .... Dr. Troy J. DOUGHERTY
43 Legal Counsel .... Mr. Josh FIGUEIRA
21 Financial Services Mng Director .... Mr. Shane WEBSTER
88 Student Development Mng Director .... Mrs. Jill EVANS
96 Purchasing & Travel Director .... Mr. Mike B. THUESON
35 Student Svcs Managing Director .... Mr. Kyle R. MARTIN
40 University Store Director .... Mr. Ryan J. BUTTARS
104 Director of International Services .... Mr. Mike R. OSWALD
36 Career and Academic Advising Dir .... Mr. Sam R. BRUBAKER
109 Auxiliary Services Mng Director .... Mr. Brett COOK
04 Admin Assistant to the President .... Mrs. Kathy L. WEBB

Carrington College - Boise (B)

1122 N Liberty Street, Boise ID 83704-8741
Telephone: (208) 377-8080 FICE Identification: 022180
Accreditation: &WJ, DA, DH, MAAB, PNUR, PTAA

† Regional accreditation is carried under the parent institution in Sacramento, CA.

College of Eastern Idaho (C)

1600 S 25th E, Idaho Falls ID 83404-5788
County: Bonneville FICE Identification: 011133
Unit ID: 142179
Telephone: (208) 524-3000 Carnegie Class: Assoc/HVT-High Trad
FAX Number: (208) 524-3007 Calendar System: Semester
URL: www.cei.edu
Established: 1969 Annual Undergrad Tuition & Fees (In-State): $3,126
Enrollment: 791 Coed
Affiliation or Control: State IRS Status: 501(c)3
Highest Offering: Associate Degree
Accreditation: NW, MAC, SURGT

01 President .... Dr. Rick AMAN
10 Vice President of Finance and Admin .... Mr. Byron MILES
05 VP Instruction/Student Affairs .... Ms. Lori BARBER
06 Registrar .... Mrs. Rae Lynn PATTERSON
21 Controller .... Mr. Don E. BOURNE
103 Mgr Workforce Trng/Cmty Education .... Ms. Michelle M. HOLT
37 Financial Aid Director .... Mr. Trevor PETERSON
04 President Administrative Assistant .... Miss Kristina BUCHAN
26 Director of College Relations .... Mr. Todd WIGHTMAN
102 Foundation Director .... Mrs. Natalie J. HEBARD
07 Director of Admissions/Placement .... Mrs. Hailey MACK
50 Business/Office/Technology Div Mgr .... Mr. Leslie JERNBERG
76 Health Care Technology Div Manager .... Ms. Kathleen NELSON
88 Trades/Industry Division Manager .... Mr. Kent E. BERGGREN
51 Adult Basic Education Div Manager .... Mrs. Sandra TAKAHASHI
09 Dir of Institutional Effectiveness .... Mr. Lee STIMPSON
13 Chief Info Technology Officer .... Mrs. Karen FOSTER
15 Chief Human Resources Officer .... Ms. Mary TAYLOR
35 Chief Student Affairs Officer .... Mr. Mike WALKER
96 Director of Purchasing .... Ms. Heidi MOORE
00 Chairman of the Board .... Mr. Park PRICE
97 Int Dean of General Education .... Mrs. Angela SACKETT
75 Dean of Career and Technical Ed .... Mr. Clint READING
32 Dean of Student Affairs .... Mr. Michael WALKER

The College of Idaho (D)

2112 Cleveland Boulevard, Caldwell ID 83605-4432
County: Canyon FICE Identification: 001617
Unit ID: 142294
Telephone: (208) 459-5011 Carnegie Class: Bac-A&S
FAX Number: (208) 454-2077 Calendar System: Other
URL: www.collegeofidaho.edu
Established: 1891 Annual Undergrad Tuition & Fees: $30,155
Enrollment: 954 Coed
Affiliation or Control: Independent Non-Profit IRS Status: 501(c)3
Highest Offering: Master's
Accreditation: NW

01 Co-President .... Mr. Doug BRIGHAM
01 Co-President .... Mr. Jim EVERETT
05 Vice President Academic Affairs .... Dr. David DOUGLASS
10 Vice Pres Finance/Administration .... Mr. Richard ERNE
32 Vice President Student Affairs .... Dr. Paul BENNION
84 Vice President for Enrollment Mgmt .... Mr. Brian BAVA
20 Associate Dean of Faculty .... Dr. Paul MOULTON
06 Registrar .... Ms. Cassandra HEATH
41 Director of Athletics .... Ms. Reagan ROSSI
26 Dir of Marketing & Communications .... Mr. Joe HUGHES
29 Director of Alumni .... Ms. Sally SKINNER
44 Director of Boone Fund .... Ms. Sarah NASH
08 Director of Library .... Ms. Christine SCHUTZ
21 Controller .... Mr. Jesse HARRIS
37 Director of Financial Services .... Ms. Jennifer WORDEN
15 Human Resources Director .... Ms. Nancy JOHNSON-CASSULO
36 Director Student Placement .... Ms. Jennifer RIDDLE
92 Director of Honors Program .... Dr. Sue SCHAPER
39 Director of Residential Life .... Ms. Jen NELSON
93 Director of Multicultural Affairs .... Mr. Arnold HERNANDEZ
42 Campus Minister/Asc Dean Students .... Dr. Phil ROGERS
19 Director of Campus Safety .... Mr. Allan LAIRD
09 Assc VP Institutional Effectiveness .... Mr. Mark HEIDRICH
110 Assoc VP of College Relations .... Mr. Jack CAFFERTY
07 Associate Director of Admissions .... Mr. Mike BURDINE
40 Bookstore Manager .... Mr. Kris PERDEW
38 Counselor .... Ms. Cynthia MAUZERALL
04 Executive Asst to President .... Ms. Ineke SEVERA

College of Southern Idaho (E)

PO Box 1238, 315 Falls Avenue,
Twin Falls ID 83303-1238
County: Twin Falls FICE Identification: 001619
Unit ID: 142559
Telephone: (208) 733-9554 Carnegie Class: Assoc/MT-VT-High Non
FAX Number: (208) 736-3015 Calendar System: Semester
URL: www.csi.edu
Established: 1965 Annual Undergrad Tuition & Fees (In-District): $3,360
Enrollment: 6,876 Coed
Affiliation or Control: Local IRS Status: 501(c)3
Highest Offering: Associate Degree
Accreditation: NW, ADNUR, DH, EMT, MAC, PTAA, RAD, SURGT

01 President .... Dr. D. Jeff FOX
00 Chairman of the Board .... Mrs. Jan MITTLEIDER
05 Exec VP/Chief Academic Officer .... Dr. Todd SCHWARZ
11 Vice President of Administration .... Mr. Jeff HARMON
13 Chief Technology Officer .... Mr. Kevin MARK
32 Vice President Student Services .... Dr. Michelle SCHUTT
09 Assoc Dean of IE/ALO .... Mr. Chris BRAGG
121 Dean of Student Success .... Mr. John HUGHES
04 Exec Admin Asst to President .... Ms. Ginger NUKAYA
10 Chief Financial Officer .... Ms. Kristy CARPENTER
20 Instructional Dean .... Ms. Tiffany SEELEY-CASE
20 Instructional Dean .... Dr. Barry PATE
20 Instructional Dean HSHS .... Mr. Jayson LLOYD
35 Dean of Students .... Mr. Jason OSTROWSKI
56 Associate Dean of Early College .... Mr. Jonathan LORD
15 Director Human Resources .... Mr. Eric NIELSON
06 Registrar .... Dr. Michele MCFARLANE
07 Director of Admissions .... Ms. Gail SCHULL
37 Director of Student Financial Aid .... Ms. Jennifer J. ZIMMERS
08 Director Library .... Ms. Teri L. FATTIG
102 Executive Director Foundation .... Ms. Debra J. WILSON
103 Exec Director Workforce Development ... Ms. Brandi TURNIPSEED
14 Dir Application/Data Architecture .... Mr. Ed DITLEFSEN
14 Dir Systems/Network Architecture .... Mr. Bruce NUKAYA
41 Athletic Director .... Mr. Joel C. BATE
18 Director Physical Plant .... Mr. Spencer CUTLER
19 Director Security & Safety .... Mr. James MUNN
26 Public Information Director .... Ms. Kim LAPRAY
40 Bookstore Manager .... Ms. Jayme KETTERLING
92 Coordinator Honors Program .... Mr. Brian DOBBS
39 Director Student Housing .... Mr. Seth SIMONSON
105 Director Web Services .... Mr. Kendall LINDLEY

College of Western Idaho (F)

6056 Birch Lane, Nampa ID 83687
County: Canyon FICE Identification: 042118
Unit ID: 455114
Telephone: (208) 562-3000 Carnegie Class: Assoc/HT-High Non
FAX Number: (888) 562-3216 Calendar System: Semester
URL: cwi.edu
Established: 2007 Annual Undergrad Tuition & Fees (In-District): $3,336
Enrollment: 10,303 Coed
Affiliation or Control: Local IRS Status: 501(c)3
Highest Offering: Associate Degree
Accreditation: NW, ACBSP, ADNUR, DA, MAC, PTAA, SURGT

01 President .... Dr. Bert GLANDON
05 Provost .... Ms. Denise ABERLE-CANNATA
11 Executive VP Operations .... Mr. Craig BROWN
86 VP College Relations .... Mr. Mark BROWNING
15 VP Human Resources .... Ms. Lillian TALLEY
10 VP Finance & Administration .... Mr. Tony MEATTE
04 Executive Asst President's Office .... Ms. Janice MCGEHEE
13 Chief Information Officer .... Mr. Michael CHACON
84 AVP Enrollment & Student Services .... Mr. Patrick TANNER
103 AVP Economic Development .... Ms. Christi ROOD
09 Exec Dir Inst Effectiveness .... Ms. Alexis MALEPEAI-RHODES
102 Executive Director CWI Foundation .... Vacant
18 Exec Dir Facilities/Plng & Mgmt .... Mr. Jeff FLYNN
32 Dean of Students .... Vacant
57 Dean Arts & Humanities .... Mr. Justin VANCE
50 Dean Business/Comm & Technology .... Ms. Kelly STEELY
76 Dean Health .... Ms. Cathleen CURRIE
54 Dean Industry/Engr & Trades .... Mr. Pat NEAL
81 Dean Math & Science .... Ms. Kae JENSEN
83 Dean Social Sciences & Public Affs ..... Ms. Courtney SANTILLAN
07 Director of Admissions & One Stop .... Mr. Luis CALOCA
121 Director Advising .... Ms. Allison MOLITOR
37 Director Financial Aid .... Ms. Jenee SNYDER
06 Registrar .... Ms. Connie BLACK
55 Director Basic Skills .... Mr. Jac WEBB
88 Director Business & Manufacturing .... Mr. Marc SWINNEY
88 Dir Center for Teaching & Learning .. Ms. Courtney COLBY BOND
88 Dir Dual Cr & College Readiness .... Mr. Stephen CRUMRINE
08 Director Library Services .... Ms. Kim REED
26 Director Mktg & Communications .... Ms. Audrey ELDRIDGE
21 Associate Controller .... Ms. Mary Jo HAYES

Idaho College of Osteopathic Medicine (G)

1311 E. Central Drive, Meridian ID 83642
County: Ada Identification: 667328
Telephone: (203) 696-4266 Carnegie Class: Not Classified
FAX Number: N/A Calendar System: Semester
URL: www.idahocom.org
Established: 2016 Annual Graduate Tuition & Fees: N/A
Enrollment: N/A Coed
Affiliation or Control: Proprietary IRS Status: Proprietary
Highest Offering: First Professional Degree; No Undergraduates
Accreditation: @OSTEO

01 President .... Dr. Tracy FARNSWORTH
05 Founding Dean & Chief Academic Ofcr .... Dr. Robert HASTY
07 Director of Admissions .... Janette MARTIN
37 Director of Financial Aid .... Nicole MCMILLIN

Idaho State University (H)

921 S 8th Ave, Pocatello ID 83209-0009
County: Bannock FICE Identification: 001620
Unit ID: 142276
Telephone: (208) 282-0211 Carnegie Class: DU-Higher
FAX Number: (208) 282-4000 Calendar System: Semester
URL: www.isu.edu
Established: 1901 Annual Undergrad Tuition & Fees (In-State): $7,420
Enrollment: 12,493 Coed
Affiliation or Control: State IRS Status: 501(c)3
Highest Offering: Doctorate
Accreditation: NW, ADNUR, ARCPA, AUD, CAATE, CACREP, CAEPN, CAHIIM, CLPSY, COARC, COMTA, DENT, DH, DIETD, DIETI, EMT, MAC, MT, MUS, NAIT, NURSE, OT, OTA, PH, PHAR, PTA, PTAA, RAD, SP, SW, THEA

01 President .... Dr. Kevin SATTERLEE
04 Executive Assistant to President .... Ms. Jennifer FORSHEE
05 Executive Vice President & Provost .... Dr. Laura WOODWORTH-NEY
10 VP Finance & Business Affairs .... Mr. Glen NELSON
111 Vice Pres of University Advancement .... Dr. Kent M. TINGEY
32 Vice Pres Student Affairs .... Ms. Lyn REDINGTON
46 Interim Vice President for Research .... Dr. Scott SNYDER
17 VP Kasiska Division Health Sciences .... Dr. Rex FORCE
43 General Counsel/Chief Comp Officer .... Ms. Joanne HIRASE-STACEY
41 Athletic Director .... Ms. Pauline THIROS
20 Vice Provo Acad Strat & Inst Effect .... Ms. Selena GRACE
20 Interim AVP for Academic Affairs .... Dr. Alan FRANTZ
84 AVP for Enrollment Management .... Vacant
30 AVP for Development .... Vacant
18 AVP for Facilities Services .... Ms. Cheryl HANSON
58 Interim Dean of Graduate School .... Ms. Karen WILSON SCOTT
54 Dean College Science & Engineering .... Dr. Scott SNYDER
67 Int Dean College of Pharmacy ..... Dr. Walter L. FITZGERALD, JR.
50 Interim Dean College of Business .... Dr. Joanne TOKLE
49 Dean College of Arts & Letters .... Dr. Kandi TURLEY-AMES
53 Dean College of Education .... Vacant
72 Dean College of Technology .... Mr. Scott RASMUSSEN
12 Dean of Academic Pgm ISU-Meridian .... Vacant
12 Director University Programs-IF .... Vacant
08 Dean & University Librarian .... Mr. Karl BRIDGES
06 Registrar & Dir of Undergrad Admiss .... Ms. Laura MCKENZIE
13 Chief Information Officer .... Mr. Randy GAINES

29 Director Alumni Relations .... Mr. Ryan SARGENT
09 Director Institutional Research .... Mr. Vince MILLER
37 Dir Student Fin Aid/Scholarships .... Mr. James R. MARTIN
15 Director Human Resources .... Mr. Brian SAGENDORF
23 Director Student Health Center .... Dr. Ronald SOLBRIG
22 Dir EEO/Affirm Action & Diversity .... Ms. Stacey GIBSON
19 Director Public Safety .... Mr. Lewis EAKINS
26 Assoc VP Marketing & Communication .... Mr. Stuart SUMMERS
86 Director Government Relations .... Mr. Kent KUNZ
88 Director Events Management .... Mr. George CASPER
35 Director of Student Life .... Mr. Kris CLARKSON
38 Director of Counseling & Testing .... Dr. Richard PONGRATZ
85 Interim Asst Dir of Intl Programs .... Mr. Shawn BASCOM
84 Director of Enrollment Services/IF .... Mr. Bradley BROSCHINSKY
07 Director Admissions & Recruitment .... Ms. Nicole JOSEPH
39 Director University Housing .... Mr. Craig THOMPSON
96 Director of Purchasing Services .... Vacant
44 Director Annual Giving .... Ms. Kallee VALENTINE
100 Chief of Staff .... Ms. Dani DUNSTAN
25 Director Contract/Grants Accounting .... Ms. Lori JOHNSON

Lewis-Clark State College (A)

500 8th Avenue, Lewiston ID 83501-2698
County: Nez Perce — FICE Identification: 001621
Unit ID: 142328
Telephone: (208) 792-5272 — Carnegie Class: Bac-Diverse
FAX Number: (208) 792-2831 — Calendar System: Semester
URL: www.lcsc.edu
Established: 1893 — Annual Undergrad Tuition & Fees (In-State): $6,618
Enrollment: 3,746 — Coed
Affiliation or Control: State — IRS Status: 501(c)3
Highest Offering: Baccalaureate
Accreditation: NW, CAEPN, EMT, IACBE, MAC, NURSE, PTAA, RAD, SW

01 President .... Dr. Cynthia L. PEMBERTON
05 Provost/VP Academic Affairs .... Dr. Lori STINSON
10 VP Finance and Administration .... Mr. Todd KILBURN
32 Vice President Student Affairs .... Dr. Andrew HANSON
75 Dean Career & Technical Education .... Mr. Jeffrey OBER
107 Dean Professional Studies .... Mr. Fred CHILSON
49 Dean Liberal Arts & Sciences .... Ms. Mary FLORES
08 Director of Library Services .... Ms. Johanna BJORK
103 Director of Workforce Training .... Dr. Linda STRICKLIN
07 Director of Admissions/Recruitment .... Ms. Soo Lee BRUCE-SMITH
06 Registrar .... Ms. Nikol ROUBIDOUX
09 Dir Planning/Research/Assessment .... Vacant
13 Chief Technology Officer .... Mr. Allen SCHMOOCK
41 Athletic Director .... Ms. Brooke CUSHMAN
15 Director of Human Resources .... Ms. Vikki SWIFT
26 Director Communications & Marketing .... Mr. Logan FOWLER
29 Director of Alumni Relations .... Ms. Renee OLSEN
37 Director of Student Financial Aid .... Ms. Laura HUGHES
30 Director of College Advancement .... Ms. Erika ALLEN
18 Director of Physical Plant .... Mr. Tom GARRISON
36 Director The Advising Center .... Ms. Debra LYBYER
96 Director of Purchasing .... Ms. Sheila KOM
19 Director Security/Safety .... Ms. JoAnn GILPIN

New Saint Andrews College (B)

PO Box 9025, Moscow ID 83843-1525
County: Latah — Identification: 666166
Unit ID: 440396
Telephone: (208) 882-1566 — Carnegie Class: Bac-A&S
FAX Number: (208) 882-4293 — Calendar System: Other
URL: www.nsa.edu
Established: 1994 — Annual Undergrad Tuition & Fees: $12,800
Enrollment: 183 — Coed
Affiliation or Control: Independent Non-Profit — IRS Status: 501(c)3
Highest Offering: Master's
Accreditation: TRACS

01 President .... Dr. Ben MERKLE
05 Academic Dean .... Dr. Timothy EDWARDS
73 Director MA Program .... Dr. Timothy EDWARDS
53 Dir Classical Christian Studies Pgm .... Mr. Christopher SCHLECT
88 Director MFA Program .... Mr. Nate WILSON
10 Chief Financial Officer .... Mr. Thomas BRAINERD
08 Head Librarian .... Mrs. Helen HOWELL
06 Registrar .... Ms. Grace BURNETT
07 Director of Admissions .... Mrs. Brenda SCHLECT
26 Marketing Manager .... Mr. Kent ATKINSON
32 Manager New Student Services .... Mr. John SAWYER
07 Manager of Recruiting .... Ms. Grace HENDRIX

North Idaho College (C)

1000 W Garden Avenue, Coeur d'Alene ID 83814-2199
County: Kootenai — FICE Identification: 001623
Unit ID: 142443
Telephone: (208) 769-3300 — Carnegie Class: Assoc/HT-Mix Trad/Non
FAX Number: (208) 765-2761 — Calendar System: Semester
URL: www.nic.edu
Established: 1933 — Annual Undergrad Tuition & Fees (In-District): $3,396
Enrollment: 5,390 — Coed
Affiliation or Control: Local — IRS Status: 501(c)3
Highest Offering: Associate Degree
Accreditation: NW, ADNUR, MAC, MLTAD, PTAA, RAD, SURGT

01 President .... Dr. Richard L. MACLENNAN
05 Vice President for Instruction .... Dr. Lita BURNS
10 VP for Finance & Business Affairs .... Mr. Christopher MARTIN
32 Vice President for Student Services .... Mr. Graydon STANLEY
88 AVP Planning Strategy/Effectiveness .... Ms. Dianna RENZ
86 Chief Communications/Govt Rels Ofcr .... Ms. Laura RUMPLER
103 Dean of Career Tech/Workforce Educ .... Ms. Kassie SILVAS
97 Dean of General Studies .... Dr. Larry BRIGGS
76 Dean of Health Prof & Nursing .... Ms. Christy DOYLE
07 Director of Admissions/Registrar .... Ms. Tami HAFT
09 Director of Inst Effectiveness .... Ms. Ann LEWIS
08 Library Director .... Mr. George MCALISTER
13 Chief Information Officer .... Mr. Ken WARDINSKY
15 Executive Director Human Resources .... Vacant
37 Director of Financial Aid .... Ms. Stephanie HOUSE
18 Director of Facilities .... Mr. Garry STARK
30 Development Director .... Ms. Rayelle ANDERSON
35 Director Student Development .... Mr. Alex HARRIS
21 Controller .... Ms. Sarah GARCIA
72 Technology Coordinator .... Mr. Andy FINNEY
29 Alumni Relations Coordinator .... Ms. Pam NOAH
04 Sr Executive Assistant .... Ms. Shannon GOODRICH
106 Director of E-learning .... Mr. Thomas SCOTT
25 Grants Development Manager .... Ms. Hannah PATON
41 Athletic Director .... Mr. Alvin WILLIAMS
19 Supervisor Security .... Mr. Patrick MURRAY

Northwest Nazarene University (D)

623 S. University Boulevard, Nampa ID 83686-5897
County: Canyon — FICE Identification: 001624
Unit ID: 142461
Telephone: (208) 467-8011 — Carnegie Class: Masters/L
FAX Number: (208) 467-8099 — Calendar System: Semester
URL: www.nnu.edu
Established: 1913 — Annual Undergrad Tuition & Fees: $29,800
Enrollment: 2,168 — Coed
Affiliation or Control: Church Of The Nazarene — IRS Status: 501(c)3
Highest Offering: Doctorate
Accreditation: NW, ACBSP, CACREP, CAEPN, MUS, NURSE, SW, THEOL

01 President .... Mr. Joel K. PEARSALL
05 Vice Pres Academic Affairs/Dean .... Dr. Brad KURTZ-SHAW
10 Vice Pres Finance & Operations .... Mr. Steve EMERSON
32 Vice President Student Life .... Dr. Carey W. COOK
88 Exec Dir for Univ Ministry & Miss .... Dr. Fred C. FULLERTON
111 Vice Pres for External Relations .... Mr. Mark WHEELER
07 Assoc Vice Pres for Admissions .... Mr. Shawn A. BLENKER
26 Assoc Vice Pres for Marketing .... Mr. Mark CORK
06 Registrar .... Mrs. Stacey BERGGREN
08 Director of the Library .... Ms. Amy RICE
29 Director of Alumni Relations .... Mr. Darl L. BRUNER
51 Dir Center for Professional Devel .... Mr. Dave R. COVINGTON
42 Dean of the Chapel .... Rev. Dustin METCALF
40 Bookstore Manager .... Ms. Gail D. WALKER
35 Assoc Vice Pres Student Engagement .... Mrs. Karen L. PEARSON
38 Director of Wellness Center .... Dr. Bryon HEMPHILL
21 Controller .... Mrs. Macey CROW
35 Director of Community Life .... Mr. Grant T. MILLER
36 Director of Career Center .... Ms. Amanda F. MARBLE
13 Exec Director of Info Technology .... Mr. Todd BAKER
37 Director of Financial Aid .... Mrs. Ann CRABB
15 Director of Human Resources .... Mrs. Larissa BUNKER
41 Athletic Director .... Ms. Kelli LINDLEY
91 Dir of Administrative Computing .... Mr. Brian C. STILLMAN
18 Chief Facilities/Physical Plant .... Mr. Eric JACKSON
04 Administrative Asst to President .... Mrs. Michelle KUYKENDALL
09 Director of Institutional Research .... Dr. Duane SLEMMER
19 Director Security/Safety .... Mr. John NORRIS

Stevens-Henager College (E)

901 Pier View Drive, Suite 105, Idaho Falls ID 83402
Telephone: (208) 522-0887 — Identification: 770573
Accreditation: ACCSC

† Branch campus of Stevens-Henager College, Ogden, UT

Stevens-Henager College-Boise (F)

1444 S. Entertainment Avenue Ste200, Boise ID 83709
Telephone: (208) 383-4540 — Identification: 666329
Accreditation: ACCSC, COARC, MAC

† Branch campus of Stevens-Henager College, Ogden, UT

University of Idaho (G)

875 Perimeter Drive, Moscow ID 83844
County: Latah — FICE Identification: 001626
Unit ID: 142285
Telephone: (208) 885-6111 — Carnegie Class: DU-Higher
FAX Number: N/A — Calendar System: Semester
URL: www.uidaho.edu
Established: 1889 — Annual Undergrad Tuition & Fees (In-State): $7,864
Enrollment: 12,072 — Coed
Affiliation or Control: State — IRS Status: 501(c)3
Highest Offering: Doctorate
Accreditation: NW, ART, CAATE, CACREP, CAEPN, CEA, CIDA, DIETC, IPSY, JOUR, LAW, LSAR, MUS, NAIT, NRPA

01 President .... Mr. C. Scott GREEN
05 Provost & Executive VP .... Dr. John M. WIENCEK
10 VP Finance and Administration .... Mr. Brian R. FOISY
111 VP University Advancement .... Ms. Mary Kay MCFADDEN
13 VP Information Technology/CIO .... Mr. Dan EWART
46 VP Research & Econ Dev .... Dr. Janet NELSON
32 VP Stdnt Affs/Dean of Students .... Dr. Blaine ECKLES
84 Vice Provost Strategic Enroll Mgmt .... Mr. Dean KAHLER
26 Executive Dir of Mktg & Comm .... Ms. Stefany BALES
41 Interim Athletic Director .... Mr. Pete ISAKSON
43 General Counsel .... Mr. Kent E. NELSON
45 Exec Spec Asst/Strategic Initiative .... Ms. Chandra ZENNER FORD
88 Special Asst/Strategy .... Ms. Toni BROYLES
86 Special Asst/State Govt Relations .... Mr. Joe STEGNER
28 Chf Diversity Ofr/Ex Dir Tribal Rel .... Dr. Yolanda BISBEE
08 Dean Library Services .... Mr. Ben HUNTER
49 Dean Col of Ltrs/Arts/Social Sci .... Dr. Sean QUINLAN
47 Dean College of Agric/Life Sci .... Dr. Michael PARRELLA
50 Dean College of Business & Econ .... Dr. Marc CHOPIN
53 Dean Col of Educ/Health/Human Sci .... Dr. Alison CARR-CHELLMAN
54 Dean College of Engineering .... Dr. Larry STAUFFER
58 Dean Graduate Studies .... Dr. Jerry MCMURTY
65 Dean College of Natural Resources .... Dr. Michael PARRELLA
61 Dean College of Law .... Mr. Jerry LONG
48 Dean College of Art & Arch .... Dr. Shauna CORRY
81 Dean College of Science .... Dr. Ginger CARNEY
20 Vice Provost for Faculty .... Dr. Torrey LAWRENCE
109 Asst VP Auxiliary Services .... Mr. Greg CAIN
15 Executive Director Human Resources .... Mr. Wesley MATTHEWS
114 Budget Director .... Ms. Trina MAHONEY
12 Executive Officer Couer d'Alene .... Dr. Charles BUCK
12 Executive Officer Boise Center .... Mr. Michael SATZ
12 Int Exec Officer Idaho Falls Ctr .... Dr. Lee OSTROM
18 Assistant Vice President Facilities .... Mr. Brian D. JOHNSON
19 Exec Dir Env Health & Safety .... Mr. Samir Shahat ABD EL-FATAH
117 Dir Emergency Mgmt & Security Sys .... Mr. Todd PERRY
108 Dir Inst Effectiveness & Accred .... Dr. Dale PIETRZAK
37 Director Student Financial Aid .... Vacant
07 Assistant Vice Provost SEM .... Ms. Bobbi J. GERRY
38 Director Counseling & Testing Ctr .... Dr. Gregory LAMBETH
42 Director Campus Christian Center .... Ms. Sharon A. KEHOE
39 Director University Residences .... Ms. Dee Dee KANIKKEBERG
44 Director Annual Giving .... Mr. Eric BILLINGS
92 Director Honors Program .... Ms. Sandra REINEKE
93 Dir Multicultural Affairs .... Mr. Jesse MARTINEZ
94 Director Women's Center .... Ms. Lysa SALSBURY
40 Director Bookstore .... Mr. Keith MCIVOR
96 Director Purchasing Services .... Ms. Julia MCILROY
36 Director Career Services .... Mr. Christopher COOK
25 Director Research Admin .... Ms. Deborah SHAVER
103 Dir Academic Support and Access Pgm .... Ms. Cynthia CASTRO
06 Registrar .... Ms. Lindsey BROWN
29 Asst VP Cmty & Alumni Relations .... Ms. Kathy BARNARD
102 Exec Director UI Foundation .... Ms. Joy FISHER
106 Dir Distance & Extended Educ .... Mr. Terry D. RATCLIFF
87 Coord Summer & Dual Credit Pgm .... Ms. Linda GOLLBERG
22 Dir Civil Rights & Investigation .... Ms. Erin AGIDIUS
105 Director Enterprise Applications .... Mr. Brian BORCHERS
104 Exec Dir International Programs .... Ms. Aryn BAXTER
100 Chief of Staff President's Office .... Ms. Brenda HELBLING

ILLINOIS

Adler University (H)

17 North Dearborn Street, Chicago IL 60602
County: Cook — FICE Identification: 020681
Unit ID: 142832
Telephone: (312) 662-4000 — Carnegie Class: Spec-4-yr-Other Health
FAX Number: (312) 662-4099 — Calendar System: Semester
URL: www.adler.edu
Established: 1952 — Annual Graduate Tuition & Fees: N/A
Enrollment: 1,097 — Coed
Affiliation or Control: Independent Non-Profit — IRS Status: 501(c)3
Highest Offering: Doctorate; No Undergraduates
Accreditation: NH, CACREP, CLPSY, IPSY, MFCD

01 President .... Dr. Raymond E. CROSSMAN
101 Board Secy/Dir Ofc of the Pres .... Ms. Mitzi NORTON
11 Vice President Administration .... Mrs. Jo Beth CUP
05 Vice President Academic Affairs .... Dr. Wendy PASZKIEWICZ
10 Vice President Finance & IT .... Mr. Jeffrey GREEN
07 Vice President Admissions .... Mr. Craig HINES
28 VP Diversity & Inclusion .... Ms. Tamara JOHNSON
26 Assoc Vice President Marketing .... Mr. Mark BRANSON
111 AVP Institutional Advancement .... Ms. Heather SCHUSTER
06 Registrar .... Ms. Sheba JONES
32 Assoc Vice President Student Affs .... Dr. Quincy PADEN
88 Ex Dir Inst Pub Safety/Soc Justice .... Dr. Elena QUINTANA
37 Director Student Financial Aid .... Mr. David NELSON
13 Sr Director Technology .... Mr. Jonathan QUACH
12 Dean Vancouver Campus .... Mr. Bradley O'HARA
106 Executive Dean Online Campus .... Dr. Sarah FORNERO
15 AVP Human Resources .... Ms. Susan YASECKO
29 Director Alumni Relations .... Vacant
04 Administrative Asst to President .... Ms. Elizabeth BLONDEL
18 Chief Facilities/Physical Plant .... Mr. Tom ROHNER
43 Dir Legal Services/General Counsel .... Ms. Julie PROSCIA
08 Director Library Services .... Ms. Ariel ORLOV
102 Dir Foundation/Corporate Relations .... Ms. Ingrid PARKER
108 Dir Institutional Effectivenes .... Ms. Katy SELINKO

Ambria College of Nursing (I)

5210 Trillium Boulevard, Hoffman Estates IL 60192
County: Cook — FICE Identification: 041247
Unit ID: 457527

Telephone: (847) 397-0300 Carnegie Class: Spec-4-yr-Other Health
FAX Number: (847) 397-0313 Calendar System: Other
URL: www.ambria.edu
Established: 2006 Annual Undergrad Tuition & Fees: N/A
Enrollment: 317 Coed
Affiliation or Control: Proprietary IRS Status: Proprietary
Highest Offering: Baccalaureate
Accreditation: ABHES

01 President .... Jon OLIVEROS

American Academy of Art (A)

332 S Michigan Avenue, Chicago IL 60604-4302
County: Cook FICE Identification: 001628
Unit ID: 142887
Telephone: (312) 461-0600 Carnegie Class: Spec-4-yr-Arts
FAX Number: (312) 294-9570 Calendar System: Semester
URL: www.aaart.edu
Established: 1923 Annual Undergrad Tuition & Fees: $34,270
Enrollment: 260 Coed
Affiliation or Control: Independent Non-Profit IRS Status: 501(c)3
Highest Offering: Baccalaureate
Accreditation: NH, ACCSC

01 President .... Mr. Richard H. OTTO
05 Academic Dean .... Mr. Duncan WEBB
06 Registrar .... Ms. Marcia R. THOMAS
36 Career Services Coordinator .... Ms. Lindsay SANDBOTHE
37 Financial Aid Director .... Ms. Ione FITZGERALD
07 Director of Admissions .... Mr. Stuart ROSENBLOOM

American InterContinental University (B)

231 North Martingale Rd, 6th Floor, Schaumburg IL 60173
County: Cook FICE Identification: 021136
Unit ID: 445027
Telephone: (877) 701-3800 Carnegie Class: Masters/L
FAX Number: N/A Calendar System: Quarter
URL: www.aiuniv.edu
Established: 1970 Annual Undergrad Tuition & Fees: $11,937
Enrollment: 9,699 Coed
Affiliation or Control: Proprietary IRS Status: Proprietary
Highest Offering: Master's
Accreditation: NH, ACBSP, CAEPT

01 President .... Mr. John KLINE
05 Provost & Chief Academic Officer .... Dr. Ruki JAYARAMAN
07 VP of Admissions .... Mrs. Trisha GANGER
32 VP of Strategic Student Operations .... Mr. Jeffrey SONNENBERG
88 VP Program Management .... Ms. April MIGEL
11 VP of Univ Policy/Administration .... Mr. Daniel SESSIONS
32 VP of Campus Operations .... Ms. Julia LEEMAN
108 Director of Inst Effectiveness .... Mr. Christopher PERRY
09 VP Educational Alliances & IRC .... Mr. Walid KAAKOUSH
12 Campus Director-Atlanta .... Ms. Sharon SMITH
12 Campus Director-Houston .... Dr. Shayan MIRABI

Augustana College (C)

639 38th Street, Rock Island IL 61201-2296
County: Rock Island FICE Identification: 001633
Unit ID: 143084
Telephone: (309) 794-7000 Carnegie Class: Bac-A&S
FAX Number: (309) 794-7422 Calendar System: 4/1/4
URL: www.augustana.edu
Established: 1860 Annual Undergrad Tuition & Fees: $42,135
Enrollment: 2,647 Coed
Affiliation or Control: Evangelical Lutheran Church In America
IRS Status: 501(c)3
Highest Offering: Baccalaureate
Accreditation: NH, MUS

01 President .... Mr. Steven C. BAHLS
05 Provost and Dean of the College .. Dr. Wendy HILTON-MORROW
10 Vice Pres of Finance and Admin .... Mr. Kirk D. ANDERSON
30 Executive VP External Relations .... Mr. W. Kent BARNDS
32 Dean of Students & VP Student Life .... Dr. Wesley BROOKS
28 VP Diversity/Equity and Inclusion .... Dr. Monica SMITH
20 Associate Dean of the College .... Dr. Michael EGAN
20 Associate Dean of the College .... Dr. Kristin DOUGLAS
20 Associate Dean of the College .... Dr. Jessica SCHULTZ
42 Chaplain .... Rev. Richard W. PRIGGIE
06 College Registrar .... Ms. Liesl A. FOWLER
09 Asst Dean/Director Inst Research .... Dr. Tsooane MOLAPO
08 Director of the Library .... Dr. Chris SCHAFER
36 Associate VP Careers & Prof Devel .... Ms. Laura KESTNER-RICKETTS
13 Director of ITS .... Mr. Chris VAUGHAN
37 Director of Student Financial Aid .... Ms. Susan STANDLEY
96 Dir Financial Plng & Procurement .... Mr. Malhar SAHEED
19 Chief of Public Safety .... Mr. Thomas M. PHILLIS
41 Director of Athletics .... Mr. Mike ZAPOLSKI
15 Director Human Resources .... Mrs. Laura C. FORD
18 Director Facilities Services .... Mr. Robert LANZEROTTI
38 Director Student Counseling .... Mr. William IAVARONE
35 Assistant Dean of Student Life .... Ms. Laura L. SCHNACK
26 Assistant VP of Comm & Marketing .... Ms. Keri RURSCH
29 Director Alumni/Parent Relations .... Ms. Kelly NOACK
07 Executive Director of Admissions .... Ms. Karen A. DAHLSTROM
04 Executive Assistant to President .... Ms. Mary KOSKI
104 Dir Intl Student & Scholar Svcs .... Ms. Xong Sony YANG
43 Dir Legal Services/General Counsel .... Ms. Sheri L. CURRAN
100 Chief of Staff .... Mr. Kai SWANSON
102 Dir Foundation/Corporate Relations .... Ms. Lori RODERICK
39 Director of Residential Life .... Mr. Christopher BEYER
105 Director Web Services & News Media .... Ms. Leslie M. DUPREE

Aurora University (D)

347 S Gladstone Avenue, Aurora IL 60506-4892
County: Kane FICE Identification: 001634
Unit ID: 143118
Telephone: (630) 892-6431 Carnegie Class: DU-Mod
FAX Number: (630) 844-5463 Calendar System: Semester
URL: www.aurora.edu
Established: 1893 Annual Undergrad Tuition & Fees: $24,260
Enrollment: 5,833 Coed
Affiliation or Control: Independent Non-Profit IRS Status: 501(c)3
Highest Offering: Doctorate
Accreditation: NH, CAATE, CAEPN, NURSE, SW

01 President .... Dr. Rebecca L. SHERRICK
32 Sr Vice President for Student Life .... Dr. Lora DE LACEY
05 Vice President for Academic Affairs .... Dr. Frank M. BUSCHER
10 Vice President for Finance .... Ms. Sharon MAXWELL
11 Vice President for Administration .... Dr. Carmella MORAN
84 Vice President for Enrollment .... Mr. James LANCASTER
30 Vice President for Development .... Ms. Meg HOWES
26 VP for Marketing and Communications .... Ms. Deb MAUE
31 Vice President Community Relations .... Ms. Sarah R. RUSSE
29 VP for Alumni Relations .... Ms. Teri TOMASZKIEWICZ
15 Vice President of Human Resources .... Ms. Mary WEIS
35 Vice President for Student Success .... Dr. Amy GRAY
37 Dean of Student Financial Services .... Ms. Heather L. GRANART
13 Chief Operating Officer .... Mr. David W. DIEHL
06 Registrar .... Ms. Melody NABORS
08 Director University Library .... Ms. Kathy CLARK
19 Senior Director of Campus Safety .... Ms. Yvonne MEYER
41 AVP Student Life/Athletic Director .... Mr. James HAMAD
38 Director of Counseling Center .... Dr. Marcie WISEMAN
66 Dean of Sch of Nursing/Allied Hlth .... Dr. Jan STROM
70 Dean School of Social Work .... Ms. Brenda BARNWELL
88 Faculty Development Liaison .... Dr. Julie HIPP
49 Dean College of Art and Sciences .... Dr. Frank BUSCHER
53 Dean School of Educ/Human Perf .... Dr. Jennifer BUCKLEY
50 Dean Dunham Sch Bus/Public Policy .... Dr. Toby ARQUETTE
106 Dean of Online Enroll/Cont Educ .... Dr. Donna LILJEGREN
20 Dean Academic Administration .... Dr. Mary TARLING
04 Executive Assistant to President .... Ms. Becca FLAMINIO
09 Director of University Analytics .... Ms. Katie THARP

Benedictine University (E)

5700 College Road, Lisle IL 60532-0900
County: DuPage FICE Identification: 001767
Unit ID: 145619
Telephone: (630) 829-6000 Carnegie Class: DU-Mod
FAX Number: N/A Calendar System: Semester
URL: www.ben.edu
Established: 1887 Annual Undergrad Tuition & Fees: $34,290
Enrollment: 5,100 Coed
Affiliation or Control: Roman Catholic IRS Status: 501(c)3
Highest Offering: Doctorate
Accreditation: NH, DIETD, DIETI, NURSE, PH

01 President .... Mr. Charles GREGORY
05 Int Provost/VP Academic Affairs .... Dr. David SONNENBERGER
10 VP Business & Finance .... Ms. Miroslava MEJIA KRUG
30 Vice President of Development .... Vacant
32 Vice Pres Student Life .... Mr. Marco MASINI
20 Assoc Provost .... Dr. Cheryl HEINZ
42 Director University Ministry .... Ms. Carrie ANKENY
06 Registrar .... Mr. Jason HEIDENFELDER
08 Director Library Services .... Mr. Jack FRITTS
37 Sr Associate Dean Financial Aid .... Ms. Diane BATTISTELLA
09 Director of Institutional Research .... Dr. Amy SHIN
36 Director Career Development .... Dr. Julie COSIMO
23 Director Health Services .... Ms. Pamela DEELY
26 Exec Dir Marketing/Communications .... Mr. Gary KOHN
50 Dean College of Business .... Dr. Darrell RADSON
81 Dean College of Science .... Dr. William LAW
49 Dean College of Lib Arts .... Dr. Joseph INCANDELA
51 VP Adult and Professional Programs .... Vacant
53 Dean Col of Educ/Health Svcs .... Dr. Christopher DUFFRIN
88 Chief Mission Officer .... Dr. Peter HUFF
124 Chief Retention Officer .... Ms. Karen CAMPANA
19 Chief of Police .... Mr. Derek FERGUSON
31 Asst to the Pres for Cmty Relations .... Ms. Patricia ARIANO
15 Director of Personnel Resources .... Ms. Betsy RHINESMITH
35 Student Activ & Commuter Svcs Coord .... Ms. Katie BUELL
13 Chief Information Officer .... Mr. Timothy HOPKINS
07 Interim Director of Admissions .... Mr. Matthew JONES
04 Administrative Asst to President .... Vacant
102 Dir Foundation/Corporate Relations .... Ms. Krissy DULEK
112 Senior Development Officer .... Mr. Eric SOLBERG
104 Director International Pgm and Svcs .... Dr. David KLEINBERG
29 Director Alumni Relations .... Mr. Jon-Pierre BRADLEY
121 Director Student Advising .... Ms. Anne BAYSINGER
39 Assoc Dean Student Life .... Mr. Jon MILLER
41 Director of Athletics .... Mr. Mark MCHORNEY
43 Chief Compliance Ofcr/Legal Counsel .... Ms. Nancy STOECKER
44 Director of Annual Giving .... Ms. Jill POSKIN
18 Exec Dir Facilities Mgmt and Plng .... Ms. Marlene LEVINE
86 Assoc Compliance Officer .... Mr. Kevin RAPPEL
40 Asst Store and Textbooks Manager .... Ms. Kelly ROE
12 Mesa Campus Dean .... Dr. Paula NORBY
38 Director Student Counseling .... Ms. Hope KEBER

Bexley Seabury (F)

1407 E 60th St, Chicago IL 60637
County: Cook FICE Identification: 037473
Unit ID: 443702
Telephone: (773) 380-6780 Carnegie Class: Spec-4-yr-Faith
FAX Number: (773) 380-6788 Calendar System: Semester
URL: www.bexleyseabury.edu
Established: 1824 Annual Graduate Tuition & Fees: N/A
Enrollment: 65 Coed
Affiliation or Control: Protestant Episcopal IRS Status: 501(c)3
Highest Offering: Doctorate; No Undergraduates
Accreditation: THEOL

01 President .... RevDr. Micah JACKSON
05 Academic Dean .... Dean Therese DELISIO
10 Chief Financial Officer .... Ms. Lisa GEE

Black Hawk College (G)

6600 34th Avenue, Moline IL 61265-5899
County: Rock Island FICE Identification: 001638
Unit ID: 143279
Telephone: (309) 796-5000 Carnegie Class: Assoc/MT-VT-High Non
FAX Number: (309) 792-5976 Calendar System: Semester
URL: www.bhc.edu
Established: 1946 Annual Undergrad Tuition & Fees (In-District): $4,470
Enrollment: 4,926 Coed
Affiliation or Control: Local IRS Status: 501(c)3
Highest Offering: Associate Degree
Accreditation: NH, ADNUR, EMT, PTAA

01 President .... Mr. Tim WYNES
05 VP of Instruction/Student Svcs .... Dr. Amy MAXEINER
10 VP Finance/Admin & Board Treasurer .... Mr. Steve FROMMELT
20 Executive Dean .... Dr. Betsey MORTHLAND
15 Director of Human Resources .... Ms. Stacey CARY
19 Chief of Police .... Mr. Shawn CISNA
09 Director Plng & Inst Effectiveness .... Ms. Kathy MALCOLM
26 Director Marketing/Public Relations .... Mr. John MEINEKE
13 Co-CIO/IT Systems Manager .... Mr. Ryan WHITE
13 Co-CIO/Manager of Admin Systems .... Ms. Sandy COX
102 Exec Dir BHC Foundation QC Campus .Ms. Maureen DICKINSON
51 Dean Adult/Continuing Educ .... Ms. Glenda NICKE
81 Academic Dean .... Mr. Ken NICKELS
04 Executive Asst to the President .... Ms. Heather BENNETT
36 Director Career Services Center .... Dr. Bruce STOREY
37 Director of Financial Aid .... Vacant
08 Librarian .... Ms. Ashtin TRIMBLE
55 Director Adult Education .... Ms. Bianca PERKINS
06 Registrar/Dean Enrollment Mgmt .... Ms. Heather BJORGAN
40 Bookstore Manager Quad Cities .... Ms. Aimee MUHLEMAN
96 Purchasing Manager .... Mr. Mike MELEG
50 Dept Chair Business & Technology .... Ms. Carrie DELCOURT
79 Dept Chair Human/Languages/Journal .... Mr. Bill DESMOND
81 Dept Chair Mathematics/Comp Science .... Ms. Connie MCLEAN
54 Dept Chair Natural Science/Engrng .... Mr. Brian GLASER
83 Dept Chair Social Sciences .... Mr. Mark ESPOSITO
47 Department Chair Agriculture .... Dr. Jeffrey HAWES
66 Dept Chair Nursing .... Ms. Trudy STARR
76 Dept Chair Allied Health/HPE .... Ms. Dianne ABELS
88 Dept Chair Counseling .... Ms. Wendy BOCK
62 Dept Chair Lrg Resource Center .... Vacant
53 Dept Chair Psych/Sociology/Educ .... Dr. Traci DAVIS
72 Dept Chair Career Technologies .... Ms. Jamie HILL
18 Chief Facilities/Physical Plant .... Mr. Bob MCCHURCH

Black Hawk College East Campus (H)

26230 Black Hawk Road, Galva IL 61434
Telephone: (309) 854-1700 Identification: 770069
Accreditation: &NH

Blackburn College (I)

700 College Avenue, Carlinville IL 62626-1498
County: Macoupin FICE Identification: 001639
Unit ID: 143288
Telephone: (217) 854-3231 Carnegie Class: Bac-A&S
FAX Number: (217) 854-5700 Calendar System: Semester
URL: www.blackburn.edu
Established: 1837 Annual Undergrad Tuition & Fees: $22,410
Enrollment: 554 Coed
Affiliation or Control: Presbyterian Church (U.S.A.) IRS Status: 501(c)3
Highest Offering: Baccalaureate
Accreditation: NH

01 President .... Dr. Julie MURRAY-JENSEN
05 Provost .... Dr. John MCCLUSKY
10 Vice Pres Administration & Finance .... Mr. Steve MORRIS
111 VP for Institutional Advancement .... Ms. Lauren DODGE
32 VP/Dean of Student Affairs .... Dr. Marsh-Allen SMITH
101 Exec Asst to Pres/Sec Bd Trustees .... Mrs. Shawna POE
07 Director of Admissions .... Mr. Justin NORWOOD
88 Director of Transfer Admissions .... Vacant

30 Sr Dir of Development/Gift Planning ... Mr. Nate RUSH
37 Director of Financial Aid ... Mrs. Alisha KAPP
08 Head Librarian ... Vacant
38 College Counselor ... Mr. Tim MORENZ
06 College Registrar ... Mrs. Dianna RUYLE
15 Director Personnel Services ... Ms. Melissa JONES
36 Director Career Services ... Mrs. Sarah STOVER
18 Director Physical Plant ... Mr. Sam HARDING
41 Dir of Athletics/Recreational Pgms ... Mr. John MALIN
42 Chaplain (Part-Time) ... Mrs. Megan BIDDLE
26 Director of Public Relations ... Vacant
09 Director of Institutional Research ... Dr. Kristi NELMS
21 Controller ... Ms. Dawn SHRYOCK
44 Exec Dir for Philanthropy ... Vacant
84 Enrollment Services Administrator ... Mrs. Kathy RUITER
19 Director Security/Safety ... Vacant
28 Director of Diversity ... Dr. Eda WATTS
13 Chief Info Technology Officer (CIO) ... Mr. Jason CLONINGER
88 Dean of Work ... Mrs. Angie MORENZ
29 Director Alumni Relations/Dev ... Mr. Stephen YEARSON
39 Assoc Dean/Director Resident Life ... Ms. Alondra OLVERA

Blessing-Rieman College of Nursing & Health Sciences (A)

11th & Oak, PO Box 7005, Quincy IL 62305-7005
County: Adams FICE Identification: 006214
Unit ID: 143297
Telephone: (217) 228-5520 Carnegie Class: Spec-4-yr-Other Health
FAX Number: (217) 223-4661 Calendar System: Semester
URL: www.brcn.edu
Established: 1891 Annual Undergrad Tuition & Fees: N/A
Enrollment: 288 Coed
Affiliation or Control: Independent Non-Profit IRS Status: 501(c)3
Highest Offering: Master's
Accreditation: NH, #COARC, NURSE

01 President/CEO ... Dr. Brenda BESHEARS
05 Academic Dean ... Dr. Jan AKRIGHT
84 Dean of Enroll Mgmt/Business Mgr ... Ms. Jenna CRABTREE
06 Registrar ... Ms. Rachel CRAMSEY

Bradley University (B)

1501 W Bradley Avenue, Peoria IL 61625-0001
County: Peoria FICE Identification: 001641
Unit ID: 143358
Telephone: (309) 676-7611 Carnegie Class: Masters/L
FAX Number: N/A Calendar System: Semester
URL: www.bradley.edu
Established: 1897 Annual Undergrad Tuition & Fees: $33,760
Enrollment: 5,844 Coed
Affiliation or Control: Independent Non-Profit IRS Status: 501(c)3
Highest Offering: Doctorate
Accreditation: NH, ART, CACREP, CAEPN, CONST, DIETD, DIETI, MUS, NURSE, PTA, SW, THEA

01 President ... Dr. Gary R. ROBERTS
05 Provost/Vice Pres Academic Affs ... Dr. Walter R. ZAKAHI
32 Vice President Student Affairs ... Mr. Nathan THOMAS
84 VP Enrollment Management ... Mr. Justin BALL
111 Vice President Advancement ... Mr. Jacob HEUSER
43 Vice Pres Legal Affairs/Gen Counsel ... Ms. Erin KASTBERG
41 VP for Intercollegiate Athletics ... Dr. Chris REYNOLDS
10 Chief Financial Officer ... Mrs. Pratima N. GANDHI
26 Associate VP Marketing ... Ms. Renee RICHARDSON
19 Chief of Campus Police ... Mr. Brian JOSCHKO
20 Interim Associate Provost ... Dr. Jobie SKAGGS
58 Assoc Provost/Dean Res/Grad School ... Dr. Jeffrey BAKKEN
20 Assistant Provost Academic Affairs ... Mrs. Linda J. PIZZUTI
114 Assistant VP Budgeting and Planning ... Mr. Demetrius L. CARMICHAEL
50 Interim Dean Foster Col Business ... Dr. Matt O'BRIEN
57 Dean Slane Col Commun/Fine Arts ... Dr. Jeffrey H. HUBERMAN
53 Interim Dean Educ & Health Sciences ... Dr. Molly CLUSKEY
54 Dean Engineering & Technology ... Dr. Lex A. AKERS
49 Dean Liberal Arts & Sciences ... Dr. Christopher JONES
106 Associate Dean Distance Education ... Dr. Molly CLUSKEY
08 Exec Director of the Library ... Ms. Barbara GALIK
39 Dir Ctr Residential Living/Ldrshp ... Mr. Ryan BAIR
36 Exec Dir Smith Career Center ... Mr. Jon NEIDY
29 Director of Alumni Relations ... Ms. Tory JENNETTEN
51 Executive Director Continuing Educ ... Ms. Janet LANGE
27 Exec Dir Public Relations ... Ms. Renee CHARLES
06 Registrar ... Mr. Andreas KINDLER
37 Director Financial Aid ... Ms. Debra JACKSON
15 Director of Human Resources ... Ms. Nena PEPLOW
18 Director Facilities Management ... Mr. Larry MCGUIRE
23 Medical Director Health Services ... Dr. Jessica HIGGS
13 Chief Information Officer ... Mr. Zach GORMAN
27 Public Relations Specialist ... Ms. Haley KRUS
78 Director Springer Center ... Mrs. Dawn KOELTZOW
87 Dir Summer/Interim Sessions ... Ms. Janet LANGE
22 Director Affirmative Action/EEO ... Ms. Nena PEPLOW
28 Exec Dir Diversity/Inclusion ... Mr. Norris CHASE
92 Director of Honors Program ... Dr. Kyle DZAPO
94 Dir of Women's Studies & Gender ... Dr. Amy SCOTT
108 Dir of Institutional Effectiveness ... Ms. Jennifer G. BURGE
40 Manager Bookstore ... Mr. Paul KROENKE
88 Dir of Health Prof Advising Ctr ... Dr. Valerie BENNETT
88 Dir Center for Legal Studies ... Ms. Jerelyn MAHER
07 Asst Dir Admissions ... Mr. Joshua JONES
104 Director Study Abroad ... Dr. Christine BLOUCH

Carl Sandburg College (C)

2400 Tom L. Wilson Boulevard, Galesburg IL 61401-9576
County: Knox FICE Identification: 007265
Unit ID: 143613
Telephone: (309) 344-2518 Carnegie Class: Assoc/MT-VT-High Non
FAX Number: (309) 344-1395 Calendar System: Semester
URL: www.sandburg.edu
Established: 1966 Annual Undergrad Tuition & Fees: $4,670
Enrollment: 1,947 Coed
Affiliation or Control: Independent Non-Profit IRS Status: 501(c)3
Highest Offering: Associate Degree
Accreditation: NH, ADNUR, DH, FUSER, PNUR

01 President ... Dr. Seamus REILLY
37 Director Financial Aid ... Ms. Lisa HANSON
07 Director of Recruitment ... Vacant
41 Athletic Director ... Mr. Mike BAILEY
06 Director of Admissions & Records ... Mr. Rick EDDY
19 Director of Public Safety ... Mr. Kipton CANFIELD
16 Director of Human Resources ... Ms. Gina KRUPPS
45 Dean of Institutional Planning ... Ms. Michelle JOHNSON
103 Dean Career & Corp Development ... Vacant
88 Director of Corporate & Leisure ... Ms. Stacey RUCKER
12 Director of Branch Campus ... Dr. Ellen HENDERSON-GASSER
81 Assoc Dean Math/Natural Sciences ... Ms. Marjorie SMOLENSKY
05 VP of Academic Services ... Ms. Carrie HAWKINSON
20 Assoc VP Academic/Student Svcs/Plng ... Ms. Misty LYON
79 Assoc Dean Humanities/Fine Arts ... Mr. James HUTCHINGS
50 Assoc Dean Social & Business Sci ... Ms. Lara ROEMER
75 Assoc Dean CTHE ... Vacant
76 Dean of Health Professions ... Ms. Kristina GRAY
04 Assistant to President & Board ... Ms. Lindsey HUBER
32 VP of Student Services ... Mr. Steve NORTON
10 Chief Financial Officer/Treasurer ... Mr. Cory GALL
15 Dean HR/Institutional Effectiveness ... Vacant
26 Director Marketing/Public Relations ... Ms. Brittany GRIMES
111 Director of Advancement ... Ms. Emily WEBEL
13 Director of Technology Services ... Mr. Rob STEVENS
84 Dean of Student Success ... Vacant
121 Director of TRIO SSS ... Ms. Autumn SCOTT
121 Director TRIO Upward Bound ... Mr. Jason STALIDES
121 Director TRIO UB Math Science ... Ms. Stephanie WOODARD

Carl Sandburg College The Branch Campus (D)

305 Sandburg Drive, Carthage IL 62321
Telephone: (217) 357-3129 Identification: 770071
Accreditation: &NH

Catholic Theological Union (E)

5401 S Cornell Avenue, Chicago IL 60615-5698
County: Cook FICE Identification: 009232
Unit ID: 143659
Telephone: (773) 371-5400 Carnegie Class: Spec-4-yr-Faith
FAX Number: (773) 324-8490 Calendar System: Semester
URL: www.ctu.edu
Established: 1968 Annual Graduate Tuition & Fees: N/A
Enrollment: 295 Coed
Affiliation or Control: Roman Catholic IRS Status: 501(c)3
Highest Offering: Doctorate; No Undergraduates
Accreditation: THEOL

01 President ... Rev. Mark R. FRANCIS, CSV
05 Vice President/Academic Dean ... Rev. Richard BENSON, CM
10 Vice Pres Administration & Finance ... Vacant
111 Vice Pres Institutional Advancement ... Ms. Colleen KENNEDY
30 Director of Development ... Ms. Rachel KUHN
08 Director of the Library ... Ms. Kristine VELDHEER
06 Registrar ... Mrs. Maria De Jesus LEMUS
07 Asst Director Admissions/Retention ... Mr. Patrick MCGOWAN
13 Director of Information Technology ... Mr. Darnell PAYNE
04 Assistant to the President ... Sr. Pam PAULOSKI, SP
84 Director Enrollment Management ... Ms. Kathryn TRNKA
104 Director Study Abroad ... Rev. Ferdinand OKORIE
105 Director Web Services ... Mr. Ron BROWN
106 Director Online Educ/E-learning ... Mr. Richard MAUNEY
18 Director Facilities ... Mr. Marty FITZGERALD
26 Communications Manager ... Ms. Kellene URBANIAK
29 Director Alumni Affairs ... Ms. Christine HENDERSON
32 Manager of Events/Student Services ... Mrs. Carmen SALAS

*Chamberlain University-Administrative Office (F)

3005 Highland Parkway, Downers Grove IL 60515
County: DuPage Identification: 667149
Telephone: (888) 556-8226 Carnegie Class: N/A
FAX Number: (630) 512-8888
URL: www.chamberlain.edu

01 President ... Dr. Karen COX
11 VP Campus Operations ... Dr. Patrick ROMBALSKI
05 Provost ... Dr. Carla SANDERSON
84 VP Enrollment Management ... Mark BUCK
32 VP Student Services ... June MARLOWE
06 University Registrar ... Abbey MCELLIGOTT
09 Assoc Prov Inst Effect/Accred/Rsrch ... Dr. Linda HOLLINGER-SMITH

*Chamberlain University-Addison (G)

1221 N. Swift Road, Addison IL 60101
County: DuPage FICE Identification: 006385
Unit ID: 454227
Telephone: (630) 953-3660 Carnegie Class: Spec-4-yr-Other Health
FAX Number: (630) 628-1154 Calendar System: Semester
URL: www.chamberlain.edu/addison
Established: 1889 Annual Undergrad Tuition & Fees: $19,375
Enrollment: 27,099 Coed
Affiliation or Control: Proprietary IRS Status: Proprietary
Highest Offering: Doctorate
Accreditation: NH, NURSE

02 Campus President ... Dr. Jan SNOW
05 Dean Academic Affairs ... Terry BRENNAN
32 Manager Student Services ... Lisa PETSCHENKO
07 Director Admissions ... Roz CASTRO

† Master's and Doctorate programs are only offered online.

**Chamberlain University-Chicago* (H)

3300 North Campbell Avenue, Chicago IL 60618
Telephone: (773) 961-3000 Identification: 770495
Accreditation: &NH, NURSE

**Chamberlain University-Tinley Park* (I)

18624 West Creek Drive, Tinley Park IL 60477
Telephone: (708) 560-2000 Identification: 770496
Accreditation: &NH, NURSE

Chicago School of Professional Psychology-Chicago (J)

325 N Wells Street, Chicago IL 60654-8158
Telephone: (312) 329-6600 Identification: 770349
Accreditation: &WC, CACREP, CLPSY

† Branch campus of Chicago School of Professional Psychology Los Angeles Campus, Los Angeles, CA

Chicago State University (K)

9501 S King Drive, Chicago IL 60628-1598
County: Cook FICE Identification: 001694
Unit ID: 144005
Telephone: (773) 995-2000 Carnegie Class: Masters/L
FAX Number: (773) 995-2563 Calendar System: Semester
URL: www.csu.edu
Established: 1867 Annual Undergrad Tuition & Fees (In-State): $10,163
Enrollment: 3,101 Coed
Affiliation or Control: State IRS Status: 501(c)3
Highest Offering: Doctorate
Accreditation: NH, ACBSP, ART, CACREP, CAEPN, CAHIIM, LIB, MUS, NRPA, NUR, OT, PHAR, SW

01 President ... Ms. Zaldwaynaka "Z" SCOTT
05 Int Provost/SVP Academic Affairs ... Dr. Leslie A. ROUNDTREE
10 Chief Finance Officer/VP DEI ... Ms. Ginger OSTRO
114 Executive Director Budget/Resource ... Mrs. Arrileen PATAWARAN
13 Chief Information Officer ... Mr. Kyle CRAMER
84 Vice Pres of Enrollment Management ... Dr. Micheal ELLISON
09 Dir Inst Effectiveness & Research ... Dr. Latrice E. EGGLESTON WILLIAMS
32 Int Dean of Student Affairs & FYE ... Mr. Michael CRAWFORD
49 Dean Col of Arts & Sciences ... Dr. LeRoy JONES, II
53 Acting Dean Col of Education ... Dr. Patrice BOYLES
67 Int Dean College of Pharmacy ... Dr. Elmer J. GENTRY
76 Actg Dean Col of Health Sciences ... Dr. Tyra L. DEAN-OUSLEY
50 Dean College of Business ... Mr. Derrick K. COLLINS
08 Dean of Library/Instruct Services ... Dr. Richard DARGA
51 Int Dean Cont Educ Nontrad Pgms ... Ms. Nelly MAYNARD
92 Interim Dean Honors College ... Dr. Kelly HARRIS
06 Interim Registrar ... Mrs. Michelle SMITH-WILLIAMS
37 Director of Financial Aid ... Ms. Rhonda SMITH
07 Int Director of Admissions Outreach ... Mr. Stephen POWENSKI
26 Director of Marketing/Communication ... Mrs. Sabrina LAND
15 Chief Talent Officer ... Ms. Lindsay HAMILTON
36 Director of Career Development ... Mrs. LaCael PALMER-PRATT
18 Director Facilities/Physical Plant ... Mr. Joseph SIMONETTI
20 Assoc Provost Academic Affairs ... Dr. Bernard ROWAN
89 Dir of First Year Experience (FYE) ... Ms. MaToya MARSH
38 Director Counseling Center ... Dr. Shenay BRIDGES-CARTER
20 Assoc Provost Academic Affairs ... Dr. Mark SUDEITH
25 Int Assoc VP of Sponsored Programs ... Dr. David KANIS
43 Assoc VP Gen Counsel/Ethics Officer ... Ms. Robin HAWKINS
19 Chief of Police ... Mr. Eddie WELCH
39 Director Student Housing ... Mr. Timothy LEE
41 Athletic Director ... Mr. Christpher ZORICH
43 General Counsel ... Ms. Stephanie KELLY
100 Chief of Staff/External Affairs ... Mr. Ryan C. GREEN
88 Deputy Chief of Staff ... Mr. Kim H. TRAN

Chicago Theological Seminary (L)

1407 East 60th Street, Chicago IL 60637-1284
County: Cook FICE Identification: 001661
Unit ID: 144014
Telephone: (773) 896-2400 Carnegie Class: Spec-4-yr-Faith
FAX Number: (773) 643-1284 Calendar System: Semester
URL: www.ctschicago.edu
Established: 1855 Annual Graduate Tuition & Fees: N/A

Enrollment: 232 Coed
Affiliation or Control: United Church Of Christ IRS Status: 501(c)3
Highest Offering: Doctorate; No Undergraduates
Accreditation: NH, THEOL

01 President .... Rev. Stephen G. RAY, JR.
05 VP Academic Affairs/Academic Dean .. Dr. Stephanie B. CROWDER
10 Vice President for Finance & Admin .... Ms. Julie FISHER
111 Vice President for Advancement .... Ms. Lisa NOTTER
06 Registrar .... Ms. Elena JIMENEZ
08 Director of the Lapp Learning Ctr .. Ms. Jasmine ABOU-EL-KHEIR
07 Director Recruitment/Admission .... Mr. Jason FREY
04 Assistant to the President .... Ms. Kim M. JOHNSON
26 Director of Communications .... Ms. Susan CUSICK
18 Facilities Coordinator .... Ms. Shauna WARREN

*City Colleges of Chicago (A)

180 N. Wabash, Suite 200, Chicago IL 60601
County: Cook FICE Identification: 001647
Unit ID: 144500
Telephone: (312) 553-2500 Carnegie Class: N/A
FAX Number: (312) 553-2699
URL: www.ccc.edu

01 Chancellor .... Mr. Juan SALGADO
05 Provost .... Dr. Mark POTTER
10 Chief Financial Officer .... Ms. Maribel RODRIGUEZ
13 Chief Information Officer .... Ms. Carmen LIDZ
43 General Counsel .... Mr. Karla GOWEN
111 Executive Vice Chancellor .... Mr. Eric LUGO
15 Chief Talent Officer .... Ms. Kimberly ROSS

*City Colleges of Chicago Harold Washington College (B)

30 E Lake Street, Chicago IL 60601-2449
County: Cook FICE Identification: 001652
Unit ID: 144209
Telephone: (312) 553-5600 Carnegie Class: Assoc/HT-Mix Trad/Non
FAX Number: (312) 553-5964 Calendar System: Semester
URL: www.ccc.edu/hwc
Established: 1962 Annual Undergrad Tuition & Fees (In-District): $3,504
Enrollment: 8,869 Coed
Affiliation or Control: State/Local IRS Status: 501(c)3
Highest Offering: Associate Degree
Accreditation: NH, ACBSP

02 President .... Dr. Ignacio LOPEZ
05 Vice Pres Academic/Student Affairs .... Vacant
10 Vice Pres Finance/Operations .... Mr. Kent LUSK
37 Director of Financial Aid .... Ms. Tenika BURNS
18 Chief Facilities/Physical Plant .... Mr. Jeremy GONZALEZ
36 Dean of College to Careers .... Mr. Paul THOMPSON, III
08 Librarian .... Mr. John KIERALDO
15 Human Resources Admin .... Mr. Thomas LINDSAY
20 Dean of Instruction .... Dr. Vincent WIGGINS
32 Dean of Student Services .... Mr. Wendell BLAIR
20 Associate Dean of Instruction .... Mr. Asif WILSON
13 Director Information Technology .... Ms. Ewa BEJNAROWICZ
35 Assoc Dean of Student Services .... Ms. Patricia CUEVAS
46 Asst Director Research/Planning .... Dr. George W. CALISTO
06 Registrar .... Ms. Courtney O'BRIEN
19 Director of Security .... Mr. Milton OWENS
09 Director Strategy/Initiatives .... Ms. Heather LABELLE

*City Colleges of Chicago Harry S Truman College (C)

1145 W Wilson Avenue, Chicago IL 60640-5691
County: Cook FICE Identification: 001648
Unit ID: 144184
Telephone: (773) 907-4700 Carnegie Class: Assoc/MT-VT-High Non
FAX Number: (773) 907-4464 Calendar System: Semester
URL: www.trumancollege.edu
Established: 1956 Annual Undergrad Tuition & Fees (In-District): $3,504
Enrollment: 8,186 Coed
Affiliation or Control: State/Local IRS Status: 501(c)3
Highest Offering: Associate Degree
Accreditation: NH

02 President .... Dr. Shawn L. JACKSON
05 VP Academic & Student Affairs .... Dr. Kate CONNOR
20 Dean of Instruction .... Dr. Susan MARCUS
06 Registrar .... Ms. My Linh TRAN
32 Dean of Student Services .... Ms. Mary Ann SOLEY
35 Associate Dean of Student Services .... Ms. Chanel BISHOP
56 Dean of Adult Education .... Mr. Armando MATA
20 Associate Dean of Instruction .... Ms. Gail GORDON-ALLEN
20 Associate Dean of Instruction .... Ms. Laura CHEATHAM
10 Exec Director Business Services .... Mr. Thomas DUNHAM
19 Director of Security .... Mr. Andres DURBAK
37 Director of Financial Aid .... Ms. Maria PINTO
15 Human Resource Business Partner .... Mr. Michael ROBERTS
13 Director Information Technology .... Mr. Nick NICHOLSON
09 Asst Dir of Research & Planning .... Mr. Sean HUDSON
21 Business Manager .... Ms. Nina CAO
53 Dean Education & Teacher Programs .... Ms. Hollie WAREJAYE
88 Dir of Student Development Projects .... Ms. Aubrey SCHEFFEY
103 Director of Workforce Development .... Ms. Danielle WALLINGTON-HARRIS
18 Director of Facilities Management .... Mr. Charles TALBERT
35 Director of Student Activities .... Ms. Denika WILSON
35 Associate Dean of Student Services .... Ms. Allison ZURES
88 Associate Dean of Adult Education .... Ms. Valerie BUSCH-ZURLENT
36 Dir of Career Planning & Placement .... Ms. Meredith GALLO-MURPHY
41 Director Intercollegiate Athletics .... Ms. Jasmine GREEN
88 Director of Disability Access Ctr .... Ms. Lauren DALEY
121 Dir Teaching & Learning Programs .... Ms. Leslie LAYMAN
04 Admin Assistant to the President .... Ms. Zsa POPIELARCZYK
07 Director Student Support Svcs-TRIO .... Mr. Anthony KWIATKOWSKI
84 Director of Enrollment Management .... Mr. Kisalan GLOVER

*City Colleges of Chicago Kennedy-King College (D)

6301 South Halsted Street, Chicago IL 60621-3798
County: Cook FICE Identification: 001654
Unit ID: 144157
Telephone: (773) 602-5000 Carnegie Class: Assoc/MT-VT-High Non
FAX Number: N/A Calendar System: Semester
URL: www.ccc.edu/colleges/kennedy
Established: 1934 Annual Undergrad Tuition & Fees (In-District): $3,504
Enrollment: 3,395 Coed
Affiliation or Control: State/Local IRS Status: 501(c)3
Highest Offering: Associate Degree
Accreditation: NH

02 President .... Dr. Gregory THOMAS
05 Vice President for Academic Affairs .... Mr. Eddie PHILLIPS
32 Dean Student Services .... Mr. Michael CRAWFORD
12 Dean-Dawson Tech Institute .... Ms. Lucretzia JAMISON
36 Dean College to Careers .... Vacant
51 Dean Adult/Continuing Education .... Mr. Henry HORACE
20 Dean of Instruction .... Ms. Darby JOHNSEN
35 Assoc Dean Student Services .... Dr. Zalika LANDRUM
35 Assoc Dean Student Services .... Vacant
88 Dean Washburne Culinary Institute .... Mr. Marshall SHAFKOWITZ
37 Director Financial Aid .... Vacant
121 Director Academic Support Services .... Ms. Shandria HOLMES
10 Exec Dir Business/Operations .... Mr. Baha AWADALLAH
06 Registrar .... Mr. Eric HAYES
09 Director of Institutional Research .... Vacant
18 Chief Facilities/Physical Plant .... Mr. Cornelius KATES
26 Marketing Director .... Mr. Daniel STERNFIELD
15 Director Human Resources .... Vacant
27 Director of Communications .... Ms. Anne KENNEDY
04 Assistant to the President .... Ms. Cris SAYRE
109 Director of Auxiliary Services .... Mr. Robert GRAHAM
45 Director Strategic Initiatives .... Mr. Patrick GIPSON
19 Director Security/Safety .... Mr. Hershey NORISE
41 Athletic Director .... Mr. Rodell DAVIS

*City Colleges of Chicago Olive-Harvey College (E)

10001 S Woodlawn Avenue, Chicago IL 60628-1645
County: Cook FICE Identification: 009767
Unit ID: 144175
Telephone: (773) 291-6100 Carnegie Class: Assoc/HT-High Non
FAX Number: (773) 291-6304 Calendar System: Semester
URL: www.ccc.edu/colleges/olive-harvey/pages/default.aspx
Established: 1970 Annual Undergrad Tuition & Fees (In-District): $3,504
Enrollment: 2,882 Coed
Affiliation or Control: State/Local IRS Status: 501(c)3
Highest Offering: Associate Degree
Accreditation: NH

02 Interim President .... Ms. Kimberly HOLLINGSWORTH
04 Executive Office Manager .... Ms. Maria PIOTROWSKI
05 Provost .... Vacant
88 Dean STEM/Ctr Teaching & Lrng .... Vacant
32 Dean Student Services .... Ms. Michelle ADAMS
51 Dean Adult & Continuing Education .... Ms. Lautauscha DAVIS
36 Assoc Dean of College to Career .... Ms. LaTonya ARMSTRONG
35 Assoc Dean of Student Services .... Ms. Inesha B. KELLY
20 Dean of Instruction .... Dr. Stephanie DECICCO
10 Exec Dir Bus/Admin/Auxiliary Svcs .... Mr. Richard SLATER
13 Director Information Technology .... Mr. Jason CAMPBELL
12 Director of South Chicago Lrng Ctr .... Vacant
37 Director Financial Aid .... Mr. Richard HAYES
06 Registrar .... Ms. Nailah WATSON
19 Director Security .... Vacant
88 Director Child Development Center .... Ms. Caroline CASILLAS
41 Director of Athletics .... Mr. Rob FLETCHER
15 Director Human Resources .... Ms. Latasha LARRY
26 Director Public Relations .... Vacant
38 Manager Wellness Center .... Vacant
18 Chief Engineer .... Mr. Tom SIEFERT

*City Colleges of Chicago Richard J. Daley College (F)

7500 S Pulaski Road, Chicago IL 60652-1299
County: Cook FICE Identification: 001649
Unit ID: 144193
Telephone: (773) 838-7500 Carnegie Class: Assoc/MT-VT-High Non
FAX Number: (773) 838-7524 Calendar System: Semester
URL: daley.ccc.edu
Established: 1960 Annual Undergrad Tuition & Fees (In-District): $3,504
Enrollment: 7,182 Coed
Affiliation or Control: State/Local IRS Status: 501(c)3
Highest Offering: Associate Degree
Accreditation: NH

02 President .... Dr. Janine E. JANOSKY
05 Vice Pres Academic/Student Affs .... Ms. Anne PANOMITROS
09 Vice Pres Institutional Effective .... Dr. Edwardo GARZA
20 Dean of Instruction .... Mr. Roberto TORRES
55 Dean Adult Education .... Vacant
32 Dean of Student Services .... Ms. Eileen LYNCH
31 Dir Community Education Programs .... Ms. Katrina PAVLIK
10 Exec Director Business Operations .... Ms. Crystal WASHINGTON
18 Chief Engineer/Physical Plant .... Mr. Kevin NOLAN
19 Director Security .... Mr. Ronald MARTIN
35 Assoc Dean Student Services .... Ms. Aneesa SALEH
06 Registrar .... Ms. Cynthia MORENO
06 Assistant Registrar .... Mr. Victor SANCHEZ
84 Director Enrollment Management .... Mr. Rafael GODINA
15 Human Resources Business Partner .... Ms. Griselda SILVA
13 Director of Information Technology .... Ms. Karen ALLEN
37 Director Student Financial Aid .... Vacant

*City Colleges of Chicago Wilbur Wright College (G)

4300 N Narragansett Avenue, Chicago IL 60634-1591
County: Cook FICE Identification: 001655
Unit ID: 144218
Telephone: (773) 777-7900 Carnegie Class: Assoc/HT-High Non
FAX Number: (773) 481-8185 Calendar System: Semester
URL: www.ccc.edu/wright
Established: 1934 Annual Undergrad Tuition & Fees (In-District): $3,504
Enrollment: 10,227 Coed
Affiliation or Control: State/Local IRS Status: 501(c)3
Highest Offering: Associate Degree
Accreditation: NH, ACBSP, OTA

01 Chancellor .... Mr. Juan SALGADO
02 President .... Dr. David POTASH
05 Int VP of Academic/Student Affairs .... Dr. James HOWLEY
32 Dean of Student Services .... Ms. Romell MURDEN
20 Interim Dean of Instruction .... Mr. Gabe ESTILL
121 Assoc Dean Student Svcs Advising .... Ms. Maria LLOPIZ
07 Assoc Dean Student Svcs Admissions .... Ms. Linda HUERTAS
20 Associate Dean of Instruction .... Vacant
10 Executive Business Director .... Ms. Phoebe WOOD
37 Director of Financial Aid .... Ms. Tammy HARRISON
09 Dir Institutional Research/Plng .... Mr. Brian TRZEBIATOWSKI
13 Director Information Technology .... Mr. Anthony GAMBOA
109 Director of Auxiliary Services .... Ms. Dina LEILER
15 Human Resources Director .... Ms. Alison GUENGERICH
38 Director of Wellness Center .... Ms. Kathryn CHAPMAN
19 Director of Security .... Mr. Jack MURPHY
06 Assistant Registrar .... Ms. Sherrea WASHINGTON
41 Athletic Director .... Mr. John MCDONNELL
51 Dean of Adult Education .... Ms. Emily ANDERSON
51 Dean Professional & Personal Dev .... Ms. Alba PEZZAROSSI
103 Dean of HPVEC .... Mr. Kenneth SANTIAGO
31 Community Affairs Liaison .... Ms. Iris MILLAN
36 Dean of College to Careers (C2C) .... Vacant
37 Assistant Director of Financial Aid .... Ms. Ashleigh BALLARD
101 Chief Advisor to the Board .... Ms. Tracey FLEMING

*Malcolm X College, One of the City Colleges of Chicago (H)

1900 W. Jackson Boulevard, Chicago IL 60612-3197
County: Cook FICE Identification: 001650
Unit ID: 144166
Telephone: (312) 850-7000 Carnegie Class: Assoc/HVT-High Non
FAX Number: (312) 850-7039 Calendar System: Semester
URL: www.ccc.edu/malcolmx
Established: 1911 Annual Undergrad Tuition & Fees (In-District): $3,504
Enrollment: 6,713 Coed
Affiliation or Control: State/Local IRS Status: 501(c)3
Highest Offering: Associate Degree
Accreditation: NH, ADNUR, COARC, DH, EMT, FUSER, PTAA, RAD

02 President .... Mr. David A. SANDERS
05 VP Academic & Student Affairs .... Dr. Cia VERSCHELDEN
32 Dean Student Services .... Mr. Mario DIAZ
15 HR Business Partner .... Mr. Seth BAKER
20 Dean Instruction .... Dr. Carleta ALSTON
20 Assoc Dean Instruction .... Ms. Glasetta BARKSDALE
13 Director Information Technology .... Dr. Ben ROOHANI
06 Registrar .... Ms. Patrice JARRETT
35 Interim Assoc Dean Student Services .... Mr. Brian HALL
37 Director Financial Aid .... Ms. Tamika CARSON
88 Director Child Care Center .... Vacant
19 Director Security/Public Safety .... Ms. Gissella LIMON
18 Chief Engineer .... Mr. John MORLEY
08 Librarian .... Vacant
21 Business Manager .... Ms. Jennifer WILLIAMS
76 Dean Health Sciences Programs .... Mr. Roy WALKER, III
56 Dean Adult Education Programs .... Mr. Jamil STEELE
51 Dean Continuing Education .... Vacant
66 Dean of Nursing .... Dr. James RICE
88 Assoc Dean Student Development .... Ms. Lisa WILLIS
88 Assoc Dean Health Careers .... Dr. Elizabeth GMITTER
36 Dir Career Planning/Placement .... Ms. Toya JOHNSON
103 Director Workforce Partnerships .... Ms. Rhonda HARDEMON

26 Director of Media Relations .... Mr. Daniel STERNFIELD
46 Director of Strategic Initiatives .... Mrs. Annie CIECHANOWSKI - ZALEWSKI
109 Director of Auxiliary Services .... Mrs. Jessica HOLLOWAY
108 VP Institutional Effectiveness .... Ms. Katonja WEBB
09 Asst Dir Research and Planning .... Mr. Steve DMARJIAN
84 Director of Enrollment Management .... Ms. Katie CURRAN
100 Executive Office Manager .... Mrs. Alanna S. WITHERSPOON

College of DuPage (A)

425 Fawell Boulevard, Glen Ellyn IL 60137-6599
County: DuPage | FICE Identification: 006656 | Unit ID: 144865
Telephone: (630) 942-2800 | Carnegie Class: Assoc/MT-VT-High Non
FAX Number: (630) 858-9399 | Calendar System: Semester
URL: www.cod.edu
Established: 1965 | Annual Undergrad Tuition & Fees (In-District): $4,080
Enrollment: 26,165 | Coed
Affiliation or Control: State/Local | IRS Status: 501(c)3
Highest Offering: Associate Degree
Accreditation: NH, ACFEI, ADNUR, ART, AT, CAHIIM, COARC, CONST, CSHSE, DH, DMS, MAC, NMT, POLYT, PTAA, RAD, SURGA, SURGT

01 President .... Dr. Brian CAPUTO
05 Provost .... Dr. Mark CURTIS-CHAVEZ
10 Int Chief Financial Ofcr/Treasurer .... Mr. Scott BRADY
45 VP Planning & Inst Effectiveness .... Mr. James BENTE
11 Int Vice Pres Administrative Affs .... Ms. Ellen ROBERTS
15 Vice Pres Human Resources .... Ms. Linda SANDS-VANKERK
111 VP Institutional Advancement .... Mr. Earl DOWLING
13 Dir Information Technology Services .... Ms. Donna BERLINER
32 Vice President Student Affairs .... Mr. Earl DOWLING
49 Dean Liberal Arts .... Dr. Sandra MARTIN
83 Dean Social & Behavioral Sci/Lib .... Ms. Marianne HUNNICUTT
51 Dean Cont Ed/Extended Learning .... Dr. Joseph CASSIDY
81 Dean Science/Tech/Engineering/Math .. Ms. Jennifer CUMPSTSON
35 Dean Student Development .... Ms. Susan JERAK
21 Controller .... Mr. Scott BRADY
18 Dir Facilities Planning and Dev .... Mr. Bruce SCHMIEDL
121 Dir Pathways for Student Success .... Ms. Jane L. SMITH
09 Director Research & Analytics .... Mr. Eugene YE
116 Internal Auditor .... Mr. James E. MARTNER
57 Director McAninch Arts Center .... Mrs. Diana MARTINEZ
41 Asst Athletic Director .... Mr. Matt FOSTER
86 Director Legislative Relations .... Ms. Mary Ann MILLUSH
19 Director & Chief COD Police Dept .... Mr. Joseph MULLIN
79 Associate Dean Humanities .... Dr. Sandra MARTINS
26 Sr Dir Public Relations/Comm/Mktg .... Ms. Wendy E. PARKS
16 Director Labor & Emp Relations .... Ms. Mia IGYARTO
07 Manager Admissions & Outreach .... Ms. Tamara MCCLAIN

College of Lake County (B)

19351 W Washington Street, Grayslake IL 60030-1198
County: Lake | FICE Identification: 007694 | Unit ID: 146472
Telephone: (847) 543-2000 | Carnegie Class: Assoc/MT-VT-High Non
FAX Number: N/A | Calendar System: Semester
URL: www.clcillinois.edu
Established: 1969 | Annual Undergrad Tuition & Fees (In-District): $3,948
Enrollment: 14,590 | Coed
Affiliation or Control: Local | IRS Status: 501(c)3
Highest Offering: Associate Degree
Accreditation: NH, ADNUR, CAHIIM, DH, MAC, RAD, SURGT

01 President .... Dr. Lori SUDDICK
11 Vice Pres Administrative Affairs .... Mr. Kenneth GOTSCH
32 Vice President Student Development .... Ms. Karen HLAVIN
05 Vice President Educational Affairs .... Vacant
06 Registrar .... Ms. Jennifer MALLER
12 Dean Southlake Campus .... Dr. Vicki CVITKOVIC
12 Interim Dean Lakeshore Campus .... Mr. Derrick HARDEN
08 Dean Library/Testing & Acad Success ..... Ms. Tanya WOLTMANN
10 Controller .... Ms. Connie KRAVITZ
50 Dean of Business/Social Science Div .... Dr. Jeffrey STOMPER
76 Dean Biological/Health Sciences .... Ms. Maureen ROBINSON
79 Dean Comm Arts/Humanities/Fine Arts .... Mr. Sheldon WALCHER
54 Dean Engr/Math/Physical Science .... Mr. Richard AMMON
51 Dean Adult Basic Education/GED/ ESL .... Dr. Arlene SANTOS-GEORGE
38 Dean Counsel/Advising/Transfer .... Ms. Sue STOCK
103 Exec Director Community Programming ...... Ms. Roneida MARTIN
26 Director Public Relations & Mktg .... Ms. Anne O'CONNELL
35 Dean Student Life .... Ms. Teresa AGUINALDO
102 Executive Director CLC Foundation .... Mr. Kurt PETERSON
15 Exec Director Human Resources .... Ms. Sue FAY
88 Exec Dir James Lumber Ctr Perf Arts ... Ms. Gwethalyn BRONNER
09 Exec Dir/Inst Effect/Plan/Research .... Vacant
41 Director of Athletics .... Vacant
86 Dir Resource Dev/Legislative Affrs .... Mr. Nick C. KALLIERIS
13 Chief Information Officer .... Mr. Greg KOZAK
14 Director User Services/User Support .... Mr. David AYKROID
96 Int Dir of Purchasing & Contracts .... Ms. Sue KILBY
88 Dir Application Svcs/Applic Develop .... Mr. Jay MEYER
35 Director Student Services Lakeshore .... Mr. David WEATHERSPOON
18 Director Facilities Administration .... Mr. Mike WELCH
88 Dir Children's Learning Center .... Ms. Carlotta CONLEY
22 Dir Ofc Students with Disabilities .... Mr. Thomas CROWE
19 Chief of Police .... Mr. Thomas GUENTHER
36 Exec Dir Career/Placement Services .... Ms. Sylvia M. JOHNSON JONES
66 Director Nursing Education .... Vacant
23 Director Health Services .... Ms. Michelle M. GRACE
37 Director Financial Aid .... Mr. Paul SCHMIDT
88 Director Educational Technology .... Mr. Scott RIAL
88 Director Professional Development .... Vacant
88 Director Technical Services .... Mr. James SENFT
100 Chief of Staff .... Mr. Derrick HARDEN
07 Director Admissions & Recruitment .... Mr. Jason SARNA
04 Admin Assistant to the President .... Ms. Karen SENASE
106 Director Online Student Success .... Ms. Meredith TUMILTY

College of Lake County Lakeshore Campus (C)

33 North Genesee Street, Waukegan IL 60085
Telephone: (847) 543-2191 | Identification: 770073
Accreditation: &NH

College of Lake County Southlake Campus (D)

1120 South Milwaukee Avenue, Vernon Hills IL 60061
Telephone: (847) 543-6501 | Identification: 770072
Accreditation: &NH

Columbia College Chicago (E)

600 S Michigan Avenue, Chicago IL 60605-1996
County: Cook | FICE Identification: 001665 | Unit ID: 144281
Telephone: (312) 369-1000 | Carnegie Class: Masters/M
FAX Number: (312) 369-8069 | Calendar System: Semester
URL: www.colum.edu
Established: 1890 | Annual Undergrad Tuition & Fees: $27,176
Enrollment: 7,312 | Coed
Affiliation or Control: Independent Non-Profit | IRS Status: 501(c)3
Highest Offering: Master's
Accreditation: NH, CIDA

01 President and CEO .... Dr. Kwang-Wu KIM
05 Provost/VP Academic Affairs .... Ms. Marcella DAVID
10 Sr VP Business Affairs/CFO .... Mr. Jerry TARRER
43 VP Legal Affairs/General Counsel .... Ms. Patricia BERGESON
30 VP Development/Alumni Relations .... Mr. Shawn WAX
84 VP Enrollment Management .... Mr. Michael JOSEPH
32 VP Student Affairs .... Dr. Sharon WILSON-TAYLOR
13 Chief Information Officer .... Ms. Kathie KOCH
85 VP Global Education .... Mr. Marcelo SABATES
20 Asst Provost Acad Services .... Mr. Brian MARTH
06 Registrar .... Ms. Keri WALTERS
120 Vice Provost for Digital Learning .... Mr. Robert GREEN
20 Senior Associate Provost .... Dr. Suzanne BLUM MALLEY
108 Assoc Provost AASL .... Mr. Neil PAGANO
15 AVP of Human Resources .... Ms. Norma DE JESUS
18 Interim AVP Fac & Construction .... Mr. Mike GUIDOTTI
37 AVP Student Financial Svcs .... Ms. Cynthia GRUNDEN
100 Chief of Staff .... Mr. Laurent PERNOT
04 Exec Assistant to the President .... Ms. Yvonne SODE
19 AVP Safety & Security .... Mr. Ronald SODINI
35 Dean of Students .... Mr. John PELRINE
57 Int Dean Sch Fine/Performing Arts .... Ms. Rosita SANDS
49 Dean School Liberal Arts/Sciences .... Dr. Steven COREY
60 Dean School of Media Arts .... Mr. Eric FREEDMAN
35 Assistant Dean of Student Life .... Ms. Sheila CARTER
36 Assoc Dean Career Development .... Mr. Erik FRIEDMAN
07 Sr Dir Admissions & Recruitment .... Mr. Derek BRINKLEY
29 Exec Director ARAG .... Ms. Miriam SMITH
09 Dir Inst Research & Reporting .... Mr. Brian CHAMBERLIN
121 Director of Academic Advising .... Mr. Keith LUSSON
123 Director Graduate Admissions .... Ms. Kara RATCLIFFE
39 Director of Residence Life .... Ms. Mary OAKES
88 Director International Admissions .... Ms. Susan STROW
08 Interim Library Director .... Mr. Dennis MCGUIRE
25 Grants & Contract Manager .... Mr. David WEINER

Concordia University Chicago (F)

7400 Augusta Street, River Forest IL 60305-1499
County: Cook | FICE Identification: 001666 | Unit ID: 144351
Telephone: (708) 771-8300 | Carnegie Class: Masters/L
FAX Number: (708) 209-3176 | Calendar System: Semester
URL: www.cuchicago.edu
Established: 1864 | Annual Undergrad Tuition & Fees: $32,078
Enrollment: 5,755 | Coed
Affiliation or Control: Lutheran Church - Missouri Synod | IRS Status: 501(c)3
Highest Offering: Doctorate
Accreditation: NH, CACREP, CAEP, CAEPN, MUS

01 President .... Dr. Russell DAWN
05 Sr Vice President for Academics .... Dr. John ZILLMAN
45 Sr VP for Planning & Research .... Vacant
10 Vice President for Finance .... Mr. Tom HALLETT
11 Vice President for Administration .... Vacant
84 Sr VP Enrollment/Student Svcs .... Ms. Evelyn P. BURDICK
32 Vice President Student Services .... Mr. Jeff HYNES
88 Asst Vice President for Enrollment .... Ms. Gwen E. KANELOS
26 Asst Vice Pres Marketing .... Mr. Eric MATANYI
49 Dean College Arts & Sciences .... Dr. Rachel EELLS
50 Dean College of Business .... Dr. Claudia SANTIN
09 Director Institutional Research .... Ms. Elizabeth OWOLABI
37 Director Student Financial Planning .... Ms. Aida ASENCIO-PINTO
08 Director of Library Services .... Ms. Yana V. SERDYUK
88 Director of Degree Completion .... Dr. Carol J. REISECK
36 Director Career Services .... Mr. Gerald PINOTTI
88 Assistant VP of Administration .... Mr. Glen D. STEINER
29 Director of Alumni Relations .... Ms. Paige CRAIG
38 Director Schmieding Counseling Ctr .... Dr. Carol A. JABS
109 Director of Auxiliary Services .... Mr. Pete D. BECKER
41 Director of Athletics .... Mr. Peter D. GNAN
21 Director of Business Services .... Ms. Aileen POL
114 Director of Budget Services .... Ms. Tina NEPOMUCENO
42 University Pastor .... Rev. Jeffrey LEININGER
24 Dir of Media Production Services .... Mr. James A. KOSINSKY
19 Director of Public Safety .... Mr. David WITKEN
121 Director of Academic Advising ...... Ms. Rosemarie GARCIA-HILLS
96 Director of Purchasing .... Ms. Denise JAMES
91 Manager of Admin Information System .... Ms. Linda C. BERRY
123 Exec Director Graduate Admission .... Ms. Deborah NESS
04 Exec Assistant to the President .... Ms. Jo Anne TERNAND

Coyne College (G)

1 N. State Street, Chicago IL 60602
County: Cook | FICE Identification: 007549 | Unit ID: 144485
Telephone: (773) 577-8100 | Carnegie Class: Assoc/HVT-High Trad
FAX Number: (312) 226-3818 | Calendar System: Other
URL: www.coynecollege.edu
Established: 1899 | Annual Undergrad Tuition & Fees: N/A
Enrollment: 422 | Coed
Affiliation or Control: Proprietary | IRS Status: Proprietary
Highest Offering: Associate Degree
Accreditation: ACCSC, MAAB

01 President .... Russell T. FREEMAN
05 Director of Education .... Virginia HANSON
07 Director of Admissions .... Claudia MACIAS-SILVERMAN
06 Registrar .... Tina FANUCCHI
08 Librarian .... Diana BARTHELEMY
36 Director of Career Services .... Jenny GONZALEZ
37 Director of Financial Aid .... Ashley TUCHTEN

Danville Area Community College (H)

2000 E Main Street, Danville IL 61832-5199
County: Vermilion | FICE Identification: 001669 | Unit ID: 144564
Telephone: (217) 443-3222 | Carnegie Class: Assoc/MT-VT-High Non
FAX Number: (217) 443-8560 | Calendar System: Semester
URL: www.dacc.edu
Established: 1949 | Annual Undergrad Tuition & Fees (In-District): $4,875
Enrollment: 2,645 | Coed
Affiliation or Control: State/Local | IRS Status: 501(c)3
Highest Offering: Associate Degree
Accreditation: NH, ADNUR, CAHIIM, RAD

01 President .... Dr. Stephen D. NACCO
04 Exec Asst to Pres/Board Sec/Grants .... Ms. Kerri L. THURMAN
05 Exec VP Instruction & Student Svcs ..... Mr. David L. KIETZMANN
15 VP Human Resources/AA Ofcr .... Ms. Jill A. CRANMORE
10 VP Finance/Chief Financial Officer . Ms. Tammy L. BETANCOURT
18 VP Administrative Services .... Mr. R. Michael CUNNINGHAM
32 Dean Student Services .... Ms. Stacy L. EHMEN
102 Foundation Executive Director .... Ms. Tonya L. HILL
26 Exec Director College Relations .... Ms. Lara L. CONKLIN
09 Exec Director Inst Effectiveness .... Mr. Bob MATTSON
103 Exec Director Workforce Dev .... Mr. Brian C. HENSGEN
21 Controller .... Ms. Debra L. KNIGHT
37 Director Financial Aid .... Ms. Janet M. INGARGIOLA
91 Programmer/Systems Administrator .... Ms. Jessica MILES
90 Director Computer & Network Svcs .... Mr. Mark BARNES
88 Director Adult Education & Literacy .... Ms. Laura M. WILLIAMS
50 Dean Business & Technology .... Ms. Terri CUMMINGS
49 Dean Liberal Arts & Library Service .... Dr. Penny J. MCCONNELL
81 Dean Math Sciences & Health Prof .... Ms. Kathy R. STURGEON
41 Director Athletics .... Mr. Tim M. BUNTON
88 Director Small Business Development .... Ms. Carol NICHOLS
07 Director Admissions & Registrar .... Mr. Timothy MORGAN
88 Director Student Support Svcs/TRIO .... Ms. Shanay M. WRIGHT
28 Asst Dean Student Services/CDO .... Ms. Carla M. BOYD
36 Dir Career Services/Veterans Center .... Mr. Nick CATLETT
88 Coordinator Campus & Comm Resources .. Ms. Dawn S. NASSER
19 Supervisor Safety & Security .... Mr. Greg FEGETT
12 Director Hoopeston Extension Site .... Ms. Karla J. COON
51 Director Community Educ/Trng Spec ...... Ms. Laura M. HENSGEN
88 Director Customized Training .... Ms. Stephanie L. YATES
88 Director Medical Imagery Programs .... Ms. Tammy L. HOWARD
88 Director Health Info Technology .... Ms. Marcie WRIGHT
66 Director Nursing .... Ms. Mary SKINNER
121 Dir Acad Advis/Couns/Transf Articu .... Ms. Stephane POTTS
88 Coordinator Recruitment .... Ms. Cristin PRINCE
18 Director Maintenance & Facilities .... Mr. Doug ADAMS

DePaul University (I)

1 E Jackson Boulevard, Chicago IL 60604-2287
County: Cook | FICE Identification: 001671 | Unit ID: 144740
Telephone: (312) 362-8610 | Carnegie Class: DU-Higher
FAX Number: (312) 362-5322 | Calendar System: Quarter
URL: www.depaul.edu
Established: 1898 | Annual Undergrad Tuition & Fees: $39,975
Enrollment: 22,769 | Coed
Affiliation or Control: Roman Catholic | IRS Status: 501(c)3

Highest Offering: Doctorate
Accreditation: NH, ANEST, CACREP, CEA, CLPSY, LAW, MUS, NURSE, PH, SPAA, SW

01 President ... Dr. A. Gabriel ESTEBAN
00 Chancellor ... Rev. Dennis H. HOLTSCHNEIDER, CM
05 Provost ... Dr. Salma GHANEM
10 Executive Vice President ... Mr. Jeffrey BETHKE
32 VP Student Affairs ... Dr. Gene ZDZIARSKI
84 Int Vice Pres Enroll Mgmt/Marketing ... Ms. Paula LUFF
111 Vice Pres for Advancement ... Dr. Daniel ALLEN
15 Vice President Human Resources ... Ms. Stephanie SMITH
18 Vice President Facilities Operation ... Mr. Robert J. JANIS
43 VP/General Counsel & Secretary ... Mr. Jose D. PADILLA
29 Assoc VP Communication & Engagement ... Ms. Tracy KRAHL
28 VP Inst Diversity & Equity ... Dr. Elizabeth F. ORTIZ
26 VP Public Relations & Communication ... Ms. Linda BLAKLEY
121 Assoc Prov Student Success/Accred ... Dr. Caryn CHADEN
106 Assoc Prov Global Eng and Online ... Dr. GianMario BESANA
100 Chief of Staff ... Mr. Steve STOUTE
13 VP Information Services ... Mr. Robert MCCORMICK
35 Assoc Vice Pres Student Affairs ... Dr. Ashley KNIGHT
35 Assoc Vice Pres Student Affairs ... Mr. Rico TYLER
09 AVP Inst Research/Market Analytics ... Dr. Liz SANDERS
36 AVP Div Planning & Mgmt/Career Ctr ... Ms. Jane MCGRATH
42 Assoc VP University Ministry ... Mr. Mark LABOE
108 AVP & COS Student Affairs ... Dr. Ellen MEENTS-DECAIGNY
27 Exec Dir News & Integrated Content ... Ms. Carol HUGHES
21 VP for Finance & Controller ... Ms. Sherri SIDLER
90 Dir Faculty Instructional Tech Svcs ... Dr. Sharon GUAN
37 Int Assoc Vice Pres Financial Aid ... Ms. Karen LEVEQUE
25 Assoc Provost for Research ... Dr. Daniela STAN RAICU
19 Director Public Safety ... Mr. Robert WACHOWSKI
38 Director Student Counseling ... Dr. Jeffery LANFEAR
39 Director of Housing & Student Ctrs ... Mr. Rick MORECI
41 Athletics Director ... Ms. Jean PONSETTO
06 Director of Registration/Records ... Ms. Patricia HUERTA
104 Director Study Abroad ... Ms. Martha MCGIVERN
123 AVP Graduate & Adult Admission ... Ms. Suzanne DEPEDER
07 Dean of Undergraduate Admission ... Ms. Carlene KLAAS
77 Dean Computing & Digital Media ... Dr. David MILLER
49 Dean Liberal Arts & Social Sciences ... Dr. Guillermo VASQUEZ DE VELASCO
50 Dean Driehaus Bus Coll/Grad Sch Bus ... Dr. Misty JOHANSON
60 Int Dean Col of Communication ... Dr. Alexandra MURPHY
64 Dean School of Music ... Dr. Ronald CALTABIANO
61 Dean College of Law ... Ms. Jennifer R. PEREA
57 Dean Theatre School ... Mr. John CULBERT
53 Dean School of Education ... Dr. Paul ZIONTS
51 Int Dean School for New Learning ... Dr. Don OPITZ
76 Dean Col of Science & Health ... Dr. Dorothy KOZLOWSKI
08 Head Librarian ... Vacant
04 Administrative Asst to President ... Ms. Phyllis GREGG
100 Deputy Chief of Staff ... Ms. Annette WILSON
86 Assoc VP Community & Govt Relations ... Mr. Peter COFFEY

*DeVry University - Home Office (A)

3005 Highland Parkway, Suite 100,
Downers Grove IL 60515
County: DuPage FICE Identification: 001672
Unit ID: 144777
Telephone: (630) 515-3000 Carnegie Class: N/A
FAX Number: (630) 571-0317
URL: www.devry.edu

01 President ... Mr. James BARTHOLOMEW
26 Chief Marketing Officer ... Mr. Remberto DEL REAL
84 VP Enrollment Management ... Ms. Elise AWWAD
05 Provost/VP Academic Affairs ... Mr. Shantanu BOSE
20 Associate Provost ... Mr. Darryl FIELD
15 VP Human Resources & Univ Relations ... Mr. David BARNETT

*DeVry University - Chicago Campus (B)

3300 N Campbell Avenue, Chicago IL 60618
County: Cook FICE Identification: 010727
Unit ID: 482477
Telephone: (773) 929-8500 Carnegie Class: Masters/L
FAX Number: (773) 348-1780 Calendar System: Semester
URL: www.devry.edu
Established: 1931 Annual Undergrad Tuition & Fees: $17,509
Enrollment: 16,964 Coed
Affiliation or Control: Proprietary IRS Status: Proprietary
Highest Offering: Master's
Accreditation: NH, ACBSP, CAHIIM

02 Center Dean ... Ms. Ruth PINEDA
05 Asst Dean Academic Excellence ... Mr. Daniel FOGARTY
07 Director Admissions Central Region ... Mr. Drew LOGAN
32 Cntrl Reg-Group Dir Student Central ... Mr. Brendan AUBIN
08 Regional Librarian ... Mr. Jason ROSSI

† Regional accreditation is carried under the parent institution in Downers Grove, IL.

Dominican University (C)

7900 W Division Street, River Forest IL 60305-1099
County: Cook FICE Identification: 001750
Unit ID: 148496
Telephone: (708) 366-2490 Carnegie Class: Masters/L
FAX Number: (708) 524-5990 Calendar System: Semester
URL: www.dom.edu
Established: 1901 Annual Undergrad Tuition & Fees: $33,434
Enrollment: 3,127 Coed
Affiliation or Control: Roman Catholic IRS Status: 501(c)3
Highest Offering: Doctorate
Accreditation: NH, #ARCPA, CAEPN, DIETC, DIETD, LIB, NURSE, SW

01 President ... Dr. Donna M. CARROLL
05 Provost ... Dr. Jeffrey CARLSON
20 Assoc Provost Strategic Initiatives ... Dr. Roberto CURCI
10 VP Finance/Business Affairs ... Mr. Mark TITZER
42 VP Mission & Ministry ... Dr. Claire NOONAN
111 VP University Advancement ... Ms. Sara ACOSTA
84 VP Enrollment Management/Marketing ... Mr. Genaro BALCAZAR
13 VP Technology & Opers/IT/CIO ... Ms. Jill ALBIN-HILL
07 AVP Enroll Mgt/Dir Undergrad Admiss ... Mr. Glenn HAMILTON
32 Dean of Students ... Ms. Norah COLLINS PIENTA
76 Dean-Borra College Health Sciences ... Dr. Kavita DHANWADA
83 Dean Applied/Social Sciences ... Dr. Jacob BUCHER
50 Dean Brennan School of Business ... Dr. Roberto CURCI
62 Int Exec Dir Sch Information Stds ... Ms. Kate MAREK
53 Interim Exec Dir School of Educ ... Dr. Colleen REARDON
70 Int Exec Dir School of Social Work ... Ms. Julie BACH
49 Interim Dean Rosary College ... Mr. Chad ROHMAN
107 Asst Prov Sch Profess/Cont Studies ... Mr. Matthew J. HLINAK
08 University Librarian ... Ms. Felice E. MACIEJEWSKI
06 Registrar ... Mr. Michael MILLER
36 Director Career Development ... Ms. Keli WOJCIECHOWSKI
29 Director Alumnae/i Relations ... Ms. Margaret RYZEWSKI
09 Dir Institutional Rsrch/Assessment ... Ms. Elizabeth SILK
07 Director Transfer/Adult Admission ... Mr. Michael MORSOVILLO
37 Director Financial Aid ... Ms. Victoria SPIVAK
23 Director Wellness Center ... Ms. Elizabeth RITZMAN
41 Director Athletics ... Mr. Erick BAUMANN
104 Director International Studies ... Dr. Sue PONREMY
121 VP Student Success & Engagement ... Dr. Barrington PRICE
28 Chief Diversity Officer ... Dr. Sheila RADFORD-HILL
15 Exec Director Human Resources ... Ms. Roberta MCMAHON
26 Director of Public Relations ... Ms. Jessica MACKINNON
27 Exec Dir of External Engagement ... Ms. Leslie RODRIGUEZ
04 Admin Assistant to the President ... Ms. Kathleen REDMOND
102 Director Foundation/Corporate Rels ... Ms. Sharon RYAN
44 Director Annual Giving ... Ms. Sarah SULLIVAN

East-West University (D)

816 S Michigan Avenue, Chicago IL 60605-2185
County: Cook FICE Identification: 021686
Unit ID: 144883
Telephone: (312) 939-0111 Carnegie Class: Bac-A&S
FAX Number: (312) 939-0083 Calendar System: Quarter
URL: www.eastwest.edu
Established: 1980 Annual Undergrad Tuition & Fees: $22,050
Enrollment: 430 Coed
Affiliation or Control: Independent Non-Profit IRS Status: 501(c)3
Highest Offering: Baccalaureate
Accreditation: NH

01 Chancellor ... Dr. M. Wasiullah KHAN
05 Provost ... Dr. Madhu JAIN
20 Academic Dean ... Vacant
30 Dean Development/Univ Relations ... Mr. Zafar A. MALIK
32 Director Counseling/Student Affairs ... Ms. Erin PANEPUCCI
37 Director of Financial Aid ... Mr. Cesar CAMPOS
06 Registrar ... Ms. Asma ADNAN
04 Assistant to the Chancellor ... Ms. Kafi KHAN
19 Director of Security ... Mr. Tasleem RAJA
10 Director of Business ... Dr. Madhu JAIN
44 Dir Devel/Univ Rels/Publications ... Ms. Barbara ABRAJANO
26 Manager Public Relations ... Vacant
18 Facilities Manager ... Mr. Tasleem RAJA
85 International Student Advisor ... Ms. Katarzyna PETEK
21 Associate Business Officer ... Ms. Deborah DEJI
84 Director Enrollment Management ... Mr. Christopher MAXWELL

Eastern Illinois University (E)

600 Lincoln Avenue, Charleston IL 61920-3099
County: Coles FICE Identification: 001674
Unit ID: 144892
Telephone: (217) 581-5000 Carnegie Class: Masters/L
FAX Number: (217) 581-2722 Calendar System: Semester
URL: www.eiu.edu
Established: 1895 Annual Undergrad Tuition & Fees (In-State): $11,803
Enrollment: 7,030 Coed
Affiliation or Control: State IRS Status: 501(c)3
Highest Offering: Beyond Master's But Less Than Doctorate
Accreditation: NH, AAFCS, ART, #CAATE, CACREP, CAEP, CAEPN, DIETD, DIETI, JOUR, MUS, NRPA, NURSE, SP, THEA

01 President ... Dr. David M. GLASSMAN
05 Provost/Vice Pres Academic Affairs ... Dr. Jay D. GATRELL
10 Vice Pres Business Affs/Treasurer ... Mr. Paul A. MCCANN
32 Int Associate VP Student Affairs ... Ms. Lynette DRAKE
111 Vice Pres University Advancement ... Dr. Ken A. WETSTEIN
35 Special Asst to VP Student Affairs ... Ms. Jennifer L. SIPES
26 AVP Integr Marketing/Communications ... Vacant
08 Dean of Library Services ... Mr. Zach NEWELL
92 Dean Honors College ... Dr. Richard ENGLAND
15 Int Director Human Resources ... Ms. Linda C. HOLLOWAY
22 Director Civil Rights ... Dr. Shawn PEOPLES
45 Dir Planning/Budget/Research ... Mr. Lakshmikara PADMARAJU
07 Director of Admissions ... Ms. Kelly MILLER
37 Int Sr Assoc Dir of Financial Aid ... Ms. Amanda STARWALT
06 Registrar ... Mr. Brad BENNINGTON
29 Director Alumni Svc/Community Rels ... Mr. Steven W. RICH
18 Dir Facilities/Planning Management ... Mr. Timothy P. ZIMMER
96 Dir Procur/Disburs/Contract Svc ... Ms. Danielle M. GREEN
38 Int Asst Dir of Counseling Center ... Ms. Lindsay WILSON
25 Director of Research & Grants ... Dr. Robert W. CHESNUT
41 Director of Athletics ... Mr. Thomas R. MICHAEL
93 Director of Minority Affairs ... Ms. Mona DAVENPORT
39 Director of Housing/Dining Service ... Mr. Mark A. HUDSON
21 Interim Director Business Services ... Ms. Linda C. HOLLOWAY
36 Director of Career Services ... Ms. Bobbi KINGERY
58 Dean Graduate School ... Dr. Ryan C. HENDRICKSON
81 Dean College Health/Human Services ... Dr. Ozlem H. ERSIN
50 Dean Lumpkin Col Bus and Tech ... Mr. William MINNIS
49 Dean College Liberal Arts/Sciences ... Dr. Anita SHELTON
53 Dean College of Education ... Mr. Doug J. BOWER
43 General Counsel ... Ms. Laura L. MCLAUGHLIN
84 Assoc VP Enrollment Management ... Mr. Josh L. NORMAN

Elgin Community College (F)

1700 Spartan Drive, Elgin IL 60123-7193
County: Kane FICE Identification: 001675
Unit ID: 144944
Telephone: (847) 697-1000 Carnegie Class: Assoc/MT-VT-Mix Trad/Non
FAX Number: (847) 214-7995 Calendar System: Semester
URL: www.elgin.edu
Established: 1949 Annual Undergrad Tuition & Fees (In-District): $3,179
Enrollment: 9,599 Coed
Affiliation or Control: Local IRS Status: 501(c)3
Highest Offering: Associate Degree
Accreditation: NH, ADNUR, COMTA, CSHSE, DA, HT, MLTAD, PTAA, RAD, RADMAG, SURGT

01 President ... Dr. David SAM
10 VP Business & Finance ... Dr. Kimberly WAGNER
05 VP Teaching/Learning/Student Dev ... Dr. Peggy HEINRICH
20 Asst VP Teach/Lrng/Stdnt Dev ... Dr. Marcy THOMPSON
20 Dean Academic Dev/Learning Resource ... Dr. Mi HU
50 Dean Sustain/Business/Career Tech ... Ms. Cathy TAYLOR
83 Dean Comm/Behavioral Sciences ... Dr. Ruixuan MAO
57 Dean Liberal/Visual/Performing Arts ... Ms. Mary HATCH
32 Asst VP/Dean of Student Services ... Dr. Gregory ROBINSON
88 Dean of Col Transitions/Partnership ... Dr. Mary PEKINS
51 Dean Adult Basic Education ... Ms. Elizabeth HOBSON
76 Dean Health Prof/Math/Science/Eng ... Dr. Wendy MILLER
88 Assoc Dean Comm/Behavioral Sciences ... Dr. Mia HARDY
106 Assoc Dean Inst Improve/Dist Lrng ... Mr. Timothy MOORE
88 Asc Dean TRIO/Reten/Stdnt Outreach ... Dr. L. Bruce AUSTIN
07 Sr Director of Admissions/Registrar ... Ms. Ann KING
18 Managing Director Facilities ... Mr. Cal BYRD
13 Chief Information Officer ... Dr. Michael CHAHINO
26 Chief Marketing/Communications Ofcr ... Ms. Toya WEBB
15 Chief Human Resources Officer ... Mr. Anthony RAY
30 Exec Dir Inst Advance/ECC Found ... Mr. David DAVIN
88 Exec Dir of TLSD Operations ... Ms. Annamarie SCHOPEN
45 VP Planning/Inst Effect/Tech ... Dr. Philip GARBER
09 Managing Dir Institutional Research ... Mr. David RUDDEN
37 Managing Dir Student Financial Svcs ... Ms. Amy PERRIN
21 Asst VP Business and Finance ... Ms. Heather SCHOLL
84 Managing Director Enrollment Svcs ... Dr. Jennifer MCCLURE
22 Paralegal/EEO/AA Title IX/FOIA Ofcr ... Ms. Marilyn PRENTICE
41 Director Athletics & Wellness ... Mr. Kent PAYNE
96 Managing Director Business Services ... Ms. Melissa TAIT
36 Assoc Dean Advising & Career Dev ... Ms. Peggy GUNDRUM
35 Director Orientation/Student Life ... Ms. Amybeth MAURER
86 Dir Cmty Engagemnt/Legislative Affs ... Ms. Paula AMENTA
04 Sr Exec Asst to Pres/Board Recorder ... Ms. Diane KERRUISH
08 Assoc Dean of Library ... Ms. Shannon POHRTE
51 Assoc Dean of Adult Educ ... Ms. Marcia LUPTAK

Elmhurst College (G)

190 Prospect, Elmhurst IL 60126-3296
County: DuPage FICE Identification: 001676
Unit ID: 144962
Telephone: (630) 279-4100 Carnegie Class: Masters/L
FAX Number: (630) 617-3282 Calendar System: 4/1/4
URL: www.elmhurst.edu
Established: 1871 Annual Undergrad Tuition & Fees: $37,055
Enrollment: 3,481 Coed
Affiliation or Control: United Church Of Christ IRS Status: 501(c)3
Highest Offering: Master's
Accreditation: NH, NURSE, OT, SP

01 President ... Dr. Troy VANAKEN
10 VP for Finance ... Ms. Cindy GONYA
05 Int VP Acad Affs/Dean of Faculty ... Dr. Connie MIXON
13 VP for Operations & Technology ... Mr. Kurt ASHLEY
111 VP of Institutional Advancement ... Ms. Valerie DAY
32 VP for Student Affairs ... Dr. Phil RIORDAN
07 VP for Admission ... Dr. Timothy RICORDATI
20 Associate Dean of Faculty ... Dr. Paul ARRIOLA
88 Exec Dir Center for Pro Excellence ... Mr. Martin GAHBAUER
18 Exec Director Facilities Management ... Mr. Michael EMERSON
26 Exec Dir of Mktg & Communication ... Mr. Jonathan SHEARER
42 Chaplain ... Rev. H. Scott MATHENEY
06 Registrar ... Ms. Linda DUFORT
27 Sr Dir Communications/Public Affs ... Ms. Desiree CHEN-MENICHINI

08 Interim Director of the Library ... Ms. Margaret COOK
36 Director of Career Education ... Ms. Julie NOSAL
38 Director of Counseling Services ... Dr. Amy SWARR
28 Director of Intercultural Education ... Dr. Michael LINDBERG
88 Advancement Services Coordinator ... Ms. Jillian BOLLOW
29 Director of Alumni Engagement ... Mr. Cameron WATKINS
15 Exec Director of Human Resources ... Vacant
19 Exec Dir of Campus Security ... Mr. Marc MOLINA
37 Director of Financial Aid ... Vacant
07 Assistant Director of Admissions ... Mr. Tim AHLBERG
123 Sr Dir Grad Admission & Enrollment ... Mr. Tim PANFIL
39 Dir of Housing & Res Life ... Ms. Sarah MEANEY
41 Director Intercollegiate Athletics ... Ms. Wendy MCMANUS
04 Executive Asst to President ... Ms. Molly NIESPO
101 Asst to President Office & Trustees ... Ms. Britney HEALD
104 Dir Intl Educ & Student Svcs ... Vacant
102 Dir of Foundation & Govt Relations ... Ms. Jill MCWILLIAMS
110 Exec Dir of Development ... Vacant
44 Director of Annual Giving ... Mr. Cameron WATKINS
50 Dir Ctr for Business & Economics ... Dr. Kathleen RUST
53 Dept Chair Education ... Dr. Lisa BURKE
96 Director of Purchasing ... Ms. Donna MALANCA
108 Asst Dean for Assessment & Accred ... Dr. A. Andrew DAS
88 Asst Dean For Faculty Development ... Dr. Kimberly LAWLER-SAGARIN
88 Asst Dean Programs & Curriculum ... Dr. Brian WILHITE
09 Inst Research/Assessment Specialist ... Dr. Yanli MA
22 Director of Diversity & Inclusion ... Ms. Jasmin ROBINSON

Erikson Institute (A)

451 N. Lasalle Street, Chicago IL 60654
County: Cook FICE Identification: 035103
Unit ID: 409254
Telephone: (312) 755-2250 Carnegie Class: Spec-4-yr-Other
FAX Number: (312) 755-0928 Calendar System: Semester
URL: www.erikson.edu
Established: 1966 Annual Graduate Tuition & Fees: N/A
Enrollment: 278 Coed
Affiliation or Control: Independent Non-Profit IRS Status: 501(c)3
Highest Offering: Master's; No Undergraduates
Accreditation: NH, SW

01 President/CEO ... Geoffrey A. NAGLE
05 Sr VP Academic Affs/Dean of Faculty ... Jie-Qi CHEN
10 Vice President Finance/CFO ... Patricia LAWSON
45 VP Inst Effectiveness and Planning ... Charles CHANG
111 Vice Pres Institutional Advancement ... Maura DALY
84 Dean of Enrollment Management ... Vacant
32 Dean of Students ... Colette DAVISON
06 Dir of Registration/Student Records ... David SAENZ
26 Dir of Communications and Marketing ... Sheila HAENNICKE
13 Chief Information Officer ... Charles CHANG
30 Dir Development/Alumni Relations ... Patricia OFFER

Eureka College (B)

300 E College Avenue, Eureka IL 61530-1500
County: Woodford FICE Identification: 001678
Unit ID: 144971
Telephone: (309) 467-3721 Carnegie Class: Bac-Diverse
FAX Number: (309) 467-6386 Calendar System: Semester
URL: www.eureka.edu
Established: 1855 Annual Undergrad Tuition & Fees: $25,390
Enrollment: 614 Coed
Affiliation or Control: Christian Church (Disciples Of Christ)
IRS Status: 501(c)3
Highest Offering: Baccalaureate
Accreditation: NH

01 President ... Dr. Jamel WRIGHT
04 Administrative Asst to President ... Mrs. Jyl ZUBIATE
05 Provost & Dean of the College ... Dr. Ann FULOP
10 Chief Financial Officer ... Mr. Craig MAYNARD
32 Dean of Student Services ... Dr. Duane BRUCE
111 SVP of Institutional Advance ... Mr. Michael MURTAGH
06 Registrar ... Ms. Kendi ONNEN
18 Director of Physical Plant ... Mr. Jeremy MISCHLER
42 Chaplain ... Rev. Bruce M. FOWLKES
36 Director of Career Development ... Ms. Kelly BAY
13 Director of Computer Services ... Dr. Kanaka VIJITHA-KUMARA
37 Director of Financial Aid ... Mrs. Tammy CROTHERS
41 Athletic Director ... Mr. Bryan MOORE
29 Director Alumni Relations ... Mrs. Shellie SCHWANKE
15 Director Personnel Services ... Mrs. Melody MOUNTS
39 Director Student Housing ... Mrs. Lisa ALLEN
28 Chief Diversity Officer ... Dr. Jamel WRIGHT
26 Director of Communications ... Ms. Brttany PARKER
84 Dean of Enrollment Management ... Mr. MacKenzie INGMIRE
108 Director Institutional Assessment ... Dr. Ann FULOP
104 Director Study Abroad ... Dr. Emily EATON
19 Director Security/Safety ... Mr. Tony M. MAXISON
44 Director Annual Giving ... Mrs. Anna CHUMBLEY

Flashpoint Chicago, a Campus of Columbia College Hollywood (C)

28 North Clark Street, Suite 500, Chicago IL 60602
Telephone: (312) 506-0600 Identification: 667083
Accreditation: &WC

Fox College (D)

6640 South Cicero Avenue, Bedford Park IL 60638
County: Cook FICE Identification: 025228
Unit ID: 145239
Telephone: (708) 444-4500 Carnegie Class: Spec 2-yr-Health
FAX Number: (708) 802-6585 Calendar System: Semester
URL: www.foxcollege.edu
Established: 1932 Annual Undergrad Tuition & Fees: $15,220
Enrollment: 433 Coed
Affiliation or Control: Proprietary IRS Status: Proprietary
Highest Offering: Associate Degree
Accreditation: NH, DH, MAAB, OTA, PTAA

01 President ... Mr. Teri TUCCI
08 Head Librarian ... Ms. Sierra CAMPBELL
36 Director Student Placement ... Ms. Lisa FENTON
37 Director Student Financial Aid ... Ms. Kerry DEMARS

Garrett-Evangelical Theological Seminary (E)

2121 Sheridan Road, Evanston IL 60201-3298
County: Cook FICE Identification: 001682
Unit ID: 145275
Telephone: (847) 866-3900 Carnegie Class: Spec-4-yr-Faith
FAX Number: (847) 866-3884 Calendar System: Semester
URL: www.garrett.edu
Established: 1853 Annual Graduate Tuition & Fees: N/A
Enrollment: 313 Coed
Affiliation or Control: United Methodist IRS Status: 501(c)3
Highest Offering: Doctorate; No Undergraduates
Accreditation: NH, THEOL

01 President ... Dr. Lallene J. RECTOR
05 Vice Pres Academic Affairs/Dean ... Dr. Mai-Anh L. TRAN
112 Senior VP for Planned Giving ... Dr. David L. HEETLAND
30 Vice President of Development ... Mr. Joe EMMICK
84 Vice Pres Student Svcs/Enrollment ... Rev. Becky J. EBERHART
10 Vice President Business Affairs/CFO ... Mr. Kevin MILLER
42 Dean of the Chapel ... Rev. Tercio JUNKER
45 Asst VP of Strategic Initiatives ... Ms. Erin B. MOORE
21 Controller ... Mr. Lee WERNER
06 Registrar/Dir of Academic Studies ... Ms. Krista MCNEIL
08 Director of United Library ... Dr. Lucy CHUNG
18 Senior Director of B&G ... Mr. Josten BERCZY
110 Director of Stewardship ... Ms. Ceciley AKINS
37 Director of Financial Aid ... Mr. Jason GILL
26 Exec Director of Communications ... Mr. Shane NICHOLS
32 Asst VP/Dean of Students ... Rev. Benjamin REYNOLDS
04 Exec Assistant to the President ... Ms. Elizabeth LWANGA
07 Director of Admissions ... Rev. Katie FAHEY

Governors State University (F)

1 University Parkway, University Park IL 60484-0975
County: Will FICE Identification: 009145
Unit ID: 145336
Telephone: (708) 534-5000 Carnegie Class: Masters/L
FAX Number: (708) 534-4107 Calendar System: Semester
URL: www.govst.edu
Established: 1969 Annual Undergrad Tuition & Fees (In-State): $12,196
Enrollment: 5,185 Coed
Affiliation or Control: State IRS Status: 501(c)3
Highest Offering: Doctorate
Accreditation: NH, CACREP, CAEPN, #HSA, NUR, OT, PTA, SP, SPAA, SW

01 President ... Dr. Elaine P. MAIMON
05 Provost/VP Academic Affairs ... Dr. Beth CADA
111 VP Advancement/CEO Foundation ... Mr. William DAVIS
13 Assoc VP/CIO Information Tech Svcs ... Mr. Chuck PUSTZ
43 Legal Counsel/VP ... Vacant
45 Director Budget Planning/Inst Rsrch ... Ms. Sandra ZURAWSKI
09 Assoc Dir of Institutional Research ... Mr. Marco KRCATOVICH, II
114 Director Budget & Financial Plng ... Vacant
29 Director of Alumni Assoc ... Vacant
50 Dean College of Business ... Dr. Jun ZHAO
49 Dean College Arts Sciences ... Dr. Andrae MARAK
76 Dean Col Health Professions ... Dr. Elizabeth BALTHAZAR
53 Dean College Education ... Dr. Shannon DERMER
32 Dean Student Affairs & Services ... Dr. Aurelio VALENTE
08 Dean University Library ... Vacant
06 Registrar ... Mr. Timothy CARROLL
37 Director Financial Aid ... Mr. John PERRY
20 Associate Provost/AVP Academic Affs ... Dr. Colleen SEXTON
15 Director Human Resources ... Vacant
18 Director Physical Plant ... Mr. Jim ZUMERCHIK
19 Director Dept Public Safety ... Mr. James MCGEE
38 Dir Student Devel/Counseling Center ... Vacant
36 Director of Career Services ... Ms. Darcie R. CAMPOS
96 Dir of Procurement/Auxiliary Svcs ... Ms. Tracy SULLIVAN
11 Chief of Administrative Operations ... Ms. Penny PERDUE
39 Director Student Housing ... Mr. Mujahid CHOUDHARY
41 Athletic Director ... Mr. Anthony BATES
86 Director Government Relations ... Ms. Maureen KELLY

Greenville University (G)

315 E College, Greenville IL 62246
County: Bond FICE Identification: 001684
Unit ID: 145372
Telephone: (618) 664-7100 Carnegie Class: Masters/S
FAX Number: (618) 664-6841 Calendar System: 4/1/4
URL: www.greenville.edu
Established: 1892 Annual Undergrad Tuition & Fees: $27,130
Enrollment: 1,235 Coed
Affiliation or Control: Free Methodist IRS Status: 501(c)3
Highest Offering: Master's
Accreditation: NH, CAEPT, SW

01 President ... Dr. Ivan FILBY
03 Executive Vice President ... Mrs. Suzanne DAVIS
101 Executive Assistant to President ... Mrs. Regina ROBART
20 Vice President for Academic Affairs ... Dr. Brian HARTLEY
111 Vice Pres for Advancement ... Mr. Scott GIFFEN
15 Vice President of Human Resources ... Mrs. Katrina LISS
28 VP and Chief Diversity Officer ... Dr. Terrell CARTER
10 Interim Associate VP/CFO ... Mrs. Barb SANDS
55 Dean of Adult Studies ... Dr. Dave HOLDEN
32 Associate VP for Community Life ... Mr. Marcos GILMORE
11 Director of Operations/Strategic Im ... Mr. Mike ADEN
19 Director of Campus Safety ... Vacant
07 Dean of Traditional Admissions ... Mr. Colin MCLAUGHLIN
08 Director of Library ... Ms. Gail HEIDEMAN
06 Registrar ... Mrs. Michelle SUSSENBACH
37 Director of Financial Aid ... Mr. David KESSINGER
112 Director of Major & Planned Gifts ... Mr. Brett BRANNON
42 Dean Chapel & Dir Spiritual Form ... Mrs. Lori GAFFNER
18 Director of Facilities ... Mr. Mark OWENS
26 Director of Marketing ... Mr. Alex STATON
49 Dean School Arts & Sciences ... Dr. Teresa HOLDEN
53 Dean School of Education ... Dr. Lisa AMUNDSON
50 Dean of School of Business ... Dr. Mark JENNER
41 Dean of Athletics ... Mr. Tom ACKERMAN

Harper College (H)

1200 W Algonquin Road, Palatine IL 60067-7398
County: Cook FICE Identification: 003961
Unit ID: 149842
Telephone: (847) 925-6000 Carnegie Class: Assoc/HT-High Non
FAX Number: (847) 925-6034 Calendar System: Semester
URL: www.harpercollege.edu
Established: 1965 Annual Undergrad Tuition & Fees (In-District): $3,684
Enrollment: 13,749 Coed
Affiliation or Control: State/Local IRS Status: 501(c)3
Highest Offering: Associate Degree
Accreditation: NH, ACBSP, ADNUR, CAHIIM, DH, DIETT, DMS, MAC, MUS, PNUR, @PTAA, RAD

01 President ... Dr. Avis PROCTOR
100 Chf of Staff/VP Inst Plng/Strat All ... Dr. Maria COONS
05 Interim Provost ... Dr. Brian KNETL
10 Exec VP Finance & Admin Services ... Dr. Ron ALLY
111 VP and Chief Advancement Officer ... Ms. Laura BROWN
103 VP Wrkfrce Solutions/Assoc Provost ... Ms. Michele' SMITH
20 Interim Assoc Provost Academics ... Dr. Kathy BRUCE
15 Chief Human Resources Officer ... Mr. Roger SPAYER
13 Chief Information Officer ... Mr. Patrick BAUER
21 Controller ... Mr. Bret BONNSTETTER
18 Exec Dir of Facilities Management ... Mr. Darryl KNIGHT
84 Asst Provost/Dean Enrollment Svcs ... Dr. Claudia MERCADO
32 Asst Provost/Dean Student Dev ... Ms. Sheryl OTTO
103 Asst VP Wrkfrce Dev/Exec Dean CE ... Dr. Mark MROZINSKI
45 Exec Dir Plng/Research/Inst Eff ... Ms. Darlene SCHLENBECKER
75 Dean Career & Technical Programs ... Ms. Joanne IVORY
76 Dean Health Careers ... Dr. Kimberly CHAVIS
08 Dean Resources for Learning ... Ms. Njambi KAMOCHE
35 Dean of Students ... Ms. Mary Kay HARTON
50 Dean Business & Social Science ... Dr. Travaris HARRIS
81 Interim Dean Mathematics & Sciences ... Ms. Kimberley POLLY
106 Dean Teaching/Learning/Distance Edu ... Dr. Michael BATES
103 Dean Workforce & Economic Devel ... Dr. Rebecca LAKE
49 Dean Liberal Arts ... Ms. Jaime LONG
102 Assoc Exec Dir Fndn/Dir Major Gifts ... Ms. Heather ZOLDAK
88 Assoc Dean Interdisc Stdnt Success ... Ms. Darice TROUT
121 Dean Student Development ... Dr. Vicki ATKINSON
27 Director Marketing Services ... Mr. Mike BARZACCHINI
36 Director Job Placement Resource Ctr ... Ms. Kathleen CANFIELD
91 Director IT Client Services ... Ms. Sue CONTARINO
09 Director Institutional Research ... Dr. Katherine COY
51 Director Adult Educational Dev ... Ms. Andrea FIEBIG
37 Dir Student Financial Assistance ... Ms. Laura MCGEE
66 Director Nursing ... Dr. Julie D'AGOSTINO
07 Dir Admissions Outreach ... Mr. Robert PARZY
121 Assoc Dean Advising Svcs ... Ms. Kristin HOFFHINES
41 Director of Athletics & Fitness ... Mr. Doug SPIWAK
88 Campus Architect ... Mr. Steve PETERSEN

Heartland Community College (I)

1500 W Raab Road, Normal IL 61761-9446
County: McLean FICE Identification: 030838
Unit ID: 384342
Telephone: (309) 268-8000 Carnegie Class: Assoc/HT-High Non
FAX Number: (309) 268-7999 Calendar System: Semester
URL: www.heartland.edu
Established: 1990 Annual Undergrad Tuition & Fees (In-District): $4,590
Enrollment: 5,193 Coed
Affiliation or Control: State/Local IRS Status: 501(c)3
Highest Offering: Associate Degree
Accreditation: NH, ADNUR, PTAA, RAD

01 President ... Dr. Keith CORNILLE
05 Provost/Vice Pres Academic Affairs ... Dr. Rick PEARCE

10 Vice Pres Business Services .... Mr. Douglas MINTER
111 Vice Pres External Affairs .... Ms. Kelli HILL
84 Vice Pres Enrollment/Student Svcs .... Dr. Sarah DIEL-HUNT
32 Assoc VP Enrollment/Student Service .... Dr. Amy PAWLIK
07 Dean Enrollment Services .... Ms. Lindsay EICKHORST
18 Executive Director of Facilities .... Mr. James HUBBARD
11 Director of Administrative Services .... Ms. Valerie CRAWFORD
13 Chief Information Officer .... Mr. Scott BROSS
21 Controller .... Ms. Sharon MCDONALD
37 Director of Financial Aid .... Mr. Todd BURNS
15 Exec Director Human Resources .... Mrs. Barb LEATHERS
41 Director of Athletics .... Mr. Ryan KNOX
121 Dean of Student Success .... Ms. Kimberly KELLEY
06 Director of Records .... Ms. Cindy ALFANO
26 Director of Marketing .... Mr. Tim BILL
35 Director of Student Engagement .... Mr. Skylar GUIMOND
36 Dir Advisement/Career Services .... Vacant
04 Executive Assistant .... Ms. Laura MAI
22 Assoc Dir Equity/Complianc/Title IX .... Mr. Terrance BOND

Hebrew Theological College (A)

7135 N Carpenter Road, Skokie IL 60077-3263
County: Cook FICE Identification: 001685
Unit ID: 145497
Telephone: (847) 982-2500 Carnegie Class: Spec-4-yr-Faith
FAX Number: (847) 674-6381 Calendar System: Semester
URL: www.htc.edu
Established: 1922 Annual Undergrad Tuition & Fees: $12,920
Enrollment: 199 Coordinate
Affiliation or Control: Independent Non-Profit IRS Status: 501(c)3
Highest Offering: Master's
Accreditation: NH

01 Chief Executive Officer .... Rabbi Shmuel SCHUMAN
05 Chief Academic Officer .... Dr. Zev ELEFF
11 Chief Operating Officer .... Mr. Sid SINGER
20 Rosh Hayeshiva .... Rabbi Avraham FRIEDMAN
11 Vice President for Administration .... Rabbi Sender KUTNER
33 Mashgiach Ruchani-Dean .... Rabbi Zvi ZIMMERMAN
20 Dean Blitstein Institute .... Dr. Chani TESSLER
34 Menahel Ruchani-Dean .... Rabbi Binyamin OLSTEIN
34 Assistant Dean Blitstein Institute .... Ms. Rita LIPSHITZ
06 Registrar .... Rabbi Gavriel BACHRACH
07 Director of Admissions .... Rabbi Joshua ZISOOK
30 Director of Development .... Vacant
44 Development Coordinator .... Rabbi Yaakov FRIEDMAN
08 Librarian .... Mr. Michael VERDERAME
125 Chancellor Emeritus .... Dr. Jerold ISENBERG

† Separate campuses for male and female students. Part of the Touro College and University System.

Highland Community College (B)

2998 W Pearl City Road, Freeport IL 61032-9341
County: Stephenson FICE Identification: 001681
Unit ID: 145521
Telephone: (815) 235-6121 Carnegie Class: Assoc/MT-VT-High Non
FAX Number: (815) 235-6130 Calendar System: Semester
URL: www.highland.edu
Established: 1962 Annual Undergrad Tuition & Fees (In-District): $4,167
Enrollment: 1,678 Coed
Affiliation or Control: State/Local IRS Status: 501(c)3
Highest Offering: Associate Degree
Accreditation: NH, MAC

01 President .... Mr. Tim HOOD
03 Executive Vice President .... Ms. Chris KUBERSKI
10 Vice Pres Administrative Services .... Ms. Jill M. JANSSEN
50 VP Business/Tech & Community Pgms . Mr. Scott R. ANDERSON
32 Vice Pres Student Dev & Support Svc ... Ms. Elizabeth L. GERBER
79 Dean Humanities/Social Sci & FA .... Mr. Jim PHILLIPS
81 Assoc Dean Natural Science & Math ...... Dr. Brendan C. DUTMER
66 Assoc Dean Nursing & Allied Health .... Ms. Jennifer GROBE
51 Director Adult Education .... Mr. Mark JANSEN
41 Director Athletics .... Mr. Peter E. NORMAN
84 Director Enrollment & Records .... Mr. Jeremy BRADT
18 Director Facilities & Safety .... Mr. Kurt SIMPSON
37 Director Financial Aid .... Ms. Kathy BANGASSER
15 Director Human Resources .... Vacant
09 Director Institutional Research .... Dr. Michelle THRUMAN
88 Dir Learning & Transitional Educ .... Ms. Carolyn PETSCHE
26 Director Marketing & Community Rel .... Ms. Leslie SCHMIDT
88 Dir Retired & Senior Volunteer Pgm .... Ms. Cindi MIELKE
88 Director Title IV Student Support .... Mr. Anthony SAGO
88 Coordinator Upward Bound Program .... Mr. Patrick JACKSON
21 Manager Accounting .... Ms. Mary J. LLOYD
40 Manager Bookstore .... Ms. Madonna KEENEY
101 Exec Asst to President/Board Sec .... Ms. Terri A. GRIMES
102 Foundation Executive Director .... Mr. Jeff REINKE
88 Foundation Director of Fundraising .... Ms. Lisa LA SALA
88 Foundation Director of Operations .... Ms. Patricia A. DUNN

Illinois Central College (C)

1 College Drive, East Peoria IL 61635-0001
County: Tazewell FICE Identification: 006753
Unit ID: 145682
Telephone: (309) 694-5422 Carnegie Class: Assoc/HT-Mix Trad/Non
FAX Number: (309) 694-5450 Calendar System: Semester
URL: www.icc.edu
Established: 1966 Annual Undergrad Tuition & Fees (In-District): $4,500
Enrollment: 9,266 Coed
Affiliation or Control: State/Local IRS Status: 501(c)3
Highest Offering: Associate Degree
Accreditation: NH, ACFEI, ADNUR, COARC, DH, EMT, MAC, MLTAD, MUS, OTA, PNUR, PTAA, RAD, SURGT

01 President .... Dr. Sheila QUIRK-BAILEY
10 Exec VP Administration/Finance .... Mr. Bruce BUDDE
26 Vice Pres of Marketing/Advancement .... Ms. Kim ARMSTRONG
05 Vice President of Academic Affairs .... Dr. Emmanuel AWUAH
102 Exec Dir Education Foundation .... Ms. Stephanie HOLMES
15 Assc Vice President Human Resources .... Ms. Michelle BUGOS
28 VP of Diversity/Intl & Adult Educ .... Dr. Rita ALI
32 Vice President Student Services .... Mr. Rocco CAPPELLO
09 Exec Dir Inst Research & Planning .... Mr. David COOK
35 Dean of Students .... Ms. Emily POINTS
84 Dean of Enrollment Management .... Vacant
51 Dean Corporate/Community Education .... Ms. Julie HOWAR
79 Dean Eng/Humanities/Lang .... Mr. Bruce BUSBY
81 Dean Math/Science/Engineering .... Mr. Joe BERGMAN
50 Dean Business/Hospitality/Info Sys ...... Ms. Michelle WEGHORST
57 Dean Arts & Communications .... Ms. Kari SCHIMMEL
47 Dean Agriculture/Industrial Tech .... Mr. Steve FLINN
76 Dean Health Careers .... Ms. Wendee GUTH
21 Director Business Services .... Ms. Kim MALCOLM
06 Registrar .... Ms. Nikisha WRIGHTANDERSON
29 Coordinator Alumni Relations .... Vacant
04 Administrative Asst to President .... Mr. Jake BEENEY
08 Director Library Services .... Ms. Cathryne KAUFMAN
19 Campus Police Chief .... Mr. Thomas LARSON
22 VP Affirmative Action/EEO .... Dr. Rita ALI
41 Athletic Director .... Ms. Heather DOTY
104 Dir International Educ Program .... Ms. Tia VAN HESTER
21 Controller .... Mr. Ed BABCOCK
101 Secretary of the Institution/Board .... Ms. Sue BULITTA

Illinois College (D)

1101 W College Avenue, Jacksonville IL 62650-2299
County: Morgan FICE Identification: 001688
Unit ID: 145691
Telephone: (217) 245-3000 Carnegie Class: Bac-A&S
FAX Number: (217) 245-3034 Calendar System: Semester
URL: www.ic.edu
Established: 1829 Annual Undergrad Tuition & Fees: $33,090
Enrollment: 959 Coed
Affiliation or Control: Independent Non-Profit IRS Status: 501(c)3
Highest Offering: Master's
Accreditation: NH

01 President .... Dr. Barbara A. FARLEY
05 Provost and Dean of the College ...... Dr. Catharine E. O'CONNELL
10 Vice President of Business Affairs .... Mr. Tim WEIS
30 Vice President Development & Alumni .... Vacant
84 Vice President of Enrollment .... Ms. Stephanie CHIPMAN
32 Dean of Students .... Vacant
20 Dean of the Faculty .... Dr. Adam PORTER
35 Dean of Student Success .... Dr. Andrew JONES
09 Exec Dir for Inst Research .... Dr. Robert A. SWEATMAN
06 Registrar .... Ms. Helen KUHN
13 Chief Info Technology Officer (CIO) .... Mr. Patrick BROWN
07 Senior Assoc Director Admissions .... Mr. Richard L. BYSTRY
37 Assoc Director of Financial Aid .... Ms. Rebecca BIRDSELL
29 Dir Annual Giving/Alumni Relations .... Vacant
26 Director Marketing/Communications .... Mr. Bryan LEONARD
08 Library Director .... Mr. Luke BEATTY
18 Director of Facilities Operations .... Mr. Al DILLOW
36 Director of Career Services .... Ms. Susan K. DRAKE
21 Controller .... Ms. Melissa J. DYSON
35 Dir Center for Student Involvement .... Ms. Karen K. HOMOLKA
42 Chaplain .... Mr. Tim MCGEE
15 Director of Human Resources .... Ms. Angela VALUCK
38 Mental Health Counselor .... Ms. Jayde JOHNSON
28 Director of Diversity .... Vacant
41 Athletic Director .... Mr. Mike SNYDER

Illinois College of Optometry (E)

3241 S Michigan Avenue, Chicago IL 60616-3878
County: Cook FICE Identification: 001689
Unit ID: 145628
Telephone: (312) 225-1700 Carnegie Class: Spec-4-yr-Other Health
FAX Number: (312) 225-1724 Calendar System: Quarter
URL: www.ico.edu
Established: 1872 Annual Undergrad Tuition & Fees: N/A
Enrollment: 599 Coed
Affiliation or Control: Independent Non-Profit IRS Status: 501(c)3
Highest Offering: First Professional Degree
Accreditation: NH, OPT, OPTR

01 President .... Dr. Mark C. COLIP
05 Vice Pres for Academic Affairs/Dean .... Dr. Stephanie MESSNER
10 VP for Finance & Business/CFO .... Mr. John BUDZYNSKI
11 Vice President for Administration .... Mrs. Laura L. ROUNCE
17 VP for Patient Care Services .... Dr. Leonard V. MESSNER
32 Dean of Student Affairs .... Dr. Erik MOTHERSBAUGH
06 Assoc Dean for Academic/Registrar ... Dr. Geoffrey GOODFELLOW
07 Director of Admissions .... Ms. Teisha JOHNSON
35 Assistant Dean for Student Success .... Ms. Beth KARMIS
84 Sr Dir of Enrollment Mgmt Tech .... Ms. Milissa BARTOLD
29 Director Alumni Relations .... Ms. Connie M. SCAVUZZO
18 Chief Facilities/Physical Plant .... Mr. Gary YOUNG
08 Chief Library Officer .... Ms. Christine WEBER
13 Chief Information Technology Office .... Mr. Amit CHOKSI

04 Chief Exec Asst to the President .... Ms. Maggie LOPEZ
19 Director Security/Safety .... Mr. Tim CAPPARELLI
36 Director of Career Development .... Ms. Daphne ANDERSON

*Illinois Eastern Community Colleges System Office (F)

233 E Chestnut Street, Olney IL 62450-2298
County: Richland FICE Identification: 009135
Unit ID: 443368
Telephone: (618) 393-2982 Carnegie Class: N/A
FAX Number: (618) 392-4816
URL: www.iecc.edu

01 Chief Executive Officer .... Mr. Terry BRUCE
05 Chief Academic Officer .... Dr. Holly MARTIN
10 Chief Finance Officer/Treasurer .... Mr. Ryan HAWKINS
103 Dean Workforce Education .... Mr. Michael THOMAS
25 Pgm Dir of Grants and Compliance .... Mr. Luke HARL
85 Pgm Dir Intl Std/Dir Dist Std Rctmt .... Ms. Pamela SWANSON-MADDEN
15 Director of Human Resources .... Mrs. Tara BUERSTER
88 Director TRIO Upward Bound .... Ms. Tiffany COWGER
88 Pgm Dir Student Learning Assessment .... Mr. Brandon WEGER
88 Director TRIO Student Support Svcs .... Mr. Wain DAVIS

*Illinois Eastern Community Colleges Frontier Community College (G)

Frontier Drive, Fairfield IL 62837-9801
County: Wayne FICE Identification: 020744
Unit ID: 403469
Telephone: (618) 842-3711 Carnegie Class: Assoc/MT-VT-High Non
FAX Number: (618) 842-4425 Calendar System: Semester
URL: www.iecc.edu/fcc
Established: 1976 Annual Undergrad Tuition & Fees (In-District): $3,970
Enrollment: 1,791 Coed
Affiliation or Control: State/Local IRS Status: 501(c)3
Highest Offering: Associate Degree
Accreditation: &NH, ADNUR

02 President .... Dr. Gerald EDGREN, JR.
05 Dean of Instruction .... Dr. Paul BRUINSMA
32 Asst Dean of Student Services .... Mrs. Jan WILES
51 Director of Adult Education .... Ms. Cheryl HOLDER
10 Director of Business .... Mrs. Mary JOHNSTON
08 Director of Learning Resource Ctr .... Ms. Merna YOUNGBLOOD
41 Interim Athletic Director .... Mrs. Jan WILES
88 Coordinator of Fire Science .... Mr. Scott MESEROLE
37 Coordinator of Financial Aid .... Ms. Lori NOE
06 Coordinator of Registration/Records .... Ms. Amy LOSS

† Regional accreditation is carried under the parent institution Illinois Eastern Community Colleges System Office in Olney, IL.

*Illinois Eastern Community Colleges Lincoln Trail College (H)

11220 State Highway 1, Robinson IL 62454-5707
County: Crawford FICE Identification: 009786
Unit ID: 403478
Telephone: (618) 544-8657 Carnegie Class: Assoc/HT-High Non
FAX Number: (618) 544-7423 Calendar System: Semester
URL: www.iecc.edu/ltc
Established: 1969 Annual Undergrad Tuition & Fees (In-District): $3,970
Enrollment: 933 Coed
Affiliation or Control: State/Local IRS Status: 501(c)3
Highest Offering: Associate Degree
Accreditation: &NH, ADNUR

02 President .... Dr. Ryan GOWER
05 Dean of the College .... Mr. Brent TODD
37 Coordinator of Financial Aid .... Ms. Amy THERIAC
32 Asst Dean of Student Services .... Ms. Julie HIGGINBOTHOM
08 Director of Learning Resource Ctr .... Ms. Vicky BONELLI
10 Director of Business .... Ms. Jamie HENRY
41 Athletic Director .... Mr. Kevin BOWERS
18 Groundskeeper .... Mr. Dan LEGGITT
26 Coord Public Information/Marketing .... Mr. Christopher FORDE

† Regional accreditation is carried under the parent institution Illinois Eastern Community Colleges System Office in Olney, IL.

*Illinois Eastern Community Colleges Olney Central College (I)

305 North West Street, Olney IL 62450-1099
County: Richland FICE Identification: 001742
Unit ID: 145707
Telephone: (618) 395-7777 Carnegie Class: Assoc/MT-VT-High Non
FAX Number: (618) 392-3293 Calendar System: Semester
URL: www.iecc.edu/occ
Established: 1962 Annual Undergrad Tuition & Fees (In-District): $3,970
Enrollment: 1,142 Coed
Affiliation or Control: State/Local IRS Status: 501(c)3
Highest Offering: Associate Degree
Accreditation: &NH, ADNUR, RAD

02 President .... Mr. Rodney RANES

05 Dean of Instruction ..... Mr. Michael CONN
32 Assistant Dean Student Services ..... Ms. Andrea PAMPE
76 Assoc Dean Nursing Allied Health ..... Dr. Theresa MARCOTTE
08 Director Learning Skills Center/LRC ..... Ms. Linda SHIDLER
88 Director Cosmetology ..... Ms. Courtney MEADOWS
10 Director Business ..... Mr. Doug SHIPMAN
41 Athletic Director/Coach ..... Mr. Dennis CONLEY
37 Financial Aid Coordinator ..... Ms. Taryn BUNTING

† Regional accreditation is carried under the parent institution Illinois Eastern Community Colleges System Office in Olney, IL.

*Illinois Eastern Community Colleges Wabash Valley College (A)

2200 College Drive, Mount Carmel IL 62863-2657
County: Wabash FICE Identification: 001779
Unit ID: 403487
Telephone: (618) 262-8641 Carnegie Class: Assoc/HVT-High Non
FAX Number: (618) 262-5347 Calendar System: Semester
URL: www.iecc.edu/wvc
Established: 1960 Annual Undergrad Tuition & Fees (In-District): $3,970
Enrollment: 3,662 Coed
Affiliation or Control: State/Local IRS Status: 501(c)3
Highest Offering: Associate Degree
Accreditation: &NH, ADNUR

02 President ..... Mr. Matt FOWLER
05 Dean of Instruction ..... Mr. Robert CONN
32 Assistant Dean Student Services ..... Mrs. Tiffany COWGER
121 Director of Academic Advising ..... Mr. Tim ZIMMER
08 Director of LRC ..... Ms. Sandy CRAIG
60 Director of Broadcasting ..... Mr. Kyle PEACH
41 Athletic Director ..... Mr. Mike CARPENTER
10 Director of Business ..... Mrs. Reilly BAUMGART
37 Financial Aid Coordinator ..... Ms. Jane OWEN
18 Groundskeeper ..... Mr. Adam ROESCH

† Regional accreditation is carried under the parent institution Illinois Eastern Community Colleges System Office in Olney, IL.

Illinois Institute of Technology (B)

10 West 35th Street, Chicago IL 60616-3793
County: Cook FICE Identification: 001691
Unit ID: 145725
Telephone: (312) 567-3000 Carnegie Class: DU-Higher
FAX Number: (312) 567-3004 Calendar System: Semester
URL: www.iit.edu
Established: 1890 Annual Undergrad Tuition & Fees: $47,646
Enrollment: 7,164 Coed
Affiliation or Control: Independent Non-Profit IRS Status: 501(c)3
Highest Offering: Doctorate
Accreditation: NH, CACREP, CEA, CLPSY, LSAR

01 President ..... Dr. Alan CRAMB
05 Provost ..... Dr. Peter KILPATRICK
84 Vice Pres Enrollment/Vice Provost ..... Dr. Mike GOSZ
10 VP Finance/CFO & Treasurer ..... Dr. Michael D. HORAN
18 VP Admin/Facilities/Pub Safety ..... Mr. Bruce WATTS
111 Vice Pres Institutional Advancement ..... Vacant
88 Vice Pres International Affairs ..... Dr. Darsh T. WASAN
86 Vice President External Affairs ..... Mr. Jess GOODE
43 Vice President General Counsel ..... Mr. Anthony D'AMATO
88 Sr VP & Dir IIT Research Inst ..... Dr. David MCCORMICK
88 VP & Dir Inst Food Safety & Health ..... Dr. Robert BRACKETT
13 CIO & Vice Provost ..... Mr. Ophir TRIGALO
28 Vice Provost Student Diversity ..... Vacant
58 Vice Provost Grad Academic Affairs ... Dr. Jamshid MOHAMMADI
46 Vice Provost for Research ..... Dr. Fred HICKERNELL
32 Vice Provost Student Affairs ..... Ms. Katherine MURPHY-STETZ
61 Dean Chicago-Kent College of Law ..... Dr. Anita K. KRUG
49 Interim Dean Col of Sci & Letters ..... Dr. Xiaofan LI
54 Dean Armour Col of Engineering ..... Dr. Natacha DEPAOLA
50 Dean Stuart School of Business ..... Vacant
48 Dean College of Architecture ..... Mr. Reed KROLOFF
83 Dean Lewis Col of Human Sciences ..... Dr. Christine HIMES
12 Dean Institute of Design ..... Mr. Denis WEIL
72 Dean School of Applied Technology ..... Dr. Bob CARLSON
08 Interim Dean of Libraries ..... Mr. Devin SAVAGE
22 Associate General Counsel ..... Ms. Candida MIRANDA
21 Assoc VP Finance & Controller ..... Mr. Ken JOHNSTON
15 Associate VP Human Resources ..... Ms. Hilary HUDSON HOSEK
88 Assoc Vice Prov Grad Acad Affs ..... Ms. Holli PRYOR HARRIS
41 AVP Director of Athletics ..... Mr. Joseph HAKES
07 Assoc Vice Pres Enrollment Svcs ..... Ms. Abigail MCGRATH
07 Asst Vice Pres UG Admissions ..... Ms. Toni RILEY
123 Asst VP Grad/Prof Admissions ..... Mr. Rishab MALHOTRA
39 AVP Residence & Greek Life ..... Vacant
14 Assoc CIO Enterprise Systems ..... Mr. Vince BATTISTA
14 Assoc CIO Technology Infrastructure ..... Mr. Ibukun OYEWOLE
14 Assoc CIO User & Technical Svcs ..... Mr. Eric BREESE
23 Assoc VP Student Health & Wellness ..... Ms. Anita OPDYCKE
29 Assoc VP Alumni & Donor Rels ..... Vacant
96 Director of Purchasing ..... Ms. Snow RUTKOWSKE
06 Interim Registrar ..... Vacant
37 Director of Financial Aid ..... Ms. Elizabeth WAHLSTROM HELGREN
22 Director Diversity/Inclusions/EE ..... Ms. Lisa MONTGOMERY
25 Director Sponsored Research ..... Mr. Robert LAPOINTE
88 Dir Environmental Health & Safety ..... Ms. Cynthia CHAFFEE
108 Director of Assessment ..... Dr. Carol-Ann EMMONS
105 Director Web Development/Services ..... Mr. Brian BAILEY
106 Dir IIT Online Tech Svcs ..... Ms. Lauren WOODS
04 Director President's Office ..... Ms. Sandra LAPORTE
90 Manager Academic Computing ..... Vacant

Illinois Institute of Technology Downtown Campus (C)

565 W Adams Street, Chicago IL 60661
Telephone: (312) 906-5000 Identification: 770075
Accreditation: &NH, LAW

Illinois Institute of Technology Rice Campus (D)

201 East Loop Road, Wheaton IL 60189
Telephone: (630) 682-6000 Identification: 770077
Accreditation: &NH

Illinois State University (E)

School and North Streets, Normal IL 61790-0001
County: McLean FICE Identification: 001692
Unit ID: 145813
Telephone: (309) 438-2111 Carnegie Class: DU-Higher
FAX Number: (309) 438-2768 Calendar System: Semester
URL: https://illinoisstate.edu/
Established: 1857 Annual Undergrad Tuition & Fees (In-State): $14,516
Enrollment: 20,784 Coed
Affiliation or Control: State IRS Status: 501(c)3
Highest Offering: Doctorate
Accreditation: NH, AAFCS, ART, AUD, CAATE, CAEPN, CAHIIM, CIDA, CONST, DIETD, DIETI, IPSY, MT, MUS, NAIT, NRPA, NURSE, SCPSY, SP, SW, THEA

01 President ..... Dr. Larry DIETZ
05 VP Academic Affairs & Provost ..... Dr. Jan MURPHY
10 VP Finance & Planning ..... Mr. Daniel STEPHENS
32 VP Student Affairs ..... Dr. Levester JOHNSON
111 VP University Advancement ..... Mr. Pat VICKERMAN
20 Associate Provost ..... Dr. Ani YAZEDJIAN
35 Assistant VP Student Affairs ..... Dr. Danielle MILLER-SCHUSTER
58 AVP Grad Stds/Research/Intl Educ ..... Dr. John BAUR
84 Assoc VP Enrollment Management ..... Ms. Jana ALBRECHT
15 Int Assoc VP Human Resources ..... Ms. Janice BONNEVILLE
13 AVP Admin Technologies/CTO ..... Mr. Charles EDAMALA
08 Interim Dean University Libraries ..... Dr. Sharon ZECK
06 University Registrar ..... Mr. Jess D. RAY
07 Director Admissions ..... Mr. Jeff MAVROS
20 Director University College ..... Ms. Amelia NOEL-ELKINS
30 Exec Director of Development ..... Ms. Joy D. HUTCHCRAFT
21 University Comptroller ..... Mr. Doug SCHNITTKER
37 Director Financial Aid ..... Ms. Bridget CURL
29 Exec Director Alumni Engagement ..... Ms. Kristin HARDING
18 Exec Director Facilities Management ..... Mr. Charles SCOTT
19 Chief University Police ..... Mr. Aaron WOODRUFF
28 Dir Ofc of Eq Opportunity & Access ..... Mr. Anthony WALESBY
23 Director Student Health Services ..... Dr. Christina NULTY
39 Director University Housing ..... Ms. Stacey MWILAMBWE
41 Director Intercollegiate Athletics ..... Mr. Larry LYONS
85 Director International Studies ..... Dr. Luis CANALES
92 Director Honors Program ..... Dr. Rocio RIVADENEYRA
94 Director Women's Studies ..... Dr. Alison BAILEY
96 Director of Purchases ..... Mr. Ernest OLSON
49 Int Dean College Arts & Sciences ..... Dr. Diane ZOSKY
50 Dean College Business ..... Mr. Ajay SAMANT
53 Int Dean College Education ..... Dr. Kevin LAUDNER
72 Dean College Applied Sci/Tech ..... Dr. Todd MCLODA
57 Dean College Fine Arts ..... Ms. Jean M K. MILLER
66 Dean Mennonite College ..... Dr. Judy NEUBRANDER
35 Dean of Students ..... Dr. John DAVENPORT
88 Assoc VP Acad Admin ..... Dr. Sam CATANZARO
88 Assoc VP Acad Fiscal Mgmt ..... Dr. Alan LACY
114 Asst VP Budget & Planning ..... Ms. Sandra CAVI
44 Senior Director Annual Giving ..... Ms. Jillian NELSON
110 Asst VP University Advancement ..... Ms. Jill JONES
27 Exec Dir University Marketing/Comm ..... Mr. Brian BEAM
45 Dir Planning/Rsch/Policy Analysis ..... Ms. Angela ENGEL
108 Director University Assessment ..... Dr. Ryan SMITH
38 Director Student Counseling ..... Dr. Sandy COLBS
43 General Counsel ..... Ms. Lisa HUSON
105 Director Web & Interactive Comm ..... Mr. Arturo RAMIREZ
86 Director State Government Relations ..... Dr. Jonathan LACKLAND
90 Assoc VP Academic Technologies ..... Dr. Mark WALBERT
04 Administrative Asst to President ..... Mr. Dave BENTLIN

Illinois Valley Community College (F)

815 N Orlando Smith Road, Oglesby IL 61348-9692
County: La Salle FICE Identification: 001705
Unit ID: 145831
Telephone: (815) 224-2720 Carnegie Class: Assoc/HVT-High Non
FAX Number: (815) 224-3033 Calendar System: Semester
URL: www.ivcc.edu
Established: 1966 Annual Undergrad Tuition & Fees (In-District): $4,000
Enrollment: 3,241 Coed
Affiliation or Control: Local IRS Status: 501(c)3
Highest Offering: Associate Degree
Accreditation: NH, ADNUR, DA, EMT

01 President ..... Dr. Jerry M. CORCORAN
05 Vice Pres for Academic Affairs ..... Dr. Deborah L. ANDERSON
10 Vice Pres Business Svcs/Finance ..... Ms. Cheryl E. ROELFSEMA
20 Assoc Vice Pres Academic Affairs ..... Ms. Bonnie L. CAMPBELL
32 Assoc Vice Pres Student Svcs ..... Mr. Mark J. GRZYBOWSKI
24 Director of Learning Resources ..... Dr. Patrice HESS
31 Director Cmty Relations & Marketing ..... Mr. Francis R. BROLLEY
13 Dir of Information Technology Svcs ..... Mr. Christopher DUNLAP
51 Dir Cont Educ/Business Svcs ..... Ms. Jennifer C. SCHERI
15 Director Human Resources ..... Ms. Leslie A. HOFER
37 Director of Financial Aid ..... Mr. Eric JOHNSON
07 Director of Admissions/Records ..... Mr. Quintin M. OVEROCKER
08 Head Librarian ..... Ms. Frances A. WHALEY
30 Director of Development ..... Mr. Francis R. BROLLEY
96 Director of Purchasing ..... Ms. Michelle L. CARBONI
18 Director of Facilities ..... Mr. Scott CURLEY
09 Director of Institutional Research ..... Mr. Matthew P. SUERTH
81 Dean Natural Science/Business ..... Mr. Ron W. GROLEAU
66 Dean of Nursing ..... Ms. Julie HOGUE
79 Dean Humanities/Fine Arts/Soc Sci ..... Dr. Robyn L. SCHIFFMAN
103 Dean Workforce Development ..... Mr. Shane LANGE

Illinois Wesleyan University (G)

PO Box 2900, 1312 Park Street, Bloomington IL 61702-2900
County: McLean FICE Identification: 001696
Unit ID: 145646
Telephone: (309) 556-1000 Carnegie Class: Bac-A&S
FAX Number: (309) 556-3411 Calendar System: Other
URL: www.iwu.edu
Established: 1850 Annual Undergrad Tuition & Fees: $47,636
Enrollment: 1,649 Coed
Affiliation or Control: Independent Non-Profit IRS Status: 501(c)3
Highest Offering: Baccalaureate
Accreditation: NH, MUS, NURSE

01 Interim President ..... Dr. Georgia NUGENT
05 Provost & Dean of Faculty ..... Dr. Mark BRODL
10 Vice President Business & Finance ..... Mr. Matt BIERMAN
30 Vice President for Advancement ..... Mr. Steve SEIBRING
27 Director for Communications ..... Ms. Ann AUBRY
32 VP Student Affairs/Dean Students ..... Dr. Karla CARNEY-HALL
84 VP of Enrollment & Marketing ..... Ms. LeAnn HUGHES
07 Dean Admissions/AVP Enrollment Mgmt ..... Mr. Greg KING
09 AVP Instl Research/Plng/Evaluation ..... Dr. Michael THOMPSON
86 Dir Government/Community Relations ..... Mr. Carl F. TEICHMAN
04 Exec Assistant to the President ..... Ms. Julie ANDERSON
20 Assoc Provost Acad Plng/Standards ..... Prof. Lynda DUKE
20 Assoc Dean Curricular/Faculty Dev ..... Prof. Kevin SULLIVAN
15 Dir Human Resources/Title IX Coord ..... Ms. Cindy LOTZ
13 Asst Provost/Chief Technology Ofcr ..... Mr. Trey SHORT
110 Asst Vice Pres for Advancement ..... Mr. Carlo ROBUSTELLI
29 Asst VP of Alumni Engagement ..... Ms. Rosetta CLAY
38 AVP/Exec Dir Counseling/Health Svcs ... Dr. Annorrah MOORMAN
35 Asst VP of Student Affairs ..... Dr. Brandon COMMON
08 University Librarian ..... Dr. Scott WALTER
06 Registrar ..... Dr. Leslie BETZ
42 Univ Chaplain/Assoc Dean Students ..... Rev. Elyse NELSON WINGER
21 Controller ..... Mr. John BRYANT
37 Director of Financial Aid ..... Mr. Scott SEIBRING
64 Director of School of Music ..... Dr. Franklin LAREY
57 Director of School of Art ..... Prof. Julie JOHNSON
57 Director of School of Theatre Arts ..... Dr. Jean KERR
66 Director of School of Nursing ..... Dr. Victoria FOLSE
41 Director of Athletics ..... Prof. Mike WAGNER
29 Director of Alumni Engagement ..... Ms. Adriane POWELL
102 Dir Grants/Foundation Relations ..... Mr. Dick FOLSE
44 Director of Wesleyan Annual Fund ..... Ms. Elizabeth CHAMBERS-KLATT
36 Director of Career Center ..... Mr. Warren KISTNER
18 Director of Physical Plant ..... Mr. James J. BLUMBERG
88 Director of Sports Information ..... Vacant
93 Director of Diversity & Inclusion ..... Mr. Kwame PATTERSON
35 Director of Student Involvement ..... Mr. Kevin CAREY
94 Dir of Women's & Gender Studies ..... Dr. Carole MYSCOFSKI
104 Director of International Office ..... Ms. Stacey SHIMIZU
40 Bookstore Manager ..... Mr. Thaddeus SUTTER
26 Director of Marketing ..... Mr. Andrew KREISS

Institute for Clinical Social Work (H)

401 South State Street, Suite 822, Chicago IL 60605
County: Cook FICE Identification: 025737
Unit ID: 145886
Telephone: (312) 935-4232 Carnegie Class: Spec-4-yr-Other Health
FAX Number: (312) 935-4255 Calendar System: Semester
URL: www.icsw.edu
Established: 1981 Annual Graduate Tuition & Fees: N/A
Enrollment: 99 Coed
Affiliation or Control: Independent Non-Profit IRS Status: 501(c)3
Highest Offering: Doctorate; No Undergraduates
Accreditation: NH

01 President ..... Dr. Michelle C. STEWART
10 Vice Pres Finance/Operations ..... Michael BAUMAN
05 Academic Dean ..... Dr. Ida ROLDAN
37 Director of Student Financial Svcs ..... Ms. Shawna JENNINGS

John A. Logan College (I)

700 Logan College Road, Carterville IL 62918-2500
County: Williamson FICE Identification: 008076
Unit ID: 146205
Telephone: (618) 985-3741 Carnegie Class: Assoc/HVT-High Non
FAX Number: (618) 985-2248 Calendar System: Semester
URL: www.jalc.edu
Established: 1967 Annual Undergrad Tuition & Fees (In-District): $3,766

Enrollment: 3,933 Coed
Affiliation or Control: State/Local IRS Status: 501(c)3
Highest Offering: Associate Degree
Accreditation: NH, DA, DMS, MLTAD, OTA, SURGT

01 President ... Dr. Ron HOUSE
05 Vice President Instruction Services ... Ms. Melanie PECORD
10 VP Business Svcs/College Facilities ... Mr. Brad MCCORMICK
32 Dean Student Services ... Mr. Tim WILLIAMS
07 Assoc Dean of Admissions ... Ms. Christy STEWART
21 Dean Financial Operations ... Ms. Stacy BUCKINGHAM
20 Dean Academic Affairs ... Dr. Stephanie HARTFORD
75 Assoc Dean of Career/Technical Educ ... Mr. Scott WERNSMAN
20 Assoc Dean of Academic Affairs ... Mr. Nathan ARNETT
103 Dean Workforce Dev/Adult Education ... Ms. Kay FLEMING
51 Dean for Continuing Education ... Dr. Barry HANCOCK
37 Director of Student Financial Asst ... Ms. Pat JACKSON
124 Dir Recruit/Retention/Acad Advisor ... Dr. Steve O'KEEFE
35 Director of Student Activities ... Ms. Adrienne BARKLEY-GIFFIN
36 Dir of Career Services and Intl Ed ... Ms. Beth STEPHENS
102 Executive Director of Foundation ... Ms. Staci SHAFER
66 Director of Nursing ... Ms. Marilyn FALASTER
88 Director of Testing Services ... Ms. Christy MCBRIDE
15 Exec Dir of Human Resources/AAO ... Dr. Clay BREWER
18 Dir Buildings and Grounds ... Mr. Tim GIBSON
09 Director Institutional Research ... Mr. Eric PULLEY
25 Grant Writer ... Ms. Tammy GWALTNEY
04 Administrative Asst to President ... Ms. Sharyl MELVIN
101 Admin Asst Pres/Board of Trustees ... Ms. Susan MAY
28 Director of Diversity & Inclusion ... Ms. Toyin FOX
41 Athletic Director ... Mr. Greg STARRICK
117 Dir of Emergency Plng & Risk Mgmt ... Vacant
88 Business Analyst ... Mr. Jason SNIDER
38 Director of Student Success ... Ms. Carolyn GALLEGLY
121 Director Academic Advisement ... Ms. Stacy HOLLOWAY
96 Dir of Purchasing/Auxiliary Svcs ... Ms. Sue ZAMORA
88 CCR & R Director ... Ms. Lori LONGUEVILLE
88 Director of ASE ... Ms. Crystal HOSSELTON
56 Director of Adult Education ... Ms. Karla TABING
50 Director of Business & Industry ... Mr. Dennis WHITE
88 Director of Corporate Education ... Ms. Michelle HAMILTON
88 Exec Dir of Integrated Technology ... Mr. Scott ELLIOTT
88 Director of CHEC ... Mr. Bradley GRIFFITH
51 Director of Continuing Education ... Mr. Greg STETTLER
18 Director of Facility Services ... Mr. Chris NAEGELE
104 Coord of International Educ ... Vacant
105 WebMaster ... Mr. Phillip LANE
106 Assoc Dean of Education Technology ... Ms. Krystal REAGAN
08 Director of Library Services ... Mr. Adam RUBIN

John Wood Community College (A)

1301 S 48th Street, Quincy IL 62305-8736
County: Adams FICE Identification: 012813
Unit ID: 146278
Telephone: (217) 224-6500 Carnegie Class: Assoc/HVT-Mix Trad/Non
FAX Number: (217) 224-4208 Calendar System: Semester
URL: www.jwcc.edu
Established: 1974 Annual Undergrad Tuition & Fees (In-District): $4,890
Enrollment: 1,896 Coed
Affiliation or Control: State/Local IRS Status: 501(c)3
Highest Offering: Associate Degree
Accreditation: NH, SURGT

01 President ... Mr. Michael ELBE
05 Vice President for Instruction ... Dr. Laurel KLINKENBERG
10 Dean Business Svcs/Inst Effective ... Mr. Joshua WELKER
32 Dean Student Services ... Vacant
49 Dean Arts and Sciences ... Ms. Stephanie PHILLIPS
75 Dean Careers/Tech/Health Education ... Mr. David HETZLER
84 Dean Enrollment Svcs/Dir Finan Aid ... Ms. Melanie LECHTENBERG
07 Director Admissions ... Vacant
06 Registrar/Dean of Students ... Mr. Cody BAGGETT
21 Director Fiscal Services ... Ms. Susan FIFER
35 Director Support Services ... Mr. Robert HODGSON
13 Director Information Technology ... Mr. Joshua BRUECK
08 Director Learning Resource Center ... Ms. Barbara LIEBER
26 Director Public Relations/Marketing ... Ms. Tracy ORNE
30 Director Advancement ... Ms. Barbara HOLTHAUS
15 Director Human Resources ... Ms. Dana KEPPNER
18 Director Physical Plant ... Mr. Lou BARTA
37 Director Financial Aid ... Ms. Melanie LECHTENBERG
19 Dean of Ops/Chief of Campus Police ... Mr. Bill LATOUR
41 Director Athletics ... Mr. Brad HOYT
40 Manager Campus Services ... Ms. Lynn BLICKHAN
96 Purchasing Coordinator ... Ms. Darla SNYDER
47 Dept Chair Ag Sciences ... Mr. Gary SHUPE
77 Dept Chair Ofc Technology/Comp Sci ... Ms. Barbara STOLL
50 Dept Chair Business ... Ms. Cathy STEPHENS
81 Department Chair Mathematics ... Ms. Brenda GRAFF
65 Dept Chair Natural Sciences ... Dr. Christopher KAELKE
79 Dept Chair Lang/Lit/Hum/Fine Arts ... Ms. Christine WIEWEL
83 Dept Chair Social/Behavior Science ... Ms. Beth REINHARDT
04 Executive Asst to President ... Ms. Leah BENZ

Joliet Junior College (B)

1215 Houbolt Road, Joliet IL 60431-8938
County: Will FICE Identification: 001699
Unit ID: 146296
Telephone: (815) 729-9020 Carnegie Class: Assoc/MT-VT-Mix Trad/Non
FAX Number: N/A Calendar System: Semester
URL: www.jjc.edu
Established: 1901 Annual Undergrad Tuition & Fees (In-District): $4,380
Enrollment: 14,910 Coed
Affiliation or Control: State/Local IRS Status: 501(c)3
Highest Offering: Associate Degree
Accreditation: NH, ACBSP, ACFEI, ADNUR, CAHIIM, DMS, MUS

01 President ... Dr. Judy MITCHELL
10 VP Administrative Services ... Mr. Rob GALICK
05 VP Academic Affairs ... Dr. Randy FLETCHER
13 Exec Dir Information Technology ... Mr. Jim SERR
32 VP Student Development ... Dr. Yolanda FARMER
07 Director Admissions & Recruitment ... Ms. Jennifer KLOBERDANZ
37 Director Financial Aid ... Ms. Deanna FISK
15 Exec Dir Human Resources ... Ms. Malinda CARTER
16 Assistant Director Human Resources ... Ms. Judy CONNELLY
06 Registrar ... Vacant
18 Sr Director Facility Services ... Mr. Patrick VAN DUYNE
109 Director Business/Auxiliary Svcs ... Ms. Janice REEDUS
26 Exec Dir Commun/External Rels ... Ms. Kelly ROHDER-TONELLI
36 Director Career Services ... Ms. Bridgett LARKIN-BEENE
41 Director Athletics ... Mr. Gregory BRAUN
21 Director Financial Svcs/Controller ... Mr. Jeffrey HEAP
19 Dir Campus Safety & Police Chief ... Mr. Peter COMANDA
111 Ex Dir Inst Adv Exec Dir JJC Found ... Ms. Kristin MULVEY
09 Director of Institutional Research ... Mr. Joseph OFFERMANN
29 Alumni Relations & Fund Manager ... Ms. Carolyn ANDERSON
49 Dean Arts & Sciences ... Ms. Sonya WILLIAMS
103 Dean Applied Arts/Wrkforce Ed & Trn ... Ms. Amy MURPHY
75 Dean CTE ... Ms. Patty ZUCCARELLO
108 Sr Director Inst Effectiveness ... Ms. Krisin CIESEMIER
88 Coord GSD ... Dr. Angie KAYSEN-LUZBETAK
04 Senior Admin Asst to President ... Ms. Jennifer TENN
101 Secretary of the Institution/Board ... Ms. Joan TIERNEY
104 Coordinator Study Abroad ... Ms. Tamara BRATTOLI
106 Dir Online Education/E-learning ... Mr. Chris OSTWINKLE
84 Dean of Enrollment Management ... Mr. Robert MORRIS
110 Asst Dir Inst Advancement ... Ms. Amanda QUINN

Judson University (C)

1151 N State Street, Elgin IL 60123-1498
County: Kane FICE Identification: 001700
Unit ID: 146339
Telephone: (847) 628-2500 Carnegie Class: Masters/S
FAX Number: (847) 628-1027 Calendar System: Semester
URL: www.judsonu.edu
Established: 1913 Annual Undergrad Tuition & Fees: $29,860
Enrollment: 1,283 Coed
Affiliation or Control: American Baptist IRS Status: 501(c)3
Highest Offering: Doctorate
Accreditation: NH

01 President ... Dr. Gene CRUME
04 Exec Assistant to the President ... Ms. Tena ROBOTHAM
05 Provost/Chief Academic Officer . Dr. A. Gillian STEWART-WELLS
10 Interim VP for Business Affairs ... Ms. Sarah TAYLOR
06 VP for Student Success & Registrar ... Ms. Virginia GUTH
28 Assoc VP Diversity & Spirit Dev ... Dr. Curtis SARTOR
20 Assoc Provost/Academic Curriculum ... Dr. Lanette POTEETE-YOUNG
20 Assoc Provost of Faculty ... Vacant
08 Library Director ... Mr. Larry WILD
37 Director of Financial Aid ... Ms. Diana WINTON
07 Director of Admissions ... Dr. Molly SMITH
26 Director of Comm & Marketing ... Ms. Mary DULABAUM
36 Career Development Coach ... Ms. Doris HAUGEN
38 Dir of Student Health & Wellness ... Vacant
18 Asst VP for Campus Operations ... Mr. Nick SALZMANN
41 Athletic Director ... Mr. Joel POPENFOOSE
124 Dir of 1st Year Exp & Persistence ... Ms. Jaimee BARTHA
85 International Advisor ... Ms. Joy KRISPIN
23 Director of Health Center ... Ms. Susan WEBER
92 Honors Director ... Dr. James HALVERSON
101 Asst Sec to Board of Trustees ... Ms. Tena ROBOTHAM
09 Director of Institutional Research ... Mr. Chad BRIGGS
39 Coordinator Student Housing ... Ms. McKenna HAAS
88 RISE Program Director ... Ms. Gineen VARGAS
111 VP for Advancement and Alumni ... Ms. Kristen EGAN
32 Dean of Student Life & Leadership ... Ms. Aubree FLICKEMA
121 Dean Student Academic Support Svcs ... Ms. Heather JOHNSON
42 Dean of University Ministries ... Mr. Chris LASH

Kankakee Community College (D)

100 College Drive, Kankakee IL 60901-6505
County: Kankakee FICE Identification: 007690
Unit ID: 146348
Telephone: (815) 802-8100 Carnegie Class: Assoc/HVT-High Non
FAX Number: (815) 802-8101 Calendar System: Semester
URL: www.kcc.edu
Established: 1966 Annual Undergrad Tuition & Fees (In-District): $4,620
Enrollment: 3,025 Coed
Affiliation or Control: State/Local IRS Status: 501(c)3
Highest Offering: Associate Degree
Accreditation: NH, ADNUR, COARC, MLTAD, PNUR, PTAA

01 President ... Dr. Michael BOYD
04 Exec Asst to Pres & BOT ... Ms. Karen SLAGER
05 VP of Academic Affairs ... Dr. David NAZE
10 VP for Finance & Administration ... Dr. Vicki GARDNER
06 Registrar ... Mr. David HERMANN
32 VP of Student Dev & Services ... Dr. Jose DA SILVA
09 Director Institutional Research ... Dr. Purva RUSHI
31 Director Adult & Community Educ ... Ms. Margaret WOLF
103 Director of Workforce Development ... Ms. Dana WASHINGTON
37 Director Financial Aid ... Ms. Michelle HASIK
41 Director Athletics ... Mr. Todd POST
15 Director Human Resources ... Mr. David CAGLE
10 Director Financial Affairs ... Ms. Beth NUNLEY
50 Assoc Dean Business & Technology ... Mr. Paul CARLSON
51 Asst Dean Cont Educ & Career Svcs ... Ms. Mary POSING
18 Dir Campus Facilities & Security ... Mr. Rich SODERQUIST
81 Assoc Dean Math/Science Division ... Dr. Francesca CATALANO
76 Assoc Dean Health Careers Div ... Ms. Sheri CAGLE
121 Director Student Advisement ... Ms. Meredith PURCELL
76 Director Respiratory Therapist Pgm ... Ms. Jaclyn CRUZ
76 Director Medical Lab Technology ... Ms. Glenda FORNERIS
66 Director Nursing ... Ms. Kellee HAYES
88 Dir Physical Therapy Asst Pgm ... Ms. Jennifer BLANCHETTE
83 Assoc Dean Humanities/Social Sci ... Ms. Jennifer HUGGINS
76 Director Radiology Technology Pgm ... Ms. Darla JEPSON
13 Director Information Tech Svcs ... Mr. Michael O'CONNOR
102 Exec Director of KCC Foundation ... Ms. Kelly MYERS
88 Director Institutional Tech/Fac Dev ... Mr. Craig KEIGHER
62 Director Learning Resource Center ... Ms. Karen BECKER
26 Director Marketing ... Ms. Kari NUGENT
101 Board Recording Secretary ... Ms. Karen SLAGER
88 Director Support Services ... Ms. Kimberlee HARPIN

Kaskaskia College (E)

27210 College Road, Centralia IL 62801-7878
County: Clinton FICE Identification: 001701
Unit ID: 146366
Telephone: (618) 545-3000 Carnegie Class: Assoc/MT-VT-High Non
FAX Number: (618) 532-1990 Calendar System: Semester
URL: www.kaskaskia.edu
Established: 1940 Annual Undergrad Tuition & Fees (In-District): $4,470
Enrollment: 3,107 Coed
Affiliation or Control: State/Local IRS Status: 501(c)3
Highest Offering: Associate Degree
Accreditation: NH, ADNUR, COARC, DA, EMT, MLTAD, PTAA, RAD

01 President ... Mr. George EVANS
11 Vice Pres Administrative Services ... Mrs. Judy HEMKER
05 Vice Pres Instructional Services ... Dr. Ashley BECKER
32 Vice President of Student Services ... Dr. Susan BATCHELOR
75 Dean Career & Technical Education ... Mr. Nicolas FARLEY
49 Dean of Arts & Sciences ... Mrs. Kellie HENEGAR
66 Dean Nursing & Health Sciences ... Mrs. Julie OBERMARK
09 Dir Institutional Effectiveness ... Mr. Bruce FISCHER
108 Associate Dean of Inst Assessment ... Mr. Alan BOERNGEN
15 Director of Human Resources ... Mrs. Jill HERCULES
18 Director Facilities/Physical Plant ... Mr. Jennings CARTER
96 Director Purchasing/Auxiliary Svcs ... Mr. Craig ROPER
37 Director of Financial Aid ... Mrs. Jill KLOSTERMANN
76 Director of Radiologic Technology ... Mrs. Mimi POLCZYNSKI
76 Program Coordinator PTA ... Mrs. Michelle WESSEL
13 Chief Information Officer ... Mr. Johnny MATTHEWS
26 Director of Marketing ... Mr. Travis HENSON
40 Bookstore Manager ... Ms. Cynthia WEBBER
07 Dean of Enrollment Services ... Ms. Amy TROUTT
88 Regional Director of Educ Centers ... Mrs. Cheryl BOEHNE
111 Dir Inst Advancement Programs ... Mrs. Suzanne CHRIST
19 Director of Public Safety ... Mr. Jeffrey BROWN
04 Admin Assistant to the President ... Mrs. Cathy QUICK
06 Registrar ... Mrs. Jenna LAMMERS
08 Chief Library Officer ... Ms. Laura VAHLKAMP

Kishwaukee College (F)

21193 Malta Road, Malta IL 60150-9600
County: De Kalb FICE Identification: 007684
Unit ID: 146418
Telephone: (815) 825-2086 Carnegie Class: Assoc/HVT-Mix Trad/Non
FAX Number: (815) 825-2072 Calendar System: Semester
URL: www.kish.edu
Established: 1968 Annual Undergrad Tuition & Fees (In-District): $4,800
Enrollment: 3,417 Coed
Affiliation or Control: State/Local IRS Status: 501(c)3
Highest Offering: Associate Degree
Accreditation: NH, ADNUR, EMT, RAD

01 President ... Dr. Laurie BOROWICZ
05 Vice President Instruction ... Dr. Joanne KANTNER
32 Vice President Student Services ... Ms. Michelle ROTHMEYER
20 Asst Vice President of Instruction ... Mr. Judson CURRY
11 Exec Director of Campus Operations ... Mr. Dave DAMMON
88 Director of Curriculum & Programs ... Ms. Terry Lyn FUNSTON
75 Exec Dean Career/Tech Education ... Ms. Bette CHILTON
121 Director of Student Success ... Ms. Sonia REISING
06 Registrar ... Ms. Tina SWIGER
49 Dean Liberal Arts/Science/Business ... Mr. Chase BUDZIAK
10 CFO ... Ms. Jill HANSEN
102 Exec Director College Relations ... Ms. Kayte HAMEL
13 Director Information Technology ... Mr. Robert MCGARRY
30 Director Development & Compliance ... Mr. Nick PIAZZA
15 Exec Dir Human Resources ... Ms. Cindy MCCLUSKEY
88 Director Student Involvement ... Mr. Scott KAWALL
04 Executive Assistant to President ... Ms. Michelle OHLINGER
66 Director of Nursing ... Ms. Melinda FINCH
09 Director of Institutional Research ... Mr. Matthew CRULL
103 Director of Business Partnerships ... Ms. LaCretia KONAN
25 Chief Contract/Grants Administrator ... Ms. Barbara LEACH
37 Manager of Financial Aid ... Mr. Adam GISSELER
96 Purchasing Accountant ... Ms. Brittney ZICK

Knox College (A)

2 E South Street, Galesburg IL 61401-4999

County: Knox FICE Identification: 001704
Unit ID: 146427

Telephone: (309) 341-7000 Carnegie Class: Bac-A&S
FAX Number: (309) 341-7090 Calendar System: Trimester
URL: www.knox.edu
Established: 1837 Annual Undergrad Tuition & Fees: $46,554
Enrollment: 1,356 Coed
Affiliation or Control: Independent Non-Profit IRS Status: 501(c)3
Highest Offering: Baccalaureate
Accreditation: NH

01 President ....Dr. Teresa L. AMOTT
101 Secretary of the College ....Ms. Peggy J. WARE
05 Provost/Dean of College ....Dr. Michael A. SCHNEIDER
10 Vice Pres for Finance & Admin Svcs ....Mr. Paul W. EISENMENGER
111 Vice President for Advancement ....Ms. Beverly HOLMES
07 Vice Pres Enrollment/Dean of Admiss ....Mr. Paul R. STEENIS
32 VP for Student Development ....Dr. Anne R. EHRLICH
26 VP Communications ....Vacant
06 Registrar ....Dr. Jerome MINER
32 Dean of Students ....Ms. Debbie SOUTHERN
20 Associate Dean of College ....Dr. Timothy J. FOSTER
37 Director Financial Aid ....Ms. Leigh T. BRINSON
08 Librarian ....Mr. Jeffrey A. DOUGLAS
36 Exec Dir Career Development ....Mr. Scott CRAWFORD
13 VP/CIO Information Technology Svcs ....Mr. Steven HALL
15 AVP Director Human Resources ....Ms. Crystal D. BOHM
18 Director Facilities Services ....Mr. Scott MAUST
21 Controller ....Ms. Bobby Jo MAURER
86 Dir Government & Community Relation ....Ms. Karrie HEARTLEIN
29 Dir Alumni & Constituent Programs ....Vacant
38 Director of Counseling Services ....Ms. Janell J. MCGRUDER
19 Director Campus Safety ....Mr. Mark A. WELKER
09 Dir Institutional Research/Assess ....Vacant
102 Dir Corporate/Foundation Relations ....Ms. Jan K. WOLBERS
44 Director Annual or Planned Giving ....Mr. Scott PARK
105 Director Web Services ....Ms. Bren TOOLEY
39 Director of Campus Life ....Ms. Eleanor KAHN
41 Director of Athletics ....Ms. Daniella J. IRLE

Lake Forest College (B)

555 N Sheridan Road, Lake Forest IL 60045-2338

County: Lake FICE Identification: 001706
Unit ID: 146481

Telephone: (847) 234-3100 Carnegie Class: Bac-A&S
FAX Number: N/A Calendar System: Semester
URL: www.lakeforest.edu
Established: 1857 Annual Undergrad Tuition & Fees: $47,064
Enrollment: 1,542 Coed
Affiliation or Control: Independent Non-Profit IRS Status: 501(c)3
Highest Offering: Master's
Accreditation: NH, IPSY

01 President ....Mr. Stephen D. SCHUTT

Lake Forest Graduate School of Management (C)

1905 W Field Court, Lake Forest IL 60045-4824

County: Lake FICE Identification: 023192
Unit ID: 146490

Telephone: (847) 234-5005 Carnegie Class: Spec-4-yr-Bus
FAX Number: (847) 295-3656 Calendar System: Semester
URL: www.lfgsm.edu
Established: 1946 Annual Graduate Tuition & Fees: N/A
Enrollment: 370 Coed
Affiliation or Control: Independent Non-Profit IRS Status: 501(c)3
Highest Offering: Master's; No Undergraduates
Accreditation: NH

01 President ....Mr. Jeffrey J. ANDERSON
05 VP and Chief Academic Officer ....Dr. Bryan J. WATKINS
10 VP Finance & CFO ....Mr. Thomas PEROZZI
20 Dean Educational Programs & Dev ....Dr. Neil HOLMAN
06 Registrar ....Ms. Diana BOOTH
07 Senior Director of Admissions ....Ms. Carolyn BRUNE
32 Director of Student Experience ....Ms. Currie GASCHE
09 Asst Dir Institutional Research ....Ms. Jeanne KUETER
37 Director of Financial Aid ....Ms. Connie ELDRIDGE
88 VP Corporate Learning ....Ms. Carrie BUCHWALD
04 Executive Assistant to President ....Ms. Dana KAECHELE

Lake Land College (D)

5001 Lake Land Boulevard, Mattoon IL 61938-9366

County: Coles FICE Identification: 007644
Unit ID: 146506

Telephone: (217) 234-5253 Carnegie Class: Assoc/HVT-High Non
FAX Number: (217) 234-5400 Calendar System: Semester
URL: https://www.lakelandcollege.edu/
Established: 1966 Annual Undergrad Tuition & Fees (In-District): $4,110
Enrollment: 4,965 Coed
Affiliation or Control: State/Local IRS Status: 501(c)3
Highest Offering: Associate Degree
Accreditation: NH, ADNUR, DH, EMT, PNUR, PTAA

01 President ....Dr. Josh BULLOCK
100 Senior Executive to the President ....Ms. Jean Anne GRUNLOH
10 VP for Business Services ....Mr. Bryan GLECKLER
05 VP for Academic Services ....Mr. Jon ALTHAUS
32 Vice President for Student Services ....Ms. Beth GERL
88 Dean of Correctional Pgms South ....Mr. Brandon YOUNG
88 Dean of Correctional Pgms North ....Ms. Jennifer BILLINGSLEY
07 Dean of Admissions Services ....Mr. Jon VAN DYKE
88 Assoc Dean Corrections Taylorville ....Mr. Robert EIFERT
88 Assoc Dean Corrections Graham ....Mr. Jeremy SWINDLE
88 Assoc Dean Corrections Western ....Ms. Malea HARNEY
88 Assoc Dean Correction IL River ....Ms. Deborah COLLINS
88 Assoc Dean Corrections Southwestern ....Mr. Harvey GROENNERT
88 Assoc Dean Corrections Jacksonville ....Vacant
88 Assoc Dean Corrections Lawrence ....Vacant
88 Assoc Dean Corrections Robinson ....Vacant
88 Assoc Dean Corrections Vandalia ....Ms. Tabitha WELCH
88 Assoc Dean Corrections Hill ....Mr. Chris WILLIAMS
111 Exec Dir College Advance/Foundation ....Ms. Jacqueline JOINES
88 Site Dir Corrections Vienna/Shawnee ....Mr. Blake MCCONNELL
21 Comptroller ....Ms. Madge SHOOT
50 Dir Center for Business & Industry ....Ms. Bonnie MOORE
08 Director of Library Services ....Mr. Scott DRONE-SILVERS
26 Dir of Marketing/Public Relations ....Mrs. Kelly ALLEE
13 Dir of Information Systems/Services ....Mr. Lee SPANIOL
37 Dir of Financial Aid/Veteran Svcs ....Ms. Paula CARPENTER
15 Director of Human Resources ....Ms. Dustha WAHLS
25 Dir Grants & Academic Operations ....Ms. Emily RAMAGE
35 Director Student Life ....Ms. Valerie LYNCH
109 Director of Auxiliary Services ....Ms. Christina KRAMER
29 Dir of Alumni Rels/Annual Giving ....Mr. Dave COX
36 Director of Career Services ....Ms. Tina MOORE
38 Chair of Counseling/Judicial Affs ....Ms. Emily HARTKE
18 Dir of Physical Plant Operations ....Mr. Scott RAWLINGS
41 Director of Athletics ....Mr. William JACKSON
09 Director of Institutional Research ....Dr. Mary BREER
84 Coordinator of Enrollment Services ....Ms. Paula SMITH
103 VP Workforce Solutions/Cmty Educ ....Dr. Jim HULL
20 Associate Dean Corrections St Ch ....Dr. Tasha DAVIS-LONG
20 Associate Dean Corrections Harris ....Ms. Tomi GRAVATT
20 Associate Dean Murphysboro ....Mr. Doung LAUMBATTUS
20 Associate Dean Corrections Sherida ....Mr. Alan MORTENSEN
20 Associate Dean Big Muddy ....Ms. Penny MURPHY
20 Associate Dean Corrections East M ....Ms. Ginger MURRAY
20 Associate Dean Pinckneyville ....Ms. Serenna OWENS
20 Associate Dean Shawnee ....Mr. Richard PATERA
103 Director Workforce Investment ....Mr. Gerry SCHLECHTE
20 Associate Dean Joilet ....Mr. Garry SCOTT
20 Associate Dean Dixon ....Mr. Keith STEVENSON
19 Chief of Police ....Mr. Jeff BRANSON

Lakeview College of Nursing (E)

903 N Logan Avenue, Danville IL 61832-3788

County: Vermilion FICE Identification: 010501
Unit ID: 146533

Telephone: (217) 709-0920 Carnegie Class: Spec-4-yr-Other Health
FAX Number: (217) 709-0954 Calendar System: Semester
URL: www.lakeviewcol.edu
Established: 1987 Annual Undergrad Tuition & Fees: N/A
Enrollment: 223 Coed
Affiliation or Control: Independent Non-Profit IRS Status: 501(c)3
Highest Offering: Baccalaureate
Accreditation: NH, NURSE

01 President ....Ms. Sheila MINGEE
05 Dean ....Ms. Lanette STUCKEY
06 Registrar/Director of Enrollment ....Ms. Connie YOUNG
08 Library Director/IT Coordinator ....Ms. Miranda SHAKE
04 Administrative Asst to President ....Ms. Karlee THOMEN

Lewis and Clark Community College (F)

5800 Godfrey Road, Godfrey IL 62035-2466

County: Madison FICE Identification: 010020
Unit ID: 146603

Telephone: (618) 468-7000 Carnegie Class: Assoc/HVT-High Non
FAX Number: (618) 466-2798 Calendar System: Semester
URL: www.lc.edu
Established: 1970 Annual Undergrad Tuition & Fees (In-District): $3,552
Enrollment: 7,000 Coed
Affiliation or Control: State/Local IRS Status: 501(c)3
Highest Offering: Associate Degree
Accreditation: NH, ADNUR, DA, DH, EMT, MAAB, OTA

01 President ....Dr. Dale T. CHAPMAN
05 Vice President Academic Affairs ....Dr. Linda CHAPMAN
84 Vice President Enrollment Services ....Mr. Kent SCHEFFEL
32 Vice Pres Student Engagement ....Dr. Sean HILL
11 Vice President Administration ....Ms. Lori ARTIS
10 Vice President Finance ....Mrs. Mary SCHULTE
114 Chief Budget Officer ....Mrs. Nancy KAISER
88 Director Corp & Comm Learning ....Mrs. Kathy WILLIS
13 Chief Information Officer ....Mr. Jeff WATSON
09 Dir Institutional Res/Library Svcs ....Mr. Dennis KRIEB
06 Registrar ....Ms. Heidi SCOTT
41 Director Athletics ....Mr. Doug STOTLER
07 Director of Enrollment Center ....Ms. Delfina DORNES
15 Director Human Resources ....Mr. Gabe SPRINGER
18 Facilities Manager ....Mr. Mike RANDALL
19 Director Security ....Mr. Brad RAISH
26 Manager Media Services ....Ms. Laura INLOW
28 Coordinator Diversity & Inclusion ....Ms. Tandra TAYLOR
30 Director of Development ....Ms. Debbie EDELMAN
37 Director Financial Aid ....Ms. Angela WEAVER

Lewis University (G)

One University Parkway, Romeoville IL 60446-2200

County: Will FICE Identification: 001707
Unit ID: 146612

Telephone: (815) 838-0500 Carnegie Class: Masters/L
FAX Number: (815) 838-9456 Calendar System: Semester
URL: www.lewisu.edu
Established: 1932 Annual Undergrad Tuition & Fees: $32,450
Enrollment: 6,506 Coed
Affiliation or Control: Roman Catholic IRS Status: 501(c)3
Highest Offering: Doctorate
Accreditation: NH, ACBSP, #CAATE, CAEPN, NURSE, SW

01 President ....Dr. David J. LIVINGSTON
05 Provost ....Dr. Christopher SINDT
32 Sr Vice President Student Services ....Mr. Joseph FALESE
10 Senior Vice Pres/CFO ....Mrs. Carolyn HEAD
84 Sr VP Enrollment Mgmt/Marketing ....Mr. Raymond KENNELLY
111 VP University Advancement ....Mr. Luigi AMENDOLA
07 Dean of Undergraduate Admission ....Mrs. Ashley SKIDMORE
35 Dean of Student Services ....Ms. Katheryn SLATTERY
88 VP Mission/Int Assoc Prov Acad Affs ....Dr. Kurt SCHACKMUTH
20 Assoc Prov for Acad Admin & Accred ....Dr. Kathy S. KREMER
49 Dean College Arts & Sciences ....Dr. Bonnie BONDAVALLI
50 Dean College Business ....Mr. Ryan BUTT
66 Co-Interim Dean CONHP GA ....Dr. Suling LI
66 Co-Interim Dean CONHP UG ....Ms. Jane TRAINOR
53 Interim Dean College of Education ....Dr. Bonnie BONDAVALLI
15 Assoc Vice Pres Human Resources ....Ms. Graciela DUFOUR
09 Assoc VP Inst Research/Planning ....Dr. Kang BAI
21 Assistant Vice Pres for Finance ....Ms. Teresa KREJCI
08 Interim Director of Library ....Mr. Andrew LENAGHAN
06 Registrar ....Mr. Gilbert MARTINEZ
37 Director of Financial Aid ....Ms. Janeen DECHARINTE
26 Director Marketing/Communications ....Dr. Ramona LAMONTAGNE
41 Director of Athletics ....Dr. John PLANEK
38 Director of Counseling Services ....Ms. Jill WHITAKER
19 Chief of Police ....Mr. James MONTANARI
42 Director of University Ministry ....Mr. Steve ZLATIC
88 Dir of Meetings/Events/Conferences ....Ms. Julie PENNER
85 Director International Student Svcs ....Mr. Michael FEKETE
91 Director of Administrative Systems ....Ms. Johanna REBMAN
13 Chief Information Officer ....Dr. LeRoy BUTLER
29 Executive Dir of Alumni Engagement ....Ms. Mary Colleen AHEARN
96 Director of Opers and Purchasing ....Ms. Jennifer SKVARLA
36 Exec Director of Career Services ....Ms. Mary MYERS
04 Administrative Asst to President ....Ms. Dawn PECKLER
102 Dir Foundation & Corp Relations ....Ms. Jennifer DOHERTY
104 Director of Intl Study Abroad ....Mr. Christopher SWANSON
105 Director of Web Development ....Mr. Sylvain GOYETTE
18 Assoc VP for Facilities ....Mr. Keith KAMERON
25 Director of Sponsored Programs ....Vacant
23 Director Health Services ....Ms. Michele RONCHETTI
39 Director of Residence Life ....Mr. Fredrick GANDY
30 Senior Development Officer ....Ms. Javonda PELMAN
44 Director Planned Giving ....Mr. Robert KANONIK

Lincoln Christian University (H)

100 Campus View Drive, Lincoln IL 62656-2167

County: Logan FICE Identification: 001708
Unit ID: 146667

Telephone: (217) 732-3168 Carnegie Class: Spec-4-yr-Faith
FAX Number: (217) 732-5914 Calendar System: Semester
URL: www.lincolnchristian.edu
Established: 1944 Annual Undergrad Tuition & Fees: $13,200
Enrollment: 789 Coed
Affiliation or Control: Christian Churches And Churches of Christ
IRS Status: 501(c)3
Highest Offering: Doctorate
Accreditation: NH, BI, CACREP, THEOL

01 President ....Dr. Donald GREEN
03 Executive Vice President ....Dr. Silas MCCORMICK
10 Vice President of Finance ....Mr. G. Steve POPENFOOSE
32 VP of Student Development ....Mrs. Jill DICKEN
05 Int Chief Academic Officer ....Dr. Barney WELLS
111 VP of University Advancement ....Vacant
29 VP of Alumni Services ....Mr. Lynn LAUGHLIN
06 Registrar ....Mr. Shawn SMITH
08 Director of Library Services ....Ms. Nancy OLSON
37 Director of Financial Aid ....Ms. Nancy SIDDENS
101 Admin Asst to Pres/Secy Bd of Gov ....Mrs. Cindy POPEJOY
13 Director of Campus Technology ....Mr. Jeremiah PROCTOR
15 Director of Human Resources ....Mrs. Marla BENNETT
41 Athletic Director ....Mr. Christian LOWRY
18 Chief Facilities/Physical Plant ....Mr. Freddie TEDRICK
26 Associate Director of Marketing ....Mr. Nathan ROBERTS
07 Director of Admissions ....Mr. Brady CREMEENS
73 Graduate and Seminary Dean ....Dr. Barney WELLS
20 Undergraduate Academic Dean ....Dr. Pete VERKRUYSE

Lincoln College (I)

300 Keokuk Street, Lincoln IL 62656-1699

County: Logan FICE Identification: 001709
Unit ID: 146676

Telephone: (217) 732-3155 Carnegie Class: Bac/Assoc-Mixed

FAX Number: (217) 732-8859 Calendar System: Semester
URL: www.lincolncollege.edu
Established: 1865 Annual Undergrad Tuition & Fees: $18,600
Enrollment: 1,121 Coed
Affiliation or Control: Independent Non-Profit IRS Status: 501(c)3
Highest Offering: Master's
Accreditation: NH, IACBE

01 President .... Dr. David M. GERLACH
05 Vice President for Academic Affairs .... Ms. Michelle BALDWIN
30 Vice President for Advancement .... Ms. Debbie ACKERMAN
84 VP for Enroll Mgmt & Student Svcs .... Ms. Susan BOEHLER
10 Vice Pres Finance & Administration .... Mr. Greg A. EIMER
07 Dean of Enrollment Management .... Mr. Jason GARBER
32 Dean of Students .... Mrs. Bridgett THOMAS
107 Exec Dir Center for Adult Learning .... Mr. Vance LAINE
88 Director of Academic Advising .... Mr. Jacob HARNACKE
06 Registrar .... Mr. Nate MCCOY
08 Head Librarian .... Mr. Derrick CASEY
13 Director of Information Technology .... Mr. Kyle LAVERY
21 Controller .... Ms. Tiffany WORTH
15 Director of Human Resources .... Mrs. Kristen ROBINSON
18 Director of Building & Grounds .... Mr. Bernard ATANUS
37 Director of Financial Aid .... Mrs. Sherry SCHONAUER
41 Athletic Director .... Mr. Mark PERDUE
40 Bookstore Manager .... Mrs. Amy RODRIGUEZ

Lincoln College of Technology (A)

8317 West North Avenue, Melrose Park IL 60160-1605
County: Cook FICE Identification: 010316
Unit ID: 146700
Telephone: (708) 344-4700 Carnegie Class: Spec 2-yr-Tech
FAX Number: (708) 345-4065 Calendar System: Semester
URL: www.lincolntech.edu
Established: 1950 Annual Undergrad Tuition & Fees: N/A
Enrollment: 719 Coed
Affiliation or Control: Proprietary IRS Status: Proprietary
Highest Offering: Associate Degree
Accreditation: ACCSC

01 Campus President .... Karen M. CLARK
05 Campus VP of Education .... Larry KESHNER
11 Director Administrative Services .... Karen STEPINA
36 Director of Career Services .... Keston EDWARDS
37 Director of Financial Aid .... Cliff DAVIS
04 Administrative Asst to President .... Mindy GUARINO
07 Director of Admissions .... Kevin FERGUSON
08 Head Librarian .... Karen MCELWAIN

Lincoln Land Community College (B)

5250 Shepherd Road, PO Box 19256,
Springfield IL 62794-9256
County: Sangamon FICE Identification: 007170
Unit ID: 146685
Telephone: (217) 786-2200 Carnegie Class: Assoc/MT-VT-High Non
FAX Number: (217) 786-2468 Calendar System: Semester
URL: www.llcc.edu
Established: 1967 Annual Undergrad Tuition & Fees (In-District): $3,372
Enrollment: 6,259 Coed
Affiliation or Control: Local IRS Status: 501(c)3
Highest Offering: Associate Degree
Accreditation: NH, ADNUR, COARC, NDT, OTA, PNUR, RAD, SURGT

01 President .... Dr. Charlotte J. WARREN
05 Vice President Academic Services .... Dr. Vern L. LINDQUIST
11 Vice President Administrative Svcs .... Vacant
103 VP Workforce Dev/Cmty Educ .... Dr. Judy JOZAITIS
32 Vice President Student Services .... Dr. Lesley J. FREDERICK
26 Exec Dir Public Relations/Marketing .... Ms. Lynn WHALEN
13 Chief Information Officer .... Mr. Esteban CRUZ
102 Exec Director LLCC Foundation .... Ms. Karen A. SANDERS
15 AVP Human Resources .... Ms. Junell A. RANSDELL
19 Police Chief .... Mr. Bradley D. GENTRY
10 AVP Finance .... Ms. Karie L. LONGHTA
121 Exec Director Academic Success .... Ms. Julie CLEVENGER
09 AVP IR and Effectiveness .... Dr. Tricia A. KUJAWA
57 Dean Language/Arts/Communication . Mr. J. Timothy HUMPHREY
76 Dean Health Professions .... Dr. Cynthia L. MASKEY
20 AVP Academic Innov & Effectiveness .... Vacant
81 Dean Mathematics/Computer Sciences .... Mr. William D. BADE
83 Dean Social Science & Business .... Dr. Victor K. BRODERICK
79 Dean English & Humanities .... Dr. Ryan ROBERTS
47 Dean Natural & Agriculture Science .... Vacant
72 Dean Applied/Engr Technologies .... Ms. Nancy SWEET
84 AVP Enrollment Services .... Ms. Shanda BYER
86 AVP Corp/Govt Trng & Econ Devel .... Ms. Paula J. LUEBBERT
08 Assoc Dean Library .... Ms. Tamara KUHN-SCHNELL
106 Dean Academic Innov/eLearning .... Ms. Becky PARTON
41 Director Athletics .... Mr. Ron RIGGLE
14 Director IT Systems .... Mr. Ben ROTH
14 Director IT Service and Support .... Ms. Joni BERNAHL
18 Director Facilities .... Mr. David BRETSCHER
91 Director IT Development .... Ms. Soodi NASSIRPOUR
66 Assoc Dean Nursing .... Ms. Sonja K. HARVEY
120 Dir Instructional Technology .... Mr. Barry P. LAMB
37 Director Financial Aid .... Ms. Allison MILLS
124 Director Student Transitions .... Mr. Chris BARRY
93 Dir Student Support Services .... Dr. Deanna M. BLACKWELL
114 Dir Budget & Fiscal Services .... Ms. Rachel N. PATAROZZI
117 Dir Construction and EHS .... Mr. Timothy R. ERVIN
109 Director Campus Services .... Mr. Andrew BLAYLOCK
35 Assistant VP Student Success .... Ms. Leslie R. JOHNSON
121 Director Student Success .... Dr. Scott E. QUEENER
88 Director Small Business Devel Ctr .... Mr. Kevin LUST
22 Dir Empl Bnft Svc/Eq Oppty Cmpl Ofc .... Ms. Nicole M. RALPH
07 Dir Admissions/Records/Registration .... Mr. Ashly THOMAS
96 Purchasing Manager .... Mr. Dwayne CURRY

Lindenwood University Belleville Campus (C)

2600 West Main Street, Belleville IL 62226
Telephone: (618) 239-6000 Identification: 770322
Accreditation: &NH, ACBSP

† Branch campus of Lindenwood University, Saint Charles, MO

Loyola University Chicago (D)

1032 W. Sheridan Road, Chicago IL 60660
County: Cook FICE Identification: 001710
Unit ID: 146719
Telephone: (773) 274-3000 Carnegie Class: DU-Higher
FAX Number: (312) 915-7003 Calendar System: Semester
URL: www.luc.edu
Established: 1870 Annual Undergrad Tuition & Fees: $44,048
Enrollment: 16,673 Coed
Affiliation or Control: Roman Catholic IRS Status: 501(c)3
Highest Offering: Doctorate
Accreditation: NH, CAEP, CLPSY, COPSY, DENT, DIETI, EMT, FEPAC, LAW, MED, NURSE, PH, SCPSY, SW, THEA, THEOL

01 President .... Dr. Jo Ann ROONEY
05 Acting Prov Academic Affairs .... Dr. Margaret F. CALLAHAN
84 VP Enrollment Management .... Mr. Paul G. ROBERTS
32 VP Student Development .... Ms. Jane NEUFELD
13 VP Information Services/CIO .... Ms. Susan M. MALISCH
88 Assoc Provost Curriculum Dev .... Dr. Jo Beth D'AGOSTINO
88 Assoc Provost Mission & Identity .... Dr. John HARDT
46 Assoc Provost Research Services .... Dr. Terri PIGOT
88 Assoc Provost Finance & Operations .... Ms. Joanna PAPPAS
08 Assoc Provost & Dir HSD Library .... Ms. Gail HENDLER
88 Asst Prov Dir Academic Business Ops .... Ms. Joanna PAPPAS
88 Asst Prov & Dir Faculty Admin .... Ms. Anne C. REULAND
88 Asst Prov Educ Resources HSD .... Rev. Keith MUCCINO, SJ
28 Asst Provost Academic Diversity .... Dr. Christopher MANNING
108 Asst Prov Inst Effectiveness .... Dr. David B. SLAVSKY
121 Asst Provost Student Academic Svcs .... Ms. Shawna COOPER-GIBSON
31 Assoc VP Campus/Community Planning .... Ms. Jennifer R. CLARK
18 Assoc VP Capital Projects .... Ms. Kana HENNING
45 Assoc VP Capital Planning .... Mr. David BEALL
88 Assoc VP Informatics/System Dev .... Mr. Ronald N. PRICE
88 Assoc VP Information Services .... Mr. Jim SIBENALLER
14 Assoc VP Information Services .... Mr. Bruce A. MONTES
16 Assoc VP Human Resources .... Ms. Joan C. STASIAK
14 Assoc VP Information Services .... Mr. Dan VONDER HEIDE
88 Asst VP Facilities .... Mr. Michael LOFTSGAARDEN
35 Asst VP & Dean of Students .... Dr. William RODRIGUEZ
39 Asst VP/Director Residence Life .... Ms. Deborah SCHMIDT-ROGERS
41 Athletic Director .... Mr. Steve WATSON
65 Dean Inst Environmental Sustain .... Dr. Nancy TUCHMAN
08 Dean Libraries .... Ms. Marianne P. RYAN
58 Dean Graduate School & Research ..... Rev. Thomas J. REGAN, SJ
49 Dean Arts & Sciences .... Rev. Thomas J. REGAN, SJ
63 Interim Dean School of Medicine .... Dr. Sam J. MARZO
66 Dean School of Nursing .... Dr. Vicki A. KEOUGH
104 Exec Dir Intl Programs .... Vacant
118 Dir Compensation & Benefits .... Vacant
19 Dir Campus Safety .... Mr. Thomas MURRAY
88 Dir of Student Complex .... Ms. Dawn M. COLLINS
27 Dir Brand Marketing .... Vacant
12 Dir Lurec Operations .... Mr. Kevin GINTY
28 Dir Student Diversity/Multicultural .... Mr. Joseph SAUCEDO
88 Dir Campus Ministry .... Ms. Ginny MCCARTHY
23 Dir of Wellness Center .... Ms. Joan HOLDEN
37 Dir of Financial Aid .... Mr. Tobyn L. FRIAR
88 Dir Faculty Center Ignatian Pedago .... Dr. Matthew THIBEAU
90 Dir System Implement & Consulting .... Vacant
42 Dir Campus Ministry .... Dr. Lisa REITER
88 Dir Global Initiatives .... Fraser S. TURNER
102 Dir of Corporate & Foundation Rels .... Vacant
09 Asst Dir Institutional Research .... Dr. Ping TSUI
07 Dir Undergraduate Admissions .... Ms. Erin T. MORIATY
36 Dir Career Development Center .... Ms. Kathryn JACKSON
28 Dir Cultural Affairs & LUMA .... Vacant
120 Dir Online Learning .... Mr. John GURNAK
88 Dir Vietnam Center .... Mr. Richard C. ALBRIGHTY

Loyola University Health Sciences Campus (E)

2160 S First Avenue, Maywood IL 60153
Telephone: (708) 216-9000 Identification: 770080
Accreditation: &NH, PAST

Loyola University Water Tower Campus (F)

820 N Michigan Avenue, Chicago IL 60611
Telephone: (312) 915-6000 Identification: 770079
Accreditation: &NH

Lutheran School of Theology at Chicago (G)

1100 E 55th Street, Chicago IL 60615-5199
County: Cook FICE Identification: 001712
Unit ID: 146728
Telephone: (773) 256-0700 Carnegie Class: Spec-4-yr-Faith
FAX Number: (773) 256-0782 Calendar System: Semester
URL: www.lstc.edu
Established: 1860 Annual Graduate Tuition & Fees: N/A
Enrollment: 201 Coed
Affiliation or Control: Evangelical Lutheran Church In America
IRS Status: 501(c)3
Highest Offering: Doctorate; No Undergraduates
Accreditation: #NH, THEOL

01 President .... Dr. James NIEMAN
04 Assistant to the President .... Ms. Patti DEBIAS
108 Exec for Assessment and Planning .... Ms. Christine YUCHA
05 Dean for Academic Affairs .... Dr. Esther MENN
88 Director of the MDiv Programs .... Dr. Kathleen BILLMAN
88 Director of the MA Programs .... Dr. Kathleen BILLMAN
58 Director of Advanced Studies .... Dr. Ben STEWART
42 Pastor to the Community .... Rev. Erik CHRISTENSEN
11 Vice President for Operations .... Mr. Bob BERRIDGE
111 Vice President for Advancement .... Mr. Clyde WALTER
10 Vice President for Finance .... Ms. Andrea FINNEGAN
32 Dean of Student Services .... Dr. Scott CHALMERS
06 Registrar .... Ms. Patricia A. BARTLEY
26 Director of Communications/Mktg .... Ms. Janet BODEN
08 Interim Director of Library .... Mr. Barry HOPKINS
13 Dir of Information Technology Svcs .... Mr. Kenesa DEBELA
15 Chief Human Resources Officer .... Mr. Aaron COPLEY-SPIVEY

MacCormac College (H)

29 E Madison Street 2nd Floor, Chicago IL 60602-4405
County: Cook FICE Identification: 001716
Unit ID: 146816
Telephone: (312) 922-1884 Carnegie Class: Spec 2-yr-Other
FAX Number: (312) 922-4286 Calendar System: Semester
URL: www.maccormac.edu
Established: 1904 Annual Undergrad Tuition & Fees: $12,660
Enrollment: 278 Coed
Affiliation or Control: Independent Non-Profit IRS Status: 501(c)3
Highest Offering: Associate Degree
Accreditation: NH

10 Dean of Finance/Operations .... Mr. Matt GAWENDA
00 Chancellor .... Dr. Marnelle ALEXIS STEPHENS
01 Interim President/Dean of Finance .... Mr. Matt GAWENDA
05 Int Dean Acad/Dean Student Affairs .... Dr. Stephen MURRAY
06 Registrar .... Ms. Mariza SILVA
37 Director of Financial Aid .... Ms. Jamieta HOSKINS
84 Dean of Admission .... Mr. Raymond KOHL
26 Dir Communications/Public Relations .... Mr. Adam HITZEMAN

MacMurray College (I)

447 E College Avenue, Jacksonville IL 62650-2590
County: Morgan FICE Identification: 001717
Unit ID: 146825
Telephone: (217) 479-7000 Carnegie Class: Bac-Diverse
FAX Number: (217) 245-0405 Calendar System: 4/1/4
URL: www.mac.edu
Established: 1846 Annual Undergrad Tuition & Fees: $27,710
Enrollment: 521 Coed
Affiliation or Control: United Methodist IRS Status: 501(c)3
Highest Offering: Baccalaureate
Accreditation: NH, NURSE, SW

01 Interim President .... Dr. Beverly RODGERS
10 VP of Business Affairs & CFO .... Ms. Kimberly STREIB
05 Interim Provost .... Dr. Gina WYANT
32 Dean of Student Life .... Ms. Beth OBERG
07 Director of Admissions .... Ms. Kristen CHENOWETH
13 Director of IT/System Administrator .... Mr. Paul YOUNKER
06 Asst Director OSSS .... Ms. Pam HARPOLE
08 Librarian .... Mr. Adam CASSELL
21 Controller .... Mr. Andrew SIDOCK
36 Director of Career Services .... Ms. Anne GODMAN
29 Dir Alumni Relations/Annual Giving .... Ms. Rikki LANGAN
09 Assoc Provost for AA & Compliance .... Vacant
18 Director of Facilities & Security .... Mr. Jonathan JUMPER
26 Director of Communications & Mktg .... Ms. Marcy JONES
04 Executive Asst to President .... Ms. Sharon SEYMOUR
41 Athletic Director .... Mr. Justin FUHLER
37 Director of One-Stop Student Svcs .... Ms. Allison DECKER
15 Director of Human Resources .... Ms. Amy TRIBBLE
19 Director Security/Safety & Housing .... Mr. Aaron EISFELDER
111 Sr Director of Inst Advancement .... Ms. Jennifer BENANTI

McCormick Theological Seminary (J)

5460 S University Avenue, Chicago IL 60615-5108
County: Cook FICE Identification: 001721
Unit ID: 146977
Telephone: (773) 947-6300 Carnegie Class: Spec-4-yr-Faith
FAX Number: (773) 288-2612 Calendar System: 4/1/4
URL: www.mccormick.edu
Established: 1829 Annual Graduate Tuition & Fees: N/A
Enrollment: 214 Coed

Affiliation or Control: Presbyterian Church (U.S.A.) IRS Status: 501(c)3
Highest Offering: Doctorate; No Undergraduates
Accreditation: NH, THEOL

01 President Mr. David CRAWFORD
00 Chair of the Board Ms. Connie LINDSEY
10 Exec Vice Pres/Chief Business Ofcr Mr. David CRAWFORD
05 Vice Pres Acad Affs/Dean Faculty Dr. Steed DAVIDSON
30 Vice Pres Seminary Rels/Development Ms. Lisa M. DAGHER
06 Registrar Ms. Chandra WADE
29 Vice Pres Alumni/ae & Church Rels Rev. Nannette BANKS
08 Director of JKM Library Dr. Christine WENDEROTH
15 Director Human Resources Ms. Ashley WOODFAULK
37 Dir Student Financial Aid/Planning Ms. Tabitha HIGHTOWER
07 Sr Director Admissions/Enrollment Ms. Veronica JOHNSON
88 Assistant to the Dean Ms. Jennifer OULD
04 Assistant to the President Ms. Joyce LEACHMAN

McHenry County College (A)

8900 US Highway 14, Crystal Lake IL 60012-2796
County: McHenry FICE Identification: 007691
Unit ID: 147004
Telephone: (815) 455-3700 Carnegie Class: Assoc/HVT-High Non
FAX Number: (815) 455-3999 Calendar System: Semester
URL: www.mchenry.edu
Established: 1967 Annual Undergrad Tuition & Fees (In-District): $3,494
Enrollment: 6,843 Coed
Affiliation or Control: State/Local IRS Status: 501(c)3
Highest Offering: Associate Degree
Accreditation: NH, CAHIIM, EMT, OTA, @PTAA

01 President Dr. Clinton E. GABBARD
04 Board Liaison Mrs. Pat KRIEGERMEIER
05 VP Academic Affairs & Workforce Dev Dr. Chris GRAY
103 Assoc VP of Workforce Development Ms. Catherine JONES
49 Assoc VP for Arts and Science Dr. Brock FISHER
11 VP Marketing/Comm & Development Ms. Christina HAGGERTY
26 Exec Dir Mktg & Creative Services Mr. Ryan KLOS
102 Exec Director MCC Foundation Mr. Brian DIBONA
25 Director of Resource Development Mr. Mark DOUGHER
88 Director of Sustainability Ms. Kim HANKINS
10 CFO/Treasurer Mr. Bob TENUTA
21 Asst VP of Finance Ms. Lynn COWLIN
19 Assoc VP Campus Public Safety Mr. Michael CLESCERI
18 Executive Director of Facilities Mr. Todd WHEELAND
40 Director Bookstore Ms. Karen SMITH
109 Director Food Services Ms. Sandra JOHNSTON
96 Director of Business Services Ms. Jennifer JONES
13 Chief Information Officer Dr. Allen P. BUTLER
119 Director Infrastructure & Security Mr. Rob RASMUSSEN
14 Director of DevOps Services Mr. Todd SMITH
09 Director of Institutional Research Dr. Amy HUMKE
15 Assoc VP of Human Resources Ms. Michelle SKINDER
88 Director Talent Management Ms. Sandra HESS MOLL
16 Director of HR Operations Ms. Anita ROEWER
108 Director of Employee Development Ms. Patricia STEJSKAL
118 Dir Employee Relations & Benefits Ms. Deetra SALLIS
32 VP Student Affairs Dr. Talia KORONKIEWICZ
06 Director of Registration & Records Ms. Amy HALLER
41 Director Athletics/Intramural & Rec Ms. Karen WILEY
88 Director Crisis Intervention Ms. Rachael BOLDMAN
88 Director of Upward Bound Program Mr. Rene GOVEA
124 Dir of Student Retention & Conduct Ms. Lisa BRNCICH
37 Interim Director of Financial Aid Ms. Marianne DEVENNY
121 Dean of Academic Development Ms. Adriane HUTCHINSON
22 Manager Access & Disability Service Ms. Lili O'CONNELL
37 Director of Financial Aid Vacant
08 Executive Director of Library Vacant
89 Dir College & Career Readiness Mr. Mike KENNEDY
20 Director of Teaching & Learning Dr. Holly LI
81 Dean of Mathematics & Sciences Dr. Maria TAYDEN
85 Dean of Humanities & Social Science Ms. Laura POWER
55 Exec Director of Adult Education Mr. Julio CAPELES-DELGADO
51 Director of Continuing Education Ms. Dori SULLINS
76 Dir Health Info Technology Programs Ms. Chris COCLANIS-LODING
66 Director Nursing Ms. Betsy SCHNOWSKE
48 Director of Urban Agriculture Ms. Alissa MOORE
88 Manager of Nursing Laboratory Ms. Ann STAUCHE
76 Dir OT Assistant Program Ms. Marlene VOGT
75 Dean Career & Technical Educ Ms. Gina MCCONOUGHEY
88 Mgr IL Small Business Development Mr. Mark BUTLER

McKendree University (B)

701 College Road, Lebanon IL 62254-9990
County: Saint Clair FICE Identification: 001722
Unit ID: 147013
Telephone: (618) 537-4481 Carnegie Class: Masters/L
FAX Number: (618) 537-6259 Calendar System: Semester
URL: www.mckendree.edu
Established: 1828 Annual Undergrad Tuition & Fees: $30,520
Enrollment: 2,676 Coed
Affiliation or Control: United Methodist IRS Status: 501(c)3
Highest Offering: Doctorate
Accreditation: NH, IACBE, NURSE

01 President Dr. James M. DENNIS
03 Senior Vice President Ms. Victoria A. DOWLING
04 Assistant to the President Ms. Patti J. DANIELS
05 Provost/Dean of the University Dr. Christine M. BAHR
10 Vice Pres Finance/Administration Dr. Marilee K. MONTANARO
07 Vice Pres Admission & Financial Aid Mr. Chris HALL
32 Vice President Student Affairs Dr. Joni BASTIAN
108 Associate Provost Inst Effective Dr. Tami EGGLESTON
88 Associate Provost for Curriculum Dr. J. Alan ALEWINE
100 Chief of Staff Mr. Daryl R. HANCOCK
13 Director Technology Information Mr. George KRISS
06 Registrar/Asst Dean Ms. Debra LARSON
08 Director of Holman Library Ms. Paula MARTIN
21 Comptroller Mrs. Hilary B. SMITH
26 Exec Dir Marketing/Communications Mrs. Krysti H. CONNELLY
29 Director Alumni Relations Mr. PJ THOMPSON
37 Director Financial Aid Mrs. Elizabeth JUEHNE
36 Director Career Services Ms. Jennifer K. PICKERELL
15 Director Human Resources Ms. Shirley A. BAUGH
27 Director Media Relations Ms. Lisa K. BRANDON
39 Director of Residence Life Mrs. Samantha ENGLAR
35 Director of Campus Activities Mr. Craig L. ROBERTSON
41 Athletic Director Mr. Chuck BRUEGGEMANN
42 Chaplain/Director Church Relations Rev Dr. B. Timothy HARRISON
40 Bookstore Director Ms. Amy BLASDEL
110 Director of Advancement Services Mr. Scott L. BILLHARTZ
19 Director Safety & Security Mr. Ranodore M. FOGGS
112 Director of Major Gifts Mrs. Whitney STRONG
113 Director of Student Accounts Ms. Kristie JAQUES-ANGLIN
28 Director of Diversity Mr. Brent W. REEVES
106 Dean of Online Dr. Melissa MEEKER
104 Director of Study Abroad Ms. Sandee POWERS
09 Director of Institutional Research Mrs. Jessica HOPKINS

Meadville Lombard Theological School (C)

610 South Michigan Avenue, Chicago IL 60605
County: Cook FICE Identification: 001723
Unit ID: 147031
Telephone: (773) 256-3000 Carnegie Class: Spec-4-yr-Faith
FAX Number: (312) 327-7002 Calendar System: Semester
URL: www.meadville.edu
Established: 1844 Annual Graduate Tuition & Fees: N/A
Enrollment: 91 Coed
Affiliation or Control: Unitarian Universalist IRS Status: 501(c)3
Highest Offering: Doctorate; No Undergraduates
Accreditation: THEOL

01 President Dr. Lee BARKER
05 Interim Provost Dr. Lee BARKER
10 Vice Pres Finance & Administration Ms. Cynthia REDMAN
06 Registrar Ms. Valencia PENN-HARGROVE

Methodist College (D)

7600 N. Academic Drive, Peoria IL 61615
County: Peoria FICE Identification: 006228
Unit ID: 147129
Telephone: (309) 672-5513 Carnegie Class: Spec-4-yr-Other Health
FAX Number: (309) 671-8303 Calendar System: Semester
URL: www.methodistcol.edu
Established: 2000 Annual Undergrad Tuition & Fees: $20,750
Enrollment: 681 Coed
Affiliation or Control: Independent Non-Profit IRS Status: 501(c)3
Highest Offering: Master's
Accreditation: NH, NURSE, @SW

01 Chancellor/President Dr. James DIRE
05 Provost/VP Academic Affairs Dr. Deborah GARRISON
10 VC Admin & Chief Financial Officer Mr. Barry SOFFIETTI
26 VC Strategic Mktg/External Affairs Ms. Anna BUEHRER
06 Registrar Ms. Melissa EARNEST
07 Director Admissions Ms. Alissa SELBURG
37 Director Financial Aid Ms. Angela ROBINSON
09 Institutional Research Coordinator Mr. Donnie JOHNSON

Midwest College of Oriental Medicine (E)

1601 Sherman Avenue, Suite 300, Evanston IL 60202
Telephone: (773) 975-1295 Identification: 666090
Accreditation: ACUP

† Branch campus of Midwest College of Oriental Medicine, Racine, WI

Midwestern Career College (F)

20 N. Wacker Dr, Ste 3800, Chicago IL 60606
County: Cook FICE Identification: 041390
Unit ID: 457536
Telephone: (312) 236-9000 Carnegie Class: Spec 2-yr-Health
FAX Number: (312) 277-1007 Calendar System: Other
URL: mccollege.edu
Established: 2004 Annual Undergrad Tuition & Fees: N/A
Enrollment: 563 Coed
Affiliation or Control: Proprietary IRS Status: Proprietary
Highest Offering: Associate Degree
Accreditation: COE, CEA

01 President/CEO Mr. Jeremy OBERFELD
07 Admissions Director Mr. Brian RULE

Midwestern University (G)

555 31st Street, Downers Grove IL 60515-1200
County: DuPage FICE Identification: 001657
Unit ID: 143853
Telephone: (630) 971-6080 Carnegie Class: Spec-4-yr-Med
FAX Number: N/A Calendar System: Quarter
URL: www.midwestern.edu
Established: 1900 Annual Undergrad Tuition & Fees: N/A
Enrollment: 2,971 Coed
Affiliation or Control: Independent Non-Profit IRS Status: 501(c)3
Highest Offering: Doctorate
Accreditation: NH, ARCPA, CLPSY, DENT, @OPT, OSTEO, OT, PHAR, PTA, SP

01 President/CEO Dr. Kathleen H. GOEPPINGER
11 Exec VP/Chief Operating Officer Vacant
10 Sr VP/Chief Financial Officer Mr. Gregory J. GAUS
21 Vice President Finance Mr. Dean P. MALONE
46 VP Research & Strategic Initiatives Dr. Theresa W. FOSSUM
26 Vice President University Relations Dr. Karen D. JOHNSON
05 VP/CAO Dental/Med/Veterinary Educ Dr. Dennis J. PAULSON
88 VP/Special Assistant to President Dr. Mary W L. LEE
05 VP/CAO Health Sci Ed & VP Clinic Op Dr. Kathleen N. PLAYER
05 VP/CAO Pharmacy/Optometry Education Dr. Joshua C. BAKER
15 VP Human Resources & Administration Ms. Angela L. MARTY
43 VP & General Counsel Ms. Barbara L. MCCLOUD
63 Dean Chicago Col of Osteo Medicine Dr. Thomas A. BOYLE
67 Dean Col Pharmacy Glendale/Chicago Dr. Mitchell R. EMERSON
76 Dean Col Health Sci Downers Grove Dr. Fred D. ROMANO
88 Dean Chicago College of Optometry Dr. Melissa A. SUCKOW
52 Dean College of Dental Medicine IL Dr. Harold J. HAERING
58 Dean College of Graduate Studies Dr. Kyle H. RAMSEY
32 Dean of Students Dr. Ross J. KOSINSKI
07 Director of Admissions Mr. Michael J. LAKEN
88 Director of Finance Mr. Gregory O'COYNE
111 Director Institutional Advancement Ms. Stacy GLASS
16 Director Human Resources Ms. Amy B. GIBSON
18 Director of Operations Mr. Kevin M. MCCORMICK
13 Director Information Technology Svc Mr. Erik P. CARROLL
08 Director Library Ms. Rebecca A. CATON
09 Director of Institutional Research Ms. Donna M. WEGLARZ
06 Registrar Ms. Elizabeth N. MORRISON
24 Director Media Resources Ms. Kathleen A M. DOOLEY
46 Director Research & Sponsored Pgms Dr. James M. WOODS
19 Director of Security/Safety Mr. Paul R. CREEKMORE
27 Director of Communications Ms. Dana FAY
37 Director Student Financial Services Mr. Nathan ERNST
21 Controller Mr. Matthew SWEENEY
14 Dir IT Applications/Clinic Svcs Mr. James RUBINSTEIN

† Tuition varies by degree program.

Millikin University (H)

1184 W Main Street, Decatur IL 62522-2084
County: Macon FICE Identification: 001724
Unit ID: 147244
Telephone: (217) 424-6211 Carnegie Class: Bac-Diverse
FAX Number: (217) 424-3993 Calendar System: Semester
URL: www.millikin.edu
Established: 1901 Annual Undergrad Tuition & Fees: $35,002
Enrollment: 2,040 Coed
Affiliation or Control: Presbyterian Church (U.S.A.) IRS Status: 501(c)3
Highest Offering: Doctorate
Accreditation: NH, ACBSP, ANEST, #CAATE, MUS, NURSE

01 President Dr. Patrick E. WHITE
05 Provost Dr. Jeffery P. APER
10 Vice Pres Finance/Business Affs Ms. Ruby F. JAMES
111 Vice Pres University Development Ms. Gina L. BIANCHI
84 Vice President Enrollment/Marketing Ms. Sarah SHUPENUS
32 VP Student Affairs/Dean of Students Mrs. Raphaella PRANGE
100 Chief of Staff/Board Secretary Ms. Marilyn S. DAVIS
49 Dean of Arts & Sciences Dr. Randy M. BROOKS
57 Dean of Fine Arts Ms. Laura LEDFORD
107 Int Dean Col of Professional Stds Dr. Pam LINDSEY
50 Dean Tabor School Business Dr. Najiba BENABESS
06 Registrar Mr. Jason WICKLINE
29 Sr Director Alumni/Donor Engagement Mrs. Alyse KNUST
102 Dir Corp & Foundation Relations Mrs. Kim MANGAN
13 Director of Technology Mrs. Amy BRILLEY
08 Director of the Library Ms. Cindy FULLER
30 Sr Director of Development Mrs. Amanda PODESCHI
41 Director of Athletics Dr. Craig WHITE
53 Director of School of Education Dr. Pamela BARNES
88 Director Kirkland Fine Arts Center Mrs. Janiece L. SADDORIS-TRAUGHBER
28 Dir Inclusion/Student Engagement Mrs. Molly BERRY
104 Int Dir Center for Intl Education Ms. Briana QUINTENZ
15 Director Human Resources Ms. Diane L. LANE
21 Director Financial Services Mrs. Vicki A. WRIGLEY
38 Director of Counseling Services Mr. Christopher MORRELL
92 Director of Honors Program Dr. Michael HARTSOCK
35 Director Student Development Mr. Z. Paul REYNOLDS
37 Director of Financial Aid Vacant
58 Director of MBA Program Dr. Najibu BENABESS
64 Director School of Music Dr. Brian K. JUSTISON
87 Director of Summer School Dr. Randy M. BROOKS
19 Dir Dept Public Safety/Chief Police Mr. Chris BALLARD
66 Director School of Nursing Dr. Elizabeth GEPHART
07 Dean of Admission Vacant
39 Director of Residence Life Mr. Paul LIDY
18 Director of Facilities Services Mr. Michael KUROPAS
26 Director of Marketing Mrs. Kylee RONEY
09 Coord of Institutional Research Mrs. Laura A. BIRCH
105 Web Developer Ms. Jessica LANDGREBE
88 Dir Ctr for Acad/Prof Perf (CAPP) Mrs. Carrie PIERSON

Monmouth College (A)

700 E Broadway, Monmouth IL 61462-1963
County: Warren FICE Identification: 001725
Unit ID: 147341
Telephone: (800) 747-2687 Carnegie Class: Bac-A&S
FAX Number: (309) 457-2141 Calendar System: Semester
URL: www.monmouthcollege.edu
Established: 1853 Annual Undergrad Tuition & Fees: $37,674
Enrollment: 1,033 Coed
Affiliation or Control: Presbyterian Church (U.S.A.) IRS Status: 501(c)3
Highest Offering: Baccalaureate
Accreditation: NH

01 President .... Dr. Clarence R. WYATT
05 Dean/Vice Pres Academic Affairs .... Dr. Mark WILLHARDT
10 Vice President Finance & Business .... Mr. Richard A. MARSHALL
32 Vice Pres Student Life/Dn Students .... Ms. Laura HUTCHINSON
84 Vice President for Enrollment Mgmt .... Ms. Kristen ENGLISH
30 Vice Pres Development/College Rels .... Mr. John OSTERLUND
07 Assoc Vice President for Enrollment .... Vacant
13 Chief Information Officer .... Mr. Daryl B. CARR
06 Registrar .... Ms. Kristi HIPPEN
08 Director Hewes Library .... Mr. Richard SAYRE
26 Exec Dir College Communications .... Mr. Duane BONIFER
15 Director of Personnel Services .... Mr. Mike MCNALL
18 Director Facilities Management .... Ms. Sarah YOUNG
20 Associate Dean of the Faculty .... Dr. Frank GERSICH
21 Controller .... Ms. Jessica R. JOHNSON
09 Director Institutional Research .... Ms. Christine D. JOHNSTON

Moody Bible Institute (B)

820 N LaSalle Boulevard, Chicago IL 60610-3263
County: Cook FICE Identification: 001727
Unit ID: 147369
Telephone: (312) 329-4000 Carnegie Class: Spec-4-yr-Faith
FAX Number: (312) 329-4109 Calendar System: Semester
URL: www.moody.edu
Established: 1886 Annual Undergrad Tuition & Fees: $13,056
Enrollment: 3,442 Coed
Affiliation or Control: Independent Non-Profit IRS Status: 501(c)3
Highest Offering: First Professional Degree
Accreditation: NH, BI, MUS, THEOL

01 President .... Dr. Mark JOBE
05 Int Provost & Dean of Education .... Dr. John JELINEK
11 Chief Operating Officer .... Mr. Mark WAGNER
10 Chief Financial Officer .... Mr. Ken HEULITT
43 VP & General Counsel .... Mrs. Janet A. STIVEN
20 VP & Associate Provost of Faculty .... Dr. Larry J. DAVIDHIZAR
13 VP of Information Systems .... Mr. Frank W. LEBER
15 VP of Human Resources .... Mrs. Debbie ZELINSKI
26 Chief Marketing Officer .... Mr. Sam CHOY
20 Int VP & Dean of Undergrad School .... Dr. Bryan O'NEAL
58 VP/Dean of Theol Sem & Grad School .... Dr. John A. JELINEK
106 VP & Dean of Dist Learning School .... Dr. Bryan O'NEAL
32 VP & Dean of Student Life .... Dr. Timothy E. ARENS
84 VP/Dean of Student/Enrollment Svcs .... Dr. Heather SHALLEY
08 Department Manager Library .... Mr. James PRESTON
06 Registrar/Director of Acad Records .... Mr. George MOSHER
29 Exec Director Alumni Association .... Mrs. Nancy HASTINGS
39 Associate Dean Residence Life .... Mr. Bruce R. NORQUIST
35 Associate Dean of Students .... Mrs. Rachel PUENTE
36 Assoc Dean of Career Development .... Mr. Patrick FRIEDLINE
38 Associate Dean Counseling Services .... Mr. Steve BRASEL
35 Associate Dean for Student Programs .... Mr. Joseph M. GONZALES, JR.
104 Dean of International Study Program .... Dr. Gregg QUIGGLE
88 Pgm Mgr of Missionary Aviation Tech .... Mr. James A. CONRAD
88 Assc Dir of Faculty Development .... Dr. Andrew BEATY
88 Dir of Instructional Design MDL .... Mr. Kevin MAHAFFY
88 Director of Student Experience MDL .... Mr. John ENGELKEMIER
44 VP of Donor Dev & Channel Strategy .... Mr. Bruce EVERHART
30 VP of Stewardship .... Mr. James ELLIOTT
96 Manager of Procurement Services .... Mr. Stephen RICHARDSON
102 Dir Foundation/Corporate Relations .... Dr. Mollie BOND
21 Controller .... Ms. Linda WAHR
37 Dean of Admissions & Financial Aid .... Mrs. Heather SHALLEY
14 Technology Services Director .... Mr. Michael JANCHENKO
18 Division Manager of Facilities .... Mr. Bill BIELAWSKI
19 Deputy Chief of Public Safety .... Mr. Brian M. STOFFER
41 Athletic Director .... Mr. Daniel DUNN
23 Admin of Health Service .... Ms. Ann MEYER
04 Executive Assistant to President .... Ms. Mary OLIVA
28 Asst Dean of Multicultural Stdnts .... Mr. Edward JONES

† Tuition is paid through donor contributions. Fees are $1,950.00 per year.

Moraine Valley Community College (C)

9000 W College Parkway, Palos Hills IL 60465-0937
County: Cook FICE Identification: 007692
Unit ID: 147378
Telephone: (708) 974-4300 Carnegie Class: Assoc/HVT-High Non
FAX Number: (708) 974-1184 Calendar System: Semester
URL: www.morainevalley.edu
Established: 1967 Annual Undergrad Tuition & Fees (In-District): $4,356
Enrollment: 14,620 Coed
Affiliation or Control: State/Local IRS Status: 501(c)3
Highest Offering: Associate Degree
Accreditation: NH, ACFEI, ADNUR, CAHIIM, COARC, MAC, POLYT, RAD

01 President .... Dr. Sylvia JENKINS
05 Vice President Academic Affairs .... Dr. Pamela HANEY
32 Vice President Student Devel .... Dr. Normah SALLEH-BARONE
11 Vice Pres Administrative Services .... Mr. Richard J. HENDRICKS
10 Vice Pres Financial & Business Svcs .... Ms. Theresa O'CARROLL
13 Chief Information Officer .... Mr. Kamlesh SANGHVI
50 Dean Science/Business/Comp Tech .... Dr. Ryen NAGLE
49 Dean Liberal Arts .... Dr. Walter FRONCZEK
124 Dean Student Engagement .... Dr. Scott FRIEDMAN
84 Dean Enrollment Services .... Dr. Darryl WILLIAMS
51 Exec Dir Corporate/Cmty & Cont Educ .... Mr. Steven PAPPAGEORGE
36 Dean Career Programs .... Ms. Kiana BATTLE
35 Dean Student Services .... Mr. Chester SHAW
88 Dean Learn Enrich & Col Readiness .... Mr. Michael MORSCHES
35 Dean of Students/Compliance Officer .... Mr. Kent MARSHALL
37 Director Financial Aid .... Vacant
09 Dir Institutional Research/Planning .... Dr. Sadya KHAN
19 Chief of Public Safety .... Mr. Patrick O'CONNOR
15 Director Human Resources .... Ms. Lynn HARRINGTON
07 Director of Admissions/Recruitment .... Mr. Andrew SARATA
18 Director Campus Operations .... Mr. Rick BRENNAN
109 Director Auxiliary Services .... Mr. Kashif SHAH
23 Director Health Education Well Ctr .... Mr. William FINN
85 Asst Dean Intl Student Admissions .... Ms. Diane VIVERITO
26 Director Marketing & Communications .... Ms. Clare BRINER
25 Dir Res Devel/Extended Programs .... Dr. Sharon KATTERMAN
21 Controller .... Mr. Michael CIPOLLA
22 Director of Disability Services .... Mr. Nathan PAYOVICH
96 Director of Purchasing .... Ms. Jane BENTLEY
102 Executive Director Foundation .... Ms. Kristy MCGREAL
20 Dean Academic Development/Outreach .... Dr. Cynthia ANDERSON
20 Dean Academic Services .... Ms. Jennifer DAVIDSON
08 Dean Learning Resource Center .... Ms. Terra JACOBSON
121 Dean Student Success .... Dr. Jo Ann JENKINS
88 Asst Dean of Enrollment Services .... Mr. Emmanuel ESPERANZA, JR.
101 Secretary of the Institution/Board .... Ms. Dawn FREDRIKSON
108 Director Institutional Assessment .... Dr. Nancy GAYLEN

Morrison Institute of Technology (D)

701 Portland Avenue, Morrison IL 61270-2959
County: Whiteside FICE Identification: 008880
Unit ID: 147396
Telephone: (815) 772-7218 Carnegie Class: Spec 2-yr-Tech
FAX Number: (815) 772-7584 Calendar System: Semester
URL: www.morrisontech.edu
Established: 1973 Annual Undergrad Tuition & Fees: $16,100
Enrollment: 102 Coed
Affiliation or Control: Independent Non-Profit IRS Status: 501(c)3
Highest Offering: Associate Degree
Accreditation: COE

01 Chief Executive Officer .... Mr. Christopher D. SCOTT
05 Vice President of Academic Affairs .... Mr. Greg J. TULLY
10 Vice President for Finance .... Mr. Richard PARKINSON
06 Registrar .... Mr. David KING
07 Admissions Director .... Ms. Jodie EAKER

Morton College (E)

3801 S Central Avenue, Cicero IL 60804-4398
County: Cook FICE Identification: 001728
Unit ID: 147411
Telephone: (708) 656-8000 Carnegie Class: Assoc/MT-VT-Mix Trad/Non
FAX Number: (708) 656-3297 Calendar System: Semester
URL: www.morton.edu
Established: 1924 Annual Undergrad Tuition & Fees (In-District): $4,372
Enrollment: 4,387 Coed
Affiliation or Control: State/Local IRS Status: 501(c)3
Highest Offering: Associate Degree
Accreditation: NH, ADNUR, PTAA

01 President .... Dr. Stanley FIELDS
05 Provost .... Dr. Keith MCLAUGHLIN
51 Dean Adult & Continuing Education .... Dr. Tom PIERCE
32 Dir Student Development .... Ms. Marisol VELASQUEZ
08 Assoc Dn Library/Instructional Tech .... Mr. Micheal KOTT
15 Director of Human Resources .... Mr. Ronald LULLO
51 Director of Continuing Education .... Ms. Susan FELICE
09 Director Institutional Research .... Ms. Magda BANDA
18 Director of Facilities & Operations .... Mr. John POTEMPA
37 Director of Financial Aid .... Ms. Yolanda FREEMON
06 Registrar .... Ms. Marlena AVALOS-THOMPSON
10 Director of Business Services/CFO .... Ms. Mireya PEREZ
11 Exec Director of Operations .... Mr. Frank MARZULLO

National Louis University (F)

122 S Michigan Avenue, Chicago IL 60603
County: Cook FICE Identification: 001733
Unit ID: 147536
Telephone: (888) 658-8632 Carnegie Class: DU-Mod
FAX Number: N/A Calendar System: Quarter
URL: www.nl.edu
Established: 1886 Annual Undergrad Tuition & Fees: $10,710
Enrollment: 4,918 Coed
Affiliation or Control: Independent Non-Profit IRS Status: 501(c)3
Highest Offering: Doctorate
Accreditation: NH, ACFEI, CACREP, CAEPN, IACBE

01 President .... Dr. Nivine MEGAHED
05 Provost .... Dr. Alison HILSABECK
111 VP Inst Advance & Communications .... Ms. Carole WOOD
15 Vice President Human Resources .... Mr. Tom BERGMANN
10 Vice Pres Finance & Administration .... Mr. Marty MICKEY
84 Vice Pres Enrollment & Marketing .... Mr. Richard YACONIS
13 VP CIO .... Mr. Michael GRAHAM
20 Vice Prov Acad Pgm & Fac Dev .... Dr. Michael CARR
06 Vice Prov Advising & Univ Registrar .... Mr. Stephen NEER
50 Dean CPSA .... Dr. Judah VIOLA
53 Dean NCE .... Dr. Robert MULLER
08 Dean University Library .... Dr. Robert MORRISON
97 Dean Undergraduate College .... Ms. Aarti DHUPELIA
28 Director of Employment/Diversity .... Vacant
37 Exec Dir Student Financial Services .... Ms. Brigid CALLAHAN
07 Director of Admissions .... Mr. Ken KASPRZAK
51 Director Outreach Academic Pgm .... Ms. Karen HAWORTH
35 Director of Student Experience .... Ms. Danielle LABAN
04 Administrative Asst to President .... Ms. Diane M. TRAUSCH
108 Director Institutional Assessment .... Ms. Mital PATEL
18 Chief Facilities/Physical Plant .... Mr. Richard SORENSON
25 Assoc Dir of Grant Operations .... Ms. Terri ATIENZA
29 Director Alumni & Outreach Programs .... Vacant
91 Technical Director .... Mr. John MAZARIEGOS
96 Purchasing Coordinator .... Ms. Caryn SMITH
102 Exec Dir of IA .... Ms. Leslie VILLASENOR
12 Florida Exec Director .... Dr. Karen O'DONNELL
103 Asst Dir Career Development .... Ms. Consiglia INTILE
45 Exec Dir Strategic Initiatives .... Mr. Andi KORITARI
44 Assoc Director Annual Giving .... Mr. Patrick BELICS
30 Dir External Funding & Grant Devel .... Ms. Arlene STRONG
36 Exec Dir Career Svcs & Placement .... Ms. Smret SMITH

National University of Health Sciences (G)

200 E Roosevelt Road, Lombard IL 60148-4583
County: DuPage FICE Identification: 001732
Unit ID: 147590
Telephone: (630) 629-2000 Carnegie Class: Spec-4-yr-Other Health
FAX Number: (630) 889-6600 Calendar System: Trimester
URL: www.nuhs.edu
Established: 1906 Annual Undergrad Tuition & Fees: N/A
Enrollment: 686 Coed
Affiliation or Control: Independent Non-Profit IRS Status: 501(c)3
Highest Offering: First Professional Degree
Accreditation: NH, ACUP, CHIRO, COMTA, NATUR

01 President .... Dr. Joseph P D. STIEFEL
05 Vice President Academic Services .... Dr. Randy L. SWENSON
10 Vice President Business Services .... Mr. Ron MENSCHING
11 Vice Pres Administrative Services .... Ms. Tracy MCHUGH
76 Dean College Allied Health Sciences .... Dr. Jerrilyn CAMBRON
51 Dean Col Postprofessional Educ .... Dr. Jenna GLENN
23 Dean of Clinics .... Dr. Theodore JOHNSON
107 Dean Col Professional Studies FL .... Dr. Daniel STRAUSS
107 Dean Col Professional Studies IL .... Dr. Sandra ROGERS
46 Dean of Research .... Dr. Gregory D. CRAMER
32 Dean of Students .... Ms. Yesenia MALDONADO
09 Dean of Institutional Effectiveness .... Dr. Nick CHANCELLOR
88 Dean Accreditation .... Vacant
08 Director Learning Resource Center .... Ms. Patricia GENARDO
06 University Registrar .... Ms. Izabela DUBAK
07 Dir Communication/Enrollment Svcs .... Ms. Victoria SWEENEY
21 Director of Financial Services .... Ms. Sue UNGER
37 Director of Financial Aid .... Mr. Marc YAMBO
18 Director Maintenance & Facilities .... Mr. Mark GALVANONI
15 Director of Human Resources .... Mr. Andrew WOZNIAK
26 Dir Communications/Enrollment Svcs .... Ms. Victoria SWEENEY
30 Dir Alumni Rels & Development .... Mrs. Tracy MCHUGH
13 Dir Management Information Services .... Mr. Ron MENSCHING
40 Bookstore Manager .... Ms. Sue ROBERTSON
39 Coordinator of Housing .... Ms. Marilyn FREAD
88 Dean of Institutional Compliance .... Mr. Daniel DRISCOLL

North Central College (H)

30 N Brainard Street, Naperville IL 60540-4607
County: DuPage FICE Identification: 001734
Unit ID: 147660
Telephone: (630) 637-5100 Carnegie Class: Masters/M
FAX Number: (630) 637-5121 Calendar System: Trimester
URL: www.northcentralcollege.edu
Established: 1861 Annual Undergrad Tuition & Fees: $38,880
Enrollment: 2,965 Coed
Affiliation or Control: United Methodist IRS Status: 501(c)3
Highest Offering: Master's
Accreditation: NH, CAATE

01 President .... Dr. Troy D. HAMMOND
04 Exec Secy/Assistant to President .... Ms. Kimberly SALZBRUNN
05 Provost/VP Academic Affairs .... Dr. Abiodun GOKE-PARIOLA
10 VP of Finance/CFO .... Ms. Maryellen SKERIK
111 VP Institutional Advancement .... Mr. Rick E. SPENCER
84 VP Enrollment Management/Athletics .... Mr. Marty R. SAUER
32 VP Student Affairs/Dean of Students .... Ms. Kimberly SLUIS
11 VP for Operations .... Mr. Michael J. HUDSON
13 VP/Chief Information Officer .... Mr. Matthew BURDEN
15 Asst Vice Pres Human Resources .... Mr. John ACARDO
26 Asst Vice Pres Mktg/Communications .... Mr. James GODO
07 Dean of Admissions .... Ms. Martha A. STOLZE
58 Dean Graduate Pgms/Continuing Educ .... Vacant

06 Registrar Mr. Timothy BROWN
08 Director of the Library Mr. John J. SMALL
36 Director of Career Development Ms. Haydee NUNEZ
37 Director of Financial Aid Ms. Kristina BONN
23 Director of the Wellness Center Ms. Tatiana SIFRI
31 Director of Cmty Educ/Conf/Camps Mr. Troy BRISTOW
41 Athletic Director Mr. James MILLER
21 AVP Finance/Controller Mr. David S. MISSURELLI
39 Director of Residence Life Ms. Sarah E. AVERY
42 Campus Chaplain Rev. Eric DOOLITTLE
09 Director of Institutional Research Mr. Peter S. BARGER
29 Director Alumni/Dev Relations Mr. Adrian M. ALDRICH
28 Director of Multicultural Affairs Ms. Dorothy J. PLEAS

North Park University (A)

3225 W Foster Avenue, Chicago IL 60625-4895
County: Cook FICE Identification: 001735
Unit ID: 147679
Telephone: (773) 244-6200 Carnegie Class: Masters/L
FAX Number: N/A Calendar System: Semester
URL: www.northpark.edu
Established: 1891 Annual Undergrad Tuition & Fees: $29,860
Enrollment: 2,937 Coed
Affiliation or Control: Evangelical Covenant Church Of America
IRS Status: 501(c)3
Highest Offering: Doctorate
Accreditation: NH, CAATE, IACBE, MUS, NURSE, THEOL

01 President Mrs. Mary K. SURRIDGE
05 Provost Dr. Michael O. EMERSON
84 Vice Pres for Enrollment/Marketing Mr. Anthony L. SCOLA
111 Vice President for Advancement Ms. Shena KEITH
32 VP for Student Engagement Vacant
10 Vice Pres Finance & Admin/CFO Mr. Scott STENMARK
73 Seminary Dean Dr. David W. KERSTEN
35 Dean of Students Ms. Elizabeth FREDEC
49 Dean of College of Arts & Sciences Dr. Gregor THUSWALDNER
107 Dean School of Professional Studies Dr. Lori SCREMENTI
50 Dean School of Business & NFP Mgmt Dr. Ann HICKS
53 Dean School of Education Dr. Rebecca NELSON
64 Dean School of Music Dr. Natalie WILLIAMS
66 Dean School of Nursing Dr. Linda DUNCAN
28 Director of Diversity Vacant
08 Dean Library & Academic Technology Ms. Kathryn MAIER-O'SHEA
07 Director Undergraduate Enrollment Mr. Brady MARTINSON
23 Director Health Services Dr. Meghan PILLOW
37 Director Financial Aid Services Ms. Carolyn LACH
13 Director of Information Technology Mr. Jeffrey K. LUNDBLAD
15 Asst VP of Human Resources Ms. Ingrid K. TENGLIN
18 Director of Physical Plant Mr. Carl H. WISTROM
19 Director of Security Mr. Daniel GOORIS
21 Director of Finance Ms. Anne MCCULLAH
26 Dir Univ Marketing & Communications Vacant
41 Asst VP for Athletics & Sports Mgmt Mr. John BORN
42 Director University Ministries Mr. Anthony ZAMBLE
36 Senior Director of Career Planning Vacant
06 Registrar Mr. Aaron D. SCHOOF
29 Alumni Relations Director Vacant
100 Exec Dir of Operations Pres Office Ms. Melissa VELEZ-LUCE
104 Director of International Office Dr. Sumie SONG
39 Director Student Housing Mr. Aidan HOWORTH
108 Assoc Prov Institutional Assessment Ms. Lisa NCUBE
106 Assoc Dean Center for Online Educ Vacant

Northeastern Illinois University (B)

5500 N Saint Louis Avenue, Chicago IL 60625-4699
County: Cook FICE Identification: 001693
Unit ID: 147776
Telephone: (773) 583-4050 Carnegie Class: Masters/L
FAX Number: (773) 442-4900 Calendar System: Semester
URL: www.neiu.edu
Established: 1867 Annual Undergrad Tuition & Fees (In-State): $11,218
Enrollment: 8,984 Coed
Affiliation or Control: State IRS Status: 501(c)3
Highest Offering: Master's
Accreditation: NH, ART, CACREP, CAEPN, MUS, SW

01 President Dr. Gloria J. GIBSON
05 Provost & VP Academic Affairs Dr. Dennis ROME
07 Director of Admissions Mr. Lamont VAUGHN
100 Chief of Staff Mr. Arnold HENNING
32 Vice President for Student Affairs Dr. Daniel LOPEZ, JR.
111 Vice President Inst Advancement Ms. Liesl V. DOWNEY
26 Chief of Staff/CMO Mr. Mike M. DIZON
35 Dean of Students Mr. Matthew F. SPECHT
84 Int Assoc VP Enrollment Services Dr. John FRAIRE
13 Chief Information Officer Mr. Sam KANN
114 Director of Univ Budgets Ms. Ann M. MCNABB
08 Dean Libraries Mr. Steven HARRIS
09 Exec Dir Inst Rsrch & Assessment Mr. Blase E. MASINI
15 Dir of HR Empl & Labor Relations Ms. Marta E. MASO
25 Director Sponsored Programs Ms. Sharon K. TODD
37 Director Financial Aid Dr. Maureen T. AMOS
50 Dean College Bus/Management Dr. Michael D. BEDELL
58 Dean College Graduate Studies & Res Dr. Michael J. STERN
53 Dean College of Education Dr. Sandra BEYDA-LORIE
49 Dean College of Arts & Sciences Dr. Katrina BELL-JORDAN
18 Asst Vice Pres Facilities Mgmt Ms. Nancy MEDINA
19 Director University Police Dept Mr. John ESCALANTE
21 Director Controller's Office Ms. Beni ORTIZ
22 Dir Equal Opportunity/AA & Ethics Ms. Natalie POTTS
86 Sr Exec Dir Government Relations Dr. Suleyma PEREZ
06 University Registrar Mr. Daniel R. WEBER
29 Director of Alumni Relations Ms. Damaris TAPIA
110 Director Institutional Advancement Mr. John L. BUTLER
96 Director Purchasing Ms. Victoria SANTIAGO
23 Director of Student Health Services Ms. Sharon HEIMBAUGH

Northern Illinois University (C)

1425 W. Lincoln Way, De Kalb IL 60115-2828
County: De Kalb FICE Identification: 001737
Unit ID: 147703
Telephone: (815) 753-1000 Carnegie Class: DU-Higher
FAX Number: (815) 753-0198 Calendar System: Semester
URL: www.niu.edu
Established: 1895 Annual Undergrad Tuition & Fees (In-State): $14,617
Enrollment: 18,045 Coed
Affiliation or Control: State IRS Status: 501(c)3
Highest Offering: Doctorate
Accreditation: NH, ART, AUD, #CAATE, CACREP, CAEP, CAEPN, CLPSY, DIETD, DIETI, IPSY, LAW, MFCD, MT, MUS, NAIT, NURSE, PH, PTA, SCPSY, SP, SPAA, THEA

01 President Lisa C. FREEMAN
05 Executive Vice Pres & Provost Beth INGRAM
20 Vice Provost Inst Effectiveness Carolinda DOUGLASS
10 VP Administration & Finance Vacant
45 Vice Prov Resource Planning Susan MINI
51 VP University Outreach Anne C. KAPLAN
46 VP Research/Innovative Partnership Jerry BLAZEY
26 VP Enroll Mgmt/Mktg/Communications Sol JENSEN
43 Acting VP/General Counsel Greg A. BRADY
111 Vice Pres University Advancement Catherine SQUIRES
13 Chief Information Officer Matt PARKS
18 AVP Facilities Mgmt/Campus Services John HECKMANN
15 Sr AVP for Human Resources Laura ALEXANDER
35 Assoc VP Stdnt Affs & Dean of Stdnt Kelly WESENER-MICHAEL
23 Director Health Services Andrew DIGATE
28 Sr AVP Academic Diversity Vernese EDGHILL-WALDEN
20 Vice Provost Omar GHRAYEB
50 Dean of Business Balaji RAJAGOPALAN
53 Dean of Education Laurie ELISH-PIPER
54 Dean of Engineering/Engr Tech Donald PETERSON
61 Interim Dean of Law Mark CORDES
49 Dean Liberal Arts & Sciences Vacant
76 Dean Health & Human Sciences Derryl BLOCK
57 Dean Visual & Performing Arts Paul KASSEL
58 Dean Grad Sch/AVP Grad Studies Bradley BOND
85 Interim Sr International Affairs Bradley BOND
88 Asst VP Outreach Rockford Rena COTSONES
12 Director Lorado Taft Field Campus Diana DENNIS
12 Director NIU Naperville Gina KENYON
06 Director Registration & Records Jerry MONTAG
09 Director of Institutional Research J. Daniel HOUSE
36 Acting Exec Dir of Career Services Brandon T. LAGANA
37 Director of Student Financial Aid Rebecca BABEL
38 Exec Dir Counseling/Consultation Brooke RUXTON
40 University Bookstore Manager Don TURK
19 Police Chief/Public Safety Thomas R. PHILLIPS, SR.
41 Athletic Director Sean FRAZIER
39 Int Sr Dir Housing/Residential Svcs Jennifer MANNING
22 Dir Disability Resources Center Debra MILLER
29 Dir Alumni Relations/Univ Advance Reggie BUSTINZA
96 Dir Procurement/Strategic Sourcing Antoinette BRIDGES
07 Acting Director of Admissions Katy SAALFELD

Northern Seminary (D)

410 Warrenville Road, Suite 300, Lisle IL 60532
County: DuPage FICE Identification: 001736
Unit ID: 147697
Telephone: (630) 620-2180 Carnegie Class: Spec-4-yr-Faith
FAX Number: (630) 620-2190 Calendar System: Quarter
URL: www.seminary.edu
Established: 1913 Annual Graduate Tuition & Fees: N/A
Enrollment: 217 Coed
Affiliation or Control: American Baptist IRS Status: 501(c)3
Highest Offering: Doctorate; No Undergraduates
Accreditation: THEOL

01 President Dr. William SHIELL
04 Executive Assistant to President Mrs. Christine KOLB
05 Dean of Academic Affairs Dr. Ingrid FARO
30 Chief Development Officer Ms. Marlene MINOR
07 Director of Enrollment Rev. Greg ARMSTRONG
06 Registrar Rev. Linda OWENS
58 Director Doctoral Studies Dr. Ingrid FARO
32 Sr Exec Director Student Services Rev. Linda OWENS
08 Director of Library and Lib Tech Mr. Blake WALTER
09 Dean of Program Dev and Innovation Dr. Jason GILE
11 Director of Operations Ms. Pamela SHELDON

Northwestern College (E)

7725 S. Harlem, Bridgeview IL 60455
County: Cook FICE Identification: 012362
Unit ID: 147749
Telephone: (708) 237-5050 Carnegie Class: Assoc/HVT-High Trad
FAX Number: (708) 237-5005 Calendar System: Quarter
URL: www.nc.edu
Established: 1902 Annual Undergrad Tuition & Fees: N/A
Enrollment: 67 Coed
Affiliation or Control: Proprietary IRS Status: Proprietary
Highest Offering: Associate Degree
Accreditation: NH, ACBSP, CAHIIM, RAD

01 President Mr. Lawrence SCHUMACHER
02 Chief Executive Officer Mr. Dimitrios KRIARAS
11 Executive VP of Operations Mrs. Gail SCHUMACHER
10 Controller Ms. Cynthia BERRYMAN
05 Chief Academic Officer Ms. Tonya TROKA
13 Exec Dir of Information Technology Mr. Omar BERNAL
86 Government and Public Relations Dir Ms. Laura POLLASTRINI
08 Director of Library Services Ms. Sarah DULAY
15 Exec Dir of Human Resources Mrs. Mona NAJIB
37 Exec Dir of Student Financial Svcs Mr. Charles WOLFE
18 Exec Dir of Project Management Ms. Lauren SCHUMACHER
66 Dean of Nursing Ms. Diann MARTIN
06 Registrar Ms. Tina MARFOE
36 Career Development Coordinator Ms. Amy BUOSCIO
04 Executive Asst to President Ms. Vilma FRANCO

Northwestern University (F)

633 Clark Street, Evanston IL 60208-3854
County: Cook FICE Identification: 001739
Unit ID: 147767
Telephone: (847) 491-3741 Carnegie Class: DU-Highest
FAX Number: (847) 491-7364 Calendar System: Quarter
URL: www.northwestern.edu
Established: 1851 Annual Undergrad Tuition & Fees: $54,568
Enrollment: 22,008 Coed
Affiliation or Control: Independent Non-Profit IRS Status: 501(c)3
Highest Offering: Doctorate
Accreditation: NH, ARCPA, AUD, CACREP, CLPSY, IPSY, LAW, MED, MFCD, OPE, PCSAS, PH, PTA, SP

01 President Dr. Morton O. SCHAPIRO
05 Provost Dr. Jonathan S. HOLLOWAY
10 Sr Vice President Business/Finance Mr. Craig JOHNSON
32 Vice President Student Affairs Dr. Patricia TELLES-IRVIN
26 Vice President University Relations Vacant
45 Vice Pres Administration & Planning Ms. Marilyn MCCOY
13 Vice Pres Information Technology Mr. Sean B. REYNOLDS
30 Vice Pres for Alumni Rel & Devel Mr. Robert MCQUINN
46 Vice President Research Mr. Joseph T. WALSH
115 Vice Pres/Chief Investment Officer Mr. William H. MCLEAN
43 Vice President/General Counsel Mr. Philip L. HARRIS
18 Int Vice Pres for Facilities Mr. Alex DARRAGH
41 Vice Pres Athletics and Recreation Mr. James J. PHILLIPS
15 Vice Pres for Human Resources Ms. Pamela BEEMER
114 Vice Pres Budget Planning Mr. Paul CASTELLUCCI
84 Dean Enrollment/AVP Stdnt Outreach Mr. Christopher WATSON
53 Associate Provost Undergrad Educ Vacant
20 Associate Provost Faculty Affairs Dr. Lindsay CHASE-LANSDALE
20 Assoc VP & Assoc Provost Academic Mr. Jake JULIA
21 Assoc Prov Budget/Facil/Analysis Ms. Jean E. SHEDD
86 Spec Asst to Pres for Govt Rels Mr. Bruce LAYTON
04 Assistant to the President Mr. Eugene Y. LOWE, JR.
100 Chief of Staff/Sr Dir President Ofc Ms. Judith V. REMINGTON
54 Dean Sch Engr/Applied Science Dr. Julio M. OTTINO
50 Dean Graduate School of Management Dr. Sally E. BLOUNT
60 Int Dean School of Journalism Dr. Charles WHITAKER
64 Dean School of Music Dr. Toni-Marie MONTGOMERY
63 Dean School of Medicine Dr. Eric G. NEILSON
107 Dean School of Professional Studies Dr. Thomas F. GIBBONS
58 Dean Graduate School Dr. Teresa WOODRUFF
60 Dean School of Communication Dr. Barbara J. O'KEEFE
53 Dean School of Educ & Social Policy Dr. David N. FIGLIO
49 Dean College Arts & Science Mr. Adrian RANDOLPH
61 Dean School of Law Dr. Daniel B. RODRIGUEZ
08 University Librarian Ms. Sarah M. PRITCHARD
36 Exec Dir of University Career Svcs Dr. Mark PRESNELL
35 Assistant VP of Student Engagement Dr. Kelly SCHAEFER
29 AVP Alumni Relations/Development Mr. David LIVELY
88 Assoc Vice President for Research Mr. Lewis SMITH
88 Assoc Vice President for Research Dr. Jian CAO
88 AVP for Rsrch/Innov & New Ventures Ms. Alicia LOFFLER
88 Assoc Vice President for Research Ms. Ann ADAMS
88 Dean for Research Dr. Rex CHISHOLM
21 Vice Pres Finance/Treasurer Vacant
07 Dean Undergrad Admiss/AVP Stdnt OR Vacant
88 Exec Dir Intl Research Partnerships Ms. Indrani MUKHARJI
23 Exec Director Health Services Dr. Robert PALINKAS
39 Asst Dean of Students Ms. Mary GOLDENBERG
38 Director of Counseling/Psych Svcs Dr. John H. DUNKLE
42 University Chaplain Dr. Timothy S. STEVENS
88 Asst VP for Information Mr. Amit PRACHAND
88 AVP Program Review/Spec Project Ms. Megan BLACKWELDER
06 University Registrar Ms. Jacqualyn CASAZZA
37 Director Financial Aid Ms. Carolyn V. LINDLEY
16 Dir HR Consulting Svcs/Staffing Ms. Caroline M. ONAGAN
19 AVP/Chief of Police & Safety Mr. Bruce LEWIS
116 Assoc VP of Audit & Compliance Ms. Marcia ISAACSON
22 Dir Equal Emply Opprty/Affirm Act Ms. Tasha SHELTON
96 Exec Director of Procurement Mr. Jim KONRAD
28 Assoc Provost Diversity & Inclusion Dr. Jabbar BENNETT

Oakton Community College (G)

1600 E Golf Road, Des Plaines IL 60016-1256
County: Cook FICE Identification: 009896
Unit ID: 147800
Telephone: (847) 635-1600 Carnegie Class: Assoc/HT-Mix Trad/Non
FAX Number: (847) 635-1992 Calendar System: Semester
URL: www.oakton.edu

Established: 1969 Annual Undergrad Tuition & Fees (In-District): $3,985
Enrollment: 8,907 Coed
Affiliation or Control: Local IRS Status: 501(c)3
Highest Offering: Associate Degree
Accreditation: NH, ADNUR, CAHIIM, MLTAD, PTAA

Code	Title	Name
01	President	Dr. Joianne L. SMITH
05	Vice President Academic Affairs	Dr. Ileo LOTT
32	Vice President Student Affairs	Dr. Karl BROOKS
10	Vice Pres Administrative Affairs	Mr. Edwin CHANDRASEKAR
20	Asst VP Acad Affs/Col Transitions	Ms. Anne BRENNAN
103	AVP Workforce Development	Mr. Marc BATTISTA
35	Asst VP Student Affs/Dean Access	Ms. Juletta PATRICK
13	Chief Information Officer	Mr. Prashant SHINDE
76	Asst Dean Health Careers	Ms. Maribel ALIMBOYOGUEN
81	Dean STEM & Health Careers	Dr. Robert SOMPOLSKI
49	Dean Liberal Arts	Ms. Linda KORBEL
50	Dean Business & Career Tech	Mr. Bradley WOOTEN
09	AVP Institutional Research	Dr. Kelly IWANAGA-BECKER
26	AVP Mktg & Comm/CAO	Ms. Katherine SAWYER
08	Assistant Dean Library	Mr. Jacob JEREMIAH
84	Dir of Admission and Enrollment	Ms. Michele BROWN
35	Director of Student Life/Inclusion	Mr. Shedrick DANIELS
121	Dean of Student Success	Mr. Sebastian CONTRERAS, JR.
124	Dir of Student Learning/Engagement	Ms. Leana CUELLAR
41	Director of Athletics	Vacant
51	Dir Cont Educ & Workforce Dev	Dr. Ruben HOWARD, II
21	Controller	Mr. Andy WILLIAMS
15	Chief Human Resources Officer	Dr. Colette HANDS
18	Director of Facilities	Mr. Joseph SCIFO
14	Director Systems & Network Svcs	Mr. John WADE
14	Dir of Software & User Svcs	Ms. Renee KOZIMOR
06	Dir of Student Fin Suppor/Registrar	Dr. Cheryl WARMANN
25	Dir of Grants & Alternative Funding	Ms. Allison GRIPPE
51	Dir of Operations and Admin	Ms. Robyn BAILEY
38	Director of Counseling	Dr. Mark KIEL
19	Chief of Police	Vacant
88	Dean Curriculum & Instruction	Ms. Ruth WILLIAMS
106	Dean Online Learning	Dr. Raymond LAWSON

Olivet Nazarene University (A)

One University Avenue, Bourbonnais IL 60914-2345
County: Kankakee FICE Identification: 001741
Unit ID: 147828
Telephone: (815) 939-5011 Carnegie Class: Masters/L
FAX Number: (815) 935-4998 Calendar System: Semester
URL: www.olivet.edu
Established: 1907 Annual Undergrad Tuition & Fees: $36,070
Enrollment: 4,986 Coed
Affiliation or Control: Church Of The Nazarene IRS Status: 501(c)3
Highest Offering: Doctorate
Accreditation: NH, CAATE, DIETD, MUS, NURSE, SW

Code	Title	Name
01	President	Dr. John C. BOWLING
10	EVP/Chief Financial Officer	Dr. David PICKERING
05	Vice President Academic Affairs	Dr. Carol SUMMERS
32	Vice President Student Development	Dr. Walter W. WEBB
111	Vice Pres Institutional Advancement	Dr. Brian ALLEN
88	Vice Pres for ONU Global	Mr. Ryan SPITTAL
29	Dir Alumni & University Relations	Mr. Erinn PROEHL
09	Dean Inst Effectiveness/Registrar	Vacant
08	Interim Dean of Library Services	Mrs. Pam GREENLEE
26	Exec Director of Univ Relations	Mrs. Susan WOLFF
37	Director of Financial Aid	Mr. Greg BRUNER
13	Chief Information Officer	Mr. Dennis SEYMOUR
41	Athletic Director	Mr. Gary NEWSOME
42	Chaplain	Rev. Mark HOLCOMB
30	Exec Director of Development	Mr. John MONGERSON
35	Director Student Activities	Mrs. Kathy STEINACKER
38	Director Student Counseling	Mrs. Lisa VANDER VEER
18	Chief Facilities/Physical Plant	Mr. Rob LALUMENDRE
40	Bookstore Manager	Mrs. Rachel PIAZZA
36	Director of Career Services	Miss Poppy MILLER
85	International Student Advisor	Dr. Mark MOUNTAIN
26	Director of Marketing	Mr. Adam ASHER
19	Director Security/Safety	Mr. Dale NEWSOME
49	Dean College of Arts & Sciences	Dr. Stephen LOWE
73	Dn Sch Theology/Christian Ministry	Dr. Mark QUANSTROM
53	Dean School of Education	Dr. Lance KILPATRICK
76	Dean School of Life/Health Sciences	Mrs. Amber RESIDORI
64	Dean School of Music	Dr. Don REDDICK
50	Dean School of Business	Dr. Glen REWERTS
54	Dean School of Engineering	Dr. Houston THOMPSON
04	Admin Assistant to the President	Ms. Marjorie VINSON
15	Director of Human Resources	Mr. Tom ASCHER

Pacific College of Oriental Medicine (B)

65 East Wacker Place 21st Floor, Chicago IL 60601
Telephone: (888) 729-4811 Identification: 666615
Accreditation: &WC, ACUP

† Branch campus of Pacific College of Oriental Medicine, San Diego CA.

Parkland College (C)

2400 W Bradley Avenue, Champaign IL 61821-1899
County: Champaign FICE Identification: 007118
Unit ID: 147916
Telephone: (217) 351-2200 Carnegie Class: Assoc/HVT-Mix Trad/Non
FAX Number: (217) 351-2581 Calendar System: Semester
URL: www.parkland.edu
Established: 1966 Annual Undergrad Tuition & Fees (In-District): $4,920
Enrollment: 7,159 Coed
Affiliation or Control: State/Local IRS Status: 501(c)3
Highest Offering: Associate Degree
Accreditation: NH, ADNUR, COARC, DH, EMT, OTA, RAD, SURGT

Code	Title	Name
01	President	Dr. Thomas R. RAMAGE
04	Asst to President/Board of Trustees	Ms. Krystal GARRETT
05	Vice President Academic Svcs	Dr. Pam LAU
32	Vice President Student Services	Dr. Mike TRAME
10	Vice Pres Administrative Svcs/ CFO	Mr. Christopher M. RANDLES
26	VP Communications/External Affairs	Ms. Stephanie STUART
35	Dean of Students	Ms. Marietta TURNER
09	Dean Institutional Effectiveness	Mr. Kevin KNOTT
50	Dept Chair Bus & Agri Industries	Mr. Jim MANSFIELD
77	Department Chair Comp Science & IT	Mr. Derek DALLAS
54	Dept Chair Engineering Science/Tech	Mr. Jim MANSFIELD
79	Dept Chair Humanities	Mr. Matt HURT
57	Dean Fine & Applied Arts	Ms. Nancy SUTTON
75	Dean Career and Technical Education	Ms. Roberta SCHOLZE
81	Department Chair Mathematics	Mr. Brian MERCER
65	Dept Chair Natural Sciences	Mr. Scott SEICHEN
83	Dept Chair Social Sci & Human Svcs	Mr. Joe WALWIK
121	Dir Center for Academic Success	Ms. Tracey HICKOX
103	Exec Director Workforce Development	Ms. Tawanna NICKENS
102	Exec Dir Foundation/Alumni Affairs	Ms. Tracy WAHFELDT
08	Director Library	Ms. Morgann QUILTY
31	Director Community Education	Ms. Triss HENDERSON
25	Grants and Contracts	Mr. Joshua BIRKY
84	Dean Enrollment Mgmt/Dir Admissions	Ms. Julie MARLATT
41	Director Athletics	Mr. Brendan MCHALE
38	Dean Counseling Services	Ms. Ellen ZIMMERMAN
07	Director Enrollment Services	Mr. Tim WENDT
19	Director Public Safety	Mr. William COLBROOK
18	Director Physical Plant	Mr. James BUSTARD
15	Director Human Resources	Ms. Kathleen MCANDREW
21	Controller	Mr. Dave DONSBACH
40	Manager of Bookstore	Ms. Connie MACEDO
108	Director Assessment Center	Mr. Michael BEHRENS
13	Chief Information Tech Officer/CIO	Mr. Amin KASSEM

Prairie State College (D)

202 S Halsted Street, Chicago Heights IL 60411-8226
County: Cook FICE Identification: 001640
Unit ID: 148007
Telephone: (708) 709-3500 Carnegie Class: Assoc/MT-VT-High Non
FAX Number: (708) 755-2587 Calendar System: Semester
URL: www.prairiestate.edu
Established: 1957 Annual Undergrad Tuition & Fees (In-District): $4,176
Enrollment: 4,403 Coed
Affiliation or Control: State/Local IRS Status: 501(c)3
Highest Offering: Associate Degree
Accreditation: NH, ADNUR, DH, SURGT

Code	Title	Name
01	President	Dr. Terri L. WINFREE
10	Vice Pres Finance & Administration	Dr. Thomas SABAN
05	Vice Pres Acad Affs/Dean Faculty	Dr. Marie C. HANSEL
103	Vice Pres Community/Economic Devel	Mr. Craig D. SCHMIDT
32	VP Student Affairs/Dean of Students	Dr. Michael D. ANTHONY
49	Dean Liberal Arts & Soc Sciences	Mr. Elighie WILSON
81	Dean Curric/Math/Nat Science	Dr. Debra L. PRENDERGAST
76	Dean Allied Health/Emerg Services	Ms. Carol FAWCETT
75	Dean Career and Tech Education	Ms. Janice KAUSHAL
15	Exec Dir Human Resources	Mr. David CRONAN
13	Exec Dir Info Technology Resources	Mr. Gregory KAIN
56	Dean Adult Education	Ms. Kim M. KUNCE
21	Controller/Dir of Business Svcs	Ms. Marina KRTINIC
08	Dean Learning Resources/Assess	Ms. Carolyn CIESLA
51	Dean Corporate/Continuing Education	Ms. Kelly LAPETINO
35	Dean Student Dev/Campus Life	Mr. Felix SIMPKINS
18	Exec Dir Facilities and Operations	Mr. Timothy J. KOSIEK
111	Exec Dir Inst Advance & Foundation	Ms. Deborah S. HAVIGHORST
07	Exec Dir Enrollment/Fin Aid Svcs	Ms. Jaime M. MILLER
19	Chief of Police	Mr. Anthony MARTIN, SR.
37	Director Financial Aid	Ms. Grace MCGINNIS
09	Director Inst Research/Planning	Dr. Adane G. KASSA
41	Director of Athletics	Mr. Christopher J. KUCHTA
04	Admin Dir Pres Office/Board	Ms. Patricia G. TROST
89	Director First Year Experience	Vacant
108	Dir Inst Effect/Plng/Accreditation	Ms. Jan BONAVIA

Principia College (E)

1 Maybeck Place, Elsah IL 62028-9799
County: Jersey FICE Identification: 001744
Unit ID: 148016
Telephone: (618) 374-2131 Carnegie Class: Bac-A&S
FAX Number: (618) 374-5500 Calendar System: Semester
URL: www.principiacollege.edu
Established: 1898 Annual Undergrad Tuition & Fees: $29,470
Enrollment: 455 Coed
Affiliation or Control: Independent Non-Profit IRS Status: 501(c)3
Highest Offering: Baccalaureate
Accreditation: NH

Code	Title	Name
01	President	Dr. Jolanda WESTERHOF
05	Dean of Academics	Dr. Meggan MADDEN
115	Chief Investment Officer	Mr. Howard E. BERNER, JR.
111	Chief Advancement Officer	Mrs. Barbara BLACKWELL
20	Associate Dean of Academics	Dr. Edith LIST
88	Dir Acad Special Programs	Mr. James HEGARTY
43	Legal Counsel	Mr. Lee BARRON
06	Registrar	Ms. Alice DERVIN
32	Dean of Students	Mrs. Maya DIETZ
08	Director of Libraries	Mrs. Lisa ROBERTS
13	Director Information Technology	Vacant
104	Director of Principia Abroad	Mrs. Stephanie LOVSETH
41	Director of Athletics	Vacant
18	Director of Facilities	Mr. Ed GOEWERT
21	Controller	Mr. Don MILLER
37	Director of Financial Aid	Mrs. Tami GAVALETZ
96	Purchasing Agent	Mrs. Susan CURRY
09	Institutional Research Officer	Ms. Roz HIBBS
27	Dir Marketing & Communications	Mrs. Laurel WALTERS
07	Director of Admissions	Mr. Brett GRIMMER

Quincy University (F)

1800 College Avenue, Quincy IL 62301-2699
County: Adams FICE Identification: 001745
Unit ID: 148131
Telephone: (217) 222-8020 Carnegie Class: Bac-Diverse
FAX Number: (217) 228-5257 Calendar System: Semester
URL: www.quincy.edu
Established: 1860 Annual Undergrad Tuition & Fees: $28,562
Enrollment: 1,067 Coed
Affiliation or Control: Roman Catholic IRS Status: 501(c)3
Highest Offering: Master's
Accreditation: NH, CACREP

Code	Title	Name
00	Chair Board of Trustees	Mr. Delmer MITCHELL
01	President	Dr. Brian R. MCGEE
05	VP for Academic Affairs	Dr. Teresa REED
42	VP for Mission & Ministry	Fr. John DOCTOR, OFM
10	VP for Business/Finance	Mr. Mark STRIEKER
84	VP Student Enrollment & Engagement	Mr. Tom OLIVER
32	VP for Student Development	Dr. Christine TRACY
41	VP for Athletics/Athletic Dir	Mr. Marty BELL
111	VP for Univ Advancement	Mrs. Julie BELL
04	Exec Assistant to the President	Mrs. Julie BUDINE
101	Corporate Secretary	Fr. John DOCTOR, OFM
21	Controller	Mrs. Randi KINDHART
20	Associate VP for Academic Affairs	Dr. Lee ENGER
06	Registrar	Ms. Nancy GEISSLER
50	Dean School of Business	Dr. Cynthia HALIEMUN
08	Dean Library/Info Resources	Ms. Patricia TOMCZAK
79	Chair Division of Humanities	Dr. Daniel STRUDWICK
81	Chair Division Science & Technology	Dr. Kimberly HALE
83	Chair Div Behavioral/Social Sci	Dr. Megan BOCCARDI
57	Chair Div Communication/Fine Arts	Mr. Karl WARMA
53	Chair School of Education	Dr. Kenneth OLIVER
13	Director of IT Services	Mr. Michael MCCABE
108	Director of Academic Assessment	Ms. Barbara ROWLAND
92	Director Honors Program	Dr. Daniel STRUDWICK
42	Director Campus Ministry	Fr. William SPENCER, OFM
30	Dir Development/Alum/Cmty Relations	Mr. Matthew BERGMAN
37	Director Financial Aid	Ms. Lisa FLACK
18	Director Facilities Management	Mr. Randy JOHNSON
39	Director Campus Programs/Res Life	Mr. Johann ST. JOHN
88	Director Housing Op/Orientation	Ms. Andrea GRUEGER
19	Director Safety & Security	Mr. Sam LATHROP
15	Director Human Resources	Mrs. Tanya MOORE
07	Director of Admissions	Mr. Brittany ELLERMAN
36	Director of Experiential Learning	Mrs. Kristen LIESEN
96	Purchasing	Ms. Jennifer TRUITT
25	Grant Writer	Vacant
40	Manager Bookstore	Mr. Ben MEANS
88	Director of Student Teaching	Dr. Glenda MCCARTY
09	Director of Institutional Research	Mr. David SHINN

Rasmussen College - Rockford (G)

6000 E. State Street, 4th Floor, Rockford IL 61108
Telephone: (815) 316-4800 Identification: 667065
Accreditation: &NH, CAHIIM, MAAB

† Regional accreditation carried under the parent institution in Saint Cloud, MN. The tuition figure is an average, actual tuition may vary.

Rasmussen College - Romeoville/Joliet (H)

1400 West Normantown Road, Romeoville IL 60446
Telephone: (815) 306-2600 Identification: 667066
Accreditation: &NH, MAAB, SURGT

† Regional accreditation carried under the parent institution in Saint Cloud, MN. The tuition figure is an average, actual tuition may vary.

Realtor University (I)

430 North Michigan Avenue, Chicago IL 60611
County: Cook Identification: 667270
Telephone: (855) 786-6546 Carnegie Class: Not Classified
FAX Number: N/A Calendar System: Semester
URL: www.realtoru.edu
Established: 2003 Annual Undergrad Tuition & Fees: N/A
Enrollment: N/A Coed
Affiliation or Control: Independent Non-Profit IRS Status: 501(c)3
Highest Offering: Master's
Accreditation: DEAC

Code	Title	Name
01	President	Bob GOLDBERG
05	Chief Academic Officer	David OVERBYE
10	Chief Financial Officer	John PIERPOINT

Rend Lake College (A)

468 N Ken Gray Parkway, Ina IL 62846-9801
County: Jefferson FICE Identification: 007119
Unit ID: 148256
Telephone: (618) 437-5321 Carnegie Class: Assoc/HVT-High Non
FAX Number: (618) 437-5677 Calendar System: Semester
URL: www.rlc.edu
Established: 1967 Annual Undergrad Tuition & Fees (In-District): $3,900
Enrollment: 2,333 Coed
Affiliation or Control: State/Local IRS Status: 501(c)3
Highest Offering: Associate Degree
Accreditation: NH, EMT, MAC, MLTAD, RAD

01 President .... Mr. Terry WILKERSON
05 VP of Instruction & Student Affairs .... Mrs. Lori RAGLAND
10 VP of Finance & Administration .... Mrs. Angie KISTNER
32 Assoc VP of Academic & Student Svcs .... Mr. Henry LEECK
26 Assoc VP of Institutional Outreach .... Mr. Chad COPPLE
121 Assoc VP of CTE & Student Support .... Mrs. Kim WILKERSON
37 Director of Financial Aid .... Ms. Cheri RUSHING
41 Athletic Director .... Mr. Tim WILLS
18 Director Physical Plant .... Mr. Donnie MILLENBINE
102 CEO of RLC Foundation .... Mrs. Kathleen ZIBBY-DAMRON
06 Director of Student Records .... Mrs. Kelly DOWNES
84 Dean of Enrollment Services .... Mrs. Vickie SCHULTE

Resurrection University (B)

1431 N. Claremont Street, 6th Floor, Chicago IL 60622
County: Cook FICE Identification: 006250
Unit ID: 149763
Telephone: (773) 252-6464 Carnegie Class: Spec-4-yr-Other Health
FAX Number: (773) 227-5134 Calendar System: Semester
URL: www.resu.edu
Established: 1982 Annual Undergrad Tuition & Fees: N/A
Enrollment: 792 Coed
Affiliation or Control: Independent Non-Profit IRS Status: 501(c)3
Highest Offering: Doctorate
Accreditation: NH, CAHIIM, NURSE, RAD

01 President .... Dr. Therese A. SCANLAN
03 Executive Vice President .... Mr. Matthew HUGHES
05 Chief Academic Officer .... Vacant
26 VP Marketing & Enrollment Mgmt .... Ms. Jeri BINGHAM
32 VP Student & Employee Affairs .... Mr. Brian BOLLENBACHER
35 Director of Student Development .... Ms. Esther WALLEN
90 Network Support Analyst .... Ms. Valarie LINDSEY
37 Student Financial Aid .... Ms. Dominique COLYER
06 Registrar .... Ms. Alicia FLEMING
84 Director of Enrollment Mgmt .... Vacant
08 Director of Library Services .... Ms. Liesl COTTRELL
66 Dean of Nursing .... Vacant
04 Administrative Asst to President .... Ms. Barbara BAILEY
13 Chief Information Technology Office .... Mr. Matthew HERTZOG
29 Director Alumni Affairs .... Ms. Vickie THORNLEY

Richland Community College (C)

One College Park, Decatur IL 62521-8513
County: Macon FICE Identification: 010879
Unit ID: 148292
Telephone: (217) 875-7200 Carnegie Class: Assoc/HVT-High Non
FAX Number: (217) 875-6961 Calendar System: Semester
URL: www.richland.edu
Established: 1971 Annual Undergrad Tuition & Fees (In-District): $4,410
Enrollment: 2,515 Coed
Affiliation or Control: State/Local IRS Status: 501(c)3
Highest Offering: Associate Degree
Accreditation: NH, ACFEI, ADNUR, CAHIIM, RAD, SURGT

01 President .... Dr. Cristobal (Cris) VALDEZ
10 Vice President of Finance & Admin .... Mr. Greg E. FLORIAN
05 Vice Pres Academic Services .... Dr. Denise CREWS
106 Director Online Learning .... Mrs. Kona JONES
30 Exec Director Foundation & Devel .... Ms. Julie MELTON
29 Dir Scholarships/Alumni Development .... Mrs. Tricia CORDULACK
15 Director Human Resources .... Ms. Robin BOLLHORST
37 Asst Dir Financial Aid/Veteran Affs .... Ms. Jody BURTNETT
81 Dean Math & Sciences/Business Div .... Dr. Andy HYNDS
76 Dean of Health Professions .... Ms. Ellen COLBECK

Robert Morris University - Illinois (D)

401 South State Street, Chicago IL 60605-1225
County: Cook FICE Identification: 001746
Unit ID: 148335
Telephone: (312) 935-6800 Carnegie Class: Masters/M
FAX Number: (312) 935-6660 Calendar System: Other
URL: www.robertmorris.edu
Established: 1913 Annual Undergrad Tuition & Fees: $28,050
Enrollment: 2,307 Coed
Affiliation or Control: Independent Non-Profit IRS Status: 501(c)3
Highest Offering: Master's
Accreditation: NH, IACBE, MAC, NURSE, SURGT

01 President .... Mablene KRUEGER
10 Sr VP/Chief Financial Officer .... Arlene REGNERUS
21 Controller .... Melanie CARLIN
15 VP of Human Resources .... Ann BRESINGHAM
88 VP of Academic Administration .... Kathleen SUHAJDA
13 VP of Information Systems .... Lisa CONTRERAS
32 VP of Student Affairs .... Angela JORDAN
05 Associate Provost .... Paul GASZAK
37 Director of Financial Services .... Michelle HAYES
21 Assoc Director of Financial Plng .... Darrell DIVINITY
41 Director of Athletics .... Jared WILLIAMSON
26 Director of Marketing .... Michelle CASINI
20 Dean of Curriculum .... Lora TIMMONS
20 Dean of Instruction .... Basim KHARTABIL
06 Dean of Student Information .... Carmen CUEVAS
58 Dean of Morris Graduate School .... Kayed AKKAWI
88 Director of MGS .... Vacant
07 Dean of Admissions .... Andy BERGER
19 Director Security/Safety .... Paul HUERTA
111 Exec Dir of Institutional Advance .... Carolyn BRANTON SMITH
35 Dir Student Professional Engagement .... Carrie ROATH
53 Director of Education .... Kimberly WARFORD
53 Director of Education .... Jane WENDORFF-CRAPS
08 Institutional Library Director .... Sue DUTLER
18 Institutional Operations Director .... Nino RANDAZZO
14 Director of Networking Services .... Adrian CEPEDA
27 Director of Public Relations .... Nancy DONOHOE
91 Director of Data Administration .... Deana MUNOZ
88 Sr Dir of Academic Administration .... Kathleen VIOLLT
121 Dir of Student Support Services .... Angelica CASTANDEA
88 Director of Grant Advancement .... Lauren MILLER
88 Dir of Upward Bound and ETS .... Carolyn BASLEY
90 Director of Academic Programming .... Vacant
27 Director of Visual Strategy & Comm .... Deanna LEE

Rock Valley College (E)

3301 N Mulford Road, Rockford IL 61114-5699
County: Winnebago FICE Identification: 001747
Unit ID: 148380
Telephone: (815) 921-7821 Carnegie Class: Assoc/MT-VT-High Trad
FAX Number: N/A Calendar System: Semester
URL: www.rockvalleycollege.edu
Established: 1964 Annual Undergrad Tuition & Fees (In-District): $3,764
Enrollment: 6,378 Coed
Affiliation or Control: Local IRS Status: 501(c)3
Highest Offering: Associate Degree
Accreditation: NH, COARC, DH, SURGT

01 President .... Dr. Douglas J. JENSEN
11 VP/Chief Operating Officer .... Mr. Jim RYAN
05 VP Academic/Student Affairs & CAO .... Mr. Ronald GEARY
10 Vice Pres Finance/CFO .... Ms. Beth YOUNG
20 Vice Pres Academic Affairs .... Dr. Lisa MEHLIG
32 VP Student Services .... Dr. Will ASHFORD
103 VP Workforce Development .... Ms. Gina CARONNA
88 VP Cmty Outreach/Strat Partnerships .... Mr. Christopher LEWIS
15 Executive Director Human Resources .... Mr. Joe SIMPSON
09 VP Inst Research/Effectiveness .... Ms. Heather SNIDER
30 Chief Development Officer .... Ms. Brittany FREIBERG
18 Director Facilities Planning & POM .... Ms. Janet TAYLOR
26 Exec Dir Col Comm/Marketing .... Mr. Dave COSTELLO
88 Director Theatre & Arts Park .... Mr. Christopher D. BRADY
19 Director Public Safety .... Vacant
06 Registrar/Director Records/Rgstn .... Ms. Stacey KOLDER
36 Manager Career Svcs/Placement .... Vacant
04 Assistant to the President .... Ms. Ann KERWITZ
04 Assistant to the President .... Ms. Kris FUCHS
41 Athletic Director .... Mr. Darin MONROE

Rockford Career College (F)

1130 S. Alpine Road, Suite 100, Rockford IL 61108
County: Winnebago FICE Identification: 008545
Unit ID: 148399
Telephone: (815) 965-8616 Carnegie Class: Assoc/HVT-Mix Trad/Non
FAX Number: (815) 965-0360 Calendar System: Quarter
URL: www.rockfordcareercollege.edu
Established: 1862 Annual Undergrad Tuition & Fees: $14,918
Enrollment: 465 Coed
Affiliation or Control: Proprietary IRS Status: Proprietary
Highest Offering: Associate Degree
Accreditation: ACCSC, MAAB

01 President/CEO .... Mr. Stephen TAVE
10 Vice President/Dir of Finance .... Mr. Guary BERNADELLE
05 Academic Dean .... Ms. Danielle HARRIOTT
12 Campus President .... Mr. Mike O'HERRON
32 Director of Student Services .... Ms. Michelle LAURIANO
06 Registrar/Director of Compliance .... Ms. Erin EGGEBRECHT
07 Director of Admissions .... Ms. Doreen STEWART
15 Director of Human Resources .... Mr. Kent SHEPLER
36 Director Career Services .... Ms. Phyllis LEE
37 Director of Financial Aid .... Ms. Mari HUFFMAN
26 Director of College Relations .... Mr. Jeff SWANBERG
08 Library/Bookstore Coordinator .... Ms. Edith HILL

Rockford University (G)

5050 E State Street, Rockford IL 61108-2393
County: Winnebago FICE Identification: 001748
Unit ID: 148405
Telephone: (815) 226-4000 Carnegie Class: Masters/S
FAX Number: (815) 226-4119 Calendar System: Semester
URL: www.rockford.edu
Established: 1847 Annual Undergrad Tuition & Fees: $30,930
Enrollment: 1,262 Coed
Affiliation or Control: Independent Non-Profit IRS Status: 501(c)3
Highest Offering: Master's
Accreditation: NH, IACBE, NUR

01 President .... Dr. Eric W. FULCOMER
05 VP of Academic Affairs/Provost .... Dr. Michael PERRY
111 VP for Institutional Advancement .... Vacant
30 AVP for Institutional Advancement .... Mrs. Denise NOE
10 VP for Finance/CFO .... Ms. Lisa CUSTARDO
21 Business Office Accounting Manager .... Mr. John DIRAIMONDO
84 VP Enrollment Management .... Mr. David HAWSEY
32 VP for Student Affairs .... Dr. Randy WORDEN
37 Assistant VP for SAS .... Mr. Todd FISCHER-FREE
11 Director of Operations .... Mr. Ed TOMASZKIEWICZ
13 Director of Information Technology .... Mr. Ryan CUSHING
123 Director of Adult & Grad Admissions .... Ms. Anissa KUHAR
06 Registrar .... Ms. Anna J. JATTKOWSKI-HUDSON
04 Exec Assistant to the President .... Ms. Jen CUNNINGHAM
41 Director of Athletics .... Mr. Jason MULLIGAN
15 Director of Human Resources .... Ms. Monique LINDSTEDT
36 Director Career Services .... Ms. Logan GLENDENNING
26 Director of Communications .... Ms. Rita ELLIOTT
09 Coordinator of IR .... Mr. Todd FISCHER-FREE
88 Director of Global Affairs .... Mr. Sam BANDY
23 Director Health Services .... Ms. Kristen CLARKE
18 Facilities Director .... Mr. Karl ALBILLAR
19 Deputy Chief of Police .... Mr. Jeffrey BOATWRIGHT
08 Head Librarian .... Ms. Kelly JAMES

Roosevelt University (H)

430 S Michigan Avenue, Chicago IL 60605-1394
County: Cook FICE Identification: 001749
Unit ID: 148487
Telephone: (312) 341-3500 Carnegie Class: DU-Mod
FAX Number: (312) 341-3655 Calendar System: Semester
URL: www.roosevelt.edu
Established: 1945 Annual Undergrad Tuition & Fees: $29,832
Enrollment: 4,457 Coed
Affiliation or Control: Independent Non-Profit IRS Status: 501(c)3
Highest Offering: Doctorate
Accreditation: NH, ACBSP, CACREP, CLPSY, MUS, PHAR

01 President .... Dr. Ali MALEKZADEH
05 Exec Vice President/Univ Provost .... Dr. Lois BECKER
10 Vice Pres of Finance/Admin and CFO .... Mr. Andrew HARRIS
84 Vice Pres Enrollment Mgmt .... Mr. Michael CASSIDY
100 Chief of Staff & Secretary to BOT .... Dr. Michael FORD
111 VP Institutional Advancement .... Vacant
30 Asst VP Institutional Advancement .... Vacant
26 VP Marketing/Communications .... Ms. Nicole BARRON
32 VP Student Affairs/Dean Students .... Mr. Jamar ORR
09 Assoc VP Inst Research .... Mr. Joseph P. REGAN
21 Acting AVP Finance/Controller .... Mr. Patrick ALFORQUE
18 Assoc VP Campus Planning & Ops .... Vacant
85 Asst Dir of International Programs .... Ms. Dawn HOUGLAND
13 Chief Information Officer/VP Tech .... Mr. Neeraj KUMAR
58 Assoc Provost Research .... Dr. Mike MALY
121 Assoc Provost Student Success .... Ms. Katrina COAKLEY
49 Dean College Arts & Sciences .... Dr. Bonnie GUNZENHAUSER
50 Dean College of Business .... Dr. Asghar SABBAGHI
64 Dean College of Performing Arts .... Mr. Rudi MARCOZZI
53 Dean College of Education .... Dr. Thomas PHILION
67 Dean College of Pharmacy .... Dr. Melissa HOGAN
88 Int CEO Auditorium Theatre .... Ms. Rachel FREUND
08 Director of Libraries .... Mr. Estavan MONTANO
06 University Registrar .... Vacant
38 Director Counseling Center .... Vacant
36 Director Career & Prof Development .... Ms. Jennifer WONDERLY
04 Exec Asst to President .... Ms. Vanessa GEORG
19 Director Campus Safety & Trans .... Mr. Tony PARKER
07 Director of Admissions .... Mr. Al NUNEZ
105 Senior Web Developer .... Mr. Eugene CHOI
96 Director of Purchasing .... Vacant

Rosalind Franklin University of Medicine & Science (I)

3333 Green Bay Road, North Chicago IL 60064-3095
County: Lake FICE Identification: 001659
Unit ID: 145558
Telephone: (847) 578-3000 Carnegie Class: Spec-4-yr-Med
FAX Number: (847) 578-3401 Calendar System: Quarter
URL: www.rosalindfranklin.edu
Established: 1912 Annual Undergrad Tuition & Fees: N/A
Enrollment: 2,145 Coed
Affiliation or Control: Independent Non-Profit IRS Status: 501(c)3
Highest Offering: Doctorate; No Lower Division
Accreditation: NH, ANEST, ARCPA, CLPSY, MED, PA, PHAR, POD, PTA

01 Interim President/CEO .... Dr. Wendy RHEAULT
05 Acting Provost .... Dr. Nancy L. PARSLEY
67 Dean College of Pharmacy .... Dr. Marc ABEL
107 Dean College Health Professions .... Dr. John VITALE
58 Dean Sch Grad PostDoc Stds .... Dr. Joseph X. DIMARIO
63 Dean Scholl Col Podiatric Med .... Dr. Nancy L. PARSLEY
63 Dean Medical School .... Dr. James RECORD
46 Exec VP Research .... Dr. Ronald S. KAPLAN
26 Senior VP University Enhancement .... Ms. Lee CONCHA
32 VP Student Success and Inclusion .... Ms. Rebecca DURKIN
88 VP Partnerships .... Dr. Sandra LARSON
20 VP Faculty Affairs .... Dr. Judith STOECKER
20 VP Academic Affairs .... Dr. Nancy L. PARSLEY
111 VP Institutional Advancement .... Mr. Chad RUBACK

10 VP Finance & Admin .... Mr. John NYLEN
43 Chief Compliance Officer .... Mr. Bret MOBERG
13 AVP Technology & Learning Resources .... Mr. Richard LOESCH
88 AVP Faculty Development .... Dr. Rea KATZ
114 AVP Financial Plng & Analysis .... Ms. Christie TIPTON
35 AVP Student Affairs .... Ms. Shelly BRZYCKI
28 AVP Diversity and Inclusion .... Dr. Tamekia SCOTT
37 AVP Student Financial Services .... Ms. Maryann DECAIRE
07 AVP Admissions/Enrollment .... Vacant
06 AVP Student Records/Registrar .... Mr. Jason CELIZ
21 Controller .... Mr. Thomas J. BUNS
29 Exec Dir Alumni Relations .... Ms. Martha KELLY BATES
30 Exec Dir of Development .... Mr. George RATTIN
30 Exec Dir of Development .... Ms. Pamela LOWE
103 Exec Dir Healthcare Workforce Dev .... Dr. William RUDMAN
09 Senior Dir Institutional Research .... Vacant
102 Dir Foundation & Grant Relations .... Ms. Shella BLUE
44 Dir Annual Giving .... Mr. Mark RUSSELL
15 Exec Dir of Human Resources .... Ms. Sally J. MADDEN
28 Dir Training/Educational Programs .... Dr. Monica CUMMINGS
121 Dir Academic Support .... Ms. Nydia STEWART
19 Dir Campus Security .... Mr. Gordon BLANCHARD
96 Dir Materials Management .... Mr. Vince BUTERA
18 Dir Facilities Management .... Mr. Robert D. JACKSON
25 Dir Sponsored Research .... Ms. Dora ESPINOSA
08 Library Director .... Mr. Scott THOMSON
16 Dir of Human Resources .... Ms. Mary TELL
04 Executive Administrative Assistant .... Ms. Jean MINA
118 Benefits Administrator .... Ms. Melissa HALEY
39 Coordinator for Residence Life .... Ms. Amber WOYAK

Rush University (A)

600 S Paulina, Chicago IL 60612-3832
County: Cook FICE Identification: 009800
Unit ID: 148511
Telephone: (312) 942-7100 Carnegie Class: Spec-4-yr-Med
FAX Number: (312) 942-2219 Calendar System: Semester
URL: www.rushu.rush.edu
Established: 1971 Annual Undergrad Tuition & Fees: N/A
Enrollment: 2,569 Coed
Affiliation or Control: Independent Non-Profit IRS Status: 501(c)3
Highest Offering: Doctorate
Accreditation: NH, ANEST, ARCPA, AUD, BBT, COARC, DIETI, DMS, HSA, IPSY, MED, MT, NURSE, OT, PAST, PERF, SP

01 President Rush University .... Dr. Sherine E. GABRIEL
00 CEO Rush Univ Medical Ctr/Rush Sys .... Dr. Larry J. GOODMAN
17 President & COO RUMC .... Mr. Michael DANDORPH
05 Provost .... Dr. Thomas A. DEUTSCH
26 Vice Pres Corp/External Affairs .... Mr. Terry PETERSON
10 Principal Business Officer .... Mr. Richard K. DAVIS
10 Senior Vice President Finance .... Mr. John MORDACH
30 Senior Vice President Philanthropy .... Ms. Diane M. MCKEEVER
13 Sr Vice Pres/Chief Information Ofcr .... Dr. Shafiq RAB
43 Vice President Legal Affairs .... Mr. Carl BERGETZ
15 Sr Vice President Human Resource .... Ms. Mary E. SCHOPP
25 Vice Pres Chief Compliance Office .... Dr. Cynthia E. BOYD
28 Int Dir Student Diversity/Multicul .... Mr. Greg MACVARISH
20 Sr Assc Provost Educational Affairs .... Dr. Gayle WARD
108 Assoc Prov Inst Res/Assess/Accred .... Dr. Rosemarie SUHAYDA
32 Chief Student Experience Officer .... Mr. Greg MACVARISH
76 Dean Col of Health Sciences .... Dr. Charlotte ROYEEN
58 Dean Graduate College .... Dr. Andrew BEAN
66 Dean College of Nursing .... Dr. Marquis D. FOREMAN
63 Dean Rush Medical College .... Dr. Ranga KRISHNAN
20 Sr Assoc Dean Medical College .... Dr. Elizabeth A. BAKER
27 Assoc VP Marketing & Comm .... Mr. Ryan NAGDEMAN
08 Director Library .... Ms. Jo CATES
35 Director Student Life & Engagement .... Ms. Angela BRANSON
37 Dir Student Financial Aid .... Ms. Jill GABLE
09 Director of Institutional Research .... Dr. Joshua JACOBS
38 Director Student Counsel Center .... Dr. Hilarie TEREBESSY
29 Director Alumni Relations .... Ms. Krista GIUFFI
96 Director of Purchasing .... Mr. Michael MULROE
18 Director University Facilities .... Mr. Chris KANAKIS
21 Manager of Financial Affairs .... Mr. Patrick MCNULTY
84 Chief Enroll Mgmt Ofcr/Registrar .... Ms. Brenda WEDDINGTON
102 Dir Foundation/Corporate Relations .... Ms. Sophia WOROBEC
105 Assoc VP IS Clinical Systems .... Mr. Steven P. WIGHTKIN
19 Director Security Services .... Mr. Lauris FREIDENFELDS
54 Director Med Ctr Engineering .... Mr. Mike WISNIEWSKI

SAE Institute Chicago (B)

820 N. Orleans St., Ste 125, Chicago IL 60610
Telephone: (312) 300-5685 Identification: 770970
Accreditation: ACCSC

† Branch campus of SAE Institute Nashville, Nashville, TN

Saint Anthony College of Nursing (C)

3301 N. Mulford Rd, Rockford IL 61114
County: Winnebago FICE Identification: 009987
Unit ID: 149028
Telephone: (815) 282-7900 Carnegie Class: Spec-4-yr-Other Health
FAX Number: (815) 282-7901 Calendar System: Semester
URL: https://www.osfhealthcare.org/sacn/
Established: 1915 Annual Undergrad Tuition & Fees: $25,948
Enrollment: 285 Coed
Affiliation or Control: Roman Catholic IRS Status: 501(c)3
Highest Offering: Doctorate
Accreditation: NH, NURSE

01 President .... Dr. Sandie S. SOLDWISCH
66 Dean Undergraduate Affairs .... Dr. Elizabeth M. CARSON
58 Dean Graduate Affairs & Research .... Dr. Shannon K. LIZER
32 Associate Dean Support Services .... Ms. Nancy A. SANDERS
08 Library Supervisor .... Ms. Heather A. KLEPITSCH
37 Financial Aid Coordinator .... Ms. Serrita WOODS
04 Administrative Asst to President .... Ms. Teresa M. DAUGHERTY
84 Enrollment Management Coordinator .... Ms. April M. LIPNITZKY
09 Inst Effectiveness/Assessment Spec .... Ms. Elizabeth R. HARP
90 Educational Technology Coordinator .... Ms. Susan K. STAAB

St. Augustine College (D)

1333-45 W Argyle Street, Chicago IL 60640-3501
County: Cook FICE Identification: 021854
Unit ID: 148876
Telephone: (773) 878-8756 Carnegie Class: Bac/Assoc-Mixed
FAX Number: (773) 878-0937 Calendar System: Semester
URL: www.staugustine.edu
Established: 1980 Annual Undergrad Tuition & Fees: $11,400
Enrollment: 1,256 Coed
Affiliation or Control: Independent Non-Profit IRS Status: 501(c)3
Highest Offering: Baccalaureate
Accreditation: NH, COARC, SW

01 President .... Dr. Reyes GONZALEZ
05 VP Academic Services & Operations .... Dr. Bruno BONDAVALLI
20 VP Academic Affairs .... Ms. Madeline ROMAN-VARGAS
10 VP Finance .... Ms. Saundra K. FLEMING
26 VP Marketing & Enrollment Mgmt .... Mr. David CORDOVA
103 VP Institute Workforce Development .... Mr. Norman RUANO
84 Vice President of Enrollment Mgmt .... Dr. Juan OJEDA
13 VP Technology/Research & Systems .... Mr. Paul HECK
37 Director of Financial Aid .... Ms. Maria ZAMBONINO
15 Director Human Resources .... Mr. Teofilo CALERO
07 Director of Admission .... Ms. Gloria QUIROZ
12 Director West Satellite .... Ms. Carmen RIVERA
12 Director South Satellite .... Dr. Beda LOPEZ SIERRA
12 Director of Southeast Satellite .... Ms. Patricia VEGA
12 Director of Aurora Satellite .... Ms. Elizabeth CARDENAS
08 Dir of Information Commons/Library .... Ms. Elizabeth MURPHY
06 Registrar .... Ms. Margarita VACA
09 Director of Institutional Research .... Mr. Robert MYERS

Saint Francis Medical Center College of Nursing (E)

511 NE Greenleaf Street, Peoria IL 61603-3783
County: Peoria FICE Identification: 006240
Unit ID: 148575
Telephone: (309) 655-2201 Carnegie Class: Spec-4-yr-Other Health
FAX Number: (309) 624-8973 Calendar System: Semester
URL: www.sfmccon.edu
Established: 1985 Annual Undergrad Tuition & Fees: N/A
Enrollment: 648 Coed
Affiliation or Control: Roman Catholic IRS Status: 501(c)3
Highest Offering: Doctorate
Accreditation: NH, NUR, NURSE

01 President of the College .... Dr. Sandie S. SOLDWISCH
05 Dean Undergraduate Program .... Dr. Sue C. BROWN
58 Dean Graduate Program .... Dr. Kimberly A. MITCHELL
32 Asst Dean of Support Services .... Mr. Kevin N. STEPHENS
07 Director of Admissions/Registrar .... Ms. Janice E. FARQUHARSON
08 Librarian .... Mr. William KOMANECKI
38 College Counselor .... Mrs. Victoria KAMHI
37 Coord Student Fin/Financial Assist .... Mrs. Nancy S. PERRYMAN
113 Coord Student Finance/Accts Rec .... Ms. Alice C. EVANS
04 Administrative Assistant .... Ms. Luann MORELOCK
108 Inst Effectiveness/Assessment Spec .... Mr. Ryan A. WILLIAMS

St. John's College (F)

729 E. Carpenter Street, Springfield IL 62702-5317
County: Sangamon FICE Identification: 030980
Unit ID: 148593
Telephone: (217) 525-5628 Carnegie Class: Spec-4-yr-Other Health
FAX Number: (217) 757-6870 Calendar System: Semester
URL: www.sjcs.edu
Established: 1991 Annual Undergrad Tuition & Fees: N/A
Enrollment: 128 Coed
Affiliation or Control: Independent Non-Profit IRS Status: 501(c)3
Highest Offering: Master's
Accreditation: NH, NUR

01 Chancellor .... Dr. Charlene S. AARON
05 Dean of Academic Affairs .... Dr. Judy SHACKELFORD
07 Admissions Officer/Registrar .... Ms. Britni CARUSO
30 Student Development Officer .... Ms. Abby MILLITELLO
37 Financial Aid/Compliance Officer .... Mr. Timothy MARTEN

Saint Xavier University (G)

3700 W 103rd Street, Chicago IL 60655-3105
County: Cook FICE Identification: 001768
Unit ID: 148627
Telephone: (773) 298-3000 Carnegie Class: Masters/L
FAX Number: (773) 779-9061 Calendar System: Semester
URL: www.sxu.edu
Established: 1846 Annual Undergrad Tuition & Fees: $33,880
Enrollment: 3,715 Coed
Affiliation or Control: Roman Catholic IRS Status: 501(c)3
Highest Offering: Master's
Accreditation: NH, CAEPN, MUS, NURSE, SP

01 President .... Dr. Laurie M. JOYNER
05 Provost .... Dr. James MACLAREN
10 Vice Pres Finance/Admin & CFO .... Mr. Daniel P. KLOTZBACH
32 VP Enrollment/Student Services .... Ms. Maureen WOGAN
09 Exec Dir Institutional Research .... Dr. Kathleen CARLSON
26 AVP Marketing/Communications .... Ms. Deb RAPACZ
111 AVP University Advancement .... Ms. Erin R. MUELLER
18 Director of Facilities Management .... Mr. Peter SKACH
20 Associate Provost .... Dr. Richard VENNERI
13 Chief Information Officer .... Ms. Molly GAIK
109 Director Auxiliary Services .... Ms. Linda MORENO
37 Director Financial Aid .... Ms. Susan SWISHER
21 Controller .... Ms. Diane STALLMANN
24 Director CIDAT .... Ms. Yue MA
08 Director Library .... Mr. David STERN
06 Director Records/Registration Svcs .... Ms. Barbara SUTTON
19 Dir Public Safety/Chief of Police .... Mr. Jack TOUHY
85 Dir Center International Education .... Ms. Kelly REIDY-FOX
36 Assoc Director Career Services .... Mr. Josh BAUGH
49 Dean Arts & Sciences .... Dr. Robin RYLAARSDAM
53 Dean School of Education .... Vacant
50 Dean Graham School of Management .... Vacant
66 Dean School of Nursing .... Dr. Peg GALLAGHER
100 Chief of Staff .... Ms. Maggie EAHEART
15 Director of Human Resources .... Mr. Gerry HORAN
29 Director Alumni Relations .... Ms. Jeanmarie GAINER
84 AVP Enrollment Management .... Mr. Brian HOTZFIELD

Sauk Valley Community College (H)

173 Illinois Route 2, Dixon IL 61021-9188
County: Lee FICE Identification: 001752
Unit ID: 148672
Telephone: (815) 288-5511 Carnegie Class: Assoc/HVT-High Non
FAX Number: (815) 288-1880 Calendar System: Semester
URL: www.svcc.edu
Established: 1965 Annual Undergrad Tuition & Fees (In-District): $4,470
Enrollment: 1,754 Coed
Affiliation or Control: State/Local IRS Status: 501(c)3
Highest Offering: Associate Degree
Accreditation: NH, RAD

01 President .... Dr. David M. HELLMICH
05 Vice Pres Academics/Student Svcs .... Mr. Jon D. MANDRELL
09 VP of Academics and Student Affairs .... Mr. Steve C. NUNEZ
76 Dean of Health Professions .... Ms. Christine L. VINCENT
10 VP of Business Services .... Mr. Kent A. SORENSON
18 Director Facilities .... Mr. Steve W. ALLERT
15 Director of Human Resources .... Ms. Kathryn C. SNOW
84 Director Enrollment Mgmt/Registrar .... Ms. Pamela S. MEDEMA
102 Dean of Institutional Advancement .... Ms. Lori A. CORTEZ
13 Dir Information Services/Security .... Mr. Eric L. EPPS
41 Director of Athletics .... Mr. Michael P. STEVENSON
37 Director of Financial Assistance .... Ms. Jennifer A. SCHULTZ
91 Learning Technology Supp Specialist .... Ms. Kathleen M. DIRKS

School of the Art Institute of Chicago (I)

37 S Wabash, Chicago IL 60603-3103
County: Cook FICE Identification: 001753
Unit ID: 143048
Telephone: (312) 899-5100 Carnegie Class: Spec-4-yr-Arts
FAX Number: (312) 263-0141 Calendar System: Semester
URL: www.saic.edu
Established: 1866 Annual Undergrad Tuition & Fees: $49,310
Enrollment: 3,648 Coed
Affiliation or Control: Independent Non-Profit IRS Status: 501(c)3
Highest Offering: Master's
Accreditation: NH, ART

01 President .... Dr. James RONDEAU
84 Vice Pres Enrollment Management .... Ms. Rose MILKOWSKI
111 VP for Institutional Advancement .... Ms. Cheryl JESSOGNE
10 Vice Pres Finance & Administration .... Mr. Brian ESKER
15 Vice President for Human Resources .... Mr. Michael NICOLAI
32 Vice Pres/Dean of Student Affairs .... Dr. Felice DUBLON
20 Vice Provost .... Mr. Paul COFFEY
18 Vice Pres Campus Operations .... Mr. Thomas BUECHELE
20 Dean of Faculty/VP Acad Affs .... Ms. Lisa WAINWRIGHT
35 Dean of Student Life .... Ms. Deborah MARTIN
21 Exec Dir Academic Accounting .... Ms. Sherry MISGEN
26 Exec Dir Enroll Mktg & Operations .... Ms. Maryann SCHAEFER
29 Exec Director Alumni Relations .... Ms. Ashley SPELL
38 Exec Director Wellness Center .... Dr. Joseph BEHEN
88 Exec Director Enrollment Services .... Ms. Jane BRUMITT
06 Director Registration & Records .... Ms. Christy MICELI
08 Exec Director of School Library .... Ms. Claire EIKE
36 Dean Career & Prof Experience .... Dr. Terri LONIER
07 Assoc Dir of Undergrad Admissions .... Mr. Dave A. MURRAY
123 Director of Graduate Admissions .... Ms. Nicole HALL
37 Director of Student Financial Svcs .... Mr. Patrick JAMES
28 Director of Multicultural Affairs .... Ms. Rashayla BROWN
88 Director of Learning Center .... Ms. Valerie ST. GERMAIN
49 Dean of Undergraduate Studies .... Ms. Tiffany HOLMES
58 Dean of Graduate Studies .... Mr. Arnold KEMP
28 Dir of Acad Affairs/Diversity/Incl .... Dr. Christina GOMEZ

Shawnee Community College (A)

8364 Shawnee College Road, Ullin IL 62992-2206
County: Pulaski FICE Identification: 007693
Unit ID: 148821
Telephone: (618) 634-3200 Carnegie Class: Assoc/MT-VT-High Non
FAX Number: (618) 634-3300 Calendar System: Semester
URL: www.shawneecc.edu
Established: 1967 Annual Undergrad Tuition & Fees (In-District): $4,000
Enrollment: 1,505 Coed
Affiliation or Control: Local IRS Status: 501(c)3
Highest Offering: Associate Degree
Accreditation: NH, MLTAD, OTA, SURGT

01 President .... Dr. Kathleen CURPHY
05 Vice President Academic Affairs .... Dr. Kathleen CURPHY
32 Vice President Student Services .... Dr. Countance ANDERSON
04 Administrative Asst to President .... Ms. Carolyn DUMAS
20 Dean Instructional Services .... Dr. Kristin SHELBY
51 Dean Adult Educ/Alternative Instruc .... Dr. Gregory MASON
10 Vice President Financial Services .... Ms. Brandy WOODS
38 Student Support Services Director .... Ms. Amber SUGGS
35 Dean of Student Services .... Ms. Dee BLAKELY
37 Dir Fin Aid/Coord Vet & Mil Personl .... Dr. Tammy CAPPS
41 Athletic Director .... Mr. John SPARKS
13 Director of Information Technology .... Mr. Chris CLARK
12 Director Metropolis Ext Center ... Ms. Jipaum ASKEW-ROBINSON
66 Director of Nursing .... Ms. Connie DRURY
08 Head Librarian .... Ms. Tracey JOHNSON
06 Registrar .... Ms. Danielle BOYD
21 Director of Business Services .... Ms. Brandy WOODS
18 Facilities Director .... Mr. Don KOCH
09 Director of Institutional Research .... Vacant
40 Bookstore Manager .... Ms. Stacy SIMPSON
88 Accessibility & Resource Coord .... Ms. Heather CASNER
88 Director Economic Development .... Vacant
26 Director of Public Relations .... Mr. Rob BETTS
36 Career Services Coordinator .... Ms. Leslie WELDON
50 Div Chair Business/Occup/Tech Dp .... Ms. Ruth SMITH
81 Division Chair Math/Science .... Ms. Lori ARMSTRONG
79 Div Chr Social Stds/Humanities/Comm .... Ms. Joella BASLER
76 Div Chair Allied Health .... Ms. Tracy LOHSTROH
15 Human Resources Director .... Ms. Emily FORTHMAN
88 Director of Learning Resources .... Mr. Russ STOUP
56 Director Anna Extension Center .... Ms. Lindsay JOHNSON
88 Education Talent Search Director .... Ms. Deborah JOHNSON

South Suburban College (B)

15800 S State Street, South Holland IL 60473-1270
County: Cook FICE Identification: 001769
Unit ID: 149365
Telephone: (708) 596-2000 Carnegie Class: Assoc/MT-VT-High Non
FAX Number: (708) 210-5710 Calendar System: Semester
URL: www.ssc.edu
Established: 1927 Annual Undergrad Tuition & Fees (In-District): $5,093
Enrollment: 3,921 Coed
Affiliation or Control: State/Local IRS Status: 501(c)3
Highest Offering: Associate Degree
Accreditation: NH, CVT, OTA

01 College President .... Dr. Lynette D. STOKES
05 Vice President Academic Services .... Dr. Tasha WILLIAMS
11 Vice Pres Administration .... Mr. Martin LAREAU
32 Vice President Student Development .... Dr. Deborah BEANESS KING
35 Dean Student Services .... Mr. Devon POWELL
09 AVP Accreditation/Inst Effective .... Mr. Ronald KAWANNA, JR.
72 Dean Science/Technology/Engr/Math .... Ms. Anna HELWIG
76 Dean Allied Health/Career Programs .... Mr. Jeff WADDY
57 Dean Fine Arts/Soc & Behav Sci/Bus .... Mr. Tom GOVAN, JR.
66 Dean Nursing/Fine Arts/English/Hum .... Ms. Miriam ANTHONY
56 Dean Adult/Continuing Education .... Mr. Matthew BEASLAND
51 Director Continuing Education .... Ms. Shirley DREWENSKI
10 Treasurer/Controller .... Mr. Tim POLLERT
26 Exec Dir Public Rels/Resource Dev .... Mr. Patrick RUSH
13 Exec Dir Information Technology .... Mr. John MCCORMACK
89 Dir New Student Ctr/Retention Svcs .... Ms. Tiffane JONES
84 Exec Director Enrollment Services .... Mrs. Robin RIHACEK
37 Director of Financial Aid .... Mr. John SEMPLE
18 Director Physical Plant Services .... Mr. Justin PAPP
24 Dir Communication Svcs/Media Design .... Mrs. Lisa MILLER
41 Athletic Director .... Mr. Steve RUZICH
09 Director of Institutional Research .... Mr. Kevin RIORDAN
15 Director Human Resources .... Ms. Kimberly PIGATTI
06 Director Registration/Records .... Ms. Tenial WHITTED
07 Director of Recruitment .... Ms. Tiffane JONES

Southeastern Illinois College (C)

3575 College Road, Harrisburg IL 62946-4925
County: Saline FICE Identification: 001757
Unit ID: 148937
Telephone: (618) 252-5400 Carnegie Class: Assoc/HVT-High Non
FAX Number: (618) 252-3156 Calendar System: Semester
URL: www.sic.edu
Established: 1960 Annual Undergrad Tuition & Fees (In-District): $3,960
Enrollment: 1,655 Coed
Affiliation or Control: State/Local IRS Status: 501(c)3
Highest Offering: Associate Degree
Accreditation: NH, MLTAD

01 President .... Dr. Jonah RICE
05 Vice President Instruction .... Dr. Karen WEISS
10 Dean Administration/Business Affs .... Ms. Lisa HITE
32 Dean Student Servicess/Enrollment .... Dr. Chad FLANNERY
103 Assoc Dean Workforce & Cmty Educ .... Mrs. Lori COX
08 Assoc Dean of Learning Commons .... Ms. Karla LEWIS
84 Director Enrollment Services .... Ms. Kyla BURFORD
26 Marketing Coordinator .... Ms. Angela WILSON
37 Financial Aid Director .... Ms. Michelle METTEN
13 Chief Information Officer .... Mr. Greg MCCULLOCH
76 Director Allied Health & Nursing .... Ms. Amy MURPHY
04 Exec Asst to President .... Mrs. Lisa DYE
18 Director of Environmental Services .... Mr. Ed FITZGERALD
15 Director of Human Resources .... Mrs. Sky FOWLER
09 Director of Institutional Research .... Mr. Chris BARR
28 Coordinator of Diversity .... Ms. Erica GRIFFIN
41 Athletic Director .... Mr. Jeremy IRLBECK

*Southern Illinois University System (D)

Stone Center - 1400 Douglas Drive, Carbondale IL 62901
County: Jackson FICE Identification: 008237
Unit ID: 149240
Telephone: (618) 536-3331 Carnegie Class: N/A
FAX Number: (618) 536-3404
URL: www.siusystem.edu

01 Interim President .... Dr. J. Kevin DORSEY
05 Acting VP Academic Affairs .... Dr. James ALLEN
10 Sr VP Financial/Admin Affs/Bd Treas .... Dr. Duane STUCKY
117 Interim Director of Risk Management .... Dr. Duane STUCKY
86 Exec Dir Governmental/Public Affs .... Mr. John CHARLES
116 Exec Dir of Internal Audits .... Ms. Kim LABONTE
43 General Counsel .... Mr. Lucas CRATER
04 Assistant to the President .... Ms. Paula S. KEITH

*Southern Illinois University Carbondale (E)

1265 Lincoln Drive, Carbondale IL 62901-6899
County: Jackson FICE Identification: 001758
Unit ID: 149222
Telephone: (618) 453-2121 Carnegie Class: DU-Higher
FAX Number: (618) 453-3250 Calendar System: Semester
URL: siu.edu
Established: 1869 Annual Undergrad Tuition & Fees (In-State): $14,704
Enrollment: 14,554 Coed
Affiliation or Control: State IRS Status: 501(c)3
Highest Offering: Doctorate
Accreditation: NH, AAB, ARCPA, ART, CACREP, CAEPN, CEA, CIDA, CLPSY, COPSY, DH, DIETD, DIETI, DMS, FUSER, IFSAC, IPSY, JOUR, LAW, MED, MUS, NAIT, PH, PTAA, RAD, RADDOS, RADMAG, RTT, SP, SPAA, SW, THEA

02 Interim Chancellor .... Dr. John M. DUNN
05 Int Provost/Vice Chanc Acad Affs .... Dr. Meera KOMARRAJU
32 Dean of Students .... Ms. Jennifer L. JONES-HALL
30 Int VC for Development/Alumni Rels .... Ms. Rae GOLDSMITH
46 Interim VC for Research .... Dr. James GARVEY
10 Vice Chanc Admin & Finance .... Ms. Judith MARSHALL
28 Interim Assoc Chancellor Diversity .... Mr. Todd BRYSON
102 CFO SIU Foundation .... Ms. Cynthia CIGANOVICH
13 Interim Chief Info Officer .... Mr. Scott D. BRIDGES
84 Assoc Chancellor for Enrollment Mgt .... Ms. Jennifer E. DEHAEMERS
20 Assoc Provost for Academic Admin .... Dr. David DILALLA
20 Assoc Provost for Academic Programs .... Dr. Lizette CHEVALIER
100 Chief of Staff .... Mr. Matthew BAUGHMAN
49 Interim Dean Liberal Arts .... Dr. Andrew BALKANSKY
50 Dean College of Business .... Dr. Terry CLARK
53 Dean Educ & Human Services .... Dr. Matthew W. KEEFER
54 Dean Engineering .... Dr. John J. WARWICK
58 Int Assoc Dean/Dir of Grad School .... Dr. Juliane WALLACE
61 Interim Dean School of Law .... Ms. Cindy G. BUYS
81 Interim Dean College of Science .... Dr. Scott ISHMAN
63 Dean School of Medicine/Provost .... Dr. Jerry E. KRUSE
47 Interim Dean Agricultural Sciences .... Ms. Karen MIDDEN
72 Dean Col Applied Sciences & Arts .... Dr. JuAn WANG
57 Interim Dean Mass Comm/Media Arts .... Dr. Deborah TUDOR
08 Dean Library Affairs .... Mr. John H. POLLITZ
37 Interim Dir Student Financial Aid .... Ms. Dee ROTOLO
09 Director Institutional Research .... Mr. Scott BRIDGES
26 Chief Marketing & Comm Officer .... Ms. Rae GOLDSMITH
15 Director Human Resources/Payroll .... Ms. Jennifer WATSON
39 Director University Housing .... Mr. Jon L. SHAFFER
36 Coordinator Career Services .... Ms. Jaime CONLEY-HOLT
85 Director International Education .... Dr. Andrew CARVER
18 Director Plant/Service Operations .... Mr. Brad DILLARD
19 Director of Public Safety .... Mr. Benjamin NEWMAN
23 Director Student Health Services .... Dr. Ted W. GRACE
41 Intercollegiate Athletic Director .... Mr. Jerry KILL
106 Executive Director Extended Campus .... Dr. Mandara SAVAGE
06 Director Registrar's Office .... Ms. Tamara WORKMAN
38 Dir Student Counseling Center .... Dr. Jaime CLARK
96 Director Procurement Services .... Ms. Debbie ABELL

*Southern Illinois University Edwardsville (F)

State Route 157, Edwardsville IL 62026
County: Madison FICE Identification: 001759
Unit ID: 149231
Telephone: (618) 650-2000 Carnegie Class: DU-Mod
FAX Number: (618) 650-2270 Calendar System: Semester
URL: www.siue.edu
Established: 1957 Annual Undergrad Tuition & Fees (In-State): $12,132
Enrollment: 13,796 Coed
Affiliation or Control: State IRS Status: 501(c)3
Highest Offering: Doctorate
Accreditation: NH, ANEST, ART, CAEPN, CONST, DENT, @DIETC, EXSC, JOUR, MUS, NURSE, PH, PHAR, SP, SPAA, SW, THEA

02 Chancellor .... Dr. Randall G. PEMBROOK
05 Provost/VC for Academic Affairs .... Dr. P. Denise COBB
10 Vice Chancellor for Admin .... Mr. Richard WALKER
111 VC Univ Adv & CEO SIUE Foundation .... Ms. Rachel C. STACK
32 Vice Chanc for Student Affairs .... Dr. Jeffrey N. WAPLE
100 Chief of Staff .... Ms. Kimberly H. DURR
22 Equal Opp/Access & Title IX .... Ms. Jamie BALL
20 Assoc Prov Rsch/Dean Grad Sch .... Dr. Jerry B. WEINBERG
35 Assoc VC Stdnt Affs/Dean of Stdnts .... Dr. James W. KLENKE
13 Assoc VC for IT & CIO .... Mr. Steven HUFFSTUTLER
28 Asc Chanc Inst Diversity/Inclusion .... Dr. Venessa BROWN
88 Interim Assistant Provost .... Dr. Jessica HARRIS
41 Asst VC Athletic Dev/Dir Athletics .... Dr. Bradley L. HEWITT
84 Assoc VC for Enrollment Management .... Dr. Scott BELOBRAJDIC
49 Dean College of Arts & Sciences .... Dr. Gregory BUDZBAN
50 Dean School of Business .... Dr. Timothy SCHOENECKER
52 Dean School of Dental Medicine .... Dr. Bruce E. ROTTER
53 Int Dean Sch of Educ/Hlth Hum Behav .... Dr. Paul ROSE
54 Dean School of Engineering .... Dr. Cem KARACAL
66 Dean School of Nursing .... Dr. Laura BERNAIX
67 Dean School of Pharmacy .... Dr. Mark S. LUER
08 Int Dean Library & Info Services .... Ms. Lydia JACKSON
114 Budget Director .... Mr. William F. WINTER, JR.
26 Exec Dir Univ Marketing & Comm .... Mr. Doug MCILHAGGA
88 Dir Grant Funded Pgm East StL Ctr .... Mr. Jesse DIXON
124 Dir Retention & Student Success .... Dr. Kevin THOMAS
07 Director Undergraduate Admissions .... Mr. Todd C. BURRELL
29 Dir Constituent Rel & Special Proj .... Ms. Cathy N. TAYLOR
36 Director Career Development Center .... Ms. Susan SEIBERT
38 Director Counseling Services .... Mr. Courtney R. BODDIE
18 Director Facilities Management .... Mr. Craig HOLAN
23 Director Health Service .... Ms. Riane B. GREENWALT
15 Director Human Resources .... Mr. Robert B. THUMITH
09 Dir Institutional Research/Studies .... Mr. Phillip M. BROWN
85 Exec Director International Affairs .... Dr. Mary WEISHAAR
96 Director of Purchasing .... Ms. Shelly ALBERT
37 Director Student Financial Aid .... Ms. Sally MULLEN
102 Dir Univ Advancement/Foundation Ops .... Mr. Kevin MARTIN
39 Director University Housing .... Mr. Michael J. SCHULTZ
19 Director University Police .... Mr. Kevin SCHMOLL
06 Registrar .... Ms. Laura A. STROM

*Southern Illinois University Carbondale School of Medicine (G)

PO Box 19620, Springfield IL 62794-9620
Telephone: (217) 545-8000 Identification: 770181
Accreditation: &NH

Southwestern Illinois College (H)

2500 Carlyle Avenue, Belleville IL 62221-5899
County: Saint Clair FICE Identification: 001636
Unit ID: 143215
Telephone: (618) 235-2700 Carnegie Class: Assoc/HVT-High Non
FAX Number: (618) 277-0631 Calendar System: Semester
URL: www.swic.edu
Established: 1946 Annual Undergrad Tuition & Fees (In-District): $3,660
Enrollment: 8,859 Coed
Affiliation or Control: State/Local IRS Status: 501(c)3
Highest Offering: Associate Degree
Accreditation: NH, ADNUR, CAHIIM, COARC, EMT, MAC, MLTAD, PTAA, RAD

01 President - District .... Mr. Nick J. MANCE
11 Chief Administrative Svcs Officer .... Mr. Bernie J. YSURSA, JR.
05 Chief Academic Officer .... Mr. Clay L. BAITMAN
15 Exec Director Human Resources .... Ms. Anna MOYER
10 CFO/Board Treasurer .... Ms. Missy ROCHE
32 Chief Student/Community Dev Officer .... Ms. Staci G. OLIVER
84 Exec Dir Enrollment Dev/Planning .... Mr. Robert TEBBE
13 Executive Director of IT .... Ms. Linda ANDRES
96 Director of Purchasing .... Mr. Mike R. THOMAS
76 Dean Health Sci/Homeland Security .... Ms. Julie A. MUERTZ
50 Acting Dean Business/Arts & Sci .... Dr. Janet S. FONTENOT
72 Dean of Technical Education .... Mr. Brad SPARKS
51 Director Adult/Continued Education .... Ms. Lisa ATKINS
35 Dean of Student Services .... Ms. Michelle L. BIRK

Spertus Institute for Jewish Learning and Leadership (I)

610 S Michigan Avenue, Chicago IL 60605-1994
County: Cook FICE Identification: 001663
Unit ID: 148982
Telephone: (312) 322-1700 Carnegie Class: Spec-4-yr-Faith
FAX Number: (312) 922-6406 Calendar System: Quarter
URL: www.spertus.edu
Established: 1924 Annual Graduate Tuition & Fees: N/A
Enrollment: 130 Coed
Affiliation or Control: Independent Non-Profit IRS Status: 501(c)3
Highest Offering: Doctorate; No Undergraduates
Accreditation: NH

01 President .... Dr. Dean P. BELL
05 Dean/CAO .... Dr. Keren FRAIMAN
10 Controller .... Mr. Doug PETERSON
37 Financial Aid Manager .... Ms. Judith WOOD

Spoon River College (A)

23235 N County Road 22, Canton IL 61520-9801
County: Fulton | FICE Identification: 001643
Unit ID: 148991
Telephone: (309) 647-4645 | Carnegie Class: Assoc/HT-High Non
FAX Number: (309) 649-6235 | Calendar System: Semester
URL: www.src.edu
Established: 1959 | Annual Undergrad Tuition & Fees (In-District): $4,950
Enrollment: 1,489 | Coed
Affiliation or Control: Local | IRS Status: 501(c)3
Highest Offering: Associate Degree
Accreditation: NH

01 President .... Mr. Curt OLDFIELD
05 Dean Instruction .... Ms. Holly NORTON
11 Vice President .... Mr. Brett STOLLER
04 Executive Asst to the President .... Ms. Julie HAMPTON
75 Dean Career & Technical Education .... Mr. Brad O'BRIEN
32 Dean Student Services .... Ms. Missy WILKINSON
66 Director Nursing .... Ms. Tamatha SCHLEICH
06 Dir of Records & Admissions .... Ms. Melissa WILKINSON
18 Director Facilities .... Mr. Bob A. HAILE
55 Dir Adult and Outreach Education .... Mr. Chad MURPHY
08 Librarian .... Ms. Marla TURGEON
13 Chief Information Officer .... Mr. Raj SIDDARAJU
41 Director Athletics/Student Life .... Mr. John BASSETT
109 Director Business & Auxil Services .... Ms. Sarah GRAY
37 Director Financial Aid .... Ms. Salinda Jo BRANSON
15 Director Human Resources .... Ms. Andrea THOMSON
14 Director Technology Services .... Mr. Dean CLARY
84 Director Enrollment Services .... Ms. Janet MUNSON
09 Coord Institutional Reporting .... Ms. Anna STINAUER
26 Director Marketing .... Ms. Sherri RADER
27 Coordinator Public Information .... Ms. Sally SHIELDS
102 Director Foundation .... Mr. Colin DAVIS

Spoon River College-Macomb Campus (B)

208 S Johnson Street, Macomb IL 61455
Telephone: (309) 837-5727 | Identification: 770097
Accreditation: &NH

Taylor Business Institute (C)

180 N. Wabash Avenue, Ste. 500, Chicago IL 60601
County: Cook | FICE Identification: 011810
Unit ID: 149310
Telephone: (312) 658-5100 | Carnegie Class: Assoc/HVT-High Trad
FAX Number: (312) 658-0867 | Calendar System: Quarter
URL: www.tbiil.edu
Established: 1962 | Annual Undergrad Tuition & Fees: $14,325
Enrollment: 127 | Coed
Affiliation or Control: Proprietary | IRS Status: Proprietary
Highest Offering: Associate Degree
Accreditation: NH

01 President .... Mrs. Janice C. PARKER
05 Dean/Chief Academic Officer .... Mr. Malik IQBAL

Telshe Yeshiva-Chicago (D)

3535 W Foster Avenue, Chicago IL 60625-5598
County: Cook | FICE Identification: 020732
Unit ID: 149329
Telephone: (773) 463-7738 | Carnegie Class: Spec-4-yr-Faith
FAX Number: (773) 463-2849 | Calendar System: Semester
Established: 1960 | Annual Undergrad Tuition & Fees: $13,500
Enrollment: 75 | Male
Affiliation or Control: Independent Non-Profit | IRS Status: 501(c)3
Highest Offering: Second Talmudic Degree
Accreditation: RABN

01 President .... Rabbi Shmuel Y. LEVIN
03 Executive Vice President .... Rabbi Yitzchok LEVIN
05 Vice President .... Rabbi Chaim D. KELLER
05 Vice President .... Rabbi Moshe SCHMELCZER
11 Administrative Director/Secretary .... Rabbi Shmuel ADLER

Toyota Technological Institute at Chicago (E)

6045 South Kenwood Avenue, Chicago IL 60637
County: Cook | Identification: 666367
Unit ID: 445054
Telephone: (773) 834-2500 | Carnegie Class: Spec-4-yr-Other Tech
FAX Number: (773) 834-9881 | Calendar System: Quarter
URL: www.ttic.edu
Established: 2003 | Annual Graduate Tuition & Fees: N/A
Enrollment: 30 | Coed
Affiliation or Control: Independent Non-Profit | IRS Status: 501(c)3
Highest Offering: Doctorate; No Undergraduates
Accreditation: NH

01 President .... Dr. Sadaoki FURUI
05 Chief Academic Officer .... Dr. Avrim BLUM
10 Chief Financial Officer .... Ms. Jessica JOHNSTON
58 Admin Director of Graduate Studies .... Ms. Christina NOVAK
15 Director of Human Resources .... Ms. Amy MINICK

Trinity Christian College (F)

6601 W College Drive, Palos Heights IL 60463-0929
County: Cook | FICE Identification: 001771
Unit ID: 149505
Telephone: (708) 597-3000 | Carnegie Class: Bac-Diverse
FAX Number: (708) 239-4826 | Calendar System: Semester
URL: www.trnty.edu
Established: 1959 | Annual Undergrad Tuition & Fees: $30,175
Enrollment: 1,192 | Coed
Affiliation or Control: Independent Non-Profit | IRS Status: 501(c)3
Highest Offering: Master's
Accreditation: NH, ACBSP, NURSE, SW

01 President .... Mr. Kurt D. DYKSTRA
05 Provost .... Dr. Aaron KUECKER
10 Vice Pres for Finance & Admin .... Mr. James E. BELSTRA
32 Vice Pres for Student Life .... Mrs. Rebekah L. STARKENBURG
26 Vice Pres for Comm & Strategic Init .... Mr. Paul BOICE
111 Vice Pres for Advancement .... Mr. Rick VAN DYKEN
110 Assoc VP for Advancement .... Mr. Dennis HARMS
42 Chaplain .... Dr. Willis VAN GRONINGEN
08 Director of Library Services .... Mrs. Cathy MAYER
15 Director of Human Resources .... Ms. Julia FOUST
06 Registrar .... Ms. Jaynn TOBIAS-JOHNSON
09 Asst Registrar for Inst Research .... Ms. Kimberly WILLIAMS
21 Controller .... Mr. Mike TROCHUCK
35 Dean of Student Life .... Mrs. Kara VAN MARION
36 Director of Career Development .... Mr. Jeff TIMMER
29 Director of Alumni Relations .... Mr. Jeremy KLYN
19 Director Security/Safety .... Mr. Tom KAZEN
13 Director of Technology Systems .... Mr. Kevin JACOBS
14 Director of Technology Support .... Mr. Doug VAN WYNGARDEN
41 AVP Student Life/Dir of Athletics .... Mr. Mark HANNA
28 Dir of Multicultural Engagement .... Mrs. Nicole SAINT-VICTOR
85 Director of Off-Campus Programs .... Dr. Burton J. ROZEMA
37 Director Financial Aid .... Mr. Michael SHIELDS
18 Director of Building/Grounds .... Mr. Tim TIMMONS
112 Director of Planned Giving .... Mr. Jeff ENFIELD
92 Director of Honors Program .... Dr. Craig MATTSON
38 Director of Counseling Services .... Dr. Stephanie GRISWOLD
04 Executive Assistant to President .... Ms. Deborah S. VINCENT
88 Senior Graphic Designer .... Mr. Pete VEGA
105 Web Developer/Social Media Manager .... Ms. Diane BRUNSTING
50 Department Chair of Business .... Mr. John WIGHTKIN
07 Director of Admissions .... Ms. Jeanine MOZIE

Trinity College of Nursing & Health Sciences (G)

2122 25th Avenue, Rock Island IL 61201-5317
County: Rock Island | FICE Identification: 006225
Unit ID: 146755
Telephone: (309) 779-7700 | Carnegie Class: Spec-4-yr-Other Health
FAX Number: (309) 779-7748 | Calendar System: Semester
URL: www.trinitycollegeqc.edu
Established: 1994 | Annual Undergrad Tuition & Fees: $27,534
Enrollment: 217 | Coed
Affiliation or Control: Independent Non-Profit | IRS Status: 501(c)3
Highest Offering: Master's
Accreditation: NH, NURSE, RAD

01 Chancellor .... Dr. Tracy L. POELVOORDE
05 Dean of Nursing & Health Sciences .... Dr. Teresa WISCHMANN
06 Registrar .... Ms. Cara BANKS

Trinity International University (H)

2065 Half Day Road, Deerfield IL 60015-1284
County: Lake | FICE Identification: 001772
Unit ID: 149514
Telephone: (847) 945-8800 | Carnegie Class: DU-Mod
FAX Number: (847) 317-8090 | Calendar System: Semester
URL: www.tiu.edu
Established: 1897 | Annual Undergrad Tuition & Fees: $32,390
Enrollment: 2,161 | Coed
Affiliation or Control: Evangelical Free Church Of America
IRS Status: 501(c)3
Highest Offering: Doctorate
Accreditation: NH, #CAATE, CACREP, THEOL

01 President .... Dr. Nicholas PERRIN
73 VP Education/Dean TEDS .... Dr. Graham COLE
05 Int VP Academic Admin/Dean TC & TGS .... Dr. Don HEDGES
32 VP Student Life & Univ Services .... Vacant
13 Sr VP for Administration & Tech .... Mr. Steven GEGGIE
111 Vice Pres University Advancement .... Mr. Carl JOHNSON
10 Vice Pres for Business Services .... Dr. Jonathan DOCKERY
26 VP for University Communication .... Mr. Mark KAHLER
27 Asst VP University Communication .... Mr. Chris DONOTO
51 Director Adult Academic Programs .... Mr. Jay SIMALA
20 Assoc Dean of TC & TGS .... Vacant
90 Director of Acad/Desktop Computing .... Mr. Chris MILLER
91 Director Administrative Computing .... Ms. Katie KEMP
61 Interim Dean of Law School .... Mr. Myron STEEVES
07 VP for Admissions .... Ms. Shawn WYNNE
19 Director of Security Services .... Mr. Aron FORCH
96 Director of Facilities .... Ms. Julie WONG
15 Director of Human Resources .... Mrs. Linda BRUNDIDGE
06 University Registrar .... Ms. Tiffany SELL
36 Director of Placement .... Dr. Phil SELL
08 University Librarian .... Ms. Rebecca DONALD
29 Director of Alumni Relations .... Mr. Garrett LUCK
92 Director of Honors Program .... Dr. Joshua HELD
35 Director of Student Activities .... Vacant
38 Director Student Care & Engagement .... Ms. Anne TOHME
04 Exec Assistant to the President .... Mrs. Jean D. MYERS
22 Dir Affirm Action/Equal Opportunity .... Ms. Linda BRUNDIDGE
41 Athletic Director .... Ms. Heather LOGUE
09 Director of Institutional Research .... Mr. Jonathan DOCKERY

Triton College (I)

2000 Fifth Avenue, River Grove IL 60171-1995
County: Cook | FICE Identification: 001773
Unit ID: 149532
Telephone: (708) 456-0300 | Carnegie Class: Assoc/MT-VT-High Non
FAX Number: (708) 583-3112 | Calendar System: Semester
URL: www.triton.edu
Established: 1964 | Annual Undergrad Tuition & Fees (In-District): $4,170
Enrollment: 10,672 | Coed
Affiliation or Control: Local | IRS Status: 501(c)3
Highest Offering: Associate Degree
Accreditation: NH, ADNUR, DMS, NMT, RAD, SURGT

01 President .... Ms. Mary-Rita MOORE
05 Vice President Academic Affairs .... Dr. Susan CAMPOS
84 Vice Pres Enroll Mgmt/Student Affs .... Dr. Jodi KOSLOW MARTIN
10 Vice President Business Services .... Mr. Sean SULLIVAN
26 Assoc VP Comm & Inst Advancement .... Mr. Derrell CARTER
101 Secretary for Brd of Trustees .... Ms. Susan PAGE
13 Assoc VP Information Systems .... Mr. Michael GARRITY
21 Assoc VP Finance & Business .... Mr. Garrick ABEZETIAN
18 Assoc VP of Facilities .... Mr. John LAMBRECHT
15 Assoc VP Human Resources .... Mr. Joe KLINGER
20 Assoc VP Academic Innov Workforce .... Mr. Paul JENSEN
35 Dean of Student Services .... Vacant
84 Dean of Enrollment Services .... Vacant
49 Dean of Arts & Sciences .... Mr. Kevin LI
72 Dean of Business & Technology .... Vacant
51 Dean of Continuing Education .... Ms. Colleen ROCKAFELLOW
121 Dean of Academic Success .... Dr. Deborah BANESS KING
55 Dean of Adult Education .... Ms. Jacqueline LYNCH
07 Assoc Dean of Enrollment Services .... Ms. Patricia ZINGA
21 Executive Director of Finance .... Mr. James REYNOLDS
27 Executive Director of Marketing .... Mr. Sam TOLIA
09 Executive Director of Research .... Dr. Kurian THARAKUNNEL
25 Exec Dir Grants Development .... Ms. Sacella SMITH
14 Sr Data and System Admin .... Ms. Elise RAPALA
86 Director Public Affairs .... Ms. Audrey JONAS
88 Special Assistant to the President .... Ms. Brenda JONES WATKINS
04 Admin Assistant to the President .... Ms. Josephine FAZIO
19 Police Chief .... Mr. Austin WEINSTOCK
41 Athletic Director .... Mr. Harry MCGINNIS

University of Chicago (J)

5801 S Ellis Avenue, Chicago IL 60637-1496
County: Cook | FICE Identification: 001774
Unit ID: 144050
Telephone: (773) 702-1234 | Carnegie Class: DU-Highest
FAX Number: N/A | Calendar System: Quarter
URL: www.uchicago.edu
Established: 1890 | Annual Undergrad Tuition & Fees: $58,230
Enrollment: 16,227 | Coed
Affiliation or Control: Independent Non-Profit | IRS Status: 501(c)3
Highest Offering: Doctorate
Accreditation: NH, CAMPEP, IPSY, LAW, MED, SW, THEOL

01 President .... Robert J. ZIMMER
03 Executive Vice President .... David B. FITHIAN
05 Provost .... Daniel DIERMEIER
17 EVP for Medical Affairs/Dean of BSD .... Kenneth S. POLONSKY
88 EVP Science/Innovation/Strategy .... Balaji SRINIVASAN
10 VP/Chief Financial Officer .... Ivan SAMSTEIN
43 Vice President & General Counsel .... Kim TAYLOR
88 VP for National Laboratories .... Juan DE PABLO
26 Vice Pres for Communications .... Paul M. RAND
45 VP for Strategic Initiatives .... Darren REISBERG
29 VP for Alumni Rels & Development .... Sharon MARINE
86 VP for Civic Engagement/Ext Affairs .... Derek DOUGLAS
101 VP and Secretary .... Katie CALLOW-WRIGHT
115 Vice Pres/Chief Investment Officer .... Mark A. SCHMID
20 Vice Provost for Acad Affairs .... Jason MERCHANT
20 Vice Provost .... Daniel ABEBE
20 Vice Provost .... Michael HOPKINS
20 Vice Provost .... Melina HALE
46 Vice Provost for Research .... Ka Yee LEE
28 Vice Provost .... Melissa GILLIAM
13 AVP/Chief Information Officer .... Kevin BOYD
22 Assoc Prov Equal Opportunity Pgms .... Bridget COLLIER
63 Dean Medicine .... Kenneth POLONSKY
54 Dean of Molecular Engineering .... Matthew TIRRELL
83 Dean Division of Social Sciences .... Amanda WOODWARD
73 Int Dean of Divinity School .... David NIRENBERG
80 Dean Harris Sch of Public Policy .... Katherine BAICKER
51 Int Dean of Graham School .... Christopher GUYMON
79 Dean of Humanities Division .... Anne ROBERTSON
70 Dean Sch of Social Svcs Admin .... Deborah GORMAN-SMITH

61 Dean of the Law School .... Thomas MILES
50 Dean of Booth School of Business .... Madhav V. RAJAN
49 Dean of the College .... John W. BOYER
65 Dean Physical Sciences Division .... Angela V. OLINTO
42 Dean Rockefeller Memorial Chapel .... Maurice CHARLES
32 Dean of Students in University .... Michele RASMUSSEN
84 Dean of College Admissions/Fin Aid .... James G. NONDORF
37 Senior Exec Director University Aid .... Amanda FIJAL
06 Registrar .... Scott CAMPBELL
57 Executive Director of UChicago Arts .... Bill MICHEL
88 Director of Oriental Institute .... Christopher WOODS

*University of Illinois System (A)

506 S Wright Street, 364 HAB, Urbana IL 61801
County: Champaign FICE Identification: 008001
Unit ID: 149587
Telephone: (217) 333-3070 Carnegie Class: N/A
FAX Number: N/A
URL: www.uillinois.edu

01 President .... Dr. Timothy L. KILLEEN
12 Chancellor/Vice President (Chicago) .... Dr. Michael AMIRIDIS
12 Chancellor/Vice President (Sprfld) .... Dr. Susan KOCH
12 Chancellor/Vice President (Urbana) .... Dr. Robert J. JONES
10 VP & Chief Financial Officer .... Mr. Avijit GHOSH
05 Exec Vice Pres and VPAA .... Dr. Barbara J. WILSON
88 Vice Pres for Econ Devel Innovation .... Dr. H. Edward SEIDEL
43 University Counsel .... Mr. Thomas R. BEARROWS
26 Exec Dir for University Relations .... Mr. Thomas P. HARDY
13 CIO & Sr Assoc VP .... Mr. Kelly J. BLOCK
15 Interim Assoc VP Human Resources .... Ms. Jami PAINTER
101 Secretary Board of Trustees/Univ .... Ms. Dedra M. WILLIAMS
102 President/CEO Univ Foundation .... Mr. James H. MOORE, JR.
29 Pres UIAA/Assoc VC for Alumni Rel .... Ms. Jennifer NEUBAUER

*University of Illinois at Chicago (B)

601 S Morgan, M/C 102, Chicago IL 60607-7128
County: Cook FICE Identification: 001776
Unit ID: 145600
Telephone: (312) 996-7000 Carnegie Class: DU-Highest
FAX Number: (312) 413-3393 Calendar System: Semester
URL: www.uic.edu
Established: 1896 Annual Undergrad Tuition & Fees (In-State): $13,764
Enrollment: 30,539 Coed
Affiliation or Control: State IRS Status: 501(c)3
Highest Offering: Doctorate
Accreditation: NH, CAHIIM, CEA, CLPSY, DENT, DIETC, DIETD, FEPAC, HSA, IPSY, MED, MIDWF, MIL, NURSE, OT, PH, PHAR, PLNG, PTA, SPAA, SW

02 Chancellor .... Dr. Michael AMIRIDIS
05 Provost/Vice Chanc Academic Affairs .... Dr. Susan POSER
32 Vice Chancellor Student Affairs .... Mr. Rex TOLLIVER
11 Vice Chanc for Admin Svcs .... Mr. John CORONADO
46 Vice Chancellor for Research .... Dr. Joanna GRODEN
26 Int Assoc Chanc Govt & Public Affs .... Ms. Theresa MINTLE
17 CEO Hospital Administration .... Dr. Michael ZENN
29 Exec Director Alumni Engagement .... Ms. Caryn KORMAN
111 Acting Vice Chanc for Advancement .... Mr. Thomas WAMSLEY
84 Vice Prov Acad/Enrollment Svcs .... Mr. Kevin BROWNE
20 Vice Provost for Faculty Affairs .... Dr. Nancy FREITAG
20 Vice Prov Undergrad Affairs .... Dr. Nikos VARELAS
88 Vice Provost for Global Engagement .... Dr. Neal R. MCCRILLIS
114 Assoc Chanc for Resource Plng/Mgmt .... Ms. Janet PARKER
35 Assoc Vice Chanc/Dean Student Affs .... Dr. Linda DEANNA
27 Senior Exec Director Public Affairs .... Ms. Sherri MCGINNIS GONZALEZ
23 Vice Chancellor Health Affairs .... Dr. Robert BARISH
10 Interim Asst VP Business/Finance .... Ms. Gloria KEELEY
48 Dean Col of Arch/Design/Arts .... Dr. Rebecca RUGG
50 Dean College of Business Admin .... Dr. Michael B. MIKHAIL
52 Dean College of Dentistry .... Dr. Clark STANFORD
53 Dean College of Education .... Dr. Alfred TATUM
54 Dean College of Engineering .... Dr. Peter C. NELSON
76 Dean Col Applied Health Sciences .... Dr. Bo FERNHALL
58 Dean Graduate College .... Dr. Karen COLLEY
92 Dean Honors College .... Dr. Ralph KEEN
49 Dean College Liberal Arts/Sciences .... Dr. Astrida O. TANTILLO
63 Exec Dean College of Medicine .... Dr. Mark ROSENBLATT
66 Dean College of Nursing .... Dr. Terri E. WEAVER
67 Dean College of Pharmacy .... Dr. Glen SCHUMOCK
70 Dean College of Social Work .... Dr. Creasie HAIRSTON
69 Dean School of Public Health .... Dr. Wayne GILES
27 Dean Urban Planning/Public Affairs .... Dr. Michael A. PAGANO
43 University Counsel .... Mr. Thomas R. BEARROWS
08 University Librarian .... Ms. Mary CASE
88 Asst Univ Librarian Health Sciences . Ms. Kathryn H. CARPENTER
07 Managing Director Admissions .... Ms. Malinda LORKOVICH
41 Director Athletics .... Mr. Garrett KLASSY
38 Director Counseling Services .... Dr. Joseph HERMES
39 Director of Campus Housing .... Ms. Susan TEGGATZ
37 Director Financial Aid .... Ms. Kiely FLETCHER
09 Director of Institutional Research .... Mr. William C. HAYWARD
16 Assoc Vice Provost Faculty Affairs .... Dr. Angela L. YUDT
22 Director Access/Equity .... Ms. Caryn A. BILLS-WINDT
36 Director Career Services .... Mr. Thy NGUYEN
13 CIO/Exec Dir Acad Computing .... Ms. Cynthia E. HERRERA LINDSTROM
56 Asst Vice Chanc Extended Campus .... Ms. Dara CROWFOOT
06 Registrar .... Mr. Robert DIXON
96 Director of Purchasing .... Ms. Debra MATLOCK
18 Exec Dir Operations/Maintenance .... Mr. Clarence F. BRIDGES
28 Assoc Chanc & VP for Diversity .... Dr. Amalia PALLARES
100 Associate Provost/Chief of Staff .... Dr. Aisha EL-AMIN
104 Executive Director of Study Abroad .... Dr. Christopher DEEGAN
88 Vice Chancellor for Innovation .... Dr. TJ AUGUSTINE

*University of Illinois at Springfield (C)

One University Plaza, Springfield IL 62703-5407
County: Sangamon FICE Identification: 009333
Unit ID: 148654
Telephone: (217) 206-6600 Carnegie Class: Masters/L
FAX Number: (217) 206-6511 Calendar System: Semester
URL: www.uis.edu
Established: 1969 Annual Undergrad Tuition & Fees (In-State): $11,813
Enrollment: 4,956 Coed
Affiliation or Control: State IRS Status: 501(c)3
Highest Offering: Doctorate
Accreditation: NH, CACREP, MT, SPAA, SW

02 Chancellor .... Dr. Susan KOCH
05 Vice Chancellor Acad Affs/Provost .... Dr. Dennis PAPINI
32 Vice Chancellor for Student Affairs .... Dr. Clarice FORD
20 Assoc Vice Chanc Undergrad Educ .... Dr. Ken MULLIKEN
29 Assoc Vice Chanc for Alumni Rels .... Mr. Charles SCHRAGE
30 Vice Chanc Dev/Sr VP UL Found .... Dr. Jeffrey D. LORBER
35 Asst Vice Chanc for Student Service .... Dr. Van VIEREGGE
18 Assoc Chanc Admin Affs/Facilities .... Mr. Charles CODERKO
22 Asc Chanc Access/Equal Opportunity .... Ms. Deanie BROWN
27 Assoc Chancellor for Public Affairs .... Ms. Kelsea GURSKI
21 Sr Assoc VP Business & Finance .... Mr. Jason BANE
49 Dean Col Liberal Arts/Science .... Dr. James ERMATINGER
50 Dean College Business/Mgmt .... Dr. Somnath BHATTACHARYA
80 Dean Col Public Affs/Admin .... Dr. Robert SMITH
53 Int Dean College Educ/Human Svcs .... Dr. James ERMATINGER
15 Sr Director HR .... Ms. Melissa MLYNSKI
43 Legal Counsel .... Ms. Rhonda PERRY
08 Dean of Library .... Dr. Piotrowski PATTIE
26 Director Public Information .... Mr. Derek SCHNAPP
114 Assc Provost Budget and Admin Plng .... Dr. Jerry JOSEPH
19 Chief Campus Police Department .... Mr. Donald MITCHELL
06 Registrar .... Mr. Brian CLEVENGER
35 Director of Student Life .... Ms. Cynthia THOMPSON
41 Interim Director of Athletics .... Dr. Clarice FORD
09 Director Institutional Research .... Ms. Laura DORMAN
96 Interim Director of Purchasing .... Ms. Janet FORD
37 Acting Dir Financial Assistance .... Ms. Carolyn SCHLOEMANN
38 Exec Director Counseling Center .... Dr. Bethany BILYEU
85 Director International Programs .. Dr. Jonathan GOLDBERGBELLE
13 Director Information Technology .... Mr. Tulio LLOSA
39 Director Campus Housing .... Mr. Brian KELLEY
07 Interim Director of Admissions .... Ms. Kathryn KLEEMAN
100 Chief of Staff .... Ms. Kelsea GURSKI
28 Director of Diversity .... Mr. Justin ROSE
36 Director Student Placement .... Ms. Katherine BATTEE-FREEMAN
84 Director Enrollment Management .... Ms. Natalie HERRING
86 Director Government Relations .... Ms. Joan SESTAK

*University of Illinois at Urbana-Champaign (D)

601 E John Street, Champaign IL 61820-5711
County: Champaign FICE Identification: 001775
Unit ID: 145637
Telephone: (217) 333-6677 Carnegie Class: DU-Highest
FAX Number: (217) 244-5352 Calendar System: Semester
URL: www.illinois.edu
Established: 1867 Annual Undergrad Tuition & Fees (In-State): $15,094
Enrollment: 48,216 Coed
Affiliation or Control: State IRS Status: 501(c)3
Highest Offering: Doctorate
Accreditation: NH, ART, AUD, CEA, CLPSY, COPSY, DANCE, DIETD, DIETI, IPSY, JOUR, LAW, LIB, LSAR, #MED, MUS, PCSAS, PH, PLNG, SP, SW, VET

00 Chief Executive Officer (President) .... Dr. Timothy L. KILLEEN
02 Chancellor .... Dr. Robert J. JONES
05 Prov/Vice Chanc Academic Affs .... Dr. Andreas CANGELLARIS
46 Interim Vice Chancellor Research .... Dr. Susan MARTINIS
32 Vice Chancellor Student Affairs .... Dr. Danita BROWN YOUNG
111 VC Inst Advancement/Found Admin .... Mr. Barry BENSON
88 Associate Chanc Corp Intl Relations .... Dr. Pradeep KHANNA
20 Vice Provost Academic Affairs .... Dr. William BERNHARD
100 Exec Associate Chancellor .... Dr. Wanda E. WARD
11 Senior Associate Chancellor .... Mr. Michael DELORENZO
88 Assoc Prov Faculty Development .... Dr. Rosa Milagros SANTOS
26 Associate Chanc Public Affairs .... Ms. Robin KALER
15 Senior Assoc Chancellor for HR .... Ms. Elyne COLE
84 Assoc Prov Enrollment Mgmt .... Mr. Daniel MANN
88 Assoc Prov Capital Planning .... Mr. Matthew TOMASZEWSKI
114 Assoc Chanc/Vice Prov for Budget .... Dr. Paul ELLINGER
104 Vice Provost Intl Pgms/Studies .... Ms. Reitumetse MABOKELA
20 Vice Provost for Undergrad Educ .... Dr. Kevin PITTS
21 Exec Assoc Provost Budget Planning .... Ms. Vicky GRESS
88 Assoc Prov Academic Pgms/Policy .... Ms. Kristi KUNTZ
09 Asst Provost Management Info .... Dr. Amy EDWARDS
49 Dean Liberal Arts & Sciences .... Dr. Feng Sheng HU
61 Dean Law .... Dr. Vikram AMAR
74 Dean Veterinary Medicine .... Dr. Peter CONSTABLE
54 Dean Engineering .... Dr. Rashid BASHIR
47 Dean Agric/Consumer/Environ Sci .... Dr. Kim KIDWELL
50 Dean Business .... Dr. Jeffrey BROWN
57 Dean Fine & Applied Arts .... Dr. Kevin HAMILTON
63 Dean Cl College of Medicine .... Dr. King LI
70 Dean School of Social Work .... Dr. Steven ANDERSON
68 Dean Col Applied Health Sciences .... Dr. Cheryl HANLEY-MAXWELL
60 Dean College of Media .... Dr. Tracy SULKIN
58 Dean Graduate College .... Dr. Wojciech CHODZKO-ZAJKO
62 Dean School of Info Sciences .... Dr. Allen H. RENEAR
53 Dean Education .... Dr. James D. ANDERSON
63 Int Reg Dean Col Med/Urbana-Champ .... Dr. Janet JOKELA
16 Dean Labor & Employment Rels .... Dr. Fritz DRASGOW
08 University Librarian & Dean .... Mr. John P. WILKIN
13 Interim Chief Information Officer .... Mr. Greg GULICK
35 Dean of Students .... Vacant
56 Int Assoc Dean Extension & Outreach .... Dr. Sharon NICKOLS
41 Director Athletics .... Mr. Josh WHITMAN
10 Asst Vice Pres Bus/Fin Affairs .... Ms. Ginger VELAZQUEZ
43 Campus Legal Counsel .... Mr. Scott RICE
14 Deputy CIO Information Technology .... Mr. Greg GULICK
22 Dir Equal Opportunity & Access .... Ms. Heidi JOHNSON
19 Director Public Safety .... Mr. Jeffrey T. CHRISTENSEN
18 Exec Director Facilities .... Dr. Mohamed ATTALLA
23 Director McKinley Health Center .... Dr. Robert D. PARKER, JR.
36 Director Career Services Center .... Ms. Jennifer NEEF
37 Director Student Financial Aid .... Ms. Michelle TRAME
38 Director Counseling Center .... Dr. Carla MCCOWAN
39 Director Housing Division .... Ms. Alma SEALINE
88 Dir Ctr Innovative Teaching/Lrng .... Dr. Michel BELLINI
06 Registrar .... Ms. Meghan HAZEN
07 Director of Admissions .... Ms. Nancy WALSH
101 Secretary of the Institution/Board .... Ms. Dedra WILLIAMS
108 Assoc Prov for Acad Effectiveness .... Dr. Staci J. PROVEZIS
100 Chief of Staff .... Ms. Laura CLOWER
86 Director Comm & Gov Relations .... Mr. Robert FLIDER

* *University of Illinois at Chicago College of Medicine at Peoria* (E)

One Illini Drive, Peoria IL 61605
Telephone: (309) 671-8402 Identification: 770182
Accreditation: &NH

* *University of Illinois at Chicago College of Medicine at Urbana* (F)

The Carle Forum, 611 West Park St, Urbana IL 61801
Telephone: (217) 333-5465 Identification: 770184
Accreditation: &NH

* *University of Illinois College of Medicine at Rockford* (G)

1601 Parkview Avenue, Rockford IL 61107
Telephone: (815) 395-0600 Identification: 770183
Accreditation: &NH, PHAR

* *UIC John Marshall Law School* (H)

315 S Plymouth Court, Chicago IL 60604-3968
Telephone: (312) 427-2737 FICE Identification: 001698
Accreditation: &NH, LAW

University of Phoenix Chicago Campus (I)

203 N. LaSalle Street, Chicago IL 60601-1210
Telephone: (312) 223-1101 Identification: 770205
Accreditation: &NH, ACBSP

† No longer accepting campus-based students.

University of St. Francis (J)

500 N Wilcox Street, Joliet IL 60435-6188
County: Will FICE Identification: 001664
Unit ID: 148584
Telephone: (815) 740-3400 Carnegie Class: DU-Mod
FAX Number: (815) 740-4285 Calendar System: Semester
URL: www.stfrancis.edu
Established: 1920 Annual Undergrad Tuition & Fees: $32,320
Enrollment: 4,166 Coed
Affiliation or Control: Roman Catholic IRS Status: 501(c)3
Highest Offering: Doctorate
Accreditation: NH, ACBSP, CAEPN, NRPA, NURSE, RTT, SW

01 President .... Dr. Arvid C. JOHNSON
05 Provost/VP Academic Affairs .... Dr. Beth ROTH
10 VP Administration & Finance .... Ms. Julee A. GARD
84 VP Admissions/Mktg/Enrollment Svcs .... Mr. Eric WIGNALL
88 VP Mission Int & Univ Ministry .... Sr. Mary Elizabeth IMLER
32 VP Student & Alumni Affairs .... Mr. Damon N. SLOAN
13 VP Operations/Planning & Technology .... Mr. Terrance L. COTTRELL
111 VP for University Advancement .... Ms. Kristin SHORT
49 Dean Col Arts & Sciences .... Dr. Elizabeth DAVIES
50 Dean Col Business/Health .... Dr. Orlando GRIEGO
53 Dean Col Education .... Dr. John S. GAMBRO
66 Dean Leach Col Nursing .... Dr. Ebere UME
20 Dean Teaching & Learning Outcomes .... Dr. Lirim NEZIROSKI
35 Dean Student Life .... Ms. Mollie ROCKAFELLOW
37 Exec Dir Financial Aid .... Mr. Bruce FOOTE
29 Dir Alumni Relations .... Ms. Aubrey L. KNIGHT
41 Dir Athletics .... Mr. Dave LAKETA
36 Dir Career Success Center .... Ms. Maribeth HEARN
38 Dir Counseling & Wellness .... Dr. Maryann ANDRADE BEKKER

28 Dir Institutional Diversity ... Ms. Allison HEARD
07 Dir Undergrad Admissions ... Mr. Eric RUIZ
123 Dir Grad/Degree Completion Admiss ... Ms. Sandra L. SLOKA
104 Dir Intl Programs Office ... Ms. Angie MAFFEO
27 Dir Marketing Services ... Ms. Julie FUTTERER
14 Dir Network Support Services ... Mr. Mark T. SNODGRASS
18 Dir Operations & Facilities ... Mr. Mike DECMAN
19 Dir Safety/Security ... Mr. Jason WILLIAMS
42 Dir University Ministry ... Ms. Jessica PEEK
06 Registrar ... Ms. Jennifer ETHRIDGE
08 Head Librarian ... Ms. Brigitte BELL
23 Coordinator of Health Services ... Ms. Phyllis M. PETERSON
09 Dir Inst Research & Planning ... Ms. Rebecca R. GARLAND
44 Director Annual Giving ... Ms. Kelly LARSON

University of Saint Mary of the Lake-Mundelein Seminary (A)

1000 E Maple Avenue, Mundelein IL 60060-1174
County: Lake FICE Identification: 001765
Unit ID: 148885
Telephone: (847) 566-6401 Carnegie Class: Spec-4-yr-Faith
FAX Number: (847) 566-7330 Calendar System: Semester
URL: www.usml.edu
Established: 1844 Annual Graduate Tuition & Fees: N/A
Enrollment: 260 Male
Affiliation or Control: Roman Catholic IRS Status: 501(c)3
Highest Offering: Doctorate; No Undergraduates
Accreditation: THEOL

00 Chancellor ... Card. Blase CUPICH
01 Rector/President ... V.Rev. John KARTJE
11 Chief Operating Officer ... Mr. James HEINEN
03 Vice Rector for Formation ... Rev. Brian WELTER
05 Vice Rector for Academic Affairs ... V.Rev. Thomas A. BAIMA
73 Pres/Pontifical Faculty of Theology ... Rev. Brendan LUPTON
10 Vice President for Finance ... Mr. John F. LEHOCKY
30 Vice President of Development ... Ms. Holly GIBOUT
20 Assoc Acad Dean Sem/Grad Sch ... Dr. Christopher MCATEE
73 Director Pre-Theology Program ... Rev. Dennis SPIES
08 Library Director ... Dr. Christopher ROGERS
06 Director of Registration & Records ... Ms. Devona SEWELL
42 Director of Spiritual Life ... Rev. Carlos RODRIGUEZ
85 Director of International Students ... Rev. Bradley ZAMORA
07 Director of Admissions ... Rev. Edward PELRINE
04 Admin Assistant to the President ... Ms. Dianne GIOVANNETTI
13 Chief Information Technology Ofcr ... Mr. Eric ALBERT
15 Chief Human Resources Officer ... Mr. Tad GEIGER
19 Director Security/Safety ... Mr. John HUINKER
38 Director Student Counseling ... Rev. Carlos RODRIGUEZ

VanderCook College of Music (B)

3140 S Federal Street, Chicago IL 60616-3731
County: Cook FICE Identification: 001778
Unit ID: 149639
Telephone: (312) 225-6288 Carnegie Class: Spec-4-yr-Other
FAX Number: (312) 225-5211 Calendar System: Semester
URL: www.vandercook.edu
Established: 1909 Annual Undergrad Tuition & Fees: $28,434
Enrollment: 158 Coed
Affiliation or Control: Independent Non-Profit IRS Status: 501(c)3
Highest Offering: Master's
Accreditation: NH, MUS

01 President ... Dr. Roseanne K. ROSENTHAL
08 Head Librarian ... Mr. Robert DELAND
05 Dean of Undergraduate Studies ... Ms. Stacey L. DOLAN
58 Dean of Graduate Studies ... Dr. Robert L. SINCLAIR
07 Director of Admissions & Alumni ... Ms. Cindy TOVAR
10 Chief Financial Officer ... Ms. Shunita RHODES
37 Director of Financial Aid ... Ms. Sirena COVINGTON
13 Director Information Technologies ... Mr. Rick MALIK
04 President's Assistant ... Ms. Cindy TOVAR
106 Dir of Continuing/Online Education ... Mr. Patrick BENSON
09 Director of Institutional Reports ... Mr. Gregor MEYER
06 Registrar/Educational Placement Dir ... Mrs. Carolyn BERGHOFF
26 Director Communications ... Vacant
29 Director Alumni Relations ... Ms. Cindy TOVAR

Waubonsee Community College (C)

Route 47 at Waubonsee Drive,
Sugar Grove IL 60554-9799
County: Kane FICE Identification: 006931
Unit ID: 149727
Telephone: (630) 466-7900 Carnegie Class: Assoc/HVT-High Non
FAX Number: (630) 466-7550 Calendar System: Semester
URL: www.waubonsee.edu
Established: 1966 Annual Undergrad Tuition & Fees (In-District): $3,264
Enrollment: 9,518 Coed
Affiliation or Control: Local IRS Status: 501(c)3
Highest Offering: Associate Degree
Accreditation: NH, ADNUR, ART, CAHIIM, EMT, MAC

01 President ... Dr. Christine J. SOBEK
05 VP Educational Affairs ... Dr. Diane NYHAMMER
10 Exec VP Finance & Operations ... Mr. David QUILLEN
45 VP Strategic Development ... Dr. Jamal SCOTT
32 Vice Pres of Student Development ... Dr. Melinda L. TEJADA
21 Asst Vice President of Finance ... Ms. Darla S. CARDINE
103 Asst VP Workforce Educ/Training ... Ms. Suzette MURRAY
121 Asst VP Transfer/Academic Support ... Vacant
13 Chief Information Officer ... Mr. Terence FELTON
35 Asst VP Student Services ... Dr. Scott PESKA
15 Exec Director Human Resources ... Ms. Michele NEEDHAM
26 Exec Dir Marketing/Communications ... Ms. Amanda GEIST
76 Dean Health Professions/Public Svc ... Dr. Jess TOUSSAINT
88 Dean Faculty Develop/Engagement ... Dr. Laura ORTIZ
79 Dean Communic/Humanities/Fine Arts ... Ms. Cynthia SPARR
81 Dean Mathematics/Sciences ... Ms. Mary Edith BUTLER
83 Dean Soc Sciences/Educ/World Lang ... Dr. Janette FUNARO
124 Dean Student Success/Retention ... Ms. Kelli SINCLAIR
56 Dean Adult Education ... Mr. Adam SCHAUER
111 Chief Advancement Officer ... Mr. Robert BARTO
50 Dean Business/Career Technologies ... Ms. Ne'Keisha STEPNEY
07 Dean for Admissions ... Ms. Faith LASHURE
31 Dean Community Education ... Vacant
04 Dir Pres Communications/Operations ... Ms. Kimberly CAPONI
37 Dir Student Financial Aid Services ... Dr. Charles BOUDREAU
09 Dean Inst Effective/Title V Proj ... Dr. Stacey RANDALL
18 Exec Dir Campus Safety/Operations ... Mr. Daniel LARSEN
06 Dir Registration/Records/Registrar ... Mr. Marc DALE
88 Dean Lrng Outcomes/Curric/Pgm Dev ... Dr. Kathleen GORSKI
88 Dean for Academic Support ... Ms. Anita MOOREBOHANNON
109 Dir/Financial/Auxiliary Services ... Mr. Lei XIE
88 Dir Employee Development ... Mr. Tim BIZOUKAS

Western Illinois University (D)

1 University Circle, Macomb IL 61455-1390
County: McDonough FICE Identification: 001780
Unit ID: 149772
Telephone: (309) 298-1414 Carnegie Class: Masters/L
FAX Number: (309) 298-2400 Calendar System: Semester
URL: www.wiu.edu
Established: 1899 Annual Undergrad Tuition & Fees (In-State): $12,951
Enrollment: 9,441 Coed
Affiliation or Control: State IRS Status: 501(c)3
Highest Offering: Doctorate
Accreditation: NH, ART, #CAATE, CACREP, CAEPN, CEA, DIETD, MUS, NAIT, NRPA, NURSE, SP, SW, THEA

01 Acting President ... Dr. Martin A. ABRAHAM
05 Interim Provost/Academic VP ... Mr. William CLOW
114 Assoc Prov Budget Planning & Per ... Dr. Russell MORGAN
20 Interim Assoc Prov/Undergrad & Grad ... Dr. Mark MOSSMAN
10 VP Administrative Services ... Dr. William J. POLLEY
32 Interim VP Student Services ... Mr. John W. SMITH
111 Vice Pres Advancement/Public Svcs ... Vacant
29 Director Alumni Programs ... Ms. Amy SPELMAN
43 General Counsel ... Mrs. Elizabeth DUVALL
39 Assoc Vice Pres Student Services ... Mr. John BIERNBAUM
45 SVP Strategic Planning & Initiative ... Dr. Joseph RIVES
86 Asst to Pres Government Relations ... Ms. Jeanette MALAFA
49 Dean College Arts/
Sciences ... Dr. Susan MARTINELLI-FERNANDEZ
50 Interim Dean College Business/Tech ... Dr. John ELFRINK
53 Interim Dean Col Educ & Human Svcs ... Dr. Katrina DAYTNER
57 Int Dean Fine Arts & Communication ... Mr. William HOON
08 Dean University Libraries ... Dr. Michael LORENZEN
92 Dean Centennial Honors Col ... Dr. Richard J. HARDY
64 Interim Director School of Music ... Dr. Jefrey BROWN
06 Registrar ... Dr. Angela LYNN
13 Int Exec Dir Univ Technology/CIO ... Ms. Rebecca SLATER
26 Exec Director Univ Communication .. Ms. Darcie R. SHINBERGER
09 Director Inst Research & Planning ... Ms. Angela BONIFAS
22 Int Dir Equal Opportunity & Access ... Ms. Andrea HENDERSON
37 Director Financial Aid ... Ms. Terri HARE
121 Dir Student Development/Success Ctr ... Ms. Samantha KLINGLER
15 Director Human Resources ... Mrs. Amelia HARTNET
18 Asst Director Physical Plant ... Mr. Troy RHOADS
19 Director Public Safety ... Mr. Derek WATTS
23 Director Health Center ... Ms. John W. SMITH
101 Exec Dir School Glob Educ & Outrch ... Dr. Jeffrey HANCKS
40 Retail Manager University Bookstore ... Mr. Jeff MOORE
41 Director Athletics ... Ms. Danielle SURPENANT
102 Director WIU Foundation ... Vacant
07 Director Undergraduate Admissions ... Mr. Doug FREED
38 Director Student Counseling ... Ms. Amy BUWICK
85 Dir Ctr International Studies ... Vacant
88 Director Budget ... Ms. Letisha TREPAC
100 Chief of Staff ... Vacant
04 Admin Assistant to the President ... Ms. Melinda A. MCFADDEN
96 Director of Purchasing ... Ms. Shannon R. REED

Western Illinois University Quad Cities (E)

3300 River Drive, Moline IL 61265
Telephone: (309) 762-9481 Identification: 770100
Accreditation: &NH

Wheaton College (F)

501 College Avenue, Wheaton IL 60187-5593
County: DuPage FICE Identification: 001781
Unit ID: 149781
Telephone: (630) 752-5000 Carnegie Class: Bac-A&S
FAX Number: (630) 752-5555 Calendar System: Semester
URL: www.wheaton.edu
Established: 1860 Annual Undergrad Tuition & Fees: $36,420
Enrollment: 2,900 Coed
Affiliation or Control: Independent Non-Profit IRS Status: 501(c)3
Highest Offering: Doctorate
Accreditation: NH, CACREP, CAEPN, CLPSY, MFCD, MUS

01 President ... Dr. Philip G. RYKEN
05 Provost ... Dr. Margaret DIDDAMS
10 Interim VP for Finance ... Mr. Ken LARSON
32 Vice President Student Development ... Mr. Paul O. CHELSEN
111 VP Advancement/Alumni Rels ... Mr. Kirk FARNEY
84 Chief Enrollment Management Officer ... Mr. Silvio E. VAZQUEZ
93 Chief Intercultural Engagement Ofcr ... Dr. Sheila CALDWELL
13 Chief Info & Campus Svc Officer ... Ms. Wendy WOODWARD
29 Sr Dir Vocation & Alum
Engagement ... Ms. Cindra STACKHOUSE TAETZSCH
04 Special Asst to the President ... Miss Marilee A. MELVIN
58 Dean of the Graduate School ... Dr. Scott MOREAU
79 Dean Biblical/Theol Studies ... Vacant
64 Dean Conservatory/Arts & Comm ... Dr. Michael WILDER
81 Dean Natural Sciences ... Dr. Becky EGGIMANN
83 Dean of Social Sciences & Education ... Dr. Bryan MCGRAW
104 Dean Global & Exper Learning ... Dr. Laura M. MONTGOMERY
83 Dean Psych/Counsel & Fam Therapy ... Dr. Terri WATSON
79 Dean Humanities ... Dr. Jeffry DAVIS
35 Dean of Student Engagement ... Dr. Steve IVESTER
08 Dean Library and Archives ... Vacant
97 Dean Curriculum and Advising ... Dr. Sarah MIGLIO
21 Controller ... Vacant
20 Exec Dir Billy Graham Ctr/Dean MML ... Dr. Ed STETZER
09 Dir Inst Research & Acad Operations ... Dr. Gary N. LARSON
06 Registrar ... Mr. Christopher HUANG
18 Director of Facilities ... Mr. Scott OKESSON
36 Dir Ctr Vocation & Career ... Ms. Dee PIERCE
15 Director of Human Resources ... Mrs. Karen TUCKER
07 Dir Undergraduate Admissions ... Mr. Jason KIRCHER
123 Dir Graduate Admissions ... Mr. Terrance CAMPBELL
37 Director Student Financial Svcs ... Ms. Karen BELLING
41 Director of Athletics ... Ms. Julie DAVIS
39 Dean of Residence Life ... Dr. Justin HETH
35 Interim Dean of Student Care ... Mrs. Carrie WILLIAMS
38 Director of Counseling ... Dr. Toussaint WHETSTONE
42 Chaplain ... Rev. Timothy BLACKMON
23 Interim Dir Student Health Services ... Ms. Beth WALSH
26 Director Marketing Communications ... Vacant
27 Director of Media Relations ... Ms. LaTonya TAYLOR
19 Chief of Public Safety ... Mr. Robert F. NORRIS
117 Director Risk Management ... Mr. Daniel CLARK
105 Director Web Communications ... Mrs. Rebecca LARSON
25 Academic Grants Officer ... Mrs. Virginia SHAFFER

Worsham College of Mortuary Science (G)

495 Northgate Parkway, Wheeling IL 60090-2646
County: Cook FICE Identification: 001783
Unit ID: 369455
Telephone: (847) 808-8444 Carnegie Class: Spec 2-yr-A&S
FAX Number: (847) 808-8493 Calendar System: Quarter
URL: www.worsham.edu
Established: 1911 Annual Undergrad Tuition & Fees: N/A
Enrollment: 87 Coed
Affiliation or Control: Proprietary IRS Status: Proprietary
Highest Offering: Associate Degree
Accreditation: FUSER

01 Director ... Ms. Leili MCMURROUGH

INDIANA

American College of Education (H)

101 West Ohio Street, Suite 1200, Indianapolis IN 46204
County: Marion Identification: 666242
Unit ID: 449889
Telephone: (800) 280-0307 Carnegie Class: Spec-4-yr-Other
FAX Number: N/A Calendar System: Other
URL: www.ace.edu
Established: 2005 Annual Undergrad Tuition & Fees: N/A
Enrollment: 4,816 Coed
Affiliation or Control: Proprietary IRS Status: Proprietary
Highest Offering: Doctorate
Accreditation: NH, CAEPT

01 President ... Dr. Shawntel D. LANDRY
05 SVP Academic Affairs ... Ms. Stephanie HINSHAW
88 Dir Regulatory Affairs & Compliance ... Mr. Tom BROUWER
07 Director of Admissions ... Ms. Jeannie TAYLOR
09 Dir Institutional Analytics ... Ms. Becky GERAMBIA
04 Executive Asst to President ... Ms. Jill ALGATE
08 Director Library ... Dr. Sandra QUIATKOWSKI
10 Chief Financial Officer ... Mr. Bryce PETERSON
26 Chief Marketing Officer ... Ms. Jill GEER
45 Chief Strategy & Innovation Officer ... Dr. Kiko SUAREZ
13 VP Information Technology ... Mr. Swapnal SHAH
15 VP Human Resources ... Ms. KK BYLAND
108 VP Continuous Improvement ... Ms. Alison WITHERSPOON
06 Registrar ... Ms. Lindsay MAY
28 Diversity & Inclusion Advisor ... Ms. Fawzia REZA
29 Alumni Engagement Officer ... Ms. Courtney SHELTON

Anabaptist Mennonite Biblical Seminary (I)

3003 Benham Avenue, Elkhart IN 46517-1999
County: Elkhart FICE Identification: 001823
Unit ID: 151865

Telephone: (574) 295-3726 Carnegie Class: Spec-4-yr-Faith
FAX Number: (574) 295-0092 Calendar System: 4/1/4
URL: www.ambs.edu
Established: 1946 Annual Graduate Tuition & Fees: N/A
Enrollment: 103 Coed
Affiliation or Control: Mennonite Church IRS Status: 501(c)3
Highest Offering: Master's; No Undergraduates
Accreditation: THEOL

01 President Dr. Sara W. SHENK
05 VP & Academic Dean Dr. Beverly K. LAPP
10 Vice President and CFO Mr. Ron RINGENBERG
111 Director of Advancement Rev. Paula KILLOUGH
06 Assistant Dean & Registrar Mr. Scott JANZEN
08 Director of Library Services Mr. Karl STUTZMAN
84 Dir Enrollment Mgmt/Financial Aid Mr. Daniel GRIMES
73 Director of Inst Mennonite Studies Dr. Jamie PITTS
04 Executive Asst to the President Ms. Karen S. STOLTZFUS
13 Director of Information Technology Mr. Brent GRABER
26 Director of Communications Ms. Melissa TROYER

Ancilla College (A)

PO Box 1, Donaldson IN 46513-0001
County: Marshall FICE Identification: 001784
Unit ID: 150048
Telephone: (574) 936-8898 Carnegie Class: Assoc/HT-High Trad
FAX Number: (574) 935-1773 Calendar System: Semester
URL: www.ancilla.edu
Established: 1937 Annual Undergrad Tuition & Fees: $17,550
Enrollment: 548 Coed
Affiliation or Control: Roman Catholic IRS Status: 501(c)3
Highest Offering: Associate Degree
Accreditation: NH

01 President Dr. Michele DVORAK
04 Assistant to the President Ms. Michelle BOUGHER
05 VP of Academic Affairs Mr. Sam SOLIMAN
10 VP of Finance & Admin Mr. Don HOLLAND
42 Vice President Mission Integration Vacant
18 Chief Facilities/Physical Plant Mr. Tom NOWAK
21 Director of Business Affairs Ms. Marcella HOPPLE
37 Director of Financial Aid Ms. Julianna LARSON
41 Athletic Director Mr. Brian PEARISON
13 Director of Information Technology Mr. John LINBACK
30 Dir Development/Alumni Relations Ms. Emily HUTSELL
06 Registrar/Institutional Research Ms. Tiffany FISHER
08 Librarian Ms. Cassaundra BASH
66 Director Nursing & Health Science Ms. Lori HUFFMAN
26 Dir of Marketing & Social Media Mr. Mitch JENSEN
39 Director Student Services Ms. Suzette KEEN
40 Bookstore Manager Sr. Carleen WRASMAN
84 Manager of Enrollment Management Vacant

Anderson University (B)

1100 E Fifth Street, Anderson IN 46012-3495
County: Madison FICE Identification: 001785
Unit ID: 150066
Telephone: (765) 649-9071 Carnegie Class: Masters/M
FAX Number: (765) 641-3851 Calendar System: Semester
URL: www.anderson.edu
Established: 1917 Annual Undergrad Tuition & Fees: $30,450
Enrollment: 1,877 Coed
Affiliation or Control: Church Of God IRS Status: 501(c)3
Highest Offering: Doctorate
Accreditation: NH, ACBSP, #CAATE, CAEP, MUS, NURSE, SW, THEOL

01 President Mr. John PISTOLE
05 Provost Dr. Marie MORRIS
10 Vice President Finance/Treasurer Mr. James RAGSDALE
111 Vice President for Advancement Ms. Jennifer HUNT
84 VP Enrollment & Marketing Mr. Ryon KAOPUIKI
73 Dean Sch of Theology/Christian Min Dr. MaryAnn HAWKINS
50 Int Dean Falls School of Business Dr. Michael COLLETTE
79 Assoc Prov/Dn Humanities/Behav Sci Dr. Joel SHROCK
64 Dean School Music/Theatre & Dance Dr. Jeffrey WRIGHT
66 Dean Sch Nursing & Kinesiology Dr. Lynn SCHMIDT
54 School of Science & Engineering Dr. Chad WALLACE
42 Campus Pastor Rev. Tamara SHELTON
32 Asst Provost/Dean of Students Mr. Chris LUEKENGA
06 University Registrar Mr. Arthur LEAK
08 Director of Libraries Dr. Janet BREWER
07 Director of Admissions Ms. Kynan SIMISON
21 Assistant Treasurer/Controller Mrs. Wendy FRANK
36 Center for Career & Calling Ms. Katie MITCHELL
13 Director of Info Technology Svcs Mr. Michael TUCKER
37 Student Financial Services Ms. Chaunta REDFIELD
18 Exec Dir Facilities & Property Mgmt Mr. Joseph ROYER
15 Director of Work Life Engagement Mr. Tim STATES
19 Director Police & Security Services Mr. Rick GARRETT
40 Bookstore Manager Mr. Dustin MARTIN
41 Athletic Director Ms. Marcie TAYLOR
38 Director Counseling Services Ms. Christal HELVERING
29 Exec Dir Alum Engage/Annual Giving Mr. Scott TILLEY
109 Manager Business & Auxiliary Svcs Mrs. Whitney JIMENEZ
04 Executive Asst to the President Mrs. Ronda REEMER
104 Director Study Abroad Mrs. Aurora DOSTER
108 Director Institutional Assessment Dr. Jaye ROGERS
39 Student Housing Coordinator Ms. Stacey CARPENTER
09 Director of Institutional Research Ms. Kim WOLFE
100 Special Assistant to the President Mr. Dan COURTNEY

105 Web Editor & Content Writer Mr. Michael BAKER
106 Asst Dir ITS/Instr Resource Center Ms. Jodie REMINDER
26 Director of Marketing Ms. Mischon HART
28 Director Cultural Resource Center Mr. Michael THIGPEN
30 Director of Development Mr. Brent BAKER

Ball State University (C)

2000 W. University Avenue, Muncie IN 47306-1099
County: Delaware FICE Identification: 001786
Unit ID: 150136
Telephone: (765) 285-5555 Carnegie Class: DU-Higher
FAX Number: (765) 285-1461 Calendar System: Semester
URL: www.bsu.edu
Established: 1918 Annual Undergrad Tuition & Fees (In-State): $9,896
Enrollment: 22,513 Coed
Affiliation or Control: State IRS Status: 501(c)3
Highest Offering: Doctorate
Accreditation: NH, ART, AUD, CAATE, CACREP, CAEP, CEA, CIDA, COARC, CONST, COPSY, DANCE, DIETD, DIETI, IPSY, JOUR, LSAR, MUS, NURSE, PLNG, RAD, SCPSY, SP, SW, THEA

01 President Mr. Geoffrey S. MEARNS
05 Provost/EVP Academic Affairs Dr. Susana RIVERA-MILLS
10 VP Business Affairs & Treasurer Mr. Alan FINN
32 VP Stdnt Aff/Enr Mgt/Dean of Stdnts Dr. Kay BALES
43 VP & General Counsel Ms. Sali K. FALLING
13 VP for IT Mr. Loren MALM
26 VP for Marketing and Comm Ms. Kathy M. WOLF
86 VP Govt Relations Cmty Engagement Mrs. Becca RICE
102 President and CEO BSU Foundation Mr. Jake LOGAN
41 Director Intercollegiate Athletics Ms. Beth GETZ
20 Int Assoc Provost/Dean Univ Col Dr. Kecia THOMPSON
28 Associate Provost Diversity Dr. Marsha MCGRIFF
50 Assoc Prov Entrepreneurial Learning Ms. Jennifer BLACKMER
108 Asst Provost Inst Effectiveness Ms. Sonia Zoe BRANDON
39 AVP Student Affairs/Dir of Housing Dr. Alan HARGRAVE
26 Assoc VP Strategic Communications Vacant
18 Assoc VP Facilities Planning/Mgmt Mr. James LOWE
109 Assoc VP Business/Auxiliary Svcs Ms. Julie HOPWOOD
14 Asst VP IT for Strategic/Fiscal Mgt Vacant
07 AVP of Enrollment/Ex Dir of Admiss Mr. Christopher T. MUNCHEL
08 Dean University Libraries Mr. Matthew SHAW
48 Dean Architecture/Planning Mr. David FERGUSON
79 Dean Col of Science/Humanities Dr. Maureen MCCARTHY
50 Dean Miller College of Business Dr. Steve FERRIS
53 Interim Dean of Teachers College Dr. Roy WEAVER
57 Dean College of Fine Arts Dr. Seth BECKMAN
58 Dean of Graduate School Dr. Adam R. BEACH
60 Dean Col of Comm/Info/Media Dr. Paaige K. TURNER
88 Founding Dean College of Health Dr. Mitchell WHALEY
92 Dean of Honors College Dr. John EMERT
88 Chief Entrepreneurship Officer Dr. Michael GOLDSBY
06 Reg/Dir Registration/Acad Pgms Mrs. Nancy L. CRONK
37 Director Scholarships/Financial Aid Dr. John MCPHERSON
15 Director of Human Resources Svcs Ms. Kate STOSS
19 Director Public Safety Mr. James DUCKHAM
25 Director Contracts & Grants Vacant
44 Director Annual or Planned Giving Vacant
30 Senior VP for Development Mr. Mark HELMUS
88 VP of Strategic Engagement & Comm Ms. Jean CROSBY
22 Assoc Dean of Students/Title IX Ms. Katie SLABAUGH
106 Dir Online Education/E-learning Ms. Staci DAVIS
38 Director Counseling/Health Services Dr. Tim HESS
88 Dir Unified Technology Support Mr. Dan LUTZ
36 Director Career Center Mr. Jim MCATEE
96 Director of Purchasing Services Mr. Roger HASSENZAHL
24 Dir of University Media Services Mr. Allen GORDON
88 Dir of Economic Development Policy Mr. David R. TERRELL
88 Dir Econ and Community Development Mr. Dick HEUPEL
104 Exec Dir International Programs Mr. Imara DAWSON
04 Exec Dir of Presidential Operations Ms. Stephanie K. ARRINGTON
101 Secretary to the Board of Trustees Ms. Anita KELSEY
45 Chief Strategy Officer Ms. Sue HODGES MOORE

Bethany Theological Seminary (D)

615 National Road W, Richmond IN 47374-4019
County: Wayne FICE Identification: 001637
Unit ID: 143233
Telephone: (800) 287-8822 Carnegie Class: Spec-4-yr-Faith
FAX Number: (765) 983-1840 Calendar System: Semester
URL: www.bethanyseminary.edu
Established: 1905 Annual Graduate Tuition & Fees: N/A
Enrollment: 47 Coed
Affiliation or Control: Church Of The Brethren IRS Status: 501(c)3
Highest Offering: Master's; No Undergraduates
Accreditation: NH, THEOL

01 President RevDr. Jeffrey W. CARTER
05 Academic Dean Dr. Steven J. SCHWEITZER
10 Exec Dir of Finance/Administration Ms. Tammy S. GLENN
30 Exec Dir Institutional Advancement Mrs. Gail CONNERLEY
20 Director of Academic Services Ms. April VANLONDEN
26 Director of Communications Ms. Jennifer L. WILLIAMS
32 Director Student Development Ms. Karen DUHAI
12 Director Brethren Academy Ms. Janet L. OBER LAMBERT
88 Dir Peace/Cross Cultural Studies Mr. Scott HOLLAND
88 Director of the MA Program Ms. Denise KETTERING-LANE
07 Exec Dir of Admissions/Student Svcs Ms. Lori M. CURRENT

Bethel University (E)

1001 Bethel Circle, Mishawaka IN 46545-5509
County: Saint Joseph FICE Identification: 001787
Unit ID: 150145
Telephone: (574) 807-7000 Carnegie Class: Masters/S
FAX Number: (574) 807-7484 Calendar System: Semester
URL: www.betheluniversity.edu
Established: 1947 Annual Undergrad Tuition & Fees: $28,590
Enrollment: 1,513 Coed
Affiliation or Control: Missionary Church IRS Status: 501(c)3
Highest Offering: Master's
Accreditation: NH, ADNUR, CAEPN, MUS, NUR

01 President Dr. Gregg A. CHENOWETH
05 VP for Academic Services Dr. Barbara K. BELLEFEUILLLE
111 VP for Advancement Mr. Matt LENTSCH
10 VP for Business Services Mr. Jerry WHITE
32 VP for Student Development Dr. Shawn M. HOLTGREN
121 Director of Student Success Mrs. Rachel A. KENNEDY
13 Senior Director of IT Ms. Patti J. FISHER
66 Dean of Nursing Dr. Deborah GILLUM
49 Dean of Arts & Sciences Dr. Janna MCLEAN
83 Dean of Humanities/Social Sciences Dr. Bradley D. SMITH
35 Dean of Students Mrs. Julie BEAM
06 Registrar Mrs. Jeanne E. FOX
36 Dir Career Devel/Global Engagement Mr. Tyler GRANT
37 Director Financial Aid Mrs. Cindi M. PEDERSEN
26 Director Public Relations Mrs. Erin C. KINZEL
41 Director Athletics Mr. Tony NATALI
08 Director Library Services Mr. Mark J. ROOT
88 Director Teacher Certification Mrs. Kimberly J. MEYER
09 Director Institutional Research Dr. Raymond E. WHITEMAN
19 Director Campus Safety Mr. Paul E. NEEL
85 Director International Students Mrs. Susan A. MATTESON
91 Director Administrative Computing Mrs. Donna FAUDREE
29 Director Alumni Services Mrs. Emily S. SHERWOOD
07 Director of Admission Mrs. Stephanie HOCHSTETLER
15 Director Human Resources Mr. Mike L. NICHOLAS
04 Administrative Asst to President Mrs. Miriam WERTZ
104 Director Global & Comm Engagement Mr. Tyler C. GRANT
112 Major Gifts Officer Mr. Jim CRAMER
108 Director Institutional Assessment Mr. Ray WHITEMAN
18 Chief Facilities/Phys Plant Ofcr Mr. Joe ZAPPIA

Butler University (F)

4600 Sunset Avenue, Indianapolis IN 46208-3443
County: Marion FICE Identification: 001788
Unit ID: 150163
Telephone: (317) 940-8000 Carnegie Class: Masters/L
FAX Number: (317) 940-9930 Calendar System: Semester
URL: www.butler.edu
Established: 1855 Annual Undergrad Tuition & Fees: $41,120
Enrollment: 5,145 Coed
Affiliation or Control: Independent Non-Profit IRS Status: 501(c)3
Highest Offering: Doctorate
Accreditation: NH, ARCPA, CACREP, CAEPN, DANCE, IPSY, MUS, PHAR, THEA

01 President Mr. James M. DANKO
05 Provost/VP Academic Affairs Dr. Kathryn MORRIS
10 Vice President for Finance Mr. Bruce E. ARICK
111 VP University Advancement Mr. Jonathan PURVIS
32 Vice President of Student Affairs Dr. Frank E. ROSS, III
41 VP & Director of Athletics Mr. Barry S. COLLIER
84 VP of Enrollment Management Ms. Lori GREENE
45 VP of Strategy and Innovation Ms. Melissa BECKWITH
43 General Counsel Ms. Claire KONOPA AIGOTTI
57 Dean Jordan College Fine Arts Dr. Michelle JARVIS
50 Dean College of Business Dr. Stephen STANDIFIRD
49 Dean Liberal Arts & Science Dr. Jay R. HOWARD
53 Dean Education Dr. Ena M. SHELLEY
67 Dean Pharmacy & Health Sciences Dr. Robert P. SOLTIS
60 Dean College of Communication Dr. Jay R. HOWARD
08 Dean of Libraries Dr. Julie L. MILLER
35 Dean Student Services Dr. Sally E. CLICK
38 Asst Dean & Director Counseling Ctr Dr. Keith B. MAGNUS
18 Executive Director of Facilities Vacant
112 Exec Dir Major Gifts/Planned Giving Mr. Michael EIKENBERRY
15 Associate VP of Human Resources Ms. Anila DIN
26 AVP Marketing & Communication Ms. Stephanie JUDGE CRIPE
88 Interim Director Butler Arts Center Mr. Aaron HURT
114 Executive Budget Director Mr. Robert J. MARCUS
37 Director Financial Aid Ms. Melissa J. SMURDON
88 Dir University Events Ms. Beth A. ALEXANDER
39 Director Residence Life Ms. Karla K. CUNNINGHAM
09 Director Institutional Research Dr. Nandini RAMASWAMY
85 Director Global Education Ms. Jill MCKINNEY
36 Director Career Services Mr. Gary R. BEAULIEU
27 Director of Creative Services Ms. Nancy LYZUN
28 Director of Diversity Programs Ms. Valerie J. DAVIDSON
86 Director of External Relations Mr. Michael KALTENMARK
07 Director of Admission Ms. Aimee SCHEUERMANN
06 Registrar Ms. Michele NEARY
13 Chief Information Officer Mr. Peter WILLIAMS
21 Controller Ms. Susan M. WESTERMEYER
40 Manager Bookstore Ms. Janine L. FRAINIER
96 Manager of Purchasing Ms. Shelly S. RABIDEAU

Calumet College of Saint Joseph (G)

2400 New York Avenue, Whiting IN 46394-2195
County: Lake FICE Identification: 001834
Unit ID: 150172

Telephone: (219) 473-7770 Carnegie Class: Masters/S
FAX Number: (219) 473-4259 Calendar System: Semester
URL: www.ccsj.edu
Established: 1951 Annual Undergrad Tuition & Fees: $19,170
Enrollment: 834 Coed
Affiliation or Control: Roman Catholic IRS Status: 501(c)3
Highest Offering: Master's
Accreditation: NH, CAEPN

01 President ....Dr. Amy MCCORMACK
84 Sr Vice President for Enrollment ....Mr. Johnny CRAIG
05 Vice President Academic Affairs ....Dr. Ginger RODRIGUEZ
111 Dir of Institutional Advancement ....Ms. Ester DIAZ
10 VP Business & Finance ....Ms. Lynn MISKUS
32 VP Student Engagement & Retention ....Dr. Dionne JONES-MALONE
06 Registrar ....Ms. Diana FRANCIS
08 Director of Library Services ....Dr. Qi CHEN
09 Institutional Researcher ....Mr. Darren HENDERSON
26 Dir of Communications & PR ....Ms. Linda GAJEWSKI
41 Athletic Director ....Mr. Enrique TORRES
37 Dir Financial Aid/Business Ofc Ops ....Mr. Michael SCHMALTZ
13 Director of Computer Services ....Mr. Kevin KRIEPS
121 Director of Academic Advising ....Mrs. Sally LOBO-TORRES
105 Director Web Services ....Mr. Dan YOUNG
07 Director of Enrollment Management ....Mr. Andy MARKS

Caris College (A)

2780 Jefferson Centre Way, Ste 102, Jeffersonville IN 47130
County: Clark Identification: 667314
Telephone: (812) 952-9791 Carnegie Class: Not Classified
FAX Number: N/A Calendar System: Quarter
URL: www.cariscollege.edu
Established: Annual Undergrad Tuition & Fees: N/A
Enrollment: N/A Coed
Affiliation or Control: Proprietary IRS Status: Proprietary
Highest Offering: Associate Degree
Accreditation: ABHES

01 President & CEO ....Mr. Bruce KEPLEY
11 Campus Director ....Ms. Brittany COTTONER
05 Director of Education ....Ms. Mandy HICKS
06 Registrar/Office Manager ....Ms. Brittany COFFEY

Chamberlain University-Indianapolis Campus (B)

9100 Keystone Crossing, Suite 300, Indianapolis IN 46240
Telephone: (317) 816-7335 Identification: 770503
Accreditation: &NH, NURSE

Christian Theological Seminary (C)

1000 W. 42nd Street, Indianapolis IN 46208-3301
County: Marion FICE Identification: 001789
Unit ID: 150215
Telephone: (317) 924-1331 Carnegie Class: Spec-4-yr-Faith
FAX Number: (317) 923-1961 Calendar System: Semester
URL: www.cts.edu
Established: 1925 Annual Graduate Tuition & Fees: N/A
Enrollment: 165 Coed
Affiliation or Control: Christian Church (Disciples Of Christ)
IRS Status: 501(c)3
Highest Offering: Doctorate; No Undergraduates
Accreditation: NH, MFCD, THEOL

01 President ....Dr. David M. MELLOTT
05 Vice Pres of Academics ....Dr. Leah GUNNING-FRANCIS
10 Vice President Finance and Business ....Mr. Curtis SHORT
30 Vice President Development ....Vacant
32 Dean of Students ....Rev. Mary HARRIS
04 Executive Administrator ....Ms. Sarah EVANS
21 Director of Business Affairs ....Mr. Scott SIMS
08 Director of Library ....Dr. Scott SEAY
06 Registrar ....Mr. Matt SCHLIMGEN
75 Director of Field Education ....Rev. Martin WRIGHT
37 Director of Student Financial Aid ....Mr. Robert FISHER
26 Director of Communications ....Rev. Nathan WILSON
13 Chief Information Tech Officer ....Mr. Jesse JOHNSON

College of Court Reporting, Inc. (D)

455 West Lincolnway, Valparaiso IN 46385
County: Lake FICE Identification: 026158
Unit ID: 150251
Telephone: (866) 294-3974 Carnegie Class: Spec 2-yr-Other
FAX Number: (219) 942-1631 Calendar System: Semester
URL: www.ccr.edu
Established: 1984 Annual Undergrad Tuition & Fees: $9,050
Enrollment: 238 Coed
Affiliation or Control: Proprietary IRS Status: Proprietary
Highest Offering: Associate Degree
Accreditation: DEAC

01 President ....Mr. Jeff T. MOODY
03 Executive Director ....Mr. Jay VETTICKAL
05 Director of Education ....Ms. Kay MOODY
07 Director of Admissions ....Ms. Nicky M. RODRIQUEZ
37 Director of Financial Aid ....Ms. Alice LEONARD
32 Director of Student Services ....Ms. Mindy BILLINGS

Concordia Theological Seminary (E)

6600 N Clinton Street, Fort Wayne IN 46825-4996
County: Allen FICE Identification: 020876
Unit ID: 150288
Telephone: (260) 452-2100 Carnegie Class: Spec-4-yr-Faith
FAX Number: (260) 452-2121 Calendar System: Quarter
URL: www.ctsfw.edu
Established: 1846 Annual Graduate Tuition & Fees: N/A
Enrollment: 290 Male
Affiliation or Control: Lutheran Church - Missouri Synod
IRS Status: 501(c)3
Highest Offering: Doctorate; No Undergraduates
Accreditation: NH, THEOL

01 President ....Dr. Lawrence R. RAST
05 Academic Dean ....Dr. Charles A. GIESCHEN
36 Chairman Pastoral Ministry/Missions ....Dr. Carl C. FICKENSCHER, II
32 Dean of Students ....Rev. Gary ZIEROTH
11 Vice President of Operations ....Rev. Jon SCICLUNA
06 Registrar ....Mrs. Barbara A. WEGMAN
07 Director of Admissions ....Rev. Matthew WIETFELDT
08 Head Librarian ....Prof. Robert V. ROETHEMEYER

DePauw University (F)

313 S Locust Street, Greencastle IN 46135-1772
County: Putnam FICE Identification: 001792
Unit ID: 150400
Telephone: (765) 658-4800 Carnegie Class: Bac-A&S
FAX Number: (765) 658-4177 Calendar System: 4/1/4
URL: www.depauw.edu
Established: 1837 Annual Undergrad Tuition & Fees: $49,704
Enrollment: 2,158 Coed
Affiliation or Control: United Methodist IRS Status: 501(c)3
Highest Offering: Baccalaureate
Accreditation: NH, MUS

01 President ....Dr. Mark MCCOY
04 Executive Assistant to President ....Ms. Elizabeth DEMMINGS
05 VP for Academic Affairs ....Dr. David BERQUE
32 VP Student Academic Life ....Mr. Alan P. HILL
10 VP for Finance/Administration ....Mr. Bob LEONARD
84 VP for Enrollment Management ....Mr. Robert ANDREWS
30 VP for Development ....Mr. Steven J. SETCHELL
20 Dean of the Faculty ....Dr. Bridget L. GOURLEY
88 Dean of Experiential Learning ....Ms. Cara L. SETCHELL
64 Dean of the School of Music ....Dr. Mellasenah MORRIS
13 Chief Information Officer ....Ms. Carol L. SMITH
35 Dean of Campus Life ....Mr. Dorian SHAGER
06 Registrar ....Dr. LaTonya BRANHAM
15 Director of Human Resources ....Ms. Jana L. GRIMES
37 Director of Financial Aid ....Mr. Elreo CAMPBELL
41 Director of Athletics ....Ms. Stevie BAKER-WATSON
21 Assoc VP for Finance ....Mr. Travis W. LINNEWEBER
08 Director of Libraries ....Mr. Rick E. PROVINE
44 Director of Annual Giving ....Ms. Rosalie BLANKENSHIP
19 Director of Public Safety ....Ms. Charlene P. SHREWSBURY
07 Director of Admission ....Ms. Amanda RYAN
18 Assoc VP for Facilities ....Mr. Warren WHITESELL
27 Director of Media Relations ....Ms. Mary DIETER
09 Director of Institutional Research ....Dr. William M. TOBIN
38 Director of Student Counseling ....Dr. Trevor YUHAS
39 Director of Housing ....Mr. Yug GILL
36 Director Student Placement ....Ms. Erin A. MAHONEY
26 VP of Communications and Marketing ....Ms. Deedie DOWDLE
105 Director Web Services ....Ms. Andrea ADAMCHAK
14 Associate CIO ....Mr. Adam HUGHES

Earlham College and Earlham School of Religion (G)

801 National Road W, Richmond IN 47374-4095
County: Wayne FICE Identification: 001793
Unit ID: 150455
Telephone: (765) 983-1200 Carnegie Class: Bac-A&S
FAX Number: (765) 983-1304 Calendar System: Semester
URL: www.earlham.edu
Established: 1847 Annual Undergrad Tuition & Fees: $46,450
Enrollment: 1,128 Coed
Affiliation or Control: Friends IRS Status: 501(c)3
Highest Offering: Master's
Accreditation: NH, THEOL

01 President ....Anne HOUTMAN
05 Vice President Academic Affairs ....Rebecca THOMAS
10 Vice President Business Affairs ....Stacy L. DAVIDSON
73 Vice President School of Religion ....Matt HISRICH
84 VP of Enrollment ....Vacant
32 Interim VP/Dean of Student Life ....Bonita WASHINGTON-LACY
20 Associate VP Academic Affairs ....Michael DEIBEL
20 Associate Academic Dean ....James LOGAN
111 Assoc VP for Institutional Advance ....Vacant
29 Director of Alumni Relations ....Alexandra PFLUG
21 Controller ....Cathy HABSCHMIDT
06 Registrar ....Vacant
121 Director Academic Support Services ....Vacant
88 Admissions School of Religion ....Julie DISHMAM
41 Athletic Director ....Julie KLINE
13 Director of Computing Services ....Brendan POST

37 Director of Financial Aid ....Katherine GOTTSCHALK
15 Director of Human Resources/Ops ....Stephanie BISHOP
85 Director of International Programs ....Vacant
18 Director of Physical Plant ....Ian SMITH
26 Director Marketing & Communications ....Jonathan GRAHAM
27 Director of Media Relations ....Brian ZIMMERMAN
19 Director of Public Safety ....Christopher LITTLE
08 Director of Library ....Neal BAKER
28 Director of Diversity & Inclusion ....Yemi MAHONEY
04 Executive Assistant ....Lyn THOMAS
39 Director Residence Life ....Shane PETERS
09 Director of Institutional Research ....Polly ALBRIGHT
38 Director Student Counseling ....Jessica SANFORD
102 Dir Foundation/Corporate Relations ....Sara PAULE
104 Director Study Abroad ....Vacant
105 Director Web Services ....David KNIGHT
44 Director Annual Giving ....Vacant

Faith Bible Seminary (H)

2000 Elmwood Ave, Lafayette IN 47904
County: Tippecanoe Identification: 667250
Telephone: (765) 448-1986 Carnegie Class: Not Classified
FAX Number: (765) 448-2985 Calendar System: Semester
URL: www.faithlafayette.org/seminary
Established: 2005 Annual Graduate Tuition & Fees: N/A
Enrollment: N/A Coed
Affiliation or Control: Independent Non-Profit IRS Status: 501(c)3
Highest Offering: Master's; No Undergraduates
Accreditation: BI

01 President ....Dr. Brent AUCOIN
84 Dean of Enrollment Management ....Mr. Kirk FATOOL

Fortis College (I)

9001 N Wesleyan Road Suite 101, Indianapolis IN 46268
Telephone: (317) 808-4800 Identification: 770574
Accreditation: ACCSC, ADNUR, MAAB

† Branch campus of Fortis College, Centreville, OH.

Franklin College of Indiana (J)

101 Branigin Boulevard, Franklin IN 46131-2623
County: Johnson FICE Identification: 001798
Unit ID: 150604
Telephone: (317) 738-8000 Carnegie Class: Bac-A&S
FAX Number: (317) 738-8013 Calendar System: 4/1/4
URL: www.franklincollege.edu
Established: 1834 Annual Undergrad Tuition & Fees: $32,010
Enrollment: 1,034 Coed
Affiliation or Control: American Baptist IRS Status: 501(c)3
Highest Offering: Master's
Accreditation: NH, #ARCPA, CAATE, CAEPN

01 President ....Dr. Thomas J. MINAR
04 Assistant to the President ....Ms. Janet D. SCHANTZ
10 Vice President and CFO ....Mr. Joseph HORNETT
05 Provost & Dean of College ....Dr. Lori SCHROEDER
07 VP/Dean of Admission/Financial Aid ....Mrs. Kathryn D. COFFMAN
30 VP for Development/Alumni Engage ....Mrs. Dana CUMMINGS
20 Associate Provost ....Dr. Denise BAIRD
32 VP Stdnt Affs/Dean of Students ....Vacant
29 Dir Alumni Engage/Campus Prtnrshps ....Ms. Emily S. WOOD
06 Associate Registrar ....Ms. Kelli JONES
18 AVP of Physical Facilities ....Mr. Thomas PATZ
39 Director of Residence Life ....Mr. Jacob E. KNIGHT
38 Director of Counseling Center ....Dr. John R. SHAFER
121 Dean Student Success/Retention ....Ms. Keri A. ELLINGTON
46 Director of Research & Grants ....Ms. Betsy SCHMIDT
44 Sr Dir Development/Planned Giving ....Mr. Thomas W. ARMOR
37 Director of Financial Aid ....Mr. James VINCENT-DUNN
42 Director of Religious Life/Chaplain ....Rev. Hannah ADAMS INGRAM
41 Director of Athletics ....Mr. Kerry N. PRATHER
13 Dir of Information Tech Services ....Mr. Larry STOFFEL
36 Director Career Development ....Mr. Kirk J. BIXLER
88 Dir Professional Dev/Employer Rels ....Ms. Jill NOVOTNY
104 Dir Office of Global Education ....Ms. Jennifer CATALDI
109 Dir of Dining Services-Parkhurst ....Vacant
44 AVP for Alumni Engage/Annual Giving ....Ms. Lee Ann JOURDAN
07 Director of Admissions ....Ms. Ashley HARDY
27 Director of Communications ....Ms. Deidra BAUMGARDNER
26 Director of Marketing ....Ms. Ann SMITH
08 Director of Library Services ....Ms. Denise SHOREY
19 Director of Campus Security ....Mr. Steve LEONARD
105 Website Administrator ....Ms. Ann SMITH
15 Manager of Employee Resources ....Ms. June HENDERSON
22 Asst Vice Pres Physical Facilities ....Mr. Thomas PATZ
40 Bookstore Manager ....Mr. Matthew NEAU
21 Business Office Manager ....Mr. Bradley JONES
23 Coordinator Student Health Center ....Ms. Catherine DECLEENE
28 Director of Diversity & Inclusion ....Ms. Terri L. ROBERTS-LEONARD
50 Head Business/Computing/Math Div ....Dr. Justin GASH
53 Head Education Division ....Dr. David MOFFETT
79 Head Humanities Division ....Dr. Susan CRISAFULLI
60 Head Journalism Division ....Mr. Joel CRAMER
65 Head Natural Sciences Division ....Dr. Sarah MORDAN-MCCOMBS
83 Head Social Sciences Division ....Dr. Kristen FLORA
57 Head Fine Arts Division ....Dr. Svetlana RAKIC

Goshen College (A)

1700 S Main Street, Goshen IN 46526-4794
County: Elkhart FICE Identification: 001799
Unit ID: 150668
Telephone: (574) 535-7000 Carnegie Class: Bac-Diverse
FAX Number: (574) 535-7060 Calendar System: Semester
URL: www.goshen.edu
Established: 1894 Annual Undergrad Tuition & Fees: $33,700
Enrollment: 950 Coed
Affiliation or Control: Mennonite Church IRS Status: 501(c)3
Highest Offering: Doctorate
Accreditation: NH, CAEPN, NURSE, SW

01 President .... Dr. Rebecca J. STOLTZFUS
03 Executive Vice President .... Vacant
05 VP Academic Affairs/Academic Dean .... Dr. Ann VENDRELY
10 Vice President for Finance .... Ms. Deanna RISSER
111 VP for Advancement .... Vacant
84 VP for Enroll Management/Marketing .... Vacant
32 Dean of Students .... Mr. Gilberto PEREZ, JR.
28 Director of Intercultural Dev .... Vacant
66 Director of Undergraduate Nursing .... Ms. Brenda SROF
66 Director of Graduate Nursing .... Dr. Ruth STOLTZFUS
70 Director of Social Work .... Dr. Jeanne M. LIECHTY
53 Director of Elementary Teacher Educ .... Dr. Kathryn MEYER REIMER
08 Library Director .... Mr. Fritz HARTMAN
82 Director of International Education .... Dr. Tom J. MEYERS
53 Director of Secondary Education .... Ms. Suzanne EHST
13 Director of Information Tech Svcs .... Mr. Michael SHERER
09 Director of Institutional Research .... Mr. Justin HEINZEKEHR
06 Registrar .... Ms. Jan KAUFFMAN
37 Director Student Financial Aid .... Mr. Joel D. SHORT
26 Director of Communications .... Ms. Jodi BEYELER
29 Director of Alumni/Parent Relations .... Mr. Dan LIECHTY
42 Campus Minister .... Rev. LaKendra HARDWARE
42 Campus Minister .... Ms. Joanne GALLARDO
36 Director of Career Services .... Mr. David KENDALL
18 Director of Facilities .... Mr. Glenn GILBERT
15 Director of Human Resources .... Vacant
106 Director of Adult/Online Pgms .... Dr. Ann VENDRELY
39 Director of Residence Life .... Mr. Chad COLEMAN
04 Exec Assistant to the President .... Ms. Kathleen YODER
108 Director Institutional Assessment .... Mr. Justin HEINZEKEHR
41 Athletic Director .... Mr. Harold WATSON
38 Director Student Counseling .... Vacant
07 Dean of Admissions .... Ms. Adela HUFFORD
102 Dir Foundation/Corporate Relations .... Vacant

Grace College and Seminary (B)

200 Seminary Drive, Winona Lake IN 46590-1294
County: Kosciusko FICE Identification: 001800
Unit ID: 150677
Telephone: (574) 372-5100 Carnegie Class: Masters/M
FAX Number: (574) 372-5139 Calendar System: Semester
URL: www.grace.edu
Established: 1937 Annual Undergrad Tuition & Fees: $24,768
Enrollment: 2,156 Coed
Affiliation or Control: Fellowship Of Grace Brethren Churches
IRS Status: 501(c)3
Highest Offering: Doctorate
Accreditation: NH, CACREP, CAEPN, THEOL

01 President .... Dr. William J. KATIP
04 Exec Assistant to the President .... Mrs. Sarah E. PRATER
05 Provost & VP of Academic Affairs .... Dr. John R. LILLIS
88 Exec Assistant to the Provost .... Mrs. Elma C. SHERMAN
20 Assistant Provost .... Mr. John M. LOMMEL
73 VP & Dean Seminary & School of Min .... Dr. Frederick CARDOZA, II
111 VP Advancement and Marketing .... Dr. Andrew R. FLAMM
11 VP Administration & Compliance .... Dr. Carrie A. YOCUM
84 Associate VP Enrollment Management .... Dr. Mark A. POHL
10 VP Financial Affairs/CFO .... Mr. Paul G. BLAIR
32 Associate VP Student Affairs .... Mr. Aaron T. CRABTREE
49 Dean of School of Arts & Sciences .... Dr. Mark M. NORRIS
83 Dean of Sch of Behavioral Science .... Dr. Thomas J. EDGINGTON
50 Dean of School of Business .... Dr. Jeffrey K. FAWCETT
53 Dean of School of Education .... Dr. Laurinda A. OWEN
106 Dean School of Prof/Online Ed .... Dr. Timothy J. ZIEBARTH
97 Dean of Core & Global Initiatives .... Mrs. Jacqueline S. SCHRAM
42 Dean of Chapel .... Mr. Brent T. MENCARELLI
06 Registrar .... Mrs. Heidi L. KANTENWEIN
08 Dir Library Services .... Mrs. Tonya L. FAWCETT
13 Dir Information Technology .... Mr. Donald W. FLUKE
23 Dir Student Health & Counseling .... Dr. Debra S. MUSSER
37 Dir Student Financial Aid .... Mrs. Charlette R. SAUDERS
15 Chief Human Resource Officer .... Mr. Norman BAKHIT
26 Dir of Marketing .... Mr. Matthew R. METZGER
18 Director Physical Plant .... Mr. Randy KLEINHANS
19 Director Security/Safety .... Mr. Glenn A. GOLDSMITH
29 Director Alumni Engagement .... Mr. Dennis L. DUNCAN
41 Director of Athletics .... Mr. Chad C. BRISCOE
36 Director Career Connections .... Mrs. Denise A. TERRY
100 Chief of Staff .... Dr. Carrie A. YOCUM
07 Director of Admissions .... Mrs. Alessa R. TRACY
30 Director of Development .... Mr. Stephen D. GERBER
39 Director Residence Life .... Mrs. Emily J. BRENNEMAN

Hanover College (C)

517 Ball Drive, Hanover IN 47243
County: Jefferson FICE Identification: 001801
Unit ID: 150756
Telephone: (812) 866-7000 Carnegie Class: Bac-A&S
FAX Number: (812) 866-2164 Calendar System: Other
URL: www.hanover.edu
Established: 1827 Annual Undergrad Tuition & Fees: $37,670
Enrollment: 1,089 Coed
Affiliation or Control: Presbyterian Church (U.S.A.) IRS Status: 501(c)3
Highest Offering: Baccalaureate
Accreditation: NH, CAEPN

01 President .... Dr. Lake LAMBERT, III
100 Chief of Staff/Exec Asst to Pres .... Shelley PREOCANIN
10 Vice President Business Affairs .... J. Michael BRUCE
41 Vice President of Athletics .... Lynn HALL
111 Vice President College Advancement .... Melba RODRIGUEZ
05 Vice President Academic Affairs .... Dr. Steve JOBE
84 Vice Pres Enrollment/Strategy .... Christopher GAGE
32 Vice President/Dean Student Life .... Dr. Dewain LEE
35 Associate Dean of Student Success .... Katy LOWE-SCHNEIDER
39 Assoc Dean Students Residence Life .... Lindsay FAULSTICK
36 Sr Dir Career/Profess Development .... Margaret KRANTZ
88 Exec Dir Business Scholars Program .... Diane MAGARY
06 Registrar .... Dr. Ken PRINCE
13 Chief Technology Officer .... Kevin STORMER
42 Chaplain .... Catherine KNOTT
29 Director of Alumni Engagement .... Christy HUGHES
19 Director of Campus Safety .... Jim HICKERSON
26 Dir of Communications & Marketing .... Vacant
08 Director of Duggan Library .... Kelly JOYCE
37 Director of Financial Aid .... Richard NASH
23 Director of Health Services .... Christy OWNBEY
15 Director of Human Resources .... Heather BUHR
18 Director of Physical Plant .... Kevin BROWN
104 Director of Study Abroad .... Uschi APPELT
38 Director of Student Counseling .... Catherine LE SAUX
96 Director of Purchasing .... Kevin BROWN

Holy Cross College (D)

PO Box 308, Notre Dame IN 46556-0308
County: Saint Joseph FICE Identification: 007263
Unit ID: 150774
Telephone: (574) 239-8400 Carnegie Class: Bac-Diverse
FAX Number: (574) 239-8323 Calendar System: Semester
URL: www.hcc-nd.edu
Established: 1966 Annual Undergrad Tuition & Fees: $30,700
Enrollment: 557 Coed
Affiliation or Control: Roman Catholic IRS Status: 501(c)3
Highest Offering: Baccalaureate
Accreditation: NH

01 President .... Rev. David D. TYSON, CSC
03 Senior Vice President .... Dr. Michael GRIFFIN
05 Provost/CAO .... Dr. Justin WATSON
10 Vice President of Finance .... Ms. Monica MARKOVICH
04 Assoc Dir of Dev/Special Events .... Ms. Jodie L. BADMAN
06 Registrar .... Mrs. Hiroko HARRISON
07 Director of Admissions .... Mr. Jordan SCHANK
38 Director of Student Counseling Svcs .... Mr. Thomas DEHORN
13 Director of Information Technology .... Mr. Doug BLAIR
32 Dean of Students/Dir of Res Life .... Mr. William MCKENNEY
08 Director of Library Services .... Mrs. Mary Ellen HEGEDUS
42 Director of Campus Ministry .... Mr. Andrew POLANIECKI
124 Dir of Recruitment and Retention .... Mr. Terron PHILLIPS
15 Director of Human Resources .... Ms. Gwen DEMAEGD
30 Director of Development .... Ms. Judeann HASTINGS
19 Chief Security Officer .... Mr. Greg RUNNELS
29 Director of Career Development .... Mr. Adam DEBECK

Horizon University (E)

7700 Indian Lake Road, Indianapolis IN 46231
County: Marion FICE Identification: 041405
Unit ID: 457226
Telephone: (800) 553-4674 Carnegie Class: Spec-4-yr-Faith
FAX Number: N/A Calendar System: Semester
URL: www.horizonuniversity.edu
Established: 1993 Annual Undergrad Tuition & Fees: $9,300
Enrollment: 16 Coed
Affiliation or Control: Independent Non-Profit IRS Status: 501(c)3
Highest Offering: Baccalaureate
Accreditation: BI

01 President .... Dr. Randall DODGE
05 Academic Dean & Exec Vice President .... Mr. Dave KOSOBUCKI
11 Dean of Administration .... Ms. Becky KIRSININKAS
10 Chief Financial Officer .... Ms. Debbie MARSHALL
32 Dean of Students .... Mr. Tracy GRAY
26 Dir Marketing/Communications .... Mr. Andrew LOCKERBIE

Huntington University (F)

2303 College Avenue, Huntington IN 46750-9986
County: Huntington FICE Identification: 001803
Unit ID: 150941
Telephone: (260) 356-6000 Carnegie Class: Masters/S
FAX Number: (260) 359-4086 Calendar System: 4/1/4
URL: www.huntington.edu
Established: 1897 Annual Undergrad Tuition & Fees: $26,158
Enrollment: 1,321 Coed
Affiliation or Control: United Brethren Church IRS Status: 501(c)3
Highest Offering: Doctorate
Accreditation: NH, CAEPN, NURSE, OT, SW

01 President .... Dr. Sherilyn R. EMBERTON
05 VP Academic Affairs/Dean Faculty .... Dr. Luke FETTERS
11 VP/Chief Operating Officer .... Dr. Russ J. DEGITZ
84 VP Enrollment Mgmt & Marketing .... Mr. Daniel SOLMS
111 Vice President for Advancement .... Dr. Stephen WEINGART
32 Vice President for Student Life .... Dr. Ron L. COFFEY
04 Administrative Asst to President .... Ms. Peg DEBOLT
42 Dean Spiritual Life/Campus Pastor .... Rev. Arthur L. WILSON
58 Dir of Grad & Professional Programs .... Mrs. Julie K. GOETZ
36 Assoc Dean Student Life/Career Dev .... Ms. Martha J. SMITH
35 Dean of Students .... Mr. Brian R. JAWORSKI
21 Controller/Dir of Fin Services .... Mrs. Connie C. BONNER
37 Director of Financial Aid .... Ms. Lisa M. MONTANY
06 Registrar .... Mrs. Sarah J. HARVEY
08 Director of Library Services .... Ms. Anita GRAY
13 Dir Information/Technology Services .... Mr. Adam L. SKILES
88 Dir Academic Center for Excellence .... Mrs. Erica MARSHALL
41 Athletic Director .... Ms. Lori L. CULLER
18 Director of Facilities .... Mrs. Marcie NOFZIGER
29 Director of Alumni Relations .... Mrs. Marcy T. HAWKINS
19 Chief of Campus Police/Safety .... Mr. Justin D. FAW
15 Human Resources Manager .... Ms. Jean COLE

Indiana State University (G)

200 N 7th Street, Terre Haute IN 47809-1902
County: Vigo FICE Identification: 001807
Unit ID: 151324
Telephone: (812) 237-6311 Carnegie Class: DU-Mod
FAX Number: (812) 237-2291 Calendar System: Semester
URL: web.indstate.edu
Established: 1865 Annual Undergrad Tuition & Fees (In-State): $9,090
Enrollment: 13,763 Coed
Affiliation or Control: State IRS Status: 501(c)3
Highest Offering: Doctorate
Accreditation: NH, ARCPA, ART, CAATE, CACREP, CAEPN, CIDA, CLPSY, CONST, DIETC, MUS, NAIT, NUR, OT, PTA, SCPSY, SP, SW

01 President .... Dr. Deborah CURTIS
100 Chief of Staff .... Ms. Teresa D. EXLINE
86 Exec Dir of Government Relations .... Mr. Greg J. GOODE
05 Provost/Vice Pres Academic Affs .... Dr. Michael J. LICARI
10 Sr VP Finance & Admin/Univ Treas .... Ms. Diann E. MCKEE
32 VP Student Affairs .... Dr. Andy MORGAN
88 Vice Pres Univ Engagement .... Dr. Nancy B. ROGERS
111 Vice Pres Univ Advancement/CEO Fndn .... Ms. Andrea L. ANGEL
43 General Counsel Legal Affairs .... Ms. Bridget K. BUTWIN
20 Assoc VP Academic Affairs .... Dr. Susan POWERS
20 Assoc VP Academic Affairs .... Dr. Mark GREEN
13 Assoc VP Chief Info Officer .... Dr. Lisa SPENCE
26 Assoc VP Comm/Marketing .... Mr. Santhana NAIDU
07 Assoc VP Enroll/Mgmt/Adm/HS Rel .... Mr. Richard J. TOOMEY
29 Exec Director of Alumni Engagement .... Mr. Rex KENDALL
15 Assoc VP Human Resources .... Mr. Rick ENYARD
14 Exec Dir Information Technology .... Mr. Yancy PHILLIPS
21 Assoc VP/Univ Controller .... Mr. Jeff JACSO
06 Registrar .... Dr. April HAY
22 Int AVP for Inclusive Excellence .... Mr. Brice YATES
28 Exec Dir Multicultural Svcs & Pgms .... Ms. Elonda ERVIN
41 Director of Athletics .... Mr. Sherard CLINKSCALES
36 Executive Director Career Svcs .... Mrs. Tradara MCLAURINE
25 Director Sponsored Programs .... Mr. Andrew SHEPARD-SMITH
09 Director of Institutional Research .... Ms. Patty MCCLINTOCK
19 Director of Public Safety .... Mr. Joseph M. NEWPORT
96 Dir Purchasing/Central Receiving .... Mr. Kevin BARR
39 Executive Dir of Residential Life .... Ms. Amanda KNERR
38 Director of Student Counseling .... Dr. Kenneth CHEW
37 Director Student Financial Aid .... Ms. Donna SIMMONDS
49 Dean of Arts & Sciences .... Dr. Christopher OLSEN
50 Interim Dean of Business .... Dr. Jack C. MAYNARD
53 Dean of Education .... Dr. Janet BUCKENMEYER
68 Dean Health & Human Svcs .... Dr. Caroline MALLORY
72 Dean of Technology .... Dr. Nesli ALP
58 Dean of Grad/Professional Studies .... Dr. Denise COLLINS
08 Dean of Library Services .... Dr. Robin CRUMRIN
56 Dean of Extended Learning .... Ms. Samantha PENNEY
35 Assoc VP Student Affairs .... Mr. Brooks MOORE

Indiana Tech (H)

1600 E Washington Boulevard, Fort Wayne IN 46803-1297
County: Allen FICE Identification: 001805
Unit ID: 151290
Telephone: (260) 422-5561 Carnegie Class: Masters/M
FAX Number: (260) 420-1453 Calendar System: Semester
URL: www.IndianaTech.edu
Established: 1930 Annual Undergrad Tuition & Fees: $26,900
Enrollment: 7,871 Coed
Affiliation or Control: Independent Non-Profit IRS Status: 501(c)3
Highest Offering: Doctorate
Accreditation: NH, CAHIIM, IACBE

01 President .... Dr. Karl W. EINOLF
10 Exec VP Finance & Administration .... Ms. Judy K. ROY
05 Vice President for Academic Affairs .... Dr. Thomas E. KAPLAN
26 VP Marketing & Communications .... Mr. Brian W. ENGELHART
32 VP for Student Affairs .... Dr. Daniel J. STOKER
84 VP for Enrollment Management .... Mr. Steve A. HERENDEEN

100 Executive Operations Director ... Ms. Jennifer A. ROSS
21 Controller ... Ms. Shelly R. MUSOLF
15 Human Resources Director ... Ms. Julie A. HENDRYX
13 AVP Information Technology ... Mr. Jeff S. LEICHTY
18 Dir Security & Facilities Mgmt ... Mr. R. Michael TOWNSLEY
37 Financial Aid Director ... Mr. Scott W. THUM
54 Dean of Engineering/Computer Sci ... Mr. David A. ASCHLIMAN
50 Dean of Business ... Dr. Kathleen WATLAND
97 Interim Dean of General Studies ... Dr. Oliver H. EVANS
58 Director Global Leadership Program ... Dr. Angie FINCANNON
09 Director of Academic Research ... Vacant
08 Director McMillen Library ... Ms. Constance E. SCOTT
06 Registrar ... Ms. Gladys A. SMITH
108 Director of Institutional Planning ... Mr. Henry D. KING
77 Assoc Dean of Computer Sciences ... Mr. Gary A. MESSICK
84 Enrollment Manager-Fort Wayne ... Mr. Yiani DEMITSAS
106 Director of Online Learning ... Dr. Y. Ben LEE
11 Associate VP for Operations ... Ms. Sharon LOKUTA
41 Athletic Director ... Ms. Debra P. WARREN
39 Assoc VP Student Services ... Mr. Chris M. DICKSON
35 Director Student Life ... Ms. Andrea G. CHECK
36 Director Career Center ... Ms. Cynthia P. VERDUCE
42 Faith Services Coordinator ... Mr. Gregory P. BYMAN
111 Associate VP Advancement ... Ms. Tracina A. SMITH
29 Dir Annual Fund & Alumni Relations ... Vacant
102 Dir Foundation/Corporate Relations ... Ms. Tracina A. SMITH
04 Admin Assistant to the President ... Ms. Shayla D. RIVERA

*Indiana University (A)

107 S. Indiana Ave., Bryan Hall 200,
Bloomington IN 47405-7000

County: Monroe
FICE Identification: 008002
Unit ID: 151351
Telephone: (812) 855-4613
Carnegie Class: N/A
FAX Number: (812) 855-9586
URL: www.indiana.edu

01 President ... Dr. Michael A. MCROBBIE
05 Exec Vice President/Provost IUB ... Ms. Lauren ROBEL
03 Exec VP IU/Chancellor IUPUI ... Dr. Nasser PAYDAR
20 Exec VP Univ Academic Affairs ... Mr. John APPLEGATE
46 Vice Pres for Research ... Dr. Fred H. CATE
28 VP Diversity/Equity/Multicult Aff ... Dr. James WIMBUSH
18 Vice Pres Capital Planning & Facil ... Dr. Thomas MORRISON
10 Vice President/CFO ... Mr. John SEJDINAJ
100 Chief of Staff ... Dr. Karen H. ADAMS
13 Vice President Info Tech/CIO ... Dr. Brad C. WHEELER
43 Vice Pres/General Counsel ... Ms. Jacqueline A. SIMMONS
104 Vice Pres for International Affairs ... Ms. Hannah BUXBAUM
86 VP Gov Relations/Econ Engagement ... Mr. William B. STEPHAN
41 VP & Dir of Intercoll Athletics ... Mr. Fred GLASS
63 EVP Univ Clinical Affs/Dean Sch Med ... Dr. Jay HESS
15 VP Human Resources ... Mr. John WHELAN
84 Vice Provost Enrollment Management ... Dr. David B. JOHNSON
21 University Treasurer ... Mr. Donald LUKES
22 Dir Office of Institutional Equity ... Ms. Emily SPRINGSTON
29 Exec Dir IU Alumni Association ... Mr. J. Thomas FORBES
102 President/CEO IU Foundation ... Dr. Dan C. SMITH
21 AVP/University Controller ... Ms. Anna K. JENSEN
116 AVP/Chief Audit Officer ... Mr. Stewart T. COBINE
04 Executive Asst to President ... Ms. Nicole TODD
25 Exec Dir Grant & Contract Services ... Mr. Jim BECKER
32 Dean of Students ... Mr. Dave O'GUINN
37 Univ Director of Financial Aid ... Ms. Jenny STEPHENS
19 Superintendent of Public Safety ... Mr. Benjamin HUNTER
06 Associate Vice Provost & Registrar ... Mr. Mark MCCONAHAY
07 Exec Director of Admissions ... Ms. Sacha THIEME
08 Dean of University Libraries ... Ms. Carolyn WALTERS
09 Exec Dir Inst Research/Reporting ... Mr. Todd J. SCHMITZ
101 Secretary of the Board ... Ms. Deborah A. LEMON
106 Director Office of Online Education ... Dr. Chris J. FOLEY
39 Exec Dir Residential Pgms & Svcs ... Mr. Pat CONNOR
44 Exec Director Annual Giving IUF ... Ms. Lindsey PEARSEY
50 Dean of Business ... Dr. Idalene F. KESNER
53 Dean of Education ... Dr. Lemuel WATSON
54 Dean Info/Computing & Engineering ... Dr. Raj ACHARYA
103 Exec Dir for Career Development ... Mr. Pat DONAHUE
96 Exec Director of Purchasing ... Ms. Tally THRASHER
26 Chief Communications Officer ... Ms. Rebecca CARL
27 Chief Marketing Officer ... Ms. Karen FERGUSON FUSON
88 Director of Media Relations ... Mr. Chuck CARNEY

*Indiana University Bloomington (B)

107 S. Indiana Avenue, Bloomington IN 47405-7000

County: Monroe
FICE Identification: 001809
Unit ID: 151351
Telephone: (812) 855-4848
Carnegie Class: DU-Highest
FAX Number: (812) 855-5678
Calendar System: Semester
URL: www.iub.edu
Established: 1820
Annual Undergrad Tuition & Fees (In-State): N/A
Enrollment: N/A
Coed
Affiliation or Control: State
IRS Status: 501(c)3
Highest Offering: Doctorate
Accreditation: NH, ART, AUD, CAATE, CAEP, CEA, #CIDA, CLPSY, COPSY, DIETD, IPSY, JOUR, LAW, LIB, MUS, NRPA, OPT, OPTR, PCSAS, PH, SCPSY, SP, SPAA, THEA

02 President ... Dr. Michael A. MCROBBIE
05 Exec VP & Provost ... Ms. Lauren ROBEL
03 Exec VP & Chanc IUPUI ... Mr. Nasser PAYDAR
05 Exec VP Univ Academic Affairs ... Mr. John S. APPLEGATE
10 VP & CFO ... Mr. John SEJDINAJ
17 Exec VP University Clinical Affairs ... Dr. Jay L. HESS
18 VP Capital Planning & Facilities ... Mr. Thomas A. MORRISON
28 VP Diversity/Equity/Multicult Affs ... Mr. James C. WIMBUSH
46 VP for Research ... Mr. Fred H. CATE
86 VP for Govt Relations ... Mr. Mike SAMPLE
88 VP for Engagement ... Mr. Bill B. STEPHAN
32 VProv Stdnt Affairs/Dean of Stdnts ... Mr. Dave O'GUINN
13 VP of IT/Comms/Mktg & CIO ... Mr. Brad WHEELER
88 Vice Prov for Research ... Mr. Rick VAN KOOTEN
20 Vice Prov for Undergraduate Educ ... Mr. Dennis GROTH
20 Vice Prov Faculty & Academic Affs ... Ms. Eliza PAVALKO
84 Vice Prov Enrollment Mgmt ... Mr. David JOHNSON
58 Vice Prov Grad Educ & Health Sci ... Mr. David DALEKE
88 Vice Prov Finance and Strategy ... Mr. Munirpallam A. VENKATARAMANAN
28 Vice Prov for Diversity/Inclusion ... Mr. John NIETO-PHILLIPS
21 Assoc VP & Univ Controller ... Ms. Anna JENSEN
15 VP Human Resources ... Mr. John WHELAN
102 Pres & CEO IU Foundation ... Mr. Daniel C. SMITH
85 Assoc VP for International Svcs ... Mr. Christopher VIERS
116 Assoc VP & Chief Audit Officer ... Mr. Stewart COBINE
49 Exec Dean College Arts & Sciences ... Mr. Larry SINGELL
08 Ruth Lilly Dean Univ Libraries ... Ms. Carolyn WALTERS
63 Int Assoc Dean of Medical Sciences ... Dr. Peter NALIN
50 Dean Kelley School of Business ... Ms. Idalene F. KESNER
53 Dean School of Education ... Mr. Lemuel WATSON
69 Dean School of Public Health ... Mr. David ALLISON
88 Dean School of Optometry ... Dr. Joseph A. BONANNO
61 Dean School of Law ... Mr. Austen L. PARRISH
64 Dean Jacobs School of Music ... Mr. Gwyn RICHARDS
60 Dean Media School ... Mr. James SHANAHAN
57 Dean School of Art/Arch & Design ... Ms. Peg FAIMON
77 Dean Sch Informatics/Comp/Eng ... Mr. Raj ACHARYA
88 Dean School of Global and Intl Stds ... Mr. Lee FEINSTEIN
80 Dean School of Pub and Env Affairs ... Mr. John D. GRAHAM
66 Assoc Dean School of Nursing ... Ms. Mary Lynn DAVIS-AJAMI
82 VP International Affairs ... Ms. Hannah BUXBAUM
92 Dean Hutton Honors College ... Mr. Andrea CICCARELLI
70 Dean School of Social Work ... Ms. Tamara DAVIS
29 CEO Alumni Association ... Mr. J.T FORBES
39 Exec Dir Residential Pgm & Svcs ... Mr. Pat CONNOR
06 Assoc Vice Provost/Registrar ... Mr. Mark MCCONAHAY
43 VP & General Counsel ... Ms. Jacqueline SIMMONS
19 Chief of Police ... Ms. Jill LEES
41 VP & Director of Athletics ... Mr. Fred GLASS
88 Dir Eskenazi Museum of Art ... Mr. David BRENNEMAN
07 Exec Director of Admissions ... Ms. Sacha THIEME
100 Chief of Staff ... Ms. Karen ADAMS
101 Secretary of the Institution/Board ... Ms. Deborah A. LEMON
106 Assoc VP & Dir Online Education ... Mr. Chris FOLEY
88 University Treasurer ... Mr. Don LUKES
88 Dir Office of Sustainability ... Mr. Andrew PREDMORE
37 Dir Student Financial Assistance ... Ms. Jackie KENNEDY-FLETCHER
04 Exec Assistant to the President ... Ms. Nicole TODD

*Indiana University East (C)

2325 Chester Boulevard, Richmond IN 47374-1289

County: Wayne
FICE Identification: 001811
Unit ID: 151388
Telephone: (765) 973-8200
Carnegie Class: Masters/S
FAX Number: N/A
Calendar System: Semester
URL: www.iue.edu
Established: 1946
Annual Undergrad Tuition & Fees (In-State): $7,344
Enrollment: 3,490
Coed
Affiliation or Control: State
IRS Status: 501(c)3
Highest Offering: Master's
Accreditation: NH, ACBSP, CAEPN, NUR

02 Chancellor ... Dr. Kathryn CRUZ-URIBE
05 Vice Chanc Academic Affairs ... Dr. Michelle MALOTT
26 Vice Chanc External Affs/Marketing ... Mr. Jason TROUTWINE
10 Vice Chancellor Admin & Finance ... Ms. Leisa JULIAN
32 Dean of Students ... Ms. Amy JARECKI
13 Director Information Technology ... Mr. Todd DUKE
30 Director of Gift Development ... Ms. Paula Kay KING
06 Registrar ... Mr. Dennis HICKS
08 Director Library/Media Services ... Dr. Frances YATES
15 Director Human Resources ... Ms. Evelyn GORDON
36 Director Career Services ... Ms. Sally SAYDSHOEV
07 Director of Admissions ... Ms. Molly VANDERPOOL
37 Dir Fin Aid & Scholarships ... Ms. Sarah SOPER
20 Director University College ... Ms. Cherie DOLEHANTY
40 Manager of Barnes & Noble Bookstore ... Ms. Kristy FRASHER
35 Director of Campus Life ... Ms. Rebeckah HESTER
113 Assistant Bursar ... Ms. Shelley DODSON
70 Director Social Work/Human Services ... Mr. Ed FITZGERALD
27 Director Communications & Marketing ... Mr. John DALTON
29 Director Alumni Relations ... Ms. Terry WIESEHAN
50 Dean Business/Technology ... Dr. Denise SMITH
83 Dean Humanities/Social Sciences ... Dr. Daren SNIDER
81 Interim Dean Natural Science & Math ... Dr. Daren SNIDER
66 Dean of Nursing ... Dr. Karen CLARK
53 Dean of Education ... Dr. Jerry WILDE
09 Director of Institutional Research ... Vacant
18 Director of Physical Facilities ... Mr. Gail SMOKER
41 Athletic Director ... Mr. Joe GRIFFIN
88 Director of Behavioral Health ... Ms. Jennifer CLAYPOOLE
19 Chief Campus Police ... Mr. Scott DUNNING
22 Dir Affirmative Action/EEOC Office ... Ms. Tracy AMYX

*Indiana University Kokomo (D)

2300 S Washington, Box 9003, Kokomo IN 46904-9003

County: Howard
FICE Identification: 001814
Unit ID: 151333
Telephone: (765) 453-2000
Carnegie Class: Bac-Diverse
FAX Number: (765) 455-9444
Calendar System: Semester
URL: www.iuk.edu
Established: 1945
Annual Undergrad Tuition & Fees (In-State): $7,344
Enrollment: 3,029
Coed
Affiliation or Control: State
IRS Status: 501(c)3
Highest Offering: Master's
Accreditation: NH, CAEP, NUR, NURSE, RAD

02 Chancellor ... Dr. Susan SCIAME-GIESECKE
05 Exec Vice Chanc Academic Affairs ... Dr. Mark CANADA
10 Vice Chancellor for Finance ... Mr. Jared HAYMAN
20 Assoc Vice Chanc Academic Affairs ... Dr. Christina DOWNEY
20 Assoc VC for Academic Affairs ... Dr. Julie SAAM
32 Vice Chanc Student Affs/Enroll Mgmt ... Dr. Todd GAMBILL
111 Vice Chancellor for Advancement ... Ms. Jan HALPERIN
72 Director Purdue Polytechnic Inst ... Mr. Jeff GRIFFIN
08 Dean of the Library ... Ms. Polly BORUFF-JONES
37 Director Financial Aid ... Ms. Dara JOHNSON
26 Dir External Rels/Public Affairs ... Ms. Catherine VALCKE
06 Registrar ... Ms. Stacey THOMAS
100 Chief of Staff ... Ms. Sarah SARBER
36 Manager Career/Accessibility Center ... Ms. Tracy SPRINGER
27 Director Media & Marketing ... Ms. Marie LINDSKOOG
07 Director of Admissions ... Ms. Angie SIDERS
28 Coord Stdnt Life & Campus Diversity ... Ms. Kate AGUILAR
35 Dean of Students ... Ms. Audra DOWLING
18 Director Facilities/Physical Plant ... Mr. John SARBER
50 Dean School of Business ... Dr. Alan KRABBENHOFT
79 Dean Sch Humanities/Social Sciences ... Dr. Eric BAIN-SELBO
66 Dean School of Nursing ... Dr. Susan HENDRICKS
53 Dean School of Education ... Dr. Leah NELLIS
81 Dean School of Sciences ... Dr. Christian CHAURET
09 Director of Institutional Research ... Ms. Angela SMITH
13 Chief Info Technology Officer (CIO) ... Mr. Nick RAY
15 Director Human Resources ... Ms. Michelle BOSWORTH
41 Athletic Director ... Mr. Greg COOPER

*Indiana University Northwest (E)

3400 Broadway, Gary IN 46408-1197

County: Lake
FICE Identification: 001815
Unit ID: 151360
Telephone: (219) 980-6500
Carnegie Class: Masters/S
FAX Number: (219) 980-6670
Calendar System: Semester
URL: www.iun.edu
Established: 1921
Annual Undergrad Tuition & Fees (In-State): $7,344
Enrollment: 4,055
Coed
Affiliation or Control: State
IRS Status: 501(c)3
Highest Offering: Master's
Accreditation: NH, CAEPN, CAHIIM, DA, DH, NUR, RAD, RTT, SPAA

02 Chancellor ... Dr. William J. LOWE
04 Dir of Executive Administration ... Mrs. Kathy MALONE
05 Exec VC Academic Affairs ... Dr. Victoria ROMAN-LAGUNAS
11 Exec Dir of Facilities/Operations ... Mr. Andrew KAPOCIUS
32 Vice Chanc Student Svcs/Enroll Mgmt ... Vacant
10 Vice Chancellor for Finance ... Ms. Michelle DICKERSON
111 Vice Chanc Advancement & Ext Affs ... Ms. Jeri Pat GABBERT
13 Chief Information Officer ... Mr. Nick RAY
20 Assoc Vice Chanc Academic Affs ... Dr. Cynthia O'DELL
09 Asst VC Inst Effectiveness & Rsrch ... Mr. John NOVAK
49 Dean College of Arts & Sciences ... Dr. Mark HOYERT
88 Dean Col of Health & Human Svcs ... Dr. Patrick BANKSTON
50 Dean School of Business & Economics ... Dr. Cynthia ROBERTS
53 Interim Dean School of Education ... Dr. Mark SPERLING
80 Dir Public & Environ Affs ... Dr. Karl BESEL
70 Director Social Work ... Dr. Darlene LYNCH
06 Registrar ... Mr. Peter ZACHOCKI
88 Director Pre-Professional Pgm ... Dr. Michael LAPOINTE
07 Director of Admissions ... Ms. Dorothy FRINK
37 Director Financial Aid ... Ms. Gina PIRTLE
36 Director Career & Placement ... Ms. Sharese DUDLEY
35 Director Student Activities ... Mr. Scott FULK
19 Director Security ... Mr. Wayne JAMES
29 Director Alumni Relations ... Vacant
66 Director Division of Nursing ... Dr. Linda DELUNAS
24 Director Instr Media ... Mr. Aaron PIGORS
08 Interim Director Library ... Ms. Latrice BOOKER
18 Director Facilities Services ... Mr. Gary GREINER
21 Director of Accounting Services ... Ms. Terri CHANCE
25 Director Research/Sponsored Pgms ... Vacant
15 Director Human Resources ... Ms. Mianta' DIMING
28 Director Diversity Programming ... Mr. James WALLACE, JR.
38 Director of Counseling Services ... Ms. Barbara A. DAHL
22 Director Affirmative Action ... Ms. Aneesah ALI
88 Dir Schlrshp in Teaching & Learning ... Dr. Christopher YOUNG
88 Dir Urban & Regional Excellence ... Dr. Ellen SZARLETA
105 Web Tech Services Manager ... Ms. Nicolle KRAUSE
106 Dir Online Education/E-learning ... Mr. Christopher YOUNG
41 Athletic Director ... Mr. Ryan SHELTON

*Indiana University-Purdue University Indianapolis (F)

301 University Blvd., Suite 5010,
Indianapolis IN 46202-5146

County: Marion
FICE Identification: 001813
Unit ID: 151111

Telephone: (317) 274-5555 Carnegie Class: DU-Higher
FAX Number: N/A Calendar System: Semester
URL: www.iupui.edu
Established: 1969 Annual Undergrad Tuition & Fees (In-State): $9,465
Enrollment: 29,791 Coed
Affiliation or Control: State IRS Status: 501(c)3
Highest Offering: Doctorate
Accreditation: NH, AA, ARCPA, ART, CAEP, CAHIIM, CAMPEP, CIDA, CLPSY, COARC, CYTO, DA, DENT, DH, DIETI, DT, EMT, FEPAC, HSA, HT, IPSY, LAW, LIB, MED, MT, MUS, NMT, NURSE, OT, PA, PAST, PH, PTA, RAD, RADDOS, RTT, SPAA, SW

02 Exec Vice Pres & Chancellor ... Dr. Nassar H. PAYDAR
100 Chief of Staff ... Ms. Margie SMITH-SIMMONS
28 Vice Chanc Diversity/Equity/Incl ... Dr. Karen L. DACE
05 Exec Vice Chanc/Chief Acad Ofcr ... Dr. Kathy E. JOHNSON
10 Vice Chanc Finance & Admin ... Ms. Camy BROEKER
30 VP for Development/Foundation ... Ms. Dee METAJ
111 Vice Chanc Community Engagement ... Ms. Amy C. WARNER
32 Vice Chancellor Student Affairs ... Dr. Eric A. WELDY
46 Interim Vice Chancellor Research ... Dr. Janice BLUM
13 Dean Information Technology ... Dr. Anastasia MORRONE
08 Dean University Library ... Ms. Kristi L. PALMER
84 Assoc Vice Chanc Enrollment Mgmt ... Mr. Boyd A. BRADSHAW
06 Registrar ... Ms. Mary Beth MYERS
113 Bursar ... Ms. Kelly SMITH-WELLER
26 Director of Communications ... Dr. Becky WOOD
22 Director Equal Opportunity ... Ms. Anne L. MITCHELL
38 Director Student Counseling ... Dr. Julie LASH
39 Director Housing/Residence Life ... Mr. Josh SKILLMAN
36 Director Career Services ... Mr. Joshua D. KILLEY
41 Director of Athletics ... Dr. Roderick D. PERRY
29 Asst VC Alumni Engagement ... Ms. Andrea SIMPSON
27 Asst Dir Strategic Communications ... Ms. Amber DENNEY
09 Asst Vice Chan Inst Research ... Dr. Michele J. HANSEN
07 Dir of Undergraduate Admissions ... Mr. Errol L. WINT
37 Director Student Financial Aid ... Mr. Marvin L. SMITH
15 Senior HR Dir/Dir Fin Services ... Ms. Julietta TOLIVER
23 Director Student Health Svcs ... Dr. Stephen F. WINTERMEYER
18 Assoc Vice Chan Campus Facility Svc ... Mr. Jeffrey PLAWECKI
19 Chief of Police ... Mr. Doug JOHNSON
92 Exec Assoc Dean Honors College ... Dr. Kristina H. SHEELER
45 Senior Advisor to the Chancellor ... Dr. Stephen P. HUNDLEY
12 Vice Chanc & Dean IUPU Columbus ... Dr. Reinhold R. HILL
57 Dean Herron School of Art & Design ... Ms. Nan GOGGIN
52 Dean School of Dentistry ... Dr. Carol A. MURDOCH-KINCH
54 Dean School of Engr/Technology ... Dr. David J. RUSSOMANNO
77 Sr Exec Asc Dn of Informatics/Comp ... Dr. Mathew J. PALAKAL
61 Dean McKinney Sch of Law ... Mr. Andrew R. KLEIN
49 Interim Dean School of Liberal Arts ... Dr. Robert REBEIN
63 Dean School of Medicine ... Dr. Jay L. HESS
66 Dean School of Nursing ... Dr. Robin P. NEWHOUSE
68 Dean Sch of Health & Human Science ... Dr. Rafael E. BAHAMONDE
81 Interim Dean School of Science ... Dr. Shiaofen FANG
70 Dean School of Social Work ... Dr. Tamara S. DAVIS
69 Dean Fairbanks Sch of Public Health ... Dr. Paul K. HALVERSON
88 Dean Lilly Fam Sch of Philanthropy ... Dr. Amir PASIC
53 Founding Dean School of Education ... Dr. Jesse P. MENDEZ
80 Exec Assoc Dean Public/Environ Affs ... Dr. Thomas D. STUCKY
85 Assoc VC International Affairs ... Dr. Hilary E. KAHN
50 Exec Assoc Dean School of Business ... Dr. Ken A. CAROW
58 Associate VC Graduate Education ... Dr. Janice S. BLUM
89 Dean University College ... Dr. James M. GLADDEN

*Indiana University South Bend (A)

1700 Mishawaka Avenue, South Bend IN 46634-7111
County: Saint Joseph FICE Identification: 001816
Unit ID: 151342
Telephone: (574) 520-4872 Carnegie Class: Masters/M
FAX Number: (574) 520-4834 Calendar System: Semester
URL: www.iusb.edu
Established: 1940 Annual Undergrad Tuition & Fees (In-State): $7,344
Enrollment: 5,385 Coed
Affiliation or Control: State IRS Status: 501(c)3
Highest Offering: Master's
Accreditation: NH, CACREP, CAEPN, DH, MUS, NURSE, RAD, SPAA

02 Chancellor ... Dr. Susan ELROD
05 Int Exec Vice Chanc Acad Affairs ... Dr. Linda CHEN
10 Vice Chanc Admin & Finance ... Mr. Philip IAPALUCCI
26 Int Vice Chanc Advance/Public Affs ... Mr. Thomas STEVICK
32 VC Stdnt Engage/Dean of Students ... Ms. Monica PORTER
13 Regional Chief Information Officer ... Mr. Nickolas RAY
20 Assoc Vice Chanc Academic Affs ... Dr. Doug MCMILLEN
84 Assoc Vice Chanc Enrollment Svcs ... Ms. Cathy M. BUCKMAN
06 Registrar ... Mr. Keith DAWSON
41 Executive Director of Athletics ... Mr. Steve BRUCE
18 Director Facilities Management ... Mr. Michael PRATER
19 Director of Safety & Security ... Mr. Kurt M. MATZ
15 Dir of Human Resources/Career Svcs ... Ms. Deb SCHMITT
24 Dir of Instructional Media Services ... Vacant
29 Dir Alumni Affs/Campus Ceremonies ... Ms. Moira DYCZKO
27 Dir Comm/Marketing/Chief of Staff ... Mr. Kenneth W. BAIERL
52 Director of Dental Auxiliary Educ ... Ms. Kristyn QUIMBY
51 Director of Extended Learning ... Mr. Mike MANCINI
38 Director Student Counseling Ctr ... Mr. Kevin GRIFFITH
07 Director of Admissions ... Ms. Connie PETERSON-MILLER
28 Dir of Diversity/Affirmative Action ... Ms. Laura HARLOW
30 Director of Development ... Ms. Dina HARRIS
39 Director of Student Housing ... Mr. Scott STRITTMATTER
21 Director of Accounting ... Ms. Kathleen PIZANA

37 Director of Financial Aid ... Ms. Lorie WILLIAMS
50 Dean of Business & Economics ... Dr. Rick KOLBE
53 Dean School of Education ... Dr. Hope DAVIS
57 Dean of the Arts ... Dr. Marvin CURTIS
76 Dean Col of Health Sciences ... Dr. Thomas FISHER
08 Dean of Library Services ... Ms. Vicki BLOOM

*Indiana University Southeast (B)

4201 Grant Line Road, New Albany IN 47150-2158
County: Floyd FICE Identification: 001817
Unit ID: 151379
Telephone: (812) 941-2333 Carnegie Class: Masters/M
FAX Number: (812) 941-2475 Calendar System: Semester
URL: www.ius.edu
Established: 1941 Annual Undergrad Tuition & Fees (In-State): $7,344
Enrollment: 5,238 Coed
Affiliation or Control: State IRS Status: 501(c)3
Highest Offering: Master's
Accreditation: NH, CAEPN, NURSE

02 Chancellor ... Dr. Ray WALLACE
05 Executive VC Academic Affairs ... Dr. Uric DUFRENE
10 VC Administration/Finance ... Mr. Dana C. WAVLE
84 VC Enrollment Mgmt/Student Affairs ... Ms. Amanda G. STONECIPHER
111 VC Advancement ... Ms. Betty S. RUSSO
20 Assoc VC Academic Affairs ... Vacant
20 Asst VC Academic Affairs ... Dr. Annette M. WYANDOTTE
13 Chief Information Officer ... Mr. Nicholas T. RAY
07 Director Admissions ... Mr. Chris CREWS
04 Exec Secretary to the Chancellor ... Ms. Jennifer N. MCBRIDE
35 Dean for Student Life ... Dr. Seuth CHALEUNPHONH
06 Registrar ... Mr. James (Jay) MCTYIER
37 Director Student Financial Aid ... Ms. Lauren GREIDER
08 Director Library Services ... Mr. C. Martin ROSEN
36 Director Career Development ... Ms. Donna REED
18 Exec Dir of Facility Operations ... Mr. Robert C. POFF
14 Dir IT Communications & Support ... Mr. Steve BENNISON
41 Director Athletics ... Mr. Joseph M. GLOVER
15 Director Human Resources ... Mr. Ray KLEIN
09 Dir Institutional Effectiveness ... Mr. Ronald E. SEVERTIS, JR.
19 Chief Safety & Security ... Mr. Stephen MILLER
38 Dir Personal Counseling ... Dr. Michael DAY
26 Dir Marketing & Communications ... Ms. Nancy J. TRAFTON
79 Dean School Arts & Letters ... Mr. James HESSELMAN
81 Dean School Natural Sciences ... Dr. Elaine HAUB
83 Dean School Social Sciences ... Dr. Kelly A. RYAN
50 Dean School Business ... Dr. David EPLION
53 Dean School Education ... Dr. Faye M. CAMAHALAN
66 Dean School Nursing ... Dr. Donna J. BOWLES
46 Dean for Research & Grad Studies ... Dr. Diane E. WILLE
28 Director Staff Equity & Diversity ... Ms. Darlene P. YOUNG
29 Dir Alumni Engagement/Annual Giving ... Mr. J. T. DOUGLAS
88 Director of Advising ... Ms. Rebecca TURNER
88 Director Academic Acctng Services ... Ms. Melissa D. HILL
113 Director Student Acctng Services ... Ms. Ashley M. MCKAY
88 Academic Information Officer ... Mr. Steven KROLAK
121 Dean Student Success & Persistence ... Dr. Donna J. DAHLGREN
30 Dir Development ... Mr. David C. DEWITT
39 Dir Residence Life & Housing ... Ms. Abbie DUPAY
100 Chief of Staff ... Mr. Dana C. WAVLE

***Indiana University-Purdue University Columbus** (C)

4601 Central Avenue, Columbus IN 47203
Telephone: (812) 348-7390 Identification: 770185
Accreditation: &NH, CAEP, NURSE

Indiana Wesleyan University (D)

4201 S Washington Street, Marion IN 46953-4999
County: Grant FICE Identification: 001822
Unit ID: 151801
Telephone: (765) 674-6901 Carnegie Class: Masters/S
FAX Number: (765) 677-2499 Calendar System: 4/1/4
URL: www.indwes.edu
Established: 1920 Annual Undergrad Tuition & Fees: $26,630
Enrollment: 3,072 Coed
Affiliation or Control: Wesleyan Church IRS Status: 501(c)3
Highest Offering: Doctorate
Accreditation: NH, ACBSP, CAATE, CACREP, CAEP, CAEPN, EXSC, MFCD, MUS, NURSE, OT, SW, THEOL

01 President ... Dr. David WRIGHT
05 Chief Academic Officer/Provost ... Dr. Stacy HAMMONS
12 Chancellor IWU-Marion ... Dr. Rod REED
12 Chancellor IWU-National & Global ... Dr. Matt LUCAS
28 VP for Multicultural Enrichment ... Ms. Diane MCDANIEL
10 Vice President Business Affs/CFO ... Mrs. Nancy SCHOONMAKER
11 President Wesley Seminary ... Dr. Colleen DERR
20 VP for Academic Affairs/CAPS ... Dr. Mike MANNING
20 VP for Academic Affairs/SON ... Dr. Barbara IHRKE
111 VP for Advancement ... Dr. Scott TURCOTT
20 Associate Provost ... Dr. Don SPROWL
26 VP Univ Communications ... Mr. Jerry SHEPHERD
84 VP Enroll Mgmt & Mktg/Non-Resident ... Mr. David ROSE
88 VP Life Calling & Integrative Lrng ... Dr. Brandon HILL
11 VP of Operations/Residential Campus ... Mr. John JONES
58 Dean Graduate School ... Dr. Joanne BARNES
73 Dean of the Seminary ... Dr. Abson JOSEPH

76 Dean School of Health Sciences ... Dr. Martin RICE
50 Dean Devoe School of Business ... Dr. Mark BROOKER
88 Dean of Developmental Learning ... Mr. Andrew PARKER
37 Associate VP Financial Aid ... Mr. Thomas RATLIFF
08 Director Library Resources ... Mrs. Shelia CARLBLOM
08 Director Off-campus Library Svcs ... Mrs. Jule KIND
29 Director of Alumni ... Vacant
07 Dir Admissions/Residential Educ ... Mr. Ian SLATER
15 Exec Director Human Resources ... Mr. Mark PEDERSON
06 University Registrar ... Mrs. Kim NICHOLSON
43 University Counsel ... Mr. Shawn MATTER
21 Controller ... Mrs. Tiffany LEWIS
41 Athletic Director ... Mr. Mark DEMICHAEL
42 Dean of the Chapel ... Dr. John BRAY
92 Dean Honors College ... Mr. David RIGGS
09 Director Institutional Research ... Mr. Tony PARANDI
18 AVP Facilities Services ... Mr. Don ROWLEY
19 Director Campus Police ... Mr. Chad BEIGHTS
25 Director of Research Support ... Vacant
13 Chief Info Technology Officer (CIO) ... Mr. Scott GILREATH
121 Dean Center for Student Success ... Mr. Nathan HERRING
102 Dir Foundation/Corporate Relations ... Dr. Michael MOFFITT
04 Exec Assistant to the President ... Ms. Lynn MUNDAY

International Business College (E)

5699 Coventry Lane, Fort Wayne IN 46804-9990
County: Allen FICE Identification: 004579
Unit ID: 151458
Telephone: (260) 459-4500 Carnegie Class: Bac/Assoc-Mixed
FAX Number: (260) 436-1896 Calendar System: Semester
URL: www.ibcfortwayne.edu
Established: 1889 Annual Undergrad Tuition & Fees: $13,960
Enrollment: 244 Coed
Affiliation or Control: Proprietary IRS Status: Proprietary
Highest Offering: Associate Degree
Accreditation: ACCSC, MAC

01 President ... Ms. Kathy CHIUDIONI
11 Campus Administrator ... Ms. Amee AUGENSTEIN
07 Admissions Manager ... Ms. Gena HOPKINS
32 Director of Student Services ... Ms. Roxanna SHULL
36 Director of Career Services ... Ms. Marty BIANSKI
06 Registrar ... Ms. Jessica BRANDEBURY

International Business College (F)

7205 Shadeland Station, Indianapolis IN 46256-3997
Telephone: (317) 813-2300 Identification: 666929
Accreditation: ACCSC, DA, MAC

*Ivy Tech Community College of Indiana-Systems Office (G)

50 W Fall Creek Parkway N Drive, Indianapolis IN 46208-5752
County: Marion FICE Identification: 008546
Unit ID: 363563
Telephone: (317) 921-4882 Carnegie Class: N/A
FAX Number: (317) 921-4753
URL: www.ivytech.edu

01 President ... Dr. Sue J. ELLSPERMANN
05 Provost/Sr Vice President ... Dr. Kara MONROE
102 Sr Vice Pres Ivy Tech Foundation ... Mr. John MURPHY
10 Sr Vice President/CFO ... Mr. Matt HAWKINS
15 Sr Vice President Human Resources ... Ms. Julie LORTON-ROWLAND
11 Sr Vice Pres & COO ... Mr. Andrew BOWNE
103 Sr VP Workforce & Career ... Mr. Chris LOWERY
20 Vice Pres Academic Affairs ... Dr. Russell D. BAKER
26 Vice Pres Marketing & Communication ... Mr. Jeff FANTER
18 Vice Pres Cap Plng & Facilities ... Ms. Amanda WILSON
86 VP Government Relations ... Ms. Mary Jane MICHALAK
88 VP K-14 Initiatives ... Vacant
28 VP Diversity/Equity & Belonging ... Mr. Doran MORELAND
88 VP Change Mgmt/Strategic Init ... Ms. Kristen MORELAND
32 Vice President Student Success ... Mr. Corey CLASEMANN-RYAN
114 VP Financial Planning & Mgmt ... Mr. William BOGARD
21 VP Finance/Sourcing/Asst Treasurer ... Mr. Dom CHASE
13 Chief Technology Officer ... Mr. Thomas RIEBE
103 Asst VP Workforce Partnerships ... Ms. Anne P. VALENTINE
35 Asst VP Student Advocacy ... Dr. Carey TREAGER-HUBER
13 Chief Information Officer ... Mr. Matt ETCHISON
06 College Registrar ... Mrs. Ann YATER
21 Asst VP Accounting & Fin Reporting ... Ms. Christy GELBACK-DIAZ
37 Asst VP Financial Aid ... Mr. Ben BURTON
19 Asst VP Statewide Security/Safety ... Mr. Jon BAREFOOT

*Ivy Tech Community College of Indiana-Indianapolis (H)

50 W Fall Creek Parkway North Drive, Indianapolis IN 46208-5752
County: Marion FICE Identification: 009917
Unit ID: 150987
Telephone: (317) 921-4882 Carnegie Class: Assoc/MT-VT-High Non
FAX Number: (317) 921-4753 Calendar System: Semester
URL: www.ivytech.edu/indianapolis/
Established: 1966 Annual Undergrad Tuition & Fees (In-State): $4,368
Enrollment: 75,486 Coed
Affiliation or Control: State IRS Status: 501(c)3

Highest Offering: Associate Degree
Accreditation: NH, ACBSP, ACFEI, ART, CAHIIM, COARC, CSHSE, FUSER, MAC, NAIT, RAD, SURGT

02 Chancellor .... Dr. Kathleen F. LEE
05 VC of Academic Affairs .... Dr. Rod BROWN
32 VC of Student Affairs/Success .... Dr. John COWLES
84 VC of Enrollment Services .... Dr. Tracy BERENS-FUNK
10 Executive Director of Finance .... Mr. Corey BACK
15 Exec Director of Human Resources .... Ms. Sara HAUGER
11 Exec Dir of Administrative Services .... Mr. Aaron ROBERTS
103 Exec Dir Workforce & Economic Devel .... Vacant
30 Exec Director of Development .... Mrs. Danielle STILES-POLK
35 Asst Vice Chanc Student Success .... Mrs. Amy GRIFFIN
37 Director of Financial Aid .... Mr. Michael COUCH
06 Registrar .... Mrs. Letha BROOKS
09 Institutional Research Analyst .... Mr. Christopher G. SLEPPPY
36 Director of Career Services .... Ms. Rebecca PATTEN-LEMONS
96 Director of Purchasing .... Vacant
20 Asst Vice Chanc Academic Support .... Ms. Rhonda ANGSMAN
26 Exec Dir Marketing/Communications .... Mrs. Tracey ALLEN

* Ivy Tech Community College of Indiana-Anderson (A)
104 West 53rd Street, Anderson IN 46013-1502
Telephone: (800) 644-4882 Identification: 770239
Accreditation: &NH, DA, DH, MAC

* Ivy Tech Community College of Indiana-Bloomington (B)
200 N Daniels Way, Bloomington IN 47404-9772
Telephone: (812) 332-1559 FICE Identification: 035213
Accreditation: &NH, ACBSP, ACFEI, COARC, CSHSE, EMT, NAIT, RTT

* Ivy Tech Community College of Indiana-Columbus (C)
4475 Central Avenue, Columbus IN 47203-1868
Telephone: (812) 372-9925 FICE Identification: 010038
Accreditation: &NH, ART, ACBSP, CSHSE, DA, MAC, NAIT, SURGT

* Ivy Tech Community College of Indiana-Evansville (D)
3501 First Avenue, Evansville IN 47710-1881
Telephone: (812) 426-2865 FICE Identification: 009925
Accreditation: &NH, ACBSP, CSHSE, EMT, MAC, NAIT, SURGT

* Ivy Tech Community College of Indiana-Fort Wayne (E)
3800 N Anthony Boulevard, Fort Wayne IN 46805-1489
Telephone: (260) 482-9171 FICE Identification: 009926
Accreditation: &NH, ACBSP, ACFEI, CAHIIM, COARC, CSHSE, EMT, MAC, NAIT

* Ivy Tech Community College of Indiana-Kokomo (F)
1815 E Morgan Street, Box 1373, Kokomo IN 46903-1373
Telephone: (765) 459-0561 FICE Identification: 010041
Accreditation: &NH, ACBSP, CSHSE, DA, EMT, MAC, NAIT, SURGT

* Ivy Tech Community College of Indiana-Lafayette (G)
3101 S Creasy Lane, Box 6299, Lafayette IN 47903-6299
Telephone: (765) 269-5000 FICE Identification: 010039
Accreditation: &NH, ACBSP, COARC, CSHSE, DA, MAC, NAIT, SURGT

* Ivy Tech Community College of Indiana-Lake County (H)
1440 E 35th Avenue, Gary IN 46409-1499
Telephone: (219) 981-1111 FICE Identification: 010040
Accreditation: &NH, ACBSP, COARC, CSHSE, FUSER, NAIT, PTAA, SURGT

* Ivy Tech Community College of Indiana-Lawrenceburg-Riverfront (I)
50 Walnut Street, Lawrenceburg IN 47025
Telephone: (812) 537-4010 Identification: 770242
Accreditation: &NH, MAC

* Ivy Tech Community College Madison (J)
590 Ivy Tech Drive, Madison IN 47250-1883
Telephone: (812) 265-2580 FICE Identification: 009923
Accreditation: &NH, ACBSP, CSHSE, EMT, MAC, NAIT

* Ivy Tech Community College of Indiana-Marion (K)
261 S Commerce Drive, Marion IN 46953
Telephone: (765) 651-3100 Identification: 770244
Accreditation: &NH, MAC

* Ivy Tech Community College of Indiana-Michigan City (L)
3714 Franklin Drive, Michigan City IN 46360
Telephone: (219) 879-9137 Identification: 770245
Accreditation: &NH, ACFEI, MAC

* Ivy Tech Community College of Indiana-Muncie (M)
4301 Cowan Road, Muncie IN 47302-9448
Telephone: (765) 289-2291 FICE Identification: 009924
Accreditation: &NH, ACBSP, ACFEI, CSHSE, MAC, NAIT, PTAA, RAD, SURGT

* Ivy Tech Community College of Indiana-Richmond (N)
2357 Chester Boulevard, Richmond IN 47374-1298
Telephone: (765) 966-2656 FICE Identification: 010037
Accreditation: &NH, ACBSP, COARC, CSHSE, MAC, NAIT

* Ivy Tech Community College of Indiana-Sellersburg (O)
8204 Highway 311, Sellersburg IN 47172-1897
Telephone: (812) 246-3301 FICE Identification: 010109
Accreditation: &NH, ACBSP, ART, COARC, CSHSE, MAC, MLTAD, NAIT, PTAA

* Ivy Tech Community College of Indiana-South Bend/Elkhart (P)
220 Dean Johnson Boulevard, South Bend IN 46601-3415
Telephone: (574) 289-7001 FICE Identification: 008423
Accreditation: &NH, ACBSP, ACFEI, ART, COARC, CSHSE, DA, DH, EMT, MAC, MLTAD, NAIT

* Ivy Tech Community College of Indiana-Terre Haute (Q)
8000 S. Education Drive, Terre Haute IN 47802-4833
Telephone: (812) 299-1121 FICE Identification: 008547
Accreditation: &NH, ACBSP, ART, COARC, CSHSE, DMS, EMT, MAC, MLTAD, NAIT, RAD, SURGT

* Ivy Tech Community College of Indiana-Valparaiso Campus (R)
3100 Ivy Tech Drive, Valparaiso IN 46383
Telephone: (219) 464-8514 Identification: 770246
Accreditation: &NH

Lincoln College of Technology (S)
7225 Winton Drive, Building 128,
Indianapolis IN 46268-4198
County: Marion FICE Identification: 007938
Unit ID: 151661
Telephone: (317) 632-5553 Carnegie Class: Spec 2-yr-Tech
FAX Number: (317) 851-3273 Calendar System: Semester
URL: www.lincolntech.edu
Established: 1962 Annual Undergrad Tuition & Fees: N/A
Enrollment: 792 Coed
Affiliation or Control: Proprietary IRS Status: Proprietary
Highest Offering: Associate Degree
Accreditation: ACCSC

01 Campus President .... Brent JENKINS
05 Academic Dean .... Rodney ALLEE
11 Director of Administrative Services .... Andy RAHIMI
37 Director Student Financial Aid .... Alison JONES
07 Director of Adult Admissions .... Shannon BIGELOW
07 Co-Dir of High School Admissions .... Charles LIVORNO
07 Co-Dir of High School Admissions .... David RITZ
36 Director of Career Services .... Christine JOYCE
13 IT Administrator .... Blake BROOKS
18 Facilities Manager .... Roger PARK
21 Business Office Coordinator .... Dawn KEMP

Manchester University (T)
604 E College Avenue, North Manchester IN 46962-1225
County: Wabash FICE Identification: 001820
Unit ID: 151777
Telephone: (260) 982-5000 Carnegie Class: Bac-Diverse
FAX Number: (260) 982-5043 Calendar System: 4/1/4
URL: www.manchester.edu
Established: 1889 Annual Undergrad Tuition & Fees: $32,758
Enrollment: 1,572 Coed
Affiliation or Control: Church Of The Brethren IRS Status: 501(c)3
Highest Offering: Doctorate
Accreditation: NH, CAATE, CAEPN, PHAR, SW

01 President .... Dr. David F. MCFADDEN
05 VP Academic Affairs .... Dr. Raylene M. ROSPOND
32 VP for Student Affairs/Student Exp .... Dr. Abby L. VAN VLERAH
10 Chief Business Officer/VP Finance .... Mr. Clair W. KNAPP
111 Vice President Advancement .... Mrs. Melanie B. HARMON
15 VP Human Res/Strategic Initiative .... Ms. Whitney A. CAUDILL
84 Asst VP for Enrollment/Marketing .... Mr. Adam R. HOHMAN
09 Asst VP Institutional Effectiveness .... Dr. Elizabeth J. BUSHNELL
13 Asst Vice Pres/Chief Tech Ofcr .... Mr. Michael CASE
20 Associate Academic Dean .... Dr. Stacy L. ERICKSON-PESETSKI
29 Director of Alumni Relations .... Ms. Kylee B. ROSENBAUM
08 Director of the Library .... Vacant
06 Registrar .... Ms. Audrey N. HAMPSHIRE
24 Instructional Design Specialist .... Mr. Justin P. LUNSFORD
38 Director of Counseling .... Ms. Danette NORMAN TILL
36 Dir Career/Professional Development .... Ms. Tish KALITA
39 Director of Residence Life .... Ms. Melanie E. LAWSON
42 University Pastor .... Mr. Bekah HOUFF
41 Athletic Director .... Mr. Rick ESPESET
19 Director of Security .... Ms. Tina L. EDWARDS
44 Director of the Manchester Fund .... Ms. Janeen W. KOOI
37 Director of Student Financial Aid .... Ms. Sherri L. SHOCKEY
85 Dir Intercultural Svcs/Chf Div Ofcr .... Mr. Michael G. DIXON
26 Asst Director Media Relations .... Ms. Anne GREGORY
18 Director of Physical Plant/Grounds .... Mr. Pieter NARAGON
23 Director of Health Services .... Ms. Anna C. RICHISON
21 Controller .... Ms. Cindy L. SEITZ
32 Director Student Activities .... Ms. Samantha A. ALLEY
96 Director of Purchasing .... Mr. Quentin J. MOUDY
40 Campus Bookstore Manager .... Ms. Heather K. GOCHENAUR
04 Administrative Asst to President .... Ms. Jill R. MANNS
25 Chief Contract/Grants Administrator .... Ms. Elena M. BOHLANDER

Marian University (U)
3200 Cold Spring Road, Indianapolis IN 46222-1997
County: Marion FICE Identification: 001821
Unit ID: 151786
Telephone: (317) 955-6000 Carnegie Class: Masters/M
FAX Number: (317) 955-6448 Calendar System: Semester
URL: www.marian.edu
Established: 1851 Annual Undergrad Tuition & Fees: $34,000
Enrollment: 3,429 Coed
Affiliation or Control: Roman Catholic IRS Status: 501(c)3
Highest Offering: Doctorate
Accreditation: NH, ANEST, CAEPN, IACBE, NURSE, OSTEO

01 President .... Mr. Daniel J. ELSENER
05 EVP & Provost/COO .... Dr. Alan SILVA
10 Sr VP Finance & Operations .... Mr. Greg GINDER
53 SVP Tchr Lrng Excel/Dn The Educ Col .... Dr. Kenith BRITT
26 VP for Marketing Communications .... Mr. Mark APPLE
45 VP Mission & Ministry .... Mr. Adam SETMEYER
32 VP Student Success & Engagement .... Ms. Ruth RODGERS
13 VP and Chief Information Officer .... Mr. Ray STANLEY
11 VP Administration/General Counsel .... Ms. Deborah LAWRENCE
111 VP Institutional Advancement .... Mr. John FINKE
63 VP and Dean College of Osteopathic .... Dr. Don SEFCIK
88 VP of Leadership Integration .... Ms. Ellen WHITT
84 VP Enrollment Management .... Dr. Paul (PJ) WOOLSTON
20 Associate Provost .... Dr. Saib OTHMAN
20 Assistant Provost .... Dr. Elizabeth OSIKA
37 Director of Financial Aid .... Ms. Monique WARE
18 Director Campus Operations .... Mr. Mike MILLER
41 Director of Athletics .... Mr. Steve DOWNING
29 Dir Alumni/Parent Engagement .... Ms. Cathy SILER
06 Registrar .... Ms. Jennifer SCHWARTZ
08 Library Director .... Ms. Jessica TRINOSKEY
35 Director Student Activities .... Ms. Sarah BALANA MOLTER
19 Chief of Police Services .... Mr. Robert RICHARDSON
27 Mgr Event Marketing & Sponsorships .... Ms. Maggie KUCIK
38 Director Academic Support Services .... Mrs. Marjorie BATIC
55 Exec Director Adult Programs .... Ms. Amy BENNETT
38 Director of Counseling Services .... Dr. Marla SMITH
09 Director of Institutional Research .... Ms. Brooke KILE
15 Director of Human Resources .... Ms. Amy KOCH
21 Director of Business Services .... Ms. Alice SHELTON
40 Bookstore Manager .... Ms. Margaret CIHLAR
04 Executive Asst to President .... Ms. Cyndi KAMP
104 Director Study Abroad .... Dr. Wendy WESTPHAL
39 Director Student Housing .... Ms. Karen CANDLISH
43 VP Administration & General Counsel .... Ms. Deborah LAWRENCE

Martin University (V)
2186 North Sherman Drive, Indianapolis IN 46218
County: Marion FICE Identification: 021408
Unit ID: 151810
Telephone: (317) 543-3235 Carnegie Class: Bac-Diverse
FAX Number: (317) 543-3257 Calendar System: Semester
URL: www.martin.edu
Established: 1977 Annual Undergrad Tuition & Fees: $13,200
Enrollment: 346 Coed
Affiliation or Control: Independent Non-Profit IRS Status: 501(c)3
Highest Offering: Master's
Accreditation: NH

10 President .... Dr. Sean L. HUDDLESTON
125 President Emeritus .... Dr. Eugene WHITE
05 Vice Pres Academic Affairs/Provost .... Dr. Lashun ARON-SMITH
09 VP of Institutional Effectiveness .... Dr. Brian STEUERWALD
10 VP Fiscal Affairs .... Mr. Michael MOOS
37 Director Financial Aid .... Ms. Virginia GOODWIN
32 Director Student & Enroll Services .... Tracey JACKSON
26 Dir of Univ Rels/Communications .... Ms. Jennifer MCCLOUD
113 Bursar .... Ms. Angela HARRINGTON-MARTIN

Mid-America College of Funeral Service (A)

3111 Hamburg Pike, Jeffersonville IN 47130-9630
County: Clark FICE Identification: 010618
Unit ID: 151962
Telephone: (812) 288-8878 Carnegie Class: Spec-4-yr-Other
FAX Number: (812) 288-5942 Calendar System: Quarter
URL: www.mid-america.edu
Established: 1980 Annual Undergrad Tuition & Fees: $11,900
Enrollment: 101 Coed
Affiliation or Control: Independent Non-Profit IRS Status: 501(c)3
Highest Offering: Baccalaureate
Accreditation: FUSER

01 President ....Dr. Mitch MITCHELL
32 Dean of Students ....Vacant
11 Office Manager ....Ms. Angela PERSINGER
37 Director of Financial Aid ....Ms. Amy BAXLEY
08 Librarian ....Ms. Sonja PIERCE
07 Director of Admissions ....Ms. Erin MURPHY

Mid-America Reformed Seminary (B)

229 Seminary Drive, Dyer IN 46311-1069
County: Lake FICE Identification: 039893
Unit ID: 373030
Telephone: (219) 864-2400 Carnegie Class: Not Classified
FAX Number: (219) 864-2410 Calendar System: Semester
URL: www.midamerica.edu
Established: 1981 Annual Graduate Tuition & Fees: N/A
Enrollment: N/A Coed
Affiliation or Control: Independent Non-Profit IRS Status: 501(c)3
Highest Offering: Master's; No Undergraduates
Accreditation: THEOL

01 President ....Dr. Cornelius VENEMA
32 Dean of Students ....Rev. Alan STRANGE
111 Vice President of Advancement ....Mr. Mike DECKINGA
11 Vice President of Operations ....Mr. Keith LEMAHIEU
36 Director of Apprenticeship Program ....Rev. Mark VANDERHART
06 Registrar ....Rev. Alan STRANGE
84 Director of Enrollment Management ....Rev. Jeffrey DEBOER
108 Director Institutional Assessment ....Rev. Marcus MININGER
08 Theological Librarian ....Rev. Alan STRANGE
26 Manager Marketing/Digital/Pubs ....Mr. Jared LUTTJEBOER

Oakland City University (C)

138 N Lucretia Street, Oakland City IN 47660-1099
County: Gibson FICE Identification: 001824
Unit ID: 152099
Telephone: (812) 749-4781 Carnegie Class: Bac-Diverse
FAX Number: (812) 749-1233 Calendar System: Semester
URL: www.oak.edu
Established: 1885 Annual Undergrad Tuition & Fees: $24,000
Enrollment: 1,303 Coed
Affiliation or Control: Baptist IRS Status: 501(c)3
Highest Offering: Doctorate
Accreditation: NH, CAEPN, IACBE, THEOL

01 President ....Dr. Ron D. DEMPSEY
11 Vice Pres Admin & Finance ....Vacant
05 Provost ....Dr. Daniel DUNIVAN
10 Chief Financial Officer ....Mr. Todd WAHL
13 Assoc VP & Chief Info Officer ....Mr. Clint WOOLSEY
111 Assoc Vice Pres of Advancement ....Mr. Brian BAKER
20 Assistant Provost ....Mrs. Ely SENA-MARTIN
50 Dean School of Business ....Dr. Cathy ROBB
53 Dean School of Education ....Dr. Rachel YARBROUGH
73 Dean Religious Studies ....Dr. Douglas LOW
49 Dean of Arts and Science ....Vacant
108 Director of Assessment ....Dr. Paul BOWDRE
32 Director of Campus Life ....Mr. Brad KNOTTS
37 Director of Financial Aid ....Mrs. Nicole SHARP
56 Coordinator Adult Extend Learning ....Dr. Cathy ROBB
22 Compliance Officer ....Ms. Patricia ENDICOTT
88 Director of Correctional Education ....Mr. Theodore PEARSON
06 Registrar ....Mrs. Linda TIPTON
08 Director of Library ....Mrs. Denise PINNICK
42 Campus Minister ....Rev. Jeffrey BRALLEY
18 Director of Maintenance ....Mr. Greg BURKE
15 Director of Human Resource ....Mrs. Cheryl YATES
19 Chief of Security ....Mr. Alec HENSLEY
29 Director of Alumni Affairs ....Ms. Susan SULLIVAN
88 Director of Student Activities ....Mr. Colin DIXON
36 Director of Directions Program ....Mrs. Charity JULIAN
35 Director Student Support Services ....Mrs. Tamara MILEY
88 Upward Bound Director ....Mr. Kyle HILL
21 Assistant Chief Financial Officer ....Mrs. Elizabeth CARLISLE
88 Supervisor of Collections ....Mrs. Anita MISKELL
88 Director of Housekeeping ....Ms. Angie WELLS
04 Administrative Asst to President ....Mrs. Mary NOSSETT
07 Director of Admissions ....Mr. Elliott SPRUELL
105 Director Web Services ....Mrs. Andrea TURNER
28 Director of Diversity ....Mrs. Elisabet SENA-MARTIN
39 Dir Resident Life/Student Housing ....Mr. Joshua BROWN
41 Athletic Director ....Vacant
13 Director of Information Technology ....Mr. Brad BURKHART
96 Director of Purchasing ....Mrs. Julie BREWSTER

Purdue University Global (D)

9000 Keystone Crossing, Ste 800, Indianapolis IN 46240
County: Marion FICE Identification: 004586
Unit ID: 260901
Telephone: (317) 208-5311 Carnegie Class: DU-Mod
FAX Number: N/A Calendar System: Quarter
URL: www.purdueglobal.edu
Established: 1937 Annual Undergrad Tuition & Fees (In-State): $14,343
Enrollment: 33,287 Coed
Affiliation or Control: State IRS Status: 501(c)3
Highest Offering: Doctorate
Accreditation: NH, ACBSP, IFSAC, NURSE

01 President ....Mr. Mitchell DANIELS, JR.
02 Chancellor ....Dr. Betty VANDENBUSH
05 Chief Academic Officer ....Dr. David STARNES
10 Chief Financial Officer ....Mr. Chris RUHL
20 VP Faculty & Academic Resources ....Dr. Carolyn NORSTROM

Purdue University Main Campus (E)

610 Purdue Mall, West Lafayette IN 47907-2040
County: Tippecanoe FICE Identification: 001825
Unit ID: 243780
Telephone: (765) 494-4600 Carnegie Class: DU-Highest
FAX Number: N/A Calendar System: Semester
URL: www.purdue.edu
Established: 1869 Annual Undergrad Tuition & Fees (In-State): $9,992
Enrollment: 42,699 Coed
Affiliation or Control: State IRS Status: 501(c)3
Highest Offering: Doctorate
Accreditation: NH, AAB, ART, AUD, CAATE, CAEPN, CIDA, CLPSY, CONST, COPSY, DIETC, DIETD, IPSY, LSAR, NAIT, NURSE, PCSAS, PHAR, SP, THEA, #VET

01 President ....Mr. Mitchell E. DANIELS, JR.
10 Exec Vice President & Treasurer ....Mr. William E. SULLIVAN
05 Provost/Exec VP for Acad Affairs ....Dr. Jay AKRIDGE
21 Sr VP Business Svcs/Asst Treas ....Mr. James S. ALMOND
26 Exec Vice Pres Communications ....Mr. Dan HASLER
13 Exe VP Information Technology ....Dr. William G. MCCARTNEY
15 Vice President Human Resources ....Mr. Bill BELL
27 Exe VP for Communication ....Mr. Dan HASLER
20 Sr Vice Prov Teaching/Learning ....Dr. Frank J. DOOLEY
28 Vice Chanc Diversity/Inclusion ....Dr. John GATES
20 Vice Pres Faculty Affairs ....Dr. Peter HOLLENBECK
08 Dean of Libraries ....Ms. Beth MCNEIL
29 President & CEO Alumni Association ....Mr. Ralph AMOS
07 Dean Admiss/VP Enrollment Mgmt ....Mr. Mitch WARREN
37 Exe Director Financial Aid ....Ms. Heidi A. CARL

Purdue University Fort Wayne (F)

2101 E Coliseum Boulevard, Fort Wayne IN 46805-1499
County: Allen FICE Identification: 001828
Unit ID: 151102
Telephone: (260) 481-6100 Carnegie Class: Masters/L
FAX Number: (260) 481-6880 Calendar System: Semester
URL: www.pfw.edu
Established: 1964 Annual Undergrad Tuition & Fees (In-State): $8,450
Enrollment: 10,414 Coed
Affiliation or Control: State IRS Status: 501(c)3
Highest Offering: Doctorate
Accreditation: NH, ART, CAEP, CAEPN, MUS, NURSE, PH, RAD, THEA

02 Chancellor ....Dr. Ronald ELSENBAUMER
05 Vice Chanc Academic Affs/Enrol Mgmt ....Dr. Carl DRUMMOND
10 Vice Chanc Financial/Admin Affairs ....Dr. David WESSE
32 Vice Chancellor Student Affairs ....Dr. Eric NORMAN
111 Vice Chancellor for Advancement ....Dr. Angie FINCANNON
26 Int Vice Chanc Marketing/Comm ....Jerry LEWIS
06 Assoc Vice Chanc/Registrar ....Dr. Cheryl HINE
07 Assoc Vice Chanc for Admissions ....Kenneth C. CHRISTMON
20 Assoc Vice Chanc Academic Programs ....Dr. Carol S. STERNBERGER
100 Chief of Staff ....Kimberly WAGNER
13 Chief Information Ofcr/Dir IT Svcs ....Mitch DAVIDSON
18 Executive Director of Facilities ....Greg JUSTICE
29 Director of Alumni Relations ....Shawna SQUIBB
08 Dean of Helmke Library ....Alexis MACKLIN
15 Dir Human Res/Institutional Equity ....Cynthia SPRINGER
41 Director of Athletics & Recreation ....Kelley HARTLEY-HUTTON
96 Director of Purchasing ....Pam THOMPSON
19 Chief of Police ....Tim POTTS
22 Director of Institutional Equity ....Christine M. MARCUCCILLI
85 Director International Programs ....Brian MYLREA
37 Director Financial Aid ....Dr. Kristina CREAGER
09 Director of Institutional Research ....Irah MODRY-CARON
51 Exec Director Continuing Studies ....Karen VANGORDER
49 Dean Arts & Sciences ....Vacant
72 Dean Engr Tech/Computer Sci ....Dr. Manoochehr ZOGHI
53 Dean Education & Public Policy ....Dr. James BURG
50 Dean Business ....Dr. Melissa GRUYS
57 Dean Visual/Performing Arts ....John O'CONNELL
04 Admin Assistant to the President ....Khin Khin GYI
39 Dir Resident Life/Student Housing ....Jordyn HOGAN

Purdue University Northwest (G)

2200 169th Street, Hammond IN 46323-2094
County: Lake FICE Identification: 001827
Unit ID: 490805
Telephone: (219) 989-2370 Carnegie Class: Masters/L
FAX Number: (219) 989-2581 Calendar System: Semester
URL: www.pnw.edu
Established: 1946 Annual Undergrad Tuition & Fees (In-State): $7,691
Enrollment: N/A Coed
Affiliation or Control: State IRS Status: 501(c)3
Highest Offering: Doctorate
Accreditation: NH, CACREP, CAEP, CEA, MFCD, NAIT, NUR, SW

01 Chancellor ....Dr. Thomas L. KEON
05 Int Vice Chanc Acad Affs & Provost ....Dr. Niaz LATIF
10 Vice Chanc Finance & Admin ....Mr. Steve TURNER
111 Vice Chanc for Inst Advancement ....Dr. Lisa GOODNIGHT
13 Vice Chanc Info Services ....Mr. Tim WINDERS
84 Int VC Enroll Mgmt & Student Affs ....Ms. Joy COLWELL
26 Assoc Vice Chanc Marketing ....Ms. Kris FALZONE
09 Assoc VCAA Inst Effectiveness ....Dr. Rebecca STANKOWSKI
21 Asst VC Finance & Business Svcs ....Ms. Kimberly THOMAS
32 Assoc Vice Chanc Stdnt Affs/EOP ....Mr. Roy HAMILTON
15 Asst Vice Chanc Human Resources ....Ms. Susan MILLLER
83 Dean College of Hum Educ & Soc Sci ....Ms. Elaine CAREY
54 Dean College of Engr & Science ....Dr. Kenneth HOLFORD
72 Interim Dean College of Technology ....Dr. Mohammad ZAHRAEE
50 Dean College of Business ....Dr. Lawrence HAMER
66 Dean College of Nursing ....Dr. Lisa HOPP
53 Dir School of Education ....Ms. Anne GREGORY
06 Registrar ....Ms. Cheryl ARROYO
20 AVC Academic Affairs/Programs ....Dr. Jonathan SWARTS
37 Exec Dir of Financial Aid ....Mr. Michael J. BIEL
41 Director of Athletics ....Mr. Richard J. COSTELLO
38 Director Counseling Center ....Dr. Kenneth JACKSON
08 Dir Research/Learning & Res Svcs ....Ms. Tammy GUERRERO
85 Exec Director of Global Engagement ....Mr. George F. KACENGA
96 Dir of Procurement/Auxiliary Svcs ....Ms. Jennifer HUPKE
39 Director Housing Residential Educ ....Ms. Scott IVERSON
92 Int Dean Honors Program ....Dr. Michael LYNN
20 Assc Vice Chan Acad Affs Supp & Dev ....Dr. Lori FELDMAN
04 Sr Exc Asst Chan Strat Initiatives ....Ms. Daphne D. ROBINSON
102 Donor Communications Specialist ....Ms. Sara SONEYE
104 Education Abroad Coordinator ....Mr. Kyle RAUSCH
105 Asst Vice Chanc Learning Tech ....Ms. Heather ZAMOJSKI
25 Exec Director CVIS ....Dr. Chenn ZHOU
28 Director Ofc Equity & Diversity ....Ms. Linda B. KNOX
36 Director Career Dev & Services ....Ms. Natalie CONNORS
90 Asst Vice Chanc Learning Technology ....Ms. Heather ZAMOJSKI
109 Dir Procurement/Auxiliary Services ....Mr. Duncan MARRIOTT
88 AVC Campus Plng/Proj & Space Mgmt ....Mr. Jacob G. LENSON
29 Exec Dir PNW Alumni Community ....Ms. Ashley GERODIMOS
18 Senior Dir of Facilities & Grounds ....Mr. Scott PARSONS
07 Exec Dir of Undergrad Admissions ....Ms. Karen L. STACHYRA
100 Chief of Staff ....Dr. Richard RUPP
19 Director of Security ....Mr. Brian E. MILLER
112 Major Gift Officer ....Ms. Jamie MANAHAN

Purdue University Northwest, Westerville Campus (H)

1401 S US 421, Westville IN 46391-9542
Telephone: (219) 785-5200 FICE Identification: 001826
Accreditation: &NH, CAEPN

† Branch Campus of Purdue University Northwest, Hammond, IN.

Radiological Technologies University-VT (I)

100 E. Wayne Street, Suite 140, South Bend IN 46601
County: St. Joseph Identification: 667156
Unit ID: 488776
Telephone: (574) 232-2408 Carnegie Class: Spec-4-yr-Other Health
FAX Number: (574) 232-2200 Calendar System: Semester
URL: www.rtuvt.com
Established: 2009 Annual Undergrad Tuition & Fees: N/A
Enrollment: 99 Coed
Affiliation or Control: Proprietary IRS Status: Proprietary
Highest Offering: Master's
Accreditation: ACCSC, RADDOS

01 President ....Brent D. MURPHY
11 Dir of Administrative Services ....Betsy DATEMA

Rose-Hulman Institute of Technology (J)

5500 Wabash Avenue, Terre Haute IN 47803-3920
County: Vigo FICE Identification: 001830
Unit ID: 152318
Telephone: (812) 877-1511 Carnegie Class: Spec-4-yr-Eng
FAX Number: (812) 877-9925 Calendar System: Quarter
URL: www.rose-hulman.edu
Established: 1874 Annual Undergrad Tuition & Fees: $49,871
Enrollment: 2,245 Coed
Affiliation or Control: Independent Non-Profit IRS Status: 501(c)3
Highest Offering: Master's
Accreditation: NH

01 President ....Mr. Robert A. COONS
10 Vice President for Finance ....Mr. Matthew D. DAVIS
05 Provost & Vice Pres Academic Affs ....Dr. Richard E. STAMPER
111 VP Inst Advancement ....Mr. Steven P. BRADY
32 VP Student Affs & Dean of Students ....Mr. Erik Z. HAYES

26 VP Communications/Marketing ... Ms. Mary W. ATTEBERRY
15 Vice Pres Human/Environmental Svcs ... Ms. Megan C. ELLIOTT
84 Vice President Enrollment Mgmt ... Dr. Thomas BEAR
88 Sr Director Venture ... Mr. Brian C. DOUGHERTY
88 Associate Dean of Innovation ... Dr. William KLINE
20 Dean of Faculty ... Dr. Russell L. WARLEY
88 Dir for Micronano Devices & Sys ... Dr. Azad SIAHMAKOUN
88 Associate Dean of Learning & Tech ... Dr. Kay C. DEE
13 Vice Pres Info Tech and CIO ... Dr. Wayne DENNISON
18 Interim Dir Facilities Operations ... Mr. Chad T. WEBER
36 Dir Career Services/Employee Rels ... Mr. Scott K. TIEKEN
07 Dean of Admissions ... Ms. Lisa M. NORTON
29 Executive Director Alumni Relations ... Mr. Brandon ZOLLNER
37 Director of Financial Aid ... Ms. Melinda L. MIDDLETON
41 Director of Athletics ... Mr. Jeffrey L. JENKINS
28 Interim Dir Center for Diversity ... Ms. Camille R. WALLACE
30 Executive Director of Development ... Mr. Chris AIMONE
110 Exec Director Advancement Service ... Ms. Jennifer KENZOR
06 Registrar ... Ms. Jan PINK
08 Sr Director Logan Library & Info ... Ms. Bernadette EWEN
19 Director of Public Safety ... Vacant
40 Bookstore Manager ... Ms. Sheryl E. FULK
85 Dir of Intl Student Services ... Ms. Karen A. DEGRANGE
04 Exec Asst to the President/BOT ... Ms. Amy TIMBERMAN
88 Director of Business Operations ... Ms. Linda L. PRICE
88 Director Administrative Services ... Mr. Bryan T. BROMSTRUP
09 Director of Institutional Research ... Dr. Timothy CHOW
102 Dir of Corp & Foundation Relations ... Vacant
35 Assoc VP & Dean of Student Affairs ... Ms. Jacqueline M. WILSON
35 Director of Student Services ... Ms. Kristen J. LOYD
44 Director of Donor Relations ... Vacant
24 Instructional Technology Manager ... Ms. Cheryl DAVIDSON
24 Emerging Digital Technologies Mgr ... Mr. Alan WARD
38 Director of Counseling Services ... Dr. Michael LATTA
108 Int Sr Dir Inst Rsrch/Plng/Assess ... Dr. Matthew D. LOVELL

St. Anthony School of Echocardiography (A)

1201 S. Main Street, Crown Point IN 46307
County: Lake — Identification: 667119
Telephone: (219) 757-6132 — Carnegie Class: Not Classified
FAX Number: (219) 681-6725 — Calendar System: Semester
URL: https://www.franciscanhealth.org/EchoSchoolNWI
Established: 2004 — Annual Undergrad Tuition & Fees: N/A
Enrollment: N/A — Coed
Affiliation or Control: Independent Non-Profit — IRS Status: 501(c)3
Highest Offering: Associate Degree
Accreditation: DMS

01 Co-Program Director ... Lori HULT
05 Co-Program Director ... Karin KOLISZ

Saint Mary-of-the-Woods College (B)

1 St Mary of Woods College,
St Mary of the Woods IN 47876-1099
County: Vigo — FICE Identification: 001835
Unit ID: 152381
Telephone: (812) 535-5151 — Carnegie Class: Masters/S
FAX Number: (812) 535-5231 — Calendar System: Semester
URL: www.smwc.edu
Established: 1840 — Annual Undergrad Tuition & Fees: $29,960
Enrollment: 959 — Coed
Affiliation or Control: Roman Catholic — IRS Status: 501(c)3
Highest Offering: Master's
Accreditation: NH, MUS, NURSE

01 President ... Dr. Dottie KING
05 VP for Academic/Student Affairs ... Dr. Janet CLARK
10 VP for Finance & Administration ... Ms. Jaclyn WALTERS
111 VP for Advancement ... Ms. Karen DYER
84 VP Enrollment Mgmt/Inst Technology ... Mr. Brennan RANDOLPH
06 Registrar ... Ms. Deanna SMITHEE
32 Associate VP of Student Affairs ... Dr. Aimee JANSSEN-ROBINSON
37 Associate VP Financial Aid ... Ms. Darla HOPPER
21 Controller ... Ms. Kari WOLFE
110 Associate VP for Advancement ... Ms. Catherine SAUNDERS
26 Exec Dir of Strategic Communication ... Ms. Dee REED
36 Director of Career Development ... Ms. Susan GRESHAM
15 Director Human Resources ... Ms. Lisa PEPPERWORTH
29 Director Advancement/Alumni Rels ... Ms. Sarah MAHADY
08 Director of the Library ... Ms. Judy TRIBBLE
07 Director of Admissions ... Mr. Chris LOZIER
20 Executive Dir Academic Affairs ... Ms. Sara BOYER
18 Director Facilities ... Mr. Josh WOOD
09 Director of Institutional Research ... Mr. Mike KING
19 Director of Campus Security ... Mr. Greg EWING
04 Admin Assistant to the President ... Ms. Peggy NASH
108 Director Institutional Assessment ... Ms. Kimberli ZORNES
38 Director Student Counseling ... Ms. Kalista LAWRENCE
41 Athletic Director ... Ms. Deanna BRADLEY

Saint Mary's College (C)

Notre Dame IN 46556
County: Saint Joseph — FICE Identification: 001836
Unit ID: 152390
Telephone: (574) 284-4000 — Carnegie Class: Bac-A&S
FAX Number: (574) 284-4716 — Calendar System: Semester
URL: www.saintmarys.edu
Established: 1844 — Annual Undergrad Tuition & Fees: $42,220
Enrollment: 1,637 — Female
Affiliation or Control: Roman Catholic — IRS Status: 501(c)3
Highest Offering: Doctorate
Accreditation: NH, CAEP, MUS, NURSE, @SP, SW

01 Interim President ... Dr. Nancy NEKVASIL
04 Special Asst to the President ... Ms. Michelle EGAN
05 Provost/Sr VP Academic Affairs ... Dr. Titilayo UFOMATA
26 Vice President College Relations ... Ms. Shari M. RODRIGUEZ
32 Vice President for Student Affairs ... Ms. Karen A. JOHNSON
10 Vice President Strategy & Finance ... Dr. Dana STRAIT
84 Vice Pres for Enrollment Management ... Ms. Mona BOWE
88 Vice President for Mission ... Ms. Judith FEAN
121 Dean of Student Academic Services ... Dr. Karen CHAMBERS
06 Dir of Academic Advising/Registrar ... Ms. Nadia EWING
07 Director of Admission ... Ms. Sarah DVORAK
08 Director of Library ... Mr. Joseph THOMAS
09 Director of Institutional Research ... Ms. Julie SISCO
29 Director of Alumnae Relations ... Ms. Kara O'LEARY
37 Director of Financial Aid ... Ms. Kathleen M. BROWN
27 Director of Media Relations ... Vacant
38 Director of Women's Health ... Ms. Elizabeth FOURMAN
13 Chief Information Officer ... Mr. Todd NORRIS
15 Director of Human Resources ... Ms. Kris URSCHEL
19 Director of Safety & Security ... Mr. Robert POST
40 Manager Bookstore ... Ms. Judith MCKEE
41 Director of Athletics ... Ms. Julie SCHROEDER-BIEK
42 Director of Campus Ministry ... Ms. Regina WILSON
18 Director of Facilities ... Mr. Benjamin BOWMAN
96 Director of Purchasing ... Ms. Kathleen CARLSON
88 Director of Student Involvement ... Vacant
85 Director of Multicultural Program ... Ms. Gloria JENKINS
43 General Counsel ... Ms. Martha MCCAMPBELL
101 Secretary to the President ... Ms. Vicki WICKIZER

Saint Meinrad School of Theology (D)

200 Hill Drive, St. Meinrad IN 47577-1030
County: Spencer — FICE Identification: 007276
Unit ID: 152451
Telephone: (812) 357-6611 — Carnegie Class: Spec-4-yr-Faith
FAX Number: (812) 357-6964 — Calendar System: Semester
URL: www.saintmeinrad.edu
Established: 1861 — Annual Graduate Tuition & Fees: N/A
Enrollment: 171 — Coed
Affiliation or Control: Roman Catholic — IRS Status: 501(c)3
Highest Offering: Master's; No Undergraduates
Accreditation: NH, THEOL

01 President & Rector ... Rev. Denis ROBINSON, OSB
03 Vice Rector ... Rev. Tobias COLGAN, OSB
05 Academic Dean ... Dr. Robert ALVIS
42 Director of Spiritual Formation ... Rev. Bede CISCO, OSB
20 Dir of Graduate Theology Programs ... Sr. Jeana VISEL, OSB
30 Vice President of Development ... Mr. Michael ZIEMIANSKI
10 Business Manager & Treasurer ... Mrs. Lisa CASTLEBURY
08 Library Director ... Dr. Daniel KOLB
06 Registrar ... Mrs. Donna BALBACH
88 Dir of Clergy Formation Pgm ... Dcn. Rick WAGNER
114 Director of Budget ... Mrs. Pam DOWLAND
37 Director of Student Financial Aid ... Mrs. Ruth KRESS
26 Director of Communications ... Mrs. Mary Jeanne SCHUMACHER
29 Director of Alumni Relations ... Mr. Joe OLIVERI
38 Director of Student Counseling Ctr ... Sr. Diane PHARO, SCN
23 Director of Health Services ... Ms. Ann ROHLEDER
04 Executive Secretary ... Mrs. Karen SCHERZER
13 Chief Info Technology Officer (CIO) ... Mr. Dave GRAMELSPACHER
110 Director of Development ... Mr. Duane SCHAEFER
105 Director Web Services ... Mrs. Mary Jeanne SCHUMACHER
106 Dir Online Education/E-learning ... Sr. Jeana VISEL, OSB
15 Director Human Resources ... Mr. Mike GRAMELSPACHER
07 Director of Admissions ... Dr. John SCHLACHTER
44 Director of Annual Giving ... Mr. Christian MOCEK
108 Director Institutional Assessment ... Dr. John SCHLACHTER
18 Chief Facilities/Physical Plant Ofc ... Mr. Mark HOFFMAN

St. Vincent College of Health Professions (E)

2001 West 86th Street, Indianapolis IN 46260
County: Marion — Identification: 667315
Telephone: (317) 338-3879 — Carnegie Class: Not Classified
FAX Number: (317) 338-3720 — Calendar System: Semester
URL: www.stvincent.org
Established: 2015 — Annual Undergrad Tuition & Fees: N/A
Enrollment: N/A — Coed
Affiliation or Control: Independent Non-Profit — IRS Status: 501(c)3
Highest Offering: Associate Degree
Accreditation: ABHES, EMT, RAD

01 President/Exec Dir Medical Educ ... Dr. Jeffrey ROTHENBERG

Taylor University (F)

West 236 Reade Avenue, Upland IN 46989-1001
County: Grant — FICE Identification: 001838
Unit ID: 152530
Telephone: (765) 998-2751 — Carnegie Class: Bac-Diverse
FAX Number: (765) 998-4910 — Calendar System: 4/1/4
URL: www.taylor.edu
Established: 1846 — Annual Undergrad Tuition & Fees: $34,114
Enrollment: 2,145 — Coed
Affiliation or Control: Independent Non-Profit — IRS Status: 501(c)3
Highest Offering: Master's
Accreditation: NH, CAEPN, CEA, MUS, SW

01 President ... Dr. Paul Lowell HAINES
100 Chief of Staff ... Ms. Sherri HARTER
45 Special Assistant to the President ... Mr. Ron SUTHERLAND
28 Spec Asst Intercultural Initiatives ... Mr. Greg DYSON
111 VP for University Advancement ... Mr. Rex BENNETT
32 VP Student Development ... Dr. Skip TRUDEAU
84 VP Enrollment Management ... Mr. Stephen MORTLAND
10 VP Business/Finance & Controller ... Mr. Stephen OLSON
05 Provost ... Dr. Michael HAMMOND
20 Vice Provost ... Dr. Jeff GROELING
13 Chief Information Officer ... Mr. Rob LINEHAN
83 Dean Sch of Soc Sci/Educ & Bus ... Dr. Rhoda SOMMERS
81 Dean Sch Natural & Applied Sciences ... Dr. Grace MILLER
49 Dean Sch Hum/Arts & Biblical Stds ... Dr. Thomas JONES
104 Dean International Programs ... Dr. Charles BRAINER
20 Dean Faculty Development/Dir BCTLE ... Dr. Barb BIRD
37 Assoc Dean Enroll Mgmt/Dir Fin Aid ... Mr. Timothy NACE
07 Exec Director Admissions ... Ms. Amy BARNETT
35 Dean of Students ... Mr. Jesse BROWN
39 Dir Residence Life ... Mr. Scott BARRETT
06 Registrar ... Ms. Janet ROGERS
08 University Librarian ... Mr. Daniel BOWELL
108 Director Assessment/Quality Improv ... Dr. Kim CASE
09 Director IR/Assoc Registrar ... Dr. Edwin WELCH
88 Exec Director for Campaigns ... Mr. David RITCHIE
110 Assoc VP for Advancement ... Mr. Mike FALDER
30 Exec Director of Development ... Ms. Kristie JACOBSON
26 Exec Director of Marketing ... Vacant
29 Exec Dir for Alumni Relations ... Mr. Brad YORDY
35 Dean Experiential Learning ... Dr. Drew MOSER
41 Director of Athletics ... Mr. Kyle GOULD
36 Director Calling and Career Office ... Mr. Jeff AUPPERLE
105 Director of Enterprise Systems ... Mr. Rod EIB
42 Campus Pastor ... Mr. Jon CAVANAGH
15 Asst Director of Human Resources ... Ms. April EVANS
106 Director of Online Learning ... Ms. Carrie MEYER
25 Dir of Sponsored Programs ... Ms. Susan GAVIN
18 Director of Facility Services ... Mr. Gregg HOLLOWAY
38 Director of Counseling Ctr ... Ms. Caroline POLAND
19 Chief of Police/Taylor Police ... Mr. Jeff WALLACE
21 Dir of Acctng/Financial Reporting ... Mr. David LLOYD
21 Director Financial Operations ... Ms. Michelle BRAGG
26 Sr Dir Parent & Community Rels ... Ms. Joyce WOOD
88 Payroll Manager ... Ms. Toni NEWLIN
114 University Bursar ... Ms. Cathy MOORMAN

TCM International Institute (G)

6337 Hollister Drive, Indianapolis IN 46224
County: Marion — Identification: 666333
Telephone: (317) 299-0333 — Carnegie Class: Not Classified
FAX Number: (317) 290-8607 — Calendar System: Semester
URL: www.tcmi.org
Established: 1991 — Annual Graduate Tuition & Fees: N/A
Enrollment: N/A — Coed
Affiliation or Control: Independent Non-Profit — IRS Status: 501(c)3
Highest Offering: Master's; No Undergraduates
Accreditation: NH

01 President ... Dr. Tony TWIST
05 VP Educational Advancement ... Mr. Richard JUSTICE
11 U.S. Director of Operations ... Ms. Carol FIELDS
10 Director of Finance ... Ms. Julie RICE

Trine University (H)

1 University Avenue, Angola IN 46703-1764
County: Steuben — FICE Identification: 001839
Unit ID: 152567
Telephone: (260) 665-4100 — Carnegie Class: Masters/M
FAX Number: (260) 665-4292 — Calendar System: Semester
URL: www.trine.edu
Established: 1884 — Annual Undergrad Tuition & Fees: $32,176
Enrollment: 4,296 — Coed
Affiliation or Control: Independent Non-Profit — IRS Status: 501(c)3
Highest Offering: Doctorate
Accreditation: NH, ACBSP, #ARCPA, CAEP, PTA

01 President ... Dr. Earl D. BROOKS, II
05 Vice President for Academic Affairs ... Dr. John SHANNON
10 Vice President Finance ... Ms. Jody GREER
84 Vice Pres Enrollment Management ... Mr. Scott GOPLIN
32 Dean of Students ... Mr. Francisco ORTIZ
26 VP Univ Marketing/Communications ... Mr. Dave JARZYNA
29 VP Alumni/Development ... Ms. Lisa MAXWELL-FRIEDEN
41 Athletic Director/Asst VP Athletics ... Mr. Matt LAND
49 Dean Jannen School of Arts & Sci ... Ms. Sarah FRANZEN
107 Asst Vice Pres Professional Studies ... Ms. Keirsten EBERTS
15 Human Resources ... Ms. Jamie NORTON
06 Registrar ... Ms. Debra F. HELMSING
04 Assistant to the President ... Ms. Gretchen MILLER
37 Director Student Financial Planning ... Ms. Kim BENNETT
08 Director of the Library ... Ms. Michelle BLANK
36 Director of Placement/Coop Educ ... Ms. Linda COOPER
09 Director Inst Planning/Analysis ... Ms. Christina ZUMBRUN

Union Bible College (I)

PO Box 900, Westfield IN 46074
County: Hamilton — Identification: 667253
Telephone: (317) 896-9324 — Carnegie Class: Not Classified

FAX Number: (317) 867-0784　Calendar System: Semester
URL: www.ubca.org
Established: 1911　Annual Undergrad Tuition & Fees: N/A
Enrollment: N/A　Coed
Affiliation or Control: Interdenominational　IRS Status: 501(c)3
Highest Offering: Baccalaureate
Accreditation: BI

01 President ... C. Adam BUCKLER
05 Vice Pres Academic Affairs ... John WHITAKER
10 Director of Finance ... Vacant
11 Director of Operations ... Greg HOBELMAN
32 Dean of Student Life ... Joe CAREY
09 Director of Institutional Research ... Isabel RUNDELL
06 Registrar ... Elizabeth DAVIS
07 Director of Admissions ... Phil HOARD

University of Evansville (A)

1800 Lincoln Avenue, Evansville IN 47722-1586
County: Vanderburgh　FICE Identification: 001795
Unit ID: 150534
Telephone: (812) 488-2000　Carnegie Class: Masters/S
FAX Number: (812) 488-2320　Calendar System: Semester
URL: www.evansville.edu
Established: 1854　Annual Undergrad Tuition & Fees: $36,416
Enrollment: 2,516　Coed
Affiliation or Control: United Methodist　IRS Status: 501(c)3
Highest Offering: Doctorate
Accreditation: NH, #ARCPA, CAATE, CAEP, MUS, NUR, PTA, PTAA

01 President ... Dr. Christopher M. PIETRUSZKIEWICZ
05 Exec VP Academic Affairs ... Dr. Michael AUSTIN
111 VP Advancement ... Ms. Abigail WERLING
10 VP Fiscal Affairs & Admin ... Ms. Donna TEAGUE
32 VP Student Affairs ... Dr. Dana CLAYTON
108 AVP Assessment/Inst Effectiveness ... Dr. Mark VALENZUELA
84 VP Enrollment/Marketing ... Dr. Shane DAVIDSON
35 Asst VP Student Affs/Dir Res Life ... Mr. Michael A. TESSIER
13 Chief Information Officer/OTS ... Mr. Michael SMITH
49 Dean of Arts & Sciences ... Dr. Ray LUTGRING
50 Int Dean of Business Administration ... Mr. Ben JOHNSON
53 Dean of Educ/Health Science ... Ms. Mary KESSLER
54 Dean Engineering/Computer Science ... Dr. Ying SHANG
51 Dir Ctr for Advancement of Lrng ... Ms. Lindsay ROBERTS
85 Exec Dir International Programs ... Dr. Wesley MILNER
41 Director of Athletics ... Mr. Mark SPENCER
88 Dir Univ Relations/Content Devel ... Ms. Amanda CAMPBELL
06 University Registrar ... Ms. Jennifer BRIGGS
08 University Librarian ... Mr. Robb WALTNER
42 University Chaplain ... Rev. Tammy GIESELMAN
11 Manager of Administrative Services ... Ms. Kim WINSETT
29 Director of Alumni/Parent Relations ... Ms. Liz RIFFERT
36 Sr Dir Ctr Career Development ... Mr. C. Gene WELLS
38 Director of Counseling/Health Educ ... Ms. Karen STENSTROM
37 Director of Student Financial Svcs ... Ms. Becky HAMILTON
15 Director of Human Resources ... Mr. Keith GEHLHAUSEN
18 Exec Dir Facilities Mgmt & Plng ... Mr. Chad MILLER
19 Director of Safety & Security ... Mr. Harold P. MATTHEWS
104 Director Educ Abroad-Harlaxton Col ... Ms. Holly CARTER
40 Director of Bookstore ... Mr. Douglas GUSTWILLER
28 Chief Diversity Officer ... Dr. Robert SHELBY
110 Director of Development ... Mr. Scott A. GILREATH
121 Director of Academic Advising ... Ms. Stacey A. SHANKS
35 Assoc Dean Student Engmt & Innov ... Mr. Geoffrey M. EDWARDS
07 Director of Admissions ... Mr. Kenton HARGIS
04 Exec Assistant to the President ... Ms. Patricia A. LIPPERT
88 Asst & Event Coord Office of Pres ... Ms. Sarah BROCK

University of Indianapolis (B)

1400 E Hanna Avenue, Indianapolis IN 46227-3697
County: Marion　FICE Identification: 001804
Unit ID: 151263
Telephone: (317) 788-3368　Carnegie Class: DU-Mod
FAX Number: (317) 788-3300　Calendar System: Semester
URL: www.uindy.edu
Established: 1902　Annual Undergrad Tuition & Fees: $29,688
Enrollment: 5,972　Coed
Affiliation or Control: United Methodist　IRS Status: 501(c)3
Highest Offering: Doctorate
Accreditation: NH, ACBSP, ART, CAATE, CAEP, CAEPN, CLPSY, COARC, COSMA, EXSC, MUS, NURSE, OT, PTA, PTAA, SW

01 President ... Dr. Robert L. MANUEL
05 Exec VP & Provost ... Dr. Stephen KOLISON
84 VP for Enrollment Services ... Mr. Ron WILKS
10 VP & CFO ... Vacant
26 VP Communications & Marketing ... Ms. Kelly HAUFLAIRE
111 Vice President for Univ Advancement ... Mr. Christopher H. MOLLOY
26 Assoc VP of External Relations ... Mr. Corey WILSON
41 VP for Intercollegiate Athletics ... Dr. Sue C. WILLEY
42 VP for Mission ... Dr. Michael G. CARTWRIGHT
43 Vice President & General Counsel ... Ms. Andrea NEWSOM
32 VP for Stdnt/Campus Affs/Dn of Std ... Ms. Kory M. VITANGELI
100 VP & Secretary to the University ... Ms. Lara G. MANN
04 Manager of Operations ... Ms. Angela PRESNELL
36 Assoc VP of Professional Edge ... Mr. Corey L. WILSON
06 Registrar ... Ms. Josh HAYES
13 VP and Chief Technology Officer ... Mr. Steven R. HERRIFORD
49 Dean College of Arts & Sciences ... Dr. Debra FEAKES
50 Dean School of Business ... Dr. Lawrence BELCHER
53 Dean School of Education ... Dr. John KUYKENDALL
66 Dean School of Nursing ... Ms. Norma HALL
76 Dean College of Health Sciences ... Dr. Stephanie KELLY
55 Dean Psychological Sciences ... Dr. Torrey WILSON
20 Assoc Provost for Academic Systems ... Dr. Mary Beth BAGG
20 Int Assoc Prov Rsrch/Grad/Acad Ptnr ... Ms. Ellen MILLER
108 Assoc VP for Accreditation ... Dr. Mary C. MOORE
07 Director of Admissions ... Mr. Ryan MCCLARNON
08 Library Director ... Vacant
15 Director Human Resources ... Mrs. Erin P. FARRELL
37 Assoc VP or Financial Aid ... Mrs. Linda B. HANDY
58 Director Graduate Business Pgms ... Mr. Stephen A. TOKAR
18 Executive Director Facilities Mgmt ... Mr. Dave STATLER
19 Director Safety & Police Services ... Mr. David K. SELBY
31 Director of Service Learning ... Dr. Marianna K. FOULKROD
42 Chaplain/Dir Lantz Center ... Rev. Jeremiah GIBBS
29 Assoc VP Alumni Engagement ... Mr. Andy M. KOCHER
85 Director International Division ... Ms. Marilyn O. CHASE
24 Asst VP of Information Systems ... Mr. Robert A. JONES
38 Director Counseling Center ... Dr. Kelly M. MILLER
40 Bookstore Manager ... Vacant

University of Notre Dame (C)

400 Main Building, Notre Dame IN 46556
County: Saint Joseph　FICE Identification: 001840
Unit ID: 152080
Telephone: (574) 631-5000　Carnegie Class: DU-Highest
FAX Number: (574) 631-6700　Calendar System: Semester
URL: www.nd.edu
Established: 1842　Annual Undergrad Tuition & Fees: $53,391
Enrollment: 12,467　Coed
Affiliation or Control: Roman Catholic　IRS Status: 501(c)3
Highest Offering: Doctorate
Accreditation: NH, ART, CLPSY, IPSY, LAW, THEOL

01 President ... Rev. John I. JENKINS, CSC
05 Provost ... Dr. Thomas G. BURISH
03 Executive Vice President ... Mr. Shannon B. CULLINAN
20 Vice Pres/Sr Associate Provost ... Dr. Christine M. MAZIAR
20 Vice Pres/Associate Provost ... Dr. Maura A. RYAN
89 Vice Pres/Associate Provost ... Dr. Hugh R. PAGE, JR.
82 VP/Provost Internationalization ... Dr. Michael PIPPENGER
32 Vice President for Student Affairs ... Ms. Erin HOFFMANN HARDING
10 Vice President for Finance ... Mr. Trent A. GROCOCK
46 Vice President for Research ... Dr. Robert J. BERNHARD
43 Vice President & General Counsel ... Ms. Marianne CORR
115 Vice Pres/Chief Investment Ofcr ... Mr. Scott C. MALPASS
41 Vice Pres & Director of Athletics ... Mr. John B. SWARBRICK, JR.
15 Vice Pres Human Resources ... Mr. Robert K. MCQUADE
26 Vice President University Relations ... Mr. Louis M. NANNI
27 VP Public Affairs/Communications ... Mr. Paul BROWNE
13 VP & Chief Information Officer ... Mr. John GOHSMAN
88 VP Mission Engagmnt/Church Affairs ... Rev. Gerald J. OLINGER, CSC
58 VP/Assoc Prov/Dean Graduate Sch ... Dr. Laura CARLSON
45 VP Strategic Planning ... Mr. David C. BAILEY
100 Vice President/Chief of Staff ... Ms. Ann M. FIRTH
19 Vice Pres Campus Safety/Univ Ops ... Mr. Mike SEAMON
28 Chief Diversity Officer ... Mr. Eric LOVE
84 Assoc VP Undergraduate Enrollment ... Mr. Donald C. BISHOP
18 VP Facilities & Design ... Mr. Douglas K. MARSH
109 Vice Pres Univ Enterprises/Events ... Ms. Micki KIDDER
06 Registrar ... Mr. Charles T. HURLEY
96 Director Procurement ... Mr. Vaibhav AGARWAL
50 Dean College of Business ... Dr. Martijn CREMERS
61 Dean of Law School ... Fr. Marcus G. COLE
54 Interim Dean College of Engineering ... Dr. Thomas E. FUJA
49 Dean of Arts & Letters ... Dr. Sarah A. MUSTILLO
81 Dean of Science ... Dr. Mary E. GALVIN
48 Dean of Architecture ... Dr. Michael N. LYKOUDIS
82 Dean School of Global Affairs ... Dr. Scott APPLEBY
29 Exec Director Alumni Assoc ... Ms. Dolly DUFFY
08 Dir of University Libraries ... Ms. Diane PARR WALKER
42 Director of Campus Ministry ... Rev. Peter M. MCCORMICK, CSC
37 Dir of Student Financial Aid ... Ms. Mary B. NUCCIARONE
36 Director of Undergrad Career Svcs ... Ms. Bridget KRIBBE
38 Director of Counseling Center ... Dr. Susan C. STEIBE-PASALICH
19 Director of Security/Police ... Ms. Keri Kei SHIBATA
07 Director of Admissions ... Ms. Christy PRATT
101 Secretary of the Institution/Board ... Ms. Beth SWIFT
09 Director of Institutional Research ... Ms. Eva NANCE
102 Dir Foundation/Corporate Relations ... Mr. Rudy REYES
104 Director Study Abroad ... Ms. Kathleen OPEL
39 Director Student Housing ... Ms. Karen M. KENNEDY
04 Administrative Asst to President ... Ms. Sarah A. GOTSCH
86 Director Government Relations ... Mr. Timothy D. SEXTON
25 Chief Contract/Grants Administrator ... Ms. Michelle JOYCE
30 Director of Development ... Ms. Jill CALDERONE
44 Director Annual Giving ... Mr. Brian DISS

University of Saint Francis (D)

2701 Spring Street, Fort Wayne IN 46808-3994
County: Allen　FICE Identification: 001832
Unit ID: 152336
Telephone: (260) 399-7700　Carnegie Class: Masters/L
FAX Number: N/A　Calendar System: Semester
URL: www.sf.edu
Established: 1890　Annual Undergrad Tuition & Fees: $30,430
Enrollment: 2,322　Coed
Affiliation or Control: Roman Catholic　IRS Status: 501(c)3
Highest Offering: Doctorate
Accreditation: NH, ACBSP, ADNUR, ANEST, ARCPA, ART, CAEP, DIETC, MLTAD, NURSE, PTAA, RAD, SURGT, SW

01 President ... Sr. M. Elise KRISS, OSF
05 VP Academic Affairs ... Dr. Lance B. RICHEY
11 VP Administration ... Mrs. Teresa A. SORDELET
111 VP Institutional Advancement ... Dr. Matthew J. SMITH
10 VP Finance and Operations ... Mr. Richard A. BIENZ
32 VP Student Affairs ... Mr. Dan A. SOLLER
84 VP Enrollment Management ... Ms. Beth M. TERRELL
20 Assoc VP Acad Affs & Dir Gen Educ ... Mrs. Trish J. BUGAJSKI, OFS
35 Associate VP Student Affairs ... Vacant
88 Assistant VP Mission Integration ... Sr. M. Anita HOLZMER, OSF
50 Dean Keith Busse School of Business ... Dr. Robert W. LEE
57 Dean School of Creative Arts ... Mrs. Colleen HUDDLESON
17 Dean School of Health Sciences ... Dr. Mindy J. YODER
49 Dean School Liberal Arts & Sciences ... Dr. Lance D. RICHEY
12 Dean Crown Point Site ... Dr. Marsha M. KING
121 Exec Dir Acad & Career Devel Ctr ... Mrs. Natalie M. WAGONER
13 Exec Dir Univ Technology ... Mrs. Kelly N. SMITH
21 Controller ... Mr. Craig M. TEETSEL
06 Registrar ... Mr. Francis P. CONNOR
42 Chaplain ... Fr. David L. MEINZEN
121 Director Academic Advising ... Ms. Melissa J. REESMAN
29 Director Alumni Relations ... Ms. Melissa S. EASTMAN
41 Director Athletics ... Mr. Michael H. MCCAFFREY
42 Director Campus Ministry ... Mr. Justin AQUILA
30 Director Development ... Mr. Matthew C. ROWAN
106 Dir Enrollment Svcs Online Learning ... Mrs. Michelle L. KUHLHORST
28 Dir Diversity & Inclusion ... Dr. Paul PORTER
14 Dir Enterprise App/Tech Services ... Mr. A. Drew REPP
37 Director Financial Aid ... Ms. Jennifer K. HULL
102 Dir Found Relations/Grant Writer ... Vacant
15 Dir Human Resources & Org Develop ... Mrs. Carol L. COFFEE
92 Dir John Duns Scotus Honors Program ... Dr. Kenneth A. BUGAJSKI
105 Director Marketing ... Mrs. Carla S. PYLE
39 Director Resident Life/Student Hous ... Vacant
88 Director Sports Information ... Mr. William J. SCOTT
88 Dir Student Service Learning/Engage ... Mrs. Katrina P. BOEDEKER
08 Assoc Dir Information/Instruc Svcs ... Mrs. Maureen E. MCMAHAN
15 Assistant Dir Human Resources ... Mr. Andy MCKEE
53 Chair Department of Education ... Dr. Mary E. REIPENHOFF
19 Supervisor Campus Safety/Security ... Mr. Edward A. LAROCQUE
18 Int Supervisor Maintenance/Grounds ... Mr. Ramon S. DEMOND
44 Senior Gift Officer ... Mrs. Tammy K. OAKES
09 Research/Assessment Analyst ... Mrs. Kim E. DIETRICH
04 Admin Liaison Office of Pres ... Miss Vicki L. JACOBS, OFS
109 Mgr Creative Dining Food Service ... Ms. Brenda CHRISTIAN
40 Mgr Barnes & Noble Campus Shoppe ... Mrs. Robin HUFFMAN

University of Southern Indiana (E)

8600 University Boulevard, Evansville IN 47712-3596
County: Vanderburgh　FICE Identification: 001808
Unit ID: 151306
Telephone: (812) 464-8600　Carnegie Class: Masters/L
FAX Number: (812) 464-1960　Calendar System: Semester
URL: www.usi.edu
Established: 1965　Annual Undergrad Tuition & Fees (In-State): $8,349
Enrollment: 11,004　Coed
Affiliation or Control: State　IRS Status: 501(c)3
Highest Offering: Doctorate
Accreditation: NH, ART, CAEP, CAEPN, CEA, COARC, COSMA, DA, DH, DIETD, DMS, EXSC, NURSE, OT, OTA, RAD, SW

01 President ... Dr. Ronald S. ROCHON
100 Exec Assistant to the President ... Mrs. Nita R. MUSICH
100 Sr Exec Assistant to the President ... Mrs. Carey BEURY
05 Provost ... Dr. Mohammed KHAYUM
10 Vice President for Finance & Admin ... Mr. Steven J. BRIDGES
84 VP for Enrollment Management ... Mr. Andrew W. WRIGHT
32 VP for Student Affairs ... Vacant
26 VP Marketing & Communications ... Mrs. Kindra L. STRUPP
20 Assoc Provost for Academic Affairs ... Dr. Shelly B. BLUNT
21 AVP for Finance & Administration ... Ms. Mary A. HUPFER
86 Chief Government/Legal Affairs Ofcr ... Mr. Aaron C. TRUMP
09 Chief Data Officer ... Dr. Katherine A. DRAUGHON
123 Interim Dir of Graduate Studies ... Dr. Michael D. DIXON
06 Registrar ... Mrs. Sandy K. FRANK
07 Director of Undergrad Admission ... Mr. Rashad E. SMITH
08 Director of Library ... Ms. Marna M. HOSTETLER
30 VP for Development/USI Foundation ... Mr. David A. BOWER
92 Director Honors Program ... Dr. Sarah E. STEVENS
38 Director of Counseling ... Dr. B. Thomas LONGWELL
29 Dir Alumni Relations/Volunteer USI ... Mrs. Janet L. JOHNSON
37 Dir Student Financial Assistance ... Mrs. Mary J. HARPER
15 Exec Director of Human Resources ... Mr. Andrew R. LENHARDT
35 Dean of Students ... Dr. Jennifer R. HAMMAT
85 Asst Provost Intl Programs & Svcs ... Ms. Heidi M. GREGORI-GAHAN
28 Director Multicultural Center ... Mrs. Pamela F. HOPSON
13 Chief Information Officer ... Mr. Richard J. TOENISKOETTER
90 Academic Services Coordinator ... Mr. Juzar AHMED
18 Dir of Facility Operations & Plng ... Mr. James E. WOLFE
96 Director Procurement Services ... Mr. Daniel R. MARTENS
27 Director of Univ Communications ... Mr. John A. FARLESS
19 Director of Public Safety ... Mr. Stephen L. BEQUETTE
39 Director of Housing/Residence Life ... Ms. Amy S. PRICE
40 Bookstore Manager ... Mr. Michael J. GOELZHAUSER

41	Athletic Director	Mr. Jon Mark HALL
50	Dean Romain College of Business	Dr. Catherine CAREY
49	Dean College of Liberal Arts	Dr. James M. BEEBY
66	Dean College Nursing/Health Prof	Dr. Ann H. WHITE
81	Dean College of Sci/Engr/Educ	Dr. Zane W. MITCHELL, JR.
51	Director of Lifelong Learning	Ms. Dawn M. STONEKING
120	Exec Dir of Online Learning	Dr. Belle COWDEN
105	Director of Web Services	Mrs. Brandi S. HESS

Valparaiso University (A)

1700 Chapel Drive, Valparaiso IN 46383-9978

County: Porter — FICE Identification: 001842
Unit ID: 152600
Telephone: (219) 464-5000 — Carnegie Class: DU-Mod
FAX Number: (219) 464-5381 — Calendar System: Semester
URL: valpo.edu
Established: 1859 — Annual Undergrad Tuition & Fees: $40,260
Enrollment: 4,026 — Coed
Affiliation or Control: Lutheran — IRS Status: 501(c)3
Highest Offering: Doctorate
Accreditation: NH, #ARCPA, CACREP, CAEPN, LAW, MUS, NURSE, SW

01	President	Dr. Mark A. HECKLER
05	Provost/Exec VP for Acad Affs	Dr. Mark BIERMANN
11	Executive VP and COO	Mr. David PHELPS
32	VP for Student Affairs	Dr. Julie DEGRAW
84	VP for Enrollment Mgmt & Mktg	Mr. Ray BROWN
58	Dean Grad School/Cont Educ	Ms. Christina GRABAREK
111	VP for Advancement	Ms. Lisa HOLLANDER
110	AVP for Advancement	Mr. Jason PETROVICH
26	Chief Communication Officer	Ms. Nicole NIEMI
43	VP University Counsel	Mr. Darron C. FARHA
10	Senior VP for Finance	Ms. Susan SCROGGINS
92	Dean of Christ College	Dr. Susan VANZANTEN
49	Dean College Arts & Sciences	Dr. Jon T. KILPINEN
61	Dean School of Law	Mr. David CLEVELAND
54	Dean College of Engineering	Dr. Eric JOHNSON
50	Dean College of Business Admin	Dr. James BRODZINSKI
66	Dean College of Nursing	Dr. Karen ALLEN
08	Dean Library Services	Ms. Trisha MILEHAM
35	Dean of Students	Dr. Timothy S. JENKINS
88	AVP Enrollment Management	Mr. David FEVIG
42	AVP for Mission & Ministry	Rev. Brian T. JOHNSON
06	Registrar	Ms. Stephanie MARTIN
19	Chief University Police	Ms. Rebecca A. WALKOWIAK
39	Asst Dean Students/Residential Life	Mr. Ryan BLEVINS
104	Assoc Dir of Study Abroad	Ms. Erin KUNERT
85	Assoc Dir of International Program	Ms. Janice LIN
29	Director Alumni Relations	Ms. Linda ROETTGER
15	Dir Human Resource Services	Mr. Scott HARRISON
18	Exec Dir of Facilities	Mr. Jason KUTCH
36	Director Career Center	Mr. Tom CATH
38	Director of Counseling Services	Dr. Stewart E. COOPER
41	Director Athletics	Mr. Mark LABARBERA
20	Asst Provost for Faculty Affairs	Dr. Rick GILLMAN
21	Controller	Ms. Tamara GINGERICH
28	Director of Multicultural Programs	Mr. Byron MARTIN
96	Exec Dir of Administration	Mr. Eric MACHARIA
09	Exec Dir Inst Effectiveness	Mr. Greg STINSON
42	Interim University Pastor	Dcs. Kristin LEWIS
42	University Pastor	Rev. James WETZSTEIN
37	Director of Financial Aid	Ms. Karen KLIMCZYK
100	Chief of Staff	Mr. Rick AMRHEIN
04	Administrative Asst to President	Ms. Gwen GRAHAM
07	Director of Admission Programs	Ms. Barb LIESKE
102	Dir Foundation/Corporate Relations	Ms. Kathy GROTH
13	Chief Info Technology Officer (CIO)	Mr. Dave SIERKOWSKI

Veritas Baptist College (B)

181 U.S. 50 East, Suite 204, Greendale IN 47025

County: Dearborn — FICE Identification: 038626
Unit ID: 482228
Telephone: (812) 221-1714 — Carnegie Class: Spec-4-yr-Faith
FAX Number: (540) 785-5441 — Calendar System: Semester
URL: www.vbc.edu
Established: 1984 — Annual Undergrad Tuition & Fees: $5,800
Enrollment: 258 — Coed
Affiliation or Control: Baptist — IRS Status: 501(c)3
Highest Offering: Master's
Accreditation: TRACS

01	President	John EDMONDS
00	Chancellor	Dr. Don FORRESTER
05	Academic Dean	Ann RILL
32	Dean of Students	Mickey CREED
10	Chief Financial Officer	Sherry DAVIS
37	Director Student Financial Aid	Lisa LUCENA
07	Director of Admissions	Michele E. CATLIN

Vincennes University (C)

1002 N First Street, Vincennes IN 47591-1504

County: Knox — FICE Identification: 001843
Unit ID: 152637
Telephone: (812) 888-8888 — Carnegie Class: Bac/Assoc-Assoc Dom
FAX Number: (812) 888-5868 — Calendar System: Semester
URL: www.vinu.edu
Established: 1801 — Annual Undergrad Tuition & Fees (In-State): $5,902
Enrollment: 18,914 — Coed
Affiliation or Control: State — IRS Status: 501(c)3
Highest Offering: Baccalaureate
Accreditation: NH, ACBSP, ADNUR, ART, CAEPN, CAHIIM, FUSER, NUR, PNUR, PTAA, SURGT

01	President	Dr. Charles R. JOHNSON
05	Provost/Vice Pres Institutional Svc	Dr. Laura TREANOR
10	Vice Pres Financial Svcs/Govt Rels	Mr. Phillip S. RATH
103	VP Workforce Dev/Comm Services	Mr. David A. TUCKER
12	Assistant VP/Dean Jasper Campus	Mr. Christian BLOME
21	Associate Vice President/Controller	Ms. Linda L. WALDROUP
32	Asst Prov Student Aff/Dean Students	Ms. Taja DAVIDSON
20	Asst Provost Curriculum & Inst	Mr. Rick A. KRIBS
35	Dean of Students	Ms. Taja DAVIDSON
26	Sr Director External Relations	Vacant
07	Director of Admissions	Ms. Heidi M. WHITEHEAD
09	Int Dir of Institutional Research	Ms. Jennifer L. HOLSCHER
13	Director of Mgmt Information Center	Mr. Carmin A. SCHNARR
88	Director of University Events	Ms. Cynthia A. BEAMAN
36	Int Dir Ctr for Career & Empl Rel	Ms. Donna TAYLOR-BOUCHIE
37	Director of Student Financial Aid	Mr. Stanley J. WERNE
22	Director Disability Services	Ms. Jill STEELE
40	Manager of Bookstore	Ms. Karen R. FAULKNER
102	Executive Director VU Foundation	Ms. Kristi R. DEETZ
41	Athletic Director	Mr. Harry L. MEEKS
88	Sr Dir Dual Credit Partnerships	Ms. Heather MOFFAT
29	Int Director of Alumni Programs	Ms. Savannah C. LINENBURG
28	Director Multicultural Affairs	Ms. Cortney L. CROSS
18	Director of Physical Plant	Mr. Andrew YOUNG
19	Director of Campus Police	Mr. Robert DUNHAM
113	Bursar	Ms. Jessica PARKER
06	Registrar	Ms. Rebecca K. LITTLE
39	Director Residential Life	Ms. Dawn M. BREWER
88	Director Marketing Services	Ms. Andrea G. TSCHERTER
96	Director of Procurement	Mr. Michael L. MORRISON
121	Director Student Success Center	Ms. Gaye WALTHALL
88	Director Architectural Services	Mr. Andrew YOUNG
15	Director Human Resources/AAO	Ms. Regina L. MCCORD-FITHIAN
76	Dean College Health Sci/Human Perf	Ms. Michelle CUMMINS
50	Dean College of Business/Public Svc	Ms. Anna MILLER
72	Dean College of Technology	Mr. Ty FREED
81	Dean College of Sc/Engr/Math	Mr. Curt COFFMAN
83	Dean Soc Sci/Perf Arts/Comm	Dr. Cynthia RAGLE
114	Budget Director	Mr. Tim EATON
79	Dean College of Humanities	Ms. Joan PUCKETT
88	Dir Avia Tech Ctr Indianapolis	Mr. Michael D. GEHRICH
108	Dir Institutional Effectiveness	Mr. Michael GRESS
88	Director Early College	Ms. Nicole SHANKLE
88	Asst VP Outreach & Engagement	Mr. Matthew J. SCHWARTZ
88	Director Veterans Affairs	Ms. Kristen PHILLIPS
88	Dir Plainfield Logistics Center	Mr. James E. DOLAN
04	Administrative Asst to President	Ms. Nancy A. IRWIN
88	Director International Recruitment	Mr. Ze (Wade) CHEN
23	Dir Univ Primary Care Clinic	Ms. Kara DOYLE
85	Director International Affairs	Vacant
51	Asst VP Lifelong Learning	Ms. Shanni E. SIMMONS

Vincennes University-Jasper Center (D)

850 College Avenue, Jasper IN 47546

Telephone: (812) 482-3030 — Identification: 770107
Accreditation: &NH

Wabash College (E)

301 W Wabash Avenue, PO Box 352,
Crawfordsville IN 47933-0352

County: Montgomery — FICE Identification: 001844
Unit ID: 152673
Telephone: (765) 361-6100 — Carnegie Class: Bac-A&S
FAX Number: (765) 361-6461 — Calendar System: Semester
URL: www.wabash.edu
Established: 1832 — Annual Undergrad Tuition & Fees: $43,650
Enrollment: 864 — Male
Affiliation or Control: Independent Non-Profit — IRS Status: 501(c)3
Highest Offering: Baccalaureate
Accreditation: NH

01	President	Dr. Gregory D. HESS
05	Dean of the College	Dr. Scott FELLER
10	Chief Financial Officer & Treasurer	Ms. Kendra COOKS
32	Dean of Students	Dr. Gregory REDDING
111	Dean for Advancement	Ms. Michelle L. JANSSEN
84	Dean for Enrollment Management	Mr. Charles (Chip) TIMMONS
07	Assoc Dean of Enroll/Dir of Admiss	Mr. Tyler WADE
28	Dean Prof Dev & Malcolm X Institute	Mr. Steven L. JONES
100	Chief of Staff	Mr. James L. AMIDON
20	Sr Associate Dean of the College	Dr. Jill LAMBERTON
08	Head Librarian & Dir Lilly Library	Mr. Jeffery BECK
06	Registrar and Assoc Dean	Dr. Jonathon D. JUMP
13	Director of IT Services	Mr. Bradley K. WEAVER
37	Director of Financial Aid	Vacant
35	Associate Dean of Students	Mr. Marc WELCH
36	Director of Career Development	Mr. Roland MORIN
29	Dir of Alumni & Parent Relations	Mr. Steve HOFFMAN
109	Director of Business Auxiliaries	Mr. Thomas E. KEEDY
41	Dir of Athletics & Campus Wellness	Mr. Matt TANNEY
110	Associate Dean for Advancement	Mr. Joseph R. KLEN
15	Director of Human Resources	Ms. Catherine A. METZ
18	Director of Campus Services	Mr. David MORGAN
21	Controller	Mr. Douglas SMITH
38	Director of Counseling Services	Mr. Kevin C. SWAIM
88	Director of Inquiries CILA	Dr. Charles F. BLAICH
88	Dir Wabash Ctr Teaching/Learning	Ms. Dena PENCE
19	Director of Safety and Security	Mr. Tom KEARNS
09	Director of Institutional Research	Mr. David DALENBERG
101	Secretary of the Institution/Board	Mr. James L. AMIDON, JR.
102	Dir Foundation/Corporate Relations	Ms. Deborah WOODS
104	Director International Programs	Ms. Amy WEIR
26	Chief Public Relations/Marketing	Ms. Kimberly JOHNSON
96	Director of Purchasing	Mr. Thomas E. KEEDY
04	Admin Assistant to the President	Ms. Beverly CUNNINGHAM
44	Director Annual Giving	Mr. Aaron SHELBY

IOWA

Allen College (F)

1825 Logan Avenue, Waterloo IA 50703-1999

County: Black Hawk — FICE Identification: 030691
Unit ID: 152798
Telephone: (319) 226-2000 — Carnegie Class: Spec-4-yr-Other Health
FAX Number: (319) 226-2010 — Calendar System: Semester
URL: www.allencollege.edu
Established: 1989 — Annual Undergrad Tuition & Fees: $18,662
Enrollment: 622 — Coed
Affiliation or Control: Independent Non-Profit — IRS Status: 501(c)3
Highest Offering: Doctorate
Accreditation: NH, DMS, MT, NURSE, OT, RAD

01	President	Dr. Jared SELIGER
05	Provost	Dr. Bob LOCH
10	Exec Director Business/Admin Svcs	Ms. Denise HANSON
66	Dean School of Nursing	Dr. Kendra WILLIAMS-PEREZ
76	Dean School of Health Sciences	Dr. Peggy FORTSCH
84	Dean Enrollment Management	Dr. Joanna RAMSDEN-MEIER
37	Director of Financial Aid	Ms. Renae CARRILLO
24	Media Specialist	Ms. Robin NICHOLSON
06	Registrar	Ms. Michelle KOEHN
08	Director of Library Services	Dr. Ruth YAN
07	Director of Admissions	Ms. Molly QUINN
09	Coord Inst Research/Effectiveness	Vacant
04	Administrative Asst to President	Ms. Rhonda GILBERT
28	Director of Diversity	Dr. Doreen MINGO

Antioch School of Church Planting and Leadership Development (G)

2400 Oakwood Road, Ames IA 50014

County: Story — Identification: 667026
Telephone: (515) 292-9694 — Carnegie Class: Not Classified
FAX Number: (515) 292-1933 — Calendar System: Other
URL: www.antiochschool.edu
Established: 2006 — Annual Undergrad Tuition & Fees: N/A
Enrollment: N/A — Coed
Affiliation or Control: Independent Non-Profit — IRS Status: 501(c)3
Highest Offering: Doctorate
Accreditation: DEAC

01	President	Jeff REED
05	Academic Dean	Stephen KEMP

*Board of Regents, State of Iowa (H)

11260 Aurora Avenue, Urbandale IA 50322-7905

County: Polk — FICE Identification: 033443
Telephone: (515) 281-3934 — Carnegie Class: N/A
FAX Number: (515) 281-6420
URL: www.iowaregents.edu

01	President	Dr. Michael J. RICHARDS
00	Executive Director & CEO	Mr. Mark J. BRAUN
05	Chief Academic Officer	Dr. Rachel L. BOON
43	Board Counsel	Mrs. Aimee K. CLAEYS
04	Executive Assistant	Mrs. Laura M. DICKSON

*Iowa State University (I)

Ames IA 50011

County: Story — FICE Identification: 001869
Unit ID: 153603
Telephone: (515) 294-4111 — Carnegie Class: DU-Highest
FAX Number: (515) 294-2592 — Calendar System: Semester
URL: www.iastate.edu
Established: 1858 — Annual Undergrad Tuition & Fees (In-State): $8,988
Enrollment: 36,158 — Coed
Affiliation or Control: State — IRS Status: 501(c)3
Highest Offering: Doctorate
Accreditation: NH, ART, CAATE, CEA, CIDA, COPSY, DIETD, DIETI, IPSY, JOUR, LSAR, MUS, NAIT, PLNG, VET

02	President	Dr. Wendy WINTERSTEEN
04	Assistant to the President	Ms. Shirley J. KNIPFEL
43	University Counsel	Mr. Michael E. NORTON
05	Sr Vice President and Provost	Dr. Jonathan A. WICKERT
10	Int Sr VP for Operations & Finance	Ms. Pam CAIN
32	Sr Vice Pres for Student Affairs	Dr. Martino HARMON
88	Int VP for Econ Dev/Business Engag	Mr. David P. SPALDING
46	Vice Pres Research	Dr. Sarah M. NUSSER
56	Vice Pres Extension/Outreach	Dr. John D. LAWRENCE
13	Int Vice Pres/Chief Info Officer	Dr. Kristin P. CONSTANT
28	Vice Pres for Diversity & Inclusion	Dr. Reginald C. STEWART

Code	Title	Name
20	Associate Provost Academic Programs	Dr. Ann Marie VANDERZANDEN
20	Assoc Prov Faculty	Dr. Dawn BRATSCH-PRINCE
18	Assoc Vice Pres Facilities Planning	Mr. Paul FULIGNI
15	Int Vice President Human Resources	Ms. Kristi DARR
35	Assoc Vice Pres & Dean of Students	Dr. Vernon J. HURTE
84	Assoc VP Stdnt Affs for Enroll Mgmt	Ms. Laura J. DOERING
38	Asst VP Stdnt Health/Wellness	Ms. Erin BALDWIN
30	President of ISU Foundation	Ms. Larissa HOLTMYER-JONES
29	President of Alumni Association	Dr. Jeffrey W. JOHNSON
41	Director of Athletics	Mr. Jamie B. POLLARD
26	Int Exec Dir Strat Rels/Comm	Ms. Jacy R. JOHNSON
06	Int Registrar	Dr. Jennifer SUCHAN
37	Director of Financial Aid	Ms. Roberta L. JOHNSON
07	Director of Admissions	Ms. Katharine JOHNSON SUSKI
22	Asst Vice Pres Equal Opportunity	Ms. Margo FOREMAN
09	Exec Director of Inst Research	Dr. Karen A. ZUNKEL
19	Asst VP and Chief of Police	Mr. Michael R. NEWTON
104	Director Study Abroad	Dr. Frank PETERS
39	Asst VP for St Aff/Dir of Residence	Dr. Peter D. ENGLIN
91	Associate CIO	Mr. David M. POPELKA
25	Assoc Director/Sponsored Pgm Admin	Ms. Tamara R. POLASKI
88	Director Ames Laboratory	Dr. Adam SCHWARTZ
96	Director of Procurement	Mr. Cory L. HARMS
40	Director University Bookstore	Ms. Rita M. PHILLIPS
58	Dean Graduate College	Dr. William R. GRAVES
08	Int Dean of Library Services	Ms. Hillary SEO
47	Dean College of Agriculture	Dr. Daniel J. ROBISON
50	Dean College of Business	Mr. David P. SPALDING
48	Dean College of Design	Mr. Luis C. RICO-GUTIERREZ
53	Dean College of Human Sciences	Dr. Laura JOLLY
54	Dean College of Engineering	Dr. W. Samuel EASTERLING
49	Dean Col of Lib Arts & Sciences	Dr. Beate SCHMITTMANN
74	Dean College of Veterinary Medicine	Dr. Daniel L. GROOMS
102	Sr Dir Dev/Corporate Relations	Mr. Mark BOECK
102	Sr Dir Dev/Foundation Relations	Ms. Donna VAN PELT
44	Exec Dir of Annual & Special Giving	Ms. Mary EVANSON
27	Director of University Marketing	Ms. Carole A. CUSTER

*University of Iowa (A)

5 W. Jefferson St, Iowa City IA 52242

County: Johnson — FICE Identification: 001892 — Unit ID: 153658

Telephone: (319) 335-3565 — Carnegie Class: DU-Highest

FAX Number: (319) 335-3560 — Calendar System: Semester

URL: www.uiowa.edu

Established: 1847 — Annual Undergrad Tuition & Fees (In-State): $9,267

Enrollment: 32,166 — Coed

Affiliation or Control: State — IRS Status: 501(c)3

Highest Offering: Doctorate

Accreditation: NH, ANEST, ARCPA, AUD, CAATE, CACREP, CEA, CLPSY, COPSY, DANCE, DENT, DMS, EMT, HSA, IPSY, JOUR, LAW, LIB, MED, MFCD, MUS, NMT, NURSE, PAST, PCSAS, PERF, PH, PHAR, PLNG, PTA, RAD, RTT, SCPSY, SP, SW, THEA

Code	Title	Name
02	President	Mr. Bruce HARRELD
05	Exec Vice President & Provost	Dr. Montserrat FUENTES
46	VP for Research	Dr. Martin SCHOLTZ
10	SVP Fin & Ops/Chief Financial Ofcr	Mr. Rod LEHNERTZ
32	Vice Pres Student Life	Dr. Melissa SHIVERS
17	VP Med Affairs/Dean College of Med	Dr. J. Brooks JACKSON
30	Vice Pres & Development Officer	Mr. David R. DIERKS
26	Asst VP External Relations	Ms. Jeneane BECK
88	Chief Innovation Officer	Mr. Jon DARSEE
27	Senior Director Marketing Comm	Mr. Ben HILL
20	Associate Provost Faculty	Dr. Kevin KREGEL
28	AVP Diversity/Equity/Inclusion	Vacant
88	Assoc Provost/Dean Univ College	Dr. Tanya UDEN-HOLMAN
45	Sr Assoc Vice President Research	Dr. Richard D. HICHWA
11	Assoc VP/Dir of Admin and Planning	Mr. Donald J. SZESZYCKI
15	Assoc VP Finance/Dir HR	Ms. Cheryl REARDON
18	Assoc VP/Dir Facilities Management	Mr. Donald J. GUCKERT
13	Assoc Vice President & CIO	Mr. Steven R. FLEAGLE
23	Assoc VP/CEO Univ Hosp & Clinics	Mr. Suresh GUNASEKARAN
25	Exec Director Sponsored Programs	Ms. Jennifer LASSNER
19	Asst VP & Director Public Safety	Mr. Scott BECKNER
85	Dean International Programs	Dr. Downing THOMAS
43	VP Legal Affairs & General Counsel	Ms. Carroll REASONER
08	University Librarian	Mr. John P. CULSHAW
102	Pres/CEO Univ Ctr for Advancement	Ms. Lynette L. MARSHALL
44	Asst VP Annual Giving	Ms. Erin ALLEN
07	Director Admissions/Enrollment	Mr. Kirk R. KLUVER
37	Director Student Financial Aid	Mr. Kathy J. BIALK
06	Registrar	Mr. Lawrence J. LOCKWOOD
36	Director Career Center	Ms. Angi MCKIE
38	Director Univ Counseling Services	Dr. Sam V. COCHRAN, III
39	Asst VP Stdnt Life/Sr Dir Hous/Din	Mr. Von STANGE
41	Director Athletics Administration	Mr. Gary BARTA
49	Dean Col of Lib Arts & Sci	Dr. Steve GODDARD
50	Dean College of Business Admin	Dr. Sarah GARDIAL
52	Dean College of Dentistry	Dr. David C. JOHNSEN
53	Dean College of Education	Dr. Daniel CLAY
54	Dean College of Engineering	Dr. Alec SCRANTON
58	Dean Graduate College	Dr. John C. KELLER
61	Dean College of Law	Dr. Kevin WASHBURN
66	Dean College of Nursing	Dr. Julie ZERWIC
67	Dean College of Pharmacy	Dr. Donald E. LETENDRE
69	Dean College of Public Health	Dr. Edith PARKER
04	Special Assistant to President	Dr. Thomas K. DEAN
22	Dir Equal Opportunity/Diversity	Ms. Jennifer A. MODESTOU
86	Director State Relations	Mr. Keith SAUNDERS
40	Director University Bookstore	Mr. George E. HERBERT
96	Assoc VP & Director Purchasing	Ms. Deborah J. ZUMBACH
92	Director Honors Program	Dr. Art L. SPISAK
87	Director Summer Session	Dr. Marlys BOOTE
35	AVP/Dean of Students	Dr. Lyn REDINGTON
84	Assoc VP/Enrollment Management	Dr. Brent GAGE
100	Chief of Staff	Mr. Peter MATTHES
104	Director Study Abroad	Mr. Douglas LEE

*University of Northern Iowa (B)

1227 W 27th Street, Cedar Falls IA 50614-0001

County: Black Hawk — FICE Identification: 001890 — Unit ID: 154095

Telephone: (319) 273-2311 — Carnegie Class: Masters/L

FAX Number: (319) 273-2885 — Calendar System: Semester

URL: https://uni.edu/

Established: 1876 — Annual Undergrad Tuition & Fees (In-State): $8,938

Enrollment: 11,861 — Coed

Affiliation or Control: State — IRS Status: 501(c)3

Highest Offering: Doctorate

Accreditation: NH, CAATE, CACREP, CEA, CIDA, MUS, NAIT, NRPA, SP, SW, THEA

Code	Title	Name
02	President	Dr. Mark A. NOOK
05	Exec VP & Provost	Dr. A. James WOHLPART
10	Sr VP Finance & Operations	Dr. Michael A. HAGER
32	Vice President for Student Affairs	Dr. Paula M. KNUDSON
111	Vice President for Univ Advancement	Mr. Jim JERMIER
84	Assoc VP for Enrollment Management	Vacant
18	Director Physical Plant Admin	Mr. Michael W. ZWANZIGER
39	Asst VP & Exec Dir of Residence	Mr. Glenn P. GRAY
20	Assoc Provost Acad Affairs	Dr. Patrick P. PEASE
20	Assoc Provost for Faculty	Dr. John F. VALLENTINE
13	Chief Information Officer	Ms. Marty L. MARK
09	Dir Inst Research & Effectiveness	Dr. Kristin M. MOSER
06	University Registrar	Ms. Joyce S. MORROW
29	Director Alumni Relations	Ms. Leslie J. PRIDEAUX
37	Director of Financial Aid	Mr. Timothy L. BAKULA
15	Dir Human Resource Services	Ms. Michelle C. BYERS
83	Dean Col Soc/Behav Sciences	Dr. Brenda L. BASS
53	Dean Col Education	Dr. Gadtane JEAN-MARIE
49	Dean Col Hum/Arts & Science	Dr. John E. FRITCH
51	Dean Cont Educ/Special Programs	Dr. Kent M. JOHNSON
58	Dean Graduate College	Dr. Jennifer WALDRON
50	Dean Col Business Admin	Dr. Leslie K. WILSON
35	Dean of Students	Ms. Allyson RAFANELLO
38	Exec Dir Health & Rec Svcs	Ms. Shelley M. O'CONNELL
22	Asst to Pres Compliance/Equity Mgmt	Ms. Leah K. GUTKNECHT
41	Athletic Director	Mr. David W. HARRIS
21	Controller/Treasurer	Ms. Tonya GERBRACHT
86	State Relations Officer	Ms. Mary C. BRAUN
104	Exec Director Intl Programs	Mr. Philip D. PLOURDE
88	Director Undergraduate Studies	Dr. Deirdre A. HEISTAD
19	Chief of Police/Dir Public Safety	Ms. Helen M. HAIRE
25	Dir Research & Sponsored Programs	Mr. Tolif R. HUNT
43	University Counsel	Mr. Timothy J. MCKENNA
88	Dir Business Operations	Ms. Christina GEWEKE
07	Director of Admissions	Vacant
28	Asst to Pres/Chief Div Officer	Ms. Gwennette C. BERRY
124	Dir Student Success and Retention	Dr. Kristin L. WOODS
112	VP for Principal Gifts	Ms. Noreen M. HERMANSEN
36	Director Career Services	Mr. Robert J. FREDERICK
101	Asst to Pres for Board & Govt Rels	Dr. Andrew MORSE

Briar Cliff University (C)

3303 Rebecca Street, Sioux City IA 51104-2324

County: Woodbury — FICE Identification: 001846 — Unit ID: 152992

Telephone: (712) 279-5321 — Carnegie Class: Bac-Diverse

FAX Number: (712) 279-5410 — Calendar System: Semester

URL: www.briarcliff.edu

Established: 1929 — Annual Undergrad Tuition & Fees: $30,970

Enrollment: 1,186 — Coed

Affiliation or Control: Roman Catholic — IRS Status: 501(c)3

Highest Offering: Doctorate

Accreditation: NH, NURSE, PTA, SW

Code	Title	Name
01	President	Ms. Rachelle L. KARSTENS
05	VP Academic Affairs	Dr. Todd KNEALING
10	Vice President Finance & Treasurer	Dr. Daisy HALVORSON
111	Vice Pres University Relations	Mrs. Tina STROUD
84	VP Enrollment Management	Mr. Matt THOMSEN
32	VP Student Dev & Inst Mission	Mrs. Louise PASKEY
06	Registrar	Mrs. Deidre ENGEL
08	Librarian/Dir Information Services	Ms. Breanne KIRSCH
13	Director Computer Center	Ms. Leah WARD
36	Director Career Development	Mr. Joshua COBBS
37	Director Financial Aid	Ms. Monica GANNON
40	Director Bookstore	Ms. Nancy WATSON
41	Athletic Director	Mr. Nic SCANDRETT
42	Director Campus Ministry	Sr. Janet MAY
18	Director Physical Plant	Ms. Angela WASHBURN
26	Director Marketing & Communications	Vacant
15	Director Human Resources	Mr. Beau SUDTELGTE
39	Director Residence Life	Mr. Dave ARENS
38	Director Student Counseling	Mrs. Jeanette TOBIN
09	Director of Institutional Research	Ms. Deidre ENGEL
30	Director of Philanthropy	Mrs. Carolyn ELLWANGER
19	Director Security/Safety	Mr. Marty POTTEBAUM
04	Admin Assistant to the President	Ms. Bernice METZ

Buena Vista University (D)

610 W Fourth Street, Storm Lake IA 50588-1798

County: Buena Vista — FICE Identification: 001847 — Unit ID: 153001

Telephone: (712) 749-2351 — Carnegie Class: Masters/M

FAX Number: (712) 749-2037 — Calendar System: 4/1/4

URL: www.bvu.edu

Established: 1891 — Annual Undergrad Tuition & Fees: $34,004

Enrollment: 1,982 — Coed

Affiliation or Control: Presbyterian Church (U.S.A.) — IRS Status: 501(c)3

Highest Offering: Master's

Accreditation: NH, #CAATE, SW

Code	Title	Name
01	President	Dr. Joshua D. MERCHANT
04	Assistant to the President	Ms. Katelyn C. ADAMS
05	VP Acad Affairs/Dean of Faculty	Dr. Brian LENZMEIER
10	Vice President Business Services	Ms. Suzette RADKE
84	Vice Pres for Enrollment Management	Mr. Kevin M. MCINTYRE
32	VP Student Success/DOS	Ms. Lucy CROFT
111	Vice Pres for Inst Advancement	Vacant
30	Assistant VP of Development	Mr. Zach RUS
81	Dean School of Science	Dr. Thom BONAGURA
50	Dean HWS School of Business	Ms. Lisa BEST
53	Dean School of Education	Dr. Ann MONROE-BAILLARGEON
49	Dean School of Liberal Arts	Dr. Dixee BARTHOLOMEW-FEIS
58	Exec Dir of Graduate Programs	Vacant
06	Registrar	Ms. Nila HOUSKA
07	Exec Director of Admissions	Mr. Nick BOONE
15	Human Resources Manager	Ms. Melissa BUTCHER
08	Actg Dir of Library/Ref Librarian	Ms. Jodie MORIN
26	Chief Marketing Officer	Mr. Rick PALLISTER
29	Director of Alumni Rels/Annual Fund	Vacant
13	Chief Information Officer	Mr. Mark LUMSDEN
18	Director Facilities Management	Mr. Keith E. SCHMIDT
36	Dir Career & Personal Development	Ms. Lori BERGLUND
37	Director of Financial Assistance	Ms. Leanne VALENTINE
28	Dir of Multicultural Engagement	Ms. Ebony KING
41	Athletic Director	Ms. Jack DENHOLM
42	Chaplain	Rev. Ken MEISSNER
19	Director of Campus Security	Ms. Jessica GARLING
09	Institutional Researcher	Mr. James E. HEWETT
96	Purchasing Administrator	Ms. Tanya LANDGRAF

Central College (E)

812 University, Pella IA 50219-1999

County: Marion — FICE Identification: 001850 — Unit ID: 153108

Telephone: (641) 628-9000 — Carnegie Class: Bac-A&S

FAX Number: (641) 628-5316 — Calendar System: Semester

URL: www.central.edu

Established: 1853 — Annual Undergrad Tuition & Fees: $37,296

Enrollment: 1,237 — Coed

Affiliation or Control: Reformed Church In America — IRS Status: 501(c)3

Highest Offering: Baccalaureate

Accreditation: NH, CAATE, MUS

Code	Title	Name
01	President	Dr. Mark L. PUTNAM
05	VP Academic Affairs/Dean of Faculty	Dr. Mary M. STREY
111	Vice President Advancement	Mrs. Sunny EIGHMY
84	VP Enrollment Mgmt & Student Devel	Mrs. Carol WILLIAMSON
10	Vice Pres for Finance & Admin	Mr. Thomas JOHNSON
20	Director of Academic Resources	Mr. Eric JONES
32	Dean of Students	Mr. Charles STREY
07	Executive Director of Admission	Mr. Chevy FREIBURGER
38	Director of Counseling	Ms. Michelle KELLAR
39	Assistant Dean of Students	Ms. Melissa SHARKEY
08	Director of Geisler Library	Ms. Beth MCMAHON
36	Director of Career & Prof Develop	Mrs. Jessica KLYN DE NOVELA
44	Dir Annual Giving & Alumni Engage	Mr. Corey FALTER
37	Director Financial Aid	Mr. Wayne DILLE
104	Associate Director of Study Abroad	Mr. Brian ZYLSTRA
13	Chief Information Officer	Ms. Debra BRUXVOORT
42	Chaplain	Rev. Joe BRUMMEL
85	Asst Dean of Intl Education	Mr. Matthew KAYE
15	Director of Human Resources	Ms. Paula RYAN
41	Athletics Director	Mr. Eric VAN KLEY
18	Dir of Facilities Management	Mr. Craig ROOSE
06	Registrar	Ms. Leslie DUININK
04	Administrative Asst to President	Ms. Carma STURTZ
09	Institutional Research Director	Vacant
96	Dir of Purchasing & Facility Svcs	Mrs. Janine FONTANA
112	Major Gifts Officer	Mr. Doyle MONSMA
112	Major Gifts Officer	Mrs. Kathy CASHEN-THOMPSON
112	Major Gifts Officer	Mrs. Michelle WILKIE
112	Major Gifts Officer	Mrs. Hannah GOURLEY
88	Director of External Engagement	Ms. Jenae JENISON

Clarke University (F)

1550 Clarke Drive, Dubuque IA 52001-3198

County: Dubuque — FICE Identification: 001852 — Unit ID: 153126

Telephone: (563) 588-6300 — Carnegie Class: DU-Mod

FAX Number: (563) 588-6789 — Calendar System: Semester

URL: www.clarke.edu

Established: 1843 — Annual Undergrad Tuition & Fees: $33,350

Enrollment: 1,039 — Coed

Affiliation or Control: Roman Catholic — IRS Status: 501(c)3

Highest Offering: Doctorate

Accreditation: NH, CAATE, MUS, NURSE, PTA, SW

01	President	Dr. Thom D. CHESNEY
04	Exec Admin Assistant to President	Ms. Kathy TEIG
05	Vice Pres Academic Affs	Dr. Susan R. BURNS
111	Vice Pres Institutional Advancement	Mr. Bill BIEBUYCK
32	Vice President Student Life	Ms. Kate ZANGER
10	Vice President Business & Finance	Ms. Elizabeth MCGRATH
84	Vice President Enrollment Mgmt	Vacant
88	Assistant to the President	Ms. Megan STULL
06	Registrar	Ms. Kristi BAGSTAD
08	Director of Library	Ms. Susanne LEIBOLD
58	Dean College of Prof & Grad Studies	Dr. Paula SCHMIDT
49	Dean College of Arts & Sciences	Dr. Norma PEREZ-KAHLER
37	Director of Financial Aid	Mr. Robert HOOVER
26	Director of Marketing	Ms. Amy ERRTHUM
13	Chief Technology Officer	Mr. Andy BELLINGS
18	Exec Dir of Facilities Management	Mr. Steven KIRSCHBAUM
38	Asst Dir of Counseling/Career Svcs	Ms. Becky HERRIG
15	Director of Human Resources	Ms. Jody PFOHL
41	Director of Athletics	Mr. Curt LONG
42	Director of Campus Ministry	Mr. Hunter DARROUZET
40	Director of the Bookstore	Ms. Sarah HAAS
23	Director of Health Services	Ms. Tammy MOORE
90	Asst Dean Acad Affairs/Inst Supp	Mr. Pat MADDUX
07	Director of Admissions	Ms. Jolene CHRISTENSEN
30	Exec Director of Development	Ms. Courtney LEONARD
29	Assoc Dir of Alumni Relations	Ms. Jodi HOOKS
85	International Students Advisor	Ms. Evelyn NADEAU

Coe College (A)

1220 1st Avenue, NE, Cedar Rapids IA 52402-5092
County: Linn — FICE Identification: 001854
Unit ID: 153144
Telephone: (319) 399-8000 — Carnegie Class: Bac-A&S
FAX Number: (319) 399-8830 — Calendar System: Semester
URL: www.coe.edu
Established: 1851 — Annual Undergrad Tuition & Fees: $44,050
Enrollment: 1,394 — Coed
Affiliation or Control: Independent Non-Profit — IRS Status: 501(c)3
Highest Offering: Baccalaureate
Accreditation: NH, CAATE, MUS, NURSE

01	President	Dr. David W. MCINALLY
05	Provost/Dean of Faculty	Dr. Paula O'LOUGHLIN
111	Vice President for Advancement	Mr. David HAYES
07	VP for Admission & Marketing	Ms. Julie STAKER
06	Registrar	Ms. Catherine ASHTON
08	Director Library Services	Ms. Jill JACK
29	Director Alumni Programs	Ms. Emily EHRHARDT
09	Director of Institutional Research	Dr. Wendy L. DUNN
37	Director of Financial Aid	Ms. Barbara HOFFMAN
20	Associate Dean	Dr. Angela ZISKOWSKI
35	Dean of Students	Mr. Marc BRADY
85	International Student Advisor	Mr. John CHAIMOV
42	Chaplain	Ms. Melea WHITE
41	Director of Athletics	Mr. Sonny TRAVIS
18	Director of Physical Plant	Ms. Lisa CIHA
36	Dir of Internships/Career Services	Ms. Barb TUPPER
15	Director of Human Resources	Ms. Kristina BRIDGES
04	Administrative Asst to President	Ms. Kim PRIBYL
13	Chief Info Technology Officer	Ms. Deb BAHR
19	Director Security/Safety	Mr. Carlos VELEZ
44	Director Annual/Planned Giving	Ms. Mary SPRINGER

Cornell College (B)

600 First Street SW, Mount Vernon IA 52314-1098
County: Linn — FICE Identification: 001856
Unit ID: 153162
Telephone: (319) 895-4000 — Carnegie Class: Bac-A&S
FAX Number: (319) 895-4492 — Calendar System: Other
URL: www.cornellcollege.edu
Established: 1853 — Annual Undergrad Tuition & Fees: $42,299
Enrollment: 1,009 — Coed
Affiliation or Control: United Methodist — IRS Status: 501(c)3
Highest Offering: Master's
Accreditation: NH

01	President	Mr. Jonathan BRAND
05	VP Acad Affairs/Dean of College	Dr. R. Joseph DIEKER
10	Vice President Business Affairs	Ms. Kay LANGSETH
84	Vice Pres Enrollment/Dn Admission	Dr. Thomas CRADY
32	Vice President Student Affairs	Mr. John W. HARP
111	VP for Alumni & College Advancement	Ms. Pam GERARD
35	Dean of Students	Dr. Gwendolyn SCHIMEK
20	Associate Dean of the College	Dr. Erin DAVIS
09	Director of Institutional Research	Vacant
37	Director of Student Financial Asst	Ms. Pamela PERRY
06	Registrar	Ms. Megan HICKS
08	College Librarian	Mr. Gregory COTTON
29	Director of Alumni & Annual Giving	Mr. RJ HOLMES-LEOPOLD
30	Senior Director of Development	Ms. Kristi COLUMBUS
26	Senior Dir Marketing/Communications	Ms. Jen VISSER
42	Chaplain	Rev Dr. Catherine M. QUEHL-ENGEL
41	Athletics Director	Mr. Keith HACKETT
18	Facilities Operations Manager	Mr. Luke FISCHER
36	Senior Dir Berry Career Institute	Ms. Jodi SCHAFER
38	Director Student Counseling	Dr. Brenda C. LOVSTUEN
15	Director of Human Resources	Ms. Stefanie BRAY
07	Director of Admission Operations	Ms. Sharon GRICE
13	Director of Information Technology	Mr. Jeff GIBSON
40	Manager Bookstore	Ms. Lee Ann GRIMLEY
04	Executive Asst to President	Ms. RuthAnn SCHEER
101	Secretary to the Board of Trustees	Ms. RuthAnn SCHEER
19	Campus Safety Director	Mr. Mark WINDER

Des Moines Area Community College (C)

2006 S Ankeny Boulevard, Ankeny IA 50023-3993
County: Polk — FICE Identification: 007120
Unit ID: 153214
Telephone: (515) 964-6200 — Carnegie Class: Assoc/HT-High Non
FAX Number: N/A — Calendar System: Semester
URL: www.dmacc.edu
Established: 1966 — Annual Undergrad Tuition & Fees (In-District): $4,680
Enrollment: 22,982 — Coed
Affiliation or Control: State/Local — IRS Status: 501(c)3
Highest Offering: Associate Degree
Accreditation: NH, ACFEI, ADNUR, COARC, DA, DH, EMT, FUSER, MAC, MLTAD, SURGT

01	President/CEO	Dr. Rob DENSON
05	Exec Vice Pres College Operations	Vacant
10	Vice President Academic Affairs	Mr. Scott OCKEN
84	Vice Pres Enrollment Management	Ms. Shelli ALLEN
13	Exec Dir Information Solutions	Mr. Mark CLARK
12	Provost Urban Campus	Dr. Anne HOWSARE
12	Provost Boone Campus	Mr. Andrew NELSON
12	Provost Carroll Campus	Mr. Joel LUNDSTROM
12	Provost Newton Campus	Dr. Joe DEHART
12	Provost West Campus	Dr. Tony PAUSTIAN
15	Executive Director Human Resources	Dr. Jenifer OWENSON
18	Executive Director Physical Plant	Mr. Greg MARTIN
102	Executive Director Foundation	Ms. Tara CONNOLLY
51	Exec Dir Continuing Education	Mr. Michael HOFFMAN
50	Exec Dir Business Resources	Ms. Kim DIDIER
36	Director Student Development	Mr. Wade ROBINSON
37	Director Financial Aid	Mr. Ean FREELS
26	Director of Marketing	Mr. Todd JONES
25	Director Grants/Contracts	Ms. Deb KOUA
19	Dir Energy Mgt/Safety/Security	Mr. Jay TIEFENTHALER
06	Registrar	Vacant
27	Media Liaison	Mr. Dan IVIS
81	Dean Sciences & Humanities	Mr. Jim STICK
72	Dean Industrial & Technology	Dr. Jennifer FOSTER
76	Dean Health Service & Science	Mr. Art BROWN
50	Dean Business/Mgmt/Information Tech	Mr. MD ISLEY
55	Dean SEMSS	Vacant
106	Dean Online Learning	Dr. Thomas AYERS
56	Assoc Dean Industry & Tech	Vacant
55	Dean Evening & Weekend College	Ms. Andrea ISEMINGER
08	Head Librarian	Ms. Rebecca FUNKE
45	Sourcing Specialist	Ms. Julie KLOCKE
41	Athletic Director	Mr. BJ MCGINN
101	Secretary of the Board	Ms. Carolyn FARLOW
04	Admin Assistant to the President	Ms. Amanda RAMSEY
09	Director of Institutional Research	Dr. Janet EMMERSON

Des Moines Area Community College Boone Campus (D)

1125 Hancock Drive, Boone IA 50036
Telephone: (515) 432-7203 — Identification: 770048
Accreditation: &NH

Des Moines Area Community College Carroll Campus (E)

906 North Grant Road, Carroll IA 51401-2525
Telephone: (712) 792-1755 — Identification: 770049
Accreditation: &NH

Des Moines Area Community College Newton Campus (F)

600 N 2nd Avenue West, Newton IA 50208
Telephone: (641) 791-3622 — Identification: 770051
Accreditation: &NH

Des Moines Area Community College Urban Campus (G)

1100 7th Street, Des Moines IA 50314
Telephone: (515) 244-4226 — Identification: 770050
Accreditation: &NH

Des Moines Area Community College West Des Moines Campus (H)

5959 Grand Avenue, West Des Moines IA 50266
Telephone: (515) 633-2407 — Identification: 770052
Accreditation: &NH

Des Moines University (I)

3200 Grand Avenue, Des Moines IA 50312-4198
County: Polk — FICE Identification: 001855
Unit ID: 154156
Telephone: (515) 271-1400 — Carnegie Class: Spec-4-yr-Med
FAX Number: (515) 271-1532 — Calendar System: Other
URL: www.dmu.edu
Established: 1898 — Annual Graduate Tuition & Fees: N/A
Enrollment: 1,575 — Coed
Affiliation or Control: Independent Non-Profit — IRS Status: 501(c)3
Highest Offering: First Professional Degree; No Undergraduates
Accreditation: NH, ARCPA, HSA, OSTEO, PH, POD, PTA

01	President/CEO	Dr. Angela L. WALKER FRANKLIN
05	Provost	Dr. Ralitsa AKINS
10	Senior Vice President & CFO	Mr. Mark PEIFFER
84	VP Enrollment Mgmt/Student Svcs	Ms. Kimberly BROWN
86	Chief External & Govt Affs Officer	Ms. Susan HUPPERT
46	Vice President for Research	Dr. Jeffrey GRAY
06	Registrar	Ms. Melinda MILLER
08	Director of Library	Ms. Natalie HUTCHINSON
15	Chief Human Resources Officer	Ms. Becky LADE
13	Chief Information Officer	Ms. Carolyn WEAVER
37	Director of Financial Aid	Ms. Mary PAYNE
18	Director of Facilities Management	Mr. John HARRIS
19	Building Services Manager	Mr. Philip BAUGHMAN
108	Chief Compliance Officer	Ms. Erika LINDEN
69	Director Public Health Program	Dr. Rachel REIMER
26	Chief Strategic Comm Officer	Mr. Mark DANES
76	Dean College Health Sciences	Dr. Jodi CAHALAN
63	Dean Col Podiatric Medicine/Surg	Dr. Robert YOHO
63	Dean Col Osteopathic Medicine	Dr. Steven HALM
04	Executive Asst to President	Ms. Christina HENDERSON
07	Director of Admissions/Recruitment	Ms. Molly MOELLER
32	Director of Student Services	Ms. Alicia LYNCH
28	Director of Multicultural Affairs	Dr. Richard SALAS
29	Director Alumni Relations	Ms. Krystal KRUSE
30	Chief Development Officer	Ms. Stephanie GREINER
101	Secretary of the Institution/Board	Ms. Linda KADING
38	Director Student Counseling	Dr. Ciara LEWIS
44	Director Annual Giving	Ms. Katie STEVENSON
22	Director/Chief Diversity Officer	Dr. Rich SALAS
25	Grants and Contract Manager	Ms. Mollie LYON

† Tuition varies by degree program.

Divine Word College (J)

102 Jacoby Drive, SW, PO Box 380,
Epworth IA 52045-0380
County: Dubuque — FICE Identification: 001858
Unit ID: 153241
Telephone: (563) 876-3353 — Carnegie Class: Spec-4-yr-Faith
FAX Number: (563) 876-3407 — Calendar System: Semester
URL: www.dwci.edu
Established: 1918 — Annual Undergrad Tuition & Fees: $13,160
Enrollment: 71 — Male
Affiliation or Control: Roman Catholic — IRS Status: 501(c)3
Highest Offering: Baccalaureate
Accreditation: NH

01	President	Fr. Thomas ASCHEMAN, SVD
05	Vice President Academic Affairs	Dr. John SZUKALSKI, SVD
11	Vice President Operations	Mr. Steven WINGER
07	Vice President for Admission	Mr. Len UHAL
10	Chief Financial/Business Officer	Ms. Marlene DECKER
32	Dean of Students	Rev. Bang TRAN, SVD
26	Public Relations Director	Ms. Sandy WILGENBUSCH
08	Librarian	Mr. Daniel C. WILLIAMS
06	Registrar	Vacant
38	Counselor	Ms. Megan SUTTON
104	Director Study Abroad	Rev. Kenneth ANICH, SVD
13	Chief Info Technology Officer (CIO)	Mr. Brad FLORENCE
30	Development Director	Rev. Linh PHAM, SVD
09	Director of Institutional Research	Mr. Paul D. STAMM
37	Student Financial Aid Coordinator	Ms. Carolyn WAECHTER
04	Admin Assistant to the President	Ms. Donna PUCCIO
29	Director Alumni Affairs	Rev. Thang HOANG, SVD

Dordt University (K)

700 7th St. NE, Sioux Center IA 51250-1697
County: Sioux — FICE Identification: 001859
Unit ID: 153250
Telephone: (712) 722-6000 — Carnegie Class: Bac-Diverse
FAX Number: (712) 722-6035 — Calendar System: Semester
URL: www.dordt.edu
Established: 1955 — Annual Undergrad Tuition & Fees: $30,840
Enrollment: 1,533 — Coed
Affiliation or Control: Christian Reformed Church — IRS Status: 501(c)3
Highest Offering: Master's
Accreditation: NH, NURSE, SW

01	President	Dr. Erik HOEKSTRA
05	Provost	Dr. Eric A. FORSETH
111	Vice President College Advancement	Mr. John BAAS
84	VP for Enrollment & Marketing	Mr. Brandon HUISMAN
106	VP for Online & Grad Programs	Dr. Leah ZUIDEMA
11	Vice President for Administration	Mr. Howard WILSON
88	Director of Global Education	Mr. Adam ADAMS
10	Exec Dir of Finance & Risk	Mrs. Stephanie BACCAM
37	Director Financial Aid	Mr. Harlan HARMELINK
06	Registrar	Mr. James BOS
88	Director for Research & Scholarship	Dr. Nathan TINTLE
58	Director Graduate Studies	Dr. Steve HOLTROP
36	Career Services Coordinator	Ms. Amy WESTRA
26	Marketing and Public Relations	Ms. Sarah MOSS
18	Director Physical Plant	Mr. Nate VAN NIEJENHUIS
32	Dean of Campus Life	Mr. Robert TAYLOR
42	Dean of Chapel	Rev. Aaron BAART
41	Director of Athletics	Mr. Ross DOUMA
40	Director Bookstore/Purchasing	Ms. Lora DEVRIES

112 Director of Planned Giving ..... Mr. Dave VANDER WERF
15 Director Human Resources ..... Mrs. Sue DROOG
96 Director of Purchasing ..... Mr. Patrick SINNEMA
91 Director of Computer Services ..... Mr. Brian VAN DONSELAAR
08 Director of Library Services ..... Ms. Jennifer BREEMS
23 Director of Health Services ..... Ms. Beth BAAS
88 Director Academic Skills Center ..... Ms. Sharon ROSENBOOM
04 Exec Admin Asst to President ..... Mrs. LeeAnn MOERMAN
07 Director of Admissions ..... Mr. Greg VAN DYKE

Drake University (A)

2507 University Avenue, Des Moines IA 50311-4505
County: Polk FICE Identification: 001860
Unit ID: 153269
Telephone: (515) 271-2011 Carnegie Class: DU-Mod
FAX Number: (515) 271-3016 Calendar System: Semester
URL: www.drake.edu
Established: 1881 Annual Undergrad Tuition & Fees: $41,396
Enrollment: 4,904 Coed
Affiliation or Control: Independent Non-Profit IRS Status: 501(c)3
Highest Offering: Doctorate
Accreditation: NH, ART, CACREP, JOUR, LAW, MUS, OT, PHAR

01 President ..... Mr. Earl F. MARTIN
05 Provost ..... Dr. Sue MATTISON
10 Interim Chief Financial Officer ..... Ms. Heather TRAVIS
11 Chief Administrative Officer ..... Ms. Venessa MACRO
111 Vice Pres University Advancement ..... Mr. John SMITH
07 Dean of Admission ..... Ms. Anne KREMER
20 Associate Provost of Curriculum ..... Mr. Art SANDERS
32 Associate Prov Student Affairs ..... Ms. Melissa STURM-SMITH
35 Dean of Students ..... Dr. Jerry PARKER
15 Human Resources Director ..... Ms. Mary Alice HILL
13 Chief Tech Information Officer ..... Mr. Chris GILL
18 Director Capital Projects ..... Ms. Jolene SCHMIDT
09 Dir of Inst Research & Assessment ..... Mr. Kevin SAUNDERS
06 Director of Student Records ..... Mr. Kevin P. MOENKHAUS
08 Dean Cowles Library ..... Ms. Gillian GREMMELS
85 Exec Dir Global Eng & Intl Pgm ..... Dr. Annique KIEL
19 Director Public Safety ..... Mr. Scott LAW
26 Director University Communications ..... Mr. Dave REMUND
29 Alumni/Parent Programs ..... Mr. Andrew VERLENGIA
49 Dean Arts & Sciences ..... Dr. Gesine GERHARD
53 Dean School Education ..... Dr. Janet M. MCMAHILL
61 Dean Law School ..... Mr. Jerry ANDERSON
50 Dean Business/Public Administration ..... Dr. Daniel CONNOLLY
67 Dean Pharmacy/Health Science ..... Dr. Renae CHESNUT
60 Dean Journ/Mass Communications ... Ms. Kathleen RICHARDSON
41 Director Intercollegiate Athletics ..... Mr. Brian HARDIN
37 Director Financial Aid ..... Mr. Ryan ZANTINGH
38 Director University Counseling Ctr ..... Dr. Mark KLOBERDANZ
92 Assistant Director Honors Program ..... Ms. Charlene SKIDMORE
94 Director Women's Studies ..... Dr. Nancy REINCKE
39 Director Office of Residence Life ..... Ms. Lorissa SOWDEN
04 Asst to President ..... Ms. Cheryle ANANIA
100 Chief of Staff ..... Mr. Nate REAGEN
30 Director of Development ..... Mr. John AMATO
96 Director of Purchasing ..... Ms. Caron FINDLEY

*Eastern Iowa Community College District (B)

101 West Third Street, Davenport IA 52801-1221
County: Scott FICE Identification: 004075
Unit ID: 153311
Telephone: (563) 336-3300 Carnegie Class: N/A
FAX Number: (563) 322-0129
URL: www.eicc.edu

01 Chancellor ..... Dr. Donald S. DOUCETTE
30 Exec Dir Resource Development ..... Dr. Ellen BLUTH
05 Vice Chanc for Education & Training ..... Dr. Joan KINDLE
27 Associate Director Communications ..... Mr. Alan CAMPBELL
10 Chief Business Officer ..... Mr. Suteesh TANDON
101 Secretary of the Institution/Board ..... Ms. Honey BEDELL
15 Director Personnel Services ..... Ms. Deb SULLIVAN
18 Chief Facilities/Physical Plant ..... Mr. Matt SCHMIT
84 Director Enrollment Management ..... Ms. Erin SNYDER

*Clinton Community College (C)

1000 Lincoln Boulevard, Clinton IA 52732-6299
County: Clinton FICE Identification: 001853
Telephone: (563) 244-7001 Carnegie Class: Not Classified
FAX Number: (563) 244-7107 Calendar System: Semester
URL: www.eicc.edu
Established: 1966 Annual Undergrad Tuition & Fees (In-District): N/A
Enrollment: N/A Coed
Affiliation or Control: State/Local IRS Status: 501(c)3
Highest Offering: Associate Degree
Accreditation: &NH, EMT

02 President ..... Dr. Karen VICKERS
05 Dean of the College ..... Mr. Gabe KNIGHT
32 Dean of Student Development ..... Ms. Lisa MILLER
102 Asst to Pres/Exec Dir Sharar Found ..... Ms. Ann EISENMAN
04 Assistant to President/Admin ..... Vacant

† Regional accreditation is carried under the parent institution Eastern Iowa Community College District in Davenport, IA.

*Muscatine Community College (D)

152 Colorado Street, Muscatine IA 52761-5396
County: Muscatine FICE Identification: 001882
Telephone: (563) 288-6001 Carnegie Class: Not Classified
FAX Number: (563) 288-6074 Calendar System: Semester
URL: www.eicc.edu
Established: 1929 Annual Undergrad Tuition & Fees (In-District): N/A
Enrollment: N/A Coed
Affiliation or Control: State/Local IRS Status: 501(c)3
Highest Offering: Associate Degree
Accreditation: &NH, EMT

02 President ..... Dr. Naomi DEWINTER
04 Assistant to the President ..... Ms. Lisa WIEGEL
05 Dean of the College ..... Dr. Jeremy PICKARD
32 Dean of Student Development ..... Ms. Shelly CRAM-RAHLF
06 Registrar ..... Ms. Robin MITCHELL
08 Library Specialist ..... Ms. Nancy LUIKART

† Regional accreditation is carried under the parent institution Eastern Iowa Community College District in Davenport, IA.

*Scott Community College (E)

500 Belmont Road, Bettendorf IA 52722-6804
County: Scott FICE Identification: 001885
Telephone: (563) 441-4001 Carnegie Class: Not Classified
FAX Number: (563) 441-4154 Calendar System: Semester
URL: www.eicc.edu
Established: 1966 Annual Undergrad Tuition & Fees (In-District): N/A
Enrollment: N/A Coed
Affiliation or Control: State/Local IRS Status: 501(c)3
Highest Offering: Associate Degree
Accreditation: &NH, CAHIIM, DA, EMT, RAD, SURGT

02 President ..... Dr. Lyn COCHRAN
32 Dean of Student Development/Affs ..... Dr. LaDrina WILSON
103 Dean Career Assistance Center ..... Dr. Scott SCHNEIDER
05 Dean of the College ..... Dr. Ann LAWLER
08 Librarian ..... Ms. Michelle BAILEY
11 Dean of Operations ..... Dr. Matt SCHMIT
37 Director Student Financial Aid ..... Ms. Katy RUSH
36 Job Placement Specialist ..... Mr. Wayne COLE

† Regional accreditation is carried under the parent institution Eastern Iowa Community College District in Davenport, IA.

Emmaus Bible College (F)

2570 Asbury Road, Dubuque IA 52001-3096
County: Dubuque FICE Identification: 023289
Unit ID: 153302
Telephone: (563) 588-8000 Carnegie Class: Spec-4-yr-Faith
FAX Number: (563) 588-1216 Calendar System: Semester
URL: www.emmaus.edu
Established: 1941 Annual Undergrad Tuition & Fees: $18,400
Enrollment: 267 Coed
Affiliation or Control: Independent Non-Profit IRS Status: 501(c)3
Highest Offering: Baccalaureate
Accreditation: NH, BI

01 President ..... Mr. Philip BOOM
10 VP for Administration and Finance ..... Mr. Mark A. PRESSON
05 Vice President for Academic Affairs ..... Mrs. Lisa L. BEATTY
111 Vice President for Advancement ..... Mr. Bill LONGSTREET
32 Dean for Student Development ..... Mr. Israel CHAVEZ
73 Chair Bible & Theology ..... Mr. Raju KUNJUMMEN
08 Librarian ..... Mr. John H. RUSH
37 Financial Aid Officer ..... Mr. Steve C. SEEMAN
21 Controller ..... Mr. Steve M. JENSEN
06 Registrar ..... Mrs. Janice G. BENNETT
106 Dir Online Education/E-learning ..... Vacant
108 Director Institutional Assessment ..... Ms. Sherri L. POPP
29 Director Alumni Relations ..... Mr. Jonathan J. ROUTLEY
41 Athletic Director ..... Mr. Chris MCHUGH
84 Director Enrollment Management ..... Ms. Laurel R. RASMUSSEN
18 Chief Facilities/Physical Plant ..... Mr. Jeremy MAU
26 Chief Public Relations/Marketing ..... Vacant
04 Administrative Asst to President ..... Ms. Laura GUERRA
50 Chair Business Department ..... Mr. Kim PARCHER
39 Dir Resident Life/Student Housing ..... Ms. Hannah LEAVITT
13 Director Technology ..... Mr. Mark NEWLAND

Faith Baptist Bible College and Seminary (G)

1900 NW 4th Street, Ankeny IA 50023-2152
County: Polk FICE Identification: 007121
Unit ID: 153320
Telephone: (515) 964-0601 Carnegie Class: Spec-4-yr-Faith
FAX Number: (515) 964-1638 Calendar System: Semester
URL: www.faith.edu
Established: 1921 Annual Undergrad Tuition & Fees: $16,876
Enrollment: 356 Coed
Affiliation or Control: Independent Non-Profit IRS Status: 501(c)3
Highest Offering: Doctorate
Accreditation: NH, BI

01 President ..... Dr. James R. TILLOTSON
03 Executive Vice President ..... Dr. Martin T. HERRON
05 VP for Academic Services ..... Dr. Kenneth D. RATHBUN
73 Dean of Seminary ..... Dr. Douglas E. BROWN
10 VP for Business/CFO ..... Mr. Paul BRAY
111 VP for Advancement/Church Rels ..... Mr. Daniel H. BJOKNE
34 Dean of Women ..... Mrs. Sandy CAPON
32 Dean of Students ..... Mr. Brandon J. FRITZ
26 Director of Communications ..... Mr. Andrew GOGERTY
06 Registrar ..... Mr. Jeff BUNJER
37 Director Student Financial Aid ..... Mr. Jordan SAUSER
08 Head Librarian ..... Dr. Paul A. HARTOG
04 Administrative Asst to President ..... Miss Briana K. HARRIER
07 VP for Enrollment and Student Life ..... Mr. Mark L. DAVIS
106 Dir Online Education/E-learning ..... Dr. Christopher E. ELLIS
41 Athletic Director ..... Mr. Brian S. FINCHAM

Graceland University (H)

1 University Place, Lamoni IA 50140-1699
County: Decatur FICE Identification: 001866
Unit ID: 153366
Telephone: (641) 784-5000 Carnegie Class: Masters/L
FAX Number: (641) 784-5480 Calendar System: Trimester
URL: www.graceland.edu
Established: 1895 Annual Undergrad Tuition & Fees: $29,240
Enrollment: 2,262 Coed
Affiliation or Control: Other IRS Status: 501(c)3
Highest Offering: Doctorate
Accreditation: NH

01 President ..... Dr. Patricia H. DRAVES
05 VP Acad Affairs/Dean of Faculty ..... Dr. Jill RHEA
108 VP Institutional Effectiveness ..... Dr. Kathleen M. CLAUSON BASH
10 Vice Pres Business/Finance ..... Mr. David SIDDALL
32 VP Student Life/Dean of Students ..... Mr. Dave SCHAAL
84 Vice Pres Enrollment ..... Mr. Scott BRIELL
111 Vice Pres Institutional Advancement ..... Mr. Kelly EVERETT
51 Director Graduate/Continuing Educ ..... Mr. Paul BINNICKER
39 Director of Residence Life ..... Ms. Deb SKINNER
06 Registrar ..... Mrs. Peggy MOTHERSHEAD
29 Director of Alumni Relations ..... Mr. Paul J. DAVIS
15 Director Human Resources ..... Mrs. Ondrea DORY
04 Executive Asst to President ..... Mrs. Jodi SEYMOUR
44 Director of Annual Fund/Stewardship ..... Ms. Paula ANDERSON
85 Director Intercultural Office ..... Ms. Diana JONES
50 Dean School of Business ..... Mr. Jeff MCELROY
53 Dean School of Education ..... Dr. Michele DICKEY-KOTZ
66 Dean School of Nursing ..... Dr. Sharon LITTLE-STOETZEL
07 Director of Admissions ..... Mr. Kevin BROWN
09 Director of Institutional Research ..... Ms. Stacy GIBBS
124 Director of Retention ..... Mrs. Nicole BRIELL

Grand View University (I)

1200 Grandview Avenue, Des Moines IA 50316-1599
County: Polk FICE Identification: 001867
Unit ID: 153375
Telephone: (515) 263-2800 Carnegie Class: Bac-Diverse
FAX Number: (515) 263-6095 Calendar System: Semester
URL: www.grandview.edu
Established: 1896 Annual Undergrad Tuition & Fees: $27,608
Enrollment: 1,836 Coed
Affiliation or Control: Evangelical Lutheran Church In America
IRS Status: 501(c)3
Highest Offering: Master's
Accreditation: NH, CAATE, NURSE, SW

01 President ..... Mr. Kent L. HENNING
04 Exec Admin Asst to the President ..... Ms. Corinna KING
05 Provost/Vice Pres Academic Affairs ..... Dr. Carl MOSES
79 Dean College of Humanities & Educ ..... Dr. Ross WASTVEDT
83 Dean College of Social/Nat Science ..... Dr. Paul RIDER
10 Vice Pres Administration & Finance ..... Mr. Adam J. VOIGTS
111 Vice President Advancement ..... Mr. William H. BURMA
84 Vice Pres Enrollment Management ..... Ms. Debbie M. BARGER
26 Vice Pres Marketing/Communications ..... Ms. Kendall DILLON
32 Vice President Student Affairs ..... Dr. Jay B. PRESCOTT
13 Vice President Information Svcs/CIO ..... Mr. Tim T. WHEELDON
37 Director Financial Aid ..... Vacant
20 Special Assistant to the Provost . Ms. Pamela M. CHRISTOFFERS
51 Dean Graduate/Adult Programs ..... Dr. Patricia A. WILLIAMS
35 Associate VP for Student Affairs ..... Mr. Jason K. BAUER
06 Registrar ..... Ms. Debbie K. GANNON
42 Senior Campus Pastor ..... Rev. Russell L. LACKEY
09 Director Inst Planning/Research ..... Ms. Debbie M. BARGER
36 Director Career Center ..... Ms. Susan M. STEARNS
08 Director of the Library ..... Ms. Pamela D. REES
40 Director Bookstore & Campus Svcs ..... Mr. Tim REGER
07 Director of Admissions ..... Mr. Ryan THOMPSON
18 Director Buildings & Grounds ..... Ms. Kim I. BUTLER
38 Director Leadership & Counseling ..... Mr. Kent A. SCHORNACK
28 Dir Multicultural & Cmty Outreach ..... Mr. Alex H. PIEDRAS
41 Athletic Director ..... Mr. Troy A. PLUMMER
15 Human Resources Manager ..... Ms. Erica L. KLUVER
88 Special Assistant to the President ..... Mr. Robert BARRON

Grinnell College (J)

1121 Park Street, Grinnell IA 50112-1690
County: Poweshiek FICE Identification: 001868
Unit ID: 153384
Telephone: (641) 269-4000 Carnegie Class: Bac-A&S
FAX Number: (641) 269-3408 Calendar System: Semester
URL: www.grinnell.edu
Established: 1846 Annual Undergrad Tuition & Fees: $52,392
Enrollment: 1,712 Coed

Affiliation or Control: Independent Non-Profit IRS Status: 501(c)3
Highest Offering: Baccalaureate
Accreditation: NH

01 President ... Raynard S. KINGTON
100 Chief of Staff/VP Planning ... Angela VOOS
05 Vice Pres Acad Affs/Dean Col ... Anne HARRIS
30 Vice President Dev/Alumni Rel ... Jaci A. THIEDE
115 Chief Investment Officer ... Jainen THAYER
10 VP for Finance/Treasurer of College ... Keith A. ARCHER
20 Senior Associate Dean of College ... Maria TAPIAS
20 Associate Dean of College ... Mark LEVANDOSKI
20 Associate Dean of the College ... Timothy ARNER
07 VP Enroll/Dean Admission & Fin Aid ... Joseph P. BAGNOLI
30 Director of Development Operations ... Adam LAUG
37 Dir Student Fin Aid & Asst VP Enrol ... Brad LINDBERG
15 Assistant VP of Human Resources ... Mary GREINER
26 Vice President for Communications ... Debra LUKEHART
06 Registrar ... Jason MAHER
08 Librarian ... Mark CHRISTEL
29 Director of Alumni Relations ... Jayn CHANEY
13 Chief Information Tech Officer ... Dave ROBINSON
09 Assoc VP Analytics/Inst Rsch ... Catherine RENNER
85 Director Intl Student Services ... Karen K. EDWARDS
40 Manager/Bookstore ... Cassandra J. WHERRY
41 Athletic Director ... Andrew HAMILTON
23 Dir Stdnt Health/Counseling Svcs ... Deb SHILL
121 Dean Student Success/Acad Advising ... Joyce STERN
18 Asst Vice Pres Facilities Mgmt ... Richard WHITNEY
19 Dir of Campus Safety ... James SHROPSHIRE
42 Chaplain/Dean of Rel Life ... Deanna SHORB
102 Director Corp/Found/Govt Rels ... Susan FERRARI
32 Assoc VP Student Affairs ... Sarah MOSCHENROSS
35 Dean of Students ... Ben NEWHOUSE
31 Dir Community Enhancement/Engagemnt . Monica CHAVEZ-SILVA
36 Dean & Dir Career Life & Service ... Mark PELTZ
04 Executive Asst to President ... Tammy PRUSHA
101 Secretary of the College ... Susan SCHOEN
104 Director of Off-Campus Study ... Alicia STANLEY
28 Asst VP and Chief Diversity Officer ... Leslie GREGG-JOLLY
39 Director Residence Life ... Joseph ROLON
44 Director Annual Giving ... Mae PARKER
96 Procurement Manager ... Amanda JONES

Hamilton Technical College (A)

1011 E 53rd Street, Davenport IA 52807-2616
County: Scott FICE Identification: 012064
Unit ID: 153427
Telephone: (563) 386-3570 Carnegie Class: Spec-4-yr-Other Tech
FAX Number: (563) 386-6756 Calendar System: Semester
URL: www.hamiltontechcollege.com
Established: 1969 Annual Undergrad Tuition & Fees: $14,250
Enrollment: 134 Coed
Affiliation or Control: Proprietary IRS Status: Proprietary
Highest Offering: Baccalaureate
Accreditation: ACCSC

01 President ... Mrs. Maryanne HAMILTON
32 Dean of Students ... Mr. Brian BEERT

Hawkeye Community College (B)

Box 8015, Waterloo IA 50704-8015
County: Black Hawk FICE Identification: 004595
Unit ID: 153445
Telephone: (319) 296-2320 Carnegie Class: Assoc/HVT-High Non
FAX Number: (319) 296-2874 Calendar System: Semester
URL: www.hawkeyecollege.edu
Established: 1966 Annual Undergrad Tuition & Fees (In-District): $5,311
Enrollment: 5,605 Coed
Affiliation or Control: State/Local IRS Status: 501(c)3
Highest Offering: Associate Degree
Accreditation: NH, COARC, DA, DH, EMT, MLTAD, #OTA, PTAA

01 President ... Dr. Todd HOLCOMB
05 Provost & VP Academic Affairs ... Dr. Jane BRADLEY
10 Vice Pres Administration & Finance ... Mr. Dan GILLEN
84 Vice Pres Enrollment Services ... Ms. Kathy A. FLYNN
111 Exec Dir Institutional Advancement ... Ms. Holly JOHNSON
15 Exec Dir Human Resource Services ... Mr. John D. CLOPTON
51 Exec Director Business & Cmty Educ ... Mr. Aaron SAUERBREI
106 Dean School of Online Learning ... Mr. Robin GALLOWAY
49 Dean Arts & Sciences ... Ms. Catharine FREEMAN
75 Dean Applied Science/Eng Technology ... Mr. David GRUNKLEE
76 Dean Interprof Health & Safety Svcs ... Mr. Eugene LEUTZINGER
32 Dean of Students ... Ms. Nancy HENDERSON
88 Dean of Transitional Programs ... Mr. Tom MUELLER
07 Dir Admiss/Recruit/Athl/Stdnt Life ... Mr. Dave BALL
21 Director Business Services ... Ms. Julie THOMAS
13 Chief Information Officer ... Mr. Brian MCCORMICK
08 Director Library Services ... Ms. Candace HAVELY
18 Director Plant & Facilities ... Mr. Terence FLYNN
06 Dir Student Records & Registration ... Mr. Tony SMOTHERS
19 Dir Public Safety/Emergency Mgr ... Mr. John KRAMER
09 Director Institutional Research ... Ms. Connie BUHR
26 Director Public Relations/Marketing ... Ms. Mary Pat MOORE
28 Director of Inclusion & Diversity ... Ms. Rhonda MCRINA
12 Director Adult Learning Center ... Ms. Sandra JENSEN
103 Dir Workforce/Career Development ... Mr. Christopher HANNAN
37 Director Student Financial Aid ... Ms. Gisella BAKER
25 Director of Grants & Resource Dev ... Ms. Constance GRIMM
35 Assoc Director of Student Life ... Ms. Meghan REILLY
04 Assistant to President ... Ms. Donna S. MCNULTY

Indian Hills Community College (C)

525 Grandview Avenue, Ottumwa IA 52501-1398
County: Wapello FICE Identification: 008403
Unit ID: 153472
Telephone: (641) 683-5111 Carnegie Class: Assoc/MT-VT-High Non
FAX Number: (641) 683-5184 Calendar System: Quarter
URL: www.indianhills.edu
Established: 1966 Annual Undergrad Tuition & Fees (In-District): $4,224
Enrollment: 4,090 Coed
Affiliation or Control: State/Local IRS Status: 501(c)3
Highest Offering: Associate Degree
Accreditation: NH, ACFEI, CAHIIM, DA, DH, EMT, MLTAD, OTA, PTAA, RAD

01 President ... Dr. Marlene SPROUSE
10 VP/Chief Financial Officer ... Mr. Bill MECK
05 Vice Pres Acad Affs/Instl Effect ... Dr. Matt THOMPSON
49 Executive Dean Arts & Sciences ... Ms. Darlas SHOCKLEY
32 Exec Dean Student Affairs/Athletics ... Mr. Brett MONAGHAN
103 Exec Dean Career/Workforce Educ ... Dr. Jill BUDDE
12 Dean Centerville Campus ... Mr. Noel GORDEN
86 Assoc Dean Govt Affs/Grants ... Ms. Martha WICK
102 Exec Dir Foundation/Development ... Ms. Blaire SIEMS
13 Prog Dir Information Technologies ... Mr. Ray RYON
15 Director Human Resources ... Mr. Zeke FLICK
18 Director Physical Facilities ... Mr. Rick FOSDYCK
06 Exec Dean Enrollment Srvs/Registrar ... Ms. Joni KELLEY
41 Athletic Director ... Mr. Brett MONAGHAN
26 Director for Media/Public Rels ... Mr. Kevin PINK
88 Asst Cheif Flight/Aviation Programs ... Mr. Brian HAMMACK
07 Director of Admissions ... Ms. Ranae MOLKENTHIN
09 Director of Institutional Research ... Dr. Stephanie HOLLIMAN-GINKENS
29 Dir Marketing & Comm Relations ... Dr. Bianca MYERS
35 Success Center ... Ms. Rhonda CONRAD

Indian Hills Community College Centerville (D)

721 N First Street, Centerville IA 52544
Telephone: (641) 856-2143 Identification: 770054
Accreditation: &NH

Iowa Central Community College (E)

One Triton Circle, Fort Dodge IA 50501
County: Webster FICE Identification: 001865
Unit ID: 153524
Telephone: (515) 576-7201 Carnegie Class: Assoc/MT-VT-High Non
FAX Number: (515) 576-7207 Calendar System: Semester
URL: www.iowacentral.edu
Established: 1966 Annual Undergrad Tuition & Fees (In-District): $5,490
Enrollment: 5,788 Coed
Affiliation or Control: Local IRS Status: 501(c)3
Highest Offering: Associate Degree
Accreditation: NH, DH, EMT, MAC, MLTAD, RAD

01 President ... Dr. Daniel P. KINNEY
04 Assistant to the President ... Mrs. Ally P. WALTER
05 Vice President of Instruction ... Dr. Stacy METZER
32 Vice Pres Enroll Mgmt/Student Devel ... Mr. Thomas J. BENEKE
10 Vice President of Business Affairs ... Mrs. Angela A. MARTIN
86 VP External Affairs/Govt Rels ... Mr. James B. KERSTEN
50 Business & Ind Technology Dean ... Mr. Neale J. ADAMS
76 Health Sciences Dean ... Mr. John HANSEN
49 Liberal Arts & Sciences Dean ... Mrs. Jennifer M. CONDON
106 Distance Learning Dean ... Mr. Timothy J. MARTIN
09 Inst Effectiveness Exec Director ... Dr. Stacy L. MENTZER
30 Development/Alumni Rels Exec Dir ... Mrs. Mary LUDWIG
103 Econ Wrkfc Dev/Cont Educ Exec Dir ... Mrs. Shelly R. BLUNK
06 Registrar ... Ms. Courtney A. KOPP
07 Enrollment Management Director ... Mrs. Sara A. SCHARF
124 Retention Center Director ... Mrs. Tracy L. CRIPPIN-HAAKE
37 Financial Aid Director ... Mrs. Lindsey M. CHRISTIE
21 Business Office Director ... Mr. Luke J. GROVE
15 Human Resources Director ... Mrs. Kimberly N. WHITMORE
16 Human Resources Coordinator ... Ms. Sandi J. PIEPER
41 Athletic Director ... Mr. Kevin TWAIT
39 Housing Director ... Mr. Jeremy D. CONLEY
38 Mental Health Counselor ... Mrs. Kelli A. REUTER
35 Student Life & Activities Director ... Mr. David L. PEARSON
88 Academic Resource Services Director ... Ms. Lori L. WALTON
18 Physical Facilities Director ... Mr. Shan L. BEECHER
12 Storm Lake Center Director ... Mr. Chris CLEVELAND
12 Webster City Center Director ... Ms. Colette BERTRAN
26 Public Information Director ... Mr. Paul A. DECOURSEY
13 Institutional Technology Director ... Mr. Jeff A. NELSEN
13 Institutional Technology Director ... Mr. Troy D. CRAMPTON
14 Sr Computer System Analyst ... Mr. Warren K. BAUER
40 Bookstore Manager ... Mrs. Samantha E. MCCLAIN

Iowa Lakes Community College (F)

19 S Seventh Street, Estherville IA 51334-2234
County: Emmet FICE Identification: 001864
Unit ID: 153533
Telephone: (712) 362-2604 Carnegie Class: Assoc/MT-VT-High Non
FAX Number: (712) 362-8363 Calendar System: Semester
URL: www.iowalakes.edu
Established: 1967 Annual Undergrad Tuition & Fees (In-District): $6,460
Enrollment: 2,011 Coed
Affiliation or Control: State/Local IRS Status: 501(c)3
Highest Offering: Associate Degree
Accreditation: NH, MAC, SURGT

01 President ... Ms. Valerie K. NEWHOUSE
11 Vice President of Administration ... Mr. Robert A. LEIFELD
12 Exec Dean Emmetsburg Campus ... Mr. Thomas S. BROTHERTON
26 Exec Director of Marketing ... Ms. Beth ELMAN
18 Exec Dir of Facilities Management ... Ms. Delaine S. HINEY
15 Exec Director Human Resources ... Ms. Kathy A. MULLER
31 Exec Dir Cmty & Business Relations ... Ms. Jolene R. ROGERS
10 Chief Financial Officer ... Mr. Jeff D. SOPER
12 Exec Dean Estherville Campus ... Mr. Scott STOKES
32 Executive Dean of Students ... Ms. Julie R. WILLIAMS

Iowa Lakes Community College Emmetsburg Campus (G)

3200 College Drive, Emmetsburg IA 50536
Telephone: (712) 852-3554 Identification: 770055
Accreditation: &NH

Iowa Lakes Community College Spencer Campus (H)

Gateway N 1900 Grand Ave, Ste B-1, Spencer IA 51301
Telephone: (712) 262-7141 Identification: 770056
Accreditation: &NH

*Iowa Valley Community College District (I)

3702 S Center Street, Marshalltown IA 50158-4760
County: Marshall FICE Identification: 033436
Telephone: (641) 752-4643 Carnegie Class: N/A
FAX Number: (641) 754-1336
URL: www.iavalley.edu

01 Chancellor ... Dr. Kristie FISHER
11 Vice Chanc Administrative Services ... Ms. Colleen SPRINGER
51 Vice Chanc Continuing Educ/Training ... Ms. Jacque GOODMAN
10 Vice Chancellor Finance/CFO ... Ms. Kathleen PINK
13 Chief Information Officer ... Mr. Mike MOSHER
12 Provost Ellsworth Community College ... Dr. Martin REIMER
12 Provost Marshalltown Community Col ... Dr. Robin SHAFFER LILIENTHAL
12 Dean of Iowa Valley Grinnell ... Ms. Mary Anne NICKLE
26 Director of Marketing ... Ms. Robin ANCTIL
09 Institutional Researcher ... Dr. Lisa BREJA
04 Asst to Chancellor/Board Secretary ... Ms. Barbara JENNINGS
86 Director of Government Affairs ... Ms. Cynthia SCHULTE

*Ellsworth Community College (J)

1100 College Avenue, Iowa Falls IA 50126-1199
County: Hardin FICE Identification: 001862
Unit ID: 153296
Telephone: (641) 648-4611 Carnegie Class: Assoc/HT-High Trad
FAX Number: (641) 648-3128 Calendar System: Semester
URL: https://www.iavalley.edu/
Established: 1890 Annual Undergrad Tuition & Fees (In-District): $4,776
Enrollment: 851 Coed
Affiliation or Control: State/Local IRS Status: 501(c)3
Highest Offering: Associate Degree
Accreditation: &NH, MAC

02 Provost ... Dr. Martin REIMER
05 Dean of Academic Affairs ... Dr. Amanda ESTEY
32 Dean of Student Affairs ... Dr. Barb KLEIN
08 Library Service Manager ... Ms. Sandra GREUFE
32 Director of Athletics/Student Life ... Mr. Nate FORSYTH
37 Director Financial Aid ... Ms. Tara MILLER
44 Dir Annual Plan Giving/Dir Alum Rel ... Ms. Kaitlyn BARTLING
07 Director of Admissions ... Ms. Adriane SIETSEMA

† Regional accreditation is carried under the parent institution Iowa Valley Community College District in Marshalltown, IA.

*Marshalltown Community College (K)

3700 S Center Street, Marshalltown IA 50158-4760
County: Marshall FICE Identification: 001875
Unit ID: 153922
Telephone: (641) 752-7106 Carnegie Class: Assoc/MT-VT-High Non
FAX Number: (641) 752-8149 Calendar System: Semester
URL: www.mcc.iavalley.edu
Established: 1927 Annual Undergrad Tuition & Fees (In-District): $4,776
Enrollment: 2,028 Coed
Affiliation or Control: State/Local IRS Status: 501(c)3
Highest Offering: Associate Degree
Accreditation: &NH, DA

02 Chancellor ... Dr. Kristie FISHER
05 Provost ... Dr. Robin SHAFFER LILIENTHAL
11 Vice Chanc Administrative Services ... Ms. Colleen SPRINGER
10 Chief Financial Officer ... Ms. Kathy PINK
20 Dean of Academic Affairs ... Mr. Patrick KENNEDY
84 Dean Enrollment/Student Life ... Ms. Angie REDMOND
20 Dean of Students/Learning Svcs/TRIO ... Mr. Nate CHUA
06 Director of Operations/Registrar ... Ms. Mandy BROWN
76 Assoc Dean of Health Occupations ... Ms. Beth JOHANNS
102 Executive Director MCC Foundation ... Ms. Carol GEIL
37 Financial Aid Administrator ... Mr. Matt DANIELS
26 Director of Marketing ... Ms. Robin ANCTIL

09 Dir of Institutional Research .... Vacant
41 Athletic Director .... Ms. Kathleen BROWN
32 Dir Student Engagement/Res Life .... Mr. Chris BREES
121 Sr Academic Advising Specialist .... Mr. Dan KEY
08 Library Services Manager .... Ms. Megan DENIS
40 MCC Bookstore Manager .... Mr. Aaron DEBOER

† Regional accreditation is carried under the parent institution Iowa Valley Community College District in Marshalltown, IA.

Iowa Wesleyan University (A)

601 N Main, Mount Pleasant IA 52641-1398
County: Henry FICE Identification: 001871
Unit ID: 153621
Telephone: (319) 385-8021 Carnegie Class: Bac-Diverse
FAX Number: (319) 385-6296 Calendar System: Semester
URL: www.iw.edu
Established: 1842 Annual Undergrad Tuition & Fees: $24,600
Enrollment: 629 Coed
Affiliation or Control: United Methodist IRS Status: 501(c)3
Highest Offering: Master's
Accreditation: NH, NUR

01 President .... Dr. Steven E. TITUS
10 VP for Finance and Treasurer .... Ms. Chris PLUNKETT
84 VP for Enrollment Management .... Dr. Nikki FENNERN
05 Provost .... Dr. DeWayne FRAZIER
26 VP for Strategic Initiatives .... Ms. Meg RICHTMAN
111 VP University Advancement .... Mr. Michael HEATON
32 Assoc VP/Dean of Students .... Dr. Rebecca BECKNER
13 Assoc VP/Chief Information Officer .... Dr. Kit NIP
06 Registrar .... Ms. Megan HILLS
37 Director of Financial Aid .... Mr. Brian JOHNSTON
07 Director of Admissions .... Ms. Kara MANDRELL
21 Controller .... Ms. Deb LILLIE
20 Asst VP for Academic Affairs .... Ms. Paula KINNEY
15 Director of Human Resources .... Ms. Kathy MOOTHART
44 Director of Wesleyan Fund .... Ms. Amy FRANTZ
27 Director of Marketing .... Vacant
88 Creative Director .... Ms. Amanda RUNDQUIST
29 Director of Alumni/Parent Relations .... Vacant
41 Athletic Director .... Mr. Derek ZANDER
18 Director of Physical Plant .... Mr. Sean GRAY
124 Coordinator of Student Engagement .... Mr. Matthew KLUNDT
36 Director of Career Development .... Ms. Katherine EVANS
40 Bookstore Director .... Ms. Amy MABEUS
04 Asst to the President .... Ms. Mary NOTESTEIN
105 Webmaster .... Ms. Cindee VANDIJK
09 Director of Institutional Research .... Vacant
30 Development Director .... Mr. Jim PEDRICK
106 Asst Dean Adult & Graduate Studies .... Ms. Barb SCHULTZ
39 Dir Resident Life/Student Housing .... Mr. Luis ARANDA

Iowa Western Community College (B)

2700 College Road, Council Bluffs IA 51503-0567
County: Pottawattamie FICE Identification: 004598
Unit ID: 153630
Telephone: (712) 325-3200 Carnegie Class: Assoc/MT-VT-High Non
FAX Number: (712) 325-3424 Calendar System: Semester
URL: www.iwcc.edu
Established: 1966 Annual Undergrad Tuition & Fees (In-District): $5,952
Enrollment: 6,080 Coed
Affiliation or Control: State/Local IRS Status: 501(c)3
Highest Offering: Associate Degree
Accreditation: NH, ACFEI, DA, DH, EMT, MAC, PTAA, SURGT

01 President .... Dr. Dan KINNEY
04 Assistant to the President .... Mrs. Erin MCKEE
05 Vice President for Academic Affairs .... Dr. Marjorie WELCH
10 Vice President of Finance .... Mr. Edwin HOLTZ
32 Vice President for Student Services .... Vacant
26 Vice Pres of Marketing/Public Rels .... Mr. Donald KOHLER
30 Vice Pres Institutional Advancement .... Mrs. Molly NOON
103 VP Economic/Workforce Devel .... Mr. Mark STANLEY
09 Dean Institutional Research/Accred .... Mrs. Tina KNAUSS
84 Dean Enrollment Services .... Vacant
121 Dean of Academic Support .... Mrs. Samantha LARSON
35 Dean Student Life/Student Success .... Ms. Kimberly HENRY
106 Dean Distance Educ/Pathway Dev .... Mr. Matthew MANCUSO
81 Dean Science/Tech/Engineering/Math .... Mrs. Barb GODDEN
79 Dean of Comm/Education/Fine Arts .... Mrs. Jenny KRUGER
76 Dean of Health & Sports Sciences .... Mrs. Barb GODDEN
51 Director of Continuing Education .... Mrs. Lisa WALKER
50 Dean Ag/Bus/Computer Info/Soc Sci .... Mrs. Aimbe DOWDELL-WHITE
06 Registrar .... Mrs. Jill CLARK
07 Director of Admissions .... Mrs. Nyssa GREER
15 Director of Human Resources .... Mrs. Robyn PORTER
29 Director of Alumni Relations .... Mrs. Sarah SAAR
37 Director of Student Financial Aid .... Ms. Lisa MORRISON
21 Director Accounting .... Ms. Randi BISSEN
13 Director Information Technology .... Mr. Bill SHELTON
41 Athletic Director .... Mr. Jeremy CAPO
39 Director of Residence Life .... Mr. Jesse OSVOLD
18 Director Physical Plant .... Mr. Brian SUTTER
96 Director of Purchasing .... Mrs. Diane OSBAHR
40 College Store Manager .... Mrs. Maggie SOBCZYK-BARRON
88 Food Service Manager .... Mr. Stephan BRYANT

Kirkwood Community College (C)

6301 Kirkwood Blvd. SW, Cedar Rapids IA 52404
County: Linn FICE Identification: 004076
Unit ID: 153737
Telephone: (319) 398-5411 Carnegie Class: Assoc/MT-VT-High Non
FAX Number: (319) 398-1037 Calendar System: Semester
URL: www.kirkwood.edu
Established: 1966 Annual Undergrad Tuition & Fees (In-District): $4,832
Enrollment: 14,049 Coed
Affiliation or Control: Local IRS Status: 501(c)3
Highest Offering: Associate Degree
Accreditation: NH, ACFEI, CAHIIM, COARC, DA, DH, DT, EMT, MAC, NDT, OTA, PTAA, SURGT

01 President .... Dr. Lori SUNDBERG
51 VP Cont Education/Training Svcs .... Dr. Kim BECICKA
10 Vice President/Chief Fin/Oper Ofcr .... Mr. Jim CHOATE
111 Vice President Advancement .... Mr. Greg NEUMEYER
05 Vice President Academic Affairs .... Dr. Bill LAMB
32 Vice President Student Services .... Mr. Jon BUSE
20 Assoc Vice President Acad Affairs .... Mr. John HENIK
12 Exec Dean Iowa City Campus .... Vacant
35 Dean of Students .... Ms. Melissa PAYNE
15 Vice President Human Resources .... Mr. Wes FOWLER
13 Vice President IT .... Mr. Jon NEFF
106 Exec Dean Distance Lrng .... Mr. Todd PRUSHA
84 Exec Dir Enrollment Services .... Mr. Patrick CLEMENCE
07 Director Admissions .... Vacant
18 VP Facilities & Security .... Mr. Troy MCQUILLEN
25 Director Grants & Fed Programs .... Ms. Doris NYAGA
41 Athletic Director .... Mr. Doug WAGEMESTER
06 Registrar .... Ms. Dena RAUCH
29 Scholarship & Alumni Director .... Ms. Jody DONALDSON
37 Financial Aid Director .... Mr. Matt FALDUTO
47 Dean Agriculture Science .... Mr. Scott ERMER
72 Dean Industrial Technology .... Mr. Dan MARTIN
79 Dean Humanities & English .... Ms. Jennifer BRADLEY
76 Dean Allied Health .... Ms. Nicky CLINE
83 Dean Social Sciences .... Dr. Brooke STRAHN-KOLLER
81 Dean Math/Science .... Vacant
66 Dean Nursing .... Dr. Kathryn DOLTER
76 Dean Health Occupations .... Dr. Mike MCLAUGHLIN
50 Dean Business & Information Tech .... Ms. Colette ATKINS
88 Dean Learning Services/Dir Library .... Mr. Arron WINGS
04 Asst to President .... Ms. Carrie ANDERSON
104 Dean International Programs .... Ms. Dawn WOOD
19 Senior Director Security/Safety .... Ms. Melissa JENSEN
26 Exec Dir Communications/Marketing .... Mr. Kevin HANSEN
112 Director Planned & Endowed Giving .... Ms. Jody PELLERIN
14 Exec Dir IT Services .... Mr. Darren ZABLOUDIL
21 Exec Director Finance .... Ms. Kris RILEY
103 Director Skills to Employment .... Ms. Carla ANDORF
108 Director Institutional Assessment .... Mr. Cort IVERSON
86 Director Government Relations .... Ms. Stephanie BREDMAN

Loras College (D)

1450 Alta Vista, Dubuque IA 52004-0178
County: Dubuque FICE Identification: 001873
Unit ID: 153825
Telephone: (563) 588-7100 Carnegie Class: Bac-Diverse
FAX Number: (563) 588-7964 Calendar System: Semester
URL: www.loras.edu
Established: 1839 Annual Undergrad Tuition & Fees: $34,184
Enrollment: 1,467 Coed
Affiliation or Control: Roman Catholic IRS Status: 501(c)3
Highest Offering: Master's
Accreditation: NH, CAATE, SW

01 President .... Mr. James E. COLLINS
05 VP Academic Affairs .... Dr. Donna N. HEALD
10 Treasurer .... Mr. Michael H. DOYLE
03 Senior Vice President .... Dr. Mary Ellen CARROLL
111 VP Institutional Advancement .... Mr. Michael H. DOYLE
32 VP Student Development .... Dr. Arthur W. SUNLEAF
04 Executive Assistant to President .... Ms. Heather L. JUNGBLUT
42 Dean of Campus Spiritual Life .... Rev. William M. JOENSEN
91 Sr Dir Technology Services .... Mr. Thomas D. KRUSE
29 Exec Dir Alumni/Communications .... Ms. Bobbi L. EARLES
15 Dir Human Resources .... Mr. Troy M. WRIGHT
09 Director of Institutional Research .... Mr. Christopher R. FEIT
38 Director Center for Counseling .... Ms. Tricia S. BORELLI
07 Admiss Dir of Recruit & Retention .. Mr. Kyle J. KLAPATAUSKAS
08 Library Director .... Vacant
35 Assistant Dean of Students .... Ms. Molly A. BURROWS-SCHUMACHER
111 Assoc VP Institutional Advance .... Mr. Joshua D. BOOTS
41 Dir Intercollegiate Athletics .... Ms. Denise A. UDELHOFEN
18 Asst VP Physical Resources .... Mr. John R. MCDERMOTT
40 Director of Bookstore .... Ms. Renee A. MENNE
23 Director of Health Center .... Ms. Tammy S. MARTI
42 Campus Ministry/P&J Coordinator .... Ms. Anastacia M. MCDERMOTT
06 Registrar .... Mr. Michael P. FRIEND
19 Dir Res Life & Campus Safety .... Ms. Molly A. BURROWS-SCHUMACHER
35 Assoc Dean of Students .... Ms. Kimberly A. WALSH
37 Director of Financial Planning .... Ms. Julie A. DUNN
26 Dir Communications/Marketing .... Mr. James R. NAPRSTEK
96 Controller for Business Office .... Ms. Rennie A. ROOT
36 Academic Internship Coordinator .... Ms. Jennifer L. WEBER

Luther College (E)

700 College Drive, Decorah IA 52101-1045
County: Winneshiek FICE Identification: 001874
Unit ID: 153834
Telephone: (563) 387-2000 Carnegie Class: Bac-A&S
FAX Number: (563) 387-2158 Calendar System: 4/1/4
URL: www.luther.edu
Established: 1861 Annual Undergrad Tuition & Fees: $42,290
Enrollment: 2,053 Coed
Affiliation or Control: Evangelical Lutheran Church In America
IRS Status: 501(c)3
Highest Offering: Baccalaureate
Accreditation: NH, CAATE, CAEPN, MUS, NURSE, SW

01 President .... Dr. Jenifer K. WARD
05 Vice Pres Acad Affs/Dean of College .... Dr. Kevin KRAUS
20 Assistant Dean .... Ms. Arleen ORVIS
30 Vice President for Development .... Mr. James JERMIER
10 Vice President for Finance & Admin .... Mr. Eric RUNESTAD
32 Vice Pres/Dean for Student Life .... Mr. Corey LANDSTROM
26 Vice Pres Communications/Marketing .... Vacant
22 VP of Inst Equity & Inclusion .... Ms. Lisa M. SCOTT
13 Exec Dir Library & Information Svcs .... Mr. Mark FRANZ
84 Int VP for Enrollment Management .... Mr. Derek HARTL
21 Controller .... Ms. Peggy LENSING
18 Director of Facilities Services .... Mr. Jay L. UTHOFF
91 Director Information Systems .... Ms. Marcia A. GULLICKSON
110 Senior Development Officer .... Mr. Doug NELSON
06 Registrar .... Dr. Richard BERNATZ
20 Associate Dean/Dir Faculty Devel .... Dr. Sean BURKE
15 Director Human Resources .... Ms. Marsha WENTHOLD
41 Director Intercollegiate Athletics .... Ms. Renae HARTL
29 Exec Director of Alumni Relations .... Ms. Sherry B. ALCOCK
27 Director of Publications & Design .... Mr. Michael BARTELS
04 Exec Assistant to the President .... Ms. Sally MING
35 Assistant Dean Student Life .... Ms. Kasey NIKKEL
36 Director Career Center .... Ms. Brenda RANUM
38 Director Counseling Service .... Ms. Meg HAMMES
37 Director Student Financial Planning .... Ms. Janice K. CORDELL
42 Dir Campus Ministry & Cong Rels .... Rev. Michael R. BLAIR
40 Director Book Shop/Union Services .... Ms. Deanna CASTERTON
39 Assistant Dean & Dir Res Life .... Ms. Kristine FRANZEN
85 Exec Dir Ctr Global Learn & Int Adm .... Mr. Jon LUND
23 Director Health Services .... Ms. Diane TAPPE
19 Director Security/Safety .... Mr. Robert HARRI
88 Director Campus Programming .... Vacant
09 Director Assessment/Inst Research .... Vacant
35 Dir Stdnt Activities and the Union .... Ms. Trish NEUBAUER
88 Student Life Assistant Dean .... Ms. Janet HUNTER
45 Dean for Inst Planning & Mission ..... Dr. Bradley CHAMBERLAIN
28 Director of Diversity Center .... Ms. Wintlett TAYLOR-BROWNE
08 Library Director .... Mr. Ryan GJERDE

Maharishi University of Management (F)

1000 N 4th Street, Fairfield IA 52557-0001
County: Jefferson FICE Identification: 011113
Unit ID: 153861
Telephone: (641) 472-7000 Carnegie Class: Masters/L
FAX Number: (641) 472-1179 Calendar System: Semester
URL: www.mum.edu
Established: 1971 Annual Undergrad Tuition & Fees: $16,530
Enrollment: 1,646 Coed
Affiliation or Control: Independent Non-Profit IRS Status: 501(c)3
Highest Offering: Doctorate
Accreditation: NH, IACBE

01 President .... Dr. John HAGELIN
05 VP Academic Affairs .... Dr. Craig PEARSON
11 Vice President of Operations .... Mr. Thomas BROOKS
30 VP Development & Alumni Relations .... Mr. Brad MYLETT
84 VP Enrollment & Student Affairs .... Mr. Rod EASON
05 Dean of Faculty .... Dr. Vicki ALEXANDER-HERRIOTT
10 Treasurer .... Mr. Michael SPIVAK
88 International Vice President .... Dr. Michael DILLBECK
88 International Vice President .... Dr. Susan DILLBECK
11 Chief Administrative Officer .... Mr. David TODT
43 Legal Counsel/Dean Global Develop .... Mr. Bill GOLDSTEIN
07 Dean of Admissions .... Mr. Ron BARNETT
32 Associate Dean of Students .... Mr. Manyu HESSE
35 Assoc Dean Enrollment/Student Affs .... Ms. Selin OZBUDAK
06 Registrar .... Ms. Taniya HALLMAN
26 Media Relations .... Mr. Jim KARPEN
106 Dir Distance Educ/Intl Programs .... Mr. Dennis HEATON
27 Director of Press .... Mr. Harry BRIGHT
39 Director of Housing .... Mr. Mahmood ALI
37 Director of Student Financial Aid .... Mr. Dan WASIELEWSKI
13 Director of Information Services .... Mr. Simon RODRIGUEZ
20 Dean Academic Programs .... Dr. Chris JONES
15 Director Human Resources .... Ms. Carol PASSOS
29 Director Alumni .... Mr. Paul STOKSTAD
111 Co-Exec Director Inst Advancement .... Mr. Nick ROSANIA
111 Co-Exec Director Inst Advancement .... Ms. Sandra ROSANIA
36 Career Development Services .... Ms. Ayesha SENGUPTA
18 Chief Facilities/Physical Plant .... Mr. Craig WAGNER
49 Dean College of Arts & Sciences .... Dr. Chris JONES
77 Dean College of Computer Sci & Math .... Mr. Gregory GUTHRIE
58 Dean of Graduate School .... Dr. Frederick TRAVIS
04 Administrative Asst to President .... Ms. Jane AIKENS
08 Director of Library .... Ms. Rouzanna VARDANYAN

41 Athletic Director ... Mr. Dustin MATTHEWS
101 Secretary of the Board of Trustees ... Ms. Susan TRACY
19 Director of Security and Safety ... Ms. Beata NACSA
106 Dir Online Education/E-learning ... Ms. Cheryl MICHIE
38 Assoc Dir Student Support Services ... Ms. Leslie DOYLE
104 Director Study Abroad ... Dr. Cathy GORINI
105 Director Web Services ... Mr. Michael MATZKIN
35 Director Student Activities ... Ms. Rachael KUNZLER

Mercy College of Health Sciences (A)

928 Sixth Avenue, Des Moines IA 50309-1239
County: Polk FICE Identification: 006273
Unit ID: 153977
Telephone: (515) 643-3180 Carnegie Class: Spec-4-yr-Other Health
FAX Number: (515) 643-6698 Calendar System: Semester
URL: www.mchs.edu
Established: 1995 Annual Undergrad Tuition & Fees: $17,952
Enrollment: 758 Coed
Affiliation or Control: Roman Catholic IRS Status: 501(c)3
Highest Offering: Baccalaureate
Accreditation: NH, ADNUR, DMS, EMT, MAC, MT, NURSE, PTAA, RAD, SURGT

01 President ... Dr. Douglas J. FIORE
05 Interim Provost & VP Acad Affairs ... Dr. Nancy K. KERTZ
10 VP of Business & Regulatory Affairs ... Dr. Thomas LEAHY
84 VP Enrollment & External Engagement ... Mr. Matthew ROMKEY
15 VP of Employee Engagement & HR ... Ms. Anne DENNIS
20 Dean Academics ... Dr. Glenda GALLISATH
08 Dir of Library and Media Services ... Ms. Jennie E. VER STEEG
06 Registrar ... Ms. Carolyn BUCKLIN
37 Director of Financial Aid ... Mr. Joe BROOKOVER
32 Dean of Student Affairs ... Ms. Lyneene RICHARDSON
13 Director of Information Technology ... Mr. David VON ARB
07 Director of Admissions ... Mr. Andrew GRESS
29 Devel & Alumni Engagement Mgr ... Ms. Ann HOEPPNER

Morningside College (B)

1501 Morningside Avenue, Sioux City IA 51106-1751
County: Woodbury FICE Identification: 001879
Unit ID: 154004
Telephone: (712) 274-5000 Carnegie Class: Masters/L
FAX Number: (712) 274-5101 Calendar System: Semester
URL: www.morningside.edu
Established: 1894 Annual Undergrad Tuition & Fees: $31,530
Enrollment: 2,788 Coed
Affiliation or Control: United Methodist IRS Status: 501(c)3
Highest Offering: Doctorate
Accreditation: NH, MUS, NURSE

01 President ... Mr. John C. REYNDERS
05 Vice President for Academic Affairs ... Dr. Christopher L. SPICER
10 Vice President Business & Finance ... Mr. Ronald A. JORGENSEN
32 Vice Pres Student Life & Enrollment ... Mrs. Terri A. CURRY
111 Vice Pres Institutional Advancement ... Mrs. Kari L. WINKLEPLECK
26 Vice Pres Marketing & Communication ... Mrs. Erin M. EDLUND
35 Dean of Students ... Dr. Karmen TEN NAPEL
20 Associate Dean for Acad Affairs ... Dr. Alden STOUT
121 Vice President Advising ... Dr. Lillian L. LOPEZ
06 Registrar ... Mrs. Jen DOLPHIN
37 Director Student Financial Planning ... Ms. Karen GAGNON
13 Exec Dir of Information Services ... Mr. Mike HUSMANN
29 Director of Alumni Relations ... Mr. Shiran NATHANIEL
07 Director of Admissions ... Ms. Steph PETERS
18 Director of Physical Plant ... Mr. Jay MALIN
19 Director of Security ... Mr. Brett LYON
23 Director of Student Health ... Ms. Carol GARVEY
36 Director of Career Services ... Ms. Stacie HAYS
40 Director of Bookstore ... Ms. Jodi STROHBEEN
41 Athletic Director ... Mr. Tim JAGER
42 Campus Ministry ... Mr. Andy NELSON
112 Director of Gift Planning ... Mr. Jonathan BLUM
15 Director Human Resources ... Ms. Cindy WELP
21 Controller ... Mr. Paul TREFT
04 Administrative Asst to President ... Mrs. Lisa KROHN
105 Digital Communications Mgr ... Ms. Kim SANGWIN
39 Asst Director Residence Life ... Ms. Sheri HINEMAN
08 Library Director ... Mr. Adam FULLERTON
38 Personal Counselor ... Ms. Bobbi MEISTER
101 Secretary of the Institution/Board ... Mrs. Lisa KROHN
91 Director Administrative Computing ... Ms. Carla GREGG
106 Dir Online Education/E-learning ... Ms. Michelle E. LAUGHLIN
84 Director Enrollment Management ... Mrs. Terri A. CURRY
30 Director of Development ... Mr. Mike FREEMAN
44 Director Annual Giving ... Ms. J.J MARLOW
53 Dean of Education ... Dr. LuAnn M. HAASE
90 Director Academic Computing ... Mr. Mike HUSMANN
96 Director of Purchasing ... Mr. Ronald A. JORGENSEN

Mount Mercy University (C)

1330 Elmhurst Drive NE, Cedar Rapids IA 52402-4797
County: Linn FICE Identification: 001880
Unit ID: 154013
Telephone: (319) 363-8213 Carnegie Class: Masters/M
FAX Number: (319) 363-5270 Calendar System: 4/1/4
URL: www.mtmercy.edu
Established: 1928 Annual Undergrad Tuition & Fees: $31,998
Enrollment: 1,848 Coed
Affiliation or Control: Roman Catholic IRS Status: 501(c)3
Highest Offering: Doctorate
Accreditation: NH, MFCD, NURSE, SW

01 President ... Ms. Laurie HAMEN
05 Provost/Vice President Academic ... Dr. Timothy LAURENT
10 VP for Business & Finance ... Ms. Anne GILLESPIE
84 VP Enrollment & Marketing ... Dr. Terri SNYDERS CRUMLEY
30 VP of Development/Alumni Relations ... Ms. Brenda HAEFNER
42 VP of Mission and Ministry ... Sr. Linda BECHEN
32 Vice Pres for Student Success ... Dr. Nate KLEIN
20 Assoc Prov/Exec Dir Acad Innovation ... Dr. Tom CASTLE
06 Registrar ... Mr. Chance MCWORTHY
08 Director of Library Services ... Ms. Kristy RAINE
36 Director of Career Services ... Ms. Cheryl TABARELLA-REDD
110 Asst VP for Development/Alumni Rel ... Ms. Lonna DREWELOW
37 Director of Financial Aid ... Ms. Bethany DAVENPORT
26 Director of Marketing ... Ms. Jamie JONES
41 Director of Athletics ... Mr. Paul GAVIN
38 Director of Counseling ... Ms. Karol WHITE
13 Asst VP/Chief Information Officer ... Mr. Brian MCDONALD
19 Interim Director of Public Safety ... Mr. Joe CERRUTO
24 Academic Technology Librarian ... Ms. Nadia GILLITZER
15 Director of Human Resources ... Mr. Thomas DOERMANN
18 Director of Facilities ... Mr. Dave DENNIS
92 Director of Honors Program ... Dr. Anna WATERMAN
40 Campus Store Manager ... Vacant
04 Assistant to the President ... Ms. Kim BLANKENHEIM
09 Exec Dir of Institutional Research ... Ms. Lori HEYING

North Iowa Area Community College (D)

500 College Drive, Mason City IA 50401-7299
County: Cerro Gordo FICE Identification: 001877
Unit ID: 154059
Telephone: (641) 423-1264 Carnegie Class: Assoc/MT-VT-High Non
FAX Number: (641) 423-1711 Calendar System: Semester
URL: www.niacc.edu
Established: 1917 Annual Undergrad Tuition & Fees (In-District): $5,408
Enrollment: 2,947 Coed
Affiliation or Control: State/Local IRS Status: 501(c)3
Highest Offering: Associate Degree
Accreditation: NH, ADNUR, MAC, PTAA

01 President ... Dr. Steven D. SCHULZ
05 Vice President Academic Affairs ... Ms. Charlene WIDENER
10 Vice Pres Administrative Services ... Ms. Noele BEAVER
32 Vice President of Student Services ... Vacant
111 Director of Inst Advancement ... Mrs. Molly H. KNOLL
88 Director of JPEC ... Mr. Timothy J. PUTNAM
15 VP Organiz Develop & Human Resource ... Dr. Shelly M. SCHMIT
06 Registrar ... Mrs. Michelle L. PETZNICK
83 Chair Humanities/Soc Sci/Nat Sci ... Mr. Joe D. DAVIS
81 Chair Math & Wellness ... Dr. Kathy M. ROGOTZKE
72 Chair Industrial Division ... Ms. Laura L. WOOD
76 Chair Health Division ... Ms. Laurie DEGROOT
50 Chair Business/Ag Division ... Ms. Laura L. WOOD
51 Dean of Continuing Education ... Mr. Terry W. SCHUMAKER
37 Director of Financial Aid ... Mrs. Mary E. BLOOMINGDALE
20 Director Learning Services ... Ms. Dalila A. SAJADIAN
13 Chief Information Officer ... Mr. Josh C. MACK
103 WIOA Title I Director Region 2 ... Ms. Patti HANSON
121 Dir Student Support Svcs/Devel ... Ms. Jennifer PATTERSON
40 Bookstore Manager ... Mrs. Rhonda K. NESHEIM-KAUFFMAN
41 Director of Athletics ... Mr. Dan J. MASON
18 Director of Facilities Management ... Mr. Tony A. PAPPAS
21 Director Business Services ... Ms. Mindy R. EASTMAN
39 Director Student Housing ... Mr. Travis J. HERGERT
08 Librarian ... Vacant
26 Dir Marketing/Public Rel/Govt Affs ... Mrs. Valerie F. ZAHORSKI-SCHMIDT
88 Director Accelerator/Incubator ... Vacant
88 Director SBDC ... Mr. Brook S. BOEHMLER
88 Director of School Partnerships ... Mr. Brian M. WOGEN
88 Dir of Operations/Continuing Educ ... Mrs. Constance J. GLANDON
88 Director of Sales & Programming ... Mrs. Jody L. EAST
09 Director of Institutional Research ... Dr. Shelly M. SCHMIT
102 Grant Writer/Inst Fund Develop Spec ... Ms. Jana T. GRZENDA
106 Instructional Tech Coordinator ... Ms. Sara UDELHOFEN
29 Director Alumni Relations ... Ms. Andrea MUJICA
07 Director of Admissions ... Dr. Rachel L. MCGUIRE
28 Director of Diversity ... Dr. Shelly M. SCHMIT
04 Administrative Asst to President ... Ms. Ilsa OTTO
22 Dir Affirmative Action/EEO ... Dr. Shelly M. SCHMIT

Northeast Iowa Community College (E)

Box 400, Calmar IA 52132-0400
County: Winneshiek FICE Identification: 004587
Unit ID: 154110
Telephone: (563) 562-3263 Carnegie Class: Assoc/HVT-High Non
FAX Number: (563) 562-3719 Calendar System: Semester
URL: www.nicc.edu
Established: 1966 Annual Undergrad Tuition & Fees (In-District): $5,820
Enrollment: 4,536 Coed
Affiliation or Control: Local IRS Status: 501(c)3
Highest Offering: Associate Degree
Accreditation: NH, CAHIIM, COARC, DA

01 President ... Dr. Liang C. WEE
10 Vice Pres Finance & Administration ... Mr. David W. DAHMS
05 Chief Acad Ofcr/VP Academic Affairs ... Dr. Kathy J. NACOS-BURDS
46 Vice Pres Bus & Community Solutions ... Dr. Wendy A. MIHM-HEROLD
11 Assoc Vice President for Operations ... Ms. Rhonda K. SEIBERT
108 VP of Institutional Effectiveness ... Ms. Wendy S. KNIGHT
15 Exec Director of Human Resources ... Ms. Connie KUENNEN
106 Assoc Dean Online Learning ... Mr. Kyle T. COLLINS
13 Director Computer Information Sys ... Mr. Craig R. MEIRICK
09 Director of Institutional Research ... Ms. Lor M. MILLER
103 Director Economic Development ... Mr. Gregory A. WILLGING
37 Director of Financial Aid ... Mr. Randy D. MASHEK
06 District Registrar ... Ms. Karla R. WINTER
84 Director of Enrollment/Retention ... Ms. Sheila R. BECKER
36 Career Services Manager ... Mr. Chris E. ENTRINGER
07 Director of Admissions ... Ms. Kristi L. STRIEF
26 Dir Marketing/News/Publications ... Ms. Shea A. HERBST

Northeast Iowa Community College Peosta Campus (F)

8342 NICC Drive, Peosta IA 52068
Telephone: (800) 728-7367 Identification: 770063
Accreditation: &NH, EMT, MAC, RAD

Northwest Iowa Community College (G)

603 W Park Street, Sheldon IA 51201-1046
County: Sioux FICE Identification: 004600
Unit ID: 154129
Telephone: (712) 324-5061 Carnegie Class: Assoc/HVT-High Non
FAX Number: (712) 324-4136 Calendar System: Semester
URL: www.nwicc.edu
Established: 1966 Annual Undergrad Tuition & Fees (In-District): $6,120
Enrollment: 1,646 Coed
Affiliation or Control: State/Local IRS Status: 501(c)3
Highest Offering: Associate Degree
Accreditation: NH, CAHIIM, RAD

01 President ... Dr. Alethea F. STUBBE
05 VP Student & Academic Services ... Dr. John HARTOG
111 Director College Advancement ... Ms. Kristi LANDIS
10 VP Operations & Finance ... Mr. Mark BROWN
49 Dean Arts & Sci/Business/Health ... Dr. Rhonda R. PENNINGS
72 Dean Applied Technology ... Mr. Steve WALDSTEIN
53 Dean Center for Teaching & Learning ... Ms. Gretchen G. BARTELSON
21 Director of Business Services ... Ms. Jessica WILLIAMS
37 Director Financial Aid ... Ms. Karna HOFMEYER
84 Director Enrollment Management ... Ms. Lisa L. STORY
08 Coordinator of Library Services ... Ms. Renee FRANKLIN
13 Director of Technology & Info Svcs ... Mr. Mike OLDENKAMP
88 Coordinator of TRIO ... Ms. Tracy GORTER
06 Registrar/Assoc Dean of Students ... Ms. Beth SIBENALLER-WOODALL
15 Director of Human Resources ... Ms. Brandi HANSEN
26 Director Community Relations ... Ms. Kristin E. KOLLBAUM
18 Director Physical Facilities ... Mr. Doug RODGER

Northwestern College (H)

101 Seventh Street, SW, Orange City IA 51041-1996
County: Sioux FICE Identification: 001883
Unit ID: 154101
Telephone: (712) 707-7000 Carnegie Class: Bac-Diverse
FAX Number: (712) 707-7247 Calendar System: Semester
URL: www.nwciowa.edu
Established: 1882 Annual Undergrad Tuition & Fees: $31,100
Enrollment: 1,243 Coed
Affiliation or Control: Reformed Church In America IRS Status: 501(c)3
Highest Offering: Master's
Accreditation: NH, #CAATE, IACBE, NURSE, SW

01 President ... Mr. Gregory E. CHRISTY
32 Dean of Student Life ... Dr. Julie VERMEER ELLIOTT
05 Vice President for Academic Affairs ... Dr. D. Nathan PHINNEY
10 Vice President Financial Affairs ... Mr. Doug D. BEUKELMAN
111 Vice President Advancement ... Mr. Jay WIELENGA
84 Dean of Enrollment Management ... Mr. Mark BLOEMENDAAL
41 Director of Athletics ... Mr. Earl WOUDSTRA
08 Director of the Library ... Ms. Greta GROND
06 Registrar ... Ms. Sandy VAN KLEY
37 Director of Financial Aid ... Mr. Eric ANDERSON
13 Director of Computing Services ... Mr. Harlan R. JORGENSEN
26 Director of Public Relations ... Mr. Duane L. BEESON
36 Director of Career Development ... Mr. William C. MINNICK
38 Dir Student Counseling Services ... Dr. Sally EDMAN
18 Director of Maintenance/Operations ... Mr. Rick SCHOLTENS
29 Director Alumni Relations ... Mr. Corky KOERSELMAN
15 Director of Human Resources ... Mrs. Deb SANDBULTE
09 Director of Institutional Research ... Mr. Michael WALLINGA
04 Administrative Asst to President ... Ms. Jill HAARSMA
19 Director Security/Safety ... Mr. Andrew VAN OMMEREN
07 Director of Admissions ... Ms. Jackie DAVIS
106 Dean of Graduate & Adult Learning ... Dr. Rebecca HOEY

Palmer College of Chiropractic (I)

1000 Brady Street, Davenport IA 52803-5287
County: Scott FICE Identification: 012300
Unit ID: 154174
Telephone: (563) 884-5000 Carnegie Class: Spec-4-yr-Other Health

FAX Number: (563) 884-5409 Calendar System: Trimester
URL: www.palmer.edu
Established: 1897 Annual Undergrad Tuition & Fees: $9,225
Enrollment: 2,237 Coed
Affiliation or Control: Independent Non-Profit IRS Status: 501(c)3
Highest Offering: First Professional Degree
Accreditation: NH, CHIRO

01 Chancellor Dr. Dennis M. MARCHIORI
05 College Provost Dr. Daniel J. WEINERT
108 Vice Chancellor for Inst Effect Dr. Robert E. PERCUOCO
32 Vice Chancellor Student Success Dr. Kevin A. CUNNINGHAM
84 Vice Chancellor for Enrollment Vacant
10 Vice Chancellor for Finance Ms. Jennifer RANDAZZO
46 Dean of Research Dr. Cynthia LONG
26 Vice Chancellor for Mktg & Comm Mr. James O'CONNOR
111 VC for Institutional Advancement Ms. Barbara MELBOURNE
20 Dean of Academic Affairs Dr. Kevin PAUSTIAN
17 Exec Dean of Clinic Affairs Dr. Ron BOESCH
20 Assoc Dean of Academic Affairs Dr. Michael TUNNING
20 Assoc Dean of Academic Affairs Dr. Michelle BARBER
110 Exec Dir Advancement Ms. Clare THOMPSON
06 Senior Director/Registrar Ms. Mindy S. LEAHY
09 Sr Dir Inst Research/Effectiveness Dr. Dustin C. DERBY
88 Sr Dir Accred & Licensure Ms. Beth BARCLAY
21 Senior Dir for Financial Affairs Ms. Kathleen GRAVES
13 Senior Dir Information Technology Mr. Mark WISELEY
15 Senior Dir of Human Resources Vacant
18 Senior Director of Facilities Mr. Michael ERNSTER
51 Sr Dir Continuing Education Dr. Mary FROST
07 Director of Campus Enrollment Mr. Erik SELLAS
37 Senior Dir of Financial Planning Ms. Abbey NAGLE-KUCH
108 Senior Director for Assessment Vacant
121 Sr Dir of Academic Support Services Dr. Alex MARGRAVE
08 Senior Director of Library Vacant
88 Sr Dir Quality Assurance/Sys Organ Ms. Earlye A. JULIEN
19 Sr Dir Campus Safety and Security Mr. Brian SHARKEY
88 Sr Dir Clinic Business Ms. Gretchen ROBINSON
27 Sr Dir Marketing Ms. Kimberly KENT
101 Exec Director Board Affairs Ms. Lynne LINDSTROM
88 Assoc Dean of Clinic Research Dr. Robert VINING

St. Ambrose University (A)

518 W Locust Street, Davenport IA 52803-2898
County: Scott FICE Identification: 001889
Unit ID: 154235
Telephone: (563) 333-6000 Carnegie Class: Masters/L
FAX Number: (563) 333-6243 Calendar System: Semester
URL: www.sau.edu
Established: 1882 Annual Undergrad Tuition & Fees: $30,894
Enrollment: 3,114 Coed
Affiliation or Control: Roman Catholic IRS Status: 501(c)3
Highest Offering: Doctorate
Accreditation: NH, ACBSP, #ARCPA, CAEPT, NURSE, OT, PTA, SP, SW

01 President Sr. Joan LESCINSKI, CSJ
05 Provost & VP Academic/Student Affs Dr. Paul KOCH
10 Vice President Finance Mr. Michael C. POSTER
42 Chaplain Rev. Thomas J. HENNEN
111 Vice President Advancement Mr. James R. STANGLE
84 Vice Pres Enrollment Management Mr. James P. LOFTUS
46 Assoc Vice Pres Assess/ Research Dr. Tracy SCHUSTER-MATLOCK
11 Director Administrative Services Ms. Carol A. GLINES
26 Director of Communications Mr. Craig J. DEVRIEZE
32 Dean of Students Mr. Christopher A. WAUGH
15 Director Human Resources Ms. Audrey D. BLAIR
13 Exec Dir of Information Resources Ms. Mary B. HEINZMAN
29 Director Alumni Rels & Spec Project Ms. Anne A. GANNAWAY
37 Director Financial Aid Ms. Julie A. HAACK
38 Director Counseling Dr. Sarah E. OLIVER
18 Director Physical Plant Mr. Jim M. HANNON
06 Registrar Mr. Dan L. ZEIMET
23 Director of Health Services Ms. Nancy A. HINES
19 Director of Security Mr. Robert CHRISTOPHER
39 Director of Residence Life Mr. Matt HANSEN
08 Director Library Ms. Mary B. HEINZMAN
36 Director Career Development Ms. Kimberly MATTESON
41 Athletic Director Mr. Michael S. HOLMES
94 Director of Women's Studies Ms. Katy A. STRZEPEK
40 Manager of Bookstore Mr. Cory W. SAMBDMAN
104 Asst VP International Education Vacant
73 Director Masters Pastoral Theology Rev. Bud GRANT
88 Director Masters Criminal Justice Dr. Chrisopher C. BARNUM
49 Dean College Arts & Sciences Dr. Paula M. MCNUTT
50 Dean College Business Dr. Maritza ESPINA
76 Dean Health & Human Services Dr. Sandra L. CASSADY
88 Dean Academic Adult & Graduate Pgm Dr. Regina M. MATHESON
54 Chair Engineering & Physical Sci Dr. Andrew J. LUTZ
57 Chair Fine Arts Ms. Kristin QUINN
88 Director Occupational Therapy Dr. Lynn J. KILBURG
88 Director Masters of Accounting Dr. Allison S. AMBROSE
58 Director MBA Pgm Dr. Russell W. WRIGHT
28 Director of Diversity Mr. Ryan C. SADDLER
04 Senior Asst to President Ms. Jana M. SEUTTER
09 Director Institutional Research Ms. Clare M. HOLLADAY
44 Assoc VP Legacy Giving/Campaign Dir Ms. Sally E. CRINO
53 Director School of Education Dr. Thomas CARPENTER
86 Dir Corporate & Community Relations Mr. Ty J. GRUNDER
101 Secretary of the Institution/Board Sr. Joan LESCINSKI, CSJ
102 Dir Foundation/Corporate Relations Ms. Nikki J. DEFAUW

106 Director Online Learning Mr. Donnie L. INGRAM
108 Director Institutional Assessment Dr. Tracy SCHUSTER-MATLOCK
96 Director of Purchasing Ms. Carol A. GLINES
22 Dir Compliance & Title IX Coord Mr. Kevin R. CARLSON

St. Luke's College (B)

2720 Stone Park Boulevard, Sioux City IA 51104-0010
County: Woodbury FICE Identification: 007291
Unit ID: 154262
Telephone: (712) 279-3149 Carnegie Class: Spec-4-yr-Other Health
FAX Number: (712) 233-8017 Calendar System: Semester
URL: www.stlukescollege.edu
Established: 1995 Annual Undergrad Tuition & Fees: $20,440
Enrollment: 274 Coed
Affiliation or Control: Independent Non-Profit IRS Status: 501(c)3
Highest Offering: Baccalaureate
Accreditation: NH, ADNUR, COARC, NURSE, PAST, RAD

01 Chancellor Mr. Michael D. STILES
05 Chief Academic Office/Provost Dr. Robert LOCH
32 Dean Student Services Ms. Danelle D. JOHANNSEN
66 Dean Nursing Education Dr. Susan BOWERS
76 Dean Health Sciences Dr. Dan JENSEN
06 Registrar Ms. Michelle FITCH
113 Bursar Ms. Lori MEIER
84 Enrollment Mgmt/Marketing Coord Ms. Sherry MCCARTHY
08 Dept Chair/Library Ms. Nancy ZUBROD
29 Alumni/Events Coordinator Vacant

Shiloh University (C)

100 Shiloh Drive, Kalona IA 52247
County: Washington Identification: 667095
Unit ID: 480499
Telephone: (319) 656-2447 Carnegie Class: Spec-4-yr-Faith
FAX Number: (319) 656-2448 Calendar System: Trimester
URL: www.shilohuniversity.edu
Established: 2006 Annual Undergrad Tuition & Fees: $4,800
Enrollment: 53 Coed
Affiliation or Control: Independent Non-Profit IRS Status: 501(c)3
Highest Offering: Doctorate
Accreditation: DEAC

00 Chancellor Vacant
01 President Mr. Christopher REEVES
05 Vice President of Academics Dr. Mark GLENN
13 Vice President of Technology Mr. James WIRTHLIN
88 Dean BA New Testament Program Ms. Amanda DEMPSTER
88 Dean BA Biblical Pastoral Program Ms. Amanda DEMPSTER
58 Dean Doctoral Studies Dr. Mark GLENN
58 Dean Graduate Programs Dr. Ana I. WOOD
06 Registrar Mr. Joshua WHEELER
07 Admissions Coordinator Mr. Jeremy RICHARDSON
08 Library Director Mrs. Julie MCPHAIL
11 Chief of Operations/Administration Vacant

Simpson College (D)

701 North C Street, Indianola IA 50125-1297
County: Warren FICE Identification: 001887
Unit ID: 154350
Telephone: (515) 961-6251 Carnegie Class: Bac-A&S
FAX Number: (515) 961-1623 Calendar System: Other
URL: www.simpson.edu
Established: 1860 Annual Undergrad Tuition & Fees: $39,144
Enrollment: 1,479 Coed
Affiliation or Control: United Methodist IRS Status: 501(c)3
Highest Offering: Master's
Accreditation: NH, #CAATE, MUS

01 President Dr. Jay K. SIMMONS
05 Vice Pres/Dean Academic Affairs Vacant
10 Vice President Business/Finance Ms. Cathy HOCH
111 Vice President College Advancement Mr. Robert J. LANE
32 Vice President Student Development Dr. Heidi LEVINE
84 Vice President Enrollment Ms. Deborah J. TIERNEY
13 VP Info Svcs/Chief Info Officer Vacant
37 Asst VP Enrollment/Financial Aid Ms. Tracie PAVON
06 Registrar & Associate Dean Ms. Jody RAGAN
35 Dean of Students Mr. Luke BEHAUNEK
26 Vice President Marketing and PR Vacant
08 Director of Library Ms. Cynthia M. DYER
15 Director of Human Resources Ms. Mary E. BARTLEY
36 Director of Career Services Ms. Bobbi SULLIVAN
07 Director of Admissions Ms. Alison SWANSON
41 Athletic Director Mr. Robert NUTGRASS
96 Director of Procurement Ms. Marilyn J. LEEK
35 Assistant Dean of Students Mr. Richard O. RAMOS
42 Chaplain Rev. Mara BAILEY
18 Director Campus Services Mr. John HARRIS
21 Controller Mr. Logan EDEL
19 Coordinator of Campus Security Mr. Chris FRERICHS
51 Associate Dean Adult Learning Ms. Amy GIESEKE
104 Director of International Education Mr. Jay WILKINSON
04 Administrative Asst to President Ms. Brenda K. WICKETT
29 Director Alumni Relations Mr. Andy ENGLISH

Simpson College West Des Moines (E)

1415 28th Street, #250, West Des Moines IA 50266
Telephone: (515) 309-3099 Identification: 770064
Accreditation: &NH

Southeastern Community College (F)

1500 W Agency Road, PO Box 180,
West Burlington IA 52655-0180
County: Des Moines FICE Identification: 001848
Unit ID: 154378
Telephone: (319) 752-2731 Carnegie Class: Assoc/MT-VT-High Non
FAX Number: (319) 752-4957 Calendar System: Semester
URL: www.scciowa.edu
Established: 1966 Annual Undergrad Tuition & Fees (In-District): $5,580
Enrollment: 2,658 Coed
Affiliation or Control: State/Local IRS Status: 501(c)3
Highest Offering: Associate Degree
Accreditation: NH, COARC, EMT, MAC

01 President Dr. Michael ASH
05 Vice Pres of Academic Affairs Dr. Janet SHEPHERD
32 Vice President of Student Services Ms. Joan WILLIAMS
11 Vice Pres Administrative Services Mr. Kevin CARR
30 Exec Director for Inst Advancement Ms. Rebecca RUMP
37 Financial Aid Officer Ms. Renae ARMENTROUT
84 Enrollment Coordinator Ms. Dana CHRISMAN
06 Registrar Mr. Dennis MARINO
15 Director Human Resources Ms. Laurie HEMPEN
49 Dean Arts and Sciences Dr. Chris SEDLACK
12 Executive Dean Dr. Teresa GARCIA
75 Dean Career/Technical Education Ms. Susan DUNEK
26 Dir Marketing/Communications Mr. Jeff EBBING

Southeastern Community College Keokuk Campus (G)

335 Messenger Road, Keokuk IA 52632
Telephone: (319) 313-1928 Identification: 770065
Accreditation: &NH

Southwestern Community College (H)

1501 W Townline Street, Creston IA 50801-1098
County: Union FICE Identification: 001857
Unit ID: 154396
Telephone: (641) 782-7081 Carnegie Class: Assoc/MT-VT-High Non
FAX Number: (641) 782-3312 Calendar System: Semester
URL: www.swcciowa.edu
Established: 1966 Annual Undergrad Tuition & Fees (In-State): $5,888
Enrollment: 1,574 Coed
Affiliation or Control: State IRS Status: 501(c)3
Highest Offering: Associate Degree
Accreditation: NH

01 President/CEO Dr. Barbara J. CRITTENDEN
03 Vice President Economic Development Mr. Thomas L. LESAN
05 Vice President Instruction Mr. Bill TAYLOR
10 Chief Financial Officer Mrs. Tia SAMO
32 Dean of Student Services Vacant
20 Asst Vice Pres of Instruction Mrs. Lindsay STOAKS
106 Director of Distance Education Mr. Doug GREENE
15 Director of Human Resources Mrs. Jolene GRIFFITH
26 Director Marketing/Enrollment Mgmt Mrs. Terri HIGGINS
08 Director Learning Resource Center Mrs. Ann COULTER
13 Director of Information Technology Mr. Scott HELM
37 Director of Financial Aid Ms. Kylee KLOMMHAUS
06 Registrar Ms. Alyssa RILEY
04 Administrative Asst to President Vacant
07 Director of Admissions Ms. Caitlyn MAITLEN

University of Dubuque (I)

2000 University Avenue, Dubuque IA 52001-5099
County: Dubuque FICE Identification: 001891
Unit ID: 153278
Telephone: (563) 589-3000 Carnegie Class: Masters/M
FAX Number: (563) 589-3682 Calendar System: 4/1/4
URL: www.dbq.edu
Established: 1852 Annual Undergrad Tuition & Fees: $34,110
Enrollment: 2,366 Coed
Affiliation or Control: Presbyterian Church (U.S.A.) IRS Status: 501(c)3
Highest Offering: Doctorate
Accreditation: NH, AAB, #ARCPA, NURSE, THEOL

01 President Dr. Jeffrey F. BULLOCK
04 Exec Assistant to the President Mrs. Sandra M. LUDESCHER
05 VPAA/Dean of the College Dr. Mark WARD
10 Vice Pres Finance/Auxiliary Svcs Mr. James D. STEINER
84 Vice Pres Enrollment/Univ Rels Mr. Peter L. SMITH
32 Vice President/Dean of Student Life Mr. Mike J. DURNIN
07 AVP & Dean of Admission Mr. Robert D. BROSHOUS
13 Director of Technology Ms. Sherry CUSICK
06 Registrar Ms. Kim WULFEKUHLE-ISAAC
08 University Librarian Mr. Christopher DOLL
15 Director of Human Resources Ms. Julie MACTAGGART
37 Dean of Student Financial Planning Ms. Teresa BRAHM
20 Dean for Academic Affairs Dr. Gail HAYES
09 Director of Institutional Research Ms. Keri SAMSON
36 Director of Vocation Dr. Amy BAUS
29 Director for Alumni Engagement Ms. Katie KRAUS
40 Director of Campus Stores Ms. Margo KETELS
41 Director of Athletics Mr. Dan RUNKLE
18 Director of Facilities Mr. Craig KLOFT
88 Executive Director Heritage Center Mr. Thomas J. ROBBINS

Upper Iowa University (A)

605 Washington, Box 1857, Fayette IA 52142-1857
County: Fayette FICE Identification: 001893
Unit ID: 154493
Telephone: (563) 425-5200 Carnegie Class: Masters/L
FAX Number: (563) 425-5271 Calendar System: Semester
URL: www.uiu.edu
Established: 1857 Annual Undergrad Tuition & Fees: $30,450
Enrollment: 4,943 Coed
Affiliation or Control: Independent Non-Profit IRS Status: 501(c)3
Highest Offering: Master's
Accreditation: NH, #CAATE, NURSE

01 President ... Dr. William R. DUFFY, II
05 Provost ... Dr. P. Joan POOR
10 Interim Chief Financial Officer ... Mr. Marty PARSONS
82 VP Student Life/International Pgms ... Mr. Ismael J. BETANCOURT VELEZ
84 VP Enrollment Management ... Ms. Kathy FRANKEN
30 VP of External Affairs ... Mr. Andrew WENTHE
36 Dean Students/Dir Residence Life ... Ms. Jean MERKLE
12 South Central Region Director ... Ms. Cynthia BENTLEY
12 Director North Central ... Ms. Jen WEBB
07 Exec Director of Admissions ... Mr. Matthew HIGGINS
06 Registrar ... Mrs. Holly STREETER
08 Director Library Services ... Mr. Rob HUDSON
41 Director Athletics ... Mr. Rick HARTZELL
04 Exec Assistant to the President ... Ms. Holly D. WOLFF
105 Director Internet Development ... Mr. Joel KUNZE
21 Controller ... Ms. Linda GEBEL
36 Director of Career Development ... Ms. Hope TRAINOR
35 Director Student Activities ... Mr. Jake BASS
26 Exec Dir for Comm and Marketing ... Mr. Karl EASTTORP
29 Director of Alumni Relations ... Mr. Andrew WENTHE
13 Director Information Technology ... Mr. Terry SMID
15 Director Human Resources ... Mr. Aaron WEDO
88 Director Sports Info Services ... Mr. Howard THOMPSON
18 Exec Director of Facilities ... Mr. Jesse PLEGGENKUHLE
40 Bookstore Manager ... Ms. Megan EIMERS
37 Director Student Financial Aid ... Ms. Kelli BELL
38 Director Student Counseling ... Ms. Crystal COLE

Waldorf University (B)

106 S 6th Street, Forest City IA 50436-1713
County: Winnebago FICE Identification: 001895
Unit ID: 154518
Telephone: (641) 585-2450 Carnegie Class: Masters/M
FAX Number: (641) 585-8194 Calendar System: Semester
URL: www.waldorf.edu
Established: 1903 Annual Undergrad Tuition & Fees: $22,076
Enrollment: 2,487 Coed
Affiliation or Control: Proprietary IRS Status: Proprietary
Highest Offering: Master's
Accreditation: NH

01 President ... Dr. Robert ALSOP
05 Dean of Col/Vice Pres Acad Affs ... Dr. Vincent BEACH
10 Vice President Business Affairs ... Vacant
04 Assistant to the President ... Ms. Cindy CARTER
32 Dean of Students ... Mr. Jason RAMAKER
92 Dean of Honors Program ... Dr. Suzanne FALCK-YI
07 Director Admissions ... Mr. Scott PITCHER
08 Library Director ... Mr. Derrick BURTON
29 Director of Alumni Affairs ... Ms. Hannah EARLL
06 Registrar ... Mr. Darrell BARBOUR
37 Director of Financial Aid ... Mr. Duane POLSDOFER
18 Director of Facilities Services ... Mr. Tim SEVERSON
26 Marketing Director ... Ms. Audrey SPARKS
44 Director of Annual Fund ... Ms. Nancy OLSON
38 Counselor ... Mr. James AMELSBERG
41 Athletic Director ... Mr. Denny JEROME
36 Director Student Placement ... Ms. Mary REISETTER
40 Bookstore Manager ... Ms. Karla SCHAEFER
15 Director Human Resources ... Ms. Dawn RAMAKER

Wartburg College (C)

PO Box 1003, 100 Wartburg Boulevard, Waverly IA 50677-0903
County: Bremer FICE Identification: 001896
Unit ID: 154527
Telephone: (319) 352-8200 Carnegie Class: Bac-A&S
FAX Number: (319) 352-8247 Calendar System: Other
URL: www.wartburg.edu
Established: 1852 Annual Undergrad Tuition & Fees: $41,280
Enrollment: 1,527 Coed
Affiliation or Control: Evangelical Lutheran Church In America
IRS Status: 501(c)3
Highest Offering: Baccalaureate
Accreditation: NH, CAEPN, MUS, SW

01 President ... Dr. Darrel D. COLSON
05 VP Acad Affairs/Dean Faculty ... Dr. Brian ERNSTING
32 VP Student Life/Dean Students ... Dr. Daniel KITTLE
10 VP for Finance and Administration ... Mr. Richard SEGGERMAN
111 Vice Pres Institutional Advancement ... Mr. Scott C. LEISINGER
84 Vice Pres Enrollment Management ... Dr. Edith J. WALDSTEIN
07 Executive Director of Admissions ... Ms. Tara WINTER
06 Registrar ... Ms. Sheree S. COVERT
26 Dir of Marketing/Communications ... Mr. Chris KNUDSON
13 Asst VP for Information Tech/CIO ... Mr. Gary L. WIPPERMAN
08 College Librarian ... Vacant
29 Dir Alumni/Parent Rel/Annual Giving ... Ms. Renee VOVES
37 Director of Financial Aid ... Ms. Jen L. SASSMAN
41 Exec Dir of Athletics and Wellness ... Mr. Eric R. WILLIS
42 Dean of Spiritual Life ... Rev.Dr. Brian BECKSTROM
18 Director of Physical Plant ... Mr. Scott SHARAR
39 Dir Res Life/Chief Student Conduct ... Ms. Cassie HALES
36 Dir of Pathways/Career Svcs ... Mr. Derek N. SOLHEIM
43 Chief Compliance Officer ... Ms. Karen THALACKER
38 Director of Counseling Svcs ... Ms. Stephanie R. NEWSOM
40 Store Mgr & Textbook Services Dir ... Ms. Janet HUEBNER
85 Dir of International Student Svcs ... Mr. Zafrul AMIN
35 Director of Student Engagement ... Ms. Lindsey LEONARD
88 Campus Pastor ... Vacant
21 Chief Business Officer & Treasurer ... Mr. Richard W. SEGGERMAN
15 Director of HR & Payroll ... Ms. Jamie HOLLAWAY
112 Senior Gift Planner ... Mr. Donald J. MEYER
92 Director Honors Program ... Dr. Leilani ZART
101 Exec Admin President Office/Sec BOR ... Ms. Janeen K. STEWART
20 Asst Dean of the Faculty ... Mr. Douglas D. KOSCHMEDER
28 Dir Multicultural Student Services ... Ms. Krystal MADLOCK
19 Director Campus Security & Safety ... Mr. Jay TOMMASIN
21 Controller ... Ms. Tracy RUCKER
09 Dir Assessment/Accreditation/Plng ... Dr. Robert STANLEY

Wartburg Theological Seminary (D)

333 Wartburg Place, Dubuque IA 52003
County: Dubuque FICE Identification: 001897
Unit ID: 154536
Telephone: (563) 589-0200 Carnegie Class: Spec-4-yr-Faith
FAX Number: (563) 589-0333 Calendar System: 4/1/4
URL: www.wartburgseminary.edu
Established: 1854 Annual Graduate Tuition & Fees: N/A
Enrollment: 121 Coed
Affiliation or Control: Evangelical Lutheran Church In America
IRS Status: 501(c)3
Highest Offering: Master's; No Undergraduates
Accreditation: NH, THEOL

01 President ... Rev. Louise N. JOHNSON
05 Academic Dean of the Seminary ... Rev.Dr. Craig L. NESSAN
10 Vice Pres for Finance & Operations ... Mr. Andy B. WILLENBORG
30 Vice President for Development ... Mr. Paul K. ERBES
07 Vice Pres for Admiss & Student Svcs ... Rev. Amy L. CURRENT
08 Library Director ... Ms. Susan J S. EBERTZ
06 Registrar/Admin Assistant to Dean ... Dr. Kevin L. ANDERSON
04 Asst to President ... Ms. Lynne BAUMHOVER
37 Director Student Financial Aid ... Ms. Barbara SIMON

Western Iowa Tech Community College (E)

PO Box 5199, 4647 Stone Avenue, Sioux City IA 51102-5199
County: Woodbury FICE Identification: 007316
Unit ID: 154572
Telephone: (712) 274-6400 Carnegie Class: Assoc/HVT-High Non
FAX Number: (712) 274-6412 Calendar System: Semester
URL: www.witcc.edu
Established: 1966 Annual Undergrad Tuition & Fees (In-District): $4,272
Enrollment: 5,731 Coed
Affiliation or Control: State/Local IRS Status: 501(c)3
Highest Offering: Associate Degree
Accreditation: NH, DA, EMT, MAC, PNUR, PTAA, SURGT

01 President ... Dr. Terry MURRELL
05 VP Learning ... Ms. Juline ALBERT
10 VP Finance/Administrative Svcs ... Mr. Troy JASMAN
15 Dean Human Resources ... Ms. Jackie PLENDL
13 Dean of Information Technologies ... Mr. Mike LOGAN
88 Dean of Students ... Ms. Janet GILL
20 Executive Dean of Instruction ... Mr. Darin MOELLER
35 Director Student Support Services ... Ms. Sara KLATT
30 Exec Director College Development ... Mr. Jim BRAUNSCHWEIG
08 Library Manager ... Ms. Sharon DYKSHOORN
88 Director Small Business Devel Ctr ... Mr. Todd RAUSCH
18 Director Physical Plant ... Mr. Kyle HUESER
06 Registrar ... Ms. Lora VANDER ZWAAG
26 Director Marketing/Publications ... Ms. Andrea ROHLENA
37 Director of Financial Aid ... Mr. Merlyn KATHOL

William Penn University (F)

201 Trueblood Avenue, Oskaloosa IA 52577-1799
County: Mahaska FICE Identification: 001900
Unit ID: 154590
Telephone: (641) 673-1001 Carnegie Class: Bac-Diverse
FAX Number: (641) 673-1396 Calendar System: Semester
URL: www.wmpenn.edu
Established: 1873 Annual Undergrad Tuition & Fees: $25,600
Enrollment: 1,339 Coed
Affiliation or Control: Friends IRS Status: 501(c)3
Highest Offering: Master's
Accreditation: NH, NURSE

01 President ... Mr. John OTTOSSON
05 Vice Pres for Academic Affairs ... Dr. Noel STAHLE
111 Vice Pres for Advancement ... Ms. Marsha RIORDAN
10 VP for Finance ... Ms. Bonnie JOHNSON
84 VP for Retention & Evening Enroll ... Ms. Kerra STRONG
32 Dean of Students ... Ms. Heidi SCHOLES
108 Director of Assessment ... Dr. Jared PEARCE
06 Registrar ... Ms. DeAnne DOLL
37 Director of Financial Aid ... Ms. Cyndi PEIFFER
36 Career Services Coordinator ... Ms. Debbie STEVENS
08 Head Librarian ... Ms. Jennifer STERLING
15 Human Resource Coordinator ... Ms. Angella DURIAN-GAMBELL
35 Director of Student Activities ... Mr. Jon HAUGEN
09 Director of Institutional Research ... Mr. Michael EDWARDS
40 Bookstore Manager ... Vacant
83 Chair Div of Social/Behavioral Sci ... Dr. Michael COLLINS
72 Co-Chair Div of Applied Technology ... Dr. Ted MCCOY
72 Co-Chair Div of Applied Technology ... Mr. Jim HOEKSEMA
53 Chair Division of Education ... Ms. Cathy WILLIAMSON
50 Chair Div of Business Admin ... Mr. David MEINERT
79 Chair Division of Humanities ... Dr. Anita MEINERT
76 Chair Div of Health & Life Sciences ... Dr. Gary CHRISTOPHER
66 Chair Div of Nursing ... Dr. Kimberley BROWN
04 Executive Asst to President ... Ms. Angella DURIAN-GAMBELL
13 Director of Information Services ... Mr. William HUGHES
19 Director of Campus Safety ... Mr. Troy BOSTON
38 Campus Counselor ... Ms. Tyne SMITH
39 Director of Residence Life ... Ms. Tanya MAMMEN
41 Athletic Director ... Mr. Nik RULE
07 Director of Admissions ... Ms. Madison STIENKE
101 Secretary of the Institution/Board ... Ms. Angella M. DURIAN-GAMBELL
29 Director Alumni Affairs ... Mr. James KOBUS

KANSAS

Allen County Community College (G)

1801 N Cottonwood, Iola KS 66749-1698
County: Allen FICE Identification: 001901
Unit ID: 154642
Telephone: (620) 901-6400 Carnegie Class: Assoc/HT-Mix Trad/Non
FAX Number: (620) 365-7406 Calendar System: Semester
URL: www.allencc.edu
Established: 1923 Annual Undergrad Tuition & Fees (In-District): $3,808
Enrollment: 2,556 Coed
Affiliation or Control: State/Local IRS Status: 501(c)3
Highest Offering: Associate Degree
Accreditation: NH

01 President ... Mr. John A. MASTERSON
05 Vice Pres for Academic Affairs ... Mr. Jon MARSHALL
10 Vice Pres for Finance & Operations ... Mr. Brian COUNSIL
32 Vice Pres Student Affairs ... Ms. Cynthia JACOBSON
12 Dean for the Iola Campus ... Mrs. Tosca HARRIS
12 Dean for the Burlingame Campus ... Vacant
106 Dean for Online Learning ... Mrs. Sherry PHELAN
08 Director of Library ... Mrs. Virginia SHAFFER
13 Director of MIS ... Mr. Doug DUNLAP
37 Director of Financial Aid ... Mrs. Kim MURRY
18 Director of Physical Plant Opers ... Mr. Tyler FREDRICKS
07 Director of Admissions ... Mrs. Kara WHEELER
41 Director of Athletics ... Mr. Doug DESMARTEAU
40 Director of Bookstore ... Mrs. Reine LOFLIN
76 Allied Health Director ... Ms. Kattia ANDREWS
85 Foreign Student Advisor ... Mrs. Nichole PETERS
09 Director Inst Research/Reporting ... Ms. Deanna MANN
35 Director Student Life ... Mr. Ryan BILDERBACK
06 Registrar ... Mrs. Bobbie HAVILAND
26 Public Relations Coordinator ... Mrs. Nancy FORD
15 Human Resources Specialist ... Mrs. Shellie REGEHR
30 Director of Development ... Mrs. Aimee THOMPSON
38 Director of Advisement ... Mrs. Nikki PETERS

Allen County Community College Burlingame Campus (H)

100 Bloomquist, Burlingame KS 66413
Telephone: (785) 654-2416 Identification: 770249
Accreditation: &NH

Baker University (I)

618 Eighth Street, Baldwin City KS 66006-0065
County: Douglas FICE Identification: 001903
Unit ID: 154688
Telephone: (785) 594-6451 Carnegie Class: DU-Mod
FAX Number: (785) 594-2522 Calendar System: 4/1/4
URL: www.bakeru.edu
Established: 1858 Annual Undergrad Tuition & Fees: $29,830
Enrollment: 2,694 Coed
Affiliation or Control: United Methodist IRS Status: 501(c)3
Highest Offering: Doctorate
Accreditation: NH, ACBSP, CAEP, EXSC, MUS, NURSE

01 President ... Dr. Lynne MURRAY
05 Interim Provost ... Dr. Tes MEHRING
84 VP of Enrollment/Marketing ... Vacant
13 CIO/VP Strategic Plng/Academic Res ... Mr. Andy JETT
10 VP of Finance & Administration ... Ms. Shelley KNEUVEAN
53 Dean School of Education ... Dr. Marc CHILDRESS
66 Dean of School of Nursing ... Dr. Bernadette M. FETTEROLF
49 Interim Dean of CAS ... Dr. Darcy RUSSELL
107 Interim Dean SPGS ... Dr. Emily FORD

41 Director Of Athletics .... Mr. Nate HOUSER
07 Director of Admissions .... Ms. Cheryl MCCRARY
26 Director of Marketing & Comm .... Ms. Dolores KITCHIN
06 University Registrar .... Ms. Ruth MILLER
21 Chief Accounting Officer/Controller .... Ms. Melissa VAN LEIDEN
18 Dir of Physical Plant/Facility Ops .... Mr. Jeremy PORTLOCK
42 Minister to the University .... Rev. Kevin HOPKINS
37 Senior Director of Financial Aid .... Ms. Jana PARKS
15 Chief Human Resources Officer .... Ms. Connie DEEL
32 Dean of Students .... Dr. Cassy BAILEY
09 Director of Institutional Research .... Mr. Eric HAYS
29 Director of Alumni Relations .... Mr. Doug BARTH
36 Director of Career Services .... Ms. Susan WADE
38 Dir of Health & Counseling Center .... Dr. Tim HODGES
08 Director of Library Services .... Mr. Ray WALLING

Baker University School of Professional and Graduate Studies (A)

7301 College Boulevard, Suite 120,
Overland Park KS 66210-1856
Telephone: (913) 491-4432 — Identification: 770250
Accreditation: &NH

Barclay College (B)

607 N Kingman, Haviland KS 67059-0288
County: Kiowa — FICE Identification: 001917
Unit ID: 155070
Telephone: (620) 862-5252 — Carnegie Class: Spec-4-yr-Faith
FAX Number: (620) 862-5242 — Calendar System: Semester
URL: www.barclaycollege.edu
Established: 1917 — Annual Undergrad Tuition & Fees: $19,000
Enrollment: 259 — Coed
Affiliation or Control: Independent Non-Profit — IRS Status: 501(c)3
Highest Offering: Master's
Accreditation: NH, BI

01 President .... Dr. Royce FRAZIER
00 Chancellor .... Dr. Adrian HALVERSTADT
05 Interim VP Academics .... Mr. Tim HAWKINS
10 VP Business Services .... Mr. Lee ANDERS
32 VP Student Services .... Mr. Ryan HAASE
111 VP Institutional Advancement .... Mr. Larry LEWIS
06 Registrar .... Mr. Mark MILLER
37 Director Student Financial Aid .... Ms. Ginger MAGGARD
84 Director Enrollment Services .... Mr. Justin KENDALL
08 Librarian .... Mrs. Jeannie ROSS
29 Alumni Relations .... Dr. Herb FRAZIER
106 Dir Online Education/E-learning .... Mr. Aaron STOKES
13 Chief Info Technology Officer (CIO) .... Mr. Trent MAGGARD
15 Director Personnel Services .... Mrs. Gayle MORTIMER
18 Chief Facilities/Physical Plant .... Mr. CD FITCH
19 Director Security/Safety .... Mr. Ryan HAASE
41 Athletic Director .... Mr. Shane SHETLEY
09 Director of Institutional Research .... Dr. Keith WHITE
25 Chief Contracts/Grants Admin .... Mr. Larry LEWIS

Barton County Community College (C)

245 NE 30th Road, Great Bend KS 67530-9107
County: Barton — FICE Identification: 004608
Unit ID: 154697
Telephone: (620) 792-2701 — Carnegie Class: Assoc/HT-High Non
FAX Number: (620) 792-5624 — Calendar System: Semester
URL: www.bartonccc.edu
Established: 1965 — Annual Undergrad Tuition & Fees (In-District): $3,584
Enrollment: 4,228 — Coed
Affiliation or Control: State/Local — IRS Status: 501(c)3
Highest Offering: Associate Degree
Accreditation: NH, ADNUR, EMT, MLTAD

01 President .... Dr. Carl R. HEILMAN
05 VP of Instruction .... Mrs. Elaine SIMMONS
10 VP of Administration .... Mr. Mark DEAN
32 VP of Student Services .... Mrs. Angela MADDY
13 Chief Information Officer .... Mrs. Michelle KAISER
20 Dean of Academics .... Mr. Brian HOWE
88 Dean of Military Academic Services .... Ms. Ashley ANDERSON
37 Assoc Dean Stdt Svcs/Dir Fin Aid .... Mrs. Myrna PERKINS
111 Exec Dir Institutional Advancement .... Mrs. Coleen CAPE
66 Exec Dir Nursing & Healthcare Educ .... Dr. Kathy KOTTAS
50 Exec Dir of Business/Tech/Cmty Educ .... Ms. Jane HOWARD
103 Exec Dir Workforce Trng & Cmty Educ .... Ms. Mary FOLEY
26 Dir of Public Relations & Marketing .... Mr. Brandon STEINERT
04 Assistant to President .... Mrs. Amye SCHNEIDER
41 Director of Athletics .... Mr. Trevor ROLFS
08 Director of Library .... Mrs. ReGina REYNOLDS-CASPER
15 Director of Human Resources .... Mrs. Julie KNOBLICH
07 Director of Admissions .... Ms. Tana COOPER
19 Coordinator of Facility Management .... Mr. Jim IRELAND
25 Director of Grants .... Ms. Cathie OSHIRO
06 Registrar .... Mrs. Lori CROWTHER
40 Bookstore Manager .... Mrs. Connie KERNS
09 Chief Inst Research Officer .... Mrs. Caicey CRUTCHER
35 Director of Student Life .... Mrs. Diane ENGLE
39 Coordinator of Student Housing .... Mr. Jonathan DIETZ
23 Nurse .... Mrs. Kathy BROCK
121 Dir Testing/Advisement/Career Svc .... Mrs. Judy JACOBS
88 Dean Fort Riley Tech Ed & Military .... Mr. Kurtis TEAL
108 Dean of Institutional Effectiveness .... Mr. Charles PERKINS
106 Assoc Dean of Distance Learning .... Mrs. Claudia MATHER

Benedictine College (D)

1020 N 2nd Street, Atchison KS 66002-1499
County: Atchison — FICE Identification: 010256
Unit ID: 154712
Telephone: (913) 367-5340 — Carnegie Class: Bac-Diverse
FAX Number: (913) 367-6566 — Calendar System: Semester
URL: www.benedictine.edu
Established: 1858 — Annual Undergrad Tuition & Fees: $29,530
Enrollment: 2,166 — Coed
Affiliation or Control: Roman Catholic — IRS Status: 501(c)3
Highest Offering: Master's
Accreditation: NH, MUS, NURSE

01 President .... Mr. Stephen D. MINNIS
05 Dean of the College .... Dr. Kimberly C. SHANKMAN
10 Chief Financial Officer .... Mr. Ronald J. OLINGER
111 Vice President Advancement .... Ms. Kelly J. VOWELS
84 Dean of Enrollment Management .... Mr. Pete HELGESEN
32 Vice President of Student Life .... Dr. Linda HENRY
35 Dean of Students .... Dr. Joseph WURTZ
41 Athletic Director .... Mr. Charles GARTENMAYER
26 Vice President for College Rels .... Mr. Tom HOOPES
20 Assoc Dean & Registrar .... Sr. Linda HERNDON, OSB
09 Director of Institutional Research .... Ms. Mary T. HYNEK
58 Exec Dir of Grad Business Programs .... Mr. Michael KING
58 Director of MASL/Asst Prof Educ .... Dr. Maureen HUPPE
37 Director of Student Financial Aid .... Mr. Tony TANKING
27 Dir of Marketing & Communications .... Mr. Steve JOHNSON
38 Director of Counseling Center .... Mrs. Grace MULCAHY
23 Director of Student Health Services .... Ms. Janet ADRIAN
18 Director of Operations .... Mr. Matt FASSERO
13 Dir of Tech & Information Sys .... Mr. Randy ROWLAND
88 Director of International Program .... Mr. Daniele MUSSO
08 Librarian .... Mr. Steven GROMATZKY
39 Director of Residence Life .... Mr. Sean MULCAHY
113 Bursar .... Ms. Becky MILLER
36 Director of Career Development .... Vacant
29 Director of Planned Giving & Alumni .... Mr. Tim ANDREWS
04 Exec Assistant to the President .... Mrs. Abby BARTLETT
15 Int Director of Human Resources .... Ms. Charo KELLEY
19 Security Account Manager .... Mr. Danny FAIRLEY
53 Chair Education Department .... Dr. Matthew RAMSEY
54 Chair Engineering Department .... Dr. Darrin MUGGLI

Bethany College (E)

335 E Swensson Street, Lindsborg KS 67456-1895
County: McPherson — FICE Identification: 001904
Unit ID: 154721
Telephone: (785) 227-3311 — Carnegie Class: Bac-Diverse
FAX Number: (785) 227-2004 — Calendar System: 4/1/4
URL: www.bethanylb.edu
Established: 1881 — Annual Undergrad Tuition & Fees: $27,850
Enrollment: 775 — Coed
Affiliation or Control: Evangelical Lutheran Church In America
IRS Status: 501(c)3
Highest Offering: Baccalaureate
Accreditation: NH, #CAATE, MUS

01 President .... Mr. William JONES
05 VP for Academic Affairs .... Dr. Elizabeth K. MAUCH
10 VP for Finance and Operations .... Mr. Martin HANIFIN
06 Registrar .... Mr. Mark BANDRE
84 Dean of Admissions/Financial Aid .... Mr. Matt PHANNENSTIEL
32 Dean of Student Development .... Mr. Ryan VAN DUSEN
111 VP for Advancement .... Mr. David EARLE
41 Dean of Athletics .... Ms. Laura MORENO
09 Director of Institutional Research .... Ms. Linda BALL
21 Controller .... Ms. Krista HARRIS
26 Exec Dir of Marketing & Comm .... Ms. Amie BAUER
07 Director of Admissions & Operations .... Ms. Vicki CORNETT
37 Director of Financial Aid .... Mr. Mark BANDRE
08 Dir of Wallerstedt Learning Center .... Ms. Denise K. CARSON
35 Asst Dean for Student Development .... Ms. Caitlin RETHORST
13 Director of Technology Services .... Mr. Joshua BIEBER
15 Director Human Resources/Title IX .... Ms. Kristi HAYS
29 Dir Alumni Relations .... Ms. Christy MAI
27 Sports Information Director .... Ms. Sara BLACKBURN
30 Director of Development .... Mr. Clair OLEEN
35 Director Campus Activities .... Ms. Tessa PETERS
38 Director of Clinical Counseling .... Ms. Ginny REYES
39 Director of Residential Education .... Ms. Anna WAUGH
88 Dir of Information Services .... Ms. Vicki CORNETT
27 Director of Publications .... Mr. Frank BALLEW
36 Director Career Services .... Ms. Caitlin RETHORST
121 Dir of Student Success Center .... Dr. Adam PRYOR
20 Asst Dean of Acad Affairs .... Vacant
108 Spec Asst to Dean Assessment .... Dr. Duke ROGERS
88 Director of Student Recruitment .... Mr. Richard STRANGE
97 Director of the Core .... Dr. Adam PRYOR
89 Dir of Ministry & 1st Yr Experience .... Dr. Tyler ATKINSON
18 Director of Campus Facilities .... Mr. Randy JIRAK
40 Bookstore Manager .... Ms. Elizabeth ALVAREZ
42 Campus Pastor .... Ms. Amy TRUHE
04 Exec Assistant to President .... Ms. Alissa JONES
57 Director of Digital & Media Arts .... Mr. Ed POGUE
53 Program Director Teacher Education .... Dr. Gretchen NORLAND
57 Chair of Theatre Department .... Mr. Greg LEGAULT
61 Chair of Criminal Justice Dept .... Mr. Randy REPP
64 Dir of Oratorio & Choral Activities .... Dr. Mark LUCAS
64 Dir of the Music Department .... Dr. Dan MASTERSON
73 Chair of Religion & Philosophy Dept .... Dr. John MULLEN

76 Athletic Training Program Director .... Ms. Laura JACKSON-STENLUND
81 Dir of Math/Science Depts .... Dr. Lucas MCCORMICK
83 Dir of Psychology Department .... Ms. Andrea RING
106 Director of Program Innovation .... Vacant
88 Director of Food Services .... Mr. Kevin MCCOY
88 Work Control Coordinator .... Vacant
92 Honors Program Coordinator .... Dr. Kristin VAN TASSEL
105 Dir Web Services & Social Media .... Ms. Molly CARVER
28 Director of Multicultural Programs .... Ms. Anna WAUGH
50 Director Business Department .... Mr. Robert CARLSON

Bethel College (F)

300 E 27th Street, North Newton KS 67117-0531
County: Harvey — FICE Identification: 001905
Unit ID: 154749
Telephone: (316) 283-2500 — Carnegie Class: Bac-Diverse
FAX Number: (316) 284-5286 — Calendar System: 4/1/4
URL: www.bethelks.edu
Established: 1887 — Annual Undergrad Tuition & Fees: $28,540
Enrollment: 503 — Coed
Affiliation or Control: Mennonite Church — IRS Status: 501(c)3
Highest Offering: Baccalaureate
Accreditation: NH, #CAATE, CAEPN, NURSE, SW

01 President .... Dr. Jonathan C. GERING
04 Assistant to the President .... Ms. Rosa M. BARRERA
05 Vice President Academic Affairs .... Dr. Robert W. MILLIMAN
32 Vice President Student Life .... Mr. Samuel C. HAYNES
41 Athletic Director .... Mr. Tony HOOPS
111 Vice President Advancement .... Mr. Bradley A. KOHLMAN
10 Vice President for Business Affairs .... Mr. Allen WEDEL
07 Vice President for Admissions .... Mr. Andrew W. JOHNSON
06 Registrar .... Ms. Marcia K. MILLER
26 Dir Marketing and Communications .... Ms. Tricia CLARK
29 Director of Alumni Engagement .... Mr. Bradley SCHMIDT
37 Director of Financial Aid .... Mr. Clark OSWALD
30 Director of Development .... Mr. Garrett WHORTON
08 Co-Director of Libraries .... Mrs. Barbara THIESEN
08 Co-Director of Libraries .... Mr. John THIESEN
42 Coordinator of Church Relations .... Mr. Benjamin LICHTI
18 Chief Facilities/Physical Plant .... Mr. Les GOERZEN
13 Chief Info Technology Officer (CIO) .... Mr. Adam HAAG
36 Dir Student Placement/Counseling .... Vacant
15 Director of HR .... Ms. Megan N. KERSHNER
28 Director of Diversity & Inclusion .... Mr. Julian GONZALEZ-SALAMANCA

Butler County Community College (G)

901 S. Haverhill Road, El Dorado KS 67042-3225
County: Butler — FICE Identification: 001906
Unit ID: 154800
Telephone: (316) 321-2222 — Carnegie Class: Assoc/HT-High Trad
FAX Number: (316) 322-3109 — Calendar System: Semester
URL: www.bc3.edu
Established: 1927 — Annual Undergrad Tuition & Fees (In-District): $3,180
Enrollment: 8,828 — Coed
Affiliation or Control: Local — IRS Status: 501(c)3
Highest Offering: Associate Degree
Accreditation: NH, ACBSP, ADNUR

01 President .... Dr. Kimberly KRULL
05 Vice President of Academics .... Ms. Lori WINNINGHAM
10 Vice President of Finance .... Mr. Kent WILLIAMS
32 Vice President of Student Services .... Mr. Bill RINKENBAUGH
111 Vice President for Inst Advancement .... Ms. Stacy COFER
08 Reference Librarian .... Ms. Judy BASTIN
06 Registrar .... Ms. Willow DEAN
09 AVP of Research/Inst Effectiveness .... Dr. Esam MOHAMMAD
15 Assoc VP of Human Resources .... Ms. Shelley STULTZ
21 Associate Business Officer .... Ms. Kim SHERWOOD
29 Director Alumni Relations .... Vacant
36 Director Student Placement .... Vacant
37 Director Student Financial Aid .... Ms. Heather WARD
35 Associate VP of Student Services .... Ms. Jessica OHMAN
26 Director of Institutional Marketing .... Ms. Kelly SNEDDEN
18 Director Facilities .... Mr. Lynn UMHOLTZ
96 Director of Purchasing .... Ms. Yolanda HACKLER
07 Director of Admissions .... Ms. Kirsten ALLEN
38 Director Student Counseling .... Ms. Jessica OHMAN
13 VP of Digital Transformation .... Mr. Bill YOUNG
19 Director Security/Safety .... Mr. Jason KENNEY
39 Director Residence Life .... Ms. Kelsey REED
41 Athletic Director .... Mr. Todd CARTER

Butler of Andover (H)

1810 N Andover Road, Andover KS 67002
Telephone: (316) 733-0071 — Identification: 770253
Accreditation: &NH

Butler of Council Grove (I)

131 West Main, Council Grove KS 66846
Telephone: (620) 382-2183 — Identification: 770254
Accreditation: &NH

Butler of Marion (J)

701 E. Main, Hill Building, Marion KS 66861
Telephone: (620) 382-2183 — Identification: 770255

Accreditation: &NH

Butler of McConnell (A)

Ed Ctr, Bldg 412, 53474 Lawrence Ct,
McConnell AFB KS 67221
Telephone: (316) 681-3522 Identification: 770257
Accreditation: &NH

Butler of Rose Hill (B)

712 Rose Hill Road, Rose Hill KS 67133
Telephone: (316) 776-0114 Identification: 770256
Accreditation: &NH

Central Baptist Theological Seminary (C)

6601 Monticello Road, Shawnee KS 66226-3513
County: Johnson FICE Identification: 001907
Unit ID: 154837
Telephone: (913) 667-5700 Carnegie Class: Spec-4-yr-Faith
FAX Number: (913) 371-8110 Calendar System: Semester
URL: cbts.edu
Established: 1901 Annual Graduate Tuition & Fees: N/A
Enrollment: N/A Coed
Affiliation or Control: Baptist IRS Status: 501(c)3
Highest Offering: Doctorate; No Undergraduates
Accreditation: NH, THEOL

01 President .... Dr. Molly T. MARSHALL
05 Provost/Dean of the Seminary .... Dr. Robert E. JOHNSON
03 Executive Vice President .... Mr. George TOWNSEND
30 VP for Institutional Advancement .... Dr. John W. GRAVLEY
06 Registrar .... Ms. Jessica C. WILLIAMS
26 Director of Seminary Relations .... Ms. Robin SANDBOTHE
85 International Student Officer .... Ms. Jessica C. WILLIAMS

Central Christian College of Kansas (D)

1200 S Main, PO Box 1403, McPherson KS 67460
County: McPherson FICE Identification: 001908
Unit ID: 154855
Telephone: (620) 241-0723 Carnegie Class: Bac-Diverse
FAX Number: (620) 241-6032 Calendar System: 4/1/4
URL: www.centralchristian.edu
Established: 1884 Annual Undergrad Tuition & Fees: $20,350
Enrollment: 865 Coed
Affiliation or Control: Free Methodist IRS Status: 501(c)3
Highest Offering: Baccalaureate
Accreditation: NH

01 President & CAO .... Dr. Leonard FAVARA, JR.
05 Academic Chief of Staff .... Dr. Jacob KAUFMAN
111 VP of Advancement .... Dr. Dean KROEKER
32 Dean of Student Life .... Mr. John WALKER
10 Controller .... Mrs. LeAnn MOORE
41 Athletic Director .... Mr. Kyle MOODY
07 Director of Admissions/Marketing .... Ms. Elizabeth CARON
06 Registrar .... Mrs. Michele AUGUST
08 Library Director .... Ms. Bev KELLEY
18 Chief Facilities/Physical Plant .... Mr. Dan BRAND
04 Executive Assistant to President .... Mrs. Hannah LITWILLER
13 Chief Info Technology Officer (CIO) .... Mr. Doug VANDERHOOF
104 Dir International Student Programs .... Ms. Hatsue AIZAWA
38 Campus Counselor .... Vacant
09 Institution Effectiveness Analyst .... Mr. Matt MALONE
102 Exec Director CCC Foundation .... Dr. David FERRELL
37 Director Student Financial Aid .... Mrs. Lois MADSEN

Cleveland University - Kansas City (E)

10850 Lowell Avenue, Overland Park KS 66210
County: Johnson FICE Identification: 020907
Unit ID: 177038
Telephone: (913) 234-0600 Carnegie Class: Spec-4-yr-Other Health
FAX Number: (913) 234-0904 Calendar System: Trimester
URL: www.cleveland.edu
Established: 1922 Annual Undergrad Tuition & Fees: $14,800
Enrollment: 492 Coed
Affiliation or Control: Independent Non-Profit IRS Status: 501(c)3
Highest Offering: First Professional Degree
Accreditation: NH, CHIRO

01 President .... Dr. Carl S. CLEVELAND, III
05 VP Academic Affairs .... Dr. Cheryl CARPENTER-DAVIS
10 Chief Operating Officer .... Mr. Jeff KARP
84 VP Enrollment Management .... Mr. Alex BACH
26 VP of Campus and Alumni Relations .... Dr. Clark BECKLEY
15 Vice Pres HR/Organizational Devel .... Mr. Dale MARRANT
111 Vice President Advancement .... Ms. Amy PIERSOL
20 Dean of Pre-Clinical Education .... Dr. Paul BARLETT
63 Dean of Chiropractic Education .... Dr. Jon WILSON
32 Dean of Student Affairs .... Mr. David FOOSE
06 Registrar .... Ms. Kathy HALE
21 Controller .... Ms. Marla COPE
37 Director of Financial Aid .... Ms. Caprice CALAMAIO
09 Director of Research .... Dr. Mark T. PFEFER
29 Director of Campus/Alumni Relations .... Ms. Jalonna BOWIE

07 Director of Admissions .... Ms. Melissa DENTON
08 Library Director .... Ms. Simone BRIAND
18 Director of Facilities Management .... Mr. Frank HANEY
04 Assistant to the President .... Ms. Carol BREWER

Cloud County Community College (F)

2221 Campus Drive, Concordia KS 66901-1002
County: Cloud FICE Identification: 001909
Unit ID: 154907
Telephone: (785) 243-1435 Carnegie Class: Assoc/HT-High Non
FAX Number: (785) 243-1459 Calendar System: Semester
URL: www.cloud.edu
Established: 1965 Annual Undergrad Tuition & Fees (In-District): $3,090
Enrollment: 1,873 Coed
Affiliation or Control: State/Local IRS Status: 501(c)3
Highest Offering: Associate Degree
Accreditation: NH, ADNUR

01 President .... Dr. Adrian H. DOUGLAS
05 VP Academic Affairs/Student Success .... Mr. Pedro LEITE
11 Vice Pres for Administrative Svcs .... Ms. Amber KNOETTGEN
13 Director of Information Technology .... Mr. Thomas ROBERTS
111 Director Institutional Advancement .... Vacant
84 Director of Enrollment Mgt .... Ms. Britni TREMBLAY
08 Director of Library Services .... Ms. Jennifer SCHROEDER
41 Athletic Director .... Mr. Matthew BECHARD
06 Registrar .... Ms. Cassie WURTZ
18 Chief Facilities/Physical Plant .... Mr. Rex E. SICARD
26 Coordinator of Marketing .... Ms. Jessica LEDUC
102 Dir Cloud County Cmty College Fndn .... Ms. Heather GENNETTE
37 Director Student Financial Aid .... Ms. Suzi KNOETTGEN
124 Director Advising & Retention .... Ms. Kris FARMER
15 Director of Human Resources .... Ms. Christine WILSON
09 Director Institutional Research .... Dr. Mitch STIMERS

Coffeyville Community College (G)

400 W 11th Street, Coffeyville KS 67337-5064
County: Montgomery FICE Identification: 001910
Unit ID: 154925
Telephone: (620) 251-7700 Carnegie Class: Assoc/HT-High Non
FAX Number: (620) 252-7098 Calendar System: Semester
URL: www.coffeyville.edu
Established: 1923 Annual Undergrad Tuition & Fees (In-District): $2,304
Enrollment: 1,802 Coed
Affiliation or Control: State/Local IRS Status: 501(c)3
Highest Offering: Associate Degree
Accreditation: NH, EMT, MAC

01 President .... Ms. Linda MOLEY
05 Vice President Academic Services .... Ms. Aron POTTER
10 Vice Pres for Operations & Finance .... Mr. Jeff MORRIS
88 VP for Innovation/Bus Initiatives .... Dr. Marlon THORNBURG
12 Director Columbus Technical Campus .... Mrs. Cindy HARROLD
102 Exec Director-CCC Foundation .... Mr. Dickie ROLLS
32 Dean of Students .... Mr. Ryan MCCUNE
09 Dean Institutional Research/Records .... Mrs. Deborah OESTMANN
26 Sr Dir of Marketing/Col Relations .... Ms. Yvonne HULL
121 Director Academic Advising/SSC .... Ms. Catie LUSBY
45 Dir Institutional Effectiveness .... Mr. Marty EVENSVOLD
37 Director of Financial Aid .... Mrs. Pam FEERER
15 Director of Human Resources .... Mrs. Kelli BAUER
41 Athletics Director .... Mr. Jeff LEIKER
18 Director of Maintenance .... Ms. Vivian FROST
106 Director of Distance Learning .... Mr. Brad WEBER
40 Bookstore Manager .... Mrs. Karen STRIMPLE
07 Admissions Representative .... Ms. Kristin HORNER

Colby Community College (H)

1255 S Range, Colby KS 67701-4099
County: Thomas FICE Identification: 001911
Unit ID: 154934
Telephone: (785) 462-3984 Carnegie Class: Assoc/MT-VT-High Non
FAX Number: (785) 460-4699 Calendar System: Semester
URL: www.colbycc.edu
Established: 1964 Annual Undergrad Tuition & Fees (In-District): $3,608
Enrollment: 1,345 Coed
Affiliation or Control: State/Local IRS Status: 501(c)3
Highest Offering: Associate Degree
Accreditation: NH, ADNUR, PTAA

01 President .... Mr. Seth M. CARTER
05 Vice President of Academic Affairs .... Mr. Bradley BENNETT
32 Vice President of Student Affairs .... Dr. George MCNULTY
10 Vice President of Business Affairs .... Ms. Carolyn KASDORF
08 Librarian .... Mrs. Tara SCHROER
26 Director of Public Information .... Mr. Doug JOHNSON
09 Dir of Institutional Effectiveness .... Mrs. Angel MORRISON
37 Director of Financial Aid .... Vacant
111 Dir of Inst Advancement/Foundation .... Ms. Jennifer SCHOENFELD
41 Athletic Director .... Mr. Mike SADDLER
13 IT Director .... Mr. Douglass MCDOWALL
04 Administrative Asst to President .... Ms. Penny CLINE

Cowley College (I)

125 S Second, PO Box 1147,
Arkansas City KS 67005-1147
County: Cowley FICE Identification: 001902
Unit ID: 154952
Telephone: (620) 442-0430 Carnegie Class: Assoc/HT-High Trad
FAX Number: (620) 441-5350 Calendar System: Semester
URL: www.cowley.edu
Established: 1922 Annual Undergrad Tuition & Fees (In-District): $3,000
Enrollment: 2,875 Coed
Affiliation or Control: Local IRS Status: 501(c)3
Highest Offering: Associate Degree
Accreditation: NH, EMT

01 President .... Dr. Dennis C. RITTLE
05 Vice President of Academic Affairs .... Dr. Michelle SCHOON
10 Vice Pres of Finance/Administration .... Dr. Gloria WALKER
13 Vice Pres Information Technology .... Mr. Paul ERDMANN
30 Vice Pres Institutional Development .... Dr. Kori GREGG
20 AVP Secondary Partnerships/Acad .... Ms. Janice STOVER
84 Exec Director Enrollment Management .... Ms. Kristi SHAW
32 Exec Director of Student Affairs .... Mr. Jason O'TOOLE
41 Athletic Director .... Mr. Shane LARSON
35 Director of Student Life .... Mr. Landon WEST
103 AVP Business/Industry Advancement .... Ms. Tina GRILLOT
106 AVP Distance Learning & Site Mgmt .... Mr. Eddie ANDREO
26 Dir Inst Comm/Public Relations .... Mr. Rama PEROO
06 Registrar .... Mr. Devin GRAVES
15 Director of Human Resources .... Ms. Jenette HANNA
11 Campus Operations Officer .... Ms. Janet GRACE
04 Admin Assistant to the President .... Ms. Tiffany VOLLMER
09 Director of Institutional Research .... Ms. Deborah PHELPS

Dodge City Community College (J)

2501 N 14th Avenue, Dodge City KS 67801-2399
County: Ford FICE Identification: 001913
Unit ID: 154998
Telephone: (620) 225-1321 Carnegie Class: Assoc/MT-VT-High Non
FAX Number: (620) 227-9366 Calendar System: Semester
URL: www.dc3.edu
Established: 1935 Annual Undergrad Tuition & Fees (In-District): $2,130
Enrollment: 1,773 Coed
Affiliation or Control: State/Local IRS Status: 501(c)3
Highest Offering: Associate Degree
Accreditation: NH, ADNUR

01 President .... Dr. Harold E. NOLTE, JR.
05 Provost Flight Program .... Dr. Adam JOHN
10 Vice Pres of Administration/Finance .... Dr. Glendon FORGEY
32 VP of Student Services .... Ms. Beverly TEMAAT
20 Vice President of Academic Affairs .... Dr. Jane HOLWERDA
102 Exec Director of DCCC Foundation .... Ms. Christina HASELHORST
24 Director Adult Learning Center .... Mrs. Brandi FERGUSON
15 Director of Human Resources .... Ms. Kristi OHLSCHWAGER
06 Registrar .... Ms. Susan GIBBS
08 Director Learning Resource Center .... Mrs. Shelly HUELSMAN
66 Director Nursing Allied Health .... Ms. Mechele HAILEY
41 Athletic Director .... Mr. Jacob RIPPLE
37 Director of Financial Aid .... Mrs. Rita BAYLESS
39 Director of Residence Life .... Ms. Margarita MORALES
18 Director of Facilities & Operations .... Mr. Russ MCBEE
04 Exec Assistant to the President .... Ms. Carla PATEE
20 Dean Workforce Development/Title V .... Mr. Ryan AUSMUS
35 Dean of Students .... Vacant
09 Dir of Inst Research/Accreditation .... Dr. Scott SEARCY
21 Comptroller .... Ms. Jessica WEST
19 Director Security/Safety .... Mr. Joshua THOMPSON
84 Director of Enrollment Management .... Mr. Lewis MIZE

Donnelly College (K)

608 N 18th Street, Kansas City KS 66102-4298
County: Wyandotte FICE Identification: 001914
Unit ID: 155007
Telephone: (913) 621-8700 Carnegie Class: Bac/Assoc-Mixed
FAX Number: (913) 621-8719 Calendar System: Semester
URL: www.donnelly.edu
Established: 1949 Annual Undergrad Tuition & Fees: $7,260
Enrollment: 360 Coed
Affiliation or Control: Roman Catholic IRS Status: 501(c)3
Highest Offering: Baccalaureate
Accreditation: NH

01 President .... Msgr. Stuart SWETLAND
05 VP of Academic & Student Affairs .... Mrs. Lisa STOOTHOFF
111 Vice President of Advancement .... Ms. Emily BUCKLEY
10 Vice President of Business Affairs .... Ms. Cheryl HICKS
09 Director of Institutional Research .... Ms. Jennifer BALES
32 Director of Student Success .... Dr. Mary PFLANZ
06 Registrar .... Ms. Jennifer BALES
08 Library Director .... Mrs. Jane BALLAGH DE TOVAR
37 Director of Financial Aid .... Mr. Michael PEPPLE
84 Enrollment Management Officer .... Mrs. Megan JORDAN

Emporia State University (L)

1 Kellogg Circle, Emporia KS 66801-5415
County: Lyon FICE Identification: 001927
Unit ID: 155025
Telephone: (620) 341-1200 Carnegie Class: Masters/L
FAX Number: (620) 341-5553 Calendar System: Semester
URL: www.emporia.edu
Established: 1863 Annual Undergrad Tuition & Fees (In-State): $6,758
Enrollment: 5,732 Coed
Affiliation or Control: State IRS Status: 501(c)3
Highest Offering: Doctorate
Accreditation: NH, ART, CAATE, CACREP, CAEP, CEA, LIB, MUS, NUR

01	President	Dr. Allison GARRETT
05	Provost/VP for Academic Affairs	Dr. David CORDLE
11	VP Admin/Fiscal Affairs	Ms. Diana E. KUHLMANN
32	Vice President Student Affairs	Dr. James E. WILLIAMS
13	Assoc Vice Pres Info Technology	Mr. Cory FALLDINE
09	Asst Provost Inst Effectiveness	Dr. JoLanna KORD
85	Dean of International Education	Mr. Mark DALY
35	Dean of Students	Ms. Lynn M. HOBSON
102	President ESU Foundation	Mr. Shane SHIVLEY
29	Director of Alumni	Mr. Jose FELICIANO, JR.
88	Director Natl Teachers Hall of Fame	Ms. Carol STRICKLAND
22	Affirmative Action Officer	Mr. Ray LAUBER
53	Interim Dean/The Teachers College	Dr. Joan BREWER
49	Dean College of Liberal Arts/Sci	Dr. R. Brent THOMAS
50	Dean School of Business	Dr. Ed BASHAW
62	Dean School of Library/Info Mgmt	Dr. Wooseob JEONG
58	Dean Graduate Studies	Dr. James SPOTSWOOD
88	Exec Dir Jones Inst Educ Excel	Dr. Roger CASWELL
06	Registrar	Ms. Sheila MARKOWITZ
08	Dean University Libraries/Archives	Dr. Michelle HAMMOND
106	Director Distance Education	Dr. James SPOTSWOOD
37	Director Student Financial Aid	Ms. Jaime MORRIS
07	Director Admissions	Dr. Kindle HOLDERBY
36	Director Career Services	Ms. June COLEMAN
38	Director Stdnt Wellness/ Counseling	Ms. Sally CRAWFORD-FOWLER
26	Exec Dir Marketing & Media Relation	Ms. Kelly HEINE
41	Director Athletics	Mr. Kent L. WEISER
18	Director Facilities/Physical Plant	Mr. Mark S. RUNGE
15	Director Human Resources	Mr. Ray LAUBER
23	Director Health Services	Ms. Mary MCDANIEL
39	Dir Residential Life/Orientation	Ms. Cass COUGHLIN
40	Manager Bookstore	Mr. Michael MCRELL
19	Director Police & Safety	Capt. Chris HOOVER
43	General Counsel	Mr. Kevin JOHNSON
21	Controller	Ms. Pamela NORTON
92	Associate Provost Honors College	Dr. Gary WYATT
28	Director Diversity & Inclusion	Vacant
04	Administrative Asst to President	Ms. Sarah MCKERNAN
86	Government Relations	Mr. Don HILL
91	Assoc CIO Academic & User Support	Dr. Rob GIBSON

Flint Hills Technical College (A)

3301 W 18th Avenue, Emporia KS 66801-5957

County: Lyon
FICE Identification: 005264
Unit ID: 155052
Telephone: (620) 343-4600
Carnegie Class: Assoc/HVT-High Non
FAX Number: (620) 343-4610
Calendar System: Semester
URL: www.fhtc.edu
Established: 1965
Annual Undergrad Tuition & Fees (In-District): $6,040
Enrollment: 1,137
Coed
Affiliation or Control: State/Local
IRS Status: 501(c)3
Highest Offering: Associate Degree
Accreditation: NH, DA, DH

01	President	Dr. Dean HOLLENBECK
05	Vice Pres Instructional Services	Mr. Steve LOEWEN
32	Vice Pres Student Services	Ms. Lisa KIRMER
10	Vice Pres Business Services	Mrs. Nancy THOMPSON
15	Director Personnel Services	Mrs. Jacinda KAHLE
37	Director Student Financial Aid	Ms. Erica CLARK
84	Director Enrollment Management	Ms. Brenda CARMICHAEL
04	Administrative Asst to President	Ms. Jacqui ANDERSON
30	Chief Development/Advancement	Mr. Mike CROUCH

Fort Hays State University (B)

600 Park Street, Hays KS 67601-4099

County: Ellis
FICE Identification: 001915
Unit ID: 155061
Telephone: (785) 628-4000
Carnegie Class: Masters/L
FAX Number: (785) 628-4096
Calendar System: Semester
URL: www.fhsu.edu
Established: 1902
Annual Undergrad Tuition & Fees (In-State): $5,130
Enrollment: 15,100
Coed
Affiliation or Control: State
IRS Status: 501(c)3
Highest Offering: Doctorate
Accreditation: NH, CAATE, CAEP, MUS, NAIT, NURSE, RAD, SP, SW

01	President	Dr. Tisa MASON
05	Provost	Dr. Jill ARENSDORF
10	Vice Pres Administration & Finance	Mr. Mike BARNETT
32	Vice Pres Student Affairs	Dr. Joseph G. LINN
35	Asst Vice Pres Student Affairs	Dr. Teresa CLOUNCH
20	Asst Provost/Learning Tech	Dr. Andrew FELDSTEIN
09	Asst VP Institutional Effectiveness	Dr. Sangki MIN
58	Interim Dean Graduate Studies	Mr. Glen MCNEIL
35	Asst Vice Pres Student Affairs	Dr. Kenton OLLIFF
06	Registrar	Mr. Craig KARLIN
07	Interim Director of Admissions	Mr. Jon ARMSTRONG
29	Exec Director Alumni & Govt Rels	Ms. Debra K. PRIDEAUX
114	Director Budget & Planning	Mr. Robert MANRY
36	Director Career Services	Ms. Karen MCCULLOUGH
37	Dir Student Financial Aid	Ms. Vanessa FLIPSE
26	Chief Communications Officer	Mr. Scott CASON
08	Dean Forsyth Library	Ms. Deborah LUDWIG
15	Director Personnel Services	Ms. Shannon LINDSEY
106	Director Virtual College	Mr. Michael MICHAELIS
53	Dean College Education	Dr. Paul ADAMS
49	Dean Col Arts/Humanities/Soc Sci	Dr. Paul W. FABER
50	Int Dean Col Bus/ Entrepreneurship	Dr. Melissa HUNSICKER-WALBURN
76	Dean Col Health & Sciences	Dr. Jeff BRIGGS
18	Co-Dir Chief Facil/Physical Plant	Mr. Jim SCHREIBER
18	Co-Dir Chief Facil/Physical Plant	Mr. Terry PFEIFER
121	Dir Acad Advise/Career Exploration	Dr. Patricia L. GRIFFIN
28	Director Inclusion and Diversity	Ms. Taylor KRILEY
19	Director University Police	Mr. Ed HOWELL
22	Univ Compliance Officer	Ms. Amy SCHAFFER
102	President/CEO Foundation	Mr. Jason WILLIBY
25	Chief Contracts/Grants Admin	Ms. Leslie PAIGE
41	Athletic Director	Mr. Curtis HAMMEKE
104	Director Study Abroad	Ms. Carol SOLKO-OLLIFF
43	General Counsel	Vacant
81	Int Dean College Science/Tech/Math	Dr. Paul DIXON
84	Asst Vice Pres Enrollment Mgmt	Mr. Dennis KING
13	Director Information Technology	Mr. Mark GRIFFIN
96	Director of Purchasing	Ms. Kathy HERRMAN
39	Director Residential Life	Ms. Christina HURTADO
04	Admin Assistant to the President	Ms. Karen ALLEN
45	Chief Institutional Planning Office	Mr. Dana CUNNINGHAM
86	Director Government Relations	Ms. Debra PRIDEAUX

Fort Scott Community College (C)

2108 S Horton, Fort Scott KS 66701-3140

County: Bourbon
FICE Identification: 001916
Unit ID: 155098
Telephone: (620) 223-2700
Carnegie Class: Assoc/MT-VT-High Non
FAX Number: (620) 223-4927
Calendar System: Semester
URL: www.fortscott.edu
Established: 1919
Annual Undergrad Tuition & Fees (In-District): $2,880
Enrollment: 1,792
Coed
Affiliation or Control: State/Local
IRS Status: 501(c)3
Highest Offering: Associate Degree
Accreditation: NH, ADNUR

01	President	Alysia JOHNSTON
05	VP of Academic Affairs	Adam BORTH
10	Vice Pres of Finance and Operations	Julie EICHENBERGER
32	Dean of Students	Tom HAVRON
13	Director of Research & Technology	Jacob REICHARD
07	Director Admissions	Matt GLADES
08	Director of Library	Susie ARVIDSON
06	Registrar	Courtney METCALF
26	Director of Strategic Communication	Kassie FUGATE-CATE
66	Director Nursing	Jordan HOWARD
14	Information Technology Director	Jason SIMON
12	Dean Crawford County	Santos MANRIQUE
12	Dean of Miami County Campus	Buddy Jo TANCK
121	VP of Student Support Services	Janet FANCHER
15	Human Resource Director	Juley MCDANIEL
30	Director of Development/Alumni	Jeff TADTMAN
37	Director Student Financial Aid	Lillie GRUBB
88	Director of Gordon Parks Museum	Kirk SHARP
21	Director Business Operations	Marianne CULBERTSON
04	Administrative Assist to President	Darlene WOOD
39	Director Student Housing	Marci MYERS
25	Director Grants & Special Projects	Ralph BEACHAM

Friends University (D)

2100 W University Avenue, Wichita KS 67213-3397

County: Sedgwick
FICE Identification: 001918
Unit ID: 155089
Telephone: (316) 295-5000
Carnegie Class: Masters/L
FAX Number: (316) 295-5060
Calendar System: Semester
URL: www.friends.edu
Established: 1898
Annual Undergrad Tuition & Fees: $28,415
Enrollment: 1,628
Coed
Affiliation or Control: Independent Non-Profit
IRS Status: 501(c)3
Highest Offering: Master's
Accreditation: NH, CAEP, MFCD, MUS

01	President	Dr. Amy CAREY
04	Executive Asst to the President	Ms. Natasha PEREZ
05	VP of Academic Affairs	Dr. Jasper LESAGE
10	VP of Finance	Mr. Vernon DOLEZAL
32	VP of Student Affairs	Dr. Guy CHMIELESKI
111	Assoc VP of University Advancement	Ms. Brie BOULANGER
11	VP of Administration	Ms. Kelley WILLIAMS
84	VP of Enrollment Management	Ms. Deb STOCKMAN
06	University Registrar	Ms. Ramah NATION
49	Academic Dean	Dr. Ken STOLTZFUS
50	Chair Business & IT	Dr. James LONG
57	Chair Fine Arts	Dr. Joan GRIFFING
81	Chair Natural Science/Math	Dr. Nora STRASSER
73	Chair Religion/Humanities	Dr. Jeremy GALLEGOS
53	Chair Teacher Education	Ms. Janet EUBANK
83	Chair Social/Behavioral Science	Dr. Tor WYNN
08	Director Library	Ms. Anne CRANE
18	Chief Facilities/Physical Plant	Mr. Roger DANLEY
07	Sr Dir Admissions & Fin Aid	Vacant
37	Director Financial Aid	Ms. Crystal ROACH
42	Pastor & Dean Campus Ministries	Dr. Guy CHMIELESKI
39	Director of Residence Life	Ms. Lacey LANDENBERGER
27	Director of Marketing	Ms. Rachel MILLARD
29	Director of Alumni Relations	Mr. Michael WALZ
12	Site Manager - Kansas City	Ms. Christy CARTER
09	Director of Institutional Research	Mr. Aidan DUNLEAVY
19	Director Security/Safety	Mr. Richard VINROE
106	Dir Online Education/E-learning	Ms. Nancy ARTAZ
41	Athletic Director	Dr. Rob RAMSEYER
91	Director Administrative Computing	Mr. Roger SCALES

Garden City Community College (E)

801 Campus Drive, Garden City KS 67846-6398

County: Finney
FICE Identification: 001919
Unit ID: 155104
Telephone: (620) 276-7611
Carnegie Class: Assoc/MT-VT-High Non
FAX Number: (620) 276-9573
Calendar System: Semester
URL: www.gcccks.edu
Established: 1919
Annual Undergrad Tuition & Fees (In-District): $3,240
Enrollment: 2,064
Coed
Affiliation or Control: Local
IRS Status: 501(c)3
Highest Offering: Associate Degree
Accreditation: #NH, ADNUR, EMT

01	President/CEO	Dr. Ryan RUDA
05	VP for Instructional Services	Mr. Marc MALONE
32	VP Student Services/Asst AD	Mr. Colin LAMB
108	Vice President IE & Accountability	Dr. Jacquelyn MESSINGER
10	Vice President Admin Services/CFO	Ms. Karla ARMSTRONG
84	Director of Enrollment Management	Ms. Tammy TABOR
06	Registrar	Ms. Nancy UNRUH
13	Dean-Technical Ed/Workforce Dev	Mr. Patrick PFEIFER
15	Director of Human Resources	Ms. Kellee MUNOZ
18	Dean Physical Plng/Facilities Mgmt	Mr. Derek RAMOS
26	Director of Public Relations	Ms. Ashley SALAZAR
37	Director Student Financial Aid	Ms. Melinda HARRINGTON
39	Director Residential Life	Ms. Christine DILLINGHAM
20	Dean of Academics	Mr. Phil TERPSTRA
04	Executive Assistant to President	Ms. Amy MCVEY
09	Director of Institutional Research	Vacant
21	Comptroller	Ms. Debra NICHOLSON
19	Campus Police Chief	Mr. Rodney DOZIER
08	Director Library Services	Mr. Trent SMITH
44	Executive Director Endowment	Mr. Jeremy GIGOT
41	Athletic Director	Mr. Greg MCVEY
121	Director of Student Success	Ms. Leslie WENZEL
22	Coord Disability Svcs & Compliance	Ms. Kari ADAMS
106	Coordinator Online Services	Ms. Vicky REYES
07	Director of Admissions	Ms. Susan MILLER

Grantham University (F)

16025 W 113th Street, Lenexa KS 66219

County: Johnson
FICE Identification: 004283
Unit ID: 442569
Telephone: (888) 947-2684
Carnegie Class: Masters/L
FAX Number: (913) 309-4949
Calendar System: Other
URL: www.grantham.edu
Established: 1951
Annual Undergrad Tuition & Fees: $6,540
Enrollment: 9,303
Coed
Affiliation or Control: Proprietary
IRS Status: Proprietary
Highest Offering: Master's
Accreditation: DEAC, IACBE, NUR

01	Int President/Chief Acad Officer	Dr. Anthony R. PETRY
22	Chief Compliance Officer	Harry DOTSON
15	Vice President Human Resources	Tracy GALLERY
13	Chief Information Officer	Baz ABOUELENEIN
37	Director Student Financial Service	Lindsay BRIDGEMAN
26	Vice President of Marketing	Aimee BROWN

Haskell Indian Nations University (G)

155 Indian Avenue, #5030, Lawrence KS 66046-4800

County: Douglas
FICE Identification: 010438
Unit ID: 155140
Telephone: (785) 749-8404
Carnegie Class: Tribal
FAX Number: (785) 749-8406
Calendar System: Semester
URL: www.haskell.edu
Established: 1884
Annual Undergrad Tuition & Fees: $480
Enrollment: 806
Coed
Affiliation or Control: Federal
IRS Status: Exempt
Highest Offering: Baccalaureate
Accreditation: NH, CAEPN

01	President	Mr. Monte MONTEITH
05	Acting Vice Pres Academic Affairs	Dr. Dan WILDCAT
11	Vice President University Services	Ms. Tonia SALVINI
10	Chief Finance Officer	Ms. Brenda RACEHORSE
13	Chief Information Officer	Mr. Joshua ARCE
111	Acting Dir Academic Support Ctr	Ms. Carrie CORNELIUS
39	Dir Resident Housing/Mgr Stdnt Life	Vacant
37	Financial Aid Officer	Ms. Carlene MORRIS
06	Registrar	Ms. Lou HARA
07	Director of Admissions	Ms. Dorothy D. STITES
09	Dir Instl Research/Sponsored Pgms	Ms. Cynthia GROUNDS
36	Career Development Specialist	Vacant
38	Director Student Counseling	Vacant
15	Human Resources Liaison	Ms. Mona FRANKLIN
96	Acquisitions	Ms. Janice BEGAY
26	Executive Asst/Public Relations	Mr. Stephen PRUE
18	Director Facilities Management	Ms. Karla VAN NOY

Hesston College (H)

301 S. Main Street, Hesston KS 67062-8901

County: Harvey
FICE Identification: 001920
Unit ID: 155177
Telephone: (620) 327-4221
Carnegie Class: Bac/Assoc-Mixed
FAX Number: (620) 327-8300
Calendar System: Semester
URL: www.hesston.edu
Established: 1909
Annual Undergrad Tuition & Fees: $26,900
Enrollment: 440
Coed

Affiliation or Control: Mennonite Church IRS Status: 501(c)3
Highest Offering: Baccalaureate
Accreditation: NH, NURSE

01 President Mr. Joseph MANICKAM
05 Vice Pres of Academics Mr. Brent YODER
07 Vice President of Admissions Mrs. Rachel S. MILLER
10 Vice Pres Finance & Auxiliary Svcs Mrs. Lisa GEORGE
32 Vice Pres Student Life Mrs. Deb ROTH
111 Vice Pres Advancement Mrs. Rachel SWARTZENDRUBER MILLER
29 Director of Alumni & Church Rels Mr. Dallas STUTZMAN
06 Registrar Mrs. Sandra HIEBERT
21 Business Manager Mr. Karl BRUBAKER

Highland Community College (A)

606 W Main, Highland KS 66035
County: Doniphan FICE Identification: 001921
Unit ID: 155186
Telephone: (785) 442-6000 Carnegie Class: Assoc/HT-High Non
FAX Number: (785) 442-6100 Calendar System: Semester
URL: www.highlandcc.edu
Established: 1858 Annual Undergrad Tuition & Fees (In-District): $3,077
Enrollment: 3,260 Coed
Affiliation or Control: Local IRS Status: 501(c)3
Highest Offering: Associate Degree
Accreditation: NH

01 President Ms. Deborah FOX
05 Vice President for Academic Affairs Dr. Erin SHAW
32 Vice President for Student Services Dr. Eric INGMIRE
10 Vice Pres for Finance/Operations Mr. Randy WILLY
72 Director of Technical Education Mr. Lucas HUNZIGER
06 Registrar Ms. Alice HAMILTON
37 Financial Aid Director Mr. Joshua NORTH
13 Co-Director of IT Mr. Marc JEAN
13 Co-Director of IT Mr. Neel PATEL
09 Director of Institutional Research Mr. Jeffrey HURN
38 Campus Counselor Vacant
41 Athletic Director Mr. Tyler NORDMAN
08 Library Director Ms. Cindy DAVIS
18 Supervisor of Buildings & Grounds Mr. Rick BLEVINS
29 Director Alumni Relations Ms. Kelly TWOMBLY
35 Director of Student Life Ms. Taylor ALLEN
15 Director of Human Resources Ms. Eileen C. GRONNIGER
40 Bookstore Coordinator Ms. Shannon WIEDMER
07 Director of Admissions Ms. Stephanie PETERSON
106 Dir Online Education/E-learning Ms. Denise PETERS
39 Director of Residence Life Mr. Tyler STOLDT
04 Admin Assistant to the President Ms. Heather FUHRMAN

Hutchinson Community College (B)

1300 N Plum Street, Hutchinson KS 67501-5894
County: Reno FICE Identification: 001923
Unit ID: 155195
Telephone: (620) 665-3500 Carnegie Class: Assoc/MT-VT-High Non
FAX Number: (620) 665-3310 Calendar System: Semester
URL: www.hutchcc.edu
Established: 1928 Annual Undergrad Tuition & Fees (In-District): $3,200
Enrollment: 5,854 Coed
Affiliation or Control: State/Local IRS Status: 501(c)3
Highest Offering: Associate Degree
Accreditation: NH, ADNUR, CAHIIM, COARC, EMT, PNUR, PTAA, RAD, SURGT

01 President Dr. Carter FILE
05 Vice President of Academic Affairs Dr. Cindy HOSS
10 Vice President Finance/Operations Ms. Julie BLANTON
103 VP Workforce Development/Outreach Mr. Steve PORTER
32 Vice President of Students Mr. Brett BRIGHT
26 Director of Marketing & Info Mr. Denny STOECKLEIN
13 Chief Information Officer Mr. Loren L. MORRIS
06 Registrar Mrs. Christina LONG
41 Athletic Director Mr. Josh GOOCH
15 Director of Personnel Mr. Brooks E. MANTOOTH
37 Financial Aid Officer Mr. Nathan BUCHE
07 Director of Admissions Mr. Corbin STROBEL
18 Director of Plant Facilities Mr. Don ROSE
39 Director of Residence Life Ms. Dana HINSHAW
29 Director Alumni Relations Mrs. Cindy KEAST
08 Coordinator of Library Services Mr. Robert KELLY
09 Coord of Institutional Research Mr. Rex CHEEVER
106 Director Online Education Dr. Rhonda CORWIN

Independence Community College (C)

1057 West College Avenue,
Independence KS 67301-0708
County: Montgomery FICE Identification: 001924
Unit ID: 155201
Telephone: (620) 331-4100 Carnegie Class: Assoc/HT-High Non
FAX Number: (620) 331-5344 Calendar System: Semester
URL: www.indycc.edu
Established: 1925 Annual Undergrad Tuition & Fees (In-District): $4,040
Enrollment: 897 Coed
Affiliation or Control: State/Local IRS Status: 501(c)3
Highest Offering: Associate Degree
Accreditation: NH

01 President Dr. Daniel W. BARWICK
10 Chief Financial Officer Mr. Jonathan SADHOO
32 VP Student Affairs/Athletics Ms. Tammie GELDENHUYS
13 Chief Information Officer Mr. Eric MONTGOMERY
26 Marketing Director Mr. Cordell JORDAN
102 Foundation Director Ms. Mandy MONROY
05 Chief Academic Officer Vacant
06 Registrar Ms. Robin WULF
08 Director Library Services Ms. Sarah OWEN
18 Maintenance/Custodial Supervisor Ms. Kris WECH
37 Financial Aid Director Ms. Laura ALLISON
09 Dir of Institutional Research Ms. Anita CHAPPUIE
04 Executive Asst to President Ms. Beverly HARRIS
40 Bookstore Manager Ms. Teresa VESTAL
88 Upward Bound Program Director Ms. Angela HOUSTON
15 Human Resources Director Ms. Lori BOOTS
106 Director of Online Education Vacant
121 Assoc Dean Tutoring/Accessibility Ms. Taylor CRAWSHAW
39 Student Housing General Manager Ms. Mary BAILEY
84 Director Enrollment Management Ms. Brittany THORNTON

Johnson County Community College (D)

12345 College Boulevard, Overland Park KS 66210-1299
County: Johnson FICE Identification: 008244
Unit ID: 155210
Telephone: (913) 469-8500 Carnegie Class: Assoc/HT-High Non
FAX Number: (913) 469-2559 Calendar System: Semester
URL: www.jccc.edu
Established: 1969 Annual Undergrad Tuition & Fees (In-District): $2,790
Enrollment: 18,638 Coed
Affiliation or Control: State/Local IRS Status: 501(c)3
Highest Offering: Associate Degree
Accreditation: NH, ACBSP, ACFEI, ADNUR, COARC, DH, EMT, IFSAC, NDT

01 President Dr. Joe SOPCICH
11 Exec Vice President Ms. Barbara LARSON
05 Vice Pres Instruction/CAO Dr. Mickey MCCLOUD
32 Vice Pres Student Success/Engagemnt Dr. Randy WEBER
13 Vice President Information Services Mr. Tom PAGANO
04 Exec Asst to the President & Board Ms. Terri SCHLICHT
10 AVP Financial Services/CFO Ms. Rachel LIERZ
18 AVP Campus Services Mr. Rex HAYS
20 AVP Instruction Dr. Gurbhushan SINGH
96 AVP Business Services Mr. Mitch BORCHERS
111 AVP Inst Advancement/Govt Affairs Ms. Kate ALLEN
14 Director Admin Computing Services Ms. Sandra WARNER
26 AVP Strategic Comm & Mktg Mr. Chris GRAY
121 Dean Student Success Mr. Paul KYLE
84 Asst Dean Enrollment Management Ms. MargE SHELLEY
35 Asst Dean Student Life/Ldrshp Dev Ms. Pam VASSAR
37 Director Student Financial Aid Ms. Christal WILLIAMS
36 Director Testing and Assessment Ms. Mary Ann DICKERSON
06 Registrar Ms. Leslie QUINN
08 Director Library Services Mr. Mark DAGANAAR
07 Director of Admissions Mr. Peter BELK
41 Director of Athletics Mr. Randy STANGE
92 Program Facilitator Honors Ms. Anna PAGE
09 Director of Institutional Research Ms. Natalie ALLEMAN-BEYERS
38 Dean Learner Engagement & Success Mr. Richard MOEHRING
103 Director Workforce Development Ms. Karen MARTLEY
108 Director Institutional Assessment Mr. John CLAYTON
15 Chief Human Resources Officer Ms. Becky CENTLIVRE
43 General Counsel Ms. Tanya WILSON

Kansas Christian College (E)

7401 Metcalf, Overland Park KS 66204-1995
County: Johnson Identification: 667134
Unit ID: 155308
Telephone: (913) 722-0272 Carnegie Class: Spec-4-yr-Faith
FAX Number: (913) 601-3826 Calendar System: Semester
URL: www.kansaschristian.edu
Established: 1938 Annual Undergrad Tuition & Fees: $7,690
Enrollment: 141 Coed
Affiliation or Control: Independent Non-Profit IRS Status: 501(c)3
Highest Offering: Baccalaureate
Accreditation: BI

01 President Mr. Chad POLLARD
00 Chairman of the Board Rev. Rodney L. DAVIS
101 Secretary of the Board Mr. Dwight PURTLE
05 Vice President of Academic Affairs Rev. Christopher W. SUMPTER
03 Executive Vice President Rev. Matthew LEE
30 Vice President of Donor Care Rev. Robert CASTILE
88 Vice Pres of Athletic Development Dr. Jim POTEET
11 Director of Operations Mr. David CARPENTER
18 Director of Facilities Mr. Harold V. CARPENTER
08 Head Librarian Mrs. Dorie SCOFIELD
09 Director of Institutional Research Mrs. Dorothy PURTLE
41 Athletic Director Mr. John JANSSEN
29 Director Alumni Affairs Vacant
37 Director Student Financial Aid Mrs. Marcia KELLEY
04 Admin Assistant to the President Ms. Terry BECKHAM

Kansas City Kansas Community College (F)

7250 State Avenue, Kansas City KS 66112-3003
County: Wyandotte FICE Identification: 001925
Unit ID: 155292
Telephone: (913) 334-1100 Carnegie Class: Assoc/MT-VT-Mix Trad/Non
FAX Number: (913) 288-7609 Calendar System: Semester
URL: www.kckcc.edu
Established: 1923 Annual Undergrad Tuition & Fees (In-District): $3,120
Enrollment: 5,825 Coed
Affiliation or Control: State/Local IRS Status: 501(c)3
Highest Offering: Associate Degree
Accreditation: NH, ACBSP, ADNUR, COARC, EMT, FUSER, MAC, PTAA

01 President Dr. Greg MOSIER
10 Chief Financial Officer Mr. Michael BEACH
05 Vice Pres Academic Affairs Dr. Beth Ann KRUEGER
32 VP Student Affairs Dr. Delfina WILSON
26 VP Strategic Initiative & Outreach Ms. Tami BARTUNEK
81 Dean Math/Science/Business Dr. Ed KREMER
84 Dean Enrollment Management Dr. Stephen TERRY
51 Exec Director Continuing Education Ms. Marisa GRAY
103 Exec Dir Entrep & Workforce Dev Ms. Alicia HOOKS
79 Dean Arts/Humanities Dr. Jerry POPE
13 Chief Information Officer Mr. Peter GABRIEL
09 Dir of Institutional Effectiveness Dr. Mihir CHAND
76 Dean of Health Professions Dr. Tiffany BOHM
75 Dean Technical Operations Vacant
36 Director Pioneer Career Ctr Ms. Marcia IRVINE
88 Director of Academic Resource Ctr Ms. Amanda WILLIAMS
41 Director of Athletics Mr. Anthony (Tony) TOMPKINS
40 Director of Bookstore Mr. Kasey MAYER
18 Director of Buildings/Grounds Mr. Jeff SIXTA
19 Director of Campus Police Chief Greg SCHNEIDER
14 Director of Computing Mr. James BENNETT
121 Dean of Student Svcs/Success Ctr Mr. Shawn DERRITT
38 Director Counseling-Advocacy Ctr Ms. Linda WARNER
37 Director of Financial Aid Ms. Mary I. DORR
21 Controller Ms. Lesley STROHSCHEIN
92 Director of Honors/Phi Theta Kappa Dr. Stacy TUCKER
28 Director of Intercultural Center Ms. Barbara CLARK-EVANS
08 Director of Learning Commons Ms. Amanda WILLIAMS
24 Director Media Services Technology Mr. Randy ROYER
106 Director of Online Services Ms. Susan STUART
35 Director of Student Activities Ms. Andrica WILCOXEN
07 Director Admissions/First Year Exp Ms. Tina CHURCH LEWANDOWSKI
06 Registrar Ms. Theresa HOLLIDAY
15 Chief Human Resources Officer Ms. Christina MCGEE
88 Director Forensic Laboratory Vacant
88 Director Wellness Center Mr. Rob M. CRANE
28 Director of Cultural Outreach Mr. Brian PATRICK
66 Int Director Nursing Ms. Susan ANDERSEN
66 Director Practical Nursing Ms. Susan K. WHITE
88 Director Technical Programs Mr. Richard PIPER
88 Director Technical Programs Perkins Ms. Donna S. SHAWN
88 Director Performing Arts Center Mr. Gary MOSBY
04 Int Exec Coordinator to President Ms. Risala ALLEN
105 Director Web Services Mr. Matthew FOWLER
22 Dir Affirmative Action/EEO Vacant
39 Director Student Housing Dr. Delfina WILSON
102 Exec Dir Foundation Ms. Mary SPANGLER
25 Chief Contract/Grants Administrator Ms. Connie NORTHRUP
90 Director Academic Computing Mr. Peter GABRIEL
96 Director of Purchasing Ms. Linda BURGESS
108 Dean Academic Support/Assessment Ms. Cecelia BREWER

Kansas State University (G)

919 Mid-Campus Drive North, Manhattan KS 66506
County: Riley FICE Identification: 001928
Unit ID: 155399
Telephone: (785) 532-6250 Carnegie Class: DU-Highest
FAX Number: (785) 532-2120 Calendar System: Semester
URL: www.k-state.edu
Established: 1863 Annual Undergrad Tuition & Fees (In-State): $10,383
Enrollment: 22,795 Coed
Affiliation or Control: State IRS Status: 501(c)3
Highest Offering: Doctorate
Accreditation: NH, ART, CAATE, CACREP, CAEPN, CEA, CIDA, CONST, DIETC, DIETD, IPSY, JOUR, LSAR, MFCD, MUS, NRPA, PH, PLNG, SP, SPAA, SW, THEA, VET

01 President Mr. Richard B. MYERS
04 Exec Asst to the President Ms. Dana M. HASTINGS
05 Provost & Executive Vice President Dr. Charles S. TABER
10 CFO & Dir Budget Planning Mr. Ethan E. ERICKSON
11 Vice President & COO Ms. Cindy A. BONTRAGER
46 VP for Research Dr. Peter K. DORHOUT
32 VP Student Life/Dean of Students Dr. Thomas A. LANE
26 VP for Communications & Marketing Mr. Jeffery B. MORRIS
15 VP Human Capital Mr. Jay W. STEPHENS
102 President/CEO of Foundation Mr. Greg WILLEMS
29 Alumni Association President Ms. Amy Button RENZ
41 Athletics Director Mr. Gene TAYLOR
100 Chief of Staff/Dir Community Rels Ms. Linda J. COOK
86 Chief Governmental Rels Officer Dr. Susan K. PETERSON
88 Exec Dir Military/Veterans Affairs Dr. Arthur S. DE GROAT, II
43 General Counsel Ms. Cheryl G. STRECKER
13 Chief Information Officer Dr. Gary L. PRATT
108 Assoc Provost Inst Effectiveness Dr. Brian A. NIEHOFF
28 Chief Diversity/Inclusion Officer Dr. Bryan D. SAMUEL
09 Director Planning & Analysis Dr. Brian A. NIEHOFF
08 Dean of Libraries Dr. Lori A. GOETSCH
47 Dean of Agriculture Dr. J. Ernest MINTON
48 Dean Architecture/Planning/Design Mr. Timothy DE NOBLE
49 Dean of Arts & Sciences Dr. Amitabha CHAKRABARTI
50 Dean of Business Admin Dr. Kevin P. GWINNER
88 Dean Global Campus Dr. Karen L. PEDERSEN

53 Dean of Education ... Dr. Debbie K. MERCER
54 Interim Dean of Engineering ... Dr. Gary A. CLARK
58 Dean of Graduate School ... Dr. Carol SHANKLIN
59 Dean of Human Ecology ... Dr. John B. BUCKWALTER
72 Int CEO/Dean Technology/Aviation ... Dr. Alysia H. STARKEY
74 Dean of Veterinary Medicine ... Dr. Bonnie R. RUSH
12 Int Dean & CEO K-State Olathe ... Dr. Jacqueline D. SPEARS
18 Assoc VP Facilities Planning/Mgmt ... Mr. Ryan F. SWANSON
19 Asst VP Univ Police & Public Safety ... Mr. Ronnie D. GRICE
96 Purchasing Manager ... Ms. Cathy OEHM
07 Assoc VP/Director of Admissions ... Mr. Lawrence E. MOEDER
06 Interim Registrar ... Ms. Susan E. COOPER
37 Assoc VP/Dir Student Fin Assistance ... Mr. Lawrence E. MOEDER
39 Assoc VP/Dir Housing & Dining Svcs ... Mr. Derek A. JACKSON
36 Exec Director Career Center ... Ms. Kerri D. KELLER

Kansas State University Polytechnic, College of Technology and Aviation (A)

2310 Centennial Road, Salina KS 67401-8196
Telephone: (785) 826-2601 FICE Identification: 004611
Accreditation: &NH, AAB

† Regional accreditation is carried under the parent institution in Manhattan, KS.

Kansas Wesleyan University (B)

100 E Claflin Avenue, Salina KS 67401-6196
County: Saline FICE Identification: 001929
Unit ID: 155414
Telephone: (785) 827-5541 Carnegie Class: Bac-Diverse
FAX Number: (785) 827-0927 Calendar System: Semester
URL: www.kwu.edu
Established: 1886 Annual Undergrad Tuition & Fees: $29,500
Enrollment: 791 Coed
Affiliation or Control: United Methodist IRS Status: 501(c)3
Highest Offering: Master's
Accreditation: NH, CAEPN, NURSE

01 President and CEO ... Dr. Matthew R. THOMPSON
04 Executive Assistant to President ... Ms. Jan M. SHIRK
05 Provost ... Dr. Damon KRAFT
32 Vice President Student Development ... Ms. Bridget R. WEISER
84 VP for Enrollment Management ... Dr. Melanie B. OVERTON
10 Chief Finance Officer ... Ms. Rhonda BETHE
06 Registrar ... Mrs. Jasmin DAUNER
30 Senior Director of Development ... Mr. Kenneth OLIVER
37 Assoc Dir Student Financial Plng ... Ms. Michelle JENSEN
07 Director of Admissions ... Mr. Esteban PAREDES
88 Admin Assistant to EVP/Provost ... Ms. Kristan HERNANDEZ
121 Director of Student Success Center ... Mr. Bryan L. MCCULLAR
26 Sr Dir Strategic Comm & Engagement ... Mrs. Paula HERMANN
08 Director of Library Services ... Ms. Kelley WEBER
24 Production Manager ... Mr. Paul GREEN
13 Director of Information Systems ... Mr. Jay C. KROB
19 Director of Emergency Management ... Dr. Lonnie BOOKER
18 Director of Plant Operations ... Mr. John SWAGERTY
40 Manager of Yotee's ... Ms. Jennifer RYAN
42 Campus Minister ... Mr. Scott JAGODZINSKE
41 Athletic Director ... Mr. Michael HERMANN
53 Director of Teacher Education ... Dr. Kristine RODRIGUEZ
79 Div Chair Humanities/Teach Educ ... Dr. Kristine RODRIGUEZ
76 Div Chair Nursing Educ & Health Sci ... Ms. Janeane HOUCHIN
83 Division Chair Social Sciences ... Dr. Steve HOEKSTRA
57 Division Chair Fine Arts ... Prof. Barbara J. NICKELL
81 Div Chair Natural Sciences/Math ... Dr. Dorothy HANNA
15 Human Resources Asst Director ... Ms. Kayla PEARSON
106 Academic Dean ... Dr. William BACKLIN
39 Resident Hall Director ... Mr. Charles STENNETT
29 Director Alumni Relations ... Ms. Kendall CARTER

Labette Community College (C)

200 S 14th, Parsons KS 67357-4299
County: Labette FICE Identification: 001930
Unit ID: 155450
Telephone: (620) 421-6700 Carnegie Class: Assoc/HVT-Mix Trad/Non
FAX Number: (620) 421-0921 Calendar System: Semester
URL: www.labette.edu
Established: 1923 Annual Undergrad Tuition & Fees (In-District): $3,060
Enrollment: 2,005 Coed
Affiliation or Control: Local IRS Status: 501(c)3
Highest Offering: Associate Degree
Accreditation: NH, ADNUR, COARC, DA, DMS, PTAA, RAD

01 President ... Dr. Mark WATKINS
04 Executive Assistant to President ... Ms. Megan A. FUGATE
05 Vice President Academic Affairs ... Mr. Joe BURKE
10 Vice President Finance & Operations ... Ms. Leanna J. DOHERTY
32 Vice President Student Affairs ... Ms. Tammy FUENTEZ
84 Assoc Dean Enrollment Mgmt ... Ms. Kathy JOHNSTON
20 Dean of Instruction ... Mr. Jason SHARP
13 Director of Information Technology ... Mrs. Jody BURZINSKI
30 Dir Resource Devel/Alumni Rels ... Mrs. Lindi D. FORBES
08 Director of Library Services ... Mr. Scott M. ZOLLARS
18 Director of Physical Plant ... Mr. Kevin DOHERTY
66 Director of Nursing ... Mrs. Delyna BOHNENBLUST
41 Athletic Director ... Mr. Aaron J. KEAL
26 Director of Public Relations ... Mrs. Bethany KENDRICK
06 Registrar/Dir Student Financial Aid ... Ms. Kathy JOHNSTON
15 Director of Human Relations ... Ms. Janice S. GEORGE
37 Director Student Financial Aid ... Ms. Kathy JOHNSTON
35 Student Life Coordinator ... Mrs. Terri LEROY
40 Bookstore Specialist ... Ms. Jessica LETTERMAN
101 Secretary of the Institution/Board ... Mrs. Megan FUGATE
103 Director Workforce Development ... Mr. Ross HARPER
29 Director Alumni Affairs ... Mrs. Lindi FORBES

Manhattan Area Technical College (D)

3136 Dickens Avenue, Manhattan KS 66503-2499
County: Riley FICE Identification: 005500
Unit ID: 155487
Telephone: (785) 587-2800 Carnegie Class: Assoc/HVT-High Non
FAX Number: (785) 587-2804 Calendar System: Semester
URL: www.manhattantech.edu
Established: 1965 Annual Undergrad Tuition & Fees (In-District): $6,750
Enrollment: 922 Coed
Affiliation or Control: State/Local IRS Status: 501(c)3
Highest Offering: Associate Degree
Accreditation: NH, ADNUR, DH, MLTAD

01 President/CEO ... Dr. Jim J. GENANDT
05 Vice Pres of Instructional Affairs ... Vacant
11 Vice Pres Operations ... Ms. Carmela JACOBS
32 VP Student Services/CAO ... Ms. Sarah PHILLIPS
30 Assoc VP Institutional Advancement ... Dr. Richard FOGG
10 Chief Financial Officer/Human Res ... Ms. Carmela JACOBS
13 Chief Information Security Officer ... Mr. Josh GFELLER
06 Registrar ... Ms. Rachel SHERLEY
07 Director of Admissions ... Mr. Neil ROSS
37 Director Financial Aid ... Ms. Laura WEISS-COOK

Manhattan Christian College (E)

1415 Anderson, Manhattan KS 66502-4081
County: Riley FICE Identification: 001931
Unit ID: 155496
Telephone: (785) 539-3571 Carnegie Class: Spec-4-yr-Faith
FAX Number: (785) 539-0832 Calendar System: Semester
URL: www.mccks.edu
Established: 1927 Annual Undergrad Tuition & Fees: $16,260
Enrollment: 282 Coed
Affiliation or Control: Christian Churches And Churches of Christ
IRS Status: 501(c)3
Highest Offering: Baccalaureate
Accreditation: NH, BI

01 President ... Mr. J. Kevin INGRAM
05 Vice President for Academic Affairs ... Dr. Greg DELORT
10 Vice President for FAS ... Mrs. Jennie JOHNSON
32 Vice President for Student Life ... Dr. Rick L. WRIGHT
06 Registrar ... Mr. Eric SANFORD
111 Director Institutional Advancement ... Mrs. Jolene K. RUPE
08 Director of Library Services ... Mr. Ron RATLIFF
41 Athletic Director ... Mr. Shawn M. CONDRA
29 Alumni Relations Director ... Mrs. Genae DENVER
04 Admin Asst to President ... Mrs. April WENDT
37 Financial Aid Director ... Mrs. Trish RUNION
07 Director of Admissions ... Mr. J. Kevin INGRAM
13 Director of Information Technology ... Mr. JT VANGILDER
39 Director of Student Development ... Mr. Ben GROGG

McPherson College (F)

1600 E Euclid, PO Box 1402, McPherson KS 67460-1402
County: McPherson FICE Identification: 001933
Unit ID: 155511
Telephone: (620) 242-0400 Carnegie Class: Bac-Diverse
FAX Number: (620) 241-8443 Calendar System: 4/1/4
URL: www.mcpherson.edu
Established: 1887 Annual Undergrad Tuition & Fees: $28,951
Enrollment: 733 Coed
Affiliation or Control: Church Of The Brethren IRS Status: 501(c)3
Highest Offering: Master's
Accreditation: NH, CAEPN

01 President ... Mr. Michael P. SCHNEIDER
05 Provost/VP Academic Affairs ... Dr. Bruce CLARY
111 Vice President for Advancement ... Mr. Roger BRIMMERMAN
32 Vice President Student Life ... Dr. Khalilah DOSS
10 Vice President for Finance ... Mr. Rick TUXHORN
84 VP Enrollment Management ... Ms. Christi HOPKINS
100 Chief of Staff ... Ms. Abby ARCHER-RIERSON
35 Dean of Students ... Mr. Ben COFFEY
36 Exec Director Career Services ... Ms. Amy BECKMAN
41 Athletic Director ... Mr. Andrew EHLING
06 Registrar ... Ms. Tricia HARTSHORN
37 Asst Director Financial Aid ... Mr. Andy OLSEN
08 Director of Library Services ... Ms. Mary HESTER
29 Director Alumni Relations ... Ms. Monica RICE
18 Director of Facilities ... Mr. Marty SIGWING

MidAmerica Nazarene University (G)

2030 E College Way, Olathe KS 66062-1899
County: Johnson FICE Identification: 007032
Unit ID: 155520
Telephone: (913) 782-3750 Carnegie Class: Masters/M
FAX Number: (913) 971-3290 Calendar System: Semester
URL: www.mnu.edu
Established: 1966 Annual Undergrad Tuition & Fees: $29,736
Enrollment: 1,888 Coed
Affiliation or Control: Church Of The Nazarene IRS Status: 501(c)3
Highest Offering: Master's
Accreditation: NH, ACBSP, CAATE, CACREP, CAEP, MUS, NURSE

01 President ... Dr. David J. SPITTAL
05 Vice Pres/Chief Academic Officer ... Dr. Nancy DAMRON
10 Vice President Finance ... Mr. Darrel ANDERSON
111 Vice Pres University Advancement ... Mr. Jon D. NORTH
32 Vice President Student Development ... Mrs. Kristi KEETON
42 University Chaplain ... Mr. Brady J. BRAATZ
88 Vice President Strategic Expansion ... Dr. Mark C. FORD
13 Associate VP for Instructional Tech ... Dr. Martin CROSSLAND
84 VP Enrollment and Marketing ... Mr. Ric BROCKMEIER
09 Dir Institutional Effectiveness ... Mrs. Patricia J. WALSH
66 Dean of the School of Nursing ... Dr. Karen D. WIEGMAN
49 Dean College of Arts & Sciences ... Vacant
06 Registrar ... Mr. James R. GARRISON
08 Director Mabee Learning Commons ... Vacant
110 Assoc VP University Advancement ... Mr. Tim KEETON
29 Director of Alumni Relations ... Mr. Pete S. BRUMBAUGH
37 Director of Student Financial Svcs ... Mr. Cathy L. COLAPIETRO
41 Athletic Director ... Mr. Todd L. GARRETT
15 Director of Human Resources ... Ms. Nancy S. MERIMEE
18 Director of Facility Services ... Mr. Jon N. SPENCE
40 Director MERC/Postmaster ... Mr. Nikos KELLEPOURIS
19 Director of Campus Safety ... Mr. Richard M. PACHECO
90 Associate VP Academic/Prof Success ... Dr. Richard HANSEN
04 Administrative Asst to President ... Mrs. Kelly GIBSON
103 Dir Workforce/Career Development ... Ms. Christine SNYDER
104 Director Study Abroad ... Mr. James GARRISON
28 Director Intercultural Engagement ... Ms. LaDonna MCCOLLOUGH
39 Director Student Housing ... Mr. Daniel RINCONES

Neosho County Community College (H)

800 W 14th Street, Chanute KS 66720-2699
County: Neosho FICE Identification: 001936
Unit ID: 155566
Telephone: (620) 431-2820 Carnegie Class: Assoc/HVT-High Non
FAX Number: (620) 431-0082 Calendar System: Semester
URL: www.neosho.edu
Established: 1935 Annual Undergrad Tuition & Fees (In-District): $4,794
Enrollment: 1,977 Coed
Affiliation or Control: Local IRS Status: 501(c)3
Highest Offering: Associate Degree
Accreditation: NH, ACBSP, ADNUR, CAHIIM, OTA, SURGT

01 President ... Dr. Brian L. INBODY
05 Vice President Student Learning ... Ms. Sarah ROBB
11 Vice President for Operations ... Mr. Kerry RANABARGAR
10 Chief Financial Officer ... Ms. Sondra K. SOLANDER
103 Dean Outreach/Workforce Development ... Ms. Brenda L. KRUMM
32 Dean of Student Services ... Ms. Kerrie COOMES
15 Director of Human Resources ... Ms. Karin JACOBSON
106 Dean for Ottawa & Online Campuses ... Ms. Marie GARDNER
13 Dean for Operations/CIO ... Mr. Jon SEIBERT
30 Director of Development/Alumni Rels ... Ms. Claudia CHRISTIANSEN
08 Coordinator of Library Services ... Mr. Todd KNISPEL
37 Director Student Financial Aid ... Ms. Jennifer DAISY
66 Director of Nursing ... Ms. Pamela COVAULT
105 Dir of Tech Services/Webmaster ... Mr. Jonathan HALE
41 Athletic Director ... Ms. Riann MULLIS
85 Dir International Student Services ... Ms. Sarah CADWALLADER
06 Registrar ... Mr. Ryan ROSE
09 Coordinator/Institutional Research ... Ms. LuAnn HAUSER
40 Chanute Bookstore Coordinator ... Vacant
40 Ottawa Bookstore Coordinator ... Ms. Sheri WOOLMAN
26 Advertising/Media Coordinator ... Ms. Nancy ISAAC
39 Director of Residence/Student Life ... Vacant
04 AA to the President/Board Clerk ... Ms. Angela ROWAN
18 Director of Facilities ... Mr. Kyle SEUFERT
07 Director of Admissions ... Ms. Amy MORRIS

Newman University (I)

3100 McCormick, Wichita KS 67213-2097
County: Sedgwick FICE Identification: 001939
Unit ID: 155335
Telephone: (316) 942-4291 Carnegie Class: Masters/L
FAX Number: (316) 942-4483 Calendar System: Semester
URL: www.newmanu.edu
Established: 1933 Annual Undergrad Tuition & Fees: $30,750
Enrollment: 3,378 Coed
Affiliation or Control: Roman Catholic IRS Status: 501(c)3
Highest Offering: Master's
Accreditation: NH, ANEST, CAEPN, COARC, NURSE, OTA, RAD, SW

01 President ... Dr. Noreen CARROCCI
04 Exec Assistant/Sec of the Corp ... Ms. Tracy MCGAREY
05 Provost & Vice Pres Acad Affairs ... Dr. Kimberly MCDOWALL LONG
111 Vice Pres University Advancement ... Mr. J.V JOHNSTON
10 Vice Pres Finance/Administration ... Ms. Jennifer GANTZ
32 Vice Pres Student Affairs ... Vacant
84 Vice Pres Enrollment Management ... Mr. Norm JONES
20 Assoc VP Academic Affairs ... Ms. Rosemary NIEDENS
42 Director of Campus Ministry ... Fr. Adam GRELINGER
29 Director of Alumni Relations ... Ms. Laura HARTLEY
41 Director of Athletics ... Ms. Joanna PRYOR
09 Director of Institutional Research ... Dr. Lori STEINER
08 Library Director ... Mr. Steve HAMERSKY

06 Registrar .... Ms. Lori GIBBON
37 Director of Financial Aid .... Ms. Myra PFANNENSTIEL
40 Director of Bookstore .... Mr. Larry WILLIAMS
13 Chief Information Officer .... Mr. Icer VAUGHAN
19 Director of Security .... Mr. Morris FLOYD
15 Director of Human Resources .... Mr. Jason POOL
21 Controller .... Ms. Diana GRIBLIN
39 Director Residence Life .... Mr. Scott MUDLOFF
35 Dean of Students .... Ms. Christine SCHNEIKERT-LUEBBE
58 Dean School of Catholic Studies .... Fr. Joseph GILE
49 Dean of Arts and Sciences .... Dr. David SHUBERT
50 Dean School of Business .... Dr. Brett ANDREWS
53 Dean of Education and Social Work .... Dr. Cameron CARLSON
104 Director Study Abroad .... Dr. Cheryl GOLDEN
18 Chief Facilities/Physical Plant .... Mr. Bruce SANDERSON
26 Chief Public Relations/Marketing .... Mr. Clark SCHAFER

North Central Kansas Technical College (A)

PO Box 507, Beloit KS 67420-0507
County: Mitchell FICE Identification: 005265
Unit ID: 155593
Telephone: (785) 738-2276 Carnegie Class: Assoc/HVT-Mix Trad/Non
FAX Number: (785) 738-2903 Calendar System: Semester
URL: www.ncktc.edu
Established: 1964 Annual Undergrad Tuition & Fees (In-District): $6,144
Enrollment: 853 Coed
Affiliation or Control: State/Local IRS Status: 501(c)3
Highest Offering: Associate Degree
Accreditation: NH, ADNUR

01 President .... Mr. Eric BURKS
05 Dean of Instruction .... Mr. Corey ISBELL
11 Dean of Administrative Services .... Mrs. Brandi ZIMMER
12 Dean of Hays Campus .... Ms. Sandy GOTTSCHALK
06 Registrar .... Ms. Judy HEIDRICK
09 Coordinator Institutional Research .... Mrs. Jennifer BROWN
32 Dean of Student Services .... Vacant
37 Director Student Financial Aid .... Ms. Leah BERGMANN
04 Administrative Asst to President .... Ms. Kelly ROBERTS
102 Dir Foundation/Marketing .... Vacant
101 Secretary of the Institution/Board .... Ms. Kelly ROBERTS
13 Chief Info Technology Officer (CIO) .... Mr. Robert MCCREIGHT

North Central Kansas Technical College (B)

2205 Wheatland Avenue, Hays KS 67601
Telephone: (785) 625-2437 Identification: 770259
Accreditation: &NH

Northwest Kansas Technical College (C)

1209 Harrison Street, PO Box 668,
Goodland KS 67735-3441
County: Sherman FICE Identification: 005267
Unit ID: 155618
Telephone: (785) 890-3641 Carnegie Class: Assoc/HVT-High Non
FAX Number: (785) 899-5711 Calendar System: Semester
URL: www.nwktc.edu
Established: 1964 Annual Undergrad Tuition & Fees (In-District): N/A
Enrollment: 896 Coed
Affiliation or Control: State/Local IRS Status: 501(c)3
Highest Offering: Associate Degree
Accreditation: NH, COARC, MAC

01 President .... Mr. Ben SCHEARS
05 Dean of Academic Advancement .... Mr. Matt POUNDS
11 Vice President of Operations .... Mrs. Sherri KNITIG
13 Vice Pres for Information Tech .... Mr. Brad BERGSMA
07 Director of Admissions .... Mrs. Kayla LUERA
41 Athletic Director .... Mr. Rory KLING
30 Director of Endowment/Career Svcs .... Mrs. Kelly JAMES

Ottawa University (D)

1001 S Cedar Street, Ottawa KS 66067-3399
County: Franklin FICE Identification: 001937
Unit ID: 155627
Telephone: (785) 242-5200 Carnegie Class: Bac-Diverse
FAX Number: (785) 229-1020 Calendar System: Semester
URL: www.ottawa.edu
Established: 1865 Annual Undergrad Tuition & Fees: $30,050
Enrollment: 727 Coed
Affiliation or Control: American Baptist IRS Status: 501(c)3
Highest Offering: Master's
Accreditation: NH, ACBSP, CAEPN, NURSE

00 Chancellor .... Mr. Kevin EICHNER
01 President .... Dr. Reggies WENYIKA
05 EVP/University Provost & CAO .... Dr. Terry HAINES
10 Exec VP & Chief Financial Officer .... Mr. J. Clark RIBORDY
107 EVP Adult Prof/Graduate Studies .... Ms. Nancy WINGERT
111 Vice Pres University Advancement .... Mr. Paul BEAN
32 Dean Student Affairs & Enrollment .... Mr. Tom TALDO
07 Director of Admissions .... Mr. Andy STILES
06 University Registrar .... Mrs. Margaret HERRON
26 Chief Marketing Officer .... Ms. Nancy WINGERT
21 Director Business Operations .... Mr. Thomas CORLEY
15 Director Human Resources .... Ms. Joanna WALTERS
37 Director Financial Aid .... Mr. Howard FISCHER
29 Director Alumni Programs .... Ms. Courtney KLAUS
08 Director Library Services .... Ms. Gloria CREED-DIKEOGU
41 Director Athletics .... Ms. Arabie CONNER
18 Chief Facilities/Physical Plant .... Mr. David BIRD
04 Executive Assistant to Chancellor .... Ms. Courtney MCCONICO
11 Chief Operations Officer .... Ms. Nancy WINGERT
20 Academic Dean .... Dr. Eric KOCH
53 Dean School of Education .... Dr. Amy HOGAN
84 Director of Enrollment Management .... Mr. Andy OTTO
50 Dean Angell Snyder Sch of Business .... Dr. Lena RODRIGUEZ
49 Dean School of Arts & Sciences .... Dr. Karen OHNESORGE
88 Director University Compliance .... Ms. Carrie STEVENS
13 Director Software Solutions .... Ms. Brandi SERVAES
28 Director of Diversity .... Mr. Donald ANDERSON
30 Director Develop/Planned Giving .... Ms. Janet PETERS
44 Director Annual Giving .... Ms. Nori HALE
104 Dean Study Abroad Program .... Dr. Marylou DEWALD
106 Director Instr Design/Academic Tech .... Dr. Carine ULLOM
19 Safety/Security Supervisor .... Mr. Kevin MOORE
36 Career Services Coordinator .... Dr. Christine CURRIER

† The Online division is included in the institution's enrollment count.

Ottawa University Kansas City (E)

4370 W. 109th Street, Suite 200,
Overland Park KS 66211-1302
Telephone: (913) 266-8600 Identification: 666083
Accreditation: &NH

† Regional accreditation is carried under the parent institution in Ottawa, KS.

Pittsburg State University (F)

1701 S Broadway, Pittsburg KS 66762-7500
County: Crawford FICE Identification: 001926
Unit ID: 155681
Telephone: (620) 231-7000 Carnegie Class: Masters/L
FAX Number: (620) 235-4080 Calendar System: Semester
URL: www.pittstate.edu
Established: 1903 Annual Undergrad Tuition & Fees (In-State): $7,298
Enrollment: 6,907 Coed
Affiliation or Control: State IRS Status: 501(c)3
Highest Offering: Doctorate
Accreditation: NH, CAEP, CAEPN, CEA, MUS, NRPA, NURSE, SW

01 President .... Dr. Steven A. SCOTT
05 Provost & VP for Academic Affairs .... Dr. Howard SMITH
11 CFO & VP Administration .... Mr. Doug BALL
111 VP University Advancement .... Ms. Kathleen FLANNERY
06 Interim Registrar .... Ms. Melinda ROELFS
32 VP Student Life .... Dr. Steve ERWIN
26 Chief Marketing & Comm Officer .... Ms. Abigail FERN
84 Assoc VP Enroll Mgmt/Stdnt Success .... Dr. Howard SMITH
51 Dean Graduate & Continuing Studies .... Dr. Pawan KAHOL
49 Dean of Arts & Sciences .... Dr. Mary Carol POMATTO
50 Dean of Business .... Dr. Paul GRIMES
53 Dean of Education .... Dr. James TRUELOVE
72 Interim Dean of Technology .... Dr. Bob FRISBEE
08 Dean of Library Services .... Mr. Randy ROBERTS
108 Director of Assessment .... Ms. Nora HATTON
27 Director of Media Relations .... Ms. Andra STEFANONI
29 Dir Alumni Rels/Constituent Svcs .... Mr. Jon A. BARTLOW
13 Chief Information Officer .... Ms. Angela NERIA
15 Director Human Resource Svcs/Budget .... Dr. Michele D. SEXTON
85 Director of International Programs .... Mr. Aaron HURT
45 Chief Strategy Officer .... Dr. Shawn NACCARATO
18 Director of Trades & Landscape Svcs .... Mr. Tom AMERSHEK
28 Dir General & Custodial Services .... Mr. Tim SENECAUT
19 Director of University Police .... Mr. Stu HITE
22 Director of Institutional Equity .... Ms. Cindy JOHNSON
37 Director of Financial Aid .... Ms. Tammy HIGGINS
41 Director Intercollegiate Athletics .... Mr. Jim JOHNSON
07 Director of Admissions .... Mr. Scott DONALDSON
36 Director Career Services .... Ms. Mindy E. CLONINGER
09 Director of Institutional Research .... Dr. Dai LI
38 Dir University Counseling Services .... Dr. Steven MAYHEW
96 Director of Purchasing .... Mr. Jim HUGHES
28 Director of Diversity .... Ms. Deatrea ROSE
10 Controller .... Ms. Barbara J. WINTER
39 Director of University Housing .... Ms. Connie D. MALLE
100 Chief of Staff .... Ms. Jaime DALTON
43 General Counsel .... Dr. Jamie BROOKSHER

Pratt Community College (G)

348 NE SR 61, Pratt KS 67124-8432
County: Pratt FICE Identification: 001938
Unit ID: 155715
Telephone: (620) 672-2700 Carnegie Class: Assoc/MT-VT-High Non
FAX Number: (620) 450-2283 Calendar System: Semester
URL: www.prattcc.edu
Established: 1938 Annual Undergrad Tuition & Fees (In-District): $3,488
Enrollment: 1,114 Coed
Affiliation or Control: State/Local IRS Status: 501(c)3
Highest Offering: Associate Degree
Accreditation: NH, ACBSP

01 President .... Dr. Mike CALVERT
05 Vice President Instruction .... Dr. Michael FITZPATRICK
10 Vice President Finance/Operations .... Mr. Kent ADAMS
84 Vice Pres Student Enroll Management .... Ms. Lisa MILLER
30 Exec Director of Inst Advancement .... Mr. Barry FISHER
41 Director of Athletics .... Mr. Tim SWARTZENDRUBER
07 Director of Admissions .... Ms. Caitlin MILLER
06 Registrar .... Mr. Joseph SALAS
13 Director of Information Technology .... Mr. Jerry SANKO
37 Director of Financial Aid .... Ms. Haley LINDSAY
08 Dir Linda Hunt Memorial Library .... Mr. Frank STAHL
15 Director of Personnel .... Ms. Rita PINKALL
21 Controller .... Ms. Christy WRIGHT
18 Director of Buildings & Grounds .... Mr. Dan PETZ
39 Director of Residence Life .... Mr. Charles KEEFER
04 Administrative Asst to President .... Ms. Donna MEIER PFEIFER
29 Director Alumni Relations .... Mr. Barry FISHER
108 Director of Planning & Assessment .... Mr. David SCHMIDT
09 Director of Institutional Research .... Ms. Amanda CORDES
26 Chief Public Relations/Marketing .... Ms. Megan MAYHEW
36 Director Student Placement .... Ms. Amy JACKSON

Rasmussen College-Kansas City/Overland Park (H)

11600 College Boulevard, Suite 100,
Overland Park KS 66210
Telephone: (913) 491-7870 Identification: 770489
Accreditation: &NH, ADNUR, MAAB

† Regional accreditation carried under the parent institution in Saint Cloud, MN. The tuition figure is an average, actual tuition may vary.

Saint Paul School of Theology (I)

4370 West 109th Street, Suite 300,
Overland Park KS 66211
County: Johnson FICE Identification: 002509
Unit ID: 179317
Telephone: (913) 253-5000 Carnegie Class: Spec-4-yr-Faith
FAX Number: (913) 253-5075 Calendar System: Semester
URL: www.spst.edu
Established: 1958 Annual Graduate Tuition & Fees: N/A
Enrollment: 116 Coed
Affiliation or Control: United Methodist IRS Status: 501(c)3
Highest Offering: Doctorate; No Undergraduates
Accreditation: NH, THEOL

01 President .... Rev. Neil B. BLAIR
05 VP Academic Affairs/Dean .... Dr. Jeanne HOEFT
111 Vice President for Inst Advancement .... Dr. Angela SIMS
32 Associate Dean of Students .... Rev. Margaretta S. NARCISSE
15 Director of Human Resources .... Mr. Matthew MILLS
06 Registrar .... Ms. Kim WARREN
37 Dir of Student Financial Services .... Ms. Kim WARREN
07 Director of Admissions .... Ms. Shannon HANCOCK
26 Director of Communications .... Mrs. Heather SNODGRASS
08 Librarian .... Ms. Maggie MUELLER
10 CFO .... Mr. Matthew MILLS
101 Secretary of the Institution/Board .... Ms. Julie A. ROBINSON
88 Chair of the Institution/Board .... Dr. Michael PARMELY
100 Director of Seminary Operations .... Ms. Melissa WHALEN
50 Assoc Director Contextual Education .... Mr. Rick BURNS

Salina Area Technical College (J)

2562 Centennial Road, Salina KS 67401
County: Saline FICE Identification: 005499
Unit ID: 155830
Telephone: (785) 309-3100 Carnegie Class: Assoc/HVT-High Non
FAX Number: (785) 309-3101 Calendar System: Semester
URL: www.salinatech.edu
Established: 1965 Annual Undergrad Tuition & Fees (In-District): $8,502
Enrollment: 598 Coed
Affiliation or Control: State/Local IRS Status: 501(c)3
Highest Offering: Associate Degree
Accreditation: NH, DA

01 President .... Mr. Gregory A. NICHOLS
05 Vice Pres of Instruction .... Ms. Stephani JOHNS-HINES
11 Vice Pres of Administrative Service .... Mrs. Jamie PALENSKE
32 Vice Pres of Student Services .... Mrs. Jennifer CALLIS
09 Director of Inst Research/Registrar .... Mrs. Denise R. HOEFFNER
15 Human Resources Coordinator .... Mrs. Tamera WILCOX
18 Director of Maintenance .... Mr. Dale CASTILLO
102 Exec Dir of SATC Foundation .... Vacant
84 Director Enrollment Management .... Vacant
37 Student Financial Aid Specialist .... Mrs. Racheal GALVAN

Seward County Community College (K)

1801 N Kansas Avenue, Liberal KS 67901-2054
County: Seward FICE Identification: 008228
Unit ID: 155858
Telephone: (620) 624-1951 Carnegie Class: Assoc/HVT-High Trad
FAX Number: (620) 417-1169 Calendar System: Semester
URL: www.sccc.edu
Established: 1967 Annual Undergrad Tuition & Fees (In-District): $3,168
Enrollment: 1,746 Coed
Affiliation or Control: State/Local IRS Status: 501(c)3
Highest Offering: Associate Degree
Accreditation: NH, ADNUR, COARC, MLTAD, SURGT

01 President .... Dr. Ken J. TRZASKA
10 VP of Finance & Operations .... Mr. Dennis M. SANDER
05 Vice President of Academic Affairs .... Dr. Joseph MCCANN
32 Vice President of Student Services .... Ms. Celeste DONOVAN
13 Chief Information Officer .... Mr. Louie S. LEMERT
06 Registrar .... Ms. Alaina M. RICE
26 Exec Dir of Marketing & PR .... Ms. Rachel C. COLEMAN
25 Exec Director of Grant Development .... Ms. Charity HORINEK
30 Chief Development Officer .... Mr. Tano TOVILLA
41 Director of Athletics .... Mr. Dan ARTAMENKO
04 Executive Assistant .... Mrs. Lois B. MAGNER
76 Dean of Allied Health .... Dr. Suzanne CAMPBELL
51 Dean Industrial Tech/Cont Educ .... Mr. Travis COMBS
20 Dean of Instruction .... Mr. Luke DOWELL
35 Dean of Students .... Ms. Annette HACKBARTH-ONSON
15 Director of Human Resources .... Vacant
09 Institutional Research/Data Analyst .... Ms. Teresa WEHMEIER
19 Security Supervisor/Asst DOF .... Mr. Wendall WEHMEIER
18 Director of Facilities .... Mr. Roger SCHEIB
39 Director of Student Living Center .... Ms. Jennifer L. MALIN
78 Director of Outreach .... Mr. Mike BAILEY
35 Dir of Student Life & Leadership .... Mr. Wade LYON
37 Director of Financial Aid .... Ms. Amy BRIDENSTINE
66 Director of Nursing .... Ms. Susan INGLAND
84 Director of Admissions .... Mr. Eric D. VOLDEN
50 Director of Business & Industry .... Mrs. Norma Jean DODGE
08 Director of Library .... Vacant
14 Network Administrator .... Mr. Doug BROWNE
40 Director of Bookstore .... Ms. Laci FURR
91 Systems Administrator .... Mr. Cecil STOLL
105 Website Specialist .... Mr. Craig DUSEK
07 Coordinator of Admissions/Recruiter .... Vacant
44 Assoc Director Annual Giving .... Mr. Chandler KIRKHART

Southwestern College (A)

100 College Street, Winfield KS 67156-2499
County: Cowley FICE Identification: 001940
Unit ID: 155900
Telephone: (620) 229-6000 Carnegie Class: Masters/M
FAX Number: (620) 229-6224 Calendar System: Semester
URL: www.sckans.edu
Established: 1885 Annual Undergrad Tuition & Fees: $30,150
Enrollment: 1,306 Coed
Affiliation or Control: United Methodist IRS Status: 501(c)3
Highest Offering: Doctorate
Accreditation: NH, #CAATE, CAEP, CAEPN, MUS, NURSE

01 President .... Dr. Bradley J. ANDREWS
03 Executive Vice President .... Mr. Dean CLARK
11 Senior Vice President .... Dr. Tracy FREDERICK
05 VP Acad Affairs/Dean of the College .... Dr. Ross PETERSON-VEATCH
10 Vice President Finance .... Ms. Shannon VARGAS
124 VP Student Retention & Success .... Dr. Dawn E. PLEAS
84 VP Enroll Mgmt Main Campus .... Mr. Adam JENKINS
45 Exec Dir Institute for Discipleship .... Dr. Stephen K. WILKE
111 Vice Pres Institutional Advancement .... Mr. Patrick WAGNER
26 Vice President Communications ... Ms. Kaydee RIGGS-JOHNSON
32 VP Student Life/Dean Students .... Mr. Dan FALK
29 Director Alumni Programs .... Ms. Jessica DIBBLE
08 Library Director .... Ms. Marjorie SNYDER
37 Director Financial Aid .... Ms. Brenda D. HICKS
06 Registrar .... Ms. Linda WEIPPERT
41 Director of Athletics .... Mr. Mike MCCOY
15 Director Human Resources .... Ms. Lonnie BOYD
04 Exec Asst to President .... Ms. Doreen FAST
42 Campus Minister .... Rev. Benjamin C. HANNE
101 Secretary of the Institution/Board .... Ms. Doreen FAST

Sterling College (B)

125 W Cooper Street, Sterling KS 67579-1533
County: Rice FICE Identification: 001945
Unit ID: 155937
Telephone: (620) 278-2173 Carnegie Class: Bac-Diverse
FAX Number: N/A Calendar System: 4/1/4
URL: www.sterling.edu
Established: 1887 Annual Undergrad Tuition & Fees: $26,000
Enrollment: 697 Coed
Affiliation or Control: Presbyterian IRS Status: 501(c)3
Highest Offering: Master's
Accreditation: NH, #CAATE, CAEPN

01 President .... Dr. Scott RICH
05 Vice President Academic Affairs .... Dr. Ken BROWN
111 Vice President for Inst Advancement .... Ms. Sheila BIRD
32 Vice President Student Life .... Mr. Jason BRIAR
11 Vice Pres Admin/Inst Initiatives .... Mr. David LANDIS
07 Vice President Enrollment .... Mr. Dennis DUTTON
41 Vice President of Athletics .... Mr. Scott DOWNING
10 CFO .... Ms. Michelle HALL
20 Assoc Vice Pres Academic Affairs .... Dr. Erin LAUDERMILK
88 Special Assistant to the President .... Mr. Scott CARTER
41 Athletic Director .... Mr. Justin MORRIS
26 Dir Marketing/Pres Communications .... Mr. Brad EVENSON
37 Director of Financial Aid .... Ms. Mitzi SUHLER
06 Registrar .... Mrs. Kendra GRIZZLE
29 Alumni & Marketing Manager .... Ms. Susie CARNEY
18 Chief Facilities/Physical Plant .... Mr. Steven CAYWOOD
42 Chaplain .... Mr. Paul BRANDES
08 Library Director .... Ms. Laurell WATNEY
36 Director of Career Services .... Mr. Terry EHRESMAN

15 Director Human Resources .... Ms. Becky VOTH
04 Administrative Asst to President .... Ms. Erica FOSS
30 Director of Development .... Mr. Aaron WEBER

Tabor College (C)

400 S Jefferson Street, Hillsboro KS 67063-1753
County: Marion FICE Identification: 001946
Unit ID: 155973
Telephone: (620) 947-3121 Carnegie Class: Bac-Diverse
FAX Number: (620) 947-2607 Calendar System: 4/1/4
URL: www.tabor.edu
Established: 1908 Annual Undergrad Tuition & Fees: $28,260
Enrollment: 770 Coed
Affiliation or Control: Mennonite Brethren Church IRS Status: 501(c)3
Highest Offering: Master's
Accreditation: NH, #CAATE, CAEPN, MUS, NURSE, SW

01 President .... Dr. Jules GLANZER
05 Exec VP of Academics & Compliance .... Dr. Frank JOHNSON
10 Vice President Business/CFO .... Mr. Michael JAMES
111 Vice President Advancement .... Mr. Ronald BRAUN
11 Exec VP of Operations .... Mr. Rusty ALLEN
32 Dean of Student Life .... Mr. Emir RUIZ-ESPARZA
06 Registrar .... Mr. Scott FRANZ
08 Director of Library Services .... Ms. Janet WILLIAMS
37 Dir of Student Financial Services .... Ms. Sadonia LANE
29 Director Alumni Relations .... Mr. Rod HAMM
26 Director of Communications .... Mr. Don RATZLAFF
18 Director Facilities/Physical Plant .... Mr. Terry ENS
121 Director Student Success .... Mrs. Aimee HENNIGH
09 Institutional Research .... Mr. David FABER
13 Director IT Infrastructure .... Mr. Chris GLANZER
14 Director of IT Operations .... Mr. Wayne KLIEWER
15 Human Resources Coordinator .... Ms. Misty SMITHSON
04 Admin Assistant to the President .... Mrs. Miriam KLIEWER
07 Director of Admissions .... Mr. Grant MYERS
36 Director Student Placement .... Mrs. Sydney FOUNTAIN

University of Kansas Main Campus (D)

1450 Jayhawk Boulevard, Room 230,
Lawrence KS 66045-7518
County: Douglas FICE Identification: 001948
Unit ID: 155317
Telephone: (785) 864-3131 Carnegie Class: DU-Highest
FAX Number: (785) 864-4120 Calendar System: Semester
URL: www.ku.edu
Established: 1866 Annual Undergrad Tuition & Fees (In-State): $11,148
Enrollment: 27,625 Coed
Affiliation or Control: State IRS Status: 501(c)3
Highest Offering: Doctorate
Accreditation: NH, ART, CAATE, CAEPN, CEA, CLPSY, COPSY, HSA, IPSY, JOUR, LAW, MUS, PH, PHAR, PLNG, SCPSY, SP, SPAA, SW

01 Chancellor .... Dr. Douglas A. GIROD
05 Interim Provost .... Dr. Carl LEJUEZ
12 Vice Chancellor/Dean Edwards Campus .... Dr. David COOK
26 Vice Chancellor for Public Affairs .... Mr. Reginald L. ROBINSON
04 Chief of Staff to Chancellor .... Ms. Julie N. MURRAY
43 General Counsel .... Mr. Brian WHITE
20 Vice Provost Faculty Development .... Dr. Christopher BROWN
10 CFO & Vice Provost for Finance .... Ms. Diane H. GODDARD
32 Vice Provost for Student Affairs .... Dr. Tammara DURHAM
46 Vice Chancellor Research .... Dr. Simon ATKINSON
28 Int Vice Provost Diversity & Equity .... Dr. Jennifer NG
84 Vice Provost Enrollment Management .... Dr. Matt MELVIN
13 Chief Information Officer .... Dr. Mary WALSH
58 Interim Dean Graduate Studies .... Dr. Audrey LAMB
104 Assoc VP International Programs .... Dr. Charles BANKART
30 President Endowment Association .... Mr. Dale SEUFERLING
29 President Alumni Association .... Mr. Heath J. PETERSON
07 Director Admissions .... Ms. Lisa P. KRESS
21 Sr Dir Financial Analysis/Reporting .... Ms. Katrina M. YOAKUM
21 Sr Assoc Vice Provost for Finance .... Mr. Jason HORNBERGER
06 University Registrar/Asst VP .... Ms. Tiffany ROBINSON
09 Chief Data Ofcr Analytics/Research .... Mr. Nick STEVENS
15 Vice Provost for Administration .... Mr. Michael ROUNDS
85 Director International Student Svcs .... Dr. Chuck OLCESE
38 Director Counseling/Psych Services .... Dr. Michael MAESTAS
88 Director Design & Construction Mgmt .... Mr. James E. MODIG
37 Director Financial Aid/Scholarships .... Ms. Angela KARLIN
36 Exec Director Career Center .... Mr. David GASTON
41 Director Intercollegiate Athletics .... Mr. Jeff LONG
18 Director Facilities Service .... Mr. Shawn HARDING
22 Director Inst Opportunity & Access .... Mr. Josh JONES
93 Director Multicultural Affairs .... Ms. Precious PORRAS
23 Int Chief of Staff Watkins Health .... Dr. Parvika SARIPALLI
14 Dir Info Tech Business Operations .... Mr. Chris CROOK
39 Director Student Housing .... Ms. Sarah WATERS
86 Director State Relations .... Ms. Kelly WHITTEN
92 Director Honors Program .... Dr. Sarah CRAWFORD-PARKER
86 Director Federal Relations .... Mr. Jack CLINE
40 Director KU Bookstore .... Ms. Jen O'CONNOR
51 Exec Dir Continuing Education .... Ms. Sharon D. GRAHAM
25 Assoc Dir Contract Negotiations .... Ms. Lucille MARINO
63 Exec Dean School of Medicine .... Dr. Robert SIMARI
49 Interim Dean Liberal Arts/Science .... Dr. John COLOMBO
61 Dean of Law .... Mr. Stephen W. MAZZA
54 Dean of Engineering .... Dr. Arvin AGAH
48 Dean Architecture/Design/Planning .... Dr. Mahesh DAAS

50 Dean of Business .... Dr. L. Paige FIELDS
67 Dean of Pharmacy .... Dr. Ron E. RAGAN
60 Dean of Journalism .... Dr. Ann M. BRILL
53 Dean of Education .... Dr. Rick GINSBERG
64 Dean of Music .... Dr. Robert L. WALZEL, JR.
70 Dean of Social Welfare .... Dr. Michelle CARNEY
08 Dean Libraries .... Mr. Kevin L. SMITH
19 Director Security/Safety .... Mr. Chris KEARY

† Medical Center and Main campus enrollments should be combined for the total institution enrollment.

University of Kansas Medical Center (E)

3901 Rainbow Boulevard, Kansas City KS 66160-0001
Telephone: (913) 588-5000 FICE Identification: 024579
Accreditation: &NH, ANEST, AUD, CAHIIM, COARC, DIETI, DMOLS, DMS, IPSY, MED, MIDWF, MT, NMT, NURSE, OT, PDPSY, PTA

† Enrollment at the Medical Center is included within the published enrollment for the University of Kansas Main Campus. Regional accreditation is carried under the parent institution in Lawrence, KS.

University of Saint Mary (F)

4100 S 4th Street, Leavenworth KS 66048-5082
County: Leavenworth FICE Identification: 001943
Unit ID: 155812
Telephone: (913) 682-5151 Carnegie Class: Masters/M
FAX Number: (913) 758-6140 Calendar System: Semester
URL: www.stmary.edu
Established: 1923 Annual Undergrad Tuition & Fees: $28,810
Enrollment: 1,310 Coed
Affiliation or Control: Roman Catholic IRS Status: 501(c)3
Highest Offering: Doctorate
Accreditation: NH, CAATE, CAEP, CAHIIM, IACBE, NURSE, PTA

01 President .... Sr. Diane STEELE
05 Academic Vice President .... Dr. Michelle METZINGER
10 Vice President for Finance .... Ms. Nancy BRAMLETT
07 VP Admissions & Marketing .... Mr. John SHULTZ
06 Registrar .... Ms. Kimberly WARREN
08 Director of the Library .... Ms. Danielle DION
09 Institutional Research Coordinator .... Ms. Christine HAMILTON
29 Director of Alumni and Constituent .... Mr. Matt ASTLEFORD
26 Director of Marketing Operations .... Ms. Katie YODER
37 Director of Financial Aid .... Ms. Heidi REID
42 Director of Campus Ministry .... Mr. Jacob HAYDEN
112 Development Officer Planned Giving .... Ms. Jane LIEBERT
41 Athletic Director .... Mr. Rob MILLER
15 Director Human Resources .... Ms. Stephanie WALKER
39 Director of Residence Life .... Ms. Kristen OWSLEY
21 Controller .... Ms. Nicole BIBLER
38 Campus Counselor .... Dr. Christina DUNN CARPENTER
18 Director of Plant Operations .... Mr. Jonathan KIRBY
40 Bookstore Manager .... Ms. Cynthia FORRESTER
12 Site Coordinator Johnson County .... Vacant
13 Director of Information Services .... Mr. Kevin GANTT
04 Executive Administrative Assistant .... Ms. Sharron LUCAS
19 Director of Public Safety .... Mr. Donald STUBBINGS

Washburn University (G)

1700 SW College Avenue, Topeka KS 66621-0001
County: Shawnee FICE Identification: 001949
Unit ID: 156082
Telephone: (785) 670-1010 Carnegie Class: DU-Mod
FAX Number: (785) 670-1089 Calendar System: Semester
URL: www.washburn.edu
Established: 1865 Annual Undergrad Tuition & Fees (In-District): $8,312
Enrollment: 6,691 Coed
Affiliation or Control: Local IRS Status: 501(c)3
Highest Offering: Doctorate
Accreditation: NH, ART, CAATE, CAEP, CAEPN, CAHIIM, CEA, COARC, DMS, LAW, MUS, NURSE, OTA, PTAA, RAD, RTT, SW

01 President .... Dr. Jerry B. FARLEY
05 Vice Pres Academic Affairs .... Dr. JuliAnn MAZACHEK
10 Vice Pres Admin & Treasurer .... Mr. Rick MARTIN
32 Vice President for Student Life .... Dr. Eric GROSPITCH
04 Special Assistant to the President .... Ms. Cynthia HOLTHAUS
84 Exec Director Enrollment Management .... Dr. Richard W. LIEDTKE
43 University Legal Counsel .... Mr. Marc FRIED
35 Assoc Vice Pres of Student Life .... Mr. Joel BLUML
20 Int Assoc Vice Pres Acad Affairs .... Dr. Jennifer BALL
102 President WU Foundation .... Mr. Marshall MEEK
06 Registrar .... Mr. Steven GRENUS
08 Dean of Libraries .... Dr. Alan BEARMAN
37 Director Student Financial Aid .... Ms. Kandace MARS
07 Director of Admissions .... Mr. Joseph TINSLEY
15 Director of Human Resources .... Ms. Teresa LEE
13 CIO/Dir Info Systems & Services .... Mr. Jim TAGLIARENI
09 Director Strategic Analysis & Rep .... Mr. William FINLEY
49 Dean College Arts/Sciences .... Dr. Laura STEPHENSON
88 Dean School Applied Studies .... Dr. Pat MUNZER
61 Dean School of Law .... Dr. Carla PRATT
50 Dean School of Business .... Dr. David SOLLARS
66 Interim Dean School of Nursing .... Dr. Jane CARPENTER
41 Director of Athletics .... Mr. Loren FERRE
22 Director Equal Opportunity .... Dr. Pam FOSTER
18 Int Director Facilities Services .... Mr. Eric JUST
23 Director Health Services .... Ms. Tiffany MCMANUS
29 Alumni Association Director .... Ms. Susie HOFFMANN

92 Dean Honors Program .... Dr. Michael J. MCGUIRE
39 Director Student Housing .... Ms. Mindy P. RENDON
40 Director Ichabod Shop .... Ms. Karen PETERSON
35 Director Student Activities .... Ms. Jessica BARRACLOUGH
38 Director Student Counseling .... Ms. Crystal LEMING
26 Director of University Relations .... Mr. Patrick EARLY
36 Director Student Placement .... Mr. Kent MCANALLY
19 Director of Police .... Mr. Chris ENOS
28 Dir of Diversity & Inclusion .....Ms. Danielle DEMPSEY-SWOPES
96 Director of Purchasing .... Ms. Sherry DRAPER

Wichita State University (A)

1845 N Fairmount, Wichita KS 67260-0001
County: Sedgwick FICE Identification: 001950
Unit ID: 156125
Telephone: (316) 978-3456 Carnegie Class: DU-Higher
FAX Number: (316) 978-3770 Calendar System: Semester
URL: www.wichita.edu
Established: 1895 Annual Undergrad Tuition & Fees (In-State): $8,270
Enrollment: 15,075 Coed
Affiliation or Control: State IRS Status: 501(c)3
Highest Offering: Doctorate
Accreditation: NH, #ARCPA, ART, AUD, CAATE, CAEP, CAEPN, CLPSY, COSMA, DANCE, DENT, DH, MT, MUS, NURSE, PTA, SP, SPAA, SW

01 Interim President .... Dr. Andy TOMPKINS
05 Provost .... Dr. Richard D. MUMA
10 VP Administration & Finance .... Mr. Werner M. GOLLING
32 VP Student Affairs .... Dr. Teri HALL
43 General Counsel .... Mr. David MOSES
26 VP Strategic Communications .... Mr. Lou HELDMAN
09 Chief Data Officer .... Dr. David WRIGHT
84 VP Enrollment Management .... Dr. Carolyn SHAW
13 Chief Information Officer .... Mr. Toney FLACK
20 Assoc VP Academic Affairs .... Dr. Linnea GLENMAYE
46 VP Research & Technology Transfer .... Dr. John S. TOMBLIN
28 Vice President for Diversity .... Dr. Marche FLEMING-RANDLE
49 Dean Liberal Arts & Sciences .... Dr. Andrew HIPPISLEY
50 Dean Barton School of Business .... Dr. Anand DESAI
53 Dean Education .... Dr. Shirley LEFEVER-DAVIS
54 Dean Engineering .... Dr. Dennis LIVESAY
57 Dean Fine Arts .... Dr. Rodney E. MILLER
76 Dean Health Professions .... Dr. Sandra BIBB
58 Interim Dean Graduate School .... Dr. Kerry WILKS
08 Dean Libraries .... Ms. Kathy DOWNES
86 Exec Director Government Relations .... Mr. Andrew SCHLAPP
24 Dir Media Resources Center .... Mr. John JONES
102 CEO & President WSU Foundation .... Ms. Elizabeth H. KING
41 Director of Athletics .... Mr. Darron BOATRIGHT
15 Director Human Resources .... Ms. Judy ESPINOZA
114 Director Budgets .... Mr. David MILLER
06 Registrar .... Ms. Gina D. CRABTREE
07 Director Admissions .... Mr. Bobby GANDU
37 Director Financial Aid .... Ms. Sheelu M. SURENDER
38 Director Counseling & Testing .... Dr. Jessica PROVINES
18 Director Physical Plant .... Mr. Bob SMITH, JR.
45 Director of Facilities Planning .... Ms. Emily A. PATTERSON
19 Chief of University Police .... Mr. Rodney E. CLARK
23 Director Student Health Services .... Ms. Camille CHILDERS
39 Director Stdnt Housing & Resid Life .... Mr. Scott JENSEN
28 Director Diversity & Inclusion .... Ms. Alicia SANCHEZ
40 Manager Bookstore .... Mr. Kevin J. KONDA
21 Assoc VP Financial Operations .... Ms. Lois TATRO
96 Director of Purchasing .... Mr. Steven WHITE
29 Executive Director Alumni Assoc .... Ms. Courtney MARSHALL
04 Assistant to President .... Ms. Anna LANIER
106 Dir Online Education/E-learning .... Mr. Mark D. PORCARO
22 Title IX Coordinator .... Ms. Sara ZAFAR
105 Director Web Services .... Mr. Tim HART
111 Chief Devel/Advancement Officer .... Dr. Keith PICKUS
44 Director Annual/Planned Giving .... Mr. Michael LAMB

Wichita State University Campus of Applied Sciences and Technology (B)

4004 N Webb Road, Wichita KS 67226-8101
County: Sedgwick FICE Identification: 005498
Unit ID: 156107
Telephone: (316) 677-9400 Carnegie Class: Assoc/HVT-High Non
FAX Number: (316) 677-9510 Calendar System: Semester
URL: www.watc.edu
Established: 1965 Annual Undergrad Tuition & Fees (In-District): $6,037
Enrollment: 4,267 Coed
Affiliation or Control: State/Local IRS Status: 501(c)3
Highest Offering: Associate Degree
Accreditation: NH, DA, SURGT

01 President .... Dr. Sheree UTASH
05 Chief of Academic Affairs .... Mr. Scott LUCAS
10 Vice Pres Finance/Administration .... Ms. Marlo DOLEZAL
20 VP General Educ/Health Sciences .... Ms. Pam DOYLE
32 Vice President Student Services .... Mr. Justin PFEIFER
26 Exec Dir Marketing/Cmty Outreach .... Mr. Andy MCFAYDEN
13 Exec Dir Tech/Inst Effectiveness .... Mr. Randy ROEBUCK
15 Exec Director Human Resources .... Ms. Judy MOUNT
09 Exec Dir Institutional Research .... Ms. Kristen MUNDAY

Wichita Technical Institute (C)

2051 South Meridian Avenue, Wichita KS 67213-1927
County: Sedgwick FICE Identification: 010503
Unit ID: 156134
Telephone: (316) 943-2241 Carnegie Class: Spec 2-yr-Tech
FAX Number: (316) 943-5438 Calendar System: Quarter
URL: www.wti.edu
Established: Annual Undergrad Tuition & Fees: N/A
Enrollment: 938 Coed
Affiliation or Control: Proprietary IRS Status: Proprietary
Highest Offering: Associate Degree
Accreditation: ACCSC

01 Director .... Mr. Rod MOORE

KENTUCKY

Alice Lloyd College (D)

Purpose Road, Pippa Passes KY 41844-9703
County: Knott FICE Identification: 001951
Unit ID: 156189
Telephone: (606) 368-2101 Carnegie Class: Bac-Diverse
FAX Number: (606) 368-6212 Calendar System: Semester
URL: www.alc.edu
Established: 1923 Annual Undergrad Tuition & Fees: $11,550
Enrollment: 598 Coed
Affiliation or Control: Independent Non-Profit IRS Status: 501(c)3
Highest Offering: Baccalaureate
Accreditation: SC

01 President .... Dr. Joe A. STEPP
03 Executive Vice President .... Dr. Jim STEPP
05 Vice President Academic Affairs .... Dr. Claude CRUM
10 Vice President of Business Affairs .... Mr. David JOHNSON
32 Dean of Students & Community Life .... Mr. Scott CORNETT
07 Director of Admissions .... Mr. Jeff CORNETT
06 Registrar .... Ms. Dana DOTSON
08 Director of Library .... Ms. Jeannie GALLOWAY
37 Director of Financial Aid .... Mrs. Tori NAIRN
88 Director of Student Work Program .... Mr. Kerry RATLIFF
53 Director of Teacher Education .... Mrs. Katrina SLONE
18 Director of Physical Plant .... Mr. Ryan GIBSON
39 Director of Student Housing .... Mr. John MILLS
29 Director of Alumni Relations .... Mrs. Teresa GRENDER
35 Director of Student Activities .... Ms. Christine STUMBO
26 Dir of Marketing & Communications .. Ms. Katelin WESTERFIELD
09 Director of Institutional Research .... Mrs. Katrina SLONE
30 Director of Development .... Mrs. Allison SOUTHARD
102 Dir Foundation/Corporate Relations .... Ms. Priscilla FRALEY
41 Athletic Director .... Mr. Gary STEPP
15 Chief Human Resources Officer .... Mr. Larry ADAMS

† Cost of tuition is guaranteed for students from 108 county territories.

American National University (E)

2376 Sir Barton Way, Lexington KY 40509-2256
County: Fayette FICE Identification: 010489
Unit ID: 157021
Telephone: (859) 253-0621 Carnegie Class: Bac/Assoc-Assoc Dom
FAX Number: (859) 254-7664 Calendar System: Quarter
URL: www.an.edu
Established: 1941 Annual Undergrad Tuition & Fees: $17,361
Enrollment: 233 Coed
Affiliation or Control: Proprietary IRS Status: Proprietary
Highest Offering: Baccalaureate
Accreditation: ABHES, SURGT, SURTEC

01 Campus Director .... Mr. Mike MCKINLEY

† Branch campus of American National University, Indianapolis, IN

American National University (F)

4205 Dixie Highway, Louisville KY 40216-4147
Telephone: (502) 447-7634 Identification: 666443
Accreditation: ABHES, CAHIIM

† Branch campus of American National University, Indianapolis, IN

American National University (G)

50 National College Boulevard, Pikeville KY 41501-3176
Telephone: (606) 478-7200 Identification: 666444
Accreditation: ABHES

† Branch campus of American National University, Indianapolis, IN

Asbury Theological Seminary (H)

204 N Lexington Avenue, Wilmore KY 40390-1199
County: Jessamine FICE Identification: 001953
Unit ID: 156222
Telephone: (859) 858-3581 Carnegie Class: Spec-4-yr-Faith
FAX Number: N/A Calendar System: 4/1/4
URL: www.asburyseminary.edu
Established: 1923 Annual Graduate Tuition & Fees: N/A
Enrollment: 1,600 Coed
Affiliation or Control: Independent Non-Profit IRS Status: 501(c)3
Highest Offering: Doctorate; No Undergraduates
Accreditation: SC, CACREP, THEOL

01 President .... Dr. Timothy C. TENNENT
05 Provost/VP of Academic Affairs .... Dr. Douglas K. MATTHEWS
10 Vice Pres Finance/Admin/CFO .... Mr. Bryan P. BLANKENSHIP
111 Vice President of Advancement .... Mr. Jay MANSUR
88 Vice President Formation .... Ms. Donna COVINGTON
84 Vice Pres Enrollment Management .... Mr. Kevin BISH
06 Registrar .... Dr. Christine L. JOHNSON
07 Director of Admissions .... Mr. Randy OZAN
37 Director of Student Financial Aid .... Mrs. Jenny BURKHART
18 Director of Physical Plant .... Mr. Brian U'REN
09 Dir Inst Effectiveness/Assessment .... Dr. Alexandra H. ANDERSON
15 Director of Human Resources .... Mrs. Barbara ANTROBUS
29 Director Alumni/Church Relations .... Ms. Tammy CESSNA
73 Dean School of Theology & Formation .... Dr. James THOBABEN
88 Assoc Prov Beeson Sch Pract Theol .... Dr. David GYERTSON
88 Dean ESJ School World of Missions .... Dr. Gregg OKESSON
88 Dean School Biblical Interpretation .... Dr. David BAUER
88 Dean Beeson School Practical Theol .... Dr. Tom TUMBLIN
88 Dean Advanced Research Programs .... Dr. Lalsangkima PACHUAU
04 Executive Asst to President .... Ms. Angela CLOYD
08 Dean Library Info & Tech Services .... Dr. Paul A. TIPPEY

Asbury University (I)

1 Macklem Drive, Wilmore KY 40390-1198
County: Jessamine FICE Identification: 001952
Unit ID: 156213
Telephone: (859) 858-3511 Carnegie Class: Masters/S
FAX Number: (859) 858-3921 Calendar System: Semester
URL: www.asbury.edu
Established: 1890 Annual Undergrad Tuition & Fees: $30,198
Enrollment: 1,990 Coed
Affiliation or Control: Independent Non-Profit IRS Status: 501(c)3
Highest Offering: Beyond Master's But Less Than Doctorate
Accreditation: SC, CAEPN, MUS, SW

01 President .... Dr. Kevin J. BROWN
05 Provost .... Dr. Timothy T. WOOSTER
10 Vice Pres Business Affs & Treasurer .... Mr. Glenn R. HAMILTON
32 Vice Pres Student Affs/Dean Stdnts .... Dr. Sarah T. BALDWIN
111 Vice Pres for Inst Advancement .... Dr. Mark R. TROYER
41 VP Intercollegiate Athletics .... Mr. Mike WHITWORTH
20 Academic Dean .... Dr. Timothy G. CAMPBELL
49 Dir of College of Arts & Sciences .... Dr. Stephen K. CLEMENTS
53 Dean School of Education .... Dr. Sharon BIXLER
60 Dean of School of Comm Arts .... Dr. James R. OWENS
106 Dean School of Adult & Online Lrng .... Mr. T. Joshua FEE
50 Dean Howard Dayton Sch Business .... Dr. Michael KANE
110 Senior Advancement Director .... Rev. Stuart A. SMITH
37 Director of Financial Aid .... Mr. Ronald M. ANDERSON
42 Assoc Dean for Campus Ministries .....Rev. Gregory K. HASELOFF
39 Assoc Dean for Residence Life .... Mr. Joe W. BRUNER
06 Registrar .... Mrs. Sheryl VOIGTS
29 Dir of Alumni Relations/Parents Pgm .... Mrs. Lisa D. HARPER
08 Director of Library Services .... Mr. Jared PORTER
13 AVP Information Tech Svcs/CIO .... Mr. Paul J. DUPREE
07 Director of Admissions .... Mr. Brandon COMBS
26 AVP Marketing & Communications .... Mr. Brad JOHNSON
18 Director of Physical Plant .... Mr. Eric C. MCMILLION
23 Supervisor of Clinic .... Ms. Heidi SUNNY
36 Dir Center for Career & Calling .... Ms. Michelle KRATZER
38 Assoc Dean of Wholeness & Wellness .... Mr. Kevin BELLEW
19 Dir of Security & Environ Safety .... Mr. David HAY
40 Manager of Bookstore .... Mr. C. David TRAMMELL
21 Associate Business Officer .... Mr. Gary E. HOWARD
04 Exec Assistant to the President .... Mrs. Michelle BUTCHER
85 Assoc Dean of Intercultural Pgms .... Rev. Esther JADHAV
09 Director of Institutional Research .... Dr. Gay HOLCOMB
15 Dir of Human Resources/Risk Mgt .... Mr. Gregory MCGEE
45 Director Institutional Planning .... Dr. Paul STEPHENS

ATA College (J)

10200 Linn Station Road, Suite 125, Louisville KY 40223
County: Jefferson FICE Identification: 040383
Unit ID: 447935
Telephone: (502) 371-8383 Carnegie Class: Spec 2-yr-Health
FAX Number: (502) 371-8598 Calendar System: Quarter
URL: www.ata.edu
Established: 1994 Annual Undergrad Tuition & Fees: $13,025
Enrollment: 289 Coed
Affiliation or Control: Proprietary IRS Status: Proprietary
Highest Offering: Associate Degree
Accreditation: ABHES

01 President/CEO .... Mr. Donald A. JONES

Baptist Seminary of Kentucky (K)

400 E. College Street, Box 358, Georgetown KY 40324
County: Scott Identification: 667211
Telephone: (502) 863-8300 Carnegie Class: Not Classified
FAX Number: (502) 863-8300 Calendar System: Semester
URL: www.bsk.edu
Established: 2002 Annual Graduate Tuition & Fees: N/A
Enrollment: N/A Coed
Affiliation or Control: Independent Non-Profit IRS Status: 501(c)3
Highest Offering: Master's; No Undergraduates
Accreditation: THEOL

01 President ... Dr. David CASSADY
05 Academic Dean ... Dr. Dalen C. JACKSON
07 Director of Admissions ... Ms. Abby SIZEMORE
06 Registrar/Academic Coordinator ... Ms. Jessalynn CORNETT

Beckfield College (A)

16 Spiral Drive, Florence KY 41042-4866
County: Boone FICE Identification: 024911
Unit ID: 247065
Telephone: (859) 371-9393 Carnegie Class: Bac/Assoc-Mixed
FAX Number: (859) 371-5096 Calendar System: Quarter
URL: www.beckfield.edu
Established: 1984 Annual Undergrad Tuition & Fees: $13,295
Enrollment: 617 Coed
Affiliation or Control: Proprietary IRS Status: Proprietary
Highest Offering: Baccalaureate
Accreditation: **ABHES**, NURSE

01 Chief Executive Officer/CFO ... Ms. Diane G. WOLFER
05 Vice Pres Education & Accreditation ... Mr. Lee FOLEY
37 Director Student Financial Services ... Ms. Kimberly VILLAVERDE
13 Vice Pres Information Technology ... Mr. Charles WILSON
07 Director Admissions ... Mr. Jeff BAKER
36 Director Career Services ... Ms. Karen SHELDON
22 Director of Compliance ... Mr. Lee FOLEY
06 Registrar ... Ms. Jocelyn ROY
08 Director of Library Services ... Ms. Gayle ECABERT
50 Dean of Business/Technology ... Dr. Erica OKERE
66 Dean of Nursing ... Dr. Deborah SMITH-CLAY
76 Dean of Allied Health ... Ms. Dolores DOMINGUEZ
97 Dean of General Education ... Ms. Mindy HODGES
88 Dean of Criminal Justice ... Ms. Brandy EXELER

Bellarmine University (B)

2001 Newburg Road, Louisville KY 40205-0671
County: Jefferson FICE Identification: 001954
Unit ID: 156286
Telephone: (502) 272-8000 Carnegie Class: DU-Mod
FAX Number: (502) 272-8033 Calendar System: Semester
URL: www.bellarmine.edu
Established: 1950 Annual Undergrad Tuition & Fees: $42,200
Enrollment: 3,757 Coed
Affiliation or Control: Independent Non-Profit IRS Status: 501(c)3
Highest Offering: Doctorate
Accreditation: **SC**, CAATE, CAEPN, COARC, MT, NURSE, PTA

01 President ... Dr. Susan M. DONOVAN
03 Senior Vice President ... Dr. Sean J. RYAN
05 Provost & Vice President ... Dr. Paul GORE
20 Vice Provost ... Dr. Graham ELLIS
20 Vice Provost Faculty Development ... Dr. Anne BUCALOS
10 Vice President for Admin & Finance ... Mr. Robert L. ZIMLICH
32 Vice President for Student Affairs ... Dr. Helen G. RYAN
30 VP for Dev & Alumni Relations ... Mr. Glenn F. KOSSE
84 VP for Enrollment/Marketing & Comm ... Dr. Mike MARSHALL
04 Administrative Asst to President ... Ms. Lucy BURNS
50 Interim Dean School of Business ... Dr. Francis RAYMOND
53 Dean Annsley Frazier Thornton Educ ... Dr. Elizabeth DINKINS
49 Dean Bellarmine College ... Dr. Mary HUFF
66 Dean Nursing & Clinical Sciences ... Dr. Nancy YORK
88 Dean Movement & Rehabilitation Sci ... Dr. Tony BROSKY
15 Chief Human Resources Officer ... Ms. Lynn M. BYNUM
21 Asst VP Business Affairs ... Ms. Denise BROWN-CORNELIUS
110 Associate VP Development ... Ms. Tina KAUFFMAN
35 Associate VP Student Affairs ... Mr. Patrick ENGLERT
85 Exec Dir Stdy Abroad & Intl Learn ... Dr. Gabriele W. BOSLEY
35 Dean of Students ... Dr. Sean MCGREEVEY
92 Director Honors Program ... Dr. Jonathan W. BLANDFORD
41 Athletic Director ... Mr. Scott P. WIEGANDT
18 Asst VP Facilities Management ... Mr. Jeffrey DEAN
07 Dean of Admission ... Mr. Timothy A. STURGEON
123 Dean of Graduate Admission ... Dr. Sara Y. PETTINGILL
08 Director of the Library ... Dr. John K. STEMMER
19 Director of Safety & Security ... Ms. Debbie FOX
06 Registrar ... Ms. Ann E. OLSEN
96 Purchasing Manager ... Mr. Patrick COONS
42 Director Campus Ministry ... Ms. Laura KLINE
39 Assoc Dean Stdnt/Dir Residence Life ... Dr. Leslie MAXIE
76 Vice Prov Col of Health Professions ... Dr. Mark WIEGAND
13 Chief Information Officer ... Mr. Eric SATTERLY
37 Director Student Financial Aid ... Ms. April TRETTER
36 Director of Career Development ... Dr. Lilly MASSA-MCKINLEY
29 Assistant VP for Alumni Relations ... Mr. Peter W. KREMER
26 Director of Media Relations ... Mr. Jason A. CISSELL
38 Director of Counseling Center ... Dr. Gary PETIPRIN
09 Director of Institutional Research ... Mr. Drew THIEMANN
45 Vice Provost for Inst Effectiveness ... Dr. James BRESLIN

Berea College (C)

101 Chestnut Street, Berea KY 40404-0003
County: Madison FICE Identification: 001955
Unit ID: 156295
Telephone: (859) 985-3000 Carnegie Class: Bac-A&S
FAX Number: N/A Calendar System: Semester
URL: www.berea.edu
Established: 1855 Annual Undergrad Tuition & Fees: $39,990
Enrollment: 1,670 Coed
Affiliation or Control: Independent Non-Profit IRS Status: 501(c)3
Highest Offering: Baccalaureate
Accreditation: **SC**, CAEPN, NURSE

01 President ... Dr. Lyle D. ROELOFS
10 Vice President Finance ... Mr. Jeff S. AMBURGEY
29 VP Alumni & College Relations ... Ms. Bernadine DOUGLAS
32 VP Labor and Student Life ... Dr. Channell BARBOUR
11 VP Operations and Sustainability ... Mr. Derrick SINGLETON
05 Provost ... Dr. Linda LEEK
45 VP Strategic Initiatives ... Ms. Teri THOMPSON
20 Dean of the Faculty ... Dr. Matthew SADERHOLM
26 Assoc VP of Int Marketing/Comm ... Ms. Kim BROWN
30 Assoc VP of Development Operations ... Ms. Joanne SINGH
35 Asst Vice Pres for Student Life ... Mr. Gus GERASSIMIDES
37 Dir of Student Financial Aid Svcs ... Ms. Theresa LOWDER
38 Dir Counseling/Psychological Svcs ... Ms. Sue REIMONDO
112 Executive Dir Major & Planned Gifts ... Ms. Teresa KASH DAVIS
108 Director of Academic Assessment ... Dr. Robert SMITH
20 Dean of Curriculum/Student Learning ... Dr. Scott STEELE
13 Chief Information Officer ... Ms. Huapei CHEN
07 Director of Admissions Operations ... Mr. Luke HODSON
88 Associate VP of Alumni Relations ... Ms. Jackie COLLIER
15 Associate VP of Human Resources ... Mr. Steve LAWSON
18 Director of Facilities Management ... Mr. Wayne ORR
88 Director of Appalachian Center ... Mr. Chris GREEN
09 Director of Inst Rsrch/Assessment ... Ms. Judith WECKMAN
27 Dir Publications/Media Relations ... Ms. Abbie DARST
08 Director of Library Services ... Mr. Calvin GROSS
41 Dir Athletics/Seabury Ctr Complex ... Mr. Mark CARTMILL
42 Director Campus Christian Center ... Rev. Loretta REYNOLDS
43 General Counsel ... Mr. Judge WILSON
19 Director of Public Safety ... Mr. V. Lavoyed HUDGINS
28 Director Black Cultural Center ... Ms. Monica JONES
88 Dean of Labor ... Ms. Sylvia ASANTE
85 Director International Center ... Dr. Richard CAHILL
40 Retail Manager College Store ... Ms. Sarah CAUDILL
96 Purchasing Manager ... Ms. Aurelia BRANDENBURG
88 Director Ctr Teaching/Learning ... Ms. Leslie ORTQUIST-AHRENS
88 Woodson Center for Interracial Educ ... Dr. Alicestyne TURLEY
88 Director of CELTS ... Ms. Ashley COCHRANE
23 Director of Health and Wellness ... Ms. Jill GURTATOWSKI
88 Director of Internships ... Ms. Esther LIVINGSTON
103 Director of Career Development ... Ms. Amanda TUDOR
104 Education Abroad Advisor ... Ms. Ann BUTWELL
06 Registrar ... Ms. Judy GINTER
100 Executive Assistant to President ... Ms. Judy MOTT
105 Director Web Design/Development ... Mr. Charlie CAMPBELL
04 Admin Assistant to the President ... Ms. Sherry THIELE
44 Director Annual Giving ... Ms. Candis ARTHUR

Brescia University (D)

717 Frederica Street, Owensboro KY 42301-3023
County: Daviess FICE Identification: 001958
Unit ID: 156356
Telephone: (270) 685-3131 Carnegie Class: Bac-Diverse
FAX Number: (270) 686-6422 Calendar System: Semester
URL: www.brescia.edu
Established: 1950 Annual Undergrad Tuition & Fees: $22,100
Enrollment: 1,231 Coed
Affiliation or Control: Roman Catholic IRS Status: 501(c)3
Highest Offering: Master's
Accreditation: **SC**, SW

01 President ... Rev. Larry HOSTETTER
05 Vice President & Academic Dean ... Dr. Cheryl CLEMONS
10 Vice President Business & Finance ... Mr. Dale CECIL
84 Vice President of Enrollment ... Mr. Christopher HOUK
111 Vice Pres Institutional Advancement ... Ms. Tracy NAYLOR
32 Vice Pres/Dean Student Development ... Mr. Joshua R. CLARY
39 Director Residence Life ... Mr. Issac DUNCAN
35 Director Stdnts Act/Leadership Dev ... Ms. Patricia LOVETT
06 Registrar ... Sr. Helena FISCHER, OSU
106 Director of BU Online ... Ms. Shanda LARUE
38 Director of Counseling Center ... Ms. Eva G. ATKINSON
08 Director of Library Services ... Sr. Judith N. RINEY, OSU
88 Director of UCTL ... Dr. Anna KUTHY
15 Director of Human Resources ... Ms. Tammy S. KELLER
13 Director of Information Technology ... Mr. Chris FORD
18 Director of Physical Plant ... Mr. Mike WARD
37 Director of Financial Aid ... Ms. Kristi EIDSON
41 Director of Athletics ... Mr. Brian SKORTZ
26 Director of Public Relations ... Ms. Rachel WHELAN
29 Director of Alumni & Donor Rels ... Mr. Jake DAVIS
44 Director of Annual Giving ... Ms. Lauren OSOWICZ
112 Director of Major Gifts ... Ms. Sydney WARREN
09 Director of Institutional Research ... Ms. Stephanie CLARY
58 Director of Graduate Program-MBA ... Dr. Sandra O. OBILADE
42 Director of Campus Ministry ... Sr. Pam MUELLER, OSU
07 Director of Admissions ... Ms. Christy ROHNER
21 Asst Director Business & Finance ... Ms. Nancy W. REYNOLDS
36 Coordinator of Career Services ... Ms. Morgan RUSSELBURG
20 Associate Academic Dean for Online ... Mr. Jeffrey BARNETTE
40 Bookstore Manager ... Ms. Beverly MCCANDLESS
25 Grants Writer/Special Asst to Pres ... Vacant
100 Chief of Staff ... Dr. Lauren MCCRARY

Campbellsville University (E)

1 Universty Drive, Campbellsville KY 42718-2799
County: Taylor FICE Identification: 001959
Unit ID: 156365
Telephone: (270) 789-5000 Carnegie Class: Masters/L
FAX Number: (270) 789-5050 Calendar System: Semester
URL: www.campbellsville.edu
Established: 1906 Annual Undergrad Tuition & Fees: $25,400
Enrollment: 7,207 Coed
Affiliation or Control: Baptist IRS Status: 501(c)3
Highest Offering: Doctorate
Accreditation: **SC**, CAEPN, IACBE, MFCD, MUS, NUR, SW

01 President ... Dr. Michael CARTER
11 Sr Vice President for Operations ... Mr. Otto TENNANT
05 Provost and VP for Academic Affairs ... Dr. Donna HEDGEPATH
30 Vice President for Development ... Mr. Benji KELLY
07 VP for Enrollment ... Dr. Shane GARRISON
41 VP for Athletics & Student Services ... Mr. Rusty HOLLINGSWORTH
20 Associate Academic Officer ... Dr. Jeanette PARKER
10 Vice President for Finance ... Mr. Tim JUDD
09 Director of Institutional Research ... Mrs. Anna PAVY
38 Director of Student Counseling ... Vacant
92 Director of Honors Program ... Dr. Craig L. ROGERS
40 Director of Bookstore ... Mrs. Donna WRIGHT
42 Director of Campus Ministries ... Mr. Edwin C. PAVY
13 Director of Computing/Communication ... Mr. Eric SMITH
37 Director of Financial Aid ... Mrs. Chris MAPES
29 Director of Alumni Relations ... Ms. Ashley FARMER
08 Director of Library Services ... Vacant
15 Director of Personnel Services ... Mr. Jason LAWSON
18 Director of Maintenance ... Mr. Steve MORRIS
26 Director of News Information ... Mrs. Joan C. MCKINNEY
06 Registrar ... Mrs. Rita A. CREASON
04 Assistant to the President ... Mrs. Kellie VAUGHN
96 Director of Purchasing ... Mrs. Lisa FERGUSON
88 Director of Custodial Services ... Mr. Bob STOTTS
19 Director Security/Safety ... Mr. Kyle DAVIS
32 Dean of Students ... Mr. Rusty WATKINS
39 Asst Dean of Stdnts/Dir Resid Life ... Mr. Andrew FRANKLIN
86 Director Government Relations ... Dr. John CHOWNING

Centre College (F)

600 W Walnut Street, Danville KY 40422-1394
County: Boyle FICE Identification: 001961
Unit ID: 156408
Telephone: (859) 238-5200 Carnegie Class: Bac-A&S
FAX Number: (859) 238-6977 Calendar System: Other
URL: www.centre.edu
Established: 1819 Annual Undergrad Tuition & Fees: $41,700
Enrollment: 1,450 Coed
Affiliation or Control: Independent Non-Profit IRS Status: 501(c)3
Highest Offering: Baccalaureate
Accreditation: **SC**

01 President ... Dr. John A. ROUSH
05 Vice Pres/Dean of College ... Dr. Ellen S. GOLDEY
10 Vice Pres/CFO & Treasurer ... Mr. Brian G. HUTZLEY
32 Vice Pres/Dean of Student Life ... Mr. Wm. Randy HAYS
30 VP Devel/Alumni Engagement ... Mr. Shawn LYONS
43 VP for Legal Affairs/Gift Planning ... Mr. James P. LEAHEY
15 VP for Human Resources/Admin Svcs ... Mrs. Kay L. DRAKE
53 Assoc Professor/Chair Education ... Dr. Sarah A. MURRAY
28 Assoc VP Diversity/Sp Asst to Pres ... Dr. Andrea C. ABRAMS
20 Assoc VP Acad Affs/Sp Asst to Pres ... Dr. Brian CUSATO
07 Dean of Admissions & Financial Aid ... Mr. Robert M. NESMITH
20 Associate Dean of the College ... Dr. Alex M. MCALLISTER
38 Director of Counseling Services ... Ms. Ann E. GOODWIN
104 Int Director of Global Citizenship ... Dr. Lori L. HARTMANN
08 Director of Library Services ... Ms. Carolyn A. FREY
04 Exec Assistant to the President ... Ms. Yvonne Y. MORLEY
37 Assoc Dean/Dir of Financial Aid ... Mr. Kevin D. LAMB
06 Registrar ... Mr. Thomas E. MANUEL
27 Chief Communications Officer ... Dr. Michael P. STRYSICK
36 Dir Ctr for Career/Professional Dev ... Ms. Joy ASHER
39 Director Student Life & Housing ... Ms. Ann S. YOUNG
41 Director of Athletics & Recreation ... Mr. W. Bradley FIELDS
19 Co-Director of Public Safety ... Mr. Kevin S. MILBY
19 Co-Director of Public Safety ... Mr. Gary D. BUGG
09 Director of Institutional Research ... Dr. Brian CUSATO
13 Chief Information Officer ... Mr. Andrew J. RYAN
24 Int Dir Ctr for Teaching/Learning ... Dr. Robyn E. CUTRIGHT
18 Director of Facilities Management ... Mr. D. Wayne KING
21 Controller ... Mr. R. Scott OWENS
42 College Chaplain ... Dr. Richard D. AXTELL
96 Asst Dir Procurement/Capital Proj ... Ms. Ann T. SMITH
29 Dir of Alumni & Family Engagement ... Ms. Megan H. MILBY
57 Director Norton Center for Arts ... Mr. Steven A. HOFFMAN
102 Dir Foundation/Corporate Relations ... Ms. Elizabeth E. GRAVES

Clear Creek Baptist Bible College (G)

300 Clear Creek Road, Pineville KY 40977-9754
County: Bell FICE Identification: 025356
Unit ID: 156417
Telephone: (606) 337-3196 Carnegie Class: Spec-4-yr-Faith
FAX Number: (606) 337-2372 Calendar System: Semester
URL: www.ccbbc.edu
Established: 1926 Annual Undergrad Tuition & Fees: $9,440
Enrollment: 138 Coed
Affiliation or Control: Southern Baptist IRS Status: 501(c)3
Highest Offering: Baccalaureate
Accreditation: **SC**, BI

01 President ... Dr. Donnie S. FOX
05 Academic Dean ... Dr. Jay SULFRIDGE
32 Dean of Student Affairs ... Vacant
11 Administrative Dean ... Mr. Jeremy ANDERSON
111 Dean of Institutional Advancement ... Mr. Matthew BLACK

08	Director of Library	Mrs. Ruth BLACK
42	Director Christian Service	Rev. Joshua SMITH
18	Director of Physical Plant	Mr. Allen SANDERS
37	Director Financial Aid	Mr. Eddie BARKER
06	Registrar	Mr. Jacob YATES
07	Director of Admissions	Mr. Douglas SAUNDERS
26	Director of College Relations	Mr. Michael DELAND
13	Dir of Information Technologies	Mr. Eric GREENE
56	Director of Distance Education	Vacant

Daymar College-Bowling Green (A)

2421 Fitzgerald Industrial Drive,
Bowling Green KY 42101-4071

Telephone: (270) 843-6750 Identification: 666439
Accreditation: ACCSC

† Branch campus of Daymar College, Nashville, TN.

Eastern Kentucky University (B)

521 Lancaster Avenue, Richmond KY 40475-3102

County: Madison FICE Identification: 001963
Unit ID: 156620
Telephone: (859) 622-1000 Carnegie Class: Masters/L
FAX Number: (859) 622-1020 Calendar System: Semester
URL: www.eku.edu
Established: 1906 Annual Undergrad Tuition & Fees (In-State): $9,666
Enrollment: 16,612 Coed
Affiliation or Control: State IRS Status: 501(c)3
Highest Offering: Doctorate
Accreditation: SC, ADNUR, CAATE, CACREP, CAEP, CAEPN, CAHIIM, CLPSY, CONST, DIETD, EMT, FEPAC, IFSAC, MT, MUS, NAIT, NRPA, NURSE, OT, PH, SP, SPAA, SW

01	President	Dr. Michael BENSON
05	Int Provost/Exec VP Acad Affairs	Dr. Jerry POGATSHNIK
10	Senior VP of Finance & Admin	Mr. Barry POYNTER
30	VP Development	Ms. Betina GARDNER
121	VP for Student Success	Dr. Eugene PALKA
11	SVP Operations/Strategic Initiative	Dr. David MCFADDIN
32	Assoc VP & Chief Student Affs Ofcr	Dr. Billy MARTIN
26	Asst VP Communications & Brand Mgmt	Mr. Doug CORNETT
35	Dean of Students	Ms. Kenna MIDDLETON
49	Interim Dean Letters/Arts/Soc Sci	Dr. Sara ZEIGLER
76	Interim Dean Health Sciences	Dr. Shelia PRESSLEY
81	Dean Science	Dr. Tom OTIENO
50	Dean Business & Technology	Dr. Thomas EREKSON
53	Dean Education	Dr. Sherry POWERS
88	Dean Justice & Safety	Dr. Victor KAPPELER
43	University Counsel	Ms. Dana FOHL
19	Chief of Police	Mr. Brian MULLINS
08	Interim Dean of Libraries	Ms. Julie GEORGE
06	Registrar	Ms. Shannon TIPTON
88	Director Advising	Mr. Benton SHIREY
07	Director Admissions	Vacant
25	Director Sponsored Programs	Mr. Gus BENSON
92	Director Honors Program	Dr. David COLEMAN
09	Asst VP Inst Effectiveness & Res	Dr. Tanalee WASSON
46	Int AVP Research	Dr. Tom MARTIN
85	Director International Student Svcs	Mr. Wenceslaus PORYEM
38	Director Counseling Center	Dr. Melissa BARTSCH
88	Int Sr Director Student Conduct	Ms. Emily DAVIS
39	Exec Dir Housing/Residence Life	Mr. Robert BROWN
37	Dir Student Financial Assistance	Mr. Bryan ERSLAN
23	Health Services Manager	Vacant
15	Chief Human Resources Officer	Vacant
14	Deputy Chief Technology Officer	Ms. Jean MARLOW
28	Vice Provost Diversity	Dr. Timothy FORDE
41	Athletic Director	Mr. Stephen LOCHMUELLER
96	Director of Purchasing & Stores	Ms. Andrea CASHELL
42	Chaplain	Vacant
04	Admin Asst to the President	Ms. Cassie MALICK
04	Special Asst to the President & SVP	Dr. Ryan WILSON
58	Dean Graduate School & AVP Rsrch	Dr. Jerry POGATSHNIK
20	Vice Provost	Dr. Sherry ROBINSON
84	Exec Director Enrollment Mgmt	Ms. Elizabeth BALLOU
14	Deputy Chief Information Officer	Mr. Jeff WHITAKER
29	Executive Director Alum Engagement	Mr. Dan MCBRIDE
19	Exec Dir Public Safety & Risk Mgmt	Mr. Bryan MAKINEN
116	Director of Internal Audit	Ms. Susan BALLARD

Frontier Nursing University (C)

195 School Street, Hyden KY 41749

County: Leslie FICE Identification: 030070
Unit ID: 156727
Telephone: (606) 672-2312 Carnegie Class: Spec-4-yr-Other Health
FAX Number: (606) 672-3776 Calendar System: Quarter
URL: www.frontier.edu
Established: 1939 Annual Graduate Tuition & Fees: N/A
Enrollment: 2,004 Coed
Affiliation or Control: Independent Non-Profit IRS Status: 501(c)3
Highest Offering: Doctorate; No Undergraduates
Accreditation: SC, MIDWF, NUR

01	President	Dr. Susan STONE
05	Associate Dean of Academic Affairs	Dr. Anne COCKERHAM
66	Dean of Nursing	Dr. Joan SLAGER
88	PM-Doctor Nursing Practice Director	Dr. Jess CALOHAN
88	Bridge Option Director	Dr. Jacquelyne BROOKS
37	Director of Financial Aid	Ms. Rainie BOGGS

Galen College of Nursing (D)

1031 Zorn Avenue, Louisville KY 40207-1064

County: Jefferson FICE Identification: 030837
Unit ID: 156471
Telephone: (502) 410-6200 Carnegie Class: Spec-4-yr-Other Health
FAX Number: N/A Calendar System: Quarter
URL: www.galencollege.edu
Established: 1989 Annual Undergrad Tuition & Fees: N/A
Enrollment: 1,703 Coed
Affiliation or Control: Proprietary IRS Status: Proprietary
Highest Offering: Master's
Accreditation: SC, ADNUR, NURSE

12	Director of Campus Operations	Mr. Marshall MOORE
106	Dean of Online Programs	Dr. Kathy BURLINGAME
66	Dean	Dr. Constance COOPER

Georgetown College (E)

400 E College Street, Georgetown KY 40324-1696

County: Scott FICE Identification: 001964
Unit ID: 156745
Telephone: (502) 863-8000 Carnegie Class: Bac-A&S
FAX Number: (502) 868-8891 Calendar System: Semester
URL: www.georgetowncollege.edu
Established: 1829 Annual Undergrad Tuition & Fees: $38,650
Enrollment: 1,767 Coed
Affiliation or Control: Baptist IRS Status: 501(c)3
Highest Offering: Master's
Accreditation: SC, #CAATE, CAEPN

01	President	Vacant
05	Provost/Dean of the College	Dr. Rosemary ALLEN
10	Vice President/CFO/Treasurer	Mr. David WILHITE
04	Executive Assistant to President	Ms. Leah STUBBS
30	Vice President for Development	Mr. John DAVIS
32	VP Student Life/Dean of Students	Dr. Curtis SANDBERG
84	Vice President for Enrollment	Dr. Jonathan SANDS WISE
13	Assoc VP for Info Tech Services	Mr. Donald L. BLAKEMAN
21	Controller	Mr. Brad KAUFMAN
06	Registrar	Mr. Jason SNIDER
15	Director of Human Resources	Ms. Debbie CLARK
53	Interim Dean of Education	Dr. Candis HASKELL
07	Director of Admissions	Vacant
37	Dir of Student Financial Planning	Mr. Bob FULTZ
30	Director of Development	Ms. Patricia GAETZ
09	Director of Institutional Research	Ms. Amber AUSTIN
08	Director of Library Services	Mr. Andrew ADLER
29	Director of Alumni Relations	Ms. Laura OWSLEY
41	Director of Athletics	Mr. Brian EVANS
26	Dir Comm/Mktg & Church Relations	Mr. H.K KINGKADE
36	Dir Graves Ctr for Calling & Career	Ms. Holly JAMES
19	Director Campus Safety	Mr. Donald LUNSFORD
38	Director of Counseling/Health Svcs	Vacant
18	Dir Facilities and Grounds	Mr. Bart HORNE
28	Asst Dean Div/Incl & Title IX Coord	Ms. Tiera MASON

Interactive College of Technology (F)

76 Caruthers Road, Newport KY 41071

Telephone: (859) 282-8989 Identification: 770535
Accreditation: COE

† Branch campus of Interactive College of Technology, Chamblee, GA

Kentucky Christian University (G)

100 Academic Parkway, Grayson KY 41143-2205

County: Carter FICE Identification: 001965
Unit ID: 157100
Telephone: (606) 474-3000 Carnegie Class: Bac-Diverse
FAX Number: (606) 474-3189 Calendar System: Semester
URL: www.kcu.edu
Established: 1919 Annual Undergrad Tuition & Fees: $19,256
Enrollment: 688 Coed
Affiliation or Control: Christian Churches And Churches of Christ
IRS Status: 501(c)3
Highest Offering: Master's
Accreditation: SC, NURSE, SW

01	President/CEO	Dr. Jeff K. METCALF
05	Executive Vice President	Dr. Marvin L. ELLIOTT
30	Director of Development	Mr. Jeffrey W. GREENE
88	Director of Church Relations	Mr. Jeff W. GREENE
06	Registrar	Mrs. Emily A. MILLER
13	Director of Campus Technology	Mr. Greg C. RICHARDSON
08	Library Director	Mrs. Naulayne R. ENDERS
108	Director Institutional Assessment	Vacant
32	Director of Student Services	Mr. William B. BAUMGARDNER
42	Campus Minister	Vacant
37	Director Financial Aid	Mrs. Jennie M. BENDER
15	Human Resource Officer	Mr. Terry L. YANKEY
38	Student Counseling Coordinator	Mrs. Lori A. SMITH-WARD
41	Athletic Director	Mr. Corey C. PHIPPS
39	Director of Residence Services	Vacant
18	Director of Facilities	Mr. John R. SEAGRAVES
29	Alumni Relations Officer	Mr. Jeff W. GREENE
58	Dean of the Graduate School	Mr. Robert G. O'LYNN
07	Director of Enrollment Services	Mrs. Sheree GREER
40	Manager of Retail Operations	Mrs. Julie M. BAUMGARDNER
105	Website Manager	Mr. David A. BENNETT
10	Director of Business	Mr. Daniel R. WHITE

*Kentucky Community and Technical College System (H)

300 N Main Street, Versailles KY 40383-1245

County: Woodford FICE Identification: 006724
Unit ID: 157854
Telephone: (859) 256-3100 Carnegie Class: N/A
FAX Number: (859) 256-3119
URL: www.kctcs.edu

01	President	Dr. Jay BOX
00	Chancellor	Dr. Kristin WILLIAMS
10	Vice President Finance	Mr. Wendell FOLLOWELL
13	Vice President Information Tech	Dr. Paul CZARAPATA
30	Vice Pres Resource Development	Mr. Benjamin MOHLER
32	Vice President Student Affairs	Dr. Gloria MCCALL
103	VC Econ Dev/Workforce Solutions	Mr. Shannon GILKEY
09	VC Research and Analysis	Dr. Alicia CROUCH
100	Chief of Staff	Ms. Hannah HODGES

*Ashland Community and Technical College (I)

1400 College Drive, Ashland KY 41101-3617

County: Boyd FICE Identification: 001990
Unit ID: 156231
Telephone: (606) 326-2000 Carnegie Class: Assoc/HVT-High Trad
FAX Number: (606) 326-2185 Calendar System: Semester
URL: www.ashland.kctcs.edu
Established: 1938 Annual Undergrad Tuition & Fees (In-State): $4,248
Enrollment: 2,603 Coed
Affiliation or Control: State IRS Status: 501(c)3
Highest Offering: Associate Degree
Accreditation: SC, ADNUR, COARC, IFSAC, SURGT

02	President	Dr. Larry FERGUSON
32	Dean Student Success/Enroll Svcs	Mr. Steven WOODBURN
10	Dean of Business Affairs	Ms. Karen BLEVINS
09	Dean Inst Plng/Research/Effective	Mr. Steve FLOUHOUSE
05	Dean of Academic Affairs	Dr. Todd BRAND
26	Director of Marketing	Ms. Allison GOBLE
08	Director of Library Services	Ms. Pamela KLINEPETER
07	Director of Admissions/Registrar	Ms. Robin LEWIS
13	Assoc Dean Information Technology	Mr. Farnoosh RAFIEE
28	Director of Cultural Diversity	Mr. Alvin BAKER
15	Director of Human Resources	Ms. Kellie ALLEN
37	Director of Financial Aid	Mr. Adam CHAPMAN
121	Director of Student Support Svcs	Ms. Megan HORNE

*Big Sandy Community and Technical College (J)

1 Bert T. Combs Drive, Prestonburg KY 41653-9502

County: Floyd FICE Identification: 001996
Unit ID: 157553
Telephone: (606) 886-3863 Carnegie Class: Assoc/MT-VT-Mix Trad/Non
FAX Number: (606) 886-2677 Calendar System: Semester
URL: www.bigsandy.kctcs.edu
Established: 1964 Annual Undergrad Tuition & Fees (In-State): $4,248
Enrollment: 4,346 Coed
Affiliation or Control: State IRS Status: 501(c)3
Highest Offering: Associate Degree
Accreditation: SC, COARC, DH

02	President/CEO	Dr. Sherry ZYLKA
32	Chief Student Affairs Officer	Mr. Jimmy WRIGHT
05	Dean of Academic Services	Ms. Myra ELLIOTT
10	Chief Business Affairs Officer	Ms. Michelle MEEK
13	Dean of IT & Facilities Management	Mr. John HERALD
08	Director of Library Services	Ms. Kathy LOWE
15	Director of Human Resources	Ms. Krystal TACKETT
06	Assistant Registrar	Ms. Carla BRANHAM
37	Director of Financial Aid	Ms. Cathy HURD-CRANK
09	Director of Inst Effectiveness	Ms. Denese ATKINSON
14	Director of Information Technology	Mr. Casey MUSIC
40	Bookstore Manager	Vacant
26	Int Dir of Strategic Communications	Ms. Greta SLONE
28	Director of Cultural Diversity	Vacant
103	Director of Workforce/Economic Dev	Ms. Rachelle BURCHETT
04	Exec Admin Asst to President	Ms. Teresa MCCOART

*Bluegrass Community and Technical College (K)

470 Cooper Drive, Lexington KY 40506-0001

County: Fayette FICE Identification: 009707
Unit ID: 156392
Telephone: (859) 246-6200 Carnegie Class: Assoc/MT-VT-High Trad
FAX Number: (859) 246-4664 Calendar System: Semester
URL: www.bluegrass.kctcs.edu
Established: 1965 Annual Undergrad Tuition & Fees (In-State): $4,328
Enrollment: 9,478 Coed
Affiliation or Control: State IRS Status: 501(c)3
Highest Offering: Associate Degree
Accreditation: SC, ADNUR, COARC, DH, IFSAC, MAC, RAD, SURGT

02	President	Dr. Koffi C. AKAKPO
05	VP of Academics/WFD	Dr. Gregory FEENEY
32	VP Student Dev/Enrollment Mgmt	Dr. Palisa WILLIAMS RUSHIN

10 VP Finance & Administration Ms. Lisa G. BELL
28 VP Multiculturalism & Inclusion Ms. Charlene WALKER
111 VP Advancement & Org Development Mr. Mark MANUEL
20 Dean Academics Dr. Karen MAYO
20 Dean Academics Ms. Tammy LILES
103 Dean of Academics/Workforce Devel Ms. Pam HATCHER
121 Dean of Academic Support Dr. Rebecca SIMMS
06 Assoc Dean of Student Records Ms. Becky HARP-STEPHENS
37 Financial Aid Director Ms. Runan EVANS
07 Admissions Director Ms. Shelbie HUGLE
110 Associate VP Institutional Develop Ms. Deborrah L. CATLETT
26 Assoc VP Strategic Communications Ms. Michelle SJOGREN
44 Assoc Vice Pres for Advancement Dr. Laurel MARTIN
79 Assistant Dean Humanities Ms. Angella KING
76 Asst Dean Allied Health/Nat Science Dr. Yasemin CONGLETON
66 Assistant Dean Nursing Dr. Melinda BAKER
81 Asst Dean Mathematics/Statistics Ms. Kausha MILLER
77 Asst Dean Business/CIS Ms. Melanie WILLIAMSON
72 Asst Dean Advanced Mfg and Trade Mr. Ralph POTTER
83 Asst Dean Comm/Hist/Lang/Social Sci Dr. Jenny JONES
08 Director Library/Tutoring Services Ms. Terry BUCKNER
51 Director Adult Education Mr. David STURGILL
106 Assistant Dean Distance Learning Dr. Kevin DUNN
18 Director of Maintenance/Operations Mr. Michael BALL
09 Director of Institutional Research Mr. Aaron GAY
96 Director of Purchasing Ms. Kimberly CAMERON

*Elizabethtown Community and Technical College (A)

600 College Street Road, Elizabethtown KY 42701
County: Hardin FICE Identification: 001991
Unit ID: 156648
Telephone: (270) 769-2371 Carnegie Class: Assoc/MT-VT-High Non
FAX Number: (270) 769-0736 Calendar System: Semester
URL: www.elizabethtown.kctcs.edu
Established: 1963 Annual Undergrad Tuition & Fees (In-State): $4,248
Enrollment: 7,115 Coed
Affiliation or Control: State IRS Status: 501(c)3
Highest Offering: Associate Degree
Accreditation: SC, ADNUR, COARC, IFSAC, RAD

02 President/CEO Dr. Juston PATE
05 Interim Provost/CAO Mr. Darrin POWELL
32 Chief Student Affairs Officer Dr. Dale BUCKLES
12 Campus Education Center Director Vacant
103 Workforce Solutions/Tech Div Chair Mr. Michael HAZZARD
10 Dean of Business Affairs Mr. Brent HOLSCLAW
20 Dean of Instruction/Prof Develop Vacant
15 Director of Human Resources Ms. Whitney TAYLOR
06 Registrar Mr. Bryan SMITH
13 Director of Information Technology Mr. Chris LEE
37 Director of Financial Aid Mr. Michael BARLOW
30 Chief Development Ms. Megan STITH
26 Director of Public Relations Ms. Mary Jo KING
24 Learning Center Coordinator Ms. Pam HARPER
36 Counselor Ms. Sharon SPRATT
38 Counselor Ms. Suzanne DARLAND
40 Bookstore Manager Ms. Stephanie JONES
108 Director Inst Effectiveness Ms. Sarah EDWARDS
18 Maintenance/Operations Supervisor Mr. Charles COBB
57 Chair Div of Arts/Humanities Ms. Jacqueline HAWKINS
81 Chair Div of Biological Science Ms. Lois CHANDLER-COUSINS
81 Chair Div of Physical Science Dr. Shawn KELLIE
75 Chair Div Occupational Technology Mr. Mike HAZZARD
83 Chair Div Social & Behavioral Sci Mr. John WALDRON
28 Director of Diversity Ms. Jerisia LAMONS
04 Exec Admin Assistant to President Ms. Emily ALLEN
105 Director Web Services Ms. Deanna YATES
08 Director of Library Services Ms. Katie MEYER
25 Dir of Grants & Sponsored Projects Ms. Stacy WESTOVER

*Gateway Community and Technical College (B)

500 Technology Way, Florence KY 41042
County: Boone FICE Identification: 005273
Unit ID: 157438
Telephone: (859) 441-4500 Carnegie Class: Assoc/MT-VT-Mix Trad/Non
FAX Number: (859) 341-6859 Calendar System: Semester
URL: www.gateway.kctcs.edu
Established: 1961 Annual Undergrad Tuition & Fees (In-State): $4,328
Enrollment: 4,201 Coed
Affiliation or Control: State IRS Status: 501(c)3
Highest Offering: Associate Degree
Accreditation: SC, CAHIIM, EMT, IFSAC

02 President/CEO Dr. Fernando FIGUEROA
05 Provost and VP Academic Affairs Dr. Teri VONHANDORF
49 Dean of Arts and Sciences Dr. Susan SANTOS
50 Dean of Business/IT/Prof Services Dr. Amy CARRINO
76 Dean of Health Professions Ms. Amber CARTER
72 Dean of Manufacturing & Trans Tech Mr. Sam COLLIER
35 Associate VP for Student Dev Ms. Mallis GRAVES
20 Associate VP Academic Services Mr. Doug PENIX
38 Director of Counseling Services Ms. Tiffany MINARD
84 Associate VP Enrollment Mr. Andre WASHINGTON
06 Registrar Mr. Andre WASHINGTON
18 Director Maintenance & Operations Mr. Mike BAKER
19 Director Security/Safety Mr. Tim CHESSER
37 Director of Financial Aid Ms. Ellen TEEGARDEN
13 Director of Information Services Ms. Melissa SEARS
66 Director of Nursing Ms. Michele SIMMS
89 Director Early College Initiatives Ms. Shelby KRENTZ
08 Director Library/Information Svcs Ms. Denise FRITSCH
110 Director of Development Ms. Sandy ORTMAN-TOMLIN
26 Asst Dir Mktg & Communications Mr. Patrick LAMPING
26 Asst Dir Mktg & Communications Ms. Erica MARYE
30 VP Devel & External Relations Ms. Adrijana KOWATSCH
10 VP Admin & Business Affairs Mr. James YOUNGER
32 VP Student Development Ms. Ingrid WASHINGTON
103 Associate VP Workforce Solutions Ms. Christi GODMAN
15 Director of Human Resources Ms. Amy HATFIELD
04 Executive Assistant to President Ms. Jane FRANTZ

*Hazard Community and Technical College (C)

One Community College Drive, Hazard KY 41701-2402
County: Perry FICE Identification: 006962
Unit ID: 156790
Telephone: (606) 436-5721 Carnegie Class: Assoc/MT-VT-High Non
FAX Number: (606) 487-3604 Calendar System: Semester
URL: www.hazard.kctcs.edu
Established: 1968 Annual Undergrad Tuition & Fees (In-State): $4,248
Enrollment: 3,305 Coed
Affiliation or Control: State IRS Status: 501(c)3
Highest Offering: Associate Degree
Accreditation: SC, CAHIIM, DMS, IFSAC, PTAA, RAD, SURGT

02 President/CEO Dr. Jennifer LINDON
05 Chief Academic Officer Dr. Sandra KIDDOO
32 Vice President of Student Affairs Ms. Germaine SHAFFER
10 Chief Financial Officer Ms. Connie WATTS
103 Dean of Workforce Solutions Mrs. Keila MILLER
13 Chief Information Officer Ms. Donna ROARK
15 Senior Director of Human Resources Ms. Vickie COMBS
18 Dean of Operations Mr. Stu FUGATE
26 Dir of Marketing & Communications Mrs. Delcie COMBS
21 Dean of Business Services Ms. Jackie HALL
08 Director Library Services Mrs. Cathy BRANSON
97 Academic Dean General Education Ms. Leila SMITH
75 Acad Dean Occupational Technologies Mr. Tony BACK
76 Acad Dean Allied Health Sci Mr. Paul CURRIE
56 Academic Dean Distance Learning Ms. Ella STRONG
37 Director of Financial Aid Mr. Charles ANDERSON, JR.
06 Registrar Ms. Libby PETERS
07 Director of Admissions Mr. Scott GROSS
09 Coord of Inst Effectiveness Ms. Lois PUFFER
28 Director of Cultural Diversity Mrs. Danielle KING

*Henderson Community College (D)

2660 S Green Street, Henderson KY 42420-4699
County: Henderson FICE Identification: 001993
Unit ID: 156851
Telephone: (270) 827-1867 Carnegie Class: Assoc/MT-VT-Mix Trad/Non
FAX Number: (270) 831-9600 Calendar System: Semester
URL: www.henderson.kctcs.edu
Established: 1960 Annual Undergrad Tuition & Fees (In-State): $4,248
Enrollment: 1,490 Coed
Affiliation or Control: State IRS Status: 501(c)3
Highest Offering: Associate Degree
Accreditation: SC, ADNUR, MAC, MLTAD

02 President Dr. Jason D. WARREN
05 Provost Dr. Reneau WAGGONER
10 Chief Business Officer Ms. Christina STINSON
08 Library Director Mr. Mike W. KNECHT
13 Director of Technology Solutions Mr. Joe HEERDINK
15 Director of Human Resources Ms. Kim JONES
57 Director of Preston Arts Center Mr. Eric KERCHNER
06 Registrar Mr. Chad PHILLIPS
66 Director of Nursing Dr. Lori DONAHOO
28 Director of Cultural Diversity Mr. William DIXON
111 Chief Advancement Officer Ms. Jennifer PRESTON
09 Dir Institutional Research & Effect Mr. Brian MCMURTRY
18 Maintenance/Oper Supervisor Mr. Lance CONYERS
36 Career Services Coordinator Ms. Angela WATSON
37 Director Financial Aid Mr. Andrew ZELLERS
84 Assoc Dean for Enrollment Mgmt Mr. Cary CONLEY
49 Div Chair Liberal Arts/Prof Studies Ms. Sharon BURTON
76 Div Chair Allied Health Dr. Carole MATTINGLY
81 Div Chair STEM Mr. Barry PHELPS
04 Administrative Asst to President Ms. Malinda S. HUDSON
103 Coordinator Workforce Solutions Ms. Stacey HOWELL

*Hopkinsville Community College (E)

720 North Drive, PO Box 2100,
Hopkinsville KY 42241-2100
County: Christian FICE Identification: 001994
Unit ID: 156860
Telephone: (270) 707-3700 Carnegie Class: Assoc/HT-Mix Trad/Non
FAX Number: (270) 886-0237 Calendar System: Semester
URL: www.hopkinsville.kctcs.edu
Established: 1965 Annual Undergrad Tuition & Fees (In-State): $4,248
Enrollment: 2,640 Coed
Affiliation or Control: State IRS Status: 501(c)3
Highest Offering: Associate Degree
Accreditation: SC, ADNUR

02 President Dr. Alissa YOUNG
04 Exec Admin Asst to President Ms. Janice JONES
05 Int Chief Academic Affairs Officer Mr. James HUNTER
10 Chief Business Affairs Officer Dr. Dale LEATHERMAN
32 Chief Student Affairs Officer Ms. Angel PRESCOTT
103 Chief Cmty/Workforce/Economic Dev Ms. Carol KIRVES
06 Registrar Ms. Tiffanie WITT
08 Director Library Services Ms. Ann NICHOLS
09 Int Dir Institutional Effectiveness Mr. James HUNTER
12 Director Fort Campbell Campus Ms. Allisha LEE
13 Director Information Technology Mr. Tony NELSON
15 Director Human Resources Ms. Yvonne GLASMAN
18 Director Maintenance/Operations Mr. Dan HAMBY
21 Associate Dean Business Affairs Ms. Ann T. HOLLAND
26 Director Marketing & Communication Ms. Rena YOUNG
28 Cultural Diversity Director Ms. Deloria SCOTT
30 Chief Institutional Advancement Ofc Ms. Yvette YONCE EASTHAM
37 Director Financial Aid Ms. Janet GUNTHER
38 Advising Center Director Ms. Deloria SCOTT
40 Bookstore Director Ms. Sheena KOCH
36 Coordinator Career Services Ms. Kanya ALLEN
19 Safety Specialist Mr. James KAUFFMAN
49 Chair Liberal Arts and Sciences Div Ms. Julia LAFFOON-JACKSON
72 Chr Professional/Technical Studies Mr. Arthur PENDLETON
66 Chair Nursing Division Ms. Joyce LAMBRUNO
81 Chair Mathematics & Sciences Div Mr. Ted H. WILSON
76 Chair Allied Health Division Dr. Beth BEVERLY

*Jefferson Community and Technical College (F)

109 E Broadway, Louisville KY 40202-2000
County: Jefferson FICE Identification: 006961
Unit ID: 156921
Telephone: (502) 213-5333 Carnegie Class: Assoc/HT-Mix Trad/Non
FAX Number: (502) 213-2115 Calendar System: Semester
URL: www.jefferson.kctcs.edu
Established: 1967 Annual Undergrad Tuition & Fees (In-State): $4,328
Enrollment: 12,250 Coed
Affiliation or Control: State IRS Status: 501(c)3
Highest Offering: Associate Degree
Accreditation: SC, ADNUR, CAHIIM, COARC, EMT, IFSAC, MAC, MLTAD, OTA, PTAA, RAD, SURGT

02 President Dr. Ty J. HANDY
05 VP of Academic & Student Affairs Dr. Diane CALHOUN-FRENCH
10 VP of Administration and CFO Mr. Gary DRYDEN
45 VP of College Advancement/Planning Mr. Don SCHIEMAN
21 Controller Ms. Norma NORTHERN
20 Dean Academic Affs Tech Pgms Dr. Telly SELLARS
97 Dean of General Education/Transfer Dr. Randy DAVIS
12 Coordinator Shelby Campus Ms. Maia LANGLEY
32 Dean Student Affs/Enrollment Mgmt Dr. Laura SMITH
08 Library Services Director Ms. Sheree WILLIAMS
13 Chief Information Technology Office Mr. Thomas ROGERS
09 Dir Inst Research/Effectiveness Dr. Brittany INGE
07 Director of Admissions Mr. Jimmy KIDD
28 Dir Diversity/Inclusion/Cmty Engage Ms. Danielle R. SIMS
06 Registrar Ms. Amanda TINDALL
26 Public Relations/Marketing Mr. Ben JACKEY
15 Human Resources Director Ms. Toni WHALEN
18 Facilities Director Ms. Pamela TURNER
37 Director of Financial Aid Ms. Angela JOHNSON
30 Inst Advance/Development Coord Ms. Karla HALL
38 Student Counseling Ms. Rhonda GUMMER
96 Director of Purchasing Ms. Pamela DUMM
12 Director of Carrollton Campus Ms. Heather YOCUM
12 Dean of Extended Campuses/Academic Ms. Donna MILLER
24 Learning Commons Ms. Hillary SORTOR
04 Administrative Asst to President Ms. Teresa B. HARPER
106 Dir Online Education/E-learning Dr. Claver HATEGEKIMANA
25 Chief Contracts/Grants Admin Ms. Joanna LYNCH
19 Int Chief Campus Safety/Security Mr. Gary DRYDEN
103 Director Workforce Development Ms. Nickie COBB
105 Director Web Services Ms. Tamie KNAEBLE

*Madisonville Community College (G)

2000 College Drive, Madisonville KY 42431-9199
County: Hopkins FICE Identification: 009010
Unit ID: 157304
Telephone: (270) 821-2250 Carnegie Class: Assoc/MT-VT-High Non
FAX Number: (270) 824-1866 Calendar System: Semester
URL: www.madisonville.kctcs.edu
Established: 1968 Annual Undergrad Tuition & Fees (In-State): $4,248
Enrollment: 3,404 Coed
Affiliation or Control: State IRS Status: 501(c)3
Highest Offering: Associate Degree
Accreditation: SC, ADNUR, COARC, EMT, IFSAC, MLTAD, OTA, PTAA, RAD, SURGA, SURGT

02 President Dr. Cynthia S. KELLEY
05 Provost Dr. Scott COOK
10 Chief Business Affairs Officer Mr. Ray GILLASPIE
11 Vice Pres Quality Assurance & Admin Dr. Jay PARRENT
32 Dean of Student Affairs Ms. Cathy A. VAUGHAN
72 Division Chair Applied Technology Mr. Matt LUCKETT
66 Div Chr Nursing/Related Tech Dr. Marsha WOODALL
79 Div Chr Humanities/Related Tech Ms. Chandy D. MELTON
83 Div Chr Social Science/Related Tech Ms. Natalie F. COOPER
81 Div Chr Mathematics and Sciences Ms. Dawn TILLEN

76 Div Chr Allied Health/Related Tech ....Ms. Tonia R. GIBSON
08 Director of Library Services ....Mr. Colin MAGEE
06 Registrar ....Ms. Casie RICHARDSON
15 Director of Human Resources ....Ms. Kim JONES
36 Director of Counseling Services ....Ms. Cathy A. VAUGHAN
111 Director of Advancement ....Ms. Raegina SCOTT
37 Director of Financial Aid ....Ms. Karen MILLER
26 Public Relations Coordinator ....Ms. Emily RAY
56 Extended Campus
Director ....Ms. Britney HERNANDEZ-STEVENSON
25 Dir Grants/Planning & Effectiveness ... Mr. David A. SCHUERMER
28 Director of Cultural Diversity ....Mr. James H. BOWLES
103 Director Workforce Solutions ....Mr. Mike DAVENPORT
20 Dean of Academic Affairs ....Ms. Lisa A. HOWERTON
21 Dean of Business Affairs ....Mr. Michael L. JOHNSON
40 Bookstore Manager ....Ms. Sonya L. PARKER
84 Dean of Enrollment Management ....Ms. Aimee J. WILKERSON
04 Sr Admin Assistant to the President . Mr. Grayson P. HAGERMAN
13 Director of Information Technology ....Mr. Joe HEERDINK
19 Director of Public Protection ....Mr. Joe BLUE

*Maysville Community and Technical College (A)

1755 US Highway 68, Maysville KY 41056-8910
County: Mason FICE Identification: 006960
Unit ID: 157331
Telephone: (606) 759-7141 Carnegie Class: Assoc/HVT-Mix Trad/Non
FAX Number: (606) 759-7176 Calendar System: Semester
URL: www.maysville.kctcs.edu
Established: 1968 Annual Undergrad Tuition & Fees (In-State): $4,248
Enrollment: 3,495 Coed
Affiliation or Control: State IRS Status: 501(c)3
Highest Offering: Associate Degree
Accreditation: SC, COARC, IFSAC, MAC, MLTAD, NAIT

02 President ....Dr. Stephen VACIK
05 Provost ....Dr. Thomas WARE
10 Chief Finance Officer ....Ms. Barbara CAMPBELL
84 Chief Ofcr Enrollment/Student Svc ....Ms. Jessica KERN
20 Assoc Dean Academic Support Svc ....Dr. Dana CALLAND
09 Assoc Dean Institutional Rsch/Plng ....Ms. Pam STAFFORD
08 Director Library Services ....Ms. Sonja EADS
13 Director Information Technology ....Mr. Brett CABLE
111 Director Advancement/Foundation ....Ms. Cara CLARKE
37 Director Financial Aid ....Ms. Sandy POWER
06 Registrar ....Ms. Lori GAUNCE
28 Director of Diversity ....Ms. Millicent HARDING
15 Director of Human Resources ....Ms. Sandi L. ESTILL
106 Coordinator Distance Learning ....Ms. Rita THOMAS
50 Div Chr Business/Info Technologies ....Ms. Natasha MADDOX
49 Div Chair Liberal Arts/Education ......Ms. Kathleen MELLENKAMP
81 Div Chair Math/Science/Agriculture ....Dr. Angela FULTZ
76 Division Chair of Health Sciences ....Ms. Deborah NOLDER
72 Division Chair Industrial Tech ....Mr. Tony WALLACE

*Owensboro Community and Technical College (B)

4800 New Hartford Road, Owensboro KY 42303-1899
County: Daviess FICE Identification: 030345
Unit ID: 247940
Telephone: (270) 686-4400 Carnegie Class: Assoc/MT-VT-High Non
FAX Number: (270) 686-4496 Calendar System: Semester
URL: www.octc.kctcs.edu
Established: 1986 Annual Undergrad Tuition & Fees (In-State): $4,248
Enrollment: 3,787 Coed
Affiliation or Control: State IRS Status: 501(c)3
Highest Offering: Associate Degree
Accreditation: SC, ACBSP, EMT, IFSAC, MAC, RAD, SURGT

02 President ....Dr. Scott WILLIAMS
04 Assistant to the President ....Ms. Kittridge MIDKIFF
05 VP of Academic Affairs ....Dr. Veena SALLAN
32 VP of Student Affairs ....Mr. Kevin BEARDMORE
10 VP of Business Affairs ....Ms. Sarah PRICE
13 VP Information Technology ....Mr. James HARTZ
103 VP Workforce Solutions ....Ms. Cynthia FIORELLA
08 Library Services Director ....Ms. Donna ABELL
06 Registrar ....Ms. Christy ELLIS
15 Director of Human Resources ....Ms. Victoria HOHIEMER
37 Dean of Student Affairs ....Dr. Andrea BORREGARD
111 Dir Institutional Advancement ....Mr. Michael RODGERS
26 Director of Public Relations ....Ms. Bernadette TOYE-HALE
28 Director of Diversity ....Dr. Ade OREDEIN
38 Director Student Counseling ....Ms. Barbara TIPMORE
96 Director of Purchasing ....Ms. Sarah PRICE
40 Bookstore Manager ....Ms. Sonya SOUTHARD
88 TV Production Manager ....Mr. John BRYENTON
07 Senior Admissions Advisor ....Ms. Linda CALHOUN
36 Career Resource/Placemnt Ctr Coord ....Ms. Katie BALLARD
79 Assoc Dean Humanities/Fine Arts ....Dr. Julia LEDFORD
49 Academic Dean Arts & Sciences ....Dr. Marc MALTBY
75 Assoc Dean Prof/Tech Studies ....Mr. Dean AUTRY
66 Associate Dean Nursing ....Ms. Terri LANHAM
20 Dean Acad Affs Prof/Tech ....Dr. Stacy EDDS-ELLIS
09 Coord Institutional Effectiveness ....Vacant
19 Director Security/Safety ....Mr. Jeff HENDRICKS

*Somerset Community College (C)

808 Monticello Street, Somerset KY 42501-2973
County: Pulaski FICE Identification: 001997
Unit ID: 157711
Telephone: (877) 629-9722 Carnegie Class: Assoc/HVT-High Trad
FAX Number: N/A Calendar System: Semester
URL: somerset.kctcs.edu
Established: 1965 Annual Undergrad Tuition & Fees (In-State): $4,248
Enrollment: 5,886 Coed
Affiliation or Control: State IRS Status: 501(c)3
Highest Offering: Associate Degree
Accreditation: SC, ADNUR, COARC, EMT, IFSAC, MLTAD, PTAA, RAD, SURGT

02 President/CEO ....Dr. Carey CASTLE
05 Senior VP of Academic Affairs ....Dr. Clint HAYES
10 Vice President of Administration ....Ms. Jill MEECE
11 Vice President of Operations ....Mr. Larry ABBOTT
76 Dean for Health Sciences ....Ms. Nancy L. POWELL
09 VP of Institutional Effectiveness ....Mr. Bruce GOVER
32 Vice President of Student Affairs ....Ms. Tracy L. CASADA
103 VP of Workforce Solutions ....Ms. Alesa JOHNSON
111 VP of Institutional Advancement ....Ms. Cindy D. CLOUSE
79 Assoc Dean Humanities/Fine Arts/SS ....Mr. Jon BURLEW
81 Assoc Dean Math/Natural Science ....Dr. Elaine KOHRMAN
50 Assoc Dean Business/Prof Services ....Mr. Kevin BRADFORD
37 Director of Financial Aid ....Mr. Patrick MAYER
06 Registrar ....Ms. Paula J. LATHAM
15 Director of Human Resources ....Ms. Jill N. MEECE
28 Director of Cultural Diversity ....Ms. Elaine WILSON
12 Director of McCreary Center ....Mr. Shawn ANDERSON
12 Director of Clinton Center ....Ms. Judy TALLENT
12 Director of Casey & Russell Centers ....Mr. J. R THOMPSON

*Southcentral Kentucky Community and Technical College (D)

1845 Loop Drive, Bowling Green KY 42101-9202
County: Warren FICE Identification: 005271
Unit ID: 156338
Telephone: (270) 901-1000 Carnegie Class: Assoc/MT-VT-Mix Trad/Non
FAX Number: (270) 901-1145 Calendar System: Semester
URL: www.bowlinggreen.kctcs.edu
Established: 1939 Annual Undergrad Tuition & Fees (In-State): $4,248
Enrollment: 4,289 Coed
Affiliation or Control: State IRS Status: 501(c)3
Highest Offering: Associate Degree
Accreditation: SC, COARC, IFSAC, RAD, SURGT

02 President & CEO ....Dr. Phillip W. NEAL
05 Provost ....Dr. James MCCASLIN
32 VP Student/Organization Success ....Ms. Brooke JUSTICE
10 Vice President Finance/Admin ....Mr. Chris CUMENS
06 Registrar ....Ms. Amy CANNON
15 Director of Human Resources ....Ms. Sherri L. FORESTER
26 Director of Public Relations ....Ms. Rebecca LEE
111 Director of Inst Advancement ....Ms. Heather ROGERS
37 Director of Financial Aid ....Ms. Jennifer WELLS
09 Director Institution Effectiveness ....Mr. Mark GARRETT

*Southeast Kentucky Community and Technical College (E)

700 College Road, Cumberland KY 40823-1099
County: Harlan FICE Identification: 001998
Unit ID: 157739
Telephone: (606) 589-2145 Carnegie Class: Assoc/HT-Mix Trad/Non
FAX Number: (606) 589-3175 Calendar System: Semester
URL: www.southeast.kctcs.edu
Established: 1960 Annual Undergrad Tuition & Fees (In-State): $4,248
Enrollment: 3,229 Coed
Affiliation or Control: State IRS Status: 501(c)3
Highest Offering: Associate Degree
Accreditation: SC, ADNUR, COARC, MLTAD, PTAA, SURGT

02 President ....Dr. Vic ADAMS
05 Chief Academic Officer ....Dr. Joel MICHAELIS
111 Chief Inst Advancement Officer .. Dr. Michele DYKES-ANDERSON
10 Chief Business Affairs Officer ....Ms. Angela SIMPSON
15 Director Human Resources ....Ms. Billie FRANKS
08 Head Librarian ....Ms. Lynn COX
13 Director of Information Technology ....Mr. Merrill GALLOWAY
28 Director of Diversity ....Dr. Carolyn SUNDY
32 Chief Student Affairs Officer ....Dr. Rebecca PARROTT
07 Director of Admissions ....Ms. Felicia CARROLL
37 Director Financial Aid ....Ms. Barbara GENT
04 Administrative Asst to President ....Mr. Paul BRYANT
06 Registrar ....Ms. Anita BARNHILL
09 Dean of Institutional Effectiveness ....Dr. Rick MASON
103 Dir Workforce/Career Development ....Ms. Sherri CLARK
18 Chief Facilities/Physical Plant ....Mr. Lige BUELL
26 Director of Public Relations ....Ms. Amy SIMPSON

*West Kentucky Community and Technical College (F)

4810 Alben Barkley Drive, Paducah KY 42002-7380
County: McCracken FICE Identification: 001979
Unit ID: 157483
Telephone: (270) 554-9200 Carnegie Class: Assoc/MT-VT-High Non
FAX Number: (270) 554-6217 Calendar System: Semester
URL: www.westkentucky.kctcs.edu
Established: 1909 Annual Undergrad Tuition & Fees (In-State): $4,248
Enrollment: 6,038 Coed
Affiliation or Control: State IRS Status: 501(c)3
Highest Offering: Associate Degree
Accreditation: SC, ACBSP, ACFEI, ADNUR, DA, DMS, IFSAC, MLTAD, PNUR, PTAA, RAD, SURGT

02 President/CEO ....Dr. Anton REECE
103 VP of Workforce Solutions ....Mr. Kevin O'NEILL
05 VP of Academic Affairs ....Dr. David HEFLIN
32 VP of Student Services ....Ms. Emily PECK
11 VP of Administrative Services ....Mr. Shay NOLAN
10 VP Business Affairs ....Ms. Susan GRAVES
111 VP Institutional Advancement ....Ms. Lee EMMONS
20 Associate VP Academic Affairs ....Dr. Karen HLINKA
08 Library Services Director ....Ms. Amy SULLIVAN
37 Financial Aid Director ....Ms. Angel RHODES
26 Public Relations Director ....Ms. Janett BLYTHE
13 Director Information Technology ....Ms. Ruby RODGERS
15 Director Human Resources ....Ms. Bridget CANTER
40 Bookstore Manager ....Mr. Todd MITCHELL
06 Registrar/Dir of Admissions ....Ms. Jess PUFFENBARGER
35 Student Activities Coordinator ....Ms. Amy ELMORE
79 Dean Humanities/Fine Arts/Soc Sci ....Mr. Britton SHURLEY
66 Dean Nursing Division ....Ms. Shari GHOLSON
76 Dean Allied Health Division ....Ms. Carrie HOPPER
75 Dean Applied Tech Division ....Ms. Stephanie MILLIKEN
81 Dean Math/Science & Computer ....Ms. Rhonda ADKINS
09 Associate VP of IE ....Dr. Renea AKIN
04 Administrative Asst to President ....Ms. Melissa ALLCOCK
19 Director Security/Safety ....Mr. David WALLACE
28 Director of Diversity ....Ms. Chevene DUNCAN-HERRING
29 Director Alumni Affairs ....Ms. Darwin TAMAR-RAMSEY
07 Director of Admissions ....Mr. Trent JOHNSON
106 Director Online Learning ....Ms. Kate SENN

Kentucky Mountain Bible College (G)

855 Highway 541, Jackson KY 41339
County: Breathitt FICE Identification: 030021
Unit ID: 157030
Telephone: (606) 693-5000 Carnegie Class: Spec-4-yr-Faith
FAX Number: (888) 742-1124 Calendar System: Semester
URL: www.kmbc.edu
Established: 1931 Annual Undergrad Tuition & Fees: $9,460
Enrollment: 83 Coed
Affiliation or Control: Interdenominational IRS Status: 501(c)3
Highest Offering: Baccalaureate
Accreditation: BI

01 President ....Dr. Philip E. SPEAS
03 Executive Vice President ....Rev. Thomas LORIMER
05 Academic Dean ....Mr. Zane DARLAND
10 Chief Business Manager/CIO ....Mr. Steve A. LORIMER
08 Head Librarian ....Ms. Patricia A. BOWEN
06 Registrar ....Dr. Richard E. ENGLEHARDT
07 Chief Admissions Counselor ....Mr. David W. LORIMER
37 Director Student Financial Aid ....Mr. Joe RITTER
32 Dean of Students ....Rev. James H. NELSON
18 Chief Facilities/Physical Plant ....Rev. Doug DUNN
20 Associate Academic Officer ....Mrs. Sara BAGBY
29 Director of Alumni Relations ....Mrs. Hannah AVERY
106 Dir Online Education/E-learning ....Rev. Jason GOBEN
88 Title 9 Coordinator ....Rev. Gary SMITH
96 Director of Purchasing ....Mr. David BOLERATZ

Kentucky State University (H)

400 E Main Street, Frankfort KY 40601-2355
County: Franklin FICE Identification: 001968
Unit ID: 157058
Telephone: (502) 597-6000 Carnegie Class: Bac-Diverse
FAX Number: (502) 597-6490 Calendar System: Semester
URL: www.kysu.edu
Established: 1886 Annual Undergrad Tuition & Fees (In-State): $8,090
Enrollment: 1,926 Coed
Affiliation or Control: State IRS Status: 501(c)3
Highest Offering: Doctorate
Accreditation: SC, ACBSP, ADNUR, CAEPN, MUS, NUR, SPAA, SW

01 President ....Dr. M. Christopher BROWN, II
10 EVP/CFO Finance & Administration ....Mr. Douglas ALLEN, II
05 Int Provost & VP Academic Affairs ....Dr. Lucian YATES, III
32 Actg VP Stdnt Engagement/Enroll
Mgt ....Dr. Jeffery T. BURGIN, JR.
26 VP Brand Identity & University Rels .....Ms. Clara ROSS STAMPS
111 VP Institutional Advancement ....Vacant
43 General Counsel ....Ms. Lisa K. LANG
20 Vice Provost of Academic Affairs ....Dr. Beverly SCHNELLER
13 Chief Information Officer ....Ms. Wendy D. DIXIE
121 Assistant VP Student Success ....Dr. Charles HOLLOWAY
35 AVP & Dean of Students ....Dr. Jeffery T. BURGIN, JR.
106 Vice Prov/Dir Online Programs ....Dr. Stashia EMANUEL
117 Safety and Compliance Officer ....Mr. Eric ROBINSON
65 Director Land Grant ....Dr. Kirk W. POMPER
47 Chair Div of Aquaculture ....Dr. James H. TIDWELL
47 Chair College of Agriculture ....Dr. John SEDLACEK
50 Chair School of Business ....Dr. Abdul M. TURAY
57 Chair Fine Arts ....Dr. Lori C. HICKS
81 Chair Math & Science ....Dr. Fariba BIGDELI JAHED
77 Chair Computer Science ....Dr. Chi SHEN
107 Chair Professional Studies ....Dr. Jo Anne RAINEY

88 Chair Literature/Language/Phil .... Mr. David SHABAZZ
83 Chair Psychology .... Dr. Tierra FREEMAN-TAYLOR
88 Acting Chair Criminal Justice .... Dr. Arthur HAYDEN
79 Chair Humanities/Social Sciences .... Dr. Cynthia GLASS
25 Dep Prov/Dir Grants Sponsored Pgms .... Mr. Derrick C. GILMORE
58 Director Graduate Studies .... Dr. James B. OBIELODAN
41 Director Athletics .... Ms. Etienne THOMAS
15 Director Human Resource Svcs .... Ms. Candace RAGLIN
04 Assistant to President .... Ms. Cheryl DUNN
21 Controller/Director Accounting Svcs .... Ms. Michelle D. SUTTON
06 Registrar .... Ms. Yolanda S. BENSON
113 Bursar .... Ms. Natalie T. TURNER
114 Director Budget .... Vacant
08 Director Library .... Ms. Sheila A. STUCKEY
121 Academic Advisor/Success Coach .... Dr. Walter MALONE
09 Dir Inst Research & Effectiveness .... Ms. Yuliana SUSANTO-ONG
07 Director Admissions .... Vacant
37 Director Financial Aid .... Ms. Russelle KEESE
96 Purchasing Manager .... Vacant
29 Director Alumni Relations .... Vacant
19 Chief of Police .... Vacant
44 Director Annual Fund and Analytics .... Mr. Michael DECOURCY
108 Dir Institutional Effectiveness .... Ms. Lauren GRAVES
86 Director Government Relations .... Ms. Rachelle JOHNSON

Kentucky Wesleyan College (A)

3000 Frederica Street, Owensboro KY 42301

County: Daviess | FICE Identification: 001969 | Unit ID: 157076

Telephone: (270) 926-3111 | Carnegie Class: Bac-Diverse
FAX Number: (270) 926-3112 | Calendar System: Semester
URL: www.kwc.edu
Established: 1858 | Annual Undergrad Tuition & Fees: $26,160
Enrollment: 716 | Coed
Affiliation or Control: United Methodist | IRS Status: 501(c)3
Highest Offering: Baccalaureate
Accreditation: SC, IACBE

01 President .... Dr. Gene TICE
05 VP Acad Affairs/Dean of the College .... Dr. Paula DEHN
10 Vice President of Finance .... Mr. Dan FRAZIER
124 VP of Exec Initiatives & Retention .... Mr. Scott E. KRAMER
32 VP of Student Services .... Ms. Rebecca MCQUEEN
13 Dir of Information Tech .... Mrs. Dena PAYNE
111 Vice President for Advancement .... Mr. Eddie KENNY
07 VP of Admissions and Financial Aid .... Mr. Matthew RUARK
06 Registrar .... Ms. Lindsey CROWE
09 Dir of Inst Effectiveness/Research .... Ms. Jenna BRASHEAR
15 Director of Human Resources .... Mrs. Linda B. KELLER
37 Director of Financial Aid .... Ms. Crystal HAMILTON
89 Director of the PLUS Center .... Vacant
08 Director of Library Learning Center .... Vacant
41 Director of Athletics .... Mr. Rob MALLORY
30 Dir of Development/Campus Relations .... Ms. Kathy RUTHERMAN
42 Director of Campus Ministries .... Mr. Shawn TOMES
110 Dir Development/Donor Rels .... Mr. M. Blake HARRISON
04 Assistant to President .... Ms. Chanda F. PRATER
106 Assoc Dean/Dir Online Education .... Mrs. Rebecca FRANCIS
36 Dir of Career Services .... Ms. Deborah JONES
39 Director of Residence Life .... Ms. Lori ETHERIDGE
29 Director Alumni Affairs .... Ms. Summer CRICK
38 Director Student Counseling .... Ms. Terri PETZOLD

Lexington Theological Seminary (B)

230 Lexington Green Circle, Ste 300, Lexington KY 40503

County: Fayette | FICE Identification: 001971 | Unit ID: 157207

Telephone: (859) 252-0361 | Carnegie Class: Spec-4-yr-Faith
FAX Number: (859) 281-6042 | Calendar System: Other
URL: www.lextheo.edu
Established: 1865 | Annual Graduate Tuition & Fees: N/A
Enrollment: 66 | Coed
Affiliation or Control: Christian Church (Disciples Of Christ) | IRS Status: 501(c)3
Highest Offering: Doctorate; No Undergraduates
Accreditation: THEOL

01 President .... Dr. Charisse L. GILLETT
05 VP Academic Affairs/Dean .... RevDr. Loida MARTELL
111 Vice President for Advancement .... Mr. Mark V. BLANKENSHIP
10 Chief Financial Officer .... Mrs. Karen C. WAGERS
06 Registrar .... Ms. Windy KIDD
08 Librarian .... Ms. Dolores YILIBUW
13 Director Information Services .... Mr. Ben WYATT
07 Director Admission .... Rev. Erin CASH
15 Director Personnel Services .... Ms. Karen C. WAGERS
18 Chief Facilities/Physical Plant .... Ms. Karen C. WAGERS
29 Director Alumni Relations .... Mr. Mark V. BLANKENSHIP
37 Director Student Financial Aid .... Ms. Windy KIDD
96 Director of Purchasing .... Ms. Robin VARNER

Lindsey Wilson College (C)

210 Lindsey Wilson Street, Columbia KY 42728-1298

County: Adair | FICE Identification: 001972 | Unit ID: 157216

Telephone: (270) 384-2126 | Carnegie Class: Masters/L
FAX Number: (270) 384-8200 | Calendar System: Semester
URL: www.lindsey.edu
Established: 1903 | Annual Undergrad Tuition & Fees: $24,850
Enrollment: 2,565 | Coed
Affiliation or Control: United Methodist | IRS Status: 501(c)3
Highest Offering: Doctorate
Accreditation: SC, CACREP, CAEP, IACBE, NURSE

01 President .... Dr. William T. LUCKEY, JR.
00 Chancellor .... Dr. John B. BEGLEY
05 Vice President Academic Affairs .... Dr. Patricia PARRISH
10 Vice President Administration .... Mr. Mark COLEMAN
111 Vice President Advancement .... Mr. Kevin A. THOMPSON
04 Executive Assistant .... Mrs. Amy THOMPSON-WELLS
32 Vice Pres Student Svcs/Enroll Mgmt .... Dr. Dean ADAMS
37 VP Educ Outreach/Stdnt Finan Svcs .... Mrs. Denise G. FUDGE
35 Dean of Students .... Mr. Christopher SCHMIDT
88 Dean of Chapel .... Dr. Terry W. SWAN
07 Dean of Admissions .... Mrs. Traci M. POOLER
07 Director of Admissions .... Mrs. Charity F. FERGUSON
55 Director of Evening College .... Vacant
41 Athletic Director .... Mr. Willis POOLER, III
06 Registrar .... Mrs. Claudia FROEDGE
15 Director of Human Resources .... Mrs. Karen F. WRIGHT
31 Dir of Civic Engagement & Std Ldrsp .... Ms. Natalie VICKOUS
36 Director Career Services .... Mrs. Laura BURWASH
08 Librarian .... Mr. Huston BARNES
18 Director of Physical Plant .... Mr. Michael L. NEWTON
109 Director of Auxiliary Services .... Mr. Jeff WILLIS
40 Bookstore Manager .... Mrs. Amy M. COOPER
35 Director of Student Activities .... Ms. Lafawn NETTLES
85 Dir International Student Programs .... Ms. Sabine EASTHAM
13 Director of Information Systems .... Mrs. Harriet B. GOLD
26 Public Relations Officer .... Mrs. Venus POPPLEWELL
29 Director of Alumni Affairs .... Ms. Hannah PECK
19 Director Safety/Security .... Mr. Michael STATEN
42 Chaplain .... Rev. Troy A. ELMORE
37 Director Student Financial Services .... Ms. Marilyn RADFORD
38 Director Student Counseling .... Dr. Jeff CRANE
66 Director of Nursing .... Mrs. Emiley BUTTON

Louisville Presbyterian Theological Seminary (D)

1044 Alta Vista Road, Louisville KY 40205-1798

County: Jefferson | FICE Identification: 001974 | Unit ID: 157298

Telephone: (502) 895-3411 | Carnegie Class: Spec-4-yr-Faith
FAX Number: (502) 895-1096 | Calendar System: 4/1/4
URL: www.lpts.edu
Established: 1853 | Annual Graduate Tuition & Fees: N/A
Enrollment: 152 | Coed
Affiliation or Control: Presbyterian Church (U.S.A.) | IRS Status: 501(c)3
Highest Offering: Doctorate; No Undergraduates
Accreditation: SC, MFCD, THEOL

01 President .... Dr. Alton POLLARD, III
111 VP Institutional Advancement .... Ms. Anne MONELL
10 Vice President & CFO .... Mr. Patrick A. CECIL
05 Interim Dean of Seminary .... Dr. Steve COOK
32 Dean of Student Engagement .... Dr. Kilen GRAY
20 Assoc Dean BCS/DMin Studies .... Dr. Angela COWSER
06 Registrar/Assoc Dean IR&E .... Dr. Steve COOK
29 Director of Church Relations .... Vacant
44 Director of Seminary Fund .... Ms. Erin HAMILTON
14 Director of Data Management .... Ms. Heather GRIFFIN
26 Director of Communications .... Mr. Chris WOOTON
08 Director of Library Services .... Vacant
21 Controller .... Ms. Angela TRAYLOR
51 Director of Continuing Educ .... Mr. Marcus HONG
07 Director of Recruitment & Admiss .... Rev. Sandra MOON
13 Director of IT Services .... Mr. Jack SHARER
18 Director of Facilities .... Mr. Tim WILLIAMS
04 Administrative Asst to President .... Ms. Susan A. DILUCA

Midway University (E)

512 E Stephens Street, Midway KY 40347-1112

County: Woodford | FICE Identification: 001975 | Unit ID: 157377

Telephone: (859) 846-4421 | Carnegie Class: Masters/S
FAX Number: (859) 846-5349 | Calendar System: Semester
URL: www.midway.edu
Established: 1847 | Annual Undergrad Tuition & Fees: $24,750
Enrollment: 1,217 | Coed
Affiliation or Control: Christian Church (Disciples Of Christ) | IRS Status: 501(c)3
Highest Offering: Master's
Accreditation: SC, ADNUR, NUR

01 President .... Dr. John P. MARSDEN
05 VP of Academic Affairs .... Dr. Mary E. STIVERS
04 Exec Assistant to the President .... Ms. Elisabet BORDT
10 Vice President of Finance .... Mrs. Leah B. RICE
111 Vice President of Advancement .... Mr. Timothy CULVER
26 Vice Pres of Marketing & Comm .... Mrs. Ellen D. GREGORY
32 Asst VP of Student Affairs .... Ms. Sarah G. MUDD
07 Director Undergraduate Admissions .... Ms. Ashley DUDGEON
13 Dean of Online Admissions & CIO .... Dr. Salah SHAKIR
06 Registrar .... Ms. Susie POWERS
08 Director of Library Services .... Dr. Ellen BLOOMFIELD
41 VP for Athletics & Admissions .... Mr. William "Rusty" KENNEDY, II
14 Technical Support Specialist .... Mr. Eric ASHCRAFT
15 Director of Human Resources .... Ms. Trish JONES
37 Director of Financial Aid .... Ms. Janet BALOK
18 Director of Facilities .... Mr. Nathan MORRIS
50 Dean Business/Equine/Sport Stds .... Dr. Mark A. GILL
49 Dean School of Arts & Sciences .... Dr. Charles H. ROBERTS
76 Dean School of Health Sciences .... Vacant
19 Director Security/Safety .... Mr. Rob SARRANTONIO
36 Director Student Placement .... Ms. Mackenzie HANES
124 Director of Advising and Retention .... Mr. Joseph RYAN
102 Dir Foundation/Corporate Relations .... Ms. Carrie BOLING
30 Director of Development .... Mr. Ben SHAFFAR

Morehead State University (F)

150 University Boulevard, Morehead KY 40351-1689

County: Rowan | FICE Identification: 001976 | Unit ID: 157386

Telephone: (800) 585-6781 | Carnegie Class: Masters/L
FAX Number: N/A | Calendar System: Semester
URL: www.moreheadstate.edu
Established: 1887 | Annual Undergrad Tuition & Fees (In-State): $9,070
Enrollment: 10,580 | Coed
Affiliation or Control: State | IRS Status: 501(c)3
Highest Offering: Doctorate
Accreditation: SC, ADNUR, ART, CAEP, COARC, DMS, MUS, NAIT, NURSE, RAD, RADMAG, SPAA, SW, THEA

01 President .... Dr. Joseph A. MORGAN
05 Interim Provost .... Dr. Robert ALBERT
10 Interim Chief Financial Officer .... Ms. Teresa C. LINDGREN
32 Vice Pres for Student Affairs .... Mr. Russell F. MAST
111 Vice Pres for Univ Advancement .... Mr. James A. SHAW
20 Assoc Provost UG Educ/Stdnt Success .... Dr. Laurie L. COUCH
88 Director of Testing Center .... Ms. Sharon S. REYNOLDS
06 Registrar .... Mr. Keith MOORE
58 Assoc Provost/Dean RSP & Grad Sch .... Dr. Michael C. HENSON
51 Asst VP Regional Educ & Outreach .... Dr. Dan J. CONNELL
84 Asst Vice Pres Enrollment Services .... Mr. Tim RHODES
45 Chief Planning Officer/AVP OPPE .... Ms. Jill C. RATLIFF
26 Asst VP Communications & Marketing .... Ms. Jami M. HORNBUCKLE
18 Asst VP Facilities & Operations .... Mr. Kim H. OATMAN
109 Interim Exec Director Auxiliary Svc .... Mr. Charles GANCIO
29 Asst VP Alumni Relations & Develop .... Ms. Melinda C. HIGHLEY
13 Chief Information Officer .... Dr. Chris HOWES
35 AVP Student Life/Dean of Students .... Mr. Maxwell J. AMMONS
08 Dean of Library Services .... Dr. David L. GREGORY
07 Dir of Undergraduate Admissions .... Ms. Holly L. POLLOCK
09 Dir Inst Research & Analysis .... Mrs. Courtney ANDREWS
15 Director of Human Resources .... Mr. Harold D. NALLY
19 Chief of Police .... Mr. Merrell J. HARRISON
21 Director Accounting/Financial Svcs .... Ms. Kelli D. OWEN
37 Director Financial Aid .... Ms. Denise M. TRUSTY
36 Interim Director Career Services .... Ms. Megan BOONE
39 Director of Housing/Residence Educ .... Mr. Alan M. RUCKER
41 Interim Director of Athletics .... Mr. James D. GORDON
43 General Counsel .... Dr. Jane FITZPATRICK
96 Director Procurement Services .... Ms. Andrea STONE
38 Int Dir of Counseling & Health Svc .... Mr. David J. LITTERAL
50 Int Dean Smith Col Business/Tech .... Dr. Gregory R. RUSSELL
53 Dean College of Education .... Dr. Chris MILLER
81 Dean College of Science .... Dr. Wayne C. MILLER
79 Dean Arts/Hum/Soc Sciences .... Dr. John P. ERNST
106 Director Distance Educ/Instr Design .... Mr. David FLORA
108 Director University Assessment .... Dr. Shannon L. HARR
88 Director of Military Initiatives .... Mr. David LITTERAL
28 Asst to Pres for Strat Initiative .... Dr. Caroline ATKINS

Murray State University (G)

102 Curris Center, Murray, KY 42071, Murray KY 42071-3318

County: Calloway | FICE Identification: 001977 | Unit ID: 157401

Telephone: (270) 809-3011 | Carnegie Class: Masters/L
FAX Number: (270) 809-3413 | Calendar System: Semester
URL: www.murraystate.edu
Established: 1922 | Annual Undergrad Tuition & Fees (In-State): $9,084
Enrollment: 10,012 | Coed
Affiliation or Control: State | IRS Status: 501(c)3
Highest Offering: Doctorate
Accreditation: SC, ANEST, ART, CACREP, CAEP, DIETD, DIETI, EXSC, JOUR, MUS, NURSE, SP, SW, THEA

01 President .... Dr. Robert JACKSON
05 Provost and VP Academic Affairs .... Dr. Mark ARANT
10 VP Finance and Administration .... Jacklyn DUDLEY
32 VP Student Affairs .... Dr. Don ROBERTSON
58 Assoc Provost for Grad Education .... Dr. Robert PERVINE
13 Chief Information Officer .... Vacant
19 Chief of Police .... Jamie HERRING
43 General Counsel .... Robert MILLER
102 President MSU Foundation .... Dr. David W. DURR
30 Executive Director of Development .... C. Tina BERNOT
29 Director of Alumni Relations .... Carrie MCGINNIS
15 Director of Human Resources .... Joyce GORDON
09 Dir Inst Effectiveness & Planning .... Dr. K. Renee FISTER
86 Dir Government and Inst Relations .... Jordan SMITH
18 Director of Facilities Management .... Jason YOUNGBLOOD
41 Director of Athletics .... Kevin SAAL
26 Director of Communication .... Shawn TOUNEY
28 Exec Dir IDEA & Title IX Coord .... Camisha DUFFY
06 Registrar .... Tracy ROBERTS
113 Bursar/Dir Student Fin Services .... Wendy CAIN
101 Sr Exec Coord for Pres/Board Sec .... T. Jill HUNT

Northern Kentucky University (A)

Nunn Drive, Highland Heights KY 41099-0000
County: Campbell FICE Identification: 009275
Unit ID: 157447
Telephone: (859) 572-5100 Carnegie Class: DU-Mod
FAX Number: (859) 572-5566 Calendar System: Semester
URL: www.nku.edu
Established: 1968 Annual Undergrad Tuition & Fees (In-State): $10,032
Enrollment: 14,456 Coed
Affiliation or Control: State IRS Status: 501(c)3
Highest Offering: Doctorate
Accreditation: SC, ANEST, CAATE, CACREP, CAEP, CAEPN, COARC, CONST, LAW, MUS, NURSE, RAD, SPAA, SW

01 President Dr. Ashish VAIDYA
05 Provost/Exec VP Academic Affairs Ms. Sue OTT ROWLANDS
32 Vice Pres Student Affairs Dr. Daniel NADLER
111 Vice Pres University Advancement Mr. Eric C. GENTRY
43 VP Legal Affairs & General Counsel Ms. Joan GATES
20 Vice Prov Undergrad Academic Affs Dr. Ande DUROJAIYE
84 VP Enrollment/Degree Management Ms. Kimberly SCRANAGE
58 Vice Prov Grad Educ/Rsrch/Outreach Ms. Samantha LANGLEY-TURNBAUGH
88 Vice Pres/Chief Strategy Officer Dr. Bonita BROWN
20 Assoc Provost Academic Affs/Admin Mr. Chad OGLE
13 Chief Information Officer Mr. Timothy FERGUSON
08 Assoc Provost Library Services Ms. Andrea FALCONE
35 AVP Student Engage/Dean of Students Mr. Arnie SLAUGHTER
29 AVP Development & Alumni Relations Vacant
49 Dean College of Arts & Sciences Dr. Diana MCGILL
50 Dean College of Business Dr. Hassan HASSABELNABY
88 Dean College of Informatics Dr. Kevin KIRBY
53 Interim Dean College of Education Dr. James ALLEN
61 Dean Chase College of Law Ms. Judith DAAR
66 Dean College of Health Professions Dr. Dale STEPHENSON
18 Asst VP Facilities Management Mr. Syed ZAIDI
18 Director Operations & Maintenance Ms. Rebecca LANTER
26 Asst VP Marketing & Communications Vacant
21 Dir Fin & Operational Auditing Mr. Larry MEYER
109 Dir BusinessOps/Auxiliary Services Mr. Andy MEEKS
88 Dir Univ Architect/Design/Const Mgt Vacant
88 Director Campus Space and Planning Ms. Mary Paula SCHUH
15 Senior Director Human Resources Ms. Lori SOUTHWOOD
21 Comptroller Mr. Russell A. KERDOLFF
19 Director University Police Mr. John GAFFIN
96 Int Director Procurement Services Mr. Blaine GILMORE
92 Dean of Honors College Mr. James BUSS
07 Director Undergraduate Admissions Ms. Melissa GORBANDT
104 Exec Dir Intl Education Center Dr. Francois LEROY
06 Registrar Mr. W. Allen COLE, III
37 AVP Enrollment & Financial Aid Ms. Leah STEWART
78 Exec Dir Ctr for Civic Engagement Mr. Mark NEIKIRK
51 Director Community Connections Vacant
25 Director Research/Grants/Contracts Ms. Mary UCCI
89 Int Director First Year Programs Ms. Tracy HART
21 Chief Financial Officer Mr. Mike HALES
09 Exec Dir Planning/Inst Research Mr. Shawn RAINEY
88 Assoc Dir Institutional Research Mr. Cori HENDERSON
88 Director Campus Recreation Mr. Shomari KEE
38 Director Health/Counseling/Prev Ms. Amy CLARK
35 Director of Student Engagement Ms. Tiffany MAYSE
36 Director Career Services Mr. Bill FROUDE
41 Dir of Intercollegiate Athletics Mr. Ken BOTHOF
22 Sr Advisor to Pres Inclusive Excell Dr. Kathleen ROBERTS

Simmons College of Kentucky (B)

1018 South 7th Street, Louisville KY 40203-3322
County: Jefferson FICE Identification: 041780
Unit ID: 461759
Telephone: (502) 776-1443 Carnegie Class: Spec-4-yr-Faith
FAX Number: (502) 776-2227 Calendar System: Semester
URL: www.simmonscollegeky.edu
Established: 1879 Annual Undergrad Tuition & Fees: $5,310
Enrollment: 216 Coed
Affiliation or Control: Baptist IRS Status: 501(c)3
Highest Offering: Baccalaureate
Accreditation: BI

01 President Dr. Kevin W. COSBY
03 Executive VP for Faith & Cmty Rels Dr. Frank M. SMITH, JR.
111 Executive VP Inst Advancement Dr. Ken B. JOBST
05 Vice Pres Academic Affairs Dr. Chris CALDWELL
32 Vice Pres Student Affs/Dir Admiss Dr. Christine COSBY-GAITHER
88 Title III Director Dr. Barbara YOUNG
06 Registrar Ms. Deborah THOMAS
08 Chief Library Officer Mr. Andrew CHALK
30 Director of Development Mr. Von PURDY

The Southern Baptist Theological Seminary (C)

2825 Lexington Road, Louisville KY 40280-2899
County: Jefferson FICE Identification: 001982
Unit ID: 157748
Telephone: (502) 897-4011 Carnegie Class: Spec-4-yr-Faith
FAX Number: (502) 899-1770 Calendar System: Other
URL: www.sbts.edu
Established: 1859 Annual Undergrad Tuition & Fees: $20,433
Enrollment: 4,083 Coed
Affiliation or Control: Southern Baptist IRS Status: 501(c)3
Highest Offering: Doctorate
Accreditation: SC, MUS, THEOL

01 President Dr. R. Albert MOHLER, JR.
100 Chief of Staff to the President Mr. Jonathan AUSTIN
04 Exec Admin Asst Office of President Mrs. Valerie GARDNER
05 Sr VP Academic Administration Dr. Matthew HALL
111 Sr VP Institutional Advancement Mr. Craig PARKER
11 Vice President of Operations Mr. Andrew VINCENT
26 Vice President Communications Mr. Kody GIBSON
13 VP Campus Technology Mr. Jason HEATH
20 Vice President Academic Services Dr. Matthew HALL
106 Assoc VP Online Education Dr. Timothy Paul JONES
108 Assoc VP Institutional Assessment Dr. Joseph C. HARROD
84 Assoc VP Enrollment Management Mr. Matt MINIER
15 Director Human Resources Mr. Brent SMALL
18 Chief Facilities/Physical Plant Mr. Henry LACHER
41 Director of Health & Recreation Mr. Michael MCCARTY
07 Director of Admissions Mr. Jeremy PELTON
08 Librarian Dr. Berry DRIVER
37 Manager of Financial Aid Mrs. Ana WILLIAMS
73 Dean of School of Theology Dr. Hershael YORK
88 Dean Missions Evang Ch Growth Dr. Paul AKIN
12 Dean Boyce College Dr. Dustin BRUCE
06 Registrar Mr. Norm CHUNG
39 Director Student Housing Mr. Tyler CLARK

Spalding University (D)

845 S Third Street, Louisville KY 40203-2213
County: Jefferson FICE Identification: 001960
Unit ID: 157757
Telephone: (502) 585-9911 Carnegie Class: DU-Mod
FAX Number: (502) 585-7158 Calendar System: Other
URL: www.spalding.edu
Established: 1814 Annual Undergrad Tuition & Fees: $24,500
Enrollment: 2,071 Coed
Affiliation or Control: Independent Non-Profit IRS Status: 501(c)3
Highest Offering: Doctorate
Accreditation: SC, #CAATE, CAEP, CLPSY, IACBE, NURSE, OT, SW

01 President Ms. Tori MURDEN MCCLURE
05 Provost Dr. John BURDEN
111 Chief Advancement Officer Vacant
58 Dean of Graduate Studies Dr. Kurt JEFFERSON
20 Dean of Undergraduate Education Dr. Tomarra ADAMS
32 Dean of Students Dr. Richard HUDSON
10 Chief Financial Officer Mr. Rush SHERMAN
43 General Counsel Ms. Emily NORRIS
84 Dean of Enrollment Management Dr. Melissa CHASTAIN
121 Director Academic Advising Center Ms. Katherine WALKER-PAYNE
06 Registrar Ms. Jennifer GOHMANN
13 Chief Information Officer Mr. Ezra KRUMHANSL
37 Director Financial Aid Ms. Michelle STANDRIDGE
15 Exec Dir of Human Resources Ms. Jennifer BROCKHOFF
09 Exec Dir of Inst Effectiveness Ms. Kay VETTER
41 Director of Athletics Mr. Roger BURKMAN
88 Admin Dir/Mstr Fine Arts in Writing Ms. Karen MANN
21 Controller Ms. Katherine WEYHING
18 JLL Facilities Manager Mr. Kevin WEBER
50 Dir Masters Business Communications Dr. Robin HINKLE
07 Director of Admissions Dr. Matthew ELDER
11 Chief of Staff/Dean of Operations Mr. Chris HART

Sullivan University (E)

3101 Bardstown Road, Louisville KY 40205-3000
County: Jefferson FICE Identification: 004619
Unit ID: 157793
Telephone: (502) 456-6504 Carnegie Class: Masters/L
FAX Number: (502) 456-0040 Calendar System: Quarter
URL: www.sullivan.edu
Established: 1962 Annual Undergrad Tuition & Fees: $12,870
Enrollment: 3,489 Coed
Affiliation or Control: Proprietary IRS Status: Proprietary
Highest Offering: Doctorate
Accreditation: SC, ARCPA, CAHIIM, COARC, COMTA, MAC, NURSE, PHAR, RAD, SURGT

00 Chancellor Dr. A. R. SULLIVAN
88 President Sullivan Univ System Mr. Glenn D. SULLIVAN
02 President/CEO Dr. Jay D. MARR
05 Sr VP for Academic Affairs/Provost Dr. Diana LAWRENCE
11 Sr Vice Pres for Administration Mr. Chris ERNST
10 Vice President Finance Mr. Shelton BRIDGES
84 VP of Enrollment Mgmt Ms. Nina MARTINEZ
86 Vice Pres of Community Partnerships Mr. David KEENE
12 VP Lexington Campus Mr. David TUDOR
58 Assoc Provost/Dean Graduate School Dr. Tim SWENSON
88 Exec Dir Natl Ctr Hospitality Stds Mr. David DODD
06 Registrar Ms. Kim MITCHELL
08 Dean of University Libraries Mr. Charles BROWN
13 Dir of IT Services Mr. Drew ARNETTE
36 Sr Dir of Career Svcs & Alumni Affs Mr. Sam MANNINO
37 Sr Dir Student Financial Planning Ms. Angela MILLER
40 Bookstore Manager Mr. Bryan NEEDY
96 Director of Purchasing Ms. Ann VEST
56 Dir of Ft Knox Extension Campus Ms. Barbara DEAN
88 University Ombudsman Mr. Jim KLEIN
29 Assoc Dir Alumni Affairs Ms. Nicole GOODIN
18 Manager Campus Facilities Mr. Mike FOWLER

Thomas More University (F)

333 Thomas More Parkway, Crestview Hills KY 41017-3495
County: Kenton FICE Identification: 002001
Unit ID: 157809
Telephone: (859) 341-5800 Carnegie Class: Masters/M
FAX Number: (859) 344-3345 Calendar System: Semester
URL: www.thomasmore.edu
Established: 1921 Annual Undergrad Tuition & Fees: $31,200
Enrollment: 2,064 Coed
Affiliation or Control: Roman Catholic IRS Status: 501(c)3
Highest Offering: Master's
Accreditation: SC, ACBSP, CAATE, CAEP, NUR

01 President Dr. Joseph L. CHILLO
04 Exec Assistant to the President Ms. Charlene BARLOW
10 CFO Mr. Robert MUNSON
05 Acting Provost Dr. Maria GARRIGA
111 Vice Pres Institutional Advancement Mr. Kevin REYNOLDS
32 Dean of Students Mr. Antwone CAMERON
09 Dir of Inst Planning/Effectiveness Ms. Kelly FRENCH
06 Registrar Ms. Michelle VEZINA
08 Director of Library Mr. Mike WELLS
37 Director of Financial Aid Mr. Mark MESSINGSCHALGER
13 Director of IT Mr. Sean KAPSAL
26 Dir Communications/Media Relations Ms. Rebecca STRATTON
38 Director of Counseling Vacant
42 Chaplain Rev. Gerald E. TWADDELL
84 VP of Enrollment Management Dr. Christopher POWERS
41 Athletic Director Mr. Terry D. CONNOR
19 Director of Campus Safety Mr. William WILSON
15 Director of Human Resources Ms. Laura CUSTER
18 Director of Facilities Mr. Errol MAYLEY
29 Director of Alumni Mrs. Bailey BUNDY
36 Dir of Career Planning/Coop Educ Ms. Robin NORTON
73 Director of Campus Ministry Mr. Andrew COLE
21 Controller Mr. Mark GOSHORN
51 Associate VP Adult & Graduate Educ Ms. Cariss SCHUTZMAN
92 Director of Honors Program Dr. Catherine SHERRON
44 Dir Annual Giving/Special Events Vacant
07 Director of Admissions Mr. Justin VOGEL
124 Director of Student Retention Ms. Becky MULLINS
39 Coordinator of Residence Life Vacant
43 University Legal Counsel Mr. Noah WELTE

Transylvania University (G)

300 N Broadway, Lexington KY 40508-1797
County: Fayette FICE Identification: 001987
Unit ID: 157818
Telephone: (859) 233-8300 Carnegie Class: Bac-A&S
FAX Number: (859) 233-8797 Calendar System: Other
URL: www.transy.edu
Established: 1780 Annual Undergrad Tuition & Fees: $38,750
Enrollment: 966 Coed
Affiliation or Control: Christian Church (Disciples Of Christ)
IRS Status: 501(c)3
Highest Offering: Baccalaureate
Accreditation: SC, CAEPN

01 President Dr. Seamus CAREY
05 Interim VP & Dean of the University Dr. Michael CAIRO
10 Vice President Finance & Business Mr. Marc MATHEWS
07 VP for Enrollment & Student Affairs Dr. Holly SHEILLEY
111 VP for Advancement Dr. Steve ANGELUCCI
13 VP for Information Technology Ms. Deepa DUBAL
26 VP for Marketing & Communications Ms. Megan MOLONEY
28 Asst VP Diversity/Inclusion Mr. Taran MCZEE
06 Registrar Ms. Michelle RAWLINGS
08 Librarian Ms. Susan M. BROWN
09 VP for Institutional Effectiveness Dr. Rhyan M. CONYERS
104 Dir Global & Intercult Engagement Ms. Courtney SMITH
20 Assistant Dean for Academic Affairs Ms. Tracy DUNN
15 Director Human Resources Ms. Alison BEGOR
18 Chief Facilities/Physical Plant Mr. Darrell BANKS
19 Director Security/Safety Mr. Gregg MURAVCHICK
96 Director of Purchasing Ms. Shawn T. SINGLETON
39 Director Residence Life Mr. Kevin FISHER
37 Director of Financial Aid Ms. Jennifer PRIEST
29 Director Alumni Relations Ms. Natasa PAJIC
04 Executive Assistant to President Ms. Kristin MILAM
41 Assistant Athletic Director Mr. Jeff CHANEY

Union College (H)

310 College Street, Barbourville KY 40906-1499
County: Knox FICE Identification: 001988
Unit ID: 157863
Telephone: (606) 546-4151 Carnegie Class: Masters/S
FAX Number: (606) 546-1217 Calendar System: Other
URL: www.unionky.edu
Established: 1879 Annual Undergrad Tuition & Fees: $27,140
Enrollment: 1,309 Coed
Affiliation or Control: United Methodist IRS Status: 501(c)3
Highest Offering: Master's
Accreditation: SC, #CAATE, CAEPN, NURSE

01 President Dr. Marcia HAWKINS
04 Assistant to the President Ms. Sherry PARTIN
31 Special Asst for External Relations Ms. Denise WAINSCOTT
42 College Minister Rev. David MILLER

Code	Title	Name
05	VP for Academic Affairs	Dr. Jim SALVUCCI
66	Dean of Nursing	Dr. Marisa GREER
53	Head of Educational Studies Dept	Dr. Jason REEVES
79	Dean School of Humanities	Dr. Karl WALLHAUSSER
58	Dean Professional and Grad Studies	Dr. David WILLIAMS
111	VP of Advancement/Communications	Mr. Brian STRUNK
29	Director of Alumni Relations	Ms. Ivana KAZIC
84	VP for Enrollment Management	Vacant
32	Dean of Students	Vacant
39	Director of Housing	Mr. Jason ELS
35	Assistant Director of Campus Life	Ms. Fernanda C. FREY
10	Chief Business Officer	Mr. Randle TEAGUE
114	Budget Director	Mr. Clark JONES
15	Exec Director of Human Resources	Ms. Lynn SMITH
118	Coordinator of Payroll/Benefits	Ms. Robin CARR
21	Controller	Ms. Jessica JUSTICE
06	Registrar	Ms. Kathy INKSTER
18	Director of Physical Plant (NMRC)	Mr. Shain SIZEMORE
41	Athletic Director	Mr. Clark JONES
09	Director of Institutional Research	Ms. Anisa JAMES
121	Associate Dean for Student Success	Ms. Stephanie SMITH
08	Head Librarian	Ms. Tara L. COOPER
37	Director of Financial Aid	Ms. Andra BUTLER
19	Safety Team Leader	Mr. Mike GRAY
13	Director of IT	Mr. Walter WAHLSTEDT
91	Director of Administrative Systems	Mr. Eric EVANS
105	Director Web Services	Mr. Phillip HORN

University of the Cumberlands (A)

6191 College Station Drive, Williamsburg KY 40769-1372

County: Whitley　　FICE Identification: 001962
Unit ID: 156541
Telephone: (606) 549-2200　　Carnegie Class: DU-Mod
FAX Number: (606) 539-4280　　Calendar System: Semester
URL: www.ucumberlands.edu
Established: 1888　　Annual Undergrad Tuition & Fees: $23,000
Enrollment: 10,097　　Coed
Affiliation or Control: Baptist　　IRS Status: 501(c)3
Highest Offering: Doctorate
Accreditation: SC, ARCPA, CACREP, CAEPN, IACBE, NURSE

Code	Title	Name
01	President	Dr. Larry L. COCKRUM
05	Vice President Academic Affairs	Dr. Christopher LESKIW
32	Vice President Student Services	Dr. Emily COLEMAN
23	Director Medical Services	Dr. Eddie PERKINS
10	Chief Financial Officer	Mr. Quentin YOUNG
11	Director of Operations	Mr. Travis WILSON
37	Director of Financial Aid	Mr. Ian FREYBERG
41	Athletic Director	Mr. Chris KRAFTICK
13	VP for Information Technology	Dr. Donnie GRIMES
84	VP for Enrollment & Communication	Dr. Jerry JACKSON
06	Registrar	Mr. Charles DUPIER
20	Associate Dean	Dr. Susan ROSE
26	Director of University Relations	Mrs. Leslie C. RYSER
35	Dean Student Life	Vacant
15	Director of Human Resources	Mr. Steve ALLEN
42	Director of Church Relations	Dr. Rick FLEENOR
36	Director of Career Services	Dr. Jamirae HOLBROOK
08	Director of Library	Ms. Jan WREN
58	Director of Graduate Advising	Mrs. Shonda POWERS
18	Director of Physical Plant	Mr. David ROOT
21	Bursar	Ms. Jo DUPIER
29	Director of Alumni Relations	Mrs. Erica HARRIS
30	Director of Development	Mr. Bill STOHLMAN

University of Kentucky (B)

101 Main Building, Lexington KY 40506-0003

County: Fayette　　FICE Identification: 001989
Unit ID: 157085
Telephone: (859) 257-1701　　Carnegie Class: DU-Highest
FAX Number: (859) 257-4000　　Calendar System: Semester
URL: www.uky.edu
Established: 1865　　Annual Undergrad Tuition & Fees (In-State): $12,245
Enrollment: 29,465　　Coed
Affiliation or Control: State　　IRS Status: 501(c)3
Highest Offering: Doctorate
Accreditation: SC, AAFCS, ARCPA, ART, CAATE, CACREP, CAEPN, CAMPEP, CIDA, CLPSY, COPSY, DENT, DIETC, DIETD, DIETI, HSA, IPSY, JOUR, LAW, LIB, LSAR, MED, MFCD, MT, MUS, NURSE, PAST, PCSAS, PH, PHAR, PTA, SCPSY, SP, SPAA, SW, THEA

Code	Title	Name
01	President	Dr. Eli I. CAPILOUTO
46	Vice President Research	Dr. Lisa A. CASSIS
05	Provost	Dr. David W. BLACKWELL
100	Chief of Staff	Dr. Bill K. SWINFORD
11	Exec VP Finance/Administration	Mr. Eric N. MONDAY
17	Executive VP for Health Affairs	Dr. Mark NEWMAN
32	Assoc Provost Student/Academic Life	Dr. Greg HEILEMAN
13	Chief Information Officer	Mr. Brian NICHOLS
35	Stdnt Affs/Dean of Students	Dr. Nicholas KEHRWALD
22	Associate VP Institutional Equity	Mr. Terry D. ALLEN
30	Vice President for Development	Dr. D. Michael RICHEY
10	VP Health Affs/Chief Financial Ofcr	Mr. Craig COLLINS
45	VP Financial Planning & CBO	Ms. Angela S. MARTIN
18	VP Facilities Mgmt & Chief Facil	Ms. Mary S. VOSEVICH
28	Assoc VP Institutional Diversity	Dr. Sonja M. FEIST-PRICE
26	VP University Relations	Mr. Thomas W. HARRIS
15	VP Human Resources Admin & CHRO	Ms. Kimberly P. WILSON
19	Asst Vice Pres Public Safety	Mr. Anthany BEATTY
109	Exec Director Auxiliary Services	Ms. Sarah F. NIKIRK
21	Assoc VP Res Admin & Fiscal Affs	Mr. Jack SUPPLEE, JR.
25	Exec Director Sponsored Projects	Ms. Kim C. CARTER
88	Assoc VP UKHC/EVPHA	Mr. Joe CLAYPOOL
58	Interim Dean of Graduate School	Dr. Brian A. JACKSON
88	Assoc Provost Faculty Advancement	Dr. Gene T. LINEBERRY
84	Assoc Provost Enroll Mgmt/Registrar	Ms. Christine HARPER
08	Interim Dean of Libraries	Dr. Deirdre SCAGGS
27	Exec Director Public Relations	Mr. Jay D. BLANTON
27	Director University Press	Ms. Leila W. SALISBURY
43	General Counsel	Mr. William E. THRO
41	Director Athletics	Mr. Mitch S. BARNHART
37	Director Student Financial Aid	Dr. Nimmi K. WIGGINS
09	Director of Institutional Research	Dr. Craig P. RUDICK
36	Asst Dean for Career & Academic Exp	Mr. Ray R. CLERE
38	Director Counseling & Testing	Dr. Mary C. BOLIN
29	Director Alumni Affairs	Mr. Timothy WALSH
21	Controller	Ms. Mary FISTER-TUCKER
47	Dean of Agriculture/Food & Envir	Dr. Nancy M. COX
19	Chief of Police	Mr. Joseph W. MONROE
88	Dean of Design	Ms. Mitzi VERNON
88	Exec Director Student Center	Mr. John H. HERBST
49	Dean of Arts & Sciences	Dr. Mark L. KORNBLUH
50	Dean of Business & Economics	Dr. Simon J. SHEATHER
53	Interim Dean of Education	Dr. Rosetta SANDIDGE
54	Dean of Engineering	Dr. Rudolph BUCHHEIT
57	Dean of Fine Arts	Mr. Mark SHANDA
60	Interim Dean of Comm/Information	Dr. Derek LANE
61	Dean of Law	Dr. David A. BRENNEN
70	Interim Dean of Social Work	Dr. Ann VAIL
76	Dean of Health Sciences	Dr. Scott M. LEPHART
52	Dean of Dentistry	Dr. Stephanos KYRKANIDES
63	Dean of Medicine/VP Clinical Affs	Dr. Robert DIPAOLA
66	Dean of Nursing	Dr. Janie H. HEATH
67	Dean of Pharmacy	Dr. Kip GUY
69	Dean Public Health	Dr. Donna ARNETT
96	Exec Director Purchasing & CPO	Mr. Barry SWANSON
108	Director of Assessment	Ms. Tara A. ROSE
44	Director Annual Giving	Ms. Anne V. LICHTENBERG

University of Louisville (C)

2301 S Third Street, Louisville KY 40292-0001

County: Jefferson　　FICE Identification: 001999
Unit ID: 157289
Telephone: (502) 852-5555　　Carnegie Class: DU-Highest
FAX Number: (502) 852-7013　　Calendar System: Semester
URL: www.louisville.edu
Established: 1798　　Annual Undergrad Tuition & Fees (In-State): $11,656
Enrollment: 21,402　　Coed
Affiliation or Control: State　　IRS Status: 501(c)3
Highest Offering: Doctorate
Accreditation: SC, AUD, CACREP, CAEP, CIDA, CLPSY, COPSY, COSMA, DENT, DH, EXSC, HSA, IPSY, LAW, MED, MFCD, MUS, NURSE, PH, PLNG, SP, SPAA, SW, THEA

Code	Title	Name
01	President	Dr. Neeli BENDAPUDI
05	Provost/EVP Academic Affairs	Dr. Beth BOEHM
17	Exec Vice Pres for Health Affairs	Vacant
46	Interim Executive VP for Research	Dr. Robert S. KEYNTON
10	Vice Pres & Chief Financial Officer	Mr. Daniel DURBIN
11	Sr Assoc VP for Operations	Mr. Mark WATKINS
111	Vice Pres Univ Advancement	Mr. Brad SHAFER
13	Vice Provost & CIO	Mr. M. Rehan KHAN
31	VP for Community Engagement	Dr. Ralph FITZPATRICK
15	Int Assoc Vice Pres HR	Mr. John ELLIOTT
41	Vice President for Athletics	Mr. Vince TYRA
18	Assoc VP Facilities/Physical Plant	Mr. Mark WATKINS
29	Asst VP for Alumni Relations	Mr. Josh HAWKINS
100	Chief of Staff for the President	Mr. Michael W. SMITH
43	General Counsel	Mr. Thomas A. HOY
58	Acting Vice Prov/Dean Grad	Dr. Paul DEMARCO
28	Vice Prov for Diversity/Intl Affs	Dr. Mordean TAYLOR-ARCHER
09	Vice Provost IR Effect & Analytics	Mr. Robert S. GOLDSTEIN
84	Vice Provost Enrollment Management	Mr. James BEGANY
106	Assoc Univ Provost Distance Ed/Delp	Dr. Gale RHODES
88	Assoc Prov for Accreditation	Ms. Connie C. SHUMAKE
21	Treasurer/Controller	Mr. Dub NEWELL
07	Executive Director Admissions	Ms. Jenny L. SAWYER
06	University Registrar	Mr. Scott A. BURKS
37	Executive Director Financial Aid	Ms. Sandra NEEL
26	Int Sr Assoc VP Comm/Marketing	Mr. John DREES
16	Dir of Staff Dev/Employee Rel	Ms. Mary E. MILES
19	Dir Public Safety/Chief of Police	Mr. Gary D. LEWIS, JR.
09	Exec Director Inst Res & Plng	Ms. Becky PATTERSON
45	Director Inst Effectiveness	Dr. Katie PARTIN
39	Director Residence Admin	Dr. Thomas HARDY
105	Director of Brand Design	Mr. Brian A. FAUST
27	Director Programming & Prod	Mr. Mark HEBERT
116	Director Audit Services	Ms. Cheri JONES
92	Exec Director of Honors Program	Dr. Joy HART
96	Director of Procurement	Ms. Sally MOLSBERGER
88	Dir Planning/Design & Construction	Mr. Kenneth DIETZ
36	Director Career Development	Mr. Bill FLETCHER
38	Director Counseling Center	Ms. Aesha UQDAH
08	Dean of University Libraries	Mr. Robert FOX
49	Dean College Arts & Sciences	Dr. Kimberly KEMPF-LEONARD
50	Dean College of Business	Dr. Todd MOORADIAN
52	Dean School of Dentistry	Dr. Thomas G. BRADLEY
53	Int Dean Col of Educ/Human Devel	Dr. Amy LINGO
70	Dean Kent School Social Work	Dr. David A. JENKINS
64	Dean School of Music	Dr. Teresa REED
61	Dean Brandeis School of Law	Mr. Colin CRAWFORD
66	Dean School of Nursing	Dr. Sonya HARDING
54	Dean Speed School Engineering	Dr. Emmanuel COLLINS
63	Dean School of Medicine	Dr. Toni GANZEL
69	Dean Public Health/Information Sci	Dr. Craig H. BLAKELY
35	Dean of Students/Vice Provost	Dr. Michael MARDIS
104	Director Study Abroad	Dr. Virginia HOSONO

University of Pikeville (D)

147 Sycamore Street, Pikeville KY 41501-1194

County: Pike　　FICE Identification: 001980
Unit ID: 157535
Telephone: (606) 218-5250　　Carnegie Class: Bac-A&S
FAX Number: (606) 218-5269　　Calendar System: Semester
URL: www.upike.edu
Established: 1889　　Annual Undergrad Tuition & Fees: $20,950
Enrollment: 2,336　　Coed
Affiliation or Control: Presbyterian Church (U.S.A.)　　IRS Status: 501(c)3
Highest Offering: Doctorate
Accreditation: SC, NUR, @OPT, OSTEO, SW

Code	Title	Name
00	Chancellor	Mr. Paul E. PATTON
01	President	Dr. Burton J. WEBB
05	Provost	Dr. Lori WERTH
49	Dean College Arts/Sciences	Dr. Jennifer DUGAN
88	Dean College of Optometry	Dr. Michael BACIGALUPI
50	Dean College of Business	Dr. Howard V. ROBERTS
53	Dean College of Education	Vacant
10	Vice Pres Finance/Business Affairs	Mr. Barry BENTLEY
111	Vice President for Advancement	Mr. David HUTCHENS
26	Director of Public Affairs	Mrs. Laura DAMRON
63	Dean KYCOM	Dr. Dana SHAFFER
32	Dean of Students	Dr. Justin OWENS
07	Director of Admissions	Mr. John YANCEY
08	Director of Library Services	Ms. Edna FUGATE
06	University Registrar	Mrs. Gia POTTER
09	Director of Institutional Research	Dr. Meg SIDLE
13	Senior Info Services Administrator	Vacant
18	Asst VP for Facilities	Mr. John HOLMAN
37	Director of Student Financial Svcs	Ms. Jennifer BATES
15	Director of Human Resources	Mr. Michael PACHECO
04	Executive Asst to President	Mrs. Sherrie MARRS
19	Director Security/Safety	Mr. Allen ABSHIRE
41	Athletic Director	Mr. Kelly WELLS
105	Coordinator of New Media	Mr. Larry EPLING
25	Chief Contracts/Grants Admin	Mrs. Tiffany THACKER
29	Director Alumni Relations	Ms. Lisa BLACKBURN
121	Director Student Success	Dr. Mathys MEYER
39	Housing Operations Supervisor	Mr. Chris ROBINSON
44	Director Annual or Planned Giving	Mr. Ronald DAMRON
90	Director Academic Computing	Mrs. Corrine BOLT
104	Director Study Abroad	Dr. Timothy WHITTIER
30	Director of Development	Mrs. Bridgette BRASHEAR

Western Kentucky University (E)

1906 College Heights Blvd, Bowling Green KY 42101-3576

County: Warren　　FICE Identification: 002002
Unit ID: 157951
Telephone: (270) 745-0111　　Carnegie Class: DU-Mod
FAX Number: (270) 745-5387　　Calendar System: Semester
URL: www.wku.edu
Established: 1906　　Annual Undergrad Tuition & Fees (In-State): $10,512
Enrollment: 20,257　　Coed
Affiliation or Control: State　　IRS Status: 501(c)3
Highest Offering: Doctorate
Accreditation: SC, ADNUR, ART, CACREP, CAEP, CAHIIM, DANCE, DH, DIETD, DIETI, JOUR, MUS, NAIT, NRPA, NURSE, PH, PTA, SP, SPAA, SW, THEA

Code	Title	Name
01	President	Dr. Timothy C. CABONI
04	Assistant to the President	Ms. Julia MCDONALD
05	Provost/VP Academic Affairs	Dr. Cheryl STEVENS
46	Assoc Provost for Research	Dr. Cheryl DAVIS
26	VP for Strategic Comm & Marketing	Vacant
30	Assoc VP Philanthropy & Alumni	Mr. John Paul BLAIR
29	Exec Director Alumni Engagement	Mr. Anthony MCADOO
84	VP Enrollment & Student Experience	Mr. Brian KUSTER
10	Exec VP StrategyOperations/Finance	Ms. Susan HOWARTH
07	Director Recruitment & Admissions	Dr. Jace T. LUX
106	Assoc VP Ext Learning & Outreach	Dr. Beth LAVES
79	Dean Arts & Letters	Dr. Larry SNYDER, JR.
50	Dean Business	Dr. Christopher SHOOK
53	Dean Education/Behavioral Sci	Dr. Corinne MURPHY
76	Dean Health & Human Services	Dr. Tania BASTA
81	Interim Dean Science & Engineering	Dr. Greg ARBUCKLE
58	Interim Dean Graduate School	Dr. Cheryl DAVIS
62	Dean Libraries	Ms. Susann DEVRIES
21	Chief Financial Officer	Mr. Jim CUMMINGS
88	Assoc VP Academic Budgets & Admin	Dr. Ladonna L. HUNTON
06	University Registrar	Ms. Jennifer HAMMONDS
13	Assistant VP Information Technology	Mr. Greg HACKBARTH
15	Director Human Resources	Mr. Tony L. GLISSON
27	Director of Media Relations	Mr. Bob SKIPPER
86	Director Govt & Community Relations	Ms. Jennifer B. SMITH
121	Assistant VP Advising & Career Dev	Mr. Christopher JENSEN
32	Assistant VP Enrollment/Student Exp	Dr. Mike REAGLE
19	Chief of Police	Mr. Mitch WALKER
102	Pres College Heights Foundation	Dr. Donald L. SMITH
37	Dir Student Financial Assistance	Mr. Bryson DAVIS
121	Director Student Support Svcs	Dr. T. Chris GEORGE
51	Dir Continuing & Professional Dev	Mr. Derek OLIVE
40	Director WKU Store	Ms. Ann FLORESCA
09	Director Institutional Research	Dr. Tuesdi HELBIG

22 Director EEO/Title IX/ADA .... Mr. Joshua HAYES
24 Dir Educational Telecommunications .... Mr. David BRINKLEY
41 Director Intercollegiate Athletics .... Mr. Todd M. STEWART
85 Assoc Provost Global Learning .... Mr. John SUNNYGARD
92 Interim Exec Dir Honors College .... Dr. Michael SMITH
96 Director Supply Chain Management .... Mr. Ken BAUSHKE
104 Dir Study Abroad & Global Learning .... Ms. Caryn LINDSAY
105 Dir Web Svcs & Digital Marketing .... Dr. Corie MARTIN
18 Chief Facilities Officer .... Mr. Bryan RUSSELL
28 Asst VP & Chief Diversity Officer .... Dr. Lynne HOLLAND
38 Director Counseling & Testing Ctr .... Dr. Peggy CROWE
43 General Counsel .... Ms. Deborah T. WILKINS

LOUISIANA

Baton Rouge School of Computers (A)

9352 Interline Avenue, Baton Rouge LA 70809-1909
County: East Baton Rouge FICE Identification: 021975
Unit ID: 158343
Telephone: (225) 923-2524 Carnegie Class: Spec 2-yr-Tech
FAX Number: (225) 923-2979 Calendar System: Other
URL: www.brsc.edu
Established: 1979 Annual Undergrad Tuition & Fees: N/A
Enrollment: 58 Coed
Affiliation or Control: Proprietary IRS Status: Proprietary
Highest Offering: Associate Degree
Accreditation: ACCSC

01 President/Director .... Mrs. Betty D. TRUXILLO
05 Chief Academic Officer .... Ms. Pauline ROBERTS
06 Registrar .... Ms. Cheryl DIFFEY

Centenary College of Louisiana (B)

PO Box 41188, Shreveport LA 71134-1188
County: Caddo FICE Identification: 002003
Unit ID: 158477
Telephone: (318) 869-5011 Carnegie Class: Bac-A&S
FAX Number: (318) 869-5010 Calendar System: Semester
URL: www.centenary.edu
Established: 1825 Annual Undergrad Tuition & Fees: $36,580
Enrollment: 588 Coed
Affiliation or Control: United Methodist IRS Status: 501(c)3
Highest Offering: Master's
Accreditation: SC, CAEPT, MUS

01 President .... Dr. Christopher HOLOMAN
04 Exec Assistant to the President .... Mrs. Connie WHITTINGTON
05 Provost & Dean of the College .... Dr. Karen SOUL
10 Vice President for Finance/Admin .... Mr. Bob BLUE
50 Dean of the School of Business .... Vacant
64 Dean of the School of Music .... Dr. Cory WIKAN
30 Vice Pres for Development .... Mr. Fred LANDRY
84 Vice President Enrollment & Mktg .... Mr. Calhoun ALLEN
20 Vice Provost for Academic Affairs .... Dr. Jeanne HAMMING
09 Assoc Prov Inst Rsrch/Regist/Record .... Dr. Katherine BEARDEN
13 Director of Information Technology .... Mr. Scott MERRITT
21 Business Manager .... Mrs. Monica POWELL
41 Director of Athletics & Recreation .... Mr. Marcus MANNING
32 Dean of Students .... Mr. Mark MILLER
38 Director of Counseling .... Ms. Tina FELDT
37 Director of Financial Aid .... Mrs. Lynette VISKOZKI
08 Librarian .... Ms. Christy WRENN
26 Dir of Strategic Communications .... Mrs. Kate PEDROTTY
29 Director Alumni/Family Relations .... Ms. Saige SOLOMON
36 Director of Professional Success .... Vacant
18 Director of Facilities .... Mr. Chris SAMPITE
25 Director Sponsored Research .... Ms. Patty J. ROBERTS
07 Assoc Dir Admissions/Recruitment .... Ms. Lauren HAWKINS
15 Human Resources Director .... Ms. Edie CUMMINGS
19 Director of Public Safety .... Mr. Eddie WALKER
104 Director Study Abroad .... Mrs. Anne-Marie BRUNER-TRACEY
39 Director Student Housing .... Mr. Montgomery MEWERS

Chamberlain University-New Orleans (C)

400 Lebarre Road, New Orleans LA 70121
Telephone: (504) 464-7995 Identification: 770983
Accreditation: &NH, NURSE

† Branch campus of Chamberlain University-Addison, Addison, IL

Dillard University (D)

2601 Gentilly Boulevard, New Orleans LA 70122-3097
County: Orleans FICE Identification: 002004
Unit ID: 158802
Telephone: (504) 283-8822 Carnegie Class: Bac-A&S
FAX Number: N/A Calendar System: Semester
URL: www.dillard.edu
Established: 1869 Annual Undergrad Tuition & Fees: $17,918
Enrollment: 1,290 Coed
Affiliation or Control: United Methodist IRS Status: 501(c)3
Highest Offering: Baccalaureate
Accreditation: SC, ACBSP, NUR

01 President .... Dr. Walter M. KIMBROUGH
111 Vice Pres Inst Advancement .... Mr. Marc BARNES
05 Provost/Sr VP for Academic Affairs .... Dr. Yolanda PAGE
32 Vice President for Student Success .... Dr. Roland BULLARD
43 VP for Legal Affairs .... Dr. Denise WALLACE
10 VP for Finance/CFO .... Mr. R. JOHNSON
84 Vice Pres Enrollment Management .... Mr. David PAGE
20 Associate Provost .... Dr. Christopher JEFFRIES
07 Dir of Recruitment & Admissions .... Ms. Monica WHITE
18 Dir of Facilities Mgmt .... Mr. Adonis WOODS
36 Director of Career/Prof Services .... Vacant
06 Dir of Records & Registration .... Mr. Robert MITCHELL, JR.
37 Dir Financial Aid/Scholarships .... Ms. Denise SPELLMAN
46 Assoc VP Research & Spons Programs .... Mr. Theodore CALLIER
30 Director of Development .... Ms. Kimberly WOODARD
04 Exec Assistant to the President .... Ms. Kathy TAYLOR
09 Director of Institutional Research .... Dr. Willie KIRKLAND
31 Director Community Development .... Mr. Nick L. HARRIS
19 Chief of Police .... Mr. Julian COAXUM
15 Director of Human Resources .... Mrs. Brittany RICHARDSON
26 Dir of Marketing/Communications .... Dr. Sheryl K. HAYDEL
08 Director of Library/Learning .... Ms. Cynthia CHARLES
49 Dean of College of Arts & Sciences .... Dr. Eartha JOHNSON
96 Purchasing Officer .... Vacant
103 Dir Workforce/Career Development .... Vacant
13 Chief Info Technology Officer (CIO) .... Mr. Cederic KONYAOLE
22 Dir Affirmative Action/EEO .... Ms. Sheila JUDGE
39 Director Student Housing .... Ms. Danette SAYLOR
41 Athletic Director .... Dr. Kiki BAKER-BARNES
50 Interim Dean of Business .... Dr. Richard IGWIKE
29 Director Alumni Relations .... Mrs. Adrian GUY-ANDERSON
44 Annual Fund Officer .... Ms. Erica DUROUSSEAU

Fortis College (E)

14111 Airline Highway, Baton Rouge LA 70817
County: East Baton Rouge FICE Identification: 034803
Unit ID: 439738
Telephone: (225) 248-1015 Carnegie Class: Spec 2-yr-Health
FAX Number: (225) 248-9517 Calendar System: Other
URL: www.fortis.edu
Established: 1991 Annual Undergrad Tuition & Fees: $14,283
Enrollment: 312 Coed
Affiliation or Control: Proprietary IRS Status: Proprietary
Highest Offering: Associate Degree
Accreditation: ABHES, MLTAD, #RAD, #SURGT, SURTEC

Franciscan Missionaries of Our Lady University (F)

5414 Brittany Drive, Baton Rouge LA 70808
County: East Baton Rouge FICE Identification: 031062
Unit ID: 160074
Telephone: (225) 768-1700 Carnegie Class: Spec-4-yr-Other Health
FAX Number: (225) 768-0811 Calendar System: Semester
URL: www.franu.edu
Established: 1923 Annual Undergrad Tuition & Fees: $13,287
Enrollment: 1,446 Coed
Affiliation or Control: Roman Catholic IRS Status: 501(c)3
Highest Offering: Doctorate
Accreditation: SC, ANEST, ARCPA, COARC, @DIETI, MT, NUR, @PTA, PTAA, RAD

01 President .... Dr. Tina HOLLAND
05 Provost/VP for Academic Affairs .... Br. Edward VIOLETT
111 VP for Institutional Advancement .... Ms. Judith ROBERSON
10 VP for Operations & Finance .... Ms. Angelia BERCEGEAY
84 VP Enrollment Mgmt/Student Affairs .... Ms. Rebecca CANNON
88 VP for Mission Identity .... Sr. Martha Ann ABSHIRE
66 Dean School of Nursing .... Dr. Amy HALL
76 Dean School of Health Professions .... Dr. Susan STEELE-MOSES
32 Dean of Students .... Dr. Alison WELLS
49 Dean School of Arts & Sciences .... Dr. Brian RASH
37 Director Financial Aid .... Mr. Terry MARTIN
06 Registrar .... Ms. Kimberly JONES-JAMES
88 Director Physician Asst Program .... Ms. Sarah DEYO
88 Director Nurse Anesthesia Program .... Dr. Aimee BADEAUX
76 Director Radiologic Technology .... Ms. Nicole ST. GERMAIN
76 Director Medical Lab Science .... Dr. Debbie FOX
76 Director Physical Therapist Asst .... Dr. Marty AIME
88 Dir Master of Health Administration .... Dr. Elaine PURDY
76 Director Respiratory Therapy .... Ms. Sue DAVIS
88 Dir Doctor of Physical Therapy Pgm .... Dr. Kirk NELSON
88 Director Learning Resource Center .... Ms. Jalan WOODWARD
13 Director of Information Systems .... Vacant
07 Director of Admissions .... Ms. Christy SEVIER
09 Dir Institutional Effectiveness .... Dr. Candi MCELHENY
04 Executive Asst to President .... Ms. Kimberly MELANCON
44 Director Annual Giving/Alumni Rels .... Mr. Corey WILLIAMS
113 Bursar .... Ms. Tracy NOVAK
42 Director Campus Ministry .... Ms. Tammy VIDRINE
90 Director Educational Technology .... Ms. Liza MAYEUX
26 Director Marketing and Comm .... Ms. Stachia MARIONEAUX
112 Director Donor Relations .... Ms. Aimee HOWARD
88 Director Service Learning .... Dr. Rhoda REDDIX
08 Co-Director Library .... Mr. Lucas HUNTINGTON
08 Co-Director Library .... Ms. Maggie MCCANN
18 Director of Operations .... Ms. Denice DORSEY
19 Director Health and Safety .... Ms. Denise GILLESPIE
38 Director Counseling .... Dr. Lynn BROWNING
30 Director of Development .... Ms. Molly SANCHEZ
88 Director Quality Enhancement Plan .... Dr. Valerie SCHLUTER
15 Human Resources Business Partner .... Ms. Jennifer STRICKLAND
25 Contract and Grants Manager .... Mr. Mark OURSO

Herzing University (G)

2500 Williams Boulevard, Kenner LA 70062
Telephone: (504) 613-4295 Identification: 666450
Accreditation: &NH, SURTEC

† Regional accreditation is carried under the parent institution in Madison, WI.

ITI Technical College (H)

13944 Airline Highway, Baton Rouge LA 70817-5998
County: East Baton Rouge FICE Identification: 021662
Unit ID: 159197
Telephone: (225) 752-4230 Carnegie Class: Spec 2-yr-Tech
FAX Number: (225) 756-0903 Calendar System: Quarter
URL: www.iticollege.edu
Established: 1973 Annual Undergrad Tuition & Fees: $11,156
Enrollment: 622 Coed
Affiliation or Control: Proprietary IRS Status: Proprietary
Highest Offering: Associate Degree
Accreditation: ACCSC

01 President .... Mr. Earl Joe MARTIN, III
03 Vice President .... Mr. Mark WORTHY
05 Dean of Education .... Ms. Lisa LAUNEY
88 Director of Compliance .... Mr. Michael CHAMPAGNE
06 Registrar .... Ms. Teresa MAYEUX
07 Director of Admissions .... Mr. Shawn NORRIS
37 Director Student Financial Aid .... Ms. Connie ROUBIQUE

Louisiana College (I)

1140 College Drive, Pineville LA 71359-0001
County: Rapides FICE Identification: 002007
Unit ID: 159568
Telephone: (318) 487-7000 Carnegie Class: Masters/S
FAX Number: (318) 487-7800 Calendar System: Semester
URL: www.lacollege.edu
Established: 1906 Annual Undergrad Tuition & Fees: $17,000
Enrollment: 1,196 Coed
Affiliation or Control: Southern Baptist IRS Status: 501(c)3
Highest Offering: Master's
Accreditation: SC, ACBSP, #CAATE, CAEPT, MUS, NURSE, PTAA, SW

01 President .... Dr. Rick BREWER
03 VP Integration Faith/Learning .... Dr. Philip CAPLES
05 Vice Pres Academic Affairs .... Dr. Cheryl CLARK
10 Vice President for Business Affairs .... Mr. Randall HARGIS
111 VP Advancement .... Dr. Jerry PIPES
32 Dean of Students .... Mr. Vince SMITH
06 Registrar .... Ms. Eileen DEBOER
84 VP Enrollment Mgmt/Admissions .... Mr. Fred HOLT
37 Director of Financial Aid .... Mr. Jeremy TREME
08 Director of the Library .... Mr. Howard TRYON
26 VP Comm/Integrative Marketing .... Mr. Norman MILLER
13 Director Computer Services .... Mr. Mark SHOEMAKER
18 Director of Physical Plant .... Mr. Randall HARGIS
21 Director of Business Office .... Ms. Beverly INGRAM
39 Director of Housing .... Ms. Hannah NYMAN
41 Athletic Director .... Mr. Reni MASON
42 Baptist Student Union Director .... Mr. Thomas WORSHAM
35 Director Student Activities .... Ms. K. B THOMAS
36 Director Career Development .... Mrs. Leneil MERCER
09 Coor of Institutional Research .... Ms. Lisa PRICE
38 Director Student Counseling .... Ms. Leneil MERCER
07 Director of Admissions .... Ms. Renee MELDER
15 Director Human Resources .... Ms. Shannon TASSIN
40 Bookstore Manager .... Ms. Linda BILLINGSLEY
29 Director of Alumni Relations .... Ms. Kathy OVERTURF
19 Chief of Safety & Security .... Mr. Clifford GATLIN
23 Coordinator of Health Services .... Ms. Janet SANDERS
04 Executive Asst to the President .... Ms. Karen WATKINS

*Louisiana Community & Technical College System (J)

265 S Foster Drive, Baton Rouge LA 70806-4104
County: East Baton Rouge Identification: 666188
Telephone: (225) 922-2800 Carnegie Class: N/A
FAX Number: (225) 922-2786
URL: www.lctcs.edu

01 President .... Dr. Monty SULLIVAN
05 Chief Academic Affairs Officer .... Dr. Rene CINTRON
10 Chief Financial Officer/COO .... Mr. Joseph F. MARIN
26 Chief Public Affairs Officer .... Mr. Quintin TAYLOR
84 Chief Enrollment Management Officer .... Dr. Emily CAMPBELL

*Baton Rouge Community College (K)

201 Community College Drive,
Baton Rouge LA 70806-4156
County: East Baton Rouge FICE Identification: 037303
Unit ID: 437103
Telephone: (225) 216-8000 Carnegie Class: Assoc/MT-VT-High Trad
FAX Number: (225) 216-8100 Calendar System: Semester
URL: www.mybrcc.edu
Established: 1998 Annual Undergrad Tuition & Fees (In-District): $4,221
Enrollment: 7,908 Coed
Affiliation or Control: State/Local IRS Status: 501(c)3
Highest Offering: Associate Degree

Accreditation: SC, ACBSP, ACFEI, ADNUR, DMS, NAIT, SURGT

02 Interim Chancellor .... Dr. Willie E. SMITH
04 Asst to the Chancellor .... Ms. Tuesday A. GRAY
26 Exec Dir of PR & Marketing .... Ms. Kizzy PAYTON
05 Vice Chanc Academic/Student Affs .... Ms. Laura YOUNGER
103 Vice Chanc for Workforce Devel .... Dr. Girard MELANCON
111 Vice Chanc for Inst Advance/Found .... Mr. Philip L. SMITH, JR.
46 Dir of Business Process Improv .... Ms. Dionne ANDRUS
10 Vice Chanc for Finance & Admin .... Vacant
21 Director of Acct & Finance .... Mr. Corlin LEBLANC
114 Director of Budgets .... Vacant
13 Chief Information Officer .... Mr. Ronald SOLOMON
15 Chief HR Officer .... Ms. Annette ARBONEAUX
19 Chief of Police .... Ms. Genoria TILLEY
25 Dir Grants Resource Center .... Ms. Ann ZANDERS
18 Chief Facilities Officer .... Mr. Larry STEPHENS
29 Alumni Relations Manager .... Ms. Georgia SCOBEE
32 Asst VC of Student Affairs .... Dr. Sarah BARLOW
35 Assoc Dean of Students .... Ms. Stacia HARDY
36 Director of Career Services .... Ms. Lisa HIBNER
37 Director of Financial Aid .... Ms. Miracle DAVIS
41 Interim Athletic Director .... Ms. Paula LEE
121 Director of Student Success .... Ms. Wendy DEVALL
88 Dir of Academic Learning Center .... Ms. Jeanne STACY
88 Upward Bound Program Director .... Ms. Darica SIMON
96 Director of Purchasing .... Ms. Hilary STEPHENSON
06 Registrar .... Ms. Erin BLAKE

*Bossier Parish Community College (A)

6220 E Texas Street, Bossier City LA 71111-6922
County: Bossier — FICE Identification: 020554
Unit ID: 158431
Telephone: (318) 678-6000 — Carnegie Class: Assoc/MT-VT-High Trad
FAX Number: (318) 678-6389 — Calendar System: Semester
URL: www.bpcc.edu
Established: 1966 — Annual Undergrad Tuition & Fees (In-District): $4,079
Enrollment: 6,734 — Coed
Affiliation or Control: State/Local — IRS Status: 501(c)3
Highest Offering: Associate Degree
Accreditation: SC, ACFEI, ADNUR, COARC, EMT, MAC, NAIT, OTA, PTAA, SURGT

02 Chancellor .... Dr. Douglas R. BATEMAN
05 VC Academic Affairs .... Ms. Lesa TAYLOR DUPREE
11 Exec VC Business Affs .... Mr. Tom WILLIAMS
32 VC of Student Services .... Ms. Karen RECCHIA
103 VC of Econ & Workforce Devl .... Dr. Gayle FLOWERS
10 Assoc VC Finance .... Mr. Raymond ABRAHAM
45 Assoc VC Inst Planning & Assessment .. Dr. Holly FRENCH-HART
20 Assoc VC Innovative Learning .... Ms. Sandra PARTAIN
51 Dean of Workforce Develop/Cont Educ .... Ms. Lisa WARGO
08 Dean of Learning Resources .... Ms. Brenda BRANTLEY
37 Director Student Financial Aid .... Ms. Vicki TEMPLE
06 Registrar .... Mr. Richard COCKERHAM
26 Director of Public Relations .... Ms. Tracy MCGILL
15 Director of Human Resources .... Ms. Teri BASHARA
35 Director of Student Life .... Ms. Marjoree HARPER
13 Chief Information Officer .... Mr. Wesley BANGE
22 Diversity/Multicultural Affairs .... Ms. Marjoree HARPER
72 Director of Educational Technology .... Mr. Charley CAMERON
18 Dir Physical Plant & Maintenance .... Mr. Chad JOHNSTON
111 Director Institutional Advancement .... Ms. Jennifer LAWRENCE
25 Director of Grants .... Dr. Jennifer LAWRENCE
96 Director of Purchasing .... Ms. Gayle DOUCET
04 Exec Assistant to Chancellor .... Ms. Christy MOORE
07 Dean of Enrollment Management .... Ms. Kathy VERCHER
108 Dir Institutional Effectiveness .... Ms. Allison MARTIN
19 Chief of Campus Police .... Mr. Jimmy STEWART
60 Dean of Comm & Performing Arts .... Dr. Ray Scott CRAWFORD
50 Dean of Business .... Ms. Peggy FULLER
54 Dean of TEM .... Ms. Megan BANGE
66 Dean of Sci/Nursing/Allied Health .... Ms. Carolyn BURROUGHS
49 Dean of Liberal Arts .... Ms. Vicki DENNIS
83 Dean of Behavioral Social Sciences .... Ms. Kay BOSTON
121 Dean of Acad Advising .... Ms. Peggy FULLER
09 Int Dir of Inst Research/Assessment .... Ms. Staci PHILLIPS
41 Athletic Director .... Mr. John RENNIE

*Central Louisiana Technical College Avoyelles Campus (B)

508 Choupique Street, Cottonport LA 71327-3743
County: Avoyelles — FICE Identification: 008317
Unit ID: 158237
Telephone: (318) 876-2401 — Carnegie Class: Not Classified
FAX Number: (318) 876-2634 — Calendar System: Semester
URL: www.cltcc.edu
Established: 1938 — Annual Undergrad Tuition & Fees (In-District): N/A
Enrollment: N/A — Coed
Affiliation or Control: State/Local — IRS Status: 501(c)3
Highest Offering: Associate Degree
Accreditation: COE

02 Interim Campus Dean .... Ms. Tiffany HOWARD

*Central Louisiana Technical Community College (C)

516 Murray St., Alexandria LA 71301
County: Rapides — FICE Identification: 005489
Unit ID: 158088
Telephone: (318) 487-5443 — Carnegie Class: Spec 2-yr-Other
FAX Number: (318) 487-5970 — Calendar System: Semester
URL: www.cltcc.edu
Established: 1965 — Annual Undergrad Tuition & Fees (In-State): $4,098
Enrollment: 2,453 — Coed
Affiliation or Control: State — IRS Status: 501(c)3
Highest Offering: Associate Degree
Accreditation: COE

02 Chancellor .... Dr. James (Jimmy) R. SAWTELLE, III
05 Vice Chanc Academic Affairs .... Mr. William TULAK
10 Vice Chanc of Finance/Admin .... Mr. Joseph BORNE
32 Exec VC Stdnt Affs/Enroll Mgmt .... Ms. Heather POOLE
103 Vice Chan Workforce .... Ms. Misty SLAYTER
04 Admin Assistant to the President .... Ms. Mary BARONET
06 Registrar .... Ms. Lynda GARVIN
08 Chief Library Officer .... Ms. Daenel VAUGHAN-TUCKER
09 Director of Institutional Research .... Dr. Stephen COX
13 Chief Information Technology Ofcr .... Dr. Sharon LAYCOCK
15 Chief Human Resources Officer .... Mr. Gregory WILLIS
37 Director Student Financial Aid .... Ms. Kelly CARUSO

*Central Louisiana Technical & Community College-Huey P. Long Campus (D)

5960 Highway 167 N, Winnfield LA 71483-5075
County: Winn — FICE Identification: 005480
Unit ID: 159090
Telephone: (318) 628-4342 — Carnegie Class: Not Classified
FAX Number: (318) 628-7768 — Calendar System: Semester
URL: www.cltcc.edu
Established: 1939 — Annual Undergrad Tuition & Fees (In-District): N/A
Enrollment: N/A — Coed
Affiliation or Control: State/Local — IRS Status: 501(c)3
Highest Offering: Associate Degree
Accreditation: COE

02 Campus Dean .... Mr. Jeff JOHNSON

*Delgado Community College (E)

615 City Park Avenue, New Orleans LA 70119-4399
County: Orleans — FICE Identification: 004625
Unit ID: 158662
Telephone: (504) 671-5000 — Carnegie Class: Assoc/MT-VT-High Trad
FAX Number: (504) 361-6699 — Calendar System: Semester
URL: www.dcc.edu
Established: 1921 — Annual Undergrad Tuition & Fees (In-District): $4,079
Enrollment: 14,239 — Coed
Affiliation or Control: State/Local — IRS Status: 501(c)3
Highest Offering: Associate Degree
Accreditation: SC, ACBSP, ACFEI, ADNUR, CAHIIM, COARC, DMS, EMT, FUSER, MLTAD, NAIT, NMT, OTA, POLYT, PTAA, RAD, RTT, SURGT

02 Chancellor .... Dr. Larissa LITTLETON STEIB
10 Int VC Business/Admin Affairs .... Mr. Ronald RUSSO
05 Int VC Acad Affs/Col Provost .... Dr. Mostafa SARWAR
103 VC Wkfrc Dev/Tech Educ/Inst Advance .... Ms. Arlanda WILLIAMS
66 Exec Dean Charity School of Nursing .... Dr. Cheryl MYERS
76 Dean Allied Health .... Mr. Harold GASPARD
50 Dean Business & Technology .... Ms. Karen MUHSIN
60 Dean Communication Division .... Ms. Emily COSPER
81 Dean Science & Math .... Dr. Jeffrey SMITH
79 Dean Arts and Humanities .... Ms. Patrice MOORE
106 Dean Distance Lrng/Instruct Tech .... Dr. Jeanne SAMUEL
12 Exec Dean West Bank Campus .... Dr. Peter CHO
12 Exec Dean City Park/VC Stdnt Affs .... Dr. Arnel COSEY
12 Exec Dean Sidney Collier .... Dr. Tamika DUPLESSIS
15 Asst Vice Chanc for Human Resources .... Ms. Carla MAJOR
13 AVC Information Technology .... Ms. Vanessa WILLIAMS
21 Asst VC Financial Services .... Mr. Ronald RUSSO
18 Asst VC Facilities & Planning .... Mr. James ROYER
21 Asst VC/Controller .... Ms. Garnette LISTI
04 Executive Asst to the Chancellor .... Ms. Traci SMOTHERS
72 Asst Dean Business & Technology .... Ms. Karen MUHSIN
09 Director Planning & Research .... Dr. Patricia ROSS
88 Exec Dir Curriculum & Pgm Devel .... Mr. Timothy STAMM
08 Dean Library .... Mr. Timothy STAMM
41 Athletic Director .... Mr. Joe SCHEUERMANN
06 College Registrar .... Ms. Maria CISNEROS
07 Director Admissions/Enrollment Svcs .... Ms. Michelle GRECO
44 Director Restricted Funds .... Ms. Sarah CAMANIA
84 Director Enrollment Management .... Mrs. Michelle GRECO
121 Director Advising & Testing .... Ms. Tania CARRADINE
96 Director Purchasing .... Ms. Tracey SHEFFIELD
19 Director Campus Police .... Mr. Henry DEAN

*L.E. Fletcher Technical Community College (F)

1407 Highway 311, Schriever LA 70395
County: Terrebonne — FICE Identification: 005761
Unit ID: 160481
Telephone: (985) 448-7900 — Carnegie Class: Assoc/HVT-Mix Trad/Non
FAX Number: (985) 446-3308 — Calendar System: Semester
URL: www.fletcher.edu
Established: 1948 — Annual Undergrad Tuition & Fees (In-State): $3,966
Enrollment: 2,221 — Coed
Affiliation or Control: State — IRS Status: Exempt
Highest Offering: Associate Degree
Accreditation: SC, ADNUR, COARC, NAIT, PNUR, SURGT

02 Chancellor .... Dr. Kristine STRICKLAND
05 Vice Chanc Academic Affairs .... Dr. Regina VERDIN
10 Vice Chanc Finance/Administration .... Vacant
103 Associate VC of Workforce .... Ms. Tandra LEMAY
06 Registrar .... Ms. Alexis KNIGHT
09 Director of Inst Research & Effect .... Dr. Carrie CORTEZ
32 Dean of Student Services .... Ms. Angie PELLEGRIN
66 Dean of Nursing and Allied Health .... Ms. Maria CAMPBELL
84 Executive Director of Enrollment .... Ms. Ana NANNEY
15 Director of Human Resources .... Ms. Gina MARCEL
04 Assistant to the Chancellor .... Mrs. Crystal GIENGER
08 Director of Library Services .... Vacant
30 Exec Dir Institutional Advancement ...... Mr. W. Chandler LEBEOUF
49 Dean Art and Sciences .... Mrs. Donna ESTRADA
25 Director Grant Writing Initiatives .... Mrs. Catherine BARBER
96 Director of Purchasing .... Ms. Nancy CLEMENT

*Louisiana Delta Community College (G)

7500 Millhaven Road, Monroe LA 71203
County: Ouachita Parish — FICE Identification: 041301
Unit ID: 483212
Telephone: (318) 345-9000 — Carnegie Class: Assoc/HVT-Mix Trad/Non
FAX Number: N/A — Calendar System: Semester
URL: www.ladelta.edu
Established: 2001 — Annual Undergrad Tuition & Fees (In-District): $4,158
Enrollment: 3,666 — Coed
Affiliation or Control: State/Local — IRS Status: 501(c)3
Highest Offering: Associate Degree
Accreditation: SC, ADNUR, EMT, NAIT

02 Chancellor .... Mr. William D. EPPS
05 Vice Chanc of Academic Affairs .... Dr. Dan CORSI
10 VC of Finance & Administration .... Mr. Wendell COPLIN
84 Exec Dir of Enrollment Mgmt .... Mr. Seth HALL
32 Vice Chanc Academics/Student Affs .... Vacant
30 Exec Dir of Dev/Alumni Relations .... Mr. James JOPLING
13 Chief Information Officer .... Mr. Bradley MASTERS
26 Director of Public Relations .... Ms. Darian ATKINS
04 Admin Assistant to the President .... Mrs. Connie L. CARR
09 Dir of IR & Effectiveness .... Ms. Stacy AINSWORTH
106 Director Online Education/E-learnin .... Mrs. Sharon BOWMAN
15 Chief Human Resources Officer .... Ms. Kendra CLEMENT
18 Chief Facilities/Physical Plant Ofc .... Mr. Mike COLVIN
38 Director Student Counseling .... Mrs. Traci CLARK
06 Registrar .... Mrs. Gwenn HALL
07 Director of Recruitment .... Mr. Michael ANDERSON
19 Director Security/Safety .... Mr. Downey BLACK
37 Director Student Financial Aid .... Mrs. Kimberly BRUCE

*Northshore Technical Community College (H)

65556 Centerpoint Blvd, Lacombe LA 70437
County: St. Tammany — FICE Identification: 006756
Unit ID: 160667
Telephone: (985) 545-1500 — Carnegie Class: Assoc/HVT-High Non
FAX Number: N/A — Calendar System: Semester
URL: www.northshorecollege.edu
Established: 1930 — Annual Undergrad Tuition & Fees (In-District): $4,103
Enrollment: 4,995 — Coed
Affiliation or Control: State/Local — IRS Status: 501(c)3
Highest Offering: Associate Degree
Accreditation: COE

02 Chancellor .... Dr. William S. WAINWRIGHT
05 Provost/Vice Chancellor of Academic .... Dr. Daniel ROBERTS
10 Vice Chancellor Finance & Admin .... Mr. Marc CHAUVIN
45 Vice Chanc Strategic Initiative .... Dr. Jim CARLSON
108 Assistant Provost Programs/Assessmt .... Dr. Paul DONALDSON
108 Director of Accreditation/Reporting .... Dr. Melandie MCGEE
32 Vice Chancellor of Student Affairs ...... Dr. Christy MONTGOMERY
06 Registrar .... Ms. Darriona LEE
76 Assoc Provost Health Sci/Nursing .... Ms. Christi MARCEAUX
75 Associate Provost Technical Studies .... Mr. Dewayne LAMBERT
12 Dean of Campus Administration .... Ms. Kim FINCH
12 Dean of Campus Administration .... Ms. Sandy YAEGER
15 Human Resources Director .... Ms. Christi BROWN
18 Director of Facilities .... Mr. Kelly PERRIN
08 Director of Library Services .... Ms. Margaret KELLER
37 Financial Aid Director .... Ms. Nichole LABAT
13 Director Information Tech/Elearning .... Mr. Khiem NGO

*Northwest Louisiana Technical Community College (I)

9500 Industrial Drive, Minden LA 71055
County: Webster — FICE Identification: 009975
Unit ID: 160010
Telephone: (318) 371-3035 — Carnegie Class: Spec 2-yr-Tech
FAX Number: (318) 371-3325 — Calendar System: Trimester
URL: www.nwltc.edu
Established: 1952 — Annual Undergrad Tuition & Fees (In-District): $2,976

Enrollment: 1,130 Coed
Affiliation or Control: State/Local IRS Status: 501(c)3
Highest Offering: Associate Degree
Accreditation: COE

02 Chancellor ... Dr. Earl MEADOR
05 Chief Academic Officer ... Ms. Dede GRIFFITH
15 Chief Human Resources Officer ... Ms. Amber SAUNDERS
10 Chief Financial Officer ... Ms. Melanie SOTAK
37 Director of Financial Aid ... Ms. Sheri BUTLER
32 Director of Student Affairs ... Mr. Stephen LONG
06 Registrar ... Ms. Stacy SHEPHERD

*Nunez Community College (A)

3710 Paris Road, Chalmette LA 70043-1297
County: Saint Bernard FICE Identification: 021661
Unit ID: 158884
Telephone: (504) 278-6200 Carnegie Class: Assoc/HVT-High Non
FAX Number: (504) 278-6480 Calendar System: Semester
URL: www.nunez.edu
Established: 1992 Annual Undergrad Tuition & Fees (In-District): $4,175
Enrollment: 2,599 Coed
Affiliation or Control: State/Local IRS Status: 501(c)3
Highest Offering: Associate Degree
Accreditation: SC, EMT, NAIT

02 Chancellor ... Dr. Tina M. TINNEY
05 Vice Chanc Academic Affairs ... Ms. Tonia LORIA
32 Vice Chanc of Student Affairs ... Ms. Becky MAILLET
10 Vice Chanc Finance & Operations ... Mr. Ronald RODRIGUEZ
15 Director Human Resources ... Ms. Pam CHARLES
20 Dean of Academic Affairs ... Dr. Lane NEVILS
51 Int Exec Dean Continuing Education ... Mr. Leonard UNBEHAGEN
103 Director Workforce Development ... Vacant
06 Registrar ... Ms. Meg GREENFIELD
07 Director of Admissions ... Mrs. Brittney BARRAS
37 Director Financial Aid ... Ms. Treasure BURTCHAELL
26 Director of Communications ... Mr. Jason LEADER
18 Coordinator of Facilities ... Ms. Dawn HART-THORE
30 Director of Development ... Ms. Katherine LEMOINE
13 IT Manager ... Mr. Jason HOSCH

*River Parishes Community College (B)

PO Box 2367, Gonzales LA 70707
County: Ascension FICE Identification: 037894
Unit ID: 436304
Telephone: (225) 743-8500 Carnegie Class: Assoc/MT-VT-High Non
FAX Number: (225) 644-8210 Calendar System: Semester
URL: www.rpcc.edu
Established: 1999 Annual Undergrad Tuition & Fees (In-District): $4,079
Enrollment: 2,342 Coed
Affiliation or Control: State/Local IRS Status: 501(c)3
Highest Offering: Associate Degree
Accreditation: SC, NAIT

02 Chancellor ... Dr. Dale DOTY
10 VC Business/Finance/Administration ... Charles CAMBRE
05 VC of Academic & Student Affairs ... Vacant
103 VC Workforce Development ... Dr. Bruce WAGUESPACK
111 Director Institutional Advancement ... Lillie MURPHY
32 Chief Student Affairs Officer ... Julian SURLA
37 Director Financial Aid ... Christina OCMAND
38 Director Student Counseling ... Shalither CUSHENBERRY
08 Director of Library Services ... Wendy JOHNSON
15 Human Resource Manager ... Francine MIGUEL
09 Director of Institutional Research ... Melba KENNEDY
06 Registrar ... Arthur GILLIS

*South Louisiana Community College (C)

1101 Bertrand Drive, Lafayette LA 70506-4124
County: Lafayette FICE Identification: 039563
Unit ID: 434061
Telephone: (337) 521-9000 Carnegie Class: Assoc/HVT-Mix Trad/Non
FAX Number: (337) 521-9061 Calendar System: Semester
URL: www.solacc.edu
Established: 1998 Annual Undergrad Tuition & Fees (In-District): $4,205
Enrollment: 6,534 Coed
Affiliation or Control: State/Local IRS Status: 501(c)3
Highest Offering: Associate Degree
Accreditation: SC, ACFEI, ADNUR, EMT, MLTAD, NAIT

02 Chancellor ... Dr. Natalie HARDER
04 Exec Assistant to the Chancellor ... Ms. Kelly GREENE
10 Vice Chanc Finance & Administration ... Mr. Bryan GLATTER
103 Assoc Vice Chanc Econ & Wrkfc Dev ... Mr. Jermaine FORD
108 Assoc Vice Chanc Inst Effectiveness ... Dr. Charles MILLER
32 Vice Chanc Acad & Student Affairs ... Dr. Vincent JUNE
37 Interim Director of Financial Aid ... Vacant
08 Director of Library Services ... Ms. Katherine ROLFES
88 Director of Student Accounts ... Ms. Wendi ROBICHEAUX
21 Director of Accounting ... Ms. Carla ORTEGO
18 Director of Facilities ... Mr. Edwin LOPEZ
15 Exec Dir Strategic Engr/Employ Svcs ... Ms. Alicia HULIN
06 Registrar ... Ms. Connie CHOPIN
19 Director Security/Safety ... Mr. Stephen NORTH
26 Communications & Marketing Director ... Ms. Christine PAYTON
84 Director Enrollment Management ... Ms. Debbie TABCHOURI

111 Vice Chanc Inst Advancement ... Ms. Lana FONTENOT
106 Director Distance Education ... Dr. Stasia HERBERT-MCZEAL
13 Chief Information Technology Office ... Mr. Brad BREAUX
28 Director Student Engagement ... Ms. Erica PRECHT
79 Dean Liberal Arts & Humanities ... Dr. John WRIGHT
81 Dean STEM/Transportation & Energy ... Dr. Darcee BEX
66 Dean of Nursing & Allied Health ... Dr. Rebecca HARRIS-SMITH
50 Dean Business/Info Tech & Tech Stds ... Mr. Sam HARB

*SOWELA Technical Community College (D)

PO Box 16950, Lake Charles LA 70616-6950
County: Calcasieu FICE Identification: 005467
Unit ID: 160579
Telephone: (337) 421-6565 Carnegie Class: Spec 2-yr-Tech
FAX Number: (337) 491-2135 Calendar System: Semester
URL: www.sowela.edu
Established: 1938 Annual Undergrad Tuition & Fees (In-District): $4,185
Enrollment: 3,347 Coed
Affiliation or Control: State/Local IRS Status: 501(c)3
Highest Offering: Associate Degree
Accreditation: SC, ACFEI, ADNUR, NAIT, SURGT

02 Chancellor ... Dr. Neil ASPINWALL
04 Assistant to the Chancellor ... Ms. Mary REEDER
05 Vice Chancellor Academic Affairs ... Dr. Paula HELLUMS
10 Vice Chancellor Finance ... Ms. Jeanine NEWMAN
103 Exec Dir of Workforce Solutions ... Mr. David HAYES
13 Chief Info Res & Tech Officer ... Dr. Martha J. SCHEXNEIDER
84 Exec Dir Enroll Mgmt/Stdnt Affs ... Ms. Pam BOERSIG
21 Controller ... Ms. Lindsey JONES
37 Director of Financial Aid ... Ms. Allison DERING
08 Director of Library Services ... Ms. Mary Frances SHERWOOD
15 Director of Human Resources ... Vacant
35 Director of Student Support Svcs ... Ms. Christine COLLINS
18 Director Facilities Planning & Mgmt ... Mr. Davidson DARBONE
09 Exec Director Planning & Analysis ... Dr. Fitzpatrick U. ANYANWU
111 Exec Dir Institutional Advancement ... Ms. Nuria R. ARIAS

*Northwest Louisiana Technical College Natchitoches Campus (E)

6587 Highway 1 Bypass, Natchitoches LA 71458-0657
Telephone: (318) 357-3162 FICE Identification: 021602
Accreditation: COE

† Branch campus of Northwest Louisiana Technical College Northwest Campus, Minden, LA.

*Northwest Louisiana Technical College Shreveport Campus (F)

Box 78527, 2010 N Market Street,
Shreveport LA 71137-8527
Telephone: (318) 676-7811 FICE Identification: 005469
Accreditation: COE

† Branch campus of Northwest Louisiana Technical College Northwest Campus, Minden, LA.

Louisiana Culinary Institute (G)

10550 Airline Highway, Baton Rouge LA 70816-4109
County: East Baton Rouge FICE Identification: 041123
Unit ID: 449612
Telephone: (225) 769-8820 Carnegie Class: Spec 2-yr-A&S
FAX Number: (225) 769-8792 Calendar System: Semester
URL: www.lci.edu
Established: 2002 Annual Undergrad Tuition & Fees: $14,575
Enrollment: 179 Coed
Affiliation or Control: Proprietary IRS Status: Proprietary
Highest Offering: Associate Degree
Accreditation: COE, ACFEI

01 Chief Executive Officer ... Keith RUSH

*Louisiana State University Administration (H)

3810 W Lakeshore Drive, Baton Rouge LA 70808-4600
County: East Baton Rouge FICE Identification: 002009
Telephone: (225) 578-2111 Carnegie Class: N/A
FAX Number: (225) 578-5524
URL: www.lsu.edu

01 President ... Dr. F. King ALEXANDER
05 Exec VP/Provost ... Dr. Stacia J. HAYNIE
17 EVP Health Affs/Med Educ Redesign ... Vacant
10 Exec VP Finance/CFO ... Mr. Daniel LAYZELL
18 System Director Facility Planning ... Mr. Danny MAHAFFEY
43 Vice Pres Legal Affairs/Gen Counsel ... Mr. Thomas SKINNER
15 System Dir Human Resource/Risk Mgt ... Ms. Sharyon LIPSCOMB
21 System Director Internal Audit ... Mr. Chad BRACKIN

*Louisiana State University and Agricultural and Mechanical College (I)

Baton Rouge LA 70803-0100
County: East Baton Rouge FICE Identification: 002010
Unit ID: 159391
Telephone: (225) 578-3202 Carnegie Class: DU-Highest
FAX Number: (225) 578-6400 Calendar System: Semester
URL: www.lsu.edu
Established: 1860 Annual Undergrad Tuition & Fees (In-State): $11,950
Enrollment: 30,861 Coed
Affiliation or Control: State IRS Status: 501(c)3
Highest Offering: Doctorate
Accreditation: SC, ART, CAATE, CACREP, CAEPN, CAMPEP, CIDA, CLPSY, CONST, COSMA, DIETD, IPSY, JOUR, LAW, LIB, LSAR, MUS, SCPSY, SP, SPAA, SW, THEA, VET

02 President ... Dr. King ALEXANDER
05 Exec Vice Pres/Provost ... Dr. Stacia HAYNIE
43 General Counsel ... Mr. Thomas SKINNER
10 Exec Vice Pres Finance & Admin/CFO ... Mr. Daniel LAYZELL
46 Vice Pres Research & Econ Dev ... Mr. Sam BENTLEY
45 Vice Pres Strategic Initiatives ... Dr. Isiah M. WARNER
32 Vice Pres Student Affairs ... Dr. Jeremiah SHINN
26 Int VP Strategic Communications ... Ms. Kristine SANDERS
102 President/CEO LSU Foundation ... Mr. Bryan BENCHOFF
28 Vice Prov Office of Diversity ... Mr. Dereck ROVARIS
20 Sr Vice Prov Academic Affairs ... Dr. Jane CASSIDY
20 Assoc Vice Pres Academic Programs ... Dr. Matt LEE
15 Int Assoc VP Human Resources Mgmt ... Mr. Tyler KEARNEY
84 VP for Enrollment Management ... Mr. Jose AVILES
85 Assoc VP International Programs ... Dr. Hector ZAPATA
37 Assoc Dir Student Aid/Scholarships ... Ms. Amy MARIX
08 Dean LSU Libraries ... Mr. Stanley WILDER
79 Int Dean of Col Hum & Soc Sciences ... Dr. Troy BLANCHARD
54 Dean College of Engineering ... Dr. Judy WORNAT
47 Dean College of Agriculture ... Dr. William RICHARDSON
50 Dean Ourso College of Business ... Dr. Richard D. WHITE
64 Dean College Music & Dramatic Arts ... Mr. Todd QUEEN
81 Dean College of Science ... Dr. Cynthia PETERSON
62 Dir Sch of Library & Info Science ... Dr. Carol BARRY
53 Int Dean College Human Sci & Educ ... Dr. Roland MITCHELL
57 Dean College of Art & Design ... Mr. Alkis TSOLAKIS
74 Dean Veterinary Medicine ... Dr. Joel D. BAINES
60 Int Dean Manship Sch of Mass Comm ... Dr. Martin JOHNSON
92 Dean Honors College ... Dr. Jonathan H. EARLE
65 Dean Sch of Coast & Environ ... Dr. Christopher D'ELIA
88 Exec Dir University College ... Ms. Andrea JONES
35 Assoc Dean of Student Affairs ... Ms. Angela GUILLORY
88 Sr Ex Dir SN Ctr Security Rsch Trng ... Mr. Jeff MOULTON
88 Exec Director Center Energy Stds ... Mr. David DISMUKES
29 President LSU Alumni Association ... Mr. Cliff VANNOY
88 Exec Director LSU Museum of Art ... Dr. Daniel STETSON
18 Assoc VP for Fac & Prop Oversight ... Mr. Tony LOMBARDO
13 Assoc VP & Chief Technology Officer ... Mr. John BORNE
75 Int Dir Sch Human Res Ed & Wk Dev ... Dr. Reid BATES
80 Director Public Admin Institute ... Dr. Jared LLORENS
88 Director LSU Press ... Ms. Alisa PLANT
41 Athletic Director ... Mr. Scott WOODWARD
06 Assoc Vice Provost & Univ Registrar ... Mr. Clayton BENTON
36 Director Olinde Career Center ... Mr. Jesse G. DOWNS
09 Director of Institutional Research ... Mr. Bernie BRAUN
93 Director Multicultural Affairs ... Ms. Andrea E. GRANT
88 Director Non-Academic/Service Area ... Ms. Summer STEIB
65 Director Museum of Natural Science ... Mr. Christopher AUSTIN
88 Director Rural Life Museum ... Mr. David FLOYD
96 Exec Director Purchasing & Property ... Ms. Sally MCKECHNIE
07 Director of Admissions ... Mr. Danny BARROW
19 Chief of LSU Police Dept ... Mr. Bart THOMPSON
39 Asst VP Residential Life ... Mr. Steve WALLER
101 Assoc Vice President for the Board ... Dr. Jason DRODDY
104 Director Study Abroad ... Mr. Harald LEDER
105 Director Info/PR/Publication/Prod ... Ms. Lori MARTIN

*Louisiana State University at Alexandria (J)

8100 Highway 71 S, Alexandria LA 71302-9121
County: Rapides FICE Identification: 002011
Unit ID: 159382
Telephone: (318) 445-3672 Carnegie Class: Bac-A&S
FAX Number: (318) 473-6418 Calendar System: Semester
URL: www.lsua.edu
Established: 1959 Annual Undergrad Tuition & Fees (In-State): $6,668
Enrollment: 3,372 Coed
Affiliation or Control: State IRS Status: 501(c)3
Highest Offering: Baccalaureate
Accreditation: SC, ACBSP, ADNUR, CAEPN, MLTAD, MT, NUR, RAD

02 Chancellor ... Dr. Paul COREIL
05 Int Prov/VC Academic Affairs ... Dr. John ROWAN
10 Vice Chanc Finance/Admin Svcs ... Mr. Deron THAXTON
111 Exec Dir Institutional Advancement ... Ms. Melinda F. ANDERSON
21 Asst VC Finance/Admin Services ... Vacant
50 Dept Chair Business Admin ... Dr. Randall DUPONT
49 Dept Chair Arts/English/Humanities ... Dr. Holly WILSON
83 Dept Chair Behavioral & Social Sci ... Dr. Jerry SANSON
81 Dept Chair Math & Physical Sciences ... Dr. Nathan PONDER
53 Department Chair Education ... Dr. Patsy JENKINS
76 Department Chair Allied Health ... Dr. Haywood JOINER
66 Department Chair Nursing ... Dr. Cathy CORMIER
49 Dept Chair Biological Sciences ... Dr. Nathan PONDER
83 Dept Chair Psychology ... Dr. Mary TREUTING
88 Dept Chair Criminal Justice ... Ms. Beth WHITTINGTON
18 Director of Facility Services ... Mr. Jerry BURNAMAN
08 Int Director Library Services ... Mr. Rusty GASPARD
37 Director of Financial Aid ... Mr. Jeff MASSEY
13 Exec Dir Info Educational Tech Svcs ... Mr. Jason NORMAND

15 Director Human Resource Management .... Ms. Lynette BURLEW
51 Director Continuing Education .... Ms. Lakeshia WILLIAMS
121 Director of Student Success .... Dr. Abbey BAIN
09 Dir Inst Research/Effectiveness .... Mr. Scott COLLEY
96 Dir Procurement Svcs/Property Mgmt .... Vacant
41 Director Athletics .... Mr. Adam JONSON
84 Dean of Enrollment Management .... Ms. Shelly KIEFFER
06 Registrar .... Vacant
19 Int Dir Public Safety/Chf of Police .... Mr. Donald COLLINS

*Louisiana State University at Eunice (A)

2048 Johnson Highway, Eunice LA 70535-6726
County: Acadia FICE Identification: 002012
Unit ID: 159407
Telephone: (337) 457-7311 Carnegie Class: Assoc/MT-VT-High Trad
FAX Number: (337) 546-6620 Calendar System: Semester
URL: www.lsue.edu
Established: 1964 Annual Undergrad Tuition & Fees (In-State): $4,730
Enrollment: 3,044 Coed
Affiliation or Control: State IRS Status: 501(c)3
Highest Offering: Associate Degree
Accreditation: SC, ADNUR, COARC, DMS, RAD

02 Chancellor .... Dr. Kimberly A. RUSSELL
05 Vice Chancellor Academic Affairs .... Dr. Renee ROBICHAUX
84 Dean of Enrollment Management .... Vacant
10 Vice Chancellor Business Affairs .... Vacant
32 Dean Student Affairs .... Dr. Kyle D. SMITH
26 Director of Public Relations .... Mr. Van REED
06 Registrar/Director of Admissions .... Vacant
37 Director of Financial Aid .... Ms. Jacqueline LA CHAPELLE
30 Dir Foundation & Inst Development .... Ms. Carey LAWSON
09 Dir Inst Effectiveness/Devel Educ .... Dr. Paul FOWLER
51 Director Continuing Education .... Mr. Launey P. GRIFFITH
18 Director Physical Plant .... Mr. Michael BROUSSARD
15 Director Personnel Services .... Ms. Angel MCGEE
81 Dean Division of Sciences/Math .... Dr. John HAMLIN
50 Dean Div Bus/Nursing/Allied Health .... Ms. Dotty MCDONALD
49 Dean Division of Liberal Arts .... Dr. Sandra MAHONEY
13 Director Information Technology .... Mr. Stephen HEYWARD
41 Athletic Director .... Mr. Jeff WILLIS
08 Director of the Library .... Ms. Cassie JOBE-GANUCHEAU
19 Director Security/Safety .... Mr. Joseph C. LALONDE
22 Affirmative Action/Equal Oppty .... Ms. Brianna WILLIAMS
39 Dir Resident Life/Student Housing .... Ms. Catherine MOLLENO

*Louisiana State University Health Sciences Center-New Orleans (B)

433 Bolivar Street, New Orleans LA 70112-2223
County: Orleans FICE Identification: 002014
Unit ID: 159373
Telephone: (504) 568-4808 Carnegie Class: Spec-4-yr-Med
FAX Number: N/A Calendar System: Semester
URL: www.lsuhsc.edu
Established: 1931 Annual Undergrad Tuition & Fees (In-State): N/A
Enrollment: 2,777 Coed
Affiliation or Control: State IRS Status: 501(c)3
Highest Offering: Doctorate
Accreditation: SC, ANEST, ARCPA, AUD, CACREP, COARC, CVT, DENT, DH, DT, IPSY, MED, MT, NURSE, OT, PH, PTA, SP

02 Chancellor .... Dr. Larry H. HOLLIER
05 Vice Chanc Acad Aff/Dean Grad Stds .... Dr. Joseph M. MOERSCHBAECHER
10 Vice Chancellor Finance/Admin .... Mr. John HARMAN
86 Vice Chanc Cmty/Minority Affairs .... Mr. Edwin MURRAY
17 Vice Chanc Clinic Affairs .... Dr. J. Chris WINTERS
43 General Counsel .... Ms. Katherine MUSLOW
63 Dean Medicine NO .... Dr. Steve NELSON
52 Dean School of Dentistry .... Dr. Henry GREMILLION
66 Dean of Nursing .... Dr. Demetrius PORCHE
69 Dean of Public Health .... Dr. Dean SMITH
76 Dean Allied Health Professions .... Dr. Jimmy R. CAIRO
04 Administrative Officer .... Mrs. Christine MANALLA
85 Director of International Services .... Ms. Remy E. ALLEN
13 Director Information Services .... Ms. Leslie L. CAPO
14 Director Computer Services .... Mr. Ken BOE
08 Director of Libraries .... Mr. J. Dale PRINCE
15 Director Human Resource Mgmt .... Dr. Rosalynn MARTIN
06 Registrar .... Mr. William Bryant FAUST
37 Dir Student Financial Aid .... Mr. Patrick GORMAN
18 Chief Facilities/Physical Plant .... Mr. John BALL
96 Exec Director of Purchasing .... Mr. Brent HEROLD

*Louisiana State University Health Sciences Center at Shreveport (C)

1501 Kings Highway, Shreveport LA 71103
County: Caddo FICE Identification: 008067
Unit ID: 435000
Telephone: (318) 675-5240 Carnegie Class: Spec-4-yr-Med
FAX Number: (318) 675-5244 Calendar System: Semester
URL: www.lsuhscshreveport.edu
Established: 1969 Annual Undergrad Tuition & Fees: N/A
Enrollment: 899 Coed
Affiliation or Control: Other IRS Status: Exempt
Highest Offering: Doctorate
Accreditation: SC, ARCPA, COARC, DENT, MED, MT, OT, PH, PTA, SP

02 Chancellor .... Dr. Ghali E. GHALI
11 Vice Chancellor Administration .... Mr. Jeff REYNOLDS
46 Vice Chancellor Research Affairs .... Dr. Chris KEVIL
05 Vice Chancellor Academic Affairs .... Dr. Jane EGGERSTEDT
10 Chief Financial Officer .... Ms. Sheila FAOUR
43 Senior Legal Counsel .... Vacant
76 Dean Sch Allied Health Prof .... Dr. Sharon DUNN
58 Dean School of Graduate Studies .... Dr. Chris KEVIL
17 Vice Chancellor Clinical Affairs .... Dr. Charles FOX
88 Exec Director of Campus Operations .... Mr. Joseph MICIOTTO
86 Interim Exec Dir Government Affairs .... Ms. Lisa BABIN
26 Exec Dir Comm/Public Relations .... Ms. Lisa BABIN
13 Chief Info Technology Officer (CIO) .... Mr. Kenneth BROWN
07 Assoc Dean for Admissions SOM .... Dr. Frank S. KENNEDY
32 Asst Dean for Student Affairs SOM .... Dr. Debbie CHANDLER
15 Exec Director of Human Resources .... Ms. Lisa EBARB
23 Executive Director Medical Services .... Ms. Leisa OGLESBY
18 Chief Facilities/Physical Plant .... Mr. Marc GIBSON
19 Interim Director Security/Safety .... Mr. Jody BLACKWELL
09 Director of Institutional Planning .... Mr. Jeffrey D. HOWELLS
25 Director of Sponsored Programs .... Ms. Annella NELSON
06 Registrar .... Ms. Kim CARMEN
08 Interim Head Librarian .... Mr. William OLMSTADT
37 Director Student Financial Aid .... Ms. Sherry GLADNEY
28 Director of Diversity .... Dr. Debbie CHANDLER
29 Director Alumni Relations .... Ms. Mary COBB
96 Director of Purchasing .... Ms. Mary A. TEMPLETON
63 Dean School of Medicine .... Dr. David F. LEWIS

† Tuition varies by degree program.

*Louisiana State University in Shreveport (D)

One University Place, Shreveport LA 71115-2399
County: Caddo FICE Identification: 002013
Unit ID: 159416
Telephone: (318) 797-5000 Carnegie Class: Masters/L
FAX Number: (318) 797-5180 Calendar System: Semester
URL: www.lsus.edu
Established: 1967 Annual Undergrad Tuition & Fees (In-State): $7,327
Enrollment: 5,996 Coed
Affiliation or Control: State IRS Status: 501(c)3
Highest Offering: Doctorate
Accreditation: SC, CACREP, CAEP, PH

02 Chancellor .... Mr. Lawrence S. CLARK
05 Interim Provost/VC Academic Affairs .... Dr. Helen TAYLOR
10 Vice Chancellor Business Affairs .... Ms. Barbie CANNON
32 Assoc VC Student Development .... Mrs. Paula ATKINS
102 Executive Director LSUS Foundation .... Ms. Laura PERDUE
29 Director Alumni Affairs .... Vacant
88 Vice Chanc Strategic Initiatives .... Dr. Julie LESSITER
06 Registrar .... Ms. Darlenna M. ATKINS
15 Director of Human Resource Mgmt .... Mr. Bill WOLFE
08 Dean Noel Memorial Library .... Mr. Brian SHERMAN
37 Director of Student Financial Aid .... Ms. Chelsea CHANCE
07 Director of Admissions .... Mrs. Mary Catherine HARVISON
38 Director Counseling Services .... Ms. Angela PELLERIN
13 Assoc VC & CIO/IT .... Mr. Shelby C. KEITH
40 Director of Bookstore .... Ms. Renee MARTIN
96 Director of Purchasing .... Mr. Bill WOLFE
26 Director of Media/Public Relations .... Mr. Wendell RILEY
04 Assistant to the Chancellor .... Ms. Shelley MOORE
19 Dir of University Police .... Mr. Donald W. WRAY
41 Athletic Director .... Mr. Lucas MORGAN
49 Dean of Arts and Sciences .... Dr. Peter SISKA
58 Dean of Graduate Studies .... Dr. Sanjay T. MENON
51 Exec Dir Continuing Education .... Mr. Brent WALLACE
53 Dean Business/Educ/Human Dev .... Dr. Nancy ALBERS
106 Director Online Learning .... Ms. Rhonda FAILEY
18 Dir Physical Plant/Facility Svcs .... Mr. Joseph LACOUR

*University of New Orleans (E)

2000 Lakeshore Drive, New Orleans LA 70148-2000
County: Orleans FICE Identification: 002015
Unit ID: 159939
Telephone: (504) 280-6000 Carnegie Class: DU-Higher
FAX Number: (504) 280-5522 Calendar System: Semester
URL: www.uno.edu
Established: 1958 Annual Undergrad Tuition & Fees (In-State): $8,771
Enrollment: 7,964 Coed
Affiliation or Control: State IRS Status: 501(c)3
Highest Offering: Doctorate
Accreditation: SC, ART, CACREP, CAEPN, MUS, PLNG, SPAA, THEA

02 President .... Dr. John W. NICKLOW
05 Provost/VP Academic Affairs .... Dr. Mahyar AMOUZEGAR
10 VP Business Affairs .... Dr. Gregg LASSEN
32 Associate VP and Dean of Students .... Dr. Carolyn GOLZ
13 Chief Information Officer .... Dr. Ray WANG
85 Asst Prov International Education .... Ms. Alea COT
19 Asst Vice Chanc for Public Safety .... Mr. Thomas HARRINGTON
50 Dean of Business Administration .... Dr. John A. WILLIAMS
54 Dean of Engineering .... Dr. Taskin KOCAK
49 Dean Liberal Arts & Education .... Dr. Kim MARTIN LONG
08 Dean Library/Information Services .... Dr. Rui WANG
81 Dean of Sciences .... Dr. Steve JOHNSON
06 University Registrar .... Mr. Rajni SOHARU
29 Director Alumni Affairs .... Ms. Rachel MASSEY
26 Chief Communications Officer .... Mr. Adam NORRIS
96 Director of Purchasing .... Ms. Susan VARBLE
41 Director Athletics .... Mr. Tim DUNCAN
39 Director Student Housing .... Ms. Amanda ROBBINS
121 Director Learning Resource Center .... Ms. Margaret WILLIAMSON
04 Exec Asst to the President .... Ms. Elizabeth LAND
09 Dir Inst Effectiveness & Research .... Dr. Colby STOEVER
15 Assoc VP Human Resource Management .... Ms. Karen PAISANT
18 Assoc VP for Facility Services .... Ms. Deborah HADDAWAY
30 Exec Director of Univ Advancement .... Mr. Anthony GREGORIO
36 Director Career Services .... Ms. Celyn BOYKIN
37 Dir Student Financial Aid & Scholar .... Ms. Ann LOCKRIDGE
38 Director Student Counseling .... Dr. Rosemond MYERS
84 Assoc VP Admissions & Enrollment .... Ms. Mary Beth MARKS

Loyola University New Orleans (F)

6363 Saint Charles Avenue, New Orleans LA 70118-6195
County: Orleans FICE Identification: 002016
Unit ID: 159656
Telephone: (504) 865-2011 Carnegie Class: DU-Mod
FAX Number: (504) 865-3851 Calendar System: Semester
URL: www.loyno.edu
Established: 1912 Annual Undergrad Tuition & Fees: $39,942
Enrollment: 3,759 Coed
Affiliation or Control: Roman Catholic IRS Status: 501(c)3
Highest Offering: Doctorate
Accreditation: #SC, CACREP, JOUR, LAW, MUS, NURSE

01 President .... Ms. Tania TETLOW
101 Exec Asst to Pres for Board Rels .... Ms. Kristine D. LELONG
04 Executive Assistant to President .... Ms. Desiree RODRIGUEZ
05 Int Prov/Vice Pres Academic Affs .... Dr. Maria CALZADA
84 SVP Enroll Mgmt/Student Affairs .... Dr. Sarah KELLY
10 Vice Pres CO Finance/Administration .... Ms. Carol MARKOWITZ
111 Vice Pres Institutional Advance .... Mr. Chris WISEMAN
88 Vice Pres for Mission & Ministry .... Fr. Justin DAFFRON
13 Vice Prov Information Tech/CIO .... Mr. Bret JACOBS
21 Int Vice Pres Financial Affairs .... Vacant
26 VP Marketing/Communications .... Ms. Rachel HOORMAN
11 Asst Vice Pres Administration .... Mr. Thomas J. RAYMOND
35 Asst Vice Pres of Student Affairs .... Mr. Robert A. REED
09 Asst Provost .... Dr. Carol Ann MACGREGOR
42 Director of University Ministry .... Mr. Kurt BINDEWALD
108 Coord Internal Reporting/Assessment .... Ms. Donna BOURGEOIS
27 Assoc Dir Public Affs/External Rels .... Ms. Patricia MURRET
43 General Counsel .... Vacant
29 Director Alumni Engagement .... Ms. Laurie LEIVA
06 Dir Stdnt Records/Registration Svcs .... Ms. Kathy R. GROS
15 Director of Human Resources .... Vacant
40 Bookstore Manager .... Ms. Maleta WILSON
41 Director Athletics & Wellness .... Mr. Brett SIMPSON
36 Director Career Development Center .... Ms. Tamara BAKER
23 Int Exec Dir of Student Affairs .... Dr. Alicia BOURQUE
19 Director University Police .... Mr. Todd W. WARREN
37 Director Scholarships/Financial Aid .... Ms. Carrie GLASS
08 Director of the Law Library .... Mr. P. Michael WHIPPLE
104 Dir Center for International Educ .... Ms. Debra DANNA
86 Dir Govt Relations & Legal Affairs .... Mr. Tommy SCREEN
38 Director Student Counseling .... Dr. Alicia BOURQUE
96 Director of Purchasing .... Mr. Robert NELSON
06 Dir Admin Services/Student Records .... Mr. Michael RACHAL
39 Director of Residential Life .... Ms. Amy BOYLE
08 Dean of Libraries .... Ms. Deborah POOLE
79 Dean Humanities/Natural Science .... Dr. Uriel QUESADA
61 Dean of Law .... Dr. Madeleine LANDRIEU
64 Dean of Music and Fine Arts .... Mr. Kern MAASS
50 Dean of Business .... Dr. Michael CAPELLA
83 Dean of Social Sciences .... Dr. Roger WHITE
88 Int Director of Service Learning .... Ms. Jennifer N. JEANFREAU
88 Director of Women's Resource Ctr .... Ms. Patricia BOYETT
92 Dir of University Honors Program .... Ms. Naomi YAVNEH
88 Dir of Common Curriculum .... Dr. Lydia VOIGT
35 Director of Student Services .... Ms. Maria MCBRIDE
109 Director of Campus Dining .... Ms. Heather BACQUE
07 Int Director of Admissions .... Mr. Nathan AMENT
18 Chief Facilities/Physical Plant .... Mr. Charles B. MARSHALL
25 Chief Contracts/Grants Admin .... Dr. Heidi L. DAVIS
28 Interim Chief Diversity Officer .... Dr. Liv KNEWMAN

McCann School of Business and Technology (G)

2319 Louisville Avenue, Monroe LA 71201-6126
Telephone: (318) 323-2889 FICE Identification: 026068
Accreditation: ACCSC

NationsUniversity (H)

650 Poydras St., Ste 1400, PMB 133, New Orleans LA 70130
County: Orleans Identification: 667257
Telephone: (866) 617-6446 Carnegie Class: Not Classified
FAX Number: N/A Calendar System: Other
URL: www.nationsu.edu
Established: 1996 Annual Undergrad Tuition & Fees: N/A
Enrollment: N/A Coed
Affiliation or Control: Independent Non-Profit IRS Status: 501(c)3
Highest Offering: Master's
Accreditation: DEAC

00 Chair of the Board .... Mr. Ernie CLEVENGER
01 Chancellor/CEO .... Dr. Mac LYNN

88 Vice Chancellor .... Dr. Herman ALEXANDER
05 Chief Academic Officer .... Dr. David B. SRYGLEY
06 Registrar .... Mrs. Mary V. MABERY
10 Chief Financial/Business Officer .... Mr. Joe SLOAN
11 Chief of Operations/Administration .... Vacant
20 Dean of Faculty .... Dr. Richard YOUNGBLOOD
32 Director of Student Services .... Mrs. Marty LYNN
38 Director of Student Advising .... Mrs. Gail HEIDERICH
26 Director of Communications .... Mr. Jon R. SLOAN
91 IT Director .... Mr. Mike BUSH
90 IT Administrator .... Mr. Glenn BEVILLE

New Orleans Baptist Theological Seminary (A)

3939 Gentilly Boulevard, New Orleans LA 70126

County: Orleans FICE Identification: 002019
Unit ID: 159948
Telephone: (504) 282-4455 Carnegie Class: Spec-4-yr-Faith
FAX Number: (504) 283-3631 Calendar System: Semester
URL: www.nobts.edu
Established: 1917 Annual Undergrad Tuition & Fees: $8,620
Enrollment: N/A Coed
Affiliation or Control: Southern Baptist IRS Status: 501(c)3
Highest Offering: Doctorate
Accreditation: SC, MUS, THEOL

01 President .... Dr. James Kenneth DEW, JR.
05 Provost .... Dr. Norris C. GRUBBS
111 Actg VP Institutional Advancement .... Mr. Mark HAGELMAN
10 Vice President for Business Affairs .... Mr. Clay L. CORVIN
30 Vice President for Development .... Vacant
15 Vice Pres of Human Resources .... Ms. Pattie SHOENER
84 Vice President Enrollment .... Mr. Larry LYON
58 Dean Graduate Studies .... Dr. Margie BUTLER
12 Dean Leavell College .... Dr. L. Thomas STRONG, III
32 AVP Student Affs/Dean of Students .... Dr. Craig GARRETT
06 Registrar .... Dr. Paul E. GREGOIRE, JR.
08 Dean of Libraries .... Dr. Jeff D. GRIFFIN
18 Associate VP of Facilities .... Dr. Jim O. PARKER
13 Assoc VP Information Technology .... Dr. Laurie S. WATTS
73 Assoc Dean Prof Doctoral Pgms .... Dr. Reggie R. OGEA
106 Associate Dean of Online Learning .... Dr. Matthew BRYANT
58 Assoc Dean Research Doctoral Pgms .... Dr. Charles A. RAY, JR.
35 Director of Student Engagement .... Mr. Conner HINTON
26 Dir Office of Communications .... Mr. Gary D. MYERS
29 Director of Alumni Relations .... Dr. Dennis L. PHELPS
36 Director of Student Enlistment .... Mr. Michael REED
37 Director of Financial Aid .... Mr. Michael WANG
38 Director of Testing & Counseling .... Dr. Jeffery W. NAVE
88 Director of Innovative Learning .... Dr. Donna B. PEAVEY
39 Director Student Housing .... Mrs. Julie BARENTINE
41 Athletic Director .... Mr. Justin SAWYER

Notre Dame Seminary, Graduate School of Theology (B)

2901 S Carrollton Avenue, New Orleans LA 70118-4391

County: Orleans FICE Identification: 002022
Unit ID: 160029
Telephone: (504) 866-7426 Carnegie Class: Spec-4-yr-Faith
FAX Number: (504) 866-3119 Calendar System: Semester
URL: www.nds.edu
Established: 1923 Annual Undergrad Tuition & Fees: N/A
Enrollment: N/A Coed
Affiliation or Control: Roman Catholic IRS Status: 501(c)3
Highest Offering: Master's
Accreditation: SC, THEOL

01 President - Rector .... V.Rev. James A. WEHNER, STD
05 Academic Dean .... Dr. Rebecca S. MALONEY
08 Director of Library .... Mr. Thomas B. BENDER, IV
09 Director IE/Planning/Faculty Devel .... Dr. Rebecca S. MALONEY
10 Business Manager .... Ms. Michelle W. KLEIN
06 Registrar .... Ms. Debora PANEPINTO

Remington College-Baton Rouge Campus (C)

4520 S Sherwood Forrest Blvd, Baton Rouge LA 70816

Telephone: (225) 236-3200 Identification: 666449
Accreditation: ACCSC

† Branch campus of Remington College, Cleveland, OH.

Remington College-Lafayette Campus (D)

303 Rue Louis XIV, Lafayette LA 70508-5700

Telephone: (337) 981-4010 FICE Identification: 005203
Accreditation: ACCSC

† Branch campus of Remington College, Cleveland, OH.

Remington College-Shreveport (E)

2106 Bert Kouns Industrial Loop, Shreveport LA 71118

Telephone: (318) 671-4000 Identification: 666302
Accreditation: ACCSC

† Branch campus of Remington College, Cleveland, OH.

Saint Joseph Seminary College (F)

75376 River Road, Saint Benedict LA 70457-9999

County: Saint Tammany FICE Identification: 002027
Unit ID: 160409
Telephone: (985) 867-2232 Carnegie Class: Spec-4-yr-Faith
FAX Number: (985) 867-2270 Calendar System: Semester
URL: www.sjasc.edu
Established: 1891 Annual Undergrad Tuition & Fees: $18,230
Enrollment: 146 Male
Affiliation or Control: Roman Catholic IRS Status: 501(c)3
Highest Offering: Baccalaureate
Accreditation: SC

01 President & Rector .... V.Rev. Gregory M. BOQUET, OSB
05 Academic Dean .... Dr. Daniel P. BURNS
03 Vice-Rector .... Rev. Matthew CLARK, OSB
08 Librarian .... Ms. Bonnie WOOD
10 Business Officer .... Mrs. Jennifer WHITEHOUSE
37 Director Financial Aid/Registrar .... Mrs. Wendy VAN DALEN
29 Director of Alumni Affairs .... Rev. Matthew CLARK, OSB
30 Director of Development .... Mr. Scott WALLACE
26 Director of Communications .... Mr. James SHIELDS
32 Dean of Students .... Rev. Jonathan WALLIS, OSB
108 Director Institutional Assessment .... Dr. Dianna LAURENT
13 Chief Info Technology Officer (CIO) .... Mr. Todd RUSSELL
18 Chief Facilities/Physical Plant .... Mr. Jim ROBEAU
04 Admin Assistant to the President .... Mrs. Cindy MARKHAM
15 Chief Human Resources Officer .... Mrs. Carla GRAVES
41 Athletic Director .... Mr. Brenton ADDISON

*Southern University and Agricultural & Mechanical College System (G)

JS Clark Admin Building, 4th Floor,
Baton Rouge LA 70813-0001

County: East Baton Rouge Parish FICE Identification: 009637
Unit ID: 160533
Telephone: (225) 771-4680 Carnegie Class: N/A
FAX Number: (225) 771-5522
URL: www.sus.edu

01 President-Chancellor .... Dr. Ray L. BELTON
12 Exec VP/Exec VC Baton Rouge Campus .. Dr. James H. AMMONS
10 System VP/Finance/Business Affairs .... Mr. Flandus MCCLINTON
05 Chief Academic Officer .... Dr. Luria YOUNG
32 VC Student Affairs/Enroll Mgmt .... Dr. Kimberly SCOTT
13 Assoc VP/Information Technology .... Dr. Gabriel FAGBEYIRO
15 Assoc VP/Human Resources .... Atty. Tracie J. WOODS
84 SUS AVP/Online Learning Services .... Dr. Moustapha DIACK
30 CEO SU System Foundation .... Mr. Alfred E. HARRELL, III
43 General Counsel to the System/Board .... Atty. Deidre D. ROBERT
04 VP of External Affairs .... Dr. Robyn M. MERRICK
26 System Director of Communications .... Mr. Henry J. TILLMAN
18 System Dir of Facilities Planning .... Mr. Eli GUILLORY
116 System Director of Internal Audit .... Ms. Linda H. CATALON
09 System Dir/Institutional Research .... Ms. Sheila D. DEROEUN
06 Interim Registrar .... Ms. Velena JOHNSON
07 Director of Admissions .... Ms. Dianna GILBERT
104 Dean of International Education .... Dr. Barbara CARPENTER
19 Director Security/Safety .... Ms. Joycelyn JOHNSON
29 Exec Dir Alumni Federation .... Mr. Derrick V. WARREN
36 Director of Career Services .... Ms. Tamara F. MONTGOMERY
37 Director Student Financial Aid .... Ms. Ursula SHORTY
38 Director Student Counseling .... Dr. ValaRay IRVIN
39 Director Student Housing .... Ms. Tracie A. ABRAHAM
41 Athletic Director .... Mr. Roman BANKS, JR.
50 Dean College of Business .... Dr. Donald ANDREWS
53 Director of Education .... Dr. VerJanis PEOPLES
54 Dean College of Sci/Engineering .... Dr. Patrick CARRIERE
96 Director of Purchasing .... Ms. Linda ANTOINE

*Southern University and A&M College (H)

Harding Boulevard, Baton Rouge LA 70813-0001

County: East Baton Rouge FICE Identification: 002025
Unit ID: 160621
Telephone: (225) 771-4500 Carnegie Class: Masters/L
FAX Number: (225) 771-2018 Calendar System: Semester
URL: www.subr.edu
Established: 1880 Annual Undergrad Tuition & Fees (In-State): $9,122
Enrollment: 6,118 Coed
Affiliation or Control: State IRS Status: 501(c)3
Highest Offering: Doctorate
Accreditation: SC, AAFCS, CACREP, CAEP, DIETI, #JOUR, MUS, NURSE, SP, SPAA, SW

02 President/Chancellor .... Dr. Ray BELTON
03 EVP/EVC BR Campus .... Dr. James H. AMMONS
100 Chief of Staff .... Ms. Katara A. WILLIAMS
10 Sys VP Finance and Admin .... Mr. Flandus MCCLINTON
45 System VP SPPIE .... Dr. Vladimir A. APPEANING
26 System VP External Affairs .... Dr. Robyn M. MERRICK
43 General Counsel .... Ms. Deidre D. ROBERT
15 AVP Human Resources .... Ms. Tracie J. WOODS
13 AVP for IT/Chief Information Ofcr .... Dr. Gabriel FAGBEYIRO
115 AVP of Finance & Treasury .... Ms. Catherine MILES
106 AVP Online Learning Services .... Dr. Moustapha DIACK
108 Exec Director Inst Effectiveness .... Dr. Toni L. MANOGIN
116 Exec Director Internal Audit .... Mr. Brian ADAMS
111 CEO SU System Foundation .... Mr. Alfred E. HARRELL
18 Exec Director Facilities .... Mr. Eli G. GUILLORY, III
29 Exec Dir SU Alumni Federation .... Mr. Derrick WARREN
114 VC Finance & Administration .... Mr. Benjamin PUGH
05 Sr Associate VC Academic Affairs .... Dr. Bijoy K. SAHOO
32 VC Student Affairs/Enroll Mgmt .... Dr. Kimberly M. SCOTT
46 VC Research & Strategic Initiatives .... Dr. Michael A. STUBBLEFIELD
41 Athletic Director .... Mr. Roman BANKS
84 AVC Enrollment Management .... Dr. Manicia FINCH
35 AVC Admissions Recruitment .... Dr. Anthony JACKSON
21 AVC Finance and Administration .... Mrs. Monica MEALIE
121 AVC Student Success .... Mr. Edward WILLIS
50 Dean College of Business .... Dr. Donald R. ANDREWS
54 Dean Col of Sciences/Engineering .... Dr. Patrick CARRIERE
80 Dean College of Government .... Dr. Damien EJIGIRI
62 Dean of Libraries .... Mrs. Emma BRADFORD-PERRY
79 Dean College of Humanities and IDS .... Dr. Cynthia D. BRYANT
51 Dean International Education .... Dr. Barbara CARPENTER
92 Dean of Honors College .... Dr. Diola BAGAYOKO
47 Interim Dean Ag Ctr Family Cons Sci .... Dr. Calvin R. WALKER
66 Interim Dean Nursing/Allied Hlth .... Dr. Jacquelinet HILL
58 Dean of the Graduate School .... Dr. Habib P. MOHAMADIAN
53 Director School of Education .... Dr. Verjanis PEOPLES
16 Director Human Resources .... Ms. Dawn HARRIS
27 Director of Communications .... Ms. Janene TATE
120 Director Online Education/E-learnin .... Ms. Tracy BARLEY
96 Director of Purchasing .... Mrs. Linda B. ANTOINE
06 Registrar .... Mrs. Dianna DEPRON
37 Director of Financial Aid .... Dr. Kelvin M. FRANCOIS
39 Director Residential Housing .... Mrs. Tracie A. ABRAHAM
07 Dir Admissions/Recruitment .... Ms. Akai SMITH
19 Chief of Police .... Ms. Joycelyn JOHNSON
36 Director Career Services .... Mrs. Tamara F. MONTGOMERY
09 Director of Institutional Research .... Mr. Srinivas R. GAVINI
25 Assoc Controller for Sponsored Pgm .... Ms. Famika SARGENT
88 Assoc Controller for Financial Op .... Mrs. Cary HOLLINS

*Southern University at New Orleans (I)

6400 Press Drive, New Orleans LA 70126-1009

County: Orleans FICE Identification: 002026
Unit ID: 160630
Telephone: (504) 286-5000 Carnegie Class: Masters/M
FAX Number: (504) 286-5131 Calendar System: Semester
URL: www.suno.edu
Established: 1956 Annual Undergrad Tuition & Fees (In-State): $7,033
Enrollment: 2,546 Coed
Affiliation or Control: State IRS Status: 501(c)3
Highest Offering: Master's
Accreditation: #SC, AAFCS, CAEPN, CAHIIM, SW

02 Chancellor .... Dr. Lisa MIMS-DEVEZIN
04 Exec Assoc to the Chancellor .... Mr. Harry DOUGHTY
05 EVC for Academic Affairs & SACS .... Dr. David S. ADEGBOYE
10 VC for Admin & Finance .... Mr. Justin JAMES
32 VC Student Affs & Enroll Management .... Vacant
46 VC for Research/Title III Programs .... Dr. Brenda W. JACKSON
111 VC Univ Advance/Community Outreach .... Mrs. Gloria B. MOULTRIE
09 Dir IR/IE & Strategic Planning .... Mrs. Ada KWANBUNBUMPEN
108 Int Lrng Outcomes/Assessment Coord .... Ms. Safia JENKINS
25 Dir Grants & Sponsored Programs .... Dr. William R. BELISLE
06 Registrar .... Ms. Gilda DAVIS
21 Comptroller .... Ms. Shawn M. CHARLES
07 Director of Recruitment .... Mr. C. Maxille MOULTRIE
08 Director of Library .... Mrs. Shatiqua A. MOSBY-WILSON
36 Dir Career Counseling & Vet Liaison .... Mr. Joseph MARION
13 Director of Information Technology .. Mr. Edmond M. CUMMINGS
15 Director of Human Resources .... Ms. Evelyn MASTERS-DUBUCLET
19 Police Captain Campus Police .... Mr. Bruce ADAMS
20 Assoc VC Academic Affairs Faculty .... Mr. Wesley T. BISHOP
41 Director of Athletics .... Mr. Bernard GRIFFITH
26 Director of Public Relations .... Ms. Tammy BARNEY
96 Director of Purchasing .... Ms. Marilyn G. MANUEL
106 Director of E-Learning .... Ms. Shelia WOOD
70 Dean School of Social Work .... Dr. Rebecca CHAISSON
50 Dean College of Business/Pub Admin .... Dr. Igwe E. UDEH
88 Director of Museum Studies .... Dr. Haitham EID
58 Director of Graduate Studies .... Ms. Deidrea JONES-HAZURE
49 Dean College of Arts & Sciences .... Dr. Evelyn HARRELL
53 Interim Dean College of Education .... Dr. Willie JONES
22 Dir Services for Students w/Disab .... Ms. Yolanda L. MIMS
32 Dir of Student Activities/Orgs .... Mrs. Mary JACKSON
38 Dir of Student Development Center .... Mrs. Josephine OKORONKWO
121 Dir Student Support Services Pgm .... Ms. Linda D. FREDERICK
88 Dir Ctr for African & American Stds .... Dr. Clyde ROBERTSON
18 Director of Facilities Management .... Mr. Derrick JAMES
37 Director Student Financial Aid .... Ms. LaCharlotte GARRETT
88 Director Quality Enhancement Plan .... Mr. Benjamin ASHU
07 Director of Admissions .... Mr. Shapiro MEADOWS

*Southern University at Shreveport-Louisiana (J)

3050 Martin Luther King Jr. Drive,
Shreveport LA 71107-4795

County: Caddo FICE Identification: 007686
Unit ID: 160649
Telephone: (318) 670-6000 Carnegie Class: Assoc/HVT-Mix Trad/Non
FAX Number: (318) 670-6374 Calendar System: Semester

URL: www.susla.edu
Established: 1964 Annual Undergrad Tuition & Fees (In-State): $4,350
Enrollment: 3,088 Coed
Affiliation or Control: State IRS Status: 501(c)3
Highest Offering: Associate Degree
Accreditation: SC, ADNUR, CAHIIM, DH, MLTAD, RAD, SURGT

02 Chancellor ....Dr. Rodney A. ELLIS
26 Spec Asst to Chanc IR/Div Univ Rels .... Mr. Theron JACKSON
05 Vice Chanc Academic Affairs .....Dr. Sharon HERRON-WILLIAMS
32 Vice Chanc Student Affairs ....Ms. Melva WILLIAMS
10 Vice Chanc Finance/Administration ....Vacant
103 VC Cmty Outreach/Workforce Devel ....Mrs. Janice B. SNEED
11 Chief Admin/Operations Officer ....Ms. Leslie R. MCCLELLON
32 Asst Vice Chanc Student Affairs ....Dr. Fatina ELLIOTT
84 Asst Vice Chanc Enrollment Mgmt ....Mr. Terence VINSON
20 Asst Vice Chanc for Academic Affs ....Dr. Regina ROBINSON
21 Chief Financial Officer ....Mrs. Brandy JACOBSEN
111 Chief Advancement Officer ....Ms. Stephanie ROGERS
113 Bursar ....Ms. Tomeka K. BROWN
06 Registrar ....Dr. Lalita ROGERS
08 Library Director ....Mrs. Jane O'RILEY
35 Director of Student Activities ....Mrs. Rebecca GILLIAM
51 Exec Director Continuing Education ....Mr. Larry FERDINAND
07 Director of Admission & Recruitment ....Vacant
37 Director of Financial Aid ....Ms. Katraya WILLIAMS
102 Exec Director SUSLA Foundation ....Mr. Frank WILLIAMS, JR.
27 Dir University Relations/Marketing ....Vacant
19 Chief University Police ....Mr. Marshall NELSON
13 Dir Information Technology Center ....Vacant
88 Director Student Support Services ....Ms. Karen COCO
75 Director Aerospace Technology ....Mr. David FOGLEMAN
38 University Counselor ....Ms. Kaye L. WASHINGTON
15 Director Human Resources ....Mr. Wayne H. BRYANT
96 Director of Purchasing ....Ms. Sophia JACKSON-LEE
18 Director Facilities & Risk ....Mr. Darrell STREET
21 University Budget Officer ....Ms. Regina WINN
72 Director Radiologic Technology ....Ms. Sheila SWIFT
88 Exec Dir TRIO Community Outreach ....Ms. Betty C. FAGBEYIRO
88 Director Dental Hygiene ....Mrs. Kheysia H. WASHINGTON
88 Director Biomedical Research Devel ....Dr. Joseph ORBAN
09 Director Inst Plng/Assessment/Rsrch ....Mr. Martin FORTNER
66 Director of Nursing ....Dr. Tiffany VARNER
79 Division Chair for Humanities ....Ms. Wanda M. WALLER
72 Dean Science & Technology/Engr ....Dr. Barry C. HESTER
76 Div Chair Allied Health Sci ....Mrs. JoAnn BROWN
83 Div Ch Behav Sci/Educ/Bus Standards ....Dr. Rosalyn J. HOLT

*Southern University Law Center (A)

PO Box 9294, Baton Rouge LA 70813
County: East Baton Rouge Identification: 667233
Unit ID: 440916
Telephone: (225) 771-2552 Carnegie Class: Spec-4-yr-Law
FAX Number: N/A Calendar System: Semester
URL: www.sulc.edu
Established: 1947 Annual Graduate Tuition & Fees: N/A
Enrollment: 576 Coed
Affiliation or Control: State IRS Status: 501(c)3
Highest Offering: First Professional Degree; No Undergraduates
Accreditation: SC, LAW

02 Chancellor ....Mr. John K. PIERRE
05 Chief Academic Officer ....Ms. Shawn VANCE
06 Director of Records & Registration ....Mrs. D'Andrea J. LEE
07 Director of Admissions/Recruitment ....Ms. Andrea LOVE
09 VC Inst Accountability/Accred ....Ms. Regina JAMES
10 Vice Chanc Finance & Administration ....Mr. Terry HALL
20 AVC Academic Support/Bar Prep ....Ms. Cynthia REED
18 Director of Facilities ....Ms. Angela GAINES
26 Director of Internal Affairs ....Ms. Jasmine HUNTER
29 Director of Alumni Affairs ....Ms. Robbin THOMAS
30 Director of Development ....Ms. Tanya FREEMAN
32 Vice Chanc Student Affairs ....Mr. Donald NORTH
36 Director of Student Placement ....Ms. Kerii LANDRY-THOMAS
37 Director of Student Financial Aid ....Ms. Calaundra CLARKE
21 Assoc Vice Chanc Finance/Budgets ....Ms. Demetria GEORGE
35 Assoc Vice Chanc Student Affairs ....Ms. Shenequa GREY

Tulane University (B)

6823 St. Charles Avenue, New Orleans LA 70118-5698
County: Orleans FICE Identification: 002029
Unit ID: 160755
Telephone: (504) 865-5000 Carnegie Class: DU-Highest
FAX Number: (504) 865-5202 Calendar System: Semester
URL: www.tulane.edu
Established: 1834 Annual Undergrad Tuition & Fees: $54,820
Enrollment: 12,384 Coed
Affiliation or Control: Independent Non-Profit IRS Status: 501(c)3
Highest Offering: Doctorate
Accreditation: SC, CAEPT, DIETI, HSA, IPSY, LAW, MED, PH, SCPSY, SW

01 President ....Mr. Michael A. FITTS
05 Sr Vice Pres Acad Affairs/Provost ....Dr. Robin FORMAN
111 Sr Vice Pres for Advancement ....Ms. Ginny WISE
108 Sr VP Strategic Init/Inst Effect ....Mr. Richard MATASAR
11 Chief Operations Officer ....Mr. Mark ALISE
63 Sr Vice Pres/Dn School of Medicine ....Dr. Lee L. HAMM
43 General Counsel ....Ms. Victoria D. JOHNSON
13 VP Information Technology/CTO ....Mr. Noel WONG
115 Chief Investment Officer ....Mr. Jeremy T. CRIGLER
32 VP Student Affairs ....Dr. J. Davison PORTER
58 Assoc Provost Graduate Studies ....Dr. Michael CUNNINGHAM
84 Vice Pres Enrollment Management ....Mr. Satya DATTAGUPTA
18 VP Facilities Management ....Mr. Randolph PHILIPSON
26 Vice Pres University Communications ....Ms. Libby ECKHARDT
46 Vice President for Research ....Dr. Giovanni PIEDIMONTE
110 Vice President Advancement ....Ms. Luann D. DOZIER
15 Vice President Human Resources ....Ms. Shantay BOLTON
117 Vice Pres Insurance & Risk Mgmt ....Ms. Joyce K. FRED
86 Assoc VP Government Relations ....Ms. Sharon P. COURTNEY
109 Assoc VP Auxiliary Svcs/Student Ctr ....Mr. Robert C. HAILEY
37 Assoc Vice President Financial Aid ....Mr. Michael GOODMAN
114 Director Budgets & Planning ....Ms. Judy VITRANO
29 VP for Alumni Affairs ....Mr. James STOFAN
21 Vice President Finance & Controller ....Mr. James WANDLING
08 Dean Library & Academic Information ....Mr. David BANUSH
38 Exec Dir Educ Resources/Couns ....Dr. Donna BENDER
36 Exec Dir Career Services Center ....Dr. Amjad AYOUBI
12 Dir Tulane Natl Primate Res Ctr ....Mr. Jay RAPPAPORT
27 Executive Director Public Relations ....Mr. Michael J. STRECKER
39 Assoc VP Housing Services/Residence ....Dr. Brian JOHNSON
96 Director Central Procurement Svcs ....Mr. William VAN CLEAVE
91 Asst VP Academic & Admin Computing ....Ms. Mary T. WALSH
41 Director Athletics ....Mr. Troy DANNEN
51 Dean Professional Advancement ....Dr. Suri DUITCH
49 Dean School of Liberal Arts ....Dr. Brian EDWARDS
49 Dean Newcomb-Tulane College ....Dr. Lee SKINNER
61 Dean School of Law ....Mr. David D. MEYER
69 Dean Sch Public Health/Trop Med ....Dr. Thomas LAVEIST
54 Dean School Science & Engineering ....Dr. Kimberly FOSTER
48 Dean School of Architecture ....Dr. Inaki ALDAY
50 Dean AB Freeman School of Business ....Dr. Ira SOLOMON
70 Dean School of Social Work ....Dr. Patrick BORDNICK
09 Director of Institutional Research ....Mr. Shawn POTTER
88 Exec Dir of CELT ....Dr. Toni WEISS
85 Assoc Dean Ctr for Global Education ....Dr. Scott PENTZER
35 Assoc VP Student Affairs ....Dr. John NONNAMAKER
88 CPS Executive Director ....Dr. Agnieszka NANCE
04 Senior Aide to the President ....Ms. Jennifer JUMONVILLE
07 Director of Admissions ....Mr. Jeffrey SCHIFFMAN
06 Registrar ....Ms. Colette RAPHEL
101 Secretary to the Board ....Ms. Cyndy ENGLISH

University of Holy Cross (C)

4123 Woodland Drive, New Orleans LA 70131-7399
County: Orleans FICE Identification: 002023
Unit ID: 160065
Telephone: (504) 394-7744 Carnegie Class: Masters/S
FAX Number: (504) 391-2421 Calendar System: Semester
URL: www.uhcno.edu
Established: 1916 Annual Undergrad Tuition & Fees: $14,180
Enrollment: 1,246 Coed
Affiliation or Control: Roman Catholic IRS Status: 501(c)3
Highest Offering: Doctorate
Accreditation: SC, CACREP, CAEP, IACBE, NDT, NUR, RAD

01 President ....Dr. David M. LANDRY
05 Provost/VP Academic Affairs ....Dr. Victoria DAHMES
10 Vice Pres for Finance & Operations ....Mrs. Arlean WEHLE
30 Vice Pres for Philanthropy/Planning ....Mr. David CATHERMAN
84 VP Enrollment Management ....Mr. Kobi SLOANE
32 VP Student Engagement/Advising ....Ms. Meredith REED
88 VP for Mission Integration ....Sr. Rochelle PERRIER
08 Director of Library Services ....Ms. Diana SCHAUBHUT
83 Dean Couns/Educ/Business ....Dr. Carolyn WHITE
66 Dean Nursing/Allied Health ....Dr. Patricia PRECHTER
49 Dean Liberal Arts and Science ....Dr. Michael LABRANCHE
32 Director Student Life ....Ms. Heather DUCHARME
06 Registrar ....Ms. Traci REES
09 Director Inst Research & Planning ....Dr. Jacques DETIEGE
42 Director of Campus Ministry ....Vacant
15 Director Human Resources ....Ms. Christine WATTS
44 Director of Annual Fund ....Mr. David CATHERMAN
13 Director of Information Services ....Ms. Rosalind CHESTER
37 Director of Financial Aid ....Mr. Hayden WAGAR
04 Administrative Asst to President ....Ms. Peggy BOURGEOIS
19 Director Security/Safety ....Mr. Bernard NELSON
26 Director Communications ....Ms. Erin SULLIVAN
29 Director Alumni Relations ....Mr. Steve MORGAN
106 Distance Education Coordinator ....Dr. Tess O'NEILL

*University of Louisiana System Office (D)

1201 N Third Street, Suite 7-300,
Baton Rouge LA 70802-5243
County: East Baton Rouge FICE Identification: 033444
Unit ID: 247083
Telephone: (225) 342-6950 Carnegie Class: N/A
FAX Number: (225) 342-6473
URL: www.ulsystem.net

01 President ....Dr. James B. HENDERSON
05 Provost and VP for Academic Affairs ....Dr. Jeannine KAHN
10 VP of Business and Finance ....Dr. Edwin LITOLFF
32 VP for Student Affairs & Governance ....Erica CALAIS
26 VP for Marketing and Communication ....Cami GEISMAN
86 Director of Governmental Affairs ....Vacant
04 Executive Asst to the President ....Sandra GREEN

*Grambling State University (E)

403 Main Street, Grambling LA 71245
County: Lincoln FICE Identification: 002006
Unit ID: 159009
Telephone: (318) 274-3811 Carnegie Class: Masters/L
FAX Number: (318) 274-6172 Calendar System: Semester
URL: www.gram.edu
Established: 1901 Annual Undergrad Tuition & Fees (In-State): $7,435
Enrollment: 5,191 Coed
Affiliation or Control: State IRS Status: 501(c)3
Highest Offering: Doctorate
Accreditation: SC, CAEPN, MUS, NRPA, NUR, SPAA, SW, THEA

02 President ....Mr. Richard GALLOT, JR.
05 Provost/VP Academic Affairs ....Dr. Ellen SMILEY
10 Int VP Finance & Administration/COO ....Mr. Martin LEMELLE, JR.
32 Vice Pres Student Affairs ....Dr. David C. PONTON, JR.
111 VP Institutional Advancement ....Mr. Marc NEWMAN
13 AVP of Info Technology ....Mrs. Peggy HANLEY
15 AVP of Human Resource Management ....Mrs. Monica BRADLEY
19 University Police Chief ....Mr. Carlos KELLY
50 Dean College of Business ....Dr. Donald WHITE
53 Dean College of Education ....Dr. Andolyn HARRISON
49 Dean College of Arts & Sci ....Dr. Stacey D. DUHON
92 Dean Honors College ....Dr. Ellen SMILEY
18 Director Facilities Management ....Mr. Fredrick CARR
09 Director of Institutional Research ....Ms. Ulrica S. EDWARDS
41 Athletic Director ....Dr. Paul BRYANT
07 Int Director of Admissions ....Ms. D'Andrea BROWN
06 Registrar/Exec Dir Enrollment Mgmt ....Mrs. Patricia J. HUTCHERSON
37 Dir Student Financial Aid ....Dr. Gavin HAMMS
29 Exec Director of Alumni Affairs ....Ms. Carolyn COLLIER
23 Director of Health Services ....Mrs. Patrice OUTLEY
38 Director Counseling Center ....Dr. Coleen SPEED
39 Director of Residential Life ....Ms. Dana K. HOWARD
42 United Campus Ministry ....Mr. Wanjiku KAMAGU
96 Director of Purchasing ....Mr. Alvin BRADLEY
40 Manager University Bookstore ....Mr. Elliot JONES
106 Director of Distance Learning ....Mr. Eldrie HAMILTON
88 Special Assistant to Provost and VP ....Mrs. JoAnn BROWN
36 Director of Career Services ....Dr. Shelia FOBBS

*Louisiana Tech University (F)

PO Box 3168, Ruston LA 71272-0001
County: Lincoln FICE Identification: 002008
Unit ID: 159647
Telephone: (318) 257-0211 Carnegie Class: DU-Higher
FAX Number: (318) 257-2928 Calendar System: Quarter
URL: www.latech.edu
Established: 1894 Annual Undergrad Tuition & Fees (In-State): $9,645
Enrollment: 12,839 Coed
Affiliation or Control: State IRS Status: 501(c)3
Highest Offering: Doctorate
Accreditation: SC, AAB, AAFCS, ADNUR, ART, AUD, CACREP, CAEP, CAEPN, CAHIIM, CIDA, COPSY, DIETD, DIETI, MUS, SP

02 President ....Dr. Leslie K. GUICE
05 Provost ....Dr. Terry M. MCCONATHY
32 EVP/VP Student Advancement ....Dr. Jim M. KING
111 Vice President for Univ Advancement ....Mr. Brooks HULL
46 Chief Research & Innovation Officer ....Dr. Davy NORRIS, JR.
10 Vice President of Finance ....Mrs. Lisa L. COLE
11 AVP of Administration & Facilities ....Mr. Sam G. WALLACE
09 AVP Inst Effect/Research & Planning ....Dr. Sheryl S. SHOEMAKER
88 AVP Acad Advancement & Partnerships ....Dr. Donna JOHNSON
58 AVP Research & Dean Grad School ....Dr. Ramu RAMACHANDRAN
88 AVP Research & Partnerships ....Dr. Sumeet DUA
35 AVP Student Advancement ....Dr. Dickie CRAWFORD
110 AVP Univ Advance & General Counsel ....Mrs. Jennifer RILEY
115 CFO & Exec Dir University Services ....Ms. Pam GILLEY
04 EA to Pres Compliance/Title IX ....Mrs. Carrie FLOURNOY
50 Dean of Business ....Dr. Chris MARTIN
53 Dean of Education ....Dr. Don N. SCHILLINGER
54 Dean of Engineering & Science ....Dr. Hisham HEGAB
65 Dean of Applied & Natural Sciences ....Dr. Gary KENNEDY
49 Dean of Liberal Arts ....Dr. Don KACZVINSKY
121 Dean Student Svcs & Acad Support ....Mrs. Stacy GILBERT
84 Dean Stdnt Engage/Undgr Recruitment ....Mr. Sam SPEED
116 Internal Auditor ....Mr. Robert GRAFTON
43 Legal Counsel ....Mr. Justin KAVALIR
26 Exec Dir University Communications ....Ms. Tonya OAKS SMITH
86 Executive Director External Affairs ....Ms. Johnette MAGNER
15 Director Human Resources ....Ms. Sheila TRAMMEL
113 Comptroller ....Ms. Courtney JARRELL
07 Director of Admissions ....Mr. Tree GEORGE
91 Director of Computer Center ....Mr. Mike COLYAR
90 Interim Dir Infrastructure & IT ....Mr. Danny SCHALES
37 Director Student Financial Aid ....Ms. Aimee F. BAXTER
06 Registrar ....Mr. Robert(Bob) D. VENTO
08 Executive Director Libraries Svcs ....Vacant
38 Dir Career Ctr/Student Counseling ....Mr. Ron CATHEY
89 Director of Freshmen Studies ....Ms. Jennifer CARTER
92 Director of Honors Program ....Dr. Ernest RUFLETH
93 Director of Multicultural Affairs ....Ms. Devonia LOVE-VAUGHN
96 Director of Procurement ....Ms. Melissa HUGHES
18 Director Physical Plant ....Mr. Joe PEEL
41 Athletics Director ....Mr. Thomas H. MCCLELLAND, II
117 Director Envir Health & Safety ....Mr. Don BRASWELL
39 Dir Resident Life & Summer Camps ....Ms. Casey INGRAM

85 Director Intl Students/Scholars ... Mr. Jay LIGON
19 Chief University Police ... Mr. Randal HERMES
40 Director Bookstore ... Mr. Michael CORBIN
118 HR Coordinator Benefits ... Ms. Taryn SOIGNIER
25 Director Sponsored Programs ... Dr. Melissa DOBSON
100 Coordinator of Planning & Advance ... Mr. Ryan W. RICHARD

*McNeese State University (A)

4205 Ryan Street, Lake Charles LA 70609-4510
County: Calcasieu FICE Identification: 002017
Unit ID: 159717
Telephone: (337) 475-5000 Carnegie Class: Masters/L
FAX Number: (337) 475-5012 Calendar System: Semester
URL: www.mcneese.edu
Established: 1939 Annual Undergrad Tuition & Fees (In-State): $7,860
Enrollment: 7,629 Coed
Affiliation or Control: State IRS Status: 501(c)3
Highest Offering: Beyond Master's But Less Than Doctorate
Accreditation: SC, ART, CACREP, CAEP, CAEPN, DIETD, DIETI, MT, MUS, NURSE, RAD

02 President ... Dr. Daryl BURCKEL
05 Provost/VP Acad Affairs/Enroll Mgmt ... Dr. C. Mitchell ADRIAN
10 VP Business Affairs ... Mr. Eddie P. MECHE
111 VP University Advancement ... Mr. Richard H. REID
32 VP Student Affairs ... Dr. Christopher THOMAS
84 Assoc VP Enrollment Management ... Dr. Toby OSBURN
20 Asst VP Academic Affairs ... Ms. Jessica HUTCHINGS
47 Dean College of Agriculture ... Dr. Frederick LEMIEUX
50 Interim Dean College of Business ... Dr. Wade ROUSSE
53 Dean College of Education ... Dr. Angelique OGEA
49 Dean College of Liberal Arts ... Dr. Michael BUCKLES
54 Dean Col of Science/Engr/Math ... Dr. Tim HALL
66 Dean Col of Nursing/Health Prof ... Dr. Peggy L. WOLFE
35 Dean Student Affairs ... Mr. Kedrick NICHOLAS
13 Chief Information Technology ... Mr. Chad THIBODEAUX
19 University Police Chief ... Mr. William SCHEUFENS
28 Chief Diversity Officer ... Dr. Michael T. SNOWDEN
41 Director of Athletics ... Mr. F. Bruce HEMPHILL
18 Director Facilities & Plant Opers ... Mr. Richard R. RHODEN
15 Dir Human Res/Student Employment ... Ms. Charlene R. ABBOTT
37 Director Student Financial Aid ... Ms. Taina J. SAVOIT
88 Director of Scholarships ... Ms. Ralynn F. CASTETE
07 Dir of Admissions and Recruiting ... Ms. Kourtney ISTRE
96 Director Purchasing/Property Cntrl ... Ms. Roxane FONTENOT
29 Director Alumni Affairs ... Ms. Joyce D. PATTERSON
92 Director of Honors College ... Dr. Scott E. GOINS
14 Director of Univ Computing Services ... Mr. Stanley HIPPLER
08 Director of Library ... Ms. Debbie L. JOHNSON-HOUSTON
85 Director of International Programs ... Ms. Preble GIRARD
26 Director Public Relations ... Ms. Candace V. TOWNSEND
31 Dir Community Service and Outreach ... Mrs. Betty H. ANDERSON
38 Director Student Counseling/Health ... Ms. Raime THIBODEAUX
106 Director of Electronic Learning ... Ms. Wendi PRATER
110 Director University Advancement ... Ms. Melissa NORTHCUTT
23 RN Supervisor-Student Health ... Ms. Ramona L. TOUPS
40 Bookstore Manager ... Ms. Donna MARTIN
06 Registrar ... Ms. Catrina BOENIG
04 Administrative Asst to President ... Ms. Deb KINGREY

*Nicholls State University (B)

906 East First Street, Thibodaux LA 70310-0001
County: Lafourche FICE Identification: 002005
Unit ID: 159966
Telephone: (985) 448-4003 Carnegie Class: Masters/L
FAX Number: (985) 448-4920 Calendar System: Semester
URL: www.nicholls.edu
Established: 1948 Annual Undergrad Tuition & Fees (In-State): $7,952
Enrollment: 6,327 Coed
Affiliation or Control: State IRS Status: 501(c)3
Highest Offering: Beyond Master's But Less Than Doctorate
Accreditation: SC, ART, CACREP, CAEPN, DIETD, DIETI, JOUR, MUS, NAIT, NURSE

02 President ... Dr. Jay CLUNE
03 Executive Vice President ... Mr. Alex ARCENEAUX
05 Provost/VP Academic & Student Affs ... Dr. Velma S. WESTBROOK
20 Vice Provost ... Dr. Todd KELLER
32 AVP Stdnt Affairs/Dean of Students ... Dr. Michele E. CARUSO
18 Superint Facility/Proj Manager ... Mr. Owen Scott WILLIAMS
10 VP for Finance & Administration ... Mr. Terry BRAUD
45 Exec Dir of Planning/Effectiveness ... Mrs. Renee G. HICKS
81 Dean of Sciences & Technology ... Dr. John DOUCET
66 Dean of Nursing ... Dr. Velma S. WESTBROOK
50 Dean Business Administration ... Dr. Marilyn MACIK-FREY
53 Dean Educ/Behavioral Sciences ... Dr. Scot RADEMAKER
121 Director of Academic Services ... Mr. David ZERANGUE
09 Dir Assess/Institutional Research ... Ms. Melanie COLLINS
08 Director of Library ... Mr. Clifton THERIOT
19 Director of University Police ... Mr. Craig M. JACCUZZO
36 Director of Career Services ... Ms. Kristie R. TAUZIN
37 Director of Student Financial Aid ... Ms. Casie TRICHE
13 Director of Computing Center ... Mr. Sam CAGLE
15 Director of Human Resources ... Mr. Steven KENNEY
26 Director of University Relations ... Mr. Jerad DAVID
51 Dir of Continuing Education ... Mrs. Elizabeth MCCURRY
41 Athletic Director ... Mr. Matt ROAN
29 Exec Dir Alumni & External Affairs ... Ms. Monique CROCHET
88 Exec Dir Leadership & Master's Pgm ... Dr. Eugene A. DIAL
06 Director Records & Registration ... Mr. Kelly J. RODRIGUE

07 Director of Admissions ... Mrs. Becky L. DUROCHER
23 Director University Health Services ... Mrs. Adrienne BOLTON
39 Director Residence Life ... Mr. Alex COAD
84 Director of Enrollment Services ... Mrs. Courtney CASSARD
96 Director of Purchasing ... Mr. Terry G. DUPRE
46 Director Research & Sponsored Pgms ... Mrs. Debra BENOIT
58 Director of Graduate Programs ... Mrs. DesLey PLAISANCE
88 Director of Printing & Design ... Mr. Bruno RUGGIERO
109 Director of Auxiliary Services ... Mrs. Brenda HASKINS
88 Coordinator of Veterans Services ... Mr. Gilberto BURBANTE
106 Dir Online Education/E-learning ... Dr. Andrew SIMONCELLI
49 Int Dean of Liberal Arts ... Mrs. Jean DONEGAN

*Northwestern State University (C)

310 Sam Sibley Drive, Suite 223,
Natchitoches LA 71497-0002
County: Natchitoches FICE Identification: 002021
Unit ID: 160038
Telephone: (318) 357-6441 Carnegie Class: Masters/L
FAX Number: (318) 357-4223 Calendar System: Semester
URL: www.nsula.edu
Established: 1884 Annual Undergrad Tuition & Fees (In-State): $7,922
Enrollment: 10,572 Coed
Affiliation or Control: State IRS Status: 501(c)3
Highest Offering: Doctorate
Accreditation: SC, ADNUR, ART, CACREP, CAEP, MUS, NURSE, RAD, SW, THEA

02 President ... Dr. Chris MAGGIO
05 Provost/VP Academic Affairs ... Dr. Greg HANDEL
11 Exec VP University & Business Affs ... Dr. Marcus JONES
26 Vice President for External Affairs ... Mr. Jerry D. PIERCE
46 VP for Tech/Innovation/Econ Dev ... Dr. Darlene WILLIAMS
10 Vice President Business Affairs ... Mr. Carl JONES
32 Dean of Students ... Mrs. Frances CONINE
53 Dean Col of Education/Human Dev ... Dr. Kimberly MCALISTER
49 Interim Dean Col of Arts & Sciences ... Dr. Francene LEMOINE
66 Dean Col of Nursing & Allied Health ... Dr. Dana CLAWSON
50 Dean Col of Business & Tech ... Dr. Margaret KILCOYNE
13 Chief Information Officer ... Mr. Ron WRIGHT
92 Director Scholars' College ... Dr. Kirsten BARTELS
12 Director CENLA Campus ... Mr. Jason PARKS
09 Director Institutional Research ... Ms. Dawn MITCHELL
84 Director of Enrollment Management ... Mrs. Jana LUCKY
06 Registrar ... Mrs. Barbara PRESCOTT
08 Director of Libraries ... Ms. Abbie LANDRY
111 Asst VP External Affs/Univ Advance ... Mr. Drake OWENS
37 Director Student Financial Aid ... Ms. Lauren JACKSON
88 Int Dir Creative & Performing Arts ... Mr. Scott BURRELL
27 Director NSU Press ... Mrs. Leah JACKSON
36 Director Counseling & Career Svcs ... Mrs. Rebecca BOONE
41 Athletic Director ... Mr. Greg BURKE
23 Director of Health Services ... Ms. Holly CAIN
07 Director of University Recruiting ... Ms. Ashlee HEWITT
15 Director Human Resources ... Mr. Cecil KNOTTS
18 Physical Plant Director ... Mr. Dale WOHLETZ
96 Director of Purchasing ... Mr. Dale MARTIN

*Southeastern Louisiana University (D)

548 Ned McGehee Drive, Hammond LA 70402-0001
County: Tangipahoa FICE Identification: 002024
Unit ID: 160612
Telephone: (985) 549-2000 Carnegie Class: Masters/L
FAX Number: (985) 549-2061 Calendar System: Semester
URL: www.southeastern.edu
Established: 1925 Annual Undergrad Tuition & Fees (In-State): $8,165
Enrollment: 14,285 Coed
Affiliation or Control: State IRS Status: 501(c)3
Highest Offering: Doctorate
Accreditation: SC, AAFCS, ART, CAATE, CACREP, CAEPN, MUS, NAIT, NURSE, SP, SW

02 President ... Dr. John L. CRAIN
05 Provost/VP Academic Affairs ... Dr. Tena GOLDING
10 VP Administration/Finance ... Mr. Sam DOMIANO
111 Vice Pres University Advancement ... Ms. Wendy LAUDERDALE
32 Vice President Student Affairs ... Dr. Eric SUMMERS
84 Asst VP Enrollment Services ... Dr. Kay MAURIN
13 Chief Information Officer ... Dr. Mike M. ASOODEH
86 Exec Asst Public & Govt Affairs ... Ms. Erin K. COWSER
21 Controller ... Ms. Khalli s. HAGAN
06 Director Records & Registration ... Ms. Paulette M. POCHE
08 Director of Library ... Mr. Eric W. JOHNSON
36 Director Career Development Svcs ... Mr. Ken W. RIDGEDELL
109 Director Auxiliary Services ... Ms. Connie DAVIS
29 Director of Alumni Services ... Ms. Michelle BIGGS
39 Dir Student Housing & Resident Svcs ... Dr. Pamela RAULT
15 Director Human Resources ... Ms. Tara DUPRE
19 Director University Police ... Vacant
46 Dir Sponsored Research/Programs ... Ms. Cheryl HALL
41 Athletic Director ... Mr. Jay ARTIGUES
18 Director Facility Planning ... Mr. Ken D. HOWE
92 Director Honors Program ... Dr. Claire PROCOPIO
23 Director Health Services ... Ms. Andrea PEEVY
38 Interim Director Counseling Center ... Dr. Peter EMERSON
37 Director Financial Aid ... Mr. Charles CAMBRE
09 Director Inst Research/Assessment ... Dr. Michelle HALL
26 Director Public Information ... Vacant
96 Dir Purchasing/Property Control ... Mr. Richard HIMBER
85 Int Dir Multicult/Intl Stdnt Affs ... Mr. Gabe WILLIS

22 Coordinator EEO/ADA ... Mr. Gene E. PREGEANT
49 Int Dn Col Arts/Human/Soc Sciences ... Dr. Karen FONTENOT
50 Int Dean of College of Business ... Dr. Antoinette PHILLIPS
53 Dean College of Education ... Dr. Paula CALDERON
66 Dean Col of Nursing & Health Sci ... Dr. Ann CARRUTH
72 Dean Col of Science & Technology ... Dr. Daniel MCCARTHY

*University of Louisiana at Lafayette (E)

104 University Circle, Lafayette LA 70503-0001
County: Lafayette FICE Identification: 002031
Unit ID: 160658
Telephone: (337) 482-1000 Carnegie Class: DU-Higher
FAX Number: (337) 482-6195 Calendar System: Semester
URL: www.louisiana.edu
Established: 1898 Annual Undergrad Tuition & Fees (In-State): $9,912
Enrollment: 17,297 Coed
Affiliation or Control: State IRS Status: 501(c)3
Highest Offering: Doctorate
Accreditation: SC, ART, CAATE, CACREP, #CAEP, CAHIIM, CIDA, JOUR, MUS, NAIT, NURSE, SP, THEA

02 President ... Dr. E. Joseph SAVOIE
05 Provost/VP for Academic Affairs ... Dr. Jaimie HEBERT
10 VP Administration & Finance ... Mr. Jerry L. LEBLANC
32 Vice President for Student Affairs ... Ms. Patricia COTTONHAM
111 VP University Advancement ... Mr. John BLOHM
46 Vice President for Research ... Dr. Ramesh KOLLURU
84 VP for Enrollment Management ... Dr. DeWayne BOWIE
13 Chief Information Officer ... Mr. Gene FIELDS
11 Director of Administrative Services ... Ms. Lisa C. LANDRY
21 Asst Vice Pres Financial Services ... Ms. Debra CALAIS
45 Asst VP Inst Effectiveness ... Dr. Blanca BAUER
20 Asst VP Academic Affairs ... Dr. Robert MCKINNEY
20 Asst VP Academic Affairs ... Dr. Fabrice LEROY
35 Dean of Students ... Dr. Margarita PEREZ
35 Assoc Dean Students/Dir Stdnt Life ... Ms. Heidie LINDSEY
25 Director of Research/Sponsored Pgms ... Vacant
91 Director of Information Systems ... Ms. Paula BREAUX
14 Director Computing Support Services ... Mr. Patrick LANDRY
08 Interim Dean University Libraries ... Ms. Susan RICHARD
07 Director of UG Admissions ... Ms. Amy DESORMEAUX
88 Director of UG Recruitment ... Vacant
88 Director Information Networks ... Mr. Stephen J. MAHLER
09 Director of Institutional Research ... Ms. Lisa LORD
55 Director University Connection ... Ms. Amanda DOYLE
37 Director of Financial Aid ... Ms. Cindy SHOWS-PEREZ
96 AVP Finance and Director Purchasing ... Ms. Marie FRANK
27 Assoc Director Publications ... Ms. Kathleen A. THAMES
36 Director Career Services ... Ms. Kim A. BILLEAUDEAU
19 Chief of Police ... Vacant
23 Director Student Health Svcs ... Ms. Madeline HUSBAND-ARDOIN
49 Dean Liberal Arts ... Dr. Jordan KELLMAN
54 Interim Dean of Engineering ... Dr. Ahmed KHATTAB
53 Dean of Education ... Dr. Nathan ROBERTS
66 Dean of Nursing ... Dr. Melinda OBERLEITNER
58 Dean of Graduate School ... Dr. Mary FARMER-KAISER
50 Interim Dean of Business Admin ... Dr. Geralyn FRANKLIN
81 Dean of Sciences ... Dr. Azmy ACKLEH
97 Dean of University College ... Dr. Bobbie DECUIR
57 Dean College of the Arts ... Mr. H. Gordon BROOKS, II
77 Director Ctr Adv Computer Studies ... Dr. Magdy A. BAYOUMI
18 Director Physical Plant ... Mr. William J. CRIST
43 Director of Operational Review ... Ms. Megan BREAUX
39 Director Housing ... Mr. Jules BREAUX
40 Manager Bookstore ... Mr. Robert RICHARD
24 Director Univ Media/Printing Svcs ... Mr. Steve MAHLER
41 Athletic Director ... Dr. Bryan MAGGARD
85 Exec Dir Global Engagement ... Dr. Gabriel CARRANZA
51 Director of Continuing Education ... Ms. Dawn PROVOST
31 Dean of Community Service ... Mr. David YARBROUGH
26 Int Chief Communications Officer ... Ms. Aimee ABSHIRE
29 Director Alumni Affairs ... Ms. Jennifer LEMEUNIER
112 Planned Giving Officer ... Mr. David P. COMEAUX
38 Director Counseling and Testing ... Mr. Brian FREDERICK
15 Chief Human Resources Officer ... Mr. Paul THOMAS
06 Registrar ... Mr. Mickey DIEZ
106 Director of Distance Learning ... Dr. Claire ARABIE
92 Director of Honors Program ... Dr. Julia FREDERICK
121 Exec Director of Student Success ... Dr. Elizabeth GIROIR
89 Director of First-Year Experience ... Vacant
28 Director of Diversity ... Ms. Taniecea MALLERY
108 Director Institutional Assessment ... Ms. Alise HAGAN
30 Exec Director of Development ... Ms. Lisa CAPONE
44 Director Annual Giving ... Ms. Claire ST. ROMAIN

*University of Louisiana at Monroe (F)

700 University Avenue, Monroe LA 71209-0001
County: Ouachita FICE Identification: 002020
Unit ID: 159993
Telephone: (318) 342-1000 Carnegie Class: DU-Mod
FAX Number: (318) 342-5161 Calendar System: Semester
URL: www.ulm.edu
Established: 1931 Annual Undergrad Tuition & Fees (In-State): $8,554
Enrollment: 9,181 Coed
Affiliation or Control: State IRS Status: 501(c)3
Highest Offering: Doctorate
Accreditation: SC, CACREP, CAEP, CAEPN, CONST, DH, EXSC, MFCD, MT, MUS, NURSE, OT, OTA, PHAR, RAD, SP, SW

02 President ..... Dr. Nick J. BRUNO
10 Vice President for Business Affairs ..... Dr. William T. GRAVES
32 Vice President for Student Affairs ..... Mr. Camile CURRIER
05 Vice President for Academic Affairs ..... Dr. Alberto RUIZ
26 Chief Communication Officer ..... Vacant
121 VP for Info Svcs/Student Success ..... Dr. Michael CAMILLE
43 Legal/Compliance Counsel ..... Ms. Sherrye CARRADINE
13 CIO/Dean of Library ..... Mr. Thomas HOOVER
84 Director Enrollment & Scholarship ..... Dr. Robyn JORDAN
41 Director of Athletics ..... Mr. Scott MCDONALD
27 Director Marketing/Communications ..... Dr. Julia LETLOW
96 Director of Purchasing ..... Ms. Cheri PERKINS
116 Internal Audit ..... Mr. Ferando CORDOVA
49 Dean Arts/Education & Sciences ..... Dr. John PRATTE
50 Dean Business and Social Sciences ..... Dr. Ronald BERRY
67 Dean Pharmacy ..... Dr. Glenn ANDERSON
76 Interim Dean College Health Science ..... Dr. Jana SUTTON
58 Dean Graduate School ..... Dr. Sushma KRISHNAMURTHY
108 Director Assessment and Evaluation ..... Mrs. Allison L. THOMPSON
09 Exec Dir Univ Planning/Analysis ..... Ms. Kelsey BOHL
08 Director Library ..... Ms. Megan LOWE
120 Interim Director ULM Online ..... Ms. Katie DAWSON
06 Registrar ..... Mr. Anthony MALTA
37 Director Financial Aid Services ..... Mr. Ralph PERRI
85 Dir Intl Student Program and Svcs ..... Ms. DeVaria HUDSON
124 Director of University Retention ..... Mrs. Barbara MICHAELIDES
102 Executive Director Foundation ..... Mrs. Susan CHAPPELL
39 Director Residential Life ..... Ms. Tresea L. BUCKHAULTS
114 Budget Officer ..... Mrs. Gail C. PARKER
21 Controller ..... Ms. Sarah WALKER
15 Director Human Resources ..... Ms. Melissa DUCOTE
14 Director Computer Center ..... Mr. Chance W. EPPINETTE
109 Exec Dir Auxiliary Enterprises ..... Mr. Tommy WALPOLE
40 Manager University Bookstore ..... Ms. Stacey CORDELL
18 Director Physical Plant Admin ..... Mr. Robert KARAM
88 Facilities Planning Officer ..... Mr. Michael DAVIS
88 Spec Projects Ofcr/Title IX Coord ..... Ms. Treina KIMBLE
38 Director Counseling Center ..... Ms. Karen FOSTER
19 Director of University Police ..... Mr. Tom TORREGROSSA
36 Director Career Center ..... Ms. Kristin CHANDLER
88 Dir Recreational Svcs/Facilities ..... Mr. Brandon BRUSCATO
88 Technology and Comm Liaison ..... Mr. Lindsey S. WILKERSON
29 Director of Alumni Affairs ..... Ms. Melissa KIPER
100 Chief Administrative Officer ..... Vacant
04 Admin Assistant to the President ..... Ms. Kathy MASTERS
25 Chief Contract/Grants Administrator ..... Dr. John SUTHERLIN
53 Director School of Education ..... Dr. Myra LOVETT
07 Exec Dir Recruitment/Admissions ..... Ms. Sami OWENS

Xavier University of Louisiana (A)

One Drexel Drive, New Orleans LA 70125-1098
County: Orleans　FICE Identification: 002032
Unit ID: 160904
Telephone: (504) 486-7411　Carnegie Class: Masters/S
FAX Number: (504) 520-7904　Calendar System: Semester
URL: www.xula.edu
Established: 1925　Annual Undergrad Tuition & Fees: $24,348
Enrollment: 3,044　Coed
Affiliation or Control: Roman Catholic　IRS Status: 501(c)3
Highest Offering: Doctorate
Accreditation: SC, ACBSP, CACREP, CAEP, MUS, PHAR, @SP

01 President ..... Dr. C. Reynold VERRET
100 Chief of Staff ..... Ms. Patrice MERCADEL
05 Provost and Sr VP Academic Affairs ..... Dr. Anne MCCALL
10 CFO and VP Fiscal Services ..... Mr. Edward J. PHILLIPS
84 VP Enrollment Management ..... Ms. Keyana SCALES
32 Vice President Student Affairs ..... Mr. Curits WRIGHT
111 Vice President Inst Advancement ..... Ms. Gia SOUBLET
13 VP Technology Administration ..... Mr. Tony MOORE
18 VP Facility Planning & Mgmt ..... Mr. Marion BRACY
15 Assoc VP Human Resources ..... Mr. Kevin WOLF
88 Dir Special Projects Pres Ofc ..... Dr. Rae BORDEN
116 Dir Office of Internal Audits ..... Mr. William BOSTICK
101 Dir Board Relations Pres Office ..... Ms. Kris POTTHARST
20 Assoc VP Academic Affairs ..... Dr. Marguerite GIGUETTE
49 Dean College of Arts & Sciences ..... Dr. Camellia M. OKPODU
67 Dean College of Pharmacy ..... Dr. Kathleen KENNEDY
46 Assoc VP Research/Sponsored Pgms ..... Vacant
88 Asst VP & Director Title III ..... Dr. Rachel THOMAS
20 Asst Provost & COO Acad Affairs ..... Ms. Shellond CHESTER
88 Spec Asst to Provost/Scholar Dev ..... Dr. Ja'Wanda GRANT
08 Director University Library ..... Ms. Tamera HANKEN
88 Dir Ctr Adv of Teaching & Fac Dev ..... Dr. Elizabeth HAMMER
45 Int Dir Inst Rsrch/Decision Support ..... Dr. Marguerite GIGUETTE
88 Dir Ctr for Equal Jus & Hum Spir ..... Dr. David ROBINSON-MORRIS
104 Interim Dir Ctr Intercult/Intl Pgm ..... Dr. Yu JIANG
36 Director Career Services ..... Ms. Tracey JACKSON
88 Dir Inst of Blk Catholic Studies ..... Dr. Kathleen D. BELLOW
116 Dir Fin Reporting/External Audit ..... Ms. Ingenue S. SCHEXNIDER-FIELDS
25 Director Grants and Contracts ..... Ms. Shirley MOSES
88 Director Payroll ..... Ms. Joyce SANDIFER
21 Director Operations ..... Ms. Lori GIE
113 Bursar ..... Ms. Patrica VAULTZ
88 Dir Environmental Health & Safety ..... Mr. Raymond BROWN
109 Exec Dir Auxiliary Services ..... Ms. LaTonya GREEN-JONES
07 Asst VP Enrollment Mgmt ..... Ms. Jazmane BROWN
37 Director Financial Aid ..... Ms. Emily LONDON-JONES
06 University Registrar ..... Mrs. Avis STUARD
19 Asst VP/Chief of Police ..... Ms. Changamire DURALL
41 Asst VP Stdnt Affairs/Dir Athletics ..... Mr. Jason HORN
22 Chf Inclusion Officer/Dep Title IX ..... Dr. Ashley BAKER
35 Asst Dean/Student Involvement ..... Mr. Darryl KELLER
88 Asst Dean/Health and Wellness ..... Ms. Virginia PELLERIN
23 Med Dir Student Health Services ..... Dr. Robert MERCADEL
38 Director Counseling Services ..... Vacant
39 Director Residential Education ..... Vacant
42 University Chaplain ..... Fr. Etido S. JEROME
88 Senior Conduct Officer ..... Ms. Judy BRACY
29 Asst VP Alum Relations & Annual Giv ..... Ms. Kimberly REESE
102 Dir Foundation/Corp Relations ..... Dr. David ROBINSON-MORRIS
14 Deputy Chief Information Officer ..... Ms. Melva D. WILLIAMS
88 Manager Datacenter Operations ..... Mr. Karl FINDORFF
26 Director Marketing & Comm ..... Ms. Diana HERNANDEZ
105 Mgr Marketing & Digital Strategy ..... Ms. Ashley DANIELS
88 Director Data Mgmt and Analytics ..... Ms. Rebecca OSAKWE
09 Director Institutional Research ..... Dr. Clair WILKINS-GREEN
108 Dir Inst Effectiv & Assessment ..... Vacant
88 Dir Inst Compliance & Plng Init ..... Dr. Treva A. LEE
121 Exec Dir Stdnt Acad Success Office ..... Dr. Nathaniel HOLMES
106 Distance Education Coordinator ..... Dr. Karen NICHOLS
40 Manager Bookstore ..... Ms. Rose NAQUIN

MAINE

Bates College (B)

2 Andrews Road, Lewiston ME 04240-6047
County: Androscoggin　FICE Identification: 002036
Unit ID: 160977
Telephone: (207) 786-6255　Carnegie Class: Bac-A&S
FAX Number: (207) 786-6123　Calendar System: Other
URL: www.bates.edu
Established: 1855　Annual Undergrad Tuition & Fees: $53,794
Enrollment: 1,787　Coed
Affiliation or Control: Independent Non-Profit　IRS Status: 501(c)3
Highest Offering: Baccalaureate
Accreditation: EH

01 President ..... Dr. A. Clayton SPENCER
05 VP Academic Affairs/Dean of Faculty ..... Dr. Malcolm HILL
10 VP Finance & Admin/Treasurer ..... Mr. Geoffrey SWIFT
08 VP for ILS & College Librarian ..... Ms. Patricia SCHOKNECHT
111 VP Advancement ..... Ms. Sarah R. PEARSON
32 Dean of Students ..... Mr. Joshua MCINTOSH
21 Asst Vice Pres Financial Planning ..... Mr. Douglas W. GINEVAN
20 Assoc Dean of Faculty ..... Ms. Aslaug ASGEIRSDOTTIR
20 Assoc Dean of Faculty ..... Dr. Margaret A. IMBER
31 Director of Community Partnerships ..... Ms. Darby K. RAY
06 Registrar ..... Ms. Mary MESERVE
09 Dir Inst Rsch/Analysis and Planning ..... Mr. Tom MCGUINNESS
15 Asst VP Human Resources ..... Vacant
18 Dir of Facilities Svcs Operations ..... Mr. Jay PHILLIPS
88 Dir Capital Planning/Construction ..... Ms. Pamela J. WICHROSKI
07 Dean of Admissions & Financial Aid ..... Ms. Leigh WEISENBURGER
19 Director Security & Campus Safety ..... Mr. Douglass MORENCY
23 Director Student Health Support ..... Vacant
26 Asst VP Communications/Media Rels ..... Mr. Sean T. FINDLEN
37 Dir Student Financial Services ..... Ms. Wendy G. GLASS
40 Dir Bookstore/Contract Officer ..... Ms. Gail S. ST. PIERRE
36 Sr Assoc Dean of PW & Career Dev ..... Mr. Allen DELONG
91 Dir Sys Development & Integration ..... Ms. Eileen P. ZIMMERMAN
88 Director of Client Services ..... Mr. Scott TINER
41 Director of Athletics ..... Mr. Jason FEIN
42 College Chaplain ..... Ms. Brittany LONGSDORF
39 Asst Dean of Students/Housing ..... Ms. Erin FOSTER ZSIGA
102 Dir Corporate/Foundation Relations ..... Ms. Rachel WRAY
104 Assoc Dean/Dir for Global Education ..... Mr. Darren GALLANT
100 Chief of Staff ..... Mr. Michael HUSSEY
28 AVP and Chief Diversity Officer ..... Ms. Noelle CHADDOCK
88 Sr Assoc Dean Admiss/Dir Intl Enrol ..... Mr. Scott ALEXANDER
04 Exec Assistant to the President ..... Ms. Claire B. SCHMOLL
101 Secretary of the Institution/Board ..... Mr. Michael HUSSEY
45 Chief Institutional Planning Office ..... Mr. Tom MCGUINNESS

† Tuition figure is a comprehensive fees figure.

Beal College (C)

99 Farm Road, Bangor ME 04401-6831
County: Penobscot　FICE Identification: 005204
Unit ID: 160995
Telephone: (207) 947-4591　Carnegie Class: Assoc/HVT-High Trad
FAX Number: (207) 947-0208　Calendar System: Other
URL: www.bealcollege.edu
Established: 1891　Annual Undergrad Tuition & Fees: N/A
Enrollment: 248　Coed
Affiliation or Control: Proprietary　IRS Status: Proprietary
Highest Offering: Associate Degree
Accreditation: ACCSC, CAHIIM, MAC

01 President ..... Ms. Sheryl L. DEWALT
03 Chief Operations Officer ..... Mr. Stephen H. VILLETT
10 Director of Finance ..... Ms. Renee DUNTON
09 Compliance Officer ..... Mr. Jeffrey BODIMER
05 Dean of Education ..... Ms. Susan HAWES
07 Admissions Representative ..... Ms. Tasha SULLIVAN
37 Director Student Financial Aid ..... Mr. Steve VILLETT
06 Registrar ..... Ms. Stephanie MISHOU
08 Chief Librarian ..... Ms. Donna BANCROFT
18 Superintendent Physical Plant ..... Mr. Kevin HARDY
36 Director Career Services ..... Ms. Robin TARDIFF
50 Director Business Studies ..... Mr. Steve VILLETT
75 Director Welding Technology ..... Mr. Jesse CROSBY
66 Director Nursing ..... Ms. Colleen KOOB

Bowdoin College (D)

255 Maine Street, Brunswick ME 04011
County: Cumberland　FICE Identification: 002038
Unit ID: 161004
Telephone: (207) 725-3000　Carnegie Class: Bac-A&S
FAX Number: (207) 725-3123　Calendar System: Semester
URL: www.bowdoin.edu
Established: 1794　Annual Undergrad Tuition & Fees: $53,922
Enrollment: 1,816　Coed
Affiliation or Control: Independent Non-Profit　IRS Status: 501(c)3
Highest Offering: Master's
Accreditation: EH

01 President ..... Dr. Clayton ROSE
10 Sr VP Finance/Admin/Treasurer ..... Mr. Matthew ORLANDO
30 Sr VP Devel & Alumni Relations ..... Mr. Scott MEIKLEJOHN
26 Sr VP Communications/Public Affairs ..... Mr. Scott W. HOOD
13 SVP/Chief Information Officer ..... Vacant
28 SVP Inclusion & Diversity ..... Vacant
15 Vice President of Human Resources ..... Ms. Tamara D. SPOERRI
32 Dean of Student Affairs ..... Ms. Janet LOHMANN
05 Dean for Academic Affairs ..... Dr. Elizabeth MCCORMACK
07 Dean of Admissions/Financial Aid ..... Ms. E. Whitney SOULE
09 VP Inst Rsrch/Analytics Consulting ..... Dr. Christina M. FINNERAN
29 Director Alumni Relations ..... Ms. Rodie F. LLOYD
08 College Librarian ..... Ms. Marjorie HASSEN
37 Director of Student Aid ..... Mr. Michael D. BARTINI
06 Registrar ..... Ms. Martina DUNCAN
19 Executive Director of Security ..... Mr. Randall NICHOLS
36 Director of Career Planning ..... Mr. Timothy DIEHL
38 Director of Counseling Service ..... Dr. Bernie HERSHBERGER
41 Director of Athletics ..... Mr. Timothy M. RYAN
23 Director of Health Services ..... Dr. Jeffrey MAHER
18 Director Facilities Ops/Maintenance ..... Mr. Theodore R. STAM
24 Instructional Media Librarian ..... Ms. Carmen M. GREENLEE
39 Director of Residential Life ..... Ms. Meadow DAVIS
109 Dir Dining & Bookstore Services ..... Ms. Mary M. KENNEDY
35 Director of Student Activities ..... Mr. Nate HINTZE
35 Dean of Students ..... Ms. Kristina Bethea ODEJIMI
88 Co-Director of the Museum of Art ..... Ms. Anne GOODYEAR
88 Co-Director of the Museum of Art ..... Mr. Frank GOODYEAR
18 Director of Capital Projects ..... Mr. Donald V. BORKOWSKI
20 Assoc Dean for Academic Affairs ..... Dr. Charles DORN

Colby College (E)

4000 Mayflower Hill, Waterville ME 04901-8840
County: Kennebec　FICE Identification: 002039
Unit ID: 161086
Telephone: (207) 859-4000　Carnegie Class: Bac-A&S
FAX Number: (207) 859-4603　Calendar System: 4/1/4
URL: www.colby.edu
Established: 1813　Annual Undergrad Tuition & Fees: $55,210
Enrollment: 1,917　Coed
Affiliation or Control: Independent Non-Profit　IRS Status: 501(c)3
Highest Offering: Baccalaureate
Accreditation: EH

01 President ..... Dr. David A. GREENE
05 Provost and Dean of Faculty ..... Dr. Margaret T. MCFADDEN
10 Vice President Admin & CFO ..... Mr. Douglas C. TERP
111 Vice Pres College Advancement ..... Ms. Jane PHILLIPS
32 Dean of the College ..... Dr. Karlene A. BURRELL-MCRAE
26 Vice President for Communications ..... Ms. Ruth JACKSON
84 Vice Pres/Dean Admiss & Fin Aid ..... Dr. Matthew PROTO
36 VP and Dean of Student Advancement ..... Dr. C. Andrew MCGADNEY
45 Vice President of Planning ..... Mr. Brian J. CLARK
43 VP/Gen Counsel/Sec of the Col ..... Mr. Richard Y. UCHIDA
20 Assoc Provost & Dean of Faculty ..... Dr. Russell R. JOHNSON
18 Asst VP Facilities and Campus Plng ..... Ms. Minakshi M. AMUNDSEN
35 Dean of Students ..... Dr. Inge-Lise AMEER
15 Asst Vice Pres Human Resources ..... Mr. Mark CROSBY
37 Asst Dean/Director Financial Aid ..... Ms. Jill A. PIERCE
06 Registrar ..... Ms. Lindsey C. NELSON
08 Director of the Colby Libraries ..... Ms. Lareese M. HALL
88 Director of Special Programs ..... Mr. Brian BRAY
19 Director of Security ..... Mr. Robert A. WILLIAMS
13 Chief Information Officer ..... Ms. Cindy J. MITCHELL
23 Medical Director ..... Dr. Paul D. BERKNER
38 Director of Counseling Services ..... Dr. Eric S. JOHNSON
41 Director of Athletics ..... Mr. Jacob OLKKOLA
09 Dir Inst Research & Assessment ..... Ms. Rebecca H. BRODIGAN
21 Controller ..... Ms. Alicia J. GARDINER
40 Director of the Bookstore ..... Ms. Barbara C. SHUTT
104 Director of Off-Campus Study ..... Dr. Nancy DOWNEY
102 Director of Grants/Sponsored Pgms ..... Mr. William C. LAYTON, III

College of the Atlantic (F)

105 Eden Street, Bar Harbor ME 04609-1198
County: Hancock　FICE Identification: 011385
Unit ID: 160959
Telephone: (207) 288-5015　Carnegie Class: Bac-A&S
FAX Number: (207) 288-3780　Calendar System: Trimester
URL: www.coa.edu
Established: 1969　Annual Undergrad Tuition & Fees: $43,542

Enrollment: 354 Coed
Affiliation or Control: Independent Non-Profit IRS Status: 501(c)3
Highest Offering: Master's
Accreditation: EH

01 President Dr. Darron COLLINS
05 Academic Dean Dr. Ken HILL
10 Administrative Dean Ms. Maureen HARRIGAN
32 Dean of Student Life Ms. Sarah LUKE
111 Dean Institutional Advancement Ms. Lynn BOULGER
07 Dean of Admission Ms. Heather ALBERT-KNOPP
06 Registrar Ms. Judy ALLEN
08 Director of Thorndike Library Ms. Jane HULTBERG
21 Comptroller Mrs. Melissa COOK
37 Int Director of Financial Aid Ms. Linda BLACK
36 Director of Internship/Career Svcs Ms. Jill BARLOW-KELLEY
26 Public Relations Mgr/Dir Comm Mr. Rob LEVIN

Husson University (A)

1 College Circle, Bangor ME 04401-2929
County: Penobscot FICE Identification: 002043
Unit ID: 487524
Telephone: (207) 941-7000 Carnegie Class: DU-Mod
FAX Number: (207) 941-7139 Calendar System: Semester
URL: www.husson.edu
Established: 1898 Annual Undergrad Tuition & Fees: $18,170
Enrollment: 3,648 Coed
Affiliation or Control: Independent Non-Profit IRS Status: 501(c)3
Highest Offering: Doctorate
Accreditation: EH, CACREP, IACBE, NURSE, OT, PHAR, PTA

01 President Dr. Robert A. CLARK
05 Sr VP for Academic Affairs/Provost Dr. Lynne COY-OGAN
10 VP Finance & Admin/Treasurer Craig HADLEY
111 Vice President for Advancement Sara C. ROBINSON
84 VP Enrollment Management Vacant
13 AVP Information Technology Garth CORMIER
50 Dean College of Business Dr. Marie HANSEN
67 Dean College of Health and Pharmacy Dr. Rhonda WASKIEWICZ
49 Dean College of Science/Humanities Dr. Patricia BIXEL
26 Exec Director of Communications Eric GORDON
32 Dean of Student Life Pamela KROPP-ANDERSON
53 Director School of Education Barbara MOODY
07 Director of Admissions Melissa ROSENBURGI
37 Director of Financial Aid Anne TABOR
06 Registrar Nancy FENDERS
09 Director of Institutional Research Dr. Gail TUDOR
108 Director Institutional Assessment Travis E. ALLEN
106 Dir Online and Extended Learning Dr. David HAUS
36 Director Career Services James WESTHOFF
41 Director of Athletics Francis PERGOLIZZI
35 Int Assoc Dean Student Life Julie GREEN
15 Exec Director Human Resources Janet KELLE
29 Director of Alumni Relations Amanda CUMMINGS
18 Director of Maintenance Gary GEROW
08 Head Librarian Susanna PATHAK
30 Director of Advancement Services Paige HOLMES
04 Executive Assistant to President Kandi HALE
100 Chief of Staff Mary Ann HAAS
19 Director Safety and Security Ray BESSETTE
38 Director of Counseling Services Colleen OWENS
105 Director Digital Communications Matthew GREEN-HAMANN
109 Assoc Vice Pres Auxiliary Services Thomas WARREN

Institute for Doctoral Studies in the Visual Arts (B)

130 Neal Street, Portland ME 04102
County: Cumberland FICE Identification: 041888
Unit ID: 462044
Telephone: (207) 879-8757 Carnegie Class: Spec-4-yr-Other
FAX Number: N/A Calendar System: Semester
URL: www.idsva.edu
Established: 2007 Annual Graduate Tuition & Fees: N/A
Enrollment: 80 Coed
Affiliation or Control: Independent Non-Profit IRS Status: 501(c)3
Highest Offering: Doctorate; No Undergraduates
Accreditation: EH

01 President George SMITH
10 Exec Vice President/CFO Amy CURTIS
05 Vice Pres Acad Affs/Dir of School Dr. Simonetta MORO

The Landing School (C)

286 River Road, Arundel ME 04046
County: York FICE Identification: 023613
Unit ID: 161208
Telephone: (207) 985-7976 Carnegie Class: Spec 2-yr-Tech
FAX Number: (207) 985-7942 Calendar System: Semester
URL: www.landingschool.edu
Established: 1978 Annual Undergrad Tuition & Fees: $21,315
Enrollment: 54 Coed
Affiliation or Control: Independent Non-Profit IRS Status: 501(c)3
Highest Offering: Associate Degree
Accreditation: ACCSC

01 President Dr. Richard J. SCHUHMANN
05 Dean of Education Mr. Sean FAWCETT
10 Dean of Administration Ms. Kristy LANK
07 Director of Admissions Ms. Abigail JOHNSON-RUSCANSKY

Maine College of Art (D)

522 Congress St, Portland ME 04101
County: Cumberland FICE Identification: 011673
Unit ID: 161509
Telephone: (207) 699-5521 Carnegie Class: Spec-4-yr-Arts
FAX Number: (207) 775-5087 Calendar System: Semester
URL: www.meca.edu
Established: 1882 Annual Undergrad Tuition & Fees: $35,050
Enrollment: 517 Coed
Affiliation or Control: Independent Non-Profit IRS Status: 501(c)3
Highest Offering: Master's
Accreditation: EH, ART

01 President Ms. Laura FREID
03 Executive Vice President Ms. Beth ELICKER
05 VP Academic Affairs/Dean of College Mr. Ian ANDERSON
30 Vice President of Development Mr. Matthew GOETTING
06 Registrar Ms. Anne DENNISON
32 Director of Student Life Ms. Jennifer DOEBLER
07 Director of Admissions Vacant
13 Director Technology Mr. Seth CLAYTER
26 Dir of Marketing & Communications Ms. Leah IGO
10 Director of Business Services Ms. Holly HIGGINS
37 Director of Financial Aid Ms. Carri FRECHETTE
51 Director Continuing Studies Ms. Nik BSULLAK
18 Director of Facilities Mr. Douglas DOERING
08 Library Director Ms. Shiva DARBANDI
04 Executive Assistant Ms. Melissa SULLIVAN
29 Director Alumni Relations Vacant
36 Director of Artists at Work Ms. Jessica TOMLINSON
101 Secretary of the Institution/Board Ms. Heather YORK
15 Chief Human Resources Officer Ms. Elizabeth ELICKER

Maine College of Health Professions (E)

70 Middle Street, Lewiston ME 04240-7027
County: Androscoggin FICE Identification: 006305
Unit ID: 161022
Telephone: (207) 795-2840 Carnegie Class: Spec 2-yr-Health
FAX Number: (207) 795-2849 Calendar System: Semester
URL: www.mchp.edu
Established: 1891 Annual Undergrad Tuition & Fees: $12,245
Enrollment: 188 Coed
Affiliation or Control: Independent Non-Profit IRS Status: 501(c)3
Highest Offering: Baccalaureate
Accreditation: EH, ADNUR, RAD

01 President Dr. Monika BISSELL
10 Vice President of Finance Ms. Lesa ROSE
05 VP of Academic/Student Affairs Dr. Alexamder CLIFFORD
88 Dean of Medical Imaging Mrs. Judith RIPLEY
07 Director of Admissions Ms. Erica WATSON
06 Registrar/Stdnt Financial Aid Couns Mrs. Nicole DEBLOIS
66 Dean of Nursing Dr. Lynne GOTJEN
88 Instructional Designer Ms. Melissa WETHERBY
22 Title 9 Coordinator Dr. Alexander CLIFFORD

*Maine Community College System (F)

323 State Street, Augusta ME 04330-7131
County: Kennebec Identification: 666092
Unit ID: 409713
Telephone: (207) 629-4000 Carnegie Class: N/A
FAX Number: (207) 629-4048
URL: www.mccs.me.edu

01 President Mr. David DAIGLER
05 Chief Academic Officer Ms. Janet SORTOR
10 Chief Financial Officer Mrs. Pamela REMIERES-MORIN
15 Chief Human Resources Officer Mr. Robert NADEAU
13 Chief Info/Technology Officer Mr. Martin GANG

*Central Maine Community College (G)

1250 Turner Street, Auburn ME 04210-6498
County: Androscoggin FICE Identification: 005276
Unit ID: 161077
Telephone: (207) 755-5100 Carnegie Class: Assoc/MT-VT-High Trad
FAX Number: (207) 755-5491 Calendar System: Semester
URL: www.cmcc.edu
Established: 1964 Annual Undergrad Tuition & Fees (In-State): $3,720
Enrollment: 2,945 Coed
Affiliation or Control: State IRS Status: 501(c)3
Highest Offering: Associate Degree
Accreditation: EH, ADNUR

02 President Dr. Scott E. KNAPP
05 Dean Academic Affairs Ms. Betsy LIBBY
06 Registrar Ms. Sonya SAMPSON
10 Dean of Finance and General Service Mr. Richard GRIFFIN
37 Director of Financial Aid Mr. John BOWIE
103 Dean Workforce & Professional Dev Ms. Michelle HAWLEY
32 Dean of Student Services Mr. Nicholas HAMEL
13 Dean Info Tech/Chief Info Security Mr. Robert BOUCHER
26 Dean of Planning & Public Affairs Mr. Roger PHILIPPON
07 Director of Admissions Mr. Andrew MORONG
08 Head Librarian Ms. Judith MORENO
18 Chief Physical Plant Mr. Raymond MASSE
22 Affirmative Action Officer Ms. Barbara OWEN
39 Director of Housing/Athletic Dir Mr. David GONYEA
15 Dean of Human Resources Ms. Barbara OWEN
27 Director of Communications Ms. Heather B. SEYMOUR
09 Director of Institutional Research Mr. Ronald BOLSTRIDGE

*Eastern Maine Community College (H)

354 Hogan Road, Bangor ME 04401-4280
County: Penobscot FICE Identification: 005277
Unit ID: 161138
Telephone: (207) 974-4600 Carnegie Class: Assoc/HVT-Mix Trad/Non
FAX Number: (207) 974-4608 Calendar System: Semester
URL: www.emcc.edu
Established: 1966 Annual Undergrad Tuition & Fees (In-State): $3,779
Enrollment: 2,567 Coed
Affiliation or Control: State IRS Status: 501(c)3
Highest Offering: Associate Degree
Accreditation: EH, ADNUR, EMT, MAC, RAD, SURGT

02 President Dr. Lisa LARSON
05 VP of Academic Affairs Ms. Elizabeth RUSSELL
10 Dir Finance & Auxiliary Services Mr. Jerry HAYMAN
32 Dean of Student Life Dr. Brian E. DOORE
09 Dean Inst Research/Enrollment Mgmt Mr. Daniel CROCKER
88 Professional Services Coordinator Mr. Shaw WEEKS
07 Director of Admissions Ms. Stacy GREEN
15 Director of Human Resources Ms. Jody MACDONALD
08 Librarian Vacant
37 Director of Financial Aid Ms. Candace WARD
13 Dean of Communication/Info Tech Vacant
18 Dir Facilities Mgmt/Student Life Vacant
111 Dir of Institutional Advancement Ms. Jenn KHAVARI
04 Admin Asst to the President Ms. Terri ADAM
19 Director of Safety & Security Ms. Ruth DOHERTY
38 Director of Student Advising Ms. Sarah SAWYER
39 Director of Residential Life Ms. Alissa GEVAIS

*Kennebec Valley Community College (I)

92 Western Avenue, Fairfield ME 04937-1367
County: Somerset FICE Identification: 009826
Unit ID: 161192
Telephone: (207) 453-5000 Carnegie Class: Assoc/HVT-Mix Trad/Non
FAX Number: (207) 453-5010 Calendar System: Semester
URL: www.kvcc.me.edu
Established: 1970 Annual Undergrad Tuition & Fees (In-State): $3,817
Enrollment: 2,554 Coed
Affiliation or Control: State IRS Status: 501(c)3
Highest Offering: Associate Degree
Accreditation: EH, ACBSP, ADNUR, CAHIIM, COARC, EMT, MAC, OTA, PTAA, RAD

02 President Dr. Richard HOPPER
05 Academic Dean Ms. Kathy ENGLEHART
13 Dean of Tech/Chief Security Officer Mr. Kevin CASEY
32 VP of Student Affairs/Public Rels Ms. Karen NORMANDIN
10 Dean of Finance & Administration Mr. Russell BEGIN
84 Asst Dean of Enrollment Management Mr. Crichton MCKENNA
06 Registrar Mr. Christian HANSEN
30 Director of Development Ms. Michelle WEBB
37 Director of Financial Aid Ms. Kathryn BLAIR
09 Director of Institutional Research Ms. Karen GLEW
04 Admin Assistant to the President Ms. Monica BRENNAN
103 Dean of Workforce Training Ms. Elizabeth FORTIN
18 Director of Operations & Compliance Ms. Brianne PUSHOR
19 Campus Safety & Security Manager Mr. Timothy MCDONALD

*Northern Maine Community College (J)

33 Edgemont Drive, Presque Isle ME 04769-2099
County: Aroostook FICE Identification: 005760
Unit ID: 161484
Telephone: (207) 768-2810 Carnegie Class: Assoc/HVT-Mix Trad/Non
FAX Number: (207) 768-2831 Calendar System: Semester
URL: www.nmcc.edu
Established: 1961 Annual Undergrad Tuition & Fees (In-State): $3,741
Enrollment: 841 Coed
Affiliation or Control: State IRS Status: 501(c)3
Highest Offering: Associate Degree
Accreditation: EH, ACBSP, ADNUR, EMT, MAC

02 President Mr. Timothy D. CROWLEY
05 Academic Dean Dr. Michael DUNLOP
32 Dean of Students Dr. William G. EGELER
10 Dean of Finance Mr. Michael WILLIAMS
51 Asst Dean Continuing Education Ms. Leah BUCK
30 Dean of Development/College Rels Dr. Dorothy MARTIN
07 Director of Admissions Ms. Wendy BRADSTREET
06 Registrar Ms. Betsy A. HARRIS
37 Director for Financial Aid Mr. Brian HALL
39 Director of Housing & Resident Life Mr. Jon A. BLANCHARD
38 Director of Counseling Ms. Tammy NELSON
18 Dean of Tech and Facilities Mr. Barry INGRAHAM
21 Business Manager Ms. Wendy CAVERHILL
40 College Store Manager Ms. Rebecca A. MAYNARD
08 Head Librarian Ms. Gail ROY
19 College Safety/Security Officer Mr. Peter GOHEEN
15 Human Resource Coordinator Ms. Beth HUMMEL

*Southern Maine Community College (A)

2 Fort Road, South Portland ME 04106-1698
County: Cumberland FICE Identification: 005525
Unit ID: 161545
Telephone: (207) 741-5500 Carnegie Class: Assoc/MT-VT-Mix Trad/Non
FAX Number: (207) 741-5751 Calendar System: Semester
URL: www.smccme.edu
Established: 1946 Annual Undergrad Tuition & Fees (In-State): $3,770
Enrollment: 5,972 Coed
Affiliation or Control: State IRS Status: 501(c)3
Highest Offering: Associate Degree
Accreditation: EH, ACFEI, ADNUR, COARC, DIETT, EMT, MAAB, RAD

02 President/CEO .... Joseph L. CASSIDY
05 Vice President & Academic Dean .... Dr. Paul CHARPENTIER
32 Dean of Student Life/Affirm Action .... Tiffanie L. BENTLEY
84 Dean Enrollment & Student Success .... Barbara CONNER
04 Exec Assistant to the President .... Lori HALL
12 Dean of the Midcoast Campus .... James WHITTEN
10 Dean of Finance .... Robert COOMBS
13 Dean of Information Technology/CIO .... Timothy DUNNE
88 Int Dean Bus & Cmty Partnerships .... Julie CHASE
06 Assoc Dean of IR/Reg/Registrar .... Jeremy DILL
20 Assoc Dean Academics/Learning .... Holly GURNEY
88 Dean of Academic & Strategic Inits .... Dr. Matthew GOODMAN
114 Director of Budget & Financial Rpt .... Shaun GRAY
37 Director of Financial Aid Systems .... Michel LUSSIER
07 Assistant Dean of Admissions .... Amy LEE
121 Associate Dean of Student Success .... Kathleen DOAN
39 Dir of Residence Life & Stdnt Dev .... Jason SAUCIER
19 Director Campus Security .... Joseph MANHARDT
41 Associate Dean of Student Life .... Matthew RICHARDS
18 Plant Maintenance Engineer III .... James RENY
40 Manager Campus Store .... Katharine DUCHETTE
113 Business Mgr Student Billing/Bursar .... Leslie GUERRETTE
15 HR & Benefits Manager .... Denise RENY
38 Dir Counseling & Disability Svcs .... Sandra LYNHAM
27 Director of Communications .... Clarke CANFIELD
102 Dir Foundation Corporate Relations .... Vacant
105 Director Web Services .... Ken POOLEY
106 Dir Online Education/E-learning .... Michael HART

*Washington County Community College (B)

One College Drive, Calais ME 04619-9704
County: Washington FICE Identification: 009231
Unit ID: 161581
Telephone: (207) 454-1000 Carnegie Class: Assoc/HVT-High Trad
FAX Number: (207) 454-1092 Calendar System: Semester
URL: www.wccc.me.edu
Established: 1969 Annual Undergrad Tuition & Fees (In-State): $3,722
Enrollment: 372 Coed
Affiliation or Control: State IRS Status: 501(c)3
Highest Offering: Associate Degree
Accreditation: EH, MAC

02 President .... Mrs. Susan MINGO
05 Dean of Academic Affairs .... Mr. Darin MCGAW
10 Dean of Finance .... Ms. Desiree THOMPSON
15 Dir of HR/Devel/Communications .... Mrs. Tina ERSKINE
84 Dean Enrollment Mgmt/Student Svcs .... Dr. Melvin ADAMS, III
103 Dean of B & I/Workforce Dev .... Ms. Nichole SAWYER
37 Financial Aid Director .... Mrs. Linda FITZSIMMONS
39 Director of Res Life .... Ms. Karen GOOKIN
04 Exec Asst to the Pres/HR Coord .... Mrs. Robyn LEIGHTON
21 Business Manager .... Mrs. Ashley MACDONALD
18 Manager Facilities .... Mr. Richard RAMSEY
13 Information Systems Specialist .... Mr. Robert FINN
06 Assistant to the Academic Dean .... Mrs. Donna GEEL
113 Student Accounts .... Mrs. Heather SMALE
08 Dir of Library & Learning Resources .... Mrs. Elizabeth PHILLIPS
22 Instructional Technologist/AAO .... Ms. Tatiana OSMOND

*York County Community College (C)

112 College Drive, Wells ME 04090-0529
County: York FICE Identification: 031229
Unit ID: 420440
Telephone: (207) 646-9282 Carnegie Class: Assoc/MT-VT-Mix Trad/Non
FAX Number: (207) 646-9675 Calendar System: Semester
URL: www.yccc.edu
Established: 1994 Annual Undergrad Tuition & Fees (In-State): $3,630
Enrollment: 1,708 Coed
Affiliation or Control: State IRS Status: 501(c)3
Highest Offering: Associate Degree
Accreditation: EH

02 Interim President .... Dr. Scott KNAPP
05 Interim Academic Dean .... Dr. Doreen ROGAN
10 Dean of Finance & Administration .... Mr. Samuel ELLIS
32 Dean of Students .... Mr. Jason AREY
09 Assoc Dean of Inst Research .... Dr. Nicholas GILL
07 Director of Admissions .... Mr. Fred QUISTGARD
08 Director Library & Learn Resources .... Ms. Amber TATNALL
30 Special Asst to the Pres & Dev Dir .... Ms. Erin HAYE
84 Director of Enrollment Services .... Ms. Jessica MASI
26 Dir of Marketing & Communications .... Ms. Stacy CHILICKI
37 Director Financial Aid .... Mr. David DAIGLE
103 Dean Workforce Dev/Community Educ .... Vacant
13 Director of Technology .... Vacant
19 Safety & Security Manager .... Mr. Mark PARADIS
21 Business Manager .... Mr. Paul GURNEY
15 Human Resources & Benefits Manager .... Vacant
18 Manager of Facilities .... Mr. Dana PETERSEN

Maine Maritime Academy (D)

1 Pleasant Street, Castine ME 04420-0001
County: Hancock FICE Identification: 002044
Unit ID: 161299
Telephone: (207) 326-4311 Carnegie Class: Bac-Diverse
FAX Number: (207) 326-2218 Calendar System: Semester
URL: www.mainemaritime.edu
Established: 1941 Annual Undergrad Tuition & Fees (In-State): $13,478
Enrollment: 1,037 Coed
Affiliation or Control: State IRS Status: 501(c)3
Highest Offering: Master's
Accreditation: EH

01 President .... Dr. William J. BRENNAN
05 Provost .... Dr. David GARDNER
10 VP Financial & Institutional Svcs .... Ms. Petra CARVER
84 VP Stdnt Svcs/Enrollment Mgmt .... Dr. Elizabeth TRUE
111 Vice President for Advancement .... Mr. Christopher HALEY
15 Human Resource Officer .... Ms. Carrie MARGRAVE
35 Dean of Student Services .... Ms. Deidra DAVIS
36 Director of Career Services .... Mr. Joe CURTIS
07 Director of Admissions .... Ms. Kelly GUALTIERI
06 Registrar .... Ms. Christina STEPHENS
29 Director Alumni Relations .... Mr. Jeff WRIGHT
37 Director Student Financial Aid .... Ms. Kathy HEATH
38 Director Student Counseling .... Mr. Paul FERREIRA
08 Head Librarian .... Ms. Lauren GARGANI
21 Director of Fiscal Operations .... Ms. Alice HERRICK
18 Director of Facilities Management .... Mr. Peter STEWART
20 Dean of Faculty .... Dr. Susan LOOMIS
26 Director of College Relations .... Ms. Jennifer DEJOY
39 Director of Residential Life .... Ms. Amanda MANNING
09 Director of Institutional Research .... Mr. Ryan KING
04 Executive Asst to President .... Ms. Rhonda VARNEY
13 Chief Technology Officer .... Ms. Lisa ROY
19 Director of Safety & Compliance .... Mr. Peter STEWART
41 Director of Athletics .... Mr. Stephen PEED

Maine Media College (E)

70 Camden St., PO Box 200, Rockport ME 04856
County: Knox Identification: 667339
Telephone: (207) 236-8581 Carnegie Class: Not Classified
FAX Number: (207) 236-2558 Calendar System: Other
URL: www.mainemedia.edu
Established: 1973 Annual Graduate Tuition & Fees: N/A
Enrollment: N/A Coed
Affiliation or Control: Independent Non-Profit IRS Status: 501(c)3
Highest Offering: Master's; No Undergraduates
Accreditation: @EH

01 President .... Margaret A. WESTON
05 Vice Pres of Academic Affairs .... Elizabeth GREENBERG
10 Dir of Finance & Administration .... Cathi FINNEMORE

Saint Joseph's College of Maine (F)

278 Whites Bridge Road, Standish ME 04084-5236
County: Cumberland FICE Identification: 002051
Unit ID: 161518
Telephone: (207) 892-6766 Carnegie Class: Masters/L
FAX Number: (207) 893-7861 Calendar System: Semester
URL: www.sjcme.edu
Established: 1912 Annual Undergrad Tuition & Fees: $35,650
Enrollment: 2,291 Coed
Affiliation or Control: Roman Catholic IRS Status: 501(c)3
Highest Offering: Master's
Accreditation: EH, CAHIIM, NURSE, SW

01 President .... Dr. James S. DLUGOS
05 VP & Chief Officer of Learning .... Dr. Michael PARDALES
30 VP & Chief Advancement Officer .... Ms. Joanne BEAN
84 AVP & Chief Enrollment Officer .... Ms. Lynne ROBINSON
88 VP for Sponsorship & Mission .... Dr. Christopher FULLER
13 AVP Chief Information Officer .... Mr. Chip STILES
32 Dean of Campus Life .... Dr. Matthew GOODWIN
35 Director of Student Engagement .... Mr. Matthew GAWEL
06 Director Academic Records/Registrar .... Mr. Kevin PAQUETTE
08 Director Library .... Ms. Shelly DAVIS
23 Director of Student Health Center .... Ms. Sheri PIERS
15 AVP/Chief Human Resources Officer .... Ms. Kristine AVERY

Thomas College (G)

180 W River Road, Waterville ME 04901-5097
County: Kennebec FICE Identification: 002052
Unit ID: 161563
Telephone: (207) 859-1111 Carnegie Class: Masters/S
FAX Number: (207) 859-1114 Calendar System: Semester
URL: www.thomas.edu
Established: 1894 Annual Undergrad Tuition & Fees: $26,900
Enrollment: 1,802 Coed
Affiliation or Control: Independent Non-Profit IRS Status: 501(c)3
Highest Offering: Master's
Accreditation: EH, COSMA

01 President .... Ms. Laurie G. LACHANCE
03 Executive Vice President .... Mr. Bernie OUELLETTE
05 Provost .... Dr. Thomas EDWARDS
10 Sr Vice Pres Financial Affairs .... Ms. Beth B. GIBBS
111 Senior Vice Pres Advancement .... Mr. Robert M. MOORE
32 Vice President Student Affairs .. Ms. Lisa DESAUTELS-POLIQUIN
13 Vice Pres Information Services/CIO .... Mr. Christopher RHODA
44 Assistant Vice Pres Advancement .... Ms. Erin BALTES
07 Asst Vice Pres Admissions .... Ms. Wendy MARTIN
35 Dean of Students .... Ms. Hannah GLADSTONE
15 Chief Human Resources Officer .... Ms. Michelle JOLER-LABBE
37 Director Student Financial Services .... Ms. Jeannine BOSSE
29 Director Alumni/Career Services .... Mr. Corey PELLETIER
18 Director Physical Plant .... Mr. Matt BRESLIN
06 Associate Registrar .... Ms. Kelsey BRAGDON
04 Executive Asst to President .... Ms. Leta BILODEAU
41 Director of Athletics .... Ms. Sara SHAW
26 Director of Publications .... Ms. Jennifer BUKER

Unity College (H)

90 Quaker Hill Road, Unity ME 04988-9502
County: Waldo FICE Identification: 006858
Unit ID: 161572
Telephone: (207) 509-7100 Carnegie Class: Bac-Diverse
FAX Number: (207) 512-1192 Calendar System: Semester
URL: www.unity.edu
Established: 1965 Annual Undergrad Tuition & Fees: $29,160
Enrollment: 733 Coed
Affiliation or Control: Independent Non-Profit IRS Status: 501(c)3
Highest Offering: Master's
Accreditation: EH

01 President .... Dr. Melik Peter KHOURY
05 Chief Academic Officer .... Dr. Erika LATTY
10 Chief Business Officer .... Ms. Holli SILVA
30 Chief Fundraising Officer .... Ms. Erica HUTCHINSON
13 Chief Information Officer .... Mr. Bert AUDETTE
111 Chief Advancement Officer .... Ms. Erica HUTCHINSON
106 Chief Distance Education Officer .... Dr. Amy ARNETT
88 Chief Sustainability Officer .... Ms. Jennifer DEHART
101 Secretary to Board .... Ms. Christine MELANSON
04 Executive Assistant .... Ms. Jo Ann REINHORN
06 Registrar .... Ms. Kelsey GILBERT
32 Dean of Student .... Mr. Ray PHINNEY
84 Dir of DE Enrollment Management .... Mr. Christopher VIGEZZI
07 Exec Dir of Admiss & Financial Aid .... Vacant
09 Dir of Institutional Effectiveness .... Ms. Elizabeth COUGHLIN
26 Director Marketing & Communications .... Ms. Alecia SUDMEYER
41 Director of Athletics & Wellness .... Vacant
109 Director Dining Services .... Ms. Lorey DUPREY
36 Director of Career Services .... Ms. Rachel KAHN
18 Dir Facilities Management Office .... Mr. James KAUPPILA
37 Director of Student Financial Svcs .... Ms. Sherry MCCOLLETT
23 Director Student Health Services .... Ms. Anna MCGALLIARD
15 Director Human Resources .... Ms. Bethany DRIGGS
121 Dean of Academic Support .... Ms. Bobette THOMAS
08 Director Library & Information Res .... Ms. Katherine RUSSELL
88 Director Outdoor Adventure Center .... Ms. Jessica STEELE
39 Director Residence Life .... Mr. Stephen S. NASON
88 ADA Coord/Learning Specialist .... Ms. Lisa BIERRE
88 Director of Curricular Innovation .... Dr. Jennifer CARTIER
27 Assoc Dir of Media Relations .... Mr. Joel CRABTREE
19 Director of Public Safety .... Mr. Jamie COOK
88 Internship Coordinator .... Ms. Kristine MCCALLISTER
40 Manager Bookstore .... Ms. Leigh JUSKEVICE
28 Chief Diversity & Inclusion Officer .... Dr. Rana JOHNSON

*University of Maine System (I)

15 Estabrooke Drive, Orono ME 04469
County: Penobscot FICE Identification: 008012
Unit ID: 161280
Telephone: N/A Carnegie Class: N/A
FAX Number: N/A
URL: www.maine.edu

01 Chancellor .... Mr. Dannel P. MALLOY
05 Vice Chancellor Academic Affairs .... Dr. Robert NEELY
10 Vice Chanc for Finance & Treasurer .... Mr. Ryan LOW
43 University Counsel .... Mr. James B. THELEN
86 Dir of Comm/Governmental Rels .... Ms. Samantha C. WARREN
101 Clerk of the Board .... Ms. Ellen DOUGHTY
32 Chief Student Affairs Officer .... Ms. Rosa REDONNETT
13 Chief Information Officer .... Dr. David DEMERS
18 Chief General Services Officer .... Mr. M. F. Chip GAVIN
15 Chief Human Resources Officer .... Vacant
26 Exec Director of Public Affairs .... Mr. Daniel DEMERITT

*University of Maine (J)

168 College Avenue, Orono ME 04469-0001
County: Penobscot FICE Identification: 002053
Unit ID: 161253
Telephone: (207) 581-1865 Carnegie Class: DU-Higher
FAX Number: (207) 581-1604 Calendar System: Semester
URL: www.umaine.edu
Established: 1865 Annual Undergrad Tuition & Fees (In-State): $11,170
Enrollment: 11,240 Coed
Affiliation or Control: State IRS Status: 501(c)3
Highest Offering: Doctorate

Accreditation: EH, ART, CAATE, CAEPN, CLPSY, DIETD, DIETI, IPSY, MUS, NURSE, SP, SW

02	President	Dr. Joan FERRINI-MUNDY
05	Exec VP Academic Affairs/Provost	Dr. Jeffrey E. HECKER
10	Vice Chanc/Chief Financial Officer	Mr. Ryan LOW
102	Pres Univ of Maine Foundation	Dr. Jeffery N. MILLS
32	VP Student Affs/Dean of Students	Dr. Robert Q. DANA
46	Vice President for Research	Dr. Kody VARAHRAMYAN
84	Vice Price Enrollment Management	Ms. Lizzie WAHAB
88	VP Innovation/Economic Development	Mr. James WARD, IV
15	Vice President of Human Resources	Mr. Chris LINDSTROM
21	Chief Business Officer	Mrs. Claire I. STRICKLAND
20	Sr Assoc Prov/Dean Undergrad Educ	Dr. Jeffrey E. ST. JOHN
100	Chief of Staff	Ms. Kimberly WHITEHEAD
08	Dean of Libraries	Ms. Joyce V. RUMERY
13	Dir ITS Project Management Office	Ms. Robin SHERMAN
18	Exec Dir Facilities/Capital Mgt Svc	Mr. Stewart A. HARVEY
26	Sr Dir Univ Relations/Operations	Ms. Margaret A. NAGLE
109	Exec Director of Auxiliary Services	Mr. Daniel H. STURRUP
25	Director Research Administration	Mr. Christopher E. BOYNTON
06	Registrar	Ms. Kimberly D. PAGE
07	Director of Transfer Admissions	Ms. Sharon M. OLIVER
37	Int Director of Financial Aid	Ms. Connie SMITH
36	Director of Career Center	Ms. Crisanne BLACKIE
09	Director Institutional Studies	Ms. Deb ALLEN
85	Sr Director International Programs	Ms. Sarah JOUGHIN
41	Athletic Director	Mr. Ken RALPH
28	Director Equal Employment Diversity	Vacant
19	Chief Police Dept	Chief Roland J. LACROIX
29	Vice Pres Alumni Association	Mr. John N. DIAMOND
40	Assoc Director of Retail Operations	Mr. Dean GRAHAM
96	Director of Procurement Services	Mr. Kevin CARR
38	Director Student Counseling	Mr. Douglas P. JOHNSON
27	Director Strategic Communications	Vacant
49	Dean Liberal Arts & Sciences	Dr. Emily A. HADDAD
50	Dean Undergrad School of Business	Ms. Faye GILBERT
50	Dean Graduate School of Business	Dr. Michael WEBER
53	Dean Educ/Human Development	Ms. Mary GRESHAN
54	Dean Engineering	Dr. Dana N. HUMPHREY
65	Dean Natural Science/Forestry/Agric	Dr. Frederick A. SERVELLO
51	Dean Lifelong Learning	Dr. Monique M. LAROCQUE
58	Dean Graduate School	Dr. Kody VARAHRAMYAN

*University of Maine at Augusta (A)

46 University Drive, Augusta ME 04330-9410

County: Kennebec — FICE Identification: 006760 — Unit ID: 161217

Telephone: (207) 621-3000 — Carnegie Class: Bac-Diverse

FAX Number: (207) 621-3116 — Calendar System: Semester

URL: www.uma.edu

Established: 1965 — Annual Undergrad Tuition & Fees (In-State): $7,988

Enrollment: 4,014 — Coed

Affiliation or Control: State — IRS Status: 501(c)3

Highest Offering: Baccalaureate

Accreditation: EH, DA, DH, NUR

02	President	Dr. Rebecca M. WYKE
05	Vice President/Provost	Dr. Joseph S. SZAKAS
10	Interim Chief Business Officer	Mr. Buster NEEL
11	Exec Director of Admin Services	Ms. Sheri R. STEVENS
111	VP for Univ Advance/Chief of Staff	Ms. Joyce BLANCHARD
84	VP Enrollment Mgmt & Marketing	Mr. Jonathan HENRY
08	Int Director of UMA Library Svcs	Ms. Stacey BROWNLIE
32	Dean of Students	Ms. Sheri FRASER
107	Dean College of Prof Studies	Ms. Brenda MCALEER
07	AVP Admission/Stdnt Financial Svcs	Ms. Brandy FINCK
06	Registrar	Ms. Ann CORBETT
15	Director of Human Resources	Ms. Amie PARKER
18	Director of Facilities/Proj Mgr	Vacant
38	Director of Counseling	Ms. Jennifer MASCARO
121	Director of Advising	Ms. Tricia DYER
40	Director Bookstore	Mr. Jerry GARTHOFF
26	Exec Dir Planning & Communications	Ms. Domna GIATAS
49	Dean College of Arts & Sciences	Mr. Greg FAHY
04	Admin Assistant to the President	Ms. Renee SHERMAN
35	Director of Student Life/Athletics	Ms. Jennifer LANEY
09	Director of Institutional Research	Dr. Hirosuke HONDA
29	Dir Annual Giving/Alumni Relations	Ms. Staci WARREN

*University of Maine at Farmington (B)

224 Main Street, Farmington ME 04938-1911

County: Franklin — FICE Identification: 002040 — Unit ID: 161226

Telephone: (207) 778-7000 — Carnegie Class: Bac-Diverse

FAX Number: (207) 778-7247 — Calendar System: Semester

URL: www.umf.maine.edu

Established: 1864 — Annual Undergrad Tuition & Fees (In-State): $9,118

Enrollment: 2,080 — Coed

Affiliation or Control: State — IRS Status: 501(c)3

Highest Offering: Master's

Accreditation: EH, CAEP

02	President	Dr. Edward SERNA
05	Assoc Provost/Dean of Education	Dr. Katherine YARDLEY
10	Exec Dir Finance & Administration	Ms. Laurie A. GARDNER
32	Vice Pres Student & Community Svcs	Ms. Christine WILSON
84	Vice Pres for Enrollment	Vacant
04	Admin Assistant to the President	Ms. Amy PERREAULT
88	Sustainability Coordinator	Dr. Lucas C. KELLETT
20	Assoc Provost	Dr. Steven QUACKENBUSH
92	Director of Honors Program	Dr. John D. MESSIER
121	Dir of Learning Assistance Center	Ms. Jessica BERRY
37	Financial Aid Director	Mr. Ronald P. MILLIKEN
21	Director of Finance	Ms. Kathleen P. FALCO
27	Assoc Director of Media Relations	Ms. April C. MULHERIN
13	IT Operations Manager	Ms. Nicole WOODHOUSE
41	Dir Athletics/Fitness & Recreation	Ms. Julie A. DAVIS
88	Dir Fitness & Recreation Center	Mr. Ben WHITE
35	Director Student Life	Mr. Brian K. UFFORD
18	Director of Facilities Management	Mr. Jeffrey MCKAY
19	Director of Public Safety	Mr. Brock E. CATON
26	Dir of Marketing and Communications	Ms. Ryan MASTRANGELO
07	Director of Admissions	Ms. Lisa ELLRICH
09	Director of Institutional Research	Mr. Nathan GRANT
111	Director of Advancement	Mr. Marc GLASS

*University of Maine at Fort Kent (C)

23 University Drive, Fort Kent ME 04743-1292

County: Aroostook — FICE Identification: 002041 — Unit ID: 161235

Telephone: (207) 834-7500 — Carnegie Class: Bac-Diverse

FAX Number: (207) 834-7503 — Calendar System: Semester

URL: www.umfk.maine.edu

Established: 1878 — Annual Undergrad Tuition & Fees (In-State): $8,115

Enrollment: 1,760 — Coed

Affiliation or Control: State — IRS Status: 501(c)3

Highest Offering: Baccalaureate

Accreditation: EH, IACBE, NURSE

02	President	Dr. Tex BOGGS
05	Vice President Academic Affairs	Vacant
10	Chief Business Officer	Mrs. Pamela ASHBY
32	Dean of Students	Mr. Matthew MORRIN
84	Exec Dir of Enrollment Management	Mr. Jason TOWERS
26	Dir Marketing & Communications	Ms. Kerri WATSON-BLAISDELL
15	HR Business Partner	Ms. Debra PELLETIER
31	Dean of Community Education	Mr. Scott A. VOISINE
08	Dir of Information Svcs/Library	Ms. Leslie E. KELLY
66	Nursing Division Director	Ms. Erin SOUCY
37	Director of Financial Aid	Ms. Lisa MICHAUD
18	Director of Facilities Management	Mr. Brian C. SCHAEFER
29	Director Alumni Relations	Vacant
07	Director of Admissions	Ms. Jill CAIRNS
121	Assistant Dean of Student Success	Vacant
09	Assoc Dir of Institutional Research	Vacant
30	Development Officer	Ms. Shannon LUGDON
06	Registrar	Mr. Alexander MYHRE
04	Admin Assistant to the President	Ms. Janna GREGORY
39	Dir Resident Life/Student Housing	Mr. Javier GONZALEZ
41	Athletic Director	Mr. Garett SHERMAN

*University of Maine at Machias (D)

116 O'Brien Avenue, Machias ME 04654-1397

Telephone: (207) 255-1200 — FICE Identification: 002055

Accreditation: &EH, NRPA

*University of Maine at Presque Isle (E)

181 Main Street, Presque Isle ME 04769-2888

County: Aroostook — FICE Identification: 002033 — Unit ID: 161341

Telephone: (207) 768-9400 — Carnegie Class: Bac-Diverse

FAX Number: (207) 768-9608 — Calendar System: Semester

URL: www.umpi.edu

Established: 1903 — Annual Undergrad Tuition & Fees (In-State): $8,035

Enrollment: 1,414 — Coed

Affiliation or Control: State — IRS Status: 501(c)3

Highest Offering: Baccalaureate

Accreditation: EH, MLTAD, PTAA, SW

02	President & Provost	Dr. Raymond J. RICE
10	Campus Business Officer	Mr. Benjamin SHAW
49	Dean of Arts and Sciences	Dr. Jason JOHNSTON
107	Dean of Professional Programs	Ms. Barbara BLACKSTONE
111	Exec Dir for University Advancement	Dr. Debbie ROARK
84	Executive Director of Enroll Mgmt	Mr. Jason TOWERS
32	Dean of Students	Mr. Matthew MORRIN
35	Associate Dean of Students	Ms. Mary Kate BARBOSA
07	Director of Admissions	Ms. Tricia ARMSTRONG
06	Registrar	Mr. Alexander MYHRE
15	Labor Relations Mgr UMPI HR Leader	Ms. Dorianna PRATT
08	Director of Library Services	Mr. Roger GETZ
36	Director of Career Preparation	Ms. Nicole FOURNIER
39	Associate Director Residence Life	Mr. Donald GIBSON
41	Director of Athletics	Mr. Daniel C. KANE
26	Director Marketing & Communications	Ms. Rachel RICE
37	Director Financial Services	Mr. Christopher BELL
18	Director of Facilities Management	Mr. Joe MOIR
19	Director Security/Safety	Mr. Frederick A. THOMAS
04	Special Assistant to the President	Ms. Lisa M. SMITH
29	Director Alumni Affairs	Mr. Craig C. CORMIER

*University of Southern Maine (F)

96 Falmouth Street, PO Box 9300, Portland ME 04101-9300

County: Cumberland — FICE Identification: 002054 — Unit ID: 161554

Telephone: (207) 780-4141 — Carnegie Class: Masters/L

FAX Number: (207) 780-4933 — Calendar System: Semester

URL: www.usm.maine.edu

Established: 1878 — Annual Undergrad Tuition & Fees (In-State): $8,918

Enrollment: 7,794 — Coed

Affiliation or Control: State — IRS Status: 501(c)3

Highest Offering: Doctorate

Accreditation: EH, ART, CAATE, CACREP, CAEPT, EXSC, LAW, MUS, NAIT, NURSE, OT, PH, SW

02	President	Dr. Glenn T. CUMMINGS
05	Provost/VPAA	Dr. Jeannine UZZI
11	Chief Operating Officer	Ms. Nancy D. GRIFFIN
29	VP Alumni/Public Engagement	Ms. Corey HASCALL
15	VP Human Resources	Ms. Natalie JONES
32	VP for Student Affairs	Mr. David ROUSSEL
84	VP Enrollment Mgmt & Marketing	Mr. Jared CASH
109	VP Corp Engagement/Auxiliary Svcs	Ms. Jeanne PAQUETTE
10	Chief Business Officer	Mr. Alexander PORTEOUS
102	President USM Foundation	Ms. Ainsely WALLACE
09	Sr Assoc Institutional Research	Ms. Patricia DAVIS
18	Exec Director Facilities Management	Mr. John SOUTHER
08	University Librarian	Mr. David NUTTY
108	Director Academic Assessment Ctr	Ms. Susan L. KING
23	Director of Health Services	Ms. Lisa BELANGER
26	Executive Director Public Affairs	Mr. Bob STEIN
37	Director Student Financial Services	Mr. Keith DUBOIS
20	Director Academic Advising	Ms. Elizabeth HIGGINS
58	Director Graduate Studies	Mr. Andrew KING
07	Director of Admissions	Ms. Rachel MORALES
06	Director of Registration	Ms. Karin PIRES
106	Director Online Teaching/Learning	Mr. Paul COCHRANE
41	Director of Athletics	Mr. Al BEAN
39	Director of Residential Life	Ms. Christina LOWERY
40	Director of USM Bookstore	Ms. Catherine JOHNSON
61	Interim Dean School of Law	Mr. Dmitry BAM
50	Dean College of Mgmt/Human Svcs	Dr. Joanne WILLIAMS
72	Dean College of Sci/Tech & Health	Dr. Jeremy QUALLS
49	Dean Arts/Humanities/Soc Sci	Dr. Adam TUCHINSKY
12	Int Dean Lewiston-Auburn College	Dr. Brian TOY
88	Director of Community-Based Lrng	Dr. Susan MCWILLIAMS
94	Director of Women & Gender Studies	Dr. Rose CLEARY
27	Director of Marketing	Ms. Traci ST. PIERRE
46	Director of Research	Ms. Kris SAHONCHIK

University of New England (G)

11 Hills Beach Road, Biddeford ME 04005-9988

County: York — FICE Identification: 002050 — Unit ID: 161457

Telephone: (207) 283-0171 — Carnegie Class: DU-Higher

FAX Number: (207) 282-6379 — Calendar System: Semester

URL: www.une.edu

Established: 1831 — Annual Undergrad Tuition & Fees: $37,620

Enrollment: 8,281 — Coed

Affiliation or Control: Independent Non-Profit — IRS Status: 501(c)3

Highest Offering: Doctorate

Accreditation: EH, ACBSP, ANEST, ARCPA, CAATE, DENT, DH, EXSC, NUR, OSTEO, OT, PH, PHAR, PTA, SW

01	President	Dr. James HERBERT
04	Executive Asst to the President	Ms. Holly HAMMOND NASS
05	Provost/Sr VP Academic Affairs	Dr. Joshua HAMILTON
06	Registrar	Ms. Kathy DAVIS
07	VP of University Admissions	Mr. Scott STEINBERG
26	VP for Strategy & Communications	Dr. Ellen BEAULIEU
18	Asst Vice President for Planning	Mr. Alan THIBEAULT
10	Senior Vice Pres Finance and Admin	Ms. Nicole TRUFANT
111	Vice Pres Institutional Advancement	Mr. Bill CHANCE
32	Asst VP of Student Affairs	Ms. Jennifer DEBURRO
21	Assoc VP of Finance	Mr. Richard KELLEY
15	Associate VP Human Resources	Vacant
82	VP Global Affairs	Dr. Anouar MAJID
121	Associate Provost Student Success	Dr. Dennis LEIGHTON
20	Associate Provost Academic Affairs	Dr. Michael SHELDON
106	Dean College of Grad/Prof Studies	Dr. Martha WILSON
49	Dean College Arts & Sciences	Dr. Jonathan MILLEN
76	Dean Health Professions	Dr. Karen PARDUE
63	Dean College Osteopathic Medicine	Dr. Jane CARREIRO
67	Dean College of Pharmacy	Dr. Robert MCCARTHY
52	Dean of College Dental Medicine	Dr. Jon RYDER
62	Dean Library Services	Mr. Andrew GOLUB
46	Associate Provost Research/Scholars	Dr. Karen HOUSEKNECHT
110	Assistant VP Inst Advancement	Ms. Amy HAILE
09	Director for Institutional Research	Ms. Kelly DUARTE
19	Director Campus Safety & Security	Mr. Jeffrey GREENE
45	Associate Director for Planning	Mr. Gregory HOGAN
08	Director Reference Services	Ms. Barbara SWARTZLANDER
28	Dir Multicultural Student Affairs	Ms. Erica ROUSSEAU
25	Director Sponsored Programs	Mr. Nicholas GERE
38	Executive Director SAC	Mr. Hahna PATTERSON
113	Asst VP Student Financial Services	Mr. Paul HENDERSON
100	Senior Advisor to President	Mr. John TUMIEL
104	Director Study Abroad/Global Educ	Ms. Emily DRAGON
13	Chief Info Technology Officer (CIO)	Mr. Craig LOFTUS
36	Director Career Services	Mr. Jeff NEVERS
102	Sr Dir Foundation/Corp Relations	Ms. Ellen RIDLEY
41	Athletic Director	Ms. Heather DAVIS
22	Title IX Coordinator	Ms. Angela SHAMBARGER
39	Assoc Dir for Housing/Resident Life	Mr. Anthony MONTALBANO
44	Associate Director Annual Giving	Ms. Anne WASHBURNE
108	Assoc Director of Assessment	Ms. Jennifer MANDEL
88	Director of Financial Planning	Mr. Matthew KOGUT
88	Dir Fin Compl/Finance & Admin	Mr. Jeffery CROCKER

MARYLAND

Allegany College of Maryland (A)

12401 Willowbrook Road, SE,
Cumberland MD 21502-2596
County: Allegany FICE Identification: 002057
Unit ID: 161688
Telephone: (301) 784-5000 Carnegie Class: Assoc/HVT-High Trad
FAX Number: (301) 784-5050 Calendar System: Semester
URL: www.allegany.edu
Established: 1961 Annual Undergrad Tuition & Fees (In-District): $4,220
Enrollment: 2,717 Coed
Affiliation or Control: Local IRS Status: 501(c)3
Highest Offering: Associate Degree
Accreditation: M, ADNUR, COARC, CSHSE, DH, MAC, MLTAD, OTA, PTAA

01 President .... Dr. Cynthia S. BAMBARA
05 Sr Vice Pres Instructional Affairs .... Dr. Kurt HOFFMAN
10 Vice President Finance/Admin .... Ms. Christina KILDUFF
30 VP Advancement/Community Rels .... Mr. David R. JONES

Ana G. Mendez University Capital Area Campus (B)

11006 Veirs Mill Road, Wheaton MD 20902
Telephone: (301) 949-2224 Identification: 770924
Accreditation: &M

† Branch campus of Universidad Ana G. Mendez, Rio Piedras, PR

Anne Arundel Community College (C)

101 College Parkway, Arnold MD 21012-1895
County: Anne Arundel FICE Identification: 002058
Unit ID: 161767
Telephone: (410) 777-2222 Carnegie Class: Assoc/HT-High Trad
FAX Number: (410) 777-2489 Calendar System: Semester
URL: www.aacc.edu
Established: 1961 Annual Undergrad Tuition & Fees (In-District): $4,670
Enrollment: 13,354 Coed
Affiliation or Control: State/Local IRS Status: 501(c)3
Highest Offering: Associate Degree
Accreditation: M, ACFEI, ADNUR, ARCPA, CAHIIM, CSHSE, EMT, MAC, MLTAD, PTAA, RAD, SURGT

01 President .... Dr. Dawn S. LINDSAY
05 VP for Learning .... Dr. Michael H. GAVIN
10 VP Learning Resources Management .... Ms. Melissa A. BEARDMORE
84 VP for Learner Support Services .... Ms. Felicia L. PATTERSON
106 Dean of Virtual Campus .... Dr. Colleen EISENBEISER
20 Associate VP for Learning .... Dr. Alycia MARSHALL
30 Director of Development .... Mr. Vollie D. MELSON
89 Dean of College Transitions .... Ms. Deneen DANGERFIELD
76 Dean School Health/Wellness/Phys Ed .... Dr. Elizabeth H. APPEL
66 Director of Nursing .... Ms. Beth Anne BATTURS
49 Dean School of Liberal Arts .... Dr. Alicia MORSE
50 Dean School of Business & Law .... Ms. Karen COOK
81 Dean School of Science & Technology .... Dr. Lance BOWEN
51 Dean Sch Cont Educ & Workforce Dev .... Dr. Kip KUNSMAN
22 Controller .... Ms. Martha D. ROTHSCHILD
21 Executive Director of Finance .... Mr. Andrew P. LITTLE
13 Chief Technology Officer/Info Svcs .... Ms. Shirin M. GOODARZI
08 Director of Library .... Ms. Cynthia K. STEINHOFF
06 Registrar .... Ms. Nancy A. BEIER
09 Dean Planning/Research/Inst Assess .... Ms. Kathy E. BOLTON
15 Exec Director of Human Resources .... Ms. Suzanne L. BOYER
26 Exec Dir Strategic Communications .... Mr. Dan B. BAUM
37 Director of Financial Aid .... Ms. Tara CAREW
07 Dir Admissions/Enroll Development .... Ms. Cassandra S. MOORE
11 Exec Dir of Administrative Services .... Mr. Maury L. CHAPUT, JR.
32 Asst Dean Student Devel & Success .... Dr. Tiffany F. BOYKIN
07 Dean Enrollment Services .... Dr. John F. GRABOWSKI
124 Dean of Student Success .... Ms. Bonnie J. GARRETT
35 Director of Student Engagement .... Mr. Leon THOMAS, III
22 Federal Compliance Officer .... Ms. Karen COOK
40 College Bookstore Manager .... Mr. Steven M. PEGG
19 Director Public Safety .... Mr. Sean KAPFHAMMER
96 Director Purchasing/Contracting .... Ms. Melanie L. SCHERER
30 Director of Development .... Ms. Wendy THOMAS
23 Coordinator Health Services .... Ms. Beth A. MAYS
41 Athletic Director .... Mr. Duane HERR
07 Assistant Director Admissions .... Mr. Brian O'NEIL
94 Coordinator of Women's Studies .... Dr. Suzanne J. SPOOR
88 Director of Environmental Center .... Dr. M. Stephen AILSTOCK
88 Director Center Study Local Issues .... Dr. Daniel D. NATAF
88 Dir Homeland Sec/Crim Justice Inst .... Dr. Tyrone POWERS
53 Director TEACH Institute .... Ms. Stacie BURCH
88 Director Hosp/Cul Arts/Tourism Inst .... Ms. Mary Ellen MASON
38 Coord Institute for the Future .... Mr. Steven T. HENICK
88 Dir Sarbanes Center/Pub & Cmty Svc .... Ms. Cathleen H. DOYLE
28 Chief Diversity Officer .... Dr. Deidra L. DENNIE
04 Executive Asst to President .... Ms. Monica RAUSA WILLIAMS
18 Dir Facilities Plng & Construction .... Mr. James TAYLOR
25 Director Sponsored Programs .... Ms. Susan GALLAGHER
101 Secretary of the Institution/Board .... Ms. Tracie THOMAS
103 Director Workforce Development .... Ms. Sonja GLADWIN
105 Director Web Services .... Ms. Amanda SACHS

Bais HaMedrash & Mesivta of Baltimore (D)

6823 Old Pimlico Road, Baltimore MD 21209
County: Baltimore FICE Identification: 041884
Unit ID: 476601
Telephone: (410) 486-0006 Carnegie Class: Spec-4-yr-Faith
FAX Number: (410) 602-9738 Calendar System: Semester
Established: 1997 Annual Undergrad Tuition & Fees: $13,000
Enrollment: 77 Male
Affiliation or Control: Independent Non-Profit IRS Status: 501(c)3
Highest Offering: First Talmudic Degree
Accreditation: RABN

01 Rosh Yeshiva .... Rabbi Chaim COHEN

Baltimore City Community College (E)

2901 Liberty Heights Avenue, Baltimore MD 21215-7893
County: Baltimore City FICE Identification: 002061
Unit ID: 161864
Telephone: (410) 462-8300 Carnegie Class: Assoc/MT-VT-High Trad
FAX Number: (410) 462-7795 Calendar System: Semester
URL: www.bccc.edu
Established: 1947 Annual Undergrad Tuition & Fees (In-State): $3,146
Enrollment: 4,188 Coed
Affiliation or Control: State IRS Status: 501(c)3
Highest Offering: Associate Degree
Accreditation: M, ACBSP, ADNUR, CAHIIM, COARC, DH, PTAA, SURGT

01 President .... Dr. Debra L. MCCURDY
10 VP Business & Finance .... Vacant
32 VP for Student Affairs .... Dr. Stanley SINGLETON
05 VP Academic Affairs .... Vacant
103 VP Workforce Dev/Cont Education .... Mr. Michael THOMAS
84 Dean of Enrollment Management .... Ms. Sylvia ROCHESTER
46 AVP Research & Strategic Planning .... Ms. Becky BURRELL
111 VP Advance/Strategic Partnership .... Ms. Dawn KIRSTAETTER
18 Dir Facilities/Plng/Operations .... Vacant
21 Controller/Chief of Accounting .... Ms. Eileen WAITSMAN
37 Director Student Financial Aid .... Vacant
13 Chief Information Tech Officer .... Mr. Stephan A. BYAM
08 Director Library/Media Services .... Mr. David-Xudong JIN
15 Director of HR .... Ms. Michelle WILLIAMS
09 Director of Institutional Research .... Ms. Eileen HAWKINS
96 Chief Procurement Officer .... Vacant
04 Executive Asst to the President .... Ms. Valerie LEVERETTE
07 Director of Admissions .... Ms. Kijaffe BUTLER
106 Director of E-Learning .... Dr. Diana ZILBERMAN
19 Director of Public Safety .... Mr. Leonard WILLIS
41 Director Intercollegiate Athletics .... Dr. Darryl POPE
86 Director Government Relations .... Vacant
29 Director Alumni Relations .... Ms. Marie HINTON
43 General Counsel/Chief of Staff .... Ms. Maria E. RODRIGUEZ
30 Director of Development .... Mr. Paul BECKHAM
20 Dean of Academic Operations .... Dr. Daphane SNOWDEN

Capitol Technology University (F)

11301 Springfield Road, Laurel MD 20708-9759
County: Prince Georges FICE Identification: 001436
Unit ID: 162061
Telephone: (301) 369-2800 Carnegie Class: Spec-4-yr-Other Tech
FAX Number: (301) 953-1442 Calendar System: Semester
URL: www.captechu.edu
Established: 1927 Annual Undergrad Tuition & Fees: $25,540
Enrollment: 736 Coed
Affiliation or Control: Independent Non-Profit IRS Status: 501(c)3
Highest Offering: Doctorate
Accreditation: M, IACBE

01 President .... Dr. Bradford L. SIMS
05 Vice President for Academic Affairs .... Vacant
10 Int VP Finance/Administration/COO .... Kathleen WERNER
84 Sr VP for Enrollment Mgmt & Mktg .... Dianne M. O'NEILL
20 Dean Academics/AVP Acad Assessment .... Dr. Nayef ABU-AGEEL
32 VP Student Engagement & Univ Devel .... Melinda A. BUNNELL-RHYNE
54 Chair Electrical Engineering .... Dr. Nayef ABU-AGEEL
06 Director of Registration & Records .... Greg HUGHES
08 Dir Library/Information Literacy .... Allen EXNER
15 VP Human Resources/Administration .... Katy DEHART
26 Asst Director Communications .... Cynthia GROSS
30 Director Development/Alumni .... Vacant
07 Director Admissions .... Vacant
37 Director of Financial Aid .... Kim WITTLER
51 Director of Continuing Education .... Vacant
18 Director of Facilities .... Casar DE LA ROSA
04 Executive Admin Asst to President .... Aletha R. WADE
103 Director of Career Services .... Constance HARRINGTON
106 Dir Online Education/E-learning .... Kim UDEH
13 Director Information Services .... Doug EDDY
39 Dir Student Life & Residential .... Brandi MCKEE

Carroll Community College (G)

1601 Washington Road, Westminster MD 21157-6913
County: Carroll FICE Identification: 031007
Unit ID: 405872
Telephone: (410) 386-8000 Carnegie Class: Assoc/HT-High Trad
FAX Number: (410) 386-8181 Calendar System: Semester
URL: www.carrollcc.edu
Established: 1993 Annual Undergrad Tuition & Fees (In-District): $4,128
Enrollment: 3,009 Coed
Affiliation or Control: Local IRS Status: 501(c)3
Highest Offering: Associate Degree
Accreditation: M, EMT, PTAA

01 President .... Dr. James D. BALL
11 Exec Vice Pres Administration .... Mr. Alan M. SCHUMAN
05 Vice Pres of Acad & Student Affs .... Dr. Rosalie MINCE
45 Vice Pres of Plng/Mktg & Assessment .... Dr. Craig A. CLAGETT
51 Vice Pres of Cont Educ/Training .... Ms. Libby TROSTLE
111 Exec Dir Inst Advance/College Fndn .... Mr. Steven WANTZ
26 Chief Communications Officer .... Ms. Patricia CARROLL
50 Div Chair Business & Technology .... Mr. Robert BROWN
60 Div Chair Communication Arts .... Ms. Siobhan WRIGHT
76 Div Chair Allied Health/Nursing .... Dr. Nancy PERRY
83 Div Chair Social Sciences/Health .... Ms. Sharon BRUNNER
54 Div Chair Mathematics/Engineer .... Ms. Brianna MCGINNIS
81 Div Chair Sciences .... Dr. Raza KHAN
53 Div Chair Educ & Trans Studies .... Ms. Susan SIES
79 Div Chair Humanities/Art/Music .... Dr. Robert YOUNG
57 Div Chair Applied & Theater Arts .... Mr. Scott GORE
32 Dean of Student Affairs .... Dr. Kristie CRUMLEY
06 Sr Dir of Records/Stdnt Data Analy .... Ms. Laurie SHIELDS
121 Sr Dir Advising/Ret/Student Place .... Dr. April HERRING
07 Sr Director Enrollment Development .... Ms. Candace EDWARDS
28 Compliance/Integrity Judge Advocate .... Mr. Jonathan ROWE
37 Director of Financial Aid .... Mr. John GAY
36 Director Career Development .... Ms. Barb GREGORY
35 Director of Student Life .... Ms. Jennifer MILAM
08 Dir Library/Media Services .... Mr. Jeremy GREEN
106 Director Online Learning .... Ms. Andrea GRAVELLE
27 Sr Director Marketing .... Dr. Maya DEMISHKEVICH
09 Director Institutional Research .... Dr. Natalie CRESPO
103 Sr Dir Corporate Svcs/Workforce Dev .... Ms. Janet LADD
45 Dir CET Research/Strategic Analysis .... Ms. Jean MARRIOTT
88 Sr Dir Career & Continuing Educ .... Mr. Steven BERRY
55 Director Lifelong Learning .... Ms. Kathy MAYAN
105 Director of Network & Tech Services .... Ms. Patti DAVIS
21 Director Fiscal Affairs .... Mr. Timothy LEAGUE
15 Director Human Resources .... Ms. Lisa KUHN
18 Director Facilities Plng Management .... Ms. Lisa AUGHENBAUGH
19 Chief of Public Safety & Security .... Vacant
88 Assoc VP Program Dev/Partnerships .... Dr. Melody MOORE
22 Director Disability Support Svcs .... Mr. Joseph TATELA
20 Assoc VP Curriculum & Assessment .... Dr. Michelle KLOSS
04 Executive Associate to President .... Ms. Marianne ANDERSON
41 Athletic Director .... Mr. Bill KELVEY

Cecil College (H)

One Seahawk Drive, North East MD 21901-1999
County: Cecil FICE Identification: 008308
Unit ID: 162104
Telephone: (410) 287-6060 Carnegie Class: Assoc/HT-High Trad
FAX Number: (410) 287-1026 Calendar System: Semester
URL: www.cecil.edu
Established: 1968 Annual Undergrad Tuition & Fees (In-District): $4,500
Enrollment: 2,468 Coed
Affiliation or Control: State/Local IRS Status: 501(c)3
Highest Offering: Associate Degree
Accreditation: M, ADNUR, EMT, MAC, PTAA

01 President .... Dr. Mary WAY BOLT
05 Vice President Academic Programs .... Dr. Christy DRYER
10 Vice President Finance .... Mr. Daniel THOMPSON
32 VP Students/Enrollment Management .... Dr. Kimberly JOYCE
13 CIO .... Mr. Maurice TYLER
111 VP Cmty/Govt Rels & College Advance .... Ms. Chris Ann SZEP
15 Executive Director Human Resources .... Ms. Lauren FLECK
20 Dean of Academic Programs .... Vacant
31 Dean of Career/Community Education .... Mr. Miles DEAN
66 Dean Nursing/Allied Hlth/Hlth Sci .... Ms. Nancy NORMAN-MARZELLA
49 Acting Dean Arts & Sciences .... Dr. Veronica DOUGHERTY
18 Director of Facilities .... Ms. Lonette DAVIS
37 Director of Financial Aid Services .... Ms. Amanda SOLECKI
26 Director of Marketing .... Ms. Amy HENDERSON
84 Director of Enrollment Management .... Vacant
93 Director Minority Student Services .... Ms. Laney HOXTER
09 Director of Institutional Research .... Mr. Dan STOICESCU
06 Director of Records & Registration .... Ms. S. Tomeka SWAN
08 Director of Library Services .... Vacant
41 Director Athletics .... Mr. Ed DURHAM
29 Coordinator Alumni Relations .... Ms. Mary MOORE
04 Exec Assistant to the President .... Ms. Sherry HARTMAN
21 Controller .... Mr. Craig WHITEFORD
19 Director Security/Safety .... Mr. John CAPOZZOLI

Chesapeake College (I)

PO Box 8, 1000 College Circle, Wye Mills MD 21679-0008
County: Queen Annes FICE Identification: 004650
Unit ID: 162168
Telephone: (410) 822-5400 Carnegie Class: Assoc/MT-VT-High Trad
FAX Number: (410) 827-5800 Calendar System: Semester
URL: www.chesapeake.edu
Established: 1965 Annual Undergrad Tuition & Fees (In-District): $3,818
Enrollment: 2,189 Coed
Affiliation or Control: State/Local IRS Status: 501(c)3
Highest Offering: Associate Degree
Accreditation: M, ADNUR, EMT, PTAA, RAD, SURGT

01 President .... Dr. Clifford COPPERSMITH

05 Vice President for Academics .... Mr. David HARPER
11 VP for Administrative Services ....Mr. Tim JONES
106 Dean for Teaching and Learning ....Ms. Chandra M. GIGLIOTTI
20 Dean for Faculty ....Dr. Juliet SMITH
32 Dean of Students ....Vacant
18 Director of Facilities ....Mr. Paul RENSHAW
15 Director of Human Resources .... Ms. Susan A. CIANCHETTA
37 Director of Financial Aid ....Ms. Princess WILLIAMS
09 Dir Inst Planning/Research & Assmnt ....Mr. Vincent MARUGGI
26 Director of Public Information ....Ms. Marcie A. MOLLOY
06 Registrar .... Mr. James A. DAVIDSON
84 Dean for Enrollment & Advising ....Ms. Joan M. SEITZER
101 Exec Assoc to President/Board ....Ms. Kate MAXWELL

College of Southern Maryland (A)

PO Box 910, La Plata MD 20646-0910

County: Charles FICE Identification: 002064

Unit ID: 162122

Telephone: (301) 934-2251 Carnegie Class: Assoc/HT-High Trad

FAX Number: (301) 934-7698 Calendar System: Semester

URL: www.csmd.edu

Established: 1958 Annual Undergrad Tuition & Fees (In-District): $3,825

Enrollment: 7,201 Coed

Affiliation or Control: Local IRS Status: 501(c)3

Highest Offering: Associate Degree

Accreditation: M, ACBSP, ADNUR, EMT, MLTAD, PNUR, PTAA

01 President .... Dr. Maureen MURPHY
05 Vice Pres Academic Affairs ....Dr. Eileen ABEL
84 VP Student Equity and Success ....Dr. Tracy HARRIS
103 VP Continuing Educ & Workforce Dev ....Vacant
10 VP Financial & Admin Services .... Mr. Tony JERNIGAN
11 VP Operations and Planning .... Dr. William COMEY
111 VP Advancement & Comm Engagement .. Ms. Michelle GOODWIN
43 Vice President/General Counsel ....Mr. Craig PATENAUDE
20 Assoc VP Academic Affairs ....Mr. Mitchell LEVY
09 Assoc VP Plng/Inst Effective/Rsrch ....Vacant
13 Assoc VP Info Management .... Mr. James FINGER
18 Director of Facilities ....Mr. Ron TOWARD
15 Assoc VP of Human Resources .... Mr. Ivan SMITH
26 Exec Dir Govt Advocacy + PIO .... Ms. Karen SMITH-HUPP
37 Director Financial Assistance ....Mr. Christian ZIMMERMANN
06 Registrar ....Ms. Carol HARRISON
08 Director of Library .... Mr. Thomas REPENNING
66 Chair Nursing Dept ....Dr. Laura POLK
41 Director of Athletics/Student Life ....Ms. Michelle RUBLE
40 General Mgr College Store .... Ms. Marcy GANNON
07 Director Admissions Department ....Vacant
96 Director of Procurement ....Mr. Joe PICCOLO
28 Exec Dir Diversity and Inclusion ....Vacant
04 Senior Exec Assoc to the President ....Ms. Larisa PFEIFFER
19 Exec Director Security/Safety ....Mr. Bill BESSETTE
25 Grants Coordinator .... Ms. Lesley QUATTLEBAUM
30 Director Development .... Ms. Chelsea BROWN

The Community College of Baltimore County (B)

7201 Rossville Blvd., Baltimore MD 21237-3899

County: Baltimore FICE Identification: 002063

Unit ID: 434672

Telephone: (443) 840-2222 Carnegie Class: Assoc/MT-VT-High Trad

FAX Number: (443) 840-1100 Calendar System: Semester

URL: www.ccbcmd.edu

Established: 1957 Annual Undergrad Tuition & Fees (In-District): $4,276

Enrollment: 19,349 Coed

Affiliation or Control: Local IRS Status: 501(c)3

Highest Offering: Associate Degree

Accreditation: M, ACBSP, ADNUR, ART, CAHIIM, COARC, COMTA, DANCE, DH, EMT, FUSER, MAC, MLTAD, MUS, OTA, POLYT, RAD, RTT, SURGT, THEA

01 President ....Dr. Sandra L. KURTINITIS
111 Vice Pres Institutional Advancement ....Mr. Kenneth WESTARY
10 Vice Pres Finance/Administration ....Ms. Melissa HOPP
05 Interim Vice Pres Instruction ....Mr. Jack MCLAUGHLIN
84 VP Enrollment & Student Services ....Dr. Richard LILLEY
26 Sr Director for Public Relations ....Ms. Mary DELUCA
15 Senior Director Human Resources ....Ms. Penny MILSOM

Faith Theological Seminary (C)

529 Walker Avenue, Baltimore MD 21212

County: Baltimore City Identification: 667016

Unit ID: 212452

Telephone: (410) 323-6211 Carnegie Class: Spec-4-yr-Faith

FAX Number: (410) 323-6331 Calendar System: Semester

URL: fts.edu

Established: 1937 Annual Undergrad Tuition & Fees: $6,760

Enrollment: 147 Coed

Affiliation or Control: Non-denominational IRS Status: 501(c)3

Highest Offering: Doctorate; No Lower Division

Accreditation: TRACS

01 President ....Rev.Dr. Norman J. MANOHAR
05 Academic Dean ....Dr. Donald M. BERGMAN
06 Registrar ....Ms. Aruna S. MANOHAR
07 Director of Admissions ....Dr. John LEPERA
08 Head Librarian ....Mrs. Anita TAYLOR
108 Director IE ....Mrs. Margaret P. PROCH
10 Business Manager ....Ms. Seo YOUNG NO
13 IT Manager/Financial Aid Advisor ....Mr. John MANOHAR

Fortis College (D)

4351 Garden City Drive, Landover MD 20785

Telephone: (301) 459-3650 Identification: 770731

Accreditation: ABHES, DH, MLTAD, RAD

† Branch campus of Fortis Institute, Erie, PA

Frederick Community College (E)

7932 Opossumtown Pike, Frederick MD 21702-2097

County: Frederick FICE Identification: 002071

Unit ID: 162557

Telephone: (301) 846-2400 Carnegie Class: Assoc/HT-Mix Trad/Non

FAX Number: (301) 846-2498 Calendar System: Semester

URL: www.frederick.edu

Established: 1957 Annual Undergrad Tuition & Fees (In-District): $3,578

Enrollment: 6,220 Coed

Affiliation or Control: State/Local IRS Status: 501(c)3

Highest Offering: Associate Degree

Accreditation: M, ADNUR, COARC, SURGT

01 President ....Ms. Elizabeth BURMASTER
11 Chief of Operations ....Mr. Eric SHULER
05 Provost/EVP Academic Affairs & CEWD ....Dr. Tony HAWKINS
10 VP for Finance ....Ms. Dana MCDONALD
32 VP for Learning Support ....Dr. Nora CLARK
111 Exec Dir Institutional Advancement .... Ms. Deborah POWELL
13 Chief Information Officer ....Mr. Joseph MCCORMICK
36 AVP/Dean of Career Programs .... Dr. Sandy MCCOMBE WALLER
84 AVP for Enrollment Services .... Ms. Laura MEARS
51 Exec Dir Adult Ed/Lifelong Learning .... Ms. Kimberly DUNCAN
15 AVP for Human Resources ....Ms. Kristi YOWELL
21 Exec Director for Finance ....Ms. Patricia HOYT
06 Exec Dir Welcome Center/Registrar ... Ms. Deirdre WEILMINSTER
49 AVP/Dean of Arts & Sciences ....Dr. Brian STIPELMAN
20 AVP Center for Teaching & Learning .... Dr. Kelly TRIGGER
35 AVP/Dean of Students .... Mr. Jerry HAYNES
124 Exec Director of Student Engagement .... Ms. Jeanni WINSTON-MUIR
09 Spec Asst to President Inst Effect .... Mr. Gerald BOYD
18 Director Facilities Planning ....Mr. John ANZINGER
08 Director of Library Services .... Ms. Colleen MCKNIGHT
108 Exec Dir Assessment and Research .... Dr. Gohar FARAHANI
26 Exec Director of Marketing and Web ....Mr. Michael BAISEY
88 Director of Special Projects .... Mr. Michael PRITCHARD
37 Exec Dir Financial Aid/Enroll Svcs .... Ms. Brenda DAYHOFF
04 Exec Assoc to the President & BOT ....Ms. Kari MELVIN
103 AVP for CEWD .... Ms. Patricia MEYER
88 Exec Director Emergency Management .... Ms. Kathy FRANCIS
14 Associate Chief Information Officer ....Mr. Adam RENO
41 Director of Athletics ....Mr. Chad SMITH
88 Director Children's Center ....Ms. Teri BICKEL
66 Director of Nursing Education .... Ms. Vanessa LOVATO
106 Exec Director Distributed Learning ....Vacant
38 Exec Dir Counseling & Advising ....Dr. Chad ADERO
88 Director Office of Adult Services ....Ms. Janice BROWN
22 Director of Disability Services ......Dr. Kate KRAMER-JEFFERSON
07 Director of Admissions ....Ms. Lisa FREEL
88 Dir Veterans and Military Services .... Ms. Rachel NACHLAS
40 Director of Bookstore .... Mr. Frederick HOCKENBERRY
88 Foundation Scholarship Manager .... Mr. Michael THORNTON
109 Business Manager .... Mr. Peter LEE
19 Director College Safety & Emergency .... Mr. Chris SASSE
28 Exec Dir Diversity/Equity/Inclusion ...Dr. Beth DOUTHIRT COHEN
88 Director Arts Center .... Mr. Wendell POINDEXTER
88 Exec Dir Open Campus & Dual Enroll ....Ms. Elizabeth DUFFY
88 Director for Testing Center ....Ms. Ina WOLF
18 Director of Plant Operations ....Mr. Greg SOLBERG
93 Director Multicultural Student Svcs ....Ms. Chianti BLACKMON
113 Director of Student Finance/Bursar ....Ms. Jane BEATTY
91 Exec Dir Network Infrastructure ....Mr. Scott REECE
90 Director Audio-Visual Tech & IT .... Mr. Bryan VALKO

Garrett College (F)

687 Mosser Road, McHenry MD 21541

County: Garrett FICE Identification: 010014

Unit ID: 162609

Telephone: (301) 387-3000 Carnegie Class: Assoc/HT-Mix Trad/Non

FAX Number: N/A Calendar System: Semester

URL: www.garrettcollege.edu

Established: 1967 Annual Undergrad Tuition & Fees (In-District): $4,088

Enrollment: 673 Coed

Affiliation or Control: State/Local IRS Status: 501(c)3

Highest Offering: Associate Degree

Accreditation: M, EMT

01 President ....Dr. Richard MIDCAP
04 Executive Assistant to President .... Ms. Marcia KNEPP
10 VP of Admin & Financial Services .... Mr. Randall BITTINGER
32 Chief Student Affairs Officer .... Mr. Robert KERNS
20 Dean of Academic Affairs ....Dr. Qing YUAN
51 Dean of Cont Educ/Workforce Devel ....Ms. Julie YODER
13 Director of IT ....Vacant
30 Dir Develop/Exec Dir Foundation ....Ms. Cherie KRUG
06 Director of Records & Registration ....Ms. Kim DEGIOVANNI
37 Director of Financial Aid ....Mr. Andrew HARVEY
08 Dir of Library/Learning Commons .... Ms. Jennifer MESLENER
21 Director of Business & Finance .... Ms. Dallas OUELLETTE
15 Director of Human Resources ....Ms. Janis BUSH
35 Director of Student Development ....Mr. Rich SCHOFIELD
65 Dir of Natural Res/Wildlife Tech .... Mr. Kevin DODGE
41 Director of Athletics .... Mr. Dennis GIBSON
18 Director of Facilities ....Ms. Kathy MEAGHER
121 Coord of Student Advis & Acad Supp ....Ms. Ashley RUBY
96 Purchasing/Accounts Payable ....Ms. Bonnie BROADWATER
40 Bookstore Manager ....Ms. Lois ANDERSON
84 Director of Enrollment Management .... Mr. Mike TUMBARELLO
108 Dean of Inst Effectiveness ....Mr. James ALLEN, JR.
105 Web Developer .... Mr. David LANTZ
88 Director of Adventure Sports ....Mr. Michael LOGSDON
106 Coordinator of Distance Learning ....Vacant
19 Coordinator of Security/Safety ....Mr. Greg SHAFFER
26 Coordinator of Marketing and PR ....Ms. Stacy HOLLER
07 Coordinator of Admissions .... Ms. Melissa WASS
25 Chief Contract/Grants Administrator ..... Ms. Kearstin HINEBAUGH
39 Director Resident Life/Student Hous ....Vacant
22 Director of Equity & Compliance ....Ms. Shelley MENEAR
09 Director of Institutional Research ....Ms. Kelli SISLER

Goucher College (G)

1021 Dulaney Valley Road, Baltimore MD 21204-2780

County: Baltimore FICE Identification: 002073

Unit ID: 162654

Telephone: (410) 337-6000 Carnegie Class: Bac-A&S

FAX Number: N/A Calendar System: Semester

URL: www.goucher.edu

Established: 1885 Annual Undergrad Tuition & Fees: $44,300

Enrollment: 2,236 Coed

Affiliation or Control: Independent Non-Profit IRS Status: 501(c)3

Highest Offering: Master's

Accreditation: M

01 President .... Mr. Kent DEVEREAUX
05 Interim Provost .... Dr. Scott SIBLEY
45 Sr VP for Strategic Initiatives ....Mr. Marty SWEIDEL
32 Vice Pres/Dean of Students ....Dr. Bryan F. COKER
111 Vice Pres Advancement ....Ms. Trishana E. BOWDEN
10 VP for Finance & Administration .... Ms. Lynne LOCHTE
26 AVP Marketing & External Relations ...... Ms. Stephanie COLDREN
13 Vice Pres for Technology ....Mr. Bill LEIMBACH
43 General Counsel .... Ms. Barbara STOB
20 Assoc Provost for Undergrad Studies ....Ms. La Jerne CORNISH
104 Assoc Prov Experiential & Ext Pgm ....Mr. Eric SINGER
88 Asst VP for Integrative Learning ....Ms. Emily PERL
15 Vice President for Human Resources ....Ms. Deborah LUPTON
21 Controller .... Mr. Alex ANTKOWIAK
41 Assoc Dean Students/Dir Athletics ....Dr. Andrew WU
07 Director of Admissions ....Vacant
08 Librarian ....Vacant
29 Exec Dir for Alumnae/i Engagement ....Ms. Jennifer PAWLO - JOHNSTONE
36 Director of Career Development ....Ms. Traci MARTIN
58 Asst Prov Grad Program in Education .... Ms. Phyllis SUNSHINE
06 Registrar .... Mr. Andrew WESTFALL
09 Senior Dir for Inst Effectiveness .... Ms. Shuang LIU
109 Dir Business/Auxiliary Services ....Vacant
18 Dir Facilities Management Services .....Mr. Terence MCCANN, JR.
37 Director Financial Aid ....Ms. Stephanie ALFORD
105 Webmaster ....Mr. John PERRELLI
106 Dir Online Education/E-learning ....Vacant
28 Asst Dean Stdnts Intercultural Affs ....Vacant
39 Director Student Housing ....Vacant
04 Executive Asst to President ....Ms. Lillian JOHNSON
19 Director of Public Safety ....Mr. David HEFFER
38 Director Student Counseling Center .... Ms. Monica NEEL

Hagerstown Community College (H)

11400 Robinwood Drive, Hagerstown MD 21742-6590

County: Washington FICE Identification: 002074

Unit ID: 162690

Telephone: (240) 500-2000 Carnegie Class: Assoc/MT-VT-Mix Trad/Non

FAX Number: (301) 393-3682 Calendar System: Semester

URL: www.hagerstowncc.edu

Established: 1946 Annual Undergrad Tuition & Fees (In-District): $4,260

Enrollment: 4,069 Coed

Affiliation or Control: State/Local IRS Status: 501(c)3

Highest Offering: Associate Degree

Accreditation: M, ADNUR, DA, DH, EMT, PNUR, RAD

01 President ....Dr. James S. KLAUBER, SR.
05 VP of Academic Affs & Student Svcs ....Dr. David WARNER
10 Vice Pres Administration/Finance ....Mr. Trevor S. JACKSON
32 Dean of Students .... Ms. Christine A. OHL-GIGLIOTTI
09 Dean of Plng/Inst Effectiveness ....Vacant
103 Dean Workforce Solutions & Cont Ed ....Ms. Theresa M. SHANK
18 Dir Facilities Management & Plng ....Mr. Jonathan G. METCALF
07 Dir of Admissions & Enrollment Mgmt . Mr. Kevin L. CRAWFORD
111 Senior Director College Advancement .... Dr. Ashley N. WHALEY
26 Dir of Public Relations & Marketing ....Ms. Elizabeth L. KIRKPATRICK
37 Director of Financial Aid ....Mr. Charles M. SCHEETZ
106 Dean of Distance Education ....Ms. Vidda P. BEACHE
21 Director of Finance ....Mr. David C. BITTORF
21 Director of Business Services ....Ms. Lita J. ORNER
66 Director of Nursing ....Ms. Karen S. HAMMOND
15 Exec Director of Human Resources .... Ms. Jennifer A. CHILDS
41 Dir Athletics/Phys Ed/Leisure Stds .... Mr. Robert C. ROHAN
13 Director of Information Technology ....Mr. Craig M. FENTRESS

Harford Community College (A)

401 Thomas Run Road, Bel Air MD 21015-1698

County: Harford | FICE Identification: 002075 | Unit ID: 162706
Telephone: (443) 412-2000 | Carnegie Class: Assoc/HT-Mix Trad/Non
FAX Number: (443) 412-2120 | Calendar System: Semester
URL: www.harford.edu
Established: 1957 | Annual Undergrad Tuition & Fees (In-District): $3,715
Enrollment: 6,109 | Coed
Affiliation or Control: Local | IRS Status: 501(c)3
Highest Offering: Associate Degree
Accreditation: M, ADNUR, EMT, HT, MAC

01	President	Dr. Dianna G. PHILLIPS
05	Vice President Academic Affairs	Dr. Karen HAYS
10	VP Finance & Administration	Vacant
32	VP Student Affs/Inst Effectiveness	Dr. Jacqueline JACKSON
100	Chief of Staff	Ms. Brenda M. MORRISON
13	Chief Information Officer	Mr. Tom ALCIDE
84	Assoc VP Enrollment Services	Mr. Patrick ELLIOTT
35	Assoc VP Student Development	Ms. Jennie TOWNER
21	AVP for Finance & Accounting	Vacant
106	Dean Teaching/Learning/Innovation	Dr. Karen M. REGE
18	Director for Campus Operations	Mr. Lou CLAYPOOLE
37	Director Financial Aid	Ms. Amy R. SPINNATO
06	Registrar	Vacant
26	Director for Communications	Ms. Nancy J. DYSARD
15	Dir Human Resources/Employee Dev	Ms. Pamela STELL
30	Director College/Alumni Development	Ms. Denise M. DREGIER
08	Director Library & Info Resources	Vacant
09	Assoc VP Analytics & Planning	Mr. Richard HARTWELL
38	Dir Advising/Career/Transfer Svcs	Ms. J. Bonnie SULZBACH
40	Coordinator College Store	Mr. Joseph BUSKIRK
07	Dir for Admissions	Ms. Jeanne GOSS
110	Asst Dir for Development	Ms. Lanell PATRICK
81	Dean Science/Tech/Engr/Math	Ms. Pamela PAPE-LINDSTROM
83	Dean Behavioral & Social Sciences	Mr. Tony WOHLERS
79	Dean of Arts & Humanities	Mr. Todd ABRAMOVITZ
50	Dean of IBAT	Ms. Kelly KOERMER
66	Dean Nursing & Allied Health Profs	Ms. Laura C. PRESTON
19	Director Security/Safety	Mr. Christopher SWAIN

Hood College (B)

401 Rosemont Avenue, Frederick MD 21701-8575

County: Frederick | FICE Identification: 002076 | Unit ID: 162760
Telephone: (301) 663-3131 | Carnegie Class: Masters/L
FAX Number: (301) 694-7653 | Calendar System: Semester
URL: www.hood.edu
Established: 1893 | Annual Undergrad Tuition & Fees: $39,492
Enrollment: 2,112 | Coed
Affiliation or Control: Independent Non-Profit | IRS Status: 501(c)3
Highest Offering: Doctorate
Accreditation: M, ACBSP, CACREP, NURSE, SW

01	President	Dr. Andrea E. CHAPDELAINE
05	Provost/VP Academic Affairs	Dr. Deborah RICKER
10	Vice Pres Finance	Mr. Charles G. MANN
111	VP for Institutional Advancement	Ms. Nancy E. GILLECE
32	VP Student Life/Dean of Students	Dr. Olivia G. WHITE
84	VP Undergrad/Grad Enrollment	Mr. William BROWN
26	VP Marketing/Communications Officer	Ms. Laurie WARD
07	Director of Admissions	Ms. Nikki BAMONTI
58	Interim Dean of Graduate School	Dr. April BOULTON
08	Interim Director of Library Service	Mr. Toby PETERSON
15	Director of Human Resources	Ms. Carol M. WUENSCHEL
13	Chief Technology Officer	Mr. Bill HOBBS
04	Executive Asst to President	Ms. Diane K. WISE
104	Director Study Abroad	Vacant
19	Director Security/Safety	Mr. Thurmond MAYNARD
39	Director Student Housing	Mr. Matthew TROUTMAN
102	Dir Foundation/Corporate Relations	Ms. Jaime CACCIOLA
06	Registrar	Ms. Ashley ANDERSON
09	Director of Institutional Research	Mr. Ross CONOVER
108	Asst Dir Institutional Assessment	Ms. Tanya WILLIAMS
28	Director of Diversity	Mr. Travis EICHELBERGER
29	Director Alumni Affairs	Ms. Kellye GREENWALD
37	Director Student Financial Aid	Ms. Melena VERITY
41	Athletic Director	Dr. Susan KOLB

Howard Community College (C)

10901 Little Patuxent Parkway, Columbia MD 21044-3197

County: Howard | FICE Identification: 008175 | Unit ID: 162779
Telephone: (443) 518-1000 | Carnegie Class: Assoc/HT-High Trad
FAX Number: N/A | Calendar System: Semester
URL: www.howardcc.edu
Established: 1966 | Annual Undergrad Tuition & Fees (In-District): $3,936
Enrollment: 9,476 | Coed
Affiliation or Control: State/Local | IRS Status: 501(c)3
Highest Offering: Associate Degree
Accreditation: M, ACFEI, ADNUR, CVT, DH, DMS, EMT, MLTAD, MUS, PNUR, PTAA, RAD

01	President	Dr. Kathleen B. HETHERINGTON
32	Vice President of Student Services	Dr. Cynthia J. PETERKA
05	Vice Pres of Academic Affairs	Dr. Jean M. SVACINA
10	Vice Pres of Administration/Finance	Ms. Lynn C. COLEMAN
13	Vice Pres Information Technology	Mr. Thomas J. GLASER
51	Associate VP Cont Ed/Workforce Dev	Ms. Minah C. WOO
84	Assoc Vice Pres Enrollment Services	Ms. Lorianna MAPPS
35	Assoc Vice Pres for Student Devel	Ms. Janice L. MARKS
15	Associate Vice Pres Human Resources	Mr. Joseph B. PETTIFORD
21	Associate Vice Pres of Finance	Mr. Chris W. HESTON
18	Exec Dir Capital Proj/Facilities	Mr. Charles W. NIGHTINGALE
101	Executive Associate to President	Ms. Linda E. EMMERICH
114	Director of Budget and Finance	Ms. Verna A. BERNOI
30	Dir of Dev/Exec Dir Educ Foundation	Ms. Melissa L. MATTEY
109	Director Auxiliary Services	Mr. L. Dewey GRIM
19	Director of Public Safety	Mr. G. William DAVIS
35	Director Student Life	Ms. Schnell R. GARRETT
04	Exec Assistant to the President	Vacant
96	Director of Procurement	Mr. Domonic A. CUSIMANO
06	Registrar	Ms. Cheryl B. CUDZILO
07	Director of Admissions & Advising	Ms. Dorothy B. PLANTZ
104	Director of International Education	Ms. Mary L. ALLEN
105	Web Enterprise Services Manager	Mr. Roger F. STOTT
37	Director of Financial Aid Services	Ms. Dawn Y. LOWE
41	Director of Athletics	Ms. Erin C. FOLEY
26	Exec Dir Public Relations/Mktg	Ms. Elizabeth S. HOMAN
09	Exec Dir Plng/Research & Org Dev	Ms. Zoe A. IRVIN
38	Director Counseling & Career Svcs	Dr. Jay J. COUGHLIN, III
20	Associate Academic Officer	Mr. Greg E. FLEISHER

Johns Hopkins University (D)

3400 N. Charles Street, Baltimore MD 21218-2680

County: Independent City | FICE Identification: 002077 | Unit ID: 162928
Telephone: (410) 516-8000 | Carnegie Class: DU-Highest
FAX Number: N/A | Calendar System: Semester
URL: www.jhu.edu
Established: 1876 | Annual Undergrad Tuition & Fees: $53,740
Enrollment: 25,151 | Coed
Affiliation or Control: Independent Non-Profit | IRS Status: 501(c)3
Highest Offering: Doctorate
Accreditation: M, BBT, CACREP, CAMPEP, DIETC, DMS, HSA, IPSY, MED, MIL, NMT, NURSE, PH

01	President	Mr. Ronald J. DANIELS
100	Vice President/Chief of Staff	Ms. Kerry A. ATES
05	Provost & Sr VP Acad Affs	Dr. Sunil KUMAR
17	CEO Johns Hopkins Medicine	Dr. Paul D. ROTHMAN
10	Sr VP Finance & Administration	Mr. Daniel G. ENNIS
29	VP for Development & Alum Relations	Mr. Fritz SCHROEDER
26	Vice Pres for Communications	Vacant
43	Vice Pres/General Counsel	Mr. Paul PINEAU
86	Vice Pres Govt/Community Affairs	Mr. Thomas LEWIS
18	Vice Pres Real Estate/Campus Svcs	Mr. Robert MCLEAN
15	Vice Pres Human Resources	Ms. Heidi CONWAY
21	Vice Pres Finance & CFO	Ms. Helene GRADY
115	Vice Pres Chief Investment Officer	Mr. Jason PERLIONI
117	Vice Provost and Chief Risk Officer	Dr. Jonathan LINKS
32	Vice Provost Student Affairs	Dr. Alanna SHANAHAN
50	Vice Provost Career Services	Dr. Farouk DEY
20	Vice Provost Faculty Affairs	Dr. Andrew DOUGLAS
07	Vice Provost Admiss & Fin Aid	Mr. David PHILLIPS
28	Chief Diversity Officer	Vacant
58	Vice Prov Grad and Prof Education	Dr. Nancy KASS
13	Vice Provost Info Technology/CIO	Ms. Stephanie REEL
22	Vice Provost Institutional Equity	Vacant
46	Vice Provost Research	Dr. Denis WIRTZ
09	Vice Provost Institutional Research	Dr. Ratna SARKAR
88	Asst Vice Prov International Svcs	Mr. James BRAILER
06	University Registrar	Mr. Tom BLACK
82	Dean Nitze School Adv Intl Studies	Dr. Eliot COHEN
49	Dean Krieger School Arts & Sciences	Dr. Beverly WENDLAND
50	Dean Carey Business School	Dr. Alexander TRIANTIS
53	Dean School of Education	Dr. Christopher MORPHEW
54	Dean Whiting Sch Engineering	Dr. Ed SCHLESINGER
63	Dean School of Medicine	Dr. Paul ROTHMAN
66	Dean School of Nursing	Dr. Patricia DAVIDSON
69	Dean Bloomberg School Public Health	Dr. Ellen MACKENZIE
08	Dean Sheridan Libraries and Museums	Mr. Winston G. TABB
64	Dean Peabody Institute	Dr. Fred BRONSTEIN
88	Director Applied Physics Lab	Mr. Ralph SEMMEL
96	Chief Procurement Officer	Mr. Brian SMITH
21	Controller	Mr. Scott JONAS
19	Exec Director Safety & Security	Ms. Christina PRESBERRY
116	Exec Director Internal Audits	Mr. James JARRELL
27	Asst Vice Pres External Relations	Ms. Karen LANCASTER
88	Exec Director JH Real Estate	Mr. Brian B. DEMBECK
104	Director Study Abroad	Dr. Lori A. CITTI
28	Chair Diversity Leadership Council	Mr. Ashley J. LLORENS
41	Athletic Director	Ms. Jennifer BAKER
101	Secretary of the Institution/Board	Ms. Maureen MARSH

Lincoln College of Technology (E)

9325 Snowden River Parkway, Columbia MD 21046

County: Howard | FICE Identification: 007936 | Unit ID: 163028
Telephone: (410) 290-7100 | Carnegie Class: Assoc/HVT-High Trad
FAX Number: (410) 290-7880 | Calendar System: Quarter
URL: www.lincolntech.com
Established: 1978 | Annual Undergrad Tuition & Fees: N/A
Enrollment: 569 | Coed
Affiliation or Control: Proprietary | IRS Status: Proprietary
Highest Offering: Associate Degree
Accreditation: ACCSC

01	Campus President	Mr. Cory HUGHES

Loyola University Maryland (F)

4501 N Charles Street, Baltimore MD 21210-2694

County: Independent City | FICE Identification: 002078 | Unit ID: 163046
Telephone: (410) 617-2000 | Carnegie Class: Masters/L
FAX Number: (410) 322-2768 | Calendar System: Semester
URL: www.loyola.edu
Established: 1852 | Annual Undergrad Tuition & Fees: $48,920
Enrollment: 5,783 | Coed
Affiliation or Control: Roman Catholic | IRS Status: 501(c)3
Highest Offering: Doctorate
Accreditation: M, CACREP, CLPSY, MACTE, SP

01	President	Rev. Brian F. LINNANE, SJ
88	VP/Special Asst to the President	Dr. Rob KELLY
05	Vice Pres Academic Affairs/Provost	Dr. Amanda THOMAS
10	VP for Finance/Admin & Treasurer	Mr. Randall GENTZLER
111	Sr Vice President Advancement	Dr. Terrence SAWYER
32	VP Student Development	Dr. Donelda COOK
84	Vice President of Enrollment Mgmt	Mr. Eric NICHOLS
09	Director of Institutional Research	Ms. Nicole JACOBS
18	Assoc VP Facilities/Campus Services	Ms. Helen SCHNEIDER
26	Dir Marketing and Communications	Ms. Rita BUETTNER
15	Assoc Vice Pres for Human Resources	Ms. Kathleen PARNELL
110	Asst Vice Pres for External Affairs	Ms. Joan FLYNN
27	Asst VP Marketing/Communications	Ms. Sharon HIGGINS
41	Asst VP/Director of Athletics	Ms. Donna WOODRUFF
07	Dean Undergraduate Admissions	Ms. Jennifer LOUDEN
123	Exec Dir of Graduate Admissions	Ms. Maureen BUSH
06	Director of Records	Ms. Rita L. STEINER
85	Dean of International Programs	Dr. Andre COLOMBAT
08	Director of Library	Ms. Barbara PREECE
42	Director of Campus Ministry	Mr. Sean BRAY
88	Dir CCSJ/York Road Initiative	Ms. Erin O'KEEFE
88	Sexual Violence Prev & Educ Coord	Ms. Melissa LEES
88	Director ALANA Services	Mr. Rodney PARKER
21	Asst VP Controller	Vacant
114	AVP Budget/Business Intelligence	Mr. Sean FRANCIS
109	Director Event Svcs/Auxiliary Mgmt	Mr. Joseph BRADLEY
88	Director Environment Health/Safety	Mr. Thomas HETTLEMAN
19	Dir of Public Safety/Campus Police	Adrian BLACK
29	Director Alumni Relations	Vacant
88	Director Advancement Services	Mr. Ian WEBSTER
49	Dean College of Arts & Sciences	Dr. Steve FOWL
50	Dean Sellinger Sch Business & Mgmt	Dr. Kathleen GETZ
83	Assoc Dean Social Sciences/Graduate	Dr. Jeffrey BARNETT
50	Asst Dean for Business Programs	Ms. Susan HASLER
88	Asst Vice Pres Student Development	Ms. Michelle CHEATEM
18	Dir Facilities Management	Ms. Kiki WILLIAMS
105	Dir Web Communications	Ms. Amy FILARDO

Maple Springs Baptist Bible College & Seminary (G)

4130 Belt Road, Capitol Heights MD 20743-5712

County: Prince Georges | FICE Identification: 038224 | Unit ID: 446394
Telephone: (301) 736-3631 | Carnegie Class: Spec-4-yr-Faith
FAX Number: (301) 735-6507 | Calendar System: Semester
URL: www.msbbcs.edu
Established: 1986 | Annual Undergrad Tuition & Fees: $5,400
Enrollment: 60 | Coed
Affiliation or Control: Baptist | IRS Status: 501(c)3
Highest Offering: Doctorate
Accreditation: TRACS

01	President/CEO	Dr. Carl KEELS
05	Vice President Academic Affairs	Dr. Betty BOOKER
11	Vice Pres Administration & Finance	Dr. Quentin COLEMAN
73	Academic Dean College Division	Dr. Carl KEELS
06	Dir Records/Admissions & Registrar	Ms. Loretta D. WALKER
09	Dir Institutional Plng/Assessment	Mr. Louis JENKINS
10	Director Business Affairs	Mr. Keith M. DUKES
32	Director Student Affairs	Mr. Jeffrey BATES
08	Dir Library/Instruc Resource Center	Mr. Darren JONES
37	Financial Aid Coordinator	Mrs. Patricia JONES
30	Director of Development	Ms. Pamela SMITH

Maryland Institute College of Art (H)

1300 W. Mount Royal Avenue, Baltimore MD 21217-4191

County: Independent City | FICE Identification: 002080 | Unit ID: 163295
Telephone: (410) 669-9200 | Carnegie Class: Spec-4-yr-Arts
FAX Number: (410) 669-9206 | Calendar System: Semester
URL: www.mica.edu
Established: 1826 | Annual Undergrad Tuition & Fees: $48,630
Enrollment: 2,128 | Coed
Affiliation or Control: Independent Non-Profit | IRS Status: 501(c)3
Highest Offering: Master's
Accreditation: M, ART

01	President	Mr. Samuel HOI
05	Vice Pres Academic Affairs/Provost	Dr. David BOGEN
10	Vice Pres Operations/Finance/COO	Mr. Douglas MANN
32	Vice Pres Student Affairs	Mr. Michael PATTERSON
07	VP Admissions/Financial Aid	Ms. Theresa BEDOYA
13	Vice Pres Technology Systems & Svcs	Ms. Alexa KIM
97	Vice Provost Open Studies	Mr. David GRACYALNY
46	Vice Provost Research/Grad Studies	Ms. Gwynne KEATHLEY

04 Executive Assistant to President .... Ms. Lisa SHEPPLEY
37 Assoc VP Financial Aid .... Ms. Diane PRENGAMAN
44 Assoc VP Dev/Constituent Rels .... Vacant
15 Human Resources Director .... Ms. Laura ROSSI
20 Assoc VP Academic Services .... Ms. Wendy PRICE
53 Dean Art Education .... Ms. Karen CARROLL
07 Assoc Dean Undergraduate Admissions .... Vacant
123 Director of Graduate Admissions .... Mr. Christopher HARRING
51 Assoc Dean Continuing/Open Studies .... Ms. Crystal SHAMBLEE
06 Assoc Dean Enrollment Svs/Registrar .... Ms. Christine PETERSON
28 Asst Dean Diversity Intercultur Dev .... Mr. Clyde JOHNSON, JR.
88 Director Budget .... Ms. Brigitte SULLIVAN
26 VP for Strategic Communications .... Ms. Debra RUBINO
39 Director Residence Life .... Mr. Scott STONE
36 Director Career Development .... Ms. Jennine STANKIEWICZ
38 Director Counseling Center .... Mr. David GOODE-CROSS
35 Director Student Activities .... Ms. Karol MARTINEZ-DOANE
88 Director Admissions Operations .... Ms. Cheryl ISSOD
08 Director & Head Librarian .... Ms. Heather SLANIA
44 Director Annual Fund .... Mr. Mansoor ALI
88 Director Advancement Services .... Ms. Dana COSTELLO
88 Research & Stewardship Manager .... Vacant
88 Director Exhibitions .... Mr. Gerald ROSS
88 Dir Data Mgmt/Registration Cont Std .... Ms. Sarah MARAVETZ
84 Dir Enroll Svcs/Stdnt Records/Rsrch .... Mr. Hadley GARBART
19 Director of Campus Safety .... Mr. Marlon BYRD
88 Director Events .... Mr. Jon LIPITZ
88 Director Operation Services .... Mr. Chris BOHASKA
102 Director Corp/Found/Govt Relations .... Ms. Sara WARREN
105 Director of Web Communications .... Mr. Justin CODD
24 Director Technical Support Services .... Mr. John RHODES
91 Director Administrative Systems .... Vacant
105 Director Network Services .... Mr. David APAW
90 Dir Instructional Advance & Tech .... Ms. Pamela STEFANUCA
40 Manager College Store .... Ms. Kerri LITZ

Maryland University of Integrative Health (A)

7750 Montpelier Road, Laurel MD 20723-6010
County: Howard | FICE Identification: 025784
Unit ID: 164085
Telephone: (410) 888-9048 | Carnegie Class: Spec-4-yr-Other Health
FAX Number: (410) 888-9004 | Calendar System: Trimester
URL: www.muih.edu
Established: 1981 | Annual Graduate Tuition & Fees: N/A
Enrollment: 1,183 | Coed
Affiliation or Control: Independent Non-Profit | IRS Status: 501(c)3
Highest Offering: Doctorate; No Undergraduates
Accreditation: M, ACUP

01 President .... Mr. Marc LEVIN
05 Provost/VP Academic Affairs .... Dr. Christina SAX
84 VP Marketing/Enrollment Management .... Mr. Nigel LONG
20 Assoc Provost Academic Operations .... Ms. Mary Ellen HRUTKA
108 Asst Provost Acad Assessment & Accr .... Ms. Deneb FALABELLA
20 Dean of Academic Affairs .... Mr. James SNOW
76 Asst Dean of Academic Affairs .... Dr. Kathleen WARNER
37 Director Student Financial Aid .... Ms. Kristina DEAN
06 Registrar .... Ms. Rhonda STOKES
13 Director IT .... Mr. Lesly ELVARD
19 Manager Security/Safety .... Ms. Jennifer YOCUM
32 Assoc VP Student & Alumni Affairs .... Dr. Tita GRAY
15 Director Human Enrichment .... Ms. Melissa L. CAHILL
04 Exec Associate to the President .... Mr. Brian LEE

McDaniel College (B)

2 College Hill, Westminster MD 21157-4390
County: Carroll | FICE Identification: 002109
Unit ID: 164270
Telephone: (410) 848-7000 | Carnegie Class: Masters/L
FAX Number: (410) 857-2279 | Calendar System: Semester
URL: www.mcdaniel.edu
Established: 1867 | Annual Undergrad Tuition & Fees: $43,260
Enrollment: 2,819 | Coed
Affiliation or Control: Independent Non-Profit | IRS Status: 501(c)3
Highest Offering: Master's
Accreditation: M, CAEPN, SW

01 President .... Dr. Roger N. CASEY
100 Chief of Staff .... Ms. Marissa CORMIER
05 Provost .... Dr. Julia JASKEN
10 Vice Pres Administration & Finance .... Mr. Thomas PHIZACKLEA
111 Vice President Advancement .... Ms. Vicky SHAFFER
84 VP Enroll Mgt/Dean of Admissions .... Ms. Janelle HOLMBOE
13 Chief Information Officer .... Mr. Andrew LAWLOR
58 Int Dean Graduate/Prof Studies .... Dr. Pam REGIS
88 Assoc Dean/Student Academic Life .... Ms. Lisa BRESLIN
89 Dir of First Year Experience .... Ms. Erin BENEVENTO
32 Dean of Students .... Ms. Elizabeth TOWLE
112 AVP Development and Leadership Gift .... Ms. Brenda FRAZIER
29 Exec Director of Alumni Relations .... Ms. Dianne THOMPSON
102 Dir Corp & Foundation Relations .... Ms. Jessica LAIRD
37 Director Financial Aid .... Dr. Karleen HOWARD
06 Registrar .... Ms. Sandra CLARK
41 Director Athletics .... Mr. Paul MOYER
36 Director Center for Exper and Opp .... Mr. Joshua AMBROSE
39 Director of Residence Life .... Mr. Michael ROBBINS
21 Director Financial Services/Treas .... Mr. Arthur S. WISNER
15 Director Human Resources .... Ms. Jennifer GLENNON
45 Dir Facility Plng/Capital Projects .... Mr. Edgar S. SELL, JR.
18 Director Physical Plant .... Mr. James COONS
19 Director of Campus Safety .... Mr. Eric IMMLER
40 Manager Bookstore .... Mr. Kyle MELOCHE
109 Dir Conferences/Auxiliary Services .... Ms. Mary J. COLBERT
28 Director of Diversity and Inclusion .... Mr. Jose MORENO
92 Director of Honors Program .... Dr. Bryn UPTON
96 Director of Purchasing/Receiving .... Ms. Ellen RUGEMER
88 Coord of Deaf Education Program .... Dr. Mark M. RUST
09 Director Institutional Research .... Ms. Robin DEWEY
86 Director of Government Relations .... Vacant
07 Dean of Admissions .... Ms. Heidi REIGEL
104 Director of International Programs .... Ms. Elizabeth DAVIS
106 Director Online Educ/E-learning .... Mr. Steve KERBY
38 Director of Wellness Center .... Ms. Heidi HUBER

Montgomery College (C)

9221 Corporate Boulevard, Rockville MD 20850
County: Montgomery | FICE Identification: 006911
Unit ID: 163426
Telephone: (240) 567-5000 | Carnegie Class: Assoc/HT-High Trad
FAX Number: (240) 567-9129 | Calendar System: Semester
URL: www.montgomerycollege.edu
Established: 1946 | Annual Undergrad Tuition & Fees (In-District): $5,178
Enrollment: 22,875 | Coed
Affiliation or Control: Local | IRS Status: 501(c)3
Highest Offering: Associate Degree
Accreditation: M, ADNUR, CAHIIM, DMS, MUS, POLYT, PTAA, RAD, SURGT

01 President .... Dr. DeRionne P. POLLARD
05 Sr VP for Academic Affairs .... Dr. Sanjay RAI
32 Sr VP for Student Affairs .... Dr. Monica R. BROWN
10 Int SVP Fiscal/Administrative Svcs .... Ms. Donna SCHENA
111 SVP Advancement/Cmty Engagement .... Mr. David SEARS
100 Chief of Staff/Chief Strategy Ofcr .... Dr. Stephen D. CAIN
88 Deputy Chief of Staff and Strategy .... Dr. Michelle T. SCOTT
35 Assoc SVP for Student Affairs .... Dr. Melissa GREGORY
21 Assoc SVP for Admin & Fiscal Svcs .... Ms. Nadine PORTER
20 Assoc SVP for Academic Affairs .... Ms. Carolyn TERRY
86 Chief Government Relations Officer .... Ms. Susan MADDEN
43 General Counsel .... Mr. Timothy D. DIETZ
04 Assistant to the President .... Ms. Ida BRITTON
101 Mgr of Bd of Trustees Svcs & Ops .... Ms. Lily LEE
12 VP & Provost Rockville Campus .... Dr. Kimberly KELLEY
12 VP & Provost Germantown Campus .... Ms. Margaret LATIMER
12 VP & Prov Takoma Pk/Silver Spring C .... Dr. Brad J. STEWART
103 VP/Prov App Tech/Tech Ed/WD&CE .... Mr. George M. PAYNE
13 Interim CIO IT .... Ms. Jane-Ellen MILLER
88 Int Dep CIO Perform Mgmt Svcs .... Mr. Patrick FEEHAN
14 Chief Technology Officer .... Mr. Anwar KARIM
15 Int Chief Human Resource Officer .... Ms. Krista WALKER
18 VP for Facilities & Public Safety .... Mr. Marvin J. MILLS
26 VP of Communications .... Mr. Ray GILMER
106 VP E-Learning/Innov/Teaching Exc .... Dr. Michael MILLS
50 Dean Acct/BusAdmin/Econ/Paralegal . Ms. Katherine MICHAELIAN
88 Dean Eng/Dev Eng/Reading .... Dr. Rodney REDMOND
83 Int Dean Anth/Cr Just/Ed/Psych/Soc .... Dr. Eric M. BENJAMIN
81 Dean Biology/Biotech/Chemistry .... Dr. James SNIEZEK
110 Assoc SVP Advance & Cmty Engagement .... Ms. Nancy NUELL
54 Dean Eng/Comp Sci/Netwk/Cyber Sec .... Dr. Muhammad KEHNEMOUYI
81 Dean Math/Dev Math/Statistics .... Mr. John HAMMAN
76 Dean Mgmt/Mental Health/Health&PE .... Ms. Angie PICKWICK
88 Dean AELP Writing/Reading/Speech .... Dr. Usha VENKATESH
79 Dean Hist/PolSci/World Lang/AmSign .... Dr. Sharon FECHTER
75 Dean Applied Tech & Gudelsky Inst .... Mr. Ed ROBERTS
50 Dean Bus Info/Tech/Safety .... Mr. Steve GREENFIELD
51 Dean Cmty Educ & Extended Learning .... Ms. Dorothy UMANS
51 Dean Adult Eng Lang & GED Programs .... Dr. Donna KINERNEY
57 Dean Visual/Perform & Media Arts .... Dr. Frank TREZZA
124 Dean Student Engagement/Affairs .... Dr. Clemmie SOLOMON
35 Dean Student Access/Affairs .... Dr. Jamin BARTOLOMEO
121 Dean Student Success/Services .... Dr. Tonya MASON
53 Dir School of Education .... Ms. Debra POESE
41 Athletic Director .... Ms. Tarlough GASQUE
102 Dir of MC Foundation/Dir of Dev .... Vacant
112 Major and Planned Gifts Director .... Ms. Francene WALKER
88 Exec Dir H. Pinkney Life Sci Park .... Ms. Martha SCHOONMAKER
09 Dir Inst Research & Effectiveness .... Dr. Robert LYNCH
96 Dir of Procurement .... Mr. Patrick JOHNSON
37 Collegewide Dir of Financial Aid .... Ms. Judith M. TAYLOR
84 Dir Enroll Svcs & College Registrar .... Mr. Ernest CARTLEDGE
19 Dir Public Safety/Emergency Mgmt .... Ms. Shawn HARRISON
28 Chief Equity & Diversity Officer .... Ms. Sharon BLAND
108 Dir of Assessment .... Dr. Cassandra JONES
25 Dir Grants & Sponsored Programs .Ms. Rose GARVIN AQUILINO
102 Interim Dir Foundation & Corp Rels .... Mr. Stuart TART
29 Alumni Coordinator .... Mr. John LIBBY
08 Dir College Libraries & Info Svcs .... Mr. Tanner WRAY
22 Dir Employee & Labor Relations .... Ms. Heather PRATT
104 Coord of Travel & Study Abroad .... Dr. Gregory MALVEAUX

Morgan State University (D)

1700 East Cold Spring Lane, Baltimore MD 21251-0001
County: Independent City | FICE Identification: 002083
Unit ID: 163453
Telephone: (443) 885-3333 | Carnegie Class: DU-Higher
FAX Number: (443) 885-3698 | Calendar System: Semester
URL: www.morgan.edu
Established: 1867 | Annual Undergrad Tuition & Fees (In-State): $7,900
Enrollment: 7,747 | Coed
Affiliation or Control: State | IRS Status: 501(c)3
Highest Offering: Doctorate
Accreditation: M, CAEPN, DIETD, LSAR, MT, MUS, NURSE, PH, PLNG, SW

01 President .... Dr. David WILSON
05 Provost/Sr VP Academic Affairs .... Dr. Lesia CRUMPTON-YOUNG
88 VP Academic Outreach and Engagement .... Dr. Maurice TAYLOR
10 Vice Pres Finance & Management .... Mr. Sidney EVANS
13 Vice Pres for Technology & CIO .... Dr. Adebisi OLADIPUPO
32 Vice Pres Student Affairs .... Dr. Kevin BANKS
30 Vice Pres Institutional Advancement .... Ms. Donna HOWARD
84 VP for Enroll Mgmt/Student Success .... Dr. Kara TURNER
21 Asst Vice President for Finance .... Vacant
35 Associate VP Student Affairs .... Ms. Tanya RUSH
100 Chief of Staff .... Dr. Don-Terry VEAL
49 Dean College of Liberal Arts .... Dr. Mbare NGOM
50 Dean School Business & Management .... Dr. Fikru BOGHOSSIAN
53 Dean School of Education .... Dr. Glenda PRIME
54 Interim Dean School of Engineering .... Dr. Craig SCOTT
58 Dean of the Graduate School .... Dr. Mark GARRISON
48 Dean School of Architecture .... Dr. Mary Anne AKERS
70 Dean School of Social Work .... Dr. Anna MCPHATTER
69 Dean School of Community Health .... Dr. Kim SYDNOR
37 Director of Financial Aid .... Ms. Tanya WILKERSON
38 Director of Counseling Services .... Ms. Nina DOBSON-HOPKINS
08 Director of Library .... Dr. Richard BRADBERRY
06 Director of Records/Registration .... Ms. Keisha CAMPBELL
07 Director of Admissions .... Ms. Shonda GRAY
36 Director of Placement .... Ms. Seana COULTER
15 Associate Vice Pres Human Resources .... Mrs. Armada GRANT
29 Director Alumni Association .... Mrs. Joyce BROWN
14 Director Computer Center .... Mr. Gilbert MORGAN
86 Director State Relations .... Mr. Claude E. HITCHCOCK
09 Director of Institutional Research .... Ms. Cheryl ROLLINS
18 Director Physical Plant .... Mr. Premdat KOKILEPERSAUD
26 Asst Vice Pres Public Relations .... Mr. Larry JONES
84 Director Enrollment Management .... Vacant
96 Director of Purchasing .... Ms. Lois WHITAKER
28 Interim Director of Diversity .... Ms. Sally SWANN
104 Director Study Abroad .... Mr. Johnson NIBA
106 Director Online Education/E-learnin .... Ms. Cynthia BROWN-LAVEIST
108 Asst VP Institutional Assessment .... Dr. Solomon ALAO
19 Chief of Police .... Mr. Lance HATCHER
39 Director Residence Life & Housing .... Dr. Douglas GWYNN
41 Athletic Director .... Dr. Edward SCOTT
43 General Counsel .... Ms. Julie GOODWIN

Mount St. Mary's University (E)

16300 Old Emmitsburg Road,
Emmitsburg MD 21727-7799
County: Frederick | FICE Identification: 002086
Unit ID: 163462
Telephone: (301) 447-6122 | Carnegie Class: Masters/M
FAX Number: (301) 447-5634 | Calendar System: Semester
URL: msmary.edu
Established: 1808 | Annual Undergrad Tuition & Fees: $41,350
Enrollment: 2,323 | Coed
Affiliation or Control: Roman Catholic | IRS Status: 501(c)3
Highest Offering: Master's
Accreditation: M, CAEPN, CEA, IACBE, THEOL

01 President .... Dr. Timothy E. TRAINOR
05 Provost .... Dr. Boyd CREASMAN
03 Vice President/Rector .... Msgr. Andrew R. BAKER
100 Chief of Staff .... Mr. Wayne A. GREEN
10 Vice Pres for Business & Finance .... Mr. William E. DAVIES
26 VP Marketing and Communications .... Mr. Jack J. CHIELLI
32 Vice President for Student Life .... Dr. Bernard FRANKLIN
22 Vice President for Equity & Success .... Dr. Paula M. WHETSEL-RIBEAU
84 Vice President of Enrollment Mgmt .... Mr. Jack J. CHIELLI
111 Vice President for Advancement .... Mr. Robert J. BRENNAN
100 Vice President University Affairs . Ms. Pauline A. ENGLESTATTER
20 Assoc Provost .... Dr. David M. MCCARTHY
58 Assoc Provost Grad/Continuing Ed .... Dr. Jennifer L. STAIGER
49 Dean College of Liberal Arts .... Dr. Peter A. DORSEY
50 Dean Richard J Bolte Sr Sch of Bus .... Dr. Michael J. DRISCOLL
81 Dean School Natural Science & Math .... Dr. Kraig E. SHEETZ
53 Dean of the Education Division .... Dr. Barbara A. MARINAK
04 Sr Exec Assistant to the President .... Ms. June B. MILLER
41 Director of Athletics .... Ms. Lynne P. ROBINSON
35 Dean of Students .... Mr. Levi ESSES
42 Chaplain/Dir of Campus Ministry .... Fr. Diego RUIZ
36 Director Career Center .... Ms. Claire M. TAURIELLO
108 Director Institutional Assessment .... Dr. Jeffrey SIMMONS
09 Director Institutional Research .... Dr. Jeffrey SIMMONS
37 Director of Financial Aid .... Mr. David C. REEDER
06 Registrar .... Mr. Christopher WEBER
07 Director of Admissions .... Mr. Eric M. DANIELSON
08 Director of the Library .... Ms. Jessica J. WHITMORE
27 Director of PR & Communications .... Ms. Donna J. KLINGER
105 Director Web Services .... Ms. Karlie A. HERBERT
30 Director of Development .... Ms. Kimberly T. JOHNSON
29 Director of Alumni Engagement .... Ms. Emily A. MYERS
112 Major Gifts Officer .... Mr. Kevin J. KALIS
88 Director of University Operations .... Ms. Danielle K. NICKAS
15 Director of Human Resources .... Ms. Kristin M. HURLEY
38 Director Student Counseling .... Mr. Gerald T. ROOTH
19 Director of Public Safety .... Mr. Rodney F. GRAYS
24 Director of Media Systems .... Mr. John B. BREWER, JR.
21 Controller .... Ms. Christine SNEERINGER
114 Director of Budget .... Ms. Tina RYDER
39 Director of Residence Life .... Ms. Abigail M. VAN ANDEN
28 Director Ctr for Student Diversity .... Mr. Leon DIXON

88 Director Office of Social Justice ... Mr. Ian C. VANANDEN
92 Director of the Honors Program ... Dr. Sarah SCOTT
18 Director of Physical Plant ... Ms. Kimberly S. KLABE
96 Purchasing Agent ... Ms. Maria L. TOPPER
40 Manager of College Store ... Ms. Margaret A. PEREGORD

Ner Israel Rabbinical College (A)

400 Mount Wilson Lane, Baltimore MD 21208-1198
County: Baltimore FICE Identification: 002087
Unit ID: 163532
Telephone: (410) 484-7200 Carnegie Class: Spec-4-yr-Faith
FAX Number: (410) 484-3060 Calendar System: Semester
URL: www.nirc.edu
Established: 1933 Annual Undergrad Tuition & Fees: $12,400
Enrollment: 450 Male
Affiliation or Control: Independent Non-Profit IRS Status: 501(c)3
Highest Offering: Doctorate
Accreditation: RABN

01 President ... Rabbi Sheftel M. NEUBERGER
05 Chief Academic Officer ... Rabbi Aharon FELDMAN
88 Executive Director ... Mr. Jerome H. KADDEN
03 Vice President ... Rabbi Boruch NEUBERGER
07 Director of Admissions ... Rabbi Beryl WEISBORD
11 Director of Administrative Services ... Mr. Larry RIBAKOW
06 Registrar ... Rabbi Chaim D. LAPIDUS
06 Registrar ... Rabbi Joseph IFRAH
85 Foreign Student Advisor ... Rabbi Eliyahu HAKKAKIAN
30 Director of Development ... Rabbi Louis HOFFMAN
45 Director of Planning ... Rabbi Leonard OBERSTEIN
37 Director Student Financial Aid ... Rabbi Shmuel SCHACHTER
18 Chief Physical Plant ... Mr. David FRIEDMAN
08 Head Librarian ... Rabbi Avrohom SHNIDMAN
39 Director of Student Housing ... Rabbi Emanuel GOLDFEIZ
29 Associate Director Alumni Relations ... Rabbi Eli GREENGART

Notre Dame of Maryland University (B)

4701 N Charles Street, Baltimore MD 21210-2404
County: Independent City FICE Identification: 002065
Unit ID: 163578
Telephone: (410) 435-0100 Carnegie Class: Masters/L
FAX Number: (410) 532-5791 Calendar System: Semester
URL: www.ndm.edu
Established: 1873 Annual Undergrad Tuition & Fees: $36,900
Enrollment: 2,475 Female
Affiliation or Control: Roman Catholic IRS Status: 501(c)3
Highest Offering: Doctorate
Accreditation: M, ACBSP, CAEPN, NURSE, PHAR

01 President ... Dr. Marylou YAM
05 Vice President Academic Affairs ... Dr. Sharon SLEAR
32 Assoc Vice President Student Life ... Vacant
111 Vice Pres Institutional Advancement ... Dr. Tanya EASTON
84 Int Vice Pres Enrollment Management ... Ms. Sharon HANDELSMAN
10 Vice Pres for Finance & Admin ... Mr. Sean DELANEY
20 Associate VP Academic Affairs ... Dr. Suzan HARKNESS
37 Assoc VP Scholarships & Fin Aid ... Vacant
100 Chief of Staff ... Mr. Gregory FITZGERALD
06 Registrar ... Ms. Susanna PRICE
36 Director Career Center ... Vacant
13 Director Information Technology ... Mr. Warren SZELISTOWSKI
29 Director of Alumnae Relations ... Ms. Aliza ROSS
08 Librarian ... Ms. Barbara PREECE
85 Director International Education ... Ms. Margo CUNNIFFE
07 Interim Director of Admissions ... Ms. Marci LEADBETER
09 Dir Inst Research/Effectiveness ... Ms. Luz CACEDA
15 Director of Human Resources ... Ms. Theresa ARNOVE
18 Director of Facility Management ... Vacant
21 Controller ... Ms. Victoria WASHINGTON
38 Director Counseling Center ... Ms. Amy PROVAN
19 Director of Public Safety ... Mr. Gene TAYLOR
40 Bookstore Manager ... Ms. Emily WARNER
41 Athletic Director ... Ms. Renee BOSTIC
42 Director Campus Ministry & Service ... Sr. Mary KERBER
67 Dean School of Pharmacy ... Dr. Anne LIN
07 Director Pharmacy Admissions ... Mr. Larry SHATTUCK
25 Chief Contracts/Grants Admin ... Mr. Carroll GALVIN
26 Chief Public Relations/Marketing ... Mr. Christian KENDZIERSKI

Prince George's Community College (C)

301 Largo Road, Largo MD 20774-2199
County: Prince Georges FICE Identification: 002089
Unit ID: 163657
Telephone: (301) 546-7422 Carnegie Class: Assoc/MT-VT-High Trad
FAX Number: N/A Calendar System: Semester
URL: www.pgcc.edu
Established: 1958 Annual Undergrad Tuition & Fees (In-District): $3,770
Enrollment: 12,113 Coed
Affiliation or Control: Local IRS Status: 501(c)3
Highest Offering: Associate Degree
Accreditation: M, ADNUR, CAHIIM, COARC, EMT, #NMT, RAD, SURGT

01 President ... Dr. Charlene M. DUKES
05 Exec Vice Pres Academic Affairs ... Dr. Clayton RILEY
32 Interim Vice Pres Student Affairs ... Ms. Cathryn CAMP
10 Vice Pres Admin/Financial Svcs ... Ms. Terri BACOTE-CHARLES
103 AVP Workforce Development/Cont Educ ... Dr. Yvette J. SNOWDEN
13 Vice Pres Enterprise Technology/CIO ... Dr. Rhonda SPELLS FENTRY
20 Sr Acad Admin to VP for Acad Affs ... Ms. Catherine LAPALOMBARA
38 Dean Student Success/Engagement ... Dr. Scheherazade W. FORMAN
84 Dean of Student Enrollment ... Ms. Carol E. MCKINNON
09 Exec Dir Research/Assessment/Effect ... Dr. Laura ARIOVICH
15 Assoc Vice Pres Human Resources ... Ms. Lark T. DOBSON
21 Exec Director Financial Affairs ... Ms. Sabrina WELLS
100 Chief of Staff ... Dr. Kim R. BOBBY
08 Director Library ... Ms. Priscilla C. THOMPSON
06 Registrar ... Dr. Juanita D. WOMACK
07 Director Recruitment ... Vacant
18 Exec Dir Facilities Planning/Mgmt ... Dr. David C. MOSBY
88 Director Physical Facilities ... Dr. Melodye BATTEN-MICKENS
86 Dir Government Affairs & Compliance ... Vacant
30 Exec Dir Institutional Advancement ... Ms. Brenda S. MITCHELL
26 Sr Dir Communications & Marketing ... Ms. Annie CREWS
96 Interim Director of Procurement ... Mrs. LaTonya HOLLAND
37 Director Financial Aid ... Ms. Thelma L. ROSS
36 Manager Career & Job Services ... Ms. Stephanie S. PAIR-CUNNINGHAM
79 Dean Humanities/English/Social Sci ... Vacant
76 Dean Health Sci/Business/Public Svc ... Ms. Angela D. ANDERSON
81 Dean Science/Tech/Engr/Math ... Dr. Christine E. BARROW

St. John's College (D)

60 College Avenue, Annapolis MD 21401
County: Anne Arundel FICE Identification: 002092
Unit ID: 163976
Telephone: (410) 263-2371 Carnegie Class: Bac-A&S
FAX Number: (410) 626-2886 Calendar System: Semester
URL: www.sjc.edu
Established: 1784 Annual Undergrad Tuition & Fees: $53,343
Enrollment: 513 Coed
Affiliation or Control: Independent Non-Profit IRS Status: 501(c)3
Highest Offering: Master's
Accreditation: M

01 President ... Mr. Peter KANELOS
05 Dean of College ... Mr. Joseph MACFARLAND
30 VP Development/Alumni Relations ... Ms. Kelly BROWN
84 Vice President of Enrollment ... Mr. Benjamin BAUM
58 Assoc Dean for Graduate Program ... Ms. Emily LANGSTON
10 Treasurer/Financial Officer ... Ms. Ally GONTANG-HIGHFIELD
06 Registrar ... Ms. Melissa STEINER
102 Director Corporate/Foundation Rels ... Ms. Susan BORDEN
37 Director of Financial Aid ... Mr. Steven BELL
08 Library Director ... Ms. Catherine DIXON
15 Director of Human Resources ... Ms. Lynn HOBBS
18 Director of Buildings and Grounds ... Mr. JR PAPPAS
19 Director of Public Safety ... Mr. Robert MUECK
23 Director of Student Health ... Ms. Nancy CALABRESE
26 Director of Communications ... Ms. Carol CARPENTER
32 Director of Student Services ... Ms. Taylor WATERS
36 Director of Career Services ... Ms. Jaime DUNN
21 Controller ... Ms. Sarah MACDONALD
29 Director of Alumni Relations ... Vacant
20 Assistant to the Dean ... Ms. Heather LATHAM
04 Executive Asst to President ... Ms. Loren ROTNER
40 Bookstore Manager ... Mr. Robin DUNN
41 Athletics & Recreation Coordinator ... Mr. Christopher KRUEGER

† See Affiliate: St. John's College at Santa Fe, NM.

St. Mary's College of Maryland (E)

47645 College Drive, Saint Mary's City MD 20686-3001
County: Saint Mary's FICE Identification: 002095
Unit ID: 163912
Telephone: (240) 895-2000 Carnegie Class: Bac-A&S
FAX Number: (240) 895-4462 Calendar System: Semester
URL: www.smcm.edu
Established: 1840 Annual Undergrad Tuition & Fees (In-State): $14,806
Enrollment: 1,598 Coed
Affiliation or Control: State IRS Status: 501(c)3
Highest Offering: Master's
Accreditation: M

01 President ... Dr. Tuajuanda C. JORDAN
05 Provost/Dean of Faculty ... Dr. Michael R. WICK
10 VP Business & Finance ... Mr. Paul A. PUSECKER
111 VP for Institutional Advancement ... Ms. Carolyn S. CURRY
84 VP Enrollment Management ... Mr. David L. HAUTANEN
21 Asst Vice President for Finance ... Mr. Christopher J. TRUE
101 Exec Assistant to President ... Ms. Betsy BARRETO
26 Asst VP of Marketing/Communication ... Mr. Michael L. BRUCKLER
29 Director Alumni Relations ... Mr. David M. SUSHINSKY
06 Registrar ... Mr. Nickolas B. TULLEY
20 Assoc Dean of Faculty ... Dr. Katherine L. GANTZ
37 Director of Financial Aid ... Mr. Rob W. MADDOX
07 Director Enrollment Operations ... Ms. Bhargavi BANDI
32 VP for Student Affairs ... Mr. Leonard E. BROWN, JR.
38 Dir of the Wellness Center ... Ms. Laurie L. SCHERER
41 Director of Athletics/Recreation ... Mr. Scott W. DEVINE
20 Assoc Dean of Curriculum ... Dr. Christine A. WOOLEY
18 Director of Physical Plant ... Ms. Annette V. ANGUEIRA
19 Director of Public Safety ... Ms. Tressa A. SETLAK
40 Director of the Campus Store ... Mr. Richard T. WAGNER
15 Director of Human Resources ... Ms. Shannon K. JARBOE
23 Director of Health Services ... Vacant
124 Assoc Dean Retention/Stdnt Success ... Ms. Joanne A. GOLDWATER
13 Asst VP of Information Technology ... Ms. Jenelle SARGENT
44 Sr Devel Ofcr Annual Giving ... Mr. Richard J. EDGAR
08 Director of the Library/Media Svcs ... Ms. Katherine E. PITCHER
102 Director of Corporate and Found ... Ms. Lauren K. SAMPSON
21 Comptroller/Director of Accounting ... Mr. Gabriel A. MBOMEH
43 Assistant Attorney General ... Ms. Allison J. BOYLE
16 Assoc Dir Human Resources ... Mr. Melvin A. MCCLINTOCK
25 Director of Sponsored Research ... Dr. Sabine DILLINGHAM
109 Procurement Ofcr/Dir of Auxiliary ... Mr. Patrick G. HUNT
92 Director DeSousa Brent Scholars Pgm ... Dr. Frederico J. TALLEY
88 Director Events and Conferences ... Ms. Linda T. JONES
30 Asst VP Development ... Ms. Karen C. RALEY
104 Director of International Education ... Ms. Danielle BARR
36 Dir of Career Development ... Ms. Kate A. SHIREY
04 Executive Asst to President ... Ms. Jennifer L. SIVAK
91 Director Administrative Computing ... Vacant
39 Exec Dir of Student Life ... Mr. Derek M. YOUNG
88 Dir of Title IX Compliance ... Mr. Michael K. DUNN
09 Director of Institutional Research ... Dr. Anne Marie BRADY
28 VP Inclusion/Diversity/Equity ... Dr. Tayo CLYBURN
105 Director Web Services ... Ms. Jeannette L. MODIC
108 Coordinator of Assessment ... Dr. Katy E. ARNETT

Saint Mary's Seminary and University (F)

5400 Roland Avenue, Baltimore MD 21210-1994
County: Baltimore City FICE Identification: 002096
Unit ID: 163842
Telephone: (410) 864-4000 Carnegie Class: Not Classified
FAX Number: (410) 864-4278 Calendar System: Semester
URL: www.stmarys.edu
Established: 1791 Annual Undergrad Tuition & Fees: N/A
Enrollment: N/A Coed
Affiliation or Control: Roman Catholic IRS Status: 501(c)3
Highest Offering: First Professional Degree
Accreditation: M, THEOL

01 President/Rector ... Rev. Phillip J. BROWN
10 Vice President for Finance ... Mr. Richard G. CHILDS
111 Vice Pres Advancement/Human Res ... Mrs. Elizabeth L. VISCONAGE
05 Dean School Theology ... Rev. Gladstone STEVENS
73 Dean St Mary's Ecumenical Institute ... Dr. D. Brent LAYTHAM
73 Dean Ecclesiastical Fac/Sch Theol ... Rev. Thomas BURKE
06 University Registrar ... Ms. Paula M. THIGPEN
113 Ecumenical Inst Billing Officer ... Ms. Marcia HANCOCK
08 Director of Knott Library ... Mr. Thomas RASZEWSKI
13 Director Information Services ... Mr. Arryn MILNE
84 Director of Recruitment ... Ms. Kaye GUIDUGLI

The SANS Technology Institute (G)

11200 Rockville Pike, Suite 200,
North Bethesda MD 20852
County: Montgomery Identification: 667006
Telephone: (301) 654-7267 Carnegie Class: Not Classified
FAX Number: (301) 951-0140 Calendar System: Other
URL: www.sans.org
Established: 2006 Annual Graduate Tuition & Fees: N/A
Enrollment: N/A Coed
Affiliation or Control: Proprietary IRS Status: Proprietary
Highest Offering: Master's; No Undergraduates
Accreditation: M

01 President ... Mr. Alan PALLER
03 Executive Director ... Mr. Eric PATTERSON
05 Provost ... Dr. Toby GOUKER

Stevenson University (H)

1525 Greenspring Valley Road,
Stevenson MD 21153-0641
County: Baltimore FICE Identification: 002107
Unit ID: 164173
Telephone: (410) 486-7000 Carnegie Class: Masters/L
FAX Number: (410) 486-3552 Calendar System: Semester
URL: www.stevenson.edu
Established: 1947 Annual Undergrad Tuition & Fees: $36,242
Enrollment: 3,876 Coed
Affiliation or Control: Independent Non-Profit IRS Status: 501(c)3
Highest Offering: Master's
Accreditation: M, CAEPN, CSHSE, MT, NURSE

01 President ... Dr. Elliot HIRSHMAN
04 Assistant to President ... Ms. Ruth HUBBARD
05 Exec VP Academic Affairs/Provost ... Dr. Susan T. GORMAN
10 Exec Vice Pres/Chief Financial Ofcr ... Mr. Timothy M. CAMPBELL
111 Vice Pres University Advancement ... Mr. Chris VAUGHAN
84 Vice Pres Enrollment Management ... Mr. Mark J. HERGAN
32 Vice President Student Affairs ... Ms. Tiffany SANCHEZ
26 VP Marketing/Digital Communications ... Mr. John BUETTNER
15 Vice Pres for Human Resources ... Mr. Dave JORDAN
100 Vice President & Chief of Staff ... Ms. Sue B. KENNEY
36 Vice President Career Services ... Ms. Sue B. GORDON
20 Asst VP for Academic Affairs ... Dr. Bridget H. BRENNAN
28 Asst VP Multicultural Experience ... Ms. Natalie GILLARD

58 Dean Graduate/Professional Studies ... Ms. Anne DAVIS
50 Interim Dean School of Business ... Mr. Aris MELISSARATOS
81 Dean School of Science ... Dr. Meredith DURMOWICZ
83 Dean Sch of Humanities/Social Sci ... Ms. Cheryl WILSON
88 Dean School of Design ... Ms. Amanda HOSTALKA
53 Dean School of Education ... Dr. Deborah KRAFT
23 Assoc Dean/Dir of Wellness Center ... Ms. Linda REYMANN
66 Associate Dean GPS Nursing ... Dr. Judith FEUSTLE
106 Associate Dean Distance Education ... Dr. Barbara ZIRKIN
18 Asst VP Facilities & Campus Svcs ... Mr. Leland R. BEITEL
21 Asst VP Financial Affs/Controller ... Ms. Melanie M. EDMONDSON
37 Director Financial Aid ... Ms. Melanie MASON
35 Assoc VP/Dean of Students ... Dr. Jeffrey M. KELLY
13 Assoc VP Information Technology/CIO ... Vacant
09 Dir Inst Research/Assessment ... Dr. Natasha MILLER
08 Director of Library Services ... Ms. Susan H. BONSTEEL
06 Registrar ... Ms. Tracy L. BOLT
19 Director of Security ... Mr. Greg CULLISON
41 Director Athletics ... Mr. Brett C. ADAMS
109 Director Auxiliary Services ... Mr. Robert REED
29 Director Alumni Relations ... Ms. Allison HUMPHRIES
22 Dir of Disability Services ... Ms. Terri MASSIE-BURRELL

Stratford University Baltimore Campus (A)

210 S. Central Avenue, Baltimore MD 21202
Telephone: (410) 762-4031 Identification: 770616
Accreditation: ACICS, ACFEI

† Branch campus of Stratford University, Falls Church, VA

*The University System of Maryland Office (B)

701 E. Pratt St., Baltimore MD 21202
County: Independent City FICE Identification: 007959
Unit ID: 164146
Telephone: (301) 445-2740 Carnegie Class: N/A
FAX Number: (301) 445-1931
URL: www.usmd.edu

01 Chancellor ... Dr. Robert L. CARET
05 Sr VC Academic Affairs ... Dr. Joann BOUGHMAN
10 Vice Chanc Admin & Finance ... Ms. Ellen HERBST
111 VC Advancement & CEO USM Foundation ... Mr. Leonard R. RALEY
86 VC Governmental Relations ... Mr. Patrick N. HOGAN
26 VC for Communications ... Mr. Timothy J. MCDONOUGH
20 Assoc Vice Chanc Academic Affairs ... Dr. Antoinette COLEMAN
13 Assoc VC & CIO ... Mr. Donald Z. SPICER
100 Chief of Staff to Chancellor ... Ms. Denise WILKERSON
116 Director Internal Audit ... Mr. David MOSCA
114 Director Budget Analysis ... Ms. Monica WEST

*University of Maryland College Park (C)

1101 Main Administration Building,
College Park MD 20742
County: Prince Georges FICE Identification: 002103
Unit ID: 163286
Telephone: (301) 405-1000 Carnegie Class: DU-Highest
FAX Number: (301) 314-9560 Calendar System: Semester
URL: www.umd.edu
Established: 1856 Annual Undergrad Tuition & Fees (In-State): $10,595
Enrollment: 40,521 Coed
Affiliation or Control: State IRS Status: 501(c)3
Highest Offering: Doctorate
Accreditation: M, AUD, CAEPN, CEA, CLPSY, COPSY, DANCE, DIETD, DIETI, IACBE, IPSY, JOUR, LIB, LSAR, MFCD, MUS, PCSAS, PH, PLNG, SCPSY, SP, SPAA

02 President ... Dr. Wallace D. LOH
05 Senior Vice President & Provost ... Dr. Mary Ann RANKIN
100 Asst President & Chief of Staff ... Ms. Michele A. EASTMAN
11 Vice President for Admin & Finance ... Mr. Carlo COLELLA
32 Vice President for Student Affairs ... Dr. Linda M. CLEMENT
111 Vice President University Relations ... Ms. Jacqueline A. LEWIS
46 Vice President for Research ... Dr. Laurie LOCASCIO
13 Vice President and CIO ... Dr. Jeffrey K. HOLLINGSWORTH
43 Vice President and General Counsel ... Mr. Michael R. POTERALA
28 Vice Pres for Diversity & Inclusion ... Dr. Georgina DODGE
47 Dean Col Agriculture/Natl Resources ... Dr. Craig BEYROUTY
48 Interim Dean School of Architecture ... Dr. Donald LINEBAUGH
79 Dean College Arts & Humanities ... Dr. Bonnie T. DILL
83 Dean Col Behavioral/Social Sciences ... Dr. Gregory F. BALL
50 Dean Smith School of Business ... Dr. Alexander J. TRIANTIS
81 Dean Col of Comp/Math/Natural Sci ... Dr. Amitabh VARSHNEY
53 Dean College of Education ... Dr. Jennifer K. RICE
54 Dean Clark School of Engineering ... Dr. Darryll J. PINES
69 Dean School of Public Health ... Dr. Boris D. LUSHNIAK
60 Dean Merrill College of Journalism ... Ms. Lucy A. DALGLISH
62 Dean College of Information Studies ... Dr. Keith MARZULLO
80 Dean School of Public Policy ... Dr. Robert C. ORR
20 Dean Undergraduate Studies ... Dr. William A. COHEN
58 Dean Graduate School ... Dr. Steve FETTER
08 Dean of the Libraries ... Dr. Adriene LIM
20 Assoc VP Innovation & Entrepreneur ... Dr. Dean CHANG
85 Assoc VP International Affairs ... Dr. Ross D. LEWIN
20 Assoc VP Acad Aff/Finance Personnel ... Ms. Cynthia R. HALE
51 Assoc VP Extended Studies ... Vacant
09 Asst VP Inst Research & Planning ... Ms. Sharon A. LA VOY
84 Assoc VP Enrollment Management ... Ms. Barbara A. GILL
20 Assoc Provost Faculty Affairs ... Dr. John BERTOT
108 Assoc Provost Acad Planning & Pgms ... Dr. Elizabeth J. BEISE
20 Assoc Provost Planning/Special Proj ... Mr. David CRONRATH
20 Assoc Provost Enterpr Resource Plng ... Dr. Jack BLANCHARD
20 Exec Dir Teach & Learn Transfrm Ctr ... Dr. Kathy TAKAYAMA
07 Exec Dir Undergraduate Admissions ... Ms. Shannon GUNDY
06 University Registrar ... Dr. Adrian R. CORNELIUS
92 Executive Director Honors College ... Dr. Susan J. DWYER
37 Director Student Financial Aid ... Mr. Dawit LEMMA
104 Dir Intl Student & Scholar Services ... Ms. Susan-Ellis DOUGHERTY
10 Assoc VP & Chief Financial Officer ... Mr. Paul S. DWORKIS
18 Assoc VP & Chief Facilities Officer ... Mr. Charles R. REUNING
96 Asst VP Procurement Str Sourcing ... Ms. Kimberly WATSON
15 Asst VP University Human Resources ... Ms. Jewel WASHINGTON
88 Asst VP for Real Estate ... Mr. Edward MAGINNIS, JR.
88 Asst VP Administration Finance ... Ms. Anne MARTENS
19 Dir Pub Safety/Chief Campus Police ... Mr. David B. MITCHELL
117 Exec Dir Env Safety/Sustain/Risk ... Ms. Maureen KOTLAS
21 Controller ... Ms. C. Christina HO
113 Bursar/Assoc Comptroller ... Ms. Alisa ABADINSKY
35 Asst VP for Student Affairs ... Dr. Mary HUMMEL
35 Asst VP for Student Affairs ... Dr. Warren KELLEY
35 Asst VP for Student Affairs ... Dr. John ZACKER
35 Asst VP for Student Affairs ... Dr. Brooke SUPPLE
36 Director University Career Center ... Mr. Kelley BISHOP
109 Director Stamp Student Union ... Dr. Marsha A. GUENZLER-STEVENS
23 Director University Health Center ... Dr. David MCBRIDE
38 Director Counseling Center ... Dr. Sharon E. KIRKLAND-GORDON
122 Director Fraternity Sorority Life ... Dr. Matt SUPPLE
39 Director Resident Life ... Vacant
26 Assoc VP Strategic Communications ... Dr. Joel SELIGMAN
30 Assoc VP University Development ... Mr. JR BLACKBURN
112 Asst VP University Relations ... Ms. Veronica MEINHARD
110 Asst VP University Relations ... Ms. Bernadette MALDONADO
29 Exec Director Alumni Association ... Ms. Amy EICHHORST
88 Assoc VP for Research ... Ms. Denise CLARK
88 Assoc VP Research Development ... Mr. Eric CHAPMAN
88 Assc VP Innovation Econ Development ... Ms. Julie LENZER
25 Director Research Administration ... Ms. Wendy MONTGOMERY
14 Asst VP Chief Technology Officer ... Ms. Tripti SINHA
14 Asst VP Academic Tech & Innovation ... Dr. Marcio A. OLIVEIRA
91 Exec Dir Enterprise Engineering ... Mr. Axel PERSAUD
119 Director Chief IT Security Officer ... Mr. Gerry SNEERINGER
90 Director Enterprise Planning ... Mr. Joseph DRASIN
86 Exec Director Government Relations ... Mr. Ross STERN
41 Director Intercollegiate Athletics ... Mr. Damon EVANS

*University of Maryland, Baltimore (D)

220 Arch Street, 14th Floor, Baltimore MD 21201-1508
County: Independent City FICE Identification: 002104
Unit ID: 163259
Telephone: (410) 706-7002 Carnegie Class: Spec-4-yr-Med
FAX Number: (410) 706-0500 Calendar System: Semester
URL: www.umaryland.edu
Established: 1807 Annual Undergrad Tuition & Fees (In-State): N/A
Enrollment: 6,703 Coed
Affiliation or Control: State IRS Status: 501(c)3
Highest Offering: Doctorate
Accreditation: M, ANEST, DENT, DH, DIETI, IPSY, LAW, MED, MT, NURSE, PA, PH, PHAR, PTA, RADDOS, SW

02 President ... Dr. Jay A. PERMAN
05 Exec VP/Prov & Dean Grad School ... Dr. Bruce E. JARRELL
11 Sr VP Opers & Inst Effect/Vice Dean ... Dr. Roger J. WARD
17 Exec VP Medical Affairs/Dean ... Dr. E. Albert REECE
10 Chief Admin & Finance Officer/VP ... Ms. Dawn M. RHODES
25 VP/Chf Enterprise & Econ Dev Ofc ... Mr. James L. HUGHES
13 VP/Chief Information Officer ... Dr. Peter J. MURRAY
46 Sr VP/Chief Acad & Research Officer ... Dr. Bruce E. JARRELL
26 Sr VP External Relations ... Ms. Jennifer B. LITCHMAN
30 Chief Philanthropy Officer/VP ... Mr. Thomas J. SULLIVAN
86 Chief Govt Affairs Officer/AVP ... Mr. Kevin P. KELLY
43 Chief University Counsel ... Ms. Susan GILLETTE
19 Chief of Police ... Ms. Alice CARY
88 Chief Accountability Officer ... Dr. Roger J. WARD
32 Sr Assoc Dean/AVP Acad & Stdnt Affs ... Dr. Flavius R. LILLY
18 Assoc VP Facilities & Operations ... Mr. Terry MORSE
15 Assoc VP Human Resources ... Mr. Matthew LASECKI
37 Assoc VP Student Financial Asst ... Ms. Patricia A. SCOTT
110 Assoc VP Development ... Mr. Larry KUSHNER
113 Assoc VP Budget & Finance ... Mr. Scott BITNER
27 Assoc VP Communications/Public Affs ... Ms. Laura A. KOZAK
88 Deputy Chief Accountability Ofc AVP ... Ms. Susan BUSKIRK
14 Asst VP Information Technology ... Mr. Christopher G. PHILLIPS
09 Asst VP Inst Rsrch & Accountability ... Mr. Gregory C. SPENGLER
96 AVP Strategic Sourcing & Acquis ... Mr. Joseph EVANS
45 AVP Real Estate Planning Space Mgt ... Mr. Stue SIROTA
88 AVP Sponsored Projects Accounting ... Ms. Laura SCARANTINO
88 AVP ORD Marketing & Operations ... Ms. Linda KENDERDINE
88 AVP ORD Sponsored Programs Admin ... Mr. Dennis PAFFRATH
88 AVP ORD Technology Transfer ... Mr. Philip ROBILOTTO
88 AVP ORD Center for Clinical Trials ... Mr. Michael ROLLOR
88 AVP ORD Economic Development ... Ms. Jane SHAAB
102 Treasurer & Dir of Operations UMBF ... Ms. Pamela HECKLER
08 Exec Dir Health Sci/Human Svc Libr ... Ms. Mary J. TOOEY
90 Exec Dir Enterprise Applications ... Mr. Michael SMITH
31 Exec Dir Cmty Initiatives/Engage ... Ms. Ashley R. VALIS
06 Director Records & Registration ... Mr. Ryan HOLTZ
88 Director Benefits & Compensation ... Ms. Patricia HOFFMAN
22 Director EEO/Affirmative Action ... Ms. Sheila GREENWOOD-BLACKSHEAR
28 Director Diversity and Inclusion ... Ms. Mikhel A. KUSHNER
85 Director International Services ... Ms. Amy RAMIREZ
38 Director Counseling ... Ms. Emilia K. PETRILLO
41 Director Univ Recreation & Fitness ... Mr. William P. CROCKETT
23 Director Student Health Center ... Dr. James BARONAS
35 Director Student Services ... Ms. Cynthia E. RICE
39 Director of UM Housing ... Ms. Margaret SCHOTTO
88 Director of Financial Services ... Mr. Larry MILLER
106 Dir Online Education/E-learning ... Dr. Flavius R. LILLY
105 Dir Web Dev Interactive Media ... Mr. Amir CHAMSAZ
52 Dean School of Dentistry ... Dr. Mark A. REYNOLDS
58 Dean Graduate School ... Dr. Bruce E. JARRELL
61 Dean School of Law ... Mr. Donald TOBIN
63 Dean School of Medicine ... Dr. E. Albert REECE
66 Dean School of Nursing ... Dr. Jane M. KIRSCHLING
67 Dean School of Pharmacy ... Dr. Natalie D. EDDINGTON
70 Dean School of Social Work ... Dr. Richard P. BARTH
04 Admin Assistant to the President ... Ms. Clara WOODLY

*University of Maryland Baltimore County (E)

1000 Hilltop Circle, Baltimore MD 21250-0001
County: Baltimore FICE Identification: 002105
Unit ID: 163268
Telephone: (410) 455-1000 Carnegie Class: DU-Higher
FAX Number: (410) 455-1210 Calendar System: 4/1/4
URL: www.umbc.edu
Established: 1966 Annual Undergrad Tuition & Fees (In-State): $11,778
Enrollment: 13,662 Coed
Affiliation or Control: State IRS Status: 501(c)3
Highest Offering: Doctorate
Accreditation: M, CAEPN, CLPSY, DANCE, DMS, EMT, IPSY, MUS, SW

02 President ... Dr. Freeman A. HRABOWSKI
05 Provost/Sr Vice Pres Academic Affs ... Dr. Philip ROUS
10 Vice Pres Finance/Administration ... Ms. Lynne SCHAEFER
32 Vice President Student Affairs ... Dr. Nancy YOUNG
111 Vice Pres Institutional Advancement ... Mr. Gregory SIMMONS
13 Vice Pres Information Technology ... Mr. Jack J. SUESS
46 Vice President of Research ... Dr. Karl V. STEINER
49 Dean Col of Arts/Humanities/Soc Sci ... Dr. Scott CASPER
81 Dean Col Natural/Math Sciences ... Dr. William LACOURSE
54 Dean College of Engr/Info Tech ... Dr. Keith BOWMAN
84 Asst Dean Graduate Enrollment Mgmt ... Ms. K. Jill BARR
20 Vice Provost/Dean Undergrad Educ ... Dr. Katharine COLE
107 Vice Provost Professional Studies ... Dr. Christopher STEELE
20 Vice Provost Academic Affairs ... Dr. Antonio R. MOREIRA
58 Dean/Vice Provost for Graduate Educ ... Dr. Janet RUTLEDGE
15 Vice Provost Faculty Affairs ... Dr. Patrice MCDERMOTT
84 Vice Provost Enrollment Management ... Dr. Yvette MOZIE-ROSS
21 Assoc VP Financial Services ... Ms. Kathy DETTLOFF
26 Assistant to Pres/Assoc VP Mktg/PR ... Ms. Lisa G. AKCHIN
11 Assoc VP Administrative Services ... Ms. Terry COOK
16 Chief HR Officer/Assoc VP ... Ms. Valerie A. THOMAS
29 Director Alumni Relations ... Ms. Stanyell BRUCE
88 Asst VP New Media/Instruction Tech ... Mr. John FRITZ
18 Asst VP Facilities Management ... Mr. Lenn CARON
04 Senior Advisor to the President ... Dr. Peter HENDERSON
96 Director of Procurement ... Dr. Elizabeth MOSS
92 Director Honors College ... Dr. Simon STACEY
41 Director Physical Educ & Recreation ... Dr. Tim HALL
19 Chief of University Police ... Mr. Paul DILLON
36 Asst VP Career & Corp Partnership ... Ms. Caroline BAKER
23 Director Health Services ... Dr. Bruce HERMAN
37 Director Financial Aid ... Ms. Jane HICKEY
25 Asst Director Sponsored Programs ... Mr. Stanley JACKSON
40 Acting Director Bookstore ... Ms. Regina THURSTON
85 Assoc Vice Prov International Educ ... Dr. David DIMARIA
08 Director Library ... Mr. Patrick DAWSON
06 Registrar ... Ms. Pamela HAWLEY
35 Director Student Life ... Dr. Daniel BARNHART
43 General Counsel ... Mr. David GLEASON
07 Asst Vice Prov Admiss/Orientation ... Mr. Dale BITTINGER
39 Director Residential Life ... Mr. John FOX
09 Director of Institutional Research ... Dr. Connie PIERSON
38 Director Student Counseling ... Dr. Bruce HERMAN
100 Chief of Staff President's Office ... Ms. Candace DODSON-REED
108 Director Institutional Assessment ... Mr. Robert CARPENTER
22 Dir Affirm Action/Equal Opportunity ... Mr. Bobbie HOYE
28 Director of Diversity ... Ms. Lisa GRAY
30 Director of Development ... Mr. Mike BUCCINO
44 Director Annual Giving ... Ms. Joanne MEREDITH
90 Director Academic Computing ... Mr. Damian DOYLE
91 Director Administrative Computing ... Mr. Joseph KIRBY
88 Dean Erickson School ... Dr. Dana BRADLEY

*University of Maryland Center for Environmental Science (F)

PO Box 775, Cambridge MD 21613
County: Dorchester Identification: 667159
Telephone: (410) 228-9250 Carnegie Class: Not Classified
FAX Number: (410) 228-3843 Calendar System: Semester
URL: www.umces.edu
Established: 1925 Annual Graduate Tuition & Fees: N/A
Enrollment: N/A Coed
Affiliation or Control: State IRS Status: 501(c)3
Highest Offering: Doctorate; No Undergraduates
Accreditation: M

02 President .... Dr. Peter GOODWIN
05 Vice Pres for Education .... Dr. Larry SANFORD
10 Vice President for Finance .... Ms. Lynn REHN

*University of Maryland Eastern Shore (A)

11868 Academic Oval, Princess Anne MD 21853-1299
County: Somerset FICE Identification: 002106
Unit ID: 163338
Telephone: (410) 651-2200 Carnegie Class: DU-Higher
FAX Number: (410) 651-6105 Calendar System: Semester
URL: www.umes.edu
Established: 1886 Annual Undergrad Tuition & Fees (In-State): $8,302
Enrollment: 3,490 Coed
Affiliation or Control: State IRS Status: 501(c)3
Highest Offering: Doctorate
Accreditation: M, CACREP, CONST, DIETD, DIETI, PHAR, PTA

02 President .... Dr. Heidi M. ANDERSON
100 Chief of Staff .... Dr. Robert C. MOCK
05 Provost/VP Academic Affairs .... Dr. Nancy S. NIEMI
10 VP Administration and Finance .... Mr. Lester S. PRIMUS
84 Vice President Enrollment Mgmt .... Mr. Hans S. COOPER
111 VP Institutional Advancement .... Mr. David A. BALCOM
13 Chief Information Officer .... Mr. Jerry WALDRON
20 Int Assoc VP Academic Affairs .... Dr. Latasha WADE
21 Associate VP Finance .... Ms. Michelle D. MARTIN
114 Budget Director .... Ms. Beatrice V. WRIGHT
15 Interim Director of Human Resources .... Ms. Ann S. MANUEL
35 Asst VP Student Affairs .... Vacant
91 Director Administrative Computing .... Mr. Kenneth GASTON
29 Director Alumni Affairs .... Mr. James G. LUNNERMON, II
08 Interim Dean Library Services .... Ms. Sharon D. BROOKS
37 Interim Director Financial Aid .... Mr. Marcel E. JAGNE-SHAW
23 Director Student Health Services .... Ms. Sharone V. GRANT
96 Director Procurement .... Ms. Jacqueline M. COLLINS
07 Director of Admissions & Enrollment .... Vacant
06 Registrar .... Ms. Cheryl HOLDEN-DUFFY
12 Int Gen Mgr Richard A Henson Center .... Ms. Ciera E. NIMMONS
36 Director Career Services .... Dr. Theresa QUEENAN
09 Director Inst Research/Plng/Assess .... Dr. Stanley M. NYIRENDA
19 Interim Director Public Safety .... Mr. Mark TYLER
18 Interim Director Physical Plant . Ms. Jicola R. JOYNES-STURGIS
39 Interim Director Residence Life .... Ms. Shannon N. WARREN
41 Athletic Director .... Mr. Keith S. DAVIDSON
21 Comptroller .... Ms. Bonita E. BYRD
46 Director Sponsored Research .... Ms. Catherine BOLEK
124 Director Student Retention .... Ms. Kimberly CLARK-SHAW
88 Director Upward Bound .... Dr. Nicole L. GALE
35 Director Student Activities .... Ms. Qiana J. DRUMMOND
88 Director Title III Program .... Dr. Frances H. MCKINNEY
26 Director Public Relations .... Mr. William ROBINSON
30 Director Development .... Vacant
111 Director Advancement Services .... Ms. Chenita R. REDDICK
51 Coordinator Continuing Education .... Ms. Gretchen M. BOGGS
38 Coordinator Counseling Services .... Dr. Patricia E. TILGHMAN
58 Interim Dean Graduate Studies .... Dr. Lakeisha L. HARRIS
47 Dean School Agric/Natural Sciences .... Dr. Moses T. KAIRO
57 Dean Sch Educ/Soc Sci/The Arts .... Dr. Marshall STEVENSON
50 Int Dean School Business & Tech .... Dr. Kate BROWN
67 Dean Sch Pharmacy/Health Prof .... Dr. Rondall E. ALLEN
28 Director of Diversity .... Mr. Jason A. CASARES
04 Exec Admin Asst to the President .... Ms. Priscilla A. LONDON
104 Director Center for Intl Education .... Dr. Lombuso S. KHOZA
105 Webmaster .... Mr. Jeremy W. TOWNSEND
106 Int Dir Online Education/E-learning .... Ms. Catherine HANSENS-PASSERI
43 General Counsel .... Mr. Matthew A. TAYLOR
86 Director Government Relations .... Mr. Jim N. MATHIAS
90 Int Director Information Technology .... Mr. Joseph R. SMITH

*University of Maryland Global Campus (B)

3501 University Boulevard East, Adelphi MD 20783-7998
County: Prince Georges FICE Identification: 011644
Unit ID: 163204
Telephone: (301) 985-7000 Carnegie Class: Masters/L
FAX Number: N/A Calendar System: Semester
URL: www.umuc.edu
Established: 1947 Annual Undergrad Tuition & Fees (In-State): $7,416
Enrollment: 59,379 Coed
Affiliation or Control: State IRS Status: 501(c)3
Highest Offering: Doctorate
Accreditation: M, CAEPN, CAHIIM, NURSE

02 President .... Mr. Javier MIYARES
05 Sr Vice Pres/Chief Academic Officer .... Dr. Alan DRIMMER
11 Sr VP Admin & Finance/CFO .... Ms. Lisa KEMP
84 Sr VP Strategic Enrollment Mgmt .... Ms. Erika ORRIS
26 Sr Vice President Communications .... Mr. Michael FREEDMAN
88 Sr VP Global Military Operations .... Mr. Lloyd MILES
45 Sr VP Institutional Effectiveness .... Vacant
88 Special Advisor to the President .... Mr. George SHOENBERGER
10 Vice Pres Financial Operations .... Mr. Eugene D. LOCKETT, JR.
43 Vice President & General Counsel .... Ms. Maureen DAVID
15 Vice President Human Resources .... Ms. JulieAnn GARCIA
86 Vice Pres Federal Govt Relations .... Vacant
111 Vice Pres Inst Advancement .... Ms. Cathy SWEET
28 VP/Chief Diversity Ofcr/Ombudsman .... Dr. Blair HAYES
07 Vice Pres Admissions .... Ms. Jamie JAYNES
18 Associate Vice President Facilities .... Mr. George TRUJILLO
86 Director of State Govt Relations .... Ms. Erin FAVAZZA
37 AVP Student Financial Aid .... Ms. Cheryl STORIE
58 Vice Provost/Dean Graduate School .... Ms. Kathryn KLOSE
08 Assoc Provost of Library Services .... Mr. Stephen MILLER
06 Assoc Vice Provost/Registrar .... Ms. Joellen SHENDY
49 Dean The Undergrad School .... Ms. Kara VAN DAM
09 Sr Director Institutional Research .... Mr. Wei ZHOU
04 Exec Assistant to the President .... Ms. Lisa JACKSON
100 Chief of Staff .... Mr. Frank PRINCIPE
19 Director Security .... Mr. William BROGAN
29 Assoc VP Alumni Programs .... Ms. Nikki SANDOVAL

*Bowie State University (C)

14000 Jericho Park Road, Bowie MD 20715-3318
County: Prince Georges FICE Identification: 002062
Unit ID: 162007
Telephone: (301) 860-4000 Carnegie Class: Masters/L
FAX Number: (301) 860-3510 Calendar System: Semester
URL: www.bowiestate.edu
Established: 1865 Annual Undergrad Tuition & Fees (In-State): $8,234
Enrollment: 6,148 Coed
Affiliation or Control: State IRS Status: 501(c)3
Highest Offering: Doctorate
Accreditation: M, ACBSP, CACREP, CAEPN, NUR, SPAA, SW

02 President .... Dr. Aminta BREAUX
05 Provost/Vice Pres Academic Affs . Dr. DeBrenna LaFa AGBENYIGA
10 VP Finance & Administration .... Mr. Anthony SAVIA
109 Assoc VP Auxiliary Services .... Mr. Wade HENLEY
21 Asst VP Finance & Administration .... Mr. Michael ATKINS
111 Vice Pres Institutional Advancement .... Mr. Brent SWINTON
32 VP Student Affairs/Campus Life .... Dr. Artie L. TRAVIS
35 Asst VP Student Affairs/Campus Life .... Dr. April JOHNSON
43 Vice Pres & General Counsel .... Ms. Karen JOHNSON SHAHEED
13 VP Office of Information Technology .... Ms. Marivic WEISS
84 VP for Enrollment Management .... Dr. Brian CLEMMONS
88 Asst VP Enrollment Management .... Vacant
88 Asst to Prov Institutional Effect .... Ms. Gayle M. FINK
06 University Registrar .... Ms. Maisha ALI
08 Assoc Library Director/Interim Dean .... Ms. Marian RUCKER-SHAMU
36 Acting Director Career Services .... Ms. Rosetta PRICE
15 Sr Director of Human Resources .... Ms. Sheila HOBSON
19 Chief of Campus Police .... Mr. Ernest WAITERS
58 Int Dean Sch of Grad Stds/Research .... Dr. Cosmos NWOKEAFOR
49 Dean College of Arts & Sciences .... Dr. George ACQUAAH
50 Int Dean College of Business .... Dr. Samuel DUAH
53 Dean College of Education .... Dr. Rhonda JETER-TWILLEY
107 Dean College Professional Studies .... Dr. Tanya SMITH BRICE
92 Director UCE Honors Program .... Dr. Monika GROSS
23 Director University Wellness Center .... Dr. Rita WUTOH
41 Director Athletics .... Mr. Clyde DOUGHTY, JR.
26 Dir University Relations/Marketing .... Ms. Cassandra M. ROBINSON
37 Director Financial Aid .... Ms. Deborah STANLEY
18 Director Facilities .... Mr. Darryl WILLIFORD
07 Director Undergraduate Admissions .... Vacant
29 Director of Alumni Relations .... Ms. Anette WEDDERBURN
96 Director of Purchasing .... Mr. Steve A. JOST
09 Director of Institutional Research .... Ms. Shama AKHTAR
04 Administrative Asst to President .... Ms. Diana MONTERO
108 Director Institutional Assessment .... Dr. Becky VERZINSKI
38 Director Student Counseling .... Dr. Tonya SWANSON
39 Interim Director Student Housing .... Mr. Rodney PETERS
44 Director Annual Giving .... Ms. Rosalind MUCHIRI
90 Director Academic Computing .... Dr. Fabio CHACON

*Coppin State University (D)

2500 W North Avenue, Baltimore MD 21216-3698
County: Baltimore City FICE Identification: 002068
Unit ID: 162283
Telephone: (410) 951-3000 Carnegie Class: Masters/S
FAX Number: (410) 333-5369 Calendar System: Semester
URL: www.coppin.edu
Established: 1900 Annual Undergrad Tuition & Fees (In-State): $8,873
Enrollment: 2,893 Coed
Affiliation or Control: State IRS Status: 501(c)3
Highest Offering: Doctorate
Accreditation: M, ACBSP, CACREP, CAEPN, CAHIIM, NURSE, SW

02 Interim President .... Dr. Mickey L. BURNIM
05 Provost/VP Academic Affairs .... Dr. Leontye LEWIS
111 VP Institutional Advancement .... Dr. Ahmed M. EL-HAGGAN
10 VP Administration & Finance .... Mr. Steve DANIK
32 VP Student Affairs/Enrollment Mgmt .... Dr. Michael FREEMAN
13 VP Information Systems/CIO .... Dr. Ahmed EL-HAGGAN
45 Asst VP Planning/Assessment .... Mr. Michael BOWDEN
20 Asst VP Academic Operations .... Dr. Rolande MURRAY
18 Asst VP Facilities Management .... Mr. Roy THOMAS
15 Asst VP of Human Resources .... Dr. Lisa EARLY
07 Director of Admissions .... Mr. Sha-Ron E. JONES
06 Registrar .... Ms. Karen BARLAND
21 Controller .... Mrs. Crystal MOSLEY
08 Director of the Library .... Dr. Mary WANZA
37 Director of Financial Aid .... Mr. Marcus BYRD
36 Director of Career Services Center .... Vacant
19 Chief of Public Safety .... Mr. Leonard HAMM
39 Director of Housing/Residence Life .... Ms. Jacquelyn WONSEY
41 Director of Athletics .... Mr. Derek CARTER
112 Donor Relations & Stewardship Coord .... Ms. Deidre JOHNSON
96 Asst Vice President of Procurement .... Mr. Thomas E. DAWSON, JR.
26 Director of University Relations .... Vacant
88 Director Client Computing Services .... Mr. Emmanuel OWUSU-SEKYERE
14 Deputy Info Technology Officer .... Vacant
105 Senior Web Developer .... Ms. Melissa C. RIGBY
92 Dean Honors College & McNair Pgms .... Mr. Ronnie L. COLLINS, SR.
58 Dean Graduate School .... Dr. Mary E. OWENS-SOUTHHALL
66 Dean of Nursing .... Dr. Tracey L. MURRAY
04 Executive Assistant to President .... Vacant
97 Chair General & Adult Education .... Dr. Jacqueline H. WILLIAMS
88 Chair Applied Psych/Rehab Counsel .... Dr. Michelle POINTER
61 Chair Crim Justice/Law Enforcement .... Dr. Jacqueline RHODEN-TRADER
53 Chair Curriculum & Instruction .... Dr. Glynis BARBER
79 Interim Chair Humanities .... Dr. Seth FORREST
50 Chair Col of Business Mgmt/Mktg .... Dr. Victoria MILLER
50 Chair Col of Bus/Sports/Ent Mgmt .... Dr. Surjeet BAIDWAN
50 Chair Col Of Business/Acct/Info Sys .... Dr. Emmanuel ANOURO
77 Chair Math & Computer Science .... Dr. Nicholas EUGENE
65 Chair Natural Sciences .... Dr. Mintesinot JIRU
83 Chair Social Sciences .... Dr. Elgin KLUGH
70 Chair Social Work .... Dr. Kesslyn BRADE-STENNIS
68 Chair Health/Physical Education .... Vacant
88 Chair Teaching and Learning .... Dr. Daniel P. JOSEPH
09 Director of Institutional Research .... Mr. Beryl HARRIS
29 Director Alumni Relations .... Ms. Marcia CEPHAS
38 Director Student Counseling .... Ms. Michelle REYNOLDS
100 Chief of Staff .... Ms. Angela GALEANO
25 Chief Contract/Grants Administrator .... Dr. Dianna J. VASS
43 Legal Counsel & Govt Rels Officer .... Mr. Matthew FRELING
44 Director Annual Giving .... Ms. Chanel NEWSOME

*Frostburg State University (E)

101 Braddock Road, Frostburg MD 21532-2303
County: Allegany FICE Identification: 002072
Unit ID: 162584
Telephone: (301) 687-4000 Carnegie Class: Masters/L
FAX Number: (301) 687-7070 Calendar System: Semester
URL: www.frostburg.edu
Established: 1898 Annual Undergrad Tuition & Fees (In-State): $9,172
Enrollment: 5,396 Coed
Affiliation or Control: State IRS Status: 501(c)3
Highest Offering: Doctorate
Accreditation: M, #ARCPA, CAATE, CAEPN, EXSC, NRPA, NURSE, SW

02 President .... Dr. Ronald NOWACZYK
05 Provost & VP Academic Affairs .... Dr. Liz THROP
32 Interim VP Student/Education Svcs .... Dr. Jeffrey GRAHAM
10 Vice President for Admin & Finance .... Mr. Leon WYDEN
111 Vice Pres University Advancement .... Mr. John SHORT
84 Vice Pres for Enrollment Management .... Ms. Arlene CASH
15 Vice President Human Resources .... Ms. Lisa HERSCH
43 University Counsel .... Mr. Bradford NIXON
20 Associate Provost .... Dr. Doris SANTAMARIA-MAKANG
35 Asst VP Student Affairs .... Vacant
45 Assoc Director Budget & Planning .... Ms. Denise MURPHY
49 Dean Col Liberal Arts/Sciences .... Dr. Kim HIXSON
50 Dean College of Business .... Dr. Sudhir SINGH
53 Interim Dean College of Education .... Dr. Boyce WILLIAMS
08 Director of the Library .... Ms. Lea MESSMAN-MANDICOTT
37 Director of Financial Aid .... Mrs. Angela L. HOVATTER
108 Director of PAIR .... Ms. SaraBeth BITTINGER
58 Director of Graduate Services .... Ms. Vickie MAZER
18 Director Facilities/Physical Plant .... Mr. Robert BOYCE
26 Director News & Media Services .... Ms. Elizabeth MEDCALF
36 Director Career Services .... Dr. Robbie L. CORDLE
38 Director Counseling & Psych Svcs .... Ms. Patricia ROBISON
40 Asst Mgr Bookstore & ID Services .... Mr. Kenneth EMERICK
41 Athletic Director .... Mr. Troy DELL
19 Chief University Police .... Col. Cynthia SMITH
13 Chief Information Officer .... Mr. Troy DONOWAY
91 Director of Technology Services .... Ms. Beth KENNEY
29 Director of Alumni .... Ms. Shannon L. GRIBBLE
22 Director of AA/EEO .... Vacant
07 Director of Admissions .... Ms. Trisha GREGORY
28 Director of Diversity .... Ms. Robin WYNDER
44 Major Gifts Officer .... Mr. Jason ANDRICK
14 Dir Networking/Telecommunications .... Mr. Gary TRENUM
96 Coord Procurement/Material Handling .... Mr. Alan R. SNYDER
23 Director Health Services .... Ms. Darlene SMITH
39 Director Residence Life .... Ms. Kimberly HINDS-BRUSH
06 Registrar .... Dr. Jay HEGEMAN
90 Director Academic Computing .... Ms. Beth KENNEY
102 Dir Foundation/Corporate Relations .... Ms. Janelle MOFFETT
104 Director Study Abroad .... Ms. Victoria GEARHART
105 Director Web Services .... Mr. Wade BLUEBAUGH
30 Director of Development .... Ms. Liz NELSON
86 Director Government Relations .... Mr. Al DELIA

*Salisbury University (F)

1101 Camden Avenue, Salisbury MD 21801-6860
County: Wicomico FICE Identification: 002091
Unit ID: 163851
Telephone: (410) 543-6000 Carnegie Class: Masters/L
FAX Number: (410) 548-2587 Calendar System: Semester
URL: www.salisbury.edu
Established: 1925 Annual Undergrad Tuition & Fees (In-State): $9,824
Enrollment: 8,714 Coed
Affiliation or Control: State IRS Status: 501(c)3

Highest Offering: Doctorate
Accreditation: M, CAATE, CAEPN, COARC, EXSC, MT, MUS, NURSE, SW

02 President .... Dr. Charles A. WIGHT
05 Provost/SVP of Academic Affairs .... Dr. Karen L. OLMSTEAD
100 Chief of Staff .... Mr. Eli J. MODLIN
10 Vice Pres Admin and Finance .... Mr. Marvin L. PYLES
32 Vice Pres of Student Affairs .... Dr. Dane R. FOUST
111 Vice Pres Advancement/External Affs .... Mr. Jason E. CURTIN
84 Asst VP of Enrollment Management .... Mr. Aaron M. BASKO
22 Assoc VP Institutional Equity .... Mr. Humberto X. ARISTIZABAL
35 Associate VP of Student Affairs .. Dr. Wallace SOUTHERLAND, III
20 Associate Provost .... Dr. Richard T. WILKENS
20 Assoc Vice Pres Academic Affairs .... Dr. Melissa M. BOOG
18 Assoc VP Facilities & Cap Mgmt .... Mr. Eric J. BERKHEIMER
35 Asst VP Student Affs/Dean Students .... Ms. Valerie J. RANDALL-LEE
13 Chief Information Officer .... Mr. Ken F. KUNDELL
26 Director of Public Relations .... Mr. Jason F. RHODES
27 Director of Marketing Strategy .... Ms. Katie M. CURTIN
41 Director of Athletics .... Dr. Gerard R. DIBARTOLO
92 Dean of Honors Program .... Dr. Andrew P. MARTINO
06 Registrar .... Vacant
07 Director of Admissions .... Ms. Elizabeth A. SKOGLUND
09 Special Asst to Pres for UARA .... Dr. Kara M. OWENS
08 Dn of Libraries/Instruct Resources .... Dr. Beatriz B. HARDY
38 Director of Counseling Center .... Vacant
36 Director of Career Services .... Dr. Kevin C. FALLON
37 Director of Financial Aid .... Mr. Mason M. WHITE
15 Assoc VP for HR .... Mr. Kevin A. VEDDER
29 Dir Alumni Relations & Gift Develop .... Mr. Jayme E. BLOCK
23 Director of Student Health Services .... Ms. Victoria A. LENTZ
35 Director Ct For Student Inv & Lead .... Ms. Tricia G. SMITH
86 Dir of Govt & Community Relations .... Mr. Eli J. MODLIN
43 General Counsel .... Ms. Karen A. TREBER
39 Director Housing/Residence Life .... Mr. David P. GUTOSKEY
19 Director of Public Safety .... Mr. Edwin L. LASHLEY
40 Director of Bookstore .... Ms. Lisa G. GRAY
18 Director of Physical Plant .... Mr. Kevin J. MANN
96 Director of Purchasing .... Mr. Jeff H. CANADA
81 Dean Henson Sch Science/Tech .... Dr. Michael S. SCOTT
50 Dean Perdue School of Business .... Dr. Christy H. WEER
49 Dean Fulton School of Liberal Arts .... Dr. Maarten L. PEREBOOM
53 Dean Seidel School of Education .... Dr. Laurie A. HENRY
76 Trnstl Dean Health/Human Svcs .... Dr. Kelly A. FIALA
58 Dean Graduate Studies/Research .... Dr. Clifton P. GRIFFIN
88 Dir Ctr for Student Achievement .... Dr. Heather W. HOLMES

*Towson University (A)

8000 York Road, Baltimore MD 21252-0001
County: Baltimore FICE Identification: 002099
Unit ID: 164076
Telephone: (410) 704-2000 Carnegie Class: DU-Mod
FAX Number: N/A Calendar System: 4/1/4
URL: www.towson.edu
Established: 1866 Annual Undergrad Tuition & Fees (In-State): $9,940
Enrollment: 22,705 Coed
Affiliation or Control: State IRS Status: 501(c)3
Highest Offering: Doctorate
Accreditation: M, ARCPA, AUD, CAATE, CAEPN, CEA, DANCE, FEPAC, IPSY, MUS, NURSE, OT, SP, THEA

02 President .... Dr. Kim SCHATZEL
05 Provost/Exec VP Academic Affs .... Dr. Melanie PERREAULT
10 Vice Pres Administration & Finance .... Mr. Benjamin LOWENTHALL
111 Vice Pres University Advancement .... Mr. Brian J. DEFILIPPIS
32 Vice President Student Affairs .... Dr. Deb MORIARTY
46 VP Innovation/Applied Research .... Dr. Daraius IRANI
26 VP Univ Marketing/Communications .... Ms. Marina COOPER
22 VP of Inclusion and Equity .... Dr. Leah COX
20 Vice Provost .... Dr. S. Maggie REITZ
84 Assoc VP Enrollment Mgmt/Registrar .... Mr. Robert GIORDANI
44 Assoc Vice President Development .... Mr. Todd LANGENBERG
29 Assoc Vice Pres Alumni Relations .... Ms. Lori B. ARMSTRONG
13 Assoc Vice President/CIO .... Mr. Jeffrey SCHMIDT
109 Assoc Vice Pres Auxiliary Svcs .... Mr. Daniel SLATTERY
18 Assoc VP Facilities Management .... Mr. Kevin PETERSEN
21 Assoc VP Fiscal Planning & Svcs .... Mr. Robert CAMPBELL
15 Assoc Vice Pres Human Resources .... Mr. C. Stephen JONES
35 Assoc Vice Pres Student Affairs .... Dr. Jana VARWIG
45 Assoc Prov Academic Res & Plng .... Dr. Gary LEVY
88 Assoc Vice President Campus Life .... Mr. Matthew LENNO
28 Assoc VP Student Affairs/Diversity .... Dr. Santiago SOLIS
39 Asst VP Housing & Residence Life .... Ms. Kelly HOOVER
37 Director for Financial Aid .... Mr. David HORNE
25 Asst VP Sponsored Programs/Research .... Ms. Nancy DUFAU
07 Director of Admissions .... Mr. David FEDORCHAK
19 AVP Public Safety/Chief of Police .... Chief Charles HERRING
53 Dean College of Education .... Dr. Laurie MULLEN
50 Dean College of Business/Economics .. Dr. Shohreh A. KAYNAMA
49 Dn Col Liberal Arts/Dir Honors Col .... Dr. Terry COONEY
81 Dean J&M Fisher Col of Science/Math .... Dr. David VANKO
57 Dean Col Fine Arts/Communication .... Ms. Susan PICINICH
76 Dean College of Health Professions .... Dr. Lisa PLOWFIELD
43 VP of Legal Affairs/HR/Gen Counsel .... Ms. Sara SLAFF
08 Dean of University Libraries .... Ms. Deborah NOLAN
104 Director Study Abroad .... Ms. Liz SHEARER
94 Chair Women's & Gender Studies .Dr. Cindy H. GISSENDANNER
09 Director Institutional Research .... Mr. Tim BIBO, JR.
27 AVP of Comm/Media Relations .... Mr. Sean WELSH
41 Director of Athletics .... Mr. Timothy LEONARD
23 Director of Health Services .... Dr. Matthias GOLDSTEIN

40 Director of University Store .... Ms. Stacy ELOFIR
96 Director of Procurement .... Mr. Jeffery SUTTON
38 Director Counseling Center .... Dr. Gregory REISING
36 Director of Career Center .... Ms. Lorie LOGAN-BENNETT
06 Assoc Director Records/Registration .... Ms. Sheena LYONS

*University of Baltimore (B)

1420 N Charles Street, Baltimore MD 21201-5779
County: Independent City FICE Identification: 002102
Unit ID: 161873
Telephone: (410) 837-4200 Carnegie Class: Masters/L
FAX Number: N/A Calendar System: Semester
URL: www.ubalt.edu
Established: 1925 Annual Undergrad Tuition & Fees (In-State): $8,958
Enrollment: 5,565 Coed
Affiliation or Control: State IRS Status: 501(c)3
Highest Offering: Doctorate
Accreditation: M, LAW, SPAA

02 President .... Mr. Kurt L. SCHMOKE
05 Executive Vice President & Provost .... Dr. Darlene B. SMITH
10 CFO/VP Administration & Finance .... Ms. Beth AMYOT
84 Dir Recruitment/Admissions/Mktg .... Vacant
111 Vice Pres Institutional Advancement .... Ms. Theresa SILANSKIS
86 VP Government & Public Affairs .... Ms. Anita HAREWOOD
18 VP Facil Mgmt/Campus Safety .... Mr. Neb SERTSU
13 Vice Pres Technology/CIO .... Mr. David BOBART
15 Assoc Vice Pres Human Resources .... Ms. Sally REED
20 Vice Provost .... Dr. Catherine ANDERSEN
09 Asst Vice Pres Institutional Rsrch .... Mr. Paul MONIODIS
31 Dir Office of Community Life .... Dr. Llatetra ESTERS
28 Dir Diversity and Culture Center .... Dr. Karla M. SHEPHERD
07 Interim AVP Admissions .... Ms. Carol DESCAK
08 Director of Library .... Mr. Jeffrey HUTSON
19 Chief of Police .... Mr. Chad ELLIS
88 AVP Enrollment Services .... Mr. Mark JACQUE
96 Director of Procurement & Supply .... Ms. Joselyn JOHNSON
44 AVP Alumni & Donor Services .... Ms. Kate CRIMMINS
36 Director Career & Internship Center .... Ms. Lakeisha MATHEWS
06 Assistant Registrar .... Ms. Brenda DER
26 Manager Public Information .... Mr. Chris HART
80 Dean College of Public Affairs .... Dr. Roger HARTLEY
49 Dean College of Arts & Sci .... Dr. Christine SPENCER
61 Dean of the School of Law .... Dr. Ronald WEICH
50 Dean School of Business .... Mr. Murray DALZIEL
88 Dir Center for Education Access .... Dr. Karyn SCHULZ
21 AVP Admin & Finance .... Ms. Barbara AUGHENBAUGH
29 Director Alumni Relations .... Ms. Kelley CHASE
37 Executive Director Financial Aid .... Mr. Terry RICHARDS

Washington Adventist University (C)

7600 Flower Avenue, Takoma Park MD 20912-7794
County: Montgomery FICE Identification: 002067
Unit ID: 162210
Telephone: (301) 891-4000 Carnegie Class: Masters/S
FAX Number: (301) 270-1618 Calendar System: Semester
URL: www.wau.edu
Established: 1904 Annual Undergrad Tuition & Fees: $23,900
Enrollment: 1,069 Coed
Affiliation or Control: Seventh-day Adventist IRS Status: 501(c)3
Highest Offering: Master's
Accreditation: M, MUS, NURSE, RAD

01 President .... Dr. Weymouth SPENCE
05 Provost .... Dr. Cheryl HARRIS KISUNZU
10 Exec Vice Pres Finance .... Mr. Patrick FARLEY
11 Chief of Operations & Compliance .... Ms. Janette NEUFVILLE
32 Vice Pres Student Life .... Ms. Amy ORTIZ-MORETTA
84 VP Marketing & Enrollment .... Mr. William JACKSON
42 Vice President Ministry .... Dr. Mark SIGUE
13 VP Information Technology .... Mr. Ricardo FLORES
15 Assoc VP of Human Resources .... Ms. Rythee JONES
58 Dean Sch Grad/Professional Studies .... Ms. Nicole CURRIER
121 Dean of Student Success .... Dr. Ralph JOHNSON
06 Registrar .... Mr. Reginald GARCON
33 Dean of Men .... Mr. Tim NELSON
34 Dean of Women .... Ms. Sabrina ETIENNE
08 Library Director .... Mr. Don ESSEX
30 Exec Dir Development/Alumni Rels .... Ms. Tanya SWEENEY
19 Director Safety & Security .... Mr. Edwin MONGE
41 Athletic Director .... Mr. Patrick CRAREY, II
07 Director of Admissions/ Recruitment .... Ms. Wanda COLON-CANALES
26 Dir Integrated Mktg/Communications .... Mr. Doug WALKER
78 Dir Coop Educ/Acad Support & Test .... Mr. Fitzroy THOMAS
18 Chief Facilities/Physical Plant .... Mr. Steve LAPHAM
37 Director Student Financial Aid .... Ms. Sharon CONWAY
38 Campus Counseling .... Dr. Grethel BRADFORD
40 Manager the College Bookstore .... Mr. Lloyd YUTUC
85 Director of International Students .... Dr. Beulah MANUEL
66 Director of Nursing .... Dr. Nancie CRESPIE
04 Executive Asst to President .... Ms. Lydée BATTLE
09 Director of Institutional Research .... Mr. Jonathan PETER

Washington College (D)

300 Washington Avenue, Chestertown MD 21620-1197
County: Kent FICE Identification: 002108
Unit ID: 164216
Telephone: (410) 778-2800 Carnegie Class: Bac-A&S
FAX Number: (410) 778-7850 Calendar System: Semester
URL: www.washcoll.edu
Established: 1782 Annual Undergrad Tuition & Fees: $46,978
Enrollment: 1,484 Coed
Affiliation or Control: Independent Non-Profit IRS Status: 501(c)3
Highest Offering: Master's
Accreditation: M

01 President .... Mr. Kurt M. LANDGRAF
05 Provost/Dean of College .... Dr. Patrice DIQUINIZO
45 VP Planning & Policy/Chief of Staff .... Mr. Victor SENSENIG
10 Vice Pres Finance .... Mrs. Laura JOHNSON
111 Vice Pres College Advancement .... Ms. Susie CHASE
84 Vice Pres Enrollment Mgmt/Marketing .... Dr. Lorna HUNTER
32 VP Student Affairs/Dean of Students .... Dr. Sarah FEYERHERM
09 Director Institutional Research .... Mr. Matthew KIBLER
20 Asst Dn First Yr Exp/Stdnt Success .... Ms. Andrea VASSAR
31 Director of Campus Special Events .... Ms. Gina RALSTON
41 Director of Athletics .... Mr. Thad MOORE
06 Registrar .... Vacant
08 Director of Miller Library .... Ms. Mary Alice BALL
21 Controller .... Vacant
18 Associate VP for Facilities .... Ms. Valerie RICHARD
15 Director of Human Resources .... Ms. Carolyn BURTON
19 Director of Public Safety .... Mr. Brandon MCFAYDEN
07 Director of Recruitment .... Mrs. Kelsey MILLER
37 Director of Financial Aid .... Ms. Jennifer RUNYON
39 Dir Res Life/Assoc Dean of Students .... Ms. Ursula HERZ
23 Clinical Director Health Services .... Mrs. Lisa M. MARX
38 Director of Counseling Center .... Ms. Miranda ALTMAN
36 Director of Career Development .... Mrs. Nanette COOLEY
28 Asst Dean Students/Dir Intcult Affs .... Mr. Jean-Pierre LAURENCEAU-MEDINA
40 Bookstore Manager .... Ms. Shannon WYBLE

Women's Institute of Torah Seminary (E)

6602 Park Heights Avenue, Baltimore MD 21215
County: Baltimore Identification: 667271
Telephone: (410) 358-3144 Carnegie Class: Not Classified
FAX Number: (866) 990-1983 Calendar System: Semester
URL: www.witbaltimore.org
Established: 1998 Annual Undergrad Tuition & Fees: N/A
Enrollment: N/A Female
Affiliation or Control: Jewish IRS Status: 501(c)3
Highest Offering: Baccalaureate
Accreditation: AIJS

01 President .... Dr. Aviva WEISBORD
05 Academic Dean .... Dr. Leslie G. KLEIN

Wor-Wic Community College (F)

32000 Campus Drive, Salisbury MD 21804-1486
County: Wicomico FICE Identification: 020739
Unit ID: 164313
Telephone: (410) 334-2800 Carnegie Class: Assoc/HVT-High Trad
FAX Number: (410) 334-2951 Calendar System: Semester
URL: www.worwic.edu
Established: 1975 Annual Undergrad Tuition & Fees (In-District): $3,240
Enrollment: 3,109 Coed
Affiliation or Control: Local IRS Status: 501(c)3
Highest Offering: Associate Degree
Accreditation: M, ACFEI, EMT, OTA, PTAA, RAD

01 President .... Dr. Murray K. HOY
05 Vice Pres Academic Affairs .... Dr. Kristin L. MALLORY
84 Vice Pres Enroll Mgmt & Student Svc .... Mr. Bryan NEWTON
10 Vice Pres Administrative Services .... Ms. Jennifer A. SANDT
26 Vice Pres Institutional Affairs .... Dr. Reenie MCCORMICK
51 Dean Continuing Education .... Mrs. Ruth E. BAKER
97 Dean General Education .... Dr. Colleen C. DALLAM
76 Dean Health Professions .... Dr. Karie SOLEMBRINO
88 Dean Occupational & Emerging Tech .... Vacant
07 Director Admissions & Records .... Ms. Angie N. HAYDEN
13 Senior Director Info Technology .... Ms. Ruth F. GILL
36 Director Career & Testing Services .... Ms. Lori SMOOT
37 Director Financial Aid .... Ms. Katie ABREU
21 Director Finance .... Mr. Thomas N. TYSON
15 Senior Director Human Resources .... Ms. Karen BERKHEIMER
121 Director of Student Success .... Ms. Amanda MESSATZZIA
27 Director Marketing .... Ms. Janet S. KENNINGTON
09 Director Inst Research & Planning .... Ms. Carol A. MENZEL
30 Director Development .... Ms. Jessica HALES
06 Registrar .... Ms. Kelly L. HEWETT
32 Sr Director of Student Development .... Dr. Deirdra G. JOHNSON
07 Sr Director Enrollment Services .... Ms. Charlene D. COOPER
08 Director of Library Services .... Ms. Cheryl MICHAEL
18 Sr Director Facilities Management .... Mr. Gregory D. GREY
96 Director Purchasing & Auxiliary Svc .... Ms. Allison M. CANADA
105 Web Developer .... Mr. Joshua W. TOWNSEND
19 Director Public Safety .... Mr. Linnie VANN, JR.
108 Director of Assessment .... Dr. Julio BIRMAN
88 Director Early College Initiative .... Mr. Richard C. WEBSTER

Yeshiva College of the Nation's Capital (G)

1216 Arcola Avenue, Silver Spring MD 20902-3408
County: Montgomery FICE Identification: 039373
Unit ID: 434937
Telephone: (301) 649-7077 Carnegie Class: Spec-4-yr-Faith
FAX Number: (301) 649-7053 Calendar System: Semester
Established: 1995 Annual Undergrad Tuition & Fees: $10,500

Enrollment: 25 Male
Affiliation or Control: Independent Non-Profit IRS Status: 501(c)3
Highest Offering: Second Talmudic Degree
Accreditation: RABN

01 President .... Rabbi Yitzchok MERKIN
05 Rosh Yeshiva .... Rabbi Aaron LOPIANSKY
37 Financial Aid Director .... Ms. Maryanna WALLS
11 Administrator .... Rabbi Yitzi LABELL

MASSACHUSETTS

American International College (A)

1000 State Street, Springfield MA 01109-3155
County: Hampden FICE Identification: 002114
Unit ID: 164447
Telephone: (413) 737-7000 Carnegie Class: Masters/L
FAX Number: (413) 205-3084 Calendar System: Semester
URL: www.aic.edu
Established: 1885 Annual Undergrad Tuition & Fees: $35,680
Enrollment: 3,283 Coed
Affiliation or Control: Independent Non-Profit IRS Status: 501(c)3
Highest Offering: Doctorate
Accreditation: EH, IACBE, NURSE, OT, PTA

01 President .... Dr. Vincent M. MANIACI
05 Exec Vice Pres Academic Affairs .... Dr. Mika NASH
11 Exec VP Administration .... Vacant
15 SVP Human Resources/Chief of Staff ..... Ms. Nicolle M. CESTERO
13 Chief Information Officer .... Ms. Mimi ROYSTON
32 VP for Student Affairs .... Mr. Brian J. O'SHAUGHNESSY
10 Vice President for Finance .... Mr. Christopher GARRITY
111 Executive Director of Institutional .... Ms. Heather GAWRON
26 VP Mktg & Communications .... Mr. Robert COLE
123 Dean of Graduate Admissions .... Ms. Kerry BARNES
07 Dean of UG Admissions .... Mr. Jonathan SCULLY
41 Athletic Director .... Mr. Matthew JOHNSON
76 Interim Dean Health Sciences .... Dr. Karen ROUSSEAU
49 Dean Business/Arts/Sciences .... Dr. Susanne SWANKER
53 Dean of Education .... Vacant
109 Associate VP for Auxiliary Services .... Mr. Jeffrey BEDNARZ
06 Interim Registrar .... Ms. Pamela ROBINSON
08 Director of Library .... Ms. Estelle H. SPENCER
35 Dean of Students .... Mr. Matthew SCOTT
38 Director Counseling Center .... Dr. Renee ROSADO
36 Dir of Career Services .... Mr. J. A. MARSHALL
76 Director Physical Therapy Program .... Vacant
66 Interim Dir of Division of Nursing .... Dr. Ellen FURMAN
50 Int Director of Business Programs .... Dr. Robyn POOLE
37 Interim Director for Financial Aid .... Ms. Nila LENNA
04 Exec Admin Asst to President .... Ms. Lani KRETSCHMAR
91 Director Academic Computing .... Mr. Ben MOJICA

Amherst College (B)

PO Box 5000, Amherst MA 01002-5000
County: Hampshire FICE Identification: 002115
Unit ID: 164465
Telephone: (413) 542-2000 Carnegie Class: Bac-A&S
FAX Number: (413) 542-2621 Calendar System: Semester
URL: www.amherst.edu
Established: 1821 Annual Undergrad Tuition & Fees: $56,426
Enrollment: 1,836 Coed
Affiliation or Control: Independent Non-Profit IRS Status: 501(c)3
Highest Offering: Baccalaureate
Accreditation: EH

01 President .... Dr. Carolyn (Biddy) A. MARTIN
05 Dean of the Faculty .... Dr. Catherine A. EPSTEIN
10 Chief Financial Officer .... Mr. Kevin C. WEINMAN
32 Chief Student Affairs Officer .... Dr. Karu KOZUMA
18 Chief of Campus Operations .... Mr. James D. BRASSORD
07 Dean Admission/Financial Aid .... Dr. Matthew MCGANN
111 Chief Advancement Officer .... Ms. Betsy CANNON SMITH
43 Chief Policy Ofcr/General Counsel ..... Ms. Lisa H. RUTHERFORD
28 Chief Diversity Officer .... Dr. Norm JONES
13 Chief Information Officer .... Mr. David L. HAMILTON
100 Chief of Staff/Sec of the Board .... Ms. Bett K. SCHUMACHTER
26 Chief Communications Officer .... Ms. Sandy GENELIUS
20 Associate Dean of the Faculty .... Dr. John CHENEY
20 Associate Dean of the Faculty .... Dr. Austin D. SARAT
37 Dean of Financial Aid .... Ms. Gail W. HOLT
09 Director of Institutional Research .... Mr. Jesse D. BARBA
21 Controller .... Mr. Stephen M. NIGRO
06 Registrar .... Vacant
08 College Librarian .... Vacant
23 Director of Student Health Services .... Dr. Emily M. JONES
15 Director of Human Resources .... Ms. Maria-Judith RODRIGUEZ
38 Director of Counseling Center .... Dr. Jacqueline ALVAREZ
41 Director of Athletics .... Mr. Donald R. FAULSTICK
36 Director of the Career Center .... Ms. Emily GRIFFEN
109 Director of Dining Services .... Mr. Joseph T. FLUECKIGER
19 Chief of Campus Police .... Mr. John B. CARTER

Anna Maria College (C)

50 Sunset Lane, Paxton MA 01612-1198
County: Worcester FICE Identification: 002117
Unit ID: 164492
Telephone: (508) 849-3333 Carnegie Class: Masters/M
FAX Number: (508) 849-3311 Calendar System: Semester
URL: www.annamaria.edu
Established: 1946 Annual Undergrad Tuition & Fees: $37,860
Enrollment: 1,445 Coed
Affiliation or Control: Roman Catholic IRS Status: 501(c)3
Highest Offering: Beyond Master's But Less Than Doctorate
Accreditation: EH, MUS, NUR, SW

01 President .... Ms. Mary Louise RETELLE
10 Vice President/Chief Financial Ofcr .... Vacant
11 Vice Pres/Chief Operations Officer .... Mr. Michael MIERS
05 VP for Academic Affairs .... Dr. Christine L. HOLMES
32 VP for Student Affairs .... Mr. Andrew O. KLEIN
111 VP for Institutional Advancement ...... Ms. Sharon M. DAVENPORT
07 VP for Enrollment .... Mr. John HAMEL
26 Director Marketing & College Rels .... Ms. Maureen HALLEY
09 Dean of Institutional Research .... Ms. Irene IRUDAYAM
06 Registrar .... Ms. Julie DIX
88 Director of the Learning Center .... Mr. Dennis VANASSE
23 Director of Health Services .... Ms. Linda ARONSON
08 Director of Library Services .... Mr. Wilfredo RIVERA-SCOTTI
29 Director of Alumni .... Ms. Patricia SCHAFFER
36 Director Career Counsel/Placement .... Ms. Brook BRIGHAM
37 Director Financial Aid .... Vacant
13 Chief Information Officer .... Mr. Michael MIERS
04 Executive Asst to the President .... Ms. Kay FLICK
18 Director Physical Plant .... Mr. Matthew SIMPSON
41 Athletic Director .... Mr. Serge DEBARI
42 Director Campus Ministry .... Ms. Melissa LANEVE
15 Interim Director of Human Resources .... Ms. Jan RUGGIERI
88 Dean of Mission Effectiveness .... Sr. Rollande QUINTAL
35 Dean of Student Life .... Vacant
51 Director Grad/Continuing Educ .... Mr. Paul VACCARO
19 Director Security/Safety .... Lt. Mark SAVASTA
102 Corporate & Foundation Rels Ofcr .... Mr. Richard RICARDI
28 Director of Diversity .... Ms. Brianna-Allyn AMISSAH
39 Director of Residence Life .... Ms. Jessica ECKSTROM

Assumption College (D)

500 Salisbury Street, Worcester MA 01609-1296
County: Worcester FICE Identification: 002118
Unit ID: 164562
Telephone: (508) 767-7000 Carnegie Class: Masters/M
FAX Number: (508) 767-7169 Calendar System: Semester
URL: www.assumption.edu
Established: 1904 Annual Undergrad Tuition & Fees: $40,958
Enrollment: 2,481 Coed
Affiliation or Control: Roman Catholic IRS Status: 501(c)3
Highest Offering: Beyond Master's But Less Than Doctorate
Accreditation: EH, CACREP

01 President .... Dr. Francesco C. CESAREO
10 VP for Finance and Administration .... Mr. Peter D. WELLS
05 Provost/Academic Vice Pres .... Dr. Gregory WEINER
32 Vice President for Student Affairs .... Dr. Catherine M. WOODBROOKS
121 Vice President for Student Success ..... Dr. Conway C. CAMPBELL
111 Vice Pres Institutional Advancement ...... Mr. Timothy R. STANTON
42 Vice President Mission .... Rev. Richard E. LAMOUREUX, AA
84 Vice Pres for Enrollment Management .... Dr. Robert MIRABILE
43 General Counsel .... Dr. Michael H. RUBINO
58 Dean School of Graduate Programs ... Dr. Kimberly A. SCHANDEL
50 Dean School of Business .... Mr. Joseph FOLEY
66 Dean School of Nursing .... Ms. Caitlin M. STOVER
49 Dean School of Liberal Arts .... Ms. Paula A. FITZPATRICK
107 Dir of Professional Studies .... Mr. Dennis BRAUN
07 Dir of Admission/Recruitment .... Mr. Michael DIPIAZZA
20 Assoc VP Academic Affairs/Grant Dev .... Dr. Eloise KNOWLTON
20 Asst VP of Academic Affairs .... Dr. Jennifer K. MORRISON
42 Director of Campus Ministry .... Mr. Paul F. COVINO
38 Director of Counseling Services .... Ms. Marta CARLSON
08 Director of Library Services .... Ms. Robin MADDALENA
10 Director of Finance .... Ms. Cathleen R. CULLEN
09 Director Inst Research and Ac Asst .... Mr. Stuart J. MUNRO
06 Registrar .... Ms. Heather PECORARO
15 Director of Human Resources .... Ms. Robin PELLEGRINO
26 Executive Director of Communication . Mr. Michael K. GUILFOYLE
88 Assistant VP for Student Success .... Ms. Mary BRESNAHAN
30 Asst VP Development/Alumni .... Ms. Linda ROSENLUND
110 Asst VP for Leadership Giving .... Ms. Melanie DEMARAIS
44 Director of Assumption Fund .... Mr. Timothy R. MARTIN
121 Director of Academic Support Center .... Dr. Allen A. BRUEHL
39 Assoc Dean Campus Life/Dir Res Life .... Mr. Joseph ZITO
41 Director of Athletics .... Ms. Jamie P. MARCOUX
19 Director of Public Safety .... Mr. Steven B. CARL
23 Director of Health Services .... Ms. Sarah K. SHERWOOD
24 Director of Media Services .... Mr. Ted HALEY
37 Director of Financial Aid .... Ms. Monica M. BLONDIN
21 Director of Business Services .... Mr. Todd DERDERIAN
86 Exec Asst for Govt/Cmty Relations .... Mr. Daniel F. DITULLIO
36 Director of Career Services .... Ms. Shannon CURTIS
04 Exec Admin Asst to President .... Ms. Sharon A. MAHONEY

Babson College (E)

231 Forest Street, Babson Park MA 02457-0310
County: Norfolk FICE Identification: 002121
Unit ID: 164580
Telephone: (781) 235-1200 Carnegie Class: Spec-4-yr-Bus
FAX Number: (781) 239-5231 Calendar System: Semester
URL: www.babson.edu
Established: 1919 Annual Undergrad Tuition & Fees: $51,104
Enrollment: 3,329 Coed
Affiliation or Control: Independent Non-Profit IRS Status: 501(c)3
Highest Offering: Master's
Accreditation: EH

01 President .... Dr. Stephen SPINELLI
12 CEO Babson Global .... Mr. David ABDOW
05 Provost .... Mr. Mark RICE
10 Chief Administrative Officer .... Ms. Katherine CRAVEN
18 AVP Facilities Mgmt & Construction .... Ms. Janet FISHSTEIN
31 VP Programming/Community Outreach .... Ms. Jane EDMONDS
111 Senior VP for Advancement .... Mr. Edward CHIU
30 Vice President of Development .... Ms. Diana P. ZAIS
45 VP Strat Initiatives/Chief of Staff .... Ms. Kelly LYNCH
15 Vice Pres Human Resources .... Ms. Donna BONAPARTE
43 VP and General Counsel .... Mr. Michael D. LAYISH
13 VP & Chief Information Officer .... Mr. Phillip KNUTEL
26 VP/Chief Marketing Officer .... Mr. Kerry SALERNO
32 VP/Dean of Students .... Dr. Lawrence P. WARD
36 Dir Graduate Center for Career Dev .... Ms. Cheri PAULSON
06 Registrar .... Ms. Linda KEAN
36 Dir Undergrad Center for Career Dev ..... Ms. Donna SOSNOWSKI
27 Director of Public Relations .... Mr. Michael CHMURA
20 Dean of Faculty .... Dr. Kenichi MATSUNO
07 Dean Undergraduate Admissions .... Ms. Courtney MINDEN
58 Dean Graduate School .... Dr. Keith ROLLAG
97 Dean Undergraduate School .... Dr. Ian LAPP
107 Dean of Babson Exec Education .... Ms. Elaine EISENMAN
37 Dir Student Financial Aid .... Ms. Meredith A. STOVER
94 Exec Dir Ctr for Wms Entrep Lship .... Dr. Susan DUFFY
28 Chief Diversity & Inclusion Officer .... Dr. Sadie BURTON-GOSS
19 Director Public Safety .... Mr. James POLLARD
41 Director of Athletics .... Mr. Michael LYNCH

Bard College at Simon's Rock (F)

84 Alford Road, Great Barrington MA 01230-9702
County: Berkshire FICE Identification: 009645
Unit ID: 167792
Telephone: (413) 644-4400 Carnegie Class: Bac/Assoc-Mixed
FAX Number: (413) 528-7365 Calendar System: Semester
URL: www.simons-rock.edu
Established: 1964 Annual Undergrad Tuition & Fees: $55,082
Enrollment: 401 Coed
Affiliation or Control: Independent Non-Profit IRS Status: 501(c)3
Highest Offering: Baccalaureate
Accreditation: EH

01 President .... Dr. Leon BOTSTEIN
05 Vice President/Provost .... Dr. Ian BICKFORD
88 Asst to Vice President & Provost .... Ms. Melanie GUERIN
20 Dean of Academic Affairs .... Dr. Patricia SHARPE
35 Vice Provost .... Dr. Sue LYON
10 Director of Finance/Admin/HR .... Mr. Philip MORRISON
111 Director Institutional Advancement .... Ms. Cathy HARDING
07 Director of Admissions .... Ms. Cindi JACOBS
06 Registrar .... Ms. Heidi ROOTS
08 Library Director .... Mr. Brian MIKESELL
37 Assoc Director of Financial Aid .... Ms. Moira BUHR
18 Director of Plant Operations .... Ms. Barb SHULTIS
38 Director Campus Wellness Center .... Ms. Sharon HARTUNIAN
19 Director of Campus Safety .... Mr. Kenneth GEREMIA
39 Dean of Students .... Dr. Moise ST. LOUIS
57 Division Head Arts .... Mr. Ben KRUPKA
81 Division Head Science/Math/Computer .... Dr. David MYERS
83 Division Head Social Studies .... Dr. Kathryn BOSWELL
79 Division Head Language/Literature .... Dr. Brendan MATHEWS
36 Dir of Academic Trans & Career Dev .... Ms. Manat WOOTEN
22 Dean of Equity & Inclusion .... Dr. Eden-Renee HAYES
04 Admin Assistant to the President .... Ms. McEvoy AMIE
09 Director of Institutional Research .... Dr. Anne O'DWYER
29 Director Alumni Affairs .... Ms. Cathy INGRAM

Bay Path University (G)

588 Longmeadow Street, Longmeadow MA 01106-2292
County: Hampden FICE Identification: 002122
Unit ID: 164632
Telephone: (413) 565-1000 Carnegie Class: Masters/L
FAX Number: (413) 565-1105 Calendar System: Semester
URL: www.baypath.edu
Established: 1897 Annual Undergrad Tuition & Fees: $34,225
Enrollment: 3,298 Female
Affiliation or Control: Independent Non-Profit IRS Status: 501(c)3
Highest Offering: Doctorate
Accreditation: EH, ARCPA, NURSE, OT

01 President .... Dr. Carol A. LEARY
05 Vice Pres Academic Affairs/Provost .... Dr. Melissa MORRISS-OLSON
10 VP Finance/Administrative Services ...... Mr. Michael GIAMPIETRO
111 VP Development/Planned Giving ... Ms. Allison GEARING-KALILL
26 VP Univ Relations & Board Liaison .... Ms. Kathleen BOURQUE
45 Chief Strategy Officer Springfield .... Ms. Caron T. HOBIN
07 Vice Prov Admissions/Mktg/Analytics ...... Ms. Rebecca CAPUANO
04 Assistant to the President .... Ms. Barbara KOCHON
88 Deputy Chief Ops Effectiveness/TAWC .... Ms. Amanda GOULD
21 Controller .... Mr. John O'ROURKE
25 Asst Dean Research/Acad Resource .... Mr. Peter TESTORI
12 Director of the Concord Campus .... Ms. Karen CARLSON
27 Director of Univ Communications ..... Ms. Kathleen WROBLEWSKI
37 Exec Dir of Student Financial Svcs .... Ms. Stephanie KING
36 Exec Dir Career & Life Planning .... Ms. Laureen CIRILLO
08 Director of the Library .... Vacant
06 Registrar .... Mr. Marshall BRADWAY
44 Associate Director of Annual Giving .... Ms. Amanda GENO

23	Director of Health Services	Ms. Deborah BAKER
15	Asst VP & Dir of Human Resources	Ms. Kathleen HALPIN-ROBBINS
18	Dir Facilities/Campus Services	Mr. Paul E. STANTON
13	Exec Dir Information Technology	Mr. Douglas SLAVAS
14	Director of IT Infrastructure	Mr. Christopher KNERR
41	Director of Athletics	Mr. Steven J. SMITH
88	Executive Director Brand Strategy	Ms. Karen WOODS
32	Dean of Students	Ms. Anne CHAPDELAINE
94	Deputy Chief Learning Officer	Ms. Maura DEVLIN
88	Dir Business Programs TAWC	Ms. Piccus MEGAN
88	Dir MBA Entrepr Thnkg/Innov Practic	Mr. Mo SATTAR
88	Dir Grad Pgms Nonprofit Mgmt/ Philan	Ms. Sylvia DE HAAS PHILLIPS
49	Vice Provost/Dean Liberal Studies	Ms. Kristine BARNETT
96	Exec Dir of Purchasing/Office Svcs	Mr. Ted LETH-STEENSEN
102	Dir Foundation/Corporate Relations	Ms. Janine MCVAY
53	Dean School Educ/Human/Hlth Sci	Dr. Elizabeth FLEMING
81	Dean School of Science & Management	Dr. Thomas LOPER
88	Dir Occupational Therapy Program	Dr. Beverly ST. PIERRE
123	Dean Graduate Admissions	Ms. Sheryl KOSAKOWSKI
57	Director MFA Program	Ms. Leanna JAMES BLACKWELL
88	Director ABA Program	Dr. Susan AINSLEIGH
88	Director PA Program	Ms. Theresa RIETHLE
77	Dir Computer Sci & Cyber Security	Mr. Matthew SMITH
88	Dir Higher Education Administration	Ms. Lauren WAY
88	Dir Finance & Accounting Program	Ms. Kara STEVENS
88	Program Director Genetic Counseling	Ms. Janice BELINER
88	Program Director Healthcare Mgmt	Ms. Theresa DEVITO
88	Director MS Leadership/Negotiation	Mr. Joshua WEISS
88	Dir Ctr Excellence Women in Science	Ms. Gina SEMPREBON
83	Director Graduate Psychology Pgm	Mr. Mark BENANDER
88	Director MS Applied Data Science	Ms. Ning JIA
88	Director Neuroscience Program	Vacant
09	Director of Institutional Research	Ms. Ashley MURACZEWSKI
39	Dir Resident Life/Student Housing	Ms. Lindsie LAVIN

Bay State College (A)

31 St. James Avenue, Boston MA 02116-2975
County: Suffolk FICE Identification: 003965
Unit ID: 164641
Telephone: (617) 217-9000 Carnegie Class: Bac-Diverse
FAX Number: (617) 249-0400 Calendar System: Semester
URL: www.baystate.edu
Established: 1946 Annual Undergrad Tuition & Fees: $22,320
Enrollment: 717 Coed
Affiliation or Control: Proprietary IRS Status: Proprietary
Highest Offering: Baccalaureate
Accreditation: EH, ADNUR, PTAA

01	Chief Executive Officer/President	Dr. Mark DEFUSCO
05	Vice President of Academic Affairs	Dr. William CARROLL
11	Vice President Operations	Jack CALARESO
32	Vice Pres Student Affs/Dean Stdnts	Kate O'HARA
07	Vice Pres of Admissions	Richard MCCARTHY
37	Director Student Financial Services	Jeanne DEVANI
06	Registrar	Sarah WOOD
08	Librarian	Jessica NEAVE
07	Int Director of Admissions	Christine MURPHY
21	Student Account Administrator	Melissa PEDERSEN
36	Director Career Services	Diann LLOYD-DENNIS
38	Director Student Counseling	Cheryl RAICHE
15	Director Human Resources	Ethel DANIEL
35	Asst Dir Student Activities	Kristin STAINE

Becker College (B)

61 Sever Street, Worcester MA 01609-2165
County: Worcester FICE Identification: 002123
Unit ID: 164720
Telephone: (508) 791-9241 Carnegie Class: Bac-Diverse
FAX Number: (508) 796-2693 Calendar System: Semester
URL: www.becker.edu
Established: 1784 Annual Undergrad Tuition & Fees: $39,200
Enrollment: 1,892 Coed
Affiliation or Control: Independent Non-Profit IRS Status: 501(c)3
Highest Offering: Master's
Accreditation: EH, ADNUR, NUR

01	President	Dr. Nancy P. CRIMMIN
10	Executive Vice President & CFO	Dr. David A. ELLIS
05	VP for Academic Affairs	Dr. Amber L. VAILL
32	VP of Student Affairs	Mr. Frank MILLERICK
30	VP of Development/Alumni Relations	Ms. Lorita WILLIAMS
84	Director of Enrollment Operations	Ms. Kelsey BRIGGS
26	Vice President for Communications	Ms. Amy DEAN
13	Executive Director of IT	Mr. Jeffrey BUTERA
19	Campus Police Chief	Mr. David J. BOUSQUET
100	Chief of Staff/Spec Asst to Pres	Vacant
15	Associate VP Human Resources	Ms. Kathleen M. GARVEY
41	VP & Athletic Director	Mr. Francis E. MILLERICK
11	Assistant VP for Administration	Mr. Kenneth CAMERON
07	Dean of Admissions	Ms. Danielle O'CONNELL
57	Dean School of Design & Technology	Mr. Alan RITACCO
66	Dean Sch of Nursing/Health Sciences	Dr. Laurie HILLSON
74	Dean Sch of Animal Stds/Natural Sci	Dr. Julie A. BAILEY
58	Dean Sch of Graduate/Prof Studies	Ms. Mary Ellen MAHONEY
88	Director of Program Development	Mr. Timothy LOEW
88	Exec Director of Global Initiatives	Dr. Debra PALLATTO-FONTAINE
36	Exec Dir Career Educ & Advising	Mr. Richard DAVINO
38	Director of Counseling Services	Rose ANDREJCZYK
114	Dir Budget & Business Services	Mr. Michael MONGEON
08	Director of the Libraries	Ms. Donna M. SIBLEY
29	Dir Planned Giving/Alumni Relations	Ms. Mary MALONEY
88	Director of Equestrian Center	Ms. Nicole EASTMAN
09	Dir Inst Research & Assessment	Ms. Vera MAUK
39	Dir Resid Life & Student Conduct	Mr. Joseph A. LOMASTRO
37	Director Financial Aid	Mr. Allen COWETT
109	Director of Auxiliary Services	Ms. Dianna JOHNSON
88	Director Yunis Social Bus Centre	Dr. Debra PALLATTO-FONTAINE
50	Director of Business Programs	Dr. Vaughn A. CALHOUN
85	Dir Intl Students & Title IX	Ms. Michelle FATCHERIC
113	Director of Student Accounts/Bursar	Mr. Alexander M. HARTMAN
23	Director of Health Services	Ms. Catherine MELOCHE
88	Manager Creative Services	Ms. Judith TONELLI-BROWN
90	Helpdesk Manager	Mr. Steven J. BIGDA
104	Coordinator of Study Abroad	Mr. Daniel W. CHAPMAN
06	Registrar	Ms. Heather PECORARO
21	Controller	Mr. Richard N. NAYLOR
04	Exec Asst to Pres/Liaison to Board	Ms. Patricia KALINOWSKI

Benjamin Franklin Institute of Technology (C)

41 Berkeley Street, Boston MA 02116-6296
County: Suffolk FICE Identification: 002151
Unit ID: 165884
Telephone: (617) 588-1368 Carnegie Class: Spec-4-yr-Other Tech
FAX Number: (617) 482-3706 Calendar System: Semester
URL: www.bfit.edu
Established: 1908 Annual Undergrad Tuition & Fees: $17,550
Enrollment: 609 Coed
Affiliation or Control: Independent Non-Profit IRS Status: 501(c)3
Highest Offering: Baccalaureate
Accreditation: EH, OPD

01	President	Anthony BENOIT
05	Dean of Academic Affairs	Dennis CAMACHO
10	Chief Financial Officer	Maureen JOYCE
100	Chief of Staff	Aisha FRANCIS
32	Dean of Student Services	Jackie CORNOG
06	Registrar	James KLASEN
08	Librarian	Sharon B. BONK
07	Dean of Recruitment	Marvin LOISEAU
111	Chief Advancement Officer	Angela JOHNSON
121	Director of Student Success	Shawn AYALA
09	Director of Institutional Research	James KLASEN
15	Director Human Resources	Diane DANIELS
19	Director of Facilities	Myftar MYRTAJ
36	Director of Career Services	Emily LEOPOLD
37	Director Student Financial Services	Jamie SANTIAGO
04	Administrative Asst to President	Vacant
13	Dean of Information Technology	Larson ROGERS

Bentley University (D)

175 Forest Street, Waltham MA 02452-4705
County: Middlesex FICE Identification: 002124
Unit ID: 164739
Telephone: (781) 891-2000 Carnegie Class: Masters/L
FAX Number: (781) 891-2569 Calendar System: Semester
URL: www.bentley.edu
Established: 1917 Annual Undergrad Tuition & Fees: $49,880
Enrollment: 5,543 Coed
Affiliation or Control: Independent Non-Profit IRS Status: 501(c)3
Highest Offering: Doctorate
Accreditation: EH

01	President	Ms. Alison DAVIS-BLAKE
43	General Counsel/Secretary to Corp	Ms. Judith MALONE
05	Interim Provost/VP Academic Affairs	Dr. Donna Maria BLANCERO
10	VP and Chief Financial Officer	Ms. Maureen FORRESTER
111	VP University Advancement	Ms. Maureen E. FLORES
32	VP Student Affairs	Dr. J. Andrew SHEPARDSON
13	VP & Chief Information Officer	Mr. Robert WITTSTEIN
84	VP Enrollment Management	Ms. Carolina FIGUEROA
49	Dean of Arts and Sciences	Dr. Eric OCHES
50	Dean of Business/Grad School	Dr. Michael JOHNSON-CRAMER
20	Associate Provost	Dr. Patrick SCHOLTEN
26	AVP Strategic Comm/Chief of Staff	Mr. Christopher J. JOYCE
121	Assoc Dean Academic Services	Ms. Catherina CARLSON
88	Director Grad Acad Advising	Ms. Colleen K. MURPHY
27	Chief Marketing Officer	Ms. Valerie FOX
15	VP of Human Resources & CHRO	Mr. George CANGIANO
21	Associate VP Finance & Operations	Ms. Nancy ANTUNES
06	Registrar	Ms. Patricia ROGERS
88	Ombudsperson	Ms. Eliane MARKOFF
38	Director of Counseling Center	Dr. Peter FORKNER
41	Director of Athletics	Mr. Robert DEFELICE
09	Director of Business Intelligence	Ms. Kelly GIARDULLO
39	Assoc Dean Student Affairs/Res Ctr	Mr. John PIGA
08	Dir Library	Ms. Hope HOUSTON
19	Executive Director of Public Safety	Mr. Ernest LEFFLER
90	Director Academic Tech Center	Mr. Gaurav SHAH
36	Assoc VP Univ Career Services	Ms. Susan BRENNAN
23	Asst Dean/Dir Health & Wellness	Ms. Geraldine TAYLOR
25	Director of Sponsored Programs	Ms. Susan RICHMAN
88	Assoc VP Enrollment Management	Ms. Donna KENDALL
07	Dean UG Admissions	Ms. Suzanne CUCCURULLO
28	Exec Dir Diversity and Inclusion	Ms. Katherine LAMPLEY
123	Int Dir Graduate Admissions	Ms. Jennifer FLAGEL
88	Director of MBA Programs	Dr. Jill A. BROWN
18	Exec Director Facilities Management	Mr. Thomas KANE
96	Exec Dir Purchasing/Adm & Camp Svcs	Ms. Julianne BRITT
44	Sr Assoc Dir Annual Giving	Mr. Brian READ
35	Dir of Student Pgm & Engagement	Ms. Nicole CHABOT-WIEFERICH
04	Exec Asst to President	Ms. Susan HAYES
104	Director of International Education	Ms. Natalie SCHLEGEL
37	Director Financial Assistance	Ms. Katherine A. ANDERSON

Berklee College of Music (E)

1140 Boylston Street, Boston MA 02215-3693
County: Suffolk FICE Identification: 002126
Unit ID: 164748
Telephone: (617) 266-1400 Carnegie Class: Spec-4-yr-Arts
FAX Number: (617) 247-6878 Calendar System: Semester
URL: www.berklee.edu
Established: 1945 Annual Undergrad Tuition & Fees: $44,140
Enrollment: 6,762 Coed
Affiliation or Control: Independent Non-Profit IRS Status: 501(c)3
Highest Offering: Master's
Accreditation: EH

01	President	Roger H. BROWN
100	Chief of Staff	Melissa HOWE
12	Exec Dir Boston Conservatory	Cathy YOUNG
05	Sr VP Academic Affairs/Provost	Lawrence J. SIMPSON
32	Sr VP Student Enrollment/Engagement	Betsy NEWMAN
106	Sr VP Online Learning/Continuing Ed	Deborah CAVALIER
84	VP Enrollment Marketing/Management	Mike KING
111	Sr VP Institutional Advancement	Cindy ALBERT LINK
10	Chief Financial Officer	Richard M. HISEY
88	VP Innovation/Strategy	Panos A. PANAY
13	VP Technology Resources	David GREGORY
15	VP Human Resources	Eileen ALVITI
88	VP Educ Outreach/Social Entrepren	Krystal BANFIELD
88	Asst Vice President Global Init	Jason CAMELIO
20	VP Academic Affairs/Vice Provost	Jay KENNEDY
26	VP for External Affairs	Tom RILEY
88	Vice Pres Academic Strategy	Carin NUERNBERG
88	Dean of Prof Performance Div	Ron SAVAGE
53	Dean of Prof Education Division	Darla S. HANLEY
06	Registrar	Jeffrey KINNAMON
39	Dir Residential/Housing Operations	Rosemary DOWLING
37	Director of Student Aid Services	Kevin FIGUEIREDO
07	Dean of Admissions	Damien S. BRACKEN
36	Assoc VP Career & Digital Strategy	Stefanie HENNING
18	Assistant VP for Facilities	Kevin ANDERSON
08	Dean of Learning Resources	Heather REID
09	Dean Inst Rrsch/Assessment/Accred	Sharon KRAMER
19	Sr Director Public Safety Services	Mark LOUNEY
28	VP Student Affs/Diversity/ Inclusion	Christopher KANDUS-FISHER
29	Sr Director of Alumni Affairs	Fritz KUHNLENZ
104	Assoc Director Study Abroad	Tracey MELLOR
27	Sr Dir Marketing/Communications	Janelle BROWNING

Boston Architectural College (F)

320 Newbury Street, Boston MA 02115-2795
County: Suffolk FICE Identification: 003966
Unit ID: 164872
Telephone: (617) 262-5000 Carnegie Class: Spec-4-yr-Arts
FAX Number: (617) 585-0111 Calendar System: Semester
URL: www.the-bac.edu
Established: 1889 Annual Undergrad Tuition & Fees: $21,924
Enrollment: 695 Coed
Affiliation or Control: Independent Non-Profit IRS Status: 501(c)3
Highest Offering: Master's
Accreditation: EH, CIDA, LSAR

01	President	Mr. Mahesh DAAS
05	Provost	Ms. Susan DUNTON
10	Vice President for Finance/Admin	Mr. Mark VIRELLO
111	VP Institutional Advancement	Mr. Ken LEMANSKI
84	VP of Enrollment Management	Mr. James RYAN
18	Director of Facilities	Ms. Ellen YEE
32	Assoc Vice Pres/Dean of Students	Mr. Richard M. GRISWOLD
88	Dean Interior Architecture	Ms. Denise RUSH
88	Dean School of Landscape Architect	Ms. Maria BELLALTA
88	Dean School of Design Studies	Mr. Donald HUNSICKER
48	Dean School of Architecture	Ms. Karen L. NELSON
88	Dean & Faculty of Practice	Mr. Len CHARNEY
13	Director of Information Technology	Mr. Jason O'BRIEN
88	Dir of Master's Thesis Arch	Mr. Ian TABERNER
88	Director of Digital Media	Mr. Peter ATWOOD
88	Dir of Applied Learning in Practice	Ms. Beth GARVER
88	Director of Media Arts	Mr. Luis MONTALVO
08	Associate Director of the Library	Vacant
07	Director of Admissions	Ms. Meredith SPINNATO
37	Director of Financial Aid	Mr. Janice WILKOS-GREENBERG
06	Registrar	Ms. Katherine KWOLEK
11	Dir of Administrative Operations	Ms. Patti VAUGHN
121	Dean of Advising Services	Ms. Rebecca CHABOT-WIEFERICH
88	Director of Foundation Studies	Mr. Lee PETERS
15	Interim Director of Human Resources	Ms. Barbara COURTEMANCHE
29	Dir of Special Events & Alumni	Ms. Jessica TANNER
21	Assoc VP for Finance & Admin	Ms. Diane MERCIER
88	Director Foundation Student Support	Mr. Michael DANIELS
04	Executive Asst to President	Ms. Ketsia FAUSTIN
26	Dir of Marketing & Communications	Ms. Nancy FINN
39	Coordinator of Student Life	Mr. Zachary TRIPSAS

Boston Baptist College (A)

950 Metropolitan Avenue, Boston MA 02136-4000
County: Suffolk FICE Identification: 032483
Unit ID: 164614
Telephone: (617) 364-3510 Carnegie Class: Spec-4-yr-Faith
FAX Number: (775) 245-1498 Calendar System: Semester
URL: www.boston.edu
Established: 1976 Annual Undergrad Tuition & Fees: $12,600
Enrollment: 80 Coed
Affiliation or Control: Baptist IRS Status: 501(c)3
Highest Offering: Baccalaureate
Accreditation: TRACS

01 President .... Rev. David V. MELTON
32 Vice President for Student Services .... Rev. Kenneth D. GILLMING
11 Vice President for Operations .... Rev. Randall WARD
84 Director of Enrollment Services .... Mrs. Rebekah BUTLER
07 Director of Admissions .... Mrs. Carolina WOUNDY
08 Head Librarian .... Mr. Fred TATRO

Boston College (B)

140 Commonwealth Avenue, Chestnut Hill MA 02467-3934
County: Middlesex FICE Identification: 002128
Unit ID: 164924
Telephone: (617) 552-8000 Carnegie Class: DU-Highest
FAX Number: (617) 552-8828 Calendar System: Semester
URL: www.bc.edu
Established: 1863 Annual Undergrad Tuition & Fees: $55,464
Enrollment: 14,628 Coed
Affiliation or Control: Roman Catholic IRS Status: 501(c)3
Highest Offering: Doctorate
Accreditation: EH, ANEST, CAEP, COPSY, LAW, NURSE, SW, THEOL

01 President .... Rev. William P. LEAHY, S.J.
05 Provost & Dean of Faculties .... Dr. David QUIGLEY
03 Executive Vice President .... Mr. Michael J. LOCHHEAD
111 Senior VP University Advancement .... Mr. James J. HUSSON
04 Vice Pres/Exec Asst to President .... Mr. Kevin J. SHEA
10 Financial Vice President/Treasurer .... Mr. John D. BURKE
32 Interim Vice Pres Student Affairs .... Ms. Joy MOORE
15 Vice President for Human Resources .... Mr. David P. TRAINOR
13 Vice Pres Information Technology .... Mr. Michael J. BOURQUE
88 Vice Pres Univ Mission & Ministry .... Rev. John T. BUTLER, S.J.
86 Vice Pres Govt/Community Affairs .... Mr. Thomas J. KEADY
18 Vice Pres Facilities Management .... Mr. Daniel F. BOURQUE
09 Vice Pres Inst Research/Assessment .... Vacant
20 Vice Provost Undergrad Acad Affairs .... Dr. Akua SARR
46 Vice Provost Research/Acad Planning .... Dr. Thomas CHILES
84 Vice Prov for Enrollment Management .. Mr. John MAHONEY, JR.
20 Vice Provost for Faculties .... Dr. Billy SOO
44 Vice President for Development .... Vacant
20 AV Provost Undergrad Acad Affairs .... Dr. J. Joseph BURNS
18 Assoc VP Capital Projects .... Ms. Mary S. NARDONE
29 Associate VP Alumni Relations .... Ms. Leah DECOSTA
16 Assoc VP Human Resources .... Mr. William MURPHY
109 Assoc VP Auxiliary Services .... Ms. Patricia A. BANDO
49 Dean Morrissey Col Arts & Sciences .... Rev. Gregory KALSCHEUR, S.J.
87 Assoc Dean of Acad Affairs/Advising ..... Mr. David M. GOODMAN
53 Dean Lynch Sch Education/Human Dev ... Dr. Stanton WORTHAM
61 Dean Law School .... Mr. Vincent D. ROUGEAU
50 Dean Carroll School of Management ...... Dr. Andrew C. BOYNTON
66 Dean Connell School of Nursing .... Dr. Susan GENNARO
70 Dean School of Social Work .... Dr. Gautam N. YADAMA
73 Dean School of Theology & Ministry .... Rev. Thomas STEGMAN, SJ
20 Dean Woods Col of Advancing Studies .. Ms. Karen MUNCASTER
35 Assoc VP Student Affairs .... Dr. Melinda STOOPS
08 University Librarian .... Dr. Thomas WALL
28 Exec Dir Institutional Diversity .... Ms. Patricia LOWE
06 Int Exec Director Student Services .... Mr. Adam KRUEKEBERG
07 Director Undergraduate Admissions .... Mr. Grant M. GOSSELIN
27 AVP Office of Univ Communications .... Mr. John B. DUNN
102 Assoc VP School Development .... Mrs. Ginger K. SAARIAHO
41 Director Athletics .... Mr. Martin JARMOND
36 Assoc VP Student Affairs .... Mr. Joseph DUPONT
42 Assoc VP Campus Ministry .... Rev. Anthony PENNA
31 Director of Community Affairs .... Mr. William R. MILLS
38 Director of Univ Counseling Svcs .... Mr. Craig D. BURNS
37 Director Financial Aid .... Ms. Mary S. MCGRANAHAN
23 Director Health Services .... Dr. Thomas I. NARY
39 Assoc VP Residential Life .... Mr. George A. AREY
25 Director Sponsored Programs .... Mrs. Sharon COMVALIUS-GODDARD
19 Dir Public Safety/Chief of Police .... Mr. William B. EVANS
40 Director Bookstore .... Mr. Robert STEWART
43 General Counsel .... Mr. Joseph M. HERLIHY
24 Director Media Technology Services .... Mr. David CORKUM
85 Dir Office of International Pgms .... Dr. Nick GOZIK
88 Dir Jesuit Inst/Pres Scholars Pgm ...... Rev. James F. KEENAN, SJ
93 Director AHANA/Intercultural Center .... Rev. Michael DAVIDSON
86 Director Governmental Relations .... Ms. Jeanne LEVESQUE
96 Director Procurement Services .... Mr. Paul MCGOWAN
09 AV Provost Assessment/Accreditation .... Dr. Jessica A. GREENE

Boston Graduate School of Psychoanalysis (C)

1581 Beacon Street, Brookline MA 02446-4602
County: Norfolk FICE Identification: 031943
Unit ID: 164915
Telephone: (617) 277-3915 Carnegie Class: Spec-4-yr-Other Health
FAX Number: (617) 277-0312 Calendar System: Semester
URL: www.bgsp.edu
Established: 1973 Annual Graduate Tuition & Fees: N/A
Enrollment: 144 Coed
Affiliation or Control: Independent Non-Profit IRS Status: 501(c)3
Highest Offering: Doctorate; No Undergraduates
Accreditation: EH

01 President .... Dr. Jane SNYDER
10 Vice President Finance .... Dr. Carol PANETTA
58 Dean of Graduate Studies .... Dr. Lynn PERLMAN
07 Director of Admissions .... Dr. Paula BERMAN
06 Registrar .... Ms. Dianne KAELI
37 Director of Financial Aid .... Ms. Stephanie WOOLBERT
21 Controller .... Ms. Gayle DOLAN
08 Head Librarian .... Ms. Amy COHEN-ROSE
88 Director of the Center for Research .... Dr. Stephen SOLDZ

Boston University (D)

One Silber Way, Boston MA 02215-1700
County: Suffolk FICE Identification: 002130
Unit ID: 164988
Telephone: (617) 353-2000 Carnegie Class: DU-Highest
FAX Number: N/A Calendar System: Semester
URL: www.bu.edu
Established: 1839 Annual Undergrad Tuition & Fees: $53,948
Enrollment: 33,355 Coed
Affiliation or Control: Independent Non-Profit IRS Status: 501(c)3
Highest Offering: Doctorate
Accreditation: EH, #ARCPA, ART, CAATE, CACREP, CAHIIM, CEA, CLPSY, COPSY, DENT, DIETD, DIETI, FEPAC, HSA, IPSY, LAW, MED, MUS, OT, PCSAS, PH, PTA, SP, SW, THEOL

01 President .... Robert A. BROWN
05 University Provost .... Jean MORRISON
17 Provost Med Campus/Dean Sch of Med .... Karen H. ANTMAN
100 VP & Chief of Staff to President .... Douglas A. SEARS
04 Exec Asst to President's Office .... Megan S. COHEN
49 Dean Col/Grad Sch Arts & Sciences .... Stan SCLAROFF
60 Dean College of Communication .... Thomas FIEDLER
53 Int Dean Wheelock Col of Educ & HD .... David CHARD
54 Dean College of Engineering .... Kenneth R. LUTCHEN
57 Dean College of Fine Arts .... Harvey YOUNG
97 Dean College General Studies .... Natalie MCKNIGHT
88 Dean School of Hospitality Admin .... Arun UPNEJA
61 Dean of School of Law .... Angela ONWUACHI-WILLIG
50 Dean Questrom School of Business .... Susan FOURNIER
42 Dean of Marsh Chapel .... Robert A. HILL
51 Dean Metropolitan College/Ext Ed .... Tanya ZLATEVA
76 Dean SAR Health & Rehab Sciences .... Christopher A. MOORE
70 Dean School of Social Work .... Jorge DELVA
73 Dean School of Theology .... Mary Elizabeth MOORE
88 Dean Pardee Sch of Global Studies .... Adil NAJAM
52 Dean Goldman Sch of Dental Medicine .... Jeffrey W. HUTTER
69 Dean School of Public Health .... Sandro GALEA
32 Associate Provost/Dean of Students .... Kenneth ELMORE
46 VP & Assoc Provost Research .... Gloria WATERS
58 Assoc Provost Graduate Affairs .... Daniel L. KLEINMAN
114 Assoc Provost Budget & Planning .... Patricia O'BRIEN
88 Chief of Staff Provost's Office .... Laura JENKS
20 Assoc Provost Undergraduate Affairs .... Elizabeth LOIZEAUX
20 Assoc Provost for Faculty Affairs .... Julie H. SANDELL
28 Assoc Provost Diversity & Inclusion .... Crystal A. WILLIAMS
106 Assoc Prov Digital Lrng/Innovation .... Chris DELLAROCAS
101 Sr VP/Sr Counsel & Board Secy .... Todd L C. KLIPP
11 Senior Vice President Operations .... Gary W. NICKSA
26 Senior VP External Relations .... Stephen P. BURGAY
30 Senior VP Devel/Alumni Relations .... Scott G. NICHOLS
10 Senior Vice Pres/CFO & Treasurer .... Martin J. HOWARD
109 Vice President Auxiliary Services .... Peter SMOKOWSKI
43 VP & General Counsel .... Erika GEETTER
86 Vice President Federal Relations .... Jennifer GRODSKY
18 VP Campus Planning & Operations .... Michael DONOVAN
45 VP Budget Planning & Business Affs .... Derek HOWE
110 Vice President Development .... Karen ENGELBOURG
88 VP/Assoc Provost Global Programs .... Willis G. WANG
13 VP Info Svcs & Tech/Chief Data Ofcr .... Tracy SCHROEDER
84 VP/Assoc Prov Enroll & Stdnt Admin .... Christine W. MCGUIRE
86 VP Government/Community Rels .... Jake SULLIVAN
29 VP Alumni Relations .... Steven A. HALL
27 VP Marketing & Creative Services .... Amy HOOK
115 Chief Investment Officer .... Lila HUNNEWELL
19 Exec Dir Pub Safety/Chief of Police .... Kelly A. NEE
103 Exec Dir Career Development .... Louis V. GAGLINI
15 VP/Chief Human Resources Officer .... Diane M. TUCKER
07 Assoc VP Enrol & Dean of Admissions .... Kelly A. WALTER
35 Assoc VP Enroll & Student Affairs .... Denise MOONEY
88 AVP Student Info Systems/Comm & PM .... Marylou OÆDONNELL-RUNDLETT
25 Assoc VP Sponsored Programs .... Diane BALDWIN
114 AVP Budget/Plng & Business Affairs .... Ines GARRANT
21 Assoc VP & University Comptroller .... Gillian EMMONS
09 Asst VP Analytical Svcs & Inst Rsch .... Linette A. DECARIE
88 Asst VP PostAward Financial Opers .... Gretchen HARTIGAN
87 Assistant Dean Summer Term .... Donna SHEA
35 Asst Dean Stdnts/Dir Stdnt Activ .... John BATTAGLINO, JR.
108 Asst Provost Academic Assessment .... Gillian PIERCE
88 Asst VP Business Affairs .... Melanie MADAIO-O'BRIEN
41 Asst VP & Director of Athletics .... Drew MARROCHELLO
06 Asst VP & University Registrar .... Christine S. PAAL
96 Asst VP/Chief Procurement Officer .... Randall MOORE
104 Exec Director Study Abroad .... Gareth MCFEELY
37 Exec Dir Financial Assistance .... Julie WICKSTROM
39 Director of Housing/Dining .... Nishmin KASHYUP
85 Mng Dir Intl Student/Scholars Ofc .... Jeanne KELLEY
28 Director Howard Thurman Center .... Katherine J. KENNEDY
22 Exec Dir Equal Opportunity .... Kim RANDALL
36 Director Student Employment .... Mary Ann FRENCH
08 University Librarian .... K. Matthew DAMES
88 Dir Ugrd Research Opportunities Pgm .... John CELENZA
88 General Manager Agganis Arena .... Kristoffer W. BRASSIL
88 Exec Director Physical Ed Rec/Dance .... Timothy MOORE
23 Director Student Health Services .... Judy T. PLATT
35 Senior Assoc Dir Student Activities .... Bryan ADAMS
102 Assoc VP Industry Engagement .... Marc SCATAMACCHIA
105 Assoc Director Web Services .... Ron YEANY
38 Director Student Counseling .... Carrie LANDA
90 Director of Research Computing .... Wayne GILMORE
91 SVP Applications & Enterprise Svcs .... Janet O'BRIEN

Brandeis University (E)

415 South Street, Waltham MA 02453
County: Middlesex FICE Identification: 002133
Unit ID: 165015
Telephone: (781) 736-2000 Carnegie Class: DU-Highest
FAX Number: (781) 736-8699 Calendar System: Semester
URL: www.brandeis.edu
Established: 1948 Annual Undergrad Tuition & Fees: $55,395
Enrollment: 5,721 Coed
Affiliation or Control: Independent Non-Profit IRS Status: 501(c)3
Highest Offering: Doctorate
Accreditation: EH

01 President .... Dr. Ronald D. LIEBOWITZ
05 Provost .... Dr. Lisa M. LYNCH
10 Exec VP for Finance/Administration .... Mr. Stewart URETSKY
111 Sr Vice Pres Inst Advancement .... Ms. Zamira KORFF
43 Sr VP and General Counsel .... Mr. Steven S. LOCKE
26 Interim VP of Communications .... Mr. Bill WALKER
21 Chief Financial Officer & Treasurer .... Mr. Samuel SOLOMON
28 Chief Diversity Officer .... Dr. Mark BRIMHALL-VARGAS
18 Interim Vice Pres for Operations .... Mr. Richard REYNOLDS
13 Chief Information Officer .... Mr. James LACRETA
15 Interim Vice Pres Human Resources .... Mr. Larry LEWELLEN
32 Vice Provost for Student Affairs .... Vacant
45 VP Planning/Institutional Research .... Mr. Dan FELDMAN
49 Dean of Arts & Sciences .... Dr. Dorothy L. HODGSON
70 Dn Heller Sch Social Pol & Mgt .... Dr. David WEIL
50 Dean International Business Sch .... Dr. Kathryn GRADDY
06 University Registrar .... Dr. Mark S. HEWITT
08 University Librarian .... Mr. Matthew SHEEHY
07 Dean of Admissions .... Ms. Jennifer WALKER
09 Director of Institutional Research .... Ms. Judith A. JAFFE
102 Asst VP Corp & Foundation Relations .... Mr. Michael DETTELBACH
36 Exec Director Hiatt Career Center .... Ms. Andrea B. DINE
37 Exec Director Student Financial Svc .... Ms. Sherri M. AVERY
100 Chief of Staff .... Mr. William R. O'REILLY, JR.

Cambridge College (F)

500 Rutherford Avenue, Boston MA 02129
County: Suffolk FICE Identification: 021829
Unit ID: 165167
Telephone: (800) 877-4723 Carnegie Class: Masters/L
FAX Number: (617) 349-3545 Calendar System: Trimester
URL: www.cambridgecollege.edu
Established: 1971 Annual Undergrad Tuition & Fees: $15,588
Enrollment: 2,261 Coed
Affiliation or Control: Independent Non-Profit IRS Status: 501(c)3
Highest Offering: Doctorate
Accreditation: EH, CAEPT

01 President .... Deborah C. JACKSON
05 Interim Provost & VP of AA .... Dr. Jerry ICE
10 CFO/VP of Finance & Administration .... John SPINARD
15 VP of Human Resources .... Lauretta SIGGERS
86 VP of Strategic Partnerships .... Phillip PAGE
45 VP of Innovation/Strat Initiatives .... Mark ROTONDO
111 VP of Institutional Advancement .... Vacant
26 VP Marketing/Communications and PR .... Jacqueline CONRAD
43 Acting General Counsel .... Judith SIZER
20 Assoc Provost Student Learning .... Dr. Tracy MCLAUGHLIN
84 Interim Assoc VP Enrollment .... Salvadore A. LIBERTO
14 Director of Information Technology .... Achal KHATRI
113 Dir of Student Financial Services .... Vacant
37 Director of Financial Aid .... Frank LAUDER
21 Controller .... Dorothy WHALEN
88 Assistant Controller .... Sharon DELESKEY
06 Registrar .... Amy CAVELIER
09 Director of Institutional Research .... Stephanie FUNDERBURG
12 Director of Puerto Rico .... Dr. Santiago MENDEZ-HERNANDEZ
12 Director of Southern California .... Rita CLEMONS
12 Asst Director of Lawrence MA .... Melissa Sue FRASCA
12 Executive Director Springfield MA .... Teresa (Terrie) FORTE
88 Senior Director SIS .... Robyn SHAHID-BELLOT
110 Managing Dir Advancement Services .... John A. BEAHM
112 Director of Major Gifts .... Alex MORR
29 Dir Annual Fund/Alumni Engagement .... Erik RYAN
88 Dir of Marketing & Digital Strategy .... Maria VASALLO
97 Dean Undergraduate Studies .... Dr. James LEE
83 Dean School of Psychology .... Dr. Niti SETH
32 Dean Student Affairs/Student Life .... Regina ROBINSON
53 Interim Dean School of Education .... Dr. Mary GARRITY

50	Dean School of Management	Vacant
88	Dir Center for Learning/Teaching	Brooks WINCHELL
88	Director of Academic Compliance	Dr. Joseph MIGLIO
121	Dir Undergrad Academic Advising	Michael DICKINSON
04	Administrative Asst to President	Robyn CARROLL
106	Dean of Online Programming	Dr. Michael E. MARRAPODI

Clark University (A)

950 Main Street, Worcester MA 01610-1477

County: Worcester FICE Identification: 002139
Unit ID: 165334
Telephone: (508) 793-7711 Carnegie Class: DU-Higher
FAX Number: (508) 793-7780 Calendar System: Semester
URL: www.clarku.edu
Established: 1887 Annual Undergrad Tuition & Fees: $45,730
Enrollment: 3,153 Coed
Affiliation or Control: Independent Non-Profit IRS Status: 501(c)3
Highest Offering: Doctorate
Accreditation: EH, CLPSY

01	President	Dr. David P. ANGEL
05	Provost & Vice Pres Academic Affs	Dr. Davis BAIRD
111	Vice Pres University Advancement	Mr. Jeffrey GILLOOLY
26	Asst Vice Pres Mktg & Communication	Mr. James KEOGH
13	Vice Pres for Information Tech/CIO	Ms. Pennie TURGEON
86	VP Government/Cmty Affs/Campus Svcs	Mr. John FOLEY
32	Dean of Students	Dr. Frances MAGEE
46	Dean of Research/Dean Grad Studies	Dr. Yuko AOYAMA
49	Assoc Provost/Dean of College	Dr. Betsy HUANG
20	Assoc Provost/Dean of the Faculty	Dr. Esther JONES
58	Dean Grad School Mgmt	Dr. Priscilla ELSASS
07	Dean of Admissions & Financial Aid	Ms. Meredith TWOMBLY
37	Director of Financial Aid	Ms. Mary Ellen SEVERANCE
08	University Librarian	Dr. Gwendolynne ARTHUR
10	Controller	Ms. Katherine CANNON
36	Director Career Development	Ms. Michelle FLINT
06	Registrar	Mr. John OHOTNICKY
15	Dir of HR/Affirm Act	Mr. David EVERITT
18	Director of Facilities Management	Mr. Daniel RODERICK
41	Director of Athletics	Ms. Trish CRONIN
114	Chief University Budget Officer	Mr. Paul WYKES
19	Chief of Campus Police	Mr. Stephen P. GOULET
23	Director of Health Services	Ms. Robin MCNALLY
28	Chief Officer Diversity/Inclusion	Ms. Sheree OHEN
04	Assistant to the President	Ms. Katrina BANKS-BINICI
115	Chief Investment Officer	Mr. James COLLINS
109	Business & Auxiliary Services Mgr	Mr. Anthony PENNY
09	Dir Strat Analytics/Inst Research	Ms. Elissa LU
104	Director Study Abroad	Ms. Alissa KRAMER
39	Director Student Housing	Mr. Tim ST. JOHN
22	Title IX Coord/Asst Dean Wellness	Ms. Lynn LEVEY
102	Dir Foundation/Corporate Relations	Ms. Jennifer HITT
105	Sr Assoc Dir of Content Mktg	Ms. Meredith KING

College of the Holy Cross (B)

1 College Street, Worcester MA 01610-2322

County: Worcester FICE Identification: 002141
Unit ID: 166124
Telephone: (508) 793-2011 Carnegie Class: Bac-A&S
FAX Number: (508) 793-3030 Calendar System: Semester
URL: www.holycross.edu
Established: 1843 Annual Undergrad Tuition & Fees: $52,770
Enrollment: 2,855 Coed
Affiliation or Control: Roman Catholic IRS Status: 501(c)3
Highest Offering: Baccalaureate
Accreditation: EH, THEA

01	President	Rev. Philip L. BOROUGHS, SJ
04	Special Assistant to the President	Ms. Jane CORR
05	VP Academic Affairs/Dean of Col	Dr. Margaret FREIJE
10	VP Admin & Finance/Treasurer	Ms. Dottie HAUVER
115	Chief Investment Officer	Mr. Timothy JARRY
32	VP Student Affairs/Dean of Students	Ms. Michelle MURRAY
30	VP for Development/Alumni Relations	Ms. Tracy BARLOK
42	Vice President for Mission	Vacant
20	Associate Dean of the College	Vacant
21	Director of Finance/Asst Treasurer	Mr. Charles ESTAPHAN
06	Registrar	Ms. Patricia RING
07	Director of Admissions	Ms. Ann B. MCDERMOTT
08	Director of Library Services	Mr. Mark SHELTON
37	Director of Financial Aid	Ms. Nicole CUNNINGHAM
25	Director of Sponsored Research	Ms. Stacy RISEMAN
42	Director Ofc of College Chaplains	Ms. Marybeth KEARNS-BARRETT
88	Director Ctr Interdisc Studies	Dr. Lorelle SEMLEY
36	Director of Career Planning	Ms. Amy MURPHY
13	Director Information Tech Services	Dr. Ellen J. KEOHANE
26	VP for Communications	Mr. Dan KIM
29	Director of Alumni Relations	Ms. Kristyn M. DYER
19	Director of Public Safety	Ms. Shawn DE JONG
35	Director of Campus Center	Mr. Jeremiah O'CONNOR
18	Director of Physical Plant	Mr. Scott M. MERRILL
41	Dir of Intercollegiate Athletics	Mr. Marcus BLOSSOM
21	Controller	Ms. Charlene BELLOWS
38	Director Counseling Center	Dr. Paul GALVINHILL
23	Director Student Health Services	Ms. Martha SULLIVAN
15	Director Human Resources	Mr. David ACHENBACH
96	Manager of Purchasing	Ms. Joan E. ANDERSON
09	Ofc of Assessment/Research	Dr. Denise BELL
86	Dir of Govt/Community Rels	Mr. Jamie D. HOAG
43	General Counsel	Ms. Elizabeth SMALL
28	Chief Diversity Officer	Mr. Amit TANEJA
104	Director Study Abroad	Dr. Brittain SMITH

College of Our Lady of the Elms (C)

291 Springfield Street, Chicopee MA 01013-2839

County: Hampden FICE Identification: 002140
Unit ID: 167394
Telephone: (413) 594-2761 Carnegie Class: Masters/M
FAX Number: (413) 592-4871 Calendar System: Semester
URL: www.elms.edu
Established: 1928 Annual Undergrad Tuition & Fees: $35,788
Enrollment: 1,580 Coed
Affiliation or Control: Roman Catholic IRS Status: 501(c)3
Highest Offering: Doctorate
Accreditation: EH, IACBE, NURSE, SW

01	President	Dr. Harry E. DUMAY
05	Vice President of Academic Affairs	Dr. Walter C. BREAU
10	Vice Pres Finance/Administration	Katie LONGLEY
84	VP Enrollment Mgmt & Marketing	Jonathan SCULLY
111	VP Institutional Advancement	Bernadette NOWAKOWSKI
32	Dean of Students	Teresa WINTERS
13	Chief Information Officer	Mary KASELOUSKAS
07	Director of Admissions	Vacant
121	Dean of Stdnt Success & Strat Init	Dr. Joyce HAMPTON
15	Director Human Resources/Personnel	Deborah METHE
110	Asst VP of Inst Advancement	Vacant
06	Registrar	Brooke BEDARD
113	Bursar	Kathleen CURRY
21	Controller	Gary RUSSETT
08	Director of Library	Anthony FONSECA
26	Director of Communications	Melinda ROSE
37	Director of Financial Aid	Richard O'CONNOR
36	Dir of Career Development	Phyllis WILLIAMS-THOMPSON
04	Executive Assistant to President	Kimberly HANNAH
09	Dir of Inst Assessment & Research	Karalee YVON
44	Dir of Annual Giving	William DZIURA
18	Dir of Campus Operations & Planning	Ron RICKEY
39	Dir of Res Life/New Student Pgms	Vacant
19	Director of Public Safety	Vacant
29	Dir of Alumni Relations	Jessica COLSON
41	Director of Athletics	Michael THEULEN
66	Dean School of Nursing	Dr. Kathleen SCOBLE
58	Dean School of Grad & Prof Studies	Dr. Elizabeth HUKOWICZ
28	Dir of Diversity & Inclusion	Alaina MACAULAY
38	Director of Counseling Center	Dr. Nicole HADDAD
23	Director of Health Center	Jessie CHENIER
42	Director of Campus Ministry	Sr. Carol ALLAN
120	Academic Technology Specialist	Sara FLINK
119	Mgr of Ntwk/Infrastructure Security	Alexander ZMACZYNSKI
24	Mgr of Media Services	Christopher PELLETIER

Conway School of Landscape Design (D)

88 Village Hill Road, Northampton MA 01060

County: Franklin FICE Identification: 022743
Unit ID: 165495
Telephone: (413) 369-4044 Carnegie Class: Spec-4-yr-Arts
FAX Number: (413) 203-6914 Calendar System: Trimester
URL: www.csld.edu
Established: 1972 Annual Graduate Tuition & Fees: N/A
Enrollment: 18 Coed
Affiliation or Control: Independent Non-Profit IRS Status: 501(c)3
Highest Offering: Master's; No Undergraduates
Accreditation: EH

01	Executive Director	Mr. Bruce STEDMAN
05	Academic Director	Mr. Ken BYRNE
10	Finance Manager	Ms. Paulina KISLYUK
11	Administrative Director	Ms. Priscilla NOVITT
06	Registrar	Ms. Nancy BRAXTON
07	Admissions Manager	Ms. Kate CHOLOKIS
29	Director Alumni Relations	Ms. Nancy BRAXTON

Curry College (E)

1071 Blue Hill Avenue, Milton MA 02186-2395

County: Norfolk FICE Identification: 002143
Unit ID: 165529
Telephone: (617) 333-0500 Carnegie Class: Masters/M
FAX Number: (617) 979-3540 Calendar System: Semester
URL: www.curry.edu
Established: 1879 Annual Undergrad Tuition & Fees: $40,070
Enrollment: 2,799 Coed
Affiliation or Control: Independent Non-Profit IRS Status: 501(c)3
Highest Offering: Master's
Accreditation: EH, IACBE, NURSE

01	President	Mr. Kenneth K. QUIGLEY, JR.
05	Vice President Academic Affairs	Dr. David SZCZERBACKI
111	VP Institutional Advancement	Ms. Sally MURRAY
10	Chief Financial Officer	Mr. David M. ROSATI
07	Associate VP and Dean of Admission	Mr. Keith ROBICHAUD
32	VP of Student Affairs	Ms. Maryellen M. KILEY
45	VP of Institutional Planning	Dr. Susan W. PENNINI
04	Assistant to the President	Ms. Amy M. BIANCHI
08	Director Library	Ms. Garrett EASTMAN
13	Chief Information Officer	Ms. Deborah GELCH
35	VP of Human Resources	Mirlen MAL
06	Registrar	Ms. June KOUKOL
18	Director of Buildings & Grounds	Mr. Robert G. O'CONNELL
110	Assoc VP of Institutional Advance	Ms. Michelle O'REGAN
36	Director of Student Placement	Ms. Kerrie ABORN
37	Assoc VP of Finance for SFS	Ms. Stephanny J. ELIAS
38	Director of Student Counseling	Dr. Alison W. MARKSON
09	Director of Institutional Research	Ms. Jennifer DUNNE
105	Director Web Services	Mr. John EAGAN
41	Athletic Director	Mr. Vincent ERUZIONE
39	Director Student Housing	Ms. Jennifer MAITINO

Dean College (F)

99 Main Street, Franklin MA 02038-1994

County: Norfolk FICE Identification: 002144
Unit ID: 165574
Telephone: (508) 541-1508 Carnegie Class: Bac/Assoc-Mixed
FAX Number: (508) 541-8726 Calendar System: Semester
URL: www.dean.edu
Established: 1865 Annual Undergrad Tuition & Fees: $39,434
Enrollment: 1,301 Coed
Affiliation or Control: Independent Non-Profit IRS Status: 501(c)3
Highest Offering: Baccalaureate
Accreditation: EH

01	President	Dr. Paula M. ROONEY
100	Chief of Staff	Ms. Sandra CAIN
05	VP Academic Affairs	Dr. Kathleen VRANOS
10	Vice Pres Financial Svcs/Treasurer	Mr. Dan MODELANE
84	VP Enrollment & Retention	Ms. Cindy T. KOZIL
111	Vice Pres Institutional Advancement	Ms. Coleen RESNICK
13	VP/Chief Information Officer	Mr. Darrell KULESZA
44	Asst VP Individual & Corporate Gift	Mr. J.J ALBERTS
21	Assoc VP/Controller/Asst Treasurer	Ms. Kathleen MCGUIRE
07	Assoc VP Enrollment/Dean Admission	Ms. Iris GODES
121	Assc VP Student Success/Career Plng	Ms. Wendy ADLER
20	Asst VP Academic Affairs	Ms. Melissa READ
18	Assoc VP Capital Plng/Facilities	Mr. Brian KELLY
26	VP Marketing & Business Development	Mr. Gregg CHALK
32	Dean of Students	Mr. David DRUCKER
51	Dean School of Continuing Studies	Mr. Paul RESTEN
50	Dean School of Business	Dr. P. Gerard SHAW
49	Dean School of Liberal Arts	Dr. Brad HASTINGS
57	Dean Palladino School of Dance/Arts	Mr. Marc ARENTSEN
06	Registrar	Ms. Louise MONAST
19	Dir Law Enforcement Services	Mr. Ken CORKRAN
08	Director of the Library	Mr. Ted BURKE
41	Athletic Director	Mr. Todd A. VASEY
39	Assistant Dean of Students	Ms. Shannon OVERCASH
35	Dir Orientation/Community Service	Ms. Jennifer POLIMER
40	Director of Bookstore	Ms. Jackie CALDERONE
37	Dean Student & Financial Plng/Svcs	Mr. Frank MULLEN
07	Director Enrollment Operations	Ms. Kathleen RYAN
36	Dir Career Planning/Internships	Ms. Thea CERIO
38	Director of Counseling Services	Ms. Mary Ann SILVESTRI
29	Director Alumni Relations	Ms. Lindsay MCHUGH

Eastern Nazarene College (G)

23 E Elm Avenue, Quincy MA 02170-2999

County: Norfolk FICE Identification: 002145
Unit ID: 165644
Telephone: (617) 745-3000 Carnegie Class: Bac-Diverse
FAX Number: (617) 745-3907 Calendar System: 4/1/4
URL: www.enc.edu
Established: 1918 Annual Undergrad Tuition & Fees: $25,598
Enrollment: 848 Coed
Affiliation or Control: Church Of The Nazarene IRS Status: 501(c)3
Highest Offering: Master's
Accreditation: EH, SW

01	President	Dr. Jack CONNELL
05	Interim Academic Dean	Dr. William MALAS, JR.
10	Vice President for Finance	Ms. Patricia CONSTANTINO
32	Vice Pres Student Development	Mr. Jeffrey KIRKSEY
111	Vice President Inst Advancement	Dr. Larry BOLLINGER
84	Vice President of Enrollment	Dr. Brad ZARGES
07	Asst Director of Admissions	Ms. Madison FLOWERS
39	Dir of Residential Life & Housing	Dr. Elizabeth MOREAU
06	Registrar	Mr. Edward WICHROWSKI
37	Director of Financial Aid	Mr. Troy MARTIN
08	Director of Library Services	Ms. Amy HWANG
19	Director Safety and Security	Mr. John GELORMINI
38	Dir Counseling & Career Services	Mr. Bradford E. THORNE
58	Assistant Dean for Adult & Graduate	Ms. Melinda SMITH
41	Director of Athletics	Mr. Bradford ZARGES
18	Director of Facilities	Mr. Jed HANNON
45	Supervisor Instructional Resources	Ms. Patricia VASQUEZ
21	Controller	Vacant
22	Director Human Resources	Ms. Christina PAUL
40	Director Bookstore	Ms. Keri LEWIS
13	Chief Information Officer	Mr. Charles BURT
04	Executive Asst to the President	Mrs. Kimberly POLSGROVE
93	Director of Multicultural Affairs	Mr. Robert BENJAMIN
09	Director of Institutional Research	Vacant
29	Alumni Relations Coordinator	Mr. Dan COMPITIELLO
36	Director Student Placement	Ms. Krista BOGERTMAN
20	Associate Dean for Academic Affairs	Dr. Linda SCOTT

Emerson College (H)

120 Boylston Street, Boston MA 02116-4624

County: Suffolk FICE Identification: 002146
Unit ID: 165662

Telephone: (617) 824-8500 Carnegie Class: Masters/L
FAX Number: (617) 824-8511 Calendar System: Semester
URL: www.emerson.edu
Established: 1880 Annual Undergrad Tuition & Fees: $46,852
Enrollment: 4,459 Coed
Affiliation or Control: Independent Non-Profit IRS Status: 501(c)3
Highest Offering: Master's
Accreditation: EH, SP

01 President .... Dr. M. Lee PELTON
43 Vice President & General Counsel .... Ms. Christine HUGHES
10 Vice President for Admin & Finance .... Ms. Maureen MURPHY
05 Provost & VP of Academic Affairs .... Dr. Michaele WHELAN
13 VP for Information Technology .... Dr. William GILLIGAN
26 AVP Communications/Marketing .... Mr. Michael SARRA
28 VP Social Justice Center .... Dr. Sylvia SPEARS
84 Vice Pres Enrollment Management .... Dr. Ruthanne MADSEN
07 Assoc VP & Dean of Admissions .... Mr. Eric SYKES
21 Assoc Vice Pres for Finance .... Mr. Robert BUTLER
15 Sr AVP for Human Resources .... Ms. Shari STIER
29 AVP Alumni Engagement .... Ms. Leigh GASPAR
86 VP Government/Community Relations .... Ms. Margaret Ann INGS
09 AVP Institutional Research .... Mr. Michael DUGGAN
58 Dean Grad Studies/AVP Acad Affairs .... Ms. Jan ROBERTS-BRESLIN
32 Vice Pres/Dean of Students .... Mr. James HOPPE
107 Exec Director Professional Studies .... Ms. Lesley NICHOLS
08 Exec Director of Library Services .... Mr. Robert FLEMING
123 Director of Graduate Admission .... Ms. Leanda FERLAND
36 Director of Career Services .... Ms. Carol SPECTOR
38 Director Counseling Center .... Dr. Elise HARRISON
41 Director Athletics .... Ms. Patricia NICOL
39 Assoc Dean Campus Life .... Mr. Erik MUURISEPP
21 Controller .... Mr. Jonathan PEARSALL
06 Registrar .... Mr. William DEWOLF
42 Campus Chaplain .... Mr. Harrison BLUM
101 AVP President's Office & BOT .... Ms. Anne SHAUGHNESSY
18 Director of Facilities .... Mr. Joseph KNOLL
37 Director Financial Aid .... Ms. Angela GRANT
04 Executive Assistant to President .... Ms. Bridget SCHULZ
104 Director Study Abroad .... Mr. David GRIFFIN
19 Chief of Police .... Mr. Robert SMITH
25 Chief Contracts/Grants Admin .... Mr. Eric ASETTA
111 VP Institutional Advancement .... Mr. Ronald KORVAS

Emmanuel College (A)

400 The Fenway, Boston MA 02115-5798
County: Suffolk FICE Identification: 002147
Unit ID: 165671
Telephone: (617) 277-9340 Carnegie Class: Bac-A&S
FAX Number: (617) 735-9877 Calendar System: Semester
URL: www.emmanuel.edu
Established: 1919 Annual Undergrad Tuition & Fees: $39,804
Enrollment: 2,083 Coed
Affiliation or Control: Roman Catholic IRS Status: 501(c)3
Highest Offering: Master's
Accreditation: EH, NURSE

01 President .... Sr. Janet EISNER, SND
100 Exec Asst to the President .... Ms. Michelle ERICKSON
04 Senior Assistant to the President .... Ms. Lori SIMMONS
10 VP of Finance/Treasurer (CFO) .... Sr. Anne DONOVAN, SND
05 VP Academic Affairs & Dean .... Dr. Josef KURTZ
32 VP of Student Affairs .... Dr. Joseph ONOFRIETTI
37 Assoc VP for Student Financial Svcs .... Ms. Jennifer PORTER
42 VP of Mission & Ministry .... Fr. John SPENCER, SJ
26 VP of College Relations .... Ms. Molly DILORENZO
84 Dean of Enrollment .... Ms. Sandra ROBBINS
35 Dean of Students .... Ms. Jennifer FORRY
09 Dean of Institutional Effectiveness .... Ms. Beth ROSS
20 Dean Academic Admin/Grad & Prof Pgm .... Ms. Cindy O'CALLAGHAN
88 Asst Dean Cmty Stdrds & Family Pgms .... Ms. Mary Beth THOMAS
121 Assoc Dean of Academic Advising .... Sr. Susan THORNELL, SND
79 Assoc Dean Humanities/Soc Science .... Ms. Lisa STEPANSKI
66 Assoc Dean Nursing .... Ms. Diane SHEA
81 Associate Dean of Natural Sciences .... Dr. Faina RYVKIN
53 Associate Dean of Education .... Sr. Karen HOKANSON, SND
08 Assoc Dn of Library/Lrng Resources .... Ms. Karen STORIN LINITZ
36 Executive Director Career Ctr .... Ms. Maureen ASHBURN
15 Director of Human Resources .... Ms. Erin FARMER NOONAN
41 Director of Athletics & Recreation .... Mr. Brendan MCWILLIAMS
38 Director of Counseling .... Dr. Brenda HAWKS
90 Director of Academic Resource Ctr .... Ms. Wendy LABRON
09 Director of Institutional Research .... Ms. Alison VALLEREUX
13 VP Information Resources/Planning .... Mr. Sean PHILPOTT
19 Director Security/Safety .... Mr. John KELLY
29 Director Alumni Relations .... Ms. Meghan BUTLER

Endicott College (B)

376 Hale Street, Beverly MA 01915-2098
County: Essex FICE Identification: 002148
Unit ID: 165699
Telephone: (978) 927-0585 Carnegie Class: Masters/L
FAX Number: (978) 927-0084 Calendar System: 4/1/4
URL: www.endicott.edu
Established: 1939 Annual Undergrad Tuition & Fees: $33,050
Enrollment: 4,795 Coed
Affiliation or Control: Independent Non-Profit IRS Status: 501(c)3
Highest Offering: Doctorate
Accreditation: EH, ART, CAATE, CIDA, COSMA, NUR

01 President .... Dr. Steven DISALVO
05 Interim Provost .... Dr. Kathleen BARNES
100 Chief of Staff .... Ms. Jillian DUBMAN
10 Vice President of Finance/CFO .... Mr. Tony FERULLO
20 VP & Dean of Undergrad College .... Dr. Laura ROSSI-LE
111 Vice Pres Institutional Advancement .... Mr. David VIGNERON
84 VP Admissions/Financial Aid .... Mr. Evan E. LIPP
26 VP Communicatons/Marketing .... Mr. Bryan CAIN
41 Asst Vice President/Dir Athletics .... Dr. Brian WYLIE
43 General Counsel .... Ms. Karen ABBOTT
32 VP Student Affairs/Dean of Students .... Ms. Brandi JOHNSON
04 Executive Administrative Assistant .... Ms. Amy ASTOLFI
45 Executive Director Research Center .... Mr. Peter L. HART
88 Exec Director Misselwood Events .... Ms. Eileen GEYER
107 Assoc Provost Grad & Prof Studies .... Dr. Chrystal PORTER
90 Assoc Dean of Academic Technology .... Mr. Kent BARCLAY
07 Associate Dean of Admission .... Mr. George M. SHERMAN
15 Director Human Resources .... Ms. Sally ARNOLD
21 Controller .... Mr. Andy VIDAL
06 Registrar .... Ms. Rosa CADENA
08 Director Library .... Mr. Brian COURTEMANCHE
37 Dean of Financial Aid .... Ms. Marcia D. TOOMEY
13 Chief Information Officer .... Ms. Amy DONOVAN
38 Director Counseling Center .... Ms. Karen TOMPKINS
36 Dean Internship and Career Center .... Ms. Dale MCLENNAN
09 Director of Institutional Research .... Mr. Donny FEMINO
96 Director of Purchasing .... Ms. Susan AYERS
85 Dean International Education .... Dr. Warren JAFERIAN
49 Dean School of Arts & Sciences .... Dr. Gene WONG
53 Dean of Education/Scholars Program .... Dr. Sara QUAY
57 Dean Visual & Performing Arts .... Mr. Mark TOWNER
59 Dean School of Hospitality Mgmt .... Dr. Todd COMEN
68 Dean Sports Science/Fitness Studies .... Dr. Deborah SWANTON
66 Director of PhD Nursing .... Dr. Kelly FISHER
50 Dean School of Business .... Dr. Michael PAIGE
60 Dean School of Communication .... Dr. Laurel HELLERSTEIN
88 Director of Internship .... Ms. Cindy RICHARD
105 Director Web Services .... Ms. Jeanne COMMETTE
19 Chief of Police/Dir Public Safety .... Mr. Charles FEMINO
104 Study Abroad Advisor .... Ms. Alicia VINAL
29 Director of Alumni Relations .... Ms. Victorya PILBIN
44 Director of Annual Giving .... Ms. Sarah EARNEST
39 Director of Housing & Student Life .... Ms. Caitlin COURTNEY-BIEDRZYCKI
121 Director Student Success .... Ms. Teresa MCGRATH
107 Dean of Professional Studies .... Ms. Laura DOUGLASS
58 Dir of Grad Education/Fellowships .... Dr. Aubry THRELKELD
58 Dir Grad Pgm in Autism/ABA Studies .... Dr. Mary Jane WEISS

FINE Mortuary College (C)

150 Kerry Place, Norwood MA 02062
County: Norfolk FICE Identification: 033164
Unit ID: 436599
Telephone: (781) 762-1211 Carnegie Class: Spec 2-yr-A&S
FAX Number: (781) 762-7177 Calendar System: Quarter
URL: www.fmc.edu
Established: 1996 Annual Undergrad Tuition & Fees: $20,520
Enrollment: 99 Coed
Affiliation or Control: Proprietary IRS Status: Proprietary
Highest Offering: Associate Degree
Accreditation: FUSER

01 President .... Mr. Kevin KOCH
03 Executive Vice President .... Mrs. Sherry JONES
05 Program Director .... Ms. Sarah STOPYRA
11 Administrative Operations Manager .... Ms. Laura HEWEY

Fisher College (D)

118 Beacon Street, Boston MA 02116-1500
County: Suffolk FICE Identification: 002150
Unit ID: 165802
Telephone: (617) 236-8800 Carnegie Class: Bac-Diverse
FAX Number: (617) 236-8858 Calendar System: Semester
URL: www.fisher.edu
Established: 1903 Annual Undergrad Tuition & Fees: $31,384
Enrollment: 1,923 Coed
Affiliation or Control: Independent Non-Profit IRS Status: 501(c)3
Highest Offering: Master's
Accreditation: EH, CAHIIM, IACBE, NURSE

01 President .... Dr. Alan RAY
03 Executive Vice President .... Ms. Ana DA CUNHA
05 Vice President Academic Affairs .... Dr. Janet KUSER
10 VP for Finance and Administration .... Mr. Steven RICH
84 VP of Enrollment Management .... Mr. Robert MELARAGNI
107 VP Div of Accelerated/Prof Studies .... Ms. Kathleen EHLERS
111 VP Advancement & Alumni Engagement .... Ms. Brenda SANCHEZ
32 Dean of Students .... Ms. Shiela LALLY
88 Dean Intl Acad Oper/Curriculum Dev .... Ms. Nancy PITHIS
49 Asst Dean School of Liberal Arts .... Mr. Willem WALLINGA
06 College Registrar .... Mr. Jesse AVALOS
41 Director of Athletics .... Ms. Catherine COURTNEY
15 Director of HR/Title IX Coord .... Ms. Ellen LYONS
26 Dir Marketing & Communications .... Mr. Michael CRAWFORD
07 Director of Admissions .... Mr. Thomas ENGLEHARDT
21 Director of Accounting .... Mr. Jeffrey CONRAD
13 Director of Information Services .... Mr. Jonathan BARTSCH
18 Director of Facilities .... Mr. Paul MCBRINE
37 Director of Financial Aid .... Ms. Jennifer WILHELM
20 Assoc Dean for Academic Services .... Ms. Barbara ZERILLO
19 Chief Dept of Public Safety .... Mr. Brian PERRIN
36 Director of Career Services .... Ms. Caroline WRIGHT
88 Director of Accessibility Service .... Dr. Wanda CAMACHO-MARON
113 College Bursar .... Ms. Kristen MARTINEZ
08 College Librarian .... Mr. Joshua MCKAIN
09 Director of Institutional Research .... Mr. Roland PEARSALL
58 Assistant Dean Grad/MBA Programs .... Dr. Neil TROTTA
39 Director Student Housing .... Ms. Shiela LALLY
124 Dir Student Engagement & Retention .... Mr. Jesse FORD
105 Webmaster & Digital Content Coord .... Mr. Thomas CARROLL
104 Director Study Abroad .... Mr. Jesse FORD
04 Special Assistant to the President .... Mr. Denny CHING

Franklin W. Olin College of Engineering (E)

Olin Way, Needham MA 02492-1200
County: Norfolk FICE Identification: 039463
Unit ID: 441982
Telephone: (781) 292-2300 Carnegie Class: Spec-4-yr-Eng
FAX Number: (781) 292-2210 Calendar System: Semester
URL: www.olin.edu
Established: 1997 Annual Undergrad Tuition & Fees: $53,736
Enrollment: 380 Coed
Affiliation or Control: Independent Non-Profit IRS Status: 501(c)3
Highest Offering: Baccalaureate
Accreditation: EH

01 President .... Dr. Richard K. MILLER
04 Asst to President .... Ms. Nancy SULLIVAN
05 Interim Provost/Dean of Faculty .... Mr. Mark SOMERVILLE
32 Dean of Student Affairs & Resources .... Ms. Rae-Anne BUTERA
06 Assoc Dean for Acad Pgms/Registrar .... Ms. Linda T. CANAVAN
07 Dean of Admission and Financial Aid .... Ms. Emily ROPER-DOTEN
37 Director of Financial Aid .... Ms. Jean RICKER
08 Library Director .... Vacant
10 VP for Financial Affairs & CFO .... Ms. Patricia GALLAGHER
13 Chief Information Officer .... Mr. Rick OSTERBERG
26 Chief Marketing Officer .... Vacant
09 Director of Inst Research .... Vacant
111 Vice President of Advancement .... Ms. Beth KRAMER
11 VP for Admin Services & Innovation .... Mr. Jeremy GOODMAN

† All admitted students who enroll at Olin College receive an Olin Scholarship covering half tuition during the eight semesters of the baccalaureate program.

Gordon College (F)

255 Grapevine Road, Wenham MA 01984-1899
County: Essex FICE Identification: 002153
Unit ID: 165936
Telephone: (978) 927-2300 Carnegie Class: Bac-A&S
FAX Number: (978) 867-4659 Calendar System: Semester
URL: www.gordon.edu
Established: 1889 Annual Undergrad Tuition & Fees: $37,400
Enrollment: 1,963 Coed
Affiliation or Control: Independent Non-Profit IRS Status: 501(c)3
Highest Offering: Master's
Accreditation: EH, MUS, SW

01 President .... Dr. D. Michael LINDSAY
03 Exec VP and Chief of Staff .... Mr. Daniel TYMANN
05 Provost .... Dr. Janel CURRY
10 VP for Finance/Business Development .... Mr. John J. TRUSCHEL
07 AVP Enrollment .... Ms. June BODONI
32 Vice President for Student Life .... Mr. Daniel TYMANN
26 VP of Marketing and Communications .... Mr. Rick SWEENEY
111 Chief Devel Ofcr/Sr VP Advancement .... Mr. Paul EDWARDS
08 Director of Library Services .... Mr. Myron SCHIRER-SUTER
06 Registrar .... Mrs. Alice A. FALCONE
13 AVP of Technology & Operations .... Mr. Christopher JONES
37 Sr Dir of Student Financial Svcs .... Mr. Daniel O'CONNELL
15 Director of Human Resources .... Vacant
18 Dir of Facilities & Sustainability .... Mr. Mark STOWELL
21 Dir of Finance and Controller .... Mr. Stephen LACORAZZA
111 AVP for Advancement .... Mrs. Britt CARLSON
36 Exec Director of Career Services .... Mr. Alexander LOWRY
96 Dir of Purchasing and Distribution .... Mr. Michael NAWOICHIK
09 AVP of Strategy & Decision Support .... Vacant
19 Chief of Police .... Mr. Glenn DECKERT
110 Dir of Advancement Service .... Mr. Rick HOUSTON
41 Director of Athletics .... Mr. Jon TYMANN
105 Creative Dir and Web Team Lead .... Mr. Stephen DAGLEY
35 Dean of Student Life .... Mr. Terry CHAREK
124 Dean of Student Engagement .... Dr. Nicholas ROWE
121 Dean of Student Success .... Mr. Christopher CARLSON
100 Deputy Chief of Staff .... Mr. William HAGEN
104 Dean Acad Init & Global Education .... Dr. Jewerl MAXWELL

Gordon-Conwell Theological Seminary (G)

130 Essex Street, South Hamilton MA 01982-2317
County: Essex FICE Identification: 009747
Unit ID: 165945
Telephone: (978) 468-7111 Carnegie Class: Spec-4-yr-Faith
FAX Number: (978) 468-6691 Calendar System: Semester
URL: www.gordonconwell.edu
Established: 1884 Annual Graduate Tuition & Fees: N/A
Enrollment: 1,734 Coed
Affiliation or Control: Independent Non-Profit IRS Status: 501(c)3
Highest Offering: Doctorate; No Undergraduates

Accreditation: EH, CACREP, THEOL

01	President	Dr. Scott W. SUNQUIST
10	Vice Pres Finance & Operations/CFO	Mr. Jay S. TREWERN
05	Vice Pres for Academic Affairs	Vacant
111	Vice President of Advancement	Vacant
112	Director Planned Giving	Mr. William FISHER
12	Dean of Boston Campus	Dr. Seong H. PARK
12	Dean of Charlotte Campus	Dr. Donald FAIRBAIRN
12	Dean of Hamilton Campus	Dr. Jeffrey ARTHURS
12	Dean of Jacksonville Campus	Dr. Bradley HOWELL
88	Chief Operations Charlotte Campus	Dr. H. Neely GASTON
32	Dean of Students	Ms. Jana HOLIDAY
15	Vice Pres of Org Effectiveness & HR	Ms. Robin HIGLE
13	Chief Information Officer	Dr. Alex KOH
18	Director of Physical Plant	Mr. Timothy INGRAHAM
08	Director of Libraries	Mr. Bob MAYER
58	Dean of Doctor of Ministry	Dr. David CURRIE
37	Director of Financial Aid	Mr. Stacey T. GLIDDEN
40	Director of Support Services	Mr. David SHOREY
19	Director of Campus Safety	Mr. Cabot W. DODGE
07	Director of Admissions	Ms. Sarah SOTELO
21	Controller & Dir Financial Svcs	Mr. Gregg HANSEN
29	Director Alumni Relations	Vacant
39	Director Student Housing	Mr. Jason STRZEPEK
04	Admin Assistant to the President	Mrs. Mia ERTEL
06	Registrar	Ms. Natalie CROWSON

Hampshire College (A)

893 West Street, Amherst MA 01002-3372

County: Hampshire FICE Identification: 004661
Unit ID: 166018
Telephone: (413) 549-4600 Carnegie Class: Bac-A&S
FAX Number: (413) 559-5584 Calendar System: 4/1/4
URL: www.hampshire.edu
Established: 1965 Annual Undergrad Tuition & Fees: $51,668
Enrollment: 1,268 Coed
Affiliation or Control: Independent Non-Profit IRS Status: 501(c)3
Highest Offering: Baccalaureate
Accreditation: EH

01	President	Mr. Edward WINGENBACK
125	President Emeritus	Dr. Jonathan LASH
101	Secretary of the College	Ms. Beth I. WARD
05	Vice President & Dean of Faculty	Dr. Eva RUESCHMANN
32	Asst VP Student Affairs	Mr. Frances ARNOLD
10	Chief Financial Officer	Mr. Peter SHEA
15	Director HR/Title IX Coord	Mr. Greg NARLESKI
111	Chief Advancement Officer	Ms. Jennifer CHRISLER
08	Interim Director of Library	Ms. Rachel BECKWITH
06	Director of Central Records	Ms. Rachael GRAHAM
37	Asst Director of Financial Aid	Ms. Jean BERG
20	AVP of Academic Affairs	Ms. Yaniris FERNANDEZ
26	Exec Dir Strategic Communications	Mr. John COURTMANCHE
29	Director Alumni & Family Relations	Ms. Melissa MILLS-DICK
36	Director Student Placement	Ms. Carin RANK
38	Director Student Counseling	Dr. Eliza MCARDLE
100	Chief of Staff	Ms. Jenny CHANDLER

Harvard University (B)

1350 Massachusetts Ave, Cambridge MA 02138-3800

County: Middlesex FICE Identification: 002155
Unit ID: 166027
Telephone: (617) 495-1000 Carnegie Class: DU-Highest
FAX Number: (617) 495-0500 Calendar System: Semester
URL: www.harvard.edu
Established: 1636 Annual Undergrad Tuition & Fees: $50,420
Enrollment: 31,120 Coed
Affiliation or Control: Independent Non-Profit IRS Status: 501(c)3
Highest Offering: Doctorate
Accreditation: EH, CAMPEP, CLPSY, DENT, IPSY, LAW, LSAR, MED, PCSAS, PH, PLNG, THEOL

01	President	Lawrence S. BACOW
05	Provost	Alan GARBER
49	Dean Arts and Sciences	Claudine GAY
58	Dean Graduate School of A&S	Emma DENCH
50	Dean Harvard Business School	Nitin NOHRIA
49	Dean Harvard College	Rakesh KHURANA
56	Dean Continuing Educ and Extension	Huntington D. LAMBERT
52	Dean School of Dental Medicine	R. Bruce DONOFF
48	Dean Graduate School of Design	Mohsen MOSTAFAVI
73	Dean Harvard Divinity School	David N. HEMPTON
53	Dean Graduate School of Education	Bridget T. LONG
54	Dean Engineering/Applied Sciences	Francis J. DOYLE
80	Dean Kennedy School of Government	Douglas ELMENDORF
61	Dean Harvard Law School	John F. MANNING
63	Dean Harvard Medical School	George Q. DALEY
69	Dean School of Public Health	Michelle A. WILLIAMS
88	Dean Inst for Advanced Studies	Tomiko BROWN-NAGIN
88	Treasurer	Paul J. FINNEGAN
03	Executive Vice President	Katherine N. LAPP
43	VP and General Counsel	Diane E. LOPEZ
29	VP Alumni Affairs/Development	Brian K. LEE
10	VP for Finance and CFO	Thomas HOLLISTER
101	VP and Secretary of the University	Marc GOODHEART
88	VP for Strategy and Programs	Leah ROSOVSKY
26	VP Public Affairs and Communication	Paul ANDREW
15	VP for Human Resources	Marilyn HAUSAMMANN
45	VP Planning and Project Management	Vacant
08	VP for the Harvard Library	Martha J. WHITEHEAD
13	VP and CIO	Anne MARGULIES
18	VP for Campus Services	Meredith WEENICK

Hebrew College (C)

160 Herrick Road, Newton Centre MA 02459-2237

County: Middlesex FICE Identification: 002157
Unit ID: 166045
Telephone: (617) 559-8600 Carnegie Class: Spec-4-yr-Faith
FAX Number: (617) 559-8601 Calendar System: Semester
URL: www.hebrewcollege.edu
Established: 1921 Annual Undergrad Tuition & Fees: N/A
Enrollment: 181 Coed
Affiliation or Control: Independent Non-Profit IRS Status: 501(c)3
Highest Offering: Beyond Master's But Less Than Doctorate
Accreditation: EH

01	President	Rabbi Sharon C. ANISFELD
10	Vice Pres Finance & Administration	Mr. Keith DROPKIN
05	Provost/Chief Academic Officer	Rabbi Michael SHIRE
26	Vice Pres Marketing/Advancement	Mr. Alan SHERMAN
32	Director of Student Services	Mr. Bob GIELOW
35	Assoc Dean Student Life	Rabbi Daniel KLEIN
06	Registrar	Ms. Marilyn JAYE
15	Director Human Resources	Ms. Steffi BOBBIN
04	Executive Asst to the President	Ms. Helaine R. FRIEDLANDER
13	Manager Information Technology	Mr. Jim KENN

Hellenic College-Holy Cross Greek Orthodox School of Theology (D)

50 Goddard Avenue, Brookline MA 02445-7496

County: Norfolk FICE Identification: 002154
Unit ID: 166054
Telephone: (617) 731-3500 Carnegie Class: Spec-4-yr-Faith
FAX Number: (617) 850-1460 Calendar System: Semester
URL: www.hchc.edu
Established: 1937 Annual Undergrad Tuition & Fees: $22,490
Enrollment: 170 Coed
Affiliation or Control: Greek Orthodox IRS Status: 501(c)3
Highest Offering: Master's
Accreditation: EH, THEOL

01	Interim President	Bishop Metropolitan METHODIOS
73	Dean School of Theology	Fr. Thomas FITZGERALD
05	Dean Hellenic College	Dr. Bruce BECK
111	VP Institutional Advancement	Vacant
32	Dean of Students	Mr. Antonios PAPATHANASIOU
10	Chief Financial Officer	Vacant
07	Director of Admissions & Records	Fr. Gregory FLOOR
08	Director Library	Rev. Joachim COTSONIS
37	Financial Aid Director	Mr. Michael KIRCHMAIER
06	Registrar	Mr. Jay OSTROSKY
13	Director Computing/Information Mgmt	Vacant
29	Director of Alumni Office	Vacant
113	Bursar	Vacant
40	Bookstore Manager	Ms. Nikoleta MAIDOU
39	Director of Housing/Security	Vacant
15	Director of Human Resources	Mr. David VOLZ
44	Director Annual or Planned Giving	Ms. Frances LEVAS
45	Director Strategic Initiatives	Mr. Gary ALEXANDER
03	Executive Vice President	Vacant

Hult International Business School (E)

One Education Street, Cambridge MA 02141-1805

County: Middlesex FICE Identification: 041432
Unit ID: 164368
Telephone: (617) 746-1990 Carnegie Class: Spec-4-yr-Bus
FAX Number: (617) 746-1991 Calendar System: Other
URL: www.hult.edu
Established: 1964 Annual Undergrad Tuition & Fees: $40,650
Enrollment: 2,798 Coed
Affiliation or Control: Proprietary IRS Status: Proprietary
Highest Offering: Doctorate
Accreditation: EH

01	President	Dr. Stephen J. HODGES
05	Chief Academic Officer	Dr. Johan ROOS
11	Chief Operating Officer	Mr. David ARTHUR
10	Chief Financial Officer	Mr. Martin ASP
13	Chief Technology Officer	Mr. John PROKOS
36	Vice President Career Development	Ms. Katharine BOSHKOFF
03	Executive Vice President UG	Dr. Jannicke ROOS
03	Executive Vice President PG	Ms. Melissa FREDETTE
88	Chief Innovation Officer	Dr. Mukul KUMAR
20	Director of Central Academics	Ms. Caroline HAYES
20	Dean of Central Academics	Dr. Ian DOUGAL
12	Senior Associate Dean Boston Campus	Ms. Mary DUTKIEWICZ
12	Dean San Francisco Campus	Dr. Mona DHILLON
84	Regional Director Enrollment	Mr. Steve WYNN
36	Dir of Career Services Boston	Ms. Maggie DALEY
32	Dir Student Services Boston	Ms. Nayeli VIVANCO
06	Registrar Boston Campus	Ms. Deanna CHAN
06	Registrar San Francisco Campus	Ms. Megan MOOSE
37	Director Student Financial Aid	Ms. Karen VAN DYNE

Laboure College (F)

303 Adams Street, Milton MA 02186-4253

County: Suffolk FICE Identification: 006324
Unit ID: 165264
Telephone: (617) 322-3500 Carnegie Class: Spec-4-yr-Other Health
FAX Number: (617) 296-7947 Calendar System: Trimester
URL: www.laboure.edu
Established: 1892 Annual Undergrad Tuition & Fees: $36,962
Enrollment: 870 Coed
Affiliation or Control: Roman Catholic IRS Status: 501(c)3
Highest Offering: Baccalaureate
Accreditation: EH, ADNUR, NDT, NURSE, RTT

01	President	Debra TOWNSLEY
10	VP of Administration and Finance	William MCDONALD
05	Vice Pres Academic Affairs	Marilyn GARDNER
32	Vice Pres Student Affairs	Matthew GREGORY
84	VP of Enrollment Management	Justin ROY
04	Executive Asst to President	Megan D. CURRIVAN
06	Registrar	John SACCO
08	Director of Library	Anicia KUCHESKY
29	Director Alumni Affairs	Katelyn DWYER
37	Director Student Financial Aid	Erin HANLON

Lasell College (G)

1844 Commonwealth Avenue, Newton MA 02466-2716

County: Middlesex FICE Identification: 002158
Unit ID: 166391
Telephone: (617) 243-2000 Carnegie Class: Masters/M
FAX Number: (617) 243-2389 Calendar System: Semester
URL: www.lasell.edu
Established: 1851 Annual Undergrad Tuition & Fees: $36,000
Enrollment: 2,055 Coed
Affiliation or Control: Independent Non-Profit IRS Status: 501(c)3
Highest Offering: Master's
Accreditation: EH, ACBSP, #CAATE, COSMA, EXSC

01	President	Michael B. ALEXANDER
05	Provost	James OSTROW
10	VP Admin & Finance/CFO	Vacant
84	VP Enrollment Management	Kathleen O'CONNOR
88	President Lasell Village	Anne DOYLE
58	VP Graduate & Prof Studies	Eric TURNER
30	VP Development & Alumni Relations	Chelsea GWYTHER
21	Assoc VP Admin & Finance	Diane PARKER
20	Assoc VP Academic Affairs	Steven BLOOM
07	Asst VP/Dean UG Admission	James TWEED
28	Asst VP/Chief Diversity Officer	Jesse TAURIAC
121	Asst VP/Dean of Academic Success	Helena SANTOS
32	Asst VP/Dean of Student Affairs	David HENNESSEY
76	Dean Health Sciences	Cris HAVERTY
57	Dean Comms & The Arts	Aaron TOFFLER
88	Dean Fashion	Anne TREVENEN
79	Dean Human/Educ/Just & Soc Sc	Lori ROSENTHAL
50	Dean Business	Matthew REILLY
37	Dir Student Financial Planning	Vacant
09	Dir Institutional Research	Eric LANTHIER
06	Registrar	Linda ARCE
18	Director Plant Operations	Wayne LAMOUREUX
26	Dir Communications	Ian MEROPOL
29	Dir Alumni Relations	Vacant
88	Dir Student Act & Orientation	Jennifer GRANGER
23	Dir Health Services	Richard ARNOLD
08	Dir Library	Anna SARNESO
41	Dir Athletics	Kristy WALTER
15	Dir Human Resources	Marymichele DELANEY
38	Dir Counseling Center	Sharon HARRINGTON-HOPE
58	Asst VP Graduate & Prof Studies	Adrienne FRANCIOSI
13	Chief Information Officer	Jonathan GORHAM
39	Dir Residential Life	Woodrow FREESE
19	Director Security/Safety	Robert WINSOR
43	Asst VP Legal Affairs	Jennifer OKEEFFE
04	Executive Asst to the President	Henry PUGH
104	Director of International Services	Sarah DRISCOLL
105	Director of Marketing	Christopher LYNETT
36	Director Career Services	Donnell TURNER

Lesley University (H)

29 Everett Street, Cambridge MA 02138-2790

County: Middlesex FICE Identification: 002160
Unit ID: 166452
Telephone: (617) 868-9600 Carnegie Class: DU-Mod
FAX Number: (617) 349-8717 Calendar System: Semester
URL: www.lesley.edu
Established: 1909 Annual Undergrad Tuition & Fees: $27,975
Enrollment: 4,732 Coed
Affiliation or Control: Independent Non-Profit IRS Status: 501(c)3
Highest Offering: Doctorate
Accreditation: EH, ACBSP, ART, CAEPT

01	President	Dr. Janet L. STEINMAYER
05	Provost	Dr. Margaret EVERETT
11	Vice President for Administration	Ms. Marylou BATT
10	Interim Vice President/CFO	Dr. Helen OUELLETTE
111	VP of Advancement	Mr. Timothy CROSS
84	VP of Enrollment Management	Mr. Timothy ROBISON
114	VP for Budgeting & Fin Planning	Ms. M. L. DYMSKI
43	General Counsel	Ms. Shirin PHILIPP
45	VP Strategy & Implementation	Dr. MaryPat LOHSE
20	Associate Provost	Dr. Lisa IJIRI
58	Int Dean Grad Sch Arts & Social Sci	Dr. Sandra WALKER
53	Interim Dean School of Education	Dr. Amy RUTSTEIN-RILEY
32	Dean of Student Life & Academic Dev	Dr. Nathaniel MAYS
49	Dean College of Liberal Arts & Sci	Dr. Steven SHAPIRO
57	Dean of College of Art and Design	Dr. Richard ZAUFT

13 Chief Information Officer .... Mr. Antonio CRESPO
123 Director of Graduate Admissions .... Ms. Barbara SELMO
15 Associate VP of Human Resources ..... Ms. Michelle POLOWCHAK
37 Director of Financial Aid .... Mr. Scott JEWELL
21 Controller .... Mr. Stephen MICARELLI
08 Dean of Libraries .... Mr. Hedi BENAICHA
07 Dir Undergrad Admissions .... Ms. Deb KOCAR
108 Director of Assessment .... Dr. Linda PURSLEY
09 Dir of Institutional Research .... Mr. Alexander WAGNER
04 Assistant to the President .... Ms. Kathleen SAMMARTINO
06 Registrar .... Ms. Adrianne ZONDERMAN
28 Chief Diversity Officer .... Mr. Amarildo BARBOSA

Longy School of Music of Bard College (A)

27 Garden Street, Cambridge MA 02138

Telephone: (617) 876-0956   Identification: 770137

Accreditation: &M

† Branch campus of Bard College, Annandale-On-Hudson, NY

*Massachusetts Board of Higher Education (B)

One Ashburton Place, Room 1401,
Boston MA 02108-1696

County: Suffolk   FICE Identification: 029283

Telephone: (617) 994-6950   Carnegie Class: N/A

FAX Number: (617) 727-6397

URL: www.mass.edu

01 Commissioner .... Dr. Carlos SANTIAGO
103 Assoc Comm Workforce Development .... Mr. David CEDRONE
45 Senior Assoc Comm Strategic Plng .... Dr. Winifred M. HAGAN
09 Sr Comm Research/Planning .... Dr. Jonathan KELLER
43 General Counsel .... Ms. Constantia PAPANIKOLAOU
10 Dep Comm Administration and Finance .... Mr. Tom SIMARD
37 Sr Dep Comm Student Financial Aid .... Dr. Clantha MCCURDY

*University of Massachusetts System Office (C)

One Beacon Street, 31st Floor, Boston MA 02108

County: Suffolk   FICE Identification: 008017

Unit ID: 166665

Telephone: (617) 287-7050   Carnegie Class: N/A

FAX Number: (617) 287-7167

URL: www.umassp.edu

01 President .... Mr. Martin T. MEEHAN
03 Executive Vice President .... Mr. James JULIAN
05 Sr VP Acad Affs/Stdnt & Intl Affs .... Dr. Katherine NEWMAN
10 Sr VP Admin/Finance & Treasurer .... Ms. Lisa CALISE
26 Vice President for Communications .... Mr. Jeff COURNOYER
11 Deputy Chief Operating Officer .... Ms. Susan KELLY
86 Special Asst to Pres Govt Relation .... Mr. David MCDERMOTT
43 General Counsel .... Mr. Gerard LEONE
13 Chief Information Officer .... Mr. John LETCHFORD
101 Secretary to Board of Trustees .... Ms. Zunilka BARRETT
116 Director for University Auditing .... Mr. Kyle DAVID
15 Chief Human Resources Officer .... Mr. Mark PREBLE
106 CEO UMass Online .... Mr. Donald KILBURN
88 VP Economic Development .... Ms. Katie STEBBINS

*University of Massachusetts (D)

Amherst MA 01003-0001

County: Hampshire   FICE Identification: 002221

Unit ID: 166629

Telephone: (413) 545-0111   Carnegie Class: DU-Highest

FAX Number: N/A   Calendar System: Semester

URL: www.umass.edu

Established: 1863   Annual Undergrad Tuition & Fees (In-State): $15,887

Enrollment: 30,340   Coed

Affiliation or Control: State   IRS Status: 501(c)3

Highest Offering: Doctorate

Accreditation: EH, ART, AUD, CAEPN, CLPSY, DIETD, DIETI, IPSY, LSAR, MUS, NURSE, PH, PLNG, SCPSY, SP

02 Chancellor .... Dr. Kumble R. SUBBASWAMY
05 Sr VC/Provost Academic Affairs .... Dr. John J. MCCARTHY
03 Deputy Chancellor/Chf Planning Ofcr .... Dr. Steven D. GOODWIN
88 Assoc Chancellor for Compliance .... Ms. Christine M. WILDA
28 Assoc Chancellor Equity & Inclusion .... Vacant
100 Chief of Staff .... Dr. Rolanda C. BURNEY
10 Vice Chancellor Admin/Finance .... Mr. Andrew P. MANGELS
111 Vice Chancellor Advancement .... Dr. Mark A. FULLER
46 Vice Chancellor Research .... Dr. Michael F. MALONE
32 Int VC Student Affairs/Campus Life .... Dr. Rolanda C. BURNEY
26 VC University Relations .... Mr. John KENNEDY
13 Int VC Information Services & CIO .... Mr. Christopher P. MISRA
41 Director of Athletics .... Mr. Ryan BAMFORD
43 Senior Counsel .... Mr. Brian W. BURKE
22 Exec Dir EO/Title IX Coord .... Ms. Debora D. FERREIRA
20 Sr Vice Provost for Acad Affairs .... Dr. Farshid HAJIR
20 Sr Vice Provost for Acad Affairs .... Dr. Tilman WOLF
20 Sr Vice Provost/Dean Ugrad Educ .... Dr. Carol A. BARR
58 Vice Provost/Dean of Grad School .... Dr. Barbara B. KRAUTHAMER
88 Assoc Provost Faculty Development .... Mr. Michael J. EAGEN
85 Assoc Provost International Pgms .... Dr. Kalpen TRIVEDI
106 Sr Vice Provost of Online Education .... Dr. John WELLS
84 Vice Provost Enrollment Management .... Dr. James ROCHE
09 Dir Strat Analysis/Decision Support .... Dr. Barb CHALFONTE
88 Assoc Provost Data & Analytics .... Dr. Ann Marie RUSSELL
108 Assoc Prov Assessment/Educ Effect .... Dr. Martha L. STASSEN
87 Director of Summer Programs .... Ms. Sarah CRAIG
123 Dir Grad Admissions/Assoc Grad Reg .... Ms. Kate C. WOODMANSEE
37 Int Dir Financial Aid Services .... Ms. Lauren LAMICA
06 University Registrar .... Dr. Patrick SULLIVAN
92 Dean Commonwealth Honors College .... Dr. Gretchen GERZINA
79 Dean Col Humanities & Fine Arts .... Dr. Julie C. HAYES
77 Dean Col Computer & Info Sci .... Dr. Laura M. HAAS
81 Dean Col Natural Science .... Dr. Tricia R. SERIO
83 Dean Col Social & Behavioral Sci .... Dr. John A. HIRD
53 Dean School of Education .... Dr. Cynthia GERSTL-PEPIN
54 Dean College of Engineering .... Dr. Sanjay RAMAN
50 Dean School of Management .... Dr. Anne MASSEY
66 Int Dean School of Nursing .... Dr. Cynthia JACELON
69 Dean Sch Public Health/Hlth Sci .... Dr. Anna Maria SIEGA-RIZ
08 Director of Libraries .... Dr. Simon NEAME
56 Director of Extension .... Ms. Jody L. JELLISON
47 Dir Stockbridge School Agriculture .... Dr. Wesley AUTIO
88 Director Fine Arts Center .... Ms. Jamilla DERIA
15 Asst Vice Chanc Human Resources .... Mr. William D. BRADY
11 Assoc Prov Admin & Finance .... Ms. Deborah M. GOULD
21 Interim Controller .... Mr. Norman GOUSY
109 Executive Dir Auxiliary Enterprises .... Mr. Kenneth K. TOONG
113 Bursar .... Ms. Erin ZUZULA
18 Assoc VC Facilities & Campus Svcs .... Mr. Shane R. CONKLIN
19 Asst Vice Chancellor/Chief Police .... Mr. Tyrone PARHAM
114 Budget Director .... Ms. Lynn C. MCKENNA
96 Director Procurement & Campus Svcs .... Mr. John O. MARTIN
40 Director Univ Store .... Mr. Scott C. WRIGLEY
35 Dean of Students .... Vacant
121 Assoc Provost Student Success .... Dr. Carolyn S. BASSETT
39 Dir Residential Life/Student Svcs .... Ms. Dawn BOND
89 Dir Assessment/Student Transition .... Dr. Marcy R. CLARK
104 Dir Educ Abroad/Adv & Stdnt Success .... Ms. Carol J. LEBOLD
122 Dir Ofc Fraternities & Sororities .... Mr. Michael D. WISEMAN
23 Exec Dir University Health Services .... Dr. George A. COREY
38 Int Co-Dir Counseling & Psych Hlth .... Dr. Melissa S. ROTKIEWICZ
38 Int Co-Dir Counseling & Psych Hlth .... Dr. Linda D. SCOTT
36 Director Career Services .... Ms. Candice J. SERAFINO
29 Asst VC/Exec Dir Alumni Relations .... Dr. JC SCHNABL
44 Exec Dir Annual Giving .... Mr. Nathan ADAMS
27 Assoc VC University Relations .... Dr. Nancy BUFFONE
88 Exec Dir News & Media Relations .... Mr. Edward F. BLAGUSZEWSKI
88 Sr Dir Executive Communications .... Ms. Amy C. GLYNN
86 Exec Dir Government Relations .... Mr. Christopher DUNN
102 Dir Foundation/Corporate Relations .... Ms. Liz M. SMITH
112 Executive Director Gift Planning .... Ms. Theresa CURRY
25 Acting Dir Grant & Contract Admin .... Ms. Carol SPRAGUE
90 Int Dir Instructional Innovation .... Dr. Robert DAVIS
14 Director of IT User Services .... Mr. Wajid CHOUDHRY
119 Chief Information Security Officer .... Mr. Matthew DALTON
105 Int Sr Director of Infrastructure .... Mr. James MILESKI
30 Assoc VC Development .... Ms. Theresa M. CURRY

*University of Massachusetts Boston (E)

100 Morrissey Boulevard, Boston MA 02125-3393

County: Suffolk   FICE Identification: 002222

Unit ID: 166638

Telephone: (617) 287-5000   Carnegie Class: DU-Higher

FAX Number: (617) 265-7173   Calendar System: Semester

URL: www.umb.edu

Established: 1964   Annual Undergrad Tuition & Fees (In-State): $14,167

Enrollment: 16,415   Coed

Affiliation or Control: State   IRS Status: 501(c)3

Highest Offering: Doctorate

Accreditation: EH, CACREP, CAEPT, CLPSY, COPSY, NURSE, SCPSY, SPAA

02 Interim Chancellor .... Dr. Katherine NEWMAN
88 Deputy Chancellor .... Mr. Garrett SMITH
05 Interim Provost .... Dr. Emily MCDERMOTT
20 Associate Provost .... Mr. Brian WHITE
10 Vice Chanc for Admin & Finance .... Ms. Kathleen KIRLEIS
111 VC for University Advancement .... Mr. Adam WISE
32 Vice Chancellor for Student Affs .... Ms. Gail DISABATINO
41 VC for Athletics & Special Projects .... Mr. Charlie TITUS
86 VC for Govt Rel/Public Aff .... Vacant
15 Vice Chanc for Human Resources .... Ms. Marie BOWEN
53 Dean Col of Educ & Human Dev .... Mr. Joseph BERGER
107 Dean Col of Advancing & Prof Stds .... Dr. Philip DISALVIO
81 Dean of Math & Science .... Dr. Andrew GROSOVSKY
79 Dean of Liberal Arts .... Dr. David TERKLA
50 Interim Dean College of Management .... Dr. Arindam BANDOPADHYAYA
66 Dean College of Nursing .... Dr. Linda THOMPSON ADAMS
80 Dean John W. McCormack Grad School .... Mr. David CASH
26 Director of Communications .... Mr. DeWayne LEHMAN
09 Assoc Prov Institutional Research .... Mr. James J. HUGHES
08 Interim Dean of Univ Libraries .... Ms. Joanne RILEY
22 Asst Chancellor/Equity & Inclusion .... Ms. Georgianna MELENDEZ
92 Dean of Honors College .... Ms. Rajini SRIKANTH
88 Dean Sch Global Incl & Social Dev .... Mr. William KIERNAN
121 Vice Prov for Academic Support Svcs .... Ms. Joan BECKER
100 Chief of Staff .... Ms. Anne RILEY
58 VP Research & Dean of Grad Studies .... Mr. Bala SUNDARAM

*University of Massachusetts Dartmouth (F)

285 Old Westport Road, North Dartmouth MA 02747-2300

County: Bristol   FICE Identification: 002210

Unit ID: 167987

Telephone: (508) 999-8000   Carnegie Class: DU-Higher

FAX Number: (508) 999-8901   Calendar System: Semester

URL: www.umassd.edu

Established: 1895   Annual Undergrad Tuition & Fees (In-State): $13,921

Enrollment: 8,406   Coed

Affiliation or Control: State   IRS Status: 501(c)3

Highest Offering: Doctorate

Accreditation: EH, ART, LAW, MT, NURSE

02 Chancellor .... Dr. Robert E. JOHNSON
11 Prov/Exec VC Acad/Stdnt Affs/COO .... Dr. Mohammad KARIM
10 VC Administration & Finance .... Mr. David GINGERELLA
111 VC University Advancement .... Ms. Jennifer CHRISLER
110 Asst VC Advancement Services .... Ms. Valerie AU
100 Senior Vice Chancellor .... Vacant
04 Executive Office Director .... Ms. Lori NICKERSON
26 Assoc VC for Public Affairs .... Mr. John HOEY
05 Vice Provost for Academic Affairs .... Dr. Magali CARRERA
58 Assoc Provost Grad Studies .... Dr. Tesfay MERESSI
86 Assoc Prov Dec & Str Initiatives .... Dr. Ramprasad BALASUBRAMANIAN
46 Assoc Provost Research & Econ Dev .... Dr. Alex FOWLER
84 Assoc VC Enrollment Management .... Mr. Robert ANDREA
21 Assoc VC Admin & Finance .... Ms. Susan AMATRUDO
18 Associate VC Facilities Management .... Mr. Peter DUFFY
88 Asst VC for Org Behavior .... Ms. Deborah MAJEWSKI
32 Vice Chancellor Student Affairs .... Dr. Shannon FINNING
13 Assoc VC IT/CIO .... Mr. Holger DIPPEL
88 Asst VC for Pgm Planning/Fiscal Mgt .... Ms. Joanne ZANELLA-LITKE
35 Assistant VC Student Success .. Ms. Carol SPENCER-MONTEIRO
49 Dean College Arts & Science .... Dr. Pauline ENTIN
50 Interim Dean Charlton Col Business .... Dr. Kathryn CARTER
54 Dean College of Engineering .... Dr. Jean VANDERGHEYNST
66 Dean College of Nursing .... Dr. Kimberly CHRISTOPHER
57 Dean College Visual Perf Arts .... Dr. A. Lawrence JENKENS
88 Dean School Marine Science/Tech .... Dr. Steven LOHRENZ
61 Dean School of Law .... Dr. Eric MITNICK
08 Dean Library Services .... Mr. Terrance BURTON
51 Asst VC Online & Continuing Educ .... Mr. David PEDRO
58 Dir Graduate Studies/Admissions .... Mr. Scott WEBSTER
96 Asst VC for Administrative Services .... Mr. Michael LAGRASSA
21 Controller .... Ms. Suzanne AUDET
88 Director Faculty Development .... Dr. Thomas STUBBLEFIELD
94 Dir Center Women/Gender/Sexuality .... Dr. Juli PARKER
121 Dir Advising/Support & Planning .... Ms. Suzanne MELLONI
06 University Registrar .... Ms. Audra CALLAHAN
07 Director of Admissions .... Ms. Hanan KHAMIS
37 Director Financial Aid .... Ms. Korinne PETERSON
09 Dir Inst Research/Assessment .... Ms. Tammy A. SILVA
19 Dir Public Safety/Chief of Police .... Col. Emil FIORAVANTI
36 Director Career Development Center .... Ms. Linda KENT DAVIS
38 Dir Counseling/Student Devel Ctr .... Dr. Catherine PERRY
90 Exec Dir IT Service Assurance .... Ms. Margaret S. DIAS
29 Director of Alumni Relations .... Ms. Nancy VANASSE
15 Sr Assoc VC Talent & Diversity .... Ms. Angela CALLAHAN
16 Asst VC Employee Relations .... Ms. Susan WILBUR
18 Director Facilities/Physical Plant .... Mr. Jeffrey LOURO
41 Director of Athletics .... Ms. Amanda VAN VOORHIS
23 Director of Health Services .... Ms. Sheila DORGAN
39 Dir Housing/Residential Education .... Ms. Lucinda POUDRIER-AARONSON
44 Asst VC for Annual Giving .... Ms. Lindsay ROTH
27 Assoc VC for Univ Marketing .... Vacant
113 Bursar .... Ms. Kathleen L. EUBANKS
35 Asst VC Student Affairs .... Ms. Cynthia CUMMINGS
35 Associate Dean of Students .... Ms. Shelly METIVIER SCOTT
104 Asst Director Study Abroad Pgms .... Ms. Gina REIS
85 Exec Dir International Education .... Ms. Christina M. BRUEN
93 Assoc Dir Fred Douglas Unity House .... Ms. Lasella HALL
88 Director Academic Resource Center .... Mr. Sokratis KOUMAS
105 Webmaster .... Mr. Donald KING
88 Director of Strategic Initiatives .... Vacant
103 Dir Experiential Learning & Intern .... Ms. Amelia ALBURN
106 Dir Center for Access & Success .... Ms. Wendi CHAKA
25 Dir Sponsored Projects Admin .... Vacant
28 Director Diversity & Inclusion .... Mr. David GOMES
45 Assoc VC Campus Master Planning .... Mr. Gregory WALTERS
103 Exec Dir Economic Development .... Mr. Hugh DUNN
88 Asst VC Civic Engagement .... Mr. Matthew ROY

*University of Massachusetts Lowell (G)

1 University Avenue, Lowell MA 01854-2881

County: Middlesex   FICE Identification: 002161

Unit ID: 166513

Telephone: (978) 934-4000   Carnegie Class: DU-Higher

FAX Number: (978) 934-3000   Calendar System: Semester

URL: www.uml.edu

Established: 1894   Annual Undergrad Tuition & Fees (In-State): $15,180

Enrollment: 18,315   Coed

Affiliation or Control: State   IRS Status: 501(c)3

Highest Offering: Doctorate

Accreditation: EH, ART, CAMPEP, @DIETC, MT, MUS, NURSE, PTA

02 Chancellor .... Dr. Jacqueline F. MOLONEY
05 Provost .... Dr. Joseph HARTMAN
10 Sr VC Financial Opers & Stat Plng ...... Ms. Joanne YESTRAMSKI
26 VC University Relations .... Ms. Patricia MCCAFFERTY
46 VC of Research & Innovation .... Dr. Julie CHEN
111 Vice Chancellor for Advancement .... Mr. John FEUDO
32 VC Student Affs/Univ Events .... Mr. Larry SIEGEL
15 Sr Assoc VC Human Resources & EOO .... Dr. Lauren TURNER
103 Vice Provost Innovation & Wkfce Dev .... Dr. Steven TELLO
18 Assoc VC Facilities Management .... Mr. Thomas DREYER
27 Assoc VC Marketing .... Mr. Bryce HOFFMAN
121 Vice Provost Student Success .... Dr. Julie NASH
84 Dean Enrollment Management .... Ms. Kerri JOHNSTON
41 Director of Athletics .... Mr. Peter CASEY
49 Dean Col Fine Arts/Hum/Soc Sci .... Dr. Luis FALCON
81 Dean Kennedy College of Sciences .... Dr. Noureddine MELIKECHI
53 Dean College of Education .... Dr. Eleanor ABRAMS
54 Interim Dean College of Engineering .... Dr. Jim SHERWOOD
76 Dean College of Health Sciences .... Dr. Shortie MCKINNEY
50 Dean Manning School of Business .. Dr. Sandra RICHTERMEYER
08 Director of Libraries .... Mr. George HART
88 Dean Academic Services .... Ms. Kerry DONOHOE
06 Registrar .... Ms. Mai NGUYEN
37 Assoc Dean Enrollment/Dir Fin Aid .... Ms. Joyce MCLAUGHLIN
38 Director of Counseling Svcs .... Dr. Deborah EDELMAN-BLANK
29 Exec Dir Alumni & Donor Relations .... Ms. Heather MAKREZ ALLEN
19 Chief Univ Police Dir Public Safety .... Mr. Randolph BRASHEARS
123 Dir Graduate Recruitment .... Dr. Shahram HAYDARI
96 Chief Procurement Officer .... Mr. Thomas HOOLE
07 Int Director Undergrad Admissions .... Ms. Christine BRYAN
119 Dir Security Tech & UCAPS .... Mr. Jon VICTORINE
22 Dir Equal Opportunity & Outreach .... Ms. Clara REYNOLDS
36 Asst Dean Student Affs/Career Dev .... Mr. Gregory DENON
88 Dir Student Disability Services .... Ms. Jody GOLDSTEIN
35 Dean Student Affairs & Enrichment .... Mr. James KOHL
23 Assoc Dir Student Health Svcs .... Ms. Diana WALKER MOYER
35 Dean Student Affairs & Event Svcs .... Ms. Brenda EVANS
13 Chief Information Officer .... Mr. Michael CIPRIANO
85 Exec Dir Intl Administration .... Ms. Maria CONLEY
104 Director Intl Exper/Study Abroad .... Ms. Fern MACKINNON
92 Dean Honors College .... Dr. Jim CANNING
100 Dir of Opers Chancellor Office .... Mr. Chris MULLIN
44 Director Annual Giving .... Ms. Deidra MILES
86 Exec Director Government Relations .... Mr. D.J CORCORAN

*University of Massachusetts Medical School (A)

55 Lake Avenue N, Worcester MA 01655-0001
County: Worcester FICE Identification: 009756
Unit ID: 166708
Telephone: (508) 856-8989 Carnegie Class: Spec-4-yr-Med
FAX Number: (508) 856-8181 Calendar System: Semester
URL: www.umassmed.edu
Established: 1962 Annual Graduate Tuition & Fees: N/A
Enrollment: 1,095 Coed
Affiliation or Control: State IRS Status: 501(c)3
Highest Offering: Doctorate; No Undergraduates
Accreditation: EH, MED, NURSE

02 Chancellor & SVP Health Sciences .... Dr. Michael F. COLLINS
05 Provost/Dean/Exec Deputy Chancellor .... Dr. Terence R. FLOTTE
10 Exec VC Administration & Finance .... Mr. John LINDSTEDT
88 Exec VC Innovation and Business Dev .... Dr. Jim GLASHEEN
111 VC for Advancement .... Mr. John J. HAYES
88 Exec Vice Chancellor MassBiologics .... Dr. Mark D. KLEMPNER
11 Exec VC Commonwealth Medicine .... Ms. Lisa COLOMBO
15 VC Diversity & Inclusion .... Dr. Deborah L. PLUMMER
86 VC for Government Relations .... Mr. John ERWIN
26 Vice Chancellor of Communications ...... Ms. Jennifer BERRYMAN
20 Vice Provost Faculty Affairs .... Dr. Luanne THORNDYKE
88 Sr Assoc Dean Educational Affs .... Dr. Anne LARKIN
63 Sr Assc Dean Clin Aff/Assc Dean GME ... Dr. Deborah DEMARCO
66 Dean Graduate School of Nursing .... Dr. Joan VITELLO
32 Vice Provost of Student Affairs .... Dr. Sonia CHIMIENTI
58 Dean Grad School Biomedical Science .... Dr. Mary Ellen LANE
06 Registrar .... Mr. Michael F. BAKER
13 Chief Information Officer .... Mr. Greg WOLF
07 Assoc Dean for Admissions .... Dr. Mariann M. MANNO
37 Director Financial Aid .... Mr. Shawn MORRISSEY
08 Director of Library .... Dr. Mary PIORUN
100 Asst VC for Mgmt/Chief of Staff .... Mr. Brendan H. CHISHOLM
04 Spec Assistant to the Chancellor .... Mr. Andrew FALACCI
46 Vice Prov Rsrch/Strat Initiatives .... Dr. Michael GREEN
88 Vice Provost for Clin/Trans Science ..... Dr. Katherine LUZURIAGA
100 Chief of Staff to Dean/Provost .... Ms. Kristen MAKI
88 Exec Asst to Dean/Prov/Exec Deputy .... Ms. Kimberly LAPERLE
04 Exec Assistant to the Chancellor .... Ms. Lisa BARRY
88 Assoc VC Management .... Mr. James HEALY
15 Assoc VC HR .... Ms. Deborah HARNOIS

*Bridgewater State University (B)

131 Summer Street, Bridgewater MA 02325-0001
County: Plymouth FICE Identification: 002183
Unit ID: 165024
Telephone: (508) 531-1000 Carnegie Class: Masters/L
FAX Number: N/A Calendar System: Semester
URL: www.bridgew.edu
Established: 1840 Annual Undergrad Tuition & Fees (In-State): $10,367
Enrollment: 11,019 Coed
Affiliation or Control: State IRS Status: 501(c)3
Highest Offering: Master's
Accreditation: EH, AAB, ART, CAATE, CACREP, CAEPN, MUS, @SP, SPAA, SW

02 President .... Mr. Frederick CLARK
05 Provost & VP Academic Affairs .... Dr. Karim ISMAILI
10 Vice President and CFO .... Mr. Doug SHROPSHIRE
32 VP Student Affs/Enrollment Mgmt .... Dr. Joseph ORAVECZ
111 VP University Advancement .... Dr. Brenda MOLIFE
15 VP Human Resources & Talent Mgmt .... Ms. Keri POWERS
26 VP Marketing & Communication .... Mr. Paul JEAN
28 VP of Student Success & Diversity .... Dr. Sabrina GENTLEWARRIOR
11 Vice President Operations .... Ms. Karen W. JASON
88 Int Vice President External Affairs .... Dr. Deniz LEUENBERGER
100 Chief of Staff .... Dr. Deniz ZEYNEP LEUENBERGER
22 Int Director EOO/Title IX .... Ms. Jocelyn FRAWLEY
15 Director HR & Talent Management .... Mr. Brian SALVAGGIO
35 Assoc VP & Dean of Students .... Ms. Denine ROCCO
84 Assoc Dean for Enrollment Services .... Mr. Todd AUDYATIS
20 Assoc Provost Faculty Affairs .... Dr. Pamela RUSSELL
45 Sr Assoc Provost/Chief Data Officer .... Dr. Michael YOUNG
79 Dean Col Humanities/Social Sci .... Dr. Arnaa ALCON
53 Int Dean Col Education/Allied Stds .... Dr. Jo HOFFMAN
51 Dean Col of Continuing Studies .... Dr. David CRANE
50 Dean Ricciardi Col of Business .... Dr. Jeanean DAVIS-STREET
07 Dean of University Admissions .... Mr. Gregg A. MEYER
13 Int VP & Chief Information Officer .... Mr. Steve ZUROMSKI
06 Registrar .... Mr. Joseph WOLK
88 Director Academic Achievement Ctr .... Vacant
29 Exec Director Alumni Relations .... Ms. Ellen CUTTLE-OLIVER
30 Director Development .... Ms. Betsy DUBUQUE
41 Director Athletics/Recreation .... Dr. Marybeth LAMB
21 Director University Services .... Dr. Margarida VIEIRA
19 Chief of Police .... Mr. David TILLINGHAST
36 Director Career Services .... Mr. John PAGANELLI
37 Director of Financial Aid .... Ms. Laura BIECHLER
23 Executive Director Wellness Center .... Dr. Christopher FRAZER
08 Director Library Administration .... Mr. Michael SOMERS
22 Director Multicultural Affairs .... Ms. Sydne M. MARROW
27 Asst Dir Creative Svcs/Publications .... Ms. Jaime KNIGHT
25 Director Grants/Sponsored Projects .... Ms. Mia ZOINO
96 Director of Procurement Services .... Dr. Jennifer PACHECO
28 Director of Institutional Diversity .... Dr. Luis F. PAREDES
81 Dean Bartlett Col Science & Math ..... Dr. Kristen PORTER-UTLEY
58 Dean College of Graduate Studies ..... Dr. Lisa KRISSOFF BOEHM
09 Director of Institutional Research .... Dr. Kate MCLAREN
88 Director Teaching and Learning .... Dr. Roben TOROSYAN
46 Asst Prov High Impact Ed Practices .... Dr. Jenny SHANAHAN
85 Assoc Dir Intl Students/Scholars .... Ms. Jennifer CURRIE
104 Director Study Abroad .... Mr. Michael SANDY
14 Int AVP Information Technology .... Ms. Kelley BARAN
105 Director of Web Development .... Ms. Eileen O'SULLIVAN
27 Asst VP & Chief Marketing Officer .... Ms. Eva GAFFNEY
27 AVP University News and Video .... Mr. David ROBICHAUD
38 Asst Clinical Dir Counseling Center .... Ms. Donna SHIAVO
39 Dir Residence Life and Housing .... Vacant
108 Director of Assessment .... Dr. Ruth SLOTNICK
88 Exec Dir Inst for Social Justice .... Dr. Kelly BROTZMAN
88 Dir Institute for Global Engagement .... Vacant
04 Staff Associate to the President .... Ms. Kelly HESS SALISBURY
43 General Counsel .... Vacant
97 Dean of Undergraduate Studies .... Dr. Rita MILLER

*Fitchburg State University (C)

160 Pearl Street, Fitchburg MA 01420-2697
County: Worcester FICE Identification: 002184
Unit ID: 165820
Telephone: (978) 345-2151 Carnegie Class: Masters/L
FAX Number: (978) 665-3693 Calendar System: Semester
URL: www.fitchburgstate.edu
Established: 1894 Annual Undergrad Tuition & Fees (In-State): $10,354
Enrollment: 7,075 Coed
Affiliation or Control: State IRS Status: 501(c)3
Highest Offering: Master's
Accreditation: EH, CAEPN, CSHSE, IACBE, NURSE

02 President .... Dr. Richard S. LAPIDUS
05 Provost/VP Academic Affairs .... Dr. Alberto CARDELLE
10 Vice Pres Finance & Administration .... Mr. Jay BRY
20 Associate VP Academic Affairs .... Dr. Catherine CANNEY
32 Vice President Student Affairs .... Dr. Laura BAYLESS
111 Vice President of Inst Advancement .... Mr. Jeffrey WOLFMAN
35 Assistant Dean for Student Devel ... Dr. Henry C. PARKINSON, III
06 Registrar .... Ms. Linda DUPELL
09 Director of Institutional Research .... Vacant
41 Director Athletics .... Mr. Matthew BURKE
07 Director of Admissions .... Ms. Jinawa MCNEIL
36 Director of Career Services .... Vacant
38 Director Counseling .... Dr. Robert HYNES
23 Director Student Health Services .... Ms. Martha FAVRE
29 Asst Director of Alumni Relations .... Ms. Emily AUSTIN-BRUNS
19 Director of Campus Police .... Chief Michael CLOUTIER
44 Director of Annual Giving .... Ms. Tanya CROWLEY
15 Asst VP of Human Resources/Payroll .... Ms. Jessica MURDOCH
18 Asst VP Capital Planning .... Mr. Joseph LOBUONO
88 Dir Capital Planning & Construction .... Mr. Doug THOMAS
25 Director Grants & Sponsored Pgm .... Ms. Karen FRANK MAYS
37 Director Financial Aid .... Ms. Denise BRINDLE
106 Dir of Digital Learning .... Ms. Nicole CHELONIS
108 Director Institutional Assessment .... Ms. Pamela MCCAFFERTY
13 Chief Info Technology Officer (CIO) .... Mr. Stephen E. SWARTZ
39 Dean of the Library .... Ms. Jacalyn KREMER
04 Special Asst to President .... Ms. Gail M. DOIRON
53 Dean of Education .... Dr. Bruno HICKS
81 Dean of Health & Natural Science .... Dr. John SCHAUMLOFFEL
58 Dean of Graduate & Cont Educ .... Dr. Becky COPPER GLENZ
49 Dean of Arts & Sciences .... Dr. Franca BARRICELLI
50 Dean of Business Technology .... Dr. Keith WILIAMSON

*Framingham State University (D)

100 State Street, PO Box 9101, Framingham MA 01701-9101
County: Middlesex FICE Identification: 002185
Unit ID: 165866
Telephone: (508) 620-1220 Carnegie Class: Masters/L
FAX Number: (508) 626-4592 Calendar System: Semester
URL: www.framingham.edu
Established: 1839 Annual Undergrad Tuition & Fees (In-State): $10,520
Enrollment: 5,691 Coed
Affiliation or Control: State IRS Status: 501(c)3
Highest Offering: Master's
Accreditation: EH, ART, CAEPN, DIETC, DIETD, IACBE, NURSE

02 President .... Dr. F. Javier CEVALLOS
03 Executive Vice President .... Dr. Dale M. HAMEL
05 Vice President Academic Affairs .... Dr. Linda VADEN-GOAD
32 Vice Pres Enrollment & Student Dev .... Dr. Lorretta HOLLOWAY
43 Vice President/General Counsel .... Ms. Ann MCDONALD
20 Associate Vice President .... Dr. Scott B. GREENBERG
13 Associate Vice President .... Mr. Patrick LAUGHRAN
18 Assistant Vice President .... Ms. Patricia WHITNEY
84 Dean of Enrollment Management .... Mr. Jeremy SPENCER
35 Dean of Students .... Dr. Meg NOWAK
39 Associate Dean Student Affairs .... Mr. Glenn COCHRAN
07 Associate Dean Undergrad Admissions .... Ms. Shayna EDDY
88 Assistant Dean Student Affairs .... Mr. David N. BALDWIN
88 Assistant Dean Student Affairs .... Dr. Christopher GREGORY
06 Executive Director/Registrar .... Mr. Mark R. POWERS
15 Director Human Resources .... Ms. Erin NECHIPURENKO
19 Chief Public Safety .... Mr. Brad MEDEIROS
121 Director Academic Support .... Ms. LaDonna BRIDGES
108 Director Assessment .... Dr. Mark NICHOLAS
41 Director Athletics .... Mr. Thomas KELLEY
36 Director Career Services .... Mrs. Dawn ROSS
37 Director Financial Aid .... Ms. Carla MINCHELLO
10 Director Financial Services .... Ms. Rachel TRANT
89 Director First Year Programs .... Mr. Benjamin J. TRAPANICK
23 Director Health Services .... Ms. Ilene HOFRENNING
104 Director International Education .... Ms. Jane DECATUR
08 Director Library Services .... Mrs. Bonnie MITCHELL
38 Director Counseling Center .... Dr. Paul WELCH
88 Director Student Involvement .... Ms. Rachel LUCKING
113 Director Student Accounts .... Mr. Gregory JACKSON
30 Director Development .... Mr. Eric GUSTAFSON
25 Director Grants Sponsored Programs .... Mr. Jonathan LEE
09 Director Institutional Research .... Ms. Ann CASO
04 Executive Assistant .... Ms. Katie HEBERT
22 Director of Equal Opportunity .... Ms. Kimberly DEXTER
58 Dean of Graduate Studies .... Dr. Yasar NAJJAR
26 Chief Public Relations Officer .... Mr. Daniel MAGAZU
28 Chief Diversity & Inclusion Officer .... Ms. Connie CABELLO
29 Director of Alumni Relations .... Ms. Jennier DEFRONZO

*Massachusetts College of Art and Design (E)

621 Huntington Avenue, Boston MA 02115-5882
County: Suffolk FICE Identification: 002180
Unit ID: 166674
Telephone: (617) 879-7000 Carnegie Class: Spec-4-yr-Arts
FAX Number: (617) 566-4034 Calendar System: Semester
URL: www.massart.edu
Established: 1873 Annual Undergrad Tuition & Fees (In-State): $13,200
Enrollment: 2,064 Coed
Affiliation or Control: State IRS Status: 501(c)3
Highest Offering: Master's
Accreditation: EH, ART

02 President .... Dr. David NELSON
11 VP of Administration & Finance .... Mr. Robert PERRY
05 Provost/VP Academic Affairs .... Dr. Kymberly PINDER
32 Vice President Student Development .... Dr. Maureen KEEFE
111 Vice Pres Institutional Advancement .... Ms. Marjorie O'MALLEY
09 Exec Dir IR/Effectiveness/Planning .... Ms. Karalynn GAU
21 Asst Vice Pres of Fiscal Affairs .... Mr. Donald ARPINO
100 Chief of Staff President's Office .... Ms. Susana SEGAT
07 Dean of Admissions/Enrollment .... Mr. Christopher WRIGHT
88 Assoc VP/Dean Multi-Cultural Affs .... Dr. Jamie COSTELLO
06 Registrar .... Mr. Jonathan RAND
37 Director of Financial Aid .... Mr. Aurelio RAMIREZ
88 Dir Curatorial Pgms/Prof Galleries .... Ms. Lisa TUNG
08 Director Library .... Ms. Rachel RESNICK
15 Director Human Resources .... Ms. Velda MCRAE-YATES
22 Dir Civil Rights Compliance/Dvrsty .... Ms. Lyssa PALU-AY
18 Exec Dir Facilities/Physical Plant .... Mr. Howie LAROSEE
88 Director of Administrative Services .... Mr. James MCDAID
26 Exec Dir Marketing/Communications .... Ms. Ellen CARR
13 Chief Info Technology Officer .... Mr. Patrick O'CONNOR
19 Director Security/Safety .... Mr. Dwayne FARLEY
104 Director Study Abroad .... Ms. Erica PUCCIO O'BRIEN
38 Director Student Counseling .... Dr. Betsy SMITH
29 Director Alumni Communications .... Ms. Darlene GILLAN
39 Director Student Housing .... Ms. Danielle LICITRA

*Massachusetts College of Liberal Arts (A)

375 Church Street, North Adams MA 01247-4100
County: Berkshire FICE Identification: 002187
Unit ID: 167288
Telephone: (413) 662-5000 Carnegie Class: Bac-A&S
FAX Number: (413) 662-5010 Calendar System: Semester
URL: www.mcla.edu
Established: 1894 Annual Undergrad Tuition & Fees (In-State): $10,559
Enrollment: 1,588 Coed
Affiliation or Control: State IRS Status: 501(c)3
Highest Offering: Master's
Accreditation: EH, CAATE, RAD

02 President .... Dr. James BIRGE
05 Interim VP Academic Affairs .... Dr. Adrienne WOOTTERS
10 VP Administration & Finance .... Mr. Lawrence BEHAN
32 VP Student Affairs .... Dr. Catherine HOLBROOK
111 VP Institutional Advancement .... Ms. Robert ZIOMEK
84 Dean Enrollment Management .... Ms. Gina PUC
28 Chief Diversity Officer ..... Dr. Christopher MACDONALD-DENNIS
15 Director Human Resources .... Ms. Barbara CHAPUT
26 Director Marketing & Communications ...... Ms. Bernadette ALDEN
20 Dean Academic Operations .... Dr. Deborah FOSS
35 Dean Student Success .... Ms. Theresa O'BRYANT
04 Executive Assistant to President .... Ms. Lisa LESCARBEAU
13 Associate Dean Information Tech .... Mr. Ian BERGERON
35 Assistant Dean Students .... Ms. Celia NORCROSS
08 Associate Dean Library Services .... Ms. Emily ALLING
51 Associate Dean DGCE .... Mr. Paul PETRITIS
06 Assistant Dean Registrar .... Mr. Steven KING
41 Director Athletics .... Ms. Laura MOONEY
37 Director Student Financial Services .... Ms. Bonnie HOWLAND
19 Director Public Safety .... Mr. Daniel COLONNO
39 Director Residential Programs .... Ms. Dianne MANNING
29 Dir Alumni Engagement .... Ms. Kate GIGLIOTTI
21 Accounting Manager .... Mr. Curt CELLANA
38 Director Counseling Services .... Ms. Heidi RIELLO
44 Director Annual Giving .... Mr. Ryan SENECAL
23 Director Health Services .... Ms. Jacki KRZANIK
09 Institutional Research Analyst .... Mr. Jason CANALES
108 Director Assessment .... Ms. Erin MILNE
07 Assistant Dir Transfer Admissions .... Ms. Erinn KENNEDY
07 Associate Dir Freshman Admissions .... Ms. Kayla HOLLINS
105 Web and Applications Manager .... Mr. Steven PESOLA
27 Creative and Brand Manager .... Ms. Francesca SHANKS
102 Grant Coordinator .... Ms. Lynette BOND
120 Associate Dir Academic Technology .... Dr. Gerol PETRUZELLA

*Massachusetts Maritime Academy (B)

101 Academy Drive, Buzzards Bay MA 02532-3400
County: Barnstable FICE Identification: 002181
Unit ID: 166692
Telephone: (508) 830-5000 Carnegie Class: Bac-Diverse
FAX Number: (508) 830-5004 Calendar System: Semester
URL: www.maritime.edu
Established: 1891 Annual Undergrad Tuition & Fees (In-State): $9,728
Enrollment: 1,780 Coed
Affiliation or Control: State IRS Status: 501(c)3
Highest Offering: Master's
Accreditation: EH, IACBE

02 President .... RADM. Francis X. MCDONALD
05 Vice President .... CAPT. Brigid PAVLONIS
10 Vice Pres Finance .... Ms. Rose CASS
32 Vice Pres Student Services .... CAPT. Edward ROZAK
84 Vice Pres External Relations .... CAPT. Elizabeth SIMMONS
13 Vice President/CIO .... Ms. Anne Marie FALLON
18 Vice President Operations .... Mr. Paul O'KEEFE
36 Assoc Dir Career/Professional Svcs ... CDR. Maryanne RICHARDS
07 Director of Admissions .... CDR. Joshua TEFFT
06 Director Student Records/Registrar .... Ms. Danielle BUMPUS
08 Director Library .... Ms. Susan BERTEAUX
108 Dir of Institutional Effectiveness .... Dr. Marlene CLAPP
15 Dean Human Resources .... Mrs. Elizabeth BENWAY
26 Chief Public Relations Officer .... Mr. Christopher RYAN
29 Director Alumni Relations .... Mr. Ian MACLEOD
37 Director Student Financial Aid .... Mrs. Cathy KEDSKI
96 Director of Purchasing .... Mr. Paul AIROZO
41 Athletic Director .... Mr. Michael KELLEY
20 Dean of Undergraduate Studies .... CAPT. Michael CUFF
58 Dean of Graduate & Continuing Educ .. CAPT. James MCDONALD

*Salem State University (C)

352 Lafayette Street, Salem MA 01970-5353
County: Essex FICE Identification: 002188
Unit ID: 167729
Telephone: (978) 542-6000 Carnegie Class: Masters/L
FAX Number: (978) 542-6970 Calendar System: Semester
URL: www.salemstate.edu
Established: 1854 Annual Undergrad Tuition & Fees (In-State): $10,642
Enrollment: 8,702 Coed
Affiliation or Control: State IRS Status: 501(c)3
Highest Offering: Master's
Accreditation: EH, ART, CAATE, CAEPN, MUS, NMT, NURSE, OT, SW, THEA

02 President .... Mr. John KEENAN
05 Provost & Academic VP .... Dr. David J. SILVA
03 Executive Vice President .... Dr. Scott JAMES
111 VP Institutional Advancement .... Ms. Cheryl CROUNSE
10 VP Finance and Facilities .... Ms. Karen HOUSE
43 General Counsel .... Ms. Rita COLUCCI
26 Asst VP Marketing/Creative Svcs .... Mr. Corey CRONIN
13 CIO-CISO .... Mr. Curt KING
100 Chief of Staff .... Dr. Nate BRYANT
21 Assoc VP Financial Svcs .... Vacant
15 Assistant VP for HR & EEO .... Mr. Mark R. QUIGLEY
20 Assoc Provost .... Dr. Neal DECHILLO
86 Senior Director External Relations .... Ms. Adria LEACH
08 Director Library .... Ms. Elizabeth MCKEIGUE
50 Dean School of Business .... Dr. Kathleen BARNES
53 Dean of Education .... Dr. Joseph CAMBONE
58 Assoc Dean Sch Grad & Prof Studies .... Dr. Barbara LAYNE
49 Dean School of Arts & Sciences .... Dr. Gail GASPARICH
32 Dean of Students .... Dr. Carla PANZELLA
110 AVP Institutional Advancement .... Ms. Mandy RAY
04 Asst to Pres/Asst Secy to BOT .... Ms. Catherine HENNESSEY
19 Director Public Safety .... Mr. Gene R. LABONTE
41 Director Athletics .... Ms. Tracey HATHAWAY
06 Registrar .... Ms. Megan M. MILLER
84 Assistant VP for Enroll Mgmt .... Ms. Bonnie GALINSKI
18 Asst VP Facilities .... Mr. Ben SZALEWICZ
28 Interim Chief Diversity Officer .... Ms. Rebecca COMAGE
37 Director of Financial Aid .... Ms. Judy CRAMER
38 Asst Dean of Students/Wellness .... Ms. Elisa CASTILLO
96 Director Purchasing & Vendor Rel .... Ms. Evelyn WILSON
25 Asst Dir Sponsored Pgms & Research .... Ms. Elaine MILO
07 Director of Admissions .... Ms. Jackie HAAS
45 Exec Dir Strategic Planning .... Dr. Chunju CHEN
39 Director Residence Life .... Ms. Rebecca JIMENEZ
88 Int Dean Col of Health & Human Svcs .... Dr. Jeanne CORCORAN
101 Secretary to the BOT .... Ms. Lynne MONTAGUE
44 Director Annual Giving .... Ms. Lori BOUDO

*Westfield State University (D)

577 Western Avenue, Westfield MA 01086-1630
County: Hampden FICE Identification: 002189
Unit ID: 168263
Telephone: (413) 572-5300 Carnegie Class: Masters/M
FAX Number: (413) 572-8147 Calendar System: Semester
URL: www.westfield.ma.edu
Established: 1839 Annual Undergrad Tuition & Fees (In-State): $10,429
Enrollment: 6,237 Coed
Affiliation or Control: State IRS Status: 501(c)3
Highest Offering: Beyond Master's But Less Than Doctorate
Accreditation: EH, #ARCPA, CAATE, CAEPN, EXSC, MUS, NURSE, SW

02 President .... Dr. Ramon S. TORRECILHA
100 Chief of Staff .... Dr. Susan LEGGETT
05 Provost/VP Academic Affairs .... Dr. Diane PRUSANK
32 Vice Pres Student Affairs .... Dr. Gloria LOPEZ
84 VP Enrollment Management .... Mr. Dan FORSTER
10 VP Administration & Finance .... Mr. Stephen TAKSAR
111 VP Institutional Advancement .... Dr. Erica BROMAN
21 Assoc VP Administration/Finance .... Ms. Lisa FREEMAN
18 Dir Facilities Capital Planningg .... Vacant
15 Asst VP Human Resources .... Dr. Jalisa D. WILLIAMS
124 Dean of Faculty .... Dr. Enrique MORALES-DIAZ
49 Interim Dean of Undergrad Studies .... Dr. Christina SWAIDAN
58 Interim Dean Graduate/Continuing Ed .... Ms. Stefanie SANCHEZ
81 Dean College of Math & Sciences .... Dr. Jennifer HANSELMAN
53 Dean College Educ/Health/Human Svcs .... Dr. Juline MILLS
79 Dean College Arts/Humanities/Soc Sc .... Dr. Emily TODD
20 Assoc Dean of Education .... Dr. Cheryl STANLEY
35 Dean of Students .... Ms. Susan LAMONTAGNE
06 Registrar .... Dr. Monique LOPEZ
09 Assoc Dean Inst Research/Assess .... Dr. Lisa PLANTEFABER
114 Assoc Dean Fiscal Mgt Budget Plng .... Ms. Michelle MAGGIO
08 Dean Acad Info Svcs/Dir Library . Mr. Thomas RAFFENSPERGER
39 Exec Director Residential Life .... Dr. Jon CONLOGUE
19 Director Public Safety .... Mr. Tony CASCIANO
36 Director Career Services .... Mr. Junior DELGADO
90 Exec Director Acad Tech Services .... Mr. Christopher HIRTLE
13 Chief Information Officer .... Mr. Alan BLAIR
91 Director Admin Systems .... Mr. Rudolph HEBERT
18 Director Facilities/Operations .... Vacant
41 Director Athletics .... Mr. Richard LENFEST
38 Director Counseling Center .... Ms. Tammy BRINGAZE
23 Director Health Services .... Ms. Patricia BERUBE
37 Director of Financial Aid .... Mr. Michael MAZEIKA
07 Director of Admissions .... Dr. Kelly HART
96 Director of Procurement .... Mr. Gary DUGGAN
25 Director Grants Sponsored Programs .... Ms. Louann D'ANGELO
102 Director of WSU Foundation .... Vacant
04 Executive Assistant to President .... Ms. Michelle LEDOUX
101 Admin Asst to Board of Trustees .... Ms. Jean BEAL
104 Director of International Program .... Ms. Cynthia SIEGLER
28 Director of Diversity & Inclusion .... Ms. Ashiah RICHEME
88 Veteran & Military Svcs Coord .... Ms. Lisa DUCHARME
106 Dir Center for Instructional Tech .... Ms. Lynn ZAYAC
22 Dir Non-Discrimination Compliance .... Dr. Jalisa D. WILLIAMS
26 Director of Campus Communications .... Ms. Tricia OLIVER
29 Director Alumni Relations .... Ms. Katheryn BRADFORD
86 Director Government Relations .... Mr. Brent BEAN

*Worcester State University (E)

486 Chandler Street, Worcester MA 01602-2597
County: Worcester FICE Identification: 002190
Unit ID: 168430
Telephone: (508) 929-8000 Carnegie Class: Masters/L
FAX Number: (508) 929-8191 Calendar System: Semester
URL: www.worcester.edu
Established: 1874 Annual Undergrad Tuition & Fees (In-State): $10,161
Enrollment: 6,434 Coed
Affiliation or Control: State IRS Status: 501(c)3
Highest Offering: Master's
Accreditation: EH, CAEPT, NURSE, OT, SP

02 President .... Mr. Barry M. MALONEY
05 Provost/VP of Academic Affairs .... Dr. Lois A. WIMS
10 Vice Pres Administration & Finance ... Ms. Kathleen EICHELROTH
32 Dean of Student Affairs .... Ms. Julie KAZARIAN
111 Vice Pres University Advancement .... Mr. Thomas MCNAMARA
84 Vice Pres for Enrollment Management .... Dr. Ryan FORSYTHE
20 Assoc VP for Academic Affairs .... Dr. Henry THERIAULT
21 Assoc VP Administration & Finance .... Ms. Robin QUILL
13 Assoc VP/CIO Univ Technology Svcs .... Dr. Anthony ADADE
58 Assoc VP CE & Dean Grad Stds .... Dr. Roberta KYLE
108 Asst VP for Assessment & Planning .... Dr. Sarah STROUT
53 Dean Sch of Educ/Hlth/Nat Sci .... Dr. Linda LARRIVEE
79 Dean Sch of Human & Social Sciences .... Dr. Russ POTTLE
88 Assoc Dean Education .... Dr. Raynold LEWIS
66 Associate Dean of Nursing .... Vacant
51 Assoc Dean of Grad/Cont Educ .... Ms. Sara GRADY
35 Assoc Dean & Dir Stdnt Ctr/Activ .... Vacant
93 Asst Dean/Dir Multicultural Affairs .... Ms. Marcela URIBE-JENNINGS
19 Chief of Campus Police .... Mr. Jason KAPURCH
86 Asst to Pres for Intl/Cmty & Govt .... Mr. Carl HERRIN
26 AVP Communications/Marketing .... Ms. Maureen O. STOKES
08 Executive Director of the Library .... Mr. Matthew BEJUNE
15 Asst VP of HR/Payroll/Aff Act/Eq .... Ms. Stacey LUSTER
18 Director of Facilities .... Ms. Sandra OLSON
37 Director of Financial Aid .... Ms. Jayne MCGINN
07 Director of Admissions .... Mr. Joseph DICARLO
39 Director Residence Life & Housing .... Mr. Adrian GAGE
113 Manager of Student Accounts .... Ms. Julie CARMEL
96 Dir Procurement/Business Manager .... Ms. Brenda BUSSEY
09 Director of Institutional Research .... Mr. Kenneth SMITH
38 Director Student Counseling .... Ms. Laura MURPHY
85 Director of International Students .... Ms. Katey PALUMBO
36 Director of Career Services .... Ms. Jillian ANDERSON
41 Director of Athletics .... Mr. Michael A. MUDD
109 Director of Admin Support Services .... Ms. Nancy M. RAMSDELL

*Berkshire Community College (F)

1350 West Street, Pittsfield MA 01201-5786
County: Berkshire FICE Identification: 002167
Unit ID: 164775
Telephone: (413) 499-4660 Carnegie Class: Assoc/MT-VT-High Trad
FAX Number: (413) 447-7840 Calendar System: Semester
URL: www.berkshirecc.edu
Established: 1960 Annual Undergrad Tuition & Fees (In-State): $5,492
Enrollment: 1,847 Coed
Affiliation or Control: State IRS Status: 501(c)3
Highest Offering: Associate Degree
Accreditation: EH, ADNUR, COARC, PTAA

02 President .... Dr. Ellen KENNEDY
05 Vice Pres for Academic Affairs .... Ms. Jennifer BERNE
10 Vice Pres Admin/Finance/CFO .... Mr. John LAW
84 Vice Pres Stdnt Affairs/Enrol Mgmt .... Mr. Adam KLEPETAR
15 Dir Human Res/Affirm Action Officer .... Ms. Melissa LOIODICE
32 Dean of Student Affairs .... Ms. Beth WALLACE
06 Registrar .... Mr. Adam EMERSON
102 Exec Dir BCC Foundation .... Vacant
13 Director Information Technology .... Mr. Arlen RAUSCHKOLB
07 Dean of Enrollment Management .... Ms. Christina WYNN
37 Director Student Financial Aid .... Ms. Anne MOORE
08 Director of the Library .... Mr. Richard FELVER
09 Dir Inst Research/Assessment .... Dr. Margaret STEPHENSON
18 Dir Facilities/Physical Plant .... Mr. David MORAN
19 Director of Safety & Security .... Mr. Ellis RICHARDSON
38 Senior Academic Counselor .... Ms. Lisa MATTILA
04 Assistant to the President .... Ms. Kim BROOKMAN
105 Director Web Services .... Mr. Douglas OLDHAM
26 Chief Public Rels/Mktg/Commun Ofcr .... Mr. Jonah SYKES
29 Director Alumni Affairs .... Ms. Toni BUCKLEY
30 Director of Development .... Ms. Shela HIDALGO
96 Director of Purchasing .... Mr. William MANNIX

*Bristol Community College (G)

777 Elsbree Street, Fall River MA 02720-7395
County: Bristol FICE Identification: 002176
Unit ID: 165033
Telephone: (508) 678-2811 Carnegie Class: Assoc/HT-High Trad
FAX Number: (508) 730-3270 Calendar System: Semester
URL: www.bristolcc.edu
Established: 1965 Annual Undergrad Tuition & Fees (In-State): $4,776
Enrollment: 7,637 Coed
Affiliation or Control: State IRS Status: 501(c)3
Highest Offering: Associate Degree
Accreditation: EH, ADNUR, CAHIIM, DH, MAC, MLTAD, OTA

02 President .... Dr. Laura L. DOUGLAS
05 Vice President of Academic Affairs .... Dr. Suzanne BUGLIONE
50 Dean of Business & Info Tech .... Mr. William BERARDI
79 Dean of Humanities & Education .... Dr. Sarah KLYBERG
83 Dean of Behavioral & Soc Sciences .... Dr. Kathleen PEARLE
76 Dean of Health Sciences .... Ms. Lynne BRODEUR
81 Dean of Math/Science & Engineering .... Dr. Sarmad SAMAN

10 VP of Administration & Finance .... Mr. Steven KENYON
84 VP of Student Svcs/Enrollment Mgmt ...... Dr. Edmund CABELLON
13 VP of Information Technology .... Ms. Jo-Ann M. PELLETIER
26 VP Marketing and Communications .... Ms. Joyce BRENNAN
103 Acting VP of Workforce Development .... Ms. Jennifer MENARD
32 Director Student/Family Engagement .... Ms. Emma MONTAGUE
07 Dean of Admissions .... Mr. John MCLAUGHLIN
12 Interim Dean of New Bedford Campus .... Mr. John MCLAUGHLIN
12 Dean of Attleboro Campus .... Mr. Rodney CLARK
06 Registrar .... Ms. Jennifer VINCENT
12 Dean of Taunton Center .... Mr. Robert REZENDES
25 Dean of Grant Development .... Ms. Jennifer MENARD
37 Interim Exec Dir Financial Aid .... Ms. Jennifer ROBERTS
38 Director Counseling Services .... Mr. Michael BENSINK
15 Interim Executive Director of HR .... Mr. Stephen HINES
30 Executive Director of Development .... Ms. Paula POPEO
18 Director of Facilities Management .... Ms. Karen PARKER
19 Director Public Safety Preparedness .... Mr. Mark NATALY
21 Comptroller .... Mr. Keith TONI
11 Associate VP of Administration .... Mr. Mark CARMODY
22 Assoc Dir of Disability Services .... Ms. Julie JODOIN
78 Director Coop Education .... Ms. Nicole HEANEY
31 Dean Ctr Workforce/Community Educ .... Ms. Carmen AGUILAR
56 Asst Dean Instructional Lrng Tech .... Ms. April BELLAFIORE
92 Director Honors Program .... Ms. Susan MCCOURT
96 Director of Purchasing .... Ms. Philicia PACHECO
41 Athletic Director .... Mr. Derek VIVEIROS
04 Executive Assistant to President .... Ms. Kathleen A. WORDELL

*Bunker Hill Community College (A)

250 New Rutherford Avenue, Boston MA 02129-2925
County: Suffolk FICE Identification: 011210
Unit ID: 165112
Telephone: (617) 228-2400 Carnegie Class: Assoc/HT-High Trad
FAX Number: (617) 228-2050 Calendar System: Semester
URL: www.bhcc.mass.edu
Established: 1973 Annual Undergrad Tuition & Fees (In-State): $4,464
Enrollment: 11,881 Coed
Affiliation or Control: State IRS Status: 501(c)3
Highest Offering: Associate Degree
Accreditation: EH, ADNUR, DMS, EMT, MLTAD, RAD, SURGT

02 President .... Dr. Pam Y. EDDINGER
10 VP of Administration and Finance .... Mr. John PITCHER
05 VP Academic Affairs/Student Service .... Dr. James F. CANNIFF
15 AVP Human Resources/Labor Relations .... Ms. Molly AMBROSE
32 Dean of Students .... Ms. Julie B. ELKINS
26 Exec Director of Communications .... Ms. Karen NORTON
18 Facilities Manager .... Mr. Ehtishamuddin QAZI
79 Dean of Humanities .... Ms. Lori A. CATALLOZZI
54 Dean of Science/Engineering/Math .... Dr. Laurie K. MCCORRY
83 Dean Behavioral/Social Sciences .... Ms. Liya ESCALERA
107 Dean of Professional Studies .... Dr. Michelle ELIAS BLOOMER
66 Director Nurse Education .... Ms. Elizabeth TOBIN
12 Associate Provost Chelsea Campus .... Dr. Alice MURILLO
21 Comptroller .... Ms. Champa NAGAGE
25 Exec Director of Grants Development .... Mr. Steven A. ROLLER
35 Director of Student Services .... Ms. Debra A. BOYER
06 Registrar .... Vacant
08 Director Library and Learning Comm .... Dr. Vivica D. PIERRE
13 Chief Information Officer .... Mr. Tim OGAWA
27 Executive Director of Marketing .... Ms. Karen M. NORTON
19 Executive Dir and Chief of Police .... Mr. Robert BARROWS
37 Exec Dir Student Financial Svcs .... Ms. Melissa HOLSTER
96 Director of Purchasing .... Mr. Mukti RAUT
84 Dean Enrollment Management .... Ms. Grace Y. YOUNG
30 Executive Director of Development .... Ms. Marilyn KUHAR
100 Exec Asst to the President .... Mr. George HALLSMITH
09 Exec Dir Institutional Research .... Mr. David LEAVITT
04 Staff Assistant to President .... Ms. Frances H. JARVIS
102 Dir Foundation/Corporate Relations .... Ms. Marilyn KUHAR
103 Director Workforce Development .... Ms. Kristen P. MCKENNA
105 Director of Digital Communications .... Ms. Nicole MORO
41 Athletic Director .... Ms. Loreto JACKSON

*Cape Cod Community College (B)

2240 Iyannough Road, West Barnstable MA 02668-1599
County: Barnstable FICE Identification: 002168
Unit ID: 165194
Telephone: (508) 362-2131 Carnegie Class: Assoc/HT-Mix Trad/Non
FAX Number: (508) 362-3988 Calendar System: Semester
URL: www.capecod.edu
Established: 1960 Annual Undergrad Tuition & Fees (In-State): $5,064
Enrollment: 3,221 Coed
Affiliation or Control: State IRS Status: 501(c)3
Highest Offering: Associate Degree
Accreditation: EH, ADNUR, DH, MAC

02 President .... Dr. John L. COX
05 Vice Pres Academic/Student Affairs .... Dr. Arlene RODRIGUEZ
10 Vice President Finance & Operations .... Ms. Lisa KOPECKY
18 Director Facilities .... Mr. Joseph MACKINNON
49 Dean Arts & Humanities .... Dr. Kathryn VRANOS
81 Dean Science/Tech/Math/Business .... Dr. Donald CRAMPTON
121 Dean Learning Res & Student Success .... Mr. David ZIEMBA
84 Dean Enroll Mgmt/Advising Services ...... Ms. Christine MCCAREY
83 Dean Health/Social Sci/Human Svcs .... Mr. Patrick PRESTON
15 Associate VP Human Resources .... Mr. Paul ALEXANDER
08 Assoc Dean Library .... Ms. Jeanmarie FRASER
13 Chief Info/Technology Officer .... Mr. Richard WIXSOM
07 Director Admissions .... Mr. Matthew CORMIER
37 Director of Financial Aid .... Ms. Sherry ANDERSEN
26 Director Communications/Marketing .... Mr. Patrick STONE
06 Registrar .... Ms. Lucina HOLMES
19 Chief Public Safety .... Ms. Maria PADILLA
04 Exec Assistant to President .... Ms. Mia HAZLETT
36 Coord Career Plng & Placement .... Vacant
09 Dir Inst Research & Effectiveness .... Ms. Maureen O'SHEA
41 Athletic Director .... Vacant

*Greenfield Community College (C)

1 College Drive, Greenfield MA 01301-9739
County: Franklin FICE Identification: 002169
Unit ID: 165981
Telephone: (413) 775-1000 Carnegie Class: Assoc/MT-VT-High Trad
FAX Number: (413) 774-4676 Calendar System: Semester
URL: www.gcc.mass.edu
Established: 1962 Annual Undergrad Tuition & Fees (In-State): $5,570
Enrollment: 1,830 Coed
Affiliation or Control: State IRS Status: 501(c)3
Highest Offering: Associate Degree
Accreditation: EH, ADNUR, EMT, MAC

02 President .... Dr. Yves SALOMON-FERNANDEZ
05 Int Chief Academic/Stdnt Affs Ofcr . Ms. Mary Ellen FYDENKEVEZ
10 Chief Financial Officer .... Ms. Karen PHILLIPS
103 Int Dean of Workforce Dev/Cmty Educ .... Mr. Mark RABINSKY
84 Dean of Enrollment Services .... Vacant
79 Dean Humanities .... Mr. Leo HWANG
81 Dean Engr/Math/Nurs & Sciences .... Vacant
30 Exec Director Resource Development .... Ms. Regina CURTIS
18 Director Physical Plant .... Mr. Jeffrey MARQUES
37 Director Financial Aid .... Ms. Linda DESJARDINS
19 Director Public Safety .... Mr. Alex WILTZ
96 Director of Purchasing .... Mr. Ryan AIKEN
08 Director Library .... Ms. Deborah CHOWN
21 Comptroller .... Mr. Mark BOUDREAU
06 Registrar .... Ms. Holly FITZPATRICK
38 Co-Coord Learning Asst Programs .... Ms. Cynthia SNOW
38 Co-Coord Learning Asst Programs .... Mr. Norman BEEBE
88 Coordinator of Student Assessment .... Ms. Catherine DEVLIN
32 Coordinator of Student Activities .... Ms. Mary MCENTEE
04 Staff Assistant to President .... Ms. Shannon LARANGE
108 Director Institutional Assessment .... Ms. Marie BREHENY
26 Chief Communications/Marketing Ofcr .... Ms. Stacy METZGER

*Holyoke Community College (D)

303 Homestead Avenue, Holyoke MA 01040-1099
County: Hampden FICE Identification: 002170
Unit ID: 166133
Telephone: (413) 538-7000 Carnegie Class: Assoc/HT-High Trad
FAX Number: (413) 552-2045 Calendar System: Semester
URL: www.hcc.edu
Established: 1946 Annual Undergrad Tuition & Fees (In-State): $4,902
Enrollment: 5,565 Coed
Affiliation or Control: State IRS Status: 501(c)3
Highest Offering: Associate Degree
Accreditation: EH, ACFEI, ADNUR, MUS, RAD

02 President .... Dr. Christina ROYAL
11 Vice Pres Administration & Finance .... Mr. William FOGARTY
05 Int VP Academic & Student Affairs .... Ms. Monica PEREZ
111 Vice Pres Institutional Advancement .... Ms. Amanda SBRISCIA
20 Assistant VP of Academic Admin .... Ms. Idelia SMITH
08 Dean Library .... Ms. Mary DIXEY
84 Dean of Enrollment Management .... Ms. Renee TASTAD
15 Dean Human Resources .... Ms. Clara ELLIOTT
36 Dean Coop Education & Career Svcs .... Vacant
06 Registrar .... Ms. Christine HOLBROOK
37 Director of Financial Aid .... Ms. Karen DEROUIN
91 Director Administrative Computing .... Vacant
18 Dir Facilities & Engineering Svcs .... Mr. Dan CAMPBELL
10 Comptroller .... Ms. Marcia MITCHELL
13 Chief Information Officer .... Ms. Linda SZALANKIEWICZ
21 Dir Business Services/Purchasing .... Ms. Karen DESJEANS
09 Director Institutional Research .... Ms. Veena DHANKHER
26 Dir of Marketing/Public Relations .... Ms. JoAnne ROME
111 Dir of Institutional Advancement .... Mr. Patrick CARPENTER
35 Dean of Student Services .... Mr. Tony SBALBI
19 Director Security/Safety .... Mr. Jose RIVERA
07 Director of Admissions .... Ms. Madeline TORRES
100 Chief of Staff .... Dr. Kathryn C. SENIE
103 Director Workforce Development .... Mr. Jeffrey HAYDEN
22 Dir Affirm Action/Equal Opportunity .... Ms. Olivia L. KYNARD
41 Athletic Director .... Mr. Thomas STEWART

*Massachusetts Bay Community College (E)

50 Oakland Street, Wellesley Hills MA 02481-5357
County: Norfolk FICE Identification: 002171
Unit ID: 166647
Telephone: (781) 239-3000 Carnegie Class: Assoc/HT-Mix Trad/Non
FAX Number: (781) 237-1061 Calendar System: Semester
URL: www.massbay.edu
Established: 1961 Annual Undergrad Tuition & Fees (In-State): $5,088
Enrollment: 4,629 Coed
Affiliation or Control: State IRS Status: 501(c)3
Highest Offering: Associate Degree
Accreditation: EH, ADNUR, EMT, RAD, SURGT

02 President .... Dr. David PODELL
04 Executive Director Ofc of the Pres .... Ms. Karen BRITTON
05 VP for Academic Affairs and Provost .... Dr. Lynn HUNTER
10 VP for Finance & Administration .... Mr. Neil BUCKLEY
15 Exec Director of Human Resources .... Ms. Samaria STALLINGS
111 VP of Inst Advance & Alumni Rels .... Ms. Mary SHIA
84 Asst VP Enrollment Management .... Ms. Lisa SLAVIN
32 VP for Student Development .... Dr. Elizabeth BLUMBERG
45 VP of Planning & Inst Effectiveness .... Dr. Courtney JACKSON
13 Chief Information Officer .... Mr. Michael LYONS
50 Dean Business & Prof Studies .... Dr. Susan MAGGIONI
88 Director of Corp Partnerships .... Ms. Cora MILLER
76 Dean Health Sciences Division .... Dr. Lynne DAVIS
20 Assistant Provost .... Dr. Christopher LA BARBERA
81 Dean STEM Division .... Dr. Chitra JAVDEKAR
06 Registrar .... Ms. Jennifer MCANDREW
21 AVP Finance & Admin .... Mr. Marcus EDWARD
88 Dir Academic Achievement Center .... Ms. Barbara BERNARD
121 Director of Academic Advising .... Ms. Sarah SALERNO
91 Director Administrative Computing .... Mr. Terry KRAMER
07 Director of Admissions .... Ms. Alison MCCARTY
36 Director of Career & Internship Svc .... Ms. Julie GINN
38 Director of Counseling .... Mr. Jon EDWARDS
37 Director of Financial Aid .... Mr. Curtis CORMIER
18 Director of Facilities .... Mr. Joseph DELISLE
08 Director of Learning Services .... Mr. Timothy RIVARD
25 Director of Grants Development .... Ms. Laura BROWN
26 Dir Marketing & Inst Communications .... Ms. Brianne MIERS
19 Director of Public Safety .... Mr. Vincent O'CONNELL
124 Associate Dean for Student Success .... Mr. Richard WILLIAMS
35 Coordinator of Student Activities .... Ms. Julie SCHLEICHER
28 Chief Diversity Officer .... Dr. Lynn MOORE
79 Int Dean Humanities/Social Sciences .... Ms. Nina KEERY
88 Dean of Automotive Technology .... Dr. Robert LILLEY
22 Director of Equity Compliance .... Ms. Lisa MACDONALD
41 Director of Athletics .... Mr. Adam NELSON

*Massasoit Community College (F)

1 Massasoit Boulevard, Brockton MA 02302-3996
County: Plymouth FICE Identification: 002177
Unit ID: 166823
Telephone: (508) 588-9100 Carnegie Class: Assoc/HVT-High Trad
FAX Number: (508) 427-1202 Calendar System: Semester
URL: www.massasoit.mass.edu
Established: 1966 Annual Undergrad Tuition & Fees (In-State): $4,824
Enrollment: 7,154 Coed
Affiliation or Control: State IRS Status: 501(c)3
Highest Offering: Associate Degree
Accreditation: EH, ADNUR, COARC, DA, EMT, MAC, RAD

02 President .... Dr. Gena GLICKMAN
05 Provost Academic/Student Services .... Dr. Deanna YAMEEN
10 VP Administration/CFO .... Mr. William MITCHELL
20 Assoc Vice Provost Academic Affairs .... Vacant
111 Chief Advancement Officer .... Mr. Paul GRAND PRÉ
28 Chief Diversity Officer .... Ms. Yolanda DENNIS
13 CIO/Dir Enterprise Systems .... Mr. William MORRISON
09 Assoc Dean Institutional Research ... Ms. Mary GOODHUE LYNCH
26 Director of Communications/PR .... Ms. Sarah YUNITS
26 Director of Marketing & Creative .... Mr. James LYNCH
84 Dean of Enrollment Management .... Ms. Shilo HENRIQUES
35 Dean of Students .... Ms. Slandie DIEUJUSTE
07 Director of Admissions .... Ms. Michelle HUGHES
37 Director Student Financial Aid .... Mr. Todd HUGHES
06 Registrar .... Ms. Jannie GILSON
121 Director of Advisement & Counseling .... Ms. Alessandra MONTEIRO
41 Director of Athletics .... Ms. Julie MULVEY
36 Director Career Placement .... Ms. Kathryn PRYLES
21 Comptroller .... Ms. Patricia MARCELLA
18 Director Facilities/Physical Plant .... Mr. Gregory HABEREK
96 Director of Purchasing .... Mr. John CAFFELLE
29 Director Alumni Relations .... Vacant
50 Dean Business & Technology .... Dr. Michael ROGGOW
79 Dean Humanities/Communication Arts .... Dr. Harriette SCOTT
76 Interim Dean Allied Health .... Ms. Susan CLOVER
83 Dean Public Svc/Social Science .... Ms. Karyn BOUTIN
81 Dean Science & Math .... Mr. Douglas BROWN
72 Exec Dean Canton/Emergent Tech .... Ms. Carine SAUVIGNON
15 VP of Human Resources .... Ms. Margaret GAZZARA HESS
103 VP of Corporate & Community Educ .... Ms. Melanie HABER
100 Chief of Staff .... Ms. Lydia CAMARA
19 Chief of Police .... Mr. Christopher CUMMINGS

*Middlesex Community College (G)

591 Springs Road, Bedford MA 01730-1197
County: Middlesex FICE Identification: 009936
Unit ID: 166887
Telephone: (781) 280-3200 Carnegie Class: Assoc/HT-High Trad
FAX Number: (781) 275-0741 Calendar System: Semester
URL: www.middlesex.mass.edu
Established: 1969 Annual Undergrad Tuition & Fees (In-State): $6,110
Enrollment: 8,206 Coed
Affiliation or Control: State IRS Status: 501(c)3
Highest Offering: Associate Degree
Accreditation: EH, ADNUR, DA, DH, DMS, DT, MAC, MLTAD, RAD

02 President .... Dr. James C. MABRY
05 Provost/VP of Academic Affairs .... Mr. Philip J. SISSON
03 Executive Vice President .... Vacant
84 VP Enrollment Svcs/Rsrch & Plng .... Vacant

15 VP Human Resources ..... Ms. Mary EMERICK
10 VP of Finance/CFO ..... Mr. Frank NOCELLA
04 Assistant to the President ..... Vacant
20 Associate Provost ..... Vacant
32 Chief Student Affs/Dean of Students ..... Ms. Pamela B. FLAHERTY
79 Dean Humanities and Social Sciences ..... Mr. Matthew OLSON
72 Dean Bus/Educ & Public Service ..... Ms. Judith HOGAN
17 Dean of Health and STEM ..... Ms. Kathleen J. SWEENEY
88 Dean Professional/Instructional Dev ..... Ms. Susan ANDERSON
22 Asst Dir HR/Affirm Action Officer ..... Mr. Reginald NICHOLS
11 Chief Administrative Officer ..... Ms. Colleen COX
96 Director of Procurement ..... Mrs. Christina KELLEY
84 Dean of Enrollment Services ..... Ms. Audrey NAHABEDIAN
111 Exec Dir Inst Advancement ..... Ms. Judith M. BURKE
07 Dean of Admissions ..... Ms. Marilynn GALLAGAN
35 Associate Dean of Students ..... Vacant
09 Dean Institutional Research ..... Ms. Linda HEINEMAN
27 Exec Director Public Affairs ..... Mr. Patrick COOK
26 Int Dir Marketing/Communication ..... Ms. Elizabeth J. NOEL
29 Director of Alumni Affairs ..... Ms. Amy LEE
37 Director of Financial Aid ..... Vacant
21 Comptroller ..... Ms. Kathy RICH
21 Bursar ..... Mr. Christopher FIORI
08 Director Library Services ..... Ms. Maryann NILES
23 Director of Health Services ..... Vacant
06 Registrar ..... Mr. Daniel MOYNIHAN
96 Coordinator of Purchasing ..... Ms. Maureen HUDSON

*Mount Wachusett Community College (A)

444 Green Street, Gardner MA 01440-1000
County: Worcester FICE Identification: 002172
Unit ID: 166957
Telephone: (978) 632-6600 Carnegie Class: Assoc/MT-VT-High Trad
FAX Number: (978) 630-9559 Calendar System: Semester
URL: www.mwcc.edu
Established: 1963 Annual Undergrad Tuition & Fees (In-State): $5,548
Enrollment: 3,854 Coed
Affiliation or Control: State IRS Status: 501(c)3
Highest Offering: Associate Degree
Accreditation: EH, ADNUR, CAHIIM, DA, DH, MAC, MLTAD, PNUR, PTAA

02 President ..... Dr. James L. VANDER HOOVEN
05 VP Academic/Student Affairs ..... Dr. Paul HERNANDEZ
103 VP Lifelong Learning/Wkfc Dev ..... Dr. Rachel FRICK CARDELLE
10 VP Finance & Administration ..... Mr. Robert LABONTE
26 VP Marketing/Communications ..... Ms. Lea Ann SCALES
111 VP Planning/Development/Inst Rsrch ..... Mr. Joseph STISO
15 VP Human Resources/Payroll ..... Mr. Peter SENNETT
20 Assistant VP of Academic Affairs ..... Dr. Michelle PARANTO
32 Sr Dean Student Affairs ..... Mr. Jason ZELESKY
12 Dean Leominster Campus ..... Mr. John WALSH
08 Dean Library and Academic Support ..... Mr. Jess MYNES
09 Asst Dean of Records/Inst Research ..... Ms. Rebecca FOREST
18 Director Maintenance/Mechanical Sys ..... Mr. William SWIFT
68 Director Mount Fitness ..... Mr. Jason SNOONIAN
19 Chief Public Safety & Security ..... Ms. Karen KOLIMAGA
35 Assistant Dean of Student Services ..... Vacant
88 Director of Enterprise Services ..... Mr. Shane MULLEN
27 Director of Media Services ..... Mr. Arthur COLLINS
04 Admin Assistant to the President ..... Ms. Jo-Ann MEAGHER
07 Director of Admissions ..... Ms. Elizabeth DALLY
37 Director Student Financial Aid ..... Ms. Deb NICHOLS
41 Athletic Director ..... Mr. Jason SNOONIAN
44 Director Annual Giving ..... Ms. Carla ZOTTOLI

*North Shore Community College (B)

1 Ferncroft Road, PO Box 3340, Danvers MA 01923-0840
County: Essex FICE Identification: 002173
Unit ID: 167312
Telephone: (978) 762-4000 Carnegie Class: Assoc/MT-VT-High Trad
FAX Number: (978) 762-4020 Calendar System: Semester
URL: www.northshore.edu
Established: 1965 Annual Undergrad Tuition & Fees (In-State): $5,184
Enrollment: 6,087 Coed
Affiliation or Control: State IRS Status: 501(c)3
Highest Offering: Associate Degree
Accreditation: EH, ADNUR, COARC, MAC, OTA, PNUR, PTAA, RAD, SURGT

02 President ..... Dr. Patricia A. GENTILE
05 Vice Pres Academic Affairs ..... Dr. Karen HYNICK
10 Vice Pres Administration/Finance ..... Ms. Janice M. FORSSTROM
32 Vice Pres Student Affairs ..... Vacant
15 Vice President Human Res/Affirm Act ..... Ms. Madeline WALLIS
103 Dean Workforce Dev/Corp Educ ..... Ms. Dianne PALTER-GILL
90 Dean Academic Technology ..... Mr. Michael BADOLATO
07 Dean of Enrollment Services ..... Mr. John DUFF
37 Asst VP Student Financial Svcs/Comp ..... Mr. Stephen CREAMER
08 Director Library/Tutoring ..... Mr. Rex KRAJEWSKI
13 Dir of Networking/Info Services ..... Mr. Gary HAM
37 Director of Financial Aid ..... Ms. Susan SULLIVAN
09 Asst Vice Pres Planning & Research ..... Ms. Laurie LACHAPELLE
18 Asst Vice Pres Facilities Mgmt ..... Mr. Richard RENEY
19 Interim Campus Police Chief ..... Mr. David COOK
21 Comptroller ..... Ms. Patricia CALLAHAN
26 Director Public Relations/New Media ..... Ms. Linda BRANTLEY
35 Chief Student Life Officer ..... Ms. Lisa MILSO
36 Director Student Placement ..... Ms. Lynn MARCUS
121 Director Student Support & Advising ..... Mr. Daniel O'NEILL
27 Director Marketing Communications ..... Ms. Samantha MCGILLOWAY
40 Bookstore Manager ..... Mr. Shawn CRONIN
06 Registrar ..... Ms. Mel POTOCZAK
04 Admin Assistant to the President ..... Ms. Susan MULVEY

*Northern Essex Community College (C)

100 Elliott Street, Haverhill MA 01830-2399
County: Essex FICE Identification: 002174
Unit ID: 167376
Telephone: (978) 556-3000 Carnegie Class: Assoc/MT-VT-High Trad
FAX Number: (978) 556-3723 Calendar System: Semester
URL: www.necc.mass.edu
Established: 1960 Annual Undergrad Tuition & Fees (In-State): $5,136
Enrollment: 5,726 Coed
Affiliation or Control: State IRS Status: 501(c)3
Highest Offering: Associate Degree
Accreditation: EH, ADNUR, COARC, CSHSE, DA, EMT, MAC, PNUR, POLYT, RAD

02 President ..... Dr. Lane A. GLENN
05 Vice President of Academic Affairs ..... Dr. William HEINEMAN
111 Vice Pres Institutional Advancement ..... Ms. Allison DOLAN WILSON
10 VP of Administration & Finance/CFO ..... Mr. Michael R. MCCARTHY
32 Asst Vice President Student Affairs ..... Vacant
12 Exec Dir of Lawrence Campus ..... Dr. Noemi CUSTODIA-LORA
09 Dean of Institutional Research ..... Ms. Kelly SARETSKY
30 Dean of Development ..... Ms. Wendy SHAFFER
121 Dean of Acad Support/Transfer ..... Vacant
103 Exec Dir Workforce Devel/Cont Educ ..... Vacant
13 Chief Information Officer ..... Mr. Jeffrey BICKFORD
06 Registrar ..... Ms. Sue SHAIN
84 Assoc Dean Enrol/Chief Fin Aid Ofcr ..... Ms. Alexis FISHBONE
26 Director of Public Relations ..... Ms. Ernestine GREENSLADE
29 Director Alumni Relations ..... Ms. Lindsey GRAHAM
18 Chief Facilities/Physical Plant ..... Mr. Paul MIEDZIONOSKI
96 Director of Purchasing ..... Ms. Elizabeth DONOVAN
100 Chief of Staff to President ..... Ms. Cheryl GOODWIN
08 Chief Library Officer ..... Mr. Michael HEARN
19 Director Security/Safety ..... Ms. Deborah CRAFTS
41 Athletic Director ..... Mr. Daniel BLAIR

*Quinsigamond Community College (D)

670 W Boylston Street, Worcester MA 01606-2092
County: Worcester FICE Identification: 002175
Unit ID: 167534
Telephone: (508) 853-2300 Carnegie Class: Assoc/MT-VT-High Trad
FAX Number: (508) 852-6943 Calendar System: Semester
URL: www.qcc.edu
Established: 1963 Annual Undergrad Tuition & Fees (In-State): $5,586
Enrollment: 7,368 Coed
Affiliation or Control: State IRS Status: 501(c)3
Highest Offering: Associate Degree
Accreditation: EH, ADNUR, COARC, CSHSE, DA, DH, EMT, MAC, OTA, PNUR, RAD, SURGT

02 President ..... Dr. Luis PEDRAJA
05 Interim VP of Academic Affairs ..... Dr. Nancy SCHOENFELD
10 VP of Administration ..... Mr. Stephen T. MARINI
32 VP of Student Enrollment/Develop ..... Dr. Lillian M. ORTIZ
15 Int Exec Dir of Human Resources ..... Ms. Elizabeth AUSTIN
20 Assistant VP Academic Affairs ..... Ms. Kathy RENTSCH
04 Executive Assistant to President ..... Ms. Selina M. BORIA
21 Asst VP for Finance/Comptroller ..... Ms. Debra A. LAFLASH
79 Dean Humanities & Education ..... Vacant
76 Dean Health Care ..... Mr. C. Pat SCHMOHL
50 Dean Business/Engineer/Technology ..... Ms. Betty LAUER
81 Dean Science & Mathematics ..... Vacant
06 Registrar ..... Ms. Barbara ZAWALICH
62 Dean of Library Services ..... Vacant
09 Dean of Inst Research/Planning ..... Dr. Ingrid SKADBERG
121 Assistant VP of Student Success ..... Ms. Michelle TUFAU-AFRIYIE
106 Dean of Digital Learning ..... Mr. Ken DWYER
56 Asst VP Ext Campus Operations ..... Mr. Victor SOMMA
35 Director Student Life & Leadership ..... Mr. Michael BEANE
18 Director of Facilities ..... Mr. James RACKI
37 Director Student Financial Aid ..... Ms. Karen GRANT
96 Purchasing Manager ..... Ms. Juliana ESPOSITO
19 Chief of Campus Police ..... Mr. Kevin RITACCO
26 Dir Institutional Communications ..... Mr. Joshua MARTIN
38 Social Worker/Mental Health Couns ..... Ms. Tina WELLS
28 Director Disability Services ..... Ms. Kristen PROCTOR
35 Dean of Students ..... Ms. Terry VECCHIO
07 Director of Admissions ..... Ms. Mishawn DAVIS-EYENE
30 Chief Development/Advancement ..... Ms. Karen RUCKS

*Roxbury Community College (E)

1234 Columbus Avenue,
Roxbury Crossing MA 02120-3423
County: Suffolk FICE Identification: 011930
Unit ID: 167631
Telephone: (617) 427-0060 Carnegie Class: Assoc/HT-High Trad
FAX Number: N/A Calendar System: Semester
URL: rcc.mass.edu
Established: 1973 Annual Undergrad Tuition & Fees (In-State): $5,848
Enrollment: 1,928 Coed
Affiliation or Control: State IRS Status: 501(c)3
Highest Offering: Associate Degree
Accreditation: EH, RAD

02 President ..... Dr. Valerie R. ROBERSON
04 Executive Asst to the President ..... Ms. Judy M. PUGH
05 VP Academic And Student Affairs ..... Ms. Cecile REGNER
111 VP Advancement/Community Engagement ..... Vacant
10 Vice President of Admin & Finance ..... Mr. Kevin HEPNER
13 Chief Information Tech Officer ..... Vacant
15 Chief Human Res/Affirm Action Ofcr ..... Ms. Patricia WEST
41 Manager of RLTAC ..... Mr. Sherman HART
08 Director of Library ..... Mr. William HOAG
23 Director of Health Services ..... Ms. Ruth HINES
30 Exec Dir Dev/Alumni/Foundation ..... Ms. Mishawn DAVIS-EYENE
06 Registrar ..... Ms. Cheryl MARTIN
32 Dean of Student Life ..... Dr. Andres OROZ
26 Director Marketing/Communications ..... Ms. Jordan SMOCK
57 Dir of Visual/Performing/Media Arts ..... Vacant
88 Director of the Writing Center Lab ..... Vacant
37 Assoc Director Financial Aid ..... Mr. Christopher LEWIS
25 Grants Research Specialist ..... Dr. Yvonne E. ANTHONY
09 Director of Institutional Research ..... Mr. Jason WRIGHT
103 Director Workforce Development ..... Mr. Salvador PINA
19 Director Security/Safety ..... Mr. David ALBENESE
81 Dean of STEM ..... Dr. Hillel SIMS
90 Director Academic Computing ..... Mr. Raymind CRUZ

*Springfield Technical Community College (F)

Armory Square, Springfield MA 01105-1296
County: Hampden FICE Identification: 008078
Unit ID: 167905
Telephone: (413) 781-7822 Carnegie Class: Assoc/HVT-High Trad
FAX Number: (413) 755-6309 Calendar System: Semester
URL: www.stcc.edu
Established: 1967 Annual Undergrad Tuition & Fees (In-State): $5,088
Enrollment: 5,343 Coed
Affiliation or Control: State IRS Status: 501(c)3
Highest Offering: Associate Degree
Accreditation: EH, ADNUR, CAHIIM, COARC, DA, DH, DMS, MAC, MLTAD, OTA, PTAA, RAD, SURGT

02 President ..... Dr. John B. COOK
05 VP of Academic Affairs ..... Dr. Geraldine DE BERLY
10 VP of Administration/CFO ..... Mr. Joseph DASILVA
32 VP Student/Multicultural Affairs ..... Mr. Kamari COLLINS
20 Dean of Academic Initiatives ..... Mr. Matthew GRAVEL
04 Assistant to the President ..... Ms. Nanette FLORES
66 Director of Nursing ..... Ms. Lisa FUGIEL
72 Dean Engineering Tech/Mathematics ..... Dr. Adrienne SMITH
76 Dean Health and Patient Simulation ..... Mr. Christopher D. SCOTT
81 Dean Sciences/Engineering Transfer ..... Dr. Robert DICKERMAN
51 Senior Director of Business Service ..... Dr. Debbie BELLUCCI
35 Asst VP Stdnt Affs/Dean of Stdnts ..... Mr. LaRue A. PIERCE
07 Dean of Admissions ..... Ms. Louisa M. DAVIS FREEMAN
06 Registrar ..... Ms. Theresa REMILLARD
41 Director of Athletics ..... Mr. J. Vincent GRASSETTI
103 Assistant VP Workforce ..... Mr. Gerardo ZAYAS, JR.
18 AVP of Administration/Facilities ..... Mrs. Maureen SOCHA
121 Director of Advising ..... Ms. Jessica HILL
26 Director of Marketing ..... Ms. Joan GRAVEL
36 Director of Coop/Career Placement ..... Ms. Pamela WHITE
15 Senior Director of Human Resources ..... Ms. Joan D. MURPHY
16 Director of Human Resources ..... Ms. Cheryl ROGERS
37 Dean of Student Financial Services ..... Mr. Jeremy GREENHOUSE
88 Fiscal/Financial Project Manager ..... Mr. Jason COHEN
35 Coord Student Activities/Devel ..... Ms. Andrea TARPEY
27 Coordinator of Media Relations ..... Mr. James DANKO
114 Senior Director Finance/Budgets ..... Mrs. Cathy OLSON
14 Sr Director of IT Applications ..... Mr. Clifton PORTER
08 Interim Dean Library Services ..... Ms. Erica EYNOUF
21 Controller ..... Mr. Jonathan TUDRYN
09 Dean of Institutional Research ..... Ms. Suzanne SMITH
108 Director of Assessment ..... Dr. Tracey TROTTIER
88 Director of Access/Student Success ..... Mr. Jose LOPES-FIGUEROA
88 Director of Gateway to College ..... Ms. Jennifer SANCHEZ
88 Director of Facilities Quality and ..... Ms. Kerri KANE
113 Director of Student Accounts ..... Ms. Dorothy UNGERER
88 Director of Grants Development & Ad ..... Ms. Kimberley BRODERICK

Massachusetts Institute of Technology (G)

77 Massachusetts Avenue, Cambridge MA 02139-4307
County: Middlesex FICE Identification: 002178
Unit ID: 166683
Telephone: (617) 253-1000 Carnegie Class: DU-Highest
FAX Number: N/A Calendar System: 4/1/4
URL: web.mit.edu
Established: 1861 Annual Undergrad Tuition & Fees: $51,832
Enrollment: 11,466 Coed
Affiliation or Control: Independent Non-Profit IRS Status: 501(c)3
Highest Offering: Doctorate
Accreditation: EH, PLNG

01 President ..... Dr. L. Rafael REIF
88 Chairman of the Corporation ..... Mr. Robert B. MILLARD
05 Provost ..... Prof. Martin A. SCHMIDT

00 Chancellor .... Prof. Cynthia BARNHART
46 Vice President for Research .... Prof. Maria T. ZUBER
106 Vice President for Open Learning .... Prof. Sanjay SARMA
10 Exec Vice President & Treasurer .... Mr. Israel RUIZ
101 VP & Secretary of the Corporation .... Ms. Suzanne GLASSBURN
30 VP for Resource Development .... Ms. Julie LUCAS
20 Chancellor for Academic Advancement .Prof. W. Eric L. GRIMSON
43 Vice President & General Counsel .... Mr. Mark DIVINCENZO
26 VP for Communications .... Vacant
29 CEO MIT Alumni Association .... Ms. Whitney T. ESPICH
115 President MIT Investment Mgmt Co .... Mr. Seth ALEXANDER
88 Deputy Executive Vice President .... Mr. Anthony P. SHARON
15 VP for Human Resources .... Vacant
13 VP for IS&T .... Mr. Mark SILIS
21 Vice President for Finance .... Mr. Glen SHOR
48 Dean Sch of Architecture & Planning .... Prof. Hashim SARKIS
54 Dean School of Engineering .... Prof. Anantha CHANDRAKASAN
79 Dean Sch Hum/Arts/Soc Sciences .... Prof. Melissa NOBLES
81 Dean School of Science .... Prof. Michael SIPSER
50 Dean Sloan School of Management .... Prof. David C. SCHMITTLEIN
20 Associate Provost .... Prof. Krystyn VAN VLIET
20 Associate Provost .... Prof. Philip S. KHOURY
20 Associate Provost .... Prof. Richard K. LESTER
08 Director of Libraries .... Ms. Chris BOURG
28 Institute Community & Equity Ofcr .... Ms. Alyce JOHNSON
88 Vice Chancellor UG & Grad Education .... Prof. Ian A. WAITZ
32 VP and Dean for Student Life .... Dr. Suzy NELSON
88 Dean for Digital Learning .... Prof. Krishna RAJAGOPAL
88 Director Lincoln Laboratory .... Dr. Eric D. EVANS
86 Director MIT Washington Office .... Mr. David GOLDSTON
07 Dean of Admissions/Student Fin Svcs .... Mr. Stuart SCHMILL
23 Medical Dir & Head MIT Medical .... Dr. Cecilia Warpinski STUOPIS
18 Director Campus Services and Chief .... Chief John DI FAVA
45 Director of Campus Planning .... Mr. Jon ALVAREZ
102 Exec Dir Foundation Relations .... Ms. Alicia SANCHEZ
25 Dir Office of Sponsored Programs .... Ms. Colleen M. LESLIE
96 Dir of Strategic Sourcing/Contracts .... Ms. Christina T. LO
41 Director of Athletics .... Ms. Julie SORIERO
09 Director of Institutional Research .... Mrs. Lydia S. SNOVER
85 Assoc Dean & Dir Intl Students Ofc .... Mr. David ELWELL
36 Director Career Services .... Ms. Deborah L. LIVERMAN
93 Associate Dean and Director OME .... Ms. DiOnetta CRAYTON
06 Registrar .... Ms. Mary CALLAHAN
88 Director MIT Press .... Ms. Amy BRAND
39 Director of Residential Services .. Ms. Jennifer HAPGOOD-WHITE
42 Chaplain to Institute .... Rev. Kirstin BOSWELL-FORD
38 Sr Assoc Dean Student Support .... Mr. David RANDALL
94 Women's and Gender Studies Director .... Prof. Helen Elaine LEE
104 Associate Dean Global Education ..... Ms. Malgorzata HEDDERICK
24 Manager Audio Visual .... Mr. Paul SHAY
90 Dir Platform & Systems Integration .... Mr. Garry P. ZACHEISS
04 Exec Assistant to the President .... Ms. Karla CASEY

Massachusetts School of Law at Andover (A)

500 Federal Street, Andover MA 01810-1094

County: Essex FICE Identification: 032353
Unit ID: 369002
Telephone: (978) 681-0800 Carnegie Class: Spec-4-yr-Law
FAX Number: (978) 681-6330 Calendar System: Semester
URL: www.mslaw.edu
Established: 1988 Annual Graduate Tuition & Fees: N/A
Enrollment: 326 Coed
Affiliation or Control: Independent Non-Profit IRS Status: 501(c)3
Highest Offering: Doctorate; No Undergraduates
Accreditation: EH

00 Dean Emeritus .... Mr. Lawrence R. VELVEL
01 Dean .... Prof. Michael COYNE
10 Chief Financial Officer .... Mr. Clifford ABELSON
37 Director of Financial Aid .... Ms. Lynn BOWAB
06 Registrar .... Ms. Rosa FIGUEIREDO
07 Director of Admissions .... Mr. Rohit BHASIN
26 Director of Media .... Ms. Kathryn VILLARE
05 Dir Academic Svcs/Career Devel .. Ms. Paula COLBY-CLEMENTS
13 Director of Technology .... Mr. Michael COYNE

MCPHS University (B)

179 Longwood Avenue, Boston MA 02115-5896

County: Suffolk FICE Identification: 002165
Unit ID: 166656
Telephone: (617) 732-2800 Carnegie Class: Spec-4-yr-Other Health
FAX Number: (617) 732-2801 Calendar System: Semester
URL: www.mcphs.edu
Established: 1823 Annual Undergrad Tuition & Fees: $33,620
Enrollment: 7,208 Coed
Affiliation or Control: Independent Non-Profit IRS Status: 501(c)3
Highest Offering: Doctorate
Accreditation: EH, ARCPA, DH, NMT, NURSE, OPT, PH, PHAR, PTA, RAD, RTT

01 President .... Mr. Charles F. MONAHAN, JR.
05 VP for Acad Affairs/Provost .... Dr. Caroline ZEIND
10 Exec Vice President/COO & CFO .... Mr. Richard J. LESSARD
111 VP for Advancement & Chief of Staff ... Ms. Marguerite JOHNSON
20 Assoc VP Academic Affs/Assoc Prov .... Vacant
20 Exec Director for Acad Affairs WM .... Ms. Sue GORMAN
20 Assoc Provost Acad & Prof Affairs .... Dr. Jeanine MOUNT
106 Assoc Provost Academic Innovation .... Dr. Barbara MACAULAY
43 VP/General Counsel & CCO .... Ms. Deborah A. O'MALLEY
32 Assoc Provost for Student Success .... Dr. Craig MACK
67 Interim Dean of Pharmacy Boston .... Dr. Stephen KERR
67 Interim CAO WM/Dean of Pharmacy WM .... Dr. Anna MORIN
08 Dean Library & Learning Resources .... Mr. Richard KAPLAN
49 Dean School of Arts and Sciences .... Dr. Delia C. ANDERSON
88 Int Dean School of Healthcare Bus .... Mr. Michael SPOONER
66 Int Dean of Nursing Worc/Manchester .... Ms. Tammy GRAVEL
107 Dean Sch of Prof Studies .... Ms. Carol STUCKEY
66 Dean School of Nursing .... Dr. Kathleen POLLEY-PAYNE
52 Int Dean Forsyth Sch of Dental Hyg .... Dr. Dianne SMALLIDGE
88 Director of Physical Therapy .... Dr. Frances KISTNER
88 Director of PA Studies Boston .... Mr. Christopher COOPER
88 Director of PA Studies Wor/Man .... Ms. Kristy ALTONGY-MAGEE
69 Director Master of Public Health .... Ms. Carly LEVY
88 Dean of Optometry .... Dr. Maryke NEIBERG
88 Dean of Acupuncture & Oriental Med .... Vacant
75 Director of Occupational Therapy .... Dr. Douglas SIMMONS
88 Director Master of Public Health .... Ms. Carly LEVY
15 Chief Human Resources Officer .... Mr. Kevin DOLAN
06 Admin Dean/University Registrar .... Ms. Stacey TAYLOR
13 Director of Information Services .... Mr. Tom SCANLON
21 Chief Business Officer .... Mr. Keith BELLUCCI
12 Exec Director Wor/Man Campuses .... Dr. Seth P. WALL
88 Title IX Coordinator .... Ms. Dawn BALLOU
84 Chief Enrollment Officer .... Ms. Kathleen RYAN
96 Director of Purchasing .... Ms. Peg CRAWFORD
38 Exec Dir Counseling Services .... Ms. Molly PAYNE
26 Director of Communications .... Mr. Michael RATTY
18 Director of Facilities .... Mr. Jeff WARD
19 Chief of Public Safety .... Mr. Kevin NOLAN
105 Manager of Web Services .... Ms. Charlene ROBERTSON
09 Exec Dir Inst Research & Assessment .... Ms. Laura UERLING
04 Special Assistant to the President .... Ms. Sheryl CHEAL
07 Senior Director of Admissions .... Mr. Rene CABRERA
25 Director Regulatory Affairs Program .... Mr. Frederick FRANKHAUSER
28 Asst Dean Diversity & Inclusion .... Ms. Julia GOLDEN-BATTLE
29 Exec Director Alumni Services .... Ms. Karen SINGLE
30 Exec Dir Development Operations .... Mr. Lawrence TOWNLEY
36 Dir Center for Prof Career Develop .... Ms. Melissa HAWKINS
36 Dir Center for Prof Career Devel WM .... Ms. Jeanette DOYLE
37 Director Student Financial Services .... Ms. Elizabeth GORHAM

MCPHS-Worcester Campus (C)

19 Foster Street, Worcester MA 01608-1715

Telephone: (508) 890-8855 Identification: 770112
Accreditation: &EH

Merrimack College (D)

315 Turnpike Street, North Andover MA 01845-5800

County: Essex FICE Identification: 002120
Unit ID: 166850
Telephone: (978) 837-5000 Carnegie Class: Masters/L
FAX Number: (978) 837-5222 Calendar System: Semester
URL: www.merrimack.edu
Established: 1947 Annual Undergrad Tuition & Fees: $41,760
Enrollment: 4,191 Coed
Affiliation or Control: Roman Catholic IRS Status: 501(c)3
Highest Offering: Master's
Accreditation: EH, CAATE

01 President .... Dr. Christopher E. HOPEY
03 Executive Vice President .... Mr. Jeffrey DOGGETT
04 Director Office of the President .... Ms. Lisa JEBALI
102 VP Corporate/Foundation Engage .... Mr. Jay CAPORALE
05 Provost & Sr VP Academic Affairs .... Dr. Allan T. WEATHERWAX
45 VP Institutional Effectiveness .... Dr. Jonathan LYON
10 SVP Finance & Administration/CFO .... Mr. Basil STEWART
04 Special Assistant to the President .... Dr. Russell MAYER
11 VP of Administration & Campus Svcs .... Mr. Mark COLLINS
84 Vice Pres Enrollment Management .... Mr. Darren CONINE
42 Vice Pres Mission & Ministry .... Rev. Raymond DLUGOS, OSA
30 Sr VP Development & Alumni Affairs .... Ms. Sara Jane BRAZDA
43 Vice President & General Counsel .... Mr. Nicholas MCDONALD
15 VP Human Resources .... Ms. Nancy MURPHY
88 Assoc VP/Chief of Staff to Provost .... Mr. Mark GOULD
86 AVP Campus Planning & Development .... Mr. Felipe SCHWARZ
20 Senior Vice Provost .... Dr. Cynthia MCGOWAN
27 VP Communications/Chief of Staff .... Ms. Bethany LO MONACO
21 Interim Controller .... Ms. Joanne FORAN
29 Assoc VP Develop & Alumni Relations .... Ms. Joanne MERMELSTEIN
32 VP Student Affairs/Dean Students .... Ms. Allison GILL
88 AVP for Wellness/Dean of Students .... Ms. Stephanie KENDALL
104 AVP Intl/Grad/Multicul Students .... Ms. Lauren BENT
36 Assoc VP Corporate & Career Engage .... Dr. Heather MAIETTA
13 AVP Information Technology/CIO .... Mr. Peter HASTINGS
07 Assoc VP/Dean of Admission .... Mr. Darren CONINE
50 Dean Girard School of Business .... Dr. Catherine USOFF
54 Dean Science & Engineering .... Dr. Cynthia MCGOWAN
49 Interim Dean of Liberal Arts .... Dr. John (Sean) CONDON
53 Dean School of Education .... Dr. Isabella CHERNEY
76 Dean School Health Sciences .... Dr. Kyle MCINNIS
37 Director Financial Aid .... Ms. Adrienne MONTGOMERY
41 Director of Athletics .... Mr. Jeremy GIBSON
09 Dir Institutional Research & Plng .... Ms. Kristen SULLIVAN
08 Director of the Library .... Ms. Kathryn GEOFFRION-SCANNELL
42 Director of Campus Ministry .... Rev. Keith HOLLIS
23 Director Hamel Health .... Ms. Katell GUELLEC
39 Director of Residence Life .... Mr. Cameron SMITH
19 Director of Police Services .... Mr. Michael DELGRECO
31 Asst Dir Stevens Svc Learning Ctr .... Ms. Katherine DONELL
24 Dir of Media Instructional Services .... Mr. Kevin SALEMME
96 Director of Purchasing .... Mr. Michael MAGNER
105 Director of Web Services .... Ms. Stacie BOWMAN
28 Director Diversity Education .... Mr. J. Scott GAGE
88 Special Asst Acad Affairs/Provost .... Mr. Michael ACCARDI

MGH Institute of Health Professions (E)

36 1st Avenue, Boston MA 02129-4557

County: Suffolk FICE Identification: 022316
Unit ID: 166869
Telephone: (617) 726-2947 Carnegie Class: Spec-4-yr-Other Health
FAX Number: (617) 726-3716 Calendar System: Semester
URL: www.mghihp.edu
Established: 1977 Annual Undergrad Tuition & Fees: N/A
Enrollment: 1,215 Coed
Affiliation or Control: Independent Non-Profit IRS Status: 501(c)3
Highest Offering: Doctorate
Accreditation: EH, #ARCPA, NURSE, OT, PTA, SP

01 President .... Dr. Paula MILONE-NUZZO
05 Provost/VP Academic Affairs .... Dr. Alex JOHNSON
10 VP Finance/Administration/COO .... Mr. Atlas EVANS
13 Assoc VP IT/Campus Svcs/Compliance ... Mr. Denis STRATFORD
100 Chief of Staff .... Ms. Elizabeth PIPES
26 Chief Communications Officer .... Mr. Paul MURPHY
30 Chief Development Officer .... Ms. Clare MCCULLY

† Tuition varies by degree program.

Montserrat College of Art (F)

23 Essex Street, Beverly MA 01915-4508

County: Essex FICE Identification: 020630
Unit ID: 166911
Telephone: (978) 921-4242 Carnegie Class: Spec-4-yr-Arts
FAX Number: (978) 922-4268 Calendar System: Semester
URL: www.montserrat.edu
Established: 1970 Annual Undergrad Tuition & Fees: $33,400
Enrollment: 368 Coed
Affiliation or Control: Independent Non-Profit IRS Status: 501(c)3
Highest Offering: Baccalaureate
Accreditation: EH, ART

01 President .... Mr. Kurt T. STEINBERG
05 Dean of Academic Affairs .... Mr. Brian PELLINEN
32 Dean of Students .... Ms. Maureen WARK
30 Director of Development .... Mr. Paul KOTAKIS
26 Dean College Rels/Spec Asst to Pres .... Ms. Jo BRODERICK
10 Chief Financial Officer .... Ms. Cara CALLANAN
13 Director of Information Technology .... Ms. Ari GROSVENOR
08 Librarian .... Ms. Cheri COE
06 Registrar .... Mrs. Theresa SKELLY
15 Human Resources Generalist .... Ms. Christin BOURANIS
07 Director of Admissions .... Mr. Jeffrey NEWELL
04 Executive Asst to the President .... Ms. Margaret WAUGH
37 Director of Financial Aid .... Mrs. Joanne RACOK
18 Facilities Manager .... Mr. James MCCARTHY
88 Dir Academic Access Studio .... Ms. Meagan GRANT
39 Director of Campus Life .... Ms. Haley MCCONVILLE

Mount Holyoke College (G)

50 College Street, South Hadley MA 01075-1424

County: Hampshire FICE Identification: 002192
Unit ID: 166939
Telephone: (413) 538-2000 Carnegie Class: Bac-A&S
FAX Number: (413) 538-2391 Calendar System: Semester
URL: www.mtholyoke.edu
Established: 1837 Annual Undergrad Tuition & Fees: $49,998
Enrollment: 2,334 Female
Affiliation or Control: Independent Non-Profit IRS Status: 501(c)3
Highest Offering: Master's
Accreditation: EH

01 President .... Sonya C. STEPHENS
05 VP Acad Affairs/Dean of Faculty .... Jon WESTERN
10 VP Finance and Administration .... Shannon GUREK
84 VP Enrollment/Dean of Admissions .... Vacant
111 VP for Advancement .... Kassandra JOLLEY
32 VP Student Life/Dean of Students .... Marcella RUNELL HALL
26 VP for Communications and Marketing ...... Charles L. GREENE, II
28 VP for Equity and Inclusion/CDO .. Kijua SANDERS-MCMURTRY
101 Secretary of the College .... Lenore REILLY
06 Registrar .... Elizabeth PYLE
13 Chief Information Officer .... Alex WIRTH-CAUCHON
100 Chief of Staff .... Kathleen C. PERTZBORN
04 Special Assistant .... Jim SHEPARD
29 Exec Director Alumnae Association .... Nancy PEREZ

New England College of Business and Finance (H)

10 High Street, Suite 204, Boston MA 02110

County: Suffolk FICE Identification: 039653
Unit ID: 164438
Telephone: (617) 603-6900 Carnegie Class: Spec-4-yr-Bus
FAX Number: (877) 469-6961 Calendar System: Other
URL: www.necb.edu
Established: 1909 Annual Undergrad Tuition & Fees: $12,120

Enrollment: 1,175 Coed
Affiliation or Control: Proprietary IRS Status: Proprietary
Highest Offering: Master's
Accreditation: EH

01 President Mr. Howard E. HORTON
05 Provost Ms. Debra LEAHY
10 Chief Financial/Admin Officer Mr. Dennis J. MADIGAN
106 VP Center for eLearning Excellence Ms. Paula BRAMANTE
21 Vice Pres of Business Development Mr. John HOPE
21 Controller Vacant
20 Associate Provost Mr. Roger PAO
88 Program Chair MBE Ms. Deborah SEMENTA
88 Program Chair MBA Dr. Carla PATALANO
49 Dean of Undergraduate Studies Dr. Donna VIENS
04 Asst to the President/Office Mgr Ms. Kathy CANTALUPA
06 Registrar Mr. Robert WAGSTAFF
32 Dean of Students Ms. Caitrin BRISSON
84 Dean of Enrollment Management Ms. Caitrin BRISSON
37 Student Finance Supervisor Ms. Renee JORDON
108 Director Institutional Assessment Ms. Lydia CAVIEUX
26 Chief Public Rels/Dir Marketing Mr. Kacey CLARK

New England College of Optometry (A)

424 Beacon Street, Boston MA 02115-1129
County: Suffolk FICE Identification: 002164
Unit ID: 167093
Telephone: (617) 266-2030 Carnegie Class: Spec-4-yr-Other Health
FAX Number: (617) 424-9202 Calendar System: Semester
URL: www.neco.edu
Established: 1894 Annual Undergrad Tuition & Fees: N/A
Enrollment: 527 Coed
Affiliation or Control: Independent Non-Profit IRS Status: 501(c)3
Highest Offering: Doctorate
Accreditation: EH, OPT, OPTR

01 President Dr. Howard B. PURCELL
125 President Emeritus Dr. Clifford SCOTT
05 Interim Dean of Academic Affairs Dr. Sandra MOHR
10 Sr VP Finance/Admin/CFO Ms. Traci LOGAN
32 Assoc Dean Students Ms. Barbara MCGINLEY
07 Director of Admissions Ms. Kristen TOBIN
37 Director Student Financial Aid Ms. Carol RUBEL
15 Exec Dir of Human Resources Ms. Elizabeth DAVIES
06 Registrar Ms. Glenda UNDERWOOD
08 Director of Library Services Ms. Heather EDMONDS
04 Executive Asst to the President Ms. Donna Marie FERRI

New England Conservatory of Music (B)

290 Huntington Avenue, Boston MA 02115-5018
County: Suffolk FICE Identification: 002194
Unit ID: 167057
Telephone: (617) 585-1100 Carnegie Class: Spec-4-yr-Arts
FAX Number: (617) 262-0500 Calendar System: Semester
URL: www.necmusic.edu
Established: 1867 Annual Undergrad Tuition & Fees: $48,750
Enrollment: 844 Coed
Affiliation or Control: Independent Non-Profit IRS Status: 501(c)3
Highest Offering: Doctorate
Accreditation: EH

01 President Ms. Andrea KALYN
05 Provost and Vice President Mr. Thomas NOVAK
10 Vice Pres for Finance Ms. Elizabeth DIONNE
111 Vice Pres Institutional Advancement Ms. Kathleen KELLY
26 Vice Pres Marketing/Communications Mr. Michael SARRA
11 Vice Pres Administration Ms. Kairyn RAINER
32 Dean of Students Mr. Nick TARTAR
07 Dean of Admissions and Fin Aid Mr. Alex POWELL
21 Controller Ms. Kristina MARTIN
18 Dir Facilities/Services/Operations Mr. Chris HAYDEN
06 Registrar/Dir of Inst Research Mr. Robert WINKLEY
08 Director of Libraries Mr. Alan KARASS
37 Associate Dean for Fin Aid Ms. Lauren URBANEK
39 Director Residence Life Vacant
29 Director of Alumni Relations Vacant
15 Director of Human Resources Mr. Nick MACKE
13 Director ITS Mr. Charles MEMBRINO
35 Sr Associate Dean of Students Ms. Rebecca TEETERS
88 Asst Dir of Student Life Ms. Robin SEARCY
38 Director of Counseling Ms. Squire PAIGE
23 Director of Health Services Ms. Leah MCKINNON-HOWE

New England Law | Boston (C)

154 Stuart Street, Boston MA 02116-5687
County: Suffolk FICE Identification: 008916
Unit ID: 167215
Telephone: (617) 451-0010 Carnegie Class: Spec-4-yr-Law
FAX Number: (617) 422-7333 Calendar System: Semester
URL: www.nesl.edu
Established: 1908 Annual Undergrad Tuition & Fees: N/A
Enrollment: 556 Coed
Affiliation or Control: Independent Non-Profit IRS Status: 501(c)3
Highest Offering: First Professional Degree
Accreditation: LAW

01 Dean/President Mr. John F. O'BRIEN
05 Associate Dean Ms. Judith GREENBERG
11 Associate Dean of Administration Ms. Susan S. CALAMARE
07 Director of Admission Ms. Michelle L'ETOILE
10 Chief Financial Officer Ms. Anne Marie MARTORANA
08 Int Director of the Law Library Ms. Kristin C. MCCARTHY
36 Director Career Services Ms. Mandie A. LEBEAU
37 Director of Financial Aid Mr. Eric A. KRUPSKI
06 Registrar Mr. David M. BERTI
18 Director of Facilities/Security Mr. Miguel ALVARADO
32 Director of Student Services Ms. Jacqueline PILGRIM
30 Dir of Development/Alumni Rels Ms. Jocelyn J. COLETTI

New England School of Acupuncture (D)

150 California Street, Newton MA 02458-1005
County: Middlesex FICE Identification: 025798
Telephone: (617) 558-1788 Carnegie Class: Spec-4-yr-Other Health
FAX Number: (617) 558-1789 Calendar System: Trimester
URL: www.nesa.edu
Established: 1975 Annual Undergrad Tuition & Fees: N/A
Enrollment: N/A Coed
Affiliation or Control: Independent Non-Profit IRS Status: 501(c)3
Highest Offering: Master's; No Lower Division
Accreditation: ACUP

01 Executive Director Susan L. GORMAN
05 Academic Dean Meredith ST. JOHN

† Affiliate of MCPHS University.

Nichols College (E)

Center Road, PO Box 5000, Dudley MA 01571-5000
County: Worcester FICE Identification: 002197
Unit ID: 167260
Telephone: (508) 213-1560 Carnegie Class: Spec-4-yr-Bus
FAX Number: N/A Calendar System: Semester
URL: www.nichols.edu
Established: 1815 Annual Undergrad Tuition & Fees: $35,000
Enrollment: 1,634 Coed
Affiliation or Control: Independent Non-Profit IRS Status: 501(c)3
Highest Offering: Master's
Accreditation: EH, COSMA, IACBE

01 President Susan WEST ENGELKEMEYER
05 Vice President for Academic Affairs Mauri S. PELTO
10 Exec Vice President Administration Michael J. STANTON
111 Vice President for Advancement William C. PIECZYNSKI
84 Vice President for Enrollment William BOFFI
32 Dean of Students Pamela J. BOGGIO
124 Assoc Dir of Enroll & Retention Katie MOULTON
13 Chief Information Officer Kevin F. BRASSARD
58 Exec Dir Graduate & Prof Studies Kerry CALNAN
04 Assistant to the President Lynn S. LOOBY
41 Interim Director of Athletics Eric GOBIEL
07 Asst Dean for Enrollment Paul O. BROWER
06 Registrar Betin ROBICHAUD
08 Director of Library Jim DOUGLAS
15 Director of Human Resources Darcy VANGEL
29 Director of Alumni Relations Molly THIENEL
21 Controller Jamie SKOWYRA
35 Dir Student Activities/Orientation Elizabeth GIONFRIDDO
36 Director of Career Services Elizabeth HORGAN
37 Director of Financial Aid Jennifer SHEEHY
38 Director Mental Health Services . Monica GOODRICH PELLETIER
27 Director of Public Relations Lorraine MARTINELLE
18 Assoc VP for Facilities Management Robert W. LAVIGNE
09 Dir of Inst Research & Reporting Emily REARDON
96 Director Procurement & Contract Svc Kay F. MORELLO
19 Director Public Safety Jack CAULFIELD
23 Director Health Services Katherine NICOLETTI
35 Assistant Dean of Students Marney BUSS
39 Director of Residence Life Amanda DESAI
104 Director Study Abroad Susan WAYMAN
105 Webmaster Dana ARMSTRONG
28 Associate Director of Diversity Tahkeya BLAKE

Northeastern University (F)

360 Huntington Avenue, Boston MA 02115-0195
County: Suffolk FICE Identification: 002199
Unit ID: 167358
Telephone: (617) 373-2000 Carnegie Class: DU-Highest
FAX Number: N/A Calendar System: Semester
URL: www.northeastern.edu
Established: 1898 Annual Undergrad Tuition & Fees: $51,522
Enrollment: 21,489 Coed
Affiliation or Control: Independent Non-Profit IRS Status: 501(c)3
Highest Offering: Doctorate
Accreditation: EH, ANEST, ARCPA, AUD, COPSY, COSMA, LAW, NURSE, PH, PHAR, PTA, SCPSY, SP, SPAA

01 President Dr. Joseph E. AOUN
03 Chancellor and SVP for Learning Mr. Ken HENDERSON
04 Exec Assistant to the President Ms. Susan CROMWELL
05 Sr VP Academic Affairs and Provost Dr. James C. BEAN
100 Chief of Staff & Counsel Mr. Nicholas BRADLEY
84 Sr VP Enroll Mgmt & CEO LLN Vacant
111 Sr VP University Advancement Ms. Diane N. MACGILLIVRAY
43 Sr VP and General Counsel Mr. Ralph C. MARTIN, II
26 Sr VP External Affairs Mr. Michael A. ARMINI
11 Sr VP & Chief Operating Officer Vacant
12 Seattle Campus Dean & CEO Mr. David THURMAN
12 Regional Dean & CEO Silicon Valley Vacant
12 Charlotte Campus Dean & CEO Dr. Cheryl RICHARDS
08 Vice Provost for Info Collaboration Dr. Dan COHEN
46 Sr Vice Prov Research Dr. David LUZZI
20 Sr Vice Prov Educ Innovation Dr. Susan AMBROSE
88 Sr Advisor Strategic Init Dr. Laura A. WANKEL
13 VP & CIO Mr. Cole CAMPLESE
88 VP Enrollment Management Mr. Sundar KUMARASAMY
32 Sr Vice Chancellor Student Affairs Ms. Madeleine A. ESTABROOK
30 VP Development Ms. Luanne KIRWIN
15 VP Human Resources Management Ms. Jane MOYER
18 VP Facilities Ms. Maria CIMILLUCA
86 VP Government Relations Mr. Tim E. LESHAN
110 VP Advancement & Campaign Director Mr. Joseph DONNELLY, JR.
31 VP City & Community Affairs Mr. John M. TOBIN
117 Director of Risk Services Ms. Sonya ROSS
45 VP & Chief Campus Planning and Dev . Ms. Kathy SPIEGELMAN
20 Sr Vice Provost Academic Affairs Ms. Debra FRANKO
114 Sr Vice Prov Budget/Planning/Admin Ms. Breean FORTIER
28 Vice Prov Inst Diversity & Inclsn Dr. John ARMENDARIZ
76 Dean Health Sciences Dr. Susan PARISH
37 Dean Student Financial Svcs Mr. Robert REDDY
36 Sr Assoc VP Employer Engagement Mr. Manny CONTOMANOLIS
88 V Provost & Deputy General Counsel Ms. Lisa SINCLAIR
58 Vice Provost Graduate Affairs Dr. Phil HE
21 VP of Finance Dr. Anthony RINI
88 AVP Research Administration Ms. Dana CARROLL
09 AVP Inst Rsrch & Data Admin Ms. Rana GLASGAL
06 Asst VP & University Registrar Ms. Linda D. ALLEN
27 VP Communications Ms. Renata NYUL
27 VP Marketing Ms. Rebecca ANZUONI
88 AVP International Advancement Mr. Robert DIETRICH
44 VP & Asst Treasurer Ms. Alysa GERLACH
92 Director University Honors Program Ms. Laurie KRAMER
42 Exec Dir Spirituality & Dialogue Mr. Alexander KERN
19 Director of Public Safety Mr. Michael DAVIS
41 Director of Athletics Mr. Jeffrey KONYA
10 Sr VP Finance & Treasurer Mr. Thomas NEDELL
77 Dean Khoury College of Computer Sci Dr. Carla E. BRODLEY
54 Interim Dean College of Engineering Dr. Jacqueline ISAACS
81 Interim Dean College of Science Dr. Michael POLLASTRI
50 Dean D'Amore-McKim School of Bus Dr. Raj ECHAMBADI
57 Dean College of Arts/Media/Design Dr. Elizabeth HUDSON
61 Dean School of Law Dr. James HACKNEY
83 Dean Col of Soc Sci & Humanities Dr. Uta POIGER
107 Dean Col Prof Studies Dr. Mary LOEFFELHOLZ
12 Dean Toronto Campus Ms. Aliza LAKHANI
106 COO Lifelong Learning Network Mr. Chris MALLETT
29 VP Alumni Relations Mr. Rick DAVIS
39 Assoc Dean Residence Life Mr. Robert JOSE

Northpoint Bible College (G)

320 South Main Street, Haverhill MA 01835
County: Essex FICE Identification: 035705
Unit ID: 217606
Telephone: (978) 478-3400 Carnegie Class: Spec-4-yr-Faith
FAX Number: (978) 478-3406 Calendar System: Semester
URL: www.northpoint.edu
Established: 1924 Annual Undergrad Tuition & Fees: $12,380
Enrollment: 365 Coed
Affiliation or Control: Assemblies Of God Church IRS Status: 501(c)3
Highest Offering: Master's
Accreditation: BI

01 President Rev Dr. David J. ARNETT
05 Academic Dean Rev Dr. Daniel HOWELL
32 Dean of Student Development Rev. Karen JACOB
10 Financial Services Manager Mrs. Carol RICCI
84 Dean of Enrollment Rev Dr. David MUNLEY
37 Director of Financial Aid Miss Patricia STAUFFER
06 Registrar Mrs. Amy MARANVILLE
13 Chief Info Technology Officer (CIO) Vacant

Pine Manor College (H)

400 Heath Street, Chestnut Hill MA 02467-2332
County: Norfolk FICE Identification: 002201
Unit ID: 167455
Telephone: (617) 731-7000 Carnegie Class: Bac-A&S
FAX Number: (617) 731-7199 Calendar System: Semester
URL: www.pmc.edu
Established: 1911 Annual Undergrad Tuition & Fees: $31,660
Enrollment: 450 Coed
Affiliation or Control: Independent Non-Profit IRS Status: 501(c)3
Highest Offering: Master's
Accreditation: EH

01 President Mr. Thomas O'REILLY
05 Dean of College Dr. Diane MELLO-GOLDNER
15 VP/Chief Human Resources Officer Ms. Shelley DROPKIN
111 VP of Advancement Ms. Janine DAILEY
32 Dean of Student Affairs Dr. Staci WEBER
84 Dean of Enrollment & Admissions Mr. Samuel WHITE
06 Registrar/Dir Inst Research Mr. Jeffrey MEI
26 Dir Publications/Media Relations Ms. Efrat ZINNAR-SHAVIT
08 Library Director Ms. MacKenzie DAVISON

Pope St. John XXIII National Seminary (A)

558 South Avenue, Weston MA 02493-2699
County: Middlesex FICE Identification: 002202
Unit ID: 167464
Telephone: (781) 899-5500 Carnegie Class: Spec-4-yr-Faith
FAX Number: (781) 899-9057 Calendar System: Semester
URL: www.psjs.edu
Established: 1964 Annual Graduate Tuition & Fees: N/A
Enrollment: 73 Male
Affiliation or Control: Roman Catholic IRS Status: 501(c)3
Highest Offering: Master's; No Undergraduates
Accreditation: THEOL

01 Rector and President .... Rev. Brian R. KIELY
03 Vice Rector .... Rev. Paul E. MICELI
05 Academic Dean .... Dr. Anthony KEATY
08 Librarian .... Mrs. Barbara NEEM
10 Business Manager .... Mrs. Kyle RYAN
06 Registrar .... Dr. Anthony KEATY
30 Chief Development Officer .... Mrs. Kate FOLAN
32 Chief Student Life Officer .... Rev. Stephen LINEHAN

Quincy College (B)

1250 Hancock Street, Quincy MA 02169-4324
County: Norfolk FICE Identification: 002205
Unit ID: 167525
Telephone: (617) 984-1700 Carnegie Class: Assoc/MT-VT-Mix Trad/Non
FAX Number: (617) 984-1779 Calendar System: Semester
URL: www.quincycollege.edu
Established: 1958 Annual Undergrad Tuition & Fees (In-District): $6,518
Enrollment: 5,343 Coed
Affiliation or Control: Local IRS Status: 501(c)3
Highest Offering: Associate Degree
Accreditation: EH, MLTAD, PTAA, SURGT

01 Acting President .... Michael G. BELLOTTI
05 Provost & SVP Academic Affairs .... Dr. Gerald P. KOOCHER
43 General Counsel .... Ms. Jessica CHERRY
04 Admin Asst to President .... Ms. Donna M. BRUGMAN
06 Dir of Student Records & Registrar .... Ms. Catherine MALONEY
66 Dean of Nursing .... Dr. Roxanne MIHAL
49 Dean of Liberal Arts .... Dr. Robert BAKER
107 Dean of Professional Programs .... Mr. William BRENNAN
81 Dean of Natural & Health Sciences .... Mr. Dennis BURKE
13 VP Technology & Mission Support .... Mr. Tom C. PHAM
37 Assoc VP for Financial Aid .... Ms. Rose M. DEVITO
10 VP of Finance .... Mr. Martin AHERN
18 Dir of Admin Services & Facilities .... Mr. William C. HALL
32 Assoc VP for Student Development .... Ms. Susan G. BOSSA
15 Director of Human Resources .... Ms. Elizabeth WALKER
26 Assoc VP of Comm & Marketing .... Mr. Taggart BOYLE
84 Director of Enrollment Management .... Mr. Craig RONDEAU
85 Director of Intl Student Services .... Ms. Lisa STACK
111 Director Institutional Advancement .... Ms. Tina CAHILL
09 AVP of Inst Research & Assessment .... Ms. Avanti SEYMOUR
35 Director of Student Development .... Ms. Amanda DECK
08 Director of Library Services .... Vacant
106 Dean Online Programs & Inst Affairs .... Mr. Daniel IBARRONDO
103 AVP Workforce Dev & Cmty Engagement .... Ms. Kate LOPCI

Regis College (C)

235 Wellesley Street, Weston MA 02493-1571
County: Middlesex FICE Identification: 002206
Unit ID: 167598
Telephone: (781) 768-7000 Carnegie Class: Spec-4-yr-Other Health
FAX Number: (781) 768-8339 Calendar System: Semester
URL: www.regiscollege.edu
Established: 1927 Annual Undergrad Tuition & Fees: $41,015
Enrollment: 2,166 Coed
Affiliation or Control: Independent Non-Profit IRS Status: 501(c)3
Highest Offering: Doctorate
Accreditation: EH, ADNUR, DMS, NMT, NUR, OT, RAD, SW

01 President .... Dr. Antoinette M. HAYS
10 Vice President Finance/Business .... Mr. Thomas G. PISTORINO
05 Vice President Academic Affairs .... Vacant
26 Vice President of Marketing & Comm .... Ms. Kelley TUTHILL
123 Vice President Grad Enrollment .... Ms. Kate SUTHERLAND
111 Vice Pres Inst Advancement .... Dr. Kimberly HOKANSON
109 AVP Auxiliary and Business Svcs .... Mr. Roger GOODE
28 AVP Inclusive Excellence/CDO .... Vacant
07 Dean of Undergraduate Admission .... Dr. Laura BERTONAZZI
37 Director of Financial Aid .... Ms. Tanya JEAN-FRANCOIS
06 Registrar .... Ms. Esther A. GHAZARIAN
09 Dean of Institutional Research .... Vacant
15 AVP of Human Resources .... Ms. Joan D. SULLIVAN
18 Director of Physical Plant .... Mr. Joseph SHAUGHNESSY
21 Director Finance & Business .... Ms. Nancy PLASKER
29 Director of Alumni Relations .... Ms. Molly ZUCCARINI
32 VP Student Affairs & UG Enrollment .... Dr. Kara KOLOMITZ
23 Director of Health Services .... Dr. Dianna JONES
08 Director of Library .... Ms. Jane PECK
13 Chief Information Officer .... Ms. Kate KORZENDORFER
41 Dean of Athletics .... Ms. Pamela ROECKER
42 Director Campus Ministry .... Mr. Daniel LEAHY
31 Director of Housing .... Ms. Bridget BUONICONTI
35 Director of Student Engagement .... Ms. Erica DEVINE
104 Director Study Abroad .... Mr. David CRISCI
19 Director of Campus Safety .... Vacant

Saint John's Seminary (D)

127 Lake Street, Brighton MA 02135-3898
County: Suffolk FICE Identification: 002214
Unit ID: 167677
Telephone: (617) 254-2610 Carnegie Class: Spec-4-yr-Faith
FAX Number: (617) 787-2336 Calendar System: Semester
URL: www.sjs.edu
Established: 1884 Annual Undergrad Tuition & Fees: $24,915
Enrollment: 178 Coed
Affiliation or Control: Roman Catholic IRS Status: 501(c)3
Highest Offering: Master's
Accreditation: EH, THEOL

01 Rector .... Msgr. James MORONEY
03 Vice Rector .... Rev. Christopher K. O'CONNOR
05 Dean of Faculty .... Prof. Paul METILLY
32 Dean of Students .... Rev. Edward RILEY
07 Director of Admissions & Records .... Mrs. Maureen DEBERNARDI
08 Librarian .... Rev. Raymond VAN DE MOORTELL
10 Director Finance and Operations .... Vacant
73 Director Pre-Theology Program .... Rev. David PIGNATO
21 Asst Finance Director .... Mr. Armand DILANDO
108 Executive Institutional Assessment .... Mr. Kieran KELLY
44 Director Annual or Planned Giving .... Ms. Sandra BARRY

Simmons University (E)

300 The Fenway, Boston MA 02115-5898
County: Suffolk FICE Identification: 002208
Unit ID: 167783
Telephone: (617) 521-2000 Carnegie Class: DU-Mod
FAX Number: (617) 521-3065 Calendar System: Semester
URL: www.simmons.edu
Established: 1899 Annual Undergrad Tuition & Fees: $40,850
Enrollment: 6,283 Coordinate
Affiliation or Control: Independent Non-Profit IRS Status: 501(c)3
Highest Offering: Doctorate
Accreditation: EH, DIETD, DIETI, LIB, NURSE, PTA, SW

01 President .... Helen G. DRINAN
04 Assistant to the President .... Marianne FIGUEIREDO
05 Provost .... Sheila (Katie) CONBOY
111 SVP Advancement .... Amy WHITE
10 Sr VP Finance/Administration .... Vacant
20 Deputy Provost .... Stefan KRUG
76 Dean Sch Nursing & Health Sciences .... Judy BEAL
50 Dean School of Management .... Patricia H. DEYTON
06 Asst VP Acad Operations & Registrar .... Vacant
08 Library Director .... Vivienne B. PIROLI
25 Director Sponsored Programs .... Jon KIMBALL
09 Director Institutional Research .... Lan GAO
36 Director Career Education Center .... Andrea WOLF
13 AVP Technology/CIO .... Debra ORR
123 Assistant VP Graduate Admissions .... Kristen HAACK
100 Chief of Staff .... Laura BRINK
42 Spiritual Life Program Manager .... Bonnie-Jeanne CASEY
38 Clinical Director Counseling Svcs .... Sherri ETTINGER
41 Director Athletics .... Ali KANTOR
32 Dean of Student Life .... Susan ANTONELLI
43 VP & General Counsel .... Kathleen R. ROGERS
15 Assistant VP Human Resources .... Vacant
28 Asst Vice President for Diversity .... Lisa SMITH-MCQUEENIE

Smith College (F)

Northampton MA 01063-0001
County: Hampshire FICE Identification: 002209
Unit ID: 167835
Telephone: (413) 584-2700 Carnegie Class: Bac-A&S
FAX Number: (413) 585-2123 Calendar System: Semester
URL: www.smith.edu
Established: 1871 Annual Undergrad Tuition & Fees: $52,404
Enrollment: 2,918 Female
Affiliation or Control: Independent Non-Profit IRS Status: 501(c)3
Highest Offering: Doctorate
Accreditation: EH, SW

01 President .... Kathleen MCCARTNEY
04 Executive Asst to the President .... Beth BERG
10 Interim Exec VP Finance & Admin .... David DESWERT
05 Provost/Dean of the Faculty .... Michael THURSTON
84 VP for Enrollment .... Audrey Y. SMITH
20 Assoc Provost Dean for Academic Dev .... Bill PETERSON
32 VP Campus Life/Dean College .... Susan ETHEREDGE
35 Dean of Students .... Julianne OHOTNICKY
70 Dean School for Social Work .... Marianne YOSHIOKA
39 Director of Residence Life .... Becky SHAW
85 Assoc Dean International Students .... Caitlin B. SZYMKOWICZ
30 VP for Development .... Beth RAFFELD
38 Director of Health and Wellness .... Pamela MCCARTHY
26 VP for Public Affairs .... Laurie FENLASON
13 VP Information Technology .... Samantha EARP
09 AVP Analytics & Inst Research .... Cate ROWEN
08 Dean of Libraries .... Susan FLISS
15 Assoc VP for Human Resources .... Vacant
07 Dean of Admission .... Deanna DIXON
37 Dir Student Financial Services .... David J. BELANGER
06 Registrar .... Gretchen B. HERRINGER
36 Director Career Development Office .... Stacie HAGENBAUGH
22 Vice President for Equity/Inclusion .... Floyd CHEUNG
20 Assoc Dean of Faculty/Academic Dev .... Patricia DIBARTOLO
18 Assoc VP for Facilities Management .... Vacant
41 Director of Athletics .... Kristin HUGHES
42 Dir of Religious/Spiritual Life .... Matilda CANTWELL
104 Dean for International Study .... Rebecca HOVEY
101 Secretary Board of Trustees/College .... Elena PALLADINO
21 AVP for Finance .... David DESWERT
100 Chief of Staff .... Joanna OLIN

Springfield College (G)

263 Alden Street, Springfield MA 01109-3797
County: Hampden FICE Identification: 002211
Unit ID: 167899
Telephone: (413) 748-3000 Carnegie Class: Masters/L
FAX Number: N/A Calendar System: Semester
URL: www.springfieldcollege.edu
Established: 1885 Annual Undergrad Tuition & Fees: $37,444
Enrollment: 3,246 Coed
Affiliation or Control: Independent Non-Profit IRS Status: 501(c)3
Highest Offering: Doctorate
Accreditation: EH, ARCPA, CAATE, CACREP, COPSY, EMT, EXSC, IACBE, NRPA, OT, PTA, SW

01 President .... Dr. Mary-Beth A. COOPER
05 Provost & VP Academic Affairs .... Dr. Martha POTVIN
111 VP Institutional Advancement .... Dr. Kathleen MARTIN
10 VP for Finance & Admin .... Mr. John MAILHOT
32 VP for Student Affairs .... Dr. Patrick LOVE
43 VP & General Counsel .... Vacant
28 VP for Inclusion & Com Engagement .... Dr. Calvin R. HILL
26 Vice President of Communications .... Mr. Stephen ROULIER
20 Assoc VP Academic Affairs .... Dr. Mary Ann COUGHLIN
20 AVP Grad Ed/Grants/Sponsored Rsrch .... Dr. James HARNSBERGER
15 Director of Human Resources .... Mr. Jonathan HOWELL
30 Sr Assoc VP/Dir of Development .... Ms. Julie TYSON
84 VP of Enrollment Management .... Mr. Stuart JONES
06 Registrar .... Mr. Keith INGALLS
08 Director of Library .... Ms. Andrea S. TAUPIER
29 Director of Alumni Relations .... Ms. Tamie KIDESS LUCEY
37 Director of Financial Aid .... Mr. Troy DAVIS
36 Director of Career Center .... Mr. Scott DRANKA
13 Chief Information Officer .... Ms. Gayle BARTON
90 Director of Network Systems .... Mr. Nadim EL-KHOURY
38 Director of Counseling Center .... Mr. Brian KRYLOWICZ
19 Exec Dir Public Safety/Chief .... Ms. Karen LEARY
85 Director of International Center .... Dr. Deborah ALM
42 Director Campus Ministry .... Mr. David MCMAHON
18 Int Dir of Facilities & Campus Svc .... Mr. Kevin ROY
41 Executive Director of Athletics .... Dr. Craig POISSON
96 Director of Purchasing .... Ms. Lita ADAMS
09 Director of Institutional Research .... Dr. Raldy LAGUILLES
102 Exec Dir Corporate Partnerships .... Mr. John WHITE
39 Director Housing & Residence Life .... Mr. Robert YANEZ
44 Senior Director Annual Giving .... Mr. Jay ANDRONACO

Stonehill College (H)

320 Washington Street, Easton MA 02357-6110
County: Bristol FICE Identification: 002217
Unit ID: 167996
Telephone: (508) 565-1000 Carnegie Class: Bac-A&S
FAX Number: (508) 565-1500 Calendar System: Semester
URL: www.stonehill.edu
Established: 1948 Annual Undergrad Tuition & Fees: $42,746
Enrollment: 2,498 Coed
Affiliation or Control: Roman Catholic IRS Status: 501(c)3
Highest Offering: Master's
Accreditation: EH

01 President .... Rev. John F. DENNING, CSC
100 Chief of Staff .... Mrs. Heather L. HEERMAN
05 Int Provost/VP for Academic Affairs .... Dr. Molly SMITH
10 Vice Pres for Finance & Treasurer .... Ms. Jeanne FINLAYSON
111 Vice President for Advancement .... Mr. Doug SMITH
32 Vice President of Student Affairs .... Ms. Pauline DOBROWSKI
21 AVP for Finance & Operations .... Mr. Craig BINNEY
35 Assoc VP for Student Affairs .... Mr. Kevin PISKADLO
37 Asst VP/Dir of Student Aid/Finance .... Mr. William C. SMITH
04 Sr Executive Asst to the President .... Mrs. Jessica L. GRACIA
20 Assoc Prov Div/Fac/Dev/Assessment .... Dr. Maria CURTIN
121 Assoc Prov for Academic Achievement .... Dr. Craig KELLEY
43 Vice President and General Counsel .... Mr. Thomas V. FLYNN
21 Controller .... Ms. Jennifer MATHEWS
84 Vice Pres for Enrollment Management .... Mr. Joe DACEY
06 Registrar .... Rev. Jeffrey L. ALLISON, CSC
09 Dir of Inst Research/Assessment .... Mr. Brian M. OLES
08 Interim Director of College Library .... Ms. Jennifer M. MACAULAY
26 Dir of Media Rels & Communications .... Mr. Martin P. MCGOVERN
29 Director of Alumni Affairs .... Ms. Anne M. SANT
15 Director of Human Resources .... Mrs. Lily A. KRENTZMAN
38 Dir of Counseling & Testing Center .... Ms. Maria A. KAVANAUGH
13 Chief Information Officer .... Ms. Tamara ANDERSON
19 Chief of Police .... Mr. David G. WORDELL
42 Director Campus Ministry .... Rev. Anthony SZAKALY, CSC
90 Manager of Instructional Technology .... Ms. Janice HARRISON
45 Director of Academic Development .... Ms. Bonnie L. TROUPE
88 Dir of Enterprise Infrastructure .... Mr. Thomas MCGRATH

23 Director of Health Services .... Mrs. Maria SULLIVAN
36 Director of Career Services .... Mrs. Christina M. BURNEY
41 Dir of Intercollegiate Athletics .... Mr. Dean R. O'KEEFE
92 Director of Honors Program .... Prof. Allyson SHECKLER
20 Int Dir Academic Services/Advising .... Mr. Zachariah D. BROWN
96 Director of Purchasing .... Mr. Gregory WOLFE
45 Asst VP for Planning & Budgeting .... Mr. Stephen BEAUREGARD
39 Director of Residence Life .... Ms. Kristen PIERCE
24 Dir of Media/Videography Services ...... Mr. Michael PIETROWSKI
40 Manager of College Bookstore .... Mrs. Mary DUNCKLEE
97 Asst Dean Gen Educ/Acad Achievement .... Dr. Todd S. GERNES
18 Director of Facilities Management .... Mr. Bruce BOYER
104 Director International Programs .... Ms. Aliki E. KARAGIANNIS
31 Campus Minister Svc Immersion Pgm .... Ms. Mary Anne CAPPELLERI
28 Director of Intercultural Affairs .... Ms. Latesha FUSSEL
49 Dean School of Arts and Sciences .... Dr. Peter N. UBERTACCIO
50 Dean of the School of Business .... Ms. Debra SALVUCCI
123 Dean of Graduate Admissions .... Ms. Melissa RATLIFF
102 Dir of Corp/Foundation & Donor Rels .... Mrs. Marie C. KELLY
07 Dean of Undergraduate Admissions .... Mr. Scott SESESKE

Suffolk University (A)

8 Ashburton Place, Boston MA 02108-2770
County: Suffolk FICE Identification: 002218
Unit ID: 168005
Telephone: (617) 573-8000 Carnegie Class: Masters/L
FAX Number: (617) 573-8353 Calendar System: Semester
URL: www.suffolk.edu
Established: 1906 Annual Undergrad Tuition & Fees: $38,566
Enrollment: 7,201 Coed
Affiliation or Control: Independent Non-Profit IRS Status: 501(c)3
Highest Offering: Doctorate
Accreditation: EH, ART, CIDA, CLPSY, HSA, IPSY, LAW, RADDOS, RTT, SPAA

01 President .... Dr. Marisa KELLY
05 Acting Provost .... Dr. Sebastian ROYO
10 Sr VP Finance/Admin/Treasurer .... Ms. Laura SANDER
30 Sr Vice Pres for Advancement .... Mr. Colm RENEHAN
09 AVP Inst Research & Assessment .... Dr. Gary FIREMAN
84 Dean of Admissions & Financial Aid ...... Ms. Donna GRAND PRE
26 VP Communications .... Mr. Greg GATLIN
86 Sr VP External Affairs .... Mr. John A. NUCCI
37 AVP/Dir of Financial Aid .... Ms. Jennifer H. RICCIARDI
32 AVP/Dean of Students .... Dr. Ann C. COYNE
06 AVP/University Registrar .... Ms. Mary LALLY
100 Chief Human Resources Officer .... Ms. Katherine WHIDDEN
28 VP Diversity/Access & Inclusion .... Ms. Joyya SMITH
13 Chief Information Officer .... Mr. Thomas LYNCH, III
43 General Counsel .... Mr. Thomas DORER
49 Dean College Arts & Science .... Dr. Maria TOYADA
61 Dean of the Law School .... Mr. Andrew PERLMAN
50 Dean Sawyer Business School .... Mr. William J. O'NEILL, JR.
88 Asst Dean for Acad Svcs Law School .... Ms. Lorraine D. COVE
19 Chief University Police .... Mr. Gerard COLETTA
04 Admin Assistant to the President .... Ms. Valerie VENTURE
25 Chief Contract/Grants Administrator .... Mr. Michael MULLAHY
44 Director Annual Giving .... Mr. John IRVIN
07 Director Undergraduate Admission .... Ms. Lark KRAJESKI
123 Director Graduate Admission .... Ms. Heather O'LEARY
29 Director Alumni Affairs/Law School .... Ms. Caitlin HAUGHEY
08 Director Law Library .... Mr. Richard BUCKINGHAM
08 Acting Director of Sawyer Library .... Ms. Sarah GRIFFIS
36 Exec Dir Career Development Center .... Vacant
41 Director of Athletics .... Mr. Cary MCCONNELL
39 Director Residence Life .... Mr. Shigeo IWAMIYA
38 Director of Health and Wellness .... Dr. Jean M. JOYCE-BRADY
35 Dir Student Ldrship & Involvement .... Mr. Dave DEANGELIS
96 Business Manager .... Mr. John KINEAVY
18 Director Construction Services .... Mr. Andre VEGA
104 Director Study Abroad .... Mr. Gregory JABAUT
106 Dean Online Education/E-learning .... Ms. Tracey RILEY

Tufts University (B)

419 Boston Avenue, Medford MA 02155
County: Middlesex FICE Identification: 002219
Unit ID: 168148
Telephone: (617) 628-5000 Carnegie Class: DU-Highest
FAX Number: N/A Calendar System: Semester
URL: www.tufts.edu
Established: 1852 Annual Undergrad Tuition & Fees: $56,382
Enrollment: 11,449 Coed
Affiliation or Control: Independent Non-Profit IRS Status: 501(c)3
Highest Offering: Doctorate
Accreditation: EH, ARCPA, ART, DENT, MED, OT, PH, PLNG, VET

01 President .... Dr. Anthony P. MONACO
100 Chief of Staff .... Mr. Michael BAENEN
03 Executive Vice President .... Mr. Michael HOWARD
05 Provost & Senior VP .... Ms. Nadine AUBRY
43 SVP Univ Relations & Gen Counsel .... Ms. Mary R. JEKA
111 SVP University Advancement .... Mr. Eric C. JOHNSON
11 Vice President for Operations .... Ms. Barbara STEIN
10 Vice President Finance/Treasurer .... Mr. Thomas S. MCGURTY
15 VP for Human Resources .... Mr. Julien C. CARTER
26 VP Communications/Marketing .... Mr. Michael RODMAN
20 Vice Provost .... Mr. Kevin DUNN
46 Associate Provost & Sr Intl Officer .... Ms. Diana CHIGAS
09 Associate Provost .... Dr. Dawn G. TERKLA
21 Administrative Associate Provost .... Ms. Celia K. CAMPBELL
110 Exec Dir University Advancement .... Ms. Margot BIGGIN
28 Assoc Prov/Chief Diversity Officer .... Dr. Joyce A. SACKEY
28 Assoc Prov/Chief Diversity Officer .... Mr. Rob MACK
23 Exec Director Health & Wellness .... Ms. Michelle D. BOWDLER
37 Director of Financial Aid .... Ms. Patricia REILLY
27 Executive Director Public Relations .... Mr. Patrick COLLINS
36 Executive Director Career Center .... Mr. Gregory J. VICTORY
08 Director Tisch Library .... Ms. Dorothy MEANEY
22 Exec Director Equal Opportunity .... Ms. Jill A. ZELLMER
38 Director Mental Health Services .... Dr. Julie S. ROSS
19 Executive Director Public Safety .... Mr. Kevin C. MAGUIRE
49 Dean Arts & Sciences .... Mr. James GLASER
54 Dean of Engineering .... Dr. Jianmin QU
60 Dean SMFA .... Ms. Nancy BAUER
58 Dean Grad School of A&S .... Mr. Robert G. COOK
61 Int Dean School of Law/Diplomacy .... Mr. Ian JOHNSTONE
52 Dean of Dental Medicine .... Dr. Nadeem KARIMBUX
74 Interim Dean Cummings Sch .... Dr. Alastair CRIBB
63 Dean Medical School .... Dr. Harris BERMAN
88 Dean Sackler School .... Dr. Daniel JAY
88 Dean Friedman School .... Dr. Dariush MOZAFFARIAN
88 Dean Tisch College .... Mr. Alan SOLOMONT
88 Dean Academic Adv & Undergrad Study .... Dr. Carmen LOWE
32 Dean of Student Affairs .... Vacant
07 Dean of Admissions/Enroll Mgmt .... Vacant
96 Sr Dir Purchasing & Strat Sourcing .... Mr. John HOMICH
41 Director Athletics .... Mr. John MORRIS
42 University Chaplain .... Rev. Gregory MCGONIGLE
102 Sr Dir Corp & Foundation Relations .... Ms. Ippolita A. CANTUTI-CASTELVETRI
104 Sr Dir Study Abroad/Global Educ .... Ms. Melanie Mala GHOSH
39 Director Res Life & Learning .... Mr. Joshua HARTMAN
112 Senior Director Gift Planning .... Ms. Brooke ANDERSON
31 Director Community Relations .... Mr. Rocco DIRICO
18 Senior Facilities Director .... Mr. Cory POULIOT

Urban College of Boston (C)

2 Boylston St, Boston MA 02116
County: Suffolk FICE Identification: 031305
Unit ID: 429128
Telephone: (617) 449-7070 Carnegie Class: Spec 2-yr-Other
FAX Number: (617) 830-3137 Calendar System: Semester
URL: www.urbancollege.edu
Established: 1993 Annual Undergrad Tuition & Fees: $7,124
Enrollment: 812 Coed
Affiliation or Control: Independent Non-Profit IRS Status: 501(c)3
Highest Offering: Associate Degree
Accreditation: EH

01 President .... Mr. Michael TAYLOR
05 Chief Academic Officer .... Ms. Clea ANDREADIS
06 Registrar .... Ms. Jasjot KAUR
84 Dean Enrollment Svcs .... Dr. Allison MATTHEWS
32 Dean of Students/Dir Student Affs .... Ms. Carmen PINEDA
37 Director of Financial Aid .... Ms. Mia TAYLOR
11 Director Operations and Finance .... Ms. Kathleen BARDELL
30 Director of Development .... Ms. Caitlin CALLAHAN
10 Chief Financial/Business Officer .... Ms. Mimoza VREKA

Wellesley College (D)

106 Central Street, Wellesley MA 02481-8203
County: Norfolk FICE Identification: 002224
Unit ID: 168218
Telephone: (781) 283-1000 Carnegie Class: Bac-A&S
FAX Number: (781) 283-3639 Calendar System: Semester
URL: www.wellesley.edu
Established: 1875 Annual Undergrad Tuition & Fees: $53,732
Enrollment: 2,508 Female
Affiliation or Control: Independent Non-Profit IRS Status: 501(c)3
Highest Offering: Baccalaureate
Accreditation: EH

01 President .... Paula A. JOHNSON
05 Provost & Dean of the College .... Andrew SHENNAN
30 VP for Resources & Public Affairs .... Mary CASEY
10 VP Finance Administration/Treasurer .... Piper ORTON
32 Vice Pres/Dean of Students .... Sheilah SHAW HORTON
18 Asst VP Facilities Management/Plng .... David CHAKRABORTY
15 Asst VP/Director Human Resources/EO .... Carolyn SLABODEN
13 Chief Information Officer .... Elizabeth GILDERSLEEVE
07 Dean of Admission/Financial Aid .... Joy ST. JOHN
42 Dean Religious/Spiritual Life .... Vacant
20 Dean of Academic Affairs .... Ann VELENCHIK
20 Dean of Faculty Affairs .... Ruth FROMMER
09 Assc Provost Institutional Planning .... Pamela L. TAYLOR
28 Assc Prov/Acad Dir Dvrsty/Inclusion .... Vacant
06 Registrar .... Carol SHANMUGARATNAM
29 Executive Director Alumnae Assn .... Missy SHEA
37 Director of Student Financial Svcs .... Kari DIFONZO
36 Assoc Prov/Dir Exec Ctr Work/Svc .... Vacant
26 Chief Public Relations Officer .... Tara MURPHY
35 Assoc Director Student Involvement .... Abigail STEVENSON
38 Administrative Counseling Svcs .... Robin COOK-NOBLES
101 Clerk Board of Trustees .... Marianne B. COOLEY
96 Purchasing Manager .... Tina M. DOLAN

Wentworth Institute of Technology (E)

550 Huntington Avenue, Boston MA 02115-5998
County: Suffolk FICE Identification: 002225
Unit ID: 168227
Telephone: (617) 989-4590 Carnegie Class: Masters/M
FAX Number: (617) 989-4591 Calendar System: Semester
URL: www.wit.edu
Established: 1904 Annual Undergrad Tuition & Fees: $33,950
Enrollment: 4,457 Coed
Affiliation or Control: Independent Non-Profit IRS Status: 501(c)3
Highest Offering: Master's
Accreditation: EH, ART, CIDA, CONST, IACBE

01 President .... Dr. Mark THOMPSON
100 VP of Exec Affairs/Chief of Staff .... Ms. Amy INTILLE
05 Sr Vice Pres of Academic Affairs .... Vacant
10 Vice President Finance .... Mr. Robert TOTINO
11 Vice President Business .... Mr. David A. WAHLSTROM
111 Vice Pres Institutional Advancement .... Ms. Paula SAKEY
84 VP Enrollment Management .... Ms. Keiko BROOMHEAD
15 Vice Pres Human Resources .... Ms. Linda SHINOMOTO
13 Vice Pres Technology Svcs/CIO .... Mr. Vish PARADKAR
88 Exec Asst to the Chief of Staff .... Ms. Rebecca COAKLEY
20 Assoc Provost .... Vacant
32 VP Student Affairs/Dean of Stdnts .... Ms. Annamaria WENNER
21 Assoc Vice President Finance .... Mr. David GILMORE
88 Assoc VP of Enrollment Management .... Ms. Dianne PLUMMER
31 Assoc VP Community Affairs .... Ms. Sandra E. PASCAL
14 Assoc VP Information Technology .... Vacant
88 AVP Innovation & Entrepreneurship .... Ms. Monique FUCHS
20 Director Acad Operations .... Ms. Kelly PARRISH
51 Dean of College of Prof & Cont Educ .... Ms. Deborah WRIGHT
07 Executive Director of Admissions .... Ms. Maureen DISCHINO
06 Registrar .... Ms. Joan ROMANO
08 Director of Library .... Mr. Kevin KIDD
113 Dir Student Financial Services .... Ms. Patricia OSGOOD
41 Director of Athletics .... Ms. Cheryl AARON
18 Associate VP Physical Facilities .... Mr. Bob BURNS
26 Chief Marketing Officer .... Ms. Michelle DAVIS
35 Assoc Vice President of Students .... Mr. Peter FOWLER
102 Dir Corp Foundation/Govt Rels .... Ms. Lori FRIEDMAN
37 Director Financial Aid .... Ms. Anne-Marie CARUSO
38 Director of Counseling .... Ms. Maura MULLIGAN
19 Director of Public Safety .... Mr. William POWERS
88 Associate Athletic Director .... Mr. William P. GORMAN
36 Dir Of Cooperative Educ/Career Svcs ... Ms. Robbin BEAUCHAMP
39 Director Housing & Residential Life .... Mr. Philip BERNARD
96 Director of Purchasing .... Vacant
09 Research and Assessment Associate .... Vacant
49 Dean for Arts & Sciences .... Dr. Patrick HAFFORD
48 Dean for Arch/Design & Const Mgmt ..... Dr. Charles HOTCHKISS
54 Dean for Engineering & Technology .... Mr. Frederick DRISCOLL
18 Director of Physical Plant .... Mr. Robert FERRO
35 Director Office of Campus Life .... Ms. Carissa DURFEE
108 Director of Institutional Effective .... Ms. Cidhinnia TORRES CAMPOS

Western New England University (F)

1215 Wilbraham Road, Springfield MA 01119-2684
County: Hampden FICE Identification: 002226
Unit ID: 168254
Telephone: (413) 782-3111 Carnegie Class: DU-Mod
FAX Number: (413) 782-1746 Calendar System: Semester
URL: www.wne.edu
Established: 1919 Annual Undergrad Tuition & Fees: $36,804
Enrollment: 3,776 Coed
Affiliation or Control: Independent Non-Profit IRS Status: 501(c)3
Highest Offering: Doctorate
Accreditation: EH, COSMA, LAW, PHAR, SW

01 President .... Dr. Anthony S. CAPRIO
04 Executive Asst to President .... Ms. Robin SAVITT-KING
05 Provost/Vice Pres Academic Affairs .... Dr. Linda E. JONES
26 Assoc VP for Media/Comm Relations .... Mrs. Barbara A. MOFFAT
10 Vice Pres Finance & Administration .... Dr. Richard WAGNER
84 VP Enrollment Mgmt/Marketing .... Mr. Bryan J. GROSS
32 VP Student Affairs/Dean of Students .... Dr. Jeanne S. HART-STEFFES
111 Vice President Advancement .... Ms. Beverly J. DWIGHT
13 Asst Vice Pres Information Tech .... Mr. Scott J. COOPEE
15 Asst VP & Dir of Human Resources .... Ms. Joanne OLLSON
61 Dean of the School of Law .... Prof. Sudha SETTY
67 Dean of the College of Pharmacy .... Dr. Evan ROBINSON
49 Dean College of Arts & Sciences .... Dr. Saeed GHAHRAMANI
50 Dean of the College of Business .... Dr. Sharianne WALKER
54 Dean of the College of Engineering ...... Dr. S. Hossein CHERAGHI
89 Dean First Year/Transfer Students .... Ms. Kerri P. JARZABSKI
08 Assoc Dean Law Library/Info Res .... Ms. Patricia NEWCOMBE
39 Asst Dean of Students and Res Life .... Mr. Jerry ROEDER
28 Asst Dean of Diversity Programs .... Mrs. Yvonne BOGLE
06 Registrar-Law .... Ms. Terese CHENIER
37 Director of Financial Aid .... Ms. Kathleen CHAMBERS
41 Director of Athletics .... Mr. Matthew LABRANCHE
36 Director Career Development Center .... Ms. Andrea ST. JAMES
38 Director of Counseling Services .... Dr. Wayne D. CARPENTER
08 Director of D'Amour Library .... Mrs. Priscilla L. PERKINS
23 Director of Health Services .... Mrs. Kathleen A. REID
18 Director of Facilities Management .... Mr. C. Michael DUNCAN
90 Dir Educational Technology Center .... Mr. Steven NARMONTAS
91 Dir of Administrative Info Systems .... Mr. Anthony MUTTI
29 Director of Alumni Engagement .... Ms. Katie DEBEER
25 Director of Grants .... Mr. Matthew VANHEYNIGEN
42 Spiritual Life Coordinator .... Ms. Sheila HANIFIN
19 Director of Public Safety .... Mr. Adam WOODROW
11 Director Administrative Services .... Ms. Arlene M. ROCK
07 Dir of Undergraduate Admissions .... Mr. Christopher WYSTEPEK
123 Director of Graduate Admissions .... Mr. Matthew FOX
20 Academic Scheduling Controller .... Dr. Linda M. CHOJNICKI

09 Director Inst Research & Planning .... Mrs. Mary GREY
43 General Counsel .... Ms. Cheryl SMITH

Wheaton College (A)

26 E Main Street, Norton MA 02766-2322
County: Bristol FICE Identification: 002227
Unit ID: 168281
Telephone: (508) 286-8200 Carnegie Class: Bac-A&S
FAX Number: (508) 286-8270 Calendar System: Semester
URL: www.wheatoncollege.edu
Established: 1834 Annual Undergrad Tuition & Fees: $52,626
Enrollment: 1,688 Coed
Affiliation or Control: Independent Non-Profit IRS Status: 501(c)3
Highest Offering: Baccalaureate
Accreditation: EH

01 President .... Dr. Dennis HANNO
05 Provost .... Dr. Renée T. WHITE
10 Exec VP Finance & Administration .... Mr. Brian DOUGLAS
111 Vice President College Advancement .... Ms. Merritt CROWLEY
84 VP of Enrollment .... Mr. Walter CAFFEY
32 VP Student Affairs/Dean of Students .... Ms. Kate E. MCCAFFREY
26 VP Marketing and Communications .... Mr. Gene P. BEGIN
37 Director of Stdnt Financial Svcs .... Ms. Susan BEARD
15 Asst VP Human Resources .... Ms. Omaira ROY
18 Asst VP Business Svcs/Phys Plant .... Mr. John M. SULLIVAN
26 Assistant VP for Communications .... Mr. Michael GRACA
13 Assistant VP Info Tech Services .... Mr. Joe LACASCIO
121 Executive Dean of Student Success .... Dr. Andrew BRERETON
06 Registrar/Dean Academic Systems .... Ms. Sally BUCKLEY
104 Dean Center for Global Education .... Ms. Gretchen YOUNG
29 Director Alumni Relations .... Ms. Courtney SHURTLEFF
44 Director Annual Fund .... Ms. Amy LAPREY
102 Dir Corporate & Foundation Rels .... Ms. Patricia DEMARCO
38 Director Counseling Center .... Ms. Valerie TOBIA
07 Director of Admission .... Ms. Judy PURDY
09 Director of Institutional Research .... Dr. Kimberly PUHALA
39 Director Stdnt Life/Housing .... Mr. Edward T. BURNETT
19 Director Public Safety .... Vacant
41 Director of Athletics & Recreation .... Vacant
14 Dir Information Tech Services .... Ms. Regina CARVELL
36 Director of Career Services .... Ms. Lisa GAVIGAN
101 Asst to President/Sec Brd Trustees .... Ms. Kelsey ANDRADE
04 Executive Asst to President .... Ms. Pam VAZ

William James College (B)

1 Wells Avenue, Newton MA 02459-3211
County: Middlesex FICE Identification: 021636
Unit ID: 166717
Telephone: (617) 327-6777 Carnegie Class: Spec-4-yr-Other Health
FAX Number: (617) 327-4447 Calendar System: Semester
URL: www.williamjames.edu
Established: 1974 Annual Graduate Tuition & Fees: N/A
Enrollment: 748 Coed
Affiliation or Control: Independent Non-Profit IRS Status: 501(c)3
Highest Offering: Doctorate; No Undergraduates
Accreditation: EH, CLPSY, IPSY, SCPSY

01 President .... Dr. Nicholas COVINO
04 Executive Asst to the President .... Ms. Lilly MANOLIS
05 Vice Pres Academic Affairs .... Dr. Stacey LAMBERT
10 VP Finance & Operations .... Mr. Daniel BRENT
111 Vice Pres Institutional Advancement .... Mr. Robert WHITTAKER
46 Assoc VP for Research .... Dr. Edward DEVOS
37 Director Financial Aid .... Ms. Hilary BAXTER
06 Registrar .... Ms. Sonji PAIGE
32 Dean of Students .... Mr. Josh COOPER
07 Director of Admissions .... Mr. Mario MURGA
51 Director Continuing Prof Education .... Mr. Dean ABBY
26 Director of Marketing/Communication .... Mrs. Katie O'HARE
13 Dir Information Technology .... Mr. Jeff CHOO
08 Head Librarian .... Ms. Julia CLEMENT
15 Human Resource Director .... Mrs. Ellen COLLINS
18 Facilities Manager .... Mr. Kevin COSTELLO
29 Director Alumni Relations .... Mr. Scott FRATZ

† Formerly Massachusetts School of Professional Psychology

Williams College (C)

880 Main Street, Williamstown MA 01267
County: Berkshire FICE Identification: 002229
Unit ID: 168342
Telephone: (413) 597-3131 Carnegie Class: Bac-A&S
FAX Number: N/A Calendar System: 4/1/4
URL: www.williams.edu
Established: 1793 Annual Undergrad Tuition & Fees: $55,450
Enrollment: 2,134 Coed
Affiliation or Control: Independent Non-Profit IRS Status: 501(c)3
Highest Offering: Master's
Accreditation: EH

01 President .... Maud S. MANDEL
05 Provost .... David LOVE
20 Dean of the Faculty .... Denise BUELL
10 VP for Fin & Admin and Treasurer .... Frederick W. PUDDESTER
32 Vice President for Campus Life .... Stephen P. KLASS
28 VP for Inst Diversity & Equity .... Leticia HAYNES
111 VP for College Relations .... Megan MOREY
26 Chief Communications Officer .... Jim REISCHE
04 Asst to Pres/Secretary of the Col .... Keli A. GAIL
20 Dean of the College .... Marlene J. SANDSTROM
18 Exec Director Facilities Management .... Robert F. WRIGHT
06 Registrar .... Kath KILVENTON
07 Director of Admission .... Sulgi LIM
37 Director of Financial Aid .... Ashley BIANCHI
08 Director of Libraries .... Jonathan MILLER
21 Controller .... Susan S. HOGAN
29 Director Alumni Relations .... Brooks L. FOEHL
15 Director of Human Resources .... Danielle GONZALEZ
36 Director of Career Center .... Donald J. KJELLEREN
109 Director of Dining Services .... Temesgen ARAYA
13 Chief Technology Officer .... Barron KORALESKY
09 Director of Institutional Research .... Courtney WADE
23 Director Integrative Wellbeing Svc .... Wendy ADAM
35 Director Office of Student Life .... Douglas J. SCHIAZZA
41 Director of Athletics/PE .... Lisa M. MELENDY
42 Chaplain .... Valerie BAILEY FISCHER

Woods Hole Oceanographic Institution (D)

266 Woods Hole Road, Woods Hole MA 02543-1535
County: Barnstable FICE Identification: 002230
Telephone: (508) 548-1400 Carnegie Class: Not Classified
FAX Number: N/A Calendar System: 4/1/4
URL: www.whoi.edu
Established: 1930 Annual Graduate Tuition & Fees: N/A
Enrollment: N/A Coed
Affiliation or Control: Independent Non-Profit IRS Status: 501(c)3
Highest Offering: Doctorate; No Undergraduates
Accreditation: EH

01 President and Director .... Dr. Mark R. ABBOTT
09 Deputy Dir/VP for Research .... Dr. Rick MURRAY
05 VP of Academic Programs and Dean .... Dr. Margaret K. TIVEY
10 VP of Operations/CFO .... Mr. Jeffrey FERNANDEZ
18 VP Marine Facilities/Operations .... Mr. Robert MUNIER
43 VP Legal Affairs/General Counsel .... Mr. Christopher LAND
111 Vice Prov Advance/Chief Mktg Ofcr .... Mr. Samuel HARP
20 Associate Dean .... Dr. Delia W. OPPO
06 Registrar .... Ms. Julia WESTWATER
08 Library Co-Director .... Ms. Lisa RAYMOND

Worcester Polytechnic Institute (E)

100 Institute Road, Worcester MA 01609-2280
County: Worcester FICE Identification: 002233
Unit ID: 168421
Telephone: (508) 831-5000 Carnegie Class: DU-Higher
FAX Number: (508) 831-5753 Calendar System: Semester
URL: www.wpi.edu
Established: 1865 Annual Undergrad Tuition & Fees: $50,530
Enrollment: 6,642 Coed
Affiliation or Control: Independent Non-Profit IRS Status: 501(c)3
Highest Offering: Doctorate
Accreditation: EH

01 President .... Dr. Laurie LESHIN
05 Interim Provost .... Dr. Winston SOBOYEJO
10 Executive Vice President & CFO .... Mr. Jeffrey S. SOLOMON
84 Senior Vice President Enrollment .... Ms. Kristin R. TICHENOR
30 VP for University Advancement .... Mr. William J. MCAVOY
26 AVP/Chief Marketing Officer .... Ms. Maureen DEIANA
13 Chief Information Officer .... Ms. Patricia PATRIA
18 Asst Vice President for Facilities .... Mr. Eric L. BEATTIE
15 VP Talent Development/CDO .... Ms. Michelle JONES-JOHNSON
20 VP Academic & Corporate Devel .... Mr. Stephen P. FLAVIN
32 Vice President of Student Affairs .... Mr. Philip N. CLAY
43 SVP/General Counsel .... Mr. David BUNIS
36 Exec Director Career Devel Center .... Mr. Stefan KOPPI
100 Vice President/Chief of Staff .... Ms. Amy MORTON
35 Asst VP & Dean of Students .... Mr. Greg SNODDY
07 Director of Admissions .... Ms. Jennifer A. CLUETT
06 University Registrar .... Ms. Sarah L. MILES
27 Director of Research Communications .... Mr. Michael W. DORSEY
96 Director of Procurement Services .... Ms. Laurie COLELLA
21 University Controller .... Mr. Patrick HITCHCOCK
09 Assistant VP of Budget Planning .... Ms. Mary CALARESE
38 Asst Dean of Stdnt Dev/Dir SDCC .... Mr. Charles C. MORSE
88 Associate Director LSBC .... Mr. Andrew BUTLER
37 Dir Student Aid & Financial Lit .... Ms. Jessica SABOURIN
19 Dir Environmental Health & Safety .... Mr. Daniel T. SARACHICK
28 Director of Multicultural Affairs .... Vacant
29 Exec Director Lifetime Engagement .... Mr. Peter A. THOMAS

MICHIGAN

Adrian College (F)

110 S Madison Street, Adrian MI 49221-2575
County: Lenawee FICE Identification: 002234
Unit ID: 168528
Telephone: (517) 265-5161 Carnegie Class: Bac-Diverse
FAX Number: (517) 264-3331 Calendar System: Semester
URL: www.adrian.edu
Established: 1859 Annual Undergrad Tuition & Fees: $37,087
Enrollment: 1,709 Coed
Affiliation or Control: United Methodist IRS Status: 501(c)3
Highest Offering: Master's
Accreditation: NH, CAATE, CAEPT, SW

01 President .... Dr. Jeffrey R. DOCKING
05 Vice Pres/Dean for Academic Affairs .... Dr. Andrea MILNER
111 Vice Pres Institutional Advancement .... Mr. James MAHONY
84 Vice President of Enrollment .... Mr. Frank J. HRIBAR
10 Vice Pres Business Affairs/CFO .... Mr. Jerry WRIGHT
32 Dean of Student Affairs .... Mrs. Melinda SCHWYN
20 Asst Dean of Academic Affairs .... Dr. Christine M. KNAGGS
30 Director of Development .... Ms. Tara GUTIERREZ
42 Chaplain/Director Church Relations .... Vacant
06 Registrar .... Ms. Kristina SCHWEIKERT
86 Dir of Govt & Foundation Relations .... Vacant
15 Director of Human Resources .... Mrs. Renee BURCK
40 Bookstore Manager .... Ms. Rachelle M. DUFFY
93 Dir Multicultural Cultural Programs .... Ms. Shantay ERNST
29 Director Alumni Relations .... Ms. Jennifer CARLSON
41 Director of Athletics .... Mr. Michael DUFFY
19 Director of Campus Safety .... Mr. Wade BIETELCHIES
36 Director of Career Planning .... Mrs. Janna D'AMICO
88 Director of Conferences .... Ms. DeAnne LEWIN
38 Director of Counseling .... Ms. Monique J. SAVAGE
08 Head Librarian .... Mr. David CRUSE
23 Director of Health Center .... Vacant
96 Director of Purchasing .... Ms. Donna WARD
37 Director of Financial Aid .... Mr. Steve BUCKLAND
18 Director of Facilities .... Mr. Chris STIVER
09 Director of Institutional Research .... Ms. Beth L. HEISS
88 Director of Academic Services .... Mr. Benjamin ERNST
88 Asst Director of Academic Services .... Vacant
100 Chief of Staff President's Office .... Mrs. Andrea BURT

Albion College (G)

611 E Porter Street, Albion MI 49224-1831
County: Calhoun FICE Identification: 002235
Unit ID: 168546
Telephone: (517) 629-1000 Carnegie Class: Bac-A&S
FAX Number: (517) 629-0509 Calendar System: Semester
URL: www.albion.edu
Established: 1835 Annual Undergrad Tuition & Fees: $45,590
Enrollment: 1,568 Coed
Affiliation or Control: United Methodist IRS Status: 501(c)3
Highest Offering: Baccalaureate
Accreditation: NH, CAEPT, MUS

01 President .... Dr. Mauri A. DITZLER
10 Vice Pres Business & Finance .... Ms. Deanna MCCORMICK
05 Provost .... Dr. Marc ROY
30 Vice Pres Institutional Advancement .... Mr. Robert ANDERSON
84 Vice Pres Enrollment Management .... Vacant
32 Vice Pres & Dean Student Affairs .... Mr. Leroy WRIGHT
13 Assoc Vice Pres Info Svcs/CIO .... Mr. Michael DEVER
07 Director of Admissions .... Ms. Mandy DUBIEL
39 Director Residential Life .... Mr. Marcus DAWSON
08 Director of Libraries .... Dr. Michael VAN HOUTEN
26 Director of Communications .... Mr. John PERNEY
29 Director of Alumni Engagement .... Vacant
38 Director of Counseling .... Dr. Frank KELEMEN
37 Director of Financial Aid .... Mr. Rob KNISS
06 Registrar .... Dr. Andrew M. DUNHAM
109 Director Dining & Hospitality Svcs .... Mrs. Pat MILLER
18 Director of Facilities Operations .... Mr. Doug LADITKA
19 Director of Campus Safety .... Mr. Kenneth SNYDER
41 Athletic Director .... Mr. Matthew AREND
42 College Chaplain .... Rev. Donald PHILLIPS
15 Director of Human Resources .... Mrs. Lisa LOCKE
09 Director of Institutional Research .... Dr. Andrew DUNHAM
96 Director of Purchasing .... Mrs. Susan CLARK
20 Associate Academic Officer .... Dr. John WOELL
28 Assoc Director Multicultural Affs .... Ms. Keena WILLIAMS
40 Manager of Bookstore .... Mr. Todd SHAYLER

Alma College (H)

614 W Superior, Alma MI 48801-1599
County: Gratiot FICE Identification: 002236
Unit ID: 168591
Telephone: (989) 463-7111 Carnegie Class: Bac-Diverse
FAX Number: (989) 463-7277 Calendar System: Other
URL: www.alma.edu
Established: 1886 Annual Undergrad Tuition & Fees: $40,258
Enrollment: 1,426 Coed
Affiliation or Control: Independent Non-Profit IRS Status: 501(c)3
Highest Offering: Baccalaureate
Accreditation: NH, CAEPT, MUS, NURSE

01 President .... Dr. Jeff ABERNATHY
05 Provost & Vice Pres for Acad Affs .... Dr. Kathleen DOUGHERTY
11 Chief Operating Officer .... Mr. Alan GATLIN
111 Vice President for Advancement .... Mr. Matt VANDENBERG
07 Vice President for Admissions .... Mrs. Amanda SLENSKI
32 Vice President for Student Life .... Dr. Karl RISHE
100 Vice Pres Planning/Chief of Staff .... Mrs. Ann HALL
04 Executive Asst to the President .... Mrs. Kelly MASLEY
06 Registrar .... Ms. Mariah ORZOLEK
20 Assistant Provost .... Ms. Susan M. DEEL
42 Chaplain .... Rev Dr. Andrew POMERVILLE
37 Director Financial Aid .... Ms. Michelle MCNIER
08 Director of Library .... Vacant
27 Associate VP for Communications .... Mr. Mike SILVERTHORN
13 Chief Technology Officer .... Vacant
18 Director Facilities & Service Mgmt .... Mr. Douglas DICE
15 Director Human Resources .... Ms. Amanda DUVAL
21 Associate VP/Controller .... Mr. Dan HENRIS

36 Director of Employment Outreach .... Vacant
35 Director of Student Affairs .... Mr. David K. BLANDFORD
38 Director Counseling & Wellness .... Ms. Anne K. LAMBRECHT
09 Director for Institutional Research .... Mr. John MACARTHUR
28 Director of Diversity & Inclusion .... Dr. Donnesha BLAKE
41 Athletic Director .... Vacant
29 Sr Dir Alumni & Family Engagement .... Mr. Bill ARNOLD
39 Director Resident Life .... Ms. Alice KRAMER

Alpena Community College (A)

665 Johnson Street, Alpena MI 49707-1495
County: Alpena FICE Identification: 002237
Unit ID: 168607
Telephone: (989) 356-9021 Carnegie Class: Bac/Assoc-Assoc Dom
FAX Number: (989) 358-7553 Calendar System: Semester
URL: www.alpenacc.edu
Established: 1952 Annual Undergrad Tuition & Fees (In-District): $4,530
Enrollment: 1,611 Coed
Affiliation or Control: Local IRS Status: 501(c)3
Highest Offering: Baccalaureate
Accreditation: NH, ADNUR, MAC, PNUR

01 President .... Dr. Donald MACMASTER
05 Vice Pres of Instruction .... Ms. Deborah BAYER
10 Vice President Admin & Finance .... Mr. Richard SUTHERLAND
32 Dean of Students .... Ms. Nancy SEGUIN
21 Controller .... Ms. Lyn KOWALEWSKY
20 Dean Learning Resource Center .... Ms. Wendy BROOKS
25 Director of TAACCT Grants .... Ms. Dawn STONE
13 Co-Director Mgmt Info Systems .... Mr. Jeff BLUMENTHAL
13 Co-Director Mgmt Info Systems .... Mr. Mark GRUNDER
26 Dir Public Information/Marketing .... Mr. Jay WALTERREIT
40 Director of ACC Bookstore .... Mr. William MATZKE
102 Dir Dev/Exec Dir ACC Foundation .... Ms. Brenda HERMAN
18 Director of Facilities Management .... Mr. Nicholas BREGE
88 Volunteer Center Director .... Ms. Cathy GUTIERREZ-ABRAHAM
06 Registrar .... Ms. Lori DZIESINSKI
15 Director Human Resources .... Ms. Carolyn DAOUST
07 Director of Admissions .... Mr. Mike KOLLIEN
37 Director Financial Aid .... Mr. Robert ROOSE
35 Director Student Life Activities .... Ms. Cynthia DEROCHER

Andrews University (B)

8975 U.S. 31, Berrien Springs MI 49104-0001
County: Berrien FICE Identification: 002238
Unit ID: 168740
Telephone: (269) 471-7771 Carnegie Class: DU-Mod
FAX Number: (269) 471-6900 Calendar System: Semester
URL: www.andrews.edu
Established: 1874 Annual Undergrad Tuition & Fees: $29,288
Enrollment: 3,300 Coed
Affiliation or Control: Seventh-day Adventist IRS Status: 501(c)3
Highest Offering: Doctorate
Accreditation: NH, CACREP, CAEPN, COPSY, DIETD, DIETI, IACBE, MT, MUS, NUR, PH, PTA, SP, SW, THEOL

01 President .... Dr. Andrea T. LUXTON
04 Executive Asst to President .... Ms. Dalry B. PAYNE
05 Provost .... Dr. Christon ARTHUR
108 Assistant Provost Inst Assessment .... Dr. Lynn MERKLIN
10 Vice Pres Financial Admin .... Mr. Glenn MEEKMA
37 Asst Vice Pres Stdt Financial Svcs .... Ms. Elynda A. BEDNEY
32 Vice Pres Student & Campus Life .... Dr. Frances M. FAEHNER
26 Spec Asst to Pres Univ/Public Affs .... Mr. Stephen D. PAYNE
84 Vice Pres Mktg/Enroll Management .... Mr. Randy K. GRAVES
27 Assoc Vice Pres Marketing .... Mr. Tony YANG
111 Vice President for Advancement .... Dr. David A. FAEHNER
30 Assoc Vice Pres Development .... Ms. Audrey CASTELBUONO
28 Vice Pres for Diversity & Inclusion .... Mr. Michael T. NIXON
43 General Counsel .... Ms. Gwendolyn POWELL BRASWELL
06 Registrar .... Ms. Aimee VITANGCOL REGOSO
20 Assoc Prov/Dean Undergrad Educ .... Dr. Keith E. MATTINGLY
49 Dean College of Arts & Sciences .... Dr. Amy ROSENTHAL
76 Dean College of Health & Human Svcs .... Dr. Emmanuel RUDATSIKIRA
50 Dean College of Professions .... Dr. Ralph TRECARTIN
73 Dean of Theological Seminary .... Dr. Jiri MOSKALA
58 Dean Graduate Studies .... Dr. Alayne THORPE
106 Dean Coll of Education/Intl Svcs .... Dr. Alayne THORPE
08 Dean of Libraries .... Ms. Paulette M. JOHNSON
46 Dean of Research .... Dr. Gary BURDICK
21 Associate Business Officer .... Vacant
13 Chief Information Officer .... Ms. Lorena L. BIDWELL
15 Director of Human Resources .... Mr. Darcy L. DE LEON
39 Dir of University Apartment Life .... Mr. Alfredo RUIZ
39 Dir of Residence Life .... Ms. Jennifer R. BURRILL
42 University Chaplain .... Ms. June M. PRICE
85 Dir of International Student Svcs .... Mr. Robert BENJAMIN
92 Director of Honors Program .... Dr. L. Monique PITTMAN
38 Dir of Counseling/Testing Center .... Dr. Judith FISHER
07 Director of University Admissions .... Ms. Jillian PANIGOT
29 Director of Alumni Services .... Mr. Andriy KHARKOVYY
19 Director of Campus Safety .... Mr. Benjamin PANIGOT
23 Director of Medical Services .... Dr. Lowell HAMEL
44 Director of Planned Giving .... Ms. Tari POPP
09 Director Institutional Research .... Mr. James R. MASSENA
18 Director of Facilities Management .... Mr. Paul ELDER
105 Manager of Web Communications .... Mr. Jason STRACK
104 Chair Intl Lang & Global Studies .... Dr. Pedro NAVIA
41 Director of Athletics .... Mr. Rob GETTYS
40 Manager of Bookstore .... Ms. Cynthia SWANSON

Aquinas College (C)

1700 Fulton St. E, Grand Rapids MI 49506-1799
County: Kent FICE Identification: 002239
Unit ID: 168786
Telephone: (616) 632-8900 Carnegie Class: Bac-A&S
FAX Number: (616) 732-4469 Calendar System: Semester
URL: www.aquinas.edu
Established: 1886 Annual Undergrad Tuition & Fees: $32,574
Enrollment: 1,716 Coed
Affiliation or Control: Roman Catholic IRS Status: 501(c)3
Highest Offering: Master's
Accreditation: NH, CAATE, CAEP

01 President .... Dr. Kevin G. QUINN
05 Interim Provost/Dean of Faculty .... Dr. Heather KESSELRING-QUAKENBUSH
102 Vice Pres Foundation .... Vacant
10 Vice Pres/Chief Financial Officer .... Ms. Lisa VANDEWEERT
84 Vice President Enrollment .... Ms. Erin CRAIG
04 Chief Exec Assistant to President .... Ms. Mary VARGAS
26 Assoc VP Marketing & Communication .... Ms. Marissa SURA
32 Assoc VP for Student Success .... Mr. Brian MATZKE
21 Controller .... Mr. Steve LUNGER
09 Dean of Institutional Effectiveness .... Vacant
53 Dean of School of Education .... Dr. Susan ENGLISH
06 Registrar .... Ms. Elizabeth FLORES
38 Dir of Career & Counseling Services .... Ms. Sharon E. SMITH
51 Director of Continuing Education .... Vacant
104 Assoc Dir International Educ Pgms .... Mr. Tim RAMSAY
94 Director of Women's Studies .... Ms. Amy DUNHAM STRAND
92 Director of Honors Program .... Dr. Michelle DEROSE
58 Director of Graduate Management .... Vacant
18 Director of Maintenance .... Mr. Dale HAISMA
39 Director of Residence Life .... Ms. Julie BLASZAK
07 Director of Admissions .... Mr. Damon BOUWKAMP
37 Director of Financial Aid .... Ms. Darcy KAMPFSCHULTE
35 Assoc VP for Student Affairs .... Mr. Nick DAVIDSON
42 Director Campus Ministry .... Mr. Robert GILMORE
13 Dir Information Technology & Svcs .... Vacant
29 Director of Alumni Engagement .... Ms. Alexa CAREY
35 Dir Student Leadership & Engagement .... Ms. Allie MARKLAND
112 Director of Major Gifts .... Ms. Cecelia CUNNINGHAM
36 Director of Career Services .... Dr. Dana HEBREARD
28 Director of Diversity & Inclusion .... Ms. Alicia LLOYD
40 Director Bookstore .... Ms. Marian TODISH
24 Media Coordinator .... Ms. Francine PAOLINI
42 Campus Chaplain .... Rev. Stanley DRONGOWSKI, OP

*Baker Professional Services, Inc. (D)

1020 S. Washington St, Owosso MI 48867
County: Shiawassee Identification: 666923
Unit ID: 419572
Telephone: (989) 729-3350 Carnegie Class: N/A
FAX Number: (810) 766-2102
URL: www.baker.edu

01 CEO .... Bart DAIG
05 Chief Academic Officer (Provost) .... Jill LANGEN

*Baker College of Flint (E)

1050 West Bristol Road, Flint MI 48507
County: Genesee FICE Identification: 004673
Unit ID: 168847
Telephone: (810) 766-4105 Carnegie Class: Masters/L
FAX Number: (810) 766-4293 Calendar System: Quarter
URL: www.baker.edu
Established: 1911 Annual Undergrad Tuition & Fees: $9,800
Enrollment: 12,018 Coed
Affiliation or Control: Independent Non-Profit IRS Status: 501(c)3
Highest Offering: Doctorate
Accreditation: NH, CAHIIM, CSHSE, IACBE, NURSE, OT, PTAA, SURGT

02 President .... Denise BANNAN

*Baker College of Allen Park (F)

4500 Enterprise Drive, Allen Park MI 48101
Telephone: (313) 425-3727 Identification: 666996
Accreditation: &NH, CAHIIM, CSHSE, IACBE, MLTAD, OTA, PTAA

*Baker College of Auburn Hills (G)

1500 University Drive, Auburn Hills MI 48326-2642
Telephone: (248) 276-8240 Identification: 666940
Accreditation: &NH, CSHSE, DMS, IACBE, PTAA

*Baker College of Cadillac (H)

9600 E 13th Street, Cadillac MI 49601-9169
Telephone: (231) 876-3107 Identification: 666941
Accreditation: &NH, CSHSE, IACBE, MAC, SURGT

*Baker College of Clinton Township (I)

34950 Little Mack, Clinton Township MI 48035-4701
Telephone: (586) 790-9591 Identification: 666942
Accreditation: &NH, CAHIIM, CSHSE, DA, DH, IACBE, MAC, RAD, SURGT

*Baker College of Jackson (J)

2800 Springport Road, Jackson MI 49202-1299
Telephone: (517) 841-4528 FICE Identification: 004680
Accreditation: &NH, CSHSE, IACBE, RTT, SURGT

*Baker College of Muskegon (K)

1903 Marquette Avenue, Muskegon MI 49442-3404
Telephone: (231) 777-5248 FICE Identification: 002296
Accreditation: &NH, ACFEI, CSHSE, IACBE, OTA, PTAA, RAD, SURGT

*Baker College of Owosso (L)

1020 South Washington, Owosso MI 48867-4400
Telephone: (989) 729-3431 Identification: 666937
Accreditation: &NH, ACFEI, CAEPT, CSHSE, DMS, IACBE, MAC, OTA, RAD

Bay College West Campus (M)

2801 N US 2, Iron Mountain MI 49801
Telephone: (906) 302-3000 Identification: 770262
Accreditation: &NH

Bay Mills Community College (N)

12214 W Lakeshore Drive, Brimley MI 49715-9750
County: Chippewa FICE Identification: 030666
Unit ID: 380359
Telephone: (906) 248-3354 Carnegie Class: Tribal
FAX Number: (906) 248-3351 Calendar System: Semester
URL: www.bmcc.edu
Established: 1984 Annual Undergrad Tuition & Fees: $3,040
Enrollment: 448 Coed
Affiliation or Control: Tribal Control IRS Status: 501(c)3
Highest Offering: Baccalaureate
Accreditation: NH

01 President .... Michael C. PARISH
05 Vice President of Academic Affairs .... Samantha CAMERON
10 Vice Pres Business & Finance .... Laura POSTMA
32 Dean of Student Services .... Debra J. WILSON
13 Director Technology/Title III .... Chet KASPER
06 Registrar/Inst Info Systems Mgr .... Sherri SCHOFIELD
37 Director Student Financial Aid .... Tina MILLER
07 Director of Admissions .... Elaine LEHRE
25 Land Grant Director .... Stephen YANNI
30 Director of Development .... Kathy ADAIR
08 Library Director .... Megan CLARKE

Bay de Noc Community College (O)

2001 N Lincoln Road, Escanaba MI 49829-2510
County: Delta FICE Identification: 002240
Unit ID: 168883
Telephone: (906) 786-5802 Carnegie Class: Assoc/MT-VT-High Trad
FAX Number: (906) 789-6952 Calendar System: Semester
URL: www.baycollege.edu
Established: 1962 Annual Undergrad Tuition & Fees (In-District): $4,788
Enrollment: 1,853 Coed
Affiliation or Control: Local IRS Status: 501(c)3
Highest Offering: Associate Degree
Accreditation: NH, ADNUR, EMT

01 President .... Dr. Laura COLEMAN
11 VP of Operations .... Ms. Christine WILLIAMS
10 VP of Finance .... Ms. Eileen SPARPANA
05 VP of Academic Affairs .... Dr. Matthew BARRON
111 VP of College Advancement .... Ms. Kim CARNE
32 VP of Student Services .... Mr. Travis BLUME
50 Dean Business/Tech/Workforce Dev .... Ms. Cindy CARTER
37 Director of Financial Aid .... Ms. Ruth CARLSON
07 Director of Admissions .... Ms. Jessica LAMARCH
15 Director of Human Resources .... Ms. Beth BERUBE
18 Director of Buildings & Grounds .... Mr. Ralph CURRY
76 Dean of Allied Health .... Mr. Mitchell CAMPBELL
49 Dean of Arts & Sciences .... Dr. Amy REDDINGER
32 Director of Student Life .... Mr. Dave LAUR
08 Head Librarian .... Mr. Oscar DELONG
04 Exec Admin Asst to President .... Mrs. Laura JOHNSON
06 Registrar .... Ms. Rebecca LANDENBERGER
106 Exec Director of Online Learning .... Mr. Joseph MOLD
19 Security Officer .... Mr. Joseph PACHECO
41 Athletic Director .... Mr. Matt JOHNSON
09 Director of Institutional Research .... Ms. Penny PAVLAT

Calvin Theological Seminary (P)

3233 Burton Street, SE, Grand Rapids MI 49546-4387
County: Kent FICE Identification: 002242
Unit ID: 169099
Telephone: (616) 957-6036 Carnegie Class: Spec-4-yr-Faith
FAX Number: (616) 957-8621 Calendar System: Semester
URL: www.calvinseminary.edu
Established: 1876 Annual Graduate Tuition & Fees: N/A
Enrollment: 341 Coed
Affiliation or Control: Christian Reformed Church IRS Status: 501(c)3
Highest Offering: Doctorate; No Undergraduates
Accreditation: THEOL

01 President .... Rev. Julius T. MEDENBLIK

05 Dean of Faculty Dr. Gary BURGE
20 Assoc Dean of Academic Programs Ms. Joan BEELEN
11 Chief of Operations/Administration Dr. Margaret MWENDA
06 Registrar Ms. Joan BEELEN
32 Dean of Students Rev. Jeff SAJDAK
08 Theological Librarian Vacant
10 Controller Mr. Chris DINH
30 Director of Development Mr. Robert KNOOR
36 Director of Vocational Ministry Rev. Geoff VANDERMOLEN
07 Dir of Admissions/Enrollment Mgmt Mr. Aaron EINFELD
37 Director of Financial Aid Mrs. Jennifer SETTERGREN

Calvin University (A)

3201 Burton Street, SE, Grand Rapids MI 49546-4388
County: Kent FICE Identification: 002241
Unit ID: 169080
Telephone: (616) 526-6000 Carnegie Class: Masters/S
FAX Number: (616) 526-8551 Calendar System: 4/1/4
URL: www.calvin.edu
Established: 1876 Annual Undergrad Tuition & Fees: $34,600
Enrollment: 3,840 Coed
Affiliation or Control: Christian Reformed Church IRS Status: 501(c)3
Highest Offering: Master's
Accreditation: NH, CAEP, CAEPT, NURSE, SP, SW

01 President Dr. Michael K. LE ROY
05 Provost Dr. Cheryl BRANDSEN
10 Vice Pres Admin/Finance Ms. Sally VANDER PLOEG
111 Vice President for Advancement Mr. Kenneth ERFFMEYER
84 Vice Pres Enrollment Strategy Mrs. Lauren J. JENSEN
32 Vice President Student Life Dr. Sarah VISSER
15 Vice President People/Strategy & IT Mr. Todd K. HUBERS
13 Assoc Vice President for IT & CIO Mr. Brian PAIGE
28 Exec Assoc for Diversity/Inclusion Dr. Michelle LOYD-PAIGE
42 College Chaplain Dr. Mary HULST
15 Director of Finance & HR Mr. Andrew L. GEORGE
08 Dean of the Library Mr. David MALONE
29 Dir of Alumni and Cmty Relations Mr. Rick J. TREUR
06 Director Academic Svcs/Registrar Mr. Thomas L. STEENWYK
35 Dean of Students Mr. John WITTE
88 Dir of Commuter Life/Assessment Vacant
88 Dean of Students for Judicial Affs Ms. Jane E. HENDRIKSMA
88 Dean of Faculty Development Dr. David WUNDER
20 Dean of Academic Administration Dr. Laura DEHAAN
83 Acad Dean Lang/Soc Sci/Context Disc Dr. Elizabeth VANDERLEI
81 Acad Dean Educ/Kinesio/Nat Sci/Math Dr. Arlene HOOGEWERF
36 Director of Career Development Ms. TaRita JOHNSON
108 Mgr Inst Effectiveness & Analytics Mrs. Lauren JENSEN
09 Assoc Dir Inst/Enroll Research Mr. Thomas A. VAN ECK
26 Dir Communications & Brand Steward Mr. Timothy L. ELLENS
27 Director of Marketing & Client Svcs Ms. Jeanne NIENHUIS
88 Director Center for Social Research Dr. Neil CARLSON
19 Director of Campus Safety Mr. William T. CORNER
18 Director Physical Plant Mr. Russell BRAY
24 Director Instruc Resources Center Vacant
38 Director Counseling and Well Center Dr. Irene KRAEGEL
23 Director Health Services Dr. Laura CHAMPION
92 Director Honors Program Dr. Amy WILSTERMANN
41 Athletic Director Dr. James TIMMER, JR.
30 Director of Development Ms. Jodi COLE
104 Director Study Abroad Dr. Cynthia SLAGTER
105 Director Web Services Mr. Luke ROBINSON
37 Director Student Financial Aid Mr. Paul R. WITTE, III
44 Director Annual Fund Ms. Melanie N. LYONS
53 Dean of Education Dr. James ROOKS
07 Director of Admissions/Counseling Vacant
101 Secretary of the Institution/Board Ms. Sharolyn J. CHRISTIANS

Career Quest Learning Center (B)

3215 S. Pennsylvania Avenue, Lansing MI 48910
County: Ingham FICE Identification: 039153
Unit ID: 446136
Telephone: (517) 318-3330 Carnegie Class: Assoc/HVT-High Non
FAX Number: (517) 318-3331 Calendar System: Other
URL: www.careerquest.edu
Established: 1995 Annual Undergrad Tuition & Fees: N/A
Enrollment: 242 Coed
Affiliation or Control: Proprietary IRS Status: Proprietary
Highest Offering: Associate Degree
Accreditation: COE

00 President & CEO Dr. Jim HUTTON
01 Campus President/VP Mollie WOODWORTH

Central Michigan University (C)

1200 S. Franklin Street, Mount Pleasant MI 48859
County: Isabella FICE Identification: 002243
Unit ID: 169248
Telephone: (989) 774-4000 Carnegie Class: DU-Higher
FAX Number: N/A Calendar System: Semester
URL: www.cmich.edu
Established: 1892 Annual Undergrad Tuition & Fees (In-State): $12,960
Enrollment: 23,257 Coed
Affiliation or Control: State IRS Status: 501(c)3
Highest Offering: Doctorate
Accreditation: NH, ART, ARCPA, AUD, CAATE, CAEP, CEA, CIDA, CLPSY, COSMA, DIETD, DIETI, EXSC, JOUR, MED, MUS, NRPA, PTA, SCPSY, SP, SPAA, SW

01 President Dr. Robert O. DAVIES
05 Executive VP/Provost Dr. Mary SCHUTTEN
20 Interim SVP Academic Affairs Dr. Ian R. DAVISON
10 Vice Pres Finance/Admin Svcs Mr. Barrie J. WILKES
86 Int Vice Pres Govt/Ext Relations Mr. Toby ROTH, JR.
84 Vice Pres Enrollment & Student Svcs Vacant
111 Interim Vice Pres Advancement Mr. Michael ALFORD
13 Vice President Info Technology/CIO Dr. Roger E. REHM
21 AVP Fin Svcs & Reporting/Controller Ms. Mary M. HILL
26 AVP University Communications Vacant
18 Assoc VP Facilities Management Mr. Jonathan D. WEBB
109 Exec Dir Auxiliary Services Mr. Calvin H. SEELYE, II
39 Director Residence Life Ms. Kathleen GARDNER
28 Vice Pres/Chief Diversity Officer Dr. A.T MILLER
15 Assoc VP Human Resources Ms. Lori L. HELLA
20 Sr Vice Provost Academic Admin Dr. Ray L. CHRISTIE
46 VP Research/Dean Graduate Studies Dr. David E. ASH
30 Dir Stewardship & Donor Rels/Advan Ms. Kelly M. BERRYHILL
08 Dean of Libraries Dr. Kathy IRWIN
32 Assoc VP Student Affairs Mr. Anthony A. VOISIN
35 Executive Director Student Affairs Mr. Shaun HOLTGREIVE
29 Exec Dir of Alumni Rels & Dev Strat Ms. Marcie M. OTTEMAN
09 Exec Dir Academic Planning/Analysis Dr. Robert M. ROE
22 Exec Dir Civil Rights/Inst Equity Vacant
07 Exec Director Admissions Ms. Lee F. FURBECK
43 Vice President & General Counsel Dr. Manuel R. RUPE
06 Registrar Mr. Keith J. MALKOWSKI
37 Director Scholarships/Financial Aid Mr. Kirk M. YATS
36 Director Career Services Ms. Julia B. SHERLOCK
38 Int Director Counseling Services Ms. Melissa M. HUTCHINSON
114 Exec Dir Financial Plng & Budgets Mr. Joseph L. GARRISON
27 Director Communications Ms. Heather L. SMITH
19 Chief of Police Mr. William YEAGLEY, JR.
40 Director CMU Bookstore Mr. Barry D. WATERS
81 Acting Dean College Sci & Engr Dr. Jane M. DAVISON
76 Dean College of Health Professions Dr. Tom J. MASTERSON
63 VP Health Aff/Dean College Medicine Dr. George E. KIKANO
49 Dean Liberal Arts & Soc Sciences Dr. Richard M. ROTHAUS
57 Dean College Arts & Media Dr. Janet HETHORN
50 Interim Dean Business Admin Dr. Karl L. SMART
53 Interim Dean Education & Human Svcs Dr. Elizabeth A. KIRBY
04 Executive Assistant to President Ms. Mary Jane FLANAGAN
96 Dir Contract & Purchasing Svcs Ms. Anne R. THRUSH
92 Director Honors Program Dr. Phame M. CAMARENA
104 Director Study Abroad Ms. Dianne S. DESALVO
116 Director Internal Audit Mr. Scott M. STRONG
110 Assoc VP of Advancement Mr. Stephen KULL
44 Director of Annual Giving Mr. Bryan L. GRIFFIN
115 Asst Controller Financial Services Ms. Kimberly A. WAGESTER
88 Asst Controller Financial Reporting Ms. Julia H. MONTROSS
117 Dir/Risk Mgmt Env Health & Safety Mr. Benjamin S. COFFMAN
121 Exec Director Student Success Dr. Evan L. MONTAGUE

Chamberlain University-Troy (D)

200 Kirts Boulevard, Suite C, Troy MI 48084
Telephone: (248) 817-4140 Identification: 770851
Accreditation: &NH, NURSE

† Branch campus of Chamberlain University-Addison, Addison, IL

Cleary University (E)

3750 Cleary Drive, Howell MI 48843
County: Livingston FICE Identification: 002246
Unit ID: 169327
Telephone: (800) 686-1883 Carnegie Class: Spec-4-yr-Bus
FAX Number: N/A Calendar System: Semester
URL: www.cleary.edu
Established: 1883 Annual Undergrad Tuition & Fees: $20,550
Enrollment: 647 Coed
Affiliation or Control: Independent Non-Profit IRS Status: 501(c)3
Highest Offering: Master's
Accreditation: NH

01 President & CEO Dr. Jayson BOYERS
05 Provost & Chief Acad Officer Ms. Emily BARNES
10 Controller Ms. Shelly HOLANDA
111 VP Institutional Advancement Dr. Matt BENNETT
109 VP Auxiliary Services Mr. Jeffrey BANE
04 Exec Director for President Ms. Darla HARGRAVES
21 Assistant Controller Ms. Megan TEMBY
09 Institutional Research Analyst Mr. Omar HABAYEB
37 Sr Financial Aid Coord Ms. Brandy AKERS
84 VP Enrollment Management Ms. Carey MONROE
40 Manager Bookstore Services Ms. Deb SOUTHERLAND
36 Director of Career Development Ms. Amy DENTON
41 Athletic Director Ms. Heather BATEMAN
15 VP Organizational Development Ms. LaRae BANE
16 Human Resources Coordinator Ms. Kathleen CONAHAN
08 Instructional Librarian Ms. Jane SCALES
18 Facilities Manager Mr. George HORN
32 Associate Dean of Students Mr. Matthew OLIVER
06 Registrar Mr. Stuart KEENAN
43 General Counsel Mr. Mike BARNES
13 Executive Director of Technology Mr. Kris TOBBE
121 Director of Academic Success Ms. Angela KUHLMAN
106 Instructional Design Manager Ms. Kirsten SHEPARD

College for Creative Studies (F)

201 East Kirby Street, Detroit MI 48202-4034
County: Wayne FICE Identification: 006771
Unit ID: 169442
Telephone: (313) 664-7400 Carnegie Class: Spec-4-yr-Arts
FAX Number: (313) 872-8377 Calendar System: Semester
URL: www.collegeforcreativestudies.edu
Established: 1906 Annual Undergrad Tuition & Fees: $44,110
Enrollment: 1,453 Coed
Affiliation or Control: Independent Non-Profit IRS Status: 501(c)3
Highest Offering: Master's
Accreditation: NH, ART, CIDA

01 President Mr. Donald L. TUSKI
100 Exec Asst to Pres & Sec to Board Ms. Sandra WILSON
04 Admin Assistant to the President Ms. Brigette NEAL
05 Provost & VP for Academic Affairs Vacant
10 Vice Pres Administration & Finance Ms. Anne D. BECK
84 Vice Pres Enrollment & Student Svcs Ms. Julie HINGELBERG
111 Vice Pres Institutional Advancement Ms. Tracy MUSCAT
58 Dean Graduate Studies Mr. Ian LAMBERT
20 Dean Undergraduate Studies Mr. Vince CARDUCCI
32 Dean of Students Mr. Daniel LONG
06 Registrar & Acad Advising Director Ms. Nadine ASHTON
123 Director Graduate Admissions Mr. Anthony MICELI
07 Director Undergraduate Admissions Ms. Carla GONZALEZ
37 Director Financial Aid Mr. Frank RAVJA
35 Director Student Life Mr. Michael COLEMAN
85 Director Intl Student Services Ms. Katherine CAMPBELL
93 Dir of Student Diversity/Inclusion Mr. Cliff HARRIS
51 Dir Continuing & Precollege Studies Ms. Jane STEWART
31 Dir of Community Arts Partnerships Mr. Mikel BRESEE
08 Director Library Ms. Beth WALKER
19 Dir of Facilities and Campus Safety Mr. Michael BRUGGEMAN
13 Director Information Technology Mr. Greg FRASER
90 Director of Academic Technologies Ms. Laurie EVANS
21 Director Business Services Ms. Kerri MCKAY
15 Director Human Resources Mr. Michael HILL
26 Director Marketing & Communications Mr. Marcus POPIOLEK
30 Sr Director Development Operations Ms. Elizabeth KLOS
36 Director Career Services Ms. Terese NEHRA
29 Asst Dir Annual Giv/Alumni Rels Mr. Anthony SPANGLER
38 Director Wellness & Counseling Ms. Valerie WEISS
40 Manager Bookstore Ms. Glen MORREN
39 Director of Residence Life Mr. Ryan HARRISON
102 Dir Foundation/Corporate Relations Ms. Shannon MCPARTLON
88 Dir of Exhibit & Public Programs Ms. Michelle PERRON

Compass College of Cinematic Arts (G)

41 Sheldon Boulevard, SE, Grand Rapids MI 49503
County: Kent FICE Identification: 041633
Unit ID: 459417
Telephone: (616) 988-1000 Carnegie Class: Spec-4-yr-Arts
FAX Number: (616) 458-4676 Calendar System: Other
URL: www.compass.edu
Established: 2003 Annual Undergrad Tuition & Fees: $15,050
Enrollment: 134 Coed
Affiliation or Control: Independent Non-Profit IRS Status: 501(c)3
Highest Offering: Baccalaureate
Accreditation: ACCSC

01 President Jay GREER
03 VP of Institutional Affairs Austin MORSE
05 Dean of Education William KAVAN
10 Finance Manager Laura COULIER
26 Director Marketing & Enrollment Alex BRADLEY
07 Admissions Manager Chuck KUHN

Concordia University Ann Arbor (H)

4090 Geddes Road, Ann Arbor MI 48105-2797
Telephone: (734) 995-7300 FICE Identification: 002247
Accreditation: &NH, CAEPN

Cornerstone University (I)

1001 E Beltline Avenue, NE, Grand Rapids MI 49525-5897
County: Kent FICE Identification: 002266
Unit ID: 170037
Telephone: (616) 949-5300 Carnegie Class: Masters/M
FAX Number: (616) 222-1540 Calendar System: Semester
URL: www.cornerstone.edu
Established: 1941 Annual Undergrad Tuition & Fees: $24,500
Enrollment: 2,361 Coed
Affiliation or Control: Independent Non-Profit IRS Status: 501(c)3
Highest Offering: Doctorate
Accreditation: NH, ACBSP, CAEPT, MUS, SW, THEOL

01 President Dr. Joseph M. STOWELL
03 Executive Vice President Dr. Peter OSBORN
05 VP Traditional Undergrad Academics Dr. Shawn NEWHOUSE
10 Chief Financial Officer Mr. Scott STEWART
88 Vice President of Broadcasting Mr. Chris LEMKE
32 VP of Student Development Mr. Gerald LONGJOHN
111 VP of Advancement Mr. Bob SACK
20 AVP Traditional Undergrad Academics Dr. Pete MUIR
73 EVP Academic/Dean Grad Theol Stdnts Dr. John VER BERKMOES
108 Assoc Dean Assessment/Stdnt Success Mrs. Emily GRATSON
35 Director of Student Services Mr. Keith DEBOER
08 Director of Miller Library Mrs. Laura WALTON
37 Director Financial Services Mrs. Carol CARPENTER
21 Director of Finance and Accounting Mr. Stephen POPP
41 Athletic Director Mr. Aaron SAGRAVES
15 Director of Human Resources Mrs. Emilie AZKOUL

18 Director of Campus Services ..... Mr. Chris BYNUM
19 Director of Campus Safety ..... Mr. Brandan BISHOP
29 Director of Alumni ..... Mr. Dennis GRAHAM
06 Registrar ..... Mrs. Gail DUHON
13 Director of Technology Support ..... Mr. Dan MILLS
38 Director of the Counseling Center ..... Mr. Scott COUREY
92 Director of Honors Program ..... Mr. Don PERINI
07 Executive Director of Admissions ..... Mrs. Lisa LINK
04 Administrative Asst to President ..... Mrs. Beth LONGJOHN
28 Dir Diversity/Multiculural Affairs ..... Mr. Kenneth RUSSELL

Cranbrook Academy of Art (A)

39221 Woodward Avenue, Bloomfield Hills MI 48304
County: Oakland FICE Identification: 002248
Unit ID: 169424
Telephone: (248) 645-3300 Carnegie Class: Spec-4-yr-Arts
FAX Number: (248) 645-3591 Calendar System: Semester
URL: www.cranbrookart.edu
Established: 1932 Annual Graduate Tuition & Fees: N/A
Enrollment: 141 Coed
Affiliation or Control: Independent Non-Profit IRS Status: 501(c)3
Highest Offering: Master's; No Undergraduates
Accreditation: NH, ART

01 Director ..... Ms. Susan EWING
05 Dir Academic Programs & Library ..... Judy DYKI
84 Mgr Enrollment & Financial Services ..... Phillip HANG
30 Senior Director of Development ..... Autumn PARROTT
44 Director of Annual Giving ..... Kelly LEWIS-GUMP

Davenport University (B)

6191 Kraft Avenue, S.E., Grand Rapids MI 49512
County: Kent FICE Identification: 002249
Unit ID: 169479
Telephone: (616) 698-7111 Carnegie Class: Masters/L
FAX Number: N/A Calendar System: Semester
URL: www.davenport.edu
Established: 1866 Annual Undergrad Tuition & Fees: $18,414
Enrollment: 7,160 Coed
Affiliation or Control: Independent Non-Profit IRS Status: 501(c)3
Highest Offering: Master's
Accreditation: NH, CAHIIM, COSMA, IACBE, MAC, NURSE, OT, PNUR

01 President ..... Dr. Richard J. PAPPAS
111 Exec VP Alumni & Development ..... Ms. Rachel RENDER
46 Exec VP of Quality & Effectiveness ..... Dr. Scott EPSTEIN
15 Exec VP Human/Organizational Devel ..... Mr. Dave VENEKLASE
32 Exec VP Admission & Student Svcs ..... Dr. Walter O'NEILL
10 Exec Vice President for Finance/CFO ..... Mr. Michael S. VOLK
05 Exec VP Academics/Provost ..... Dr. Gilda GELY
07 VP Admissions/Strategic Partnership ..... Mr. David LAWRENCE
09 VP for Institutional Research ..... Dr. Kathy ABOUFADEL
12 Vice President Detroit Campuses ..... Ms. Lisa HOWZE
18 VP Facilities Management ..... Mr. Damon P. GONZALES
50 Dean College of Business & Tech ..... Vacant
76 Dean College of Health Professions ..... Dr. Karen DALEY
49 Dean College of Arts and Sciences ..... Ms. Patty BRECHBIEL
106 Dean Global Campus ..... Mr. Brian MILLER
107 Dean College of Urban Education ..... Dr. Susan GUNN
37 Exec Director Financial Aid ..... Mr. David DE BOER
26 EVP for Univ Relations & Comm ..... Ms. Deb COOPER
29 Exec Dir of Alumni & Development ..... Vacant
21 Controller ..... Mr. Michael SLEVA
06 University Registrar ..... Mr. Christopher MARX
41 Director of Athletics ..... Mr. Paul LOWDEN
04 Administrative Asst to President ..... Ms. Rose KARSTEN
28 Exec Dir Diversity/Equity/Inclusion ..... Vacant
39 Exec Dir Campus Life ..... Mr. Joseph BISHOP
27 Exec Dir Communications & PR ..... Ms. Amy MILLER

Davenport University Holland (C)

643 S Waverly Road, Holland MI 49423
Telephone: (616) 395-4600 Identification: 770266
Accreditation: &NH

Davenport University Lansing (D)

200 S. Grand Avenue, Lansing MI 48933
Telephone: (517) 484-2600 Identification: 770268
Accreditation: &NH, MAC

Davenport University Midland (E)

3555 E Patrick Road, Midland MI 48642
Telephone: (989) 835-5588 Identification: 770270
Accreditation: &NH

Davenport University Warren (F)

27650 Dequindre Road, Warren MI 48092
Telephone: (586) 558-8700 Identification: 770272
Accreditation: &NH

Delta College (G)

1961 Delta Rd., University Center MI 48710-0001
County: Bay FICE Identification: 002251
Unit ID: 169521
Telephone: (989) 686-9000 Carnegie Class: Assoc/MT-VT-High Trad
FAX Number: (989) 667-0620 Calendar System: Semester
URL: www.delta.edu
Established: 1961 Annual Undergrad Tuition & Fees (In-District): $4,010
Enrollment: 8,677 Coed
Affiliation or Control: Local IRS Status: 501(c)3
Highest Offering: Associate Degree
Accreditation: NH, ADNUR, COARC, DA, DH, DMS, PTAA, RAD, SURGA, SURGT

01 President ..... Dr. Jean GOODNOW
10 Vice President Finance/Treasurer ..... Ms. Sarah DUFRESNE
32 Vice President Student & Educ Svcs ..... Ms. Margarita MOSQUEDA
05 VP Instruction/Learning Svcs ..... Dr. Reva CURRY
111 Ex Dir Delta Col Found/Inst Advance ..... Ms. Pam CLARK
20 Dean of Teaching & Learning ..... Dr. Martha CRAWMER
35 Dean of Students ..... Mr. Jonathan MILLER
36 Dean Career Educ/Learning Part ..... Ms. Ginny PRZYGOCKI
84 Dean of Enrollment Management ..... Dr. Russell CURLEY
26 Marketing & Public Info Director ..... Ms. Leanne GOVITZ
108 Ex Dir Admin Svcs & Inst Effective ..... Ms. Andrea L. URSUY
101 Assistant to Pres/Board Secretary ..... Ms. Andrea URSUY
13 Director of Information Technology ..... Mr. Bill WESOLEK
25 Director of Corporate Services ..... Ms. Jennifer CARROLL
37 Director of Student Financial Aid ..... Ms. Lisa BAKER
15 Director of Human Resources ..... Mr. Scott LEWLESS
18 Director of Facilities Management ..... Mr. Nicholas BOVID
07 Dir of Admissions & Recruitment ..... Mr. Zachary WARD
19 Director of Public Safety ..... Mr. Robert BATTINKOFF
88 Director of Learning Centers ..... Ms. Kristy NELSON
124 Associate Dean of Retention ..... Ms. Michelle RAUBE
49 Associate Dean Arts & Letters Div ..... Mr. Jonathan GARN
50 Associate Dean Business & Tech Div ..... Ms. Susan ROCHE
88 Associate Dean Health/Wellness Div ..... Dr. Pete FOX
81 Associate Dean Science & Math Div ..... Ms. Colleen THOMAS
83 Associate Dean Social Sciences Div ..... Dr. Daniel ALLEN
21 Business Services Director ..... Mr. Jonathan FOCO
09 Director of Institutional Research ..... Mr. Wm. Michael WOOD
06 Registrar ..... Ms. Terri GOULD
13 Chief Information Officer ..... Mr. Adam DICKINSON
40 Assistant Bookstore Manager ..... Mr. Daniel FRANCKE
08 Mgr of Library Programs & Services ..... Ms. Michele PRATT

Eastern Michigan University (H)

900 Oakwood St, Ypsilanti MI 48197-2207
County: Washtenaw FICE Identification: 002259
Unit ID: 169798
Telephone: (734) 487-1849 Carnegie Class: DU-Higher
FAX Number: (734) 481-1095 Calendar System: Semester
URL: www.emich.edu
Established: 1849 Annual Undergrad Tuition & Fees (In-State): $12,508
Enrollment: 20,525 Coed
Affiliation or Control: State IRS Status: 501(c)3
Highest Offering: Doctorate
Accreditation: NH, ARCPA, ART, CAATE, CACREP, CAEP, CAEPN, CEA, CIDA, CLPSY, CONST, DIETC, MT, MUS, NURSE, OPE, OT, PLNG, SP, SPAA, SW

01 President ..... Dr. James M. SMITH
05 Provost and Executive VP ..... Dr. Rhonda LONGWORTH
10 Chief Financial Officer ..... Mr. Michael VALDES
26 Vice President Communications ..... Mr. Walter KRAFT
111 VP Advance/Exec Dir Foundation ..... Mr. William SHEPARD
101 VP & Sec to the Board of Regents ..... Ms. Vicki REAUME
41 Vice President/Dir Athletics ..... Mr. Scott WETHERBEE
84 Vice Pres/Chief Enrollment Officer ..... Mr. Kevin KUCERA
86 Int VP Govt/Cmty Relations ..... Ms. Vicki REAUME
18 VP for Operations ..... Mr. John P. DONEGAN
15 VP for University Human Resources ..... Mr. David TURNER
43 General Counsel ..... Ms. Lauren LONDON
13 Asst VP & Chief Information Officer ..... Mr. Ron WOODY
19 Exec Dir Public Safety ..... Mr. Robert HEIGHES
100 Chief of Staff ..... Mr. Leigh GREDEN
114 Assoc Prov/Assoc VP Budget/Op ..... Dr. James J. CARROLL, III
20 Assoc Prov/Assoc VP Acad Pgm Svcs ..... Mr. Michael TEW
49 Dean Col of Art & Sciences ..... Dr. Dana HELLER
50 Dean Col of Business ..... Dr. Kenneth LORD
53 Dean Col of Education ..... Dr. Michael SAYLER
69 Dean Col Health & Human Svcs ..... Dr. Murali NAIR
72 Dean Col of Technology ..... Dr. Mohamad QATU
58 Int Assc Prov/AVP Grad Studies/Rsrc ..... Dr. Wade TORNQUIST
08 University Librarian ..... Ms. Rhonda FOWLER
23 Asst VP of Student Well-Being ..... Ms. Ellen GOLD
09 Asst VP & Exec Dir Inst Rsrch/Info ..... Dr. Bin NING
20 Asst VP Academic Affairs/AHR ..... Dr. David WOIKE
21 Asst VP Business Oper/Student Svcs ..... Mr. Brian KULPA
102 Exec Dir Foundation Operations/CFO ..... Ms. Laura WILBANKS
88 Asst VP Acad & Student Affs/Ombuds ..... Dr. Chiara HENSLEY
32 Assoc Vice Pres Student Affairs ..... Mr. Calvin PHILLIPS
27 Executive Director Media Relations ..... Mr. Geoffrey LARCOM
88 Dir Charter Schools Program ..... Dr. Malverne WINBORNE
92 Interim Asst VP Honors College ..... Dr. Mary K. RAMSEY
39 Dir Housing & Residence Life ..... Ms. Jeanette ZALBA
114 Exec Dir Financial Plng & Budget ..... Mr. Todd OHMER
88 Dir University Convocation Center ..... Mr. Mark MONAHAN
112 Dir Planned Giving/Foundation ..... Ms. Susan RINK
102 Assoc VP Advancement/Foundation ..... Ms. Jill HUNSBERGER
88 Exec Dir Integrated Content ..... Ms. Darcy GIFFORD
88 Gen Mgr WEMU-FM Public Rad ..... Ms. Mary MOTHERWELL
06 Registrar ..... Ms. Christina SHELL
37 Director Financial Aid ..... Ms. Donna HOLUBIK
28 Dir Diversity & Cmty Involvement ..... Mr. Steven P. BRYANT
22 Dir Diversity & Affirmative Action ..... Ms. Sharon ABRAHAM
96 Director Purchasing ..... Mr. Travis TEMEYER
88 Title IX Coordinator ..... Dr. Melody A. WERNER
88 Title IX Investigator ..... Ms. Anika AWAI-WILLIAMS
88 Senior Assoc to CFO ..... Mr. Daniel KELLY
88 Controller ..... Ms. Doris M. CELIAN
88 Asst Controller/Student Bus Svcs ..... Ms. Beth HARDCASTLE
88 Dir Business Systems Support ..... Mr. Kenneth R. ADKINS
97 Dir Undergrad Studies/Prov Office ..... Dr. Doris FIELDS

Ecumenical Theological Seminary (I)

2930 Woodward Avenue, Detroit MI 48201-3035
County: Wayne FICE Identification: 040024
Unit ID: 247162
Telephone: (313) 831-5200 Carnegie Class: Spec-4-yr-Faith
FAX Number: (313) 831-1353 Calendar System: Quarter
URL: www.etseminary.edu
Established: 1980 Annual Undergrad Tuition & Fees: N/A
Enrollment: 54 Coed
Affiliation or Control: Independent Non-Profit IRS Status: 501(c)3
Highest Offering: Doctorate
Accreditation: THEOL

01 President ..... Dr. Kenneth E. HARRIS
05 Vice Pres Academic Affs/Acad Dean ..... Dr. Kenneth E. HARRIS
32 Vice Pres Administration/Stdnt Svcs ..... Dr. Genetta Y. HATCHER
04 Executive Asst to the President ..... Mrs. Barbara PYE
10 Finance Officer/Business Mgmt ..... Ms. Jacquelyn HINES
07 Dir of Admissions/Enrollment Mgmt ..... Mr. LaRon MOORE
73 Director Doctor of Ministry Program ..... Dr. Constance SIMON
58 Director of Masters Program ..... Dr. James WADDELL
73 Director of Urban Ministry Program ..... Dr. Brandon GRAFIUS

Ferris State University (J)

1201 S. State Street, Big Rapids MI 49307-2295
County: Mecosta FICE Identification: 002260
Unit ID: 169910
Telephone: (231) 591-2000 Carnegie Class: DU-Mod
FAX Number: (231) 591-3592 Calendar System: Semester
URL: www.ferris.edu
Established: 1884 Annual Undergrad Tuition & Fees (In-State): $11,788
Enrollment: 13,798 Coed
Affiliation or Control: State IRS Status: 501(c)3
Highest Offering: First Professional Degree
Accreditation: NH, ACBSP, CAEPT, CAHIIM, CEA, COARC, CONST, DH, DMS, MLTAD, MT, NMT, NUR, NURSE, OPT, OPTR, PHAR, RAD, SW

01 President ..... Dr. David L. EISLER
05 Provost & VPAA ..... Dr. Paul A. BLAKE
43 Vice President & General Counsel ..... Mr. Miles J. POSTEMA
10 Interim VP Administration & Finance ..... Mr. Mike HUGHES
111 VP of Advancement & Mktg ..... Ms. Shelly PEARCY
32 Vice President Student Affairs ..... Dr. Jeanine WARD-ROOF
12 Interim President KCAD ..... Ms. Tara MCCRACKIN
56 Dean Extended and Intl Operations ..... Dr. Steve REIFERT
28 VP for Diversity and Inclusion ..... Dr. David PILGRIM
88 Int Assoc Provost Accreditation ..... Ms. Mandy SEIFERLEIN
109 Assoc VP of Auxiliary Enterprises ..... Ms. Gheretta HARRIS
21 Assistant VP of Finance ..... Mr. Mike GRANDY
110 Assoc VP for Advancement ..... Mr. Bob MURRAY
15 Assoc VP Human Resources ..... Vacant
18 Assoc VP Physical Plant ..... Mr. Mike HUGHES
84 Associate Dean Enrollment Services ..... Ms. Kathy LAKE
07 Dean of Enrollment Services ..... Dr. Kristen SALOMONSON
114 Director Budget Planning/Analysis ..... Ms. Sally DEPEW
13 Interim Chief Technology Officer ..... Mr. Ralph WILLIAMS
19 Director of Public Safety ..... Mr. Bruce BORKOVICH
88 Mgr Stdnt Empl & Financial Aid Adv ..... Mr. John RANDLE
88 Director of University Center ..... Mr. Mark SCHUELKE
38 Director Counseling & Health Center ..... Ms. Lindsay BARBER
35 Dean of Student Life ..... Ms. Joy PUFHAL
88 Dir Multicultural Student Svcs ..... Dr. Matthew CHANEY
88 Director for CLACS ..... Ms. Angela ROMAN
88 Director University Recreation ..... Ms. Cindy HORN
29 Assoc VP for External Relations ..... Mr. Jeremy MISHLER
09 Dir of Inst Research & Testing ..... Ms. Mitzi DAY
39 Director Residential Life ..... Mr. Brian MARQUARDT
40 Director Bookstore ..... Ms. Karen BOHREN
41 Director of Athletics ..... Mr. Perk WEISENBURGER
44 Dir Annual Giving & Advance Svcs ..... Ms. Jennifer YONTZ
49 Dean of Arts & Sciences ..... Dr. Kristi HAIK
50 Dean of Business ..... Dr. David NICOL
53 Dean Educ & Human Svcs ..... Mr. Arrick JACKSON
67 Dean of Pharmacy ..... Dr. Steve DURST
76 Dean of Health Professions ..... Dr. Lincoln GIBBS
63 Dean Michigan College Optometry ..... Dr. David DAMARI
72 Dean of Engineering Technology ..... Mr. Richard GOOSEN
08 Interim Dean of FLITE ..... Dr. Jason BENTLEY
04 Executive Asst to the President ..... Ms. Terri COOK
101 Secretary to the Board of Trustees ..... Ms. Karen HUISMAN
37 Director Financial Aid ..... Ms. Heidi WISBY
06 Registrar ..... Ms. Elise GRAMZA
104 Executive Dir Office of Intl Educ ..... Dr. Piram PRAKASAM
105 Web Content Manager ..... Mr. Theodore HALM
22 Director of Equal Opportunity ..... Ms. Kylie PIETTE
106 Director Online Education ..... Dr. Amy L. GREENE

Finlandia University (K)

601 Quincy Street, Hancock MI 49930-1882
County: Houghton FICE Identification: 002322
Unit ID: 172440
Telephone: (906) 482-5300 Carnegie Class: Bac-Diverse
FAX Number: (906) 487-7366 Calendar System: Semester
URL: www.finlandia.edu

Established: 1896 Annual Undergrad Tuition & Fees: $22,758
Enrollment: 402 Coed
Affiliation or Control: Evangelical Lutheran Church In America
IRS Status: 501(c)3
Highest Offering: Baccalaureate
Accreditation: NH, MAC, NURSE, PTAA

01 President ... Dr. Philip JOHNSON
10 Chief Financial Officer ... Ms. Angela PRICE
05 VP Academic Affairs ... Dr. Fredi DE YAMPERT
111 VP External Relations & Advancement ... Ms. Karin VAN DYKE
04 Executive Administrative Assistant ... Ms. Doreen KORPELA
26 Director Marketing/Communications ... Mr. Michael BABCOCK
08 Head Librarian ... Ms. Rebecca DALY
32 Dean of Students & Enrollment ... Ms. Erin BARNETT
42 Campus Pastor ... Mr. Corbin EDDY
06 Registrar ... Mr. Jason SULLIVAN
13 Director Information Technology ... Mr. Scott BLAKE
41 Athletic Director ... Mr. Curtis WITTENBERG
18 Director of Plant and Facilities ... Mr. Curt HAHKA
37 Director Financial Services ... Ms. Sandra TURNQUIST
40 Bookstore Manager ... Ms. Alana NOLAN
96 Purchaser ... Ms. Janine NOTTKE
15 Human Resources Manager ... Ms. Alyson DELANDSHEER
07 Director of Admissions ... Mr. Collin SAINT-ONGE
19 Director of Campus Safety/Security ... Mr. Jim HARDEN
39 Director of Residence Life ... Ms. Leann FOGLE
49 Dean College of Arts & Sciences ... Dr. Jason OYADOMARI
57 Dean Intl School of Art & Design ... Ms. Denise VANDEVILLE
76 Dean College of Health Science ... Dr. Fredi DEYAMPERT
50 Dean Intl School of Business ... Mr. Kevin MANNINEN
88 Title IX Coordinator ... Ms. Alyson DELANDSHEER

Glen Oaks Community College (A)

62249 Shimmel Road, Centreville MI 49032-9719
County: Saint Joseph FICE Identification: 002263
Unit ID: 169974
Telephone: (269) 467-9945 Carnegie Class: Assoc/MT-VT-High Non
FAX Number: (269) 467-4114 Calendar System: Semester
URL: www.glenoaks.edu
Established: 1965 Annual Undergrad Tuition & Fees (In-District): $3,552
Enrollment: 1,207 Coed
Affiliation or Control: Local IRS Status: 501(c)3
Highest Offering: Associate Degree
Accreditation: NH, MAC

01 President ... Dr. David DEVIER
05 Dean of Academics/Extended Learning ... Dr. Patricia MORGENSTERN
10 Dean of Finance/Administrative Svcs ... Mr. Bruce ZAKRZEWSKI
32 Dean of Student Services ... Ms. Tonya HOWDEN
66 Dean of Nursing ... Mr. Bill LEDERMAN
08 Director Learning Resources Center ... Ms. Trista NELSON
21 Accountant ... Ms. Jennifer DODSON
18 Director of Buildings/Grounds ... Mr. Larry DIEKMAN
07 Director of Admissions ... Ms. Adrienne SKINNER
37 Dir of Financial Aid/Scholarships ... Ms. Jean ZIMMERMAN
41 Director of Athletics ... Ms. Courtney IVAN
09 Inst Effectiveness/Research Analyst ... Dr. Tammy RUSSELL
15 Personnel Coordinator ... Ms. Candy BOHACZ
26 Public Relations/Marketing ... Ms. Valorie JUERGENS
04 Admin Assistant to the President ... Ms. Diane ZINSMASTER
06 Registrar ... Ms. Amy YOUNG
103 Director Workforce Development ... Mr. Paul AIVARS
39 Dir Resident Life/Student Housing ... Ms. April YOST

Gogebic Community College (B)

E4946 Jackson Road, Ironwood MI 49938-1366
County: Gogebic FICE Identification: 002264
Unit ID: 169992
Telephone: (906) 932-4231 Carnegie Class: Assoc/HVT-High Trad
FAX Number: (906) 932-5541 Calendar System: Semester
URL: www.gogebic.edu
Established: 1931 Annual Undergrad Tuition & Fees (In-District): $4,924
Enrollment: 1,042 Coed
Affiliation or Control: Local IRS Status: 501(c)3
Highest Offering: Associate Degree
Accreditation: NH, MAC

01 President ... Dr. George MCNULTY
05 Vice Pres of Academic Affairs ... Mr. David DARROW
10 Vice Pres of Business Services ... Mr. Erik M. GUENARD
32 Vice Pres of Student Services ... Ms. Jeanne GRAHAM
37 Director Financial Aid ... Mr. Marc MADIGAN
76 Director of Allied Health Program ... Ms. Nicole ROWE
88 Director of Ski Area Management ... Mr. James VANDERSPOEL
08 Dir Learning Resource Center ... Vacant
13 Director of Computer Services ... Mr. Steve SPETS
07 Dir of Admission/Public Information ... Ms. Kim ZECKOVICH
30 Dir of Institutional Development ... Ms. Kelly MARZCAK
15 Director of Human Resources ... Ms. Ashley PAQUETTE
88 Transfer Coord/Veterans Services ... Ms. Tara TREGEMBO
09 Institutional Researcher ... Ms. Miranda LAWVER
04 Administrative Asst to President ... Ms. Kari KLEMME

Grace Christian University (C)

1011 Aldon Street, SW, Grand Rapids MI 49509-1998
County: Kent FICE Identification: 002265
Unit ID: 170000
Telephone: (616) 538-2330 Carnegie Class: Spec-4-yr-Faith
FAX Number: (616) 538-0599 Calendar System: Semester
URL: www.gracechristian.edu
Established: 1939 Annual Undergrad Tuition & Fees: $13,945
Enrollment: 888 Coed
Affiliation or Control: Independent Non-Profit IRS Status: 501(c)3
Highest Offering: Master's
Accreditation: NH, BI

01 President ... Dr. Kenneth B. KEMPER
05 Provost ... Mrs. Kim PILIECI
20 Assistant Provost ... Mr. Timothy RUMLEY
10 Vice Pres Finance/Business Opers ... Mr. Douglas VRIESMAN
11 Exec Vice President ... Mr. Brian P. SHERSTAD
32 Assoc Vice Pres Student Affairs ... Mr. Kyle BOHL
04 Executive Assistant to President ... Mrs. Joyce A. STORMS
06 Registrar ... Mrs. Linda K. SILER
111 Vice Pres Institutional Advancement ... Mr. Stephen GOWDY
08 Director Library Services ... Mr. Jeff BRODRICK
37 Director of Financial Aid ... Mr. Kurt POSTMA
13 Director of Information Technology ... Mr. Mark LOVE
18 Director of Maintenance ... Mr. Nathan JOHNSON
41 Athletic Director ... Mr. Gary BAILEY
42 Campus Ministry Coordinator ... Mr. Jim GAMBLE
26 Assoc Vice President of Marketing ... Mr. Zak SORENSEN
15 Assoc Vice Pres of Human Resources ... Mrs. Sherea LACY
29 Alumni Services Coordinator ... Mrs. Julianne PRIOLO
07 Director of Admissions on Campus ... Mr. Alex BRADLEY
07 Director of Admissions Online ... Mr. Joshua WILLIAMS
07 Director of Admissions Online ... Mrs. Erin ANDERSON
38 Director Student Counseling ... Mrs. Ineke WILKINSON

† Name changed from Grace Bible College on July 1, 2018.

Grand Rapids Community College (D)

143 Bostwick Avenue NE, Grand Rapids MI 49503-3295
County: Kent FICE Identification: 002267
Unit ID: 170055
Telephone: (616) 234-4000 Carnegie Class: Assoc/MT-VT-High Trad
FAX Number: (616) 234-4005 Calendar System: Semester
URL: www.grcc.edu
Established: 1914 Annual Undergrad Tuition & Fees (In-District): $3,833
Enrollment: 14,269 Coed
Affiliation or Control: Local IRS Status: 501(c)3
Highest Offering: Associate Degree
Accreditation: NH, ACFEI, ADNUR, ART, DA, DH, MAC, MUS, OTA, PNUR, RAD

01 President ... Dr. Bill PINK
05 Prov/Exec VP Academic Affairs ... Vacant
10 Exec VP Business/Financial Services ... Ms. Lisa FREIBURGER
13 VP & CIO Lrng Res/Tech Solutions ... Mr. David ANDERSON
111 AVP Advancement/Exec Dir Foundation ... Dr. Kathryn MULLINS
28 Chief Equity & Inclusion Officer ... Dr. Afeni MCNEELY COBHAM
124 Dean of Student Success & Retention ... Mr. Eric MULLEN
32 Dean Student Affairs ... Dr. Tina OEN-HOXIE
09 Dean Inst Research & Planning ... Ms. Donna KRAGT
49 Dean School of Arts & Sciences ... Dr. Michael VARGO
103 Dean Workforce Development ... Dr. Amy MANSFIELD
26 Director of Communications ... Mr. David MURRAY
37 Director of Financial Aid ... Ms. Ann ISACKSON
15 Executive Director Human Resources ... Ms. Cathy KUBIAK
06 Registrar ... Ms. Valerie BUTTERFIELD
35 Director Student Activities ... Ms. Caroline BLAIR
88 Assoc Director Student Employment ... Ms. Luann WEDGE
08 Director of Library Services ... Mr. Brian BEECHER
18 Executive Director of Facilities ... Mr. Thomas J. SMITH
19 Chief of Campus Police ... Ms. Rebecca R. WHITMAN
43 General Counsel ... Ms. Kathy KEATING
96 Director Purchasing ... Mr. Mansfield MATTHEWSON
12 Dean of Lakeshore Campus & Outreach ... Mr. Daniel CLARK

Grand Valley State University (E)

1 Campus Drive, Allendale MI 49401-9403
County: Ottawa FICE Identification: 002268
Unit ID: 170082
Telephone: (616) 331-5000 Carnegie Class: Masters/L
FAX Number: (616) 331-3503 Calendar System: Semester
URL: www.gvsu.edu
Established: 1960 Annual Undergrad Tuition & Fees (In-State): $12,484
Enrollment: 25,049 Coed
Affiliation or Control: State IRS Status: 501(c)3
Highest Offering: Doctorate
Accreditation: NH, ARCPA, ART, CAATE, CAEPN, CAHIIM, CARTE, CVT, @DIETC, DMS, IPSY, MT, MUS, NURSE, OT, PH, PTA, RADDOS, RTT, SP, SPAA, SW

01 President ... Dr. Philomena V. MANTELLA
05 Provost/Exec VP Acad & Student Affs ... Dr. Maria C. CIMITILE
26 Vice President University Relations ... Mr. Matthew E. MCLOGAN
10 Vice President for Finance & Admin ... Dr. Greg SANIAL
84 Vice President Enrollment Develop ... Ms. Lynn M. BLUE
30 Vice President for Development ... Ms. Karen M. LOTH
28 Vice President Inclusion and Equity ... Dr. Jesse M. BERNAL
43 Vice President and General Counsel ... Mr. Thomas A. BUTCHER
100 Exec Assoc to the President ... Vacant
32 Vice Provost & Dean of Students ... Dr. Loren RULLMAN
88 Vice Prov for Research Admin ... Dr. Robert SMART
20 Vice Prov Instruct Dev & Innovation ... Dr. Christine RENER
23 Vice Prov for Health ... Dr. Jean NAGELKERK
20 Assoc VP Academic Affairs ... Dr. Edward ABOUFADEL
20 Assoc VP Academic Affairs ... Dr. Ellen SCHENDEL
20 Assoc VP Academic Affairs ... Dr. Suzeanne BENET
20 Senior Assoc VP Academic Affairs ... Dr. Chris PLOUFF
20 Assoc VP Academic Affairs ... Ms. Bonnie BOWEN
21 Assoc VP Business/Finance ... Mr. Brian COPELAND
114 Director of University Budgets ... Ms. Jennifer SCHICK
15 Assoc VP Human Resources ... Ms. Maureen WALSH
88 Assoc VP Institutional Marketing ... Ms. Rhonda LUBBERTS
27 Assoc VP for Univ Communications ... Ms. Mary Eilleen LYON
88 Assoc VP for Strategic Initiatives ... Mr. James BACHMEIER
18 Assoc VP Facilities Services ... Mr. Timothy THIMMESCH
88 Assoc VP for Facilities Planning ... Ms. Karen INGLE
12 Assoc VP Fac Svcs GR & Reg Ctrs ... Ms. Lisa HAYNES
22 Assoc VP for Inclusion & Equity ... Ms. Kathleen VANDERVEEN
35 Assoc VP Inclusion & Student Affs ... Dr. Marlene KOWALSKI-BRAUN
88 Assoc VP for Charter Schools ... Dr. Robert KIMBALL
49 Dean Col of Liberal Arts & Sciences ... Dr. Frederick ANTCZAK
50 Dean Seidman Col of Business ... Dr. Diana LAWSON
70 Dean College of Cmty/Public Service ... Dr. George GRANT
53 Interim Dean College of Education ... Dr. Sherril SOMAN
54 Dean Padnos Col Engr & Computing ... Dr. Paul PLOTKOWSKI
76 Dean College of Health Professions ... Dr. Roy OLSSON
88 Interim Dean Col Interdisc Studies ... Dr. Mark SCHAUB
66 Dean Kirkhof College of Nursing ... Dr. Cynthia MCCURREN
58 Dean Graduate School ... Dr. Jeffrey POTTEIGER
08 Dean University Libraries ... Dr. Annie BELANGER
07 Assoc VP for Admissions ... Ms. Jodi CHYCINSKI
29 Director of Alumni Relations ... Mr. Chris BARBEE
36 Director of Career Center ... Mr. Troy FARLEY
37 Assoc VP for Financial Aid ... Ms. Michelle RHODES
88 Director of Hauenstein Center ... Mr. Gleaves WHITNEY
39 Director of Housing & Res Life ... Dr. Andrew BEACHNAU
13 Assoc VP Information Tech & CIO ... Ms. Sue KORZINEK
09 Assoc VP Institutional Analysis ... Dr. Philip BATTY
22 Director AA/EEO Equity Officer ... Mr. Scott AYOTTE
96 Director of Procurement Services ... Mr. Kim PATRICK
19 Director Public Safety/Police Chief ... Mr. Brandon DEHAAN
38 Director Univ Counseling Center ... Dr. Amber ROBERTS
41 Athletic Director ... Ms. Keri BECKER
85 Interim Chief International Officer ... Mr. Mike VROOMAN
88 Controller ... Ms. Pam BRENZING
88 General Manager WGVU ... Mr. Ken KOLBE
06 Assoc VP & Registrar ... Ms. Pam WELLS
88 Title IX Coordinator ... Ms. Theresa ROWLAND
88 Assoc VP & Deputy General Counsel ... Ms. Pat SMITH

Great Lakes Christian College (F)

6211 Willow Highway, Lansing MI 48917-1299
County: Eaton FICE Identification: 002269
Unit ID: 170091
Telephone: (517) 321-0242 Carnegie Class: Spec-4-yr-Faith
FAX Number: (517) 321-5902 Calendar System: Semester
URL: www.glcc.edu
Established: 1949 Annual Undergrad Tuition & Fees: $17,220
Enrollment: 129 Coed
Affiliation or Control: Christian Churches And Churches of Christ
IRS Status: 501(c)3
Highest Offering: Baccalaureate
Accreditation: NH

01 President ... Mr. Lawrence L. CARTER
10 Vice President Finance/Operations ... Mr. Timothy J. WYNSMA
05 Vice President of Academic Affairs ... Mr. Michael B. HARRISON
111 Vice Pres Institutional Advancement ... Mr. Philip E. BEAVERS
84 Vice Pres Enrollment Mgmt ... Mr. Gregory STAUFFER
06 Registrar ... Dr. Esther A. HETRICK
08 Director of Library Services ... Mrs. Heather BUNCE
37 Financial Aid Director ... Prof. Ryan APPLE
32 Dean of Students/Dir Student Life ... Mr. Ryan BUSHNELL
41 Athletic Director ... Mr. Richard WESTERLUND
88 Director of Outreach Ministries ... Mrs. Judy BEAVERS
18 Maintenance Supervisor ... Mr. Chris ADLEMAN
04 Administrative Secretary ... Ms. Marie A. RIGGS

Henry Ford College (G)

5101 Evergreen Road, Dearborn MI 48128-1495
County: Wayne FICE Identification: 002270
Unit ID: 170240
Telephone: (313) 845-9615 Carnegie Class: Bac/Assoc-Assoc Dom
FAX Number: (313) 845-9658 Calendar System: Semester
URL: www.hfcc.edu
Established: 1938 Annual Undergrad Tuition & Fees (In-District): $3,124
Enrollment: 12,786 Coed
Affiliation or Control: Local IRS Status: 501(c)3
Highest Offering: Baccalaureate
Accreditation: NH, ACFEI, ADNUR, COARC, EMT, MAC, PTAA, RAD, SURGT

01 President ... Dr. Russell A. KAVALHUNA
10 Vice President Financial Services ... Dr. John SATKOWSKI
32 Vice President Student Affairs ... Dr. Daniel R. HERBST
05 Vice Pres Academic/Career Education ... Dr. Michael NEALON
111 Vice Pres of Inst Advancement ... Mr. A. Reginald BEST, JR.
11 VP Admin Services/Chief of Staff ... Vacant
45 VP Inst Research and Planning ... Dr. Lori GONKO
06 Exec Director Registration/Enroll ... Ms. Holly DIAMOND
38 Assoc Dean Counseling ... Mr. Atallah IBRAHIM
50 Dean Business/Entrepreneurship/PD ... Ms. Patricia CHATMAN
08 Director Library ... Vacant
13 Dir Network and Infrastructure ... Mr. Joseph ZITNIK
27 Dir Marketing/Communications ... Mr. Rhonda DELONG
37 Exec Director Student Financial Aid ... Mr. Kevin J. CULLER
92 Director Honors Program ... Dr. Michael DAHER

96 Director Purchasing .... Mr. Fred STEINER
40 Manager of College Store .... Ms. Pamela HALL
04 Administrative Asst to President .... Ms. Kathy DIMITRIOU
09 Director of Institutional Research .... Mr. Chris BUCZYNSKI
15 Director Personnel Services .... Vacant
19 Director Security/Safety .... Ms. Karen SCHOEN
41 Athletic Director .... Ms. Rochelle TAYLOR
43 Dir Legal Services/General Counsel .... Dr. Amy CLARK

Hillsdale College (A)

33 East College Street, Hillsdale MI 49242-1298
County: Hillsdale FICE Identification: 002272
Unit ID: 170286
Telephone: (517) 437-7341 Carnegie Class: Bac-A&S
FAX Number: (517) 437-3923 Calendar System: Semester
URL: www.hillsdale.edu
Established: 1844 Annual Undergrad Tuition & Fees: $27,578
Enrollment: 1,556 Coed
Affiliation or Control: Independent Non-Profit IRS Status: 501(c)3
Highest Offering: Doctorate
Accreditation: NH

01 President .... Dr. Larry ARNN
05 Provost .... Dr. Chris VANORMAN
11 VP & Chief Administrative Officer .... Mr. Rich PEWE
43 VP & General Counsel .... Mr. Robert NORTON
07 VP Admissions/Business Development .... Mr. Doug BANBURY
26 VP External Affairs .... Mr. Douglas JEFFREY
10 VP Finance .... Mr. Patrick FLANNERY
111 VP Institutional Advancement .... Mr. John CERVINI
88 VP Marketing .... Mr. Matt SCHLIENTZ
32 VP Student Affairs/Dean of Women .... Ms. Diane PHILIPP
27 Associate VP External Affairs .... Mr. Timothy CASPAR
100 Chief Staff Officer .... Mr. Mike HARNER
36 Executive Director Career Services .... Mr. Ken KOOPMANS
15 Executive Director HR .... Ms. Janet MARSH
13 Executive Director ITS .... Mr. Jason SHERRILL
29 Director Alumni Affairs .... Mr. Grigor HASTED
41 Director Athletics .... Mr. Don BRUBACHER
19 Director Campus Security .... Mr. William WHORLEY
40 Director College Bookstore .... Ms. Cindy WILLING
37 Director Financial Aid .... Mr. Rich MOEGGENBERG
23 Director Health Services .... Mr. Brock LUTZ
08 Director Library .... Ms. Maurine MCCOURRY
09 Director Institutional Research .... Mr. George ALLEN
18 Director Facilities .... Mr. Dave BILLINGTON
35 Director Student Activities .... Ms. Ashlyn LANDHERR
42 Chaplain .... Rev. Adam RICK
21 Controller .... Ms. LeAnn CREGER
33 Dean of Men .... Mr. Aaron PETERSEN
06 Registrar .... Mr. Douglas MCARTHUR
04 Exec Assistant to the President .... Ms. Madison MOORE
88 Assistant to the Provost .... Mr. Mark MAIER

Hope College (B)

141 E 12th Street, Holland MI 49423-3607
County: Ottawa FICE Identification: 002273
Unit ID: 170301
Telephone: (616) 395-7000 Carnegie Class: Bac-A&S
FAX Number: (616) 395-7922 Calendar System: Semester
URL: www.hope.edu
Established: 1866 Annual Undergrad Tuition & Fees: $34,010
Enrollment: 3,150 Coed
Affiliation or Control: Reformed Church In America IRS Status: 501(c)3
Highest Offering: Baccalaureate
Accreditation: NH, ART, CAATE, CAEPT, DANCE, MUS, NURSE, SW, THEA

01 President .... Mr. Matthew A. SCOGIN
05 Provost .... Dr. Cady SHORT-THOMPSON
10 Vice Pres and Chief Fiscal Officer .... Mr. Thomas W. BYLSMA
07 Vice President for Admissions .... Mr. William VANDERBILT
30 VP for Develop & Alumni Engagement .... Mr. Jeffrey PUCKETT
32 VP Student Devel/Dean of Students .... Dr. Richard A. FROST
26 VP Public Affairs & Marketing .... Mrs. Jennifer FELLINGER
08 Librarian .... Ms. Kelly G. JACOBSMA
39 Dir of Residential Life & Housing .... Dr. John E. JOBSON
22 Assc Dn Stdnts/Dir Ctr Div & Incl .... Ms. Vanessa GREENE
94 Director of Women's/Gender Studies .... Dr. Virginia BEARD
81 Dean for Natural Sciences .... Dr. David G. VAN WYLEN
79 Dean for Arts & Humanities .... Dr. Sandra L. VISSER
83 Dean for Social Sciences .... Dr. Scott D. VANDER STOEP
88 Dean of the Chapel .... Rev Dr. Trygve D. JOHNSON
37 Director of Financial Aid .... Ms. Jill NUTT
36 Assoc Dean for the Career Dev Ctr .... Mr. Dale F. AUSTIN
21 Director of Finance & Business Svcs .... Mr. Douglas VAN DYKEN
11 Director of Operations .... Ms. Kara SLATER
88 Director of Process and Innovation .... Mr. Carl E. HEIDEMAN
15 Director of Human Resources .... Mrs. Lori MULDER
40 Manager of Hope-Geneva Bookstore .... Mr. Craig THELEN
29 Exec Director of Alumni Engagement .... Mr. Scott TRAVIS
41 Director of Athletics .... Mr. Tim SCHOONVELD
42 Senior Chaplain .... Rev. Paul H. BOERSMA
38 Asst Dean/Director Counseling Ctr .... Dr. Kristen GRAY
04 Executive Asst to the President .... Mrs. Jan SOMMERVILLE
19 Director Security/Safety .... Mr. Jeffrey HERTEL
13 Dir Computing/Info Technology .... Mr. Jeff PESTUN
100 Chief of Staff .... Mrs. Mary REMENSCHNEIDER
06 Registrar .... Mrs. Carol DE JONG
105 Director Web Communications .... Mr. Jason CASH
28 Chief Officer for Culture & Incl .... Dr. Sonja TRENT-BROWN
44 Dir of Leadership & Annual Giving .... Ms. Dana GILL

Jackson College (C)

2111 Emmons Road, Jackson MI 49201-8399
County: Jackson FICE Identification: 002274
Unit ID: 170444
Telephone: (517) 787-0800 Carnegie Class: Bac/Assoc-Assoc Dom
FAX Number: (517) 796-8630 Calendar System: Semester
URL: www.jccmi.edu
Established: 1928 Annual Undergrad Tuition & Fees (In-District): $6,298
Enrollment: 4,798 Coed
Affiliation or Control: Local IRS Status: 501(c)3
Highest Offering: Baccalaureate
Accreditation: NH, ACBSP, COARC, DH, DMS, EMT, MAC, RAD

01 President/CEO .... Dr. Daniel J. PHELAN
05 Vice President for Instruction .... Ms. Kate THIROLF
10 Vice President of Finance/CFO .... Mr. Darrell NORRIS
32 Vice Pres of Student Services .... Mr. Jeremy FREW
11 Vice Pres of Administration .... Ms. Cindy ALLEN
102 President of JCC Foundation .... Mr. Jason VALENTE
06 Registrar .... Mr. Zakary MCNITT
07 Asst Director of Admissions .... Ms. Victoria SNYDER
08 Library Director .... Ms. Jennifer ADAMS
09 Exec Director of Inst Effectiveness .... Vacant
100 Chief of Staff .... Ms. Sara PERKIN
103 Dir Workforce/Career Development .... Ms. Tina MATZ
18 Chief Facilities/Physical Plant .... Mr. Jim JONES
19 Security/Safety Manager .... Mr. Jeffrey WHIPPLE
28 Director of Diversity .... Mr. Lee HAMPTON
29 Director Alumni Relations .... Ms. Brigette ROBINSON
37 Director Student Financial Aid .... Mr. Andrew SPOHN
39 Director of Housing .... Ms. Elizabeth ANDREWS
41 Athletic Director .... Ms. Heather BATEMAN

Kalamazoo College (D)

1200 Academy Street, Kalamazoo MI 49006-3295
County: Kalamazoo FICE Identification: 002275
Unit ID: 170532
Telephone: (269) 337-7000 Carnegie Class: Bac-A&S
FAX Number: (269) 337-7251 Calendar System: Quarter
URL: www.kzoo.edu
Established: 1833 Annual Undergrad Tuition & Fees: $48,666
Enrollment: 1,436 Coed
Affiliation or Control: Independent Non-Profit IRS Status: 501(c)3
Highest Offering: Baccalaureate
Accreditation: NH

01 President .... Dr. Jorge G. GONZALEZ
05 Associate Provost .... Dr. Laura L. FURGE
10 Interim VP Business & Finance .... Ms. Catherine BONNES
111 Vice President College Advancement .... Mr. Albert J. DESIMONE
32 VP Student Devel & Dean of Students .... Dr. Sarah B. WESTFALL
85 Associate Provost for Intl Pgms .... Dr. Margaret WIEDENHOEFT
13 Chief Information Officer .... Mr. Gregory S. DIMENT
09 Director of Inst Support/Research .... Ms. Tara WEBB
35 Assoc Dean of Stdnts/1st Yr Exper .... Ms. Dana JANSMA
06 Registrar .... Ms. Nicole KRAGT
15 Human Resources Manager .... Ms. Renee E. BOELCKE
07 Dean of Admission and Financial Aid .... Mr. Eric P. STAAB
37 Director of Financial Aid .... Ms. Becca MURPHY
26 Director of College Communication .... Ms. Kate WORSTER
18 Director of Facilities Management .... Ms. Susan K. LINDEMANN
40 Director Bookstore .... Ms. Deborah L. THOMPSON
29 Director of Alumni Relations .... Ms. Kimberly J. ALDRICH
38 Director of Student Counseling .... Dr. Kenlanna FERGUSON
121 Director of Advising .... Ms. Lesley J. CLINARD
36 Interim Dir Ctr Career/Prof Dev .... Ms. Valerie MILLER
04 Administrative Asst to President .... Ms. Melanie K. WILLIAMS
08 Head Librarian .... Dr. Stacy A. NOWICKI
102 Dir Foundation/Corporate Relations .... Ms. Ann M. JENKS
19 Director Security/Safety .... Mr. Timothy YOUNG
41 Athletic Director .... Ms. Rebecca S. HALL
88 Enrollment Data Specialist .... Ms. Linda WIRGAU
30 Director of Development .... Mr. Andrew M. MILLER
44 Director Annual Giving .... Ms. Laurel S. PALMER

Kalamazoo Valley Community College (E)

6767 West O Avenue, PO Box 4070,
Kalamazoo MI 49003-4070
County: Kalamazoo FICE Identification: 006949
Unit ID: 170541
Telephone: (269) 488-4400 Carnegie Class: Assoc/HT-High Trad
FAX Number: (269) 488-4220 Calendar System: Semester
URL: www.kvcc.edu
Established: 1966 Annual Undergrad Tuition & Fees (In-District): $3,446
Enrollment: 8,316 Coed
Affiliation or Control: Local IRS Status: 501(c)3
Highest Offering: Associate Degree
Accreditation: NH, ACFEI, COARC, DH, EMT, MAC

01 President .... Dr. L. Marshall WASHINGTON
05 Provost and VP Instr Student Succ .... Dr. Peter LINDEN
11 EVP Enrollment/Campus Operations .... Mr. Michael COLLINS
10 Vice President Finance & Business .... Mr. Brian LUETH
15 Vice President for Human Resources .... Mr. Aaron HILLIARD
13 Vice Pres for Admin Svc/Info Tech .... Mr. Tim WELSH
31 VP for Strategic Business/Cmty Dev .... Mr. Craig JBARA
121 Dean of Student Success .... Ms. Laura COSBY

108 AVP for Analytics/Res/Compliance .... Ms. Kathy JOHNSON
19 Director of Public Safety .... Mr. Richard IVES
08 Director of Libraries .... Mr. Mark WALTERS
07 Dir Admissions/Registration/Records .... Ms. Sarah HUBBELL
09 Dir Planning/Research/Accred/Compl .... Mr. Dan MONDOUX
30 Director Development .... Mr. Steve DOHERTY
37 Director Financial Aid .... Ms. Alisha CEDERBERG
26 Director of Marketing .... Ms. Linda DEPTA
18 Dir Facilities/Construction Mgmt .... Mr. Dannie ALEXANDER
96 Mgr of Purchasing .... Mr. Paul O'CONNELL
21 Director of Business Services .... Ms. Muriel HICE
28 Director of Diversity .... Mr. Trice BATSON
41 Athletic Director .... Mr. Russ PANICO
84 Director Enrollment Management .... Mr. EJ BAST
124 Dir of Student Retention Completion .... Mr. Evan PAUKEN
04 Admin Assistant to the President .... Ms. Sherry SMURR
29 Director Alumni Affairs .... Ms. Kathy JOHNSON

Kellogg Community College (F)

450 North Avenue, Battle Creek MI 49017-3397
County: Calhoun FICE Identification: 002276
Unit ID: 170550
Telephone: (269) 965-3931 Carnegie Class: Assoc/MT-VT-High Trad
FAX Number: (269) 962-4290 Calendar System: Semester
URL: www.kellogg.edu
Established: 1956 Annual Undergrad Tuition & Fees (In-District): $3,928
Enrollment: 4,814 Coed
Affiliation or Control: Local IRS Status: 501(c)3
Highest Offering: Associate Degree
Accreditation: NH, ADNUR, DH, EMT, NDT, PTAA, RAD

01 President .... Mr. Mark P. O'CONNELL
05 Vice President Instruction .... Dr. Paul WATSON
32 Vice Pres Student & Community Svcs .... Dr. Kay KECK
10 Chief Financial Officer .... Mr. Richard SCOTT
57 Chair Arts & Communication Dept .... Ms. Barbara SUDEIKIS
81 Chair Math & Science Dept .... Ms. Carole DAVIS
49 Dean Arts and Sciences .... Ms. Tonya FORBES
102 Executive Director KCC Foundation .... Ms. Teresa DURHAM
96 Director Purchasing .... Ms. Angela CLEVELAND
06 Registrar .... Ms. Colleen WRIGHT
08 Dn Inst Effectiveness/Library Svcs .... Dr. Michele REID
41 Director Athletics & PE .... Mr. Tom SHAW
12 Director of Grahl Center .... Ms. Shari DEEVERS
12 Director of Fehsenfeld Center .... Mr. Colin MCCALEB
15 Director Human Resources .... Ms. Ali ROBERTSON
18 Dir Inst Facilities .... Mr. Brad FULLER
51 Director Lifelong Learning .... Ms. Mary GREEN
09 Director Inst Compliance Reporting .... Ms. Naomi LIVENGOOD
21 Director of Finance .... Ms. Tracy BEATTY
12 Director Regional Mfg Tech Center .... Ms. Kimberly ANDREWS-BINGHAM
35 Dean Student & Community Services .... Ms. Terah ZAREMBA
26 Dir Public Information & Marketing .... Mr. Eric GREENE
07 Director of Fin Aid & Admissions .... Ms. Nikki JEWELL
40 Bookstore Manager .... Ms. Catherine JAMES
28 Director of Diversity .... Dr. Jorge ZEBALLOS
04 Manager President's Office .... Ms. Pauline ROMBAUGH
103 Dean Workforce Development .... Dr. Jan KARAZIM
36 Director Career & Emp Services .... Mr. Patrick CASEY
37 Director Financial Aid .... Ms. Nikki JEWELL
121 Manager Academic Advising .... Ms. Donna MALASKI
19 Chief of Public Safety .... Mr. Austin SIMONS

Kendall College of Art & Design of Ferris State University (G)

17 Fountain Street, NW, Grand Rapids MI 49503
Telephone: (800) 676-2787 Identification: 770273
Accreditation: &NH, ART, CIDA

Kettering University (H)

1700 University Avenue, Flint MI 48504-6214
County: Genesee FICE Identification: 002262
Unit ID: 169983
Telephone: (810) 762-9500 Carnegie Class: Masters/M
FAX Number: (810) 762-9837 Calendar System: Semester
URL: www.kettering.edu
Established: 1919 Annual Undergrad Tuition & Fees: $43,490
Enrollment: 2,311 Coed
Affiliation or Control: Independent Non-Profit IRS Status: 501(c)3
Highest Offering: Master's
Accreditation: NH, ACBSP

01 President .... Dr. Robert K. MCMAHAN
04 Executive Assistant to President .... Ms. Evelyn YAEGER
04 Assistant to President .... Ms. Megan HANSON
05 Provost & VP Academic Affairs .... Dr. James ZHANG
10 VP Administration & Finance .... Mr. Tom AYERS
84 VP Enrollment Services .... Mr. Kip DARCY
32 VP Student Life & Dean of Students .... Ms. Betsy E. HOMSHER
111 VP Univ Advancement/Ext Relations .... Ms. Susan DAVIES
13 VP Instruct/Admin & Info Technology .... Ms. Viola SPRAGUE
106 VP Kettering Global .... Ms. Christine WALLACE
20 Associate Provost .... Dr. Kathryn SVINARICH
15 Director of Human Resources .... Ms. Camilla KEMP
102 Dir of Philanthropy Corp/Found .... Mr. Thomas SOMMER
29 Dir of Alumni Engagement .... Mr. Steven BANDURSKI
44 Dir of Philanthropy Indiv Giving .... Mr. David TINDALL
19 Director of Campus Safety .... Mr. Paul CRANE

37 Director Student Financial Aid ....Ms. Diane K. KIMES
21 Controller ....Ms. Nancy FIKE
09 Director of Institutional Research ....Dr. Mark WOODS
58 Dean Grad Studies & Research ....Mr. Scott REEVE
18 Director Physical Plant ....Mr. Joseph ASPERGER
08 Director Library Services ....Ms. Dina MEIN
07 Director of Admissions ....Mr. Scott TRAVIS
41 Director Athletics/Rec Service ....Mr. Michael L. SCHAAL
93 Director Minority Student Affairs ....Mr. L.B MCCUNE
104 Director International Office ....Ms. Laura ALLEN
109 Director Auxiliary Services ....Ms. Nadine L. THOR
26 Dir of Media & Public Relations ....Ms. Jeanne POLYDORIS
06 Registrar ....Ms. Judi LANGOLF
23 Director Wellness Center ....Ms. Cristina REED
39 Director Residence Life ....Ms. Sybil JACOB
78 Director Coop Educ & Career Svcs ....Ms. Venetia PETTEWAY
88 MI SBDC Regional Director ....Ms. Janis MUELLER
96 Purchasing Manager ....Ms. Kathleen A. REMENDER
14 Director of IT Operations ....Mr. Daniel GARCIA
25 Contract/Grant Specialist ....Ms. Jodi L. DORR
105 Webmaster ....Ms. Donna WICKS
88 Dir Enrollment Events/Visitor Rels .....Ms. Sheila ADAMS COWES
88 Director Special Events ....Ms. Michele LOPER
121 Asst Dir Academic Success Center ....Ms. Sam KLASKOW
54 Dean Engineering ....Mr. Craig HOFF
49 Dean Sciences/Liberal Arts ....Dr. Kathryn SVINARICH

Keweenaw Bay Ojibwa Community College (A)

111 Beartown Rd, PO Box 519, Baraga MI 49908
County: Baraga FICE Identification: 041647
Unit ID: 461315
Telephone: (906) 353-4640 Carnegie Class: Tribal
FAX Number: (906) 353-8107 Calendar System: Semester
URL: www.kbocc.edu
Established: 1975 Annual Undergrad Tuition & Fees (In-District): $3,140
Enrollment: 98 Coed
Affiliation or Control: Local IRS Status: 501(c)3
Highest Offering: Associate Degree
Accreditation: NH

01 President ....Ms. Lori Ann SHERMAN
10 Vice Pres of Operations ....Ms. Cherie DAKOTA
05 Dean of Instruction ....Dr. B. Louise VIRTANEN
32 Dean of Students ....Ms. Liz JULIO
07 Admissions Officer ....Ms. Betti SZAROLETTA
37 Director Financial Aid ....Mr. Patrick RACETTE

Kirtland Community College (B)

4800 W. 4 Mile Road, Grayling MI 49738
County: Crawford FICE Identification: 007171
Unit ID: 170587
Telephone: (989) 275-5000 Carnegie Class: Assoc/HVT-Mix Trad/Non
FAX Number: (989) 563-5915 Calendar System: Semester
URL: www.kirtland.edu
Established: 1966 Annual Undergrad Tuition & Fees (In-District): $4,170
Enrollment: 1,528 Coed
Affiliation or Control: Local IRS Status: 501(c)3
Highest Offering: Associate Degree
Accreditation: NH, CAHIIM, CVT, EMT, SURGT

01 President ....Dr. Thomas QUINN
05 Vice Pres of Instructional Services ....Dr. Julie LAVENDER
32 Vice Pres of Student Svcs/Registrar ....Ms. Michelle VYSKOCIL
10 Vice Pres of Business Services ....Mr. Jason BROGE
13 Chief Info Ofcr/Title III Proj Dir ....Mr. Matt BIERMANN
75 Dean of Occupational Programs ....Mr. Steven FOSGARD
08 Director of Library & Tutoring Svcs ....Ms. Deb SHUMAKER
37 Director of Financial Aid ....Ms. Christin BATES
18 Director of Facilities ....Mr. Ron SHARPE
15 Dir of Human Resources/Talent Dev ....Mr. Nathan SUTTON
09 Director of Institutional Research ....Mr. Nick BAKER
102 Foundation Director ....Mr. David LEPPER
26 Director of Public Information ....Vacant
07 Admissions Coordinator ....Mr. Ryan MADDIS
19 Director Security/Safety ....Mr. Glenn GUTIERREZ
21 Director of Finance ....Ms. Kristin BARNHART
00 Chair Board of Trustees ....Ms. MaryAnn FERRIGAN
103 Director Workforce Development ....Ms. Kathleen FOX
105 Director Web Services ....Ms. Marj ESCH

Kuyper College (C)

3333 East Beltline Avenue, NE,
Grand Rapids MI 49525-9749
County: Kent FICE Identification: 002311
Unit ID: 171881
Telephone: (616) 222-3000 Carnegie Class: Bac-Diverse
FAX Number: (616) 988-3608 Calendar System: Semester
URL: www.kuyper.edu
Established: 1939 Annual Undergrad Tuition & Fees: $21,989
Enrollment: 184 Coed
Affiliation or Control: Independent Non-Profit IRS Status: 501(c)3
Highest Offering: Master's
Accreditation: NH, BI, SW

01 President ....Dr. Patricia HARRIS
05 Academic Dean ....Dr. Jeff FISHER
06 Registrar ....Ms. Sarah BEHM
10 Controller/CFO ....Ms. Christine MULKA
111 Vice Pres for College Advancement ....Mr. Ken CAPISCIOLTO
07 Director of Admissions ....Mr. Kevin GILLIAM
37 Financial Aid Director ....Ms. Agnes M. RUSSELL
44 Manager of the Annual Fund ....Ms. Lisa RUSTICUS
04 Assistant to the President ....Ms. Alyssa BLOM
08 Director of Library Services ....Ms. Michelle NORQUIST
32 Dean of Students/Workforce Dev ....Mr. Curt ESSENBURG
18 Maintenance Supervisor ....Mr. Tim CHUPP
29 Manager of Alumni Relations ....Ms. Lisa RUSTICUS
15 Director of Human Resources ....Ms. Annie FIELDS
13 Director Computing/Info Management ....Mr. Keith TORNO
49 Arts and Sciences ....Mr. Andrew ZWART
70 Social Work ....Mr. Greg SCOTT
73 Theology ....Dr. Branson PARLER
85 International Student Services ....Ms. Jana POSTMA
50 Director of Business Leadership ....Mr. Marc ANDREAS
106 Director of Online Learning ....Mr. Darwin GLASSFORD

Lake Michigan College (D)

2755 E Napier, Benton Harbor MI 49022-1899
County: Berrien FICE Identification: 002277
Unit ID: 170620
Telephone: (269) 927-1000 Carnegie Class: Bac/Assoc-Assoc Dom
FAX Number: N/A Calendar System: Semester
URL: www.lakemichigancollege.edu
Established: 1946 Annual Undergrad Tuition & Fees (In-District): $4,500
Enrollment: 3,477 Coed
Affiliation or Control: Local IRS Status: 501(c)3
Highest Offering: Baccalaureate
Accreditation: NH, ADNUR, DA, DMS, MAC, RAD

01 President ....Dr. Trevor A. KUBATZKE
11 VP Administrative Services ....Ms. Anne C. ERDMAN
10 Chief Financial Officer ....Ms. Kelli HAHN
04 Exec Assistant to the President ....Ms. Rebecca STEFFEN
05 VP Academics ....Dr. Leslie KELLOGG
103 Dean Career Education Workforce ....Dr. Ken FLOWERS
49 Dean Arts & Sciences ....Dr. Gary ROBERTS
76 Dean Health Sciences ....Ms. Marla CLARK
84 VP of Enrollment & Community Engage ......Mr. Doug SCHAFFER
56 VP Regional Campuses ....Ms. Barbara CRAIG
88 Manager Mainstage Services ....Mr. Mike NADOLSKI
18 Director Facilities Management ....Ms. Sara VANDERVEEN
13 Exec Dir Informational Technology ....Vacant
26 Director Marketing & Communications ....Ms. Candice ELDERS
06 Registrar ....Ms. Sara SKINNER
102 Exec Director College Foundation ....Ms. Mary KLEMM
96 Purchasing Manager ....Mr. Nathan MAIN
90 Director Teaching/Learning Center ....Mr. Mark KELLY
08 Head Librarian ....Ms. Diane BAKER
09 Director of Institutional Research ....Mr. Daniel KMITTA
19 Director Security/Safety ....Mr. Steve SILCOX
39 Director Student Housing ....Vacant
41 Athletic Director ....Mr. Melissa GRAU
37 Director Financial Aid ....Ms. Kemmoree DUNCOMBE
07 Director Admission & Recruitment ....Mr. Jeremy SCHAEFFER

Lake Superior State University (E)

650 W Easterday Avenue,
Sault Sainte Marie MI 49783-1699
County: Chippewa FICE Identification: 002293
Unit ID: 170639
Telephone: (906) 632-6841 Carnegie Class: Bac-Diverse
FAX Number: (906) 635-2111 Calendar System: Semester
URL: www.lssu.edu
Established: 1946 Annual Undergrad Tuition & Fees (In-State): $11,895
Enrollment: 1,963 Coed
Affiliation or Control: State IRS Status: 501(c)3
Highest Offering: Baccalaureate
Accreditation: NH, ACBSP, CAEPT, EMT, MT, NURSE

01 President ....Dr. Rodney S. HANLEY
05 Provost/VP Academic Affairs ....Dr. Lynn GILLETTE
32 Vice Pres Student Affairs ....Dr. Michael BEAZLEY
10 Vice President Finance ....Mr. Morrie WALWORTH
84 Vice President Enrollment/Mktg & IT ....Mr. John KAWAUCHI
102 Executive Director of Foundation ....Mr. Tom COATES
81 Interim Dean Sci & the Environment ....Dr. Steven JOHNSON
49 Interim Dean of Educ & Liberal Arts ....Dr. Barb LIGHT
66 Dean Health and Behavior ....Dr. Ronald HUTCHINS
50 Dean Innovations & Solutions ....Dr. Kimberly MULLER
18 Interim Director Physical Plant ....Mr. Todd SALO
06 Registrar ....Ms. Nancy NEVE
07 Interim Director of Admissions ....Ms. Stacy POST
15 Director of Human Resources ....Ms. Wendy BEACH
36 Director of Academic Services ....Ms. Geralyn NARKIEWICZ
37 Interim Director of Financial Aid ....Ms. Katelynn COON
38 Director of Counseling ....Ms. Kristin LARSON
28 Diversity Ofcr/Asst Dir Housing ....Mr. Derric KNIGHT
29 Director Alumni Relations ....Ms. Susan FITZPATRICK
96 Purchasing Manager ....Ms. Stacy CHARLES
23 Director Health Services ....Ms. Karen STOREY
28 Dir Native American Ctr/Diversity ....Ms. Stephanie SABATINE
41 Director of Athletics ....Dr. David PAITSON
35 Director Student Life ....Ms. Sharmay WOOD
40 Bookstore Manager ....Ms. Amber MCLEAN
09 Institutional Research Analyst ....Mr. Deepak PATNALA

Lansing Community College (F)

610 N Capitol Avenue, Lansing MI 48933
County: Ingham FICE Identification: 002278
Unit ID: 170657
Telephone: (517) 483-1200 Carnegie Class: Assoc/MT-VT-High Trad
FAX Number: (517) 483-1845 Calendar System: Semester
URL: www.lcc.edu
Established: 1957 Annual Undergrad Tuition & Fees (In-District): $3,530
Enrollment: 12,882 Coed
Affiliation or Control: Local IRS Status: 501(c)3
Highest Offering: Associate Degree
Accreditation: NH, ADNUR, COMTA, DH, DMS, EMT, IFSAC, NDT, #RAD, SURGT

01 President ....Dr. Brent KNIGHT
05 Provost ....Ms. Elaine POGONCHEFF
10 Exec VP Finance/Admin & Advancement ....Dr. Lisa WEBB SHARPE
21 Chief Financial Officer ....Mr. Don WILSKE
13 Chief Information Officer ....Mr. Kevin BUBB
11 Exec Dir Administrative Svcs ....Mr. Chris MACKERSIE
20 Associate VP Academic Affairs ....Dr. Sally WELCH
30 Assoc VP External Affs/Development ....Dr. Toni GLASSCOE
88 Dean Health & Human Services ....Ms. Margie CLARK
103 Dean Community Educ/Workforce Dev ....Mr. Bo GARCIA
49 Dean Arts & Sciences ....Ms. Andrea HOAGLAND
32 Dean Student Affairs ....Ms. Ronda MILLER
72 Dean Technical Careers ....Mr. Mark COSGROVE
15 Exec Director Human Resources ....Ms. Ann KRONEMAN
28 Chief Diversity Officer ....Ms. Tonya BAILEY
26 Director Public Affairs ....Ms. Marilyn TWINE
09 Exec Dir Center for Data Science ....Mr. Matt FALL

Lawrence Technological University (G)

21000 W Ten Mile Road, Southfield MI 48075-1058
County: Oakland FICE Identification: 002279
Unit ID: 170675
Telephone: (248) 204-4000 Carnegie Class: Masters/L
FAX Number: (248) 204-3727 Calendar System: Semester
URL: www.ltu.edu
Established: 1932 Annual Undergrad Tuition & Fees: $33,570
Enrollment: 3,069 Coed
Affiliation or Control: Independent Non-Profit IRS Status: 501(c)3
Highest Offering: Doctorate
Accreditation: NH, ACBSP, ART, CIDA, IACBE

01 President and CEO ....Dr. Virinder K. MOUDGIL
04 Exec Assistant to the President ....Ms. Karen MCARDLE
05 Provost & VP Academic Affairs ....Dr. Maria J. VAZ
88 Exec Dir Marburger STEM Center ...Dr. Sibrina Nichelle COLLINS
10 Vice Pres Finance/Admin ....Ms. Linda L. HEIGHT
111 Vice Pres University Advancement ....Ms. Christine MEOLA
26 Vice Pres Mktg & Public Affairs ....Mr. Bruce J. ANNETT, JR.
20 Assistant Provost ....Mr. Jim JOLLY
84 Asst Provost Enrollment Management ....Ms. Lisa R. KUJAWA
48 Dean of Architecture & Design ....Mr. Karl DAUBMANN
49 Interim Dean of Arts & Sciences ....Mr. Glen BAUER
54 Dean of Engineering ....Dr. Nabil F. GRACE
50 Dean of Management ....Dr. Bahman MIRSHAB
32 Dean of Students & Diversity Dir ....Mr. Kevin FINN
13 Chief Information Officer/IT Svcs ....Mr. Tim CHAVIS
07 Director of Admissions ....Ms. Jane T. ROHRBACK
06 University Registrar ....Ms. Noreen FERGUSON
08 Director Library ....Mr. Gary R. COCOZZOLI
18 Director of Campus Facilities ....Mr. Carey G. VALENTINE
14 Director Help Desk/Services ....Ms. Charlene RAMOS
37 Director of Financial Aid ....Ms. Susie POLI-SMITH
41 Dir of Rec/Athletics & Wellness ....Mr. Scott TRUDEAU
36 Director of Career Services ....Ms. Peg PIERCE
35 Assistant Dean of Students ....Ms. Cyndi SPOTTS
39 Director of Residence Life ....Ms. Kimberly JERDINE
86 Exec Dir Corp & Comm Partnerships ....Mr. Mark J. BRUCKI
102 Dir of Corp & Foundations Relations .....Ms. Nadia FADEL-BAZZI
112 Director of Major Gifts ....Ms. Julie VULAJ
15 Exec Director of Human Resources ....Ms. Deshawn JOHNSON
40 Manager Campus Bookstore ....Ms. Adria RAHN
109 Director of Dining Services ....Ms. Nancy THOMAS
27 Dir of Univ Comm & Academic Editor ....Ms. Renee TAMBEAU
88 Managing Editor Univ News Bureau ....Mr. Matt ROUSH
19 Director of Campus Safety ....Mr. Steven J. BOGDALEK
44 Director of Annual Giving ....Ms. Lauren N. SEEBOLD
31 Exec Dir of Outreach & Spec Events ....Ms. Robin LECLERC
110 Coordinator of Advancement Services ....Ms. Brande' OLIVER
88 University Architect ....Mr. Joseph C. VERYSER
121 Dir of Academic Achievement Center ....Dr. Gladys M. AVILES
09 Dir of Inst Research/Academic Plng ....Ms. Noreen FERGUSON
96 Purchasing Supervisor ....Ms. Michelle BUTKOVICH
105 Director of Web Services ....Mr. Christian FORREST
106 eLearning Architect & Pgm Producer ....Dr. Lynn MILLER-WIETECHA
29 Director Alumni Affairs ....Ms. Krysta COLEMAN

Macomb Community College (H)

14500 Twelve Mile Road, Warren MI 48088-3896
County: Macomb FICE Identification: 008906
Unit ID: 170790
Telephone: (586) 445-7241 Carnegie Class: Assoc/MT-VT-Mix Trad/Non
FAX Number: (586) 445-7886 Calendar System: Semester
URL: www.macomb.edu

Established: 1954 Annual Undergrad Tuition & Fees (In-District): $3,375
Enrollment: 21,014 Coed
Affiliation or Control: Local IRS Status: 501(c)3
Highest Offering: Associate Degree
Accreditation: NH, ACFEI, ADNUR, CAHIIM, COARC, EMT, IFSAC, MAC, OTA, PTAA, SURGT

01 President ... Dr. James SAWYER
05 Interim VP/Provost Learning Unit ... Dr. Donald RITZENHEIN
10 Vice President for Business ... Ms. Elizabeth ARGIRI
15 Vice President for Human Resources ... Ms. Denise WILLIAMS
111 VP College Adv/Community Relations ... Vacant
26 Dean University Relations ... Mr. Kevin CHANDLER
32 Vice President for Student Services . Ms. Jill M. THOMAS-LITTLE
49 Dean Arts & Sciences ... Dr. Marie PRITCHETT
76 Dean Health/Public Services ... Dr. Nara MIRIJANIAN
54 Dean Engineering & Adv Tech ... Mr. Donald HUTCHISON
50 Dean Business & Info Technology ... Mr. David CORBA
35 Dean of Student Success ... Dr. Susan BOYD
115 Director Finance & Investments ... Ms. Kathi POINDEXTER
88 Director Public Service Institute ... Mr. Michael LOPEZ
27 Director Marketing & Recruitment ... Ms. Audrey TAKACS
09 Director Institutional Research ... Ms. Deirdre SYMS
88 Director Special Research Projects ... Dr. Randall HICKMAN
06 Registrar/Dir Enrollment Services ... Dr. Carrie JEFFERS
102 Director MCC Foundation ... Ms. Christina AYAR
38 Dir Counseling & Academic Advising ... Ms. Michelle KOSS
96 Purchasing Administrator ... Mr. Dennis COSTELLO
41 Director of Athletics ... Mr. Bryan RIZZO
18 Director Facilities Management ... Mr. Cleveland SIMMONS
37 Director of Financial Aid ... Mr. Douglas LEVY
36 Director Career Employment Services ... Mr. Robert PENKALA
51 Dir Workforce Continuing Education ... Ms. Elise JOHNSON
13 CIO ... Mr. Michael ZIMMERMAN
08 Dean Libraries/Learning Resources ... Mr. Michael BALSAMO
43 General Counsel ... Mr. Jeffrey STEELE

Madonna University (A)

36600 Schoolcraft Road, Livonia MI 48150-1176
County: Wayne FICE Identification: 002282
Unit ID: 170806
Telephone: (734) 432-5300 Carnegie Class: Masters/L
FAX Number: (734) 432-5333 Calendar System: Semester
URL: www.madonna.edu
Established: 1937 Annual Undergrad Tuition & Fees: $21,900
Enrollment: 3,086 Coed
Affiliation or Control: Roman Catholic IRS Status: 501(c)3
Highest Offering: Doctorate
Accreditation: NH, ACBSP, CAEP, DIETD, DMS, FEPAC, NURSE, SW

01 President ... Dr. Michael GRANDILLO
05 Provost and VP for Academic Admin ... Dr. James O'NEILL
11 Exec Vice President & COO ... Dr. Cameron CRUICKSHANK
10 Vice Pres for Finance/Operations ... Vacant
32 Vice President for Student Affairs ... Dr. Connie TINGSON-GATUZ
42 Director of Campus Ministry ... Mr. Jesse COX
84 Asst VP Enrollment Svc & Registrar ... Ms. Dina DUBUIS
07 Director of Admissions ... Mr. Mark SHROEDER
28 Chief Diversity Officer ... Vacant
08 Librarian ... Vacant
37 Director of Financial Aid ... Mr. Phillip HANG
13 Chief Info Technology Officer ... Mr. John MONTGOMERY
15 Director of Human Resources ... Ms. Tracey DURDEN
36 Director of Career Development ... Mrs. Lenore KOWALSKI
88 Director of Special Events ... Ms. Katie ALEXANDER
19 Director Public Safety ... Mr. Gary MANN
41 Director of Athletics ... Mr. Scott KENNELL
40 Bookstore Manager ... Ms. Debbie MITCHELL
39 Director Residence Hall ... Ms. Sarah GOMBAR
24 Interim Dir Broadcast & Cinema ... Ms. Susan BOYD
88 Director Nursing Simulation Lab ... Ms. Laura VAN HORN
09 Institutional Research Coordinator ... Mr. David PIASECKI
18 Chief Facilities/Physical Plant ... Ms. Jody BATWAY
29 Alumni and Annual Fund Officer ... Ms. Kaitlyn DOUGHERTY
26 Director of Marketing ... Ms. Jennifer KENNEDY
79 Int Dean/Chair Arts & Humanities ... Dr. Kevin EYSTER
50 Interim Dean School of Business ... Dr. Deborah DUNN
58 Dean Graduate Studies ... Dr. Deborah DUNN
66 Dean Nursing & Health ... Dr. Judith MCKENNA
83 Dean Natural & Social Sciences ... Dr. Karen ROSS
53 Dean Education ... Dr. Karen OBSNIUK
101 Secretary Board of Trustees ... Mr. Matthew BEATTIE
30 Director of Development ... Mr. John DOYLE
104 Asst VP Academic Plng/Study Abroad ... Mr. John MAGEE
106 Associate Dean of Online Education ... Dr. Elena QURESHI
04 Executive Asst to President ... Ms. Nancy BUNTON
100 Chief of Staff ... Mr. Neil NEIDHARDT

MIAT College of Technology (B)

2955 South Haggerty Road, Canton MI 48188
County: Wayne FICE Identification: 020603
Unit ID: 169655
Telephone: (734) 423-2139 Carnegie Class: Spec 2-yr-Tech
FAX Number: (734) 858-5000 Calendar System: Other
URL: www.miat.edu
Established: Annual Undergrad Tuition & Fees: $12,833
Enrollment: 700 Coed
Affiliation or Control: Proprietary IRS Status: Proprietary
Highest Offering: Associate Degree
Accreditation: ACCSC

01 Campus President ... Mr. Kevin BURCHETT

Michigan School of Psychology (C)

26811 Orchard Lake Road,
Farmington Hills MI 48334-4512
County: Oakland FICE Identification: 021989
Unit ID: 169220
Telephone: (248) 476-1122 Carnegie Class: Spec-4-yr-Other Health
FAX Number: (248) 476-1125 Calendar System: Semester
URL: www.msp.edu
Established: 1981 Annual Graduate Tuition & Fees: N/A
Enrollment: 173 Coed
Affiliation or Control: Independent Non-Profit IRS Status: 501(c)3
Highest Offering: Doctorate; No Undergraduates
Accreditation: NH, CLPSY

01 President/Chief Executive Officer ... Dr. Fran BROWN
03 Vice President/Chief Operating Ofcr ... Ms. Diane ZALAPI
05 Program Director/Chief Academic Ofc ... Dr. Shannon CHÁVEZ-KORELL
13 Dir of Info Tech & Campus Security ... Mr. Jeffrey CROSS
08 Head Academic Librarian ... Ms. Michelle WHEELER
06 Registrar ... Ms. Amanda MING
07 Admissions/Recruitment Coordinator ... Ms. Carrie HAUSER
11 Dir of Administrative Operations ... Ms. Laura LANE
23 Director of Clinical Training ... Dr. Heidi MARTIN

Michigan State University (D)

426 Auditorium Road, East Lansing MI 48824-1046
County: Ingham FICE Identification: 002290
Unit ID: 171100
Telephone: (517) 355-1855 Carnegie Class: DU-Highest
FAX Number: N/A Calendar System: Semester
URL: www.msu.edu
Established: 1855 Annual Undergrad Tuition & Fees (In-State): $14,460
Enrollment: 50,019 Coed
Affiliation or Control: State IRS Status: 501(c)3
Highest Offering: Doctorate
Accreditation: NH, ANEST, CAATE, CACREP, CAEPT, CEA, CIDA, CLPSY, CONST, DIETD, DIETI, FEPAC, IPSY, JOUR, LAW, LSAR, MED, MFCD, MT, MUS, NURSE, OSTEO, PLNG, SCPSY, SP, SW, VET

01 President ... Dr. Samuel L. STANLEY
05 Provost/Exec VP Academic Affairs ... Vacant
11 Exec Vice Pres for Administration ... Dr. Satish UDPA
101 Secretary to Board ... Ms. Nakia BARR
46 Vice Pres Research/Graduate Studies ... Dr. Stephen HSU
32 VP Student Affairs & Services ... Dr. Denise B. MAYBANK
86 Vice President Governmental Affairs ... Dr. Kathleen WILBUR
10 VP Finance Operations/Treasurer ... Mr. Mark P. HAAS
111 Vice Pres Univ Advancement ... Ms. Marti HEIL
43 VP Legal Affairs/General Counsel ... Mr. Bob YOUNG
18 Assc VP Infrastructure Plng & Facil ... Mr. Dan BOLLMAN
109 Vice President Auxiliary Services ... Mr. Vennie GORE
26 VP Communication & Brand Strategy ... Ms. Heather C. SWAIN
27 Vice Pres & Univ Spokesperson . Ms. Emily GERKIN GUERRANT
22 Dir Inclusion/Intercult Initiatives ... Ms. Paulette GRANBERRY-RUSSELL
88 Assoc VP Research/Graduate Studies ... Dr. Paul M. HUNT
58 Assoc Prov and Dean Grad School ... Dr. Judith STODDART
20 Assoc Prov/Dean Undergrad Educ ... Dr. Sekhar CHIVUKULA
31 Assoc Prov Univ Outreach/ Engagement ... Dr. Hiram E. FITZGERALD
84 Assoc Provost Acad Svcs/Enroll Mgt ... Dr. John D. GABOURY
16 Assoc Prov/VP Academic Human Res ... Mr. Theodore H. CURRY, II
45 Asst VP & Director of Plng/Budgets ... Mr. David S. BYELICH
15 Asst Vice Pres for Human Resources ... Ms. Sharon BUTLER
13 Chief Information Officer ... Vacant
88 Asst VP Ofc of Sponsored Programs ... Dr. Twila REIGHLEY
21 Controller ... Mr. Greg DEPPONG
07 Director of Admissions ... Vacant
29 Assoc VP for Alumni Relations ... Mr. Bob THOMAS
25 Director Contract & Grant Admin ... Mr. Daniel T. EVON
36 Assoc Dir Career Services/Placement ... Dr. Phil GARDNER
38 Director Counseling Center ... Dr. Scott BECKER
88 Dir MI AgBioResearch ... Dr. Doug BUHLER
56 Assoc Dir MSU Extension ... Dr. Jeff DWYER
37 Director of Financial Aid ... Mr. Richard SHIPMAN
06 Registrar ... Mr. Steve SHABLIN
85 Director Intl Students/Scholars ... Mr. James DORSETT
23 Director MSU Student Health Ctr ... Dr. Glynda M. MOORER
92 Dean Honors College ... Dr. Cynthia JACKSON-ELMOORE
41 Int Dir Intercollegiate Athletics ... Mr. William R. BEEKMAN
08 Director of Libraries ... Mr. Clifford H. HAKA
88 Dir Natl Supercond Cyclotron Lab ... Dr. Brad SHERRILL
19 Police Chf/Dir Police & Pub Safety ... Ms. Kelly ROUDEBUSH
47 Dean Col Agricul/Natural Resources ... Dr. Ronald HENDRICK
79 Dean College Arts & Letters ... Dr. Christopher P. LONG
79 Dean Res Col Arts/Humanities ... Dr. Stephen L. ESQUITH
50 Dean Eli Broad Col of Business ... Dr. Sanjay GUPTA
60 Dean Col Communications/Arts & Sci ... Dr. Prabu DAVID
53 Dean College of Education ... Dr. Robert FLODEN
54 Dean College of Engineering ... Dr. Leo KEMPEL
63 Dean College Human Medicine ... Dr. Norman BEAUCHAMP
82 Dean James Madison College ... Dr. Sherman W. GARNETT
61 Dean College of Law ... Mr. Lawrence PONOROFF
81 Dean Lyman Briggs College ... Dr. Michele H. JACKSON
64 Dean College of Music ... Mr. James FORGER
81 Int Dean College Natural Science ... Ms. Cheryl SISK
66 Dean College of Nursing ... Dr. Randolph RASCH
63 Int Dean Col Osteopathic Medicine ... Dr. Andrea AMALFITANO
83 Dean College of Social Sciences ... Dr. Rachel CROSEN
74 Dean College Veterinary Medicine ... Dr. John C. BAKER
82 Dean Intl Studies & Programs ... Dr. Steven D. HANSON
04 Administrative Asst to President ... Ms. Marnie GOODWIN
100 Chief of Staff ... Mr. Michael ZEIG
09 Director of Institutional Research ... Mr. Stephen HSU
102 Dir Foundation/Corporate Relations ... Ms. Deepa SRIKANTA
105 Director Web Services ... Mr. Randy BROWN
30 Chief Development Officer ... Mr. Bob GROVES
39 Dir Resident Life/Student Housing ... Ms. Kathy COLLINS
44 Director Annual Giving ... Ms. Kathleen DENEAU
96 Director of Purchasing ... Ms. Kim WATSON
104 Director Study Abroad ... Dr. Opal LEEMAN BARTZIS

Michigan Technological University (E)

1400 Townsend Drive, Houghton MI 49931-1295
County: Houghton FICE Identification: 002292
Unit ID: 171128
Telephone: (906) 487-1885 Carnegie Class: DU-Higher
FAX Number: (906) 487-2935 Calendar System: Semester
URL: www.mtu.edu
Established: 1885 Annual Undergrad Tuition & Fees (In-State): $15,646
Enrollment: 7,292 Coed
Affiliation or Control: State IRS Status: 501(c)3
Highest Offering: Doctorate
Accreditation: NH, CEA, CONST, MT

01 President ... Dr. Richard J. KOUBEK
05 Provost/Sr Vice Pres Acad Affairs ... Dr. Jacqueline E. HUNTOON
86 Vice Pres Governmental Relations ... Mr. William R. KORDENBROCK
46 Vice President for Research ... Dr. David D. REED
84 Vice Pres Univ Relations/Enrollment ... Dr. John B. LEHMAN
111 VP Advancement & Alumni Engagement ... Dr. Bill ROBERTS
32 Dean of Students/Assoc Provost ... Dr. Bonnie B. GORMAN
10 CFO/Senior VP for Administration ... Ms. Susan E. KERRY
92 Dean Pavlis Honors College ... Dr. Lorelle MEADOWS
26 Asst VP Univ Mktg/Communications ... Mr. Ian REPP
08 Director of the Library ... Mr. Joshua OLSON
09 Institutional Analysis ... Mr. Richard ELENICH
29 Asst VP of Alumni Engagement ... Ms. Brenda RUDIGER
06 Registrar ... Ms. Theresa K. JACQUES
07 Director Undergraduate Recruitment ... Ms. Allison A. CARTER
15 Director Human Resources ... Ms. Renee HILLER
37 Director of Financial Aid ... Mr. Joe J. COOPER
36 Director Career Services ... Ms. Beth WILLIAMS
18 Exec Director Facilities Management ... Vacant
114 Exec Director Budget and Planning ... Ms. Debbie L. SHELDON
38 Director Counseling Services ... Ms. Amber BENNETT
19 Director and Chief Public Safety ... Mr. Brian J. CADWELL
22 Exec Director Affirmative Programs ... Ms. Beth LUNDE-STOCKERO
96 Director of Purchasing ... Ms. Danielle CYRUS
58 Assoc Provost/Dean Graduate School ... Dr. Pushpalatha MURTHY
50 Dean School of Business & Economics ... Dr. Dean L. JOHNSON
54 Dean College of Engineering ... Dr. Janet CALLAHAN
65 Dean School of Forestry ... Dr. Andrew J. STORER
49 Dean College of Sciences/Arts ... Dr. David HEMMER
77 Dean College of Computing ... Dr. Adrienne MINERICK
13 Chief Information Officer ... Mr. Joshua OLSON
41 Athletic Director ... Dr. Suzanne SANREGRET
25 Chief Contracts/Grants Admin ... Ms. Julie SEPPALA
39 Chief Housing Officer/Director ... Mr. Travis L. PIERCE
04 Dir Presidential Communications ... Ms. Heather L. HERMAN
28 Director of Diversity/Asst Dean ... Ms. Kellie RAFFAELLI
43 General Counsel ... Ms. Sarah H. SCHULTE

Mid Michigan College (F)

1375 S Clare Avenue, Harrison MI 48625-9447
County: Clare FICE Identification: 006768
Unit ID: 171155
Telephone: (989) 386-6622 Carnegie Class: Assoc/MT-VT-Mix Trad/Non
FAX Number: (989) 386-2411 Calendar System: Semester
URL: www.midmich.edu
Established: 1965 Annual Undergrad Tuition & Fees (In-District): $4,744
Enrollment: 4,048 Coed
Affiliation or Control: State/Local IRS Status: 501(c)3
Highest Offering: Associate Degree
Accreditation: NH, MAC, PTAA, RAD

01 President ... Dr. Christine M. HAMMOND
05 Vice President of Academic Services ... Dr. Jennifer FAGER
32 Vice President of Student Services ... Dr. Matt MILLER
111 VP Community Outreach/Advancement ... Dr. Scott MERTES
10 VP of Finance & Facilities ... Ms. Lillian K. FRICK
04 Exec Asst to President & Trustees ... Ms. Amy LINCE
15 Associate VP Human Resources ... Ms. Lori FASSETT
13 CIO/Associate VP Tech Services ... Mr. Anthony FREDS
26 Assoc VP Strategic Communications ... Ms. Jessie GORDON
103 Assoc VP Economic & Workforce Dev ... Mr. Scott GOVITZ
19 Assoc VP of Security Ops/Systems ... Ms. Kim BARNES
09 Assoc VP Institutional Research ... Dr. Peter VELGUTH
102 Assoc VP of the Mid Foundation ... Mr. Thomas OLVER

Monroe County Community College (G)

1555 S Raisinville Road, Monroe MI 48161-9746
County: Monroe FICE Identification: 002294
Unit ID: 171225
Telephone: (734) 242-7300 Carnegie Class: Assoc/MT-VT-Mix Trad/Non
FAX Number: (734) 242-9711 Calendar System: Semester

URL: www.monroeccc.edu
Established: 1964 Annual Undergrad Tuition & Fees (In-District): $3,965
Enrollment: 3,109 Coed
Affiliation or Control: Local IRS Status: 170(c)1
Highest Offering: Associate Degree
Accreditation: NH, ADNUR, COARC

01 President Dr. Kojo QUARTEY
05 Vice President of Instruction Dr. Grace B. YACKEE
10 Vice Pres of Admin Ms. Suzanne M. WETZEL
32 Vice Pres Student & Information Svc Mr. Randell W. DANIELS
72 Dean of Applied Sci & Eng Tech Mr. Parmeshwar COOMAR
50 Dean of Business Mr. Paul L. KNOLLMAN
76 Dean of Health Sciences Ms. Kimberly LINDQUIST
79 Dean of Humanities/Social Science Vacant
81 Dean of Science/Mathematics Mr. Kevin COOPER
06 Registrar Ms. Tracy VOGT
07 Director of Admissions/Guidance Vacant
88 Director of Upward Bound Mr. Anthony QUINN
88 Director of Respiratory Therapy Mr. Ijaz AHMED
21 Director of Financial Services Mr. Andrew FISCHER
18 Director Physical Plant Mr. Jack BURNS
109 Dir Auxiliary Services/Purchasing Ms. Kelly HEINZERLING
14 Director Data Processing Services Mr. James A. ROSS
37 Director of Financial Aid Ms. Valerie CULLER
36 Dir Business Devel/Employment Svcs Mr. Barry C. KINSEY
51 Director of Lifelong Learning Ms. Tina PILLARELLI
13 Manager Information Services Mr. Brian K. LAY
26 Director of Marketing/Communication Mr. Joseph VERKENNES
15 Director of Human Resources Ms. Linda TORBET
04 Executive Asst to President Ms. Penny R. DORCEY
09 Coord Inst Research/Eval & Assess Ms. Quri WYGONIK
102 Exec Director Foundation Mr. Joshua MYERS

Montcalm Community College (A)

2800 College Drive, Sidney MI 48885-9723
County: Montcalm FICE Identification: 002295
Unit ID: 171234
Telephone: (989) 328-2111 Carnegie Class: Assoc/MT-VT-High Trad
FAX Number: (989) 328-2950 Calendar System: Semester
URL: www.montcalm.edu
Established: 1965 Annual Undergrad Tuition & Fees (In-District): $4,530
Enrollment: 1,691 Coed
Affiliation or Control: Local IRS Status: 501(c)3
Highest Offering: Associate Degree
Accreditation: NH, MAC

01 President Mr. Robert C. FERRENTINO
05 Vice Pres for Academic Affairs Mr. Robert SPOHR
10 VP Administrative Services Ms. Connie STEWART
102 Executive Director of Foundation Ms. Lisa LUND
32 Dean Student & Enrollment Svcs Ms. Debra ALEXANDER
37 Director of Financial Aid Ms. Jessica HERRICK
13 Director Information Tech Svcs Mr. Rodney C. MIDDLETON
09 Research Analyst Mr. Vladimir EDELMAN
26 Communications Director Ms. Shelly STRAUTZ-SPRINGBORN
15 Director of Human Resources Ms. Riki JENSEN
21 Director of Accounting Ms. Kire WIERDA
18 Director of Facilities Mr. Taylor MALE
66 Dean of Nursing & Health Careers Ms. Danielle ANDERSON
07 Recruitment Director Ms. Emily CARMEY
103 Dean Industrial Ed & Workforce Trng Ms. Susan HATTO
30 Development Director Ms. Melissa CHRISTENSEN
08 Librarian Ms. Katie ARWOOD

Moody Theological Seminary-Michigan (B)

41550 E Ann Arbor Trail, Plymouth MI 48170-4308
Telephone: (734) 207-9581 FICE Identification: 031353
Accreditation: &NH, THEOL

† Regional accreditation is carried under the parent institution Moody Bible Institute, Chicago, IL.

Mott Community College (C)

1401 E Court Street, Flint MI 48503-2089
County: Genesee FICE Identification: 002261
Unit ID: 169275
Telephone: (810) 762-0200 Carnegie Class: Assoc/HT-High Trad
FAX Number: (810) 762-0257 Calendar System: Semester
URL: www.mcc.edu
Established: 1923 Annual Undergrad Tuition & Fees (In-District): $4,080
Enrollment: 7,689 Coed
Affiliation or Control: Local IRS Status: 501(c)3
Highest Offering: Associate Degree
Accreditation: NH, ACBSP, ADNUR, COARC, DA, DH, OTA, PTAA

01 President Dr. Beverly WALKER-GRIFFEA
05 Int Vice Pres Academic Affairs Ms. Michelle GLENN
32 VP Student Success Mr. Jason WILSON
10 Chief Financial Officer Mr. Larry GAWTHROP
111 Assoc VP Institutional Advancement Mr. Dale WEIGHILL
15 Associate Vice President of HR Mr. Philip ESPINOSA
103 Assoc VP Workforce & Economic Dev Mr. Robert MATTHEWS
37 Exec Dir Student Financial Svcs Mr. Richard BORUSZEWSKI
81 Dean of Math & Science Mr. Todd TROUTMAN
76 Dean of Health Sciences Dr. Rebecca MYSZENSKI
83 Dean Social Sciences & Fine Arts Ms. Mary CUSACK
50 Dean of Business Mr. Stephen SHUBERT
72 Interim Dean of Technology Dr. Madonna JACKSON
13 Chief Technology Officer Ms. Cheryl SHELTON
06 Registrar Dr. Chris ENGLE
36 Int Dir Career Center/Job Placement Mr. Aron GERICS
62 Executive Director Library Mrs. Jill SODT
18 Exec Director Physical Plant Mr. Chad STIRRETT
41 Director Athletics/Campus Rec Mr. Al PERRY
09 Exec Dir Institutional Research Vacant
35 Student Life Coordinator Ms. Alexandria DOWDALL
96 Director of Purchasing Ms. Jody MICHAEL
04 Executive Asst to President Ms. Melody BARTHOLOMEW
101 Board Relations Coordinator Mr. Michael SIMON

Muskegon Community College (D)

221 S Quarterline Road, Muskegon MI 49442-1493
County: Muskegon FICE Identification: 002297
Unit ID: 171304
Telephone: (231) 773-9131 Carnegie Class: Assoc/MT-VT-Mix Trad/Non
FAX Number: (231) 777-0440 Calendar System: Semester
URL: www.muskegoncc.edu
Established: 1926 Annual Undergrad Tuition & Fees (In-District): $6,090
Enrollment: 4,311 Coed
Affiliation or Control: Local IRS Status: Exempt
Highest Offering: Associate Degree
Accreditation: NH, ADNUR, COARC, MAC

01 President Dr. Dale K. NESBARY
03 Provost/Executive Vice President Dr. John SELMON
05 VP for Academic Affairs Ms. Kelley CONRAD
32 Dean of Student Svcs & Registrar Ms. Jean ROBERTS
20 Dean of Instruction & Assessment Dr. Edward BREITENBACH
31 Dean of Community Outreach Ms. Trynette Lottie HARPS
10 Director of Finance Mr. Kenneth LONG
13 Chief Information Officer Mr. Mike ALSTROM
37 Director Financial Aid Mr. Bruce WIERDA
09 Dir Institutional Research & Grants Mr. Eduardo BEDOYA
45 Director of Strategic Initiatives Ms. Tina DEE
15 Executive Director of HR Ms. Kristine ANDERSON
41 Dean of College Svcs & AD Mr. Marty MCDERMOTT
18 Physical Plant Director Mr. David STURGEON
29 Alumni & Donor Relations Manager Ms. Rachel STEWART
04 Executive Assistant to President Ms. Cindy S. DEBOEF

North Central Michigan College (E)

1515 Howard Street, Petoskey MI 49770-8717
County: Emmet FICE Identification: 002299
Unit ID: 171395
Telephone: (231) 348-6600 Carnegie Class: Assoc/HT-Mix Trad/Non
FAX Number: (231) 348-6628 Calendar System: Semester
URL: www.ncmich.edu
Established: 1958 Annual Undergrad Tuition & Fees (In-District): $3,857
Enrollment: 2,527 Coed
Affiliation or Control: Local IRS Status: 501(c)3
Highest Offering: Associate Degree
Accreditation: NH, EMT

01 President Dr. David R. FINLEY
05 VP Academic Affairs/Student Success Dr. Peter OLSON
10 VP of Finance & Facilities David HARTNETT
32 VP of Student Services Renee DEYOUNG
102 Executive Director Foundation Chelsea PLATTE
08 Librarian Vacant
37 Director of Financial Aid Virginia PANOFF
18 Director of Physical Plant Ernst RUSCHE
84 Dir Enrollment Services/Registrar Joseph BALINSKI
21 Director of Business Services Troy SLATER
39 Director of Campus Housing Leon NASH
15 Director of Human Resources Diana SOUZA
40 Bookstore Manager Noah MOORE-GOAD
09 Assoc Dean Research & Assessment Dr. Robert MARSH
49 Dean Liberal Arts Dr. Sara GLASGOW
66 Dean Nurs/Allied Hlth/Sci Dr. Jamie PAGELS
50 Dean Business/Manuf/Tech Charles HAYES
26 Director of College Communications Carol LAENEN
07 Director of Student Outreach Corey LANSING
13 Director of Information Services David BORING
88 Director of Resource Center Dallas CULVAHOUSE
04 Administrative Asst to President Megan VAN HORN
06 Registrar Joseph BALINSKI

Northern Michigan University (F)

1401 Presque Isle Avenue, Marquette MI 49855-5301
County: Marquette FICE Identification: 002301
Unit ID: 171456
Telephone: (906) 227-1000 Carnegie Class: Masters/M
FAX Number: (906) 227-2204 Calendar System: Semester
URL: www.nmu.edu
Established: 1899 Annual Undergrad Tuition & Fees (In-State): $10,729
Enrollment: 7,612 Coed
Affiliation or Control: State IRS Status: 501(c)3
Highest Offering: Doctorate
Accreditation: NH, CAATE, CAEP, CGTECH, DMOLS, MLTAD, MT, MUS, NURSE, RAD, SURGT, SW

01 President Dr. Fritz J. ERICKSON
05 Provost/VP Academic Affairs Dr. Kerri SCHUILING
10 VP for Finance & Administration Mr. R. Gavin LEACH
102 CEO NMU Foundation Mr. Brad CANALE
09 Assoc VP for Inst Research Mr. Jason NICHOLAS
106 VP Extended Lrng/Cmty Engagement Dr. Steve VANDENAVOND
20 Asc Provost Acad Affs/Undergrad Pgm Dr. Dale P. KAPLA
58 Interim Dir Graduate Education Dr. Lisa ECKERT
08 Dean Library/Instructional Support Dr. Leslie A. WARREN
32 Assistant VP/Dean of Students Dr. Christine G. GREER
49 Dean of Arts & Sciences Dr. Rob WINN
50 Dean Walker L Cisler Col Bus Prof. Carol JOHNSON
72 Dean Col of Technology/Occ Science Mr. Robert ESLINGER
06 Registrar Ms. Kim M. ROTUNDO
45 Asst to Pres Strategic Initiatives Ms. Cindy L. PAAVOLA
36 Dir of Acad & Career Advisement Mr. James G. GADZINSKI
37 Director of Financial Aid Mr. Michael R. ROTUNDO
38 Director Counseling Center Vacant
88 Director Glenn T Seaborg Center Mr. Chris STANDERFORD
41 Athletic Director Mr. Forrest KARR
19 Dir Public Safety/Police Services Mr. Michael J. BATH
39 Director Housing/Residence Life Mr. Jeff KORPI
07 Director of Admissions Ms. Gerri L. DANIELS
23 Chief of Staff/Physician Dr. Christopher KIRKPATRICK
15 Director of Human Resources Ms. Rhea DEVER
26 Asst VP Marketing & Communications Dr. Derek HALL
93 Dir Multicult Educ/Resource Center Ms. Shirley A. BROZZO
92 Director of Honors Program Dr. David H. WOOD
88 Director of Support/Consulting Svcs Ms. Felecia J. FLACK
24 Director Broadcast & AV Services Mr. Eric L. SMITH
29 Exec Dir Alumni Ops/Annual Giving Ms. Robyn L. STILLE
40 Bookstore Manager Mr. Paul WRIGHT
18 Associate VP Eng & Plan/Facilities Ms. Kathy A. RICHARDS
13 Chief Technology Officer Mr. David W. MAKI
96 Manager of Purchasing Mr. Steven D. BROWN
86 Exec Dir of BOT & Govt Relations Ms. Deanna HEMMILA
04 Executive Assistant to President Ms. Laura GLOVER
101 Secretary Board of Trustees Ms. Cathy NIEMI
22 Dir Affirmative Action/EEO Ms. Janet KOSKI
53 Dean Teacher Educ/Dir of Educ Dr. Joe LUBIG
28 Chief Diversity Officer Dr. Jessica CRUZ
103 Director Workforce Development Ms. Stephanie ZADROGA-LANGLOIS
105 Web Systems Director Mr. Eric JOHNSON
25 Director Grants & Contracts Ms. Erica GOFF

Northwestern Michigan College (G)

1701 E Front Street, Traverse City MI 49686-3061
County: Grand Traverse FICE Identification: 002302
Unit ID: 171483
Telephone: (231) 995-1000 Carnegie Class: Bac/Assoc-Assoc Dom
FAX Number: (231) 995-1339 Calendar System: Semester
URL: www.nmc.edu
Established: 1951 Annual Undergrad Tuition & Fees (In-District): $4,174
Enrollment: 3,954 Coed
Affiliation or Control: Local IRS Status: 501(c)3
Highest Offering: Baccalaureate
Accreditation: NH, ACFEI, ADNUR, DA, PNUR, SURGT

01 President Mr. Timothy J. NELSON
100 Chief of Staff to President & Board Ms. Holly J. GORTON
05 VP for Educational Services Dr. Stephen N. SICILIANO
10 VP of Finance & Administration Ms. Vicki COOK
15 Associate VP of Human Resources Mr. Mark LIEBLING
13 VP for Student Svcs & Technology Mr. Todd NEIBAUER
102 Assoc VP of Resource Dev & Found Ms. Rebecca M. TEAHEN
88 Exec Dir of Dennos Museum Center Mr. Eugene A. JENNEMAN
107 VP Lifelong/Professional Learning Ms. Marguerite C. COTTO
88 Director Training & Research Mr. Richard R. WOLIN
75 Director of Technical Division Mr. Ed BAILEY
88 Director of Aviation Mr. Alex BLOYE
29 Director Alumni Relations Mr. Cameron PENNY
32 Dean of Students Ms. Lisa THOMAS
37 Director of Financial Aid Ms. Linda BERLIN
90 Director of Systems and LAN Mgmt Mr. Dan WASSON
50 Director of the Hagerty Center Mr. Chad SCHENKELBERGER
20 Dir Academic Affairs/Business Div Mr. Brian HEFFNER
08 Director of Library Services Vacant
92 Director of Learning Services Ms. Kari L. KAHLER
21 Controller Mr. Troy KIERCZYNSKI
24 Director Educational Media Tech Ms. Terri GUSTAFSON
26 Exec Dir of PR/Marketing/Comm Ms. Diana FAIRBANKS
56 Director Extended Educ Services Ms. Laura MATCHETT
18 Director of Campus Services Mr. Paul PERRY
12 Supt Great Lakes Maritime Academy RAdm. Gerard ACHENBACH, USMS
06 Registrar Ms. Sheila RUPP
07 Director of Admissions Ms. Cathryn CLAERHOUT
09 Dir Research Planning Effectiveness Ms. Joy EVANS GOODCHILD
30 Director of Development Ms. Paris MORSE
88 Director of Water Studies Institute Mr. Hans VANSUMEREN
64 Director of Music Programs Mr. Jeffrey COBB
104 Director of International Services Mr. Jim BENSLEY
66 Director of Nursing Programs Ms. Laura SCHMIDT
23 Director of Health Services Ms. Renee R. JACOBSON
88 Director of Police Academy Mr. Brian HEFFNER
39 Associate Dean of Campus & Res Life Dr. Marcus BENNETT
12 Director Great Lakes Culinary Inst Ms. Les ECKERT
36 Director of Advising Ms. Lindsey DICKINSON

Northwood University (H)

4000 Whiting Drive, Midland MI 48640-2398
County: Midland FICE Identification: 004072
Unit ID: 171492
Telephone: (989) 837-4200 Carnegie Class: Spec-4-yr-Bus
FAX Number: (989) 837-4111 Calendar System: Semester
URL: www.northwood.edu
Established: 1959 Annual Undergrad Tuition & Fees: $27,060

Enrollment: 3,353 Coed
Affiliation or Control: Independent Non-Profit IRS Status: 501(c)3
Highest Offering: Master's
Accreditation: NH, ACBSP

01 President & Chief Executive Officer ....Dr. Keith A. PRETTY
05 EVP/CAO/COO ....Dr. Kristin STEHOUWER
10 Vice President Finance/CFO ....Mr. W. Karl STEPHAN
88 SVP Strategic/Corporate Alliances ....Dr. Timothy G. NASH
84 VP Enrollment Management ....Ms. Rhonda ANDERSON
30 VP University Advancement & Alumni .Mr. Justin W. MARSHALL
88 VP Exec Educ/Corp Pgm/Bus Ofcr ....Dr. Kevin G. FEGAN
26 VP Marketing/Communications/PR ....Ms. Rachel VALDISERRI
85 AVP/Dean International Programs ....Ms. Mamiko REEVES
51 Associate Dean Adult Degree Program ....Ms. Rhonda C. ANDERSON
32 Dean of Students ....Mr. Andy CRIPE
96 Director of Asset Management ....Mr. David L. BENDER
06 Registrar ....Dr. Marisa L. TOSCHKOFF
07 Director of Admissions ....Mr. Michael SULLIVAN
37 Financial Aid Systems Director ....Mr. Mark A. MARTIN
15 Director of Human Resources ....Ms. Pamela L. CHRISTIE
21 Business Office Mgr/System Director ....Ms. Susan M. RIDGWAY
29 Executive Director Alumni Relations ....Ms. Julie L. ADAMCZYK
41 Athletic Director ....Mr. David F. MARSH
19 Director Security/Safety ....Ms. April OWENS
35 Director Student Life ....Ms. Teresa GEORGE

Oakland Community College (A)

2480 Opdyke Road, Bloomfield Hills MI 48304-2266
County: Oakland FICE Identification: 002303
Unit ID: 171535
Telephone: (248) 341-2000 Carnegie Class: Assoc/HT-High Non
FAX Number: (248) 341-2099 Calendar System: Semester
URL: www.oaklandcc.edu
Established: 1964 Annual Undergrad Tuition & Fees (In-District): $2,408
Enrollment: 17,116 Coed
Affiliation or Control: State/Local IRS Status: 501(c)3
Highest Offering: Associate Degree
Accreditation: NH, ACFEI, ADNUR, COARC, DH, DMS, MAC, RAD, SURGT

01 Chancellor ....Mr. Peter PROVENZANO
05 Vice Chanc for Academic Affairs ....Dr. Mary C. MAZE
11 Vice Chanc Administrative Services ....Ms. Bobbie REMIAS
32 Vice Chanc for Student Services ....Ms. Lori PRZYMUSINSKI
15 Vice Chancellor for Human Resources ....Ms. Karen L. BATHANTI
13 Vice Chanc Info Technologies/CIO ....Mr. Robert MONTGOMERY
43 Vice Chanc for Legal Affairs ....Ms. Eileen K. HUSBAND
26 Int Vice Chanc for Marketing & Comm ....Mr. Dan J. JENUWINE
20 Assoc Vice Chanc Academic Affairs ....Dr. Timothy SHERWOOD
20 Assoc Vice Chanc Academic Affairs ....Mr. Joseph L. PETROSKY
04 Exec Administrator to Chancellor ....Ms. Cherie A. FOSTER
27 Exec Dir of Marketing & Comm ....Ms. Janet E. ROBERTS
108 Exec Director Inst Effectiveness ....Dr. Sooyeon LEE
35 Dean of Student Services ....Mr. Jahquan C. HAWKINS
35 Dean of Student Services ....Mr. Robert T. SPANN
35 Dean of Student Services ....Ms. Janice L. BROWN-WILLIAMS
66 Int Acad Dean Nursing/Health Prof ....Ms. Mary E. MILES
14 Exec Dir IT Infrastructure ....Mr. Chuck S. FLAGG
06 Registrar ....Mr. Stephen M. LINDEN
18 Director Physical Facilities ....Mr. Daniel P. CHEREWICK
19 Chief of Public Safety ....Mr. Paul J. MATYNKA
21 Controller ....Ms. Sharon K. CONVERSE
114 Director Budget & Financial Plng ....Mrs. Renee OSZUST
102 Exec Director OCC Foundation ....Mr. Daniel JENUWIN
36 Director of Career Svcs & Coop Ed ....Ms. Donna L. DUHAME-SCHMIDT
41 Athletic Director ....Ms. Jamie L. CORONA
96 Dir Purchasing/Auxiliary Svcs ....Ms. Sarah L. ROWLEY
37 Director Financial Res/Scholarships ....Ms. Wilma B. PORTER
81 Academic Dean Math/Nat Life Sci ....Mr. Ken M. WILLIAMS
80 Academic Dean Public Services/CREST ....Mr. David F. CECI
62 Academic Dean Learning Resources ....Ms. Mary Ann SHEBLE
83 Academic Dean Soc Sci & Human Svcs ....Mr. Kevin BRATTON
79 Acad Dean Humanities/Art & Design ....Ms. Cindy L. CARBONE
88 Academic Dean College Readiness ....Ms. Beverly J. STANBROUGH
60 Academic Dean English/Lit/Comm ....Ms. Cindy L. CARBONE
50 Acad Dean Bus & Info Technologies ....Mr. Tom M. HENDRICKS
88 Interim Academic Dean EMIT ....Mr. Tom M. HENDRICKS
106 Academic Dean of Distance Learning ....Ms. Kayla S. LEBLANC
88 Foundation Coordinator ....Ms. Candy GEETER
88 Director Law Enforcement Training ....Mr. David F. CECI
07 Director of Admissions ....Ms. Laurie G. HUBER
86 Exec Dir Govt & Cmty Relations ....Mr. Doug J. SMITH

Oakland Community College Auburn Hills (B)

2900 Featherstone Road, Auburn Hills MI 48326-2845
Telephone: (248) 232-4100 Identification: 770281
Accreditation: &NH, EMT

Oakland Community College Highland Lakes (C)

7350 Cooley Lake Road, Waterford MI 48327-4187
Telephone: (248) 942-3100 Identification: 770285
Accreditation: &NH

Oakland Community College Orchard Ridge (D)

27055 Orchard Lake Road,
Farmington Hills MI 48334-4579
Telephone: (248) 522-3400 Identification: 770282
Accreditation: &NH

Oakland Community College Royal Oak (E)

739 South Washington Avenue, Royal Oak MI 48067-3898
Telephone: (248) 246-2400 Identification: 770283
Accreditation: &NH

Oakland Community College Southfield (F)

22322 Rutland Drive, Southfield MI 48075-4793
Telephone: (248) 341-2000 Identification: 770284
Accreditation: &NH

Oakland University (G)

371 Wilson Boulevard, Rochester MI 48309-4400
County: Oakland FICE Identification: 002307
Unit ID: 171571
Telephone: (248) 370-2100 Carnegie Class: DU-Higher
FAX Number: N/A Calendar System: Semester
URL: www.oakland.edu
Established: 1957 Annual Undergrad Tuition & Fees (In-State): $12,606
Enrollment: 19,333 Coed
Affiliation or Control: State IRS Status: 501(c)3
Highest Offering: Doctorate
Accreditation: NH, ANEST, CACREP, CAEPT, DANCE, MED, MUS, NURSE, PH, PTA, RAD, SPAA, SW, THEA

01 President ....Dr. Ora PESCOVITZ
05 Sr VP Academic Affairs/Provost ....Dr. James P. LENTINI
32 VP Stdnt Affs/Chief Diversity Ofcr ....Mr. Glenn MCINTOSH
11 Chief Operating Officer ....Mr. Scott G. KUNSELMAN
111 VP University Advancement ....Mr. Michael WESTFALL
10 VP Finance & Administration ....Mr. John W. BEAGHAN
86 VP Government & Comm Relations ....Ms. Rochelle A. BLACK
12 Exec Dir Macomb Outreach ....Ms. Julie DICHTEL
66 Dean School of Nursing ....Dr. Judy A. DIDION
54 Dean Engineering & Computer Science ....Dr. Louay M. CHAMRA
76 Dean School Health Sciences ....Dr. Kevin A. BALL
53 Dean Educ & Human Services ....Dr. Jon MARGERUM-LEYS
49 Dean College Arts & Sciences ....Dr. Kevin J. CORCORAN
50 Dean School of Business Admin ....Dr. Michael A. MAZZEO
63 Interim Dean School of Medicine ....Dr. Duane MEZWA
08 Interim Dean University Library ....Ms. Mariela A. HRISTOVA
20 Interim Associate Provost ....Dr. Anne HITT
46 Assoc VP for Research ....Dr. David A. STONE
24 Mgr Classroom Support/Tech Service ....Mr. John J. REESER
20 Asst VP Academic Affairs ....Ms. Peggy S. COOKE
88 Director Center for Excellence ....Dr. Judith ABLESER
88 Dir Eye Research Institute ....Dr. Frank GIBLIN
88 Director FAJRI ....Dr. Sayed NASSAR
21 Assoc VP Finance & Administration ....Mr. Thomas P. LEMARBE
18 Assoc VP Facilities Management ....Ms. Patricia A. ENGLE
15 Assoc VP University Human Resources ....Mr. Ronald P. WATSON
102 Sr Director of Campaign Management .Ms. Alison K. GAUDREAU
35 Dean of Students ....Mr. Michael WADSWORTH
19 Chief of Police ....Mr. Mark B. GORDON
06 Registrar ....Ms. Tricia WESTERGAARD
44 Dir Annual Giving Program ....Ms. Kelly N. BRAULT
37 Director of Financial Aid ....Ms. Cindy L. HERMSEN
29 Sr Dir of Engagement/Alumni ....Ms. Sue HELDEROP
26 VP Communications & Marketing ....Mr. John O. YOUNG
41 Athletics Director ....Mr. Steven WATERFIELD
16 AVP Academic Human Resources ....Ms. Joi M. CUNNINGHAM
39 Director of University Housing ....Mr. James R. ZENTMEYER
36 Senior Director Career Services ....Mr. Wayne J. THIBODEAU
38 Director Counseling Center ....Dr. David J. SCHWARTZ
85 Director International Students ....Mr. David J. ARCHBOLD
22 Director Disability Support Svcs ....Mr. Sarah GUADALUPE
96 Director of Purchasing ....Ms. Paula S. REYES
101 VP Legal Affairs & General Counsel ....Mr. Victor A. ZAMBARDI
13 Chief Information Officer ....Ms. Theresa M. ROWE
84 Assoc VP Enrollment Management ....Ms. Dawn M. AUBRY
58 Acting Dean Graduate Education ....Dr. Susan M. AWBREY
45 Chief Strategy Officer ....Dr. Claudia A. PETRESCU
09 Director of Institutional Research ....Ms. Song YAN
104 Exec Director Global Engagement ....Ms. Rosemary MAX
106 Director of e-learning ....Dr. Shaun A. MOORE

Olivet College (H)

320 S Main Street, Olivet MI 49076-9406
County: Eaton FICE Identification: 002308
Unit ID: 171599
Telephone: (269) 749-7000 Carnegie Class: Bac-Diverse
FAX Number: (269) 749-7600 Calendar System: Semester
URL: www.olivetcollege.edu
Established: 1844 Annual Undergrad Tuition & Fees: $27,680
Enrollment: 1,224 Coed
Affiliation or Control: Independent Non-Profit IRS Status: 501(c)3
Highest Offering: Master's
Accreditation: NH

01 President ....Dr. Steven M. COREY
05 Provost and Dean of the College ....Dr. Maria DAVIS
10 Interim CFO ....Mr. Mark DERUITER
07 Vice Pres Admissions ....Ms. Lisa LEHMAN
32 Vice Pres/Dean Student Life ....Dr. Amy POPP-RADFORD
111 Vice Pres Advancement ....Mr. William HULL
13 Asst Vice President Technology ....Mr. Suresh ACHARYA
06 Registrar ....Ms. Leslie SULLIVAN
41 Athletic Director ....Mr. Ryan SHOCKEY
42 Director of Campus Ministries ....Mr. Michael F. FALES
36 Dir Career Services Network ....Vacant
37 Director of Student Financial Aid ....Ms. Libby JEAN
18 Interim Director of Facilities ....Mr. Larry COLVIN
94 Director of Women's Resource Center ....Ms. Cynthia NOYES
39 Student Housing ....Ms. Shawn HAGADON
15 Director of Human Resources ....Mrs. Terri GLASGOW
29 Director of Alumni Engagement ....Ms. Samantha PEARL
04 Executive Asst to President ....Ms. Barbara SPENCER
08 Head Librarian ....Ms. Julia FALES
19 Director Security/Safety ....Mr. Phil REED

Puritan Reformed Theological Seminary (I)

2965 Leonard Street NE, Grand Rapids MI 49525
County: Kent Identification: 667099
Telephone: (616) 977-0599 Carnegie Class: Not Classified
FAX Number: (616) 285-3246 Calendar System: Semester
URL: www.prts.edu
Established: 1995 Annual Graduate Tuition & Fees: N/A
Enrollment: N/A Coed
Affiliation or Control: Independent Non-Profit IRS Status: 501(c)3
Highest Offering: Doctorate; No Undergraduates
Accreditation: THEOL

01 President ....Dr. Joel R. BEEKE
05 Academic Dean/VP Academic Affairs ....Dr. Michael BARRETT
06 Registrar/Director of Admissions ....Mr. Jonathon BEEKE
10 Vice President for Operations ....Mr. Henk KLEYN
38 Dean of Students/Spiritual Form ....Rev. Mark KELDERMAN
04 Administrative Asst to President ....Ms. Ann C. DYKEMA
26 Chief Public Relations/Marketing ....Mr. Chris HANNA
08 Head Librarian ....Mrs. Laura LADWIG
106 Dir Online Education/E-learning ....Mr. Chris ENGELSMA
13 IT Director ....Mr. Seth HUCKSTEAD
24 Video Producer & Editor ....Mr. Darryl BRADFORD

Rochester University (J)

800 W Avon Road, Rochester Hills MI 48307-2764
County: Oakland FICE Identification: 002288
Unit ID: 170967
Telephone: (248) 218-2000 Carnegie Class: Bac-Diverse
FAX Number: (248) 218-2025 Calendar System: Semester
URL: www.rc.edu
Established: 1959 Annual Undergrad Tuition & Fees: $23,282
Enrollment: 1,168 Coed
Affiliation or Control: Independent Non-Profit IRS Status: 501(c)3
Highest Offering: Master's
Accreditation: NH, NURSE

01 President ....Dr. Brian L. STOGNER
05 Provost ....Dr. Remylin BRUDER
101 Sr VP/Special Asst to President ....Mr. Klint A. PLEASANT
10 Exec VP/Chief Financial Officer ....Mr. Thomas D. RELLINGER
07 Vice President ....Mr. Scott SAMUELS
21 Controller ....Ms. Susan IDE
18 Director Operational Support ....Mr. Jacob LAWLESS
50 Dir School of Business/Prof Studies ....Mrs. Danny CAGNET
79 Dean School of Humanities ....Dr. Catherine PARKER
15 Director of Human Resources ....Mrs. Ginny MAY
26 Dir of Communication Services ....Mr. Elliot JONES
32 Dean of Students ....Dr. Sharia HAYS
37 Director of Student Financial Svcs ....Ms. Jessica ARCHAMBEAU
08 Director of Library Services ....Mrs. Allison JIMENEZ
06 Registrar ....Ms. Rebekah PINCHBACK
108 Director of Assessment ....Dr. J. Mark MANRY
29 Director of Alumni ....Mr. Larry STEWART
121 Director of Advising ....Mrs. Debi RUTLEDGE
41 Director of Athletics ....Mr. Klint PLEASANT
42 Director of Spiritual Life ....Mr. Evan GREEN
19 Director of Safety & Security ....Mr. Jacob LAWLESS
04 Executive Assistant ....Mrs. Allyson STINNETT
13 Chief Information Technology Office ....Mr. Eric CAMPBELL
30 Director of Development ....Mrs. Jennifer PORTER
09 Director of Institutional Research ....Dr. Mark MANRY
104 GEO Coordinator ....Dr. Keith HUEY
53 Dean School of Education ....Mr. Melvin BLOHM
43 General Counsel ....Mr. Dennis VEARA

Sacred Heart Major Seminary (K)

2701 Chicago Boulevard, Detroit MI 48206-1799
County: Wayne FICE Identification: 002313
Unit ID: 172033
Telephone: (313) 883-8501 Carnegie Class: Spec-4-yr-Faith
FAX Number: (313) 883-8685 Calendar System: Semester
URL: www.shms.edu
Established: 1919 Annual Undergrad Tuition & Fees: $19,900
Enrollment: 496 Coed
Affiliation or Control: Roman Catholic IRS Status: 501(c)3
Highest Offering: Master's
Accreditation: NH, THEOL

01 Rector & President .... Msgr. Todd LAJINESS
32 Vice Rector/Dean of Seminarians .... Rev. Stephen BURR
05 Dean of Studies .... Rev. Timothy LABOE
73 Dean of the Inst for Lay Ministry .... Dr. Matthew GERLACH
10 Director Finance/Treasurer .... Ms. Ann Marie CONNOLLY
06 Registrar .... Dr. David TWELLMAN
35 Director Undergraduate Seminarians .... Rev. Clint MCDONELL
88 Graduate Spiritual Director .... Rev. Daniel TRAPP
08 Library Director .... Mr. Christopher SPILKER
58 Dir Graduate Pastoral Formation .... Rev. John VANDENAKKER
111 Director Institutional Advancement .... Mr. David ZANITSCH
18 Facilities Director .... Mr. John DUNCAN
07 Director of Admissions .... Mr. Ryan CAHILL
106 Dir of Distance Ed/Online Learning .... Dr. John GRESHAM
88 Director of Graduate Seminarians .... Rev. Charles FOX

Saginaw Chippewa Tribal College (A)

2274 Enterprise Drive, Mount Pleasant MI 48858-2335
County: Isabella FICE Identification: 037723
Unit ID: 441070
Telephone: (989) 317-4760 Carnegie Class: Tribal
FAX Number: (989) 317-4781 Calendar System: Semester
URL: www.sagchip.edu
Established: 1998 Annual Undergrad Tuition & Fees: $2,040
Enrollment: 154 Coed
Affiliation or Control: Tribal Control IRS Status: 501(c)3
Highest Offering: Associate Degree
Accreditation: NH

01 President .... Ms. Carla SINEWAY
05 Dean of Instruction .... Ms. Cheryl SWARTHOUT
32 Dean of Student Services .... Ms. Amanda FLAUGHER
07 Admissions Officer/Registrar .... Ms. Jacqueline GRAVERATTE
37 Financial Aid Officer .... Ms. Patricia ALONZO
09 Dean of Research .... Ms. Tracy REED
25 Grants and Special Projects Coord .... Ms. Gena QUALLS

Saginaw Valley State University (B)

7400 Bay Road, University Center MI 48710-0001
County: Saginaw FICE Identification: 002314
Unit ID: 172051
Telephone: (989) 964-4000 Carnegie Class: Masters/L
FAX Number: (989) 964-0180 Calendar System: Semester
URL: www.svsu.edu
Established: 1963 Annual Undergrad Tuition & Fees (In-State): $10,308
Enrollment: 8,617 Coed
Affiliation or Control: State IRS Status: 501(c)3
Highest Offering: Doctorate
Accreditation: NH, CAATE, CAEP, CEA, MT, MUS, NURSE, OT, SW

01 President .... Dr. Donald J. BACHAND
05 Provost/VP Academic Affairs .... Dr. Deborah R. HUNTLEY
10 Exec VP Admin & Business Affairs .... Mr. James G. MULADORE
29 Executive Director Alumni Relations .... Mr. James P. DWYER
32 Assoc Provost Student Affairs .... Dr. Sidney R. CHILDS
28 Spec Asst to Pres/Diversity Pgms .... Dr. Mamie T. THORNS
83 Assoc Dean Arts/Behavioral Sciences .... Dr. Carlos RAMET
49 Dean Arts/Behavioral Sciences .... Dr. Marc H. PERETZ
21 Assoc VP Admin & Business Affairs .... Mr. Ronald E. PORTWINE
43 AVP Legal Affairs/Athletic Director .... Mr. John DECKER
114 AVP for Admin & Business Affairs .... Ms. Susan L. CRANE
15 General Counsel & HR Director .... Ms. Ellen E. CRANE
13 Exec Dir Information Tech Svcs .... Mr. Larry K. EMMONS
07 Director of Admissions .... Ms. Jennifer K. PAHL
06 Registrar .... Dr. Clifford DORNE
36 Interim Director Career Services .... Mr. Thomas E. BARNIKOW
21 Director Business Services .... Ms. Connie J. SCHWEITZER
08 Dir of Melvin J Zahnow Library .... Ms. Anita DEY
25 Dir Sponsored Pgms/IRB Rsrch Compl .... Ms. Janet M. RENTSCH
15 Human Resources Manager .... Ms. Jennifer NEITZEL
37 Director Scholarships/Financial Aid .... Mr. Robert L. LEMUEL
38 Dir Student Counseling Center .... Mr. Eddie V. JONES
50 Dean College of Business/Management .... Dr. Anthony R. BOWRIN
88 Dir Environmental Health & Safety .... Mr. Robert J. TUTSOCK
88 Asst Registrar .... Dr. Shawn WILSON
102 Executive Director SVSU Foundation .... Mr. Andrew J. BETHUNE
96 Purchasing Manager .... Mr. Joshua M. WEBB
76 Dean of Health & Human Services .... Dr. Judith P. RULAND
09 Director of Institutional Research .... Dr. Nicholas J. WAGNER
101 Exec Asst to the Pres/Sec to Board .... Mrs. Mary A. KOWALESKI
20 Assoc Provost for Academic Affairs .... Dr. Joshua J. ODE
86 Director of Governmental Affairs .... Mr. John L. KACZYNSKI

St. Clair County Community College (C)

323 Erie Street, PO Box 5015, Port Huron MI 48061-5015
County: St. Clair FICE Identification: 002310
Unit ID: 172291
Telephone: (810) 984-3881 Carnegie Class: Assoc/HT-Mix Trad/Non
FAX Number: (810) 984-4730 Calendar System: Semester
URL: www.sc4.edu
Established: 1923 Annual Undergrad Tuition & Fees (In-District): $4,582
Enrollment: 3,601 Coed
Affiliation or Control: Local IRS Status: 501(c)3
Highest Offering: Associate Degree
Accreditation: NH, ADNUR, CAHIIM, #COARC, EMT, MAC, RAD

01 President .... Dr. Deborah SNYDER
04 Exec Assistant to the President .... Ms. Mary HAWTIN
11 Exec VP/Chief Operating Officer .... Mr. Kirk KRAMER
05 Chief Academic Officer .... Ms. Julie ARMSTRONG
32 VP of Student Services .... Mr. Pete LACEY
10 Chief Financial Officer .... Ms. Mary Kay BRUNNER
15 VP of Human Resources .... Ms. Bethany MAYEA
26 VP of Marketing & Communication .... Ms. Kristin COPENHAVER
09 VP of Institutional Effectiveness .... Ms. Linda DAVIS
37 Dir of Financial Assistance/Svcs .... Ms. Josephine CASSAR
06 Registrar .... Ms. Carrie BEARSS
41 Director of Athletics .... Mr. Dale VOS
08 Assoc Dean Library Services .... Ms. Kendra LAKE

Schoolcraft College (D)

18600 Haggerty Road, Livonia MI 48152-2696
County: Wayne FICE Identification: 002315
Unit ID: 172200
Telephone: (734) 462-4400 Carnegie Class: Bac/Assoc-Assoc Dom
FAX Number: (734) 462-4507 Calendar System: Semester
URL: www.schoolcraft.edu
Established: 1961 Annual Undergrad Tuition & Fees (In-District): $3,850
Enrollment: 10,558 Coed
Affiliation or Control: Local IRS Status: 501(c)3
Highest Offering: Baccalaureate
Accreditation: NH, ACFEI, ADNUR, CAHIIM, EMT, MAC, PNUR

01 President .... Dr. Conway A. JEFFRESS
10 Vice Pres/Chief Financial Officer .... Dr. Glenn CERNY
05 Vice Pres/CAO .... Dr. Cheryl HAWKINS
32 Vice Pres/Chief Student Affs Ofcr .... Dr. Cheryl M. HAGEN
26 VP & Chief Information Officer .... Mr. Patrick TURNER
49 Dean Liberal Arts & Sciences .... Dr. Michele KELLY
75 Dean Occupational Prog/Econ Dev .... Dr. Robert LEADLEY
20 Assoc Dean Stdnt Success/Retention .... Ms. Melissa SCHULTZ
88 Assoc Dean College Centers .... Dr. Bonnie HECKARD-FARMER
51 Assoc Dean Cont Educ/Prof Develop .... Dr. Leslie PETTY
38 Assoc Dean Counseling/Student Sppt .... Dr. Michael OLIVER
11 Assoc Dean Opers/Curriculum/Assess .... Ms. Cindy CICCHELLI
35 Dean of Students .... Mr. Martin HEATOR
53 Assoc Dean Occupational/Educ Pgms .... Dr. Dennis GENIG
88 Assoc Dean Public Safety Programs .... Mr. Gerald CHAMPAGNE
88 Assoc Dean Advising & Partnerships .... Dr. Laurie KATTUAH-SNYDER
72 Asst Dean Occupational Programs .... Ms. Amy JONES
15 Exec Director of Human Resources .... Ms. Laura SENSING
88 Assoc Dean of Student Relations .... Ms. Nicole WILSON-FENNELL
37 Director of Financial Aid .... Mr. Michael WILLIAMS
19 Chief of Police .... Mr. Steven KAUFMAN
96 Dir of Purchasing/Business Ops .... Mr. Matthew WILSON
21 Controller/Director of Finance .... Mr. Jon LAMB
84 Dean of Enrollment Services .... Ms. Stacey STOVER
88 Exec Dir Info Security & Networking .... Mr. Jeffrey BORTON
88 Exec Dir Academic/Admin Info Sys .... Ms. Laura CULLEN
04 Executive Asst to President .... Ms. Karla W. FRENTZOS
18 Exec Dir/Facilities Operations .... Mr. John WRIGHT
27 Exec Dir Marketing & Advancement .... Ms. Van NGUYEN
41 Director of Athletics .... Mr. Sidney FOX
44 Exec Director of Development .... Ms. Dawn MAGRETTA
06 Registrar .... Ms. Tracy MILLER

Siena Heights University (E)

1247 Siena Heights Drive, Adrian MI 49221-1796
County: Lenawee FICE Identification: 002316
Unit ID: 172264
Telephone: (517) 263-0731 Carnegie Class: Masters/S
FAX Number: (517) 264-7704 Calendar System: Semester
URL: www.sienaheights.edu
Established: 1919 Annual Undergrad Tuition & Fees: $27,124
Enrollment: 2,464 Coed
Affiliation or Control: Roman Catholic IRS Status: 501(c)3
Highest Offering: Beyond Master's But Less Than Doctorate
Accreditation: NH, ART, CAEPT, NURSE, SW

01 President .... Dr. Peg ALBERT, OP
10 Sr Vice Pres for Business/Finance .... Dr. J. Lee JOHNSON
111 Vice President for Advancement .... Mr. Daniel PENA
05 Vice President for Academic Affairs .... Dr. Sharon R. WEBER, OP
84 Vice Pres of Enrollment Mgmt Svcs .... Mr. George WOLF
107 Dean of Professional Studies/Grad .... Dr. Cheri BETZ
49 Dean College of Arts and Science .... Dr. Matthew DRAUD
32 Dean for Students .... Mr. Michael ORLANDO
06 Registrar .... Vacant
07 Director of Admissions .... Ms. Trudy MOHRE
08 Director of Library .... Mrs. Melissa SISSEN
13 Chief Information Officer .... Mr. Robert C. METZ
41 Director of Athletics .... Ms. Susan SYLJEBECK
15 Human Resource Director .... Mr. Michael L. KARABETSOS
42 Director of Campus Ministry .... Sr. Mary JONES, OP
38 Director of Counseling Services .... Mrs. Sandy MORLEY
121 Director of Academic Advising .... Mrs. Ashley WISNIEWSKI
18 Supt of Buildings & Grounds .... Mr. Brian BERTRAM
09 Director of Institutional Research .... Mr. Jason YOUNG
39 Director of Residence Life .... Ms. Samantha THACKER
19 Director of Campus Security .... Mrs. Cindy A. BIRDWELL
23 Director of Health Services .... Sr. Sharon SPANBAUER
29 Director of Alumni Relations .... Mrs. Kate HAMILTON
36 Director of Career Services .... Ms. Sarah A. CHRENKO
28 Director of Immersion & Diversity .... Mrs. Sharese MATHIS
26 Dir of Integrated Univ Marketing .... Mr. Doug GOODNOUGH
37 Director Student Financial Aid .... Mrs. Lori KOSARUE
21 Controller .... Ms. Mary KRUSE
44 Coordinator of Annual Fund .... Mrs. Shawna WILSON
04 Executive Assistant to President .... Mrs. Deborah KELLER

Southwestern Michigan College (F)

58900 Cherry Grove Road, Dowagiac MI 49047-9793
County: Cass FICE Identification: 002317
Unit ID: 172307
Telephone: (269) 782-1000 Carnegie Class: Assoc/HT-High Trad
FAX Number: (269) 782-8414 Calendar System: Semester
URL: www.swmich.edu
Established: 1964 Annual Undergrad Tuition & Fees (In-District): $5,145
Enrollment: 2,330 Coed
Affiliation or Control: State/Local IRS Status: 501(c)3
Highest Offering: Associate Degree
Accreditation: NH, ADNUR, CAHIIM

01 President .... Dr. David MATHEWS
100 Chief of Staff .... Mr. Brent BREWER
10 Vice President/Chief Business Ofcr .... Ms. Susan COULSTON
05 Vice President of Instruction .... Dr. David FLEMING
26 Vice President of Mktg/Enrollment .... Mr. Michael O'BRIEN
32 Vice President of Student Services .... Dr. Joseph ODENWALD
12 Executive Director of Niles Campus .... Mr. Jason SMITH
13 Director of IT and CIO .... Mr. Mic VALERIS
50 Dean NAC/School of Business .... Dr. Stacy YOUNG
66 Dean School Nursing/Human Services .... Ms. Rebecca JELLISON
49 Dean of Arts and Sciences .... Dr. Keith HOWELL
07 Director of Admissions .... Dr. Lucian LEONE
18 Director of Buildings & Grounds .... Mr. John EBERHART
19 Director of Campus Security/Conduct .... Mr. Lyndon PARRISH
88 Dir Educational Talent Search Pgm .... Ms. Maria KULKA
37 Director of Financial Aid .... Ms. Lauren MOW
15 Director of Human Resources .... Ms. Heather HESS
09 Director of Institutional Research .... Dr. Angela EVANS
08 Director of Library Services .... Ms. Colleen WELSCH
06 Director of Records/Registrar .... Mr. Steven CARLSON
121 Director of Student Support Svcs .... Ms. Angela PALSAK
39 Director of Student Housing .... Mr. Jeffery HOOKS
21 Controller .... Ms. Michelle KITE
88 Manager of Accounting .... Ms. Christy MANGUS
88 Manager of Academic Advising .... Ms. Kathie GRIES
89 Manager of First Year Experience .... Ms. Katie HANNAH
26 Manager of Marketing .... Ms. Michelle BOGUE
88 Manager of Student Activity Center .... Mr. William ROGGEMAN
88 Manager of Testing Center .... Ms. Kristen LOWNDS

Southwestern Michigan College Niles Area Campus (G)

33890 U.S. Highway 12, Niles MI 49120
Telephone: (800) 456-8675 Identification: 770286
Accreditation: &NH

Spring Arbor University (H)

106 E Main Street, Spring Arbor MI 49283-9799
County: Jackson FICE Identification: 002318
Unit ID: 172334
Telephone: (517) 750-1200 Carnegie Class: Masters/L
FAX Number: (517) 750-6620 Calendar System: 4/1/4
URL: www.arbor.edu
Established: 1873 Annual Undergrad Tuition & Fees: $28,810
Enrollment: 3,342 Coed
Affiliation or Control: Free Methodist IRS Status: 501(c)3
Highest Offering: Master's
Accreditation: NH, CACREP, #CAEP, CAEPN, MUS, NURSE, SW

01 University President .... Dr. Brent ELLIS
03 Executive Vice President .... Dr. Douglas A. WILCOXSON
05 VP for Academic Affairs .... Dr. Carol C. GREEN
10 VP for Finance & Administration .... Mr. Kevin W. ROSE
32 VP Student Success & Calling .... Mr. Corey ROSS
84 VP Enroll & Marketing .... Mr. Jon BAHR
15 Assistant VP for Human Resources .... Mrs. Kerry J. KLEE-TIESMAN
88 Chief Strategy Officer .... Dr. Kimberly RUPERT
04 Assistant to the President .... Mrs. Rhonda R. SAURBEK
13 Chief Technology Officer .... Mr. Randy G. MELTON
49 Dean School Arts & Sciences .... Vacant
50 Dean Gainey School of Business .... Dr. Caleb K. CHAN
53 Dean School of Education .... Vacant
35 Asst VP Student Development .... Mr. Dan VANDERHILL
06 Registrar .... Mrs. Sherri HENDRIX
07 Director of Enrollment Operations .... Vacant
21 Assistant VP Financial Services .... Mrs. Dawn I. SCHNITKEY
30 Executive Director of Development .... Mrs. Linda SCHAUB
26 Exec Dir Mktg & Communication .... Ms. Bethany L. LANDIS
41 Athletic Director .... Mr. Ryan T. COTTINGHAM
42 Chaplain .... Dr. Brian S. KONO
37 Director of Financial Aid .... Mr. Herbert K. ROTICH
09 Director Institutional Research .... Mr. Thomas P. KORMAN
121 Dir of Student Success Initiative .... Mrs. Laura S. BRECKNER
108 Director of Assessment .... Vacant
08 Director Library .... Vacant
18 Director of Physical Plant .... Mr. Marty FORTRESS
124 Director Retention & Fresh Programs .... Mrs. Carrie L. WILLIAMS
104 Director Cross Cultural Studies .... Mrs. Diane L. KURTZ
23 Exec Dir Student Health/Wellness .... Mrs. Mary BRODA
39 Associate Dean of Students .... Mr. Robert C. PRATT
36 Career Development Advisor .... Mr. Chad W. MELTON
19 Director Campus Safety .... Mr. Scott L. KREBILL

106 Assoc Dean External/SAUonline .... Mr. Gary R. TUCKER
28 Chief Diversity Officer .... Mr. Kevin BROWN
29 Director Alumni Relations .... Vacant
105 Web Architect .... Mr. Ryan J. KELLY

SS. Cyril and Methodius Seminary (A)

3535 Indian Trail, Orchard Lake MI 48324-1623
County: Oakland FICE Identification: 037384
Unit ID: 260211
Telephone: (248) 683-0310 Carnegie Class: Not Classified
FAX Number: (248) 738-6735 Calendar System: Semester
URL: www.sscms.edu
Established: 1885 Annual Graduate Tuition & Fees: N/A
Enrollment: N/A Coed
Affiliation or Control: Roman Catholic IRS Status: 501(c)3
Highest Offering: Master's; No Undergraduates
Accreditation: THEOL

01 Rector/President .... V.Rev. Michael WORONIEWICZ
05 Dean Intellectual Formation .... Rev.Fr. Leonard OBLOY
42 Dean Pastoral Formation .... RevMsg. Francis KOPER
06 Registrar .... Ms. Joanna OLEJNICZAK-CAUSHAJ

University of Detroit Mercy (B)

4001 W McNichols Road, Detroit MI 48221-3038
County: Wayne FICE Identification: 002323
Unit ID: 169716
Telephone: (313) 993-1000 Carnegie Class: DU-Mod
FAX Number: (313) 993-1229 Calendar System: Semester
URL: www.udmercy.edu
Established: 1877 Annual Undergrad Tuition & Fees: $28,000
Enrollment: 5,113 Coed
Affiliation or Control: Roman Catholic IRS Status: 501(c)3
Highest Offering: Doctorate
Accreditation: NH, ANEST, ARCPA, CACREP, CAEP, CAHIIM, CLPSY, DENT, DH, NURSE, SW

01 President .... Dr. Antoine M. GARIBALDI
05 Provost and VP for Academic Affairs .... Ms. Pamela ZARKOWSKI
10 Int VP for Business & Finance/CFO .... Mr. Thomas MANCEOR
111 VP for University Advancement .... Mr. Arnold D'AMBROSIO
84 VP Enrollment & Student Affairs .... Ms. Deborah STIEFFEL
101 University Secretary & Senior Atty .... Ms. Monica BARBOUR
18 Assoc Vice Pres Facil Management .... Ms. Tamara BATCHELLER
15 Associate Vice Pres Human Resources .... Ms. April LYNCH
26 Assoc VP Marketing & Communications .... Mr. Gary ERWIN
13 Associate Vice President ITS .... Mr. Edward TRACY, II
06 Associate VP/Registrar .... Ms. Diane M. PRAET
44 Exec Director of Annual Giving .... Ms. Judy WERNETTE
112 Exec Director of Major Gifts .... Mr. Dennis CARLESSO
32 Dean of Students .... Ms. Monica WILLIAMS
08 Dean of Libraries .... Ms. Jennifer DEAN
09 Director of Institutional Research .... Ms. Shelley WAGNON
37 Director Scholarships & Fin Aid .... Ms. Caren BENDES
35 Associate Director of Student Life .... Ms. Dorothy STEWART
41 Director of Athletics .... Mr. Robert VOWELS
49 Dean College of Liberal Arts/Ed .... Dr. Mark DENHAM
61 Dean School of Law .... Ms. Phyllis CROCKER
54 Interim Dean College Engr & Science .... Dr. Katherine SNYDER
48 Dean School of Architecture .... Mr. Daniel PITERA
50 Dean Col Business Admin .... Dr. Joseph EISENHAUER
52 Dean School of Dentistry .... Dr. Mert AKSU
76 Dean CHP/Nursing .... Dr. Neal ROSENBERG
36 Dir Center for Career & Prof Devel .... Vacant
39 Director Residence Life .... Ms. Lanae GILL
04 Exec Asst to the President .... Ms. Lisa MACDONNELL
85 Dir of International Services .... Vacant
38 Director of Wellness Center .... Ms. Annamaria SILVERI
92 Co-Director of Honors Program .... Dr. Evan PETERSON
92 Co-Director of Honors Program .... Dr. Nicholas ROMBES
88 Coordinator of Advancement Systems .... Ms. Stephanie JONES
07 Executive Director of Admissions .... Ms. Tyra ROUNDS
108 Director of Assessment .... Vacant
19 Director Public Safety .... Mr. Joel GALLIHUGH
25 Dir of Sponsored Research .... Vacant
53 Chair Education Department .... Dr. Alan GRIGG
106 Dir Online Education/E-learning .... Ms. Jennifer DEAN
102 Dir Foundation/Corporate Relations .... Ms. Yvonne LINDSTROM
22 Title IX & Equity/Compliance Coord .... Ms. Marjorie LANG
29 Director Alumni Relations .... Ms. Margaret PATTISON

University of Detroit Mercy Corktown Campus (C)

2700 Martin Luther King Jr. Blvd, Detroit MI 48208-2576
Telephone: (313) 494-6700 Identification: 770291
Accreditation: &NH

University of Detroit Mercy School of Law (D)

651 E Jefferson Avenue, Detroit MI 48226-4349
Telephone: (313) 596-0200 Identification: 770292
Accreditation: &NH, LAW

University of Michigan-Ann Arbor (E)

500 S. State Street, Ann Arbor MI 48109
County: Washtenaw FICE Identification: 002325
Unit ID: 170976
Telephone: (734) 764-1817 Carnegie Class: DU-Highest
FAX Number: N/A Calendar System: Trimester
URL: umich.edu
Established: 1817 Annual Undergrad Tuition & Fees (In-State): $15,262
Enrollment: 46,002 Coed
Affiliation or Control: State IRS Status: 501(c)3
Highest Offering: Doctorate
Accreditation: NH, ART, CAATE, CAEPT, CLPSY, DANCE, DENT, DH, DIETD, DIETI, HSA, IPSY, LAW, LIB, LSAR, MED, MIDWF, MUS, NURSE, PDPSY, PH, PHAR, PLNG, SW

01 President .... Dr. Mark S. SCHLISSEL
05 Provost .... Dr. Martin A. PHILBERT
10 Exec Vice President/CFO .... Mr. Kevin P. HEGARTY
17 Exec VP Medical Affairs/Dean Med .... Dr. Marschall S. RUNGE
30 Vice President Development .... Mr. Thomas A. BAIRD
32 Vice President Student Life .... Dr. E. Royster HARPER
46 Interim Vice President for Research .... Dr. Rebecca M. CUNNINGHAM
86 Vice Pres Governmental Relations .... Ms. Cynthia H. WILBANKS
26 Vice Pres Communications .... Ms. Kallie B. MICHELS
43 Vice Pres/General Counsel .... Mr. Timothy G. LYNCH
101 Vice Pres/Sec of the University .... Ms. Sally J. CHURCHILL
04 Exec Asst to the President .... Ms. Erika J. HRABEC
100 Special Counsel to the Provost .... Ms. Christine M. GERDES
114 Vice Provost Acad/Budget Affairs .... Ms. Amy DITTMAR
20 Vice Provost Acad & Faculty Affairs .... Dr. Lori J. PIERCE
20 Vice Provost Acad & Faculty Affairs .... Dr. Sara B. BLAIR
58 V Prov Acad Affs/Dean Grad Studies .... Dr. Michael J. SOLOMON
104 Vice Provost Global & Engaged Educ .... Vacant
28 Vice Prov Diversity/Eqty/Inclusion .... Dr. Robert M. SELLERS
08 V Prov Acad Innov & Univ Librarian .... Dr. James L. HILTON
84 Vice Provost for Enrollment Mgmt .... Dr. Kedra B. ISHOP
09 Assoc Vice Provost & Exec Dir OBP .... Ms. Tammy C. BIMER
07 Director Undergrad Admissions .... Ms. Erica L. SANDERS
15 Int Assoc VProv/Sr Dir Acad HR/OIE .... Mr. Jeffery R. FRUMKIN
18 Assoc VP Facilities/Operations .... Mr. Henry D. BAIER
21 Assoc VP Finance .... Vacant
115 Chief Investment Officer .... Mr. Erik LUNDBERG
88 AVP Research Nat Sciences/Engr .... Dr. Volker SICK
88 Asst VP and Chief of Staff Research .... Dr. Nicholas WIGGINTON
46 Assoc VP for Research .... Dr. Michael J. IMPERIALE
88 Asst VP Reg and Comp Oversight .... Ms. Lois BRAKO
46 Assoc VP for Research .... Dr. Stephanie J. ROWLEY
88 Asst VP Animal Resources .... Dr. William KING
88 Asst VP Animal Pgm Comp Oversight .... Mr. William GREER
46 Assoc VP for Research .... Dr. Eric MICHIELSSEN
88 Asst VP Fed Rel for Research .... Ms. Kristina KO
46 Assoc VP Research .... Dr. Kelly B. SEXTON
35 Assoc VP Student Life/Dean Stdnts .... Ms. Laura B. JONES
35 Assoc VP Student Life .... Ms. Anjali N. ANTURKAR
35 Assoc VP Student Life .... Dr. Simone HIMBEAULT-TAYLOR
35 Assoc VP Student Life .... Mr. Kambiz KHALILI
16 Assoc VP for Human Resources .... Ms. Laurita E. THOMAS
13 Chief Information Officer .... Dr. Ravi PENDSE
06 University Registrar .... Mr. Paul A. ROBINSON
96 Director Procurement Services .... Vacant
38 Director Counseling & Psych Service .... Dr. Todd D. SEVIG
39 Director University Housing .... Vacant
23 Exec Dir University Health Service .... Dr. Robert D. ERNST
19 Exec Dir Pub Safety/Security .... Mr. Eddie L. WASHINGTON
37 Exec Director Financial Aid .... Ms. Pamela W. FOWLER
41 Director of Athletics .... Mr. Warde MANUEL
48 Dean Col Architecture/Urban Plng .... Dr. Jonathan MASSEY
49 Int Dn Col Literature/Science/Arts .... Dr. Elizabeth R. COLE
54 Dean College of Engineering .... Dr. Alec D. GALLIMORE
61 Dean Law School .... Mr. Mark D. WEST
67 Dean College of Pharmacy .... Dr. James T. DALTON
65 Dean Sch Natural Resources/Environ .... Dr. Jonathan T. OVERPECK
64 Dean School Music/Theatre & Dance .... Dr. David GIER
57 Dean School of Art & Design .... Dr. Gunalan L. NADARAJAN
50 Dean School of Business .... Mr. Scott DERUE
52 Dean School of Dentistry .... Dr. Laurie K. MCCAULEY
53 Dean School of Education .... Dr. Elizabeth B. MOJE
62 Dean School of Information .... Dr. Thomas A. FINHOLT
68 Dean School of Kinesiology .... Dr. Lori PLOUTZ-SNYDER
66 Dean School of Nursing .... Dr. Patricia D. HURN
80 Dean School of Public Policy .... Mr. Michael S. BARR
70 Dean School of Social Work .... Dr. Lynn VIDEKA
69 Dean School of Public Health .... Dr. Fredrick BOWMAN
29 President Alumni Association .... Mr. Steve C. GRAFTON
102 Director Foundation/Corporate Rels .... Ms. Maureen MARTIN
44 Director Annual Giving .... Ms. Megan F. DOUD

University of Michigan-Dearborn (F)

4901 Evergreen Road, Dearborn MI 48128-1491
County: Wayne FICE Identification: 002326
Unit ID: 171137
Telephone: (313) 593-5000 Carnegie Class: Masters/L
FAX Number: (313) 593-5452 Calendar System: Trimester
URL: www.umd.umich.edu
Established: 1959 Annual Undergrad Tuition & Fees (In-State): $12,930
Enrollment: 9,330 Coed
Affiliation or Control: State IRS Status: 501(c)3
Highest Offering: Doctorate
Accreditation: NH, CAEPT, CEA

01 Chancellor .... Dr. Dominico GRASSO
05 Prov/Vice Chanc Academic Affairs .... Dr. Catherine A. DAVY
10 Vice Chancellor Business Affairs .... Mr. Jeffrey L. EVANS
84 Vice Chanc Enrollment Management .... Vacant
111 Vice Chanc Inst Advancement .... Dr. Casandra ULBRICH
26 Vice Chanc for External Relations .... Mr. Kenneth KETTENBEIL
21 Director of Financial Services .... Mr. Noel HORNBACHER
06 Registrar .... Mr. Timothy TAYLOR
27 Director Communications/Marketing .... Ms. Beth MARMARELLI
86 Government Relations Manager .... Mr. Mike LATVIS
15 Director of Human Resources .... Ms. Rima BERRY-HUNG
29 Alumni Engagement .... Ms. Cristina FRENDO
20 Associate Provost Undergraduate .... Dr. Mitchel SOLLENBERGER
58 Associate Provost Graduate .... Dr. Ilir MITEZA
13 Dir IT Strategy/Operations .... Ms. Carrie SHUMAKER
08 Interim Director of Library .... Dr. Maureen LINKER
09 Int Dir of Institutional Research .... Dr. Mitchel SOLLENBERGER
07 Director of Admissions .... Ms. Deb PEFFER
32 Dean of Students .... Dr. Amy FINLAY
37 Director of Financial Aid .... Ms. Katherine ALLEN
38 Director of Counseling .... Dr. Sara BYCZEK
36 Director of Career Services .... Ms. Regina M. STORRS
85 Director of International Affairs .... Mr. Francisco LOPEZ
18 Exec Dir of Facilities Operations .... Ms. Carol GLICK
19 Chief of Police .... Mr. Gary GORSKI
22 Director Institutional Equity .... Ms. Pam HEATLIE
28 Sp Counsel to Chanc for Inclusion .... Dr. Ann LAMPKIN-WILLIAMS
49 Dean Col Arts/Science/Letters .... Dr. Martin HERSHOCK
54 Dean Col of Engr/Computer Science .... Dr. A. W. ENGLAND
50 Dean College of Business .... Dr. Raju BALAKRISHNAN
53 Dean College of Educ/Health/HS .. Dr. Ann LAMPKIN-WILLIAMS
88 Director of Enrollment Research .... Mr. Dan MERIAN
41 Athletic Director .... Mr. Matt BEAUDRY
102 Dir Foundation/Corporate Relations .... Ms. Cheryl DONOHOE
44 Director Annual Giving .... Ms. Eva GOGOLA
90 Director Academic Computing .... Ms. Carrie SHUMAKER

University of Michigan-Flint (G)

303 E Kearsley Street, Flint MI 48502-1950
County: Genesee FICE Identification: 002327
Unit ID: 171146
Telephone: (810) 762-3000 Carnegie Class: DU-Mod
FAX Number: (810) 762-5725 Calendar System: Semester
URL: www.umflint.edu
Established: 1956 Annual Undergrad Tuition & Fees (In-State): $11,304
Enrollment: 7,836 Coed
Affiliation or Control: State IRS Status: 501(c)3
Highest Offering: Doctorate
Accreditation: NH, ANEST, CAEPN, CEA, #COARC, MUS, NURSE, PTA, RTT, SW

01 Chancellor .... Dr. Susan E. BORREGO
05 Provost/VC Academic Affairs .... Dr. Susan ALCOCK
32 VC Campus Inclusion & Student Life .... Dr. Christopher GIORDANO
10 VC Business and Finance .... Mr. Michael J. HAGUE
111 Interim VC University Advancement .... Dr. Mary Jo SEKELSKY
121 Asst VC for Student Success .... Vacant
35 Assoc VC & Dean of Students .... Dr. Julie SNYDER
84 VC for Enrollment Management .... Dr. Kristi HOTTENSTEIN
58 Int Assoc Provost/Dean Grad Pgms .... Dr. Stephen TURNER
20 Asst Prov/Dean Undergrad Studies .... Vacant
26 Exec Dir Communications & Marketing .... Mr. Jim PECK
86 Director Government Relations .... Ms. Mia MCNEIL
28 Director of Educational Oppty .... Vacant
08 Director of Library & Dean of EAS .. Mr. Robert L. HOUBECK, JR.
06 Registrar .... Ms. Karen A. ARNOULD
07 Admissions Director .... Ms. Karen CUZYDLO
37 Director Financial Aid .... Ms. Lori VEDDER
15 Director Human Res/Affirm Action .... Ms. Beth MANNING
49 Dean College of Arts & Sciences .... Dr. Susan GANO-PHILLIPS
50 Dean School of Management .... Dr. Scott JOHNSON
66 Dean School of Nursing .... Dr. Margaret ANDREWS
76 Dean College of Health Studies .... Dr. Donna FRY
53 Dean Sch Education & Human Svcs .... Dr. Robert BARNETT
51 Director of Extended Learning .... Mr. Nicholas GASPAR
19 Director of Public Safety .... Mr. Raymond D. HALL
18 Dir Facilities Mgmt/Auxiliary Svcs .... Mr. George HAKIM
13 Director Info Technology Services .... Mr. Scott ARNST
121 Director Student Success Center .... Dr. Dawn MARKELL
46 Director of Research .... Dr. Kenneth SYLVESTER
21 Director of Financial Svcs & Budget .... Mr. Gerald GLASCO
88 Director University Outreach .... Ms. Paula NAS
96 Procurement Agent Senior .... Ms. Brenda ROTH
09 Director of Institutional Analysis .... Ms. Fawn SKARSTEN
38 Director CAPS .... Vacant
39 Assoc Director Student Housing .... Mr. Clark DAWOOD
100 Chief of Staff .... Dr. Tess BARKER
04 Executive Asst to the Chancellor .... Ms. Dru A. DORAN
29 Exec Director Alumni Relations .... Dr. Mary Jo SEKELSKY
30 Interim Director of Development .... Dr. Mary Jo SEKELSKY
92 Director Honors Program .... Dr. Maureen THUM
88 Sr Dir of Student Involv & Ldrship .... Vacant
91 Dir of Adm Info Mgmt Services .... Ms. Jay GANDHI
88 Dir Center Gender & Sexuality .... Ms. Heather JOHNSON
88 Dir Thompson Center for T&L .... Dr. Tracy WACKER

Van Andel Institute Graduate School (H)

333 Bostwick Avenue NE, Grand Rapids MI 49503
County: Kent Identification: 667085
Telephone: (616) 234-5708 Carnegie Class: Not Classified
FAX Number: (616) 234-5709 Calendar System: Semester
URL: vaigs.vai.org
Established: 2005 Annual Graduate Tuition & Fees: N/A
Enrollment: N/A Coed
Affiliation or Control: Independent Non-Profit IRS Status: 501(c)3
Highest Offering: Doctorate; No Undergraduates

Accreditation: NH

01 President/Dean of VAIGS .... Dr. Steven J. TRIEZENBERG
05 Assistant Dean of Graduate School .... Dr. Brian HAAB
06 Enrollment and Records Admin .... Ms. Christy MAYO
04 Executive Asst to
President .... Mrs. Susanne MILLER-SCHACHINGER
32 Chief Student Affairs/Student Life .. Ms. Nancy SCHAPERKOTTER
04 Administrative Assistant .... Ms. Kathy BENTLEY

Walsh College of Accountancy and Business Administration (A)

3838 Livernois Road, Box 7006, Troy MI 48007-7006
County: Oakland FICE Identification: 004071
Unit ID: 172608
Telephone: (248) 689-8282 Carnegie Class: Spec-4-yr-Bus
FAX Number: (248) 689-9066 Calendar System: Semester
URL: www.walshcollege.edu
Established: 1922 Annual Undergrad Tuition & Fees: N/A
Enrollment: 2,299 Coed
Affiliation or Control: Independent Non-Profit IRS Status: 501(c)3
Highest Offering: Doctorate
Accreditation: NH, ACBSP

01 President & CEO .... Ms. Marsha KELLIHER
05 Executive VP/Chief Academic Ofc .... Dr. Michael A. RINKUS
10 Vice President/CFO/Treasurer . Ms. Helen C. KIEBA-TOLKSDORF
15 VP/Chief Human Resources/Admin
Ofcr .... Ms. Elizabeth A. BARNES
26 VP/Chief Marketing & Enrollment Ofc .... Ms. Patti SWANSON
30 Vice President/Chief Dev Officer .... Ms. Susan FOLEY
04 Exec Assistant to the President .... Ms. Stephanie M. WHEELER
20 Asst VP Accreditation and Acad Adm .... Ms. Victoria R. SCAVONE
09 Asst VP Institutional Research .... Ms. Kelly PEREZ-VERGARA
106 Director Office of Online Learning .... Mr. Drew SMITH
20 Director Academic Administration .... Ms. Monique CARDENAS
37 Director Financial Aid .... Ms. Catherine BERRAHOU
18 Director Facilities/Auxiliary Svcs .... Ms. Chris STOUT
21 Controller .... Mr. Ryan KUNZELMAN
07 Director Admissions/Acad Advising .... Ms. Heather RIGBY
06 Director of Records/Registrar .... Ms. Stacy JOHNSON
13 Exec Dir Ofc of Info Technology .... Mr. Jacob KLEIN
12 Director Novi Campus .... Mr. Jason SWEET
36 Director Career Services .... Ms. Brenda PAINE
88 Chair Management .... Dr. Ann SAURBIER
88 Chair Business Comm .... Dr. Jenny TATSAK
88 Chair Marketing .... Dr. Michael LEVENS
29 Manager of Alumni Relations .... Ms. Melanie ESLAND
88 Chair Accounting .... Mr. John BLACK
88 Chair Finance & Economics .... Mr. John MOORE
88 Chair Decision Sciences .... Mr. Dave SCHIPPERS
88 Chair Taxation .... Mr. Richard DAVIDSON
08 Chief Library Officer .... Ms. Caryn NOEL

Washtenaw Community College (B)

4800 E Huron River Dr, Ann Arbor MI 48105-4800
County: Washtenaw FICE Identification: 002328
Unit ID: 172617
Telephone: (734) 973-3300 Carnegie Class: Assoc/HT-Mix Trad/Non
FAX Number: (734) 677-5413 Calendar System: Semester
URL: www.wccnet.edu
Established: 1965 Annual Undergrad Tuition & Fees (In-District): $2,520
Enrollment: 12,335 Coed
Affiliation or Control: Local IRS Status: 501(c)3
Highest Offering: Associate Degree
Accreditation: NH, ACFEI, ADNUR, DA, PTAA, RAD, SURGT

01 President .... Dr. Rose B. BELLANCA
10 Exec VP & Chief Financial Officer .... Mr. William JOHNSON
05 VP for Instruction .... Dr. Kimberly HURNS
15 VP Human Resources & Labor .... Mr. Samuel VELTRI
32 Exec VP Student & Academic Services .... Ms. Linda BLAKEY
111 AVP of College Advancement .... Mr. Phil SNYDER
26 VP Economic/Community & College
Dev .... Ms. Michelle MUELLER
84 AVP Recruitment & Enrollment .... Mr. Aamer CHAUDRI
45 Exec Dir Inst Effect Plng & Accred .... Dr. Julie MORRISON
121 Dean Supp Svcs & Student Advocacy .... Dr. Elizabeth ORBITS
50 Dean Business & Computer Tech .... Ms. Eva SAMULSKI
81 Dean Math/Sciene/Engineering .... Vacant
76 Dean Health Science .... Dr. Valerie GREAVES
36 Dean Career Svc/UA Programs .... Ms. Marilyn DONHAM
28 Dean Diversity & Inclusion .... Vacant
88 Dean Adv Tech/Public Service .... Mr. Brandon TUCKER
10 Controller .... Ms. Lynn GRACE
114 Dir Budget/Purchasing/Auxiliary Svc .... Ms. Barbara FILLINGER
16 Director Human Resource Svcs .... Ms. Christine MIHALY
37 Director Financial Aid .... Ms. Lori TRAPP
09 Director Institutional Research .... Dr. Roger MOURAD
19 Chief Public Safety .... Mr. Scott HILDEN
35 Dir Student Development/Activities .... Mr. Peter LESHKEVICH
86 Dir of Government Relations .... Vacant
43 General Counsel .... Mr. Larry BARKOFF
04 Dir of President and Board Affairs .... Ms. Vanessa BROOKS
100 Chief of Staff .... Vacant
06 Dir of Records/Registrar .... Ms. Kathy CURRIE
106 Exec Director Online Education .... Mr. Peter BACCILE

Wayne County Community College District (C)

801 W Fort Street, Detroit MI 48226-3010
County: Wayne FICE Identification: 009230
Unit ID: 172635
Telephone: (313) 496-2600 Carnegie Class: Assoc/HT-Mix Trad/Non
FAX Number: (313) 961-9439 Calendar System: Semester
URL: www.wcccd.edu
Established: 1967 Annual Undergrad Tuition & Fees (In-District): $2,886
Enrollment: 14,806 Coed
Affiliation or Control: State/Local IRS Status: 501(c)3
Highest Offering: Associate Degree
Accreditation: NH, AT, DA, DH, EMT, SURGT

01 Chancellor .... Dr. Curtis L. IVERY
05 Dist VC Curriculum/Learning Pgm .... Dr. Patrick J. MCNALLY
88 Dist VC Acad Accountability/Policy .... Ms. CharMaine HINES
103 Dist VC Sch Cont Ed/Wrkforce Dev .... Dr. Shawna FORBES
10 Executive VC & Chief Fiscal Officer .... Ms. Kim DICARO
15 Dist VC HR/Accountability .... Mr. Furquan AHMED
09 Dist VC IE & Research .... Ms. Johnesa HODGE
32 Asst to Chancellor for Student Svcs .... Mr. Brian SINGLETON
12 Campus President Downriver .... Mr. Anthony ARMINIAK
12 Campus President Downtown .... Ms. Denise SHANNON
12 Campus President Ted Scott Campus ...... Mr. Anthony ARMINIAK
12 Campus President Northwest .... Vacant
12 Campus President Eastern .... Mr. Mark SANFORD
17 Provost Health Sciences .... Dr. Abby FREEMAN
26 Asst to Chanc for Communication .... Ms. Unbreen AMIR
28 Provost Diversity & Inclusion .... Dr. Fidelis D'CUNHA
13 Chief Technology Officer .... Mr. Yoseph DEMISSIE
19 Chief District Police Authority .... Mr. Darrick D. MUHAMMAD
44 Chief Dev Ofcr/Scholarship Giving .... Ms. Carolyn CARTER
104 Dist Dean International Programs .... Mr. David C. BUTTY

Wayne County Community College District Downriver Campus (D)

21000 Northline Road, Taylor MI 48180
Telephone: (734) 946-3500 Identification: 770297
Accreditation: &NH

Wayne County Community College District Downtown Campus (E)

1001 West Fort Street, Detroit MI 48226
Telephone: (313) 496-2758 Identification: 770926
Accreditation: &NH

Wayne County Community College District Eastern Campus (F)

5901 Conner, Detroit MI 48213
Telephone: (313) 922-3311 Identification: 770295
Accreditation: &NH

Wayne County Community College District Northwest Campus (G)

8200 West Outer Drive, Detroit MI 48219
Telephone: (313) 943-4000 Identification: 770296
Accreditation: &NH

Wayne County Community College District Ted Scott Campus (H)

9555 Haggerty Road, Belleville MI 48111
Telephone: (734) 699-7008 Identification: 770294
Accreditation: &NH, SURGA

Wayne State University (I)

656 W. Kirby Street, Room # 4070, Detroit MI 48202-4095
County: Wayne FICE Identification: 002329
Unit ID: 172644
Telephone: (313) 577-2424 Carnegie Class: DU-Highest
FAX Number: (313) 577-8154 Calendar System: Semester
URL: www.wayne.edu
Established: 1868 Annual Undergrad Tuition & Fees (In-State): $13,097
Enrollment: 27,064 Coed
Affiliation or Control: State IRS Status: 501(c)3
Highest Offering: Doctorate
Accreditation: NH, ANEST, ARCPA, AUD, CACREP, CAEP, CAMPEP, CEA, CLPSY, DANCE, DIETC, EXSC, FUSER, LAW, LIB, MED, MIDWF, MT, MUS, NURSE, OT, PA, PH, PHAR, PLNG, PTA, RAD, RTT, SP, SPAA, SW, THEA

01 President .... Dr. M. Roy WILSON
100 Chief of Staff/VP Marketing & Comm ..... Mr. Michael G. WRIGHT
05 Provost .... Dr. Keith WHITFIELD
10 VP Finance & Business/Treasurer/CFO ...... Mr. William DECATUR
43 Vice President and General Counsel .... Mr. Louis A. LESSEM
46 Vice President for Research .... Dr. Stephen M. LANIER
30 VP Development and Alumni Affairs .... Ms. Susan E. BURNS
86 VP Government and Community Affairs ... Mr. Patrick O. LINDSEY
20 Assoc Provost for Academic Affairs .... Dr. R. Darin ELLIS
88 VP for Economic Development .... Mr. Ned STAEBLER
84 Assoc VP for Enrollment Mgmt .... Ms. Dawn MEDLEY
101 VP & Secretary to the BOG .... Ms. Julie H. MILLER
04 Assistant to the President .... Ms. Allison GUILLIOM
29 Assoc VP Alumni Relations .... Mr. Peter CABORN
15 Assoc VP of Human Resources .... Ms. Debra WILLIAMS
18 Assoc VP Facilities/Planning/Mgmt .... Vacant
114 Assoc VP Budget .... Mr. Jeff BOLTON
44 Associate VP of Individual Gifts .... Dr. Stephen E. HENRIE
32 Dean of Students .... Dr. David J. STRAUSS
07 Director Undergraduate Admissions .... Ms. Ericka JACKSON
26 Director of Communications .... Mr. Matthew T. LOCKWOOD
25 Asst VP Sponsored Program Admin .... Ms. Gail L. RYAN
37 Director of Student Financial Aid .... Ms. Catherine KAY
62 Dean University Library System .... Dr. Jon G. CAWTHORNE
06 University Registrar .... Mr. Kurt KRUSCHINSKA
49 Dean College of Liberal Arts/Sci .... Dr. Stephanie HARTWELL
61 Dean Law School .... Mr. Richard BIERSCHBACH
63 Dean School of Medicine .... Dr. Jack SOBEL
66 Dean College of Nursing .... Dr. Laurie LAUZON CLABO
54 Dean College of Engineering .... Dr. Farshad FOTOUHI
50 Dean Ilitch School of Business .... Dr. Robert E. FORSYTHE
70 Dean School of Social Work .... Dr. Sheryl KUBIAK
67 Interim Dean College of Pharmacy .... Dr. Catherine LYSACK
53 Dean College of Education .... Dr. Anita WELCH
57 Dean College Fine/Perf & Comm Arts .... Dr. Matthew SEEGER
92 Dean Honors College .... Dr. John CORVINO
58 Interim Dean Graduate School .... Dr. Ingrid GUERRA-LOPEZ
96 Assistant VP of Procurement .... Mr. Kenneth DOHERTY
104 Associate VP Outreach & Intl Pgms .... Dr. Ahmad EZZEDDINE
109 Assoc VP Business & Auxiliary Ops .... Mr. Timothy MICHAEL
88 Assoc VP Tech Commercialization .... Dr. Joan DUNBAR
13 Associate VP CIO .... Mr. Daren HUBBARD
41 Director of Athletics .... Mr. Robert FOURNIER
105 Director of Web Communications .... Mr. Nick DENARDIS
19 Chief of Police .... Mr. Anthony HOLT
22 Director Equal Opportunity .... Ms. Nikki WRIGHT
28 Assoc Provost Diversity & Inclusion ...... Dr. Marquita CHAMBLEE
36 Director of Career Services .... Mr. Ronald KENT
39 Director Housing & Residential Life .... Ms. Nikki DUNHAM
108 Director Institutional Assessment .... Dr. Catherine BARRETTE
38 Director Student Counseling .... Dr. Jeffrey KUENTZEL
09 Assoc VP Institutional Research .... Dr. Meihua ZHAI
102 Assoc VP Principal Gifts .... Ms. Tracy UTECH
21 Controller .... Ms. Tamaka BUTLER
44 Director of Annual Giving .... Ms. Joye CLARK
106 Manager Online Education/E-Learnin .... Ms. Stacy N. JACKSON
90 Director Academic Computing .... Mr. Rob THOMPSON

West Shore Community College (J)

3000 N. Stiles Road, Scottville MI 49454-0277
County: Mason FICE Identification: 007950
Unit ID: 172671
Telephone: (231) 845-6211 Carnegie Class: Assoc/MT-VT-Mix Trad/Non
FAX Number: (231) 843-5803 Calendar System: Semester
URL: www.westshore.edu
Established: 1967 Annual Undergrad Tuition & Fees (In-District): $2,930
Enrollment: 1,120 Coed
Affiliation or Control: Local IRS Status: 501(c)3
Highest Offering: Associate Degree
Accreditation: NH

01 President .... Mr. Scott WARD
04 Executive Assistant to President .... Ms. Lisa STANKOWSKI
26 Exec Director of College Relations .... Mr. Thomas A. HAWLEY
11 VP of Administrative Services .... Dr. Mark KINNEY
49 Dean of Arts and Sciences .... Dr. Brooke PORTMANN
13 Director of Information Technology .... Ms. Debra HINTZ
24 Media Svcs & Learning Tech Coord .... Mr. Craig PETERSON
119 Network Administrator .... Mr. Terrence JOHNSON
75 Dean of Occupational Programs .... Ms. Christy CHRISTMAS
32 Dean of Student Services .... Mr. Chad E. INABINET
06 Registrar .... Ms. Jill SWEET
09 Director of Institutional Research .... Mr. Steve SPARLING
40 Director of Bookstore & Food Svcs .... Ms. Cheryl HOGAN
37 Director Financial Aid .... Ms. Rebekah SCHAUB
91 Manager of Adm Computing Systems .... Mr. Ryan GREGORSKI
61 Director of Criminal Justice .... Mr. Dan DELLAR
18 Director of Facilities & Recreation .... Mr. Michael A. MOORE
15 Director of Human Resources .... Ms. Debra CAMPBELL
16 Human Resources Specialist .... Ms. Sarah WAGNER
88 Director Student Resources .... Vacant
08 Director of Library Services .... Ms. Renee SNODGRASS
23 Director of Wellness Center .... Ms. Julie PAGE-SMITH
10 Director of Accounting .... Ms. Kristen BIGGS
84 Director of Enrollment Services .... Ms. Annie JACOBSON
88 Administrative Assistant .... Ms. Tasha DAULT
103 Dir of Business Opportunity Center .... Ms. Crystal YOUNG
120 Learning Management Systems Analyst .... Mr. Tom ALWAY
66 Director of Nursing .... Ms. Shelley BOES
105 Webmaster/Computer Technician .... Mr. Tim FINK

Western Michigan University (K)

1903 West Michigan Avenue, Kalamazoo MI 49008-5202
County: Kalamazoo FICE Identification: 002330
Unit ID: 172699
Telephone: (269) 387-1000 Carnegie Class: DU-Higher
FAX Number: (269) 387-0958 Calendar System: Semester
URL: wmich.edu
Established: 1903 Annual Undergrad Tuition & Fees (In-State): $12,483
Enrollment: 22,869 Coed
Affiliation or Control: State IRS Status: 501(c)3
Highest Offering: Doctorate

Accreditation: NH, AAB, ARCPA, ART, AUD, #CAATE, CACREP, CAEPN, CEA, CIDA, CLPSY, COPSY, DANCE, DIETD, DIETI, MUS, NURSE, OT, @PTA, SP, SPAA, SW, THEA

01 President .... Dr. Edward B. MONTGOMERY
05 Provost/Vice Pres Academic Affairs .... Dr. Jennifer P. BOTT
10 Vice Pres Business & Finance/CFO .... Ms. Jan VAN DER KLEY
32 VP Student Affairs .... Dr. Diane K. ANDERSON
46 Vice President for Research .... Dr. Terri G. KINZY
30 VP Development/Alumni Relations .... Ms. Kristen DEVRIES
43 General Counsel .... Dr. Carrick CRAIG
28 VP for Diversity and Inclusion .... Dr. Candy MCCORKLE
108 Assoc Prov Assessment/UG Studies .... Dr. David S. REINHOLD
21 Assoc Vice Pres Business & Finance .... Ms. Patti VAN WALBECK
15 Assoc Vice Pres Human Resources .... Dr. Warren L. HILLS
18 Assoc Vice Pres Facilities Mgmt .... Mr. Peter J. STRAZDAS
35 Assoc VP of SA & Dean of Students .... Dr. Suzie NAGEL
35 Assoc VP for Student Affairs .... Mr. Vernon PAYNE
114 Exec Dir University Budgets .... Ms. Colleen SCARFF
101 Secretary Board of Trustees .... Mr. Kahler B. SCHUEMANN
58 Dean Graduate College .... Dr. Susan R. STAPLETON
49 Dean of Arts & Sciences .... Dr. Carla M. KORETSKY
88 Dean of Aviation .... Capt. David M. POWELL
50 Dean of Business .... Dr. Satish DESHPANDE
53 Dean of Education & Human Dev .... Dr. Ming LI
54 Dean of Engineer & Applied Sciences ..... Dr. Houssam TOUTANJI
57 Dean of Fine Arts .... Mr. Daniel GUYETTE
76 Dean Health & Human Services .... Dr. Earlie WASHINGTON
92 Dean of Lee Honors College .... Dr. Gary H. BISCHOF
08 Dean of Libraries .... Ms. Julie A. GARRISON
26 Vice Pres Marketing & Strategic Com .... Mr. Tony PROUDFOOT
27 Exec Dir of University Relations .... Ms. Paula M. DAVIS
06 Registrar .... Ms. Carrie CUMMING
07 Director Admissions/Orientation .... Vacant
37 Dir Student Financial Aid .... Ms. Shashanta JAMES
38 Dir Counseling Services .... Dr. Brian J. FULLER
41 Dir Athletics .... Ms. Kathy B. BEAUREGARD
88 Assoc Prov for Global Education .... Dr. Paulo ZAGALO-MELO
85 Int Dir Intl Admissions & Services .... Ms. Soong Min CHOW
14 Chief Technology Officer .... Mr. Thomas WOLF, JR.
22 Exec Dir Institutional Equity .... Dr. Evelyn B. WINFIELD-THOMAS
104 Director Study Abroad .... Dr. Lee M. PENYAK
19 Dir Public Safety/Chief of Police .... Mr. Scott R. MERLO
25 Dir Grants/Contracts .... Ms. Betty J. MCKAIN
39 Director Residence Life .... Mr. Steven C. PALMER

Western Michigan University Cooley Law School (A)

300 S Capitol Avenue, Lansing MI 48933
County: Ingham	FICE Identification: 012627
Unit ID: 172477
Telephone: (517) 371-5140	Carnegie Class: Spec-4-yr-Law
FAX Number: (517) 334-5718	Calendar System: Semester
URL: www.cooley.edu
Established: 1972	Annual Graduate Tuition & Fees: N/A
Enrollment: 1,279	Coed
Affiliation or Control: Independent Non-Profit	IRS Status: 501(c)3
Highest Offering: First Professional Degree; No Undergraduates
Accreditation: NH, LAW

01 President and Dean .... James MCGRATH
04 Executive Asst to the President .... Cherie BECK
10 Chief Financial Officer/COO .... Kathleen CONKLIN
08 Associate Dean Library/Info Svcs .... Duane STROJNY
20 Associate Dean Lansing Campus .... Michael MCDANIEL
108 Assoc Dean Planning/Accreditation .... Laura LEDUC
32 Assoc Dean Students/Professionalism .... Amy TIMMER
43 Assoc Dean External Aff/Gen Counsel .... James ROBB
13 Assoc Dean for Information Tech/CIO .... Charles MICKENS
84 Assoc Dean for Enrollment Services .... Paul ZELENSKI
12 Associate Dean Grand Rapids .... Tracey BRAME
12 Associate Dean Tampa Bay .... Dan MATTHEWS
12 Associate Dean Auburn Hills Campus .... Joan VESTRAND
88 Assistant Dean Auburn Hills Campus .... Lisa HALUSHKA
88 Assistant Dean Lansing Campus .... Mable MARTIN-SCOTT
88 Assistant Dean Grand Rapids Campus .... Victoria VULETICH
88 Assistant Dean Tampa Bay Campus .... Katherine GUSTAFSON
07 Asst Dean Admissions/Financial Aid .... Lena BAILEY
36 Asst Dean Career/Professional Devel .... Lisa FADLER
06 Registrar/Dir of Student Records .... Danielle HALL
40 Bookstore Manager .... Joelle TOPP
21 Controller .... Ronda BECK
29 Director Alumni Donor Relations .... Pamela HEOS
26 Director Communications .... Terry CARELLA

Western Michigan University Cooley Law School Auburn Hills Campus (B)

2630 Featherstone Road, Auburn Hills MI 48326
Telephone: (248) 751-7800	Identification: 770288
Accreditation: &NH

Western Michigan University Cooley Law School Grand Rapids Campus (C)

111 Commerce Avenue, SW, Grand Rapids MI 49503
Telephone: (606) 301-6800	Identification: 770289
Accreditation: &NH

Western Michigan University Homer Stryker MD School of Medicine (D)

1000 Oakland Dr, Kalamazoo MI 49008-8010
County: Kalamazoo	Identification: 667287
Telephone: (269) 337-4400	Carnegie Class: Not Classified
FAX Number: N/A	Calendar System: Semester
URL: med.wmich.edu
Established: 2012	Annual Graduate Tuition & Fees: N/A
Enrollment: N/A	Coed
Affiliation or Control: Independent Non-Profit	IRS Status: 501(c)3
Highest Offering: Doctorate; No Undergraduates
Accreditation: NH, MED

01 Founding Dean .... Dr. Hal B. JENSON
05 Assoc Dean for Faculty Affairs .... Dr. Lisa GRAVES
10 Assoc Dean Administration/Finance .... Ms. Lori STRAUBE
32 Assoc Dean Student Affairs .... Dr. Peter ZIEMKOWSKI

Western Theological Seminary (E)

101 E 13th Street, Holland MI 49423-3622
County: Ottawa	FICE Identification: 002331
Unit ID: 172705
Telephone: (616) 392-8555	Carnegie Class: Spec-4-yr-Faith
FAX Number: (616) 392-7717	Calendar System: Semester
URL: www.westernsem.edu
Established: 1866	Annual Graduate Tuition & Fees: N/A
Enrollment: 347	Coed
Affiliation or Control: Reformed Church In America	IRS Status: 501(c)3
Highest Offering: Doctorate; No Undergraduates
Accreditation: THEOL

01 President .... Dr. Felix THEONUGRAHA
03 Executive Vice President .... Rev. Jeffrey MUNROE
05 Academic Dean/VP Academic Affairs .... Dr. Alvin PADILLA
10 Vice President of Finance .... Mr. Norman DONKERSLOOT
08 Director of the Library .... Dr. Daniel FLORES
06 Registrar .... Mr. Kyle WIGBOLDY
07 Director of Admissions .... Ms. Jill ENGLISH
15 Dir of Administration & Human Res .... Ms. Rayetta PEREZ
04 Executive Asst to the President . Ms. Lannette ZYLMAN-TENHAVE
30 Director of Development .... Mr. Andy BAST

Yeshiva Beth Yehuda - Yeshiva Gedolah of Greater Detroit (F)

24600 Greenfield, Oak Park MI 48237-1544
County: Oakland	FICE Identification: 023638
Unit ID: 247773
Telephone: (248) 968-3360	Carnegie Class: Spec-4-yr-Faith
FAX Number: (248) 968-8613	Calendar System: Semester
Established: 1985	Annual Undergrad Tuition & Fees: $6,800
Enrollment: 66	Male
Affiliation or Control: Independent Non-Profit	IRS Status: 501(c)3
Highest Offering: Doctorate
Accreditation: RABN

01 Dean .... Rabbi Y. BAKST
05 Assistant Dean .... Rabbi M. S. BAKST
11 Executive Administrator .... Rabbi P. RUSHNAWITZ
37 Director of Financial Aid .... Rabbi Y. BLITZ

MINNESOTA

Academy College (G)

1600 W. 82nd Street, Suite 100, Bloomington MN 55431
County: Hennepin	FICE Identification: 020503
Unit ID: 172866
Telephone: (952) 851-0066	Carnegie Class: Spec-4-yr-Other Tech
FAX Number: (952) 851-0094	Calendar System: Quarter
URL: www.academycollege.edu
Established: 1936	Annual Undergrad Tuition & Fees: $17,661
Enrollment: 65	Coed
Affiliation or Control: Proprietary	IRS Status: Proprietary
Highest Offering: Baccalaureate
Accreditation: ACCSC

01 President .... Nancy GRAZZINI-OLSON
37 Director of Financial Aid .... Kellye MACLEOD

Adler Graduate School (H)

10225 Yellow Circle Dr, Minnetonka MN 55423
County: Hennepin	FICE Identification: 030519
Unit ID: 374024
Telephone: (612) 861-7554	Carnegie Class: Spec-4-yr-Other Health
FAX Number: (612) 861-7559	Calendar System: Semester
URL: www.alfredadler.edu
Established: 1969	Annual Graduate Tuition & Fees: N/A
Enrollment: 317	Coed
Affiliation or Control: Independent Non-Profit	IRS Status: 501(c)3
Highest Offering: Master's; No Undergraduates
Accreditation: NH

01 President .... Dr. Jeffrey ALLEN
05 Director of Academics .... Dr. Solange RIBEIRO
32 Director of Student Success Svcs .... Dr. Meg WHISTON
10 VP for Finance & Administration .... Ms. Kathy BENGTSON
07 Dir of Admissions/Alumni Relations .... Ms. Evelyn HAAS
37 Director of Student Financial Aid .... Ms. Jeanette MAYNARD NELSON
06 Registrar .... Ms. Debbie VELASCO
08 Head Librarian .... Ms. Nicole MARCHAND

American Academy of Acupuncture and Oriental Medicine (I)

1925 W County Road B2, Roseville MN 55113-2703
County: Ramsey	FICE Identification: 038333
Unit ID: 446002
Telephone: (651) 631-0204	Carnegie Class: Spec-4-yr-Other Health
FAX Number: (651) 631-0361	Calendar System: Trimester
URL: www.aaaom.edu
Established: 1997	Annual Graduate Tuition & Fees: N/A
Enrollment: 98	Coed
Affiliation or Control: Proprietary	IRS Status: Proprietary
Highest Offering: Master's; No Undergraduates
Accreditation: ACUP

01 President .... Dr. Changzhen GONG
11 Administrative Director .... Leila NIELSEN
37 Financial Aid Officer .... Cate LARSON

Association Free Lutheran Bible School and Seminary (J)

3134 East Medicine Lake Blvd, Plymouth MN 55441
County: Hennepin	Identification: 667235
Telephone: (763) 544-9501	Carnegie Class: Not Classified
FAX Number: (763) 412-2047	Calendar System: Semester
URL: www.aflbs.org
Established: 1964	Annual Graduate Tuition & Fees: N/A
Enrollment: N/A	Coed
Affiliation or Control: Independent Non-Profit	IRS Status: 501(c)3
Highest Offering: Master's; No Undergraduates
Accreditation: TRACS

01 President .... Wade MOBLEY
03 Vice President/Dean .... Vacant
03 Vice President/Dean .... James MOLSTRE
05 Vice President Academic Affairs .... Mark OLSON
11 Vice President of Operations .... Larry MYHRER

Augsburg University (K)

2211 Riverside Avenue, Minneapolis MN 55454-1398
County: Hennepin	FICE Identification: 002334
Unit ID: 173045
Telephone: (612) 330-1000	Carnegie Class: Masters/L
FAX Number: (612) 330-1649	Calendar System: Semester
URL: www.augsburg.edu
Established: 1869	Annual Undergrad Tuition & Fees: $38,800
Enrollment: 3,562	Coed
Affiliation or Control: Evangelical Lutheran Church In America
IRS Status: 501(c)3
Highest Offering: Doctorate
Accreditation: NH, ARCPA, MUS, NURSE, SW

01 President .... Dr. Paul C. PRIBBENOW
05 Provost and Chief Academic Officer .... Dr. Karen KAIVOLA
10 Interim CFO/VP Finance & Admin .... Ms. Rebecca JOHN
111 VP Institutional Advancement .... Ms. Heather RIDDLE
32 VP Student Affairs .... Ms. Ann L. GARVEY
26 VP Marketing/Communication .... Ms. Rebecca JOHN
45 VP & Chief Strategy Officer .... Mr. Leif B. ANDERSON
110 AVP Institutional Advancement .... Ms. Amy ALKIRE
107 Dean of Professional Studies .... Dr. Monica C. DEVERS
49 Interim Dean of Arts & Sciences .... Dr. David MATZ
88 Asst Provost of Global Education .... Mr. Patrick MULVIHILL
35 Dean of Students .... Dr. Sarah GRIESSE
12 Director Rochester Program .... Mr. Jeremy UPDIKE
41 Athletic Director .... Mr. Jeffrey F. SWENSON
42 Campus Pastor .... Rev. Sonja HAGANDER
28 Chief Diversity Officer/Dir CAO .... Ms. Joanne REECK
37 Director of Financial Aid .... Ms. Gina JONES
06 Registrar .... Ms. Marah JACOBSON-SCHULTE
07 Director Undergraduate Admissions .... Mr. Devon G. ROSS
84 AVP Enrollment Management .... Mr. Nathan GORR
18 Director of Facilities Mgmt .... Mr. Doug SHELLUM
13 Chief Information Officer .... Mr. Scott KRAJEWSKI
38 Director Ctr Wellness & Counseling . Ms. Nancy G. GUILBEAULT
15 Interim HR Director .... Ms. Dawn MILLER
08 Director Library Services .... Ms. Mary HOLLERICH
19 Director Public Safety & Risk Mgmt .... Mr. Scott BROWNELL
31 Director Community Relations .... Mr. Steve PEACOCK
88 Director StepUp Program .... Vacant
85 Director International Student Svc .... Mr. James TRELSTAD-PORTER
114 Director of Budget .... Mr. Tom CARROLL
88 Director Event & Conf Planning .... Vacant
20 Director of Academic Administration .... Dr. Nathan HALLANGER
27 Dir Public Rel & Internal Comm .... Ms. Gita SITARAMIAH
27 Director Marketing Communication .... Mr. Stephen JENDRASZAK
36 Exec Director Strommen Center .... Mr. Lee GEORGE
39 Director Residence Life .... Ms. Amanda ERDMAN
104 Director Global Initiatives .... Ms. Leah SPINOSA DE VEGA

25 Director Sponsored Programs .... Vacant
04 Executive Assistant to President .... Ms. Cyndi BERG
88 Dir Enrollment Systems & Analytics .... Ms. Stephanie RUCKEL
40 Bookstore Manager .... Ms. Chanti MILLER
09 Dir Inst Research & Effectiveness .... Ms. Kathryn HAHN
96 Manager of Purchasing/Central Svcs .... Mr. Doug ROSENBERG

Bethany Global University (A)

6820 Auto Club Road, Suite C, Bloomington MN 55438
County: Hennepin Identification: 667136
Unit ID: 486284
Telephone: (952) 222-0699 Carnegie Class: Spec-4-yr-Faith
FAX Number: (952) 829-2753 Calendar System: Semester
URL: https://bethanygu.edu/
Established: 1948 Annual Undergrad Tuition & Fees: $14,270
Enrollment: 312 Coed
Affiliation or Control: Interdenominational IRS Status: 501(c)3
Highest Offering: Master's
Accreditation: BI

01 President .... Dan BROKKE
03 Executive Vice President .... Tim FREEMAN
04 Executive Asst to President .... Petra HARBOUR
05 Provost/Executive VP/Professor .... Dave HASZ
88 VP of Global Training .... Paul HARTFORD
20 Dean of Academic Affairs .... Jason HACHE
84 Director of Enrollment .... Ken FREIRE
08 Head Librarian .... Roger VANOOSTEN
101 Secretary of the Institution/Board .... Theresa HARTFORD
58 Dean of Graduate Studies .... Jim RAYMO
13 Network and Computer Administrator .... Chris ERICKSON
15 Director Personnel Services .... Chelsey HOFFMEISTER
18 Chief Facilities/Physical Plant .... Mike MORCOMB
19 Director Security/Safety .... Matt ADAIR
26 Chief Public Relations/Marketing .... Dan SANCHEZ
29 Donor Communications Specialist .... Holly WARD
30 Chief Development/Advancement .... Randy DIRKS
33 Dean of Men/Student Life .... Derek BROKKE
34 Dean of Women/Student Life .... Bethany FREIRE
37 Director Student Financial Aid .... Aaron HARRIS
06 Registrar .... Hannah LEVIN

Bethany Lutheran College (B)

700 Luther Drive, Mankato MN 56001-6163
County: Blue Earth FICE Identification: 002337
Unit ID: 173142
Telephone: (507) 344-7000 Carnegie Class: Bac-A&S
FAX Number: (507) 344-7376 Calendar System: Semester
URL: www.blc.edu
Established: 1911 Annual Undergrad Tuition & Fees: $27,780
Enrollment: 651 Coed
Affiliation or Control: Evangelical Lutheran Synod IRS Status: 501(c)3
Highest Offering: Baccalaureate
Accreditation: NH, NURSE

01 President .... Dr. Gene R. PFEIFER
42 Dir Campus Spiritual Life/Chaplain .... Rev. Donald L. MOLDSTAD
05 Vice President of Academic Affairs .... Dr. Jason H. LOWREY
32 Vice President of Student Affairs .... Dr. Theodore E. MANTHE
10 VP of Finance & Administration .... Mr. Daniel L. MUNDAHL
111 Vice President of Advancement .... Mr. Arthur P. WESTPHAL
37 Director of Financial Aid .... Mr. Jeffrey W. YOUNGE
06 Registrar .... Mr. Sergio SALGADO
07 VP of Admissions & Enrollment .... Dr. Jeffrey C. LEMKE
15 Manager of Human Resources .... Mr. Joshua PEDERSON
08 Director of Library Services .... Ms. Alyssa K. INNIGER
13 Director of Information Technology .... Mr. John M. SEHLOFF
26 Dir of Institutional Communication .... Mr. Lance W. SCHWARTZ
41 Director of Athletics .... Mr. Donald M. WESTPHAL
29 Manager of Alumni Relations .... Mr. Jacob C. KRIER
09 Mgr Acad & Institutional Research .... Ms. Lisa A. SHUBERT
40 Bookstore Manager .... Mr. Daniel GERDTS
21 Controller .... Mr. Gregory W. COSTELLO
28 Coord Ctr for Intercultural Develop .... Vacant
38 Coord of Student Counseling .... Vacant
18 Director of Facilities .... Mr. Patrick E. HULL
108 Director of Assessment .... Dr. Theodore E. MANTHE
04 Executive Asst to President .... Mrs. Barbara J. DRESSEN
106 Director Online Learning .... Mr. Kevin ZIMMERMAN

Bethel University (C)

3900 Bethel Drive, Saint Paul MN 55112-6999
County: Ramsey FICE Identification: 009058
Unit ID: 173160
Telephone: (651) 638-6400 Carnegie Class: DU-Mod
FAX Number: (651) 638-6001 Calendar System: Semester
URL: www.bethel.edu
Established: 1871 Annual Undergrad Tuition & Fees: $37,300
Enrollment: 3,797 Coed
Affiliation or Control: Baptist IRS Status: 501(c)3
Highest Offering: Doctorate
Accreditation: NH, ACBSP, ARCPA, CAATE, CAEPT, MFCD, MIDWF, NURSE, SW, THEOL

01 President .... Dr. James H. BARNES, III
100 Special Assistant to President .... Dr. John A. ADDLEMAN
05 Executive Vice Pres and Provost .... Dr. Debra HARLESS
10 Chief Financial Officer .... Ms. Amy BLAZ
20 Associate Provost .... Dr. Randy BERGEN
26 Chief Enrollment/Marketing Officer .... Mr. Michael VEDDERS
111 Chief Advancement Officer .... Mr. Jim BENDER
46 Chief Inst Data/Research Officer .... Mr. Daniel NELSON
90 Chief Facilities/Technology Officer .... Mr. Mark POSNER
29 Exec Minister for Church Relations .... Mr. Ralph GUSTAFSON
32 Vice President Student Life .... Dr. William WASHINGTON
20 Assoc Provost of CAS .... Dr. Deborah SULLIVAN-TRAINOR
73 Dean of Seminary .... Dr. Peter VOGT
79 Dean Arts & Humanities .... Dr. Barrett FISHER
108 Assoc Dean Inst Assess/Accred .... Dr. Joel FREDERICKSON
81 Dean Natural/Behavioral Sci .... Dr. Carole YOUNG
107 Dean Faculty Dev/Professional Pgms .... Vacant
104 Assoc Dean Off-Campus Programs .... Mr. Vincent PETERS
35 Dean of Students .... Ms. Miranda POWERS
08 Director of Libraries .... Mr. David R. STEWART
15 Chief Human Resources/Strategy Ofcr .... Ms. Cara WALD
41 Athletic Director .... Mr. Robert B. BJORKLUND
37 Financial Aid Officer .... Mr. Jeffery D. OLSON
42 AVP Christian Formation/Church Rels .... Ms. Laurel BUNKER
07 Director of CAS Admissions .... Mr. Bret HYDER
07 Dir Seminary/CAPS/GS Admissions .... Ms. Kate GUNDERSON
06 University Registrar .... Ms. Diane KRUSEMARK
36 Director Career Counsel/Placement .... Mr. Dave BROZA
19 Director Risk Mgmt/Safety/Security .... Mr. Zach HILL
40 Director Campus Stores .... Ms. Jill SONSTEBY
23 Director of Health Services .... Mrs. Elizabeth K. MILLER
96 Director of Purchasing .... Vacant
38 Director Student Counseling .... Dr. Miriam HILL
18 Int Dir of Facilities Admin Ops .... Mr. Barry HOLST
18 Director Facilities Tech Ops .... Mr. Glenn HOFER
28 Chief Diversity Officer .... Dr. Ruben RIVERA
29 Director Alumni & Family Relations .... Ms. Jennifer SCOTT
110 Assoc Vice Pres of Development .... Ms. Jeanne OSGOOD

† The marriage and family therapy master's program at Bethel Seminary San Diego is accredited by the Commission on Accreditation for Marriage and Family Therapy Education (COAMFTE) of the American Association for Marriage and Family Therapy (AAMFT)

Bethlehem College & Seminary (D)

720 13th Avenue South, Minneapolis MN 55415
County: Hennepin Identification: 667249
Unit ID: 486053
Telephone: (612) 455-3420 Carnegie Class: Spec-4-yr-Faith
FAX Number: N/A Calendar System: Semester
URL: bcsmn.edu
Established: 2009 Annual Undergrad Tuition & Fees: $6,560
Enrollment: 186 Coed
Affiliation or Control: Independent Non-Profit IRS Status: 501(c)3
Highest Offering: Master's
Accreditation: BI

01 President .... Dr. Timothy TOMLINSON
05 Academic Dean .... Dr. Brian TABB
11 VP of Administration .... Jason ABELL
111 VP of Advancement .... Rick SEGAL
07 Director of Admissions .... Daniel KLEVEN
04 Assistant to President .... Lance M. KRAMER
06 Registrar/Bursar & Dir Inst Rsrch .... Connie KOPISCHKE

Capella University (E)

225 S 6th Street, 9th Floor, Minneapolis MN 55402-4319
County: Hennepin FICE Identification: 032673
Unit ID: 413413
Telephone: (888) 227-3552 Carnegie Class: DU-Mod
FAX Number: (612) 977-5066 Calendar System: Other
URL: www.capella.edu
Established: 1993 Annual Undergrad Tuition & Fees: $14,579
Enrollment: 36,284 Coed
Affiliation or Control: Proprietary IRS Status: Proprietary
Highest Offering: Doctorate
Accreditation: NH, ACBSP, CACREP, CAEP, MFCD, NURSE, SW

01 President .... Dr. Richard SENESE
05 VP Academic Affairs/CAO .... Dr. Constance ST. GERMAIN
66 VP and General Manager .... Jennifer HOFF
50 VP and General Manager .... Tonia TEASLEY

Carleton College (F)

1 N College Street, Northfield MN 55057-4001
County: Rice FICE Identification: 002340
Unit ID: 173258
Telephone: (507) 222-4000 Carnegie Class: Bac-A&S
FAX Number: (507) 222-4204 Calendar System: Trimester
URL: www.carleton.edu
Established: 1866 Annual Undergrad Tuition & Fees: $54,759
Enrollment: 2,078 Coed
Affiliation or Control: Independent Non-Profit IRS Status: 501(c)3
Highest Offering: Baccalaureate
Accreditation: NH

01 President .... Mr. Steven G. POSKANZER, JR.
05 Dean of the College .... Ms. Beverly NAGEL
10 VP Business & Finance/Treasurer .... Mr. Fred A. ROGERS
111 Vice President External Relations .... Mr. Tommy BONNER
32 VP for Student Dev/Dean of Students .. Ms. Carolyn LIVINGSTON
07 VP and Dean of Admissions/Fin Aid .... Mr. Paul THIBOUTOT
100 Vice President/Chief of Staff .... Ms. Elise ESLINGER
26 Assoc VP Ext Relations/Dir Col Comm .... Mr. Joe HARGIS
20 Associate Dean of the College .... Ms. Gretchen HOFMEISTER
20 Associate Dean of the College .... Mr. Andrew FISHER
88 Dir of Advising/Fac Div Rctmnt .... Mr. Alfred MONTERO
88 Director of Student Fellowships .... Ms. Marynel RYAN VAN ZEE
35 Associate Dean of Students .... Mr. Joseph BAGGOT
35 Associate Dean of Students .... Ms. Cathy CARLSON
37 Assoc Dean Admiss/Dir Stdnt Fin Svc .... Mr. Rod M. OTO
42 Chaplain .... Rev. Carolyn FURE-SLOCUM
06 Registrar .... Ms. Emy FARLEY
08 College Librarian .... Mr. Bradley SCHAFFNER
09 Asst VP Inst Research & Assessment .... Mr. Todd JAMISON
44 Asst VP Alum/Par Rel/Annual Giving .... Ms. Becky ZRIMSEK
29 Director of Alumni Relations .... Mr. Michael THOMPSON
88 Director of Alumni Annual Fund .... Ms. Nicole SCHROEDER
110 Assoc VP for Development .... Mr. Dan RUSTAD
112 Director of Gift Planning .... Ms. Lynne WILMOT
13 Chief Technology Officer .... Ms. Janet SCANNELL
105 Dir Marketing Comm/Content Dvlpmt .... Vacant
27 Director of Public Relations/Media .... Ms. Helen CLARKE EBERT
15 Director of Human Resources .... Ms. Kerstin CARDENAS
39 Director of Residential Life .... Ms. Andrea ROBINSON
85 Dir Intercult/International Life .... Ms. Briza ZUBIA
104 Director of Off-Campus Studies .... Ms. Helena KAUFMAN
36 Director of the Career Center .... Mr. R.J HOLMES-LEOPOLD
23 Dir Student Health and Counseling .... Ms. Marit LYSNE
18 Dir of Facilities/Capital Planning .... Mr. Steven SPEHN
21 Comptroller .... Ms. Linda THORNTON
102 Dir Corporate/Foundation Relations .... Mr. Mark GLEASON
88 Dir of Educational Research .... Ms. Andrea NIXON
88 Dir Center for Learning/Teaching .... Ms. Melissa EBLEN-ZAYAS
109 Director of Auxiliary Services .... Mr. Jesse CASHMAN
41 Athletic Director .... Mr. Gerald YOUNG
19 Director of Security/Emergency Mgmt .... Mr. John BERMEL
105 Director of Web Services .... Ms. Julie ANDERSON
88 Dir of Enterprise Information Svcs .... Ms. Julie CREAMER
88 Director of Technology Support .... Mr. Austin ROBINSON-COOLIDGE

CenterPoint Massage and Shiatsu Therapy School & Clinic (G)

5300 West 35th Street, Minneapolis MN 55416
County: Hennepin FICE Identification: 041488
Unit ID: 457651
Telephone: (952) 562-5200 Carnegie Class: Not Classified
FAX Number: (952) 562-5201 Calendar System: Semester
URL: www.centerpointmn.com
Established: 2001 Annual Undergrad Tuition & Fees: N/A
Enrollment: 93 Coed
Affiliation or Control: Proprietary IRS Status: Proprietary
Highest Offering: Associate Degree
Accreditation: COMTA

Central Baptist Theological Seminary of Minneapolis (H)

900 Forestview Lane N, Plymouth MN 55441-5934
County: Hennepin Identification: 666050
Telephone: (763) 417-8250 Carnegie Class: Not Classified
FAX Number: (763) 417-8258 Calendar System: Semester
URL: www.centralseminary.edu
Established: 1956 Annual Undergrad Tuition & Fees: N/A
Enrollment: N/A Coed
Affiliation or Control: Baptist IRS Status: 501(c)3
Highest Offering: Doctorate
Accreditation: THEOL

01 President .... Dr. Matthew D. MORRELL
05 Provost/EVP .... Dr. Brett J. WILLIAMS
111 Vice Pres of Advancement .... Mr. Ron GOTZMAN
07 Director Recruitment/Retention .... Mr. Dan JOHNSON
06 Registrar .... Dr. Jeff STRAUB
08 Chief Library Officer .... Mr. Adam KEIM

*College of Medicine, Mayo Clinic (I)

200 First Street, Rochester MN 55905-3712
County: Olmsted Identification: 666719
Telephone: (507) 284-2511 Carnegie Class: N/A
FAX Number: (507) 284-0999
URL: www.mayo.edu

01 Chief Executive Officer .... Dr. John H. NOSEWORTHY
05 Exec Dean for Education Mayo Clinic .... Dr. Frederick B. MEYER
46 Exec Dean for Research Mayo Clinic .... Dr. Greg GORES
15 Chair of Human Resources .... Ms. Cathy FRASER
30 Exec Dean of Development .... Dr. Michael CAMILLERI
86 Chair Government Relations .... Vacant
37 Financial Aid Officer .... Mr. David L. DAHLEN
08 Executive Director of Libraries .... Ms. Anna Beth MORGAN
29 Director Mayo Clinic Alumni Center .... Ms. Judith ANDERSON

*Mayo Medical School (J)

200 1st Street, SW, Rochester MN 55905-0001
County: Olmsted FICE Identification: 011732
Unit ID: 173957
Telephone: (507) 538-4897 Carnegie Class: Spec-4-yr-Med
FAX Number: (507) 284-2634 Calendar System: Other
URL: www.mayo.edu/mms
Established: 1971 Annual Undergrad Tuition & Fees: N/A
Enrollment: 264 Coed

Affiliation or Control: Independent Non-Profit IRS Status: 501(c)3
Highest Offering: First Professional Degree
Accreditation: NH, MED

02 Dean .... Dr. Fredric B. MEYER
05 Assoc Dean Academic Affairs .... Dr. Darcy A. REED
32 Assoc Dean Student Affairs .... Dr. Alexandra P. WOLANSKYJ
20 Assoc Dean Faculty Affairs .... Dr. Geoffrey B. THOMPSON
11 Administrator for Mayo Med School .... Ms. Marcia ANDRESEN REID
22 Chief Human Resources .... Ms. Cathryn FRASER
26 Chief Mktg Ofcr/Chair Public Affs .... Mr. Chris W. GADE
88 Internatl Personnel Practice Group .... Ms. Ann H. LANCE
37 Director of Financial Aid .... Mr. David L. DAHLEN
08 Head Librarian .... Ms. Anna Beth MORGAN
06 Registrar .... Ms. Delores L. BENNETT

* *Mayo Clinic College of Medicine-Mayo Graduate School* (A)

200 First Street, SW, Rochester MN 55905-0001
Telephone: (507) 538-1160 FICE Identification: 011516
Accreditation: &NH, DENT, PDPSY

† Regional accreditation is carried under College of Medicine, Mayo Clinic.

* *Mayo Clinic School of Health Sciences* (B)

200 First St. SW, Siebens Bldg 3,
Rochester MN 55905-0001
Telephone: (507) 284-3293 FICE Identification: 008182
Accreditation: &NH, ANEST, COARC, CVT, CYTO, DIETI, DMS, EMT, MT, NDT, NMT, PAST, PTA, RAD, RTT, SURGA

† Regional accreditation is carried under College of Medicine, Mayo Clinic.

College of Saint Benedict (C)

37 S College Avenue, Saint Joseph MN 56374-2099
County: Stearns FICE Identification: 002341
Unit ID: 174747
Telephone: (320) 363-5011 Carnegie Class: Bac-A&S
FAX Number: (320) 363-6099 Calendar System: Semester
URL: www.csbsju.edu
Established: 1913 Annual Undergrad Tuition & Fees: $45,264
Enrollment: 1,937 Coordinate
Affiliation or Control: Roman Catholic IRS Status: 501(c)3
Highest Offering: Baccalaureate
Accreditation: NH, DIETD, MUS, NURSE

01 President .... Dr. Mary HINTON
05 Provost Academic Affairs .... Dr. Richard ICE
32 Vice President Student Development .... Ms. Mary A. GELLER
111 VP Institutional Advancement .... Ms. Kathy HANSEN
10 Vice Pres Finance/Administration .... Ms. Susan M. PALMER
07 VP Admission & Financial Aid .... Mr. Nate DEHNE
18 Exec Director Facilities .... Mr. Ryan GIDEON
20 Academic Dean .... Dr. Barbara MAY
34 Dean of Students .... Ms. Jody L. TERHAAR
06 Registrar .... Ms. Julie E. GRUSKA
08 Director Library .... Ms. Kathy PARKER
37 Exec Director Financial Aid .... Mr. Stuart PERRY
15 Director Human Resources .... Ms. Carol ABELL
38 Director of Counseling .... Dr. Mike J. EWING
42 Director of Campus Ministry .... Sr. Sharon NOHNER, OSB
41 Athletic Director .... Ms. Glennis WERNER
13 Director of Info Technology Svc .... Ms. Casey GORDON
19 Director of Security .... Mr. Darren SWANSON
21 Controller .... Ms. Anne OBERMAN
36 Executive Director XPD .... Ms. Angie SCHMIDT WHITNEY
09 Assoc Dir of Institutional Research .... Ms. Karen KNUTSON
40 Director of Bookstores .... Ms. Tina STREIT
100 Chief of Staff/Lead Title IX Coord .... Dr. Kathryn ENKE
88 Director Student Human Rights .... Mr. Brandyn WOODARD
110 Assoc VP Institutional Advancement .... Ms. Heather PIEPER-OLSON

The College of Saint Scholastica (D)

1200 Kenwood Avenue, Duluth MN 55811-4199
County: Saint Louis FICE Identification: 002343
Unit ID: 174899
Telephone: (218) 723-6000 Carnegie Class: DU-Mod
FAX Number: (218) 723-6290 Calendar System: Semester
URL: www.css.edu
Established: 1912 Annual Undergrad Tuition & Fees: $37,212
Enrollment: 4,276 Coed
Affiliation or Control: Roman Catholic IRS Status: 501(c)3
Highest Offering: Doctorate
Accreditation: NH, #ARCPA, CAATE, CAEP, CAEPT, CAHIIM, NURSE, OT, #PTA, SW

01 President .... Dr. Colette GEARY
10 Vice President Finance .... Ms. Susan KERRY
05 Vice Pres Academic Affairs .... Dr. Wolfgang NATTER
30 Int Vice Pres College Advancement .... Mr. Del CASE
32 Vice President for Student Affairs .... Mr. Steve LYONS
13 Chief Information Officer .... Mr. Xavier KNIGHT

Concordia College (E)

901 8th Street S, Moorhead MN 56562-0001
County: Clay FICE Identification: 002346
Unit ID: 173300
Telephone: (218) 299-4000 Carnegie Class: Bac-A&S
FAX Number: (218) 299-3947 Calendar System: Semester
URL: www.cord.edu
Established: 1891 Annual Undergrad Tuition & Fees: $39,878
Enrollment: 2,059 Coed
Affiliation or Control: Evangelical Lutheran Church In America
IRS Status: 501(c)3
Highest Offering: Master's
Accreditation: NH, CAEP, DIETD, DIETI, MUS, NURSE, SW

01 President .... Dr. William J. CRAFT
05 VP Academic Affairs .... Dr. Eric J. ELIASON
10 Vice Pres Finance/Treasurer .... Ms. Linda J. BROWN
84 Vice Pres Enrollment and Marketing .... Mr. Karl A. STUMO
111 Vice Pres Advancement .... Ms. Teresa L. HARLAND
32 VP Student Dev and Campus Life .... Dr. Lisa SETHRE-HOFSTAD
28 Chief Diversity Officer .... Dr. Edward ANTONIO
20 Dean of the College .... Dr. Susan J. LARSON
100 Deputy to the President .... Dr. Jill M. ABBOTT
13 Exec Dir of Information Technology .... Mr. Erik RAMSTAD
07 Dir of Admission Operations .... Ms. Samantha AXVIG
06 Registrar .... Ms. Lisa M. SJOBERG
37 Assoc VP Enrollment & Financial Aid .... Mr. Eric J. ADDINGTON
08 Library Director .... Mrs. Laura K. PROBST
15 Director Human Resources .... Ms. Peggy L. TORRANCE
29 Director Alumni Relations .... Mr. Eric P. JOHNSON
26 Assoc VP Comm/Chief Mktg Officer .... Mr. Josh D. LYSNE
18 Director of Facilities Management .... Mr. Dallas FOSSUM
41 Athletic Director .... Ms. Rachel D. BERGESON
42 Director Dovre Center .... Dr. Larry A. PAPENFUSS
42 Minister of Word and Sacrament .... Vacant
42 Minister Faith & Spirituality .... Mr. Jon LEISETH
19 Director of Public Safety .... Mr. William MACDONALD
04 Exec Asst to the President .... Ms. DeeAnn M. KRUGLER
104 Assoc Dean Global Learning .... Dr. Per M. ANDERSON
108 Dir Institutional Effectiveness .... Dr. Jasi O'CONNOR
25 Dir Found Rels/Research Grants .... Ms. Jillain VEIL-EHNERT
30 Director of Development .... Ms. Trina PISK HALL
39 Director Residence Life .... Ms. Mikal C. KENFIELD
117 Director Risk Management .... Mr. Roger T. OLSON
44 Director Annual Fund .... Ms. Rachel M. CLARKE
36 Director of Career Center .... Ms. Kris OLSON
38 Director of Counseling Center .... Mr. Matthew RUTTEN

Concordia University, St. Paul (F)

1282 Concordia Ave, Saint Paul MN 55104-5494
County: Ramsey FICE Identification: 002347
Unit ID: 173328
Telephone: (651) 641-8278 Carnegie Class: Masters/L
FAX Number: (651) 659-0207 Calendar System: Semester
URL: www.csp.edu
Established: 1893 Annual Undergrad Tuition & Fees: $22,275
Enrollment: 4,817 Coed
Affiliation or Control: Lutheran Church - Missouri Synod
IRS Status: 501(c)3
Highest Offering: Doctorate
Accreditation: NH, NURSE, OPE, PTA

01 President .... Rev.Dr. Thomas Karl RIES
03 Executive Vice President .... Dr. Cheryl T. CHATMAN
05 Vice President Academic Affairs .... Dr. Marilyn REINECK
10 Vice President for Finance .... Rev.Dr. Michael H. DORNER
111 Vice President for Advancement .... Mr. Mark HILL
11 Provost/SVP for Administration .... Dr. Eric E. LAMOTT
84 VP Cohort Enrollment Management .... Dr. Kimberly CRAIG
07 Assoc Dir Undergraduate Admissions .... Mrs. Kelly A. MACIK
32 Assoc VP Student Life .... Mr. Jason M. RAHN
108 Assoc VP for Assessment/Accred .... Dr. Miriam LUEBKE
53 Dean College of Education .... Mr. Lonn MALY
79 Dean Coll of Humanities/Social Sci .... Dr. Paul HILLMER
58 Dean of Graduate School .... Dr. Michael WALCHESKI
50 Dean College of Business .... Dr. Kevin HALL
76 Dean College of Health & Science .... Dr. Katie J. FISCHER
28 Dean of Diversity .... Dr. Cheryl T. CHATMAN
39 Asst Director of Residence Life .... Mr. Jake WAKEM
06 Registrar .... Ms. Lynn LUNDQUIST
08 Director of Library Services .... Mr. Jonathan B. NEILSON
26 Dir Univ Communications/Mrktng .... Mr. Brian EVANS
15 Director of Human Resources .... Ms. Milissa M. BECKER
37 Director of Financial Aid .... Ms. Jeanie PECK
04 Executive Assistant to President .... Ms. Jill K. SIMON
42 University Pastor .... Rev. Thomas GUNDERMANN
88 Director of Traditional Advising .... Ms. Gretchen WALTHER
09 Director of Institutional Research .... Ms. Beth C. PETER
29 Director of Alumni Relations .... Mrs. Rhonda K. PALMERSHEIM
41 Director of Athletics .... Mrs. Regan M. MCATHIE
18 Director of Operations .... Mr. James P. ORCHARD
40 Bookstore Manager .... Mr. Chad L. MASTEL
90 Director of Computer Services .... Mr. Jonathan S. BREITBARTH
91 Director Administrative Computing .... Ms. Beth C. PETER
19 Risk Manager .... Mr. David GALLOWAY
24 Help Desk Coordinator .... Mr. Cristopher A. GIBSON

Crown College (G)

8700 College View Drive, Saint Bonifacius MN 55375-9001
County: Carver FICE Identification: 002383
Unit ID: 174862
Telephone: (952) 446-4100 Carnegie Class: Masters/S
FAX Number: (952) 446-4149 Calendar System: Semester
URL: www.crown.edu
Established: 1916 Annual Undergrad Tuition & Fees: $26,200
Enrollment: 1,353 Coed
Affiliation or Control: The Christian And Missionary Alliance
IRS Status: 501(c)3
Highest Offering: Master's
Accreditation: NH, NURSE

01 President .... Dr. David J. WIGGINS
04 Exec Assistant to the President .... Mrs. Emily HONEBRINK
10 VP Finance .... Dr. Scott MOATS
05 VP Academic Affairs/Provost .... Dr. Scott MOATS
32 VP Student Development .... Dr. Bill KUHN
84 VP Enrollment & Marketing Svcs .... Mr. Bruce SNYDER
30 VP External Relations .... Ms. Jill OSBORN
20 Dean for Undergraduate Pgms .... Dr. Scott MOATS
66 Director of Nursing .... Mrs. Teresa NEWBY
21 Controller .... Mr. Ronald STRAKA
41 Athletic Director .... Mr. Jamison ROSS
08 Director of Media Services .... Vacant
06 Registrar .... Dr. Cheryl FISK
37 Director of Financial Aid .... Mr. Jon ERICKSON
35 Director Student Engagement .... Mrs. Martha SWIFT
07 Director of Graduate Admissions .... Ms. Maggie UNGER
18 Director of Facilities Services .... Mr. Rick LARSON
40 Director of Campus Store .... Mrs. Sharie THOELKE
58 AVP Sch Online Studies/Grad School .... Dr. Fawn MCCRACKEN
42 Chaplain .... Mr. Bill KUHN
15 Director of Human Resources .... Mrs. Amy LUESSE
36 Dir Counseling & Career Services .... Mr. Bill JOHNSON
13 Director of Technology Services .... Mr. Paul FLAGSTAD
26 Marketing/Communications Manager .... Mrs. Tara ANDERSON
29 Manager of Alumni Relations .... Mrs. Sarah BENBOW

Dunwoody College of Technology (H)

818 Dunwoody Boulevard, Minneapolis MN 55403-1192
County: Hennepin FICE Identification: 004641
Unit ID: 175227
Telephone: (612) 374-5800 Carnegie Class: Bac/Assoc-Mixed
FAX Number: (612) 381-9620 Calendar System: Semester
URL: www.dunwoody.edu
Established: 1914 Annual Undergrad Tuition & Fees: $22,046
Enrollment: 1,301 Coed
Affiliation or Control: Independent Non-Profit IRS Status: 501(c)3
Highest Offering: Baccalaureate
Accreditation: NH, CIDA, RAD

01 President .... Dr. Rich WAGNER
05 Provost .... Mr. Jeff YLINEN
84 Vice President Enrollment Mgmt .... Ms. Cynthia OLSON
111 VP of Institutional Advancement .... Mr. Brian NELSON
15 Vice President of Human Resources .... Ms. Patricia EDMAN
10 VP of Administrative Svcs & CFO .... Ms. Tammy MCGEE

Gustavus Adolphus College (I)

800 W College Avenue, Saint Peter MN 56082-1498
County: Nicollet FICE Identification: 002353
Unit ID: 173647
Telephone: (507) 933-8000 Carnegie Class: Bac-A&S
FAX Number: (507) 933-7041 Calendar System: Semester
URL: www.gustavus.edu
Established: 1862 Annual Undergrad Tuition & Fees: $45,400
Enrollment: 2,181 Coed
Affiliation or Control: Evangelical Lutheran Church In America
IRS Status: 501(c)3
Highest Offering: Baccalaureate
Accreditation: NH, CAATE, NURSE

01 President .... Ms. Rebecca M. BERGMAN
05 Provost and Dean of the College .... Dr. Brenda S. KELLY
10 VP for Finance/Treasurer/CFO .... Mr. Curtis J. KOWALESKI
07 AVP and Dean of Admission .... Mr. Richard S. AUNE
07 AVP for Enrollment .... Mr. Kirk CARLSON
111 VP for Institutional Advancement .... Mr. Thomas W. YOUNG
32 VP for Student Life .... Dr. JoNes R. VANHECKE
26 VP Marketing & Communication .... Mr. Timothy R. KENNEDY
88 VP Mission/Strategy/Innovation .... Dr. Kathi TUNHEIM
28 Director Diversity Center .... Mr. Thomas G. FLUNKER
09 Director Institutional Research .... Mr. David A. MENK
08 Head Librarian .... Ms. Michelle TWAIT
88 Director Church Relations .... Rev. Grady I. ST. DENNIS
29 Dir Alumni and Parent Engagement .... Ms. Angela ERICKSON
36 Exec Director Career Development .... Vacant
06 Registrar .... Ms. Kristianne R. WESTPHAL
13 Dir Gustavus Technology Services .... Ms. Tami AUNE
18 AVP Facilities .... Mr. Travis JORDAN
37 AVP and Dean of Financial Aid .... Mr. Doug O. MINTER
39 Director Residential Life .... Mr. Anthony BETTENDORF
42 Chaplain .... Rev. Siri C. ERICKSON
35 Assistant VP for Student Life .... Ms. Megan RUBLE
35 Assistant VP for Student Life .... Mr. Charlie POTTS
41 Athletics Director .... Mr. Thomas W. BROWN
15 Director Human Resources .... Vacant
19 Director Campus Security .... Ms. Carol A. BREWER
40 Manager Book Mark .... Ms. Molly L. YONKERS
27 Dir Media Relations/Internal Comm .... Mr. Jacob J. AKIN
04 Asst to the Pres & Sec of the Board .... Ms. Jolene D. CHRISTENSEN

Hamline University (A)

1536 Hewitt Avenue, Saint Paul MN 55104-1284
County: Ramsey FICE Identification: 002354
Unit ID: 173665
Telephone: (651) 523-2800 Carnegie Class: Masters/L
FAX Number: (651) 523-2899 Calendar System: 4/1/4
URL: www.hamline.edu
Established: 1854 Annual Undergrad Tuition & Fees: $41,290
Enrollment: 3,734 Coed
Affiliation or Control: United Methodist IRS Status: 501(c)3
Highest Offering: Doctorate
Accreditation: NH, CAEPN, MUS

01 President ... Dr. Fayneese S. MILLER
05 Provost ... Dr. John MATACHEK
10 Sr VP Business/Finance/Technology ... Ms. Margaret TUNGSETH
111 VP Institutional Advancement ... Mr. Mike TOMPOS
32 Dean of Students ... Ms. Patti KLEIN
43 VP HR/General Counsel ... Ms. Catherine WASSBERG
84 Vice Pres Enrollment Management ... Ms. Mai Nhia XIONG-CHAN
13 Assoc VP/Dir IT ... Vacant
26 Assoc VP Marketing/Communications ... Ms. Lynn FARMER
18 Assoc VP Facilities/Physical Plant ... Mr. Lowell BROMANDER
50 Dean School of Business ... Ms. Anne MCCARTHY
49 Dean College Liberal Arts ... Ms. Marcela KOSTIHOVA
85 Ast Dn/Dir Multicult/Intl Stdt Affs ... Mr. Carlos SNEED
06 Registrar Undergrad/Grad Schools ... Ms. Gwen SHERBURNE
29 Exec Dir of Hamline Alumni Assn ... Ms. Elizabeth L. RADTKE
37 Director Financial Aid ... Ms. Lynette WAHL
07 Director Undergraduate Admission ... Ms. Holly COLLINS
15 Director Human Resources ... Ms. Lisa TODD
36 Interim Dir Career Development ... Mr. Terry MIDDENDORF
41 Athletic Director ... Mr. Jason VERDUGO
19 Director of Safety & Security ... Ms. Melinda HEIKKINEN
23 Director Counseling & Health Center ... Ms. Hussein RAJPUT
35 Dir Student Leadership & Activities ... Vacant
42 Chaplain & Director ... Ms. Nancy M. VICTORIN-VANGERUD
96 Director of Purchasing ... Ms. Susan BORNUS
04 Exec Assistant to the President ... Vacant
09 Director of Institutional Research ... Ms. Tracy WILLIAMS
08 Head Librarian ... Mr. Terry METZ
39 Director Student Housing ... Mr. Javier GUTIERREZ

Hazelden Betty Ford Graduate School of Addiction Studies (B)

PO Box 11 (CO9), Center City MN 55012-0011
County: Chisago FICE Identification: 040443
Unit ID: 173683
Telephone: (651) 213-4175 Carnegie Class: Spec-4-yr-Other Health
FAX Number: (651) 213-4710 Calendar System: Semester
URL: www.hazeldenbettyford.org
Established: 1999 Annual Graduate Tuition & Fees: N/A
Enrollment: 177 Coed
Affiliation or Control: Independent Non-Profit IRS Status: 501(c)3
Highest Offering: Master's; No Undergraduates
Accreditation: NH

01 President and CEO ... Mr. Mark MISHEK
05 Vice Pres Education/Research ... Dr. Valerie SLAYMAKER
88 Asst to the Chief Academic Officer ... Ms. Denell BELLE ISLE
20 Dean ... Dr. Roy KAMMER
07 Mgr Enrollment & Student Services ... Ms. LeAnn BROWN
06 Registrar ... Ms. Debra MATTISON
88 Registrar of Administrative Service ... Ms. Twyla RAMSDELL

Herzing University (C)

435 Ford Rd, St. Louis Park MN 55426
Telephone: (763) 535-3000 FICE Identification: 011017
Accreditation: &NH, DA, DH, NURSE, OTA, @PTAA

† Regional accreditation is carried under the parent institution in Madison, WI.

Institute of Production and Recording (D)

300 N. 1st Avenue, Suite 500, Minneapolis MN 55401
County: Hennepin FICE Identification: 041302
Unit ID: 454616
Telephone: (612) 351-0631 Carnegie Class: Spec-4-yr-Arts
FAX Number: (612) 244-2801 Calendar System: Other
URL: www.ipr.edu
Established: 2002 Annual Undergrad Tuition & Fees: $19,776
Enrollment: 212 Coed
Affiliation or Control: Proprietary IRS Status: Proprietary
Highest Offering: Baccalaureate
Accreditation: ACCSC

01 Campus Director ... Stacy SEVERSON
05 Dean of Education ... Tracy WODELE
07 Assoc Director of Admissions ... Stacy SEVERSON
36 Director of Career Services ... Diana WELTER
08 Librarian ... Tina HALFMANN

Leech Lake Tribal College (E)

6945 Little Wolf Rd., NW, Cass Lake MN 56633
County: Cass FICE Identification: 030964
Unit ID: 413626
Telephone: (218) 335-4200 Carnegie Class: Tribal
FAX Number: (218) 335-4282 Calendar System: Semester
URL: www.lltc.edu
Established: 1990 Annual Undergrad Tuition & Fees: $4,198
Enrollment: 181 Coed
Affiliation or Control: Tribal Control IRS Status: 501(c)3
Highest Offering: Associate Degree
Accreditation: #NH

01 President ... Raymond BURNS
05 Dean Academics/Chief Academic Ofcr ... Vikki HOWARD
10 Director of Finance ... Genny LOWRY
32 Dean of Student Services ... Michelle SABOO
09 Dir Institutional Rsrch/Assessment ... Tracy HENDRICKSON
84 Dir Enrollment Services/Registrar ... Stacey LUNDBERG

Luther Seminary (F)

2481 Como Avenue, Saint Paul MN 55108-1496
County: Ramsey FICE Identification: 002357
Unit ID: 173896
Telephone: (651) 641-3456 Carnegie Class: Spec-4-yr-Faith
FAX Number: (651) 641-3425 Calendar System: Semester
URL: www.luthersem.edu
Established: 1869 Annual Graduate Tuition & Fees: N/A
Enrollment: 459 Coed
Affiliation or Control: Evangelical Lutheran Church In America
IRS Status: 501(c)3
Highest Offering: Doctorate; No Undergraduates
Accreditation: NH, THEOL

01 President ... Rev.Dr. Robin STEINKE
05 VP of Academic Affairs ... Dr. Dirk LANG
10 VP Administration & Finance ... Mr. Michael MORROW
26 VP Seminary Relations ... Ms. Heidi DROEGEMUELLER
32 Dean of Students ... Ms. Sarah LUEDTKE-JONES
15 Director of Human Resources ... Vacant
07 Director of Admissions ... Vacant
06 Registrar ... Ms. Diane DONCITS
27 Marketing/Communications Manager ... Vacant
84 Director of Enrollment Services ... Ms. Jessi LECLEAR VACHTA

Lutheran Brethren Seminary (G)

1036 Alcott Avenue W, Fergus Falls MN 56537
County: Otter Tail Identification: 666644
Telephone: (218) 739-3375 Carnegie Class: Not Classified
FAX Number: N/A Calendar System: Semester
URL: www.lbs.edu
Established: 1903 Annual Graduate Tuition & Fees: N/A
Enrollment: N/A Coed
Affiliation or Control: Other IRS Status: 501(c)3
Highest Offering: Master's; No Undergraduates
Accreditation: TRACS

01 President ... Dr. David VEUM
05 Dean of the Seminary/CAO ... Dr. Brad PRIBBENOW
06 Registrar/Director of Admissions ... Dr. Gaylan MATHIESEN

Macalester College (H)

1600 Grand Avenue, Saint Paul MN 55105-1801
County: Ramsey FICE Identification: 002358
Unit ID: 173902
Telephone: (651) 696-6000 Carnegie Class: Bac-A&S
FAX Number: (651) 696-6689 Calendar System: Semester
URL: www.macalester.edu
Established: 1874 Annual Undergrad Tuition & Fees: $54,344
Enrollment: 2,136 Coed
Affiliation or Control: Presbyterian Church (U.S.A.) IRS Status: 501(c)3
Highest Offering: Baccalaureate
Accreditation: NH

01 President ... Dr. Brian C. ROSENBERG
05 Dean of the Faculty & Provost ... Dr. Karine F. MOE
115 Chief Investment Officer ... Mr. Gary D. MARTIN
111 VP Advancement ... Mr. Andrew BROWN
32 Vice President Student Affairs ... Ms. Donna LEE
10 Vice President for Admin/Finance ... Mr. David M. WHEATON
13 Associate VP ITS/CIO ... Ms. Jennifer HAAS
07 Vice President Admissions Fin Aid ... Mr. Jeffrey S. ALLEN
85 Dean Annan Inst Global Citizenship ... Dr. Donna K. MAEDA
20 Director of Academic Programs ... Ms. Ann M. MINNICK
28 Dean of Multicultural Life ... Ms. Marjorie TRUEBLOOD
35 Dean of Students ... Ms. DeMethra BRADLEY
37 Director Student Financial Aid ... Ms. Jenae A. SCHMIDT
06 Registrar ... Mr. Timothy S. TRAFFIE
35 Assoc Dean of Students ... Mr. Andrew WELLS
15 Director Employment Services ... Mr. Bob GRAF
18 Director Facilities Management ... Mr. Nathan P. LIEF
41 Athletic Director ... Mr. Donnie A. BROOKS
04 Assistant to the President ... Ms. Cynthia L. HENDRICKS
21 Assistant Vice President Finance ... Ms. Patricia M. LANGER
26 Associate VP Comm and Marketing ... Ms. Julie T. HURBANIS
29 Asst VP Alumni Engagement ... Ms. Katie LADAS
38 Director Health and Wellness Center ... Ms. Denise WARD
96 Dir Purchasing/Accounts Payable ... Mr. Matthew D. RUMPZA
105 Dir Digital Engagement & Ext Rel ... Ms. Sara C. SUELFLOW
84 Manager of Enrollment Systems ... Mr. Abraham NOEL
08 Head Librarian ... Ms. Teresa FISHEL
102 Dir Foundation/Corporate Relations ... Ms. Michelle EPP
36 Dean of Career Exploration ... Ms. Mindy J. DEARDURFF
19 Assoc Director Security/Safety ... Mr. Bill S. COLLUMBIEN
09 Director Institutional Research ... Dr. Polly A. FASSINGER

Martin Luther College (I)

1995 Luther Court, New Ulm MN 56073-3300
County: Brown FICE Identification: 002361
Unit ID: 173452
Telephone: (507) 354-8221 Carnegie Class: Spec-4-yr-Other
FAX Number: (507) 354-8225 Calendar System: Semester
URL: www.mlc-wels.edu
Established: 1995 Annual Undergrad Tuition & Fees: $15,410
Enrollment: 981 Coed
Affiliation or Control: Wisconsin Evangelical Lutheran Synod
IRS Status: 501(c)3
Highest Offering: Master's
Accreditation: NH

01 President ... Rev. Mark G. ZARLING
05 Vice President for Academics ... Dr. Jeffery P. WIECHMAN
11 Vice President for Administration ... Prof. Scott D. SCHMUDLACH
32 Vice President Student Life ... Prof. Jeffrey L. SCHONE
53 Academic Dean Educational Ministry ... Prof. Benjamin P. CLEMONS
73 Academic Dean Pastoral Ministry ... Prof. Daniel N. BALGE
10 Director of Finance ... Mrs. Carla J. HULKE
08 Director of Library Services ... Mrs. Linda KRAMER
37 Director of Financial Aid ... Mr. Mark D. BAUER
07 Director of Admissions ... Prof. Mark A. STEIN
58 Director Graduate Studies/Cont Educ ... Dr. John E. MEYER
88 Director of Clinical Experiences ... Prof. Paul A. TESS
41 Director of Athletics ... Prof. James M. UNKE
42 Campus Pastor ... Dr. John C. BOEDER
13 Director of Technology ... Mr. James A. RATHJE
26 Director of Public Relations ... Prof. William A. PEKRUL
40 Bookstore Manager ... Mrs. Linette M. SCHARLEMANN
90 Director of Academic Computing ... Prof. Rachel M. FELD
29 Director Alumni Relations ... Mr. Stephen J. BALZA
108 Director Institutional Assessment ... Prof. Rebecca L. COX
06 Registrar ... Mrs. Gwen L. KRAL
09 Director of Institutional Research ... Prof. Steven R. THIESFELDT
15 Chief Human Resources Officer ... Mrs. Andrea E. WENDLAND

Minneapolis Business College (J)

1711 W County Road B, Roseville MN 55113-4056
County: Ramsey FICE Identification: 004645
Unit ID: 174118
Telephone: (651) 636-7406 Carnegie Class: Assoc/HVT-High Trad
FAX Number: (651) 636-8185 Calendar System: Semester
URL: www.minneapolisbusinesscollege.edu
Established: 1874 Annual Undergrad Tuition & Fees: $15,120
Enrollment: 177 Coed
Affiliation or Control: Proprietary IRS Status: Proprietary
Highest Offering: Associate Degree
Accreditation: ACCSC, MAC

01 President ... Mr. David WHITMAN
05 Director of Education ... Ms. Kate ADAMS
32 Director of Student Services ... Mrs. Marie MARTIN
36 Int Director of Placement ... Ms. Kelley RILEY

† In teach-out mode. Closing Dec 2019.

Minneapolis College of Art and Design (K)

2501 Stevens Avenue, Minneapolis MN 55404-4343
County: Hennepin FICE Identification: 002365
Unit ID: 174127
Telephone: (612) 874-3700 Carnegie Class: Spec-4-yr-Arts
FAX Number: (612) 874-3704 Calendar System: Semester
URL: www.mcad.edu
Established: 1886 Annual Undergrad Tuition & Fees: $39,120
Enrollment: 774 Coed
Affiliation or Control: Independent Non-Profit IRS Status: 501(c)3
Highest Offering: Master's
Accreditation: NH, ART

01 President ... Mr. Sanjit SETHI
04 Exec Asst to President/Sec Board ... Ms. Sarah HARDING
05 Vice President Academic Affairs ... Ms. Karen WIRTH
10 VP Finance/Chief Financial Officer ... Ms. Joy BRATHWAITE
11 Vice President Administration ... Ms. Pam NEWSOME
111 VP Institutional Advancement ... Ms. Cindy THEIS
84 Vice Pres Enrollment Management ... Ms. Melissa HUYBRECHT
32 Vice President of Student Affairs ... Ms. Jen ZUCCOLA
18 Assoc VP Facilities/Public Safety ... Mr. Brock RASMUSSEN
13 Assoc Vice President Technology ... Mr. R. Hal WELLS
06 Registrar ... Mr. River GORDON
51 Director of Continuing Education ... Ms. Lara ROY
08 Director of Library ... Ms. Amy BECKER
24 Director Media Technology Services ... Mr. Scott BOWMAN
36 Director of Career Services ... Ms. Meghana SHROFF
29 Director Alumni and Annual Giving ... Mr. Seth GOODSPEED
39 Director Student Housing ... Mr. Nate K. LUTZ
26 Director Communications ... Vacant
37 Director Student Financial Aid ... Ms. Laura LINK
108 Director Accreditation & Assessment ... Ms. Melissa RANDS
19 Director of Public Safety ... Mr. Steve MCLAUGHLIN

*Minnesota State Colleges and Universities System Office (A)

30 7th Street East, Suite 350, Saint Paul MN 55101-4901
County: Ramsey FICE Identification: 009346
Unit ID: 428453
Telephone: (651) 201-1800 Carnegie Class: N/A
FAX Number: (651) 297-5550
URL: https://www.minnstate.edu/

01 Interim Chancellor .... Devinder MALHOTRA
15 Vice Chancellor Human Resources .... Eric DAVIS
05 Sr Vice Chanc Academic/Student Affs .... Ron ANDERSON
10 Int Vice Chancellor of Finance CFO .... William MAKI
13 Vice Chanc Information Tech/CIO .... Ramon PADILLA
26 Chief Marketing/Communications Ofcr .... Noelle HAWTON
18 Assoc Vice Chancellor Facilities .... Brian D. YOLITZ
46 Assoc Vice Chanc Research/Planning .... Vacant
32 Assoc Vice Chanc Student Affairs .... Brent GLASS
100 Interim Chief of Staff .... Jaime SIMONSEN
16 Asst Dir Human Resources .... Jessica WHITE
28 Chief Diversity Officer .... Clyde WILSON PICKETT
102 Exec Dir System/Foundation Rels .... Vacant
43 General Counsel .... Gary CUNNINGHAM
45 Program Dir Academic Planning .... Todd HARMENING

*Alexandria Technical & Community College (B)

1601 Jefferson Street, Alexandria MN 56308-2796
County: Douglas FICE Identification: 005544
Unit ID: 172918
Telephone: (320) 762-4600 Carnegie Class: Assoc/HVT-High Non
FAX Number: (320) 762-4501 Calendar System: Semester
URL: www.alextech.edu
Established: 1961 Annual Undergrad Tuition & Fees (In-State): $5,416
Enrollment: 2,794 Coed
Affiliation or Control: State IRS Status: 501(c)3
Highest Offering: Associate Degree
Accreditation: NH, MLTAD

02 President .... Mr. Michael SEYMOUR
41 Vice Pres/Athletic Director .... Vacant
51 Dean of Customized Training .... Vacant
10 Chief Financial Officer .... Mr. David BJELLAND
05 Sr Dean Academic Affairs & Students .... Mr. Gregg RAISANEN
32 Dean of Student Affairs .... Vacant
72 Dean of Technology .... Mr. Steve RICHARDS
66 Dean of Nursing and Health .... Ms. Merilee RETZLOFF
19 Dean of Law Enforcement .... Mr. Scott BERGER
37 Financial Aid Director .... Mr. Steve RICHARDS
22 Human Rights Officer .... Ms. Tamzin BUKOWSKI
36 Director Student Placement .... Mr. Patrick RUNNING
102 Foundation Executive Director .... Ms. Amy ALLEN
06 Registrar .... Mr. Patrick RUNNING
18 Director of Facilities .... Mr. Joel SEELA
15 Chief Human Resources Officer .... Ms. Shari MALONEY
09 Director of Institutional Research .... Ms. Rebekah SUMMER
07 Director of Admissions .... Ms. Lynn ARNQUIST
35 Director of Student Activities .... Ms. Michelle AHLQUIST
88 Director of K-12 Initiatives .... Ms. Mary LENZ
04 Asst to Pres/Dir of Office Services .... Ms. Annette PAVEK
21 Director of Financial Operations .... Ms. Julie FENLASON
40 Bookstore Manager .... Ms. Missy DOEBBER-BREVER
30 Development Officer .... Ms. Linda DOLAN
121 Director of Support Services .... Ms. Kaye MADIGAN
28 Chief Diversity Officer .... Ms. Merilee RETZLOFF

*Anoka-Ramsey Community College (C)

11200 Mississippi Boulevard NW,
Coon Rapids MN 55433-3470
County: Anoka FICE Identification: 002332
Unit ID: 172963
Telephone: (763) 433-1100 Carnegie Class: Assoc/HT-High Non
FAX Number: (763) 433-1121 Calendar System: Semester
URL: www.anokaramsey.edu
Established: 1965 Annual Undergrad Tuition & Fees (In-State): $5,073
Enrollment: 8,954 Coed
Affiliation or Control: State IRS Status: 501(c)3
Highest Offering: Associate Degree
Accreditation: NH, ACBSP, ADNUR, MUS, PTAA

02 President .... Dr. Kent HANSON
10 VP Finance & Administration .... Mr. Don LEWIS
05 Int VP Academic/Student Affairs .... Mr. Steve CRITTENDEN
32 Dean of Student Affairs .... Ms. Lisa HARRIS
35 Dean of Students .... Mr. Steve CRITTENDEN
18 Physical Plant Manager .... Mr. Roger FREEMAN
15 Chief HR Director .... Mr. Jay NELSON
57 Dean of Arts & Letters .... Mr. Greg RATHERT
88 Dean CE/CT/Bus/Tech/Wellness .... Ms. Luanne KANE
35 Dean Student Life .... Vacant
76 Dean of Allied Health .... Ms. Natasha BAER
21 Director Fiscal & Auxiliary Svcs .... Ms. Marilyn SMITH
81 Interim Dean of STEM .... Ms. Melissa MILLS
09 Dean of Research & Assessment .... Ms. Nora MORRIS
28 Director of Multicultural Affairs .... Ms. Venoreen BROWNE-BOATSWAIN
102 Interim Director of Foundations .... Mr. Jamie BARTHEL
26 Director of Mktg/Public Relations .... Ms. Mary JACOBSON
19 Director of Safety & Security .... Mr. Cliff ANDERSON
35 Director of Student Life .... Ms. Joyce TRACZYK
13 Interim Director of Technology .... Mr. Tim ZONDLO
21 Business Manager .... Ms. Kim BIENFANG
37 Interim Director Financial Aid .... Ms. Brittany TWEED
04 Administrative Asst to President .... Ms. Margie SCHLUETER
06 Registrar .... Vacant

*Anoka Technical College (D)

1355 W Highway 10, Anoka MN 55303-1590
County: Anoka FICE Identification: 007350
Unit ID: 172954
Telephone: (763) 576-4700 Carnegie Class: Assoc/HVT-High Trad
FAX Number: (763) 576-4715 Calendar System: Semester
URL: www.anokatech.edu
Established: 1967 Annual Undergrad Tuition & Fees (In-District): $5,584
Enrollment: 1,864 Coed
Affiliation or Control: State/Local IRS Status: 501(c)3
Highest Offering: Associate Degree
Accreditation: NH, CAHIIM, MAC, OTA, SURGT

02 President .... Dr. Kent HANSON
05 Vice Pres of Acad/Student Affs .... Dr. Elaina BLEIFIELD
13 Chief Information Officer .... Richard MALOTT
10 Vice Pres Finance & Admin .... Donald LEWIS
20 Academic Dean .... Dina HUMBLE
04 Assistant to the President .... Margie SCHLUETER
15 Chief Human Resource Officer .... Jay NELSON
26 Director of Marketing .... Mary JACOBSON
06 Director of Records .... Susan RUMPCA
32 Dean of Student Affairs .... Sean JOHNS
37 Interim Financial Aid Director .... Brittany TWEED
08 Head Librarian .... Jill HOLMAN
18 Chief Facilities/Physical Plant .... Kenneth KARR
19 Director Security/Safety .... Clifford ANDERSON
84 Director of Enrollment Services .... LeAnna WANGERIN
09 Director of Institutional Research .... Nora MORRIS
28 Director of Diversity .... Venoreen BROWNE-BOATSWAIN

*Bemidji State University (E)

1500 Birchmont Drive NE, Bemidji MN 56601-2699
County: Beltrami FICE Identification: 002336
Unit ID: 173124
Telephone: (218) 755-2001 Carnegie Class: Masters/S
FAX Number: N/A Calendar System: Semester
URL: www.bemidjistate.edu
Established: 1919 Annual Undergrad Tuition & Fees (In-State): $8,696
Enrollment: 5,195 Coed
Affiliation or Control: State IRS Status: 501(c)3
Highest Offering: Master's
Accreditation: NH, IACBE, MUS, NAIT, NURSE, SW

02 President .... Dr. Faith C. HENSRUD
05 Provost/VP Acad & Stdnt Affairs .... Dr. Tony PEFFER
10 VP Finance & Administration .... Ms. Karen SNOREK
84 Exec Dir of Enrollment Management .... Ms. Michelle FRENZEL
22 Int Affirm Action & Accreditation .... Dr. Debra PETERSON
20 Assoc VP Academic Affairs .... Dr. Allen BEDFORD
08 Library & Library Services .... Mr. Pete MCDONNELL
09 Director Inst Rsrch/Effectiveness .... Vacant
88 Dir Center for Professional Devel .... Dr. Debbie GUELDA
92 Director Honors Program .... Dr. Season ELLISON
85 Director International Program Ctr .... Mr. Patrick LIU
88 Co-Director Leadership Studies .... Dr. Dennis LUNT
88 Co-Director Leadership Studies .... Dr. Virgil BAKKEN
88 Dean Individual & Community Health .... Dr. Joseph RITTER
50 Dean Business/Math & Sciences .... Dr. Marilyn YODER
88 Exec Dir MN Adv Manuf Ctr of Excell .... Mr. Jeremy LEFFELMAN
50 Director MARS Program .... Dr. Kelly LA VENTURE
79 Dean Arts/Education & Humanities .... Dr. Jim BARTA
32 Assoc VP for Student Life & Success .... Vacant
93 Director American Indian Ctr .... Mr. Bill BLACKWELL
28 Dir Ctr for Diversity/Equity & Incl .... Dr. Ye (Solar) HONG
88 Director Campus Recreation .... Ms. Kierstin HOVEN
88 Director Hobson Memorial Union .... Ms. Nina JOHNSON
39 Director Housing & Res Life .... Dr. Randall LUDEMAN
38 Director Ctr for Health-Counseling .... Vacant
106 Director Distance Learning .... Ms. Lynn JOHNSON
21 Business Manager .... Mr. Ron BECKSTROM
18 Physical Plant Manager .... Mr. Travis BARNES
19 Director Public Safety .... Mr. Casey J. MCCARTHY
15 Chief Human Resources Officer .... Ms. Megan ZOTHMAN
13 Acting Chief Information Officer .... Ms. Karen SNOREK
07 Director Admissions .... Mr. Paul MULLER
37 Director Financial Aid .... Ms. Lesa LAWRENCE
06 Registrar .... Ms. Kim GOURNEAU
121 Director Advising Success Center .... Mr. Zak JOHNSON
36 Director Career Services .... Ms. Margie T. GIAUQUE
88 TRIO/SSS/UB/McNair .... Ms. Kelli STEGGALL
88 Disability Services .... Mr. Christian BRECZINSKI
26 Exec Dir Communications & Mktg .... Mr. Andy BARTLETT
41 Athletic Director .... Mr. Tracy DILL
111 Exec Dir for University Advancement .... Mr. Joshua CHRISTIANSON
29 Director Alumni Relations .... Mr. Brett BAHR
58 Director Graduate Studies .... Mr. George MCCONNELL

*Central Lakes College (F)

501 W College Drive, Brainerd MN 56401-3900
County: Crow Wing FICE Identification: 002339
Unit ID: 173203
Telephone: (218) 855-8000 Carnegie Class: Assoc/MT-VT-High Non
FAX Number: (218) 855-8057 Calendar System: Semester
URL: www.clcmn.edu
Established: 1938 Annual Undergrad Tuition & Fees (In-State): $5,493
Enrollment: 3,784 Coed
Affiliation or Control: State IRS Status: 501(c)3
Highest Offering: Associate Degree
Accreditation: NH, DA, MAC

02 President .... Dr. Hara D. CHARLIER
05 VP Academic & Student Affairs .... Ms. Joy BODIN
11 VP Administrative Services .... Ms. Kari CHRISTIANSEN
12 Dean Staples Campus/CTE/Grants .... Ms. Tara KARELS
12 Dean Brainerd CTE/Cus Trng .... Ms. Rebekah KENT
47 Dean of Agricultural Studies .... Mr. Keith OLANDER
84 Dean of Enrollment/Student Success .... Mr. Paul PREIMESBERGER
49 Dean of Liberal Arts .... Ms. Martha KUEHN
30 Director of Res Develop/CLC Found .... Ms. Jana SHOGREN
15 Director of Human Resources .... Ms. Sharon MOHR
07 Director of Enrollment Services .... Mr. Nick HEISSERER
06 Registrar .... Ms. Susan STUDNISKI
08 Librarian .... Mr. David BISSONETTE
37 Director Financial Aid .... Mr. Mike BARNABY
14 Director of Technology/Support .... Mr. Scott STREED
26 Director Marketing .... Mr. Kenn DOLS
109 Director of Business/Auxil Services .... Ms. Christina ANDERSON
88 Director of Trio Programs .... Mr. Charles BLACKLANCE
18 Director Physical Plant/Facilities .... Mr. James MCARDELL
28 Dean of Students/Equity/Inclusion .... Ms. Mary SAM
04 Executive Asst to President .... Ms. Jody LONGBELLA
09 Director of Institutional Research .... Ms. Wendy ADAMSON
88 Director Small Business Dev Center .... Mr. Greg BERGMAN
19 Director Security/Safety .... Mr. Matthew KRUEGER
32 Director of Student Life .... Mr. Erich HEPPNER

*Century College (G)

3300 Century Avenue North,
White Bear Lake MN 55110-1894
County: Ramsey FICE Identification: 010546
Unit ID: 175315
Telephone: (651) 779-3200 Carnegie Class: Assoc/MT-VT-High Trad
FAX Number: N/A Calendar System: Semester
URL: www.century.edu
Established: 1967 Annual Undergrad Tuition & Fees (In-State): $5,435
Enrollment: 8,745 Coed
Affiliation or Control: State IRS Status: 501(c)3
Highest Offering: Associate Degree
Accreditation: NH, ADNUR, DA, DH, EMT, MAC, MUS, RAD

02 President .... Ms. Angelia MILLENDER
05 Vice President Academic Affairs .... Ms. Jenni SWENSON
32 Vice President Student Affairs .... Ms. Pakou YANG
10 VP Finance & Administration .... Mr. Patrick OPATZ
13 Assoc VP Information Tech/Admn Svcs .... Mr. John ROHLEDER
84 Assoc Dean Enrollment Management .... Ms. Ali PICKENS-OPOKU
96 Buyer Supervisor .... Ms. Suzanne WENNEN
21 Director of Finance .... Ms. Marilyn SMITH
102 Executive Director Foundation .... Ms. Jill GREENHALGH
06 Registrar .... Ms. Kirsten FABOZZI
15 Director of Human Resources .... Ms. Mary NIENABER
07 Interim Director of Admissions .... Mr. Robert BEAVER
88 Director Academic Partnerships .... Ms. Sue DION
37 Director of Financial Aid .... Ms. Pam ENGEBRETSON
18 Physical Building Supervisor .... Mr. Michael HOUFER
19 Director of Public Safety .... Mr. Jason PHILIPP
66 Academic Dean .... Ms. Beth HEIN
50 Dean Business/Industry/Design .... Vacant
72 Academic Dean .... Ms. Monica RAMIREZ
81 Academic Dean .... Mr. Andrew NESSET
83 Academic Dean .... Ms. Julie ZALOUDEK
35 Dean of Student Affairs .... Vacant
35 Dean of Student Affairs .... Ms. Kristin HAGEMAN
09 Dean of Institutional Effectiveness .... Ms. Nichole PETERSEN
04 Executive Assistant to President .... Ms. Christine MCGING
26 Director of Marketing .... Mr. James STUMNE
28 Chief Diversity Officer .... Ms. Rosa RODRIGUEZ

*Dakota County Technical College (H)

145th Street E, Rosemount MN 55068-2999
County: Dakota FICE Identification: 010402
Unit ID: 173416
Telephone: (651) 423-8000 Carnegie Class: Assoc/HVT-High Trad
FAX Number: (651) 423-8775 Calendar System: Semester
URL: www.dctc.edu
Established: 1970 Annual Undergrad Tuition & Fees (In-District): $5,713
Enrollment: 2,478 Coed
Affiliation or Control: State/Local IRS Status: 501(c)3
Highest Offering: Associate Degree
Accreditation: NH, DA, MAC

02 Interim President .... Mr. Michael BERNDT
05 VP Academic & Student Affairs .... Dr. Mike OPP
09 VP Strategic Alignment .... Vacant
10 VP/Chief Financial Officer .... Mr. Patrick JACOBSON-SCHULTE
09 Assoc VP Strategic Initiatives .... Ms. Carrie SCHNEIDER

32 Assoc VP Student Affairs ... Ms. Anne JOHNSON
88 Dean Transportation/Construct/Manuf ... Mr. Scott DETERMAN
49 Dean Academic Ops/Arts & Sciences ... Ms. Gayle LARSON
13 Chief Information Officer ... Mr. Todd JAGERSON
121 Director Student Success ... Vacant
06 Registrar/Enrollment Director ... Ms. Jodie SWEARINGEN
18 Director of Operations ... Mr. Paul DEMUTH
35 Director Student Life/Activities ... Ms. Nicole MEULEMANS
103 Dean Customized Training/Cont Educ ... Mr. Pat MCQUILLAN
07 Admissions Outreach Coordinator ... Ms. Karianne LOULA
111 Director Institutional Advancement ... Ms. Erin EDLUND
37 Director Financial Aid ... Mr. Scott ROELKE
15 Int Chief Human Resource Officer ... Ms. Laina CARLSON
26 Dir Strategic Mktg/Communication ... Ms. Lise FREKING

*Fond du Lac Tribal and Community College (A)

2101 14th Street, Cloquet MN 55720-2984

County: Carlton | FICE Identification: 031291 | Unit ID: 380368
Telephone: (218) 879-0800 | Carnegie Class: Tribal
FAX Number: (218) 879-0814 | Calendar System: Semester
URL: www.fdltcc.edu
Established: 1987 | Annual Undergrad Tuition & Fees (In-State): $5,319
Enrollment: 1,946 | Coed
Affiliation or Control: State | IRS Status: 501(c)3
Highest Offering: Associate Degree
Accreditation: NH

02 Interim President ... Ms. Stephanie HAMMITT
05 Vice President of Academics ... Dr. Anna FELLEGY
10 Interim Chief Financial Officer ... Mr. Bret BUSAKOWSKI
32 Dean of Student Affairs ... Ms. Anita HANSON
26 Director of Public Information ... Mr. Tom URBANSKI
06 Registrar ... Ms. Leah TOLLEFSON
88 Disability Services/Student Service ... Ms. Nancy OLSEN
13 Information Technology Specialist ... Mr. Loran WAPPES
37 Director of Financial Aid ... Mr. David SUTHERLAND
07 Director of Admissions ... Ms. Susan BUMANN
09 Director of Institutional Research ... Mr. James EISENHAUER
35 Dir of Student Support Services ... Ms. Peggy POITRA
62 Library Services ... Ms. Nancy BROUGHTON
30 Director of Development ... Ms. Stephanie HAMMITT
39 Director of Housing ... Mr. Jesse STIREWALT
15 Director of Human Resources ... Ms. Marisa HAGGY
18 Chief Facilities/Physical Plant ... Mr. Mark BERNHARDSON
40 Bookstore Coordinator ... Ms. Bonnie BERNHARDSON
04 Executive Assistant to President ... Ms. Mary SOYRING

*Hennepin Technical College (B)

9000 Brooklyn Boulevard, Brooklyn Park MN 55445-2399

County: Hennepin | FICE Identification: 010491 | Unit ID: 173708
Telephone: (952) 995-1300 | Carnegie Class: Assoc/HVT-High Trad
FAX Number: (763) 488-2956 | Calendar System: Semester
URL: www.hennepintech.edu
Established: 1972 | Annual Undergrad Tuition & Fees (In-District): $5,248
Enrollment: 5,078 | Coed
Affiliation or Control: State/Local | IRS Status: 501(c)3
Highest Offering: Associate Degree
Accreditation: NH, ACBSP, ACFEI, DA, MAC

02 President ... Dr. Merrill IRVING, JR.
10 Vice Pres Finance and Operations ... Mr. Craig ERICKSON
06 Registrar ... Ms. Julie HIGDEM
15 Chief Human Resources Officer ... Ms. Marybeth CHRISTENSON-JONES
28 Vice Pres of of Diversity ... Ms. Jean MAIERHOFER
09 Dir of Institutional Effectiveness ... Ms. Debra NEWGARD
111 Chief Advancement/Comm Officer ... Ms. Nairobi ABRAMS
37 Director of Financial Aid ... Mr. Tim JACOBSON
84 VP Enrollment Services ... Dr. Amanda TURNER
121 Interim VP Student Success ... Ms. Jess LAURITSEN
04 Administrative Asst to President ... Ms. Lisa YEAGER
13 Chief Info Technology Officer (CIO) ... Mr. Jason KOPP
08 Head Librarian ... Ms. Jennie SIMNING
22 Dir Affirmative Action/EEO ... Ms. Jean MAIERHOFER
19 Director Security/Safety ... Mr. Randy ROEHRICK
32 Director Student Life ... Ms. Sue SCHMITZ
18 Director of Operations/Facilities ... Mr. Joe WIGHTKIN
05 VP Academic Affairs ... Ms. Leanne ROGSTAD

*Hibbing Community College, A Technical and Community College (C)

1515 E 25th Street, Hibbing MN 55746-3300

County: Saint Louis | FICE Identification: 002355 | Unit ID: 173735
Telephone: (218) 262-7200 | Carnegie Class: Assoc/HVT-Mix Trad/Non
FAX Number: (218) 262-6717 | Calendar System: Semester
URL: www.hibbing.edu
Established: 1916 | Annual Undergrad Tuition & Fees (In-State): $5,310
Enrollment: 1,208 | Coed
Affiliation or Control: State | IRS Status: 501(c)3
Highest Offering: Associate Degree
Accreditation: NH, ADNUR, DA, MLTAD

02 Interim President ... Dr. Michael RAICH
05 Interim Provost ... Mr. Aaron REINI
20 Interim Dean of Academics ... Ms. Jessalyn SABIN
10 VP Finance & Administration ... Ms. Karen KEDROWSKI
09 Institutional Research ... Ms. Tracey ROY
37 Director Student Financial Aid ... Ms. Jodi PONTINEN
18 Plant Maintenance Engineer ... Mr. David OLDS
26 Marketing Specialist/Public Info ... Ms. Jessica MATVEY
06 Registrar ... Ms. Kari DOUCETTE
13 Chief Info Technology Officer (CIO) ... Mr. Don BREARLEY
39 Director Student Housing ... Vacant
41 Athletic Director ... Mr. Mike FLATEN
08 Head Librarian ... Ms. Rachel MILANI
28 Director of Diversity ... Ms. Jane BARRICK
07 Director of Admissions ... Ms. Sarah MERHAR
121 Student Success Director ... Ms. Jen BOBEN
15 Chief Human Resource/Diversity Ofcr ... Ms. Carmen BRADACH
19 Safety & Emergency Management Coord ... Ms. Gina GODEEN

*Inver Hills Community College (D)

2500 80th Street E, Inver Grove Heights MN 55076-3224

County: Dakota | FICE Identification: 009740 | Unit ID: 173799
Telephone: (651) 450-3000 | Carnegie Class: Assoc/HT-Mix Trad/Non
FAX Number: (651) 450-3679 | Calendar System: Semester
URL: www.inverhills.edu
Established: 1970 | Annual Undergrad Tuition & Fees (In-State): $5,332
Enrollment: 4,479 | Coed
Affiliation or Control: State | IRS Status: 501(c)3
Highest Offering: Associate Degree
Accreditation: NH, ACBSP, ADNUR, EMT

02 Interim President ... Dr. Michael BERNDT
05 Provost/VP Academic Affs ... Dr. Tia ROBINSON-COOPER
11 Vice Pres Administrative Services ... Mr. Patrick JACOBSON-SCHULTE
32 Vice Pres Student Affairs ... Dr. Wendy ROBINSON
10 Vice Pres/Chief Financial Officer ... Mr. Patrick JACOBSON-SCHULTE
06 Registrar ... Mr. Scott KLAEHN
36 Dean of Career Programs ... Ms. Janica AUSTAD
79 Dean of Liberal Arts ... Dr. Barb CURCHACK
81 Dean of STEM/Social Sciences ... Dr. Stephen L. STROM
102 Exec Dir Foundation & Advancement ... Mrs. Michelle BOE
15 Int Chief Human Resources Officer ... Ms. Laina CARLSON
103 Dean Ctr Prof/Workforce Development ... Vacant
08 Librarian ... Ms. Julie BENOLKEN
124 Dean of Student Success & Retention ... Ms. Kari RUSCH-CURL
88 Dir Paralegal Pgm/Ofc Sys-Legal ... Ms. Sally DAHLQUIST
90 Director Acad Tech/Computing Svcs ... Vacant
18 Director Facilities Plng/Management ... Mr. Paul DEMUTH
88 Int Dir Emergency Health Svcs ... Mr. Kevin JOHNSON
28 Director of Equity & Inclusion ... Vacant
37 Int Director of Financial Aid ... Mr. Scott ROELKE
09 Director of Institutional Research ... Ms. Wendy MARSON
26 Dir of Inst Advance/Mktg & PR ... Vacant
35 Director of Student Life ... Ms. Nicole MEULEMANS
13 Chief Information Technology Office ... Mr. Todd JAGERSON

*Itasca Community College (E)

1851 E Highway 169, Grand Rapids MN 55744-3397

County: Itasca | FICE Identification: 002356 | Unit ID: 173805
Telephone: (800) 996-6422 | Carnegie Class: Assoc/HT-Mix Trad/Non
FAX Number: (218) 322-2332 | Calendar System: Semester
URL: www.itascacc.edu
Established: 1922 | Annual Undergrad Tuition & Fees (In-State): $5,325
Enrollment: 1,211 | Coed
Affiliation or Control: State | IRS Status: 501(c)3
Highest Offering: Associate Degree
Accreditation: NH

02 Chief Executive Officer ... Mr. William D. MAKI
03 Executive Vice President ... Ms. Karen KEDROWSKI
05 Provost ... Dr. Bart JOHNSON
20 Academic Dean ... Dr. Bart JOHNSON
10 Accounting Officer Finance ... Ms. Karen KEDROWSKI
84 Dir of Enrollment Mgmt/Admissions ... Mr. William MARSHALL
06 Registrar ... Ms. Becky BOURQUIN
29 Director of Alumni Relations ... Ms. Susan LYNCH
30 Director of College Development ... Ms. Susan LYNCH
37 Director of Student Financial Aid ... Ms. Allison GEISLER
08 Head Librarian ... Mr. Steve BEAN
18 Director of Facilities & Info Tech ... Mr. Chad HAATVEDT
40 Bookstore Manager ... Ms. Faith MCBRIDE
28 Director of Diversity ... Mr. Harold ANNETTE
09 Director of Institutional Research ... Ms. Tracey ROY
39 Director Student Housing ... Mr. Weldon BRAXTON
32 Dean of Student & Admin Services ... Mr. Richard KANGAS

*Lake Superior College (F)

2101 Trinity Road, Duluth MN 55811-3399

County: Saint Louis | FICE Identification: 005757 | Unit ID: 173461
Telephone: (218) 733-7600 | Carnegie Class: Assoc/MT-VT-High Non
FAX Number: (218) 733-5937 | Calendar System: Semester
URL: www.lsc.edu
Established: 1995 | Annual Undergrad Tuition & Fees (In-State): $5,166
Enrollment: 5,059 | Coed
Affiliation or Control: State | IRS Status: 501(c)3
Highest Offering: Associate Degree
Accreditation: NH, ADNUR, COARC, DH, MAC, MLTAD, PNUR, PTAA, RAD, SURGT

02 President ... Dr. Patricia L. ROGERS
05 VP Academic/Student Affairs ... Ms. Hanna ERPESTAD
11 VP Administration ... Mr. Al FINLAYSON
50 Dean of Business/Industry ... Mr. Brad VIETHS
49 Interim Dean Liberal Arts/Sciences ... Mr. Jamal ADAM
76 Interim Dean Allied Health/ Nursing ... Ms. Anna SACKETTE-URNESS
103 Dean of Workforce & Community Dev ... Ms. Tamara ARNOTT
09 IR/Accred Assessment/Research ... Ms. Denise MILLS-LEMIRE
07 Director of Admissions ... Ms. Kayti STOLP
15 Director of Human Resources ... Vacant
111 Dir of Institutional Advancement ... Mr. Daniel FANNING
06 Registrar ... Ms. Melissa LENO
18 Building Maintenance Foreman ... Mr. Mark CARDINAL
32 Dean of Student Affairs ... Mr. Wade GORDON
36 Director Career Services ... Vacant
37 Director Student Financial Aid ... Ms. LaNita ROBINSON
21 Director Business Services ... Ms. Nickoel ANDERSON
13 Director Information Technology ... Mr. Steve FUDALLY
121 Director of Advising ... Mr. Keith TURNER
96 Purchasing Agent ... Mr. Michael FRANCISCO
04 Executive Asst to President ... Ms. Debbie JOHNSON

*Mesabi Range College (G)

1001 West Chestnut Street, Virginia MN 55792-3401

County: Saint Louis | FICE Identification: 004009 | Unit ID: 173993
Telephone: (218) 741-3095 | Carnegie Class: Assoc/MT-VT-High Non
FAX Number: (218) 748-2419 | Calendar System: Semester
URL: www.mesabirange.edu
Established: 1918 | Annual Undergrad Tuition & Fees (In-State): $5,329
Enrollment: 1,248 | Coed
Affiliation or Control: State | IRS Status: Exempt
Highest Offering: Associate Degree
Accreditation: NH, EMT

02 Interim President ... Mr. Michael RAICH
05 Provost/CAO ... Mrs. Shelly MCCAULEY JUGOVICH
10 Vice Pres Finance/Administration ... Mrs. Karen KEDROWSKI
32 Dir Student Support Services ... Ms. Jennifer WILLARD
15 Director Human Resources ... Mrs. Carmen BRADACH
37 Director Student Financial Aid ... Ms. Jodi PONTINEN
06 Registrar ... Mrs. Rebecca STEVINSON
07 Director of Admissions ... Ms. Brenda KOCHEVAR
09 Director of Institutional Research ... Ms. Tracey ROY
38 Student Counseling ... Ms. Kelly BAKK
36 Student Placement ... Ms. Shari CHRISTENSON
13 Chief Info Technology Officer (CIO) ... Mrs. Shelly MCCAULEY-JUGOVICH
41 Athletic Director ... Mr. Brad SCOTT

*Metropolitan State University (H)

700 E 7th Street, Saint Paul MN 55106-5000

County: Ramsey | FICE Identification: 010374 | Unit ID: 174020
Telephone: (651) 793-1300 | Carnegie Class: DU-Mod
FAX Number: (651) 793-1235 | Calendar System: Semester
URL: www.metrostate.edu
Established: 1971 | Annual Undergrad Tuition & Fees (In-State): $7,879
Enrollment: 8,148 | Coed
Affiliation or Control: State | IRS Status: 501(c)3
Highest Offering: Doctorate
Accreditation: NH, ACBSP, NURSE, SW

02 President ... Ms. Virginia ARTHUR
05 Prov/Exec VP Acad & Student Affs ... Dr. Amy GORT
10 VP for Finance and Operations/CFO ... Ms. Tracy HATCH
111 VP for University Advancement ... Ms. Rita DIBBLE
84 Actg Exec Dir Enrollment Services ... Ms. Sarah KOEPKE
32 Dean of Students ... Dr. Maya SULLIVAN
13 VP & CIO IT Services ... Mr. Stephen REED
21 Business Manager ... Mr. Ondara NYANG'AU
15 Director Human Resources ... Ms. Deb GEHRKE
06 Registrar ... Mr. Daryl JOHNSON
37 Director Financial Aid ... Ms. Lois LARSON
26 VP for Marketin/Comm & Recruitment ... Ms. Audrey BERGENGREN
29 Director Alumni Relations ... Ms. Kristine HANSEN
28 Chief Diversity Officer ... Mr. Craig MORRIS
09 Director Institutional Research ... Ms. Cynthia DEVORE
07 Actg Executive Director Admissions ... Ms. Sarah KOEPKE
81 Dean College of Sciences ... Dr. Kyle SWANSON
58 Dean College of Management ... Dr. Rassoule HADIDI
88 Int Dean Col Cmty Stds/Urban Affs ... Dr. Francis SCHWEIGERT
88 Int Dean Col Individualized Stds ... Dr. Charles TEDDER
88 Dean School of Urban Education ... Dr. Rene ANTROP-GONZALEZ
49 Dean College of Liberal Arts ... Dr. Craig HANSEN
66 Dean College of Nursing/Health Sci ... Vacant
08 Dean Library/Information Services ... Ms. Beth CLAUSEN
121 Assoc Provost for Student Success ... Ms. Roberta (Bobbie) ANDERSON

*Minneapolis Community and Technical College (I)

1501 Hennepin Avenue, Minneapolis MN 55403-9810

County: Hennepin | FICE Identification: 002362 | Unit ID: 174136
Telephone: (612) 659-6000 | Carnegie Class: Assoc/MT-VT-High Trad

FAX Number: N/A Calendar System: Semester
URL: www.minneapolis.edu
Established: 1996 Annual Undergrad Tuition & Fees (In-State): $5,396
Enrollment: 7,486 Coed
Affiliation or Control: State IRS Status: 501(c)3
Highest Offering: Associate Degree
Accreditation: NH, ADNUR, DA, POLYT

02 President Dr. Sharon PIERCE
05 Vice Pres Academic Affairs Dr. Gail O'KANE
10 Vice Pres Finance/Operations Mr. Christopher RAU
32 Vice President Student Affairs Mr. Patrick TROUP
84 Dean of Enrollment Management Mr. Matthew CRAWFORD
49 Dean of Liberal Arts Dr. Derrick LINDSTROM
81 Dean of Science & Mathematics Dr. Ben WENG
103 Director of Workforce Development Ms. Deanna KOENIG
66 Dean of Nursing & Allied Health Vacant
35 Dean of Students Ms. Becky NORDIN
15 Chief Human Resources Officer Ms. Dianna CUSICK
13 Chief Information Officer Ms. Tiffni DEEB
06 Registrar Ms. Michele COPELAND
08 Librarian Mr. Tom ELAND
37 Financial Aid Director Ms. Angela CHRISTENSEN
09 Dir of Institutional Effectiveness Mr. Fernando FURQUIM
18 Director Facilities Mr. Roger BROZ
19 Director of Public Safety Mr. Curt SCHMIDT
26 Chief Public Relations Officer Ms. Deanna SHEELY
35 Director Student Life Ms. Tara MARTINEZ

*Minnesota State College Southeast (A)

1250 Homer Road, Winona MN 55987-4897
County: Winona FICE Identification: 002393
Unit ID: 175263
Telephone: (507) 453-2700 Carnegie Class: Assoc/HVT-Mix Trad/Non
FAX Number: (507) 453-2715 Calendar System: Semester
URL: www.southeastmn.edu
Established: 1949 Annual Undergrad Tuition & Fees (In-District): $5,628
Enrollment: 1,920 Coed
Affiliation or Control: State/Local IRS Status: 501(c)3
Highest Offering: Associate Degree
Accreditation: NH, MLTAD, PNUR, RAD

02 Interim President Dr. Larry LUNDBLAD
10 Vice Pres Finance/Administration Mr. Mike KROENING
05 Vice President of Academic Affairs Ms. Jennifer ECCLES
13 Chief Information Officer Mr. Rick NAHRGANG
49 Dean of Liberal Arts & Sciences Ms. Jolene PONCELET
72 Dean of Trade & Technology Mr. Travis THUL
15 Chief Human Resource Officer Ms. Maryellen KANZ
84 Director of Recruitment Ms. Shannon SCHELL
37 Director Financial Aid Dr. Tammy VONDRASEK
18 Chief Facilities/Physical Plant Mr. Thomas HOFFMAN
29 Director of Alumni Relations Ms. Casie JOHNSON
26 Director of Marketing Ms. Joanne THOMPSON
103 Director of Customized Training Vacant
27 Director of Communications Ms. Katryn CONLIN
21 Accounting Supervisor Ms. Lisa POZANC
16 Associate Human Resources Officer Ms. Kim NESS
19 Director of Security Mr. Chris CICHOSZ
04 Assistant to President Ms. Amy DRAZKOWSKI
32 Dean Of Students Mr. Josiah LITANT

*Minnesota State Community and Technical College (B)

1414 College Way, Fergus Falls MN 56537-1000
County: Otter Tail FICE Identification: 005541
Unit ID: 173559
Telephone: (218) 736-1500 Carnegie Class: Assoc/HVT-Mix Trad/Non
FAX Number: (218) 736-1510 Calendar System: Semester
URL: www.minnesota.edu
Established: 1960 Annual Undergrad Tuition & Fees (In-State): $5,335
Enrollment: 6,422 Coed
Affiliation or Control: State IRS Status: 501(c)3
Highest Offering: Associate Degree
Accreditation: NH, CAHIIM, DA, MLTAD, RAD

02 President Dr. Carrie BRIMHALL
05 Chief Academic Officer Vacant
15 Chief of Human Resources Mrs. Dacia JOHNSON
32 VP of Student Devel & Marketing Dr. Peter WIELINSKI
06 Registrar Ms. Sharlene ALLEN
13 Chief Information Officer Mr. Dan KNUDSON
10 Chief Finance Officer Mr. Pat NORDICK
121 Dean of Student Success Mr. Shawn ANDERSON
18 Director of College Facilities Mr. Joel KOTSCHEVAR
20 Int Assoc Dean of Acad & Stdnt Affs Ms. Karen BUBOLTZ
12 Academic Dean-Detroit Lakes Vacant
12 Acad Dean Lib Arts/Sci-Fergus Falls Mr. Matthew BORCHERDING
12 Academic Dean-Wadena Vacant
103 Dean of CTS/BES Mr. G.L TUCKER
76 Dean of Health Careers Mrs. Jennifer JACOBSON
72 Dean of Acad Affs for Tech Programs Ms. Carrie WARD
09 Dean of Inst Eff/Tech Programs Mr. Steve ERICKSON
121 Dean of Academic Support Ms. Angela MATHERS
49 Assoc Dean of Liberal Arts & Sci Ms. Anne THURMER
66 Associate Dean/Director of Nursing Ms. Amber REED
07 Director of Admissions Vacant

28 Chief Diversity Officer Vacant
30 Chief Development & Alum Officer Vacant
36 Career Services Director Ms. Sue ZURN
08 Head Librarian Ms. Kari OANES
04 Exec Assistant to the President Ms. Karen REILY
19 Director Safety & ER Preparedness Ms. Paula PEDERSON
37 Director of Financial Aid Ms. Wendy OLDS
39 Dir of Campus Housing & Resid Life Ms. Victoria MCWANE-CREEK

*Minnesota State University, Mankato (C)

309 Wigley Administration Center, Mankato MN 56001-6062
County: Blue Earth FICE Identification: 002360
Unit ID: 173920
Telephone: (507) 389-1111 Carnegie Class: Masters/L
FAX Number: (507) 389-6200 Calendar System: Semester
URL: www.mnsu.edu
Established: 1868 Annual Undergrad Tuition & Fees (In-State): $8,184
Enrollment: 14,712 Coed
Affiliation or Control: State IRS Status: Exempt
Highest Offering: Doctorate
Accreditation: NH, AAB, ART, CAATE, CACREP, CAEP, CAEPN, CONST, DH, DIETD, MUS, NRPA, NURSE, SP, SPAA, SW

02 President Dr. Richard DAVENPORT
05 Provost/Sr Vice Pres Academic Affs Dr. Marilyn WELLS
10 Vice Pres Finance & Administration Mr. Richard STRAKA
111 VP University Advancement Mr. Kent STANLEY
13 VP Technology/CIO Mr. Mark JOHNSON
88 VP Strategic/Bus/Ed/Reg Prtrshps Mr. Robert FLEISCHMAN
32 VP for Student Affairs Dr. David JONES
20 VP for Academic Affairs Dr. Brian MARTENSON
09 VP of Institutional Research Ms. Lynn AKEY
100 Chief of Staff Ms. Sheri SARGENT
04 Exec Assistant to the President Ms. Juanita MILBRETT
20 Interim AVP for Undergrad Education Ms. Terry WALLACE
28 Dean Institutional Diversity Mr. Henry MORRIS
18 Facilities Service Director Mr. David COWAN
06 University Registrar Mr. Marcius BROCK
07 Director of Admissions Mr. Brian JONES
08 Interim Dean Library Services Ms. Daardi MIXON
15 Director of Human Resources Mr. Steve BARRETT
36 Director Career Development Ms. Pamela WELLER-DENGEL
26 Director Media Relations Mr. Daniel BENSON
41 Dir of Intercollegiate Athletics Mr. Kevin BUISMAN
29 Director of Alumni Relations Mr. Ramon PINERO
22 Director Affirmative Action Ms. Linda ALVAREZ
37 Director Student Financial Services Ms. Jan MARBLE
58 AVP Graduate Studies/Research Dr. Stephen STOYNOFF
79 Dean of Arts & Humanities Dr. Matt CECIL
53 Dean of Education Dr. Jean HAAR
50 Dean of Business Dr. Brenda FLANNERY
76 Dean Allied Health/Nursing Dr. Kristine RETHERFORD
81 Dean Science/Engineering/Technology Dr. Brian MARTENSEN
83 Dean Social/Behavioral Science Dr. Matt LAOYZA
104 Acting Dean Global Education Ms. Anne DAHLMAN
56 Dean University Extended Education Dr. Tom NORMAN
38 Director Student Counseling Ms. Kari MUCH
18 AVP Facilities Management Mr. Paul CORCORAN
114 AVP for Budget & Business Services Mr. Steve SMITH
19 Director Security/Safety Ms. Sandi SCHNORENBERG
39 Director Student Housing Ms. Cindy JANNEY
51 Dir Cont Educ & Prof Development Ms. Lou DICKMEYER

*Minnesota State University Moorhead (D)

1104 7th Avenue S, Moorhead MN 56563-2996
County: Clay FICE Identification: 002367
Unit ID: 174358
Telephone: (218) 477-4000 Carnegie Class: Masters/M
FAX Number: (218) 477-2168 Calendar System: Semester
URL: www.mnstate.edu
Established: 1887 Annual Undergrad Tuition & Fees (In-State): $8,496
Enrollment: 6,005 Coed
Affiliation or Control: State IRS Status: 501(c)3
Highest Offering: Doctorate
Accreditation: NH, ART, #CAATE, CACREP, CAEPN, CONST, MUS, NAIT, NURSE, SP, SW

02 President Dr. Anne BLACKHURST
05 VP Academic Affairs Dr. Arrick L. JACKSON
10 VP Finance & Administration Ms. Jean HOLLAAR
84 VP Enrollment Mgmt/Student Affairs Dr. Brenda AMENSON-HILL
29 VP Alumni Foundation Mr. Gary HAUGO
04 Assistant to the President Ms. Kathleen J. MCNABB
20 AVP Academic Affairs Vacant
28 Chief Diversity Officer Dr. Donna L. BROWN
09 Dir Institutional Effectiveness Vacant
41 Director of Athletics Mr. Doug D. PETERS
13 Chief Information Officer Mr. Daniel A. HECKAMAN
21 Comptroller Ms. Karen K. LESTER
50 Int Dean Business & Innovation Mr. Josh J. BEHL
49 Dean Arts/Media/Communication Dr. Earnest LAMB
53 Dean Educ/Human Svcs/Grad Stds Dr. Ok-Hee LEE
83 Int Dean Sciences/Health/Environmnt Dr. Lisa NAWROT
79 Dean of Col Humanities/Soc Sci Dr. Annette L. MORROW
106 Dean Graduate/Extended Learning Dr. Lisa KARCH

32 Dean of Students Ms. Kara GRAVLEY-STACK
15 Director Human Resources Ms. Ann HIEDEMAN
06 Registrar Ms. Heather M. SOLEIM
26 Chief Marketing Officer Mrs. Kirsten JENSEN
19 Director of Public Safety Mr. Ryan NELSON
37 Dir Financial Aid & Scholarships Ms. Melissa DINGMANN
23 Dir Hendrix Counseling Ctr Ms. Angela BELLANGER
22 Director of Accessibility Resources Ms. Kari KLETTKE
36 Director of Career Development Vacant
07 Director of Admissions Mr. Tom REBURN
35 Exec Dir Student Union Mr. Layne ANDERSON
39 Dir Housing & Residential Life Ms. Heather PHILLIPS
85 Director International Student Affs Ms. Janet M. HOHENSTEIN
18 Interim Manager Physical Plant Ms. Jean HOLLAAR
40 Bookstore Supervisor Ms. Kim M. SAMSON

*Minnesota West Community and Technical College (E)

1450 Collegeway, Worthington MN 56187
County: Nobles FICE Identification: 005263
Unit ID: 173638
Telephone: (800) 658-2330 Carnegie Class: Not Classified
FAX Number: (507) 372-5803 Calendar System: Semester
URL: www.mnwest.edu
Established: 1985 Annual Undergrad Tuition & Fees (In-State): N/A
Enrollment: N/A Coed
Affiliation or Control: State IRS Status: 501(c)3
Highest Offering: Associate Degree
Accreditation: NH, ADNUR, DA, MAC, MLTAD, RAD, SURGT

02 President Dr. Terry GAALSWYK
05 College Provost Dr. Jeff WILLIAMSON
10 Vice Pres Finance/Facilities Ms. Jodi LANDGAARD
106 Dean Technology/Distance Learning Ms. Kayla WESTRA
66 Dean Science/Nursing Ms. Dawn GORDON
07 Director Admissions/Registration Ms. Katie HERONIMUS
18 Chief Facilities/Physical Plant Mr. Gordon HEITKAMP
37 Director Financial Aid Ms. Katie HERONIMUS
15 Director Human Resources Ms. Karen MILLER
102 Foundation Director Mr. Michael VAN KEULEN
08 Library Director Mr. Kip THORSON
10 Business Manager Ms. Kayla RICHTER
26 Dir Marketing/Enrollment/Comm Ms. Amber LUINENBURG

*Normandale Community College (F)

9700 France Avenue S, Bloomington MN 55431-4399
County: Hennepin FICE Identification: 007954
Unit ID: 174428
Telephone: (952) 358-8200 Carnegie Class: Assoc/HT-Mix Trad/Non
FAX Number: (952) 358-8101 Calendar System: Semester
URL: www.normandale.edu
Established: 1968 Annual Undergrad Tuition & Fees (In-State): $5,791
Enrollment: 9,844 Coed
Affiliation or Control: State IRS Status: 501(c)3
Highest Offering: Associate Degree
Accreditation: NH, ACBSP, ADNUR, ART, DH, DIETT, MUS, THEA

02 President Dr. Joyce C. ESTER
04 Executive Assistant to President Mrs. Kris CRAIG
10 Vice President Finance & Operations Dr. Lisa WHEELER
05 Provost/Vice Pres of Academic Affs Dr. Kristina KELLER
32 Vice President of Student Affairs Mrs. Dara HAGEN
15 Chief Human Resources Officer Vacant
111 Chief Inst Advancement Officer Ms. Andrea SPECHT
09 Dir of Research & Planning Dr. Mark LEWIS
50 Dean of Business & Social Sci Mr. Michael KIRCH
79 Dean of Humanities Dr. Jeffrey JUDGE
81 Dean of STEM Dr. Cary KOMOTO
76 Dean of Health Sciences Dr. Colleen BRICKLE
08 Dean of Academic Svcs & Library Mrs. Erin DALY
21 Assoc VP Finance & Accounting Ms. Norma KONSCHAK
13 Chief Information Officer Mr. Stephen WINCKELMAN
16 Assistant Human Resources Director Ms. Victoria SCHWAB
18 Assoc Vice Pres of Operations Mr. Patrick BUHL
102 Executive Director of Foundation Ms. Jody SKENDERIAN
84 Dean Outreach & Enrollment Mr. Torrion AMIE
35 Dean of Students Mr. Jason CARDINAL
26 Chief Public Relations Officer Mr. Steve GELLER
06 Registrar Ms. Tonya HANSON
07 Director of Admissions Ms. Nancy PATES
37 Director of Financial Aid & Scholar Mrs. Susan ANT
38 Assoc Director of Advising & Couns Ms. Kari RUSCH-CURL
19 Director of Public Safety Mr. Erik BENTLEY
106 Director of Online Learning Vacant
27 Director of Marketing Communication Mrs. Jennifer LEFLER
88 Accounting Supervisor Mrs. Cindy LADD
40 Bookstore Manager Mr. Chris PETERSON
25 Grant Development Director Mrs. Angela ARNOLD
22 Equity & Inclusion Officer Mr. John PARKER-DER BOGHOSSIAN

*North Hennepin Community College (G)

7411 85th Avenue N, Brooklyn Park MN 55445-2299
County: Hennepin FICE Identification: 002370
Unit ID: 174376
Telephone: (763) 424-0702 Carnegie Class: Assoc/HT-Mix Trad/Non
FAX Number: (763) 424-0929 Calendar System: Semester
URL: www.nhcc.edu
Established: 1966 Annual Undergrad Tuition & Fees (In-State): $4,433

Enrollment: 6,550 Coed
Affiliation or Control: State IRS Status: 501(c)3
Highest Offering: Associate Degree
Accreditation: NH, ACBSP, ADNUR, MLTAD

02 Interim President Dr. Jeffery WILLIAMSON
05 Provost Dr. Jesse MASON
10 VP Finance & Facilities Mr. Stephen KENT
13 Chief Information Officer Mr. Joseph COLLINS
32 Int Dean Student Development Ms. Lindsay FORT
08 Librarian Mr. Craig LARSON
06 Director of Admissions & Records Ms. Melissa LEIMBEK
15 Chief Human Resources Officer Ms. Victoria DEFORD
18 Director of Plant Services Mr. Phillip STIER
102 Foundation Executive Director Mr. Dale FAGRE
28 Director Diversity/Multiculturalism Vacant
26 Dir Marketing/Communications Ms. Liz HOGENSON
09 Director of Institutional Research Ms. Dena COLEMER
19 Director of Public Safety Mr. Ibuchwa KISONGO
21 Business Manager Ms. Dawn BELKO
49 Int Dean of Liberal Arts Mr. Anthony MILLER
50 Dean Business & Career Programs Ms. Nerita HUGHES
81 Dean of Math/Science Mr. Jayant ANAND
76 Dean of Nursing & Allied Health Ms. Doris HILL
60 Int Dean of Comm/Language/Fine Arts Ms. Shirley JOHNSON
121 Director Student Advising Ms. Sarah DOMAN-FLYGARE
04 Executive Assistant to President Ms. Nicole CARLSON
36 Director Student Placement Ms. Deb ATKINS
37 Int Director Student Financial Aid Ms. Kristi L'ALLIER

*Northland Community and Technical College (A)

1101 Highway One East, Thief River Falls MN 56701
County: Pennington FICE Identification: 002385
Unit ID: 174473
Telephone: (218) 683-8800 Carnegie Class: Assoc/HVT-Mix Trad/Non
FAX Number: (218) 683-8980 Calendar System: Semester
URL: www.northlandcollege.edu
Established: 1965 Annual Undergrad Tuition & Fees (In-State): $5,549
Enrollment: 3,416 Coed
Affiliation or Control: State IRS Status: 501(c)3
Highest Offering: Associate Degree
Accreditation: NH, ADNUR, COARC, EMT, OTA, PTAA, RAD, SURGT

02 President Dr. Dennis BONA
10 VP of Admin Services/CFO Ms. Shannon JESME
04 Asst to President Ms. Julie FENNING
05 Provost Dr. Brian HUSCHLE
20 Dean Thief River Falls Campus Mr. Mike CURFMAN
103 Dean Workforce & Econ Development Mr. James RETKA
102 Executive Director NCTC Foundation Mr. Lars DYRUD
121 Academic Success Ctr Director Vacant
38 Counselor Ms. Kelsy BLOWERS
84 Dir of Enrollment Mgmt & Admission Ms. Nicki CARLSON
37 Director Student Financial Aid Ms. Lisa BOTTEM
09 Director of Institutional Research Dr. Mary FONTES
15 Chief Human Resource Officer Ms. Kristi LANE
18 Chief Facilities/Physical Plant Mr. Clinton CASTLE
26 Director of Marketing/Communication Mr. Chad SPERLING
06 Registrar Mr. Ben HOFFMAN
13 Director of Technology Ms. Stacey HRON
41 Director of Athletics Mr. James RETKA
19 Director Security/Safety Mr. Cory FELLER

*Northwest Technical College (B)

905 Grant Avenue, SE, Bemidji MN 56601-4907
County: Beltrami FICE Identification: 005759
Unit ID: 173115
Telephone: (218) 333-6600 Carnegie Class: Assoc/HVT-High Non
FAX Number: (218) 333-6694 Calendar System: Semester
URL: www.ntcmn.edu
Established: 1966 Annual Undergrad Tuition & Fees (In-State): $5,488
Enrollment: 941 Coed
Affiliation or Control: State IRS Status: 501(c)3
Highest Offering: Associate Degree
Accreditation: NH, DA

02 President Dr. Faith HENSRUD
05 Chief Academic Officer Mr. Darrin STROSAHL

*Pine Technical and Community College (C)

900 Fourth Street, SE, Pine City MN 55063-2198
County: Pine FICE Identification: 005535
Unit ID: 174570
Telephone: (320) 629-5100 Carnegie Class: Assoc/HVT-High Non
FAX Number: (320) 629-5101 Calendar System: Semester
URL: www.pine.edu
Established: 1965 Annual Undergrad Tuition & Fees (In-State): $4,066
Enrollment: 1,969 Coed
Affiliation or Control: State IRS Status: 501(c)3
Highest Offering: Associate Degree
Accreditation: NH, MAC

02 President Mr. Joe MULFORD
05 Vice Pres Academic/Student Affairs Ms. Denine ROOD
13 Chief Information Officer Ms. Janis WEGNER
10 Chief Financial Officer Ms. Janis WEGNER
51 Dean of Continuing Edu/Custom Trng Mr. Jason SPAETH
66 Dean Nursing/Health Science Dr. Connie FRISCH
36 Exec Dir Employment/Training Ctr Mr. Dwayne GREEN
06 Registrar Ms. Darla CAVERLEY
15 Chief Human Resources Officer Ms. Amy KRUSE
26 Director Marketing/Enrollment Ms. Katie KOPPY
32 Director Student Affairs Mr. Shawn REYNOLDS
18 Physical Plant Supervisor Mr. Steven LANGE
04 Executive Asst to President Ms. Sandi CARLISLE

*Rainy River Community College (D)

1501 Highway 71, International Falls MN 56649-2187
County: Koochiching FICE Identification: 006775
Unit ID: 174604
Telephone: (218) 285-7722 Carnegie Class: Assoc/HT-High Non
FAX Number: (218) 285-2239 Calendar System: Semester
URL: www.rainyriver.edu
Established: 1967 Annual Undergrad Tuition & Fees (In-State): $5,325
Enrollment: 269 Coed
Affiliation or Control: State IRS Status: 501(c)3
Highest Offering: Associate Degree
Accreditation: NH

02 Interim President Dr. Michael RAICH
05 Provost Dr. Roxanne KELLY
06 Registrar Ms. Stephanie TURBAN
37 Director of Financial Aid Ms. Jodi PONTINEN
13 Dir Information Technology Ms. Shelly JUGOVICH
10 Business Manager Mrs. Emily AHRENS

*Ridgewater College (E)

PO Box 1097, 2101 15th Ave NW, Willmar MN 56201-1097
County: Kandiyohi FICE Identification: 005252
Unit ID: 175236
Telephone: (320) 222-5200 Carnegie Class: Assoc/HVT-Mix Trad/Non
FAX Number: (320) 222-5212 Calendar System: Semester
URL: www.ridgewater.edu
Established: 1961 Annual Undergrad Tuition & Fees (In-State): $5,765
Enrollment: 3,366 Coed
Affiliation or Control: State IRS Status: 501(c)3
Highest Offering: Associate Degree
Accreditation: NH, ADNUR, CAHIIM, EMT, MAC, PNUR

02 President Dr. Craig JOHNSON
05 Vice Pres Student Success Mr. Mike KUTZKE
10 Vice President Finance & Operations Mr. Daniel F. HOLTZ
51 Dean of Cust Trng & Cont Education Mr. Sam BOWEN
20 Dean of Instruction/Technical Pgms Mr. Matthew FEUERBORN
20 VP Student Success Mr. Mike KUTZKE
20 Dean Instruction/Liberal Arts/Sci Mr. Jeff MILLER
32 Dean of Student Services Ms. Heidi L. OLSON
21 Director of Business Services Ms. Cheryl A. NORLIEN
15 Int Chief Human Resource Officer Mr. Keith BALASKI
66 Director of Nursing Ms. Faith JOHNSON
37 Director of Financial Aid Mr. James W. RICE
07 Admissions/Academic Advisor Ms. Amy BIRKLAND
41 Athletic Director Mr. Todd M. THORSTAD
06 Registrar Ms. Kelli S. KIENITZ
13 Chief Information Officer Mr. Timothy L. FURR
26 Dir Communications/Mktg/Admissions Ms. Laura KUVAAS
102 Foundation Executive Director Ms. Kelly J. MAGNUSON
09 Director of Institutional Research Dr. Ellen ROSTER
28 Multicultural Outreach/Academic Adv Ms. Jehana SCHWANDT
18 Physical Plant Director Mr. Kip R. OVESON

*Riverland Community College (F)

1900 8th Avenue, NW, Austin MN 55912-1473
County: Mower FICE Identification: 002335
Unit ID: 173063
Telephone: (507) 433-0600 Carnegie Class: Assoc/HT-High Non
FAX Number: (507) 433-0665 Calendar System: Semester
URL: www.riverland.edu
Established: 1940 Annual Undergrad Tuition & Fees (In-State): $5,570
Enrollment: 3,108 Coed
Affiliation or Control: State IRS Status: 501(c)3
Highest Offering: Associate Degree
Accreditation: NH, ACBSP, ADNUR, MAC, PNUR, RAD

02 President Dr. Adenuga ATEWOLOGUN
05 VP of Academic & Student Affairs Ms. Barbara EMBACHER
10 Chief Financial Officer Mr. Brad DOSS
15 Chief Human Resources Officer Ms. Karen IRWIN
66 Director of Nursing Ms. Laura BEASLEY
49 Dean Arts/Public Service & Business Mr. Kelly MCCALLA
75 Dean Science/Tech/Trade & Industry Mr. Ryan LANGEMEIER
32 Dean of Student Affairs Ms. Chelsea ANDERSON
111 Dean for Institutional Advancement Ms. Janelle KOEPKE
06 Dir of Enrollment Svcs/Registrar Ms. Sue JECH
07 Dir of Admissions & New Student Rel Ms. Nel ZELLAR
26 Exec Dir Communications/Media/Mktg Mr. James DOUGLASS
37 Director of Financial Aid Ms. Patty HEMANN
36 Dir of College Partnerships & Trans Ms. Jean KYLE
13 VP Technology & Learning Resources Mr. Mark BAAS
18 Facilities Supervisor Mr. Shawn O'CONNOR
96 Purchasing Agent Ms. Page PETERSEN
28 Reg DiversityTrainer/Investgtr Ms. Ricki WALTERS
08 Librarian Ms. Jeannie (Carol) DIGGS
19 Safety Administrator Mr. Mike HOWE
29 Director Grants/Alumni Relations Ms. Kim NELSON
41 Athletic Director Ms. Helen JAHR

*Rochester Community and Technical College (G)

851 30th Avenue, SE, Rochester MN 55904-4999
County: Olmsted FICE Identification: 002373
Unit ID: 174738
Telephone: (507) 285-7210 Carnegie Class: Assoc/MT-VT-High Trad
FAX Number: (507) 285-7496 Calendar System: Semester
URL: www.rctc.edu
Established: 1915 Annual Undergrad Tuition & Fees (In-State): $5,639
Enrollment: 5,115 Coed
Affiliation or Control: State IRS Status: 501(c)3
Highest Offering: Associate Degree
Accreditation: NH, ACBSP, ADNUR, CAHIIM, DA, DH, PNUR, SURGT

02 President Dr. Jeffery BOYD
05 Interim VP of Academic Affairs Ms. Michelle PYFFEREOEN
10 Vice Pres Finance and Facilities Mr. Steve SCHMALL
81 Interim Dean Sciences Dr. Teresa BROWN
49 Dean of Liberal Arts Dr. Brenda FRAME
75 Interim Dean of Career/Technical Ms. Lori JENSEN
15 Chief Human Resource Officer Vacant
13 Chief Information Officer Mr. Mir QADER
32 Chief Student Affairs Officer Vacant
103 Dir of Business/Workforce Dev Dr. Jennifer WILSON
35 Director of Student Life Ms. Laura ENGELMAN
06 Registrar Ms. Melanie CALLISTER
07 Director Admissions and Enrollment Ms. Alicia ZEONE
37 Director Financial Aid Ms. Beth DIEKMANN
09 Director of Institutional Research Dr. Priyank SHAH
04 Executive Assistant to President Mrs. Judy KINGSBURY
21 Business Office Supervisor Ms. Kelly PYFFEREOEN
26 Chief Public Relations Officer Mr. Nate STOLTMAN
19 Director of Campus Safety/Security Mr. Scott MCCULLOUGH
40 Bookstore Coordinator Ms. Michelle DANIELSON
96 Purchasing Manager Ms. June MEITZNER
102 Foundation Executive Director Vacant
18 Chief Facilities/Physical Plant Mr. Mark FASS
08 Head Librarian Ms. Diane POLLOCK
22 Dir Affirmative Action/EEO Vacant
41 Athletic Director Mr. Mike LESTER
105 Director Web Services Mr. Darin HOFFMAN
45 Chief Inst Effect/Planning Officer Mr. Peter WRUCK

*St. Cloud State University (H)

720 4th Avenue S, Saint Cloud MN 56301-4498
County: Stearns FICE Identification: 002377
Unit ID: 174783
Telephone: (320) 308-0121 Carnegie Class: Masters/L
FAX Number: N/A Calendar System: Semester
URL: www.stcloudstate.edu
Established: 1869 Annual Undergrad Tuition & Fees (In-State): $8,265
Enrollment: 14,975 Coed
Affiliation or Control: State IRS Status: 501(c)3
Highest Offering: Doctorate
Accreditation: NH, ART, #CAATE, CACREP, CAEPN, JOUR, MFCD, MT, MUS, NAIT, NURSE, SP, SW, THEA

02 President Dr. Robbyn WACKER
04 Executive Asst to President Ms. Meredith L. ATHMAN
05 Provost/VP for Academic Affairs Dr. Dan GREGORY
10 Vice Pres for Finance/Admin Vacant
84 VP Enrollment Management Mr. Jason L. WOODS
45 VP for Planning & Engagement Ms. Lisa H. FOSS
111 Vice Pres University Advancement Mr. Matthew ANDREW
32 Vice Pres Student Life Development Dr. Wanda OVERLAND
43 Special Advisor to the President Dr. Judith P. SIMINOE
86 Director Univ/Legislative Relations Mr. Bernie OMANN
22 Equity & Access Officer Dr. Ellyn BARTGES
41 Director of Athletics Ms. Heather WEEMS
15 Chief Human Resource Officer Mr. Michael FREER
13 Deputy Chief Information Officer Mr. Phil THORSON
21 Director of Business Services Mr. Jeff WAGNER
26 Exec Dir Marketing & Communications Mr. Adam HAMMER
50 Dean Herberger Business School Dr. David HARRIS
53 Dean School of Education Dr. Jennifer MUELLER
76 Dean School of Health/Human Service Dr. Shonda M. CRAFT
49 Dean College of Liberal Arts Dr. Mark SPRINGER
80 Dean School of Public Affairs Dr. King BANAIAN
81 Interim Dean Science & Engineering Dr. Adel ALI
08 Dean University Library Ms. Rhonda HUISMAN
46 Int AP for Research/Sponsored Pgms Dr. Latha RAMAKRISHNAN
88 Interim Dean University College Dr. Glenn DAVIS
20 Exec Dir of Academic Resources Dr. Michele MUMM
35 AP Faculty/Student Affairs Dr. LaVonne CORNELL-SWANSON
07 AVP Student Recruit & Enrollment Vacant
06 Registrar and Student Records Ms. Sue BAYERL
29 Director of Constituent Engagement Ms. Terri MISCHE
36 Executive Director Career Center Ms. Michelle SCHMITZ
37 Director of Financial Aid Mr. Mike T. URAN
38 Director of Counseling Dr. John M. EGGERS
117 AVP Safety/Risk Management Vacant
09 Dir Analytics/Business Intelligence Mr. Brent DONNAY
18 AVP Facilities Management Mr. Phil MOESSNER
88 Director American Indian Center Vacant
88 Director LGBT Resource Center Mr. Seth KAEMPFER
88 Director Lindgren Child Care Center Mr. Dennis MERGEN

22 Director Student Accessibility Svcs ... Ms. Andria BELISLE
23 Director Student Health Services ... Ms. Corie BECKERMANN
88 Director Womens Center ... Ms. Jane OLSEN
19 Director Public Safety ... Mr. Kevin WHITLOCK
88 Int AVP Intl Studies/Dir MSS ... Mr. Shahzad AHMAD

*Saint Cloud Technical and Community College (A)

1540 Northway Drive, Saint Cloud MN 56303-1240
County: Stearns FICE Identification: 005534
Unit ID: 174756
Telephone: (320) 308-5000 Carnegie Class: Assoc/MT-VT-High Trad
FAX Number: (320) 308-5981 Calendar System: Semester
URL: www.sctcc.edu
Established: 1948 Annual Undergrad Tuition & Fees (In-State): $5,377
Enrollment: 4,218 Coed
Affiliation or Control: State IRS Status: 501(c)3
Highest Offering: Associate Degree
Accreditation: NH, CAHIIM, CVT, DA, DH, DMS, EMT, PNUR, SURGT

02 President ... Dr. Annesa CHEEK
05 VP of Academic & Student Affairs ... Ms. Lisa STICH
04 Assistant to the President ... Ms. Karen A. HIEMENZ
10 Vice Pres Admin/Chief Financial Ofc ... Ms. Lori KLOOS
22 Vice Pres Equity & Inclusion ... Vacant
75 Dean Trade/Industry ... Mr. Mike MENDEZ
81 Dean of Liberal Arts & Trans Stds ... Ms. Melissa LINDSEY
50 Dean of Business/Comm/Humanities ... Ms. Sally DUFNER
66 Dean of Nursing/Health ... Mr. Robert MUSTER
06 Registrar ... Ms. Bretta EDWARDS
15 Dir Personnel Svcs/Affirm Action ... Ms. Deb A. HOLSTAD
84 Dir of Enroll Management/Admissions ... Ms. Jodi M. ELNESS
08 Head Librarian ... Ms. Patricia AKERMAN
19 Security/Safety Officer ... Mr. Christopher LOOS
37 Director Student Financial Aid ... Ms. Anita G. BAUGH
36 Director Student Placement ... Ms. Jackie BAUER
40 Director Bookstore ... Mr. Aquirre REESE
35 Activ Dir/Chief Student Life Ofcr ... Vacant
18 Chief Facilities/Physical Plant ... Mr. Jason THEISEN
13 Chief Information Officer ... Ms. Viola BERGQUIST
21 Business Officer ... Ms. Diane ILLIES
96 Director of Purchasing ... Ms. Susan MEYER
14 Director Library & Info Technology ... Ms. Viola BERGQUIST
22 Director Affirm Action/Equal Oppty ... Ms. Deb HOLSTAD
30 Chief Devel/Dir Annual/Planned Giv ... Ms. Arlene WILLIAMS
84 Dean of Enrollment Management ... Ms. Amie ANDERSON
09 Director of Institutional Research ... Mr. Christopher THOMS

*Saint Paul College-A Community & Technical College (B)

235 Marshall Avenue, Saint Paul MN 55102-1800
County: Ramsey FICE Identification: 005533
Unit ID: 175041
Telephone: (651) 846-1703 Carnegie Class: Assoc/MT-VT-Mix Trad/Non
FAX Number: (651) 846-1451 Calendar System: Semester
URL: www.saintpaul.edu
Established: 1910 Annual Undergrad Tuition & Fees (In-State): $5,561
Enrollment: 6,940 Coed
Affiliation or Control: State IRS Status: 501(c)3
Highest Offering: Associate Degree
Accreditation: #NH, ACBSP, ACFEI, CAHIIM, COARC, MLTAD, PNUR, SURGT

02 Interim President ... Dr. Deidra PEASLEE
10 Vice President Finance & Operations ... Mr. Scott WILSON
32 Vice President of Student Affairs ... Dr. Laura KING
05 Vice President of Academic Affairs ... Dr. Kristen RANEY
27 Director of TRIO ... Ms. Mary VANG
103 Dean Workforce Trng/Continuing Educ ... Dr. Tracy WILSON
84 Int Dean Enrollment Management ... Ms. Tarah BJORKLUND
15 Chief Human Resources Officer ... Ms. Rachelle M. SCHMIDT
06 Int Dir Admissions/Registration ... Ms. Laura KITTELSON
09 Dean of Inst Research/Plng/Grants ... Ms. Nichole SORENSON
29 Director of Alumni Relations ... Mr. Logan SPINDLER
36 Director Student Placement ... Ms. Sheryl SAUL
38 Director Student Counseling ... Dr. Lisa HANES-GOODLANDER
96 Director of Purchasing ... Ms. Teresa SORENSEN
18 Director Facilities/Physical Plant ... Mr. Ben MARTINSON
21 Business Manager ... Ms. Liz SCHMIDT
22 Director Equity/Inclusion ... Ms. Wendy ROBERSON
37 Director of Student Financial Aid ... Mr. Adam JOHNSON
102 Exec Dir of Foundation/Alumni Rels ... Mr. David KLINE
13 Chief Information Officer ... Mr. Najam SAEED
26 Int Dir Marketing/Recruitment ... Mr. Rick SMITH
76 Dean of Health Sciences/Services ... Dr. Brendan ASHBY
81 Dean Science/Technology/Eng & Math ... Dr. Enyinda ONUNWOR
50 Dean Business/Career Tech Educ ... Dr. Rainer HAARBUSCH
57 Dean Liberal & Fine Arts ... Dr. Andrew KUBAS
19 Director Security/Safety ... Mr. Thomas BERGS
108 Dean of Academic Effectiveness ... Ms. Sarah CARRICO
88 Interim Dir OneStop Services ... Mr. Adam JOHNSON

*South Central College (C)

1920 Lee Boulevard, PO Box 1920,
North Mankato MN 56003
County: Nicollet FICE Identification: 005537
Unit ID: 173911
Telephone: (507) 389-7200 Carnegie Class: Assoc/MT-VT-Mix Trad/Non
FAX Number: (507) 388-9951 Calendar System: Semester
URL: www.southcentral.edu
Established: 1946 Annual Undergrad Tuition & Fees (In-District): $5,491
Enrollment: 2,787 Coed
Affiliation or Control: State/Local IRS Status: 501(c)3
Highest Offering: Associate Degree
Accreditation: NH, ADNUR, DA, EMT, MAC, MLTAD, PNUR

02 President ... Dr. Annette PARKER
04 Exec Assistant to the President ... Ms. Susan JAMESON
05 Vice Pres Student/Academic Affs ... Dr. DeAnna BURT
10 VP Finance/Operations ... Ms. Roxy TRAXLER
15 CHRO ... Ms. Dawn PEARSON
103 VP of Economic Development ... Ms. Marsha DANIELSON
09 VP Research & Inst Effectiveness ... Dr. Narren BROWN
32 Dean of Student Affairs ... Ms. Judy ENDRES
49 Dean of LAS ... Dr. Rick KURTZ
75 Dean of Career & Technical Educ ... Ms. Kellie MCELROY HOOPER
47 Dean of Agriculture ... Mr. Brad SCHLOESSER
66 Dean of Allied Health & Nursing ... Dr. Kim JOHNSON
26 Public Relations/Marketing Director ... Ms. Shelly MEGAW
28 Chief Diversity Officer ... Vacant
37 Director of Financial Aid ... Ms. Jayne DINSE
08 Librarian ... Ms. Heather BIEDERMANN
06 Registrar ... Ms. Deann SCHLOESSER
102 Exec Director N Mankato Foundation ... Ms. Erin AANENSON
40 Bookstore Manager ... Ms. Katie HOBSON
19 Director of Safety & Security ... Vacant

*Southwest Minnesota State University (D)

1501 State Street, Marshall MN 56258-1598
County: Lyon FICE Identification: 002375
Unit ID: 175078
Telephone: (507) 537-7678 Carnegie Class: Masters/M
FAX Number: (507) 537-7154 Calendar System: Semester
URL: www.smsu.edu
Established: 1963 Annual Undergrad Tuition & Fees (In-State): $8,612
Enrollment: 7,154 Coed
Affiliation or Control: State IRS Status: 501(c)3
Highest Offering: Master's
Accreditation: NH, MUS, NURSE, SW

02 President ... Dr. Kumara JAYASURIYA
05 Provost ... Dr. Teri WALLACE
10 VP Finance and Admin ... Ms. Debra KERKAERT
32 AVP Stdnt Affairs/Dean of Students ... Mr. Scott CROWELL
111 VP Advance/Foundation Ex Dir ... Mr. William MULSO
49 Dean Arts/Letters/Sciences ... Dr. Aimee SHOUSE
50 Dean Bus/Ed/Grad/Prof Studies ... Dr. Raphael ONYEAGHALA
41 Athletic Director ... Mr. Christopher HMIELEWSKI
13 Chief Information Officer ... Mr. Dan BAUN
07 VP EMSS ... Vacant
14 Director of Computer Services ... Mr. Shawn HEDMAN
06 Registrar ... Ms. Patricia CARMODY
19 Director University Public Safety ... Mr. Michael MUNFORD
28 Director Diversity & Inclusion ... Mr. Jay LEE
15 Chief Human Resources/Affirm Action ... Ms. Nancy OLSON
29 Director of Alumni ... Mr. Michael VANDREHLE
18 Facilities & Physical Plant Manager ... Ms. Cyndi HOLM
36 Director of Career Services ... Ms. Melissa SCHOLTEN
37 Director of Financial Aid ... Mr. David VIKANDER
38 University Counselor ... Ms. Sara FIER
96 Buyer Supervisor ... Ms. Barb BERKENPAS
21 Business Manager ... Ms. Jackie TAUER
26 Dir Communications/Marketing ... Mr. James TATE
04 Exec Admin Asst to President ... Ms. Chris ANDERSON
09 Director of Institutional Research ... Mr. Alan MATZNER
30 Director Development ... Ms. Stacy FROST
44 Director Annual Giving ... Mr. Erik VOGEL

*Vermilion Community College (E)

1900 E Camp Street, Ely MN 55731-1998
County: Saint Louis FICE Identification: 002350
Unit ID: 175157
Telephone: (218) 365-7200 Carnegie Class: Assoc/HT-Mix Trad/Non
FAX Number: (218) 235-2173 Calendar System: Semester
URL: www.vcc.edu
Established: 1922 Annual Undergrad Tuition & Fees (In-State): $5,325
Enrollment: 724 Coed
Affiliation or Control: State IRS Status: 501(c)3
Highest Offering: Associate Degree
Accreditation: NH

02 Provost/Chief Academic Officer ... Mr. Shawn BINA
07 Director of Admissions/Student Affs ... Mr. Jeff NELSON
09 Director of Institutional Research ... Ms. Heather HOHENSTEIN
32 Dir Student Life/Facil/Phy Plant ... Mr. Dave MARSHALL
36 Director of Student Placement ... Ms. Molly JOHNSTON
37 Director of Student Financial Aid ... Ms. Shannan HARDING
38 Director of Student Counseling ... Ms. Kate COWLEY
29 Director Alumni Relations ... Ms. Patti ZUPANCICH
28 Director of Diversity ... Ms. Patti ZUPANCICH
26 Chief Pub Rel Officer/Enrollment ... Mr. Jeff NELSON
06 Registrar/Instructional Services ... Ms. Chris HEGENBARTH

*Winona State University (F)

PO Box 5838, Winona MN 55987-0838
County: Winona FICE Identification: 002394
Unit ID: 175272
Telephone: (507) 457-5000 Carnegie Class: Masters/S
FAX Number: (507) 457-5586 Calendar System: Quarter
URL: www.winona.edu
Established: 1858 Annual Undergrad Tuition & Fees (In-State): $9,425
Enrollment: 7,981 Coed
Affiliation or Control: State IRS Status: 501(c)3
Highest Offering: Doctorate
Accreditation: NH, CAATE, CACREP, CAEPN, MUS, NURSE, SW, THEA

02 President ... Dr. Scott R. OLSON
05 Int Provost/VP Academic Affairs/CAO ... Dr. Edward REILLY
10 VP Finance & Administration ... Mr. Scott ELLINGHUYSEN
111 VP University Advancement ... Vacant
32 VP Enrollment & Student Life & Dev ... Ms. Denise MCDOWELL
13 AVP Academic Affairs/CIO ... Mr. Kenneth JANZ
26 Asst VP Marketing & Communications ... Vacant
38 Director of Counseling Services ... Dr. Benedict EZEOKE
54 Dean College of Science/Engineering ... Dr. Charla MIERTSCHIN
49 Dean College of Liberal Arts ... Dr. Peter MIENE
50 Dean College of Business ... Dr. Hamid AKBARI
53 Dean College of Education ... Dr. Daniel KIRK
66 Dean Col of Nursing/Health Science ... Dr. Julie ANDERSON
35 Dean of Students ... Ms. Karen JOHNSON
06 Sr Associate Registrar ... Ms. Tania SCHMIDT
84 Director Warrior Success Center ... Mr. Ron STREGE
37 Assistant Director of Financial Aid ... Ms. Charlene KREUZER
36 Associate Director Career Services ... Ms. Deanna GODDARD
07 Director of Admissions ... Mr. Brian JICINSKY
39 Residential College Program Coord ... Ms. Sarah OLCOTT
51 Exec Dir Outreach/Continuing Educ ... Ms. Linda KINGSTON
29 Associate Director Alumni Relations ... Mr. Mark REITAN
40 Bookstore Manager ... Ms. Karen KRAUSE
44 Director Development ... Ms. Debbie BLOCK
88 Director of International Svcs ... Ms. Kemale PINAR
19 Director of Security ... Mr. Christopher CICHOSZ
41 Athletic Director ... Mr. Eric SCHOH
18 Asst VP for Facilities Management ... Mr. James GOBLIRSCH
27 Director University Public Info ... Ms. Andrea NORTHAM
94 Director of Women's Studies ... Dr. Tamara BERG
96 Director of Purchasing ... Ms. Laura MANN
28 Director of Cultural Diversity ... Mr. Jonathan LOCUST
15 Director of Human Resources ... Ms. Lori REED

*Anoka-Ramsey Community College Cambridge Campus (G)

300 Spirit River Drive South, Cambridge MN 55008-5704
Telephone: (763) 433-1100 Identification: 770298
Accreditation: &NH

*Hennepin Technical College (H)

131000 College View, Eden Prairie MN 55347
Telephone: (952) 995-1300 Identification: 770299
Accreditation: &NH

*Mesabi Range College Eveleth (I)

1100 Industrial Park Drive, Eveleth MN 55734
Telephone: (218) 741-3095 Identification: 770300
Accreditation: &NH

*Minnesota State Community and Technical College Detroit Lakes (J)

900 Highway 34 E, Detroit Lakes MN 56501
Telephone: (218) 846-3700 Identification: 770303
Accreditation: &NH

*Minnesota State Community and Technical College Moorhead (K)

1900 28th Avenue S, Moorhead MN 56560
Telephone: (218) 299-6500 Identification: 770304
Accreditation: &NH, CVT, DH, SURGT

*Minnesota State Community and Technical College Wadena (L)

405 Colfax Avenue SW, Wadena MN 56482
Telephone: (213) 631-7800 Identification: 770305
Accreditation: &NH

*Minnesota West Community and Technical College Canby Campus (M)

1011 First Street West, Canby MN 56220
Telephone: (507) 223-7252 Identification: 770306
Accreditation: &NH

*Minnesota West Community and Technical College Granite Falls Campus (N)

1593 11th Avenue, Granite Falls MN 56241
Telephone: (320) 564-5000 Identification: 770307
Accreditation: &NH

*Minnesota West Community and Technical College Jackson Campus (O)

401 West Street, Jackson MN 56143
Telephone: (547) 847-7920 Identification: 770308
Accreditation: &NH

*** *Minnesota West Community and Technical College Pipestone Campus*** **(A)**

1314 North Hiawatha Avenue, Pipestone MN 56164

Telephone: (507) 825-6800 Identification: 770309

Accreditation: &NH, CAHIIM

*** *Minnesota West Community and Technical College Worthington Campus*** **(B)**

1450 Collegeway, Worthington MN 56187

Telephone: (507) 372-3464 Identification: 770310

Accreditation: &NH

*** *Northland Community and Technical College East Grand Forks Campus*** **(C)**

2022 Central Avenue NE, East Grand Forks MN 56721

Telephone: (218) 793-2800 Identification: 770311

Accreditation: &NH, @DIETT

*** *Riverland Community College Albert Lea Campus*** **(D)**

2200 Riverland Drive, Albert Lea MN 56007

Telephone: (507) 379-3300 Identification: 770313

Accreditation: &NH

*** *South Central College Faribault Campus*** **(E)**

1225 Third Street SW, Faribault MN 55021

Telephone: (507) 332-5800 Identification: 770314

Accreditation: &NH

*** *Winona State University-Rochester*** **(F)**

859 30th Avenue SE, Rochester MN 55904

Telephone: (800) 366-5418 Identification: 770317

Accreditation: &NH

Mitchell Hamline School of Law (G)

875 Summit Avenue, Saint Paul MN 55105-3076

County: Ramsey FICE Identification: 002391

Unit ID: 175281

Telephone: (651) 227-9171 Carnegie Class: Spec-4-yr-Law

FAX Number: (651) 290-6414 Calendar System: Semester

URL: www.mitchellhamline.edu

Established: 1900 Annual Graduate Tuition & Fees: N/A

Enrollment: 1,095 Coed

Affiliation or Control: Independent Non-Profit IRS Status: 501(c)3

Highest Offering: First Professional Degree; No Undergraduates

Accreditation: LAW

01 Interim President & Dean .... Mr. Peter KNAPP
04 Exec Asst to President & Board .... Ms. Mirdalys TWEETON
05 Vice Dean Academic & Faculty Affs .... Ms. Kate KRUSE
30 VP of Development .... Ms. Jodi GLASER
15 Director Human Resources .... Ms. Andrea BIEN
13 Director of Information Technology .... Mr. Andrew ALLEN
10 VP Finance & Administration .... Mr. Art BERMAN
11 VP Cmty Relations & Operations .... Ms. Christine SZAJ
08 Interim Director of Law Library .... Ms. Lisa HEIDENREICH
28 Program Mgr/Diversity & Inclusion .... Ms. Sharon VAN LEER
36 Dean for Career Development .... Ms. Leanne FUITH
07 Interim Dean of Admissions .... Ms. Ann GEMMELL
06 Registrar .... Ms. Colleen CLISH
37 Director of Financial Aid .... Mr. Nick ANDERSON
96 Purchasing Manager .... Ms. Paula B. MERTH
19 Director Security .... Mr. David HELLERMANN
32 Dean of Student Affairs .... Ms. Lynn LEMOINE
121 Dean of Academic Excellence .... Ms. Dena SONBOL
26 Asst Director of Marketing .... Mr. Doug BELDEN

North Central University (H)

910 Elliot Avenue, Minneapolis MN 55404-1391

County: Hennepin FICE Identification: 002369

Unit ID: 174437

Telephone: (612) 343-4400 Carnegie Class: Bac-Diverse

FAX Number: (612) 343-4778 Calendar System: Semester

URL: www.northcentral.edu

Established: 1930 Annual Undergrad Tuition & Fees: $24,240

Enrollment: 1,109 Coed

Affiliation or Control: Assemblies Of God Church IRS Status: 501(c)3

Highest Offering: Master's

Accreditation: NH, SW

01 President .... Rev. Scott A. HAGAN
03 Executive Vice President .... Dr. Andrew C. DENTON
04 Executive Assistant to President .... Mrs. Kristie KERR
05 Provost .... Dr. Don L. TUCKER
10 Chief Financial Officer .... Mr. Brian LI
42 Vice President of Spiritual Life .... Dr. Doug GRAHAM
106 VP Strategy & Online Education .... Mr. Greg LEEPER
57 Dean of the College of Fine Arts .... Mr. Larry C. BACH
50 Dean of College of Business & Tech .... Mr. Bill TIBBETTS
49 Dean of College of Arts & Sciences .... Dr. Desiree LIBENGOOD
88 Dean of Col of Church Leadership .... Dr. Allen TENNISON
21 Director of Accounting .... Mr. Bruce W. WHEELER
32 Dean of Students .... Mr. Jeremiy WILLIAMSON
41 Director of Athletics .... Mr. Greg L. JOHNSON
37 Director of Financial Aid .... Mr. Alex HINTZ
08 Library Director .... Mrs. Judy PRUITT
13 Director of Information Technology .... Mr. Steve D. KRAHN
06 Registrar .... Ms. Mary MURPHY
09 Dir Inst Research/Effectiveness .... Ms. Erin WHITE
07 Director of Admissions .... Mrs. Beth HARSHBARGER
121 Exec Dir of Student Development .... Mr. Todd MONGER
18 Executive Director of Operations .... Mr. Steve TEBBS
58 Dean College of Grad & Prof Educ ... Dr. Renea C. BRATHWAITE
15 Director of Human Resources .... Ms. Kate KETTERLING
19 Director Security/Safety .... Mr. Brent PETERS
111 Executive Director of Advancement .... Ms. Aimee ROBERTSON
30 Director of Development .... Rev. Trent REDMANN
108 Dean of Assessment & Accreditation .... Ms. LaToya BURRELL
26 Director of Communications .... Ms. Nancy ZUGSCHWERT
29 Director Alumni Affairs .... Ms. Tabby FINTON
84 Chief Enrollment Officer .... Mr. Mike PRICE

Northwestern Health Sciences University (I)

2501 W 84th Street, Bloomington MN 55431-1599

County: Hennepin FICE Identification: 012328

Unit ID: 174507

Telephone: (952) 888-4777 Carnegie Class: Spec-4-yr-Other Health

FAX Number: (952) 888-6713 Calendar System: Trimester

URL: www.nwhealth.edu

Established: 1941 Annual Undergrad Tuition & Fees: $10,996

Enrollment: 826 Coed

Affiliation or Control: Independent Non-Profit IRS Status: 501(c)3

Highest Offering: First Professional Degree

Accreditation: NH, ACUP, CHIRO, COMTA, MAC, MLTAD, MT, RTT

01 President and CEO .... Dr. Deborah BUSHWAY
05 Int Sr Dean Academic/Student Affs .... Dr. Dale HEALEY
10 Chief Financial Officer .... Ms. Jakki EDWARDS
32 Dean of Students and Alumni Service .... Ms. Joan MAZE
15 VP of Human Resources .... Ms. Mary GALE
26 VP of Marketing & Events .... Ms. Kathy HAGENS
30 VP of Development .... Mr. Brendan BANNIGAN
07 Director of Admissions .... Ms. Erin KAHN
08 Director of Library Services .... Ms. Anne MACKERETH
29 Manager Alumni Services .... Ms. Lilly MOKAMBA
51 Director of Continuing Education .... Dr. Nancy RUBIN
13 Chief Information Officer .... Mr. Chad JOHNSON
38 University Counselor .... Ms. Becky LAWYER
18 Director Facilities Management .... Mr. Kevin WOLPERN
96 Director Bookstore & Purchasing .... Ms. Jan HALLEEN
04 Administrative Asst to President .... Ms. Nancy JOHNSON
37 Director of Student Financial Svcs .... Ms. Karen SAMSTAD
76 Dean College of Health & Wellness .... Dr. Dale HEALEY
88 Dean College of Chiropractic .... Dr. Trevor FOSHANG
06 Registrar .... Ms. Susan NEPPL
108 Dir Assessment & Inst Effectiveness .... Mr. Yung-Chi SUNG

Oak Hills Christian College (J)

1600 Oak Hills Road SW, Bemidji MN 56601-8826

County: Beltrami FICE Identification: 009992

Unit ID: 174525

Telephone: (218) 751-8670 Carnegie Class: Spec-4-yr-Faith

FAX Number: (218) 751-8825 Calendar System: Semester

URL: www.oakhills.edu

Established: 1946 Annual Undergrad Tuition & Fees: $17,314

Enrollment: 103 Coed

Affiliation or Control: Interdenominational IRS Status: 501(c)3

Highest Offering: Baccalaureate

Accreditation: BI

01 President .... Dr. Martin GIESE
05 Sr VP of Academics & Administration .... Dr. Susan GLIDDEN
111 VP of Institutional Advance & Mktg .... Ms. Leesa DRURY
84 VP Enrollment Management .... Mr. Michael RASCH
32 Dean Student Life/Security Officer .... Mr. Brad DEJAGER
06 Registrar .... Ms. Tammy MCCRAY
08 Library Director/IT Director .... Mr. Keith BUSH
37 Director of Financial Aid .... Ms. Mishele MCKAIN
04 Administrative Asst to President .... Ms. Stacy NORVOLD
10 Chief Business Officer .... Mr. Bruce KAEHNE
41 Athletic Director .... Mr. Jeremy ANDERSON
18 Chief Facilities/Physical Plant Ofc .... Mr. Chuck ALLEN

* Rasmussen College Corporate Office (K)

8300 Norman Center Drive, Suite 300,
Bloomington MN 55437

County: Hennepin Identification: 667034

Unit ID: 17501405

Telephone: (952) 806-3910 Carnegie Class: N/A

FAX Number: (952) 831-0624

URL: www.rasmussen.edu

01 President .... Dr. Trenda BOYUM-BREEN
06 Registrar .... Ms. Juliana KLOCEK
07 Director of Admissions .... Mr. Dwayne BERTOTTO
37 Director Student Financial Aid .... Ms. Cappy BREUER

* Rasmussen College - St. Cloud (L)

226 Park Avenue South, Saint Cloud MN 56301-3713

County: Stearns FICE Identification: 008694

Unit ID: 175014

Telephone: (320) 251-5600 Carnegie Class: Bac/Assoc-Mixed

FAX Number: (320) 251-3702 Calendar System: Quarter

URL: www.Rasmussen.edu

Established: 1902 Annual Undergrad Tuition & Fees: $10,935

Enrollment: 4,509 Coed

Affiliation or Control: Proprietary IRS Status: Proprietary

Highest Offering: Master's

Accreditation: NH, ADNUR, CAHIIM, MAAB, NURSE, PNUR, SURGT

02 Campus Director .... Ms. Mary SWINGLE

† Regional accreditation carried under the parent institution in Lake Elmo, MN.

*** *Rasmussen College - Bloomington*** **(M)**

4400 W 78th St, 6th Floor, Bloomington MN 55435

Telephone: (952) 545-2000 FICE Identification: 011686

Accreditation: &NH, ADNUR, CAHIIM, MAAB

† Regional accreditation carried under the parent institution in Saint Cloud, MN. The tuition figure is an average, actual tuition may vary.

*** *Rasmussen College - Eagan*** **(N)**

3500 Federal Drive, Eagan MN 55122-1346

Telephone: (651) 687-9000 FICE Identification: 004648

Accreditation: &NH, CAHIIM, MAAB

† Regional accreditation carried under the parent institution in Saint Cloud, MN. The tuition figure is an average, actual tuition may vary.

*** *Rasmussen College - Mankato*** **(O)**

1400 Madison Ave, Suite 510, Mankato MN 56001

Telephone: (507) 625-6556 FICE Identification: 025033

Accreditation: &NH, ADNUR, CAHIIM, MAAB, PNUR

† Regional accreditation carried under the parent institution in Saint Cloud, MN.

Red Lake Nation College (P)

15480 Migizi Dr PO Box 576, Red Lake MN 56671

County: Beltrami Identification: 667311

Telephone: (218) 679-2860 Carnegie Class: Not Classified

FAX Number: (218) 679-3870 Calendar System: Semester

URL: www.rlnc.edu

Established: 2014 Annual Undergrad Tuition & Fees: N/A

Enrollment: N/A Coed

Affiliation or Control: Tribal Control IRS Status: 501(c)3

Highest Offering: Associate Degree

Accreditation: @NH

01 President .... Dan KING
05 Vice Pres Ops & Academic Affairs .... Mandy SCHRAM
32 Vice Pres Student Success .... Nokomis PAIZ
10 CFO .... Tami NISWANDER
08 Dir Library Svcs/Tribal Archives .... Lea PERKINS
06 Registrar .... Brandon SPEARS

St. Catherine University **(Q)**

601 25th Avenue S, Minneapolis MN 55454

Telephone: (651) 690-6000 Identification: 770315

Accreditation: &NH, RTT

St. Catherine University (R)

2004 Randolph Avenue, Saint Paul MN 55105-1789

County: Ramsey FICE Identification: 002342

Unit ID: 175005

Telephone: (651) 690-6000 Carnegie Class: DU-Mod

FAX Number: (651) 690-6024 Calendar System: 4/1/4

URL: www.stkate.edu

Established: 1905 Annual Undergrad Tuition & Fees: $39,554

Enrollment: 4,724 Female

Affiliation or Control: Roman Catholic IRS Status: 501(c)3

Highest Offering: Doctorate

Accreditation: NH, ARCPA, COARC, DIETD, DMS, EXSC, LIB, NUR, OT, OTA, PTA, PTAA, RAD, SW

01 President .... Ms. ReBecca K. ROLOFF
05 EVP and Provost .... Dr. Anita THOMAS
10 EVP and CFO .... Ms. Angela RILEY
111 EVP and Chief Advancement Officer .... Ms. Elizabeth HALLORAN
04 Exec Assistant to the President .... Ms. Bryonie MOON
49 Dean Sch Humanities/Arts/Sci .... Dr. Tarshia STANLEY
76 Dean Health Sciences .... Dr. Lisa DUTTON
66 Dean Nursing .... Dr. Laura FERO
32 Dean of Students .... Dr. Seth SNYDER
08 Library Director .... Ms. Emily ASCH
84 SVP Enrollment Management/Athletics .. Mr. Andrew MELENDRES
30 Director of Development .... Ms. Elizabeth RIEDEL CARNEY
21 VP for Finance & Controller .... Ms. Tracey GRAN
13 VP and CIO .... Ms. Jean GUEZMIR
15 SVP for HR/Equity & Inclusion .... Ms. Patricia PRATT-COOK

06 Registrar ... Ms. Cynthia EGENESS
29 Director of Alumnae Relations ... Ms. Mandy IVERSON
26 VP Marketing & Communications ... Dr. Toccara STARK
07 Associate VP of Admissions ... Ms. Cory PIPER-HAUSWIRTH
37 AVP Enrollment/Financial Aid ... Ms. Elizabeth STEVENS
27 AVP Admission/Market Development ... Mr. Greg STEENSON
36 Director of Career Development ... Ms. Tina WAGNER
35 Associate Dean of Students ... Ms. Ellen RICHTER-NORGEL
16 Director of Human Resources ... Ms. Sarah SCHNELL
38 Director of Student Counseling ... Ms. Heide MALAT
92 Director of Honors Program ... Dr. Rafael CERVANTES
94 Director of Women's Studies ... Dr. Sharon DOHERTY
96 Director of Purchasing ... Mr. Michael HARA
09 Dir Inst Rsrch/Plng/Assessment . Dr. Jennifer ROBINSON KLOOS
18 VP Public Safety & Facilities ... Mr. Mark JOHNSON
28 Dir Multicultural/Intl Pgms & Svcs ... Ms. Donna HAUER
41 Athletic Director ... Mr. Eric STACEY
19 Director of Public Safety ... Mr. Victor JURAN

Saint John's University (A)

2850 Abbey Plaza, Box 2000, Collegeville MN 56321-2000
County: Stearns FICE Identification: 002379
Unit ID: 174792
Telephone: (320) 363-2011 Carnegie Class: Bac-A&S
FAX Number: (320) 363-2504 Calendar System: Semester
URL: www.csbsju.edu
Established: 1857 Annual Undergrad Tuition & Fees: $44,990
Enrollment: 1,815 Male
Affiliation or Control: Roman Catholic IRS Status: 501(c)3
Highest Offering: Master's
Accreditation: NH, DIETD, MUS, NURSE, THEOL

01 Interim President ... Dr. Eugene MCALLISTER
100 Chief of Staff ... Ms. Patti EPSKY
05 Provost Academic Affairs ... Dr. Richard ICE
20 Academic Dean ... Dr. Barbara MAY
88 Dean of the Faculty ... Dr. Terence CHECK
111 Vice President for Inst Advancement ... Mr. Rob CULLIGAN
32 Interim Vice Pres Student Dev ... Mr. Michael CONNOLLY
84 Vice Pres Enrollment Mgmt/Marketing ... Mr. Nathan DEHNE
10 Vice Pres Finance/Admin Services ... Mr. Richard ADAMSON
73 Dean School Theology ... Fr. Dale LAUNDERVILLE, OSB
35 Dean of Students ... Mr. Michael CONNOLLY
08 Director of Library ... Ms. Kathleen PARKER
06 Registrar ... Ms. Julie GRUSKA
26 Exec Director of Public Relations ... Mr. Michael HEMMESCH
37 Exec Director of Financial Aid ... Mr. Stuart PERRY
29 Director of Alumni Relations ... Mr. Adam HERBST
15 Director Human Resources ... Ms. Carol ABELL
13 Director of Info Technology Svcs ... Ms. Casey GORDON

Saint Mary's University of Minnesota (B)

700 Terrace Heights, Winona MN 55987-1399
County: Winona FICE Identification: 002380
Unit ID: 174817
Telephone: (507) 452-4430 Carnegie Class: Masters/L
FAX Number: (507) 457-1633 Calendar System: Semester
URL: www.smumn.edu
Established: 1912 Annual Undergrad Tuition & Fees: $35,110
Enrollment: 5,754 Coed
Affiliation or Control: Roman Catholic IRS Status: 501(c)3
Highest Offering: Doctorate
Accreditation: NH, ANEST, COPSY, IACBE, MFCD, MUS, NMT, NURSE

01 President ... Rev. James P. BURNS, IVD
18 Vice President of Facilities ... Mr. James BEDTKE
111 VP for Advancement & Communication ... Ms. Audrey KINTZI
32 VP for Student Affairs/Student Life ... Dr. Timothy GOSSEN
10 Senior VP for Finance & Operations ... Mr. Ben MURRAY
43 General Counsel & Univ Secretary ... Ms. Ann E. MERCHLEWITZ
05 Chief Academic Office & VP for SGPP ... Bro. Robert SMITH
20 Academic Dean/Assoc Vice President ... Dr. Sarah FERGUSON
35 Assistant VP for Student Life ... Ms. Marisa QUINN
04 Exec Assistant to the President ... Ms. Peggy WALTERS
06 Registrar ... Mr. Christopher VERCH
07 Vice President for Admissions ... Vacant
37 Director of Financial Aid ... Ms. Paul TERRIO
88 Director of Conferencing & Camps ... Ms. Kathy PEDERSON
36 Dir Career Services & Internships ... Mr. Michael HAGARTY
38 Director of Counseling Center ... Vacant
08 Director of Library ... Ms. Laura OANES
19 Director of Campus Security ... Vacant
18 Facilities Manager ... Mr. Timothy STENSGARD
23 Director of Health Services ... Ms. Christina URIBE NITTI
29 Director Alumni Relations ... Mr. Robert FISHER
41 Director of Athletics ... Mr. Brian SISSON
15 Assistant VP for Human Resources ... Mr. David MILIOTIS
09 Director of Institutional Research ... Ms. Kara WENER
53 Dean School of Education ... Dr. Rebecca HOPKINS
79 Dean of Arts & Humanities ... Dr. Michael CHARRON
108 Director Accreditation & Compliance ... Dr. Robin HEMENWAY
50 Dean School of Business ... Vacant
83 Dean Sciences & Health Professions ... Dr. Todd REINHART
91 Director Administrative Computing ... Ms. Tianna JOHNSON
44 Director Annual Giving ... Vacant
100 Chief of Staff ... Mr. Andrew DIRKSEN

St. Olaf College (C)

1520 St. Olaf Avenue, Northfield MN 55057-1098
County: Rice FICE Identification: 002382
Unit ID: 174844
Telephone: (507) 786-2222 Carnegie Class: Bac-A&S
FAX Number: N/A Calendar System: 4/1/4
URL: wp.stolaf.edu
Established: 1874 Annual Undergrad Tuition & Fees: $47,840
Enrollment: 3,035 Coed
Affiliation or Control: Evangelical Lutheran Church In America
IRS Status: 501(c)3
Highest Offering: Baccalaureate
Accreditation: NH, ART, DANCE, MUS, NURSE, SW, THEA

01 President ... Dr. David R. ANDERSON
05 Provost & Dean of the College ... Dr. Marci J. SORTOR
10 Vice Pres & Chief Financial Officer ... Ms. Janet K. HANSON
111 Vice Pres for Advancement ... Mr. Enoch BLAZIS
32 Vice Pres for Student Life ... Dr. Hassel Andre MORRISON
84 Vice Pres Enrollment/Col Relations ... Mr. Michael KYLE
88 Vice Pres for Mission ... Dr. Jo M. BELD
15 Vice Pres for Human Resources ... Mr. Michael GOODSON
43 General Counsel ... Mr. Carl CROSBY LEHMANN
28 Asst to the Pres for Inst Diversity ... Mr. Bruce KING
20 Associate Provost ... Dr. Dan DRESSEN
06 Asst VP/Registrar ... Ms. Ericka K. PETERSON
89 Assoc Dean Interdisciplin/Gen Stds ... Dr. Dana GROSS
81 Assoc Dean Natural Sciences & Math ... Dr. Mary WALCZAK
79 Assoc Dean Humanities ... Dr. Corliss SWAIN
57 Assoc Dean Fine Arts ... Mr. Kent MCWILLIAMS
83 Assoc Dean Social Sciences ... Dr. Rebecca JUDGE
115 Asst VP/Chief Investment Officer ... Mr. Mark GELLE
114 Asst VP/Budget & Auxiliary Ops ... Ms. Angela MATHEWS
07 Dean of Admissions & Financial Aid ... Mr. Chris GEORGE
35 Dean of Students ... Dr. Rosalyn EATON
35 Assoc Dean of Students ... Mr. Justin FLEMING
35 Assoc Dean of Students ... Mr. Timothy SCHROER
42 Campus Pastor ... Dr. Matthew MAROHL
13 Director of IT and Libraries ... Ms. Roberta LEMBKE
19 Director of Public Safety ... Mr. Fred C. BEHR
41 Director of Athletics ... Mr. Ryan A. BOWLES
29 Dir of Engage/Alum/Parent Relations ... Mr. Brad HOFF
44 Director of Annual Giving ... Ms. Steph MCCLUSKEY
38 Director of Counseling ... Dr. Stephen O'NEILL
26 Chief Marketing Officer ... Ms. Katie WARREN
75 Dir Piper Ctr for Vocation & Career ... Ms. Leslie MOORE
36 Sr Assoc Dir Career Educ & Coaching ... Ms. Kirsten CAHOON
108 Assoc Dir of Eval & Assessment ... Ms. Kelsey THOMPSON
09 Director of Institutional Research ... Ms. Susan CANON
39 Director of Residence Life ... Ms. Pamela MCDOWELL
37 Director of Student Financial Aid ... Ms. Carly EICHHORST
102 Dir of Govt/Fndtn & Corp Relations ... Ms. Helen WARREN
104 Dir of Intl & Off-Campus Studies ... Dr. Jodi MALMGREN
04 Exec Assistant to the President ... Ms. Jennifer WHITSON

United Theological Seminary of the Twin Cities (D)

767 Eustis Street, Suite 140, St. Paul MN 55114
County: Ramsey FICE Identification: 002386
Unit ID: 175139
Telephone: (651) 633-4311 Carnegie Class: Spec-4-yr-Faith
FAX Number: (651) 633-4315 Calendar System: Trimester
URL: www.unitedseminary.edu
Established: 1962 Annual Graduate Tuition & Fees: N/A
Enrollment: 83 Coed
Affiliation or Control: United Church Of Christ IRS Status: 501(c)3
Highest Offering: Doctorate; No Undergraduates
Accreditation: NH, THEOL

01 President ... Dr. Lewis P. ZEIDNER
05 VP for Academic Affairs/Dean ... Dr. Kyle ROBERTS
10 VP for Finance and Administration ... Mr. Jeff SWENSON
111 VP for Advancement ... Ms. Cindy SCHRIEVER
26 VP for Marketing ... Ms. Amee MCDONALD
121 VP for Student Formation/Vocation ... Rev. Karen HUTT
84 VP for Student Enrollment ... Mr. Silas MORGAN
08 Director of the Library ... Mr. Dale DOBIAS
37 Director Fin Aid & Inst Assessment ... Dr. Ken REYNHOUT
88 Dir of Advanced Studies ... Mr. Demian WHEELER
73 Director of Theology and the Arts ... Ms. Jennifer AWES-FREEMAN
29 Dir of Alum Engagement/Giving ... Dr. Cindi Beth JOHNSON
88 Dir Ctr Faith/Justice/Social Trans ... Mr. Steve NEWCOM
15 Dir Human Resources & Operations ... Ms. Vonda PEARSON
20 Dir Academic Ops & Distance Educ ... Mr. Matt STOLLENWERK
88 Dir of Formation ... Rev. John LEE
88 Dir Student Mentoring and Context ... Ms. Sara SMALLEY
13 Director of Information Services ... Mr. Adam PFUHL
06 Registrar and Academic Advisor ... Ms. Hillary VAMSTAD
88 Operational Logistics/Special Event ... Ms. Trisha FRANCE

University of Minnesota (E)

100 Church Street SE, 202 Morrill, Minneapolis MN 55455
County: Hennepin FICE Identification: 003969
Unit ID: 174066
Telephone: (612) 626-1616 Carnegie Class: DU-Highest
FAX Number: (612) 625-3875 Calendar System: Semester
URL: www.umn.edu
Established: 1851 Annual Undergrad Tuition & Fees (In-State): $14,760
Enrollment: 51,848 Coed
Affiliation or Control: State IRS Status: 501(c)3
Highest Offering: Doctorate
Accreditation: NH, ANEST, AUD, CAMPEP, CEA, CIDA, CLPSY, CONST, COPSY, DANCE, DENT, DH, DIETC, DIETD, DIETI, FUSER, HSA, IPSY, JOUR, LAW, LSAR, MED, MFCD, MIDWF, MT, MUS, NURSE, OT, PCSAS, PH, PHAR, PLNG, PTA, RTT, SCPSY, SP, SPAA, SW, VET

01 President ... Dr. Joan T. GABEL
100 Senior Assistant to President ... Dr. Bill HALDEMAN
05 EVP Academic Affairs/Provost ... Dr. Karen HANSEN
10 Sr VP Finance & Operations ... Mr. Brian BURNETT
46 Vice President for Research ... Dr. Chris J. CRAMER
58 Vice Prov/Dean Graduate Education ... Dr. Scott LANYON
20 Vice Prov/Dean Undergrad Education ... Dr. Robert MCMASTER
15 Vice President Human Resources ... Ms. Kathryn F. BROWN
88 Vice Pres for University Services ... Mr. Michael BERTHELSEN
28 Vice Pres Equity and Diversity ... Dr. Michael GOH
13 VP/Chief Info Officer ... Mr. Bernard GULACHEK
43 General Counsel ... Mr. Doug PETERSON
102 President Univ Minnesota Foundation ... Ms. Katherine SCHMIDLKOFER
25 Assoc VP Sponsored Projects Admin ... Ms. Pamela WEBB
26 Vice Pres for University Relations ... Mr. Matt KRAMER
18 Assoc VP/Chief of Facilities ... Mr. Bill PAULUS
32 Int Vice Provost Student Affairs ... Ms. Maggie TOWLE
19 Chief of Police ... Mr. Matthew CLARK
08 University Librarian ... Dr. Wendy P. LOUGEE
06 Assoc Vice Provost/Registrar ... Ms. Sue N. VAN VOORHIS
07 Exec Director of Admissions ... Ms. Heidi MEYER
09 Director of Institutional Research ... Dr. John KELLOGG
22 Director Equal Oppty/Affirm Action ... Ms. Tina MARISAM
37 Director of Student Finance ... Ms. Tina FALKNER
40 Director of the U of M Bookstores ... Mr. Ross ROSATI
39 Dir of Housing & Residential Life ... Ms. Laurie L. MCLAUGHLIN
48 Dean College of Design ... Ms. Carol STROHECKER
86 Chief Government Relations Officer ... Mr. J.D BURTON
29 CEO Alumni Association ... Ms. Lisa LEWIS
38 Dir of Student Counseling Services ... Dr. Vesna HAMPEL-KOZAR
114 Associate VP for Budget/Finance ... Ms. Julie A. TONNESON
96 Director of Purchasing ... Ms. Beth TAPP
49 Dean of the College of Liberal Arts ... Mr. John COLEMAN
51 Dean Cont/Professional Studies ... Dr. Bob A. STINE
61 Dean of the Law School ... Mr. Garry JENKINS
74 Dean College of Veterinary Medicine ... Dr. Trevor R. AMES
63 Dean of the Medical School ... Dr. Jakub TOLAR
66 Dean of the School of Nursing ... Dr. Connie J. DELANEY
53 Dean College Education/Human Devel ... Dr. Jean K. QUAM
52 Dean of the School of Dentistry ... Dr. Gary ANDERSON
69 Dean of the School Public Health ... Dr. John FINNEGAN
54 Dean College of Science/Engineering ... Dr. Mostafa KAVEH
67 Dean of the College Pharmacy ... Dr. Lynda WELAGE
50 Dean Carlson School of Management ... Dr. Srilata A. ZAHEER
80 Dean Humphrey Sch of Pub Aff ... Dr. Laura BLOOMBERG
81 Dean College of Biological Science ... Dr. Valery E. FORBES
47 Dean Col Food/Agric/Natural Res Sci ... Mr. Brian BUHR
41 Director Intercollegiate Athletics ... Mr. Mark COYLE
27 Chief Public Relations Officer ... Mr. Chuck TOMBARGE
27 Chief Marketing Officer ... Ms. Ann ARONSON
21 Associate VP of Finance/Asst CFO ... Mr. Michael D. VOLNA
101 Secretary of the Institution/Board ... Mr. Brian STEEVES

University of Minnesota Duluth (F)

1049 University Drive, Duluth MN 55812-3011
County: Saint Louis FICE Identification: 002388
Unit ID: 174233
Telephone: (218) 726-8000 Carnegie Class: Masters/M
FAX Number: (218) 726-6254 Calendar System: Semester
URL: www.d.umn.edu
Established: 1947 Annual Undergrad Tuition & Fees (In-State): $13,366
Enrollment: 11,168 Coed
Affiliation or Control: State IRS Status: 501(c)3
Highest Offering: Doctorate
Accreditation: NH, ART, MUS, SP, SW

01 Chancellor ... Dr. Lendley C. BLACK
05 Exec Vice Chanc Acad Affairs ... Dr. Fernando DELGADO
32 Vice Chanc Stdnt Life/Dean Stdnts ... Dr. Lisa ERWIN
10 Vice Chanc Finance/Operations ... Mr. Stephen W. KETO
06 Registrar ... Ms. Carla L. BOYD
08 Director of Library ... Mr. Matt ROSENDAHL
37 Director Financial Aid ... Ms. Brenda H. HERZIG
36 Director Career Services ... Ms. Julie A. WESTLUND
13 Director Info Tech Sys/Services ... Dr. Jason DAVIS
09 Director Institutional Research ... Ms. Mary KEENAN
25 Senior Grant Administrator ... Ms. Elizabeth RUMSEY
41 Athletic Director ... Mr. Josh BERLO
15 Director Human Resources ... Mr. Mark YURAN
07 Director Admissions ... Mr. Scott SCHULZ
18 Dir Facilities/Physical Plant ... Mr. John RASHID
29 Director Alumni Relations ... Mr. Matthew DUFFY
30 Director Development ... Ms. Tricia BUNTEN
114 Director of Budget and Analysis ... Mr. Greg SATHER
86 Dir University Marketing Public Rel ... Ms. Lynne WILLIAMS
63 Dean School of Medicine ... Dr. Paula TERMUHLEN
81 Dean College Science/Engineering ... Dr. Wendy REED
49 Dean College Liberal Arts ... Dr. Jeremy YOUDE
53 Dean Col Education/Human Svc Prof ... Dr. Jill PINKNEY-PASTRANA
50 Dean School of Business & Economics ... Dr. Amy HIETAPELTO
57 Dean School Fine Arts ... Mr. Robert KASE
67 Dean School of Pharmacy ... Dr. Mike SWANOSKI
58 Director of Grad Programs ... Dr. Erik BROWN

19 Chief of Police .... Mr. Sean HULS
88 Dir Educ for Inclusive Excellence .... Ms. Paula PEDERSEN
04 Executive Asst to the Chancellor .... Ms. Jean CONNER
104 Director Study Abroad .... Mr. Karl MARKGRAF
39 Dir Resident Life/Student Housing .... Mr. Jeremy LEIFERMAN

University of Minnesota-Crookston (A)

2900 University Avenue, Crookston MN 56716-5001
County: Polk FICE Identification: 004069
Unit ID: 174075
Telephone: (218) 281-6510 Carnegie Class: Bac-Diverse
FAX Number: (218) 281-8040 Calendar System: Semester
URL: www.crk.umn.edu
Established: 1965 Annual Undergrad Tuition & Fees (In-State): $11,822
Enrollment: 2,834 Coed
Affiliation or Control: State IRS Status: 501(c)3
Highest Offering: Baccalaureate
Accreditation: NH

01 Chancellor .... Dr. Mary HOLZ-CLAUSE
05 VC for Academic & Student Affairs .... Dr. John HOFFMAN
32 Assoc VC Student Affs/Enrollment .... Dr. Lisa SAMUELSON
18 Director Facilities/Operations .... Mr. Dave DANFORTH
10 Dir of Finance/University Services .... Ms. Tricia SANDERS
15 Director Human Resources .... Mr. Les JOHNSON
37 Director Financial Aid .... Vacant
26 Director of Communications .... Mrs. Elizabeth TOLLEFSON
30 Dir Development/Alumni Relations .... Ms. Brandy CHAFFEE
08 Director Library .... Ms. Keri YOUNGSTRAND
36 Director Career/Counseling .... Mr. Tim MENARD
49 Head of Arts/Humanities/Soc Sci ... Dr. Soo-Yin LIM-THOMPSON
47 Head Agriculture & Nat Resources .... Dr. Harouna MAIGA
81 Head Math/Science/Technology .... Dr. Tony KERN
50 Head Business .... Dr. Kevin THOMPSON
51 Director of Outreach .... Ms. Michelle CHRISTOPHERSON
06 Registrar .... Dr. Ken MYERS
07 Director of Admissions .... Ms. Carola THORSON
28 Director of Diversity .... Ms. Lorna HOLLOWELL
85 Dir of International Programs .... Dr. Kimberly GILLETTE

University of Minnesota-Morris (B)

600 E 4th Street, Morris MN 56267-2132
County: Stevens FICE Identification: 002389
Unit ID: 174251
Telephone: (320) 589-6035 Carnegie Class: Bac-A&S
FAX Number: (320) 589-6399 Calendar System: Semester
URL: www.morris.umn.edu
Established: 1959 Annual Undergrad Tuition & Fees (In-State): $13,314
Enrollment: 1,627 Coed
Affiliation or Control: State IRS Status: 501(c)3
Highest Offering: Baccalaureate
Accreditation: NH, CAEPN

01 Chancellor .... Dr. Michelle BEHR
05 Interim Vice Chanc Acad Affs/ Dean .... Dr. Janet SCHRUNK ERICKSEN
32 Vice Chanc for Student Affairs .... Ms. Sandra OLSON-LOY
10 Vice Chanc for Finance & Facilities .... Mr. Bryan HERRMANN
21 Finance Manager .... Ms. Melissa WROBLESKI
08 Head Librarian .... Ms. LeAnn DEAN
06 Registrar's Office .... Ms. Judy KORN
26 Director of Communications .... Vacant
29 Director of Alumni Relations .... Vacant
09 Director of Institutional Research .... Ms. Nancy HELSPER
36 Director Career Center .... Vacant
13 Director Information Technology .... Mr. Matt SENGER
37 Director of Financial Aid .... Ms. Jill BEAUREGARD
93 Interim Dir Multi Ethnic Stdnt Pgm .... Ms. Tammy BERBERI
24 Director Educational Media .... Mr. Michael CIHAK
07 Director of Admissions .... Ms. Jennifer ZYCH HERRMANN
108 Director of Institutional Effective .... Ms. Melissa BERT
53 Chair of Education Division .... Dr. Gwen RUDNEY
81 Chair of Science/Math Division .... Dr. Peh NG
79 Chair of Humanities Division .... Dr. Stacey ARONSON
83 Chair of Social Science Division .... Dr. Arne KILDEGAARD

University of Minnesota Rochester (C)

111 South Broadway, Suite 300, Rochester MN 55904
Telephone: (800) 947-0117 Identification: 770316
Accreditation: &NH, OT

University of Northwestern - St. Paul (D)

3003 Snelling Avenue N, Saint Paul MN 55113-1598
County: Ramsey FICE Identification: 002371
Unit ID: 174491
Telephone: (651) 631-5100 Carnegie Class: Masters/M
FAX Number: (651) 628-3339 Calendar System: Semester
URL: www.unwsp.edu
Established: 1902 Annual Undergrad Tuition & Fees: $31,540
Enrollment: 3,521 Coed
Affiliation or Control: Independent Non-Profit IRS Status: 501(c)3
Highest Offering: Master's
Accreditation: NH, MUS, NURSE

01 President .... Dr. Alan S. CURETON
05 Senior Vice Pres Academic Affairs .... Dr. Janet B. SOMMERS
26 Senior Vice President Media .... Mr. Jason R. SHARP
32 Vice Pres Student Life .... Ms. Nina M. BARNES
111 Vice President for Advancement .... Mrs. April L. MORETON
10 Vice President Finance/CFO .... Mr. Bryon D. KRUEGER
15 Vice President of Human Resources .... Mr. Timothy A. RICH
84 Vice President Enrollment Mgmt .... Vacant
18 Assoc VP Facility Ops & Planning .... Mr. Brian L. HUMPHRIES
79 Dean College of Arts & Humanities .. Dr. Jeremy W. KOLWINSKA
83 Dean College Behavioral/Natural Sci .... Dr. Daniel R. CRANE
107 Dean College Professional Studies .... Dr. Susan E. JOHNSON
58 Dean Graduate/Online & Adult .... Vacant
20 Sr Dean Academic Administration .... Dr. Fengling M. JOHNSON
13 CIO .... Mr. Chad N. MILLER
21 Controller .... Mr. Marcus D. SARAZIN
09 Institutional Researcher Rprt Spec .... Mr. Russell E. ERICKSON
38 Director of Counseling/Student Svcs . Ms. Dannette C. WILFAHRT
88 Director of Disability Services .... Mrs. Ruth A. FRIES
37 Director of Financial Aid .... Ms. Hannah K. BLAHNIK
23 Director of Health Services .... Vacant
08 Director of Library Services .... Mrs. Ruth A. MCGUIRE
19 Director of Public Safety .... Mr. Peter L. SOLA
96 Manager of Purchasing .... Ms. Cheryl A. GLASS
40 Manager Campus Store .... Mrs. Julienne N. ENTINGER
101 Exec Secy to Pres & Bd of Trustees .... Mrs. Kathy M. SPARKS
04 Executive Admin Asst to President .... Mrs. Rachel A. MORGAN
102 Asst VP Advance/VP of NW Foundation .... Mr. Kirby R. STOLL
103 Director of Career Development .... Mrs. April C. STENSGARD
26 Director Marketing .... Mrs. Sheri V. LUNN
108 Director of Assessment .... Mrs. Cheryl R. NORMAN
06 Registrar .... Mr. Andy L. SIMPSON
110 Sr Director Advancement Relations .... Mr. Rich A. BRANHAM
29 Director Alumni & Public Relations .... Mr. Scott D. ANDERSON
07 Dir Trad Enrollment Management .... Mr. Erick P. KLEIN

† Formerly Northwestern College

University of Saint Thomas (E)

2115 Summit Avenue, Saint Paul MN 55105-1096
County: Ramsey FICE Identification: 002345
Unit ID: 174914
Telephone: (651) 962-5000 Carnegie Class: DU-Mod
FAX Number: (651) 962-6360 Calendar System: 4/1/4
URL: www.stthomas.edu
Established: 1885 Annual Undergrad Tuition & Fees: $42,736
Enrollment: 9,878 Coed
Affiliation or Control: Roman Catholic IRS Status: 501(c)3
Highest Offering: Doctorate
Accreditation: NH, COPSY, HSA, IPSY, LAW, MUS, SW, THEOL

01 President .... Dr. Julie H. SULLIVAN
05 EVP & Provost .... Dr. Richard G. PLUMB
20 Rector/VP School of Divinity .... Fr. Joseph C. TAPHORN
32 VP For Student Affairs .... Dr. Karen M. LANGE
10 VP For Business Affairs/CFO .... Mr. Mark D. VANGSGARD
100 Chief of Staff .... Ms. Amy G. MCDONOUGH
13 CIO/VP Info Resources & Technology .... Dr. Edmund U. CLARK
20 Vice Provost for Academic Affairs .... Dr. Wendy N. WYATT
84 VP Enrollment Management .... Mr. Allan L. COTRONE
21 AVP & Controller .... Ms. Melissa K. PELLAND
18 AVP for Facilities .... Mr. James M. BRUMMER
109 Director Dining Services .... Dr. Pamela L. PETERSON
49 Dean College Arts & Sciences .... Dr. Yohuru R. WILLIAMS
50 Dean Opus College of Business .... Dr. Stefanie A. LENWAY
53 Dean School of Education .. Dr. Kathlene L. HOLMES CAMPBELL
70 Int Dean School of Social Work .... Dr. Corrine I. CARVALHO
73 Academic Dean School of Divinity .... Dr. Christopher J. THOMPSON
61 Dean School of Law .... Mr. Robert K. VISCHER
35 Dean of Students .... Ms. Linda M. BAUGHMAN
88 Chair Grad School Prof Psychology .... Dr. Christopher S. VYE
58 Dir Graduate Programs/Business Comm .. Dr. Michael C. PORTER
54 Dean School of Engineering .... Dr. Donald H. WEINKFAUF
30 VP Development & Alumni Relations .... Mr. Erik J. THURMAN
06 AVP of Student Data & Registrar .... Ms. Karen M. JULIAN
37 Director of Financial Aid .... Ms. Kristin A. ROACH
35 Director Campus Life .... Ms. Margaret D. CAHILL
36 Director Career Development Center .... Ms. Linda M. SLOAN
26 VP/Chief Marketing Officer .... Ms. Kymm MARTINEZ
41 VP/Director of Athletics .... Mr. Phil J. ESTEN
40 Director Bookstore .... Mr. Stephen L. GRIFFIN
42 Director Campus Ministry .... Fr. Lawrence BLAKE
19 Director Public Safety .... Mr. Daniel J. MEUWISSEN
38 Int Dir Counseling & Psych Svcs .... Dr. Debra J. BRODERICK
96 AVP Procurement Services .... Ms. Karen M. HARTHORN
88 Dean Dougherty Family College .... Mr. Alvin V. ABRAHAM
88 VP For Mission .... Fr. Larry J. SNYDER
15 AVP For Human Resources .... Ms. Michelle THOM
43 General Counsel .... Ms. Sara E. GROSS METHNER
125 President Emeritus .... Fr. Dennis J. DEASE
39 Director Residence Life .... Dr. Aaron M. MACKE

Walden University (F)

100 Washington Ave S, Suite 900, Minneapolis MN 55401
County: Hennepin FICE Identification: 025042
Unit ID: 125231
Telephone: (866) 492-5336 Carnegie Class: DU-Mod
FAX Number: (612) 338-5092 Calendar System: Other
URL: www.waldenu.edu
Established: 1970 Annual Undergrad Tuition & Fees: $12,120
Enrollment: 49,680 Coed
Affiliation or Control: Proprietary IRS Status: Proprietary
Highest Offering: Doctorate
Accreditation: NH, ACBSP, CACREP, CAEP, NURSE, SW

01 President .... Dr. Ward ULMER
11 Sr VP Commercial Operations .... Mr. Jeff TOGNOLA
88 Chief Strategy/Transformation Ofcr .... Mr. Steven TOM
05 Provost and Chief Academic Officer .... Dr. Eric RIEDEL
13 CIO .... Mr. Karthik VENKATESH
10 CFO .... Mr. Roger MCKINNEY
20 Vice Provost .... Dr. Savitri DIXON-SAXON
20 Vice Provost .... Dr. Andrea LINDELL
20 Vice Provost .... Dr. Marilyn POWELL
20 Vice Provost .... Dr. Sue SUBOCZ
28 VP of Diversity/Equity & Inclusion .... Dr. Denise BOSTON
86 VP Government Relations .... Ms. Jennifer BLUM
06 Registrar & Assoc Vice Provost .... Ms. Devon EDMUND
88 Assoc Vice Provost & Director .... Dr. Maleka INGRAM
121 Sr Exec Director Student Success .... Ms. Susanna DAVIDSEN
107 Exec Dir Global/Prof Applied Lrng .... Dr. Mary RAEKER-REBEK
88 Exec Dir Ctr for Faculty Excel .... Dr. Annie MORGAN
46 Exec Dir Inst Research/Assessment .... Mr. Jim LENIO
32 Exec Dir & Dean of Student Affairs .... Dr. Walter MCCOLLUM
15 Exec Dir of Human Resources .... Ms. Ivanie BRONSON
88 Exec Dir Ctr for Research Quality .... Dr. Laura LYNN
72 Dean College of Management and Tech ... Dr. Karlyn BARILOVITS
82 Dean Sch of Psych & Sch Pub Pol/Adm .... Dr. Shana GARRETT
83 Dean Sch of Counseling & Human Svcs .... Dr. Bill BARKLEY
76 Dean School of Health Sciences .... Dr. Jorg WESTERMANN
70 Dean School of Social Work .... Dr. Lisa MOON
53 Dean Sch of Education & Prof Lic .... Vacant
106 Dean Competency Based Education .... Dr. Martha CHENEY
53 Dean Sch Higher Ed/Ldrshp & Policy .... Dr. Kelly COSTNER
97 Exec Dir Ctr for Gen Education .... Dr. Steven DANVER
37 Director of Financial Aid .... Ms. Melvina JOHNSON
108 Dir of University Assessment .... Dr. Shari JORISSEN
88 Director Academic Initiatives .... Dr. William SCHULZ
08 Director of Library Services .... Ms. Michelle HAJDER
121 Sr Director Academic Advising .... Ms. Mandy OLSEN
43 Dir Legal Services/General Counsel .... Ms. Staci SHELLEY
26 Director of External Relations .... Ms. Sabrina RAM
29 Director of Alumni Relations .... Vacant
07 Director of Admissions .... Vacant
113 Bursar .... Ms. Linda ANTHONY
09 Assoc Dir of Institutional Rsrch .... Ms. Laura RIBICH

White Earth Tribal and Community College (G)

PO Box 478, Mahnomen MN 56557-0478
County: Mahnomen FICE Identification: 039214
Unit ID: 434751
Telephone: (218) 935-0417 Carnegie Class: Tribal
FAX Number: (218) 936-5814 Calendar System: Semester
URL: www.wetcc.edu
Established: 1997 Annual Undergrad Tuition & Fees: $4,593
Enrollment: 90 Coed
Affiliation or Control: Tribal Control IRS Status: 501(c)3
Highest Offering: Associate Degree
Accreditation: NH

01 President .... Lorna J. LAGUE
04 Executive Assistant .... Luke WARNSHOLZ
88 Special Projects Director .... Jen MCDOUGALL
10 Finance Director .... Eric FLYEN
05 Academic Dean .... Melinda RUSTAD
32 Dean of Student Services .... Vacant
56 Director of Extension .... Kim ANDERSON
07 Admissions Coordinator .... Amber FOX
06 Registrar .... Lorraine LUFKINS
37 Financial Aid Coordinator .... Michelle WARREN
15 Human Resources Technician .... Vacant
18 Facilities Manager .... Paul PEMBERTON
13 IT Director .... Sharon BUERMANN
19 Security Coordinator .... Kurt HALVORSON
26 Marketing/Communications Specialist .... Vacant
08 Head Librarian .... Tammi JALOWIEC

MISSISSIPPI

Alcorn State University (H)

1000 ASU Drive, #359, Lorman MS 39096-7500
County: Claiborne FICE Identification: 002396
Unit ID: 175342
Telephone: (601) 877-6100 Carnegie Class: Masters/M
FAX Number: (601) 877-2975 Calendar System: Semester
URL: www.alcorn.edu
Established: 1871 Annual Undergrad Tuition & Fees (In-State): $7,084
Enrollment: 3,716 Coed
Affiliation or Control: State IRS Status: 501(c)3
Highest Offering: Doctorate
Accreditation: SC, AAFCS, ACBSP, ADNUR, CAEP, MUS, NAIT, NUR, SW

01 President .... Dr. Felecia M. NAVE
05 Int Provost/EVP Academic Affairs .... Dr. John IGWEBUIKE
11 Sr VP for Univ Operations/COO .... Vacant
04 Exec Asst to the President .... Mrs. Karen R. SHEDRICK
116 Director of Internal Audit .... Ms. Tomeka L. MOORE
46 Chief Research Officer .... Dr. Babu P. PATLOLLA
10 VP for Finance & Administrative Svc .... Mrs. Carolyn DUPRE
32 VP for Student Affairs .... Mr. Tracy M. COOK
10 Associate VP for Fiscal Affairs .... Ms. Lucreta TRIBUNE

111 VP Institutional Advancement ... Mr. Marcus D. WARD
26 VP Marketing/Communications ... Mr. Marcus D. WARD
20 Int VProv Academic Affs/Grad Stds ... Dr. Donna WILLIAMS
18 Assoc VP for Facilities Management ... Dr. Jeff POSEY
39 Director of Residence Life ... Ms. Aimee REYNOLDS
28 Dir of Educational Equity/Inclusion ... Mrs. Lljuna WEIR
21 Director of Accounting ... Ms. Cora FULLER
96 Purchasing Agent ... Ms. Mertha V. GEORGE
07 Director of Admissions/Recruiting ... Mrs. Katangela TENNER
37 Director of Financial Aid ... Mrs. Juanita RUSSELL-EDWARDS
06 Registrar ... Dr. Tracee SMITH
08 Dean University Libraries ... Dr. Blanche SANDERS
47 Dean School of Agriculture ... Dr. Edmond BUCKNER
49 Dean School of Arts & Science ... Dr. Babu P. PATLOLLA
50 Dean School of Business ... Dr. Donna WILLIAMS
53 Dean School of Education ... Dr. Ivan BANKS
66 Dean School of Nursing ... Dr. Debra SPRING
88 Dean University College ... Dr. Valerie THOMPSON
13 CIO for Ctr for Info Tech Svcs ... Dr. Willie B. BENSON, JR.
15 Director of Human Resources ... Dr. Wanda FLEMING
36 Director Career Services ... Mrs. Felecia PITTMAN
23 Director of Health & Disab Services ... Ms. Dorothy G. JACKSON-DAVIS
41 Director of Athletics ... Mr. Derek HORNE
40 Manager Barnes and Noble ... Ms. Roshae LACEY
38 Director of Counseling & Testing ... Dr. Barbara MARTIN
09 Int Dir Institutional Rsrch/Assess ... Dr. LaDonna EANOCHS
108 Dir Institutional Effectiveness ... Dr. LaToya HART
19 Chief of Campus Police ... Mr. Douglas STEWART
88 General Manager Sodexo ... Mr. Gretchen FAVORS
102 Exec Dir ASU Foundation ... Mr. Marcus D. WARD
31 Dir Ctr Rural Life/Econ Dev ... Mr. Alfred GALTNEY
92 Director of Pre-Prof/Honors Program ... Dr. Thomas C. STURGIS
25 Grants/Contract Administrator ... Ms. Sallie GRIFFIN
88 Sp Asst to Pres Cmty & Econ Dev ... Dr. Ruth R. NICHOLS
88 Exec Dir Online/Vicksburg Exp Ctr ... Dr. Tamia HERNDON
104 Director Study Abroad ... Dr. Dovi ALIPOE
88 Asst VP Athletic Compl/Acad Svc ... Mr. Cyrus R. CABLE
100 Chief of Staff ... Vacant
106 Dir Distance Learning/Online Educ ... Dr. Tamia HERNDON

Antonelli College (A)

1500 N 31st Avenue, Hattiesburg MS 39401-3056
Telephone: (601) 583-4100 Identification: 666517
Accreditation: ACCSC

† Branch campus of Antonelli College, OH.

Antonelli College (B)

460 Briarwood Drive, Suite 200, Jackson MS 39206-3053
Telephone: (601) 362-9991 Identification: 666518
Accreditation: ACCSC

† Branch campus of Antonelli College, OH.

Belhaven University (C)

1500 Peachtree Street, Jackson MS 39202-1798
County: Hinds FICE Identification: 002397
Unit ID: 175421
Telephone: (601) 968-5940 Carnegie Class: Masters/L
FAX Number: (601) 968-9998 Calendar System: Semester
URL: www.belhaven.edu
Established: 1883 Annual Undergrad Tuition & Fees: $25,300
Enrollment: 4,458 Coed
Affiliation or Control: Presbyterian Church (U.S.A.) IRS Status: 501(c)3
Highest Offering: Doctorate
Accreditation: SC, ART, DANCE, IACBE, MUS, NURSE, SW, THEA

01 President ... Dr. Roger PARROTT
05 Provost/Vice Pres Academic Affairs ... Dr. Bradford SMITH
05 VP of Online Academic Affairs ... Dr. Audrey KELLEHER
84 VP of Enrollment and Marketing ... Mr. Kevin RUSSELL
10 CFO & VP Business Affairs ... Mr. David TARRANT
41 VP Student Dev/Athletic Director ... Mr. Scott LITTLE
11 Asst VP Campus Operations ... Mr. David POTVIN
32 Asst VP Enrollment/Student Services ... Mrs. Suzanne SULLIVAN
12 Assoc VP of Regional Campuses ... Dr. Rick UPCHURCH
106 Assoc VP Online Studies ... Dr. Aaron METZCAR
20 Assoc VP of Academic Support ... Dr. Vicki WOLFE
50 Dean of the School of Business ... Dr. Chip MASON
53 Dean of the School of Education ... Dr. David HAND
66 Dean of the School of Nursing ... Dr. Barbara JOHNSON
79 Dean of Worldview Studies ... Dr. Tracy FORD
88 Dean Regional Campuses ... Dr. Paul CRISS
88 Dean of Curriculum ... Dr. Ken ELLIOTT
35 Dean of Student Life ... Dr. Greg HAWKINS
06 Registrar ... Mrs. Donna WEEKS
26 Director of University Relations ... Mr. Bryant BUTLER
13 Director Information Technology ... Mr. Bo MILLER
19 Director Security ... Mr. Steve FARMER
07 Director of Admissions ... Mr. Jake DONALD
09 Dir Inst Research/Academic Systems ... Mrs. Lea Ann BETHANY
08 Director of Libraries ... Mr. Chris CULLNANE, II
15 Director of Human Resources ... Mrs. Sherry OVERBY
37 Director of Financial Aid ... Mrs. Debbi BRASWELL
121 Director of Student Care ... Mrs. Sandra KELLY
111 Director of Advancement/Alumni ... Mr. Frank LAWS
40 Bookstore Manager ... Ms. Ashli JONES
88 Military Sponsorship Administrator ... Mr. Bo JONES

Blue Mountain College (D)

201 W Main Street, PO Box 160,
Blue Mountain MS 38610-0160
County: Tippah FICE Identification: 002398
Unit ID: 175430
Telephone: (662) 685-4771 Carnegie Class: Bac-Diverse
FAX Number: (662) 685-4776 Calendar System: Semester
URL: www.bmc.edu
Established: 1873 Annual Undergrad Tuition & Fees: $12,584
Enrollment: 601 Coed
Affiliation or Control: Southern Baptist IRS Status: 501(c)3
Highest Offering: Master's
Accreditation: SC

01 President ... Dr. Barbara C. MCMILLIN
04 Admin Assistant to the President ... Mrs. Pam BOWMAN
05 Provost and Vice President ... Dr. Sharon B. ENZOR
53 Dean of Education ... Dr. Jenetta WADDELL
59 Dean of Business ... Dr. Anthony BULLARD
09 Director of Institutional Research ... Mr. Robert E. RUCKER
08 Director of Library Services ... Ms. Hannah JOHNSON
06 Registrar ... Mrs. Sheila D. FREEMAN
88 Director Teaching & Learning Center ... Dr. Delise TEAGUE
32 Dean of Students ... Mr. Philip RITCHEY
07 Vice Pres for Enrollment Services ... Mr. Lynn GIBSON
30 VP Community Rels/Dir BMC Found ... Mr. Jody HILL
37 Director of Financial Aid ... Mrs. Beverly HICKEY
10 Chief Financial Officer ... Mr. Steve ROBBINS
11 Chief Operating Officer ... Mrs. Joyce PETERS
40 Campus Store Manager ... Mrs. Dot M. LOCKE
41 Athletic Director ... Mr. Will LOWREY
42 Director Baptist Student Union ... Mrs. Tracy S. MOSER
13 Director of Information Services ... Mr. Kevin BAREFIELD
26 Dir of PR/Publications ... Ms. Emma L. AINSWORTH
29 Director of Alumni Relations ... Mrs. Kayce BRAGG
88 Director of Church Relations ... Dr. Ronald MEEKS

Coahoma Community College (E)

3240 Friars Point Road, Clarksdale MS 38614-9700
County: Coahoma FICE Identification: 002401
Unit ID: 175519
Telephone: (662) 627-2571 Carnegie Class: Assoc/HVT-High Trad
FAX Number: (662) 627-9451 Calendar System: Semester
URL: www.coahomacc.edu
Established: 1949 Annual Undergrad Tuition & Fees (In-District): $3,003
Enrollment: 1,954 Coed
Affiliation or Control: State/Local IRS Status: 501(c)3
Highest Offering: Associate Degree
Accreditation: SC, ADNUR, COARC, EMT, POLYT

01 President ... Dr. Valmadge T. TOWNER
05 Dean of Academics ... Dr. Rolanda BROWN
10 Chief Financial Officer ... Ms. Deborah VALENTINE
32 Director of Student Services ... Mrs. Karen DONE
09 Dir Inst Effectiveness/SACS Liaison ... Mrs. Margaret DIXON
30 Coordinator for Federal Programs ... Mrs. Marilyn STARKS
75 Dean of Career & Technical Educ ... Mrs. Anne SHELTON-CLARK
06 Interim Registrar ... Mr. Michael HOUSTON
08 Dir Library/Instructional Resources ... Mrs. Rose LOCKETT
13 Director Computer Services ... Mr. Rob STALDER
19 Director of Safety ... Mr. Charles JONES
26 Chief Communication Officer ... Mr. Marriel HARDY
37 Director of Financial Aid ... Dr. Luke HOWARD
15 Director of Employee Services ... Mr. Michael HOUSTON
51 Director of Educational Outreach ... Ms. Letha RICHARDS
29 Director Alumni Relations ... Vacant
36 Director Student Placement ... Mrs. Trina COX
38 Coordinator of Student Counseling ... Ms. Renee HALL
04 Administrative Asst to President ... Ms. Yolanda D. MILLER
100 Chief of Staff ... Mr. Jerone SHAW
103 Dir Workforce/Career Development ... Mr. Steven JOSSELL
105 Director Web Services ... Mr. Ezra HOWARD
106 Dir Online Education/E-learning ... Mr. Joseph MCKEE
41 Interim Athletic Director ... Mr. Reggie HANKERSON

Concorde Career College (F)

7900 Airways Boulevard, Suite 103, Southaven MS 38671
Telephone: (662) 429-9909 Identification: 770540
Accreditation: COE

† Branch campus of Concorde Career College, Memphis, TN

Copiah-Lincoln Community College (G)

PO Box 649, Wesson MS 39191-0649
County: Copiah FICE Identification: 002402
Unit ID: 175573
Telephone: (601) 643-5101 Carnegie Class: Assoc/HT-High Trad
FAX Number: (601) 643-8212 Calendar System: Semester
URL: www.colin.edu
Established: 1928 Annual Undergrad Tuition & Fees (In-State): $3,180
Enrollment: 3,075 Coed
Affiliation or Control: State IRS Status: 501(c)3
Highest Offering: Associate Degree
Accreditation: SC, ADNUR, COARC, MLTAD, RAD

01 President ... Dr. Jane G. HULON
04 Assistant to the President ... Mrs. Amber N. BRITT
10 Vice President Business Affairs ... Mr. Richard BAKER
12 VP of the Simpson County Center ... Dr. Dewayne MIDDLETON
12 Vice Pres of the Natchez Campus ... Vacant
05 Assoc Vice President of Instruction ... Mrs. Jackei MARTIN
20 Dean of Academic Instructions ... Dr. Stephanie DUGUID
32 Dean of Student Services ... Mr. Chris WARREN
75 Dean Career & Technical Educ ... Mr. Brent DUGUID
31 Dean of Community Programs ... Dr. Brenda B. ORR
41 Athletic Director ... Mr. Bryan NOBILE
07 Director of Enrollment Services ... Mrs. Samantha SPEGG
35 Assistant Dean of Students ... Mr. Bryan NOBILE
37 Director Student Financial Aid ... Mrs. Leslie SMITH
40 Director Bookstore ... Mr. Charles HART
08 Director of Library Resources ... Mrs. Jacqueline QUINN
26 Director of Public Relations ... Mrs. Natalie DAVIS
13 Information Systems Specialist ... Ms. Deemie LETCHWORTH
19 Director of Security ... Mr. Alvin STARKEY
09 Dir Inst Effectiv/Facilities Plng ... Mrs. Tiffany PERRYMAN
35 Dean of Students ... Mr. Chris WARREN
102 Director of Foundation & Alumni Svc ... Mrs. Angela FURR
18 Director of Physical Plant ... Mr. Daniel CASE
66 Director of Assoc Degree Nursing ... Ms. Mary Ann FLINT
06 Student Records Manager ... Mrs. Gay LANGHAM
57 Chair Fine Arts Division ... Ms. Juanita PROFFITT
50 Chair Business Division ... Mr. Richard BAKER
68 Chair Physical Education Division ... Mrs. Brenda SMITH
81 Chair Math/Computer Science Div ... Mr. Eddie BRITT
79 Chair Humanities Division ... Mrs. Mary WARREN
82 Chair Social Science Division ... Mr. Keith STOVALL
88 Chair Science Division ... Dr. Kevin MCKONE
96 Director of Purchasing ... Mrs. Erin LIKENS
106 Director of E-learning ... Dr. Amanda HOOD
108 QEP Director ... Ms. Glenda SILVERII
15 Human Resources Director ... Ms. Julia PARKER
39 Director Student Housing ... Mr. Allen KENT
91 Director of Technology/Info Systems ... Mr. James P. MCINNIS

Delta State University (H)

1003 W. Sunflower Rd., Cleveland MS 38733
County: Bolivar FICE Identification: 002403
Unit ID: 175616
Telephone: (662) 846-3000 Carnegie Class: Masters/L
FAX Number: (662) 846-4014 Calendar System: Semester
URL: www.deltastate.edu
Established: 1924 Annual Undergrad Tuition & Fees (In-State): $7,246
Enrollment: 3,785 Coed
Affiliation or Control: State IRS Status: 501(c)3
Highest Offering: Doctorate
Accreditation: SC, AAB, AAFCS, ACBSP, ART, CACREP, CAEPN, #DIETC, MUS, NURSE, SW

01 President ... Mr. William (Bill) LAFORGE
05 Provost/VP Academic Affairs ... Dr. Charles MCADAMS
10 Vice President for Finance ... Mr. James RUTLEDGE
32 Vice President for Student Affairs ... Dr. Vernell BENNETT
111 Vice Pres Univ Advance & Ext Rels ... Mr. Rick MUNROE
100 Chief of Staff/VP Univ Relations ... Dr. Michelle A. ROBERTS
15 Director of Human Resources ... Ms. Lisa GIGER
41 Director of Athletics ... Mr. Mike KINNISON
49 Dean College of Arts & Sciences ... Dr. David BREAUX
50 Dean College of Business ... Dr. Billy MOORE
53 Dean College of Education ... Dr. Leslie GRIFFIN
66 Dean School of Nursing ... Dr. Vicki L. BINGHAM
08 Dean Library Services ... Mr. Jeff SLAGELL
58 Dean Graduate/Continuing Studies ... Dr. Beverly MOON
06 Registrar/Dir Inst Research & Plng ... Ms. Emily C. DABNEY
13 Chief Information Officer ... Mr. Edwin CRAFT
21 Comptroller/Accounting ... Mrs. Beverly LINDSEY
116 Internal Auditor ... Mrs. Mary Helen VARNER
88 Executive Director BPAC ... Ms. Laura HOWELL
121 Executive Director Student Success ... Ms. Christy RIDDLE
88 Dir of Athlete Support Services ... Ms. Tricia KILLEBREW
37 Dir Student Financial Assistance ... Dr. Megan SMITH
38 Director Counsel/Stdnt Health Svcs ... Dr. Richard HOUSTON
36 Director Career Services ... Ms. Nakikke JOHNSON
19 Director of Police Dept ... Mr. Jeffrey JOHNS
39 Director of Housing ... Ms. Julie JACKSON
26 Dir of Communications & Marketing ... Mr. Peter SZATMARY
29 Director of Alumni Affairs ... Ms. Amanda ROBINSON
25 Director Institutional Grants ... Ms. Heather MILLER
113 Director Student Business Svcs ... Mr. Kelvin DAVIS
106 Dir of Clinical Exper/Licens/Acct ... Mrs. Anjanette POWERS
31 Director Delta Center Culture Learn ... Dr. Rolando HERTS
18 Director of Facilities Mgmt ... Mr. Gerald FINLEY
35 Director of Student Development ... Mr. Michael LIPFORD
40 Manager of Bookstore ... Ms. Mallory KENDALL
102 Special Asst to Pres for Donor Rels ... Mr. Keith FULCHER
104 Director Study Abroad/QEP ... Mrs. Michelle JOHANSEN
88 Director of Food Services ... Mr. Gerald FYRE
07 Director of Admissions ... Mr. Merritt DAIN

East Central Community College (I)

PO Box 129, Decatur MS 39327-0129
County: Newton FICE Identification: 002404
Unit ID: 175643
Telephone: (601) 635-2111 Carnegie Class: Assoc/MT-VT-High Trad
FAX Number: (601) 635-4011 Calendar System: Semester
URL: www.eccc.edu
Established: 1928 Annual Undergrad Tuition & Fees (In-District): $2,870
Enrollment: 2,560 Coed
Affiliation or Control: Local IRS Status: 501(c)3

Highest Offering: Associate Degree
Accreditation: SC, ADNUR, SURGT

01 President Dr. Billy W. STEWART
05 Vice President for Instruction Dr. Teresa L. MACKEY
10 Vice Pres for Business Operations Mr. Mickey VANCE
32 Vice President for Student Services Dr. Randall LEE
09 VP Institutional Research/Effective Mr. David CASE
26 VP for Public Information Mr. Bill WAGNON
106 Dean of eLearning Education Dr. Christa WILHITE
08 Dean of Learning Resources Mr. Leslie HUGHES
121 Director of Success Center/Testing Ms. Misty SMITH
51 Director of Adult Education/HSE Ms. Alfreda THOMPSON
103 Director of Career & Tech Education Mr. Wayne EASON
07 Director Admissions and Records Dr. Stacey HOLLINGSWORTH
15 Director of Human Resources Mrs. Julie ROWZEE
18 Superintendent of Physical Plant Mr. Artie FOREMAN
13 Dean of Information Technology Mr. Derek PACE
14 Assoc Dir Information Technology Mrs. Regena BOYKIN
37 Director of Financial Aid Mrs. Brenda B. CARSON
19 Chief of Police Mr. John HARRIS
39 Director of Hous/Student Activities Dr. Amanda WALTON
29 Dir of Alumni Relations/Foundation Vacant
57 Chairperson Fine Arts Division Mr. Chas EVANS
81 Chair Mathematics/Computer Science Ms. Cathryn MAY
83 Chairperson Social Sciences Mrs. Wanda HURLEY
76 Dean of Healthcare Education Dr. Sheryl ALLEN
81 Chairperson Science Mr. Curt SKIPPER
60 Chairperson Communications/Language Mrs. Carol SHACKELFORD
04 Administrative Asst to President Ms. Carole H. GERMANY
41 Director of Athletics Mr. Paul NIXON

East Mississippi Community College (A)

PO Box 158, Scooba MS 39358-0158
County: Kemper FICE Identification: 002405
Unit ID: 175652
Telephone: (662) 476-5000 Carnegie Class: Assoc/MT-VT-Mix Trad/Non
FAX Number: (662) 476-5058 Calendar System: Semester
URL: www.eastms.edu
Established: 1927 Annual Undergrad Tuition & Fees (In-District): $3,440
Enrollment: 3,908 Coed
Affiliation or Control: State/Local IRS Status: 501(c)3
Highest Offering: Associate Degree
Accreditation: SC, ADNUR, EMT, FUSER

01 President Dr. Scott ALSOBROOKS
12 Vice President for GT Campus Dr. Paul MILLER
12 Vice President for Scooba Campus Mr. Mickey STOKES
10 Chief Financial Officer Ms. Melissa MOSLEY
103 VP Workforce & Cmty Services Dr. Raj SHAUNAK
04 Administrative Asst to President Mrs. Christina VERNON
09 Director IR/E Mr. Mark ALEXANDER
13 Director of Info Technology Mr. Michael TVARKUNAS
18 Director of Physical Plant Mr. Kyle YOUNGER
37 Director of Financial Aid Mr. Garry JONES
06 Registrar Mrs. Melinda SCIPLE
07 Director of Admissions Vacant
40 Bookstore Manager Mrs. Ginnie CODY
26 Director of Public Information Mr. Rocky HIGGINBOTHAM
32 Dean of Students SC Campus Mr. Tony MONTGOMERY
32 Dean of Students GT Campus Dr. Melanie SANDERS
41 Athletic Director Mr. Mickey STOKES
12 Director Columbus Air Force Base Vacant
19 Chief of Police Mr. Archer SALLIS
15 Director Human Resources Ms. Theresa HARPOLE
111 Exec Director College Advancement Mr. Marcus WOOD
20 Associate Dean of Instruction SC Mr. James RUSH
20 Associate Dean of Instruction GT Mrs. Gina THOMPSON
20 Associate Dean of Instruction CT Dr. Michael BUSBY
106 Associate Dean of E-learning Mrs. Chris SQUARE

Hinds Community College (B)

PO Box 1100, Raymond MS 39154-1100
County: Hinds FICE Identification: 002407
Unit ID: 175786
Telephone: (601) 857-5261 Carnegie Class: Assoc/HVT-High Trad
FAX Number: (601) 857-3518 Calendar System: Semester
URL: www.hindscc.edu
Established: 1917 Annual Undergrad Tuition & Fees (In-District): $3,130
Enrollment: 12,061 Coed
Affiliation or Control: State/Local IRS Status: 501(c)3
Highest Offering: Associate Degree
Accreditation: SC, ADNUR, CAHIIM, COARC, DA, DMS, EMT, MLTAD, PTAA, RAD, SURGT

01 President Dr. Clyde MUSE
10 Vice President Business Services Mr. Vic PARKER
12 VP Raymond/NSG/AH/Parallel Pgm Dr. Keri COLE
12 VP Rankin/Jackson/Dir Occup Pgm Dr. Norman SESSION
12 Vice President for Vicksburg-Warren Mr. Marvin MOAK
12 Vice President for Utica and Admin Mrs. Sherry FRANKLIN
18 VP Physical Plant/Auxiliary Svcs Mr. Thomas WASSON
111 VP Advancement Mr. Randall HARRIS
103 Vice Pres Workforce Development Dr. Chad STOCKS
84 Director of Enrollment Services Ms. Kathryn B. COLE
08 Dean of Learning Resources Ms. Mary Beth APPLIN
05 Academic Dean Dr. Benjamin G. CLOYD
15 Director of Human Resources Ms. Gay Lynn CASTON
37 Dir of Financial Aid & VA Affairs Mrs. Louanne LANGSTON
38 Director of Counseling Services Dr. Kashanta JACKSON
41 Athletic Director Mr. Gene MURPHY
09 Director of Institutional Research Ms. Carley DEAR
26 Public Relations Director Ms. Cathy C. HAYDEN
96 Director of Purchasing Mr. Samuel LEMONIS
04 Executive Secretary to President Mrs. Alesia PORCH
106 Dean Online Education/E-learning Mrs. Keri COLE
13 Chief Info Technology Officer (CIO) Mr. Hamp SHIVE
29 Alumni Coordinator Ms. Libby POSEY
39 Director Student Housing Mr. DeAndre HOUSE
07 Director of Admissions Dr. Stephanie HUDSON
102 Dir Foundation/Corporate Relations Mrs. Jackie GRANBERRY
19 Director Security/Safety Mr. Joey JAMISON
86 Director Government Relations Mrs. Colleen HARTFIELD

Holmes Community College (C)

Hill Street, PO Box 369, Goodman MS 39079-0369
County: Holmes FICE Identification: 002408
Unit ID: 175810
Telephone: (662) 472-2312 Carnegie Class: Assoc/HVT-Mix Trad/Non
FAX Number: (662) 472-9152 Calendar System: Semester
URL: www.holmescc.edu
Established: 1925 Annual Undergrad Tuition & Fees (In-District): $3,110
Enrollment: 5,789 Coed
Affiliation or Control: Local IRS Status: 501(c)3
Highest Offering: Associate Degree
Accreditation: SC, ADNUR, EMT, OTA, PTAA, SURGT

01 President Dr. Jim HAFFEY
03 Executive Vice President Mr. Sonny SPARKS
09 VP Inst Research & Student Affairs Dr. Lindy MCCAIN
05 Vice Pres for Academic Programs Dr. Jenny B. JONES
12 Vice President Ridgeland Campus Dr. Don BURNHAM
12 Vice President Grenada Center Dr. Michelle BURNEY
72 Vice President Technical Education Dr. Amy WHITTINGTON
10 Vice Pres of Financial Services Mr. Sonny SPARKS
07 Director of Admissions & Records Mrs. Kay BATES
08 Librarian Mr. James THOMPSON
26 Director of Communications & Assoc Mr. Steve DIFFEY
103 Vice President of Workforce Develop Dr. Mike BLANKENSHIP
37 Director Student Financial Aid Mr. Clate HOLLEMAN
15 Director Personnel Services Ms. Julia BROWN
09 Director of Institutional Research Dr. Stephanie DIFFEY
18 Chief Facilities/Physical Plant Vacant
96 Director of Purchasing Mrs. Rosemary SELF
06 Registrar Mrs. Kay BATES
29 Director Alumni Relations Mrs. Katherine ELLARD
21 Business Manager Mr. Matt SURRELL
04 Exec Assistant to the President Mrs. Angie S. BURRELL
105 Director Marketing/Recruiting Mrs. Bronwyn MARTIN
106 Director Online Education/E-learnin Mrs. Tish STEWART
108 Director Institutional Research Dr. Stephanie DIFFEY
13 Director of Information Technology Mr. Kevin BAKER
19 Director of Public Safety Mr. Chris DILL
38 Director Student Counseling Mrs. Terri J. BANKS
39 Dir Resident Life/Student Housing Mr. Terry FANCHER
41 Vice Pres/Director of Athletics Mr. Andy WOOD
50 Academic Dean-Goodman Dr. Jenny BAILEY-JONES
53 Academic Dean-Ridgeland Dr. Tonya LAWRENCE

Itawamba Community College (D)

602 W Hill Street, Fulton MS 38843-1022
County: Itawamba FICE Identification: 002409
Unit ID: 175829
Telephone: (662) 862-8000 Carnegie Class: Assoc/HT-High Trad
FAX Number: (662) 862-8036 Calendar System: Semester
URL: www.iccms.edu
Established: 1948 Annual Undergrad Tuition & Fees (In-District): $3,160
Enrollment: 5,019 Coed
Affiliation or Control: Local IRS Status: 501(c)3
Highest Offering: Associate Degree
Accreditation: SC, ADNUR, CAHIIM, COARC, EMT, OTA, PTAA, RAD, SURGT

01 President Mr. Jay S. ALLEN
05 Vice President of Instruction Dr. Michelle SUMEREL
10 Exec Director of Finance Ms. Sandi SOUTH
07 Dean of Enrollment Dr. Melissa HAAB
32 Dean of Students Dr. Brad BOGGS
26 Director Community Relations Ms. Nina STROTHER
37 Director of Financial Aid Mr. Terry BLAND
24 Director of Learning Resources Ms. Janet ARMOUR
08 Librarian/Tupelo Ms. Holly GRAY
51 Director of Adult & Continuing Educ Vacant
41 Athletic Director Ms. Carrie BALL-WILLIAMSON
102 Director of Foundation Mr. Jim INGRAM
18 Chief Facilities/Physical Plant Mr. Thomas BONDS
09 Director of Institutional Research Mrs. Elizabeth EDWARDS
15 Exec Director of Human Resources Mr. Timothy C. SENTER
106 Dean of eLearning Ms. Denise GILLESPIE
76 Dean of Health Sciences Ms. Rilla JONES
75 Dean of Career & Technical Educ Mr. Barry EMISON
108 Director Strategic Planning and IE Mrs. Amy CAPPLEMAN
39 Director Student Housing Mr. Chad CASE
06 Registrar Mr. Bobby SOLOMON

Jackson State University (E)

1400 J. R. Lynch Street, Jackson MS 39217
County: Hinds FICE Identification: 002410
Unit ID: 175856
Telephone: (601) 979-2121 Carnegie Class: DU-Higher
FAX Number: (601) 979-2358 Calendar System: Semester
URL: www.jsums.edu
Established: 1877 Annual Undergrad Tuition & Fees (In-State): $8,051
Enrollment: 8,558 Coed
Affiliation or Control: State IRS Status: 501(c)3
Highest Offering: Doctorate
Accreditation: SC, ART, CACREP, CAEPN, CLPSY, MUS, NAIT, PH, PLNG, SP, SPAA, SW

01 President Dr. William BYNUM, JR.
05 Provost/Vice Pres Academic Affairs Dr. Lynda BROWN-WRIGHT
100 Vice President & Chief of Staff Dr. Debra MAYS-JACKSON
10 VP Business & Finance/CFO Dr. Daarel E. BURNETTE
111 VP Institutional Advancement Ms. Veronica M. COHEN
41 VP & Director of Athletics Mr. Ashley ROBINSON
46 Assoc Prov Research & Economic Dev Dr. Joseph A. WHITTAKER
84 AVP Enrollment Management Mr. Warren JOHNSON
28 Spec Asst to Pres/Chief Diver Ofcr Mr. Thomas HUDSON
32 Assoc Provost for Student Affairs Dr. Susan E. POWELL
114 Exec Dir Budget & Fin Analysis Mrs. Tammiko HARRISON
21 Exec Dir Actg/Fin Rpts/Fisc Com Mrs. Tracy STAPLETON
13 Chief Information Officer Dr. Deborah DENT
15 Executive Director Human Resources Mrs. Robin SPANN-PACK
43 General Counsel Mr. Edward WATSON
50 Int Dean College of Business Dr. Sheila PORTERFIELD
53 Int Dean College Educ/Human Devel Dr. Locord D. WILSON
49 Dean College of Liberal Arts Dr. Mario AZEVEDO
72 Dean College of Sci/Engr/Tech Dr. Wilbur WALTERS
80 Dean College of Public Service Dr. Roosevelt SHELTON
69 Int Dean School of Public Health Dr. Mohammad SHABAZZI
58 Dean Division of Graduate Studies Dr. Preselfannie MCDANIELS
106 Dean JSU Online Ms. Andrea JONES
08 Dean Div of Library & Info Res Dr. Melissa DRUCKREY
88 Interim Dean University College Dr. Marie O'BANNER-JACKSON
92 Assoc Dean Div of Honors College Dr. Loria BROWN GORDAN
88 Assoc VP/Director of Title III Dr. Mitchell SHEARS
14 Assoc VP Information Tech Dr. Michael ROBINSON
35 Assoc VP Student Life/Dean Students Dr. Laquala COLEMAN
51 Director of Lifelong Learning Dr. Carlos WILSON
110 Asst VP Institutional Advancement Mrs. Gwen CAPLES
116 Internal Auditor Mr. Christopher THOMAS
85 Director JSU Global Dr. Thomas CALHOUN
29 Dir Alumni/Constituency Relations Ms. Tabatha TERRELL-BROOKS
18 Exec Dir for Fac/Construct Mgmt Mr. Robert WATTS
88 Associate University Physician Dr. Robert SMITH
37 Director of Financial Aid Mrs. Glenda LATTIMORE
39 Exec Director Housing & Residence Ms. Tammy TIMBERS
06 Registrar Mr. Alfred B. JACKSON
23 Director of Health Services Dr. Samuel JONES
89 Director of First Year Experience Mrs. Meshonya WREN-COLEMAN
88 Int Director MS Urban Research Ctr Dr. Sam MOZEE, JR.
19 Director Public Safety Mr. Thomas ALBRIGHT
26 Exec Director Communications Ms. Maxine GREENLEAF
22 Int Director for ADA Services Mr. Aaron RICHARDSON
40 Manager Bookstore Ms. Dyonne CONNER
09 Dir Inst Research/Planning/Effect Dr. Shemeka MCCLUNG
36 Executive Director Career Services Ms. Lashanda JORDAN
38 Director Student Counseling Ms. Shanice WHITE
21 Executive Director Business Office Ms. Jewell HARRIS
22 Chief Diversity/EEO-AA Officer Mr. Thomas HUDSON
07 Assoc Dir Undergraduate Admissions Ms. Janieth ADAMS
84 Assoc Director Student Recruitment Ms. Keiona MILLER
105 Webmaster Mr. Gerard L. HOWARD
90 Director Academic IT Ms. Emily A. BISHOP
109 Director Auxiliary Services Ms. Kameshia HILL
89 Director Division Undergrad Studies Dr. Floressa HANNAH-JEFFERSON
88 Director Veteran & Military Center Ms. Latoya REED

Jones County Junior College (F)

900 S Court Street, Ellisville MS 39437-3999
County: Jones FICE Identification: 002411
Unit ID: 175883
Telephone: (601) 477-4000 Carnegie Class: Assoc/MT-VT-High Trad
FAX Number: (601) 477-4875 Calendar System: Semester
URL: www.jcjc.edu
Established: 1927 Annual Undergrad Tuition & Fees (In-District): $3,480
Enrollment: 4,517 Coed
Affiliation or Control: State/Local IRS Status: Exempt
Highest Offering: Associate Degree
Accreditation: SC, ACBSP, ADNUR, EMT, RAD

01 President Dr. Jesse R. SMITH
05 EVP/Chief Academic & Financial Ofcr Mr. Rick YOUNGBLOOD
32 Executive VP Student Affairs Ms. Gwen MAGEE
111 VP of Advancement Mr. Charlie GARRETSON
84 VP of Enrollment Management Mr. Rick HAMILTON
13 Director of Information Technology Mr. Paul SPELL
26 EVP/CMO/CIO/CEMO Ms. Finee RUFFIN
100 Asst to the Pres Cabinet Operations Ms. Beth MCDANIEL
18 Asst to the Pres Facilities Mgmt Mr. Michael BRADSHAW
86 Asst to the Pres Govt Relations Mr. Jim WALLEY
88 Asst to the Pres Leadership Dr. Sam JONES
88 Asst to the Pres Office Operations Ms. Teresa WELCH
35 Dean of Student Affairs Mr. Mark EASLEY
20 Dean of Academic Affairs Dr. Jason DEDWYLER
103 Dir of the Advanced Tech Center Mr. Greg BUTLER
37 Director of Student Financial Aid Ms. Jennifer SUBER

39 Director of Housing ... Mr. Chuck ROBERTSON
40 Bookstore Manager ... Mr. Kevin KUHN
41 Director of Athletics ... Mr. Joel CAIN
15 Director of Human Resources ... Mr. Luke HAMMONDS
96 Director of Purchasing ... Ms. Daphne YEAGER
106 Dean of eLearning ... Ms. Ashley BEARD
08 Head Librarian ... Mr. Andrew SHARP
19 Chief Campus Police ... Mr. Stan LIVINGSTON

Meridian Community College (A)

910 Highway 19 North, Meridian MS 39307-5890
County: Lauderdale FICE Identification: 002413
Unit ID: 175935
Telephone: (601) 483-8241 Carnegie Class: Assoc/HVT-High Trad
FAX Number: (601) 481-1305 Calendar System: Semester
URL: www.meridiancc.edu
Established: 1937 Annual Undergrad Tuition & Fees (In-District): $3,054
Enrollment: 3,555 Coed
Affiliation or Control: Local IRS Status: 501(c)3
Highest Offering: Associate Degree
Accreditation: SC, ADNUR, CAHIIM, COARC, DA, DH, EMT, MAC, MLTAD, PNUR, PTAA, RAD, SURGT

01 President ... Dr. Thomas HUEBNER, JR.
10 Chief Financial Officer ... Mrs. Pam HARRISON
11 Vice President of Operations ... Ms. Soraya WELDEN
05 Dean of Academic Affairs ... Mr. Michael THOMPSON
103 VP for Workforce Solutions ... Mr. Joseph KNIGHT
111 VP Advancement/Exec Dir Foundation ... Mrs. Leia HILL
04 Executive Assistant to President ... Mrs. Lauren CLAY
103 Dean of Workforce Education ... Mrs. Lori SMITH
76 Asst VP Nursing/Health Education ... Dr. Lara COLLUM
18 Director Physical Plant ... Mr. Adam FOREMAN
09 Dir Institutional Effectiveness ... Mrs. Cathy PARKER
07 Director of Admissions ... Dr. Angela PAYNE
32 Dean of Student Services ... Mrs. Deanna SMITH
37 Director Financial Aid ... Ms. Nedra BRADLEY
15 Director Human Resources ... Ms. Angie PICKARD
41 Athletic Director ... Mr. Sander ATKINSON
19 Chief of Campus Police ... Mr. Nick KIRKLAND
40 Bookstore Manager ... Mrs. Cher WARREN
26 Director of Public Information ... Mrs. Kay THOMAS
36 Career Center Development Director ... Ms. Katrina GARRETT
06 Registrar ... Ms. Deborah OLDHAM
105 Webmaster ... Ms. Inga BASS
13 Director of Telecommunications ... Mr. Chris EDWARDS
39 Director Student Housing ... Mr. Calvin BENNETT
106 Director of E-Learning ... Ms. Marie ROBERTS

Millsaps College (B)

1701 N State Street, Jackson MS 39210-0001
County: Hinds FICE Identification: 002414
Unit ID: 175980
Telephone: (601) 974-1000 Carnegie Class: Bac-A&S
FAX Number: (601) 974-1059 Calendar System: Semester
URL: www.millsaps.edu
Established: 1890 Annual Undergrad Tuition & Fees: $39,910
Enrollment: 859 Coed
Affiliation or Control: United Methodist IRS Status: 501(c)3
Highest Offering: Master's
Accreditation: SC, CAEP

01 President ... Dr. Rob PEARIGEN
05 Provost & Dean of the College ... Dr. Keith DUNN
10 Vice Pres of Finance ... Vacant
111 VP for Institutional Advancement ... Ms. Hope CARTER
32 VP Student Life/Dean Students ... Dr. Brit KATZ
50 Dean of the School of Management ... Dr. Kimberly G. BURKE
84 Vice Pres Enrollment/Communications ... Dr. Robert ALEXANDER
79 Assoc Dean Arts & Humanities ... Dr. Laura FRANEY
28 Assoc Dean Intercul Affs/Cmty Life ... Mr. Demetrius BROWN
81 Associate Dean Sciences Division ... Dr. Stan GALICKI
82 AVP for International Initiatives ... Ms. Molly WEST
37 Director of Financial Aid ... Mrs. Isabelle HIGBEE
20 Director Academic Support Services ... Ms. Kia SMITH
51 Director of Continuing Education ... Dr. Nola R. GIBSON
08 College Librarian ... Ms. Jamie B. WILSON
36 Director of Career Center ... Mr. Ryan COLVIN
41 Director of Athletics ... Mr. Donnie BROOKS
15 Dir of Human Resource Services ... Ms. Julie DANIELS
42 Chaplain ... Dr. Joey SHELTON
21 Controller ... Mrs. Whitney EMRICH
06 Registrar ... Dr. Ken THOMPSON
09 Director of Institutional Research ... Mr. Ken THOMPSON
18 Director of Physical Plant ... Mr. Michael SWITZER
29 Director Alumni Relations ... Ms. Maribeth KITCHINGS
19 Director Security/Safety ... Mr. John CONWAY
26 Director of Communications & Market ... Mr. John SEWELL
04 Executive Asst to President ... Mrs. Penta MOORE
100 Chief of Staff ... Mr. Kenneth TOWNSEND
102 Dir Foundation/Corporate Relations ... Mr. Lloyd GRAY
44 Director Annual Giving ... Mr. Jim BURKE

Mississippi College (C)

200 W College Street, Clinton MS 39058-0001
County: Hinds FICE Identification: 002415
Unit ID: 176053
Telephone: (601) 925-3000 Carnegie Class: DU-Mod
FAX Number: (601) 925-3276 Calendar System: Semester
URL: www.mc.edu
Established: 1826 Annual Undergrad Tuition & Fees: $18,026
Enrollment: 5,036 Coed
Affiliation or Control: Southern Baptist IRS Status: 501(c)3
Highest Offering: Doctorate
Accreditation: SC, ARCPA, CACREP, CAEPN, CIDA, LAW, MUS, NURSE, SW

01 President ... Dr. Blake THOMPSON
04 Sr Exec Assistant to President ... Ms. Shelia CARPENTER
10 Chief Financial Officer ... Ms. Donna LEWIS
05 Interim Provost/VPAA ... Dr. Debbie NORRIS
32 VP Enrollment Svcs/Dean of Students ... Dr. Jim TURCOTTE
45 Vice President Planning/Assessment ... Dr. Debbie NORRIS
42 Vice Pres Christian Development ... Vacant
111 Chief Advancement Officer ... Vacant
11 Vice Pres Admin/Government Rels ... Dr. Steve STANFORD
84 Director Enrollment Services ... Vacant
06 Registrar ... Ms. Megan PRITCHETT
09 Director of Institutional Research ... Vacant
08 Director of Library ... Dr. Ron HOWARD
21 Controller ... Ms. Allison ROOKER
13 Chief Information Officer ... Mr. Bill CRANFORD
38 Director Counseling/Testing Center ... Dr. Morgan BRYANT
15 Director Human Resources ... Ms. Donna SMITH
29 Exec Director of Alumni Affairs ... Dr. Jim TURCOTTE
26 Director Public Relations ... Ms. Tracey HARRISON
18 Director of Physical Plant ... Dr. Tom WILLIAMS
39 Coordinator of Residence Life ... Ms. Julie KERR
37 Director Student Financial Aid ... Ms. Karon MCMILLAN
07 Director of Admissions ... Mr. Kyle BRANTLEY
35 Assoc Dir of Student Engagement ... Ms. Becca BENSON
19 Director of Public Safety ... Mr. Mike WARREN
41 Director of Athletics ... Mr. Mike JONES
96 Director of Purchasing ... Ms. Dana ELMORE
40 Manager Bookstore ... Mr. Daniel HOWARD
36 Director of Career Services ... Ms. Taylor ORMON
81 Dean School of Science/Mathematics ... Dr. Stan BALDWIN
50 Dean School of Business Admin ... Dr. Marcelo EDUARDO
79 Dean School of Humanities ... Dr. Jonathan RANDLE
53 Dean School of Education ... Dr. Cindy MELTON
73 Dean Sch Christian Studies/Fine Art ... Dr. Wayne VAN HORN
61 Dean School of Law ... Dr. Patricia BENNETT
58 Dean Grad School/Special Programs ... Dr. Debbie NORRIS
66 Dean School of Nursing ... Dr. Kimberly SHARP
86 Director Government Relations ... Dr. Steve STANFORD
30 Director of Development ... Ms. Barbara BROWN
43 Legal Counsel ... Dr. Bill TOWNSEND

Mississippi Delta Community College (D)

PO Box 668, Moorhead MS 38761-0668
County: Sunflower FICE Identification: 002416
Unit ID: 176008
Telephone: (662) 246-6322 Carnegie Class: Assoc/MT-VT-High Trad
FAX Number: (662) 246-6321 Calendar System: Semester
URL: www.msdelta.edu
Established: 1926 Annual Undergrad Tuition & Fees (In-District): $3,030
Enrollment: 2,320 Coed
Affiliation or Control: Local IRS Status: 501(c)3
Highest Offering: Associate Degree
Accreditation: SC, ADNUR, DH, MLTAD, RAD

01 President ... Dr. Tyrone JACKSON
05 Vice President of Instruction ... Mrs. Teresa WEBSTER
10 Vice President of Business Services ... Mrs. Marsha LEE
32 Vice President of Student Services ... Dr. Edward RICE
88 Dean of GHEC Operations ... Ms. Linda CLARK
103 VP of Workforce ... Mr. Todd DONALD
111 Assoc VP College Advancement ... Mr. Reed ABRAHAM
15 Director of Human Resources ... Ms. Brenda VANLANDINGHAM
37 Director of Financial Aid ... Ms. Deborah MARTIN
07 Director of Admissions ... Mr. Jay GARY
13 Director Computer & Info Tech Svcs ... Mr. Jim AYCOCK
08 Director of Library Services ... Mrs. Kristi BARIOLA
88 Director Counseling/Recruiting ... Mrs. Kate FAILING
18 Director of Maintenance ... Mr. Don LEE
88 Director of Special Events ... Mrs. Corey SMITH
09 Director of Institutional Research ... Dr. Rosemary LAMB
04 Admin Asst to the President ... Mrs. Debra BAKER
41 Athletic Director ... Mr. Jeff TATUM
19 Director Security/Safety ... Mr. Clifton KING
76 Dean of Allied Health ... Mrs. Patricia KELLY
75 Dean of Career/Technical Education ... Mrs. Suzanne THOMPSON
106 Coordinator of E-learning ... Mrs. Brenda BRIDGERS
29 Director Alumni Affairs ... Mr. Jim AYCOCK

Mississippi Gulf Coast Community College (E)

PO Box 609, Perkinston MS 39573-0012
County: Stone FICE Identification: 002417
Unit ID: 176071
Telephone: (601) 928-5211 Carnegie Class: Assoc/MT-VT-High Trad
FAX Number: (601) 928-6386 Calendar System: Semester
URL: www.mgccc.edu
Established: 1911 Annual Undergrad Tuition & Fees (In-District): $3,670
Enrollment: 8,888 Coed
Affiliation or Control: Local IRS Status: Exempt
Highest Offering: Associate Degree
Accreditation: SC, ACFEI, ADNUR, #COARC, EMT, MAC, MLTAD, PNUR, RAD, SURGT

01 President ... Dr. Mary S. GRAHAM
05 Exec VP Teaching/Lrng/Cmty Campus ... Dr. Jonathan WOODWARD
10 Exec VP Administration/Finance ... Dr. Jason PUGH
12 VP Perkinston Campus (PC) ... Dr. Ladd TAYLOR
12 VP Jefferson Davis Campus (JDC) ... Dr. Cedric BRADLEY
12 VP Jackson County Campus (JCC) ... Dr. Tammy FRANKS
32 Exec VP Enroll Mgmt/Student Service ... Dr. Phil BONFANTI
30 Exe VP Institutional Advancement ... Dr. Suzi BROWN
103 AVP Cmty Campus/Career Tech Educ ... Mr. John SHOWS
15 Assoc VP Human Resources ... Mr. Jared BURNS
09 AVP Inst Research & Effectiveness ... Mr. Adam SWANSON
26 AVP Institutional Relations ... Ms. Christen DUHE
110 AVP Institutional Advancement ... Ms. Kady PIETZ
106 Director of eLearning ... Ms. Jennifer LEIMER
96 Dir of Purchasing & Property Ctrl ... Mr. Jay NEWTON
50 Dean of Business Services ... Mr. Wayne KUNTZ
50 Dean of Business Services - PC ... Ms. Rebecca LAYTON
50 Dean of Business Services-JC ... Mr. Jason FERGUSON
50 Dean of Business Services-JD ... Ms. Blythe KING
66 College Dean of Health Sciences ... Dr. Joan HENDRIX
75 Dean of Teaching & Learning-PCC ... Mr. Bobby GHOSAL
75 Dean of Teaching & Learning-JD ... Dr. Erin RIGGINS
75 Dean of Teaching & Learning-JCC ... Ms. Lisa RHODES
75 Dean of Career/Tech and Wkforce-JCC ... Mr. Brock CLARK
32 Dn Stdnt Svcs/Enroll Mgmt - PC ... Dr. Jason BEVERLY
32 Dn Stdnt Svcs/Enroll Mgmt - JCC ... Ms. Michelle SEKUL
32 Dn Stdnt Svcs/Enroll Mgmt - JDC ... Vacant
88 Dean George County Center ... Vacant
39 Director Residential/Student Life ... Mr. Trey ROBERTSON
07 Director of Admissions/Rec - JCC ... Mr. William EVERITT
07 Director of Admissions/Rec - JDC ... Mr. Christopher BAGWELL
07 Director of Admissions/Rec-PCC ... Ms. Mollie BARGAR
37 Financial Aid Director - JCC ... Ms. Angela BRADLEY
37 Financial Aid Director-PCC ... Ms. Heather DEARMAN
37 Financial Aid Director - JDC ... Ms. LaShanda CHAMBERLAIN
84 Director of Enrollment Services-JCC ... Ms. Beth LOVORN
84 Director of Enrollment Services-JD ... Ms. Dawn BUCKLEY
84 Director of Enrollment Services-PCC ... Ms. Paula RAINEY
04 Exec Assistant to the President ... Ms. Natasha BAUCUM
21 Assoc VP Finance/Comptroller ... Ms. Shelly FORD

Mississippi State University (F)

Lee Boulevard, Mississippi State MS 39762-5708
County: Oktibbeha FICE Identification: 002423
Unit ID: 176080
Telephone: (662) 325-2323 Carnegie Class: DU-Highest
FAX Number: (662) 325-7455 Calendar System: Semester
URL: www.msstate.edu
Established: 1878 Annual Undergrad Tuition & Fees (In-State): $8,650
Enrollment: 21,883 Coed
Affiliation or Control: State IRS Status: 501(c)3
Highest Offering: Doctorate
Accreditation: SC, AAFCS, ART, CACREP, CAEPN, CIDA, CLPSY, DIETD, DIETI, LSAR, MUS, SCPSY, SPAA, SW, VET

01 President ... Dr. Mark E. KEENUM
05 Provost/Executive VP ... Dr. David SHAW
46 VP Research & Economic Development ... Vacant
88 VP Agric/Forestry & Veterinary Med ... Dr. Reuben MOORE
10 VP for Budget and Planning ... Mr. Don ZANT
32 VP for Student Affairs ... Dr. Regina HYATT
30 VP for Development and Alumni ... Mr. John P. RUSH
18 VP for Campus Services ... Ms. Amy TUCK
07 Assistant VP Enrollment ... Dr. John DICKERSON
41 Athletic Director ... Mr. John COHEN
43 General Counsel ... Ms. Joan LUCAS
28 Chief Diversity Officer ... Ms. Rasheda BODDIE-FORBES
15 Interim Chief Human Resources Ofcr ... Dr. Darrell EASLEY
26 Exec Dir External Affairs ... Mr. Kyle STEWARD
27 Chief Communications Officer ... Mr. Sid SALTER
86 Director Government Relations ... Mr. Lee WEISKOPF
20 Assoc Provost Academic Affairs ... Dr. Peter RYAN
13 Chief Information Officer ... Mr. Steve PARROTT
88 Exec Dir International Institute ... Dr. Julie JORDAN
48 Dean of Architecture/Art/Design ... Dr. Angi BOURGEOIS
49 Dean Arts & Sciences ... Dr. Rick TRAVIS
50 Dean College Business ... Dr. Sharon OSWALD
53 Dean of Education ... Dr. Richard L. BLACKBOURN
58 Interim Dean of Graduate Studies ... Dr. Peter RYAN
54 Dean College of Engineering ... Dr. Jason KEITH
65 Dean of Forest Resources ... Dr. George M. HOPPER
47 Dean College Agriculture & Life Sci ... Dr. George M. HOPPER
74 Dean of Veterinary Medicine ... Dr. Kent H. HOBLET
12 Admin Dir & Head of Meridian Campus ... Dr. Terry CRUSE
08 Dean of Libraries ... Ms. Frances N. COLEMAN
92 Dean Honors College ... Dr. Christopher SNYDER
56 Dir University Extension Service ... Dr. Gary JACKSON
88 Dir Agricultural Experiment Station ... Dr. George M. HOPPER
06 Registrar ... Dr. John R. DICKERSON
106 Director Distance Education ... Dr. Susan SEAL
36 Director Career Services/Coop Educ ... Ms. Angie CHRESTMAN
35 Dean of Students ... Dr. Thomas BOURGEOIS
38 Director Counseling Services ... Ms. Luellyn SWITZER
37 Director Student Financial Aid ... Mr. Paul MCKINNEY
39 Exec Director Housing/Res Life ... Ms. Dei ALLARD
09 Director Institutional Research ... Dr. Tim CHAMBLEE
23 Exec Director Univ Health Services ... Dr. Clifton STORY
29 Director of Alumni Association ... Mr. Jeffrey DAVIS
112 Director of Planned Giving ... Mr. Wes GORDON
25 Director Sponsored Projects ... Mr. Kevin ENROTH
116 Director Internal Audit ... Ms. Leisa ERVIN
96 Director Procurement/Contracts ... Mr. Don BUFFUM
19 Police Chief ... Mr. Vance RICE

Mississippi University for Women (A)

1100 College Street, Columbus MS 39701-5800

County: Lowndes FICE Identification: 002422
Unit ID: 176035
Telephone: (877) 462-8439 Carnegie Class: Masters/M
FAX Number: (662) 329-7297 Calendar System: Semester
URL: www.muw.edu
Established: 1884 Annual Undergrad Tuition & Fees (In-State): $6,940
Enrollment: 2,789 Coed
Affiliation or Control: State IRS Status: 501(c)3
Highest Offering: Doctorate
Accreditation: SC, ACBSP, ADNUR, ART, CAEPN, MUS, NURSE, SP

01 President .... Ms. Nora R. MILLER
05 Provost/VP Academic Affairs .... Dr. Scott TOLLISON
10 Sr Vice Pres Administration & CFO .... Mr. Mark D. ELLARD
26 Exec Dir of University Relations .... Ms. Anika M. PERKINS
32 Vice Pres for Student Affairs .... Dr. Jennifer MILES
20 Assoc Vice Pres Academic Affairs .... Dr. Martin HATTON
43 University Counsel .... Ms. Karen CLAY
49 Dean College Arts/Sciences .... Dr. Brian ANDERSON
50 Int Dean Business & Profess Studies .... Dr. Marty A. BROCK
66 Dean College Nursing/SLP .... Dr. Tammie M. MCCOY
08 Dean of Library Services .... Ms. Amanda C. POWERS
58 Director Graduate Studies .... Dr. Martin HATTON
88 Director Outreach & Innovation .... Ms. Melinda LOWE
27 Chief Information Officer .... Ms. Carla LOWERY
06 Registrar .... Ms. Lynn DOBBS
09 Director Inst Research & Assessment .... Ms. Jennifer MOORE
92 Director Honors College .... Dr. Kim WHITEHEAD
25 Director Sponsored Programs .... Ms. Ashley GILLESPIE
29 Director Alumni Relations .... Ms. Lyndsay CUMBERLAND
30 Exec Dir Development/Alumni Rels .... Ms. Andrea N. STEVENS
44 Director Annual Giving .... Ms. Brandy WILLIAMS
105 Dir Web Development/Univ Webmaster .... Mr. Rich SOBOLEWSKI
21 Director University Accounting .... Ms. Susan SOBLEY
116 Internal Auditor .... Mr. Kenneth WIDNER
13 Director of Information Systems .... Mr. Aaron BROOKS
07 Director Admissions .... Ms. Shelley MCNEES MOSS
37 Director Financial Aid .... Ms. Nicole PATRICK
15 Interim Director Human Resources .... Ms. Laura QUINN
19 Chief of Police .... Mr. Randy G. VIBROCK
18 Director of Facilities Management .... Mr. Jody KENNEDY
96 Director Resources Management .... Ms. Angie S. ATKINS
35 Director Student Life .... Ms. Jessica HARPOLE
35 Dean of Students .... Ms. Sirena CANTRELL
41 Dir Athletics & Recreation .... Mr. Jason TRUFANT
40 Director Bookstore .... Ms. Rita ROBINSON
121 Director Student Success Center .... Dr. David BROOKING
109 General Manager of MUW Dining Svcs .... Vacant
84 Enrollment Certification Officer .... Ms. Jody PETERS
14 Director of Systems & Networks .... Mr. Rodney GODFREY
104 Director Study Abroad .... Dr. Kim WHITEHEAD
39 Director Housing & Residence Life .... Mr. Andrew MONEYMAKER

Mississippi Valley State University (B)

14000 Highway 82 W, Itta Bena MS 38941-1400

County: Leflore FICE Identification: 002424
Unit ID: 176044
Telephone: (662) 254-9041 Carnegie Class: Masters/S
FAX Number: (662) 254-6709 Calendar System: Semester
URL: www.mvsu.edu
Established: 1950 Annual Undergrad Tuition & Fees (In-State): $6,550
Enrollment: 2,385 Coed
Affiliation or Control: State IRS Status: 501(c)3
Highest Offering: Master's
Accreditation: SC, ACBSP, ART, CAEPN, MUS, SW

01 President .... Dr. Jerryl BRIGGS, SR.
05 Interim VP Academic Affairs .... Dr. Elizabeth EVANS
32 Vice Pres for Student Affairs .... Dr. Jacqueline GIBSON
20 Assoc VP Academic Affairs .... Vacant
09 Asst VP for IRE/Strat Planning .... Dr. Sharon FREEMAN
10 VP Business & Finance/CFO .... Ms. Joyce A. DIXON
100 Chief of Staff/Legislative Liaison .... Mrs. LaShon F. BROOKS
111 Int Vice Pres for Univ Advancement .... Mr. Dameon SHAW
106 Asst VP for Distance & Online .... Dr. Kenneth DONE
84 Sr Exec Dir Enrollment Management .... Mr. Michael TAYLOR
39 Director Residence Life .... Mr. Raynaldo GILLUS
41 Director of Athletics .... Mrs. Dianthia FORD-KEE
06 Director of Student Records .... Mr. Jeffery LOGGINS
07 Director Admission/Recruitment .... Dr. Danisha WILLIAMS
08 Head Librarian .... Ms. Mantra HENDERSON
15 Director of Human Resources .... Mrs. Elizabeth HURSSEY
13 Director of Information Technology .... Mr. Torrey MOORE
37 Director of Financial Aid .... Mr. Letherio ZEIGLER
29 Manager of Alumni Relations .... Ms. Evonna LUCAS
26 Director of Comm/Mktg .... Mrs. Brittany D. GREEN
19 Chief/Director University Police .... Mr. Xavier REDMOND
18 Director Facilities/Capital Project .... Mr. Terrence HURSSEY
36 Director Career Development .... Ms. Essie L. BRYANT
38 Dean of Student Development .... Dr. Yolanda JONES
50 Acting Chair of Business Department .... Dr. Curressia BROWN
53 Chair of Education Dept .... Vacant
88 Chair English/Foreign Language .... Dr. John ZHENG
57 Acting Chair Fine Arts Department .... Dr. Kimberly BROADWATER
68 Chair Health/Phys Ed/Rec Dept .... Dr. Gloria ROSS
81 Chair of Math/Computer Science Dept .... Dr. Latonya GARNER
54 Acting Chair of Engineering Tech .... Mr. Antonio BROWNLOW
60 Chair Mass Communication Dept .... Dr. Samuel OSUNDE
88 Chair Criminal Justice .... Dr. Emmanual AMADI
70 Chair Social Work Department .... Dr. Catherine SINGLETON-WALKER
96 Director of Purchasing .... Ms. Carla M. WILLIAMS
04 Executive Asst to President .... Mrs. Auguster WALLACE
25 Director Sponsored Pgm/Title III .... Mr. Samuel MELTON, JR.
30 Director of Development .... Mr. Kendall TANNER

Northeast Mississippi Community College (C)

101 Cunningham Boulevard, Booneville MS 38829-1731

County: Prentiss FICE Identification: 002426
Unit ID: 176169
Telephone: (662) 728-7751 Carnegie Class: Assoc/MT-VT-High Trad
FAX Number: (662) 728-1165 Calendar System: Semester
URL: www.nemcc.edu
Established: 1948 Annual Undergrad Tuition & Fees (In-District): $3,596
Enrollment: 3,501 Coed
Affiliation or Control: State/Local IRS Status: 501(c)3
Highest Offering: Associate Degree
Accreditation: SC, ADNUR, COARC, DH, MAC, MLTAD, RAD

01 President .... Ricky G. FORD
03 Executive Vice President .... Craig-Ellis SASSSER
103 VP Workforce Training/Economic Dev .... Nadara L. COLE
26 Vice President of Marketing .... Will KOLLMEYER
10 Vice President of Finance .... Chris MURPHY
26 Assoc Vice Pres of Public Info .... Tony FINCH
05 Vice President of Instruction .... Michelle BARAGONA
32 Vice President of Students .... Ray SCOTT
35 Assoc Dean of Student Activities .... Rod COGGIN
08 Director Learning Resources .... Glenice STONE
96 Director of Purchasing .... Amber GARNER
37 Director of Financial Aid .... Greg WINDHAM
38 Director Student Counseling .... Joey WILLIFORD
13 Director Computer Center .... Gregory SMITH
18 Director Facilities/Maintenance .... Mark HATFIELD
39 Director Residential Housing .... Rod COGGIN
75 Director of Vocational Tech Educ .... Jason MATTOX
84 Dir of Enrollment Svcs/Registrar .... Chassie KELLY
15 Human Resources Officer .... Wesley FLOYD
04 Administrative Asst to President .... Misty DEVAUGHN
102 Dir Foundation/Corporate Relations .... Patrick D. EATON
106 Dir Online Education/E-learning .... Kim HARRIS
19 Director Security/Safety .... Randy A. BAXTER

Northwest Mississippi Community College (D)

4975 Highway 51 N, Senatobia MS 38668-1703

County: Tate FICE Identification: 002427
Unit ID: 176178
Telephone: (662) 562-3200 Carnegie Class: Assoc/MT-VT-High Trad
FAX Number: (662) 562-3911 Calendar System: Semester
URL: www.northwestms.edu
Established: 1927 Annual Undergrad Tuition & Fees (In-State): $3,000
Enrollment: 7,654 Coed
Affiliation or Control: State IRS Status: 501(c)3
Highest Offering: Associate Degree
Accreditation: SC, ADNUR, COARC, EMT, FUSER

01 President .... Dr. Michael J. HEINDL
10 Vice President for Fiscal Affairs .... Mr. Jeff HORTON
32 VP Student Affairs/Chief of Staff .... Mr. Dan SMITH
05 Vice Pres for Educational Affairs .... Dr. Matthew DOMAS
103 Dean Career Tech Ed/Wrkfce Dev Trng .... Mr. David CAMPBELL
84 Dean Enrollment Mgmt & Registrar .... Mrs. Aime ANDERSON
22 Director of Student Disability Svcs .... Mr. Gerald BEARD
26 Director of Communications .... Mrs. Julie BAUER
37 Director of Financial Aid .... Ms. LeKeisha MURRY
36 Dir Student Development Center .... Ms. Meg ROSS
08 Director of Learning Resources .... Dr. Melissa WRIGHT
13 Director Management Information Sys .... Mrs. Amy LATHAM
07 Director of Recruiting .... Mrs. Jere HERRINGTON
09 Director Planning/Inst Research .... Dr. Carolyn WARREN
18 Director of Physical Plant Building .... Mrs. Mary AYERS
19 Chief of Campus Security .... Mr. Zabe DAVIS
30 Director of Development/Alumni Rels .... Ms. Patti GORDON
39 Director of Campus Life and Housing .... Ms. Tara DUNN
40 Director Bookstore .... Mr. Joel BOYLES
41 Director of Athletics/Intramurals .... Vacant
96 Director of Purchasing .... Mrs. Ruth DUNLAP
15 Personnel Officer .... Mrs. Erica STANFORD
21 Business Manager .... Vacant

Pearl River Community College (E)

101 Highway 11 N, Poplarville MS 39470-2298

County: Pearl River FICE Identification: 002430
Unit ID: 176239
Telephone: (601) 403-1000 Carnegie Class: Assoc/MT-VT-Mix Trad/Non
FAX Number: (601) 403-1339 Calendar System: Semester
URL: www.prcc.edu
Established: 1909 Annual Undergrad Tuition & Fees (In-District): $3,500
Enrollment: 4,829 Coed
Affiliation or Control: State/Local IRS Status: 501(c)3
Highest Offering: Associate Degree
Accreditation: SC, ADNUR, COARC, DA, DH, MLTAD, OTA, PTAA, RAD, SURGT

01 President .... Dr. Adam J. BREERWOOD
05 VP for Poplarville Campus & Instruc .... Dr. Martha L. SMITH
11 VP for College Operations .... Mr. Roger A. KNIGHT
09 VP for Planning & Inst Research .... Dr. Jennifer SEAL
12 VP for Forrest County Operations .... Dr. Jana CAUSEY
08 Director of College Libraries .... Ms. Tracy SMITH
07 Director of Admissions and Records .... Ms. Tonia SEAL
18 Director of Physical Plant .... Mr. Craig TYNES
30 Director Development/Alumni Rels .... Mr. Ernest L. LOVELL, JR.
37 Director Student Financial Aid .... Ms. Tyia BROOKS
41 Athletic Director .... Mr. Jeff LONG
26 Director of Recruitment/Marketing .... Ms. Delana HARRIS
04 Administrative Asst to President .... Ms. Marilyn DILLARD
105 Webmaster .... Mr. Eric REID
13 Chief Info Technology Officer (CIO) .... Mr. Matt LOGAN
108 Dean of Workforce/Com Dev .... Ms. Terri CLARK
15 Director of Human Resources .... Ms. Kelly REID

Reformed Theological Seminary (F)

5422 Clinton Boulevard, Jackson MS 39209-3099

County: Hinds FICE Identification: 009193
Unit ID: 176284
Telephone: (601) 923-1600 Carnegie Class: Not Classified
FAX Number: (601) 923-1654 Calendar System: 4/1/4
URL: www.rts.edu
Established: 1965 Annual Graduate Tuition & Fees: N/A
Enrollment: N/A Coed
Affiliation or Control: Independent Non-Profit IRS Status: 501(c)3
Highest Offering: Doctorate; No Undergraduates
Accreditation: SC, THEOL

00 Chancellor Emeritus .... Dr. Robert C. CANNADA, JR.
01 Chancellor/CEO .... Dr. J. Ligon DUNCAN
10 Chief Operations Financial Officer .... Mr. Bradley TISDALE
05 Provost and Chief Academic Officer .... Dr. Robert CARA
108 Chief Institutional Assessment Ofcr .... Ms. Polly STONE
30 Sr Vice President for Development .... Mr. Matthew S. BRYSON
12 President Charlotte Campus .... Dr. Michael J. KRUGER
12 President Orlando Campus .... Dr. Scott R. SWAIN
12 President Jackson Campus .... Dr. Guy L. RICHARDSON
12 Executive Director Atlanta Campus .... Dr. Guy RICHARD
106 Exec Dir RTS Global/Distance Educ .... Mr. David R. JOHN, III
12 President Washington DC .... Dr. Scott REDD
12 Executive Director Dallas Campus .... Dr. Mark MCDOWELL
12 Executive Director Houston Campus .... Dr. Robert ARENDALE
12 Executive Director NYC Campus .... Dr. Jay HARVEY
26 Director of Comm and Marketing .... Mr. Phillip HOLMES

Rust College (G)

150 Rust Avenue, Holly Springs MS 38635-2328

County: Marshall FICE Identification: 002433
Unit ID: 176318
Telephone: (662) 252-8000 Carnegie Class: Bac-A&S
FAX Number: (662) 252-6107 Calendar System: Semester
URL: www.rustcollege.edu
Established: 1866 Annual Undergrad Tuition & Fees: $9,900
Enrollment: 860 Coed
Affiliation or Control: United Methodist IRS Status: 501(c)3
Highest Offering: Baccalaureate
Accreditation: SC, SW

01 President .... Dr. David L. BECKLEY
111 Vice President for College Relation .... Dr. Ishmell H. EDWARDS
10 Vice President for Finance .... Mr. Donald MANNING-MILLER
05 Vice President for Academic Affairs .... Dr. Paul C. LAMPLEY
06 Registrar .... Ms. Eleanor CLAYBORN
08 Library Director .... Mrs. Anita W. MOORE
13 Director Computer Center .... Mrs. Barbara NAYLOR MOORE
32 Dean of Administrative Services .... Vacant
35 Director Student Activities .... Mrs. Maryanne OGUTU
37 Director of Financial Aid .... Ms. Arlisha WALTON
25 Director Contracts & Grants .... Dr. Vida MAYS
29 Director Alumni Development .... Ms. Jo Ann SCOTT
89 Chair First Year Experience .... Mrs. Carolyn HYMON
21 Comptroller .... Mrs. Sandra C. DAWKINS
84 Dean of Enrollment Services .... Dr. Braque TALLEY
23 Director Student Health Services .... Ms. Jannie LUELLEN
39 Director Student Housing .... Ms. Tanya K. KIRK
36 Director of Career Pathways .... Ms. Sandra BURKE
18 Director Physical Plant .... Mr. Robert CURRY
83 Division Chair Social Science .... Dr. Alfred J. STOVALL
15 Director Personnel Services .... Ms. Patricia PEGUES
19 Chief of Security .... Mr. Eric SCOTT
30 Director of Development .... Ms. Jo Ann SCOTT
40 Bookstore Manager .... Mrs. Patricia HARRIS
42 College Chaplain .... Rev. Annie TRAVIS
96 Director of Purchasing .... Ms. Ollie BOWENS
50 Division Chair Business .... Mr. Richard FREDERICK
53 Division Chair Education .... Dr. Leon HOWARD
79 Division Chair Humanities .... Dr. Margaret DELASHMIT
81 Chair Division Science & Math .... Dr. Doris WARD
70 Chair Department of Social Work .... Mrs. Debra BUTLER
105 Director Web Services .... Vacant
41 Athletic Director .... Mr. Stanley STUBBS
101 Secretary of the Institution/Board .... Mrs. Willa TERRY
106 Dir Online Education/E-learning .... Dr. Helen OLIVER
38 Director Student Counseling .... Dr. Rosetta HOWARD
09 Director of Institutional Research .... Dr. Charles WILLIAMS
90 Director Academic Computing .... Vacant
91 Director Administrative Computing .... Mrs. Barbara N. MOORE
04 Admin Assistant to the President .... Mrs. Willa J. TERRY
22 Dir Affirm Action/Equal Opportunity .... Ms. Patricia PEGUES
26 Director of Public Relations .... Mrs. Rasheedah JACKSON
44 Director Annual Giving .... Ms. Lillie M. BOLTON

Southeastern Baptist College (A)

4229 Highway 15 N, Laurel MS 39440-1096

County: Jones FICE Identification: 002435
Unit ID: 176336
Telephone: (601) 426-6346 Carnegie Class: Spec-4-yr-Faith
FAX Number: (601) 426-6347 Calendar System: Semester
URL: www.southeasternbaptist.edu
Established: 1948 Annual Undergrad Tuition & Fees: $6,025
Enrollment: 38 Coed
Affiliation or Control: Baptist IRS Status: 501(c)3
Highest Offering: Baccalaureate
Accreditation: BI

01 President ... Dr. Scott CARSON
05 Academic Dean ... Mrs. Janice WALKER
06 Registrar ... Mrs. Emma BOND
07 Director of Admissions ... Ms. Rhonda SIMS
37 Director of Financial Aid ... Mrs. Ginny SINGLETON
08 Director of Library ... Mrs. Amy HINTON
41 Director of Athletics ... Mr. Buddy DUKE
13 Director Information Technology ... Mr. Hubert DYESS

Southwest Mississippi Community College (B)

1156 College Drive, Summit MS 39666-9029

County: Pike FICE Identification: 002436
Unit ID: 176354
Telephone: (601) 276-2000 Carnegie Class: Assoc/MT-VT-High Trad
FAX Number: (601) 276-3888 Calendar System: Semester
URL: www.smcc.edu
Established: 1918 Annual Undergrad Tuition & Fees (In-District): $3,280
Enrollment: 1,959 Coed
Affiliation or Control: Local IRS Status: 501(c)3
Highest Offering: Associate Degree
Accreditation: SC, ADNUR, CAHIIM

01 President ... Dr. Steve BISHOP
05 Vice President of Academic Affairs ... Ms. Alicia SHOWS
10 Vice President of Financial Affairs ... Mr. Andrew ALFORD
32 Vice President of Student Affairs ... Dr. Brent GREGORY
18 Vice Pres Physical Resources ... Mr. Bill TUCKER
06 Vice President Admissions/Registrar ... Mr. Matthew CALHOUN
75 Asst VP for CTE ... Dr. Addie BOONE
37 Director Financial Aid ... Ms. Amber KELLY
09 Director of Institutional Research ... Mr. Matthew CALHOUN
08 Librarian ... Ms. Laura RIDDLE
39 Dir Student Activities/Housing ... Mrs. Lauren WOODWORTH

Tougaloo College (C)

500 West County Line Road, Tougaloo MS 39174-9999

County: Madison FICE Identification: 002439
Unit ID: 176406
Telephone: (601) 977-7730 Carnegie Class: Bac-A&S
FAX Number: (601) 977-7739 Calendar System: Semester
URL: www.tougaloo.edu
Established: 1869 Annual Undergrad Tuition & Fees: $10,600
Enrollment: 809 Coed
Affiliation or Control: United Church Of Christ IRS Status: 501(c)3
Highest Offering: Master's
Accreditation: SC

01 President ... Dr. Carmen J. WALTERS
05 Provost/VP Academic Affairs ... Dr. Bianca GARNER
111 VP Institutional Advancement ... Vacant
32 Vice Pres of Student Affairs ... Dr. Eric W. JACKSON
10 Vice Pres Finance Administration ... Vacant
18 Vice Pres for Facilities Management ... Mr. Kelle MENOGAN
110 Asst VP Institutional Advancement ... Dr. Linda DANIELS
08 Int Director of Library Services ... Ms. Susan SPRINGER
13 Interim Chief Information Officer ... Mr. Derrick CALDWELL
37 Director of Student Financial Aid ... Ms. Maria THOMAS
06 Registrar ... Ms. Carolyn L. EVANS
15 Director Human Resources ... Ms. Doretha PRESLEY
29 Director of Alumni Affairs ... Mrs. Doris BRIDGEMAN
36 Director of Career Services ... Ms. Whitney MCDOWELL
46 Int Dir of Sponsored Pgms/Research ... Mr. Kerry THOMAS
88 Director of TRiO ... Dr. Valvia WILSON
38 Director of Counseling Services ... Dr. Rosie HARPER
96 Purchasing Agent ... Ms. Tracey MINOR
19 Director Security/Safety ... Ms. Edna DRAKE
39 Director Student Housing ... Ms. Tracey PAUL
104 Director Study Abroad Education ... Dr. Loye ASHTON
105 Director Web Services ... Ms. Virginia VARDAMAN
41 Athletic Director ... Mr. Keith BARNES

University of Mississippi (D)

P.O. Box 1848, University MS 38677

County: Lafayette FICE Identification: 002440
Unit ID: 176017
Telephone: (662) 915-7211 Carnegie Class: DU-Highest
FAX Number: (662) 915-7010 Calendar System: Semester
URL: www.olemiss.edu
Established: 1844 Annual Undergrad Tuition & Fees (In-State): $8,660
Enrollment: 23,136 Coed
Affiliation or Control: State IRS Status: 501(c)3
Highest Offering: Doctorate
Accreditation: SC, ART, CACREP, CAEPN, CEA, CLPSY, DIETC, DIETD, FEPAC, JOUR, LAW, MUS, NRPA, PHAR, SP, SW, THEA

01 Chancellor ... Dr. Glenn BOYCE
05 Senior Associate Provost ... Dr. Noel E. WILKIN
10 Vice Chanc Administration & Finance ... Vacant
32 Vice Chancellor for Student Affairs ... Dr. Brandi HEPHNER LABANC
46 VC Research/Sponsored Programs ... Dr. Josh GLADDEN
28 VC Diversity/Community Engagement ... Ms. Katrina M. CALDWELL
30 Vice Chanc Development ... Mrs. Charlotte PARKS
26 Chief Marketing/Communications Ofcr ... Mr. Jim ZOOK
35 Asst VC Student Affs/Dean Students ... Dr. Brent MARSH
51 Assoc Prov/Dir Outreach/Cont Stds ... Dr. Tony AMMETER
06 Asst Provost & Registrar ... Dr. Charlotte Fant PEGUES
08 Dean of Libraries ... Ms. Cecilia BOTERO
13 Chief Information Officer ... Mr. Nishanth RODRIGUES
110 Exec Director Development ... Mr. Denson HOLLIS
29 Exec Director of Alumni Affairs ... Mr. Kurt PURDOM
37 Director of Financial Aid ... Mrs. Laura DIVEN-BROWN
36 Director of Career Center ... Ms. Toni D. AVANT
41 Interim Director of Athletics ... Mr. Keith CARTER
15 AVC/Dir of Human Res & Contr Svcs ... Mr. Clayton H. JONES
18 Director of Facilities Management ... Mr. Dean HANSEN
19 Dir/Chief Univ Police/Campus Safety ... Mr. Ray HAWKINS
38 Dir of University Counseling Center ... Dr. Quinton T. EDWARDS, JR.
23 Director University Health Services ... Mr. Alex LANGHART
39 AVC Student Affs/Dir Stdnt Housing ... Mr. Lionel MATEN
09 Director Institutional Research ... Dr. Katie BUSBY
22 Dir Equal Oppty/Reg Compliance ... Ms. Rebecca B. BRESSLER
100 Chief of Staff to the Chancellor ... Mrs. Sue T. KEISER
43 General Counsel ... Ms. Erika MCKINLEY
96 Director of Procurement Services ... Ms. Rachel R. BOST
06 Associate Registrar ... Mrs. Denise KNIGHTON
21 Controller ... Mrs. Nina JONES
07 Interim Director of Admissions ... Mrs. Jody LOWE
50 Dean School of Business Admin ... Dr. Kendall B. CYREE
49 Dean College of Liberal Arts ... Dr. Lee COHEN
81 Dean School of Applied Sciences ... Dr. Peter W. GRANDJEAN
53 Dean School of Education ... Dr. David ROCK
54 Dean School of Engineering ... Dr. David PULEO
61 Dean School of Law ... Dr. Susan DUNCAN
67 Dean of the School of Pharmacy ... Dr. David D. ALLEN
88 Dean School of Accountancy ... Dr. W. Mark WILDER
60 Dean Meek Sch Journalism/New Media ... Dr. H. Will NORTON
58 Dean of the Graduate School ... Dr. Annette KLUCK
92 Dean of SM Barksdale Honors College ... Dr. Douglass SULLIVAN-GONZALEZ
86 Associate General Counsel ... Mr. Perry SANSING
88 University Ombudsman ... Mr. Paul CAFFERA
116 Director of Audit ... Ms. Tanya SATTERFIELD
104 Director Study Abroad ... Mrs. Blair MCELROY
44 Director Annual Giving ... Mrs. Maura LANGHART

University of Mississippi Medical Center (E)

2500 N State Street, Jackson MS 39216-4505

County: Hinds FICE Identification: 004688
Unit ID: 17601701
Telephone: (601) 984-1000 Carnegie Class: Not Classified
FAX Number: (601) 984-1013 Calendar System: Semester
URL: www.umc.edu
Established: 1955 Annual Undergrad Tuition & Fees (In-State): N/A
Enrollment: N/A Coed
Affiliation or Control: State IRS Status: 501(c)3
Highest Offering: Doctorate
Accreditation: SC, CAHIIM, DENT, DH, IPSY, MED, MT, NMT, NURSE, OT, PHAR, PTA, RAD, RADMAG

01 Vice Chancellor Health Affairs ... Dr. LouAnn WOODWARD
05 Assoc VC for Academic Affairs ... Dr. Ralph H. DIDLAKE
23 Assoc Vice Chanc Clinical Affairs ... Dr. Charles O'MARA
46 Associate Vice Chanc Research ... Dr. Richard SUMMERS
17 Health System Chief Exec Officer ... Mr. Kevin COOK
10 Chief Financial Officer ... Mr. Nelson WEICHOLD
111 Chief Inst Advancement Officer ... Mr. Thomas H. FORTNER
15 Chief Human Resources Officer ... Ms. Paula M. HENDERSON
63 Vice Dean for Medical Educ SOM ... Dr. Loretta JACKSON-WILLIAMS
28 Chief Diversity & Inclusion Officer ... Dr. Juanyce TAYLOR
100 Chief of Staff to Vice Chancellor ... Dr. Brian RUTLEDGE
43 Interim Chief Legal Officer ... Mr. William C. SMITH, III
11 Chief Administrative Officer ... Dr. Jonathan WILSON
76 Dean Sch Health Related Professions ... Dr. Jessica H. BAILEY
88 Dean School Population Health ... Dr. Bettina BEECH
58 Dean Sch Grad Stds Health Sciences ... Dr. Joey GRANGER
66 Dean School of Nursing ... Dr. Julie SANFORD
52 Dean of School of Dentistry ... Dr. David A. FELTON
67 Assoc Dean for Clinical Affs/SOPH ... Dr. Leigh A. ROSS

University of Southern Mississippi (F)

118 College Drive, #5001, Hattiesburg MS 39406-0001

County: Forrest FICE Identification: 002441
Unit ID: 176372
Telephone: (601) 266-1000 Carnegie Class: DU-Highest
FAX Number: (601) 266-5756 Calendar System: Semester
URL: www.usm.edu
Established: 1910 Annual Undergrad Tuition & Fees (In-State): $8,624
Enrollment: 14,478 Coed
Affiliation or Control: State IRS Status: 501(c)3
Highest Offering: Doctorate
Accreditation: SC, AAFCS, ANEST, ART, AUD, CAATE, CAEPN, CIDA, CLPSY, CONST, COPSY, DANCE, DIETD, DIETI, JOUR, KIN, LIB, MFCD, MT, MUS, NURSE, PH, SCPSY, SP, SW, THEA

01 President ... Dr. Rodney D. BENNETT
04 Assistant to the President ... Mr. Houston ERNST
05 Provost & VP for Academic Affairs ... Dr. Steven MOSER
10 Int VP Finance & Administration ... Ms. Allyson EASTERWOOD
12 VP for Gulf Coast Campus ... Dr. Steven G. MILLER
108 Assoc Prov Institutional Effect ... Dr. Doug MASTERSON
53 Dean College Education/Psychology ... Dr. Trent GOULD
50 Dean College Business ... Vacant
66 Dean College Nursing ... Dr. Kathy MASTERS
72 Dean College Science/Technology ... Dr. Chris WINSTEAD
92 Dean of Honors College ... Dr. Ellen WEINAUER
76 Interim Dean College Health ... Dr. Trent GOULD
58 Dean Graduate School ... Dr. Karen COATS
08 Dean/University Librarian ... Dr. John EYE
18 Asst VP Planning & Facilities Mgmt ... Dr. Chris CRENSHAW
13 Chief Information Officer ... Mr. David SLIMAN
06 Registrar ... Mr. Greg PIERCE
25 Asst VP for Research Administration ... Ms. Marcia LANDEN
45 Dir of Institutional Effectiveness ... Mrs. Kathryn LOWERY
29 Alumni Activities/Exec Director ... Mr. Jerry DEFATTA
36 Director Career Services ... Mr. Russell ANDERSON
21 Asc VP for Finance & Controller ... Ms. Allyson EASTERWOOD
22 Title IX Coordinator ... Dr. Rebecca MALLEY
38 Director of Counseling Center ... Dr. Deena CRAWFORD
23 Director of Health Services ... Dr. Melissa ROBERTS
39 Director of Residence Life ... Dr. Scott BLACKWELL
15 Associate VP of Human Resources ... Mrs. Krystyna VARNADO
96 Director Procurement & Contracts ... Mr. Steve BALLEW
07 Interim Director of Admissions ... Ms. Susan W. SCOTT
88 Asst to Pres Military/Vet Stdnt Aff ... Gen. Jeff HAMMOND
102 Exec Dir USM Foundation ... Ms. Stace L. MERCIER
104 Assoc VP for Intl Programs ... Dr. Daniel NORTON
106 Dir Learn Enhancement Ctr ... Dr. Tom HUTCHINSON
43 Dir Legal Services/General Counsel ... Mr. Robert D. GHOLSON
86 Vice President for External Affairs ... Mr. Chad DRISKELL
37 Director Student Financial Aid ... Mr. David WILLIAMSON

Wesley Biblical Seminary (G)

1880 E County Line Rd, Ridgeland MS 39175

County: Hinds FICE Identification: 025162
Unit ID: 176451
Telephone: (601) 366-8880 Carnegie Class: Spec-4-yr-Faith
FAX Number: (601) 366-8832 Calendar System: Semester
URL: www.wbs.edu
Established: 1974 Annual Graduate Tuition & Fees: N/A
Enrollment: 76 Coed
Affiliation or Control: Interdenominational IRS Status: 501(c)3
Highest Offering: Master's; No Undergraduates
Accreditation: THEOL

01 President ... Dr. John E. NEIHOF, JR.
05 VP Academic Affairs/Academic Dean ... Dr. Chris LOHRSTORFER
07 Exec VP Recruitment/Student Svcs ... Rev. Rob POCAI
30 Vice President Development ... Mr. Joshua FREIDEMAN
10 Director Business Affairs ... Ms. Peggy PRICE
08 Director of Library Services ... Ms. Grace ANDREWS
06 Registrar/Director Financial Aid ... Mr. Karl LUMAN

William Carey University (H)

710 William Carey Parkway, Hattiesburg MS 39401

County: Forrest FICE Identification: 002447
Unit ID: 176479
Telephone: (601) 318-6051 Carnegie Class: DU-Mod
FAX Number: N/A Calendar System: Trimester
URL: www.wmcarey.edu
Established: 1892 Annual Undergrad Tuition & Fees: $12,600
Enrollment: 4,839 Coed
Affiliation or Control: Southern Baptist IRS Status: 501(c)3
Highest Offering: Doctorate
Accreditation: SC, CAEPN, CAHIIM, IACBE, MUS, NURSE, OSTEO, @PHAR, @PTA

01 President/Chief Executive Officer ... Dr. Tommy KING
03 Provost ... Dr. Scott HUMMEL
05 Vice President of Academic Affairs ... Dr. Garry M. BRELAND
10 Vice Pres Business Affs/CFO ... Mr. Grant GUTHRIE
32 Vice Pres for Student Support ... Mrs. Valerie BRIDGEFORTH
46 Vice President Inst Effectiveness ... Dr. Bennie R. CROCKETT
63 Dean College Osteopathic Medicine ... Dr. Italo SUBBARAO
12 Admin/Acad Dean Tradition Campus ... Dr. Cassandra CONNER
50 Dean School of Business ... Dr. Cheryl DALE
53 Dean School of Education ... Dr. Benjamin BURNETT
83 Dean Sch Natural/Behavioral Science ... Dr. Frank BAUGH
66 Dean School of Nursing ... Dr. Alicia LUNDSTROM
49 Dean School of Arts & Letters ... Dr. Myron NOONKESTER
64 Dean School of Music ... Dr. Wes DYKES
73 Chair School of Ministry Studies ... Dr. Daniel CALDWELL
84 Dean of Enrollment Management ... Mr. William N. CURRY
58 Dean of Graduate Studies ... Dr. Frank BAUGH
09 Director of Institutional Research ... Mrs. Susan CURRY
06 Registrar ... Mrs. Deborah HILL
08 Dean Libraries & Learning Resource ... Mr. Reese POWELL
29 Alumni Director ... Mrs. Pam SHEARER
26 Coordinator of Media Relations ... Ms. Suzanne MONK
13 Chief Information Officer ... Mr. Jeff ANDREWS
92 Director of Honors Program ... Dr. Jay RICHARDSON

114 Director of Budget Management .... Mr. Grant GUTHRIE
41 Athletic Director .... Mr. D. J PULLEY
18 Dir Facilities/Grounds/Maintenance .... Mr. Robert BLEVINS
12 Director of Keesler Center .... Ms. Amanda KNESAL
15 Associate VP of Human Resources .... Dr. Deidre SHOWS
19 Director Campus Security .... Mr. Tim SLADE
07 Director of Admissions .... Mrs. Alissa KING
04 Administrative Asst to President .... Mrs. Charlotte GREEN
106 E-Learning Coordinator .... Ms. Shanna MURRAY-LUKE
102 Assoc VP for University Enhancement .... Dr. Angela HOUSTON
37 Director Student Financial Aid .... Mr. William CURRY
39 Director of Housing .... Mrs. Anna STERLING-HINTON
43 General Legal Counsel .... Mrs. Julie HAWKINS
44 Annual Fund Director .... Mr. Dean PACE

MISSOURI

A. T. Still University of Health Sciences (A)

800 W Jefferson Street, Kirksville MO 63501-1497
County: Adair FICE Identification: 002477
Unit ID: 177834
Telephone: (660) 626-2391 Carnegie Class: Spec-4-yr-Med
FAX Number: (660) 626-2672 Calendar System: Semester
URL: www.atsu.edu
Established: 1892 Annual Graduate Tuition & Fees: N/A
Enrollment: 3,723 Coed
Affiliation or Control: Independent Non-Profit IRS Status: 501(c)3
Highest Offering: First Professional Degree; No Undergraduates
Accreditation: NH, DENT, OSTEO, PH

01 President .... Dr. Craig PHELPS
05 Sr VP Academic Affairs .... Dr. Norman GEVITZ
63 Dean KCOM .... Dr. Margaret WILSON
32 VP Student Affairs .... Mrs. Lori HAXTON
111 VP University Advancement .... Dr. Shaun SOMMERER
43 VP & General Counsel .... Mr. Matthew HEEREN
46 VP Inst Res Grants & Info Systems .... Dr. John HEARD
52 Dean MO Sch of Dentistry/Oral Hlth .... Dr. Dwight MCLEOD
58 Dean Col of Graduate Hlth Studies .... Dr. Don ALTMAN
52 Dean AZ Sch of Dentistry/Oral Hlth .... Dr. Robert TROMBLY
76 Dean AZ Sch of Health Sciences .... Dr. Ann Lee BURCH
63 Dean Sch of Osteo Med in AZ .... Dr. Jeffrey MORGAN
10 VP Finance & Administration/CFO .... Mr. Rick RIEDER
35 Assoc VP AZ Student Affairs .... Dr. Beth POPPRE
13 Asst VP Info Technologies/Services .... Mr. Bryan KRUSNIAK
07 Asst VP Admissions .... Dr. David KOENECKE
88 VP Univ Strat Partnershps/Diversity .... Dr. Gary CLOUD
45 Sr VP Strat Planning & Univ Init .... Dr. O.T WENDEL
25 Associate VP Sponsored Programs .... Mrs. Gaylah SUBLETTE
04 Asst to Pres & Secretary to BoT .... Mrs. Norine EITEL
06 Registrar .... Dr. Deanna HUNSAKER
08 University Librarian .... Mr. Harold BRIGHT
15 Asst VP Human Resources/AA Ofcr . Mrs. Donna BROWN WYATT
18 Director Facilities/Plant Operation .... Mr. Robert EHRLICH
38 Director Student Counseling .... Mr. Thomas VAN VLECK
96 Director Purchasing .... Mr. Corey LOUDER
19 Director Security .... Mr. Bob FRAIZER
28 Director of Diversity .... Mr. Clinton NORMORE
20 Associate VP Academic Affairs .... Dr. Ann BOYLE
110 Associate VP University Advancement .... Mr. Bob BEHNEN
88 Assistant VP CED .... Dr. Leonard GOLDSTEIN
21 Assistant VP for Finance .... Mrs. Tonya GRIMM
09 Director AT Still Research Inst .... Dr. Brian DEGENHARDT
29 Assoc Director Alumni Relations .... Mrs. Melody CHAMBERS

† Arizona campus accreditation includes ARPCA, AUD, CAATE, DENT, OSTEO, OT, PTA.

American Business & Technology University (B)

1018 West Saint Maartens Drive, Saint Joseph MO 64506
County: Buchanan FICE Identification: 041187
Unit ID: 457688
Telephone: (816) 279-7000 Carnegie Class: Bac/Assoc-Mixed
FAX Number: (888) 890-8190 Calendar System: Other
URL: www.abtu.edu
Established: 2001 Annual Undergrad Tuition & Fees: N/A
Enrollment: 890 Coed
Affiliation or Control: Proprietary IRS Status: Proprietary
Highest Offering: Master's
Accreditation: DEAC

01 President & CEO .... Mr. Ramsey ATIEH
11 Vice President .... Mr. Lute ATIEH
88 VP of Strategic Initiatives .... Mr. Eddie COLON
37 VP of Financial Aid/Compliance .... Dr. Michael CAMPBELL
05 Chief Academic Officer .... Dr. Luanne HAGGARD
13 Chief Information Officer .... Mr. Ramsey ATIEH
10 Chief Financial Officer .... Mr. Dan MARLOW
20 Program Development Officer .... Dr. Donald LADER
108 Accreditation/Compliance Officer .... Mr. Chad BREAZILE
06 Registrar .... Mrs. Kourtney DRAKE
07 Director of Admissions .... Mr. Richard LINGLE
29 Director Alumni/Career Services .... Ms. Debra HAYES

American Trade School (C)

3925 Industrial Drive, Saint Ann MO 63074
County: Saint Louis FICE Identification: 041748
Unit ID: 461573
Telephone: (314) 423-1900 Carnegie Class: Spec 2-yr-Tech
FAX Number: (314) 423-1911 Calendar System: Quarter
URL: www.americantradeschool.edu
Established: 2003 Annual Undergrad Tuition & Fees: N/A
Enrollment: 80 Coed
Affiliation or Control: Proprietary IRS Status: Proprietary
Highest Offering: Associate Degree
Accreditation: ACCSC

01 Chief Executive Officer/President .... Mr. John VATTEROTT, JR.

Aquinas Institute of Theology (D)

23 S Spring Avenue, Saint Louis MO 63108-3323
County: City of Saint Louis FICE Identification: 001632
Unit ID: 176600
Telephone: (314) 256-8800 Carnegie Class: Spec-4-yr-Faith
FAX Number: N/A Calendar System: Semester
URL: www.ai.edu
Established: 1951 Annual Graduate Tuition & Fees: N/A
Enrollment: 132 Coed
Affiliation or Control: Roman Catholic IRS Status: 501(c)3
Highest Offering: Doctorate; No Undergraduates
Accreditation: THEOL

01 President .... Rev. Mark WEDIG, OP
05 Academic Dean .... Rev. Michael MASCARI, OP
06 Registrar .... Mrs. Erin HAMMOND
84 Director Recruitment and Admissions .... Mrs. Amelia BLANTON HIBNER
32 Director Institutional Integrity .... Vacant
29 Director Alumni .... Mr. David WERTHMANN
37 Director Financial Aid .... Ms. Clare BEHRMANN
90 Director Instructional Technology .... Mr. Daniel MOORE
04 Admin Assistant to the President .... Mrs. Paula KAINTZ
10 Chief Financial/Business Officer .... Mrs. Donna THRO
30 Director of Development .... Mrs. Kathy LUTHER

Assemblies of God Theological Seminary (E)

1111 N Glenstone Avenue, Springfield MO 65802-2131
County: Greene FICE Identification: 012120
Unit ID: 176619
Telephone: (417) 268-1000 Carnegie Class: Spec-4-yr-Faith
FAX Number: (417) 268-1001 Calendar System: Semester
URL: www.agts.edu
Established: 1972 Annual Graduate Tuition & Fees: N/A
Enrollment: N/A Coed
Affiliation or Control: Assemblies Of God Church IRS Status: 501(c)3
Highest Offering: Doctorate; No Undergraduates
Accreditation: THEOL

05 Vice President/Dean of AGTS .... Dr. Timothy A. HAGER
20 Associate Dean .... Dr. Paul W. LEWIS
58 Dir Intercultural Doctoral Studies .... Dr. DeLonn L. RANCE
58 Dir PhD Biblical Interp & Theol .... Dr. Paul W. LEWIS
58 Director DMin Program .... Dr. John A. BATTAGLIA
42 Spiritual Life Coordinator .... Mrs. Christina M. VINCENT
88 Director of Veteran Center .... Mrs. Stormy M. DAVIS
08 Seminary Librarian .... Mr. Matthew CLARK
06 Seminary Registration/Degree Audit .... Mrs. Kathy L. HARRISON
37 Financial Aid Coordinator .... Mr. Trevor O'BRYAN
29 Alumni & Development Coordinator .... Vacant
04 Executive Assistant to VP/Dean .... Mrs. Deborah L. GEHRIS

† The Seminary continues to offer its educational programs as a distinct unit within the consolidated Evangel University, Springfield, MO.

Avila University (F)

11901 Wornall Road, Kansas City MO 64145-9990
County: Jackson FICE Identification: 002449
Unit ID: 176628
Telephone: (816) 942-8400 Carnegie Class: Masters/M
FAX Number: (816) 942-3362 Calendar System: Semester
URL: www.avila.edu
Established: 1916 Annual Undergrad Tuition & Fees: $19,900
Enrollment: 1,703 Coed
Affiliation or Control: Roman Catholic IRS Status: 501(c)3
Highest Offering: Master's
Accreditation: NH, CAEP, IACBE, NURSE, RAD, SW

01 President .... Dr. Ron SLEPITZA
05 Provost/VP of Academic Affairs .... Dr. Sue WILLCOX
10 Vice Pres for Finance/Admin Svcs .... Mr. Tim KLOCKO
84 VP for Enrollment & Athletics .... Ms. Alexandra ADAMS
32 AVP Student Development/Success .... Ms. Darby GOUGH
13 Coordinator Information Management .... Mr. Jon GAMBILL
26 Sr Dir Marketing/Communications .... Mr. Darren ROUBINEK
30 Sr Director Development .... Ms. Deanna NELSON
06 Registrar/Director Student Records .... Ms. Michelle DRISCOLL
08 Director of Library .... Vacant
37 Director of Financial Aid .... Mr. Paul GORDON
42 Dir Mission Effect & Campus Ministr .... Mr. David M. ARMSTRONG
21 Controller .... Mr. Joseph H. SJUTS
29 Director Alumni .... Mrs. Bailey CARR
41 Athletic Director .... Mr. Sean SUMME
15 Director of Human Resources .... Ms. Susie MATHERS
18 Director Campus Services .... Mr. Mike STUCKEY
40 Bookstore Manager .... Mr. John A. TARANTO
38 Coord Counseling & Career Services .... Ms. Elizabeth MCKINLEY
04 Admin Assistant to the President .... Mrs. Tracy D. OWENS
07 Director of Admissions .... Mr. Josh PARISSE

Baptist Bible College (G)

628 E Kearney St, Springfield MO 65803-3498
County: Greene FICE Identification: 013208
Unit ID: 176664
Telephone: (417) 268-6000 Carnegie Class: Spec-4-yr-Faith
FAX Number: (800) 819-8330 Calendar System: Semester
URL: www.gobbc.edu
Established: 1950 Annual Undergrad Tuition & Fees: $14,150
Enrollment: 297 Coed
Affiliation or Control: Baptist IRS Status: 501(c)3
Highest Offering: First Professional Degree
Accreditation: NH, BI

01 President .... Mr. Mark L. MILIONI
05 Academic Dean .... Mr. Terry A. ALLCORN
10 Vice President of Financial Affairs .... Mr. Jason L. TODD
32 Vice President of Student Affairs .... Mr. Nathaniel S. HARMON
18 Chief Facilities/Physical Plant .... Mr. Chris C. WILLIAMS
06 Registrar .... Mr. Terry A. ALLCORN
07 Director of Enrollment Services .... Mr. Nathaniel S. HARMON
37 Director of Financial Aid .... Mr. Brian RAINS
33 Dean of Men .... Mr. Bill J. LEVERGOOD
34 Dean of Women .... Mrs. Tina L. EBERT
15 Director of Human Resources .... Miss Emily MILIONI
19 Director of Security/Safety .... Mr. Glenn COZZENS
08 Director of Library Services .... Mr. Jon JONES
04 Administrative Asst to President .... Mrs. Barbara MILIONI
09 Director of Institutional Research .... Mr. Shannon L. MULFORD
108 Dir of Institutional Effectiveness .... Mr. Roland Q. DUDLEY
41 Athletic Director .... Mr. Darin MEINDERS

Bolivar Technical College (H)

1135 North Oakland Avenue, Bolivar MO 65613
Telephone: (417) 777-5062 Identification: 667033
Accreditation: ABHES

Brookes Bible College (I)

10257 St. Charles Rock Road, St. Ann MO 63074
County: St. Louis Identification: 667137
Telephone: (314) 773-0083 Carnegie Class: Not Classified
FAX Number: (314) 736-6293 Calendar System: Semester
URL: www.brookes.edu
Established: 1909 Annual Undergrad Tuition & Fees: N/A
Enrollment: N/A Coed
Affiliation or Control: Independent Non-Profit IRS Status: 501(c)3
Highest Offering: Associate Degree
Accreditation: BI

01 President .... Rev. Robert D. THURMAN, JR.
00 Chairman of the Board .... Dr. James CLARK
05 VP Academic Affs and Enrollment .... Rev. Joshua CLUTTERHAM
10 Chief Financial Officer .... Mr. Brian TOENNIES
08 Librarian .... Ms. Kathleen B. MILLIGAN

Bryan University (J)

4255 Nature Center Way, Springfield MO 65804
County: Greene FICE Identification: 030663
Unit ID: 369516
Telephone: (417) 862-5700 Carnegie Class: Bac/Assoc-Mixed
FAX Number: (417) 865-7144 Calendar System: Other
URL: www.bryanu.edu
Established: 1982 Annual Undergrad Tuition & Fees: $15,400
Enrollment: 296 Coed
Affiliation or Control: Proprietary IRS Status: Proprietary
Highest Offering: Master's
Accreditation: ACICS

01 Executive Director .... Mr. Scott HAAR

Calvary University (K)

15800 Calvary Road, Kansas City MO 64147-1341
County: Cass FICE Identification: 002450
Unit ID: 176789
Telephone: (816) 322-0110 Carnegie Class: Spec-4-yr-Faith
FAX Number: (816) 331-4474 Calendar System: Semester
URL: www.calvary.edu
Established: 1932 Annual Undergrad Tuition & Fees: $11,164
Enrollment: 267 Coed
Affiliation or Control: Independent Non-Profit IRS Status: 501(c)3
Highest Offering: First Professional Degree
Accreditation: NH, BI

01 President/CEO .... Dr. Christopher CONE
10 Chief Operating Officer/VP .... Mr. Randy GRIMM
05 Chief Academic Officer/VP .... Dr. Teddy BITNER
111 Chief Development Officer/VP .... Mr. Bill STEBBINS
32 Vice President of Student Develop .... Mr. Cory D. TROWBRIDGE
41 Athletic Director .... Miss Jeanette REGIER
100 Director of the President's Office .... Mr. John OGLESBY
97 Dean of the College .... Dr. Luther SMITH
73 Dean of the Seminary .... Dr. Thomas BAURAIN

58 Dean of the Graduate School .... Dr. Skip HESSEL
06 Registrar .... Mr. Gary ROGERS
13 Director Information Technology .... Mr. Aaron HEATH
84 VP of Enrollment Services .... Mrs. Tania EDWARDS
19 Director of Security .... Mr. Glenn WILLIAMS
37 Director of Financial Aid .... Mr. Robert CRANK
08 Head Librarian .... Miss Tiffany SMITH
108 Director of Institutional Effective .... Ms. Rose HENNESS
15 Human Resources Director .... Mrs. Gwen ALLEN
29 Alumni Relations Coordinator .... Mrs. Sara KLAASSEN
121 Director of The Academic Center .... Ms. Rose HENNESS
88 Director of Christian Ministries .... Mr. Joe EVERETT
109 Director of Food Service .... Mr. Joe DAPRA
105 Director Web Services .... Vacant
35 Asst Director of Student Services .... Mrs. Melony DYKMANN
26 VP of Marketing & Communications .... Mr. Shaun LEPAGE
18 Director of Maintenance .... Mr. Doug DRISKELL
88 VP of Western Initiatives .... Mr. Jeff CAMPA
39 Residence Life Coordinator .... Miss Rachel HONTZ
88 VP of Eastern Initiatives .... Dr. Allan HENDERSON
12 Int Dir of the Innovation Center .... Mr. Bill GEORGE

Central Christian College of the Bible (A)

911 E Urbandale Drive, Moberly MO 65270-1997
County: Randolph FICE Identification: 022664
Unit ID: 176910
Telephone: (660) 263-3900 Carnegie Class: Spec-4-yr-Faith
FAX Number: (660) 263-3936 Calendar System: Semester
URL: www.cccb.edu
Established: 1957 Annual Undergrad Tuition & Fees: $13,900
Enrollment: 239 Coed
Affiliation or Control: Christian Churches And Churches of Christ
IRS Status: 501(c)3
Highest Offering: Baccalaureate
Accreditation: BI

01 President .... Dr. David B. FINCHER
05 Vice President of Academics .... Dr. Jim ESTEP
10 VP of Business & Finance .... Mrs. Lara LAWRENCE
07 Director of Admissions .... Mr. Brent CROSSWHITE
88 Director of Stewardship .... Mr. Alan G. WILSON
04 Exec Assistant to the President .... Mrs. Sherry L. WALLIS
32 Exec Dir of Student Development .... Mr. Darryl C. AMMON
121 Dean of Student Success .... Dr. Eric A. STEVENS
35 Dean of Students/Assessment Coord .... Ms. Anne P. MENEAR
41 Athletic Director .... Mr. Jack DEFREITAS
08 Head Librarian .... Mrs. Patty A. AGEE
06 Registrar .... Mrs. Rhonda J. DUNHAM
37 Director of Financial Aid .... Mr. Rocky CHRISTENSEN
13 Director of Information Technology .... Mr. James WILLIAMSON
18 Physical Plant Manager .... Mr. Mark E. DUNHAM
40 Bookstore Manager .... Mrs. Kelly HARDING
35 Director of Student Services .... Mrs. Lori PETER
39 Residence Director - Women .... Mrs. Anne MENEAR
39 Residence Director - Men .... Mr. Rocky CHRISTENSEN
33 Dean of Men .... Mr. Darryl AMMON
101 Secretary of the Institution/Board .... Mr. Ronald SELF
106 Director Online Education .... Mr. James FRANKE
30 Director of Development .... Mr. Kevin BROWN
107 Assoc Dean of Professional Studies .... Mr. Brandon BRADLEY

† Onsite students accepted into a degree or certificate program will receive Full-Tuition Scholarship which equals cost of tuition up to 18 hrs/semester. Scholarship may be reduced from deficiencies in grades, Christian service, or chapel attendance.

Central Methodist University (B)

411 Central Methodist Square, Fayette MO 65248-1198
County: Howard FICE Identification: 002453
Unit ID: 445267
Telephone: (660) 248-3391 Carnegie Class: Masters/S
FAX Number: (660) 248-2287 Calendar System: Semester
URL: www.centralmethodist.edu
Established: 1854 Annual Undergrad Tuition & Fees: $5,760
Enrollment: 3,999 Coed
Affiliation or Control: United Methodist IRS Status: 501(c)3
Highest Offering: Master's
Accreditation: NH, CAATE, CACREP, MUS, NURSE, OTA, PTAA

01 President .... Dr. Roger D. DRAKE
05 Provost .... Dr. Rita GULSTAD
13 VP Technology & Planning .... Mr. Chad GAINES
111 VP Advancement/Alumni Rels .... Dr. Joshua JACOBS
32 VP Student Engagement .... Mr. Kenneth R. OLIVER
84 VP Enrollment Management .... Dr. Joseph PARISI
10 VP Finance & Administration .... Ms. Julee SHERMAN
08 Director of Information Resources .... Ms. Cynthia DUDENHOFFER
37 Director of Financial Assistance .... Ms. Karen EBBESMEYER
44 Asst Director of Affinity Giving .... Mr. Josh MCCARROLL
07 Director of Admissions .... Ms. Aimee SAGE
106 Asst Dean Online Programs .... Ms. Stephanie BRINK
09 Coordinator Institutional Research .... Ms. Amber MONNIG
26 Exec Dir Marketing Communications .... Mr. Scott QUEEN
04 Administrative Asst to President .... Ms. Mary LAY
15 Director of Human Resources .... Ms. Kimberly THOMSON
06 Registrar .... Ms. Brianne HILGEDICK
18 Chief Facilities/Physical Plant .... Mr. Derry WISWALL
19 Safety Coordinator .... Vacant
36 Director Student Placement .... Ms. Nicolette YEVICH
40 Bookstore Manager .... Ms. Jill BARRINGHAUS
39 Associate Dean of Students .... Mr. Brad DIXON

Chamberlain University-St. Louis (C)

11830 Westline Industrial, Ste 106, St. Louis MO 63146
Telephone: (314) 991-6200 Identification: 770494
Accreditation: &NH, NURSE

† Branch campus of Chamberlain University-Addison, Addison, IL

City Vision University (D)

1100 E 11th Street, Kansas City MO 64106-3028
County: United States FICE Identification: 041191
Unit ID: 457697
Telephone: (816) 960-2008 Carnegie Class: Spec-4-yr-Other Health
FAX Number: (816) 256-8471 Calendar System: Other
URL: www.cityvision.edu
Established: 1998 Annual Undergrad Tuition & Fees: $5,600
Enrollment: 113 Coed
Affiliation or Control: Other IRS Status: 501(c)3
Highest Offering: Master's
Accreditation: DEAC

01 Executive Director/President .... Dr. Andrew SEARS
05 Chief Academic Officer .... Dr. Joshua REICHARD
83 Addiction Studies Department Chair .... Mrs. Lynda MITTON
10 Financial Aid/Accounting Manager .... Mrs. Traci HEDLUND
07 Director of Admissions .... Ms. Nancy YOUNG

† Mail address is 31 Torrey St, Dorchester, MA 02124-3543.

College of the Ozarks (E)

PO Box 17, Point Lookout MO 65726-0017
County: Taney FICE Identification: 002500
Unit ID: 178697
Telephone: (417) 334-6411 Carnegie Class: Bac-Diverse
FAX Number: N/A Calendar System: Semester
URL: www.cofo.edu
Established: 1906 Annual Undergrad Tuition & Fees: $19,360
Enrollment: 1,508 Coed
Affiliation or Control: Independent Non-Profit IRS Status: 501(c)3
Highest Offering: Baccalaureate
Accreditation: NH, ACFEI, DIETD, NURSE, @TRACS

01 President .... Dr. Jerry C. DAVIS
03 Vice President .... Dr. Howell W. KEETER
05 VP Academic Affairs/Dean of College .... Dr. Eric BOLGER
10 Chief Financial Officer .... Mr. Sam KETCHER
21 Actg VP Voc Pgms/Business Affairs .... Dr. Weston T. WIEBE
88 VP Cultural Affs/Dean Character Ed .... Dr. Sue HEAD
07 VP Patriotic Activities/Dean Admiss .... Dr. Marci LINSON
42 VP Christian Ministries/Dean Chapel .... Dr. Justin CARSWELL
30 Dean of Development .... Mrs. Natalie RASNICK
11 Dean of Work Education/Admin .... Dr. Marvin SCHOENECKE
32 Dean of Students .... Dr. Nick SHARP
06 Registrar .... Mrs. Lacey MATTHEIS
29 Director of Alumni Affairs .... Mrs. Angela WILLIAMSON
36 Director of Career Center .... Mr. Jim FREEMAN
37 Director of Financial Aid .... Mr. Jeff FORD
26 Director of Public Relations .... Mrs. Valorie COLEMAN
96 Director of Purchasing .... Mr. Andy MCNEILL
38 Student Counseling .... Mrs. Pat MCLEAN
04 Assistant to the President .... Mrs. Tamara J. SCHNEIDER
04 Assistant to President Research .... Mrs. Elizabeth BLEVINS
13 Chief Info Technology Officer .... Mr. Jeffrey K. SCHNEIDER
18 Chief Facilities/Physical Plant .... Mr. Jody BRASWELL
41 Athletic Director .... Mr. Steve SHEPHERD
08 Librarian/Library Science .... Ms. Gwen SIMMONS
19 Director of Security .... Mr. Robert BRIDGES

Columbia College (F)

1001 Rogers Street, Columbia MO 65216-0001
County: Boone FICE Identification: 002456
Unit ID: 177065
Telephone: (573) 875-8700 Carnegie Class: Masters/L
FAX Number: (573) 875-7209 Calendar System: Semester
URL: www.ccis.edu
Established: 1851 Annual Undergrad Tuition & Fees: $22,704
Enrollment: 13,492 Coed
Affiliation or Control: Christian Church (Disciples Of Christ)
IRS Status: 501(c)3
Highest Offering: Master's
Accreditation: NH, MAC, NURSE

01 President .... Dr. Scott DALRYMPLE
04 Sr Exec Assistant to the President .... Ms. Mary BROWN
05 Provost/Vice Pres Academic Affairs .... Dr. Piyusha SINGH
51 VP Adult Higher Education .... Dr. Jeff MUSGROVE
11 SVP/Chief Operations Officer .... Mr. Kevin PALMER
106 VP Online Educ/Online Campus .... Vacant
111 Vice President of Advancement .... Ms. Suzanne ROTHWELL
10 Chief Financial Officer .... Mr. Bruce E. BOYER
32 Dean of Student Affairs .... Mr. Dave ROBERTS
18 Exec Director of Plant/Facilities .... Mr. Cliff JARVIS
26 AVP of Marketing .... Mr. Brad WUCHER
07 AVP of Admissions .... Ms. Stephanie JOHNSON
06 Registrar .... Ms. Jennifer THORPE
29 Director of Alumni Relations .... Ms. Ann MERRIFIELD
27 Exec Director of Public Relations .... Ms. Suzanne ROTHWELL
37 Director of Financial Aid .... Ms. Sharon A. ABERNATHY
08 Director of Stafford Library .... Ms. Janet CARUTHERS
35 Director of Student Activities .... Ms. Kim COKE
36 Director Career Services Center .... Mr. Dan GOMEZ-PALACIO
15 Executive Director Human Resources .... Ms. Patty FISCHER
23 Director of Health Services .... Ms. Judy WOOD
13 Chief Information Officer .... Mr. Gary STANOWSKI
55 Sr Dir Adult Higher Educ Acad Spprt .... Mr. Eric CUNNINGHAM
58 Associate Dean Graduate Studies .... Vacant
41 Athletic Director .... Mr. James ARNOLD
09 Director Institutional Research .... Ms. Misty HASKAMP
19 Director of Campus Safety .... Mr. Robert KLAUSMEYER
21 Bursar .... Mr. Randal SCHENEWERK

Conception Seminary College (G)

37174 State Highway VV, PO Box 502,
Conception MO 64433-0502
County: Nodaway FICE Identification: 002467
Unit ID: 177083
Telephone: (660) 944-3105 Carnegie Class: Spec-4-yr-Faith
FAX Number: (660) 944-2829 Calendar System: Semester
URL: www.conception.edu
Established: 1883 Annual Undergrad Tuition & Fees: $22,379
Enrollment: 75 Male
Affiliation or Control: Roman Catholic IRS Status: 501(c)3
Highest Offering: Baccalaureate
Accreditation: NH

01 Rector & President .... Rev. Brendan MOSS
11 Director of Administration .... Mrs. Amy K. SCHIEBER
32 Dean of Students .... Rev. Victor SCHINSTOCK
05 Dean of Academic Affairs .... Bro. Thomas SULLIVAN
10 Business Manager/Dir Auxiliary Svcs .... Bro. Jacob KUBAJAK
30 Development Director .... Mrs. Jenny HUARD
07 Director of Admissions/Registrar .... Mrs. Jeanette SCHIEBER
37 Director of Student Financial Aid .... Bro. Justin J. HERNANDEZ
29 Director of Alumni .... Bro. Thomas SULLIVAN
08 Librarian .... Mr. Chris BRITE
26 Director of Communications .... Mrs. Kaity HOLTMAN
13 Director of Information Technology .... Mr. Tony MEISTER
38 Director of Counseling Services .... Rev. Duane REINERT
41 Director of Wellness Program .... Mr. Skip SHEAR
18 Chief Facilities/Physical Plant .... Mr. Mark WIEDERHOLT

Concorde Career College (H)

3239 Broadway Boulevard, Kansas City MO 64111-2407
County: Jackson FICE Identification: 023616
Unit ID: 155283
Telephone: (816) 531-5223 Carnegie Class: Spec-4-yr-Other Health
FAX Number: (816) 756-3231 Calendar System: Other
URL: www.concorde.edu
Established: 1986 Annual Undergrad Tuition & Fees: N/A
Enrollment: 516 Coed
Affiliation or Control: Proprietary IRS Status: Proprietary
Highest Offering: Baccalaureate
Accreditation: ACCSC, COARC, DH, #PTAA

01 Campus President .... Katherin PACKARD
05 Academic Dean .... Heather NICKEL
07 Director of Admissions .... Monte SCHAICH
32 Director of Student Affairs .... Dan GURULE
37 Director of Financial Aid .... Sharon BALDWIN

Concordia Seminary (I)

801 Seminary Place, Saint Louis MO 63105-3168
County: Saint Louis FICE Identification: 002457
Unit ID: 177092
Telephone: (314) 505-7000 Carnegie Class: Spec-4-yr-Faith
FAX Number: (314) 505-7001 Calendar System: Semester
URL: www.csl.edu
Established: 1839 Annual Graduate Tuition & Fees: N/A
Enrollment: 532 Coed
Affiliation or Control: Lutheran Church - Missouri Synod
IRS Status: 501(c)3
Highest Offering: Doctorate; No Undergraduates
Accreditation: NH, THEOL

01 President .... Rev Dr. Dale A. MEYER
03 Executive Vice President/COO .... Mr. Michael LOUIS
05 Provost .... Rev Dr. Douglas L. RUTT
10 Sr VP for Finance/Administration .... Mr. Chad A. CATTOOR
111 Senior VP for Advancement .... Mrs. Vicki BIGGS
58 Dean of Advanced Studies .... Rev Dr. Gerhard BODE
06 Registrar .... Mrs. Beth R. MENNEKE
110 Executive Director Seminary Support .... Rev. John L. BUSH
08 Associate Provost/Dir Library Svcs .... Rev Dr. Benjamin HAUPT
88 Director Center for Hispanic Study .... Rev Dr. Leopoldo A. SANCHEZ
15 Director of Human Resources .... Mr. Thomas MYERS
18 Director Campus Facilities .... Mr. Martin HAGUE
36 Director of Placement .... Rev Dr. Glenn NIELSEN
37 Director of Student Financial Aid .... Mrs. Laura HEMMER
13 Chief Information Officer .... Mr. John KLINGER
29 Sr Coord Alumni Relations .... Ms. Melodie BOSTIC
04 Executive Asst to President .... Mrs. Pamela K. DAVITZ
07 Director of Admissions .... Rev. William WREDE
09 Director of Institutional Research .... Rev Dr. Alan BORCHERDING
44 Director Gift Operations .... Mrs. Valerie SOMMER

51 Director Continuing Education .... Ms. Erika BENNETT
88 Managing Editor of Seminary Public ...... RevDr. Travis J. SCHOLL

Cottey College (A)

1000 W Austin Boulevard, Nevada MO 64772-2763
County: Vernon FICE Identification: 002458
Unit ID: 177117
Telephone: (417) 667-8181 Carnegie Class: Bac/Assoc-Mixed
FAX Number: (417) 667-8103 Calendar System: Semester
URL: www.cottey.edu
Established: 1884 Annual Undergrad Tuition & Fees: $21,160
Enrollment: 270 Female
Affiliation or Control: Independent Non-Profit IRS Status: 501(c)3
Highest Offering: Baccalaureate
Accreditation: NH, MUS

01 President .... Dr. Jann WEITZEL
05 VP Academic Affs/Dean of Faculty .... Dr. Joann BANGS
88 Dir Center Women's Leadership .... Ms. Denise C. HEDGES
36 Coord Career & Transfer Planning .... Ms. Renee HAMPTON
04 Executive Asst to President .... Mrs. Tricia BOBBETT
10 VP for Administration & Finance .... Mrs. Amy RUETTEN
111 Int VP Institutional Advancement .... Ms. Sherri TAYLOR
32 VP for Student Life .... Mr. Landon ADAMS
42 Dir Spiritual Life & Diversity .... Ms. Erica SIGAUKE
30 Director of Development .... Ms. Staci KEYS
07 Director of Admissions .... Ms. Angela MOORE
06 Registrar .... Mr. William STANFILL
08 Library Director .... Ms. Courtney TRAUTWEILER
18 Director Physical Plant/Security .... Mr. T.J TUBBS
19 Dir Campus Security & Title IX .... Mr. Mark BURGER
27 Director of Public Information .... Mr. Steve E. REED
15 Director of Human Resources .... Ms. Betsy A. MCREYNOLDS
91 Director Administrative Computing .... Mr. Keith J. SPENCER
120 Instructional Technology Specialist .... Mr. Mike DOMBROSKI
37 Director of Financial Aid .... Mrs. Sherry R. PENNINGTON
90 Director Academic Computing .... Mr. Adam S. DEAN
39 Interim Director of Housing .... Blaklee SANDERS
41 Director of Athletics .... Ms. Stephanie BEASON
40 Bookstore Manager .... Mrs. Lois J. WITTE
09 Coordinator Institutional Research .... Mrs. Nancy KERBS
29 Director of Alumnae Relations .... Ms. Christi ELLIS
38 Coordinator of Counseling .... Ms. Jeanna SIMPSON
88 Director of PEO Relations .... Ms. Margaret HAVERSTIC
121 Coordinator Academic Advising .... Ms. Stephanie MCGHEE
85 Coord International Student Svcs .... Ms. Megan CORRIGAN

Covenant Theological Seminary (B)

12330 Conway Road, Saint Louis MO 63141-8697
County: Saint Louis FICE Identification: 004707
Unit ID: 177126
Telephone: (314) 434-4044 Carnegie Class: Spec-4-yr-Faith
FAX Number: (314) 434-4819 Calendar System: 4/1/4
URL: www.covenantseminary.edu
Established: 1956 Annual Graduate Tuition & Fees: N/A
Enrollment: 517 Coed
Affiliation or Control: Presbyterian Church In America IRS Status: 501(c)3
Highest Offering: Doctorate; No Undergraduates
Accreditation: NH, THEOL

01 President .... Dr. Mark DALBEY
05 VP of Academics .... Dr. Jay SKLAR
10 VP of Business and Finance .... Ms. Alice EVANS
111 VP of Advancement .... Mr. John RANHEIM
88 VP at Large .... Dr. Daniel M. DORIANI
08 Library Director .... Rev. James C. PAKALA
20 Dean of Academic Administration .... Ms. Jessica SWIGART
32 Dean of Students .... Rev. Michael HIGGINS
18 Director of Facilities & Operations .... Mr. David BROWN
07 Director of Admissions .... Mr. Mark SANDVIG
88 Senior Director of Business Develop .... Mr. Ken MCDONALD
37 Director of Financial Aid .... Ms. Melinda CONN
13 Director of Information Technology .... Mr. Ryan JOHNS
06 Registrar .... Ms. Betsy GASOSKE
29 Alumni/Placement Services Director .... Dr. Joel HATHAWAY
21 Controller .... Mr. Jason ROBEY
88 Director of Field Education .... Mr. Jeremy MAIN
26 Director of Communications .... Mr. Kent NEEDLER
38 Associate Dean of Counseling .... Mrs. Sabrina HICKEL
35 Associate Dean of Student Life .... Mr. Mark MCELMURRY
35 Associate Dean of Student Life .... Ms. Suzanne BATES
88 Associate Dean of Academic Services .... Ms. Diane PRESTON
15 Assoc Director of Human Resources .... Mrs. Betty BRADLEY
106 Assoc Director of Online Learning .... Mr. Aaron GOLDSTEIN

Cox College (C)

1423 N Jefferson Avenue, Springfield MO 65802-1917
County: Greene FICE Identification: 020682
Unit ID: 176770
Telephone: (417) 269-3401 Carnegie Class: Spec-4-yr-Other Health
FAX Number: (417) 269-3581 Calendar System: Semester
URL: www.coxcollege.edu
Established: 1907 Annual Undergrad Tuition & Fees: $11,920
Enrollment: 904 Coed
Affiliation or Control: Independent Non-Profit IRS Status: 501(c)3
Highest Offering: Master's
Accreditation: NH, ADNUR, DIETI, DMS, NURSE, OT, RAD

01 President .... Dr. Amy DEMELO
05 Vice Pres Acad Affairs/Inst Effect .... Vacant
10 Vice Pres Business/Finance .... Jayne BULLARD
32 VP Student Affs/Marketing/Comm/Dev .... Dr. Sonya HAYTER
58 Dean Interprof Graduate Studies .... Vacant
37 Director of Financial Aid .... Steve NICHOLS
07 Director of Admissions .... Antoinette MURPHY
08 Director Library Services .... Wilma BUNCH

Crowder College (D)

601 Laclede Avenue, Neosho MO 64850-9165
County: Newton FICE Identification: 002459
Unit ID: 177135
Telephone: (417) 451-3223 Carnegie Class: Assoc/HT-Mix Trad/Non
FAX Number: (417) 455-5702 Calendar System: Semester
URL: www.crowder.edu
Established: 1963 Annual Undergrad Tuition & Fees (In-District): $2,856
Enrollment: 4,960 Coed
Affiliation or Control: Local IRS Status: 501(c)3
Highest Offering: Associate Degree
Accreditation: NH, ADNUR, EMT, OTA

01 President .... Dr. Glenn COLTHARP
10 Vice President of Finance .... Ms. Amy RAND
05 Vice President of Academic Affairs .... Dr. Adam MORRIS
32 Vice President of Student Affairs .... Mrs. Tiffany SLINKARD
26 Assoc VP of Information Services .... Mrs. Mickie MAHAN
75 Assoc VP of Careers & Tech Educ .... Dr. Phillip WITT
20 Assoc VP of Academic Affairs .... Mr. Keith ZOROMSKI
07 Director of Admissions .... Mr. JP DICKEY
09 Director of Institutional Research .... Mr. Chett DANIEL
08 Director of Lee Library .... Mr. Eric DEATHERAGE
27 Director of Public Information .... Mrs. Cindy BROWN
41 Athletic Director .... Mr. John SISEMORE
37 Director of Financial Aid .... Mrs. Stephanie FERGUSON
15 Director of Human Resources .... Mrs. Michelle PAUL
111 Dir of Institutional Advancement .... Mr. Jim CULLUMBER
40 Bookstore Manager .... Ms. Colleen HOLLAND
36 Career Services Coordinator .... Ms. Abby TRIBBLE
13 Director of Information Technology .... Mr. Mitch CORDRAY

Culver-Stockton College (E)

One College Hill, Canton MO 63435-1257
County: Lewis FICE Identification: 002460
Unit ID: 177144
Telephone: (573) 288-6000 Carnegie Class: Bac-Diverse
FAX Number: (573) 288-6611 Calendar System: Semester
URL: www.culver.edu
Established: 1853 Annual Undergrad Tuition & Fees: $26,680
Enrollment: 1,134 Coed
Affiliation or Control: Christian Church (Disciples Of Christ)
IRS Status: 501(c)3
Highest Offering: Master's
Accreditation: NH, CAATE, IACBE, MUS

01 President .... Dr. Kelly M. THOMPSON
05 VPAA/Dean of College .... Dr. Lauren SCHELLENBERGER
32 Dean of Student Life .... Dr. D. Christopher GILL
07 Interim Director of Admission .... Ms. Erica MITCHELL
111 VP for Advancement .... Dr. Bill SHEEHAN
06 Registrar/Director Inst Research .... Mrs. Chris HUEBOTTER
08 Librarian .... Dr. Katherine MARNEY
26 Marketing and PR Coordinator .... Mr. Brian KROEGER
37 Director Financial Aid .... Mrs. Tina WISEMAN
29 Director of Alumni Programs .... Mrs. Melissa DUBUQUE
91 Exec Dir Admin Systems/Services .... Dr. Joseph LIESEN
10 Chief Financial Officer .... Mrs. Diane BOZARTH
15 Director of Human Resources .... Mrs. Amy BAKER
35 Coordinator of Student Activities .... Mr. Bill BOXDORFER
42 Chaplain .... Rev. Amanda SORENSON
41 Athletic Director .... Mr. Patrick ATWELL
40 Wildcat Warehouse Manager .... Mrs. Sharon FARR
04 Assistant to the President .... Ms. Cindy FREELS
19 Director Campus Security & Facil .... Mr. Michael BRINGER
49 Chair Applied Liberal Arts/Sciences .... Dr. Scott GILTNER
50 Chair Business Education & Law .... Mrs. Julie STRAUS
57 Chair Fine Applied & Literary Arts .... Dr. Dylan MARNEY
20 Assoc Dean for Exp Ed/External Rels .... Dr. Dell Ann JANNEY
92 Director of Honors Program .... Dr. Haidee HEATON
24 Media Coordinator .... Mrs. Julie WRIGHT
44 Director of the Annual Fund .... Mr. Steve MILLER
36 Dir of Career Services/Internship .... Ms. Robin JARVIS
39 Director of Residential Life .... Ms. Megan CATALANO
121 Associate Dean Academic Success .... Dr. Kim GAITHER
38 Dir Counseling/Student Wellness .... Ms. Susan MOON
09 Director of Institutional Research .... Mrs. Karla MCREYNOLDS
110 Director of Advancement Operations .... Mrs. Marjorie ELLISON
104 Director Study Abroad .... Dr. Melissa HOLT

Drury University (F)

900 N Benton Avenue, Springfield MO 65802-3791
County: Greene FICE Identification: 002461
Unit ID: 177214
Telephone: (417) 873-7879 Carnegie Class: Masters/M
FAX Number: (417) 873-7529 Calendar System: Semester
URL: www.drury.edu
Established: 1873 Annual Undergrad Tuition & Fees: $28,515
Enrollment: 3,512 Coed
Affiliation or Control: Independent Non-Profit IRS Status: 501(c)3
Highest Offering: Master's
Accreditation: NH, CAEPN, MUS

01 President .... Dr. Timothy CLOYD
05 Provost .... Dr. Beth HARVILLE
10 Vice President for Admin & CFO .... Ms. Chelsey DOLLARHIDE
32 EVP Student Affs/Dean of Students .... Dr. Tijuana S. JULIAN
111 Executive VP for Advancement .... Mr. Wayne CHIPMAN
30 EVP Development & Campaign Director .... Ms. Amy AMASON
13 Executive Vice President/CIO .... Mr. David J. HINSON
20 Assoc VP Academic Affairs Quality .... Dr. Peter K. MEIDLINGER
84 EVP Enrollment Management .... Mr. Kevin KROPF
26 EVP Marketing and Communications .... Ms. Wendy FLANAGAN
51 EVP Enrollment Mgt & Ops - CCPS .... Ms. Kimbrea BROWNING
43 Exec VP Univ Rels/General Counsel .... Mr. Aaron JONES
06 Registrar .... Mrs. Cindy M. JONES
14 AVP Tech Svcs/Sr Dir Info Svcs .... Mr. Val SERAFIMOV
37 Director of Financial Aid .... Ms. Rebecca AHRENS
08 Director of FW Olin Library .... Mr. William GARVIN
36 Dir Career Planning & Development .... Ms. Emily BUCKMASTER
15 Director of Human Resources .... Ms. Marilyn HARRIS
09 Director of Institutional Research .... Dr. Justin LEINAWEAVER
18 Director of Facilities Operations .... Mr. Brandon GAMMILL
38 Dir Counseling/Disability/Testing .... Mr. Ed DERR
19 Executive Director Safety/Security .... Ms. Sarene DEEDS
35 Director of Orientation .... Ms. Jennifer STEWART
39 Dir of Student Housing .... Ms. Holly BINDER
40 Director Univ Bookstore .... Ms. Valerie RAINS
41 Director of Athletics .... Mr. Corey BRAY
42 Chaplain .... Dr. Peter BROWNING
04 Executive Asst to President .... Ms. Bonnie WILCOX
104 Associate Dean Intl Programs .... Dr. Thomas RUSSO
106 Dean Online Education .... Dr. Leah BLAKEY
50 Dean School of Business .... Dr. Clifton PETTY
53 Dean School of Education .... Dr. Shannon CUFF
102 Dir Foundation/Corporate Relations .... Ms. Emma RUZICKA
28 Director of Diversity .... Ms. Rosalyn THOMAS
29 Director Alumni Relations .... Ms. Andrea BATTAGLIA
07 Director of Admissions .... Ms. Lindsay TOBIN
30 Director of Development .... Vacant
44 Director Annual Giving .... Ms. Melanie EARL-REPLOGLE

Drury University Ft. Leonard Wood Campus (G)

4904 Constitution Drive, Ft. Leonard Wood MO 65473
Telephone: (573) 329-4400 Identification: 770319
Accreditation: &NH

Drury University Lebanon Campus (H)

122 E. Commercial Street, Lebanon MO 65536
Telephone: (417) 532-9828 Identification: 770320
Accreditation: &NH

Drury University Rolla Campus (I)

1034 S. Bishop Avenue, Rolla MO 65401
Telephone: (573) 368-4959 Identification: 770321
Accreditation: &NH

East Central College (J)

1964 Prairie Dell Road, Union MO 63084-0529
County: Franklin FICE Identification: 008862
Unit ID: 177250
Telephone: (636) 584-6500 Carnegie Class: Assoc/HT-Mix Trad/Non
FAX Number: (636) 583-1897 Calendar System: Semester
URL: www.eastcentral.edu
Established: 1968 Annual Undergrad Tuition & Fees (In-District): $2,592
Enrollment: 2,897 Coed
Affiliation or Control: Local IRS Status: 501(c)3
Highest Offering: Associate Degree
Accreditation: NH, ACFEI, ART, CAHIIM, EMT, MAC, MUS, NAIT, OTA

01 President .... Dr. C. Jon BAUER
10 Vice Pres Finance/Administration .... Vacant
05 Vice President Academic Affairs .... Ms. Robyn WALTER
32 Vice President Student Development .... Mr. Heath MARTIN
26 VP External Relations .... Mr. Joel DOEPKER
12 Director ECC Rolla .... Ms. Christina M. AYRES
102 Exec Director Foundation .... Vacant
18 Director Facilities & Grounds .... Mr. Tot PRATT
08 Director of Library Services .... Ms. Lisa M. FARRELL
96 Purchasing Manager .... Ms. Melissa D. POPP
79 Dean of Instruction .... Ms. Ann BOEHMER
81 Div Chair Math/Engineering/Science .... Dr. Isaiah KELLOGG
75 Dean of Career & Technical Educ .... Mr. Richard HUDANICK
83 Division Chair Social Sciences .... Dr. William CUNNINGHAM
64 Division Chair Music .... Mr. Timothy SEXTON
15 Director Human Resources .... Ms. Wendy HARTMANN
76 Dean of Health Sciences .... Ms. Nancy MITCHELL
37 Director Financial Aid .... Ms. Karen GRIFFIN
06 Registrar .... Ms. Sarah SCROGGINS
21 Director Financial Svcs/Comptroller .... Ms. Annette MOORE
09 Director of Institutional Research .... Ms. Bethany L. LOHDEN
27 Director of Public Relations .... Mr. Jay SCHERDER
13 Director Information Technology .... Mr. Doug HOUSTON
40 Bookstore/Mail/Imaging Coordinator .... Mr. Doug A. AGEE
121 Coordinator Advisement Services .... Mr. Paul LAMPE
103 Executive Director Workforce Devel .... Mr. Edward SHELTON
51 Coordinator Adult Educ & Literacy .... Ms. Alice WHALEN
24 Coordinator Instructional Design .... Mr. R. Chad BALDWIN
35 Coordinator Student Activities .... Ms. Courtney HENRICHSEN
04 Executive Asst to President .... Ms. Bonnie S. GARDNER

41 Athletic Director .... Mr. Jay MEHRHOFF
101 Secretary of the Institution/Board .... Ms. Bonnie GARDNER

Eden Theological Seminary (A)

475 E Lockwood Avenue,
Webster Groves MO 63119-3192

County: Saint Louis — FICE Identification: 002462
Unit ID: 177278
Telephone: (314) 961-3627 — Carnegie Class: Spec-4-yr-Faith
FAX Number: (314) 962-9918 — Calendar System: 4/1/4
URL: www.eden.edu
Established: 1850 — Annual Graduate Tuition & Fees: N/A
Enrollment: 136 — Coed
Affiliation or Control: United Church Of Christ — IRS Status: 501(c)3
Highest Offering: Doctorate; No Undergraduates
Accreditation: NH, THEOL

01 President .... Dr. David M. GREENHAW
05 Academic Dean .... Dr. Sharon TAN
06 Registrar .... Ms. Michelle WOBBE
07 Director of Admissions .... Rev. Ray ROBINSON
04 Admin Asst to the President .... Ms. Danita CARTER
32 Dean of Students .... Rev. Carol SHANKS
10 Chief Financial Officer .... Ms. Tammy CRAIG
30 Director of Development .... Ms. Sandi LAFATA
15 Chief Human Resources Officer .... Ms. Trina OWENS
26 Chief Public Rels/Mktg/Comm Ofcr .... Ms. Lisa BROWN
101 Secretary of the Institution/Board .... Ms. Denise D. STAUFFER
18 Chief Facilities/Physical Plant .... Ms. Heather SHAW

Evangel University (B)

1111 N Glenstone, Springfield MO 65802-2191

County: Greene — FICE Identification: 002463
Unit ID: 177339
Telephone: (417) 865-2815 — Carnegie Class: Masters/M
FAX Number: (417) 865-9599 — Calendar System: Semester
URL: www.evangel.edu
Established: 1955 — Annual Undergrad Tuition & Fees: $23,421
Enrollment: 2,112 — Coed
Affiliation or Control: Assemblies Of God Church — IRS Status: 501(c)3
Highest Offering: Doctorate
Accreditation: NH, ACBSP, CAATE, CACREP, MUS, SW

01 President .... Dr. Carol A. TAYLOR
10 Vice Pres for Business/Finance .... Ms. Linda ALLEN
32 VP for Student Development .... Dr. Sheri PHILLIPS
30 VP for University Advancement .... Dr. Michael KOLSTAD
05 VP for Academic Affairs/Provost .... Dr. Michael MCCORCLE
84 Vice Pres Enrollment Management .... Mr. Chris BELCHER
18 Director of Physical Plant .... Mr. Brian HAUFF
41 Director of Athletics .... Dr. Dennis MCDONALD
06 Registrar .... Mrs. Cathy WILLIAMS
08 Librarian .... Mr. Richard OLIVER
19 Director of Public Safety .... Mr. Todd REVELL
38 Director of Counseling Services .... Mr. Brian UPTON
29 Director Alumni Relations .... Mr. Doug JENKINS
37 Dir of Student Financial Services .... Mrs. Valerie SHARP
36 Career Development/Placement .... Mrs. Shannon MCCLURE
42 Campus Pastor .... Rev. Greg JOHNS
26 Director of Public Relations .... Mr. Paul LOGSDON
27 Chief Communications/Marketing Ofcr .... Ms. Patricia HANSEN
23 Director of Health Services .... Ms. Susan BRYAN
21 Controller .... Mr. Dan EDWARDS
35 Director Student Life .... Miss Gina RENTSCHLER
15 Director of Human Resources .... Mrs. Samantha TYLER
39 Housing Coordinator .... Mrs. Pamela SMALLWOOD
09 Director of Institutional Research .... Dr. Linda WELLBORN
04 Executive Asst to President .... Mrs. Angela DENSE
101 Secretary of the Institution/Board .... Mrs. Angela DENSE

Fontbonne University (C)

6800 Wydown Boulevard, Saint Louis MO 63105-3098

County: Saint Louis — FICE Identification: 002464
Unit ID: 177418
Telephone: (314) 862-3456 — Carnegie Class: Masters/L
FAX Number: (314) 889-1451 — Calendar System: Semester
URL: www.fontbonne.edu
Established: 1923 — Annual Undergrad Tuition & Fees: $26,340
Enrollment: 1,375 — Coed
Affiliation or Control: Roman Catholic — IRS Status: 501(c)3
Highest Offering: Doctorate
Accreditation: NH, ACBSP, CAEP, DIETD, SP, SW

01 President .... Dr. J. Michael PRESSIMONE
05 Vice President Academic Affairs .... Dr. Carey ADAMS
30 Vice President Advancement .... Mrs. Kitty LOHRUM
32 Vice President Student Affairs .... Mr. Joseph DEIGHTON
10 Vice President Finance & Admin/CFO .... Ms. Lisa VANSICKLE
84 Vice President Enrollment Mgt .... Vacant
13 Director of Information Technology .... Mr. Robert HUDSON
35 Associate Vice Pres Student Affairs .... Mrs. Carla HICKMAN
20 Associate VP Acad Affairs .... Dr. Corinne WOHLFORD
49 Dean Arts & Sciences .... Dr. Adam WEYHAUPT
50 Dean Global Business/Prof Studies .... Vacant
76 Dean Educ/Allied Health Prof .... Dr. Gale RICE
06 Interim Registrar .... Ms. Ann KAUFFMAN
15 Director Human Resources .... Mrs. Linda PIPITONE
08 University Librarian .... Dr. Sharon MCCASLIN
45 Acad/Disabilities Resources Coord .... Mrs. Regina WADE JOHNSON
09 Director Inst Research & Assessment .... Mrs. Meaghan ONG
26 Exec Dir Communications/Marketing .... Vacant
106 Director Online Programs .... Ms. Joanne MATTSON
88 Director Academic Advising .... Ms. Lee DELAET
85 Director International Affairs .... Mrs. Rebecca BAHAN
29 Director Alumni Relations .... Ms. Kate FLATLEY
41 Director Athletics .... Mrs. Maria BUCKEL
28 Director Multicultural Affairs .... Mr. James WILLIAMS
88 Dir Ldrshp Educ & Stdnt Activities .... Dr. Janelle JULIAN
19 Director Public Safety .... Mr. Larry VERTREES
07 Associate VP Admission .... Ms. Jenny CHISM
18 Director Physical Plant .... Mr. Brent SPIES
04 Exec Asst Office of Pres/Board .... Mrs. Yvonne FARMER
121 Dir Student Success/Engagement .... Ms. Amy SIMONS
36 Director Career Development .... Ms. Christine KELLER
38 Director Counseling and Wellness .... Vacant

Global University (D)

1211 South Glenstone Avenue,
Springfield MO 65804-1894

County: Greene — Identification: 666687
Unit ID: 247296
Telephone: (800) 443-1083 — Carnegie Class: Not Classified
FAX Number: (417) 865-7167 — Calendar System: Other
URL: www.globaluniversity.edu
Established: 2000 — Annual Undergrad Tuition & Fees: N/A
Enrollment: N/A — Coed
Affiliation or Control: Assemblies Of God Church — IRS Status: 501(c)3
Highest Offering: Doctorate
Accreditation: NH

01 President .... Dr. Gary SEEVERS, JR.
03 Executive Vice President .... Rev. Keith HEERMANN
05 Provost .... Dr. David L. DEGARMO
20 Vice Provost Academic Effectiveness .... Rev. D. Bradley AUSBURY
58 Dean Graduate School/Theology .... Dr. Randy J. HEDLUN
73 Dean UG School Bible & Theology .... Dr. Kevin FOLK
13 VP Info Tech/Media Dept .... Mr. Wade W. PETTENGER
10 Vice President Finance .... Mr. Mark PERRY
111 Vice President Advancement .... Dr. Steve TOURVILLE
07 Director of Enrollment Services .... Rev. Todd WAGGONER
06 Registrar .... Mrs. Lynne KROH
15 Director of Human Resources .... Ms. Jami NEMETI
04 Administrative Asst to President .... Mr. Gabriel RICHNER
08 Head Librarian .... Rev. Russ LANGFORD
09 Director of Institutional Research .... Rev. Brad AUSBURY
18 Chief Facilities/Physical Plant .... Mr. Bruce HAVENS

Goldfarb School of Nursing at Barnes-Jewish College (E)

4483 Duncan Avenue, Stop: 90-36-697,
Saint Louis MO 63110-1111

County: Saint Louis — FICE Identification: 006389
Unit ID: 177719
Telephone: (314) 454-7055 — Carnegie Class: Spec-4-yr-Other Health
FAX Number: (314) 362-9250 — Calendar System: Trimester
URL: www.barnesjewishcollege.edu
Established: 1902 — Annual Undergrad Tuition & Fees: N/A
Enrollment: 633 — Coed
Affiliation or Control: Independent Non-Profit — IRS Status: 501(c)3
Highest Offering: Doctorate
Accreditation: NH, ANEST, NURSE

01 President/Dean .... Dr. Nancy RIDENOUR
10 Vice Dean for Finance/Admin .... Mr. Djuan COLEMAN
32 Vice Dean Student Affairs/Diversity .... Dr. Michael WARD
15 Vice Dean Human Resources .... Ms. Rosalynn BRYANT
05 Dean Academic Affairs .... Dr. Mayola ROWSER
46 Associate Dean for Research .... Vacant
08 Library & Info Services Director .... Ms. Renee GORRELL
13 Director Information System .... Mr. Carlos PARDO
06 Registrar .... Ms. Terri MONTGOMERY
84 Director Enrollment Management .... Ms. Stacy BOGIER
04 Administrative Asst to President .... Ms. Beth HOOK
29 Director Alumni Relations .... Dr. June COWELL-OATES

Graceland University (F)

1401 West Truman Road, Independence MO 64050-3434

Telephone: (816) 833-0524 — Identification: 666262
Accreditation: &NH, NURSE

† Regional accreditation is carried under the parent institution in Lamoni, IA.

Graduate School of the Stowers Institute for Medical Research (G)

1000 East 50th Street, Kansas City MO 64110

County: Jackson — Identification: 667369
Telephone: (816) 926-4400 — Carnegie Class: Not Classified
FAX Number: N/A — Calendar System: Other
URL: www.stowers.org/gradschool
Established: 2012 — Annual Graduate Tuition & Fees: N/A
Enrollment: N/A — Coed
Affiliation or Control: Independent Non-Profit — IRS Status: 501(c)3
Highest Offering: Doctorate; No Undergraduates
Accreditation: @NH

01 President .... Dr. Betty DREES

Hannibal-LaGrange University (H)

2800 Palmyra Road, Hannibal MO 63401-1999

County: Marion — FICE Identification: 009089
Unit ID: 177542
Telephone: (573) 221-3675 — Carnegie Class: Bac-Diverse
FAX Number: (573) 221-6594 — Calendar System: Semester
URL: www.hlg.edu
Established: 1858 — Annual Undergrad Tuition & Fees: $22,750
Enrollment: 974 — Coed
Affiliation or Control: Southern Baptist — IRS Status: 501(c)3
Highest Offering: Master's
Accreditation: NH, ADNUR, NURSE

01 President .... Dr. Anthony W. ALLEN
05 VP for Academic Administration .... Dr. Miles S. MULLIN, II
45 VP for Institutional Effectiveness .... Dr. Raymond W. CARTY
10 VP for Business & Finance .... Mrs. Betty L. ANDERSON
84 VP for Enrollment Management .... Dr. Raymond W. CARTY
32 Dir Student Life/Int Dean of Stdnts .... Mr. Josh PIERCE
26 Director Public Relations .... Vacant
06 Registrar/Director of Records .... Mr. Jeremy WALLACE
37 Director of Financial Aid .... Mr. Brice D. BAUMGARDNER
29 Dir Alumni Rels/Development .... Ms. Lauren YOUSE
36 Assoc Dean Academic/Career Services .... Dr. Karry D. RICHARDSON
08 Library Director .... Mrs. Julie A. ANDRESEN
18 Chief Facilities/Physical Plant .... Vacant
19 Chief Public Safety/Compliance Ofcr .... Mr. Kyle BRENNEMANN
39 Director of Residential Life .... Mr. Joshua PIERCE
41 Athletic Director .... Mr. Jason D. NICHOLS
40 Campus Store Manager .... Mrs. Susan A. BOOTH
07 Director of Admissions .... Mr. Sean C. FREEMAN
30 Director of Development .... Mr. David DEXHEIMER
106 Dir Graduate and Online Division .... Dr. Jill ARNOLD

Harris-Stowe State University (I)

3026 Laclede Avenue, Saint Louis MO 63103-2199

County: Independent City — FICE Identification: 002466
Unit ID: 177551
Telephone: (314) 340-3366 — Carnegie Class: Bac-Diverse
FAX Number: (314) 340-3399 — Calendar System: Semester
URL: www.hssu.edu
Established: 1857 — Annual Undergrad Tuition & Fees (In-State): $5,388
Enrollment: 1,442 — Coed
Affiliation or Control: State — IRS Status: 501(c)3
Highest Offering: Baccalaureate
Accreditation: NH, ACBSP, CAEP

01 Interim President .... Dr. Dwyane SMITH
05 Vice President Academic Affairs .... Dr. Dwyane SMITH
10 VP Administration & Finance Affs .... Mr. Brian HUGGINS
13 Vice President IT Services .... Mr. James FOGT
111 Exec Dir Inst Adv/Spec Asst to Pres .... Vacant
06 Registrar .... Ms. Chauvette MCELMURRY
07 Dir Admissions/Advise/Retention .... Ms. Loretta MCDONALD
08 Interim Director Library Services .... Ms. Linda ORZEL
37 Director Financial Assistance .... Mr. James GREEN
15 Director of Human Resources .... Mr. Rodney GEE
38 Director Counseling Services .... Mrs. Vicki BERNARD
25 Exec Dir Title III/Sponsored Pgms .... Mrs. Heather BOSTIC
20 Interim Dir of Academic Success .... Dr. LaTonia COLLINS-SMITH
41 Interim Director of Athletics .... Ms. Shontele ALLEN
88 Director of Business Services .... Ms. Barbara A. MORROW
36 Director of Career Services .... Ms. Victoria HARRIS
21 Vice President & CFO .... Mr. Brian HUGGINS
53 Dean College of Education .... Dr. Quincy ROSE
50 Dean Busch School of Business .... Ms. Fatemeh ZAKERY
49 Dean College of Arts & Sciences .... Dr. Sudarsan KANT
19 Director Security/Safety .... Vacant
32 Vice President of Student Affairs .... Dr. Shawn BAKER
04 Executive Asst to the President .... Ms. Connie ZENTZ
26 Exe Dir of Communications & Mktg .... Dr. Alandrea STEWART
39 Asst Dean/Director Resident Life .... Ms. Sarah UPHOFF
84 Dean of Enrollment Management .... Mr. Reynolda BROWN

Heartland Christian College (J)

500 New Creation Rd, Newark MO 63458

County: Knox — Identification: 667091
Telephone: (660) 284-4800 — Carnegie Class: Not Classified
FAX Number: (680) 284-4098 — Calendar System: Semester
URL: www.heartlandcollege.edu
Established: 1992 — Annual Undergrad Tuition & Fees: N/A
Enrollment: N/A — Coed
Affiliation or Control: Non-denominational — IRS Status: 501(c)3
Highest Offering: Associate Degree
Accreditation: BI

01 President .... Kris R. PALMER
05 Chief Academic Officer .... Martha PALMER
10 CFO .... David BARTON
06 Registrar .... Crystin RUTHERFORD
08 Head Librarian .... Molly NICKERSON

Jefferson College (A)

1000 Viking Drive, Hillsboro MO 63050-2441
County: Jefferson FICE Identification: 002468
Unit ID: 177676
Telephone: (636) 797-3000 Carnegie Class: Assoc/MT-VT-High Trad
FAX Number: (636) 789-4012 Calendar System: Semester
URL: www.jeffco.edu
Established: 1963 Annual Undergrad Tuition & Fees (In-District): $3,330
Enrollment: 4,439 Coed
Affiliation or Control: State/Local IRS Status: 501(c)3
Highest Offering: Associate Degree
Accreditation: NH, CAHIIM, EMT, OTA, PTAA, RAD

01 President ... Dr. Raymond V. CUMMISKEY
02 President-Elect ... Dr. Dena MCCAFFREY
04 Exec Asst to the President & Board ... Ms. Lisa VINYARD
05 VP Instruction ... Vacant
10 VP Finance & Administration ... Mr. Daryl GEHBAUER
32 VP Student Services ... Dr. Kimberly HARVEY
101 Sr Dir Online Educ/Assess/CAO ... Mr. Allan WAMSLEY
20 Dean of Instruction ... Mr. Chris DEGEARE
21 Controller ... Mr. Mark JANIESCH
15 Director of Human Resources ... Ms. Tasha WELSH
30 Exec Director of Development ... Ms. Karen WICKS
26 Director of PR & Marketing ... Mr. Roger BARRENTINE
13 Director Information Technology ... Mr. Tracy JAMES
45 Dir Financial Reporting/Analysis ... Ms. Kathy KUHLMANN
06 Registrar ... Ms. Stacey WILSON
50 Assoc Dean Business/Social Science ... Dr. Terry KITE
79 Assoc Dean Humanities ... Dr. Michael BOOKER
76 Assoc Dean Science & Health ... Mr. Kenny WILSON
81 Assoc Dean Math/Physics/Technology ... Vacant
37 Director Student Financial Services ... Ms. Sarah BRIGHT
84 Director Enrollment Services ... Ms. Holly LINCOLN
96 Director of Purchasing ... Ms. Sheree BELL
08 Director Library Services ... Ms. Lisa PRITCHARD
41 Director Athletics ... Mr. Robert DEUTSCHMAN
31 Director Business/Community Develop ... Mr. Bryan HERRICK
18 Director Buildings & Grounds ... Mr. Dale RICHARDSON
19 Director Public Safety Programs ... Ms. Diane SCANGA
66 Director of Nursing ... Ms. Amy MCDANIEL
121 Director Advising & Retention ... Ms. Kathy JOHNSTON
124 Director Student Support Services ... Ms. Diane ARNZEN
45 Dir Institutional Effec/Strat Plng ... Ms. Patricia AUMANN
74 Director Veterinary Technology ... Ms. Dana NEVOIS
88 Director Child Care Center ... Ms. Stephanie CAGE
39 Director Residential & Student Life ... Ms. Kristen YELTON
55 Director Adult Educ/Literacy ... Ms. Julie JOHNS

Kansas City Art Institute (B)

4415 Warwick Boulevard, Kansas City MO 64111-1874
County: Jackson FICE Identification: 002473
Unit ID: 177746
Telephone: (816) 472-4852 Carnegie Class: Spec-4-yr-Arts
FAX Number: (816) 472-3493 Calendar System: Semester
URL: www.kcai.edu
Established: 1885 Annual Undergrad Tuition & Fees: $38,400
Enrollment: 663 Coed
Affiliation or Control: Independent Non-Profit IRS Status: 501(c)3
Highest Offering: Baccalaureate
Accreditation: NH, ART

01 The Nerman Family President ... Mr. Tony JONES
10 EVP for Administration/CFO ... Vacant
05 EVP for Academic Affairs ... Dr. Bambi BURGARD
111 Senior VP for Advancement ... Ms. Nicolle RATLIFF
20 VP for Academic Affairs ... Dr. Milton KATZ
15 VP of Human Resources ... Vacant
13 Vice Pres/Chief Information Officer ... Vacant
32 Dean of Student Affairs ... Ms. Gina GOLBA
84 VP for Enrollment ... Ms. Karen TOWNSEND
20 Senior Academic Affairs Specialist ... Ms. Julia WELLES
26 Director of Communications and PR ... Mr. Whit BONES
51 Dir Continuing/Professional Studies ... Ms. Cambria POTTER
06 Registrar ... Ms. Nancy EASTMAN
35 Assistant Dean of Student Affairs ... Mr. Joe TIMSON
38 Psychologist and Counseling Coord ... Ms. Elisabeth SUNDERMEIER
18 Facilities Director/Plant Services ... Ms. Roxie CURTIS
29 Director of Alumni Relations ... Ms. Charlotte MATTHEWS
37 Director of Financial Aid ... Ms. Lori BAER
36 Dir of Acad Advising & Career Svcs ... Ms. Amanda HADJU
08 Director of Library ... Ms. M.J POEHLER
24 Director of Creative Media ... Mr. Aldo BACCHETTA
19 Director of Safety & Security ... Mr. Erik HULSE
109 Director of Auxiliary Services ... Ms. Jennifer BOE
88 Director of H&R Block Artspace ... Ms. Raechell SMITH
21 Director of Finance & Accounting ... Vacant
04 Administrative Asst to President ... Ms. Marjorie BRADSHAW
39 Asst Dir of Housing & Student Activ ... Mr. Dexter EARNEY
102 Dir Foundation/Corporate Relations ... Mr. Randy WILLIAMS

Kansas City University of Medicine & Biosciences (C)

1750 East Independence Avenue, Kansas City MO 64119
County: Jackson FICE Identification: 002474
Unit ID: 179812
Telephone: (816) 654-7000 Carnegie Class: Spec-4-yr-Med
FAX Number: (816) 654-7101 Calendar System: Semester
URL: www.kcumb.edu
Established: 1916 Annual Graduate Tuition & Fees: N/A
Enrollment: 1,190 Coed
Affiliation or Control: Independent Non-Profit IRS Status: 501(c)3
Highest Offering: First Professional Degree; No Undergraduates
Accreditation: NH, OSTEO

01 President & CEO ... Dr. Marc B. HAHN
05 EVP Academic & Rsrch Affs/Provost ... Dr. Edward R. O'CONNOR
10 Exec VP Finance/Operations ... Mr. Joseph MASSMAN
31 Vice Pres Community Engagement ... Dr. Jane LAMPO
30 VP for Institutional Advancement ... Dr. Jane LAMPO
84 Vice Prov Student/Enrollment Svcs ... Dr. Richard P. WINSLOW
45 Assoc Prov IE/Accred/Inclusion ... Mr. Adrian R. CLARK
32 Assoc Provost Student Services ... Ms. Sara E. SELKIRK
17 Exec Dean Col of Osteopathic Med ... Dr. Darrin D'AGOSTINO
12 Dean Joplin Campus ... Dr. Laura ROSCH
76 Dean College of Biosciences ... Dr. Robert WHITE
20 Vice Dean/COM KCU ... Dr. G. Michael JOHNSON
35 Director Student Activities ... Dr. Catherine DOBSON
100 Chief of Staff/Dir Govt Relations ... Dr. Brooke YODER
26 Manager Public Relations/Outreach ... Ms. Elizabeth ALEX
08 University Library Director ... Ms. Lori FITTERLING
88 Director of Strategic Initiatives ... Mr. Pete STOBIE
15 Director Human Resources ... Ms. Julie DEANE
06 Registrar ... Ms. Freda STRACK
18 Facilities Manager ... Ms. Anna GRAETHER
13 Director of Information Technology ... Mr. Lance HUGGINS
37 Director of Financial Aid ... Ms. Kristi NICHOL
88 Associate Dean of Clinical Educ ... Dr. Josh COX
88 Dir Clinical Education Development ... Ms. Valorie MILLICAN
19 Director Campus Operations ... Mr. James HERRINGTON
38 Director Counseling and Support Svc ... Dr. James DUGAN
29 Dir Alumni Dev/Annual Giving ... Mr. Stuart HOFFMAN
07 Director of Admissions ... Ms. Patricia HARPER

Kenrick-Glennon Seminary, Kenrick School of Theology (D)

5200 Glennon Drive, Saint Louis MO 63119-4399
County: Saint Louis FICE Identification: 002476
Unit ID: 177816
Telephone: (314) 792-6100 Carnegie Class: Spec-4-yr-Faith
FAX Number: (314) 792-6500 Calendar System: Semester
URL: www.kenrick.edu
Established: 1893 Annual Undergrad Tuition & Fees: $21,590
Enrollment: 130 Male
Affiliation or Control: Roman Catholic IRS Status: 501(c)3
Highest Offering: Master's
Accreditation: NH, THEOL

01 President/Rector ... Rev. James MASON
03 Vice Rector for Formation ... Rev. Paul HOESING
73 Dir Pre-Theol & Asst Vice Rector ... Rev. Fadi AURO
88 Director of Spiritual Formation ... Rev. Kristian TEATER
08 Director of Library ... Ms. Mary Ann AUBIN
42 Director of Worship ... Rev. Don ANSTOETTER
30 Director of Development ... Mrs. Kate SAUERBURGER
06 Registrar/Financial Aid ... Deacon Carl SOMMER
10 Chief Business Officer ... Mr. Greg NOVAK

Lincoln University (E)

820 Chestnut Street, Jefferson City MO 65101-3537
County: Cole FICE Identification: 002479
Unit ID: 177940
Telephone: (573) 681-5000 Carnegie Class: Bac-Diverse
FAX Number: (573) 681-5566 Calendar System: Semester
URL: www.lincolnu.edu
Established: 1866 Annual Undergrad Tuition & Fees (In-State): $7,632
Enrollment: 2,619 Coed
Affiliation or Control: State IRS Status: 501(c)3
Highest Offering: Beyond Master's But Less Than Doctorate
Accreditation: NH, ACBSP, ADNUR, CAEPN, NUR, SW

01 President ... Dr. Jerald WOOLFOLK
32 Vice President Student Affairs ... Dr. Marcus CHANAY
05 VP Academic Affairs/Provost ... Dr. Alphonso SANDERS
10 Vice Pres Administration/Finance ... Mrs. Sandy KOETTING
30 Director Philanthropy ... Vacant
83 Dean College of Arts & Sciences ... Dr. Jennifer BENNE
20 Asst Vice Pres Academic Affs ... Dr. Benjamin ARNOLD
47 Dean of Ag/Natural Sciences ... Dr. Majed EL-DWEIK
08 University Librarian ... Vacant
15 Director Human Resources ... Vacant
18 Director of Facilities and Planning ... Mr. Jeffrey TURNER
19 Chief of Police ... Mr. Gary HILL
41 Director of Athletics ... Mr. John MOSELEY
29 Director Alumni Relations ... Ms. Elizabeth MORROW
26 Director of University Relations ... Ms. Misty YOUNG
06 Registrar ... Ms. Adrienne WYATT
36 Director Career & Academic Support ... Mrs. Ruth CANADA
09 Director Ctr Assess/Inst Rsrch ... Mrs. Beth NOLTE
23 Director Student Health Services ... Mr. James SMITH
43 Legal Counsel ... Ms. Jacqueline SHIPMA
37 Director Financial Aid ... Ms. Kala SMITH
96 Director of Purchasing ... Vacant
13 Chief Information Officer ... Mr. John BAX
35 Assoc VP Stdnt Affs/Dean of Stdnts ... Dr. Miron BILLINGSLEY
12 Director Fort Leonard Wood Site ... Mrs. Barbara LANE
56 Dir Educational/Innovation/Extended ... Dr. Rachel SALE
100 Exec Asst to Pres/Chief of Staff ... Mr. Carlos GRAHAM
85 International Student Coordinator ... Ms. Jeanne CULBERSON
22 Dir Affirmative Action/EEO ... Vacant
66 Dean of the School of Nursing ... Dr. Ann MCSWAIN
50 Dean of the School of Business ... Dr. Eric BURGESS
53 Dean of the School of Education ... Dr. Marrix SEYMORE, SR.
07 Director of Admissions ... Ms. Tammy NOBLES
25 Director of Grants/Sponsored Rsrch ... Ms. Tiffany NOLAN

Lindenwood University (F)

209 S Kingshighway, Saint Charles MO 63301-1695
County: Saint Charles FICE Identification: 002480
Unit ID: 177968
Telephone: (636) 949-2000 Carnegie Class: DU-Mod
FAX Number: (636) 949-4910 Calendar System: Semester
URL: www.lindenwood.edu
Established: 1827 Annual Undergrad Tuition & Fees: $17,600
Enrollment: 10,025 Coed
Affiliation or Control: Independent Non-Profit IRS Status: 501(c)3
Highest Offering: Doctorate
Accreditation: NH, ACBSP, CAATE, CAEPT, NURSE, SW

01 President ... Mr. John R. PORTER
100 Chief of Staff & Asst Secy to BOD ... Mrs. Stefani SCHUETTE
05 Provost/VP Acad & Student Affairs ... Dr. Marilyn ABBOTT
30 Vice Pres University Relations ... Mrs. Lisa O'BRIEN ENGER
15 Vice Pres Human Resources ... Dr. Deb AYRES
84 SVP Enroll Mgmt/Student Engagement ... Mr. Terry WHITTUM
108 Chief Assessment Officer ... Dr. Bethany ALDEN-RIVERS
06 Registrar ... Ms. Christine HANNAR
10 Chief Financial Officer ... Mr. Frank SANFILIPPO
11 Vice Pres Operations ... Dr. Diane MOORE
41 Vice Pres Athletics ... Mr. Brad WACHLER
13 Vice Pres Information Technology ... Mr. TJ RAINS
26 Director of Communications ... Mr. Chris DUGGAN
08 Dean of Library Services ... Ms. Elizabeth MACDONALD
37 Director of Financial Aid ... Ms. Jamie SHAHIN
35 Dir of Student Involvement ... Ms. Angela ROYAL
28 Assoc VP Student Life & Diversity ... Ms. Shane WILLIAMSON
07 Asst VP University Admissions ... Ms. Kara SCHILLI
39 Director of Residential Life ... Mr. Terry RUSSELL
92 Director of Honors Program ... Mr. Zachary ALLEY
88 Asst Athletic Dir/Compliance ... Ms. Anna GIRDWOOD
89 Director of First Year Programs ... Mrs. Sarah LEASSNER
42 Chaplain ... Dr. Nichole TORBITZKY
79 Dean School of Humanities ... Dr. Kathi VOSEVICH
81 Dean School of Sciences ... Dr. Ricardo DELGADO
53 Dean School of Education ... Dr. Anthony SCHEFFLER
57 Dean Fine & Performing Arts ... Dr. Jason LIVELY
50 Dean Business/Entrepreneurship ... Dr. Roger ELLIS
51 Dean Evening/Adult Programs ... Dr. Gina GANAHL
76 Dean School of Health Sciences ... Dr. Cynthia SCHROEDER
106 Dean Online Education/E-learning ... Dr. Joe ALSOBROOK
19 Director Security/Safety ... Mr. Ryan ANDERSON
105 Webmaster ... Mr. Jason WAACK
22 Coordinator Title IX ... Ms. Kelly MOYICH
38 Director Student Counseling ... Mr. Jonathan HUNN
104 Director Study Abroad ... Dr. Molly HUDGINS

Logan University (G)

1851 Schoettler Road, Chesterfield MO 63017
County: Saint Louis FICE Identification: 004703
Unit ID: 177986
Telephone: (636) 227-2100 Carnegie Class: Spec-4-yr-Other Health
FAX Number: N/A Calendar System: Trimester
URL: www.logan.edu
Established: 1935 Annual Undergrad Tuition & Fees: $6,800
Enrollment: 1,371 Coed
Affiliation or Control: Independent Non-Profit IRS Status: 501(c)3
Highest Offering: First Professional Degree
Accreditation: NH, CHIRO

01 President ... Dr. Clay MCDONALD
30 VP Chiropractic/Alumni Relations ... Dr. Ralph BARRALE
111 VP Institutional Advancement ... Ms. Theresa FLECK
13 VP Information Tech/CIO ... Dr. Brad HOUGH
10 VP Admin Services/CFO ... Mr. Adil KHAN
05 Exec VP Academic Affairs ... Dr. Kimberly PADDOCK-O'REILLY
09 VP Strategic Perf/Cont Improv ... Dr. Lee VAN DUSEN

Maryville University of Saint Louis (H)

650 Maryville University Drive, Saint Louis MO 63141-7299
County: Saint Louis FICE Identification: 002482
Unit ID: 178059
Telephone: (314) 529-9300 Carnegie Class: DU-Mod
FAX Number: (314) 529-9900 Calendar System: Semester
URL: www.maryville.edu
Established: 1872 Annual Undergrad Tuition & Fees: $28,470
Enrollment: 7,689 Coed
Affiliation or Control: Independent Non-Profit IRS Status: 501(c)3
Highest Offering: Doctorate
Accreditation: NH, ACBSP, ART, CACREP, CAEPN, CIDA, MUS, NURSE, OT, PTA, SP

01 President ... Dr. Mark LOMBARDI
05 Vice Pres Academic Affairs ... Dr. Cherie FISTER
10 Vice Pres Finance & Facilities ... Dr. Steve MANDEVILLE
84 Vice President Enrollment ... Ms. Shani LENORE
30 VP Development and Alumni Relations ... Ms. Margaret ONKEN
32 VP for Student Life ... Dr. Nina CALDWELL
121 VP for Student Success ... Dr. Jennifer MCCLUSKEY

26 VP Integrated Mktg & Communications ..... Ms. Marcia SULLIVAN
20 Associate VP Academic Affairs ..... Dr. Tammy GOCIAL
46 VP Strategic Trends ..... Mr. Jeff MILLER
100 Chief of Staff ..... Ms. Jessica NORRIS
50 Interim Dean School of Business ..... Dr. Tammy GOCIAL
53 Dean School of Education ..... Dr. Mascheal SCHAPPE
76 Dean School Health Professions ..... Ms. Michelle JENKINS-UNTERBERG
49 Int Dean College Arts & Sciences ..... Ms. Jennifer YUKNA
08 Dean University Library ..... Ms. Sandra HARRIS
106 Dean Adult & Online Education ..... Ms. Katherine LOUTHAN
88 VP for Operational Excellence ..... Dr. Stephanie ELFRINK
07 Asst Vice Pres Enrollment ..... Ms. Melissa MACE
29 Director of Alumni Affairs ..... Mr. Andrew FOX
42 Dir Campus Ministry & Comm Service ..... Mr. Stephen DISALVO
35 Dean of Students ..... Dr. Kathy QUINN
36 Director Career & Prof Development ..... Ms. Erin BOSWELL
21 Controller/Dir Finance ..... Ms. Nikki PAYNE
37 Director of Financial Aid ..... Ms. Martha HARBAUGH
23 Director of Health & Wellness ..... Ms. Lisa MUNCH
28 Asst Dean Diversity/Inclusion ..... Mr. Turan MULLINS
13 Chief Technology Officer ..... Mr. Doug GLAZE
09 Dir Info Resources/Data Analytics ..... Mr. Jonathan SCHLERETH
90 Dir Learning Design & Technology ..... Ms. Pamela BRYAN WILLIAMS
18 Senior Project Manager ..... Ms. Angela WARNER
112 Director of Planned Gifts ..... Mr. Mark ROOCK
102 Dir Foundation/Corp Relations ..... Ms. Peggy MICHELSON
19 Director of Public Safety ..... Mr. Jair KOLLASCH
39 Director of Residential Life ..... Mr. Ryan MCDONNELL
104 Assoc VP/Dir Ctr for Global Educ ..... Dr. James HARF
88 Asst Athletic Dir Communications ..... Mr. Charles YAHNG
88 AVP Ops Systems/Quality Assurance ..... Ms. Elizabeth STACEY
88 Director Fresh Ideas Food Services ..... Ms. Linda THACKER
38 Director Personal Counseling ..... Ms. Jennifer HENRY
88 Chief of Staff for Development ..... Ms. Fay FETICK
88 Assoc VP Ctr for Institution Values ..... Dr. Alden CRADDOCK
04 Executive Asst to President ..... Ms. Maria KNIERIM
109 Director of Auxiliary Operations ..... Ms. Laura STEVENS
06 Assistant Registrar ..... Ms. Danielle MCCALL
105 Assoc Director Web Strategy ..... Ms. Kate BOELHAUF
41 Director of Athletics & Recreation ..... Mr. Lonnie FOLKS

Metro Business College (A)

1732 N Kingshighway, Cape Girardeau MO 63701-2122
County: Cape — FICE Identification: 021802
Unit ID: 178110
Telephone: (573) 334-9181 — Carnegie Class: Assoc/HVT-High Non
FAX Number: (573) 334-0617 — Calendar System: Other
URL: www.metrobusinesscollege.edu
Established: 1981 — Annual Undergrad Tuition & Fees: $11,375
Enrollment: 61 — Coed
Affiliation or Control: Proprietary — IRS Status: Proprietary
Highest Offering: Associate Degree
Accreditation: ACICS

01 VP of Operations ..... Ms. Mary BUCKLEY
12 Campus Director ..... Mrs. Jan REIMANN
05 Education Director ..... Mrs. Leslie WATKINS
37 Financial Aid Director ..... Mrs. Janie WARNE
36 Career Services Coordinator ..... Mrs. Diane JORDAN
07 Director of Admissions ..... Mrs. Denise ACEY

Metro Business College (B)

210 El Mercado Plaza, Jefferson City MO 65109
Telephone: (573) 635-6600 — Identification: 666454
Accreditation: ACICS

† Branch campus of Metro Business College, Cape Girardeau, MO.

Metro Business College (C)

1202 E Highway 72, Rolla MO 65401-3938
Telephone: (573) 364-8464 — Identification: 666455
Accreditation: ACICS

† Branch campus of Metro Business College, Cape Girardeau, MO.

*Metropolitan Community College - Kansas City Administrative Center (D)

3200 Broadway, Kansas City MO 64111-2429
County: Jackson — FICE Identification: 009137
Unit ID: 177995
Telephone: (816) 604-1000 — Carnegie Class: N/A
FAX Number: (816) 759-1158
URL: www.mcckc.edu

01 Chancellor ..... Dr. Kimberly BEATTY
101 Chancellor's Asst/Board Secretary ..... Ms. Cindy K. JOHNSON
12 President Penn Valley/Maple Woods ..... Dr. Tyjaun LEE
12 President Blue River/Bus & Tech ..... Dr. Thomas MEYER
12 President Longview ..... Dr. Utpal GOSWAMI
05 Vice Chanc of Academic Affairs ..... Dr. Caron DAUGHTERTY
32 Vice Chanc Student Success/Engagmnt ..... Dr. Kathrine SWANSON
10 Vice Chanc Admin Svcs/CFO ..... Dr. Donald CHRUSCIEL
13 Vice Chanc Inst Effect/Research/Tec ..... Dr. John CHAWANA
100 Chief Legal Officer ..... Ms. Sandra GARCIA
20 AVC Academic Affairs ..... Dr. Dreand JOHNSON
35 AVC Student Serv/Enrollment ..... Dr. Karen MOORE
18 Chief Facilities Officer ..... Mr. Jeffrey ULLMANN
15 AVC/Chief Human Resources Officer ..... Dr. Bill DIAL
103 AVC Workforce & Economic Dev ..... Vacant
37 AVC Student Financial Services ..... Ms. Dena NORRIS
21 AVC Financial Svcs & Admin Sys ..... Ms. Patricia A. AMICK
111 AVC of Advancement ..... Ms. Jessica RAMIREZ
108 Exec Dir Curriculum & Assessment ..... Ms. Tammie MAY
19 Chief of Campus Police ..... Mr. Londell JAMERSON, JR.
28 Executive Director Inclusion & Eng ..... Ms. Chocoletta SIMPSON
88 Director of Resource Dev ..... Ms. Kendra EDWARDS
13 Exec Dir Information Technology ..... Mr. Gary W. SCHIEBER
106 VP Online Instruction/Student Svcs ..... Ms. Deanna SNYDER
09 Executive Director Inst Research ..... Mrs. Melissa GIESE
88 Dir of Support Services PS ..... Mr. Domenick R. BROUILLETTE
114 Director Budget and Planning ..... Vacant
88 Director Student Disability Svcs ..... Ms. Kim FERNANDES
36 Director Career Education ..... Mr. Rusty SULLIVAN
88 Dir of CTE Accountability & Comp ..... Ms. Teresa A. LONEY
96 Executive Director of Procurement ..... Mr. Mitch BORCHERS
06 Registrar ..... Mr. Ryan MEADOR
41 Athletic Director ..... Mr. Brian BECHTEL

*Metropolitan Community College - Blue River (E)

20301 E 78 Highway, Independence MO 64057-2053
County: Jackson — FICE Identification: 032613
Telephone: (816) 604-1000 — Carnegie Class: Not Classified
FAX Number: N/A — Calendar System: Semester
URL: www.mcckc.edu
Established: 1997 — Annual Undergrad Tuition & Fees (In-District): N/A
Enrollment: N/A — Coed
Affiliation or Control: State/Local — IRS Status: 501(c)3
Highest Offering: Associate Degree
Accreditation: &NH

02 President ..... Dr. Thomas W. MEYER
03 Vice President ..... Dr. Warren E. HAYNES
04 Sr Exec Admin Asst to the President ..... Mrs. Kimberly A. MORICONI
05 Dean of Instruction ..... Mr. Steven JOHNSON
32 Dean of Student Development/Enroll ..... Dr. Jonathan L. BURKE
11 Director of Campus Operations ..... Mrs. Kimberly POINDEXTER
19 Campus Police Sergeant ..... SGT. Larry MCCREA
18 Facilities Superintendent ..... Mr. Clint JOHNSON

† Regional accreditation is carried under the parent institution Metropolitan Community College-Kansas City Administrative Center in Kansas City, MO.

*Metropolitan Community College - Business and Technology (F)

1775 Universal Avenue, Kansas City MO 64120-2429
County: Jackson — Identification: 666295
Telephone: (816) 604-1000 — Carnegie Class: Not Classified
FAX Number: (816) 482-5256 — Calendar System: Semester
URL: www.mcckc.edu/btc
Established: 1995 — Annual Undergrad Tuition & Fees (In-District): N/A
Enrollment: N/A — Coed
Affiliation or Control: Local — IRS Status: 501(c)3
Highest Offering: Associate Degree
Accreditation: &NH

02 President ..... Dr. Thomas MEYER
05 VP Instruction/Student Services ..... Dr. Warren HAYNES
20 Dean of Instruction ..... Dr. Steven JOHNSON
32 Dean Student Development/Enrollment ..... Dr. Jon BURKE
10 Director of Campus Operations ..... Mrs. Kim POINDEXTER
103 Exec Dir Workforce Development ..... Vacant
04 Admin Assistant to the President ..... Ms. Letonia (LT) TORRENCE

† Regional accreditation is carried under the parent institution Metropolitan Community College-Kansas City Administrative Center in Kansas City, MO.

*Metropolitan Community College - Longview (G)

500 SW Longview Road, Lee's Summit MO 64081-2105
County: Jackson — FICE Identification: 009140
Telephone: (816) 604-1000 — Carnegie Class: Not Classified
FAX Number: (816) 672-2025 — Calendar System: Semester
URL: www.mcckc.edu
Established: 1969 — Annual Undergrad Tuition & Fees (In-District): N/A
Enrollment: N/A — Coed
Affiliation or Control: Local — IRS Status: 501(c)3
Highest Offering: Associate Degree
Accreditation: &NH

02 President ..... Dr. Utpal K. GOSWAMI
03 Vice President ..... Dr. David C. OEHLER
05 Dean of Instruction ..... Dr. Ryan E. CRIDER
32 Dean Student Devel/Enrollment Mgmt ..... Dr. Diana BOYD MCELROY
11 Director Campus Operations ..... Mrs. Lisa BRAY
37 Financial Aid Manager ..... Ms. Lisa L. FANNAN
18 Physical Facilities Superintendent ..... Mr. Lloyd HALE
36 Career Services Coordinator ..... Mrs. Maggie GARCIA
38 Director Student Counseling ..... Ms. Gretchen S. BLYTHE

† Regional accreditation is carried under the parent institution Metropolitan Community College-Kansas City Administrative Center in Kansas City, MO.

*Metropolitan Community College - Maple Woods (H)

2601 NE Barry Road, Kansas City MO 64156-1299
County: Clay — FICE Identification: 009139
Telephone: (816) 604-1000 — Carnegie Class: Not Classified
FAX Number: (816) 437-3049 — Calendar System: Semester
URL: www.mcckc.edu
Established: 1968 — Annual Undergrad Tuition & Fees (In-District): N/A
Enrollment: N/A — Coed
Affiliation or Control: Local — IRS Status: 501(c)3
Highest Offering: Associate Degree
Accreditation: &NH

02 President ..... Dr. Tyjuan A. LEE
03 Executive Vice President ..... Dr. Ellen CROWE
05 Dean Instruction ..... Dr. Micheal STROHSCHEIN
32 Dean Student Devel/Enrollment ..... Mr. Terrell TIGNER
11 Director of Campus Operations ..... Ms. Rene BENNETT
08 Librarian ..... Mrs. Linda CARTER
41 Athletic Director ..... Dr. Brian BECHTEL
37 Financial Aid Manager ..... Mrs. Robin STIMAC
18 Physical Facilities Superintendent ..... Vacant
31 Community Relations Coordinator ..... Mr. Adam KISLER
36 Student Employment Service Coord ..... Ms. Mary Lynn MUNGER

† Regional accreditation is carried under the parent institution Metropolitan Community College-Kansas City Administrative Center in Kansas City, MO.

*Metropolitan Community College - Penn Valley (I)

3201 Southwest Trafficway, Kansas City MO 64111-2764
County: Jackson — FICE Identification: 002484
Telephone: (816) 604-1000 — Carnegie Class: Not Classified
FAX Number: (816) 759-4161 — Calendar System: Semester
URL: www.mcckc.edu
Established: 1915 — Annual Undergrad Tuition & Fees (In-District): N/A
Enrollment: N/A — Coed
Affiliation or Control: Local — IRS Status: 501(c)3
Highest Offering: Associate Degree
Accreditation: &NH, ADNUR, CAHIIM, DA, EMT, OTA, PTAA, RAD, SURGT

02 President ..... Dr. Tyjaun LEE
05 Dean of Instruction ..... Ms. Christine HOWELL
32 Dean of Student Development ..... Mr. Eric THOMPSON
84 Dean of Enrollment Services ..... Vacant
23 Director of Nursing Program ..... Ms. Evelyn CLAIBORNE
08 Librarian ..... Mr. Michael KORKLAN
13 NUS Department Director ..... Vacant
18 Facilities Services Superintendent ..... Mr. Robert BURKEY
19 Campus Police Captain ..... Cpt. Ronald REILLY
84 Enrollment Manager ..... Mr. Carlton FOWLER
41 Athletic Programs Manager ..... Mr. Marcus HARVEY
37 Student Financial Aid Manager ..... Vacant
10 Business Office Supervisor ..... Ms. Michele ALLEN
26 Community & Public Relations Coord ..... Mr. Jordan WILLIAMS
36 Career Coordinator ..... Vacant
11 Director of Campus Operations ..... Mr. Basil LISTER

† Regional accreditation is carried under the parent institution Metropolitan Community College-Kansas City Administrative Center in Kansas City, MO.

Midwest Institute (J)

2 Soccer Park Road, Fenton MO 63026
County: St. Louis — FICE Identification: 021211
Unit ID: 178183
Telephone: (314) 965-8363 — Carnegie Class: Spec 2-yr-Health
FAX Number: N/A — Calendar System: Other
URL: www.midwestinstitute.com
Established: 1965 — Annual Undergrad Tuition & Fees: N/A
Enrollment: 270 — Coed
Affiliation or Control: Proprietary — IRS Status: Proprietary
Highest Offering: Associate Degree
Accreditation: #ABHES

05 Director of Education ..... Vacant

Midwest Institute-Earth City (K)

4260 Shoreline Drive, Earth City MO 63045
County: Saint Louis — Identification: 667074
Telephone: (314) 344-4440 — Carnegie Class: Not Classified
FAX Number: (314) 344-0495 — Calendar System: Other
URL: www.midwestinstitute.com
Established: 1970 — Annual Undergrad Tuition & Fees: N/A
Enrollment: N/A — Coed
Affiliation or Control: Proprietary — IRS Status: Proprietary
Highest Offering: Associate Degree
Accreditation: ABHES, SURTEC

01 President ..... Vacant

Midwest University (L)

851 Parr Road, Wentzville MO 63385-0365
County: Saint Charles — FICE Identification: 035283
Telephone: (636) 327-4645 — Carnegie Class: Not Classified
FAX Number: (636) 327-4715 — Calendar System: Semester
URL: www.midwest.edu
Established: 1986 — Annual Undergrad Tuition & Fees: N/A

Enrollment: N/A Coed
Affiliation or Control: Independent Non-Profit IRS Status: 501(c)3
Highest Offering: Doctorate
Accreditation: BI

01 President ... Dr. James SONG
11 Executive Assistant to President ... Ms. Taylor BUMILLER
05 Academic Dean ... Dr. Hee Cheol LEE
09 Dir of Institutional Effectiveness ... Mr. Rolfe E. KIEHNE
42 Chaplain ... Dr. Myeong H. OH
06 Registrar/Admission ... Mr. Jeoung H. HAM
08 Director of Library Services ... Mrs. Mi Kyoung HWANG
10 Director of Finance ... Mr. Kyong S. YEOM
21 Business Office Manager ... Mrs. Bok H. SONG
45 Director of Planning & Marketing ... Mr. Jae P. SONG
13 Director of Information Technology ... Dr. Hee C. LEE
12 Korea Office Regional Director ... Dr. Jae M. SONG
12 Washington DC Regional Director ... Dr. Yoo K. KO
07 Admission Counselor ... Mr. Sang Bae SEO
85 International Student Officer ... Mr. Kyong S. YEOM
85 International Student Officer ... Dr. Yoo K. KO
104 Director of International Devel ... Dr. Hee C. LEE
88 Dir Sch of Intl Aviation/Bus Ldrshp ... Dr. Soon C. BYEON
73 Director of Theology ... Dr. Myeong Hwan OH
64 Director School of Music ... Dr. Jee Y. SHIN
12 Dir International Research Center ... Dr. Christina JOUNG

Midwestern Baptist Theological Seminary (A)

5001 N Oak Trafficway, Kansas City MO 64118-4697
County: Clay FICE Identification: 002485
Unit ID: 178208
Telephone: (816) 414-3700 Carnegie Class: Spec-4-yr-Faith
FAX Number: (816) 414-3724 Calendar System: Semester
URL: www.mbts.edu
Established: 1957 Annual Undergrad Tuition & Fees: $7,920
Enrollment: 2,239 Coed
Affiliation or Control: Southern Baptist IRS Status: 501(c)3
Highest Offering: Doctorate
Accreditation: NH, THEOL

01 President ... Dr. Jason K. ALLEN
05 Provost ... Dr. Jason DUESING
10 VP for Inst Administration/Fin Svcs ... Mr. James KRAGENBRING
30 VP of Institutional Relations ... Mr. Charles SMITH
20 Dean Midwestern College ... Dr. Samuel BIERIG
58 Dean of Graduate Studies ... Dr. Thor MADSEN
09 Dean of Institutional Effectiveness ... Dr. Rodney A. HARRISON
73 Dean of Postgraduate Studies ... Dr. Rodney A. HARRISON
32 Dean of Students ... Dr. John Mark YEATS
20 Associate Dean ... Dr. Rustin UMSTATTD
13 Director of Info Technology ... Mr. David MEYER
06 Registrar ... Dr. Mike HAWKINS
08 Librarian ... Ms. Kenette HARDER
04 Exec Assistant to the President ... Mr. Patrick HUDSON
18 Director of Campus Operations ... Mr. Merv CHAPMAN
84 Dir Student Recruitment & Admission ... Mr. Camden PULLIAM

Mineral Area College (B)

5270 Flat River Road, Park Hills MO 63601-2224
County: Saint Francois FICE Identification: 002486
Unit ID: 178217
Telephone: (573) 431-4593 Carnegie Class: Assoc/HT-High Trad
FAX Number: (573) 518-2164 Calendar System: Semester
URL: www.mineralarea.edu
Established: 1922 Annual Undergrad Tuition & Fees (In-District): $3,670
Enrollment: 3,700 Coed
Affiliation or Control: Local IRS Status: 501(c)3
Highest Offering: Associate Degree
Accreditation: NH, EMT, PTAA, #RAD

01 President ... Dr. Joe GILGOUR
75 Dean Career/Tech Educ ... Mr. Roger MCMILLIAN
49 Dean of Arts & Sciences ... Dr. Diana STUART
32 Dean Student Services ... Ms. Julie SHEETS
10 Chief Financial Officer ... Ms. Lori CRUMP
13 Chief Information Officer ... Dr. Amy HENSON
06 Registrar ... Ms. Connie HOLDER
07 Director of Admissions ... Ms. Julie SHEETS
09 Director of Institutional Research ... Ms. Lisa EDBURG
26 Director of College Communications ... Ms. Danielle BASLER
29 Director Alumni Relations ... Mr. Kevin THURMAN
30 Director of Development ... Mr. Kevin THURMAN
15 Director Human Resources ... Ms. Kathryn NEFF
37 Director Student Financial Aid ... Ms. Denise SEBASTIAN
38 Director Student Counseling ... Mr. Michael EASTER
18 Facilities Manager ... Mr. Barry WILFONG
21 Director Payroll ... Ms. Sarah DEMENT
04 Administrative Asst to President ... Ms. Amy MCKENNA-JONES
08 Director of the Library ... Ms. Melissa HOPKINS
19 Director Security/Safety ... Mr. Rich FLOTRON
39 Director Student Housing ... Ms. Debi BAYLESS
41 Athletic Director ... Mr. Jim GERWITZ

Missouri Baptist University (C)

One College Park Drive, Saint Louis MO 63141-8698
County: Saint Louis FICE Identification: 007540
Unit ID: 178244
Telephone: (314) 434-1115 Carnegie Class: Masters/L
FAX Number: (314) 434-7596 Calendar System: Semester
URL: www.mobap.edu
Established: 1964 Annual Undergrad Tuition & Fees: $27,124
Enrollment: 5,488 Coed
Affiliation or Control: Baptist IRS Status: 501(c)3
Highest Offering: Doctorate
Accreditation: NH, CAEP, CAEPN, EXSC, MUS

01 President ... Dr. Keith L. ROSS
04 Assistant to the President ... Mrs. Janet MAYFIELD
05 Senior VP of Academic Affs/Provost ... Dr. Andy CHAMBERS
26 VP of Enroll/Mktg/Communications ... Mr. Bryce CHAPMAN
32 VP of Student Development ... Dr. Benjamin LION
10 Senior VP for Business Affairs ... Mr. Ken REVENAUGH
20 Assoc VP for Academic Affs & Accred ... Dr. Lydia THEBEAU
58 Assoc VP for Grad Affairs ... Dr. Melanie BISHOP
29 Director for Alumni Relations ... Mr. Brian KNAPP
85 Director of International Services ... Ms. Lauren REPP
09 Director Institutional Research ... Mrs. Heather BRASE
08 Librarian ... Mrs. Rebekah MCKINNEY
37 Director Financial Services ... Mr. Zach GREENLEE
111 Exec Dir for Univ Advancement ... Mrs. Ashlee JOHNSON
35 Assoc Dean Students ... Ms. Kimberly GREY
41 Assoc VP & Director of Athletics ... Dr. Thomas SMITH
18 Director Campus Operations ... Mr. Andy HOUGH
06 Director of Records ... Mrs. Thea ABRAHAM
15 Director Personnel Services ... Mrs. Laurie WALLACE
13 Director of Information Systems ... Mr. Jerry MCKITTRICK
19 Director Public Safety ... Mr. Stephen HEIDKE
21 Controller ... Mrs. Pam SAVAGE
30 Development Officer ... Mrs. Ashlee JOHNSON
07 Exec Director of Admissions ... Mrs. Cynthia SUTTON
28 Diversity/Inclusion Initiative ... Vacant
66 Dean of School of Nursing ... Dr. Amber PYATT

Missouri Southern State University (D)

3950 E Newman Road, Joplin MO 64801-1595
County: Jasper FICE Identification: 002488
Unit ID: 178341
Telephone: (417) 625-9300 Carnegie Class: Bac-Diverse
FAX Number: (417) 625-3121 Calendar System: Semester
URL: www.mssu.edu
Established: 1965 Annual Undergrad Tuition & Fees (In-State): $6,503
Enrollment: 6,174 Coed
Affiliation or Control: State IRS Status: 501(c)3
Highest Offering: Master's
Accreditation: NH, ACBSP, CAEP, COARC, DH, EMT, NUR, RAD, SW

01 President ... Dr. Alan MARBLE
05 Provost/Vice Pres Academic Affairs ... Dr. Paula CARSON
32 Vice Pres Stdnt Affs/Enrollment ... Mr. Darren S. FULLERTON
10 Vice President Business Affairs ... Mr. Rob YUST
30 Exec Vice Pres for Development ... Dr. Brad HODSON
20 Prov/Vice Pres Academic Affairs ... Dr. Wendy MCGRANE
06 Registrar ... Ms. Cheryl DOBSON
08 Library Director ... Mr. James CAPECI
37 Director Student Financial Aid ... Ms. Becca L. DISKIN
21 Treasurer ... Mrs. Linda EIS
15 Director Human Resources ... Mr. Evan JEWSBURY
18 Director Facilities/Physical Plant ... Mr. Bryan GOODWIN
76 Dean School Health Sciences ... Dr. Richard SCHOOLER
49 Dean School of Arts & Sciences ... Dr. Marsi ARCHER
53 Interim Dean School of Education ... Dr. Lorinda HACKETT
50 Int Dean Plaster School of Business ... Dr. Jeff ZIMMERMAN
04 Administrative Asst to President ... Ms. Laura BOYD
07 Director of Admissions ... Mr. Michael SANDERS
104 Director Study Abroad ... Dr. Chad STEBBINS
106 Director Distance Learning ... Mr. Scott SNELL
108 Dir Institutional Effectiveness ... Dr. Josie WELSH
19 Chief of Campus Police ... Mr. Kenneth KENNEDY
41 Director of Athletics ... Mr. Jared BRUGGEMAN
44 Director of Annual Giving ... Ms. Elisa BRYANT
114 Dir Budget & Operations ... Mr. Jeff GIBSON
26 Dir University Relations/Marketing ... Ms. Heather LESMEISTER
29 Director Alumni Relations ... Ms. Lee ELLIFF POUND
28 Director of Diversity ... Ms. Faustina ABRAHAMS
13 Chief Info Technology Officer (CIO) ... Mr. Albert E. STADLER
39 Director Student Housing ... Mr. Joshua M. DOAK

Missouri State University (E)

901 S National Avenue, Springfield MO 65897-0027
County: Greene FICE Identification: 002503
Unit ID: 179566
Telephone: (417) 836-8500 Carnegie Class: DU-Mod
FAX Number: (417) 836-7669 Calendar System: Semester
URL: www.missouristate.edu
Established: 1905 Annual Undergrad Tuition & Fees (In-State): $7,376
Enrollment: 23,697 Coed
Affiliation or Control: State IRS Status: 501(c)3
Highest Offering: Doctorate
Accreditation: NH, ADNUR, ANEST, ARCPA, AUD, CAATE, CACREP, CAEPN, CEA, CONST, DIETD, @DIETI, MUS, NRPA, NURSE, OT, PH, PLNG, PTA, SP, SW, THEA

01 President ... Mr. Clifton M. SMART, III
05 Provost ... Dr. Frank E. EINHELLIG
12 Chancellor West Plains Campus ... Dr. Shirley A. LAWLER
46 VP for Research/Economic Devel ... Dr. James P. BAKER
11 Vice Pres Administrative Services ... Mr. Matthew MORRIS
111 Vice Pres University Advancement ... Mr. W. Brent DUNN
32 VP Student Affairs & Dean of Stdts ... Dr. Dee SISCOE
26 VP Marketing and Communications ... Ms. Suzanne SHAW
20 Deputy Provost ... Dr. Christopher J. CRAIG
20 Associate Provost ... Dr. Rachelle DARABI
20 Associate Provost ... Dr. Joye NORRIS
58 Dean of Grad College ... Dr. Julie J. MASTERSON
10 Chief Financial Officer ... Mr. Steve FOUCART
84 Associate VP Enrollment Mgmt & Svcs ... Mr. Rob HORNBERGER
08 Dean Library Services ... Mr. Thomas A. PETERS
28 Chief Diversity Officer ... Mr. H. Wes PRATT
09 Director of Institutional Research ... Dr. Michelle D. OLSEN
29 Exec Dir of Alumni Relations ... Ms. Lori FAN
15 Director of Human Resources ... Mr. Tamaria FEW
37 Director of Student Financial Aid ... Mr. Rob MOORE
19 Director of University Safety ... Mr. David A. HALL
36 Director of the Career Center ... Dr. Kelly E. RAPP
13 Chief Information Officer ... Mr. Jeff P. COINER
100 Chief of Staff ... Mr. Ryan DEBOEF
23 Director of Health & Wellness Svcs ... Dr. Dave MUEGGE
92 Director Honors College ... Dr. John F. CHUCHIAK
18 Director Facilities Management ... Mr. Brad B. KIELHOFNER
96 Director of Procurement ... Mr. Mike WILLS
07 Director of Admissions ... Ms. Nechell T. BONDS
06 Asst VP Enrollment Mgmt/Registrar ... Vacant
49 Dean College Arts & Letters ... Dr. Shawn T. WAHL
79 Dean Col Humanities/Public Affairs ... Dr. Victor MATTHEWS
76 Dean Col Health/Human Services ... Dr. Mark SMITH
81 Dean Col Natural/Applied Science ... Dr. Tamera S. JAHNKE
53 Dean College of Education ... Dr. David HOUGH
50 Dean College of Business ... Dr. David B. MEINERT
85 Director of International Services ... Mr. Patrick M. PARNELL
105 Dir of Web Strategy and Devel ... Ms. Jessica J. HEINZ
41 Athletic Director ... Mr. Kyle MOATS
43 General Counsel ... Ms. Rachael M. DOCKERY
04 Exec Assistant to the President ... Ms. Rowena A. STONE
101 Secretary of the Board ... Ms. Kristan E. GOCHENAUER

Missouri State University - West Plains (F)

128 Garfield, West Plains MO 65775-2715
County: Howell FICE Identification: 031060
Unit ID: 179344
Telephone: (417) 255-7255 Carnegie Class: Assoc/HT-Mix Trad/Non
FAX Number: (417) 255-7962 Calendar System: Semester
URL: www.wp.missouristate.edu
Established: 1963 Annual Undergrad Tuition & Fees (In-State): $4,305
Enrollment: 1,918 Coed
Affiliation or Control: State IRS Status: 501(c)3
Highest Offering: Associate Degree
Accreditation: NH

01 Chancellor ... Dr. Drew A. BENNETT
05 Dean of Academics ... Dr. Dennis LANCASTER
32 Dean of Student Services ... Dr. Angela TOTTY
20 Assistant Dean of Academic Affairs ... Dr. Michael ORF
10 Director of Business/Support Svcs ... Mr. Scott SCHNEIDER
30 Director of Development ... Ms. Melody HUBBELL
27 Director of Univ Communications ... Mrs. Cheryl CALDWELL
31 Director of Univ/Community Pgms ... Ms. Brenda POLYARD
06 Registrar ... Mrs. Laurie WALL
26 Chief Public Relations Officer ... Mrs. Cheryl CALDWELL
13 Dir Information Technology Services ... Mr. David YOUNG
18 Chief Facilities/Physical Plant ... Mr. Ron HENSLEY
04 Executive Asst to Chancellor ... Mrs. Debra MOSLEY
08 Director Library Services ... Mrs. Sylvia KUHLMEIER
15 Procurement/Human Resources Spec ... Mrs. Alyssa D. COLLINS
07 Coord of Admissions ... Mrs. Melissa JETT
09 Coord of Institutional Research ... Ms. Carrie STEEN
39 Coord Student Life and Development ... Mr. Jared CATES

Missouri Valley College (G)

500 E College, Marshall MO 65340-3197
County: Saline FICE Identification: 002489
Unit ID: 178369
Telephone: (660) 831-4000 Carnegie Class: Bac-Diverse
FAX Number: (660) 831-4039 Calendar System: Semester
URL: www.moval.edu
Established: 1889 Annual Undergrad Tuition & Fees: $20,600
Enrollment: 1,820 Coed
Affiliation or Control: Presbyterian Church (U.S.A.) IRS Status: 501(c)3
Highest Offering: Master's
Accreditation: NH, NURSE

01 President ... Dr. Bonnie HUMPHREY
00 Chancellor Emeritus ... Dr. Earl J. REEVES
111 Vice Pres Institutional Advancement ... Mr. Eric SAPPINGTON
32 Vice Pres Student Affairs ... Dr. Heath MORGAN
05 VP Academic Affairs/Chief Acad Ofcr . Dr. Diane BARTHOLOMEW
18 Vice Pres of Operations ... Mr. Tim SCHULTE
10 Chief Financial Officer ... Mr. Richard GOZIA
07 Admissions Director ... Mr. Greg SILVEY
06 Registrar ... Ms. Marsha LASHLEY
21 Business Officer ... Mrs. Tonia BARTEL
08 Head Librarian ... Mr. Bryan CARSON
41 Executive Vice President/AD ... Mr. Tom FIFER
42 Director Campus Ministry ... Rev. Pam SEBASTIAN
09 Director of Institutional Research ... Dr. Tonia COMPTON
37 Director Student Financial Aid ... Mr. Paul GORDON
38 Director Student Counseling ... Ms. Teresa CESELSKI
13 Director of Systems Administration ... Mr. Jason RINNE
26 Dir of Marketing & Media Relations ... Ms. Danielle DURHAM
04 Administrative Asst to President ... Ms. Brandy SCHULTE

Missouri Western State University (A)

4525 Downs Drive, Saint Joseph MO 64507-2294
County: Buchanan FICE Identification: 002490
Unit ID: 178387
Telephone: (816) 271-4200 Carnegie Class: Masters/M
FAX Number: N/A Calendar System: Semester
URL: www.missouriwestern.edu
Established: 1915 Annual Undergrad Tuition & Fees (In-State): $7,960
Enrollment: 5,533 Coed
Affiliation or Control: State IRS Status: 501(c)3
Highest Offering: Master's
Accreditation: NH, CAEPN, CAHIIM, MUS, NURSE, PTAA, SW, THEA

Code	Title	Name
01	President	Mr. Matthew J. WILSON
05	Provost/VP Academic Affairs	Dr. Doug DAVENPORT
111	Vice Pres University Advancement	Vacant
10	VP Financial Planning and Admin	Mr. Darrell MORRISON
32	Vice Pres for Student Affairs	Ms. Shana MEYER
20	Assoc Vice Pres Academic Affairs	Vacant
21	Assoc VP Financial Plng/Admin	Ms. Carey MCMILLIAN
84	AVP Enrollment Mgmt & Retention	Mr. Paul ORSCHELN
107	Interim Dean Professional Studies	Dr. Crystal HARRIS
57	Dean of Fine Arts	Vacant
49	Dean Liberal Arts & Science	Dr. Joel HYER
51	Dean of Western Institute	Vacant
50	Dean of Business	Dr. Logan JONES
35	Dean of Students	Vacant
06	Registrar	Ms. Susan BRACCIANO
08	Director of Library	Ms. Sally GIBSON
37	Director Student Financial Aid	Ms. Marilyn BAKER
13	Director of Information Technology	Vacant
38	Director Student Counsel & Testing	Mr. H. David BROWN
18	Director Physical Plant	Mr. Bryan ADKINS
41	Vice President Intercol Athletics	Mr. Josh LOONEY
15	Director of Human Resources	Ms. Sara FREEMYER
86	Director of External Relations	Mr. Steve JOHNSTON
26	Dir of Public Relations & Marketing	Ms. Jomel NICHOLS
29	Director of Alumni Services	Ms. Colleen KOWICH
96	Director of Purchasing	Ms. Letha NOLD
04	Executive Associate to President	Ms. Kim SIGRIST
36	Career Development Director	Dr. Vince BOWHAY
39	Director Student Housing	Mr. Nathan ROBERTS
19	Chief of University Police	Ms. Jill VOLTMER

Moberly Area Community College (B)

101 College Avenue, Moberly MO 65270-1304
County: Randolph FICE Identification: 002491
Unit ID: 178448
Telephone: (660) 263-4100 Carnegie Class: Assoc/HT-Mix Trad/Non
FAX Number: (660) 263-6252 Calendar System: Semester
URL: www.macc.edu
Established: 1927 Annual Undergrad Tuition & Fees (In-District): $3,390
Enrollment: 4,898 Coed
Affiliation or Control: State/Local IRS Status: 501(c)3
Highest Offering: Associate Degree
Accreditation: NH, MLTAD, OTA

Code	Title	Name
01	President	Dr. Jeffery LASHLEY
10	Vice President for Finance	Ms. Susan SPENCER
05	Vice President for Instruction	Dr. Todd MARTIN
75	Dean Workforce Dev/Technical Educ	Ms. Jo FEY
32	Dean Student Affairs & Enrollment	Ms. Michele MCCALL
20	Dean of Academic Affairs	Dr. Jacqueline FISCHER
09	Dir Inst Reporting & Compliance	Ms. Meghan HOLLERAN
21	Director Business Services	Ms. Sandra MACHETTA
26	Dir Marketing and Public Relations	Mr. Chase STAMP
18	Director of Plant Operations	Mr. Eric ROSS
13	Chief Information Officer	Mr. Robert WIDEMAN
08	Dir Library & Academic Resources	Ms. Donna MONNIG
15	Director of Human Resources	Ms. Ann PARKS
14	Dir of Instructional Technology	Ms. Susan BURDEN
37	Director of Financial Aid	Ms. Amy HAGER
06	Registrar	Ms. Julie PERKINS
29	Dir Inst Development & Alumni Svcs	Ms. Susan ARMENT
36	Dir Career and Technical Programs	Ms. Suzi MCGARVEY
88	Director of Academic Services	Ms. Katelyn BRANDKAMP
04	Administrative Asst to President	Ms. Cheryl SHOEMYER
103	Exec Dir of Workforce Development	Ms. Brandi GLOVER
19	Director Security & Residence Life	Ms. Lori PERRY
76	Dean of Health Sciences	Ms. Michelle FREY

Nazarene Theological Seminary (C)

1700 E Meyer Boulevard, Kansas City MO 64131-1263
County: Jackson FICE Identification: 002494
Unit ID: 178518
Telephone: (816) 268-5400 Carnegie Class: Spec-4-yr-Faith
FAX Number: (816) 268-5500 Calendar System: Semester
URL: www.nts.edu
Established: 1945 Annual Graduate Tuition & Fees: N/A
Enrollment: 210 Coed
Affiliation or Control: Church Of The Nazarene IRS Status: 501(c)3
Highest Offering: Doctorate; No Undergraduates
Accreditation: THEOL

Code	Title	Name
01	President	Dr. Jeren ROWELL
05	Dean of the Faculty	Dr. Josh SWEEDEN
11	Dean for Administration	Dr. Glenn MILLER
08	Director Library Service	Mrs. Debra BRADSHAW
06	Registrar/Director of Admissions	Ms. Megan ZIRKLE
37	Financial Aid Coordinator	Mrs. Cindy HOWARD
26	Director of Communications	Rev. Jason VEACH
111	Dean for Advancement	Rev. Timothy MCPHERSON
04	Admin Assistant to the President	Mrs. Nancy MCPHERSON
13	Chief Information Technology Ofcr	Rev. Stephen PORTER
123	Director of Graduate Admissions	Dr. Levi JONES
07	Director of Admissions	Mr. Derek DAVIS
101	Secretary of the Institution/Board	Mr. Allen BROWN
18	Chief Facilities/Physical Plant	Ms. Carol NOLTING
29	Director Alumni Affairs	Rev. Dana PREUSCH
38	Director Student Counseling	Dr. William KIRKEMO

North Central Missouri College (D)

1301 Main Street, Trenton MO 64683-1824
County: Grundy FICE Identification: 002514
Unit ID: 179715
Telephone: (660) 359-3948 Carnegie Class: Assoc/MT-VT-High Non
FAX Number: (660) 359-2211 Calendar System: Semester
URL: www.ncmissouri.edu
Established: 1925 Annual Undergrad Tuition & Fees (In-District): $3,600
Enrollment: 1,832 Coed
Affiliation or Control: Local IRS Status: 501(c)3
Highest Offering: Associate Degree
Accreditation: NH, DH, OTA

Code	Title	Name
01	President	Dr. Lenny KLAVER
03	Executive Vice President	Dr. Tristan LONDRE
10	Chief Financial Officer	Mr. Tyson OTTO
32	Dean of Student Services	Dr. Kristen ALLEY
05	Dean of Instruction	Dr. Mitchell HOLDER
06	Registrar	Ms. Linda BROWN
13	Chief Information Officer	Mr. Alan BARNETT
08	Librarian	Ms. Beth CALDARELLO
37	Director of Financial Aid	Ms. Kimberly MEEKER
30	Director Development	Ms. Alicia ENDICOTT
40	Director Bookstore	Ms. Cecilia MARSH
39	Director Student Housing	Mr. Donnie HILLERMAN
41	Athletic Director	Mr. Steve RICHMAN
18	Director of Facilities	Mr. Randy YOUNG
105	Director Web Services	Ms. Tami CAMPBELL
09	Director of Institutional Research	Ms. Tara NOAH
04	Administrative Asst to President	Ms. Kristi HARRIS
07	Director of Admissions	Ms. Kristie CROSS

Northwest Missouri State University (E)

800 University Drive, Maryville MO 64468-6015
County: Nodaway FICE Identification: 002496
Unit ID: 178624
Telephone: (660) 562-1212 Carnegie Class: Masters/L
FAX Number: (660) 562-1900 Calendar System: Trimester
URL: www.nwmissouri.edu
Established: 1905 Annual Undergrad Tuition & Fees (In-State): $7,844
Enrollment: 6,338 Coed
Affiliation or Control: State IRS Status: 501(c)3
Highest Offering: Beyond Master's But Less Than Doctorate
Accreditation: NH, ACBSP, CAEPN, DIETD, @DIETI, MUS, NRPA

Code	Title	Name
01	President	Dr. John JASINSKI
05	Provost	Dr. Jamie HOOYMAN
10	Vice Pres of Finance	Ms. Stacy CARRICK
32	Vice Pres Student Affairs	Dr. Matt BAKER
30	VP External Relations	Dr. Lonelle RATHJE
88	VP of Culture	Mr. Clarence GREEN
58	Assoc Prov for Grad & Prof Studies	Dr. Gregory HADDOCK
49	Assoc Prov Dean Col of Arts & Sci	Dr. Michael STEINER
20	Assoc Prov Academic Ops & Dev	Dr. Jay JOHNSON
53	Dean School of Education	Dr. Timothy WALL
26	Exec Dir Marketing/Communications	Mr. Brandon STANLEY
41	Director Athletics	Mr. Andy PETERSON
15	Director of Human Resources	Ms. Krista BARCUS
13	Director of IT	Mr. Jeffrey THOMAS
09	Director Institutional Research	Mr. Egon HEIDENDAL
96	Director of Purchasing	Ms. Alyssa PULLEY
21	Asst VP of Finance	Ms. Mary COLLINS
18	AVP Capital Pgms & Facil Svcs	Mr. Allen MAYS
60	Director School of Comm/Mass Media	Dr. Matt WALKER
76	Dir School of Health Sci & Wellness	Dr. Terry LONG
47	Director School of Agriculture	Mr. Rodney BARR
50	Director School of Business	Dr. Stephen LUDWIG
77	Director School of Computer Science	Dr. Doug HAWLEY

Ozark Christian College (F)

1111 N Main Street, Joplin MO 64801-4804
County: Jasper FICE Identification: 022027
Unit ID: 178679
Telephone: (417) 626-1234 Carnegie Class: Spec-4-yr-Faith
FAX Number: (417) 624-0090 Calendar System: Semester
URL: www.occ.edu
Established: 1942 Annual Undergrad Tuition & Fees: $12,620
Enrollment: 587 Coed
Affiliation or Control: Independent Non-Profit IRS Status: 501(c)3
Highest Offering: Baccalaureate
Accreditation: @NH, BI

Code	Title	Name
01	President	Matt PROCTOR
04	Executive Asst to the President	Kathy BOWERS
03	Executive Vice President	Damien SPIKEREIT
111	Exec VP of College Advancement	Jim DALRYMPLE
29	Director of Alumni	Troy NELSON
30	Director of Development	Alex FOLLETT
05	Executive VP of Academics	Doug ALDRIDGE
20	Assistant Academic Dean	Chad RAGSDALE
20	Assoc Academic Dean	Shane WOOD
106	Assc Dean Online Learning/Acad Tech	Shawn LINDSAY
88	Director Academic Operations	Lisa WITTE
06	Registrar	Jennifer MCMILLIN
90	Director Academic Resource Commons	Jessica SCHEUERMANN
08	Director of Library	Derek MOSER
09	VP Inst Research & Effectiveness	Teresa WELCH
32	VP of Student Affairs	Andy STORMS
19	Sr Dir Community Stds/Campus Safety	Monte SHOEMAKE
42	Campus Minister	Julie GARISS
42	Campus Minister	Randy GARISS
23	Campus Nurse	Sara WOOD
109	Director of Dining Services	Teresa BAKER
41	Director of Athletics	Chris LAHM
88	Director of Ministry Center	Kevin GREER
28	Director of Diversity	Matthew MCBIRTH
11	VP of Campus Operations	David MCMILLIN
84	VP of Enrollment Management	Robert WITTE
07	Director of Admissions	Jesse FURST
37	Dir Student Financial Services	Kim BALENTINE
15	Director of Human Resources	Whitney MORGAN
26	Director Marketing & Communications	Amy STORMS
64	Director Worship & Creative Arts	Matt STAFFORD
64	Chapel Minister/Frontline Director	Isaac SCHADE
13	Director of IT Dept	Mitchell PIERCY
40	Director of Bookstore	Bob HEATH
18	Director Physical Plant	Tim RUNYON
43	General Counsel	Doug MILLER

Ozarks Technical Community College (G)

1001 E Chestnut Expressway, Springfield MO 65802-3625
County: Greene FICE Identification: 030830
Unit ID: 177472
Telephone: (417) 447-7500 Carnegie Class: Assoc/MT-VT-High Trad
FAX Number: N/A Calendar System: Semester
URL: www.otc.edu
Established: 1990 Annual Undergrad Tuition & Fees (In-District): $3,392
Enrollment: 12,692 Coed
Affiliation or Control: State/Local IRS Status: 501(c)3
Highest Offering: Associate Degree
Accreditation: NH, ACFEI, ADNUR, CAHIIM, COARC, DA, DH, EMT, IFSAC, MLTAD, OTA, PTAA, SURGT

Code	Title	Name
01	Chancellor	Dr. Hal L. HIGDON
100	Chief of Staff	Ms. Stephanie SUMNERS
101	Secretary to the Chancellor	Ms. Janel GRASSI
05	Vice Chancellor Academic Affairs	Dr. Tracy MCGRADY
11	Vice Chancellor Admin Services	Mr. Rob RECTOR
32	Vice Chancellor Student Affairs	Ms. Joan BARRETT
10	Vice Chancellor Finance	Ms. Marla MOODY
12	President Table Rock Campus	Dr. Cliff DAVIS
12	President Richwood Valley Campus	Dr. Jeff JOCHEMS
13	Chief Technology Officer	Mr. David ESPING
15	Assoc VC Human Resources/Workforce	Ms. Ocki HAAS
20	Dean of Academic Services	Dr. Vivian ELDER
76	Dean of Allied Health Programs	Dr. Sherry TAYLOR
97	Dean of General Education	Dr. Lance RENNER
72	Dean of Technical Education	Dr. Matthew HUDSON
103	Exec Dir Workforce Development	Ms. Sherry COKER
06	Asst Registrar Records/Registration	Ms. Amy BERGANT
38	Director of Counseling Services	Mr. James CARPENTER
26	College Dir Comm & Marketing	Mr. Mark MILLER
18	College Director Facilities/Grounds	Mr. Rickie TAYLOR
28	College Dir Equity & Compliance	Mr. Kevin LUEBBERING
37	College Director of Financial Aid	Ms. Kim CARY
08	Director College Library	Ms. Sarah FANCHER
88	Director College Library RVC/TRC	Ms. Angela SWIFT
36	Director of Career Employment Svcs	Ms. Kathy CHRISTY
102	Exec Director of OTC Foundation	Ms. Amy BACON
30	Development Coordinator	Ms. Sarah BARGO
09	College Dir Research/Strategic Plng	Mr. Matthew SIMPSON
19	College Director Safety & Security	Mr. Scott LEVEN
35	Dean of Students	Ms. Joyce BATEMAN
88	Director Dual Credit/HS Admissions	Ms. Piper WILSON
105	Director Web Services	Mr. George LAMELZA
106	Dir Online Education/E-learning	Mr. Matthew HARRIS
25	Director of Grant Development	Dr. Abigail BENZ
96	Director of Procurement	Ms. J'Neal MCCOY
07	Director of Admissions/Registrar	Mr. Scott FIEDLER
88	Exec Dir Ctr for Advanced Mfg	Mr. Robert RANDOLPH

Ozarks Technical Community College Richwood Valley (H)

3369 W Jackson Street, Nixa MO 65714
Telephone: (417) 447-7700 Identification: 770324
Accreditation: &NH

Ozarks Technical Community College Table Rock Campus (I)

10698 Historic Highway, MO 165, Hollister MO 65672
Telephone: (417) 336-6239 Identification: 770325
Accreditation: &NH

Park University (A)

8700 River Park Drive, Parkville MO 64152-3795
County: Platte FICE Identification: 002498
Unit ID: 178721
Telephone: (816) 741-2000 Carnegie Class: Masters/L
FAX Number: (816) 746-6423 Calendar System: Semester
URL: www.park.edu
Established: 1875 Annual Undergrad Tuition & Fees: $11,572
Enrollment: 11,457 Coed
Affiliation or Control: Independent Non-Profit IRS Status: 501(c)3
Highest Offering: Master's
Accreditation: NH, ACBSP, NURSE, SW

01 President .... Dr. Greg GUNDERSON
11 VP and Chief Operating Officer .... Mr. Shane SMEED
05 Provost .... Dr. Michelle MYERS
10 Chief Financial Officer .... Mr. Brian BODE
111 Chief Advancement Officer .... Mr. Nathan MARTICKE
20 Associate Provost .... Dr. Emily SALLEE
29 Assoc VP for External Relations .... Mr. Erik BERGRUD
32 Associate VP/Dean of Student Life .... Dr. Jayme UDEN
58 Director Graduate Student Success .... Ms. Joslyn CREIGHTON
06 Registrar .... Dr. Cynthia OTTS
37 Director Student Financial Service .... Ms. Brynn BOLOGNA
08 Director of Library Systems .... Mr. Brent SHORT
44 Dir Advancement Svcs/Annual Fund .... Ms. Jessica GREASON
15 Chief Human Resources Officer .... Mr. Roger DUSING
41 Director of Athletics .... Mr. Claude ENGLISH
66 Director of Nursing Program .... Ms. Teresa CROWDER
85 Sr Director International Students .... Mr. Kevin VICKER
13 Chief Information Officer .... Mr. David WHITTAKER
19 Director of Campus Safety .... Mr. William LONDON
50 MBA Gen Concentration Coordinator .... Dr. Nick KOUDOU
04 Executive Asst to the President .... Ms. Ami WISDOM
50 Dean College of Management .... Mr. Kirby BROWN
20 Associate VP Academic Operations .... Dr. Kathryn ERVIN
49 Int Dean Liberal Arts & Sciences .... Dr. James PASLEY
53 Interim Dean School for Education .... Dr. Timothy WESTCOTT
101 Asst Secretary to Board of Trustees .... Ms. Ami WISDOM
100 Chief of Staff .... Ms. Laure CHRISTENSEN
88 Assoc Dir International Recruitment .... Ms. Lora ZAIDARHZAUVA
105 Web Manager .... Ms. Gariela SA TELES
18 Manager Facilities Maintenance .... Mr. Kevin MARTINEAU
26 Dir Communications/Public Relations .... Mr. Brad BILES
36 Director of Career Development .... Ms. Leah FLETCHER
38 Director of Counseling Center .... Mr. Dustin WALL
39 Director Student Housing .... Mr. Isaac BARBER
21 Senior Director Financial Report .... Ms. Donna BAKER
09 Dir Institutional Effectiveness .... Ms. Jennifer HELLER
121 Sr Director Student Success .... Mr. Andrew DAVIS

Pinnacle Career Institute (B)

10301 Hickman Mills Drive, Kansas City MO 64137
County: Jackson FICE Identification: 010405
Unit ID: 177302
Telephone: (816) 331-5700 Carnegie Class: Assoc/HVT-High Trad
FAX Number: (816) 331-2026 Calendar System: Quarter
URL: www.pcitraining.edu
Established: 1953 Annual Undergrad Tuition & Fees: N/A
Enrollment: 248 Coed
Affiliation or Control: Proprietary IRS Status: Proprietary
Highest Offering: Associate Degree
Accreditation: ACCSC

01 Executive Vice President .... Rebecca CLOTHIER
05 Director of Education .... Jean LASCOE

Pinnacle Career Institute (C)

10301 Hickman Mills Drive, Kansas City MO 64137
Telephone: (816) 331-5700 Identification: 770737
Accreditation: ACCSC

Purdue University Global-St. Louis (D)

1807 Park 270 Drive, St. Louis MO 63146
Telephone: (314) 205-7900 Identification: 770988
Accreditation: &NH, ACBSP

† Regional accreditation is carried under Purdue University Global in Indianapolis, IN.

Ranken Technical College (E)

4431 Finney Avenue, Saint Louis MO 63113-2898
County: Saint Louis FICE Identification: 012500
Unit ID: 178891
Telephone: (314) 371-0236 Carnegie Class: Bac/Assoc-Assoc Dom
FAX Number: (314) 371-0241 Calendar System: Semester
URL: ranken.edu/
Established: 1907 Annual Undergrad Tuition & Fees: $14,457
Enrollment: 1,644 Coed
Affiliation or Control: Independent Non-Profit IRS Status: 501(c)3
Highest Offering: Baccalaureate
Accreditation: NH, ACBSP

01 President .... Mr. Don POHL
10 Vice President for Finance & Admin .... Mr. Peter T. MURTAUGH
00 Chief Executive Officer .... Mr. Stan SHOUN
22 VP Diversity/Student Success .... Ms. Crystal HERRON
51 Dean of Continuing Education .... Mr. Keyvan GERAMI
05 Dean Academic Affairs .... Mr. Dan KANIA
84 Dean of Enrollment Management/Mktg .... Ms. Frank MILLER
111 Dir Institutional Advancement .... Mr. Tony PISCIOTTA
07 Admissions Director .... Ms. Ann FARAJALLAH
06 Registrar .... Ms. Cody DUNLAP
18 Director Buildings & Grounds .... Mr. David CADLE
29 Director of Alumni Relations .... Vacant
37 Director Financial Aid .... Ms. Michelle L. WILLIAMS
21 Business Office Manager .... Ms. Sara M. DAMINSKI
36 Career Services Coordinator .... Ms. Janie K. SUMMERS
15 Human Resources Coordinator .... Ms. Janice A. BOLLMANN
04 Administrative Asst to President .... Ms. Patricia CAPPS

Research College of Nursing (F)

2525 E Meyer Boulevard, Kansas City MO 64132-1133
County: Jackson FICE Identification: 006392
Unit ID: 178989
Telephone: (816) 995-2800 Carnegie Class: Spec-4-yr-Other Health
FAX Number: (816) 995-2817 Calendar System: Semester
URL: www.researchcollege.edu
Established: 1980 Annual Undergrad Tuition & Fees: N/A
Enrollment: 306 Coed
Affiliation or Control: Proprietary IRS Status: Proprietary
Highest Offering: Master's
Accreditation: NH, NURSE

01 President .... Dr. Thad R. WILSON
05 Dean .... Dr. Julie NAUSER
07 Director Admissions .... Ms. Leslie BURRY
32 Director Student Affairs .... Ms. Amanda GRAY
37 Director Financial Aid .... Ms. Stacie WITHERS
24 Director LRC .... Ms. Tobey STOSBERG
13 Senior Technology Analyst .... Mr. Bill HAMPSON
04 Administrative Asst to President .... Mrs. Sherry L. OWEN
06 Registrar .... Ms. Camelia WILLIAMS
08 Head Librarian .... Ms. Kitty SERLING
106 Dir Online Education/E-learning .... Ms. Sheryl MAX
26 Advancement & Development Officer .... Ms. Tiffany HAMLETT
39 Asst Director of Student Affairs .... Ms. Erica RAMIREZ
112 Coordinator of Student Accounts .... Ms. Marcy SACKMAN
88 Director of Resources .... Mr. Daniel ODER
09 Director of Institutional Research .... Ms. Christine HAMMOND

Rockbridge Seminary (G)

3111 East Battlefield Street, Springfield MO 65804
County: Greene Identification: 667151
Telephone: (866) 931-4300 Carnegie Class: Not Classified
FAX Number: (866) 931-4300 Calendar System: Semester
URL: www.rockbridge.edu
Established: 2002 Annual Graduate Tuition & Fees: N/A
Enrollment: N/A Coed
Affiliation or Control: Independent Non-Profit IRS Status: 501(c)3
Highest Offering: Doctorate; No Undergraduates
Accreditation: DEAC

01 President .... Dr. Daryl ELDRIDGE
05 Chief Academic Officer .... Dr. Mark SIMPSON
08 Head Librarian .... Seth ALLEN
04 Administrative Asst to President .... Heather WILLIAMSON
29 Director Alumni Relations .... Linda GRABER

Rockhurst University (H)

1100 Rockhurst Road, Kansas City MO 64110-2561
County: Jackson FICE Identification: 002499
Unit ID: 179043
Telephone: (816) 501-4000 Carnegie Class: Masters/L
FAX Number: (816) 501-4588 Calendar System: Semester
URL: www.rockhurst.edu
Established: 1910 Annual Undergrad Tuition & Fees: $37,590
Enrollment: 3,043 Coed
Affiliation or Control: Roman Catholic IRS Status: 501(c)3
Highest Offering: Doctorate
Accreditation: NH, CAEPT, OT, PTA, SP

01 President .... Rev. Thomas B. CURRAN
111 Vice President for Advancement .... Ms. Mary MOONEY BURNS
10 Chief Financial Officer .... Mr. Gerald MOENCH
05 Provost & Senior VP Acad Affairs .... Dr. Douglas N. DUNHAM
88 Vice Pres Mission & Ministry .... Ms. Cindy SCHMERSAL
32 VP Student Development/Athletics .... Dr. Matthew D. QUICK
13 Assoc VP Information Technology .... Mr. Bart KLEIN
18 Assoc VP Facilities Operations .... Mr. Jason RIORDAN
84 Assoc Provost Enrollment Services .... Mr. Matthew ELLIS
45 Assoc Provost Inst Effectiveness .... Dr. Paula SHORTER
35 Associate Dean of Students .... Ms. Melinda PETTEGREW
35 Director of Student Life .... Ms. Angie CARR ROBINETT
39 Assoc Dean of Students/Dir Res Life .... Mr. Mark HETZLER
04 Exec Assistant to the President .... Ms. Decla TYLER-SIMPSON
50 Interim Dean College of Business .... Dr. Myles GARTLAND
49 Dean Arts & Sciences .... Dr. Jennifer FRIEND
88 Dean College Health/Human Services .... Ms. Kris VACEK
66 Pres Research College of Nursing .... Dr. Thad WILSON
08 Director Library .... Ms. Laurie E. HATHMAN
06 Registrar .... Ms. Brenda LANEY
37 Director Student Financial Aid .... Ms. Maureen MCKINNON
41 Director of Athletics .... Mr. Gary BURNS
15 Director of Human Resources .... Ms. Barbra UPTON-GARVIN
13 Director of Infrastructure Services .... Mr. Michael CRAIG
36 Director of Career Center .... Mr. Michael J. THEOBALD
30 Exec Director of Development .... Ms. Paula MOSS
26 Director of University Relations .... Ms. Katherine FROHOFF
110 Assistant Director Advancement .... Mr. Brent BLAZEK
42 Director of Campus Ministry .... Mr. Bill KRIEGE
19 Director Security/Safety .... Mr. Randy HOPKINS
38 Director of Student Counseling .... Dr. Elbert DARDEN
31 Dir Community Relations & Outreach .... Ms. Alicia R. DOUGLAS
07 Director of Operations/Admission .... Ms. Annie LEHWALD
40 Director Bookstore .... Ms. Jami CADE
108 Director Assessment & Accreditation .... Ms. Annalisa GRAMLICH
09 Project Manager Inst Data/Analytics .... Ms. Wendy PICKEL
14 Support Manager Computer Services .... Mr. Darnell JONES
21 Controller .... Ms. Kris PACE
66 Dean Research College of Nursing .... Dr. Julie NAUSER
105 Web Development Director .... Mr. Jeremiah BARBER
104 Study Abroad Advisor .... Ms. Paivi BYBEE
106 Director of Online Learning .... Ms. Melissa MESSINA
27 Director of Marketing .... Mr. Dave HUNT
22 Chief Inclusion Officer .... Dr. Leslie DOYLE
88 Director of the Learning Center .... Mr. Kirk SKOGLUND
88 Director Center for Svc Learning .... Dr. Julia VARGAS

St. Charles Community College (I)

4601 Mid Rivers Mall Drive, Cottleville MO 63376-2865
County: Saint Charles FICE Identification: 025306
Unit ID: 262031
Telephone: (636) 922-8000 Carnegie Class: Assoc/HT-High Trad
FAX Number: (636) 922-8352 Calendar System: Semester
URL: www.stchas.edu
Established: 1986 Annual Undergrad Tuition & Fees (In-District): $2,664
Enrollment: 6,563 Coed
Affiliation or Control: State/Local IRS Status: 501(c)3
Highest Offering: Associate Degree
Accreditation: NH, ADNUR, CAHIIM, CSHSE, EMT, OTA

01 President .... Dr. Barbara KAVALIER
04 Exec Assistant .... Ms. Julie PARCEL
05 VP Academic Affairs .... Dr. John BOOKSTAVER
11 VP Administrative Services/COO .... Mr. Todd GALBIERZ
15 VP Human Resources .... Ms. Donna DAVIS
26 VP Marketing/Student Life .... Ms. Heather MCDORMAN
18 Director of Facilities/Construction .... Mr. Al KOEHLER
20 AVP Academic Affairs .... Dr. Michael B. DOMPIERRE
08 Interim Dean LRC/Acad Support .... Ms. Karen GEORGE
09 Director Institutional Research .... Dr. Chris JACKSON
13 Chief Information Officer .... Mr. Chad SHEPHERD
124 AVP Col Transitions/Support Svcs .. Ms. Kathy BROCKGREITENS
19 Director Public Safety .... Mr. Bob RONKOSKI
90 Director Technology Support .... Ms. Lisa MOUSER
32 Exec Dean Student Life .... Mr. Boyd COPELAND
51 Assoc Dean Continuing Education .... Ms. Lauren DICKENS
50 Int Dean Bus/Sci/Ed/Math/CompSci .... Dr. Darren OSBURN
57 Dean Arts/Humanities/Soc Sci .... Dr. Mara VORACHEK-WARREN
40 Asst Director Bookstore .... Mr. Daniel GRANZOW
41 Director Athletics .... Mr. Timothy BRIX
96 Director Purchasing .... Vacant
91 Director Administrative Computing .... Mr. Don POPHAM
06 Dir Enrollment Svcs/Registrar .... Vacant
10 Asst VP Financial Services .... Ms. Susan RUBEMEYER
36 Career Services Manager .... Ms. Jenny HAHN SCHNIPPER
31 AVP Corporate & Community Dev .... Ms. Amanda SIZEMORE
21 Director Financial Services .... Ms. Barbara FUERST
109 Asst Director Food Services .... Ms. Laura GRANT
88 Exec Dir/Special Assistant .... Ms. Betsy SCHNEIDER

Saint Louis Christian College (J)

1360 Grandview Drive, Florissant MO 63033-6499
County: Saint Louis FICE Identification: 012580
Unit ID: 179256
Telephone: (314) 837-6777 Carnegie Class: Spec-4-yr-Faith
FAX Number: (314) 837-8291 Calendar System: Semester
URL: https://stlchristian.edu/
Established: 1956 Annual Undergrad Tuition & Fees: $11,560
Enrollment: 82 Coed
Affiliation or Control: Other Protestant IRS Status: 501(c)3
Highest Offering: Baccalaureate
Accreditation: BI

01 President .... Mr. Terry STINE
10 VP of Finance/Administration .... Dr. Ron COOK
05 VP of Academics .... Dr. Scott WOMBLE
32 VP of Student Life .... Mr. Steve NAGLAK
111 VP of Advancement .... Mr. Rick CHAMP
04 Assistant to the President .... Ms. Deb PABARCUS
07 Director of Admissions .... Ms. Kelsey FORD
06 Registrar .... Ms. Cindy BINGAMON
37 Director of Financial Aid .... Ms. Cathi WILHOIT
08 Librarian .... Ms. Karen GALLACCI
13 Technical Services Specialist .... Mr. Joshua BETTISON
40 Bookstore Manager .... Ms. Jeri Ann JERALDS

Saint Louis College of Health Careers-Fenton Campus (K)

1297 N Highway Drive, Fenton MO 63026-1909
Telephone: (636) 529-0000 Identification: 666274
Accreditation: ABHES, COARC, OTA, PTAA

† Branch campus of Saint Louis College of Health Careers-South Taylor, Saint Louis, MO.

Saint Louis College of Health Careers-South Taylor (A)

909 S Taylor Avenue, Saint Louis MO 63110-1511
County: Saint Louis FICE Identification: 023405
Unit ID: 179511
Telephone: (314) 652-0300 Carnegie Class: Spec 2-yr-Health
FAX Number: (314) 884-2838 Calendar System: Semester
URL: www.slchc.edu
Established: 1981 Annual Undergrad Tuition & Fees: N/A
Enrollment: 258 Coed
Affiliation or Control: Proprietary IRS Status: Proprietary
Highest Offering: Associate Degree
Accreditation: **ABHES**

11 Chief of Administration .... Dr. Rush ROBINSON
06 Registrar .... Ms. Teresa JACKSON
05 Director of Education .... Mr. Michael TRAAS
36 Director Student Placement .... Ms. Hannah PFLANZ

St. Louis College of Pharmacy (B)

4588 Parkview Place, Saint Louis MO 63110-1088
County: Independent City FICE Identification: 002504
Unit ID: 179265
Telephone: (314) 367-8700 Carnegie Class: Spec-4-yr-Other Health
FAX Number: (314) 446-8304 Calendar System: Semester
URL: www.stlcop.edu
Established: 1864 Annual Undergrad Tuition & Fees: $29,981
Enrollment: 1,309 Coed
Affiliation or Control: Independent Non-Profit IRS Status: 501(c)3
Highest Offering: First Professional Degree
Accreditation: **NH**, PHAR

01 President .... Dr. John A. PIEPER
111 Vice Pres Devel/Alumni Relations .... Ms. Kathy GARDNER
10 VP Finance/Administration/CFO .... Vacant
84 VP Enrollment Services/Marketing .... Ms. Beth KESERAUSKIS
13 Vice Pres Info Technology & CIO .... Mr. Todd FINOCH
28 Vice Pres Diversity & Inclusion .... Dr. Isaac BUTLER
32 Vice President of Student Affairs .... Dr. Heather FRENCH
46 Vice President of Research .... Dr. Thomas BURRIS
18 AVP College Services .... Mr. Eric KNOLL
108 AVP Institutional Effectiveness .... Mr. George VINEYARD
49 Dean Arts & Science/Student Affairs .... Dr. Kimberly J. KILGORE
67 Dean of Pharmacy .... Dr. Bruce CANADAY
15 Director of Human Resources .... Mr. Daniel C. BAUER
30 Senior Development Officer .... Ms. Colleen WATERMON
06 Registrar .... Ms. Laura KLOS
08 Library Director .... Ms. Jill NISSEN
37 Director of Financial Aid .... Mr. Daniel J. STIFFLER
41 Director of Athletics .... Ms. Jill HARTER
88 Special Assistant to the President .. Sr. Mary Louise DEGENHART
88 Special Assistant to the President .... Mr. Michael SASS
07 Director of Admissions .... Ms. Jill GEBKE
19 Director Security/Safety .... Mr. Scott PATTERSON
29 Director Alumni Relations .... Ms. Stephanie MAUZY
38 Director Counseling Center .... Ms. Michelle HASTINGS
43 General Counsel .... Mr. Kenneth FLEISCHMANN
44 Annual Giving Officer .... Mr. Vincent PIAZZA
04 Admin Assistant to the President .... Ms. Lynn FALLERT

*Saint Louis Community College - Cosand Center (C)

3221 McKelvey Road, Bridgeton MO 63044
County: Saint Louis FICE Identification: 002471
Unit ID: 179308
Telephone: (314) 539-5000 Carnegie Class: N/A
FAX Number: (314) 539-5170
URL: www.stlcc.edu

01 Chancellor .... Dr. Jeff PITTMAN
05 Vice Chanc Academic Affairs .... Dr. Andrew LANGREHR
10 Vice Chanc Finance/Administration .... Mr. Paul ZINCK
32 Vice Chanc Student Affairs .... Dr. Anthony CRUZ
103 Assoc VC Workforce Solutions .... Mr. Hart NELSON
13 Chief Information Officer .... Mr. Keith HACKE
15 Assoc Vice Chanc Human Resources .... Ms. Deborah BARRON
102 Executive Director STLCC Foundation .... Ms. Jo-Ann DIGMAN
26 Exec Dir Marketing/Communication .... Ms. Kedra TOLSON
09 Director of Institutional Research .... Ms. Kelli BURNS
112 Director of Grants .... Vacant
06 Registrar .... Ms. Melanie STEGEMAN
04 Administrative Asst to Chancellor .... Ms. Yvonne BLOOM
101 Secretary of the Board .... Ms. Rebecca GARRISON
106 Mgr Online Student Services .... Ms. Stacey FOSTER
37 Dir Dist Financial Aid/Scholarships . Ms. Regina G. BLACKSHEAR
96 Assistant Controller .... Ms. Cindy GREEN
19 Director Public Safety .... LtCol. Alfred ADKINS
41 Director Athletics .... Vacant
43 Dir Legal Services/General Counsel .... Ms. Mary NELSON

*Saint Louis Community College at Florissant Valley (D)

3400 Pershall Road, Saint Louis MO 63135-1499
Telephone: (314) 513-4200 FICE Identification: 002470
Accreditation: **&NH**, ADNUR, ART, DIETT

*Saint Louis Community College at Forest Park (E)

5600 Oakland Avenue, Saint Louis MO 63110-1393
Telephone: (314) 644-9100 Identification: 667353
Accreditation: **NH**, ACFEI, ADNUR, CAHIIM, COARC, DA, DH, DMS, EMT, FUSER, MLTAD, RAD, SURGT

*Saint Louis Community College at Meramec (F)

11333 Big Bend Road, Kirkwood MO 63122-5799
Telephone: (314) 984-7500 FICE Identification: 002472
Accreditation: **&NH**, ADNUR, ART, OTA, PTAA

*Saint Louis Community College at Wildwood (G)

2645 Generations Drive, Wildwood MO 63040-1168
Telephone: (636) 422-2000 Identification: 667084
Accreditation: **&NH**

Saint Louis University (H)

One Grand Boulevard, Saint Louis MO 63103-2097
County: Independent City FICE Identification: 002506
Unit ID: 179159
Telephone: (314) 977-2500 Carnegie Class: DU-Higher
FAX Number: (314) 977-3874 Calendar System: Semester
URL: www.slu.edu
Established: 1818 Annual Undergrad Tuition & Fees: $43,884
Enrollment: 14,581 Coed
Affiliation or Control: Roman Catholic IRS Status: 501(c)3
Highest Offering: Doctorate
Accreditation: **NH**, AAB, ARCPA, ART, CAATE, CAEP, CAEPN, CAHIIM, CLPSY, DENT, DIETD, DIETI, HSA, LAW, MED, MFCD, MT, NMT, NURSE, OT, PH, PTA, RADMAG, RTT, SP, SW

01 President .... Dr. Fred P. PESTELLO
05 Interim Provost .... Dr. Chester GILLIS
10 Vice Pres/Chief Financial Officer .... Mr. David F. HEIMBURGER
18 Assoc VP Facilities Management .... Mr. Michael LUCIDO
84 VP Enrollment/Retention Management .... Ms. Kathleen DAVIS
12 Director Madrid Campus .... Dr. Paul VITA
15 VP Human Resources .... Mr. Mickey LUNA
26 VP Marketing and Communications .... Mr. Jeffrey FOWLER
43 Vice President/General Counsel .... Mr. William R. KAUFFMAN
32 Vice President Student Development .... Dr. Kent PORTERFIELD
30 VP Development .... Ms. Sheila M. MANION
42 Spec Asst to Pres Mission/Identity .. Fr. Christopher COLLINS, SJ
13 Vice Pres Information Tech Svcs/CIO .... Mr. David HAKANSON
23 Vice President for Medical Affairs .... Dr. Kevin BEHRNS
27 Asst VP Marketing & Communications .... Ms. Laura GEISER
29 Exec Development Director .... Ms. Mary CONNOLLY
21 Assistant Controller .... Mr. Fred R. WINKLER
35 Associate VP and Dean of Students .... Dr. Mona HICKS
54 Dean Parks Col Engr/Aviation .... Dr. Michelle SABICK
49 Dean Arts & Sciences .... Dr. Christopher DUNCAN
50 Dean Cook School of Business .... Dr. Mark HIGGINS
61 Dean of Law .... Mr. William P. JOHNSON
63 Dean of Medical School .... Dr. Kevin BEHRNS
79 Dean Philosophy & Letters .... Bro. William REHG, SJ
53 Int Dean College of Education .... Dr. Molly SCHALLER
08 University Librarian .... Mr. David CASSENS
88 Exec Dir Ctr for Health Care Ethics .... Dr. Jeffrey BISHOP
52 Exec Dir Ctr Advanced Dental Educ .... Dr. John HATTON
46 Vice President for Research .... Dr. Kenneth OLLIFF
19 Asst VP Pub Safety & Emergency Prep .... Mr. James MORAN
06 University Registrar .... Mr. Jay HAUGEN
07 Interim Director of Admission .... Ms. Heidi BUFFINGTON
37 Director Financial Aid .... Ms. Cari S. WICKLIFFE
41 Athletics Director .... Mr. Christopher V. MAY
85 Director International Center .... Vacant
92 Director Honors Program .... Mr. Robert PAMPEL
31 Pgm Mgr Leadership Community Svcs .... Dr. Bryan SOKOL
100 Chief of Staff .... Mr. Bob GAGNE
88 Director Univ Museums/Galleries .... Dr. Petruta LIPAN
44 Exec Development Dir Planned Giving .... Mr. Kent G. LEVAN
20 Asst Academic Vice President .... Dr. Steven SANCHEZ
96 Director of Business Services .... Mr. Jeff HOVEY
22 Dir Ofc of Inst Equity & Diversity .... Ms. Michelle LEWIS
86 Director Government Relations .... Mr. Marc SCHEESSELE
28 VP Diversity/Community Engagement .... Dr. Jonathan C. SMITH
103 Executive Dir Workforce Development .... Ms. Katherine CAIN
105 Director Web Services .... Mr. Mark RIMAR
38 Director Student Counseling .... Dr. Steve BYRNES
09 Director of Institutional Research .... Ms. Stacey HARRINGTON
101 Board & Council Administrator .... Ms. Amelia ARNOLD

Saint Luke's College of Health Sciences (I)

624 Westport Road, Kansas City MO 64111
County: Jackson FICE Identification: 009782
Unit ID: 179450
Telephone: (816) 936-8700 Carnegie Class: Spec-4-yr-Other Health
FAX Number: N/A Calendar System: Semester
URL: www.saintlukescollege.edu
Established: 1903 Annual Undergrad Tuition & Fees: N/A
Enrollment: 554 Coed
Affiliation or Control: Independent Non-Profit IRS Status: 501(c)3
Highest Offering: Master's
Accreditation: **NH**, NURSE

01 President/CEO .... Dr. Hubert BENITEZ
05 Provost/Chief Academic Officer .... Dr. Carlos G. PENALOZA
66 Dean of Nursing .... Dr. Victoria GRANDO
32 Chief Student Affairs Officer .... Ms. Marcia LADAGE
09 Dir Institutional Effectiveness .... Ms. Tere NAYLOR
10 Chief Financial Officer .... Ms. Rebecca PECK
30 Chief Development Officer .... Dr. Melody MESSNER
26 Director of Communications .... Ms. Laurie DELONG
84 Director Enrollment Management .... Mr. Josh RICHARDS
06 Registrar/Dir Records Management .... Ms. Jill LENOX

Southeast Missouri Hospital College of Nursing and Health Sciences (J)

2001 William Street, Cape Girardeau MO 63703-5815
County: Cape Girardeau FICE Identification: 030709
Unit ID: 417734
Telephone: (573) 334-6825 Carnegie Class: Spec-4-yr-Other Health
FAX Number: (573) 339-7805 Calendar System: Semester
URL: www.sehcollege.edu
Established: 1990 Annual Undergrad Tuition & Fees: $16,636
Enrollment: 206 Coed
Affiliation or Control: Independent Non-Profit IRS Status: 501(c)3
Highest Offering: Baccalaureate
Accreditation: **NH**, ADNUR, MT, NURSE, RAD, SURGT

01 President .... Dr. Steven D. LANGDON
05 Dean General Education/Student Svcs .... Dr. Dedria A. BLAKELY
66 Dean of Nursing .... Dr. Tonya BUTTRY
06 Registrar .... Ms. Debbie HOWEY
37 Financial Aid Director .... Ms. Cassandra HICKS
09 Inst Research Officer/Admissions .... Ms. Rhonda VANDERGRIFF
10 Business Officer .... Ms. Deanna SELLS

Southeast Missouri State University (K)

One University Plaza, Cape Girardeau MO 63701-4799
County: Cape Girardeau FICE Identification: 002501
Unit ID: 179557
Telephone: (573) 651-2000 Carnegie Class: Masters/L
FAX Number: (573) 651-2200 Calendar System: Semester
URL: www.semo.edu
Established: 1873 Annual Undergrad Tuition & Fees (In-State): $7,418
Enrollment: 11,486 Coed
Affiliation or Control: State IRS Status: 501(c)3
Highest Offering: Beyond Master's But Less Than Doctorate
Accreditation: **NH**, ART, CAATE, CACREP, CAEP, CEA, CIDA, COSMA, DANCE, DIETD, DIETI, JOUR, MUS, NAIT, NRPA, NURSE, SP, SW, THEA

01 President .... Dr. Carlos VARGAS
05 Provost .... Dr. Michael GODARD
10 VP Finance & Administration .... Mrs. Kathy M. MANGELS
84 VP Enrollment Mgmt/Student Success .... Dr. Debbie BELOW
111 Int VP University Advancement .... Mrs. Trudy LEE
09 Director of Institutional Research .... Mr. Eric CHAMBERS
100 Chief of Staff & Asst to the Pres .... Mr. Chris MARTIN
22 Asst to Pres Equity & Diversity .... Ms. Sonia RUCKER
13 Asst Vice Pres Information Tech .... Mr. Floyd DAVENPORT
32 AVP for Student Life .... Dr. Bruce SKINNER
50 Dean Harrison Col of Bus & Comp .... Dr. Alberto DAVILA
53 Int Dean Col of Educ/Hlth/Hum Stds .... Dr. Joe PUJOL
76 Int Dean Col of Humanities & Soc Sc .... Dr. Hamner HILL
79 Dean College of Arts & Media ... Ms. Rhonda WELLER STILSON
81 Dean Col of Sci/Tech/Engr/Math .... Dr. Tamela RANDOLPH
35 Dean of Students .... Ms. Sonia RUCKER
08 Dean of Kent Library .... Ms. Barbara GLACKIN
07 Director of Admissions .... Ms. Lenell HAHN
35 Director of Campus Life & Event Svc .... Ms. Michele IRBY
26 Dir Univ Marketing .... Ms. Tonya WELLS
41 Director of Athletics .... Mr. Brady L. BARKE
29 Director Alumni Services .... Mr. George GASSER
85 Exec Dir Intl Education & Svcs .... Mr. Kevin TIMLIN
12 Dean of Regional Campuses .... Ms. Marsha L. BLANCHARD
18 Director of Facilities Management .... Ms. Angela MEYER
37 Director of Student Financial Svcs .... Mr. Matt KEARNEY
27 Director of Univ Communications .... Ms. Ann K. HAYES
15 Director of Human Resources .... Ms. Alissa VANDEVEN
19 Dir of Public Safety/Trans .... Ms. Beth GLAUS
06 Registrar .... Ms. Sandy L. HINKLE
88 Director of Show Me Center .... Mr. Wil GORMAN
92 Dir Jane Stephens Honors Pgm .... Dr. Jim MCGILL
38 Dir Counseling & Disability Svcs .... Ms. Janice BUNCH
21 Controller & Asst Treasurer .... Ms. Pam SANDER
39 Director of Residence Life .... Dr. Kendra SKINNER

Southwest Baptist University (L)

1600 University Avenue, Bolivar MO 65613-2597
County: Polk FICE Identification: 002502
Unit ID: 179326
Telephone: (417) 328-5281 Carnegie Class: Masters/M
FAX Number: (417) 328-1514 Calendar System: Semester
URL: www.sbuniv.edu
Established: 1878 Annual Undergrad Tuition & Fees: $24,078
Enrollment: 3,592 Coed
Affiliation or Control: Southern Baptist IRS Status: 501(c)3
Highest Offering: Doctorate

Accreditation: NH, ACBSP, ADNUR, CAATE, MUS, NUR, PTA, RAD, SW

01 President ... Dr. Eric TURNER
05 Provost ... Dr. Lee SKINKLE
45 Vice Pres for Strategic Planning ... Dr. Allison LANGFORD
32 Vice Pres for Student Development ... Dr. Rob HARRIS
11 Vice President Administration ... Mrs. Tara PARSON
30 Vice President University Relations ... Dr. Brad JOHNSON
41 Athletic Director ... Mr. Mike PITTS
84 Dean of Enrollment Management ... Mr. Darren CROWDER
20 Assistant Provost ... Dr. Dana STEWARD
57 Dean Music/Arts/Letters ... Dr. Jeff WATERS
73 Dean College Theology/Ministry ... Dr. Rodney REEVES
53 Dean Education/Social Sciences ... Dr. Kevin SCHRIVER
81 Dean Science/Math ... Dr. Perry TOMPKINS
50 Dean College Business/Computer Sci ... Dr. Troy BETHARDS
08 Dean of University Libraries ... Dr. Ed WALTON
66 Dean of College Nursing/Health Sci .. Dr. Brittney HENDRICKSON
13 Chief Technology Officer ... Mr. David BOLTON
37 Dir Student Financial Assistance ... Mr. Brad GAMBLE
91 Network Administrator ... Mr. Kevin KELLEY
19 Director Campus Security ... Mr. Mark GRABOWSKI
106 Director of Online Learning ... Dr. Scott MCNEAL
42 Director University Ministries ... Mr. Kurt CADDY
18 Director Physical Plant ... Mr. Robbie BRYANT
06 Registrar ... Mrs. Roberta RASOR
39 Director Residence Life ... Ms. Landee NEVILLS
07 Director Admissions ... Mrs. Becky VAN STAVERN
36 Director of Career Services ... Mrs. Suzanne POWERS
29 Director of Alumni Engagement ... Mrs. Holly BRIDGE
35 Director Student Activities ... Dr. Nathan PENLAND
04 Executive Coordinator to President ... Mrs. Brittany EARL
108 Dir of Institutional Effectiveness ... Mr. Levi FOX
26 Chief Public Relations Officer ... Mrs. Charlotte MARSCH
123 Director of Graduate Admissions ... Mr. Todd EARL
38 Director Counseling Services ... Mrs. Debbie WALKER
10 Controller ... Ms. Terri ROGERS
15 Director of Human Resources ... Mrs. Sunny FULLER
40 Book Store Manager ... Vacant

Southwest Baptist University Mountain View Center (A)

PO Box 489, Mountain View MO 65548
Telephone: (417) 934-2999 Identification: 770326
Accreditation: &NH

Southwest Baptist University Salem (B)

501 S Grand, Salem MO 65560
Telephone: (573) 729-7071 Identification: 770327
Accreditation: &NH

Southwest Baptist University Springfield (C)

4431 S Fremont, Springfield MO 65804
Telephone: (417) 820-2069 Identification: 770328
Accreditation: &NH

State Fair Community College (D)

3201 W 16th Street, Sedalia MO 65301-2199
County: Pettis FICE Identification: 008080
Unit ID: 179539
Telephone: (660) 596-7222 Carnegie Class: Assoc/HT-High Trad
FAX Number: (660) 596-7335 Calendar System: Semester
URL: www.sfccmo.edu
Established: 1968 Annual Undergrad Tuition & Fees (In-District): $3,000
Enrollment: 4,742 Coed
Affiliation or Control: Local IRS Status: 501(c)3
Highest Offering: Associate Degree
Accreditation: NH, CAHIIM, CONST, DH, DMS, OTA, RAD

01 President ... Dr. Joanna ANDERSON
05 VP for Educ/Student Support Svcs ... Dr. Brent BATES
10 VP for Finance/Administration & HR ... Mr. Keith ACUFF
20 Dean of Academic Affairs ... Mr. Jim CUNNINGHAM
75 Dean Vocational/Technical Studies ... Vacant
121 Dean Student/Academic Support ... Dr. Autumn PORTER
13 Chief Information Officer ... Mr. Mark HAVERLY
102 Exec Director SFCC Foundation ... Ms. Mary TREUNER
06 Registrar ... Mrs. Jennifer WILBANKS
37 Director of Financial Aid ... Mrs. Angel MEFFORD
18 Chief Facilities/Physical Plant ... Mr. Justin O'NEAL
21 Controller Business Officer ... Mrs. Diane BROCKMAN
26 Exec Dir Marketing/Communication ... Mr. Brad HENDERSON
07 Director of Admissions ... Dr. Ty NANCE
04 Executive Asst to President ... Vacant
41 Athletic Director ... Mr. Darren PANNIER
15 Exec Director Human Resources ... Ms. Rachel DAWSON

State Technical College of Missouri (E)

One Technology Drive, Linn MO 65051-0479
County: Osage FICE Identification: 004711
Unit ID: 177977
Telephone: (573) 897-5000 Carnegie Class: Assoc/HVT-High Trad
FAX Number: N/A Calendar System: Semester
URL: www.statetechmo.edu
Established: 1961 Annual Undergrad Tuition & Fees (In-State): $6,120
Enrollment: 1,256 Coed
Affiliation or Control: State IRS Status: 501(c)3
Highest Offering: Associate Degree
Accreditation: NH, DA, NAIT, PTAA, RAD

01 President ... Dr. Shawn STRONG
101 Board of Regents Secretary ... Ms. Nichole ENGELHARDT
05 Vice President of Academic Affairs ... Ms. Vicki SCHWINKE
32 Vice President of Student Affairs ... Dr. Chris BOWSER
10 Vice President of Finance ... Ms. Jenny JACOBS
111 Vice President of Advancement ... Ms. Shannon GRUS
100 Chief of Staff ... Ms. Amy AMES
04 Executive Asst to the President ... Ms. Nichole ENGELHARDT
18 Director of Facilities ... Mr. Brad CREDE
13 Director of IT ... Mr. Mike ELY
26 Director of Marketing ... Mr. Brandon MCELWAIN
103 Director of Professional Dev ... Ms. Angie GAINES
20 Dean ... Ms. Janet CLANTON
56 Dean ... Mr. Aaron KLIETHERMES

Stephens College (F)

1200 E Broadway, Columbia MO 65215-0001
County: Boone FICE Identification: 002512
Unit ID: 179548
Telephone: (573) 442-2211 Carnegie Class: Masters/S
FAX Number: (573) 876-7248 Calendar System: Semester
URL: www.stephens.edu
Established: 1833 Annual Undergrad Tuition & Fees: $30,950
Enrollment: 862 Female
Affiliation or Control: Independent Non-Profit IRS Status: 501(c)3
Highest Offering: Master's
Accreditation: NH, #ARCPA, CAHIIM

01 President ... Dr. Dianne LYNCH
10 Vice Pres Finance/Business/CFO ... Mr. Dane FUHRMAN
05 Vice Pres Academic Affairs ... Dr. Leslie WILLEY
111 Vice Pres Institutional Advancement ... Ms. Gina SHOLTIS
32 Vice Pres Student Development ... Dr. Laura NUNNELLY
26 VP of Marketing/Public Relations ... Ms. Rebecca KLINE
84 Vice President Enrollment Mgmt ... Dr. Brian SAJKO
06 Registrar ... Ms. Linda SHARP
13 IT Director ... Mr. Mark BRUNNER
41 Athletic Director ... Vacant
37 Director of Financial Aid ... Ms. Alexandria MILLER
04 Executive Asst to President ... Ms. Lita PISTONO
07 Director of Admissions ... Ms. Tiffany GOALDER
08 Head Librarian ... Mr. Dan KAMMER
18 Director of Facilities Mgmt ... Mr. Ken ROBERTS
19 Director Security/Safety ... Mr. Ken HAMMOND
39 Director of Residence Life ... Ms. Alissa PEI
104 Study Abroad Coordinator ... Dr. James TERRY
108 Director Institutional Assessment ... Dr. Sharon SCHATTGEN
15 Director of Human Resources ..Ms. Kimberly SCHELLENBERGER

Stevens Institute of Business & Arts (G)

1521 Washington Avenue, Saint Louis MO 63103
County: Saint Louis FICE Identification: 008552
Unit ID: 178767
Telephone: (314) 421-0949 Carnegie Class: Spec-4-yr-Bus
FAX Number: (314) 421-0304 Calendar System: Quarter
URL: www.siba.edu
Established: 1947 Annual Undergrad Tuition & Fees: $12,960
Enrollment: 121 Coed
Affiliation or Control: Proprietary IRS Status: Proprietary
Highest Offering: Baccalaureate
Accreditation: ACCSC

01 President ... Ms. Cynthia A. MUSTERMAN
05 Academic Dean & Registrar ... Ms. Emilee SCHNEFKE
37 Financial Aid Director ... Ms. Christa SIAMPOS
07 Director of Admissions ... Ms. Sara DORN
36 Career Services Director ... Vacant

Texas County Technical College (H)

6915 S Highway 63 PO Box 314, Houston MO 65483
County: Texas FICE Identification: 035793
Unit ID: 441487
Telephone: (417) 967-5466 Carnegie Class: Spec 2-yr-Health
FAX Number: (417) 967-4604 Calendar System: Semester
URL: www.texascountytech.edu
Established: 1986 Annual Undergrad Tuition & Fees: $17,277
Enrollment: 54 Coed
Affiliation or Control: Independent Non-Profit IRS Status: 501(c)3
Highest Offering: Associate Degree
Accreditation: ABHES

01 President ... Ms. Charlotte GRAY
07 Director of Admissions/Registrar ... Ms. Clarice CASEBEER
37 Financial Aid Liaison ... Ms. Clarice CASEBEER

Three Rivers College (I)

2080 Three Rivers Boulevard,
Poplar Bluff MO 63901-2350
County: Butler FICE Identification: 004713
Unit ID: 179645
Telephone: (573) 840-9600 Carnegie Class: Assoc/HT-High Trad
FAX Number: (573) 840-9604 Calendar System: Semester
URL: www.trcc.edu
Established: 1966 Annual Undergrad Tuition & Fees (In-State): $3,960
Enrollment: 3,226 Coed
Affiliation or Control: State IRS Status: 501(c)3
Highest Offering: Associate Degree
Accreditation: NH, ACBSP, ADNUR, EMT, MLTAD, OTA

01 President ... Dr. Wesley A. PAYNE
10 Chief Financial Officer ... Ms. Charlotte EUBANK
05 Chief Academic Officer ... Dr. Justin HOGGARD
08 Director Library Services ... Ms. Kathy SANDERS
37 Director Financial Aid ... Ms. Regina MORRIS
06 Registrar ... Ms. Melanie HAMANN
32 Dean of Student Services ... Ms. Ann MATTHEWS
09 Dean of Institutional Effectiveness ... Dr. Maribeth PAYNE
18 Chief Facilities/Physical Plant ... Mr. Rob TOMLINSON
15 Director Human Resources ... Ms. Kristina D. MCDANIEL
26 Chief Public Relations Officer ... Ms. Teresa JOHNSON
30 Chief Development/Dir Alumni Rels ... Ms. Michelle REYNOLDS
84 Director Enrollment Management ... Mr. Chris ADAMS
96 Dir Procurement/Risk Management ... Ms. Cambrea HALCUMB
04 Administrative Asst to President ... Ms. Janine HEATH
103 Dir Workforce/Career Development ... Mr. Kevin SWAN
13 Chief Info Technology Officer (CIO) ... Mr. Steve ATWOOD
22 Dir Affirmative Action/EEO ... Ms. Kristina D. MCDANIEL
39 Director Student Housing ... Ms. Laura MILLIGAN
19 Director Security/Safety ... Mr. Chuck STRATTON

Truman State University (J)

100 E Normal, Kirksville MO 63501-4221
County: Adair FICE Identification: 002495
Unit ID: 178615
Telephone: (660) 785-4000 Carnegie Class: Masters/M
FAX Number: (660) 785-4030 Calendar System: Semester
URL: www.truman.edu
Established: 1867 Annual Undergrad Tuition & Fees (In-State): $7,749
Enrollment: 6,272 Coed
Affiliation or Control: State IRS Status: 501(c)3
Highest Offering: Master's
Accreditation: NH, CAATE, CAEP, MUS, NURSE, SP

01 President ... Dr. Susan L. THOMAS
05 Exec VP Acad Affairs & Provost ... Dr. Janet GOOCH
111 Vice Pres for Univ Advancement ... Dr. Ernie HUGHES
10 VP for Admin Finance & Planning ... Mr. David RECTOR
84 VP for Enrollment Mgmt & Marketing ... Dr. Tyana LANGE
32 VP for Student Affairs ... Mrs. Janna STOSKOPF
43 General Counsel ... Mr. Warren WELLS
21 Comptroller ... Mr. Michael GARZANELLI
41 Athletic Director ... Mr. Jerry WOLLMERING
15 Executive Dir of Human Resources ... Ms. Sally HERLETH
07 Assoc Director of Admission ... Ms. Dawn HOWD
37 Financial Aid Director ... Ms. Marla FERNANDEZ
06 Registrar ... Ms. Nancy ASHER
13 Director Information Technology ... Mrs. Donna LISS
26 Director of Public Relations ... Mrs. Heidi TEMPLETON
20 Associate Provost ... Dr. Kevin MINCH
38 Dir Student Health/Counseling Svcs ... Dr. Brenda HIGGINS
83 Dean Sch Social & Cultural Studies ... Dr. Elizabeth CLARK
50 Dean School of Business ... Dr. Debra KERBY
81 Dean Sch of Science & Math ... Dr. Timothy WALSTON
53 Dean Sch of Health Sci & Educ ... Dr. Lance RATCLIFF
49 Int Dean School of Arts & Letters ... Ms. Jeanne HARDING

University of Central Missouri (K)

Administration Building, Room 101,
Warrensburg MO 64093-5299
County: Johnson FICE Identification: 002454
Unit ID: 176965
Telephone: (660) 543-4255 Carnegie Class: Masters/L
FAX Number: (660) 543-4200 Calendar System: Semester
URL: www.ucmo.edu
Established: 1871 Annual Undergrad Tuition & Fees (In-State): $7,673
Enrollment: 12,333 Coed
Affiliation or Control: State IRS Status: 501(c)3
Highest Offering: Beyond Master's But Less Than Doctorate
Accreditation: NH, AAB, AAFCS, ART, #CAATE, CACREP, CAEPN, CEA, CIDA, DIETD, MUS, NAIT, NURSE, SP, SW, THEA

01 President ... Dr. Roger BEST
101 Exec Asst to Pres/Asst Sec to Board ... Ms. Monica R. HUFFMAN
43 General Counsel ... Ms. Lindsay CHAPMAN
05 Provost & VP of Academic Affairs ... Dr. Phillip BRIDGMON
32 VP Student Experience/Engagement ... Dr. Sharlene GARBER BAX
10 Vice President Finance & Operations ... Mr. Bill HAWLEY
41 Vice Pres Intercollegiate Athletics ... Mr. Jerry M. HUGHES
20 Vice Prov Academic Program/Services ... Dr. Doug KOCH
35 Assoc VP Student Services/Title IX ... Dr. Corey L. BOWMAN
84 Interim Vice Provost Enroll Mgmt ... Dr. Karen GOOS
111 Vice Pres Advancement & Ext Engage ... Ms. Courtney GODDARD
08 University Librarian ... Dr. Gail STAINES
49 Int Dean Arts/Humanities/Soc Sci ... Dr. Mike SAWYER
72 Dean College of Health/Science/Tech ... Dr. Alice L. GREIFE
50 Dean Business & Prof Studies ... Dr. Jose MERCADO
53 Dean of College of Education ... Dr. Robert LEE
13 Vice Provost for Technology & CIO ... Dr. James F. GRAHAM
06 Director of Registrar ... Dr. Lisa RUNYAN
26 Dir Marketing & Promotions ... Ms. Kelly WALDRAM CRAMER
121 Director Academic Success Advisor ... Mr. Kenneth SCHUELLER
37 Dir Student Financial Assistance ... Mr. Tony LUBBERS
19 Director of Public Safety ... Mr. Scott RHOAD
109 AVP Student Auxiliary Services ... Mr. Patrick J. BRADLEY
18 Assoc VP Capital Plng/Fac Mgmt ... Mr. Timothy CASTILAW

96 Director Purchasing .... Ms. Lisa BUTLER
15 Assoc VP Human Resources .... Ms. Ranea TAYLOR
40 Director of Univ Store & Textbooks .... Mr. Charles D. RUTT
56 Vice Provost of Extended Studies .... Dr. Laurel HOGUE
07 Asst Vice Prov Admissions/Fin Aid .... Mr. Drew GRIFFIN
38 Interim Director Counseling Center .... Dr. Jeanne WOON
24 Director CentralNET .... Mr. Michael JEFFRIES
36 Director Career Services .... Ms. Amber GOREHAM
09 Director of Institutional Research .... Dr. Meng CHEN

*University of Missouri System Administration (A)

321 University Hall, Columbia MO 65211-3020
County: Boone FICE Identification: 002515
Unit ID: 178439
Telephone: (573) 882-2011 Carnegie Class: N/A
FAX Number: (573) 882-2721
URL: www.umsystem.edu

01 President .... Mr. Mun Y. CHOI
100 Chief of Staff .... Ms. Christine HOLT
10 Vice President Finance/CFO .... Ryan RAPP
28 Chief Diversity/Equity/Incl Ofcr .... Dr. Kevin G. MCDONALD
09 Vice Pres Research/Econ Development .... Mr. Mark MCINTOSH
13 Vice President Info Technology .... Dr. Gary K. ALLEN
15 Vice Pres Human Resource Svcs .... Ms. Marsha FISCHER
20 Sr Assoc Vice Pres Academic Affairs .... Dr. Steven W. GRAHAM
43 General Counsel .... Mr. Stephen J. OWENS
26 Chief Communications Officer .... Ms. Kamrhan FARWELL
17 CEO/COO UM Health Care .... Mr. Jonathan CARTRIGHT
21 Treasurer .... Mr. Tom F. RICHARDS
21 Controller .... Mr. Eric VOGELWEID
04 Executive Asst to President .... Ms. Janet WAIBEL
101 Secretary of the Board of Curators .... Ms. Cindy S. HARMON

*University of Missouri - Columbia (B)

Columbia MO 65211-0001
County: Boone FICE Identification: 002516
Unit ID: 178396
Telephone: (573) 882-2121 Carnegie Class: DU-Highest
FAX Number: (573) 882-9907 Calendar System: Semester
URL: www.missouri.edu
Established: 1839 Annual Undergrad Tuition & Fees (In-State): $9,972
Enrollment: 30,844 Coed
Affiliation or Control: State IRS Status: 501(c)3
Highest Offering: Doctorate
Accreditation: NH, CAATE, CAEPT, CAMPEP, CEA, CIDA, CLPSY, COARC, COPSY, DIETC, DMS, HSA, IPSY, JOUR, LAW, LIB, MED, MUS, NMT, NRPA, NURSE, OT, PCSAS, PH, PHAR, PTA, RAD, SCPSY, SP, SPAA, SW, VET

02 Chancellor .... Dr. Alexander N. CARTWRIGHT
100 Chief of Staff .... Dr. Marty OETTING
05 Provost & Exec Vice Chanc Acad Affs .... Dr. Latha RAMCHAND
111 Vice Chanc Advancement .... Dr. Tom S. HILES
28 Vice Chanc Diversity .... Dr. NaTashua R. DAVIS
56 Vice Chanc Extension .... Dr. Marshall M. STEWART
10 Vice Chanc Finance & CFO .... Ms. Rhonda K. GIBLER
15 Vice Chanc Human Resources .... Ms. Patty A. HABERBERGER
11 Vice Chanc Operations .... Mr. Gary L. WARD
46 Vice Chanc Research/Econ Dev .... Dr. Mark A. MCINTOSH
29 Assoc Vice Chanc Alumni Relations .... Mr. Todd A. MCCUBBIN
28 Asst V Chanc Civil Rights/Title IX .... Ms. Andrea (Andy) S. HAYES
84 Vice Prov Enrollment Mgmt .... Ms. Kim A. HUMPHREY
09 Vice Prov Institutional Rsrch & QI .... Dr. Mardy T. EIMERS
85 Interim Vice Prov Intl Pgms .... Dr. Mary A. STEGMAIER
08 Vice Prov Libraries/Univ Librarian .... Ms. Ann C. RILEY
32 Vice Provost Student Affairs .... Dr. William B. STACKMAN
106 Vice Prov Undergrad Studies/eLearn .... Dr. James N. SPAIN
17 Chief Executive Officer .... Dr. Jonathan W. CURTRIGHT
13 Interim Chief Information Officer .... Ms. Beth C. CHANCELLOR
26 Chief Marketing & Comm Officer .... Dr. Kamrhan M. FARWELL
19 Police Chief University Police .... Mr. Robert (Doug) D. SCHWANDT
35 Dean of Students .... Dr. Jeffrey R. ZEILENGA
38 Exec Dir Stdnt Health & Well-Being .... Dr. Jamie L. SHUTTER
06 University Registrar .... Ms. Brenda V. SELMAN
47 Dean Agri/Food & Natural Resources .... Dr. Christopher R. DAUBERT
49 Dean Arts & Science .... Dr. Patricia A. OKKER
50 Dean Business .... Dr. Ajay S. VINZE
53 Dean Education .... Dr. Kathryn B. CHVAL
54 Dean Engineering .... Dr. Elizabeth G. LOBOA
58 Dean Graduate School .... Dr. Jeni L. HART
76 Dean Health Professions .... Dr. Kristofer HAGGLUND
59 Dean Human Environmental Sciences .... Dr. James (Sandy) S. RIKOON
60 Dean Journalism .... Dr. David D. KURPIUS
61 Dean Law .... Dr. Lyrissa B. LIDSKY
63 Interim Dean Medicine .... Dr. Steven C. ZWEIG
66 Dean Nursing .... Dr. Sarah A. THOMPSON
74 Dean Veterinary Medicine .... Dr. Carolyn J. HENRY
07 Director Admissions .... Mr. Charles A. MAY
41 Director Athletics .... Mr. Jim STERK
40 Director Campus Retail .... Ms. Sherry L. POLLARD
36 Director Career Center .... Dr. Rob M. MCDANIELS
105 Director Digital Service .... Mr. Kevin S. BAILEY
92 Director Honors College .... Dr. Jerome (J.D.) D. BOWERS
25 Director Sponsored Program Admin .... Mr. Craig A. DAVID
37 Int Director Student Financial Aid .... Ms. Lynn K. STICHNOTE

*University of Missouri - Kansas City (C)

5100 Rockhill Road, Kansas City MO 64110-2499
County: Jackson FICE Identification: 002518
Unit ID: 178402
Telephone: (816) 235-1000 Carnegie Class: DU-Higher
FAX Number: (816) 235-1717 Calendar System: Semester
URL: www.umkc.edu
Established: 1929 Annual Undergrad Tuition & Fees (In-State): $8,178
Enrollment: 16,372 Coed
Affiliation or Control: State IRS Status: 501(c)3
Highest Offering: Doctorate
Accreditation: NH, AA, ANEST, ARCPA, CAEP, CAEPN, CEA, CLPSY, COPSY, DANCE, DENT, DH, EMT, IPSY, LAW, MED, MUS, NURSE, OTA, PHAR, SPAA, SW, THEA

02 Chancellor .... Dr. C. Mauli AGRAWAL
05 Provost/Executive Vice Chancellor .... Dr. Barbara BICHELMEYER
28 Vice Chanc Diversity & Inclusion .... Dr. Susan WILSON
10 Vice Chanc Finance/Administration .... Ms. Sharon LINDENBAUM
21 Director Budgeting and Planning .... Ms. Karen D. WILKERSON
113 Director of Cashier/Collections .... Mr. Paul SCHWARTZ
18 Assoc Vice Chanc Campus Facilities .... Mr. Robert A. SIMMONS
104 Dir International Academic Programs .... Dr. Joy STEVENSON
102 Pres UMKC Foundation .... Ms. Lisa BARONIO
111 Vice Chanc University Advancement .... Mr. Curt J. CRESPINO
41 Athletic Director .... Mr. Brandon MARTIN
13 Chief Information Officer .... Mr. Andrew GOODENOW
119 Information Security Officer .... Mr. Justin MALYN
15 Vice Chanc Human Resources .... Ms. Carol HINTZ
118 Employee Services .... Mr. Ted STAHL
20 Deputy Prov for Academic Affairs .... Dr. Cynthia L. PEMBERTON
121 Assoc Vice Provost Univ College .... Dr. Kim MCNELEY
106 Asst Vice Provost Acad Innovation .... Dr. Molly MEAD
49 Int Dean College of Arts & Sciences .... Dr. Jennifer LUNDGREN
50 Dean Bloch School of Management .... Dr. Brian KLAAS
81 Dean Sch Bio and Chemical Sciences .... Dr. Theodore WHITE
92 Dean Honors College .... Dr. Jim MCKUSICK
64 Dean Conservatory of Music & Dance .... Dr. Diane PETRELLA
52 Dean School of Dentistry .... Dr. Marsha A. PYLE
53 Dean School of Education .... Dr. Justin PERRY
54 Dean Sch of Computing/Engineering .... Dr. Kevin Z. TRUMAN
61 Dean School of Law .... Ms. Barbara GLESNER FINES
63 Interim Dean School of Medicine .... Dr. Mary Anne JACKSON
66 Dean Sch of Nursing & Health Stds .... Dr. Ann CARY
67 Dean School of Pharmacy .... Dr. Russell B. MELCHERT
08 Dean University Libraries .... Dr. Bonnie POSTLETHWAITE
58 Dean of Graduate Studies .... Dr. Jennifer LUNDGREN
20 Vice Provost Inst Effectiveness .... Dr. Kelli COX
108 Director of Assessment .... Dr. Ruth CAIN
09 Director Institutional Research .... Dr. Ali KORKMAZ
84 Asst Vice Prov Enroll Management .... Mr. Doug SWINK
32 Interim Dean of Students .... Dr. Chris BROWN
35 Director Student Conduct .... Ms. Keishea BOYD
88 Director Student Involvement .... Dr. Todd WELLS
26 Vice Chanc Strategic Market & Comm .... Ms. Anne SPENNER
27 Director Media Relations .... Mr. John MARTELLARO
29 Director Alumni & Constituent Rels .... Ms. Kathryn HOUSTON
86 Asst Vice Chanc External Relations .... Mr. Troy LILLEBO
22 Title IX Coordinator .... Dr. Sybil WYATT
121 Dir Academic Support & Mentoring .... Dr. Julie COLLINS
07 Director of Admissions .... Ms. Alice ARREDONDO
37 Director Student Financial Aid .... Mr. Scott YOUNG
06 Registrar .... Ms. Amy COLE
19 Chief Campus Police .... Mr. Michael BONGARTZ
40 Director Bookstore .... Mr. Pete EISENTRAGER
38 Dir Counseling/Health/Disability .... Dr. Arnold ABELS
88 Director Women's Center .... Dr. Brenda BETHMAN
36 Int Director Career Services .... Ms. Tess SURPRENANT
39 Int Director Residential Life .... Mr. Troy LILLEBO
93 Dir Multicultural Student Affairs .... Ms. Keichanda DEES-BURNETT
109 Director Student Union .... Mr. Jody JEFFRIES
25 Business Manager for Admin Services .... Mr. Jeffery ROSS

*University of Missouri - Saint Louis (D)

1 University Boulevard, Saint Louis MO 63121-4400
County: Saint Louis FICE Identification: 002519
Unit ID: 178420
Telephone: (314) 516-5000 Carnegie Class: DU-Higher
FAX Number: (314) 516-5378 Calendar System: Semester
URL: www.umsl.edu
Established: 1963 Annual Undergrad Tuition & Fees (In-State): $9,792
Enrollment: 16,715 Coed
Affiliation or Control: State IRS Status: 501(c)3
Highest Offering: Doctorate
Accreditation: NH, CACREP, CAEPN, CLPSY, IPSY, MUS, NURSE, OPT, OPTR, SPAA, SW

02 Interim Chancellor .... Dr. Kristin SOBOLIK
05 Provost/Vice Chanc Acad Affairs .... Dr. Kristin SOBOLIK
10 Vice Chanc Finance/Admn & CFO .... Mr. Rick BANIAK
111 Interim VC Univ Advancement .... Ms. Beth KRUMM
26 Assoc Vice Chanc Marketing/Comm .... Mr. Robert D. SAMPLES
28 Dir Diversity/Equity/Inclusion .... Ms. Deborah J. BURRIS
46 Vice Provost Research Admin .... Dr. Christopher SPILLING
32 Vice Provost Student Affairs .... Dr. Curtis C. COONROD
58 Dean Graduate School .... Dr. Teresa THIEL
13 CIO .... Dr. Jane L. WILLIAMS
88 Dir Center for Teaching & Learning .... Dr. J. Andy GOODMAN
21 Sr Dir Financial Planning .... Ms. Tanika BUSCH
85 Director International Studies .... Dr. George T. SIPOS
49 Dean College Arts & Sciences .... Dr. Andrew KERSTEN
50 Interim Dean College Business Admin .... Mr. Charles E. HOFFMAN
53 Dean College of Education .... Dr. Ann TAYLOR
66 Dean College of Nursing .... Dr. Susan DEAN-BAAR
92 Dean Honors College .... Dr. Edward MUNN SANCHEZ
88 Dean College of Optometry .... Dr. Larry J. DAVIS
08 Dean of Libraries .... Mr. Christopher DAMES
54 Dean Engineering Program .... Dr. Joseph O'SULLIVAN
88 Asst to the Chancellor .... Ms. Elizabeth VAN UUM
35 Assoc Vice Provost Campus Life .... Dr. D'Andre BRADDIX
93 Asst Dean of Stdnts/MultiCultural .... Dr. Natissia SMALL
41 Director of Athletics .... Ms. Lori FLANAGAN
84 Dean of Enrollment Mgmt .... Mr. Alan BYRD
40 Manager Bookstore .... Ms. Stephanie EATON
36 Director Career Services .... Ms. Teresa A. BALESTRERI
06 Registrar .... Ms. Theresa KEUSS
39 Director Residential Life .... Ms. Jacquelyn WARREN
37 Director Student Financial Aid .... Dr. Anthony C. GEORGES
88 Dir Scientific & Computing/ITE .... Dr. William J. LEMON
88 Dir MO Inst of Mental Health .... Dr. Robert H. PAUL
18 Assoc Vice Chanc Facilities Mgmt .... Mr. Larry A. EISENBERG
114 Director Budget Services .... Ms. Joann F. WIILKINSON
88 Director of Finance & Accounting .... Mr. Randall VOGAN
113 Director Cashiers/Student Accounts .... Mr. Mitchell R. HESS
15 Executive Director Human Resources .... Mr. James W. HERTEL
19 Director Institutional Safety .... Mr. Dan FREET
09 Manager Institutional Research .... Dr. Carol S. SHOLY
88 Director St Louis Public Radio .... Mr. Tim J. EBY
44 Assoc VC Engagement/Annual Giving .... Ms. Jennifer JEZEK-TAUSSIG
70 Dean Social Work .... Dr. Sharon JOHNSON
88 Dir Performing Arts Center .... Mr. John R. CATTANACH
88 Dir Des Lee Collaborative Vision .... Ms. Patricia ZAHN
88 Dir Student Support/SUCCEED .... Mr. Jonathan LIDGUS
88 Dir Recreation/Wellness .... Ms. Yvette KELL

*Missouri University of Science & Technology (E)

300 W 13th Street, Rolla MO 65409-0001
County: Phelps FICE Identification: 002517
Unit ID: 178411
Telephone: (573) 341-4111 Carnegie Class: DU-Higher
FAX Number: (573) 341-4307 Calendar System: Semester
URL: www.mst.edu
Established: 1870 Annual Undergrad Tuition & Fees (In-State): $9,440
Enrollment: 8,883 Coed
Affiliation or Control: State IRS Status: 501(c)3
Highest Offering: Doctorate
Accreditation: NH, CEA

02 Chancellor .... Dr. Mohammad DEHGHANI
05 Interim Provost/Exec Vice Chanc .... Dr. Stephen ROBERTS
10 Interim Vice Chanc Finance/Ops .... Ms. Cuba PLAIN
111 Vice Chanc University Advancement .... Ms. Joan M. NESBITT
32 Vice Chancellor Student Affairs .... Dr. Debra A G. ROBINSON
35 Assoc Vice Chanc Student Affairs .... Dr. James H. MURPHY
20 Int Deputy Provost Acad Excellence .... Dr. Richard K. BROW
121 Vice Provost Academic Support .... Dr. Jeffrey CAWLFIELD
84 Acting Vice Prov/Dean Enroll Mgt .... Ms. Brooke M. DURBIN
54 VP/Dean Col Engr & Computing .... Dr. Richard WLEZIEN
49 Int VP/Dean Arts/Sciences/Business .... Dr. Kate DROWNE
08 Director of Library .... Dr. Oliver CHEN
13 Interim Co-CIO .... Mr. Mark BOOKOUT
13 Interim Co-CIO .... Ms. Cathy ALLISON
06 Registrar .... Ms. Deanne JACKSON
38 AVC Student Affairs/Support Svcs .... Dr. Edna GROVER-BISKER
41 Director of Athletics .... Mr. Mark E. MULLIN
23 Senior Dir Student Health Services .... Dr. Dennis S. GOODMAN
36 Dir Career Opportunities Center .... Mr. William ZWIKELMAIER
85 AP International/Cultural Affairs .... Dr. Jeanie HOFER
35 Director Student Life .... Mr. John GALLAGHER
39 Director Residential Life .... Dr. Dorie PAINE
07 Interim Director of Admissions .... Ms. Cathy TIPTON
29 Asst Vice Chanc Advancement Svcs .... Ms. Darlene RAMSAY
37 Director Student Financial Aid .... Ms. Bridgette K. BETZ
26 Executive Director Communications .... Mr. Andrew P. CAREAGA
18 Asst Vice Chanc Facilities Svcs .... Mr. Ted RUTH
40 Manager of University Bookstore .... Mr. Mark GALLARDO
19 Director University Police .... Mr. Douglas P. ROBERTS
27 Assoc Dir Strategic Communications .... Ms. Cheryl A. MCKAY
112 Director Planned Giving .... Mr. John HELD, II
28 Chief Diversity Officer .... Mr. Neil OUTAR
15 Director Human Resources .... Ms. Rhonda BYERS

*Missouri University of Science & Technology Global-St. Louis (F)

12837 Flushing Meadows Dr., Ste 210,
St. Louis MO 63131
Telephone: (314) 835-9822 Identification: 770323
Accreditation: &NH

Urshan Graduate School of Theology (G)

1151 Century Link Dr., Wentzville MO 63385
County: St. Charles FICE Identification: 041461
Unit ID: 455099
Telephone: (314) 838-8858 Carnegie Class: Spec-4-yr-Faith

FAX Number: (314) 838-8848 Calendar System: Semester
URL: www.ugst.edu
Established: 2001 Annual Undergrad Tuition & Fees: N/A
Enrollment: 91 Coed
Affiliation or Control: Other Protestant IRS Status: 501(c)3
Highest Offering: Master's
Accreditation: @NH, THEOL

01 President Dr. Brent COLTHARP
03 Executive Vice President Rev. Jennie RUSSELL
05 Academic Dean Rev. David JOHNSON
32 Dean of Student Services Rev. David REID
10 CFO Mrs. Jill CRUMPACKER
06 Registrar Ms. Brook CROW
08 Head Librarian Dr. Gary ERICKSON
106 Director of Distance Learning Ms. Vinessa D'SA
26 Director of Marketing and Events Mr. David MOLINA
07 Director of Admissions Ms. Dinecia GATES
15 Chief Human Resources Officer Mrs. Marsha JOHNSTON
30 Development Officer Mr. Christopher BRAINOS
36 Director Student Placement Ms. Amber WILLEFORD
37 Director Student Financial Aid Mr. Grant POLLARD
39 Director Student Housing Mrs. Rachel CARSON
101 Secretary of the Institution/Board Rev. Darrell JOHNS
108 Dir Institutional Effectiveness Mrs. Wanda BAKER
44 Director Annual Giving Mr. Christopher BRAINOS
09 Director of Institutional Research Dr. Cindy MILLER
13 Chief Information Technology Ofcr Mr. Kameron GOODMAN
18 Chief Facilities/Physical Plant Rev. Timothy SIMONEAUX

Washington University in St. Louis (A)

One Brookings Drive, Saint Louis MO 63130-4899
County: Saint Louis FICE Identification: 002520
Unit ID: 179867
Telephone: (314) 935-5100 Carnegie Class: DU-Highest
FAX Number: N/A Calendar System: Semester
URL: www.wustl.edu
Established: 1853 Annual Undergrad Tuition & Fees: $53,399
Enrollment: 15,303 Coed
Affiliation or Control: Independent Non-Profit IRS Status: 501(c)3
Highest Offering: Doctorate
Accreditation: NH, ART, AUD, CLPSY, LAW, LSAR, MED, OT, PCSAS, PH, PTA, SW

01 Chancellor Dr. Andrew D. MARTIN
05 Int Provost/Exec VC Acad Affairs Dr. Marion G. CRAIN
11 Exec VC Admin & Chief Adm Officer Mr. Henry S. WEBBER
63 Exec Vice Chanc/Dean of Medicine Dr. David H. PERLMUTTER
43 Vice Chanc/General Counsel Ms. Monica J. ALLEN
111 Exec VC Alumni & Development Ms. Pamella A. HENSON
10 Vice Chancellor for Finance/CFO Ms. Amy B. KWESKIN
46 Vice Chancellor for Research Dr. Jennifer K. LODGE
15 Vice Chanc for Human Resources Ms. Legail P. CHANDLER
13 Vice Chanc & Chief Info Officer Mr. Chris KIELT
32 Vice Chancellor for Student Affairs Dr. Lori S. WHITE
26 Vice Chanc for Public Affairs Ms. Jill D. FRIEDMAN
86 VC Government & Community Relations Ms. Pamela S. LOKKEN
115 Chief Investment Officer Mr. Scott L. WILSON
21 Assoc VC for Finance and Treasurer Mr. Mark N. AMIRI
49 Dean Faculty of Arts & Sciences Dr. Barbara A. SCHAAL
61 Dean School of Law Dr. Nancy STAUDT
54 Dean McKelvey School of Engineering Dr. Aaron F. BOBICK
57 Dean Sam Fox Sch Design/Visual Arts Prof. Carmon COLANGELO
57 Dir College & Grad Sch of Art Prof. Amy G. HAUFT
50 Dean Olin School of Business Prof. Mark P. TAYLOR
58 Dean The Graduate School Prof. William F. TATE
70 Dean Brown School of Social Work Prof. Mary M. MCKAY
55 Interim Dean University College Prof. Heather A. CORCORAN
48 Dir College of Architecture & Grad Prof. Heather WOOFTER
100 Assoc Vice Chanc/Chief of Staff Ms. Rebecca L. BROWN
101 Secretary to the Board of Trustees Ms. Ida H. EARLY
07 Vice Provost for Admissions & Fin Ms. Ronne P. TURNER
20 Vice Provost/Assoc VC Academic Affs Prof. Gerhild S. WILLIAMS
29 Sr VC Alumni & Development Programs Mr. William S. STOLL
26 Assoc VC Medical Public Affairs Ms. Joni L. WESTERHOUSE
28 Vice Provost Prof. Adrienne D. DAVIS
85 VC for International Affairs Prof. Kurt T. DIRKS
08 Vice Provost & University Librarian Ms. Denise STEPHENS
35 Assoc Vice Chanc for Students/Dean Dr. Robert M. WILD
92 Assoc VC & Dean Scholar Pgm Ms. Robyn S. HADLEY
14 Asst VC for Enterprise Applications Mr. Scott TAYLOR
27 Assoc VC for Univ Communications Ms. Julie A. FLORY
85 Asst VC/Dir International Students Ms. Kathy STEINER-LANG
96 Assoc VC Resource Management Mr. Alan S. KUEBLER
36 Assoc VC/Director Career Center Mr. Mark W. SMITH
18 Assoc VC Facilities Planning/Mgmt Mr. JD LONG, II
88 Asst VC Environ Health & Safety Mr. Bruce D. BACKUS
88 Assoc VC Real Estate Ms. Mary B. CAMPBELL
72 Director OTM Ms. Nichole R. MERCIER
90 Asst VC for Enterprise Appl Service Ms. Denise R. HIRSCHBECK
23 Exec Dir Habif Health & Wellness Dr. Cheri LEBLANC
37 Director Student Financial Services Mr. Michael J. RUNIEWICZ
41 Director of Athletics Mr. Anthony J. AZAMA
19 Chief of Police Mr. Mark R. GLENN
07 Director of Admissions Ms. Emily L. ALMAS
06 University Registrar Ms. Susan E. HOSACK
38 Director of Mental Health Services Dr. Thomas M. BROUNK

Washington University in St. Louis-School of Medicine (B)

660 Euclid Avenue, Saint Louis MO 63110
Telephone: (314) 360-5000 Identification: 770329
Accreditation: &NH

Webster University (C)

470 E Lockwood, Webster Groves MO 63119-3141
County: Saint Louis FICE Identification: 002521
Unit ID: 179894
Telephone: (800) 981-9801 Carnegie Class: Masters/L
FAX Number: N/A Calendar System: Semester
URL: www.webster.edu
Established: 1915 Annual Undergrad Tuition & Fees: $27,900
Enrollment: 12,736 Coed
Affiliation or Control: Independent Non-Profit IRS Status: 501(c)3
Highest Offering: Doctorate
Accreditation: NH, ACBSP, ANEST, CACREP, CAEPN, MUS, NUR

01 President Dr. Elizabeth J. STROBLE
05 Provost Dr. Julian Z. SCHUSTER
84 Vice Pres Enrollment Vacant
10 Interim Chief Financial Officer Mr. Richard MEYER
13 Chief Information Officer Ms. Margie MUTHUKUMARU
101 University Secretary Ms. Jeanelle WILEY
20 Vice Provost Ms. Nancy HELLERUD
58 Asst Provost for Graduate Studies Dr. Elizabeth RUSSELL
04 Executive Assistant to President Ms. Dana SPREHE
50 Dean School Business/Technology Dr. Simone CUMMINGS
53 Interim Dean School of Education Dr. Thomas CORNELL
57 Dean Leigh Gerdine Col of Fine Arts Mr. Paul STEGER
49 Dean Col of Arts & Sciences Dr. Anton WALLNER
60 Dean School of Communications Dr. Eric ROTHENBUHLER
08 Dean of University Library Ms. Eileen CONDON
32 Int AVP Stdnt Affs/Dean of Students Mr. John BUCK
56 Dean of Extended Education Ms. Thao DANG-WILLIAMS
106 AVP/Military and Online Education Dr. Michael COTTAM
82 AVP Academic Affairs Intl Pgms Vacant
15 Int Chief Human Resources Officer Ms. Douglas RAU
27 AVP & Chief Comm Officer Mr. Rick ROCKWELL
12 AVP Extended US Campuses Dr. Donavan OUTTEN
37 AVP UG Admiss/Dir Financial Aid Mr. James MYERS
28 AVP Diversity & Inclusion Vacant
06 Registrar Mr. Don MORRIS
20 Director of Academic Advising Mr. Kim KLEINMAN
19 Director Public Safety Mr. Rick GERGER
26 Dir Public Relations/Global Mktg Mr. Patrick GIBLIN
24 Dir of Media & Acad Tech Services Mr. Dewey MARTIN
36 Dir Career Planning & Dev Center Mr. John LINK
29 Director of Alumni Programs Vacant
41 Director Athletics Mr. Scott KILGALLON
23 Director Student Health Svcs Ms. Ann BROPHY
35 Director Student Engagement Ms. Jennifer STEWART
38 Director Counsel & Life Development Dr. Patrick STACK
96 Director of Procurement Services Mr. Kenneth CREEHAN
09 Director of Inst Effectiveness Mr. Justin BITNER
18 Director Facilities Planning Vacant
104 Director of Study Abroad Ms. Kelly HEATH
111 AVP Advancement Ms. Andrea SOTO
07 Dir UG Admissions/Int Grad Admiss Mr. Andrew LAUE

WellSpring School of Allied Health-Kansas City (D)

9140 Ward Pkwy Ste 100, Kansas City MO 64114
County: Jackson FICE Identification: 039704
Unit ID: 447999
Telephone: (816) 523-9140 Carnegie Class: Spec 2-yr-Health
FAX Number: (816) 523-0741 Calendar System: Other
URL: www.wellspring.edu
Established: 1988 Annual Undergrad Tuition & Fees: N/A
Enrollment: 176 Coed
Affiliation or Control: Proprietary IRS Status: Proprietary
Highest Offering: Associate Degree
Accreditation: ABHES

01 President Donald FARQUHARSON
11 VP of Campus Operations Robin O'CONNELL
05 Education Director Tracy HOUTZ

Westminster College (E)

501 Westminster Avenue, Fulton MO 65251-1230
County: Callaway FICE Identification: 002523
Unit ID: 179946
Telephone: (573) 642-3361 Carnegie Class: Bac-A&S
FAX Number: (573) 592-5227 Calendar System: Semester
URL: www.wcmo.edu
Established: 1851 Annual Undergrad Tuition & Fees: $27,600
Enrollment: 767 Coed
Affiliation or Control: Independent Non-Profit IRS Status: 501(c)3
Highest Offering: Baccalaureate
Accreditation: NH, ACBSP

01 President Dr. Fletcher LAMKIN
05 VP of Academic Affairs Dr. David ROEBUCK
111 VP for Advancement Vacant
10 Vice Pres Business/Chief Fin Ofcr Mr. Bob FESSLER
26 VP & Chief Communications Officer Ms. Lana POOLE
32 Dean of Student Life Dr. Kasi LACEY
84 VP of Enrollment Services Mr. Ted KULAWIAK
18 VP of Campus Operations Mr. Dan HASLAG
20 Associate Dean of Faculty Dr. Cinnamon BROWN
121 Associate Dean of Student Success Dr. Ingrid ILINCA
06 Registrar Mrs. Phyllis MASEK
07 Director of Admissions Ms. Amy MAREK
13 Executive Director of IT Mr. Matt VORE
37 Senior Director of Financial Aid Ms. Aimee BRISTOW
111 Director of Advancement Services Ms. Gina CAMPAGNA
15 Director of Human Resources Ms. Mandy MARCH
19 Director of Campus Safety/Security Mr. Jack BENKE
41 Athletic Director Mr. Matt MITCHELL
23 Exec Director Wellness Center Dr. Kasi LACEY
27 Director Media & Public Relations Mr. Robert CROUSE
29 Dir Alumni Engagement Ms. Sarah MUNNS
08 Director of Library Services Ms. Angela GROGAN
36 Director of Career Services Ms. Meg LANGLAND
09 Director of Institutional Research Vacant
42 Chaplain Rev. Kiva NICE-WEBB
04 Executive Asst to the President Ms. Amy LOWE

William Jewell College (F)

500 College Hill, Liberty MO 64068-1896
County: Clay FICE Identification: 002524
Unit ID: 179955
Telephone: (816) 781-7700 Carnegie Class: Bac-Diverse
FAX Number: (816) 415-5027 Calendar System: Semester
URL: www.jewell.edu
Established: 1849 Annual Undergrad Tuition & Fees: $34,400
Enrollment: 933 Coed
Affiliation or Control: Independent Non-Profit IRS Status: 501(c)3
Highest Offering: Master's
Accreditation: NH, MUS, NURSE

01 President Dr. Elizabeth MACLEOD WALLS
05 Provost Dr. Anne C. DEMA
10 Vice Pres for Finance & Operations Mr. Brian CLEMONS
111 Vice Pres Institutional Advancement Mr. Clark MORRIS
84 Vice Pres Enrollment & Marketing Mr. Eric BLAIR
32 Dean of Student Life Ms. Shelly KING
07 Director of Admission Services Mr. Brian HAINES
06 Registrar Dr. Edwin H. LANE
08 Director of Library Services Ms. Rebecca HAMLETT
21 Director of Accounting and Finance Ms. Barb WALTERS
13 Director of Information Technology Ms. Lan GUO
97 Assoc Dean Core Curriculum Dr. Gary ARMSTRONG
37 Director of Financial Aid Mr. Daniel HOLT
15 Director of Human Resources Ms. Julie DUBINSKY
18 Director of Facilities Management Ms. Stephany GUEST
57 Executive Director Harriman-Jewell Mr. Clark W. MORRIS
41 Director of Athletics Mr. Thomas EISENHAUER
36 Director of Career Development Ms. Marissa BLAND
38 Director of Counseling Services Ms. Tricia HAGER
29 Director of Alumni Relations Ms. Andrea MELOAN
104 Director of Global Studies Ms. Sara ROUND
04 Executive Asst to President Ms. Tiffany POLLARD
19 Director of Campus Safety Mr. Landon JONES
26 Director of Marketing Ms. Cara DAHLOR
39 Director of Residence Life Mr. Ernie STUFFLEBEAN
44 Director of Annual Giving Ms. Laura HANAVAN
90 Director of Teaching/Learning Tech Mr. Heath HASE
50 Chair Comm in Business & Leadership Dr. Kelli SCHUTTE
53 Chair Education Dr. Donna GARDNER

William Woods University (G)

One University Avenue, Fulton MO 65251-1098
County: Callaway FICE Identification: 002525
Unit ID: 179964
Telephone: (800) 995-3159 Carnegie Class: DU-Mod
FAX Number: (573) 592-1146 Calendar System: Semester
URL: www.williamwoods.edu
Established: 1870 Annual Undergrad Tuition & Fees: $24,110
Enrollment: 2,284 Coed
Affiliation or Control: Christian Church (Disciples Of Christ)
IRS Status: 501(c)3
Highest Offering: Doctorate
Accreditation: NH, ACBSP, SW

01 President Dr. Jahnae H. BARNETT
03 University Vice President Scott GALLAGHER
84 Vice President of Enrollment Kathy GROVES
32 Vice President/Dean of Student Life Dr. Venita MITCHELL
26 Vice President of Strategic Comm John FOUGERE
108 Vice President Inst Effectiveness Dr. Michael WESTERFIELD
05 Vice President/Dean for Acad Affs Dr. Aimee SAPP
111 Vice President of Advancement Lisa COLE EIMERS
10 Chief Financial Officer Julie HOUSEWORTH
13 Chief Information Officer Vacant

MONTANA

Aaniiih Nakoda College (H)

PO Box 159, Harlem MT 59526-0159
County: Blaine FICE Identification: 025175
Unit ID: 180203
Telephone: (406) 353-2607 Carnegie Class: Tribal
FAX Number: (406) 353-2898 Calendar System: Semester
URL: www.ancollege.edu
Established: 1984 Annual Undergrad Tuition & Fees: $2,410

Enrollment: 122 Coed
Affiliation or Control: Tribal Control IRS Status: 501(c)3
Highest Offering: Associate Degree
Accreditation: NW

01 President Dr. Carole FALCON-CHANDLER
05 Int Dean of Academic Affairs Dr. Sean CHANDLER
32 Dean of Student Affairs Ms. Clarena BROCKIE
10 Comptroller Ms. Debra EVE
06 Registrar/Admissions Officer Mrs. Dixie BROCKIE
37 Financial Aid Director Ms. Toma CAMPBELL-HOOPS
08 Library Director Ms. Eva ENGLISH
25 Sponsored Programs Director Mr. Scott FRISKICS
13 Manager Information Systems Mr. Harold H. HEPPNER
40 Bookstore Manager Ms. Kimberly BROCKIE
04 Assistant to the President Ms. Michele BROCKIE
09 Institutional Research Assistant Ms. Danielle JACKSON

Apollos University (A)

600 Central Avenue, Ste 215, Great Falls MT 59401
County: Cascade Identification: 667096
Telephone: (406) 604-4300 Carnegie Class: Not Classified
FAX Number: (866) 287-1938 Calendar System: Quarter
URL: apollos.edu
Established: 2005 Annual Undergrad Tuition & Fees: N/A
Enrollment: N/A Coed
Affiliation or Control: Proprietary IRS Status: Proprietary
Highest Offering: Doctorate
Accreditation: DEAC

00 CEO Dr. Paul EIDSON
01 President Dr. Scott EIDSON
05 EVP/Provost and CAO Dr. Robin WESTERIK
32 Exec Vice Pres Student Services Dr. Michelle FOX
10 Sr Vice Pres Administration/CFO Dr. Kelly LANCASTER
15 Vice President Human Resources Dr. Amanda CERAR-DERBISH
07 Dir Admissions/Student Engagement Ms. Laura TOVAR
06 Registrar Ms. Rebekah SANDERS

Blackfeet Community College (B)

Box 819, Browning MT 59417-0819
County: Glacier FICE Identification: 025106
Unit ID: 180054
Telephone: (406) 338-5441 Carnegie Class: Tribal
FAX Number: (406) 338-3272 Calendar System: Semester
URL: www.bfcc.edu
Established: 1974 Annual Undergrad Tuition & Fees: $3,370
Enrollment: 375 Coed
Affiliation or Control: Independent Non-Profit IRS Status: 501(c)3
Highest Offering: Associate Degree
Accreditation: NW

01 President Dr. Karla BIRD
05 Dean Academic Affairs Mrs. Carol MURRAY
32 Dean Student Services Vacant
10 Finance Director Vacant
37 Director of Financial Aid Mrs. Gaylene DUCHARME
06 Registrar/Dir of Admissions Ms. Helen HORN
09 Director of Institutional Research Mr. Brad R. HALL
18 Chief Facilities/Physical Plant Mr. Smokey HENRIKSEN
15 Human Resources Director Ms. Shannon CONNELLY

Carroll College (C)

1601 N Benton Avenue, Helena MT 59625-0002
County: Lewis And Clark FICE Identification: 002526
Unit ID: 180106
Telephone: (406) 447-4300 Carnegie Class: Bac-Diverse
FAX Number: (406) 447-4533 Calendar System: Semester
URL: www.carroll.edu
Established: 1909 Annual Undergrad Tuition & Fees: $35,486
Enrollment: 1,362 Coed
Affiliation or Control: Roman Catholic IRS Status: 501(c)3
Highest Offering: Baccalaureate
Accreditation: NW, IACBE, NURSE

01 President Dr. John CECH
04 Executive Asst to the President Ms. Hannah VANHOOSE
05 Interim Sr VP for Academic Affairs Ms. Cathy DAY
10 VP for Finance & Administration Ms. Lori PETERSON
84 VP of Enrollment and Marketing Dr. Chato HAZELBAKER
111 VP for Institutional Advancement Mr. Michael MCMAHON
42 Director Campus Ministry-Chaplain Rev. Marc LENNEMAN
41 Athletic Director Mr. Charles GROSS
32 Dean of Students & Retention Ms. Beth GROMAN
09 Director of Institutional Research Mr. Erik ROSE
06 Registrar Ms. Cassie HALL
26 Director of Public Relations Ms. Sarah LAWLOR
37 Financial Aid Director Ms. Janet RIIS
36 Career Services & Internships Mr. Wes FEIST
15 Dir Human Resources & Admin Svcs Ms. Renee M. MCMAHON
18 Director of Facilities Mr. Walter H. BISKUPIAK
35 Dir Student Activities/Leadership Mr. Patrick HARRIS
21 Controller Ms. Kari BRUSTKERN
13 Campus Computing/Info Tech Director Ms. Loretta ANDREWS
29 Director Alumni Relations Ms. Renee WALL

Chief Dull Knife College (D)

One College Drive, PO Box 98, Lame Deer MT 59043
County: Rosebud FICE Identification: 025452
Unit ID: 180160
Telephone: (406) 477-6215 Carnegie Class: Tribal
FAX Number: (406) 477-6219 Calendar System: Semester
URL: www.cdkc.edu
Established: 1975 Annual Undergrad Tuition & Fees: $2,260
Enrollment: 186 Coed
Affiliation or Control: Independent Non-Profit IRS Status: 501(c)3
Highest Offering: Associate Degree
Accreditation: NW

01 President/Int Dean Cultural Affairs Dr. Richard LITTLEBEAR
03 Vice President Mr. William WERTMAN
05 Dean Academic Affairs Mr. William BRIGGS
32 Dean Student Affairs Mr. Zane SPANG
37 Director Financial Aid Mr. Jody JENSON
08 Library Director M. Jerusha SHIPSTEAD

Dawson Community College (E)

P.O. Box 421, Glendive MT 59330-0421
County: Dawson FICE Identification: 002529
Unit ID: 180151
Telephone: (406) 377-3396 Carnegie Class: Assoc/HT-High Non
FAX Number: (406) 377-8132 Calendar System: Semester
URL: www.dawson.edu
Established: 1940 Annual Undergrad Tuition & Fees (In-District): $3,720
Enrollment: 329 Coed
Affiliation or Control: State/Local IRS Status: 501(c)3
Highest Offering: Associate Degree
Accreditation: NW

01 President Dr. Scott R. MICKELSEN
05 VP Academic & Student Affairs Ms. Traci MASAU
06 Registrar Ms. Virginia BOYSUN
08 Library Director Mr. Nasir AWILL
37 Director of Financial Aid Mr. Justin BEECH
13 Director of Information Technology Mr. Mark ROE
15 VP of Advancement & Human Resources Ms. Leslie WELDON
103 Dir Workforce/Career Development Ms. Sara ENGLE
84 Director Enrollment Management Ms. Suela CELA
04 Assistant to the President Ms. Randi JOHNSON
10 Chief Financial/Business Officer Ms. Jennifer KING
41 Athletic Director Mr. Joe PETERSON
07 Director of Admissions Ms. Suela CELA
102 Exec Director of the Foundation Mr. Dennis HARP
18 Chief Facilities/Phys Plant Ofcr Mr. Todd THOMPSON
25 Chief Contract/Grants Administrator Ms. Sarah BROCKEL
26 Dir Marketing & Public Relations Ms. Janelle OLBERDING
39 Director Residence Life Mr. Jon LANGLOIS
96 Director of Purchasing Ms. Tammy REED

Flathead Valley Community College (F)

777 Grandview Drive, Kalispell MT 59901
County: Flathead FICE Identification: 006777
Unit ID: 180197
Telephone: (406) 756-3822 Carnegie Class: Assoc/MT-VT-High Non
FAX Number: (406) 756-3815 Calendar System: Semester
URL: www.fvcc.edu
Established: 1967 Annual Undergrad Tuition & Fees (In-District): $4,808
Enrollment: 2,307 Coed
Affiliation or Control: Local IRS Status: 501(c)3
Highest Offering: Associate Degree
Accreditation: NW, EMT, MAC, PTAA, SURGT

01 President Dr. Jane A. KARAS
05 Vice President Academic Affairs Dr. Chris CLOUSE
10 VP Administration & Finance/CFO Ms. Beckie CHRISTIAENS
12 Director Lincoln County Campus Mr. Chad SHILLING
32 Dean of Student Affairs Ms. Brenda HANSON
51 Exec Dir Economic Dev/Cont Educ Mr. Chris PARSON
111 Exec Dir Institutional Advancement Ms. Colleen UNTERREINER
13 Exec Dir Mgmt Information Systems Mr. Duane ANDERSON
15 Exec Director of Human Resources Ms. Karen GLASSER
06 Registrar Ms. Sharon NAU
37 Director Financial Aid Ms. Cindy KIEFER
88 Director of Adult Basic Education Ms. Andrea AUS
21 Controller/Business Services Ms. Dawn STEELE
26 Director Marketing & Communication Mr. Christopher DEMANCHE
96 Director of Purchasing Mr. Steve LARSON
18 Manager Maintenance Service Mr. David EVANS
24 Coord Instructional Media Services Ms. Malinda CRAWFORD
36 Career Advisor Ms. Cathy ALLARD
04 Administrative Asst to President Ms. Monica SETTLES

Fort Peck Community College (G)

PO Box 398, Poplar MT 59255-0398
County: Roosevelt FICE Identification: 023430
Unit ID: 180212
Telephone: (406) 768-6300 Carnegie Class: Tribal
FAX Number: (406) 768-6301 Calendar System: Semester
URL: www.fpcc.edu
Established: 1978 Annual Undergrad Tuition & Fees: $2,250
Enrollment: 358 Coed
Affiliation or Control: Tribal Control IRS Status: 501(c)3
Highest Offering: Associate Degree
Accreditation: NW

01 President Ms. Haven GOURNEAU
05 Vice President Academic Affairs Mr. Wayne TWO BULLS
32 Vice President Student Services Mr. Elijah HOPKINS
30 Director Institutional Development Mr. Craig SMITH
10 Business Manager Ms. Rose ATKINSON
06 Registrar Ms. Michelle DAY
37 Financial Aid Officer Ms. Lanette CLARK
40 Bookstore Manager Vacant
08 Head Librarian Mrs. Anita A. SCHEETZ

Little Big Horn College (H)

PO Box 370, Crow Agency MT 59022-0370
County: Big Horn FICE Identification: 022866
Unit ID: 180328
Telephone: (406) 638-3104 Carnegie Class: Tribal
FAX Number: (406) 638-3169 Calendar System: Semester
URL: www.lbhc.edu
Established: 1980 Annual Undergrad Tuition & Fees: $3,200
Enrollment: 243 Coed
Affiliation or Control: Tribal Control IRS Status: 501(c)3
Highest Offering: Associate Degree
Accreditation: NW

01 President Dr. David YARLOTT, JR.
05 Dean of Academics Miss Frederica LEFTHAND
32 Dean of Student Affairs Miss Patricia WHITEMAN
11 Dean of Administration Ms. Shaleen OLD COYOTE
06 Registrar Mr. William OLD CROW
08 Director of Library Mr. Tim BERNARDIS
13 Chief Information Officer Mr. Franklin COOPER
10 Chief Finance Officer Ms. Aldean GOOD LUCK
15 Director Human Resources Ms. Robin VALLIE
97 Dept Head/General Stds/Crow Stds Dr. Tim MCCLEARY
81 Dept Head/Math/Science/Technology Vacant
25 Chief Contracts/Grants Admin Miss Eva FLYING
37 Financial Aid Director Ms. Beverly SNELL

Miles Community College (I)

2715 Dickinson, Miles City MT 59301-4799
County: Custer FICE Identification: 002528
Unit ID: 180373
Telephone: (406) 874-6100 Carnegie Class: Assoc/MT-VT-Mix Trad/Non
FAX Number: (406) 874-6282 Calendar System: Semester
URL: www.milescc.edu
Established: 1939 Annual Undergrad Tuition & Fees (In-District): $4,230
Enrollment: 459 Coed
Affiliation or Control: State/Local IRS Status: 501(c)3
Highest Offering: Associate Degree
Accreditation: NW, ADNUR

01 President Aaron CLINGINGSMITH
05 Vice Pres of Academic Affairs Dr. Rita KRATKY
84 Dean of Enrollment Services Erin NIEDGE
32 Dean of Student Engagement Richard DESHIELDS
08 Director of Library Mr. George DICKIE
13 Director Information Technology Mr. Donald D. WARNER
37 Director Student Financial Aid Ms. Danielle DINGES
18 Chief Facilities/Physical Plant Mr. Ross LAWRENCE
21 Business Services Director Ms. Nancy AABERGE
06 Registrar Ms. Lisa BLUNT
15 Dean of Admn Svcs & Human Resources Ms. Kylene PHIPPS
66 Director Nursing Ms. Pauline FLOTKOETTER
20 Associate Academic Officer Mr. Garth SLEIGHT
40 Manager Bookstore Ms. Michele TRIMBLE
04 Administrative Asst to President Ms. Candy LANEY

Montana Bible College (J)

3625 South 19th Avenue, Bozeman MT 59718-9108
County: Gallatin FICE Identification: 041403
Unit ID: 262165
Telephone: (406) 586-3585 Carnegie Class: Spec-4-yr-Faith
FAX Number: (406) 586-3585 Calendar System: Semester
URL: www.montanabiblecollege.edu
Established: 1987 Annual Undergrad Tuition & Fees: N/A
Enrollment: N/A Coed
Affiliation or Control: Independent Non-Profit IRS Status: 501(c)3
Highest Offering: Baccalaureate
Accreditation: BI

01 President Mr. Ryan WARD
05 Academic Dean Vacant
06 Registrar Mrs. Louise TURNER
07 Admissions Director Mrs. Susan JACKSON
08 Librarian Mrs. Larissa ORMAN
32 Dean of Students Mr. Danny JOHNSON
10 Business Manager Mrs. Leota FRED
84 Director of Enrollment Management Mr. Dan HOVESTOL
30 Advance & Devel Dir/Dean of Women Ms. Jenni O'BRIAN
13 Information Technology Director Mr. Austin RUHL
88 Discipleship Director Mr. Micah FORSYTHE

*Montana University System Office (K)

2500 Broadway, Helena MT 59601-3201
County: Lewis And Clark FICE Identification: 029072
Unit ID: 180470
Telephone: (406) 449-9124 Carnegie Class: N/A
FAX Number: (406) 449-9171
URL: www.mus.edu

01 Commissioner Higher Education .... Mr. Clayton T. CHRISTIAN
05 Deputy Cmsr Academic/Student Affs .... Dr. Brock TESSMAN
45 Deputy Cmsr Budget & Planning .... Mr. Tyler TREVOR
15 Deputy Cmsr Human Resources .... Mr. Kevin MCRAE
43 Chief Legal Counsel/Deputy Comm .... Ms. Viv HAMMILL
100 Chief of Staff .... Mr. Tyler TREVOR
118 Director of Benefits .... Mrs. Mary LACHENBRUCH
117 Director of Work Comp Risk Mgmt .... Ms. Leah Jo TIETZ
93 Dir Minority/Amer Ind Achievement .... Ms. Angela MCLEAN
13 OCHE IT Manager .... Ms. Edwina MORRISON

*University of Montana - Missoula (A)

32 Campus Drive, Missoula MT 59812-0001
County: Missoula FICE Identification: 002536
Unit ID: 180489
Telephone: (406) 243-2311 Carnegie Class: DU-Higher
FAX Number: (406) 243-2797 Calendar System: Semester
URL: www.umt.edu
Established: 1893 Annual Undergrad Tuition & Fees (In-State): $7,244
Enrollment: 11,865 Coed
Affiliation or Control: State IRS Status: 501(c)3
Highest Offering: Doctorate
Accreditation: NW, ART, CAATE, CACREP, CAEPN, CEA, CLPSY, COARC, JOUR, LAW, MUS, PH, PHAR, PTA, SCPSY, SP, SPAA, SW, THEA

02 President .... Mr. Seth BODNAR
05 Executive VP and Provost .... Dr. Jon HARBOR
100 Chief of Staff .... Ms. Kelly WEBSTER
10 Vice Pres for Operations & Finance .... Mr. Paul LASITER
84 VP Enroll/Strategic Communications .... Dr. Cathy COLE
46 Vice Pres Research/Development .... Dr. Scott WHITTENBURG
45 AVP for Plng/Budget Analysis .... Ms. Dawn RESSEL
15 AVP Human Resource Services .... Ms. Terri PHILLIPS
20 Vice Provost for Academic Affairs .... Dr. Nathan LINDSAY
121 Vice Provost for Student Success .... Ms. Sarah SWAGER
43 Legal Counsel .... Ms. Lucy FRANCE
12 Interim Director Mansfield Center .... Ms. Deena MANSOUR
88 Dir Broadcast Media Center .... Mr. Ray EKNESS
22 Int Dir Equal Oppty/Affirm Action .... Ms. Alicia ARANT
06 Registrar .... Mr. Joseph HICKMAN
18 Director Facilities Svcs .... Mr. Kevin KREBSBACH
13 CIO .... Ms. Renae SCOTT
38 Director Counseling .... Mr. Mike FROST
36 Int Dir Exper Lrng/Career Success .... Dr. Andrea VERNON
37 Director of Financial Aid .... Ms. Emily WILLIAMSON
29 Director of Alumni Office .... Mr. Jed LISTON
102 President & CEO/UM Foundation .... Ms. Cindy WILLIAMS
19 Director of Public Safety .... Mr. Martin LUDEMANN
23 Director Curry Health Center .... Dr. Rick CURTIS
39 Director Residence Life .... Ms. Sandra CURTIS
41 Athletic Director .... Mr. Kent HASLAM
88 Exec Director of Global Engagement .... Dr. Donna ANDERSON
21 Director Business Services .... Vacant
88 Exec Director Student Success .... Mr. Brian FRENCH
08 Interim Dean Mansfield Library .... Dr. Barry BROWN
49 Int Dean Coll Humanities/Sciences .... Dr. Jenny MCNULTY
61 Dean School of Law .... Mr. Paul KIRGIS
65 Dean College Forestry/Conservation .... Dr. Thomas DELUCA
50 Interim Dean College of Business .... Dr. Suzanne TILLEMAN
76 Dean Col Health Prof & Biomed Sci .... Dr. Reed HUMPHREY
53 Dean College of Education .... Dr. Adrea LAWERANCE
57 Int Dean Col of Arts/Media .... Dr. John DEBOER
75 Dean Missoula College .... Dr. Thomas GALLAGHER
92 Dean Honors College .... Dr. Timothy NICHOLS

*The University of Montana Western (B)

710 S Atlantic St, Dillon MT 59725-3598
County: Beaverhead FICE Identification: 002537
Unit ID: 180692
Telephone: (406) 683-7011 Carnegie Class: Bac-Diverse
FAX Number: (406) 683-7493 Calendar System: Other
URL: www.umwestern.edu
Established: 1893 Annual Undergrad Tuition & Fees (In-State): $5,717
Enrollment: 1,538 Coed
Affiliation or Control: State IRS Status: 501(c)3
Highest Offering: Baccalaureate
Accreditation: NW, CAEP, IACBE

02 Chancellor .... Dr. Beth WEATHERBY
05 Provost .... Dr. Deborah HEDEEN
10 Vice Chanc Administration/Finance .... Mr. Michael REID
26 Director of Communications .... Mr. Matt RAFFETY
20 Dean of Outreach .... Ms. Anneliese RIPLEY
06 Registrar .... Ms. Charity WALTERS
07 Director of Admissions .... Mr. Matt ALLEN
08 Librarian .... Ms. Anne KISH
36 Director of Field Learning .... Vacant
41 Director of Athletics .... Mr. Bill WILSON
13 Director of Information Technology .... Mr. Chad BAVER
32 Dean of Students .... Ms. Nicole HAZELBAKER
30 Director of Devel/Alumni Relations .... Ms. Roxanne ENGELLANT
37 Director of Student Financial Aid .... Ms. Louise DRIVER
38 Director Student Counseling .... Mr. Jerry GIRARD
15 Human Resources .... Ms. Patti LAKE
04 Administrative Asst to Chancellor .... Ms. Hillary LOWELL
22 Dir Affirmative Action/EEO .... Ms. Liane FORRESTER

*Helena College University of Montana (C)

1115 N Roberts, Helena MT 59601-3098
County: Lewis and Clark FICE Identification: 007570
Unit ID: 180276
Telephone: (406) 447-6900 Carnegie Class: Assoc/HVT-Mix Trad/Non
FAX Number: (406) 447-6397 Calendar System: Semester
URL: www.HelenaCollege.edu
Established: 1939 Annual Undergrad Tuition & Fees (In-State): $3,359
Enrollment: 1,422 Coed
Affiliation or Control: State IRS Status: 501(c)3
Highest Offering: Associate Degree
Accreditation: NW, ADNUR, IFSAC

02 Dean/CEO .... Dr. Daniel BINGHAM
04 Exe Assistant to Dean/CEO .... Ms. Paige PAYNE
05 Assoc Dean Academic & Student Affs .... Dr. Sandra BAUMAN
07 Director of Admissions and Records .... Ms. Sarah DELLWO
08 Director of Library Services .... Ms. Della DUBBE
51 Director of Continuing Education .... Ms. Mary LANNERT
18 Interim Dir of Facilities .... Mr. Tommi HAIKKA
13 Director of IT .... Mr. Mike HAUSLER
40 Bookstore Manager .... Ms. Cherise HECHT
26 Director of Marketing .... Ms. Donna BREITBART
37 Acting Dean of Admin Affairs .... Ms. Valerie CURTIN
37 Interim Dir of Financial Aid .... Ms. Traci MERZIAK
15 Director of Human Resources .... Ms. Therese COLLETTE
09 Director of Institutional Research .... Mr. Michael BROWN
106 Director eLearning .... Ms. Amy KONG

*Montana State University (D)

PO Box 172190, Bozeman MT 59717-2190
County: Gallatin FICE Identification: 002532
Unit ID: 180461
Telephone: (406) 994-2452 Carnegie Class: DU-Highest
FAX Number: (406) 994-1923 Calendar System: Semester
URL: www.montana.edu
Established: 1893 Annual Undergrad Tuition & Fees (In-State): $7,277
Enrollment: 16,613 Coed
Affiliation or Control: State IRS Status: 501(c)3
Highest Offering: Doctorate
Accreditation: NW, ART, CACREP, CAEP, DIETD, DIETI, IPSY, MT, MUS, NURSE

02 President .... Dr. Waded CRUZADO
05 Exec VP Academic Affairs/Provost .... Dr. Robert MOKWA
20 Senior Vice Provost .... Dr. David SINGEL
88 Vice Provost .... Dr. Ron LARSEN
10 Vice Pres Admin/Finance .... Mr. Terry LEIST
32 Vice Pres Student Success .... Dr. Chris KEARNS
56 Executive Director Extension .... Dr. Cody STONE
46 VP Research & Econ Development .... Dr. Renee REIJO PERA
18 Assoc Vice Pres University Services .... Mr. Daniel STEVENSON
15 Assoc VP HR/Chief HR Officer .... Ms. Jeanette GREY GILBERT
102 President/CEO MSU Foundation .... Mr. Christopher D. MURRAY
104 Assoc Prov International Programs .... Dr. Miley GONZALEZ
26 Exec Director Univ Communications .... Mr. Tracy ELLIG
88 Exec Director Museum of the Rockies .... Mr. Chris DOBBS
50 Dean Business .... Mr. Mark RANALLI
53 Dean Education/Health/Human Dev .... Dr. Alison HARMON
54 Dean Engineering .... Dr. Brett GUNNINK
49 Dean Letters & Science .... Dr. Nicol RAE
66 Dean Nursing .... Dr. Sarah SHANNON
08 Dean Libraries .... Mr. Kenning ARLITSCH
35 Dean Students .... Dr. Matthew CAIRES
58 Dean Graduate School .... Dr. Karlene HOO
92 Dean Honors College .... Dr. Ilses-Mari LEE
47 VP and Dean Agriculture .... Dr. Sreekala BAJWA
48 Dean Arts/Architecture .... Dr. Royce SMITH
63 Dir WWAMI Medical Educ Program .... Dr. Martin TEINTZE
07 Director Admissions .... Ms. Ronda RUSSELL
22 Director Institutional Equity .... Ms. Emily STARK
41 Director Athletics .... Mr. Leon COSTELLO
109 Assoc VP Auxiliary Services .... Mr. Tom STUMP
36 Dir Allen Yarnell Center .... Dr. Carina BECK
38 Dir Counseling/Psych Services .... Dr. Elizabeth ASSERSON
56 Exec Director Extended University .... Dr. Kim OBBINK
37 Director Financial Aid .... Mr. James BROSCHEIT
43 Legal Counsel .... Ms. Kellie PETERSON
45 Director Planning & Analysis .... Dr. Chris FASTNOW
96 Director Procurement .... Mr. Brian O'CONNOR
06 Registrar .... Mr. Tony CAMPEAU
27 Director Marketing/Creative Service .... Ms. Julie KIPFER
19 Chief of University Police .... Mr. Frank PARRISH, JR.
100 Asst to the President .... Ms. Maggie HAYES
105 Director Web Communications .... Vacant
13 Vice Pres for Information Tech .... Mr. Jerry SHEEHAN
25 Asst Vice Pres for Research .... Ms. Leslie SCHMIDT
39 Director Housing/Residence Life .... Mr. Jeff BONDY
14 Assoc Chief IT/CSO .... Mr. Adam EDELMAN
88 Dir Employee & Labor Relations .... Ms. Susan ALT
114 Dir University Budget Office .... Ms. Kathy ATTEBURY
88 Director Women's Center .... Ms. Elizabeth DANFORTH

*Montana State University Billings (E)

1500 University Drive, Billings MT 59101-0245
County: Yellowstone FICE Identification: 002530
Unit ID: 180179
Telephone: (406) 657-2011 Carnegie Class: Masters/M
FAX Number: (406) 657-2302 Calendar System: Semester
URL: www.msubillings.edu
Established: 1927 Annual Undergrad Tuition & Fees (In-State): $5,928
Enrollment: 4,401 Coed
Affiliation or Control: State IRS Status: 501(c)3
Highest Offering: Master's
Accreditation: NW, ART, CAATE, CACREP, CAEP, EMT, IFSAC, MUS, NURSE

02 Chancellor .... Dr. Daniel EDELMAN
10 Vice Chanc Administration/Finance .... Vacant
05 Academic Vice Chancellor & Provost .... Dr. Melinda ARNOLD
32 Vice Chanc Student Access & Success .Dr. Kimberly HAYWORTH
20 Interim Associate Provost .... Dr. Christine SHEARER
102 President/CEO Foundation .... Mr. Bill KENNEDY
29 Director Alumni Relations .... Ms. Gillette VAIRA
08 Director Library Services .... Ms. Darlene HERT
06 Records & Registrar .... Dr. Cheri JOHANNES
07 Director Admissions .... Ms. Tammi WATSON
15 Interim Director Human Resources .... Ms. Jody STAHL
36 Director Advising/Career Services .... Dr. Becky LYONS
13 Interim Chief Information Officer .... Mr. Brett WEISZ
25 Dir Grants & Sponsored Pgms .... Ms. Cindy BELL
26 Director University Relations .... Ms. Shannon WILCOX
09 Director Institutional Research .... Ms. Joann STRYKER
18 Director Facility Services .... Mr. Christopher EAGAN
58 Director Graduate Studies .... Vacant
41 Athletic Director .... Ms. Krista MONTAGUE
19 Chief of Campus Police .... Mr. Denis OTTERNESS
37 Interim Director Financial Aid .... Ms. Kalie PORTER
40 Director Bookstore .... Mr. Ed BROWN
35 Dean of Student Engagement .... Ms. Kathy KOTECKI
114 University Budget Director .... Vacant
96 Director of Business Services .... Ms. Barb SHAFER
121 Director Academic Support Center .... Mr. Stephen FOGGATT
28 Dir Montana Ctr for Inclusive Educ .... Dr. Tom MANTHEY
89 Director New Student Services .... Ms. Kristin PETERMAN
88 Director American Indian Outreach .... Ms. Reno CHARETTE
85 Exec Dir Intl Studies/Outreach .... Dr. Paul FOSTER
106 Director e-Learning .... Dr. Susan BALTER-REITZ
92 Dir of University Honors Program .... Dr. David CRAIG
104 Specialist Intl Marketing/Outreach .... Mr. Neil BEYER
49 Dean of Arts & Sciences .... Dr. Christine SHEARER
53 Dean of Education .... Dr. Roberto NAVA
50 Dean College of Business .... Dr. Elaine LABACH
12 Dean City College .... Dr. Vicki TRIER
97 Associate Dean City College .... Dr. Florence GARCIA
76 Int Dean College Allied Health Prof .... Dr. Kurt TOENJES
04 Admin Assistant to the President .... Ms. Evelyn NOENNIG
39 Director Student Engagement .... Ms. Brandee SOENS

*Montana State University - Northern (F)

PO Box 7751, Havre MT 59501-7751
County: Hill FICE Identification: 002533
Unit ID: 180522
Telephone: (406) 265-3700 Carnegie Class: Bac-Diverse
FAX Number: N/A Calendar System: Semester
URL: www.msun.edu
Established: 1929 Annual Undergrad Tuition & Fees (In-State): $5,955
Enrollment: 1,236 Coed
Affiliation or Control: State IRS Status: 501(c)3
Highest Offering: Master's
Accreditation: NW, ADNUR, NUR

02 Chancellor .... Mr. Gregory D. KEGEL
05 Provost/VC Academic Affairs .... Dr. Neil MOISEY
10 VC Finance & Administration .... Vacant
102 Executive Director of Foundation .... Vacant
72 Dean College Technical Sciences .... Dr. Dave KRUEGER
32 Dean of Students .... Dr. Steven WISE
53 Int Dean Col Educ/Arts & Sciences .... Dr. Darlene SELLERS
06 Director Admissions/Student Records .... Ms. Alisha SCHROEDER
66 Dean of College of Health Sciences .... Ms. Jaime DUKE
21 Controller .... Mr. Chris WENDLAND
41 Athletic Director .... Mr. Christian OBERQUELL
36 Director Career Center .... Ms. Mary HELLER
13 Interim Chief Info Tech Officer .... Ms. Marianne HOPPE
37 Director of Financial Aid .... Ms. Cindy SMALL
26 Director of University Relations .... Mr. James POTTER
08 Director of Library .... Ms. Vicki GIST
38 Director Student Support Services .... Ms. Maura GATCH
84 Exec Director Enrollment Mgmt .... Ms. Maura GATCH
15 Director of Human Resources .... Ms. Suzanne HUNGER
18 Facilities Manager .... Mr. Dan ULMEN
29 Outreach Specialist .... Ms. Lee LOUNDER
100 Chief of Staff .... Ms. Rachel DEAN

*Great Falls College Montana State University (G)

2100 16th Avenue South, Great Falls MT 59405-4909
County: Cascade FICE Identification: 009314
Unit ID: 180249
Telephone: (406) 771-4300 Carnegie Class: Assoc/MT-VT-Mix Trad/Non
FAX Number: (406) 771-4317 Calendar System: Semester
URL: gfcmsu.edu
Established: 1969 Annual Undergrad Tuition & Fees (In-State): $3,386
Enrollment: 1,691 Coed
Affiliation or Control: State IRS Status: 501(c)3
Highest Offering: Associate Degree
Accreditation: NW, CAHIIM, COARC, DA, DH, EMT, PTAA, SURGT

02 CEO/Dean .... Dr. Susan J. WOLFF

05 Chief Academic Officer ... Dr. Heidi PASEK
32 Chief Student Affairs & HR Officer ... Ms. Mary Kay BONILLA
26 Communications & Marketing Manager .. Ms. Taylor ALEXANDER
13 Chief Technology Officer ... Mr. David BONILLA
18 Director of Facilities Services ... Mr. Gary SMART
36 Director Advising & Career Center ... Mr. Troy STODDARD
37 Director Student Financial Aid ... Ms. Leah HABEL
40 Bookstore Manager ... Mr. Steve HALSTED
11 Operations & Finance Manager ... Ms. Carmen ROBERTS
09 Research Analyst ... Ms. Eleazar ORTEGA
08 Director of Library Services ... Ms. Laura WIGHT
88 Trades Division Director ... Mr. Joel SIMS
97 Director of General Studies ... Ms. Leanne FROST
76 Director of Health Sciences ... Mr. Russell MOTSCHENBACHER
06 Registrar ... Ms. Dena WAGNER-FOSSEN
84 Director Recruitment & Enrollment ... Ms. Shannon MARR

*Montana Technological University (A)

1300 W Park Street, Butte MT 59701-8997
County: Silver Bow — FICE Identification: 002531
Unit ID: 180416
Telephone: (800) 445-8324 — Carnegie Class: Masters/S
FAX Number: (406) 496-4710 — Calendar System: Semester
URL: www.mtech.edu
Established: 1893 — Annual Undergrad Tuition & Fees (In-State): $7,412
Enrollment: 1,909 — Coed
Affiliation or Control: State — IRS Status: 501(c)3
Highest Offering: Doctorate
Accreditation: NW, IACBE, NURSE

02 Chancellor ... Dr. Les COOK
05 Provost ... Dr. Douglas M. ABBOTT
10 Business Officer/Controller ... Ms. Carleen CASSIDY
11 VC for Administration & Finance ... Vacant
30 VC for Development & Univ Relations ... Mr. Joseph MCCLAFFERTY
84 Assoc VC for Enrollment Management ... Dr. Carrie VATH
46 VC Research & Dean Grad Sch ... Dr. Beverly HARTLINE
65 Director Bureau of Mines & Geology ... Dr. John J. METESH
88 Dir Inst of Educational Opportunity ... Ms. Amy VERLANIC
36 Director Career Services ... Ms. Sarah RAYMOND
08 Director Library ... Mr. Scott JUSKIEWICZ
37 Director of Financial Aid ... Ms. Shauna SAVAGE
18 Director of Physical Facilities ... Mr. Douglas EVANS
29 Director Alumni Affairs ... Ms. Peggy S. MCCOY
41 Athletic Director ... Mr. Matt STEPAN
72 Dean College of Technology ... Dr. David GURCHIEK
81 Dean Col Letters/Sci/Prof Studies ... Dr. Steven GAMMON
54 Dean School of Mines & Engineering ... Dr. Dan TRUDNOWSKI
110 Director of Development ... Mr. Michael BARTH
39 Director Residence Life ... Mr. Scott FORTHOFER
26 Director Public Relations ... Ms. Amanda BADOVINAC
40 Bookstore Director ... Ms. Laurie VANDEL
09 Director Institutional Research ... Ms. Melissa KUMP
06 Registrar ... Ms. Leslie DICKERSON
07 Director of Recruiting ... Ms. Stephanie CROWE
105 Webmaster ... Ms. Diane WARTHEN
106 Director of Distance Learning ... Vacant
13 Director of Information Technology ... Ms. Jennifer SIMON
96 Dir Purchasing & Budgets ... Ms. Marissa BENTLEY
15 Dir Human Resources ... Ms. Vanessa VAN DYK
04 Assistant to the Chancellor ... Ms. Victoria PAGAN
25 Dir of Sponsored Programs ... Ms. Joanne LEE
38 Director Student Counseling ... Ms. Amy LORANG

*City College at Montana State University Billings (B)

3803 Central Avenue, Billings MT 59102-4398
Telephone: (406) 247-3000 — FICE Identification: 010166
Accreditation: &NW

† Regional accreditation is carried under the parent institution Montana State University-Billings, Billings, MT.

*Highlands College of Montana Tech (C)

25 Basin Creek Road, Butte MT 59701-9704
Telephone: (406) 496-3701 — FICE Identification: 009282
Accreditation: &NW

† Regional accreditation is carried under the parent institution Montana Tech of The University of Montanna, Butte, MT.

*Missoula College-University of Montana (D)

1205 East Broadway Street, Missoula MT 59802
Telephone: (406) 243-7811 — FICE Identification: 007561
Accreditation: &NW, ACFEI, ADNUR, SURGT

† Regional accreditation is carried under the parent institution The University of Montana-Missoula, Missoula, MT.

Rocky Mountain College (E)

1511 Poly Drive, Billings MT 59102-1796
County: Yellowstone — FICE Identification: 002534
Unit ID: 180595
Telephone: (406) 657-1000 — Carnegie Class: Masters/S
FAX Number: (406) 259-9751 — Calendar System: Semester
URL: www.rocky.edu
Established: 1878 — Annual Undergrad Tuition & Fees: $28,572
Enrollment: 991 — Coed
Affiliation or Control: Interdenominational — IRS Status: 501(c)3
Highest Offering: Master's
Accreditation: NW, AAB, ARCPA

01 President ... Dr. Robert WILMOUTH
05 Provost/Academic Vice President ... Dr. Stephen A. GERMIC
32 Vice President for Student Life ... Mr. Bradley A. NASON
111 Vice President of Advancement ... Mr. Tyler WILTGEN
10 Chief Financial Officer ... Ms. Melodie CHARETTE
88 Director of Educational Leadership ... Dr. Stevie SCHMITZ
08 Director of the Library ... Ms. Bobbi OTTE
112 Director of Major Gifts ... Ms. Heather OHS
13 Director of Information Technology ... Mr. Daniel WOLTERS
18 Director of Campus Facilities ... Mr. Keith NORTH
41 Director of Athletics ... Mr. Jeff MALBY
44 Director of Annual Fund ... Ms. Jill HIRSCHI
09 Institutional Research Analyst ... Miss Erica WALL
06 Registrar ... Dr. Jennifer BRATZ
37 Director of Financial Assistance ... Ms. Jessica FRANCISCHETTI
39 Director of Residence Life ... Ms. Shaydean SAYE
04 Executive Assistant to the Pres ... Ms. Tracy DAVIDSON
29 Director of Alumni Relations ... Ms. Sarah CLARK
84 Dean of Enrollment Services ... Mr. Austin MAPSTON
19 Director Security/Safety ... Ms. Amberly TANZOSH
91 Director Administrative Computing ... Ms. Kellee PIERCE
15 Chief Human Resources Officer ... Ms. Marcella BUSTER

Salish Kootenai College (F)

PO Box 70, Pablo MT 59855-0070
County: Lake — FICE Identification: 021434
Unit ID: 180647
Telephone: (406) 275-4800 — Carnegie Class: Tribal
FAX Number: (406) 275-4801 — Calendar System: Quarter
URL: www.skc.edu
Established: 1977 — Annual Undergrad Tuition & Fees: $4,220
Enrollment: 809 — Coed
Affiliation or Control: Independent Non-Profit — IRS Status: 501(c)3
Highest Offering: Baccalaureate
Accreditation: NW, ADNUR, DA, NUR, SW

01 President ... Dr. Sandra BOHAM
05 Vice President of Academic Affairs ... Mr. Dan DURGLO
10 Vice Pres Business Affairs ... Ms. Audrey PLOUFFE
06 Registrar ... Ms. Cleo KENMILLE
07 Director of Admissions ... Ms. Raelyn DUMONTIER
08 Library Director ... Mr. Fred NOEL
37 Financial Aid Director ... Ms. Jackie SWAIN
09 Dir Institutional Effectiveness ... Dr. Stacey SHERWIN
15 Human Resources/Title IX Coord . Ms. Rachel ANDREWS-GOULD
102 College Foundation Director ... Ms. Karen DELANY
32 Dean of Students ... Ms. Tracie MCDONALD
13 Chief Information Officer ... Mr. Al ANDERSON
18 Physical Plant Operations Manager ... Mr. Michael BIG CRANE
04 Admin Assistant to President ... Ms. Anita BIG SPRING

Stone Child College (G)

8294 Upper Box Elder Road, Box Elder MT 59521-9796
County: Hill — FICE Identification: 026109
Unit ID: 366340
Telephone: (406) 395-4875 — Carnegie Class: Tribal
FAX Number: (406) 395-4836 — Calendar System: Semester
URL: www.stonechild.edu/
Established: 1984 — Annual Undergrad Tuition & Fees: $2,645
Enrollment: 554 — Coed
Affiliation or Control: Tribal Control — IRS Status: 501(c)3
Highest Offering: Associate Degree
Accreditation: NW

01 President ... Ms. Cory SANGREY-BILLY
05 Dean of Academics ... Ms. Wilma TYNER
32 Dean of Student Services ... Ms. Helen WINDY BOY
10 Chief Financial Officer ... Ms. Tiffany GALBARY
04 Admin Asst/Personnel ... Ms. Wanda ST. MARKS
06 Registrar ... Ms. Gaile TORRES
13 Network Systems Administrator ... Mr. Paul GARCIA
40 Bookstore Manager ... Mr. Colton GALBAVY
37 Financial Aid Officer ... Ms. Jolin SUN CHILD
18 Facilities/Maintenance Supervisor ... Mr. Gus BACON
08 Head Librarian ... Ms. Joy BRIDWELL
41 Athletic Director ... Mr. Cameron BILLY

University of Providence (H)

1301 20th Street S, Great Falls MT 59405-4996
County: Cascade — FICE Identification: 002527
Unit ID: 180258
Telephone: (800) 856-9544 — Carnegie Class: Bac-Diverse
FAX Number: (406) 791-5209 — Calendar System: Semester
URL: www.uprovidence.edu
Established: 1932 — Annual Undergrad Tuition & Fees: $25,168
Enrollment: 1,066 — Coed
Affiliation or Control: Roman Catholic — IRS Status: 501(c)3
Highest Offering: Master's
Accreditation: NW, CACREP, NURSE

01 Interim President ... Rev. Oliver J. DOYLE
05 Provost ... Dr. Matthew REDINGER
10 Exec VP/COO/CFO ... Dr. Gaby HAWAT
17 VP School of Health Professions ... Dr. Deborah BURTON
03 VP for Mission Integration ... Vacant
41 VP for Athletics ... Mr. Dave GANTT
111 VP for Advancement ... Dr. Lisa FLOWERS
32 VP for Student Development ... Vacant
84 VP for Enrollment Management ... Vacant
13 Chief Technology Officer ... Mr. Jamie SCHULTZ
121 Sr Dir of Academic Success Center ... Mrs. Twila CROFT
88 Exec Dir Business Operations ... Ms. Kylie CARRANZA
21 Financial Controller ... Ms. Jillian EHNOT
79 Div Chair Arts & Humanities ... Mr. Bryan SLAVIK
81 Div Chair Sciences ... Dr. Katrina STARK
58 Div Chair Grad & Prof Studies ... Mr. Jim CROFT
35 Dean of Students ... Mr. Jake CLARK
07 Director of Admissions Operations ... Ms. Melanie HOUGE
06 Registrar ... Ms. Brittany BUDESKI
97 Core Director ... Dr. Sarah SPANGLER
51 Dir Teaching & Learning Excellence ... Ms. Karen LEE
09 Director of Institutional Research ... Dr. Gregory MADSON
121 Director Student Support Services ... Mr. Matthew HAUK
106 Director of Distance Learning ... Mr. Jim GRETCH
39 Director of Residential Life ... Mr. Aaron STUCKER
15 Director of Human Resources ... Ms. Kila SHEPHERD
108 Director of Inst Effectiveness ... Ms. Leslie MILLS
37 Director Financial Aid ... Ms. Kelli ENGELHARDT
36 Director of Career Services ... Mr. Rod JOHANSON
113 Director of Student Accounts ... Ms. Amber HERIGON
18 Director Physical Plant ... Mr. Chet PIETRYKOWSKI
88 Director of Campus Ministry ... Mr. Nicolas ESTRADA
25 Database & Grants Program Manager ... Ms. Jennifer LEHMAN
08 Senior Librarian ... Ms. Susan LEE
88 Sports Information Director ... Vacant
88 Providence Formation Director ... Ms. Stephanie SCHNIDER
04 Exec Assistant to the President ... Ms. Trudi COLE
88 Sr Admin Assistant to the Provost ... Ms. Lindsay BERG
29 Director Alumni Affairs ... Ms. Katelyn FARRINGTON

Yellowstone Christian College (I)

1515 S. Shiloh Road, Billings MT 59106
County: Yellowstone — Identification: 667254
Telephone: (406) 656-9950 — Carnegie Class: Not Classified
FAX Number: N/A — Calendar System: Semester
URL: www.yellowstonechristian.edu
Established: 1974 — Annual Undergrad Tuition & Fees: N/A
Enrollment: N/A — Coed
Affiliation or Control: Independent Non-Profit — IRS Status: 501(c)3
Highest Offering: Baccalaureate
Accreditation: BI

01 President ... Vacant
05 Provost & Dean of Academics ... Mr. John RAMOS
84 Dean of Enrollment ... Mr. Max SOFT
10 Chief Financial Officer ... Dr. Robert ESHLEMAN
32 Associate Dean of Students ... Miss Miranda CARTER
06 Registrar ... Mrs. Cheryl ANDERSON
41 Athletic Director ... Mr. Brandon ROGERS

NEBRASKA

Bellevue University (J)

1000 Galvin Road S, Bellevue NE 68005-3098
County: Sarpy — FICE Identification: 009743
Unit ID: 180814
Telephone: (402) 293-2000 — Carnegie Class: Masters/L
FAX Number: (402) 293-2020 — Calendar System: Other
URL: www.bellevue.edu
Established: 1966 — Annual Undergrad Tuition & Fees: $7,827
Enrollment: 8,655 — Coed
Affiliation or Control: Independent Non-Profit — IRS Status: 501(c)3
Highest Offering: Doctorate
Accreditation: NH, CACREP, IACBE, NURSE

01 President ... Dr. Mary B. HAWKINS
88 Exec VP Operations ... Mr. Jim GROTRIAN
11 Exec VP Administrative Services ... Mr. Matthew DAVIS
18 Vice President Facilities ... Mr. Jerry A. BLASIG
72 Dean of College of Science & Tech ... Dr. Mary DOBRANSKY
50 Dean College of Business ... Dr. Rebecca MURDOCK
49 Dean College of Arts & Sciences ... Dr. Clif MASON
51 Dean Continuing/Professional Educ ... Dr. Michelle EPPLER
04 Exec Assistant to the President ... Ms. Christine HOW
32 AVP Community & Student Affairs ... Mr. Scott BIERMAN
37 Director Student Financial Aid ... Ms. Janet SOLBERG
08 Sr Dir Library Services ... Ms. Robin BERNSTEIN
102 Foundation CEO ... Mr. Russ RUPIPER
41 Director of Athletics ... Mr. Ed LEHOTAK
40 Director Bookstore ... Mr. Mark RIGGERT
88 Director of Buildings & Grounds ... Mr. Ralph (Sam) J. BORER
30 VP Development Programs ... Ms. Dorothy MORROW
21 Controller ... Ms. Brooke LAMBERT
19 Director of Security/Safety ... Mr. Greg ALLEN
108 Quality Assurance Programs Director ... Mr. Pete HEINEMAN
26 Sr Dir Marketing Operations ... Ms. Geri MASON
06 Registrar ... Ms. Colette LEWIS

Bryan College of Health Sciences (K)

1535 S 52nd St., Lincoln NE 68506
County: Lancaster — FICE Identification: 006399
Unit ID: 180878
Telephone: (402) 481-3801 — Carnegie Class: Spec-4-yr-Other Health
FAX Number: N/A — Calendar System: Semester
URL: www.bryanhealthcollege.edu

Established: 2001 Annual Undergrad Tuition & Fees: $17,282
Enrollment: 679 Coed
Affiliation or Control: Independent Non-Profit IRS Status: 501(c)3
Highest Offering: Doctorate
Accreditation: NH, ANEST, CVT, DMS, NUR

01 President .... Dr. Richard LLOYD
05 Provost .... Dr. Kelsi ANDERSON
97 Dean of Educational Development .... Dr. Kristy PLANDER
11 Dean of Operations .... Dr. Bill EVANS
66 Dean of Undergraduate Nursing .... Dr. Theresa DELAHOYDE
66 Dean of Graduate Nursing .... Dr. Marcia KUBE
76 Dean of Healthcare Studies .... Dr. Amy KNOBBE
88 Dean of Nurse Anesthesia .... Dr. Sharon HADENFELDT
32 Dean of Students .... Dr. Alethea STOVALL
08 Director of Library Services .... Ms. Jan RICE
06 Registrar .... Ms. Pam MCMASTER
29 Director of Student/Alumni Services .... Ms. Brenda NEEMANN
37 Director of Student Financial Aid .... Ms. Maggie HACKWITH
113 Bursar .... Mr. Larry MORRISON
106 Distance Education Director .... Ms. Deb MAEDER
84 Dean of Enrollment Management .... Ms. Stacy DAM

Central Community College (A)

PO Box 4903, Grand Island NE 68802-4903
County: Hall FICE Identification: 020995
Unit ID: 180902
Telephone: (308) 398-4222 Carnegie Class: Assoc/HVT-High Non
FAX Number: (308) 398-7398 Calendar System: Semester
URL: www.cccneb.edu
Established: 1966 Annual Undergrad Tuition & Fees (In-District): $3,000
Enrollment: 6,082 Coed
Affiliation or Control: Local IRS Status: 501(c)3
Highest Offering: Associate Degree
Accreditation: NH, ADNUR, CAHIIM, DA, DH, EMT, MAC, MLTAD, OTA

01 College President .... Dr. Matthew GOTSCHALL
03 VP of Innovation & Instruction .... Dr. Candace WALTON
10 Vice President of Admin Services .... Mr. Joel KING
15 Vice President of Human Resources .... Dr. Chris WADDLE
12 Grand Island Campus President .... Dr. Marcie KEMNITZ
12 Columbus Campus President .... Dr. Kathy FUCHSER
12 Hastings Campus President .... Dr. Jerry WALLACE
102 Foundation Executive Director .... Mr. Dean MOORS
05 Dean of Academic Education .... Dr. Beverly CLARK, III
50 Dean of Business & Entrepreneurship .... Ms. Roxann HOLLIDAY
76 Dean of Health Sciences .... Ms. Paulette WOODS-RAMSEY
88 Dean of Skilled & Technical Science .... Dr. Nate ALLEN
84 Dean of Enrollment Management .... Ms. Janel WALTON
32 Dean of Student Success .... Dr. Beth PRZYMUS
56 Dean of Ext Learning Services .... Mr. Ron KLUCK
75 Dean of Training .... Dr. Kelly CHRISTENSEN
13 IT Services Manager .... Mr. Tom PETERS
06 Registrar .... Ms. Barb LARSON
29 Director Alumni Relations .... Ms. Cheri BEDA
37 Area Director Student Financial Aid .... Ms. Victoria KUCERA
41 Interim Athletic Director .... Ms. Mary YOUNG
09 Director Institutional Research .... Mr. Brian MCDERMOTT
28 Equity and Compliance Manager .... Ms. Lauren SLAUGHTER
26 Public Relations/Marketing Director .... Mr. Scott MILLER
07 Admissions Director Columbus .... Ms. Kristin HOESING
07 Admissions Director Grand Island .... Ms. Erin LESIAK
07 Admissions Director Hastings .... Ms. Regina SOMER
96 Purchasing Manager .... Ms. Carmen TAYLOR
04 Communications Asst to President .... Ms. Joni RANSOM

Central Community College Columbus Campus (B)

PO Box 1027, 4500 63rd Street,
Columbus NE 68602-1027
Telephone: (402) 564-7132 Identification: 770331
Accreditation: &NH

Central Community College Hastings Campus (C)

550 S Technical Blvd, PO Box 1024,
Hastings NE 68902-1024
Telephone: (402) 463-9811 Identification: 770332
Accreditation: &NH

CHI Health School of Radiologic Technology (D)

6901 North 72nd Street, Omaha NE 68122
County: Douglas FICE Identification: 008492
Unit ID: 181145
Telephone: (402) 572-3650 Carnegie Class: Spec 2-yr-Health
FAX Number: (402) 398-6650 Calendar System: Semester
URL: www.chihealth.com/school-of-radiologic-technology
Established: 1953 Annual Undergrad Tuition & Fees: N/A
Enrollment: 15 Coed
Affiliation or Control: Independent Non-Profit IRS Status: 501(c)3
Highest Offering: Associate Degree
Accreditation: RAD

01 Program Director .... Robert A. HUGHES
10 Chief Financial Officer .... Jeanette WOJTALEWICZ
05 Chief Academic Officer .... Dr. Michael WHITE

Clarkson College (E)

101 S 42nd Street, Omaha NE 68131-2739
County: Douglas FICE Identification: 009862
Unit ID: 180832
Telephone: (402) 552-3100 Carnegie Class: Spec-4-yr-Other Health
FAX Number: (402) 552-3369 Calendar System: Semester
URL: www.clarksoncollege.edu
Established: 1888 Annual Undergrad Tuition & Fees: $13,392
Enrollment: 1,273 Coed
Affiliation or Control: Independent Non-Profit IRS Status: 501(c)3
Highest Offering: Doctorate
Accreditation: NH, ANEST, CAHIIM, NUR, PTAA, RAD

01 Interim President .... Dr. Aubray ORDUNA
05 VP of Academic Affairs .... Dr. Andriea NEBEL
11 Vice Pres Operations .... Jina PAUL
10 Controller .... Megan WICKLESS-MULDER
06 Registrar .... Natalie VRBKA
15 Director Human Resources .... Daniel WOJTALEWICZ
13 Director Technology .... Ryan SCHURMAN
28 Director Diversity Services .... Aubray D. ORDUNA
37 Director Student Financial Services .... Laura THAYER-MENCKE
08 Director Library Services .... Anne HEIMANN
38 Director Success Center .... Julie TAYLOR-COSTELLO
97 Director General Education .... Lori BACHLE
66 Dean Nursing/Dir BS & Grad Nursing .... Dr. Aubray ORDUNA
50 Dir of Business & HIM .... Carla DIRKSCHNEIDER
76 Dir Medical Imaging/Radiologic Tech .... Ellen COLLINS
76 Dir Physical Therapist Asst Pgm .... Jessica NIEMANN
07 Director Admissions .... Ken ZEIGER
51 Director of Professional Dev .... Judi B. DUNN
29 Coordinator Alumni Relations .... Rita VANFLEET
106 Coordinator Online Education .... Vacant
09 Coord Inst Effect/Quality Assurance .... Chris SWANSON

College of Saint Mary (F)

7000 Mercy Road, Omaha NE 68106-2606
County: Douglas FICE Identification: 002540
Unit ID: 181604
Telephone: (402) 399-2400 Carnegie Class: Masters/M
FAX Number: (402) 399-2647 Calendar System: Semester
URL: www.csm.edu
Established: 1923 Annual Undergrad Tuition & Fees: $20,350
Enrollment: 1,140 Female
Affiliation or Control: Roman Catholic IRS Status: 501(c)3
Highest Offering: Doctorate
Accreditation: NH, #ARCPA, NUR, OT

01 President .... Dr. Maryanne STEVENS, RSM
05 Provost .... Dr. Sarah KOTTICH
10 Vice Pres Finance/Administration .... Ms. Bridgette RENBARGER
32 Vice President Student Success .... Dr. Tara KNUDSON-CARL
84 Vice President Enrollment .... Ms. Sara HANSON
111 Vice Pres Alumnae/Donor Relations .... Ms. Terri CAMPBELL
26 Vice President Marketing .... Mr. Nate NEUFIND
08 Director of Library .... Ms. Sara WILLIAMS
19 Director Security/Safety .... Mr. David FERBER
06 Registrar .... Sr. Marie ANGELE
37 Chief Student Financial Aid Officer .... Ms. Beth SISK
28 Director of Multicultural Affairs .... Ms. Alexis SHERMAN
27 AVP for Marketing/Public Relations .... Ms. Brittney LONG
21 Controller .... Ms. Susan WAGONER
11 Chief of Administration .... Ms. Kim SAVICKY
15 Chief HR Officer .... Ms. Jessica HOCHSTEIN
40 Director Bookstore .... Mr. Steve WESTENBROEK
35 Assoc Dean Student Affairs .... Ms. Katty PETAK
39 Director Residence Life .... Mr. Matthew CROONQUIST
112 Director of Major Gifts and Alumna .... Ms. Elizabeth GILBERT
44 Director of Annual Giving & Alumna .... Ms. Megan COLE
41 Athletic Director .... Mr. Peter HARING
18 Director Physical Plant .... Mr. Dan SPARGEN
42 Director Campus Ministry .... Ms. Carla GERRIETS
13 Chief IT Officer .... Mr. Kevin SHOLL
04 Executive Asst to the President .... Ms. Robyn KNIFFEN

Concordia University (G)

800 N Columbia Avenue, Seward NE 68434-1599
County: Seward FICE Identification: 002541
Unit ID: 180984
Telephone: (402) 643-3651 Carnegie Class: Masters/L
FAX Number: (402) 643-4073 Calendar System: Other
URL: www.cune.edu
Established: 1894 Annual Undergrad Tuition & Fees: $32,220
Enrollment: 2,520 Coed
Affiliation or Control: Lutheran Church - Missouri Synod
IRS Status: 501(c)3
Highest Offering: Master's
Accreditation: NH, CAEPN, IACBE, MUS

01 President .... Rev Dr. Brian L. FRIEDRICH
05 Provost .... Dr. Timothy PREUSS
111 Vice President Inst Advancement .... Mr. Kurth BRASHEAR
26 Sr VP Enrollment/Marketing .... Mr. Scott SEEVERS
32 VP for Student Affairs & Athletics .... Mr. Gene BROOKS
10 Chief Financial Officer .... Mr. David KUMM
53 Dean of Educ/Health & Human Science .... Dr. Lorinda SANKEY
49 Dean of Arts & Sciences .... Dr. Brent ROYUK
13 Chief Information Officer .... Dr. Kent EINSPAHR
50 Dean College of Business .... Mr. Jonathon MOBERLY
08 Director of Library Services .... Mr. Philip HENDRICKSON
88 Dir of Education/Synodical Careers .... Mr. William SCHRANZ
29 Director Alumni/University Rels .... Mrs. Jennifer FURR
36 Dir Career Development & Retention .... Mr. Corey GRAY
41 Athletic Director .... Mr. Devin SMITH
42 Campus Pastor .... Rev. Ryan MATTHIAS
37 Director of Financial Aid .... Mr. Scott JENKINS
18 Facilities Director/Maintenance .... Mr. Dale NOVAK
15 Director of Human Resources .... Mrs. Connie BUTLER
07 Director Enrollment Operations .... Mr. Aaron ROBERTS
27 Director of Marketing/Communication .... Mr. Seth MERANDA
115 Sr Dir Strategic Initiatives/Invest .... Mr. Curt SHERMAN
110 Sr Dir of Advancement Operations .... Mrs. Leigh LEWIS
106 Dir Classroom Innov & Online Educ .... Ms. Angie WASSENMILLER
06 Associate Registrar Undergraduate .... Mr. Brad WOODRUFF
121 Sr Director of Student Success Ctr .... Mrs. Lori READ
84 Director of Enrollment Mgmt .... Mr. Jeremy GEIDEL
19 Director Security/Safety .... Mr. Ron DOWN
35 Director Student Development .... Ms. Rebekah FREED
43 Dir Legal Services/Gen Counsel .... Mr. Kurth BRASHEAR
28 Multicult Spec/Asst Dir Stdnt Life .... Mr. Von THOMAS
110 Director of Advancement .... Mrs. Amy JURGENS

Creative Center (H)

10850 Emmet Street, Omaha NE 68164-2911
County: Douglas FICE Identification: 031643
Unit ID: 430485
Telephone: (402) 898-1000 Carnegie Class: Spec-4-yr-Arts
FAX Number: (402) 898-1301 Calendar System: Semester
URL: www.creativecenter.edu
Established: 1993 Annual Undergrad Tuition & Fees: $27,700
Enrollment: 51 Coed
Affiliation or Control: Proprietary IRS Status: Proprietary
Highest Offering: Baccalaureate
Accreditation: ACCSC

01 President .... Mr. Ray DOTZLER
05 Director .... Ms. Kim GUYER
07 Director of Admissions .... Mr. Richard CALDWELL
37 Director Student Financial Aid .... Ms. Sandy LAROCCA

Creighton University (I)

2500 California Plaza, Omaha NE 68178-0001
County: Douglas FICE Identification: 002542
Unit ID: 181002
Telephone: (402) 280-2700 Carnegie Class: DU-Mod
FAX Number: N/A Calendar System: Semester
URL: www.creighton.edu
Established: 1878 Annual Undergrad Tuition & Fees: $39,916
Enrollment: 8,654 Coed
Affiliation or Control: Roman Catholic IRS Status: 501(c)3
Highest Offering: Doctorate
Accreditation: NH, ARCPA, CAEP, CAMPEP, CEA, DENT, EMT, LAW, MED, NURSE, OT, PHAR, PTA, SW

01 President .... Rev. Daniel S. HENDRICKSON, SJ
00 Chairman Creighton University Board .... Mr. Michael R. MCCARTHY
05 Provost .... Dr. Thomas F. MURRAY
100 Spec Asst to Pres & Board Liaison .... Mr. John W. DARWIN
04 Sr Exec Assistant President Office .. Ms. Lori L. VANDER MOLEN
04 Exec Assistant President Office .... Mr. David L. BARNUM
101 Corporate Secretary .... Mr. James S. JANSEN
03 Executive Vice President .... Ms. Jan E. MADSEN
88 Vice Provost Mission & Ministry .... Dr. Eileen C. BURKE-SULLIVAN
88 Sr Dir Ignation Formation/Ministry .... Ms. Susan NAATZ
42 Director Campus Ministry .... Mr. Kyle C. LIERK
88 Director Ctr for Service & Justice .... Mr. Kenneth REED-BOULEY
88 Director Retreat Center .... Ms. Amy K. HOOVER
111 Vice President University Relations .... Mr. Matthew C. GERARD
110 Assistant VP Principal Gifts .... Mr. Mike T. FINDLEY
110 Asst VP University Relations .... Fr. Tom MERKEL, SJ
110 AVP Development AZ HSC Campus .... Ms. Meghan S. FROST
30 Assistant VP of Development .... Ms. Cortney A. BAUER
88 AVP Athletic Development .... Mr. Adrian E. DOWELL
30 Int AVP Advancement Svcs & Dev Prog .... Ms. Amy M. MCELHANEY
29 Assistant VP Alumni Relations .... Ms. Diane G. STORMBERG
88 Sr Philanthropic Advisor .... Mr. Steven A. SCHOLER
45 Chair President's Plng Committee .... Dr. Mary E. CHASE
08 University Librarian .... Vacant
106 Assoc VP Teaching & Learning Center .... Dr. Debra FORD
09 Director Institutional Research .... Dr. Ying VUTHIPADADON
06 Registrar .... Ms. Melinda J. STONER
88 Director Disability Accommodations .... Ms. Denise Y. LE CLAIR
36 Director Career Center .... Mr. Jeremy M. FISHER
43 General Counsel .... Mr. James S. JANSEN
32 Vice Provost Student Life .... Dr. Tanya C. WINEGARD
35 Assoc VP Student Development .... Dr. Wayne YOUNG
35 Assoc VP Student Engagement .... Dr. Michele K. BOGARD
41 Athletic Director .... Mr. Bruce D. RASMUSSEN
39 Sr Dir Housing & Auxiliary Service .... Mr. Lucas NOVOTNY
39 Director of Residential Life .... Ms. Michael LORENZ
88 Sr Dir Community Stdrds & Wellbeing .... Ms. Desiree NOWNES
93 Dir Creighton Intercultural Center .... Ms. Becky NICKERSON
88 Director of Recreation and Wellness .... Mr. Steve WOITA
89 Dir Student Ldshp & Involvement Ctr .... Ms. Katie M. KELSEY
84 VP Enrollment Mgmt & Univ Planning .... Dr. Mary E. CHASE

07 Director Admissions/Scholarships .... Ms. Sarah D. RICHARDSON
123 Dir Graduate and Adult Recruitment ....Ms. Linsay JOHNSON
124 Director Retention ....Ms. Katie CHRISTENSON
37 Director Student Financial Aid ....Ms. Paula S. KOHLES
121 Dir Acad Success & Educ Opportunity .... Dr. Joe ECKLUND
49 Dean College of Arts & Sciences ....Dr. Bridget M. KEEGAN
50 Dean Heider College of Business .... Dr. Anthony R. HENDRICKSON
107 Dean College Professional Studies .... Dr. Gail M. JENSEN
52 Dean School of Dentistry .... Dr. Mark A. LATTA
58 Dean Graduate School .... Dr. Gail M. JENSEN
61 Dean School of Law .... Mr. Joshua P. FERSHEE
63 Dean School of Medicine .... Dr. Robert W. DUNLAY
66 Dean College of Nursing ....Dr. Catherine M. TODERO
67 Dean Sch of Pharmacy & Health Prof ....Dr. Evan T. ROBINSON
26 Interim Leader Univ Comm & Mkt .... Ms. Pam MORTENSON
27 Director Communication ....Mr. Rick C. DAVIS
105 Director Web Strategy ....Vacant
18 Asst VP Facility Mgmt & Planning ....Mr. Derek SCOTT
19 Director Public Safety ....Mr. Michael D. REINER
10 Vice President Finance ....Vacant
21 Assoc VP Finance .... Mr. John J. JESSE, III
113 Assoc Director Business Office ....Ms. Ann M. O'DOWD
114 Dir Budget/Planning & Analysis .... Ms. Tara S. MCGUIRE
116 Director Internal Audit ....Mr. T. Paul TOMOSER
117 Risk Manager ....Ms. Katie BOOTON
88 Manager of Tax and GAAP ....Mr. Jason T. MCGILL
96 Sr Director Procurement .... Mr. Eric J. GILMORE
15 Assoc VP Human Resources ....Ms. Janel T. ALLEN
118 Sr Director Benefits & Compensation ....Ms. Molly BILLINGS
13 Vice Provost IT and Library Science ....Vacant
14 AVP Digital Transformation ....Dr. David RAMCHARAN
90 AVP Digital Experience ....Dr. Ryan M. CAMERON
91 Senior Director IT ....Mr. Mark MONGAR
119 Information Security Officer ....Mr. Bryan S. MCLAUGHLIN
24 IT Solutions Architect Learning Env .... Mr. Charles LENOSKY
22 Exec Director Equity & Inclusion ....Ms. Allison S. TAYLOR
23 Medical Dir Student Health Services .... Dr. Nathan HAECKER
25 Director Sponsored Programs Admin ....Ms. Beth J. HERR
28 VP Institution Diversity/Inclusion .... Dr. Christopher M. WHITT
38 Director Counseling Services .... Dr. Jennifer PETER
40 Bookstore Manager ....Mr. Sam GUNTER
85 VP Global Engagement ....Dr. Rene L. PADILLA
86 Director Comm & Govt Relationships ....Mr. Chris T. RODGERS
92 Director Honors Program .... Dr. Jeffrey P. HAUSE
104 Global Programs Coordinator .... Ms. Lizzy E. CURRAN
104 Global Programs Coordinator .... Ms. Krista CUPICH
20 VP Academic Admin & Partnerships ....Ms. Tricia A. BRUNDO SHARRAR
20 VP Learning & Assessment .... Dr. Gail M. JENSEN

Doane University (A)

1014 Boswell Avenue, Crete NE 68333
County: Saline FICE Identification: 002544
Unit ID: 181020
Telephone: (800) 333-6263 Carnegie Class: Bac-A&S
FAX Number: (402) 826-8600 Calendar System: 4/1/4
URL: www.doane.edu
Established: 1872 Annual Undergrad Tuition & Fees: $33,800
Enrollment: 1,069 Coed
Affiliation or Control: United Church Of Christ IRS Status: 501(c)3
Highest Offering: Doctorate
Accreditation: NH, CAEPN, MUS, NURSE

01 President ....Dr. Jacque CARTER
05 Provost/VP of Academic Affairs .... Dr. Paul SAVORY
10 Vice President of Finance & Admin .... Ms. Julie SCHMIDT
111 Vice President for Advancement .... Mr. Marty FYE
32 Vice President Student Affairs ....Dr. Carrie LOVELACE PETR
13 VP for Information Technology ....Mr. Mike CARPENTER
07 VP for Enrollment Svcs & Marketing ....Vacant
53 Interim Dean College of Education .... Dr. Tim FREY
107 Dean College of Prof Studies .... Dr. Lorie COOK-BENJAMIN
49 Dean College of Arts/Sciences .... Dr. Pedro MALIGO
106 Assoc VP Online/Adult Educ ....Ms. Andrea BUTLER
06 Registrar .... Ms. Denise ELLIS
37 Director of Financial Aid ....Ms. Peggy TVRDY
08 Director of the Library .... Ms. Melissa GOMIS
21 Controller ....Mr. Ned TUCKER
88 Asst Dean/Dir Hansen Leadership .... Ms. Abby VOLLMER
26 Sr Director of Strategic Comm ....Vacant
29 Director of Alumni Relation ....Ms. Anne ZIOLA
15 Director of Human Resources .... Ms. Laura NORTHUP
18 Dir of Facilities & Constr Proj ....Mr. Brian FLESNER
12 Director of Lincoln Campus .... Ms. Angie KLASEK
12 Director of Omaha Campus ....Ms. Ann GREIMAN
12 Director of Grand Island Campus ....Vacant
41 Athletic Director .... Mr. Matthew FRANZEN
42 Dir of Religious & Spiritual Life .....Dr. Leah REDIGER-SCHULTE
28 Director Multicultural Pgm & Educ .... Dr. Wilma JACKSON
23 Director of Health and Wellness ....Ms. Kelly JIROVEC
35 Director of Student Support Service .... Ms. Anita HARKINS
09 Director of Institutional Research ....Dr. Raja TAYEH
19 Dir of Campus Safety/Assoc Dean ....Mr. Russ HEWITT
04 Executive Assistant to President ....Ms. Marsha SCHRADER

Doane University (B)

3180 W U.S. Highway 34, Grand Island NE 68801
Telephone: (308) 398-0800 Identification: 770333
Accreditation: &NH

Doane University (C)

303 North 52nd Street, Lincoln NE 68504
Telephone: (402) 466-4774 Identification: 770334
Accreditation: &NH

Hastings College (D)

710 N Turner Avenue, Box 269, Hastings NE 68902-0269
County: Adams FICE Identification: 002548
Unit ID: 181127
Telephone: (402) 463-2402 Carnegie Class: Bac-Diverse
FAX Number: (402) 461-7490 Calendar System: 4/1/4
URL: www.hastings.edu
Established: 1882 Annual Undergrad Tuition & Fees: $30,050
Enrollment: 1,202 Coed
Affiliation or Control: Presbyterian Church (U.S.A.) IRS Status: 501(c)3
Highest Offering: Master's
Accreditation: NH, CAEP, MUS

01 President ....Dr. Travis FEEZELL
00 Chairman of the Board ....Mr. Glen MOSS
102 Executive Director of Foundation ....Mr. Gary FREEMAN
10 VP for Finance .... Mr. Tony BEATA
84 EVP Enrollment/Student Experience .... Ms. Susan MEESKE
05 VP of Academic Affairs .... Dr. Barbara SUNDERMAN
20 Assoc VP for Academic Affairs ....Vacant
100 Chief of Staff ....Vacant
41 Athletic Director .... Mr. B.J PUMROY
32 Assoc VP for Student Affairs ....Vacant
112 Assoc VP for Planned & Major Gifts ....Mr. Michael KARLOFF
110 Assoc VP for Development ....Ms. Judee L. KONEN
06 Registrar .... Mr. Jim BOEVE
37 Director of Financial Aid ....Ms. Traci BOEVE
18 Director of Facilities ....Mr. John MABUS
15 Director of Human Resources .... Ms. Kari FLUCKEY
26 Director of Marketing ....Mr. Michael HOWIE
08 Director of Libraries ....Ms. Susan FRANKLIN
29 AVP of External Relations ....Mr. Matt FONG
13 Director of IT ....Ms. Patty KINGSLEY
14 Network Administrator ....Mr. Josh KELLEY
90 Acad Computer Support Specialist ....Mr. Erik NIELSEN
18 Director Physical Plant Services .... Mr. Ron GRIGGS
93 Minority Students ....Dr. Moses DOGBEVIA
28 Pushkin Institute Director ....Dr. Rob BABCOCK
36 Director of Career Services .... Ms. Kimberly K. GRAVIETTE
23 Director Campus Health Services .... Ms. Beth LITTRELL
42 Chaplain ....Vacant
21 Director of Accounting ....Vacant
35 Dean of Student Engagement .... Dr. Lisa SMITH
19 Director of Security/Safety .... Mr. Brian HESSLER
38 Director of Counseling Services ....Mr. Jon LOETTERLE
40 Bookstore Manager ....Ms. Brianna WEICHEL
88 Graphic Designer/Publisher ....Mrs. Camille KASTL
85 International Program Director ....Mr. Grant HUNTER
04 Executive Asst to President & VPAA ....Ms. Marin SUHR
07 Director of Admissions ....Ms. Chris SCHUKEI
09 Director of Institutional Research ....Dr. Kristin CHARLES
44 Director Annual Giving ....Ms. Alicia O'DONNELL

Little Priest Tribal College (E)

601 East College Drive, PO Box 270, Winnebago NE 68071-0270
County: Thurston FICE Identification: 033233
Unit ID: 434016
Telephone: (402) 878-2380 Carnegie Class: Tribal
FAX Number: (402) 878-2355 Calendar System: Semester
URL: www.littlepriest.edu
Established: 1996 Annual Undergrad Tuition & Fees: $5,140
Enrollment: 141 Coed
Affiliation or Control: Independent Non-Profit IRS Status: 501(c)3
Highest Offering: Associate Degree
Accreditation: NH

01 President .... Mr. Maunka MORGAN
05 VP of Academic & Student Affairs .... Mr. Manoj PATIL
10 Director of Finance ....Mr. Mark VASINA
07 Director of Admissions .... Ms. Maria GARCIA
37 Director of Financial Aid .... Ms. Yatty MOHAMMAD
15 Human Resources ....Vacant
41 Director of Athletics ....Mr. Keith HANKS, SR.
32 Director of Student Support Service .... Mr. Wambli DOLEZAL
13 IT Director ....Mr. Morri CONWAY
25 Director of Grants & Inst Contracts ....Ms. Angela MILLER
06 Registrar ....Vacant
09 Director of Institutional Research ....Vacant
04 Exec Assistant to the President .... Ms. Insey PARKER
19 Director Security/Safety ....Mr. Justin MCCAULEY

Mary Lanning Healthcare School of Radiology (F)

715 North St. Joseph Avenue, Hastings NE 68901
County: Adams FICE Identification: 004431
Unit ID: 181251
Telephone: (402) 461-5177 Carnegie Class: Not Classified
FAX Number: (402) 460-5059 Calendar System: Other
URL: www.marylanning.org
Established: 1952 Annual Undergrad Tuition & Fees: N/A
Enrollment: N/A Coed
Affiliation or Control: Independent Non-Profit IRS Status: 501(c)3
Highest Offering: Associate Degree
Accreditation: RAD

01 President/Medical Director ....Eric BARBER
10 Chief Financial Officer .... Shawn NORDBY
11 Chief Operating Officer ....Mark CALLAHAN
15 Vice Pres Human Resources ....Bruce CUTRIGHT

McCook Community College (G)

1205 East Third Street, McCook NE 69001
Telephone: (308) 345-8100 Identification: 770337
Accreditation: &NH, EMT

Metropolitan Community College (H)

PO Box 3777, Omaha NE 68103-0777
County: Douglas FICE Identification: 012586
Unit ID: 181303
Telephone: (531) 622-2400 Carnegie Class: Assoc/HT-High Non
FAX Number: (402) 457-2395 Calendar System: Quarter
URL: www.mccneb.edu
Established: 1974 Annual Undergrad Tuition & Fees (In-District): $3,105
Enrollment: 14,954 Coed
Affiliation or Control: Local IRS Status: 501(c)3
Highest Offering: Associate Degree
Accreditation: NH, ACBSP, ACFEI, ADNUR, CAHIIM, COARC, CSHSE, DA, EMT, MAC

01 President .... Mr. Randy SCHMAILZL
05 Vice President Academic Affairs ....Dr. Tom MCDONNELL
28 Assoc Vice Pres Equity/Diversity . Dr. Cynthia GOOCH-GRAYSON
15 Assoc Vice Pres of Human Resources ....Ms. Melissa BEBER
45 VP for Strategic Initiatives ....Mr. William OWEN
32 Vice Pres for Student Affairs .... Dr. Marie VAZQUEZ
11 Vice President for Admin Services ....Mr. Dave KOEBEL
26 Assoc VP Marketing Brand & Commun .... Ms. Nannette RODRIGUEZ
18 Director Facilities Management .... Mr. Bernard SEDLACEK
37 Director of Financial Aid ....Ms. Wilma HJELLUM
96 Director Administrative Management ...... Mr. Richard HANNEMAN
19 Chief of Police/Dir Emergency Mgmt .... Mr. Donald THORSON
84 Dean of Enrollment Management ....Dr. Charles CHEVALIER
27 Chief Information Officer ....Mr. Chad LYNCH
06 Registrar .... Ms. Albertha SCHMID
43 Dir Legal Services/General Counsel .... Mr. Jim THIBODEAU
30 Director of Development .... Dr. Jacqueline ALMQUIST
91 Director Administrative Computing ....Ms. Jodie SNIDER
04 Executive Assistant to President ....Ms. Rita EYERLY
100 Senior Aide to the President .... Ms. Patricia CRISLER

Metropolitan Community College Elkhorn Valley Campus (I)

829 North 204th Street, Elkhorn NE 68022
Telephone: (531) 622-5231 Identification: 770335
Accreditation: &NH

Metropolitan Community College South Omaha Campus (J)

2909 Edward Babe Gomez Avenue, Omaha NE 68107
Telephone: (531) 622-5231 Identification: 770336
Accreditation: &NH

Mid-Plains Community College (K)

601 W State Farm Road, North Platte NE 69101-9491
County: Lincoln FICE Identification: 002557
Unit ID: 181312
Telephone: (800) 658-4308 Carnegie Class: Assoc/MT-VT-High Non
FAX Number: (308) 535-3794 Calendar System: Semester
URL: www.mpcc.edu
Established: 1926 Annual Undergrad Tuition & Fees (In-District): $3,210
Enrollment: 2,221 Coed
Affiliation or Control: State/Local IRS Status: 501(c)3
Highest Offering: Associate Degree
Accreditation: NH, ADNUR, DA, MLTAD

01 President ....Mr. Ryan PURDY
12 VP North Platte Community College ....Dr. Jody TOMANEK
12 Vice Pres McCook Community College ....Ms. Kelly RIPPEN
10 Area Business Officer ....Mr. Michael STEELE
05 Area VP for Academic Affairs ....Dr. Jody TOMANEK
09 Area Dir Instl Effectiveness .... Mr. Tad PFEIFER
32 Area Dean of Student Life ....Dr. Brian OBERT
56 Area Director of Outreach ....Ms. Gail KNOTT
36 Area Dean of Career Services ....Ms. Becky BARNER
84 Area Dean of Enrollment Management ....Ms. Kelly RIPPEN
06 Area Registrar ....Ms. Lana STEWART
26 Area Dir Public Inform/Marketing ....Mrs. Lauren GRABAU
15 Area Director of Human Resources .... Ms. Rebecca WRAGE
13 Int Area Director Information Svcs ....Mr. Trent WIESE
37 Area Dir of Student Financial Aid ....Ms. Erinn BROWN

Midland University (L)

900 N Clarkson, Fremont NE 68025-4395
County: Dodge FICE Identification: 002553
Unit ID: 181330
Telephone: (402) 721-5480 Carnegie Class: Masters/S
FAX Number: (402) 721-0250 Calendar System: 4/1/4
URL: www.midlandu.edu
Established: 1883 Annual Undergrad Tuition & Fees: $32,598

Enrollment: 1,793 Coed
Affiliation or Control: Evangelical Lutheran Church In America
IRS Status: 501(c)3
Highest Offering: Master's
Accreditation: NH, CAATE, COARC, NUR

01 President ... Ms. Jody HORNER
05 Vice Pres Academic Affairs ... Ms. Susan KRUML
32 Vice Pres Student Affairs ... Mr. Lawrence CHATTERS
10 Vice Pres Finance & Administration ... Ms. Jodi BENJAMIN
30 Vice Pres for Inst Advancement ... Ms. Jessica JANSSEN
84 VP Enrollment Management/Marketing ... Mr. Merritt NELSON
15 Director Human Resources ... Ms. Caryl JOHANNSEN
06 Director Academic Services ... Mr. Eric MACZKA
07 Asst Director of Admissions ... Mr. Kyle PEACOCK
37 Director of Financial Aid ... Mr. Douglas WATSON
21 Controller & AVP Finance/Fac Plng ... Mr. Joe HARNISCH
41 Athletic Director ... Mr. Dave GILLESPIE
66 Director of Nursing ... Dr. Linda QUINN
13 Chief Information Officer ... Mr. Shane PERRIEN
18 Director Facilities Management ... Mr. Shawn NELSON
44 Annual Giving Officer ... Ms. Katie CHATTERS

Myotherapy Institute (A)

4001 Pioneer Woods Drive, Lincoln NE 68506-7547
County: Lancaster FICE Identification: 032793
Unit ID: 434432
Telephone: (402) 421-7410 Carnegie Class: Spec 2-yr-Health
FAX Number: (402) 421-6736 Calendar System: Other
URL: www.myotherapy.edu
Established: 1992 Annual Undergrad Tuition & Fees: $16,750
Enrollment: 23 Coed
Affiliation or Control: Proprietary IRS Status: Proprietary
Highest Offering: Associate Degree
Accreditation: ACCSC

01 Director ... Ms. Sue KOZISEK

Nebraska Indian Community College (B)

1111 Hwy 75 - PO Box 428, Macy NE 68039-0428
County: Thurston FICE Identification: 025508
Unit ID: 181419
Telephone: (402) 494-2311 Carnegie Class: Tribal
FAX Number: (402) 837-4183 Calendar System: Semester
URL: www.thenicc.edu
Established: 1973 Annual Undergrad Tuition & Fees: $4,080
Enrollment: 180 Coed
Affiliation or Control: Tribal Control IRS Status: Exempt
Highest Offering: Associate Degree
Accreditation: NH

01 President ... Dr. Michael OLTROGGE
05 Academic Dean ... Dr. Kristine SUDBECK
32 Dean Student Services ... Dawne PRICE
13 Chief Information Officer ... Justin KOCIAN
06 Registrar ... Troy MUNHOFEN
15 Human Resource Director ... Cheryl HANSEN
08 Library Director ... Wanda HENKE

Nebraska Methodist College (C)

720 N 87th Street, Omaha NE 68114-2852
County: Douglas FICE Identification: 006404
Unit ID: 181297
Telephone: (402) 354-7000 Carnegie Class: Spec-4-yr-Other Health
FAX Number: (402) 354-7090 Calendar System: Semester
URL: www.methodistcollege.edu
Established: 1891 Annual Undergrad Tuition & Fees: $16,308
Enrollment: 1,167 Coed
Affiliation or Control: Independent Non-Profit IRS Status: 501(c)3
Highest Offering: Doctorate
Accreditation: NH, COARC, DMS, MAC, NURSE, OT, PTAA, RAD, SURGT

01 President ... Dr. Deb CARLSON
03 Executive Vice President ... Dr. Deb CARLSON
05 Vice President Academic Affairs ... Dr. Amy CLARK
10 VP Business & Operations ... Dr. Dean TICKLE
84 VP Enrollment & Student Success ... Dr. Lori GIGLIOTTI
66 Dean of Nursing ... Dr. Susan WARD
58 Program Director Master's Nursing ... Dr. Linda FOLEY
66 Pgm Director Undergrad Nursing ... Ms. Nellie JOHNSON
88 Director of Special Pgms Nursing ... Dr. Susie WARD
76 Dean Health Professions ... Ms. Kendra CRAVEN
49 Dean of Arts & Sciences ... Dr. Dean MANTERNACH
76 Director Physical Therapist Asst ... Ms. Shannon STRUBY
76 Director Respiratory Care ... Ms. Lisa FUCHS
88 Director Radiologic Technology ... Ms. Kate ROLLINS
88 Program Director Sonography ... Ms. Jody BERG
88 Director Surgical Technology ... Ms. Christy GRANT
08 Director John Moritz Library ... Ms. Emily MCILLECE
42 Dir Spiritual Dev/Campus Ministry ... Mr. Craig ZIMMER
29 Alumni Engagement Director ... Ms. Angela HEESACKER-SMITH
07 Director Enrollment Services ... Ms. Megan MARYOTT
06 Dir Student Records/Registration ... Mr. Shawn BAKER
37 Director Financial Aid ... Ms. Penny JAMES
107 Exec Dir Professional Development ... Ms. Jillian SISSON
121 Chf Stdnt/Institutional Success Ofc ... Ms. Lindsay SNIPES
04 Administrative Asst to President ... Ms. Cathy BECK
18 Chief Facilities/Physical Plant ... Dr. Dean TICKLE

*Nebraska State College System (D)

1327 H Street, Suite 200, Lincoln NE 68508
County: Lancaster FICE Identification: 033441
Telephone: (402) 471-2505 Carnegie Class: N/A
FAX Number: (402) 471-2669
URL: www.nscs.edu

01 Chancellor ... Dr. Paul D. TURMAN
43 General Counsel/VC for Empl Rels ... Ms. Kristin PETERSEN
10 Vice Chancellor Finance/Admin ... Ms. Carolyn MURPHY
32 VC Student Affairs & Risk Mgmt ... Ms. Angela MELTON
18 Vice Chanc Facilities & Info Tech ... Mr. Steve HOTOVY
05 VC Acad Planning/Partnerships ... Dr. Jodi KUPPER
21 Director of Financial Operations ... Mr. Matthew EASH
21 Director of Systemwide Accounting . Ms. Christina WUNDERLICH
13 System Data Analyst/Reports Devel ... Mr. Mike DUNKLE
26 Sys Dir Ext Rels/Communications ... Ms. Judi YORGES
22 System Director for Title IX ... Ms. Taylor SINCLAIR
15 Human Resource Specialist ... Ms. Kara VOGT

*Chadron State College (E)

1000 Main Street, Chadron NE 69337-2690
County: Dawes FICE Identification: 002539
Unit ID: 180948
Telephone: (308) 432-6000 Carnegie Class: Masters/M
FAX Number: (308) 432-6464 Calendar System: Semester
URL: www.csc.edu
Established: 1911 Annual Undergrad Tuition & Fees (In-State): $7,384
Enrollment: 2,737 Coed
Affiliation or Control: State IRS Status: 501(c)3
Highest Offering: Master's
Accreditation: NH, ACBSP, CAEPN, MUS, SW

02 President ... Dr. Randy RHINE
05 Vice President Academic Affairs ... Dr. Charles SNARE
10 Vice Pres Administration & Finance ... Ms. Kari GASWICK
84 Vice Pres Enrollment Mgmt & Mktg ... Mr. Jon HANSEN
13 Chief Information Officer ... Ms. Ann M. BURK
58 Dean Graduate Studies/BEAMS ... Vacant
49 Dean Essential Studies/Liberal Art ... Dr. James MARGETTS
107 Dean Prof Studies/Applied Sciences ... Dr. James POWELL
21 Comptroller ... Ms. Melany HUGHES
09 Director Institutional Research ... Ms. Malinda LINEGAR
102 Chief Exec Officer CS Foundation ... Mr. Ben WATSON
06 Registrar ... Ms. Melissa MITCHELL
32 Assoc VP Student Services ... Ms. Sherry L. DOUGLAS
07 Director of Admissions ... Ms. Lisa STEIN
15 Assoc VP Human Resources ... Ms. Anne DEMERSSEMAN
39 Director of Housing ... Mr. Austen STEPHENS
41 Athletics Director ... Mr. Joel SMITH
36 Director of Internships/Career Svcs ... Ms. Deena KENNELL
114 Budget Director ... Ms. Jordan HEITING
26 Director College Relations ... Mr. Alex HELMBRECHT
18 Director Facilities ... Mr. Harold MOWRY

*Peru State College (F)

PO Box 10, Peru NE 68421-0010
County: Nemaha FICE Identification: 002559
Unit ID: 181534
Telephone: (402) 872-3815 Carnegie Class: Masters/M
FAX Number: (402) 872-2375 Calendar System: Semester
URL: www.peru.edu
Established: 1867 Annual Undergrad Tuition & Fees (In-State): $7,512
Enrollment: 2,349 Coed
Affiliation or Control: State IRS Status: 501(c)3
Highest Offering: Master's
Accreditation: NH, CAEPN

02 President ... Dr. Daniel HANSON
05 Vice Pres Academic Affairs ... Dr. Tim BORCHERS
10 Vice Pres Administration & Finance ... Ms. Debbie WHITE
32 Vice Pres Enroll Mgmt & Stdnt Affs ... Dr. Jesse DORMAN
102 Exec Director PSC Foundations ... Mr. Todd SIMPSON
41 Director of Athletics ... Mr. Wayne ALBURY
26 Dir of Marketing & Communications ... Mr. Jason HOGUE
06 Dir Student Records/Coll Registrar ... Ms. Deann BAYNE
37 Director of Financial Aid ... Vacant
08 Director of Library ... Ms. Veronica MEIER
15 Director of Human Resources ... Ms. Eulanda CADE
18 Director Campus Services ... Ms. Jill MCCORMICK
21 Director of Business Services ... Ms. Erin RIESCHICK
07 Director of Admissions ... Ms. Cindy CAMMACK
38 Licensed Student Counselor ... Ms. Jamie EBERLY
108 Director Institutional Assessment ... Ms. Kristin BUSCHER
13 Chief Info Technology Officer (CIO) ... Mr. Gene BEARDSLEE
19 Director Security/Safety ... Mr. Tim ROBERTSON
04 Admin Assistant to the President ... Ms. Amy MINCER

*Wayne State College (G)

1111 Main Street, Wayne NE 68787-1172
County: Wayne FICE Identification: 002566
Unit ID: 181783
Telephone: (402) 375-7000 Carnegie Class: Masters/M
FAX Number: (402) 375-7204 Calendar System: Semester
URL: www.wsc.edu
Established: 1909 Annual Undergrad Tuition & Fees (In-State): $7,172
Enrollment: 3,292 Coed
Affiliation or Control: State IRS Status: 501(c)3
Highest Offering: Beyond Master's But Less Than Doctorate
Accreditation: NH, ART, CACREP, #CAEP, CSHSE, IACBE, MUS

02 President ... Dr. Marysz RAMES
05 Vice President Academic Affairs ... Mr. Steven ELLIOTT
10 Vice Pres Admin/Finance ... Ms. Angela FREDRICKSON
102 CEO Foundation Office ... Mr. Kevin ARMSTRONG
32 Vice President of Student Affairs ... Vacant
13 VP for Information Technology ... Mr. John DUNNING
37 Director Financial Aid ... Ms. Annette KAUS
07 Director of Admissions ... Mr. Kevin HALLE
38 Director of Counseling ... Ms. Alicia DORCEY MCINTOSH
39 Director of Residence Life ... Vacant
36 Director of Career Services ... Ms. Jason BARELMAN
26 Director College Relations ... Mr. Jay COLLIER
41 Director of Athletics ... Mr. Mike POWICKI
18 Director of Facility Services ... Mr. Kyle NELSEN
08 Director of Library Services ... Mr. David GRABER
06 Registrar ... Ms. Rebeka WILSON
112 Director of Major Gifts ... Ms. Deb LUNDAHL
29 Director of Alumni Relations ... Ms. Laura ROBINETT
15 Director of Human Resources ... Ms. Candace TIMMERMAN
79 Dean School of Arts & Humanities ... Dr. Yasuko TAOKA
50 Dean Sch of Business & Technology ... Dr. Vaughn BENSON
53 Dean Sch of Educ & Couns ... Dr. Nicholas SHUDAK
83 Dean Sch of Natural/Social Sci ... Dr. Tammy EVETOVICH
93 Dir of Multicultural/Intl Programs ... Dr. Leah KEINO
09 Research Analyst ... Ms. Jeannette BARRY
108 Director of Assessment ... Ms. Sue SYDOW
91 Director Administrative Computing ... Vacant
04 Secretary to the President ... Ms. Joni BACKER
19 Campus Security Manager ... Mr. Jason MRSNY
51 Dir of Continuing Educ & Outreach ... Ms. Judith SCHERER CONNEALY

Nebraska Wesleyan University (H)

5000 St. Paul Avenue, Lincoln NE 68504-2794
County: Lancaster FICE Identification: 002555
Unit ID: 181446
Telephone: (402) 466-2371 Carnegie Class: Masters/M
FAX Number: (402) 465-2179 Calendar System: Semester
URL: www.nebrwesleyan.edu
Established: 1887 Annual Undergrad Tuition & Fees: $34,202
Enrollment: 2,064 Coed
Affiliation or Control: United Methodist IRS Status: 501(c)3
Highest Offering: Master's
Accreditation: NH, CAATE, CAEPN, MUS, NURSE, SW

01 President ... Dr. Darrin S. GOOD
05 Provost ... Dr. Graciela CANEIRO-LIVINGSTON
10 Vice Pres Finance/Administration ... Ms. Tish GADE-JONES
84 Vice President Enrollment Mgmt ... Mr. Bill MOTZER
111 Vice President Advancement ... Mr. John GREVING
32 Vice President Student Life ... Dr. Sarah KELEN
42 University Minister/Church Relation ... Rev. Eduardo BOUSSON
58 Dean of Graduate Programs ... Dr. Jennifer ZIEGLER
20 Dean of Undergraduate Programs ... Dr. Kathy WOLFE
20 Assoc Prov Integral/Exper Learning ... Dr. Patrick HAYDEN-ROY
21 Asst VP & Controller ... Mr. Greg D. MASCHMAN
41 Athletic Director ... Dr. Ira A. ZEFF
06 Asst Provost & Univ Registrar ... Ms. Brooke GLENN
08 University Librarian ... Ms. Julie PINNELL
09 Data Analyst/IR Specialist ... Mr. Ricky HULL
38 Director Counseling Services ... Dr. Kimberly CORNER
07 Director of Admissions ... Ms. Staci BELL
104 Director of Global Engagement ... Ms. Sarah BARR
102 Director of Foundation Relations ... Ms. Tara GREGG
23 Director Student Health Services ... Ms. Nancy J. NEWMAN
24 Director Instructional Technology ... Mr. Jay L. KAHLER
14 Director Administrative Systems ... Mr. Mark MURPHY
92 Director Wesleyan Honors Academy ... Dr. Marian BORGMANN-INGWERSEN
44 Director Archway Fund ... Ms. Erika PASCHOLD
07 Director of Admissions ... Mr. Gordie COFFIN
36 Director Career Development ... Ms. Kim AFRANK
37 Director of Financial Aid ... Mr. Tom J. OCHSNER
13 Director of Computer Services ... Mr. Steven R. DOW
15 Director of Human Resources ... Ms. Maria HARDER
18 Director of Physical Plant ... Mr. Jim RUZICKA
26 Director of Marketing ... Ms. Peggy S. HAIN
27 Director of Public Relations ... Ms. Sara M. OLSON
29 Director of Alumni Relations ... Ms. Shelley MCHUGH
121 Asst Dean Stdnt Success/Engagement ... Ms. Karri SANDERSON
124 Asst Dean Stdnt Success/Persistence ... Ms. Candice HOWELL
39 Asst Dean Stdnt Success/Res Educ ... Ms. Brandi SESTAK
88 Asst Dean Stdnt Success/Campus Comm .. Ms. Janelle ANDREINI
04 Special Asst to President ... Ms. P. J. RABEL
105 Director Web Services ... Mr. Eric ASPEGREN
28 Asst Director Diversity & Inclusion ... Ms. Wendy HUNT

North Platte Community College-North Campus (I)

1101 Halligan Drive, North Platte NE 69101
Telephone: (308) 535-3600 Identification: 770338
Accreditation: &NH

Northeast Community College (J)

801 E Benjamin, PO Box 469, Norfolk NE 68702-0469
County: Madison FICE Identification: 011667
Unit ID: 181491
Telephone: (402) 371-2020 Carnegie Class: Assoc/MT-VT-High Non
FAX Number: (402) 844-7400 Calendar System: Semester
URL: www.northeast.edu

Established: 1973 Annual Undergrad Tuition & Fees (In-District): $3,480
Enrollment: 5,086 Coed
Affiliation or Control: Local IRS Status: 501(c)3
Highest Offering: Associate Degree
Accreditation: NH, ADNUR, CAHIIM, EMT, PTAA

01 President .... Vacant
03 Executive Vice President .... Mr. John V. BLAYLOCK
05 Vice President Educational Services .... Vacant
10 Vice Pres of Finance and Facilities .... Vacant
32 Vice President of Student Services .... Mrs. Amanda NIPP
13 Vice President of Technology .... Mr. Derek BIERMAN
88 Associate VP of Ctr for Enterprise .... Mr. Eric JOHNSON
30 Assoc VP of Devel/External Affairs .... Dr. Tracy L. KRUSE
15 Associate VP of Human Resources .... Vacant
47 Dean Ag/Health/Sciences .... Mrs. Corinne MORRIS
49 Dean Humanities/Arts/Social Sci .... Mrs. Faye KILDAY
50 Dean of Business/Math/Tech .... Dr. Wade HERLEY
76 Dean of Health/Wellness .... Dr. Michele GILL
11 Dean of Administrative Services .... Mrs. Coleen BRESSLER
75 Dean of Applied Technology .... Vacant
45 Dean of Institutional Planning .... Mrs. Michela KEELER-STROM
84 Dean of Enrollment Services .... Ms. Lori TROWBRIDGE
18 Exec Director of Physical Plant .... Mr. Brandon MCLEAN
06 Registrar .... Mrs. Makala MAPLE
37 Financial Aid Director .... Ms. Stacy DIECKMAN
36 Director of Career Services .... Mrs. Terri HEGGEMEYER
66 Director of Nursing Programs .... Mrs. Karen K. WEIDNER
96 Director of Purchasing .... Mr. Chris RUTTEN
41 Dean of Student Life and Athletics .... Mr. Kurt KOHLER
39 Director of Residence Life .... Ms. Jessica FANTINI
88 Director of Analytics Services .... Mr. Mike AUTEN
08 Director of Library Services .... Mrs. Mary Louise FOSTER
26 Director of Public Relations .... Mr. James CURRY
40 College Store Manager .... Mrs. Julie CARLSON
35 Director of Student Conduct .... Mrs. Maureen BAKER
09 Data Scientist .... Ms. Julie MELNICK
35 Director of Student Activities .... Ms. Carissa KOLLATH
27 Exec Dir of Marketing/Recruitment .... Mrs. Jennifer GREVE
07 Director of Recruitment .... Mr. Bradley RANSLEM
104 Dir of Ctr for Global Engagement .... Ms. Pam SAALFELD
16 Dir of HR/Talent and HR Compliance .... Mrs. Jessica DVORAK
04 Executive Assistant to President .... Mrs. Diane REIKOFSKI

Saint Gregory the Great Seminary (A)

800 Fletcher Road, Seward NE 68434-8145
County: Seward Identification: 667027
Unit ID: 486114
Telephone: (402) 643-4052 Carnegie Class: Not Classified
FAX Number: (402) 643-6964 Calendar System: Semester
URL: www.sggs.edu
Established: 1998 Annual Undergrad Tuition & Fees: N/A
Enrollment: N/A Male
Affiliation or Control: Roman Catholic IRS Status: 501(c)3
Highest Offering: Baccalaureate
Accreditation: NH

01 Rector/President .... VRev. Jeffrey EICKHOFF
05 Academic Dean .... Rev. Lawrence STOLEY
13 Vice Rector/Director of Technology .... Rev. John ROONEY

Southeast Community College (B)

4771 West Scott Road, Beatrice NE 68310-7042
Telephone: (402) 228-3468 Identification: 770341
Accreditation: &NH

Southeast Community College (C)

301 S 68 Street Place, Lincoln NE 68510-2449
County: Lancaster FICE Identification: 025083
Unit ID: 181640
Telephone: (402) 323-3400 Carnegie Class: Assoc/MT-VT-High Non
FAX Number: (402) 323-3420 Calendar System: Quarter
URL: www.southeast.edu
Established: 1973 Annual Undergrad Tuition & Fees (In-District): $3,128
Enrollment: 9,412 Coed
Affiliation or Control: State/Local IRS Status: 501(c)3
Highest Offering: Associate Degree
Accreditation: NH, ACBSP, ACFEI, ADNUR, COARC, CSHSE, DA, EMT, MAC, MLTAD, PNUR, POLYT, PTAA, RAD, SURGT

01 President .... Dr. Paul ILLICH
05 Vice President Instruction .... Dr. Dennis HEADRICK
22 Vice Pres Access/Equity/Diversity .... Mr. Jose SOTO
11 VP Administrative Svcs/Res Devel .... Ms. Amy G. JORGENS
32 Vice Pres Student Services .... Ms. Bev CUMMINS
46 VP Research/Planning/Technology .... Mr. Ed KOSTER
15 Vice Pres Human Resources/Safety .... Mr. Bruce TANGEMAN
88 Dean of Instruction Assessment .... Mr. Bruce EXSTROM
35 Dean of Students .... Ms. Theresa WEBSTER
84 Dean Student Enrollment .... Mr. Mike PEGRAM
37 Director of Financial Aid .... Ms. Melissa TROYER
26 Dir of Public Information/Marketing .... Mr. Stu OSTERTHUN
09 Dir Institutional Effect/Research .... Ms. Robin MOORE
102 Foundation Director .... Mr. Jack HUCK
90 Information Services Manager .... Mr. Alan BRUNKOW

Southeast Community College (D)

600 State Street, Milford NE 68405-8498
Telephone: (402) 761-2131 Identification: 770342
Accreditation: &NH

Summit Christian College (E)

2025 21st Street, Gering NE 69341
County: Scotts Bluff Identification: 667209
Unit ID: 181543
Telephone: (308) 632-6933 Carnegie Class: Spec-4-yr-Faith
FAX Number: (308) 632-8599 Calendar System: Semester
URL: www.summitcc.net
Established: 1951 Annual Undergrad Tuition & Fees: $6,726
Enrollment: 30 Coed
Affiliation or Control: Independent Non-Profit IRS Status: 501(c)3
Highest Offering: Baccalaureate
Accreditation: BI

01 President .... David K. PARRISH
05 Academic Dean .... Aaron PROHS
06 Registrar .... Andi GRANT
07 Director of Admissions .... Emilie YATES
11 Chief of Operations/Administration .... Scott GRIBBLE

Union College (F)

3800 S 48th Street, Lincoln NE 68506-4300
County: Lancaster FICE Identification: 002563
Unit ID: 181738
Telephone: (402) 486-2600 Carnegie Class: Bac-Diverse
FAX Number: (402) 486-2895 Calendar System: Semester
URL: www.ucollege.edu
Established: 1891 Annual Undergrad Tuition & Fees: $23,780
Enrollment: 868 Coed
Affiliation or Control: Seventh-day Adventist IRS Status: 501(c)3
Highest Offering: Master's
Accreditation: NH, ARCPA, CAEPN, NURSE, SW

01 President .... Dr. Vinita SAUDER
05 Vice President for Academic Admin .... Dr. Frankie ROSE
10 Vice President for Financial Admin .... Mr. Steve TRANA
32 Vice President Student Life .... Dr. Kim CANINE
111 Vice President for Advancement .... Ms. LuAnn DAVIS
42 Vice President for Spiritual Life .... Dr. Rich CARLSON
08 Library Director .... Ms. Melissa HORTEMILLER
13 Director of Information Systems .... Mr. Richard HENRIQUES
33 Dean of Men .... Mr. Daniel FORCE
06 Director Records/Registrar .... Ms. Kim HAZELTON
07 Director Enrollment & Admissions .... Mr. Kevin ERICKSON
26 Director of Public Relations .... Mr. Ryan TELLER
29 Director Alumni Relations .... Ms. Kenna Lee CARLSON
37 Director Student Financial Aid .... Ms. Laurie WHEELER
15 Human Resources Director .... Ms. Lisa R. FORBES
36 Career Center Coordinator .... Ms. Trina CRESS
09 Director of Institutional Research .... Ms. Salli JENKS
104 Director Study Abroad .... Ms. Elena CORNWELL
19 Director Security/Safety .... Mr. Mark ELDRIDGE
39 Dir Resident Life/Student Housing .... Mr. Chris CANINE

Universal College of Healing Arts (G)

8702 N 30th Street, Omaha NE 68112-1810
County: Douglas FICE Identification: 038214
Unit ID: 446598
Telephone: (402) 556-4456 Carnegie Class: Spec 2-yr-Health
FAX Number: (402) 561-0635 Calendar System: Semester
URL: www.ucha.edu
Established: 1995 Annual Undergrad Tuition & Fees: $10,566
Enrollment: 46 Coed
Affiliation or Control: Proprietary IRS Status: Proprietary
Highest Offering: Associate Degree
Accreditation: ABHES

01 President .... Ms. Paulette GENTHON

*University of Nebraska Central Administration (H)

3835 Holdrege, Lincoln NE 68583-0745
County: Lancaster FICE Identification: 008025
Unit ID: 181747
Telephone: (402) 472-8636 Carnegie Class: N/A
FAX Number: (402) 472-1237
URL: www.nebraska.edu

01 President .... Dr. Hank BOUNDS
05 Exec Vice President & Provost .... Dr. Susan M. FRITZ
10 Sr Vice Pres Business & Finance .... Mr. Chris KABOUREK
43 VP/General Counsel .... Mr. James POTTORFF
47 VP Agriculture/Natural Res .... Dr. Michael J. BOEHM
100 Chief of Staff .... Mr. Phillip BAKKEN
13 Assoc VP/CIO .... Mr. Bret R. BLACKMAN
101 Corporation Secretary .... Ms. Carmen K. MAURER
86 Interim VP University Affairs .... Mr. Heath M. MELLO
18 Asst VP/Dir Facility Plng/Mgmt .... Vacant
09 Asst VP/Dir Inst Research/Planning .... Dr. Kristin YATES
88 Asst VP P-16 Initiatives .... Dr. Gabrielle A. BANICK
88 Asst VP Global Strategy/Intl Init .... Dr. Steven T. DUKE
26 Asst VP Univ Affs/Dir Comm & Mktg .... Ms. Jacqueline M. OSTROWICKI
04 Special Assistant to the President .... Mr. Bradley G. STAUFFER
22 Chief Compliance Officer .... Mr. Preetham JEYARAM
28 Assistant VP Diversity/Inclusion .... Ms. Stancia J. JENKINS

*University of Nebraska at Kearney (I)

2504 9th Avenue, Kearney NE 68849
County: Buffalo FICE Identification: 002551
Unit ID: 181215
Telephone: (308) 865-8208 Carnegie Class: Masters/L
FAX Number: (308) 865-8665 Calendar System: Semester
URL: www.unk.edu
Established: 1903 Annual Undergrad Tuition & Fees (In-State): $7,512
Enrollment: 6,644 Coed
Affiliation or Control: State IRS Status: 501(c)3
Highest Offering: Beyond Master's But Less Than Doctorate
Accreditation: NH, CAATE, CACREP, CAEP, CIDA, MUS, NAIT, SP, SW

02 Chancellor .... Mr. Douglas A. KRISTENSEN
05 Sr VC Academic & Student Affairs .... Dr. Charles J. BICAK
10 Vice Chanc Business & Finance .... Mr. Jon C. WATTS
84 VC for Enrollment Mgmt & Marketing .... Ms. Kelly H. BARTLING
30 Vice President Development .... Mr. Lucas DART
13 Int Asst Vice Chanc Info Technology .... Ms. Jane PETERSEN
21 Assoc Vice Chanc Business & Finance .... Ms. Jane SHELDON
49 Dean Arts & Sciences .... Dr. Ryan L. TETEN
50 Dean Business/Technology .... Dr. Tim E. JARES
53 Interim Dean of Education .... Dr. Grace MIMS
58 Dean Graduate Studies .... Dr. Mark ELLIS
32 Dean of Student Affairs .... Dr. Gilbert HINGA
04 Exec Assistant to the Chancellor .... Vacant
06 Dir Student Records/Registration .... Ms. Kim SCHIPPOREIT
08 Dean of the Library .... Ms. Janet S. WILKE
36 Director Academic & Career Services .... Ms. Amy L. RUNDSTROM
07 Dir UG Recruitment/Admissions .... Mr. Dusty NEWTON
18 Dir Facilities Mgmt & Planning .... Mr. Lee MCQUEEN
19 Director Police .... Mr. James F. DAVIS
22 Dir Affirm Action/Equal Opportunity .... Ms. Mary J. CHINNOCK PETROSKI
09 Director Institutional Research .... Ms. Lisa NEAL
09 Director Academic Resources .... Ms. Megan M. FRYDA
26 Sr Dir Communications & Marketing .... Mr. Todd GOTTULA
29 Director Alumni Services .... Mr. Lucas DART
35 Director Student Life .... Ms. Sharon PELC
23 Director Counseling & Health Care .... Ms. Wendy L. SCHARDT
39 Director Residence Life .... Mr. George HOLMAN
40 Director Bookstore .... Mr. Len J. FANGMEYER
41 Director Intercollegiate Athletics .... Mr. Marc BAUER
88 Director Finance .... Ms. Jill PURDY
108 Director Assessment .... Dr. Beth D. HINGA
25 Asst Vice Chanc Sponsored Programs .... Mr. Richard A. MOCARSKI
85 Asst Vice Chanc for Intl Affairs .... Dr. Tim J. BURKINK
114 Director Budget .... Ms. Jean MATTSON
96 Director Procurement Services .... Mr. Scott A. BENSON
37 Director Financial Aid .... Ms. Mary SOMMERS
93 Director Multicultural Affairs .... Mr. Juan GUZMAN
92 Director Honors Program .... Dr. John FALCONER
15 Director Human Resources .... Mr. Scott A. BENSON
88 Director Business Services .... Mr. Michael T. CHRISTEN

*University of Nebraska - Lincoln (J)

14th and R Streets, Lincoln NE 68588-0002
County: Lancaster FICE Identification: 002565
Unit ID: 181464
Telephone: (402) 472-7211 Carnegie Class: DU-Highest
FAX Number: (402) 472-2410 Calendar System: Semester
URL: www.unl.edu
Established: 1869 Annual Undergrad Tuition & Fees (In-State): $9,242
Enrollment: 26,079 Coed
Affiliation or Control: State IRS Status: 501(c)3
Highest Offering: Doctorate
Accreditation: NH, ART, AUD, CAATE, CAEP, CIDA, CLPSY, CONST, COPSY, DANCE, DIETD, DIETI, IPSY, JOUR, LAW, LSAR, MFCD, MUS, PLNG, SCPSY, SP, THEA

02 Chancellor .... Dr. Ronnie D. GREEN
05 Int EVC for Academic Affairs .... Dr. Richard MOBERLY
10 VC Business & Finance .... Dr. William NUNEZ
32 Interim VC Student Affairs .... Dr. Laurie BELLOWS
65 Vice Chanc Agric/Nat Resources .... Dr. Michael BOEHM
46 VC Researc/Economic Development .... Mr. Robert WILHELM
13 VC Information Technology & CIO .... Mr. Mark ASKREN
28 Vice Chanc Diversity/Inclusion .... Dr. Marco BARKER
86 Asst to Chanc Govt & Mil Relations .... Ms. Michelle WAITE
15 Asst Vice Chanc for Human Resources .... Mr. Bruce A. CURRIN
20 Sr Assoc Vice Chanc & Dean .... Dr. Amy GOODBURN
84 Asst VC for Enrollment Mgmt .... Ms. Amber S. WILLIAMS
08 Dean University Libraries .... Ms. Claire STEWART
58 Assoc VC & Dean Grad Studies .... Dr. Timothy CARR
49 Dean Arts & Sciences .... Dr. Mark BUTTON
54 Dean Engineering .... Dr. Lance PEREZ
61 Acting Dean of Law .... Dr. Anna SHAVERS
47 Dean Agric Science/Nat Resources .... Dr. Tiffany HENG-MOSS
50 Dean Business .... Dr. Kathy FARRELL
60 Int Dean Journ/Mass Communications .... Dr. Amy STRUTHERS
53 Dean Education & Human Sciences .... Dr. Sherri JONES
48 Dean College Architecture .... Dr. Katherine ANKERSON
47 Dean Agricultural Research Division .... Dr. Archie CLUTTER
56 Dean & Dir Cooperative Extens .... Dr. Charles HIBBERD
93 Director Educ Access & TRIO Pgms .... Ms. Catherine YAMAMOTO
57 Dean Fine & Performing Arts .... Dr. Charles D. O'CONNOR
37 Dir Scholarships/Financial Aid .... Mr. Justin C. BROWN
09 Dir Research/Analytics .... Mr. Heath TUTTLE
88 Asst Dean Acad Svcs & Enrollment .... Mr. James VOLKMER

92 Director Honors Program ....Dr. Patrice MCMAHON
94 Director Women's Studies ....Dr. Marie-Chantal KALISA
06 University Registrar ....Mr. Steven BOOTON
36 Director Career Services Center ....Mr. Bill WATTS
19 Chief University Police Services ....Mr. Owen YARDLEY
22 Assoc to Chanc Equity & Compliance .. Ms. Tamiko STRICKMAN
23 Director University Health Center ....Ms. Jill LYNCH-SOSA
39 Int Director Housing Office ....Mr. Charlie FRANCIS
41 Director of Athletics ....Mr. William MOOS
106 Dir Distance Education Services ....Dr. Nancy ADEN-FOX
29 Exec Director Alumni Association ....Ms. Shelley ZABOROWSKI
26 Chief Communication/Mktg Ofcr ....Ms. Deb FIDDELKE
30 Chief Development ....Mr. Brian HASTINGS
38 Director Student Counseling ....Dr. Robert N. PORTNOY
96 Director of Procurement Services ....Ms. Maggie L. WITT
07 Director of Admissions ....Ms. Abby FREEMAN
100 Chief of Staff ....Dr. Michael ZELENY
28 Director Staff Diversity ....Ms. Karen KASSEBAUM
104 Director Education Abroad ....Ms. Rebecca BASKERVILLE

*University of Nebraska Medical Center (A)

987020 Nebraska Medical Center, Omaha NE 68198-7020
County: Douglas FICE Identification: 006895
Unit ID: 181428
Telephone: (402) 559-4000 Carnegie Class: Spec-4-yr-Med
FAX Number: (402) 559-4396 Calendar System: Semester
URL: www.unmc.edu
Established: 1869 Annual Undergrad Tuition & Fees (In-State): N/A
Enrollment: 3,908 Coed
Affiliation or Control: State IRS Status: 501(c)3
Highest Offering: Doctorate
Accreditation: NH, ARCPA, CYTO, DENT, DH, DMS, MED, MT, NURSE, PERF, PH, PHAR, PTA, RAD, RADMAG, RTT

02 Chancellor ....Dr. Jeffery P. GOLD
05 Sr Vice Chancellor Acad Affairs ....Dr. H. Dele O. DAVIES
10 Vice Chanc Business/Fin & Bus Dev ....Mr. Douglas EWALD
46 Vice Chancellor Research ....Dr. Jennifer LARSEN
86 Vice Chancellor External Affairs ....Mr. Robert BARTEE
32 Vice Chanc Student Success/Acad Aff ....Dr. Daniel SHIPP
20 Assoc Vice Chanc Academic Affairs ....Dr. Gary YEE
20 Assoc Vice Chancellor iEXCEL ....Dr. Pamela BOYERS
20 Assoc Vice Chanc Global/Stdnt Supp ....Dr. Jane MEZA
88 Assoc Vice Chanc Basic Sci Rsch ....Dr. Kenneth BAYLES
88 Assoc Vice Chancellor Research ....Dr. Christopher KRATOCHVIL
88 Assoc Vice Chanc Bus Development ....Dr. Rodney MARKIN
18 Assoc Vice Chanc Facilities ....Mr. Kenneth HANSEN
13 Assoc Vice Chancellor ITS ....Dr. Michael ASH
20 Asst Vice Chanc Acad Affs/Reg Comp ....Dr. Bruce GORDON
88 Asst VC Health Security Train/Educ ....Dr. John-Martin LOWE
88 Asst Vice Chanc Campus Wellness ....Dr. Steven WENGEL
20 Asst Vice Chanc Acad Affs ....Dr. Philip COVINGTON
21 Asst Vice Chanc Business & Finance ....Mr. William LAWLOR
15 Asst Vice Chanc for Human Resources ....Ms. Aileen WARREN
08 Asst Vice Chanc & Director Library ....Ms. Emily J. MCELROY
58 Dean Graduate Studies ....Dr. H. Dele O. DAVIES
52 Dean College of Dentistry ....Dr. Janet GUTHMILLER
63 Dean College of Medicine ....Dr. Bradley E. BRITIGAN
66 Dean College of Nursing ....Dr. Juliann SEBASTIAN
67 Dean College of Pharmacy ....Dr. Keith OLSEN
69 Dean College of Public Health ....Dr. Ali KHAN
76 Dean College of Allied Health Prof ....Dr. Kyle P. MEYER
88 Dir Eppley Cancer Research Inst ....Dr. Kenneth H. COWAN
88 Director Munroe-Meyer Institute ....Dr. Karoly MIRNICS
43 Assoc Gen Counsel Hlth Sci ....Ms. Tara SCROGIN
37 Director Financial Aid Office ....Ms. Judith D. WALKER
26 Director of Public Relations ....Mr. William O'NEILL
29 Director Alumni Relations ....Ms. Catherine MELLO
38 Exec Dir Counseling & Student Dev ....Dr. David S. CARVER
28 Director of Diversity ....Ms. Linda CUNNINGHAM
96 Director Procurement & Mtrls Mgt ....Mr. Robert JENNINGS
09 Director Institutional Research ....Ms. Jeanne FERBRACHE
19 Asst Vice Chanc/Chief of Police ....Ms. Charlotte EVANS

*University of Nebraska at Omaha (B)

6001 Dodge Street, Omaha NE 68182-0001
County: Douglas FICE Identification: 002554
Unit ID: 181394
Telephone: (402) 554-2200 Carnegie Class: DU-Higher
FAX Number: (402) 554-3555 Calendar System: Semester
URL: www.unomaha.edu
Established: 1908 Annual Undergrad Tuition & Fees (In-State): $7,790
Enrollment: 15,731 Coed
Affiliation or Control: State IRS Status: 501(c)3
Highest Offering: Doctorate
Accreditation: NH, AAB, ART, CAATE, CACREP, CAEPN, CEA, MUS, SP, SPAA, SW

02 Chancellor ....Dr. Jeffrey P. GOLD
05 Sr Vice Chanc Acad/Student Affs ....Dr. Sacha E. KOPP
10 Vice Chanc Business & Finance ....Mr. Doug A. EWALD
13 Chief Information Officer ....Mr. Bret BLACKMAN
21 Assoc Vice Chanc Business & Finance ....Vacant
32 Vice Chanc Student Affairs ....Dr. Daniel SHIPP
84 Assoc Vice Chanc Enroll Mgmt Svcs ....Mr. Omar CORREA
58 Dean Graduate Studies ....Dr. Deb SMITH-HOWELL
57 Dean Fine Arts/Communication/Media ....Dr. Michael HILT
53 Dean of Education ....Dr. Nancy EDICK
50 Dean of Business Administration ....Dr. Lou POL
49 Dean of Arts & Sciences ....Dr. David J. BOOCKER
88 Associate Vice Chancellor Global ....Ms. Jane L. MEZA
72 Dean Info Science/Technology ....Dr. Hesham ALI
80 Dean Public Affairs/Community ....Dr. John R. BARTLE
62 Dean of Library Services ....Mr. David E. RICHARDS
09 Dir Institutional Effectiveness ....Dr. T. Hank ROBINSON
35 Chief Student Life Officer ....Vacant
15 Director Human Resources ....Mr. Cecil HICKS, JR.
18 Director Facilities Mgmt/Planning ....Mr. John AMEND
06 Interim Registrar ....Mr. Matt SCHILL
07 Director of Admissions ....Mr. Lena STOVER
37 Director Financial Aid ....Mr. Marty HABROCK
88 Director Student Testing Center ....Mr. John GOLKA
41 Vice Chanc Athletic Leadership/Mgmt ....Mr. Trev ALBERTS
29 President/CEO Alumni Association ....Mr. Lee DENKER
26 Exec Dir University Communications ....Ms. Makayla MCMORRIS
96 Procurement Systems Coordinator ....Ms. Lynn MCALPINE
40 Manager Book Store ....Mr. Eric HAGER
19 Director of Public Safety ....Ms. Charlotte EVANS

*University of Nebraska - Nebraska College of Technical Agriculture (C)

404 E 7th Street, Curtis NE 69025-9502
County: Frontier FICE Identification: 007358
Unit ID: 181765
Telephone: (308) 367-4124 Carnegie Class: Spec 2-yr-Other
FAX Number: (308) 367-5203 Calendar System: Semester
URL: www.ncta.unl.edu
Established: 1913 Annual Undergrad Tuition & Fees (In-State): $5,228
Enrollment: 317 Coed
Affiliation or Control: State IRS Status: 501(c)3
Highest Offering: Associate Degree
Accreditation: NH

02 Dean ....Dr. Ron ROSATI
10 Assoc Dean Finance/Ops/Student Svcs ....Mrs. Jennifer A. MCCONVILLE
21 Business Manager/Human Resources ....Ms. Jan GILBERT
04 Administrative Asst to President ....Ms. Catherine M. HAUPTMAN
06 Registrar ....Mrs. Victoria LUKE
08 Head Librarian ....Mr. Mo KHAMOUNA
09 Director of Institutional Research ....Ms. Mary RITTENHOUSE
13 Chief Info Technology Officer (CIO) ....Vacant
39 Director Student Housing ....Ms. Erika ARAMBULA
84 Asst Vice Chanc Enrollment Mgmt ....Ms. Amber WILLIAMS

Western Nebraska Community College (D)

1601 E 27th Street, Scottsbluff NE 69361-1815
County: Scotts Bluff FICE Identification: 002560
Unit ID: 181817
Telephone: (308) 635-3606 Carnegie Class: Assoc/MT-VT-High Non
FAX Number: (308) 635-6100 Calendar System: Semester
URL: www.wncc.edu
Established: 1926 Annual Undergrad Tuition & Fees (In-District): $2,820
Enrollment: 1,905 Coed
Affiliation or Control: State/Local IRS Status: 501(c)3
Highest Offering: Associate Degree
Accreditation: NH, CAHIIM, PNUR, SURGT

01 President ....Dr. Todd R. HOLCOMB
05 Executive Vice President ....Dr. Kim KUSTER-DALE
15 Executive Director of HR ....Ms. Kathy AULT
32 Vice President Student Services ....Ms. Nina GRANT
10 Vice Pres Administrative Services ....Mr. William D. KNAPPER
20 Dean of Instruction ....Ms. Hallie FEIL
35 Dean of Students ....Mr. Norman COLEY, JR.
12 Sidney Campus Director ....Ms. Paula J. ABBOTT
88 Assoc Dean Instruct Support Svcs ....Ms. Ellen M. DILLON
102 Foundation Executive Director ....Ms. Jennifer REISIG
06 Registrar ....Mr. Roger S. HOVEY
37 Financial Aid Director ....Ms. Sheila R. JOHNS
26 Public Relations & Marketing Dir ....Ms. Allison JUDY
38 Counseling Director ....Mr. Norman J. STEPHENSON
21 Accounting Services Director ....Mr. David KOEHLER
41 Athletic Director ....Mr. Ryan C. BURGNER
51 Lifelong Learning Director ....Ms. Lori S. STROMBERG
07 Admissions Director ....Ms. Gretchen K. FOSTER
39 Residence Life Director ....Ms. Molly BONUCHI
13 Information Technology Director ....Mr. Joe W. DEER
40 Bookstore Operations Director ....Mr. Rich RIDDICK
19 Safety/Environmental Mgmt Director ....Mr. Josh VESPER
09 Institutional Research Director ....Ms. Nino KALATOZI
88 Academic Testing & Tutoring Coord ....Ms. Tammie KLEICH
39 Student Engagement Director ....Ms. Megan WESCOAT
50 Int Div Chair Business/Applied Tech ....Dr. Charlie GREGORY
79 Div Chair Acad Enrich/Lang/Fine Art ....Ms. Jennifer L. PEDERSEN
66 Nursing Program Director ....Ms. Rebecca KAUTZ
81 Division Chair Math & Science ....Ms. Laurie ALKIRE
88 Health Info Technology Program Dir ....Ms. Peg A. WOLFF
76 Division Chair Health Sciences ....Dr. Ronda KINSEY
29 Director Alumni Relations/Steward ....Ms. Jennifer R. SIBAL
106 Instructional Tech Coordinator ....Ms. Heidi JACKSON

York College (E)

1125 E 8th Street, York NE 68467-2699
County: York FICE Identification: 002567
Unit ID: 181853
Telephone: (402) 363-5600 Carnegie Class: Bac-Diverse
FAX Number: (402) 363-5623 Calendar System: Semester
URL: www.york.edu
Established: 1890 Annual Undergrad Tuition & Fees: $19,310
Enrollment: 462 Coed
Affiliation or Control: Churches Of Christ IRS Status: 501(c)3
Highest Offering: Master's
Accreditation: NH, CAEP

01 President ....Dr. Steven W. ECKMAN
05 Provost ....Dr. Shane MOUNTJOY
10 Vice President Finance & Operations ....Mr. Todd SHELDON
111 Vice Pres Advancement ....Mr. Brent MAGNER
41 VP for Athletics and Enrollment ....Mr. Jared STARK
42 VP for Spiritual Development ....Dr. Sam GARNER
32 Dean of Student Development ....Mrs. Catherine SEUFFERLEIN
21 Business Manager ....Mr. Dan COLE
06 Registrar ....Mr. Jared LEINEN
35 Dean of Students ....Ms. Meghan SHRUCK
08 Director of Library ....Mrs. Ruth CARLOCK
26 Director of Publications ....Mr. Steddon L. SIKES
37 Financial Aid Director ....Mr. Brien ALLEY
40 Campus Store Manager ....Mrs. Janet RUSH
18 Supervisor Buildings & Grounds ....Mr. Bob GAVER
73 Chair Bible ....Dr. Frank E. WHEELER
88 Chair History ....Mr. Tim D. MCNEESE
50 Chair English ....Dr. Jennifer DUTCH
81 Chair Math/Sciences ....Dr. Alex WILLIAMS
57 Chair Performing Arts/Communication ....Dr. Clark A. ROUSH
29 Dir Alumni & Community Relations ....Mrs. Chrystal HOUSTON
04 Executive Asst to President ....Mrs. Gayle A. GOOD
13 Chief Info Technology Officer (CIO) ....Mr. Joel COEHOORN
39 Director Student Housing ....Mr. Collin TUCKER
106 Dir Online Education/E-learning ....Dr. Kirk MALLETTE
07 Director of Admissions ....Mr. David ODOM

NEVADA

The Art Institute of Las Vegas (F)

2350 Corporate Circle, Henderson NV 89074-7737
County: Clark FICE Identification: 030846
Unit ID: 182111
Telephone: (702) 369-9944 Carnegie Class: Spec-4-yr-Arts
FAX Number: (702) 992-8564 Calendar System: Quarter
URL: www.artinstitutes.edu/las-vegas/
Established: 1983 Annual Undergrad Tuition & Fees: $17,316
Enrollment: 683 Coed
Affiliation or Control: Proprietary IRS Status: Proprietary
Highest Offering: Baccalaureate
Accreditation: #ACICS, ACFEI, CIDA

Career College of Northern Nevada (G)

1421 Pullman Drive, Sparks NV 89434
County: Washoe FICE Identification: 026215
Unit ID: 181941
Telephone: (775) 241-4445 Carnegie Class: Assoc/HVT-High Trad
FAX Number: (775) 856-0935 Calendar System: Quarter
URL: www.ccnn.edu
Established: 1984 Annual Undergrad Tuition & Fees: N/A
Enrollment: 401 Coed
Affiliation or Control: Proprietary IRS Status: Proprietary
Highest Offering: Associate Degree
Accreditation: ACCSC

01 President ....Mr. L. Nathan N. CLARK

Carrington College - Las Vegas (H)

5740 S Eastern Avenue, Suite 140, Las Vegas NV 89119
Telephone: (702) 688-4300 Identification: 770742
Accreditation: &WJ, COARC, PTAA

† Regional accreditation is carried under the parent institution in Sacramento, CA.

Carrington College - Reno (I)

5580 Kietzke Lane, Reno NV 89511
Telephone: (775) 335-2900 Identification: 770743
Accreditation: &WJ, ADNUR

† Regional accreditation is carried under the parent institution in Sacramento, CA.

Chamberlain University-Las Vegas (J)

9901 Covington Cross Drive, Las Vegas NV 89144
Telephone: (702) 786-1660 Identification: 770852
Accreditation: &NH, NURSE

† Branch campus of Chamberlain University-Addison, Addison, IL

*Nevada System of Higher Education (K)

2601 Enterprise Road, Reno NV 89512-1666
County: Washoe FICE Identification: 008026
Unit ID: 182519
Telephone: (775) 784-4901 Carnegie Class: N/A
FAX Number: (775) 784-1127
URL: www.nevada.edu

01 Chancellor .... Mr. Thom REILLY
05 VC Academic & Student Affairs .... Ms. Crystal ABBA
10 Chief Financial Officer .... Mr. Andrew CLINGER
101 Chief of Staff of Board of Regents .... Mr. Dean J. GOULD
43 Chief General Counsel .... Mr. Joseph REYNOLDS
86 VC Govt and Community Affairs .... Ms. Constance BROOKS
12 VC Community Colleges .... Mr. Nate MACKINNON

*College of Southern Nevada (A)

6375 W Charleston Boulevard, Las Vegas NV 89146-1139
County: Clark FICE Identification: 010362
Unit ID: 182005
Telephone: (702) 651-5000 Carnegie Class: Bac/Assoc-Assoc Dom
FAX Number: N/A Calendar System: Semester
URL: www.csn.edu
Established: 1971 Annual Undergrad Tuition & Fees (In-State): $3,492
Enrollment: 33,914 Coed
Affiliation or Control: State IRS Status: 501(c)3
Highest Offering: Baccalaureate
Accreditation: NW, ACBSP, ACFEI, ADNUR, CAHIIM, CEA, COARC, DA, DH, DMS, EMT, MAC, MT, OPD, PNUR, PTAA, SURGT

02 President .... Dr. Federico ZARAGOZA
04 Executive Assistant .... Ms. Annette LORD
10 VP for Finance & Administration .... Ms. Mary Kaye BAILEY
32 VP for Student Affairs .... Ms. Juanita CHRYSANTHOU
05 VP for Academic Affairs .... Dr. Margo MARTIN
12 VP/Provost Henderson Campus .... Ms. Patricia A. CHARLTON
12 VP/Provost Charleston Campus .... Dr. Sonya PEARSON
12 VP/Provost North Las Vegas Campus .... Dr. Clarissa COTA
102 Exec Director CSN Foundation .... Ms. Barbara TALISMAN
18 Assoc VP Facilities/Opers/Maint .... Ms. Sherri PAYNE
43 Legal Counsel .... Mr. Richard HINCKLEY
06 Int Dir Student Affairs/Registrar .... Ms. Bernadette LOPEZ-GARRETT
103 Exec Dir Workforce Education .... Dr. Ricardo VILLALOBOS
72 Dean Adv & Applied Technologies .... Dr. Michael SPANGLER
81 Interim Dean Science & Math .... Dr. Pete LANAGAN
83 Dean Social Sciences & Education .... Dr. Charles OKEKE
79 Interim Dean Arts & Letters .... Mr. Lester TANAKA
76 Interim Dean Health Sciences .... Ms. Janice GLASPER
50 Dean of Business .... Dr. Marcus JOHNSON
96 Associate VP of Purchasing .... Mr. Rolando MOSQUEDA
41 Director of Athletics .... Mr. L. Dexter IRVIN
114 Assoc Vice Pres Budget Services .... Ms. Lisa BAKKE
09 Exec Dir of Institutional Research .... Mr. John BEARCE
62 Director Library Services .... Ms. Caprice ROBERSON
37 Associate VP for Financial Aid .... Ms. Victoria GOEKE
19 Chief of Police .... Mr. Darryl CARABALLO
13 Technology CIO .... Mr. Mugunth VAITHYLINGAM
15 Interim Chief HR Officer .... Ms. Ayesha KIDD
28 Executive Director of Diversity .... Ms. Maria MARINCH
106 Dir Online Education/E-learning .... Mr. Terry NORRIS
22 Director of Institutional Equity .... Dr. Armen ASHERIAN

*Great Basin College (B)

1500 College Parkway, Elko NV 89801-5032
County: Elko FICE Identification: 006977
Unit ID: 182306
Telephone: (775) 738-8493 Carnegie Class: Bac/Assoc-Mixed
FAX Number: (775) 738-8771 Calendar System: Semester
URL: www.gbcnv.edu
Established: 1967 Annual Undergrad Tuition & Fees (In-State): $3,128
Enrollment: 3,244 Coed
Affiliation or Control: State IRS Status: 501(c)3
Highest Offering: Baccalaureate
Accreditation: NW, ADNUR, CSHSE, NUR, RAD

02 President .... Ms. Joyce HELENS
05 Vice President for Academic Affairs .... Vacant
10 Vice President for Business Affairs .... Ms. Sonja SIBERT
106 Associate VP for Distance Education .... Vacant
04 Assistant to the President .... Ms. Mardell WILKINS
32 Vice President for Student Affairs .... Dr. Jake RIVERA
09 Dir Institutional Rsrch/Effective .... Dr. William BROWN
37 Dir Student Financial Svcs & VA .... Mr. Scott NIELSEN
07 Director of Admissions/Registrar .... Ms. Melissa RISI
49 Dean of Arts and Letters .... Vacant
75 Dean of Applied Science .... Mr. Bret MURPHY
76 Dean of Health Sciences/Human Svcs .... Dr. Amber DONNELLI
12 Director Ely Center .... Ms. Veronica NELSON
12 Director Winnemucca Center .... Ms. Lisa CAMPBELL
12 Director Pahrump Valley Center .... Ms. Diane WRIGHTMAN
51 Director Continuing Education .... Mrs. Angie DEBRAGA
102 Director Foundation .... Mr. Matt MCCARTY
19 Director Safety and Security .... Ms. Patricia ANDERSON
25 Director Grants .... Ms. Jeannie BAILEY
43 General Counsel .... Mr. John ALBRECHT
26 Assoc Dir Marketing/Communication .... Ms. Kayla MCCARSON

*Nevada State College (C)

1300 Nevada State Drive, Henderson NV 89002-9455
County: Clark FICE Identification: 041143
Unit ID: 441900
Telephone: (702) 992-2000 Carnegie Class: Bac-Diverse
FAX Number: (702) 992-2226 Calendar System: Semester
URL: www.nsc.edu
Established: 2002 Annual Undergrad Tuition & Fees (In-District): $5,438
Enrollment: 4,216 Coed
Affiliation or Control: State/Local IRS Status: 501(c)3
Highest Offering: Master's
Accreditation: NW, NURSE, SP

02 President .... Bart PATTERSON
05 Provost/Exec Vice President .... Dr. Vickie SHIELDS
10 Vice Pres Finance & Administration .... Kevin BUTLER
08 Director of Library Services .... Nathaniel KING
09 Director of Institutional Research .... Dr. Sandip THANKI
28 AVP/Director of Diversity .... Dr. Edith FERNANDEZ
121 Assoc Vice Provost Student Success .... Gregory ROBINSON
37 Director Student Financial Aid .... Anthony MORRONE
53 Dean of Education .... Dr. Dennis POTTHOFF
06 Registrar .... Adelfa SULLIVAN

*Truckee Meadows Community College (D)

7000 Dandini Boulevard, Reno NV 89512-3999
County: Washoe FICE Identification: 021077
Unit ID: 182500
Telephone: (775) 673-7000 Carnegie Class: Assoc/MT-VT-Mix Trad/Non
FAX Number: (775) 673-7108 Calendar System: Semester
URL: www.tmcc.edu
Established: 1971 Annual Undergrad Tuition & Fees (In-State): $2,963
Enrollment: 10,720 Coed
Affiliation or Control: State IRS Status: 501(c)3
Highest Offering: Associate Degree
Accreditation: NW, ACFEI, ADNUR, DA, DH, DIETT, EMT, RAD

02 President .... Dr. Karin HILGERSOM
04 Executive Assistant to President .... Ms. Lisa FARMER
05 VP Academic Affairs .... Dr. Marie MURGOLO
26 Assoc VP Research/Mktg & Web Svcs .... Ms. Elena BUBNOVA
09 Director Institutional Research .... Ms. Cheryl SCOTT
32 VP Student Services & Diversity .... Ms. Estela LEVARIO GUTIERREZ
10 VP Finance & Admin Services .... Mr. Jim NEW
102 Exec Dir Foundation/Development .... Mrs. Gretchen SAWYER
07 Director Admissions & Records .... Mr. Andrew HUGHES
21 Controller Accounting Services .... Mr. Rich WILLIAMS
37 Executive Director Financial Aid .... Ms. Sharon WURM
124 Exec Dir Retention and Support Svcs .... Ms. Joan STEINMAN
15 Director Human Resources .... Ms. Roni FOX
18 Exec Director Facilities Services .... Mr. Dave ROBERTS
103 Dir Workforce Devel/Cmty Education .... Ms. Bruncha MILASZEWSKI
08 Learning Commons Director .... Ms. Maura HADAWAY

† Granted candidacy at the Baccalaureate level.

*University of Nevada, Las Vegas (E)

4505 S Maryland Parkway, Las Vegas NV 89154-1001
County: Clark FICE Identification: 002569
Unit ID: 182281
Telephone: (702) 895-3201 Carnegie Class: DU-Highest
FAX Number: (702) 895-1088 Calendar System: Semester
URL: www.unlv.edu
Established: 1957 Annual Undergrad Tuition & Fees (In-State): $7,985
Enrollment: 30,471 Coed
Affiliation or Control: State IRS Status: 501(c)3
Highest Offering: Doctorate
Accreditation: NW, ART, CAATE, CAMPEP, CIDA, CLPSY, CONST, DENT, DIETD, DIETI, HSA, IPSY, LAW, LSAR, #MED, MFCD, MUS, NURSE, PH, PTA, RAD, SPAA, SW

02 President .... Dr. Marta MEANA
100 Chief of Staff .... Dr. Fred TREDUP
05 Executive Vice President & Provost .... Dr. Chris HEAVEY
10 Vice Pres Finance & Business & CFO .... Mrs. Jean VOCK
41 Director of Athletics .... Mrs. Desiree REED-FRANCOIS
32 Vice President for Student Affairs .... Dr. Juanita FAIN
46 VP Research & Economic Development .. Dr. Mary S. CROUGHAN
30 VP Philanthropy & Alumni .... Vacant
86 VP Government Affairs & Compliance .... Mr. Luis VALERA
26 VP Brand & Chief Marketing Officer .... Mr. Vince ALBERTA
28 Chief Diversity Officer .... Dr. Barbee OAKES
43 General Counsel .... Mrs. Elda SIDHU
07 AVP Enrollment & Student Services .... Dr. Brent DRAKE
35 Assoc VP for Student Affairs .... Dr. Renee WATSON
29 Sr Assoc VP Alumni Relations .... Mr. Chad WARREN
31 Int Exec Dir of Community Relations .... Mrs. Sue DIBELLA
15 VP Human Resources Officer .... Dr. Ericka SMITH
87 Vice Provost Educational Outreach .... Mr. Joseph MIERA
20 Vice Provost Academic Programs .... Dr. Javier RODRIGUEZ
20 Vice Provost for Undergraduate Educ .... Dr. Laurel PRITCHARD
09 Vice Provost Decision Support .... Dr. Brent DRAKE
13 Vice Provost Information Technology .... Dr. Lori TEMPLE
58 Dean of Graduate College .... Dr. Kate H. KORGAN
50 Dean Business .... Dr. Brent A. HATHAWAY
49 Dean Liberal Arts .... Dr. Jennifer KEENE
53 Dean of Education .... Dr. Kim K. METCALF
54 Dean of Engineering .... Dr. Rama VENKAT
66 Dean of Nursing .... Dr. Angela AMAR
63 Interim Dean School of Medicine .... Dr. John FILDES
52 Dean School of Dental Medicine .... Dr. Karen P. WEST
61 Dean School of Law .... Mr. Daniel W. HAMILTON
81 Dean of Sciences .... Dr. Eric CHRONISTER
88 Dean College of Hotel Admin .... Dr. Stowe SHOEMAKER
57 Dean Fine Arts .... Dr. Nancy USCHER
08 Dean of Libraries .... Ms. Maggie FARRELL
88 Dean Urban Affairs .... Dr. Robert R. ULMER
92 Interim Dean Honors College .... Dr. Andrew HANSON
121 Dean Academic Success Center .... Dr. Ann MCDONOUGH
88 Dean Community Health Sciences . Dr. Shawn GERSTENBERGER
76 Dean Sch Allied Health Sciences .... Dr. Ronald T. BROWN
06 Registrar .... Dr. Sam FUGAZZOTTO
37 Dir Financial Aid & Scholarships .... Mr. Norm BEDFORD
19 AVP & Dir Univ Police Services .... Mr. Adam GARCIA
39 Executive Director Residential Life .... Mr. Richard CLARK
38 AVP Student Wellness .... Dr. Jamie DAVIDSON
23 Director Student Health .... Ms. Kathy A. UNDERWOOD
96 Director Purchasing .... Ms. Sharrie MAYDEN
85 Dir International Students/Scholars .... Ms. Marianna PANOSSI
25 Director Sponsored Programs .... Ms. Lori CICCONE

*University of Nevada, Reno (F)

1664 N. Virginia Street, Reno NV 89557
County: Washoe FICE Identification: 002568
Unit ID: 182290
Telephone: (775) 784-1110 Carnegie Class: DU-Highest
FAX Number: (775) 784-1300 Calendar System: Semester
URL: www.unr.edu
Established: 1874 Annual Undergrad Tuition & Fees (In-State): $7,599
Enrollment: 21,657 Coed
Affiliation or Control: State IRS Status: 501(c)3
Highest Offering: Doctorate
Accreditation: NW, #ARCPA, CACREP, CAEPN, CEA, CLPSY, DIETD, DIETI, JOUR, MED, MUS, NURSE, PH, SP, SW

02 President .... Dr. Marc JOHNSON
05 Exec Vice Pres & Provost .... Dr. Kevin CARMAN
11 Vice Pres Administration & Finance .... Mr. Victor REDDING
63 VP Health Sci/Dean Sch of Medicine .... Dr. Thomas L. SCHWENK
30 Vice President Devel/Alumni Rels .... Mr. John CAROTHERS
32 Vice President for Student Services .... Dr. Shannon ELLIS
46 Vice President for Research .... Dr. Mridul GAUTAM
08 Dean of Libraries .... Dr. Kathlin D. RAY
20 Vice Prov Instr/Undergrad Programs .... Dr. David SHINTANI
20 Vice Provost Faculty Affairs .... Dr. Jill HEATON
58 Vice Provost/Dean Grad School .... Dr. David ZEH
51 Vice Provost for Extended Studies .... Dr. Fred B. HOLMAN
10 Assoc VP Business & Finance .... Ms. Sheri MENDEZ
84 Assoc VP Enrollment Services .... Dr. Melisa N. CHOROSZY
121 Assoc VP Student Success Services .... Dr. Jerry MARCZYNSKI
45 Assoc VP Plng/Budget/Analysis .... Mr. Rashawn NORMAN
18 Asst Vice Pres Facilities Svcs .... Mr. Sean MCGOLDRICK
21 Controller .... Ms. Kara GRIFFIN
41 Director Athletics .... Mr. Doug KNUTH
96 Director Purchasing .... Mr. Raymond MORAN
19 Int Director University Police Svcs .... Mr. Todd RENWICK
22 Dir Equal Opportunity & Title IX .... Ms. Maria DOUCETTPERRY
37 Director Student Financial Svcs .... Mr. Timothy WOLFE
39 Director Resident Life & Housing . Mr. Rodney L. AESCHLIMANN
23 Director Student Health Svcs .... Dr. Cheryl HUG-ENGLISH
09 Director Institutional Analysis .... Dr. Serge HERZOG
86 Spec Asst to Pres External Affairs .... Ms. Heidi GANSERT
65 Dir Mackay Sch Mines/Earth Science .... Dr. Russell FIELDS
66 Dean of Nursing .... Dr. Debera THOMAS
57 Director School of the Arts .... Dr. Larry ENGSTROM
25 Director Sponsored Projects .... Ms. Charlene HART
40 Director Wolf Shop .... Mr. Steve DUBEY
49 Dean Liberal Arts .... Dr. Debra MODDELMOG
47 Dean Agriculture/Biotech/Nat Res .... Dr. William PAYNE
50 Dean Business Administration .... Dr. Gregory MOSIER
53 Dean of Education .... Dr. Donald EASTON-BROOKS
54 Dean Engineering .... Dr. Emmanuel MARAGAKIS
60 Dean School of Journalism .... Mr. Alan STAVITSKY
81 Dean College of Science .... Dr. Jeffrey S. THOMPSON
07 Director of Admissions .... Dr. Stephen MAPLES
29 Director Alumni Relations .... Ms. Amy CAROTHERS
06 Associate Registrar .... Ms. Heather TURK FIECOAT
26 Int Exec Dir Marketing & Comm .... Ms. Kerri GARCIA
04 Executive Asst to President .... Ms. Aubrey FLORES
100 Chief of Staff .... Ms. Patricia RICHARD
104 Dir/CEO Univ Study Abroad Consort .... Dr. Carmelo URZA
13 Chief Info Technology Officer (CIO) .... Mr. Steven SMITH
28 Dir Ctr for Student Cultural Dev .... Mr. Jose M. PULIDO LEON
43 General Counsel .... Ms. Mary DUGAN
112 Director of Planned Giving .... Ms. Lisa RILEY
69 Dean School of Community Health Sci .... Dr. Trudy LARSON

*Western Nevada College (G)

2201 W College Parkway, Carson City NV 89703-7316
County: Carson FICE Identification: 010363
Unit ID: 182564
Telephone: (775) 445-3000 Carnegie Class: Bac/Assoc-Assoc Dom
FAX Number: (775) 445-3051 Calendar System: Semester
URL: www.wnc.edu
Established: 1971 Annual Undergrad Tuition & Fees (In-State): $3,158
Enrollment: 3,642 Coed
Affiliation or Control: State IRS Status: 501(c)3
Highest Offering: Baccalaureate
Accreditation: NW, ADNUR

02 President .... Dr. Vincent R. SOLIS
04 Assistant to the President .... Ms. Deb CONRAD
05 VP Instruction/Inst Effectiveness .... Dr. Kyle DALPE
10 Chief Financial Officer .... Ms. Darla DODGE
43 Vice President/Legal Counsel .... Mr. Mark GHAN
20 Dean of Instruction .... Vacant
84 Chief Enroll/Student Success Ofcr .... Mr. Jeffrey DOWNS
21 Controller .... Ms. Coral LOPEZ
88 Director Child Development Center .... Ms. Anna Lisa ACOSTA

38 Director of Counseling/Advising .... Ms. Piper MCCARTHY
18 Director Facilities Mgmt/Planning .... Mr. Kevin GAFFNEY
37 Director Financial Aid .... Mr. John (JW) LAZZARI
26 Director Information & Marketing .... Ms. Jamie MCNINCH
08 Director of Learning & Innovation .... Ms. Denise FROHLICH
06 Registrar/Director of Admissions .... Ms. Dianne HILLIARD
30 Director of Development .... Ms. Niki GLADYS
09 Director of Institutional Research .... Ms. Cathy FULKERSON
13 Director of Computing Services .... Mr. Ryan SWAIN
114 Budget Officer .... Ms. Darla DODGE
15 Director Human Resources .... Ms. Melody DULEY
35 Student Life Coordinator .... Ms. Heather RIKALO
49 Academic Director Liberal Arts .... Mr. Scott MORRISON
72 Academic Director Career & Tech Div .... Dr. Georgia WHITE
66 Academic Dir Nursing/Allied Health .... Dr. Judith CORDIA
41 Athletic Director .... Vacant
19 Police Services Commander .... Mr. Tod MILLER

Northwest Career College (A)

7398 Smoke Ranch Road, Las Vegas NV 89128
County: Clark FICE Identification: 038385
Unit ID: 445948
Telephone: (702) 254-7577 Carnegie Class: Spec 2-yr-Other
FAX Number: (702) 256-9181 Calendar System: Other
URL: www.northwestcareercollege.edu
Established: 1997 Annual Undergrad Tuition & Fees: N/A
Enrollment: 756 Coed
Affiliation or Control: Proprietary IRS Status: Proprietary
Highest Offering: Associate Degree
Accreditation: ABHES

01 President/Founder .... Dr. John KENNY
05 Director of Education .... Dr. Thomas KENNY
11 COO .... Patrick KENNY
10 CFO .... Stephanie KENNY
37 Financial Aid Officer .... Guillermo BALDERAS
36 Director of Career Services .... Jilian LOPEZ
09 Director of Compliance .... Thomas KENNY
07 Director of Admissions .... Grace PEREA
13 Director of Technology .... Michael KENNY
06 Registrar .... Cheryl DADEY

Pima Medical Institute-Las Vegas (B)

3333 E Flamingo Road, Las Vegas NV 89121-4329
Telephone: (702) 458-9650 Identification: 666273
Accreditation: ABHES, COARC, OTA, PTAA, RAD

† Branch campus of Pima Medical Institute, Tucson, AZ.

Roseman University of Health Sciences (C)

11 Sunset Way, Henderson NV 89014-2333
County: Clark FICE Identification: 040653
Unit ID: 445735
Telephone: (702) 990-4433 Carnegie Class: Spec-4-yr-Other Health
FAX Number: (702) 990-4435 Calendar System: Other
URL: www.roseman.edu
Established: 1999 Annual Undergrad Tuition & Fees: N/A
Enrollment: 1,580 Coed
Affiliation or Control: Independent Non-Profit IRS Status: 501(c)3
Highest Offering: Doctorate
Accreditation: NW, DENT, IACBE, NURSE, PHAR

01 President .... Dr. Renee COFFMAN
12 Chancellor Summerlin Campus .... Dr. Mark A. PENN
12 Chancellor Henderson Campus .... Dr. Eucharia E. NNADI
10 VP Business & Finance .... Mr. Ken WILKINS
11 VP of Operations .... Mr. Terrell SPARKS
03 Vice President Executive Affairs .... Dr. Charles F. LACY
26 Vice President Communications & PR .... Mr. Jason ROTH
09 VP Qual Assurance/Intercampus Cons .... Dr. Thomas METZGER
32 VP for Student Services .... Dr. Michael DEYOUNG
67 Dean College of Pharmacy .... Dr. Larry FANNIN
66 Dean College of Nursing .... Dr. Mable H. SMITH
52 Dean College of Dental Medicine .... Dr. Frank LICARI
50 Director MBA Program .... Dr. Okeleke NZEOGWU
37 Director of Financial Aid .... Ms. Sally MICKELSON
88 Assoc Dean Clinical Affairs .... Dr. Kenneth KING
07 Assoc Dean Admissions/Student Svcs .... Dr. William HARMAN
15 Director of Human Resources .... Ms. Saralyn BARNES
08 Director of Library Services .... Ms. Karen CANEPI
06 Registrar/Director of Student Svcs .... Ms. Angela D. BIGBY

Sierra Nevada College (D)

999 Tahoe Boulevard, Incline Village NV 89451-9500
County: Washoe FICE Identification: 009192
Unit ID: 182458
Telephone: (775) 831-1314 Carnegie Class: Masters/M
FAX Number: (775) 832-1696 Calendar System: Semester
URL: www.sierranevada.edu
Established: 1969 Annual Undergrad Tuition & Fees: $34,241
Enrollment: 965 Coed
Affiliation or Control: Independent Non-Profit IRS Status: 501(c)3
Highest Offering: Master's
Accreditation: NW

00 Chairman Board of Trustees .... Dr. Atam LALCHANDANI
01 Interim President .... Dr. Ed ZSCHAU
05 Executive Vice President/Provost .... Ms. Shannon BEETS
111 Interim VP for Advancement .... Ms. Dianne SEVERANCE
10 VP for Finance/Administration .... Ms. Susan JOHNSON
32 Dean of Students .... Mr. Will HOIDA
07 Interim Director of UG Admissions .... Ms. Abby STEVENS
20 Associate Provost .... Dr. Dan O'BRYAN
37 Director of Financial Aid .... Ms. Judy ROBERTS
26 Director of Marketing .... Mr. Daniel KELLY
09 Director of Institutional Research .... Ms. Annamarie JONES
15 Director of Human Resources .... Mr. Tyler YOUNG
18 Chief Facilities/Physical Plant .... Mr. Layne SESSIONS
06 Registrar .... Ms. Rose WEHBY
53 Statewide Dir Teacher Education .... Ms. Beth TALIAFERRO
13 Director Information Technology .... Vacant
16 Human Resources Coordinator .... Ms. Dana HOFFELT
21 Controller .... Ms. Victoria LOBOSCO
04 Executive Asst to the President .... Ms. Kristine YOUNG
41 Athletic Director .... Mr. Christian DELEON
08 Chief Library Officer .... Ms. Lara SCHOTT
101 Secretary of the Institution/Board .... Ms. Kristine K. YOUNG

Touro University Nevada (E)

874 American Pacific Drive, Henderson NV 89014
Telephone: (702) 777-8687 Identification: 770966
Accreditation: &WC, ARCPA, NURSE, OSTEO, OT, PTA

† Branch campus of Touro University California, Vallejo, CA

University of Phoenix Las Vegas Campus (F)

3755 Breakthrough Way, Ste. 100,
Las Vegas NV 89135-3047
Telephone: (702) 352-2944 Identification: 770220
Accreditation: &NH, ACBSP

† Branch campus of University of Phoenix, Tempe, AZ

Wongu University of Oriental Medicine (G)

8620 S Eastern Avenue, Las Vegas NV 89123
County: Clark Identification: 667262
Unit ID: 488907
Telephone: (702) 463-2122 Carnegie Class: Spec-4-yr-Other Health
FAX Number: (702) 946-5050 Calendar System: Quarter
URL: www.wongu.org
Established: 2012 Annual Graduate Tuition & Fees: N/A
Enrollment: 35 Coed
Affiliation or Control: Independent Non-Profit IRS Status: 501(c)3
Highest Offering: Master's; No Undergraduates
Accreditation: ACUP

01 President .... Dr. Daniel DAVIES
05 Academic Dean .... Dr. Chalaiporn IAMSIRITHAWORN
10 Chief Financial Officer .... Carolyn YANAI
06 Registrar .... Chau NGUYEN
07 Director Admissions/HR Officer .... Lisa SEQUERA

NEW HAMPSHIRE

Colby-Sawyer College (H)

541 Main Street, New London NH 03257-7835
County: Merrimack FICE Identification: 002572
Unit ID: 182634
Telephone: (603) 526-3000 Carnegie Class: Bac-Diverse
FAX Number: (603) 526-3500 Calendar System: Semester
URL: www.colby-sawyer.edu
Established: 1837 Annual Undergrad Tuition & Fees: $42,398
Enrollment: 995 Coed
Affiliation or Control: Independent Non-Profit IRS Status: 501(c)3
Highest Offering: Master's
Accreditation: EH, ACBSP, CAATE, NURSE

01 President .... Dr. Susan D. STUEBNER
05 Academic Vice Pres/Dean of Faculty .... Dr. Laura A. SYKES
10 Vice Pres for Finance and Admin .... Ms. Karen BONEWALD
32 Vice President and Dean of Students .... Ms. Robin BURROUGHS DAVIS
111 Vice President Advancement .... Mr. Daniel B. PARISH
07 Vice Pres Admissions/Financial Aid .... Ms. Anna D. MINER
26 Vice Pres Marketing/Communications .... Mr. Gregg MAZZOLA
101 Secretary of the College .... Ms. Rachel A. PARSONS
21 Controller/Assistant Treasurer .... Ms. Megan MILLER
09 Director Institutional Research .... Vacant
39 Director Residential Education .... Ms. Mary MCLAUGHLIN
37 Director of Financial Aid .... Ms. Beth W. RENZULLI
08 Director Library .... Ms. Malia EBEL
06 Registrar .... Ms. Diane H. DRISCOLL
13 Director Information Technology .... Mr. William ST. CYR
41 Director of Athletics .... Mr. Bill FOTI
41 Director of Athletics .... Mr. George MARTIN
88 Dir Student Lrng Collaborative .... Ms. Caren BALDWIN-DIMEO
44 Dir Annual Giving/Operations .... Mr. Luke GORMAN
29 Dir Alumni Relations .... Ms. Tracey M. AUSTIN
19 Director of Campus Safety .... Mr. Peter L. BERTHIAUME
18 Director of Facilities .... Mr. Domenic GIOIOSO
40 Bookstore Manager .... Ms. Alison SEWARD
23 Dir of Baird Health & Counsel Ctr .... Ms. Pamela SPEAR
92 Director Wesson Honors Program .... Ms. Ann Page STECKER

*Community College System of New Hampshire (I)

26 College Drive, Concord NH 03301-7407
County: Merrimack Identification: 666462
Telephone: (603) 230-3500 Carnegie Class: N/A
FAX Number: (603) 271-2725
URL: www.ccsnh.edu

01 Chancellor .... Dr. Ross GITTELL
03 Vice Chancellor .... Vacant
10 Chief Operating Officer .... Charles ANSELL
15 Chief Human Resources Officer .... Vacant
26 Director of Communications .... Shannon REID
13 Chief Info Technology Officer (CIO) .... Susan BROUILLET

*Great Bay Community College (J)

320 Corporate Drive, Portsmouth NH 03801-2879
County: Rockingham FICE Identification: 002583
Unit ID: 183150
Telephone: (603) 427-7600 Carnegie Class: Assoc/MT-VT-Mix Trad/Non
FAX Number: (603) 334-6308 Calendar System: Semester
URL: www.greatbay.edu
Established: 1945 Annual Undergrad Tuition & Fees (In-State): $7,680
Enrollment: 1,846 Coed
Affiliation or Control: State IRS Status: 501(c)3
Highest Offering: Associate Degree
Accreditation: EH, ACBSP, ADNUR, SURGT

02 President .... Dr. Pelema MORRICE
05 Vice President Academic Affairs .... Ms. Lisa MCCURLEY
32 Int VP Student Success/Enroll Mgmt .... Ms. Deanna FRIEDMAN
10 Chief Financial Officer .... Ms. Joanne BERRY
06 Registrar .... Ms. Sandra HO
07 Director Admissions .... Ms. Carey WALKER
09 Director Institutional Research .... Ms. Fran CHICKERING

*Lakes Region Community College (K)

379 Belmont Road, Laconia NH 03246-1364
County: Belknap FICE Identification: 007555
Unit ID: 183123
Telephone: (603) 524-3207 Carnegie Class: Assoc/HVT-Mix Trad/Non
FAX Number: (603) 527-2042 Calendar System: Semester
URL: www.lrcc.edu
Established: 1967 Annual Undergrad Tuition & Fees (In-District): $7,168
Enrollment: 827 Coed
Affiliation or Control: State/Local IRS Status: 501(c)3
Highest Offering: Associate Degree
Accreditation: EH, ADNUR

02 President .... Dr. Larissa BAIA
05 VP of Academic & Student Affairs .... Mr. Patrick CATE
10 Chief Financial Officer .... Ms. Marsha BOURDON
04 Executive Asst to President .... Ms. Elizabeth LAWTON
06 Registrar .... Ms. Laura LEMIEN
07 Director of Admissions .... Mr. Wayne FRASER
37 Director Student Financial Aid .... Ms. Kristen PURRINGTON
26 Public Information Officer .... Mr. Max BROWN

*Manchester Community College (L)

1066 Front Street, Manchester NH 03102-8518
County: Hillsborough FICE Identification: 002582
Unit ID: 183132
Telephone: (603) 206-8000 Carnegie Class: Assoc/MT-VT-Mix Trad/Non
FAX Number: (603) 668-5354 Calendar System: Semester
URL: www.mccnh.edu
Established: 1945 Annual Undergrad Tuition & Fees (In-State): $7,520
Enrollment: 2,766 Coed
Affiliation or Control: State IRS Status: 501(c)3
Highest Offering: Associate Degree
Accreditation: EH, ACBSP, ADNUR, CAHIIM, MAC

02 President .... Dr. Susan D. HUARD
05 Vice President Academic Affairs .... Dr. Brian BICKNELL
32 VP Students/Community Development .... Kim KEEGAN
07 Director of Admissions .... Miho BEAN
26 Director of Marketing .... Victoria JAFFE
37 Financial Aid Officer .... Stephanie J. WELDON
06 Registrar .... Evelyn R. PERRON
08 Library Director .... Deb BAKER
09 Director Institutional Research .... Dr. Jere TURNER
10 Business Affairs Officer .... Kelly CHAPMAN
15 Human Resources Officer .... Jeannette DIBELLA
40 Bookstore Manager .... Cindy CORLISS
66 Nursing Director .... Charlene WOLFE-STEPRO
21 Accountant I .... Carol DESPATHY
13 Director Information Technology .... Jean POTILLO
35 Director Student Life .... Aileen CLAY
113 Bursar .... Nathalie FERNS
04 Administrative Asst to President .... Karen KEELER
103 Dir Workforce/Career Development .... Kristine DUDLEY
106 Dir Online Education/E-learning .... Brian CHICK
18 Chief Facilities/Physical Plant .... Joshua MURPHY
19 Director Security/Safety .... Jeff NYHAN
29 Director Alumni Relations .... Vacant

*Nashua Community College (A)

505 Amherst Street, Nashua NH 03063-1092

County: Hillsborough | FICE Identification: 009236
Unit ID: 183141
Telephone: (603) 578-8900 | Carnegie Class: Assoc/MT-VT-Mix Trad/Non
FAX Number: (603) 882-8690 | Calendar System: Semester
URL: www.nashuacc.edu
Established: 1967 | Annual Undergrad Tuition & Fees (In-State): $7,616
Enrollment: 1,791 | Coed
Affiliation or Control: State | IRS Status: 501(c)3
Highest Offering: Associate Degree
Accreditation: EH, ACBSP, ADNUR

02 President .... Ms. Lucille A. JORDAN
05 Interim Vice Pres Academic Affairs .... Robyn GRISWOLD
32 Vice Pres Student & Community Affs .... Ms. Lizbeth GONZALEZ
09 Assoc VP Inst Research/Acad Affs .... Mr. Phil FRANKLAND
10 Business Affairs Officer .... Vacant
06 Registrar-Nashua .... Ms. Jennifer OLISZCZAK
37 Financial Aid Officer .... Ms. Anne EULE
08 Director Library Services .... Ms. Maggie BERO
15 Human Resources Director .... Ms. Catherine BARRY
18 Plant Maintenance Engineer .... Mr. Scott BIENVENUE
19 Director of Security .... Ms. Jennifer CRUZ
26 Director Marketing/Public Relations .... Mr. Barry MEEHAN
04 Administrative Asst to President .... Ms. Lucy JENKINS

*NHTI-Concord's Community College (B)

31 College Drive, Concord NH 03301-7412

County: Merrimack | FICE Identification: 002581
Unit ID: 183099
Telephone: (603) 271-6484 | Carnegie Class: Assoc/MT-VT-High Trad
FAX Number: (603) 230-9311 | Calendar System: Semester
URL: www.nhti.edu
Established: 1965 | Annual Undergrad Tuition & Fees (In-State): $7,680
Enrollment: 3,666 | Coed
Affiliation or Control: State | IRS Status: 501(c)3
Highest Offering: Associate Degree
Accreditation: EH, ACBSP, ADNUR, DA, DH, DMS, EMT, RAD, RTT

02 President .... Dr. Gretchen MULLIN-SAWICKI
32 VP Student Affairs .... Dr. Laura PANTANO
05 Vice President Academic Affairs .... Dr. Fiona MCDONNELL
20 Assoc Vice Pres of Academic Affairs .... Vacant
10 Business Operations Officer .... Ms. Stephanie MILENDER
08 Director Library .... Mr. Stephen AMBRA
07 Director of Admissions .... Mr. Steven GORMAN
06 Registrar .... Ms. Michele KARWOCKI
13 Enterprise Technology Manager .... Mr. Todd BEDELL
26 Director of Communications .... Vacant
36 Dir Residence Life/Career Counsel .... Ms. Trish LORING
38 Dir Student Dev & Counseling .... Mr. Luis ROSA
37 Financial Aid Director .... Ms. Sheri GONTHIER
19 Dir of Campus Safety & Maintenance .... Mr. Jason BISHOP
41 Athletic Director .... Mr. Paul HOGAN
15 Director Human Resources .... Ms. Susan MAKEE
28 Dir Cross-Cultural Education/ESOL .... Ms. Dawn HIGGINS
96 Director of Purchasing .... Ms. Elizabeth CORLISS
105 Website Coordinator .... Ms. Christine METCALF
106 Dir Online Learning .... Ms. Trisha DIONNE
09 Director of Institutional Research .... Mr. Gary GONTHIER
29 Director Alumni & Development .... Ms. Laura A. SCOTT
39 Director Student Housing .... Ms. Trish LORING

*River Valley Community College (C)

1 College Place, Claremont NH 03743-9707

County: Sullivan | FICE Identification: 007560
Unit ID: 183114
Telephone: (603) 542-7744 | Carnegie Class: Assoc/HVT-Mix Trad/Non
FAX Number: (603) 543-1844 | Calendar System: Semester
URL: www.rivervalley.edu
Established: 1968 | Annual Undergrad Tuition & Fees (In-State): $7,298
Enrollment: 859 | Coed
Affiliation or Control: State | IRS Status: 501(c)3
Highest Offering: Associate Degree
Accreditation: EH, ACBSP, ADNUR, COARC, MAC, MLTAD, OTA, PTAA, RAD

02 President .... Alfred WILLIAMS
05 VP of Academic and Student Affairs .... Jennifer COURNOYER
103 VP of Strategy and Workforce Dev .... Joshua LAMOUREUX
04 Exec Assistant to the President .... Anna BATTYE

*White Mountains Community College (D)

2020 Riverside Drive, Berlin NH 03570-3799

County: Coos | FICE Identification: 005291
Unit ID: 183105
Telephone: (603) 752-1113 | Carnegie Class: Assoc/HVT-High Non
FAX Number: (603) 752-6335 | Calendar System: Semester
URL: www.wmcc.edu
Established: 1966 | Annual Undergrad Tuition & Fees (In-State): $7,970
Enrollment: 698 | Coed
Affiliation or Control: State | IRS Status: 501(c)3
Highest Offering: Associate Degree
Accreditation: EH, MAC

02 President .... Dr. Charles LLOYD
05 Vice Pres Academic Affairs .... Kristen MILLER
32 Vice President Student Affairs .... Martha LAFLAMME
10 Chief Financial Officer .... Scott FIELDS
06 Registrar .... Laura PROVOST
08 Director of Library Services .... Melissa LAPLANTE
18 Chief Facilities/Physical Plant .... Stephen DEROSIER
13 Director Computer Center .... Vacant
91 Director Administrative Computing .... Donald WEEKS
22 Dir Affirmative Action/Equal Oppty .... Vacant
40 Director Bookstore .... Stacia ROBERGE
07 Director of Admissions .... Amanda GAEB
09 Director of Institutional Research .... Suzanne WASILESKI
37 Asst Director Student Financial Aid .... Angela LABONTE
105 Director Web Services .... Milton CAMILLE
15 Director Personnel Services .... Gretchen TAILLON
38 Director Student Counseling .... Jeff SWAYZE
88 Director of Academic Centers .... Melanie ROBBINS
04 Admin Assistant to the President .... Gretchen TAILLON
19 Director Security/Safety .... Michael WEBSTER

Dartmouth College (E)

Hanover NH 03755-4030

County: Grafton | FICE Identification: 002573
Unit ID: 182670
Telephone: (603) 646-1110 | Carnegie Class: DU-Highest
FAX Number: N/A | Calendar System: Quarter
URL: www.dartmouth.edu
Established: 1769 | Annual Undergrad Tuition & Fees: $55,453
Enrollment: 6,509 | Coed
Affiliation or Control: Independent Non-Profit | IRS Status: 501(c)3
Highest Offering: Doctorate
Accreditation: EH, CAMPEP, IPSY, MED, PAST, PH

01 President .... Dr. Philip J. HANLON
03 Executive Vice President .... Mr. Richard G. MILLS
101 Secretary to Board of Trustees .... Ms. Laura H. HERCOD
05 Provost .... Dr. Joseph J. HELBLE
111 Sr Vice President for Advancement .... Mr. Robert W. LASHER
46 Vice Provost for Research .... Dr. Dean R. MADDEN
10 CFO and Vice Pres Finance .... Mr. Michael F. WAGNER
26 VP Communications .... Mr. Justin ANDERSON
28 Vice Pres for Inst Diversity/Equity .... Dr. Evelynn ELLIS
15 Chief Human Resources Officer .... Mr. Scot R. BEMIS
29 Vice President Alumni Relations .... Ms. Cheryl A. BASCOMB
63 Dean Geisel Sch of Medicine .... Dr. Duane A. COMPTON
18 VP of Campus Services .... Mr. Steven C. MOORE
43 General Counsel .... Ms. Sandhya L. IYER
20 Dean of the College .... Dr. Kathryn J. LIVELY
06 Registrar .... Ms. Meredith BRAZ
07 VProv Enroll/Dean Admiss & Fin Aid .... Mr. Lee A. COFFIN
37 Director of Financial Aid .... Mr. Gordon D. KOFF
13 VP and Chief Information Officer .... Mr. Mitchel W. DAVIS
08 Dean of Libraries .... Ms. Susanne MEHRER
49 Dean of Faculty of Arts & Sciences .... Dr. Elizabeth F. SMITH
50 Dean of Amos Tuck School .... Dr. Matthew J. SLAUGHTER
54 Dean of the Thayer School .... Dr. Alexis R. ABRAMSON
58 Dean of Graduate Studies .... Dr. F. Jon KULL
102 Dean of Tucker Foundation .... Rabbi Daveen H. LITWIN
41 Director of Athletics .... Mr. Harry SHEEHY
117 Dir Risk/Internal Control Svcs .... Ms. Catherine LARK
23 Director of the Health Services .... Dr. Mark H. REED
36 Director Center for Prof Dev .... Mr. Roger W. WOOLSEY
25 Dir Office of Sponsored Projects .... Ms. Jill M. MORTALI
32 Vice Provost for Student Affairs .... Vacant
19 Interim Director Safety & Security .... Mr. Keiselim A. MONTAS
09 Assoc Pro of Institutional Research .... Ms. Alicia M. BETSINGER
38 Dir Counseling/Human Development .... Dr. Heather A. EARLE
22 Dir Equal Opportunity/Affirm Action .... Ms. Theodosia S. COOK
96 Director of Procurement .... Ms. Tammy L. MOFFATT
115 Chief Investment Officer .... Ms. Alice A. RUTH
35 Sr Assoc Dean for Student Affairs .... Vacant
21 Controller .... Ms. Gail C. GOODNESS
04 Senior Executive Asst to President .... Ms. Jennifer A. SHEPHERD
100 Chief of Staff .... Ms. Laura H. HERCOD
103 Dir Workforce/Career Development .... Mr. Roger W. WOOLSEY
104 Director Study Abroad .... Ms. John G. TANSEY
105 Director Web Services .... Mr. Jonathan CHIAPPA
106 Dir Digital Learning Initiatives .... Mr. Joshua M. KIM
39 Director Residential Life .... Mr. Michael W. WOOTEN
86 Director Government Relations .... Ms. Martha F. AUSTIN
90 Dir Academic Computing/Campus Tech .... Mr. Alan R. CATTIER

Franklin Pierce University (F)

40 University Drive, Rindge NH 03461-5046

County: Cheshire | FICE Identification: 002575
Unit ID: 182795
Telephone: (603) 899-4000 | Carnegie Class: Masters/M
FAX Number: (603) 899-6448 | Calendar System: Semester
URL: www.franklinpierce.edu
Established: 1962 | Annual Undergrad Tuition & Fees: $36,900
Enrollment: 2,303 | Coed
Affiliation or Control: Independent Non-Profit | IRS Status: 501(c)3
Highest Offering: Doctorate
Accreditation: EH, #ARCPA, IACBE, NUR, PTA

01 President .... Dr. Kim MOONEY
05 Interim VP Academic Affairs/Provost .... Dr. David STARRETT
10 Vice President Finance & CFO .... Ms. Sandra QUAYE
111 VP for University Advancement .... Ms. Julie ZAHN
84 VP Enrollment & Univ Communications .... Ms. Linda QUIMBY
32 Dean of Student Affairs .... Dr. Andrew POLLOM
37 Assoc VP for Student Financial Svcs .... Mr. Kenneth FERREIRA
41 Athletic Director .... Ms. Rachel BURLESON
15 Interim Director of Human Resources .... Ms. Dawn BROUSSARD
06 University Registrar .... Ms. Charlee EATON
08 University Librarian .... Dr. Paul JENKINS
20 Exec Dean Assessment and Acad Aff .... Dr. Sarah DANGELANTONIO
09 Executive Director of IR .... Dr. Karen J. BROWN
79 Dean Coll Liberal Arts & Social Sci .... Dr. Matthew KONIECZKA
76 Dean Coll of Health & Natural Sci .... Dr. Maria R. ALTOBELLO
50 Dean College of Business .... Dr. Norman FAIOLA
36 Exec Director of Career Services .... Mr. Pierre MORTON
29 Assc VP for University Advancement .... Ms. Crystal NEUHAUSER
26 Director University Communication .... Mr. Kenneth PHILLIPS
88 Asst Dean of Student Involvement .... Mr. Scott ANSEVIN-ALLEN
39 Asst Dean Res Life & Comm Standard .... Ms. Kathleen DOUGHERTY
21 Director of Finance & Accounting .... Ms. Suzanne CARPENTER
18 Director of Plant Operations .... Mr. Doug LEAR
124 Dir of Diversity & Retention .... Mr. Derek SCALIA
96 Director of Purchasing .... Ms. Chere HALLETT-ADAMS
104 Director Study Abroad .... Ms. Patti VORFELD
13 Director of IT .... Mr. Thomas TOLBERT
04 Executive Asst to the President .... Ms. Heather RINGWALD

MCPHS-Manchester Campus (G)

1260 Elm Street, Manchester NH 03101

Telephone: (603) 314-0210 | Identification: 770113
Accreditation: &EH, #ARCPA, OT, PHAR

† Branch campus of MCPHS University, Boston, MA

New England College (H)

98 Bridge Street, Henniker NH 03242-3244

County: Merrimack | FICE Identification: 002579
Unit ID: 182980
Telephone: (603) 428-2000 | Carnegie Class: Masters/L
FAX Number: (603) 428-7230 | Calendar System: Semester
URL: www.nec.edu
Established: 1946 | Annual Undergrad Tuition & Fees: $37,914
Enrollment: 2,832 | Coed
Affiliation or Control: Independent Non-Profit | IRS Status: 501(c)3
Highest Offering: Doctorate
Accreditation: EH

01 President .... Dr. Michele D. PERKINS
05 VP of Academic Affairs .... Dr. Wayne LESPERANCE
88 Sr VP Academic Alliances .... Dr. James MURTHA
10 Sr Vice President/CFO .... Dr. Paula A. AMATO
08 Library Director .... Ms. Chelsea HANRAHAN
20 Dean of Accreditation/Acad Effect .... Dr. Nelly LEJTER
04 Assistant to President .... Ms. Betsy MEDVETZ
13 VP Technology & Mktg Communications .... Ms. Carol THOMAS
32 VP of Student Affairs .... Mr. Mike TABERSKI
06 Registrar .... Ms. Beth DOWLING
37 Director Student Financial Svcs .... Ms. Kristen BLASE
21 Controller .... Mr. Brian BOYER
36 Director Career/Life Planning .... Mr. Gene DURKEE
111 VP for Advancement .... Mr. Nicholas ZAHARIAS
15 Human Resources Manager .... Ms. Tanya GUAY
102 Dir Corp & Foundation Relations .... Mr. Gregory PALMER
18 AVP of Capital and Facilities Mgmt .... Mr. Dan GEARAN
19 Director Campus Safety .... Mr. Scott LANE
39 Director Res Life & Student Housing .... Ms. Doreen LONG
41 Athletic Director .... Mr. Dave DECEW
09 Director of Institutional Research .... Mr. Frank HALL
104 Director Study Abroad .... Mr. Jason BUCK
105 Director Web Services .... Mr. Chris BOGLE
108 Director Institutional Assessment .... Ms. Nelly LEJTER
38 Director Student Counseling .... Ms. Erin BROOKS
53 Assoc Dean Education .... Ms. Patricia CORBETT
86 Director Government Relations .... Mr. Tom HORGAN
14 Director Technology Services .... Mr. Eric SAWYER
07 Director of Admissions .... Dr. Ashley BATTLE
28 Director of Diversity .... Ms. India BARROWS
29 Director Alumni Affairs .... Ms. Lorella VOLPE
44 Director Annual Giving .... Mr. Matt KENNEDY
50 Assoc Dean of Management .... Dr. Erin WILKINSON HARTUNG

New Hampshire Institute of Art (I)

148 Concord Street, Manchester NH 03104-4858

County: Hillsborough | FICE Identification: 031823
Unit ID: 430810
Telephone: (603) 623-0313 | Carnegie Class: Spec-4-yr-Arts
FAX Number: (603) 641-1832 | Calendar System: Semester
URL: www.nhia.edu
Established: 1898 | Annual Undergrad Tuition & Fees: $28,080
Enrollment: 351 | Coed
Affiliation or Control: Independent Non-Profit | IRS Status: 501(c)3
Highest Offering: Master's
Accreditation: EH, ART

01 President .... Mr. Kent DEVEREAUX
10 Vice President of Finance .... Vacant
30 Vice President of Development .... Vacant
84 Vice President of Enrollment .... Mr. Jonathan LINDSAY
12 Manchester Campus Director .... Dr. James MURTHA
12 Sharon Arts Campus Director .... Ms. Camellia SOUSA
04 Executive Assistant to President .... Ms. Sara DADIAN PEREZ

05 Dean of Undergrad Studies .... Mr. Bill SCHAAF
58 Dean of Graduate Studies .... Ms. Lucinda BLISS
08 Library Director .... Ms. Betsy HOLMES
88 Director of Advising .... Ms. Tricia GIBBS
06 Registrar .... Ms. Siobhan SWANSON
20 Academic Affairs Administrator .... Ms. Claire SHEA
113 Bursar .... Vacant
32 Dean of Student Affairs .... Ms. Michele TRACIA
37 Interim Director Financial Aid .... Ms. Amy HOSS
31 Assoc Dean Community Education .... Mr. Chris ARCHER
15 Director of Human Resources .... Ms. Katrina KRAMER
21 Accounting Manager .... Ms. Nancy JORDAN
18 Facilities Director .... Mr. Paul GYMZIAK
13 Director Information Technologies .... Mr. John FALLAVOLLITA
38 Counselor .... Ms. Tanya POPOLOSKI
88 Academic Support Center Coordinator .... Ms. Kristen DRONEY

† Merging with New England College on 12/1/2018.

Northeast Catholic College (A)

511 Kearsarge Mountain Road, Warner NH 03278-4012
County: Merrimack FICE Identification: 022233
Unit ID: 182917
Telephone: (603) 456-2656 Carnegie Class: Bac-A&S
FAX Number: (603) 456-2660 Calendar System: Semester
URL: www.NortheastCatholic.edu
Established: 1973 Annual Undergrad Tuition & Fees: $24,000
Enrollment: 71 Coed
Affiliation or Control: Roman Catholic IRS Status: 501(c)3
Highest Offering: Baccalaureate
Accreditation: EH

01 President .... Dr. George A. HARNE
05 Academic Dean .... Dr. Brian FITZGERALD
10 Chief Operating Officer .... Mr. R. Daniel PETERSON
32 Dean of Students .... Ms. Mazel BELT
07 Dir of Admissions/Communications .... Mr. Michael BEECHER
37 Director Financial Aid/Librarian .... Mrs. Marie LASHER

Rivier University (B)

420 S Main Street, Nashua NH 03060-5086
County: Hillsborough FICE Identification: 002586
Unit ID: 183211
Telephone: (603) 888-1311 Carnegie Class: Masters/L
FAX Number: (603) 897-8811 Calendar System: Semester
URL: www.rivier.edu
Established: 1933 Annual Undergrad Tuition & Fees: $32,140
Enrollment: 2,431 Coed
Affiliation or Control: Roman Catholic IRS Status: 501(c)3
Highest Offering: Doctorate
Accreditation: EH, ADNUR, NUR, PSPSY

01 President .... Sr. Paula Marie BULEY
05 Vice President for Academic Affairs .... Dr. Douglas HOWARD
10 Vice Pres Finance & Administration .... Dr. John PARKER
32 Vice President Student Affairs .... Mr. Kurt STIMELING
84 Vice Pres Enrollment Management .... Ms. Karen SCHEDIN
111 Vice Pres University Advancement .... Ms. Karen COOPER
35 Asst Vice Pres Student Affairs .... Ms. Paula RANDAZZA
13 Chief Information Officer .... Ms. Heidi CROWELL
21 Controller .... Ms. Megan PRITCHARD
06 Registrar .... Ms. Dina BROWN
08 Library Director .... Mr. Daniel SPEIDEL
36 Exec Dir Career Development Center .... Ms. Patricia ANTONELLI
37 Director Student Financial Aid .... Ms. Valerie PATNAUDE
15 Human Resources Manager .... Ms. Jane CLAVETTE
18 Director Facilities Management .... Mr. Richard PERRINE
14 Director Instructional Computing .... Sr. Martha VILLENEUVE
41 Athletic Director .... Ms. Joanne MERRILL
42 Chaplain Campus Ministry .... Bro. Paul DEMERS
28 Director Multicultural Affairs .... Vacant
29 Dir Alumni Relations/Special Events .... Ms. Joanne YOUNG
26 Director Marketing/Communication .... Ms. Sky CROSWELL

Saint Anselm College (C)

100 Saint Anselm Drive, Manchester NH 03102-1310
County: Hillsborough FICE Identification: 002587
Unit ID: 183239
Telephone: (603) 641-7000 Carnegie Class: Bac-A&S
FAX Number: (603) 641-7116 Calendar System: Semester
URL: www.anselm.edu
Established: 1889 Annual Undergrad Tuition & Fees: $41,200
Enrollment: 1,964 Coed
Affiliation or Control: Roman Catholic IRS Status: 501(c)3
Highest Offering: Baccalaureate
Accreditation: EH, NURSE

01 President .... Dr. Joseph A. FAVAZZA
05 Vice Pres Academic Affairs .... Br. Isaac MURPHY, OSB
111 Sr VP College Advancement .... Mr. James P. FLANAGAN
125 President Emeritus .... Fr. Jonathan P. DEFELICE
26 Exec Dir Col Comm & Mktg .... Vacant
10 Chief Financial Ofcr/Sr VP Finance .... Vacant
28 Chief Diversity Officer .... Dr. Ande DIAZ
29 Assistant VP Alumni & Programs .... Ms. Patrice RUSSELL
06 Registrar .... Ms. Tracy MORGAN
07 Dean of Admissions/VP Enrollment .... Vacant
08 Librarian .... Mr. Charles M. GETCHELL, JR.
37 Director of Financial Aid .... Ms. Elizabeth KEUFFEL
35 Dean of Students .... Dr. Alicia A. FINN
89 Dean of Freshmen .... Ms. Stephanie M. FERNANDEZ
66 Exec Director of Nursing .... Dr. Maureen A. O'REILLY
04 Assistant to the President .... Ms. Janet L. POIRIER
18 Director of Physical Plant .... Mr. Donald MOREAU
23 Director of Health Services .... Ms. Maura MARSHALL
41 Director of Athletics .... Mr. Daron MONTGOMERY
42 Director of Campus Ministry .... Dr. Susan S. GABERT
09 Director of Institutional Research .... Vacant
13 Chief Information Officer .... Vacant
15 Director Human Resources .... Ms. Molly MCKEAN
19 Director Security/Safety .... Mr. Donald DAVIDSON
53 Director Education Planning .... Dr. Laura WASIELEWSKI
28 Director Multicultural Center .... Dr. Wayne CURRIE
39 Director Student Housing .... Ms. Susan WEINTRAUB
104 Assoc Dir Study Abroad .... Vacant
25 Dir Sponsored Programs & Research .... Ms. Mary MADER
44 Asst VP Individual Giving .... Mr. John DAVIS
86 Director Government Relations .... Mr. Neil LEVESQUE
36 Director Student Placement .... Mr. Samuel ALLEN
102 Dir Foundation/Corporate Rels .... Ms. Sharon SWEET

Southern New Hampshire University (D)

2500 North River Road, Manchester NH 03106-1045
County: Hillsborough FICE Identification: 002580
Unit ID: 183026
Telephone: (603) 626-9100 Carnegie Class: Masters/L
FAX Number: (603) 645-9665 Calendar System: Semester
URL: www.snhu.edu
Established: 1932 Annual Undergrad Tuition & Fees: $31,136
Enrollment: 90,955 Coed
Affiliation or Control: Independent Non-Profit IRS Status: 501(c)3
Highest Offering: Doctorate
Accreditation: EH, ACBSP, CAEPT, CAHIIM, NURSE

00 Chairman Board of Trustees .... Mr. Mark OUELLETTE
01 President .... Dr. Paul LEBLANC
04 Executive Assistant to President .... Ms. Alycia AVERY
11 Chief Operating Officer .... Ms. Amelia MANNING
97 President University College .... Dr. Patricia LYNOTT
88 President Global Campus .... Dr. Gregory FOWLER
45 Chief Strategy & Innovation Officer .... Dr. William ZEMP
15 Exec VP Human Resources .... Ms. Danielle STANTON
13 Exec VP Technology & Transformation .... Mr. Thomas DIONISIO
54 Exec VP College of Engr/Tech/Aero .... Dr. Kirk KOLENBRANDER
100 Sr VP/Chief of Staff .... Dr. Adrian HAUGABROOK
103 Sr VP Workforce Partnerships .... Mr. Scott DURAND
10 Chief Financial Officer .... Mr. Kenneth LEE
05 Sr VP/Chief Academic Officer .. Dr. Kimberly BOGLE JUBINVILLE
43 Sr VP General Counsel .... Ms. Yvette CLARK
26 Sr VP External Affairs/Comm .... Ms. Libby MAY
111 Sr VP Institutional Advancement .... Mr. Donald BREZINSKI
86 Chief Diversity & Inclusion Officer .... Ms. Jada HEBRA
88 VP Global Education Movement .... Dr. Chrystina RUSSELL
27 Chief Marketing Officer .... Ms. Alana BURNS
20 VPAA University College .... Dr. Michael EVANS
20 VP Academic Programs Global Campus .... Dr. Jennifer BATCHELOR
06 VP & University Registrar .... Ms. Deanna BECHARD
32 Chief Std Exp Officer Global Campus .... Ms. Jamie JAMES
32 VP Student Affairs Univ College .... Dr. Heather LORENZ
37 Chief Financial Services Officer .... Ms. Susan NATHAN
84 VP Enroll Mgmt/Std Success Univ Col .... Ms. Carey GLINES
88 VP Strategic Enablement & Analytics .... Mr. Nicholas EREMITA
08 VP/Dean of the Library .... Vacant

The Thomas More College of Liberal Arts (E)

6 Manchester Street, Merrimack NH 03054-4805
County: Hillsborough FICE Identification: 030431
Unit ID: 183275
Telephone: (603) 880-8308 Carnegie Class: Bac-A&S
FAX Number: (603) 880-9280 Calendar System: Semester
URL: www.thomasmorecollege.edu
Established: 1978 Annual Undergrad Tuition & Fees: $21,600
Enrollment: 90 Coed
Affiliation or Control: Independent Non-Profit IRS Status: 501(c)3
Highest Offering: Baccalaureate
Accreditation: EH

01 President .... Dr. William E. FAHEY
30 Director Institutional Advancement .... Mr. Paul JACKSON
05 Academic Dean .... Dr. Walter THOMPSON
32 Dean of Students .... Mr. Denis KITZINGER
44 Director Institutional Advancement .... Mr. Paul JACKSON
10 Director of Business .... Ms. Pamela BERNSTEIN
35 Director of Collegiate Life .... Dr. Sara KITZINGER
04 Executive Asst President's Office .... Ms. Valerie BURGESS
06 Registrar .... Ms. Pamela BERNSTEIN
07 Director of Admissions .... Mr. Zachary NACCASH
08 Librarian .... Ms. Alexis ROHLFING

*University System of New Hampshire (F)

5 Chenell Drive, Suite 301, Concord NH 03301
County: Merrimack FICE Identification: 008027
Unit ID: 183327
Telephone: (603) 862-0700 Carnegie Class: N/A
FAX Number: (603) 862-0908
URL: usnh.edu

01 Chancellor .... Dr. Todd J. LEACH
10 VC Financial Affairs & Treasurer .... Ms. Catherine A. PROVENCHER
43 General Counsel .... Mr. Ronald F. RODGERS
09 Dir of Institutional Research .... Ms. Heidi HEDEGARD
15 Chief Human Resource Officer .... Mr. James MCGRAIL
04 Admin Assistant to the President .... Ms. Tia MILLER
13 Chief Information Technology Office .... Mr. Russ BATTISTA

*University of New Hampshire (G)

105 Main Street, Durham NH 03824
County: Strafford FICE Identification: 002589
Unit ID: 183044
Telephone: (603) 862-1234 Carnegie Class: DU-Highest
FAX Number: N/A Calendar System: Semester
URL: www.unh.edu
Established: 1866 Annual Undergrad Tuition & Fees (In-State): $18,499
Enrollment: 15,363 Coed
Affiliation or Control: State IRS Status: 501(c)3
Highest Offering: Doctorate
Accreditation: EH, ACFEI, #CAATE, CAEP, CAEPT, CARTE, DIETD, DIETI, IPSY, LAW, MFCD, MT, MUS, NRPA, NURSE, OT, PH, SP, SW

02 President .... Dr. James W. DEAN, JR.
100 Chief of Staff .... Ms. Megan W. DAVIS
05 Provost & VP for Academic Affairs .... Dr. Wayne E. JONES, JR.
10 VP Finance/Administration .... Mr. Christopher D. CLEMENT
84 Int VP Enrollment Management .... Mr. Robert P H. MCGANN
111 VP Advancement .... Ms. Deborah DUTTON COX
46 Vice Provost for Research .... Dr. Kevin GARDNER
26 Assoc VP Univ Communications .... Mr. Mica B. STARK
43 General Counsel .... Mr. Ronald F. RODGERS
20 Assoc Prov Academic Administration .... Ms. Leigh Anne MELANSON
28 Int Assoc VP Cmty/Equity/Diversity .... Dr. Monica E. CHIU
20 Sr Vice Prov Academic Affairs .... Dr. Palligarnai T. VASUDEVAN
15 Assoc VP/Chief HR Officer .... Ms. Kathleen A. NEILS
29 AVP Advancement/Exec Dir Alumni .... Ms. Susan ENTZ
88 Sr VProv Engagement & Faculty Dev .... Dr. Julie E. WILLIAMS
90 Asst Vice Prov Digital Lrng & Comm .... Ms. Terri S. WINTERS
21 Assoc VP for Finance .... Ms. Kerry L. SCALA
13 Asst VP Enterprise Comp & Int CIO .... Mr. William J. HALL
40 Manager of UNH Bookstore .... Mr. Frank MOORE
16 Asst VP Human Resources .... Ms. Sari M. BENNETT
21 Assoc VP Business Affairs .... Mr. David J. MAY
18 Assoc VP Facilities .... Mr. William P. JANELLE
32 Sr Vice Provost & Dean of Students .... Dr. John T. KIRKPATRICK
39 Director Residential Life .... Ms. Ruth E. ABELMANN
23 Exec Director Health & Wellness .... Dr. Kevin E. CHARLES
25 Dir Sponsored Programs .... Mr. Victor G. SOSA
47 Dean Life Sciences/Agriculture .... Dr. Jon M. WRAITH
49 Dean Liberal Arts .... Dr. Michele M. DILLON
50 Dean Paul College of Business .... Dr. Deborah M. MERRILL-SANDS
58 Dean Graduate School .... Dr. Cari A. MOORHEAD
76 Dean Health & Human Services .... Dr. Michael FERRARA
54 Int Dean Engineering/Physical Sci .... Dr. Charles K. ZERCHER
61 Dean UNH School of Law .... Ms. Megan M. CARPENTER
12 Dean UNH at Manchester .... Dr. Michael P. DECELLE
08 Dean University Library .... Dr. Tara Lynn FULTON
56 Dean/Dir Cooperative Extension .... Dr. Kenneth J. LAVALLEY
22 Dir Affirmative Action & Equity .... Ms. Donna Marie SORRENTINO
07 Sr Assoc Dir Admissions/Recruit .... Ms. Tara E. SCHOLDER
06 Registrar .... Mr. Andrew G. COLBY
37 Dir Financial Aid .... Mr. Joel B. CARSTENS
41 Dir Intercollegiate Athletics .... Mr. Martin SCARANO
38 Dir Psychological Services .... Dr. Shari A. ROBINSON
110 Sr Exec Director of Advance/Finance .... Mr. Erik E. GROSS
88 Dir Housing/Conf Services .... Ms. Katherine M. IRLA-CHESNEY
19 Asst VP Public Safety & Risk Mgt .... Chief Paul M. DEAN
85 Dir Intl Students & Scholars .... Ms. Leila L. PAJE-MANALO
92 Dir Honors Program .... Dr. Catherine M. PEEBLES
09 Dir Inst Research & Assessment .... Dr. Anne SHATTUCK
88 Dir Writing Program .... Dr. Edward A. MUELLER
91 Sr Director for Center of Data .... Ms. Jackie SNOW

*Granite State College (H)

25 Hall Street, Concord NH 03301-7317
County: Merrimack FICE Identification: 031013
Unit ID: 183257
Telephone: (603) 228-3000 Carnegie Class: Masters/S
FAX Number: (603) 513-1389 Calendar System: Quarter
URL: www.granite.edu
Established: 1972 Annual Undergrad Tuition & Fees (In-State): $7,761
Enrollment: 2,019 Coed
Affiliation or Control: State IRS Status: 501(c)3
Highest Offering: Master's
Accreditation: EH, CAEPT, NURSE

02 President .... Dr. Mark RUBINSTEIN
05 Provost/VP Academic Affairs .... Dr. Scott A. STANLEY
10 VP Finance & Administration .... Ms. Lisa L. SHAWNEY
84 VP Enrollment Management .... Ms. Tara PAYNE
53 Dean of School of Education .... Mr. Nick MARKS
24 Director of Educational Technology .... Ms. Reta CHAFFEE
08 Assistant Dean of Library Services .... Ms. Patricia ERWIN-PLOOG
04 Administrative Asst to Provost .... Ms. Susan L. ORR
15 Asst VP of Human Resources .... Ms. Maggie HYNDMAN
21 Asst VP of Finance .... Mr. Steve PERROTTA
18 Dir of Facilities/Safety/Sustain .... Mr. Peter CONKLIN

07 Asst VP of Enrollment Operations .... Ms. Christine WILLIAMS
07 VP of Enrollment Management .... Ms. Tara PAYNE
121 Sr Dir of Advising/Stdnt Engagement .... Ms. Nicole HORNE
37 Director Student Financial Aid .... Mr. Mac BRODERICK
36 Director of Career Services .... Ms. Jan COVILLE
06 Registrar .... Ms. Cortney FRENCH
108 Dir Inst Effectiveness/Compliance .... Mr. Todd SLOVER
124 Director of Student Affairs .... Ms. Tiffany DOHERTY

*Keene State College (A)

229 Main Street, Keene NH 03435-0001
County: Cheshire FICE Identification: 002590
Unit ID: 183062
Telephone: (603) 352-1909 Carnegie Class: Bac-Diverse
FAX Number: (603) 358-2257 Calendar System: Semester
URL: www.keene.edu
Established: 1909 Annual Undergrad Tuition & Fees (In-State): $14,212
Enrollment: 3,866 Coed
Affiliation or Control: State IRS Status: 501(c)3
Highest Offering: Master's
Accreditation: EH, CAATE, CAEPN, DIETD, DIETI, MUS, NURSE

02 President .... Dr. Melinda TREADWELL
05 Provost/VP Academic Affairs .... Dr. Nancy FEY-YENSAN
32 VP Student Affairs .... Dr. Kemal ATKINS
10 VP Finance & Administration .... Dr. Susan LAPANNE
84 VP Enrollment/Marketing & Comm .... Mr. Jeff HOLEMAN
111 Executive Director Advancement .... Ms. Veronica ROSA
28 AVP Inst Diversity & Equity .... Dr. Dottie MORRIS
81 Dean of Sciences/Sustain & Health .... Dr. Karrie KALICH
57 Dean Arts/Education & Culture .... Dr. Kirsti SANDY
35 Dean of Students .... Dr. Gail ZIMMERMAN
13 Chief Information Officer .... Ms. Laura SERAICHICK
15 Director Human Resources .... Ms. Karen CRAWFORD
08 Dean of Library .... Dr. Celia E. RABINOWITZ
39 Assoc Dean Students/Dir Res Life .... Mr. Kent DRAKE-DEESE
07 Director of Admissions .... Ms. Margaret RICHMOND
06 Registrar .... Ms. Barbara CORMIER
26 Director Strategic Communications .... Ms. Kelly RICAURTE
18 Director Physical Plant .... Mr. Frank MAZZOLA
09 Dir Inst Effectiveness & IR .... Mr. George SMEATON
38 Director of Counseling Center .... Dr. Brian QUIGLEY
96 Campus Purchasing Director .... Ms. Renee HARLOW

*Plymouth State University (B)

17 High Street, Plymouth NH 03264-1595
County: Grafton FICE Identification: 002591
Unit ID: 183080
Telephone: (603) 535-5000 Carnegie Class: Masters/L
FAX Number: (603) 535-2654 Calendar System: Semester
URL: www.plymouth.edu
Established: 1871 Annual Undergrad Tuition & Fees (In-State): $14,099
Enrollment: 5,046 Coed
Affiliation or Control: State IRS Status: 501(c)3
Highest Offering: Doctorate
Accreditation: EH, ACBSP, CAATE, CACREP, #CAEP, CAEPN, NURSE, @PTA, SW

02 President .... Dr. Donald L. BIRX
05 Provost/VP for Academic Affairs .... Mr. Robin H. DORFF
10 VP for Finance & Administration .... Ms. Tracy L. CLAYBAUGH
111 VP for University Advancement .... Ms. Paula L. HOBSON
26 Int VP of Comm/Enroll/Student Life .. Mr. Marlin COLLINGWOOD
13 Chief Information Officer .... Mr. Richard G. GROSSMAN
20 Assoc VP Undergraduate Studies .... Dr. David ZEHR
21 Assoc VP Finance & Administration .... Ms. Laurie WILCOX
07 Interim Director of Admissions .... Mr. Matthew L. WALLACE
39 Dir Residence Life/Dining Svcs .... Ms. Amanda GRAZIOSO
32 Dean of Students .... Mr. Jeffrey C. FURLONE
108 Dir Institutional Effectiveness .... Ms. Melissa K. CHRISTENSEN
06 Registrar .... Ms. Tonya B. LABROSSE
30 Director of Development/Major Gifts .... Mr. John E. SCHEINMAN
29 Director of Alumni Relations .... Mr. Rodney EKSTROM
113 Director Student Financial Services .... Vacant
15 Director of Human Resources .... Ms. Caryn L. INES
19 Dir Public Safety and Emer Planning . Mr. Steven H. TEMPERINO
41 Director of Athletics .... Ms. Kim M. BOWNES
18 Director of Physical Plant .... Vacant
38 Dir of Counseling/Human Rel Center .... Mr. Robert G. HLASNY
88 Coordinator Title IX/504 .... Ms. Janette T. WIGGETT
08 Outreach Librarian .... Ms. Anne M. JUNG-MATHEWS
40 Bookstore Manager .... Mr. Steve RHEAUME

NEW JERSEY

Assumption College for Sisters (C)

200A Morris Avenue, Denville NJ 07834
County: Morris FICE Identification: 002595
Unit ID: 183600
Telephone: (973) 957-0188 Carnegie Class: Assoc/HT-High Trad
FAX Number: (973) 957-0190 Calendar System: Semester
URL: www.acs350.org
Established: 1953 Annual Undergrad Tuition & Fees: $5,716
Enrollment: 47 Female
Affiliation or Control: Roman Catholic IRS Status: 501(c)3
Highest Offering: Associate Degree
Accreditation: M

01 President/Chief of Development .... Sr. Joseph SPRING, SCC
05 Academic Dean .... Sr. Teresa BRUNO, SC
10 Treasurer/Institutional Advancement .... Mrs. Patricia MCGRADY
32 Chief Student Life Officer .... Sr. Marie Cecelia LANDIS, SCC
06 Registrar .... Mrs. Barbara KELLY-VERGONA
13 Chf Information Technology Officer .... Mrs. Jean WEDEMEIER

Atlantic Cape Community College (D)

5100 Black Horse Pike, Mays Landing NJ 08330-2699
County: Atlantic FICE Identification: 002596
Unit ID: 183655
Telephone: (609) 343-4900 Carnegie Class: Assoc/HT-High Trad
FAX Number: (609) 343-4917 Calendar System: Semester
URL: www.atlantic.edu
Established: 1964 Annual Undergrad Tuition & Fees (In-District): $4,818
Enrollment: 5,528 Coed
Affiliation or Control: State/Local IRS Status: 501(c)3
Highest Offering: Associate Degree
Accreditation: M, ACFEI, ADNUR

01 President .... Dr. Barbara GABA
05 Vice President Academic Affairs .... Dr. Josette KATZ
11 Chief Business Officer .... Mr. August DAQUILA
100 Chief of Staff .... Ms. Jean MCALISTER
10 Chief Financial Officer .... Ms. Leslie JAMISON
46 Dean Institutional Research .. Dr. Vanessa O'BRIEN-MCMASTERS
32 Dean Student Affairs .... Ms. Paula DAVIS
26 Executive Director Marketing .... Ms. Laura BATCHELOR
12 Dean Worthington Atlantic City .... Ms. Donna VASSALLO
12 Dean Cape May County Campus .... Ms. Maria KELLETT
88 Dean Academy of Culinary Arts .... Ms. Kelly MCCLAY
49 Dean Liberal Studies .... Dr. Denise COULTER
06 Registrar .... Ms. Heather PETERSON
07 Director Admissions & Recruitment .... Mr. Joseph ROONEY
37 Director Financial Aid .... Ms. Linda DESANTIS
35 Dir Student Dev & Judicial Officer .... Ms. Nancy PORFIDO
09 Director Institutional Research .... Mr. Luis MONTEFUSCO
96 Director Business Services .... Ms. Dorie KEENER
18 Director Facilities Management .... Mr. Russell WAUGH

Bais Medrash Mayan Hatorah (E)

101 Milton Street, Lakewood NJ 08701
County: Ocean Identification: 667280
Unit ID: 490513
Telephone: (732) 367-9900 Carnegie Class: Spec-4-yr-Faith
FAX Number: N/A Calendar System: Other
Established: Annual Undergrad Tuition & Fees: $10,650
Enrollment: 53 Male
Affiliation or Control: Independent Non-Profit IRS Status: 501(c)3
Highest Offering: First Talmudic Degree
Accreditation: AIJS

05 Dean .... Rabbi Abraham NEWMAN

Bais Medrash Toras Chesed (F)

910 Monmouth Avenue, Lakewood NJ 08701-1921
County: Ocean FICE Identification: 040813
Unit ID: 449658
Telephone: (732) 364-1220 Carnegie Class: Spec-4-yr-Faith
FAX Number: (732) 886-2323 Calendar System: Semester
Established: 1999 Annual Undergrad Tuition & Fees: $6,400
Enrollment: 105 Male
Affiliation or Control: Independent Non-Profit IRS Status: 501(c)3
Highest Offering: Baccalaureate
Accreditation: RABN

01 Dean .... Rabbi N. STEIN
37 Director of Financial Aid .... Mrs. H. WEISS

Bais Medrash Zichron Meir (G)

1500 Vermont Ave, Lakewood NJ 08701
County: Ocean Identification: 667259
Telephone: (732) 370-1560 Carnegie Class: Not Classified
FAX Number: (732) 363-7864 Calendar System: Semester
Established: 2013 Annual Undergrad Tuition & Fees: N/A
Enrollment: N/A Male
Affiliation or Control: Independent Non-Profit IRS Status: 501(c)3
Highest Offering: First Talmudic Degree
Accreditation: @RABN

01 CEO .... Zev MINTZ
10 CFO .... Nissim BASALA
37 Dir Student Financial Aid/Registrar .... Lipa EIDELMAN

Bergen Community College (H)

400 Paramus Road, Paramus NJ 07652-1595
County: Bergen FICE Identification: 004736
Unit ID: 183743
Telephone: (201) 447-7100 Carnegie Class: Assoc/HT-High Trad
FAX Number: (201) 447-9042 Calendar System: Semester
URL: www.bergen.edu
Established: 1965 Annual Undergrad Tuition & Fees (In-District): $4,500
Enrollment: 14,062 Coed
Affiliation or Control: State/Local IRS Status: 501(c)3
Highest Offering: Associate Degree
Accreditation: M, ADNUR, COARC, DH, DMS, EMT, MAC, RAD, RTT, SURGT

01 President .... Dr. Michael REDMOND
03 Executive Vice President .... Dr. Brian AGNEW
05 Vice President of Academic Affairs .... Dr. Brock FISHER
32 Interim VP Student Services .... Ms. Priscilla KLYMENKO
50 Dean Business/Arts/Social Science .... Dr. Victor BROWN
79 Dean of Humanities .... Mr. Adam GOODELL
76 Dean Health Professions .... Dr. Susan BARNARD
81 Dean Science/Math & Technology .... Ms. Emily VANDALOVSKY
51 Exec Dir of Continuing Education .... Ms. Christine GILLESPIE
08 Dean Library Services .... Mr. David MARKS
35 Dean of Student Affairs at Ciarco .... Vacant
121 Dean of Student Support Services .... Ms. Jennifer REYES
15 Director of Human Resources .... Ms. Gwendolyn HAREWOOD
18 Managing Director Physical Plant .... Mr. Michael HYJECK
19 VP Fac Ops/Plng & Public Safety .... Mr. William CORCORAN
13 Executive Dir of Info Technology .... Vacant
06 Managing Dir Registration/Records .... Ms. Jacqueline OTTEY
31 Director of Community/Cultural Affs .... Mr. Peter LEDONNE
101 Exec Asst Board of Trustees/Pres .... Ms. Maria FERRARA
29 Managing Director of Alumni Affairs .... Vacant
37 Managing Dir Stdnt Financial Ops .... Ms. Caroline OFODILE
102 Exec Dir Foundation/Development .... Mr. Ronald MILLER
25 Dir Grants Admin/Inst Effectiveness .... Dr. William YAKOWICZ
96 Director of Purchasing & Services .... Ms. Barbara HAMILTON-GOLDEN
26 Exec Dir Pub Rels & Community Cult ... Dr. Lawrence HLAVENKA

Berkeley College (I)

44 Rifle Camp Road, Woodland Park NJ 07424-3367
County: Passaic FICE Identification: 007502
Unit ID: 183789
Telephone: (973) 278-5400 Carnegie Class: Bac-Diverse
FAX Number: (973) 278-0282 Calendar System: Semester
URL: www.berkeleycollege.edu
Established: 1931 Annual Undergrad Tuition & Fees: $25,900
Enrollment: 3,477 Coed
Affiliation or Control: Proprietary IRS Status: Proprietary
Highest Offering: Master's
Accreditation: M, CIDA, IACBE, MAC, SURGT

00 Chairman of the Board .... Mr. Kevin L. LUING
01 President .... Mr. Michael J. SMITH
05 Provost .... Dr. Marsha POLLARD
84 Executive VP .... Mr. Tim LUING
32 Senior VP Student Success .... Dr. Diane RECINOS
10 VP Finance .... Mr. Dino KASAMIS
88 Vice President .... Mr. Brian MAHER
43 VP & Chief Compliance Officer .... Mr. Randy LUING
35 VP Student Development/Campus Life .... Dr. Dallas F. REED
36 VP Career Services .... Ms. Amy SORICELLI
37 VP Financial Aid Compliance .... Mr. Howard LESLIE
114 VP Budget & Student Accounts .... Ms. Eileen LOFTUS-BERLIN
13 Senior VP/Chief Information Officer .... Mr. Leonard DE BOTTON
20 Associate Provost Faculty Affairs .... Dr. Judith KORNBERG
20 Assoc Provost Student Engagement .... Mr. Paul KLESCHICK
106 Dean Online .... Dr. Joseph SCURALLI
58 Dean School of Graduate Studies .... Vacant
50 Dean School of Business .... Dr. Elana ZOLFO
76 Dean School Health Studies .... Dr. Eva SKUKA
107 Dean School of Professional Studies .... Dr. Marianne VAKALIS
49 Dean School of Liberal Arts .... Dr. Don KIEFFER
88 Dean Developmental Education .... Dr. Gerald IACULLO
08 VP Library Services .... Ms. Marlene DOTY
15 VP Human Resources .... Ms. Karen J. CARPENTIERI
26 VP Marketing .... Mr. William DIMASI
11 VP Campus Operations .... Mr. Will MOYA
31 VP Communications & Ext Relations .. Ms. Angela HARRINGTON
86 Senior VP Government Relations NJ .... Ms. Teri DUDA
121 Associate VP Academic Advisement .... Mr. Joseph GIUFFRE
06 Registrar .... Ms. Deborah PALICIA
29 AVP Alumni Relations & Career Svcs .... Mr. Michael IRIS
22 Director Disability Services .... Dr. Sharon MCLENNON-WIER
88 Asst VP Military & Veterans Affairs .... Mr. Edward J. DENNIS
38 Sr Director Personal Counseling .... Dr. Sandra COPPOLA
41 Director Athletics .... Mr. Andrew DESTEPHANO
07 VP Undergraduate Enrollment .... Mr. David J. BERTONE
85 VP International Operations .... Dr. Nori JAFFER
123 Director Graduate Admissions .... Mr. Michael LINCOLN
18 Sr Vice President Operations .... Mr. Thomas ALESSANDRELLO
19 Asst VP Pub Safety/Emergency Mgmt .... Mr. Robert MAGUIRE
109 Senior Director Auxiliary Services .... Mr. Luis COLLAZO
27 Director Media Relations .... Ms. Ilene GREENFIELD
119 Info Systems Security Manager .... Mr. Steven BECKER
09 Director of Institutional Research .... Ms. Rebecca J. DRENNEN

Beth Medrash Govoha (J)

617 Sixth Street, Lakewood NJ 08701-2797
County: Ocean FICE Identification: 007947
Unit ID: 183804
Telephone: (732) 367-1060 Carnegie Class: Spec-4-yr-Faith
FAX Number: (732) 367-7487 Calendar System: Semester
URL: www.yeshivanotices.org
Established: 1943 Annual Undergrad Tuition & Fees: N/A
Enrollment: 6,479 Male
Affiliation or Control: Independent Non-Profit IRS Status: 501(c)3
Highest Offering: Beyond Master's But Less Than Doctorate
Accreditation: RABN

01 President/Chief Executive Officer .... Rabbi Aaron KOTLER
05 Chairman Academic Council .... Rabbi A. Malkiel KOTLER
10 Chief Financial Officer .... Mr. Isaac LEVINE

43 VP Finance/Corporate/Legal Affairs .... Rabbi Eli KUPERMAN
11 Vice President Admin/Campus Life .... Rabbi Yitzchok S. KOTLER
33 Dean of Students .... Rabbi Mattisyahu SALOMON
58 Dean of Graduate Studies .... Rabbi Yisroel NEUMAN
30 Vice President of Fundraising .... Rabbi Mordechai HERSKOWITZ
86 Director Government Affairs .... Mrs. Chanie JACOBOWITZ
06 Registrar .... Rabbi Moshe ROCKOVE
84 Director Enrollment Management .... Rabbi Gedalya A. GREEN
07 Director of Admissions .... Rabbi Avraham FEUER
08 Director Library/Research Programs .... Rabbi Benjamin SPIEGEL
36 Director of Placement .... Rabbi Yaakov SHULMAN
39 Director of Residence Halls .... Rabbi Yosef HOUSMAN
15 Director of Human Resources .... Mrs. Dina YELLIN
18 Director of Facilities .... Mr. Mottie MOSESON

Bloomfield College (A)

467 Franklin Street, Bloomfield NJ 07003-3425
County: Essex FICE Identification: 002597
Unit ID: 183822
Telephone: (973) 748-9000 Carnegie Class: Bac-A&S
FAX Number: (973) 743-3998 Calendar System: Semester
URL: www.bloomfield.edu
Established: 1868 Annual Undergrad Tuition & Fees: $29,950
Enrollment: 1,842 Coed
Affiliation or Control: Presbyterian Church (U.S.A.) IRS Status: 501(c)3
Highest Offering: Master's
Accreditation: M, CAEPT, NURSE

01 President .... Dr. Marcheta P. EVANS
10 Vice President Finance/Admin .... William A. MCDONALD
04 Administrative Asst to President .... Christina M. NOLAN
05 Vice President Academic Affairs .... Tresmaine R. GRIMES
84 VP Enrollment Mgmt .... Kevin CAVANAGH
32 VP Student Affairs/Dean of Students .... Patrick J. LAMY
111 Interim VP for Advancement .... Nicole QUINN
107 VP Global Affairs/Prof Studies .... Peter K. JEONG
21 AVP for Finance and Administration .... Vacant
06 Registrar and Director of Advising .... Annette RAYMOND
09 Director Inst Research/Assessment .... Vacant
20 Associate Dean for Faculty .... Carolyn I. SPIES
79 Chair Div of Humanities .... Brandon FRALIX
83 Chair Div Social/Behavioral Science .... Dunja TRUNK
66 Chair Div of Nursing .... Neddie SERRA
81 Chair Div of Natural Science/Math .... Jim MURPHY
57 Chair Div Creative Arts Technology .... Yuichiro NISHIZAWA
50 Chair Div Accounting/Business/CIS .... Steven KREUTZER
53 Chair Div of Education .... Karen FASANELLA
08 Library Director .... Gregory REID
13 Director Enterprise Tech Services .... Andrew GERSTMAYR
36 Director of Ctr for Career Develop .... Elaine FRAZIER
37 Interim Director of Financial Aid .... Quincina LITTLEJOHN
35 Asst VP for Student Affairs .... Rose MITCHELL
15 Assoc Director Human Resources .... Susan DACEY
07 Assoc Director Of Admissions .... Julia DELBAGNO
18 Supervisor of Buildings & Grounds .... Jack V. MCGRANE
85 Coord Intl Admissions/Student Svcs .... Jamilah MOUDIAB
38 Director Personal Counseling .... Nicole PALAGANO
26 Director Public Rels/Advancemnt Mkt .... Alicia COOK
42 Dir Spiritual Life/College Chaplain .... Vacant
88 Director Teacher Education .... Mary PORCELLI
41 Director of Athletics .... Sheila WOOTEN
121 Director Center Academic Develop .... Leah BROWN-JOHNSON
19 Director of Security .... Jack CORTEZ
39 Director Res Educ & Housing .... Sandy DAWOUD
105 Webmaster .... Matt SHILLITANI
24 Director of Media Center .... Barbara ISACSON
14 Director Institutional Technology .... Yifeng BAI
40 Store Manager .... Vacant

Brookdale Community College (B)

Newman Springs Road, Lincroft NJ 07738-1597
County: Monmouth FICE Identification: 008404
Unit ID: 183859
Telephone: (732) 842-1900 Carnegie Class: Assoc/MT-VT-High Trad
FAX Number: (732) 224-2242 Calendar System: Other
URL: www.brookdalecc.edu
Established: 1967 Annual Undergrad Tuition & Fees (In-District): $4,869
Enrollment: 12,790 Coed
Affiliation or Control: State/Local IRS Status: 501(c)3
Highest Offering: Associate Degree
Accreditation: M, ACFEI, ADNUR, CAHIIM, COARC, CSHSE, RAD

01 President .... Dr. David M. STOUT
05 Vice President for Learning .... Dr. Matthew REED
10 Dir of Finance & Operations .... Ms. Teresa MANFREDA
86 Exec Dir Govt & Comm Rels .... Mr. Edward JOHNSON
32 Assoc VP of Student Affairs .... Dr. Yesenia MADAS
15 Assoc VP HR & Organizational Safety .... Ms. Patricia SENSI
08 Director of Library .... Mr. Steven CHUDNICK
45 Assoc VP Plng & Inst Effectiveness .... Dr. Nancy KEGELMAN
26 Int Exec Director College Relations .... Ms. Kathy KAMATANI
102 Exec Dir Foundation/Alumni Affs .... Mr. Timothy ZEISS
35 Dir of Student Life & Activities .... Ms. Lauren BRUTSMAN
37 Director of Financial Aid .... Ms. Stephanie FITZSIMMONS
25 Director Grants & Institutional Dev .... Ms. Laura V. QAISSAUNEE
38 Director Student Services .... Dr. Stephen A. CURTO
06 Registrar .... Ms. Kimberly HEUSER
09 Dir of Institutional Research/Evalu .... Dr. Laura LONGO
27 Dir of Marketing/Creative Services .... Ms. Suzanne ALTSHULER
28 Mgr Diversity/Inclusion/Compliance .... Vacant
104 Director of International Center .... Ms. Janice THOMAS
13 Chief Information Officer (CIO) .... Mr. George SOTIRION
19 Police Chief .... Mr. Robert KIMLER
41 Dir Athletics & Recreation .... Ms. Katelyn AMUNDSON
50 Dean Business & Social Science .... Dr. Patricia GALLO
81 Dean of STEM .... Dr. Anoop AHLUWALIA
106 Assoc VP Educ Access/Innovation .... Dr. William BURNS
79 Dean Humanities Inst .... Ms. Margaret NATTER
04 Senior Asst to President & BOT .... Ms. Cynthia GRUSKOS
18 Dir Facilities Mgmt & Construction .... Vacant
07 Director of Admissions .... Ms. Mary Beth REILLY
51 Dean of Cont & Prof Studies .... Ms. Joan SCOCCO
43 Exec Assoc of Legal Services .... Ms. Bonnie PASSARELLA

Brookdale Community College Freehold Campus (C)

3680 US Highway 9 South, Freehold NJ 07728
Telephone: (732) 780-0020 Identification: 770125
Accreditation: &M

Caldwell University (D)

120 Bloomfield Avenue, Caldwell NJ 07006-5310
County: Essex FICE Identification: 002598
Unit ID: 183910
Telephone: (973) 618-3000 Carnegie Class: Masters/M
FAX Number: (973) 618-3300 Calendar System: Semester
URL: www.caldwell.edu
Established: 1939 Annual Undergrad Tuition & Fees: $34,715
Enrollment: 2,206 Coed
Affiliation or Control: Roman Catholic IRS Status: 501(c)3
Highest Offering: Doctorate
Accreditation: M, ACBSP, CACREP, CAEPT, NURSE

01 President .... Dr. Nancy BLATTNER
05 Vice President for Academic Affairs .... Dr. Barbara CHESLER
15 VP Institutional Effectiveness .... Mrs. Sheila N. O'ROURKE
32 Vice President for Student Affairs .... Sr. Kathleen TUITE
84 Acting VP for Enrollment Management .... Mr. Stephen QUINN
30 Vice Pres Development/Alumni Affs .... Mr. Kevin BOYLE
50 Associate Dean School of Business .... Ms. Virginia RICH
53 Associate Dean School of Education .... Dr. Joan MORIARTY
85 Director International Student Svcs .... Mr. Maulin JOSHI
110 AVP Development/Alumni Affairs .... Ms. Lori FUNICELLO
112 Director of Gift Planning .... Vacant
06 University Registrar .... Mr. Ian K. WHITE
08 Head Librarian .... Ms. Ellen JOHNSTON
07 Asst Vice President Enrollment .... Mr. Stephen QUINN
58 Associate VP for Academic Affairs .... Dr. Ellina CHERNOBILSKY
38 Executive Director of Counseling .... Ms. Robin DAVENPORT
39 Assistant Dean Residence Life .... Ms. Crystal LOPEZ
13 Exec Director Information Tech .... Mr. Donald O'HAGAN
36 Dir Career Plng & Development .... Ms. Geraldine PERRET
37 Director Financial Aid .... Ms. Eileen FELSKE
41 Asst Vice Pres & Dir of Athletics .... Mr. Mark A. CORINO
26 Director News and Media Relations .... Ms. Colette LIDDY
19 Executive Director Campus Safety .... Mr. Glenn GATES
91 Director Administrative Technology .... Mr. David BOHNY
16 Director of Human Resources .... Mrs. Michelle STAUSS
35 Asst Dean Student Engagement .. Mr. Timothy KESSLER-CLEARY
106 Dir Online Education/E-learning .... Ms. Soheila KOBLER
04 Administrative Asst to President .... Ms. Sharon KIEVIT
09 Director of Institutional Research .... Ms. Susan HAYES
124 Asst Dean Advisement and Retention .... Ms. Henrieta GENFI
102 Dir Foundation/Corporate Relations .... Ms. Pat LEVINS
105 Director Web Services .... Mr. Anthony YANG
42 Director of Campus Ministry .... Ms. Colleen O'BRIEN
10 Chief Financial/Business Officer .... Mr. Shin MOON
29 Director Alumni Affairs .... Ms. Meghan MORAN

Camden County College (E)

PO Box 200, Blackwood NJ 08012-0200
County: Camden FICE Identification: 006865
Unit ID: 183938
Telephone: (856) 227-7200 Carnegie Class: Assoc/MT-VT-Mix Trad/Non
FAX Number: (856) 374-4894 Calendar System: Semester
URL: www.camdencc.edu
Established: 1967 Annual Undergrad Tuition & Fees (In-District): $4,320
Enrollment: 10,492 Coed
Affiliation or Control: State/Local IRS Status: 501(c)3
Highest Offering: Associate Degree
Accreditation: M, CAHIIM, DA, DH, DIETT, OPD

01 President .... Mr. Donald BORDEN
45 VP Institutional Effectiveness .... Dr. Jacquelyn GALBIATI
05 Vice Pres Academic Affairs .... Dr. David EDWARDS
84 Exec Dean Enrollment/Student Svcs .... Dr. James CANONICA
10 Exec Dir Finance & Planning .... Ms. Helen ANTONAKAKIS
11 Exec Dir Financial Admin Svcs .... Mr. Maris KUKAINIS
15 Executive Director Human Resources .... Ms. Kathleen KANE
51 Exec Dean School/Comm Academic Pgm .... Ms. Margo VENABLE
13 Chief Info Technology Officer (CIO) .... Mr. Jack POST
43 Dir Legal Services/General Counsel .... Mr. Karl MCCONNELL
108 Dean Academic Affairs .... Dr. Teresa A. SMITH
09 Dean Inst Research/Plng/ Grants .... Dr. Rebecca FIDLER-SHEPPARD
81 Dean Math Science Health Careers .... Vacant
79 Dean Arts/Humanities/Soc Science .... Mr. Michael NESTER
12 Exec Dean Camden City Campus .... Vacant
07 Dir Admissions/Registration Svcs .... Mr. Steve D'AMBROSIO
37 Executive Director of Financial Aid .... Ms. Felicia BRYANT
19 Director Public Safety .... Mr. John SCHUCK
29 External Resources Develop Assoc .... Ms. Melissa DALY
88 Director of Testing .... Mr. Daniel MCMASTERS
26 Director of Communications .... Ms. Julie YANKANICH
06 Dir Student System Records .... Ms. Bunny KOHL
08 Director Library Services .... Ms. Isabel GRAY
41 Athletic Director .... Mr. William BANKS

Camden County College Camden City Campus (F)

200 N Broadway, Camden NJ 08102-1185
Telephone: (856) 338-1817 Identification: 770126
Accreditation: &M

Centenary University (G)

400 Jefferson Street, Hackettstown NJ 07840-2100
County: Warren FICE Identification: 002599
Unit ID: 183974
Telephone: (908) 852-1400 Carnegie Class: Masters/M
FAX Number: (908) 850-9508 Calendar System: Semester
URL: www.centenaryuniversity.edu
Established: 1867 Annual Undergrad Tuition & Fees: $32,998
Enrollment: 1,990 Coed
Affiliation or Control: Independent Non-Profit IRS Status: 501(c)3
Highest Offering: Doctorate
Accreditation: M, CAEPT, IACBE, SW

01 Interim President .... Dr. Rosalind REICHARD
05 VP for Academic Affairs .... Dr. Amy D'OLIVO
10 VP for Business & Finance .... Mr. Denton STARGEL
84 VP for Enrollment Mgmt & Marketing . Dr. Robert L. MILLER, JR.
32 VP for Student Life Dean Students .... Ms. Kerry MULLINS
15 Director for Human Resources .... Ms. Christine ROSADO
18 Director of Facilities .... Mr. Jonathan MIRABEL
09 Coordinator Institutional Research .... Ms. Ying WANG
35 Sr Director Student Engagement .... Ms. Tiffany KUSHNER
06 Registrar .... Ms. Christine VANDENBERG
08 Int Dir Taylor Memorial Library .... Ms. Maryanne FEGAN
36 Director Career Development Center .... Mr. Joshua D. WALKER
41 Director of Athletics .... Mr. Travis SPENCER
19 Chief of Campus Safety .... Mr. Leonard KUNZ
38 Director of Counseling Center .... Ms. Lorna FARMER
13 Chief Information Officer .... Ms. Sharon AINSLEY
04 Exec Assistant to the President .... Ms. Diane LYNCH

Chamberlain University-North Brunswick (H)

630 US Highway One, North Brunswick NJ 08902
Telephone: (732) 875-1300 Identification: 770850
Accreditation: &NH, NURSE

† Branch campus of Chamberlain University-Addison, Addison, IL

The College of New Jersey (I)

2000 Pennington Road, Ewing NJ 08628-1104
County: Mercer FICE Identification: 002642
Unit ID: 187134
Telephone: (609) 771-1855 Carnegie Class: Masters/L
FAX Number: (609) 637-5191 Calendar System: Semester
URL: www.tcnj.edu
Established: 1855 Annual Undergrad Tuition & Fees (In-State): $16,551
Enrollment: 7,552 Coed
Affiliation or Control: State IRS Status: 501(c)3
Highest Offering: Master's
Accreditation: M, ART, CACREP, CAEPN, MUS, NURSE

01 President .... Dr. Kathryn A. FOSTER
05 Int Provost/VP Academic Affairs .... Dr. William KEEP
11 Vice Pres for Administration .... Vacant
10 Vice President & Treasurer .... Mr. Lloyd RICKETTS
43 Vice President & General Counsel .... Mr. Thomas MAHONEY
111 Vice Pres for College Advancement .... Mr. John DONOHUE
32 Int Vice President Student Affairs .... Mr. Sean STALLINGS
15 Vice Pres Human Resources .... Dr. Gregory POGUE
84 Vice Pres Enrollment Management .... Ms. Lisa ANGELONI
13 CIO & VP for Info Technology .... Dr. Sharon BLANTON
100 Chief of Staff/Secy to Board .... Ms. Heather FEHN
18 Assoc VP Facilities & Admin Svcs .... Ms. Maritza MCGRAW
30 Assoc Vice President of Development .... Mr. Charles WRIGHT
35 Asst VP for Student Affairs/Engage .... Ms. Elizabeth BAPASOLA
35 Int Asst Vice Pres Student Affairs .... Dr. Kelly HENNESSY
20 Vice Provost .... Dr. Timothy CLYDESDALE
57 Dean School of The Arts & Comm .... Dr. Maurice HALL
50 Interim Dean School of Business .... Dr. Bozena LEVEN
79 Dean Sch Humanities/Soc Sci .... Dr. Jane WONG
53 Dean School of Education .... Dr. Suzanne MCCOTTER
54 Dean School of Engineering .... Dr. Steven SCHREINER
66 Dean Nursing/Health/Exercise Sci .... Dr. Carole KENNER
81 Dean School of Science .... Dr. Jeffrey OSBORN
58 Dir Grad & Intersession Programs .... Dr. Susan HYDRO
37 Exec Dir of Student Fin Assistance .... Mr. Wil CASAINE
09 Assoc Provost Ctr Inst Effective .... Dr. Mosen AURYAN
41 Exec Director of Athletics .... Ms. Amanda DEMARTINO
29 Executive Director Alumni Affairs .... Mr. John CASTALDO
26 Assoc VP Comm/Mktg/Brand Mgmt .... Mr. David MUHA
18 Director of Campus Construction .... Mr. William RUDEAU
23 Director for Health Services .... Ms. Janice VERMEYCHUK
06 Exec Director Records/Registration .... Mr. Frank COOPER
19 Interim Dir Campus Police .... Chief Timothy GRANT

96 Exec Dir Procurement Services .... Mr. Anup KAPUR
28 Assoc VP/Chief Diversity Officer .... Ms. Kerri TILLETT
07 Exec Dir Admissions/Enrollment Mgmt ...... Ms. Grecia MONTERO
36 Director Career Center .... Ms. Debra KELLY
38 AVP/Director Counseling/Psych Svcs .... Dr. Mark FOREST

College of Saint Elizabeth (A)

2 Convent Road, Morristown NJ 07960-6989

County: Morris FICE Identification: 002600
Unit ID: 186618

Telephone: (973) 290-4000 Carnegie Class: Masters/M
FAX Number: N/A Calendar System: Semester
URL: www.cse.edu
Established: 1899 Annual Undergrad Tuition & Fees: $33,596
Enrollment: 1,141 Coed
Affiliation or Control: Roman Catholic IRS Status: 501(c)3
Highest Offering: Doctorate
Accreditation: M, CAEPT, DIETD, DIETI, NUR, SW

01 President .... Dr. Helen J. STREUBERT
05 VP for Academic Affairs .... Dr. Monique GUILLORY
32 VP Student Life .... Ms. Katherine BUCK
10 VP Finance Admin/Treasurer .... Mr. Michael FESCOE
111 Vice Pres Institutional Advancement .... Ms. Sally CLEARY
84 VP Enrollment Management .... Ms. Joanne LANDERS
21 Controller .... Mr. Eric S. FENCHEL
06 Registrar .... Ms. Marybeth OBRYCKI
09 Dir Inst Research & Acad Assessment .... Dr. Michele YURECKO
08 Director Mahoney Library .... Mr. Mark FERGUSON
42 Campus Minister .... Ms. Clare ETTENSOHN
18 Director of Facilities & Security .... Mr. James GERRISH
37 Director of Financial Aid .... Ms. Rebecca E. REES
26 Director Marketing/ Communications .... Ms. Denise G. PANYIK-DALE
22 Director EOF Program .... Mr. Clifford WOODWARD
36 Dir Experiential Lrng & Career Svcs ... Mr. Michael PENNINGTON
38 Director of Counseling .... Ms. Zsuzsanna NAGY
88 Dir Volunteerism & Svc Learning .... Ms. Jayne I. MURPHY-MORRIS
35 Director of Student Engagement .... Ms. Naima K. RICKS
41 Director of Athletics .... Ms. Juliene SIMPSON
30 Senior Director Development .... Vacant
29 Dir Alumni Engagement/Alumni Assoc .... Ms. Carol Ann KOERT
15 Director Human Resources .... Ms. Kristi RUSSO
40 C-Store/Dining Services .... Mr. Dean PIACENTINI
110 Asst VP Institutional Advancement .... Ms. Janice HILL
105 Director IT-Web .... Mr. David B. RABINOWITZ
04 Administrative Asst to President .... Ms. MaryAnn RICCIOTTI
13 Chief Info Technology Officer .... Ms. Margie ROHR
107 Dean of Professional Studies .... Dr. Patricia HEINDEL
49 Dean of Arts and Sciences .... Dr. Anthony SANTAMARIA
104 Coord Acad Internships & Study Away ... Ms. Periana STAGGERS
19 Director Security/Safety .... Mr. Richard WALL
39 Asst Director Residence Life .... Mr. Jason J. GREENHOUSE
04 Exec Asst to President .... Ms. Meghan AITKEN

County College of Morris (B)

214 Center Grove Road, Randolph NJ 07869-2086

County: Morris FICE Identification: 007729
Unit ID: 184180

Telephone: (973) 328-5000 Carnegie Class: Assoc/HT-High Trad
FAX Number: (973) 328-1282 Calendar System: Semester
URL: www.ccm.edu
Established: 1965 Annual Undergrad Tuition & Fees (In-District): $4,920
Enrollment: 7,949 Coed
Affiliation or Control: State/Local IRS Status: 501(c)3
Highest Offering: Associate Degree
Accreditation: M, ACBSP, ADNUR, COARC, RAD

01 President .... Dr. Anthony J. IACONO
05 Vice President of Academic Affairs .... Dr. John MARLIN
10 Vice President of Business/Finance .... Ms. Karen VANDERHOOF
32 VP of Student Development .... Dr. Bette M. SIMMONS
102 Exec Dir Foundation .... Ms. Katie OLSEN
15 VP Human Resources & Labor Rels .... Mr. Thomas BURK
09 Dean Inst Research .... Ms. Phebe SOLIMAN
114 Director Budget & Business Services .... Mr. John YOUNG
25 Director Resource Development .... Dr. Katrina BELL
07 Admissions Officer .... Ms. Donna TATARKA
37 Director Financial Aid .... Mr. Harvey WILLIS
06 Registrar .... Ms. Laura Lee BOWENS
26 Chief Public Relations Officer .... Ms. Kathleen BRUNET
29 Director Alumni Office .... Ms. Barbara CAPSOURAS
13 VP Institutional Effectiveness/CIO .... Mr. Robert STIRTON
08 Dean Learning Resource Ctr .... Ms. Heather CRAVEN
36 Director Career Svcs/Coop Education .... Ms. Denise SCHMIDT
38 Counseling Services Coordinator .... Ms. Janique CAFFIE
49 Dean Liberal Arts .... Vacant
76 Dean Health/Natural Sciences .... Ms. Monica MARASKA
103 VP Workforce Dev/Prof Studies .... Mr. Patrick ENRIGHT
19 Director Security & Safety .... Vacant
41 Director Athletics .... Mr. Jack SULLIVAN
23 Health Services Coordinator .... Ms. Elizabeth HOBAN
18 Director of Plant & Maintenance .... Mr. Joseph PONTURO
96 Director of Purchasing .... Ms. Joanne KEARNS
40 Bookstore Manager .... Mr. Jeff LUBNOW

Drew University (C)

36 Madison Avenue, Madison NJ 07940-1493

County: Morris FICE Identification: 002603
Unit ID: 184348

Telephone: (973) 408-3000 Carnegie Class: Bac-A&S
FAX Number: N/A Calendar System: 4/1/4
URL: www.drew.edu
Established: 1866 Annual Undergrad Tuition & Fees: $39,800
Enrollment: 2,117 Coed
Affiliation or Control: Independent Non-Profit IRS Status: 501(c)3
Highest Offering: Doctorate
Accreditation: M, CAEPT, THEOL

01 President .... Dr. MaryAnn BAENNINGER
05 Chief Academic Officer .... Dr. Debra LIEBOWITZ
84 Int Vice Pres for Enrollment .... Mr. Colby MCCARTHY
111 Vice Pres Advancement .... Mr. Bret SILVER
10 Vice Pres Finance/Business Affairs .... Mr. John VITALI
73 Dean Theological School .... Dr. Javier VIERA
08 University Librarian .... Mr. Andrew BONAMICI
32 Vice President Student Life .... Dr. Frank MERCKX
26 VP Communications & Marketing .... Ms. Kristen WILLIAMS
07 Exec Dir College Admissions .... Mr. Jim SKIFF
15 Director of Human Resources .... Ms. Maria FORCE
22 Title IX Coordinator .... Dr. Frank MERCKX
21 Controller .... Ms. Renee LISCHIN
96 Director Purchasing .... Ms. Deborah TAVERA
18 Director Facilities Operations .... Mr. Greg SMITH
37 Director Financial Assistance .... Ms. Colby MCCARTHY
19 Director Public Safety .... Mr. Andy ENGEMANN
23 Director Health Services .... Ms. Joan GALBRAITH
35 Director Student Activities .... Ms. Michelle BRISSON
38 Director Counseling Services .... Dr. Jim MANDALA
07 Director Theological Admissions .... Mr. Kevin D. MILLER
07 Director Graduate Admissions .... Mr. Amo KUBEYINJE
09 Director Institutional Research .... Mr. Alex MCCLUNG
41 Director Athletics .... Ms. Christa RACINE
06 Registrar .... Ms. Stephanie CALDWELL
40 Manager Bookstore .... Ms. Marie JOYNER
04 Administrative Asst to President .... Ms. Kathleen SUTHERLAND
100 Chief of Staff .... Ms. Barb BRESNAHAN
104 Director Study Abroad .... Ms. Stacy FISCHER
105 Webmaster .... Mr. Justin JACKSON
13 Interim Chief Technology Officer .... Mr. Christopher DARRELL
29 Director Alumni Relations .... Ms. Carol BASSIE
43 Director Legal Services .... Ms. Meredith PALMER
108 Director Institutional Assessment .... Dr. Michael FRIED
39 Dir Resident Life/Student Housing .... Ms. Stephanie PELHAM
44 Interim Director Annual Giving .... Ms. Kaitlin CASEY
20 Assoc Prov Exp Educ & Career ..... Dr. Daniel PASCOE AGUILAR
84 Director Enrollment Management .... Mr. Robert HERR

Eastern International College (D)

684 Newark Avenue, Jersey City NJ 07306

County: Hudson FICE Identification: 031226
Unit ID: 421878

Telephone: (201) 216-9901 Carnegie Class: Spec-4-yr-Other Health
FAX Number: (201) 533-1027 Calendar System: Semester
URL: www.eicollege.edu
Established: 1990 Annual Undergrad Tuition & Fees: $21,225
Enrollment: 230 Coed
Affiliation or Control: Proprietary IRS Status: Proprietary
Highest Offering: Baccalaureate
Accreditation: @M, ACCSC, ADNUR, CVT, DH

01 CEO/President .... Dr. Bashir MOHSEN
05 Vice President of Academic Affairs .... Dr. Mustafa MUSTAFA
06 Registrar .... Mrs. Tina HAMILTON
12 Campus Director .... Ms. Agnieszka DRUPKA
36 Corporate Director of Career Svcs .... Ms. Jennifer GONZALEZ
37 Director Student Financial Aid .... Ms. Iren BRODSKIY
20 Dean of Education .... Mrs. Kimberly MORSE
13 Chief Info Technology Officer (CIO) .... Ms. Brynn DEPREY
32 Student Life Coordinator .... Ms. Jennifer GONZALEZ
38 Student Counseling Officer .... Ms. Maria BILLINGS
08 Head Librarian .... Ms. Lisa BOGART
22 Chief EEO Officer & Legal Liaison .... Mr. George CACERES

Eastern International College-Belleville Campus (E)

251 Washington Avenue, Belleville NJ 07109
Telephone: (973) 751-9051 Identification: 770580
Accreditation: ACCSC

Eastwick College (F)

250 Moore Street, Hackensack NJ 07601

County: Bergen Identification: 667131
Unit ID: 183488

Telephone: (201) 488-9400 Carnegie Class: Assoc/HVT-High Non
FAX Number: (201) 488-1007 Calendar System: Quarter
URL: www.eastwick.edu
Established: 1985 Annual Undergrad Tuition & Fees: $14,832
Enrollment: 399 Coed
Affiliation or Control: Proprietary IRS Status: Proprietary
Highest Offering: Associate Degree
Accreditation: ACCSC, ACICS, FUSER

01 President .... Thomas M. EASTWICK
11 Director Hackensack Campus .... Joyce MARCHIONE-TRAINA
05 Dean of Academics .... Dawood GUIRGUIS

Eastwick College (G)

103 Park Avenue, Nutley NJ 07110

County: Essex FICE Identification: 020923
Unit ID: 185721

Telephone: (973) 661-0600 Carnegie Class: Assoc/HVT-Mix Trad/Non
FAX Number: (973) 661-2954 Calendar System: Quarter
URL: www.eastwick.edu
Established: 2014 Annual Undergrad Tuition & Fees: $15,305
Enrollment: 486 Coed
Affiliation or Control: Proprietary IRS Status: Proprietary
Highest Offering: Associate Degree
Accreditation: ACCSC, ACICS

01 President .... Thomas EASTWICK
11 Vice Pres of Operations .... Bhavna TAILOR
05 Dean of Academics .... Sameh FARAGALLA

Eastwick College (H)

10 South Franklin Turnpike, Ramsey NJ 07446

County: Bergen FICE Identification: 020537
Unit ID: 184959

Telephone: (201) 327-8877 Carnegie Class: Spec-4-yr-Other Health
FAX Number: (201) 327-9054 Calendar System: Other
URL: www.eastwick.edu
Established: 1968 Annual Undergrad Tuition & Fees: $15,881
Enrollment: 772 Coed
Affiliation or Control: Proprietary IRS Status: Proprietary
Highest Offering: Baccalaureate
Accreditation: ACCSC, ACICS, CVT, OTA, SURGT

01 President .... Thomas EASTWICK
03 Executive Vice President .... Rafael CASTILLA
05 Vice President Academic Affairs .... Joyce TRAINA
11 Vice Pres Operations .... Bhavna TAILOR
07 Director of Admissions .... Letitia BURKE
36 Director Career Development .... Jennifer BATE
37 Corp Director of Financial Aid .... Christy DELAGUERRA

Essex County College (I)

303 University Avenue, Newark NJ 07102-1798

County: Essex FICE Identification: 007107
Unit ID: 184481

Telephone: (973) 877-3000 Carnegie Class: Assoc/MT-VT-High Trad
FAX Number: (973) 877-3044 Calendar System: Other
URL: www.essex.edu
Established: 1966 Annual Undergrad Tuition & Fees (In-District): $4,995
Enrollment: 8,997 Coed
Affiliation or Control: State/Local IRS Status: 501(c)3
Highest Offering: Associate Degree
Accreditation: M, ACBSP, ADNUR, OPD, PTAA, RAD

01 President .... Dr. Anthony MUNROE
05 Vice Pres/Chief Academic Officer .... Dr. Jeffrey LEE
04 Admin Asst to the President .... Ms. Jonell CONGLETON
10 VP Business Operations .... Mr. Julio IZQUIERDO
81 Dean STEM .... Dr. Jill STEIN
108 Exec Dir Inst Planning/Assessment .... Mr. John RUNFELDT
13 Exec Dean/CIO Admin & Learning Tech ... Mr. Mohamed SEDDIKI
32 Dean Student Affairs .... Dr. Keith KIRKLAND
106 Assoc Dean Online Learning Resource .... Dr. Leigh BELLO-DECASTRO
25 Director Management Grant Funds .... Ms. Yvette JEFFERIES
09 Director Institutional Research .... Dr. Jinsoo PARK
51 Dean Community & Continuing Educ .... Dr. Elvira VIEIRA
08 Director MLK Library .... Mrs. Gwendolyn SLATON
35 Assoc Dean Student Life/Development .... Ms. Patricia SLADE
18 Director Facilities Mgmt .... Mr. Jeff SHAPIRO
19 Director Public Safety .... Mr. Anthony CROMARTIE
96 Director Purchasing .... Mr. Marvin SMITH
37 Director Financial Aid .... Mr. David SMEDLEY
113 Director Bursar's Office .... Ms. Darlene MILLER
36 Director Student Development .... Dr. S. Aisha STEPLIGHT JOHNSON
88 Director Child Development Center .... Ms. Virginia FLANIGAN
41 Director Athletics .... Mr. Michael DOUGHTIE
24 Chief of Operations Media Prod Tech .... Mr. Eugene JACKSON
00 President Emeritus .... Dr. A. Zachary YAMBA
06 Registrar .... Mrs. Zewdnesh KASSA
38 Director Student Counseling .... Dr. Stephanie A. STEPLIGHT JOHNSON
43 General Counsel .... Ms. Joy TOLLIVER
84 Director Enrollment Management .... Mr. Sanjay RAMDATH

Essex County College-West Essex Branch Campus (J)

730 West Bloomfield Avenue, West Caldwell NJ 07006
Telephone: (973) 877-6590 Identification: 770127
Accreditation: &M

Fairleigh Dickinson University (K)

1000 River Road, Teaneck NJ 07666-1996

County: Bergen FICE Identification: 002607
Unit ID: 184603

Telephone: (201) 692-2000 Carnegie Class: Masters/L
FAX Number: N/A Calendar System: Semester
URL: www.fdu.edu
Established: 1942 Annual Undergrad Tuition & Fees: $40,732
Enrollment: 7,846 Coed

Affiliation or Control: Independent Non-Profit IRS Status: 501(c)3
Highest Offering: Doctorate
Accreditation: M, CACREP, CAEPT, CLPSY, NURSE, PHAR

01 President ... Dr. Christopher CAPUANO
43 Int University Counsel/Secretary ... Ms. Elizabeth JOYCE
05 University Provost/Sr VP Acad Affs ... Dr. Gillian SMALL
111 Sr Vice Pres University Advancement ... Mr. Richard REISS
10 Senior VP for Finance & COO ... Ms. Hania FERRARA
18 VP for Facilities & Auxiliary Svcs ... Mr. Richard A. FRICK
84 VP Enrollment/Planning & Effect ... Dr. Luke D. SCHULTHEIS
13 VP/Chief Information Officer ... Mr. Neal M. STURM
07 AVP Admissions/Fin Aid/Enrollment ... Ms. Traci BANKS
26 Associate VP Communications ... Mr. Angelo CARFAGNA
15 Associate VP Human Resources ... Ms. Rose D'AMBROSIO
06 AVP Enrollment Services/Registrar ... Ms. Carol CREEKMORE
21 Assoc VP for Finance ... Mr. Frank BARRA
104 Vice Provost for International Affs ... Dr. Jason SCORZA
29 Exec Director Alumni Relations ... Ms. Karin HAMILTON
51 Dean Petrocelli Col of Cont Stds ... Dr. Lisa BRAVERMAN
49 Dean Becton Col of Arts & Sci ... Dr. Geoffrey WEINMAN
50 Dean College Business Admin ... Dr. Andrew ROSMAN
20 Interim Dean University College ... Dr. Vicki COHEN
32 Dean of Students Metro ... Mr. Vidal LOPEZ
32 Dean of Students Florham ... Dr. Robin M. WILLIAMSON
08 Assoc University Librarian-Florham ... Ms. Brigid BURKE
08 Assoc University Librarian-Metro ... Ms. Kathy STEIN-SMITH
51 Director Continuing Education ... Dr. Thomas SWANZEY
88 Dir Public Administration Institute ... Dr. William ROBERTS
116 Director Internal Audit ... Ms. Agnes SCAGLIONE
53 Interim Dir School of Education ... Dr. Miriam SINGER
66 Director Sch of Nurs/Allied Health ... Dr. Minerva GUTTMAN
41 Director of Athletics-Metro ... Mr. Bradford D. HURLBUT
41 Director of Athletics-Florham ... Ms. Jennifer NOON
07 Univ Dir of Undergrad Admissions ... Mr. Andrew IPPOLITO
09 Director of Institutional Research ... Dr. Sam MICHALOWSKI
37 University Director Financial Aid ... Ms. Renee VOLAK
19 Dir Public Safety-Florham Campus ... Mr. Joseph VITIELLO
19 Director Public Safety-Metro Campus ... Mr. David A. MILES
12 Campus Executive-Metro Campus ... Dr. Steven NELSON
12 Campus Executive-Florham Campus ... Dr. Brian MAURO
96 Director of Purchasing ... Ms. Juliette BROOKS
04 Assistant to the President ... Ms. Jeanne MAZZOLLA
25 Univ Dir Grants/Sponsored Projects ... Ms. Jane TSAMBIS
36 University Dir Career Development ... Ms. Donna ROBERTSON
117 Risk Manager ... Ms. Gail LEMAIRE
39 Assoc Dean of Stdnts/Residence Life ... Mr. Ruben FLORES

Felician University (A)

262 S Main Street, Lodi NJ 07644-2198
County: Bergen FICE Identification: 002610
Unit ID: 184612
Telephone: (201) 559-6000 Carnegie Class: Masters/M
FAX Number: (201) 559-6188 Calendar System: Semester
URL: www.felician.edu
Established: 1942 Annual Undergrad Tuition & Fees: $34,320
Enrollment: 1,996 Coed
Affiliation or Control: Roman Catholic IRS Status: 501(c)3
Highest Offering: Doctorate
Accreditation: M, CAEPT, IACBE, NURSE

01 President ... Dr. Anne PRISCO
05 Vice Pres Acad Affairs ... Dr. Sylvia MCGEARY
20 Asst VP Academic Support Services ... Dr. Ann V. GUILLORY
10 Int VP for Business/Finance/CFO ... Mr. Thomas TRUCHAN
84 VP Enroll Mgmt & Student Affairs ... Ms. Francine ANDREA
04 Admin Assistant to the President ... Ms. Meggan O'NEILL
06 Registrar ... Ms. Priscilla KLYMENKO
123 Assoc Vice Pres Grad & Intl Enroll ... Mr. Michael SZAREK
15 Director of Human Resources ... Ms. Virginia TOPOLSKI
37 Exec Director Student Financial Aid ... Ms. Cynthia MONTALVO
39 Director of Residence Life ... Ms. Laura PIEROTTI
36 Director of Career Development Ctr ... Ms. Tiffany AUSTIN
13 Asst VP of Information Technology ... Mr. Christopher FINCH
24 Director A-V Center ... Mr. Anthony KLYMENKO
88 Assoc Director Center for Learning ... Mr. Hamdi SHAHIN
53 Dean School of Education ... Dr. Stephanie MCGOWAN
49 Dean School of Arts/Science ... Dr. George E. ABAUNZA
108 Dean Assessment/Fac Excellence ... Dr. Dolores HENCHY
23 Director Health Services ... Ms. Carolyn LEWIS
41 Director of Athletics ... Mr. Benjamin DINALLO, JR.
92 Director Honors Program ... Dr. Jeffrey BLANCHARD

Georgian Court University (B)

900 Lakewood Avenue, Lakewood NJ 08701-2697
County: Ocean FICE Identification: 002608
Unit ID: 184773
Telephone: (732) 987-2200 Carnegie Class: Masters/M
FAX Number: N/A Calendar System: Semester
URL: www.georgian.edu
Established: 1908 Annual Undergrad Tuition & Fees: $32,976
Enrollment: 2,390 Coed
Affiliation or Control: Roman Catholic IRS Status: 501(c)3
Highest Offering: Master's
Accreditation: M, ACBSP, CACREP, CAEPT, NURSE, SW

01 President ... Dr. Joseph R. MARBACH
05 Interim Provost ... Dr. Janice WARNER
10 Chief Financial Officer/VP Finance ... Mr. James TRUSDELL
111 Vice Pres Institutional Advancement ... Mr. Matthew MANFRA
20 Assoc Provost Academic Pgm Devel ... Dr. Michael GROSS
84 Interim VP for Enrollment/Retention ... Ms. Kathleen BOODY
32 Dean of Students ... Dr. Amani JENNINGS
42 Director of Campus Ministry ... Mr. Jeff SCHAFFER
41 Director Athletics/Recreation ... Ms. Laura LIESMAN
50 Dean School of Business ... Dr. Jennifer EDMONDS
53 Dean of School of Education ... Dr. Christopher CAMPISANO
49 Dean School of Arts & Sciences ... Dr. Mary CHINERY
09 Director of Institutional Research ... Mr. Wayne ARNDT
08 Director of Library Services ... Mr. Jeffrey DONNELLY
06 Registrar ... Ms. Corinne MITCHELL
21 Controller ... Ms. Maureen RYAN-HOFFMAN
15 Director of Human Resources ... Vacant
13 Chief Information Officer ... Mr. Steve CAROL
37 Director of Financial Aid ... Ms. Cynthia MCCARTHY
26 Exec Dir of Marketing & Comm ... Ms. Gail TOWNS
88 Dir Conferences & Special Events ... Ms. Mary CRANWELL
29 Director of Alumni Relations ... Ms. ToniAnn MCLAUGHLIN
36 Director Career Services ... Ms. Ceceilia O'CALLAGHAN
38 Director of Counseling ... Dr. Robin SOLBACH
23 Director of Health Services ... Ms. Robin SOLBACH
18 Director of Facilities ... Mr. Michael PUTNAM
19 Director of Security ... Mr. Thomas ZAMBRANO
123 Director Graduate Admissions ... Mr. Patrick GIVENS
39 Director of Residence Life ... Ms. Stephanie ABDALLA
04 Executive Asst to President ... Ms. Stephanie TEDESCO
105 Web Administrator ... Mr. Richard BERARDI
108 Asst VP for University Assessment ... Sr. Janet THIEL
96 Purchasing Coordinator ... Ms. Julie PARLACOSKI
30 Asst Vice Pres for Development ... Vacant
101 Spec Asst to Pres/Sec to Board ... Ms. Stephanie TEDESCO
102 Dir Foundation/Corporate Relations ... Ms. Lori THOMAS

Hudson County Community College (C)

70 Sip Avenue, Jersey City NJ 07306
County: Hudson FICE Identification: 012954
Unit ID: 184995
Telephone: (201) 714-7100 Carnegie Class: Assoc/HT-High Trad
FAX Number: (201) 656-1799 Calendar System: Semester
URL: www.hccc.edu
Established: 1974 Annual Undergrad Tuition & Fees (In-District): $5,718
Enrollment: 8,864 Coed
Affiliation or Control: State/Local IRS Status: 501(c)3
Highest Offering: Associate Degree
Accreditation: M, ACFEI, ADNUR, RAD

01 President ... Dr. Christopher M. REBER
05 Exec Vice Pres and Provost ... Dr. Eric FRIEDMAN
10 Vice Pres Business/Finance & CFO ... Ms. Veronica ZEICHNER
111 Vice Pres Planning/Development ... Dr. Nicholas CHIARAVALLOTI
15 Vice President Human Resources ... Ms. Anna KRUPITSKIY
09 Assoc Dean Institutional Rsrch/Plng ... Vacant
32 VP for Student Affairs/Enrollment ... Mrs. Lisa DOUGHERTY
50 Assoc Dean Business and Science ... Ms. Catherine SIRANGELO-ELBADAWY
20 Assistant VP Academic Affairs ... Mr. Christopher WAHL
16 Asst Vice Pres Employee Relations ... Ms. Vivyen RAY
37 Executive Director Financial Aid ... Ms. Sylvia F. MENDOZA
88 Assoc Dean English and ESL ... Ms. Elizabeth NESIUS
06 Registrar ... Ms. Victoria ORELLANA
13 Chief Information Officer ... Ms. Patricia CLAY
07 Director of Admissions ... Mr. Matthew FESSLER
81 Dean of Instruction/Sciences ... Mr. John MARLIN
88 Director Testing & Assessment ... Ms. Darlery FRANCO
88 Executive Director Culinary Arts ... Mr. Paul DILLON
51 Dean of Cont Educ & Workforce Dev ... Ms. Lori MARGOLIN
21 Controller ... Mr. Geoffrey SIMS
25 Director of Grants ... Mr. Sean KERWICK
08 Librarian ... Ms. Ellen RENAUD
35 Director Student Activities ... Ms. Veronica ZEROSIMO
26 Director of Communications ... Ms. Jennifer CHRISTOPHER
121 Associate Dean Student Success ... Dr. Sheila DYNAN
40 Manager HCCC Bookstore ... Ms. Tom COLBAN
96 Dir of Contracts and Procurement ... Mr. Jeff ROBERSON
19 Director Security/Safety ... Mr. John QUIGLEY
04 Executive Admin Asst to President ... Ms. Jennifer OAKLEY
18 Exec Dir Engineering Operations ... Mr. Ilya ASHMYAN
08 Dean of Libraries ... Ms. Jennie PU
106 Dir Online Education/E-learning ... Mr. Robert KHAN

Jersey College (D)

546 US Highway 46, Teterboro NJ 07608
County: Bergen FICE Identification: 041341
Unit ID: 455196
Telephone: (201) 489-5836 Carnegie Class: Not Classified
FAX Number: (201) 525-0986 Calendar System: Quarter
URL: jerseycollege.edu
Established: 2003 Annual Undergrad Tuition & Fees: N/A
Enrollment: N/A Coed
Affiliation or Control: Proprietary IRS Status: Proprietary
Highest Offering: Associate Degree
Accreditation: COE, ADNUR

00 Chancellor ... Greg KARZHEVSKY
01 President ... Steven B. LITVACK

Kean University (E)

1000 Morris Avenue, Union NJ 07083-0411
County: Union FICE Identification: 002622
Unit ID: 185262
Telephone: (908) 737-5326 Carnegie Class: Masters/L
FAX Number: (908) 737-4636 Calendar System: Semester
URL: www.kean.edu
Established: 1855 Annual Undergrad Tuition & Fees (In-State): $12,348
Enrollment: 14,226 Coed
Affiliation or Control: State IRS Status: 501(c)3
Highest Offering: Doctorate
Accreditation: M, ART, CAATE, CACREP, CAEP, CAEPN, CIDA, MUS, NUR, OT, PSPSY, PTA, SP, SW, THEA

01 President ... Dr. Dawood FARAHI
10 VP Administration & Finance ... Mr. Andrew BRANNEN
05 Provost/VP Academic Affairs ... Dr. Jeffrey TONEY
20 Associate Provost ... Dr. Suzanne BOUSQUET
111 Acting VP Institutional Advancement ... Ms. Audrey KELLY
32 VP for Student Affairs ... Ms. Janice MURRAY-LAURY
26 VP University Relations ... Ms. Karen SMITH
100 Chief of Staff ... Ms. Audrey KELLY
45 Special Counsel & VP Planning ... Ms. Felice VAZQUEZ
12 Exec Vice Chancellor WKU ... Vacant
43 Assoc VP/Chief University Counsel ... Vacant
84 VP Enrollment Services ... Ms. Marsha MCCARTHY
12 Assoc VP/Dean Kean Ocean ... Dr. Stephen KUBOW
12 Assoc VPAA Kean Wenzhou ... Vacant
20 Asst VP Academic Affairs ... Ms. Joy MOSKOVITZ
39 Asst VP Residential Stdnt Services ... Ms. Maximina RIVERA
18 Asst VP for Operations ... Vacant
08 Assoc VP University Library ... Mr. Paul CROFT
37 Asst VP Student Financial Services ... Mr. Faruque CHOWDHURY
58 Dean Nathan Weiss Grad Col ... Dr. Christine THORPE
53 Dean Col Education ... Dr. Anthony PITTMAN
79 Acting Dean Col Liberal Arts ... Dr. Jonathan MERCANTINI
50 Dean Col Business & Public Mgt ... Vacant
81 Dean Col Nat & Appl Hlth Sci ... Dr. George CHANG
48 Dean Michael Graves Col ... Dr. David MOHNEY
106 Assoc Dean Online Learning ... Mr. Corey VIGDOR
15 Dir Human Resources ... Ms. Jennifer PETERS
108 Assoc Dir Accredit & Assessment ... Mrs. Agata WOLFE
09 Dir Institutional Research ... Dr. Shiji SHEN
07 Dir of Admissions ... Mr. Carlos NAZARIO
13 Dir Office for Computer/Inform Svcs ... Mr. Anthony SANTORA
114 Director Budget ... Mrs. Alyce FRANKLIN-OWENS
21 Dir General Accounting ... Mr. Joseph ANTONOWICZ
37 Dir Financial Aid ... Ms. Sherrell WATSON-HALL
06 Registrar ... Vacant
25 Dir Research & Sponsored Pgms ... Ms. Susan GANNON
27 Dir University Relations ... Ms. Margaret MCCORRY
84 Exec Dir Enroll Mgmt Operations ... Mr. Chad AUSTEIN
96 Dir for Purchasing ... Vacant
38 Dir Counseling & Disability Svcs ... Mr. Vincent KIEFNER
65 Director for Sustainability ... Dr. Feng QI
104 Dir Center International Studies ... Mrs. Jessica BARZILAY
41 Dir for Athletics ... Mr. Jack MCKIERNAN
35 Dir Ctr for Student Lead & Svcs ... Mr. Scott SNOWDEN
19 Dir of Campus Police ... Mr. Mark FARSI
23 Dir for Health Services ... Ms. Robin MANSFIELD
88 Dir Veterans Student Services ... Mr. Vito ZAJDA
22 Dir Affirmative Action ... Dr. Charlie WILLIAMS
42 Chaplain for Campus Ministry ... Ms. Miranda ROLDAN

Mercer County Community College (F)

1200 Old Trenton Road, PO Box 17202,
West Windsor NJ 08550
County: Mercer FICE Identification: 004740
Unit ID: 185509
Telephone: (609) 586-4800 Carnegie Class: Assoc/MT-VT-High Trad
FAX Number: (609) 570-3870 Calendar System: Semester
URL: www.mccc.edu
Established: 1966 Annual Undergrad Tuition & Fees (In-District): $4,206
Enrollment: 7,630 Coed
Affiliation or Control: State/Local IRS Status: 501(c)3
Highest Offering: Associate Degree
Accreditation: M, AAB, ADNUR, FUSER, MACTE, MLTAD, PTAA, RAD

01 President ... Dr. Jianping WANG
111 Vice President College Advancement ... Mr. Joseph CLAFFEY
05 Interim VP for Academic Affairs ... Dr. Robert SCHREYER
10 Vice President for Admin & Finance ... Dr. Mark HARRIS
32 Vice President for Student Affairs ... Dr. Diane CAMPBELL
76 Dean Health Professions ... Mr. Kevin DUFFY
49 Dean Liberal Arts ... Dr. Robert KLEINSCHMIDT
50 Dean Business/Technology and STEM ... Dr. Farah BENNANI
12 Dean of James Kerney Campus ... Dr. Tonia PERRY-CONLEY
13 Chief Information Officer ... Mr. Chuck KEELER
21 Exec Dir of Finance ... Mr. Brian MCCLOSKEY
26 Director Marketing ... Mr. Francis PAIXAO
15 Exec Dir Compliance/Human Resources ... Vacant
06 Registrar ... Ms. Shannon KRAUSE
37 Director of Financial Aid ... Mr. Jason TAYLOR
09 Senior Dir Institutional Research ... Ms. Nina MAY
18 Chief Facilities/Physical Plant ... Mr. Bryon MARSHALL
96 Director of Purchasing ... Mr. Stephen GREGOROWICZ
84 Asst Dean Strategic Enrollment Svcs ... Ms. Savita BAMBHROLIA
08 Director of Library Services ... Ms. Pam PRICE
101 Exec Asst to the President/Board ... Ms. Beth BROWER
51 Dean Division of Lifelong Learning ... Vacant
104 Coord of Global Education ... Prof. Andrea LYNCH
106 Dean Innov/Online Educ/Stdnt Suc ... Dr. Alexandra SALAS
25 Chief Contracts/Grants Admin ... Ms. Kami ABDALA
36 Director Transfer & Career Services ... Ms. Laurene JONES
41 Athletic Director ... Mr. John SIMONE
108 Dean Inst Effectiveness ... Dr. Elizabeth ANDERSON
19 Director Security/Safety ... Mr. Bryon MARSHALL
29 Director Alumni Affairs ... Ms. Ilyndove HEALY

Middlesex County College (A)

2600 Woodbridge Avenue, Edison NJ 08818-3050
County: Middlesex FICE Identification: 002615
Unit ID: 185536
Telephone: (732) 548-6000 Carnegie Class: Assoc/MT-VT-High Trad
FAX Number: (732) 494-8244 Calendar System: Semester
URL: www.middlesexcc.edu
Established: 1964 Annual Undergrad Tuition & Fees (In-District): $3,516
Enrollment: 11,381 Coed
Affiliation or Control: State/Local IRS Status: 501(c)3
Highest Offering: Associate Degree
Accreditation: M, ADNUR, DH, DIETT, MLTAD, RAD

01 President ... Dr. Mark MCCORMICK
05 Acting VP Acad & Student Affairs ... Dr. Jeffrey HERRON
10 Chief Financial Officer ... Vacant
111 VP for Institutional Advancement ... Ms. Michelle CAMPBELL
32 Dean Student Affairs ... Ms. Marla BRINSON
107 Dean Professional Studies ... Vacant
51 Dean Continuing Education ... Dr. Roseann BUCCIARELLI
18 Exec Director Facilities Management ... Mr. Donald DROST
13 Exec Director Information Tech ... Mr. Bradley MORTON
21 Controller ... Ms. Lori WILKIN
07 Director Admissions & Recruitment ... Ms. Lisa RODRIGUEZ-GREGORY
06 Registrar ... Mr. Richard COLE
37 Financial Aid Director ... Mr. Christopher RODRIGUEZ
26 Chief Public Relations Officer ... Mr. Thomas PETERSON
96 Director of Purchasing ... Mr. David FRICKE
09 Director of Institutional Research ... Ms. Meghan ALAI
25 Director Grants Development ... Ms. Yamillet FEBO-GOMEZ
29 Dir Development & Alumni Relations ... Ms. Veronica CLINTON
04 Administrative Asst to President ... Ms. Sally D'ALOISIO
15 Exec Director of Human Resources ... Vacant
08 Director Library ... Ms. Marilyn OCHOA

Monmouth University (B)

400 Cedar Avenue, West Long Branch NJ 07764-1898
County: Monmouth FICE Identification: 002616
Unit ID: 185572
Telephone: (732) 571-3400 Carnegie Class: Masters/L
FAX Number: (732) 571-3629 Calendar System: Semester
URL: www.monmouth.edu
Established: 1933 Annual Undergrad Tuition & Fees: $38,138
Enrollment: 6,340 Coed
Affiliation or Control: Independent Non-Profit IRS Status: 501(c)3
Highest Offering: Doctorate
Accreditation: M, #ARCPA, CACREP, CAEPN, NURSE, SP, SW

01 President ... Mr. Grey J. DIMENNA
04 Exec Asst to President & BOT ... Ms. Annette GOUGH
05 Provost/VP Academic Affairs ... Dr. Laura MORIARTY
58 Vice Provost for Graduate Studies ... Dr. Michael PALLADINO
20 Vice Provost for Global Educ ... Dr. Jon STAUFF
20 Vice Provost for Transform Lrng ... Dr. Kathryn KLOBY
20 Vice Provost for Plng & Dec Support ... Ms. Christine BENOL
20 Vice Provost for Acad & Fac Affs ... Dr. Nicolle PARSONS-POLLARD
06 Registrar ... Mrs. Lynn REYNOLDS
49 Dean Sch Humanities/Social Science ... Dr. Kenneth WOMACK
50 Dean Leon Hess Business Sch ... Dr. Donald MOLIVER
53 Dean School of Education ... Dr. John HENNING
81 Dean Sch of Science ... Dr. Steven BACHRACH
66 Dean School of Nursing/Health Stds ... Dr. Janet MAHONEY
70 Dean School of Social Work ... Dr. Robin MAMA
92 Dean Honors School ... Dr. Nancy MEZEY
08 University Librarian ... Mr. Kurt WAGNER
10 Vice President Finance ... Mr. William G. CRAIG
21 Assoc VP for Finance/Budgets ... Mr. Joseph PINGITORE
96 Director of Purchasing ... Mr. Mark MIRANDA
43 Vice President & General Counsel ... Mr. John J. CHRISTOPHER
117 Dir of Compliance/Risk Mgr ... Mr. Michael WUNSCH
22 Director Equity and Diversity ... Ms. Nina ANDERSON
11 Vice President Administrative Svcs ... Mrs. Patricia SWANNACK
18 Assoc VP Campus Plng/Construction ... Mr. Robert CORNERO
19 Director/Chief of Police ... Capt. William MCELRATH
15 Director of Human Resources ... Ms. Robyn SALVO
32 VP Student Life & Ldrshp Engagement ... Mrs. Mary Anne NAGY
35 Assoc VP for Student Life ... Mr. James PILLAR
35 Dir Student Activities/Student Ctr ... Ms. Amy BELLINA
111 Vice Pres University Advancement ... Mr. Jonathan MEER
26 Assoc VP Univ Mktg/Communications ... Ms. Tara PETERS
30 Assoc VP for Development ... Ms. Wendy PARSONS
84 Vice Pres Enrollment Management ... Dr. Robert MC CAIG
37 Assoc VP Enr Mgmt/Dir Fin Aid ... Ms. Claire ALASIO
07 Assoc VP for UG & GR Admission ... Ms. Lauren VENTO-CIFELLI
41 Vice Pres & Director of Athletics ... Dr. Marilyn MCNEIL
13 Vice Pres Information Management ... Dr. Edward CHRISTENSEN
97 Assoc Vice Prov/Acad Found/Gen Ed ... Dr. Judith NYE
09 Director of Institutional Research ... Mr. Bin CHENG
36 Assistant Dean for Career Services ... Mr. William HILL
86 Dir of Government & Community Rels ... Mr. Paul DEMENT
27 Chief Univ Editor/Dir Exec Comm ... Mr. Michael MAIDEN
25 Director of Grants & Contracts ... Mr. Tony LAZROE
39 Assoc Dir Res Life/Housing Ops ... Ms. Megan JONES
29 Exec Director Of Alumni Engagement ... Ms. Amanda KLAUS
38 Director Counseling & Psych Svcs ... Mr. Andrew LEE

Montclair State University (C)

1 Normal Avenue, Montclair NJ 07043-9987
County: Essex and Passaic FICE Identification: 002617
Unit ID: 185590
Telephone: (973) 655-4000 Carnegie Class: DU-Higher
FAX Number: N/A Calendar System: Semester
URL: www.montclair.edu
Established: 1908 Annual Undergrad Tuition & Fees (In-State): $12,790
Enrollment: 21,013 Coed
Affiliation or Control: State IRS Status: 501(c)3
Highest Offering: Doctorate
Accreditation: M, ART, AUD, CAATE, CACREP, CAEPN, DANCE, DIETD, DIETI, MUS, NURSE, PH, SP, @SW, THEA

01 President ... Dr. Susan A. COLE
05 Provost/Vice Pres Academic Affairs ... Dr. Willard P. GINGERICH
10 Vice Pres Finance & Treasurer ... Mr. Jon ROSENHEIN
32 Vice Pres Student Devel/Campus Life ... Dr. Karen L. PENNINGTON
18 Vice Pres Univ Facilities ... Mr. Shawn M. CONNOLLY
13 Vice Pres Info Technology ... Ms. Candace C. FLEMING
30 Vice Pres Development ... Ms. Colleen COPPLA
26 Vice Pres Communications/Marketing ... Dr. Joseph A. BRENNAN
15 Vice Pres Human Resources ... Mr. David VERNON
114 Exec Director Budget and Planning ... Mr. David JOSEPHSON
43 University Counsel ... Mr. Mark FLEMING
46 Vice Prov Research/Dean Grad School ... Dr. Scott HERNESS
89 Assoc Prov UG Ed/Dean Univ College ... Dr. David HOOD
79 Dean Col Humanities & Soc Sciences ... Dr. Peter KINGSTONE
81 Dean Col Science & Mathematics ... Dr. Lora BILLINGS
53 Dean Col Education & Human Svcs ... Dr. Tamara F. LUCAS
57 Dean College of the Arts ... Mr. Daniel A. GURSKIS
50 Dean School of Business ... Dr. Alan G. CANT
66 Dean School of Nursing ... Dr. Janice SMOLOWITZ
60 Dir School of Communication & Media ... Dr. Keith STRUDLER
64 Acting Dir School of Music ... Dr. Thomas MCCAULEY
08 Dean Library Services ... Dr. Judith L. HUNT
35 Dean of Students ... Ms. Margaree COLEMAN-CARTER
20 Assoc Provost Academic Affairs ... Dr. Kenneth SUMNER
20 Assoc Provost Academic Affairs ... Dr. Joanne F. COTE-BONANNO
21 Associate VP Finance ... Mr. Michael GALVIN
121 Assoc VP Student Acad Services ... Dr. Allyson STRAKER-BANKS
88 Assoc VP Campus Planning/Proj Mgmt ... Mr. Michael ZANKO
14 Assoc VP Enterprise Tech Services ... Mr. Jeff GIACOBBE
14 Assoc VP Enterprise Application Svc ... Ms. Donna SADLON
88 Assoc VP Project Management Office ... Mr. Samir BAKANE
110 Assoc VP Development ... Ms. Lisa HOYT
102 Assoc VP Foundation Adm & Finance ... Mr. Jeffrey CAMPO
88 Assoc University Counsel ... Ms. Maria ANDERSON
07 Director Undergraduate Admissions ... Mr. Jeffrey D. GANT
37 Director Financial Aid ... Mr. James T. ANDERSON
09 Director Institutional Research ... Vacant
06 University Registrar ... Ms. Leslie SUTTON-SMITH
19 Chief of Police ... Mr. Paul M. CELL
41 Athletic Director ... Mr. Robert CHESNEY
100 Chief of Staff ... Mr. Keith D. BARRACK
86 Director Government Relations ... Ms. Shantí PALMER
04 Exec Asst to President ... Ms. Karen M. AIELLO

New Brunswick Theological Seminary (D)

35 Seminary Place, New Brunswick NJ 08901
County: Middlesex FICE Identification: 002619
Unit ID: 185758
Telephone: (732) 247-5241 Carnegie Class: Spec-4-yr-Faith
FAX Number: (732) 249-5412 Calendar System: Semester
URL: www.nbts.edu
Established: 1784 Annual Graduate Tuition & Fees: N/A
Enrollment: 148 Coed
Affiliation or Control: Reformed Church In America IRS Status: 501(c)3
Highest Offering: Doctorate; No Undergraduates
Accreditation: @M, THEOL

01 President ... Dr. Micah L. MCCREARY
04 Assistant to the President ... Ms. Alycia BENCIVENGO
10 Exec VP Operations/CFO ... Mr. Kenneth TERMOTT
13 VP Communications/Technology ... Mr. Steve MANN
05 Dean of Academic Affairs ... Dr. Beth LANEEL TANNER
21 Manager/Bursar ... Ms. Tara HAMILL
30 Co-Director of Advancement ... Ms. Carol Lynn PATTERSON
30 Co-Director of Advancement ... Mr. Scott SHELDON
08 Int Director of the Library ... Mr. John COAKLEY
06 Registrar ... Ms. Yasha PEOPLE
32 Dean of Students/Title IX Coord ... Ms. Joan MARSHALL
108 Assoc Dean of Assessment ... Dr. Terry SMITH
07 Director of Admissions ... Dr. JerQuentin SUTTON
18 Facilities Manager ... Mr. Paul KUHN
36 Director of Field Education ... Dr. Faye TAYLOR

New Jersey City University (E)

2039 Kennedy Boulevard, Jersey City NJ 07305-1597
County: Hudson FICE Identification: 002613
Unit ID: 185129
Telephone: (201) 200-2000 Carnegie Class: Masters/L
FAX Number: (201) 200-2352 Calendar System: Semester
URL: www.njcu.edu
Established: 1927 Annual Undergrad Tuition & Fees (In-State): $12,052
Enrollment: 8,283 Coed
Affiliation or Control: State IRS Status: 501(c)3
Highest Offering: Doctorate
Accreditation: M, ACBSP, ART, CACREP, CAEP, MUS, NURSE

01 President ... Dr. Sue HENDERSON
05 Provost/Sr VP Academic Affairs ... Dr. Tamara JHASHI
11 Vice Pres & Chief Operating Officer ... Dr. Aaron ASKA
111 Vice Pres & Chief Strategy Officer ... Mr. Jason KROLL
100 Chief of Staff ... Dr. Guillermo DE VEYGA
10 Vice Pres & Chief Financial Officer ... Mr. James WHITE
32 Assoc Vice Pres for Student Affairs ... Ms. Jodi BAILEY
07 Assoc VP Admissions/Enrollment Mgmt ... Mr. Benjamin ROHDIN
26 Assoc VP of Communications ... Dr. Sherrie MADIA
15 Assoc VP for Human Resources ... Ms. Julia BASILE
20 Assoc Provost for Academic Affairs ... Dr. Nurdan S. DUZGOREN-AYDIN
20 Interim Assistant Provost ... Dr. Karen MORGAN
13 Assoc VP Information Technology ... Ms. Phyllis SZANI
102 Executive Director Foundation ... Mr. Kwi BRENNAN
88 Asst VP for Global Initiatives ... Ms. Tamara CUNNINGHAM
21 Controller ... Ms. Rosemary TAVARES
49 Dean Arts & Sciences ... Dr. Joao SEDYCIAS
53 Int Dean Education & Prof Studies ... Dr. Deborah WOO
50 Dean School of Business ... Dr. Bernard MCSHERRY
107 Dean Prof Educ & Lifelong Learning ... Dr. Michael EDMONDSON
108 AVP Institutional Effectiveness ... Dr. Sue GERBER
08 Director of Library Services ... Mr. Frederick SMITH
06 Registrar ... Mr. Navin SAIBOO
36 Director Career Planning/Placement ... Dr. Jennifer JONES
16 Director Talent Management ... Mr. Robert PIASKOWSKY
19 Assoc VP of Public Safety ... Dr. Ronald HURLEY
41 Assoc VP & Athletics Director ... Mr. Shawn TUCKER
22 Director Affirmative Action/EEO/AA ... Ms. Lisa NORCIA
29 Director of Donor/Alumni Relations ... Ms. Jane MCCLELLAN
38 Director Counseling & Wellness Svcs ... Dr. Abisola GALLAGHER
96 Assoc VP of Business Services ... Ms. Edie DELVECCHIO
43 University Counsel ... Mr. Alfred E. RAMEY, JR.
85 Director of International Programs ... Mr. Craig KATZ
37 Director of Financial Aid ... Mr. Robert MACAULEY
117 Budget Officer & Risk Manager ... Mr. Luis R. MORALES
39 Assistant Dean of Residence Life ... Ms. Jennifer K. LUCIANO
106 Director of Online Learning ... Dr. Michael KOSKINEN
25 Executive Director Grants Office ... Dr. Ashok VASEASHTA
30 Director NJCU Fund ... Mr. Richard A. RODNEY

New Jersey Institute of Technology (F)

University Heights, Newark NJ 07102-1982
County: Essex FICE Identification: 002621
Unit ID: 185828
Telephone: (973) 596-3000 Carnegie Class: DU-Highest
FAX Number: (973) 642-4380 Calendar System: Semester
URL: www.njit.edu
Established: 1881 Annual Undergrad Tuition & Fees (In-State): $17,338
Enrollment: 11,446 Coed
Affiliation or Control: State IRS Status: 501(c)3
Highest Offering: Doctorate
Accreditation: M, ART, CIDA

01 President ... Dr. Joel S. BLOOM
05 Provost and Senior Executive VP ... Dr. Fadi P. DEEK
10 Sr VP Finance/CFO ... Mr. Edward J. BISHOF, SR.
30 VP Development & Alumni Relations ... Dr. Kenneth ALEXO, JR.
46 Sr VP Tech & Bus Dev/Pres NJII ... Dr. Donald H. SEBASTIAN
88 VP for Real Estate & Capital Dev ... Mr. Andrew P. CHRIST
15 Interim VP Human Resources ... Ms. Holly C. STERN
43 General Counsel/VP Legal Affairs ... Ms. Holly C. STERN
20 V Provost Acad Affs & Student Svcs ... Dr. Basil BALTZIS
54 Dean Newark College of Engineering ... Dr. Moshe KAM
48 Dean Col Arch & Design ... Dr. Branko R. KOLAREVIC
49 Dean Col Sci/Liberal Arts ... Dr. Kevin D. BELFIELD
50 Dean School of Management ... Ms. Oya I. TUKEL
92 Dean A Dorman Honors College ... Dr. Louis I. HAMILTON
77 Dean Ying Wu College of Computing ... Dr. Craig GOTSMAN
46 Vice Provost for Research ... Dr. Atam P. DHAWAN
21 AVP Accounting & Treasury Mgmt ... Mr. Brian J. KIRKPATRICK
58 Vice Provost Graduate Studies ... Dr. Sotirios G. ZIAVRAS
13 Interim CIO ... Mr. Gregg M. CHOTTINER
45 Assoc VP for Business & Econ Devel ... Dr. Timothy V. FRANKLIN
84 AVP Enrollment Mgmt/Academic Svcs ... Dr. Wendy LIN-COOK
44 Assoc VP for Development ... Ms. Jacqueline G. RHODES
41 Asst VP/Director of Athletics ... Mr. Leonard I. KAPLAN
32 Dean of Students & Campus Life ... Dr. Marybeth BOGER
35 Assoc Dean of Students Cmty Dev ... Dr. Sharon E. MORGAN
29 Assoc VP for Constituent Relations ... Mr. Michael A. WALL
04 Sr Assistant to President ... Ms. Renee WATKINS
88 Exec Dir Ctr for Pre-College Pgms ... Dr. Jacqueline L. CUSACK
36 Exec Director Career Devel Svcs ... Mr. Gregory MASS
09 Exec Dir Ofc of Inst Effectiveness ... Dr. Charles R. BROOKS
08 University Librarian ... Ms. Ann D. HOANG
06 Registrar ... Dr. Jerry TROMBELLA
37 Dir Student Financial Aid Services ... Ms. Ivon NUNEZ
22 Director EOP ... Dr. Crystal SMITH
38 Dir Counseling & Psych Services ... Dr. Phyllis BOLLING
19 Chief of Police ... Mr. Joseph S. MARSWILLO
24 Dir Media & Technology Support Svcs ... Mr. Joseph BONCHI
85 Director Global Initiatives ... Ms. Cristiana A. KUNYCZKA
88 Sr Dir Events & Conference Svcs ... Ms. Lorie BROWN
96 Director Purchasing ... Ms. Eugenia REGENCIO
86 Chief External Affairs Officer ... Ms. Angela R. GARRETSON
105 Director Web Services ... Mr. Ersal ASLAM
07 Exec Dir of University Admissions ... Mr. Stephen M. ECK
106 Executive Director Digital Learning ... Mr. Blake HAGGERTY
25 Director Sponsored Research ... Dr. Eric D. HETHERINGTON
39 Director Resident Life ... Mr. Sean R. DOWD

Ocean County College (A)

PO Box 2001, Toms River NJ 08754-2001
County: Ocean FICE Identification: 002624
Unit ID: 185873
Telephone: (732) 255-0400 Carnegie Class: Assoc/HT-Mix Trad/Non
FAX Number: (732) 255-0444 Calendar System: Semester
URL: www.ocean.edu
Established: 1964 Annual Undergrad Tuition & Fees (In-District): $4,555
Enrollment: 8,377 Coed
Affiliation or Control: State/Local IRS Status: 501(c)3
Highest Offering: Associate Degree
Accreditation: M, ADNUR, EMT

01 President .... Dr. Jon H. LARSON
10 Exec VP of Finance & Administration .... Ms. Sara WINCHESTER
32 VP Student Affairs .... Dr. Gerald RACIOPPI
05 VP of Academic Affairs .... Dr. Joseph KONOPKA
15 Asst VP Human Resources .... Ms. Tracey DONALDSON
20 Asst VP for Academic Affairs .... Dr. Antoinette M. CLAY
18 Asst VP Facilities .... Mr. Matthew KENNEDY
04 Senior Aide to the President .... Vacant
57 Dean Language and the Arts .... Ms. Heidi SHERIDAN
81 Dean Math/Science & Tech .... Dr. Sylvia RIVIELLO
66 Dean of Nursing .... Ms. Teresa WALSH
83 Dean of Social Science .... Ms. Rosann BAR
88 Assoc VP of International Programs .... Dr. Maysa HAYWARD
102 Exec Dir OCC Foundation .... Mr. Kenneth MALAGIERE
103 Dir Cont Educ/Workforce Devel .... Ms. Kaitlin EVERETT
106 Interim Assoc VP of e-Learning .... Mr. Hatem AKL
106 Assistant Dean of e-Learning .. Ms. Christine WEBSTER-HANSEN
08 Director of Library Services .... Ms. Donna ROSINSKI-KAUS
13 Chief Information Officer .... Mr. James ROSS
37 Director of Financial Aid .... Ms. Yessica GARCIA-GUZMAN
06 Registrar .... Ms. Janine EMMA
121 Dir of Academic Advising Services .... Ms. Anna REGAN
19 Director of College Security .... Mr. John LOPEZ
26 Exec Director of College Relations .... Ms. Jan KIRSTEN
07 Director of Admissions .... Mr. A.J TRUMP
93 Director of EOF & OMS .... Ms. Laura RICKARDS
18 Director of Facilities .... Mr. James CALAMIA
41 Exec Dir of Athletics .... Ms. Ilene COHEN
45 Exec Dir of Institutional Planning .... Ms. Alexa BESHARA
21 Exec Dir of Strategic Projects .... Vacant
124 Dean of Academic Services .... Ms. Lori HARRIS-RANSOM
35 Director of Student Life .... Ms. Jennifer FAZIO
29 Alumni & Advancement Director .... Ms. Kimberly MALONEY
38 Dir Counseling/Student Development .... Dr. Kathryn PANDOLPHO
84 Director Enrollment Services .... Ms. Sheenah HARTIGAN
105 Asst Director Web Services .... Ms. Maureen CONLON
25 Manager of Grants .... Ms. Kayci CLAYTON
96 Director Purchasing & Payables .... Ms. Christine HEALEY
106 Dean of e-Learning .... Ms. Vivian LYNN

Passaic County Community College (B)

1 College Boulevard, Paterson NJ 07509-1179
County: Passaic FICE Identification: 009994
Unit ID: 186034
Telephone: (973) 684-6868 Carnegie Class: Assoc/MT-VT-High Trad
FAX Number: (973) 684-5843 Calendar System: Semester
URL: www.pccc.edu
Established: 1968 Annual Undergrad Tuition & Fees (In-District): $5,070
Enrollment: 6,975 Coed
Affiliation or Control: State/Local IRS Status: 501(c)3
Highest Offering: Associate Degree
Accreditation: M, ADNUR, CAHIIM, RAD

01 President .... Dr. Steven ROSE
05 Vice Pres Academic/Student Affairs .... Dr. Jacqueline KINEAVY
10 Vice Pres Finance/Adm Services .... Mr. Steven HARDY
12 Vice Pres Passaic Academic Center .... Ms. Patricia HARDY
13 Vice Pres Information Technology .... Mr. Robert MONDELLI
15 Associate Vice Pres Human Resources .... Mr. Jose FERNANDEZ
20 Dean Academic Affairs .... Dr. Bassel STASSIS
08 Associate Dean Learning Resources .... Mr. Greg FALLON
66 Assoc Dean Nurse Educ/Health Scis ... Ms. Donna STANKIEWICZ
121 Assoc Dean Academic Support Svc .... Mr. Peter HYNES
09 Dir Institutional Research .... Mr. Justin HULL
88 Ex Dir Cultural Affs/The Poetry Ctr .... Ms. Maria GILLAN
111 Vice President Inst Advancement .... Mr. Todd SORBER
84 Dean Enrollment Management .... Vacant
88 Dn Academic Initiative Policy Mgmt .... Ms. Betsy MARINACE
18 Assoc VP Facilities/Planning .... Mr. Brian EGAN
37 Director Financial Aid .... Ms. Linda GAYTON
06 Registrar .... Ms. Lorriane SMITH
19 Director Security .... Mr. Glenn BROWN
35 Director Student Activities .... Ms. Maria MARTE
41 Athletic Director .... Mr. Wayne MARTIN
07 Director of Admissions .... Ms. Stephanie DECKER
29 Director Alumni Relations .... Vacant
32 Chief Student Life Officer .... Dr. Sharon GOLDSTEIN
26 Chief Public Relations Officer .... Mr. Todd SORBER
96 Director of Purchasing .... Mr. Michael D'AGATI
101 Dir Board Affairs/Asst to President .... Ms. Evelyn DEFEIS
103 Actg Exec Dir Workforce/Career Dev .... Ms. Janet ALBRECHT

Pillar College (C)

60 Park Place, Suite 701, Newark NJ 07102
County: Essex FICE Identification: 036663
Unit ID: 440794
Telephone: (973) 803-5000 Carnegie Class: Spec-4-yr-Faith
FAX Number: (973) 242-3282 Calendar System: Semester
URL: www.pillar.edu
Established: 1908 Annual Undergrad Tuition & Fees: $21,700
Enrollment: 543 Coed
Affiliation or Control: Other IRS Status: 501(c)3
Highest Offering: Master's
Accreditation: M, BI

01 President .... Dr. David E. SCHROEDER
30 VP Business Development/Operations .... Mr. Kelvin THOMAS
05 VP Academic Affairs/Dean of College .... Dr. Mark HARDEN
11 Chf Operating Ofcr/Exec Vice Pres .... Mr. Rupert A. HAYLES, JR.
32 VP Student Engagement .... Ms. Amy HUBER
10 Vice Pres Business/Finance .... Ms. Julia PEREZ
111 VP Institutional Outreach .... Ms. Keyla PAVIA
104 VP International Program Admin .... Ms. Linda SCHMITT
88 VP Strategic Alliances .... Dr. Wayne R. DYER
58 Vice Pres MBA Development .... Dr. Ralph GRANT
20 Assoc Vice Pres Academic Affairs .... Mrs. Amy HUBER
06 Registrar .... Mr. Brian SCHROEDER
37 Assistant Director of Financial Aid .... Ms. Eboni CRAWFORD
07 Director of Admissions .... Mr. Dominic DIGIOACCHINO
08 Director of Library .... Ms. Lorraine HODGES
26 Director of Marketing .... Mr. Kelvin THOMAS
110 Director of Advancement .... Ms. Cathy PROCTOR
42 Coordinator of Spiritual Formation .... Mr. Nishanth THOMAS

Princeton Theological Seminary (D)

PO Box 821, 64 Mercer Street, Princeton NJ 08542-0803
County: Mercer FICE Identification: 002626
Unit ID: 186122
Telephone: (609) 497-7990 Carnegie Class: Spec-4-yr-Faith
FAX Number: (609) 924-2973 Calendar System: Semester
URL: www.ptsem.edu
Established: 1812 Annual Graduate Tuition & Fees: N/A
Enrollment: 502 Coed
Affiliation or Control: Presbyterian Church (U.S.A.) IRS Status: 501(c)3
Highest Offering: Doctorate; No Undergraduates
Accreditation: M, THEOL

01 President .... Dr. M. Craig BARNES
03 Executive Vice President .... Dr. Shane A. BERG
10 SVP/Chief Financial Ofcr/Treasurer .... Mr. John W. GILMORE
111 VP for Advancement .... Ms. Jaime ZAMPARELLI
11 VP of Operations .... Mr. Kurt A. GABBARD
26 VP for External Relations .... Ms. Anne WHITAKER STEWART
05 Dean and VP of Academic Affairs .... Dr. Jacqueline E. LAPSLEY
32 Dean Student Life & VP Stdnt Rels .... Rev. John E. WHITE
20 Senior Assoc Academic Dean .... Dr. Shawn OLIVER
35 Assoc Dean Stdnt Life/Dir Sr Plcmnt .. RevDr. Catherine C. DAVIS
51 Assoc Dean of Continuing Educ .... Rev. Dayle G. ROUNDS
06 Registrar .... Ms. Brenda D. WILLIAMS
84 Director of Enrollment Management .... Mr. Matthew R. SPINA
08 Managing Dir of the Library .... Ms. Evelyn FRANGAKIS
110 Assoc VP for Advancement .... Rev. J. Thomas KORT
15 Director of Human Resources .... Ms. Barbara MECCIA
13 Director of Information Tech/CIO .... Mr. Jeffrey SIEBEN
18 Director of Facilities/Construction .... Mr. German MARTINEZ
88 Director of Campus Relations .... Rev. Joicy BECKER-RICHARDS
39 Director of Housing/Auxiliary Svcs .... Mr. Stephen CARDONE
20 Assoc Dean for Academic Admin .... Dr. Rose Ellen DUNN
38 Director of Student Counseling .... Rev. Nancy L. SCHONGALLA-BOWMAN
42 Minister of the Chapel .... Rev. Janice S. AMMON
28 Assoc Dean of Inst Diversity .... Rev. Victor ALOYO, JR.
04 Deputy to the President .... Ms. Catherine AHMAD
37 Assoc Director Financial Aid .... Mr. Michael D. LIVIO
44 Director of Annual Giving .... Ms. Cheryl ALI
44 Director of Planned Giving .... Vacant
29 Director of Alumni Relations .... Rev. Ann-Henley SAUNDERS

Princeton University (E)

Princeton NJ 08544-1098
County: Mercer FICE Identification: 002627
Unit ID: 186131
Telephone: (609) 258-3000 Carnegie Class: DU-Highest
FAX Number: N/A Calendar System: Semester
URL: www.princeton.edu
Established: 1746 Annual Undergrad Tuition & Fees: $50,340
Enrollment: 8,273 Coed
Affiliation or Control: Independent Non-Profit IRS Status: 501(c)3
Highest Offering: Doctorate
Accreditation: M, CAEPT

01 President .... Cristopher L. EISGRUBER
03 Executive Vice President .... Treby WILLIAMS
05 Provost .... Deborah PRENTICE
04 Vice President & Secretary .... Hilary PARKER
10 Vice Pres for Finance & Treasurer .... Jim MATTEO
111 Vice President for Advancement .... Kevin B. HEANEY
26 Vice Pres Comm/Public Affairs .... Brent COLBURN
32 Vice President of Campus Life .... Rochelle CALHOUN
18 Vice President for Facilities .... KyuJung E. WHANG
13 Vice President Info Technology/CIO .... Jay DOMINICK
15 Vice President for Human Resources .... Lianne C. SULLIVAN-CROWLEY
109 VP for University Services .... Chad L. KLAUS
20 Vice Provost Academic/Budget Plng .... Richard MYERS
22 Vice Provost Inst Equity/Diversity .... Michelle MINTER
09 Vice Provost Institutional Research .... Jed MARSH
88 Vice Prov Space Programming/Plng .... Paul LAMARCHE
114 Budget Dir/Vice Provost Finance .... Steven GILL
116 Chief Audit & Compliance Officer .... Nilufer K. SHROFF
20 Actg Vice Provost Intl Initiatives .... Aly KASSAM-REMTULLA
29 Deputy Vice President Alumni Affs .... Margaret M. MILLER
44 Exec Director Annual Giving .... Sue WALSH
88 AVP Facilities Design/Construction .... Anne ST. MAURO
88 Assoc Vice Pres University Services .... Andrew KANE
46 Chair Univ Rsrch Bd/Dean Research .... Pablo DEBENEDETTI
43 General Counsel .... Ramona E. ROMERO
88 President PRINCO .... Andrew K. GOLDEN
58 Dean of the Graduate School .... Sarah-Jane LESLIE
88 Dean of the Faculty .... Sanjeev KULKARNI
49 Dean of the College .... Jill S. DOLAN
54 Dean of School of Engineering .... Emily CARTER
82 Dean of WW Sch of Public/Intl Affs .... Cecilia ROUSE
48 Dean of School of Architecture .... Monica PONCE DE LEON
42 Dean of Religious Life .... Alison BODEN
35 Dean of Undergraduate Students .... Kathleen DEIGNAN
07 Dean of Admission .... Karen RICHARDSON
17 Exec Director Health Services .... John KOLLIGIAN
08 University Librarian .... Anne JARVIS
06 Registrar .... Polly WINFREY GRIFFIN
37 Dir Undergraduate Financial Aid .... Robin A. MOSCATO
86 Director Government Affairs .... Joyce A. RECHTSCHAFFEN
31 Dir Community & Regional Affairs .... Kristin APPELGET
41 Director of Athletics .... Mollie D. MARCOUX
96 Director of Purchasing .... Donald E. WESTON, JR.
38 Dir of Counseling & Psych Services .... Anita MCLEAN
16 Director Human Resources .... Claire JACOBS ELSON
85 Director Davis International Center .... Jackie LEIGHTON
90 Assoc CIO/Dir Academic Services OIT .... Serge J. GOLDSTEIN
14 Assoc CIO/Dir Support Services OIT .... Steven M. SATHER
91 Dir Enterprise Infrastructure OIT .... Donna E. TATRO
30 AVP for Development .... Kerstin LARSEN
104 Sr Assoc Dean for Intl Pgms .... Karen KRAHULIK
39 Director Housing .... Andrew KANE
19 Executive Director Public Safety .... Paul OMINSKY
36 Director Student Placement .... Kimberly BETZ

Rabbi Jacob Joseph School (F)

1 Plainfield Avenue, Edison NJ 08817-4494
County: Middlesex FICE Identification: 030775
Unit ID: 384421
Telephone: (732) 985-6533 Carnegie Class: Spec-4-yr-Faith
FAX Number: (732) 985-6553 Calendar System: Semester
Established: 1982 Annual Undergrad Tuition & Fees: $11,900
Enrollment: 86 Male
Affiliation or Control: Independent Non-Profit IRS Status: 501(c)3
Highest Offering: Baccalaureate
Accreditation: RABN

01 President .... Dr. Marvin SCHICK
03 Rosh Yeshiva .... Rabbi Yaakov BUSEL
05 Rosh Yeshiva .... Rabbi Joseph EICHENSTEIN
37 Financial Aid Director .... Rabbi Yitzchok WEINTRAUB

Rabbinical College of America (G)

226 Sussex Avenue, Morristown NJ 07960-3600
County: Morris FICE Identification: 008609
Unit ID: 186186
Telephone: (973) 267-9404 Carnegie Class: Spec-4-yr-Faith
FAX Number: (973) 553-6957 Calendar System: Trimester
URL: www.rca.edu
Established: 1956 Annual Undergrad Tuition & Fees: $11,500
Enrollment: 227 Male
Affiliation or Control: Independent Non-Profit IRS Status: 501(c)3
Highest Offering: Baccalaureate
Accreditation: RABN

01 Dean .... Rabbi Moshe HERSON
04 Admin Assistant to the Dean .... Rabbi Mendy HERSON
26 Public Relations Officer .... Mrs. Chana TUNK
06 Registrar .... Mrs. Shoshana SOLOMON
88 Director New Direction Program .... Rabbi Zalman DUBINSKY
10 Chief Business Officer .... Vacant
37 Director Student Financial Aid .... Rabbi Yisroel GOLDBERG
08 Chief Librarian .... Rabbi Sholom SPALTER
51 Dir Continuing Educ/Alumni Rels .... Rabbi Boruch HECHT
88 Director Semicha Program .... Rabbi Chaim SCHAPIRO
18 Director Building and Grounds .... Rabbi Hershel LIPSKIER

Ramapo College of New Jersey (H)

505 Ramapo Valley Road, Mahwah NJ 07430-1680
County: Bergen FICE Identification: 009344
Unit ID: 186201
Telephone: (201) 684-7500 Carnegie Class: Masters/M
FAX Number: (201) 684-7508 Calendar System: Semester
URL: www.ramapo.edu
Established: 1969 Annual Undergrad Tuition & Fees (In-State): $14,374
Enrollment: 6,120 Coed
Affiliation or Control: State IRS Status: 501(c)3
Highest Offering: Master's
Accreditation: M, CAEPT, NUR, SW

01 President .... Dr. Peter P. MERCER
05 Provost/VP Academic Affairs .... Dr. Stefan BECKER
10 VP Admin & Fin/Chief of Operations . Ms. Kirsten LOEWRIGKEIT
43 VP and General Counsel .... Mr. Michael A. TRIPODI

111 VP Inst Advance/Dir Found/Chief Dev .... Ms. Cathleen DAVEY
84 Assoc VP of Enrollment Mgmt .... Mr. Christopher ROMANO
45 Chief Planning Officer .... Dr. Dorothy ECHOLS TOBE
100 Chief of Staff/Board Liaison .... Dr. Brittany A. WILLIAMS-GOLDSTEIN
116 Director of Internal Audit .... Ms. Patricia CHAVEZ
20 Vice Prov Curriculum & Assessment .... Dr. Susan GAULDEN
45 Director of Capital Planning .... Mr. Daniel ROCHE
13 Interim Chief Information Officer .... Mr. Robert DOSTER
86 Government Relations Officer .... Mr. Patrick W. O'CONNOR
105 Asst VP Mktg/Comm & Web Admin .... Ms. Melissa HORVATH-PLYMAN
08 College Librarian/Dean .... Vacant
06 Interim Registrar .... Ms. Fernanda PAPALIA
07 Director of Admissions .... Mr. Peter RICE
37 Director of Financial Aid .... Mr. F. Shawn O'NEILL
21 Controller .... Ms. Colleen O'KEEFE
15 Asst VP of HR & Benefits .... Ms. Viriginia GALDIERI
78 Dir Exper Learning/Career Svcs .... Ms. Beth RICCA
32 Dean of Students .... Ms. Melissa VAN DER WALL
41 Director of Athletics .... Mr. Harold CROCKER
18 Director of Facilities .... Mr. Michael CUNNINGHAM
19 Director Public Safety .... Mr. Vincent MARKOWSKI
88 Director Educ Opportunity Program .... Ms. Barbara HARMON-FRANCIS
50 Dean Anisfield School of Business .... Dr. Edward PETKUS
82 Interim Dean Salameno Sch Hum/Glob .... Dr. Susan HANGEN
57 Interim Dean Sch of Contemp Arts .... Mr. Peter CAMPBELL
83 Dean Sch Soc Science & Human Svc .... Dr. Aaron S. LORENZ
81 Dean Sch Theoretical/Applied Sci .... Dr. Edward SAIFF
53 Asst Dean for Teacher Education .... Dr. Brian CHINNI
38 Director Ctr for Health/Counseling .... Dr. Judith GREEN
29 Dir Alumni Relations .... Ms. Joanne FAVATA
04 Executive Assistant to President .... Ms. Sara GAZZILLO
23 Coordinator Health Services .... Ms. Debbie LUKACSKO
09 Director of Institutional Research .... Dr. Gurvinder KHANEJA
22 Dir Affirmative Action/EEO .... Vacant
40 Bookstore Manager .... Ms. Theresa KING
85 Dir Intl Education/Study Abroad .... Mr. Ben LEVY
36 Asst Dir Career Dev & Placement .... Ms. Debra STARK
96 Director of Purchasing .... Mr. Michael T. D'AGATI
103 Manager of Learning/Devel & Perf .... Mr. Roger JANS
25 Asst VP of Grants/Sponsor Programs .... Ms. Angela CRISTINI
28 Chief Diversity & Equity Officer .... Ms. Nicole MORGAN AGARD
35 Director of Student Conduct .... Ms. Kathleen HALLISSEY
121 Asst VP of Student Success .... Mr. Joseph CONNELL
114 Chief Budget Officer .... Ms. Beth WALKLEY
113 Director of Student Accounts .... Ms. Debra SCHULTES
118 Benefits Manager .... Ms. Valerie HUNTER
119 Network Administrator .... Ms. Joelisio DOSANJOS
39 Dir Resident Life/Student Housing .... Ms. Lisa GONSISKO

Raritan Valley Community College (A)

118 Lamington Road, Branchburg NJ 08876
County: Somerset — FICE Identification: 007731
Unit ID: 186645
Telephone: (908) 526-1200 — Carnegie Class: Assoc/MT-VT-High Trad
FAX Number: (908) 526-0253 — Calendar System: Semester
URL: www.raritanval.edu
Established: 1966 — Annual Undergrad Tuition & Fees (In-District): $4,612
Enrollment: 8,079 — Coed
Affiliation or Control: State/Local — IRS Status: 501(c)3
Highest Offering: Associate Degree
Accreditation: M, ADNUR, CAHIIM, MAC, OPD

01 President .... Dr. Michael MCDONOUGH
05 Provost & VP Academic Affairs .... Dr. Deborah PRESTON
10 Vice President Finance/Facilities .... Mr. John TROJAN
15 Exec Dir HR & Labor Relations .... Ms. Cheryl WALLACE
32 VP for Student Affairs & Outreach .... Ms. Jacki BELIN
49 Dean of Liberal & Fine Arts .... Dr. Patrice MARKS
81 Dean of STEM .... Dr. Sarah IMBRIGLIO
20 Dean Academic Support & Ed Partners .... Dr. Audrey LOERA
18 Exec Director Facilities/Grounds .... Mr. Brian O'ROURKE
38 Dir of Student Advising & Couns .... Mr. Greg DESANCTIS
24 Director Media Relations .... Ms. Donna STOLZER
88 Director Conference Services .... Ms. Karen VAUGHAN
72 Executive Director Inst Technology .... Mr. Michael E. MACHNIK
102 Executive Director Foundation .... Mr. Michael MARION
14 Exec Dir Technology Services .... Mr. Robert PESCINSKI
21 Controller/Exec Dir of Finance .... Ms. Violet J. WILLENSKY
57 Director of Theatre .... Mr. Alan C. LIDDELL
09 Dir of Inst Research/Assessment .... Ms. Sarah DONNELLY
88 Director of Planetarium .... Ms. Amie GALLAGHER
88 Director of Child Care Center .... Ms. Cathy GRIFFIN
37 Director of Financial Aid .... Mr. Lenny MESONAS
06 Registrar .... Mr. John WHEELER
96 Director of Purchasing .... Mr. Michael DEPINTO
35 Director of Student Life .... Mr. Russell BAREFOOT
36 Director Transfer/Career Services .... Mr. Paul MICHAUD
26 Executive Director Marketing .... Ms. Janet THOMPSON
84 Exec Dir Enrollment Management .... Ms. Carolyn WHITE
35 Dean of Student Affairs .... Mr. Jason FREDERICKS
103 Dir Workforce Training Ctr .... Ms. Joananne COFFARO
19 Director Security/Safety .... Mr. Robert SZKODNEY
41 Athletic Director .... Mr. George EVERSMANN

Rider University (B)

2083 Lawrenceville Road, Lawrenceville NJ 08648-3099
County: Mercer — FICE Identification: 002628
Unit ID: 186283
Telephone: (609) 896-5000 — Carnegie Class: Masters/L
FAX Number: (609) 895-5681 — Calendar System: Semester
URL: www.rider.edu
Established: 1865 — Annual Undergrad Tuition & Fees: $42,860
Enrollment: 5,073 — Coed
Affiliation or Control: Independent Non-Profit — IRS Status: 501(c)3
Highest Offering: Master's
Accreditation: M, CACREP, CAEPN, MUS, NURSE

01 President .... Dr. Gregory DELL'OMO
05 Provost/Vice Pres Academic Affairs .... Dr. DonnaJean A. FREDEEN
10 Vice President Finance/Treasurer .... Mr. James HARTMAN
111 Vice Pres University Advancement .... Ms. Karin KLIM
32 Vice President Student Affairs .... Dr. Leanna FENNEBERG
84 Vice Pres Enrollment Management .... Mr. Drew C. AROMANDO
13 Assoc VP Information Technologies .... Vacant
21 Associate Vice President/Controller .... Mr. Peter BIHUNIAK
09 Director Institutional Analysis .... Dr. Brad LITCHFIELD
18 VP Facilities/Auxiliary Services .... Mr. Michael F. RECA
45 VP Strategic Initiatives & Planning .... Ms. Debbie STASOLLA
26 Assoc VP for Univ Mktg/Comm .... Ms. Kristine A. BROWN
20 Associate Provost/Legal Counsel .... Dr. Matt STIEGLITZ
12 Dean Westminster Choir College .... Dr. Marshall ONOFRIO
07 Dean of Enrollment .... Ms. Susan C. CHRISTIAN
51 Dean College of Cont Studies .... Mr. Boris VILIC
49 Dean College Liberal Arts & Science .... Dr. Kelly BIDLE
53 Dean College of Educ & Human Svcs .... Dr. Sharon SHERMAN
50 Interim Dean College Business Admin .... Dr. Gene KUTCHER
06 Registrar .... Ms. Susan A. STEFANICK
08 Sr Assoc Provost & Dean Libraries .... Dr. Richard L. RICCARDI
15 VP HR/Affirmative Action .... Mr. Robert STOTO
19 Director of Public Safety .... Mr. James WALDON
29 Director of Alumni Relations .... Ms. Natalie M. POLLARD
41 Director of Athletics .... Mr. Donald P. HARNUM
37 Exec Dir Student Financial Svcs .... Mr. Jim CONLON
40 Manager College Store .... Ms. Deana REED
04 Director of Office of the President .... Vacant
36 Director of Career Placement .... Ms. Kim BARBERICH
28 Director Equity Diversity Inclusion .... Dr. Pamela PRUITT
35 AVP Student Affairs/Dean of Stdnts .... Ms. Cindy THREATT
38 Director of Counseling .... Dr. Nadine HEITZ
96 Director of Procurement .... Ms. Ann Marie MEAD

Rowan College at Burlington County (C)

900 College Circle, Mt. Laurel NJ 08054
County: Burlington — FICE Identification: 007730
Unit ID: 183877
Telephone: (856) 222-9311 — Carnegie Class: Assoc/HT-Mix Trad/Non
FAX Number: (609) 894-0183 — Calendar System: Semester
URL: www.rcbc.edu
Established: 1966 — Annual Undergrad Tuition & Fees (In-District): $4,725
Enrollment: 8,951 — Coed
Affiliation or Control: State/Local — IRS Status: 501(c)3
Highest Offering: Associate Degree
Accreditation: M, ADNUR, CAHIIM, DH, DMS, RAD

01 President .... Dr. Michael A. CIOCE
04 Exec Asst to the President .... Ms. Lynne Marie DEVERICKS
05 Sr Vice President/Provost .... Dr. David SPANG
03 Sr VP Admin and Operations .... Mr. Thomas J. CZERNIECKI
103 VP WDI and Lifelong Learning .... Ms. Anna PAYANZO COTTON
84 VP Enroll Mgmt and Student Success .... Dr. Karen ARCHAMBAULT
13 Chief Information Officer .... Mr. Mark MEARA
15 Exec Dir Budget/Purchasing/HR .... Mr. Harry METZINGER
11 Chief Operations Officer .... Mr. Matthew FARR
102 Exec Dir Foundation .... Vacant
26 Exec Dir Marketing/Communications .... Mr. Greg VOLPE
15 Asst Director of HR .... Ms. Michelle RUSSELL
49 Dean of Liberal Arts .... Dr. Donna VANDERGRIFT
81 Dean of STEM .... Dr. Edem TETTEH
76 Dean of Health Sciences .... Dr. Karen MONTALTO
106 Dean of Learning Resources .... Dr. Martin A. HOFFMAN, SR.
07 Dean of Enrollment Management .... Mr. Michael YAKUBOV
32 Dean of Student Success .... Dr. Catherine R. BRIGGS
06 Registrar .... Ms. LacyJane RYMAN-MESCAL
41 Director of Athletics .... Ms. Heather CONGER
88 Director of Culinary Arts .... Mr. James BRUDNICKI
88 Director of EOF Program .... Ms. Edith CORBIN
25 Director Educ Programs & Grants .... Dr. Nicole SCOTT
19 Director of Public Safety .... Mr. Andrew EATON

Rowan College of South Jersey (D)

1400 Tanyard Road, Sewell NJ 08080-9518
County: Gloucester — FICE Identification: 006901
Unit ID: 184791
Telephone: (856) 468-5000 — Carnegie Class: Assoc/HT-High Trad
FAX Number: N/A — Calendar System: 4/1/4
URL: www.rcsj
Established: 1966 — Annual Undergrad Tuition & Fees (In-District): $4,470
Enrollment: 7,158 — Coed
Affiliation or Control: State/Local — IRS Status: 501(c)3
Highest Offering: Associate Degree
Accreditation: M, ADNUR, DMS, NMT, PTAA

01 President .... Dr. Frederick KEATING
05 VP Academic Services .... Dr. Brenden RICKARDS
11 Vice President & COO .... Mr. Dominick BURZICHELLI
32 Vice President Student Svcs .... Ms. Judith ATKINSON
13 Vice President/CIO .... Mr. Josh R. PIDDINGTON
10 Exec Director Financial Services .... Mrs. Elizabeth HALL
15 Exec Director Human Resource .... Mrs. Marlene LOGLISCI
04 Sr Exec Assistant to the President .... Ms. Meg RESUE
28 Exec Dir Diversity and Equity .... Mrs. Almarie JONES
09 Dean Inst Research & Assessment .... Ms. Karen DURKIN
66 Dean Nursing & Allied Health .... Dr. Susan HALL
49 Dean Liberal Arts .... Dr. Paul RUFINO
81 Dean STEM .... Dr. Christina NASE
20 Dean Academic Compliance .... Dr. Danielle ZIMECKI-FENNIMORE
61 Dean Law and Justice .... Mr. Fred H. MADDEN
50 Dean Business Studies .... Ms. Patricia CLAGHORN
07 Exec Director Admissions/Registrar .... Ms. Sandra HOFFMAN
36 Director Career & Academic Planning .... Mr. John ORTIZ
35 Exec Director Student Engagement .... Ms. Samantha VAN KOOY
08 Director Library Services .... Mrs. Jane S. CROCKER
111 Exec Director Inst Advancement .... Ms. Randee DAVIDSON
19 Director Security/Safety .... Mr. Joseph GETSINGER
37 Exec Dir Financial Aid & Admission .... Mr. Michael CHANDO
96 Controller/Purchasing .... Mr. Mark ZORZI

Rowan University (E)

201 Mullica Hill Road, Glassboro NJ 08028-1700
County: Gloucester — FICE Identification: 002609
Unit ID: 184782
Telephone: (856) 256-4000 — Carnegie Class: DU-Higher
FAX Number: (856) 256-4929 — Calendar System: Semester
URL: www.rowan.edu
Established: 1923 — Annual Undergrad Tuition & Fees (In-State): $13,697
Enrollment: 18,484 — Coed
Affiliation or Control: State — IRS Status: 501(c)3
Highest Offering: Doctorate
Accreditation: M, ART, CAATE, CACREP, CAEPN, CLPSY, DIETC, MED, MUS, NURSE, OSTEO, THEA

01 President .... Dr. Ali HOUSHMAND
05 Provost .... Dr. Anthony LOWMAN
10 Senior Vice Pres of Finance/CFO .... Mr. Joseph F. SCULLY
111 Senior VP University Advancement .... Mr. John ZABINSKI
11 SVP Administration/Operations .... Mr. Robert ZAZZALI
32 Int VP Student Life/Dean Students .... Dr. Drew TINNIN
86 EVP Policy/External Relationships .... Mr. Steve WEINSTEIN
18 VP for Facilities & Operations .... Dr. Joseph CAMPBELL
44 VP Advance/Deputy Exec Dir Fndn .... Mr. Ronald J. TALLARIDA
20 VP Academic Affairs .... Dr. Roberta HARVEY
46 VP Research .... Dr. Beena SUKUMARAN
13 VP Information Resources/CIO .... Dr. Mira LALOVIC-HAND
26 VP for University Relations .... Dr. Joe CARDONA
84 SVP Strategic Enrollment Management .... Dr. Jeffrey HAND
19 Asst VP Public Safety/Emerg Mgmt .... Mr. Michael KANTNER
15 Asst VP Labor Relations .... Mr. Kenneth KUERZI
38 Sr Dir Counseling/Psych Services .... Dr. David RUBENSTEIN
91 Asst VP of EIS .... Mr. James HENDERSON
63 Dean of Cooper Medical School of RU .... Dr. Annette REBOLI
08 Assoc Provost Library Info Services .... Mr. Scott MUIR
50 Dean Rohrer College of Business .... Dr. Susan LEHRMAN
81 Dean College of Science/Mathematics .... Dr. Christian BOTEZ
53 Dean of Education .... Vacant
57 Dean of Performing Arts .... Dr. Rick DAMMERS
58 VP Global Learning & Partnerships .... Dr. Horacio SOSA
54 Interim Dean of Engineering .... Dr. Stephanie FARRELL
60 Dean Communication & Creative Arts .... Dr. Sanford M. TWEEDIE
83 Dean Humanities & Social Sciences .... Dr. Nawal H. AMMAR
88 Dean School of Osteopathic Medicine .... Dr. Thomas CAVALIERI
88 AVP Global Learning & Partnerships .... Dr. Lorraine RICCHEZZA
16 CHRO/VP Human Resources .... Ms. Theresa DRYE
22 SVP Diversity/Equity/Inclusion .... Dr. Monika SHEALEY
41 Director of Athletics .... Dr. John GIANNINI
88 Dir Distinguished Events/Spec Proj .... Vacant
07 Director of Admissions .... Dr. Albert BETTS
36 Asst Dir Ofc Career Advancement .... Dr. Alicia MONROE
96 Sr Dir Contracting & Procurement .... Ms. Christina BRASTETER
27 Asst VP University Relations .... Ms. Lori MARSHALL
105 Dir Strategic Planning/Management .... Dr. Rihab SAADEDDINE
85 Assoc Director International Center .... Ms. Ghina MAHMOUD
100 Chief of Staff/BOT Liaison .... Dr. Joanne M. CONNOR

Rowan University of South Jersey Cumberland Campus (F)

3322 College Drive, PO Box 1500,
Vineland NJ 08362-1500
Telephone: (856) 691-8600 — FICE Identification: 002601
Accreditation: &M, ADNUR, RAD

Rutgers University - Camden (G)

303 Cooper Street, Camden NJ 08102
County: Camden — FICE Identification: 004741
Unit ID: 186371
Telephone: (856) 225-6095 — Carnegie Class: DU-Higher
FAX Number: (856) 225-6495 — Calendar System: Semester
URL: www.camden.rutgers.edu
Established: 1926 — Annual Undergrad Tuition & Fees (In-State): $14,835
Enrollment: 6,853 — Coed
Affiliation or Control: State — IRS Status: 501(c)3
Highest Offering: Doctorate
Accreditation: &M, CAEPT, LAW, NURSE, PTA, SPAA

00 President Rutgers University .... Dr. Robert BARCHI
02 Chancellor Rutgers Camden .... Ms. Phoebe A. HADDON
05 Exec Vice Chancellor and Provost .... Dr. Michael PALIS
11 Sr Vice Chancellor Admin & Finance .... Mr. Larry GAINES

32 Vice Chancellor Student Affairs ... Ms. Mary Beth DAISEY
111 Vice Chancellor Advancement ... Mr. Philip T. ELLMORE
20 Vice Chancellor Student Acad Succ ... Dr. Jason RIVERA
84 Vice Chancellor Enroll Mgmt ... Dr. Craig WESTMAN
26 Assoc Chancellor for Ext Relations ... Mr. Michael J. SEPANIC
31 Assoc Chancellor Civic Engage ... Ms. Nyemma WATSON
121 Asst Chancellor Student Success ... Dr. Marsha BESONG
46 Assoc Provost Research ... Dr. Benedetto PICCOLI
06 Assoc Registrar ... Ms. Diana KEOUGH
61 Co-Dean Rutgers Law School ... Mr. David LOPEZ
61 Co-Dean Rutgers Law School ... Ms. Kimberly MUTCHERSON
35 Dean of Students ... Mr. Thomas J. DIVALERIO
50 Dean School of Business ... Dr. Jaishankar GANESH
49 Dean Fac Arts & Sciences ... Dr. Howard MARCHITELLO
66 Dean School of Nursing ... Dr. Donna NICKITAS
85 Assoc Dean International Students ... Ms. Elizabeth A. ATKINS
58 Assoc Dean Grad School ... Dr. Michelle MELOY
39 Assoc Dean Housing and Res Life ... Ms. Allison WISNIEWSKI
36 Asst Dean Career Center ... Ms. Cheryl A. HALLMAN
37 Exec Director Financial Aid ... Ms. Danielle BARBEE
18 Exec Director Facilities ... Mr. Christopher PYE
30 Sr Director Development ... Ms. Kate BRENNAN
110 Director of Development ... Ms. Akua ASIAMAH-ANDRADE
53 Director MA Teaching Program ... Dr. Sara M. BECKER
94 Director Gender Studies ... Dr. Gail A. CAPUTO
41 Director Athletics & Recreation ... Mr. Jeffrey L. DEAN
88 Director Economic Development ... Mr. Gregory GAMBLE
08 Director Paul Robeson Library ... Ms. Regina KOURY
92 Director Honors College ... Dr. Timothy MARTIN
25 Director Sponsored Research ... Ms. Cammie MORRISON
29 Director Alumni Relations ... Mr. Scott D. OWENS
07 Director Enrollment Communications ... Ms. Yosmeriz ROMAN
10 Director Finance and Administration ... Ms. Rosa M. RIVERA
13 Director Information Technology ... Mr. Thomas J. RYAN
09 Director Data Analytics ... Dr. Jason C. SCHWEITZER
104 Asst Director International Student ... Ms. Marissa AMOS
103 Asst Director Continuing Studies ... Ms. Dalynn KNIGGE
38 Staff Psychologist Health Services ... Dr. Rachel THUER
88 Chair Childhood Studies Dapartment ... Dr. Daniel COOK
82 Chair Political Science Department ... Dr. Maureen DONAGHY
57 Chair Fine Arts Department ... Dr. Kenneth ELLIOTT
88 Chair English Department ... Dr. Richard EPSTEIN
81 Acting Chair Mathematics Department ... Dr. Siqi FU
88 Chair Chemistry Department ... Dr. Catherine GRGICAK
83 Chair Psychology Department ... Dr. Naomi MARMORSTEIN
80 Chair Public Policy Department ... Dr. Lorraine MINNITE
54 Chair Physics ... Dr. Sean M. OÆMALLEY
77 Chair Computer Science Department ... Dr. Suneeta RAMASWAMI
88 Chair Foreign Languages Department ... Dr. James RUSHING
88 Chair Biology Department ... Dr. Daniel SHAIN
88 Chair Sociology/Anthro Department ... Dr. Jane SIEGEL
88 Chair History Department ... Dr. Lorrin THOMAS
73 Chair Philosophy and Religion Dept ... Dr. John WALL
88 Chair Economic Department ... Dr. Tetsuji YAMADA
19 Chief Campus Police ... Mr. Richard DINAN
23 Director Health Services ... Dr. Neuza SERRA
15 Sr Associate Human Resources ... Ms. Jennifer WILLIAMS
96 Sr Analyst University Procurement ... Mr. Christian AHA
100 Chief of Staff to the Chancellor ... Ms. Loree JONES

† Regional accreditation is carried under Rutgers the State University of New Jersey New Brunswick.

Rutgers University - New Brunswick (A)

83 Somerset Street, New Brunswick NJ 08901

County: Middlesex FICE Identification: 002629
Unit ID: 186380
Telephone: (848) 932-7821 Carnegie Class: DU-Highest
FAX Number: (732) 932-5532 Calendar System: Semester
URL: https://newbrunswick.rutgers.edu/
Established: 1766 Annual Undergrad Tuition & Fees (In-State): $14,974
Enrollment: 49,577 Coed
Affiliation or Control: State IRS Status: 501(c)3
Highest Offering: Doctorate
Accreditation: M, ART, CACREP, CAEPT, CEA, CLPSY, DANCE, DIETD, IPSY, LIB, LSAR, MUS, PCSAS, PH, PHAR, PLNG, SCPSY, SPAA, SW

00 President Rutgers University ... Dr. Robert BARCHI
02 Chancellor Rutgers New Brunswick ... Dr. Christopher MOLLOY
17 Chancellor Rutgers RBHS ... Dr. Brian J. STROM
05 Interim Provost New Brunswick ... Dr. Wanda BLANCHETT
76 Provost Biomedical and Health Sci ... Dr. Jeffrey CARSON
76 Provost Biomedical and Health Sci ... Dr. Patricia FITZGERALD-BOCARSLY
11 Exec Vice Chancellor Admin/Plng ... Dr. Felicia MCGINTY
10 Sr Vice Chancellor Finance & Admin ... Ms. Kathleen BRAMWELL
23 Sr Vice Chancellor Clinical Affairs ... Dr. Vicente H. GRACIAS
21 Vice Chancellor Finance ... Ms. Romayne BOTTI
111 Vice Chancellor Advancement ... Ms. Lavinia BOXILL
26 Vice Chancellor Comm & Marketing ... Ms. Jennifer HOLLINGSHEAD
88 Vice Chancellor Cancer Pgms RBHS ... Dr. Steven K. LIBUTTI
84 Vice Chancellor Enroll Management ... Mr. Courtney MCANUFF
32 Vice Chancellor Student Affairs ... Dr. Salvador MENA
46 Vice Chancellor Research/Innovation ... Dr. Prabhas V. MOGHE
88 Vice Chanc Translational Medicine ... Dr. Reynold PANETTIERI
88 Vice Chanc Interpretive Pgm RBHS ... Dr. Denise V. RODGERS
20 Vice Chancellor UG Academic Affairs ... Dr. Ben SIFUENTES-JÁUREGUI
27 Assoc Vice Chancellor Communication ... Mr. Zach HOSSEINI
88 CEO Univ Behavioral Health Care ... Dr. Frank GHINASSI
06 University Registrar ... Ms. Kelley BRENNAN-SOKOLOWSKI
47 Exec Dean Sch Enviro/Biological Sci ... Dr. Robert M. GOODMAN
49 Exec Dean SAS ... Dr. Peter MARCH
67 Dean Ernest Mario Sch Pharm ... Dr. Joseph BARONE
53 Int Dean Graduate School of Educ ... Dr. Clark A. CHINN
83 Dean Grad School Applied/Prof Psych ... Dr. Francine CONWAY
88 Dean Life Sciences SAS ... Dr. Lori COVEY
88 Dean Sch Mgmt Labor Relations ... Dr. Adrienne EATON
54 Dean School of Engineering ... Dr. Thomas N. FARRIS
52 Dean Rutgers School of Dental Med ... Dr. Cecile FELDMAN
92 Admn Dean New Brunswick Honors Col ... Dr. Paul GILMORE
69 Dean School of Public Health ... Dr. Perry N. HALKITIS
66 Dean School of Nursing ... Dr. William L. HOLZEMER
63 Dean New Jersey Medical School ... Dr. Robert JOHNSON
58 Dean School of Graduate Studies ... Dr. Jerome J. KUKOR
50 Dean Sch of Business Newark/NB ... Dr. Lei LEI
97 Dean Douglass Residential College ... Dr. Jacquelyn S. LITT
76 Dean School of Health Professions ... Dr. Gwendolyn M. MAHON
12 Dean College Avenue Campus ... Dr. Matthew K. MATSUDA
12 Dean Busch Campus ... Dr. Thomas PAPATHOMAS
70 Dean School of Social Work ... Dr. Cathryn C. POTTER
62 Dean Sch Communication & Info ... Dr. Jonathan POTTER
75 Dean University College Community ... Dr. Dona SCHNEIDER
57 Dean Mason Gross School of Art ... Dr. George B. STAUFFER
12 Dean Livingston Campus ... Dr. Lea P. STEWART
12 Dean Cook Campus ... Dr. Judith STORCH
80 Dean EJB Sch Plng/Public Policy ... Dr. Piyushimita THAKURIAH
58 Vice Dean School of Graduate Stds ... Dr. Kathleen SCOTTO
19 Exec Director Police Services/Chief ... Mr. Kenneth B. COP
36 Exec Director Career Services ... Mr. Rick HEARIN
39 Exec Director of Residence Life ... Mr. Dan MORRISON
88 Exec Director Center Org Dev & Lead ... Dr. Brent D. RUBEN
18 Exec Director Facilities ... Mr. Christopher PYE
105 Sr Director Office of Creative Svcs ... Ms. Joanne DUS-ZASTROW
109 Sr Director Student Centers ... Mr. William OÆBRIEN
31 Sr Director Community Affairs ... Ms. Melissa SELESKY
91 Univ Dir Enterprise Svcs Del ... Mr. Frank J. REDA
122 Dir Fraternity & Sorority Affairs ... Ms. JoAnn ARNHOLT
87 Director NB Summer Session ... Ms. Elizabeth BEASLEY
37 Director Financial Aid ... Mr. Brian BERRY
64 Director Music Education ... Dr. William BERZ
88 Dir Advanced Biotech/Medicine ... Dr. Martin J. BLASER
123 Director Graduate Admissions ... Ms. Linda J. COSTA
88 Director Inst Health/Health Policy ... Dr. XinQi DONG
13 Interim Director of IT & Info Pgm ... Dr. Michael DOYLE
91 Director Information Technology ... Ms. Keri BUDNOVITCH
09 Director Institutional Research ... Ms. Tina GRYCENKOV
41 Director Intercollegiate Athletics ... Mr. Patrick E. HOBBS
08 Director New Brunswick Libraries ... Ms. Dee MAGNONI
07 Director Applicant Services ... Ms. Phyllis MICKETTI
60 Director UG Studies Journalism ... Mr. Steven MILLER
25 Director Grant & Contract Acc ... Mr. Lamar OGLESBY
85 Dir International Student Services ... Ms. Urmi OTIV
106 Director Teaching with Technology ... Mr. William PAGAN
22 Director SAS Equal Opp Fund Program ... Dr. Michelle SHOSTACK
38 Interim Director of CAPS ... Dr. Steven SOHNLE
104 Director Study Abroad ... Mr. Dan WAITE
88 Dir Occupational Hlth Sciences Inst ... Dr. Helmut ZARBL
74 Program Director Animal Sciences ... Dr. Aparna M. ZAMA
102 Assoc Director Economic Development ... Ms. Lori DARS
103 Asst Director Continuing Studies ... Ms. Dalynn KNIGGE
15 Business Manager HR ... Ms. Carey MURRAY
96 Manager University Procurement ... Ms. Kathryn KUHNERT
65 Chair Dept of Ecol/Evol/Natural Res ... Dr. Henry JOHN-ALDER
73 Chair Dept of Religion ... Dr. Tia M. KOLBABA
82 Chair Political Sciences Dept ... Dr. Richard LAU
81 Chair Math Department ... Dr. Michael SAKS
94 Chair Dept Women's/Gender Studies ... Dr. Mary TRIGG
29 Sr Alumni Engagement Associate ... Mr. Elijah ROSENTHAL
28 Admin Coord Diversity/Inclusion ... Ms. Cynthia CHURCH
04 Assistant to the Chancellor ... Ms. Susan ENGLISH

Rutgers University - Newark (B)

123 Washington St., Newark NJ 07102

County: Essex FICE Identification: 002631
Unit ID: 186399
Telephone: (973) 353-5541 Carnegie Class: DU-Higher
FAX Number: (973) 353-1048 Calendar System: Semester
URL: https://www.newark.rutgers.edu/
Established: 1908 Annual Undergrad Tuition & Fees (In-State): $14,409
Enrollment: 12,768 Coed
Affiliation or Control: State IRS Status: 501(c)3
Highest Offering: Doctorate
Accreditation: &M, ANEST, CAEPT, IPSY, LAW, NURSE, SPAA, SW

00 President Rutgers University ... Dr. Robert BARCHI
02 Chancellor Rutgers Newark ... Dr. Nancy E. CANTOR
03 Exec Vice Chancellor ... Dr. Sherri-Ann P. BUTTERFIELD
05 Exec Vice Chancellor & Provost ... Dr. Jerome D. WILLIAMS
26 Sr Vice Chancellor Public Affairs ... Mr. Peter ENGLOT
10 Sr Vice Chancellor Finance/CFO ... Ms. Amber RANDOLPH
86 Vice Chancellor Extern & Govt Rels ... Dr. Marcia W. BROWN
20 Vice Chancellor Acad Pgms & Svcs ... Dr. John GUNKEL
30 Vice Chancellor for Development ... Dr. Irene O'BRIEN
46 Vice Chancellor Research ... Dr. Piotr PIOTROWIAK
32 Vice Chancellor for Student Affairs ... Dr. Corlisse THOMAS
45 Vice Chancellor Plng & Implement ... Dr. Bonita M. VEYSEY
84 AVC Enroll Svcs & Exp ... Dr. Bil LEIPOLD
07 Asst Chancellor Enrollment Mgmt ... Ms. LaToya BATTLE-BROWN
31 Asst Chancellor Comm Partner ... Dr. Diane HILL
114 Asst Prov for Budget Admin ... Dr. Mary TAMASCO
06 Registrar ... Ms. Marie DIAZ-TORRES
88 Dean School Criminal Justice ... Dr. Rod BRUNSON
58 Dean Graduate School Newark ... Dr. Kyle W. FARMBRY
69 Dean School of Public Health ... Dr. Perry N. HALKITIS
66 Dean School of Nursing ... Dr. William L. HOLZEMER
50 Dean Business Newark/New Bruns ... Dr. Lei LEI
61 Co-Dean Rutgers Law School ... Mr. David LOPEZ
61 Co-Dean Rutgers Law School ... Ms. Kimberly MUTCHERSON
80 Dean Sch Pub Aff & Admin ... Dr. Charles MENIFIELD
49 Acting Dean Arts & Science ... Dr. Denis PARE
70 Dean School of Social Work ... Dr. Cathryn C. POTTER
88 Sr Assoc Dean Faculty ... Dr. Eva GILOI
39 Assoc Dean Housing & Residence Life ... Dr. Angelita BONILLA
18 Exec Director Facilities ... Mr. Christopher PYE
21 Exec Dir Business & Financial Svcs ... Mr. Sanjana RIMAL
36 Exec Director Career Services ... Ms. Bernadette SO
85 Exec Director Glob Eng Exp Lrng ... Dr. Clayton WALTON
13 University Dir Enterprise Svcs Del ... Mr. Frank J. REDA
96 Director Procurement Admin ... Ms. Ida ANGELONE
08 Director Dana Library ... Ms. Consuella A. ASKEW
15 Director Human Resources ... Ms. Arleska CASTILLO
88 Director Express Newark ... Mr. Victor DAVSON
60 Director Journalism Program ... Ms. Robin GABY FISHER
41 Director of Athletics & Recreation ... Mr. Mark GRIFFIN
64 Director RU Chorus ... Mr. Brian HARLOW
19 Director Public Safety Newark ... Mr. Carmelo V. HUERTAS
88 Director of Global Affairs ... Dr. Gabriela KUETTING
90 Director Acad Technology Services ... Ms. Joy MCDONALD
37 Director Financial Aid ... Ms. Natalia MORISSEAU
25 Director Grant & Contract Acc ... Mr. Lamar OGLESBY
106 Director Teaching with Technology ... Mr. William PAGAN
88 Director Center for Metro Research ... Dr. Charles M. PAYNE
92 Director Honors College ... Dr. Brian PHILLIPS MURPHY
88 Director LGBTQ & Div Res Center ... Ms. Yoleidy ROSARIO
23 Director Health Services ... Dr. Sandra SAMUELS
94 Director Women's & Gender Studies ... Dr. Whitney STRUB
38 Director Student Counseling ... Dr. Anice THOMAS
104 Director Study Abroad ... Mr. Dan WAITE
29 Director Alumni Relations ... Ms. Gloria T. WALKER
87 Director Summer Session ... Ms. Amber WILLIAMS
27 Director Public Relations ... Ms. Kimberlee S. WILLIAMS
09 Research Project Manager ... Mr. Chengbo YIN
102 Assoc Director Economic Development ... Ms. Lori DARS
103 Asst Director Continuing Studies ... Ms. Dalynn KNIGGE
83 Chair Sociology Department ... Dr. Christopher DUNCAN
81 Chair Mathematics and Computer Sci ... Dr. Li GUO
82 Chair Political Science Department ... Dr. Jyl JOSEPHSON
88 Chair African American Studies ... Mr. John KEENE
53 Chair Urban Education Program ... Dr. Arthur B. POWELL
57 Chair Fine Arts Program ... Mr. Ian WATSON
91 Manager Information Technology ... Mr. David EDWARD
22 Program and Acad Coordinator EOF ... Ms. Devendra BENI
28 Admin Coordinator Diversity and Inc ... Ms. Cynthia CHURCH
04 Sr Exec Associate to Chancellor ... Ms. Carla HAILEY PENN

† Regional accreditation is carried under Rutgers the State University of New Jersey New Brunswick.

Rutgers New Jersey Medical School (C)

185 South Orange Avenue, Newark NJ 07103
Telephone: (973) 972-4538 FICE Identification: 002620
Accreditation: &M, MED

Rutgers - Robert Wood Johnson Medical School (D)

675 Hoes Lane West, Piscataway NJ 08854
Telephone: (732) 235-6300 FICE Identification: 024549
Accreditation: &M, CAMPEP, IPSY, MED, PAST

Rutgers School of Dental Medicine (E)

110 Bergen Street, Suite B812, Newark NJ 07103
Telephone: (973) 972-4440 FICE Identification: 024635
Accreditation: &M, DENT

Rutgers School of Health Professions (F)

65 Bergen Street, Room 149, Newark NJ 07107
Telephone: (973) 972-4276 FICE Identification: 020668
Accreditation: &M, ARCPA, CACREP, CAHIIM, CYTO, DIETC, DIETI, DMS, MT, NMT, OTA, PTA

Rutgers School of Nursing (G)

180 University Avenue, Newark NJ 07102
Telephone: (973) 353-5293 Identification: 666970
Accreditation: &M, MIDWF, NURSE

Rutgers School of Public Health (H)

683 Hoes Lane West, Piscataway NJ 08854
Telephone: (732) 235-9700 Identification: 666991
Accreditation: &M, PH

Saint Peter's University (I)

2641 Kennedy Boulevard, Jersey City NJ 07306-5997
County: Hudson FICE Identification: 002638
Unit ID: 186432
Telephone: (201) 761-6000 Carnegie Class: Masters/L
FAX Number: (201) 761-7801 Calendar System: Semester
URL: www.saintpeters.edu
Established: 1872 Annual Undergrad Tuition & Fees: $37,486

Enrollment: 3,524 Coed
Affiliation or Control: Roman Catholic IRS Status: 501(c)3
Highest Offering: Doctorate
Accreditation: M, CAEPT, IACBE, NURSE

01 President Dr. Eugene J. CORNACCHIA
45 Spec Asst to Pres for Inst Plng Dr. Virginia BENDER
100 Special Assistant to the President Dr. Eileen POIANI
04 Administrative Asst to President Ms. Dorene E. WILLIAMS
05 Provost/VP Academic Affairs Dr. Frederick BONATO
10 VP of Finance & Business Mr. Hector O. PAREDES
32 VP Stdnt Life & Development Mr. Anthony SKEVAKIS
42 Vice Pres for Mission & Ministry Fr. Rocco DANZI, SJ
84 VP Enrollment Mgmt & Marketing Ms. Elizabeth SULLIVAN
13 VP & Chief Information Officer Mr. Milos TOPIC
111 Vice President Advancement Ms. Leah LETO
07 Assoc VP and Dean of Admissions Vacant
20 Asst VP Academic Affairs/Assessment Dr. Mildred A. MIHLON
66 Dean of Nursing Dr. Lauren O'HARE
50 KPMG Dean School of Business Dr. Mary Kate NAATUS
53 Dean Caufield School of Education Dr. Joseph DORIA
49 Dean College of Arts & Sciences Dr. WeiDong ZHU
78 Exec Dir Career Engagement/Exp Lrng Ms. Laura PAKHMANOV
123 Exec Dir Admission Graduate Mr. Ben SCHOLZ
26 Exec Dir University Communications Ms. Sarah MALINOWSKI-FERRARY
37 Director of Student Fin Aid Ms. Jennifer RAGSDALE
08 Director of the Library Ms. Daisy DECOSTER
09 Director of Institutional Research Mr. Lamberto C. NIEVES
19 Director of Campus Safety Mr. Scott TORRE
15 Director of Human Resources Ms. Elena SERRA
29 Director Alumni Engagement Ms. Claudia POPE-BAYNE
44 Director of Annual Giving Mr. Scott DONOVAN
38 Dir of Counseling & Psyc Service Mr. Ronald BECKER
39 Interim Director of Residence Life Mr. Willie LEE
41 Director of Athletics Mr. Bryan FELT
42 Director of Campus Ministry Ms. Christine BOYLE
14 Director of Network Services Mr. Bert VABRE
51 Director of Center Global Learning Mr. Scott KELLER
18 Dir of Facility & Univ Services Ms. Anna DE PAULA
102 Dir Foundation/Corp & Govt Rels Mr. Emory EDWARDS
105 Dir of Web Strategies & Comm Mr. Kyle RIVERS
36 Director of Student Placement Ms. Laura PAKHMANOV
06 Registrar Ms. Kamla SINGH
43 General Counsel Mr. Eugene T. PAOLINO

Salem Community College (A)

460 Hollywood Avenue, Carneys Point NJ 08069-2799
County: Salem FICE Identification: 005461
Unit ID: 186469
Telephone: (856) 299-2100 Carnegie Class: Assoc/MT-VT-High Trad
FAX Number: (856) 351-2634 Calendar System: Semester
URL: www.salemcc.edu
Established: 1972 Annual Undergrad Tuition & Fees (In-District): $5,070
Enrollment: 916 Coed
Affiliation or Control: State/Local IRS Status: 501(c)3
Highest Offering: Associate Degree
Accreditation: M, ADNUR

01 President Dr. Michael GORMAN
05 Dean of Academic Affairs Mr. Kenneth ROBEL
10 Chief Financial/Business Ofcr Mr. Kevin KUTCHER
04 Admin Asst Office to the President Ms. Maria FANTINI
20 Assoc Dean of Academic Affairs Mrs. Maura CAVANAGH-DICK
84 Dean of Enrollment/Admissions Mr. Kevin CATALFAMO
06 Registrar Ms. Jill JAMES
108 Dir of Institutional Effectiveness Mr. Marc ROY
19 Director of Security/Safety Mr. John MORRISON
09 Dir of Inst Research & Planning Mr. Ronald BURKHARDT
30 Dir of Inst Advancement/Alumni Mr. William CLARK
37 Director of Financial Aid Mrs. Dana MOORE
66 Dir of Nursing/Allied Health Vacant
88 Director of Academic & Info Svcs Ms. Jennifer PIERCE
13 Director of Information Technology Mr. Larry MCKEE
102 Executive Director SCC Foundation Ms. Ceil SMITH
21 Manager of Finance Ms. Catherine PRIEST
88 Accounts Manager Ms. Maureen DOUGHERTY
07 Interim Manager of Admissions Mrs. Ashley MARKLEY
15 Manager Human Resources Ms. Barbara QUAILE
41 Athletic Director Mr. Bob BUNNELL

Seton Hall University (B)

400 S Orange Avenue, South Orange NJ 07079-2697
County: Essex FICE Identification: 002632
Unit ID: 186584
Telephone: (973) 761-9000 Carnegie Class: DU-Higher
FAX Number: N/A Calendar System: Semester
URL: www.shu.edu
Established: 1856 Annual Undergrad Tuition & Fees: $42,170
Enrollment: 9,801 Coed
Affiliation or Control: Roman Catholic IRS Status: 501(c)3
Highest Offering: Doctorate
Accreditation: M, ARCPA, CAATE, CAEP, CAEPN, COPSY, HSA, LAW, #MED, MFCD, NURSE, OT, PTA, SP, SPAA, SW, THEOL

01 President Dr. Joseph E. NYRE
05 Interim Provost and Executive VP Dr. Karen A. BOROFF
20 Senior Associate Provost Dr. Joan GUETTI
20 Associate Vice Provost Msgr. Robert COLEMAN
10 Vice Pres for Finance/CFO Mr. Stephen A. GRAHAM
11 EVP Operations & Chief of Staff Mr. Patrick G. LYONS
43 Vice President & General Counsel Ms. Catherine A. KIERNAN
111 Interim Vice Pres Univ Advancement Mr. Matthew BOROWICK
32 Int Vice Pres for Student Services Dr. Robin CUNNINGHAM
84 Sr Vice Pres for Enrollment Mgmt Dr. Alyssa MCCLOUD
42 Vice Pres for Mission & Ministry Msgr. C. Anthony ZICCARDI
15 Assoc Vice Pres Human Resources Mr. Michael SILVESTRO
29 Assoc VP Alumni/Engage/Philanthropy Mr. Anthony D. BELLUCCI
112 Sr Dir Principal Gifts/Gift Plng Mr. Joseph GUASCONI
26 Assoc VP Public Relations & Mktg Mr. Dan P. KALMANSON
18 Assoc VP for Facilities & Operation Mr. John SIGNORELLO
35 Assoc VP/Dean of Students Ms. Karen VAN NORMAN
45 Assoc Provost Dr. Gregory A. BURTON
88 Assoc Provost for Strategy/Finance Mr. Erik LILLQUIST
19 Asst VP Security Mr. Patrick LINFANTE
49 Dean of Arts & Sciences Dr. Peter SHOEMAKER
50 Dean School of Business Dr. Joyce A. STRAWSER
60 Dean Communication & the Arts Ms. Deirdre YATES
66 Dean of Nursing Dr. Marie FOLEY
53 Dean College Education Svcs Dr. Maureen GILLETTE
73 Rector/Dean School of Theology Msgr. Joseph R. REILLY
63 Dean School of Health & Med Science Dr. Brian SHULMAN
82 Dean Diplomacy/Intl Relations Dr. Andrea BARTOLI
63 Dean Medical School Dr. Bonita STANTON
61 Dean of Law School Ms. Kathleen BOOZANG
08 Dean of University Libraries Dr. John E. BUSCHMAN
51 Dean Cont Educ/Professional Studies Ms. Karen PASSARO
88 Assoc Dean/Director of EOP Dr. Majid WHITNEY
88 Director Upward Bound Ms. Shanetta S. LILLARD
21 Director of Business Affairs Mr. Peter TRUNK
13 Chief Information Officer Dr. Stephen LANDRY
28 Director Compliance & Risk Mgmt Ms. Lori A. BROWN
37 Director for Financial Aid Ms. Javonda ASANTE
39 Director of Housing/Residence Life Mr. Timothy MORAN
06 University Registrar Ms. Mary Ellen FARRELL
36 Director of the Career Center Ms. Reesa GREENWALD
41 Dir Athletics/Recreational Services Mr. Bryan FELT
18 Director of Facilities Engineering Mr. Leon VANDEMEULEBROEKE
38 Director of Counseling Dr. Dianne AGUERO-TROTTER
42 Director of Campus Ministry Rev. Colin KAY
88 Minister to Priest Community Msgr. Robert M. COLEMAN
09 Dir Plng Inst Research & Assessment Ms. Connie L. BEALE
07 Dir of Undergraduate Admissions Ms. Mary Clare CULLUM
96 Director of Procurement Mr. Martin E. KOELLER
23 Director Health Services Ms. Diane LYNCH
88 Director Core Curriculum Dr. Nancy ENRIGHT
102 Dir Foundation/Corporate Relations Mr. Steven SMITH
104 Director International Programs Ms. Maria BOUZAS
58 Director Graduate Affairs/Info Svcs Mr. Israel CHIA
88 Asst Provost for Academic Affairs Dr. Christopher CUCCIA
86 Director Government Relations Mr. Matthew BOROWICK

Stevens Institute of Technology (C)

Castle Point on Hudson, Hoboken NJ 07030-5991
County: Hudson FICE Identification: 002639
Unit ID: 186867
Telephone: (201) 216-5000 Carnegie Class: DU-Higher
FAX Number: (201) 216-8341 Calendar System: Semester
URL: www.stevens.edu
Established: 1870 Annual Undergrad Tuition & Fees: $52,202
Enrollment: 6,916 Coed
Affiliation or Control: Independent Non-Profit IRS Status: 501(c)3
Highest Offering: Doctorate
Accreditation: M

01 President Dr. Nariman FARVARDIN
04 Exec Assistant to the President Ms. Phyllis RUIZ
05 Provost/University Vice President Dr. Christophe PIERRE
30 Assoc Vice Pres for Development Ms. Dawn DA SILVA
10 CFO/VP for Finance/Treasurer Dr. Louis MAYER
84 VP Enrollment Mgt/Student Affairs Ms. Marybeth MURPHY
15 Vice President Human Resources Mr. Warren PETTY
43 Vice President General Counsel Ms. Kathy L. SCHULZ
13 VP for Information Technology & CIO Mr. David DODD
26 VP Communications & Marketing Mr. Edward STUKANE
18 VP for Facilities/Campus Operations Mr. Robert MAFFIA
32 Assistant VP Student Affairs Ms. Sara KLEIN
21 AVP for Financial Planning/Budgets Ms. Theresa PASCOE
35 Dean of Students Mr. Kenneth NILSEN
39 Dean for Residence Life Ms. Trina BALLANTYNE
20 Assoc Dean Undergraduate Academics Dr. Erol CESMEBASI
29 AVP Alumni Engagement & ED/SAA Mr. Matthew GWIN
36 Exec Director of Career Services Ms. Lynn INSLEY
19 Chief & Director of Campus Police Mr. Timothy GRIFFIN
41 Athletic Director Mr. Russell ROGERS
85 Assoc Dean/Intl Student & Scholars Vacant
38 Director of Student Counseling Dr. Eric D. ROSE
25 Exec Director Sponsored Research Ms. Barbara DEHAVEN
54 Dean School of Engr & Science Dr. Jean ZU
50 Dean School of Business Dr. Gregory PRASTACOS
49 Dean College of Arts & Letters Dr. Kelland THOMAS
77 Dean School Systems/Enterprise Dr. Yehia MASSOUD
09 Director of Institutional Research Ms. Minghui WANG
100 VP for Gov/Cmty Rels/Chief of Staff Ms. Beth MCGRATH
28 Exec Director Diversity & Inclusion Ms. Susan METZ
58 Vice Provost for Graduate Education Dr. Constantin CHASSAPIS
46 Vice Provost for Research Dr. Dilhan KALYON
06 Registrar Ms. Anna-Lize HARRIS
08 Director of Library & Info Svcs Ms. Linda BENINGHOVE
104 Director International Programs Ms. Susan RACHOUH
106 Assistant Dean WebCampus Mr. Robert ZOTTI
37 AVP for Financial Aid/UG Admissions Ms. Susan GROSS
96 Director of Procurement Mr. Brian SEABOLD
108 Asst Director for Assessment Dr. Jie ZHANG

Stockton University (D)

101 Vera King Farris Drive, Galloway NJ 08205-9441
County: Atlantic FICE Identification: 009345
Unit ID: 186876
Telephone: (609) 652-1776 Carnegie Class: Masters/L
FAX Number: N/A Calendar System: Semester
URL: www.stockton.edu
Established: 1969 Annual Undergrad Tuition & Fees (In-State): $13,739
Enrollment: 9,216 Coed
Affiliation or Control: State IRS Status: 501(c)3
Highest Offering: Doctorate
Accreditation: M, CAEPT, NURSE, OT, PTA, SP, SW

01 President Dr. Harvey KESSELMAN
05 Provost & VP for Academic Affairs Dr. Lori VERMEULEN
100 Exec VP and Chief of Staff Dr. Susan C. DAVENPORT
10 Vice Pres Administration & Finance Mr. Michael ANGULO
32 Vice President Student Affairs Dr. Christopher C. CATCHING
20 Assoc Provost Programs & Planning Dr. Carra HOOD
20 Chief Academic Officer for AC Dr. Michelle MCDONALD
96 Dir Procurement & Contracting Ms. Margaret QUINN
13 Chief Information Officer Mr. Scott HUSTON
21 Assoc VP ADFI Ms. Jennifer POTTER
18 VP Facilities & Operations Mr. Donald M. HUDSON
28 Chief Ofcr Inst Diversity/Equity Dr. Valerie HAYES
88 Int Ex Dir WJ Hughes Ctr Pub Plcy Mr. John FROONJIAN
30 Chief Dev Ofcr/Exec Dir Found Mr. Daniel P. NUGENT
26 Exec Dir Univ Relations/Marketing Mr. Geoffrey PETTIFER
84 Chief Enrollment Management Officer Mr. Robert HEINRICH
07 Assoc Dean Enrollment Management Ms. Alison HENRY
45 Asst VP Div Admin Strategic Init Dr. Pedro SANTANA
06 Registrar Mr. Joseph LOSASSO
53 Dean School of Education Dr. Claudine KEENAN
97 Dean School of General Studies Dr. Robert S. GREGG
79 Dean School Arts & Humanities Dr. Lisa HONAKER
50 Dean School of Business Dr. Alphonso OGBUEHI
58 Dir of Graduate Studies Ms. AmyBeth GLASS
81 Dean School of Natural Sci/Math Dr. Peter STRAUB
83 Dean Sch Social/Behav Sciences Dr. Marissa LEVY
76 Dean School of Health Sciences Dr. Margaret SLUSSER
15 Associate VP for Human Resources Mr. Rahmaan SIMPKINS
09 Director Institutional Research Dr. Xiangping KONG
08 Director of Library Services Mr. Joseph TOTH
88 Director SRI & ETTC Ms. Patricia WEEKS
37 Director of Financial Aid Ms. Heidi KOVALICK
19 Director of Campus Public Safety Mr. Adrian WIGGINS
88 Manager Performing Arts Center Ms. Suze DIPIETRO-STEWART
41 Exec Dir Athletics & Recreation Mr. Kevin MCHUGH
39 Executive Director Residential Life Mr. Steven E. RADWANSKI
124 Asst VP Transitions & Retention Mr. Walter L. TARVER, III
43 General Counsel Mr. Brian KOWALSKI
121 Dir Academic Advis/Assoc Dean GENS Dr. Peter HAGEN
114 Associate Director of Budget Mr. Michael WOOD
29 Director Alumni Relations Ms. Sara FAUROT
110 Assoc Chf Devel Ofcr/Campaign Mgr Ms. Cindy CRAGER
12 COO Atlantic City Campus Mr. Brian K. JACKSON
04 Admin Assistant to the President Ms. Kathryn MASON
25 Exec Dir Research & Spons Programs Mr. Todd REGN
45 Chief Institutional Planning Office Mr. Peter BARATTA

Sussex County Community College (E)

One College Hill Road, Newton NJ 07860-1146
County: Sussex FICE Identification: 025688
Unit ID: 247603
Telephone: (973) 300-2100 Carnegie Class: Assoc/HT-High Trad
FAX Number: (973) 579-9351 Calendar System: Semester
URL: www.sussex.edu
Established: 1982 Annual Undergrad Tuition & Fees (In-District): $6,750
Enrollment: 2,529 Coed
Affiliation or Control: State/Local IRS Status: 501(c)3
Highest Offering: Associate Degree
Accreditation: M, MAC

01 President Dr. Jon H. CONNOLLY
04 Asst to President/Board of Trustees Wendy FULLEM
10 CFO/Vice Pres Administrative Svcs Ketan GANDHI
05 VP of Academic Affairs/CAO Dr. Mercedes AGUIRRE BATTY
32 Vice Pres Student Services Dr. Kathleen OKAY
15 Exec Dir of Human Resources Michael GALLEGLY
26 Dir of Marketing/Public Info Kathleen PETERSON
24 Assoc Dean of Learning Resources Vacant
09 Assoc Dean Institutional Research Cory HOMER
41 Dir of Athletics/Dean Student Affs John KUNTZ
21 Director of Accounting Manal MESEHA
19 Director Campus Safety & Security Fred MAMAY
113 Dir of Bursar/Financial Services Tatsiana SHUMSKAYA
08 Director of College Library Stephanie COOPER
07 Director of Admissions Todd POLTERSDORF
37 Director of Financial Aid Diane PIENTA-LETTA
06 Registrar Solweig DIMINO
108 Director Institutional Assessment Cory HOMER
04 Assistant to the President Patricia SHATSOFF
102 Director of Foundation Monica LEMPERLE
13 Director Information Technology Judy LOVAS
38 Director Student Counseling Kathy GALLICHIO

Talmudical Academy of New Jersey (A)

Route 524, Adelphia NJ 07710-9999
County: Monmouth FICE Identification: 011989
Unit ID: 186900
Telephone: (732) 431-1600 Carnegie Class: Spec-4-yr-Faith
FAX Number: (732) 431-3951 Calendar System: Semester
URL: taofnj@gmail.com
Established: 1971 Annual Undergrad Tuition & Fees: $13,700
Enrollment: 60 Male
Affiliation or Control: Independent Non-Profit IRS Status: 501(c)3
Highest Offering: Baccalaureate
Accreditation: RABN

01 President .... Mr. Charles SEMAH
05 Dean/Registrar .... Rabbi Yeruchim SHAIN
10 Chief Financial/Business Officer .... Mr. Neal GOTTLIEB

Thomas Edison State University (B)

111 W State Street, Trenton NJ 08608-1176
County: Mercer FICE Identification: 021922
Unit ID: 187046
Telephone: (609) 984-1100 Carnegie Class: Masters/M
FAX Number: (609) 292-9000 Calendar System: Other
URL: www.tesu.edu
Established: 1972 Annual Undergrad Tuition & Fees (In-State): $7,519
Enrollment: 11,945 Coed
Affiliation or Control: State IRS Status: 501(c)3
Highest Offering: Doctorate
Accreditation: M, ACBSP, CAEPT, NURSE, POLYT

01 President .... Dr. Merodie A. HANCOCK
05 Vice President & Provost .... Vacant
10 Vice President & CFO .... Mr. Christopher STRINGER
26 Vice President Public Affairs .... Mr. John P. THURBER
31 Vice Pres Cmty & Govt Affairs .... Ms. Robin WALTON
84 VP Enrollment Management .... Dr. Dennis DEVERY
51 Vice Prov/Dean Watson Sch Cont Stds .... Dr. Joseph YOUNGBLOOD
88 Assoc VP Military/Veteran Education .... Mr. Louis MARTINI
09 Assoc VP for Planning & Research .... Dr. Ann Marie SENIOR
27 Senior Director of Communications ... Ms. Victoria A. MONAGHAN
88 Assoc Provost Learning Technology .... Mr. Matthew COOPER
21 Treasurer .... Mr. Steve D. ALBANO
100 Chief of Staff .... Mr. Michael MANCINI
27 Director Market Research/ Assessment .... Ms. Marie R. POWER-BARNES
43 General Counsel .... Ms. Barbara KLEVA
66 Dean School of Nursing .... Dr. Phyllis MARSHALL
49 Dean Heavin Sch of Arts & Sciences .... Dr. John WOZNICKI
50 Dean School of Business & Mgmt .... Dr. Michael WILLIAMS
06 Assoc Vice Pres/Univ Registrar .... Ms. Catharine PUNCHELLO-COBOS
72 Dean School of Applied Sci/Tech .... Dr. John AJE
21 Controller .... Mr. John SCHAIBLE
13 Chief Information Officer .... Mr. Drew W. HOPKINS
88 Senior Dir Office of Testing .... Mr. Maureen WOODRUFF
29 Director of Alumni Affairs .... Ms. Meg FRANTZ
37 Director of Financial Aid .... Mr. James OWENS
18 Director Facilities & Operations .... Ms. Mary C. HACK
30 Associate VP for Development .... Ms. Misty ISAK
102 Director Corporate Relations .... Mr. Frederick BRAND
08 State Librarian .... Ms. Mary CHUTE
105 Dir Website/Multimedia Productivity ...... Mr. Jeffery LUSHBAUGH
88 Director of Advancement Services .... Ms. Erica SPIZZIRRRI
44 Dir Annual Fund/Donor Relations .... Ms. Jennifer GUERRERO
88 Executive Director Watson Institute .... Ms. Barbara JOHNSON
88 ADA Coordinator .... Ms. Laura BRENNER-SCOTTI
88 Sr Fellow/Dir Ctr Leadership/Govt ...... Ms. Melissa A. MASZCZAK

† The Thomas Edison State University 12-month enrollment is 17,511.

Union County College (C)

1033 Springfield Avenue, Cranford NJ 07016-1598
County: Union FICE Identification: 002643
Unit ID: 187198
Telephone: (908) 709-7000 Carnegie Class: Assoc/HT-High Trad
FAX Number: (908) 709-0527 Calendar System: Semester
URL: www.ucc.edu
Established: 1933 Annual Undergrad Tuition & Fees (In-District): $5,140
Enrollment: 9,711 Coed
Affiliation or Control: State/Local IRS Status: 501(c)3
Highest Offering: Associate Degree
Accreditation: M, PTAA

01 President .... Dr. Margaret M. MCMENAMIN
05 Vice President Academic Affairs .... Dr. Maris LOWN
10 Vice Pres Financial Affs/Treasurer .... Ms. Lynne A. WELCH
32 Vice President Student Development .. Dr. Demond T. HARGROVE
11 Vice President Admin Services .... Dr. Athos BREWER
11 Associate VP Administration .... Mr. Vincent LOTANO
21 Associate VP Finance .... Vacant
20 Assoc VPAA & Dean Scotch Plains .... Dr. Bernard POLNARIEV
09 Exec Dir of Institutional Research .... Dr. Elizabeth COONER
102 Exec Director Foundation .... Mr. Douglas ROUSE
51 Exec Dir Cont Educ & Workforce Dev .... Dr. Lisa HISCANO
26 Board Sec & Exec Dir Col Relations .... Dr. Jaime M. SEGAL
12 Dean Plainfield Campus .... Dr. Victoria UKACHUKWU
12 Dean Elizabeth Campus .... Dr. Lester SANDRES RAPALO
79 Dean of Humanities .... Dr. Melissa SANDE
81 Dean of STEM .... Dr. Liesl JONES
83 Dean Social Sciences & Business .... Dr. Carlos BARREZUETA
08 Dean of Learning Resources .... Vacant
43 Associate General Counsel .... Dr. Marlene WHITE
114 Dir Financial Reporting & Budget .... Ms. Marlene SOUSA
116 Dir Financial Operations & Grants .... Ms. Jane KANE
96 Director of Purchasing .... Mr. Mark ANDERSON
13 Chief Information Officer .... Mr. Eric WINCH
18 Director Facilities .... Mr. Robert HOGAN
19 Director Public Safety .... Mr. Joseph HINES
25 Director of Grants .... Ms. Cheryl SHIBER
15 Director of Human Resources .... Vacant
41 Dean of College Life .... Ms. Tamalea SMITH
35 Dean of Students .... Mr. Mensah PETERSON
35 Dean of Student Success .... Ms. Rebecca ROYAL
06 Registrar .... Ms. Nina HERNANDEZ
121 Director Advising/Career/Transfer .... Ms. Heather KEITH
37 Director of Financial Aid .... Mr. Dayne CHANCE
113 Director of Student Accounts .... Ms. Kathryn VELLIOS
28 Director EOF .... Mr. Ruben MELENDEZ
84 Director Enrollment Services .... Ms. Beatriz RODRIGUEZ
41 Director of Athletics .... Mr. Shawn NOEL
24 Director Media Services .... Mr. Patrick GALLAGHER
106 Director of Instructional Design .... Dr. Jeffrey GUTKIN
88 Asst Dir Acad Learning Center .... Mr. Jose PAEZ-FIGUEROA
14 Technical Director .... Mr. Kevin TSAKONAS
14 Enterprise Applications Director .... Mr. Wisam SHAHIN
04 Executive Assistant to President .... Ms. Susan MATIKA
40 Manager Bookstore .... Ms. Christine SALZMAN

Union County College Elizabeth Campus (D)

40 W Jersey Street, Elizabeth NJ 07202-2314
Telephone: (908) 965-6000 Identification: 770134
Accreditation: &M, EMT

Union County College Plainfield Campus (E)

232 E 2nd Street, Plainfield NJ 07060
Telephone: (908) 412-3599 Identification: 770135
Accreditation: &M, #COARC

University of Phoenix Jersey City Campus (F)

88 Town Square Place, Jersey City NJ 07310-1756
Telephone: (201) 610-1408 Identification: 770218
Accreditation: &NH, ACBSP

† No longer accepting campus-based students.

Warren County Community College (G)

475 Route 57 W, Washington NJ 07882-4343
County: Warren FICE Identification: 025039
Unit ID: 245625
Telephone: (908) 835-9222 Carnegie Class: Assoc/HT-High Non
FAX Number: (908) 689-9262 Calendar System: Semester
URL: www.warren.edu
Established: 1981 Annual Undergrad Tuition & Fees (In-District): $4,980
Enrollment: 3,348 Coed
Affiliation or Control: State/Local IRS Status: 501(c)3
Highest Offering: Associate Degree
Accreditation: M, ADNUR, MAC

01 President .... Dr. William AUSTIN
10 Vice Pres Finance & Operations .... Ms. Barbara PRATT
51 Vice Pres Corporate/Continuing Educ .... Ms. Eve AZAR
11 Dean of Administration .... Mr. Dennis FLORENTINE
07 VP of Student Services .... Mr. Jeremy BEELER
05 VP of Academics .... Dr. Marianne VANDEURSEN
37 Director of Financial Aid .... Ms. Jacqueline DALY
15 Director Human Resources .... Ms. Sharon HINTZ
04 Administrative Asst to President .... Ms. Genevieve VASKO
08 Head Librarian .... Ms. Lisa STOLL
09 Director of Institutional Research .... Ms. Nikki DADARRIA
102 Dir Foundation/Corporate Relations ...... Ms. Samir ELBASSIOUNY

Westminster Choir College (H)

101 Walnut Lane, Princeton NJ 08540
Telephone: (609) 921-7100 Identification: 770128
Accreditation: &M

William Paterson University of New Jersey (I)

300 Pompton Road, Wayne NJ 07470-2152
County: Passaic FICE Identification: 002625
Unit ID: 187444
Telephone: (973) 720-2000 Carnegie Class: Masters/L
FAX Number: N/A Calendar System: Semester
URL: www.wpunj.edu
Established: 1855 Annual Undergrad Tuition & Fees (In-State): $13,060
Enrollment: 10,252 Coed
Affiliation or Control: State IRS Status: 501(c)3
Highest Offering: Doctorate
Accreditation: M, ART, CAATE, CACREP, CAEPN, CLPSY, MUS, NURSE, PH, SP

01 President .... Dr. Richard HELLDOBLER
05 Senior Vice President/Provost .... Dr. Joshua POWERS
100 Chf of Staff to Pres/Board of Trust .... Dr. Shelley BANNISTER
10 Vice Pres Administration/Finance .... Mr. Stephen BOLYAI
111 Vice Pres Institutional Advancement .... Ms. Pamela FERGUSON
32 Vice President Student Development .... Dr. Miki CAMMARATA
84 VP of Enrollment Management .... Dr. Reginald ROSS
88 Assoc Provost Academic Development ..... Ms. Danielle LIAUTAUD
114 Assoc VP Finance Budget/Fiscal Plng .... Vacant
11 Assoc VP for Administration .... Mr. Kevin GARVEY
26 VP Mktg & Public Relations .... Mr. Stuart GOLDSTEIN
15 Vice Pres Human Resources .... Ms. Allison BOUCHER-JARVIS
19 Dir Public Safety & Univ Police .... Mr. Charles LOWE
35 Associate VP for Campus Life .... Mr. Francisco DIAZ
35 Assoc VP/Dean Student Development .... Dr. Glen SHERMAN
60 Dean Col Arts/Comm .... Mr. Daryl MOORE
53 Dean College of Education .... Dr. Amy GINSBERG
66 Dean College of Science & Health .... Dr. Venkatanarayanan SHARMA
79 Dean Human & Social Science .... Dr. Kara M. RABBITT
50 Interim Dean College of Business .... Dr. Susan GODAR
08 Dean D & L Cheng Library .... Dr. Edward OWUSU-ANSAH
21 Assoc VP Finance & Controller .... Ms. Samantha GREEN
28 Dir Empl Rels/Equity/Title IX Coord .... Ms. Regina A. TINDALL
51 Exec Dir Cont Educ/Distance Lrng .... Dr. Bernadette TIERNAN
20 Associate Provost Academic Affairs .... Dr. Sandra B. HILL
20 Assoc Prov for Curriculum & Intl Ed .... Dr. Jonathan LINCOLN
86 Assoc VP Govt & External Relations .... Mr. Patrick DEDEO
27 Director Public Information .... Ms. Mary Beth ZEMAN
29 Executive Director Alumni .... Ms. Janis SCHWARTZ
108 Director Inst Research & Assessment .... Dr. Sesime ADANU
13 Chief Information Officer .... Mr. Eric ROSENBERG
43 General Counsel .... Ms. Laura HERTZOG
16 Director of Human Resources ...... Ms. Denise ROBINSON-LEWIS
07 Assoc Vice President Admissions .... Mr. Ken SCHNEIDER
37 Director Financial Aid .... Mr. Michael CORSO
06 Registrar .... Ms. Susan ASTARITA
41 Director Athletics .... Ms. Sabrina GRANT
36 Director of Career Dev & Advisement ... Ms. Sharon ROSENGART
39 Interim Director of Residence Life .... Ms. Rebecca BAIRD
23 Dir Counseling/Health & Wellness .... Dr. Jill GUZMAN
40 Director Bookstore .... Mr. Scott DUNLAP
18 Director Capital Plng/Design/Constr .... Vacant
85 Director International Student Svcs .... Ms. Cinzia RICHARDSON
94 Director of Women's Center .... Ms. Librada SANCHEZ
96 Director of Purchasing .... Mr. Stephen SONDEY
89 Director of New Student Programs .... Ms. Amanda VASQUEZ
92 Director of Honors College .... Dr. Barbara ANDREW
35 Dir Campus Activ/Svc & Leadership .... Ms. Donna MINNICH SPUHLER
88 Assoc Dir Instruction/Research Tech .... Mr. Patrick RYAN
04 Sr Admin Assistant to President .... Ms. Rachel RODRIGUEZ

Yeshiva Bais Aharon (J)

905 Park Avenue, Lakewood NJ 08701
County: Ocean Identification: 667291
Unit ID: 490319
Telephone: (732) 367-7604 Carnegie Class: Spec-4-yr-Faith
FAX Number: (732) 367-1777 Calendar System: Semester
Established: 2012 Annual Undergrad Tuition & Fees: $9,075
Enrollment: 44 Male
Affiliation or Control: Independent Non-Profit IRS Status: 501(c)3
Highest Offering: First Talmudic Degree
Accreditation: AIJS

Yeshiva Chemdas Hatorah (K)

950 Massachusetts Avenue, Lakewood NJ 08701
County: Ocean Identification: 667281
Telephone: (732) 363-7110 Carnegie Class: Not Classified
FAX Number: (732) 961-5220 Calendar System: Other
Established: Annual Undergrad Tuition & Fees: N/A
Enrollment: N/A Male
Affiliation or Control: Independent Non-Profit IRS Status: 501(c)3
Highest Offering: First Talmudic Degree
Accreditation: AIJS

01 Administrator .... Rabbi Menachen OPPENHEIM

Yeshiva Gedolah of Cliffwood (L)

200 Center Street, Keyport NJ 07735
County: Monmouth Identification: 667322
Telephone: (732) 765-9126 Carnegie Class: Not Classified
FAX Number: (732) 865-7247 Calendar System: Semester
Established: 2004 Annual Undergrad Tuition & Fees: N/A
Enrollment: N/A Male
Affiliation or Control: Independent Non-Profit IRS Status: 501(c)3
Highest Offering: First Talmudic Degree
Accreditation: RABN

01 CEO .... Samuel ALSTER
06 Registrar .... Baruch SEGEL
10 CFO .... Shimon ALSTER
37 Financial Aid Administrator .... Aryeh BRODSKY

Yeshiva Gedolah Keren Hatorah (M)

1083 Brook Road, Lakewood NJ 08701
County: Ocean Identification: 667282
Telephone: (732) 942-1811 Carnegie Class: Not Classified
FAX Number: (732) 994-4222 Calendar System: Other
URL: yeshivagedolahkerenhatorah.com

Established: 2009 Annual Undergrad Tuition & Fees: N/A
Enrollment: N/A Male
Affiliation or Control: Independent Non-Profit IRS Status: 501(c)3
Highest Offering: First Talmudic Degree
Accreditation: AIJS

01 CEO/Executive Director .... Vacant

Yeshiva Gedolah Shaarei Shmuel (A)

511 Ocean Ave, Lakewood NJ 08701
County: Ocean Identification: 667260
Unit ID: 488350
Telephone: (732) 363-2164 Carnegie Class: Spec-4-yr-Faith
FAX Number: (732) 364-3331 Calendar System: Other
Established: 2008 Annual Undergrad Tuition & Fees: $8,800
Enrollment: 81 Male
Affiliation or Control: Independent Non-Profit IRS Status: 501(c)3
Highest Offering: First Talmudic Degree
Accreditation: @RABN

Yeshiva Gedolah Tiferes Boruch (B)

21 Rockview Avenue, North Plainfield NJ 07060
County: Union Identification: 667283
Telephone: (908) 753-2600 Carnegie Class: Not Classified
FAX Number: (908) 753-4243 Calendar System: Semester
URL: yeshivagedolahtiferesboruch.com
Established: 1989 Annual Undergrad Tuition & Fees: N/A
Enrollment: N/A Male
Affiliation or Control: Independent Non-Profit IRS Status: 501(c)3
Highest Offering: First Talmudic Degree
Accreditation: AIJS

05 Dean .... Rabbi Eliyohu SOROTZKIN

Yeshiva Gedolah Zichron Leyma (C)

2035 Vauxhall Road, Union NJ 07083
County: Union FICE Identification: 041924
Unit ID: 476692
Telephone: (908) 587-0502 Carnegie Class: Spec-4-yr-Faith
FAX Number: (908) 349-3111 Calendar System: Semester
URL: www.yzl.edu
Established: 1999 Annual Undergrad Tuition & Fees: $10,750
Enrollment: 21 Male
Affiliation or Control: Independent Non-Profit IRS Status: 501(c)3
Highest Offering: First Talmudic Degree
Accreditation: RABN

Yeshiva Toras Chaim (D)

999 Ridge Avenue, Lakewood NJ 08701-2120
County: Ocean FICE Identification: 041311
Unit ID: 451398
Telephone: (732) 414-2834 Carnegie Class: Spec-4-yr-Faith
FAX Number: (732) 414-2838 Calendar System: Semester
Established: 2000 Annual Undergrad Tuition & Fees: $12,250
Enrollment: 222 Male
Affiliation or Control: Independent Non-Profit IRS Status: 501(c)3
Highest Offering: Baccalaureate
Accreditation: RABN

05 Chief Academic Officer .... Rabbi Mendel SLOMOVITS
06 Registrar .... Mrs. Devoiry DURST
10 Bookkeeper .... Mrs. Michal GROSSMAN

Yeshiva Yesodei Hatorah (E)

2 Yesodei Court, Lakewood NJ 08701
County: Ocean Identification: 667109
Unit ID: 481438
Telephone: (732) 370-3360 Carnegie Class: Spec-4-yr-Faith
FAX Number: (732) 886-2659 Calendar System: Semester
Established: 1995 Annual Undergrad Tuition & Fees: $13,000
Enrollment: 65 Male
Affiliation or Control: Independent Non-Profit IRS Status: 501(c)3
Highest Offering: First Talmudic Degree
Accreditation: RABN

05 Dean .... Rabbi Shaya TREFF
10 Chief Financial/Business Officer .... Rabbi Shaya UNGAR
20 Associate Academic Officer .... Rabbi Yisroel Meir TREFF

Yeshivas Be'er Yitzchok (F)

1391 North Avenue, Elizabeth NJ 07208-2480
County: Union FICE Identification: 041234
Unit ID: 451370
Telephone: (908) 354-6057 Carnegie Class: Spec-4-yr-Faith
FAX Number: (908) 820-0431 Calendar System: Semester
Established: 1999 Annual Undergrad Tuition & Fees: $10,900
Enrollment: 43 Male
Affiliation or Control: Independent Non-Profit IRS Status: 501(c)3
Highest Offering: Baccalaureate
Accreditation: AIJS

01 Chief Executive Officer .... Rabbi Avrohom SCHULMAN
37 Director of Student Financial Aid .... Mrs. Chana MILLER

NEW MEXICO

Brookline College (G)

4201 Central Avenue NW Ste J,
Albuquerque NM 87105-1649
Telephone: (505) 880-2877 Identification: 666724
Accreditation: ABHES

† Branch campus of Brookline College, Phoenix, AZ

Burrell College of Osteopathic Medicine (H)

3501 Arrowhead Drive, Las Cruces NM 88001
County: Dona Ana Identification: 667248
Unit ID: 488554
Telephone: (575) 674-2266 Carnegie Class: Not Classified
FAX Number: (575) 674-2267 Calendar System: Semester
URL: www.bcomnm.org
Established: 2013 Annual Graduate Tuition & Fees: N/A
Enrollment: 320 Coed
Affiliation or Control: Other IRS Status: Proprietary
Highest Offering: Doctorate; No Undergraduates
Accreditation: @OSTEO

01 President .... Mr. John L. HUMMER
05 Dean and Chief Academic Officer .... Dr. Don N. PESKA
10 CFO/VP Admin & Finance .... Ms. Jennifer TAYLOR
13 Chief Information Officer/AVP Admin .... Mr. Jeff HARRIS
06 Registrar .... Ms. Marisella REYES
07 Director of Admissions .... Ms. Courtney LEWIS
08 Library Director .... Ms. Erin PALAZZOLO
15 Director of Human Resources .... Ms. Dawn M. LEAKE
26 Dir Communications & Marketing .... Ms. Nadia WHITEHEAD
32 Int Exec Dir of Student Affairs .... Ms. Vanessa RICHARDSON
37 Director of Financial Aid .... Dr. Marlene MELENDEZ
35 Director of Student Life .... Mr. Brett NEWCOMER

Carrington College - Albuquerque (I)

1001 Menaul Boulevard NE, Albuquerque NM 87107
Telephone: (505) 254-7777 Identification: 666014
Accreditation: &WJ

† Regional accreditation is carried under the parent institution in Sacramento, CA.

Central New Mexico Community College (J)

525 Buena Vista, SE, Albuquerque NM 87106-4096
County: Bernalillo FICE Identification: 004742
Unit ID: 187532
Telephone: (505) 224-3000 Carnegie Class: Assoc/HT-Mix Trad/Non
FAX Number: N/A Calendar System: Semester
URL: www.cnm.edu
Established: 1965 Annual Undergrad Tuition & Fees (In-District): $1,626
Enrollment: 24,442 Coed
Affiliation or Control: State/Local IRS Status: 501(c)3
Highest Offering: Associate Degree
Accreditation: NH, ACBSP, ACFEI, ADNUR, CAHIIM, COARC, CONST, DA, DMS, EMT, MLTAD, #PTAA, RAD, SURGT

01 President .... Dr. Katharine W. WINOGRAD
05 Vice President for Academic Affairs .... Dr. Sydney D. GUNTHORPE
32 Vice President for Student Services .... Mr. Eugene PADILLA
10 Vice Pres for Finance & Operations .... Ms. Tracy HARTZLER
84 Assoc Vice Pres Enrollment Mgmt .... Vacant
35 Dean of Students .... Mr. Christopher CAVAZOS
08 Director Learning Resources .... Ms. Poppy JOHNSON RENVALL
13 Chief Information Officer .... Mr. Victor LEON
103 Program Management Director .... Ms. Evelyn DOW
36 Job Connection Services .... Ms. Stacey COOLEY
30 Exec Director of Development .... Mr. Clinton WELLS
07 Director Enrollment Services .... Mr. Glenn DAMIANI
26 Exec Dir Mktg & Public Relations .... Mrs. Angela SIMS
27 Dir Communications/Media Relations .... Mr. Brad MOORE
37 Director Student Financial Aid .... Mr. Lee CARRILLO
15 Executive Director Human Resources .... Ms. Juliane ZITER
81 Interim Dean Sch of Math/Sci/Engr .... Mr. Philip CARMAN
50 Dean School of Bus/Info Technology .... Ms. Donna DILLER
72 Dean School of Applied Technologies .... Ms. Kristen BENEDICT
97 Dean Sch of Adult & Gen Educ .... Ms. LouAnne LUNDGREN
83 Dean Comm/Humanities/Soc Sci .... Ms. Erica VOLKERS BARREIRO
76 Interim Dean Health/Well/Pub Safety .... Ms. Carol ASH
06 Registrar .... Ms. Rosenda MINELLA
18 Exec Dir Physical Plant .... Mr. Marvin MARTINEZ
21 Exec Dir Fiscal Ops/Comptroller .... Ms. Wanda HELMS
35 Director of Student Life .... Mr. Kristofer GAUSSOIN
96 Director of Purchasing .... Ms. Gerrie BECKER
19 Chief of Safety & Security .... Mr. John CORVINO
04 Administrative Asst to President .... Ms. Erin BRADSHAW
09 Dir Assess/Institutional Research .... Ms. Linda MARTIN
29 Director Alumni Relations .... Vacant
43 Dir Legal Svcs/General Counsel .... Mr. Michael ANAYA

Clovis Community College (K)

417 Schepps Boulevard, Clovis NM 88101-8381
County: Curry FICE Identification: 004743
Unit ID: 187639
Telephone: (575) 769-2811 Carnegie Class: Assoc/MT-VT-High Non
FAX Number: (575) 769-4190 Calendar System: Semester
URL: www.clovis.edu
Established: 1971 Annual Undergrad Tuition & Fees (In-State): $1,376
Enrollment: 3,114 Coed
Affiliation or Control: State IRS Status: 501(c)3
Highest Offering: Associate Degree
Accreditation: NH, ADNUR, #PTAA, RAD

01 Interim President .... Dr. Robin KUYKENDALL
03 Executive Vice President .... Dr. Robin JONES
10 VP of Administration & Finance .... Dr. Adrien BENNINGS
13 VP of IT and Operations .... Mr. Norman KIA
21 Director of Finance .... Ms. Heather LOVATO
07 Dir Admissions/Records/Registrar .... Ms. Marlee STEPHENSON
37 Director of Financial Aid .... Ms. April CHAVEZ
08 Director Library/Learning Resources .... Ms. Kelly GRAY
121 Dir Center for Student Success .... Ms. Emily GLIKAS
86 Dir of Advising & Govt Relations .... Mr. Marcus SMITH
15 Director of Human Resource Services .... Ms. Gay GOETTSCH
88 Director Small Business Development .... Ms. Sandra TAYLOR-SAWYER
91 Director of Administrative Info Sys .... Mr. David BURCH
56 Director Extended Learning .... Ms. Robin KUYKENDALL
36 Director Student Placement .... Vacant
111 Dir of Institutional Advancement .... Ms. Desiree MARKHAM
18 Director of Physical Plant .... Mr. Paul ARAGON
76 Div Chair Allied Health Programs .... Ms. Shawna MCGILL
88 Div Chair Languages/History/Theater .... Ms. Janett JOHNSON
50 Div Chair Business Admin/Accounting .... Ms. Monica SANCHEZ
81 Div Chair Math/Science/Hum/HPE .... Mr. Don SCROGGINS
77 Div Chair CIS/Art/Comm .... Mr. Ray WALKER
04 Executive Asst to President .... Ms. Beverly ARAGON
09 Director of Institutional Research .... Ms. Courtney TEMPEL
19 Director of Campus Security .... Mr. Freddie SALAZAR
102 Exec Director of CCC Foundation .... Ms. Natalie DAGGETT
105 Marketing & Website Manager .... Ms. Esther MOHRMANN
25 Chief Contract and Grants Admin .... Dr. Mindy WATSON
36 Career & Development Coordinator .... Ms. Alexis NOON
90 Director of User Services .... Mr. Ricky FUENTES
96 Director of Purchasing .... Mr. Corey ISAACS

Dine College Shiprock Branch (L)

1228 Yucca St., PO Box 580, Shiprock NM 87420
Telephone: (505) 368-3500 Identification: 770007
Accreditation: &NH

† Branch campus of Dine College, Tsaile, AZ

Eastern New Mexico University Main Campus (M)

1500 S Avenue K, Portales NM 88130-7400
County: Roosevelt FICE Identification: 002651
Unit ID: 187648
Telephone: (575) 562-1011 Carnegie Class: Masters/L
FAX Number: (575) 562-2980 Calendar System: Semester
URL: www.enmu.edu
Established: 1927 Annual Undergrad Tuition & Fees (In-State): $6,326
Enrollment: 6,023 Coed
Affiliation or Control: State IRS Status: 501(c)3
Highest Offering: Master's
Accreditation: NH, ACBSP, MUS, NUR, SP, SW

01 President .... Dr. Jeffery ELWELL
05 Vice President Academic Affairs .... Dr. Jamie LAURENZ
10 Vice President Business Affairs .... Mr. Scott SMART
32 Vice President for Student Affairs .... Dr. Jeff LONG
13 Vice President of Technology .... Mr. Clark ELSWICK
45 VP Planning/Analysis/Inst Research .... Dr. Patrice CALDWELL
20 Asst Vice Pres for Academic Affairs .... Dr. Suzanne BALCH-LINDSAY
20 Asst Vice Pres Academic Affairs .... Dr. John MONTGOMERY
111 Assoc Vice Pres Advancement .... Ms. Noelle BARTL
26 Asst Vice Pres of Communications .... Mr. John HOUSER
21 Comptroller .... Mrs. Carol FLETCHER
53 Dean Education/Technology .... Dr. Penny A. GARCIA
50 Interim Dean Business .... Dr. John MONTGOMERY
57 Dean Fine Arts .... Dr. Jeff GENTRY
49 Dean Liberal Arts & Science .... Dr. Mary AYALA
58 Dean Graduate School .... Dr. John MONTGOMERY
22 Affirmative Action Officer .... Ms. Jessica SMALL
08 Director of Library .... Ms. Melveta WALKER
06 Registrar .... Ms. DeLynn BARGAS
37 Director Student Financial Aid .... Mr. Brent SMALL
07 Director Enrollment Services .... Mr. Cody SPITZ
15 Director of Human Resources .... Mr. Benito GONZALES
88 Director of Broadcasting .... Mr. Duane RYAN
18 Director Physical Plant .... Mr. John KANMORE
41 Athletic Director .... Vacant
19 Chief of University Police .... Mr. Brad MAULDIN
36 Dir Counseling Center/Career Svcs .... Ms. Susan LARSEN
39 Director Student Housing .... Mr. Steven ESTOCK
09 Director Institutional Research .... Mr. Brendan HENNESSEY
96 Director of Purchasing .... Mr. Scott DAVIS
29 Coordinator of Alumni .... Ms. Annamaria SHORT

106 Dir of Distance Learning/Outreach .... Mr. Ryan ROARK
35 Director Campus Life .... Vacant

Eastern New Mexico University-Roswell (A)

PO Box 6000, Roswell NM 88202-6000
County: Chaves FICE Identification: 002661
Unit ID: 187666
Telephone: (575) 624-7000 Carnegie Class: Assoc/HVT-High Non
FAX Number: (575) 624-7342 Calendar System: Semester
URL: www.roswell.enmu.edu
Established: 1958 Annual Undergrad Tuition & Fees (In-State): $2,256
Enrollment: 2,686 Coed
Affiliation or Control: State IRS Status: 501(c)3
Highest Offering: Associate Degree
Accreditation: NH, ADNUR, COARC, EMT, MAC, OTA

01 President .... Dr. Shawn POWELL
05 VP for Academic Affairs .... Vacant
10 VP for Business Affairs .... Vacant
32 VP for Student Affairs .... Mr. Mike MARTINEZ
21 Controller .... Ms. Karen FRANKLIN
35 Asst VP for Student Affairs .... Vacant
08 Director Learning Resource Center .... Mr. Rollah ASTON
37 Director Financial Aid .... Mr. Chris MEEKS
30 Director College Development .... Ms. Donna ORACION
07 Director Admissions and Records .... Ms. Linda NEEL
13 Director of Computer Services .... Vacant
15 Director of Human Resources .... Ms. Rebecca SCHNEIDER
18 Director of Physical Plant .... Mr. Derek DUBIEL
19 Director of Security .... Mr. Bard MCFADIN
96 Director of Purchasing .... Mr. Cole COLLINS
09 Director Institutional Research .... Mr. Todd DEKAY
04 Administrative Asst to President .... Mrs. Linde NEWMAN
49 AVP of Arts & Science Education .... Ms. Annemarie OLDFIELD
76 AVP of Health Education .... Dr. Laurie JENSEN
72 AVP of Technical Education .... Mr. Chad SMITH

EC-Council University (B)

101C Sun Avenue NE, Albuquerque NM 87109
County: Bernalillo Identification: 667232
Telephone: (505) 922-2889 Carnegie Class: Not Classified
FAX Number: (505) 856-8267 Calendar System: Other
URL: www.eccu.edu
Established: 2003 Annual Undergrad Tuition & Fees: N/A
Enrollment: N/A Coed
Affiliation or Control: Proprietary IRS Status: Proprietary
Highest Offering: Master's
Accreditation: DEAC

00 CEO .... Sanjay BAVISI
01 President .... Lata BAVISI
03 Vice President .... David OXENHANDLER
05 Dean .... Charline NIXON
06 Registrar .... David VALDEZ

Institute of American Indian Arts (C)

83 Avan Nu Po Road, Santa Fe NM 87508-1300
County: Santa Fe FICE Identification: 021464
Unit ID: 187745
Telephone: (505) 424-2300 Carnegie Class: Tribal
FAX Number: (505) 424-4500 Calendar System: Semester
URL: www.iaia.edu
Established: 1962 Annual Undergrad Tuition & Fees: $4,980
Enrollment: 659 Coed
Affiliation or Control: Federal IRS Status: Exempt
Highest Offering: Master's
Accreditation: NH, ART

01 President .... Dr. Robert MARTIN
05 Academic Dean .... Ms. Charlene TETERS
10 Chief Financial Officer .... Mr. Larry MIRABAL
32 Dean of Student Life .... Ms. Carmen HENAN
84 Chief Enrollment & Retention Ofcr .... Ms. Nena ANAYA
111 Dir of Institutional Advancement .... Ms. Danyelle MEANS
26 Dir of Marketing and Communication .... Mr. Eric DAVIS
88 Dir of IAIA Museum .... Ms. Patsy PHILLIPS
25 Dir of Sponsored Programs .... Ms. Laurie BRAYSHAW
09 Dir of Institutional Research .... Dr. William SAYRE

Luna Community College (D)

366 Luna Drive, Las Vegas NM 87701-1510
County: San Miguel FICE Identification: 009962
Unit ID: 363633
Telephone: (505) 454-2500 Carnegie Class: Assoc/MT-VT-High Non
FAX Number: (505) 454-2519 Calendar System: Semester
URL: www.luna.edu
Established: 1970 Annual Undergrad Tuition & Fees (In-District): $962
Enrollment: 1,356 Coed
Affiliation or Control: State/Local IRS Status: 501(c)3
Highest Offering: Associate Degree
Accreditation: #NH, ACBSP, ADNUR, DA

01 Acting President .... Dr. Sharon LALLA
05 VP of Instruction/Student Services .... Dr. Sharon LALLA
10 Vice Pres of Finance/Administration .... Ms. Donna FLORES-MEDINA
09 Director Institutional Research .... Vacant
07 Director of Admissions .... Mr. Moses MARQUEZ
06 Registrar .... Ms. Henrietta MAESTAS
18 Manager Physical Plant .... Mr. Matthew CORDOVA
37 Director Student Financial Aid .... Mr. Michael MONTOYA
15 Director Human Resources .... Ms. Carolyn CHAVEZ
30 Director Development .... Ms. Elaina LUNA
13 Director of Computer Services .... Mr. Matthew BOWIE

Mesalands Community College (E)

911 S 10th Street, Tucumcari NM 88401-3352
County: Quay FICE Identification: 032063
Unit ID: 188261
Telephone: (505) 461-4413 Carnegie Class: Assoc/MT-VT-High Non
FAX Number: (505) 461-1901 Calendar System: Semester
URL: www.mesalands.edu
Established: 1980 Annual Undergrad Tuition & Fees (In-District): $1,812
Enrollment: 1,005 Coed
Affiliation or Control: State/Local IRS Status: 501(c)3
Highest Offering: Associate Degree
Accreditation: NH

01 President .... Dr. John D. GROESBECK
04 Executive Asst to President .... Ms. Consuelo E. CHAVEZ
32 Vice President Student Affairs .... Dr. Aaron KENNEDY
05 Vice President of Academic Affairs .... Ms. Natalie GILLARD
11 Vice President of Admin Affairs .... Ms. Amanda HAMMER
37 Director Financial Aid .... Ms. Jessica ELEBARIO
26 Director Public Relations .... Ms. Kimberly HANNA
72 Director of NAWRTC .... Mr. Jim MORGAN
84 Director of Enrollment Management .... Ms. Amber MCCLURE
13 Director of IT .... Mr. Larry WICKHAM
09 Dir Inst Research and Development .... Dr. Forrest KAATZ
15 HR Specialist .... Ms. Tammy HALL
20 Director of Academic Affairs .... Ms. Donna GARCIA
08 Library Director .... Vacant

National College of Midwifery (F)

1041 Reed Street, Suite C, Taos NM 87571
County: Taos Identification: 666251
Telephone: (575) 758-8914 Carnegie Class: Not Classified
FAX Number: N/A Calendar System: Trimester
URL: www.midwiferycollege.edu
Established: 1989 Annual Undergrad Tuition & Fees: N/A
Enrollment: N/A Coed
Affiliation or Control: Independent Non-Profit IRS Status: 501(c)3
Highest Offering: Doctorate
Accreditation: MEAC

01 CEO/President .... Marcy ANDREW
11 Chief Operations Officer .... Clorinda ROMERO
30 Chief Development Officer .... Cassaundra JAH

Navajo Technical University (G)

PO Box 849, Crownpoint NM 87313-0849
County: McKinley FICE Identification: 023576
Unit ID: 187596
Telephone: (505) 786-4100 Carnegie Class: Tribal
FAX Number: (505) 786-5644 Calendar System: Semester
URL: www.navajotech.edu
Established: 1979 Annual Undergrad Tuition & Fees: $4,070
Enrollment: 1,772 Coed
Affiliation or Control: Tribal Control IRS Status: 501(c)3
Highest Offering: Master's
Accreditation: NH, ACFEI

01 President .... Dr. Elmer GUY
32 Dean of Student Services .... Ms. Jerlynn HENRY
10 Chief Financial Officer .... Ms. Geraldine GAMBLE
05 Dean of Undergraduate Studies .... Dr. Casmir AGBARAJI
06 Registrar/Director of Admissions .... Ms. Nathalie BECENTI
09 Data Assessment Director .... Vacant
25 Contracts & Grant Officer .... Vacant
37 Student Financial Aid Officer .... Mr. Tyrrell HARDY
08 Head Librarian .... Mr. Darwin C. HENDERSON
04 Executive Assistant .... Ms. Tonilee BECENTI
13 IT Director .... Mr. Jason ARVISO
41 Athletic Director .... Mr. George LAFRANCE
15 Human Resource Director .... Mr. Ralph ROANHORSE

† Tuition figure is for a student enrolled in a federally recognized Indian tribe.

New Mexico Highlands University (H)

PO Box 9000, Las Vegas NM 87701-9000
County: San Miguel FICE Identification: 002653
Unit ID: 187897
Telephone: (877) 850-9064 Carnegie Class: Masters/L
FAX Number: N/A Calendar System: Semester
URL: www.nmhu.edu
Established: 1893 Annual Undergrad Tuition & Fees (In-State): $6,150
Enrollment: 3,098 Coed
Affiliation or Control: State IRS Status: 501(c)3
Highest Offering: Master's
Accreditation: NH, ACBSP, CACREP, CAEPN, NURSE, SW

01 President .... Dr. Sam MINNER
05 Provost/VP for Academic Affairs .... Dr. Roxanne GONZALES
10 VP Finance & Admin .... Mr. Max BACA
84 Interim VP for Strat Enroll Mgmt .... Dr. Edward MARTINEZ
32 Dean of Students .... Dr. Kimberly BLEA
07 Dir of Student Recruitment/Admiss .... Mrs. Jessica HURTADO
06 Co-Acting Registrar .... Ms. Andrea CRESPIN
06 Co-Acting Registrar .... Ms. Inca CRESPIN
09 Dir Inst Effectiveness & Research .... Dr. Lee ALLARD
13 Director of Information Technology .... Mr. Joe GIERI
15 Director Human Resources .... Ms. Denise MONTOYA
18 Director of Facilities Mgmt .... Ms. Sylvia BACA
19 Chief Police/Security .... Mr. Clarence ROMERO
26 Director of University Relations .... Mr. Sean WEAVER
29 Alumni Director .... Ms. Juli SALMAN
111 Vice President for Advancement .... Ms. Theresa LAW
36 Director of Career Services .... Mr. Tranquilino HURTADO
37 Director of Financial Aid .... Ms. Susan CHAVEZ
40 Bookstore Manager .... Ms. Naomi VILLANUEVA
50 Interim Dean School of Business .... Dr. Keith TUCKER
53 Interim Dean School of Education .... Dr. Sheree JEDERBERG
39 Director Student Housing .... Ms. Yvette WILKES
04 Admin Assistant to the President .... Ms. Carolina MARTINEZ
08 Chief Library Officer .... Mr. Ruben ARAGON
106 Director Online/Extended Learning .... Mr. Patrick WILSON
41 Interim Athletic Director .... Mr. Craig SNOW
96 Director of Purchasing .... Mr. Adam BUSTOS

New Mexico Institute of Mining and Technology (I)

801 Leroy Place, Socorro NM 87801-4796
County: Socorro FICE Identification: 002654
Unit ID: 187967
Telephone: (575) 835-5434 Carnegie Class: Masters/S
FAX Number: (575) 835-6329 Calendar System: Semester
URL: www.nmt.edu
Established: 1889 Annual Undergrad Tuition & Fees (In-State): $7,770
Enrollment: 2,009 Coed
Affiliation or Control: State IRS Status: 501(c)3
Highest Offering: Doctorate
Accreditation: NH

01 President .... Dr. Stephen G. WELLS
10 Vice Pres Administration & Finance .... Mr. Cleve MCDANIEL
05 Vice President Academic Affairs .... Dr. Doug WELLS
46 Vice Pres Research/Economic Devel .... Dr. Van D. ROMERO
32 Vice Pres Student/Univ Affairs .... Ms. Melissa JARAMILLO-FLEMING
20 Assoc Vice Pres Academic Affairs .... Dr. Peter MOZLEY
45 Assoc VP Research/Econ Development .... Mr. Carlos REY ROMERO
58 Dean of Graduate Studies .... Dr. Aly EL-OSERY
08 Librarian .... Mr. David COX
15 Director of Human Resources .... Ms. JoAnn SALOME
06 Registrar .... Mr. Scott ZEMAN
07 Director of Admission .... Mr. Anthony ORTIZ
37 Director of Financial Aid .... Mr. Kenneth AERTS
30 Director Office for Advancement .... Ms. Colleen FOSTER
22 Director Affirm Action & Compliance .... Mr. Randy SAAVEDRA
13 Director of Information Services .... Mr. Joseph FRANKLIN
65 Director Bur Geology & Mineral Res .... Dr. Nelia DUNBAR
12 Director Petro Recovery Res Ctr .... Dr. Robert BALCH
18 Director Facilities Management .... Ms. Yvonne MANZANO
38 Dir Counseling/Disabilities Svcs .... Ms. Angela GAUTIER
96 Chief Procurement Officer .... Ms. Kimela MILLER
09 Institutional Researcher .... Ms. Stephany MOORE
26 Chief Public Relations Officer .... Mr. Dave LEPRE

New Mexico Junior College (J)

1 Thunderbird Circle, Hobbs NM 88240-9123
County: Lea FICE Identification: 002655
Unit ID: 187903
Telephone: (575) 392-4510 Carnegie Class: Assoc/HT-Mix Trad/Non
FAX Number: (575) 492-2732 Calendar System: Semester
URL: www.nmjc.edu
Established: 1965 Annual Undergrad Tuition & Fees (In-District): $1,320
Enrollment: 2,310 Coed
Affiliation or Control: Local IRS Status: 501(c)3
Highest Offering: Associate Degree
Accreditation: NH, ADNUR

01 President .... Dr. Kelvin SHARP
05 Vice President Instruction .... Dr. Larry SANDERSON
10 Vice President Finance .... Dan HARDIN
32 Vice President Student Services .... Cathy MITCHELL
103 Vice President Training & Outreach .... Jeff MCCOOL
43 General Counsel/Admin Services .... Scotty HOLLOMAN
13 Dir Computer Information System .... Bill KUNKO
26 Director of Communications .... Susan FINE
04 Executive Asst to the President .... Norma FAUGHT
37 Director Financial Aid .... Kerrie MITCHELL
66 Director of Allied Health/Nursing .... Misty STINE
18 Chief Facilities/Physical Plant .... Dr. Charley CARROLL
81 Dean Applied Sciences .... Dr. Stephanie FERGUSON
08 Dean Academic Studies/Library .... Dianne MARQUEZ
40 Director of Bookstore Services .... Robert ADAMS
19 Director of Public Safety .... Walter COBURN
08 Director of Library Services .... Vacant
96 Coordinator of Purchasing .... JoeMike GOMEZ
41 Director of Athletics .... Deron CLARK
102 Acct/Controller-NMJC Foundation .... Christina KUNKO

21 Controller Joshua MORGAN
39 Director Student Housing Marisol ARENIVAS
88 Interim Director WHM/LCCHF Erin ANDERSON
88 Dir NMJC Research Foundation Vacant
06 Registrar Rebecca WHITLEY
19 Director of Campus Security/Safety Dennis KELLEY
30 Director of Development Dan SOCOLOFSKY

New Mexico Military Institute (A)

101 W College, Roswell NM 88201-5173

County: Chaves
FICE Identification: 002656
Unit ID: 187912
Telephone: (575) 622-6250
Carnegie Class: Assoc/HT-High Trad
FAX Number: (575) 624-8058
Calendar System: Semester
URL: www.nmmi.edu
Established: 1891
Annual Undergrad Tuition & Fees (In-State): $4,530
Enrollment: 419
Coed
Affiliation or Control: State
IRS Status: 501(c)3
Highest Offering: Associate Degree
Accreditation: NH

01 Superintendent/President MGen. Jerry W. GRIZZLE
32 Commandant LtCol. Jonathan K. GRAFF
100 Chief of Staff Col. David WEST
10 Chief Financial Officer Col. Judy SCHARMER
05 Dean BGen. Douglas J. MURRAY
41 Athletic Director/Dir Physical Educ Col. Jose BARRON
30 Development and Advancement Officer Maj. Kris WARD
116 Internal Auditor Capt. Ma Eva HEACOX
88 Professor of Military Science LtCol. Aaron JOHNSON
20 Vice Dean & High School Princ Col. George BRICK
15 Assistant Human Resources Director Ms. Carmen BELL
50 Assoc Dean Social Science/Business LtCol. Philip BACA
81 Assoc Dean Science/Mathematics Col. John R. MCVAY
79 Associate Dean Humanities Maj. Joel DYKSTRA
64 Director of Music Mr. Matthew BRADY
08 Director of the Library LtCol. Kalith SMITH
26 Marketing & Communication Director Vacant
18 Chief Facilities/Physical Plant Mr. Kent TAYLOR
06 Registrar Maj. Chris WRIGHT
37 Director of Financial Aid Maj. Sonya F. RODRIGUEZ
88 Mil Services Academies Prep Dir SCPO. Charles SCOTT
19 Chief of Campus Police Mr. Jerrold LONOWSKI
38 Director of Cadet Counseling Center Maj. Chance MACE
29 Director Alumni Association LtCol. Danny ARMIJO
04 Executive Secretary to President Ms. Bernadette BEATTY
09 Director of Institutional Research Ms. Michele BATES
102 Dir Foundation/Corporate Relations Mr. Jimmy BARNES
13 Chief Info Technology Officer Mr. Todd LUPIEN
07 Director of Admissions LtCol. Darius DOUGLAS

New Mexico State University Main Campus (B)

Box 30001, Las Cruces NM 88003-8001

County: Dona Ana
FICE Identification: 002657
Unit ID: 188030
Telephone: (575) 646-2035
Carnegie Class: DU-Higher
FAX Number: (575) 646-6334
Calendar System: Semester
URL: www.nmsu.edu
Established: 1888
Annual Undergrad Tuition & Fees (In-State): $6,686
Enrollment: 14,432
Coed
Affiliation or Control: State
IRS Status: 501(c)3
Highest Offering: Doctorate
Accreditation: NH, CAATE, CACREP, CAEP, CAEPN, COPSY, DIETD, DIETI, IPSY, MUS, NURSE, PH, SP, SPAA, SW

00 Chancellor Dr. Dan ARVIZU
01 President Dr. John FLOROS
05 Provost & Exec VP Ms. Carol PARKER
10 Sr VP Administration/Finance Dr. Andrew BURKE
111 VP Univ Advance/Pres NMSU Found Ms. Tina BYFORD
32 VP Student Success/Enroll Mgmt Dr. Renay SCOTT
85 Int Assoc Provost Intl/Border Pgm Dr. Rod MCSHERRY
26 Assoc VP Marketing & Comm Mr. Justin BANNISTER
21 Assoc VP Admin & Finance Ms. D'Anne STUART
15 Asst VP Human Resources Svcs Ms. Gena W. JONES
20 Assoc VP/Deputy Provost Dr. Greg FANT
09 Int Asst VP Institutional Analysis Ms. Natalie KELLNER
86 Asst VP Government Relations Mr. Ricardo REL
49 Dean College of Arts & Sciences Dr. Enrico PONTELLI
50 Dean Business College Dr. James HOFFMAN
53 Dean College of Education Dr. Susan BROWN
54 Dean College of Engineering Dr. Lakshmi REDDI
58 Dean Graduate School Dr. Luis CIFUENTES
76 Int Dean Col Health & Social Svcs Dr. Sonya COOPER
35 Dean of Students Dr. Ann GOODMAN
13 Chief Information Officer Ms. Norma GRIJALVA
06 University Registrar Ms. Dacia SEDILLO
43 General Counsel Mr. Roy COLLINS
08 Dean University Library Dr. Elizabeth TITUS
29 AVP Alumni Engagement/Participation Ms. Leslie CERVANTES
21 University Controller Ms. Norma NOEL
39 Acting Director Student Housing Ms. Ophelia WATKINS
23 Exec Director Health & Wellness Ms. Lori MCKEE
38 Interim Director Counseling Center Ms. Lori MCKEE
41 Director Athletics Mr. Mario MOCCIA
35 Asst VP Student Affairs Dr. Anthony S. MARIN
96 Dir Procurement Services Ms. Javier CORDERO
22 Dir Institutional Equity/EEO Ms. Laura CASTILLE
07 Director Admissions Ms. Seth MINER
18 Int Assoc VP Facilities Services Mr. Alton LOONEY
27 Dir of Marketing/Creative Svcs Ms. Ellen J. CASTELLO
47 Dean College of Agric Dr. Rolando FLORES
92 Dean Honors College Dr. Miriam CHAIKEN
12 President NMSU-DACC Dr. Monica TORRES
12 President NMSU Alamogordo Dr. Ken VAN WINKLE
12 President NMSU-Carlsbad Dr. John GRATTON
12 President NMSU-Grants Dr. Mickey BEST
100 Chief of Staff Mr. J. Leonard MARTINEZ
37 Director Student Financial Aid Dr. Vandeen MCKENZIE

New Mexico State University at Alamogordo (C)

2400 N Scenic Drive, Alamogordo NM 88310-4239

County: Otero
FICE Identification: 002658
Unit ID: 187994
Telephone: (575) 439-3600
Carnegie Class: Assoc/HT-High Non
FAX Number: (575) 439-3643
Calendar System: Semester
URL: www.nmsua.edu
Established: 1958
Annual Undergrad Tuition & Fees (In-State): $2,064
Enrollment: 1,710
Coed
Affiliation or Control: State
IRS Status: 501(c)3
Highest Offering: Associate Degree
Accreditation: NH

01 President Dr. Ken VAN WINKLE
05 Vice President for Academic Affairs Dr. Mark CAL
32 Vice President for Student Services Mrs. Anne RICKSECKER
10 Vice President for Business/Finance Mr. Antonio SALINAS
56 Assoc Vice Pres Extended Programs Mrs. Michelle PERRY
26 Marketing Representative Dr. Ken VAN WINKLE
13 Chief Info Technology Officer (CIO) Mr. David SANDERS
08 Librarian Dr. Sharon JENKINS
07 Director of Admissions/Registrar Mrs. Anne RICKSECKER
37 Financial Aid Representative Ms. Doris VALDESPINO
09 Director of Institutional Research Mr. Greg HILLIS
15 Director Human Resources Mrs. Brenda W. GARCIA
18 Director Facilities/Physical Plant Ms. Nancy WILKSON
96 Senior Buyer Mr. Lee M. KINNEY
04 Administrative Asst to President Ms. Mary FECHNER
106 Dir Online Education/E-learning Mrs. Sherrell WHEELER
105 Director Web Services Mr. David HILLE
108 Director Institutional Assessment Dr. Joyce HILL
19 Director Security/Safety Mr. Richard KOMMER
30 Director of Development Dr. Juan GARCIA

New Mexico State University at Carlsbad (D)

1500 University Drive, Carlsbad NM 88220-3598

County: Eddy
FICE Identification: 002659
Unit ID: 188003
Telephone: (575) 234-9200
Carnegie Class: Assoc/MT-VT-High Non
FAX Number: (575) 885-4951
Calendar System: Semester
URL: www.carlsbad.nmsu.edu
Established: 1950
Annual Undergrad Tuition & Fees (In-State): $1,276
Enrollment: 1,952
Coed
Affiliation or Control: State
IRS Status: 501(c)3
Highest Offering: Associate Degree
Accreditation: NH, ADNUR

01 Campus President Dr. John GRATTON
05 Chief Academic Officer/Provost Dr. Andrew I. NWANNE
32 Vice Pres Student Services Ms. Juanita GARCIA
10 VP Business & Finance Ms. Karla VOLPI
37 Director Financial Aid Ms. Diana CAMPOS
15 Human Resources Specialist Ms. Judith COX TINDOL
26 Director Marketing & Publications Ms. Sky KLAUS
04 Administrative Asst to President Ms. Janice CARNATHAN
18 Chief Facilities/Physical Plant Mr. Jeff NEAL

New Mexico State University Dona Ana Community College (E)

2800 Sonoma Ranch Boulevard, Las Cruces NM 88011

County: Dona Ana
Identification: 666649
Unit ID: 187620
Telephone: (575) 527-7500
Carnegie Class: Assoc/MT-VT-Mix Trad/Non
FAX Number: (575) 528-7300
Calendar System: Semester
URL: dacc.nmsu.edu
Established: 1973
Annual Undergrad Tuition & Fees (In-State): $1,770
Enrollment: 7,917
Coed
Affiliation or Control: State
IRS Status: 501(c)3
Highest Offering: Associate Degree
Accreditation: NH, ACBSP, ADNUR, COARC, DA, DH, DMS, EMT, IFSAC, RAD

01 President Dr. Monica TORRES
05 Interim VP Academic Affairs Dr. Susan WOOD
10 VP Business & Finance Ms. Kelly BROOKS
32 VP Student Services Mr. Amadeo LEDESMA
26 VP External Relations Mr. Arthur BINDER
20 AVP Acad Affairs/Assessment & Accr Dr. Susan WOOD
84 Assoc VP Acad Affairs/Enroll Mgt Dr. Rusty FOX
49 Division Dean Arts/Hum/Social Sci Dr. Martin WORTMAN
50 Division Dean Business/Public Svcs Ms. Lydia BAGWELL
76 Division Dean Health Sciences Ms. Josefina CARMONA
72 Division Dean Advanced Technologies Ms. Saundra CASTILLO
103 Exec Director Workforce Dev/Trng Dr. Fred OWENSBY
62 Director Library Services Ms. Tammy POWERS
121 Director Academic Advising Mr. Brad MAZDRA
09 Director Institutional Analysis Ms. Mary Beth WORLEY
55 Director Adult Education Ms. Maria ETHIER
31 Director Community Education Ms. Mary ULRICH
88 Director South County Centers Ms. Jacqueline KIEFER
21 Manager Business Office Ms. Diane PIERCE
15 Manager Human Resources Operation Ms. Yvette BENITIZ
90 Director Computer Support Ms. Lori ALLEN
18 Manager Facilities Services Mr. Michael LUCHAU
07 Director Admissions Ms. Geraldine MARTINEZ
37 Director Financial Aid Ms. Michelle LUKESH
22 Director Student Accessibility Svcs Mr. Jesse HAAS

New Mexico State University Grants (F)

1500 Third Street, Grants NM 87020-2025

Telephone: (505) 287-6678
FICE Identification: 008854
Accreditation: &NH

† Regional accreditation is carried under the parent institution in Las Cruces, NM.

Northern New Mexico College (G)

921 N Paseo de Onate, Espanola NM 87532-2649

County: Rio Arriba
FICE Identification: 020839
Unit ID: 188058
Telephone: (505) 747-2100
Carnegie Class: Bac/Assoc-Mixed
FAX Number: (505) 747-2170
Calendar System: Semester
URL: www.nnmc.edu
Established: 1909
Annual Undergrad Tuition & Fees (In-State): $4,952
Enrollment: 948
Coed
Affiliation or Control: State
IRS Status: 501(c)3
Highest Offering: Baccalaureate
Accreditation: NH, ACBSP, ADNUR, CAEPN, NURSE

01 President Dr. Richard J. BAILEY, JR.
10 Vice Pres for Finance & Admin Mr. Ricky BEJARANO
05 Provost/VP Academic Affairs Dr. Ivan LOPEZ-HURTADO
32 Interim Dean of Students Mr. Frank ORONA
06 Registrar Mr. Gerald WHEELER
08 Head Librarian Ms. Courtney BRUCH
84 Director of Recruitment Mr. Frank ORONA
37 Director of Financial Aid Mr. Jacob PACHECO
13 Director Information Technologies Mr. Jimi MONTOYA
15 Director of Human Resources Vacant
07 Director of Admissions Mr. Frank ORONA
102 Dir Foundation/Corporate Relations Dr. Richard J. BAILEY, JR.
28 Director of Equity & Diversity Dr. Patricia TRUJILLO
18 Director of Facilities/Security Mr. Andy ROMERO
09 Director of Institutional Research Ms. Carmella SANCHEZ
21 Dir Small Business Development Ms. Julianna BARBEE
121 Dir Inst Advise/Coord Stdnt Advise Ms. Lisa WILSON
41 Athletic Director/Coach Mr. Ryan CORDOVA
101 Exec Asst to Pres/Board of Regents Ms. Amy E. PENA
51 Coordinator Continuing Education Ms. Cecilia ROMERO
53 Interim Dean College of Education Dr. Sandra RODRIGUEZ
49 Dean College of Arts and Sciences Dr. Ulises RICOY
76 Dean of College of Health Sciences Ms. Ellen TRABKA
50 Dean Col of Business Administration Dr. Lori BACA
54 Int Dean Engineering & Technology Dr. Sadia AHMED
26 Creative Dir Communications/Mktg Ms. Sandy KROLICK

Pima Medical Institute-Albuquerque (H)

4400 Cutler Avenue NE, Albuquerque NM 87110-3935

Telephone: (505) 881-1234
FICE Identification: 036783
Accreditation: ABHES, COARC, DH, PTAA, RAD

† Branch campus of Pima Medical Institute-Tucson, Tucson, AZ

Ruidoso Branch Community College (I)

709 Mechem Drive, Ruidoso NM 88345

Telephone: (575) 257-2120
Identification: 770345
Accreditation: &NH

St. John's College (J)

1160 Camino de la Cruz Blanca, Santa Fe NM 87505-4599

County: Santa Fe
FICE Identification: 002093
Unit ID: 245652
Telephone: (505) 984-6000
Carnegie Class: Bac-A&S
FAX Number: (505) 984-6003
Calendar System: Semester
URL: www.sjc.edu
Established: 1964
Annual Undergrad Tuition & Fees: $54,118
Enrollment: 386
Coed
Affiliation or Control: Independent Non-Profit
IRS Status: 501(c)3
Highest Offering: Master's
Accreditation: NH

01 President Mr. Mark ROOSEVELT
05 Dean of the College Mr. J. Walter STERLING
30 Vice Pres for Dev/Alumni Affairs Ms. Phelosha COLLAROS
10 Treasurer/Financer Officer Mr. Michael DURAN
58 Assoc Dean Graduate Programs Mr. David MCDONALD
06 Registrar Mrs. Marline MARQUEZ-SCALLY
08 Library Director Ms. Jennifer SPRAGUE
07 Director of Admissions Mr. Yvette SHAFFER
09 Director of Institutional Research Vacant
15 Director of Human Resources Mr. Aaron YOUNG

18 Chief Facilities/Physical Plant ....Mr. Pat HOLMAN
26 Dir of Communications/External Rels ....Mr. Gabe GOMEZ
29 Assoc Dir of Alumni Relations ....Ms. Chris AAMOT
36 Director Career Services ....Ms. Margaret ODELL
37 Director Student Financial Aid ....Mr. Mike RODRIQUEZ

† Affiliated with St. John's College, Maryland.

San Juan College (A)

4601 College Boulevard, Farmington NM 87402-4699
County: San Juan FICE Identification: 002660
Unit ID: 188100
Telephone: (505) 326-3311 Carnegie Class: Assoc/HVT-Mix Trad/Non
FAX Number: (505) 566-3385 Calendar System: Semester
URL: www.sanjuancollege.edu
Established: 1956 Annual Undergrad Tuition & Fees (In-District): $1,546
Enrollment: 7,030 Coed
Affiliation or Control: Local IRS Status: 501(c)3
Highest Offering: Associate Degree
Accreditation: NH, ADNUR, CAHIIM, COARC, DH, EMT, OTA, PTAA, SURGT

01 President ....Dr. Toni PENDERGRASS
03 Executive Vice President ....Mr. Edward DESPLAS
05 Vice Pres for Learning ....Dr. Adrienne FORGETTE
32 Vice Pres for Student Services ....Dr. Boomer APPLEMAN
04 Executive Asst to President ....Ms. Jeanne NOTSON
20 Assoc VP for Learning ....Ms. Sandy GILPIN
15 AVP Human Resources and Legal Act ....Ms. Kerri LANGONI
102 Executive Director Foundation ....Ms. Gayle DEAN
21 Controller ....Mr. Kristie ELLIS
26 Director Marketing/Public Relations ....Ms. Rhonda SCHAEFER
124 Director of Retention ....Dr. Jenniffer VALORA
84 Sr Dir Enrollment Management ....Mr. Jon BETZ
50 Dean Sch Business & IT ....Dr. Brad PURDY
79 Dean School of Humanities ....Mr. John BOGGS
76 Int Dean Sch of Health Sciences ....Ms. Sherrie PAXSON
65 Int Dean School of Energy ....Ms. Alicia CORBELL
72 Int Dean School Trades & Technology ....Mr. Ron JERNIGAN
81 Dean Math/Science & Engineering ....Dr. Michael OTTINGER
16 Asst Dir HR Equity/Diversity ....Ms. Stacey ALLEN
88 Director Native American Programs ....Mr. Byron TSABETSAYE
08 Director Library Services ....Vacant
37 Sr Director of Financial Aid ....Ms. Mindi-Kim SCHRUM
18 Director Physical Plant ....Mr. Chris HARRELSON
19 Director Security/Safety ....Mr. Kenneth HIBNER
35 Director Student Activities ....Ms. Amanda ROBLES
96 Director Purchasing ....Mr. Frank COLE
38 Director Student Advising Center ....Ms. Christy FERRATO
74 Director Vet-Tech Program ....Dr. David WRIGHT
06 Registrar ....Ms. Sherri GAUGH
09 Int Dir of Institutional Research ....Ms. Carrie TSOSIE-JIM
13 Chief Info Technology Officer (CIO) ....Mr. Roy LYTLE
103 Dean of Workforce & Economic Devel ....Dr. Lorenzo REYES

Santa Fe Community College (B)

6401 Richards Avenue, Santa Fe NM 87508-4887
County: Santa Fe FICE Identification: 022781
Unit ID: 188137
Telephone: (505) 428-1000 Carnegie Class: Assoc/MT-VT-High Non
FAX Number: (505) 428-1296 Calendar System: Semester
URL: www.sfcc.edu
Established: 1983 Annual Undergrad Tuition & Fees (In-State): $1,755
Enrollment: 4,581 Coed
Affiliation or Control: State IRS Status: 501(c)3
Highest Offering: Associate Degree
Accreditation: NH, ADNUR, COARC, DA, EMT, MAC

01 President ....Dr. Becky ROWLEY
05 Vice Pres Academic Affairs ....Ms. Margaret PETERS
10 Vice Pres Finance ....Mr. Nick TELLES
09 VP Planning & Inst Effectiveness ....Mr. Yash MORIMOTO
84 Assoc VP Enrollment & Student Svcs ....Ms. Thomasinia ORTIZ-GALLEGOS
51 Director Cont Educ/Workforce Dev ....Ms. Kris SWEDIN
26 Exec Dir Marketing/Public Rels ....Mr. Todd LOVATO
102 Exec Dir SFCC Foundation ....Ms. Deborah BOLDT
06 Registrar ....Ms. Kathleen SENA
13 Chief Information Officer ....Mr. Jeremy LOVATO
37 Financial Aid Director ....Ms. Kelly DURBIN
66 Director of Nursing Education ....Ms. Terri TEWART
08 Library Director ....Ms. Valerie NYE
15 Interim Director of Human Resources ....Mr. Yash MORIMOTO
88 Director Small Business Development ....Mr. Brian DUBOFF
18 Exec Dir Plant & Operations Mgmt ....Mr. Henry MIGNARDOT
12 Executive Director HEC ....Ms. Rebecca ESTRADA
49 Dean School of Liberal Arts ....Dr. Bernadette JACOBS
54 Dean Sch Health/Engineering & Math ....Dr. Jenny LANDEN
76 Dean School of Fitness Education ....Dr. Jenny LANDEN
57 Dean Sch Arts/Design & Media Arts ....Dr. Bernadette JACOBS
75 Dean Trades/Tech/Sustainability ....Dr. Camilla BUSTAMANTE
50 Dean School of Business & Educ ....Dr. Camilla BUSTAMANTE
101 Executive Asst to the President ....Ms. Donna WELLS
96 Director of Purchasing ....Mr. John APODACA
25 Chief Contracts/Grants Admin ....Ms. Ann BLACK

Southwest Acupuncture College (C)

1622 Galisteo Street, Santa Fe NM 87505-6351
County: Santa Fe FICE Identification: 026220
Unit ID: 366605
Telephone: (505) 438-8884 Carnegie Class: Spec-4-yr-Other Health
FAX Number: (505) 438-8883 Calendar System: Semester
URL: www.acupuncturecollege.edu
Established: 1980 Annual Undergrad Tuition & Fees: N/A
Enrollment: 37 Coed
Affiliation or Control: Proprietary IRS Status: Proprietary
Highest Offering: Master's; No Lower Division
Accreditation: ACUP

01 CEO ....Dr. Anthony ABBATE
03 Executive Director ....Dr. Skya ABBATE
10 Chief Fiscal Officer ....Mr. Jim KUTSKO
12 Campus Director Santa Fe ....Dr. Paul ROSSIGNOL
17 Clinical Director Santa Fe ....Dr. Pamela BARRETT
05 Academic Dean Santa Fe ....Ms. Susan CHANEY
37 Director of Financial Aid ....Ms. Angela ANAYA
07 Director of Admissions ....Ms. Sophia BUNGAY

Southwest University of Visual Arts (D)

5000 Marble Avenue, NE, Albuquerque NM 87110-6344
Telephone: (505) 254-7575 Identification: 666524
Accreditation: &NH, CIDA

† Regional accreditation is carried under the parent institution in Tucson, AZ.

Southwestern College (E)

3960 San Felipe Road, Santa Fe NM 87507
County: Santa Fe FICE Identification: 030761
Unit ID: 188207
Telephone: (505) 471-5756 Carnegie Class: Spec-4-yr-Other Health
FAX Number: (505) 471-4071 Calendar System: Quarter
URL: www.swc.edu
Established: 1979 Annual Graduate Tuition & Fees: N/A
Enrollment: 178 Coed
Affiliation or Control: Independent Non-Profit IRS Status: 501(c)3
Highest Offering: Master's; No Undergraduates
Accreditation: NH

01 President ....Dr. Ann FILEMYR
12 Exec VP/Dir New Earth Institute SWC ....Ms. Katherine NINOS
05 Vice Pres Academic Affairs/Dean ....Dr. Jamal GRANICK
84 Director of Enrollment Services ....Ms. Dru PHOENIX
06 Registrar ....Ms. Andrea PACHECO
10 Chief Finance Officer ....Ms. Allison FRANK
13 Chief Technology Officer ....Ms. Donna HARRINGTON
32 Director Student/Career Services ....Ms. Emilah DAWN DETORO

Southwestern Indian Polytechnic Institute (F)

9169 Coors Boulevard, NW, Albuquerque NM 87120
County: Bernalillo FICE Identification: 025110
Unit ID: 188216
Telephone: (505) 346-2348 Carnegie Class: Tribal
FAX Number: (505) 346-2343 Calendar System: Trimester
URL: www.sipi.edu
Established: 1971 Annual Undergrad Tuition & Fees: $1,095
Enrollment: 366 Coed
Affiliation or Control: Federal IRS Status: 501(c)3
Highest Offering: Associate Degree
Accreditation: NH, OPD, OPLT

01 President ....Dr. Sherry ALLISON
10 Vice Pres College Operations ....Mr. Eric CHRISTENSEN
05 Vice President Academic Programs ....Ms. Valerie MONTOYA
09 Dir Institutional Rsch/Effect/Plng ....Mr. Edward HUMMINGBIRD
32 Acting Director of Student Services ....Dr. Cecelia COMETSEVAH
07 Director Admissions/Registrar ....Mr. Joseph CARPIO
15 Human Resources Specialist ....Ms. Dawn AMI
18 Facilities Director ....Ms. Renee ALLEN
37 Director Student Financial Aid ....Mr. Joseph CARPIO

University of New Mexico Main Campus (G)

1 University of New Mexico, Albuquerque NM 87131-0001
County: Bernalillo FICE Identification: 002663
Unit ID: 187985
Telephone: (505) 277-0111 Carnegie Class: DU-Highest
FAX Number: (505) 277-6019 Calendar System: Semester
URL: www.unm.edu
Established: 1889 Annual Undergrad Tuition & Fees (In-State): $7,633
Enrollment: 26,221 Coed
Affiliation or Control: State IRS Status: 501(c)3
Highest Offering: Doctorate
Accreditation: NH, ARCPA, CAATE, CACREP, CAEPN, CAMPEP, CLPSY, CONST, DANCE, DENT, DH, DIETD, DIETI, EMT, IPSY, JOUR, LAW, LSAR, MED, MIDWF, MT, MUS, NMT, NURSE, OT, PH, PHAR, PLNG, PTA, SP, SPAA, THEA

01 President ....Dr. Garnett S. STOKES
05 Provost ....Dr. James HOLLOWAY
17 Chancellor of Health Sciences Ctr ....Dr. Paul B. ROTH
10 SVP Finance & Administration ....Dr. Teresa COSTANTINIDIS
100 Chief of Staff ....Dr. Terry BABBITT
12 Special Asst for Branch Affairs ....Dr. Wynn M. GOERING
20 Int Sr Vice Prov for Acad Affairs ....Dr. Barbara L. RODRIGUEZ
46 Vice President Research ....Dr. Gabriel J. LOPEZ
25 AVP Research Administration ....Patricia HENNING
32 Vice President Student Affairs ....Dr. Eliseo S. TORRES
28 Vice Chancellor HSC Diversity ....Dr. Valerie ROMERO-LEGGOTT
84 Vice Prov Enrollment & Analytics ....Dan GARCIA
15 Vice President Human Resources ....Dorothy ANDERSON
21 University Controller ....Elizabeth METZGER
13 Chief Information Officer ....Duane ARRUTTI
14 Int Deputy Chief Information Ofcr ....Brian PIETREWICZ
43 Chief Legal Counsel ....Loretta MARTINEZ
29 AVP Alumni Relations ....Dana ALLEN
20 Dir Financial Ops Academic Affairs ....Nicole DOPSON
35 AVP Student Life ....Dr. Walter C. MILLER
35 AVP Student Services ....Dr. Tim GUTIERREZ
50 Dean Anderson School of Mgmt ....Dr. Craig WHITE
48 Dean Sch of Architecture & Planning ....Dr. Geraldine FORBES ISAIS
49 Dean College of Arts & Sciences ....Dr. Mark PECENY
53 Interim Dean College of Education ....Dr. Deborah RIFENBARY
54 Dean School of Engineering ....Dr. Christos CHRISTODOULOU
57 Interim Dean College of Fine Arts ....Dr. Regina CARLOW
61 Dean School of Law ....Sergio PAREJA
63 Exec Vice Dean School of Medicine ....Dr. Martha MCGREW
66 Dean College of Nursing ....Dr. Christine KASPER
67 Dean College of Pharmacy ....Dr. Donald A. GODWIN
80 Dir School of Public Admin ....Dr. Bruce J. PERLMAN
92 Dean University College ....Dr. Kate KRAUSE
58 Dean Office of Graduate Studies ....Dr. Julie COONROD
51 Int Director Continuing Education ....Audrey ARNOLD
08 Dean University Libraries ....Dr. Richard CLEMENT
26 Chief Univ Marketing & Comm Officer ....Cinnamon BLAIR
27 HSC Exec Dir Comm & Marketing ....William O. SPARKS
27 University Media Relations Officer ....Daniel JIRON
105 Mgr University Web Communications ....Matt CARTER
86 Interim Director Government Affairs ....Connie BEIMER
09 Director Institutional Analytics ....Dr. Heather S. MECHLER
88 University Architect ....Amy COBURN
18 Director Physical Plant ....Al SENA
19 Chief of Police ....Kevin MCCABE
96 Chief Procurement Officer ....Bruce E. CHERRIN
23 Director Student Health Center ....Dr. Beverly KLOEPPEL
22 Director Equal Opportunity ....Francie CORDOVA
56 Dir Extended Learning ....Debby KNOTTS
35 Dean of Students ....Nasha TORREZ
07 Director Admissions and Recruitment ....Matt HULETT
06 Registrar ....Sheila JURNAK
37 Director Student Financial Aid ....Brian MALONE
36 Director Career Services ....Dr. Jenna S. CRABB
39 Director Student Housing & Res Life ....Wayne SULLIVAN
40 Director Bookstore ....Carrie MITCHELL
108 Director of Assessment ....Vacant
102 UNM Foundation President and CEO ....Henry NEMCIK
30 VP University Development ....Larry RYAN
30 VP Development Health Sciences Ctr ....Bill UHER
88 CEO UNM Hospital ....Steve MCKERNAN
04 Administrative Asst to President ....Mitch GARRITY
101 Secretary of the Institution/Board ....Mallory REVIERE

University of New Mexico-Gallup (H)

705 Gurley Avenue, Gallup NM 87301
Telephone: (505) 863-7500 FICE Identification: 006881
Accreditation: &NH, ADNUR, CAHIIM, DA, MLTAD

† Regional accreditation is carried under the parent institution in Albuquerque, NM.

University of New Mexico-Los Alamos (I)

4000 University Drive, Los Alamos NM 87544-2233
Telephone: (505) 662-5919 Identification: 666742
Accreditation: &NH

† Regional accreditation is carried under the parent institution in Albuquerque, NM.

University of New Mexico-Taos (J)

1157 Country Road 110, Ranchos de Taos NM 87557
Telephone: (575) 737-6215 Identification: 666743
Accreditation: &NH, ADNUR

† Regional accreditation is carried under the parent institution in Albuquerque, NM.

University of New Mexico-Valencia (K)

280 La Entrada Road, Los Lunas NM 87031-7633
Telephone: (505) 925-8500 Identification: 666741
Accreditation: &NH, ADNUR

† Regional accreditation is carried under the parent institution in Albuquerque, NM.

University of Phoenix New Mexico Campus (L)

5700 Pasadena Avenue, NE, Albuquerque NM 87113-1570
Telephone: (505) 821-4800 Identification: 770219
Accreditation: &NH, ACBSP

† No longer accepting campus-based students.

University of St. Francis (M)

1500 N. Renaissance Blvd, NE, Ste C, Albuquerque NM 87107
Telephone: (505) 266-5565 Identification: 770099

Accreditation: &NH, ARCPA

† Branch campus of University of St. Francis, Joliet, IL

University of the Southwest (A)

6610 Lovington Highway, Hobbs NM 88240-9129
County: Lea | FICE Identification: 002650
Unit ID: 188182
Telephone: (575) 392-6561 | Carnegie Class: Masters/M
FAX Number: (575) 392-6006 | Calendar System: Semester
URL: www.usw.edu
Established: 1962 | Annual Undergrad Tuition & Fees: $16,200
Enrollment: 1,026 | Coed
Affiliation or Control: Independent Non-Profit | IRS Status: 501(c)3
Highest Offering: Doctorate
Accreditation: NH

01 President ... Dr. Quint THURMAN
05 Provost ... Dr. Ryan TIPTON
10 VP for Financial Services/CFO ... Mr. Steven RACHEL
37 Vice President of Student Finance ... Mrs. Dawny KRINGEL
18 Campus Steward ... Dr. David ARNOLD
41 Acting Athletic Director ... Mr. Steve APPEL
32 Director of Student Affairs ... Ms. Amanda GUZMAN
15 Asst VP HR & Regulatory Compliance ... Mrs. Veronica TORREZ
49 Dean College of Arts & Sciences ... Vacant
50 Dean College of Business ... Dr. Ryan TIPTON
53 Dean College of Education ... Dr. Elyn PALMER
06 University Registrar ... Ms. Lissete TERRAZAS
84 Enrollment Counselor ... Ms. Donna ROBBINS
58 Director of Graduate Center ... Mrs. Sandy WILKINSON
35 Director of Student Life ... Ms. Shelbie FAUGHT
39 Director Student Housing ... Mr. Cory HITCHCOCK
30 Coord of Development & Fundraising ... Vacant
38 University Counselor ... Mr. Brian ARNOLD
42 Campus Pastor ... Mr. Mark ROHRER
105 Instructional Design Technician ... Mr. David WILLIS
26 Stakeholder Relations Coordinator ... Ms. RaeLynn DUNLAP
04 Administrative Asst to President ... Mrs. Linda WOODFIN
08 Library & Student Lrng Resources ... Ms. Paige SULLIVAN
88 Maintenance Supervisor ... Mr. Lonnie HARRISON

Western New Mexico University (B)

PO Box 680, Silver City NM 88062-0680
County: Grant | FICE Identification: 002664
Unit ID: 188304
Telephone: (575) 538-6238 | Carnegie Class: Masters/L
FAX Number: (575) 538-6364 | Calendar System: Semester
URL: wnmu.edu
Established: 1893 | Annual Undergrad Tuition & Fees (In-State): $6,066
Enrollment: 3,088 | Coed
Affiliation or Control: State | IRS Status: 501(c)3
Highest Offering: Beyond Master's But Less Than Doctorate
Accreditation: NH, ACBSP, CAEPN, NURSE, SW

01 President ... Dr. Joseph SHEPARD
05 Provost/Vice Pres Academic Affairs ... Dr. Jack CROCKER
32 VP Student Affairs/Enrollment Mgmt ... Dr. Isaac BRUNDAGE
10 VP Business Affairs ... Ms. Kelley RIDDLE
30 VP External Affairs ... Dr. Magdaleno MANZANAREZ
20 Assoc Vice Pres Academic Affairs ... Dr. Steven CHAVEZ
06 Registrar ... Ms. Betsy MILLER
08 University Librarian ... Dr. Gilda BAEZA-ORTEGO
37 Director Student Financial Aid ... Ms. Cheryl HAIN
07 Director Admissions & Recruitment ... Mr. Andrew LUNT
09 Director of Institutional Research ... Vacant
15 Director of Human Resources ... Ms. Maura GONSIOR
18 Asst VP of Facilities ... Mr. Kevin MATTHES
26 Director of Marketing ... Mr. Mario SANCHEZ
29 Director of Alumni Affairs ... Ms. Amanda MOFFETT LANE
36 Coord of Career/Student Svcs ... Ms. Janine SOHLER
35 Asst Dean of Student Life & Develop ... Ms. Jessica MORALES
96 Director Materials/Resources ... Ms. Amy BACA
100 Chief of Staff ... Ms. Julie MORALES
19 Director Campus Police ... Mr. Eddie FLORES
41 Athletic Director ... Mr. Scott NOBLE
49 Dean of College of Arts and Science ... Vacant
53 Interim Dean of Education ... Dr. Debra DIRKSEN
04 Admin Assistant to the President ... Ms. Mary Rae MCDONALD
22 Affirmative Action/Equal Oppty ... Ms. Debra NOBLE

NEW YORK

Adelphi University (C)

1 South Avenue, PO Box 701,
Garden City NY 11530-0701
County: Nassau | FICE Identification: 002666
Unit ID: 188429
Telephone: (516) 877-3000 | Carnegie Class: DU-Mod
FAX Number: (516) 877-3545 | Calendar System: Semester
URL: www.adelphi.edu
Established: 1896 | Annual Undergrad Tuition & Fees: $38,740
Enrollment: 7,978 | Coed
Affiliation or Control: Independent Non-Profit | IRS Status: 501(c)3
Highest Offering: Doctorate
Accreditation: M, AUD, CAEPN, CLPSY, IPSY, NURSE, SP, SW

01 President ... Dr. Christine M. RIORDAN
05 Provost/Exec VP ... Dr. Steve EVERETT
10 Executive VP of Finance & Admin ... Mr. James J. PERRINO
28 VP of Diversity and Inclusion ... Dr. Perry GREENE
111 Int VP of University Advancement ... Ms. Patrice REGAN-PANZA
84 VP of Enrollment Management ... Ms. Kristen CAPEZZA
26 AVP Branding Strategy & Univ Comm .. Ms. Joanna TEMPLETON
100 Chief of Staff/Assoc VP Ext Rel ... Ms. Maggie GRAFER
20 Deputy Provost ... Dr. Audrey S. BLUMBERG
32 Assoc Provost for Student Success ... Dr. Peter WEST
20 Assoc Provost Fac Adv & Research ... Dr. Chris K. STORM, JR.
21 CFO & Assoc VP ... Mr. Robert L. DECARLO
13 Chief Information Officer/CIO ... Ms. Carol A. BOYLE
15 Chief Human Resource Officer ... Ms. Lucinda J. DONNELLY
19 Chief Admin Officer & Assoc VP ... Mr. Eugene PALMA
09 Assistant Provost for IR ... Dr. Nava LERER
18 Asst VP for Facilities Management ... Mr. Robert J. SHIPLEY
37 Asst VP Student Financial Services ... Ms. Sheryl L. MIHOPULOS
49 Dean College of Arts & Sciences ... Dr. Vincent WANG
53 Dean Col of Educ & Health Sciences ... Dr. Xiao-lei WANG
66 Dean Col of Nursing & Public Health ... Dr. Elaine L. SMITH
70 Int Dean School of Social Work ... Ms. Diann E. CAMERON-KELLY
83 Dean GF Derner Sch of Psychology ... Dr. Jacques BARBER
50 Dean RB Willumstad Sch of Business ... Dr. Rajib N. SANYAL
92 Dean Honors College ... Dr. Susan DINAN
107 Dean Col of Prof & Cont Studies ... Mr. Andy ATZERT
08 Interim Dean University Libraries ... Ms. Debbi SMITH
35 Dean of Student Affairs/Asst VP ... Mr. Jeffrey A. KESSLER
16 Dir Talent Mgmt & Labor Relations ... Ms. Jane FISHER
41 Director of Athletics ... Mr. Daniel MCCABE
36 Exec Dir Center Career & Prof Dev ... Mr. Thomas J. WARD, JR.
06 University Registrar ... Mr. Steven E. SMITH
104 Director International Education ... Ms. Shannon HARRISON
23 Director Health Services ... Ms. Jacqueline JOHNSTON
38 Director Counseling & Support Svcs ... Dr. Carol A. LUCAS
39 Director Residential Life/Housing ... Mr. Guy SENEQUE
29 Exec Director Alumni Relations ... Ms. Jodie SPERICO
114 Dir of Financial Ops & Assoc VP ... Mr. Michael J. MCLEOD
96 Director of Procurement ... Ms. Elizabeth F. KASH
108 Director Institutional Assessment ... Vacant
105 Director of Web Development ... Ms. Tara A. COYLE
101 Director of Board Relations ... Ms. Mary ALDRIDGE
91 Director of Postmodern ERP ... Mr. Michael DICRESCIO
44 Director of Participation ... Ms. Jennifer WALSH
88 Spec Asst to Provost for Strat Init ... Dr. Sam GROGG
46 Director Research & Sponsored Pgms ... Ms. Mary CORTINA
88 Dir Faculty Ctr for Prof Excellence ... Ms. Nathalie ZARISFI

Albany College of Pharmacy and Health Sciences (D)

106 New Scotland Avenue, Albany NY 12208-3492
County: Albany | FICE Identification: 002885
Unit ID: 188526
Telephone: (518) 694-7200 | Carnegie Class: Spec-4-yr-Other Health
FAX Number: (518) 694-7202 | Calendar System: Semester
URL: www.acphs.edu
Established: 1881 | Annual Undergrad Tuition & Fees: $35,105
Enrollment: 1,384 | Coed
Affiliation or Control: Independent Non-Profit | IRS Status: 501(c)3
Highest Offering: Doctorate
Accreditation: M, CYTO, MT, PHAR

01 President ... Greg DEWEY
05 Interim Dean/VP of Academic Affairs ... Anuja GHORPADE
46 Director of Research ... Martha HASS
12 Associate Dean for Vermont Campus ... Jennifer MATHEWS
32 VP of Student Success ... Susan IWANOWICZ
10 VP of Finance ... Michele VIEN
111 VP of Institutional Advancement ... Vicki DILORENZO
84 VP of Enrollment Management ... Tiffany GUTIERREZ
13 Chief Information Officer ... Joshua SINGLETARY
11 VP of Administrative Operations ... Packy MCGRAW
07 Director of Admissions ... Nicholas BALK
06 Registrar ... Jeff DUFOUR
26 Exec Director of Marketing/Comm ... Vacant
41 Director of Athletics & Rec ... Christine KANAWADA
15 Director of Human Resources ... Susan KARAVOLAS
110 AVP of Development ... Deanna ENNELLO-BUTLER
37 Director of Financial Aid ... Kathleen MONTAGUE

Albany Law School (E)

80 New Scotland Avenue, Albany NY 12208-3494
County: Albany | FICE Identification: 002886
Unit ID: 188535
Telephone: (518) 445-2311 | Carnegie Class: Spec-4-yr-Law
FAX Number: (518) 445-2315 | Calendar System: Semester
URL: www.albanylaw.edu
Established: 1851 | Annual Undergrad Tuition & Fees: N/A
Enrollment: 435 | Coed
Affiliation or Control: Independent Non-Profit | IRS Status: 501(c)3
Highest Offering: First Professional Degree
Accreditation: @M, LAW

01 President & Dean ... Dean Alicia OUELLETTE
05 Assoc Dean Acad Affairs ... Dean Connie MAYER
10 Vice President Finance & Business ... Mr. Victor E. RAUSCHER
08 Director of Library ... Mr. David WALKER
111 Vice President Inst Advancement ... Dr. Jeffrey SCHANZ
32 Associate Dean for Student Affairs ... Prof. Rosemary QUEENAN
06 Assistant Dean and Registrar ... Ms. Joanne FITZSIMMONS
36 Asst Dean Career Center ... Ms. Mary WALSH FITZPATRICK
26 Director Communications ... Mr. Chris COLTON
04 Executive Assistant to the Dean ... Ms. Barbara JORDAN-SMITH
07 Assistant Dean of Admissions ... Ms. Amy MANGIONE
88 Director Clinical Program ... Prof. Connie MAYER
13 Assoc Dir Enterprise Info Systems ... Vacant
29 Director Alumni Engage/Inst Events ... Mr. Geoffrey SEBER
15 Director Human Resources ... Ms. Sherri DONNELLY
37 Director Student Financial Aid ... Ms. Andrea WEDLER
18 Director of Facilities & Admin Svcs ... Mr. Brian LAPLANTE
36 Director of Career Services ... Ms. Joanne CASEY
106 Dir Online Learning/Instruct Tech ... Dr. Patricia BAIA

Albany Medical College (F)

47 New Scotland Avenue, Mail #34,
Albany NY 12208-3479
County: Albany | FICE Identification: 002887
Unit ID: 188580
Telephone: (518) 262-6008 | Carnegie Class: Spec-4-yr-Med
FAX Number: (518) 262-6515 | Calendar System: Semester
URL: www.amc.edu
Established: 1839 | Annual Graduate Tuition & Fees: N/A
Enrollment: 840 | Coed
Affiliation or Control: Independent Non-Profit | IRS Status: 501(c)3
Highest Offering: Doctorate; No Undergraduates
Accreditation: M, ANEST, ARCPA, IPSY, MED, PAST

01 Dean/Exec VP Health Affairs ... Dr. Vincent P. VERDILE
10 EVP/Chief Financial Officer ... Ms. Frances SPREER-ALBERT
05 Vice Dean for Academic Admin ... Dr. Henry S. POHL
17 Vice Dean Clinical Affairs ... Dr. Ferdinand VENDITTI
32 Assoc Dean for Acad & Student Affs ... Vacant
63 Assoc Dean Graduate Medical Educ ... Dr. Joel BARTFIELD
22 Assoc Dean Cmty Outreach/Medical Ed ... Dr. Ingrid M. ALLARD
08 Asc Dn Info Resrcs/Tech/Dir Library ... Ms. Enid GEYER
88 Asst Dean Medical Education ... Dr. Rebecca KELLER
58 Assoc Dean for Graduate Studies ... Dr. Peter VINCENT
06 Registrar ... Ms. Krista REYNOLDS-STUMP
88 Director Graduate Medical Education ... Ms. Catherine RIDDLE
76 Director Physician Asst Program ... Dr. David IRVINE
29 Executive Director Alumni Relations ... Ms. Sandra DINOTO
26 Director Public Relations ... Mr. Jeffrey GORDON
30 Chief Development ... Ms. Molly NICHOL
51 Director Cont Medical Education ... Ms. Jennifer PRICE
15 Director Human Resources ... Ms. Darleen SOUZA
37 Director Student Financial Aid ... Ms. Ann LOUGHMAN
96 Director of Purchasing ... Ms. Ann CRISLIP
27 Marketing Specialist ... Ms. Nicolette VISCUSI
03 Executive Assoc Dean ... Mr. John DEPAOLA
09 Director of Institutional Research ... Dr. Paul FEUSTEL
85 Director Foreign Students ... Ms. Marianne R. WILLIAMS
13 Chief Info Technology Officer (CIO) ... Mr. George HICKMAN
18 Chief Facilities Physical Plant ... Mr. Donald STICHTER
19 Director Security/Safety ... Mr. John HERRITAGE
38 Director Student Counseling ... Dr. Jeffrey WINSEMAN
43 Dir Legal Services/General Counsel ... Mr. Lee HESSBERG
45 Chief Institutional Planning ... Ms. Courtney BURKE
88 Director Nurse Anesthesia Pgm ... Dr. Jodi DELLA ROCCA

Albert Einstein College of Medicine (G)

1300 Morris Park Avenue, Bronx NY 10461
FICE Identification: 042797
Telephone: (718) 430-2000 | Carnegie Class: Not Classified
FAX Number: N/A | Calendar System: Semester
URL: www.einstein.yu.edu
Established: 1953 | Annual Undergrad Tuition & Fees: N/A
Enrollment: N/A | Coed
Affiliation or Control: Independent Non-Profit | IRS Status: 501(c)3
Highest Offering: First Professional Degree
Accreditation: @M, MED

01 Dean ... Dr. Gordon F. TOMASELLI
63 Executive Dean ... Dr. Edward R. BURNS
10 Assoc Dean Admin & Finance ... Dr. Gregg T. TARQUINIO
32 Assoc Dean for Student Affairs ... Dr. Allison LUDWIG
07 Associate Dean of Admissions ... Ms. Noreen KERRIGAN

Alfred University (H)

One Saxon Drive, Alfred NY 14802-1205
County: Allegany | FICE Identification: 002668
Unit ID: 188641
Telephone: (607) 871-2111 | Carnegie Class: Masters/L
FAX Number: (607) 871-2339 | Calendar System: Semester
URL: www.alfred.edu
Established: 1836 | Annual Undergrad Tuition & Fees: $29,188
Enrollment: 2,354 | Coed
Affiliation or Control: Independent Non-Profit | IRS Status: 501(c)3
Highest Offering: Doctorate
Accreditation: M, ART, CAATE, CACREP, SCPSY

01 President ... Dr. Mark A. ZUPAN
05 Int Provost/VP for Academic Affairs ... Dr. Elizabeth A. DOBIE
10 VP for Business & Finance/Treasurer ... Ms. Giovina LLOYD
30 VP for University Relations ... Mr. Jason AMORE
84 VP for Enrollment Management ... Mr. Brian DALTON
32 VP for Student Affairs ... Ms. Kimberly GUYER
57 Dean School of Art & Design ... Mr. Gerar EDIZEL

49 Int Dean Col of Lib Arts & Sciences .... Mr. G. David TOOT
107 Dean College of Business .... Mr. Mark LEWIS
54 Dean School of Engineering .... Dr. Gabrielle G. GAUSTAD
35 Int Dean of Students .... Mrs. Del Rey HONEYCUTT
29 Alumni Engagement Officer .... Ms. Janet MARBLE
37 Exec Dir Student Financial Aid Svcs .... Ms. Jane A. GILLILAND
07 Director of Admissions .... Mr. Jacob M. YALE
06 Registrar .... Mr. Pontus NIKLASSON
19 Chief of Public Safety .... Mr. John R. ZLOMEK
26 Exec Dir of Mktg & Communication ..... Mr. Michael KOZLOWSKI
39 Director of Residence Life .... Ms. Vicky GEBEL
13 Director Information Tech Svcs .... Mr. Gary O. ROBERTS
36 Director Career Development Ctr .... Ms. Amanda BAKER
41 Athletic Director .... Mr. Paul VECCHIO
23 Dir Counseling & Wellness Center .... Dr. Del Ray HONEYCUTT
08 Dean of Libraries .... Mr. Brian T. SULLIVAN
08 Director of Libraries .... Mrs. Mechele C. ROMANCHOCK
15 Director of Human Resources .... Mr. Mark A. GUINAN
21 Controller .... Ms. Amanda R. AZZI
92 Director of the Honors Program .... Dr. Julianna R. GRAY
94 Dir of Women's Leadership Center .... Ms. Abby GRIFFITH
43 Dir Physical Plants .... Mr. James T. BABCOCK
101 Secretary to the Corporation .... Ms. Mary C. MCALLISTER
104 Dir Study Abroad Programs .... Ms. Jeanne V. MARION
40 Bookstore Manager .... Mrs. Marcy K. BRADLEY
87 Dir of Summer/Parent Programs .... Mrs. Bonnie J. DUNGAN
09 Director of Institutional Research .... Mr. Frederick B. RODGERS
28 Director of Diversity .... Mr. Daniel J. NAPOLITANO
102 Dir Foundation/Corporate Relations .... Mr. Brian SHANAHAN
96 Director of Procurement .... Mrs. Melissa BADEAU

American Academy of Dramatic Arts (A)

120 Madison Avenue, New York NY 10016-7089

County: New York FICE Identification: 007465
Unit ID: 188678
Telephone: (212) 686-9244 Carnegie Class: Spec 2-yr-A&S
FAX Number: (212) 545-7934 Calendar System: Other
URL: www.aada.edu
Established: 1884 Annual Undergrad Tuition & Fees: $35,160
Enrollment: 269 Coed
Affiliation or Control: Independent Non-Profit IRS Status: 501(c)3
Highest Offering: Associate Degree
Accreditation: M, THEA

01 President .... Ms. Susan ZECH
111 Sr VP Institutional Advancement .... Vacant
10 Chief Financial Officer .... Mr. Joel BLOCK
05 Director of Instruction .... Mr. Constantine SCOPAS
07 Director of Admissions .... Ms. Kerin REILLY
27 Sr Director of Marketing .... Mr. James LUBIN
08 Librarian .... Ms. Deborah PICONE
21 Controller .... Ms. Linda VIALA
11 Senior Director of Operations .... Mr. Peter TUFEL
26 Director External Affairs .... Vacant
37 Director of Financial Aid .... Ms. Lisa SHAHEEN
04 Exec Assistant to the President .... Mr. Jimmy WILSON

American Academy McAllister Institute of Funeral Service (B)

619 W 54th Street, 2nd Floor, New York NY 10019

County: New York FICE Identification: 010813
Unit ID: 188687
Telephone: (212) 757-1190 Carnegie Class: Spec 2-yr-A&S
FAX Number: (212) 765-5923 Calendar System: Semester
URL: www.aami.edu
Established: 1926 Annual Undergrad Tuition & Fees: $17,085
Enrollment: 480 Coed
Affiliation or Control: Independent Non-Profit IRS Status: 501(c)3
Highest Offering: Associate Degree
Accreditation: FUSER

01 President .... Dr. George CONNICK
11 Program Director .... Ms. Tracy LENTZ
10 Bursar .... Mr. Jay TSO
37 Financial Aid Officer .... Ms. Natalie GIVAN
06 Registrar .... Mr. Andre RAMPAUL
07 Dir of Admissions/Enrollment Mgmt .... Ms. Tracy LENTZ
20 Academic Advisor .... Ms. Charlotte RERRICK
20 Academic Advisor .... Ms. Karen CARR
43 Legal Counsel .... Mr. Charles MAURER

ASA College (C)

151 Lawrence Street, Brooklyn NY 11201

County: Kings FICE Identification: 030955
Unit ID: 404994
Telephone: (718) 522-9073 Carnegie Class: Assoc/MT-VT-High Trad
FAX Number: (718) 532-1433 Calendar System: Semester
URL: www.asa.edu
Established: 1985 Annual Undergrad Tuition & Fees: $12,920
Enrollment: 4,686 Coed
Affiliation or Control: Proprietary IRS Status: Proprietary
Highest Offering: Baccalaureate
Accreditation: M, MAC, @PTAA

01 President .... Mr. Jose F. VALENCIA
05 Provost .... Dr. Shanthi KONKOTH
26 Vice President Marketing/Admissions .. Ms. Victoria KOSTYUKOV
29 VP Placement/Alumni Svcs .... Ms. Lesia WILLIS
37 VP Financial Aid Svcs .... Ms. Victoriya SHTAMLER
11 VP Planning & Operations .... Ms. Maritza MERCADO
86 VP Govt & Community Rels .... Mr. Roberto DUMAUAL
10 Controller .... Mr. Mark MIRENBERG
20 Academic Dean .... Dr. Edward KUFUOR
106 Director of Distance Learning .... Mr. Joel ALMORADIE
08 Head Librarian .... Mr. Brook STOWE
06 Registrar .... Ms. Mariana ZINDER
13 IT Director .... Mr. David ESTRIN
108 Director Institutional Assessment .... Ms. Ksenia KASIMOVA
09 Director Institutional Research .... Ms. Anna BOUKHMAN
15 Director of Human Resources .... Vacant
18 Chief Facilities/Physical Plant .... Mr. Walter KRUMER
50 Dean of Business .... Ms. Bridget UDEH
88 Dean of Legal Studies .... Vacant
49 Dean of Arts and Sciences .... Mr. Lizhi (Frank) ZHU
88 Director for Language Studies .... Ms. Ludmilla DRAGUSHANSKAYA
36 Director College/Career Prep .... Ms. Denise DUBRON
76 Dean of Health Disciplines .... Dr. Nasser SEDHOM
66 Dean of Nursing .... Ms. Donna M. REID
54 Dean Div Engineering & Technology .... Vacant
20 Dean Academic & Program Development ... Ms. Deborah HUGHES
88 Ombudsperson .... Dr. Jennifer ROSS
32 Asst Dean for Student Success .... Ms. Lillian GRANILLO
16 Title IX Coordinator .... Dr. Jayne WEINBERGER
38 Director Student Counseling ..... Ms. Tatyana KRYZHANOVSKAYA
41 Athletic Director .... Mr. Kenneth WILCOX
39 Director Student Housing .... Vacant

Bais Binyomin Academy, Inc (D)

51 Carlton Road, Monsey NY 10952

County: Rockland FICE Identification: 029120
Unit ID: 128586
Telephone: (845) 207-0330 Carnegie Class: Spec-4-yr-Faith
FAX Number: N/A Calendar System: Semester
Established: 1976 Annual Undergrad Tuition & Fees: $8,450
Enrollment: 25 Male
Affiliation or Control: Independent Non-Profit IRS Status: 501(c)3
Highest Offering: First Talmudic Degree
Accreditation: RABN

01 Rosh Hayeshiva .... Rabbi Meyer HERSHKOWITZ
04 Associate Rosh Hayeshiva .... Rabbi Yeruchom ZEILBERGER
05 Dean .... Rabbi Michael BENDER

Bais Medrash Ateres Shlomo (E)

220 Bennett Avenue, New York NY 10040

County: New York Identification: 667321
Telephone: (212) 419-5758 Carnegie Class: Not Classified
FAX Number: (914) 736-1055 Calendar System: Semester
URL: baismedrashateresshlomo.com
Established: 2016 Annual Undergrad Tuition & Fees: N/A
Enrollment: N/A Male
Affiliation or Control: Jewish IRS Status: 501(c)3
Highest Offering: First Talmudic Degree
Accreditation: AIJS

Bank Street College of Education (F)

610 W 112 Street, New York NY 10025-1898

County: New York FICE Identification: 002669
Unit ID: 189015
Telephone: (212) 875-4400 Carnegie Class: Spec-4-yr-Other
FAX Number: (212) 875-4759 Calendar System: Semester
URL: www.bankstreet.edu
Established: 1916 Annual Graduate Tuition & Fees: N/A
Enrollment: 704 Coed
Affiliation or Control: Independent Non-Profit IRS Status: 501(c)3
Highest Offering: Master's; No Undergraduates
Accreditation: M

01 President .... Shael POLAKOW-SURANSKY
100 Chief of Staff .... Katherine CONNELLY
10 Chief Financial Officer .... Alpha CONTEH
11 Chief Operating Officer .... Justin TYACK
30 VP Development .... Marcela HAHN
86 VP Governance/Community Engagement .... Akilah ROSADO
58 Dean of the Graduate School .... Cecelia TRAUGH
88 Dean of Children's Programs .... Jed LIPPARD
123 Director of Graduate Admissions .... Stephen OSTENDORFF
06 Registrar .... Ann COX
37 Director of Student Financial Aid .... Emmett COOPER
29 Director of Alumni Relations .... Linda REING
15 Chief Human Resources Officer .... Elyse MATTHEWS
13 Chief Information Officer .... Judith JOHNSON
18 Dir of Facilities/Security/Safety .... Carlos ESQUIVEL
08 Director of Library Services .... Kristin FREDA
36 Director of Student Placement .... Susan LEVINE
09 Director of Institutional Research .... Amy KLINE
04 Executive Assistant to President .... Regina WRIGHT

Bard College (G)

PO Box 5000, Annandale-On-Hudson NY 12504-5000

County: Dutchess FICE Identification: 002671
Unit ID: 189088
Telephone: (845) 758-6822 Carnegie Class: Bac-A&S
FAX Number: (845) 758-4294 Calendar System: Semester
URL: www.bard.edu
Established: 1860 Annual Undergrad Tuition & Fees: $54,680
Enrollment: 2,293 Coed
Affiliation or Control: Independent Non-Profit IRS Status: 501(c)3
Highest Offering: Doctorate
Accreditation: M, #CAEP

01 President .... Dr. Leon BOTSTEIN
03 Executive Vice President of College .... Dr. Dimitri B. PAPADIMITRIOU
45 Vice Pres for Strategic Initiatives .... Mr. Taun TOAY
30 Vice Pres Alumni/ae Affairs/Devel .... Ms. Debra PEMSTEIN
10 VP for Admin & Finance/CFO .... Dr. James BRUDVIG
11 Vice President for Administration .... Ms. Coleen MURPHY ALEXANDER
05 Associate Dean of the College .... Ms. Deirdre D'ALBERTIS
20 VP Acad Affairs/Dir Civic Engagemnt .... Dr. Jonathan BECKER
20 Associate VP for Academic Affairs .... Dr. David SHEIN
100 Chief of Staff .... Ms. Malia DU MONT
32 VP for Student Affairs .... Ms. Erin CANNAN
09 VP for Institutional Research .... Dr. Mark D. HALSEY
35 Dean of Student Affairs .... Ms. Bethany NOHLGREN
57 Dir Milton Avery Grad Sch of Arts .... Mr. Arthur GIBBONS
88 Dir Bard Grad Ctr Decorative Arts .... Dr. Susan WEBER
88 Exec Dir Ctr Curatorial Studies .... Mr. Tom ECCLES
110 Asst VP Dir of Inst Support .... Ms. Karen UNGER
88 Director Ctr Environmental Policy .... Dr. Eban GOODSTEIN
37 Director Financial Aid .... Ms. Denise ACKERMAN
06 Registrar .... Mr. Peter GADSBY
26 Associate VP of Communications .... Mr. Mark PRIMOFF
15 Director of Human Resources .... Ms. Kimberly ALEXANDER
21 Associate VP for Finance .... Vacant
88 Director Inst Writing/Thinking .... Ms. Erica KAUFMAN
18 Director of Buildings & Grounds .... Mr. Randy CLUM
13 Director Mgmt Info Systems .... Mr. Michael TOMPKINS
29 Director Alumni/ae Affairs .... Ms. Jane BRIEN
36 Director Career Development .... Ms. Elizabeth GIGLIO
19 Director Safety & Security .... Mr. John GOMEZ
09 Director of Institutional Research .... Mr. Joseph F. AHERN
24 Director of Audio/Video Services .... Mr. Paul LABARBERA
28 Director of Multicultural Affairs .... Dr. Ann SEATON
41 Director of Athletics .... Ms. Kristin E. HALL
40 Bookstore Manager .... Ms. Merry MEYER
23 Director Student Health Services .... Ms. Marsha DAVIS
38 Director Student Counseling .... Ms. Tamara TELBERG
07 Director of Admission .... Ms. Mackie SIEBENS
39 Director of Housing .... Ms. Nancy W. SMITH
90 Chief Information Officer .... Mr. David BRANGAITIS

Bard High School Early College Manhattan (H)

525 East Houston Street, New York NY 10002

Telephone: (212) 995-8479 Identification: 770114
Accreditation: &EH

† Branch campus of Bard College at Simon's Rock, Great Barrington, MA

Bard High School Early College Queens (I)

30-20 Thomson Avenue, Long Island City NY 11101

Telephone: (718) 361-3133 Identification: 770115
Accreditation: &EH

† Branch campus of Bard College at Simon's Rock, Great Barrington, MA

Barnard College (J)

3009 Broadway, New York NY 10027-6598

County: New York FICE Identification: 002708
Unit ID: 189097
Telephone: (212) 854-5262 Carnegie Class: Bac-A&S
FAX Number: (212) 854-6220 Calendar System: Semester
URL: www.barnard.edu
Established: 1889 Annual Undergrad Tuition & Fees: $55,032
Enrollment: 2,544 Female
Affiliation or Control: Independent Non-Profit IRS Status: 501(c)3
Highest Offering: Baccalaureate
Accreditation: M

01 President .... Sian L. BEILOCK
43 VP Legal Affairs/Chief of Staff .... Jomysha STEPHEN
05 Provost & Dean of Faculty .... Linda BELL
03 Chief Operating Officer .... Robert GOLDBERG
30 Vice President for Development .... Lisa YEH
26 Vice Pres Communications .... Gabrielle SIMPSON
10 Vice President for Finance .... Eileen M. DI BENEDETTO
11 Vice Pres Campus Services .... Roger MOSIER
13 Vice Pres Information Technology .... Carol KATZMAN
15 Vice President for Human Resources .... Catherine GEDDIS
84 Vice President for Enrollment .... Jennifer FONDILLER
28 VP Diversity Equity and Inclusion ..... Ariana GONZÁLEZ STOKAS
32 Dean of the College .... Leslie GRINAGE
20 Dean of Studies .... Natalie FRIEDMAN
06 Registrar .... Jennifer SIMMONS
37 Director of Financial Aid .... Nanette DILAURO
35 Associate Dean for Student Life .... Emy CARDOZA
39 Exec Dir Res Life and Housing .... Alicia LAWRENCE
23 Exec Director of Student Health Svc .... Mary Joan MURPHY
36 Asst Dean Beyond Barnard .... A-J ARONSTEIN
29 Exec Director of Alumnae Relations .... Karen SENDLER
08 Dean of the Library .... Jennifer GREEN
101 Secretary to the Board of Trustees .... Alyssa SCHIFFMAN
19 Exec Director Public Safety .... Antonio GONZALEZ
109 Director of Business Operations .... Douglas MAGET

18 Director Facilities Services .... Daniel DAVIS
09 Dir Institutional Research .... Vacant
04 Special Assistant to the President .... Katelyn DUTTON
102 Exec Dir Institutional Giving .... Dorothy WEAVER
104 Assoc Provost Inst Initiatives .... Giorgio DIMAURO
108 Act Dir Institutional Assessment .... Carolina TAMARA
38 Director Student Counseling .... Mary COMMERFORD
44 Director Annual Giving .... Amy LEVEEN
96 Director of Purchasing .... Douglas MAGET
100 Chief of Staff .... Jomysha STEPHEN

† Affiliated with Columbia University in the City of New York.

Be'er Yaakov Talmudic Seminary (A)

12 Jefferson Avenue, Spring Valley NY 10977
County: Rockland
FICE Identification: 041928
Unit ID: 476717
Telephone: (845) 362-3053
Carnegie Class: Spec-4-yr-Faith
FAX Number: (845) 406-9699
Calendar System: Semester
Established: 1995
Annual Undergrad Tuition & Fees: $10,220
Enrollment: 510
Male
Affiliation or Control: Independent Non-Profit
IRS Status: 501(c)3
Highest Offering: First Talmudic Degree
Accreditation: RABN

01 CEO .... Mr. Jacob UNGAR
05 Dean .... Rabbi Israel EISENBERGER
06 Registrar/Administrator .... Rabbi Yitzchok SOIFER
37 Financial Aid Administrator .... Mrs. Chana NOTIS

Beis Medrash Heichal Dovid (B)

211 Beach 17th Street, Far Rockaway NY 11691-4433
County: Queens
FICE Identification: 037133
Unit ID: 444413
Telephone: (718) 868-2300
Carnegie Class: Spec-4-yr-Faith
FAX Number: (718) 868-0517
Calendar System: Semester
Established: 1999
Annual Undergrad Tuition & Fees: $9,500
Enrollment: 125
Male
Affiliation or Control: Independent Non-Profit
IRS Status: 501(c)3
Highest Offering: Second Talmudic Degree
Accreditation: RABN

01 Dean .... Rabbi Yaakov BENDER
05 Rosh Yeshiva .... Rabbi Shlomo Avidgor ALTUSKY
37 Financial Aid Officer .... Rabbi Aaron STEINBERG

The Belanger School of Nursing (C)

650 McClellan Street, Schenectady NY 12304
County: Schenectady
FICE Identification: 006448
Unit ID: 190956
Telephone: (518) 243-4471
Carnegie Class: Spec 2-yr-Health
FAX Number: (518) 243-4470
Calendar System: Other
URL: www.ellisbelangerschoolofnursing.org
Established: 1903
Annual Undergrad Tuition & Fees: $10,523
Enrollment: 114
Coed
Affiliation or Control: Independent Non-Profit
IRS Status: 501(c)3
Highest Offering: Associate Degree
Accreditation: ADNUR

01 Director .... Ms. Michele HEWITT
05 Chief Academic Officer .... Ms. Michele HEWITT
37 Student Financial Aid Coordinator .... Ms. Patricia BRUNDIGE
88 ADA Coordinator .... Ms. Amy TESSITORE
08 Head Librarian .... Ms. Emily SPINNER

Berkeley College (D)

3 East 43rd Street, New York NY 10017-4604
County: New York
FICE Identification: 007394
Unit ID: 189228
Telephone: (212) 986-4343
Carnegie Class: Spec-4-yr-Bus
FAX Number: (212) 818-1169
Calendar System: Semester
URL: www.berkeleycollege.edu
Established: 1931
Annual Undergrad Tuition & Fees: $25,900
Enrollment: 3,635
Coed
Affiliation or Control: Proprietary
IRS Status: Proprietary
Highest Offering: Baccalaureate
Accreditation: M, IACBE

00 Chairman of the Board .... Mr. Kevin L. LUING
01 President .... Mr. Michael J. SMITH
05 Provost .... Dr. Marsha POLLARD
84 Executive VP .... Mr. Tim LUING
32 Senior VP Student Success .... Dr. Diane RECINOS
10 VP Finance .... Mr. Dino KASAMIS
03 Vice President .... Mr. Brian MAHER
43 VP & Chief Compliance Officer .... Mr. Randy LUING
35 VP Student Development/Campus Life .... Dr. Dallas REED
36 VP Career Services .... Ms. Amy SORICELLI
37 VP Financial Aid Compliance .... Mr. Howard LESLIE
114 VP Budget & Student Accounts .... Ms. Eileen LOFTUS-BERLIN
13 Senior VP/Chief Information Officer .... Mr. Leonard DE BOTTON
20 Associate Provost Faculty Affairs .... Dr. Judith KORNBERG
20 Assoc Provost Student Engagement .... Mr. Paul KLESCHICK
106 Dean Online .... Dr. Joseph SCURALLI
50 Dean School of Business .... Dr. Elana ZOLFO
76 Dean School Health Studies .... Dr. Eva SKUKA
107 Dean School of Professional Studies .... Dr. Marianne VAKALIS
49 Dean School of Liberal Arts .... Dr. Don KIEFFER
88 Dean Developmental Education .... Dr. Gerald IACULLO
08 VP Library Services .... Ms. Marlene DOTY
15 VP Human Resources .... Ms. Karen J. CARPENTIERI
26 VP Marketing .... Mr. William DIMASI
11 VP Campus Operations .... Mr. Will MOYA
31 VP Communications & Ext Relations .. Ms. Angela HARRINGTON
86 VP Government Relations NY .... Mr. Gbubemi OKOTIEURO
121 Assistant VP Academic Advisement .... Mr. Joseph GIUFFRE
06 Registrar .... Ms. Deborah PALICIA
29 AVP Alumni Relation & Career Svcs .... Mr. Michael IRIS
22 Director Disability Services ...... Dr. Sharon M. MCLENNON-WIER
88 Asst VP Military & Veterans Affairs .... Mr. Edward J. DENNIS
38 Sr Director Personal Counseling .... Dr. Sandra E. COPPOLA
41 Director Athletics .... Mr. Andrew DESTEPHANO
07 VP Undergraduate Enrollment .... Mr. David J. BERTONE
85 VP International Operations .... Dr. Nori JAFFER
18 Sr Vice Pres Operations .... Mr. Thomas ALESSANDRELLO
19 Assistant VP Public Safety .... Mr. Robert MAGUIRE
109 Senior Director Auxiliary Services .... Mr. Luis COLLAZO
27 Director Media Relations .... Ms. Ilene GREENFIELD
119 Info Systems Security Manager .... Mr. Steven BECKER
09 Director Institutional Research .... Ms. Rebecca J. DRENNEN

Bet Medrash Gadol Ateret Torah (E)

901 Quentin Road, Brooklyn NY 11223
County: Kings
Identification: 667146
Unit ID: 485999
Telephone: (347) 394-1036
Carnegie Class: Spec-4-yr-Faith
FAX Number: (347) 394-1096
Calendar System: Semester
Established: 1992
Annual Undergrad Tuition & Fees: $10,050
Enrollment: 93
Male
Affiliation or Control: Independent Non-Profit
IRS Status: 501(c)3
Highest Offering: Second Talmudic Degree
Accreditation: @RABN

01 President/CEO .... Rabbi Joseph HARARI-RAFUL
10 Chief Financial/Business Officer .... Irwin SHAMAH
06 Registrar .... Mrs. Ruchana MANSOUR
11 Chief of Operations/Administration .... Zev KLEINER

Beth Hamedrash Shaarei Yosher Institute (F)

4102-10 16th Avenue, Brooklyn NY 11204-1099
County: Kings
FICE Identification: 011192
Unit ID: 189273
Telephone: (718) 854-2290
Carnegie Class: Spec-4-yr-Faith
FAX Number: (718) 436-9045
Calendar System: Semester
Established: 1962
Annual Undergrad Tuition & Fees: $9,350
Enrollment: 54
Male
Affiliation or Control: Independent Non-Profit
IRS Status: 501(c)3
Highest Offering: Second Talmudic Degree
Accreditation: RABN

05 Chief Academic Officer .... Rabbi Chaim ROSENBERG
10 Chief Business Officer .... Rabbi Pinches KAFF
29 Director Alumni Association .... Rabbi Eliyohu ROSENBLUM
15 Director Personnel Services .... Rabbi Mordechai MARGULIES
37 Director Student Financial Aid .... Rabbi Aaron ROTTENBERG
06 Registrar .... Rabbi Sol ROSENBERG

Beth Medrash Meor Yitzchok (G)

65 Dykstra's Way East, Monsey NY 10952
County: Rockland
Identification: 667111
Unit ID: 486196
Telephone: (845) 426-3488
Carnegie Class: Spec-4-yr-Faith
FAX Number: (845) 425-5415
Calendar System: Semester
Established: 2007
Annual Undergrad Tuition & Fees: $9,550
Enrollment: 129
Male
Affiliation or Control: Independent Non-Profit
IRS Status: 501(c)3
Highest Offering: First Talmudic Degree
Accreditation: RABN

Bill and Sandra Pomeroy College of Nursing at Crouse Hospital (H)

736 Irving Avenue, Syracuse NY 13210
County: Onondaga
FICE Identification: 006445
Unit ID: 190451
Telephone: (315) 470-7481
Carnegie Class: Spec 2-yr-Health
FAX Number: (315) 470-5774
Calendar System: Semester
URL: www.crouse.org/nursing
Established: 1913
Annual Undergrad Tuition & Fees: $15,125
Enrollment: 265
Coed
Affiliation or Control: Independent Non-Profit
IRS Status: 501(c)3
Highest Offering: Associate Degree
Accreditation: ADNUR

05 Dean .... Patricia MORGAN
20 Assistant Dean for Faculty .... David FALCI
07 Assistant Dean for Enrollment .... Amy GRAHAM
32 Assistant Dean for Students .... Ryan BARKER
06 Registrar/Bursar .... Jeanne CELSO
37 Financial Affairs Officer .... Kenny KENDALL
88 Instruction/Technology Coordinator .... Kelly DUFFY
08 Head Librarian .... Ellen OWENS

Boricua College (I)

3755 Broadway, New York NY 10032-1599
County: New York
FICE Identification: 013029
Unit ID: 189413
Telephone: (212) 694-1000
Carnegie Class: Bac-Diverse
FAX Number: (212) 694-1015
Calendar System: Semester
URL: www.boricuacollege.edu
Established: 1974
Annual Undergrad Tuition & Fees: $11,025
Enrollment: 883
Coed
Affiliation or Control: Independent Non-Profit
IRS Status: 501(c)3
Highest Offering: Master's
Accreditation: M, CAEPT

01 President .... Dr. Victor G. ALICEA
04 Exec Assistant to the President .... Ms. Sandra BELLAMY
05 VP Academic Affairs .... Dr. Shivaji SENGUPTA
13 VP Information & Tech/Facil Mgmt .... Mr. Irving RAMIREZ
20 VP Academic Planning & Programming .... Dr. John GUZMAN
15 VP Personnel/Human Resources .... Ms. Francia L. CASTRO
43 Legal Counsel .... Mr. Jorge BATISTA
10 Director Finance .... Mr. Elias OYOLA
113 Director Bursar .... Mr. Jose R. MANSO
07 Dir Admissions Bronx Campus Ctr .... Mr. Teofilo SANTIAGO
07 Dir Admissions Manhattan Campus .... Mr. Ismael SANCHEZ
07 Dir Admissions Brooklyn Cam Ctr .... Ms. Aurea MORALES
06 Director Registration & Assessments .... Ms. Beatriz AHORRIO
37 Director Financial Aid .... Ms. Rosalia CRUZ
08 Director Library/Learning Resources .... Ms. Liza RIVERA
18 Dir Environment Svcs Manhattan Camp .... Mr. Carlos ANDUJAR
18 Dir Environment Svcs Brooklyn .... Mr. Juan RIVERA PAGAN
18 Dir Environment Svcs Bronx Camp .... Mr. Jose VAZQUEZ
30 Director of Development .... Vacant
20 Dean Academic Affairs Manhattan Ctr .... Mr. Moises PEREYRA
20 Dean of Generic Studies Bronx Ctr .... Mr. Jose Israel LOPEZ

Brooklyn Law School (J)

250 Joralemon Street, Brooklyn NY 11201-3798
County: Kings
FICE Identification: 002677
Unit ID: 189501
Telephone: (718) 625-2200
Carnegie Class: Spec-4-yr-Law
FAX Number: (718) 780-0393
Calendar System: Semester
URL: www.brooklaw.edu
Established: 1901
Annual Graduate Tuition & Fees: N/A
Enrollment: 1,151
Coed
Affiliation or Control: Independent Non-Profit
IRS Status: 501(c)3
Highest Offering: First Professional Degree; No Undergraduates
Accreditation: LAW

00 Dean and President Emerita .... Dean Joan G. WEXLER
01 President/Dean .... Dean Michael T. CAHILL
05 Vice Dean of Academic Affairs .... Dean Christina MULLIGAN
20 Assoc Dean for Experiential Educ .... Dean Stacy CAPLOW
20 Assoc Dn Faculty/Rsrch/Scholarship .... Dean Edward JANGER
32 Dean of Students .... Dean Jennifer R. LANG
10 Chief Financial Officer .... Ms. Laurie H. NEWITZ
21 Treasurer .... Ms. Shoshanna M. CAMPBELL
07 Dean of Admissions .... Dean Eulas BOYD, JR.
36 Dean of Career Development .... Dean Karen EISEN
08 Director of Library .... Prof. Janet SINDER
30 Director of Development .... Mr. Sean MORIARTY
29 Director of Alumni Relations .... Ms. Caitlin MONCK
06 Registrar .... Mr. Christian BESTER
37 Director of Financial Aid .... Ms. Nancy L. ZAHZAM
11 Chief Operating Officer .... Ms. Linda HARVEY
18 Facilities Manager .... Mr. Salvatore DECANDIA
15 Human Resources Manager .... Mr. Matthew BURNS
13 Chief Info Technology Officer (CIO) .... Mr. Steven MARKS
19 Director of Public Safety .... Ms. Mercedes RAVELO
43 Gen Counsel/Chf Compliance Officer .... Ms. Stephanie VULLO

*Bryant & Stratton College System Office (K)

200 Redtail Rd., Orchard Park NY 14127
County: Erie
Identification: 666828
Telephone: (716) 250-7500
Carnegie Class: N/A
FAX Number: (716) 250-7510
URL: www.bryantstratton.edu

01 President & CEO .... Dr. Francis J. FELSER
11 VP/Chief Operating Officer .... Mr. David VADEN
10 VP/Chief Financial Officer .... Mr. Christopher GERACE
13 VP/Online Division and CIO .... Ms. Doreen JUSTINGER
84 VP/Chief Enrollment Officer .... Ms. Tracy NANNERY
108 Exec Dir Strat Plng & Assessment .... Ms. Anne LORIA

*Bryant & Stratton College (L)

465 Main Street, Suite 400, Buffalo NY 14203-1795
County: Erie
FICE Identification: 002678
Unit ID: 189583
Telephone: (716) 884-9120
Carnegie Class: Bac/Assoc-Mixed
FAX Number: (716) 884-0091
Calendar System: Semester
URL: www.bryantstratton.edu
Established: 1854
Annual Undergrad Tuition & Fees: $17,216
Enrollment: 491
Coed
Affiliation or Control: Proprietary
IRS Status: Proprietary
Highest Offering: Baccalaureate
Accreditation: M, MAC

02 Campus Director Dr. Marvel E. ROSS-JONES
05 Dean of Instruction Mr. Michael MCKINLEY
07 Director of Admissions Mr. Kevin MUSE
36 Director of Career Services Mrs. Angelette BODDIE
10 WNY Business Office Director Ms. Kathleen OWCZARCZAK

* Bryant & Stratton College (A)

1259 Central Avenue, Albany NY 12205-5230
Telephone: (518) 437-1802 FICE Identification: 004749
Accreditation: &M, MAC

* Bryant & Stratton College (B)

854 Long Pond Road, Rochester NY 14612-3049
Telephone: (585) 720-0660 FICE Identification: 012470
Accreditation: &M, MAC, OTA

* Bryant & Stratton College (C)

953 James Street, Syracuse NY 13203-2502
Telephone: (315) 472-6603 FICE Identification: 008276
Accreditation: &M, MAC, OTA, PTAA

Canisius College (D)

2001 Main Street, Buffalo NY 14208-1098
County: Erie FICE Identification: 002681
Unit ID: 189705
Telephone: (716) 883-7000 Carnegie Class: Masters/L
FAX Number: (716) 888-2525 Calendar System: Semester
URL: www.canisius.edu
Established: 1870 Annual Undergrad Tuition & Fees: $28,488
Enrollment: 3,464 Coed
Affiliation or Control: Roman Catholic IRS Status: 501(c)3
Highest Offering: Master's
Accreditation: M, CAATE, CACREP, CAEP

01 President Mr. John J. HURLEY
05 Interim VP Academic Affairs Dr. Sara R. MORRIS
10 Vice President Business & Finance Mr. Marco F. BENEDETTI
32 VP Student Affs & Dean of Students Dr. Daniel A. DENTINO
111 VP Institutional Advancement Mr. William COLLINS, II
84 VP for Enrollment Management Mr. Ian S. DAY
20 Assoc VP for Academic Affairs Vacant
113 Asst VP/Dir Stdnt Rec & Fin Svcs Mr. Kevin M. SMITH
26 Asst VP Mktg & Communications Mr. Matther Z. WOJICK
88 Assoc Dean/Director Griff Center Dr. Mark R. HARRINGTON
08 Director of Library Ms. Kristine E. KASBOHM
07 Director Undergrad Admissions Mr. Justin P. ROGERS
112 Director of Principal Gifts Mr. J. Patrick GREENWALD
21 Controller Mr. Ronald J. HABERER
50 Dean School of Business Dr. Denise M. ROTONDO
37 Assoc Dir of Stdnt Records/Fin Svcs Ms. Mary A. KOEHNEKE
06 Registrar/Asst Dir Stdnt Rec & FA Ms. Deborah W. PROHN
26 Chief Communications Officer Ms. Eileen C. HERBERT
15 Assoc VP for HR and Compliance Ms. Linda M. WALLESHAUSER
53 Interim Dean School Educ/Human Svcs Dr. Nancy WALLACE
25 Director of Sponsored Programs Ms. Mary Ann LANGLOIS
18 Director Facilities Management Mr. Thomas E. CIMINELLI
23 Director Student Health Center Ms. Patricia H. CREAHAN
38 Director Counseling Center Ms. Eileen A. NILAND
39 Assoc Dean of Stdnts/Dir Resid Life Mr. Matthew H. MULVILLE
104 Director Study Abroad Mr. Brian SMITH
40 Course Materials Manager/Bookstore Mr. Andrew J. THOMAS
41 Director Athletics Mr. William J. MAHER
42 Director Campus Ministry Mr. Michael F. HAYES, JR.
90 Director of User Services Mr. Scott D. CLARK
94 Dir of Women's Business Center Ms. Sara L. VESCIO
92 Director of All College Honors Pgm Dr. Bruce J. DIERENFIELD
88 Director of Multi Cultural Programs Mr. Sababu C. NORRIS
13 Chief Information Officer Mr. Lawrence DENI
24 Director Media Center Mr. Daniel J. DREW
96 Director of Purchasing Mr. Gary B. LEW
04 Assistant to the President Ms. Erica C. SAMMARCO
91 Director Administrative Computing Ms. Michele FOLSOM
108 Dir Inst & Research Effectiveness Ms. Lauren YOUNG
102 Dir Foundation/Corporate Relations Mrs. Sandy A. MILLER
19 Director Public Safety Mrs. Kimberly L. BEATY
29 Director Alumni Engagement Ms. Erin M. ZACK
44 Director Canisius Fund Ms. Summer L. HANDZLIK

Cayuga Community College (E)

197 Franklin Street, Auburn NY 13021-3099
County: Cayuga FICE Identification: 002861
Unit ID: 189839
Telephone: (315) 255-1743 Carnegie Class: Assoc/HT-High Non
FAX Number: (315) 255-2117 Calendar System: Semester
URL: www.cayuga-cc.edu
Established: 1953 Annual Undergrad Tuition & Fees (In-District): $5,290
Enrollment: 3,784 Coed
Affiliation or Control: State/Local IRS Status: 501(c)3
Highest Offering: Associate Degree
Accreditation: M, ADNUR, OTA

01 President Mr. Brian M. DURANT
04 Assistant to President/Board Ms. Pamela A. HELEEN
05 Provost/Vice Pres Academic Affairs Dr. Anne J. HERRON
32 Vice President Student Affairs Mr. Jeffrey E. ROSENTHAL
10 Vice Pres Administration/Treasurer Dr. Dan DOBELL
102 Executive Director Foundation Mr. Guy T. COSENTINO
07 Director of Admissions Mr. Bruce M. BLODGETT
09 Director Institutional Research Ms. Virginia RUDNICK
08 Library Director Ms. Sara DAVENPORT
41 Director Athletics Mr. Peter E. LIDDELL
15 Director Human Resources Mr. Thomas CORCORAN
35 Director Student Activities Mr. Norman LEE
19 Director Public Safety Mr. Doug KINNEY

Cazenovia College (F)

22 Sullivan Street, Cazenovia NY 13035
County: Madison FICE Identification: 002685
Unit ID: 189848
Telephone: (800) 654-3210 Carnegie Class: Bac-Diverse
FAX Number: (315) 655-4143 Calendar System: Semester
URL: www.cazenovia.edu
Established: 1824 Annual Undergrad Tuition & Fees: $34,630
Enrollment: 893 Coed
Affiliation or Control: Independent Non-Profit IRS Status: 501(c)3
Highest Offering: Baccalaureate
Accreditation: M, IACBE

01 President Dr. Ronald D. CHESBROUGH
05 VP Academic Affs/Dean of Faculty Dr. Sharon A. DETTMER
32 Vice Pres for Student Affairs Dr. Karey PINE
10 VP Financial Affs/Chief Fin Officer Mr. Mark H. EDWARDS
45 VP for Planning/Inst Effectiveness Dr. David BERGH
30 Executive Director of Development Ms. Julie PALMER
89 Dean First Year Program Mr. Jesse LOTT
08 Director of Library Services Ms. Heather C. WHALEN-SMITH
37 Assoc Dean Financial Aid Ms. Christine MANDEL
26 Director Marketing/Communications Mr. Timothy D. GREENE
15 Director Human Resources Ms. Janice ROMAGNOLI
23 Director Health Services Ms. Deborah FRANK
36 Dir Career/Extended Learning Svcs Ms. Christine RICHARDSON
41 Director Intercollegiate Athletics Mr. Pete WAY
13 Director of Technology Development Mr. David PALMER
06 Registrar Ms. Christine MANDEL
09 Dir Institutional Rsrch/Assessment Dr. Jon C. DALY
18 Dir of Physical Plant Operations Mr. Jeff SLOCUM
29 Director Alumni Relations Ms. Shari WHITAKER
07 Sr Assoc Director of Admissions Ms. Kristen BOWERS
04 Exec Assistant to the President Ms. Judy L. PAPAYANAKOS

Central Yeshiva Beth Joseph (G)

1502 Avenue N, Brooklyn NY 11230
County: Kings Identification: 667157
Unit ID: 488004
Telephone: (718) 269-4080 Carnegie Class: Spec-4-yr-Faith
FAX Number: (718) 269-4080 Calendar System: Semester
Established: 1942 Annual Undergrad Tuition & Fees: N/A
Enrollment: 40 Male
Affiliation or Control: Independent Non-Profit IRS Status: 501(c)3
Highest Offering: First Talmudic Degree
Accreditation: RABN

01 Chief Executive Officer Rabbi Moshe JOFEN
37 Director Student Financial Aid Rabbi Yechezkel MOSCOVITZ
06 Registrar Rabbi Baruch MILLER

Central Yeshiva Tomchei Tmimim Lubavitch America (H)

841-853 Ocean Parkway, Brooklyn NY 11230-2798
County: Kings FICE Identification: 004776
Unit ID: 189857
Telephone: (718) 774-3430 Carnegie Class: Spec-4-yr-Faith
FAX Number: N/A Calendar System: Semester
Established: 1941 Annual Undergrad Tuition & Fees: $7,700
Enrollment: 544 Male
Affiliation or Control: Independent Non-Profit IRS Status: 501(c)3
Highest Offering: Second Talmudic Degree
Accreditation: AIJS, RABN

01 President Rabbi Shloime ZARCHI
05 Dean Rabbi Zalman LABKOWSKI
06 Registrar Rabbi Joseph WILMOWSKY
37 Financial Aid Director Rabbi Moshe M. GLUCKOWSKY
26 Director Public Relations Mr. Shaya BOYMELGREEN
10 Treasurer Rabbi Moshe BOGOMILSKY

Christ the King Seminary (I)

711 Knox Road, P.O. Box 607,
East Aurora NY 14052-0607
County: Erie FICE Identification: 002822
Unit ID: 189981
Telephone: (716) 652-8900 Carnegie Class: Spec-4-yr-Faith
FAX Number: (716) 652-8903 Calendar System: Semester
URL: www.cks.edu
Established: 1974 Annual Graduate Tuition & Fees: N/A
Enrollment: 78 Coed
Affiliation or Control: Roman Catholic IRS Status: 501(c)3
Highest Offering: Master's; No Undergraduates
Accreditation: M, THEOL

01 Rector/President Rev. Kevin G. CREAGH, CM
03 Vice Rector Rev. Robert A. WOZNIAK
05 Academic Dean Mr. Michael SHERRY
10 Comptroller Mrs. Nancy M. EHLERS
111 Director Institutional Advancement Mrs. Susan LANKES
08 Library Director Ms. Teresa LUBIENECKI
06 Registrar Mrs. Julie GALEY
04 Administrative Asst to President Ms. Nadine OATES
19 Director Security/Safety Rev. John ADAMS
26 Marketing/Communications Officer Mrs. Pamela SIERACKI

Christie's Education, New York (J)

1230 Avenue of the Americas, Fl 20, New York NY 10020
County: New York FICE Identification: 036654
Unit ID: 475510
Telephone: (212) 355-1501 Carnegie Class: Spec-4-yr-Arts
FAX Number: (212) 355-7370 Calendar System: Quarter
URL: www.christies.edu
Established: 1993 Annual Graduate Tuition & Fees: N/A
Enrollment: 83 Coed
Affiliation or Control: Proprietary IRS Status: Proprietary
Highest Offering: Master's; No Undergraduates
Accreditation: NY

01 Academic Director Dr. Veronique CHAGNON-BURKE
08 Learning Resources Manager Ms. Karen MAGUIRE
07 Assoc Dir Admissions/Recruitment Ms. Hilary SMITH
10 Dir Business and Student Services Mrs. Margaret CONKLIN
37 Academic/Financial Aid Coordinator Ms. Amanda MUSCATO
21 Sr Business/Student Services Coord Ms. Lindsay SCHWARTZ
36 Career Services Officer Mrs. Suzanne JULIG
51 Continuing Education Coordinator Ms. Sarah BUCCARELLI

* City University of New York (K)

205 E. 42nd Street, New York NY 10017
County: New York FICE Identification: 025061
Unit ID: 190035
Telephone: (646) 664-9100 Carnegie Class: N/A
FAX Number: (646) 664-3868
URL: www2.cuny.edu

01 Chancellor Dr. Felix V. MATOS RODRIGUEZ
05 Exec VC/University Provost Dr. Jose LOUIS CRUZ
10 Sr Vice Chancellor Budget/Finance Mr. Matthew SAPIENZA
101 Secretary of the Board of Trustees Ms. Gayle HORWITZ
43 Int General Counsel/SVC Legal Affs Ms. Pamela S. SILVERBLATT
11 Exec VC/Chief Operating Officer Mr. Hector BATISTA
18 VC Facility Plng/Construction Mgmt Ms. Judy BERGTRAUM
13 VC/Chief Information Officer Mr. Brian COHEN
32 Interim VC Student Affairs Dr. Chris ROSA
88 Sr Vice Chanc for Labor Relations Ms. Pamela S. SILVERBLATT
09 Interim Associate VC for Research Mr. Dan E. MCCLOSKEY
15 Interim VC for Human Resources Mgmt Ms. Margaret EGAN
111 Int VC for Univ Advancement Ms. Andrea SHAPIRO DAVIS
20 Sr Dean for Academic Affairs Mr. John MOGULESCU
84 AVC of Enrollment Strategy/Mgmt Ms. Laura BRUNO
09 Dean Institutional Research Mr. David CROOK
28 Dean Diversity/Recruitment Ms. Arlene TORRES
26 Vice Chanc Communications/Marketing Ms. Maite JUNCO
88 Assoc VC for Academic Strategy Ms. Amy MCINTOSH

* Baruch College/City University of New York (L)

One Bernard Baruch Way, New York NY 10010-5526
County: New York FICE Identification: 007273
Unit ID: 190512
Telephone: (646) 312-1000 Carnegie Class: Masters/L
FAX Number: N/A Calendar System: Semester
URL: www.baruch.cuny.edu
Established: 1968 Annual Undergrad Tuition & Fees (In-District): $7,262
Enrollment: 18,289 Coed
Affiliation or Control: State/Local IRS Status: 501(c)3
Highest Offering: Doctorate
Accreditation: M, IPSY, SPAA

02 President Dr. Mitchel B. WALLERSTEIN
05 Int Provost/SVP Academic Affairs Dr. James MCCARTHY
20 Assoc Provost Dr. Dennis SLAVIN
10 Vice Pres Administration/Finance Ms. Katharine COBB
84 VP Enroll Mgmt/Strategic Init Ms. Mary GORMAN
111 VP for College Advancement Mr. David SHANTON
13 VP for Information Services Mr. Arthur DOWNING
26 VP for Comm/Ext Rels & Econ Dev Ms. Christina LATOUF
32 VP Student Affairs/Dean of Students Dr. Art KING
21 Asst Vice President Finance Ms. Mary FINNEN
43 Asst VP Legal Counsel Ms. Olga DAIS
102 President Baruch College Fund Vacant
50 Dean Zicklin School of Business Dr. Fenwick HUSS
49 Dean Weissman School Arts & Science Dr. Aldemaro ROMERO, JR.
80 Dean School Public/Intl Affairs Dr. David BIRDSELL
08 Dean of Library Mr. Arthur DOWNING
58 Executive Officer Doctoral Program Dr. Joseph WEINTROP
100 Chief of Staff Ms. Kenya N. LEE
25 Director of Sponsored Programs Vacant
15 Exec Dir of Human Resources Ms. Andrea CAVINESS
36 Director Career Development Center Ms. Ellen STEIN
90 Asst Dir Client Svcs/Fac Liaison Vacant
85 Director Intl Student Office Ms. Rosa KELLEY
19 Director Public Safety Mr. Henry J. MCLAUGHLIN
09 Dir Institutional Rsrch/Pgm Assess Mr. John CHOONOO

29 Director Alumni Relations .... Ms. Janet ROSSBACH
96 Director of Purchasing .... Dr. Diane OQUENDO
22 Chief Diversity Officer .... Ms. Mona JHA
41 Athletic Director .... Ms. Heather MACCULLOCH
86 Dir of Govt and Community Relations .... Mr. Eric LUGO
06 Senior Registrar .... Mr. Edward ADAMS
104 Director Study Abroad .... Dr. Richard MITTEN
37 Director of Financial Aid Services .... Ms. Elizabeth RIQUEZ
07 Dir of Undergraduate Admissions .... Ms. Marisa DELACRUZ
108 Asst Provost for Assessment/Accred .... Dr. Rachel FESTER

*City University of New York Borough of Manhattan Community College (A)

199 Chambers Street, New York NY 10007-1047
County: New York FICE Identification: 002691
Unit ID: 190521
Telephone: (212) 220-1230 Carnegie Class: Assoc/HT-High Trad
FAX Number: (212) 220-1244 Calendar System: Semester
URL: www.bmcc.cuny.edu
Established: 1963 Annual Undergrad Tuition & Fees (In-District): $5,170
Enrollment: 26,932 Coed
Affiliation or Control: State/Local IRS Status: 501(c)3
Highest Offering: Associate Degree
Accreditation: M, ADNUR, CAHIIM, COARC, EMT

02 Interim President .... Dr. Karrin E. WILKS
05 Int Provost/SVP Academic Affairs .... Dr. Erwin WONG
11 Vice President Administration/Plng .... Vacant
43 Spec Legal Counsel/Labor Designee .... Ms. Meryl R. KAYNARD
32 Vice President of Student Affairs .... Dr. Marva CRAIG
30 Vice Pres of Development .... Ms. Doris HOLZ
84 Vice Pres Enrollment Management .... Dr. Diane WALLESER
10 Asst Vice Pres of Finance .... Ms. Elena SAMUELS
51 Dean Ctr for Cont Ed/Workforce Dev .... Mr. Sunil GUPTA
25 Dean Office of Sponsored Programs .... Mr. John MONTANEZ
20 Dean for Instruction/Curriculum .... Vacant
20 Assoc Dean of Faculty .... Dr. James BERG
121 Asst Dean Academic Support .... Ms. Janice ZUMMO
37 Interim Director Financial Aid .... Ms. Albina KHASIDOVA
15 Director Human Resources .... Ms. Gloria CHAO
07 Director of Admissions .... Ms. Lisa KASPER
06 Senior Registrar .... Mr. Mohammad ALAM
08 Dir Learning Resource Center .... Mr. Gregory FARRELL
09 Dean Inst Effective/Strategic Plng .... Dr. Christopher SHULTS
28 Chief Diversity Officer .... Ms. Odelia LEVY
18 Asst VP Planning/Facilities .... Mr. Jorge YAFAR
26 Exec Director Public Affairs .... Mr. Manuel ROMERO
41 Director of Athletics .... Vacant
102 Dir Foundation/Corporate Relations .... Mr. Bryan HALLER
36 Dir Academic Advise/Transfer Center .... Ms. Carei THOMAS
38 Director Counseling Center .... Vacant
96 Acting Director of Procurement .... Ms. Leonore GONZALEZ

*City University of New York Bronx Community College (B)

2155 University Avenue, Bronx NY 10453-2895
County: Bronx FICE Identification: 002692
Unit ID: 190530
Telephone: (718) 289-5100 Carnegie Class: Assoc/HT-High Trad
FAX Number: (718) 289-6011 Calendar System: Semester
URL: www.bcc.cuny.edu
Established: 1957 Annual Undergrad Tuition & Fees (In-District): $5,206
Enrollment: 10,935 Coed
Affiliation or Control: State/Local IRS Status: 501(c)3
Highest Offering: Associate Degree
Accreditation: M, ACBSP, ADNUR, MLTAD, NMT, RAD

02 President .... Dr. Thomas A. ISEKENEGBE
05 Int VP/Provost Academic Affairs .... Dr. Luis MONTENEGRO
86 Government Rels and Ext Affairs Dir .... Mr. David W. LEVERS
32 VP for Student Affairs .... Ms. Irene R. DELGADO
111 VP for Advance/Comm & Ext Rels .... Dr. Eddy BAYARDELLE
26 Asst VP Comm & Marketing .... Mr. Richard GINSBERG
35 Dean of Student Services .... Mr. Bernard GANTT
11 AVP for Campus Operations .... Mr. David A. TAYLOR
30 Asst VP for Development .... Ms. Angela WAMBUGU COBB
103 Dean for Workforce & Econ Develop .... Mr. Kenneth ADAMS
45 Dean for Research/Plng & Assessment .... Dr. Nancy RITZE
20 Assoc Dean AA for Curr & Fac Dev .... Dr. Alexander OTT
10 Dir for Financial & Business Svcs .... Ms. Gina UGARTE
06 Registrar/Dir Enrollment .... Ms. Karen THOMAS
13 Chief Information Officer .... Mr. Loic AUDUSSEAU
37 Financial Aid Director .... Ms. Margaret NELSON
07 Director for Admission/Recruitment .... Ms. Patricia A. RAMOS
15 Human Resources Director .... Ms. Marta CLARK
08 Chief Librarian .... Prof. Michael J. MILLER
19 Public Safety Director .... Mr. James VERDICCHIO
41 Student Athletics Director .... Mr. Ryan MCCARTHY
18 Chief Super Physical Plant Svcs .... Vacant
29 Alum Rel/Plan Giv/Indiv Donors Mgr .... Mr. Robert WHELAN
88 Mgr of College Discovery .... Ms. Cynthia SUAREZ-ESPINAL
43 Exe Counsel & Deputy to President .... Ms. Karla R. WILLIAMS
96 Director of Purchasing .... Vacant
28 Chief Diversity/Affirm Act Ofcr .... Ms. Jessenia PAOLI
14 Deputy Chief Technology Officer .... Ms. Luisa MARTICH
108 Academic Assessment Manager .... Dr. Richard LAMANNA
20 Dean for Academic Affairs .... Dr. Luis MONTENEGRO
90 Dir for Academic Comp Svcs Desk .... Ms. Wanda SANTIAGO
91 Manager of Admin Systems & Svcs .... Mr. Rolly WILTSHIRE
51 Manager Continuing/Prof Education .... Vacant
25 Dir of Grants Development .... Ms. Judith EISENBERG
22 Affirmative Action Specialist .... Mr. Oluwafemi AKINSANYA
102 Dev Corp and Foundation Rel Mgmt .... Ms. Julia OLIVA
104 Dir Intl Educ and Study Abroad Pgm .... Vacant
09 OIR Inst Research Specialist .... Mrs. Chelsea RAMOS
46 Director of Research & Testing .... Mr. Chris EFTHIMIOU
106 Dir IT Academic App/CTLT .... Mr. Mark LENNERTON
36 Dir Transfer and Job Placement .... Mr. Alan FUENTES
04 Administrative Asst to President .... Ms. Amirah COUSINS
100 Chief of Staff .... Ms. Karla Renee WILLIAMS
38 Director Student Counseling .... Vacant

*City University of New York Brooklyn College (C)

2900 Bedford Avenue, Brooklyn NY 11210-2889
County: Kings FICE Identification: 002687
Unit ID: 190549
Telephone: (718) 951-5000 Carnegie Class: Masters/L
FAX Number: N/A Calendar System: Semester
URL: www.brooklyn.cuny.edu
Established: 1930 Annual Undergrad Tuition & Fees (In-District): $7,240
Enrollment: 17,803 Coed
Affiliation or Control: State/Local IRS Status: 170(c)1
Highest Offering: Master's
Accreditation: M, AUD, CACREP, DIETD, DIETI, SP

02 President .... Ms. Michelle J. ANDERSON
05 Provost/Sr Vice Pres Acad Affairs .... Dr. Anne LOPES
10 Sr VP for Finance & Administration .... Mr. Alan GILBERT
111 Vice Pres Institutional Advancement .... Mr. Todd GALITZ
32 Vice President for Student Affairs .... Dr. Ronald JACKSON
84 VP Enroll Management and Retention .... Ms. Lillian O'REILLY
26 AVP Communications and Marketing .... Mr. Jason CAREY
100 Chief of Staff to Pres & Exec Dir .... Ms. Nicole HAAS
43 Chief Legal/Labor Relations Officer .... Mr. Tony THOMAS
108 Assoc Prov & AVP Inst Effectiveness .... Dr. Tammie CUMMING
20 Assoc Provost for Faculty & Admin .... Dr. Tammy LEWIS
53 Dean School of Education .... Dr. April BEDFORD
57 Dean Schl Visual Media & Perf Arts .... Dr. Maria A. CONELLI
83 Int Dean Sch Humanities & Soc Sci .... Dr. Kenneth GOULD
81 Dean Schl Natural & Behav Sciences .... Dr. Kleanthis PSARRIS
50 Interim Dean Koppelman Sch Business .... Dr. Susanne SCOTT
13 Asst VP Info Technology Services .... Mr. Mark GOLD
08 Assoc Dean Lib/Ex Dir Acd Info Tech .... Dr. Mary MALLERY
88 Interim Assoc Dean Sch of Business .... Dr. Herve QUENEAU
88 Asst Dean Academic Programs .... Dr. Lucas RUBIN
35 Assistant Dean for Student Services .... Mr. Dave BRYAN
35 Assistant Dean for Student Life .... Ms. Moraima SMITH
28 Interim Chief Diversity Officer .... Mr. Anthony BROWN
113 Exec Dir Student Fin Svcs & Bursar .... Ms. Yasmin ALI
07 Exec Director Enrollment Services .... Ms. Natalie COOMBS
45 Exec Director Budget & Planning .... Mr. Emir GANIC
121 Exec Dir Student Success Center .... Ms. Tracy NEWTON
88 Exec Dir Sci & Resilience Institute .... Mr. Adam PARRIS
18 Executive Director of Operations .... Mr. Michael ROGOVIN
21 Comptroller .... Ms. Beatrice GILLING RAYNOR
15 Exec Dir Human Resource Services .... Ms. Renita WHITE SIMMONS
112 Managing Dir Campaign & Leader Gift .... Ms. Emily MOQTADERI
09 Sr Dir Inst Rsrch & Data Analysis .... Dr. Michael AYERS
25 Dir Research & Sponsored Programs .... Ms. Sabrina CEREZO
96 Dir Procurement & Support Services .... Ms. Madonna CHARLES
88 Assoc Director Academic Assessment .... Dr. Fredrik DEBOER
29 Director of Alumni Affairs .... Ms. Lisa DICCE
06 Registrar .... Mr. Richard FELTMAN
41 Dir Rec Intramurals/Intercol Athl .... Mr. Bruce FILOSA
36 Dir Magner Ctr/Career Dev & Interns .... Ms. Natalia GUARIN-KLEIN
38 Director Personal Counseling .... Dr. Gregory KUHLMAN
114 Director of Budget .... Mr. Michael LANZA
37 Director Financial Aid .... Mr. Marcus RICHARDSON
88 Testing & Transfer Evaluation Ofcr .... Ms. Monica RIVERA
92 Dir Scholars Pgm & Honors Academy .... Dr. Lisa SCHWEBEL
90 Dir Acad Information Technologies .... Mr. Howard SPIVAK
19 Director Safety & Security .... Mr. Donald A. WENZ

*City University of New York The City College (D)

160 Convent Avenue, New York NY 10031-9198
County: New York FICE Identification: 002688
Unit ID: 190567
Telephone: (212) 650-7000 Carnegie Class: DU-Higher
FAX Number: (212) 650-7680 Calendar System: Semester
URL: www.ccny.cuny.edu
Established: 1847 Annual Undergrad Tuition & Fees (In-District): $7,140
Enrollment: 16,001 Coed
Affiliation or Control: State/Local IRS Status: 501(c)3
Highest Offering: Doctorate
Accreditation: M, ARCPA, CAEPN, CLPSY, LSAR, #MED

02 President .... Dr. Vincent G. BOUDREAU
05 Int Provost/Sr VP Academic Affairs .... Mr. Tony LISS
111 Exec Dir Inst Advancement/Fndn .... Ms. Dee Dee MOZELESKI
29 Executive Director Alumni Affairs .... Mr. David COVINGTON
10 Vice Pres Finance & CFO .... Mr. Felix LAM
84 Assistant Vice President CUNYfirst .... Ms. Celia P. LLOYD
18 AVP Facilities Mgmt .... Mr. David ROBINSON
86 VP Governmental/Community Affairs .... Ms. Karen WITHERSPOON
32 Int Vice Pres for Student Devel .... Ms. Wendy J. THORNTON
13 AVP Information Technology/CIO .... Mr. Kenneth IHRER
26 Sr Advisor to Pres for External Aff .... Ms. Dee Dee MOZELESKI
63 Interim Dean CUNY Sch of Medicine .... Ms. Erica FRIEDMAN
54 Dean of Engineering .... Dr. Gilda BARABINO
53 Dean School of Education .... Ms. Mary E. DRISCOLL
47 Acting Dean School of Architecture .... Mr. Gordon GEBERT
88 Dean of CWE-Div of Interdiscip Stds .... Dr. Juan Carlos MERCADO
81 Acting Dean of Science .... Mr. V. Parameswaran NAIR
82 Dean School of Civic/Global Ldrshp .... Dr. Andrew RICH
79 Dean of Humanities & The Arts .... Mr. Erec KOCH
43 Executive Counsel to the President .... Mr. Paul F. OCCHIOGROSSO
15 Asst Vice Pres of Human Resources .... Vacant
23 Exec Director Health and Wellness .... Ms. Teresa WALKER
06 Senior Registrar .... Vacant
35 Exec Dir of Student Affairs at CWE .... Ms. Sophia DEMETRIOU
08 Assoc Dean & Chief Librarian .... Dr. Charles STEWART
25 Dir for Grants & Sponsored Pgms .... Dr. Alan SHIH
09 Director of Institutional Research .... Mr. Edward SILVERMAN
37 Director of Financial Aid .... Ms. Arshaw RAMKARAN
27 Public Relations Coordinator .... Ms. Ashley AROCHO
28 Chf Diversity Ofcr/Dean Faculty Rel .... Vacant
90 Computer Systems Manager Level IV .... Mr. Curtis RIAS
36 Director of Career Services .... Ms. Katie NAILLER
19 Exec Dir Public Safety/Security .... Mr. Pat MORENA
24 Director of Instructional Media .... Mr. Nana ABEYIE
07 Exec Director of Admissions .... Mr. Joseph FANTOZZI
96 Director of Business Services .... Vacant

*College of Staten Island CUNY (E)

2800 Victory Boulevard, Staten Island NY 10314-6600
County: Richmond FICE Identification: 002698
Unit ID: 190558
Telephone: (718) 982-2000 Carnegie Class: Masters/L
FAX Number: N/A Calendar System: Semester
URL: www.csi.cuny.edu
Established: 1976 Annual Undergrad Tuition & Fees (In-District): $7,290
Enrollment: 13,594 Coed
Affiliation or Control: State/Local IRS Status: 501(c)3
Highest Offering: Doctorate
Accreditation: M, ADNUR, CAEP, MT, NUR, PTA, SW

02 President .... Dr. William J. FRITZ
05 Sr VP Acad Affairs/Provost .... Dr. Michael PARRISH
32 VP Student & Enrollment Services .... Ms. Jennifer S. BORRERO
111 Executive Dir Inst Advancement .... Ms. Cheryl ADOLPH
10 AVP for Finance & Budget/CFO .... Mr. Carlos A. SERRANO
86 VP Econ Dev/Cont Stds/Govt Rels .... Mr. Kenichi IWAMA
18 Int VP Campus Planning/Facilities .... Ms. Hope BERTE
15 Deputy Director of Human Resources .... Ms. Manuela ALONGI
84 AVP for Enrollment Services .... Vacant
20 Assoc Provost for Undergrad Studies .... Dr. Ralf PEETZ
13 AVP & CIO Info Technology Services .... Dr. Patricia KAHN
81 Dean of Science & Technology .... Dr. Vivian INCERA
79 Dean Humanities & Social Sci .... Dr. Sarolta A. TAKACS
08 Associate Dean & Chief Librarian .... Ms. Amy STEMPLER
100 Chief of Staff/Deputy to President .... Mr. Robert WALLACE
35 Interim Executive Dir Student Svcs .... Ms. Danielle E. DIMITROV
50 Dean School of Business .... Dr. Susan L. HOLAK
76 Dean School of Health Sciences .... Dr. Marcus TYE
53 Dean School of Education .... Dr. Kenneth GOLD
58 Assoc Provost Grad Studies/Research .... Dr. Margaret-Ellen (Mel) PIPE
28 Int Chief Diversity & Title IX Ofcr .... Ms. Catherine FERRARA
16 Dir Employee Rels/Labor Designee .... Ms. Jessica COLLURA

*City University of New York Graduate Center (F)

365 Fifth Avenue, New York NY 10016-4309
County: New York FICE Identification: 004765
Unit ID: 190576
Telephone: (212) 817-7000 Carnegie Class: DU-Highest
FAX Number: N/A Calendar System: Semester
URL: www.gc.cuny.edu
Established: 1961 Annual Undergrad Tuition & Fees (In-District): N/A
Enrollment: 7,674 Coed
Affiliation or Control: State/Local IRS Status: 501(c)3
Highest Offering: Doctorate
Accreditation: M, AUD, CAHIIM, CLPSY, @DIETI, JOUR, NURSE, PH, SCPSY

02 Interim President .... Dr. James MUYSKENS
05 Interim Provost and Sr VP Acad Affs .... Dr. Julia WRIGLEY
10 Sr VP Finance and Administration .... Dr. Sebastian T. PERSICO
13 VP Information Technology .... Mr. Robert D. CAMPBELL
111 VP Institutional Advancement .... Mr. Jay GOLAN
26 VP Communications .... Ms. Wendy DEMARCO FUENTES
32 VP Student Affairs .... Mr. Matthew G. SCHOENGOOD
21 Asst Vice President Finance .... Mr. Stuart B. SHOR
81 Dean for Science .... Dr. Joshua BRUMBERG
20 Assoc Provost & Dean Academic Affs .... Dr. David OLAN
08 Chief Librarian .... Ms. Polly THISTLETHWAITE
100 Chief of Staff .... Vacant
19 Exec Dir Security & Public Safety .... Mr. John FLAHERTY
15 Exec Dir of Human Resources .... Mr. David BOXILL
46 Exec Dir Research & Sponsored Pgm .... Dr. Edith GONZALEZ
37 Exec Dir Fellowships/Financial Aid .... Ms. Phyllis SCHULZ
20 Exec Director of Academic Affairs .... Ms. Stacie TIONGSON
06 Dir Stdnt Services/Senior Registrar .... Mr. Vincent J. DELUCA
85 Director International Students .... Ms. Linda ASARO

43 Legal Counsel & Labor Designee .... Ms. Lynette M. PHILLIPS
18 Director Facilities .... Mr. Charles SCOTT
22 Chief Diversity Officer .... Ms. Pinar OZGU
07 Director Admissions .... Mr. Les GRIBBEN
25 Director Sponsored Research .... Ms. Hilry FISHER
38 Dir Well Ctr/Psy Coun Svc/Adult Dev .... Dr. Robert HATCHER
04 Administrative Asst to President .... Ms. Alexandra ROBINSON

*City University of New York Herbert H. Lehman College (A)

250 Bedford Park Boulevard W, Bronx NY 10468-1589
County: Bronx FICE Identification: 007022
Unit ID: 190637
Telephone: (718) 960-8000 Carnegie Class: Masters/L
FAX Number: N/A Calendar System: Semester
URL: www.lehman.edu
Established: 1968 Annual Undergrad Tuition & Fees (In-District): $7,210
Enrollment: 14,130 Coed
Affiliation or Control: State/Local IRS Status: 501(c)3
Highest Offering: Master's
Accreditation: M, CACREP, CAEPN, DIETD, DIETI, NURSE, SP, SW

02 Interim President .... Dr. Daniel LEMONS
100 Deputy to President Strategic Init .... Ms. Gladys MALDOON
05 Provost/SVP Academic Affairs .... Dr. Peter O. NWOSU
84 Assoc Provost/VP Enroll Mgmt .... Dr. Reine SARMIENTO
10 Interim VP Administration/Finance .... Ms. Rene M. ROTOLO
111 Vice Pres Institutional Advancement .... Ms. Susan EBERSOLE
32 Vice President Student Affairs .... Vacant
13 Vice Pres/Chief Info Officer .... Mr. Ronald BERGMANN
79 Dean School of Arts/Humanities .... Dr. James MAHON
83 Int Dean School of Nat & Soc Sci .... Dr. Pamela MILLS
20 Dean of Academic Affairs .... Dr. Daniel LEMONS
76 Int Dean Sch Hlth Sci/Hum Svc/Nurs .... Dr. Elin WARING
51 Dean School Cont Educ/Prof Studies .... Dr. Jane MACKILLOP
53 Int Dean School of Education .... Dr. Gaoyin QIAN
08 Chief Librarian .... Dr. Kenneth SCHLESINGER
43 Counsel to Pres/Labor Designee .... Mr. Esdras TULIER
28 Chief Diversity Officer .... Ms. Dawn EWING-MORGAN
18 Asst VP Campus Planning/Facilities .... Ms. Rene M. ROTOLO
45 AVP Strategy/Policy & Analytics .... Dr. Jonathan GAGLIARDI
26 AVP for Marketing & Communications .... Ms. Karen CROWE
35 Dean of Student Affairs .... Dr. Stanley BAZILE
21 Asst VP for Financial Operations .... Ms. Gina HARWOOD
14 Asst VP Information Technology .... Ms. Ediltrudys RUIZ
06 Senior Registrar .... Ms. Yvette ROSARIO
07 Director of Admissions .... Ms. Laurie AUSTIN
29 Assoc Director of Alumni Relations .... Mr. Robert PAGAN
88 Director of the Art Gallery .... Mr. Bartholomew F. BLAND
36 Interim Director Career Services .... Ms. Bascilla TOUSSAINT
38 Director Counseling Center .... Ms. Karen SMITH MOORE
37 Director Financial Aid .... Ms. Elvira SENESE
89 Director Freshman Year Initiative .... Dr. Steven WYCKOFF
46 Dir Research & Sponsored Programs .... Mr. Brandon J. BEGARLY
92 Director of Honors College Program .... Dr. Gary SCHWARTZ
15 Director of Human Resources .... Mr. Eric WASHINGTON
09 Director of Institutional Research .... Mr. Raymond GALINSKI
121 Dir Instruct Support Services Pgm .... Ms. Althea FORDE
27 Dir Media Relations & Publications .... Vacant
88 Director Performing Arts Center .... Ms. Eva BORNSTEIN
19 Director of Public Safety .... Mr. Fausto RAMIREZ
109 Director of Auxiliary Services .... Ms. Andrea PINNOCK
41 Athletic Director .... Dr. Martin ZWIREN
40 Bookstore Manager .... Ms. Caitlin NEWSOME
120 Dir Online Education/E-learning .... Dr. Olena ZHADKO
114 Director of Budget .... Ms. Bethania ORTEGA
44 Director Advancement Initiatives .. Ms. Tara REGIST TOMLINSON

*Hostos Community College-City University of New York (B)

500 Grand Concourse, Bronx NY 10451-5323
County: Bronx FICE Identification: 008611
Unit ID: 190585
Telephone: (718) 518-4300 Carnegie Class: Assoc/HT-High Trad
FAX Number: (718) 518-4294 Calendar System: Semester
URL: www.hostos.cuny.edu
Established: 1970 Annual Undergrad Tuition & Fees (In-District): $5,208
Enrollment: 7,211 Coed
Affiliation or Control: State/Local IRS Status: 501(c)3
Highest Offering: Associate Degree
Accreditation: M, DH, RAD

02 President .... Dr. David GOMEZ
05 Provost/VP for Academic Affairs .... Dr. Christine MANGINO
10 Senior Vice Pres for Admin/ Finance .... Ms. Esther RODRIGUEZ-CHARDAVOYNE
32 VP Student Development/Enroll Mgmt .... Mr. Nathaniel CRUZ
100 Deputy to President .... Vacant
111 Vice Pres Institutional Advancement .... Ms. Ana MARTINEZ
103 VP for Cont Educ & Workforce Dev .... Mr. Peter MERTENS
13 Asst Vice Pres Info Technology .... Mr. Varun SEHGAL
114 Finance/Budget Director .... Ms. Fanny DUMANCELA
18 Exec Dir Facil Plng Des Mgmt .... Ms. Elizabeth FRIEDMAN
04 Associate Dean for Community Rels .. Ms. Ana I. GARCIA-REYES
20 Asst Dean of Academic Affairs .... Mr. Felix CARDONA
84 Asst Dean of Enrollment Management .... Dr. Johana RIVERA
35 Assistant Dean of Student Life .... Ms. Johanna GOMEZ
43 Exec Counsel & Labor Designee .... Mr. Eugene SOHN
26 Director of Communication .... Ms. Soldanela RIVERA LOPEZ
38 Director of Counseling .... Ms. Linda ALEXANDER-WALLACE
15 Director Human Resources .... Ms. Shirley SHEVACH
86 Dir Government/External Affairs .... Mr. Joshua RIVERA
06 Registrar .... Ms. Nelida PASTORIZA
07 Dir of Admissions & Recruitment .... Mr. Carlos RIVERA
37 Director of Financial Aid .... Ms. Leslie KING
19 Director of Campus Security .... Mr. Arnaldo BERNABE
25 Director Grants & Contracts .... Ms. Kelba SOSA
09 Director Institutional Research .... Mr. Piotr KOCIK
08 Head Librarian .... Ms. Madeline FORD
22 Chief Diversity Officer .... Ms. Lauren GRETINA
29 Development/Alumni Relations Mgr .... Mr. Felix SANCHEZ
36 Director Student Career Programs .... Ms. Lisanette ROSARIO
35 Director Student Activities .... Mr. Jerry ROSA
96 Director of Procurement .... Mr. Kevin CARMINE
108 Asst Dn Inst Eff/Strat Plng/Assess .... Ms. Babette AUDANT
21 Exec Director Business & Finance .... Mr. Ken ACQUAH

*City University of New York Hunter College (C)

695 Park Avenue, New York NY 10065
County: New York FICE Identification: 002689
Unit ID: 190594
Telephone: (212) 772-4000 Carnegie Class: Masters/L
FAX Number: N/A Calendar System: Semester
URL: www.hunter.cuny.edu
Established: 1870 Annual Undergrad Tuition & Fees (In-District): $7,182
Enrollment: 23,005 Coed
Affiliation or Control: State/Local IRS Status: 501(c)3
Highest Offering: Doctorate
Accreditation: M, AUD, CACREP, CAEPN, CYTO, DIETD, DIETI, NURSE, PLNG, PTA, SP, SW

02 President .... Ms. Jennifer J. RAAB
100 Chief of Staff .... Ms. Anne LYTLE
10 Acting Vice Pres Finance/Budget .... Ms. Livia CANGEMI
05 Provost/Vice Pres Academic Affairs .... Mr. Lon KAUFMAN
32 VP Student Affs/Dean of Stdnts .... Ms. Eija AYRAVAINEN
43 General Counsel/Dean of Faculty ...... Ms. Carol ROBLES-ROMAN
26 Asst VP & Dir Communication .... Vacant
13 Asst Vice Pres Information Tech .... Mr. Mitch AHLBAUM
21 Executive Director Business Svcs .... Ms. Livia CANGEMI
21 Asst Vice Pres Business Services .... Vacant
35 Asst Vice Pres of Student Affairs .... Vacant
28 Dean Diversity and Compliance .... Mr. John ROSE
49 Dean School of Arts & Sciences .... Dr. Andrew POLSKY
70 Acting Dean School of Social Work .... Ms. Mary CAVANAUGH
53 Dean School of Education .... Mr. Michael MIDDLETON
66 Dean School of Nursing .... Dr. Gail C. MCCAIN
08 Dean of Libraries/Chief Librarian .... Mr. Brian LYM
06 Registrar .... Vacant
09 Director of Institutional Research .... Ms. Joan LAMBE
15 Director of Human Resources .... Ms. Galia GALANSKY
35 Director Student Advising .... Mr. Bryan MAASJO
36 Director Student Placement .... Ms. Susan MCCARTY
29 Director Alumni Relations .... Vacant
19 College Security Director .... Mr. Joseph FOELSCH
07 Director of Admissions .... Ms. Lori JANOWSKI
104 Director Study Abroad .... Ms. Elizabeth SACHS
108 Dir Institutional Assessment .... Ms. Maureen ERICKSON
41 Athletic Director .... Ms. Terry WANSART
84 Dir Enrollment Mgmt/Recruit .... Ms. Sarah FARSAD

*City University of New York John Jay College of Criminal Justice (D)

524 West 59th Street, New York NY 10019-1093
County: New York FICE Identification: 002693
Unit ID: 190600
Telephone: (212) 237-8000 Carnegie Class: Masters/L
FAX Number: (212) 237-8607 Calendar System: Semester
URL: www.jjay.cuny.edu
Established: 1964 Annual Undergrad Tuition & Fees (In-District): $7,270
Enrollment: 14,834 Coed
Affiliation or Control: State/Local IRS Status: 501(c)3
Highest Offering: Master's
Accreditation: M, CLPSY, FEPAC, SPAA

02 President .... Ms. Karol V. MASON
05 Provost .... Dr. Yi LI
32 Int VP Student Affairs .... Ms. Ellen HARTIGAN
111 Vice Pres Institutional Advancement .... Ms. Robin MERLE
84 Int VP Enrollment Management .... Ms. Ellen HARTIGAN
04 Executive Assoc to President .... Ms. Raeanne DAVIS
121 Acad Advis Dir/Sr Co-Curric Admin .... Ms. Rulisa GALLOWAY-PERRY
46 Associate Provost/Dean of Research .... Dr. Anthony CARPI
10 SVP Finance/Administration .... Mr. Steven TITAN
20 Assoc Prov & Dean of Undergrad Stds .... Dr. Dara BRYNE
08 Chief Librarian .... Dr. Lawrence SULLIVAN
37 Director of Financial Aid .... Ms. Sylvia CRESPO-LOPEZ
30 Director of Development .... Vacant
35 Director Student Activities .... Ms. Danielle OFFICER
25 Director of Funded Research .... Ms. Susy MENDES
09 Director of Institutional Research .... Mr. Ricardo ANZALDUA
89 Director of First Year Experience .... Ms. Katalin SZUR
06 Registrar .... Mr. Daniel MATOS
88 Director of CRJ Research & Eval .... Dr. Jeffrey BUTTS
07 Director of Admissions .... Mr. Vincent PAPANDREA
13 Chief Information Officer .... Mr. Joe LAUB
19 Director of Public Safety .... Mr. Diego REDONDO
24 Director of Media Services .... Vacant
27 Chief Communications Officer .... Ms. Rama SUDHAKAR
36 Dir of Career Development Svcs .... Ms. Chantelle WRIGHT
38 Director of Counseling .... Dr. Gerard BRYANT
41 Athletic Director .... Ms. Carol KASHOW
21 Associate Business Officer .... Ms. Emily KARP
29 Director Alumni Relations .... Ms. Jerylle KEMP
96 Director of Purchasing .... Mr. Daniel DOLAN
88 Senior International Officer .... Ms. Mayra NIEVES
18 Director Facilities/Physical Plant .... Mr. Anthony BRACCO
43 Assistant Vice President & Counsel .... Ms. Marjorie SINGER
86 Exec Dir of External Relations .... Ms. Mindy BOCKSTEIN
121 Director of Academic Advisement .... Dr. Sumaya VILLANUEVA
22 Int Dir of Accessibility Services .... Ms. Malanie CLARKE
104 Director Study Abroad .... Mr. Kenneth YANES
28 Director of Diversity .... Ms. Silvia MONTALBAN
39 Director Student Housing .... Ms. Jessica CARSON
102 Dir Foundation/Corporate Relations .... Vacant
106 Dir Online Education/E-learning .... Ms. Judith CAHN
15 Exec Director of Human Resources .... Mr. Jared HERST

† The Clinical Psychology PhD is awarded through the CUNY Graduate Center.

*City University of New York Kingsborough Community College (E)

2001 Oriental Boulevard, Brooklyn NY 11235-2333
County: Kings FICE Identification: 002694
Unit ID: 190619
Telephone: (718) 368-5109 Carnegie Class: Assoc/HT-Mix Trad/Non
FAX Number: (718) 368-5003 Calendar System: Other
URL: www.kbcc.cuny.edu
Established: 1963 Annual Undergrad Tuition & Fees (In-District): $5,252
Enrollment: 15,034 Coed
Affiliation or Control: State/Local IRS Status: 501(c)3
Highest Offering: Associate Degree
Accreditation: M, ADNUR, EMT, POLYT, PTAA, SURGT

02 President .... Dr. Claudia V. SCHRADER
05 Vice Pres Academic Affs/Provost .... Dr. Joanne RUSSELL
10 Vice Pres Finance/Administration .... Mr. Eduardo RIOS
100 Executive Chief of Staff .... Dr. Tasheka SUTTON-YOUNG
32 Vice Pres of Student Affairs .... Mr. Peter COHEN
51 Dean Continuing Education .... Ms. Christine BECKNER
35 Director of Student Life .... Ms. Maria PATESTAS
84 Vice Pres Enrollment Management .... Dr. Johana RIVERA
09 Vice Pres Inst Effectiveness .... Dr. Richard FOX
30 Vice Pres Institutional Advancement .... Dr. Elizabeth BASILE
15 Director of Human Resources .... Ms. Micheline DRISCOLL
22 Dir Affirmative Action/EO Officer .... Mr. Michael VALENTE
19 Director of Security & Safety .... Mr. James CAPOZZI
08 Chief Librarian .... Ms. Josephine MURPHY
06 Registrar .... Mr. Michael KLEIN
18 Campus Facilities Officer .... Mr. Anthony CORAZZA
37 Financial Aid Officer .... Mr. Sinu JACOB
13 Chief Information Officer .... Mr. Asif HUSSAIN
36 Director Career Services .... Ms. Melissa MERCED
24 Director of Educational Media .... Mr. Michael ROSSON
41 Director of Athletics .... Mr. Damani THOMAS
96 Director of Purchasing .... Ms. Kiesha STEWART
29 Director Alumni Relations .... Ms. Laura GLAZIER-SMITH
38 Director Student Counseling .... Ms. Dasha GORINSHTEYN

*LaGuardia Community College/ City University of New York (F)

31-10 Thomson Avenue, Long Island City NY 11101-3083
County: Queens FICE Identification: 010051
Unit ID: 190628
Telephone: (718) 482-7200 Carnegie Class: Assoc/HT-High Trad
FAX Number: (718) 609-2000 Calendar System: Semester
URL: www.lagcc.cuny.edu
Established: 1971 Annual Undergrad Tuition & Fees (In-District): $5,218
Enrollment: 19,373 Coed
Affiliation or Control: State/Local IRS Status: 501(c)3
Highest Offering: Associate Degree
Accreditation: M, ADNUR, DIETT, EMT, OTA, PTAA

02 Interim President .... Dr. Paul ARCARIO
05 Int Provost/Senior Vice President .... Dr. Nireata D. SEALS
04 Senior Advisor to President .... Mr. Robert JAFFE
11 Vice President of Administration .... Mr. Shahir ERFAN
111 VP of Institutional Advancement .... Ms. Janet CORCORAN
13 Vice Pres Information Technology .... Mr. Henry SALTIEL
32 Int Vice President Student Affairs .... Dr. Bart GRACHAN
51 Vice Pres Continuing Education .... Mr. Mark C. HEALY
20 Assoc Dean for Academic Affairs .... Mr. Bret EYNON
20 Assoc Dean for Academic Affairs .... Ms. Dion MILLER
84 Asst Dean Enrollment Services .... Vacant
103 Asst Dean of Workforce Development .... Vacant
18 Exec Dir Facilities Mgmt/Planning .... Mr. Kenneth CAMPANELLI
15 Exec Director of Human Resources .... Mr. Oswald FRASER
10 Exec Director Finance & Business .... Mr. Thomas HLADEK
08 Chief Librarian .... Mr. Scott WHITE
37 Director Student Financial Services .... Ms. Gail BAKSH-JARRETT
07 Director of Admissions .... Ms. LaVora DESVIGNE
26 Dir Marketing/Communications .... Mr. Charles ELIAS
21 Associate Business Manager .... Ms. Carmen LUONG
36 Director Employment/Career Svc Ctr .... Ms. Claudia BALDONEDO
96 Director Procurement & Contracts .... Mr. Mitchell HENDERSON
86 Government Relations Manager .... Ms. Claudia CHAN

*City University of New York Medgar Evers College (A)

1650 Bedford Avenue, Brooklyn NY 11225-2010
County: Kings FICE Identification: 010097
Unit ID: 190646
Telephone: (718) 270-4900 Carnegie Class: Bac/Assoc-Mixed
FAX Number: (718) 270-5126 Calendar System: Semester
URL: www.mec.cuny.edu
Established: 1970 Annual Undergrad Tuition & Fees (In-District): $7,152
Enrollment: 6,652 Coed
Affiliation or Control: State/Local IRS Status: 501(c)3
Highest Offering: Baccalaureate
Accreditation: M, ACBSP, ADNUR, CAEPN, NUR, #SW

02 President Dr. Rudolph F. CREW
11 Chief Operating Officer Mr. Jerald POSMAN
05 Provost/Senior Vice President Dr. Augustine OKEREKE
10 VP Finance & Administration Ms. Jacqueline CLARK
20 Asst VP & Assoc Provost Dr. Heyward M. DREHER
32 Dean of Students Dr. Alexis MCLEAN
20 Dean of Academic Affairs Dr. Hollie JONES
51 Dean Sch Professional & Comm Dev Dr. Evelyn CASTRO
50 Dean of the School of Business Dr. Jo-Ann ROLLE
49 Dean of the School of Liberal Arts Dr. Ethan GOLOGAR
72 Dean School of Science/Health/Tech Dr. Mohsin PATWARY
100 Chief of Staff Ms. Lakisha MURRAY
43 Chief Legal Officer Mr. Johnathon HARDAWAY
04 Exec Assistant to the President Mrs. Lisa ANDERSON
22 Director of Affirmative Action Ms. Tanya ISAACS
06 Registrar Vacant
86 Exec Dir Govt Affs/Comm & Mktg Ms. Jennifer N. JAMES
13 Asst VP/CIO Vacant
37 Director of Financial Aid Vacant
38 Director of Counseling Dr. JoAnn JOYNER-GRAHAM
19 Director of Security Mr. Nolan BRIGGS
41 Director of Athletics Ms. Chetara MURPHY
25 Grants Officer Mr. Chi KOON
89 Dir Freshman Year Program Ms. Nicole BERRY
55 Director Evening/Weekend Programs Ms. Yvette WALL
36 Sr Director of Career Development Ms. Antoinette ROBERSON
111 Vice Pres Inst Advancement Vacant
18 Supt of Buildings & Grounds Mr. Dave ADEBANJO
84 Exec Dir Enrollment Management Mrs. Shannon CLARKE-ANDERSON
29 Director of Alumni Relations Ms. Marsha ESCAGY
07 Director Admissions Ms. Jo-Ann JACOBS
09 Director of Institutional Research Dr. Eva CHAN
08 Interim Chief Librarian Dr. Judith SCHWARTZ
66 Chair Dept of Nursing Dr. Jean GUMBS
50 Chair Dept of Business Admin Ms. Sambhavi LAKSHMINARAYANAN
53 Chair Multi-Early Child & Elem Educ Dr. Rupam SARAN
60 Chair Dept of Mass Comm Dr. Clinton CRAWFORD
88 Chair Department Accounting Dr. Rosemary WILLIAMS
81 Chair Department of Mathematics Dr. Joshua SUSSAN
77 Chair Dept Physics/Computer Sci Dr. Armando HOWARD
81 Chair Department of Biology Dr. Carolle BOLNET
83 Chair Dept of Social/Behavioral Sci Dr. Maria DELONGORIA
88 Chair Department of Psychology Dr. Maudry LASHLEY
88 Chair Dept of Public Administration Dr. Zulema BLAIR
88 Chair Computer Info Systems Dr. David AHN
88 Chair Department Economics/Finance Dr. Emmanuel EGBE
88 Chair Department of English Dr. Keming LIU
88 Chair Dept of Philosophy & Religion Dr. Vivaldi JEAN MARIE
88 Chair Dept of World Lang & Culture Dr. Maria-Luisa RUIZ
88 Chair Chemistry/Environmental Sci Dr. Alicia REID
88 Chair Dev & Special Education Dr. Donna WRIGHT
35 Director of Student Life Ms. Amani REECE
15 Executive Dir of Human Resources Ms. Tanya ISAACS
113 Director Office of the Bursar Ms. Thais PILIERI
28 Chief Diversity Officer Ms. Tanya ISAACS
104 Director Study Abroad Ms. Rachelle TAYLOR

*New York City College of Technology/City University of New York (B)

300 Jay Street, Brooklyn NY 11201-1909
County: Kings FICE Identification: 002696
Unit ID: 190655
Telephone: (718) 260-5000 Carnegie Class: Bac/Assoc-Mixed
FAX Number: (718) 260-5198 Calendar System: Semester
URL: www.citytech.cuny.edu
Established: 1946 Annual Undergrad Tuition & Fees (In-District): $7,120
Enrollment: 17,279 Coed
Affiliation or Control: State/Local IRS Status: 501(c)3
Highest Offering: Baccalaureate
Accreditation: M, ADNUR, ART, CSHSE, DH, DT, NUR, OPD, RAD

02 President Dr. Russell K. HOTZLER
05 Provost Dr. Bonne AUGUST
10 Vice Pres Finance/Administration Dr. Miguel CAIROL
84 VP Enrollment/Student Affairs Mr. Michel HODGE
20 Associate Provost Academic Affairs Dr. Pamela BROWN
22 Counsel/Affirmative Action Officer Ms. Gilen CHAN
07 Director of Admissions Ms. Alexis CHACONIS
06 Registrar Ms. Tasha RHODES
37 Director of Financial Aid Ms. Sandra HIGGINS
08 Librarian Ms. Maura SMALE
13 Director of Computer Center Ms. Rita UDDIN
107 Dean of Professional Studies Mr. David SMITH
72 Dean of Technology Vacant
49 Dean of Arts & Science Mr. Justin VASQUEZ-PORITZ
51 Dean Continuing Education Dr. Carol SONNENBLICK
55 Director Evening Session Mr. James LAP
15 Director of Human Resources Ms. Sandra GORDON
25 Grants Officer Ms. Barbara BURKE
24 Director of Inst Tech/Media Svcs Ms. Karen LUNDSTREM
09 Director of Assessment Vacant
26 Exec Dir Public Relations Ms. Faith CORBETT
29 Director Alumni Relations Vacant
38 Director Student Counseling Ms. Cynthia BINK
96 Director of Purchasing Mr. Wayne ROBINSON
18 Chief Facilities/Physical Plant Mr. James VASQUEZ
30 Chief Development/Spec Asst to Pres Dr. Stephen SOIFFER
21 Executive Dir of Business Mgmt Mr. Wayne ROBINSON

*City University of New York Queens College (C)

65-30 Kissena Boulevard, Flushing NY 11367-1597
County: Queens FICE Identification: 002690
Unit ID: 190664
Telephone: (718) 997-5000 Carnegie Class: Masters/L
FAX Number: (718) 997-5598 Calendar System: Semester
URL: www.qc.cuny.edu
Established: 1937 Annual Undergrad Tuition & Fees (In-District): $7,338
Enrollment: 19,866 Coed
Affiliation or Control: State/Local IRS Status: 501(c)3
Highest Offering: Master's
Accreditation: M, #CAEP, CAEPN, CLPSY, DIETD, DIETI, LAW, LIB, SP

02 President Dr. William TRAMONTANO
05 Provost & VP Academic Affairs Dr. Elizabeth HENDREY
10 VP Finance/Administration Mr. William KELLER
32 Vice President for Student Affairs Dr. Adam ROCKMAN
26 VP Comm & Senior Adv to Pres Mr. Jay HERSHENSON
84 VP Enrollment & Student Retention Mr. Richard ALVAREZ
111 VP Inst Adv & Alumni Relations Ms. Laurie DORF
43 AVP/General Counsel Ms. Sandy A. CURKO
100 Chief of Staff Ms. Meghan MOORE-WILK
27 Director of Communications Ms. Leslie JAY
13 AVP/CIO Information Tech Mr. Troy HAHN
20 Assoc Provost Res/Faculty Programs Dr. Alicia ALVERO
20 Assoc Provost Res and Intl Programs Dr. Yongwu RONG
21 AVP Budget and Finance Mr. Joseph LOUGHREN
88 Assistant Provost Dr. Eva FERNANDEZ
57 Dean of Arts & Humanities Dr. William MCCLURE
81 Dean of Math & Natural Sciences Vacant
53 Dean of Education Dr. Craig MICHAELS
58 Dean of Graduate Studies Dr. Glenn BURGER
83 Dean of Social Sciences Dr. Michael WOLFE
15 AVP Human Resources Ms. Lee KELLY
41 Director of Athletics Mr. Robert TWIBLE
88 Director of Events Ms. Sylvia HERNANDEZ
18 AVP Facilities Mr. Zeco KRCIC
07 Executive Director for the QC Hub Mr. Vincent ANGRISANI
38 Director of Counseling & Advisement Vacant
06 Co-Director QC Hub/Registrar Vacant
09 Dean of Inst Effectiveness Ms. Cheryl LITTMAN
08 Chief Librarian Ms. Kristin HART
37 Co-Director QC Hub/Financial Aid Mr. Clifford COULOUTE
29 Manager Alumni Affairs Ms. Laura ABRAMS
19 Director of Security/Safety Dr. Beth A. LAMANNA
22 Director of Compliance & Diversity Ms. Sharon SHULMAN
96 Director of Purchasing Mr. Surinder VIRK
86 AVP Ext Affairs & Govt Relations Mr. Jeffrey ROSENSTOCK
26 Director of Marketing Ms. Lillian ZEPEDA
100 Deputy Chief of Staff Dr. Odalys DIAZ PIÑEIRO
104 Director of Study Abroad Vacant
25 Chief Contract/Grants Administrator Ms. Poline PAPOULIS
39 Director of Student Housing Mr. Sean PIERCE

† The Clinical Psychology PhD is awarded through the CUNY Graduate Center.

*City University of New York Queensborough Community College (D)

222-05 56th Avenue, Bayside NY 11364-1497
County: Queens FICE Identification: 002697
Unit ID: 190673
Telephone: (718) 631-6262 Carnegie Class: Assoc/HT-High Trad
FAX Number: N/A Calendar System: Semester
URL: www.qcc.cuny.edu
Established: 1958 Annual Undergrad Tuition & Fees (In-District): $5,210
Enrollment: 15,400 Coed
Affiliation or Control: State/Local IRS Status: 501(c)3
Highest Offering: Associate Degree
Accreditation: M, ACBSP, ADNUR, ART, THEA

02 President Dr. Timothy LYNCH
11 Sr Vice Pres/Chief Operating Ofcr Ms. Sherri NEWCOMB
05 Int Provost/VP Academic Affairs Dr. Sandra PALMER
10 Vice Pres Finance & Admin Mr. William FAULKNER
111 Vice Pres Institutional Advancement Ms. Rosemary S. ZINS
32 Vice President Student Affairs Dr. Brian KERR
15 Dean Human Resource/Labor Rels Ms. Liza LARIOS
51 VP Continuing Ed/Workforce Dev Vacant
108 VP Strategic Plng/Assessment Vacant
26 VP/Chief Communications/Mktg Ofcr Mr. Stephen DI DIO
88 Dean Accred Assessment Dr. Arthur CORRADETTI
13 Chief Information Technology Ofcr Mr. George SHERMAN
08 Chief Librarian Ms. Jeanne GALVIN
06 Registrar Vacant
84 Dean of Enrollment Management Ms. Veronica LUKAS
07 Asst Dean of New Student Enrollment Ms. Linda EVANGELOU
09 Director of Institutional Research Ms. Elisabeth LACKNER
16 Director of Human Resources Ms. Ellen ADAMS
19 Director of Safety & Security Mr. John TRIOLO
22 Chief Diversity Officer Ms. Josephine PANTALEO
04 Executive Asst to President Ms. Elaine IOANNOU
104 Dir Ctr for Intl Stds/Study Abroad Ms. Lampeto (Betty) EFTHYMIOU
18 Chief Admin Superintendent Mr. Joseph CARTOLANO
36 Director of Career Services Ms. Constance PELUSO
30 Development Officer Ms. Saji SHEERAZI
21 Exec Dir Finance/Admin Operations Mr. David WASSERMAN
45 Exec Dir Budget/Resource Planning Mr. Mark CARPENTIER
20 Dean of Faculty Vacant
35 Asst Dean of Student Dev/Conduct Ms. Tikola RUSSELL
88 Asst Dean Ctr Excell in Teach/Lrng Dr. Kathleen LANDY
103 Dean Continuing Educ/Workforce Dev Ms. Hui-Yin HSU

*City University of New York Stella and Charles Guttman Community College (E)

50 West 40th Street, New York NY 10018
County: New York Identification: 667126
Unit ID: 475565
Telephone: (646) 313-8000 Carnegie Class: Assoc/HT-High Trad
FAX Number: N/A Calendar System: Semester
URL: www.guttman.cuny.edu
Established: 2011 Annual Undergrad Tuition & Fees (In-District): $5,194
Enrollment: 1,066 Coed
Affiliation or Control: State/Local IRS Status: 501(c)3
Highest Offering: Associate Degree
Accreditation: M

02 President Scott EVENBECK
05 Provost and Vice President Howard M. WACH
10 Vice Pres Admin & Finance Mary COLEMAN
45 Dean Strategic Plng & Effectiveness Stuart COCHRAN
09 Director of Institutional Research Elisa HERTZ
100 Chief of Staff Linda MERIANS
13 Chief Info Technology Officer (CIO) John STROUD
15 Director Human Resources Nila BHAUMIK
18 Director Facilities Planning Shirley LAW
19 Director Public Safety Anastasia KOUTSIDIS
37 Director Student Financial Aid Cristina ORTIZ-HARVEY
06 Registrar Cortes MARISOL
07 Director of Admissions So SOPHEA
86 Director Government Relations Lavita MCMATH-TURNER
04 Administrative Asst to President Nina CONROY
102 Dir Foundation/Corporate Relations Bruce LYONS
29 Director Alumni Relations LaToya JACKSON
32 Dean of Student Engagement Charles PRYOR

*City University of New York York College (F)

94-20 Guy Brewer Boulevard, Jamaica NY 11451-0001
County: Queens FICE Identification: 004759
Unit ID: 190691
Telephone: (718) 262-2000 Carnegie Class: Bac-Diverse
FAX Number: (718) 262-2352 Calendar System: Semester
URL: www.york.cuny.edu
Established: 1966 Annual Undergrad Tuition & Fees (In-District): $7,158
Enrollment: 8,533 Coed
Affiliation or Control: State/Local IRS Status: 501(c)3
Highest Offering: Master's
Accreditation: M, ARCPA, CAEPN, EXSC, MT, MT, NUR, OT, SW

02 President Dr. Marcia V. KEIZS
05 Provost/Sr VP for Academic Affs Dr. Panayiotis MELETIES
10 VP of Administration & Finance/COO Mr. Ronald C. THOMAS
32 Vice Pres for Student Development Dr. Vincent BANREY
111 VP Institutional Advancement Mr. Shereitte STOKES
49 Dean School of Arts & Sciences Dr. Donna CHIRICO
83 Dean Sch of Health Sci & Prof Pgms Dr. Maureen BECKER
50 Dean Sch of Business & Info Systems Vacant
43 Labor & Legal Affairs Mr. Russell PLATZEK
15 Exec Director HR Ms. Sabrina JOHNSON-CHANDLER
13 Interim Chief Information Officer Mr. Claudio LINDOW
09 AVP Inst Effective/Strategic Plng Dr. Lori HOEFFNER
06 Registrar Ms. Sharon DAVIDSON
08 Chief Librarian Ms. Njoki KINYATTI
90 Director of Academic Computing Dr. Che-Tsao HUANG
86 Exec Dir Govt/Strategic Initiative Dr. Earl G. SIMONS
19 Director of Security Chief Rufus MASSIAH
37 Director of Financial Aid Ms. Beverly BROWN
18 Director Campus Planning Mr. Noel GAMBOA
35 Director Student Activities Dr. Jean PHELPS
36 Director Career Services Ms. Linda H. CHESNEY
25 Dir Research/Sponsored Programs Ms. Dawn HEWITT
38 Interim Director of Counseling Dr. Jayoung CHOI
41 Director of Athletics & Recreation Ms. Denee BARRACATO
04 Executive Assoc to the President Ms. Sandra BELL ADAMS
84 Exec Dir Enrollment Mgmt Dr. Latoro YATES
29 Manager Alumni Affairs Ms. Mondell SEALY

28 Director of Diversity Ms. Alicia FRANQUI
96 Director of Purchasing Ms. Rashmi MALESH
07 Director of Admissions Mr. Anthony DAVIS
103 Director Workforce Development Vacant
44 Manager Annual Giving Ms. Geneen MCCAULEY

Clarkson University (A)

8 Clarkson Ave, Potsdam NY 13699
County: St. Lawrence FICE Identification: 002699
Unit ID: 190044
Telephone: (315) 268-6400 Carnegie Class: DU-Higher
FAX Number: (315) 268-7647 Calendar System: Semester
URL: www.clarkson.edu
Established: 1896 Annual Undergrad Tuition & Fees: $49,444
Enrollment: 4,233 Coed
Affiliation or Control: Independent Non-Profit IRS Status: 501(c)3
Highest Offering: Doctorate
Accreditation: M, ARCPA, HSA, OT, PTA

01 President Dr. Anthony G. COLLINS
05 Provost Dr. Robyn HANNIGAN
111 VP External Relations Dr. Kelly O. CHEZUM
10 Chief Financial Officer Mr. Robert CREE
84 VP Enrollment & Student Advancement Mr. Brian T. GRANT
30 VP Development & Alumni Relations Mr. Matthew DRAPER
18 Director Facilities & Services Mr. Ian HAZEN
15 Chief Human Resources Officer Ms. Amy MCGAHERAN
41 Athletics Director Mr. Scott J. SMALLING
13 Chief Information Officer Mr. Joshua A. FISKE
45 Exec Dir of Institutional Planning Ms. Shannon ROBINSON
28 Chief Inclusion Officer Dr. Jennifer BALL
49 Dean of Arts & Sciences Dr. Charles E. THORPE
50 Dean of Business Dr. Augustine LADO
54 Dean of Engineering Dr. William JEMISON
65 Dir Inst for a Sustainable Environ Dr. Susan POWERS
58 Dean of Graduate School Dr. Kerop JANOYAN
12 Pres & CEO Beacon Institute Mr. Michael WALSH
88 Dir of Inst for STEM Education Dr. Peter TURNER
08 Dean of Libraries Ms. Michelle L. YOUNG
92 Director Honors Program Dr. Jonathan D. GOSS
20 Exec Dir Academic Affairs Ms. Amanda PICKERING
88 Managing Director Clarkson Ignite Ms. Erin DRAPER
21 Controller Mr. Keith ROSSER
114 Director Budget & Planning Ms. Paula STURGE
117 Dir Legal Affairs/Compliance/Risk Ms. Debra DRESCHER
37 Director Financial Aid Ms. Pamela NICHOLS
88 Dir Student Administrative Services Ms. Suzanne E. DAVIS
06 Registrar Ms. Jen J. STOKES
07 Director of Admissions Ms. Trish DOBBS
88 Dir of Clarkson School Admission Mr. Matthew RUTHERFORD
121 AVP Stdnt Success Ctr & Int Rel Ms. Cathy MCNAMARA
32 Dean of Students Mr. James PITTMAN
35 AVP Student Affairs & Global Init Mr. Jeffrey D. TAYLOR
19 Director Campus Safety & Security Mr. David W. DELISLE
23 Director Student Health Services Ms. Susan KNOWLES
36 Director Career Center Ms. Margo JENKINS
104 Study Abroad Advisor Ms. Christine BAILEY
38 Director Counseling Services Ms. Aleta NIMS
85 Director Intl Students & Scholars Ms. Tess C. CASLER
29 AVP Engagement & Operations Ms. Teresa PLANTY
110 AVP Development Mr. Steven SMALLING
102 Director Foundation Relations Ms. Erin LONDRAVILLE
44 Director Annual Giving Programs Ms. Nichole THOMAS
91 Director Administrative Computing Mr. Chris CUTLER
90 Manager Academic Technology Ms. Laura PERRY
105 Director Web Development Ms. Julie DAVIS
09 Assoc Dir Institutional Research Ms. Jenna STONE
25 Contract & Grant Administrator Ms. Anna Marie DAWLEY
26 Director of Media Relations Ms. Melissa M. LINDELL
27 Director of Interactive Marketing Ms. Jessica CARISTA
04 Assistant to the President Ms. Carrie CAPELLA
40 Bookstore Manager Ms. Amanda STOPA GOLDSTEIN

Clinton Community College (B)

136 Clinton Point Drive, Plattsburgh NY 12901-9573
County: Clinton FICE Identification: 006787
Unit ID: 190053
Telephone: (518) 562-4200 Carnegie Class: Assoc/HT-Mix Trad/Non
FAX Number: (518) 561-4890 Calendar System: Semester
URL: www.clinton.edu
Established: 1966 Annual Undergrad Tuition & Fees (In-District): $6,202
Enrollment: 1,547 Coed
Affiliation or Control: State/Local IRS Status: 501(c)3
Highest Offering: Associate Degree
Accreditation: M, ADNUR

01 President Mr. Ray DI PASQUALE
05 Vice President for Academic Affairs Dr. John KOWAL
10 Vice Pres for Admin/Business Affs Vacant
32 Dean of Student Affairs Mr. John BORNER
111 Vice Pres Institutional Advancement Mr. Steven G. FREDERICK
20 Assoc Vice Pres Academic Affairs Vacant
37 Director of Financial Aid Ms. Mary LA PIERRE
84 Dean of Enrollment Management Mrs. Anna MIARKA-GRZELAK
06 Registrar Vacant
13 Director Information Technology Mr. Rick BATCHELDER
15 Human Resource/Affirm Act Officer Vacant
18 Director of Buildings/Grounds Mr. Robert TROMBLEY
04 Administrative Asst to President Mrs. Tammy M. VILLANUEVA
21 Controller Mrs. Mary LAVALLEY-BLAINE

Cochran School of Nursing (C)

967 North Broadway, Yonkers NY 10701-1399
County: Westchester FICE Identification: 006443
Unit ID: 190071
Telephone: (914) 964-4282 Carnegie Class: Spec 2-yr-Health
FAX Number: (914) 964-4266 Calendar System: Semester
URL: www.cochranschoolofnursing.us
Established: 1894 Annual Undergrad Tuition & Fees: N/A
Enrollment: 120 Coed
Affiliation or Control: Independent Non-Profit IRS Status: 501(c)3
Highest Offering: Associate Degree
Accreditation: ADNUR

01 Dean Dr. Annemarie MCALLISTER
08 Learning Resources Director Ms. Paula GRAHAM
32 Dir Student Services/Finances Ms. Brandy HAUGHTON

Cold Spring Harbor Laboratory/ Watson School of Biological Sciences (D)

PO Box 100, One Bungtown Road,
Cold Spring Harbor NY 11724-0100
County: Suffolk FICE Identification: 034563
Unit ID: 436377
Telephone: (516) 367-6890 Carnegie Class: Not Classified
FAX Number: (516) 367-6919 Calendar System: Other
URL: www.cshl.edu
Established: 1890 Annual Graduate Tuition & Fees: N/A
Enrollment: N/A Coed
Affiliation or Control: Independent Non-Profit IRS Status: 501(c)3
Highest Offering: Doctorate; No Undergraduates
Accreditation: NY

01 President Dr. Bruce STILLMAN
05 Dean of Academic Affairs Dr. Terri I. GRODZICKER
10 Chief Financial Officer Ms. Lari C. RUSSO
30 VP Development/Cmty Relations Mr. Charles V. PRIZZI
13 VP Information Technology/CIO Mr. Hans-Erik ARONSON
15 Vice Pres Human Resources Ms. Katherine G. RAFTERY
26 Vice Pres Communications Ms. Dagnia ZEIDLICKIS
43 Vice Pres General Counsel Ms. Debra ARENARE
81 Dean Dr. Alexander GANN

Colgate Rochester Crozer Divinity School (E)

1100 S Goodman Street, Rochester NY 14620-2589
County: Monroe FICE Identification: 002700
Unit ID: 190080
Telephone: (585) 271-1320 Carnegie Class: Spec-4-yr-Faith
FAX Number: (585) 271-8013 Calendar System: Semester
URL: www.crcds.edu
Established: 1817 Annual Graduate Tuition & Fees: N/A
Enrollment: 50 Coed
Affiliation or Control: Independent Non-Profit IRS Status: 501(c)3
Highest Offering: Doctorate; No Undergraduates
Accreditation: THEOL

01 President Dr. Angela D. SIMS
05 VP Academic Life & Dean of Faculty Prof. Stephanie L. SAUVE
10 Chief Financial Officer Ms. Patty KEENAHAN
07 Director of Admissions Ms. Deanna PFLUKE
111 VP Institutional Advancement Dr. Courtney WILEY-HARRIS
94 Dean of Women & Gender Studies Vacant
06 Registrar Mr. Max KURZDORFER
08 Director of Library Services Ms. Margaret A. NEAD
26 Communications Coordinator Vacant
32 Dir Student Services/Financial Aid Ms. Polly BUSH
29 Director of Alumni Ms. Lisa BORS

Colgate University (F)

13 Oak Drive, Hamilton NY 13346-1386
County: Madison FICE Identification: 002701
Unit ID: 190099
Telephone: (315) 228-1000 Carnegie Class: Bac-A&S
FAX Number: (315) 228-7798 Calendar System: Semester
URL: www.colgate.edu
Established: 1819 Annual Undergrad Tuition & Fees: $55,870
Enrollment: 2,894 Coed
Affiliation or Control: Independent Non-Profit IRS Status: 501(c)3
Highest Offering: Master's
Accreditation: M

01 President Brian W. CASEY
05 Dean of Faculty & Provost Tracey E. HUCKS
10 Sr VP for Finance & Admin Joseph S. HOPE
100 Chief of Staff/Sec to the BOT Hanna RODRIGUEZ-FARRAR
88 Sr Advisor to the President Christopher WELLS
32 VP & Dean of the College Paul J. MCLOUGHLIN, II
41 VP & Director of Athletics Nicki MOORE
101 Interim VP for Advancement Robert L. TYBURSKI
07 VP of Admission & Fin Aid Gary L. ROSS
26 VP for Communications Laura JACK
111 VP for Advancement Vacant
04 Assistant to the President Debbie PILS
21 Associate Vice Pres/Controller Thomas O'NEILL
21 Assoc VP Budget & Financial Plg John COLLINS
21 AVP for Finance & Administration Dan PARTIGIANONI
18 Assoc VP for Facilities Stephen HUGHES
20 Associate Dean of the Faculty Doug JOHNSON
20 Associate Dean of the Faculty Lesleigh CUSHING
20 Associate Dean of the Faculty Martin WONG
88 Vice Provost Admin & Planning Trish ST. LEGER
28 Assoc Provost Equity & Diversity Marilyn RUGG
06 Registrar Neil ALBERT
07 Dean of Admission Tara BUBBLE
08 University Librarian Courtney YOUNG
13 Chief Information Officer Niranjan DAVRAY
110 AVP for Advancement Doug CHIARELLO
112 AVP Advancement/Planned Giving Andrew CODDINGTON
88 Assoc VP Advancement Admin & Plg Thirza MORREALE
88 Asst VP Advancement/Dir Prof Net Jennifer STONE
29 AVP Advancement/Alumni Relations Tim MANSFIELD
88 Senior Philanthropic Advisor Patty CAPRIO
37 Director of Financial Aid Gina M. SOLIZ
109 AVP Cmty Affairs/Auxiliary Services Joanne BORFITZ
19 Assoc VP for Campus Safety Daniel GOUGH
36 Assoc VP for Career Initiatives Michael SCIOLA
40 Dir Off-Campus Retail Operations Leslie PASCO
42 University Chaplain Corey MACPHERSON
38 Director Counseling/Psych Services Dawn LAFRANCE
96 Director of Purchasing Simon FRITZ
23 Director Student Health Services Merrill MILLER
94 Director Women's Studies Susan THOMSON
44 Director Relationship Development Sara GROH
88 Director Advancement Operations Lindsey HOHAM
44 Director Annual Giving Catherine MARHENKE
39 Director of Residential Housing Stacey MILLARD
09 Dir Institutional Planning/Research Neil ALBERT
22 Dir EEO & Affirmative Action Tamala FLACK
102 Dir of Corp Foundation & Govt Rels Bruce MOSELEY
104 Director of Off-Campus Study Joanna HOLVEY BOWLES

College of Mount Saint Vincent (G)

6301 Riverdale Avenue, Riverdale NY 10471-1093
County: Bronx FICE Identification: 002703
Unit ID: 193399
Telephone: (718) 405-3200 Carnegie Class: Masters/S
FAX Number: (718) 601-6392 Calendar System: Semester
URL: www.mountsaintvincent.edu
Established: 1847 Annual Undergrad Tuition & Fees: $38,180
Enrollment: 1,910 Coed
Affiliation or Control: Independent Non-Profit IRS Status: 501(c)3
Highest Offering: Master's
Accreditation: M, ACBSP, CAEPT, NURSE

01 President Dr. Charles L. FLYNN, JR.
05 Provost/Dean of Faculty Dr. Sarah STEVENSON
20 Dean of the College Dr. Lynne BONGIOVANNI
07 Sr VP for Admission/External Rels Ms. Madeleine MELKONIAN
10 Executive VP/Treasurer/CFO Mr. Abed ELKESHK
11 VP for Operations Mr. Kevin DEGROAT
13 VP Information Technology/CIO Mr. Adam WICHERN
32 Dean of Students Ms. Kelli BODRATO
88 Director Mission Integration Mr. Matthew SHIELDS
06 Registrar Mrs. Jeannette PICHARDO
08 Director of Library Mr. Joseph LEVIS
09 Director of Institutional Research Sr. Carol M. FINEGAN, SC
36 Director Career Education Mr. Robson CHERETTA
37 Director of Financial Aid Vacant
42 Dir Campus Ministry/Act Dir Mission Mr. Mathew SHIELDS
35 Dir of Student Affairs/Assoc Dean Dr. Gabrielle OCCHIOGROSSO
41 Dir Athletics & Recreation Mr. Barima YEBOAH
38 Director Counseling Services Ms. Rebecca HALPERIN
23 Director of Health Services Mrs. Eileen MCCABE
26 Director for Public Relations/Mktg Ms. Leah MUNCH
19 Dir Campus Safety/Security Mr. Thomas VASSALLO
66 Director of Nursing Dr. Judith ERICKSON
44 Assoc Dir Alumnae Rels/Annual Giv Ms. Kristin YANNIELLO
15 Director of Human Resources Ms. Melissa SAMUELS
21 Controller Mr. James WONG
04 Assistant to the President Ms. Mary BAUER
18 Director of Facilities Mr. Ryan ANDERSON
07 Director of Admissions Ms. Curt DIRCKS
92 Director of Honors Program Dr. Rosita VILLAGOMEZ
97 Director of Core Curriculum Dr. Robert JACKLOSKY

The College of Saint Rose (H)

432 Western Avenue, Albany NY 12203-1490
County: Albany FICE Identification: 002705
Unit ID: 195234
Telephone: (518) 454-5111 Carnegie Class: Masters/L
FAX Number: (518) 438-3293 Calendar System: Semester
URL: www.strose.edu
Established: 1920 Annual Undergrad Tuition & Fees: $32,574
Enrollment: 3,929 Coed
Affiliation or Control: Independent Non-Profit IRS Status: 501(c)3
Highest Offering: Master's
Accreditation: M, ACBSP, ART, CAEPN, MUS, SP, SW

01 President Dr. Carolyn J. STEFANCO
100 Chief of Staff Ms. Lisa HALEY-THOMSON
05 Int Provost/VP Academic Affairs Dr. Margaret MCLANE
32 Vice President for Student Affairs Mr. Dennis MCDONALD
84 Vice Pres of Enrollment Mgmt & Mktg Mrs. Mary M. GRONDAHL

111 Vice Pres Institutional Advancement ... Mr. Ian FARRELL
15 Assoc Vice Pres Human Res/Risk Mgt ... Mr. Jeffrey KNAPP
10 Assoc VP Financial Planning and Aux ... Ms. Valerie MYERS
07 Asst VP Undergrad Recruit/Admission ... Ms. Kathleen LESKO
123 Asst VP of Grad Recruit/Enrollment ... Ms. Cris MURRAY
37 Asst VP of Financial Aid ... Mr. Steven W. DWIRE
110 Asst VP for Advancement Operations ... Ms. Lisa MCKENZIE
35 Asst VP Student Affairs ... Ms. Mary R. MCLAUGHLIN
42 Dean of Spiritual Life/Pfaff Endow ... Dr. Michael BRANNIGAN
86 Exec Dir of Govt Community Affairs ... Mr. Michael D'ATTILIO
13 Interim Assoc VP for IT/Facilities ... Mr. John ELLIS
21 Assoc VP Financial Reporting/Comptr ... Ms. Beatrice DIEHL
06 Registrar ... Mr. Craig TYNAN
08 Director of Library Services ... Mr. Andrew URBANEK
39 Director Residence Life ... Ms. Jennifer RICHARDSON
36 Director of the Career Center ... Ms. Michele OSBORNE
38 Clinical Dir Counseling/Psych Svcs ... Mr. Ronald J. HAMER
41 Director Athletics & Recreation ... Ms. Catherine A. HAKER
91 Director Infrastructure/Programming ... Mr. William TRAVER
31 Director Community Services ... Mr. Kenneth SCOTT
42 Director of Campus Ministry ... Ms. Joan HORGAN
23 Director of Health Services ... Ms. Sandra FRESE
19 Director of Safety/Security ... Mr. Steven STELLA
121 VP for Student Success & Engagement ... Dr. Shai BUTLER
88 Director of Academic Advisement ... Dr. Kelly MEYER
23 Director of Clinical Services ... Ms. Jacqueline KLEIN
96 Director Purchasing/Auxiliary Svcs ... Ms. Patricia BUCKLEY
09 Assoc VP of Institutional Effective ... Mrs. Lisa KEATING
40 Manager of Campus Store ... Ms. Emily IVES
24 Dir of Computer/Media Services ... Mr. Michael STRATTON
04 Exec Admin Asst to the President ... Mrs. Julie KOCHAN
101 Board Liaison/General Counsel Asst ... Ms. Maria RUSSO
102 Dir Corporate & Foundation Relation ... Ms. Devon STEIN
106 Dir Online Learning Services ... Mr. Thomas ROSENBERGER
43 General Counsel ... Ms. Nancy WILLIAMSON
50 Interim Dean School of Business ... Dr. K. Michael MATHEWS
79 Interim Dean Arts & Humanities ... Dr. Jeffrey MARLETT
81 Interim Dean Math & Sciences ... Dr. Ian MACDONALD
112 Director of Principal & Major Gifts ... Ms. Therese STILLMAN
26 AVP of Marketing & Communications ... Ms. Jennifer GISH
104 Asst VP for Global Affairs ... Emin HAJIYEV
28 Chief Diversity Officer ... Dr. Shai BUTLER

The College of Westchester (A)

325 Central Avenue, White Plains NY 10606
County: Westchester — FICE Identification: 005208 — Unit ID: 197285
Telephone: (914) 948-4442 — Carnegie Class: Bac/Assoc-Mixed
FAX Number: (914) 948-5441 — Calendar System: Semester
URL: www.cw.edu
Established: 1915 — Annual Undergrad Tuition & Fees: $21,015
Enrollment: 916 — Coed
Affiliation or Control: Proprietary — IRS Status: Proprietary
Highest Offering: Baccalaureate
Accreditation: M

01 President & CEO ... Mrs. Mary Beth DEL BALZO
05 Provost/VP Academic Affairs ... Dr. Warren ROSENBERG
88 Vice President Special Projects ... Mr. Dale T. SMITH
84 VP of Enrollment Management ... Mr. Matt CURTIS
36 Director of Career Services ... Ms. Joann SONDEY
121 Dean of Student Success & Retention ... Mrs. Maria GANGI
37 Dir of Student Financial Services ... Mrs. Dianne PEPITONE

Columbia-Greene Community College (B)

4400 Route 23, Hudson NY 12534-9543
County: Columbia — FICE Identification: 006789 — Unit ID: 190169
Telephone: (518) 828-4181 — Carnegie Class: Assoc/HT-Mix Trad/Non
FAX Number: (518) 822-2015 — Calendar System: Semester
URL: www.sunycgcc.edu
Established: 1966 — Annual Undergrad Tuition & Fees (In-District): $5,094
Enrollment: 1,620 — Coed
Affiliation or Control: State/Local — IRS Status: 501(c)3
Highest Offering: Associate Degree
Accreditation: M, ADNUR

00 Chairman of the Board ... Dr. Edward SCHNEIER
01 President ... Dr. Carlee DRUMMER
05 VP/Dean of Academic Affairs ... Dr. George TIMMONS
10 VP/Dean of Administration ... Ms. Dianne TOPPLE
32 VP/Dean of Students/Enrollment Mgmt ... Dr. Joseph WATSON
38 Counselor ... Ms. Diane JOHNSON
18 Director Building & Grounds ... Ms. Allison MURPHY
26 Director Public Relations ... Ms. Jaclyn STEVENSON
37 Director of Financial Aid ... Ms. Joel PHELPS
06 Registrar ... Ms. Ann BRUNO
13 Director Information Systems ... Mr. Gino RIZZI
15 Director of Human Resources ... Ms. Melissa FANDOZZI
22 Affirmative Action Officer ... Ms. Melissa FANDOZZI
09 Assistant Dean of Planning & IE ... Dr. Casey O'BRIEN
31 Director of Community Services ... Mr. Robert BODRATTI
41 Athletic Director ... Mr. Nicolas DYER
121 Director Academic Support Center ... Dr. Mary-Teresa HEATH
103 Director of Workforce Development ... Ms. Maureen BOUTIN
07 Director of Admissions ... Ms. Rachel KAPPEL
30 Dir of Development & Alumni Svcs ... Ms. Joan KOWEEK
20 Assistant Dean of Academic Affairs ... Ms. Carol DOERFER
113 Bursar ... Ms. Christy WARD

19 Director of Security ... Mr. John LEONE
96 Purchasing Officer ... Ms. Patricia DAY
04 Assistant to the President ... Ms. Mary GARAFALO

Columbia University in the City of New York (C)

615 West 131st Street, New York NY 10027-6902
County: New York — FICE Identification: 002707 — Unit ID: 190150
Telephone: (212) 854-1754 — Carnegie Class: DU-Highest
FAX Number: (212) 851-7022 — Calendar System: Semester
URL: www.columbia.edu
Established: 1754 — Annual Undergrad Tuition & Fees: $59,430
Enrollment: 30,454 — Coed
Affiliation or Control: Independent Non-Profit — IRS Status: 501(c)3
Highest Offering: Doctorate
Accreditation: M, ANEST, CAMPEP, CEA, DENT, HSA, IPSY, JOUR, LAW, MED, MIDWF, NURSE, OT, PH, PLNG, PTA, SPAA, SW

01 President ... Mr. Lee C. BOLLINGER
05 Provost ... Dr. John COATSWORTH
03 Senior Exec Vice President ... Mr. Gerald M. ROSBERG
49 Interim EVP Arts & Sciences ... Ms. Maya TOLSTOY
76 Exec VP Health/Biomed Sciences ... Dr. Lee GOLDMAN
09 Exec Vice President Research ... Dr. G. Michael PURDY
43 General Counsel ... Ms. Jane E. BOOTH
26 Exec Vice President Public Affairs ... Ms. Shailagh J. MURRAY
101 Secretary of the University ... Mr. Jerome DAVIS
10 Exec Vice President for Finance ... Ms. Anne R. SULLIVAN
18 Exec Vice President Facilities ... Mr. David GREENBERG
88 Exec Vice President Global ... Mr. Safwan M. MASRI
30 Exec Vice Pres Development & Alumni ... Ms. Amelia J. ALVERSON
32 Exec Vice President University Life ... Ms. Suzanne B. GOLDBERG
41 Athletic Director ... Mr. Peter E. PILLING
88 Ombuds Officer ... Ms. Joan WATERS
100 Chief of Staff to President ... Ms. Susan K. GLANCY
20 Vice Provost Academic Programs ... Dr. Melissa D. BEGG
20 Vice Provost Faculty Affairs ... Ms. Latha VENKATARAMAN
11 Vice Provost Administration ... Mr. Troy EGGERS
88 Vice Provost Teaching & Learning ... Mr. Soulaymane KACHANI
28 Vice Provost Diversity & Inclusion ... Dr. Dennis MITCHELL
08 Vice Provost & Univ Librarian ... Ms. Ann D. THORNTON
48 Dean Grad School Arch/Plng/Preserv ... Ms. Amale ANDRAOS
57 Dean School of the Arts ... Dr. Carol BECKER
58 Dean Grad School of Arts & Science ... Dr. Carlos J. ALONSO
50 Dean Graduate School of Business ... Dr. R. Glenn HUBBARD
49 Dean Columbia College ... Dr. James J. VALENTINI
107 Dean School of Professional Studies ... Mr. Jason M. WINGARD
54 Dean Sch Engr/Applied Science ... Dr. Mary C. BOYCE
82 Dean School Intl/Public Affairs ... Ms. Merit E. JANOW
97 Dean School General Studies ... Dr. Lisa ROSEN-METSCH
60 Dean Graduate School Journalism ... Mr. Stephen W. COLL
61 Dean School of Law ... Ms. Gillian LESTER
70 Interim Dean School of Social Work ... Dr. Irwin GARFINKEL
63 Dean Faculty of Medicine ... Dr. Lee GOLDMAN
52 Dean Sch Dental & Oral Surgery ... Dr. Christian S. STOHLER
66 Dean School of Nursing ... Dr. Bobbie BERKOWITZ
69 Dean School of Public Health ... Dr. Linda P. FRIED
38 Exec Director Student Counseling ... Dr. Richard EICHLER
37 Assoc VP Student Financial Svcs ... Ms. Jane HOJAN-CLARK
06 Assoc Vice Pres & Registrar ... Mr. Barry S. KANE
07 Dean of Undergraduate Admissions ... Ms. Jessica MARINACCIO

† Parent institution of Barnard College and Teachers College, Columbia University.

Concordia College (D)

171 White Plains Road, Bronxville NY 10708-1923
County: Westchester — FICE Identification: 002709 — Unit ID: 190248
Telephone: (914) 337-9300 — Carnegie Class: Masters/S
FAX Number: (914) 395-4500 — Calendar System: Semester
URL: www.concordia-ny.edu
Established: 1881 — Annual Undergrad Tuition & Fees: $32,900
Enrollment: 1,597 — Coed
Affiliation or Control: Lutheran Church - Missouri Synod — IRS Status: 501(c)3
Highest Offering: Master's
Accreditation: #M, CAEP, IACBE, NURSE, RAD, SW

01 President ... Rev.Dr. John A. NUNES
03 Executive Vice President ... Dr. James BURKEE
05 Provost ... Dr. Sherry J. FRASER
10 Chief Financial/Operations Officer ... Ms. Lea EMERY
111 Vice President Advancement ... Ms. Kathleen SUSS
45 VP Strategic Planning & Management ... Mr. Theodore FRANCAVILLA
42 VP Leadership/Campus Pastor ... Rev Dr. Victor BELTON
43 General Counsel ... Ms. Arlene TORRES
79 Vice Prov Undergraduate Acad Affs ... Dr. Mandana NAKHAI
84 Sr Director of Enrollment ... Mr. John MCLOUGHLIN
66 Interim Dean Division of Nursing ... Dr. Karen BOURGEOIS
51 Dean of Adult Education & Business ... Dr. William M. SALVA
32 Dir Academic/Student Services ... Vacant
06 Registrar Coordinator ... Vacant
08 Library Director ... Mr. William L. PERRENOD
41 Athletic Director ... Ms. Kathy LAOUTARIS
23 Director Student Health Services ... Ms. Susan CRANE
88 Assoc Dean Academic Operations ... Mr. Christopher D'AMBROSIO

18 Director Facilities/Campus Services ... Mr. Paul A. SCHULZ
26 Director of Marketing/Webmaster ... Ms. Holly MAGNANI
42 Director of Church Relations ... Ms. Kathy DRESSER
31 Sr Director Community Relations ... Ms. Joyce KENNEDY
92 Director of Fellows Program ... Dr. Kate E. BEHR
15 Director of Human Resources ... Ms. Terry VIDAL
13 Dir Information Technology Services ... Mr. Gary GOLLENBERG
21 Controller ... Ms. Kathleen DUNLEAVY
121 Director of Student Success ... Ms. Johanna L. PERRY
36 Director of Career Development ... Ms. Laura GREVI
53 Dean of Teacher Education ... Dr. Stephanie SQUIRES
102 Dir of Alumni/Donor Relations ... Ms. Lois MONTORIO
09 Dir Institutional Effect/Research ... Ms. Kimberly GARGIULO
19 Director of Campus Safety ... Mr. Stephen BONURA
106 Dean Online Education/E-learning ... Ms. Susan KRAUSS

Cooper Union (E)

30 Cooper Square, New York NY 10003-7120
County: New York — FICE Identification: 002710 — Unit ID: 190372
Telephone: (212) 353-4100 — Carnegie Class: Bac-Diverse
FAX Number: (212) 353-4244 — Calendar System: Semester
URL: www.cooper.edu
Established: 1859 — Annual Undergrad Tuition & Fees: $46,700
Enrollment: 946 — Coed
Affiliation or Control: Independent Non-Profit — IRS Status: 501(c)3
Highest Offering: Master's
Accreditation: M, ART

01 President ... Laura SPARKS
10 Vice President Finance and Admin ... John RUTH
07 Dean of Admissions ... Vacant
30 Actg Vice President of Development ... Nicole KIDSTON
57 Dean School of Art ... Michael (Mike) ESSL
48 Dean School of Architecture ... Nader TEHRANI
79 Actg Dean Humanities/Social Sci ... Peter BUCKLEY
54 Dean School of Engineering ... Barry SHOOP
32 Dean of Students ... Christopher CHAMBERLIN
15 Chief Talent Officer ... Natalie BROOKS
88 Creative Director ... Mindy LANG
45 Dir of Strategic Initiatives & Eff ... Antoinette (Toni) TORRES
26 Dir Governance & External Affairs ... Danielle COOPER DAUGHTRY
27 Media Relations Manager ... Kim NEWMAN

† Every student receives a full-tuition scholarship.

Cornell University (F)

Day Hall, Ithaca NY 14850
County: Tompkins — FICE Identification: 002711 — Unit ID: 190415
Telephone: (607) 255-2000 — Carnegie Class: DU-Highest
FAX Number: (607) 255-5396 — Calendar System: Semester
URL: www.cornell.edu
Established: 1865 — Annual Undergrad Tuition & Fees: $55,188
Enrollment: 23,016 — Coed
Affiliation or Control: Independent Non-Profit — IRS Status: 501(c)3
Highest Offering: Doctorate
Accreditation: M, CIDA, DIETD, DIETI, HSA, LAW, LSAR, PLNG, VET

01 President ... Martha E. POLLACK
05 Provost ... Michael I. KOTLIKOFF
63 Prov Medical Affairs/Dean Med Col ... Augustine M.K CHOI
20 Deputy Provost ... John A. SILICIANO
10 Executive VP Financial Affairs/CFO ... Joanne M. DESTEFANO
46 Vice Provost Research/Tech Transfer ... Emmanuel P. GIANNELLIS
58 Senior Vice Prov & Dean Grad School ... Barbara A. KNUTH
88 Vice Prov for International Affairs ... Wendy WOLFORD
20 Vice Provost ... Katherine MCCOMAS
114 Vice Pres Budget & Planning ... Paul STREETER
29 VP Alumni Affairs/Development ... Fred VAN SICKLE
15 VP and Chief Human Resources ... Mary George OPPERMAN
32 VP Student & Campus Life ... Ryan T. LOMBARDI
26 Vice Pres for University Relations ... Joel M. MALINA
86 Associate VP for Govt Relations ... Charles KRUZANSKY
72 Dean/Vice Prov Cornell NYC Tech ... Daniel S. HUTTENLOCHER
43 University Counsel & Secretary Corp ... Madelyn F. WESSEL
21 Vice President Financial Affairs ... Gerald HECTOR
13 VP & CIO for Info Technology ... David LIFKA
115 Chief Investment Officer ... Kenneth M. MIRANDA
18 Vice Pres Infrastructure/Property ... Frederick BURGESS
97 Vice Provost Undergrad Educ ... Lisa NISHI
84 Assoc Vice Provost Enrollment ... Jason LOCKE
21 Interim University Controller ... Kim YEOH
21 Assoc Vice President/Treasurer ... Harper WATTERS
116 University Auditor ... Glen C. MUELLER
20 Dean of Faculty ... Charles VAN LOAN
47 Dean Col Agriculture/Life Sciences ... Kathryn J. BOOR
48 Dean College Arch/Art/Planning ... Kent KLEINMAN
49 Dean College Arts & Science ... Gretchen RITTER
54 Dean College of Engineering ... Lance R. COLLINS
88 Interim Dean School Hotel Admin ... Kate D. WALSH
59 Int Dean College Human Ecology ... Rachel DUNIFUN
50 Dean SC Johnson College of Business ... L. Joseph THOMAS
88 Dean Dyson School Applied Economics ... Lynn PERRY WOOTEN
50 Dean Industrial/Labor Rels ... Kevin F. HALLOCK
61 Dean Law School ... Eduardo M. PEÑALVER
74 Dean College Veterinary Medicine ... Lorin D. WARNICK
77 Dean of Computing and Info Science ... Gregory J. MORRISETT
51 Dean Cont Education/Summer Session ... Glenn C. ALTSCHULER
50 Dean of the Weill Graduate School ... Gary KORETZKY

08 University Librarian .... Anne R. KENNEY
88 Interim Dir Africana Stds/Research .... Noliwe L. ROOKS
07 Dir Undergraduate Admissions .... Shawn FELTON
37 Interim Director Financial Aid .... Colleen WRIGHT
35 Dean of Students .... Vijay PENDAKUR
06 University Registrar .... Cassandra C. DEMBOSKY
41 Director Athletics/Physical Educ .... J. Andrew NOEL, JR.
36 Director of Cornell Career Services .... Rebecca M. SPARROW
22 Assoc VP Wrkfrce Dvrsty & Inclusion .... Lynette CHAPPELL-WILLIAMS
23 Assoc Vice Pres Campus Health .... Janet L. CORSON-RIKERT
28 Assoc Vice Prov Faculty Diversity .... Yael LEVITTE
42 Dir Cornell United Religious Works .... Rev. Kenneth I. CLARKE
25 Sr Director Sponsored Fin Svcs .... Jeffrey A. SILBER
19 Chief Cornell Police .... Kathy R. ZONER
96 Sr Dir Procurement and Bus Svcs .... Thomas W. ROMANTIC
29 Assoc Vice Pres Alumni Affairs .... James A. MAZZA
09 AVP Inst Research/Planning .... Marin E. CLARKBERG
80 Dean Johnson Grad School of Mgmt .... Mark W. NELSON
08 Carl A Kroch University Librarian .... Gerald R. BEASLEY
104 Exec Dir Office of Global Learning .... Uttiyo RAYCHAUDHURI

† Parent institution of Weill Medical College of Cornell University.

The Culinary Institute of America (A)

1946 Campus Drive, Hyde Park NY 12538-1499

County: Dutchess FICE Identification: 007304
Unit ID: 190503
Telephone: (845) 905-4288 Carnegie Class: Spec-4-yr-Other
FAX Number: (845) 452-0165 Calendar System: Semester
URL: www.ciachef.edu
Established: 1946 Annual Undergrad Tuition & Fees: $32,720
Enrollment: 3,131 Coed
Affiliation or Control: Independent Non-Profit IRS Status: 501(c)3
Highest Offering: Master's
Accreditation: M

01 President .... Dr. Tim RYAN
10 VP Finance and Administration .... Ms. Maria KRUPIN
111 VP Advancement .... Mr. Kevin ALLAN
05 Provost .... Mr. Mark ERICKSON
20 VP Academic Affairs .... Dr. Michael SPERLING
26 VP Mktg & Communications .... Mr. Dan VINH
45 VP Strategic Init & Industry Ldrsp .... Mr. Greg DRESCHER
32 AVP & Dean of Student Affairs .... Dr. Kathleen MERGET
35 Assistant Director Student Life .... Mr. Nathan FLINTJER
38 Director Counseling & Psych Svcs .... Ms. Mueller CHRISTIANE
09 Dir Inst Research & Effectiveness .... Ms. Betsy CARROLL
23 Director Health Services .... Ms. Margot SCHINELLA
21 Director Finance .... Mr. Steven STROM
96 Director Purchasing & Storeroom .... Mr. Gower LANE
18 Director Facilities .... Mr. Evin LEDERMAN
19 Director Campus Safety .... Mr. William CAREY
37 Director Student Financial Planning .... Ms. Kathleen GAILOR
110 Senior Advancement Officer .... Ms. Denise ZANCHELLI
88 Dean Academic Engagement & Admin .... Ms. Carolyn TRAGNI
12 AVP Branch Campuses .... Ms. Susan CUSSEN
88 Dean School of Culinary Arts .... Mr. Brendan WALSH
88 Dean School of Baking & Pastry Arts .... Vacant
49 Dean School of Lib Arts & Food Std .... Ms. Denise BAUER
108 Dir Accreditation and Assessment .... Ms. Maureen ERICKSON
06 Registrar .... Mr. Chet KOULIK
36 Director Career & Academic Advising .... Ms. Crystal DECAROLIS
08 Director Library & Information Sys .... Mr. Jon GRENNAN
100 Associate VP/Chief of Staff .... Mr. Rick TIETJEN
15 Senior Director Human Resources .... Ms. Shay GARRIOCH
04 Executive Asst to President .... Ms. Shannon CAMPER
110 Senior Advancement Officer .... Ms. Elly ERICKSON
50 Dean School of Business & Mgmt Stds .... Ms. Annette GRAHAM
88 Acting Dean School of Cul Science .... Mr. Ted RUSSIN
88 Sr Director Faculty Relations .... Mr. Joe MORANO
84 Assoc VP Enrollment Mgmt .... Ms. Rachel BIRCHWOOD
88 Director Creative Services .... Ms. Terri TOTTEN
39 Assoc Dean Campus Life/Stdnt Dev .... Mr. James MANLEY
41 Asst Dir Recreation & Wellness .... Mr. Serge NALYWAYKO

Daemen College (B)

4380 Main Street, Amherst NY 14226-3592

County: Erie FICE Identification: 002808
Unit ID: 190725
Telephone: (716) 839-3600 Carnegie Class: DU-Mod
FAX Number: (716) 839-8516 Calendar System: Semester
URL: www.daemen.edu
Established: 1947 Annual Undergrad Tuition & Fees: $28,580
Enrollment: 2,635 Coed
Affiliation or Control: Independent Non-Profit IRS Status: 501(c)3
Highest Offering: Doctorate
Accreditation: M, ARCPA, CAATE, CYTO, @DIETI, IACBE, NUR, #PTA, SW

01 President .... Dr. Gary A. OLSON
05 SVP Academic Affs/Dean of College .... Dr. Michael S. BROGAN
10 VP for Business Affairs & Treasurer .... Dr. Robert ROOD
30 VP Institutional Advancement .... Ms. Mary GLENN
32 VP Student Affairs .... Dr. Greg J. NAYOR
20 Assoc VP Academic Affairs .... Ms. Doris MURPHY
21 VP for Business Affairs/Comptroller .... Ms. Lisa A. ARIDA
13 VP Information Technology .... Ms. Kelly DURAN
09 Director of Institutional Research .... Ms. Karen MORONSKI-CHAPMAN
35 Dean of Students .... Ms. Kerry SPICER
108 Assoc VP of Inst Effectiveness .... Ms. Irene HOLOHAN-MOYER
08 Director of RIC and Library Service .... Ms. Melissa PETERSON
06 Registrar .... Ms. Tiffany SHADDEN
100 Chief of Staff .... Ms. Amanda R. GROSS
121 Asst Dean for Academic Advisement .... Ms. Sabrina FENNELL
37 Director of Financial Aid .... Mr. Jeffrey M. PAGANO
15 Director of Human Resources .... Ms. Tracy MASSE
26 Dir of Institutional Communications .... Ms. Paula WITHERELL
44 Director of Development .... Ms. Amanda REBECK
39 Dir of Housing & Residence Life .... Ms. Danielle WEAVER
35 Director of Student Activities .... Mr. Michael PAGLICCI
18 Director of Facilities .... Mr. Don PHILLIPS
19 Director of Campus Safety .... Mr. Douglas SMITH
41 Director of Athletics .... Ms. Traci MURPHY
96 Dir of Purchasing/Central Services .... Ms. Annette BITTERMAN
92 Director of Honors Program .... Mr. Jay WENDLAND
29 Director Alumni Relations .... Ms. Katie M. GRAF
40 Bookstore Manager .... Ms. Jaclyn HERNE
88 Dir of New Program Development .... Ms. Susan M. MARCHIONE
04 Admin Assoc Office of the President .... Ms. Sarah PORZUCEK
104 Director Study Abroad .... Ms. Ann ROBINSON
106 Exec Dir of Web Communications .... Mr. Thomas WOJCIECHOWSKI
38 Director of Counseling Services .... Ms. Shannon SCHMITT

Davis College (C)

400 Riverside Drive, Johnson City NY 13790-2714

County: Broome FICE Identification: 021691
Unit ID: 194569
Telephone: (607) 729-1581 Carnegie Class: Spec-4-yr-Faith
FAX Number: (607) 729-2962 Calendar System: Semester
URL: www.davisny.edu
Established: 1900 Annual Undergrad Tuition & Fees: $17,150
Enrollment: 288 Coed
Affiliation or Control: Independent Non-Profit IRS Status: 501(c)3
Highest Offering: Baccalaureate
Accreditation: #M, BI

01 Interim President .... Dr. Doug BLANC
00 Chancellor .... Dr. Dino J. PEDRONE
05 Vice Pres Academic Affairs .... Dr. George SNYDER, JR.
32 Vice Pres of Student Affairs .... Vacant
35 Dir Student Support Services .... Mr. Sherman MCELWAIN
11 Operating Officer .... Vacant
10 Financial Officer .... Mr. Larry ELLIS
04 Assistant to the President .... Ms. Naomi SARAVANAPAVAN
06 Registrar .... Mrs. Susan VANDEVENTER
08 Librarian .... Mrs. Shelley BYRON
37 Director Financial Aid .... Mrs. Sandra CONKLIN
07 Director of Admissions .... Mrs. Sandra CONKLIN
108 Director Institutional Assessment .... Dr. George SNYDER
18 Chief Facilities/Physical Plant .... Vacant
41 Athletic Director .... Vacant
106 Dir Online Education/E-learning .... Mrs. JoAnna OSTER

Dominican College of Blauvelt (D)

470 Western Highway, Orangeburg NY 10962-1210

County: Rockland FICE Identification: 002713
Unit ID: 190761
Telephone: (845) 848-7800 Carnegie Class: Masters/S
FAX Number: (845) 359-2313 Calendar System: Semester
URL: www.dc.edu
Established: 1952 Annual Undergrad Tuition & Fees: $29,000
Enrollment: 1,954 Coed
Affiliation or Control: Independent Non-Profit IRS Status: 501(c)3
Highest Offering: Doctorate
Accreditation: M, CAATE, IACBE, NURSE, OT, PTA, SW

01 President .... Sr Dr. Mary Eileen O'BRIEN
00 Chancellor .... Sr. Kathleen SULLIVAN
05 Vice Pres/Dean Academic Affairs .... Dr. Thomas S. NOWAK
84 Vice Pres of Enrollment Management .... Mr. Brian FERNANDES
32 Dean of Students .... Mr. John BURKE
10 Director of Fiscal Affairs .... Mr. Anthony CIPOLLA
06 Registrar .... Ms. Mary MCFADDEN
07 Director of Admissions .... Mr. Joseph AHLSTRIN
08 Librarian .... Ms. Jennifer SHELTON
111 Director of Inst Advancement .... Mr. Joseph VALENTI
15 Director Human Resources .... Ms. Marybeth BRODERICK
26 Chief Public Relations Officer .... Ms. Susan CERRA
29 Director Alumni Relations .... Ms. Mary MCHUGH
35 Director Student Activities .... Ms. Rachel MCGINTY
09 Inst Research/Plng/Assessment Ofcr .... Dr. Shao-Wei WU
37 Director Student Financial Aid .... Ms. Stacy SALINAS
36 Director Student Placement .... Ms. Evelyn FISKAA
38 Director Student Counseling .... Ms. Alise COHEN
21 Controller .... Ms. Roxanne DROWN
13 Director Information Technology .... Mr. Russell DIAZ
18 Chief Facilities/Physical Plant .... Mr. Agron GASHI
20 Associate Academic Officer .... Ms. Ann VAVOLIZZA
39 Director Student Housing .... Mr. Joseph DRATCH
41 Athletic Director .... Mr. Joseph CLINTON
42 Director Campus Ministry .... Sr. Barbara MCENEANY
96 Director of Purchasing .... Vacant
28 Director of Diversity .... Vacant
19 Director of Security/Safety .... Mr. John LENNON
42 Chaplain .... Vacant
31 Dir Cmty Engagemt/Ldrship Develop .... Ms. Melissa GRAU

Dutchess Community College (E)

53 Pendell Road, Poughkeepsie NY 12601-1595

County: Dutchess FICE Identification: 002864
Unit ID: 190840
Telephone: (845) 431-8000 Carnegie Class: Assoc/HT-Mix Trad/Non
FAX Number: (845) 431-8984 Calendar System: Semester
URL: www.sunydutchess.edu
Established: 1957 Annual Undergrad Tuition & Fees (In-District): $4,404
Enrollment: 9,061 Coed
Affiliation or Control: State/Local IRS Status: 501(c)3
Highest Offering: Associate Degree
Accreditation: M, ADNUR, EMT, MLTAD

01 President .... Dr. Pamela R. EDINGTON
05 Provost and VP AA and Student Svcs .... Dr. Ellen M. GAMBINO
32 Dean of Student Services .... Dr. Colleen M. TROGISCH
10 VP & Dean of Administration .... Vacant
20 Dean of Academic Affairs .... Dr. Holly MOLELLA
20 Associate Dean of Academic Affairs .... Ms. Susan ROGERS
20 Associate Dean of Academic Affairs .... Ms. Maria BOADA
31 Assoc VP & Dean Comm Svcs Spec Pgms .... Vacant
21 Associate VP Administration .... Ms. Donna ROCAP
06 Registrar .... Ms. Angela ROMANO
84 Assoc Dean Stdnt Svcs/Enrollment .... Mr. Michael ROE
08 Director of the Library .... Ms. Cathy CARL
111 Exec Dir Institutional Advancement .... Ms. Diana POLLARD
09 Director Planning/Inst Research .... Mr. Scott SCHNACKENBERG
37 Director Financial Aid .... Ms. Susan MEAD
36 Director Counseling/Career Svcs .... Mr. Mark BALABAN
15 Director Human Resources Mgmt .... Ms. Esther COURET
18 Assoc VP of Admin Facilities Mgmt .... Ms. Bridgette ANDERSON
19 Director Campus Security .... Mr. Ed COX
13 Assoc Dean Admin Info Technology .... Vacant
35 Director of Student Life .... Ms. Debra A. WALLER
26 Director Comm & Public Relations .... Ms. Judi STOKES
88 Assoc Dir Teaching Learning Center .... Ms. Chrisie MITCHELL
88 Director of Scheduling .... Ms. Danielle WILLIAMS
12 Director DCC South Branch .... Mr. Timothy DECKER
04 Exec Assistant to the President .... Ms. AnneMarie ANDREWS
101 Secretary to the Board of Trustees .... Ms. Linda M. BEASIMER
22 Dir Affirmative Action/EEO .... Ms. Esther COURET
39 Director Residence Life .... Ms. Adrianna GRECO
25 Chief Contract and Grants Administr .... Mr. Martin SCHNEIDER
28 Director of Diversity .... Dr. Wazir JEFFERSON
96 Director of Purchasing .... Mr. Thomas DUFFY

D'Youville College (F)

320 Porter Avenue, Buffalo NY 14201-1084

County: Erie FICE Identification: 002712
Unit ID: 190716
Telephone: (716) 829-8000 Carnegie Class: DU-Mod
FAX Number: (716) 829-7820 Calendar System: Semester
URL: www.dyc.edu
Established: 1908 Annual Undergrad Tuition & Fees: $26,750
Enrollment: 3,021 Coed
Affiliation or Control: Independent Non-Profit IRS Status: 501(c)3
Highest Offering: Doctorate
Accreditation: M, ARCPA, CHIRO, DIETC, IACBE, NURSE, OT, PHAR, PTA

01 President .... Dr. Lorrie CLEMO
11 Exec VP of Administrative Affairs .... Vacant
05 VP for Academic Affairs .... Dr. Mimi STEADMAN
10 VP for Financial Affairs .... Mr. John GARFOOT
45 VP for Inst Effectiveness and Plng .... Mr. Joggeshwar DAS
84 VP Enrollment Mgmt/Student Life .... Dr. Randyll BOWEN
18 VP of Operations .... Mr. Nathan MARTON
111 VP of Institutional Advancement .... Ms. Kathleen CHRISTY
88 VP for Mission Integration .... Vacant
66 Dean School of Nursing .... Dr. Christine VERNI
49 Dean Sch of Arts/Sciences & Educ .... Vacant
35 Dean of Students .... Mr. James STURM
67 Dean School of Pharmacy .... Dr. Canio MARASCO
76 Dean School of Health Professions .... Dr. Maureen FINNEY
88 Assistant VP for Enrollment Mgt .... Mr. Matthew METZ
85 Assoc VP for Global Education .... Ms. Laryssa PETRYSHYN
29 Assoc VP for Alumni Engagement .... Ms. Meg RITTLING
25 Assoc VP Grants & Spec Developments .... Ms. Molly FLYNN
110 Assoc VP for Advancement Svcs .... Ms. Aimee PEARSON
32 Assistant VP for Student Life .... Mr. Anthony SPINA
21 Assistant VP of Finance .... Mr. Timothy KORN
88 Artistic Director Kavinoky Theater .... Mr. David LAMB
13 Chief Information Officer .... Mr. Roozbeh TAVAKOLI
06 Registrar .... Mr. Daryl SMITH
113 Bursar .... Ms. Andrea ADDISON
09 Director Inst Rsrch/Assess Support .... Mr. Mark ECKSTEIN
108 Assistant Dean of Assessment .... Mr. Salvatore D'AMATO
91 Director Administrative Computing .... Mr. Robert HALL
44 Director Annual Giving .... Ms. Kelly BIEHLS
41 Director Athletics .... Mr. Brian CAVANAUGH
42 Director Campus Ministry .... Vacant
36 Director Career Services Center .... Ms. Denise HARRIS
88 Director College Center .... Ms. Deborah E. OWENS
14 Director Computer & Network Svcs .... Ms. Mary SPENCE
102 Director Foundation Relations .... Mr. William P. MCKEEVER
23 Director Health Center .... Ms. Nicole CONROE
15 Director Human Resources .... Ms. Linda MORETTI
88 Director Learning Center .... Ms. Christina SPINK-FORMANSKI
08 Director Library Services .... Mr. Rand BELLAVIA
28 Director Multicultural Affairs .... Ms. Yolanda WOOD
38 Director Personal Counseling .... Ms. Kimberly ZITTEL
26 Director Marketing & Communications .... Vacant

19 Director Security .... Mr. Keith BOVA
37 Director Student Financial Aid .... Mr. James NOWAK
07 Director of Transfer Admissions .... Ms. Meghan HARMON
07 Director of Freshman Admissions .... Ms. Allison NEWMAN
124 Director Retention Services .... Ms. Amy YODER
123 Director of Graduate Admissions .... Mr. Zachary RHODES
88 Director Veterans Affairs Office .... MSGT. Robert T. WARD
120 Director E-Learning Services ..... Ms. Kristen HORTMAN-FOWLER
88 Director CRPASH .... Dr. Renee CADZOW
88 Director Ctr Health Behav Rsrch .... Dr. Brian WROTNIAK
88 Dir of Int Aff VA & Mil Rsrch Ctr .... Dr. Bonnie FOX-GARRITY
88 Dir of Ext Aff VA & Mil Rsrch Ctr .... Dr. Dion DALY
04 Senior Exec Asst to the President .... Ms. Holly CARPENTER
120 Director of Teaching Innovations .... Dr. Leah MACVIE
39 Director Residence Life .... Vacant
106 Dean of Online Education .... Mr. Jeremiah GRABOWSKI
96 Director of Purchasing .... Ms. Tammy DISTEFANO

Elim Bible Institute and College (A)

7245 College Street, Lima NY 14485
County: Livingston — Identification: 667245
Unit ID: 488305
Telephone: (585) 582-1230 — Carnegie Class: Spec 2-yr-Other
FAX Number: (585) 582-8130 — Calendar System: Semester
URL: www.elim.edu
Established: 1924 — Annual Undergrad Tuition & Fees: $9,934
Enrollment: 97 — Coed
Affiliation or Control: Independent Non-Profit — IRS Status: 501(c)3
Highest Offering: Associate Degree
Accreditation: TRACS

01 President .... Michael CAVANAUGH
05 Vice President of Academic Affairs .... Danuta CASE
32 Dean of Students .... Stacy CLINE
10 Chief Financial Officer .... Mary Lynne KNILEY
07 Director of Admissions .... Matthew DRAKE
73 Program Chair .... John MILLER
35 Campus Life Director .... Emily SANDERS
18 Facilities Director .... Terry KELLEY
06 Registrar .... Leah WILSON

The Elmezzi Graduate School of Molecular Medicine (B)

350 Community Drive, Manhasset NY 11030-3828
County: Nassau — Identification: 666671
Unit ID: 486080
Telephone: (516) 562-3405 — Carnegie Class: Spec-4-yr-Other Health
FAX Number: (516) 562-1022 — Calendar System: Other
URL: www.elmezzigraduateschool.org
Established: 1999 — Annual Graduate Tuition & Fees: N/A
Enrollment: 11 — Coed
Affiliation or Control: Independent Non-Profit — IRS Status: 501(c)3
Highest Offering: Doctorate; No Undergraduates
Accreditation: NY

01 President .... Dr. Kevin J. TRACEY
03 Provost .... Dr. Bettie M. STEINBERG
05 Dean .... Dr. Annette LEE
20 Associate Dean .... Dr. Christine METZ
10 Chief Financial Officer .... Ms. Diane QUINN
101 Secretary of the Institution/Board .... Mr. Laurence KRAEMER
11 Chief of Administration .... Ms. Emilia HRISTIS
19 Director Security/Safety .... Mr. Robert KIKEL
25 Director Contracts/Grants Admin .... Ms. Diane MARBURY

Elmira Business Institute (C)

4100 Vestal Rd Vestal Exec Park, Vestal NY 13850
County: Broome — FICE Identification: 009043
Unit ID: 190974
Telephone: (607) 729-8915 — Carnegie Class: Assoc/HVT-Mix Trad/Non
FAX Number: (607) 729-8916 — Calendar System: Semester
URL: www.ebi.edu
Established: 1858 — Annual Undergrad Tuition & Fees: $21,700
Enrollment: 205 — Coed
Affiliation or Control: Proprietary — IRS Status: Proprietary
Highest Offering: Associate Degree
Accreditation: ABHES, MAC

01 President .... Mr. Brad C. PHILLIPS
10 Sr Vice President of Administration .... Ms. Kathleen HAMILTON
05 Chief Academic Officer .... Vacant
11 Campus Director .... Ms. Angela WOOD
07 Regional Director of Admissions .... Vacant

Elmira College (D)

One Park Place, Elmira NY 14901-2099
County: Chemung — FICE Identification: 002718
Unit ID: 190983
Telephone: (607) 735-1800 — Carnegie Class: Bac-Diverse
FAX Number: (607) 735-1758 — Calendar System: Other
URL: www.elmira.edu
Established: 1855 — Annual Undergrad Tuition & Fees: $41,900
Enrollment: 1,012 — Coed
Affiliation or Control: Independent Non-Profit — IRS Status: 501(c)3
Highest Offering: Master's
Accreditation: M, NUR

01 President .... Dr. Charles W. LINDSAY
10 VP of Finance and Administration .... Mr. John C. ADAMS
05 Provost .... Dr. Corey E. STILTS
30 Vice Pres of External Relations .... Mr. Michael B. ROGERS
84 Vice Pres of Enrollment Management .... Dr. Elizabeth LAMBERT
09 VP of IR/Planning & Assessment .... Ms. Karen L. JOHNSON
20 Dean of Academic Affairs .... Dr. Lynn L. GILLIE
37 Director of Financial Aid .... Mrs. Lorraine MOTHERSHED
06 Registrar .... Mr. Michael HALPERIN
51 Director of Prof & Continuing Educ .... Mr. Alan YECK
08 Dir of the Gannett-Tripp Library .... Ms. Margaret KAPPANADZE
41 Director of Athletics .... Ms. Renee CARLINEO
36 Director of Career Services .... Ms. Brenna WESTON
50 Chair of Business/Economics .... Dr. Mariam KHAWAR
79 Chair of Creative Arts/Humanities .... Dr. Mitchell R. LEWIS
81 Chair of Math/Natural Sciences .... Dr. Daniel KJAR
83 Chair of Soc/Behavioral Science .... Dr. Christopher TERRY
53 Chair of Teacher Ed/Dir of Grad Ed .... Dr. Deborah D. OWENS
88 Dir of Comm Sciences/Disorders .... Prof. Cathy M. THORNTON
66 Director of Nurse Education .... Dr. Milissa VOLINO
29 Director of Alumni Relations .... Ms. Ellen HIMMELREICH
26 Dir of Communications & Marketing .... Ms. Jennifer L. SWAIN
39 Director of Residence Life .... Mr. Nathan FRIESEMA
40 Dir of Bookstore & Special Projects .... Ms. Shannon MOYLAN
15 Director of Human Resources .... Ms. Jessica CARPENTER
13 Chief Information Officer .... Vacant
19 Director of Campus Safety .... Mr. Steve VANN
112 Director of Major and Planned Gifts .... Ms. Adriana GIANCOLI
44 Director of Annual Giving .... Vacant
102 Director of Grants .... Mrs. Valerie R. ROSPLOCK
23 Director of Health Services .... Mrs. Wendy FISCUS
04 Exec Assistant to the President .... Mrs. Mary C. BARRETT
38 Assoc Dean of Students .... Dr. Kevin MURPHY
90 Director of User Services .... Ms. Kim WIEHE
96 Purchasing Coordinator .... Ms. Kathy KNAPP

Elyon College (E)

1400 West 6th Street, Brooklyn NY 11204
County: Kings — Identification: 667290
Unit ID: 490346
Telephone: (718) 259-5600 — Carnegie Class: Spec 2-yr-Other
FAX Number: (218) 259-8024 — Calendar System: Trimester
URL: elyoncollege.org
Established: — Annual Undergrad Tuition & Fees: $13,720
Enrollment: 29 — Coed
Affiliation or Control: Independent Non-Profit — IRS Status: 501(c)3
Highest Offering: Associate Degree
Accreditation: CNCE

01 President .... Chaim A. WALDMAN

Erie Community College (F)

121 Ellicott Street, Buffalo NY 14203-2698
County: Erie — FICE Identification: 010684
Unit ID: 191083
Telephone: (716) 842-2770 — Carnegie Class: Assoc/MT-VT-High Non
FAX Number: (716) 851-1129 — Calendar System: Semester
URL: www.ecc.edu
Established: 1971 — Annual Undergrad Tuition & Fees (In-District): $5,575
Enrollment: 11,135 — Coed
Affiliation or Control: State/Local — IRS Status: 501(c)3
Highest Offering: Associate Degree
Accreditation: M, ACFEI, ADNUR, CAHIIM, COARC, DH, DIETT, DT, EMT, MAC, MLTAD, OPD, OTA, RTT

01 President .... Dr. Dan HOCOY
111 EVP Inst Advancement & Efficiency .... Mr. Michael PIETKIEWICZ
11 EVP Administration and Finance .... Ms. Penelope HOWARD
05 Provost/EVP Academic Affairs .... Dr. Douglas SCHEIDT
84 Vice President Enrollment Mgmt .... Dr. Steve SMITH
32 VP Student Affairs .... Vacant
35 Dean of Students City .... Ms. Petrina HILL-CHEATOM
35 Dean of Students North .... Mr. Jason PERRI
35 Dean of Students South .... Vacant
13 Chief Information Officer .... Ms. F. Meena LAKHAVANI
76 Vice Provost Health Sciences .... Mr. Patrick J. WILES
14 Director of ERP Sys & Info Svcs .... Mr. David L. ARLINGTON
18 Vice President Facilities/Security .... Mr. Tracy GAST
109 Coordinator Institutional Services .... Mr. Joel J. DAMIANI
15 Associate Vice Pres Human Resources .... Ms. Tracey CLEVELAND
16 Director Talent Mgmt & Empl Engmt .... Ms. Maria CARROLL
49 Dean Liberal Arts & Science North .... Dr. Jamie SMITH
49 Dean Liberal Arts & Science South .... Ms. Joanne COLMERAUER
50 Dean Business/Public Service .... Mr. Juan MARTINEZ
56 Director Dist Learning/Altern Pgm .... Mr. Patrick RYAN
72 Dean Engineering/Technology .... Ms. Adiam TSEGAI
28 Chief Diversity Officer .... Ms. Tracey ARCHIE
06 Director of Registration .... Mr. Paul A. LAMANNA
07 Director of Admissions .... Mr. Philip STRUEBEL
08 Librarian City .... Ms. Kathleen POWERS
08 Librarian North .... Mr. Matthew BEST
08 Librarian South .... Ms. Taheera SHAHEED-SONUBI
40 Bookstore Manager City .... Ms. Susan SCHMITTENDORF
40 Bookstore Manager North .... Ms. Teresa KALINOWSKI
40 Bookstore Manager South .... Mr. Michael FOX
88 Health Services Nurse South .... Ms. Frances WILLIAMS
88 Health Services Nurse North .... Ms. Lisa GRAZIANO
88 Health Services Nurse City .... Ms. Kelly ROCKWELL
36 Career Resource Center Director .... Ms. Katherine MARSHALL
09 Director Institutional Research .... Ms. Marlene ARNO
45 Vice Provost IRAAP .... Dr. Fabio ESCOBAR
27 Public Information Officer .... Mr. Michael FARRELL
41 Director of Athletics .... Mr. Peter J. JEREBKO
88 Assistant Director Athletics .... Mr. Steve L. MULLEN
37 Director of Financial Aid .... Mr. Scott WELTJEN
21 Business Manager .... Mr. Paul F. DANIEU
24 Audio Visual Coordinator City .... Mr. Mark DZIELSKI
24 Audio Visual Coordinator North .... Mr. Ryan NOGLE
24 Audio Visual Coordinator North .... Mr. Nicholas SONRICKER
24 Audio Visual Coordinator South .... Mr. David SEIFERT
88 Coordinator of Corporate Training .... Mr. John P. SLISZ
25 Grants Coordinator .... Mr. Michael J. BIGGANE
29 Director of Alumni Relations .... Vacant
88 Dir of Student Access/Veteran Affs .... Mr. Daniel FRONTERA
88 Advanced Studies Coordinator .... Ms. Deborah F. SCHMITT

Excelsior College (G)

7 Columbia Circle, Albany NY 12203-5156
County: Albany — FICE Identification: 002834
Unit ID: 196680
Telephone: (518) 464-8500 — Carnegie Class: Masters/L
FAX Number: (518) 464-8777 — Calendar System: Other
URL: www.excelsior.edu
Established: 1971 — Annual Undergrad Tuition & Fees: N/A
Enrollment: 34,022 — Coed
Affiliation or Control: Independent Non-Profit — IRS Status: 501(c)3
Highest Offering: Master's
Accreditation: M, ADNUR, IACBE, NUR

01 President .... Dr. James BALDWIN
43 General Counsel .... Ms. Karen HALACO
05 Chief Academic Officer/Provost .... Dr. Debbie SOPCZYK
11 Chief Operating Officer .... Mr. James LETTKO
117 Exec Dir of Risk Management .... Mr. James COX
20 Assoc Provost .... Ms. Emilsen HOLGUIN
20 Assoc Provost .... Dr. Laurie CARBO-PORTER
13 Chief Technology Officer .... Mr. Saul MORSE
15 VP Human Resources .... Mr. Mark HOWE
10 CFO/VP Finance .... Mr. Richard HANNMANN
46 AVP Analytics/Decision Support .... Dr. Lisa DANIELS
108 Exec Dir Outcomes Assessment .... Mr. Andre FOISY
88 AVP Center for Military & Veteran .... Ms. Susan DEWAN
21 Controller .... Ms. Hillary KOLDIN
96 Dean of Undergraduate Studies .... Dr. Li-Fang SHIH
66 Dean of Nursing .... Dr. Mary Lee POLLARD
58 Dean of Graduate Studies .... Vacant
88 Ombudsperson .... Ms. Kathy MORAN
06 Registrar .... Ms. Lori MORANO
88 Exec Dir of Test Development .... Ms. Mika HOFFMAN
26 Chief Marketing Officer .... Ms. Dawn GERRAIN
88 Deputy CIO of Enterprise Systems .... Mr. Donn AIKEN
88 Exec Dir Enterprise Ops .... Mr. Dan MERKT
88 Director of Creative Services .... Ms. Maria SPARKS
27 Chief Communications Officer .... Mr. Michael LESCZINSKI
28 Diversity Coordinator .... Ms. Toby HAMLIN
37 Exec Dir Financial Aid .... Ms. Susan MERCHANT
14 Chief Operations Officer for IT .... Ms. Andrea LALA
88 Exec Dir of Enterprise Apps Support .... Mr. Jim WALL
88 Exec Director Transcript Analysis .... Ms. Kat MCGRATH
07 Exec Director of Admissions .... Ms. Patti HOEG
101 Asst to Pres for Trustee .... Ms. Laurie KEENAN

Fashion Institute of Technology (H)

Seventh Avenue at 27 Street, New York NY 10001-5992
County: New York — FICE Identification: 002866
Unit ID: 191126
Telephone: (212) 217-7999 — Carnegie Class: Masters/S
FAX Number: N/A — Calendar System: Semester
URL: www.fitnyc.edu
Established: 1944 — Annual Undergrad Tuition & Fees (In-District): $5,740
Enrollment: 8,846 — Coed
Affiliation or Control: State/Local — IRS Status: 501(c)3
Highest Offering: Master's
Accreditation: M, ACBSP, ART, CIDA

01 President .... Dr. Joyce F. BROWN
10 Treasurer/VP Finance/Administration .... Ms. Sherry F. BRABHAM
101 Secy of College/General Counsel .... Mr. Stephen P. TUTTLE
05 Vice President Academic Affairs .... Dr. Giacomo OLIVA
26 Vice Pres Comm/External Rels .... Ms. Loretta LAWRENCE KEANE
84 VP Enrollment/Student Success .... Ms. Catherine O'ROURKE
15 VP Human Res Mgmt/Labor Rels .... Dr. Cynthia M. GLASS
30 VP Advancemt/Exec Director FIT Fdn .... Mr. Philips R. MCCARTY
13 Acting VP of Information Technology .... Mr. Laurence A. BAACH
88 Deputy to Pres Industry/Partnership .... Ms. Joanne ARBUCKLE
100 Deputy to the President .... Ms. Jennifer LOTURCO
28 Chief Diversity Officer .... Dr. Ronald A. MILON
88 Acting Exec Dir Strategic Planning .... Ms. Jacqueline JENKINS
88 Associate General Counsel .... Mr. Eric ODIN
20 Assoc Vice Pres Academic Operations .... Dr. Sidney A. GRIMES
20 Assoc VP Academic Affairs .... Dr. Yasemin JONES
21 Assoc Vice Pres Finance/Accounting .... Mr. Bayard KING
27 Assistant VP Comm/External Rels .... Ms. Carol LEVEN
14 AVP Business Intelligence .... Doris BERGER
88 Asst VP Enrollment Management .... Mr. Terence PEAVY
32 Asst VP Student Success/Dean Stdnts .... Dr. Shadia A. SACHEDINA
119 AVP & Chief Info Security Officer .... Mr. Walter KERNER
58 Dean School of Graduate Studies .... Dr. Mary E. DAVIS
50 Dean School Business & Technology .... Mr. Steven FRUMKIN
49 Dean School of Liberal Arts .... Dr. Patrick KNISLEY

104 Dean for International Education ... Dr. Deirdre C. SATO
51 Exec Dir Continuing & Prof Studies ... Mr. Daniel GERGER
57 Dean School of Art & Design ... Mr. Troy RICHARDS
121 Assoc Dean Student Acad Support ... Dr. Tardis JOHNSON
88 Acting Associate Dean Art & Design ... Ms. Melanie REIM
09 Asst Dean Inst Research & Effect ... Dr. Darrell GLENN
88 Asst Dean Curriculum & Instruction ... Ms. Deborah KLESENSKI-RISPOLI
88 Assistant Dean of Students ... Ms. Suzanne MCGILLICUDDY
88 Assistant Dean for International Ed ... Dr. Helen GAUDETTE
08 Director Gladys Marcus Library ... Mr. NJ BRADEEN
88 Director of The Museum at FIT ... Dr. Valerie STEELE
88 Exec Dir FIT/Infor DTech Lab ... Mr. Michael FERRARO
18 Executive Director of Facilities ... Mr. George JEFREMOW
108 Exec Dir Management Analysis ... Mr. Joseph IANNINI
88 Director Special Events ... Vacant
07 Director of Admissions ... Mr. Richard S. SUNDAY
22 Affirmative Action Officer ... Ms. Deliwe KEKANE
38 Director Counseling Center ... Dr. Susan BRETON
39 Director of Residential Life ... Christina DIGGS
37 Acting Director of Financial Aid ... Mr. Barry FISCHER
06 Director of Registration & Records ... Ms. Rita CAMMARATA
36 Director Career & Internship Svcs ... Mr. Frantz L. ALCINDOR
35 Director of Student Life ... Ms. Michelle VAN-ESS
19 Director of Public Safety ... Mr. Mario CABRERA
86 Director Govt & Community Relations ... Ms. Lisa WAGER
41 Director Athletics & Recreation ... Mr. Keith HERON
96 Director of Budget ... Ms. Nancy SU
88 Dir of Educational Opportunity Pgms ... Ms. Taur D. ORANGE
21 Controller ... Ms. Shelci GRAHAM
88 Dir Envir Health/Safety Compliance ... Mr. Paul DEBIASE
29 Dir Alumni Engagement/Giving/Fndn ... Ms. Amy GARAWITZ
105 Manager Digital Strategy ... Ms. Taryn REJHOLEC
55 Dir Evening/Weekend/Pre-College Pgm ... Ms. Michele NAGEL
96 Director of Procurement Services ... Mr. Walter WINTER
85 Director International Student Svcs ... Ms. Erika ROHRBACH
90 Director Educ Tech/Desktop Svcs ... Ms. Meredith PERKINS
106 Director Online Learning ... Tamara CUPPLES
35 Assistant Dean of Students ... Vacant
16 Asst Vice Pres Human Res/Labor Rels ... Vacant
92 Exec Dir President'l Scholars Pgm ... Ms. Yasemin C. LEVINE
88 Director of Policy and Compliance ... Ms. Griselda GONZALEZ
88 Internal Auditor ... Mr. Harold LEDERMAN
04 Assistant to the President ... Ms. Beverly SOLOCHEK
04 Special Assistant to the President ... Ms. Arlene SPIVACK

Fei Tian College (A)

140 Galley Hill Road, Cuddebackville NY 12729
County: Orange — Identification: 667205
Telephone: (845) 672-0550 — Carnegie Class: Not Classified
FAX Number: (845) 977-0481 — Calendar System: Semester
URL: www.feitian.edu
Established: — Annual Undergrad Tuition & Fees: N/A
Enrollment: N/A — Coed
Affiliation or Control: Independent Non-Profit — IRS Status: 501(c)3
Highest Offering: Master's
Accreditation: NY

01 President ... Ms. Vina LEE

Finger Lakes Community College (B)

3325 Marvin Sands Drive, Canandaigua NY 14424-8405
County: Ontario — FICE Identification: 007532
Unit ID: 191199
Telephone: (585) 394-3522 — Carnegie Class: Assoc/HT-High Non
FAX Number: (585) 394-5005 — Calendar System: Semester
URL: www.flcc.edu
Established: 1965 — Annual Undergrad Tuition & Fees (In-District): $5,158
Enrollment: 6,356 — Coed
Affiliation or Control: State/Local — IRS Status: 501(c)3
Highest Offering: Associate Degree
Accreditation: M, ADNUR

01 President ... Dr. Robert NYE
05 Provost ... Mr. Jonathan M. KEISER
10 Sr Vice President of Admin/Finance ... Mr. J.R DEMPSEY
84 Vice Pres Enrollment Management ... Ms. Carol S. URBAITIS
32 Assoc Vice Pres of Student Affairs ... Ms. Sarah WHIFFEN
108 VP Strategic Init/Assessment ... Ms. Debora ORTLOFF
20 Assoc VP Instruction & Assessment ... Dr. Cassy KENT
20 Assoc VP Academic Affairs ... Mr. Jacob E. AMIDON
15 Director of Human Resources ... Ms. Grace H. LOOMIS
111 Chief Advancement Officer ... Mr. Louis NOCE
19 Dir of Campus Security Operations ... Mr. Jason R. MAITLAND
21 Controller ... Mr. Joseph L. DELFORTE
18 Director of Facilities & Grounds ... Ms. Catherine AHERN
07 Director of Admissions ... Ms. Bonnie B. RITTS
06 Registrar ... Mr. Michael FISHER
25 Director of Grants Development ... Ms. Kal A. WYSOKOWSKI
37 Director of Financial Aid ... Ms. Dawn LANGDON
35 Director of Student Life ... Ms. Jennie ERDLE
13 Chief Information Officer ... Mr. John TAYLOR
38 Dir Educ Planning/Career Services ... Ms. Tomas GONZALEZ
36 Career Services Coordinator ... Ms. Tammie WOODY
08 Director Library Learning Resources ... Ms. Sarah MOON
26 Director of Marketing ... Ms. Heidi C. MARCIN
23 Director of Student Health Services ... Ms. Janette ARUK
24 Dir Instructional Technology ... Mr. Daniel P. FARSACI
29 Director of Alumni Relations ... Ms. Lisa L. SCOTT
72 Chair Science & Technology ... Ms. Jennifer CARNEY
50 Interim Chair Business ... Mr. Gary SLOAN
65 Chair Environment Conservation Hort ... Mr. John FOUST
57 Chair Visual/Performing Arts ... Ms. Catherine JOHNSON
66 Chair Nursing ... Ms. Mary CORIALE
68 Chair Physical Education ... Mr. Eric MARSH
81 Chair Computer Science ... Mr. William MCLAUGHLIN
79 Chair Humanities ... Ms. Maureen MASS-FEARY
83 Chair Social Science ... Mr. Joshua W. HELLER
81 Chair Mathematics ... Ms. Theresa GAUTHIER
09 Director of Institutional Research ... Ms. Debora ORTLOFF
103 Director Workforce Development ... Mr. Todd SLOANE
106 Director of Online Learning ... Mr. Ryan MCCABE
28 Chief Diversity Officer ... Mr. Sim COVINGTON

Finger Lakes Health College of Nursing and Health Sciences (C)

196 North Street, Geneva NY 14456
County: Ontario — Identification: 667154
Unit ID: 475422
Telephone: (315) 787-4005 — Carnegie Class: Spec 2-yr-Health
FAX Number: (313) 787-4275 — Calendar System: Semester
URL: www.flhcon.edu
Established: 2008 — Annual Undergrad Tuition & Fees: $11,585
Enrollment: 126 — Coed
Affiliation or Control: Independent Non-Profit — IRS Status: 501(c)3
Highest Offering: Associate Degree
Accreditation: ABHES, ADNUR, PNUR, SURGT, SURTEC

01 Dean ... Susan CARLSON
32 Student Services Coordinator ... Ann SPAYD

Five Towns College (D)

305 North Service Road, Dix Hills NY 11746-6055
County: Suffolk — FICE Identification: 012561
Unit ID: 191205
Telephone: (631) 656-2157 — Carnegie Class: Bac-Diverse
FAX Number: (631) 656-2172 — Calendar System: Semester
URL: www.ftc.edu
Established: 1972 — Annual Undergrad Tuition & Fees: $21,280
Enrollment: 670 — Coed
Affiliation or Control: Proprietary — IRS Status: Proprietary
Highest Offering: Doctorate
Accreditation: M, CAEPN

01 President ... Mr. David COHEN
05 Provost ... Ms. Carolann MILLER
10 Vice Pres Finance/Administration ... Mr. Hubert STACHURA
32 Dean of Students ... Mr. Jerry COHEN
06 Registrar ... Ms. Jessica ROTOLO
37 Director of Financial Aid ... Mr. Jason LABONTE
08 Library Director ... Mr. John VANSTEEN
38 College Counselor ... Ms. Carolyn NEWMAN
64 Chair of Music Division ... Prof. Jill MILLER-THORN
50 Chair of Business Division ... Ms. Kate KIMMEL
49 Chair of Liberal Arts Division ... Mr. Joseph KUHL
53 Chair of Education Division ... Mr. William FORTGANG
88 Chair of Theatre Arts ... Dr. David KRASNER
36 Director Student Placement ... Ms. Krysti O'ROURKE
18 Chief Facilities/Physical Plant ... Mr. Mark SHAUGHNESSY
19 Director of Public Safety ... Mr. Howard GRAY
39 Director of Residential Life ... Mr. Thomas O'BOYLE
07 Director of Admissions ... Ms. Kathryn REILLY

Fordham University (E)

441 East Fordham Road, Bronx NY 10458-9993
County: Bronx — FICE Identification: 002722
Unit ID: 191241
Telephone: (718) 817-1000 — Carnegie Class: DU-Higher
FAX Number: (718) 817-4925 — Calendar System: Semester
URL: www.fordham.edu
Established: 1841 — Annual Undergrad Tuition & Fees: $52,687
Enrollment: 16,037 — Coed
Affiliation or Control: Independent Non-Profit — IRS Status: 501(c)3
Highest Offering: Doctorate
Accreditation: M, CAEPN, CLPSY, COPSY, LAW, SCPSY, SW

01 President ... Rev. Joseph M. MCSHANE, S.J.
100 Assoc VP Pres Operations ... Mrs. Dorothy MARINUCCI
04 Asst Univ Sec/Spec Asst to Pres ... Mr. Michael R. TREROTOLA
05 Provost/SVP ... Dr. Dennis C. JACOBS
10 SVP/CFO and Treasurer ... Ms. Martha K. HIRST
32 Sr Vice President Student Affairs ... Mr. Jeffrey L. GRAY
84 Sr Vice President for Enrollment ... Dr. Peter A. STACE
21 Vice President for Finance ... Mr. Nicholas B. MILOWSKI
13 Interim CIO ... Mr. Shaya PHILLIPS
12 Vice President for Lincoln Center ... Mr. Frank SIMIO
30 Vice President for Development ... Mr. Roger A. MILICI, JR.
88 Vice President for Mission ... Rev. Michael C. MCCARTHY, S.J.
18 VP for Facilities Management ... Mr. Marco VALERA
15 Vice President for HR ... Ms. Kay TURNER
101 Secretary of the University ... Ms. Margaret T. BALL
20 Vice Provost ... Dr. Jonathan CRYSTAL
20 Assoc Vice Pres Academic Affairs ... Dr. Benjamin CROOKER
20 Assoc Vice Pres Academic Affairs ... Dr. Ellen FAHEY-SMITH
28 CDO/AVP Academic Affairs ... Mr. Rafael ZAPATA
20 Assoc Vice Pres Academic Affairs ... Dr. Ron JACOBSON
29 AVP/Director of Alumni Relations ... Mr. Michael GRIFFIN
37 Vice Pres Financial Aid/Admission ... Mr. John W. BUCKLEY
06 Asst Vice Pres Enrollment/Registrar ... Dr. Gene FEIN
86 Assoc Vice Pres for Government Rels ... Ms. Lesley A. MASSIAH-ARTHUR
43 General Counsel ... Ms. Elaine CROSSON
35 Asst VP and Dean of Students ... Mr. Christopher RODGERS
35 Asst VP & Dean of Student Services ... Mr. Gregory J. PAPPAS
12 Dean Fordham College at Rose Hill ... Dr. Maura B. MAST
49 AVP Arts & Sci Educ/Dean A&S Fac ... Dr. Eva BADOWSKA
58 Interim Dean Grad Arts and Sciences ... Dr. Melissa LABONTE
73 Dean Graduate Religious Education ... Rev. Faustino M. CRUZ, S.M.
50 Dean Gabelli School of Business ... Dr. Donna RAPACCIOLI
107 Dean Sch of Prof and Cont Studies ... Dr. Anthony R. DAVIDSON
12 Dean Fordham College LC ... Dr. Laura AURICCHIO
53 Dean Graduate Education LC ... Dr. Virginia ROACH
61 Dean School of Law LC ... Mr. Matthew DILLER
70 Dean Graduate Social Service LC ... Dr. Debra MCPHEE
09 Director Institutional Research ... Dr. Peter FEIGENBAUM
42 Executive Director Campus Ministry ... Rev. Jose-Luis SALAZAR, S.J.
21 Controller ... Mr. Anthony GRONO
19 AVP Public Safety ... Mr. John CARROLL
22 Title IX Coordinator ... Mr. Kareem PEAT
46 Chief Research Officer/AVP ... Dr. Z. George HONG
08 Director of University Libraries ... Ms. Linda LOSCHIAVO
24 Director Media Center ... Mr. Jerry GREEN
23 Director of Health Center ... Ms. Maureen KEOWN
35 Asst Dean Student Involvement ... Mr. Cody ARCURI
88 AVP of Athletic Alumni Relations ... Mr. Francis X. MCLAUGHLIN
96 Director of Strategic Sourcing ... Ms. Diana LULGJURAJ
38 Director of Psychological Svcs ... Dr. Jeffrey NG
28 Asst Dean/Dir Multicultural Affairs ... Mr. Juan Carlos MATOS
36 Director Career Services ... Ms. Annette MCLAUGHLIN
39 Asst Dean/Dir Residential Life ... Mr. Alex FISCHER
07 Dean of Admission ... Dr. Patricia PEEK
41 Athletic Director ... Mr. Dave ROACH

Fulton-Montgomery Community College (F)

2805 State Highway 67, Johnstown NY 12095-3790
County: Montgomery — FICE Identification: 002867
Unit ID: 191302
Telephone: (518) 736-3622 — Carnegie Class: Assoc/HT-High Trad
FAX Number: (518) 762-5693 — Calendar System: Semester
URL: www.fmcc.edu
Established: 1963 — Annual Undergrad Tuition & Fees (In-District): $5,170
Enrollment: 2,403 — Coed
Affiliation or Control: State/Local — IRS Status: 501(c)3
Highest Offering: Associate Degree
Accreditation: M, ADNUR, RAD

01 President ... Dr. Greg TRUCKENMILLER
05 Provost/Vice Pres Academic Affairs ... Ms. Diana PUTNAM
10 Vice Pres Finance & Administration ... Mr. David M. MORROW
32 Vice President of Student Affairs ... Ms. Jane KELLEY
20 Dean of Academic Affairs ... Vacant
20 Associate Dean of Academic Affairs ... Ms. Ronalyn WILSON
20 Associate Dean of Academic Affairs ... Ms. Jacqueline SNYDER
21 Director of Business Affairs ... Mr. Gregg WILBUR
13 Director of Information Technology ... Vacant
18 Director of Facilities ... Mr. Joshua FLEMING
07 Associate Dean for Admissions ... Ms. Laura LAPORTE
06 Registrar ... Mr. Scott COLLINS
08 Librarian ... Ms. Mary DONOHUE
36 Director of Career Planning ... Ms. Andrea SCRIBNER
121 Director Advisement/Counseling/Test ... Ms. Mary-Jo FERRAUILO-DAVIS
30 Chief Development ... Ms. Lesley LANZI
09 Director of Institutional Research ... Vacant
37 Coordinator Financial Aid ... Ms. Rebecca COZZOCREA
04 Administrative Asst to President ... Ms. Paula WEAVER
15 Director of Human Resources ... Mr. Jason RAUCH
19 Director of Public Safety ... Mr. Mark PIERCE
124 Assoc Dean Student Success & Reten ... Ms. Jean KARUTIS
26 Coordinator Public Relations ... Vacant
39 Director Student Housing ... Mr. Nicoy PUSEY
41 Athletic Director ... Mr. Kevin JONES
90 IT Infrastructure Administrator ... Mr. William BONNER
91 Associate Director of IT ... Mr. Paul PUTMAN
38 Director Student Counseling ... Ms. Mary-Jo FERRAUILO-DAVIS

General Theological Seminary (G)

440 West 21st Street, New York NY 10011-2981
County: New York — FICE Identification: 002726
Unit ID: 191320
Telephone: (212) 243-5150 — Carnegie Class: Spec-4-yr-Faith
FAX Number: (212) 727-3907 — Calendar System: Semester
URL: www.gts.edu
Established: 1817 — Annual Graduate Tuition & Fees: N/A
Enrollment: 45 — Coed
Affiliation or Control: Protestant Episcopal — IRS Status: 501(c)3
Highest Offering: Master's; No Undergraduates
Accreditation: THEOL

01 President and Dean ... Rev. Kurt DUNKLE
05 VP & Dean of Academic Affairs ... Dr. Michael DELASHMUTT
10 VP & Controller ... Mr. Robert ELLIOT
11 Vice President of Operations ... Mr. Anthony KHANI
111 VP for Institutional Advancement ... Ms. Donna ASHLEY
07 Director of Admissions ... Ms. Logan POLLARD
06 Director of Acad Mgmt & Registrar ... Ms. Stacie WARING

15 Director of HR & Financial Aid ... Ms. Trecia O'SULLIVAN
26 Director of Communications ... Mr. Joshua BRUNER
30 Director of Development ... Mr. Jonathan SILVER
04 Exec Asst to the President & Dean ... Mr. Joseph BARNES

Genesee Community College (A)

One College Road, Batavia NY 14020-9704
County: Genesee FICE Identification: 006782
Unit ID: 191339
Telephone: (585) 343-0055 Carnegie Class: Assoc/MT-VT-High Non
FAX Number: (585) 343-4541 Calendar System: Semester
URL: www.genesee.edu
Established: 1966 Annual Undergrad Tuition & Fees (In-District): $4,640
Enrollment: 5,906 Coed
Affiliation or Control: State/Local IRS Status: 501(c)3
Highest Offering: Associate Degree
Accreditation: M, ADNUR, COARC, POLYT, PTAA

01 President ... Dr. James SUNSER
05 Provost/Exec VP Academic Affairs ... Dr. Kathleen SCHIEFEN
81 Dean Math/Science/Career Education ... Dr. Rafael ALICEA-MALDONADO
83 Dean Human Communication/Behavior ... Mr. Timothy TOMCZAK
56 Dean of Distributed Learning ... Dr. Craig LAMB
20 Asc Dean Accelerated Col Enrol Pgms ... Mr. Edward LEVINSTEIN
06 Registrar ... Mr. Terrence REDING
57 Director Fine & Performing Arts ... Ms. Maryanne ARENA
68 Director of Health & Physical Educ ... Ms. Rebecca DZIEKAN
10 Exec VP for Finance & Operations ... Mr. William T. EMM
09 Assoc VP Inst Rsrch & Assessment ... Ms. Carol MARRIOTT
15 Assoc VP for Human Resources ... Ms. Gina WEAVER
25 Director of Grants Services ... Mr. James DONSBACH
88 Director Business Skills Training ... Mr. John MCGOWAN
21 Controller ... Ms. Kristin L. YUNKER
13 Director of Computer Services ... Ms. Cindy DELMAR
18 Director of Buildings & Grounds ... Mr. Levi OLSEN
32 VP for Student & Enrollment Svcs ... Dr. Shelitha WILLIAMS
35 Dean of Students ... Ms. Patricia CHAYA
07 Assistant Dean of Admissions ... Ms. Lyndsay GERHARDT
37 Director of Financial Aid ... Mr. Joseph A. BAILEY
88 Director of Student Activities ... Ms. Kristen MRUK
41 Director of Athletics ... Ms. Kristen SCHUTH
30 VP Devel & External Affairs ... Vacant
04 Administrative Asst to President ... Ms. Bethany ARADINE
19 Director Security/Safety ... Mr. Stephen WISE
08 Chief Library Officer ... Ms. Jessica OLIN
29 Director Alumni Affairs ... Ms. Tammy ARNETH

Glasgow Caledonian New York College (B)

64 Wooster Street, New York NY 10012
County: New York Identification: 667340
Telephone: (646) 768-5300 Carnegie Class: Not Classified
FAX Number: N/A Calendar System: Semester
URL: www.gcnyc.com
Established: Annual Graduate Tuition & Fees: N/A
Enrollment: N/A Coed
Affiliation or Control: Independent Non-Profit IRS Status: 501(c)3
Highest Offering: Master's; No Undergraduates
Accreditation: ⊕M

01 President ... Dr. Pamela GILLIES
03 Vice President ... Ms. Cara SMYTH
05 Interim Provost ... Dr. Walter ROETTGER
06 Registrar ... Mr. Stephen LOPEZ
30 Dir of Bus Development/Fin Aid ... Mr. Carlos AMADOR
32 Dir Student Services & Operation . Ms. Jessica CHANG-RUSSELL
07 Dir Admissions/Recruitment ... Ms. Dominique STUDER

Hamilton College (C)

198 College Hill Road, Clinton NY 13323-1218
County: Oneida FICE Identification: 002728
Unit ID: 191515
Telephone: (315) 859-4011 Carnegie Class: Bac-A&S
FAX Number: (315) 859-4991 Calendar System: Semester
URL: www.hamilton.edu
Established: 1812 Annual Undergrad Tuition & Fees: $54,620
Enrollment: 1,901 Coed
Affiliation or Control: Independent Non-Profit IRS Status: 501(c)3
Highest Offering: Baccalaureate
Accreditation: M

01 President ... David WIPPMAN
05 VPAA/Dean of Faculty ... Suzanne KEEN
11 Vice Pres Administration/Finance ... Karen L. LEACH
30 Vice Pres Communication/Development ... Lori R. DENNISON
13 Vice Pres Information Technology ... Joseph SHELLEY
07 VP/Dean Admission & Financial Aid ... Monica C. INZER
32 Vice Pres/Dean of Students ... Terry MARTINEZ
20 Associate Dean of Faculty ... Nathan GOODALE
41 Athletic Director ... Jonathan T. HIND
39 Director Residential Life ... Travis R. HILL
10 AVP of Finance and Controller ... Carol GABLE
08 Dir of Library/Info Technology ... Joe SHELLEY
27 Director Strategic Communications ... Stacey J. HIMMELBERGER
37 Director of Financial Aid ... K. Cameron FEIST
36 Int Exec Director Career Center ... Sam WELCH
06 Registrar ... Kristin M. FRIEDEL
15 Director of Human Resources ... Stephen STEMKOSKI
18 Associate VP for Facilities ... Roger F. WAKEMAN
19 Director of Campus Safety ... Frank COOTS
38 Director Counseling/Psych Services ... David WALDEN
42 Newman Chaplain ... John CROGHAN
24 Director Audiovisual Services ... Timothy J. HICKS
09 Director of Institutional Research ... Gordon J. HEWITT
26 Associate VP of Communications ... Michael J. DEBRAGGIO
28 Chief Diversity Officer ... Terry MARTINEZ
29 Director Alumni Relations ... Fred ROGERS
96 Director of Purchasing ... Vacant
40 Manager College Store ... Jennifer PHILLIPS
100 Chief of Staff ... Gillian M. KING

Hartwick College (D)

One Hartwick Drive, Oneonta NY 13820-1790
County: Otsego FICE Identification: 002729
Unit ID: 191533
Telephone: (607) 431-4000 Carnegie Class: Bac-A&S
FAX Number: (607) 431-4206 Calendar System: 4/1/4
URL: www.hartwick.edu
Established: 1797 Annual Undergrad Tuition & Fees: $45,510
Enrollment: 1,201 Coed
Affiliation or Control: Independent Non-Profit IRS Status: 501(c)3
Highest Offering: Master's
Accreditation: M, ART, MUS, NURSE

01 President ... Dr. Margaret L. DRUGOVICH
05 Executive Vice President & Provost ... Dr. William EHMANN
10 Vice President Finance/CFO ... Dr. Dorothy LEWIS
111 Int VP Institutional Advancement ... Ms. Peg LUY
32 Vice Pres for Student Experience ... Ms. Karen MCGRATH
84 Vice Pres for Enrollment Management ... Ms. Karen MCGRATH
04 Senior Assistant to the President ... Ms. Lisa CORBETT
15 Director Human Resources ... Ms. Suzanne JANITZ
39 Director Residence Life ... Mr. Zachary BROWN
06 Registrar ... Mr. Matthew SANFORD
20 Dean of Academic Affairs ... Dr. Kellie BEAN
37 Director of Financial Aid ... Ms. Melissa ALLEN
08 Interim Director of Libraries ... Mr. David HEYDUK
85 Director International Pgms ... Dr. Godlove FONJWENG
13 Director Inst Info Systems Services ... Ms. Deb B. HILTS
91 Director Technologies Services ... Ms. Suzanne GAYNOR
18 Director of Facilities Services ... Mr. Joseph MACK
41 Director of Athletics ... Mr. John CZARNECKI
38 Director of Counseling Services ... Mr. Gary ROBINSON
23 Director of Student Health Center ... Ms. Amy GARDNER
26 Marketing Communications Manager ... Mr. David LUBELL
29 Exec Dir of Donor & Alumni Rels ... Vacant
07 Director Admissions ... Ms. Lisa STARKEY-WOODS
12 Director Pine Lake Campus ... Ms. Erin TOAL
21 Director Financial Svcs/Controller ... Ms. Karen ZUILL
09 Director of Institutional Research ... Mr. J. R BJERKLIE
29 Executive Director of Engagement ... Vacant
19 Director of Campus Safety ... Mr. Terry SHULTZ
40 Manager of B&N Bookstore ... Mr. Frank WERDANN
102 Dir Foundation/Corporate Relations ... Ms. Lisa IANNELLO
105 Director Web Services ... Ms. Stephanie BRUNETTA

Hebrew Union College-Jewish Institute of Religion (E)

1 West 4th Street, New York NY 10012-1186
County: New York FICE Identification: 004054
Unit ID: 203067
Telephone: (212) 674-5300 Carnegie Class: Spec-4-yr-Faith
FAX Number: (212) 388-1720 Calendar System: Semester
URL: www.huc.edu
Established: 1875 Annual Graduate Tuition & Fees: N/A
Enrollment: 317 Coed
Affiliation or Control: Jewish IRS Status: 501(c)3
Highest Offering: Doctorate; No Undergraduates
Accreditation: M, PAST

01 President ... Dr. Andrew REHFELD
05 Provost/Dean ... Rabbi Andrea WEISS
111 Vice President Inst Advancement ... Ms. Lissie DIRINGER
10 Chief Financial Officer ... Ms. Barbara M. TELEK
101 Exec Sec to Board of Governors ... Ms. Andrea KANN
26 AVP National Dir Public Affs/Comm ... Ms. Jean B. ROSENSAFT
44 Director of Institutional Giving ... Ms. Cheryl SLAVIN
08 Librarian ... Mr. Yoram BITTON
79 Director American Jewish Archives ... Dr. Gary ZOLA
09 Manager Institutional Research ... Mr. Sutanu MAJUMDAR
07 Director Recruitment/Admission ... Mr. Adam ALLENBERG
13 Director of Information Systems ... Mr. John H. BRUGGEMAN
15 Director of HR ... Ms. Marviette JOHNSON
37 National Director of Financial Aid ... Ms. Roseanne ACKERLEY

Helene Fuld College of Nursing (F)

24 East 120th Street, New York NY 10035
County: New York FICE Identification: 010153
Unit ID: 191597
Telephone: (212) 616-7200 Carnegie Class: Spec-4-yr-Other Health
FAX Number: (212) 616-7299 Calendar System: Quarter
URL: www.helenefuld.edu
Established: 1945 Annual Undergrad Tuition & Fees: N/A
Enrollment: 480 Coed
Affiliation or Control: Independent Non-Profit IRS Status: 501(c)3
Highest Offering: Baccalaureate
Accreditation: M, ADNUR, NURSE

01 President ... Dr. Joyce P. GRIFFIN-SOBEL
03 Exec Vice President ... Dr. Sandy CAROLLO
10 Head of Finance ... Mrs. Galina VILKINA
100 Chief of Staff ... Ms. Leslie FOUNTAIN WILLIAMS
32 Director of Student Services ... Mrs. Sandra SENIOR
08 Director of Library ... Mr. Indrajeet SINGH CHAUHAN
35 Assoc Director of Student Services ... Ms. Gladys PINEDA
26 Director of External Affairs ... Ms. Michelle HERNANDEZ
37 Financial Aid Counselor ... Ms. Andrine THOMAS
15 Director Human Resources ... Ms. Alysha WILLIS
38 College Counselor ... Ms. Dana GOLIN
04 Executive Assistant ... Ms. Kadia DARBY
13 Director Information Technology ... Mr. Eickel ORTIZ
84 College Recruiter ... Ms. Alphonsa ITTOOP
07 Admissions Assistant ... Ms. Celia OLIVER
29 Director Alumni Relations ... Vacant

Herkimer County Community College (G)

100 Reservoir Road, Herkimer NY 13350-1598
County: Herkimer FICE Identification: 004788
Unit ID: 191612
Telephone: (315) 866-0300 Carnegie Class: Assoc/HT-Mix Trad/Non
FAX Number: (315) 866-5539 Calendar System: Semester
URL: www.herkimer.edu
Established: 1966 Annual Undergrad Tuition & Fees (In-District): $5,320
Enrollment: 2,632 Coed
Affiliation or Control: State/Local IRS Status: 501(c)3
Highest Offering: Associate Degree
Accreditation: M, PTAA

01 President ... Dr. Cathleen C. MCCOLGIN
10 Sr VP for Admin & Finance ... Mr. Nicholas LAINO
05 Provost ... Mr. Michael ORIOLO
32 Dean of Students ... Mr. Donald DUTCHER
20 Associate Dean Academic Affairs BH ... Mr. William MCDONALD
83 Assoc Dean Academic Affs Social Sci ... Dr. Robin RIECKER
20 Assoc Dean of Academic Affairs ... Mrs. Linda LAMB
15 Director of Human Resources ... Mr. James SALAMY
41 Director of Athletics ... Mr. Donald DUTCHER
08 Director of Library Services ... Mr. Alfred BEROWSKI
09 Director Institutional Research ... Ms. Karen AYOUCH
100 Assistant to the President ... Mr. Daniel SARGENT
18 Director Facilities Operations ... Mr. Robert WOUDENBERG
37 Director Student Financial Aid ... Mrs. Susan TRIPP
26 Director of Public Relations ... Ms. Rebecca RUFFING
36 Career Services Counselor ... Mrs. Suzanne PADDOCK
96 Purchasing Agent ... Mr. Jeremy CINGRANELLI
102 Dir Foundation/Corporate Relations ... Mr. Robert FOWLER
19 Director of Campus Safety ... Mr. Timothy ROGERS
39 Director Residence Life ... Mr. Jason RATHBUN
04 Admin Assistant to the President ... Ms. Shari HUNT
07 Director of Admissions ... Dr. Denver STICKROD
38 Director Student Counseling ... Ms. Wendy MARCHESE

Hilbert College (H)

5200 South Park Avenue, Hamburg NY 14075-1597
County: Erie FICE Identification: 002735
Unit ID: 191621
Telephone: (716) 649-7900 Carnegie Class: Bac-Diverse
FAX Number: (716) 649-0702 Calendar System: Semester
URL: www.hilbert.edu
Established: 1957 Annual Undergrad Tuition & Fees: $22,350
Enrollment: 792 Coed
Affiliation or Control: Independent Non-Profit IRS Status: 501(c)3
Highest Offering: Master's
Accreditation: M

01 President ... Dr. Michael S. BROPHY
05 Provost/Vice Pres Academic Affs ... Dr. Kristina LANTZKY-EATON
111 Vice Pres Inst Advancement ... Ms. Kathleen CHRISTY
10 Vice President Business/Finance ... Mr. Richard J. PINKOWSKI, JR.
13 Vice President Information Services ... Mr. Michael MURRIN
84 VP Enrollment Management ... Mr. Dwight SANCHEZ
32 VProv Leadership Dev/Dean of Stdnts ... Mr. Gregory ROBERTS
26 Dir Marketing & Communications ... Mr. Matthew HEIDT
92 Director Honors Program ... Dr. Amy E. SMITH
39 Dir Residence Life/Judicial Affairs ... Ms. Jill COLE
41 Athletic Director ... Ms. Megan VALENTINE
19 Director Security/Safety ... Mr. Vito CZYZ
29 Asst Dir Annual Giving/Alum Engage ... Vacant
42 Dir Mission Intgrtn/Campus Ministry ... Ms. Mamie SMITH
08 Director of McGrath Library ... Ms. Colleen DIPPOLD
07 Director of Admissions ... Mr. Brian FILJONES
36 Director Placement/Career Services ... Ms. Katie MARTOCHE
37 Interim Director Financial Aid ... Ms. Nicole GRIFFO
06 Director of Student Records ... Ms. Katelyn LETIZIA
38 Director Student Counseling ... Ms. Phyllis K. DEWEY
09 Director of Institutional Research ... Dr. John WISE
15 Director of Human Resources ... Ms. Maura FLYNN
28 Director of Multicultural Affairs ... Ms. Tanya DUTSON
35 Director of Student Activities ... Ms. Jessica TODD
96 Director of Purchasing ... Mr. Gary DILLSWORTH
21 Asst Vice Pres Business/Finance ... Mr. Anthony WIERTEL
18 Chief Facilities/Physical Plant ... Mr. Gary DILLSWORTH
04 Administrative Asst to President ... Ms. Eileen STACK
102 Dir Corp Foundation/Govt Relations ... Ms. Elizabeth SIMONS

Hobart and William Smith Colleges (A)

300 Pulteney Street, Geneva NY 14456-3397
County: Ontario FICE Identification: 002731
Unit ID: 191630
Telephone: (315) 781-3000 Carnegie Class: Bac-A&S
FAX Number: (315) 781-3654 Calendar System: Semester
URL: www.hws.edu
Established: 1822 Annual Undergrad Tuition & Fees: $55,255
Enrollment: 2,244 Coordinate
Affiliation or Control: Independent Non-Profit IRS Status: 501(c)3
Highest Offering: Master's
Accreditation: M, CAEPT

01 President .... Dr. Joyce P. JACOBSEN
04 Exec Assistant to the President .... Ms. Valerie VISTOCCO
05 Interim Provost & Dean of Faculty .... Dr. Dwayne LUCAS
10 VP for Finance & Administration/CFO .... Ms. Carolee WHITE
32 Vice President for Campus Life .... Mr. Robert FLOWERS
100 Chief of Staff President's Office .... Ms. Kathleen REGAN
111 Vice President for Advancement .... Mr. Robert O'CONNOR
15 Vice President for Human Resources .... Ms. Sonya WILLIAMS
84 Dean of Admission/Interim VP .... Mr. John YOUNG
26 VP for Marketing & Communications .... Ms. Cathy WILLIAMS
13 VP for Strategic Initiatives/CIO .... Mr. Fred DAMIANO
43 Vice President and General Counsel .... Mr. Louis GUARD
19 Associate VP of Campus Safety .... Mr. Martin CORBETT
20 Assoc VP Faculty & Development .... Dr. Joseph RUSINKO
35 Asst VP/Dean Student Engagement .... Mr. Brandon BARILE
42 Chaplain .... Rev. Nita BYRD
14 Deputy CIO/Dir Enterprise Solutions .... Mr. Jeremy TRUMBLE
08 Colleges' Librarian .... Mr. Vincent BOISSELLE
06 Registrar .... Mr. Peter SARRATORI
104 Dean of Global Education .... Dr. Thomas D'AGOSTINO
108 Dean Teach/Learn & Assessment .... Dr. Susan PLINER
41 Director Womens Athletics .... Ms. Deborah STEWARD
41 Interim Director Mens Athletics .... Mr. Brian MILLER
33 Interim Dean of Hobart College .... Dr. Khuram HUSSAIN
34 Dean of William Smith College .... Ms. Lisa KAENZIG
110 Associate VP for Advancement .... Ms. Leila RICE
29 Associate VP for Alumni Relations .... Mr. Jared WEEDEN
21 Interim Controller .... Ms. Carol GROVER
20 Assoc VP for the Curriculum .... Dr. David GALLOWAY
114 Assoc VP Budget & Finance .... Mr. Damian BOLSTER
36 Director Center for Career Services .... Ms. Brandi FERRARA
07 Director of Admissions .... Mr. William WARDER
37 Director of Financial Aid .... Ms. Beth NEPA
39 Assistant Dean Student Engagement .... Ms. Shelle BASILIO
35 Director of Student Activities .... Ms. Kristen TOBEY
88 Director of Intercultural Affairs .... Dr. Alejandra MOLINA
88 Director Conferences/Events .... Ms. Erica COONEY-CONNOR
16 Associate Director Human Resources .... Ms. Peggy FERRAN
38 Director Counseling Center .... Mr. Michael SIEMBOR
85 Director of International Students .... Mr. David GAGE
102 Dir Corp/Foundation Rels/Legal Affs .... Mr. Gerard BUCKLEY
113 Assoc Controller/Student Accounts .... Ms. Rebecca BARNES
88 Dir Network/Systems Infrastructure .... Mr. Derek LUSTIG
106 Director of Digital Learning .... Ms. Juliet BOISSELLE
27 Associate VP of Communications .... Ms. Mary LECLAIR
88 Director of Publications .... Ms. Margaret KOWALIK
105 Director Web Development .... Mr. Michael DIMAURO
88 Director Athletic Communications .... Mr. Ken DEBOLT
12 Director Finger Lakes Institute .... Dr. Lisa CLECKNER
31 Dir Community Engagement .... Ms. Kathleen FLOWERS
88 Director Academic Opportunity Pgm .... Mr. James BURRUTO
88 Director of Parent Program .... Ms. Jennifer MURRAY
88 Director Stewardship Programs .... Ms. Kelly YOUNG
44 Director Annual & Athletic Giving .... Ms. Dulcie MEYER
96 Director Procurement/Auxiliary Svcs .... Ms. Claudette KILLIAN
88 Sr Dir Development for Athletics .... Mr. Michael CRAGG
27 Director of Marketing .... Ms. Gina KANE
25 Director of Sponsored Programs .... Ms. Roberta TRUSCELLO
30 Director Advancement Services .... Ms. Karen REUSCHER

Hofstra University (B)

100 Hofstra University, Hempstead NY 11549-1000
County: Nassau FICE Identification: 002732
Unit ID: 191649
Telephone: (516) 463-6600 Carnegie Class: DU-Mod
FAX Number: (516) 463-4848 Calendar System: Semester
URL: www.hofstra.edu
Established: 1935 Annual Undergrad Tuition & Fees: $45,700
Enrollment: 11,131 Coed
Affiliation or Control: Independent Non-Profit IRS Status: 501(c)3
Highest Offering: Doctorate
Accreditation: M, ARCPA, AUD, CAATE, CACREP, CAMPEP, CLPSY, IPSY, JOUR, LAW, MED, NURSE, OT, PH, SCPSY, SP

01 President .... Mr. Stuart RABINOWITZ
05 Provost/Sr VP for Academic Affairs .... Dr. Herman A. BERLINER
45 Sr VP for Planning and Admin .... Ms. M. Patricia ADAMSKI
10 VP Financial Affairs/Treasurer .... Ms. Catherine HENNESSY
32 Vice President for Student Affairs .. Mr. W. Houston DOUGHARTY
30 Vice President for Development .... Mr. Alan J. KELLY
26 Vice President University Relations .... Ms. Melissa A. CONNOLLY
43 VP Legal Affairs & General Counsel .... Ms. Dolores FREDRICH
13 VP Digital Innovation & Technology .... Mr. Steve FABIANI
18 VP for Facilities and Operations .... Mr. Joseph BARKWILL
84 Vice Pres Enrollment Management .... Ms. Jessica L. EADS
91 Asst VP for Information Technology .... Ms. Linda J. HANTZSCHEL
09 Exec Dir Inst Rsrch/Admin Assessmnt .... Ms. Chavon STUPARICH
20 Special Advisor to the Provost .... Dr. Margaret ABRAHAM
114 Assoc Provost Budget & Planning .... Mr. Richard M. APOLLO
25 Assoc Provost Rsrch/Sponsored Pgms .... Ms. Sofia KAKOULIDIS
07 VP Admissions & Financial Aid .... Ms. Jessica L. EADS
50 Dean Zarb Sch of Business .... Dr. Janet A. LENAGHAN
54 Dean School of Engineering .... Dr. Sina Y. RABBANY
60 Dean School of Communication .... Mr. Mark LUKASIEWICZ
49 Dean College Liberal Arts/Science .... Dr. Benjamin RIFKIN
08 Director Library & Info Services .... Mr. Howard E. GRAVES
121 Dean for University Advisement .... Ms. Anne M. MONGILLO
61 Dean Law School .... Hon. A. Gail PRUDENTI
63 Dean Medical School .... Dr. Lawrence SMITH
66 Dean Sch/Grad Nursing & Health Prof .... Dr. Kathleen GALLO
35 Dean of Students .... Ms. Gabrielle ST. LEGER
29 Senior Director Alumni Affairs .... Ms. Amy R. REICH
39 Associate Director Residential Programs .... Ms. Novia P. WHYTE
38 Dir Student Counseling Services .... Dr. John C. GUTHMAN
22 Equal Rights/Opportunity Ofcr .... Ms. Jennifer MONE
23 Dir Health & Wellness Center .... Dr. Donna WILLENBROCK
41 Director Intercollegiate Athletics .... Mr. Rick COLE, JR.
15 Director of Human Resources .... Ms. Denise S. CUNNINGHAM
40 Manager Bookstore .... Mr. Steven BABBITT
19 Director Public Safety .... Ms. Karen O'CALLAGHAN
96 Director of Purchasing Contracts .... Mr. David DALE
92 Dean Honors College .... Dr. Warren FRISINA
06 Registrar/Dir of Academic Records .... Mr. Evan S. KOEGL
04 Admin Assistant to the President .... Ms. Isabel D. FREY
37 Director Student Financial Aid .... Ms. Sandra MERVIUS
36 Exec Dir Career Center .... Ms. Michelle KYRIAKIDES
44 Director Annual Giving .... Ms. Julia C. PALMEDO
28 Chief Diversity & Inclusion Officer .... Mr. Cornell CRAIG

Holy Trinity Orthodox Seminary (C)

PO Box 36, Jordanville NY 13361-0036
County: Herkimer FICE Identification: 002733
Telephone: (315) 858-0945 Carnegie Class: Not Classified
FAX Number: (315) 858-0945 Calendar System: Semester
URL: www.hts.edu
Established: 1948 Annual Undergrad Tuition & Fees: N/A
Enrollment: N/A Male
Affiliation or Control: Russian Orthodox IRS Status: 501(c)3
Highest Offering: Master's
Accreditation: NY

01 Rector/CEO .... V.Rev. Luke MURIANKA
05 Dean .... V.Rev. Alexander WEBSTER
20 Assistant Dean .... Rev. Ephraim WILLMARTH
32 Dean of Students .... Rev. Cyprian ALEXANDROU
06 Registrar .... Rev. Ephraim WILLMARTH
07 Director of Admissions .... Rev. Ephraim WILLMARTH
08 Librarian .... Mr. Michael PEREKRESTOV

Houghton College (D)

One Willard Avenue, Houghton NY 14744-0128
County: Allegany FICE Identification: 002734
Unit ID: 191676
Telephone: (585) 567-9200 Carnegie Class: Bac-A&S
FAX Number: (585) 567-9572 Calendar System: Semester
URL: www.houghton.edu
Established: 1883 Annual Undergrad Tuition & Fees: $32,488
Enrollment: 1,043 Coed
Affiliation or Control: Wesleyan Church IRS Status: 501(c)3
Highest Offering: Master's
Accreditation: M, MUS

01 President .... Dr. Shirley A. MULLEN
05 Chief Academic Ofcr/Dean of Faculty .... Dr. Paul YOUNG
32 Dean of Student Life .... Mr. Marc SMITHERS
10 Vice President for Finance .... Mr. Dale WRIGHT
111 Vice President for Advancement .... Mr. Karl SISSON
84 Vice President for Enrollment .... Vacant
04 Dir of Operations Ofc of the Pres .... Ms. Betsy SANFORD
06 Registrar .... Mr. Kevin KETTINGER
37 Director of Financial Aid .... Ms. Marianne LOPER
08 Director of the Library .... Mr. David STEVICK
29 Dir Alumni & Community Relations .... Ms. Phyllis GAERTE
42 Dean of the Chapel .... Dr. Michael JORDAN
09 Assoc Dean Institutional Research .... Mr. Mark ALESSI
36 Director of VOCA .... Vacant
15 Director of Human Resources .... Ms. Nancy STANLEY
26 Dir Marketing & Communications .... Mr. Jeff BABBITT
13 Director of Technology .... Mr. Donald HAINGRAY
18 Director of Facilities .... Mr. Chad PLYMALE
19 Chief Security Officer .... Mr. Ray M. PARLETT
23 Director of Health Services .... Dr. David BRUBAKER
41 Executive Director of Athletics .... Mr. Matthew WEBB
21 Controller .... Ms. Danae FORREST
39 Director Residence Life .... Mr. Marc SMITHERS
38 Director Counseling Services .... Dr. William BURRICHTER
92 Director of Honors Program .... Dr. Benjamin LIPSCOMB

Hudson Valley Community College (E)

80 Vandenburgh Avenue, Troy NY 12180-6096
County: Rensselaer FICE Identification: 002868
Unit ID: 191719
Telephone: (518) 629-4822 Carnegie Class: Assoc/MT-VT-Mix Trad/Non
FAX Number: (518) 629-4576 Calendar System: Semester
URL: www.hvcc.edu
Established: 1953 Annual Undergrad Tuition & Fees (In-District): $5,812
Enrollment: 11,020 Coed
Affiliation or Control: State/Local IRS Status: 501(c)3
Highest Offering: Associate Degree
Accreditation: M, ADNUR, COARC, DH, DMS, EMT, FUSER, POLYT, SURGT

01 President .... Dr. Roger A. RAMSAMMY
04 Executive Asst to the President .... Ms. Suzanne K. KALKBRENNER
11 VP for Administration and Finance .... Mr. William D. REUTER
05 Interim VP Academic Affairs .... Ms. Judith DILORENZO
32 Vice President for Student Affairs .... Mr. Louis COPLIN
49 Dean School of Busines/Liberal Arts .... Dr. Fabian VEGA
81 Interim Dean of STEM .... Dr. Jonathan ASHDOWN
103 Dean Econ/Workforce Development .... Ms. Penny HILL
76 Int Dean School of Health Sciences .... Dr. Patricia KLIMKEWICZ
08 Dir of College Learning Centers .... Ms. Marcy PENDERGAST
07 Director of Admissions .... Ms. Julie PANZANARO
06 Registrar .... Mr. Ian LACHANCE
13 Chief Information Officer .... Mr. Jonathan BRENNAN
18 Director Physical Plant .... Mr. Richard EDWARDS
38 Exec Dir Student Development .... Dr. Kathleen SWEENER
45 Exec Dir Institutional Effective .... Ms. Kathleen PETLEY
37 Director of Financial Aid .... Ms. Lisa VAN WIE
36 Dir Center For Careers & Transfer .... Ms. Gayle HEALY
15 Exec Director of Human Resources .... Ms. Karen PAQUETTE
19 Director of Public Safety .... Mr. Fred ALIBERTI
23 Coordinator Health Services .... Ms. Claudine POTVIN-GIORDANO
22 Director of Disability Resources .... Ms. DeAnne MARTOCCI
09 Director Planning & Research .... Mr. James F. MACKLIN
35 Director of Student Life .... Mr. Alfredo BALARIN
85 International Student Advisor .... Dr. Jay DEITCHMAN
40 Bookstore Manager .... Ms. Stephanie DANZ
41 Director of Athletics .... Mr. Justin HOYT
20 Asst VP of Academics .... Vacant
124 Dean Retention/Instruct Support .... Ms. Karen FERRER-MUNIZ
96 Dir Business Services/Purchasing .... Ms. Patricia GASTON
21 Comptroller .... Mr. John BRAUNGARD
26 Exec Dir Communications/Marketing .... Mr. Dennis KENNEDY
86 Exec Dir External & Govt Affairs .... Ms. Regina LAGATTA
51 Assoc Dean Continuing Education .... Mr. Richard F. BENNETT, II
25 Director of Grants .... Ms. Cheryl L. BEAUCHAMP
29 Alumni Relations/Annual Giving .... Ms. Jana PUTZIG
88 Scholarship & Operations Coord .... Ms. Kimberly G. BERRY
106 Interim Dir of Distance Learning .... Ms. Linda RYDER
108 Dean Institutional Assessment .... Dr. Margaret GEEHAN
105 Web Coordinator .... Ms. Sandra EYERMAN
28 Chief Diversity Officer .... Mr. Ainsley THOMAS
30 Dir of Development/Donor Relations .... Ms. Angela D. O'NEAL
16 Director of Human Resources .... Ms. Deborah RICHEY

Icahn School of Medicine at Mount Sinai (F)

One Gustave L. Levy Place, New York NY 10029-6500
County: New York FICE Identification: 007026
Unit ID: 193405
Telephone: (212) 241-6500 Carnegie Class: Spec-4-yr-Med
FAX Number: (212) 241-7146 Calendar System: Other
URL: www.icahn.mssm.edu
Established: 1963 Annual Graduate Tuition & Fees: N/A
Enrollment: 1,208 Coed
Affiliation or Control: Independent Non-Profit IRS Status: 501(c)3
Highest Offering: Doctorate; No Undergraduates
Accreditation: M, DENT, IPSY, MED, PH

01 President & CEO .... Dr. Kenneth L. DAVIS
05 Exec Vice Pres/Dean Sch of Medicine .... Dr. Dennis S. CHARNEY
10 Sr Vice Pres for Finance .... Mr. Stephen HARVEY
63 Dean for Medical Education .... Dr. David MULLER
11 Dean for Operations .... Mr. Jeffrey SILBERSTEIN
04 Administrative Asst to President .... Ms. JoAnn L. FINK
28 Director of Diversity .... Dr. Gary BUTTS
90 Director Academic Computing .... Mr. Paul LAWRENCE

Iona College (G)

715 North Avenue, New Rochelle NY 10801-1890
County: Westchester FICE Identification: 002737
Unit ID: 191931
Telephone: (914) 633-2000 Carnegie Class: Masters/L
FAX Number: (914) 633-2642 Calendar System: Semester
URL: www.iona.edu
Established: 1940 Annual Undergrad Tuition & Fees: $38,812
Enrollment: 3,792 Coed
Affiliation or Control: Independent Non-Profit IRS Status: 501(c)3
Highest Offering: Master's
Accreditation: M, CAEPN, JOUR, MFCD, SP, SW

01 President .... Dr. Seamus CAREY
05 Provost/Sr VP Academic Affairs .... Dr. Darrell WHEELER
10 Sr Vice President Finance & Admin .... Ms. Anne Marie SCHETTINI-LYNCH
111 Sr VP Advancement/External Affairs .... Mr. Paul J. SUTERA
100 VP/Chief of Staff & Board Secy .... Ms. MaryEllen CALLAGHAN
84 Interim VP Enrollment Management .... Ms. Rebecca ECKSTEIN
13 Vice Provost Info Technology/CIO .... Ms. Joanne STEELE
32 Vice Provost Student Life .... Ms. Denise HOPKINS-POSELLE
37 Assoc VP Student Financial Services .... Ms. Eileen DOYLE
14 Asst Vice Provost for Info Tech .... Mr. Dimitris HALARIS
20 Assoc Vice Provost Academic Affairs .... Dr. Michael JORDAN
88 Assc Prov Strategic Acad Initiative .... Dr. Tricia MULLIGAN
35 Asst Vice Prov Student Development .... Ms. Elizabeth OLIVIERI-LENAHAN
49 Dean School Arts & Sciences .... Dr. Joseph STABILE
50 Interim Dean School of Business .... Dr. Richard HIGHFIELD
43 General Counsel .... Ms. Kathleen MCELROY

18 Director of Facilities Management ... Mr. Richard MURRAY
39 Director Residential Life ... Ms. Courtney FERRICK
15 Director of HR & Title IX Coord ... Ms. Tracey WILMOT
38 Director of Counseling Center ... Dr. Brielle STARK-ADLER
36 Assoc Vice Prov Career Development ... Mr. Matthew CARDIN
08 Director of Libraries ... Mr. Richard PALLADINO
42 Director of Campus Ministries ... Mr. Carl PROCARIO-FOLEY
06 Registrar ... Mr. Thomas MURASSO
41 Director of Athletics ... Mr. Matthew T. GLOVASKI
86 Director of Govt Relations/Grants ... Vacant
09 Dir of Inst Effectiveness/Planning ... Mr. Jason DIFFENDERFER
21 Director of Business Services ... Ms. Nancy MORANO
26 Director of Public Relations ... Ms. Mary Clare REILLEY
19 Dir Campus Safety and Security ... Mr. Adrian NAVARRETE
23 Director of Health Services ... Ms. Robin SCHAFER
96 Asst Director of Business Services ... Ms. Carol Ann KENNY
92 Director of Honors Program ... Dr. Kim PAFFENROTH
123 Director of Graduate Admissions ... Vacant
04 Executive Asst to President ... Ms. Laura PROSTANO
105 Webpage Designer/Developer ... Mr. Peter MACELI
29 Director Alumni Relations ... Vacant

Island Drafting and Technical Institute (A)

128 Broadway, Amityville NY 11701-2704
County: Suffolk FICE Identification: 007375
Unit ID: 191959
Telephone: (631) 691-8733 Carnegie Class: Spec 2-yr-Tech
FAX Number: (631) 691-8738 Calendar System: Semester
URL: www.idti.edu
Established: 1957 Annual Undergrad Tuition & Fees: $16,650
Enrollment: 90 Coed
Affiliation or Control: Proprietary IRS Status: Proprietary
Highest Offering: Associate Degree
Accreditation: ACCSC

01 President ... Mr. James G. DI LIBERTO
03 Vice President ... Mr. John G. DI LIBERTO
05 Dean ... Ms. Patricia HAUSFELD

Ithaca College (B)

953 Danby Road, Ithaca NY 14850-7001
County: Tompkins FICE Identification: 002739
Unit ID: 191968
Telephone: (607) 274-3011 Carnegie Class: Masters/L
FAX Number: N/A Calendar System: Semester
URL: www.ithaca.edu
Established: 1892 Annual Undergrad Tuition & Fees: $43,978
Enrollment: 6,516 Coed
Affiliation or Control: Independent Non-Profit IRS Status: 501(c)3
Highest Offering: Doctorate
Accreditation: M, CAATE, MUS, NRPA, OT, PTA, SP, THEA

01 President ... Dr. Shirley M. COLLADO
100 Chief of Staff ... Ms. Melissa DALY
05 Provost/Sr VP Academic Affairs ... Dr. La Jerne T. CORNISH
10 VP of Finance & Admin ... Mr. William GUERRERO
43 VP & General Counsel ... Mr. Guilherme COSTA
84 VP Marketing & Enrollment Strategy ... Ms. Laurie KOEHLER
111 VP Institutional Advancement ... Ms. Wendy KOBLER
15 VP Human & Org Development/Plng ... Ms. Hayley HARRIS
20 Asst Prov/Dean Interdis/Intl Stds ... Dr. Tanya R. SAUNDERS
26 Exec Director of Strategic Comm ... Mr. Robert WAGNER
13 Assoc VP Information Technology ... Mr. David WEIL
18 Assoc VP for Facilities Management ... Mr. Tim CAREY
32 VP Student Affairs/Campus Life ... Dr. Rosanna FERRO
20 Associate Provost Academic Program ... Dr. Jeane COPENHAVER-JOHNSON
49 Dean School Humanities/Sci ... Dr. Melanie STEIN
64 Dean of School of Music ... Dr. Karl PAULNACK
76 Dean Sch Health Sciences/Human Perf ... Ms. Linda PETROSINO
50 Dean School of Business ... Mr. Sean REID
60 Dean School of Communications ... Ms. Diane GAYESKI
06 Registrar ... Ms. Vikki LEVINE
09 Chief Analytics Officer ... Dr. Yuko MULUGETTA
07 Director of Admission ... Ms. Nicole EVERSLEY BRADWELL
12 Director London Center ... Ms. Thorunn LONSDALE
38 Director Counseling/Health/Wellness ... Dr. Vivian LORENZO
37 Dir of Student Financial Services ... Mrs. Lisa HOSKEY
35 Dean of Students ... Ms. Bonnie S. PRUNTY
08 College Librarian ... Ms. Lisabeth CHABOT
41 Dir Intercol Athletics/Rec Sports ... Ms. Susan BASSETT
114 Director of Budget ... Mr. Michael HOWZE
27 Senior Assoc Dir for Campus Comm ... Mr. David C. MALEY
40 Manager of College Stores ... Mr. Rick WATSON
42 Dir Religious & Spiritual Life ... Mr. Hierald OSORTO
28 Dir Inclusion/Diversity/Equity ... Dr. Sean EVERSLEY BRADWELL
85 Dir International Student Services ... Ms. Diana DIMITROVA
88 Dir Center for Faculty Excellence ... Mr. Gordon ROWLAND
04 Exec Assistant to the President ... Ms. Jaimie M. VOORHEES

Jamestown Business College (C)

7 Fairmount Avenue, Box 429, Jamestown NY 14702-0429
County: Chautauqua FICE Identification: 008495
Unit ID: 192004
Telephone: (716) 664-5100 Carnegie Class: Spec-4-yr-Bus
FAX Number: (716) 664-3144 Calendar System: Quarter
URL: www.jbc.edu
Established: 1886 Annual Undergrad Tuition & Fees: $12,645
Enrollment: 323 Coed
Affiliation or Control: Proprietary IRS Status: Proprietary
Highest Offering: Baccalaureate
Accreditation: M

01 President ... Mr. David CONKLIN
05 Dean ... Ms. Pamela REESE
07 Director Admissions ... Ms. Christina CONKLIN
06 Registrar ... Ms. Cynthia CARTWRIGHT
37 Director of Financial Aid ... Mrs. Kelly OLMSTED
26 Communications ... Ms. Emily BUTCHER

Jamestown Community College (D)

525 Falconer Street, Jamestown NY 14701
County: Chautauqua FICE Identification: 002869
Unit ID: 191986
Telephone: (716) 338-1000 Carnegie Class: Assoc/HT-High Non
FAX Number: (716) 338-1466 Calendar System: Semester
URL: www.sunyjcc.edu
Established: 1950 Annual Undergrad Tuition & Fees (In-District): $5,850
Enrollment: 4,463 Coed
Affiliation or Control: State/Local IRS Status: 501(c)3
Highest Offering: Associate Degree
Accreditation: M, ADNUR, OTA

01 President ... Dr. Daniel T. DEMARTE
05 Vice Pres of Academic Affairs ... Dr. Marilyn A. ZAGORA
11 Vice Pres of Administration ... Mr. Michael MARTELLO
32 Vice Pres of Student Affairs ... Mr. Kirk YOUNG
103 Vice Pres of Workforce Readiness ... Mr. Holger EKANGER
12 Exec Dir of Catt County Campus ... Ms. Paula SNYDER
09 Dean Research & Planning ... Ms. Barbara RUSSELL
06 Registrar ... Ms. Tracy KELLY
07 Interim Director Admission ... Ms. Corrine CASE
08 Library Director ... Mr. Timothy ARNOLD
37 Exec Dir Student Finance/Records ... Ms. Jill COLBURN
15 Exec Director Human Resources ... Ms. Nicolette RICZKER
41 Athletic Director ... Mr. George SISSON
43 Legal Counsel ... Mr. Stephen ABDELLA
18 Director Facilities/Physical Plant ... Mr. David JOHNSON
04 Administrative Asst to President ... Ms. Marsha L. HERN
19 Director Security/Safety ... Mr. Barry SWANSON
30 Chief Development/Advancement ... Mr. Tim SMEAL
39 Director Student Housing ... Mr. Tyler SILAGYI
105 Director Web Services ... Ms. Karli CHAMP
13 Chief Info Technology Officer (CIO) ... Ms. Denise BURBEY
29 Director Alumni Relations ... Ms. Heather MORRIS
21 Director Administrative Services ... Ms. Karen FULLER
96 Financial Analyst/Business Office ... Ms. Jennifer BEEBE
36 Director Student Placement ... Mr. Ron TURAK
38 Director Student Counseling ... Ms. Tammy SMITH

Jamestown Community College Cattaraugus County Campus (E)

260 North Union Street, PO Box 5901,
Olean NY 14760-5901
Telephone: (716) 376-7504 Identification: 770138
Accreditation: &M

Jefferson Community College (F)

1220 Coffeen Street, Watertown NY 13601-1897
County: Jefferson FICE Identification: 002870
Unit ID: 192022
Telephone: (315) 786-2200 Carnegie Class: Assoc/HT-Mix Trad/Non
FAX Number: (315) 786-0158 Calendar System: Semester
URL: www.sunyjefferson.edu
Established: 1961 Annual Undergrad Tuition & Fees (In-District): $5,424
Enrollment: 3,460 Coed
Affiliation or Control: State/Local IRS Status: 501(c)3
Highest Offering: Associate Degree
Accreditation: M, ADNUR

01 President ... Dr. Ty A. STONE
05 Vice President Academic Affairs ... Mr. Thomas FINCH
10 Vice President Admin/Finance ... Mr. Daniel DUPEE
32 Vice President for Student Affairs ... Dr. Corey CAMPBELL
49 Associate VP for Liberal Arts ... Ms. Jerilyn FAIRMAN
81 Associate VP for Math/Science ... Ms. Linda DITTRICH
121 Dean of Student Success ... Ms. Rebecca SMALL KELLOGG
103 Assoc P for Workforce Dev/Business ... Mr. Terrence HARRIS
32 Dean of Students ... Vacant
04 Assistant to the President ... Ms. Edie ROGGIE
08 Library Director ... Ms. Connie HOLBERG
07 Dean of Enrollment Services ... Mr. James AMBROSE
26 Sr Dir Government Affs/Public Rels ... Ms. Karen FREEMAN
37 Director Financial Aid ... Vacant
06 Registrar ... Ms. Deborah M. ELLIOTT
88 Director Small Business Center ... Mr. Eric F. CONSTANCE
09 Director of Planning/IR/Grants ... Ms. Megan STADLER
18 Chief Facilities/Physical Plant ... Mr. Bruce ALEXANDER
29 Alumni Development Officer ... Vacant
35 Director Student Devel/Activities ... Vacant
36 Director Career Planning/Placement ... Ms. Michele D. GEFELL
88 Director of Advising ... Mr. Craig MCNAMARA
27 Dir of Marketing/Communications ... Vacant
15 Exec Dir Finance/Human Resources ... Ms. Kerry A. YOUNG
30 College Development Officer ... Vacant
31 Director Community Services ... Ms. Kathleen MORRIS
119 Chief Security Information Officer ... Mr. Donald HORTON
19 Director Security/Safety ... Mr. Wesley HISSONG
41 Athletic Director ... Mr. Jeffrey WILEY

Jewish Theological Seminary of America (G)

3080 Broadway, New York NY 10027-4649
County: New York FICE Identification: 002740
Unit ID: 192040
Telephone: (212) 678-8000 Carnegie Class: Spec-4-yr-Faith
FAX Number: (212) 678-8947 Calendar System: Semester
URL: www.jtsa.edu
Established: 1886 Annual Undergrad Tuition & Fees: $56,778
Enrollment: 368 Coed
Affiliation or Control: Independent Non-Profit IRS Status: 501(c)3
Highest Offering: Doctorate
Accreditation: M, PAST

01 Chancellor ... Dr. Arnold M. EISEN
03 Exec VC/Chief Operating Officer ... Mr. Marc GARY
30 Vice Chanc/Chief Development Ofcr ... Ms. Bonnie EPSTEIN
05 Provost ... Dr. Shuly SCHWARTZ
10 Chief Financial Officer ... Mr. Jeffrey JACOB
43 General Counsel ... Mr. Keath BLATT
49 Dean List College Jewish Studies ... Dr. Amy KALMANOFSKY
53 Dean Davidson School of Education ... Dr. Shira EPSTEIN
58 Dean of The Graduate School ... Dr. Shuly SCHWARTZ
64 Director Miller Cantorial School ... Cantor Nancy ABRAMSON
73 Dean of Religious Leadership ... Rabbi Daniel NEVINS
32 Dean of Student Life ... Ms. Sara HOROWITZ
08 Librarian ... Dr. David KRAEMER
15 Director of Human Resources ... Ms. Diana TORRES-PETRILLI
18 Director of Operations ... Mr. James ESPOSITO
13 Director Information Technology ... Mr. Ray MORALES
26 Chief Communications Officer ... Ms. Elise DOWELL
06 Registrar/Director Financial Aid ... Ms. Amy HERSH
39 Director of Residence Life ... Mr. Bradley MOOT
84 Director of Enrollment Management ... Ms. Melissa PRESENT
35 Director of Student Life ... Ms. Ruth DECALO
38 Director Student Counseling ... Dr. David DAVAR
29 Director of Alumni Affairs ... Mrs. Melissa FRIEDMAN
20 Associate Provost ... Dr. Stephen GARFINKEL
37 Director of Financial Aid ... Ms. Amy HERSH
88 Director of Community Engagement ... Rabbi Julia ANDELMAN
04 Executive Asst to Chancellor ... Ms. Michelle MEHRING
19 Director Security/Safety ... Chief Anthony VAUGHAN

The Juilliard School (H)

60 Lincoln Center Plaza, New York NY 10023-6588
County: New York FICE Identification: 002742
Unit ID: 192110
Telephone: (212) 799-5000 Carnegie Class: Spec-4-yr-Arts
FAX Number: (212) 724-0263 Calendar System: Semester
URL: www.juilliard.edu
Established: 1905 Annual Undergrad Tuition & Fees: $45,110
Enrollment: 927 Coed
Affiliation or Control: Independent Non-Profit IRS Status: 501(c)3
Highest Offering: Doctorate
Accreditation: M

01 President ... Mr. Damian WOETZEL
05 Provost & Dean ... Mr. Ara GUZELIMIAN
10 Vice Pres/Chief Financial Officer ... Ms. Christine TODD
08 VP for Library/Info Resources ... Ms. Jane GOTTLIEB
111 VP & Chief Advancement Officer ... Ms. Alexandra WHEELER
18 Vice Pres for Facilities Management ... Mr. Joseph MASTRANGELO
84 VP Enrollment Mgmt/Student Dev ... Ms. Joan D. WARREN
43 Vice Pres Admin/General Counsel ... Mr. Maurice F. EDELSON
100 Vice President & Chief of Staff ... Ms. Jacqueline SCHMIDT
26 Vice Pres for Public Affairs ... Ms. Rosalie CONTRERAS
88 Special Projects Producer ... Ms. Kathryn KOZLARK
32 Dean for Student Development ... Mr. Barrett HIPES
20 Dean of Academic Affairs ... Mr. Jose GARCIA-LEON
64 Assoc Dean/Director Music Division ... Mr. Adam MEYER
64 Asst Dean/Dir of Chamber Music ... Ms. Barli NUGENT
35 Asst Dean of Student Affairs ... Ms. Sabrina TANBARA
57 Dir Richard Rodgers Drama Div ... Mr. Evan YIONOULIS
57 Artistic Director of Dance Division ... Ms. Alicia Graf MACK
88 Artistic Director of Vocal Arts ... Mr. Brian ZEGER
88 Artist in Residence/Artistic Advise ... Ms. Monica HUGGETT
88 Director of Performance Activities ... Ms. Monica THAKKAR
88 Artistic Dir Pre-College Division ... Ms. Yoheved KAPLINSKY
06 Registrar ... Ms. Katherine GERTSON
07 Assoc Dean Enrollment Management ... Dr. Kathleen TESAR
112 Director of Major Gifts ... Ms. Katie MURTHA
15 Director of Human Resources ... Ms. Caryn G. DOKTOR
38 Director of Counseling Services ... Mr. William BUSE
37 Director Student Financial Aid ... Ms. Tina GONZALEZ
88 Director of Juilliard Jazz ... Mr. Wynton MARSALIS
96 Director of Office Services ... Mr. Scott A. HOLDEN
36 Director Career Services ... Vacant
13 Chief Information Officer ... Mr. Carl YOUNG
14 Chief Technology Officer ... Mr. Steve DOTY
04 Executive Asst to the President ... Ms. Denise CRAWFORT
19 Director Security/Safety ... Mr. Adam GAGAN
29 Director Alumni Relations ... Ms. Rebecca VACCARELLI
39 Director of Residence Life ... Mr. Todd PORTER

Kehilath Yakov Rabbinical Seminary (I)

638 Bedford Avenue, Brooklyn NY 11211-8007
County: Kings FICE Identification: 010549
Unit ID: 192165

Telephone: (718) 963-1212 Carnegie Class: Spec-4-yr-Faith
FAX Number: (718) 387-8586 Calendar System: Semester
Established: 1948 Annual Undergrad Tuition & Fees: $9,800
Enrollment: 159 Male
Affiliation or Control: Independent Non-Profit IRS Status: 501(c)3
Highest Offering: First Talmudic Degree
Accreditation: RABN

01 President .... Mr. Sandor SCHWARTZ

Keuka College (A)

141 Central Avenue, Keuka Park NY 14478
County: Yates FICE Identification: 002744
Unit ID: 192192
Telephone: (315) 279-5000 Carnegie Class: Masters/M
FAX Number: (315) 279-5216 Calendar System: Semester
URL: www.keuka.edu
Established: 1890 Annual Undergrad Tuition & Fees: $32,044
Enrollment: 1,953 Coed
Affiliation or Control: Independent Non-Profit IRS Status: 501(c)3
Highest Offering: Master's
Accreditation: M, CAEPT, IACBE, NURSE, OT, SW

01 President .... Mrs. Amy STOREY
05 Int Prov/VP for Academic Affairs .... Dr. Bradley FUSTER
10 VP for Finance/Administration .... Mr. Robert BAUMET
84 VP for Enroll Mgmt/Student Devel .... Mr. Mark PETRIE
111 AVP for Advancement/External Affs .... Mr. Peter BEKISZ
20 Assoc Provost for Acad Innovation .... Dr. Timothy SELLERS
20 Assistant Provost .... Dr. Laurel HESTER
08 Director of Library .... Ms. Linda PARK
29 Sr Dir Alumni Relations/Advancement .... Mrs. Billy Jo JAYNE
15 Director of Human Resources .... Mrs. Deborah DRAIN
37 Director Financial Aid .... Ms. Catherine BUZANSKI
21 Controller .... Mr. Philip CATALANO
13 Asst VP/Chief Information Officer .... Ms. Andrea CAMPBELL
32 AVP for Student Affairs/Dean Stdnts .... Dr. Tracy MCFARLAND
19 Director of Campus Safety .... Mr. James CUNNINGHAM
23 Coordinator of Health Services .... Ms. Cindy CHRISTIE
38 Director of Counseling Services .. Ms. Mary MARTINI-HAUSNER
07 Director of Admissions on Campus .... Ms. Megan PERKINS
41 Director of Athletics .... Mr. David M. SWEET
42 College Chaplain .... Mr. Eric DETAR
06 Registrar .... Ms. Jill BIRD
26 Director Mktg Analytics/Proj Mgmt .... Ms. Christen ACCARDI
96 Purchasing Liaison .... Ms. Brenda DEUCK
76 Div Chair Occupational Therapy .... Dr. Christopher ALTERIO
83 Div Chair Basic Soc & Applied Sci .... Dr. Tom TREMER
50 Div Chair Business & Management .... Dr. Ed SILVERMAN
53 Div Chair of Education .... Dr. Klaudia LORINCZOVA
79 Div Chair Humanities/Fine Arts .... Dr. Jennie JOINER
81 Div Chair Natural Sciences/Math .... Dr. Mark SUGALSKI
66 Div Chair Nursing .... Dr. Elizabeth RUSSO
70 Div Chair Social Work .... Dr. Jason MCKINNEY
112 Major Gift Officer .... Ms. Maryanne CAMERON
88 Senior Dir of Conference Services .... Ms. Karen MANN
104 Assoc Director Intercultural Affs .... Ms. Jamyra YOUNG
85 Dean of International Program/Asia .... Mr. Gary GISS
119 Director of Info Systems & Security .... Mr. Thomas FLICKER
27 Director of Comm & Media Relations .... Mr. Kevin FRISCH
31 Dir of Community Relations/Events .... Ms. Katharine WAYE
88 Director of Field Prd Pgm/Intern .... Ms. Tara BLOOM
21 Senior Accountant .... Ms. Kayla ROBINSON
08 Director of HEOP .... Ms. Lisa THOMPSON
113 Director of Student Accounts .... Ms. Mary Ellen GRIFFITHS
35 Dir Student Activities/New Students .... Ms. Eva ROBBINS
88 Program & Org Management .... Dr. Deborah GREGORY
09 Director of Institutional Research .... Vacant

The King's College (B)

56 Broadway, New York NY 10004-1613
County: New York FICE Identification: 040953
Unit ID: 454184
Telephone: (212) 659-7200 Carnegie Class: Bac-A&S
FAX Number: (212) 659-7210 Calendar System: Semester
URL: www.tkc.edu
Established: 1938 Annual Undergrad Tuition & Fees: $36,450
Enrollment: 555 Coed
Affiliation or Control: Independent Non-Profit IRS Status: 501(c)3
Highest Offering: Baccalaureate
Accreditation: M

00 Chairman of the Board of Trustees .... Mr. Timothy DUNN
01 President .... Dr. Tim GIBSON
03 Executive Vice President .... Mr. Brian BRENBERG
05 Provost .... Dr. Mark HIJLEH
10 Vice President Finance/CFO .... Mr. Frank TORINO
45 Vice Pres Strategic Planning .... Dr. Kimberly THORNBURY
32 Vice President Student Development .... Mr. Eric BENNETT
35 Dean of Students .... Mr. David LEEDY
21 Controller .... Ms. Judy BARRINGER
06 Registrar .... Mr. Paul MIDDLEKAUFF
37 Director of Financial Aid .... Ms. Anna PETERS
04 Executive Asst to President .... Ms. Megan STARNES
09 Director of Institutional Research .... Dr. Kimberly THORNBURY
07 Director Admissions .... Mr. Noah HUNTER
18 Chief Facilities/Physical Plant .... Mr. Rich SWITZER
26 Chief Public Relations Officer .... Ms. Natalie NAKAMURA
30 Director Development Services .... Ms. Tonnie CHEN
36 Director Career Development .... Mr. Matthew PERMAN
38 Director Student Counseling .... Ms. Esther THUN
84 Director Enrollment Management .... Mr. Noah HUNTER
08 Director Library Services .... Ms. Christina ROGERS
39 Director Resident Life .... Ms. Leticia MOSQUEDA
41 Athletic Director .... Mr. Bryan FINLEY
15 Director Human Resources .... Ms. Grace GLEASON
102 Director Grants and Foundation .... Mr. Michael TOSCANO
13 Director of Information Technology .... Mr. Bracey FUENZALIDA

Le Moyne College (C)

1419 Salt Springs Road, Syracuse NY 13214-1301
County: Onondaga FICE Identification: 002748
Unit ID: 192323
Telephone: (315) 445-4100 Carnegie Class: Masters/L
FAX Number: (315) 445-4540 Calendar System: Semester
URL: www.lemoyne.edu
Established: 1946 Annual Undergrad Tuition & Fees: $34,625
Enrollment: 3,431 Coed
Affiliation or Control: Independent Non-Profit IRS Status: 501(c)3
Highest Offering: Doctorate
Accreditation: M, ARCPA, NURSE, OT

01 President .... Dr. Linda M. LEMURA
05 Provost & VP Acad Affairs .... Rev. Joseph G. MARINA
10 Senior VP Fin & Admin & Treasurer .... Mr. Roger W. STACKPOOLE
111 Vice Pres Comm & Advancement .... Mr. Bill BROWER
32 Vice Pres Student Development ... Dr. Deborah M. CADY MELZER
84 Vice Pres of Enrollment .... Dr. Timothy LEE
88 Vice Pres Mission Integration & Dev .... Rev. David C. MCCALLUM, SJ
88 Rector of the Jesuit Community .... Rev. Donald KIRBY, SJ
49 Interim Dean of Arts & Sciences .... Dr. James HANNAN
50 Dean School of Business .... Mr. James E. JOSEPH
58 Dean of Graduate & Prof Studies .... Dr. Meega WELLS
20 Assoc Provost .... Dr. Mary K. COLLINS
21 Assoc VP for Finance & Controller .... Mr. Brian M. LOUCY
15 Asst VP for HR and Org Dev .... Ms. Karin BOTTO
41 Interim Director of Athletics .... Mr. Tim FENTON
18 Asst VP Facilities Mgmt & Planning .... Mr. Jed S. SCHNEIDER
26 Assoc VP for Marketing .... Mr. Peter S. KILLIAN
35 Dean of Students .... Ms. Anne E. KEARNEY
35 Asst Dean for Student Development .... Mr. Mark G. GODLESKI
121 Asst Dean for Academic Advising .... Ms. Allison FARRELL
88 Asst Dean/Dir CSTEP & STEP .... Ms. Darshini ROOPNARINE
84 Sr Dir Enrollment Management .... Ms. Kristen P. TRAPASSO
07 Senior Director of Admission .... Ms. Mary CHANDLER
51 Director of Continuing Education .... Ms. Patricia J. BLISS
88 Dir of Transfer Admission .... Ms. Cathy ANDERSON
13 Director of Info Technology .... Mr. Shaun C. BLACK
09 Director of Institutional Research .... Dr. Daniel L. SKIDMORE
22 EEO/Affirmative Action Officer .... Ms. Karin BOTTO
06 Registrar/Sr Director Enrollment .... Ms. Cynthia A. ALIBRANDI
08 Director of the Library .... Ms. Inga BARNELLO
42 Director of Campus Ministry .... Mr. Thomas ANDINO
27 Director of Communications .... Mr. Joseph B. DELLA POSTA
88 Director Campus Life & Leadership .... Mr. John R. HALEY
19 Director of Security .... Mr. Mark J. PETTERELLI
112 Senior Dir Leadership Giving .... Ms. Kimberly B. MCAULIFF
39 Dir of Campus Life & Leadership .... Mr. John HALEY
36 Director Career Advising/Devpment .... Ms. Meredith TORNABENE
04 Assistant to the President .... Ms. Carly J. COLBERT
28 Asst to the Provost for Diversity .... Dr. Tabor FISHER
44 Sr Dir Annual Giving/Stewardship .... Ms. Katherine COGSWELL
86 Director Govt/Foundation Relations .... Mr. Steven W. KULICK
110 Director of Advancement Services .... Mr. Paul F. LYNCH
29 Director of Alumni Engagement .... Ms. Kasha GODLESKI
23 Dir Wellness Ctr for Health & Couns .... Ms. Maria RANDAZZO
88 Director of HEOP and AHANA .... Ms. Kelsi-Leandra LANE
40 Bookstore Manager .... Ms. Jessica L. MANNINO

LIM College (D)

12 E 53rd Street, New York NY 10022-5268
County: New York FICE Identification: 007466
Unit ID: 192271
Telephone: (212) 752-1530 Carnegie Class: Spec-4-yr-Bus
FAX Number: (212) 832-6109 Calendar System: Semester
URL: www.limcollege.edu
Established: 1939 Annual Undergrad Tuition & Fees: $27,030
Enrollment: 1,713 Coed
Affiliation or Control: Proprietary IRS Status: Proprietary
Highest Offering: Master's
Accreditation: M, ACBSP

01 President .... Elizabeth S. MARCUSE
05 Provost .... Lisa SPRINGER
10 Exec VP Finance & Operations/Treas .... Michael T. DONOHUE
26 VP for Marketing and Communications .... Victoria FULLARD
84 VP for Enrollment Services .... Kristina ORTIZ
86 VP for Govt Relations/Cmty Affairs .... Christopher E. BARTO
21 AVP of Finance/Accounting .... Haroon AHMED
58 Chair of Graduate Studies .... John KEANE
20 Assoc Dean of Academic Affairs .... Patricia FITZMAURICE
08 Director of Library Services .... Lou ACIERNO
06 College Registrar .... Carolyn DISNEW
36 AVP for Career and Internship Svcs .... Tammy J. SAMUELS
35 Dean of Student Affairs .... Michael RICHARDS
38 Sr Dir Counseling & Accessibility .... Jodi N. LICHT
39 Residence Director .... Chanelle SEARS
07 Director of Admissions .... Maura LA HARA
88 Asst Director of Online Admissions .... Antoinette LIQUET
09 Director of Institutional Research .... Nikisha WILLIAMS
21 Accounting Manager .... Svetlana KANEVSKAYA
96 Purchasing Director .... Eric MARTIN
37 Sr Dir of Student Financial Svcs .... Dorothy MARTIN-HATCHER
30 Sr VP for External Relations .... Gail NARDIN
27 Director of Communications .... Meredith FINNIN
27 Director of Marketing .... Laura CIOFFI
13 Chief Technology Officer .... Maurice MORENCY
14 Director of Information Technology .... Nelson LEON
18 Director of Facilities .... Jonathan ABREU
108 Assoc Dean Assessment/Acred/Plng .... Jacqueline LEBLANC
40 Director of the Bookstore .... Kerri ZIEMBA
124 Dir of Retention & Student Success .... Erin LYNN
16 Asst Dir of Human Resources .... Carolyn HIGGINS
104 Study Abroad Coordinator .... Vacant
85 Coord of International Student Svcs .... Kate LEVY
88 Director of Faculty Development .... Mitchell KASE
123 Asst Dir of Graduate Admissions .... George TOLEDO
35 Director of Student Life .... M.T TELOKI

Long Island Business Institute (E)

6500 Jericho Turnpike, Commack NY 11725
Telephone: (631) 499-7100 Identification: 770746
Accreditation: NY

Long Island Business Institute (F)

136-18 39th Avenue, Flushing NY 11354
County: Queens FICE Identification: 020937
Unit ID: 192509
Telephone: (718) 939-5100 Carnegie Class: Spec 2-yr-Other
FAX Number: (718) 939-9235 Calendar System: Semester
URL: www.libi.edu
Established: 1968 Annual Undergrad Tuition & Fees: $14,475
Enrollment: 717 Coed
Affiliation or Control: Proprietary IRS Status: Proprietary
Highest Offering: Associate Degree
Accreditation: NY

01 President .... Ms. Monica W. FOOTE
05 Provost .... Ms. Stacey JOHNSON
11 Asst Campus Program Director .... Ms. Michelle HOUSTON
10 Assoc Dir Administration/Finance .... Mr. Li ZHU
37 Financial Aid Director .... Ms. Cynthia YUN LIN
08 Librarian Commack Campus .... Ms. Terry CANAVAN
08 Sr Librarian Flushing Campus .... Ms. Adrianna ARGUELLES

*Long Island University (G)

700 Northern Boulevard, Brookville NY 11548-1327
County: Nassau FICE Identification: 002751
Unit ID: 192457
Telephone: (516) 299-2501 Carnegie Class: N/A
FAX Number: N/A
URL: www.liu.edu

01 President .... Dr. Kimberly R. CLINE
13 VP for Information Technology & CIO .... Mr. George BAROUDI
10 Vice President Finance & Treasurer ... Mr. Christopher N. FEVOLA
07 VP of Admissions .... Ms. Deirdre WHITMAN
43 Chief University Counsel .... Mr. Michael BEST
09 Chief Institutional Effectiveness .... Mr. Andy PERSON
15 Chief Talent/HR Officer .... Ms. Denise DICK
16 Executive Director Human Resources .... Ms. Lisa AROJO
96 Dir Sourcing/Procurement Svcs .... Mr. Allan HOWELL
05 Senior VP for Academic Affairs .... Dr. Randy BURD
21 Assoc Vice Pres/Controller .... Mr. Mark SCHMOTZER
111 Vice President of Univ Advancement .... Mr. Charles RASBERRY
11 Chief Administrative Officer .... Mr. Joseph SCHAEFER

*Long Island University - LIU Post (H)

720 Northern Boulevard, Brookville NY 11548
County: Nassau FICE Identification: 002754
Unit ID: 192448
Telephone: (516) 299-2900 Carnegie Class: DU-Mod
FAX Number: (516) 299-2137 Calendar System: Semester
URL: www.liu.edu/post
Established: 1954 Annual Undergrad Tuition & Fees: $37,763
Enrollment: 8,499 Coed
Affiliation or Control: Independent Non-Profit IRS Status: 501(c)3
Highest Offering: Doctorate
Accreditation: M, CACREP, CAHIIM, CLPSY, DIETD, DIETI, LIB, MT, NURSE, PERF, RAD, SP, SPAA, SW

02 President .... Dr. Kimberly R. CLINE
05 Vice President for Academic Affairs .... Dr. Ed WEIS
07 VP of Admissions .... Ms. Deirdre WHITMAN
49 Dean College Lib Arts/Science .... Dr. Nathaniel BOWDITCH
66 Dean Sch Health Prof/Nursing .... Dr. Lori KNAPP
50 Dean College of Management .... Dr. Robert VALLI
53 Dean College of Educ/Info & Tech .... Dr. Albert INSERRA
88 Dean of School of Comm & Design .... Dr. Steven BREESE
32 Dean of Students/LIU Promise .... Mr. Michael BERTHEL
41 Director of Athletics .... Ms. Debbie DEJONG
18 University Facilities Officer .... Mr. Roy FERGUS
19 University Dir of Public Safety .... Mr. Michael FEVOLA

* *Long Island University - LIU Brentwood* (A)

Grant Campus, 1001 Crooked Hill Rd,
Brentwood NY 11717
Telephone: (631) 287-8500 Identification: 666076
Accreditation: &M

* *Long Island University - LIU Brooklyn* (B)

1 University Plaza, Brooklyn NY 11201
Telephone: (718) 488-1011 FICE Identification: 004779
Accreditation: &M, ARCPA, #CAATE, CLPSY, COARC, DMS, NURSE, OT, PH, PHAR, PTA, #SP, SPAA, SW

* *Long Island University - LIU Hudson* (C)

735 Anderson Hill Road, Purchase NY 10577
Telephone: (914) 831-2700 Identification: 666078
Accreditation: &M

* *Long Island University - LIU Riverhead* (D)

121 Speonk-Riverhead Road - LIU Bld,
Riverhead NY 11901-3499
Telephone: (631) 287-8010 Identification: 666174
Accreditation: &M, CAEPT

Louis V. Gerstner Jr. Graduate School of Biomedical Sciences, Memorial Sloan Kettering Cancer Center (E)

1275 York Avenue, P.O. Box 441, New York NY 10065
County: New York Identification: 666643
Telephone: (646) 888-6639 Carnegie Class: Not Classified
FAX Number: (646) 422-2351 Calendar System: Semester
URL: www.sloankettering.edu
Established: 2004 Annual Graduate Tuition & Fees: N/A
Enrollment: N/A Coed
Affiliation or Control: Independent Non-Profit IRS Status: 501(c)3
Highest Offering: Doctorate; No Undergraduates
Accreditation: NY

01 President .... Dr. Craig B. THOMPSON
05 Provost .... Dr. Joan MASSAGUE
20 Dean .... Dr. Michael H. OVERHOLTZER
88 Associate Dean .... Ms. Linda BURNLEY
06 Registrar .... Mr. David L. MCDONAGH
08 Director of Library Services .... Ms. Donna S. GIBSON
88 Assistant Dean .... Dr. Thomas G. MAGALDI

Machzikei Hadath Rabbinical College (F)

5407 16th Avenue, Brooklyn NY 11204-1805
County: Kings FICE Identification: 013026
Unit ID: 192624
Telephone: (718) 854-8777 Carnegie Class: Spec-4-yr-Faith
FAX Number: (718) 851-1265 Calendar System: Semester
URL: WWW.MHRC.EDU
Established: 1956 Annual Undergrad Tuition & Fees: $11,500
Enrollment: 146 Male
Affiliation or Control: Independent Non-Profit IRS Status: 501(c)3
Highest Offering: First Talmudic Degree
Accreditation: RABN

01 President .... Mr. Alexander SCHAECHTER

Mandl School - The College of Allied Health (G)

254 W 54th Street, 9th Floor, New York NY 10019
County: New York FICE Identification: 007401
Unit ID: 192688
Telephone: (212) 247-3434 Carnegie Class: Spec 2-yr-Health
FAX Number: (212) 247-3617 Calendar System: Semester
URL: www.mandl.edu
Established: 1924 Annual Undergrad Tuition & Fees: $14,070
Enrollment: 598 Coed
Affiliation or Control: Proprietary IRS Status: Proprietary
Highest Offering: Associate Degree
Accreditation: ABHES, COARC, SURTEC

01 President .... Mr. Melvyn P. WEINER
05 Vice President of Academic Affairs .... Dr. Orsete DIAS
11 VP Operations/Dir Financial Aid .... Mr. Stuart WEINER
36 Vice President of Career Services .... Mr. James FLANAGAN
06 Vice Pres Records & Registration .... Mr. Marc WEINER
84 Vice Pres Enrollment Management .... Ms. Randie SENSER
10 Chief Financial Officer .... Mrs. Nettie WEINER
06 Registrar .... Ms. Tina PAPULI
07 Director of Recruitment .... Ms. Racquel GARCIA
08 Director of the Library .... Ms. Melissa AARONBERG
32 Assistant Dean Student Support Svcs .. Dr. Karlene RICHARDSON

Manhattan College (H)

Manhattan College Parkway, Bronx NY 10471-4099
County: Bronx FICE Identification: 002758
Unit ID: 192703
Telephone: (718) 862-8000 Carnegie Class: Masters/L
FAX Number: (718) 862-8014 Calendar System: Semester
URL: www.manhattan.edu
Established: 1853 Annual Undergrad Tuition & Fees: $42,608
Enrollment: 4,242 Coed
Affiliation or Control: Independent Non-Profit IRS Status: 501(c)3
Highest Offering: Master's
Accreditation: M, NMT

01 President .... Dr. Brennan O'DONNELL
05 Executive Vice President & Provost .... Dr. William CLYDE
10 VP for Finance & CFO .... Mr. Matthew S. MCMANNESS
32 Vice President Student Life .... Dr. Richard SATTERLEE
111 Vice President College Advancement ..... Mr. Thomas MAURIELLO
15 Vice President for Human Resources .... Ms. Barbara A. FABE
18 Vice President for Facilities .... Mr. Andrew RYAN
84 Vice President Enrollment Mgmt .... Dr. William J. BISSET
88 Vice President for Mission .... Br. Jack CURRAN
20 Associate Provost .... Dr. Rani ROY
35 Assistant VP of Student Life .... Dr. Emmanuel AGO
35 Dean of Students .... Dr. Michael CAREY
06 Registrar .... Mr. Carlos TONCHE
07 Dir of Undergraduate Admissions .... Ms. Tara FAY-REILLY
08 Director of Libraries .... Dr. William WALTERS
13 Director of Information Tech Svcs .... Mr. Jake HOLMQUIST
19 Director of Public Safety .... Mr. Peter DECARO
29 Director of Alumni Relations .... Mr. Louis CALVELLI
26 Director of Mktg & Communications .... Mrs. Lydia E. GRAY
36 Director Ctr Career Development .... Ms. Rachel CIRELLI
38 Dir of Counseling & Health Services .... Ms. Jennifer MCARDLE
39 Director of Residence Life .... Mr. Charles CLENCY
41 Director of Athletics .... Ms. Marianne REILLY
42 Director of Campus Ministry .... Ms. Lois HARR
30 Director of Development/Advancement .... Mr. Stephen WHITE
78 Director Opportunity Pgms .... Mr. Andrew BURNS
40 Director of Campus Bookstore .... Mr. Henry CASTILLO
22 Dir of Personnel/Affirm Action Ofcr .... Ms. Vickie M. COWAN
09 Dir Inst Research/Assessment .... Ms. Bridget MILLER
21 Controller .... Mr. Dennis LONERGAN
21 Business Manager .... Mr. Kenneth WALDHOF
85 International Student Advisor .... Ms. Debra L. DAMICO
37 Director of Financial Aid Admin .... Ms. Denise SCALZO
49 Dean of Liberal Arts .... Dr. Keith BROWER
50 Dean of O'Malley School of Business .... Dr. Donald GIBSON
53 Dean of Education & Health .... Dr. Karen NICHOLSON
54 Dean of Engineering .... Dr. Tim WARD
51 Dean of Sch Cont & Prof Studies .... Dr. Cheryl HARRISON
121 Director Ctr for Academic Success .... Ms. Marisa PASSAFIUME
81 Dean of Science .... Dr. Constantine THEODOSIOU
88 Dir of Specialized Resource Center .... Ms. Anne VACCARO
88 Dir Grad & Fellowship Advisement .... Vacant
123 Director of Graduate Admissions .... Ms. Suzana PAVISIC
88 Director of Transfer Admissions .... Mr. Troy COGBURN
88 Dir Comm Svcs & Outreach .... Ms. Marilyn CARTER-STEVENS
104 Assistant Director Study Abroad .... Ms. Erinn KEHOE
43 General Counsel .... Ms. Tamara BRITT
28 Director Equity/Diversity/Title IX .... Ms. Sheetal KALE
88 Sr Advisor Strategic Partnerships .... Mr. Robert WALSH
108 Dir Institutional Effectiveness .... Dr. Bridget MILLER
104 Director Study Abroad .... Dr. Ricardo DELLO BUONO

Manhattan School of Music (I)

130 Claremont Avenue, New York NY 10027-4631
County: New York FICE Identification: 002759
Unit ID: 192712
Telephone: (212) 749-2802 Carnegie Class: Spec-4-yr-Arts
FAX Number: (212) 749-5471 Calendar System: Semester
URL: www.msmnyc.edu
Established: 1917 Annual Undergrad Tuition & Fees: $47,300
Enrollment: 1,007 Coed
Affiliation or Control: Independent Non-Profit IRS Status: 501(c)3
Highest Offering: Doctorate
Accreditation: M

01 President .... Dr. James GANDRE
05 Executive VP and Provost .... Dr. Joyce GRIGGS
10 Sr VP and CFO .... Mr. Gary MEYER
111 VP for Advancement .... Ms. Susan MADDEN
26 VP for Media and Communications .... Mr. Jeff BREITHAUPT
84 Dean of Enrollment Management .... Ms. Amy A. ANDERSON
32 Dean of Students .... Dr. Monica CHRISTENSEN
15 VP for Human Relations & Admin .... Ms. Carol MATOS
106 Dean of Dist Learning & Rec Arts .... Ms. Christianne ORTO
100 Chief of Staff .... Ms. Alexa SMITH
20 Dean of Academic Operations .... Mr. Bryan GREANEY
06 Registrar .... Mr. Thomas ZARKOS
13 Chief Information Officer .... Mr. Ray MORALES
14 Assistant IT Director .... Mr. Seth JANNIFER
37 Director of Financial Aid .... Ms. Anna CHRISSOTIMOS
35 Director of Student Engagement .... Ms. Melanie DORSEY
39 Director of Residence Life .... Ms. Samantha TYMCHYN
31 Director of Educational Outreach .... Ms. Rebecca CHARNOW
29 Assoc Dir for Alumni Engagement .... Ms. Lauren FRANKOVICH
08 Director of Library Services .... Mr. Peter CALEB
102 AVP Advance/Inst/Individual Giving .... Mr. Edward SIEN
40 Campus Store Manager .... Ms. Katherine COPLAND
85 Director Intl Student Services .... Mr. Michael LOCKHART
88 Dir Ctr for Music Entrepreneurship .... Mr. Casey MOLIN-DUNN
88 Dean of Performance/Production Ops .... Mr. Henry VALORIS
21 Director of Accounting & Controller .... Ms. Susan FINK
18 Dir of Facilities & Campus Safety .... Mr. Luis PLAZA
04 Admin Asst to the President .... Ms. Courtney SAMS

Manhattanville College (J)

2900 Purchase Street, Purchase NY 10577-2132
County: Westchester FICE Identification: 002760
Unit ID: 192749
Telephone: (914) 694-2200 Carnegie Class: Masters/L
FAX Number: (914) 694-2386 Calendar System: Semester
URL: www.mville.edu
Established: 1841 Annual Undergrad Tuition & Fees: $38,820
Enrollment: 2,690 Coed
Affiliation or Control: Independent Non-Profit IRS Status: 501(c)3
Highest Offering: Doctorate
Accreditation: M, CAEP, CAEPN, IACBE

01 President .... Dr. Michael E. GEISLER
04 Exec Admin Asst to the President .... Ms. Deborah A. FALLONE
05 Int Provost/VP of Academic Affairs .... Dr. Louise H. FEROE
10 VP Finance/Administration .... Mr. Erik PAULSON
84 Vice Pres Admissions/Enrollment .... Mr. Peter BURNS
111 Int Vice Pres Inst Advancement .... Ms. Tracy H. MUIRHEAD
18 Director of Physical Plant .... Mr. Daniel HANNON
32 Vice Pres of Student Affairs .... Ms. Cindy L. PORTER
13 CIO/VP Digital Strategy & Planning .... Mr. Jim RUSSELL
107 Assoc Dean School of Prof Studies .... Ms. Laura PERSKY
53 Dean School of Education .... Dr. Shelley WEPNER
26 AVP for Communications & Marketing .... Ms. Cara CEA
06 Registrar .... Ms. Jeneen KELLY
08 Director of the Library .... Mr. Jeff ROSEDALE
37 Director of Financial Aid .... Mr. Robert GILMORE
38 Assoc Dean Stdnt Health/Counseling .... Ms. Melissa BOSTON
35 Dean of Students .... Ms. Sharlise SMITH-RODRIGUEZ
41 Director of Athletics .... Mr. Edward MANETTA
42 Actg Dir Ctr Religion/Soc Justice .... Ms. Nicole HYLTON-PATTERSON
36 Director Center for Career Devel .... Ms. Meghan MAKARCZUK
19 Director of Security .... Mr. Anthony HERRMANN
07 Director of Admissions .... Mr. Peter BURNS
15 Director of Human Resources .... Mr. Don DEAN
35 Asst Dir Student Involvement/Ldrshp ...... Mr. Alexander BARKLEY
96 Director of Purchasing .... Mr. Matthew HYLAND
104 Dir Intl Student Svcs/Study Abroad .... Ms. L.A ADAMS
23 Assoc Dn Student Health/Counseling .... Ms. Melissa BOSTON

Maria College of Albany (K)

700 New Scotland Avenue, Albany NY 12208-1798
County: Albany FICE Identification: 002763
Unit ID: 192785
Telephone: (518) 438-3111 Carnegie Class: Spec-4-yr-Other Health
FAX Number: (518) 438-7170 Calendar System: 4/1/4
URL: www.mariacollege.edu
Established: 1958 Annual Undergrad Tuition & Fees: $15,140
Enrollment: 855 Coed
Affiliation or Control: Independent Non-Profit IRS Status: 501(c)3
Highest Offering: Baccalaureate
Accreditation: M, ADNUR, NUR, OTA

01 President .... Dr. Thomas J. GAMBLE
05 Vice Pres Academic Administration ... Mr. Joseph M. MCDONALD
10 VP for Finance & Administration .... Mr. Joel NUDI
32 VP Student Life/Mission Integr .... Ms. Victoria L. BATTELL
111 Assoc VP Advancement .... Mr. Paul MCAVOY
37 Director Financial Aid .... Ms. Karen CONRAD
21 Director of Business Affairs .... Mrs. Frances BERNARD
06 Registrar/Dir Inst Research .... Ms. Kari BENNETT
07 Director of Admissions .... Mr. John RAMOSKA
08 Librarian .... Ms. Marisa GITTO
13 Director of Information Technology .... Ms. Robin DELORENZO
18 Superintendent Physical Plant .... Mr. Andrew PEREZ
36 Director Career Services .... Mr. Andrew LEDOUX
15 Chief Human Resources Officer .... Mr. Joel D. NUDI
20 Dean of College .... Dr. Anne JUNG

Marist College (L)

3399 North Road, Poughkeepsie NY 12601-1387
County: Dutchess FICE Identification: 002765
Unit ID: 192819
Telephone: (845) 575-3000 Carnegie Class: Masters/L
FAX Number: (845) 471-6213 Calendar System: Semester
URL: www.marist.edu
Established: 1929 Annual Undergrad Tuition & Fees: $39,600
Enrollment: 6,657 Coed
Affiliation or Control: Independent Non-Profit IRS Status: 501(c)3
Highest Offering: Doctorate
Accreditation: M, #ARCPA, CAATE, MT, @PTA, SPAA, SW

01 Interim President .... Dr. Dennis J. MURRAY
03 EVP/Chief Strategy/Innovation Ofcr ...... Dr. Geoffrey L. BRACKETT
05 Vice President for Academic Affairs ...... Dr. Thomas S. WERMUTH
84 VP Enrollment/Mktg & Communications ...... Mr. Sean P. KAYLOR
111 Vice President College Advancement .... Mr. Christopher M. DELGIORNO
13 VP Information Technology/CIO .... Mr. Michael CAPUTO
32 VP/Dean for Student Affairs .... Mrs. Deborah A. DICAPRIO
10 Vice President Business Affairs/CFO .... Mr. John P. PECCHIA
15 VP for Human Resources .... Mrs. Christina DANIELE
20 Assoc VP/Dean Academic Affairs .... Dr. John RITSCHDORFF
07 Asst VP Enroll Mgmt/Dean UG Admiss ... Mr. Kent W. RINEHART
123 Dean Graduate Admission .... Ms. Kelly HOLMES
35 Assoc Dean of Student Affairs .... Mr. Steve SANSOLA
43 College Counsel .... Ms. Sima Saran AHUJA

29 Executive Director Alumni Relations .... Ms. Amy K. WOODS
09 Director Inst Research & Planning ....Dr. Judith STODDARD
06 Assoc Dean Stdnt Acad Aff/Registrar ....Mrs. Judith IVANKOVIC
37 Exec Dir Student Financial Services ....Mr. Joseph R. WEGLARZ
08 Director of Library .... Ms. Becky ALBITZ
18 Director of Physical Plant ....Mr. Justin BUTWELL
26 Asst VP Marketing & Communications .... Mrs. Elisabeth W. TAVAREZ
96 Director of Purchasing ....Mr. Stephen J. KOCHIS
36 Director Career Services ....Dr. Mary O. JONES
19 Director of Safety & Security ....Mr. John BLAISDELL
39 Director of Housing & Resident Life ....Mrs. Sarah H. ENGLISH
41 Director of Athletics ....Mr. Timothy S. MURRAY
24 Director of Media & Instruct Tech ....Ms. Joey WALL
23 Director of Health Services ....Dr. Melissa SCHISKIE
38 Director of Counseling ....Dr. Naomi A. FERLEGER
42 Director Campus Ministry ....Bro. Francis E. KELLY
44 Director of Annual Giving ....Ms. Hannah ALLEY-KELLER
105 Director Web Services ....Vacant
50 Dean School of Management ....Mr. Larry G. SINGLETON
60 Dean School of Communication/Arts ....Dr. Lyn R. LEPRE
77 Dean School of Comp Sci/Mathematics ......Dr. Roger L. NORTON
49 Dean School of Liberal Arts ....Dr. Martin B. SHAFFER
81 Dean School of Science ....Dr. Linda SLATER
107 Dean School of Professional Pgms ....Dr. Daniel SZPIRO
83 Dean Sch of Social/Behavioral Sci .... Dr. Deborah GATINS
104 Dean International Programs ....Mr. John PETERS
101 Chief of Staff & Secy to Board ....Mrs. Emily V. SALAND
25 Director of Academic Grants ....Mrs. Donna S. BERGER
28 Diversity/Inclusion/Engagement Ofcr ....Vacant

Marymount Manhattan College (A)

221 E 71st Street, New York NY 10021-4597

County: New York FICE Identification: 002769
Unit ID: 192864

Telephone: (212) 517-0400 Carnegie Class: Bac-A&S
FAX Number: (212) 517-0541 Calendar System: Semester
URL: www.mmm.edu
Established: 1936 Annual Undergrad Tuition & Fees: $33,778
Enrollment: 2,150 Coed
Affiliation or Control: Independent Non-Profit IRS Status: 501(c)3
Highest Offering: Master's
Accreditation: M

01 President .... Dr. Kerry WALK
05 VP for Acad Aff/Dean of Faculty ....Dr. Sharon MEAGHER
32 VP Student Affairs ....Dr. Carol JACKSON
10 Vice Pres Admin & Finance ....Vacant
111 VP Institutional Advancement ....Vacant
84 VP for Enrollment Mgmt ....Mr. Todd HEILMAN
15 Associate VP for Human Resources .... Ms. Bree BULLINGHAM
45 Associate VP Strategic Initiatives .... Dr. Kathleen LEBESCO
21 Associate VP Admin & Controller .... Mr. Wayne SANTUCCI
20 AVP for Academic Administration ....Mr. Richard SHELDON
13 Chief Information Officer ....Ms. Dale HOCHSTEIN
28 Chief Diversity Off/Title IX Coord . Ms. Rebecca MATTIS-PINARD
36 Exec Dir of Career Svcs ....Ms. Robin E. NACKMAN
88 Assoc Controller for Financial Oper ....Mr. Jonathan MADOR
07 Dean of Admissions .... Mr. Christian ANDRADE
121 Asst VP and Dean of CAE .... Mr. Michael SALMON
88 Associate VP Enrollment Management .... Ms. Maria DEINNOCENTIIS
06 Registrar .... Ms. Regina CHAN
09 Dir Institutional Research ....Ms. Cheryl GOLDSTEIN
35 Dir of Student Dev and Activities ....Dr. Dayne HUTCHINSON
89 Asst Dean of Academic Advisement ....Ms. Melissa WEEKES
08 Director of the Library ....Mr. Brian ROCCO
22 Dir of Acad Access/Disability Srvs ....Ms. Diana NASH
38 Dir Counseling & Psychological Svcs .... Ms. Neda HAJIZEDAH
88 Dir of the Ctr for Acad Support .... Ms. Monica COLBERT
12 Dir of Bedford Hills College Prog .... Ms. Aileen BAUMGARTNER
96 Director of Administrative Services .... Ms. Maria MARZANO
114 Asst Controller for Recon/Reporting ....Ms. Rachel KATZ
19 Director of Campus Safety .... Mr. James CAMBRIA
26 Director of Multimedia Comm .... Ms. Carly LYNCH
35 Dean of Students .... Ms. Emmalyn YAMRICK
109 Exec Dir of Business Operations .... Ms. Diana ZAMBROTTA
102 Sr Dir Inst Giving/Advance Svcs .... Ms. Kayla MCCAFFREY
44 Sr Dir Indiv Giving/Donor Rel .... Ms. Lisha BODDEN
112 Director of Major Gifts/Parent Prog ....Ms. Rita MURRAY
39 Director of Residence Life .... Mr. Michael ZAKARIAN
04 Admin Assistant to the President ....Ms. Tunisia WRAGG

Mechon L'Hoyroa (B)

168 Maple Avenue, Monsey NY 10952

County: Rockland FICE Identification: 042615
Unit ID: 490328

Telephone: (845) 425-9565 Carnegie Class: Spec-4-yr-Faith
FAX Number: (845) 425-2094 Calendar System: Other
Established: 1990 Annual Undergrad Tuition & Fees: $8,500
Enrollment: 40 Male
Affiliation or Control: Jewish IRS Status: 501(c)3
Highest Offering: First Talmudic Degree
Accreditation: AIJS

01 President ....Vacant

Medaille College (C)

18 Agassiz Circle, Buffalo NY 14214-2695

County: Erie FICE Identification: 002777
Unit ID: 192925

Telephone: (716) 880-2000 Carnegie Class: Masters/L
FAX Number: (716) 884-0291 Calendar System: Semester
URL: www.medaille.edu
Established: 1875 Annual Undergrad Tuition & Fees: $29,500
Enrollment: 2,198 Coed
Affiliation or Control: Independent Non-Profit IRS Status: 501(c)3
Highest Offering: Doctorate
Accreditation: M, CACREP, CAEPT, CAHIIM, IACBE

01 President .... Dr. Kenneth M. MACUR
05 Vice President Academic Affairs .... Dr. Lori V. QUIGLEY
10 Vice President Business/Finance ....Mr. Robert S. MCDOW
30 Vice Pres for College Relations ....Mr. John P. CRAWFORD
07 VP Enroll Mgmt/Marketing/Admiss .Mr. Christopher P. LARUSSO
09 Director of Institutional Research ....Dr. Mary M. TODD
32 VP for Student Development .... Ms. Amy M. DEKAY
44 Dir of Major Gifts & Planned Giving .... Ms. Jeanine PURCELL
41 Athletic Director .... Ms. Amy DEKAY
36 Director Career Planning/Placement .... Ms. Carol CULLINAN
13 Chief Information Officer .... Mr. Robert D. CHYKA
06 Registrar ....Ms. Tracey KONGATS
08 Library Director ....Mr. Andrew YEAGER
37 Director Financial Aid ....Mr. James P. AYERS
15 Director of Human Resources ....Ms. Barbara J. BILOTTA
35 Director of Student Involvement .... Mr. Daniel P. PUCCIO
38 Director Counseling Services ....Ms. Rosalina B. RIZZO
19 Director of Campus Public Safety ....Ms. Debra D. KELLY
29 Coordinator of Alumni Relations ....Mr. John P. CRAWFORD

Medaille College Rochester Branch Campus (D)

1880 S Winston Road, Suite 1, Rochester NY 14618

Telephone: (585) 272-0030 Identification: 770140
Accreditation: &M

Memorial College of Nursing (E)

714 New Scotland, 111 Marian Hall, Albany NY 12208

County: Albany FICE Identification: 012203
Unit ID: 192961

Telephone: (518) 525-6850 Carnegie Class: Spec 2-yr-Health
FAX Number: (518) 525-6852 Calendar System: Semester
URL: www.sphp.com/memorial-college-of-nursing
Established: 1901 Annual Undergrad Tuition & Fees: $12,979
Enrollment: 124 Coed
Affiliation or Control: Independent Non-Profit IRS Status: 501(c)3
Highest Offering: Associate Degree
Accreditation: ADNUR

01 Acting Director .... Dr. Patricia CANNISTRACI
32 Director Student Services ....Ms. Angela COX
07 Admissions Coordinator ....Ms. Dalia NEGRON

† Relocated to Maria College of Albany Campus

Mercy College (F)

555 Broadway, Dobbs Ferry NY 10522-1189

County: Westchester FICE Identification: 002772
Unit ID: 193016

Telephone: (800) 637-2969 Carnegie Class: Masters/L
FAX Number: (914) 674-5978 Calendar System: Semester
URL: www.mercy.edu
Established: 1950 Annual Undergrad Tuition & Fees: $19,042
Enrollment: 9,506 Coed
Affiliation or Control: Independent Non-Profit IRS Status: 501(c)3
Highest Offering: Doctorate
Accreditation: M, #ARCPA, CAEP, CAEPN, EXSC, MT, NURSE, OT, OTA, PTA, SP, SW

01 President ....Mr. Timothy HALL
05 Provost & Vice Pres Acad Affairs .... Dr. Jose HERRERA
20 Associate Provost for Acad Affairs ....Dr. Lucretia MANN
32 Vice President of Student Affairs .... Mr. Kevin JOYCE
50 Dean School of Business ....Dr. Lloyd GIBSON
53 Interim Dean School of Education ....Dr. Eric MARTONE
83 Dean School Soc/Behavioral Sci .... Dr. Karol DEAN
76 Dean School Health/Natural Sci ....Dr. Joan TOGLIA
49 Interim Dean School Liberal Arts ....Mr. Stephen WARD
15 Exec Dir of Human Resources ....Ms. Anne GILMARTIN
11 VP Operations & Facilities ....Mr. Thomas SIMMONDS
07 VP of Admissions & Recruitment ....Mr. Adam CASTRO
10 Interim Chief Financial Officer ....Mr. Richard AKS
84 VP Enrollment Services ....Ms. Margaret MCGRAIL
111 Chief Advancement Officer ....Ms. Bernadette WADE
100 Chief of Staff ....Ms. Irene BUCKLEY
04 Exec Assistant Office of President .... Ms. Grace CREIGHTON
88 Director of Learning Assessment .... Ms. Victoria FERRARA
43 General Counsel ....Ms. Kristen BOWES
07 Executive Director of Admissions ....Mrs. Allison GURDINEER
09 Exec Dir Institutional Research ....Mr. Edward HARTWELL
39 Assistant Dean of Student Affairs ....Mr. Jason ALT
13 Chief Information Officer ....Mr. Daniel ZELEM
14 Director of Information Technology .... Mr. Todd PRATTELLA
06 Exec Director of Registrar .... Ms. Debra KENNEY
45 Asst VP of Inst Assess/Plng/Analy .... Ms. Jessica HABER
113 Sr Director of Student Accounts .... Ms. Felicia BRANDON
21 Controller .... Ms. Narda ROMERO
19 Exec Dir Safety & Emergency Mgmt ....Mr. Konrad MOTYKA
114 Exec Dir of Budgets & Planning .... Mr. Timothy LEVER
18 Dir Facilities Services Mgmt .... Mr. Thomas LAMERE
96 Director of Purchasing ....Ms. Patricia SABATINO
08 Director of Mercy College Libraries ....Mr. Mustafa SAKARYA
41 Director of Athletics .... Mr. Matt KILCULLEN
26 Director of Communications .... Ms. Jessica BAILY
30 Exec Director of Development ....Ms. Katherine COPPINGER
29 Director of Alumni Relations ....Ms. Alexis MCGRATH-ROTHENBERG
25 Dir Sponsored Programs .... Ms. Janet PARTENZA
104 Director Center Global Engagement ....Dr. Sheila GERSH
106 Director Online Learning ....Dr. Mary LOZINA
103 Exec Director of Career & Prof Dev ....Ms. Jill HART
101 Secretary of the Institution/Board .... Ms. Irene BUCKLEY
112 Major Gifts Officer ....Mrs. Christina BROCCOLI
88 AVP Marketing & Analytics ....Mr. Christian CONNELLY
23 Director Health & Wellness ....Ms. Colleen POWERS
38 Director Student Counseling Center .... Dr. Ori SHINAR

Mesivta of Eastern Parkway Rabbinical Seminary (G)

510 Dahill Road, Brooklyn NY 11218-5559

County: Kings FICE Identification: 009335
Unit ID: 193061

Telephone: (718) 438-1002 Carnegie Class: Spec-4-yr-Faith
FAX Number: (718) 438-2591 Calendar System: Semester
Established: 1947 Annual Undergrad Tuition & Fees: $9,450
Enrollment: 32 Male
Affiliation or Control: Independent Non-Profit IRS Status: 501(c)3
Highest Offering: Second Talmudic Degree
Accreditation: RABN

01 President ....Rabbi Issac HEIMOVITZ
32 Dean of Students ....Rabbi Shlomo Z. EPSTEIN
37 Director of Student Financial Aid ....Rabbi Ira LIBERMAN
46 Director of Research ....Rabbi Hersch BASCH
10 Chief Fiscal Officer ....Rabbi Joseph HALBERSTADT

Mesivta Tifereth Jerusalem of America (H)

145 E Broadway, New York NY 10002-6301

County: New York FICE Identification: 003974
Unit ID: 193070

Telephone: (212) 964-2830 Carnegie Class: Spec-4-yr-Faith
FAX Number: (212) 349-5213 Calendar System: Semester
Established: 1907 Annual Undergrad Tuition & Fees: $11,500
Enrollment: 69 Male
Affiliation or Control: Independent Non-Profit IRS Status: 501(c)3
Highest Offering: Second Talmudic Degree
Accreditation: RABN

01 President & Dean Faculties ....Rabbi David FEINSTEIN
06 Registrar .... Chana YAMPOLSKY
37 Director Student Financial Aid ....E. GOLD

Mesivta Torah Vodaath Seminary (I)

425 E Ninth Street, Brooklyn NY 11218-5299

County: Kings FICE Identification: 007264
Unit ID: 193052

Telephone: (718) 941-8000 Carnegie Class: Spec-4-yr-Faith
FAX Number: (718) 941-8032 Calendar System: Semester
Established: 1918 Annual Undergrad Tuition & Fees: $11,960
Enrollment: 366 Male
Affiliation or Control: Independent Non-Profit IRS Status: 501(c)3
Highest Offering: Second Talmudic Degree
Accreditation: AIJS, RABN

01 Dean ....Rabbi Yisroel REISMAN
03 Executive Director ....Rabbi Yitzchok GOTTDIENER
06 Registrar ....Rabbi Shmuel KUTTEN
33 Dean of Men ....Rabbi Elya KATZ
31 Director Community Services ....Mr. Shraga WERNER

Metropolitan College of New York (J)

60 West Street, New York NY 10006

County: New York FICE Identification: 009769
Unit ID: 190114

Telephone: (212) 343-1234 Carnegie Class: Masters/L
FAX Number: (212) 343-7399 Calendar System: Semester
URL: www.metropolitan.edu
Established: 1964 Annual Undergrad Tuition & Fees: $19,454
Enrollment: 1,113 Coed
Affiliation or Control: Independent Non-Profit IRS Status: 501(c)3
Highest Offering: Master's
Accreditation: M, ACBSP, CAEPN

01 President .... Dr. Joanne PASSARO
10 Interim VP Finance & Admin/CFO ... Ms. Michelle BLANKENSHIP
05 Chief Academic Officer ....Dr. Tilokie DEPOO
84 Vice Pres for Enrollment Management ....Dr. Collette GARRITY
12 Exec Director of MCNY Bronx Campus ....Mr. John EDWARDS
07 Interim Director of Admissions ....Mr. Steebo VARGHESE
80 Dean School Public Affairs & Admin .... Dr. Humphrey CROOKENDALE
50 Dean School for Business .... Dr. Tilokie DEPOO
88 Interim Dean ACSHSE ....Dr. Joanne ARDOVINI
32 Dean of Students ....Ms. Clotilde IBARRA
37 Director of Financial Aid ....Mr. Douane CAMPBELL
06 Registrar ....Ms. Noreen SMITH

08 Director of Library Services .... Ms. Kate ADLER
09 Dir Institutional Rsrch/Assessment .... Mr. Anthony WILLIAMS
15 Director Human Resources .... Ms. Judith SANTIAGO
30 Chief Development Officer .... Ms. Mary MARTEL
26 Chief Public Relations Officer .... Ms. Tina GEORGIOU
13 Chief Information Officer .... Mr. Adrian SMITH
113 Bursar .... Mr. Taurean KENNEDY
04 Exec Assistant to the President .... Ms. Isabel CABRERA
29 Director Alumni Relations .... Ms. Tina GEORGIOU
36 Exec Dir College-Wide Career Dev .... Mr. John EDWARDS

Mildred Elley (A)

855 Central Avenue, Albany NY 12206
County: Albany FICE Identification: 022195
Unit ID: 193201
Telephone: (518) 786-0855 Carnegie Class: Assoc/HVT-High Trad
FAX Number: (518) 786-0898 Calendar System: Other
URL: www.mildred-elley.edu
Established: 1917 Annual Undergrad Tuition & Fees: $12,934
Enrollment: 521 Coed
Affiliation or Control: Proprietary IRS Status: Proprietary
Highest Offering: Associate Degree
Accreditation: ABHES

01 Chairwoman of the Board .... Ms. Faith A. TAKES

Mildred Elley-New York City (B)

25 Broadway, 16th Floor, New York NY 10004
Telephone: (212) 380-9004 Identification: 770747
Accreditation: ABHES

Mirrer Yeshiva Central Institute (C)

1795 Ocean Parkway, Brooklyn NY 11223-2010
County: Kings FICE Identification: 004798
Unit ID: 193247
Telephone: (718) 645-0536 Carnegie Class: Spec-4-yr-Faith
FAX Number: (718) 645-9251 Calendar System: Semester
Established: 1947 Annual Undergrad Tuition & Fees: $8,570
Enrollment: 183 Male
Affiliation or Control: Independent Non-Profit IRS Status: 501(c)3
Highest Offering: Second Talmudic Degree
Accreditation: RABN

00 Chancellor .... Rabbi Avrohom Yaakov NELKENBAUM
01 President and Dean .... Rabbi Osher KALMANOWITZ
05 Vice President & Dean .... Rabbi Asher BERENBAUM
33 Dean of Men .... Rabbi Esrael ERLANGER
03 Executive Director .... Rabbi Pinchas HECHT
06 Registrar-Administrator .... Mrs. Devorah BERENBAUM
08 Director of the Library .... Rabbi Aaron SAPOZNICK
38 Director of Guidance .... Rabbi Yisroel FISHMAN
37 Financial Aid Director .... Mrs. Rachel BERENBAUM

Mohawk Valley Community College (D)

1101 Sherman Drive, Utica NY 13501-5394
County: Oneida FICE Identification: 002871
Unit ID: 193283
Telephone: (315) 792-5400 Carnegie Class: Assoc/HT-Mix Trad/Non
FAX Number: (315) 792-5666 Calendar System: Semester
URL: www.mvcc.edu
Established: 1946 Annual Undergrad Tuition & Fees (In-District): $5,266
Enrollment: 6,506 Coed
Affiliation or Control: State/Local IRS Status: 501(c)3
Highest Offering: Associate Degree
Accreditation: M, ADNUR, CAHIIM, COARC, RAD, SURTEC

01 President .... Dr. Randall J. VAN WAGONER
04 Assistant to the President .... Ms. Gloria KAROL
88 Exec Dir Org Culture & Wellness .... Ms. Jill HEINTZ
09 Dir Institutional Research/Analysis .... Ms. Marie MIKNAVICH
05 Vice Pres Learning/Academic Affairs .... Mr. Lewis J. KAHLER
88 Asst Vice Pres Bus/Educ/Lib Arts .... Vacant
53 Assoc Dean Educ & Lang Studies .... Ms. Julie DEWAN
88 Asst Vice Pres STEM/Health/Soc Sci .... Dr. Kathleen LINAKER
54 Assoc Dean Phys Sci/Engr/App Tech .... Mr. Timothy THOMAS
57 Assoc Dean Art .... Mr. Todd BEHRENDT
77 Assoc Dean Bus/Cyber/Comp Sci .... Mr. Jake MIHEVC
81 Assoc Dean Math & Natural Sci .... Dr. Robert WOODROW
79 Assoc Dean Humanities .... Mr. Jim ROBERTS
76 Assoc Dean Health Professions .... Ms. Melissa COPPERWHEAT
83 Assoc Dean Soc Sci & Public Svc .... Mr. Mark MONTGOMERY
88 Dean Emergency Prep & Public Svc .... Ms. Marianne BUTTENSCHON
08 Director College Libraries .... Mr. Stephen FRISBEE
88 Exec Dean Academic Dev & Innovation .... Mr. James LYNCH
10 Vice Pres Administrative Services .... Mr. Thomas SQUIRES
32 VP Student Affairs/Dean of Students .... Ms. Stephanie C. REYNOLDS
84 Assoc Dean Enrollment & Advisement .... Mrs. Jennifer DEWEERTH
36 Assoc Dean Development & Transition .... Mr. James MAIO
39 Assoc Dean Student & Residence Life .... Mr. Dennis GIBBONS
103 Assoc VP of Workforce Development .... Ms. Franca ARMSTRONG
111 VP Cmty Devel/Exec Dir MVCC Found .... Mr. Frank DUROSS
44 Dir of Donor & Resource Development .... Ms. Deanna FERRO
96 Coord Expend/Fixed Asset Procure .... Ms. Joyce PALMER
13 Exec Dir of Information Technology .... Mr. Paul KATCHMAR
88 Dir Ctr Community/Economic Dev .... Ms. Kristen SKOBLA
15 Exec Director of Human Resources .... Mrs. Kimberly EVANS-DAME
26 Director Marketing/Communications .... Mr. Alen SMAJIC
07 Director of Admissions .... Mr. Daniel IANNO
37 Director of Financial Aid .... Mr. Michael PEDE
06 Dir of Student Records/Registrar .... Mrs. Rosemary V. SPETKA
18 Dir of Facilities and Operations .... Mr. Michael MCHARRIS
19 Exec Dir Pub Safety/Emergency Mgmt .... Mr. David AMICO
21 Business Office Controller .... Mr. Brian MOLINARO
41 Athletic Director .... Mr. Gary BROADHURST

Mohawk Valley Community College Rome Campus (E)

1101 Floyd Avenue, Rome NY 13440
Telephone: (315) 339-3470 Identification: 770141
Accreditation: &M

Molloy College (F)

1000 Hempstead Avenue, PO Box 5002, Rockville Centre NY 11571-5002
County: Nassau FICE Identification: 002775
Unit ID: 193292
Telephone: (516) 323-3000 Carnegie Class: Masters/L
FAX Number: N/A Calendar System: 4/1/4
URL: www.molloy.edu
Established: 1955 Annual Undergrad Tuition & Fees: $31,490
Enrollment: 4,980 Coed
Affiliation or Control: Independent Non-Profit IRS Status: 501(c)3
Highest Offering: Doctorate
Accreditation: M, CACREP, CAEP, CAEPN, COARC, CVT, MUS, NMT, NURSE, SP, SW

01 President .... Dr. Drew BOGNER
05 VP Academic Affairs/Dean of Faculty .... Dr. Ann Z. BRANCHINI
10 Vice Pres for Finance & Treasurer .... Ms. Susan WILLIAMS
84 Vice Pres Enrollment Management .... Ms. Linda ALBANESE
111 VP for Advancement .... Mr. Edward J. THOMPSON
32 VP for Student Affairs .... Dr. Janine BRANCINI
45 VP Tech & Inst Effectiveness .... Mr. Michael TORRES
42 VP for Mission & Ministry .... Ms. Catherine MUSCENTE
30 Dir Development & Special Projects .... Ms. Angela ZIMMERMAN
37 Director Student Financial Services .... Ms. Debra OCONNOR
36 Director of Career Development .... Ms. Mary BROSNAN
41 Director of Athletics .... Ms. Susan CASSIDY
07 Asst VP for Enrollment Management .... Ms. Marguerite LANE
37 Director of Financial Aid .... Mrs. Ana C. LOCKWARD
21 Asst VP for Finance .... Ms. Barbara CALISSI
06 Registrar .... Ms. Susan FORTMAN
09 Sr Dir Institutional Effectiveness .... Ms. Christina CAPPELLANO
15 Asst VP for HR & Title IX Coord .... Ms. Lisa MILLER
18 Asst VP for Facilities .... Mr. James MULTARI
26 Asst VP of Marketing & PR .... Mr. Ken YOUNG
29 Director of Alumni Relations .... Ms. Mary Jane REILLY
19 Director of Public Safety .... Mr. Brian CONNORS
85 Director of International Education .... Vacant
105 Director Web Technologies .... Vacant
20 Asst VP for Academic Affairs .... Dr. Barbara T. SCHMIDT
13 Sr Director of IT .... Mr. Michael OLIVO
88 Director of Networking & Infra .... Mr. Sean LAURIE
08 Head Librarian .... Ms. Judith BRINK-DRESCHER
100 Chief of Staff .... Ms. Diane K. FORNIERI
106 Dean Innovative Delivery Methods .... Ms. Amy GAIMARO
04 Executive Asst to the President .... Ms. Ann Marie LUONGO

Monroe College (G)

2501 Jerome Avenue, Bronx NY 10468-5407
County: Bronx FICE Identification: 004799
Unit ID: 193308
Telephone: (718) 933-6700 Carnegie Class: Masters/L
FAX Number: (718) 295-5861 Calendar System: Semester
URL: www.monroecollege.edu
Established: 1933 Annual Undergrad Tuition & Fees: $15,428
Enrollment: 6,310 Coed
Affiliation or Control: Proprietary IRS Status: Proprietary
Highest Offering: Master's
Accreditation: M, ACBSP, ACFEI, ADNUR, NUR, PNUR

01 President .... Marc M. JEROME
03 Senior Vice President .... David DIMOND
05 SVP Academic of Affairs .... Dr. Karenann CARTY
21 Controller .... Olesia TIAGI
84 Senior Vice President .... Anthony ALLEN
26 Executive Director Public Affairs .... Jacqueline RUEGGER
58 Dean of Graduate Programs .... Alex CANALS
12 Vice President Academic Affairs .... Carol GENESE
86 Asst Vice Pres Governmental Affairs .... Dr. Donald E. SIMON
108 Asst VP Inst Research & Effective .... Dr. Edward S. SCHNEIDERMAN
26 Executive Director of Marketing .... Lauren ROSENTHAL
06 Registrar .... Abigail THORPE
09 Dir Institutional Research .... Peter NWAKEZE
07 Dean Admissions NR Campus .... Michael NIEDZWIECKI
21 AVP Student Financial Services .... Daniel SHARON
113 Bursar .... Scott STERN
35 Dean of Intl Student Services .... Mark SONNENSTEIN
07 Dean of International Admissions .... Gersom LOPEZ
07 Vice President Online Admissions .... Craig PATRICK
37 Director Student Financial Aid .... Calette FAGAN-MURDOCK
36 VP Corporate & Community Outreach .... Pamela DELLAPORTA
08 Director of Library Services BX .... Christine ARTIS
08 Director of Library Services NR .... Tom GORDON
39 Director of Residential Life .... Romario DACOSTA
29 Director of Alumni Relations .... Leslie JEROME
13 Chief Info Technology Officer (CIO) .... Terrance MCGOWAN
04 Executive Assistant to President .... Jennifer NACCARI
15 Director of Human Resources .... Kerry MCLAUGHLIN
19 Director of Public Safety .... Clifford HOLLINGSWORTH
41 Athletic Director .... Luis MELENDEZ

Monroe Community College (H)

1000 E Henrietta Road, Rochester NY 14623-5780
County: Monroe FICE Identification: 002872
Unit ID: 193326
Telephone: (585) 292-2000 Carnegie Class: Assoc/HT-Mix Trad/Non
FAX Number: (585) 427-2749 Calendar System: Semester
URL: www.monroecc.edu
Established: 1961 Annual Undergrad Tuition & Fees (In-District): $5,336
Enrollment: 12,907 Coed
Affiliation or Control: State/Local IRS Status: 501(c)3
Highest Offering: Associate Degree
Accreditation: M, ADNUR, CAHIIM, DH, EMT, MLTAD, RAD, SURGT

01 President .... Dr. Anne M. KRESS
05 Provost & VP Academic Svcs .... Dr. Andrea C. WADE
84 Assoc VP Enrollment Mgmt .... Ms. Christine CASALINUOVO-ADAMS
32 Vice President Student Services .... Dr. Lloyd A. HOLMES
10 CFO and VP Administrative Svcs .... Mr. Hezekiah N. SIMMONS
103 VP Econ Dev/Workforce Svc .... Mr. Todd M. OLDHAM
102 Exec Director MCC Foundation .... Ms. Gretchen D. WOOD
12 Exec Dean Downtown Campus .... Dr. Joel L. FRATER
35 Assoc Vice Pres Student Services .... Mr. John J. DELATE
13 Asst VP/CIO Educational Tech Svcs .... Ms. Eileen M. WIRLEY
18 Assoc Vice Pres Facilities .... Mr. Blaine D. GRINDLE
88 Assoc Vice Pres Instructional Svc .... Mr. Terrance KEYS
20 Assoc Vice Pres Academic Services .... Ms. Kimberley COLLINS
37 Director Financial Aid Compliance .... Mr. Jerome S. ST. CROIX
09 Director Institutional Research .... Mr. William DIXON
08 Director ETS Libraries .... Ms. Katherine E. GHIDIU
36 Director Career & Veteran Services .... Ms. Michelle P. MAYO
21 Assoc Vice President Admin Svcs .... Mr. Darrell K. JACHIM-MOORE
28 Chief Diversity Officer .... Dr. Calvin J. GANTT
06 Director Registrar & Records .... Ms. Elizabeth R. RIPTON
30 Director of Development .... Mr. Mark J. PASTORELLA
38 Dir Counseling & Disability Svcs .... Ms. Aubrey ZAMIARA
19 Director Public Safety .... Mr. Melvin (Tony) A. PEREZ
41 Director Athletics .... Mr. Aaron M. BOUYEA
25 Director Grants .... Ms. Remegia A. MITCHELL
35 Director of Student Life .... Ms. Elizabeth J. STEWART
23 Director of Health Services .... Ms. Jacqueline M. CARSON
21 Controller .... Mr. Michael G. QUINN
79 Dean Humanities & Social Services .... Mr. Michael JACOBS
81 Dean STEM and Health .... Ms. Margaret I. KAMINSKY
88 Dean Academic Foundations .... Ms. Medea RAMBISH
19 Dean Public Safety Training Ctr .... Mr. Michael S. KARNES
35 Director Student Svcs DC .... Ms. Kimberly F. DELARGE
20 Dean Acad Svcs DC .... Dr. Kimberly MCKINSEY-MABRY
15 Asst to President HR/Affirm Act Ofc .... Ms. Melissa A. FINGAR
40 Manager Bookstore .... Ms. Charlene SUTER
22 Director Educ Opportunity Program .... Ms. Brenda A. SMITH
88 Director Advise/Transfer Services .... Ms. Marlene A. FINE
43 Legal Counsel .... Vacant
88 Dir Financial Aid Opers .... Ms. Melissa M. JARKOWSKI
96 Director of Purchasing .... Mr. Patrick M. BATES
39 Director Housing/Residence Life .... Ms. Jamia DANZY
04 Executive Asst to President .... Ms. Sheila M. STRONG
07 Director of Admissions .... Ms. Sarah HAGREEN
101 Secy to the Board of Trustees/Pres .... Ms. Linda M. HALL
108 Asst Director Assess and Curriculum .... Dr. Susan L. HALL
29 Coord Alumni & Annual Giving .... Ms. Karen A. SHAW
45 Director Institutional Planning .... Ms. Valarie L. AVALONE
90 Assoc Dir Comm and Network Services .... Mr. James F. CLEMENT
86 Asst to the Pres Govt/Cmty Rels .... Mr. Clayton W. JONES

Montefiore School of Nursing (I)

53 Valentine Street, Mount Vernon NY 10550
County: Westchester FICE Identification: 022178
Unit ID: 193380
Telephone: (914) 361-6221 Carnegie Class: Not Classified
FAX Number: (914) 665-7047 Calendar System: Semester
URL: www.montefioreschoolofnursing.org
Established: 2014 Annual Undergrad Tuition & Fees: $12,076
Enrollment: N/A Coed
Affiliation or Control: Independent Non-Profit IRS Status: 501(c)3
Highest Offering: Associate Degree
Accreditation: ADNUR

05 Dean .... Dr. Rebecca GREER
07 Director of Admissions/Registrar .... Chanelle HYDE

Mount Saint Mary College (J)

330 Powell Avenue, Newburgh NY 12550-3412
County: Orange FICE Identification: 002778
Unit ID: 193353
Telephone: (845) 561-0800 Carnegie Class: Masters/M
FAX Number: (845) 562-6762 Calendar System: Semester
URL: www.msmc.edu
Established: 1959 Annual Undergrad Tuition & Fees: $31,118
Enrollment: 2,365 Coed

Affiliation or Control: Independent Non-Profit IRS Status: 501(c)3
Highest Offering: Master's
Accreditation: M, CAEP, CAEPN, IACBE, NURSE

Code	Title	Name
01	President	Dr. Jason N. ADSIT
05	Vice President for Academic Affairs	Dr. Michael OLIVETTE
10	Vice Pres Finance & Admin/Treasurer	Mr. Art GLASS
111	Vice Pres for College Advancement	Mrs. Nikki KHURANA-BAUGH
32	Vice President for Students	Mrs. Elaine O'GRADY
84	Dean of Admissions	Mrs. Susana BRISCOE-ALBA
35	Dean of Students	Vacant
38	Asst Dean of Support Services	Dr. Orin STRAUCHLER
20	Asst Vice Pres Academic Affairs	Dr. Yasmine L. KALKSTEIN
06	Registrar	Ms. Jannelle HAUG
07	Director of Admissions	Ms. Eileen BARDNEY
08	Director of the Library	Mrs. Barbara W. PETRUZZELLI
37	Director of Financial Aid	Ms. Jacqueline PEREZ
09	Asst VP of Inst Research/CDO	Mr. Ryan WILLIAMS
15	Director of Human Resources	Mrs. Sharnie CANARY
42	Chaplain	Fr. Gregoire J. FLUET
35	Director of Student Activities	Ms. Barbara MULLIGAN
39	Exec Dir of Operations and Housing	Mr. Michael O'KEEFE
29	Director of Alumni Affairs	Ms. Michelle A. IACUESSA
41	Director of Athletics & Recreation	Ms. Jessica MUSHEL
36	Director of the Career Center	Mrs. Kathleen O'KEEFE
13	Chief Information Officer	Mr. Dennis RUSH
96	Purchasing Manager	Mr. Brian MOORE
106	Director of Online Learning	Ms. Kristen DELLASALA
39	Director of Residence Life	Ms. Maxine MONROE
18	Exec Director of Facilities & Space	Ms. Maryann PILON
26	Exec Dir of Marketing/Communication	Mr. Dean DIMARZO
04	Executive Asst to the President	Ms. Barbara CONNOLLY
104	Study Abroad Advisor	Ms. Ingrid MORALES
19	Director Security/Safety	Mr. Matthew BYRNE
44	Director Annual Giving	Ms. Margaret TREACY
66	Dean School of Nursing	Dr. Susan LAROCCO
88	Asst to Pres Mission Integration	Dr. Charles ZOLA

Nassau Community College (A)

1 Education Drive, Garden City NY 11530-6793
County: Nassau FICE Identification: 002873
Unit ID: 193478
Telephone: (516) 572-7501 Carnegie Class: Assoc/HT-High Trad
FAX Number: (516) 572-7750 Calendar System: Semester
URL: www.ncc.edu
Established: 1959 Annual Undergrad Tuition & Fees (In-District): $5,880
Enrollment: 19,059 Coed
Affiliation or Control: State/Local IRS Status: 501(c)3
Highest Offering: Associate Degree
Accreditation: M, ADNUR, COARC, FUSER, MLTAD, PTAA, RTT, SURGT

Code	Title	Name
01	President	Dr. Jermaine F. WILLIAMS
05	Interim VP Academic Affairs	Dr. Valerie H. COLLINS
18	VP Facilities Management	Dr. Joseph V. MUSCARELLA
10	VP Finance/CFO	Vacant
32	VP Academic Student Services	Ms. Maria P. CONZATTI
111	VP Institutional Advancement	Vacant
22	Assoc VP Equity/Inclusion & AA/CDO	Dr. Craig J. WRIGHT
43	General Counsel	Ms. Donna M. HAUGEN
103	Asst Vice Pres Workforce Devel	Dr. Janet CARUSO
21	Treasurer	Ms. Lisa HAHN
88	Asst VP Maintenance/Operations	Mr. Robert FOLEY
15	Associate VP Human Resources	Ms. Dorlena DUNBAR
113	Assoc VP Student Financial Affairs	Ms. Sandra V. FRIEDMAN
46	AVP Inst Effectiveness & Strat Plng	Dr. John D. OSAE-KWAPONG
96	Director Procurement	Mr. Phillip CAPPELLO
35	Dean of Students	Ms. Charmian SMITH
79	Dean Arts & Humanities	Ms. Melanie HAMMER
97	Acting Dean Gen Educ & Soc Sciences	Ms. Genette ALVAREZ-ORTIZ
81	Acting Dean Math & Science	Mr. Thomas FERNANDEZ
66	Dean Nursing & Health Sciences	Dr. Kenya BEARD
107	Interim Dean Professional Studies	Dr. Jerry KORNBLUTH
37	Director Financial Aid	Ms. Patricia NOREN
07	Dean of Admissions	Mr. David FOLLICK
25	Asst VP Sponsored Programs	Mr. Edmund KOEPPEL
16	Asst VP HR Operations	Ms. Deborah REED-SEGRETI
88	Asst VP Design & Construction	Ms. Carol FRIEDMAN
106	Asst VP Distance Education	Ms. Deborah SPIRO
51	Associate Dean Lifelong Learning	Ms. Elizabeth HAWLEY
88	Asst VP Labor Relations	Ms. Laurie PEZZULLO
26	Interim Dir Marketing/Communication	Ms. Charmian SMITH
08	Chairperson Library	Ms. Christine FARADAY
41	Director Athletics/PED	Ms. Kerri-Ann MCTIERNAN
06	Registrar	Mr. Chester BARKAN
19	Director Public Safety	Mr. Martin RODDINI
23	Coordinator Student Health Services	Ms. Margaret MCGOVERN
121	Director Academic Advisement	Ms. Amanda FOX
13	Asst VP/CIO	Mr. Richard LAWLESS
102	Executive Dir NCC Foundation	Ms. Joy DEDONATO
04	Exec Asst to Pres/Board of Trustees	Ms. Anne E. BRANDI
112	Director Administration & Benefits	Ms. Nardos HAMILTON
09	Asst Dir Institutional Effectivenes	Ms. Tina S. WYNDER
85	Acting Dean International Education	Ms. Rosemary ORTLIEB

Nazareth College of Rochester (B)

4245 East Avenue, Rochester NY 14618-3790
County: Monroe FICE Identification: 002779
Unit ID: 193584
Telephone: (585) 389-2525 Carnegie Class: Masters/L
FAX Number: (585) 586-2452 Calendar System: Semester
URL: www.naz.edu
Established: 1924 Annual Undergrad Tuition & Fees: $34,505
Enrollment: 2,900 Coed
Affiliation or Control: Independent Non-Profit IRS Status: 501(c)3
Highest Offering: Doctorate
Accreditation: M, ART, MT, MUS, NURSE, OT, PTA, SP, SW

Code	Title	Name
01	President	Mr. Daan BRAVEMAN
04	Executive Assistant to President	Ms. Cathleen M. STEVENS
05	Vice President Academic Affairs	Dr. Andrea TALENTINO
111	Vice Pres Institutional Advancement	Ms. Kelly GAGAN
10	Vice President Finance & Admin	Mr. Patrick RICHEY
84	Vice Pres Enrollment & Student Exp	Ms. Meaghan ARENA
28	Vice President Diversity/Inclusion	Dr. Diane ARIZA
29	Director of Alumni Relations	Ms. Donna BORGUS
15	Assoc VP Human Resources	Mrs. JoEllen PINKHAM
20	Asst VP Academic Affairs	Dr. Lisa DURANT JONES
06	Registrar	Ms. Alison TEETER
37	Director Student Financial Aid	Ms. Janice SCHEUTZOW
26	Director Marketing & Communications	Ms. Elizabeth CRONIN
13	Director Information Tech Svcs	Ms. Karen KUPPINGER
08	Director of Library	Ms. Catherine DOYLE
19	Director of Security	Ms. Terri STEWART
39	Director of Campus Life	Ms. Carey BACKMAN
41	Director of Athletics	Mr. Peter G. BOTHNER
42	Director Center for Spirituality	Mr. Jamie FAZIO
36	Director of Career Services	Mr. Michael D. KAHL
18	Director Buildings/Grounds	Mr. Peter LANA
09	Director of Institutional Research	Dr. Nicholas LAMENDOLA
23	Director of Health Services	Ms. Susan QUINN
121	Director of Academic Advisement	Ms. Linda SEARING
88	Director of the Arts Center	Ms. Rita J. MANNELLI
113	Bursar	Mr. John GARBE
49	Dean of Col of Arts and Sciences	Dr. Dianne OLIVER
76	Dean School of Health & Human Svcs	Dr. Brigid NOONAN
53	Dean School of Education	Dr. Kathleen DABOLL-LAVOIE
50	Dean Sch of Business & Leadership	Dr. Kenneth RHEA
88	Exec Dir of Ctr International Educ	Dr. Nevan FISHER
88	Dir of Center for Service Learning	Dr. David STEITZ
89	Dir Stdnt Transition/First Year Ctr	Mr. Andrew MORRIS
96	Director of Purchasing	Ms. Joanne FITZGERALD
88	Dir Center for Civic Engagement	Ms. Nuala BOYLE
123	Dir Graduate Admissions/Transfer	Ms. Judith G. BAKER
86	Director Government Relations	Ms. Mary Kay BISHOP

The New School (C)

66 W 12th Street, New York NY 10011-8603
County: New York FICE Identification: 020662
Unit ID: 193654
Telephone: (212) 229-5600 Carnegie Class: DU-Higher
FAX Number: N/A Calendar System: Semester
URL: www.newschool.edu
Established: 1919 Annual Undergrad Tuition & Fees: $49,064
Enrollment: 10,389 Coed
Affiliation or Control: Independent Non-Profit IRS Status: 501(c)3
Highest Offering: Doctorate
Accreditation: M, ART, CLPSY, SPAA

Code	Title	Name
01	President	Dr. David VAN ZANDT
100	Chief of Staff to President	Ms. Deborah BOGOSIAN
04	Executive Assistant to President	Ms. Lindsey WARFORD
05	Provost and Chief Academic Officer	Mr. Tim MARSHALL
48	Exec Dean Parsons School for Design	Dr. Rachel SCHREIBER
82	Exec Dean School for Public Engage	Dr. Mary WATSON
64	Exec Dean Perf Arts and Dean Mannes	Mr. Richard KESSLER
83	Dean New School for Social Research	Dr. William MILBERG
49	Dean Eugene Lang College	Dr. Stephanie BROWNER
12	Dean Parsons Paris	Ms. Florence LECLERC-DICKLER
51	Sr VP and Dean Open Campus	Dr. Helen WUSSOW
84	Chief Enrollment & Success Officer	Mr. Donald RESNICK
88	Sr VP Corporate Partnerships	Ms. Deborah GIBB
11	Chief Operating Officer	Mr. Tokumbo SHOBOWALE
30	Chief Development Officer	Mr. Mark GIBBEL
26	Chief Marketing Officer	Ms. Anne ADRIANCE
15	Chief Legal & Human Resource Ofcr	Mr. Jerry CUTLER
32	Sr VP for Student Success	Ms. Michelle RELYEA
28	Sr VP for Social Justice	Ms. Maya WILEY
13	Sr VP & Chief Information Officer	Mr. Lin ZHOU
10	VP Finance/Business & Treasurer	Mr. Steve STABILE
88	VP Buildings	Ms. Lia GARTNER
20	Dep Provost & Sr VP Academic Affs	Dr. Bryna SANGER
20	Vice Provost Acad Planning Admin	Ms. Jin KIM
88	VP Transdisciplinary Initiative	Dr. Jamer HUNT
46	Vice Provost Research	Dr. Michael SCHOBER
88	Sr Vice Pres Global Partnerships	Ms. Carol KIM
07	VP Strat Enrollment Mgmt	Vacant
88	Assoc Dean/Dean Fashion	Mr. Burak CAKMAK
88	Assoc Dean/Dean Milano School	Dr. John CLINTON
88	Assc Dn/Dean Art/Design Hist/Theory	Dr. Rhonda GARELICK
88	Assoc Dean/Dean Art/Media & Tech	Ms. Anne GAINES
48	Assoc Dean/Dean Constructed Envir	Mr. Robert KIRKBRIDE
88	Assoc Dean/Dean Media Studies	Mr. Vladan NIKOLIC
48	Assoc Dean/Dean Design Strategies	Ms. Jane PIRONE
88	Assoc Dean/Dean Undergrad Stds	Vacant
88	Assoc Dean/Dean School of Drama	Mr. Pippin PARKER
64	Assoc Dean/Dean School of Jazz	Mr. Keller COKER
88	Director Creative Writing	Mr. Luis JARAMILLO
20	Assoc Provost Faculty Affairs	Dr. Eleni LITT
09	Assoc Provost Inst Rsrch	Dr. Paula MAAS
108	Assoc Provost Inst Effect & Accred	Dr. Michaela ROME
25	Assoc Provost Research	Mr. David NGO
121	Assoc VP Student Success	Dr. Monique RINERE
124	Assoc VP Student Success	Ms. Ann Marie KLOTZ
06	Assoc VP & Registrar	Ms. Rebecca HUNTER
27	Assoc VP Strategic Marketing	Ms. Lisa PRESTON
35	Asst VP and Dean of Students	Mr. Kevin WILLIAMS
88	Assoc VP Foundation Technology	Mr. Chris BREZIL
21	Asst VP & Controller	Ms. Natalie PRESSEY
114	Asst VP Budget & Planning	Ms. Loretta FERRARI
14	Senior Director Operations (IT)	Ms. Jennifer SMITH
16	Asst VP Human Resources	Mr. Irwin KROOT
88	Asst VP Design & Construction	Ms. Jo GOLDBERGER
88	Asst VP Capital Infrastructure	Mr. Silviu HERSCHER
88	Asst VP Process Improvement	Ms. Lisa BONNER
110	Asst VP Develop & Alumni	Mr. Ryan BAGLEY
102	Exec Dir Devel/Corp & Foundation	Ms. Laura CRONIN
112	Campaign Director	Ms. Tanya MÚJICA KEENAN
08	University Librarian	Mr. Ed SCARCELLE
23	Asst VP Student Health	Ms. Tracy ROBIN
39	Sr Director Student and Campus Life	Mr. Travis WHISLER
19	Director Security	Mr. Thomas ILICETO
37	Director Financial Aid	Ms. Laverne WALKER
18	Asst VP Facilities Management	Mr. Thomas WHALEN
38	Director Counseling Services	Dr. Jerry FINKELSTEIN
22	Director Student Disability Svcs	Mr. Nicholas FARANDA
88	Director Events IT	Mr. Mark FITZPATRICK
101	Asst Secretary to the Corporation	Ms. Lori SINGER

New York Academy of Art (D)

111 Franklin Street, New York NY 10013
County: New York FICE Identification: 026001
Unit ID: 366368
Telephone: (212) 966-0300 Carnegie Class: Spec-4-yr-Arts
FAX Number: N/A Calendar System: Semester
URL: www.nyaa.edu
Established: 1982 Annual Graduate Tuition & Fees: N/A
Enrollment: 119 Coed
Affiliation or Control: Independent Non-Profit IRS Status: 501(c)3
Highest Offering: Master's; No Undergraduates
Accreditation: M, ART

Code	Title	Name
01	President	Mr. David KRATZ
05	Dean of Academic Affairs	Mr. Peter DRAKE
10	Chief Financial Officer	Mr. Stephan KORSAKOV
11	Director of Operations	Mr. Michael SMITH
06	Registrar	Ms. Katie HEMMER
30	Director of Development	Ms. Lisa KIRK

New York Automotive and Diesel Institute (E)

178-18 Liberty Avenue, Jamaica NY 11433
County: Queens FICE Identification: 035373
Telephone: (917) 720-4847 Carnegie Class: Not Classified
FAX Number: (718) 658-4044 Calendar System: Semester
URL: nyadi.edu
Established: Annual Undergrad Tuition & Fees: N/A
Enrollment: N/A Coed
Affiliation or Control: Proprietary IRS Status: Proprietary
Highest Offering: Associate Degree
Accreditation: ACCSC

Code	Title	Name
01	College President	Patrick HART

New York Chiropractic College (F)

2360 State Route 89, Seneca Falls NY 13148-0800
County: Seneca FICE Identification: 012277
Unit ID: 193751
Telephone: (315) 568-3000 Carnegie Class: Spec-4-yr-Other Health
FAX Number: (315) 568-3012 Calendar System: Trimester
URL: www.nycc.edu
Established: 1919 Annual Undergrad Tuition & Fees: N/A
Enrollment: 926 Coed
Affiliation or Control: Independent Non-Profit IRS Status: 501(c)3
Highest Offering: First Professional Degree
Accreditation: M, ACUP, CHIRO

Code	Title	Name
01	President	Dr. Michael A. MESTAN
05	Exec Vice Pres of Academic Affairs	Dr. Anne KILLEN
10	Vice Pres of Finance/Admin Svcs	Mr. Sean ANGLIM
111	VP Inst Advance & Special Proj	Dr. J. Todd KNUDSEN
84	Vice Pres Enrollment & Planning	Dr. Jen SESSLER
96	Assoc VP Admin Svcs/Dir Purchasing	Mr. Richard B. WORDEN
13	Assoc VP Informational Tech	Mr. Christophe MCQUEENEY
76	Dean School of Health Sciences & Ed	Dr. J. Nicolas POIRIER
88	Dean of Chiropractic	Dr. Karen A. BOBAK
06	Registrar	Mr. Kevin MCCARTHY
37	Director Financial Aid	Mr. Darrin ROOKER
107	Director of Bachelor Prof Studies	Dr. Erica CALLAHAN
46	Dean of Research	Dr. Jeanmarie R. BURKE
12	Depew Health Center Administrator	Dr. Ana STEARNS
12	Levittown Health Ctr Chief of Staff	Ms. Melissa MURPHY
17	Assoc Dean for Chiro Clinical Educ	Dr. Wendy L. MANERI
51	Director Post Grad & Cont Educ	Dr. Owen PAPUGUA
08	Director of the Library	Ms. Bethyn BONI
88	Dir Academy Admc Excl Stdnt Success	Mr. Peter THOMPSON
41	Dir Health & Fitness Education	Mr. Rhett TICCONI
32	Director Ofc of Student Engagement	Vacant
36	Dir Ctr Career Dev Prof Success	Ms. Susan D. PITTENGER
29	Director of Alumni Relations	Ms. Diane ZINK
45	Director Accreditation	Dr. Beth DONOHUE

09 Quality Engineer Ms. Patricia MERKLE
15 Human Resources Manager Ms. Christine MCDERMOTT
14 Information Tech Administrator Mr. Shane SHOWERS
19 Director Facilities/Security Mr. William WAYNE
40 Bookstore Manager Ms. Helen STUCK
76 Dir Applied Clinical Nutrition Pgm Dr. Peter NICKLESS
88 Dean of FL Sch Acup/Oriental Med Dr. Phil GARRISON
88 Dir MS Diagnostic Imaging Program Dr. Chad WARSHEL
12 Rochester Hlth Ctr Chf of Staff Dr. Ryan NADEAU
90 Systems Administrator Ms. Shelly STUCK
24 Educational Tech Administrator Mr. Bernard CECCHINI
23 Director Health Center Operations Mrs. Melissa BAXTER
21 Controller Ms. Karen QUEST
88 Dir MS Hum Anat Phys Instructn Pgm Dr. William GERMANO

New York College of Health Professions (A)

6801 Jericho Turnpike, Syosset NY 11791-4413

County: Nassau
FICE Identification: 025994
Unit ID: 418126
Telephone: (516) 364-0808
Carnegie Class: Spec-4-yr-Other Health
FAX Number: (516) 364-6645
Calendar System: Trimester
URL: www.nycollege.edu
Established: 1981
Annual Undergrad Tuition & Fees: $14,226
Enrollment: 485
Coed
Affiliation or Control: Independent Non-Profit
IRS Status: 501(c)3
Highest Offering: Master's
Accreditation: NY, ACUP

01 President Dr. A Li SONG
10 Chief Financial Officer Mr. Errol VIRASAWMI
63 Dean Grad Sch Oriental Medicine Dr. James SHINOL
05 Dean of Academic Affairs Vacant
06 Registrar Mr. Timothy BOUDREAU
07 Associate Director of Admissions Mrs. Mary RODAS
08 Dir Library/Information Services Ms. Cynthia CAYEA
09 Director of Institutional Research Vacant
113 Bursar Ms. Jacqueline MCINTYRE
13 Manager Information Technology Mr. Peter WANG
32 Student Services Administrator Mr. Brian ALVAREZ
88 Dean Sch of Massage Therapy Dr. Jian YANG

New York College of Podiatric Medicine (B)

53 E 124th Street, New York NY 10035-1815

County: New York
FICE Identification: 002749
Unit ID: 194073
Telephone: (212) 410-8000
Carnegie Class: Spec-4-yr-Med
FAX Number: (212) 876-7670
Calendar System: Semester
URL: www.nycpm.edu
Established: 1911
Annual Undergrad Tuition & Fees: N/A
Enrollment: 396
Coed
Affiliation or Control: Independent Non-Profit
IRS Status: 501(c)3
Highest Offering: First Professional Degree
Accreditation: POD

01 President Mr. Louis L. LEVINE
05 Vice Pres Academic Affairs/Dean Dr. Michael J. TREPAL
11 Chief Operating Ofcr/VP Admin Mr. Joel STURM
10 Chief Financial Officer Mr. Greg ONAIFO
13 Vice Pres Info Systems & Technology Mr. Aman SAFAEI
63 VP Medical Education/Medical Dir Dr. Mark SWARTZ
20 Dean Clinical Educ/Dir Res Pgms Dr. Ronald SOAVE
09 Dean Institutional Research Dr. Eileen CHUSID
32 Dean Student Affairs Ms. Lisa LEE
07 Asst Dean Academic Administration Mr. Alain SILVERIO
88 Asst Dean Clinical Clerkships/Affls Ms. Judith QUINTANA
26 Director Public Affairs/Development Ms. Ellen LUBELL
08 Director of Library Mr. Paul TREMBLAY
37 Director Financial Aid Ms. Eve TRAUBE
06 Registrar Ms. Doreen D'AMICO
19 Director Security/Safety Mr. James WARREN
39 Housing Manager Ms. Susan MARANDI

New York College of Traditional Chinese Medicine (C)

200 Old Country Road, Suite 500, Mineola NY 11501-4204

County: Nassau
FICE Identification: 034433
Unit ID: 439783
Telephone: (516) 739-1545
Carnegie Class: Spec-4-yr-Other Health
FAX Number: (516) 873-9622
Calendar System: Trimester
URL: www.nyctcm.edu
Established: 1996
Annual Undergrad Tuition & Fees: N/A
Enrollment: 196
Coed
Affiliation or Control: Independent Non-Profit
IRS Status: 501(c)3
Highest Offering: Master's
Accreditation: ACUP

01 President Dr. Yemeng CHEN
10 Administrative Dean Ms. Megan HAUNGS
05 Academic Dean Dr. Sunny SHEN
07 Admissions Manager Ms. Lynn BAI
23 Clinic Director Ms. Mona LEE-YUAN
88 Clinic Manager Ms. Yiping ZHAO
06 Records Manager Ms. Susan SU
37 Financial Aid/Admin Coordinator Ms. Elise MA
21 Financial Manager Ms. Lily ZOU
08 Operations Manager Ms. Ling Ling CHANG

The New York Conservatory for Dramatic Arts (D)

39 West 19th Street, New York NY 10011

County: New York
FICE Identification: 031207
Unit ID: 421841
Telephone: (212) 645-0030
Carnegie Class: Spec 2-yr-A&S
FAX Number: (212) 645-0039
Calendar System: Semester
URL: www.nycda.edu
Established: 1980
Annual Undergrad Tuition & Fees: $32,742
Enrollment: 237
Coed
Affiliation or Control: Proprietary
IRS Status: Proprietary
Highest Offering: Associate Degree
Accreditation: THEA

00 CEO Mike Vishol DABIDAT
01 President/Artistic Director Richard OMAR
05 Director of Education Jay GOLDENBERG
20 Assoc Director of Education Sara BUFFAMANTI
06 Registrar Stefon SIMMONS
08 Head Librarian Martha REPETTO
07 Director of Admissions Bryce RUSSELL
10 Chief Business Officer Emily CHOU
37 Director Student Financial Aid Alexander VO
39 Residence Director Deanna BERTINI

New York Graduate School of Psychoanalysis (E)

16 West Tenth Street, New York NY 10011

Telephone: (212) 260-7050
Identification: 770116
Accreditation: &EH

† Branch campus of Boston Graduate School of Psychoanalysis, Brookline, MA

New York Institute of Technology (F)

Northern Boulevard, Old Westbury NY 11568-8000

County: Nassau
FICE Identification: 004804
Unit ID: 194091
Telephone: (516) 686-7516
Carnegie Class: Masters/L
FAX Number: (516) 686-7613
Calendar System: Semester
URL: www.nyit.edu
Established: 1955
Annual Undergrad Tuition & Fees: $36,890
Enrollment: 7,403
Coed
Affiliation or Control: Independent Non-Profit
IRS Status: 501(c)3
Highest Offering: Doctorate
Accreditation: M, ARCPA, CACREP, CAEP, CIDA, NURSE, OSTEO, OT, PTA

01 President Dr. Henry FOLEY
05 Provost/Vice Pres Academic Affairs Dr. Junius GONZALEZ
20 Associate Provost Dr. Lou REINISCH
84 Vice Pres for Enrollment & EA Dr. Mark HAMPTON
111 Vice Pres Development/Alumni Rels Mr. Patrick MINSON
26 Vice Pres Strategic Communications Dr. Nada ANID
10 CFO & Treasurer Ms. Barbara HOLAHAN
21 Controller Ms. Eileen VALERIO
43 General Counsel Ms. Catherine FLICKINGER
06 Registrar Ms. Kristen SMITH
76 Dean School of Health Professions Dr. Gordon SCHMIDT
48 Dean Sch Architecture & Design Ms. Maria PERBELLINI
54 Dean School of Engr/Computer Sci Dr. Babak DASTGHEIB-BEHESHTI
49 Dean School Arts & Sciences Dr. Daniel QUIGLEY
50 Dean School of Management Dr. Jess BORONICO
36 Int Director Career Services Ms. Laurie HOLLISTER
75 Sr Dr Vocational Independence Pgm Mr. Paul CAVANAGH
88 Ex Director Global Academic Program Ms. Emily RUKOBO
09 Director Inst Research & Assessment Mr. Michael LANE
88 Director Environmental Health/Safe Mr. Kristen PANELLA
22 Director Compliance Title IX Coord Ms. Cheryl MONTICCIOLO
07 Dean Admissions & Financial Aid Ms. Karen VAHEY
27 Senior Director of Communications Ms. Bobbie DELL'AQUILO
29 Asst Director of Alumni Relations Ms. Sabrina POLIDORO
18 Sr Director Facilities Operations Mr. William MARCHAND
37 Senior Director of Financial Aid Ms. Rosemary FERRUCCI
19 Director Security Mr. John ESPINA
41 Director Athletics Mr. Dan VELEZ ORTIZ
25 Asst Provost Grants Office Dr. Allison ANDORS
116 Senior Director of Internal Audit Ms. Rachel BERTHOUMIEUX
121 Asst Dean Advising & Enrichment Ms. Monika ROHDE
15 Executive Director Human Resources Ms. Carol JABLONSKY
13 Acting CITO Ms. Laurie HARVEY
91 Director Systems & Network Mr. Brian MAROLDO
35 Associate Dean Campus Life Ms. Zennabelle SEWELL
63 Vice Pres/Dean Health Sci/Med Affs Dr. Jerry BALENTINE
04 Executive Admin to President Ms. Elizabeth FREDERICKS

New York Law School (G)

185 West Broadway, New York NY 10013-2959

County: New York
FICE Identification: 002783
Unit ID: 193821
Telephone: (212) 431-2100
Carnegie Class: Spec-4-yr-Law
FAX Number: (212) 965-8838
Calendar System: Semester
URL: www.nyls.edu
Established: 1891
Annual Graduate Tuition & Fees: N/A
Enrollment: 995
Coed
Affiliation or Control: Independent Non-Profit
IRS Status: 501(c)3
Highest Offering: Doctorate; No Undergraduates
Accreditation: LAW

01 Dean and President Dean Anthony CROWELL
05 Assoc Dean Academic & Student Engag Dean William P. LAPIANA
10 Executive Vice President & CFO Mr. Stuart KLEIN
11 Assoc Dean for Inst Accountability Dean Joan R. FISHMAN
26 VP of Marketing & Communications Ms. Elizabeth THOMAS
111 VP of Institutional Advancement Ms. Marcey GRIGSBY
08 Director of Law Library/Assoc Dean Prof. Camille BROUSSARD
84 Assoc Dean Admissions & Prof Dev Mr. Jeffery BECHERER
07 Asst Dean of Admissions & Finan Aid Ms. Ella Mae ESTRADA
36 Asst Dean of Advising & Prof Dev Ms. Courtney FITZGIBBONS
21 Sr Asst VP Financial Plng & Mgmt Ms. Susan REDLER
18 Chief Maintenance/Operations/Secur Mr. Paul REPETTO
15 Asst Vice President Human Resources Ms. Jody PARIANTE
09 VP Institutional Research Dr. Joanne INGHAM
32 Assistant Dean for Student Life Ms. Sally HARDING
88 Senor Asst VP Project Management Mr. George HAYES
30 Director of Development Vacant
20 Asst Dean Academic Program Develop Ms. Erin BOND
06 Assistant Dean and Registrar Mr. Oral HOPE
13 Chief Information Officer Mr. Thomas SOCASH
35 Sr Director of Student Life Ms. Shani DARBY
96 Purchasing Coordinator Mr. Norman DAWKINS
104 Director Study Abroad Mr. Michael RHEE
86 Director Government Relations Mr. Ariel DVORKIN
37 Director Student Financial Aid Mr. Christopher CLARKE
04 Admin Assistant to the President Mr. Frank CHIAPPETTA
29 Director Alumni Affairs Ms. Marcey GRIGSBY
43 Asst Dean & General Counsel Mr. Matthew GEWOLB

New York Medical College (H)

40 Sunshine Cottage Road, Valhalla NY 10595-1690

County: Westchester
FICE Identification: 002784
Unit ID: 193830
Telephone: (914) 594-4900
Carnegie Class: Spec-4-yr-Med
FAX Number: (914) 594-4145
Calendar System: Other
URL: www.nymc.edu
Established: 1860
Annual Graduate Tuition & Fees: N/A
Enrollment: 1,498
Coed
Affiliation or Control: Jewish
IRS Status: 501(c)3
Highest Offering: Doctorate; No Undergraduates
Accreditation: M, DENT, MED, PAST, PH, PTA, SP

01 President Dr. Alan H. KADISH
00 Chancellor and CEO Dr. Edward C. HALPERIN
100 Chief of Staff Ms. Vilma BORDONARO
63 Dean School of Medicine Dr. Jerry NADLER
10 Vice Pres Financial Operations Mr. Adam D. HAMMERMAN
11 Vice President Operations Mr. Michael ROGOVIN
26 Vice Pres Communications Ms. Jennifer RIEKERT
46 Vice President for Research Dr. Salomon AMAR
58 Dean Grad Sch Basic Medical Science Dr. Marina HOLZ
76 Dean Sch Health Sciences & Practice Dr. Robert W. AMLER
30 Chief Development Officer Ms. Bess CHAZHUR
86 Vice President Government Affairs Dr. Robert W. AMLER
21 Controller Ms. Irene CRASTRO-BOLIN
13 Sr Dir Information Tech Services Mr. Luis MONTES
63 Vice Dean Grad Med Ed/Affiliations Dr. Richard G. MCCARRICK
32 Sr Assoc Dean Student Affairs Dr. Jane PONTERIO
37 Asc Dn Stdnt Affs/Dir Finan Plng Mr. Anthony M. SOZZO
08 Assoc Dean/Dir Health Sci Library Ms. Marie ASCHER
07 Director of Admissions Ms. Karen MURRAY
06 College Registrar Ms. Eileen ROMERO
39 Director Student Housing Ms. Katherine E. DILLON
18 Dir Capital Planning/Facilities Ms. Sarah COTTET
19 Director of Security Mr. William ALLISON
85 Intl Student/Scholar Advisor Ms. Elizabeth WARD
23 Director Health Services Ms. Marisa MONTECALVO
38 Director Student Counseling Dr. Mark SINGER
105 Director Web Communications Mr. Kevin R. CUMMINGS
24 Head Educational Media Mr. Michael COTTER
14 Coord of Instruct Computing Tech Mr. Jason DI NARDI
04 Admin Assistant to the President Ms. Ashley MCCARRICK

New York School of Interior Design (I)

170 East 70th Street, New York NY 10021-5110

County: New York
FICE Identification: 020690
Unit ID: 194116
Telephone: (212) 472-1500
Carnegie Class: Spec-4-yr-Arts
FAX Number: (212) 472-3800
Calendar System: 4/1/4
URL: www.nysid.edu
Established: 1916
Annual Undergrad Tuition & Fees: $24,834
Enrollment: 541
Coed
Affiliation or Control: Independent Non-Profit
IRS Status: 501(c)3
Highest Offering: Master's
Accreditation: M, ART, CIDA

01 President Mr. David SPROULS
05 VP Academic Affairs/Dean Dr. Ellen FISHER
10 VP for Finance & Administration Ms. Jane CHEN
32 Dean of Students Ms. Karen HIGGINBOTHAM
04 Assistant to the President Ms. Jeanne KO
06 Registrar Ms. Jennifer MELENDEZ
08 Director of the Library Mr. Billy KWAN
07 Director of Admissions Mr. Brett CIONE
37 Financial Aid Assistant Ms. Kimberley TELLUS
15 Director of Personnel Services Ms. Yvonne MORAY
18 Chief Facilities/Physical Plant Mr. Zeke KOLENOVIC
20 Associate Dean Ms. Barbara LOWENTHAL
13 Dir of Network & Tech Support Svcs Mr. Dan TRUONG
38 Director Student Counseling Dr. Penny MORGANSTEIN

09 Director of Institutional Research .... Mr. Christopher VINGER
30 Director of Development .... Ms. Joy COOPER
100 Chief of Staff .... Mr. David OWENS-HILL

New York Theological Seminary (A)

475 Riverside Drive, Suite 500, New York NY 10115-0083
County: New York FICE Identification: 002674
Unit ID: 193894
Telephone: (212) 870-1211 Carnegie Class: Spec-4-yr-Faith
FAX Number: (212) 870-1236 Calendar System: Semester
URL: www.nyts.edu
Established: 1900 Annual Graduate Tuition & Fees: N/A
Enrollment: 359 Coed
Affiliation or Control: Independent Non-Profit IRS Status: 501(c)3
Highest Offering: Doctorate; No Undergraduates
Accreditation: THEOL

01 President .... Dr. LaKeesha WALROND
30 VP Development/Inst Advancement .... Vacant
05 VP Academic Affairs/Dean .... Dr. Efrain AGOSTO
10 Chief Financial Officer/Controller .... Mr. Craig KING
08 Librarian .... Dr. Rafael REYES
06 Registrar .... Ms. Lydia R. BUMGARDNER
37 Director Financial Aid .... Ms. Tamisia WHITE
26 Coordinator Publications/Marketing ..... Ms. Angelica C. MORALES
105 Director Web Services .... Mr. Ahsan RAZA
108 Director Institutional Assessment .... Vacant
29 Director Alumni Relations .... Ms. Cynthia GARDNER-BRIM
38 Director Student Counseling .... Dr. Edward L. HUNT

New York University (B)

70 Washington Square S, New York NY 10012-1092
County: New York FICE Identification: 002785
Unit ID: 193900
Telephone: (212) 998-1212 Carnegie Class: DU-Highest
FAX Number: N/A Calendar System: Semester
URL: www.nyu.edu
Established: 1831 Annual Undergrad Tuition & Fees: $51,828
Enrollment: 51,123 Coed
Affiliation or Control: Independent Non-Profit IRS Status: 501(c)3
Highest Offering: Doctorate
Accreditation: M, CAEPT, COPSY, DENT, DH, DIETD, DIETI, HSA, IPSY, JOUR, LAW, MED, MIDWF, NURSE, OT, PAST, PH, PLNG, PTA, SP, SPAA, SURGT, SW

01 President .... Dr. Andrew HAMILTON
05 Provost .... Dr. Katherine FLEMING
10 Executive VP for Finance/IT .... Dr. Martin DORPH
26 Sr VP for Univ Rels/Pub Affairs .... Dr. Lynne BROWN
30 Sr VP Development/Alumni Relations .... Mr. Robert CASHION
32 Sr Vice Pres for Student Affairs .... Dr. Marc L. WAIS
43 General Counsel & Secretary .... Mr. Terrance NOLAN
46 Sr Vice Provost for Research .... Dr. Paul M. HORN
35 VC Global Pgms/Univ Life at NYU .... Dr. Linda G. MILLS
18 VP Facilities & Construction Mgmt .... Mr. David ALONSO
27 Sr Vice Pres for Public Affairs .... Mr. John H. BECKMAN
84 Vice Pres Enrollment .... Ms. MJ KNOLL-FINN
15 Vice Pres Human Resources .... Ms. Sabrina ELLIS
13 VP and Chief Information Officer .... Mr. Len PETERS
45 Vice Provost for Resource Planning .... Mr. Anthony JIGA
21 Sr VP Finance and Budget/CFO .... Ms. Stephanie PIANKA
19 Sr VP Global Campus Safety .... Mr. Marlon LYNCH
06 University Registrar .... Ms. Elizabeth A. KIENLE-GRANZO
20 Deputy Provost .... Dr. C. Cybele RAVER
88 VP for Global Programs .... Dr. Nancy J. MORRISON
07 Asst VP for Undergrad Admissions .... Vacant
20 Asst Provost Academic Pgm Review .... Dr. Diana L. KARAFIN
41 Asst VP Stdnt Affairs/Dir Athletics .... Mr. Christopher BLEDSOE
23 Assoc VP Stdnt Hlth/Exec Dir SHC .... Dr. Carlo CIOTOLI
37 Asst VP Financial Aid .... Ms. Lynn E. HIGINBOTHAM
22 Exec Dir Ofc of Equal Opportunity .... Ms. Mary SIGNOR
08 Dean of Libraries .... Ms. Carol A. MANDEL
39 Sr Director Housing Services .... Mr. Neil S. HANRAHAN
09 Director of Institutional Research .... Mr. David P. VINTINNER

Niagara County Community College (C)

3111 Saunders Settlement Road, Sanborn NY 14132-9460
County: Niagara FICE Identification: 002874
Unit ID: 193946
Telephone: (716) 614-6200 Carnegie Class: Assoc/MT-VT-High Trad
FAX Number: (716) 614-6700 Calendar System: Semester
URL: www.niagaracc.suny.edu
Established: 1962 Annual Undergrad Tuition & Fees (In-District): $4,923
Enrollment: 5,439 Coed
Affiliation or Control: State/Local IRS Status: 501(c)3
Highest Offering: Associate Degree
Accreditation: M, ACFEI, ADNUR, MAC, PTAA, RAD, SURGT

01 Interim President .... Dr. William MURABITO
05 Int Vice President Academic Affairs .... Ms. Lydia ULATOWSKI
103 VP Workforce Development .... Ms. Karen KWANDRANS
10 Interim VP of Finance/Info Tech .... Mr. John EICHNER
32 Vice President of Student Services .... Ms. Julia PITMAN
11 Interim Vice President Operations .... Mr. Wayne LYNCH
09 Director Planning and Research .... Vacant
15 Director of Human Resources .... Ms. Catherine BROWN
84 Asst VP of Enrollment Management .... Mr. Robert MCKEOWN
21 Director of Business Services .... Vacant
04 Assistant to President .... Ms. Barbara WALCK
06 Registrar .... Ms. Julie SCHUCKER
35 Director of Student Development .... Vacant
37 Director of Financial Aid .... Mr. James TRIMBOLI
26 Director Public Relations .... Ms. Barbara DESIMONE
18 Assistant Director of Facilities .... Mr. Donald SAPH
08 Head Librarian .... Ms. Nancy KENNEDY
105 Director Web Services .... Mr. Cory WRIGHT
106 Dir Online Education/E-learning .... Ms. Lisa DUBUC
13 Chief Info Technology Officer .... Mr. Dennis MICHAELS
19 Director Security/Safety .... Mr. Ross ANNABLE
102 Foundation Director .... Ms. Deborah BREWER
39 Assistant Director Student Housing .... Ms. Jill FADDOUL
41 Athletic Director .... Ms. Amanda HASELEY
91 Dir User & Administrative Tech .... Mr. Brian ZELLI
29 Alumni Development Specialist .... Ms. Allison KORTA
07 Director of Admissions .... Mr. Douglas MCNABB
108 Director Institutional Assessment .... Vacant
25 Director of Grants .... Mr. Brian MICHEL
104 Director Study Abroad .... Ms. Britani PRUNER
36 Interim Director Student Placement .... Ms. Alissa SHUGATS-CUMMINGS
38 Director Student Counseling .... Vacant

Niagara University (D)

5795 Lewiston Road, Niagara University NY 14109
County: Niagara FICE Identification: 002788
Unit ID: 193973
Telephone: (716) 285-1212 Carnegie Class: Masters/L
FAX Number: (716) 286-8710 Calendar System: Semester
URL: www.niagara.edu
Established: 1856 Annual Undergrad Tuition & Fees: $33,180
Enrollment: 3,949 Coed
Affiliation or Control: Independent Non-Profit IRS Status: 501(c)3
Highest Offering: Doctorate
Accreditation: M, CACREP, CAEP, NURSE, SW

01 President .... Rev. James MAHER, CM
03 Executive Vice President .... Dr. Debra COLLEY
05 Provost/VP for Academic Affairs .... Dr. Timothy IRELAND
10 Senior VP Operations & Finance .... Ms. Mary E. BORGOGNONI
84 SVP Enrollment Mgmt/Strategic Init .... Mr. Robert MURPHY
32 AVP Student Affs/Inst Effectiveness .... Mr. Christopher R. SHEFFIELD
88 VP for International Relations .... Vacant
111 VP for Institutional Advancement .... Dr. Derek M. WESLEY
42 VP Mission Integration .... Rev. Aidan R. ROONEY, CM
20 Associate Provost .... Dr. Henrik C. BORGSTROM
26 AVP of Public/External/Govt Rels .... Mr. Thomas BURNS
110 Assoc VP for Inst Advancement .... Mr. David GREENMAN
43 General Counsel .... Mr. Kevin HINKLEY
21 Chief Financial/Innovation Ofcr .... Mr. Robert MORREALE
35 Dean of Student Affairs .... Mr. Jason JAKUBOWSKI
49 Dean Col of Arts & Science .... Dr. Peter BUTERA
50 Dean Col of Business Admin .... Dr. Mark FRASCATORE
53 Dean Col of Education .... Dr. Chandra FOOTE
88 Dean Col Hospitality/Tourism Mgt .... Dr. Kurt A. STAHURA
09 Director of Institutional Research .... Dr. Vennessa L. WALKER
88 Facility Planner .... Mr. Daniel MCMANN
07 Director of Admissions Operations .... Mr. Harry S. GONG
07 Director of Admissions .... Mr. Mark E. WOJNOWSKI
08 Director of Libraries .... Mr. David SCHOEN
19 Director of Campus Safety .... Mr. John F. BARKER
37 Director of Financial Aid .... Ms. Katie L. KOCSIS
39 Director of Residence Life .... Ms. Kimberly FENTON
35 Director of Campus Activities .... Mrs. Mati ORTIZ
13 Director Information Technology .... Mr. Richard P. KERNIN
88 Director of Art Museum .... Ms. Kate KOPERSKI
15 Director of Human Resources .... Ms. Donna MOSTILLER
23 Dir of Student Health & Wellness .... Ms. Adrienne KASBAUM
41 Director of Athletics .... Mr. Simon GRAY
18 Director of Facility Services .... Mr. Daniel M. GUARIGLIA
88 Dean of Academic Services .... Ms. Antonia KNIGHT
121 Director of Academic Support .... Mrs. Diane STOELTING
88 Exec Dir Inst for Civic Engagement .... Mrs. Patricia WROBEL
88 Dir Rec & Intramurals/Kiernan Ctr .... Mr. Derek PUFF
29 Director Alumni Relations .... Ms. Jaclyn ROSSI
21 Controller .... Mr. Donald E. SMITH
88 Assoc Dir Acad Affs/Grad Recruit .... Mr. Evan F. PIERCE
92 Honors Program Coordinator .... Dr. Michael BARNWELL
93 Dir Multicultural Affairs .... Ms. Averl HARBIN
28 Assoc Dir Equity & Inclusion .... Mr. Ryan THOMPSON
06 University Registrar .... Mr. R. Ryan KENDRICK
113 Director of Student Accounts .... Ms. Martie HOWELL
25 Dir Sponsored Pgms & Fndn Rels .... Ms. Jill SHUEY
102 Asst VP Spons Pgms & Found Rels .... Ms. Adrienne STANFILL
36 Director of Career Services .... Ms. Stephanie MORRIS
104 Exec Dir Brennan Ctr & Intl Rels .... Dr. Deborah CURTIS
88 Director of IMPACT .... Mr. Thomas LOWE
88 Veterans Services Coordinator .... Mr. Robert HEALY
04 Executive Asst to President .... Mrs. Ashley MISKO

North Country Community College (E)

23 Santanoni Avenue, PO Box 89,
Saranac Lake NY 12983-0089
County: Essex FICE Identification: 007111
Unit ID: 194028
Telephone: (518) 891-2915 Carnegie Class: Assoc/HVT-High Non
FAX Number: (518) 891-2915 Calendar System: Semester
URL: www.nccc.edu
Established: 1967 Annual Undergrad Tuition & Fees (In-District): $6,008
Enrollment: 2,006 Coed
Affiliation or Control: State/Local IRS Status: 501(c)3
Highest Offering: Associate Degree
Accreditation: M

01 President .... Mr. Joe KEEGAN
05 Vice Pres of Academic Affairs .... Mrs. Sarah MAROUN
10 Vice Pres for Administration/CFO .... Mr. Robert FARMER
07 Dean of Admissions .... Vacant
06 Registrar/Records Officer .... Mrs. Shelly ST. LOUIS
09 Asst Dean Inst Research/Support .... Mr. Scott HARWOOD
32 Dean of Campus & Student Life .... Ms. Kim IRLAND
29 Director Alumni Relations .... Ms. Diana FORTUNE
04 Executive Asst to the President .... Mrs. Stacie HURWITCH
37 Director Student Financial Aid .... Mr. Matthew SANCHEZ
41 Athletic Director .... Mr. Chad LADUE

Northeastern Seminary (F)

2265 Westside Drive, Rochester NY 14624-1932
County: Monroe FICE Identification: 034194
Unit ID: 439817
Telephone: (585) 594-6800 Carnegie Class: Spec-4-yr-Faith
FAX Number: (585) 594-6801 Calendar System: Semester
URL: www.nes.edu
Established: 1998 Annual Graduate Tuition & Fees: N/A
Enrollment: 124 Coed
Affiliation or Control: Independent Non-Profit IRS Status: 501(c)3
Highest Offering: Doctorate; No Undergraduates
Accreditation: M, THEOL

01 President .... Dr. Deana L. PORTERFIELD
05 Academic Vice President and Dean .... Dr. Douglas CULLUM
32 VP for Student and Organ Dev .... Mrs. Ruth LOGAN
07 AVP for Seminary Enrollment .... Mr. JP ANDERSON
11 Exec Director of Seminary Admin .... Ms. Kristen BROWN
04 Administrative Asst to President .... Mrs. Mimi WHEELER
06 Registrar .... Ms. Lesa KOHR
10 Chief Business Officer .... Mrs. Laurie LEO
111 VP for Institutional Advancement .... Mr. Darrell BELL
13 AVP Information Technology .... Mr. Peter SAXENA
102 Dir Foundation/Corporate Relations .... Ms. Lisa TIFFIN

† The Seminary is affiliated with Roberts Wesleyan College.

Nyack College (G)

1 South Boulevard, Nyack NY 10960-3698
County: Rockland FICE Identification: 002790
Unit ID: 194161
Telephone: (845) 675-4400 Carnegie Class: Masters/L
FAX Number: (845) 358-1751 Calendar System: Semester
URL: www.nyack.edu
Established: 1882 Annual Undergrad Tuition & Fees: $25,350
Enrollment: 2,455 Coed
Affiliation or Control: The Christian And Missionary Alliance
IRS Status: 501(c)3
Highest Offering: Doctorate
Accreditation: M, CAEP, MFCD, MUS, NURSE, SW

01 President .... Dr. Michael G. SCALES
04 Assistant to the President .... Mrs. Bonita D'AMIL
10 Exec Vice President & Treasurer .... Mr. David C. JENNINGS
05 Provost/VP for Academic Affairs .... Dr. David F. TURK
84 Vice President for Enrollment .... Mr. Jeff RICKEY
111 Vice President of Advancement .... Rev. Jeffery QUINN
73 Dean Seminary .... Dr. Ronald WALBORN
50 Dean School of Business & Ldrshp .... Dr. Anita UNDERWOOD
64 Dean School of Music .... Dr. Sue Lane TALLEY
53 Dean School of Education .... Dr. JoAnn LOONEY
66 Dean School of Nursing .... Mrs. Inseon HWANG
121 Assoc Dean Student Success .... Dr. Gwen PARKER AMES
32 Vice Pres of Student Development .... Mrs. Wanda VELEZ
88 Vice President of Church Relations .... Mr. Charles HAMMOND
06 Institutional Registrar .... Ms. Evangeline COUCHEY
07 Dir of Admissions Undergrad .... Mr. Andres VALENZUELA
37 Dir of Fin Svcs Undergrad .... Mr. Isaac FOSTER
41 Director of Athletics .... Mr. Keith A. DAVIE
15 Director of Human Resources .... Mrs. Karen DAVIE
13 Director of Information Technology .... Mr. Kevin A. BUEL
09 Director of Institutional Research .... Mr. Greg BEEMAN
18 Director of Operations/Aramark .... Mr. Doug WALKER
26 Dir of Public & Media Relations .... Mrs. Deborah WALKER
105 Webmaster .... Mr. Joshua WAY
108 Director Institutional Assessment .... Ms. Kristen LUBA

Nyack College Manhattan Center (H)

2 Washington Street, New York NY 10004
Telephone: (212) 625-0500 Identification: 770143
Accreditation: &M, THEOL

Ohr Hameir Theological Seminary (I)

141 Furnace Woods Road,
Cortlandt Manor NY 10567-6112
County: Westchester FICE Identification: 011984
Unit ID: 194189
Telephone: (914) 736-1500 Carnegie Class: Spec-4-yr-Faith
FAX Number: (914) 736-1055 Calendar System: Semester
Established: 1962 Annual Undergrad Tuition & Fees: $11,750
Enrollment: 101 Male
Affiliation or Control: Independent Non-Profit IRS Status: 501(c)3
Highest Offering: Second Talmudic Degree

Accreditation: RABN

01 President .... Rabbi E. KANAREK
30 Chief Devel Ofcr/Dir Financial Aid .... Rabbi Jacob ROTHBERG
06 Registrar .... Rabbi Berel KANAREK

Ohr Somayach Tanenbaum Educational Center (A)

244 Route 306, Monsey NY 10952-0334
County: Rockland FICE Identification: 023201
Unit ID: 243805
Telephone: (845) 425-1370 Carnegie Class: Not Classified
FAX Number: (845) 425-8865 Calendar System: Trimester
URL: www.os.edu
Established: 1979 Annual Undergrad Tuition & Fees: N/A
Enrollment: N/A Coordinate
Affiliation or Control: Independent Non-Profit IRS Status: 501(c)3
Highest Offering: First Professional Degree
Accreditation: RABN

01 Director .... Rabbi Avrohom ROKOWSKY
05 Dean .... Rabbi Israel ROKOWSKY
06 Registrar .... Mrs. Miriam GROSSMAN
10 Chief Business Officer .... Rabbi Moshe HASS

Onondaga Community College (B)

4585 West Seneca Turnpike, Syracuse NY 13215-4585
County: Onondaga FICE Identification: 002875
Unit ID: 194222
Telephone: (315) 498-2622 Carnegie Class: Assoc/HT-Mix Trad/Non
FAX Number: (315) 492-9208 Calendar System: Semester
URL: www.sunyocc.edu
Established: 1962 Annual Undergrad Tuition & Fees (In-District): $5,484
Enrollment: 10,659 Coed
Affiliation or Control: State/Local IRS Status: 501(c)3
Highest Offering: Associate Degree
Accreditation: M, ADNUR, CAHIIM, PTAA, SURGT

01 President .... Dr. Casey CRABILL
05 Provost and SVP Educational Svcs .... Vacant
10 Sr Vice Pres & CFO .... Mr. Mark MANNING
32 SVP Student Engage & Learning Supp .... Vacant
03 VP Governance and Compliance .... Ms. Anastasia URTZ
30 Vice President Development .... Ms. Lisa MOORE
84 VP Enrollment Development & Comm .... Ms. Amy KREMENEK
09 VP Inst Planning/Assess/Research .... Dr. Agatha AWUAH
13 Chief Information Officer .... Mr. Dwight FISCHER
21 SVP & Chief Financial Officer .... Mr. Mark MANNING
124 AVP Student Engagement .... Ms. Rebecca HODA-KEARSE
20 Asst VP Academic & Support Svcs .... Ms. Kathleen D'APRIX
28 VP/Chief Diversity Officer .... Ms. Eunice WILLIAMS
18 VP Property Management .... Vacant
37 Director Financial Aid .... Vacant
41 Athletic Director .... Mr. Michael BORSZ
08 Chair Library .... Ms. Pauline SHOSTACK
19 VP Campus Safety & Security .... Mr. David WALL
22 Director Disability Services .... Ms. Nancy CARR
06 Registrar .... Vacant
113 Assistant Director Student Accounts .... Ms. Sally LUTON
96 Assistant VP Management Services .... Mr. Michael MCMULLEN
38 Director Advising & Counseling .... Ms. Jeanine ECKENRODE
18 Director of Sustainability .... Mr. Sean VORMWALD
04 Assistant to the President .... Ms. Julie HART
103 AVP Economic & Workforce Dev .... Mr. Michael METZGAR
25 AVP Research & Grants .... Ms. Nicole SCHLATER
29 Assistant Director Alumni Comm .... Mr. Russ CORBIN
45 AVP Inst Effectiveness & Planning .... Ms. Wendy TARBY
26 AVP Advancement Communications .... Ms. Susan TORMEY
43 Interim General Counsel .... Dr. Kevin MOORE
15 Chief Human Resources Officer .... Ms. Bridget SCHOLL
44 Director Annual Giving .... Mr. Shawn EDIE

Orange County Community College (C)

115 South Street, Middletown NY 10940-6437
County: Orange FICE Identification: 002876
Unit ID: 194240
Telephone: (845) 344-6222 Carnegie Class: Assoc/HT-High Trad
FAX Number: (845) 343-1228 Calendar System: Semester
URL: www.sunyorange.edu
Established: 1950 Annual Undergrad Tuition & Fees (In-District): $5,580
Enrollment: 6,601 Coed
Affiliation or Control: State/Local IRS Status: 501(c)3
Highest Offering: Associate Degree
Accreditation: M, ACBSP, ADNUR, DH, MLTAD, OTA, PTAA, RAD

01 President .... Dr. Kristine M. YOUNG
05 Vice Pres Academic Affairs .... Ms. Erika HACKMAN
32 Vice Pres Student Services .... Ms. Gerianne BRUSATI
10 VP Administration/Finance .... Ms. Linda DAUER
30 Vice Pres Institutional Advancement .... Mr. Vinnie CAZZETTA
13 Chief Information Officer .... Mr. Michael THARP
84 Assoc VP for Enrollment Management .... Vacant
76 Assoc VP Health Professions .... Dr. Michael GAWRONSKI, JR.
102 Int Executive Director Foundation .... Ms. Dawn ANSBRO
50 Assoc VP Business/Math/Sci/Tech .... Ms. Anne PRIAL
35 Assoc Vice Pres Stdnt Engagemt/Comp .... Ms. Madeline TORRES-DIAZ
15 Assoc Vice Pres Human Resources .... Ms. Wendy HOLMES
08 Library Director .... Mr. Andrew HEIZ
51 Dir Continuing/Professional Educ .... Mr. David KOHN
19 Int Director Campus Security/Safety .... Mr. Anthony JACKLITSCH
09 Inst Plng/Assessment/Research Ofcr .... Ms. Christine WORK
18 Director Administrative Services .... Mr. Michael WORDEN
37 Director of Financial Aid .... Vacant
06 Registrar .... Ms. Darlene BENZENBERG
26 Communications Officer .... Mr. Mike ALBRIGHT
88 Director Academic Advising .... Ms. Talia LLOSA
07 Director of Admissions .... Mr. Maynard SCHMIDT
35 Director Student Activities .... Mr. Steve HARPST
04 Exec Asst to President .... Ms. Carol MURRAY
41 Athletic Director .... Mr. Wayne SMITH
28 Chief Diversity Officer .... Ms. Lorraine LOPEZ-JANOVE
29 Dir Alumni Engagement/Cmty Rels .... Ms. Jennifer D'ANDREA

Orange County Community College Newburgh Branch Campus (D)

1 Washington Center, Newburgh NY 12550
Telephone: (845) 562-2454 Identification: 770144
Accreditation: &M

Pace University (E)

1 Pace Plaza, New York NY 10038-1598
County: New York FICE Identification: 002791
Unit ID: 194310
Telephone: (212) 346-1200 Carnegie Class: DU-Mod
FAX Number: (212) 346-1933 Calendar System: Semester
URL: www.pace.edu
Established: 1906 Annual Undergrad Tuition & Fees: $45,280
Enrollment: 12,986 Coed
Affiliation or Control: Independent Non-Profit IRS Status: 501(c)3
Highest Offering: Doctorate
Accreditation: M, ARCPA, CACREP, #CAEP, CAEPN, @DIETC, IPSY, LAW, NURSE, PSPSY, @SP

01 President .... Mr. Marvin KRISLOV
10 Exec Vice President/CFO .... Mr. Robert C. ALMON
05 Provost .... Dr. Vanya QUINONES
84 Vice Pres Enrollment/Placement .... Ms. Robina C. SCHEPP
111 VP Development/Alumni Relations .... Mr. Gary LAERMER
13 VP Information Tech/CIO .... Mr. Paul DAMPIER
26 VP/Chief Marketing Ofcr Univ Rels .... Mr. James STERNGOLD
15 Assoc Vice Pres Human Resources .... Vacant
09 Asst Vice Pres Plng/Assess/Inst Res .... Ms. Nancy DERIGGI
86 Asst Vice Pres Govt/Community Rels .... Ms. Vanessa J. HERMAN
19 Associate VP General Services .... Mr. Frank MCDONALD
50 Dean Lubin School of Business .... Mr. Neil S. BRAUN
49 Acting Dean Dyson College Arts/Sci .... Dr. Richard SCHLESINGER
53 Acting Dean School of Education .... Dr. Xiao-lei WANG
76 Dean College Health Professions .... Dr. Harriet R. FELDMAN
77 Dean School of CSIS .... Dr. Jonathan H. HILL
32 Dean of Students New York .... Dr. Marijo RUSSELL-OÆGRADY
32 Dean of Students Westchester .... Dr. Lisa BARDILL MOSCARITOLO
61 Dean School of Law .... Mr. David YASSKY
107 Asst VP Continuing/Professional Ed .... Dr. Christine SHAKESPEARE
06 Graduate Registrar .... Ms. Margaret JONES
06 Law School Registrar .... Ms. Nilda RODRIGUEZ
06 Associate University Registrar .... Ms. Barbara MCCARTHY
88 Asst Director Adult Education NY .... Ms. Nicola FOSTER
21 Interim Comptroller .... Mr. William VOLL
43 University Counsel .... Mr. Stephen BRODSKY
113 University Bursar .... Ms. Susan WEYGANT
07 Dir of Admissions NY/Westchester .... Ms. Joanna BRODA
22 Affirmative Action Officer .... Ms. Arletha MILES
14 Asst VP Information Technology Svcs .... Mr. Chris ELARDE
84 Director Adult Enroll Svcs/New York .... Ms. Janet KIRTMAN
38 Director Counseling Services .... Dr. Richard SHADICK
39 Director of Residential Life .... Mr. A. Patrick ROGER-GORDON
40 Executive Director Bookstore .... Ms. Mary LIETO
85 Assoc Dir Intl Pgms & Services .... Mr. Kraig WALKUP
96 Director of Purchasing - Contracts .... Ms. Alice SEIFERT
18 Director Facilities/Physical Plant .... Mr. Abdul JABAR
28 Director of Diversity .... Ms. Shanelle HENRY ROBINSON

Pacific College of Oriental Medicine (F)

110 William Street, 19th Floor, New York NY 10038
Telephone: (212) 982-3456 Identification: 666139
Accreditation: &WC, ACUP, NUR

† Branch campus of Pacific College of Oriental Medicine, San Diego CA.

Paul Smith's College (G)

PO Box 265, Paul Smiths NY 12970-0265
County: Franklin FICE Identification: 002795
Unit ID: 194392
Telephone: (518) 327-6000 Carnegie Class: Bac-Diverse
FAX Number: N/A Calendar System: Trimester
URL: www.paulsmiths.edu
Established: 1937 Annual Undergrad Tuition & Fees: $28,452
Enrollment: 771 Coed
Affiliation or Control: Independent Non-Profit IRS Status: 501(c)3
Highest Offering: Master's
Accreditation: M

01 President .... Dr. Cathy S. DOVE
05 Provost .... Dr. Nicholas HUNT-BULL
111 Vice President Inst Advancement .... Mr. F. Raymond AGNEW
84 VP of Enrollment Management .... Mr. David PLACEY
32 VP Student Affairs/Campus Life .... Dr. Terry LINDSAY
29 Director of Alumni Relations .... Ms. Heather TUTTLE
13 Dir Library Svcs/Info Technology .... Mr. Michael BECCARIA
06 Registrar .... Dr. Jeffrey WALTON
19 Lead Campus Safety Officer .... Ms. Holly PARKER
09 Director Institutional Research .... Dr. Jeffrey WALTON
22 Director HEOP .... Ms. Kate MULLEN
41 Director of Athletics .... Mr. James TUCKER
10 Comptroller .... Mr. Alexander BRYDEN
40 Manager of College Store .... Ms. Diana L. LYNG-GLIDDI
96 Purchasing Coordinator .... Ms. Cynthia LEMERY
36 Career Services Coordinator .... Ms. Debra DUTCHER
20 Assoc Academic Officer/Provost .... Dr. Catherine LALONDE
04 Admin Assistant to the President .... Ms. Bianca BETTGER
15 Director of Human Resources .... Ms. Gwen GOODMAN
26 Chief Marketing Officer .... Ms. Shannon OBORNE
37 Director Student Financial Aid .... Ms. Sonya STEIN
38 Director Student Counseling .... Ms. Shakirra JONES
39 Director Residence Life .... Ms. Amanda JONES

Phillips School of Nursing at Mount Sinai Beth Israel (H)

776 Sixth Avenue, 4th Floor, New York NY 10001-6354
County: New York FICE Identification: 006438
Unit ID: 189282
Telephone: (212) 614-6110 Carnegie Class: Spec-4-yr-Other Health
FAX Number: (212) 614-6109 Calendar System: Semester
URL: www.pson.edu
Established: 1904 Annual Undergrad Tuition & Fees: $36,795
Enrollment: 178 Coed
Affiliation or Control: Independent Non-Profit IRS Status: 501(c)3
Highest Offering: Baccalaureate
Accreditation: NY, ADNUR, NURSE

01 Dean .... Dr. Todd AMBROSIA
05 Sr Associate Dean .... Dr. Laly JOSEPH
32 Asst Dean Student Svcs/Inst Effect .... Mrs. Bernice PASS-STERN
88 Assistant Dean for BAC Programs .... Ms. Carleen GRAHAM
30 Dir Development/Communications .... Ms. Linda FABRIZIO

Plaza College (I)

118-33 Queens Boulevard, Forest Hills NY 11375
County: Queens FICE Identification: 012358
Unit ID: 194499
Telephone: (718) 779-1430 Carnegie Class: Bac/Assoc-Mixed
FAX Number: (718) 779-7423 Calendar System: Semester
URL: www.plazacollege.edu
Established: 1916 Annual Undergrad Tuition & Fees: $12,450
Enrollment: 909 Coed
Affiliation or Control: Proprietary IRS Status: Proprietary
Highest Offering: Baccalaureate
Accreditation: M, CAHIIM, DH, MAC

01 President .... Charles E. CALLAHAN, III
10 Vice Pres of Financial Services .... Vacant
11 Chief Operating Officer .... Charles E. CALLAHAN, IV
05 Dean of Academic Affairs .... Marie DOLLA
06 Registrar .... Carol GARCIA
21 Comptroller .... Linda ROCKHILL
07 Director of Admissions .... Vanessa LOPEZ
20 Dean Curriculum Development .... Marianne C. ZIPF
08 College Librarian .... Eva BABALIS
23 Director Health Services .... Candice CALLAHAN
37 Director Financial Aid .... Peggy CHUNG
32 Dean of Students .... Dawn VETRANO
35 Dean of Student Activities .... Jonathan HOWLE
15 Director of HR/HR Officer .... Correne CAVALIERI
09 Assoc Dean Institutional Research .... Edward DEE
13 Chief Technology Officer .... David COLUCCI
88 Director of ARC/Library .... Allison KRAMPF
14 Manager Information Technology .... Norman ALVARADO
76 Program Director Medical Assisting .... Daryl ANDERSON
26 Director of Communications .... Brittany TRAVIS
38 Freshman Counseling .... Caroline CALLAHAN
36 Director of Career Services .... Regina POKIDAYLO

Pratt Institute (J)

200 Willoughby Avenue, Brooklyn NY 11205-3899
County: Kings FICE Identification: 002798
Unit ID: 194578
Telephone: (718) 636-3600 Carnegie Class: Spec-4-yr-Arts
FAX Number: (718) 636-3670 Calendar System: Semester
URL: www.pratt.edu
Established: 1887 Annual Undergrad Tuition & Fees: $51,870
Enrollment: 5,035 Coed
Affiliation or Control: Independent Non-Profit IRS Status: 501(c)3
Highest Offering: Master's
Accreditation: M, ART, CAEPT, CIDA, LIB, PLNG

01 President .... Ms. Frances BRONET
00 President Emeritus .... Dr. Thomas F. SCHUTTE
05 Provost .... Dr. Kirk E. PILLOW
32 Vice President for Student Life .... Dr. Helen MATUSOW-AYRES
10 Vice Pres Finance/Administration .... Ms. Cathleen KENNY

111 Vice Pres for Inst Advancement .... Ms. Daphne HALPERN
84 Vice President for Enrollment .... Ms. Judith AARON
28 VP for Diversity/Equity/Inclusion .... Ms. Nsombi B. RICKETTS
26 Vice Pres Communications/Marketing .... Mr. James KEMPSTER
20 Associate Provost Academic Affairs .... Dr. Donna HEILAND
88 Assoc Provost Strat Partnerships .... Dr. Allison DRUIN
11 Assistant to Pres Administration .... Ms. Josie CAPORUSCIO
06 Registrar .... Mr. Luke PHILLIPS
08 Director of the Library .... Mr. Russ ABELL
15 Director Human Resources .... Mr. Steve RICCOBONO
51 Dean Continuing Education .... Ms. Maira SEARA
36 Director of Career Services .... Ms. Rhonda SCHALLER
37 Director Student Financial Aid .... Mr. Nedzad GOGA
09 Exec Dir Strat Planning & Inst Eff .... Vacant
43 Director of Legal Affairs .... Mr. Thomas GREENE
96 Director of Purchasing .... Ms. Mitzi BRYAN
57 Interim Dean of Art .... Mr. Jorge OLIVER
49 Dean Liberal Arts/Science .... Dr. Andrew BARNES
48 Dean School of Architecture .... Mr. Thomas HANRAHAN
62 Dean Information/Library Sci .... Dr. Anthony COCCIOLO
88 Dean of Design .... Ms. Anita COONEY
13 Chief Info Technology Officer (CIO) .... Mr. Joseph HEMWAY
18 Chief Facilities Officer .... Mr. Christopher GAVLICK
19 Director Security/Safety .... Mr. Dennis MAZONE
39 Director Student Housing .... Mr. Christopher KASIK
41 Athletic Director .... Mr. Walter RICKARD
90 Director Academic Computing .... Mr. Ellery MATTHEWS

Rabbinical Academy Mesivta Rabbi Chaim Berlin (A)

1605 Coney Island Avenue, Brooklyn NY 11230-4715
County: Kings — FICE Identification: 003976
Unit ID: 194657
Telephone: (718) 377-0777 — Carnegie Class: Spec-4-yr-Faith
FAX Number: (718) 338-5578 — Calendar System: Semester
Established: 1939 — Annual Undergrad Tuition & Fees: $12,450
Enrollment: 290 — Male
Affiliation or Control: Independent Non-Profit — IRS Status: 501(c)3
Highest Offering: Second Talmudic Degree
Accreditation: RABN

01 Provost .... Rabbi Abraham H. FRUCHTHANDLER
05 President of the Faculty .... Rabbi Aaron M. SCHECHTER
03 Executive Director .... Rabbi Y. Mayer LASKER
29 Director of Alumni Association .... Mendel SCHECHTER
45 Chief Planning Officer .... Rabbi Tuvia M. OBERMEISTER
20 Associate Director .... Eli RABINOWITZ
37 Financial Aid Administrator .... Michael A. REISS

Rabbinical College Beth Shraga (B)

28 Saddle River Road, Monsey NY 10952-3035
County: Rockland — FICE Identification: 010943
Unit ID: 194693
Telephone: (845) 356-1980 — Carnegie Class: Spec-4-yr-Faith
FAX Number: (845) 425-2604 — Calendar System: Semester
Established: 1965 — Annual Undergrad Tuition & Fees: $13,550
Enrollment: 39 — Male
Affiliation or Control: Independent Non-Profit — IRS Status: 501(c)3
Highest Offering: Second Talmudic Degree
Accreditation: RABN

01 President .... Rabbi Emanuel SCHIFF

Rabbinical College Bobover Yeshiva B'nei Zion (C)

1577 48th Street, Brooklyn NY 11219-3293
County: Kings — FICE Identification: 008614
Unit ID: 194666
Telephone: (718) 438-2018 — Carnegie Class: Spec-4-yr-Faith
FAX Number: (718) 871-9031 — Calendar System: Semester
Established: 1947 — Annual Undergrad Tuition & Fees: $7,750
Enrollment: 342 — Male
Affiliation or Control: Independent Non-Profit — IRS Status: 501(c)3
Highest Offering: First Talmudic Degree
Accreditation: RABN

01 President .... Rabbi Boruch Avrohom HOROWITZ

Rabbinical College of Long Island (D)

205 W Beech Street, Long Beach NY 11561-0630
County: Nassau — FICE Identification: 010378
Unit ID: 194736
Telephone: (516) 255-4700 — Carnegie Class: Spec-4-yr-Faith
FAX Number: (516) 255-4701 — Calendar System: Semester
Established: 1965 — Annual Undergrad Tuition & Fees: $8,800
Enrollment: 143 — Male
Affiliation or Control: Independent Non-Profit — IRS Status: 501(c)3
Highest Offering: First Talmudic Degree
Accreditation: RABN

01 President .... Rabbi Yitzchok FEIGELSTOCK
06 Registrar .... Rabbi Dovid N. ROTHSCHILD
32 Dean of Students .... Rabbi Yeruchem PITTER
07 CEO and Director of Admissions .... Rabbi Chaim HOBERMAN
37 Financial Aid Administrator .... Rabbi Shlomo TEICHMAN
06 Assistant Registrar .... Mrs. Sora CENSON

Rabbinical College Ohr Shimon Yisroel (E)

215-217 Hewes Street, Brooklyn NY 11211-8102
County: Kings — FICE Identification: 031292
Unit ID: 405854
Telephone: (718) 855-4092 — Carnegie Class: Spec-4-yr-Faith
FAX Number: (718) 855-8479 — Calendar System: Semester
Established: — Annual Undergrad Tuition & Fees: $13,600
Enrollment: 227 — Male
Affiliation or Control: Independent Non-Profit — IRS Status: 501(c)3
Highest Offering: First Talmudic Degree
Accreditation: RABN

01 President .... Rabbi Shulem WALTER

Rabbinical College Ohr Yisroel (F)

8800 Seaview Avenue, Brooklyn NY 11236
County: Kings — Identification: 667145
Unit ID: 484871
Telephone: (718) 633-4715 — Carnegie Class: Spec-4-yr-Faith
FAX Number: (347) 702-5436 — Calendar System: Semester
Established: 2009 — Annual Undergrad Tuition & Fees: $9,000
Enrollment: 116 — Male
Affiliation or Control: Independent Non-Profit — IRS Status: 501(c)3
Highest Offering: First Talmudic Degree
Accreditation: @RABN

01 President .... Rabbi Daniel GELDZAHLER

Rabbinical Seminary of America (G)

76-01 147th Street, Flushing NY 11367-3148
County: Queens — FICE Identification: 003978
Unit ID: 194763
Telephone: (718) 268-4700 — Carnegie Class: Spec-4-yr-Faith
FAX Number: (718) 268-4684 — Calendar System: Semester
Established: 1933 — Annual Undergrad Tuition & Fees: $9,800
Enrollment: 454 — Male
Affiliation or Control: Independent Non-Profit — IRS Status: 501(c)3
Highest Offering: Second Talmudic Degree
Accreditation: RABN

01 President .... Rabbi David HARRIS
01 President .... Rabbi Akiva GRUNBLATT
03 Executive Vice President .... Rabbi Hayim SCHWARTZ
11 Director of Operation .... Rabbi Meir GLAZER
06 Registrar .... Rabbi Abraham SEMMEL
05 Executive Director .... Rabbi Yehuda JEGER
30 Director Development .... Rabbi Yossi SINGER
37 Director of Financial Aid .... Mrs. Laya EISENSTEIN
18 Chief Physical Plant .... Mr. Ariel WOLFARTH
88 Director of Special Projects .... Vacant
91 Director of Admin Computing .... Mr. Jonathan PLATOVSKY
39 Director Student Housing .... Rabbi Elisha FEINBERG
46 Director Research & Development .... Vacant

Relay Graduate School of Education (H)

40 West 20th Street, 7th Floor, New York NY 10011
County: New York — Identification: 667117
Unit ID: 475033
Telephone: (212) 228-1888 — Carnegie Class: Spec-4-yr-Other
FAX Number: (212) 228-1855 — Calendar System: Other
URL: www.relayschool.org
Established: 2011 — Annual Graduate Tuition & Fees: N/A
Enrollment: 3,186 — Coed
Affiliation or Control: Independent Non-Profit — IRS Status: 501(c)3
Highest Offering: Master's; No Undergraduates
Accreditation: M, CAEPN

01 Co-Founder/President .... Mr. Norman ATKINS
05 Provost .... Dr. Brent MADDIN
10 Chief Financial Officer .... Ms. Piper EVANS
11 Chief Operating Officer .... Ms. Pamela INBASEKARAM
32 Chief Student Services Officer .... Ms. Kelly BOUCHER MORRIS
20 Dean .... Ms. Jennifer RAMOS

Rensselaer Polytechnic Institute (I)

110 8th Street, Troy NY 12180-3590
County: Rensselaer — FICE Identification: 002803
Unit ID: 194824
Telephone: (518) 276-6000 — Carnegie Class: DU-Highest
FAX Number: N/A — Calendar System: Semester
URL: www.rpi.edu
Established: 1824 — Annual Undergrad Tuition & Fees: $53,880
Enrollment: 7,592 — Coed
Affiliation or Control: Independent Non-Profit — IRS Status: 501(c)3
Highest Offering: Doctorate
Accreditation: M

01 President .... Dr. Shirley Ann JACKSON
05 Provost .... Dr. Prabhat HAJELA
11 Vice President for Administration .... Mr. Claude ROUNDS
26 VP Strategic Comm/External Rels .... Ms. Richie C. HUNTER
10 Vice President for Finance/CFO .... Ms. Barbara J. HOUGH
45 Vice Pres for Research .... Vacant
111 Vice Pres Institutional Advancement .... Mr. Graig R. EASTIN
32 Vice President Student Life .... Dr. Peter KONWERSKI
15 Vice Pres Human Resources .... Mr. Curtis N. POWELL
13 Vice Pres for Info Services & CIO .... Mr. John E. KOLB
84 Vice Pres Enrollment Management .... Dr. Jonathan D. WEXLER
43 Secretary of Inst/General Counsel .... Mr. Craig A. COOK
27 Assoc VP Marketing/Communications .... Ms. Pamela S. SMITH
41 Assoc Vice Pres/Director Athletics .... Dr. Lee MCELROY
19 AVP Public Safety/Emergency Mgmt .... Mr. Vadim THOMAS
21 Asst Vice Pres for Administration .... Mr. Paul W. MARTIN
29 Asst Vice Pres Alumni Relations .... Vacant
35 Asst Vice Pres & Dean of Students .... Mr. Travis APGAR
121 Asst Vice Pres of Student Success .... Ms. Lisa TRAHAN
54 Dean School of Engineering .... Dr. Shekhar GARDE
81 Dean School of Science .... Dr. Curt BRENEMAN
79 Dean Sch of Humanities/Arts/Soc Sci .... Dr. Mary SIMONI
50 Acting Dean Lally School Management .... Dr. Chanaka EDIRISINGHE
48 Dean School of Architecture .... Mr. Evan DOUGLIS
107 Dean Acad & Admin Affs Hartford .... Dr. Aric KRAUSE
58 Vice Provost/Dean Graduate Educ .... Dr. Stanley DUNN
20 Vice Provost/Dean Undergrad Educ .... Dr. Keith MOO-YOUNG
06 Registrar .... Vacant
37 Director Financial Aid .... Mr. Martin C. DANIELS
09 Director of Institutional Research .... Vacant
08 Director of Libraries .... Mr. Andrew C. WHITE
25 Director of Research Administration .... Ms. Javeria KAZI
36 Director Career Development Center .... Mr. Philip BRUCE
07 Director Undergrad Admissions .... Ms. Karen S. LONG
123 Director Graduate Admissions .... Mr. Jarron P. DECKER
18 Director Physical Plant .... Mr. Ernest J. KATZWINKEL
23 Exec Director Student Health Center .... Dr. Leslie LAWRENCE
38 Director Student Counseling .... Vacant
96 Director Procurement Services .... Mr. Ron MORASKI
04 Executive Asst to the President .... Vacant
105 Director Web Services .... Mr. Andrew C. WHITE
44 Director Annual Giving .... Ms. Silvia R. EDMONDS
90 Director Client Info Services .... Ms. Jacqueline B. STAMPALIA
91 Director Enterprise Info Services .... Ms. Mary Alice O'BRIEN
39 Dean Student Living & Learning .... Mr. John LAWLOR

Richard Gilder Graduate School at the American Museum of Natural History (J)

Central Park West at 79th Street, New York NY 10024
County: New York — Identification: 667003
Unit ID: 458548
Telephone: (212) 769-5055 — Carnegie Class: Not Classified
FAX Number: (212) 769-5257 — Calendar System: Other
URL: www.amnh.org/our-research/richard-gilder-graduate-school
Established: 2006 — Annual Graduate Tuition & Fees: N/A
Enrollment: N/A — Coed
Affiliation or Control: Independent Non-Profit — IRS Status: 501(c)3
Highest Offering: Doctorate; No Undergraduates
Accreditation: NY, CAEP

01 Dean .... Dr. John J. FLYNN

Roberts Wesleyan College (K)

2301 Westside Drive, Rochester NY 14624-1997
County: Monroe — FICE Identification: 002805
Unit ID: 194958
Telephone: (585) 594-6000 — Carnegie Class: Masters/L
FAX Number: (585) 594-6371 — Calendar System: Semester
URL: www.roberts.edu
Established: 1866 — Annual Undergrad Tuition & Fees: $31,568
Enrollment: 1,740 — Coed
Affiliation or Control: Independent Non-Profit — IRS Status: 501(c)3
Highest Offering: Doctorate
Accreditation: M, ART, IACBE, MUS, NURSE, PSPSY, SW

01 President .... Dr. Deana L. PORTERFIELD
05 Sr VP & Chief Academic Officer .... Dr. David BASINGER
10 Sr Vice President & Treasurer .... Ms. Laurie LEO
32 VP for Student & Org Development .... Mrs. Ruth LOGAN
111 VP Institutional Advancement .... Mr. Darrell BELL
84 VP for Enrollment Management .... Mrs. Kimberley WIEDEFELD
07 Exec Director of UG Admissions .... Ms. Mary SASSO
112 Assoc VP for Major Gifts .... Mr. Maurice (Max) MCGINNIS
26 AVP for Brand/Marketing Comm .... Ms. Donna MCLAREN
13 Assoc VP for Information Technology .... Mr. Pradeep SAXENA
40 Director of Bookstore Services .... Mr. Darren WALTON
41 Director of Athletics .... Mr. Robert SEGAVE
37 Director of Student Financial Svcs .... Ms. Tayler KREUTTER
09 Dir Institutional Research/Assess .... Dr. Paul W. KENNEDY
42 Chaplain .... Rev. Gerald COLEMAN
06 Registrar .... Mrs. Lesa J. KOHR
04 Administrative Asst to President .... Mrs. Mimi WHEELER
15 Director Personnel Services .... Mrs. Amy PORPILIA
18 Chief Facilities/Physical Plant .... Mr. T. Richard GREER
19 Director Security/Safety .... Mr. Rick BILLITIER
25 Chief Contracts/Grants Admin .... Mrs. Lisa TIFFIN
29 Director Alumni Relations .... Mr. Kirk KETTINGER
103 Dir Workforce/Career Development .... Ms. Mary FLAHERTY
104 Director International Engagement .... Ms. Julie RUSHIK
50 Dean School of Business .... Dr. Steven BOVEE

† Parent institution of Northeastern Seminary.

Rochester Institute of Technology (A)

1 Lomb Memorial Drive, Rochester NY 14623-5604
County: Monroe FICE Identification: 002806
Unit ID: 195003
Telephone: (585) 475-2411 Carnegie Class: DU-Higher
FAX Number: (585) 475-7049 Calendar System: Quarter
URL: www.rit.edu
Established: 1829 Annual Undergrad Tuition & Fees: $42,345
Enrollment: 16,584 Coed
Affiliation or Control: Independent Non-Profit IRS Status: 501(c)3
Highest Offering: Doctorate
Accreditation: M, #ARCPA, ART, CAEPT, CEA, CIDA, DIETD, DMS, IPSY

01 President .... Dr. David C. MUNSON, JR.
05 Int Provost/SVP Academic Affairs .... Dr. Christine M. LICATA
100 Chief of Staff .... Mrs. Karen A. BARROWS
10 Sr Vice Pres Finance/Administration .... Dr. James H. WATTERS
84 VP Enrollment Management .... Mr. Ian MORTIMER
32 Sr Vice President Student Affairs .... Dr. Sandra S. JOHNSON
46 President NTID/RIT Vice Pres & Dean .... Dr. Gerard J. BUCKLEY
12 President RIT Dubai .... Dr. Yousef AL-ASSAF
30 VP for Development & Alumni Rels .... Dr. Lisa CAUDA
86 Vice President Govt/Cmty Relations .... Ms. Deborah M. STENDARDI
46 Vice President Research .... Dr. Ryne RAFFAELLE
28 VP Diversity & Inclusion .... Dr. Keith JENKINS
12 Int Pres/Dn of Fac AUK/Kosovo Pgms .... Dr. Kamal SHAHRABI
76 VP/Dean Coll Health Sciences/Tech .... Dr. Daniel B. ORNT
46 Vice Provost .... Dr. Christine M. LICATA
36 Director Coop Educ/Career Svcs .... Ms. Maria RICHART
26 Chief Communications Officer .... Mr. Robert FINNERTY
20 Assoc Provost and Director CIMS .... Dr. Nabil NASR
08 Director of RIT Libraries .... Ms. Marcia TRAVERNICHT
12 President-RIT Croatia .... Mr. Donald HUDSPETH
29 Exec Director Alumni Relations .... Mr. Jon RODIBAUGH
21 Asst VP/Controller/Asst Treasurer .... Ms. Lyn KELLY
18 Asst VP Facilities Management Svs .... Mr. John MOORE
06 Assoc VP/Registrar .... Mr. Joe LOFFREDO
07 Director of Admissions .... Ms. Marian NICOLETTI
37 Asst VP & Dir Fin Aid & Scholarship .... Mr. Larry CHAMBERS
84 Assoc VP & Dir Grad/PT Enroll Svc .... Ms. Diane ELLISON
112 Assoc VP for Campaigns & Const Dev .... Vacant
09 Asst VP Inst Rsrch/Policy Studies .... Dr. Joan E. GRAHAM
15 Assoc VP/Director Human Resources .... Ms. Judy BENDER
44 Executive Director Annual Giving .... Ms. Marisa PSAILA
35 Assoc VP Student Development .... Dr. Heath BOICE-PARDEE
85 Director International Student Svcs .... Mr. Jeffrey W. COX
96 Exec Director Procurement Services .... Ms. Debra KUSSE
102 Sr Director Foundation Relations .... Vacant
102 Exec Dir Corp/Foundation Relations .... Mr. Paul HARRIS
101 Secretary of the Institute .... Mrs. Karen A. BARROWS
50 Dean of Business .... Dr. Jacqueline MOZRALL
54 Dean of Engineering .... Dr. Doreen EDWARDS
72 Dean of Engineering Technology .... Dr. S. Manian RAMKUMAR
49 Dean of Liberal Arts .... Dr. James J. WINEBRAKE
81 Dean of Science .... Dr. Sophia MAGGELAKIS
57 Int Dean College of Art & Design .... Dr. Robin CASS
77 Dean Col Computer/Info Science .... Dr. Anne HAAKE
58 Dean Graduate Education .... Dr. Twyla CUMMINGS
04 Exec Admin Asst to President .... Ms. Sonia RODRIGUEZ
11 Chief of Administration .... Mrs. Karen A. BARROWS
13 Chief Info Technology Officer (CIO) .... Ms. Jeanne CASARES
41 Exec Dir Intercollegiate Athletics .... Mr. Louis SPIOTTI
26 Chief Marketing Officer .... Mr. John K. TRIERWEILER
103 Assoc Dir Organizational Dev .... Ms. Joeann M. HUMBERT
104 Assoc Provost Intl Ed/Global Pgms .... Dr. James A. MYERS
105 Director Web Services .... Mr. Raman S. BHALLA
106 Exec Director Innovative Learning .... Dr. Neil F. HAIR
108 Asst Provost Assmt/Accreditation .... Dr. Anne G. WAHL
19 Director Public Safety .... Mr. Gary D. MOXLEY
38 Director Counseling & Psych Svcs .... Dr. David R. REETZ
39 AVP Stdnt Aux Svcs/Housing Ops .... Dr. Howard WARD

Rockefeller University (B)

1230 York Avenue, New York NY 10065-6399
County: New York FICE Identification: 002807
Unit ID: 195049
Telephone: (212) 327-8000 Carnegie Class: DU-Higher
FAX Number: (212) 327-8699 Calendar System: Trimester
URL: www.rockefeller.edu
Established: 1901 Annual Graduate Tuition & Fees: N/A
Enrollment: 232 Coed
Affiliation or Control: Independent Non-Profit IRS Status: 501(c)3
Highest Offering: Doctorate; No Undergraduates
Accreditation: NY

01 President .... Dr. Richard P. LIFTON
03 Executive Vice President .... Dr. Timothy O'CONNOR
43 Vice President & General Counsel .... Ms. Deborah YEOH
05 Vice President Academic Affairs .... Mr. Michael W. YOUNG
10 Vice President Finance .... Mr. James H. LAPPLE
30 Sr Vice President Development .... Ms. Maren E. IMHOFF
17 Vice President for Medical Affairs .... Dr. Barry S. COLLER
20 Dean & Vice Pres of Educ Affairs .... Dr. Sidney STRICKLAND
15 Vice President Human Resources .... Ms. Virginia A. HUFFMAN
18 Assoc Vice Pres Plant Operations .... Mr. Alexander KOGAN
45 Assoc Vice Pres Plng & Constr .... Mr. George B. CANDLER
13 Chief Information Officer .... Mr. Anthony CARVALLOZA
25 Dir Pgm Dev & Sponsored Research .... Ms. Collette L. RYDER
08 University Librarian .... Dr. Matthew V. COVEY
19 Director Security .... Mr. James ROGERS
26 Assoc VP Communications/Public Affs .... Mr. Franklin HOKE

Rockland Community College (C)

145 College Road, Suffern NY 10901-3699
County: Rockland FICE Identification: 002877
Unit ID: 195058
Telephone: (845) 574-4000 Carnegie Class: Assoc/HT-High Trad
FAX Number: (845) 574-4463 Calendar System: Semester
URL: www.sunyrockland.edu
Established: 1959 Annual Undergrad Tuition & Fees (In-District): $5,182
Enrollment: 6,950 Coed
Affiliation or Control: State/Local IRS Status: 501(c)3
Highest Offering: Associate Degree
Accreditation: M, ADNUR, OTA

01 President .... Dr. Michael A. BASTON
10 Int Chief Financial Officer .... Dr. Daniel DOBELL
05 Provost/Exec Vice President .... Dr. Susan DEER
32 VP Enrollment & Student Affairs .... Dr. Helen BREWER
21 Assoc VP Finance/Administration .... Mr. Joseph MARRA
88 AVP Academic/Community Partnershp .... Mr. Thomas DELLA TORRE
84 AVP of Enrollment Management .... Ms. Dana STILLEY
35 Dean Student Development .... Ms. Sutonia BOYKIN
37 Director Financial Aid .... Ms. Debra BOUABIDI
06 Registrar .... Ms. Robin CONKLIN
13 Director of Information Services .... Dr. Steven FERRES
18 Chief Facilities/Physical Plant .... Mr. Douglas SCHMIDT
28 Dir Equity/Compliance/Affirm Act .... Ms. Melissa ROY
09 Director of Institutional Research .... Dr. Jim ROBERTSON
20 Asst to Vice Pres Academic Affairs .... Ms. Patricia KOBES
26 Chief Public Relations Officer .... Ms. Tzipora REITMAN
04 Administrative Asst to President .... Mr. Ben NAYLOR
07 Director of Admissions .... Mr. Jude FLEURISMOND
101 Secretary of the Board .... Mr. Ben NAYLOR
106 Dir Online Education/E-learning .... Ms. Lilia JUELE
11 Chief of Administration .... Mr. Dennis CALLINAN
15 Int Director Human Resources .... Mr. Wayne TAYLOR
19 Director Public Safety .... Mr. William MURPHY
25 Assoc VP for Resource Development .... Ms. Elizabeth KENDALL
41 Athletic Director .... Mr. Dan KEELEY
90 Director Academic Computing .... Ms. Lilia JUELE

The Sage Colleges (D)

65 First Street, Troy NY 12180-4199
County: Rensselaer FICE Identification: 002810
Unit ID: 195128
Telephone: (518) 244-2000 Carnegie Class: DU-Mod
FAX Number: (518) 244-2460 Calendar System: Semester
URL: www.sage.edu
Established: 1916 Annual Undergrad Tuition & Fees: $30,857
Enrollment: 2,525 Coed
Affiliation or Control: Independent Non-Profit IRS Status: 501(c)3
Highest Offering: Doctorate
Accreditation: M, ART, DIETD, DIETI, IACBE, NURSE, OT, PTA

01 President .... Dr. Christopher AMES
05 Interim Provost .... Dr. Theresa HAND
111 VP for Institutional Advancement .... Ms. Kate ADAMS
84 Interim VP Marketing/Enroll Mgmt .... Ms. Susan REANTILLO
12 Dean Sage College of Albany .... Dr. Deborah LAWRENCE
12 Dean Russell Sage College .... Dr. Deborah LAWRENCE
10 VP for Finance & Treasurer .... Mr. Rick BARTHELMAS
32 Vice Pres for Campus Life .... Ms. Patricia CELLEMME
11 VP Administration & Planning .... Ms. Deirdre ZARRILLO
35 Dean of Students-RSC .... Ms. Stacy GONZALEZ
35 Dean of Students-SCA .... Ms. Sharon MURRAY
76 Dean of Health Sciences .... Dr. Kathleen KELLY
06 Registrar .... Ms. Kathy SCOVILLE
07 Director of UG Admission .... Ms. Sarah BARRETT
88 Dean School of Management .... Dr. Kimberly FREDERICKS
53 Dean School of Education .... Dr. John PELIZZA
29 Dir of Alumni Relations SCA/SGS .... Ms. Katie FALSO
29 Director Alumnae Relations RSC .... Ms. Joan CLIFFORD
123 Dir of Graduate & Adult Admissions .... Mr. Michael JONES
37 Director of Financial Aid .... Ms. Kelley ROBINSON
15 Director of Human Resources .... Ms. Laura D'AGOSTINO
09 Director of Institutional Research .... Ms. Lori PIZER
18 Director Facilities Management .... Mr. John ZAJACESKOWSKI
121 Dir of Academic Advisement-SCA .... Ms. Karen SCHELL
121 Dir of Academic Advisement-RSC .... Ms. Beth MANEY
26 Dir of Communications & Marketing .... Ms. Heidi WEBER
92 Director of Honors Programs .... Dr. Tonya MOUTRAY
96 Dir of Purchasing/Accts Payable .... Ms. Paula SELMER
04 Administrative Asst to President .... Ms. Rose L. GRIGNON
08 Head Librarian .... Ms. Lisa C. BRAINARD
105 Webmaster .... Mr. Kurt EYE
108 Director Institutional Assessment .... Vacant
19 Director Security/Safety .... Mr. Michael TREMBLAY
39 Director of Residence Life .... Ms. Shylah ADDANTE
41 Athletic Director .... Ms. Sandy AUGESTINE-COLLINS
44 Sr Director of Annual Giving .... Ms. Kathleen DANICA
91 Director of IT/Network Services .... Mr. John HARRIS
106 Director of Online Education .... Ms. Kimberly TAYLOR
28 Director of Diversity & Inclusion .... Dr. David B. GREEN, JR.

Saint Bernard's School of Theology & Ministry (E)

120 French Road, Rochester NY 14618-3822
County: Monroe FICE Identification: 002815
Unit ID: 195155
Telephone: (585) 271-3657 Carnegie Class: Spec-4-yr-Faith
FAX Number: (585) 271-2045 Calendar System: Semester
URL: www.stbernards.edu
Established: 1893 Annual Graduate Tuition & Fees: N/A
Enrollment: 77 Coed
Affiliation or Control: Roman Catholic IRS Status: 501(c)3
Highest Offering: Master's; No Undergraduates
Accreditation: THEOL

01 Acting President .... Dr. Matthew KUHNER
11 Office Manager .... Ms. Corinne DERCOLA
10 Controller .... Mr. Jim PUDETTI
07 Director of Recruitment .... Mr. Matthew BROWN

St. Bonaventure University (F)

P.O. Box 2450, St. Bonaventure NY 14778
County: Cattaraugus FICE Identification: 002817
Unit ID: 195164
Telephone: (716) 375-2000 Carnegie Class: Masters/M
FAX Number: N/A Calendar System: Semester
URL: www.sbu.edu
Established: 1858 Annual Undergrad Tuition & Fees: $34,331
Enrollment: 2,084 Coed
Affiliation or Control: Roman Catholic IRS Status: 501(c)3
Highest Offering: Master's
Accreditation: M, CACREP, CAEPN, JOUR

01 President .... Dr. Dennis R. DEPERRO
05 Provost and VP for Academic Affairs .... Dr. Joseph ZIMMER
32 Vice Pres for Student Affairs .... Ms. Kathryn O'BRIEN
10 VP Finance & Administration/CFO .. Mr. H. Daniel HUNGERFORD
26 Int Vice Pres University Relations .... Mr. Thomas MISSEL
42 Exec Dir University Ministries .... Fr. Francis J. DISPIGNO, OFM
111 Vice Pres for Advancement .... Mr. Robert VAN WICKLIN
84 Vice President for Enrollment .... Mr. Bernard VALENTO
57 Exec Dir of Q Arts Center .... Mr. Ludwig BRUNNER
20 Assoc Vice Pres Academic Affairs .... Ms. Ann LEHMAN
100 Assoc VP & Chief of Staff .... Ms. Ann LEHMAN
11 Exec Assistant to the President .... Ms. Sarah STANGLE
15 Director Human Resources .... Mr. Erik SEASTEDT
07 Director of Recruitment .... Mr. Douglas BRADY
37 Director of Financial Aid .... Mr. Christopher CARTMILL
06 Registrar .... Mr. George B. SWINDOLL
39 Exec Dir Residential Living/Conduct .... Ms. Nichole GONZALEZ
13 Assoc Provost/Chief Info Officer .... Dr. Michael HOFFMAN
08 Director Friedsam Memorial Library .... Ms. Ann TENGLUND
101 Director of Board/Govt/Cmty Rels .... Mr. Thomas BUTTAFARRO, JR.
41 Director of Athletics .... Mr. Tim KENNEY
29 Director of Alumni Services .... Mr. Joseph FLANAGAN
36 Director of Career Services .... Ms. Pamela FERMAN
43 University Counsel .... Mr. Jeff REISNER
23 Director Wellness Center .... Mr. Christopher ANDERSON
18 Director of Facilities Operations .... Mr. Rob HURLBURT
21 Controller .... Ms. Nancy K. TAYLOR
19 Director of Safety and Security .... Mr. Gary SEGRUE
40 Manager Bookstore .... Ms. Annette DONAVON
44 Director Annual Giving Program .... Ms. Karen HEITZINGER
92 Director of Honors Program .... Dr. Darryl MAYEAUX
49 Dean School of Arts & Sci .... Dr. David HILMEY
50 Dean School of Business .... Dr. Matricia JAMES
58 Dean School of Graduate Studies .... Dr. Lisa BUENAVENTURA
53 Dean School of Education .... Dr. Lisa BUENAVENTURA
60 Dean Jandoli Sch of Communication .... Mr. Aaron CHIMBLE
76 Dean School of Allied Health .... Dr. Douglas PISANO
26 Director Marketing and Promotions .... Mr. Seth JOHNSON

St. Elizabeth College of Nursing (G)

2215 Genesee Street, Utica NY 13501-5998
County: Oneida FICE Identification: 006461
Unit ID: 195702
Telephone: (315) 798-8144 Carnegie Class: Spec 2-yr-Health
FAX Number: (315) 798-8271 Calendar System: Semester
URL: www.secon.edu
Established: 1904 Annual Undergrad Tuition & Fees: $16,630
Enrollment: 202 Coed
Affiliation or Control: Independent Non-Profit IRS Status: 501(c)3
Highest Offering: Associate Degree
Accreditation: M, ADNUR

01 President .... Dr. Varinya SHEPPARD
32 Co-Dean of Students/Faculty Devel .... Mrs. Beverly PLANTE
32 Co-Dean of Students/Faculty Devel .... Mrs. Jessica ELDRED
06 Registrar & Bursar .... Mr. Joseph CASCELLA
10 Director of Finance & Enrollment .... Ms. Sherry WOJNAS

St. Francis College (H)

180 Remsen Street, Brooklyn NY 11201-4398
County: Kings FICE Identification: 002820
Unit ID: 195173
Telephone: (718) 522-2300 Carnegie Class: Bac-Diverse
FAX Number: (718) 522-1274 Calendar System: Semester
URL: www.sfc.edu
Established: 1859 Annual Undergrad Tuition & Fees: $26,188
Enrollment: 2,362 Coed
Affiliation or Control: Independent Non-Profit IRS Status: 501(c)3
Highest Offering: Master's
Accreditation: M, NURSE

01 President .... Dr. Miguel MARTINEZ-SAENZ
10 Vice President of Financial Affairs .... Mr. John RAGNO

26 Vice Pres Govt/Community Relations .... Ms. Linda WERBEL DASHEFSKY
30 Vice President of Development .... Mr. Thomas FLOOD
84 Vice Pres Enrollment Mgmt Svcs .... Vacant
18 VP Facilities Mgmt/Capital Projects .... Mr. Kevin O'ROURKE
104 VP Internationalization Initiative .... Mr. Reza FAKHARI
05 Vice President Academic Affairs .... Dr. Jennifer LANCASTER
20 Academic Dean .... Dr. Kathleen GRAY
58 Assoc Dean Grad Pgms/Adult Educ .... Vacant
121 Assoc Dean for Student Success .... Ms. Monica MICHALSKI
15 Director of Human Resources .... Mr. Richard GRASSO
13 Chief Information Officer .... Ms. Madalyn HANLEY
06 Registrar .... Ms. Susan E. WEISMAN
32 Dean of Students .... Dr. Jose RODRIGUEZ
08 Director Library Services .... Ms. Mona WASSERMAN
36 Director of Career Development .... Ms. Naomi KINLEY
29 Director of Alumni Relations .... Vacant
41 Director of Athletics .... Ms. Irma GARCIA
42 Director Campus Ministry .... Vacant
09 Director of Institutional Research .... Mr. Steven CATALANO
07 Director Admissions .... Mr. Robert OLIVA
100 Chief of Staff .... Ms. Monique PRYOR
105 Director Web Services .... Ms. Tearanny STREET
106 AVP of Online Learning & Program .... Dr. Gale GIBSON-GAYLE
19 Asst Director of Campus Security .... Mr. Edward EVANS
25 Chief Contract/Grants Administrator .... Ms. Emily WARD
23 Director of Student Health Services .... Ms. Natasha EDWARDS
39 Dir Student Engagement/Resid Life .... Ms. Anilsa NUNEZ

St. John Fisher College (A)

3690 East Avenue, Rochester NY 14618-3597

County: Monroe FICE Identification: 002821
Unit ID: 195720
Telephone: (585) 385-8000 Carnegie Class: DU-Mod
FAX Number: (585) 899-3870 Calendar System: Semester
URL: www.sjfc.edu
Established: 1948 Annual Undergrad Tuition & Fees: $34,310
Enrollment: 3,776 Coed
Affiliation or Control: Independent Non-Profit IRS Status: 501(c)3
Highest Offering: Doctorate
Accreditation: M, CACREP, CAEPN, COSMA, NURSE, PHAR

01 President .... Dr. Gerard J. ROONEY
04 Senior Executive Assistant .... Ms. Mary M. MCGOWAN
05 Provost .... Dr. Kevin RAILEY
84 VP Enrollment Management .... Mr. Jose J. PERALES
10 VP Finance/CFO .... Ms. Linda M. STEINKIRCHNER
32 VP Student Affairs .... Dr. Matha THORNTON
111 VP Institutional Advancement .... Mr. Phillip CASTLEBERRY
49 Int Dean School of Arts/Sciences .... Dr. Ann Marie FALLON
50 Dean School of Business .... Dr. Rama YELKUR
53 Dean School of Education .... Dr. Michael WISCHNOWSKI
66 Dean School of Nursing .... Dr. Dianne C. COONEY MINER
67 Dean School of Pharmacy .... Dr. Christine R. BIRNIE
28 Director Multicultural Affairs .... Mr. Yantee SLOBERT
06 Registrar .... Ms. Julia M. THOMAS
15 Asst Vice Pres Human Resources .... Ms. Elizabeth SKRAINAR
26 Director Marketing & Communications .... Ms. Kate M. TOROK
06 Associate Registrar .... Ms. Cheryl O. EVANS
08 Director of the Library .... Ms. Melissa JADLOS
13 Chief Information/Computing Officer .... Mr. Stacy S. SLOCUM
16 Director of Payroll & Benefits .... Ms. Mary R. POWLEY
37 Director Student Financial Aid .... Ms. Marie FICO
42 Director Campus Ministry .... Fr. Kevin MANNARA
19 Director of Safety & Security .... Mr. David DICARO
41 Athletic Director .... Mr. Robert A. WARD
18 Director of Physical Plant .... Mr. Kenneth WIDANKA
21 Controller .... Ms. Diane MARTZ
23 Dir of Health & Wellness Center .... Ms. Rebecca KIEFFER
104 Int Dir of Cmty Svc & Study Abroad .... Ms. Maria S. PLUTINO
07 Director of Freshman Admissions .... Ms. Stacy A. LEDERMANN
123 Assoc Dir of Transfer/Grad Admiss .... Ms. Michelle GOSIER
09 Dir Inst Research/Assessment .... Ms. Elizabeth A. LACHANCE
35 Director Student Affairs .... Ms. Amanda METZGER
36 Director Career Services .... Dr. Julia OVERTON-HEALY
105 Webmaster .... Ms. Jody C. BENEDICT
96 Director of Purchasing .... Ms. Susan WISNIEWSKI
101 Secretary to the Board .... Ms. Stephanie WILLIAMS

St. John's University (B)

8000 Utopia Parkway, Queens NY 11439-0001

County: Queens FICE Identification: 002823
Unit ID: 195809
Telephone: (718) 990-6161 Carnegie Class: DU-Mod
FAX Number: (718) 990-2314 Calendar System: Semester
URL: www.stjohns.edu
Established: 1870 Annual Undergrad Tuition & Fees: $41,760
Enrollment: 21,340 Coed
Affiliation or Control: Roman Catholic IRS Status: 501(c)3
Highest Offering: Doctorate
Accreditation: M, ARCPA, ART, AUD, CACREP, CLPSY, EMT, LAW, LIB, MT, PHAR, RAD, SCPSY, SP

01 President .... Dr. Conrado M. GEMPESAW
04 Presidential Asst Administration .... Ms. Carolyn MADAIO
03 Executive VP Mission .... Rev. Bernard M. TRACEY, CM
05 Provost/VP Academic Affairs .... Dr. Simon MOLLER
10 VP Business Affairs/CFO/ Treasurer .... Ms. Sharon HEWITT WATKINS
11 VP Admin/Secretary & Gen Counsel .... Mr. Joseph E. OLIVA
32 VP Student Affairs .... Dr. Kathryn T. HUTCHINSON
84 Vice Provost & Chief Enroll Officer .... Mr. Jorge RODRIGUEZ
111 VP University Advancement/Relations .... Dr. Christian P. VAUPEL
15 Assoc VP HR/Chf Div Ofcr/Dep GC .... Ms. Nada` M. LLEWELLYN
13 Chief Information Officer .... Ms. Anne R. PACIONE
41 Director of Athletics .... Mr. Michael CRAGG
49 Dean St John's College .... Dr. Jeffrey W. FAGEN
53 Dean School of Education .... Dr. David BELL
61 Dean School of Law .... Mr. Michael A. SIMONS
50 Dean Tobin College of Business .... Dr. Norean R. SHARPE
67 Dean Pharmacy/Health Sciences .... Dr. Russell J. DIGATE
107 Dean College Prof Studies .... Dr. Katia PASSERINI
08 Dean University Libraries .... Dr. Valeda F. DENT
12 Vice Provost - SI .... Dr. James O'KEEFE
31 VP Community Relations .... Mr. Joseph A. SCIAME
18 Assoc VP Campus Facilities/Services .... Mr. Brian BAUMER
91 Assoc VP Information Technology .... Ms. Maura A. WOODS
27 Assoc VP Marketing & Communications .... Ms. Caren BATZER
42 Assoc VP University Ministry .... Ms. Victoria R. SANTANGELO
21 Asst VP Business Affairs .... Ms. Judy CHEN
88 Asst VP University Events .... Ms. Nunziatina A. MANULI
20 Vice Provost Acad Support Services .... Dr. Andre A. MCKENZIE
106 Vice Provost Digital Learning .... Dr. Elizabeth CIABOCCHI
11 Assoc Provost Admin/Inst Accred .... Ms. Linda A. SHANNON
104 Assoc Provost Global Studies .... Dr. Matthew PUCCIARELLI
121 Assoc Provost Student Success .... Dr. Jacqueline H. GROGAN
20 Asst Provost Acad Res & Mgmt Plng .... Ms. Geraldine AMERA
19 Exec Dir Public Safety/Risk Mgt .... Ms. Denise VENCAK
36 Exec Dir University Career Services .... Ms. Paulette B. GONZALEZ
86 Exec Dir Univ Rel/Asst VP Gov Rels .... Mr. Brian BROWNE
90 Exec Director User Services .... Mr. Kenneth J. MAHLMEISTER
88 Exec Director Vincentian Center .... Rev. Patrick J. GRIFFIN, CM
06 University Registrar .... Ms. Joanne A. LLERANDI
39 Sr Director Residence Life .... Mr. Eric M. FINKELSTEIN
07 Director Admissions .... Mrs. Samantha R. WRIGHT
29 Director Alumni Relations .... Mr. Mark A. ANDREWS
38 Director Counseling Center .... Dr. Tow Y. YAU
88 Director Ctr for Teaching/Learning .... Dr. Cynthia R. PHILLIPS
105 Director Digital Communications .... Ms. Linda ROMANO
37 Director Financial Aid/Research .... Ms. Maryanne H. TWOMEY
25 Dir Grants & Sponsored Research .... Mr. Jared E. LITTMAN
92 Director Honors Program .... Dr. Robert J. FORMAN
16 Director Human Resources Services .... Ms. Cynthia F. SIMPSON
09 Director Institutional Research .... Ms. Christine M. GOODWIN
116 Director Internal Audit .... Mr. Alex J. HOEHN
85 Dir Int Students/Scholar Svcs .... Ms. Amy R. SCHOENFELD
112 Director Planned Giving .... Ms. Susan M. DAMIANI
88 Dir Pre-Admin/Asst to VP S&O P .... Mrs. Cecelia M. RUSSO
96 Director Purchasing .... Mr. Jeffery I. WEISS
23 Director Queens Health Services .... Mrs. Pauline TUMMINO
20 Assoc Provost Academic - SI .... Dr. Robert FANUZZI
35 Assoc Dean Student Affairs - SI .... Mr. David GACHIGO
07 Sr Asst Director Admissions - SI .... Mr. David A. PIERRE
38 Associate Dir Counseling Ctr - SI .... Dr. Erin RYAN
37 Asst Director Financial Aid - SI .... Mr. Thomas J. MARLOW
39 Assoc Dir of Res Life - SI .... Dr. Jason T. BARTLETT
40 Manager of Bookstore .... Mrs. Denise SERVIDIO

Saint Joseph's College, New York (C)

245 Clinton Avenue, Brooklyn NY 11205-3688

County: Kings FICE Identification: 002825
Unit ID: 195544
Telephone: (718) 940-5300 Carnegie Class: Masters/M
FAX Number: (718) 636-7245 Calendar System: Semester
URL: www.sjcny.edu
Established: 1916 Annual Undergrad Tuition & Fees: $27,830
Enrollment: 1,176 Coed
Affiliation or Control: Independent Non-Profit IRS Status: 501(c)3
Highest Offering: Master's
Accreditation: M, ADNUR, NRPA, NUR

01 President .... Dr. Donald R. BOOMGAARDEN
05 Provost .... Dr. Robert RILEY
26 VP of Marketing and Communications .... Ms. Jessica MCALEER
10 Chief Financial Officer .... Mr. John C. ROTH
20 Interim Executive Dean - BK .... Dr. Raymond D'ANGELO
13 VP IT and Chief Information Officer .... Ms. Michelle PAPAJOHN
32 VP for Student Life - BK .... Ms. Sherrie VAN ARNAM
111 VP for Institutional Advancement .... Ms. Rory SHAFFER-WALSH
84 VP for Enrollment Management - BK .... Ms. Christine MURPHY
41 AVP and Senior Athletics Director .... Ms. Shantey HILL
19 Director Security/Safety .... Mr. Michael MCGRANN
88 Director of Child Study Center .... Dr. Susan STRAUT COLLARD
90 Exec Director Client Services .... Ms. Lichele ABEAR
37 Director of Financial Aid .... Ms. Amy THOMPSON
36 Exec Director Career Development .... Ms. Ellen BURTI
15 Exec Director of Human Resources .... Ms. D'adra CRUMP
18 Interim Director Physical Plant .... Ms. Linda VIGNATO
21 Controller .... Mr. Matthew BRELLIS
14 Exec Director Network Operations .... Mr. Ted DEC
06 College Registrar .... Mr. Robert PERGOLIS
08 Director of Library .... Dr. Elizabeth POLLICINO MURPHY
88 Director of Public Affairs .... Mr. Michael BANACH
28 Coordinator of Diversity .... Vacant
112 Planned Giving Officer .... Ms. Susan LOUCKS
38 Director Student Counseling .... Dr. Anissa MOODY
29 Associate Director Alumni Relations .... Ms. Dee KAYALAR
09 Director of Institutional Research .... Ms. Allison LIST
102 Director Foundation Relations .... Ms. Amy ENGEL
86 Director Government Relations .... Mr. Michael BANACH
04 Executive Admin Asst to President .... Ms. Kimberly MAILLEY

St. Joseph's College of Nursing (D)

206 Prospect Avenue, Syracuse NY 13203-1806

County: Onondaga FICE Identification: 006467
Unit ID: 195191
Telephone: (315) 448-5040 Carnegie Class: Spec 2-yr-Health
FAX Number: (315) 448-5745 Calendar System: Semester
URL: www.sjhcon.org
Established: 1898 Annual Undergrad Tuition & Fees: $20,095
Enrollment: 298 Coed
Affiliation or Control: Independent Non-Profit IRS Status: 501(c)3
Highest Offering: Associate Degree
Accreditation: M

01 VP/Dean .... Mrs. Marianne MARKOWITZ

Saint Joseph's Seminary (E)

Dunwoodie, #201 Seminary Avenue, Yonkers NY 10704-1852

County: Westchester FICE Identification: 002826
Telephone: (914) 968-6200 Carnegie Class: Not Classified
FAX Number: (914) 376-2019 Calendar System: Semester
URL: www.dunwoodie.edu
Established: 1896 Annual Graduate Tuition & Fees: N/A
Enrollment: N/A Coed
Affiliation or Control: Roman Catholic IRS Status: 501(c)3
Highest Offering: Master's; No Undergraduates
Accreditation: M, THEOL

01 Rector .... Msgr. Peter I. VACCARI
05 Academic Dean .... Rev. Kevin P. O'REILLY
32 Dean of Students/Admissions .... Rev. Nicholas A. ZIENTARSKI
08 Director Library Services .... Mr. Connor FLATZ
06 Registrar .... Ms. Roenice GONZALEZ
38 Director of Psychological Services .... Dr. Richard GALLAGHER
18 Director of Buildings & Grounds .... Mr. Joseph DI LELLO
26 Dir of Communications/Technology .... Ms. Cynthia F. HARRISON
07 Director of Admissions .... Fr. Thomas BERG
108 Director Institutional Assessment .... Msgr. Michael CURRAN

St. Lawrence University (F)

23 Romoda Drive, Canton NY 13617-1423

County: St. Lawrence FICE Identification: 002829
Unit ID: 195216
Telephone: (315) 229-5011 Carnegie Class: Bac-A&S
FAX Number: (315) 229-5502 Calendar System: Other
URL: www.stlawu.edu
Established: 1856 Annual Undergrad Tuition & Fees: $54,846
Enrollment: 2,493 Coed
Affiliation or Control: Independent Non-Profit IRS Status: 501(c)3
Highest Offering: Master's
Accreditation: M, CAEPT

01 President .... Dr. William L. FOX
05 Vice Pres/Dean Academic Affairs .... Dr. Karl K. SCHONBERG
111 Vice Pres University Advancement .... Mr. Thomas PYNCHON
10 VP Finance/Administration & Treas .... Mr. Stephen HIETSCH
32 Vice Pres/Dean Student Life .... Mr. Earlhagi BRADLEY
07 VP & Dean for Admissions/Fin Aid .... Ms. Florence HINES
26 VP for Employee/Community Relations .... Mrs. Lisa M. CANIA
89 Associate Dean of the First-Year .... Dr. Sarah BARBER
35 Associate Dean of Student Life .... Mr. Rance DAVIS
06 Registrar .... Ms. Lorie MACKENZIE
37 Director of Financial Aid .... Mrs. Patricia J B. FARMER
08 VP Libraries & Information Tech .... Mr. Justin SIPHER
36 Director of Career Services .... Mr. Ronald G. ALBERTSON
09 Director of Institutional Research .... Ms. Christine ZIMMERMAN
18 Chief Facilities/Physical Plant .... Mr. Daniel B. SEAMAN
20 Assoc Dean of Academic Admin .... Ms. Lorie R. MACKENZIE
29 Director Alumni Relations .... Mr. Joseph C. KENISTON
39 Director Residence Life .... Mr. Christopher MARQUARDT
23 Director of Health & Counseling .... Mr. Timothy CORBITT
84 Exec Director Enrollment Management .... Mr. Jeremy FREEMAN
96 Director of Purchasing .... Mr. Nickolas ORMASEN
15 Director Personnel Services .... Mrs. Colleen MANLEY
38 Director Student Counseling .... Mr. Timothy CORBITT
04 Admin Assistant to the President .... Ms. Dayle BURGESS
19 Director Security/Safety .... Mr. Patrick GAGNON
28 Director of Diversity .... Dr. Kimberly FLINT-HAMILTON
41 Athletic Director .... Mr. Robert DUROCHER

St. Paul's School of Nursing (G)

97-77 Queens Boulevard, Queens NY 11374

County: Queens FICE Identification: 012364
Unit ID: 189811
Telephone: (718) 357-0500 Carnegie Class: Spec 2-yr-Health
FAX Number: (718) 357-4683 Calendar System: Semester
URL: www.stpaulsschoolofnursing.edu
Established: 1969 Annual Undergrad Tuition & Fees: $21,823
Enrollment: 582 Coed
Affiliation or Control: Proprietary IRS Status: Proprietary
Highest Offering: Associate Degree
Accreditation: ABHES

01 President .... Dr. Eric RICIOPPO

Saint Paul's School of Nursing-Staten Island (A)

2 Teleport Dr Ste 203, Corp Comm 2, Staten Island NY 10311
County: Richmond
FICE Identification: 009479
Unit ID: 195784
Telephone: (718) 818-6470
Carnegie Class: Spec 2-yr-Health
FAX Number: (718) 818-6020
Calendar System: Semester
URL: www.stpaulsschoolofnursing.edu
Established: 1904
Annual Undergrad Tuition & Fees: $17,395
Enrollment: 532
Coed
Affiliation or Control: Proprietary
IRS Status: Proprietary
Highest Offering: Associate Degree
Accreditation: ABHES

01 President ... Mr. David SMITH
05 Director of Education ... Dr. Chris SCHNUPP
66 Dean of Nursing ... Ms. Genevieve JENSEN
06 Registrar ... Mr. Jeff NAMIAN
10 Business Office Manager ... Ms. Olga FORINA
07 Director of Admissions ... Mr. Otis HALL
32 Director of Career Services ... Ms. Lynn SALVAGE
37 Director of Financial Aid ... Ms. Nayamka WARD
08 LRC Manager ... Ms. Judy LEE

St. Thomas Aquinas College (B)

125 Route 340, Sparkill NY 10976-1050
County: Rockland
FICE Identification: 002832
Unit ID: 195243
Telephone: (845) 398-4000
Carnegie Class: Masters/S
FAX Number: (845) 359-8136
Calendar System: 4/1/4
URL: www.stac.edu
Established: 1952
Annual Undergrad Tuition & Fees: $31,950
Enrollment: 1,915
Coed
Affiliation or Control: Independent Non-Profit
IRS Status: 501(c)3
Highest Offering: Master's
Accreditation: M, CAEPN, IACBE

01 President ... Dr. Margaret M. FITZPATRICK, SC
03 Senior Vice President ... Mr. Joseph DONINI
10 Vice Pres Administration & Finance ... Mr. Joseph DONINI
05 Provost/Vice Pres Academic Affairs ... Dr. Robert MURRAY
32 Vice Pres/Dean Student Development ... Dr. Kirk MANNING
30 Vice Pres Institutional Advancement ... Mrs. Karen WRIGHT
15 Director Human Resources ... Mrs. Maria COUPE
07 Director Admissions ... Ms. Samantha BAZILE
09 Dir Inst Research/Program Develop ... Dr. Renee QUINTYNE
21 Controller ... Ms. Jennifer MAZZA
44 Dir Annual Giving & Alumni Affairs ... Mrs. Jennifer TANIS
35 Director Student Activities ... Mr. Nicholas MIGLIORINO
38 Director Student Counseling ... Dr. Louis MUGGEO
06 Registrar ... Ms. Eileen MURPHY
36 Director Career Development ... Mrs. Maureen MULHERN
37 Director Financial Aid ... Mrs. Joanne SULLIVAN
13 Director of Computing Services ... Mr. Sunny ANTHWAL
18 Dir Facilities & Construction ... Mr. Patrick LAMBERT
26 Dir Campus Communications/Enr Mktg ... Ms. Annie LOMBARDI
50 Dean School of Business ... Mr. Michael MURPHY
53 Dean School of Education ... Dr. Meenakshi GAJRIA
49 Dean School of Arts & Sciences ... Dr. Heath BOWEN
04 Executive Asst to President ... Ms. Lee TAUSSI

Saint Vladimir's Orthodox Theological Seminary (C)

575 Scarsdale Road, Yonkers NY 10707
County: Westchester
FICE Identification: 002833
Unit ID: 195580
Telephone: (914) 961-8313
Carnegie Class: Spec-4-yr-Faith
FAX Number: (914) 961-4507
Calendar System: Semester
URL: www.svots.edu
Established: 1938
Annual Graduate Tuition & Fees: N/A
Enrollment: 89
Coed
Affiliation or Control: Independent Non-Profit
IRS Status: 501(c)3
Highest Offering: Doctorate; No Undergraduates
Accreditation: THEOL

01 President ... V.Rev. Chad HATFIELD
05 Academic Dean ... Dr. Ionut Alexandru TUDORIE
10 Chief Financial Officer ... Mrs. Melanie RINGA
13 Chief Technology Officer ... Mr. Georgios KOKONAS
32 Assoc Dean for Student Affairs ... RevDr. David MEZYNSKI
06 Registrar ... Vacant
08 Librarian ... Ms. Eleana SILK
35 Student Affairs Administrator ... Ms. Gabrielle RUSSIN
108 Dir Institutional Assessment ... Dr. Peter BOUTENEFF
111 Sr Advisor Advancement ... Mr. Ted BAZIL
26 Director of Marketing ... Ms. Sarah WERNER
29 Director Alumni Affairs ... Ms. Robyn HATRAK
30 Director of Development ... Ms. Sharon ROSS
04 Admin Assistant to President ... Mrs. Ann SANCHEZ

Salvation Army College for Officer Training (D)

201 Lafayette Avenue, Suffern NY 10901-4707
County: Rockland
Identification: 666020
Telephone: (845) 368-7200
Carnegie Class: Not Classified
FAX Number: (845) 357-6644
Calendar System: Other
URL: www.use.salvationarmy.org
Established: 1905
Annual Undergrad Tuition & Fees: N/A
Enrollment: N/A
Coed
Affiliation or Control: Independent Non-Profit
IRS Status: 501(c)3
Highest Offering: Associate Degree
Accreditation: NY

01 Principal ... LtCol. David E. KELLY
11 Asst Principal for Administration ... Major Jongwoo KIM
05 Director of Curriculum ... Major Eva GEDDES
06 Registrar ... Vacant
09 Coord Inst Research/Accred Liaison ... Dr. Dennis A. VANDER WEELE
10 Chief Business Officer ... Major Ronald STARNES
15 Director Personnel Services ... Major Alberto SUAREZ
20 Associate Academic Officer ... Capt. Sheila WILLIAMS-GAGE
21 Associate Business Officer ... Mrs. Robin FRASER
32 Director Student Affairs ... Vacant
72 Education Tech Coordinator ... Mr. Marcos A. LOPEZ

Samaritan Hospital School of Nursing (E)

1300 Massachusetts Avenue, Troy NY 12180
County: Rensselaer
FICE Identification: 009248
Unit ID: 195289
Telephone: (518) 268-5010
Carnegie Class: Spec 2-yr-Health
FAX Number: (518) 268-5040
Calendar System: Semester
URL: www.nehealth.com
Established: 1903
Annual Undergrad Tuition & Fees: $13,936
Enrollment: 144
Coed
Affiliation or Control: Independent Non-Profit
IRS Status: 501(c)3
Highest Offering: Associate Degree
Accreditation: ADNUR, PNUR

01 Director ... Ms. Susan BIRKHEAD

Sarah Lawrence College (F)

1 Meadway, Bronxville NY 10708-5999
County: Westchester
FICE Identification: 002813
Unit ID: 195304
Telephone: (914) 337-0700
Carnegie Class: Bac-A&S
FAX Number: N/A
Calendar System: Semester
URL: www.slc.edu
Established: 1926
Annual Undergrad Tuition & Fees: $55,900
Enrollment: 1,696
Coed
Affiliation or Control: Independent Non-Profit
IRS Status: 501(c)3
Highest Offering: Master's
Accreditation: M

01 President ... Dr. Cristle COLLINS JUDD
05 Provost and Dean of Faculty ... Dr. Kanwal SINGH
10 Vice Pres Finance/Operations ... Stephen SCHAFER
111 VP for Advancement/External Rels ... Patricia GOLDMAN
11 Vice President for Administration ... Thomas L. BLUM
84 VP Enrollment & Dean of Admission ... Kevin MCKENNA
20 Associate Dean of the College ... Melissa FRAZIER
32 Dean of Studies & Student Life ... Daniel TRUJILLO
22 Dean of Equity and Inclusion ... Vacant
35 Dean of Student Affairs ... Dr. Paige CRANDALL
58 Dean Graduate Studies ... Kim FERGUSON
06 Registrar ... Daniel LICHT
08 Director of Libraries ... Bobbie SMOLOW
13 Chief Technology Officer ... Sean JAMESON
29 Director of Alumni ... Vacant
36 Director Career Counseling ... Angela CHERUBINI
44 Individual Giving Officer ... Elisa BALESTRA
28 Director of Diversity ... Vacant
18 Asst Vice President of Facilities ... Maureen GALLAGHER
19 AVP of Public Safety/Purchasing ... Vacant
04 Executive Asst to President ... Karen SANDERS
100 Chief of Staff ... Thomas BLUM
104 Asst Dean Study Abroad ... Prema SAMUEL
37 Director Student Financial Aid ... Nick SALINAS
102 Director Foundation/Corporate Rels ... Joseph TOMARAS
15 Director Human Resources ... Danielle COSCIA
41 Athletic Director ... Kristin MAILE
96 Director of Purchasing ... Jennifer MELENDEZ

Schenectady County Community College (G)

78 Washington Avenue, Schenectady NY 12305
County: Schenectady
FICE Identification: 006785
Unit ID: 195322
Telephone: (518) 381-1200
Carnegie Class: Assoc/MT-VT-High Non
FAX Number: (518) 346-0379
Calendar System: Semester
URL: www.sunysccc.edu
Established: 1967
Annual Undergrad Tuition & Fees (In-District): $4,944
Enrollment: 6,588
Coed
Affiliation or Control: State/Local
IRS Status: 501(c)3
Highest Offering: Associate Degree
Accreditation: M, ACFEI, MUS

01 President ... Dr. Steady MOONO
05 VP for Acad/Student Affs & Provost ... Dr. Penny A. HAYNES
11 Vice President of Administration ... Mr. Patrick RYAN
30 Executive Director of Development ... Ms. Stacy MCILDUFF
103 VP Workforce Development/Cmty Educ ... Ms. Denise ZIESKE
13 Chief Information Officer ... Mr. Ron MARZITELLI
20 Assistant VP Academic Affairs ... Vacant
32 Dean of Students ... Mr. Stephen FRAGALE
37 Director of Financial Aid ... Mr. Mark BESSETTE
06 Registrar ... Ms. Cynthia ZIELASKOWSKI
07 Director of Admissions ... Mr. Thomas BREEN
08 Director Library Services ... Ms. Jacqueline KELEHER-HUGHES
18 Director of Facilities ... Mr. Anthony SCHWARTZ
36 Exec Dir SUNY Col/Career Coun Ctr ... Dr. DeShawn MCGARRITY
15 Human Resources Specialist ... Ms. Carianne TROTTA
88 Recruitment Specialist ... Ms. Sandra TROIANO
09 Coordinator Institutional Research ... Mr. Dale MILLER
28 Dir Educ Opportunity Pgms/Access ... Ms. Angela WEST-DAVIS
10 Controller ... Ms. Aimee S. WARFIELD
100 Chief of Staff ... Ms. Paula OHLHOUS
26 Director Marketing/Public Relations ... Mr. David REGAN WHITE
27 Public Rels/Publications Specialist ... Ms. Heather L. MEANEY

School of Visual Arts (H)

209 E 23rd Street, New York NY 10010-3994
County: New York
FICE Identification: 007468
Unit ID: 197151
Telephone: (212) 592-2000
Carnegie Class: Spec-4-yr-Arts
FAX Number: (212) 725-3587
Calendar System: Semester
URL: www.sva.edu
Established: 1947
Annual Undergrad Tuition & Fees: $39,900
Enrollment: 4,393
Coed
Affiliation or Control: Proprietary
IRS Status: Proprietary
Highest Offering: Master's
Accreditation: M, ART, CIDA

01 President ... David J. RHODES
03 Executive Vice President ... Anthony P. RHODES
05 Provost ... Christopher J. CYPHERS
10 Chief Financial Officer ... Gary SHILLET
32 Exec Dir of Student Affairs/Admiss ... Javier VEGA
26 Exec Director of External Relations ... Susan MODENSTEIN
13 Chief Information Officer ... Cosmin TOMESCU
06 Registrar ... Jason KOTH
07 Director Admission ... Matthew R. FARINA
35 Director of Student Affairs ... Bill MARTINO
08 Director Visual Arts Library ... Caitlin KILGALLEN
37 Director Financial Aid ... William BERRIOS
36 Director Career Development ... Angie WOJAK
30 Director Development/Alumni Affairs ... Jane NUZZO
19 Director Security ... Nick AGJMURATI
15 Exec Director of Human Resources ... Frank AGOSTA
09 Director of Institutional Research ... Jerold DAVIS
26 Director of Communication ... Joyce KAYE

Sh'or Yoshuv Rabbinical College (I)

1 Cedar Lawn Avenue, Lawrence NY 11559-1714
County: Nassau
FICE Identification: 025059
Unit ID: 195438
Telephone: (516) 239-9002
Carnegie Class: Spec-4-yr-Faith
FAX Number: (516) 239-9003
Calendar System: Semester
URL: www.shoryoshuv.org
Established: 1963
Annual Undergrad Tuition & Fees: $9,460
Enrollment: 144
Male
Affiliation or Control: Independent Non-Profit
IRS Status: 501(c)3
Highest Offering: Second Talmudic Degree
Accreditation: RABN

01 Dean ... Rabbi Naftalie JAEGER
05 Executive Director ... Mr. Moshe RUBIN
32 Director of Student Affairs ... Rabbi Elysha SANDLER
06 Registrar ... Mrs. Sheila FLEISCHER
37 Director SFA ... Rabbi Chaim MAJEROVIC

Siena College (J)

515 Loudon Road, Loudonville NY 12211-1462
County: Albany
FICE Identification: 002816
Unit ID: 195474
Telephone: (518) 783-2300
Carnegie Class: Masters/S
FAX Number: (518) 783-4293
Calendar System: Semester
URL: www.siena.edu
Established: 1937
Annual Undergrad Tuition & Fees: $36,975
Enrollment: 3,226
Coed
Affiliation or Control: Independent Non-Profit
IRS Status: 501(c)3
Highest Offering: Master's
Accreditation: M, NURSE, SW

01 President ... Bro. F. Edward COUGHLIN, OFM
05 Vice President for Academic Affairs ... Dr. Margaret MADDEN
32 Vice President for Student Life ... Dr. Maryellen GILROY
10 Vice President for Finance & Admin ... Mr. Paul T. STEC
84 VP for Enrollment Management ... Mr. Ned J. JONES
30 VP for Development & Ext Affairs ... Mr. David B. SMITH
100 VP & Chief of Staff ... Vacant
41 VP & Director of Athletics ... Mr. John D'ARGENIO
13 Chief Information Officer ... Mr. Mark A. BERMAN
49 Dean of Liberal Arts ... Dr. Lara WHELAN
50 Dean of Business ... Dr. Charles SEIFERT
81 Dean of Science ... Dr. John CUMMINGS
124 Assoc VP Stdnt Retention & Success ... Dr. Tamara DURANT
37 Assoc Vice Pres Financial Aid ... Ms. Mary K. LAWYER
35 Assoc VP Student Life ... Mr. John R. FELIO
15 Asst VP for Human Resources ... Ms. Cynthia B. KING-LEROY
21 Asst VP for Finance & Admin ... Ms. Mary C. STRUNK
18 Asst VP for Facilities Management ... Mr. Mark FROST

19 Asst VP Stdnt Life/Dir Public Safe ... Mr. Michael PAPADOPOULOS
20 Asst VP Academic Affairs ... Ms. Laurie FAY
06 Registrar ... Mr. James SERBALIK
07 Director of Admissions ... Ms. Katie SZALDA
08 Dir of Library/Audio Visual Svcs ... Ms. Loretta EBERT
92 Director of Honors Program ... Dr. Lois K. DALY
35 Dean of Students ... Ms. Jabrina ROBINSON
39 Director of Community Living ... Mr. Adam CASLER
36 Dir Ofc of Career Dev & Prof Educ ... Ms. Debra DELBELSO
26 Deputy Chief Information Officer ... Ms. Mary W. PARLETT-SWEENEY
42 Chaplain of the College ... Fr. Lawrence ANDERSON, OFM
38 Director of Counseling Center ... Dr. Nathan PRUITT
29 Director of Alumni Relations ... Ms. Mary Beth FINNERTY
09 Dir of Institutional Research ... Ms. Tara COPE
117 Dir of Risk Analysis/Project Mgmt ... Ms. Sandy SERBALIK
94 Dir Sr Thea Bowman Ctr for Women ... Ms. Beth DEANGELIS
23 Director of Health Services ... Ms. Carrie HOGAN
40 Bookstore Manager ... Mr. Richard IVES
110 Director of Development ... Mr. Brad R. BODMER
28 Dir of Damietta Cross-Cultural Ctr ... Ms. Christa J. GRANT
104 Director of Study Abroad/Intl Pgms ... Br. Brian C. BELANGER, OFM
109 Dir of Auxiliary Svcs & Procurement ... Ms. Laura S. ZOCCO
43 Legal Services/General Counsel ... Ms. Rose SEGGOS
35 Director of Student Activities ... Ms. Karen KEIS
20 Director of Academic Programs ... Ms. Lynn ROGERS
121 Dir of Siena Enhanced Edu Dev/SEED ... Ms. Holly CHEVERTON
88 Director HEOP ... Ms. Carol SANDOVAL
25 Dir Grants & Sponsored Pgms ... Ms. Sally SOUTHWICK
22 Title IX Coord/EEO Specialist ... Ms. Lois GOLAND
88 Dir Office of Accessibility ... Ms. Julie GOLD
04 Admin Assistant to the President ... Mrs. Kathleen S. KIERNAN
101 Secretary of the Institution/Board ... Ms. Kathleen ROBETOR
108 Dir Institutional Effectiveness ... Dr. Mohua ROSE

Skidmore College (A)

815 N Broadway, Saratoga Springs NY 12866-1632
County: Saratoga FICE Identification: 002814
Unit ID: 195526
Telephone: (518) 580-5000 Carnegie Class: Bac-A&S
FAX Number: (518) 580-5936 Calendar System: Semester
URL: www.skidmore.edu
Established: 1911 Annual Undergrad Tuition & Fees: $54,420
Enrollment: 2,684 Coed
Affiliation or Control: Independent Non-Profit IRS Status: 501(c)3
Highest Offering: Baccalaureate
Accreditation: M, ART, SW

01 President ... Dr. Philip A. GLOTZBACH
05 VP Academic Affairs/Dean of Faculty ... Dr. Michael T. ORR
10 Vice Pres Finance/Admin/Treasurer ... Ms. Donna NG
111 Vice President for Advancement ... Mr. Sean CAMPBELL
15 Chief HR Officer/AVP Fin & Admin ... Mr. Brett LAST
32 Dean of Students and Vice President ... Ms. Cerri A. BANKS
35 Sr Assoc Dean of Stdnts/Asst VP SA ... Vacant
07 VP & Dean of Admiss & Fin Aid ... Ms. Mary Lou W. BATES
88 Int Exec Dir of Special Programs ... Dr. Auden THOMAS
06 Registrar ... Mr. David DECONNO
20 Assoc Dean for Stdnt Acad Affairs ... Dr. Ronald SEYB
28 Assoc Dn for Diversity/Faculty Affs ... Dr. Janet G. CASEY
88 Assoc Dn Infrastruc & Fac Affs ... Dr. Patricia FEHLING
89 Dir of First Year Experience ... Vacant
35 Assoc Dean Student Affs/Campus Life ... Ms. Mariel MARTIN
39 Assoc Dean Res Life/Student Conduct ... Ms. Ann Marie PRZYWARA
88 Dir Student Academic Services ... Mr. Jamin TOTINO
45 VP Strategic Plng & Inst Diversity ... Dr. Joshua C. WOODFORK
26 VP Communications & Mktg ... Mr. Martin A. MBUGUA
09 Director of Institutional Research ... Mr. Joseph STANKOVICH
102 Dir Foundation & Corporate Rels ... Mr. Barry PRITZKER
46 Director of Sponsored Research ... Ms. Mary HOEHN
13 Chief Technology Officer ... Mr. Dwane M. STERLING
105 Print & Web Project Specialist ... Mr. Andy CAMP
88 Dir Acad Pgm/Resid/Inst & Cmty Pgms ... Dr. Auden THOMAS
88 Dir Ctr for Leadership/Teach/Lrng ... Dr. Kristie A. FORD
22 Asst Dir EEO & Workforce Diversity ... Ms. Saytra GREEN
91 Director IT-Enterprise Systems ... Mr. Kevin L. CRIDER
104 Dir of Off-Campus Study & Exchanges ... Ms. Cori FILSON
44 Senior Director Donor Relations ... Ms. Mary L. SOLOMONS
30 Assoc VP Advancement & Campaign Dir ... Ms. Lori EASTMAN
29 Exec Dir Alumni Rels/Col Events ... Mr. Michael SPOSILI
36 Assoc Dean Stdnt Affs/Career Dev ... Ms. Kim CRABBE
37 Director of Financial Aid ... Ms. Beth POST
38 Assoc Dn Stdnt Affs/Health/Wellness ... Dr. Julia C. ROUTBORT
21 Asst VP for Finance & Controller ... Mr. Kyle BERNARD
109 Asst VP for Fin Planning & Aux Svcs ... Ms. Kelley A. PATTON-OSTRANDER
23 Director of Health Services ... Ms. Patricia BOSEN
18 Director of Facilities Services ... Mr. Daniel RODECKER
19 Director of Campus Safety ... Mr. Timothy J. MUNRO
08 College Librarian ... Ms. Marta BRUNNER
96 Director of Purchasing ... Mrs. Carol N. SCHNITZER
42 Dir Religious & Spiritual Life ... Ms. Parker DIGGORY
24 Director of Media Services ... Mr. Michael G. FORBES
40 Skidmore Shop Sales Manager ... Ms. Dawn J. ARIA
88 Special Assistant to the President ... Ms. Jeanne M. SISSON
101 Board Coordinator ... Ms. Susan W. KOPPI
41 Assoc Dean Stdnt Affs/Athletics Dir ... Ms. Gail L. CUMMINGS-DANSON
108 Inst Effectiveness Specialist ... Dr. Amy J. TWEEDY

Sotheby's Institute of Art (B)

570 Lexington Ave, 6th Floor, New York NY 10022
County: New York Identification: 667007
Unit ID: 481094
Telephone: (212) 517-3929 Carnegie Class: Spec-4-yr-Arts
FAX Number: (212) 517-6568 Calendar System: Semester
URL: www.sothebysinstitute.com
Established: 2006 Annual Graduate Tuition & Fees: N/A
Enrollment: 268 Coed
Affiliation or Control: Proprietary IRS Status: Proprietary
Highest Offering: First Professional Degree; No Undergraduates
Accreditation: ART

01 Director/CEO ... Ms. Christine KUAN
07 Senior Dir of Global Admissions ... Ms. Susan ROTH
10 Global Director Finance ... Ms. Rebecca STILES
21 Associate Financial/Business Ofcr ... Ms. Karen CHANG
08 Head Librarian ... Mr. Eric WOLF
32 Chief Student Affairs/Student Life ... Ms. Sara MOORE
06 Registrar ... Mr. Giovanni PALOMO
88 Director Non-Degree Programs ... Ms. Kay CHUBBUCK

*State University of New York System Office (C)

State University Plaza, Albany NY 12246-0001
County: Albany FICE Identification: 008788
Unit ID: 195827
Telephone: (518) 320-1100 Carnegie Class: N/A
FAX Number: (518) 320-1561
URL: www.suny.edu

01 Chancellor ... Dr. Kristina JOHNSON
11 Sr Vice Chancellor & COO ... Mr. Robert L. MEGNA
28 SVC Strat Init/Chief Diversity Ofcr ... Ms. Teresa MILLER
05 Vice Provost & VC for Acad Affairs ... Dr. Elizabeth BRINGSJORD
10 Vice Chancellor for Finance and CFO .. Ms. Eileen MCLOUGHLIN
46 Vice Chanc Research & Econ Devel ... Dr. Grace WANG
43 VC Legal Affairs & General Counsel ... Ms. Elizabeth GARVEY
22 System Affirmative Action Officer ... Ms. Jennie Marie DURAN
18 VC for Cap Facil/GM Constr Fund ... Mr. Robert HAELEN
15 Vice Chancellor for Human Resources ... Mr. Curtis LLOYD
17 Chief Ofcr Acad Health & Univ Hosp ... Dr. Ricardo AZZIZ
26 Asst VC for Communications ... Ms. Casey VATTIMO
88 Sr VC for Cmty Col & Educ Pipeline ... Ms. Johanna DUNCAN-POITIER
11 Assistant VC for Operations ... Ms. Kellie J. DUPUIS
88 Pres Faculty Council of Cmty Col ... Ms. Nina TAMROWSKI
88 University Faculty Senate President ... Ms. Gwen KAY
20 Sr Assoc VC and Vice Prov Acad Affs ... Vacant
84 Assoc VC for Enrollment Management ... Vacant

*University at Albany, SUNY (D)

1400 Washington Avenue, Albany NY 12222-1000
County: Albany FICE Identification: 002835
Unit ID: 196060
Telephone: (518) 442-3300 Carnegie Class: DU-Highest
FAX Number: N/A Calendar System: Semester
URL: www.albany.edu
Established: 1844 Annual Undergrad Tuition & Fees (In-State): $10,011
Enrollment: 17,743 Coed
Affiliation or Control: State IRS Status: 501(c)3
Highest Offering: Doctorate
Accreditation: M, CAEPT, CLPSY, COPSY, IPSY, LIB, PH, PLNG, SCPSY, SPAA, SW

02 President ... Havidán RODRÍGUEZ
05 Provost/Sr VP Academic Affairs ... Carol KIM
46 Vice President for Research ... James DIAS
10 Vice Pres Finance & Administration ... Todd FOREMAN
30 VP Univ Dev & Exec Dir UA Found ... Fardin SANAI
32 Vice President Student Affairs ... Michael N. CHRISTAKIS
41 Director of Athletics ... Mark BENSON
43 Senior Counsel ... Janet THAYER
28 Asst VP Diversity/Inclusion ... Tamra MINOR
86 VP Govt & Community Relations ... Sheila SEERY
21 Assoc VP Office of Risk Mgmt ... Kevin WILCOX
35 Assoc VP Enrollment Mgmt ... Ed ENGELBRIDE
100 Chief of Staff ... Bruce SZELEST
21 Associate VP Finance & Business ... John GIARRUSSO
88 Vice Provost Acad Resource Plng ... Jack D. MAHONEY
49 Int Dean College of Arts & Sciences ... Jeanette ALTARRIBA
53 Interim Dean School of Education ... Jason E. LANE
50 Dean School of Business ... Sen NILANJAN
69 Dean School of Public Health ... David HOLTGRAVE
61 Dean of Criminal Justice ... William A. PRIDEMORE
80 Dean Rockefeller Col of Pub Affs ... R. Karl RETHEMEYER
70 VProv Pub Eng/Dean Sch Social Welf ... Lynn WARNER
54 Dean Engineering & Applied Sci ... Kim L. BOYER
58 Vice Provost & Dean Grad Educ ... Kevin WILLIAMS
08 Dean of Libraries ... Rebecca MUGRIDGE
06 College Registrar ... Karen CHICO HURST
29 Exec Director Alumni Association ... Lee SERRAVILLO, JR.
38 Dir Counsel/Psych Svcs/Asst VP SA ... Estela RIVERO
20 Sr Vice Prov/AVP Academic Affairs ... William B. HEDBERG
104 VP Ctr for Intl Educ/Global Strat ... Harvey CHARLES
88 Asst Vice Prov Faculty/Acad Affairs ... Benjamin WEAVER
106 Assoc Provost for Online Education ... Peter J. SHEA
100 Vice Provost and Chief of Staff ... Ann Marie MURRAY

*State University of New York at Binghamton (E)

Vestal Parkway E, Box 6000, Binghamton NY 13902-6000
County: Broome FICE Identification: 002836
Unit ID: 196079
Telephone: (607) 777-2000 Carnegie Class: DU-Highest
FAX Number: (607) 777-4000 Calendar System: Semester
URL: www.binghamton.edu
Established: 1946 Annual Undergrad Tuition & Fees (In-State): $9,808
Enrollment: 17,351 Coed
Affiliation or Control: State IRS Status: 501(c)3
Highest Offering: Doctorate
Accreditation: M, CLPSY, MUS, NURSE, @PHAR, SPAA, SW

02 President ... Dr. Harvey G. STENGER, JR.
100 Chief of Staff ... Ms. Darcy FAUCI
05 Exec VP for Academic Affs/Provost ... Dr. Donald NIEMAN
10 Vice President Operations ... Ms. JoAnn NAVARRO
32 Vice President Student Affairs ... Mr. Brian T. ROSE
46 Vice President for Research ... Dr. Bahgat SAMMAKIA
111 Vice President Advancement ... Mr. John KOCH
104 Exec Vice Prov Intl Initiatives ... Dr. Hari SRIHARI
20 Senior Vice Provost ... Dr. Michael F. MCGOFF
58 Vice Prov/Dean of Graduate School ... Dr. Aondover TARHULE
18 Assoc VP Facilities Management ... Mr. Lawrence J. ROMA
35 Interim Dean of Students ... Dr. Randall EDOUARD
102 Exec Dir of Bing Foundation ... Ms. Sheila DOYLE
26 Assoc Vice Pres Univ Comm/Mktg ... Mr. Gregory DELVISCIO
13 Chief Information Officer ... Dr. Niyazi BODUR
04 Exec Assistant to the President ... Ms. Laura L. O'NEIL
15 Asst Vice Pres for Human Resources ... Mr. Joseph P. SCHULTZ
07 Int Asst Vice Prov & Dir of Admiss ... Ms. Krista MEDIONTE-PHILIPS
08 Dean of Libraries ... Dr. Curtis KENDRICK
85 Director Intl Students/Scholar Svcs ... Ms. Patricia MARRAPESE
37 Dir Financial Aid/Stdnt Records ... Ms. Amber STALLMAN
38 Director Health & Counseling ... Ms. Johann FIORE CONTE
36 Director Career Development Center ... Ms. Kelli SMITH
19 Director Public Safety ... Mr. Timothy FAUGHANAN
41 Director Athletics ... Mr. Patrick ELLIOTT
88 Director Educ Opportunities Pgm ... Mr. Calvin GANTT
22 Int Dir Diversity/Equity/Inclusive ... Ms. Nicole SIRJU-JOHNSON
28 Director Multi-Cultural Res Ctr ... Ms. Nicole SIRJU-JOHNSON
92 Director Binghamton Univ Scholars ... Dr. William ZIEGLER
94 Exec Director of Women's Studies ... Ms. Dara J. SILBERSTEIN
96 Director of Procurement ... Mr. Matthew SCHOFIELD
09 Asst Provost Institutional Research ... Ms. Nasrin FATIMA
49 Dean Arts & Science Harpur Col ... Dr. Elizabeth CHILTON
50 Dean School of Management ... Dr. Upinder S. DHILLON
54 Dn Watson Sch Engr/Applied Science ... Dr. Hari SRIHARI
66 Dean Decker School of Nursing ... Dr. Mario ORTIZ
31 Dean Community & Public Affairs ... Dr. Laura BRONSTEIN
106 Dir Center for Innov/Cont Educ ... Mr. Thomas KOWALIK
43 Campus Atty/General Counsel ... Ms. Barbara SCARLETT

*University at Buffalo-SUNY (F)

3435 Main Street, Buffalo NY 14214
County: Erie FICE Identification: 002837
Unit ID: 196088
Telephone: (716) 645-2000 Carnegie Class: DU-Highest
FAX Number: N/A Calendar System: Semester
URL: www.buffalo.edu
Established: 1846 Annual Undergrad Tuition & Fees (In-State): $10,099
Enrollment: 30,648 Coed
Affiliation or Control: State IRS Status: 501(c)3
Highest Offering: Doctorate
Accreditation: M, ANEST, AUD, CACREP, CAMPEP, CEA, CLPSY, DA, DENT, DIETI, IPSY, LAW, LIB, MED, MT, NMT, NURSE, OT, PCSAS, PH, PHAR, PLNG, PSPSY, PTA, SP, SW

02 President ... Dr. Satish K. TRIPATHI
05 Provost/Exec VP Academic Affs ... Dr. Charles F. ZUKOSKI
10 Vice Pres Finance & Administration ... Ms. Laura E. HUBBARD
32 Vice President Student Life ... Dr. A. Scott WEBER
17 Vice President Health Sciences ... Dr. Michael E. CAIN
111 Vice Pres Univ Advancement ... Mr. Rodney M. GRABOWSKI
46 Vice Pres for Research/Econ Develop ... Dr. Venu GOVINDARAJU
84 Vice Provost of Enrollment ... Mr. Lee H. MELVIN
15 Assoc VP Human Resources ... Mr. Mark COLDREN
58 Vice Provost Educational Affairs ... Dr. Graham L. HAMMILL
20 Vice Provost for Faculty Affairs ... Dr. Robert GRANFIELD
104 Interim Vice Provost for Intl Educ ... Dr. John J. WOOD
08 VP for Univ Libraries ... Ms. Evviva WEINRAUB
13 VP & Chief Information Officer ... Mr. Brice BIBLE
37 Director Financial Aid ... Mr. John GOTTARDY
09 Assoc Vice Pres/Dir Inst Research ... Mr. Craig W. ABBEY
88 Assoc VP Academic Planning ... Mr. William J. MCDONNELL
96 Asst Vice Pres Procurement Services ... Mr. Daniel VIVIAN
26 Interim VP Univ Communications ... Mr. John DELLACONTRADA
22 Vice Provost Inclusive Excellence . Dr. Despina M. STRATIGAKOS
28 Dir Equity/Diversity/Inclusion ... Ms. Sharon E. NOLAN-WEISS
41 Director of Athletics ... Mr. Mark M. ALNUTT
91 Director Enterprise Application Svc ... Ms. Susan A. HUSTON
07 Director of UG Admissions ... Mr. Troy A. MILLER
19 Chief of Police ... Mr. Chris J. BARTOLOMEI
39 Director of Campus Living ... Mr. Tom R. TIBERI
38 Director of Counseling Services ... Dr. Sharon L. MITCHELL
23 Director Health Services ... Ms. Susan M. SNYDER
36 Director Career Services ... Ms. Arlene F. KAUKUS
85 Director Intl Students/Scholar Svc ... Ms. Kathryn E. TUDINI

40 Manager University Bookstores Mr. Gregory NEUMANN
92 Director Univ Honors College Dr. Dalia A. MULLER
29 Assoc VP Alumni Eng & Annual Giving Ms. Cynthia KHOO-ROBINSON
27 Assoc VP Marketing & Digital Comm Mr. Jeffrey N. SMITH
48 Dean School Arch & Planning Dr. Robert G. SHIBLEY
49 Dean College of Arts/Sciences Dr. Robin G. SCHULZE
52 Dean School Dental Medicine Dr. Joseph J. ZAMBON
53 Dean Graduate Sch of Education Dr. Suzanne N. ROSENBLITH
54 Dean School Engr/Applied Sci Dr. Liesl FOLKS
61 Dean School of Law Ms. Aviva ABRAMOVSKY
50 Dean School of Management Dr. Paul E. TESLUK
63 Dean School Medicine/Biomed Sci Dr. Michael E. CAIN
66 Dean School of Nursing Dr. Marsha L. LEWIS
67 Dean School Pharmacy/Pharm Sciences Dr. James O'DONNELL
76 Dean Sch Public Hlth/Hlth Prof Dr. Jean WACTAWSKI-WENDE
70 Dean School of Social Work Dr. Nancy J. SMYTH
97 Dean Undergraduate Education Dr. Ann M. BISANTZ
06 Registrar Dr. Kara C. SAUNDERS
88 Exec Dir Educ Opportunity Ctr Dr. Julius G. ADAMS

*State University of New York at Fredonia (A)

280 Central Avenue, Fredonia NY 14063-1136
County: Chautauqua FICE Identification: 002844
Unit ID: 196158
Telephone: (716) 673-3111 Carnegie Class: Masters/M
FAX Number: N/A Calendar System: Semester
URL: www.fredonia.edu
Established: 1826 Annual Undergrad Tuition & Fees (In-State): $8,488
Enrollment: 4,630 Coed
Affiliation or Control: State IRS Status: 501(c)3
Highest Offering: Master's
Accreditation: M, ART, CAEP, MUS, SP, SW, THEA

02 President Dr. Virginia S. HORVATH
05 Provost & VP for Acad Affairs Dr. Terry BROWN
10 VP for Finance and Admin Mr. Michael D. METZGER
84 VP for Enrollment & Student Svcs Dr. Cedric B. HOWARD
102 Exec Dir for the College Foundation Ms. Betty GOSSETT
20 Assoc VP Curriculum/Assessment/Ac Vacant
49 Dean College of Liberal Arts & Sci Dr. Andy KARAFA
88 VP Engagement & Economic Dev Dr. Kevin KEARNS
57 Dean College of Visual & Perf Arts Vacant
58 Assoc Provost for Graduate Studies Dr. Judy HOROWITZ
50 Interim Dean School of Business Dr. Mojtaba SEYEDIAN
53 Dean College of Education Dr. Christine E. GIVNER
18 Director Facilities Services Mr. Kevin P. CLOOS
06 Registrar Mr. Scott D. SAUNDERS
07 Director of Admissions Mr. Cory M. BEZEK
08 Director Library Services Mr. Randolph Lee GADIKIAN
09 Dir Institutional Research/Planning Dr. Xiao Y. ZHANG
36 Director of Career Development Ms. Tracy COLLINGWOOD
19 Chief University Police Ms. Ann K. BURNS
39 Director Residence Life Mrs. Kathy FORSTER
41 Athletic Director Mr. Gerald FISK
23 Director of Health Services Ms. Deborah A. DIBBLE
38 Director Counseling Center Dr. Tracy L. STENGER
13 CIO/Associate VP Mr. Stephen J. RIEKS
15 Director of Human Resources Mr. Michael D. DALEY
26 Director of Public Relations Mr. Jeffrey WOODARD
85 Director of Intercultural Center Dr. Khristian J. KING
92 Director of Honors Program Dr. Natalie GERBER
94 Coordinator of Women's Studies Mr. Jeffry J. IOVANNONE
96 Director of Purchasing Mrs. Shari K. MILLER
28 Chief Diversity Officer Vacant
29 Director Alumni Affairs Ms. Patricia A. FERALDI
04 Administrative Asst to President Mrs. Denise M. SZALKOWSKI
104 Director Office International Educ Dr. Naomi BALDWIN
105 Web Content Manager Mr. Jonathan WOOLSON
106 Online Learning Coordinator Ms. Lisa MELOHUSKY
22 Dir Affirm Action/Equal Opportunity Vacant
37 Director of Financial Aid Mr. Brandon M. GILLILAND

*State University of New York at New Paltz (B)

1 Hawk Drive, New Paltz NY 12561-2443
County: Ulster FICE Identification: 002846
Unit ID: 196176
Telephone: (845) 257-7869 Carnegie Class: Masters/L
FAX Number: (845) 257-3009 Calendar System: Semester
URL: www.newpaltz.edu
Established: 1823 Annual Undergrad Tuition & Fees (In-State): $8,254
Enrollment: 7,565 Coed
Affiliation or Control: State IRS Status: 501(c)3
Highest Offering: Beyond Master's But Less Than Doctorate
Accreditation: M, ART, CAEPN, MUS, SP, THEA

02 President Dr. Donald P. CHRISTIAN
100 Chief of Staff/VP Communication Ms. Shelly A. WRIGHT
05 Provost Dr. Lorin Basden ARNOLD
10 Vice Pres Administration & Finance Ms. Michele HALSTEAD
30 VP Development/Alumni Relations Ms. Erica MARKS
32 Student Affairs Vice President Dr. Stephanie BLAISDELL
84 Vice Pres Enrollment Management Mr. L. David EATON
20 Assoc Provost Dr. Laurel GARRICK DUHANEY
13 Asst Vice Pres Tech/Info Systems Mr. John REINA
21 Asst Vice President Administration Ms. Julieta MAJAK
114 Asst VP Budget Ms. Julie WALSH
09 Asst VP Inst Research/Planning Ms. Lucy WALKER
18 Asst VP Facilities Management Mr. John SHUPE
58 Assistant VP Grad & Ext Learning Ms. Shala MILLS
53 Dean of Education Dr. Michael ROSENBERG
57 Dean Fine & Performing Arts Dr. Jennifer MOKREN
49 Dean Liberal Arts & Sciences Dr. Laura BARRETT
50 Dean School of Business Dr. Kristin BACKHAUS
54 Dean Science and Engineering Dr. Daniel FREEDMAN
07 Dean of Admissions Ms. Lisa JONES
08 Dean Sojourner Truth Library Mr. W. Mark COLVSON
86 Ex Dir Compliance/Camp Clm/Title IX Ms. Tanhena PACHECO DUNN
07 Assoc Dean/Dir Freshmen Admissions Ms. Kimberly STRANO
15 Director Human Resources Ms. Tanhena PACHECO DUNN
37 Director of Financial Aid Ms. Maureen LOHAN-BREMER
06 Registrar Ms. Stella TURK
29 Director Alumni Relations Ms. Shana CIRCE
38 Director Student Counseling Dr. Gweneth LLOYD
26 Media Relations Manager Ms. Melissa KACZMAREK
96 Director of Purchasing/Procurement Mr. David FARBANIEC
19 Chief of Police Ms. Mary RITAYIK
41 Athletic Director Mr. Stuart ROBINSON

*State University of New York at Oneonta (C)

108 Ravine Parkway, Oneonta NY 13820-4015
County: Otsego FICE Identification: 002847
Unit ID: 196185
Telephone: (607) 436-3500 Carnegie Class: Masters/M
FAX Number: N/A Calendar System: Semester
URL: www.oneonta.edu
Established: 1889 Annual Undergrad Tuition & Fees (In-State): $8,421
Enrollment: 6,358 Coed
Affiliation or Control: State IRS Status: 501(c)3
Highest Offering: Master's
Accreditation: M, AAFCS, DIETD, DIETI, IPSY, MUS, THEA

02 President Dr. Barbara MORRIS
100 Chief of Staff Ms. Colleen E. BRANNAN
05 Provost/Vice Pres Academic Affairs Dr. Leamor KAHANOV
10 VP Finance/Administration Ms. Julie PISCITELLO
32 Vice President Student Development Dr. Franklin D. CHAMBERS
111 Vice President College Advancement Mr. Paul J. ADAMO
09 Assoc Prov Inst Assessment & Eff Vacant
20 Assoc Provost Academic Programs Dr. Eileen MORGAN-ZAYACHEK
83 Dean School of Liberal Arts Dr. Elizabeth DUNN
50 Dean School of Econ & Business Dr. Wade THOMAS
53 Dean School of Educ & Human Ecology Dr. Jan BOWERS
81 Interim Dean School of Science Dr. Tracy ALLEN
58 Director of Graduate Studies Vacant
84 Chief Enrollment Services Officer Mr. Kevin JENSEN
35 Assoc Vice Pres Student Development Ms. Amanda FINCH
18 Chief Facilities/Safety Officer Mr. Lachlan SQUAIR
19 Chief of Police Ms. Jennifer FILA
15 Sr Exec Employee Services Officer Ms. Lisa M. WENCK
26 Chief Communication/Mktg Officer Mr. Hal S. LEGG
07 Director of Admissions Ms. Karen A. BROWN
29 Director of Alumni Engagement Ms. Laura MADELONE LINCOLN
110 Director Advancement Services Mr. Benjamin WENDROW
44 Director Fund for Oneonta Ms. Kim NOSTROM
41 Athletic Director Ms. Tracey M. RANIERI
114 Budget Control Officer/Budget Dir Vacant
25 Director Business Services Ms. Betty M. TIRADO
36 Director Career Development Ms. Melissa MARIETTA
13 Chief Information Officer Mr. Steven MANISCALCO
90 Director IT Customer Support Mr. Steven J. MANISCALCO
23 Dir Health & Counseling Services Dr. Melissa A. FALLON-KORB
24 Director Creative Media Services Mr. David W. GEASEY
37 Associate Director Financial Aid Ms. Barbara PLEDGER
09 Dir Institutional Research Vacant
85 Int Director International Educ Ms. Katherine STANLEY
89 Director Orientation/First Year Exp Ms. Monica C. GRAU
96 Procurement/Travel Office Manager Ms. Terri THOMAS
06 College Registrar Ms. Maureen P. ARTALE
39 Director Residential Community Life Mr. Tyler MILLER
93 Director Access/Opportunity Pgms Ms. Pathy LEIVA
28 Chief Diversity Officer Vacant
22 Affirmative Action Officer Mr. Andrew STAMMEL

*Stony Brook University (D)

310 Administration Building, Stony Brook NY 11794-0701
County: Suffolk FICE Identification: 002838
Unit ID: 196097
Telephone: (631) 632-6265 Carnegie Class: DU-Highest
FAX Number: (631) 632-6621 Calendar System: Semester
URL: www.stonybrook.edu
Established: 1957 Annual Undergrad Tuition & Fees (In-State): $9,625
Enrollment: 25,989 Coed
Affiliation or Control: State IRS Status: 501(c)3
Highest Offering: Doctorate
Accreditation: M, ARCPA, CAATE, CAEPN, CAMPEP, CLPSY, COARC, COARCP, DENT, DIETI, EMT, IPSY, JOUR, MED, MIDWF, MT, NURSE, OT, PCSAS, PH, POLYT, PTA, RADDOS, SW

02 President/CEO Dr. Samuel L. STANLEY
05 Provost Dr. Michael BERNSTEIN
63 Sr VP HSC/Dean School of Medicine Dr. Kenneth KAUSHANSKY
11 Sr VP for Administration/Finance Ms. Kathleen BYINGTON
46 Vice President Research Dr. Richard REEDER
32 Int VP Student Aff/Dean of Students Dr. Richard GATTEAU
10 VP Finance Mr. Lyle GOMES
111 Sr VP University Advancement Vacant
100 Chief Deputy Ms. Judith GREIMAN
114 Associate VP for Budget Vacant
26 VP Comm & Mktg/Chief Comm Officer Mr. Nicholas SCIBETTA
39 Asst Vice Pres Campus Residences Dr. Dallas BAUMAN
17 Interim CEO University Hospital Ms. Carol GOMES
84 Assoc Prov Enrollment/Retent Mgmt Mr. Rodney MORRISON
13 CIO Ms. Melissa WOO
45 Vice President Strategic Initiative Dr. Matthew WHELAN
43 Senior Counsel in Charge Ms. Susan BLUM
49 Int Dean College Arts & Sciences Dr. Nicole SAMPSON
88 Dean School of Marine & Atmos Sci Dr. Paul SHEPSON
52 Dean School of Dental Medicine Dr. Mary R. TRUHLAR
68 Athletic Director Mr. Shawn R. HEILBRON
58 Int Dean Grad Sch/VProv Grad Stds Dr. Richard J. GERRIG
76 Int Dean School Health Tech & Mgmt Dr. Lisa JOHNSON
66 Dean School of Nursing Dr. Lee XIPPOLITOS
70 Dean School of Social Welfare Dr. Jacqueline MONDROS
08 Int Dean of Libraries Mr. Shafeek FAZAL
86 SVP Government & Community Rel Ms. Judith GREIMAN
88 Exec Dir LI State Vets Home Mr. Fred SGANGA
19 Chief of Police Mr. Robert LENAHAN
15 VP Human Resource Svcs Ms. Lynn JOHNSON
28 Dir Diversity/AA/Equal Employ Oppty Ms. Marjolie LEONARD
09 AVP Inst Rsrch/Plng/Effectiveness Dr. Braden J. HOSCH
85 Dean International Programs Dr. Jun LIU
102 Int Exec Dir of Stony Brook Found Mr. Jason HSIUH
29 Director Alumni Relations Mr. Matthew COLSON
23 Director University Health Services Dr. Rachel BERGESON
38 Int Dir Counseling/Psych Services Dr. Julian PESSIER
36 Director Career Placement Center Ms. Marianna SAVOCA
06 Registrar Ms. Diane BELLO
37 Financial Aid/Scholarships Ms. Jacqueline PASCARIELLO
50 Dean College of Business Dr. Manuel LONDON
27 University Media Relations Officer Ms. Lauren SHEPROW
96 Director of Purchasing/Procurement Vacant
60 Int Dean School of Journalism Ms. Laura LINDENFELD
04 Executive Asst to President Ms. Carol LONDOIRO

*SUNY Downstate Medical Center (E)

450 Clarkson Avenue, Brooklyn NY 11203-2098
County: Kings FICE Identification: 002839
Unit ID: 196255
Telephone: (718) 270-1000 Carnegie Class: Spec-4-yr-Med
FAX Number: (718) 270-4092 Calendar System: Semester
URL: www.downstate.edu
Established: 1860 Annual Undergrad Tuition & Fees (In-State): N/A
Enrollment: 1,792 Coed
Affiliation or Control: State IRS Status: 501(c)3
Highest Offering: Doctorate
Accreditation: M, ARCPA, DMS, MED, MIDWF, NURSE, OT, PH, PTA

02 President Dr. Wayne J. RILEY
10 Chief Financial Officer Dr. Richard MILLER
11 COO/Exec VP Administration Ms. Heidi J. ARONIN
05 Sr Vice Pres for Academic Affairs Dr. Pascal IMPERATO
32 VP Academic & Student Affairs Dr. Jeffrey S. PUTMAN
26 AVP Communications & Marketing Ms. Dawn SKEETE-WALKER
13 Chief Information Officer Ms. Michele SCAGGIANTE
121 AVP Academic Support Services Dr. Seth LANGLEY
07 Director of Admissions Dr. Shushawna DEOLIVEIRA
06 Registrar Ms. Anne SHONBRUN
37 Director Student Financial Aid Ms. Farah BURNETT
27 Dir Media & Public Relations Mr. John GILLESPIE
04 Executive Asst to President Ms. Reina ALFRED
08 Interim Librarian Dr. Mohamed HUSSAIN
09 Director of Institutional Research Ms. Charis NG
15 VP Human Resources Ms. Judith DORSEY
18 VP Facilities Management & Dev Mr. James MINTO
19 Interim Chief University Police Mr. Israel MALDONADO
22 AVP Diversity & Inclusion Ms. Victoria AJIBADE
25 Chief Contracts/Grants Admin Ms. Maureen CRYSTAL
39 Director Student Housing Ms. Margaret O'SULLIVAN
43 Dir Legal Services/General Counsel Mr. Kevin O'MARA
45 Chief Institutional Planning Vacant
63 Interim Dean College of Medicine Dr. Michael LUCCHESI
53 Dean College of Nursing Dr. Lori A. ESCALLIER
76 Dean School of Health Professions Dr. Allen LEWIS
69 Dean School of Public Health Dr. Kitaw DEMISSIE
58 Dean School of Graduate Studies Dr. Mark STEWART
86 Director Government Relations Mr. Jelanie DESHONG
90 Asst Director Academic Computing Dr. Jim NEILL
96 Exec Dir of Contracts & Purchasing Mr. Raul TOSADO
113 Bursar Mr. Peter LJUTIC
100 Chief of Staff Dr. Keydron GUINN
108 Director Institutional Assessment Dr. Bonnie GRANAT
36 Director Student Placement Vacant

*State University of New York Upstate Medical University (F)

750 E Adams Street, Syracuse NY 13210-2375
County: Onondaga FICE Identification: 002840
Unit ID: 196307
Telephone: (315) 464-5540 Carnegie Class: Spec-4-yr-Med
FAX Number: (315) 464-8823 Calendar System: Semester
URL: https://www.upstate.edu
Established: 1834 Annual Undergrad Tuition & Fees (In-State): N/A
Enrollment: 1,484 Coed
Affiliation or Control: State IRS Status: 501(c)3

Highest Offering: Doctorate
Accreditation: M, ARCPA, COARC, DENT, DMOLS, EMT, IPSY, MED, MT, NURSE, PAST, PERF, PH, PTA, RAD, RTT

02 Interim President .... Dr. Mantosh DEWAN
63 Dean College of Medicine .... Dr. Julio LICINIO
17 CEO University Hospital .... Dr. Robert CORONA
10 Vice President Finance & Management .... Mr. Eric SMITH
05 Vice President Academic Affairs .... Dr. Lynn CLEARY
46 Interim Vice President for Research .... Dr. Mark SCHMITT
58 Dean College Graduate Studies .... Dr. Mark SCHMITT
66 Dean College of Nursing .... Dr. Tammy AUSTIN-KETCH
76 Dean College of Health Professions .... Dr. Katherine BEISSNER
102 Exec Director HSC Foundation .... Ms. Eileen PEZZI
100 Interim Chief of Staff .... Ms. Linda VEIT
32 Dean Student Affairs .... Dr. Julie R. WHITE
43 Senior Managing Counsel .... Ms. Lisa ALEXANDER
29 Director of Medical Alumni Affairs .... Mr. Paul W. NORCROSS
15 Assoc VP Human Resources .... Mr. Chris FROST
13 Chief Information Officer .... Mr. Mark ZEMAN
28 Interim Chief Diversity Officer .... Dr. Malika CARTER
108 Director Evaluation and Assessment .... Dr. Lauren GERMAIN
06 Registrar/Dir Inst Research .... Ms. Jennifer MARTIN TSE
08 Director of Libraries .... Ms. Christina POPE
07 Assoc Dean Admissions/Financial Aid .... Ms. Jennifer C. WELCH
106 Director E-Learning .... Dr. Pamela YOUNGS-MAHER
18 Chief Facilities/Physical Plant .... Mr. Bob LOTKOWICTZ
21 Assistant Vice President Finance .... Mr. David ANTHONY
37 Director Student Financial Aid .... Ms. Nicole MORGANTE

*SUNY Broome Community College (A)

PO Box 1017, Binghamton NY 13902-1017
County: Broome FICE Identification: 002862
Unit ID: 189547
Telephone: (607) 778-5000 Carnegie Class: Assoc/HT-Mix Trad/Non
FAX Number: (607) 778-5310 Calendar System: Semester
URL: www.sunybroome.edu
Established: 1946 Annual Undergrad Tuition & Fees (In-District): $5,355
Enrollment: 5,624 Coed
Affiliation or Control: State/Local IRS Status: 501(c)3
Highest Offering: Associate Degree
Accreditation: M, ADNUR, CAHIIM, DH, MAC, MLTAD, PTAA, RAD

02 President .... Dr. Kevin DRUMM
05 Exec VP/Chief Academic Officer .... Dr. Francis BATTISTI
11 Vice Pres Admin/Financial Affairs .... Mr. Michael SULLIVAN
32 VP Student Development & CDO .... Dr. Carol ROSS-SCOTT
10 Associate Vice Pres & Controller .... Ms. Jeanette TILLOTSON
50 Assoc VP & Dean Bus/Public Svcs .... Ms. Elizabeth MOLLEN
76 Assoc VP & Dean of Health Sciences .... Dr. Amy BRANDT
49 Assoc VP & Dean of Liberal Arts .... Dr. Michael KINNEY
51 Dir Continuing Educ & Workforce Dev .... Ms. Janet HERTZOG
81 Assoc Vice Pres & Dean STEM .... Dr. Michele SNYDER
35 Dean of Students .... Mr. Scott SCHUHERT
102 Executive Director BCC Foundation .. Ms. Catherine R. WILLIAMS
08 Director Learning Resource Center .... Ms. Robin PETRUS
07 Director of Admissions .... Mrs. Elisabeth COSTANZO
15 Human Resources Officer .... Ms. Lynn FEDORCHAK
06 Registrar .... Mr. Martin GUZZI
36 Director of Placement Services .... Vacant
108 Dean Institutional Effectiveness .... Dr. Sesime ADANU
18 Interim Campus Operations Director .... Mr. David LIGEIKIS
37 Director of Financial Aid .... Ms. Laura HODEL
13 Dir Information Technology Services .... Mr. John PETKASH
23 Director of Health Services .... Mr. Joseph O'CONNOR
25 Director of Sponsored Programs .... Ms. Shelli CORDISCO
41 Director of Athletics .... Mr. Brett CARTER
19 Dir of Campus Safety & Security .... Mr. Joseph O'CONNOR
29 Director Alumni Affairs .... Mr. Anthony ZOSTANT
40 Bookstore Manager .... Ms. Kristin DEMPSEY
88 Dir Educational Opportunity Pgm .... Ms. Venessa RODRIGUEZ
96 Director of Purchasing .... Mr. Randy CAMPBELL
26 Dir of Marketing/Communications .... Mr. Jesse WELLS
85 Ast Dir Intl Admiss/Intl Stdnt Stds .... Ms. Susan WELLINGTON
104 Coordinator Study Abroad Program .... Ms. Maria BASUALDO
38 Student Counseling .... Mr. Joseph SPENCE
22 Dir Affirmative Action/EEO .... Ms. Paige SEDLACEK
39 Director Student Housing .... Ms. Amy ZIEZIULA
04 Assistant to the President .... Ms. Diana D. LENZO
84 Exec Enrollment Management Officer .... Mr. Jesse WELLS
103 Director Workforce Development .... Ms. Janet M. HERTZOG
30 Director of Development .... Ms. Lisa SCHAPPERT

*State University of New York, The College at Brockport (B)

350 New Campus Drive, Brockport NY 14420-2914
County: Monroe FICE Identification: 002841
Unit ID: 196121
Telephone: (585) 395-2211 Carnegie Class: Masters/L
FAX Number: (585) 395-2401 Calendar System: Semester
URL: www.brockport.edu
Established: 1835 Annual Undergrad Tuition & Fees (In-State): $8,412
Enrollment: 8,313 Coed
Affiliation or Control: State IRS Status: 501(c)3
Highest Offering: Master's
Accreditation: M, CAATE, CACREP, CAEP, DANCE, EXSC, NRPA, NURSE, SPAA, SW, THEA

02 President .... Dr. Heidi R. MACPHERSON
05 Provost & VP Academic Affairs .... Dr. Katy HEYNING
10 VP Administration & Finance .... Mr. James WALL
84 VP Enrollment Mgmt/Student Affairs .... Dr. Kathryn WILSON
111 VP Advancement .... Mr. Michael ANDRIATCH
26 VP for University Relations .... Mr. David MIHALYOV
20 Vice Provost .... Dr. Eileen DANIEL
28 Chief Diversity Officer .... Dr. Cephas ARCHIE
18 Director of Physical Plant .... Mr. Kevin RICE
32 AVP EMSA - Student Affairs .... Ms. Lorraine ACKER
21 Asst VP Finance & Management .... Ms. Karen M. RIOTTO
13 CIO .... Mr. Robert CUSHMAN
49 Dean Arts and Sciences .... Dr. Jose MALIEKAL
50 Int Dean Business and Management .... Dr. Susan STITES-DOE
53 Dean Educ/Health & Hum Svcs .... Dr. Thomas J. HERNANDEZ
14 Director of Info Tech System .... Mr. Stephen COOK
07 Dir of Undergrad Admissions .... Mr. Robert WYANT
58 Int Dir Center for Grad Studies .... Mr. Michael HARRISON
104 Int Dir Global Educ and Engagement .... Ms. Lindsay CRANE
37 Int Dir Financial Aid Daily Ops .... Ms. Nora BELL-OWENS
36 Director of Career Services .... Ms. Jill WESLEY
19 Chief of University Police .... Mr. Daniel VASILE
06 College Registrar .... Mr. Peter DOWE
15 Director of Human Resources .... Ms. Wendy CRANMER
22 Affirmative Action Officer .... Ms. Tammy GOUGER
124 AVP EMSA - Plng/Assess/Retention .... Dr. Sara KELLY
23 Director Student Health/Counseling .... Ms. Cheryl VAN LARE
39 Int Dir Residential Life .... Ms. Monique REW-BIGELOW
41 Director of Athletics .... Mr. Erick HART
25 Director of Grants Development .... Ms. Justine BRIGGS
92 Director of Honors Program .... Dr. Austin BUSCH
09 Dir Inst Research & Analysis .... Mr. Richard DIRMYER
96 Director of Procurement & Payment .... Mr. Mark W. STACY
94 Chair Women and Gender Studies .... Dr. Milo OBOURN
29 Director Alumni Relations .... Mr. Kerry GOTHAM
04 Assistant to the President .... Ms. Julie A. PRUSS
08 Director of Library Services .... Ms. Diane FULKERSON
88 Title IX & College Compliance Ofcr .... Ms. Denine CARR

*State University of New York College at Buffalo (C)

1300 Elmwood Avenue, Buffalo NY 14222-1091
County: Erie FICE Identification: 002842
Unit ID: 196130
Telephone: (716) 878-4000 Carnegie Class: Masters/L
FAX Number: (716) 878-3039 Calendar System: Semester
URL: www.buffalostate.edu
Established: 1871 Annual Undergrad Tuition & Fees (In-State): $8,210
Enrollment: 9,516 Coed
Affiliation or Control: State IRS Status: 501(c)3
Highest Offering: Master's
Accreditation: M, ART, CAEPN, CIDA, DIETC, DIETD, FEPAC, JOUR, MUS, NAIT, SP, SW, THEA

02 President .... Dr. Katherine S. CONWAY-TURNER
100 Chief of Staff/Secretary to Board .... Ms. Crystal J. RODRIGUEZ
05 Interim Provost .... Dr. James MAYROSE
10 Vice President Finance & Management .... Mrs. Laura J. BARNUM
32 Vice President Student Affairs .... Dr. Timothy W. GORDON
111 VP Inst Advance & FNDN Exec Dir .... Dr. James M. FINNERTY
28 Chief Diversity Officer .... Dr. Karen A. CLINTON JONES
13 CIO/VP Enrollment/Marketing/Comm .... Dr. Jacquelyn L. MALCOLM
19 Chief University Police .... Mr. Peter M. CAREY
21 Assoc Vice President & Comptroller .... Mr. James A. THOR
15 Assoc VP Human Resource Management . Ms. Susan J. EARSHEN
20 Special Adv to Provost for Educ .... Vacant
88 Int AVP Inst Effectiveness .... Dr. Eric J. KRIEG
14 AVP Data and Analytics/IT .... Ms. Judith B. BASINSKI
108 Associate Provost .... Dr. Amitra A. WALL
26 Assoc VP College Relations .... Mr. Timothy J. WALSH
08 Special Asst to CIO .... Ms. Maryruth F. GLOGOWSKI
30 Assoc VP Development .... Mr. R. Scott BURNS
86 AVP Govt Rels/Alumni Engagement .... Mr. William J. BENFANTI
51 Assoc VP Continuing Prof Studies .... Dr. Margaret A. SHAW-BURNETT
53 Dean School of Education .... Dr. Wendy A. PATERSON
49 Dean School of Arts & Humanities .... Mr. Benjamin C. CHRISTY
83 Dean Natural & Social Sciences .... Dr. Mark W. SEVERSON
107 Int Dean School of the Professions .... Dr. Rita M. ZIENTER
58 Dean Graduate School .... Dr. Kevin J. MILLER
88 Resident Manager Chartwells .... Mr. Glenn R. BUCELLO
88 Director Liberty Partnership .... Ms. Patrice A. CATHEY
88 Director STEP .... Mr. Darryl CARTER
88 Director Upward Bound .... Mr. Donald A. PATTERSON
36 Director of Career Development .... Ms. Stephanie B. ZUCKERMAN-AVILES
27 Director Public Relations .... Mr. Jerod T. DAHLGREN
07 Director Undergraduate Admissions .... Mr. David P. LORETO
06 Registrar .... Dr. Nigel R. MARRINER
37 Director of Financial Aid .... Ms. Connie F. COOKE
39 Asst Dean Residence Life .... Dr. Philip BADASZEWSKI
113 Dir Student Accounts/Parking Svcs .... Ms. Jayme S. RITER
41 Director Intercollegiate Athletics .... Mr. Jerry S. BOYES
88 Dir New Student & Family Programs .... Mr. Daniel HEIMS
23 AVP Weigel Wellness Center .... Dr. Rock D. DOYLE
35 Dean of Students .... Ms. Sarah M. YOUNG
85 Asst Prov Student Global Engagement .... Dr. Robert SUMMERS
88 Director of Business Services .... Vacant
25 AVP for Sponsored Program Operation .... Mrs. Donna L. SCUTO
35 Asst Dean Student Ldrshp/Engagement .... Mr. David W. COX
09 Director Institutional Research .... Mr. Yves M. GACHETTE
29 Director of Alumni Engagement .... Ms. Mary-Jo JAGORD
96 Director of Contract Management .... Mr. Steven M. OLSEN
40 Manager College Bookstore .... Ms. Lynn M. PUMA
88 Operations Manager .... Mr. Dominic HANNON
22 Director Assessibility Service .... Ms. Lisa T. MORRISON-FRONCKOWIAK
88 Director Student Conduct .... Ms. Janelle BROOKS
18 Dir Facilities/Constr/Maintenance .... Mr. Steven E. SHAFFER

*State University of New York College at Cortland (D)

PO Box 2000, Cortland NY 13045-0900
County: Cortland FICE Identification: 002843
Unit ID: 196149
Telephone: (607) 753-2011 Carnegie Class: Masters/L
FAX Number: (607) 753-5999 Calendar System: Semester
URL: www.cortland.edu
Established: 1868 Annual Undergrad Tuition & Fees (In-State): $8,536
Enrollment: 6,913 Coed
Affiliation or Control: State IRS Status: 501(c)3
Highest Offering: Master's
Accreditation: M, CAATE, CAEP, CAEPN, NRPA, PH, SP

02 President .... Dr. Erik J. BITTERBAUM
05 Provost .... Dr. Mark PRUS
32 Vice Pres Student Affairs .... Mr. C. Gregory SHARER
111 Vice Pres Inst Advancement .... Mr. Peter PERKINS
10 Vice Pres for Finance & Admin .... Ms. Anna ADDONISIO
21 Assoc VP for Finance .... Vacant
13 Assoc Provost for Info Resources .... Ms. Amy BERG
18 Assoc VP Facilities Management .... Mr. Zach NEWSWANGER
20 Assoc Prov for Academic Affairs .... Dr. Carol VAN DER KARR
84 Asst Vice Pres Enrollment Mgmt .... Mr. Mark YACAVONE
108 Vice Pres for Policy/Accreditation .... Dr. Virginia LEVINE
09 Director Inst Rsrch/Assessment .... Mr. Stephen CUNNINGHAM
08 Director of Libraries .... Ms. Jennifer KRONENBITTER
06 Registrar .... Mr. Thomas HANFORD
36 Director of Career Services .... Ms. Nanette PASQUARELLO
15 Asst VP Human Resources .... Mr. Gary EVANS
29 Int Director Alumni Engagement .... Ms. Erin BOYLAN
38 Dir Counseling/Student Devel .... Dr. Carolyn BERSHAD
37 Dir of Student Financial Aid .... Ms. Karen GALLAGHER
19 Chief of University Police .... Mr. Mark DEPAULL
91 Director Admin Computing Svcs .... Mr. Daniel SIDEBOTTOM
90 Director Campus Technology Services .... Ms. Lisa KAHLE
107 Dean Professional Studies .... Dr. John COTTONE
49 Dean Arts & Sciences .... Dr. Bruce MATTINGLY
26 Director of Communications .... Mr. Frederic PIERCE
53 Dean of Education .... Dr. Andrea LACHANCE
93 Dir Educational Opportunity Program .. Dr. Lewis ROSENGARTEN
92 Director of Honors Program .... Dr. Frank ROSSI
94 Coordinator of Women's Studies .... Dr. Jena CURTIS
96 Director of Purchasing .... Ms. Melissa FOX
22 Affirmative Action Officer .... Ms. Melanie WOODWARD
28 Director Multicult Life/Diversity .... Ms. AnnaMaria CIRRINCIONE
41 Athletic Director .... Mr. Mike URTZ
104 Director International Programs .... Dr. Mary SCHLARB
25 Assoc Dir Research & Sponsored Pgms .... Mr. Thomas FRANK
39 Director Student Housing .... Mr. Ralph CARRASQUILLO
07 Director of Admissions .... Mr. Mark YACAVONE

*State University of New York College at Geneseo (E)

1 College Circle, Geneseo NY 14454-1401
County: Livingston FICE Identification: 002845
Unit ID: 196167
Telephone: (585) 245-5000 Carnegie Class: Masters/S
FAX Number: (585) 245-5005 Calendar System: Semester
URL: www.geneseo.edu
Established: 1871 Annual Undergrad Tuition & Fees (In-State): $8,651
Enrollment: 5,652 Coed
Affiliation or Control: State IRS Status: 501(c)3
Highest Offering: Master's
Accreditation: M, CAEPN

02 President .... Dr. Denise A. BATTLES
05 Provost .... Dr. Stacey ROBERTSON
20 Vice Provost for Academic Affairs .... Dr. Glenn GEISER-GETZ
11 Vice President for Finance & Admin .... Ms. Julie BUEHLER
32 Vice Pres for Student & Campus Life .... Vacant
111 Interim VP of College Advancement .... Mr. Justin JOHNSTON
84 Vice Pres Enrollment Mgmt .... Dr. Costas SOLOMOU
10 Assoc VP Administration/Controller .... Mr. Brice M. WEIGMAN
26 Chief Comm & Marketing Officer .... Ms. Gail GLOVER
100 Senior Associate to the President .... Ms. Wendi KINNEY
15 Asst Vice Pres Human Resources .... Ms. Julie A. BRIGGS
29 Interim Director Alumni Relations .... Ms. Rose LINFOOT
20 Int Asst Provost Curric & Assess .... Mr. William HARRISON
35 Dean of Students .... Dr. Leonard SANCILIO
07 Director of Admissions .... Ms. Kimberly HARVEY
08 Library Director .... Mr. Benjamin RAWLINS
13 Director Computing/Info Technology .. Ms. Susan E. CHICHESTER
37 Director of Financial Aid .... Ms. Susan ROMANO
25 Director of Sponsored Research .... Dr. Anne E. BALDWIN
09 Director of Institutional Research .... Dr. Julie M. RAO
06 Registrar .... Ms. Kimberley WILLIS
36 Director of Career Development .. Ms. Jessie STACK LOMBARDO
28 Chief Diversity Officer .... Robbie ROUTENBERG
88 Director of Multicul Pgm & Services .... Dr. Sasha ELOI-EVANS
19 Chief of University Police .... Mr. Thomas KILCULLEN
18 Interim Asst VP for Fac & Planning .... Mr. Robert M. AMES
114 Dir of Acct & Budgeting Services .... Mr. Jeffrey NORDLAND

38 Clinical Dir Counseling Services Dr. Alex CARLO
38 Clinical Dir S Village Couns Svcs Dr. Beth K. CHOLETTE
96 Director of Purchasing Ms. Rebecca E. ANCHOR
04 Asst to President Ms. Teresa SEXTON
121 Dean of Acad Planning & Advising Dr. Celia A. EASTON
41 Dir of Intercollegiate Athletics Mr. Michael C. MOONEY
50 Dean of School of Business Dr. Mary Ellen ZUCKERMAN
53 Interim Dir School of Education Dr. Dennis SHOWERS
88 Dir Research Tech & Strategic Proj Mr. Kirk ANNE
14 Assoc Director & Manager Info Sys Mr. Paul JACKSON

*State University of New York College at Old Westbury (A)

P.O. Box 210, 223 Store Hill Road,
Old Westbury NY 11568-0210

County: Nassau
FICE Identification: 007109
Unit ID: 196237
Telephone: (516) 876-3000
Carnegie Class: Masters/S
FAX Number: (516) 876-3209
Calendar System: Semester
URL: www.oldwestbury.edu
Established: 1965
Annual Undergrad Tuition & Fees (In-State): $8,143
Enrollment: 4,910
Coed
Affiliation or Control: State
IRS Status: 501(c)3
Highest Offering: Master's
Accreditation: M, CAEPN, PH

02 President Dr. Calvin O. BUTTS, III
100 Chief of Staff Ms. Mona G. RANKIN
05 Provost/Sr VP Academic Affairs Dr. Patrick O'SULLIVAN
84 Acting VP for Enrollment Services Mr. Frank PIZZARDI
32 VP Stdnt Affs/Chief Diversity Ofcr Mr. Usama SHAIKH
10 Sr VP Div Business & Finance/CFO Mr. Len L. DAVIS
15 Asst to Pres for Admin/Dir HR Mr. William P. KIMMINS
111 VP Inst Advance/Exec Dir Foundation Dr. Wayne EDWARDS
26 Vice Pres Communications Mr. Michael G. KINANE
21 Assoc VP Business Affs/Controller Mr. Pat LETTINI
20 Acting Associate Provost Dr. Duncan QUARLESS
21 Assoc VP of Business Compliance Mr. Arthur H. ANGST, JR.
20 Asst Vice Pres Academic Affairs Mr. Anthony BARBERA
09 Asst VP AA/Inst Rsrch/Assessment Dr. Jacob HELLER
49 Dean School of Arts & Sciences Dr. Barbara HILLERY
50 Dean School of Business Dr. Raj DEVASAGAYAM
35 Dean of Students Ms. Claudia L. MARIN ANDRADE
53 Dean School of Education Dr. Nancy BROWN
107 Director School of Prof Studies Dr. Edward BEVER
19 Chief of Police Mr. Steven SIENA
13 Chief Information Officer Mr. Evan KOBOLAKIS
06 Registrar Ms. Patricia A. SMITH
88 Director of Advancement Initiatives Mr. Rossano ROVELLO
89 Director First-Year Experience Dr. Laura M. ANKER
31 Director of Community Relations Ms. Carolyn BENNETT
38 Dir Counseling/Psych Wellness Svcs Dr. Trisha BILLARD
29 Director of Alumni Affairs Ms. Penny J. CHIN
22 Dir Ofc Svcs for Stdnts/Disability Ms. Stacey DEFELICE
92 Director Honors College Dr. Anthony L. DELUCA
08 Library Director Ms. Antonia DIGREGORIO
88 Coordinator of Scholarships Ms. Pritpal KAINTH
108 Dir Inst Research & Assessment Ms. Sandra KAUFMANN
109 Exec Dir Auxiliary Svc Corp Ms. Carol KAUNITZ
88 Director of Capital Planning Mr. Ray MAGGIORE
88 Dir Spec Programs Acad Affairs Mr. Yves M. MAGLOIRE
36 Dir Career Plng & Development Ms. Jerilyn MARINAN
18 Director of Facilities Mr. Timothy MCGARRY
35 Director of Student Activities Ms. Suzanne MCLOUGHLIN
25 Director of Sponsored Programs Mr. Thomas MURPHY
96 Director of Purchasing Mr. James MWAURA
37 Director Financial Aid Ms. Mildred O'KEEFE
07 Director of Admissions Mr. Frank PIZZARDI
88 Dir Educational Opportunity Program Mr. Jerrell W. ROBINSON
88 Dir Ofc of Student Conduct Mr. Brian SCHWIRZBIN
39 Director Residential Life Mr. Gareth SHUMACK
23 Dir Student Health Services Ms. Cristine TESORIERO
88 Dir Orientation & Special Events Ms. Jaclyn VENTO
41 Director of Athletics Ms. Lenore J. WALSH

*State University of New York College at Oswego (B)

7060 State Route 104, Oswego NY 13126-3501

County: Oswego
FICE Identification: 002848
Unit ID: 196194
Telephone: (315) 312-2500
Carnegie Class: Masters/L
FAX Number: (315) 312-5799
Calendar System: Semester
URL: www.oswego.edu
Established: 1861
Annual Undergrad Tuition & Fees (In-State): $8,440
Enrollment: 8,026
Coed
Affiliation or Control: State
IRS Status: 501(c)3
Highest Offering: Master's
Accreditation: M, ART, CACREP, CAEPN, MUS, THEA

02 President Dr. Deborah F. STANLEY
05 VP Academic Affairs/Provost Dr. Scott R. FURLONG
10 VP Admin/Finance Mr. Nicholas A. LYONS
84 VP Student Affairs/Enrollment Mgmt Dr. Jerri HOWLAND
30 VP Devel/Alumni Relations Ms. Mary CANALE
100 Chief of Staff Ms. Kristi ECK
88 Dep to the Pres Ext Prtnr Econ Dev Ms. Pamela CARACCIOLI
32 Interim Dean of Students Dr. Kathleen EVANS
28 Chief Diversity & Inclusion Officer Dr. Rodmon KING
18 Asst VP for Facilities Services Mr. Mitch FIELDS
21 Asst VP for Finance & Budget Ms. Vicki FURLONG
20 Associate Provost Dr. Rameen MOHAMMADI
04 Exec Asst to Pres/Affrm Action Ofcr Dr. Mary TOALE
26 Chief Communication Officer Mr. Wayne WESTERVELT
25 Assoc Provost Research Dev & Admin Mr. William BOWERS
94 Director Gender & Women's Studies Dr. Joanna GOPLEN
06 Registrar Mr. Jerret LEMAY
08 Director of Libraries Ms. Sarah CONRAD WEISMAN
91 Assoc Dir Campus Tech Services Mr. Michael C. PISA
37 Interim Director of Financial Aid Ms. Jennie HOFFMAN
09 Director Inst Research & Assessment Dr. Deborah FURLONG
36 Director Career Services Mr. Gary MORRIS
38 Director Counseling Services Center Ms. Katherine WOLFE-LYGA
15 Director Human Resources Ms. Amy PLOTNER
19 University Police Chief Mr. John ROSSI
23 Director of Walker Health Center Ms. Angela BROWN
39 Asst VP Residence Life & Housing Mr. Shaun N. CRISLER
41 Interim Director of Athletics Ms. Susan VISCOMI
96 Purchasing Associate Vacant
13 Chief Technology Officer Mr. Sean MORIARTY
29 Director Alumni Relations Ms. Laura KELLY
07 Interim Director of Admissions Ms. Vicki FURLONG
40 College Store Manager Ms. Susan RABY
49 Dean Col Lib Arts & Science Dr. Kristin CROYLE
53 Dean School of Education Dr. Pamela MICHEL
58 Dean Grad Studies Dr. Kristen C. EICHHORN
50 Dean School of Business Dr. Prabakar KOTHANDARAMAN
51 Dean of Extended Learning Ms. Jill PIPPIN
88 Dean of Comm/Media & the Arts Dr. Julie PRETZAT
35 Asst VP Student Development Dr. Kathleen EVANS
109 General Manager Auxiliary Services Mr. Michael FLAHERTY
104 Assoc Provost Intl Educ & Programs Dr. Joshua S. MCKEOWN

*State University of New York College at Plattsburgh (C)

101 Broad Street, Plattsburgh NY 12901-2637

County: Clinton
FICE Identification: 002849
Unit ID: 196246
Telephone: (518) 564-2000
Carnegie Class: Masters/M
FAX Number: (518) 564-3932
Calendar System: Semester
URL: www.plattsburgh.edu
Established: 1889
Annual Undergrad Tuition & Fees (In-State): $8,369
Enrollment: 5,719
Coed
Affiliation or Control: State
IRS Status: 501(c)3
Highest Offering: Master's
Accreditation: M, CACREP, DIETD, NURSE, SP, SW

02 President Dr. John ETTLING
05 Int Provost/VP Academic Affairs Dr. David HILL
10 Vice President for Administration Ms. Josee LAROCHELLE
111 Vice Pres Institutional Advancement Ms. Anne W. HANSEN
32 Vice President for Student Affairs Mr. Bryan G. HARTMAN
49 Dean of Arts & Sciences Dr. Andrew S. BUCKSER
53 Int Dean Educ/Health/Human Svcs Dr. Denise SIMARD
50 Dean of Business/Economics Dr. Rowena ORTIZ-WALTERS
12 Dean Branch Campus at Queensbury Mr. Stephen DANNA
08 Dean Library/Info Services Ms. Holly B. HELLER-ROSS
22 Director of Affirmative Action Vacant
88 Title IX Coordinator Ms. Butterfly L. BLAISE
20 Assistant Provost Ms. Diane K. MERKEL
11 Asst to Vice Pres Administration Mr. Sean B. DERMODY
15 Asst VP for Human Resources Ms. Susan T. WELCH
110 Asst VP for Institutional Advanc Mr. David P. GREGOIRE
06 Registrar Ms. Pamela MUNSON
11 Assoc VP for Admin & Finance Vacant
114 Budget Officer Ms. Magen M. RENADETTE
19 Chief University Police Mr. Patrick RASCOE
109 Exec Dir College Auxiliary Services Mr. Wayne A. DUPREY
26 Exec Dir Communication/Public Affs Mr. Kennith KNELLY
121 Director of Academic Advising Ms. Suzanne L. DALEY
29 Director of Alumni Relations Ms. Kerry CHAPIN LAVIGNE
41 Director of Athletics Mr. Michael P. HOWARD
36 Director of Career Development Ctr Vacant
40 Director of College Store Ms. Michelle MARCIL
30 Director of Development Ms. Faith M. LONG
18 Director of Facilities Mr. William A. CIRCELLI
37 Director of Financial Aid Mr. Todd A. MORAVEC
39 Director of Housing Mr. Stephen P. MATTHEWS
09 Dir of Institutional Effectiveness Vacant
96 Director of Purchasing Vacant
46 Dir Sponsored Research/Programs Mr. Michael E. SIMPSON
88 Director of Student Conduct Mr. Larry K. ALLEN
23 Dir Ctr for Stdnt Hlth & Psych Svcs Dr. Kathleen M. CAMELO
91 Programming Manager Mr. Thomas J. HIGGINS
04 Executive Asst to the President Vacant
13 Chief Info Technology Officer (CIO) Ms. Holly B. HELLER ROSS

*State University of New York College at Potsdam (D)

44 Pierrepont Avenue, Potsdam NY 13676-2294

County: Saint Lawrence
FICE Identification: 002850
Unit ID: 196200
Telephone: (315) 267-2000
Carnegie Class: Masters/M
FAX Number: (315) 267-2496
Calendar System: Semester
URL: www.potsdam.edu
Established: 1816
Annual Undergrad Tuition & Fees (In-State): $8,462
Enrollment: 3,587
Coed
Affiliation or Control: State
IRS Status: 501(c)3
Highest Offering: Master's
Accreditation: M, CAEPN, MUS, THEA

02 President Dr. Kristin G. ESTERBERG
05 Provost Dr. Bette S. BERGERON
10 Vice President for Business Affairs Mr. Eric JOHNSTON-ORTIZ
111 VP College Advancement Mr. Sal CANIA
84 Assoc VP Enroll Mgmt/Inst Effect Vacant
04 Executive Asst to the President Mrs. Nicole A. CONANT
20 Associate Provost Dr. Jill R. PEARON
18 Asst Vice Pres for Facilities Vacant
13 Chief Information Officer Vacant
53 Dean Educ & Prof Studies Dr. Allen C. GRANT
49 Dean of Arts and Sciences Dr. Gretchen GALBRAITH
64 Dean of Music Dr. Michael R. SITTON
08 Director of Libraries Ms. Jenica P. ROGERS
06 Registrar Ms. Stephanie L. CLAXTON
07 Director of Admissions Mr. Thomas W. NESBITT
37 Director of Financial Aid Ms. Susan E. GODREAU
36 Director of Career Planning Vacant
38 Director of Counseling Center Mrs. Gena C. NELSON
15 Director of Human Resources Ms. Melissa PROULX
19 Chief of University Police Mr. Tim M. ASHLEY
29 Director of Alumni Relations Ms. Mona O. VROMAN
109 Executive Dir of Auxiliary Corp Mr. Daniel J. HAYES
23 Director of Health Services Ms. Tracy J. HARCOURT
32 Interim Dean of Students Mr. Eric D. DUCHSCHERER
40 Director of College Bookstore Mr. Lyndon J. LAKE
41 Athletic Director Mr. Sharief HASHIM
25 Director Research & Sponsored Pgms Mr. Jack MCGUIRE
92 Director of Honors Program Dr. Thomas N. BAKER
94 Director of Women's Studies Vacant
27 Asst VP Marketing/Communications Mrs. Mindy E. THOMPSON
86 Community/Govt Rels Associate Mrs. Nicole A. CONANT
58 Director of Graduate and Cont Educ Mr. Joshua J. LAFAVE
28 Chief Diversity Officer Dr. Bernadette S. TIAPO
09 Director of Institutional Research Mrs. Judith R. SINGH
104 Director Study Abroad Mrs. Krista M. LAVACK
96 Director of Purchasing Mr. Mark E. MARTINCHEK
39 Director of Residence Life Ms. Julie DOLD
44 Director Annual Giving Mr. Peter J. CUTLER

*Purchase College, State University of New York (E)

735 Anderson Hill Road, Purchase NY 10577-1402

County: Westchester
FICE Identification: 006791
Unit ID: 196219
Telephone: (914) 251-6000
Carnegie Class: Bac-A&S
FAX Number: (914) 251-6014
Calendar System: Semester
URL: www.purchase.edu
Established: 1967
Annual Undergrad Tuition & Fees (In-State): $8,698
Enrollment: 4,167
Coed
Affiliation or Control: State
IRS Status: 501(c)3
Highest Offering: Master's
Accreditation: M, ART

02 Interim President Mr. Dennis J. CRAIG
19 Chief of University Police Mr. Dayton TUCKER
10 CFO/VP Operations Ms. Judy NOLAN
05 Provost/VP Academic Affairs Dr. Barry PEARSON
32 Int VP Student Affs & Enroll Mgmt Ms. Patty BICE
111 VP of Institutional Advancement Ms. Catherine BROD
57 Director Conservatory Theatre Arts Vacant
51 Exec Dir Liberal Stds/Cont Educ Ms. Trudy MILBURN
81 Dean Sch Natural/Social Sciences Dr. Linda BASTONE
79 Chair School of Humanities Dr. Aviva TAUBENFELD
20 Assoc Provost Academic Affairs Dr. Gregory TAYLOR
88 Dir Performing Arts Center Mr. Seth SOLOWAY
88 Director Neuberger Museum of Art Dr. Tracy FITZPATRICK
08 Interim Director of the Library Mr. Keith LANDA
64 Dir Conservatory of Music Dr. Jennifer UNDERCOFLER
57 Dean School of Arts Dr. Lorenzo CANDELARIA
13 Director Campus Technology Services Mr. Bill JUNOR
37 Director Student Financial Services Corey YORK
38 Director of Counseling Center Dr. Cathie CHESTER
36 Director Career Development Ms. Wendy MOROSOFF
15 Director of Human Resources Ms. Kathleen FARRELL
41 Athletic Director Mr. Chris BISIGNANO
39 Director Community Engagement Mr. Mario RAPETTI
96 Director of Purchasing Mr. Edward HERRAN
35 Dean of Student Affairs Ms. Patricia BICE
09 Director of Institutional Research Ms. Barbara MOORE
18 Sr Dir Capital Facilities Planning Mr. Michael KOPAS
22 Title IX Officer/Affirm Action Ofcr Ms. Jerima DEWESE
88 Environmental Health/Safety Officer Mr. Edward MUSAL
44 Director Annual Giving Ms. Carla WEILAND-ZALEZNAK
26 Dir Communications/Creative Svcs Ms. Sandy DYLAK
86 Dir of Govt Relations/Spec Projects Ms. Elizabeth C. ROBERTSON
04 Assistant to President Ms. Carrie K. BIANCHI
104 Director Study Abroad Ms. Suzanne NEARY
29 Exec Director Alumni Engagement Ms. Nadege ROC

*State University of New York College of Agriculture and Technology at Cobleskill (F)

Route 7, Knapp Hall, Cobleskill NY 12043

County: Schoharie
FICE Identification: 002856
Unit ID: 196033
Telephone: (518) 255-5011
Carnegie Class: Bac-Diverse
FAX Number: (518) 255-5333
Calendar System: Semester
URL: www.cobleskill.edu
Established: 1911
Annual Undergrad Tuition & Fees (In-State): $8,654

Enrollment: 2,291 Coed
Affiliation or Control: State IRS Status: 501(c)3
Highest Offering: Baccalaureate
Accreditation: M, ACFEI, EMT, HT

02	President	Dr. Marion TERENZIO
05	Provost & Vice Pres Academic Affs	Dr. Susan ZIMMERMANN
100	Chief of Staff	Ms. Amy HEALY
32	VP for Student Affairs	Dr. Anne HOPKINS-GROSS
10	Vice Pres Business & Finance	Ms. Wendy GILMAN
11	Vice Pres Operations	Ms. Bonnie MARTIN
30	Vice Pres for Development	Mr. John J. ZACHAREK
47	Dean Agriculture/Natural Res	Mr. Timothy MOORE
49	Dean Liberal Arts & Sciences	Vacant
08	Dean Library/Information Svcs	Ms. Elizabeth ORGERON
26	Director of Communications	Mr. James FELDMAN
16	Director Employee Relations	Ms. Lynn BERGER
06	Registrar	Ms. Christine JOHANNESEN
21	Chief Business Officer	Ms. Carol VOSATKA
84	Chief Enrollment Officer	Vacant
29	Dir Alumni Relations/Annual Giving	Ms. Marie O. GERHARDT
07	Assistant Director of Admissions	Mr. Caleb GRANT
39	Director of Residential Life	Mr. Matthew LALONDE
36	Director of Student Success Ctr	Ms. Donna PESTA
23	Co-Director Wellness Center	Ms. Mary RADLIFF
23	Co-Director Wellness Center	Ms. Lynn ONTL
37	Director of Financial Aid	Ms. Louise BIRON
35	Director Student Life Center	Mr. Jeffrey C. FOOTE
41	Director of Athletics	Ms. Marie CURRAN-HEADLEY
13	Director Information Tech Services	Vacant
19	Chief University Police Dept	Vacant
09	Chief Strat Plng/Inst Effectiveness	Dr. Tara WINTER
15	Director of Human Resources	Ms. Lynn BERGER
18	Director Facilities/Physical Plant	Mr. Joseph BATCHELDER
40	Manager Bookstore	Ms. Jeri USATCH
85	Director of International Programs	Dr. Susan JAGENDORF
96	Director of Purchasing	Ms. Laura GROSS
25	Dir of Grants and Sponsored Program	Mr. Barry GELL
22	Director of EOP	Mr. Derwin BENNETT
88	Dir of Student Accounts	Ms. Sarah LEDERMANN
105	Webmaster	Vacant

*State University of New York College of Environmental Science and Forestry (A)

1 Forestry Drive, Syracuse NY 13210-2778
County: Onondaga FICE Identification: 002851
Unit ID: 196103
Telephone: (315) 470-6500 Carnegie Class: DU-Higher
FAX Number: (315) 470-6779 Calendar System: Semester
URL: www.esf.edu
Established: 1911 Annual Undergrad Tuition & Fees (In-State): $8,874
Enrollment: 2,213 Coed
Affiliation or Control: State IRS Status: 501(c)3
Highest Offering: Doctorate
Accreditation: M, LSAR

02	Interim President	Dr. David C. AMBERG
05	Provost/Exec Vice President	Dr. Nosa EGIEBOR
10	CFO/Vice Pres for Administration	Mr. Joseph RUFO
100	Chief of Staff/Chief Sust Officer	Mr. Mark LICHTENSTEIN
04	Asst to the President	Ms. Ragan A. SQUIER
86	VP for Govt & External Relations	Dr. Maureen O. FELLOWS
30	Asst VP for Development	Ms. Brenda T. GREENFIELD
46	Vice Provost for Research	Dr. Christopher T. NOMURA
58	Assoc Prov & Dean Grad School	Mr. S. Scott SHANNON
32	Vice Provost/Dean Student Affairs	Dr. Anne E. LOMBARD
21	Director Business Affairs	Mr. David R. DZWONKOWSKI
13	Chief Information Officer	Vacant
15	Director Human Resources	Ms. Marcia A. BARBER
26	Director of Communications	Mrs. Claire B. DUNN
19	Chief of University Police	Mr. Thomas LEROY
28	Chief Diversity Officer	Dr. Malika CARTER
08	Director of College Libraries	Mr. Matthew R. SMITH
07	Director of Admissions	Mrs. Susan H. SANFORD
37	Director of Financial Aid	Mr. Mark J. HILL
29	Director of Alumni Affairs	Ms. Debbie J. CAVINESS
18	Dir Facil Planning/Design & Constr	Mr. Gary S. PEDEN
36	Dir of Career Services	Mr. John TURBEVILLE
38	Dir of Counseling Services	Ms. Ruth LARSON
35	Dir Stdnt Involvement & Leadership	Mrs. Laura CRANDALL
41	Dir of Intercollegiate Athletics	Mr. Daniel RAMIN
43	Associate Counsel	Mr. Kevin HAYDEN
104	Asst Dir International Education	Mr. Thomas E. CARTER
44	Development Officer - Annual Giving	Ms. Tammy SCHLAFER
91	Manager of Information Systems	Mr. Kenneth J. STVAN

*State University of New York College of Optometry (B)

33 W 42nd Street, New York NY 10036-8003
County: New York FICE Identification: 009929
Unit ID: 196228
Telephone: (212) 938-4000 Carnegie Class: Spec-4-yr-Other Health
FAX Number: (212) 938-5696 Calendar System: Semester
URL: www.sunyopt.edu
Established: 1971 Annual Graduate Tuition & Fees: N/A
Enrollment: 413 Coed
Affiliation or Control: State IRS Status: 501(c)3
Highest Offering: Doctorate; No Undergraduates
Accreditation: M, OPT, OPTR

02	President	Dr. David A. HEATH
05	Dean/VP Academic Affairs	Dr. David TROILO
10	VP For Administration and Finance	Mr. David A. BOWERS
32	Vice Pres Student Affairs	Dr. Guilherme ALBIERI
17	Vice Pres for Clinical Admin	Ms. Liduvina MARTINEZ-GONZALEZ
111	Vice Pres Institutional Advancement	Ms. Dawn RIGNEY
04	Assistant to the President	Ms. Karen DEGAZON
09	Dir Institutional Research/Planning	Dr. Steven SCHWARTZ
08	Director Library Services	Ms. Elaine WELLS
15	Director of Human Resources	Mr. Douglas SCHADING
37	Financial Aid Officer	Mr. Vito CAVALLARO
06	Registrar	Ms. Jacqueline MARTINEZ
58	Assoc Dean Rsrch/Graduate Studies	Dr. Stewart BLOOMFIELD
26	Director of Communications	Ms. Amber HOPKINS-JENKINS
13	Chief Info Technology Officer (CIO)	Mr. Robert PELLOT
84	Director Enrollment Management	Dr. Guilherme ALBIERI
96	Director of Purchasing	Ms. Maureen MORLEY

*Alfred State College (C)

10 Upper College Drive, Alfred NY 14802-1196
County: Allegany FICE Identification: 002854
Unit ID: 196006
Telephone: (607) 587-4010 Carnegie Class: Bac/Assoc-Mixed
FAX Number: N/A Calendar System: Semester
URL: www.alfredstate.edu
Established: 1908 Annual Undergrad Tuition & Fees (In-State): $8,570
Enrollment: 3,686 Coed
Affiliation or Control: State IRS Status: 501(c)3
Highest Offering: Baccalaureate
Accreditation: M, ADNUR, CAHIIM, CONST, FEPAC, NURSE, RAD

02	President	Dr. Irby (Skip) SULLIVAN
05	Provost	Ms. Kristin POPPO
32	Vice President Student Affairs	Mr. Gregory S. SAMMONS
111	Sr Dir Institutional Advancement	Ms. Danielle M. WHITE
09	Institutional Research Analyst	Mr. Daniel D. JARDINE
84	VP for Enrollment Mgmt	Ms. Betsy PENROSE
13	Director Computer Services	Mr. Michael A. CASE
100	Chief of Staff	Ms. Wendy DRESSER-RECKTENWALD
37	Dir Student Financial Services	Mrs. Julie ROSE
29	Director Alumni Relations	Ms. Colleen ARGENTIERI
18	Interim Director of Facilities	Mr. John NICKERSON
14	Asst Director of Computing Services	Mr. Carl H. RAHR, JR.
23	Sr Director Health Svcs/Wellness	Ms. Hollie M. HALL
121	Assoc VP of Academic Services	Ms. Kathleen EBERT
19	Chief of University Police	Mr. Matthew D. HELLER
96	Director of Purchasing	Mrs. Michelle MCCARTHY
10	Chief Financial Officer	Mr. Joseph T. GREENTHAL
36	Director of Career Services	Ms. Elaine MORSMAN
49	Dean School of Arts & Sciences	Mr. Dan KATZ
54	Dean School of Mgmt & Engr Tech	Dr. John WILLIAMS
75	Int Dean Sch Applied Technology	Mr. Jeff STEVENS
41	Athletic Director	Mr. Jason DOVIAK

*SUNY Adirondack (D)

640 Bay Road, Queensbury NY 12804-1498
County: Warren FICE Identification: 002860
Unit ID: 188438
Telephone: (518) 743-2200 Carnegie Class: Assoc/HT-High Trad
FAX Number: (518) 745-1433 Calendar System: Semester
URL: www.sunyacc.edu
Established: 1960 Annual Undergrad Tuition & Fees (In-District): $5,340
Enrollment: 3,892 Coed
Affiliation or Control: State/Local IRS Status: 501(c)3
Highest Offering: Associate Degree
Accreditation: M, ADNUR

02	President	Dr. Kristine DUFFY
05	Vice Pres Academic Affairs	Mr. John JABLONSKI
10	Vice Pres Admin Services/Treasurer	Vacant
20	Dean for Academic Initiatives	Ms. Diane WILDEY
32	Dean for Student Affairs	Vacant
84	VP for Enrollment & Student Affairs	Mr. Rob PALMIERI
09	Director of Inst Research/Planning	Ms. Carol RUNGE
13	Chief Information Officer	Ms. Mary HAND
15	Director of Human Resources	Ms. Mindy WILSON
51	Asst Dean Cont Educ & Workforce	Mrs. Caelynn PRYLO
40	Director Bookstore	Mr. Tom KENT
21	Director of Business Affairs	Ms. Lisa DESTER
18	Director Facilities	Mr. Anthony PALANGI
37	Director Financial Aid	Ms. Colleen WISE
06	Registrar	Ms. Mary ALDOUS
07	Director of Admissions	Ms. Sarah J. LINEHAN
08	Director of Library Services	Ms. Teresa RONNING
35	Dir of Student Life & Diversity	Vacant
101	Secretary to the Board of Trustees	Ms. Kathy DRISLANE
19	Asst Director of Public Safety	Mr. Richard CONINE
39	Director of Residence Life	Ms. Phylicia COLEY

*SUNY Canton-College of Technology (E)

34 Cornell Drive, Canton NY 13617-1098
County: Saint Lawrence FICE Identification: 002855
Unit ID: 196015
Telephone: (315) 386-7011 Carnegie Class: Bac-Diverse
FAX Number: (315) 386-7930 Calendar System: Semester
URL: www.canton.edu
Established: 1906 Annual Undergrad Tuition & Fees (In-State): $8,389
Enrollment: 3,180 Coed
Affiliation or Control: State IRS Status: 501(c)3
Highest Offering: Baccalaureate
Accreditation: M, ADNUR, FUSER, NUR, PNUR, PTAA

02	President	Dr. Zvi SZAFRAN
05	Provost	Dr. Peggy A. DE COOKE
11	Vice Pres for Administration	Ms. Shawn MILLER
10	Chief Financial Officer	Ms. Shawn MILLER
111	Vice Pres for Advancement	Ms. Tracey THOMPSON
32	Vice President for Student Affairs	Ms. Courtney D. BISH
35	Dean of Students	Ms. Courtney D. BISH
72	Dean Canino Sch Eng Tech	Mr. Michael J. NEWTOWN
76	Dean Sch Sci/Health/Crim Justice	Dr. Kenneth M. ERICKSON
50	Dean Sch Business/Liberal Arts	Dr. Phil NEISSER
20	Associate Provost	Dr. Molly MOTT
88	Dean Acad Support Svcs/Instr Tech	Dr. Molly A. MOTT
41	Director of Athletics	Mr. Randy B. SIEMINSKI
100	Exec Dir for University Relations	Dr. Lenore VANDERZEE
101	College Council Secretary	Ms. Michaela J. YOUNG
04	Exec Assistant to the President	Ms. Michaela J. YOUNG
35	Director Student Activities	Ms. Priscilla LEGGETTE
28	Co-Chief Diversity Officer/AAO	Ms. Lashawanda T. INGRAM
28	Co-Chief Diversity Officer/AAO	Ms. Emily HAMILTON-HONEY
96	Director of Purchasing	Ms. Bethany A. MARTIN
37	Director of Financial Aid	Ms. Kerrie L. COOPER
21	College Accountant	Ms. Amanda CRUMP
15	Director of Human Resources	Ms. Suzan MCDERMOTT
36	Director of Career Services	Ms. Julie PARKMAN
06	Registrar	Ms. Memorie L. SHAMPINE
08	Director of Library Services	Ms. Cori WILHELM
18	Director of Physical Plant	Mr. Patrick G. HANSS
18	Plant Superintendent	Mr. Martin D. AVERY
19	Chief of University Police	Mr. Alan MULKIN
23	Director of Health Services	Ms. Shanna WHITE
26	Dir Public Rels/Web Coord	Mr. Travis SMITH
40	Manager Campus Store	Mr. Corey JORDAN
39	Director of Residence Life	Mr. John M. KENNEDY
09	Dir of Inst Research/Assessment	Ms. Sarah E. TODD
13	Assistant VP IT/CIO	Mr. Kyle BROWN
29	Director of Alumni Affairs	Ms. Peggy S. LEVATO
38	Director of Counseling	Ms. Melinda A. MILLER
07	Director of Admissions	Ms. Melissa EVANS
88	Director of Facilities	Mr. Michael R. MCCORMICK
30	Director of Development	Ms. Peggy S. LEVATO
90	Int Help Desk Coordinator	Mr. Benjamin MATOTT
104	Coord Intl Student Initiatives	Ms. Erin LASSIAL
103	Dir of Workforce Development	Mr. Art GARNO
25	Grants Coordinator	Ms. Betsy ROHR ADAMS

*SUNY Corning Community College (F)

One Academic Drive, Corning NY 14830-3297
County: Steuben FICE Identification: 002863
Unit ID: 190442
Telephone: (607) 962-9000 Carnegie Class: Assoc/HT-Mix Trad/Non
FAX Number: (607) 962-9456 Calendar System: Semester
URL: www.corning-cc.edu
Established: 1956 Annual Undergrad Tuition & Fees (In-District): $5,442
Enrollment: 3,834 Coed
Affiliation or Control: State/Local IRS Status: 501(c)3
Highest Offering: Associate Degree
Accreditation: M, ADNUR

01	President	Dr. William P. MULLANEY
11	Vice President Admin Svcs/CFO	Mr. Todd GARNIER
05	Provost	Dr. L. Dean FISHER
30	Exec Dir CCC Development Foundation	Ms. Angela FLEMING
08	Asst Dean Learning Resources	Dr. Sabrina JOHNSON-TAYLOR
06	Registrar	Ms. Loretta HENDRICKSON
07	Director of Recruitment	Mr. David EMPET
15	Exec Dir of HR and Ch Div Officer	Ms. Connie PARK
18	Chief Facilities/Physical Plant	Mr. Calvin WILLIAMS
37	Director Student Financial Aid	Mr. Troy MARTIN
09	Research Analyst	Mr. Paul ANDREWS
04	Executive Office Manager	Ms. Jina TORIBIO
103	Exec Dir Workforce Development	Ms. Jeanne ESCHBACH
19	Director Public Safety	Mr. David BURDICK

*State University of New York College of Technology at Delhi (G)

454 Delhi Drive, Delhi NY 13753-4454
County: Delaware FICE Identification: 002857
Unit ID: 196024
Telephone: (607) 746-4000 Carnegie Class: Bac/Assoc-Mixed
FAX Number: (607) 746-4208 Calendar System: Semester
URL: www.delhi.edu
Established: 1913 Annual Undergrad Tuition & Fees (In-State): $8,360
Enrollment: 3,511 Coed
Affiliation or Control: State IRS Status: 501(c)3
Highest Offering: Master's
Accreditation: M, ACFEI, ADNUR, CONST, NUR, NURSE

02	President	Dr. Michael R. LALIBERTE
05	Provost	Dr. Kelli H. LIGEIKIS
32	VP for Student Life	Mr. Tomas A. AGUIRRE
10	VP for Finance & Administration	Ms. Carol M. BISHOP
111	Vice Pres for College Advancement	Mr. Michael A. SULLIVAN
36	Career Planning & Devel Associate	Ms. Kristin A. DEFOREST
07	Director of Admissions	Mr. Robert C. PIUROWSKI
13	Chief Information Officer	Mr. Shawn P. BRISLIN
19	Chief of University Police	Mr. Martin A. PETTIT

35 Asst Vice Pres for Student Life ... Mr. John J. PADOVANI
08 Director of the Resnick Library ... Ms. Carrie J. FISHNER
36 Dir Career & Business Development ... Ms. Glenda V. ROBERTS
31 Sr Staff Assoc Ctr for Cmty Engage ... Ms. Michele T. DEFREECE
18 Director of Physical Plant ... Mr. David A. LOVELAND
41 Director of Athletics ... Mr. Robert H. BACKUS
06 Registrar ... Ms. Nancy L. SMITH
37 Director of Financial Aid ... Ms. Elizabeth D. BERRY
38 Director Counseling & Health Svcs ... Ms. Lori BARNES
29 Alumni/Annual Giving Coordinator ... Ms. Lucinda C. BRYDON
21 Controller ... Ms. Amy L. BROWN
26 Vice Pres Communications/Marketing ... Ms. Dawn R. SOHNS
09 Asst for Institutional Research ... Ms. JoAnna M. BROSNAN
04 Administrative Asst to President ... Mr. George L. SPIELMAN
102 Exec Dir College Foundation ... Mr. Joel M. SMITH
22 Dir Human Resources/Affirm Action ... Ms. Mary B. MORTON
25 Grants Specialist ... Ms. Ellen A. LIBERATORI

*State University of New York Empire State College (A)

2 Union Avenue, Saratoga Springs NY 12866-4390
County: Saratoga
FICE Identification: 010286
Unit ID: 196264
Telephone: (518) 587-2100
Carnegie Class: Masters/L
FAX Number: (518) 587-2886
Calendar System: Other
URL: www.esc.edu
Established: 1971
Annual Undergrad Tuition & Fees (In-State): $7,405
Enrollment: 10,977
Coed
Affiliation or Control: State
IRS Status: 501(c)3
Highest Offering: Master's
Accreditation: M, IACBE, NURSE

02 President ... Dr. Jim MALATRAS
100 Chief of Staff ... Mr. Aaron GLADD
05 Interim Provost/Vice Pres AA ... Dr. Meg BENKE
111 VP of Advancement ... Mr. Walter WILLIAMS
11 Executive VP Admin & ITT ... Mr. Joseph GARCIA
84 VP for Enrollment Management ... Dr. Clayton STEEN
09 VP for Decision Support ... Dr. Mitchell S. NESLER
20 Interim VP Academic Administration ... Dr. Tai ARNOLD
26 AVP for Communications ... Mr. Kyle ADAMS
15 Asst VP for Human Resources ... Ms. Tracey MEEK
97 Interim Vice Provost ... Dr. Nikki SHRIMPTON
20 Dean Academic/Instructional Svcs ... Dr. Lisa D'ADAMO-WEINSTEIN
20 Interim Vice Provost ... Dr. John LAWLESS
70 Associate Dean Social Science ... Dr. Frank VANDER VALK
50 Associate Dean Business ... Dr. Julie GEDRO
79 Associate Dean Humanities ... Dr. Megan MULLEN
58 Assoc Dean School for Grad Studies ... Dr. Nathan GONYEA
66 Dean School of Nursing ... Dr. Bridget NETTLETON
28 Chief Diversity Officer ... Mr. Elliott DAWES
12 Co-Int Exec Director Metro Center ... Dr. Christopher WHANN
91 Director Admin Applications ... Mr. Mark CLAVERIE
110 Director Advancement Services ... Ms. Vicki SCHAAKE
29 Dir Alumni and Student Relations ... Ms. Maureen WINNEY
44 Director of the Fund ... Ms. Stephanie CORP
21 Director Business Office ... Ms. Becky PALMIERI
108 Dir Collegewide Academic Review ... Dr. Nan TRAVERS
27 Director of Communications ... Mr. David HENAHAN
88 Director of Academic Development ... Mr. Brian GOODALE
88 Dir Compliance/Environment Sustain ... Ms. Sadie ROSS
18 Senior Director of Facilities ... Mr. Rick REIMANN
30 Director of Development ... Mr. Toby TOBROCKE
88 Director College Project Management ... Mr. Walter LEWIS
96 Director Procurement ... Mr. Charley SUMMERSELL
24 Director Publications ... Mr. Kirk STARCZEWSKI
19 Director of Safety & Security ... Mr. Mark JANKOWSKI
21 Director Student Accounts ... Ms. Pamela MALONE
88 Int Dir Veteran & Military Educ ... Ms. Desiree DRINDAK
06 Registrar ... Ms. Pamela ENSER
07 Director Admissions ... Ms. Jennifer D'AGOSTINO

*Farmingdale State College (B)

2350 Broadhollow Road, Farmingdale NY 11735-1021
County: Suffolk
FICE Identification: 002858
Unit ID: 196042
Telephone: (631) 420-2000
Carnegie Class: Bac-Diverse
FAX Number: N/A
Calendar System: Semester
URL: www.farmingdale.edu
Established: 1912
Annual Undergrad Tuition & Fees (In-State): $8,306
Enrollment: 9,574
Coed
Affiliation or Control: State
IRS Status: 501(c)3
Highest Offering: Master's
Accreditation: M, AAB, DH, MLTAD, MT, NAIT, NURSE

02 President ... Dr. John S. NADER
05 Provost/Vice Pres for Academic Affs ... Dr. Laura JOSEPH
10 Vice Pres Admin/Finance and CFO ... Mr. Gregory O'CONNOR
32 Vice Pres Student Affairs ... Dr. Tom CORTI
111 VP Inst Advancement/Enrollment Mgmt ... Mr. Patrick CALABRIA
30 VP for Development/Philanthropy ... Ms. Nancy CONNORS
20 Associate Provost ... Dr. Michael GOODSTONE
11 Director of Admin Services ... Ms. Dorothy HUGHES
35 Dean of Students ... Ms. Terry ESNES-JOHNSON
84 Dir Enrollment Svc/Partnership Pgm ... Mr. Jim HALL
19 Interim Chief University Police ... Mr. Daniel DAUGHERTY
18 Director of Physical Plant ... Mr. John S. DZINANKA
26 Sr Director of Communications ... Ms. Kathryn S. COLEY
06 Registrar ... Ms. Cindy MCCUE
08 Head Librarian ... Ms. Karen GELLES
15 Director Human Resources ... Ms. Marybeth INCANDELA
90 Director of Information Technology ... Mr. Jeffrey BORAH
36 Director Career Development ... Ms. Dolores CIACCIO
37 Director Student Financial Services ... Ms. Diane KAZANECKI-KEMPTER
09 Chief Inst Research Officer ... Ms. Patricia LIND-GONZALEZ
23 Director Student Health Services ... Mr. Kevin MURPHY
41 Dir Athletics Admin & Ext Affairs ... Mr. Michael HARRINGTON
41 Dir of Athletics Comp & Operations ... Mr. Tom AZZARA
39 Dir Student Activities/Campus Ctr ... Ms. Eunice RO
102 President Farmingdale Foundation ... Mr. Robert VAN NOSTRAND
24 Director Media Resources ... Mr. Martin BRANDT
29 Director Alumni Relations ... Ms. Michelle JOHNSON
28 Chief Diversity Officer ... Dr. Kevin JORDAN
40 Manager Bookstore ... Ms. Roberta MIRRO
21 Controller ... Ms. Ellen WEBER
96 Purchasing Associate ... Ms. Lisa BRUNS
75 Exec Dir LI Educ Opportunity Center ... Dr. Elsa-Sofia MOROTE
50 Dean School of Business ... Dr. Richard VOGEL
76 Dean School Health Sciences ... Dr. Denny RYMAN
49 Dean School of Arts & Sciences ... Dr. Charles ADAIR
104 Study Abroad Advisor ... Ms. Agata ADAMCZUK
105 Director Web Services ... Ms. Sylvia NAVARRO-NICOSIA
53 Dean International Education ... Dr. Lorraine GREENWALD
04 Administrative Asst to President ... Ms. Carolyn FEDDER

*State University of New York Maritime College (C)

6 Pennyfield Avenue, Throggs Neck NY 10465-4198
County: Bronx
FICE Identification: 002853
Unit ID: 196291
Telephone: (718) 409-7200
Carnegie Class: Masters/S
FAX Number: (718) 409-7392
Calendar System: Semester
URL: www.sunymaritime.edu
Established: 1874
Annual Undergrad Tuition & Fees (In-State): $8,283
Enrollment: 1,794
Coed
Affiliation or Control: State
IRS Status: 501(c)3
Highest Offering: Master's
Accreditation: M

02 President ... RADM. Michael A. ALFULTIS
04 Executive Assistant to President ... Ms. Claudine TAVIN-WARKENTHIEN
05 Provost/Vice Pres Academic Affairs ... Dr. Joseph HOFFMAN
10 Vice Pres Finance/Admin ... Mr. Scott DIETERICH
26 Vice President University Relations ... Ms. Aimee BERNSTEIN
32 Commandant of Cadets/Master TSES ... CAPT. Richard S. SMITH
20 Academic Dean ... Dr. Gilbert TRAUB
100 Chief of Staff ... CAPT. Mark WOOLLEY
07 Dean of Admissions ... Mr. Rohan HOWELL
35 Assoc Provost/Dean of Students ... Mr. William IMBRIALE
27 Exec Director of External Affairs ... Ms. Mary MUECKE
15 AVP Human Resources/Chief Div Ofcr ... Ms. LuAnn AUGUSTINE-PLAISANCE
19 University Police Chief ... Mr. Myron PRYJMAK
37 Director Financial Aid ... Ms. Andrea DAMAR
41 Director of Athletics ... Mr. Kristofer SCHNATZ
06 Registrar ... Ms. Sarah GRADY
09 Dir Inst Research/Assessment ... CAPT. Mark WOOLLEY
08 Library Director ... Ms. Corey HALAYCHIK
88 Dean of Maritime Educ/Training ... CAPT. Ernest FINK

*SUNY Morrisville (D)

PO Box 901, Morrisville NY 13408-0901
County: Madison
FICE Identification: 002859
Unit ID: 196051
Telephone: (315) 684-6000
Carnegie Class: Bac/Assoc-Mixed
FAX Number: (315) 684-6116
Calendar System: Semester
URL: www.morrisville.edu
Established: 1908
Annual Undergrad Tuition & Fees (In-State): $8,670
Enrollment: 3,063
Coed
Affiliation or Control: State
IRS Status: 501(c)3
Highest Offering: Baccalaureate
Accreditation: M, ACBSP, ADNUR, DIETT, NUR

02 President ... Dr. David E. ROGERS
05 Provost ... Dr. Barry A. SPRIGGS
10 Vice Pres for Administration ... Dr. Roberta H. SLOAN
84 Chief Enrollment Officer ... Dr. Robert C. BLANCHET
32 Dean of Students ... Mr. Geoffrey S. ISABELLE
47 Dean School Agric/Business/Tech ... Dr. Stevie WATSON
49 Dean Liberal Arts/Sciences/Society ... Dr. Anibal TORRES
111 Exec Dir Advancement & PR ... Ms. Theresa R. KEVORKIAN
07 Director of Admission ... Ms. Kaylynn C. INGLESIAS
37 Director of Financial Aid ... Ms. Dacia L. BANKS
09 Director of Institutional Research ... Ms. Marian D. WHITNEY
08 Director of Library ... Ms. Christine A. RUDECOFF
23 Director Student Health Center ... Ms. Debra P. BABOWICZ
15 Dir HR/Affirmative Action ... Dr. Mary H. BONDEROFF
29 Alumni Engagement Coordinator ... Ms. Rhiannon L. DACUNHA
26 Exec Director Communication Mktg ... Mr. Graham GARNER
06 Associate Registrar ... Ms. Erin R. LONGO
13 Chief Info Technology Officer (CIO) ... Dr. Roberta H. SLOAN
18 Exec Director of Facilities ... Mr. Christopher S. MARONEY
19 Chief of Police ... Mr. Paul G. FIELD
36 Career Planning/Development Ofcr ... Ms. Barbara A. ROBACK
39 Director Student Housing ... Ms. Elizabeth R. ACKMAN
41 Athletic Director ... Vacant
14 Asst Dir of Technology Services ... Mr. Jeff GAY
04 Administrative Asst to President ... Ms. JoAnn GODFREY
108 Associate Provost of Assessment ... Dr. Jason P. ZBOCK

*SUNY Polytechnic Institute (E)

100 Seymour Road, Utica NY 13502
County: Oneida
FICE Identification: 011678
Unit ID: 196112
Telephone: (315) 792-7100
Carnegie Class: Masters/M
FAX Number: (315) 792-7222
Calendar System: Semester
URL: www.sunypoly.edu
Established: 1966
Annual Undergrad Tuition & Fees (In-State): $8,238
Enrollment: 2,912
Coed
Affiliation or Control: State
IRS Status: 501(c)3
Highest Offering: Doctorate
Accreditation: M, CAHIIM, NURSE

02 President ... Dr. Grace WANG
11 Chief Operating Officer ... Mr. Michael FRAME
04 Assistant to the President ... Ms. Laurie HARTMAN
46 VP for Research Advancement ... Dr. Shadi SHAHEDIPOUR-SANDVIK
15 VP for Human Resources ... Ms. Rhonda HAINES
32 VP for Student Affairs ... Ms. Marybeth LYONS
30 AVP for Development ... Mrs. Andrea LAGATTA
05 Provost ... Dr. Steven SCHNEIDER
84 AVP for Enrollment Mgmt ... Ms. Maryrose RAAB
49 Dean Arts & Sciences ... Dr. Andrew RUSSELL
50 Dean Business Management ... Dr. Arthur LU
54 Dean Engineering ... Dr. Michael CARPENTER
81 Dean Nanoscale Science & Engr ... Dr. Andres MELENDEZ
76 Dean Health Professions ... Dr. Kathleen ROURKE
19 Chief of Police ... Mr. Gary BEAN
18 Director of Facilities ... Mr. Matt PUTNAM
26 Director University Communications ... Mr. Steve FERRENCE
41 Director Athletics ... Mr. Kevin M. GRIMMER
21 Associate VP of Business Affairs ... Ms. Susan HEAD
88 Director of Student Conduct ... Ms. Megan WYETT
36 Director Career Services ... Mr. Jose Miguel LONGO
23 Director Health & Wellness Center ... Ms. Jo RUFFRAGE
09 Assistant VP Institutional Research ... Ms. Valerie FUSCO
35 AVP Student Affairs ... Mrs. Jennifer ADAMS
37 Director Student Financial Aid ... Mr. Michael ALSHEIMER
06 Registrar ... Mrs. Meghan GETMAN
123 Coordinator Graduate Center ... Ms. Alicia FOSTER
43 Associate Counsel ... Mr. Mark LEMIRE
108 Director Institutional Assessment ... Dr. Joanne JOSEPH
13 Chief Information Officer ... Mr. Andrew BELLINGER
07 Director of Admissions ... Ms. Gina LISCIO
08 Director of Library Services ... Ms. Rebecca HEWITT
120 Dir Online Education/E-learning ... Mr. Rick SHELTON
29 Director Alumni Relations ... Vacant
96 Director of Purchasing ... Mr. David MANORE

*Suffolk County Community College Central Administration (F)

533 College Road, Selden NY 11784-2899
County: Suffolk
Identification: 666658
Unit ID: 366395
Telephone: (631) 451-4000
Carnegie Class: N/A
FAX Number: (631) 451-4715
URL: www.sunysuffolk.edu

01 EVP/Officer in Charge ... Mr. Louis J. PETRIZZO
27 College Communications Director ... Mr. Drew BIONDO
43 College General Counsel ... Mr. Louis J. PETRIZZO
05 VP Academic Affairs ... Dr. Paul M. BEAUDIN
10 VP Business Financial Affairs ... Ms. Gail VIZZINI
30 Vice Pres Institutional Advancement ... Ms. Mary Lou ARANEO
45 VP Planning/Inst Effectiveness ... Dr. Jeffrey M. PEDERSEN
32 VP of Student Affairs ... Dr. Christopher J. ADAMS
13 VP Computer Information Systems ... Mr. Shady AZZAM-GOMEZ
103 Assoc VP Workforce/Econ Development ... Mr. John LOMBARDO
84 College Dean Enrollment Management ... Ms. Joanne E. BRAXTON
06 Assoc Dean Master Sched/Registrar ... Ms. Anna FLACK
35 Campus Assoc Dean Student Services ... Mr. Charles BARTOLOTTA
37 College Director of Financial Aid ... Ms. Nancy A. BREWER
28 Col Coord Multicultural Affairs ... Mr. James W. BANKS
102 Executive Director Foundation ... Dr. Sylvia DIAZ
30 Col Assoc Dean Inst Advancement ... Mr. Andrew FAWCETT
104 Col Assoc Dean Spec Prog & Ext Part ... Dr. Iaroslava BABENCHUK
106 Asst Dean Instructional Technology ... Mr. Douglas KAHN
14 Assoc Dean Computer Info Systems ... Mr. Gary RIS
19 Director Fire/Public Safety ... Mr. Baycan FIDELI
22 Chief Diversity Officer/Title IX ... Ms. Christina VARGAS
25 Col Asst Dean Grants Development ... Dr. William T. TUCKER
26 Dir College Relations/Publications ... Ms. Mary M. FEDER
29 Director Alumni Relations ... Mr. Russell MALBROUGH
41 College Director of Athletics ... Mr. Kevin FOLEY
86 Col Director Legislative Affairs ... Mr. Benjamin ZWIRN
96 Admin Director Business Operations ... Ms. Beatriz CASTANO
36 Director Career Services ... Ms. Tania VELAZQUEZ
18 Executive Director Facilities ... Mr. Paul COOPER

*Suffolk County Community College (G)

533 College Road, Selden NY 11784-2899
County: Suffolk
FICE Identification: 002878
Telephone: (631) 451-4000
Carnegie Class: Not Classified

FAX Number: (631) 451-4015 Calendar System: Semester
URL: www.sunysuffolk.edu
Established: 1959 Annual Undergrad Tuition & Fees (In-District): N/A
Enrollment: N/A Coed
Affiliation or Control: State/Local IRS Status: 501(c)3
Highest Offering: Associate Degree
Accreditation: M, ADNUR, CAHIIM, DIETT, EMT, OTA, PNUR, PTAA

02 Executive Dean/Campus CEO .... Mr. P. Wesley LUNDBURG
05 Assoc Dean of Academic Affairs .... Dr. Sandra SPROWS
32 Assoc Dean of Student Services .... Dr. Edward MARTINEZ
37 Director of Financial Aid .... Ms. Renee NUNZIATO
35 Assistant Dean of Student Services .... Dr. Katherine AGUIRRE
08 Head Librarian .... Ms. Susan LIEBERTHAL
13 Asst Dir of Application Development .... Mr. Christopher T. BLAKE
18 Director Facilities/Physical Plant .... Vacant
36 Dir Career Svcs/Cooperative Educ .... Ms. Tania VELAZQUEZ
92 Coordinator Honors Program .... Mr. Albin COFONE
10 Admin Director of Business Affairs .... Mr. John P. CIENSKI
90 Coord of Instructional Technology .... Mr. Paul BASILEO
91 Data Control Supervisor .... Mr. Paul MATUS

Sullivan County Community College (A)

112 College Road, Loch Sheldrake NY 12759-5721
County: Sullivan FICE Identification: 002879
Unit ID: 195988
Telephone: (845) 434-5750 Carnegie Class: Assoc/MT-VT-Mix Trad/Non
FAX Number: (845) 434-4806 Calendar System: Semester
URL: www.sunysullivan.edu
Established: 1962 Annual Undergrad Tuition & Fees (In-District): $5,690
Enrollment: 1,565 Coed
Affiliation or Control: State/Local IRS Status: 501(c)3
Highest Offering: Associate Degree
Accreditation: M, ACBSP, COARC

01 President .... Mr. John (Jay) QUAINTANCE
05 Vice Pres Academic & Student Affs .... Dr. Keith POMAKOY
10 Chief Financial Officer/Controller .... Vacant
45 Assoc VP for Planning/HR & Facil .... Vacant
32 Dean Student Development Services .... Mr. Chris DEPEW
49 Dean of Liberal Arts & Sciences .... Ms. Rose HANOFEE
45 Dean of Community Outreach ... Ms. Cindy BENNEDUM-KASHAN
07 Director Admissions & Recruiting .... Mr. Steve ALHONA
35 Director Student Activities .... Mr. Frank SINIGAGLIA
41 Director of Athletics .... Mr. Chris DEPEW
15 Asst Director of Human Resources .... Ms. Stephanie SMART
09 Director Institutional Research .... Ms. Janet HALPRIN
38 Director Student Counseling .... Vacant
13 Director Information Technology .... Mr. James SAMMANN
19 Director Security/Safety .... Mr. Matt LASPISA
06 Dir Registration Services/Registrar .... Ms. Anne MARCHAL
26 Coord of Public & Alumni Relations .... Vacant
04 Exec Assistant to the President .... Ms. Maura CAYCHO
37 Director Student Financial Aid .... Ms. Keri WHITEHEAD

Swedish Institute-College of Health Sciences (B)

226 W 26th Street, New York NY 10001-6700
County: New York FICE Identification: 021700
Unit ID: 196389
Telephone: (212) 924-5900 Carnegie Class: Spec 2-yr-Health
FAX Number: (212) 924-7600 Calendar System: Semester
URL: www.swedishinstitute.edu
Established: 1916 Annual Undergrad Tuition & Fees: $21,725
Enrollment: 733 Coed
Affiliation or Control: Proprietary IRS Status: Proprietary
Highest Offering: Associate Degree
Accreditation: ACCSC, ADNUR

01 President .... Ms. Erin SHEA
10 Director of Finance .... Mr. Nathan FIELDS
05 Director of Education .... Dr. Joseph BALATBAT
07 Director of Admissions .... Vacant
88 VP for Program Development .... Mr. John KATOMSKI
88 Dean of Advanced Personal Training .... Mr. Vincent METZO
88 Dean for Massage Therapy .... Ms. Ericka CLINTON
66 Dean of Nursing .... Ms. Hillory THORPE
13 Director of Information Technology .... Mr. Rob SIEFKEN
32 Director of Student Services .... Ms. Theresa ROBBINSON
26 Director of Public Relations .... Vacant
37 Financial Aid Director .... Ms. Desire DEJESUS-AVILES
08 Director of Library Services .... Mr. Matthew FORTINO
06 Registrar .... Ms. Qiana HORTON
113 Bursar .... Ms. Beatriz ACEVEDO
51 Director of Continuing Education .... Ms. Tania OGULLUKIAN
40 Bookstore Manager .... Mr. Dan YUEN
36 Director of Career Services .... Mr. Richard GARDNER

Syracuse University (C)

900 South Crouse Avenue, Syracuse NY 13244
County: Onondaga FICE Identification: 002882
Unit ID: 196413
Telephone: (315) 443-1870 Carnegie Class: DU-Highest
FAX Number: (315) 443-3503 Calendar System: Semester
URL: www.syr.edu
Established: 1870 Annual Undergrad Tuition & Fees: $51,853
Enrollment: 22,484 Coed
Affiliation or Control: Independent Non-Profit IRS Status: 501(c)3
Highest Offering: Doctorate
Accreditation: M, ART, AUD, CACREP, CIDA, CLPSY, DIETD, DIETI, FEPAC, JOUR, LAW, LIB, MFCD, MUS, PH, SCPSY, SP, SPAA, SW

01 Chancellor & President .... Mr. Kent SYVERUD
05 Vice Chanc/Prov Academic Affs .... Dr. Michele WHEATLY
10 Executive Vice President & CFO .... Dr. Amir RAHNAMAY-AZAR
43 Sr VP and General Counsel .... Mr. Daniel J. FRENCH
100 Sr VP and Chief of Staff .... Ms. Candace CAMPBELL JACKSON
111 Chief Advancement Ofcr/Sr VP .... Mr. Matthew TER MOLEN
32 Sr VP/Enroll and the Student Exp .... Mr. Dolan EVANOVICH
88 SVP for Academic Operations .... Mr. Steve BENNETT
41 Athletic Director .... Mr. John WILDHACK
26 SVP & Chief Marketing/Comm Officer .... Ms. Dara J. ROYER
21 Comptroller .... Ms. Jean B. GALLIPEAU
15 Sr VP/Chief Human Resources Officer .... Mr. Andrew GORDON
20 Assoc Provost Faculty Affairs .... Ms. LaVonda REED
20 Assoc Prov for Academic Affairs .... Dr. Chris JOHNSON
13 VP Information Technology/CIO .... Mr. Samuel SCOZZAFAVA
46 Vice Pres for Research .... Dr. John LIU
101 Secretary Board of Trustees .... Ms. Lisa A. DOLAK
48 Dean School of Architecture .... Dr. Michael A. SPEAKS
49 Dean College of Arts & Sciences .... Dr. Karin RUHLANDT
58 Assoc Prov Grad Stds/Dean Grad Sch .... Dr. Peter VANABLE
08 Dean of University Libraries .... Mr. David SEAMAN
53 Dean School of Education .... Dr. Joanna O. MASINGILA
76 Dean Col of Sport & Human Dynamics .... Dr. Diane LYDEN MURPHY
54 Dean Col Engineering/Computer Sci .... Dr. J. Cole SMITH
62 Interim Dean iSchool .... Mr. David SEAMAN
61 Dean College of Law .... Dr. Craig M. BOISE
50 Dean Whitman School of Management .... Dr. Eugene ANDERSON
60 Int Dean Newhouse Sch Public Comm .... Ms. Amy FALKNER
57 Dean Col Visual & Performing Arts .... Dr. Michael TICK
51 Dean University College .... Dr. Michael FRASCIELLO
07 Dean of Admissions .... Dr. Maurice A. HARRIS
42 Dean Hendricks Chapel .... Rev. Brian KONKOL
88 Vice Chancellor Strat Init & Innov .... Mr. Michael HAYNIE
18 VP and Chief Facilities Officer .... Mr. Pete SALA
19 Sr VP Safety/Chief Law Enforc Ofc .... Mr. Anthony CALLISTO
28 Chief Diversity Officer .... Dr. Keith ALFORD
31 VP for Community Engagement .... Ms. Bea GONZALEZ

Talmudical Institute of Upstate New York (D)

769 Park Avenue, Rochester NY 14607-3046
County: Monroe FICE Identification: 025506
Unit ID: 196440
Telephone: (585) 473-2810 Carnegie Class: Spec-4-yr-Faith
FAX Number: (585) 442-0417 Calendar System: Semester
URL: tiuny.org
Established: 1974 Annual Undergrad Tuition & Fees: $6,150
Enrollment: 16 Male
Affiliation or Control: Independent Non-Profit IRS Status: 501(c)3
Highest Offering: Second Talmudic Degree
Accreditation: RABN

01 Dean .... Rabbi Menachem DAVIDOWITZ
03 Executive Vice President .... Rabbi Shlomo NOBLE

Talmudical Seminary of Bobov (E)

5120 New Utrecht Avenue, Brooklyn NY 11204-1108
County: Kings FICE Identification: 041155
Unit ID: 451404
Telephone: (718) 854-8700 Carnegie Class: Spec-4-yr-Faith
FAX Number: (718) 854-8707 Calendar System: Semester
Established: 2005 Annual Undergrad Tuition & Fees: $10,200
Enrollment: 406 Male
Affiliation or Control: Independent Non-Profit IRS Status: 501(c)3
Highest Offering: First Talmudic Degree
Accreditation: RABN

01 Dean .... Rabbi Joshua RUBIN
37 Director Student Financial Aid .... Josef DEUTSCH
06 Registrar .... Solomon GORDON

Talmudical Seminary Oholei Torah (F)

667 Eastern Parkway, Brooklyn NY 11213-3397
County: Kings FICE Identification: 012011
Unit ID: 196431
Telephone: (718) 774-5050 Carnegie Class: Spec-4-yr-Faith
FAX Number: (718) 778-0784 Calendar System: Semester
Established: 1956 Annual Undergrad Tuition & Fees: $9,800
Enrollment: 300 Male
Affiliation or Control: Independent Non-Profit IRS Status: 501(c)3
Highest Offering: First Talmudic Degree
Accreditation: RABN

01 Chief Executive Officer .... Mr. Zalman CHEIN
05 Dean .... Elchonon LESCHES
10 Business Officer .... Gary SUSSKIND
37 Financial Aid Officer .... Sholom ROSENFELD

Teachers College, Columbia University (G)

525 West 120th Street, New York NY 10027
County: New York FICE Identification: 003979
Unit ID: 196468
Telephone: (212) 678-3000 Carnegie Class: DU-Higher
FAX Number: (212) 678-4048 Calendar System: Semester
URL: www.tc.columbia.edu
Established: 1887 Annual Graduate Tuition & Fees: N/A
Enrollment: 4,701 Coed
Affiliation or Control: Independent Non-Profit IRS Status: 501(c)3
Highest Offering: Doctorate; No Undergraduates
Accreditation: M, CLPSY, COPSY, DIETI, PH, SCPSY, SP

01 President .... Dr. Thomas R. BAILEY
05 Provost & VP for Academic Affairs .... Dr. Stephanie ROWLEY
100 Secretary to College/Chief of Staff .... Dr. Katie CONWAY
10 Vice Pres Finance & Administration .... Ms. JoAnne WILLIAMS
30 Vice Pres Devel/External Affairs .... Ms. Suzanne MURPHY
22 Vice Pres for Diversity/Cmty Affs .... Ms. Janice S. ROBINSON
88 VP Sch/Cmty Partnshp/Spec Advis .... Dr. Nancy STREIM
21 Assoc Vice Pres/Controller .... Mr. Henry PERKOWSKI
18 Asst VP Facilities .... Mr. Brian ALFORD
84 Vice Provost Enrollment Services .... Ms. Amy GREENSTEIN
06 Registrar .... Mr. Sam FUGAZZOTTO
13 Chief Information Officer .... Mr. Dan ARACENA
08 Library Director .... Vacant
15 Director Human Resources .... Vacant
19 Director Public Safety .... Mr. John DE ANGELIS
43 General Counsel .... Mr. Michael FEIERMAN
09 Director of Institutional Research .... Ms. Haley ROSENFELD
29 Director Alumni Relations .... Ms. Rosella GARCIA
39 Director Student Housing .... Mr. Dewayne WHITE

† Affiliated with Columbia University in the City of New York.

Tompkins Cortland Community College (H)

170 North Street, PO Box 139, Dryden NY 13053-8504
County: Tompkins FICE Identification: 006788
Unit ID: 196565
Telephone: (607) 844-8211 Carnegie Class: Assoc/HT-High Non
FAX Number: (607) 844-9665 Calendar System: Semester
URL: www.TompkinsCortland.edu
Established: 1968 Annual Undergrad Tuition & Fees (In-District): $6,046
Enrollment: 2,632 Coed
Affiliation or Control: State/Local IRS Status: 501(c)3
Highest Offering: Associate Degree
Accreditation: M, ADNUR

01 President .... Dr. Orinthia T. MONTAGUE
05 Provost and VP of Academic Affairs .... Dr. Paul REIFENHEISER
32 Vice President for Student Services .... Mr. Greg MCCALLEY
20 Associate Provost .... Dr. Malvika TALWAR
08 Library Director .... Mr. Gregg KIEHL
84 Dean Operations & Enrollment Mgmt .... Ms. Blixy K. TAETZSCH
88 Associate Dean for Enrollment Mgmt .... Ms. LaSonya GRIGGS
121 Director of Student Success Service . Ms. Michelle NIGHTINGALE
14 Director of Technology Support .... Mr. Tony DEFRANCO
37 Director of Financial Aid .... Ms. Tamara OLIVER
26 Director of Communications .... Mr. Bryan CHAMBALA
15 Human Resources Administrator .... Ms. Sharon CLARK
07 Director of Admissions .... Mr. Sandy DRUMLUK
10 Director of Budget & Finance .... Ms. Susan DEWEY
13 Chief Information Officer .... Mr. Timothy DENSMORE
19 Director of Safety & Security .... Mr. J. Beau SAUL
41 Athletic Director .... Mr. Mick R. MCDANIEL
39 Director Residence Life .... Ms. Darese DOSKAL
38 Director of Mental Health Services .... Ms. Alison BEACH
18 Director of Facilities .... Mr. Adam POTTER
28 Chief Diversity Officer/Dir ODESS .... Mr. Seth THOMPSON
101 Asst to President/Clerk of Board .... Ms. Cathy NORTHROP
102 Development Coordinator .... Ms. Julie GERG

Torah Temimah Talmudical Seminary (I)

507 Ocean Parkway, Brooklyn NY 11218-5913
County: Kings FICE Identification: 021916
Unit ID: 196583
Telephone: (718) 853-8500 Carnegie Class: Spec-4-yr-Faith
FAX Number: (718) 438-5779 Calendar System: Semester
Established: 1978 Annual Undergrad Tuition & Fees: $11,050
Enrollment: 66 Male
Affiliation or Control: Independent Non-Profit IRS Status: 501(c)3
Highest Offering: Second Talmudic Degree
Accreditation: RABN

01 President & Dean .... Rabbi L. MARGULIES
03 Executive Director .... Rabbi L. MARGULIES
05 Chief Academic Officer .... Rabbi Lipa GELDWORTH
37 Financial Aid Administrator .... Mr. Martin WALDMAN
38 Director of Guidance .... Rabbi Yirmiya GUGENHEIMER
11 Administrator .... Rabbi Yisroel KLEINMAN

Touro College (J)

500 7th Avenue, New York NY 10018
County: New York FICE Identification: 010142
Unit ID: 196592
Telephone: (646) 565-6000 Carnegie Class: DU-Mod
FAX Number: N/A Calendar System: Semester
URL: www.touro.edu
Established: 1970 Annual Undergrad Tuition & Fees: $19,870
Enrollment: 11,908 Coed
Affiliation or Control: Independent Non-Profit IRS Status: 501(c)3
Highest Offering: Doctorate

Accreditation: M, ARCPA, CAEPT, DENT, LAW, NURSE, OSTEO, OT, PHAR, PTA, RAD, SP, SW

01 President/Chief Executive Officer .... Dr. Alan KADISH
04 Executive Asst to the President .... Mr. Clifford METH
03 Executive Vice President .... Rabbi Moshe D. KRUPKA
10 Senior Vice President & CFO .... Mr. Melvin M. NESS
11 Sr Vice Pres/Chief Admin Officer .... Mr. Jeffrey ROSENGARTEN
111 Vice Pres Institutional Advancement .... Mr. Paul GLASSER
05 VP Undergrad Acad Affs/Dean of Fac .... Dr. Stanley L. BOYLAN
58 Vice Pres of Grad Studies .... Dr. Nadja GRAFF
32 VP Plng & Assessment/Dean of Stdnts .... Dr. Robert GOLDSCHMIDT
13 VP of Operations & Info Systems .... Dr. Franklin STEEN
84 VP Student Administrative Services .... Mr. Matthew BONILLA
53 Dean Grad School Education .... Dr. Jacob EASLEY, II
56 Vice President IPE/Dean NYSCAS .... Dr. Judah WEINBERGER
106 VP Online Educ/Dn Women's Division .... Dr. Marian STOLTZ-LOIKE
09 Director Institutional Research .... Mr. Evan HOBERMAN
43 Senior VP of Legal Affairs .... Mr. Michael NEWMAN
58 Provost Graduate/Professional Div .... Ms. Patricia SALKIN
52 Dean College of Dental Medicine .... Dr. Ronnie MYERS
63 Dean Col of Osteopathic Med .... Dr. Kenneth STEIER
63 Dean Col of Osteopathic Med Harlem .... Dr. David FORSTEIN
67 Dean College of Pharmacy .... Dr. Henry COHEN
76 Dean of School of Health Sciences .... Dr. Louis H. PRIMAVERA
58 Dean Grad School Jewish Studies .... Dr. Michael A. SHMIDMAN
72 Dean Grad School of Technology .... Dr. Issac HERSKOWITZ
70 Dean Graduate School of Social Work .... Dr. Steven HUBERMAN
12 Dean Lander College for Men .... Dr. Moshe Z. SOKOL
50 Dean Grad School of Business .... Dr. Mary LO RE
38 Dean of Advising & Counseling .... Dr. Avery HOROWITZ
51 Asst Dean School Lifelong Education .... Dr. Briendy STERN
06 University Registrar .... Ms. Lidia MEINDL
37 Dir Reg Compliance/Financial Aid .... Mr. Matthew LIEBERMAN
08 Director of Libraries .... Ms. Bashe SIMON
07 Director of Admissions .... Mr. Benjamin ENOMA
76 Director Physician Asst Program .... Dr. Joseph TOMMASINO
75 Director of Occupational Therapy .... Dr. Stephanie DAPICE-WONG
76 Director of Physical Therapy .... Ms. Jill HORBACEWICZ
88 Pgm Dir Speech Lang Path/Grad Pgm .... Ms. Hindy LUBINSKY
110 AVP Inst Advancement .... Ms. Beth GORIN
110 AVP Institutional Advancement .... Ms. Linda HOWARD-WEISSMAN
91 Chief Info Security Officer .... Ms. Patricia CIUFFO
19 Director of Security .... Ms. Lydia PEREZ
19 Dir of Emergency Preparedness .... Ms. Shoshana YEHUDAH
15 Director of Human Resources .... Mr. Thomas MODERO
96 Director of Purchasing .... Ms. Wanda HERNANDEZ
18 Dir of Facilities/Real Estate .... Mr. Mark GOODMAN
21 Controller .... Mr. Stuart LIPPMAN
26 Dir of Communication/External Rels .... Ms. Elisheva SCHLAM
36 Director Student Placement .... Mr. Stuart ANSEL
25 Director Office Sponsored Pgm .... Mr. Glenn DAVIS
04 Administrative Asst to President .... Ms. Elaine GOLDBERG
104 Director Study Abroad .... Dr. Chana SOSEVSKY
105 Director Web Services .... Ms. Lisa HALBERSTAM
41 Athletic Director .... Mr. Irv BADER
114 Director of Budget & Planning .... Mr. David BELL

Touro College Bay Shore (A)

1700 Union Boulevard, Bay Shore NY 11706
Telephone: (631) 665-1600 Identification: 770145
Accreditation: &M, ARCPA, OT, PTA

Touro College Flatbush (B)

1602 Avenue J, Brooklyn NY 11230
Telephone: (718) 252-7800 Identification: 770146
Accreditation: &M

Touro College, Jacob D. Fuchsberg Law Center (C)

225 Eastview Drive, Central Islip NY 11722
Telephone: (631) 761-7000 Identification: 770148
Accreditation: &M

Trocaire College (D)

360 Choate Avenue, Buffalo NY 14220-2094
County: Erie FICE Identification: 002812
Unit ID: 196653
Telephone: (716) 826-1200 Carnegie Class: Spec-4-yr-Other Health
FAX Number: (716) 828-6107 Calendar System: Semester
URL: www.trocaire.edu
Established: 1958 Annual Undergrad Tuition & Fees: $17,650
Enrollment: 1,399 Coed
Affiliation or Control: Independent Non-Profit IRS Status: 501(c)3
Highest Offering: Baccalaureate
Accreditation: M, ADNUR, CAHIIM, MAC, NUR, PNUR, RAD, SURGT

01 President .... Dr. Bassam M. DEEB
03 Senior Vice President .... Dr. Richard T. LINN
10 VP for Finance .... Mr. John J. HUDACK
05 Vice President for Academic Affairs .... Dr. Allyson LOWE
32 Chief Student Affairs Officer .... Ms. Kathleen SAUNDERS
30 VP Development & Cmty Engagement .... Vacant
21 Associate VP for Finance .... Mr. Edward JOHNSON
13 AVP Technology/Information Svcs .... Mr. Jim POULOS
84 Chief Enrollment Officer .... Ms. Jacqueline MATHENY
66 Int Dean C. McAuley School Nursing .... Dr. Linda KERWIN
15 Chief Human Resources Officer .... Ms. Janet PETERS
37 Director of Financial Aid .... Mr. Sean HUDSON
25 Grant Coordinator .... Ms. Rachel FLAMMER
26 Director of Public Relations .... Ms. Emily Burns PERRYMAN
06 Associate Registrar .... Mrs. Theresa HORNER
121 Dir Advisement & Student Support .... Dr. Christine RYAN
88 Director Learning Center .... Ms. Bridget HODGES
124 Director of Student Engagement .... Mr. Thomas VANE
88 Director Wellness Center .... Ms. Jennifer EHLINGER-SAJ
18 Facilities Director .... Mr. Richard MCGILVRAY
110 Director of Development .... Vacant
07 Dean of Admissions .... Mrs. Mollie A. BALLARO
40 Manager Bookstore .... Mr. Shawn HENRIS
76 Dean of Allied Health & Professions .... Dr. Linda KERWIN
108 Coordinator of Assessment/Research .... Vacant
88 Director of Mission & Service .... Mr. Robert SHEARN
103 VP for Innovation/Workforce Devel .... Dr. Gary SMITH

Ulster County Community College (E)

491 Cottekill Road, PO Box 557, Stone Ridge NY 12484
County: Ulster FICE Identification: 002880
Unit ID: 196699
Telephone: (845) 687-5000 Carnegie Class: Assoc/HT-High Non
FAX Number: (845) 687-5083 Calendar System: Semester
URL: www.sunyulster.edu
Established: 1961 Annual Undergrad Tuition & Fees (In-District): $5,340
Enrollment: 3,560 Coed
Affiliation or Control: State/Local IRS Status: 501(c)3
Highest Offering: Associate Degree
Accreditation: M, ADNUR

01 President .... Dr. Alan P. ROBERTS
84 Sr Vice Pres Enrollment Mgmt .... Ms. Ann MARROTT
05 VP for Academic Affairs .... Mr. Kevin STONER
51 Dean of Continuing & Prof Educ .... Mr. Christopher MARX
10 VP Admin Svcs/Chief Business Ofcr .... Mr. Christopher NGUYEN
111 Exec Dir of Inst Advance & Ext Rels .... Ms. Lorraine SALMON
04 Assistant to President .... Ms. Jennifer ZELL
08 Director of Library Services .... Ms. Kari MACK
37 Director of Financial Aid .... Mr. Christopher CHANG
06 Registrar .... Ms. Debra MILLER
41 Athletic Director .... Mr. Matthew BRENNIE
19 Director of Safety & Security .... Mr. Wayne FREER
07 Asst Dean Enrollment & Dir Admiss .... Mr. Matthew GREEN
26 Chief Public Relations Officer .... Ms. Ann MARROTT
36 Dir Student Place/Acad Support Svcs .... Ms. Jane KITHCART
32 Director Student Affairs .... Ms. Ann MARROTT
18 Director of Plant Operations .... Vacant
09 Director of Institutional Research .... Mr. Clarence (Hank) MILLER
103 Workforce Development .... Mr. Christopher MARX
15 Coordinator of Personnel Services .... Mrs. Debra DELANOY
21 Asst Dean of Admin Services .... Ms. Amy WINTERS
96 Coord Procurement/General Services .... Mr. Stephen GALLART
101 Secretary of the Institution/Board .... Ms. Jennifer ZELL
38 Assistant Dean of Student Success .... Ms. Wendy MCCORRY

Unification Theological Seminary (F)

4 West 43rd Street 2nd Floor, New York NY 10036
County: Manhattan FICE Identification: 032163
Unit ID: 246789
Telephone: (212) 563-6647 Carnegie Class: Spec-4-yr-Faith
FAX Number: (212) 563-6431 Calendar System: Semester
URL: www.uts.edu
Established: 1975 Annual Undergrad Tuition & Fees: N/A
Enrollment: 133 Coed
Affiliation or Control: Unification Church IRS Status: 501(c)3
Highest Offering: Doctorate
Accreditation: M

01 President .... Dr. Hugh SPURGIN
05 Academic Dean .... Dr. Keisuke NODA
11 Vice President .... Dr. Michael MICKLER
88 Director of Field Education .... Dr. Jacob DAVID
10 Director of Finances .... Mr. Frank ZOCHOL
06 Registrar .... Mrs. Ute DELANEY
08 Librarian .... Mr. Robert WAGNER
37 Student Financial Aid Director .... Mr. Henry CHRISTOPHER
18 Plant Director .... Mr. Carl VERDERBER
07 Director of Admissions .... Mr. Henry CHRISTOPHER
30 Dir for Development & Alumni Rels .... Mr. Robin GRAHAM
32 Chief Student Affairs/Student Life .... Mrs. Joy THERIOT
13 Chief Info Technology Officer (CIO) .... Mr. Robert PUMPHREY
84 Director Enrollment Management .... Dr. Drissa KONE

Union College (G)

807 Union Street, Schenectady NY 12308-3181
County: Schenectady FICE Identification: 002889
Unit ID: 196866
Telephone: (518) 388-6000 Carnegie Class: Bac-A&S
FAX Number: (518) 388-6800 Calendar System: Trimester
URL: www.union.edu
Established: 1795 Annual Undergrad Tuition & Fees: $55,290
Enrollment: 2,267 Coed
Affiliation or Control: Independent Non-Profit IRS Status: 501(c)3
Highest Offering: Baccalaureate
Accreditation: M

01 President .... Dr. David R. HARRIS
05 VP Academic Affs/Dean Faculty .... Dr. Strom THACKER
111 Vice President College Relations .... Ms. Terri A. CERVENY
10 Vice President for Finance & Admin .... Ms. Michele GIBSON
07 VP Admissions/Fin Aid/Enrollment .... Mr. Matthew J. MALATESTA
100 Chief of Staff .... Ms. Darcy CZAJKA
22 Chief Diversity Officer .... Dr. Gretchel L. HATHAWAY
32 VP Student Affairs/Dean of Students .... Dr. Fran 'Cee BROWN-MCCLURE
20 Dean of Studies .... Dr. Michelle ANGRIST
13 Chief Information Officer .... Ms. Ellen YU
06 Registrar .... Ms. Penelope S. ADEY
08 College Librarian .... Ms. Frances J. MALOY
26 Director of Media and Public Rels .... Mr. Phillip J. WAJDA
37 Director of Financial Aid .... Ms. Linda M. PARKER
38 Director of Student Counseling .... Mr. Marcus S. HOTALING
36 Director of Career Center .... Mr. Robert C. SOULES
15 Director of Human Resources .... Vacant
41 Director of Athletics .... Mr. James MCLAUGHLIN
19 Director Campus Safety .... Mr. Christopher M. HAYEN
39 Director Residence Life .... Ms. Amanda J. BINGEL

† Tuition figure is a comprehensive fees figure.

Union Theological Seminary (H)

3041 Broadway, New York NY 10027-5792
County: New York FICE Identification: 002890
Unit ID: 196884
Telephone: (212) 662-7100 Carnegie Class: Spec-4-yr-Faith
FAX Number: (212) 280-1416 Calendar System: Semester
URL: www.utsnyc.edu
Established: 1836 Annual Graduate Tuition & Fees: N/A
Enrollment: 217 Coed
Affiliation or Control: Independent Non-Profit IRS Status: 501(c)3
Highest Offering: Doctorate; No Undergraduates
Accreditation: M, THEOL

01 President .... Dr. Serene JONES
03 Executive Vice President .... Mr. Fred DAVIE
10 Int VP Finance & Operations .... Mr. Brent DICKMAN
30 Interim VP for Development .... Ms. Emily ODOM
05 VP of Academic Affairs and Dean .... Dr. Pamela COOPER-WHITE
32 Interim Assoc Dean Student Affairs .... Mr. William CRAWFORD
88 Senior Director of Integrative Educ .... Dr. Su Y. PAK
07 VP for Admissions and Financial Aid .... Ms. Vanessa HUTCHINSON
06 Registrar .... Ms. Nicole MIRANDO
18 Deputy Vice Pres Building/Grounds .... Mr. Michael MALONEY
39 Director Housing/Campus Services .... Mr. Michael ORZECHOWSKI
15 Director Personnel Services .... Ms. Diana TORRES-PETRILLI
100 Chief of Staff .... Mr. Jody WEST
13 Chief Info Technology Officer (CIO) .... Mr. Donald JOSHUA
29 Director Alumni Affairs .... Ms. Emily ODOM
37 Director Student Financial Aid .... Ms. Melissa DESRAVINES

United Talmudical Seminary (I)

191 Rodney Street, Brooklyn NY 11211-7900
County: Kings FICE Identification: 011189
Unit ID: 197018
Telephone: (718) 963-9770 Carnegie Class: Spec-4-yr-Faith
FAX Number: (718) 963-9775 Calendar System: Semester
Established: 1949 Annual Undergrad Tuition & Fees: $13,962
Enrollment: 2,722 Male
Affiliation or Control: Independent Non-Profit IRS Status: 501(c)3
Highest Offering: Second Talmudic Degree
Accreditation: RABN

01 Dean .... Rabbi Zalman TEITLBAUM
05 Assoc Dean Scholastic Services .... Rabbi Yeruchem DEUTSCH
37 Financial Aid Administrator .... Mr. Bernard KATZ
10 Business Officer .... Mr. Solomon GREENFELD

University of Rochester (J)

500 Joseph C. Wilson Boulevard, Rochester NY 14627
County: Monroe FICE Identification: 002894
Unit ID: 195030
Telephone: (585) 275-2121 Carnegie Class: DU-Highest
FAX Number: (585) 275-0359 Calendar System: Semester
URL: www.rochester.edu
Established: 1850 Annual Undergrad Tuition & Fees: $53,909
Enrollment: 11,648 Coed
Affiliation or Control: Independent Non-Profit IRS Status: 501(c)3
Highest Offering: Doctorate
Accreditation: M, CACREP, CAEPN, CLPSY, DENT, IPSY, MED, MFCD, MT, MUS, NURSE, PAST, PDPSY, PH

01 President .... Mrs. Sarah C. MENGELSDORF
05 Provost & Sr Vice Pres for Research .... Mr. Rob CLARK
10 Sr Vice Pres Admin & Fin/CFO .... Ms. Holly CRAWFORD
17 Sr Vice Pres Health Sci/Med Ctr CEO .... Dr. Mark B. TAUBMAN
115 Sr Vice Pres/Chief Investment Ofcr .... Mr. Douglas PHILLIPS
111 SVP & Chief Advancement Officer .... Mr. Thomas FARRELL
43 Vice Pres & General Counsel .... Ms. Donna G. PAYNE
28 Vice Pres Equity & Inclusion/CDO .... Mrs. Mercedes RAMÍREZ FERNÁNDEZ
26 Vice Pres Communications .... Ms. Elizabeth STAUDERMAN
13 Vice Pres/CIO for the University .... Mr. David E. LEWIS
15 Assoc Vice Pres Human Resources .... Mr. Tony KINSLOW

58 Vice Provost/Univ Dean of Grad Ed ..... Ms. Melissa STURGE-APPLE
100 General Secy/Pres Chief of Staff ..... Ms. Lamar R. MURPHY
88 Vice Provost Fac Devel & Diversity ..... Dr. Vivian LEWIS
32 Dean of Students ..... Mr. Matthew BURNS
08 Dean River Campus Libraries ..... Ms. Mary Ann MAVRINAC
49 Dean of School of Arts & Sciences ..... Ms. Gloria CULVER
88 Dean of Arts/Sci & Engr Faculty ..... Mr. Donald HALL
54 Dean of Hajim Engineering School ..... Ms. Wendi HEINZELMAN
07 Dir of AS&E Undergrad Admissions ..... Mr. Jason NEVINGER
37 Director of Financial Aid ..... Ms. Samantha VEEDER
108 Assoc Provost Academic Admin ..... Ms. Jane Marie SOUZA
114 Sr AVP Budgets & Planning ..... Mr. Michael ANDREWS
63 Dean of School of Medicine & Dent ..... Dr. Mark B. TAUBMAN
64 Dean of Eastman School of Music ..... Mr. Jamal ROSSI
66 Dean of School of Nursing ..... Ms. Kathy RIDEOUT
50 Dean of Simon Business School ..... Mr. Andrew AINSLIE
53 Dean Warner Grad Sch Educ & Hum Dev ..... Vacant
35 Assoc Dean Students Arts/Sci & Engr ..... Ms. Anne-Marie ALGIER
23 Chief Medical Officer ..... Dr. Michael J. APOSTOLAKOS
52 Dir Eastman Institute Oral Health ..... Dr. Eli ELIAV
25 AVP Research & Project Admin ..... Ms. Gunta LIDERS
18 Assoc Vice Pres Facilities/Services ..... Vacant
29 AVP Alumni/Constituent Relations ..... Dr. Karen CHANCE MERCURIUS
86 Executive Director Govt Relations ..... Mr. Peter J. ROBINSON
96 Assoc Vice Pres Purchasing & Supply ..... Mr. Carl TIETJEN
04 Executive Asst to the President ..... Ms. Deb DALE
06 University Registrar ..... Ms. Nancy SPECHT
19 Director of Public Safety ..... Mr. Mark T. FISCHER
88 Dir of the Memorial Art Gallery ..... Mr. Jonathan BINSTOCK
41 Director of Athletics & Recreation ..... Mr. George VANDERZWAAG
39 Exec Dir Res Life & Housing Svcs ..... Ms. Laurel CONTOMANOLIS
36 Assoc Vice Provost Career Education ..... Mr. Joe TESTANI
101 Administrator to Board of Trustees ..... Ms. Jackie E. KING
42 Director Religious & Spiritual Life ..... Rev. Denise YARBROUGH
104 Director Study Abroad ..... Ms. Tynelle STEWART
22 Equal Op Dir/Title IX Coordinator ..... Ms. Morgan LEVY
09 Sr Univ Dir Institutional Research ..... Mr. John PODVIN

U.T.A. Mesivta of Kiryas Joel (A)

PO Box 2009, Monroe NY 10949-8509

County: Orange — FICE Identification: 038023 — Unit ID: 446604
Telephone: (845) 783-9901 — Carnegie Class: Spec-4-yr-Faith
FAX Number: (845) 782-3620 — Calendar System: Semester
Established: 1999 — Annual Undergrad Tuition & Fees: $12,000
Enrollment: 1,864 — Male
Affiliation or Control: Independent Non-Profit — IRS Status: 501(c)3
Highest Offering: First Talmudic Degree
Accreditation: RABN

00 Chief Executive Officer ..... David GOLDBERGER
01 President ..... Elias HOROWITZ
05 Rosh Yeshiva ..... Rabbi Aharon TEITELBAUM
37 Financial Aid Director ..... David SCHWARTZ

Utica College (B)

1600 Burrstone Road, Utica NY 13502-4892

County: Oneida — FICE Identification: 002883 — Unit ID: 197045
Telephone: (315) 792-3111 — Carnegie Class: Masters/L
FAX Number: (315) 792-3292 — Calendar System: Semester
URL: www.utica.edu
Established: 1946 — Annual Undergrad Tuition & Fees: $21,382
Enrollment: 5,258 — Coed
Affiliation or Control: Independent Non-Profit — IRS Status: 501(c)3
Highest Offering: Doctorate
Accreditation: M, ACBSP, CAEPT, CONST, DIETC, NURSE, OT, PTA

01 President ..... Dr. Laura CASAMENTO
05 Provost & Vice Pres Academic Aff ..... Dr. Todd PFANNESTIEL
10 Vice Pres Financial Affs/Treasurer ..... Ms. Pamela SALMON
32 Vice Pres Student Affairs ..... Mr. Jeffrey GATES
04 Executive Assistant to President ..... Ms. Kim D. LAMBERT
111 VP of Advancement ..... Mr. George NEHME
84 Vice President for Enrollment Mgmt ..... Mr. Jeffrey GATES
20 Associate Provost ..... Dr. Robert M. HALLIDAY
26 Asst VP Marketing/Communication ..... Mr. Kelly L. ADAMS
76 Dean for Health Professions/Educ ..... Dr. Patrice HALLOCK
49 Dean for Arts & Sciences ..... Dr. Sharon H. WISE
50 Dean for Business & Justice Studies ..... Dr. John CAMEY
53 Dean for Education ..... Dr. Patrice HALLOCK
35 Dean of Students ..... Ms. Alane P. VARGA
113 Director of Student Acct Operation ..... Ms. Rosanna FALCHER
29 Director Alumni & Parent Relations ..... Mr. Mark C. KOVACS
36 Director Career Services ..... Ms. Halina LOTYCZEWSKI
37 Director of Financial Aid ..... Ms. Karolina HOLL
06 Registrar ..... Mr. Craig DEWAN
30 Director of Development ..... Mr. Athony VILLANTI
41 Director of Physical Educ/Athletics ..... Mr. David FONTAINE
39 Director of Residence Life ..... Mr. Scott NONEMAKER
13 Dir College Info & Application Svcs ..... Mr. Scott HUMPHREY
15 Director of Human Resources ..... Ms. Lisa GREEN
24 Dir Computer User Svcs ..... Mr. Daniel SLOAN
107 Exec Dir Corp/Professional Pgms ..... Ms. Joni L. PULLIAM
51 Director of Credit Programs ..... Ms. Evelyn FAZEKAS
85 Dean of International Education ..... Ms. Deborah WILSON-ALLAM
18 Director Facilities Management ..... Mr. Donald L. HARTER
19 Director of Campus Safety ..... Mr. Wayne SULLIVAN
92 Director Honors Program ..... Dr. Lawrence DAY
28 Dir Office of Opportunity Programs ..... Mr. John OSSOWSKI
96 Manager of Purchasing ..... Ms. Bobbie H. SMOROL
09 Assoc VP IT & Inst Research ..... Mr. Matthew S. CARR
101 Secretary of the Institution/Board ..... Ms. Jacqueline LYNCH
108 Dean of Academic Assessment ..... Ms. Ann DAMIANO
38 Director Student Counseling ..... Ms. Alison FRANKLIN
07 Asst VP UG Admissions ..... Ms. Donna SHAFFNER
08 Head Librarian ..... Mr. James K. TELIHA
106 Assoc Prov/VP E-learning ..... Dr. Polly SMITH
43 Dir Legal Services/General Counsel ..... Mr. Andrew W. BEAKMAN

† Utica College maintains an academic tie with Syracuse University that allows undergraduates to receive a Syracuse University degree.

Vassar College (C)

124 Raymond Avenue, Poughkeepsie NY 12604-0001

County: Dutchess — FICE Identification: 002895 — Unit ID: 197133
Telephone: (845) 437-7000 — Carnegie Class: Bac-A&S
FAX Number: (845) 437-7187 — Calendar System: Semester
URL: www.vassar.edu
Established: 1861 — Annual Undergrad Tuition & Fees: $56,960
Enrollment: 2,353 — Coed
Affiliation or Control: Independent Non-Profit — IRS Status: 501(c)3
Highest Offering: Master's
Accreditation: M

01 President ..... Dr. Elizabeth BRADLEY
05 Dean of the Faculty ..... Mr. William HOYNES
20 Dean of the College ..... Mr. Carlos ALAMO
10 Actg Vice Pres for Finance & Admin ..... Mr. Stephen DAHNERT
13 VP CIS/Chief Information Officer ..... Mr. Carlos GARCIA
07 Dean Admission/Financial Aid ..... Ms. Sonya SMITH
49 Dean of Studies ..... Dr. Benjamin LOTTO
20 Sr Assoc Dean College Prof Dev ..... Mr. Edward L. PITTMAN
35 Assoc Dean Col/Dir Campus Activit ..... Ms. Teresa QUINN
06 Registrar ..... Ms. Colleen MALLET
08 Director of the Libraries ..... Mr. Andrew ASHTON
36 Director Career Development Center ..... Ms. Stacy Lee SCHNEIDER BINGHAM
15 AVP Human Resources ..... Ms. Ruth SPENCER
18 Exec Dir of Facilities Operations ..... Mr. William PEABODY
38 Director of Psychological Services ..... Dr. Wendy A. FREEDMAN
96 Director of Purchasing ..... Ms. Rosaleen CARDILLO
04 Administrative Asst to President ..... Ms. Ilene COOKE
104 Director Study Abroad ..... Dr. Tracey HOLLAND
19 Director Security/Safety ..... Ms. Arlene SABO
29 VP Alumni Relations/Exe Dir AAVC ..... Ms. Lisa TESSLER
41 Athletic Director ..... Ms. Michelle WALSH

Vaughn College of Aeronautics and Technology (D)

86-01 23rd Avenue, Flushing NY 11369

County: Queens — FICE Identification: 002665 — Unit ID: 188340
Telephone: (718) 429-6600 — Carnegie Class: Bac/Assoc-Mixed
FAX Number: (718) 429-0671 — Calendar System: Semester
URL: www.vaughn.edu
Established: 1932 — Annual Undergrad Tuition & Fees: $25,260
Enrollment: 1,502 — Coed
Affiliation or Control: Independent Non-Profit — IRS Status: 501(c)3
Highest Offering: Master's
Accreditation: M, IACBE

01 President ..... Dr. Sharon B. DEVIVO
10 Vice Pres for Business & Finance ..... Mr. Robert G. WALDMANN
84 Vice President Enrollment Services ..... Mr. Ernie SHEPELSKY
15 Assoc VP College Services/Human Res ..... Ms. Mary DURKIN
05 Vice Pres of Academic Affairs ..... Dr. Paul LAVERGNE
32 VP Student Affairs ..... Ms. Kelli SMITH
35 Assoc VP/Dean Student Affairs ..... Ms. Elaine T. WHITE
30 Asst VP Development/Alumni Affair ..... Vacant
37 Director of Financial Aid ..... Ms. Tameika BENNETT
06 Registrar/Assoc VP Enrollment ..... Mrs. Beatriz CRUZ
08 Librarian ..... Mr. Curt FRIEHS
26 Director of Public Affairs ..... Ms. Maureen KIGGINS
96 Coordinator of Purchasing ..... Mr. Manuel ADRIANZEN
09 Manager of Inst Effectiveness ..... Ms. Rebekah CHOW
07 Assoc VP Enrollment ..... Mr. Celso ALVAREZ
18 Director of Facilities ..... Mr. Justin BURMEISTER
38 Dir Student Counseling/Wellness ..... Ms. Stacey DUTIL
13 Asst Director Computer Operations ..... Mr. Hamwant (Neil) SINGH
88 Vice Pres Training ..... Mr. Domenic PROSCIA
04 Administrative Asst to President ..... Ms. Barbara LOCKE
103 Dir Workforce/Career Development ..... Mr. Phil MEADE
106 Dir Online Education/E-learning ..... Vacant
41 Athletic Director ..... Mr. Ricky MCCOLLUM
29 Director Alumni Relations ..... Vacant
19 Director Security/Safety ..... Mr. Martin CAPUNAY

Villa Maria College of Buffalo (E)

240 Pine Ridge Road, Buffalo NY 14225-3999

County: Erie — FICE Identification: 002896 — Unit ID: 197142
Telephone: (716) 896-0700 — Carnegie Class: Bac/Assoc-Mixed
FAX Number: (716) 896-0705 — Calendar System: Semester
URL: www.villa.edu
Established: 1960 — Annual Undergrad Tuition & Fees: $23,010
Enrollment: 596 — Coed
Affiliation or Control: Independent Non-Profit — IRS Status: 501(c)3
Highest Offering: Baccalaureate
Accreditation: M, CIDA, MUS, OTA, PTAA

01 President ..... Dr. Matthew GIORDANO
05 Vice President for Academic Affairs ..... Dr. Ryan HARTNETT
10 Vice President for Finance ..... Mr. Richard PINKOWSKI
30 Vice President for Development ..... Mrs. Mary ROBINSON
32 VP for Enrollment Management ..... Mr. Brian EMERSON
88 Vice Pres for Mission Integration ..... Dr. Donald MONNIN
06 Registrar ..... Ms. Darby RATLIFF
07 Director of Admissions ..... Ms. Becky STRATHEARN
08 Director of Library ..... Ms. Lucy WAITE
37 Dir Financial Aid & Veteran Affairs ..... Ms. Aimee MURCH
09 Director of Institutional Research ..... Sr. Mary Albertine STACHOWSKI
38 Director of Care Center ..... Ms. Jessica M. SIEGEL
13 Director of Computer Services ..... Vacant
18 Plant & Grounds Manager ..... Mr. David WISNER
25 Director of Grants ..... Mrs. Mary ROBINSON
88 Instructional Design & Program Dev ..... Dr. Ryan HARTNETT
36 Dir Career Svcs & Internships ..... Mrs. Judith PISKUN
42 Campus Minister ..... Rev. Augustine AYAGA
85 Director of Foreign Students ..... Vacant
26 Communications Specialist ..... Ms. Kristen SCHOBER
35 Director of Student Life ..... Mr. DJ (Donald) SCHIER
88 Archivist ..... Vacant
22 Affirmative Action Officer ..... Ms. Diane M. HANDZLIK
29 Director of Alumni Relations ..... Ms. Tracy ROZLER
121 Director Student Success Center ..... Ms. Elizabeth KERR
57 Art Department Chair ..... Mr. Robert GRIZANTI
64 Music Department Chair ..... Mr. Anthony CASUCCIO
49 LiberalArts/Prof Studies Chair ..... Vacant
108 Director Institutional Assessment ..... Dr. Matthew GIORDANO
04 Administrative Asst to President ..... Ms. Michaeline KARPINSKI
103 Dir Workforce/Career Development ..... Dr. Ryan HARTNETT
41 Athletic Director ..... Ms. Amanda JANOSKY
15 Chief Human Resources Officer ..... Dr. Carleen FLOREA

Wagner College (F)

1 Campus Road, Staten Island NY 10301-4479

County: Richmond — FICE Identification: 002899 — Unit ID: 197197
Telephone: (718) 390-3100 — Carnegie Class: Masters/M
FAX Number: (718) 390-3467 — Calendar System: Semester
URL: www.wagner.edu
Established: 1883 — Annual Undergrad Tuition & Fees: $47,090
Enrollment: 2,271 — Coed
Affiliation or Control: Independent Non-Profit — IRS Status: 501(c)3
Highest Offering: Doctorate
Accreditation: M, ACBSP, ARCPA, NUR

01 President ..... Dr. Joel W. MARTIN
05 Provost/VP Academic Affairs ..... Dr. Jeffrey KRAUS
84 Sr VP for Planning & Enrollment ..... Mr. Angelo G. ARAIMO
11 VP Administration ..... Vacant
04 Assistant to the President ..... Ms. Ria CARNAVAS
88 VP Internationalization ..... Ms. Ruta SHAH-GORDON
10 CFO and VP for Finance & Business ..... Mr. John CARRESCIA
108 Assoc Provost for Assessment ..... Vacant
20 Assoc Provost for Academic Affairs ..... Dr. Nicholas RICHARDSON
06 Registrar ..... Ms. Athena TURNER-FREDERICK
13 Chief Information Officer ..... Mr. Frank CAFASSO
42 Chaplain ..... Ms. Elaine SCHENK
29 Director Alumni Relations ..... Ms. Karen MORAN
39 Director Residential Educ ..... Mr. Thomas TRESSLER-GELOK
30 Chief Development Officer ..... Vacant
18 Director of Campus Operations ..... Mr. Daniel SWITZER
41 Director of Athletics ..... Mr. Walter HAMELINE
23 Assistant Dean Health & Wellness ..... Ms. Kathleen OBERFELDT
19 Director of Public Safety ..... Mr. Edwin MOSS
15 Chief HR Officer & Title IX Coord ..... Ms. Jazzmine CLARKE-GLOVER
37 Director of Financial Aid ..... Ms. Theresa WEIMER
58 Dean of Graduate Studies ..... Vacant
07 Dean of Enrollment ..... Vacant
09 IR Director/Asst Dir of Enrollment ..... Ms. Patricia CLANCY
32 Assistant Dean Campus Life ..... Ms. Ange CONCEPCION
36 Dean & Director CACE ..... Dr. Matthew KUBACKI
08 Director of the Horrman Library ..... Mr. Dennis SCHAUB
101 Secretary to the Board of Trustees ..... Mr. David MARTIN

Webb Institute (G)

298 Crescent Beach Road, Glen Cove NY 11542-1398

County: Nassau — FICE Identification: 002900 — Unit ID: 197221
Telephone: (516) 671-2213 — Carnegie Class: Spec-4-yr-Eng
FAX Number: (516) 674-9838 — Calendar System: Semester
URL: www.webb.edu
Established: 1889 — Annual Undergrad Tuition & Fees: $50,175
Enrollment: 98 — Coed
Affiliation or Control: Independent Non-Profit — IRS Status: 501(c)3
Highest Offering: Baccalaureate
Accreditation: M

01 President ..... Mr. R. Keith MICHEL
05 Dean ..... Prof. Matthew R. WERNER
20 Assistant Dean ..... Prof. Richard C. HARRIS
08 Librarian ..... Ms. Patricia M. PRESCOTT
30 Chief Development ..... Mr. Anthony ZIC
10 Director of Financial Affairs ..... Ms. Rhonda LIGHTCAP
09 Director of Institutional Research ..... Prof. Richard A. ROYCE
32 Director of Student Affairs ..... Vacant

18	Director of Facilities	Mr. John FERRANTE
84	Dir Enrollment Mgmt/Admissions	Ms. Lauren CARBALLO
29	Director of Alumni Relations	Ms. Gailmarie SUJECKI
26	Chief Public Relations Officer	Ms. Kerri ALLEGRETTA
13	Director of Communications and IT	Mr. Peter MILLER
06	Registrar	Ms. Jocelyn M. WILSON
37	Director of Financial Aid	Ms. Jocelyn M. WILSON
04	Administrative Asst to President	Ms. Gailmarie SUJECKI
15	Director Personnel Services	Ms. Svetlana MILLER

Weill Cornell Medicine (A)

1300 York Avenue, New York NY 10065-4805
Telephone: (212) 746-5454 FICE Identification: 004762
Accreditation: &M, ARCPA, DENT, IPSY, MED

† Regional accreditation is carried under the parent institution Cornell University, Ithaca, NY.

Wells College (B)

170 Main Street, Aurora NY 13026-0500
County: Cayuga FICE Identification: 002901
Unit ID: 197230
Telephone: (315) 364-3266 Carnegie Class: Bac-A&S
FAX Number: (315) 364-3227 Calendar System: Semester
URL: www.wells.edu
Established: 1868 Annual Undergrad Tuition & Fees: $40,700
Enrollment: 488 Coed
Affiliation or Control: Independent Non-Profit IRS Status: 501(c)3
Highest Offering: Baccalaureate
Accreditation: #M

01	President	Dr. Jonathan GIBRALTER
05	Provost and Dean of the College	Dr. Cindy SPEAKER
10	Vice President and CFO	Mr. Robert A. CREE
21	Controller	Ms. Susan WEATHERBY
111	Vice President for Advancement	Vacant
32	Dean of Students	Dr. Charles B. KENYON
84	Vice President for Enrollment Svcs	Vacant
06	Registrar and Dir Inst Research	Mr. Paul APPLEBEE
08	Library Director	Ms. Carol HENDERSON
37	Director Financial Aid	Ms. Laura BURNS
44	Director of Annual Giving	Ms. Pamela SHERADIN
26	Dir of Communications/Marketing	Mr. Christopher POLLOCK
29	Dir Alumnae & Alumni Engagement	Ms. Jennifer JANES
19	Director of Campus Safety	Mr. Anthony PLURETTI
18	Dir of Facilities/Physical Plant	Mr. Brian BROWN
15	Manager of Human Resources	Ms. Kit VAN ORMAN

Westchester Community College (C)

75 Grasslands Road, Valhalla NY 10595-1636
County: Westchester FICE Identification: 002881
Unit ID: 197294
Telephone: (914) 606-6600 Carnegie Class: Assoc/HT-Mix Trad/Non
FAX Number: (914) 606-6780 Calendar System: Semester
URL: www.sunywcc.edu
Established: 1946 Annual Undergrad Tuition & Fees (In-District): $4,836
Enrollment: 12,571 Coed
Affiliation or Control: State/Local IRS Status: 501(c)3
Highest Offering: Associate Degree
Accreditation: M, COARC, #DIETT, EMT, RAD

01	President	Dr. Belinda S. MILES
05	Provost & VP Academic Affairs	Dr. Vanessa MOREST
32	VP Stdnt Access/Involve/Success	Dr. Sara THOMPSON-TWEEDY
10	Vice Pres Administrative Services	Mr. Brian MURPHY
102	VP Ext Affairs/Exec Dir Foundation	Ms. Eve LARNER
103	VP Workforce Dev & Comm Education	Ms. Teresita WISELL
81	Dean School of Math/Science/Engr	Dr. Raymond HOUSTON
76	Dean School of Health Careers/Tech	Dr. Ronald BLOOM
50	Dean School of Bus & Prof Careers	Dr. Carmen Leonor MARTINEZ-LOPEZ
79	Dean School Arts/Hum/Soc Science	Dr. Karen TAYLOR
22	Associate Dean & Director of EOC	Dr. Gina GAINES
35	Assoc Dean Student Personnel Svcs	Ms. Ellen ZENDMAN
08	Asc Dn Lrng Res/Dist Lrng/Inst Tech	Ms. Pamela POLLARD
26	Director of College/Cmty Relations	Mr. Patrick HENNESSEY
06	Registrar	Mr. Christopher WESTBY
37	Dir of Student Financial Assistance	Mr. Jason FRANKY
13	Vice President of IT	Mr. Anthony SCORDINO
07	Director of Admissions	Ms. Gloria DE LA PAZ
84	Assoc Dean Enrollment Management	Dr. Ruben BARATO
15	Director Human Resources	Ms. Aurora WORKMAN
88	Dir Faculty Student Assoc	Mr. Joseph POPPA
45	Asst Dean Planning and Inst Effect	Ms. Yelizaveta ADAMS
19	Director of Security	Mr. Scott SULLIVAN
24	Director Media Services	Mr. Gennaro MASELLI
41	Athletic Director	Mr. Michael BELFIORE
21	Assoc Business Officer/Controller	Ms. Dawn GILLINS
18	Director Physical Plant	Mr. Robert CIRILLO
96	Deputy Purchasing Agent	Mr. John-Paul IANNACE
27	Publications Manager	Mr. Edward TATTON
23	Coordinator Student Health Services	Ms. Janice GILROY
88	Coord of Transfer Services	Ms. Robin GRAFF
100	Chief of Staff	Dr. Shawn BROWN
101	Secretary of the Institution/Board	Ms. Yolanda HOWELL
105	Director Web Services	Mr. Patrick DANNENHOFFER
25	Chief Contract/Grants Administrator	Dr. Laurie MILLER-MCNEILL
28	Director of Diversity	Vacant
29	Director Alumni Affairs	Ms. Michelle SCHLEIBAUM
44	Director Annual Giving	Ms. Jessica DENARO

Yeshiva Derech Chaim (D)

1573 39th Street, Brooklyn NY 11218-4413
County: Kings FICE Identification: 022651
Unit ID: 197647
Telephone: (718) 438-5476 Carnegie Class: Spec-4-yr-Faith
FAX Number: (718) 435-9285 Calendar System: Semester
Established: 1975 Annual Undergrad Tuition & Fees: $12,100
Enrollment: 138 Male
Affiliation or Control: Independent Non-Profit IRS Status: 501(c)3
Highest Offering: Second Talmudic Degree
Accreditation: RABN

01	President	Rabbi Chaim RENNERT
01	President	Rabbi Yisroel PLUTCHOK

Yeshiva D'Monsey Rabbinical College (E)

2 Roman Boulevard, Monsey NY 10952-3106
County: Rockland FICE Identification: 031473
Unit ID: 420325
Telephone: (845) 426-3276 Carnegie Class: Spec-4-yr-Faith
FAX Number: (845) 352-1119 Calendar System: Semester
Established: 1984 Annual Undergrad Tuition & Fees: $7,300
Enrollment: 76 Male
Affiliation or Control: Independent Non-Profit IRS Status: 501(c)3
Highest Offering: Second Talmudic Degree
Accreditation: RABN

01	Rosh Yeshiva	Rabbi Moishe GREEN
05	Rosh Yeshiva	Rabbi Ruvain GREEN
37	Financial Aid Director	Rabbi Aron BERGER

Yeshiva of Far Rockaway (F)

802 Hicksville Road, Far Rockaway NY 11691-5219
County: Queens FICE Identification: 041196
Unit ID: 190752
Telephone: (718) 327-7600 Carnegie Class: Spec-4-yr-Faith
FAX Number: (718) 327-1430 Calendar System: Semester
Established: 1969 Annual Undergrad Tuition & Fees: $11,750
Enrollment: 33 Male
Affiliation or Control: Independent Non-Profit IRS Status: 501(c)3
Highest Offering: First Talmudic Degree
Accreditation: RABN

01	President	Rabbi Yechiel I. PERR
03	Executive Director	Rabbi Shayeh KOHN
32	Dean of Students	Rabbi Dovid KLEINKAUFMAN
06	Registrar	Mrs. Tamara MASLOW

Yeshiva Gedolah Imrei Yosef D'Spinka (G)

1466 56th Street, Brooklyn NY 11219-4696
County: Kings FICE Identification: 030001
Unit ID: 375230
Telephone: (718) 851-8721 Carnegie Class: Spec-4-yr-Faith
FAX Number: (718) 686-8849 Calendar System: Semester
Established: 1987 Annual Undergrad Tuition & Fees: $9,500
Enrollment: 105 Male
Affiliation or Control: Independent Non-Profit IRS Status: 501(c)3
Highest Offering: First Talmudic Degree
Accreditation: RABN

01	President	Joseph SOLOMON

Yeshiva Gedolah Kesser Torah (H)

50 Cedar Lane, Monsey NY 10952
County: Rockland Identification: 667112
Unit ID: 481410
Telephone: (845) 406-4308 Carnegie Class: Spec-4-yr-Faith
FAX Number: (845) 406-4199 Calendar System: Semester
Established: 2004 Annual Undergrad Tuition & Fees: $11,300
Enrollment: 71 Male
Affiliation or Control: Independent Non-Profit IRS Status: 501(c)3
Highest Offering: First Talmudic Degree
Accreditation: RABN

00	CEO	Rabbi David FISHMAN
01	President	David BERNSTEIN
06	Registrar	Rabbi Ephraim SALB
37	Director Student Financial Aid	Yaakov BERGER

Yeshiva Gedolah Ohr Yisrael (I)

2899 Nostrand Avenue, Brooklyn NY 11229
County: Kings Identification: 667077
Unit ID: 486017
Telephone: (718) 382-8702 Carnegie Class: Spec-4-yr-Faith
FAX Number: (718) 382-8703 Calendar System: Semester
Established: 1999 Annual Undergrad Tuition & Fees: $7,600
Enrollment: 39 Male
Affiliation or Control: Independent Non-Profit IRS Status: 501(c)3
Highest Offering: First Talmudic Degree
Accreditation: RABN

01	Rosh Yeshiva	Avraham ZUCKER
10	Treasurer	Avi KAHN

Yeshiva Karlin Stolin Beth Aaron V'Israel Rabbinical Institute (J)

1818 54th Street, Brooklyn NY 11204-1545
County: Kings FICE Identification: 025058
Unit ID: 197601
Telephone: (718) 232-7800 Carnegie Class: Spec-4-yr-Faith
FAX Number: (718) 331-4833 Calendar System: Semester
Established: 1948 Annual Undergrad Tuition & Fees: $12,800
Enrollment: 151 Male
Affiliation or Control: Independent Non-Profit IRS Status: 501(c)3
Highest Offering: First Talmudic Degree
Accreditation: RABN

01	Chief Executive Officer	Rabbi Yochanan PILCHICK
05	Dean Theology/Chief Acad Officer	Rabbi Chaim WOLPIN, OBM
06	Registrar	Rabbi Aryeh WOLPIN
08	Librarian	Rabbi Yochanan GOLDHABER
10	Fiscal Officer	Rabbi Irving PERRES
37	Financial Aid Director	Rabbi David STEIN
33	Dean of Men	Rabbi Gedelyah MACHLIS

Yeshiva Kollel Tifereth Elizer (K)

1227 47th Street, Brooklyn NY 11219
County: Kings Identification: 667367
Telephone: (718) 600-8897 Carnegie Class: Not Classified
FAX Number: (718) 889-7033 Calendar System: Semester
Established: 1987 Annual Undergrad Tuition & Fees: N/A
Enrollment: 79 Male
Affiliation or Control: Independent Non-Profit IRS Status: 501(c)3
Highest Offering: First Talmudic Degree
Accreditation: RABN

01	Chief Executive Officer	Rabbi Avrum Yehuda LOW
10	Chief Financial Officer	Rabbi Hershel LOW
37	Financial Aid Administrator	Rabbi Yesoscher MEISELS
06	Registrar	Mrs. Rochel LOW

Yeshiva of Machzikai Hadas (L)

1301 47th Street, Brooklyn NY 11219
County: Kings FICE Identification: 041381
Unit ID: 455257
Telephone: (718) 853-2442 Carnegie Class: Spec-4-yr-Faith
FAX Number: (718) 853-2504 Calendar System: Semester
Established: 2001 Annual Undergrad Tuition & Fees: $9,200
Enrollment: 413 Male
Affiliation or Control: Independent Non-Profit IRS Status: 501(c)3
Highest Offering: First Talmudic Degree
Accreditation: RABN

01	Rosh Yeshiva	Rabbi Yidel MONHEIT

Yeshiva of Nitra Rabbinical College (M)

194 Division Avenue, Brooklyn NY 11211-7199
County: Kings FICE Identification: 011670
Unit ID: 197674
Telephone: (718) 387-0422 Carnegie Class: Spec-4-yr-Faith
FAX Number: (718) 387-9400 Calendar System: Semester
Established: 1946 Annual Undergrad Tuition & Fees: $8,500
Enrollment: 209 Male
Affiliation or Control: Independent Non-Profit IRS Status: 501(c)3
Highest Offering: Second Talmudic Degree
Accreditation: RABN

01	President	Mr. Alfred SCHOENBERGER
03	Vice President	Mr. Mendel KLEIN
05	Dean	Rabbi Samuel D. UNGAR
11	Administrative Officer	Mr. Ernest SCHWARTZ

Yeshiva Ohr Naftoli (N)

701 Blooming Grove Turnpike, New Windsor NY 12553
County: Orange Identification: 667284
Unit ID: 490504
Telephone: (845) 784-4020 Carnegie Class: Spec-4-yr-Faith
FAX Number: (845) 784-2028 Calendar System: Other
URL: www.ohrnaftoli.org
Established: Annual Undergrad Tuition & Fees: $9,500
Enrollment: 24 Male
Affiliation or Control: Independent Non-Profit IRS Status: 501(c)3
Highest Offering: First Talmudic Degree
Accreditation: AIJS

01	Executive Director	Rabbi Yitzchok KRAUSZ

Yeshiva Shaar Ephraim (O)

178 Maple Avenue, Monsey NY 10952
County: Rockland FICE Identification: 042590
Unit ID: 490276
Telephone: (845) 426-3110 Carnegie Class: Spec-4-yr-Faith
FAX Number: (845) 425-4721 Calendar System: Semester

URL: shaarephraim.org
Established: 2012 Annual Undergrad Tuition & Fees: $13,675
Enrollment: N/A Male
Affiliation or Control: Independent Non-Profit IRS Status: 501(c)3
Highest Offering: First Talmudic Degree
Accreditation: RABN

01 President Rabbi Yehuda OSHRY
33 Dean of Men Rabbi Moshe GREENBURG
37 Director of Financial Aid Mr. Dow KRESCH

Yeshiva Shaar HaTorah-Grodno (A)

83-96 117th Street, Kew Gardens NY 11415
County: Queens FICE Identification: 021520
Unit ID: 197692
Telephone: (718) 846-1940 Carnegie Class: Spec-4-yr-Faith
FAX Number: (718) 850-7916 Calendar System: Semester
Established: 1976 Annual Undergrad Tuition & Fees: $15,760
Enrollment: 111 Male
Affiliation or Control: Independent Non-Profit IRS Status: 501(c)3
Highest Offering: Second Talmudic Degree
Accreditation: RABN

01 Administrator Rabbi Yoel YANKELEWITZ

Yeshiva Shaarei Torah of Rockland (B)

91 W Carlton Road, Suffern NY 10901-4013
County: Rockland FICE Identification: 034963
Unit ID: 441609
Telephone: (845) 352-3431 Carnegie Class: Spec-4-yr-Faith
FAX Number: (845) 352-3433 Calendar System: Semester
Established: 1977 Annual Undergrad Tuition & Fees: $12,500
Enrollment: 93 Male
Affiliation or Control: Independent Non-Profit IRS Status: 501(c)3
Highest Offering: First Talmudic Degree
Accreditation: AIJS

01 President Dr. Don ZWICKLER
05 Rosh Hayeshiva Rabbi Mordechai WOLMARK
37 Financial Aid Administrator Mr. Elimelech SCHWARTZ
06 Registrar Mrs. Rachel CELNIK

Yeshiva Sholom Shachna (C)

401 Elmwood Avenue, Brooklyn NY 11230
County: Kings Identification: 667147
Unit ID: 486026
Telephone: (718) 252-6333 Carnegie Class: Spec-4-yr-Faith
FAX Number: (718) 338-2536 Calendar System: Semester
URL: yeshivasholomshachna.com
Established: 2005 Annual Undergrad Tuition & Fees: $10,750
Enrollment: 105 Male
Affiliation or Control: Independent Non-Profit IRS Status: 501(c)3
Highest Offering: First Talmudic Degree
Accreditation: @RABN

01 Chief Executive Officer Rabbi Meir Chaim GUTFREUND
10 Chief Financial/Business Officer Mrs. Dina GUTFREUND
05 Chief Academic Officer/Registrar Rabbi Simcha OLEN
37 Director Student Financial Aid Mrs. Esty FARKAS

Yeshiva of the Telshe Alumni (D)

4904 Independence Avenue, Riverdale NY 10471
County: Bronx FICE Identification: 025463
Unit ID: 431983
Telephone: (718) 601-3523 Carnegie Class: Spec-4-yr-Faith
FAX Number: (718) 601-2141 Calendar System: Semester
Established: 1981 Annual Undergrad Tuition & Fees: $9,850
Enrollment: 116 Male
Affiliation or Control: Independent Non-Profit IRS Status: 501(c)3
Highest Offering: First Talmudic Degree
Accreditation: RABN

01 President Rabbi Avrohom AUSBAND
03 Executive Director Rabbi Noson JOSEPH
29 Director Alumni Relations Rabbi Moshe FERBER

Yeshiva University (E)

500 W 185th Street, New York NY 10033-3201
County: New York FICE Identification: 002903
Unit ID: 197708
Telephone: (212) 960-5400 Carnegie Class: DU-Higher
FAX Number: (212) 960-0055 Calendar System: Semester
URL: www.yu.edu
Established: 1886 Annual Undergrad Tuition & Fees: $43,500
Enrollment: 6,330 Coordinate
Affiliation or Control: Independent Non-Profit IRS Status: 501(c)3
Highest Offering: Doctorate
Accreditation: M, CAEPT, CLPSY, DENT, IPSY, LAW, PSPSY, @SP, SW

01 President Dr. Ari BERMAN
05 Provost/Sr VP Academic Affairs Dr. Selma BOTMAN
88 Chief of Staff to the Provost Dr. Timothy STEVENS
100 Sr Vice Pres/Chief of Staff Mr. Josh JOSEPH
10 Vice Pres/Chief Financial Officer Mr. Jacob HARMAN
111 Vice Pres Institutional Advancement Mr. Adam GERDTS
11 Vice President University Affairs Dr. Herbert C. DOBRINSKY
13 Chief Information Officer Mr. Jim VASQUEZ
43 VP Legal Affs/Secretary/Gen Counsel Mr. Andrew J. LAUER
32 Int Vice Pres Univ & Cmty Life Rabbi Josh JOSEPH
26 Exec Dir Communications/Public Affs Mr. Doron STERN
04 Exec Assistant to President Ms. Linda DOS SANTOS
08 Director of University Libraries Mr. Paul GLASSMAN
35 Dean of Students Dr. Chaim NISSEL
73 Dn Undergrad Torah Stds/REITS Rabbi Yosef KALINSKY
49 Dean YU Undergrad Fac Arts Sci Dr. Karen BACON
50 Dean Sy Syms School of Business Dr. Noam WASSERMAN
58 Dean Ferkauf Graduate School Psych Vacant
58 Dean Bernard Revel Graduate School Dr. David BERGER
58 Dean Azrieli Grad Sch Jewish Educ Dr. Rona NOVICK
70 Dean Wurzweiler School Social Work Dr. Danielle WOZNIAK
58 Dean Katz School Grad & Prof Stds Dr. Paul RUSSO
37 Director of Student Finances Mr. Robert FRIEDMAN
07 Director Undergraduate Admissions Ms. Geri MANSDORF
29 Director University Alumni Affairs Ms. Dina BURCAT
06 University Registrar Ms. Jeannine ENGLERT
09 Director of Institutional Research Mr. Yuxiang LIU
96 Director of Procurement Mr. Thomas CANNON
15 Chief Human Resources Officer Ms. Julie AUSTER
38 Director Student Counseling Dr. Yael MUSKAT
22 Dir Affirmative Action/EEO Ms. Renee COKER
41 Athletic Director Mr. Joe BENDARSH
19 Director Security/Safety Mr. Donald SOMMERS
36 Executive Director Career Center Ms. Susan BAUER
18 Chief Facilities & Admin Officer Mr. Randy APFELBAUM

Yeshiva Yesoda Hatorah Vetz Chaim (F)

505 Bedford Avenue, Brooklyn NY 11211
County: Kings Identification: 667368
Telephone: (718) 302-7500 Carnegie Class: Not Classified
FAX Number: N/A Calendar System: Semester
Established: 2013 Annual Undergrad Tuition & Fees: N/A
Enrollment: N/A Male
Affiliation or Control: Independent Non-Profit IRS Status: 501(c)3
Highest Offering: First Talmudic Degree
Accreditation: RABN

01 President Mr. Samuel FISCHER
37 Director of Financial Aid Mr. Getzel FALKOWITZ

Yeshiva Zichron Aryeh (G)

1213 Bay 25th Street, Far Rockaway NY 11691
County: Queens Identification: 667110
Unit ID: 487746
Telephone: (347) 619-9074 Carnegie Class: Spec-4-yr-Faith
FAX Number: (516) 295-5737 Calendar System: Semester
Established: 1992 Annual Undergrad Tuition & Fees: $8,750
Enrollment: 24 Male
Affiliation or Control: Independent Non-Profit IRS Status: 501(c)3
Highest Offering: Second Talmudic Degree
Accreditation: RABN

03 Executive Vice President Rabbi Shaya COHEN
10 Controller Rabbi Ari DERDIK
06 Registrar/Dir of Admissions Rabbi Yehuda COHEN
37 Financial Aid Admin Mr. Yaakov JAFFE
18 Chief Facilities Mr. Danny SCHUSTER
08 Head Librarian Mr. Yechezkel MOSKOWITZ

Yeshivas Maharit Dsatmar (H)

475 County Rt. 105, Monroe NY 10950
County: Orange Identification: 667204
Unit ID: 488101
Telephone: (845) 782-1380 Carnegie Class: Spec-4-yr-Faith
FAX Number: (845) 302-1093 Calendar System: Semester
Established: 2011 Annual Undergrad Tuition & Fees: $11,500
Enrollment: 99 Male
Affiliation or Control: Independent Non-Profit IRS Status: 501(c)3
Highest Offering: First Talmudic Degree
Accreditation: @RABN

01 CEO Yitzchok TYRNAUER
06 Registrar Joel BRAVER
10 Associate Business Officer Libi WITRIOL
37 Director of Financial Aid Yoel KESTENBAUM

Yeshivas Novominsk (I)

1690 60th Street, Brooklyn NY 11204-2138
County: Kings FICE Identification: 031271
Unit ID: 405058
Telephone: (718) 438-2727 Carnegie Class: Spec-4-yr-Faith
FAX Number: (718) 438-2472 Calendar System: Semester
Established: 1988 Annual Undergrad Tuition & Fees: $10,000
Enrollment: 154 Male
Affiliation or Control: Independent Non-Profit IRS Status: 501(c)3
Highest Offering: First Talmudic Degree
Accreditation: RABN

01 Executive Director Rabbi Lipa BRENNAN
32 Dean of Students Rabbi Yaakov PERLOW
11 Administrator Rabbi Boruch TWERSKI

Yeshivath Viznitz (J)

PO Box 446, Monsey NY 10952-0446
County: Rockland FICE Identification: 013027
Unit ID: 197735
Telephone: (845) 731-3700 Carnegie Class: Spec-4-yr-Faith
FAX Number: (845) 356-7359 Calendar System: Semester
Established: 1946 Annual Undergrad Tuition & Fees: $10,100
Enrollment: 690 Male
Affiliation or Control: Independent Non-Profit IRS Status: 501(c)3
Highest Offering: Second Talmudic Degree
Accreditation: RABN

01 President Gershon NEIMAN
10 Chief Fiscal Officer Rabbi David ROSENBERG

Yeshivath Zichron Moshe (K)

PO Box 580, South Fallsburg NY 12779-0580
County: Sullivan FICE Identification: 011821
Unit ID: 197744
Telephone: (845) 434-5240 Carnegie Class: Spec-4-yr-Faith
FAX Number: (845) 434-1009 Calendar System: Semester
Established: 1969 Annual Undergrad Tuition & Fees: $13,450
Enrollment: 199 Male
Affiliation or Control: Independent Non-Profit IRS Status: 501(c)3
Highest Offering: Second Talmudic Degree
Accreditation: AIJS

01 President Rabbi Ephraim Y. SHER
37 Director Student Financial Aid Rabbi Dov PERECMAN
06 Registrar Mrs. Miryom R. MILLER

NORTH CAROLINA

Apex School of Theology (L)

1701 T. W. Alexander Drive, Durham NC 27703-8024
County: Durham FICE Identification: 035134
Unit ID: 441511
Telephone: (919) 572-1625 Carnegie Class: Spec-4-yr-Faith
FAX Number: (919) 572-1762 Calendar System: Other
URL: www.apexsot.edu
Established: 1995 Annual Undergrad Tuition & Fees: $5,100
Enrollment: 824 Coed
Affiliation or Control: Independent Non-Profit IRS Status: 501(c)3
Highest Offering: Doctorate
Accreditation: TRACS

01 President Dr. Joseph E. PERKINS
03 Executive Vice President Dr. Herbert R. DAVIS
05 Academic Dean/Graduate Dean Dr. Lafayette MAXWELL
06 Registrar Mr. Joseph A. PERKINS
08 Head Librarian Ms. Cynthia RUFFIN
10 Chief Financial Officer Mrs. Yolanda DEAVERS
20 Undergraduate Dean Dr. Gladys LONG
88 Dean Master of Arts Christian Couns Dr. Tonya ARMSTRONG
73 Dean Doctor of Ministry Dr. Lafayette MAXWELL
32 Director Student Affairs Dr. George T. DANIELS
45 Dir of Institutional Effectiveness Dr. Henry D. WELLS, JR.
04 Executive Admin Asst to President Ms. Rolanda J. HOLLAND
07 Admissions Coordinator Ms. Sandra J. MANNING
13 Dir of Educational Technology Dr. Clarence BURKE
18 Chief Facilities/Physical Plant Mr. Anthony PATTERSON
37 Director Student Financial Aid Ms. Floya COTTEN-BROWN
04 Executive Asst to the President Dr. Reginald HIGH
88 Academic Student Advisor Dr. Sharon LEE

Barton College (M)

400 Atlantic Christian College Dr, Wilson NC 27893
County: Wilson FICE Identification: 002908
Unit ID: 197911
Telephone: (252) 399-6300 Carnegie Class: Bac-Diverse
FAX Number: (252) 399-6374 Calendar System: Semester
URL: www.barton.edu
Established: 1902 Annual Undergrad Tuition & Fees: $30,880
Enrollment: 960 Coed
Affiliation or Control: Christian Church (Disciples Of Christ)
IRS Status: 501(c)3
Highest Offering: Master's
Accreditation: SC, NURSE, SW

01 President Dr. Douglas N. SEARCY
05 Vice President Academic Affairs Dr. Gary DAYNES
10 Vice Pres Finance & Administration Mr. David A. BROWNING
111 Int Vice Pres Inst Advancement Mr. Michael STRADER
84 Vice President for Enrollment Mgmt Mr. Dennis T. MATTHEWS
32 Vice President Student Engagement Dr. Chrissy COLEY
07 Asst VP of Admissions Ms. Amanda METTS
30 Asst VP for Development Mr. Tom MAZE
50 Dean School of Business Mr. Ron EGGERS
66 Dean School of Nursing Dr. Sharon SARVEY
53 Dean School of Education Dr. Jackie ENNIS
79 Dean School of Humanities Dr. Liz KISER
81 Dean School of Sciences Dr. Kevin PENNINGTON
76 Dean Allied Health & Sport Studies Dr. Steve FULKS
88 Dean School of Social Work Dr. Barbara CONKLIN
57 Dean Visual/Performing & Comm Arts Ms. Susan FECHO
58 Dean Graduate/Professional Studies Dr. Susan BANE

41 Athletic Director Mr. Todd WILKINSON
106 Dir Online Education/E-learning Ms. Lorraine RAPER
121 Asst Dean of Student Success Ms. Angie WALSTON
06 Registrar Ms. Sheila MILNE
37 Director Student Financial Aid Mr. Thomas WELCH
26 Director of Public Relations Mrs. Kathy DAUGHETY
08 Director of the Library Mr. Robert CAGNA
15 Asst VP of Human Resources Mrs. Vicky MORRIS
23 Director of Health Services Mrs. Jennifer HIGH
44 Dir Annual Giving & Digital Mktg Mr. Archie BANE
14 Director Technology Mr. David GRAYBEAL
18 Director of Physical Plant Mr. Michael AVERETT
42 Chaplain Rev. David FINNEGAN-HOSEY
40 Bookstore Manager Ms. Candice MOORE
04 Executive Asst to President Mrs. Sheila WILSON
39 Assistant Dean Student Development Mr. Joseph DLUGOS
88 Director of Publications Mr. Keith TEW
105 Director Web Services Mr. Ken DOZIER
91 Director Administrative Computing Vacant
09 Director of Institutional Research Ms. Lorie A. DALOLA

Belmont Abbey College (A)

100 Belmont Mount Holly Road, Belmont NC 28012-1802
County: Gaston FICE Identification: 002910
Unit ID: 197984
Telephone: (704) 461-6701 Carnegie Class: Bac-Diverse
FAX Number: (704) 461-6670 Calendar System: Semester
URL: belmontabbeycollege.edu/
Established: 1876 Annual Undergrad Tuition & Fees: $18,500
Enrollment: 1,555 Coed
Affiliation or Control: Roman Catholic IRS Status: 501(c)3
Highest Offering: Baccalaureate
Accreditation: SC

01 President Dr. William K. THIERFELDER
10 SVP Finance/Admin/Operations Mr. Allan MARK
05 Vice Provost for Academic Affairs Dr. David WILLIAMS
26 VP Col Relations & General Counsel Mr. Gregory SWANSON
20 Assoc Dean for Academic Affairs Dr. Joseph WYSOCKI
30 Development Officer Ms. Chris PEELER
29 Director of Alumni Relations Ms. Bridget CONBOY
08 Director of the Library Mr. Donald BEAGLE
06 Registrar Ms. Margot RHOADES
09 Vice Prov Assessment/Rsrch/Accred Ms. Karen PRICE
36 Director Career Counseling/Placemnt Ms. Stephannie MILES
27 Exec Dir Marketing/Communications Mr. Rolando RIVAS
37 Dir Student Financial Services Mrs. Elisa FISHER
38 Wellness Center Counselor Mrs. Melanie ECKSTEIN
41 Athletic Director Mr. Stephen MISS
21 Controller Ms. Beth RUNSER
19 Chief of Campus Police Mr. Andy LEONARD
42 Director of Campus Ministry Mr. Patrick FORD
15 Director of Human Resources Ms. Cheryl TROTTER
18 Chief Facilities/Physical Plant Vacant
07 Dean of Admissions Ms. Nicole FOCARETO
13 Chief Info Technology Officer (CIO) Mr. Nash HASAN
32 Dean of Student Life Mr. Tom MACALESTER
04 Sr Executive Assistant Ms. Trudi MALO

Bennett College (B)

900 E Washington Street, Greensboro NC 27401-3239
County: Guilford FICE Identification: 002911
Unit ID: 197993
Telephone: (336) 273-4431 Carnegie Class: Bac-A&S
FAX Number: (336) 370-8688 Calendar System: Semester
URL: www.bennett.edu
Established: 1873 Annual Undergrad Tuition & Fees: $18,513
Enrollment: 493 Female
Affiliation or Control: United Methodist IRS Status: 501(c)3
Highest Offering: Baccalaureate
Accreditation: #SC, CAEPN, SW

01 President Dr. Phyllis W. DAWKINS
05 Int Provost & VP Academic Affairs Dr. Michelle LINSTER
10 Interim VP Business & Finance Mr. John KOVATCH
111 Vice Pres Inst Advancement Mr. LaDaniel GATLING, II
88 Sr Advisor/Assoc VP Admin Services Dr. Anne C. HAYES
21 Assoc VP Business & Finance Ms. Latonya FLAMER
84 Assoc VP Enrollment Mgmt/Registrar Ms. Gisele ABRON
32 Assoc VP Student Affairs Dr. Lorraine ACKER
26 Dir Public Relations & Publication Vacant
09 Dir Institutional Rsrch & Testing Ms. Karen JAMES
08 Director of Holgate Library Ms. Joan WILLIAMS
07 Director of Admissions Mr. James CRAWFORD
37 Director of Financial Aid Ms. Pam DOUGLAS
29 Exec Director Alumnae Affairs Ms. Audrey FRANKLIN
36 Director Career Services Mr. Darryl JOHNSON
38 Dir Coun Svcs/Supervisor Health Svc Ms. Robin CAMPBELL
15 Director of Human Resources Ms. Linda DIAMOND
42 Chaplain/Director Campus Ministry Rev Dr. Natalie MCLEAN
88 Chair Curriculum & Instruction Dr. Annette WILSON
79 Interim Chair Humanities Ms. Penny SPEAS
81 Int Chair Biological & Chemical Sci Dr. Michael COTTON
19 Director Campus Safety Mr. Keifer BRADSHAW
13 Assoc Dir Information Tech Svcs Mr. William MORRIS
04 Executive Asst to the President Vacant
104 Director Center for Global Studies Ms. Kelly MALLARI
106 Dean or Director Online Education Mr. Tom LIPSCOMB
108 Director Institutional Assessment Dr. Sonya RICKS
25 Dir Title III & Sponsored Programs Ms. Sylvia NICHOLSON
39 Dir Campus Life/Student Activities Ms. Rachel PRIDGEN
50 Dept Chair Bus/Econ & Entre Studies Dr. Christopher WALSON
20 Dean of Faculty Dr. Annette WILSON

Brevard College (C)

One Brevard College Drive, Brevard NC 28712-3306
County: Transylvania FICE Identification: 002912
Unit ID: 198066
Telephone: (828) 883-8292 Carnegie Class: Bac-Diverse
FAX Number: (828) 884-3790 Calendar System: Semester
URL: www.brevard.edu
Established: 1853 Annual Undergrad Tuition & Fees: $28,640
Enrollment: 677 Coed
Affiliation or Control: United Methodist IRS Status: 501(c)3
Highest Offering: Baccalaureate
Accreditation: SC, MUS

01 President Dr. David C. JOYCE
05 VP Academic Affairs/Dean of Faculty Dr. Roy S. SHEFFIELD
10 VP for Finance & Operations Mr. Juan C. MASCARO
30 VP for Alumni Affairs & Development Ms. Kathryn HOLTEN
84 Vice Pres Admissions/Financial Aid Mr. Ryan C. HOLT
32 VP Student Success & Services Mrs. Debora D'ANNA
04 Executive Asst to the President Ms. Katherine T. PARNELL
13 Dir of Information Technology Mr. Jay TRUSSELL
06 Registrar Mrs. Amy HERTZ
21 Associate VP Finance/Controller Mr. Mitchell RADFORD
08 Director of Library Dr. Marie JONES
30 Director of Development Mr. Jeff JOYCE
19 Dir of Safety/Security/Risk Mgmt Mr. Stan JACOBSEN
41 Director of Athletics Ms. Myranda NASH
18 Director of Facilities/Grounds Mr. Burke ULREY
121 Director Academic Enrichment Ctr Ms. Shirley E. ARNOLD
36 Director of Career Exploration/Dev Ms. Nacole POTTS
92 Director of Honors Program Dr. Robert J. CABIN
38 Assoc Dean/Dir of Counseling Ms. Deanne DASBURG
57 Chair Division of Fine Arts Dr. Kathryn GRESHAM
79 Chair Division of Humanities Dr. Tom J. BELL
83 Chair Div of Social Sciences Dr. Laura VANCE
81 Chair Div Env Stds/Math/Nat Science Dr. Jennifer E. FRICK-RUPPERT
88 Chair Division of WLEE Dr. Jennifer L. KAFSKY
26 Director of Public Information Ms. Christie CAUBLE
39 Associate Dean of Housing/Res Life Mr. Michael COHEN
07 Director of Admissions & Fin Aid Mr. David VOLRATH
15 Director of Human Resources Mrs. Myra COOPER
09 Director of Institutional Research Mr. Scott NIKOLAI
29 Director Alumni Affairs Mr. David BORMAN

Cabarrus College of Health Sciences (D)

401 Medical Park Drive, Concord NC 28025-3959
County: Cabarrus FICE Identification: 006477
Unit ID: 198109
Telephone: (704) 403-1555 Carnegie Class: Spec-4-yr-Other Health
FAX Number: (704) 403-1764 Calendar System: Semester
URL: www.cabarruscollege.edu
Established: 1942 Annual Undergrad Tuition & Fees: $13,194
Enrollment: 453 Coed
Affiliation or Control: Independent Non-Profit IRS Status: 501(c)3
Highest Offering: Master's
Accreditation: SC, ADNUR, MAC, NURSE, OT, OTA, SURGT

01 Acting President Dr. Meg PATCHETT
05 Acting Provost Dr. Lisa ALLISON-JONES
32 Dean Student Affs/Enrollment Mgmt Ms. Christine L. CORSELLO
10 Chief Financial Officer Mr. David CANNON
66 ADN Program Chair Mrs. Kim PLEMMONS
88 OT Assistant Program Chair Ms. Nancy GREEN
88 Master OT Program Chair Dr. Nancy MURPHY
88 Medical Assisting Program Chair Ms. Rachel HOUSTON
88 Surgical Technology Program Chair Mrs. Michelle GAY
88 Medical Imagining Program Chair Mrs. Rhonda WEAVER
88 Associate in Science Program Chair Mrs. Zinat HASSANPOUR
88 Pharmacy Technology Program Chair Mrs. Annette SIMMONS
97 General Education Program Chair Mrs. Stacey WILSON
66 Dean of Nursing Dr. Delores BENN
88 Coord Campus & Community Outreach Mrs. Cara LURSEN
26 Coord of Marketing & Graduate Educ Mrs. Melanie GASS
37 Director of Financial Aid Mrs. Valerie RICHARD
06 Dir Student Records & Info Mgmt Mrs. Mary ELMORE
07 Director of Recruitment & Retention Mrs. Lorri B. CONNOR
04 Administrative Asst to President Mrs. Amy DRY
08 Head Librarian Mrs. Cassie DIXON

Campbell University (E)

PO Box 127, Buies Creek NC 27506-0097
County: Harnett FICE Identification: 002913
Unit ID: 198136
Telephone: (910) 893-1200 Carnegie Class: DU-Mod
FAX Number: (910) 893-1424 Calendar System: Semester
URL: www.campbell.edu
Established: 1887 Annual Undergrad Tuition & Fees: $32,500
Enrollment: 6,604 Coed
Affiliation or Control: Baptist IRS Status: 501(c)3
Highest Offering: Doctorate
Accreditation: SC, ACBSP, ARCPA, #CAATE, CACREP, CAEP, LAW, NURSE, OSTEO, PH, PHAR, PTA, SW, THEOL

00 Chancellor Dr. Jerry WALLACE
01 President Dr. J. Bradley CREED
03 Executive Vice President Dr. John ROBERSON
05 Vice Pres Academic Affs & Provost Dr. Mark HAMMOND
111 Vice President for Advancement Mr. Britt DAVIS
32 Vice President for Student Life Dr. Dennis BAZEMORE
84 Vice Pres Enrollment Management Vacant
07 Asst Vice Pres of Admissions Mr. Jason HALL
49 Dean of College of Arts & Science Dr. Michael WELLS
61 Dean of the Law School Mr. J. Rich LEONARD
50 Dean Lundy-Fetterman Sch Business Mr. Kevin O'MARA
53 Dean School of Education Dr. Karen NERY
67 Dean College of Pharmacy/Health Sci Dr. Michael ADAMS
63 Dean of Osteopathic Medical School Dr. John M. KAUFFMAN, JR.
54 Dean School of Engineering Dr. Jenna CARPENTER
35 Dean of Campus Life Vacant
06 Registrar Ms. Karen PORE
21 Assistant VP for Business Mr. Al HARDISON
29 AVP of Alumni Engagement Ms. Sarah SWAIN
08 Dean of Library Ms. Alexia RIGGS
37 Director of Financial Aid Ms. Mary OTTO
13 Int Director of Computing Services Mr. John R. SKUCE
26 AVP Communications/Marketing Ms. Haven HOTTEL
15 Director Human Resources Mr. Trent ELMORE
18 Chief Facilities/Physical Plant Mr. J. Scot PHILLIPS
38 Director Student Counseling Mrs. Laura RICH
96 Director of Purchasing Mr. Win QUAKENBUSH
92 Director of Honors Program Dr. Sherry TRUFFIN
09 Asst Provost for Inst Effectiveness Mrs. Maren HESS
106 Dean of Adult & Online Education Dr. Beth RUBIN
41 Interim Athletic Director Ms. Wanda WATKINS
43 Dir Legal Services/General Counsel Mr. Bob COGSWELL

Carolina Christian College (F)

PO Box 777, Winston-Salem NC 27102
County: Forsyth FICE Identification: 035703
Unit ID: 199971
Telephone: (336) 744-0900 Carnegie Class: Spec-4-yr-Faith
FAX Number: (336) 744-0901 Calendar System: Semester
URL: www.carolina.edu
Established: 1945 Annual Undergrad Tuition & Fees: $8,800
Enrollment: 42 Coed
Affiliation or Control: Independent Non-Profit IRS Status: 501(c)3
Highest Offering: Master's
Accreditation: BI

01 President Dr. LaTanya V. TYSON
05 VP of Academics/Graduate Studies Dr. Derrick THORPE
32 Dean of Students Mr. Tyrone TYSON
10 Chief Business Officer Ms. Amy BARNHART
08 Library Director Ms. Sarah TAYLOR
37 Financial Aid Director Ms. LaJada CREWS
06 Registrar Ms. Debra BRADSHAW
26 Chief Public Relations Officer Mr. MacArthur DAVIS
09 Director of Institutional Research Vacant

Carolina College of Biblical Studies (G)

817 S. McPherson Church Road, Fayetteville NC 28303
County: Cumberland FICE Identification: 041542
Unit ID: 461032
Telephone: (910) 323-5614 Carnegie Class: Spec-4-yr-Faith
FAX Number: (910) 323-0425 Calendar System: Quarter
URL: www.ccbs.edu
Established: 1973 Annual Undergrad Tuition & Fees: $6,320
Enrollment: 193 Coed
Affiliation or Control: Non-denominational IRS Status: 501(c)3
Highest Offering: Master's
Accreditation: BI

01 President Dr. Bill KORVER
05 Provost Dr. Chris DICKERSON
30 Vice Pres Strategic Development Dr. Bill BOYD
10 Vice Pres of Finance Ms. Aby CURLEY
84 VP Enrollment/Student Services Dr. Rodney PHILLIPS

Carolinas College of Health Sciences (H)

1200 Blythe Boulevard, Charlotte NC 28203
County: Mecklenburg FICE Identification: 031042
Unit ID: 433174
Telephone: (704) 355-5043 Carnegie Class: Spec 2-yr-Health
FAX Number: (704) 355-9336 Calendar System: Semester
URL: www.CarolinasCollege.edu
Established: 1990 Annual Undergrad Tuition & Fees (In-District): $13,932
Enrollment: 444 Coed
Affiliation or Control: State/Local IRS Status: 501(c)3
Highest Offering: Baccalaureate
Accreditation: SC, ADNUR, HT, MT, RAD, RTT

01 President Dr. T. Hampton HOPKINS
05 Provost Dr. Lori BEQUETTE
10 Dean Administrative/Financial Svcs Mr. David CANNON
32 Dean Student Affs/Enrollment Mgmt Dr. Karen LEWIS
06 Dir Student Records & Information Ms. Chrisanne RANCATI
30 Dir Development/Alumni Relations Ms. Ruthie MIHAL
07 Director Admissions & Recruitment Mr. Jameson DONNELL

37	Director Financial Aid	Ms. Kirstie CLARK
90	Director Teaching/Learning & Tech	Mr. Jared SMITH
09	Institutional Research Coordinator	Ms. Cheryl PULLIAM
04	Admin Assistant to President	Ms. Pat LEWIS

Catawba College (A)

2300 W Innes Street, Salisbury NC 28144-2488
County: Rowan FICE Identification: 002914
Unit ID: 198215
Telephone: (704) 637-4111 Carnegie Class: Bac-Diverse
FAX Number: (704) 637-4444 Calendar System: Semester
URL: www.catawba.edu
Established: 1851 Annual Undergrad Tuition & Fees: $30,520
Enrollment: 1,336 Coed
Affiliation or Control: United Church Of Christ IRS Status: 501(c)3
Highest Offering: Master's
Accreditation: SC, ACBSP, #CAATE, CAEPN

01	President	Mr. Brien LEWIS
42	Senior Vice President/Chaplain	Dr. Kenneth W. CLAPP
05	Provost	Dr. Constance ROGERS-LOWERY
30	VP of Development	Ms. Meg K. DEES
07	Vice Pres for Admissions	Ms. Elaine P. HOLDEN
04	Assistant to President	Mrs. Amy H. WILLIAMS
09	Dir Institutional Research	Ms. Steffanie WEST
10	Chief Financial Officer	Mr. Nelson MURPHY
15	Chief Human Resources Officer	Mr. Drew H. DAVIS
13	Chief Information Tech Officer	Ms. Joanna L. JASPER
32	Senior VP/Dean of Students	Mr. Jared TICE
88	Director of Student Conduct	Ms. Laura GILLAND
08	Library Director	Mr. Earl GIVENS
06	Registrar	Ms. Kim SMITH
37	Director of Financial Assistance	Ms. Kelli HAND
36	Director of Placement	Ms. Shelley TYLER-SMITH
88	Director Sports Info & Promotion	Mr. Jim D. LEWIS
40	Director Bookstore	Mrs. Stephanie TAYLOR
41	Athletic Director	Mr. Larry W. LECKONBY
18	Chief Facilities/Physical Plant	Ms. Frances F. TAYLOR
29	Director Alumni Relations	Ms. Erin STRINGER
19	Director Security/Safety	Mr. David NAJARIAN
44	Director Annual Giving	Ms. Mindy MILLER

Chamberlain University-Charlotte (B)

2015 Ayrsley Town Blvd, Ste 204, Charlotte NC 28273
Telephone: (980) 939-6241 Identification: 770979
Accreditation: &NH, NURSE

† Branch campus of Chamberlain University-Addison, Addison, IL

Charlotte Christian College and Theological Seminary (C)

PO Box 790106, Charlotte NC 28206-7901
County: Mecklenburg FICE Identification: 038273
Unit ID: 444778
Telephone: (704) 334-6882 Carnegie Class: Spec-4-yr-Faith
FAX Number: (704) 334-6885 Calendar System: Semester
URL: www.charlottechristian.edu
Established: 1996 Annual Undergrad Tuition & Fees: $10,368
Enrollment: 97 Coed
Affiliation or Control: Independent Non-Profit IRS Status: 501(c)3
Highest Offering: Doctorate
Accreditation: TRACS

01	President	Dr. Eddie G. GRIGG
05	Vice President of Academic Affairs	Dr. Adiaha STRANGE
32	Vice President of Student Affairs	Vacant
111	Director of Advancement	Vacant
06	Registrar/Dir International Student	Ms. Nancy RAY
08	Head Librarian	Ms. Kathryn HARMON
07	Director of Admissions	Mr. George SHEARS, III
10	Business Office Manager	Mr. Al WITT
37	Financial Aid Officer	Mr. Kenneth ROACH

Chowan University (D)

One University Place, Murfreesboro NC 27855-1844
County: Hertford FICE Identification: 002916
Unit ID: 198303
Telephone: (252) 398-6500 Carnegie Class: Bac-A&S
FAX Number: (252) 398-1190 Calendar System: Semester
URL: www.chowan.edu
Established: 1848 Annual Undergrad Tuition & Fees: $24,980
Enrollment: 1,503 Coed
Affiliation or Control: Baptist IRS Status: 501(c)3
Highest Offering: Master's
Accreditation: SC, MUS

01	President	Dr. Kirk E. PETERSON
05	Vice President Academic Affairs	Dr. Danny B. MOORE
20	Associate Provost Academic Affairs	Dr. John DILUSTRO
20	Assoc Provost External Relations	Dr. Brenda S. TINKHAM
10	Vice President Business Affairs	Mr. Danny R. DAVIS
21	Comptroller	Vacant
32	Vice President Student Affairs	Dr. Montrose STREETER
30	Vice President Development	Mr. John TAYLOE
15	Director of Human Resources	Mr. Timothy STEINROCK
07	Vice President Admissions	Ms. Kimberly BAILEY
13	Assistant VP Information Technology	Mr. James R. HOWELL
06	Registrar	Ms. Jennifer HUMPHREY
26	Director of Public Relations	Mrs. Brooke REICH
08	Head Librarian	Mrs. Georgia E. WILLIAMS
37	Director of Financial Aid	Ms. Ruth CASPER
42	Campus Minister	Ms. Mari E. WILES
18	Director Physical Plant	Vacant
19	Chief of Security	Mr. Derek A. BURKE
35	Director Student Life	Mr. Bradley CASH
36	Director Counseling/Career Services	Ms. Yolanda MAJETTE
39	Director Housing & Residence Life	Vacant
41	Athletics Director	Mr. Patrick M. MASHUDA
09	Director Institutional Research	Vacant
88	Director Upward Bound	Mr. E. Frank STEPHENSON
21	Director Business Services	Mrs. Julie W. EMORY
29	Director Alumni Services	Mrs. Kay M. THOMAS
49	Dean School of Arts and Sciences	Dr. Jennifer PLACE
50	Dean School of Business	Dr. Hunter TAYLOR
53	Dean School of Education	Dr. Ella E. BENSON
57	Dean School Fine and Applied Arts	Mrs. Christina RUPSCH
58	Dean School of Graduate Studies	Dr. John DILUSTRO
40	Bookstore Manager	Vacant

Daoist Traditions College of Chinese Medical Arts (E)

382 Montford Avenue, Asheville NC 28801
County: Buncombe FICE Identification: 041464
Unit ID: 455178
Telephone: (828) 225-3993 Carnegie Class: Spec-4-yr-Other Health
FAX Number: (828) 255-3306 Calendar System: Semester
URL: www.daoisttraditions.edu
Established: 2003 Annual Graduate Tuition & Fees: N/A
Enrollment: 84 Coed
Affiliation or Control: Proprietary IRS Status: Proprietary
Highest Offering: Doctorate; No Undergraduates
Accreditation: ACUP

01	President/Financial Director	Dr. Mary Cissy MAJEBE
04	Administrative Asst to President	Jennifer MOORE
07	Director of Admissions/Financial Ai	Juliet DANIEL

Davidson College (F)

PO Box 5000, Davidson NC 28035-5000
County: Mecklenburg FICE Identification: 002918
Unit ID: 198385
Telephone: (704) 894-2000 Carnegie Class: Bac-A&S
FAX Number: (704) 894-2005 Calendar System: Semester
URL: www.davidson.edu
Established: 1837 Annual Undergrad Tuition & Fees: $51,447
Enrollment: 1,810 Coed
Affiliation or Control: Independent Non-Profit IRS Status: 501(c)3
Highest Offering: Baccalaureate
Accreditation: SC

01	President	Dr. Carol E. QUILLEN
05	Vice Pres Acad Affs/Dean of Faculty	Dr. Philip N. JEFFERSON
26	Vice President College Relations	Ms. Eileen M. KEELEY
10	Vice Pres Finance & Administration	Vacant
32	VP Student Life/Dean of Students	Dr. Byron P. MCCRAE
07	VP & Dean Admissions/Financial Aid	Mr. Christopher J. GRUBER
09	VP Planning/Institutional Research	Ms. Linda M. LEFAUVE
43	VP and General Counsel	Ms. Sarah L. PHILLIPS
111	Exec Dir of Advancement Opers	Ms. Kim CLINE
20	Assoc Dean Academic Administration	Vacant
45	VP for Strategic Initiatives	Vacant
20	Assoc Dean of Faculty	Dr. Fuji P. LOZADA
30	Assoc VP of Development	Mr. Brad MARTIN
31	Assoc VP Campus/Community Relations	Ms. Stephanie GLASER
06	Registrar	Ms. Angela B. DEWBERRY
13	Chief Information Officer	Mr. Kevin DAVIS
37	Director Financial Aid	Mr. David GELINAS
15	Director of Human Resources	Dr. Kim BALL
41	Director of Athletics	Mr. Chris CLUNIE
08	Director of the Library	Ms. Lisa FORREST
29	Director Alumni Relations	Ms. Marya L. HOWELL
21	Controller/Director Business Svcs	Ms. Lori GASTON
18	Director Facilities & Engineering	Mr. David M. HOLTHOUSER
19	Chief of Campus Police	Mr. Todd D. SIGLER
36	Exec Dir Career Development	Mr. Jamie STAMEY
35	Director of College Union	Mr. Mike GOODE
39	Dir Resid Life/Assoc Dean Students	Mr. Jason S. SHAFFER
42	College Chaplain	Dr. Robert C. SPACH
88	Dir Ctr for Interdisciplinary Stds	Dr. Hilton KELLY
82	Assoc Dean Intl Programs/Studies	Dr. Jonathan BERKEY
25	Director of Grants & Contracts	Dr. Mary W. MUCHANE
24	Director of Digital Innovation	Ms. Kristen ESHLEMAN
38	Director Student Counseling Center	Vacant
44	Exec Dir of Engagement	Ms. Lisa H. COMBS
96	Director of Purchasing	Vacant
40	College Store General Manager	Mr. William T. REILLY
04	Executive Asst to President	Mrs. Traci L. RUSS-WILSON
27	Chief Comm and Marketing Officer	Mr. Mark JOHNSON

Duke University (G)

Durham NC 27706-8001
County: Durham FICE Identification: 002920
Unit ID: 198419
Telephone: (919) 684-8111 Carnegie Class: DU-Highest
FAX Number: (919) 684-3200 Calendar System: Semester
URL: www.duke.edu
Established: 1838 Annual Undergrad Tuition & Fees: $55,695
Enrollment: 16,130 Coed
Affiliation or Control: Independent Non-Profit IRS Status: 501(c)3
Highest Offering: Doctorate
Accreditation: SC, ANEST, ARCPA, CAEP, CAMPEP, CLPSY, DIETI, IPSY, LAW, MED, NURSE, PA, PAST, PCSAS, PTA, THEOL

01	President	Vincent PRICE
05	Provost	Sally KORNBLUTH
17	Chancellor for Health Affairs	A. Eugene WASHINGTON
11	Exec Vice Pres for Administration	Tallman TRASK, III
10	Vice President Financial Services	Timothy WALSH
15	Vice President for Administration	Kyle CAVANAUGH
07	Dean Undergraduate Admissions	Christoph O. GUTTENTAG
21	Exec Vice Provost Finance & Admin	Jennifer FRANCIS
13	Vice Prov Information Technology	Tracy FUTHEY
88	Vice Prov Interdisciplinary Studies	Edward BALLEISEN
88	Vice Provost Faculty Advancement	Abbas BENMAMOUN
46	Vice Provost for Research	Lawrence CARIN
88	Vice Prov Innov/Entrepreneurship	Eric TOONE
08	Librarian/Vice Prov Library Affairs	Deborah JAKUBS
37	Asst Vice Provost/Dir Financial Aid	Alison RABIL
65	Dean Sch of the Environment	Toddi R. STEELMAN
61	Dean of Law School	David F. LEVI
63	Dn Sch Med/Sr Vice Chanc Acad Affs	Mary E. KLOTMAN
50	Dean Fuqua School of Business	William BOULDING
73	Dean of the Divinity School	L. Gregory JONES
58	Dean Grad Sch/Vice Prov Grad Educ	Paula D. MCCLAIN
49	Dean Faculty Arts/Science	Valerie ASHBY
66	Dean School of Nursing	Marion BROOME
54	Dean of Engineering	Ravi BELLAMKONDA
88	Dean Sanford Sch of Public Policy	Judith KELLEY
88	Director Duke University Press	Dean SMITH
18	Vice President for Facilities	John NOONAN
06	Registrar	Frank BLALARK
09	Director of Institutional Research	David JAMIESON-DRAKE
04	Executive Asst to the President	Lisa JORDAN
101	VP and University Secretary	Richard RIDDELL
102	Asst VP Foundation Relations	Beth EASTLICK
105	Senior Manager Web Services	Ryn NASSER
22	Vice President Institutional Equity	Kimberly HEWITT
26	Chief Public Relations/Marketing	Michael SCHOENFELD
29	Director Alumni Relations	Sterly WILDER
32	Vice President Student Affairs	Mary Pat MCMAHON
36	Director Career Center	William WRIGHT-SWADEL
41	VP and Director Athletics	Kevin WHITE
43	Vice President and General Counsel	Pamela BERNARD
44	Asst VP Annual Giving	Jennifer SPISAK-CAMERON
53	Vice Provost Undergraduate Educ	Gary BENNETT
86	Assoc VP Federal Relations	Christopher SIMMONS
96	Assoc VP Procurement	Jane PLEASANTS
104	Executive Director Global Education	Amanda KELSO
30	VP Alumni Affairs/Development	David KENNEDY

ECPI University-Charlotte (H)

4800 Airport Center Pkwy #100, Charlotte NC 28208
Telephone: (704) 399-1010 Identification: 770951
Accreditation: &SC, MAAB

† Branch campus of ECPI University, Virginia Beach, VA

ECPI University-Greensboro (I)

7802 Airport Center Drive, Greensboro NC 27409
Telephone: (336) 792-7594 Identification: 770952
Accreditation: &SC, MAAB

† Branch campus of ECPI University, Virginia Beach, VA

ECPI University-Raleigh (J)

4101 Doie Cope Road, Raleigh NC 27613
Telephone: (919) 283-5748 Identification: 770953
Accreditation: &SC, MAAB

† Branch campus of ECPI University, Virginia Beach, VA

Elon University (K)

2700 Campus Box, Elon NC 27244-2010
County: Alamance FICE Identification: 002927
Unit ID: 198516
Telephone: (336) 278-2000 Carnegie Class: DU-Mod
FAX Number: N/A Calendar System: 4/1/4
URL: www.elon.edu
Established: 1889 Annual Undergrad Tuition & Fees: $35,319
Enrollment: 6,791 Coed
Affiliation or Control: Independent Non-Profit IRS Status: 501(c)3
Highest Offering: Doctorate
Accreditation: SC, ARCPA, CAEPN, JOUR, LAW, PTA

01	President	Dr. Connie LEDOUX BOOK
05	Provost/Exec VP Academic Affairs	Dr. Steven D. HOUSE
100	Chief of Staff/Sec to the Board	Mr. Jeff STEIN
07	VP of Admissions/Financial Planning	Mr. Greg ZAISER
10	SVP Bus/Fin/Tech & Sp Asst to Pres	Mr. Gerald O. WHITTINGTON
111	Vice Pres University Advancement	Mr. James B. PIATT
32	Vice Pres/Dean of Student Life	Dr. Jon DOOLEY
26	Vice Pres University Communications	Mr. Daniel J. ANDERSON
21	VP for Business/Finance/Tech	Mr. Bob SHEA
108	Assoc Prov Curriculum & Assessment	Dr. Maurice LEVESQUE

27 Asst Provost for Comm & Operations .... Dr. Paul MILLER
20 Int Assoc Prov Acad Excellence .... Dr. Maureen VANDERMAAS-PEELER
20 Sr Assoc Provost for Faculty Affs .... Dr. Tim PEEPLES
21 Asst VP for Business and Finance .... Ms. Susan M. KIRKLAND
49 Dean College of Arts & Sci .... Dr. Gabie SMITH
50 Dean Love School of Business .... Dr. Raghu TADEPALLI
60 Dean of School of Communications .... Dr. Rochelle FORD
53 Dean of School of Education .... Dr. Ann BULLOCK
61 Dean of School of Law .... Mr. Luke BIERMAN
76 Dean of School of Health Sciences .... Dr. Becky NEIDUSKI
85 Dean of Global Studies .... Mr. Woody PELTON
35 Associate VP of Student Life .... Mrs. Jana Lynn F. PATTERSON
08 Dean and University Librarian .... Ms. Joan RUELLE
41 Director of Athletics .... Mr. Dave L. BLANK
06 Registrar .... Dr. Rodney PARKS
42 University Chaplain .... Dr. Janet FULLER
37 Director of Financial Planning .... Dr. M. Patrick MURPHY
29 Sr Dir of Alumni Engagement .... Mr. Brian FEELEY
121 Assoc Dean of Academic Support .... Dr. Becky OLIVE-TAYLOR
36 Exec Director of Std Prof Dev Ctr .... Mr. Tom BRINKLEY
88 Dir of Planning/Design/Construction .... Mr. Brad D. MOORE
18 Asst VP of Physical Plant .... Mr. Tom FLOOD
15 Exec Director of Human Resources .... Vacant
109 Director of Auxiliary Services .... Ms. Carrie RYAN
19 Director Campus Safety/Police .... Mr. Dennis FRANKS
23 Dir Student Health/Univ Physician .... Dr. Ginette ARCHINAL
38 Director Counseling Services .... Ms. Marie SHAW
11 Assistant VP for Admin Svcs .... Mr. Christopher D. FULKERSON
09 Exec Director Institutional Rsch .... Dr. Robert I. SPRINGER
13 Assistant VP for Technology and CIO .... Mr. Christopher C. WATERS
25 Director of Sponsored Programs .... Ms. Bonnie BRUNO
22 Assoc VP for Inclusive Excellence .... Dr. Randy WILLIAMS
92 Director of Honors Program .... Dr. Lynn HUBER
94 Director Women's Stds/Gender Stds .... Dr. Sarah GLASCO
96 Director of Purchasing .... Mr. Jeff HENDRICKS
88 Director of Sustainability .... Ms. Elaine DURR
04 Admin Assistant to the President .... Dr. Smith JACKSON
101 Secretary of the Institution/Board .... Mr. Patrick NOLTEMEYER
102 Director Foundation/Corporate Rels .... Ms. Sylvia DURANT
104 Director Study Abroad .... Ms. Rhonda WALLER
28 Director of Diversity .... Ms. Leigh-Anne ROYSTER
30 Director of Development .... Mr. Brian BAKER
39 Director Residence Life .... Ms. MarQuita BARKER
44 Director Annual Giving .... Mr. Steve CODNER

Gardner-Webb University (A)

PO Box 897 (110 South Main Street), Boiling Springs NC 28017-0897

County: Cleveland | FICE Identification: 002929 | Unit ID: 198561
Telephone: (704) 406-2361 | Carnegie Class: DU-Mod
FAX Number: (704) 406-4329 | Calendar System: Semester
URL: www.gardner-webb.edu
Established: 1905 | Annual Undergrad Tuition & Fees: $32,000
Enrollment: 3,818 | Coed
Affiliation or Control: Baptist | IRS Status: 501(c)3
Highest Offering: Doctorate
Accreditation: SC, ACBSP, ADNUR, #ARCPA, #CAATE, CACREP, CAEPN, EXSC, MUS, NUR, THEOL

01 President .... Dr. William M. DOWNS
05 Provost & Executive Vice President .... Dr. Benjamin C. LESLIE
04 Sr Assistant to the President .... Mrs. Stephanie L. STEARNS
11 Vice President for Administration .... Mr. Mike W. HARDIN
26 VP of Marketing .... Mr. Richard K. MCDEVITT
111 VP for External Affairs/Advancement .... Mr. H. Woodrow FISH
32 Vice Pres Student Development .... Ms. Sarah CURRIE
84 Vice Pres Enrollment Management .... Ms. Kristen SETZER
41 Vice President for Athletics .... Mr. Chuck S. BURCH
45 VP Planning & Inst Effectiveness .... Dr. Jeffrey L. TUBBS
18 Assoc Vice Pres for Operations .... Mr. Wayne E. JOHNSON
13 Assoc VP for Technology Services .. Mr. Gregory G. HUMPHRIES
20 Assoc Provost Prof/Graduate Studies .... Dr. Bruce BOYLES
49 Assoc Provost for Arts & Sciences .... Dr. David YELTON
21 Assoc VP for Business & Finance .... Ms. Robin G. HAMRICK
07 Assoc VP for Undergrad Admissions .... Ms. Annie FREEMAN
37 Asst VP for Financial Planning .... Ms. Anita ELLIOTT
06 Registrar- .... Mrs. LouAnn P. SCATES
20 Assoc Provost Academic Development .... Ms. Carmen BUTLER
19 Chief of University Police .... Mr. Barry JOHNSON
27 Assoc VP for Marketing/Comm .... Mr. Noel T. MANNING
08 Director of the Library .... Ms. Pam DENNIS
38 Director of Counseling Services .... Ms. Cindy WALLACE
89 Director of Freshmen Programs .... Ms. Jessica HERRNDON
58 Dean of Graduate School .... Dr. Elizabeth PACK
73 Dean of Divinity School .... Dr. Robert W. CANOY
66 Dean of Nursing School .... Dr. Nicole WATERS
92 Director of Honors Program .... Dr. Thomas H. JONES
88 Director Program for Blind/Deaf .... Mrs. Cheryl J. POTTER
21 Comptroller .... Ms. Haley KENDRICK
35 Director Student Activities .... Mr. Brian ARNOLD
42 Minister to the University .... Dr. Tracy C. JESSUP
39 Director of Residence Life .... Mr. John R. JOHNSON, JR.
50 Dean of Business School .... Ms. Mischia TAYLOR
15 Director Human Resources .... Mr. W. Scott WHITE
09 Director of Institutional Research .... Ms. Lisa KINDLER
29 Director Alumni Relations .... Mrs. Leah CLEVENGER
44 Director of Annual Campaign .... Ms. Sara MCCALL
27 Asst Dir University Media Relations .... Vacant
40 Bookstore Manager .... Ms. Cary CALDWELL

109 Director of Operations Support .... Mr. Brian SPEER
102 Dir Foundation/Corporate Relations .... Mr. Aaron HINTON
103 Director Workforce Development .... Mr. Micah MARTIN
106 Director of Digital Learning .... Dr. Emily ROBERTSON
108 Director Institutional Assessment .... Dr. Lucas STERN
28 Director of Diversity .... Mrs. Jackie LEACH
53 Dean School of Education .... Dr. Prince BULL

Grace College of Divinity (B)

5117 Cliffdale Road, Fayetteville NC 28314

County: Cumberland | FICE Identification: 041737 | Unit ID: 461528
Telephone: (910) 221-2224 | Carnegie Class: Spec-4-yr-Faith
FAX Number: N/A | Calendar System: Semester
URL: www.gcd.edu
Established: 2000 | Annual Undergrad Tuition & Fees: $6,100
Enrollment: 144 | Coed
Affiliation or Control: Other Protestant | IRS Status: 501(c)3
Highest Offering: Baccalaureate
Accreditation: BI

01 President .... Dr. Steven CROWTHER
11 Vice President of Administration .... Ms. Cathy LUCAS
05 Academic Dean .... Mr. Ron MCBRIDE
84 Dean of Enrollment Management .... Mr. John MCINTYRE
32 Dean of Students .... Mrs. Stefanie ERTEL
106 Dean of Online Education/E-Learning .... Mr. Tom JOHNSON
10 Chief Financial Officer .... Ms. Omayra COON
30 Director of Development .... Ms. Diane SHARP
08 Librarian .... Mr. David ASPINALL
108 Director of Assessment & Planning .... Ms. Sharyn J. TEAGUE
06 Registrar .... Ms. Nakiya SMITH

Grace Communion Seminary (C)

3120 Whitehall Park Drive, Charlotte NC 28273-3335

County: Mecklenburg | Identification: 667115
Telephone: (980) 495-3978 | Carnegie Class: Not Classified
FAX Number: (844) 350-3419 | Calendar System: Semester
URL: www.gcs.edu
Established: 2008 | Annual Graduate Tuition & Fees: N/A
Enrollment: N/A | Coed
Affiliation or Control: Independent Non-Profit | IRS Status: 501(c)3
Highest Offering: Master's; No Undergraduates
Accreditation: DEAC

01 President/CEO .... Dr. Gary DEDDO
05 Dean of Faculty .... Dr. Michael MORRISON
06 Registrar .... Ms. Georgia MCKINNON
10 CFO/Liaison Officer .... Dr. Russell DUKE

Greensboro College (D)

815 W Market Street, Greensboro NC 27401-1875

County: Guilford | FICE Identification: 002930 | Unit ID: 198598
Telephone: (336) 272-7102 | Carnegie Class: Bac-Diverse
FAX Number: (336) 217-6634 | Calendar System: Semester
URL: www.greensboro.edu
Established: 1838 | Annual Undergrad Tuition & Fees: $29,140
Enrollment: 1,081 | Coed
Affiliation or Control: United Methodist | IRS Status: 501(c)3
Highest Offering: Master's
Accreditation: SC, ACBSP, MUS

00 Chairman of the Board .... Mr. Kevin GREEN
01 President .... Dr. Lawrence D. CZARDA
04 Exec Asst to President/Clerk to BoT .... Ms. Susan J. BARRINGER
05 Senior VP Chief Academic Officer .... Dr. Paul L. LESLIE
11 Exec VP Chief Operations Officer .... Dr. Robin L. DANIEL
10 VP Chief Financial Officer .... Mr. Chris ELMORE
111 VP Chief Advancement Officer .... Ms. Anne J. HURD
20 Assoc VP Academic Admin .... Ms. Martha M. BUNCH
20 Dean of the Faculty .... Dr. Richard A. MAYES
57 Dean School of Arts .... Dr. David SCHRAM
50 Dean School of Business .... Dr. William K. MACREYNOLDS
53 Dean School of Soc Sci & Education .... Dr. Rebecca BLOMGREN
79 Dean School of Humanities .... Dr. Daniel MALOTKY
81 Dean School of Science & Mathematic .... Dr. Jessica G. SHARPE
07 Dean of Admissions .... Ms. Julianne SCHATZ
13 Asst VP Information Technology .... Dr. Larry BURTON
37 Financial Aid Director .... Ms. Lindsay S. LATHAM
113 Student Accounts Director .... Ms. Marilyn WOODS
26 Communications Director .... Mr. Lex ALEXANDER
26 Marketing Director .... Mr. Tom SAITTA
06 Registrar .... Mr. Travis MICKEY
32 Dean of Students .... Ms. Shana PLASTERS
39 Residence Life Coordinator .... Ms. Megan WHITCOMB
89 First Year Experience Director .... Ms. Jenna AVENT
36 Career Services Director .... Ms. Caryn ATWATER
104 Study Abroad Director .... Ms. Georgiann BOGDAN
09 Institutional Research Director .... Mr. Travis MICKEY
108 Director Institutional Assessment .... Ms. Patricia ALBERT
121 Academic Success Director .... Ms. Tica D. GREEN
124 Student Retention Director .... Ms. D'andre HARDY
15 Human Resources Director .... Ms. Sonia HOFFMAN
18 Facilities Director .... Mr. Justin LISZKA
19 Security Director .... Mr. Calvin L. GILMORE
23 Student Health Director .... Ms. Lauren T. CHILDREY
38 Counseling Services Director .... Ms. Emily HOLMES
92 George Ctr/Honors Studies Director .... Mr. Neill CLEGG

30 Asst VP Development .... Ms. Ellie P. YEARNS
29 Alumni Engagement Director .... Ms. Kaleigh HEMSTOCK
08 Library Director .... Mr. Will RITTER
41 Interim Athletic Director .... Dr. Robin L. DANIEL
42 Campus Chaplain .... Rev. Robert W. BREWER
40 Bookstore Manager .... Mr. Cliff BRALY, JR.
21 Controller .... Ms. Michelle STILES
88 Title IX Coordinator .... Ms. Emily SCOTT

Guilford College (E)

5800 W Friendly Avenue, Greensboro NC 27410-4173

County: Guilford | FICE Identification: 002931 | Unit ID: 198613
Telephone: (336) 316-2000 | Carnegie Class: Bac-A&S
FAX Number: (336) 316-2950 | Calendar System: Semester
URL: www.guilford.edu
Established: 1837 | Annual Undergrad Tuition & Fees: $37,120
Enrollment: 1,680 | Coed
Affiliation or Control: Friends | IRS Status: 501(c)3
Highest Offering: Master's
Accreditation: SC, ACBSP

01 President .... Dr. Jane K. FERNANDES
05 Provost/Academic Dean .... Dr. Frank BOYD
100 Chief of Staff .... Ms. Erin BROWNLEE DELL
10 Vice Pres Finance/Administration .... Mr. Len SIPPEL
26 Vice Pres Marketing/Enrollment .... Mr. Roger DEGERMAN
111 Vice Pres Advancement .... Mr. Ara SERJOIE
22 VP Diversity/Equity/Inclusion .... Dr. Barbara LAWRENCE
29 Assoc VP Alumni/Constituent Rels .... Mr. R. Ty BUCKNER
28 Assoc VP Diversity/Equity/Inclusion .... Dr. Krishauna HINES-GAITHER
32 Assoc Dean of Students .... Mr. Steven MENCARINI
20 Associate Academic Dean .... Dr. Kathryn SHIELDS
20 Associate Academic Dean .... Dr. Kyle DELL
37 Director Student Financial Svcs .... Vacant
06 Registrar .... Mr. Alfred MOORE
08 Director of the Library .... Ms. Suzanne M. BARTELS
41 Director of Athletics .... Ms. Susan BOWER
19 Director of Public Safety .... Mr. William ANDERSON
15 Director Human Resources .... Ms. Alisa QUICK
09 Dir Inst Research/Assessment .... Dr. Stephanie HARGRAVE
13 Director Info Technology & Services .... Mr. Chuck CURRY, JR.
42 WR Rogers Dir of Friends Center .... Dr. C. Wess DANIELS
38 Director Student Counseling .... Mr. Keilan RICKARD
92 Director Honors Program .... Dr. Heather HAYTON
96 Director of Purchasing .... Ms. Tracy A. HALL
104 Director Study Abroad .... Mr. Daniel DIAZ
04 Executive Coordinator .... Ms. Rachel WIESELQUIST
44 Director Annual Giving .... Ms. Kellie DENTLER

Heritage Bible College (F)

PO Box 1628, Dunn NC 28335-1628

County: Harnett | FICE Identification: 030893 | Unit ID: 198677
Telephone: (910) 892-3178 | Carnegie Class: Spec-4-yr-Faith
FAX Number: (910) 491-9790 | Calendar System: Semester
URL: www.heritagebiblecollege.edu
Established: 1971 | Annual Undergrad Tuition & Fees: $8,328
Enrollment: 42 | Coed
Affiliation or Control: Other | IRS Status: 501(c)3
Highest Offering: Baccalaureate
Accreditation: TRACS

01 President .... Dr. Randy BARKER
05 Academic Dean .... Mr. Stephen RZONCA
32 Dean Student Services .... Vacant
06 Registrar .... Mr. Stephen RZONCA
10 Business Administrator .... Mrs. LeAnne PAGE
108 Director of Inst Effectiveness .... Ms. Janet PARKER
37 Director of Financial Aid/Admission . Mr. Sterling THARRINGTON
13 Chief Info Technology Officer (CIO) .... Mr. Wesley JOHNSON

High Point University (G)

One University Parkway, High Point NC 27268-0001

County: Guilford | FICE Identification: 002933 | Unit ID: 198695
Telephone: (336) 841-9000 | Carnegie Class: Bac-Diverse
FAX Number: (336) 841-4599 | Calendar System: Semester
URL: www.highpoint.edu
Established: 1924 | Annual Undergrad Tuition & Fees: $35,118
Enrollment: 4,951 | Coed
Affiliation or Control: United Methodist | IRS Status: 501(c)3
Highest Offering: Doctorate
Accreditation: SC, #ARCPA, ART, CAATE, CAEP, CIDA, @PHAR, @PTA

01 President .... Dr. Nido R. QUBEIN
05 Provost .... Dr. Dennis G. CARROLL
10 Sr VP for Business Affairs .... Mr. Brad CALLOWAY
84 Sr VP for Enrollment .... Mr. Andy BILLS
26 Sr VP for Communications .... Mr. Roger D. CLODFELTER, JR.
32 Sr VP for Student Life .... Mrs. Gail C. TUTTLE
30 Sr VP for Development .... Mr. Christopher H. DUDLEY
46 VP for Research and Planning .... Dr. Jeffrey M. ADAMS
18 VP for Facilities & Auxiliary Svcs .... Mr. Stephen L. POTTER
10 VP for Financial Affairs .... Ms. Debi S. BUTT
88 VP for Exp Learning & Career Dev .... Dr. Stephanie O. CROFTON
07 VP for Undergrad Admissions .... Mr. Kerr C. RAMSAY
13 VP for Enterprise IT .... Mr. Curtis BARKER

41 VP for Athletics and AD Mr. Dan HAUSER
31 VP for Community Relations Mr. Barry S. KITLEY
123 Assoc VP of Graduate Admissions Mr. Andrew S. MODLIN
35 Asst VP for Student Life Dr. Tara K. SHOLLENBERGER
35 Asst VP for Student Life Mr. Scott WOJCIECHOWSKI
35 Asst VP for Student Life Ms. Erica D. LEWIS
88 Asst VP for Graduate Admissions Mr. Lars C. FARABEE
24 Asst VP for Communication Mgt Ms. Hillary C. KOKAJKO
27 Asst VP for Communications Ms. Pamela J. HAYNES
30 Asst VP for Development Mr. McKennon SHEA
88 Asst VP for Facility Operations Mr. Troy J. THOMPSON
49 Dean of College of Arts & Science Dr. Carole B. STONEKING
57 Dean of School of Art and Design Dr. John C. TURPIN
50 Dean of School of Business Dr. James B. WEHRLEY
60 Dean of School of Communication Dr. Virginia M. MCDERMOTT
53 Dean of School of Education Dr. Mariann W. TILLERY
54 Dean of the School of Engineering Dr. Michael OUDSHOORN
76 Dean of School of Health Sciences Dr. Daniel E. ERB
81 Dean of School of Natural Sciences Dr. Angela C. BAUER
67 Dean of School of Pharmacy Dr. Earl W. LINGLE
20 Assistant Dean Academic Services Ms. Karen C. NAYLON
08 Director of Library Services Mr. David L. BRYDEN
23 Medical Director Dr. Marnie S. MARLETTE
19 Chief of Security Mr. Jeff A. KARPOVICH
06 Registrar Mr. Danny K. BROOKS
15 Sr Director of Human Resources Mr. Marc SEARS
88 Sr Director of University Events Ms. Melissa L. ANDERSON
29 Director of Alumni Engagement Mr. Bradley G. TAYLOR
37 Dir of Student Financial Planning Mr. Ronald ELMORE
25 Director of Sponsored Programs Ms. Leanna NICKS
38 Director of Counseling Services Dr. M.J RALEIGH
09 Dir of Inst Research & Assessment Mr. James S. LOWREY
113 Assoc Director of Student Accounts Ms. Megan INCH
96 Mgr Contracts & Procurement Mr. Gene BUNTING
40 Manager Bookstore Mr. William HOLSTON
85 Director of International Students Ms. Marjorie R. CHURCH
36 Director of Career Development Dr. William A. GENTRY
104 Director of Global Education Dr. Jeffrey M. PALIS
88 Director of Service Learning Dr. Joseph D. BLOSSER
88 Director of Undergraduate Research Dr. Joanne D. ALTMAN
04 Admin Assistant to President Ms. Judy K. RAY
88 Manager of University Mail Center Mr. Michael R. HALL

Hood Theological Seminary (A)

1810 Lutheran Synod Drive, Salisbury NC 28144-5768
County: Rowan FICE Identification: 036633
Unit ID: 443076
Telephone: (704) 636-7611 Carnegie Class: Spec-4-yr-Faith
FAX Number: (704) 636-7699 Calendar System: Semester
URL: www.hoodseminary.edu
Established: 1904 Annual Undergrad Tuition & Fees: N/A
Enrollment: 142 Coed
Affiliation or Control: African Methodist Episcopal Zion Church
IRS Status: 501(c)3
Highest Offering: Doctorate
Accreditation: THEOL

01 President Dr. Vergel L. LATTIMORE
05 Academic Dean Dr. Trevor EPPEHIMER
32 Dean of Students Dr. Dora R. MBUWAYESANGO
10 Chief Financial Officer Rev.Dr. Regina M. DANCY
26 Dir Communication/Info/Pub Ms. Kelly BRYANT
111 Dir Institutional Advancement Mr. John C. EVERETT
06 Registrar Ms. Nancy BAKER
15 Director Human Resources RevDr. Regina M. DANCY
19 Chief of Security Mr. James MILTON
07 Director of Admissions Rev.Dr. Reginald BOYD
08 Director of the Library Ms. Patricia COMMANDER
37 Director Student Financial Aid Ms. Angela DAVIS-BAXTER

Hosanna Bible College (B)

3519 Fayetteville St, Durham NC 27707
County: Durham Identification: 667373
Telephone: (919) 267-1640 Carnegie Class: Not Classified
FAX Number: (888) 392-4968 Calendar System: Semester
URL: www.hosannabc.org
Established: 1992 Annual Undergrad Tuition & Fees: N/A
Enrollment: N/A Coed
Affiliation or Control: Independent Non-Profit IRS Status: 501(c)3
Highest Offering: Doctorate
Accreditation: @TRACS

01 President Dr. John T. CHAPMAN
05 Provost Dr. Shannon R. TRIBBLE

Johnson & Wales University-Charlotte (C)

801 W Trade Street, Charlotte NC 28202-1122
Telephone: (980) 598-1000 Identification: 666375
Accreditation: &EH

† Regional accreditation is carried under the parent institution in Providence, RI.

Johnson C. Smith University (D)

100 Beatties Ford Road, Charlotte NC 28216-5398
County: Mecklenburg FICE Identification: 002936
Unit ID: 198756
Telephone: (704) 378-1000 Carnegie Class: Bac-A&S
FAX Number: (704) 372-1242 Calendar System: Semester
URL: www.jcsu.edu
Established: 1867 Annual Undergrad Tuition & Fees: $18,236
Enrollment: 1,483 Coed
Affiliation or Control: Independent Non-Profit IRS Status: 501(c)3
Highest Offering: Master's
Accreditation: SC, LC, SW

01 President Mr. Clarence (Clay) D. ARMBRISTER
10 Vice Pres for Finance Mr. Greg PETZKE
111 Vice President for Inst Advancement Ms. Tami SIMMONS
86 VP Government Sponsored Pgms Dr. Diane BOWLES
15 VP Administrative Services/CHRO Ms. Latrelle P. MCALLISTER
81 Dean of STEM Vacant
49 Dean of Arts and Letters Dr. Brian JONES
70 Dean of School of Social Work Dr. Helen CALDWELL
32 Dean of Students Mr. Takeem DEAN
89 Associate Dean of First-Year Exper Dr. Cathy JONES
88 Dean of the University College Dr. Antonio HENLEY
107 Dean Metro College Prof Studies Dr. Laura MCLEAN
121 Dean of Academic Support Services Mr. John NORRIS
08 Director of the Library Ms. Monika RHUE
07 Director of Admissions Mr. Vory BILLUPS
13 Director Information Technology Mr. John NORRIS
09 Dir Plng/Assess/Effect/Rsrch Mrs. Sharell CANNADY
26 Director of Comm and Marketing Ms. Sherri BELFIELD
29 Director Alumni Affairs Mrs. Wanda FOY-BURROUGHS
37 Director Financial Aid Ms. Shelline WARREN
41 Athletic Director Mr. Stephen JOYNER, SR.
06 Registrar Mrs. Keisha WILSON
39 Coordinator of Housing Services Ms. Ashley SMITH
40 Manager of Bookstore Ms. Robin SORENSEN
117 Manager Risk Management Mrs. Debra HOLLIS
23 Health Center Coordinator Ms. Marian JONES
19 Director Security/Safety Mr. Jermaine CHERRY

Lees-McRae College (E)

191 Main Street, Banner Elk NC 28604-0128
County: Avery FICE Identification: 002939
Unit ID: 198808
Telephone: (828) 898-5241 Carnegie Class: Bac-Diverse
FAX Number: (828) 898-8814 Calendar System: Semester
URL: www.lmc.edu
Established: 1900 Annual Undergrad Tuition & Fees: $25,878
Enrollment: 921 Coed
Affiliation or Control: Presbyterian Church (U.S.A.) IRS Status: 501(c)3
Highest Offering: Master's
Accreditation: SC, NURSE

01 President Dr. Herbert L. KING
04 Secretary to the President Ms. Vicki FOSTER
05 Provost & Dean of Faculty Dr. Todd LIDH
10 VP Finance/Business Affairs Mr. Jon KOKOS
32 Dean of Students Mr. Justin KITTS
45 VP Strategic Planning/Effectiveness Mr. Blaine J. HANSEN
41 VP Athletics/Club Sports Mr. Craig MCPHAIL
84 VP Enrollment Management Ms. Erin HEALEY
111 VP for Institutional Advancement Mr. Edward ROBERTS
66 Dean Nursing/Health Sciences Dr. Kimberly S. PRIODE
79 Dean Arts/Humanities/Education Dr. Pamela VESELY
81 Dean Natural & Behavioral Sciences Dr. Billy CARVER
50 Dean Business & Management Ms. Amy ANDERSON
111 Director of Advancement Services Ms. Mary TAYLOR
121 Dir Burton Ctr for Student Success Ms. Keri MAGANA
08 Director Libraries Ms. Jess BELLEMER
06 Registrar Ms. Lynn HINSHAW
19 Director Security/Safety Mr. H.D STEWART
13 Director Technology Services Mr. Ben HOLTSCLAW
15 Director Human Resources Ms. Mary FURST
21 Controller Ms. Susan STEPHENSON
35 Associate Dean of Students Ms. Kelsey TAYLOR
26 Director Marketing & Design Ms. Lauren FOSTER
07 Director Admissions Ms. Beverly HAGUE
37 Director Financial Aid Ms. Cathy SHELL
36 Director Career Services Ms. Laura PELL
38 Director Counseling Services Ms. Marla GENTILE
113 Bursar Ms. Rachel FREDERICK
23 Director of Health Services Mr. Carl GRIEWISCH
121 Director of Tutoring Services Ms. Sue MCGUIRE
112 Major Gifts Officer Mr. Samuel STEPHENSON

Lenoir-Rhyne University (F)

625 7th Avenue NE, Hickory NC 28601-3984
County: Catawba FICE Identification: 002941
Unit ID: 198835
Telephone: (828) 328-1741 Carnegie Class: Masters/L
FAX Number: (828) 328-7368 Calendar System: Semester
URL: www.lr.edu
Established: 1891 Annual Undergrad Tuition & Fees: $36,400
Enrollment: 2,557 Coed
Affiliation or Control: Evangelical Lutheran Church In America
IRS Status: 501(c)3
Highest Offering: Master's
Accreditation: SC, ACBSP, #ARCPA, CAATE, CACREP, DIETI, NURSE, OT, PH, THEOL

01 President Dr. Fred WHITT
05 Provost Dr. Gary JOHNSON
10 Sr Vice President Finance/Admin Mr. Peter KENDALL
111 Vice Pres Institutional Advancement Mrs. Catherine NIEKRO
84 Vice President for Enrollment Mgmt Ms. Rachel NICHOLS
32 Asst Provost/Dean of Students Dr. Katie FISHER
104 Assoc Dean Global Learning Ms. Charlotte WILLIAMS
58 Dean Grad Studies/Lifelong Learning Dr. Amy WOOD
06 Registrar Mr. Stacey BRACKETT
08 Librarian Mr. Frank QUINN
15 Director of Human Resources Mr. Rick NICHOLS
40 Director of Bookstore Ms. Lucy MANZANARES
18 Director of Facilities/Plant Mr. Otis PITTS
41 Athletic Director Ms. Kim PATE
42 Campus Pastor Rev. Andrew WEISNER
19 Director of Security Mr. Norris YODER
92 Director of Honors Program Dr. Joshua RING
13 Interim Chief Information Officer Mr. Anthony WILLIAMS
26 Dir of Marketing/Communication Vacant
88 Director of Conferences & Events Ms. Janet MATTHEWS
07 Director of Enrollment Services Mr. Eric BRANDON
09 Dir of Inst Research/Assess Dr. Debra TEMPLETON
37 Director Student Financial Aid Ms. Courtney THOMPSON-BALLARD
38 Dir Student Counseling/Placement Ms. Jenny SMITH
88 Dir Liberal Arts/Visiting Writers Dr. Rand BRANDES
28 Director Multicultural Affairs Ms. Emma SELLERS
88 Institute on Obesity Ms. Kimberly PENNINGTON
65 Institute on Conservation Dr. John BRZORAD
85 Dir of International Programs Dr. Laura DOBSON
53 College of Education/Human Services Dr. Hank WEDDINGTON
73 College of Theology Rev.Dr. David RATKE
76 College of Health Sciences Dr. Michael MCGEE
49 College of Arts & Sciences Dr. Dan KISER
81 Col of Professional/Math Studies Dr. Mary LESSER
36 Director Student Placement Ms. Katie WOHLMAN
39 Director Student Housing Mr. Jonathan RINK
43 Dir of Compliance/Title IX Ms. Dawn FLOYD

Living Arts College @ School of Communication Arts (G)

3000 Wakefield Crossing Drive, Raleigh NC 27614-7076
County: Wake FICE Identification: 031090
Unit ID: 421832
Telephone: (919) 488-8500 Carnegie Class: Bac-Diverse
FAX Number: (919) 488-8490 Calendar System: Quarter
URL: www.living-arts-college.edu
Established: 1992 Annual Undergrad Tuition & Fees: $16,600
Enrollment: 263 Coed
Affiliation or Control: Proprietary IRS Status: Proprietary
Highest Offering: Baccalaureate
Accreditation: ACICS, MAC

01 President Mr. Roger KLIETZ

Livingstone College (H)

701 W Monroe Street, Salisbury NC 28144-5298
County: Rowan FICE Identification: 002942
Unit ID: 198862
Telephone: (704) 216-6000 Carnegie Class: Bac-Diverse
FAX Number: (704) 216-6217 Calendar System: Semester
URL: www.livingstone.edu
Established: 1879 Annual Undergrad Tuition & Fees: $18,296
Enrollment: 1,150 Coed
Affiliation or Control: African Methodist Episcopal Zion Church
IRS Status: 501(c)3
Highest Offering: Baccalaureate
Accreditation: SC, CAEPN, IACBE, SW

01 President Dr. Jimmy R. JENKINS, SR.
04 Exec Asst to the President Dr. State W. ALEXANDER
05 Vice Pres Academic Affairs Dr. Kelli V. RANDALL
10 Vice Pres Business & Finance/Ops Mr. Reginald DICKENS
32 Vice President Student Affairs Dr. Orlando LEWIS
30 Vice Pres Inst Advance/College Rels Vacant
35 Assoc Vice Pres of Student Affairs Dr. Tony BALDWIN
20 Asst Vice Pres Academic Affairs Vacant
38 Dean of Counseling Services Mrs. Elizabeth ALSTON-PINCKNEY
06 Registrar Mrs. Wendy JACKSON
08 Director Library Services Ms. Laura JOHNSON
26 Vice Pres Communications & PR Dr. State W. ALEXANDER
37 Director of Financial Aid Ms. Stephanie MCNEIL
36 Director of Career Services Ms. Sereyna WALLACE
13 Director of Computer Info Systems Mr. Chong DAN
15 Director of Human Resources Mr. Avery STALEY
29 Director Alumni Affairs Ms. Vincia MILLER
09 Director of Institutional Research Mr. Robert L. MCINNIS
84 Director of Enrollment Management Dr. Tony BALDWIN
07 Director of Admissions Vacant
40 Bookstore Director Mr. Keith ANDERSON
41 Athletic Director Mr. Lamonte J. MASSEY-SAMPSON
96 Director of Purchasing Ms. Debra WOOD
18 Director of Physical Plant Mr. Weldon SPENCER
23 Health Services Manager Vacant
27 Asst Director Public Relations Ms. Kimberly HARRINGTON

Louisburg College (I)

501 N. Main Street, Louisburg NC 27549-7705
County: Franklin FICE Identification: 002943
Unit ID: 198871
Telephone: (919) 496-2521 Carnegie Class: Assoc/HT-High Trad
FAX Number: (919) 496-7141 Calendar System: Semester
URL: www.louisburg.edu
Established: 1787 Annual Undergrad Tuition & Fees: $18,581
Enrollment: 624 Coed
Affiliation or Control: United Methodist IRS Status: 501(c)3

Highest Offering: Associate Degree
Accreditation: SC

01 President ... Dr. Gary M. BROWN
05 VP of Academic Life ... Dr. Bonnie SUDERMAN
111 VP of Institutional Advancement ... Mr. J. Lea CALLAWAY
10 Chief Financial Officer ... Ms. Debra SMITH
84 Senior VP of Enrollment Management ... Ms. Stephanie B. TOLBERT
44 Director of Annual Giving ... Ms. Jamie PATRICK
06 Registrar ... Vacant
08 Librarian ... Ms. Kristine JONES
38 Director of Counseling Services ... Ms. Fonda PORTER
37 Director of Financial Aid ... Ms. Tracy POTTER
18 Associate VP of Facilities ... Mr. Nathan BIEGENZAHN
04 Administrative Asst to President ... Ms. Terry PISANO
07 Director of Admissions ... Ms. Maura DICOLLA
09 Director of Institutional Research ... Vacant
19 Campus Police Chief ... Vacant
41 Athletic Director ... Mr. Mike HOLLOMAN
13 Chief Technology Officer ... Mr. Farooq AGHA
15 Director of Human Resources ... Ms. Terry WRIGHT

Mars Hill University (A)

PO Box 370, Mars Hill NC 28754-0370
County: Madison FICE Identification: 002944
Unit ID: 198899
Telephone: (828) 689-1307 Carnegie Class: Bac-Diverse
FAX Number: (828) 689-1478 Calendar System: Semester
URL: www.mhu.edu
Established: 1856 Annual Undergrad Tuition & Fees: $32,968
Enrollment: 1,277 Coed
Affiliation or Control: Independent Non-Profit IRS Status: 501(c)3
Highest Offering: Master's
Accreditation: SC, #CAATE, CAEPN, MUS, NURSE, SW

01 President ... Dr. Tony FLOYD
111 Vice President for Inst Advancement ... Mr. Harold (Bud) G. CHRISTMAN
05 Vice Pres for Academic Affairs ... Dr. John OMACHONU
10 Vice Pres Finance/Facilities Mgmt ... Mr. Neil TILLEY
32 AVP Student Dev/Dean of Stdnts ... Dr. David ROZEBOOM
20 Asst Vice Pres for Academic Admin ... Vacant
07 Director of Admissions ... Ms. Kristie VANCE
06 Dean Academic Records/Registrar ... Ms. Marie NICHOLSON
08 Director of Library Services ... Ms. Beverly ROBERTSON
26 Sr Director of Marketing ... Ms. Samantha FENDER
42 Campus Chaplain ... Rev. Stephanie MCLESKEY
41 Director of Athletics ... Mr. Rick BAKER
37 Director of Financial Aid ... Ms. Nichole BUCKNER
29 Director of Alumni & Donor Rels ... Ms. Amy GARRISON
85 Director International Education ... Mr. Gordon HINNERS
09 Director Institutional Research ... Dr. Kim REIGLE
38 Director Student Counseling ... Ms. Cassandra PAVONE
15 AVP Human Resources/Strategic Init ... Dr. Joy KISH
13 Director Information Technology Svc ... Mr. Ted BRUNER
18 Director of Facilities ... Mr. Donald EDWARDS
40 Director of Bookstore ... Mr. Darryl R. NORTON
51 Dean of Adult & Graduate Studies ... Vacant
97 Chair of General Studies ... Ms. Cathy L. ADKINS
19 Director Security/Safety ... Mr. Kevin WEST
28 Director of Diversity ... Mrs. Alaysia HACKETT

Meredith College (B)

3800 Hillsborough Street, Raleigh NC 27607-5298
County: Wake FICE Identification: 002945
Unit ID: 198950
Telephone: (919) 760-8600 Carnegie Class: Bac-A&S
FAX Number: (919) 760-2828 Calendar System: Semester
URL: www.meredith.edu
Established: 1891 Annual Undergrad Tuition & Fees: $37,176
Enrollment: 1,980 Female
Affiliation or Control: Independent Non-Profit IRS Status: 501(c)3
Highest Offering: Master's
Accreditation: SC, CAEPN, CIDA, DIETD, DIETI, MUS, SW

01 President ... Dr. Jo ALLEN
05 Sr Vice Pres and Provost ... Dr. Matthew POSLUSNY
30 Vice Pres Institutional Advancement ... Dr. Charles (Lennie) BARTON
10 Vice Pres for Business & Finance ... Mr. Craig BARFIELD
32 Vice President for College Programs ... Dr. Jean JACKSON
26 Vice President of Marketing ... Ms. Kristi EAVES-MCLENNAN
35 Dean of Students ... Ms. Ann C. GLEASON
58 Director of Graduate Programs ... Dr. Monica MCKINNEY
06 Registrar ... Ms. Evie ODOM
09 Dir Research/Planning & Assessment ... Dr. C. Dianne RAUBENHEIMER
08 Director Library Info Services ... Ms. Laura DAVIDSON
07 Director of Admissions ... Ms. Shery BOYLES
37 Director of Financial Assistance ... Mr. Kevin MICHAELSEN
35 Dir Student Activ/Leadership Devel ... Ms. Cheryl S. JENKINS
28 Assistant Dean of Students ... Ms. Tomecca SLOANE
36 Director Office of Career Planning ... Ms. Dana SUMNER
29 Dir of Alumnae & Parent Relations ... Ms. Hilary ALLEN
38 Director of Counseling Center ... Ms. Beth A. MEIER
39 Director Resident Life/Housing ... Ms. Heidi LECOUNT
20 Director of Academic Advising ... Mr. Alex DAVIS
31 Director Campus Events ... Mr. Bill BROWN
23 Director Health Services ... Dr. Mary JOHNSON
42 Campus Minister ... Rev. Donna BATTLE

13 Chief Information Officer ... Mr. Jeffrey HOWLETT
19 Chief Campus Police ... Mr. Al WHITE
15 Director of Human Resources ... Ms. Pamela GALLOWAY
18 Chief Facilities/Physical Plant ... Ms. Sharon CAMPBELL
21 Director of Accounting ... Ms. Susan WILLIAMS
88 Director of Learning Center ... Dr. Carmen CHRISTOPHER
104 Director of International Programs ... Dr. Brooke SHURER
124 Dir Retention & Student Success ... Mr. Brandon STOKES
88 Director of Strong Points ... Ms. Candice WEBB

Methodist University (C)

5400 Ramsey Street, Fayetteville NC 28311-1498
County: Cumberland FICE Identification: 002946
Unit ID: 198969
Telephone: (910) 630-7005 Carnegie Class: Masters/S
FAX Number: (910) 630-7317 Calendar System: Semester
URL: www.methodist.edu
Established: 1956 Annual Undergrad Tuition & Fees: $33,852
Enrollment: 2,259 Coed
Affiliation or Control: United Methodist IRS Status: 501(c)3
Highest Offering: Doctorate
Accreditation: SC, ACBSP, ARCPA, #CAATE, NURSE, PTA, SW

01 President ... Dr. Stanley T. WEARDEN
05 Provost ... Vacant
10 VP Business Affairs/Controller ... Ms. Dawn AUSBORN
32 Vice Pres for Student Affairs ... Mr. William WALKER
11 VP Planning and Administration ... Ms. Sheila C. KINSEY
108 VP Planning and Evaluation ... Dr. Donald L. LASSITER
84 Vice Pres Enrollment Management ... Mr. Rick D. LOWE
42 VP Campus Ministry/Cmty Engagement ... Rev. Kelli W. TAYLOR
26 Director University Relations ... Mrs. Kim HASTY
41 Vice Pres/Director of Athletics ... Mr. Dave EAVENSON
20 Associate VP for Academic Affairs ... Ms. Beth CARTER
20 Associate VP for Academic Affairs ... Dr. Lori BROOKMAN
35 Assoc Dean Student Services ... Mr. Todd D. HARRIS
36 Assoc Dean Student/Career Services . Ms. Antoinette P. BELLAMY
29 Director Alumni Affairs ... Ms. Kirbie DOCKERY
07 Dean of Admissions ... Mr. Jamie W. LEGG
37 Director of Financial Aid ... Ms. Bonnie J. ADAMSON
06 Registrar ... Ms. Jasmin K. BROWN
08 Head Librarian ... Ms. Tracey PEARSON
104 Dir Intl Programs/Study Abroad ... Mr. Lyle SHEPPARD
19 Director Police/Public Safety ... Mr. Mark BREWINGTON
15 Director Personnel Services ... Mrs. Debra YEATTS
18 Director of Facilities ... Mr. Bill YOUNG
38 Director Student Counseling ... Dr. Deirdre JACKSON
96 Director of Purchasing ... Ms. Mckenzie JACKSON
04 Admin Assistant to the President ... Ms. Jessica W. HOBBS
105 Director Web Services ... Mr. Michael MOLTER
25 Chief Contract/Grants Administrator ... Ms. Wendy HUSTWIT

Mid-Atlantic Christian University (D)

715 N Poindexter, Elizabeth City NC 27909-4054
County: Pasquotank FICE Identification: 022809
Unit ID: 199458
Telephone: (252) 334-2000 Carnegie Class: Spec-4-yr-Faith
FAX Number: (252) 334-2071 Calendar System: Semester
URL: www.macuniversity.edu
Established: 1948 Annual Undergrad Tuition & Fees: $15,300
Enrollment: 192 Coed
Affiliation or Control: Churches Of Christ IRS Status: 501(c)3
Highest Offering: Baccalaureate
Accreditation: SC

01 President ... Mr. John W. MAURICE, JR.
05 Vice President Academic Affairs ... Dr. Kevin W. LARSEN
32 Vice President Student Life ... Dr. E. Jay BANKS
84 Vice President Enrollment Services ... Mr. Marty RILEY
111 Director Inst Advancement ... Mrs. Elizabeth H. CROSS
10 Vice President Finance ... Mrs. Sara SHEPHERD
09 Director of Institutional Research ... Dr. Kevin W. LARSEN
06 Registrar ... Miss Yolanda K. TESKE
08 Director of Library ... Vacant
38 Counselor ... Dr. David S. KING
37 Financial Aid Administrator ... Mrs. Jenny ROWLAND
35 Student Life Administrator ... Mrs. Vicki F. RILEY
49 Chair of Arts and Sciences ... Dr. Robert W. SMITH
73 Chair of Biblical Studies ... Dr. Lee M. FIELDS
42 Chair of Christian Ministry ... Dr. Claudio F. DIVINO
88 Chair of Marketplace Ministry ... Dr. David S. KING
41 Athletic Director ... Mr. J. Andy MENEELY

Miller-Motte College (E)

2205 Walnut Street, Cary NC 27518
Telephone: (919) 325-7443 Identification: 770726
Accreditation: ACCSC

† Branch campus of Platt College, Tulsa, OK.

Miller-Motte College (F)

3725 Ramsey Street, Fayetteville NC 28311
Telephone: (910) 354-1900 Identification: 770728
Accreditation: ACCSC

† Branch campus of Platt College, Tulsa, OK.

Miller-Motte College (G)

105 New Frontier Way, Jacksonville NC 28546
Telephone: (910) 778-9304 Identification: 770729
Accreditation: ACCSC

† Branch campus of Platt College, Tulsa, OK.

Miller-Motte College (H)

3901 Capital Boulevard, Suite 151, Raleigh NC 27604
Telephone: (919) 230-6471 Identification: 770727
Accreditation: ACCSC, DA, MAC

† Branch campus of Platt College, Tulsa, OK.

Miller-Motte Technical College (I)

5000 Market Street, Wilmington NC 28405-3430
Telephone: (910) 392-4660 FICE Identification: 030632
Accreditation: ACCSC, DA, MAC

† Branch campus of Platt College, Tulsa, OK.

Montreat College (J)

PO Box 1267, 310 Gaither Circle,
Montreat NC 28757-1267
County: Buncombe FICE Identification: 002948
Unit ID: 199032
Telephone: (828) 669-8012 Carnegie Class: Masters/S
FAX Number: (828) 669-9554 Calendar System: Semester
URL: www.montreat.edu
Established: 1916 Annual Undergrad Tuition & Fees: $26,920
Enrollment: 917 Coed
Affiliation or Control: Non-denominational IRS Status: 501(c)3
Highest Offering: Master's
Accreditation: SC, CACREP

01 President ... Dr. Paul J. MAURER
10 VP for Finance and Administration ... Mr. Jack HEINEN
58 VP and Dean for Adult/Grad Studies ... Mr. Rob SAUM
05 VP and Dean for Academic Affairs ... Dr. Greg KERR
84 VP for Enrollment and Management ... Ms. Kristin JANES
32 VP and Dean for Student Services ... Dr. Daniel BENNETT
111 Chief Advancement Officer ... Mr. Joe KIRKLAND
26 Exec Dir Marketing/Communications ... Ms. Sara BAUGHMAN
09 Assoc Dean of Academics & Inst Eff ... Vacant
108 Director of Assessment ... Mr. Brad FAIRCLOTH
41 Athletic Director ... Mr. Jose LARIOS
29 Director Alumni Relations ... Vacant
37 Director of Student Financial Svcs ... Mr. Jeremy HURSE
38 Director of Counseling ... Vacant
110 Director for Advancement Services .... Ms. Kristine BUCKWALTER
08 Library Director ... Mr. Nathan KING
21 Controller ... Mrs. Patti GUFFEY
04 Executive Assistant to President ... Mrs. Laura BUCKWALTER
42 Dean of Spiritual Formation ... Rev. Rachel TOONE
06 Registrar ... Vacant
40 Bookstore Manager ... Ms. Carly BRAENDEL
19 Director of Campus Security ... Mr. Jamie DOUGLASS
18 Chief Facilities/Physical Plant ... Mr. Chris DUFFY
13 Chief Information Technology Office ... Mr. Paul HAWKINSON

Native American Bible College (K)

PO Box 248, Shannon NC 28386
County: Hoke Identification: 667092
Telephone: (910) 843-5304 Carnegie Class: Not Classified
FAX Number: N/A Calendar System: Semester
URL: nabc.edu
Established: 1968 Annual Undergrad Tuition & Fees: N/A
Enrollment: N/A Coed
Affiliation or Control: Assemblies Of God Church IRS Status: 501(c)3
Highest Offering: Baccalaureate
Accreditation: BI

01 President ... James A. KEYS
05 Chief Academic Officer ... Vacant
32 Chief Student Development Officer ... John DAVIS
08 Chief Librarian ... T. Liisa KELLY
04 Administrative Asst to President ... Misa D. LOWERY
06 Registrar ... Isabel LOPEZ

*North Carolina Community College System (L)

200 W Jones Street, 5001 MSC, Raleigh NC 27699-5001
County: Wake FICE Identification: 033445
Telephone: (919) 807-7100 Carnegie Class: N/A
FAX Number: (919) 807-7166
URL: www.nccommunitycolleges.edu

01 President ... Mr. Peter HANS
05 Interim Chief Academic Officer ... Mr. Wesley BEDDARD
100 Chief of Staff ... Ms. Jennifer HAYGOOD
10 Vice Pres/Chief Financial Officer ... Ms. Elizabeth GROVENSTEIN
13 VP Technology Solutions ... Mr. Jim PARKER
46 Assoc VP for STEM Innovation ... Dr. Matthew MEYER
101 Exec Director State Board Affairs ... Mr. Bryan JENKINS
04 Special Assistant to the President ... Vacant

*Alamance Community College (A)

1247 Jimmie Kerr Road/PO Box 8000,
Graham NC 27253-8000

County: Alamance FICE Identification: 005463
Unit ID: 199786
Telephone: (336) 578-2002 Carnegie Class: Assoc/MT-VT-Mix Trad/Non
FAX Number: (336) 578-1987 Calendar System: Semester
URL: www.alamancecc.edu
Established: 1958 Annual Undergrad Tuition & Fees (In-District): $2,036
Enrollment: 4,184 Coed
Affiliation or Control: State/Local IRS Status: 501(c)3
Highest Offering: Associate Degree
Accreditation: SC, ACFEI, DA, EMT, MAC, MLTAD

02 President .... Dr. Algie C. GATEWOOD
03 Executive Vice President .... Mr. Scott QUEEN
10 VP Admin & Fiscal Svcs .... Vacant
111 VP Institutional Advancement .... Ms. Carolyn RHODE
05 VP of Instruction .... Ms. Constance WOLFE
103 VP Workforce Development .... Mr. Gary SAUNDERS
32 VP Student Success .... Dr. Carol DISQUE
50 Dean Business/Arts & Sciences .... Ms. Sonya MCCOOK
72 Dean Industrial Technologies .... Mr. Justin SNYDER
69 Dean Health & Public Svcs .... Mr. David FRAZEE
21 Controller .... Mr. Matthew BANKO
06 Registrar .... Mr. Kenneth DOBBINS
11 Director Administrative Services .... Mr. Thomas HARTMAN
15 Director Human Resources .... Ms. Lorri ALLISON
13 Director Information Services .... Mr. Winfield HENRY
08 Director Learning Resources Center .... Ms. Sheila STREET
26 Director Public Information/Mktg .... Mr. Edward WILLIAMS
56 Director Occupational Ext Program .... Vacant
84 Director Enrollment Management .... Ms. Elizabeth BREHLER
37 Director Financial Aid .... Ms. Sabrina DEGAIN
36 Director Counseling & Career Svcs .... Ms. Ilona OWENS
38 Special Needs/Counseling Svcs Coord .... Ms. Monica ISBELL
121 Academic Support Specialist .... Ms. Jennifer BROWNELL
09 Institutional Researcher .... Dr. Jessica HARRELL
19 Director Security/Safety .... Mr. David PREVATTE
04 Admin Assistant to the President .... Ms. Logan SAVITS

*Asheville - Buncombe Technical Community College (B)

340 Victoria Road, Asheville NC 28801-4897

County: Buncombe FICE Identification: 004033
Unit ID: 197887
Telephone: (828) 398-7900 Carnegie Class: Assoc/MT-VT-High Non
FAX Number: (828) 281-9696 Calendar System: Semester
URL: www.abtech.edu
Established: 1959 Annual Undergrad Tuition & Fees (In-District): $2,632
Enrollment: 7,262 Coed
Affiliation or Control: State/Local IRS Status: 501(c)3
Highest Offering: Associate Degree
Accreditation: SC, ACFEI, DA, DH, DMS, EMT, MAC, MLTAD, OTA, RAD, SURGT

02 President .... Dr. Dennis KING
10 VP Business & Finance/CFO .... Dr. Dirk WILMOTH
13 Vice Pres Information Technology .... Mr. Brian WILLIS
05 VP Instructional Services .... Dr. Beth STEWART
20 Associate VP Instructional Services .... Dr. Gene LOFLIN
32 VP Student Services .... Dr. Terry BRASIER
15 Exec Dir Human Resources & OD .... Ms. Shanna CHAMBERS
103 VP Econ Workforce Dev/Cont Educ .... Dr. Shelley WHITE
04 Executive Administrative Assistant .... Ms. Carolyn RICE
111 Exec Director College Advancement .... Ms. Amanda EDWARDS
49 Dean Arts & Sciences .... Mr. Kenet ADAMSON
50 Dean Business & Hospitality Educ .... Ms. Brenda MCFARLAND
54 Dean Engineering & Applied Tech .... Mr. Vernon D. DAUGHERTY
35 Director Student Life/Development .... Ms. Michele HATHCOCK
21 Director Business Services .... Ms. Lisa LANKFORD
37 Director of Financial Aid .... Ms. Cynthia ANDERSON
06 Registrar .... Mr. Aaron RICHMAN
84 Director Enrollment Services .... Ms. Lisa F. BUSH
24 Director Library Services .... Mr. Russell TAYLOR
12 Director Madison County Campus .... Ms. Sherri DAVIS
18 Director Plant Operations .... Mr. Clarence TATE
19 Chief of Police/Security .... Ms. Kara WALKER
31 Director Community Services Program .... Ms. Brinda W. CALDWELL
08 Librarian .... Mr. Russell TAYLOR
09 Exec Director Research & Planning .... Mr. David B. WHITE
26 Exec Dir Community Rels/Marketing .... Ms. Kerri GLOVER
28 Director of Diversity .... Vacant
40 Bookstore Manager .... Mr. Kevin MILLS
96 Purchasing Agent .... Ms. Rebecca R. WATKINS
72 Dir Cust Rels/Technology Services .... Mr. Cris HARSHMAN

*Beaufort County Community College (C)

5337 US Hwy 264 East, Washington NC 27889-7889

County: Beaufort FICE Identification: 008558
Unit ID: 197966
Telephone: (252) 946-6194 Carnegie Class: Assoc/HT-High Trad
FAX Number: (252) 940-6234 Calendar System: Semester
URL: www.beaufortccc.edu
Established: 1967 Annual Undergrad Tuition & Fees (In-District): $2,518
Enrollment: 1,500 Coed
Affiliation or Control: State/Local IRS Status: 501(c)3
Highest Offering: Associate Degree
Accreditation: SC, MLTAD

02 President .... Dr. David LOOPE
05 VP of Academics .... Dr. Jay SULLIVAN
10 VP of Administrative Services .... Mr. Mark NELSON
32 VP of Student Services .... Vacant
51 VP of Continuing Education .... Mrs. Stacey GERARD
111 VP of Institutional Advancement .... Ms. Serena SULLIVAN
09 Dean Inst Effectiveness .... Ms. Erica S. CARACOGLIA
26 Mktg & PR Coordinator .... Mr. Attila NEMECZ
31 Dir of Community Partnerships .... Mr. Clay CARTER
66 Dean of Nursing & Allied Health .... Mr. Kent DICKERSON
49 Dean Arts & Sciences .... Mrs. Lisa HILL
50 Dean of Business & Industrial Tech .... Mr. Ben MORRIS
08 Director of Library .... Mrs. Paula HOPPER
14 Network Administrator .... Mr. Whiting TOLER
91 System Administrator .... Mr. Brandon BUNCH
15 Director of Human Resources .... Mrs. Nicole HAM
19 Chief of Campus Police .... Mr. Todd ALLIGOOD
37 Director of Financial Aid .... Ms. Crystal TAYLOR
06 Registrar .... Ms. Melissa A. FRANCIS
07 Director of Admissions .... Mrs. Michele MAYO
103 Dir of Business & Industry Svcs .... Mr. Lentz STOWE
04 Executive Asst to President & Board .... Mrs. Jennie SINGLETON
96 Purchasing Coordinator .... Ms. Rebecca ADAMS
38 Director of Counseling .... Mrs. Kimberly JACKSON
105 Webmaster .... Vacant
18 Dir Campus Operations .... Mr. Jason SQUIRES
13 Chief Technology Officer/Info Tech .... Mr. Arthur RICHARD
21 Controller .... Ms. Gay EDWARDS

*Bladen Community College (D)

PO Box 266, Dublin NC 28332-0266

County: Bladen FICE Identification: 007987
Unit ID: 198011
Telephone: (910) 879-5500 Carnegie Class: Assoc/MT-VT-Mix Trad/Non
FAX Number: (910) 879-5564 Calendar System: Semester
URL: www.bladencc.edu
Established: 1967 Annual Undergrad Tuition & Fees (In-State): $2,532
Enrollment: 1,141 Coed
Affiliation or Control: State IRS Status: 501(c)3
Highest Offering: Associate Degree
Accreditation: SC

02 President .... Dr. Amanda LEE
04 Exec Admin Asst to the President .... Ms. Melissa HESTER
05 Executive VP and Chief Acad Officer .... Mr. Jeffrey KORNEGAY
51 VP for Continuing Education .... Ms. Sondra GUYTON
20 Assoc VP for Academic Services .... Ms. Cynthia MCKOY
32 Vice President for Student Services .... Mr. Barry PRIEST
10 Vice President for Finance .... Mr. Jay STANLEY
88 Assoc VP for Program Services .... Mr. Lynn KING
21 Controller .... Ms. Lacie JACOBS
08 Director Student Resource Center .... Ms. Sherwin RICE
09 Dir Institutional Effect & Planning .... Vacant
37 Director of Financial Aid .... Ms. Samantha BENSON
106 Director of Distance Learning .... Mr. Ray SHEPPARD
15 Director of Human Resources .... Ms. Tiina MUNDY
18 Director of Facilities .... Mr. Junior RIDEOUT
26 POI/Marketing Coordinator .... Ms. Joy GRADY
102 Foundation Director .... Ms. Linda BURNEY
06 Registrar .... Ms. Andrea CARTER-FISHER

*Blue Ridge Community College (E)

180 W Campus Drive, Flat Rock NC 28731-4728

County: Henderson FICE Identification: 009684
Unit ID: 198039
Telephone: (828) 694-1700 Carnegie Class: Assoc/MT-VT-Mix Trad/Non
FAX Number: (828) 694-1690 Calendar System: Semester
URL: www.blueridge.edu
Established: 1969 Annual Undergrad Tuition & Fees (In-District): $2,601
Enrollment: 2,122 Coed
Affiliation or Control: State/Local IRS Status: 501(c)3
Highest Offering: Associate Degree
Accreditation: SC, EMT, SURGT

02 President .... Dr. Laura B. LEATHERWOOD
05 VP for Instruction .... Ms. Katherine ALLEN
32 VP for Student Services .... Ms. Kirsten BUNCH
103 VP Workforce Dev/Cont Education .... Dr. Chris ENGLISH
10 AVP for Finance/CFO .... Ms. Carolyn W. ALLEY
11 Vice Pres General Administration .... Dr. Chad MERRILL
49 Dean for Arts and Sciences .... Mr. Aaron COOK
72 Dean for Advanced Technology .... Mr. Joe SHOOK
76 Dean for Health Sciences .... Ms. Leigh ANGEL
97 Dean for Basic Skills .... Ms. Robin NORRIS-PAULISON
50 Dean for Business/Service Careers .... Ms. Brenda BLACKBURN
102 Executive Director Foundation .... Ms. Ann F. GREEN
44 Institutional Advance/Rsrch Coord .... Ms. Carol Ann LYDON
06 Registrar .... Ms. Sara SCHUMACHER
08 Director for Library Services .... Ms. Ali NORVELL
37 Director Financial Aid .... Ms. Lisanne MASTERSON
13 Assoc Vice President/CIO .... Mr. Steve YOUNG
18 Director of Facilities .... Mr. Peter HEMANS
26 Dir of Marketing & Communications .... Ms. Lee Anna HANEY
84 Director of Enrollment Management .... Ms. Laura SIMMONS
15 Director of Human Resources .... Vacant
19 Chief of Police/Dir Public Safety .... Mr. Daran DODD

*Brunswick Community College (F)

50 College Road, Bolivia NC 28422

County: Brunswick FICE Identification: 021707
Unit ID: 198084
Telephone: (910) 755-7300 Carnegie Class: Assoc/HT-High Non
FAX Number: (910) 754-9609 Calendar System: Semester
URL: www.brunswickcc.edu
Established: 1979 Annual Undergrad Tuition & Fees (In-State): $2,532
Enrollment: 1,425 Coed
Affiliation or Control: State IRS Status: 501(c)3
Highest Offering: Associate Degree
Accreditation: SC, CAHIIM, MAC

02 President .... Dr. Gene SMITH
05 Exec Vice Pres/Chief Academic Ofcr .... Dr. Lois SMITH
10 Vice President Budget and Finance .... Ms. Sheila GALLOWAY
32 Vice Pres of Student Affairs .. Dr. Denise A. HOUCHEN-CLAGETT
09 Director of Institutional Planning .... Dr. Michael COBB
08 Dir Learning Resources/Acad Support .... Mrs. Carmen ELLIS
06 Registrar .... Ms. Christine DYE
15 Director Human Resources .... Ms. Nicole WILLIAMS
19 Public Safety/Police Director .... Mr. Lindsay WALTON
18 AVP/Physical Plant Director .... Mr. Jack LUCIANO
102 Director Resource Development .... Ms. Elina DICOSTANZO
26 Director of Marketing & Public Info .... Ms. London SCHMIDT
37 Financial Aid/Veterans Affs Coord .... Ms. Tracy SOMERLAD
72 Dean Professional Technical Service .... Mr. Eric HOLLOMAN
49 Dean Arts & Sciences .... Dr. John GRAY
04 Executive Asst to President .... Ms. Cynthia STERLING
13 Chief Info Officer .... Mr. Ronnie BRYANT
41 Athletic Director .... Mr. Robert ALLEN
36 Career Counselor .... Ms. Leslie WILDER

*Caldwell Community College and Technical Institute (G)

2855 Hickory Boulevard, Hudson NC 28638-1399

County: Caldwell FICE Identification: 004835
Unit ID: 198118
Telephone: (828) 726-2200 Carnegie Class: Assoc/HT-High Non
FAX Number: (828) 726-2216 Calendar System: Semester
URL: www.cccti.edu
Established: 1964 Annual Undergrad Tuition & Fees (In-District): $2,522
Enrollment: 3,495 Coed
Affiliation or Control: State/Local IRS Status: 501(c)3
Highest Offering: Associate Degree
Accreditation: SC, ADNUR, DMS, EMT, MAC, #NMT, PTAA, RAD

02 President .... Dr. Mark POARCH
32 Vice President Student Services .... Mrs. Dena HOLMAN
103 Dean Cont Ed/Workforce Development .... Ms. Brandy DUNLAP
11 Vice President of Operations .... Mr. Donnie BASSINGER
12 Executive Director Watauga Campus .... Mr. Steve MELTON
05 Vice President of Instruction .... Mr. Randy LEDFORD, JR.
84 Dir Enrollment Mgmt Services .... Mr. Dennis SEAGLE
08 Director Learning Resources Center .... Ms. Alison BEARD
37 Director Financial Aid .... Ms. Julie AHOUSE
36 Dir Custom Training/Work Based Lrng .... Mr. Rick SHEW
15 Director Human Resources .... Ms. Pamela ROMANO
10 Controller .... Mrs. Rashelle PENLEY
09 Dir Inst Effectiveness/Research .... Mrs. Liz SILVERS
27 Public Relations Officer .... Mr. Edward TERRY
102 Director Foundation Office .... Ms. Marla CHRISTIE
38 Director Student Counseling .... Mr. Shannon BROWN
96 Purchasing Agent .... Mr. Vincent LINNEY
40 Director of College Stores .... Mrs. Trina CURTIS
04 Exec Assistant to the President .... Mrs. Donna CHURCH
19 Director Security/Safety .... Mr. Donnie BASSINGER
18 Director Facility Services .... Mr. Jeff HERMAN
06 Registrar .... Ms. Beth HOLLAND
13 Chief Info Technology Officer (CIO) .... Ms. Susan WOOTEN

*Cape Fear Community College (H)

411 N Front Street, Wilmington NC 28401-3993

County: New Hanover FICE Identification: 005320
Unit ID: 198154
Telephone: (910) 362-7000 Carnegie Class: Assoc/HT-High Trad
FAX Number: (910) 763-2279 Calendar System: Semester
URL: www.cfcc.edu
Established: 1958 Annual Undergrad Tuition & Fees (In-District): $2,748
Enrollment: 8,317 Coed
Affiliation or Control: State/Local IRS Status: 501(c)3
Highest Offering: Associate Degree
Accreditation: SC, ADNUR, DA, DH, DMS, OTA, RAD, SURGT

02 President .... Mr. James P. MORTON
03 Executive Vice President .... Ms. Melissa SINGLER
32 VP Student Svcs & Enrollment Mgmt .... Ms. Joanne CERES
05 Vice Pres Academic Affairs .... Dr. Jason CHAFFIN
10 Vice President Business Services .... Ms. Christina GREENE
06 Registrar .... Ms. Angela MURPHY
102 Exec Director CFCC Foundation .... Ms. Veronica GODWIN
31 Director Community Relations .... Vacant
84 Dean of Enrollment Management .... Ms. Jackie FOSTER
08 Dean Learning Resources Center .... Ms. Catherine LEE
37 Director of Financial Aid .... Ms. Rachel CAVANAUGH
13 Director Information Technology Svc .... Mr. Kumar LAKHAVANI
26 Director of Creative Services .... Vacant
15 Exec Dir Human Resources .... Ms. Sharon SMITH

35 Dean of Student Affairs ... Mr. Robby MCGEE
96 Director of Purchasing & Inventory ... Mr. Clarence ROGERS
51 Dean of Continuing Education ... Mr. John DOWNING
75 Dean Vocational/Technical Education ... Mr. Mark COUNCIL
49 Dean Arts & Sciences ... Ms. Lynn CRISWELL
76 Dean Health Sciences ... Dr. Angela BALLENTINE
105 Web Services Analyst ... Ms. Christina HEIKKILA
04 Sr Exec Assistant to President ... Ms. Michelle LEE
19 Campus Safety Coordinator ... Ms. Lynn SYLVIA
79 Dir Humanities & Fine Arts Center ... Mr. Shane FERNANDO
25 Director of Grant Development ... Ms. Val CLEMMONS
22 Dir of Disability Support Services ... Ms. Aimee HELMUS
41 Dir Student Activities/Athletics ... Mr. Ryan MANTLO
18 Exec Dir Capital Projects & Maint ... Mr. David KANOY
106 Online Learning Coordinator ... Vacant
14 Manager Infrastructure Team ... Mr. Jakim FRIANT
101 Secretary of the Institution/Board ... Ms. Michelle LEE
103 Director Workforce Development ... Mr. Koshua DAVIS

*Carteret Community College (A)

3505 Arendell Street, Morehead City NC 28557-2989
County: Carteret FICE Identification: 008081
Unit ID: 198206
Telephone: (252) 222-6000 Carnegie Class: Assoc/MT-VT-High Trad
FAX Number: (252) 222-2514 Calendar System: Semester
URL: www.carteret.edu
Established: 1963 Annual Undergrad Tuition & Fees (In-District): $2,696
Enrollment: 1,536 Coed
Affiliation or Control: State/Local IRS Status: 501(c)3
Highest Offering: Associate Degree
Accreditation: SC, ADNUR, COARC, MAC, RAD

02 President ... Dr. John D. HAUSER
05 VP for Instruction/Student Support ... Dr. Tracy MANCINI
10 VP Finance/Administrative Services ... Mr. Steven DAVIS
31 VP Corp/Community Education ... Mr. Perry L. HARKER
04 Exec Dir Office of the President ... Ms. Logan L. OKUN
08 Director of the Library ... Ms. Elizabeth BAKER
32 Dean of Student Services ... Mr. Dana MERCK
84 Enrollment Advisor ... Mr. Rick HILL
13 Dir Network/Info Systems/Security ... Mr. John GREEN
15 Director of Human Resources ... Ms. Amanda BRYANT
102 Exec Director of the Foundation ... Ms. Brenda REASH
49 Dean Arts & Sciences ... Ms. Doree HILL
76 Dean of Health Sciences ... Ms. Laurie A. FRESHWATER
88 Dean of Applied Science ... Ms. Catherine LASSITER
37 Director/Financial Aid Officer ... Ms. Brenda J. LONG
06 Director Enrollment Svcs/Registrar ... Ms. Tammi COBLE
09 Exec Dir Inst Rsrch/Effectiveness ... Ms. Kristy CRAIG
18 VP of Plant Operations/Facilities ... Mr. Steve SPARKS
26 Director of Marketing/Public Affs ... Ms. Alize PROISY
96 Director of Business Operations ... Ms. Donna L. CUMBIE
106 Dir of Instruct Support/Dist Lrng ... Mr. Ed LADENBURGER

*Catawba Valley Community College (B)

2550 Highway 70, SE, Hickory NC 28602-9699
County: Catawba FICE Identification: 005318
Unit ID: 198233
Telephone: (828) 327-7000 Carnegie Class: Assoc/HT-Mix Trad/Non
FAX Number: (828) 327-7276 Calendar System: Semester
URL: www.cvcc.edu
Established: 1960 Annual Undergrad Tuition & Fees (In-District): $2,347
Enrollment: 4,827 Coed
Affiliation or Control: State/Local IRS Status: 501(c)3
Highest Offering: Associate Degree
Accreditation: SC, ADNUR, CAHIIM, COARC, DH, EMT, IFSAC, NDT, POLYT, RAD, SURGT

02 President ... Dr. Garrett D. HINSHAW
05 Exec Vice President of Instruction ... Dr. Keith MACKIE
10 Sr VP Business Affairs-Operations ... Mr. Wes BUNCH
32 Dean of Student Access/Development ... Mrs. Cindy COULTER
15 Director Human Resources ... Mr. Roger IRVIN
07 Director of Admissions/Records ... Ms. Kelly PLUMLEY
21 Controller ... Ms. Jennifer HAMM
37 Director Scholarships/Financial Aid ... Ms. Carolyn BRANDON
09 Ofc Accountability/Efficienc/Effect ... Mr. Kevin ROUSE
88 Director Industrial Training ... Ms. Crystal GLENN
88 Director Small Business Center ... Mr. Jeff NEUVILLE
50 Director Business/Technology Ext ... Ms. Susan KILLIAN
88 Director Hosiery Technology Center ... Mr. Daniel C. ST. LOUIS
13 Director Information Technologies ... Mr. Daniel CLANTON
19 Director Campus Safety/Security ... Mr. Steve HUNT
31 Director Community Education ... Ms. Chanell MORELLO
36 Counselor/Job Placement Svcs Coord ... Ms. Tammy MULLER
76 Dean Sch of Health & Public Service ... Ms. Robin ROSS
04 Administrative Asst to President ... Ms. Sherry WILLIAMS
29 Director Alumni Relations ... Ms. Mary REYNOLDS
41 Athletic Director ... Mr. Nick SCHROEDER

*Central Carolina Community College (C)

1105 Kelly Drive, Sanford NC 27330-9000
County: Lee FICE Identification: 005449
Unit ID: 198251
Telephone: (919) 775-5401 Carnegie Class: Assoc/MT-VT-Mix Trad/Non
FAX Number: (919) 718-7380 Calendar System: Semester
URL: www.cccc.edu
Established: 1958 Annual Undergrad Tuition & Fees (In-District): $2,544
Enrollment: 5,188 Coed
Affiliation or Control: State/Local IRS Status: 501(c)3
Highest Offering: Associate Degree
Accreditation: SC, DA, DH, EMT, MAC

02 President ... Dr. Lisa M. CHAPMAN
05 Vice Pres Learning/Wrkfce Dev/CAO ... Dr. Brian MERRITT
11 Vice Pres of Administrative Svcs ... Mr. Philip PRICE
32 Vice President Student Services ... Mr. Ken R. HOYLE
09 VP Assessment/Planning/Research ... Dr. Linda SCUILETTI
108 VP Assessment/Planning/Research ... Ms. Linda NOKES SCUILETTI
26 Assoc VP Marketing/External Rels ... Dr. Marcie DISHMAN
12 Provost Chatham Campus ... Mr. Mark HALL
04 Exec Asst to Pres/Secretary to BOT ... Ms. Lorraine WHITAKER
12 Provost Harnett Campus ... Dr. Jon MATTHEWS
08 Director of Library Services ... Ms. Tara LUCAS
15 Assoc Director of Human Resources ... Ms. Valerie BENN
102 Exec Director of CCCC Foundation ... Ms. Emily HARE
06 Dean of Enrollment/Registrar ... Ms. Jamie TYSON-CHILDRESS
07 Director of Admissions ... Mr. Adam WADE
37 Director Financial Aid ... Ms. Zilma LOPES
18 Physical Plant Manager ... Mr. Ronnie MEASAMER
75 Dean Career/Technical Programs ... Mr. Drew GOODSON
76 Dean Health Sciences/Human Services ... Ms. Lisa GODFREY
49 Dean Arts & Sciences/Advising ... Mr. Scott BYINGTON

*Central Piedmont Community College (D)

PO Box 35009, Charlotte NC 28235-5009
County: Mecklenburg FICE Identification: 002915
Unit ID: 198260
Telephone: (704) 330-2722 Carnegie Class: Assoc/HT-High Trad
FAX Number: (704) 330-5045 Calendar System: Semester
URL: www.cpcc.edu
Established: 1963 Annual Undergrad Tuition & Fees (In-District): $2,792
Enrollment: 19,100 Coed
Affiliation or Control: State/Local IRS Status: 501(c)3
Highest Offering: Associate Degree
Accreditation: SC, ACFEI, ADNUR, CAHIIM, COARC, CSHSE, CVT, CYTO, DA, DH, EMT, MAC, MLTAD, OTA, PTAA, SURGT

02 President ... Dr. Kandi W. DEITEMEYER
32 VP Student & Enrollment Services ... Dr. Marcia CONSTON
10 VP Finance & Admin Services ... Mr. Mike WHITEMAN
13 VP for Technology & CIO ... Mr. David KIM
111 VP for Institutional Advancement ... Dr. Kevin MCCARTHY
04 Special Assistant to the President ... Dr. Tracie CLARK
26 VP Comm/Marketing/Public Relations ... Mr. Jeffrey LOWRANCE
18 Assoc VP Facilities & Construction ... Ms. Vicki SAVILLE
116 Exec Director Compliance/Audit ... Ms. Kelley HORTON
15 Chief Human Resources Officer ... Mr. Mark SHORT
25 Assoc VP Government Rels & Grants ... Mr. Michael HORN
21 AVP Finance/Admin Services ... Ms. Jessica BOYCE
102 AVP Foundation/Inst Advancement ... Ms. Katie JONES
12 Dean Levine Campus ... Dr. Edith MCELROY
12 Dean Merancas Campus ... Ms. Tamara WILLIAMS
12 Dean Central Campus ... Dr. Paul KOEHNKE
12 Dean Cato Campus ... Mr. George HENDERSON
12 Dean Harris Campus/AVP Corp Dev ... Ms. Mary VICKERS-KOCH
103 AVP of Workforce Development ... Dr. Kelly TRAINOR
54 Dean STEM-S ... Mr. Chris PAYNTER
124 Dean Retention Services ... Dr. Clint MCELROY
35 Dean Student Life/Service Learning ... Mr. Mark HELMS
84 Dean Enrollment Management ... Dr. Daniel (JJ) MCEACHERN
08 Dean Libraries ... Ms. Gloria KELLEY
121 Dean College & Career Readiness ... Ms. Karen PAULY
07 Dean Enrollment Services ... Dr. April JONES
22 Dir Affirmative Action/EEO ... Mr. Leon MATTHEWS
06 Dean Admissions & Registration ... Mr. Greg STANLEY
19 Exec Dir College Security ... Mr. Charles WRIGHT
76 Dean Health Professions ... Ms. Maureen BUMBA

*Cleveland Community College (E)

137 S Post Road, Shelby NC 28152-6296
County: Cleveland FICE Identification: 008082
Unit ID: 198321
Telephone: (704) 669-6000 Carnegie Class: Assoc/MT-VT-Mix Trad/Non
FAX Number: (704) 669-4202 Calendar System: Semester
URL: www.clevelandcc.edu
Established: 1965 Annual Undergrad Tuition & Fees (In-District): $2,552
Enrollment: 2,700 Coed
Affiliation or Control: State/Local IRS Status: 501(c)3
Highest Offering: Associate Degree
Accreditation: SC, EMT, MAC, RAD, SURGT

02 President ... Dr. Jason HURST
05 Vice President of Academic Programs ... Dr. Becky SAIN
32 Vice President of Student Services ... Dr. Andy GARDNER
10 Vice Pres Business Operations/CFO ... Mr. Bruce COLE
51 Vice Pres of Continuing Education ... Mr. Ken MOONEY
30 Sr Dean Devel/Governmental Rels ... Vacant
102 Executive Director CCC Foundation ... Dr. Mary CARLSON
09 Dean of Plng & Institutional Effect ... Dr. Laura BOWEN
88 Director CECHS Relations ... Ms. Nedra MADDOX
84 Director of Enrollment Services ... Dr. Emily HURDT
08 Dean of Learning Resources ... Mrs. Barbara MCKIBBIN
96 Purchasing Officer ... Mr. Lance ASHLEY
18 Director of Physical Plant ... Mr. Mark FOX
19 Director of Security ... Mr. Richard FIELDS
15 Human Resources & Safety Manager ... Mr. Allen KNICELEY
13 Chief Information Officer ... Mr. Jonathan DAVIS
14 Network Administrator ... Mr. Robin DYER
24 Audiovisual Coordinator ... Mr. Rodger PERRY
26 Public Info/Marketing Coordinator ... Mrs. Paula VESS
07 Director Records/Educ Partnerships ... Ms. Emily AREY
49 Dean Arts & Sciences ... Ms. Betty STACK
50 Dean Business & Allied Health ... Dr. John LATTIMORE
103 VP Econ/Workforce Development ... Mr. Bruce MACK
88 Dean Learning Center ... Dr. Chris NANNEY

*Coastal Carolina Community College (F)

444 Western Boulevard, Jacksonville NC 28546-6816
County: Onslow FICE Identification: 005316
Unit ID: 198330
Telephone: (910) 455-1221 Carnegie Class: Assoc/HT-Mix Trad/Non
FAX Number: (910) 455-7027 Calendar System: Semester
URL: www.coastalcarolina.edu
Established: 1963 Annual Undergrad Tuition & Fees (In-District): $2,462
Enrollment: 4,030 Coed
Affiliation or Control: State/Local IRS Status: 501(c)3
Highest Offering: Associate Degree
Accreditation: SC, DA, DH, EMT, MLTAD, SURGT

02 President ... Mr. David L. HEATHERLY
05 VP for Instruction ... Ms. Ginger TUTON
09 VP Inst Eff/Research/Innovation ... Ms. Sharon R. MCGINNIS
11 VP for Administrative Supp Svcs ... Dr. Annette HARPINE
32 Division Chair for Student Services ... Mr. Matthew HERRMANN
15 Personnel Officer ... Ms. Cindy BURKHART
26 Pub Info Ofcr/Ex Dir Col Foundation ... Ms. Krystal PHILLIPS
07 Director of Admissions ... Dr. Jessica RANERO-RAMIREZ
18 Dir Physical Plant/Auxiliary Svcs ... Ms. Carol LURZ
37 Director for Financial Aid Services ... Ms. Tammy LYON
88 Director for Veterans Services ... Mr. Christopher P. SABIN
88 Director Economic Development ... Ms. Anne C. SHAW
04 Assistant to the President and BOT ... Ms. Tonya L. MORTON
06 Registrar ... Ms. Mishelle DUPUIS

*College of the Albemarle (G)

1208 North Road Street, Elizabeth City NC 27906-2327
County: Pasquotank FICE Identification: 002917
Unit ID: 197814
Telephone: (252) 335-0821 Carnegie Class: Assoc/HT-High Non
FAX Number: (252) 335-2011 Calendar System: Semester
URL: www.albemarle.edu
Established: 1960 Annual Undergrad Tuition & Fees (In-District): $2,239
Enrollment: 2,507 Coed
Affiliation or Control: State/Local IRS Status: 501(c)3
Highest Offering: Associate Degree
Accreditation: SC, ADNUR, MAC, MLTAD, SURGT

02 Interim President ... Dr. Travis TWIFORD
10 Chief Financial Officer ... Mrs. Susan GENTRY
05 Vice President for Learning ... Dr. Evonne CARTER
11 VP Business & Admin Services ... Mr. John IVES
32 VP for Student Suc & Enr Mgmt ... Ms. Lynn HURDLE-WINSLOW
12 Dean Dare County Campus ... Mr. Timothy SWEENEY
30 Executive Director Foundation & Dev ... Mrs. Amy ALCOCER
37 Director Admissions & Financial Aid ... Ms. Angela R. GODFREY-DAWSON
35 Coord Student Life & Leadership ... Ms. Alicia STOKLEY
06 Registrar ... Ms. Andrea DANCE
88 Director Small Business Center ... Ms. Ginger H. O'NEAL
78 Work-Based Learning Liaison ... Mrs. Lynn JENNINGS
04 Exec Assistant to the President ... Mrs. Valerie MUELLER
08 Director Library ... Mr. Rodney WOOTEN
12 Campus Admin Edenton-Chowan Campus ... Mrs. Robin ZINSMEISTER
13 Director Mgmt Information Services ... Mr. Wayman WHITE
15 Director Human Resources ... Ms. Ella BUNCH
18 Director Physical Facilities ... Mr. Patrick CUTHRELL
40 Administrative Services Manager ... Mr. William DEFEO
09 Director of Inst Effectiveness ... Vacant
88 Coord Prison Education Programs ... Mr. Andre WILLIAMS
88 Coordinator Secondary Education ... Mr. Derek MEREDITH
49 Dean Arts and Sciences ... Mr. Dean ROUGHTON
50 Dean Business & Applied Tech ... Mrs. Michelle WATERS
76 Dean Health & Wellness ... Ms. Robin HARRIS
81 Dept Chair Sciences ... Mr. Todd KRUEGER
83 Department Chair Social Sciences ... Mr. Brian EDWARDS
60 Dept Chair English & Comm ... Mrs. Laura MORRISON
81 Dept Chair Math and Engineering ... Ms. Rhonda WATTS
76 Dept Chair Allied Health ... Mr. Jeffrey CARTER
77 Dept Chair Bus & Computer Sys Tech ... Ms. Sharon BROWN
57 Department Chair Human & Fine Arts ... Ms. Ekaterina YOUNGER
66 Dept Chair ADN ... Mrs. Katie MILLER
19 Director Public Safety & Preparedns ... Mr. Dennis SMITH
88 Dir Basic Skills/Workforce Reading ... Mrs. Wanda FLETCHER
121 Director Advising & Student Success ... Mrs. Eushekia HEWITT
103 Dean Workforce Dev/Pub Svc/Career ... Mrs. Robin ZINSMEISTER
106 Coordinator Distance Education ... Dr. Susan PECK

*Craven Community College (H)

800 College Court, New Bern NC 28562-4984
County: Craven FICE Identification: 006799
Unit ID: 198367
Telephone: (252) 638-7200 Carnegie Class: Assoc/MT-VT-Mix Trad/Non
FAX Number: (252) 638-4232 Calendar System: Semester
URL: www.cravencc.edu

Established: 1965 Annual Undergrad Tuition & Fees (In-District): $2,023
Enrollment: 3,021 Coed
Affiliation or Control: State/Local IRS Status: 501(c)3
Highest Offering: Associate Degree
Accreditation: SC, ACBSP, CAHIIM, MAC, PTAA

02 President .... Dr. Raymond STAATS
05 VP for Instruction .... Dr. Kathleen GALLMAN
11 VP for Administrative Services .... Mr. Jim MILLARD
32 VP for Students .... Mr. Gery BOUCHER
49 Dean Liberal Arts & Univ Transfer .... Dr. Betty K. HATCHER
36 Dean Career Programs .... Mr. Ricky MEADOWS
09 Exec Director Inst Effectiveness .... Dr. David L. TOWNSEND
06 Registrar .... Ms. Yuko BOYD
111 Executive Director Inst Advancement .. Mr. Charles WETHINGTON
12 Dean Havelock-Cherry Point Campus .... Mr. Walter CALABRESE
37 Executive Director Financial Aid .... Ms. Leslie M. LLOYD
31 Dir Community Workforce Relations .... Mr. Greg SINGLETON
88 Director Basic Skills Programs .... Ms. Sandy BAYLISS-CARR
08 Director Library Services .... Mrs. Catherine C. CAMPBELL
10 Exec Dir Financial Services .... Mrs. Cynthia A. PATTERSON
88 Director TRIO Student Support Svcs .... Ms. Donna MARSHALL
15 Exec Director Human Resources .... Ms. Denise HORNE
103 Dean Workforce Development .... Mr. Robin MATTHEWS
18 Executive Director Facilities .... Mr. John MELVILLE
13 Dean Technology Services .... Dr. Julia HAMILTON
96 Procurement & Fixed Assets Officer .... Mr. Hiram Todd MURPHREY
84 Dean Enrollment Management .... Ms. Zomar PETER
25 Director Grants/Strategic Partners .... Ms. Monica MINUS
04 Exec Asst to Pres/Board of Trustees .... Ms. Cynthia ENSLEY
19 Executive Director Security .... Mr. Paul DAMICO
121 Exec Director Academic Support .... Ms. Jennifer BUMGARNER
76 Dean Health Programs .... Dr. J. Alec NEWTON
07 Director Admissions & Records .... Mrs. Tina PROCTOR
26 Director Communications .... Mr. Craig RAMEY

*Davidson County Community College (A)

PO Box 1287, Lexington NC 27293-1287
County: Davidson FICE Identification: 002919
Unit ID: 198376
Telephone: (336) 249-8186 Carnegie Class: Assoc/MT-VT-Mix Trad/Non
FAX Number: (336) 249-0379 Calendar System: Semester
URL: www.davidsonccc.edu
Established: 1958 Annual Undergrad Tuition & Fees (In-District): $2,588
Enrollment: 3,627 Coed
Affiliation or Control: State/Local IRS Status: 501(c)3
Highest Offering: Associate Degree
Accreditation: SC, ADNUR, CAHIIM, EMT, MAC, MLTAD, SURGT

02 President .... Dr. Darrin L. HARTNESS
05 VP Academic Programs & Services .... Dr. Margaret H. ANNUNZIATA
32 VP Student Affairs .... Dr. Rhonda Q. COATS
10 VP Financial/Administrative Svcs .... Ms. Laura L. YARBROUGH
102 VP Ext Affairs/Exec Dir Foundation .... Ms. Jenny M. VARNER
76 Dean Health/Wellness/Pub Safety .... Ms. Rose MCDANIEL
97 Dean Gen Studies & Acad Support .... Dr. Christy FORREST
50 Dean Business Engineering Technical .... Vacant
12 Dean Davie Campus .... Ms. Teresa KINES
35 Dean Student Services .... Ms. Jane BIRKHOLZ
121 VP Student Success & Communications ... Ms. Susan BURLESON
26 Director Marketing & Communications .... Ms. DeeDe PINCKNEY
06 Dir Student Records/Registration .... Mr. Bryan MCCULLOUGH
36 Director Career Development .... Mr. Charles MAYER
18 Director Physical Plant Services .... Mr. Keith RAKER
15 Director Personnel Services .... Vacant
04 Administrative Asst to President .... Ms. Carleen TERRELL
08 Head Librarian .... Mr. Jason SETZER
37 Director Student Financial Aid .... Ms. Lori BLEVINS
41 Athletic Director .... Mr. Kenneth KIRK
07 Director of Admissions .... Mr. Antonio JORDAN
09 Director of Institutional Research .... Mr. Mark PUTERBAUGH
19 Director Security/Safety .... Ms. Rita MATHEWS
111 Chief Development/Advancement .... Ms. Kristin BRIGGS
124 Dean Student Engagement/Completion .... Ms. Keisha JONES

*Durham Technical Community College (B)

1637 Lawson Street, Durham NC 27703-5023
County: Durham FICE Identification: 005448
Unit ID: 198455
Telephone: (919) 536-7200 Carnegie Class: Assoc/MT-VT-Mix Trad/Non
FAX Number: (919) 686-3601 Calendar System: Semester
URL: www.durhamtech.edu
Established: 1961 Annual Undergrad Tuition & Fees (In-District): $1,958
Enrollment: 5,415 Coed
Affiliation or Control: State/Local IRS Status: 501(c)3
Highest Offering: Associate Degree
Accreditation: SC, ADNUR, CAHIIM, CEA, COARC, DT, EMT, MAC, OPD, OTA, PNUR, SURGT

02 President .... Dr. William G. INGRAM
32 Exec VP Academics/Stdnt Engagement .... Mr. Tom JAYNES
05 VP/Chief Academic Officer .... Ms. Susan PARIS
10 VP Finance and Administration .... Mr. Matt WILLIAMS
51 VP Corp/Continuing Education .... Dr. Peter WOOLDRIDGE
32 VP Student Engage/Dev/Support .... Dr. Christine KELLY KLEESE
100 Chief of Staff .... Ms. Tina B. RUFF
04 Executive Secy to the President .... Ms. Gloria GAY
35 Dean Student Development/Support .... Ms. Lisa D. INMAN
06 Asst Dean Student Records/Registrar .... Mr. Abraham DONES
13 Exec Dir Information Tech Svcs .... Mr. Patrick HINES
09 Dir Institutional Research/Eval .... Dr. Melanie RIESTER
15 Executive Director Human Resources .... Ms. Kathy MCKINLEY
08 Director Library .... Ms. Julie HUMPHREY
37 Dir Financial Aid/Veteran Svcs .... Ms. Nadine FORD
109 Director Auxiliary Services .... Ms. Yolanda V. MOORE-JONES
07 Director Admissions .... Mr. Abraham DONES
18 Director Facility Services .... Mr. Marshall R. FULLER
26 Dir Marketing/Comm/Public Info Ofcr .... Mr. Nathan HARDIN

*Edgecombe Community College (C)

2009 W Wilson Street, Tarboro NC 27886-9399
County: Edgecombe FICE Identification: 008855
Unit ID: 198491
Telephone: (252) 823-5166 Carnegie Class: Assoc/MT-VT-High Trad
FAX Number: N/A Calendar System: Semester
URL: www.edgecombe.edu
Established: 1967 Annual Undergrad Tuition & Fees (In-District): $2,640
Enrollment: 2,198 Coed
Affiliation or Control: State/Local IRS Status: 501(c)3
Highest Offering: Associate Degree
Accreditation: SC, ADNUR, CAHIIM, COARC, MAC, PNUR, RAD, SURGT

02 President .... Dr. Gregory MCLEOD
05 Vice President of Instruction .... Dr. Harry STARNES
11 Vice Pres Administrative Services .... Ms. Debbie BATTEN
32 Vice President Student Services .... Mr. Michael J. JORDAN
84 Dean Enrollment Management .... Mr. Tony ROOK
35 Dean of Students .... Ms. Samanthia PHILLIPS
108 Director of Inst Effectiveness .... Ms. Sheila HOSKINS
26 Director of Public Information .... Ms. Mary T. BASS
08 Director of Library Services .... Ms. Deborah PARISHER
06 Registrar .... Ms. Cathy P. DUPREE
15 Director Personnel Services .... Ms. Susan BARKALOW
18 Chief Facilities/Physical Plant .... Mr. John BUTZ
37 Director Student Financial Aid .... Mr. Sherlock MCDOUGALD
04 Executive Asst to President .... Ms. Phyllis TALBOT
13 Director Computer Services .... Mr. Neil BAKER
43 Dir Legal Services/General Counsel .... Mr. Mark S. LORENCE

*Fayetteville Technical Community College (D)

PO Box 35236, 2201 Hull Road, Fayetteville NC 28303-0236
County: Cumberland FICE Identification: 007640
Unit ID: 198534
Telephone: (910) 678-8400 Carnegie Class: Assoc/MT-VT-Mix Trad/Non
FAX Number: (910) 678-8269 Calendar System: Semester
URL: www.faytechcc.edu
Established: 1961 Annual Undergrad Tuition & Fees (In-State): $2,544
Enrollment: 11,660 Coed
Affiliation or Control: State IRS Status: 501(c)3
Highest Offering: Associate Degree
Accreditation: SC, ADNUR, COARC, DA, DH, EMT, FUSER, PTAA, RAD, SURGT

02 President .... Dr. Larry KEEN
05 Sr VP Academic/Student Svcs .... Dr. Mark SORRELLS
10 Sr VP Business and Finance .... Mrs. Robin DEAVER
15 VP Human Res/Inst Effect/Assessment .... Mr. Carl MITCHELL
11 VP for Administrative Services .... Mr. Joseph W. LEVISTER, JR.
13 VP Learning Technologies .... Vacant
43 VP for Legal Services .... Mr. David SULLIVAN
26 Exec Dir Marketing/Public Relations .... Ms. Wanda DAIL
102 Executive Director of Foundation .... Ms. Lauren ARP
84 Dean Enrollment Mgmt/Financial Aid . Mr. Harper SHACKELFORD
51 Assoc Vice Pres for Cont Educ .... Dr. Jolee MARSH
32 Assoc Vice Pres Student Services .... Dr. Rosemary KELLY
06 Registrar .... Ms. Melissa A. JONES
21 Assoc Vice Pres Business & Finance .... Mr. Charles SMITH
07 Director of Admissions .... Dr. Louanna CASTLEMAN
20 Assoc Vice Pres of Academic Support .... Ms. DeSandra WASHINGTON
14 Director Management Information Svc .... Mrs. Pamela SCULLY
18 Director of Facility Services .... Mr. Steven ARNDT
96 Procurement Manager Business/Financ .... Ms. Amy SAMPERTON
50 Dean of Business Programs .... Mrs. Cindy BURNS
49 Dean of Arts/Humanities .... Mr. Antonio JACKSON
76 Dean of Health Programs .... Mrs. Susan ELLIS
54 Dean Engr/Applied Tech Pgms .... Mrs. Pamela GIBSON
81 Dean of Sciences & Mathematics .... Mr. Chris DIORIETES
88 Dean of Public Service .... Mrs. Linda NOVAK
77 Dean of Computer Technologies .... Mrs. Tenette PREVATTE
08 Chief Library Officer .... Mr. Laurence GAVIN
09 Dean of Institutional Effectiveness .... Dr. Vincent CASTANO
19 Director Security/Safety .... Mr. Joseph BAILER
37 Director Student Financial Aid .... Mrs. Regina ANGLIN
41 Athletic Director .... Mr. Michael NEAL

*Forsyth Technical Community College (E)

2100 Silas Creek Parkway, Winston-Salem NC 27103-5197
County: Forsyth FICE Identification: 005317
Unit ID: 198552
Telephone: (336) 723-0371 Carnegie Class: Assoc/MT-VT-High Trad
FAX Number: (336) 761-2399 Calendar System: Semester
URL: www.forsythtech.edu
Established: 1960 Annual Undergrad Tuition & Fees (In-State): $2,199
Enrollment: 7,756 Coed
Affiliation or Control: State IRS Status: 501(c)3
Highest Offering: Associate Degree
Accreditation: SC, COARC, CVT, DA, DH, DMS, MAC, NMT, RAD, RTT

02 President .... Dr. Janet N. SPRIGGS
05 Provost .... Dr. Joel WELCH
32 VP Educational Support Services .... Dr. Jewel B. CHERRY
31 VP for Community Engagement .... Mr. William GREEN
10 VP Business Services & CFO .... Ms. Wendy R. EMERSON
103 Vice Pres Economic & Workforce Dev .... Mr. Alan K. MURDOCK
15 VP Human Resources .... Ms. Anna Marie SMITH
13 VP Information Technology .... Mr. Chris PEARCE
45 VP for Strategic Innovation .... Mr. Kevin OSBORNE
100 Executive Director Administration .... Ms. Sherri W. BOWEN
50 Dean Business & Info Tech .... Ms. Pamela SHORTT
81 Dean Math/Sciences & Tech .... Dr. Torry REYNOLDS
79 Dean of Humanities/Social Sci .... Ms. Anu WILLIAMS
54 Dean of Engineering Tech Div .... Mr. John CARSTENS
17 Dean of Health Technologies .... Ms. Linda LATHAM
31 Dean Community/Economic Development .... Ms. Sharon D. ANDERSON
08 Dean Learning Resources .... Mr. J. Randel CANDELARIA
88 Dean College and Career Readiness .... Ms. Sydney RICHARDSON
66 Director Nursing .... Ms. Sharon MOORE
76 Director Imaging .... Ms. Tamara BECK
76 Director Health Services .... Ms. Jean E. MIDDLESWARTH
21 Dean Financial Services .... Ms. Melanie L. NUCKOLS
121 Director Student Success Center .... Ms. Masonne SAWYER
15 Director Human Resources .... Vacant
88 Dir Recruiting/Student Support Svcs .... Mr. Edwin B. WADDELL
37 Director Student Financial Services .... Mr. Ricky C. HODGES
06 Director Records/Registrar .... Ms. Gwen D. WHITAKER
07 Director of Admissions .... Vacant
18 Director Physical Plant Services .... Mr. Scott BOOTH
19 Chief of Police .... Ms. Carolyn MCMACKIN
88 Director Small Business Center .... Mr. Allan YOUNGER
35 Director Student Life & Engagement .... Ms. Beverly N. LEWIS
96 Director Purchasing/Equipment .... Mr. Keith BLYTHE
109 Director Auxiliary Services .... Mr. Brian A. HICKS
12 Sr Director Off Campus Centers .... Ms. Kristie F. HENDRIX
12 Director National Ctr Biotech .... Mr. Russel READ
12 Director Divisional Ops & Support .... Ms. Michelle DIXON
12 Director Stokes County Center .... Ms. Sally ELLIOTT
88 Director Educational Partnerships .... Ms. Kimberly BRYANT
88 Dean Business and Industry .... Ms. Jennifer B. COULOMBE
88 Dean Health and Emergency Programs .... Mr. Wesley D. HUTCHINS
88 Dir Transportation Technology Ctr .... Ms. Kristen SEAMSTER
88 Dean Transformative Learning Center .... Mr. James COOK
44 Director Donor Relations .... Ms. Angela COOK
04 Special Projects & Policy Admin .... Ms. Dawn P. MITCHELL
25 Director Grant Writing & Dev .... Mr. Mike MASSOGLIA
44 Director Development & Annual Fund .... Ms. Patricia VAUGHN
34 Director Shugarts Women's Center .... Ms. Kenyetta RICHMOND
36 Director Career Services .... Ms. Jessica LONG
26 Manager of Public Relations .... Ms. Judi SAINT SING

*Gaston College (F)

201 Highway 321 South, Dallas NC 28034-1499
County: Gaston FICE Identification: 002973
Unit ID: 198570
Telephone: (704) 922-6200 Carnegie Class: Assoc/MT-VT-High Trad
FAX Number: (704) 922-2323 Calendar System: Semester
URL: www.gaston.edu
Established: 1964 Annual Undergrad Tuition & Fees (In-District): $2,704
Enrollment: 5,172 Coed
Affiliation or Control: State/Local IRS Status: 501(c)3
Highest Offering: Associate Degree
Accreditation: SC, ACBSP, ADNUR, DIETT, EMT, IFSAC, MAC, PNUR

02 President .... Dr. Patricia A. SKINNER
05 VP Academic Affairs .... Dr. Dewey DELLINGER
103 VP Economic & Workforce Develop .... Dr. Dennis MCELHOE
10 VP Finance/Facilities/Operations .... Ms. Cynthia MCCRORY
32 VP Student Affairs/Enrollment Mgmt .... Dr. Silvia Patricia RIOS-HUSAIN
11 Chief Administrative Officer .... Mr. Todd BANEY
102 Interim Chief Dev Ofcr/Dir Fdn .... Mr. Luke UPCHURCH
04 Exec Admin Assistant to Pres .... Ms. Mary Ellen DILLON
21 Assoc VP Fin/Oper/Fac & Controller .... Vacant
20 Assoc VP Academic Affairs .... Dr. Heather WOODSON
103 Assoc VP Economic/Workforce Devel .... Dr. Justin ARNOLD
35 Assoc VP Student Affairs .... Dr. Audrey SHERRILL
12 Dean Kimbrell Campus .... Dr. Heather WOODSON
12 Dean Lincoln Campus .... Dr. John MCHUGH
50 Dean Business & Information Tech .... Vacant
72 Interim Dean Engr Technologies .... Dr. George HENDRICKS
72 Interim Dean Indus Technologies .... Mr. Eric RHOM
76 Dean Health & Human Services .... Dr. Allison ABERNATHY
49 Dean Arts & Sciences .... Ms. Tonia BROOME
07 Dir Admissions .... Dr. Jennifer NICHOLS
38 Interim Director of Counseling .... Dr. Audrey SHERRILL
40 Dir Bookstore/Vending Services .... Mr. Charles WILSON
78 Interim Dir Educational Ptnrshp .... Dr. Jennifer NICHOLS
18 Dir Facilities Management .... Mr. Russell SMYRE
37 Dir Financial Aid/Veterans Affairs .... Ms. Ungina PERKINS
25 Dir Grants/Special Projects .... Mr. Luke UPCHURCH
09 Dir Institutional Effectiveness .... Dr. Rex CLAY
121 Dir Student Success/Learning .... Mr. Damon MURRAY

08 Dir Libraries ... Dr. Harry COOKE
26 Dir Marketing/Public Relations ... Ms. Stephanie MICHAEL-PICKETT
96 Mgr Purch/Ship/Rec & Equipment ... Mr. Manraj SINGH
06 Dir Registration/Records ... Ms. Alisa ROY
75 Dir Textile Technology Ctr ... Mr. Sam BUFF
19 Chief Campus Police & Security ... Mr. Billy LYTTON
13 Chief Technology Services Officer ... Ms. Savonne MCNEILL
15 Mgr HR/Envir/Health/Safety/Prof Dev ... Ms. Carol DENTON
106 Director of Distance Education ... Ms. Kim GELSINGER

*Guilford Technical Community College (A)

PO Box 309, Jamestown NC 27282-0309
County: Guilford FICE Identification: 004838
Unit ID: 198622
Telephone: (336) 334-4822 Carnegie Class: Assoc/MT-VT-High Trad
FAX Number: (336) 454-2745 Calendar System: Semester
URL: www.gtcc.edu
Established: 1958 Annual Undergrad Tuition & Fees (In-State): $2,319
Enrollment: 10,072 Coed
Affiliation or Control: State IRS Status: 501(c)3
Highest Offering: Associate Degree
Accreditation: SC, ACFEI, DA, DH, EMT, IFSAC, MAC, PTAA, RAD, SURGT

02 President ... Dr. Anthony CLARKE
05 Sr Vice Pres of the College/CAO ... Dr. Beth PITONZO
32 Interim VP Student Support Services ... Mr. Kirby MOORE
11 AVP Facility Operations & Safety ... Mr. Mitchell JOHNSON
10 VP of Business & Finance/CFO ... Ms. Nancy B. SOLLOSI
20 Int AVP Student Support Services ... Dr. Chris CHAFIN
51 Assoc VP Corp & Continuing Educ ... Ms. Martha BERGMAN
12 Dean Greensboro Campus ... Dr. Manuel DUDLEY
12 Dean High Point Campus ... Dr. Mark HARRIS
50 Dir Business & Industry Training ... Mr. Stephen CASTELLOE
15 Director of Human Resources ... Ms. Cheryl BRYANT-SHANKS
13 Chief Information Officer ... Mr. Ron HORN
18 Director of Construction ... Mr. Charles YOUNG
09 Director of Institutional Research ... Ms. Kristen CORBELL
07 Director of Admissions ... Mr. Jesse CROSS
35 Director of Student Life ... Ms. Berri V. CROSS
37 Director Financial Aid ... Ms. Lisa A. KORETOFF
19 Chief of Campus Police ... Mr. James PHILLIPS
06 Registrar ... Mr. Joe ROWBOTTOM
21 AVP Business & Finance/Controller ... Ms. Angela M. CARTER
40 Bookstore Manager ... Mr. Shawn G. DEE
36 Coordinator Career Services ... Vacant
38 Director Counseling & Assessment ... Dr. Chris CHAFIN
30 Director of Development ... Ms. Nancy CALKINS
08 Dir of Library Services ... Ms. Monica YOUNG
41 Athletic Director ... Mr. Kirk CHANDLER
96 Director of Purchasing ... Mr. Michael STOUT
88 Dir of Organizational Development ... Ms. Jackie GREENLEE

*Halifax Community College (B)

PO Drawer 809, Weldon NC 27890-0809
County: Halifax FICE Identification: 007986
Unit ID: 198640
Telephone: (252) 536-2551 Carnegie Class: Assoc/MT-VT-High Non
FAX Number: (252) 536-4144 Calendar System: Semester
URL: www.halifaxcc.edu
Established: 1967 Annual Undergrad Tuition & Fees (In-District): $2,608
Enrollment: 1,113 Coed
Affiliation or Control: State/Local IRS Status: 501(c)3
Highest Offering: Associate Degree
Accreditation: SC, DH, MLTAD

02 President ... Dr. Michael A. ELAM
04 Exec Assistant to the President ... Ms. Kimberly J. MACK
05 Vice Pres Academic Affairs ... Dr. Jeffery B. FIELDS
10 Vice President Admin Services ... Mr. David FORESTER
111 VP Inst Effectiveness/Advancement ... Dr. Edwin IMASUEN
32 VP Student Svcs & Enrollment Mgmt ... Dr. Barbara BRADLEY-HASTY
20 Dean of Curriculum Programs ... Vacant
06 Registrar ... Ms. Dawn VELIKY
07 Director of Admissions/Enrol Mgmt ... Vacant
08 Director Learning Resources ... Ms. Lynn ALLEN
09 Dir of Institutional Research ... Mr. Marcus LEWIS
26 Dir Public Relations & Marketing ... Ms. Molly WALLACE
38 Director Counseling Services ... Ms. Charice ROSSER
18 Facilities/Physical Plant ... Mr. Jeremy WEBB
36 Director Career/College Promise ... Ms. Jennifer JONES
37 Director of Financial Aid ... Mrs. Tara KEETER
96 Purchasing Agent ... Ms. Sarah CHAMBLEE
15 Human Resources Manager ... Mrs. Margaret MURGA
13 Int Information Systems Manager ... Ms. Caroline HARRIS
49 Div Chair Arts & Sciences/Business ... Vacant
76 Div Chr Health Sciences/Humanities ... Ms. Allisha HICKS
75 Div Chair Vocation/Industrial Tech ... Vacant
106 Dir Online Education/E-learning ... Ms. Ellen GRANT
19 Chief Campus Security ... Lt. Emmett SMITH
25 Chief Contracts/Grants Admin ... Mr. Victor MARROW
30 Director of Development ... Mr. Allen PURSER
103 Director Workforce Development ... Mr. Jerry EDMONDS, III

*Haywood Community College (C)

185 Freedlander Drive, Clyde NC 28721-9453
County: Haywood FICE Identification: 008083
Unit ID: 198668
Telephone: (828) 627-2821 Carnegie Class: Assoc/MT-VT-High Trad
FAX Number: (828) 627-3606 Calendar System: Semester
URL: www.haywood.edu
Established: 1965 Annual Undergrad Tuition & Fees (In-State): $2,580
Enrollment: 1,344 Coed
Affiliation or Control: State IRS Status: 501(c)3
Highest Offering: Associate Degree
Accreditation: SC, MAC

02 President ... Dr. Barbara PARKER
05 Vice President of Instruction ... Mrs. Wendy HINES
32 Vice President Student Services ... Dr. Michael COLEMAN
10 Vice President Business Operations ... Mrs. Karen DENNEY
18 Director of Campus Development ... Mr. Brek LANNING
111 Dir Institutional Advancement ... Mrs. Pam HARDIN
26 Director Marketing & Communications ... Vacant
15 Director of Human Resources ... Mrs. Marsha STINES
84 Dir of Enrollment Mgmt/Registrar ... Mrs. Danielle HARRIS
37 Sr Dir Student Enrollment/Fin Aid ... Mrs. Tracy RAPP
09 Dir Inst Excellence/Research/Grants ... Mr. David ONDER
103 Dean of Workforce Dev/Cont Educ ... Mr. Doug BURCHFIELD

*Isothermal Community College (D)

PO Box 804, Spindale NC 28160-0804
County: Rutherford FICE Identification: 002934
Unit ID: 198710
Telephone: (828) 395-1292 Carnegie Class: Assoc/MT-VT-High Non
FAX Number: (828) 286-1120 Calendar System: Semester
URL: www.isothermal.edu
Established: 1964 Annual Undergrad Tuition & Fees (In-District): $2,542
Enrollment: 1,929 Coed
Affiliation or Control: State/Local IRS Status: 501(c)3
Highest Offering: Associate Degree
Accreditation: SC

02 President ... Mr. Walter H. DALTON
11 COO & Vice Pres ... Mr. Stephen MATHENY
05 Vice Pres Academic & Student Svcs ... Dr. Dolly HORTON
103 Vice Pres Cmty/Workforce Educ ... Mr. Thad HARRILL
32 Dean of Student Affairs ... Ms. Sandra LACKNER
50 Dean of Business Sciences ... Ms. Kim WAWZYSKO
49 Dean of Arts & Sciences ... Dr. Kathy ACKERMAN
75 Dean of Applied Science & Engr ... Mr. Joe LOONEY
51 Dean of Continuing Education ... Mrs. Donna HOOD
12 Director of Polk Campus ... Mrs. Kate BARKSCHAT
20 Director Academic Development ... Mrs. Debbie PUETT
08 Director Library Services ... Mr. Charles WIGGINS
10 Controller ... Mrs. Amy M. PENSON
37 Financial Aid Officer ... Mrs. Pamela ELLIS
26 Dir Marketing/Community Relations ... Mr. Mike GAVIN
18 Dir Plant Operations/Maintenance ... Mr. Bill DOLL
121 Director Advising & Success Center ... Dr. Kashanda RAY
84 Director of Enrollment Management ... Ms. Diane DICKERSON
06 Registrar ... Ms. Rachel MERCANTINI
96 Director of Purchasing ... Ms. Trish HUNTSINGER
13 Director of Information Technology ... Mr. Robby WALTERS
40 Bookstore Manager ... Mrs. Danielle ALEY
04 Executive Asst to President ... Mrs. DeeDee BARNARD
15 Director Personnel Services ... Ms. Amy HARPER
09 Director of Institutional Research ... Ms. Anne L. OXENREIDER

*James Sprunt Community College (E)

PO Box 398, Kenansville NC 28349-0398
County: Duplin FICE Identification: 007687
Unit ID: 198729
Telephone: (910) 296-2400 Carnegie Class: Assoc/MT-VT-High Trad
FAX Number: (910) 296-1636 Calendar System: Semester
URL: www.jamessprunt.edu
Established: 1964 Annual Undergrad Tuition & Fees (In-State): $2,570
Enrollment: 1,219 Coed
Affiliation or Control: State IRS Status: 501(c)3
Highest Offering: Associate Degree
Accreditation: SC

02 President ... Dr. Jay CARRAWAY
05 VP of Curriculum Services ... Ms. June DAVIS
51 AVP of Continuing Education ... Mr. Anthony THOMAS
10 VP of Admin & Fiscal Services ... Mr. John HARDISON
32 Associate VP of Student Services ... Mr. Brian JONES
111 VP Col Advance/Inst Effectiveness ... Mr. Stanley TURBEVILLE
06 Registrar ... Ms. Kelly MICAL
07 Admissions Specialist ... Ms. Wanda EDWARDS
37 Director Financial Aid/Vet Affairs ... Ms. Tracy WARD
38 Director of Student Counseling ... Ms. Amber FERRELL
08 Director Library Services ... Ms. Christine VASICA
15 Dir Human Resources/Campus Safety ... Ms. Debbie MARTIN
97 Director of General Education ... Mr. Andy CAVENAUGH
09 Dir Research/Plng/Inst Effective ... Mrs. Norma Jean HATCHER
26 Director of Public Info/Print Media ... Ms. Cheryl HEMRIC
18 Chief Facilities/Physical Plant ... Mr. Dennis SUTTON
96 Director of Purchasing ... Ms. Toni HENDERSON
55 Instr/Coord Evening/Weekend Svcs ... Mr. James THOMAS
13 Chief Info Technology Officer (CIO) ... Vacant
19 Director Security/Safety ... Mr. Richard WHITMAN
04 Admin Assistant to the President ... Mrs. Stephanie STUART

*Johnston Community College (F)

PO Box 2350, 245 College Road, Smithfield NC 27577-2350
County: Johnston FICE Identification: 009336
Unit ID: 198774
Telephone: (919) 934-3051 Carnegie Class: Assoc/MT-VT-High Non
FAX Number: (919) 209-2142 Calendar System: Semester
URL: www.johnstoncc.edu
Established: 1969 Annual Undergrad Tuition & Fees (In-District): $2,657
Enrollment: 4,152 Coed
Affiliation or Control: State/Local IRS Status: 501(c)3
Highest Offering: Associate Degree
Accreditation: SC, ADNUR, DMS, EMT, MAC, RAD

02 President ... Dr. David N. JOHNSON
10 VP Admin/Financial & IT Resources ... Dr. Darryl MCGRAW
05 Vice Pres of Instruction ... Mrs. Dee Dee D. DAUGHTRY
32 Vice Pres of Student Services ... Dr. Pamela J. HARRELL
09 Exec Dir of Research and IE ... Dr. Terri S. LEE
102 Executive Director of Foundation ... Dr. Twyla C. WELLS
13 Chief Information Officer ... Mr. Jeff PICKERING
08 Lead Librarian ... Ms. Jennifer SEAGRAVES
105 Student Services Data & Application ... Mr. Dustin H. GURLEY
06 Registrar ... Ms. Deena H. HENRY
37 Director Financial Aid ... Mrs. Betty C. WOODALL
109 Assoc VP of Auxiliary Enterprises ... Mr. Ken H. MITCHELL
15 Director of Human Resources ... Mr. Harlan FRYE
07 Dir of Enrollment & Student Success ... Mrs. Megan L. SHANER
103 Dean Workforce Dev/Advanced Tech ... Mrs. Joy T. CALLAHAN
76 Dean Health/Wellness & Human Svcs ... Dr. Linda D. SMITH
49 Dean University Studies/Educ Tech ... Mrs. Dawn S. DIXON
50 Int Dean Business/Advanced Tech ... Mrs. Jennifer SERVI-ROBERTS
26 Senior Director of Communications ... Mrs. Traci D. ASHLEY
18 Maintenance Director ... Mr. Michael MASSEY
96 Purchasing and Equipment Director ... Ms. Cassandra HAIRE
88 Secy and Emer Preparedness Coord ... Ms. Sarah GIBBS
04 Exec Asst to the President ... Ms. Sandy MILLARD

*Lenoir Community College (G)

231 Highway 58 South, Kinston NC 28502-0188
County: Lenoir FICE Identification: 002940
Unit ID: 198817
Telephone: (252) 527-6223 Carnegie Class: Assoc/MT-VT-High Non
FAX Number: (252) 233-6879 Calendar System: Semester
URL: www.lenoircc.edu
Established: 1958 Annual Undergrad Tuition & Fees (In-District): $2,558
Enrollment: 2,664 Coed
Affiliation or Control: State/Local IRS Status: 501(c)3
Highest Offering: Associate Degree
Accreditation: SC, ACFEI, EMT, MAC, POLYT, RAD, SURGT

02 President ... Dr. Rusty HUNT
51 VP Continuing Education ... Mrs. Renee SUTTON
11 Senior VP Administrative Services ... Ms. Deborah SUTTON
05 SVP Instruction/Student Services ... Dr. Deborah GRIMES
10 Chief Financial Officer ... Ms. Deborah SUTTON
06 Registrar ... Ms. Shelia WIGGINS
84 Director Enrollment Mgmt/Admissions ... Mrs. Kimberly HILL
32 Dean of Student Services ... Dr. John Paul BLACK
37 Director of Student Financial Aid ... Mr. J. D GIBBS
13 Chief Info Ofcr/Dean Admin Svcs ... Mr. Lee WETHERINGTON
09 Director Innovation & Effectiveness ... Mr. Jonathan TYNDALL
15 Director Human Resources ... Mrs. Tasha JOHNSON
18 Director of Maintenance ... Mr. Reed LOVICK
41 Athletic Director ... Mrs. Shelly BARNES
21 Director of Financial Services ... Ms. Jessica MCMAHON
96 Purchasing Agent ... Ms. Rhonda DEAVER
26 Director of Mktg/Recruiting/Comm ... Ms. Richy HUNEYCUTT
111 Director Institutional Advancement ... Mrs. Jeanne KENNEDY
103 Work-Based Lrng Coord ... Mrs. Sherry IRSIK
08 Director of Learning Resources ... Mr. Rich GARAFOLO
50 Dean of Business/Technologies ... Mr. Gary CLEMENTS
49 Dean of Arts & Sciences ... Dr. Timothy MADDOX
76 Dean of Health Sciences & Nursing ... Dr. Alexis WELCH
72 Dean of Industrial Technologies ... Dr. Maggie BROWN
72 Dean of Administrative Services ... Mr. Lee WETHERINGTON
51 Dean of Workforce Development & CE ... Dr. Dustin WALSTON
35 Director Student Activities ... Mrs. Shelly BARNES
07 Director of Admissions ... Mrs. Kimberly HILL

*Martin Community College (H)

1161 Kehukee Park Road, Williamston NC 27892-9988
County: Martin FICE Identification: 007988
Unit ID: 198905
Telephone: (252) 792-1521 Carnegie Class: Assoc/MT-VT-High Non
FAX Number: (252) 792-0826 Calendar System: Semester
URL: www.martincc.edu
Established: 1967 Annual Undergrad Tuition & Fees (In-State): $1,886
Enrollment: 837 Coed
Affiliation or Control: State IRS Status: 501(c)3
Highest Offering: Associate Degree
Accreditation: SC, DA, MAC, PTAA

02 President ... Dr. Ken BOHAM
03 Executive Vice President ... Dr. Brian BUSCH
05 Dean of Academic Affairs ... Dr. Tabitha MILLER
10 Chief Financial Officer ... Ms. Tammy BAILEY
04 Asst to Pres for Business/Industry ... Mr. Billy BARBER
37 Financial Aid Director ... Ms. Terri LEGGETT
07 Counselor and Admissions ... Ms. Vanessa TRIPP
06 Registrar ... Ms. Eileen JARMUL
51 Dean Continuing Education ... Vacant
18 Director of Facilities ... Mr. Walter WHEELER
15 Human Resource Director ... Vacant
13 Director of IT ... Mr. Elijah T. FREEMAN

09 Director of Institutional Research .... Ms. Maureen GREEN
96 Director of Purchasing .... Ms. Jennifer CHERRY
12 Director of Bertie Campus .... Mr. Norman CHERRY
08 Library Director .... Ms. Mary Anne CAUDLE
101 Exec Asst to President and BOT .... Ms. Kismet MATTHEWS
26 Dir Communications/PIO .... Ms. Judy JENNETTE

*Mayland Community College (A)

PO Box 547, Spruce Pine NC 28777-0547
County: Mitchell FICE Identification: 011197
Unit ID: 198914
Telephone: (828) 765-7351 Carnegie Class: Assoc/MT-VT-Mix Trad/Non
FAX Number: (828) 765-0728 Calendar System: Semester
URL: www.mayland.edu
Established: 1971 Annual Undergrad Tuition & Fees (In-District): $2,558
Enrollment: 986 Coed
Affiliation or Control: State/Local IRS Status: 501(c)3
Highest Offering: Associate Degree
Accreditation: SC, MAC

02 President .... Dr. John C. BOYD
04 Assistant to the President .... Ms. Brooke BURLESON
10 Vice President Administrative Svcs .... Mrs. Amanda BUCHANAN
05 Vice Pres Academics & Workforce Dev .... Mrs. Rita EARLEY
32 Dean of Students .... Ms. Michelle MUSICH
76 Dean of Health Sciences Programs .... Mrs. Kim BURR
49 Dean of Arts & Sciences .... Ms. Sherry SHERMAN
72 Dean of Career Technologies .... Ms. Brenda MCFEE
08 Director Learning Resources Center .... Mr. Jon WILMESHERR
09 Dir Institutional Effectiveness .... Mr. Ryan RAY
06 Registrar .... Vacant
88 Dean of Basic Skills Programs .... Mr. Steve GUNTER
12 Dean Avery County EWD .... Mrs. Melissa C. PHILLIPS
12 Dean Mitchell County EWD .... Mr. Chris HELMS
12 Dean Yancey County EWD .... Dr. Monica S. CARPENTER
37 Director Student Financial Aid .... Ms. Sonja PETERSON
18 Director Facilities/Physical Plant .... Mr. Lee WHITTINGTON
13 Dir Management Information Systems .... Mr. Tommy R. LEDFORD
15 Director Personnel Services .... Mr. Judy MCCLURE
96 Coordinator of Purchasing/Equipment .... Mr. Eddie BUCHANAN

*McDowell Technical Community College (B)

54 College Drive, Marion NC 28752-8728
County: McDowell FICE Identification: 008085
Unit ID: 198923
Telephone: (828) 652-6021 Carnegie Class: Assoc/MT-VT-High Non
FAX Number: (828) 652-1014 Calendar System: Semester
URL: www.mcdowelltech.edu
Established: 1964 Annual Undergrad Tuition & Fees (In-District): $1,926
Enrollment: 1,043 Coed
Affiliation or Control: State/Local IRS Status: 501(c)3
Highest Offering: Associate Degree
Accreditation: SC, CAHIIM

02 President .... Dr. John GOSSETT
05 Vice Pres for Learning/Student Svcs .... Dr. Penny CROSS
10 Vice Pres Finance/Administration .... Mr. Ryan GARRISON
20 Dean Curriculum Programs .... Dr. James BENTON
09 Director of Inst Effectiveness .... Mr. Ladelle HARMON
26 Director of External Relations .... Mr. Michael K. LAVENDER
13 Director of Technology/Info Systems .... Mr. Elmer R. MACOPSON
08 Int Director of Library Services .... Ms. Pat TALLENT
88 Director of Industrial Training .... Mr. Eddie SHUFORD
76 Director of Health Sciences .... Mrs. Judy MELTON
06 Registrar .... Ms. Kelly HAMLIN
37 Director Student Financial Aid .... Ms. Kim M. LEDBETTER
36 Director of Student Enrichment Ctr .... Mrs. Donna SHORT
88 Director Adult Basic Skills .... Mrs. Teresa VALENTINO
88 Counselor/VA Director .... Mrs. Donna SHORT
51 Director of Continuing Education .... Mr. Brad LEDBETTER
88 Director Basic Law Enforcement Trng .... Mr. Stacy BUFF
07 Director of Admissions .... Mr. Wingate CAIN
15 Human Resources Manager .... Ms. Breanna ROSE
30 Foundation Resource Devel Officer .... Vacant
106 Coordinator of Distance Education .... Mrs. Joan WEILER
18 Coord Maintenance/Custodial Svcs .... Mr. Carl COSTNER
88 Director MTCC Small Business Center .... Mr. Frank SILVER
04 Exec Assistant to the President .... Ms. Madalyn GAITO

*Mitchell Community College (C)

500 W Broad Street, Statesville NC 28677-5293
County: Iredell FICE Identification: 002947
Unit ID: 198987
Telephone: (704) 878-3200 Carnegie Class: Assoc/HT-High Non
FAX Number: (704) 878-0872 Calendar System: Semester
URL: www.mitchellcc.edu
Established: 1852 Annual Undergrad Tuition & Fees (In-State): $2,651
Enrollment: 3,204 Coed
Affiliation or Control: State IRS Status: 501(c)3
Highest Offering: Associate Degree
Accreditation: SC, ADNUR, MAC, MUS

02 President .... Dr. Tim BREWER
05 Vice President of Instruction .... Dr. Camille REESE
10 Vice Pres of Finance/Administration .... Mr. Gerald HYDE
103 Vice Pres Workforce Development/CEC .... Ms. Carol JOHNSON
111 Vice President for Advancement .... Mr. James HOGAN
32 Vice Pres Student Services .... Dr. Porter BRANNON
12 Exec Director of Mooresville Campus .... Mr. Robert LESLIE
09 Exec Director Research & Planning .... Ms. Eva EISNAUGLE
121 Director Student Academic Success .... Dr. Sandra LANDRY
37 Director of Financial Aid .... Ms. Candace COOPER
18 Director of Facilities .... Mr. Chad LACKEY
88 Director of Educational Partnership .... Ms. Amanda RHEA
06 Registrar .... Ms. Erin DUBEA
19 Director of Public Safety .... Mr. David BULLINS
121 Director of Academic Advising .... Ms. Myra LEWIS
15 Director of Human Resources .... Mr. Paul SANTOS
97 Dean of College Transfer .... Ms. Tia COLEMAN
50 Dean of Bus/Agriculture/Public Svc .... Mr. Mark SMALLEY
66 Dean of Nursing and Sciences .... Ms. Linda WIERSCH

*Montgomery Community College (D)

1011 Page Street, Troy NC 27371-0787
County: Montgomery FICE Identification: 008087
Unit ID: 199023
Telephone: (910) 898-9600 Carnegie Class: Assoc/HVT-High Non
FAX Number: (910) 576-2176 Calendar System: Semester
URL: www.montgomery.edu
Established: 1967 Annual Undergrad Tuition & Fees (In-District): $2,537
Enrollment: 925 Coed
Affiliation or Control: State/Local IRS Status: 501(c)3
Highest Offering: Associate Degree
Accreditation: SC, CSHSE, DA, MAC

02 President .... Dr. Chad A. BLEDSOE
05 Vice Pres of Instruction .... Lee PROCTOR
11 VP of Administrative Services .... Jeanette MCBRIDE
32 VP of Student Services .... Beth SMITH
51 Dean of Continuing Education .... Andrew GARDNER
102 Executive Director Foundation/Grant .... Korrie ERVIN
26 Public Information Officer .... Michele HAYWOOD
09 Dir Institutional Effectiveness .... Carol HOLTON
13 Dir of Information Technology .... Cindy ELLISON
04 Assistant to the President .... Courtney B. ATKINS
38 Counseling Services .... Vacant
07 Admissions Officer .... Karen FRYE
37 Director of Financial Aid .... Doni S. HATCHEL
15 Director Of Human Resources .... Melisa BOND
10 Accountant .... Tonya LUCK
18 Director of Facilities .... Wanda FRICK
35 Student Activities Coordinator .... Jessica BLAKE
08 Head Librarian .... Deborah ASHBY

*Nash Community College (E)

522 N Old Carriage Road, Rocky Mount NC 27804-0488
County: Nash FICE Identification: 008557
Unit ID: 199087
Telephone: (252) 443-4011 Carnegie Class: Assoc/MT-VT-Mix Trad/Non
FAX Number: (252) 451-8201 Calendar System: Semester
URL: www.nashcc.edu
Established: 1967 Annual Undergrad Tuition & Fees (In-District): $2,632
Enrollment: 2,966 Coed
Affiliation or Control: State/Local IRS Status: 501(c)3
Highest Offering: Associate Degree
Accreditation: SC, MAC, PTAA

02 President .... Dr. William S. CARVER, II
04 Admin Asst to President/Board .... Mrs. Odell P. HOLLIDAY
103 VP Corporate/Economic Dev .... Mrs. Wendy C. MARLOWE
111 VP Institutional Advancement .... Mrs. Pamela H. BALLEW
05 Vice President for Instruction .... Dr. Tammie L. CLARK
10 Vice President of Finance .... Mrs. Adrienne S. COVINGTON
13 Vice President Technology & CIO .... Dr. Jonathan S. VESTER
32 VP Student & Enrollment Svcs .... Mr. Mike LATHAM
26 Dean of Marketing .... Mrs. Kelley P. DEAL
88 Assoc VP/Transfer Initiatives .... Ms. Deana L. GUIDO
09 Assoc Dean Institutional Effective .... Ms. Farley A. PHILLIPS
88 Director Small Business Center .... Ms. Theresa R. PEADEN
07 Director of Admissions/Recruitment .... Dr. Daniel O. WILSON
37 Director of Financial Aid .... Ms. Tammy LESTER
15 Director Human Resources .... Ms. Morgan R. BLAND
18 Director of Facilities .... Mr. Greg DEANS
06 Registrar/Director of Records .... Mrs. Kathy S. ADCOX

*Pamlico Community College (F)

PO Box 185, Grantsboro NC 28529-0185
County: Pamlico FICE Identification: 007031
Unit ID: 199263
Telephone: (252) 249-1851 Carnegie Class: Assoc/MT-VT-Mix Trad/Non
FAX Number: (252) 249-2377 Calendar System: Semester
URL: www.pamlicocc.edu
Established: 1962 Annual Undergrad Tuition & Fees (In-District): $1,867
Enrollment: 462 Coed
Affiliation or Control: State/Local IRS Status: 501(c)3
Highest Offering: Associate Degree
Accreditation: SC, MAC, NDT

02 President .... Dr. Jim ROSS
10 CFO .... Ms. Sherry RABY
05 Vice Pres Instructional Svcs .... Ms. Michelle WILLIS KRAUSS
32 Vice Pres of Student Services .... Mr. Jamie GIBBS
13 CIO .... Mr. Scott FRAZER
09 Dir of Institutional Effectiveness .... Ms. Rebecca PESKO
15 Director of Human Resources .... Ms. Brandy FILLINGAME
06 Interim Registrar .... Ms. Gretchen STEIGER
37 Director of Financial Aid .... Ms. Meredith BEEMAN
21 Controller .... Ms. Susan MCROY
26 Director of Public Affairs .... Mr. Sandy WALL
04 Administrative Asst to President .... Ms. Michelle NOEVERE
106 Coordinator of Distance Learning .... Ms. Kathy MAYO

*Piedmont Community College (G)

1715 College Dr, Roxboro NC 27573-1197
County: Person FICE Identification: 009646
Unit ID: 199324
Telephone: (336) 599-1181 Carnegie Class: Assoc/MT-VT-Mix Trad/Non
FAX Number: (336) 597-3817 Calendar System: Semester
URL: www.piedmontcc.edu
Established: 1970 Annual Undergrad Tuition & Fees (In-District): $2,544
Enrollment: 1,311 Coed
Affiliation or Control: State/Local IRS Status: 501(c)3
Highest Offering: Associate Degree
Accreditation: SC, EMT, MAC

02 President .... Dr. Pamela G. SENEGAL
05 Vice Pres Instruction/CAO .... Dr. Barbara BUCHANAN
51 Vice Pres Continuing Education .... Dr. Doris W. CARVER
11 Vice Pres Administrative Services .... Ms. Beverly J. MURPHY
32 Vice President Student Development .... Ms. Shelly T. STONE-MOYE
106 Dean Distance Education .... Vacant
88 Dean Adult Basic Skills .... Ms. Debra B. HARLOW
103 Dean Occupational Ext & Corr Ed .... Mr. Benjamin FOTI
76 Dean Health Sciences and Human Svcs .... Ms. Alisa L. MONTGOMERY
08 Dean Learning Commons .... Mr. Don M. MILLER
72 Dean Tech/Occupational Programs .... Mr. Walter C. MONTGOMERY
105 Webmaster/Graphics Designer .... Mr. Kevin R. TYBURSKI
88 Director TRiO Programs .... Ms. Samantha G. AARON
103 Dean Workforce Development .... Mr. Jody B. BLACKWELL
06 Registrar .... Ms. Susan L. GREINER
37 Dir Financial Aid/Veterans Affairs .... Ms. Paulita N. WILLIAMS
18 Director Buildings and Grounds .... Vacant
25 Director Grants .... Vacant
15 Director Human Resources .... Ms. Shaundria WILLIAMS
88 Director QEP .... Ms. Lisa K. COOLEY
26 Director Public Information .... Ms. Elizabeth R. TOWNSEND
09 Dir Research/Inst Effectiveness .... Vacant
13 Chief Information Officer .... Vacant
19 Director College Safety .... Mr. Adam W. IRBY
29 Director Events and Resource Mgmt .... Ms. Patricia I. CLAYTON
96 Purchasing Officer/Accountant .... Ms. Jovana AMARO
04 Executive Asst to President .... Ms. Tammy W. DUNCAN
10 Controller .... Vacant
102 Executive Director PCC Foundation .Ms. Allison D. SATTERFIELD
49 Dean Arts/Sciences Univ Trsf .... Ms. Karen SANDERS
12 Dean Caswell County .... Vacant

*Pitt Community College (H)

PO Drawer 7007, Greenville NC 27835-7007
County: Pitt FICE Identification: 004062
Unit ID: 199333
Telephone: (252) 493-7200 Carnegie Class: Assoc/MT-VT-Mix Trad/Non
FAX Number: (252) 321-4458 Calendar System: Semester
URL: www.pittcc.edu
Established: 1961 Annual Undergrad Tuition & Fees (In-State): $1,930
Enrollment: 8,256 Coed
Affiliation or Control: State IRS Status: 501(c)3
Highest Offering: Associate Degree
Accreditation: SC, ADNUR, CAHIIM, COARC, CSHSE, DMS, EMT, MAC, OTA, POLYT, RAD, RADDOS, RTT

02 President .... Dr. Lawrence L. ROUSE
05 VP Academic Affairs & Student Svcs .... Dr. Thomas GOULD
11 Vice Pres Administrative Services .... Mr. Rick OWENS
26 Vice Pres Strategic Initiatives .... Dr. Johnny SMITH
111 Vice Pres Institutional Advancement .... Mrs. Marianne COX
20 Asst Vice Pres Academic Affairs .... Ms. Lori PREAST
13 AVP Information Technology/Services .... Mr. Ernest SIMONS
10 Vice President of Finance .... Mr. Ricky BROWN
04 Executive Admin Asst to President .... Mrs. Kathy M. CARNES
08 Director Library .... Ms. Leigh RUSSELL
09 Exec Dir of Planning & Research .... Dr. Brian MILLER
15 Vice President of Human Resources .... Dr. Ina RAWLINSON
91 Director of Admin Computing .... Mr. Wes WOOTEN
06 Registrar .... Ms. Angela CLINE
38 Director of Counseling .... Dr. Kimberly WILLIAMSON
88 Director Basic Skills Program .... Ms. Laurie WESTON
18 Director of Facilities .... Mr. Timothy STRICKLAND
41 Athletic Director .... Ms. Dawn MANNING
29 Director of Alumni Relations .... Mr. John BACON
96 Director of Purchasing .... Ms. Jane ALLIGOOD
19 Chief Public Safety/Campus Police .... Mr. Tyronne TURNAGE
88 Director Small Business Svcs .... Mr. Jerry ENSOR
104 Director Study Abroad .... Vacant
37 Director Financial Aid .... Ms. Lee BRAY
40 Manager of College Store .... Ms. Holly BARBEE
106 Coord Instructional Tech/Dist Educ .... Mr. Mike CLENDENEN
55 Coord/Counselor Evening Programs .... Mr. Alton WADFORD
50 Division Dean of Business .... Ms. Katherine CLYDE
76 Division Dean Health Sciences .... Ms. Donna V. NEAL
49 Division Dean of Art & Sciences ... Dr. Stephanie MANLEY-ROOK
75 Div Dean Construct/Indus Tech .... Mr. Stephen MATHEWS
61 Div Dean Legal Sci/Public Svc .... Dr. Dan MAYO

07 Director of Admissions ....Ms. Shakenna WHITE
102 Dir Foundation/Corporate Relations ....Ms. Georgia SIGMON
105 Director Web Services ....Mr. Kris ANDERSON
25 Director Grants Management ....Ms. Julia CRIPPEN
26 Marketing Director ....Ms. Jane POWER

*Randolph Community College (A)

629 Industrial Park Avenue, Asheboro NC 27205
County: Randolph FICE Identification: 005447
Unit ID: 199421
Telephone: (336) 633-0200 Carnegie Class: Assoc/HT-Mix Trad/Non
FAX Number: (336) 629-4695 Calendar System: Semester
URL: www.randolph.edu
Established: 1962 Annual Undergrad Tuition & Fees (In-District): $2,373
Enrollment: 2,747 Coed
Affiliation or Control: State/Local IRS Status: 501(c)3
Highest Offering: Associate Degree
Accreditation: SC, MAC, RAD

02 President ....Dr. Robert S. SHACKLEFORD, JR.
10 Vice Pres Administrative Services ....Ms. Daffie H. GARRIS
05 Vice Pres Instructional Services ....Ms. Suzanne Y. ROHRBAUGH
32 Vice President Student Services ....Mr. Chad WILLIAMS
103 VP Workforce Development/Cont Educ ....Mr. Elbert J. LASSITER
111 VP Institutional Advancement ....Ms. Shelley W. GREENE
08 Dean Library Services ....Ms. Deborah S. LUCK
12 Director Archdale Center ....Ms. Tonya C. MONROE
21 Dir Financial Services/Controller ....Ms. Susan I. RICE
26 Director Marketing ....Ms. Felicia R. BARLOW
18 Director Facilities Operations ....Ms. Cindi J. GOODWIN
13 Director Information Tech Svcs ....Ms. Tara A. WILLIAMS
09 Planning & Assessment Specialist ....Ms. Stacy C. SCHMITT
15 Director of Human Resources ....Ms. Melanie AVELINO
37 Director Financial Aid & Veteran Af ....Mr. Joel TROGDON
07 Dir Admissions/Records & Registrar ..Ms. Hillary D. PRITCHARD
106 Director Distance Education ....Mr. Devin A. SOVA
88 Director of ABE and AHS ....Ms. Jordan H. WILLIAMSON
88 Director Public Safety Programs ....Ms. Regina L. BREWER
96 Purchasing Agent ....Mr. Christopher G. HUSSEY
27 Asst Director Public Information ....Ms. Cathy D. HEFFERIN
04 Exec Asst to Pres/Board of Trustees ..Ms. Heather O. CLOUSTON
19 Dir Safety/Emergency Preparedness ....Mr. Matthew R. NEEDHAM
30 Director of Development ....Ms. Lorie L. MCCROSKEY

*Richmond Community College (B)

Box 1189, Hamlet NC 28345-1189
County: Richmond FICE Identification: 005464
Unit ID: 199449
Telephone: (910) 410-1700 Carnegie Class: Assoc/MT-VT-Mix Trad/Non
FAX Number: (910) 582-7028 Calendar System: Semester
URL: www.richmondcc.edu
Established: 1964 Annual Undergrad Tuition & Fees (In-District): $2,516
Enrollment: 2,528 Coed
Affiliation or Control: State/Local IRS Status: 501(c)3
Highest Offering: Associate Degree
Accreditation: SC, MAC

02 President ....Dr. W. Dale MCINNIS
32 Vice President for Student Services ....Ms. Sharon GOODMAN
05 Vice President for Instruction/CAO ....Mr. Kevin PARSONS
10 Executive VP and CFO ....Mr. Brent BARBEE
103 VP for Workforce & Economic Develop ....Vacant
08 Dean of Learning Resources ....Vacant
88 Director of Basic Skills ....Mr. John KESTER
26 Assoc VP of Mktg & Strategic Plng ... Ms. Sheri DUNN-RAMSAY
09 Director of Institutional Research ....Ms. Chihoko TERRY
15 Director of Human Resources ....Ms. Gaye CLARK
27 Dir of Marketing & Communications ....Ms. Wylie BELL
21 Controller ....Ms. Debbie CASHWELL
36 Director of Career and Transfer Svc ....Ms. Patsy STANLEY
37 Director Student Financial Aid ....Ms. Andrea DANIELS
96 Purchasing Officer ....Mr. Martin BRIDGES
18 Director of Facility Services ....Mr. Scotty MABE
38 Director Student Counseling ....Mr. Chris GARDNER
04 Executive Asst to President ....Ms. Teena PARSONS
06 Registrar ....Ms. Cayce HOLMES
106 Director of Distance Learning ....Mr. Alan QUESTELL
13 Chief Information Officer ....Mr. Lee MONTROSE
54 Dean of Applied Sciences & Engr ....Dr. Devon HALL
49 Dean of Arts & Sciences ....Mr. Lee BALLENGER

*Roanoke-Chowan Community College (C)

109 Community College Road, Ahoskie NC 27910
County: Hertford FICE Identification: 008613
Unit ID: 199467
Telephone: (252) 862-1200 Carnegie Class: Assoc/HT-High Non
FAX Number: (252) 862-1358 Calendar System: Semester
URL: www.roanokechowan.edu
Established: 1967 Annual Undergrad Tuition & Fees (In-District): $2,642
Enrollment: 791 Coed
Affiliation or Control: State/Local IRS Status: 501(c)3
Highest Offering: Associate Degree
Accreditation: #SC

02 President ....Dr. Stanley J. ELLIOTT
05 Dean of Academic Affairs ....Dr. Adriane LECHE
76 Director Allied Health Programs ....Ms. Jamie BURNS
32 Dean of Student Services ....Dr. LaTanya M. NIXON
10 Dean of Administrative Fiscal Svcs ....Vacant
21 Controller ....Ms. Belinda SMITH
18 Foreman ....Mr. Timothy LASSITER
106 Director Distance Learning ....Ms. Melanie TEMPLE
37 Director Financial Aid ....Mrs. Ruchelle RICKS
13 Director of Information Systems ....Dr. Mary LEARY
84 Director Enrollment Svcs/Curric Reg ....Mrs. Amy F. WIGGINS
121 Director Student Support Services ....Dr. Tanya OLIVER
15 Interim Director Human Resources ....Mrs. Nicole BOONE
06 Registrar/Continuing Educ/Workforce ....Ms. Shirley GAY
102 Director R-CCC Foundation ....Vacant
09 Director of Institutional Research ....Mrs. Jaime P. HECKSTALL
103 Dean Continuing Ed/Workforce Devel ....Mr. Charles H. PURSER
96 Purchasing Agent/Equipment Coord ....Ms. Susan B. MELTON
04 Admin Assistant to the President ... Ms. Joanne JOHNSON-SHAW
08 Chief Library Officer ....Mrs. Bonnie BURKETT
19 Director Security/Safety ....Ms. Tamara ALLEN

*Robeson Community College (D)

PO Box 1420, Lumberton NC 28359-1420
County: Robeson FICE Identification: 008612
Unit ID: 199476
Telephone: (910) 272-3700 Carnegie Class: Assoc/MT-VT-Mix Trad/Non
FAX Number: (910) 272-3328 Calendar System: Semester
URL: www.robeson.edu
Established: 1965 Annual Undergrad Tuition & Fees (In-District): $2,563
Enrollment: 1,935 Coed
Affiliation or Control: State/Local IRS Status: 501(c)3
Highest Offering: Associate Degree
Accreditation: SC, COARC, RAD, SURGT

02 President ....Dr. Kimberly GOLD
05 VP Instruction/Sppt Svcs/CAO ....Mr. Bill MAUNEY
51 Vice Pres Adult & Continuing Educ ....Vacant
10 Vice President Business Services ....Mrs. Tami B. GEORGE
55 Asst VP Public Svc/Appl Tech Pgms ...Mr. William L. LOCKLEAR
88 Asst VP Univ Transfer/Bus/Hlth Pgms ....Ms. Connie IVEY
32 Asst Vice Pres Student Services ....Mr. Ronnie LOCKLEAR
13 Asst VP/Chief Information Officer ....Mr. Dustin LONG
07 Director of Admissions/Enroll Svcs ....Ms. Patricia LOCKLEAR
08 Director of Learning Resource Svcs ....Mrs. Maryellen O'BRIEN
06 Dir Records/Registration/Registrar ....Mrs. Beth CARMICAL
37 Financial Aid Director ....Ms. Teresa TUBBS
18 Director of Facilities ....Mr. Kenny DAVIS
102 Director Foundation & Development ....Ms. Rebekah R. LOWRY
36 Counseling & Career Services ....Mr. Ronnie SAMPSON
15 Personnel Services Specialist ....Ms. Pam ROMANO
96 Purchasing Officer ....Ms. Christy MUSSELWHITE
04 Administrative Asst to President ....Ms. Regina L. BRANCH
09 Director of Institutional Effective ....Ms. Toni SACRY
19 Director Security ....Ms. Patricia CLARK

*Rockingham Community College (E)

PO Box 38, Wentworth NC 27375-0038
County: Rockingham FICE Identification: 002958
Unit ID: 199485
Telephone: (336) 342-4261 Carnegie Class: Assoc/HT-High Trad
FAX Number: (336) 349-9986 Calendar System: Semester
URL: www.rockinghamcc.edu
Established: 1963 Annual Undergrad Tuition & Fees (In-District): $1,966
Enrollment: 1,931 Coed
Affiliation or Control: State/Local IRS Status: 501(c)3
Highest Offering: Associate Degree
Accreditation: SC, COARC, SURGT

02 President ....Dr. Mark O. KINLAW
05 Vice President for Academic Affairs ....Ms. Sheila REGAN
11 VP of Administrative Services ....Mr. Steven W. WOODRUFF
32 Vice Pres for Student Development ..Dr. Robert S. LOWDERMILK
88 Assoc VP Administrative Services ....Dr. E. Anthony GUNN
103 Dean of Workforce Development & CE ....Vacant
49 Dean of Arts & Sciences ....Ms. Celeste H. ALLIS
76 Dean of Health & Public Services ....Ms. Vickie CHITWOOD
88 Director Testing Services ....Ms. Kimberly SHIREMAN
13 AVP Technology/Inst Effectiveness ....Ms. Gretchen PARRISH
06 Registrar ....Ms. Carla MOORE
08 Director Library Services/Archivist ....Ms. Mary GOMEZ
30 Director Development/Foundation ....Dr. Cindy SARWI
37 Director of Financial Aid ....Ms. Carol PERRY
84 Director of Enrollment Services ....Mr. Derick SATTERFIELD
35 Director Student Life ....Ms. Maggie MURRAY
40 Bookstore Manager ....Ms. Della J. GASTON
15 Director Human Resources ....Ms. Joy G. CHAPPELL
26 Director Public Information ....Ms. Gerri HUNT
96 Purchasing Officer/Equip Coord ....Mr. Caleb RORRER

*Rowan-Cabarrus Community College (F)

1333 Jake Alexander Blvd., South, Salisbury NC 28145
County: Rowan FICE Identification: 005754
Unit ID: 199494
Telephone: (704) 216-7222 Carnegie Class: Assoc/HT-Mix Trad/Non
FAX Number: N/A Calendar System: Semester
URL: www.rccc.edu
Established: 1963 Annual Undergrad Tuition & Fees (In-State): $2,626
Enrollment: 5,819 Coed
Affiliation or Control: State IRS Status: 501(c)3
Highest Offering: Associate Degree
Accreditation: SC, ADNUR, DA, OTA, PNUR, @PTAA, RAD

02 President ....Dr. Carol SPALDING
05 Academic Vice President ....Dr. Michael D. QUILLEN
51 VP Corporate & Continuing Education ....Mr. Craig LAMB
121 Vice Pres Student Success ....Ms. Natasha LIPSCOMB
13 Chief Information Officer ....Mr. Kenneth G. INGLE, III
18 Chief Officer College Environment .. Mr. Jonathan CHAMBERLAIN
20 Assoc Academic Vice President ....Ms. Debra NEESMITH
20 Assoc Academic Vice President ....Mr. Angelo MARKANTONAKIS
21 Assoc Chief Financial Officer ....Ms. Kizzy LEA
76 Dean Health Programs ....Dr. Wendy BARNHARDT
49 Dean Arts and Sciences ....Ms. Carol SCHERCZINGER
54 Dean Engineering Tech/Public Svcs ....Mr. Van MADRAY
106 Director Distance Learning ....Mrs. Faith JELLEY
36 Exec Dir College & Career Readiness ....Mr. Jay TAYLOR
08 Director Learning Resource Center ....Mr. Timothy HUNTER
25 Director Grants Development ....Ms. Rebecca HOOKS
121 Exec Dir Students Success Svc ....Ms. Lisa LEDBETTER
96 Director of Purchasing ....Ms. Kathy PIPER
37 Director of Student Financial Aid ....Ms. Allison SCOTT
06 Registrar/Dir Admission & Records ....Mr. Phillip LOPP
35 Director Student Life & Leadership ....Mrs. Barb MEIDL
15 Assoc Chief Human Resources Officer ....Mrs. Nekita EUBANKS
28 Dir Diversity & Compliance Training ....Dr. Steve CATHCART
09 Exec Dir Inst Effectiveness & Rsch ....Ms. Catherine GARCIA
19 Director Campus Safety & Security ....Mr. Paul DUPREE
26 Exec Dir Marketing & Recruiting ....Ms. Paula DIBLEY

*Sampson Community College (G)

PO Box 318, Clinton NC 28329-0318
County: Sampson FICE Identification: 007892
Unit ID: 199625
Telephone: (910) 592-8081 Carnegie Class: Assoc/MT-VT-High Trad
FAX Number: (910) 592-8048 Calendar System: Semester
URL: www.sampsoncc.edu
Established: 1967 Annual Undergrad Tuition & Fees (In-District): $2,783
Enrollment: 1,443 Coed
Affiliation or Control: State/Local IRS Status: 501(c)3
Highest Offering: Associate Degree
Accreditation: SC, ADNUR, MAC, PNUR

02 President ....Dr. Bill STARLING
05 Vice Pres Academic Affairs ....Mrs. Wanda CAPPS
10 Vice Pres Finance/Auxiliary Svcs ....Mrs. Kelly JACKSON
32 Dean of Student Services ....Ms. Blair HAIRR
103 Dean of Wkfc Dev/Continuing Educ ....Mrs. Amanda BRADSHAW
07 Director of Admissions ....Ms. Holly BREWINGTON
09 Director of Academic Svcs/IE ....Mr. Marvin RONDON
13 Director of Information Technology ....Ms. Angela TOUSEY
06 Registrar ....Ms. Betsy LLOYD
26 Public Information Office ....Mr. Dan GRUBB
37 Dir Financial Aid/Veteran Services ....Ms. Marleen POWELL
08 Director Library Services ....Ms. Donna ODOM
102 Foundation Executive Director ....Mrs. Lisa TURLINGTON
15 Dir Personnel/Exec Asst to Pres ....Mrs. Frankie SUTTER

*Sandhills Community College (H)

3395 Airport Road, Pinehurst NC 28374-8283
County: Moore FICE Identification: 002961
Unit ID: 199634
Telephone: (910) 692-6185 Carnegie Class: Assoc/MT-VT-Mix Trad/Non
FAX Number: (910) 695-1823 Calendar System: Semester
URL: www.sandhills.edu
Established: 1963 Annual Undergrad Tuition & Fees (In-State): $2,598
Enrollment: 4,206 Coed
Affiliation or Control: State IRS Status: 501(c)3
Highest Offering: Associate Degree
Accreditation: SC, COARC, EMT, MLTAD, RAD, SURGT

02 President ....Dr. John R. DEMPSEY
03 Executive Vice President ....Ms. Brenda JACKSON
05 VP of Academic Affairs ....Dr. Rebecca ROUSH
32 VP of Student Services ....Mrs. Kellie SHOEMAKE
51 VP of Continuing Education ....Ms. Andrea KORTE
88 VP College Initiatives ....Mr. Ron LAYNE
15 Assoc VP Human Resources ....Ms. Wendy B. DODSON
35 Dean of Student Services ....Mr. David FARMER
04 Exec Assistant to the President ....Ms. Heather LYONS
20 Dean of Instruction ....Ms. Linda CHANDLER
09 Dean of Planning & Research ....Ms. Lindsey FARMER
102 VP of Institutional Advancement ....Ms. Germaine ELKINS
08 Dean of Learning Resources ....Vacant
06 Director of Records & Registration ....Ms. Jean BLUE
37 Director of Financial Aid ....Ms. Carmeline MORRIS
106 Dean of Academic Support ....Ms. Wendy KAUFFMAN
13 Chief Information Officer ....Mr. Roderick BROWER
19 Director of Security/Safety ....Mr. Dwight THREET
18 Director of Facilities ....Mr. Doug SMITH
21 Dir Finance & Student Accounts ....Mr. Joseph BROWN
26 Director of Marketing and PR ....Ms. Karen MANNING
40 Bookstore Manager ....Ms. Sandra DALES
07 Director of Admissions ....Ms. Cary GREENE

*South Piedmont Community College (I)

PO Box 126, Polkton NC 28135-0126
County: Anson/Union FICE Identification: 007985
Unit ID: 197850
Telephone: (704) 272-5300 Carnegie Class: Assoc/MT-VT-High Non
FAX Number: (704) 272-5350 Calendar System: Semester

URL: www.spcc.edu
Established: 1999 Annual Undergrad Tuition & Fees (In-District): $1,995
Enrollment: 2,980 Coed
Affiliation or Control: State/Local IRS Status: 501(c)3
Highest Offering: Associate Degree
Accreditation: SC, DMS, EMT, MAC

02 President ... Dr. Maria PHARR
05 Vice Pres Academic Affairs/CAO ... Mr. Carl BISHOP
10 VP Finance/Administrative Svcs/CFO ... Ms. Michelle BROCK
32 Vice Pres Student Services ... Mrs. Elaine CLODFELTER
111 VP Inst Advancement/SPCC Foundation ... Mrs. Julie SIKES
04 Exec Assistant to President ... Mrs. Elizabeth HAMRICK
15 Assoc VP Human Res/Payroll/Org Dev ... Ms. Lauren SELLERS
21 Assoc Vice Pres Finance/Admin Svcs ... Mr. Richard ASHLEY
13 Assoc VP Info Tech Svcs/CIO ... Ms. Natisha GIVENS
18 Executive Director of Facilities ... Mr. Thomas SUGGS
108 Assoc VP Planning/IE ... Ms. Jill MILLARD
49 Dean School of Arts & Science ... Mr. James MINOR
76 Dean Health & Public Safety ... Mr. Phil KLEIN
72 Dean Applied Science & Technology ... Dr. Maria LANDER
84 Dean of Enrollment Services ... Mr. John RATLIFF
20 Assoc VP of Academic Affairs ... Dr. Makena STEWART
06 Registrar ... Ms. Cathy HORNE
08 Director Library Services ... Mr. Grant LEFOE
88 Dean College & Career Readiness ... Ms. Kelly STEGALL
36 Director of Advising/QEP ... Ms. Jessica YOUNG
07 Director of Admissions ... Ms. Amanda SECREST
19 Campus Safety Director ... Mr. Mike WILSON
37 Director Student Financial Aid ... Ms. Emily JARRELL

*Southeastern Community College (A)

4564 Chadbourn Highway, PO Box 151,
Whiteville NC 28472-0151
County: Columbus FICE Identification: 002964
Unit ID: 199722
Telephone: (910) 642-7141 Carnegie Class: Assoc/MT-VT-Mix Trad/Non
FAX Number: (910) 642-5658 Calendar System: Semester
URL: www.sccnc.edu
Established: 1964 Annual Undergrad Tuition & Fees (In-State): $2,595
Enrollment: 1,450 Coed
Affiliation or Control: State IRS Status: 501(c)3
Highest Offering: Associate Degree
Accreditation: SC, MLTAD

02 President ... Dr. Anthony CLARKE
10 Vice President Administrative Svcs ... Mr. Daniel FIGLER
05 Vice Pres Academic Affairs ... Dr. Michael AYERS
103 VP Workforce & Cmty Development ... Ms. Beverlee S. NANCE
32 VP Student Services/Title IX Deputy ... Dr. Sylvia COX
76 Dean Allied Hlth/Sci/Fine Arts/Math ... Dr. James HUTCHERSON
08 Librarian ... Ms. Kay HOUSER
30 Director Institutional Advancement ... Ms. Lisa CLARK
15 Director Human Resources ... Mr. Bill MAULTSBY
21 Controller ... Ms. Donna TURBEVILLE
26 Interim Dir Marketing & Outreach ... Ms. Haylee DAMATO
13 Director of Information Technology ... Mr. Jason STRICKLAND
51 Director of Continuing Education ... Ms. Brenda ORDERS
37 Director of Financial Aid ... Ms. Sheila DOCKERY
06 Dir of Student Records/Registrar ... Ms. Sylvia MCQUEEN
36 Director of Counseling ... Ms. Julia ROBERTS

*Southwestern Community College (B)

447 College Drive, Sylva NC 28779-8581
County: Jackson FICE Identification: 008466
Unit ID: 199731
Telephone: (828) 339-4000 Carnegie Class: Assoc/MT-VT-Mix Trad/Non
FAX Number: (828) 586-3129 Calendar System: Semester
URL: www.southwesterncc.edu
Established: 1964 Annual Undergrad Tuition & Fees (In-District): $2,213
Enrollment: 2,464 Coed
Affiliation or Control: State/Local IRS Status: 501(c)3
Highest Offering: Associate Degree
Accreditation: SC, CAHIIM, COARC, DMS, EMT, MAC, MLTAD, OTA, PTAA, RAD

02 President ... Dr. Don L. TOMAS
05 Exec VP Instructional/Student Svcs ... Dr. Thom R. BROOKS
10 VP for Financial & Admin Services ... Mr. William BROTHERS
13 VP Information Technology ... Mr. Scott BAKER
103 Dean of Workforce/Cont Education ... Mr. Scott SUTTON
12 Dean Macon Campus ... Dr. Cheryl DAVIDS
32 Dean of Students ... Ms. Cheryl CONTINO-CONNER
06 Dir Student Records/Registrar ... Ms. Clyanne HYDE
08 Library Director ... Mrs. Dianne LINDGREN
09 Director Inst Research & Planning ... Mr. Jonathan E. DEAN
37 Financial Aid Director ... Ms. Melody L. LAWRENCE
26 Director of Public Relations ... Mr. Tyler GOODE
102 Director of SCC Foundation ... Mr. Brett WOODS
84 Director of Enrollment Management ... Dr. Mark ELLISON
18 Chief Facilities/Physical Plant ... Ms. Lisa SIZEMORE

*Stanly Community College (C)

141 College Drive, Albemarle NC 28001-7458
County: Stanly FICE Identification: 011194
Unit ID: 199740
Telephone: (704) 982-0121 Carnegie Class: Assoc/MT-VT-Mix Trad/Non
FAX Number: (704) 982-0819 Calendar System: Semester
URL: www.stanly.edu
Established: 1971 Annual Undergrad Tuition & Fees (In-District): $2,673
Enrollment: 2,540 Coed
Affiliation or Control: State/Local IRS Status: 501(c)3
Highest Offering: Associate Degree
Accreditation: SC, COARC, EMT, MAC, MLTAD, RAD

02 President ... Dr. John ENAMAIT
11 Executive VP/COO ... Vacant
45 VP of Strategic Planning/Compliance ... Mrs. Carmen NUNALEE
05 VP of Academic Affairs/CAO ... Dr. Heather HILL
32 VP Student Success/Dean of Students ... Dr. Myra FURR
10 VP Administrative Services/CFO ... Mrs. Kimberly BRADSHAW
23 Assoc VP Health & Public Svcs ... Dr. Tammy CRUMP
20 Assoc VP Transfer ... Mrs. Tammi MCILWAINE
20 Assoc VP AMIT ... Mr. Jeff PARSONS
13 Chief Technical Officer ... Mr. Jeff DRAKE
14 Director of Enterprise Applications ... Mr. Joel ALLEN
119 Director of Network Services ... Mr. Heath LUQUIRE
90 Director of Desktop Services ... Mr. Terry MCMANUS
120 Coordinator e-Learning Activities ... Mr. Joe POLLARD
04 Exec Aide to President ... Mrs. Ashley SMITH
103 Director of Econ/Workforce Dev ... Mrs. Krista BOWERS
37 Dean Financial Aid Management ... Ms. Petra FIELDS
84 Dean of Enrollment Management ... Mr. Patrick HOLYFIELD
36 Asst Dean Students/Career Placement ... Mr. Marcus PRYOR
121 Assoc Dean of Academic Support ... Mrs. Jennifer HATLEY
06 Curriculum Associate Registrar ... Ms. Michelle POPLIN
38 Director Counseling/Special Svcs ... Ms. Megan BREHUN
26 Dean of Marketing ... Mr. Thomas GEORGE
27 Director Marketing ... Mrs. Michelle PEIFER
07 Director of Admissions ... Ms. April HARPER
21 Dean of Business Services ... Mrs. Catherine BIBY
18 Director Admin/Facilities Services ... Mr. Blake BOSTIC
102 Exec Director of SCC Foundation ... Ms. Jeania MARTIN
15 Director of Human Resources ... Mrs. Lori POPLIN
08 LRC Director ... Mr. Joel FERDON
24 Director of Media Services ... Mr. Mark SAMPLE
96 Purchasing Agent ... Mrs. Shelley OSBORNE
19 Director of Security ... Mr. Mike MARTIN
09 Director Inst Research/Planning ... Dr. Cindy DEAN

*Surry Community College (D)

630 S Main Street, Dobson NC 27017-0304
County: Surry FICE Identification: 002970
Unit ID: 199768
Telephone: (336) 386-8121 Carnegie Class: Assoc/MT-VT-Mix Trad/Non
FAX Number: (336) 386-8951 Calendar System: Semester
URL: www.surry.edu
Established: 1964 Annual Undergrad Tuition & Fees (In-State): $2,540
Enrollment: 3,236 Coed
Affiliation or Control: State IRS Status: 501(c)3
Highest Offering: Associate Degree
Accreditation: SC, EMT, MAC, PTAA

02 President ... Dr. David R. SHOCKLEY
05 VP Academic Affairs ... Dr. Jami WOODS
10 VP of Finance ... Mr. Tony L. MARTIN
13 VP Technology Services ... Dr. Candace HOLDER
09 Exec Dir of Analytics & Research ... Mr. Michael FAULKNER
15 Director Personnel Services ... Ms. Melonie WEATHERS
18 Chief Facilities/Physical Plant ... Mr. Randy ROGERS
19 Director Security/Safety ... Mr. Marty SHROPSHIRE
26 Chief Public Relations/Marketing ... Ms. Julie PHARR
41 Athletic Director ... Mr. Mark TUCKER

*Tri-County Community College (E)

21 Campus Circle, Murphy NC 28906-7919
County: Cherokee FICE Identification: 009430
Unit ID: 199795
Telephone: (828) 837-6810 Carnegie Class: Assoc/HT-High Non
FAX Number: (828) 837-0028 Calendar System: Semester
URL: www.tricountycc.edu
Established: 1964 Annual Undergrad Tuition & Fees (In-State): $2,363
Enrollment: 1,026 Coed
Affiliation or Control: State IRS Status: 501(c)3
Highest Offering: Associate Degree
Accreditation: SC, EMT

02 President ... Dr. Donna TIPTON-ROGERS
05 VP Instruction/Inst Effectiveness ... Dr. Steve WOOD
10 VP for Business & Finance ... Mr. Bill VESPASIAN
45 VP College & Community Initiatives ... Mr. Bo GRAY
13 Dir of Computing & Information Mgt ... Mr. Jason OUTEN
124 Coordinator Recruitment/Retention ... Ms. Samantha Major JONES
103 Dir Economic/Workforce Development ... Mr. Paul WORLEY
09 Dean Research & Planning/EC Liaison ... Dr. Jason CHAMBERS
15 Director of Human Resources ... Ms. Connie IVEY
91 Systems Administrator/Data Base Mgr ... Mr. Randy GUYETTE
106 Learning Mgt Systems Administrator ... Mr. Donnie MORROW
111 Coord Institutional Advancement ... Mr. Roarke ARROWOOD
06 Registrar Curriculum ... Ms. Holly HYDE
37 Director of Financial Aid ... Ms. Diane OWL
96 Purchasing Agent ... Ms. Judy OWENBY
84 Director of Enrollment Management ... Ms. Lee BEAL
18 Coordinator of Facility Services ... Mr. Tim NICHOLSON
04 Admin Assistant to the President ... Ms. Sallie C. BAKER

*Vance-Granville Community College (F)

PO Box 917, Henderson NC 27536-0917
County: Vance FICE Identification: 009903
Unit ID: 199838
Telephone: (252) 492-2061 Carnegie Class: Assoc/MT-VT-Mix Trad/Non
FAX Number: (252) 430-0460 Calendar System: Semester
URL: www.vgcc.edu
Established: 1969 Annual Undergrad Tuition & Fees (In-State): $1,948
Enrollment: 3,329 Coed
Affiliation or Control: State Related IRS Status: 501(c)3
Highest Offering: Associate Degree
Accreditation: SC, CSHSE, MAC, RAD

02 President ... Dr. Rachel M. DESMARAIS
05 VP of Learning ... Dr. Levy BROWN
10 VP for Finance & Operations ... Mr. Steve GRAHAM
103 VP Workforce & Cmty Engagement ... Vacant
09 VP of Institutional Research & Tech ... Dr. Kenneth A. LEWIS, JR.
12 Dean Franklin County Campus ... Ms. Bobbie Jo C. MAY
12 Dean South Campus ... Ms. Tanya WEARY
12 Dean K12 Partnerships/Warren Campus ... Mr. Lyndon HALL
124 Dean Student Retention/Success ... Mr. Jeff ALLEN
27 Director of Marketing ... Mr. Chris LA ROCCA
37 Director of Financial Aid ... Mr. Randall THORNTON
15 Director of Human Resources ... Ms. Tanvi GOEL
08 Director Learning Resources Center ... Ms. Elaine STEM
09 Director of Planning & Research ... Ms. Julie HICKS
18 Director of Plant Operations ... Mr. Ashley ROBERSON
121 Dir of Advising & College Success ... Ms. Amy O'GEARY
36 Director of Career Services ... Ms. Linda FLETCHER
06 Registrar ... Ms. Kathy KTUL
40 Bookstore Manager ... Ms. Sandra NEWTON
84 Dean Student Access/Support ... Ms. Kali BROWN

*Wake Technical Community College (G)

9101 Fayetteville Road, Raleigh NC 27603-5696
County: Wake FICE Identification: 004844
Unit ID: 199856
Telephone: (919) 866-5000 Carnegie Class: Assoc/HT-High Trad
FAX Number: (919) 779-3360 Calendar System: Semester
URL: www.waketech.edu
Established: 1958 Annual Undergrad Tuition & Fees (In-District): $2,768
Enrollment: 22,494 Coed
Affiliation or Control: State/Local IRS Status: 501(c)3
Highest Offering: Associate Degree
Accreditation: SC, ACFEI, ADNUR, DA, DH, MAC, MLTAD, RAD

02 President ... Dr. Scott RALLS
03 Executive Vice President ... Dr. Gayle GREENE
30 VP of Devel & Strategic Partnership ... Mr. Matthew B. SMITH
05 VP Curriculum Education Svcs ... Mrs. Sandra L. DIETRICH
32 SVP Enrollment & Student Services ... Dr. Willa H. JERMAN
103 VP Workforce Continuing Education ... Mr. Anthony CAISON
10 VP of Financial & Business Svcs ... Mrs. Marla L. TART
26 VP Communications/Public Relations ... Mrs. Laurie C. CLOWERS
15 VP Human Resources/College Safety ... Ms. Benita I. CLARK
18 Vice Pres Facilities ... Mr. Jeffrey J. CARTER
13 VP Information Technology Svcs ... Dr. Ryan SCHWIEBERT
84 AVP Enrollment Services ... Mr. John W. SAPARILAS
35 AVP Student Services ... Mr. Kevin A. BROWN
88 AVP CE Open Enrollment ... Mrs. Monica P. GEMPERLEIN
04 Strategic Projects Coord/Exec Asst ... Mrs. Savannah VINCE
19 Chief of Police ... Mr. Michael A. PENRY
46 Dean IE/Accreditation & Research ... Dr. John B. BOONE
30 Sr Dir Foundation Rels/Admin ... Mrs. Stephanie S. LAKE
25 Dean Sponsored Programs ... Mrs. Amy MACDONALD
06 Dean/Curriculum Registrar ... Ms. Holly Elaine SWART
72 Dean Tech Training & Career Dev ... Mr. Jeffrey MERRITT
37 Dean Financial Aid/Veterans Affairs ... Mrs. Regina M. HUGGINS
88 Sr Dean Strat Innovations Sp Proj ... Mrs. Karen B. PHINAZEE
07 Associate Dean Admissions ... Ms. Tina P. CARTER
27 Dir Communications Ops/Brand Mgmt ... Mrs. Francie W. SANDERSON
36 Assoc Dean Career & Empl Resources ... Mrs. Lynn E. KAVCSAK
12 Dean Public Safety Education Campus .. Mr. Jeffrey B. ROBINSON
76 Provost Health Sci Campus ... Dr. Angela BALLENTINE
81 Dean Mathematics/Sciences Div ... Ms. Sharon L. WELKER
79 Dean Arts/Humanities/Soc Sci Div ... Dr. Elizabeth (Beth) LEWIS
50 Dean Business & Public Svcs Tech ... Ms. Catherine LASSITER
75 Dean Applied Engr & Technologies ... Ms. Patricia A. GODIN
77 Dean Computer Technologies ... Mr. Keith BABUSZCZAK
88 Sr Dean Instructional Support ... Mr. James A. ROBERSON

*Wayne Community College (H)

3000 Wayne Memorial Drive Box 8002,
Goldsboro NC 27533-8002
County: Wayne FICE Identification: 002980
Unit ID: 199892
Telephone: (919) 735-5151 Carnegie Class: Assoc/MT-VT-High Trad
FAX Number: (919) 739-7137 Calendar System: Semester
URL: www.waynecc.edu
Established: 1957 Annual Undergrad Tuition & Fees (In-District): $2,524
Enrollment: 3,426 Coed
Affiliation or Control: State/Local IRS Status: 501(c)3
Highest Offering: Associate Degree
Accreditation: SC, ADNUR, DA, DH, MAC, MLTAD, PNUR

02 President ... Dr. Thomas A. WALKER, JR.
05 VP Academic/Student Services ... Dr. Patty PFEIFFER
10 VP Finance/Chief Financial Officer ... Mrs. Joy KORNEGAY
11 AVP Administrative Services ... Mr. Derek HUNTER
45 AVP Inst Effectiveness/Innovation ... Mrs. Dorothy MOORE
32 AVP Academic and Student Services ... Ms. Joanna MORRISETTE
51 AVP Continuing Education Services ... Ms. Renita DAWSON

15 AVP Human Res/Safety/Compliance ... Mr. Charles GAYLOR, IV
72 Division Dean Applied Technologies ... Dr. Ernie WHITE
49 Division Dean Arts & Sciences ... Dr. Brandon JENKINS
101 Asst Sec to the Board of Trustees ... Mrs. Leasa O. HOLMES
50 Div Dean Business & Computer Tech ... Ms. Tracy SCHMELTZER
76 Div Dean Allied Health/Public Svc ... Mrs. Janeil MARAK
88 Division Dean Public Safety ... Ms. Beverly DEANS
08 Director Library Services ... Dr. Ruth Aletha ANDREW
12 Coordinator Seymour Johnson AFB ... Mrs. Dori FRASER
92 Honors Program Coordinator ... Mrs. Deniz TUCK
106 Distance Education Specialist ... Mr. Randall SHEARON
26 Director Office of Communications ... Mr. Ken JONES
13 Director Information Technology ... Mr. Matt BAUER
18 Facility Operations Superintendent ... Mr. Chris SCHOTT
19 Chief Campus Police & Security ... Chief Willie L. BRINSON
40 Manager Bookstore ... Mrs. Cheryl MCBEE
103 Ex Dir Wayne Bus/Indus Ctr & WORKS ... Mr. Craig FOUCHT
07 Director Admissions & Records ... Ms. Jennifer MAYO
37 Director Student Financial Aid ... Mrs. Brenda D. MERCER-BURGESS
36 Director College & Career Promise ... Mrs. Lorie WALLER
78 Director Cooperative Programs ... Ms. Lorie WALLER
35 Student Activities Coordinator ... Ms. Paige HAM
96 Director of Purchasing ... Mr. Wade QUINN
102 Executive Director of Foundation .. Mrs. Adrienne NORTHINGTON
26 Public Information Officer ... Ms. Tara HUMPHRIES
15 Director Human Resources ... Ms. Melanie BELL
04 Senior Executive Asst to President ... Mrs. Leasa O. HOLMES
38 Interim Director Student Counseling ... Mr. Carl BROW
04 Executive Administrative Assistant ... Mrs. Shelbra JACKSON
88 Director of Inventory Management ... Mr. Mark JOHNSON
88 Director College Transfer Advising ... Mrs. Kaycee INGRAM

*Western Piedmont Community College (A)

1001 Burkemont Avenue, Morganton NC 28655-4504
County: Burke FICE Identification: 002982
Unit ID: 199908
Telephone: (828) 438-3500 Carnegie Class: Assoc/HT-Mix Trad/Non
FAX Number: (828) 438-6015 Calendar System: Semester
URL: www.wpcc.edu
Established: 1964 Annual Undergrad Tuition & Fees (In-State): $2,577
Enrollment: 1,834 Coed
Affiliation or Control: State IRS Status: 501(c)3
Highest Offering: Associate Degree
Accreditation: SC, ADNUR, DA, MAC, MLTAD

02 President ... Dr. Michael S. HELMICK
05 VP Academic & Student Success ... Ms. Rhia M. CRAWFORD
10 VP Admin Svcs/Chief Financial Ofcr ... Ms. Sandra K. HOILMAN
26 VP External Affairs & Workforce Dev ... Vacant
103 Dean Workforce Dev & Cont Educ ... Mr. Lee KISER
32 Dean of Student Services ... Ms. Susan WILLIAMS
08 Library Director ... Ms. Nancy DANIEL
54 Dean Applied Technologies ... Mr. Michael DANIELS
49 Dean Arts & Sciences ... Ms. Ann Marie MCNEELY
50 Dean Business/PS/Academic Support ... Vacant
06 Director Records & Registration ... Mrs. Joan P. HOGAN
15 Director Human Resources ... Ms. Lisa H. SESSIONS
84 Director Enrollment Management ... Mrs. Jennifer PROPST
37 Director Student Financial Aid ... Ms. Dori BARRON
13 Director Management Info Systems ... Ms. Nancy E. NORRIS
09 Director Inst Research/Eval ... Ms. Susan A. BERLEY
96 Director of Purchasing ... Ms. Linda CARSWELL
18 Director of Maintenance ... Vacant
04 Exec Admin Asst to President ... Ms. Kathy F. DURHAM
19 Director Security/Safety ... Vacant

*Wilkes Community College (B)

1328 S Collegiate Drive, Wilkesboro NC 28697-0120
County: Wilkes FICE Identification: 002983
Unit ID: 199926
Telephone: (336) 838-6100 Carnegie Class: Assoc/MT-VT-Mix Trad/Non
FAX Number: (336) 903-3219 Calendar System: Semester
URL: www.wilkescc.edu
Established: 1965 Annual Undergrad Tuition & Fees (In-State): $2,572
Enrollment: 2,665 Coed
Affiliation or Control: State IRS Status: 501(c)3
Highest Offering: Associate Degree
Accreditation: SC, COARC, DA, MAC, RAD

02 President ... Dr. Jeff A. COX
05 VP of Instruction ... Ms. Blair HANCOCK
10 Senior VP of Administration ... Mr. D. Morgan FRANCIS, JR.
32 VP of Instr Support/Student Svcs ... Ms. Kim E. FAW
103 Applied Career Technologies ... Mr. Ronald DOLLYHITE
13 Assoc VP Information Technology ... Mr. Mike WINGLER
51 VP WDCE/Ashe Campus ... Mr. Christopher D. ROBINSON
12 Director Alleghany Center ... Ms. Susan NILO
09 Inst Effectiveness Exec Director ... Ms. Nicole FOGLE
50 Dean Business/Public Svc Tech Div ... Mrs. Kristen MACEMORE
76 Dean Health Sciences Division ... Mr. Billy WOODS
18 Exec Director/Facilities Services ... Mr. Morgan FRANCIS
30 Exec Director Development ... Ms. Allison PHILLIPS
15 Director of Human Resources ... Ms. Sherry P. COX
06 Registrar ... Mr. Michael WARD
35 Dean of Student Services ... Mr. Scott JOHNSON
37 Director of Financial Aid ... Ms. Roberta HARLESS
38 Director Counseling & Career Svcs ... Dr. Lynda K. BLACK
16 Director Career & Talent Develop ... Mr. Curt MILLER
08 Director Learning Resources ... Ms. Christy EARP
38 Director SAGE ... Mr. Thomas SCHLITT
40 Bookstore Manager ... Ms. Kelly CHURCH
26 Public Info & Relations Officer ... Ms. Patty PARSONS
19 Chief of Police/Campus Police Dept ... Mr. Jamie MCGUIRE
04 Executive Asst to President ... Ms. Cynthia ALFORD
96 Purchasing Agent ... Ms. Amber BLACKBURN
07 Director of Admissions ... Ms. Elisabeth BLEVINS

*Wilson Community College (C)

PO Box 4305, Wilson NC 27893-0305
County: Wilson FICE Identification: 004845
Unit ID: 199953
Telephone: (252) 291-1195 Carnegie Class: Assoc/MT-VT-High Non
FAX Number: (252) 243-7148 Calendar System: Semester
URL: www.wilsoncc.edu
Established: 1958 Annual Undergrad Tuition & Fees (In-State): $2,572
Enrollment: 1,806 Coed
Affiliation or Control: State IRS Status: 501(c)3
Highest Offering: Associate Degree
Accreditation: SC, SURGT

02 President ... Dr. Tim WRIGHT
05 Vice Pres for Academic Affairs ... Mr. Robert HOLSTEN
10 Vice Pres for Finance & Admin Svcs ... Ms. Jessica JONES
09 Director of Institutional Effective ... Mr. Andrew WALKER
51 Exec Dean of Cont Educ ... Ms. Kim GAMLIN
32 Exec Dean of Student Development ... Ms. Amy NOEL
76 Dean of Allied Health & Sciences ... Ms. Becky STRICKLAND
50 Dean of Business & Applied Tech ... Mr. Wes HILL
72 Dean of Industrial Technologies ... Ms. Margie NORFLEET
15 Director of Human Resources ... Ms. Kathy WILLIAMSON
08 Head Librarian ... Mr. Gerry J. O'NEILL
21 Controller ... Vacant
06 Dir of Enrollment Svcs/Registrar ... Ms. Jennifer GONYEA
07 Director of Admissions ... Mr. Joshua HARRIS
18 Director of Facilities ... Mr. Ray OWENS
37 Dir of Financial Aid/Vet Affairs ... Ms. Lisa BAKER
111 Director Institutional Advancement ... Ms. Jessica BAILEY
13 Director of IT ... Ms. Susan WEEKLEY
96 Purchasing & Capital Projects Mgr ... Ms. Donna A. TURNER
40 Bookstore Manager ... Ms. Kaschia SPELLS
04 Exec Asst to the President ... Ms. Tracy LANE
106 Director of DL/Web Services ... Ms. Angela HERRING

North Carolina Wesleyan College (D)

3400 N Wesleyan Boulevard,
Rocky Mount NC 27804-8630
County: Nash FICE Identification: 002951
Unit ID: 199209
Telephone: (252) 985-5100 Carnegie Class: Bac-Diverse
FAX Number: (252) 985-5231 Calendar System: 4/1/4
URL: www.ncwc.edu
Established: 1956 Annual Undergrad Tuition & Fees: $30,750
Enrollment: 2,093 Coed
Affiliation or Control: United Methodist IRS Status: 501(c)3
Highest Offering: Master's
Accreditation: SC, CAEPN, EXSC

01 President ... Dr. Dewey CLARK
05 Interim Provost/VP Academic Affairs ... Dr. Evan DUFF
10 Vice President of Finance ... Ms. Suzanne BRACKETT
111 Vice President of Advancement ... Mr. Eddie COATS
84 Vice President of Enrollment ... Mrs. Judy ROLLINS
32 VP Student Affairs/Dean of Students ... Mr. Edward NAYLOR
15 Vice President of Human Services ... Mr. Tim OZMENT
09 Chief Planning & Research Officer ... Dr. Larry H. KELLEY
06 Registrar ... Mrs. Candace CASHWELL
08 Director of Library ... Ms. Esther BURGESS
26 Director of Communications ... Vacant
23 Director Health Services ... Ms. Jessica BRYS-WILSON
36 Director of Career Services ... Mr. Kenny DICKERSON
19 Director of Campus Security ... Mr. J. W. SEARS
41 Director of Athletics ... Mr. John THOMPSON
29 Director Alumni Rels/Annual Fund ... Vacant
21 Controller ... Mr. Andrew VOTIPKA
37 Director of Financial Aid ... Vacant
16 Director of Human Resources ... Mr. Darrell S. WHITLEY
18 Director of Facilities ... Mr. Raymond THOMPSON
07 Assistant Director of Admissions ... Mr. Ben LILLEY
38 Director of Counseling and DSS ... Vacant
40 Manager College Store ... Mr. Marcus RICH
20 Associate Academic Officer ... Dr. Molly WYATT
108 Director Institutional Assessment ... Dr. Larry H. KELLEY
13 Chief Info Technology Officer (CIO) ... Mr. Gregory BOYKIN
39 Director Student Housing ... Ms. Jesse LANGLEY
50 Chair Business ... Dr. Jackie LEWIS

Pfeiffer University (E)

48380 US Highway 52 N / PO Box 960,
Misenheimer NC 28109-0960
County: Stanly FICE Identification: 002955
Unit ID: 199306
Telephone: (704) 463-1360 Carnegie Class: Masters/L
FAX Number: (704) 463-1363 Calendar System: Semester
URL: www.pfeiffer.edu
Established: 1885 Annual Undergrad Tuition & Fees: $30,234
Enrollment: 1,306 Coed
Affiliation or Control: United Methodist IRS Status: 501(c)3
Highest Offering: Master's
Accreditation: SC, ACBSP, CAEPN, MFCD, MUS, NURSE

01 President ... Dr. Scott W. BULLARD
04 Executive Assistant to President ... Ms. Teena P. MAULDIN
13 CIO ... Vacant
10 Vice President for Finance/CFO ... Mrs. Robin LESLIE
05 Provost/VP Academic Affairs ... Dr. Tracy Y. ESPY
32 VP Student Affairs/Dean of Students ... Mr. Ron LAFFITTE
111 Vice Pres Inst Advancement ... Vacant
84 Vice Pres for Enrollment ... Vacant
41 Vice Pres Athletics ... Vacant
06 Registrar ... Ms. Lourdes SILVA
84 Director of Enrollment Operations ... Vacant
15 Director of Human Resources ... Ms. Twyla KIDD
09 Exec Director IR/Plng & Research ... Mrs. Julia KENNEDY
26 Director of Inst Communications ... Mr. Casey HABICH
38 Director of Counseling ... Vacant
08 Director of the Library ... Ms. Lara LITTLE
37 Director of Financial Aid ... Ms. Jill POWELL
14 Director Information Technology ... Vacant
07 Director of Undergrad Admissions ... Vacant
121 Dir of Academic Support Services ... Dr. Jim E. GULLEDGE
19 Dir of Campus Safety & Security ... Mr. Erik MCGINNIS
18 Director of Facilities ... Ms. Sharon K. BARD
42 University Chaplain ... Rev. Maegan HABICH
36 Director of Career Development ... Ms. Caroline SAWYER
39 Director of Residence Life ... Ms. Regina SIMMONS
58 Director of MCE Program ... Vacant
110 Exec Dir of Institutional Advance ... Ms. JoEllen NEWSOME
29 Director of Alumni Affairs ... Vacant
112 Advisor Planned Giving ... Mr. John LELFER
39 Asst Director of Residence Life ... Vacant
40 Bookstore Manager ... Ms. Dechelle ELLIS
104 Coord of Intl Studies/Study Abroad ... Ms. Rebecca HRACZO
50 Int Dean Division of Business ... Dr. Dawn LUCAS
53 Dean Division of Education ... Dr. Dawn LUCAS
49 Dean Division of Arts & Sciences ... Dr. Marilyn SUTTON-HAYWOOD
76 Dean Div of Applied Health Science ... Ms. Vernease MILLER

Piedmont International University (F)

420 S Broad Street, Winston-Salem NC 27101-5197
County: Forsyth FICE Identification: 002956
Unit ID: 489937
Telephone: (336) 725-8344 Carnegie Class: Spec-4-yr-Faith
FAX Number: (336) 725-5522 Calendar System: Semester
URL: www.piedmontu.edu
Established: 1945 Annual Undergrad Tuition & Fees: $9,920
Enrollment: 669 Coed
Affiliation or Control: Independent Non-Profit IRS Status: 501(c)3
Highest Offering: Doctorate
Accreditation: TRACS

01 President ... Dr. Charles W. PETITT
05 Executive VP for Academic Affairs ... Dr. Sandeep GOPALAN
00 Chancellor ... Dr. Steve CONDON
20 Provost ... Dr. Beth D. ASHBURN
11 Director of Operations ... Mr. Chris RONK
73 Vice Pres Temple Baptist Seminary ... Dr. Barkev TRACHIAN
20 VP of Academic Initiatives ... Dr. Byron EDENS
20 Associate Provost ... Dr. Alex GRANADOS
06 Registrar ... Mr. Jeremy BONTRAGER
08 Librarian ... Mr. Jason SEYMOUR
32 Dean of Campus and Spiritual Life ... Mr. Jeff CLAWSON
34 Dean of Women ... Mrs. Rebecca BOTTOMS
42 Director of Church Relations ... Mr. Tony WILSON
04 Administrative Asst to President ... Mrs. Stephanie PRICE
07 Director of Admissions ... Ms. Angela HOOVER
37 Financial Aid Director ... Mrs. Mandy MCLAIN
45 Institutional Effectiveness Dir ... Mr. Jeremy PATTISALL
41 Athletic Director ... Dr. Steve CONDON
108 Director Institutional Assessment ... Mr. Jeremy PATTISALL
30 Director of Development ... Mr. Kurtis THOMPKINS

Queens University of Charlotte (G)

1900 Selwyn Avenue, Charlotte NC 28274-0001
County: Mecklenburg FICE Identification: 002957
Unit ID: 199412
Telephone: (704) 337-2200 Carnegie Class: Masters/L
FAX Number: (704) 337-2517 Calendar System: Semester
URL: www.queens.edu
Established: 1857 Annual Undergrad Tuition & Fees: $34,684
Enrollment: 2,507 Coed
Affiliation or Control: Presbyterian Church (U.S.A.) IRS Status: 501(c)3
Highest Offering: Master's
Accreditation: SC, CAEPN, MUS, NURSE

01 President ... Dr. Daniel G. LUGO
05 VP Academic Affairs & Provost ... Dr. Sarah FATHERLY
30 VP Univ Advancement & Athletics ... Mr. James BULLOCK
26 VP Student Egmt/Dean of Students ... Ms. Maria FLORES-MILLS
10 CFO & VP for Administration ... Mr. Matthew PACKEY
13 AVP/Chief Information Officer ... Mr. Brian BAUTE
49 Dean Col Arts & Sci & Cato Sch Educ ... Dr. John SISKO
50 Dean of McColl School of Business ... Dr. Rick MATHIEU
60 Dean Knight School of Communication ... Dr. Timothy J. BROWN
76 Dean Blair College of Health ... Dr. Tama MORRIS
06 Registrar ... Ms. Linda FLEISCHMAN
15 Director of Human Resources ... Ms. Teri ORSINI, SPHR

Reformed Theological Seminary (A)

2101 Carmel Road, Charlotte NC 28226-6399
Telephone: (704) 366-5066 Identification: 666785
Accreditation: &SC, THEOL

† Regional accreditation is carried under the parent institution in Jackson, MS.

St. Andrews University (B)

1700 Dogwood Mile, Laurinburg NC 28352-5598
Telephone: (910) 277-5555 FICE Identification: 002967
Accreditation: &SC

† Regional accreditation is carried under the parent institution, Webber International University, Babson Park, FL.

Saint Augustine's University (C)

1315 Oakwood Avenue, Raleigh NC 27610-2298
County: Wake FICE Identification: 002968
Unit ID: 199582
Telephone: (919) 516-4000 Carnegie Class: Bac-Diverse
FAX Number: (919) 828-0817 Calendar System: Semester
URL: www.st-aug.edu
Established: 1867 Annual Undergrad Tuition & Fees: $17,890
Enrollment: 974 Coed
Affiliation or Control: Protestant Episcopal IRS Status: 501(c)3
Highest Offering: Baccalaureate
Accreditation: SC

01 Interim President ..... Dr. Gaddius FAULCON
04 Exec Assistant to the President ..... Ms. Audrey IVORY
111 VP Institutional Advancement & COO ..... Vacant
100 Chief of Staff ..... Ms. Sharon G. LAISURE
05 Int Provost/VP Academic Affairs ..... Dr. Wanda B. CONEAL
10 VP for Fiscal Affairs ..... Mr. Edward PATRICK
84 VP Enrollment Mgmt & Student Svcs ..... Dr. Ronald H. BROWN
11 VP for Administration ..... Vacant
09 Vice Provost for Academic Services ..... Dr. Orlando E. HANKINS
21 Chief Financial Officer ..... Ms. Tonya JACKSON
20 Vice Provost/ADA Coordinator ..... Dr. Linda H. CURTIS
15 Director Human Resources ..... Ms. Chanda DOUGLAS-WARD
32 Dean of Students ..... Mr. Paul A. NORMAN
35 Director of Student Activity ..... Ms. Ann BROWN
42 Chaplain ..... Vacant
13 Chief Information Officer ..... Ms. Llewellyn FAMBLES
41 Director Athletics ..... Mr. George D. WILLIAMS
06 Interim Registrar ..... Ms. Jeanese M. OUTLAW
50 Dean Business/Mgmt & Technology ..... Mr. Van SAPP
83 Dean Social and Behavioral Sciences ..... Vacant
81 Dean Sciences/Math/Public Health ..... Dr. Mark A. MELTON
79 Int Dean Humanities/Educ/Soc Sci ..... Mr. James E. LYONS
97 Dean General College ..... Dr. Kengie R. BASS
37 Interim Director Financial Aid ..... Ms. Sharon R. GRIFFIN
08 Director of Library Service ..... Ms. Tiawanna S. NEVELS
36 Director of Professional Management ..... Dr. Cindy LOVE
19 Director of Public Safety ..... Ms. Sharon HERMON
18 Director Physical Plant ..... Mr. Hector F. GALLEGO
29 Director Alumni Affairs ..... Ms. Sheryl H. XIMINES
22 Dir Affirmative Action/EEO ..... Vacant
30 Director of Development ..... Ms. Candice MURRAY
39 Dir Resident Life/Student Housing .. Ms. Barbara D. BROADAWAY
90 Director Academic Computing ..... Ms. Carlene J. MORGAN
07 Director of Admissions ..... Mr. Paul VANDERGRIFF
106 Director Online Education ..... Dr. Michael BOONE
25 Chief Contract/Grants Administrator ..... Ms. Linda GUNN-JONES
26 Dir Ofc Marketing & Communications ..... Ms. Kimberly MOORE

Salem College (D)

601 South Church Street, Winston-Salem NC 27101
County: Forsyth FICE Identification: 002960
Unit ID: 199607
Telephone: (336) 721-2600 Carnegie Class: Bac-A&S
FAX Number: (336) 917-5339 Calendar System: 4/1/4
URL: www.salem.edu
Established: 1772 Annual Undergrad Tuition & Fees: $29,166
Enrollment: 984 Female
Affiliation or Control: Moravian Church IRS Status: 501(c)3
Highest Offering: Master's
Accreditation: #SC, MUS

01 Interim President ..... Ms. Sandra J. DORAN
05 Int VP Acad/Stdnt Aff & Dean of Col ..... Dr. Susan HENKING
111 VP for Inst Advancement ..... Ms. Kathryn M. BARNES
45 VP for Strategic Planning ..... Ms. Katherine K. WATTS
10 VP Finance & Admin/CFO ..... Mr. Ken BUCHANAN
32 Dean of Students ..... Dr. Krispin W. BARR
58 Dean of Graduate Studies ..... Dr. Sheryl LONG
51 Interim Dean Adult Education ..... Ms. Betty TELFORD
20 Dean Undergraduate Studies ..... Dr. Richard VINSON
08 Director of Libraries ..... Ms. Elizabeth NOVICKI
44 Director Annual Giving ..... Ms. Felicia CAREY
13 Director Information Technology ..... Mr. Kris KELLEY
15 Director of Payroll & Benefits ..... Ms. Debbie SULLIVAN
38 Director Counseling Services ..... Vacant
37 Director Student Financial Aid ..... Mr. Paul COSCIA
36 Director Career Devel/Internships ..... Ms. Monica BOYD
06 Interim Registrar/Dir Inst Research ..... Dr. Richard VINSON
18 Director Facilities/Physical Plant ..... Vacant
29 Director Alumnae Relations ..... Ms. Jenny STOKES
04 Executive Asst to President ..... Ms. Rosemary LOFTUS WHEELER
41 Athletic Director ..... Ms. Patricia HUGHES
07 Director of Admissions ..... Ms. Julie HANES

Shaw University (E)

118 East South Street, Raleigh NC 27601
County: Wake FICE Identification: 002962
Unit ID: 199643
Telephone: (919) 546-8300 Carnegie Class: Bac-Diverse
FAX Number: (919) 546-8301 Calendar System: Semester
URL: www.shawu.edu
Established: 1865 Annual Undergrad Tuition & Fees: $16,480
Enrollment: 1,660 Coed
Affiliation or Control: Baptist IRS Status: 501(c)3
Highest Offering: Master's
Accreditation: SC, CAEPN, SW, THEOL

01 President ..... Dr. Paulette DILLARD
11 VP for University Operations & COO ..... Dr. Michael T. WEST
05 VP for Academic Affairs ..... Dr. Renata DUSENBURY
10 VP for Finance & Administration ..... Mr. David BYRD
111 VP Institutional Advancement ..... Ms. Marilyn RICHARDS
32 VP for Student Affairs ..... Dr. Keith POWELL
84 Chief Enrollment Management Officer ..... Mr. Anthony BROOKS
13 Chief Information Officer ..... Mr. David ALEXANDER
73 Dean Divinity School ..... Dr. Johnny HILL
101 Special Asst to Pres/Board Liaison ..... Vacant
15 Director Human Resources/Title IX ..... Mr. Lee WOOD
07 Director Admissions/Recruitment ..... Vacant
06 Registrar ..... Ms. Jody HAMILTON
51 Exec Director Adult Degree Programs ..... Dr. Michael T. WEST
88 Assoc Director Adult Degree Pgms ..... Dr. Oscar A. RODRIQUEZ
08 Director of Library Services ..... Mr. Larry TREADWELL
41 Director of Athletics ..... Dr. Alfonza CARTER
38 Director Counseling Center ..... Ms. Jerelene CARVER
88 Director Judicial Services ..... Ms. Agnes BAXTER
121 Director Academic Success ..... Ms. Rishard WEDDERBURN
36 Dir Exper Learning/Career Devel ..... Dr. Sharon HUNTER-RAINEY
50 Dean Business/Entrepreneurship/Tech ..... Vacant
49 Dean Arts & Sciences ..... Vacant
88 Dean Social/Political/Educational ..... Vacant
88 Dean Academic Support ..... Dr. Vanessa RAYNOR
53 Dept Head Education & Child Develop ..... Dr. Lucy WILSON
81 Dept Head General/Interdisciplinary ..... Mr. Jason MORGAN
76 Dept Head Health/Human/Life Science ..... Dr. Kimberly RAIFORD
60 Dept Head Mass Comm & Digital Tech ..... Dr. Cassandra MITCHELL
83 Dept Head Social & Justice Studies ..... Ms. MaNina MCNEILL
19 Chief Campus Police & Security ..... Mr. Steven LESANE
18 Facilities Manager ..... Mr. Donald SCUOTTO
09 Sr Data Analyst/Inst Rsrch Coord ..... Mr. Brian CUMBERBATCH
26 Director Public Relations ..... Ms. Lucera PARKER
105 Digital Media Manager ..... Ms. Renee SADDLER
25 Dir Sponsored Programs/Title III ..... Ms. Tori WILLIS
124 Director Student Retention ..... Ms. Doris BULLOCK
29 Director Alumni Relations ..... Dr. Lamont JOHNSON
37 Director Student Financial Aid ..... Mr. Ibrahim BAH
106 Dir Digital Teaching & Learning ..... Dr. Alesheia BACCOUS
96 Director Procurement ..... Ms. Dana MONROE
102 Dev Officer Corp/Found Relations ..... Mr. Brian ALLEN
108 Senior Assessment Coordinator ..... Dr. Bernice CAMPBELL
30 Senior Director Development ..... Ms. Dianne PLEDGER
44 Annual Giving Director ..... Mr. Charles CLARK
45 Chief Institutional Planning Office ..... Dr. Michael T. WEST

Shepherds Theological Seminary (F)

6051 Tryon Road, Cary NC 27518-9316
County: Wake FICE Identification: 041730
Unit ID: 461485
Telephone: (919) 573-5350 Carnegie Class: Spec-4-yr-Faith
FAX Number: (919) 573-1438 Calendar System: Semester
URL: www.shepherds.edu
Established: 2003 Annual Graduate Tuition & Fees: N/A
Enrollment: 93 Coed
Affiliation or Control: Independent Non-Profit IRS Status: 501(c)3
Highest Offering: Master's; No Undergraduates
Accreditation: THEOL

01 President ..... Dr. Stephen DAVEY
05 Provost/Dean ..... Dr. Tim M. SIGLER
20 Vice Pres Academic Affairs/CAO ..... Mr. Thomas PITTMAN
111 Vice President of Advancement ..... Dr. Alan POTTER
10 Chief Financial Officer ..... Mr. Ewart HODGINS
07 Director Student Recruitment ..... Dr. Douglas BOOKMAN
32 Dean of Students ..... Dr. Peter GOEMAN
06 Registrar/Financial Aid Officer ..... Mrs. Lucy BURGGRAFF
08 Director Library Services ..... Mr. William COBERLY
94 Director of Women's Programs ..... Dr. Karen SMITH
26 Director of Church Relations ..... Dr. Les LOFQUIST
56 Director of Laramie Teaching Site ..... Dr. Clayton SCHULTZ
56 Director of Texas Teaching Site ..... Dr. Thomas BABER
27 Director of Communications ..... Mrs. Marilyn FITCH
108 Director of Assessment ..... Mr. Ed GELB
19 Director Security/Safety ..... Mrs. Karen FOUNTAINE

Southeastern Baptist Theological Seminary (G)

Box 1889, Wake Forest NC 27588-1889
County: Wake FICE Identification: 002963
Unit ID: 199759
Telephone: (919) 761-2100 Carnegie Class: Masters/L
FAX Number: N/A Calendar System: Semester
URL: www.sebts.edu
Established: 1950 Annual Undergrad Tuition & Fees: $9,394
Enrollment: 2,638 Coed
Affiliation or Control: Southern Baptist IRS Status: 501(c)3
Highest Offering: Doctorate
Accreditation: SC, THEOL

01 President ..... Dr. Daniel L. AKIN
05 Provost/Dean of Faculty ..... Dr. Bruce R. ASHFORD
10 Executive VP for Operations ..... Mr. Ryan HUTCHINSON
20 VP Academic Administration ..... Dr. Keith WHITFIELD
111 Vice Pres Institutional Advancement ..... Mr. Art RAINER
32 VP Student Services/Dean Students ..... Dr. Mark LIEDERBACH
04 Administrative Asst to President ..... Mrs. Kim HUMPHREY
06 Registrar ..... Mr. Cody OLDARCE
07 Director of Admissions ..... Dr. Larry LYON
29 Dir Financial/Alumni Development ..... Mr. Jonathan SIX
37 Director of Financial Aid ..... Mr. Jesse PARKER
08 Director Library Services ..... Mr. Jason FOWLER
106 Dir Online Education ..... Mr. Jerry LASSETTER
09 Coord Institutional Research ..... Mr. Ben BABER
13 Director Information Technologies ..... Mr. Wayne JENKS
15 Director Human Resources ..... Mrs. Dawn SATTERWHITE
28 Spec Asst Pres for Diversity ..... Mr. Walter STRICKLAND
39 Director Student Housing ..... Mr. Doug NALLEY
43 General Counsel ..... Mr. George HARVEY

Southeastern Free Will Baptist College (H)

532 Eagle Rock Rd, Box 1960, Wendell NC 27591
County: Wake Identification: 667309
Telephone: (919) 365-7711 Carnegie Class: Not Classified
FAX Number: (919) 365-4940 Calendar System: Semester
URL: sfwbc.edu
Established: 1983 Annual Undergrad Tuition & Fees: N/A
Enrollment: N/A Coed
Affiliation or Control: Free Will Baptist IRS Status: 501(c)3
Highest Offering: Baccalaureate
Accreditation: @TRACS

01 President ..... Rev. Nate ANGE
05 College Dean ..... Dr. Danny BAER
30 Director of Development ..... Rev. Steve BERRY
32 Dean of Students ..... Mr. Timothy GAYNOR
06 Academic Dean ..... Mr. Marc HOLLOMAN
10 Business Manager ..... Mr. Daniel OSBORNE

Southern Evangelical Seminary (I)

15015 Lancaster Hwy, Charlotte NC 28277
County: Union FICE Identification: 036115
Telephone: (704) 847-5600 Carnegie Class: Not Classified
FAX Number: (704) 845-1747 Calendar System: Semester
URL: www.ses.edu
Established: 1992 Annual Undergrad Tuition & Fees: N/A
Enrollment: N/A Coed
Affiliation or Control: Independent Non-Profit IRS Status: 501(c)3
Highest Offering: Doctorate
Accreditation: TRACS

01 President & COO ..... Dr. Richard D. LAND
05 Academic Dean ..... Dr. J. Thomas BRIDGES
07 Director of Admissions ..... Ms. Dianna WILLIAMS
10 Business Manager ..... Mrs. Jennifer DRAKE
08 Library Director ..... Mr. Ronald I. JORDAHL
06 Registrar ..... Dr. Douglas E. POTTER
32 Director Student Services ..... Ms. Dianna WILLIAMS
13 Dir of Information Technology ..... Mr. Timothy BURKETT
26 Director Communications ..... Mr. Jeff LENHART
04 Executive Asst to President ..... Mrs. Christina S. WOODSIDE
35 Dean of Students ..... Dr. Mel WINSTEAD
88 Director Missions ..... Mr. Adam TUCKER
106 Dir Online Education/E-learning ..... Mr. Jeff LENHART
30 Dir of Institutional Advancement ..... Mr. Eric GUSTAFSON
12 Director of Bible College ..... Dr. Floyd ELMORE

University of Mount Olive (J)

634 Henderson Street, Mount Olive NC 28365-1263
County: Wayne FICE Identification: 002949
Unit ID: 199069
Telephone: (919) 658-2502 Carnegie Class: Masters/S
FAX Number: (919) 658-7180 Calendar System: Semester
URL: www.umo.edu
Established: 1951 Annual Undergrad Tuition & Fees: $20,600
Enrollment: 3,451 Coed
Affiliation or Control: Original Free Will Baptist Church IRS Status: 501(c)3
Highest Offering: Master's
Accreditation: SC, ACBSP, NURSE

01 President ..... Dr. David POOLE
03 Executive Vice President ..... Dr. Carol G. CARRERE
05 VP for Academic Affairs ..... Dr. Kenneth D. HINES
10 VP for Finance & Administration ..... Mr. Jeremy SHREVE
84 VP for Enrollment ..... Mr. Tim WOODARD
32 VP for Student Affairs ..... Dr. Dan SULLIVAN
111 VP for Institutional Advancement ..... Vacant
20 AVP Acad Affairs/Dean Grad Studies ..... Dr. David DOMMER
49 Dean School of Arts and Sciences ..... Dr. Burt LEWIS

50 Dean Tillman School of Business ... Dr. Kathy BEST
51 AVP for Adult & Graduate Operations ... Dr. Lisa M. NUESELL
08 Director of Library Services ... Ms. Pamela R. WOOD
12 Regional Director ... Ms. Christy COX
12 Regional Director ... Mr. Stuart BLOUNT
12 Regional Director ... Dr. John P. RUTTER
84 Executive Director Enrollment Dev ... Mr. Oscar RODRIGUEZ
09 Director Inst Research & Planning ... Dr. Juliane SANTIAGO
108 Director of Assessment ... Dr. Ron STEVENS
06 Registrar ... Mr. David L. BOURGEOIS
35 Director of Campus Life ... Ms. Nicole L. GARRETT
36 Director of Career Center ... Ms. Laurica YANCEY
39 Director of Housing/Resident Life ... Ms. Katelyn REINKE
26 Director of Public Relations ... Ms. Rhonda E. JESSUP
102 Dir Foundations & Sponsored Program ... Mr. Dustin BANNISTER
29 Director of Alumni Relations . Ms. Hope S. MCPHERSON FIELDS
44 Director of Annual Fund ... Ms. Melinda HOLLAND
37 Director of Financial Aid ... Ms. Katrina K. LEE
15 Director of Human Resources ... Ms. Cordelia A. WILCOX
23 Student Health Services ... Ms. Joanne L. MORGAN
04 Assistant to the President ... Ms. Katherine B. GARDNER
18 Director Building & Grounds ... Mr. Jeff D. BROGDEN
13 Director Technology Services ... Mr. Kenneth M. DAVIS, JR.
14 Director Technology Support ... Mr. Robert R. PRUETT
92 Director Honors Program ... Dr. Brenda B. CATES
41 VP for Athletics ... Mr. Jeffrey M. EISEN

*University of North Carolina General Administration (A)

Box 2688, 910 Raleigh Road, Chapel Hill NC 27515-2688
County: Orange FICE Identification: 002971
Unit ID: 199175
Telephone: (919) 962-1000 Carnegie Class: N/A
FAX Number: (919) 962-2751
URL: www.northcarolina.edu

01 Interim President ... Dr. William L. ROPER
05 Sr Vice Pres Academic Affairs/CAA ... Dr. Kimberly VAN NOORT
11 Sr Vice Pres Finance/Operations ... Vacant
100 Chief of Staff/Sr Vice President ... Ms. Meredith DIDIER
10 Int Sr Vice Pres Finance/Budget ... Mr. Rick WHITFIELD
20 VP Academic/Student Affairs ... Vacant
13 Vice Pres Data & Analytics ... Mr. Dan COHEN-VOGEL
43 Sr VP Govt/Legal/Risk/Gen Counsel ... Mr. Thomas SHANAHAN
46 VP Academic Pgms/Faculty/Research ... Vacant
101 Sr Assoc VP/Sec of the University ... Ms. Andrea POOLE
86 Vice Pres State Govt Relations ... Mr. Drew MORETZ
86 Vice Pres Federal Relations ... Ms. Elizabeth MORRA
26 Vice President for Communications ... Vacant
15 Vice Pres for Human Resources ... Mr. Matthew BRODY
31 Sr VP for External Affairs ... Mr. Kevin HOWELL

*Appalachian State University (B)

287 Rivers Street, Boone NC 28608-0001
County: Watauga FICE Identification: 002906
Unit ID: 197869
Telephone: (828) 262-2000 Carnegie Class: Masters/L
FAX Number: (828) 262-2347 Calendar System: Semester
URL: www.appstate.edu
Established: 1899 Annual Undergrad Tuition & Fees (In-State): $7,364
Enrollment: 18,811 Coed
Affiliation or Control: State IRS Status: 501(c)3
Highest Offering: Doctorate
Accreditation: SC, ART, CAATE, CACREP, CAEPN, CIDA, DANCE, DIETD, DIETI, IPSY, MFCD, MUS, NRPA, NURSE, PH, SP, SPAA, SW, THEA

02 Chancellor ... Dr. Sheri N. EVERTS
100 Chief of Staff/Vice Chancellor ... Mr. Hank T. FOREMAN
05 Provost/Exec Vice Chancellor ... Dr. Darrell P. KRUGER
10 Vice Chanc Business Affairs ... Mr. Paul D. FORTE
32 Vice Chanc Student Development ... Mr. J.J BROWN
111 Vice Chanc Univ Advancement ... Dr. Randy EDWARDS
20 Vice Provost for Undergrad Educ ... Dr. Mark GINN
46 Interim Vice Provost for Research ... Dr. Ece KARATAN
26 Assc VC Advance/Chief Comm Ofcr ... Mrs. Megan HAYES
84 Assoc VC for Enrollment Management ... Ms. Cindy BARR
29 Exec Director of Alumni Affairs ... Vacant
43 General Counsel ... Mr. Paul MEGGETT
13 Chief Information Officer ... Mr. David E. HAYLER
06 University Registrar ... Ms. Debbie RACE
38 Dir Counseling/Psychological Svcs ... Dr. Christopher J. HOGAN
37 Director of Financial Aid ... Mr. Wesley ARMSTRONG
15 Director of Human Resources ... Mr. Mark BACHMEIER
09 Exec Dir Inst Research/Planning ... Mrs. Heather H. LANGDON
51 Exec Director of Distance Education ... Dr. Terry RAWLS
41 Director of Athletics ... Mr. Douglas P. GILLIN
49 Dean for College of Arts & Sciences ... Dr. Neva J. SPECHT
50 Dean for College of Business ... Dr. Heather NORRIS
53 Dean for College of Education ... Dr. Melba C. SPOONER
57 Dean for College Fine/Applied Arts ... Ms. Phyllis KLODA
64 Dean for the School of Music ... Dr. James DOUTHIT
58 Dean of Graduate School ... Dr. Michael MCKENZIE
08 Dean of Libraries ... Dr. Dane WARD
18 Dir of the Physical Plant ... Mr. Jeff PIERCE
114 Budget Director ... Mr. John E. ADAMS
96 Director of Materials Management ... Mr. John WALL
28 Dir Multicultural Student Devel ... Vacant

*East Carolina University (C)

1000 East Fifth Street, Greenville NC 27858-4353
County: Pitt FICE Identification: 002923
Unit ID: 198464
Telephone: (252) 328-6212 Carnegie Class: DU-Higher
FAX Number: (252) 328-4155 Calendar System: Semester
URL: www.ecu.edu
Established: 1907 Annual Undergrad Tuition & Fees (In-State): $7,188
Enrollment: 29,131 Coed
Affiliation or Control: State IRS Status: 501(c)3
Highest Offering: Doctorate
Accreditation: SC, AAFCS, ANEST, ARCPA, ART, AUD, CAATE, CACREP, CAEPN, CAHIIM, CAMPEP, CARTE, CEA, CIDA, CLPSY, CONST, DENT, DIETD, DIETI, LIB, MED, MFCD, MIDWF, MT, MUS, NAIT, NRPA, NURSE, OT, PH, PLNG, PTA, SCPSY, SP, SPAA, SW, THEA

02 Acting Chancellor ... Dr. Ron MITCHELSON
100 Chief of Staff ... Mr. Jim HOPF
05 Provost & Sr VC Academic Affairs ... Dr. Ron MITCHELSON
32 Vice Chancellor for Student Affairs ... Dr. Virginia HARDY
17 Vice Chancellor Health Sciences ... Dr. Mark STACY
10 Vice Chanc Administration & Finance ... Ms. Sara THORNDIKE
111 Vice Chanc Univ Advancement ... Mr. Christopher DYBA
46 VC Research/Econ Dev/Engagement ... Dr. Jay GOLDEN
29 Assoc VC for Alumni Relations ... Vacant
39 Assoc VC Camp Liv/Dining ... Mr. William L. MCCARTNEY, JR.
35 Assoc Vice Chanc & Dean of Stdnts ... Dr. Lynn M. ROEDER
22 Assoc Provost Equity/Diversity ... Ms. Lakesha ALSTON FORBES
43 Vice Chancellor for Legal Affairs ... Ms. Donna G. PAYNE
09 Associate Provost IPAR ... Dr. Ying ZHOU
41 Athletic Director ... Mr. Jon GILBERT
13 CIO and Assoc Vice Chanc ITCS ... Mr. Don SWEET
15 Assoc VC Human Resources ... Ms. Kitty WETHERINGTON
18 Assoc VC for Campus Opers ... Mr. William BAGNELL
21 Int Assoc VC for Business Services ... Mr. Kevin CARRAWAY
88 Assoc VC Environ Health & Safety ... Mr. Bill KOCH
88 Assistant VC of Global Affairs ... Dr. Jon REZEK
20 Dir of Institutional Plng & Accred ... Dr. Cynthia BELLACERO
88 Dir of Campus Rec & Wellness ... Mr. William EHLING
84 Assoc Provost for Enrollment Svcs ... Dr. John FLETCHER
26 Int Exec Dir Comm/Public Affs/Mktg ... Ms. Jeannine HUTSON
07 Director of Admissions ... Vacant
06 Registrar ... Ms. Angela R. ANDERSON
08 Director JY Joyner Library ... Ms. Jan LEWIS
88 Dir Health Sciences Library ... Ms. Beth KETTERMAN
101 Asst Secretary to Board of Trustees ... Ms. Megan AYERS
37 Director of Financial Aid ... Ms. Julie POORMAN
19 Chief of Police ... Mr. Jon R. BARNWELL
51 Exec Dir Acad Out/Cont & Dist Educ ... Dr. Regis M. GILMAN
27 Asst VC for University Marketing ... Mr. Clint BAILEY
27 Director of Publications ... Mr. Jimmy ROSTAR
88 Director of Military Programs ... Mr. Tim WISEMAN
96 Director of Purchasing ... Mr. Kevin CARRAWAY
36 Director Career Center ... Ms. Leslie ROGERS
116 Chief Audit Officer ... Mr. Wayne B. POOLE
21 AVC for Financial Services ... Ms. Dee BOWLING
49 Dean College of Arts & Sciences ... Dr. William DOWNS
76 Dean College of Allied Health ... Dr. Robert ORLIKOFF
68 Dean Col Health/Human Performance ... Dr. Anisa ZVONKOVIC
66 Dean College of Nursing ... Dr. Sylvia BROWN
50 Dean College of Business ... Dr. Paul SCHWAGER
57 Dean Col Fine Arts/Comm ... Dr. Christopher BUDDO
53 Dean College of Education ... Dr. B. Grant HAYES
72 Dean Col of Engineering and Tech ... Dr. Harry PLOEHN
58 Dean Graduate School ... Dr. Paul GEMPERLINE
92 Dean Honors College ... Dr. David WHITE
63 Dean Brody School of Medicine ... Dr. Mark STACY
52 Dean School of Dental Medicine ... Dr. Gregory CHADWICK
04 Assistant to Chancellor ... Ms. Christy DANIELS
25 Dir of Grants and Contracts ... Ms. Julie COLE
86 Director of Strategic Initiatives ... Vacant
102 President/CEO ECU Foundation ... Mr. Chris DYBA
54 Chairperson Engineering ... Dr. Barbara MULLER-BORER
108 Director Institutional Assessment ... Ms. Kristen DREYFUS

*Elizabeth City State University (D)

1704 Weeksville Road, Elizabeth City NC 27909-7806
County: Pasquotank FICE Identification: 002926
Unit ID: 198507
Telephone: (252) 335-3400 Carnegie Class: Bac-Diverse
FAX Number: (252) 335-3731 Calendar System: Semester
URL: www.ecsu.edu
Established: 1891 Annual Undergrad Tuition & Fees (In-State): $3,194
Enrollment: 1,411 Coed
Affiliation or Control: State IRS Status: 501(c)3
Highest Offering: Master's
Accreditation: SC, CAEP, CAEPN, MUS, SW

02 Chancellor ... Dr. Karrie G. DIXON
05 Provost/VC Acad Affairs ... Dr. Farrah J. WARD
03 Vice Chanc/Chief of Staff ... Dr. Derrick L. WILKINS
11 VC for Operations/General Counsel ... Mr. Alyn GOODSON
10 VC for Business & Finance/CFO ... Mr. Joshua LASSITER
32 Vice Chancellor for Student Affairs ... Mr. Gary L. BROWN
111 Interim VC University Advancement ... Ms. Letitia L. EVANS
116 Director of Internal Audit ... Ms. Sharnita I. WILSON-PARKER
84 Assoc VC Enrollment Mgmt/Registrar ... Dr. Althea A. RIDDICK
86 Special Asst Government Relations ... Mr. Carson D. RICH
101 Secretary of the Institution/Board ... Ms. Gwendolyn SANDERS
04 Executive Asst to Chancellor ... Ms. Alexxis D. HUTCHINSON
13 Chief Information Officer ... Mr. Suresh B. MURUGAN
41 Athletic Director ... Mr. George L. BRIGHT
15 Interim Chief HR Officer ... Ms. Paula G. BOWE
26 Exec Dir Strategic Comm ... Ms. Michelle L. BALL
20 Interim Assoc VC Academic Affairs ... Dr. Gloria E. PAYNE
20 Interim Assoc VC Academic Affairs ... Dr. Melinda R. ANDERSON
21 Controller ... Ms. Gina R. KNIGHT
96 Director of Business Services ... Ms. Rachael M. HAINES
114 Director of Budget ... Mr. Robert J. THIBEAULT
109 Director of Auxiliary Services ... Ms. Sherron D. WHITE
113 Accountant/Bursar ... Ms. Thelma R. WILLIAMS
14 Deputy Chief Information Officer ... Mr. Eric V. ZARGHAMI
90 IT Client Services Manager ... Ms. Samantha STEVENS
91 IT Systems Administrator ... Ms. Angela W. BAILEY
09 Dir Institutional Effectiveness ... Dr. Fred M. OKANDA
35 Assoc Vice Chanc Student Affairs ... Mr. Kevin J. WADE
08 Director of Library Services ... Dr. Juanita M. SPENCE
07 Interim Director of Admissions ... Mr. Darius D. EURE
38 Director Counseling Center ... Ms. Jody GRANDY
36 Director of Career Services ... Vacant
37 Director Student Financial Aid ... Mr. Jeremi WATKINS
102 Dir Foundation and Corp Relations ... Vacant
29 Dir Alumni Relations and Engagement ... Vacant
112 Major and Planned Gifts Officer ... Ms. Teresa C. LASSITER
18 Interim Dir of Facilities/Planning ... Mr. Harley G. GRIMES
26 Director of Marketing ... Ms. Rhonda HAYES
87 Director of Summer School ... Dr. Chyna N. CRAWFORD
58 Director of Graduate Education ... Dr. Timothy A. GOODALE
106 Dir Distance/Continuing Educ ... Dr. Kimberley N. STEVENSON
19 Director of Public Safety ... Mr. John MANLEY
39 Interim Dir Housing and Res Life ... Ms. Sabrina R. WILLIAMS
121 Chair of University Studies ... Dr. Tarsha M. ROGERS
23 Director of Student Health Services ... Ms. Gloria M. BROWN
25 Director of Sponsored Programs ... Ms. AnneMarie DELGADO

*Fayetteville State University (E)

1200 Murchison Road, Fayetteville NC 28301-4298
County: Cumberland FICE Identification: 002928
Unit ID: 198543
Telephone: (910) 672-1111 Carnegie Class: Masters/M
FAX Number: (910) 672-1769 Calendar System: Semester
URL: www.uncfsu.edu
Established: 1867 Annual Undergrad Tuition & Fees (In-State): $5,249
Enrollment: 6,226 Coed
Affiliation or Control: State IRS Status: 501(c)3
Highest Offering: Doctorate
Accreditation: SC, ART, CAEPN, FEPAC, MUS, NURSE, SW

02 Chancellor ... Dr. James A. ANDERSON
100 Vice Chancellor and Chief of Staff ... Dr. Jon YOUNG
05 Int Prov/Vice Chanc Academic Affs ... Dr. Pamela JACKSON
10 Vice Chancellor Business/Finance ... Mr. Carlton SPELLMAN
32 Vice Chancellor Student Affairs ... Dr. Janice HAYNIE
111 Vice Chanc Inst Advancement ... Ms. Lorna RICOTTA
13 Vice Chanc Info Technology/CIO ... Mr. Nick GANESAN
35 Assoc Vice Chanc Student Affairs ... Dr. Juanette COUNCIL
18 Assoc Vice Chanc Facilities Mgmt ... Mr. Jon PARSONS
15 Assoc Vice Chanc Human Resources ... Ms. Terri TIBBS
88 Senior Assoc Vice Chancellor ... Dr. Perry A. MASSEY
45 Assoc VC Pgms/Plng/Assessment ... Vacant
92 Acting Program Director Honors ... Dr. Erin WHITE
06 Registrar ... Ms. Sarah BAKER
26 Director Public Relations ... Mr. Jeff WOMBLE
08 Director of Library Services ... Vacant
07 Director of Admissions ... Ms. Ulisa BOWLES
39 Interim Director of Residence Life ... Ms. Adrina RUSSELL
37 Director Student Financial Aid ... Mrs. Kamesia HOUSE
43 General Counsel ... Mrs. Wanda LESSANE JENKINS
41 Athletic Director ... Mr. Anthony T. BENNETT
96 Director of Purchasing ... Ms. Willie MCINTYRE
28 Director of Diversity ... Vacant
88 Dean University College ... Dr. John I. BROOKS
66 Department Chair Nursing ... Dr. Afua ARHIN
50 Int Dean Sch Business/Economics ... Dr. J. Lee BROWN
53 Dean School of Education ... Dr. Marion GILLIS-OLION
49 Dean College Arts and Sciences ... Dr. Samuel ADU-MIREKU
101 Secretary of Univ/Board Liaison ... Ms. Suzetta M. PERKINS
04 Administrative Asst to President ... Mrs. Ann ZOMERFELD
86 Director Government Relations ... Mr. Wesley FOUNTAIN
25 Chief Contracts/Grants Admin . Ms. Chrystal COOPER-JOHNSON
84 AVC Director Enrollment Management ... Dr. Thalia WILSON

*North Carolina Agricultural and Technical State University (F)

1601 East Market Street, Greensboro NC 27411-0001
County: Guilford FICE Identification: 002905
Unit ID: 199102
Telephone: (336) 334-7500 Carnegie Class: DU-Higher
FAX Number: (336) 334-7136 Calendar System: Semester
URL: www.ncat.edu
Established: 1891 Annual Undergrad Tuition & Fees (In-State): $6,612
Enrollment: 11,877 Coed
Affiliation or Control: State IRS Status: 501(c)3
Highest Offering: Doctorate
Accreditation: SC, AAFCS, CACREP, CAEPN, CONST, JOUR, LSAR, MUS, NAIT, NUR, SW, THEA

02 Chancellor ... Dr. Harold L. MARTIN, SR.
05 Provost/Exec VC Academic Affairs ... Dr. Beryl MCEWEN
10 VC Business & Finance ... Mr. Robert POMPEY, JR.

100 Chief of Staff Ms. Erin HART
46 Interim VC Research & Economic Dev Dr. Sanjiv SARIN
32 VC Student Affairs Dr. Melody C. PIERCE
15 Interim VC Human Resources Ms. Erickia ELBERT
13 VC ITS & CIO Mr. Tom JACKSON
43 General Counsel Ms. Melissa HOLLOWAY
111 VC University Advancement Mr. Kenneth E. SIGMON, JR.
20 VP Academic Strat & Operations Ms. Nicole PRIDE
26 AVC University Relations Mr. Todd H. SIMMONS
114 AVC for Budget & Planning Mrs. Chartarra JOYNER
58 Interim Dean Graduate College Dr. Clay GLOSTER
45 VP Strategic Planning & Inst Effect Dr. Muktha B. JOST
18 AVC for Bus/Finance/Facilities Mr. Andrew M. PERKINS, JR.
19 AVC Police/Public Safety Mr. Charles E. WILSON, JR.
08 Dean Library Services Ms. Vicki COLEMAN
47 Dean Agriculture/Environmental Sci Dr. Mohamed AHMEDNA
49 Dean Arts/Human/Soc Sciences Dr. Frances WARD-JOHNSON
53 Interim Dean College of Education Dr. Miriam WAGNER
54 Dean College of Engineering Dr. Robin N. COGER
66 Dean College Health & Hum Sci Dr. Lenora CAMPBELL
50 Dean College of Business/Economics Dr. Kevin L. JAMES
72 Dean College Science and Technology Dr. Abdellah AHMIDOUCH
54 Dean Joint Sch Nanosci/Nanoeng Dr. Sherine O. OBARE
06 University Registrar Mrs. Kelly A. ROWETT JAMES
84 Int AVP for Enrollment Management Ms. Jacque POWERS
37 Director Financial Aid Mrs. Sherri M. AVENT
36 Exec Director Career Services Ms. Cynthia DOWNING
29 AVC for Alumni Relations Ms. Teresa DAVIS
85 Dir International Student Affairs Ms. Loreatha D. GRAVES
88 Dir Multicultural Student Center Mr. Gerald SPATES
41 Director of Athletics Mr. Earl M. HILTON, III
39 Interim Exec Dir Housing Ms. Elfrida MENSAH
23 Dir Student Health Services Dr. David H. WAGNER
38 Director of Counseling Service Dr. Vivian D. BARNETTE
25 Director of Contracts/Grants Ms. Natalie TEAGLE
92 Director of Honors Program Dr. Margaret KANIPES
96 Director of Procurement Services Ms. Martinique WILLIAMS
27 Director of Media Relations Ms. Tiffany S. JONES
40 Bookstore Manager Ms. Michaele WIGGINS
106 Dir of ITS/Distance Education Dr. Tracie O. LEWIS
108 Director Institutional Research Dr. Khoi D. TO
22 Director Affirmative Action/EEO Ms. Linda MANGUM
112 AVC for Major Gifts/Annual Giving Mr. P. Kevin WILLIAMSON
86 Director External Affairs Mr. Ray TRAPP
07 Interim Director of Admissions Ms. Jameia TENNIE
101 Secretary to the Board Ms. Shannon BENNETT

*North Carolina Central University (A)

1801 Fayetteville Street, Durham NC 27707-3129

County: Durham FICE Identification: 002950
Unit ID: 199157
Telephone: (919) 530-6100 Carnegie Class: Masters/L
FAX Number: (919) 530-5014 Calendar System: Semester
URL: www.nccu.edu
Established: 1910 Annual Undergrad Tuition & Fees (In-State): $6,464
Enrollment: 8,097 Coed
Affiliation or Control: State IRS Status: 501(c)3
Highest Offering: Doctorate
Accreditation: SC, #CAATE, CACREP, CAEPN, DIETD, DIETI, LAW, LIB, NRPA, NUR, SP, SW, THEA

02 Chancellor Dr. Johnson O. AKINLEYE
05 Interim Provost & VCAA Dr. Patrick R. LIVERPOOL
100 Chief of Staff Dr. Al ZOW
43 General Counsel Mrs. Hope TYEHIMBA
10 Vice Chanc Admin & Finance Dr. Cornelius WOOTEN
32 VC for Student Affairs Dr. Angela COLEMAN
111 Vice Chanc Inst Advancement Dr. Harriet F. DAVIS
20 Assoc Provost for Academic Programs Dr. Michelle L. MAYO
11 Assoc VC Administration/Finance Ms. Akua MATHERSON
20 Assoc VC Faculty Develop Dr. Yolanda B. ANDERSON
15 Chief Human Resources Ms. Sylvia ANDERSON
88 Assoc VC Innovat/Engaged & Global Dr. Ontario S. WOODEN
88 Director Student Union Mr. Orok OROK
45 Director Strategic Planning Mr. Johnnie SOUTHERLAND
35 Assistant VC of Student Affairs Dr. Toya CORBETT
13 Chief Information Officer Mrs. Leah KRAUS
07 Director Undergraduate Admissions Dr. Nicole GIBBS
88 Director of External Affairs Dr. Michael PAGE
06 Registrar Dr. Jerome GOODWIN
91 Student Systems Manager Ms. Billie HANES
29 Director of Alumni Relations Mrs. LaMisa M. FOXX
26 Assoc VC for Public Relations Mrs. Ayana D. HERNANDEZ
37 Director of Financial Aid Ms. Sharon J. OLIVER
08 Director Library Services Dr. Theodosia T. SHIELDS
19 Chief of University Police Mr. Fred HAMMETT
121 Interim Associate Dean Univ College Dr. Kesha T. LEE
88 Director Art Museum Vacant
39 Director Residential Life Mr. James B. LEACH
41 Director Athletics Dr. Ingrid L. WICKER-MCCREE
09 Assoc VC Inst Research/Eval/Plng Dr. Jeanette BARKER
96 Director of Purchasing Vacant
92 Director of Honors Program Dr. Ansel E. BROWN
38 Exec Director of Counseling Center Dr. Ruth GILLIAM PHILLIPS
22 Director of EEO & Employee Relation Ms. Ann PENN
84 Assoc VC Enrollment Management Dr. Monica T. LEACH
109 Dir Auxiliaries/Business Services Mr. Timothy J. MOORE
40 Manager Bookstore Ms. Jacqueline MCDOWELL
58 Dean Sch Grad Stds/Asc VC Grad Rsch Dr. Jaleh REZAIE
61 Interim Dean of the Law School Mrs. Elaine M. O'NEAL
62 Dean School of Library/Info Science Dr. Jon P. GANT
50 Dean School of Business Mr. Anthony C. NELSON
88 Interim Dean of University College Mr. William R. MOULTRIE
49 Dean College of Arts and Sciences Dr. Carlton E. WILSON
83 Dean College Behavioral/Social Scis Dr. Debra O. PARKER
53 Dean School of Education Dr. Audrey W. BEARD
04 Executive Asst to Chancellor Ms. Zelda STANFIELD
102 Executive Director NCCU Foundation Mr. Ernest JENKINS
104 Asst Director International Affairs Dr. Olivia JONES
105 Director Web Services Mr. Damond NOLLAN
106 Director Division Extended Studies Mrs. Kimberly C. PHIFER-MCGHEE
108 Director of Assessment Ms. Tia M. DOXEY
25 Director Contracts/Grants Admin Vacant
36 Director Career Services Mrs. Catrina S. DOSREIS
44 Director Annual Giving Ms. Kara ENDSLEY

*North Carolina State University (B)

20 Watauga Club Drive, Raleigh NC 27695

County: Wake FICE Identification: 002972
Unit ID: 199193
Telephone: (919) 515-2011 Carnegie Class: DU-Highest
FAX Number: (919) 515-7740 Calendar System: Semester
URL: www.ncsu.edu
Established: 1887 Annual Undergrad Tuition & Fees (In-State): $9,101
Enrollment: 34,432 Coed
Affiliation or Control: State IRS Status: 501(c)3
Highest Offering: Doctorate
Accreditation: SC, ART, CACREP, CAEP, IPSY, LSAR, NRPA, SCPSY, SPAA, SW, VET

02 Chancellor Dr. William Randy WOODSON
05 Provost/Exec Vice Chancellor Dr. Warwick A. ARDEN
43 Vice Chanc & General Counsel Ms. Allison NEWHART
10 Interim Vice Chanc Finance & Admin Ms. Mary PELOQUIN-DODD
46 Vice Chanc Research & Innovation Dr. Mladen VOUK
32 Vice Chan/Dean Div Acad & Stdnt Aff Dr. Michael D. MULLEN
111 Vice Chanc Univ Advancement Mr. Brian C. SISCHO
13 Vice Chanc Information Technology Dr. Marc I. HOIT
101 Secretary of the University Ms. P. J. TEAL
88 Sr Vice Provost for Acad Strategy Dr. Duane K. LARICK
106 Sr Vice Prov Acad Outreach/Entrepre Dr. Thomas K. MILLER
08 Vice Provost/Director of Libraries Mr. Greg RASCHKE
22 Int VP Inst Equity & Diversity Ms. Sheri SCHWAB
18 Assoc Vice Chanc Facilities Mr. Doug MORTON
39 Assoc Vice Chanc Housing and Living Dr. Barry OLSON
26 Assoc Vice Chanc Univ Communication Mr. Brad BOHLANDER
29 Assoc Vice Chanc Alumni Relations Mr. Benny SUGGS
15 Assoc Vice Chanc Human Resources Ms. Marie WILLIAMS
19 Chief of Public Safety Mr. Jack W. MOORMAN
09 Sr Vice Prov Inst Rsrch & Planning Ms. Mary K. LELIK
07 AVP & Director of UG Admissions Mr. Jon WESTOVER
06 Sr Vice Provost & Univ Registrar Dr. Louis D. HUNT
25 Director Contracts & Grants Mr. Justo TORRES
37 Director of Financial Aid Ms. Krista RINGLER
38 Director of Counseling Center Dr. Monica OSBURN
41 Director Athletics Mr. Boo CORRIGAN
21 Assoc Vice Chancellor & Treasurer Ms. Mary T. PELOQUIN-DODD
88 Director of Materials Management Mrs. Sharon LOOSMAN
79 Dean Humanities/Social Sciences Dr. Jeffery P. BRADEN
48 Dean of Design Dr. Mark HOVERSTEN
54 Dean of Engineering Dr. Louis A. MARTIN-VEGA
47 Dean Agriculture/Life Sciences Dr. Richard H. LINTON
65 Dean of Natural Resources Dr. Mary WATZIN
53 Dean of Education Dr. Mary Ann DANOWITZ
50 Dean of Poole College of Management Dr. Frank BUCKLESS
81 Dean College of Sciences Dr. Chris MCGAHAN
88 Dean of Textiles Dr. David HINKS
74 Dean of Veterinary Medicine Dr. D. Paul LUNN
58 Interim Dean of Graduate School Dr. Peter J. HARRIES
86 VC Ext Affs/Partnerships/Econ Dev Mr. Kevin D. HOWELL

*University of North Carolina at Asheville (C)

1 University Heights, Asheville NC 28804-8503

County: Buncombe FICE Identification: 002907
Unit ID: 199111
Telephone: (828) 251-6600 Carnegie Class: Bac-A&S
FAX Number: (828) 251-6495 Calendar System: Semester
URL: www.unca.edu
Established: 1927 Annual Undergrad Tuition & Fees (In-State): $7,145
Enrollment: 3,852 Coed
Affiliation or Control: State IRS Status: 501(c)3
Highest Offering: Master's
Accreditation: SC, CAEPN

02 Chancellor Dr. Nancy J. CABLE
100 Chief of Staff Ms. Shannon C. EARLE
05 Provost/VC Academic Affairs Dr. Kai CAMPBELL
10 Vice Chancellor Admin & Finance Mr. John PIERCE
111 Vice Chancellor Advancement Vacant
32 Vice Chanc for Student Affairs Dr. Bill HAGGARD
41 Director of Athletics Ms. Janet R. CONE
43 University General Counsel Mr. Clifton WILLIAMS
15 Dir Human Res/Affirmative Action Ms. Nicole NORIAN
09 Dir Inst Research/Effect/Plng Dr. Michael GASS
20 Asst Provost Academic Admin Vacant
81 Dean Natural Science Dr. Herman HOLT
79 Dean Humanities Dr. Wiebke STREHL
83 Dean Social Science Vacant
08 University Librarian Ms. Leah DUNN
13 Chief Information Officer Mr. Scott COWDREY
07 Sr Dir Admissions/Financial Aid Mr. Steve MCKELLIPS
58 Dir Graduate Studies/Continuing Ed Dr. Gerard VOOS
06 Registrar Ms. Lynne HORGAN
21 Assoc VC of Finance/Controller Ms. Mary HALL
19 Asst VC for Public Safety Mr. Eric BOYCE
96 Purchasing Officer Mr. Joel KNISLEY
26 Chief Communication & Mktg Ofc Ms. Sarah BROBERG
27 Public Communication Spec Mr. Steve PLEVER
23 Dir Student Health/Counseling Mr. John CUTSPEC
88 Assoc Dean of Students Dr. Melanie FOX
39 Dir of Housing/Student Life Opers Mr. Vollie BARNWELL
36 Dir Ctr for Career Development Ms. Lisa TANDAN
35 Dean of Students Ms. Jackie MCHARGUE
04 Exec Asst to Chancellor Ms. Jennifer MENNELL

*University of North Carolina at Chapel Hill (D)

Chapel Hill NC 27599-0001

County: Orange FICE Identification: 002974
Unit ID: 199120
Telephone: (919) 962-2211 Carnegie Class: DU-Highest
FAX Number: (919) 962-5604 Calendar System: Semester
URL: www.unc.edu
Established: 1789 Annual Undergrad Tuition & Fees (In-State): $8,987
Enrollment: 29,911 Coed
Affiliation or Control: State IRS Status: 501(c)3
Highest Offering: Doctorate
Accreditation: SC, ACAE, #ARCPA, AUD, CAATE, CACREP, CAEPN, CLPSY, DENT, DH, DIETC, DMOLS, HSA, IPSY, JOUR, LAW, LC, LIB, MED, MT, NMT, NURSE, OT, PAST, PCSAS, PH, PHAR, PLNG, PTA, RAD, RADDOS, RTT, SCPSY, SP, SPAA, SW

02 Interim Chancellor Dr. Kevin GUSKIEWICZ
05 Provost & Exec Vice Chancellor Dr. Bob A. BLOUIN
20 Exec Vice Provost/Chief Intl Ofcr Dr. Ronald STRAUSS
10 Vice Chancellor Finance/Operations Mr. Jonathan PRUITT
32 Int Vice Chancellor Student Affairs Ms. Christi HURT
13 VC Info Technology/Chief Info Ofcr Mr. Chris KIELT
46 Vice Chancellor for Research Dr. Terry MAGNUSON
17 CEO UNC Health Care/VC Medical Affs Dr. A. Welsley BURKS
26 Assoc VC University Communications Mr. Rick WHITE
90 Asst VC Rsch Computing/Learng Tech Dr. Michael BARKER
08 Assoc Prov/University Librarian Ms. Sarah MICHALAK
21 Senior Assoc Vice Chancellor & CFO Vacant
20 Vice Provost Academic Initiatives Dr. Carol TRESOLINI
18 Assoc Vice Chanc Facilities Plng Ms. Anna WU
31 Director Community Relations Ms. Linda DOUGLAS
28 Vice Prov Diversity/Multicultural Ms. G. Rumay ALEXANDER
11 Provost Administration Dr. Lynn E. WILLIFORD
39 Dir Housing & Residential Education Mr. Alan BLATTNER
41 Director of Athletics Mr. Lawrence (Bubba) R. CUNNINGHAM
06 Int Asst Vice Prov/Univ Registrar Ms. Allison LEGGE
07 Vice Prov Enroll/Undergrad Admiss Dr. Stephen M. FARMER
29 Pres/Director General Alumni Assoc Mr. Douglas S. DIBBERT
37 Assoc Prov/Dir Scholar/Student Aid Ms. Shirley A. ORT
36 Director University Career Services Mr. Gary Alan MILLER
38 Dir Counseling & Psychological Svcs Dr. Allen H. O'BARR
44 Exec Director of Annual Giving Ms. Darlene GOOCH
19 Dir Public Safety/Chief of Police Chief Jeff B. MCCRACKEN
51 Director Center for Cont Education Mr. Rob BRUCE
27 Director University Relations Mr. Mike MCFARLAND
96 Director Procurement Services Ms. Martha PENDERGRASS
35 Assoc Vice Chanc Student Affairs Dr. Bettina SHUFORD
87 Dean of the Summer School Ms. Jan YOPP
49 Dean College Arts & Sciences Dr. Kevin GUSKIEWICZ
61 Dean School of Law Mr. Martin BRINKLEY
63 Dean School of Medicine Dr. A. Wesley BURKS
52 Dean School of Dentistry Dr. Scott S. DE ROSSI
58 Dean of Graduate School Dr. Steven W. MATSON
50 Dean Kenan-Flagler Business School Mr. Douglas SHACKLEFORD
70 Dean School of Social Work Dr. Gary L. BOWEN
67 Int Dean School of Pharmacy Dr. Dhiren THAKKER
60 Dean School of Journalism/Mass Comm Ms. Susan R. KING
62 Dean School of Info/Library Science Dr. Gary MARCHIONINI
69 Dean School of Public Health Dr. Barbara K. RIMER
53 Dean School of Education Dr. Fouad ABD-EL-KHALICK
80 Dean School of Government Dr. Michael R. SMITH
23 Exec Dir Campus Health Services Dr. Mary COVINGTON
92 Associate Dean for Honors Dr. James L. LELOUDIS

*University of North Carolina at Charlotte (E)

9201 University City Boulevard, Charlotte NC 28223-0001

County: Mecklenburg FICE Identification: 002975
Unit ID: 199139
Telephone: (704) 687-8622 Carnegie Class: DU-Higher
FAX Number: N/A Calendar System: Semester
URL: https://www.uncc.edu/
Established: 1946 Annual Undergrad Tuition & Fees (In-State): $6,853
Enrollment: 29,317 Coed
Affiliation or Control: State IRS Status: 501(c)3
Highest Offering: Doctorate
Accreditation: SC, ANEST, ART, CACREP, CAEPN, CEA, CLPSY, #COARC, DANCE, EXSC, HSA, IPSY, MUS, NURSE, PH, POLYT, SPAA, SW, THEA

02 Chancellor ... Dr. Philip L. DUBOIS
100 Chief of Staff ... Ms. Kim S. BRADLEY
05 Provost/Vice Chanc Acad Affairs ... Dr. Joan F. LORDEN
20 Senior Associate Provost ... Dr. Jay RAJA
88 Int Assc Prov Met Stds/Ext Acad Pgm ... Mr. Curt WALTON
10 Vice Chancellor Business Affairs ... Ms. Elizabeth A. HARDIN
111 Vice Chancellor Univ Advancement ... Mr. Niles F. SORENSEN
86 Spec Asst for Constituent Relations ... Ms. Betty DOSTER
32 Vice Chancellor Student Affairs ... Dr. Kevin BAILEY
46 Vice Chanc Research/Econ Dev ... Dr. Richard A. TANKERSLEY
13 Vice Chanc Info Tech Svcs/CIO ... Dr. Michael CARLIN
18 Assoc Vice Chanc Facilities Mgmt ... Mr. Jon VARNELL
08 Dean Atkins Library ... Dr. Anne C. MOORE
88 Assoc Prov Budget & Personnel ... Ms. Lori MCMAHON
82 Asst Provost for Intl Programs ... Mr. Joel A. GALLEGOS
88 Assistant Provost ... Dr. Leslie ZENK
26 Assoc VC for Univ Communications ... Vacant
106 Dir Distance Educ/Summer School ... Mr. Jody CEBINA
51 Dir Continuing Education ... Mr. Asher HAINES
31 Sr Dir Community Relations ... Ms. Jeanette SIMS
39 Assoc Vice Chanc/Dir Residence Life ... Dr. Aaron HART
21 Assoc Vice Chancellor for Finance ... Ms. Anne BROWN
21 Assoc Vice Chanc Business Svcs ... Mr. Keith N. WASSUM
58 Assoc Provost/Dean Graduate School . Dr. Thomas L. REYNOLDS
84 Assoc Provost for Enrollment Mgmt ... Ms. Tina M. MCENTIRE
43 VC for Inst Integrity/Gen Counsel .. Mr. James E. HUMPHREY, IV
07 Director Undergraduate Admissions ... Ms. Claire J. KIRBY
35 Dean of Students/Assoc VC Stdnt Aff ... Ms. Christine REED DAVIS
37 Director of Financial Aid ... Mr. Bruce BLACKMON
38 Assoc VC Health Programs & Services ... Dr. David B. SPANO
36 Director University Career Center ... Dr. Patrick MADSEN
40 Bookstore Manager ... Ms. Cheryl GRIFFITH-KLINE
29 Exec Director Alumni Affairs ... Ms. Sallie HUTTON SISTARE
88 Assoc VC Safety and Security ... Mr. John BOGDAN
19 Chief/Dir Police & Public Safety ... Mr. Jeffrey A. BAKER
09 Asst Provost Institutional Research ... Mr. Stephen A. COPPOLA
41 Director of Athletics ... Mr. Mike HILL
96 Director of Purchasing ... Mr. Randy DUNCAN
93 Dir Acad Diversity/Inclusion ... Mrs. Regena BROWN
23 Admin Director Student Health Svcs ... Mr. David ROUSMANIERE
15 Assoc Vice Chanc Human Res/Aff Act ... Mr. Gary W. STINNETT
85 Dir Intl Student/Scholar Svcs ... Mr. Tarek A. ELSHAYEB
104 Director Study Abroad ... Mr. Brad SEKULICH
48 Dean College of Arts/Architecture ... Mr. Brook MULLER
50 Dean College of Business ... Dr. Steven H. OTT
54 Dean College of Engineering ... Dr. Robert E. JOHNSON
53 Dean College of Education ... Dr. Ellen C. MCINTYRE
49 Dean Col of Liberal Arts & Sciences ... Dr. Nancy A. GUTIERREZ
76 Dean Col of Health & Human Svcs ... Dr. Catrine TUDOR-LOCKE
72 Dean College Computing/Informatics ... Dr. Fatma MILI
97 Dean University College ... Dr. John SMAIL
92 Exec Director of Honors College ... Dr. Malin PEREIRA
06 University Registrar ... Mr. Jonathan REECE
44 Director of Planning Giving ... Ms. Amy SHEHEE
44 Director of Annual Giving ... Ms. Stacie G. YOUNG
04 Executive Asst to President ... Ms. Shari DUNN
108 Exec Dir Assessment & Accreditation ... Dr. Christine ROBINSON
25 Exec Dir Contracts/Grants Admin ... Ms. Valerie CRICKARD
28 Director Faculty Affairs/Diversity ... Dr. Yvette HUET

*University of North Carolina at Greensboro (A)

PO Box 26170, Greensboro NC 27402-6170

County: Guilford | FICE Identification: 002976 | Unit ID: 199148
Telephone: (336) 334-5000 | Carnegie Class: DU-Higher
FAX Number: (336) 256-0408 | Calendar System: Semester
URL: www.uncg.edu
Established: 1891 | Annual Undergrad Tuition & Fees (In-State): $7,331
Enrollment: 19,922 | Coed
Affiliation or Control: State | IRS Status: 501(c)3
Highest Offering: Doctorate
Accreditation: SC, ANEST, CAATE, CACREP, CAEPN, CIDA, CLPSY, DANCE, DIETD, DIETI, LIB, MUS, NRPA, NURSE, PH, SP, SPAA, SW, THEA

02 Chancellor ... Dr. Franklin D. GILLIAM
100 Chief of Staff ... Ms. Waiyi TSE
05 Provost/Exec VC Academic Affairs ... Dr. Dana L. DUNN
10 Vice Chancellor Business Affairs ... Mr. Charles A. MAIMONE
13 Vice Chanc Info Tech Services ... Ms. Donna R. HEATH
32 Vice Chanc for Student Affairs ... Dr. Cathy AKENS
84 Vice Chancellor Enrollment Mgmt ... Vacant
111 VC University Advancement ... Dr. Beth FISCHER
26 VC Strategic Communications ... Mr. Jeff S. SHAFER
43 University General Counsel ... Mr. Jerry D. BLAKEMORE
20 Senior Vice Provost ... Dr. Alan J. BOYETTE
97 Dir Univ Teaching/Learning Commons ... Dr. David J. TEACHOUT
46 Vice Chanc Research & Engagement ... Dr. Terri L. SHELTON
104 Assoc Provost Intl Programs ... Dr. Penelope J. PYNES
15 Assoc VC Human Resources ... Ms. Jeanne MADORIN
35 Assoc VC/Dean Students ... Dr. Brett CARTER
21 Associate VC Financial Services ... Mr. Steven W. RHEW
88 Assoc VC Learning Tech Client Svs ... Mr. Todd SUTTON
18 Associate Vice Chanc for Facilities ... Mr. Jorge QUINTAL
09 Assoc Vice Prov/Director Research ... Dr. Larry D. MAYES
88 Assoc Dir Opers & Ext Reporting ... Dr. William B. ZHANG
35 Associate VC for Student Affairs ... Dr. Jim S. SETTLE
91 Assoc VC for Admin Systems ... Mr. Lee NORRIS
45 Assoc VC Strategy & Policy ... Dr. Julia JACKSON-NEWSOM
20 Assoc VP Dean Undergrad Studies ... Dr. Andrew HAMILTON
58 Vice Prov/Dean Graduate Education ... Dr. Kelly J. BURKE
49 Dean of Arts & Sciences ... Dr. John Z. KISS
50 Dean of Business & Economics ... Dr. McRae BANKS
53 Dean of Education ... Dr. Randall D. PENFIELD
68 Dean of Health & Human Sciences ... Dr. Carl G. MATTACOLA
64 Dean of Visual & Performing Arts ... Dr. Bruce D. MCCLUNG
66 Dean of Nursing ... Dr. Robin E. REMSBURG
54 Dean Joint Sch NanoScience/Engineer ... Dr. Sherine O. OBARE
08 Dean of University Libraries ... Mr. Martin HALBERT
06 Interim University Registrar ... Ms. Elizabeth CRANFORD
108 Dir Assessment and Accreditation ... Dr. Jodi E. PETTAZZONI
07 Director of Admissions ... Mr. Christopher J. KELLER
29 Dir Alumni Assn & Annual Giving ... Ms. Mary G. LANDERS
88 Director of Recreation and Wellness ... Dr. Jill BEVILLE
23 Director Student Health Services ... Ms. Kathy BABER
36 Director Career Services Ctr ... Ms. Nicole HALL
106 Dean Division of Online Learning ... Dr. James M. EDDY
92 Dean Lloyd International Honors Col ... Mr. Omar ALI
25 Dir Contracts and Grants ... Mr. William D. WALTERS
37 Director of Financial Aid ... Ms. Deborah TOLLEFSON
39 Director Housing & Residence Life ... Mr. Timothy JOHNSON
41 Director Intercollegiate Athletics ... Ms. Kim RECORD
89 Dir New Student Transitions & FYE ... Dr. Kim SOUSA-PEOPLES
19 Assoc VC for Safety/Emergency Mgmt ... Mr. Rollin DONELSON
28 Director Multicultural Affairs ... Vacant
96 Director Purchasing ... Mr. Michael F. LOGAN
40 University Bookstore Manager ... Mr. Brad LIGHT
04 Exec Assistant to the Chancellor ... Ms. Kimberly N. PARIS
105 University Webmaster ... Mr. Chris WATERS
38 Director Counseling Center ... Dr. Jennifer M. WHITNEY
44 Director Annual Giving ... Ms. Michelle R. DOEBLER
86 Dir Federal & External Affairs ... Ms. Nikki M. BAKER
90 Director Tech Support & Svcs ... Ms. Sherry L. WOODY
86 Dir State & External Affairs ... Mr. Andrew R. CAGLE
22 Dir Affirm Action/Equal Opportunity ... Ms. Patricia LYNCH

*University of North Carolina at Pembroke (B)

One University Drive, PO Box 1510, Pembroke NC 28372-1510

County: Robeson | FICE Identification: 002954 | Unit ID: 199281
Telephone: (910) 521-6000 | Carnegie Class: Masters/L
FAX Number: (910) 521-6176 | Calendar System: Semester
URL: www.uncp.edu
Established: 1887 | Annual Undergrad Tuition & Fees (In-State): $3,418
Enrollment: 6,252 | Coed
Affiliation or Control: State | IRS Status: 501(c)3
Highest Offering: Master's
Accreditation: SC, ART, CAATE, CACREP, CAEPN, MUS, NURSE, SW

02 Chancellor ... Dr. Robin G. CUMMINGS
43 General Counsel ... Mr. Joshua MALCOLM
05 Provost/VC Academic Affairs ... Dr. David WARD
100 Chief of Staff ... Mr. Mark GOGAL
10 Vice Chanc Finance & Admin ... Dr. William THOMAS
116 Chief Audit Officer ... Ms. Megan FEES
32 Vice Chanc Student Affairs ... Dr. Lisa L. SCHAEFFER
41 Director of Athletics ... Mr. Dick CHRISTY
111 Vice Chanc for Advancement ... Mr. Bryan ROBINSON
26 Dir University Communications/Mktg ... Ms. Jodi PHELPS
88 Director Title IX and Clery Act Co ... Ms. Ronette SUTTON GERBER
88 Int Asst to Chancellor Rsrch/Comm ... Ms. Tabi CAIN
04 Executive Asst to the Chancellor ... Ms. Jocelyn GRAHAM
20 Assoc Vice Chancellor ... Dr. Scott BILLINGSLEY
85 Assoc VC Global Engagement ... Ms. Cathy Lee ARCUINO
84 Assoc Vice Chanc for Enrollment Mgt ... Ms. Lois H. WILLIAMS
45 Assoc VC for Planning/Accreditation ... Dr. Elizabeth NORMANDY
25 Assoc VC Research and Sponsored ... Vacant
53 Interim Dean of School of Education ... Dr. Zoe LOCKLEAR
50 Dean of School of Business ... Dr. Barry O'BRIEN
49 Dean of Arts & Sciences ... Dr. Jeff FREDERICK
08 Dean of Library Services ... Dr. Dennis SWANSON
58 Dean of The Graduate School ... Dr. Irene AIKEN
89 Dean of University College ... Ms. Beth HOLDER
92 Dean of Honors College ... Dr. Mark MILEWICZ
76 Dean College of Health Sciences ... Vacant
88 Director for Academic Resources ... Ms. Leslie T. BELL
09 Director Institutional Research ... Dr. Chunmei YAO
06 Registrar ... Ms. Christina REEVES
07 Director of Admissions ... Mrs. Elizabeth HUNTER
37 Director Financial Aid ... Ms. Jenelle HANDCOX
121 Dir Center for Student Success ... Dr. Derek OXENDINE
88 Director Accessibility Resource ... Dr. Nicolette CAMPOS
106 Int Dir Online/Distance Education ... Dr. Ki Byung CHAE
25 Dir Sponsored Research/Grant ... Ms. Lisa HUNT
21 Assoc Vice Chancellor for Finance ... Vacant
13 Int Assoc VC Info Resources/CIO ... Mr. Kevin PAIT
15 Asst Vice Chanc for Human Resources ... Ms. Angela REVELS-BULLARD
18 Asst VC for Facilities ... Vacant
16 Assoc Dir Human Resources ... Ms. Donna STRICKLAND
16 Dir Employee Relations and Dev ... Mr. Benjamin SIMMONS
88 Facilities Superintendent ... Mr. Mark VESELY
119 Chief Information Security Officer ... Mr. Don BRYANT
14 Deputy CIO Infrastructure and Opers ... Mr. Kevin PAIT
14 Dir IT Support Services ... Ms. Liz CUMMINGS
96 Director of Business Services ... Ms. Karen SWINEY
21 Controller ... Ms. Jennifer ADDISON
113 Bursar ... Ms. Cynthia REVELS
114 Director Budget & Planning ... Ms. Kristy NANCE
35 Asst Vice Chanc Student Affairs ... Ms. Cynthia OXENDINE
38 Director Counseling/Testing Center ... Ms. LynnDee HORNE
32 Dir of Campus Engagement/Leadership ... Mr. Abdul GHAFFAR
39 Director Housing and Resident Life ... Mr. Paul POSENER
28 Dir Multicultural/Minority Affairs ... Mr. Robert L. CANIDA, II
36 Director Career Services Center ... Dr. Marlane A. MOWITZ
88 Sports Information Director ... Mr. Todd ANDERSON
80 Director Public Administration Pgm ... Dr. Emily NEFF-SHARUM
23 Director of Student Health Services ... Ms. Cora BULLARD
29 Director of Alumni Engagement ... Ms. Alexis LOCKLEAR
44 Assistant Director of Annual Fund ... Mr. Paris ROEBUCK
110 Dir Advancement Services ... Vacant
27 Director of Creative Services ... Mr. David YBARRA
31 Director of Community Relations ... Mr. Paul JOLICOEUR
19 Director Security/Safety ... Mr. McDuffie CUMMINGS, JR.
88 Faculty Senate Chair ... Dr. Mitu ASHRAF
104 Director Study Abroad ... Mr. Alexander BRANDT

*University of North Carolina Wilmington (C)

601 S College Road, Wilmington NC 28403-5931

County: New Hanover | FICE Identification: 002984 | Unit ID: 199218
Telephone: (910) 962-3030 | Carnegie Class: DU-Higher
FAX Number: (910) 962-4050 | Calendar System: Semester
URL: www.uncw.edu
Established: 1947 | Annual Undergrad Tuition & Fees (In-State): $7,091
Enrollment: 16,487 | Coed
Affiliation or Control: State | IRS Status: 501(c)3
Highest Offering: Doctorate
Accreditation: SC, CAATE, CAEPN, CEA, MUS, NURSE, PH, SPAA, SW

02 Chancellor ... Dr. Jose V. SARTARELLI
05 Provost/Vice Chanc Academic Affairs ... Dr. Marilyn SHEERER
10 Vice Chancellor Business Affairs ... Mr. Miles LACKEY
32 Vice Chanc for Student Affairs ... Ms. Patricia L. LEONARD
111 Vice Chanc University Advancement ... Mr. Eddie STUART
110 Assoc Vice Chanc Univ Advancement ... Ms. Missy KENNEDY
21 Assoc Vice Chanc Business Services ... Ms. Sharon H. BOYD
21 Assoc VC Business Affs/Facilities ... Mr. Mark D. MORGAN
106 Assoc VC for Distance Education ... Dr. Jeremy DICKERSON
46 Assoc Provost for Research ... Dr. Stuart BORRETT
28 Chief Diversity Officer ... Dr. Kent GUION
26 Chief Communications Officer ... Ms. Janine IAMUNNO
09 Assoc Provost Inst Research/Plng ... Dr. Andy MAUK
35 Assoc VC/Dean of Students ... Dr. Michael A. WALKER
84 Director Enrollment Management ... Mr. Marcio MORENO
85 Assoc VC International Programs ... Dr. Michael WILHELM
15 Assoc VC Human Resources ... Ms. Elizabeth GRIMES
100 Chief of Staff ... Mr. Bradley BALLOU
06 University Registrar ... Ms. Amanda FLEMING
08 University Librarian ... Ms. Lucy HOLMAN
37 Director Financial Aid/Scholarships ... Mr. Frederick HOLDING
18 Director of Physical Plant ... Mr. David OLSON
19 Assoc Dir Envir Health & Safety ... Ms. Deb TEW
23 Dir Student Health/Wellness Center ... Ms. Katrin WESNER
109 Director of Auxiliary Services ... Mr. Brian DAILEY
41 Director of Athletics ... Mr. Jimmy BASS
36 Interim Director Career Center ... Ms. Nadirah PIPPEN
29 Director of Alumni Relations ... Mrs. Lindsay LEROY
96 Director of Purchasing ... Mr. John ROBINSON
38 Dir Counseling Center/Univ Testing ... Dr. Mark PEREZ-LOPEZ
40 Manager Bookstore ... Ms. Mee So YIM
49 Dean Col Arts & Sciences ... Dr. Aswani VOLETY
50 Dean Cameron School of Business ... Dr. Robert BURRUS
53 Dean Watson School of Education ... Dr. Van O. DEMPSEY
66 Director School of Nursing ... Dr. Linda HADDAD
58 Dean of Graduate School ... Dr. Chris FINELLI
76 Dean Col Health & Human Svcs ... Dr. Charles HARDY
04 Executive Assistant to the Chanc ... Ms. Carolyn S. HARTMAN
07 Director Admissions ... Mr. Marcio MORENO
13 Chief Info Technology Officer (CIO) ... Ms. Sharyne MILLER
25 Dir Sponsored Pgms/Rsrch/Compliance ... Ms. Panda POWELL
43 General Counsel ... Mr. John SCHERER
54 Director Engineering ... Dr. Amy REAMER
90 Consulting Services Support Dir ... Ms. Beverly VAGNERINI
101 Asst to the Chancellor/Trustees ... Mr. Mark LANIER
39 Director Housing/Residence Life ... Mr. Peter GROENENDYK
108 Dir Office of Inst Effectiveness ... Dr. Kelly CHARLES
30 Director of Development ... Ms. Dawn CARTER

*University of North Carolina School of the Arts (D)

1533 S Main Street, Winston-Salem NC 27127-2738

County: Forsyth | FICE Identification: 003981 | Unit ID: 199184
Telephone: (336) 770-3399 | Carnegie Class: Spec-4-yr-Arts
FAX Number: (336) 770-3375 | Calendar System: Semester
URL: www.uncsa.edu
Established: 1963 | Annual Undergrad Tuition & Fees (In-State): $9,371
Enrollment: 1,014 | Coed
Affiliation or Control: State | IRS Status: 501(c)3
Highest Offering: Master's
Accreditation: SC

02 Interim Chancellor ... Mr. Brian COLE
05 Interim Provost and EVC ... Dr. Karin PETERSON
10 Vice Chanc for Finance & Admin ... Mr. Michael SMITH
111 Vice Chanc for Advancement ... Mr. Edward LEWIS
18 Assoc VC Facilities ... Mr. Michael O'CONNOR
26 Vice Chanc Strategic Communication ... Ms. Claire MACHAMER

09 Director of Institutional Research Mr. Jeff PATON
07 Director of Admissions Mr. Paul RAZZA
08 University Librarian Ms. Sarah FALLS
27 Director of Communications Ms. Marla CARPENTER
06 Registrar Ms. Erin MORIN
15 Director of Human Resources Ms. Angela MAHONEY
37 Director of Financial Aid Mrs. Jane KAMIAB
49 Dean of Liberal Arts Mr. Dean WILCOX
64 Dean School of Music Mr. Brian COLE
57 Dean School of Dance Ms. Susan JAFFE
48 Dean Sch of Design/Production Mr. Michael KELLEY
88 Dean School of Drama Mr. Scott ZIGLER
13 Chief Technology Officer Mr. Terrence HARMON
19 Chief of Police Mr. Frank BRINKLEY
38 Dir of Counseling & Testing Svcs Vacant
32 Vice Provost & Dean Student Affairs Dr. Tracey FORD
96 Director of Purchasing Ms. Jeanette VALENTINE
88 Dir Ctr for Design Innovation Mr. Jim DECRISTO
57 Exec Dir Kenan Inst for the Arts Ms. Corey MADDEN
88 Interim Dean School of Filmmaking Mr. Henry GRILLO
88 Headmaster/Dean HS Academic Program Mr. Martin FERRELL
35 Director of Student Engagement Mr. Steve GALLAGHER
87 Dir Educ Outreach & Summer Programs Ms. Suzanna WATKINS
39 Assistant Dean & Dir of RLPH Mr. Joseph RICK
23 Director of Health Services Ms. Sharon SUMMER
100 Chief of Staff Mr. James DECRISTO
43 General Counsel Mr. David HARRISON
102 Foundation Director Ms. Cynthia LIBERTY
108 Director of Inst Effectiveness Mr. Jeff PATON

*Western Carolina University (A)

One University Way, HFR 501, Cullowhee NC 28723-9646
County: Jackson FICE Identification: 002981
Unit ID: 200004
Telephone: (828) 227-7100 Carnegie Class: Masters/L
FAX Number: (828) 227-7176 Calendar System: Semester
URL: www.wcu.edu
Established: 1889 Annual Undergrad Tuition & Fees (In-State): $3,926
Enrollment: 11,034 Coed
Affiliation or Control: State IRS Status: 501(c)3
Highest Offering: Doctorate
Accreditation: SC, ANEST, ART, CAATE, CACREP, CAEPN, CARTE, CIDA, CONST, DIETD, DIETI, EMT, IPSY, MUS, NURSE, PTA, SP, SPAA, SW, THEA

02 Chancellor Dr. Kelli R. BROWN
05 Vice Provost for Academic Affairs Dr. Carol BURTON
10 Vice Chanc Admin & Finance Mr. Mike BYERS
32 Vice Chancellor/Student Affairs Dr. H. Samuel MILLER, JR.
121 Asst Vice Chanc Student Success Dr. Lowell K. DAVIS
35 Asst Vice Chanc/Student Affairs Ms. Kellie MONTEITH
111 Vice Chancellor Advancement Mrs. Lori LEWIS
20 Assoc Provost Academic Affairs Dr. Brandon SCHWAB
18 Assoc VC for Facilities Management Mr. Joe WALKER
100 Chief of Staff Dr. Melissa WARGO
04 Acting Assistant to the Chancellor Ms. Jessica WOODS
43 Legal Counsel Mr. Shea BROWNING
38 Director of Counseling Services Dr. Kimberly GORMAN
06 Registrar Mr. Larry HAMMER
07 Director of Student Recruitment Mr. Phil CAULEY
09 Asst Vice Chancellor of OIPE Mr. Tim METZ
37 Director of Financial Aid Ms. Trina ORR
15 Assoc VC of Human Resources Dr. Cory CAUSBY
13 Chief Information Officer Mr. Craig FOWLER
29 Director of Alumni Affairs Mr. Marty RAMSEY
08 Dean of Library Services Dr. Farzaneh RAZZAGHI
88 Exec Director Education Outreach Dr. Susan FOUTS
109 Director Campus Services Mr. Bryant BARNETT
41 Athletic Director Mr. Randy EATON
23 Director University Health Services Ms. Pamela BUCHANAN
96 Director of Purchasing Ms. Cindy NICHOLSON
40 Director Book & Supply Store Ms. Pamela DEGRAFFENREID
38 Director of Advising Center Mr. Travis BULLUCK
36 Director of Career Services Ms. Theresa PAUL
26 Chief Communications Officer Mr. Bill STUDENC
57 Dean of Fine & Performing Arts Dr. George H. BROWN
58 Dean Grad School & Research Dr. Brian KLOEPPEL
49 Dean Arts & Sciences Dr. Richard STARNES
72 Dean Kimmel School Constr Mgmt/Tech Dr. Jeffrey RAY
53 Dean Educ & Allied Professions Dr. Kim WINTER
76 Dean Health & Human Sciences Dr. Douglas R. KESKULA
92 Dean of Honors College Dr. Jill GRANGER
88 Director Content Strategy Ms. Donna GALLO
86 Director of External Relations Ms. Meredith WHITFIELD
27 Director of Marketing & Brand Ms. Stacy MACGREGOR

*Winston-Salem State University (B)

601 MLK Jr. Drive, 200 Blair Hall,
Winston-Salem NC 27110-0001
County: Forsyth FICE Identification: 002986
Unit ID: 199999
Telephone: (336) 750-2000 Carnegie Class: Masters/M
FAX Number: (336) 750-2049 Calendar System: Semester
URL: www.wssu.edu
Established: 1892 Annual Undergrad Tuition & Fees (In-State): $5,904
Enrollment: 5,098 Coed
Affiliation or Control: State IRS Status: 501(c)3
Highest Offering: Doctorate
Accreditation: SC, CACREP, CAEPN, MT, MUS, NRPA, NURSE, OT, PTA, SW

02 Chancellor Dr. Elwood L. ROBINSON

05 Provost/VC Academic Affairs Dr. Anthony GRAHAM
32 Assoc Prov/VC Student Development Dr. Melvin NORWOOD
20 Associate Provost Dr. Carolynn BERRY
45 Assoc Prov Administration/Plng Mrs. Letitia C. WALL
10 Vice Chanc Finance & Admin Mrs. Constance MALLETTE
111 Vice Chanc Univ Advancement Mrs. LaTanya D. AFOLAYAN
100 Vice Chancellor/Chief of Staff Mrs. Camille KLUTTZ-LEACH
18 Assoc Vice Chanc Facilities Mgmt Mr. Timothy MCMULLEN
13 Assoc Prov/Chief Information Ofcr Dr. Derrick MURRAY
116 Director Internal Audit/Compliance Ms. Shannon B. HENRY
19 Chief of Campus Police Mrs. Patricia D. NORRIS
08 Director of Library Services Ms. Wanda BROWN
39 Director Hous/Residence Life Ms. Chantal BOUCHEREAU
37 Director of Financial Aid Mr. Robert MUHAMMED
15 Assoc Vice Chanc Human Resources Vacant
26 VC Communication/Chief Marketing Ms. Jamie HUNT
84 Dir Enrollment Communications Ms. Cathy HOOTS
102 Exec Director Univ Donor Events Mrs. Kimberly REESE
35 Director Student Activities Ms. Heather DAVIS
23 Dir of Student Health Center Vacant
41 Interim Athletic Director Mr. George KNOX
07 Director of Admissions Dr. Kerwin GRAHAM
43 Chief Legal Counsel Mr. Ivey BROWN
96 Director Purchasing Mr. Alan IRELAND
90 Director Academic Computer Center Mr. Cuthrell JOHNSON
79 Dean University College LLL Dr. Darryl SCRIVEN
76 Interim Dean School of Health Sci Dr. Celia HOOPER
88 Director of Title III Dr. Everette L. WITHERSPOON
06 Registrar Ms. Sharon STODDARD
108 Director Institutional Assessment Dr. Becky MUSSAT-WHITLOW

University of Phoenix Charlotte Campus (C)

3800 Arco Corporate Drive, Charlotte NC 28273-3409
Telephone: (704) 504-5409 Identification: 770216
Accreditation: &NH, ACBSP

† No longer accepting campus-based students.

Wake Forest University (D)

1834 Wake Forest Road, Winston-Salem NC 27109-8758
County: Forsyth FICE Identification: 002978
Unit ID: 199847
Telephone: (336) 758-5000 Carnegie Class: DU-Higher
FAX Number: (336) 758-6074 Calendar System: Semester
URL: www.wfu.edu
Established: 1834 Annual Undergrad Tuition & Fees: $53,322
Enrollment: 8,116 Coed
Affiliation or Control: Independent Non-Profit IRS Status: 501(c)3
Highest Offering: Doctorate
Accreditation: SC, ANEST, ARCPA, CACREP, CAEP, DENT, IPSY, LAW, MED, THEOL

01 President Dr. Nathan O. HATCH
43 SVP/General Counsel/Sec BOT Mr. J. Reid MORGAN
10 Exec Vice Pres/Chief Financial Ofcr Mr. B. Hofler MILAM
05 Provost Mr. Rogan KERSH
11 Vice President for Administration Vacant
111 Vice Pres University Advancement Mr. Mark A. PETERSEN
32 Vice Pres Campus Life Dr. Penny RUE
115 Vice Pres/Chief Investment Officer Mr. James J. DUNN
100 Chief of Staff Ms. Mary E. PUGEL
35 Assoc VP/Dean of Student Services Mr. Adam GOLDSTEIN
44 Ast VP/Dir Parent/Donor Relations Ms. Minta A. MCNALLY
30 Asst VP/Director of Development Mr. Robert T. BAKER
13 CIO/Assoc Provost for Tech/IS Mr. Muchane MUCHANE
46 Assoc Provost for Research Dr. S. Bruce KING
49 Dean of the College Dr. Michele K. GILLESPIE
61 Dean School of Law Mr. Suzanne REYNOLDS
50 Dean of Business Mr. Charles IACOVOU
73 Dean of Divinity Dr. Jill Y. CRAINSHAW
09 Dir Inst Research/Academic Admin Mr. Phil HANDWERK
08 Dir of the Z Smith Reynolds Library Mr. Tim PYATT
07 Director of Admissions Ms. Martha B. ALLMAN
37 Director of Financial Aid Mr. William T. WELLS
36 VP Office of Personal & Career Dev Mr. Andy CHAN
06 Registrar Mr. Harold PACE
41 Director of Athletics Mr. Ronald D. WELLMAN
15 Chief Human Resources Officer Ms. Carmen I. CANALES
18 Director Facilities Management Mr. John SHENETTE
38 Dir University Counseling Center Dr. Marianne A. SCHUBERT
23 Director Student Health Service Dr. Cecil D. PRICE
39 Dean Residence Life & Housing Ms. Donna MCGALLIARD
42 Chaplain Rev. Timothy L. AUMAN
19 Chief University Police Ms. Regina G. LAWSON
22 EEO Mgr/Diversity & Compliance Dir Ms. Angela CULLER
94 Director Women's & Gender Studies Dr. Wanda BALZANO
26 Chief Public Relations Officer Mr. Brett EATON
104 Director Study Abroad Mr. David F. TAYLOR
29 Director Alumni Engagement Mrs. Kelly MCCONNICO

Warren Wilson College (E)

PO Box 9000, Asheville NC 28815-9000
County: Buncombe FICE Identification: 002979
Unit ID: 199865
Telephone: (828) 771-2000 Carnegie Class: Bac-A&S
FAX Number: (828) 771-7097 Calendar System: Semester
URL: www.warren-wilson.edu
Established: 1894 Annual Undergrad Tuition & Fees: $36,280
Enrollment: 661 Coed
Affiliation or Control: Presbyterian Church (U.S.A.) IRS Status: 501(c)3
Highest Offering: Master's
Accreditation: SC, SW

01 President Dr. Lynn M. MORTON
05 Int Vice Pres Academic Affairs Dr. Paul J. BARTELS
10 VP Administration & Finance/CFO Ms. Belinda BURKE
111 Vice Pres for Advancement Mr. Zanne GARLAND
32 Vice Pres Student Life Mr. Paul C. PERRINE
84 Vice President Enrollment Mr. Matt EDLUND
88 Vice Pres Applied Learning Ms. Cathy KRAMER
37 Director Financial Aid Ms. Lori LEWIS
44 Director Annual Fund Ms. Mary HAY
26 Director of Media Relations Vacant
38 Director of Counseling Mr. Arthur SHUSTER
36 Director Career Services Ms. Wendy SELIGMANN
42 Dir of Spiritual Life & Chaplain Rev. Brian AMMONS
07 Director of Admission Mr. Brian LIECHTI
15 Director Human Resources Ms. Mandy KUTSHIED
19 Director Public Safety Mr. Justin GILDNER
28 Inclusion/Diversity/Equity Director Ms. Clarissa HARRIS
31 Assoc Director Community Engagement Ms. Brooke MILLSAPS

William Peace University (F)

15 E Peace Street, Raleigh NC 27604-1194
County: Wake FICE Identification: 002953
Unit ID: 199272
Telephone: (919) 508-2000 Carnegie Class: Bac-Diverse
FAX Number: (919) 508-2326 Calendar System: Semester
URL: www.peace.edu
Established: 1857 Annual Undergrad Tuition & Fees: $30,500
Enrollment: 930 Coed
Affiliation or Control: Presbyterian Church (U.S.A.) IRS Status: 501(c)3
Highest Offering: Baccalaureate
Accreditation: SC

01 President Dr. Brian C. RALPH
100 Dir of Presidential Operations Ms. Kelley DIETZ
05 Vice President for Academic Affairs Dr. Charles DUNCAN
111 Vice Pres University Advancement Ms. Jodi STAMEY
32 Vice President for Student Services Mr. Frank RIZZO
10 Vice Pres Finance & Administration Mr. George A. YEARWOOD
84 Int VP Enrollment Mgmt/Marketing Ms. Colleen MURPHY
15 Assoc Vice Pres for Human Resources Ms. Kathy LAMBERT
18 Assoc VP for Buildings and Grounds Mr. John B. CRANHAM
13 Chief Information Officer Mr. Josh FRANK
06 Registrar Ms. Melanie FULLER
09 Director of Institutional Research Ms. Carolyn BLATTNER
37 Director of Financial Aid Ms. Michelle HEMMER
41 Exec Director of Athletics Mr. Philip ROWE

Wingate University (G)

220 N. Camden Road, Wingate NC 28174-0159
County: Union FICE Identification: 002985
Unit ID: 199962
Telephone: (704) 233-8000 Carnegie Class: DU-Mod
FAX Number: (704) 233-8014 Calendar System: Semester
URL: www.wingate.edu
Established: 1896 Annual Undergrad Tuition & Fees: $33,166
Enrollment: 3,620 Coed
Affiliation or Control: Southern Baptist IRS Status: 501(c)3
Highest Offering: Doctorate
Accreditation: SC, ACBSP, ARCPA, CAATE, COSMA, MUS, NUR, PHAR, PTA

01 President Dr. T. Rhett BROWN
05 Provost Dr. Helen TATE
41 VP & Director of Athletics Mr. R. Stephen POSTON
10 SVP Business and Finance Mr. J. Craig ADDISON
26 SVP for External Relations Dr. Heather C. MILLER
11 VP for Operations Mr. Scott E. HUNSUCKER
111 Vice President for Advancement Ms. Hannah DICKERSON
15 VP for Human Resources Ms. Dori ARMSTEAD
88 VP Strategic Partnerships Mr. Vincent TILSON
115 VP Business Mr. William H. DURHAM
110 Assoc VP for Advancement Mr. Roy Lee RAGSDALE, JR.
109 AVP for Auxiliary Services Mr. Cameron JACKSON
121 Dean of Academic Support Programs Mrs. Glenda H. BEBBER
67 Dean School of Pharmacy Dr. Robert B. SUPERNAW
49 Dean School Arts & Sciences Dr. H. Donald MERRILL
50 Dean School of Business Dr. Peter FRANK
53 Dean School of Education Dr. Annette DIGBY
08 Director of Library Mrs. Amee M. ODOM
39 Assoc Dean Res Life & Involvement Ms. Brandy SHOTT
37 Director Student Financial Planning Ms. Teresa G. WILLIAMS
88 AVP Strategic Partnerships Mr. Jeffrey ATKINSON
91 Director Administrative Computing Mr. Timothy D. HERRIN
29 Asst Director of Alumni Relations Ms. Brittany BUMGARNER
42 Minister to Stdnts/Sr Dir CVICS Rev. A. Dane JORDAN
40 Director of Campus Store Mrs. Sherri SHANK
19 Campus Safety Chief Mr. Mike EASLEY
38 Director of Counseling Services Ms. Lori HINNANT
13 Director of Information Technology Ms. Jeanette K. BUJAK
36 Dir of Internships and Career Svcs Ms. Sharon ROBINSON
32 Dean of Campus Life/Student Life Mr. Michael REYNOLDS
06 Registrar Ms. Maria TAYLOR
07 Director of Admissions Ms. Elizabeth BIGGERSTAFF
04 Executive Assistant to President Ms. Tammy T. BRITT
13 CIO Mr. Steve SHANK
20 Vice Provost Student Engagement Dr. Nancy RANDALL

NORTH DAKOTA

Cankdeska Cikana Community College (A)

PO Box 269, 214 First Avenue,
Fort Totten ND 58335-0269

County: Benson
FICE Identification: 022365
Unit ID: 200208
Telephone: (701) 766-4415
Carnegie Class: Tribal
FAX Number: (701) 766-4077
Calendar System: Semester
URL: www.littlehoop.edu
Established: 1974
Annual Undergrad Tuition & Fees: $3,300
Enrollment: 242
Coed
Affiliation or Control: Independent Non-Profit
IRS Status: 501(c)3
Highest Offering: Associate Degree
Accreditation: NH

01 President ... Dr. Cynthia A. LINDQUIST
05 Academic Dean ... Mrs. Teresa HARDING
10 CFO ... Mrs. Chelly VEER
11 Dean of Administration ... Mr. Stuart YOUNG
06 Registrar ... Ms. DeShawn LAWRENCE

*North Dakota University System Office (B)

600 E Boulevard Avenue, Dept. 215,
Bismarck ND 58505-0230

County: Burleigh
FICE Identification: 033434
Telephone: (701) 328-2960
Carnegie Class: N/A
FAX Number: (701) 328-2961
URL: www.ndus.edu

01 Chancellor ... Mark HAGEROTT
100 Chief of Staff ... Terry MEYER
05 Interim VC Acad/Student Affairs ... Lisa JOHNSON
10 VC Administrative Affairs/CFO ... Tammy DOLAN
13 VC IT/Chief Information Officer ... Darin KING
45 VC Strategy/Strategic Engagement ... James WISECUP
37 Director of Financial Aid ... Brenda ZASTOUPIL
21 Director of Finance ... David KREBSBACH
09 Dir of Institutional Research ... Jennifer WEBER
26 Dir of Communications & Media Rels ... Billie Jo LORIUS
88 Director of Financial Reporting ... Robin PUTNAM
20 Director of Academic Affairs ... Lisa JOHNSON
32 Director of Student Affairs ... Katie FITZSIMMONS
18 Director Facilities Planning ... Rick TONDER
15 Director of Human Resources ... Jane GRINDE

*University of North Dakota (C)

264 Centennial Drive, Grand Forks ND 58202

County: Grand Forks
FICE Identification: 003005
Unit ID: 200280
Telephone: (701) 777-3000
Carnegie Class: DU-Higher
FAX Number: (701) 777-2696
Calendar System: Semester
URL: www.und.edu
Established: 1883
Annual Undergrad Tuition & Fees (In-State): $8,695
Enrollment: 14,406
Coed
Affiliation or Control: State
IRS Status: 501(c)3
Highest Offering: Doctorate
Accreditation: NH, AAB, ANEST, ARCPA, ART, CAATE, CAEPN, CLPSY, COPSY, DIETC, HT, LAW, MED, MT, MUS, NURSE, OT, PH, PTA, SP, SPAA, SW, THEA

02 Interim President ... Dr. Joshua WYNNE
100 Chief of Staff ... Vacant
29 CEO Alumni Assoc & Foundation ... Ms. DeAnna CARLSON-ZINK
05 Vice Pres Academic Affairs/Provost ... Dr. Thomas DILORENZO
10 Vice Pres Finance/Operations & CFO ... Mr. Jed SHIVERS
32 Int Vice Pres Stdnt Affs/Diversity ... Dr. Cara HALGREN
17 Vice President Health Affairs ... Dr. Joshua WYNNE
46 VP Research/Economic Devel ... Dr. John MIHELICH
26 VP Marketing/Communications ... Ms. Meloney LINDER
27 Director of Communications ... Mr. David L. DODDS
27 Dir of Marketing & Creative Svcs ... Ms. Jennifer SWANGLER
21 Assoc VP Finance ... Ms. Karla MONGEON-STEWART
18 Assoc VP Facilities ... Mr. Michael PIEPER
45 AVP Research & Economic Dev/RDC ... Dr. Barry MILAVETZ
88 AVP Rsrch & Econ Dev/Capacity Bldg ... Dr. Mark HOFFMANN
20 Asst VP Student Academic Services ... Ms. Lisa BURGER
84 Int Vice Provost Enrollment Mgmt ... Ms. Janelle KILGORE
13 Chief Information Officer ... Dr. Madhavi MARASINGHE
20 Senior Vice Provost ... Dr. Debbie STORRS
28 Assoc VP Diversity & Inclusion ... Vacant
08 Dean of Libraries & Info Res ... Ms. Stephanie WALKER
06 Registrar ... Mr. Scott CORRELL
15 AVP Human Resources/Payroll Svcs ... Ms. Peggy VARBERG
19 AVP Public Safety/Police Chief ... Mr. Eric PLUMMER
38 Director Univ Counseling Center ... Mr. Thomas SOLEM
36 Director Career Services ... Ms. Ilene ODEGARD
20 Director Instructional Development ... Dr. Anne KELSCH
22 Director EEO/Affirmative Action ... Ms. Donna SMITH
37 Int Director Student Financial Aid ... Ms. Chelsea LARSON
39 Director Housing ... Mr. Troy NOELDNER
23 Director of Student Health ... Ms. Rosy DUB
43 General Counsel ... Mr. Jason JENKINS
41 Director Athletics ... Mr. William CHAVES
85 Director International Programs ... Ms. Katie DAVIDSON
21 Controller ... Ms. Sharon LOILAND
88 Dir Student Rights/Responsibilities ... Mr. Alex POKORNOWSKI
94 Director Women's Center ... Vacant
96 Director Financial Operations ... Ms. Jana THOMPSON
92 Int Director Honors Program ... Dr. A. Rebecca ROZELLE-STONE
28 Dir Multicultural Student Services ... Dr. Stacey BORBOA-PETERSON
114 Assoc Dir Resource Plng/Alloc ... Ms. Cindy FETSCH
49 Dean of Arts & Sciences ... Dr. Brad RUNDQUIST
58 Int Dean School of Graduate Studies ... Dr. John MIHELICH
61 Dean School of Law ... Mr. Michael MCGINNISS
66 Int Dn Col Nursing/Prof Discipline ... Dr. Diana KOSTRZEWSKI
50 Dean Business/Public Admin ... Dr. Amy HENLEY
54 Int Dean College of Engr/Mines ... Dr. Brian TANDE
53 Dean Col Education/Human Devel ... Dr. Cindy JUNTUNEN
88 Dean of Aerospace Sciences ... Dr. Paul LINDSETH
63 Dean Sch Medicine/Health Science ... Dr. Joshua WYNNE
35 Assoc Dean of Students ... Dr. Cassie GERHARDT
88 Executive Director Memorial Union ... Ms. Cheryl GREW-GILLEN
109 Director Dining Services ... Mr. Orlynn ROSAASEN
88 Dir Children's Learning Center ... Ms. Dawnita NILLES
13 Dir App/Integration Support ... Ms. Sherry LAWDERMILT
22 Dir Disability Svcs for Students ... Ms. Debrah GLENNEN
88 Director TRIO Programs ... Mr. Derek SPORBERT
88 Student Account Relations Mgr ... Mr. Matt LUKACH
07 Director Admissions ... Ms. Jennifer AAMODT
09 Dir University Analytics/Planning ... Ms. Amanda MOSKE
105 Director Web Services ... Ms. Tera BUCKLEY
106 Vice Prov Online Educ/Strat Plng ... Dr. Jeffrey HOLM
25 Export Control/Contract Officer ... Mr. Michael SADLER
86 Chief Liaison Officer ... Mr. Peter B. JOHNSON

*Dickinson State University (D)

291 Campus Drive, Dickinson ND 58601-4896

County: Stark
FICE Identification: 002989
Unit ID: 200059
Telephone: (701) 483-2507
Carnegie Class: Bac-Diverse
FAX Number: (701) 483-2006
Calendar System: Semester
URL: www.dickinsonstate.edu
Established: 1918
Annual Undergrad Tuition & Fees (In-State): $6,768
Enrollment: 1,425
Coed
Affiliation or Control: State
IRS Status: 501(c)3
Highest Offering: Master's
Accreditation: NH, CAEP, IACBE, MUS, NUR, PNUR

02 President ... Dr. Thomas MITZEL
05 Interim Provost/VP Academic Affairs ... Ms. Marilyn LEE
10 Interim VP for Finance/Admin ... Ms. Laura NELSON
26 VP University Relations/Recruitment ... Ms. Marie MOE
20 Int Assoc Provt/Dean of Instruction ... Dr. Kenneth HAUGHT
29 Exec Dir Alumni Assoc/Foundation ... Mr. Ty ORTON
41 Director of Intercollege Athletics ... Mr. Pete STANTON
56 Director of Extended Learning ... Mr. Anthony WILLER
12 Director of DSU Bismarck/Williston ... Ms. Annette MARTEL
06 Director of Academic Records ... Ms. Kathy MEYER
08 Head of Library Services ... Ms. Staci GREEN
13 Director of Information Technology ... Mr. Todd HAUF
37 Director of Financial Aid ... Mr. Christopher MEEK
84 Asst Dean Enrollment Management ... Ms. Heidi KIPPENHAN
35 Asst Dean of Student Services ... Ms. Jennifer WITHERS
109 Director of Food Service ... Mr. Aaron ZUMMER
40 Manager University Store ... Ms. Symonne GESSELE
36 Dir Career Dev/Disability Services ... Ms. Ashley TILLMAN
85 Intl/Multicultural Affairs Coord ... Ms. Wynter MILLER
39 Housing Coordinator ... Ms. Jennifer WITHERS
15 Director of Human Resources ... Ms. Krissy KILWEIN
18 Chief Facilities/Physical Plant ... Mr. Mick RIESINGER
19 Interim Director of Public Safety ... Mr. Ed STRIEFEL
04 Executive Asst to President ... Ms. Kari HANSTAD
22 Affirmative Action Officer/Title IX ... Mr. Jarelle LEWIS

*Mayville State University (E)

330 3rd Street, NE, Mayville ND 58257-1299

County: Traill
FICE Identification: 002993
Unit ID: 200226
Telephone: (701) 788-2301
Carnegie Class: Bac-Diverse
FAX Number: (701) 788-4748
Calendar System: Semester
URL: www.mayvillestate.edu
Established: 1889
Annual Undergrad Tuition & Fees (In-State): $6,666
Enrollment: 1,140
Coed
Affiliation or Control: State
IRS Status: 501(c)3
Highest Offering: Master's
Accreditation: NH, CAEPN, NURSE

02 President ... Dr. Brian VAN HORN
05 Vice President for Academic Affairs ... Dr. Keith A. STENEHJEM
10 Vice President for Business Affairs ... Ms. Jami HOVET
32 Vice President for Student Affairs ... Dr. Andrew J. PFLIPSEN
102 Executive Foundation Director ... Mr. John J. KLOCKE
09 Exec Dir Institution Effectiveness ... Ms. Maren A. JOHNSON
41 Athletic Director ... Mr. Ryan HALL
04 Exec Assistant to the President ... Ms. Mary L. TRUDEAU
26 Assoc Dir Found/Dir PR & Marketing ... Ms. Beth I. SWENSON
07 Director of Admissions ... Mr. James R. MOROWSKI
06 Dir Academic Records/Registrar ... Ms. Heather HOYT
106 Director of Extended Learning ... Ms. Misti L. WUORI
37 Director of Financial Aid ... Ms. Shirley M. HANSON
08 Director of Library Services ... Ms. Kelly J. KORNKVEN
35 Director of Student Life ... Dr. Jeffrey A. POWELL
40 Director of Bookstore ... Ms. Pam B. SOHOLT
18 Director of Physical Plant ... Mr. Dan P. LORENZ
18 Director of Facilities Services ... Mr. Bob J. KOZOJED
15 Director of Human Resources ... Ms. Sarah GASEVIC
13 Chief Information Officer ... Mr. Patrick W. STEELE
21 Controller ... Ms. Courtney PETERSON
38 Dir Counseling/Freshmen Retention ... Ms. Kristi L. LENTZ
121 Dir Student Success/Disability Svc ... Ms. Katie J. RICHARDS
28 Dir Cultural Diversity/ Inclusion ... Ms. Dina ZAVALA-PETHERBRIDGE
36 Director of Career Services ... Mr. Jay A. HENRICKSON
27 Dir Strategic Student Communication ... Mr. Catlin E. SOLUM
50 Division Chair Business ... Ms. Rhonda L. NELSON
53 Dean/Div Chair Education ... Dr. Andi L. DULSKI-BUCHOLZ
68 Division Chair Physical Education ... Dr. Jeremiah T. MOEN
81 Division Chair Science/Math ... Dr. Joseph MEHUS
66 Division Chair Nursing ... Ms. Tami L. SUCH
49 Division Chair Liberal Arts ... Dr. Lynn DILIVIO

*Minot State University (F)

500 University Avenue W, Minot ND 58707-0001

County: Ward
FICE Identification: 002994
Unit ID: 200253
Telephone: (701) 858-3000
Carnegie Class: Masters/M
FAX Number: (701) 839-6933
Calendar System: Semester
URL: www.minotstateu.edu
Established: 1913
Annual Undergrad Tuition & Fees (In-State): $7,064
Enrollment: 3,216
Coed
Affiliation or Control: State
IRS Status: 501(c)3
Highest Offering: Beyond Master's But Less Than Doctorate
Accreditation: NH, #CAATE, CAEP, IACBE, MUS, NUR, SP, SW

02 President ... Dr. Steven SHIRLEY
05 VP for Academic Affairs ... Dr. Laurie GELLER
10 Vice President for Finance/Admin ... Mr. Brent WINIGER
111 Vice President for Advancement ... Mr. Rick HEDBERG
32 Vice President for Student Affairs ... Mr. Kevin HARMON
21 AVP Business Services/Controller ... Ms. Jonelle WATSON
07 Admissions ... Ms. Katie TYLER
18 Facilities Management ... Mr. Brian SMITH
06 Registrar ... Ms. Rebecca RINGHAM
08 Chair of Library Services ... Ms. Jane LAPLANTE
23 Director of Student Wellness ... Mr. Paul BREKKE
37 Director of Financial Aid ... Ms. Laurie WEBER
50 AVP CEL/Graduate ... Dr. Jacek MROZIK
29 Director Alumni Relations ... Ms. Janna MCKECHNIE
13 Director Computer Services ... Mr. George WITHUS
40 Director Bookstore ... Ms. Tiffany HETH
41 Athletic Director ... Mr. Andy CARTER
26 Director University Communications ... Mr. Michael LINNELL
15 Director of Human Resources ... Dr. Marc WACHTFOGEL
12 Dean of Dakota College at Bottineau ... Dr. Jerry MIGLER
36 Director of Campus Career Services ... Ms. Lynda BERTSCH
25 Grants & Contracts Accountant ... Ms. Sheila LATHAM
09 Director of Institutional Research ... Ms. Cari OLSON
04 Executive Asst to President ... Ms. Deb WENTZ
39 Director Student Housing ... Ms. Karina STANDER
27 Director of Marketing ... Ms. Teresa LOFTESNES
104 Director International Programs ... Ms. Libby CLAERBOUT
19 Director Security/Safety ... Mr. Gary ORLUCK
88 Director of Veterans Services ... Mr. Andrew HEITKAMP
88 Title IX Coordinator ... Ms. Lisa DOOLEY
108 Director Institutional Assessment ... Dr. Michael BROOKS

*North Dakota State University Main Campus (G)

P.O. Box 6050, Fargo ND 58108-6050

County: Cass
FICE Identification: 002997
Unit ID: 200332
Telephone: (701) 231-8011
Carnegie Class: DU-Higher
FAX Number: (701) 231-8722
Calendar System: Semester
URL: www.ndsu.edu
Established: 1890
Annual Undergrad Tuition & Fees (In-State): $9,414
Enrollment: 14,358
Coed
Affiliation or Control: State
IRS Status: 501(c)3
Highest Offering: Doctorate
Accreditation: NH, ART, CAATE, CACREP, CAEPN, CIDA, COARC, CONST, DIETC, DIETD, EXSC, LSAR, MUS, NURSE, PH, PHAR, THEA

02 President ... Dr. Dean BRESCIANI
05 Provost ... Dr. Ken GRAFTON
10 Vice President Business & Finance ... Mr. Bruce BOLLINGER
46 Vice Pres Research & Creative Act ... Dr. Jane SCHUH
88 Vice President Ag/Univ Extension ... Dr. Ken GRAFTON
30 Int Pres/CEO Dev/Fdn/Alum Assn ... Mr. John GLOVER
13 Chief Information Officer ... Mr. Marc WALLMAN
84 Vice Prov Student Affs/Enroll Mgmt ... Ms. Laura OSTER-AALAND
20 Vice Provost for Academic Affairs ... Vacant
88 Vice Provost Faculty/Title IX ... Ms. Canan BILEN-GREEN
25 Assoc VP Sponsored Programs Admin ... Ms. Valrey V. KETTNER
26 Assoc VP University Relations ... Ms. Laura MCDANIEL
06 University Registrar ... Ms. Rhonda KITCH
88 Director Administrative Systems ... Mr. Viet DOAN
08 Dean of Libraries ... Mr. Joe MOCNIK
51 Dir Distance/Continuing Educ ... Ms. Jill MOTSCHENBACHER
37 Director Financial Aid/Scholarships ... Mr. Jeff JACOBS
36 Director Career Center ... Ms. Rhonda KITCH
27 Communication Coordinator ... Ms. Ann ROBINSON-PAUL
50 Dean Business ... Dr. Scott BEAULIER
54 Dean Engineering/Architecture ... Dr. Michael KESSLER
59 Dean Human Development & Family Sci ... Dr. Margaret FITZGERALD

49 Dean Arts/Humanities/Social Science ....Dr. David BERTOLINI
81 Dean of Science & Math ....Dr. Scott WOOD
67 Dean of Pharmacy/Nursing/Allied Sci ...Dr. Charles D. PETERSON
47 Dean of Agric/Food Sys & Nat Res ....Dr. David BUCHANAN
58 Dean Graduate School ....Dr. Claudia TOMANY
114 Director of Budget ....Ms. Cynthia ROTT
18 Director Facilities Management ....Mr. Mike ELLINGSON
19 Dir of Univ Police/Safety Officer ....Mr. Mike BORR
38 Director Counseling Center ....Dr. William BURNS
23 Director Wellness Center ....Mr. Jobey LICHTBLAU
39 Director of Residence Life ....Mr. Rian NOSTRUM
40 Director Bookstore ....Ms. Kimberly ANVINSON
41 Director of Athletics ....Mr. Matt LARSEN
57 Director Fine Arts ....Dr. E. John MILLER
09 Dir Institutional Research/Analysis ....Ms. Emily BERG
96 Director of Purchasing ....Ms. Stacey O. WINTER
07 Director of Admissions ....Ms. Merideth SHERLIN
04 Executive Asst to President ....Ms. Stephanie WAWERS
15 Director HR/Payroll ....Ms. Jill SPACEK
88 Dir Grant & Contract Accounting ....Ms. Ann YONG
100 Chief of Staff ....Mr. Christopher WILSON
104 Director Study Abroad ....Ms. Alicia KAUFFMAN

*Valley City State University (A)

101 College Street, SW, Valley City ND 58072-4098
County: Barnes FICE Identification: 003008
Unit ID: 200572
Telephone: (701) 845-7122 Carnegie Class: Bac-Diverse
FAX Number: (701) 845-7104 Calendar System: Semester
URL: www.vcsu.edu
Established: 1889 Annual Undergrad Tuition & Fees (In-State): $7,626
Enrollment: 1,522 Coed
Affiliation or Control: State IRS Status: 501(c)3
Highest Offering: Master's
Accreditation: NH, #CAATE, CAEPN, MUS

02 President ....Dr. Alan LAFAVE
05 Vice Pres Academic Affairs ....Dr. Margaret DAHLBERG
10 Vice President Business Affairs ....Mr. Wesley WINTCH
32 Vice President Student Affairs ....Mr. Pete SMITHHISLER
53 Dean Sch of Educ/Graduate Stds ....Dr. Sheri OAKLAND
08 Library Director ....Ms. Jennier JENNESS
20 Int Learning Center Coordinator ....Ms. Jackie OWEN
37 Director Student Financial Aid ....Ms. Marcia PRITCHERT
13 Chief Information Officer ....Mr. Joseph TYKWINSKI
41 Athletic Director ....Ms. Jill DEVRIES
84 Director of Enrollment Services ....Ms. Charlene STENSON
30 Director of University Advancement ....Mr. Larry J. ROBINSON
18 Asst Director Facilities Services ....Mr. Pat HORNER
15 Human Resources Director ....Ms. Jennifer LARSON
44 Asst Dir Univ Advance/Alumni Rels ....Ms. Kim HESCH
38 Director of Student Counseling ....Ms. Erin KLINGENBERG
26 Director Marketing/Communications ....Mr. Greg VANNEY
40 Director Bookstore ....Mr. Todd ROGELSTAD
06 Registrar ....Ms. Jody KLIER
09 Dir Institutional Rsch/Assessment ....Ms. Kerry GREGORYK
36 Career Services Coordinator ....Ms. Kari BODINE

*Bismarck State College (B)

PO Box 5587, Bismarck ND 58506-5587
County: Burleigh FICE Identification: 002988
Unit ID: 200022
Telephone: (701) 224-5400 Carnegie Class: Bac/Assoc-Assoc Dom
FAX Number: (701) 224-5550 Calendar System: Semester
URL: bismarckstate.edu
Established: 1939 Annual Undergrad Tuition & Fees (In-State): $3,992
Enrollment: 3,756 Coed
Affiliation or Control: State IRS Status: 501(c)3
Highest Offering: Baccalaureate
Accreditation: NH, ADNUR, EMT, MLTAD, SURGT

02 President ....Dr. Larry C. SKOGEN
10 VP Operations/CFO ....Ms. Rebecca COLLINS
05 VP Academic Affairs ....Mr. Dan LEINGANG
111 VP College Advance/Exec Dir Found ....Ms. Kari KNUDSON
88 Dean Nat Energy Ctr of Excell ....Mr. Bruce EMMIL
84 Dean of Enrollment Management ....Ms. Karen ERICKSON
88 Dean Current & Emerging Technology ....Ms. Carla HIXON
32 Dean of Students ....Mr. Jay MEIER
13 Chief Information Officer ....Ms. Carol FLAA
15 Chief Human Resources Officer ....Ms. Rita LINDGREN
106 Chief Dist Learning/Military Affs ....Mr. Lane HUBER
26 Chief College Relations Officer ....Ms. Marnie PIEHL
51 Director Continuing Education ....Ms. Sara VOLLMER
08 Director of Library Services ....Ms. Marlene ANDERSON
18 Chief Buildings/Grounds Officer ....Mr. Don ROETHLER
41 Director of Athletics ....Mr. Buster GILLISS
37 Director of Financial Aid ....Mr. Scott LINGEN
39 Director Student & Residence Life ....Ms. Heather SHEEHAN
06 Director Academic Records/Registrar ....Mr. Tom LENO
36 Dir Counseling & Advising Services ....Ms. Kate MILLNER
108 Director IE & Strategic Planning ....Dr. John CARROLL
88 Program Manager NECE ....Mr. Dan SCHMIDT
88 Program Manager NECE ....Mr. Kyren MILLER
88 Training & Program Manager NECE ....Ms. Alicia UHDE
30 Resource Development Manager ....Vacant
29 Alumni Coordinator ....Ms. Rita NODLAND
40 Bookstore Manager/Purchasing Coord ....Ms. Debra SANDNESS
04 Executive Assistant to President ....Ms. Janell CAMPBELL
19 Campus Safety & Security Manager ....Mr. Matthew GIDDINGS

*Dakota College at Bottineau (C)

105 Simrall Boulevard, Bottineau ND 58318-1198
County: Bottineau FICE Identification: 002995
Unit ID: 200314
Telephone: (701) 228-2277 Carnegie Class: Assoc/HT-High Non
FAX Number: (701) 228-5468 Calendar System: Semester
URL: www.dakotacollege.edu
Established: 1906 Annual Undergrad Tuition & Fees (In-State): $4,568
Enrollment: 909 Coed
Affiliation or Control: State IRS Status: 501(c)3
Highest Offering: Associate Degree
Accreditation: NH, EMT

02 Campus Dean ....Dr. Jerry MIGLER
10 Director of Business Affairs ....Ms. Lisa MOCK
32 Assoc Dean for Student Affairs ....Mr. Larry BROOKS
05 Assoc Dean for Academic Affairs ....Mr. Larry BROOKS
08 Librarian ....Ms. Hattie ALBERTSON
06 Registrar ....Ms. Leisha LUNNIE
37 Director Financial Aid ....Ms. April ABRAHAMSON
41 Athletic Director ....Mr. Dan DAVIS
30 Director of Development ....Ms. Leslie STEVENS
39 Housing Director ....Ms. Michelle DAVIS
28 Director of Diversity ....Dr. Zahra MOSS
40 Bookstore Manager ....Ms. Janeen POLLMAN
18 Chief Facilities/Physical Plant ....Mr. Darrell WATERS
38 Director Student Counseling ....Ms. Corey GORDER
04 Administrative Asst to President ....Ms. Sandy HAGENESS
106 Dir Online Education/E-learning ....Ms. Kayla O'TOOLE
25 Chief Contracts/Grants Admin ....Dr. Indrani SASMAL
07 Director of Admissions ....Ms. Beth MACDONALD
13 Chief Information Technology Ofcr ....Mr. Brad GANGL

*Lake Region State College (D)

1801 College Drive N, Devils Lake ND 58301-1598
County: Ramsey FICE Identification: 002991
Unit ID: 200192
Telephone: (701) 662-1600 Carnegie Class: Assoc/MT-VT-High Non
FAX Number: (701) 662-1570 Calendar System: Semester
URL: www.lrsc.edu
Established: 1941 Annual Undergrad Tuition & Fees (In-State): $4,475
Enrollment: 1,972 Coed
Affiliation or Control: State IRS Status: 501(c)3
Highest Offering: Associate Degree
Accreditation: NH, ADNUR

02 President ....Dr. Douglas D. DARLING
05 VP Academic/Student Affairs ....Mr. Lloyd HALVORSON
10 VP Administrative Affairs ....Mr. Corry G. KENNER
12 Director of Branch Campus ....Mr. John COWGER
102 Executive Director Foundation ....Ms. Elonda NORD
84 Director of Enrollment Management ....Mr. Steven SHARK
37 Dir Student Finan Aid/Placemnt Svcs ....Ms. Katie NETTELL
109 Director Food Service ....Ms. Rosalie SEIBEL
18 Director Physical Plant ....Mr. Chad ESTENSON
08 Librarian ....Ms. Sheila COLLINS
41 Director Athletics ....Mr. Daniel MERTENS
13 Director of Information Technology ....Mr. Gary HAUGHLAND
15 HR Risk Mgmt/Placement Svcs ....Mrs. Sandi LILLEHAUGEN
40 Director of Bookstore ....Ms. Melissa STOTTS
06 Registrar ....Mr. Daniel JOHNSON
26 Director of Public Relations/Mktg ....Ms. Erin WOOD
31 Director Community Education ....Mr. Daniel DRIESSEN
09 Director of Institutional Research ....Ms. Brandi NELSON
28 Director of Diversity ....Mrs. Kristi HERNANDEZ
38 Director Counseling Services ....Mrs. Brigitte GREYWATER
07 Director of Admissions ....Mr. Steven SHARK
21 Controller ....Ms. Joann KITCHENS
04 Administrative Asst to President ....Ms. Bobbi J. LUNDAY
29 Director Alumni Relations ....Ms. Elonda NORD
39 Director Student Housing ....Dr. Randall FIXEN

*North Dakota State College of Science (E)

800 N Sixth Street, Wahpeton ND 58076-0002
County: Richland FICE Identification: 002996
Unit ID: 200305
Telephone: (800) 342-4325 Carnegie Class: Assoc/HVT-Mix Trad/Non
FAX Number: (701) 671-2145 Calendar System: Semester
URL: www.ndscs.edu
Established: 1903 Annual Undergrad Tuition & Fees (In-State): $5,132
Enrollment: 2,985 Coed
Affiliation or Control: State IRS Status: 501(c)3
Highest Offering: Associate Degree
Accreditation: NH, ADNUR, CAHIIM, DA, DH, EMT, OTA, PNUR

02 President ....Dr. John RICHMAN
05 VP Academic & Student Affairs ....Mr. Harvey LINK
11 Vice Pres Administrative Affairs ....Mr. Dennis GLADEN
32 Vice Pres Student Affairs ....Dr. Jane VANGSNESS FRISCH
103 Vice Pres Workforce Development ....Mr. Tony GRINDBERG
10 Chief Financial Officer ....Mr. Keith JOHNSON
13 Chief Information Officer ....Mr. Cloy TOBOLA
37 Director Financial Aid ....Mrs. Shelley BLOME
29 Exec Dir of Alumni Foundation ....Mrs. Kim NELSON
41 Athletic Director ....Mr. Stuart ENGEN
15 Exec Dir Human Resources ....Mrs. Sandi GILBERTSON
18 Director Facilities/Physical Plant ....Mr. Dallas FOSSUM

20 Academic Services Chair ....Ms. Maria KADUC
39 Exec Director of Residence Life ....Mrs. Melissa JOHNSON
07 Director of Admissions & Records ....Mrs. Barb MUND
06 Asst Director Admissions & Records ....Mr. Justin GRAMS
38 Counseling Center ....Mr. Vince PLUMMER
49 Dean Arts Sciences/Business ....Mr. Ken KOMPELIEN
64 Director of Music ....Mr. Bryan POYZER

*Williston State College (F)

1410 University Avenue, Williston ND 58801-1326
County: Williams FICE Identification: 003007
Unit ID: 200341
Telephone: (701) 774-4200 Carnegie Class: Assoc/HT-Mix Trad/Non
FAX Number: (701) 774-4211 Calendar System: Semester
URL: www.willistonstate.edu
Established: 1961 Annual Undergrad Tuition & Fees (In-State): $5,304
Enrollment: 1,098 Coed
Affiliation or Control: State IRS Status: 501(c)3
Highest Offering: Associate Degree
Accreditation: NH

02 President ....Dr. John MILLER
05 Vice President Academic Affairs ....Kimberli WRAY
32 Vice President Student Affairs ....Kaylyn BONDY
10 Chief Financial Officer ....Riley YADON
102 Exec Director WSC Foundation ....Terry OLSON
103 Regional Director for Technical Pgm ....Kenley NEBEKER
37 Coord for Student Financial Aid ....Andrea CARVER

Nueta Hidatsa Sahnish College (G)

PO Box 490, New Town ND 58763-0490
County: Mountrail FICE Identification: 025537
Unit ID: 200086
Telephone: (701) 627-4738 Carnegie Class: Tribal
FAX Number: (701) 627-3609 Calendar System: Semester
URL: www.nhsc.edu
Established: 1973 Annual Undergrad Tuition & Fees: $3,870
Enrollment: 228 Coed
Affiliation or Control: Independent Non-Profit IRS Status: 501(c)3
Highest Offering: Baccalaureate
Accreditation: NH

01 President ....Dr. Twyla BAKER-DEMARAY
05 Academic Dean ....Dr. Kerry HARTMAN
32 Vice Pres Student Services ....Dr. Constance FRANKBERRY
10 Interim Chief Financial Officer ....Dr. Stacey MORTENSEN
25 Director Grants/Accreditation ....Dr. Stacey MORTENSEN
06 Registrar ....Ms. Alicia REED
37 Int Director Financial Aid ....Mr. Tim OLSON
08 Director Library Services ....Ms. Amy SOLIS
124 Student Devel Retention Counselor ....Ms. Deanna RAINBOW
40 Bookstore Manager ....Ms. Iona LITTLE WHITEMAN

Rasmussen College - Fargo/Moorhead (H)

4012 19th Avenue, South, Fargo ND 58103-7196
Telephone: (701) 277-3889 FICE Identification: 004846
Accreditation: &NH

† Regional acrreditation is carried under parent institution in Saint Cloud, MN. The tuition figure is an average, actual tuition may vary.

Sitting Bull College (I)

9299 Highway 24, Fort Yates ND 58538-9706
County: Sioux FICE Identification: 021882
Unit ID: 200466
Telephone: (701) 854-8000 Carnegie Class: Tribal
FAX Number: (701) 854-8197 Calendar System: Semester
URL: www.sittingbull.edu
Established: 1971 Annual Undergrad Tuition & Fees: $4,010
Enrollment: 317 Coed
Affiliation or Control: Tribal Control IRS Status: 501(c)3
Highest Offering: Master's
Accreditation: NH

01 President ....Dr. Laurel VERMILLION
11 Vice President of Operations ....Dr. Koreen RESSLER
37 Director Financial Student Aid ....Ms. Donna SEABOY
06 Registrar ....Ms. Melody AZURE
08 Head Librarian ....Mr. Mark HOLMAN
40 Director of Bookstore ....Mrs. Tracy MAHER

Trinity Bible College & Graduate School (J)

50 S 6th Avenue, Ellendale ND 58436-7150
County: Dickey FICE Identification: 012059
Unit ID: 200484
Telephone: (701) 349-3621 Carnegie Class: Spec-4-yr-Faith
FAX Number: (701) 349-5786 Calendar System: Semester
URL: www.trinitybiblecollege.edu
Established: 1948 Annual Undergrad Tuition & Fees: $16,320
Enrollment: 235 Coed
Affiliation or Control: Assemblies Of God Church IRS Status: 501(c)3
Highest Offering: Doctorate
Accreditation: BI

01 President ....Dr. Paul ALEXANDER

03 Executive Vice President .... Rev. Ian O'BRIEN
05 Vice President of Academic Affairs .... Dr. Bill HENNESSY
32 Vice President of Student Affairs .... Ms. Twyla KUNTZ
84 Director of Enrollment .... Rev. Matthew PAYNE
58 Dean of Graduate School .... Dr. Carol ALEXANDER
106 Director of Distance Education .... Dr. Todd DIEDRICH
06 Academic Registrar .... Ms. Sara BEST
08 Librarian .... Mrs. Phyllis KUNO
18 Director of Facility Services .... Mr. Mike FERGEL
41 Athletic Director .... Mr. Jordan NOWELL
04 Admin Assistant to the President .... Mrs. Jessica M. SAYLOR
26 Director of Marketing .... Mrs. Maggie PAYNE
38 Director Student Counseling .... Ms. Amanda BELMONT

Turtle Mountain Community College (A)

Box 340, Belcourt ND 58316-0340
County: Rolette FICE Identification: 023011
Unit ID: 200527
Telephone: (701) 477-7862 Carnegie Class: Tribal
FAX Number: (701) 477-7870 Calendar System: Semester
URL: www.tm.edu
Established: 1972 Annual Undergrad Tuition & Fees: $2,250
Enrollment: 567 Coed
Affiliation or Control: Independent Non-Profit IRS Status: 501(c)3
Highest Offering: Baccalaureate
Accreditation: NH, MLTAD

01 Interim President .... Dr. Kellie M. HALL
03 Vice President .... Dr. Kellie M. HALL
05 Academic Dean .... Dr. Terri MARTIN-PARISIEN
32 Dean of Student Affairs .... Wanda LADUCER
10 Comptroller .... Tracy AZURE
75 Director Vocational/Education .... Sheila TROTTIER
06 Registrar .... Angel GLADUE
51 Dir of Community/Adult Education .... Sandra LAROCQUE
07 Admissions Records Officer .... Joni LAFONTAINE
15 Director Personnel Services .... Holly CAHILL
37 Financial Aid Director .... Sheila MORIN
40 Director of Bookstore .... Shirley MORIN
18 Chief Facilities/Physical Plant .... Wesley DAVIS
88 Title III Director .... Dave RIPLEY
04 Executive Assistant to President .... Zachery KING
101 Secretary of the Institution/Board .... Candace LONGIE
38 Director Student Counseling .... Dr. Andrea LAVERDURE
41 Athletic Director .... Pete DAVIS
09 Director of Institutional Research .... Ace CHARETTE
19 Safety/Compliance Officer .... Chris PARISIEN
08 Library Director .... Laisee ALLERY
13 IT Director .... Chad DAVIS
36 Placement Center Coordinator .... Mike VANDAL
53 Director of Teacher Education .... Dr. Teresa DELORME

United Tribes Technical College (B)

3315 University Drive, Bismarck ND 58504-7596
County: Burleigh FICE Identification: 022429
Unit ID: 200554
Telephone: (701) 255-3285 Carnegie Class: Tribal
FAX Number: (701) 530-0605 Calendar System: Semester
URL: www.uttc.edu
Established: 1969 Annual Undergrad Tuition & Fees: $4,252
Enrollment: 315 Coed
Affiliation or Control: Independent Non-Profit IRS Status: 501(c)3
Highest Offering: Baccalaureate
Accreditation: NH

01 President .... Dr. Leander MCDONALD
05 Vice Pres Academic Affairs .... Dr. Lisa AZURE
11 Vice Pres Campus Services .... Mr. Jolene DECOTEAU
10 Finance Director .... Mrs. Katina DECOTEAU
07 Admissions Director .... Ms. Vicki ALBERTS
06 Registrar .... Ms. Alicia REED
15 Human Resources Director .... Mrs. Rae GUNN
41 Athletic Director .... Mr. Pete CONWAY
13 IT Director .... Mr. Christopher BAILLIE
19 Safety and Security Director .... Mr. Joely HEAVY RUNNER
04 Exec Assistant to the President .... Ms. Merle BOTONE
08 Librarian .... Mrs. Charlene WEIS
20 Dean of Instruction .... Ms. Leah HAMANN
37 Financial Aid Director .... Mr. Scott SKARRO
106 Dir Online Education/E-learning .... Ms. Leah HAMANN
09 Director Institutional Research .... Ms. Leah WOODKE
39 Director Student Housing .... Ms. Melissa PLENTY CHIEF

University of Jamestown (C)

6000 College Lane, Jamestown ND 58405-0001
County: Stutsman FICE Identification: 002990
Unit ID: 200156
Telephone: (701) 252-3467 Carnegie Class: Bac-Diverse
FAX Number: (701) 253-4318 Calendar System: Semester
URL: www.uj.edu
Established: 1883 Annual Undergrad Tuition & Fees: $21,976
Enrollment: 1,135 Coed
Affiliation or Control: Presbyterian Church (U.S.A.) IRS Status: 501(c)3
Highest Offering: Doctorate
Accreditation: NH, NURSE, PTA

01 President .... Dr. Polly PETERSON
05 Provost .... Dr. Paul OLSON
32 Assoc Dean of Engage/Student Affs .... Mr. Dustin JENSEN
84 Vice President of Enrollment Mgmt .... Mr. Greg ULLAND
30 VP Development and Alumni Relations .... Mr. Brett MOSER
26 Executive VP .... Ms. Tena LAWRENCE
101 Asst to Pres/Secy to Bd of Trustees .... Ms. Erin KLEIN
06 Registrar .... Mr. Michael P. WOODLEY
37 Director of Financial Aid .... Ms. Judy HAGER
08 Librarian .... Mrs. Phyllis K. BRATTON
36 Director Experiential Education .... Ms. Heidi LARSON
27 Director of Design & Publications .... Ms. Donna SCHMITZ
41 Athletic Director .... Mr. Sean JOHNSON
13 Director Computer Center .... Mr. Chris HOKE
18 Chief Facilities/Physical Plant .... Vacant
105 Director Web Services .... Mr. Dallas ROSIN
19 Director Security/Safety .... Ms. Nicole HEINLE
22 Dir Affirmative Action/EEO .... Ms. Becky KNODEL
39 Director Student Housing .... Mr. Eric THORSON
27 Director of Marketing .... Ms. Karen H. CRANE

University of Mary (D)

7500 University Drive, Bismarck ND 58504-9652
County: Burleigh FICE Identification: 002992
Unit ID: 200217
Telephone: (701) 255-7500 Carnegie Class: DU-Mod
FAX Number: (701) 255-7687 Calendar System: Other
URL: www.umary.edu
Established: 1959 Annual Undergrad Tuition & Fees: $18,444
Enrollment: 3,396 Coed
Affiliation or Control: Roman Catholic IRS Status: 501(c)3
Highest Offering: Doctorate
Accreditation: NH, CAATE, COARC, EXSC, IACBE, MUS, NURSE, OT, PTA, @SP, SW

01 President .... Msgr. James P. SHEA
03 Executive Vice President .... Mr. Gregory A. VETTER
05 Vice President for Academic Affairs .... Dr. Diane FLADELAND
10 Vice President Financial Affairs .... Ms. Christi SCHAEFBAUER
32 Vice President Student Development .... Dr. Timothy SEAWORTH
84 Vice President Enrollment Services .... Vacant
26 Vice President for Public Affairs .... Mr. Jerome J. RICHTER
30 Director of Mission Advancement .... Vacant
06 Registrar .... Ms. Melissa MCDOWALL
08 Librarian .... Mr. David GRAY
37 Director of Financial Aid .... Mrs. Karrie K. HUBER
07 Director of Admissions .... Mr. Richard HINTON
09 Director of Institutional Research .... Mr. Phil REESE
15 Director Human Resources .... Mrs. Bonnie L. DAHL
18 Chief Facilities/Physical Plant .... Mr. Luke SEIDLING
20 Associate Academic Officer .... Dr. Alyssa MARTIN
35 Associate Student Affairs Officer .... Mrs. Sarah D. EBERLE

OHIO

Allegheny Wesleyan College (E)

2161 Woodsdale Road, Salem OH 44460-8920
County: Columbiana FICE Identification: 034573
Unit ID: 200873
Telephone: (330) 337-6403 Carnegie Class: Spec-4-yr-Faith
FAX Number: (424) 228-3006 Calendar System: Semester
URL: www.awc.edu
Established: 1956 Annual Undergrad Tuition & Fees: $7,000
Enrollment: 84 Coed
Affiliation or Control: Wesleyan Church IRS Status: 501(c)3
Highest Offering: Baccalaureate
Accreditation: BI

01 President .... Rev. Daniel R. HARDY, SR.
05 Academic Dean .... Mrs. Jeanne W. ZVARITCH
10 Business Manager .... Miss Katrina KAUFMAN
32 Dean of Students .... Rev. Timothy FORRIDER
30 Director of Development .... Mr. Tom SANDERS
06 Registrar & Director Admissions .... Mr. James DENTLER
08 Head Librarian .... Mrs. Crystal WHITHAM
37 Financial Aid Administrator .... Mrs. Esther PHELPS
09 Dir of Institutional Effectiveness .... Mrs. Jeanne ZVARITCH
40 Bookstore Manager .... Rev. Daniel GILES
33 Dean of Men .... Mr. Stefan LETONEK
34 Dean of Women .... Miss Heidi MCINTIRE
07 Director of Admissions .... Mr. James DENTLER
18 Chief Facilities/Physical Plant .... Mr. Darrin PATTERSON
29 Director Alumni Relations .... Rev. John DYE
38 Director Student Counseling .... Mrs. Kimberly FORD
04 Admin Assistant to the President .... Ms. Suzie A. ZEIGLER
13 Chief Information Tech Officer .... Mr. Matt DAVIS

American Institute of Alternative Medicine (F)

6685 Doubletree Avenue, Columbus OH 43229-1113
County: Franklin FICE Identification: 035344
Unit ID: 441636
Telephone: (614) 825-6255 Carnegie Class: Spec-4-yr-Other Health
FAX Number: (614) 825-6279 Calendar System: Quarter
URL: www.aiam.edu
Established: 1994 Annual Undergrad Tuition & Fees: $14,338
Enrollment: 395 Coed
Affiliation or Control: Proprietary IRS Status: Proprietary
Highest Offering: Master's
Accreditation: ACCSC, ACUP

00 Chief Executive Officer .... Diane SATER-WEE
01 Campus President .... Dr. Ralynn ERNEST
10 Chief Financial Officer .... Helen YEE
05 Academic Dean .... Dr. Elaine HIATT
36 Dir of Student Success .... LeeAnn POLLITT
20 Director Academic & Business Admin .... Jennifer BREDELL
21 Controller .... Barry COOK
37 Financial Aid Officer .... Ulrike ROSSER
06 Registrar .... James BROOKS
66 Director of Nursing .... Frances HUTCHISON
08 Chief Library Officer .... Melissa FISCHER

Antioch College (G)

One Morgan Place, Yellow Springs OH 45387
County: Greene Identification: 667214
Unit ID: 483018
Telephone: (937) 767-1286 Carnegie Class: Bac-A&S
FAX Number: N/A Calendar System: Quarter
URL: www.antiochcollege.edu
Established: 1853 Annual Undergrad Tuition & Fees: $35,568
Enrollment: 133 Coed
Affiliation or Control: Independent Non-Profit IRS Status: 501(c)3
Highest Offering: Baccalaureate
Accreditation: NH

01 President .... Dr. Thomas MANLEY
05 Provost/Vice Pres Acad Affairs .... Dr. Lori COLLINS-HALL
111 Vice Pres Advancement .... Ms. Susanne HASHIM
28 Vice Pres Diversity & Inclusion .... Ms. Mila COOPER
07 Dean of Admission & External Rels .... Dr. Gariot LOUIMA
06 Registrar .... Mr. Ron NAPOLI
09 Dir Innovation & Inst Effectiveness .... Ms. Hannah SPIRRISON
13 Dir Information Technology .... Mr. Kevin STOKES
04 Administrative Asst to President .... Ms. Nancy WUEBBEN

*Antioch University (H)

900 Dayton Street, Yellow Springs OH 45387-1635
County: Greene FICE Identification: 003010
Unit ID: 442392
Telephone: (937) 769-1800 Carnegie Class: N/A
FAX Number: (937) 769-1806
URL: www.antioch.edu

01 Chancellor .... Mr. William GROVES
10 Vice Chancellor/CFO .... Dr. Allan GOZUM
05 AVC Academic Affairs/Student Svcs .... Dr. Iris WEISMAN
30 Int Vice Chanc Inst Advancement .... Mr. Tim FORBESS
26 Vice Chancellor for Marketing .... Dr. MB LUFKIN
15 Chief Human Resources Officer .... Ms. Suzette CASTONGUAY
91 Director IT/Chief Information Ofcr .... Mr. Rodney FOWLKES
04 Exec Asst to the Executive Team .... Ms. Judy OWENS
06 Registrar .... Ms. Maureen HEACOCK
08 Head Librarian .... Ms. Dana KNOTT
101 Exec Asst to Chanc/Sec to the Board .... Vacant
29 Director Alumni Relations .... Ms. Carol KRUMBACH
37 Director Student Financial Aid .... Mr. Donald RONAN

† Parent institution of Antioch University Midwest in OH; Antioch University Seattle in WA; Antioch University New England in NH; and Antioch University Los Angeles and Antioch University Santa Barbara in CA.

*Antioch University Midwest (I)

900 Dayton Street, Yellow Springs OH 45387-1745
Telephone: (937) 769-1800 Identification: 666811
Accreditation: NH

Antonelli College (J)

124 E Seventh Street, Cincinnati OH 45202-2592
County: Hamilton FICE Identification: 012891
Unit ID: 201016
Telephone: (800) 505-4338 Carnegie Class: Assoc/HVT-High Non
FAX Number: (513) 241-9396 Calendar System: Semester
URL: www.antonellicollege.edu
Established: 1947 Annual Undergrad Tuition & Fees: $15,980
Enrollment: 117 Coed
Affiliation or Control: Proprietary IRS Status: Proprietary
Highest Offering: Associate Degree
Accreditation: ACCSC

01 Campus President .... Dr. Mary Ann DAVIS
05 Director Of Education .... Ms. Andrea MILLETTE
32 Dean of Students .... Mr. Corey BJARNSON
06 Registrar .... Vacant
36 Career Services Coordinator .... Ms. Charlene SMITH
07 Director of Admissions .... Ms. Nikki CONLEY
37 Director Student Financial Aid .... Ms. Leah C. ELKINS

Art Academy of Cincinnati (K)

1212 Jackson Street, Cincinnati OH 45202-7106
County: Hamilton FICE Identification: 003011
Unit ID: 201061
Telephone: (513) 562-6262 Carnegie Class: Spec-4-yr-Arts
FAX Number: (513) 562-8778 Calendar System: Semester
URL: www.artacademy.edu
Established: 1869 Annual Undergrad Tuition & Fees: $33,450
Enrollment: 181 Coed
Affiliation or Control: Independent Non-Profit IRS Status: 501(c)3

Highest Offering: Master's
Accreditation: NH, ART

01 President Mr. Joe GIRANDOLA
05 VP for Academic Affairs/CAO Ms. Paige WILLIAMS
10 CFO Ms. Anna DOWELL
30 Director of Development Ms. Jennifer SPURLOCK
37 Director of Financial Aid Ms. Rebecca CARR
06 Director of Registrar Services Mr. Alex SIEBERT
21 Accounting Manager Ms. Danielle MACALUSO
84 Dir of Enrollment Management Ms. Amanda PARKER-WOLERY
15 Human Resources Generalist Ms. Linda KOLLMANN
32 Director of Student Services Ms. Kelsey NIHISER
31 Director of Community Education Ms. Jennifer SPURLOCK
04 Executive Assistant to President Ms. Lacey HASLAM
105 Digital Media Specialist Mr. Jimmy BAKER
13 Lead Systems Engineer Mr. Kyle GRIZZELL
26 Marketing/Communications Specialist Ms. Amanda PARKER-WOLERY

Ashland University (A)

401 College Avenue, Ashland OH 44805
County: Ashland FICE Identification: 003012
Unit ID: 201104
Telephone: (419) 289-4142 Carnegie Class: Masters/L
FAX Number: N/A Calendar System: Semester
URL: www.ashland.edu
Established: 1878 Annual Undergrad Tuition & Fees: $21,342
Enrollment: 6,471 Coed
Affiliation or Control: Brethren Church IRS Status: 501(c)3
Highest Offering: Doctorate
Accreditation: NH, ACBSP, CAATE, CACREP, #CAEP, CAEPN, DIETD, MUS, NURSE, SW, THEOL

01 President Dr. Carlos CAMPO
73 Exec Dean/VP Theological Seminary Dr. Juan MARTINEZ
05 Provost Dr. Amiel JARSTFER
32 Vice President Student Affairs Dr. Robert POOL
111 Vice Pres Development & Inst Advanc Mrs. Margaret POMFRET
84 Vice President Enrollment Mgmt/Mktg Vacant
18 Vice Pres Facilities/Mgmt & Plng Mr. Rick M. EWING, II
10 CFO Mr. Marc PASTERIS
13 Chief Tech & Info Officer Dr. Donald THARP
42 Director Religious Life Vacant
37 Director Student Financial Aid Mr. Stephen C. HOWELL
29 Director Alumni/Parent Relations Mr. Jeff ALIX
26 Director Marketing/Communications Mrs. Rhonda PEMBER
15 Director of Human Resources/Legal Mr. Joshua A. HUGHES
36 Executive Director Career Services Mr. Lenroy JONES
26 Director Public Relations Mr. Steven M. HANNAN
41 Director Athletics Mr. Albert KING
88 Exec Dir Ashbrook Ctr Mr. Christopher FLANNERY
09 Director Inst Research & Assessment Dr. Larry BUNCE
07 Director Admissions Mr. W.C VANCE
123 Director Graduate Admissions Mr. Bernard BANNIN
49 Dean College Arts & Sciences Dr. Dawn WEBER
106 Dean Online & Adult Studies Dr. Dean GOON
50 Dean College Business/Econ Dr. Elad GRANOT
53 Dean College Education Dr. Donna BREAULT
66 Dean Col Nursing & Health Sci Dr. Carrie KEIB
51 Exec Director Prof Development Dr. James POWELL
19 Director Security/Safety Mr. David B. MCLAUGHLIN
38 Director Counseling Dr. Oscar MCKNIGHT
112 Director Planned Giving Ms. Amanda MIDDIS
39 Director Residence Life Ms. Kimberly LAMMERS
102 Chief Corporate Relations Officer Dr. Dan LAWSON
104 Director Study Abroad Ms. Rebecca PARILLO
122 Assistant Director Greek Life Mr. Dustin HARGIS
25 Director University Grants Mrs. Sharon LOWE
06 Registrar Mr. Mark BRITTON
08 Director Library Mr. Scott SAVAGE
109 Director Auxiliary Services Mr. Matthew PORTNER
40 Bookstore Manager Ms. Amanda BROWN
85 Director Foreign Students Mr. Scott PARILLO
121 Director Academic Support Ms. Megan SHERAR
04 Admin Assistant to the President Ms. Heather KRUPA
28 Director Diversity Ms. Terri LINK

ATA College (B)

225 Pictoria Drive Suite 200, Cincinnati OH 45246
Telephone: (513) 671-1920 Identification: 666673
Accreditation: ABHES

† Branch campus of ATA College, Florence, KY.

Athenaeum of Ohio (C)

6616 Beechmont Avenue, Cincinnati OH 45230-5900
County: Hamilton FICE Identification: 003013
Unit ID: 201140
Telephone: (513) 231-2223 Carnegie Class: Spec-4-yr-Faith
FAX Number: (513) 231-3254 Calendar System: Semester
URL: www.athenaeum.edu
Established: 1829 Annual Graduate Tuition & Fees: N/A
Enrollment: 195 Coed
Affiliation or Control: Roman Catholic IRS Status: 501(c)3
Highest Offering: Master's; No Undergraduates
Accreditation: NH, THEOL

01 President & Rector V.Rev. Anthony R. BRAUSCH
05 Academic Dean of Athenaeum Rev. David ENDRES
10 Vice Pres Finance/Administration Mr. Dennis K. EAGAN
111 VP Development/Advancement Mr. Kyle ISAACK
08 Head Librarian Mrs. Connie SONG
06 Registrar Mr. Nicholas JOBE
42 Dir Lay Pastoral Ministry Program Dr. Susan MCGURGAN
108 Director of Assessment Mr. Nicholas JOBE
13 Chief Information Technology Office Vacant

Aultman College of Nursing and Health Sciences (D)

2600 Sixth Street SW, Canton OH 44710-1799
County: Stark FICE Identification: 006487
Unit ID: 201177
Telephone: (330) 363-6347 Carnegie Class: Spec-4-yr-Other Health
FAX Number: (330) 580-6654 Calendar System: Semester
URL: www.aultmancollege.edu
Established: 2004 Annual Undergrad Tuition & Fees: $18,510
Enrollment: 394 Coed
Affiliation or Control: Independent Non-Profit IRS Status: 501(c)3
Highest Offering: Baccalaureate
Accreditation: NH, ADNUR, NURSE, RAD, @SW

01 President Dr. Jean PADDOCK
10 VP Business & Student Affairs Jeannine SHAMBAUGH
05 VP Academic Affairs Dr. Brock REIMAN
30 VP Community Engagement Vi LEGGETT
09 Director IE and Compliance Lyn SABINO
06 Registrar Christine COURT
13 Chief Information Technology Office Jacqui KRUMPELMAN
84 Director Enrollment Management Sue SHEPHERD

Baldwin Wallace University (E)

275 Eastland Road, Berea OH 44017-2088
County: Cuyahoga FICE Identification: 003014
Unit ID: 201195
Telephone: (440) 826-2900 Carnegie Class: Masters/L
FAX Number: (440) 826-3777 Calendar System: Semester
URL: www.bw.edu/
Established: 1845 Annual Undergrad Tuition & Fees: $32,586
Enrollment: 3,791 Coed
Affiliation or Control: Independent Non-Profit IRS Status: 501(c)3
Highest Offering: Master's
Accreditation: NH, ARCPA, CAATE, CAEP, CAEPN, EXSC, MUS, NURSE, SP

01 President Dr. Robert C. HELMER
03 Senior Vice President Mr. Richard L. FLETCHER
05 Provost Dr. Stephen D. STAHL
10 Vice President for Finance & Admin Mr. William M. RENIFF
32 VP Student Affairs/Dean of Students Dr. Trina DOBBERSTEIN
84 Vice Pres of Enrollment Management Dr. Scott SCHULZ
111 Vice Pres for Advancement Mr. Patrick DUNLAVY
26 Asst VP/Director College Relations Mr. Dan KARP
20 Associate Provost Dr. Lisa HENDERSON
89 Dean of First Year Students Mr. Marc WEST
51 Director of Adult Learning Ms. Nancy JIROUSEK
08 Director of Ritter Library Mr. John DIGENNARO
13 Chief Information Officer Mr. Greg G. FLANIK
44 Director Annual Giving Ms. Ann MILLER
29 Director Alumni Relations Mrs. Christine DAVENPORT
30 Senior Advancement Officer Mrs. Ellen ZEGARRA
37 Director of Financial Aid Dr. George ROLLESTON
15 Asst VP for Human Resources Mr. Sam RAMIREZ
38 Director of Counseling Services Ms. Sophia D. KALLERGIS
121 Coordinator of Academic Advising Ms. Dianna SPYCHER
06 Registrar Mr. Tim SEITZ
07 Dir Undergraduate Admission Dr. Scott A. SCHULZ
123 Dir of Tr/Adult & Grad Admission Ms. Winifred GERHARDT
18 Director of Buildings & Grounds Mr. Don DUBENA
88 Director of Intercultural Education Dr. Javier MORALES-ORTIZ
96 Director of Purchasing Ms. Karen STENGER
28 Director Campus Diversity Affairs Mr. Charles HARKNESS
04 Administrative Asst to President Ms. Kimberlee A. KUHAJDA
09 Director of Institutional Research Ms. Susan T. WARNER
104 Director Study Abroad Ms. Christy L. SHREFLER
39 Director Student Housing Mr. Robin W. GAGNOW
102 Dir Foundation/Corporate Relations Ms. Annie HEIDERSBACH
19 Director Security/Safety Mr. Gary BLACK
41 Athletic Director Mr. Kris DIAZ
50 Dean of School of Business Dr. Frank BRAUN
53 Dean of School of Education Dr. Michael SMITH
36 Director Career Services Mr. Patrick KEEBLER

Belmont College (F)

68094 Hammond Road, Saint Clairsville OH 43950-9766
County: Belmont FICE Identification: 009941
Unit ID: 201283
Telephone: (740) 695-9500 Carnegie Class: Assoc/HVT-Mix Trad/Non
FAX Number: (740) 695-2247 Calendar System: Semester
URL: www.belmontcollege.edu
Established: 1969 Annual Undergrad Tuition & Fees (In-State): $4,310
Enrollment: 1,150 Coed
Affiliation or Control: State IRS Status: 501(c)3
Highest Offering: Associate Degree
Accreditation: NH, EMT, MAC

01 President & CEO Dr. Paul GASPARRO
05 VP of Academics & Student Affairs Dr. Jeremy VITTEK
11 Vice Pres of Administrative Affairs Mr. John S. KOUCOUMARIS
111 Vice Pres of Advancement/ Marketing Mr. Raymond J. KONKOLESKI, II
32 Dean of Stdnt Affs/Enrollment Mgmt Vacant
20 Dean of Instruction Dr. Jesse GIPKO
09 Dir of Institutional Research/Plng Vacant
06 Registrar Ms. Jennifer NIPPERT
15 VP Human Resources/Sustainability Vacant
37 Assoc Dean of Financial Aid Ms. Susan NELSON-HENSLEY
121 Transfer/Articulat/Academic Advisor Vacant
13 Exec Dir of Information Services Mr. Troy CALDWELL
04 Exec Asst to President Ms. Kristy KOSKY
11 Director of Operations Vacant
26 Public Relations Coordinator Ms. Julie KECK

Bluffton University (G)

1 University Drive, Bluffton OH 45817-2104
County: Allen FICE Identification: 003016
Unit ID: 201371
Telephone: (419) 358-3000 Carnegie Class: Bac-Diverse
FAX Number: (419) 358-3323 Calendar System: Semester
URL: www.bluffton.edu
Established: 1899 Annual Undergrad Tuition & Fees: $32,766
Enrollment: 815 Coed
Affiliation or Control: Mennonite Church IRS Status: 501(c)3
Highest Offering: Master's
Accreditation: NH, CAEP, DIETD, MUS, SW

01 President Dr. Jane WOOD
10 Vice President for Fiscal Affairs Mr. Kevin A. NICKEL
111 Vice President for Inst Advancement Dr. Hans HOUSHOWER
05 Vice Pres & Dean Academic Affairs Dr. Lamar NISLY
84 VP for Enrollment Mgmt Mrs. Robin BOWLUS
32 VP for Student Life/Dean of Stdnts Vacant
41 Int VP for Student Life & Ath Dir Mr. Phillip TALAVINIA
08 Director of Libraries Ms. Mary Jean JOHNSON
06 Registrar Ms. Iris NEUFELD
26 Chief Public Relations Officer Mrs. Robin BOWLUS
29 Alumni Relations Mgr & Mktg Coord Ms. Claire CLAY
07 Director of UG Admissions Vacant
18 Director Building/Grounds Mr. Mustaq AHMED
15 Director Human Resources Mr. Scott A. SHARIK
04 Administrative Asst to President Ms. Amanda DAVIS
13 Chief Info Technology Officer (CIO) Ms. Deb TURNER
36 Director Student Placement Ms. Shari AYERS
38 Director Student Counseling Ms. Rae STATON
39 Director of Residence Life Mr. Tyson GOINGS
44 Annual Fund Coordinator Mr. Brett SCHROEDER
105 Director Web Services Ms. Sara KISSEBERTH
37 Director of Financial Aid Mr. Lawrence MATTHEWS

Bowling Green State University (H)

220 McFall Center, Bowling Green OH 43403-0001
County: Wood FICE Identification: 003018
Unit ID: 201441
Telephone: (419) 372-2211 Carnegie Class: DU-Higher
FAX Number: (419) 372-8446 Calendar System: Semester
URL: www.bgsu.edu
Established: 1910 Annual Undergrad Tuition & Fees (In-State): $11,105
Enrollment: 17,357 Coed
Affiliation or Control: State IRS Status: 501(c)3
Highest Offering: Doctorate
Accreditation: NH, ART, CACREP, CAEPN, CLPSY, CONST, COSMA, DIETD, DIETI, EXSC, IPSY, JOUR, MT, MUS, NAIT, NURSE, PH, SP, SPAA, SW, THEA

01 President Dr. Rodney K. ROGERS
05 Sr VP Academic Affairs/Provost Dr. Joe B. WHITEHEAD
10 CFO/VP Finance & Admin Ms. Sherideen S. STOLL
100 VP Partnerships/Chief of Staff Dr. Sue HOUSTON
32 Vice President Student Affairs Dr. Tom GIBSON
04 Executive Asst to President Ms. Laurel E. ZAWODNY
111 VP Univ Advancement Ms. Pam CONLIN
84 VP Enrollment Management Ms. Cecilia CASTELLANO
20 Assoc Professor/Assoc Dean Dr. Sheila J. ROBERTS
35 Dean of Students Mr. Chris BULLINS
11 Asst VP for Campus Operations Dr. Andrea DEPINET
26 Chief Marketing & Comm Officer Mr. David KIELMEYER
29 AVP Alumni/Dev/Annual Giving Vacant
46 VP Research & Econ Engagement Dr. Michael Y. OGAWA
88 Asst VP Student Affs/Dir Rec Sports Dr. Stephen KAMPF
41 Director of Athletics Mr. Bob MOOSBRUGGER
15 Chief Human Resources Officer Ms. Viva MCCARVER
39 Director of Residence Life Mr. Joshua LAWRIE
45 Int VP Capital Planning & Design Dr. Bruce A. MEYER
13 Chief Information Officer Mr. John M. ELLINGER
43 Vice President & General Counsel Vacant
58 Dean Graduate College Dr. Margaret BOOTH
49 Dean College Arts/Sciences Dr. Raymond CRAIG
50 Dean College Business Admin Mr. Raymond BRAUN
88 Director Service Learning Dr. Virginia J. ROSSER
53 Dean Col of Educ & Human Dev Dr. Dawn SHINEW
12 Dean Firelands College Dr. Andrew KURTZ
69 Dean College Hlth/Human Svcs Dr. James CIESLA
08 Dean University Libraries Ms. Sara BUSHONG
64 Dean College of Musical Arts Dr. William MATHIS
72 Dean College of TAAE Dr. Jennie GALLIMORE
57 Director of School of Art Mr. Charlie KANWISCHER
60 Dir Sch of Media & Communication Dr. Laura STAFFORD
88 Dir Sch Human Move/Sport/Leisure Dr. Ray SCHNEIDER
88 Dir Sch Family & Consumer Sciences Dr. Deborah G. WOOLDRIDGE

53 Dir Sch Educ Fnds/Leadership/Policy ... Dr. Patrick PAUKEN
53 Dir Sch of Teaching & Learning ... Dr. Mark SEALS
92 Dean Honors College ... Dr. Simon MORGAN-RUSSELL
106 Assoc Director eCampus ... Dr. Sheri ORWICK OGDEN
85 Exec Dir International Student Svcs ... Dr. Marcia SALAZAR-VALENTINE
21 Exec Dir of Business Operations ... Mr. Bradley K. LEIGH
07 Director Admissions ... Ms. Adrea SPOON
114 Dir Budgeting & Resource Planning ... Ms. Sharon SWARTZ
06 University Registrar ... Vacant
40 Int Director Bookstore ... Ms. Amy THOMSON
19 Director Public Safety ... Mr. Michael A. CAMPBELL
36 Director Career Center ... Ms. Danielle DIMOFF
38 Director Counseling Center ... Dr. Garrett GILMER
37 Dir Student Financial Aid ... Dr. Betsy JOHNSON
23 Asst Director Center for Health ... Ms. Marlene REYNOLDS
44 Director of Annual Giving ... Ms. Jenny WENSINK
101 Secretary to the Board ... Dr. Patrick PAUKEN
88 Co-Gen Manager WBGU Public Media ... Vacant
88 Co-Gen Manager WBGU Public Media ... Ms. Tina L. SIMON
88 Director Trio Programs ... Ms. Victoria AMPIAW
116 Internal Auditing & Adv Svcs ... Mr. James LAMBERT
88 Director Women's Center ... Vacant
22 Director Accessibility Svcs ... Ms. Peggy DENNIS
88 President's Leadership Academy ... Dr. Jacob E. CLEMENS
109 Director Dining Services ... Mr. Michael L. PAULUS
96 Director of Business Operations ... Mr. Phillip WORLEY
88 Director Student Employment ... Ms. Dawn CHONG
88 Director Learning Commons ... Mr. Travis BROWN
121 Director Advising Services ... Mr. Dermot M. FORDE
88 Asst VP Non-Trad & Transfer Svcs ... Dr. Barbara L. HENRY
09 Vice Provost for Inst Effectiveness ... Dr. Julia MATUGA
65 Dir Sch Earth/Environ & Society ... Dr. Jeffrey SNYDER
112 AVP Major Giving ... Ms. Christine HANSEN
88 AVP Eq Div In/Title IX Coord ... Ms. Jennifer Q. MCCARY
35 Assoc VP Student Affairs ... Ms. Jodi WEBB
18 AVP Capital Planning/Campus Ops ... Dr. Bruce A. MEYER

Bowling Green State University Firelands College (A)

One University Drive, Huron OH 44839-9719
Telephone: (419) 433-5560 FICE Identification: 007856
Accreditation: &NH, COARC, DMS

† Regional accreditation is carried under the parent institution in Bowling Green, OH.

Bradford School (B)

2469 Stelzer Road, Columbus OH 43219-3129
County: Franklin FICE Identification: 004853
Unit ID: 202161
Telephone: (614) 416-6200 Carnegie Class: Assoc/HVT-High Trad
FAX Number: (614) 416-6210 Calendar System: Semester
URL: www.bradfordschoolcolumbus.edu
Established: 1985 Annual Undergrad Tuition & Fees: $13,980
Enrollment: 368 Coed
Affiliation or Control: Proprietary IRS Status: Proprietary
Highest Offering: Associate Degree
Accreditation: ACCSC, ACFEI, MAC, PTAA

01 President ... Mr. Dennis BARTELS
05 Director of Education ... Ms. Beth WOOD
07 Director of Admissions ... Ms. Raeann LEE

Bryant & Stratton College (C)

12955 Snow Road, Parma OH 44130-1013
Telephone: (216) 265-3151 FICE Identification: 022744
Accreditation: &M, ADNUR, MAC, NURSE, PNUR, PTAA

† Regional accreditation is carried under the parent institution (corporate office) in Buffalo, NY.

Capital University (D)

1 College and Main Street, Columbus OH 43209-2394
County: Franklin FICE Identification: 003023
Unit ID: 201548
Telephone: (614) 236-6011 Carnegie Class: Masters/M
FAX Number: N/A Calendar System: Semester
URL: www.capital.edu
Established: 1850 Annual Undergrad Tuition & Fees: $35,466
Enrollment: 3,384 Coed
Affiliation or Control: Evangelical Lutheran Church In America
IRS Status: 501(c)3
Highest Offering: First Professional Degree
Accreditation: NH, ACBSP, CAATE, CAEP, LAW, MUS, NURSE, SW, THEOL

01 President ... Dr. Elizabeth L. PAUL
05 Provost & VP for Learning ... Dr. Jody FOURNIER
10 Vice President Business & Finance ... Mr. William MEA
43 University Counsel & Vice President ... Dr. Tanya J. POTEET
26 VP Integrated Marketing & Comm ... Ms. Tina GUEGOLD
84 VP Strategic Enrollment Mgmt ... Mr. Jean-Paul SPAGNOLO
111 Vice Pres Inst Advancement ... Ms. Jennifer PATTERSON
100 Exec Asst to Pres/Board Liaison ... Ms. Nona S. MCGUIRE
20 Sr Assoc Provost ... Dr. Terry D. LAHM
21 Asst VP Business & Finance ... Mr. Erin DELFFS
27 Asst VP IMC ... Ms. D. Nichole JOHNSON
07 Asst VP Enrollment Services ... Ms. Susan E. KANNENWISCHER
30 Asst Vice President Development ... Ms. April NOVOTNY
88 Director Public Relations & Mktg ... Ms. Denise RUSSELL
09 Director of Institutional Research ... Dr. Larry T. HUNTER
06 Registrar ... Mr. Brent KOERBER
07 Director of Admissions ... Mr. Garien HUDSON
29 Sr Director of Alumni Engagement ... Ms. Amanda RITCHEY
36 Director of Career Services ... Mr. Eric R. ANDERSON
08 University Librarian/Director IMC ... Ms. Rachel RUBIN
121 Director Academic Success ... Mr. Bruce EPPS
41 Athletic Director ... Mr. Roger INGLES
13 Director Information Technology ... Vacant
85 Director Intl Education & ESL ... Ms. Jennifer ADAMS
32 Dean Engagement & Success ... Ms. Deanna WAGNER
18 Director Facilities Management ... Mr. Paul MATTHEWS
15 Director Human Resources ... Mr. Mark PRINGLE
38 Dir Univ Counseling/Health Svcs ... Dr. Cathy MCDANIELS WILSON
28 Director Diversity and Inclusion ... Mr. Almar WALTER
92 Honors Program ... Dr. Stephanie GRAY WILSON
40 Manager Bookstore ... Ms. Kelsey WAITE
42 University Pastor ... Mr. Andrew TUCKER
61 Dean of Law School ... Ms. Rachel JANUTIS
64 Interim Dean of the Conservatory ... Dr. Tom ZUGGER
53 Chair Department of Education ... Dr. James WIGHTMAN
66 Dean School of Nursing ... Vacant
102 Dir Foundation/Corporate Relations ... Mr. Gregory WINSLOW
108 Assoc Provost Accred & Analytics ... Dr. Jens HEMMINGSEN
22 Asst Provost/Title IX Coordinator ... Ms. Jennifer SPEAKMAN
04 Administrative Asst to President ... Ms. Victoria MCGRAW-ROWE
19 Director Security/Safety ... Mr. Frank FERNANDEZ
105 Assoc Director Web & Digital Svcs ... Mr. Russel PEPPER
39 Director Residential & Comm Life ... Mr. Jon GEYER
50 Dean School of Management & Ldrshp ... Mr. John GENTNER
37 Director Financial Aid ... Mr. John BROWN

Capital University Law School (E)

303 East Broad Street, Columbus OH 43215
Telephone: (614) 236-6500 Identification: 770347
Accreditation: &NH

Case Western Reserve University (F)

10900 Euclid Avenue, Cleveland OH 44106-7001
County: Cuyahoga FICE Identification: 003024
Unit ID: 201645
Telephone: (216) 368-2000 Carnegie Class: DU-Highest
FAX Number: N/A Calendar System: Semester
URL: www.case.edu
Established: 1826 Annual Undergrad Tuition & Fees: $49,042
Enrollment: 11,824 Coed
Affiliation or Control: Independent Non-Profit IRS Status: 501(c)3
Highest Offering: Doctorate
Accreditation: NH, AA, ANEST, #ARCPA, CAEPT, CLPSY, DENT, DIETD, DIETI, IPSY, LAW, MED, MIDWF, MUS, NURSE, PH, SP, SW

01 President ... Ms. Barbara R. SNYDER
100 Chief of Staff ... Katie M. BRANCATO
05 Provost/Executive Vice President ... Dr. Ben VINSON, III
10 Senior Vice Pres for Finance & CFO ... Mr. John F. SIDERAS
11 Senior Vice Pres for Administration ... Ms. Elizabeth J. KEEFER
30 Sr VP Univ Relations & Development ... Ms. Carol L. MOSS
17 Sr VP Medical Affairs/Dean Medicine ... Dr. Pamela B. DAVIS
46 Vice President for Research ... Dr. Suzanne M. RIVERA
13 VP for Information Services/CIO ... Ms. Sue B. WORKMAN
84 Vice Pres for Enrollment ... Mr. Richard W. BISCHOFF
32 Vice President for Student Affairs ... Mr. Louis W. STARK
18 VP Campus Planning/Facilities Mgmt ... Mr. Stephen M. CAMPBELL
15 Vice President for Human Resources ... Ms. Carolyn GREGORY
43 Sr Vice Pres/Gen Counsel/Secretary ... Ms. Elizabeth J. KEEFER
19 Vice President for Campus Services ... Mr. Richard J. JAMIESON
26 VP Univ Marketing & Communications ... Ms. Chris SHERIDAN
86 VP Government/Foundation Relations ... Dr. Julie M. REHM
88 Exec Director Government Relations ... Ms. Jennifer RUGGLES
31 Exec Dir Local Govt & Community Rel ... Mr. Julian ROGERS
29 Sr Exec Director Alumni Relations ... Mr. Bradford CREWS
45 Assoc VP Univ Plng & Administration ... Ms. Victoria WRIGHT
28 Int VP Inclusion/Diver/Equal Oppty ... Dr. Joy R. BOSTIC
22 Asst Vice Pres & Director of Equity ... Mr. Christopher JONES
27 Dir Media Relations/Communications ... Mr. Bill LUBINGER
21 Treasurer ... Mr. Michael J. LEE
115 Deputy Chief Investment Officer ... Mr. Timothy R. MILANICH
20 Vice Provost Undergrad Education ... Dr. Donald L. FEKE
82 Vice Prov International Affairs ... Mr. David FLESHLER
88 Dean of Undergraduate Studies ... Dr. Jeffrey WOLCOWITZ
21 Controller ... Ms. Patricia L. KOST
06 Registrar ... Ms. Amy S. HAMMETT
37 Director of Financial Aid ... Ms. Venus PULIAFICO
07 Director Undergraduate Admissions ... Mr. Robert R. MCCULLOUGH
08 University Librarian & Assoc Prov ... Mr. Arnold HIRSHON
121 Vice Provost of Student Success ... Dr. Thomas MATTHEWS
85 Dir International Student Svcs ... Ms. Marielena MAGGIO
38 Exec Dir Univ Health & Counsel Svcs ... Jenna MCCARTHY
09 Director of Institutional Research ... Ms. Jean E. GUBBINS
96 Dir Procurement/Distribution Svcs ... Ms. Mandy CARTE
41 Athletic Director ... Ms. Amy BACKUS
61 Co-Dean of Law ... Mr. Michael P. SCHARF
61 Co-Dean of Law ... Ms. Jessica W. BERG
49 Int Dean of Arts & Sciences ... Dr. Timothy BEAL
63 Dean of Medicine ... Dr. Pamela B. DAVIS
66 Dean of Nursing ... Dr. Carol M. MUSIL
52 Dean of Dental Medicine ... Dr. Kenneth B. CHANCE
50 Dean of Management ... Dr. Manoj MALHOTRA
70 Dean Applied Social Science ... Dr. Grover C. GILMORE
54 Dean of Engineering ... Dr. Venkataramanan BALAKRISHNAN
58 Dean of Graduate Studies ... Dr. Charles E. ROZEK
04 Executive Asst to President ... Ms. Jane M. VONDRAK
102 Asst VP Corporate Rels ... Ms. Anne M. BORCHERT
25 Associate VP for Research ... Ms. Stephanie ENDY

Cedarville University (G)

251 N Main Street, Cedarville OH 45314-0601
County: Greene FICE Identification: 003025
Unit ID: 201654
Telephone: (937) 766-2211 Carnegie Class: Masters/S
FAX Number: (937) 766-2760 Calendar System: Semester
URL: www.cedarville.edu
Established: 1887 Annual Undergrad Tuition & Fees: $30,270
Enrollment: 3,886 Coed
Affiliation or Control: Baptist IRS Status: 501(c)3
Highest Offering: Doctorate
Accreditation: NH, ACBSP, CAATE, CAEPN, MUS, NURSE, PHAR, SW

01 President ... Dr. Jerry T. WHITE
05 Vice President for Academics ... Dr. Thomas MACH
10 Vice President for Business ... Mr. Christopher SOHN
111 Vice President for Advancement ... Dr. Rick MELSON
32 VP Stdnt Life/Christian Ministries ... Dr. Jon WOOD
26 VP for Marketing and Communications ... Dr. Janice SUPPLEE
84 Vice President for Enrollment Mgmt ... Dr. Scott VAN LOO
41 Athletic Director ... Dr. Alan GEIST
43 General Counsel ... Mr. John HART
20 Assistant VP for Academics ... Dr. Randall MCKINION
15 Associate VP for Human Resources ... Mr. John DAVIS
21 Associate VP for Finance/Controller ... Mr. Phillip GRAFTON
18 Associate VP for Operations ... Mr. Rodney JOHNSON
13 Associate VP for Technology/CIO ... Mr. Micah COOPER
42 Associate VP Christian Ministries ... Mr. Jim CATO
06 University Registrar ... Mrs. Fran CAMPBELL
97 Dean Undergraduate Programs ... Dr. Pamela D. JOHNSON
08 Dean Library Services ... Mr. Josh MICHAEL
73 Dean School of Biblical/Theological ... Dr. Jason LEE
53 Dean School of Education ... Dr. Jeremy ERVIN
50 Dean School of Business ... Dr. Jeffrey HAYMOND
67 Dean School of Pharmacy ... Dr. Marc SWEENEY
66 Dean School of Nursing ... Mrs. Angelia MICKLE
54 Dean School Engineering/Comp Sci ... Dr. Robert CHASNOV
34 Director Stdt Dvlpmnt/Dean of Women ... Miss Mindy MAY
33 Assc Dean Stdnt Dvlpmt/Dean of Men ... Mr. Brad D. SMITH
26 Exec Director of Public Relations ... Mr. Mark WEINSTEIN
37 Exec Director of Financial Aid ... Mr. Kim JENERETTE
29 Exec Director Alumni ... Mr. Jeff BESTE
19 Director of Campus Safety ... Mr. Douglas W. CHISHOLM
105 Director Web Services ... Mr. Mark MAZELIN
108 Director Assessment & Accreditation ... Mr. Tom BETCHER
36 Director Career Services ... Mr. Jeff REEP
40 Manager of Retail Services ... Mrs. Tammy L. SLONE
04 Executive Asst to the President ... Dr. Zach BOWDEN
101 Admin Assoc to Pres/Asst Secy BOT ... Mrs. Angela MCINTOSH

Central Ohio Technical College (H)

1179 University Drive, Newark OH 43055-1767
County: Licking FICE Identification: 011046
Unit ID: 201672
Telephone: (740) 366-1351 Carnegie Class: Assoc/HVT-High Non
FAX Number: (740) 366-5047 Calendar System: Semester
URL: www.cotc.edu
Established: 1971 Annual Undergrad Tuition & Fees (In-State): $4,536
Enrollment: 3,479 Coed
Affiliation or Control: State IRS Status: 501(c)3
Highest Offering: Associate Degree
Accreditation: NH, ACBSP, ACFEI, ADNUR, CSHSE, DMS, EMT, IFSAC, RAD, SURGT

01 President ... Dr. John BERRY
10 Vice President Business & Finance ... Mr. David BRILLHART
05 Dean for General Educ/Transfer Pgms ... Dr. Chad WEIRICK
32 Dean of Students ... Ms. Holly MASON
15 VP for Inst Planning & HR Devel ... Dr. Jacqueline PARRILL
08 Director of Library ... Ms. Katie BLOCKSIDGE
06 Records Manager/Registrar ... Ms. Veronica RINE
26 Director Marketing/Public Relations ... Ms. Suzanne BRESSOUD
37 Director Financial Aid/Veteran Affs ... Ms. Faith PHILLIPS
19 Director Public Safety ... Mr. Adam FEATHERLING
111 Director of Advancement ... Ms. Kim MANNO
35 Asst Dean of Students ... Mr. Justin KHOL
13 Chief Information Officer ... Vacant
22 Program Mgr Learn Asst Ctr Disabled ... Ms. Connie ZANG
96 Manager of Purchasing ... Ms. Kimberley SIBERT
18 Facilities Superintendent ... Mr. Brian BOEHMER
51 Coord of Community Svc/Learning ... Ms. Vorley TAYLOR
36 Dir Career Dev & Experiential Lrng ... Mr. Derek THATCHER
04 Assistant to the President ... Ms. Jan TOMLINSON
09 Director of Institutional Research ... Mr. Christopher DOLL
50 Dean for Business/Engineering/IT ... Vacant
84 Dean of Enrollment Management ... Ms. Sarah MORRISON
101 Secretary of the Institution/Board ... Ms. Jan TOMLINSON
103 VP Econ Dev/Workforce Solutions ... Ms. Vicki MAPLE

Central Ohio Technical College Coshocton Campus (A)

200 North Whitewoman Street, Coshocton OH 43812
Telephone: (740) 622-1408 Identification: 770348
Accreditation: &NH

Central Ohio Technical College Knox Campus (B)

236 South Main Street, Mount Vernon OH 43050
Telephone: (740) 392-2526 Identification: 770350
Accreditation: &NH

Central Ohio Technical College Pataskala Campus (C)

8660 East Broad Street, Reynoldsburg OH 43068
Telephone: (740) 755-7090 Identification: 770351
Accreditation: &NH

Central State University (D)

PO Box 1004, 1400 Brush Row Road, Wilberforce OH 45384-1004
County: Greene FICE Identification: 003026
Unit ID: 201690
Telephone: (937) 376-6332 Carnegie Class: Bac-Diverse
FAX Number: (937) 376-6138 Calendar System: Semester
URL: www.centralstate.edu
Established: 1887 Annual Undergrad Tuition & Fees (In-State): $6,346
Enrollment: 1,784 Coed
Affiliation or Control: State IRS Status: 501(c)3
Highest Offering: Master's
Accreditation: NH, ACBSP, ART, MUS, SW

01 President .... Dr. Cynthia JACKSON-HAMMOND
100 Chief of Staff .... Mrs. Wendy HAYES
05 Provost/VP Academic Affairs .... Dr. Pedro L. MARTINEZ
10 Vice President Admin & Finance .... Mr. Curtis PETTIS
111 Vice Pres Institutional Advancement .... Mr. Jahan CULBREATH
32 Vice President Student Affairs .... Dr. B. Sherrance RUSSELL
13 Director/Chief Information Officer .... Dr. Tonjia COVERDALE
20 Assoc Vice Pres Academic Affairs .... Vacant
06 University Registrar .... Ms. Felicia HARRIS
08 Director of Hallie Q Brown Library .... Ms. Carolin STERLING
89 Exec Director of University College .... Dr. Gene MOORE
12 Director of CSU Dayton .... Mrs. Lesa DEVOND
09 Director Assessment/Inst Research .... Mr. Mohammad ALI
19 Chief of Police .... Chief Stephanie HILL
26 Director Public Relations .... Vacant
23 Medical Director .... Dr. Karen MATHEWS
29 Director Alumni Relations .... Mr. Keith PERKINS
36 Director Career Services .... Ms. Karla HARPER
37 Director Student Financial Aid .... Mrs. Demarus CRAWFORD-WHITE
39 Interim Director of Residence Life .... Mr. Justyn FRY
41 Athletic Director .... Ms. Tara OWENS
42 Director Campus Ministry .... Rev. Kima CUNNINGHAM
46 Director Sponsored Pgms/Research .... Mr. Morakinyo KUTI
49 Dean Coll Humanities/Arts & Sci .... Dr. George ARASIMOWICZ
50 Dean College of Business .... Dr. Fidelis M. IKEM
53 Interim Dean College of Education .... Dr. Zaki SHARIF
15 Director of Human Resources .... Vacant
21 Director Business Svcs/Capital Dev .... Ms. Cynthia MICHAEL
25 Director Grants Accounting .... Vacant
92 Director Honors Program .... Dr. Fred A. AIKENS
21 Controller .... Ms. Candy CARR
114 Budget Director .... Ms. Sheila BROWN
38 Director Student Counseling .... Mr. NseAbasi EKPO
104 Director of Global Education .... Dr. Fahmi ABBOUSHI
106 Dir Online Learning .... Dr. Jean-Jacques MEDASTIN
18 Director Facilities/Physical Plant .... Mr. Milton THOMPSON
43 General Counsel .... Ms. Laura WILSON
54 Dean Col of Science and Engineering .... Dr. Alton JOHNSON
86 Chief Ofcr of Government Relations .... Mr. Charles SHAHID
07 Director of Admissions .... Mr. James BURRELL
108 Director Institutional Assessment .... Dr. Rebecca ERTEL

Chamberlain University-Cleveland (E)

6700 Euclid Avenue, Suite 201, Cleveland OH 44103
Telephone: (216) 361-6005 Identification: 770505
Accreditation: &NH, NURSE

† Branch campus of Chamberlain University-Addison, Addison, IL

Chamberlain University-Columbus (F)

1350 Alum Creek Drive, Columbus OH 43209
Telephone: (614) 252-8890 Identification: 770499
Accreditation: &NH, NURSE

† Branch campus of Chamberlain University-Addison, Addison, IL

Chatfield College (G)

20918 State Route 251, Saint Martin OH 45118-9059
County: Brown FICE Identification: 010880
Unit ID: 201751
Telephone: (513) 875-3344 Carnegie Class: Assoc/HT-High Non
FAX Number: (513) 875-3912 Calendar System: Semester
URL: www.chatfield.edu
Established: 1971 Annual Undergrad Tuition & Fees: $12,031
Enrollment: 294 Coed
Affiliation or Control: Independent Non-Profit IRS Status: 501(c)3
Highest Offering: Associate Degree
Accreditation: NH

01 President .... Mr. John P. TAFARO
11 Vice President/COO .... Mr. Robert ELMORE
05 Chief Academic Officer/Dean .... Mr. Peter HANSON
10 Director of Finance .... Ms. Mary R. JACOBS
111 Director of Advancement .... Mrs. Kelly WATSON
07 Director of Admissions .... Mr. John PENROSE
20 Associate Dean/Site Director .... Mr. Matthew LONG
26 Director of Marketing Communication .... Ms. Brianna HOUCHENS
04 Administrative Asst to President .... Ms. Cheryl A. KERN
06 Registrar .... Mr. Gordon GILES
08 Head Librarian .... Ms. Emilia KNISELY
37 Financial Aid Counselor .... Ms. Chazeray EWING
37 Financial Aid Counselor .... Ms. Becki BROWN

The Christ College of Nursing and Health Sciences (H)

2139 Auburn Avenue, Cincinnati OH 45219
County: Hamilton FICE Identification: 006489
Unit ID: 201821
Telephone: (513) 585-2401 Carnegie Class: Spec-4-yr-Other Health
FAX Number: (513) 585-3540 Calendar System: Semester
URL: www.thechristcollege.edu
Established: 2006 Annual Undergrad Tuition & Fees: $16,203
Enrollment: 914 Coed
Affiliation or Control: Independent Non-Profit IRS Status: 501(c)3
Highest Offering: Baccalaureate
Accreditation: NH, ADNUR, NURSE

01 President .... Dr. Gail E. KIST-KLINE
05 Dean of Academics .... Vacant
121 Dean of Student Success .... Dr. Meghan E. HOLLOWELL
84 Dean of Enrollment Management .... Mr. Bradley A. JACKSON
04 Executive Assistant to President .... Ms. Jessica L. DUNKLEY
11 Lead Project Consultant .... Ms. Carolyn HUNTER
10 Senior Financial Analyst .... Ms. Laura WEHBY
37 Director of Financial Aid .... Mr. Tim RING

Cincinnati Christian University (I)

2700 Glenway Avenue, Cincinnati OH 45204-3200
County: Hamilton FICE Identification: 003029
Unit ID: 201858
Telephone: (513) 244-8100 Carnegie Class: Spec-4-yr-Faith
FAX Number: (513) 244-8140 Calendar System: Semester
URL: www.ccuniversity.edu
Established: 1924 Annual Undergrad Tuition & Fees: $17,228
Enrollment: 750 Coed
Affiliation or Control: Christian Churches And Churches of Christ
IRS Status: 501(c)3
Highest Offering: First Professional Degree
Accreditation: NH, CACREP, CAEPT

01 Chief Executive Officer .... Mr. Ronald E. HEINEMAN
05 Chief Academic Officer .... Mr. Paul FRISKNEY
11 VP Finance/Administration .... Mr. Randy KOEHLER, II
111 Dir of Advancement & Development .... Vacant
51 Dir of Center for Adult Learning .... Dr. Aaron BURGESS
84 Director of Adult Enrollment .... Vacant
83 Dean Education/Behavioral Sciences .... Dr. Sandra BEAM
50 Dean of School of Business .... Dr. Aaron BURGESS
20 Director of Faculty Development .... Dr. James A. SMITH
113 Bursar .... Mrs. Linda WAUGH
06 Registrar .... Mrs. Amanda DERICO
08 Director of Library Services .... Mr. James LLOYD
32 Director of Student Life .... Mr. Ray HORTON
37 Associate Director of Financial Aid .... Ms. Marcella FARMER
41 Director of Athletics .... Mr. John TAYLOR
18 Director of Operations .... Mr. Nathan CHESNUT
15 Director of Human Resources .... Vacant
13 Director of Information Technology .... Vacant
19 Director of Security .... Vacant
104 Director Study Abroad .... Vacant
28 Director of Diversity .... Mr. Jonathan GARRETT
96 Director of Purchasing .... Mrs. Sharon KNISLEY

Cincinnati College of Mortuary Science (J)

645 W North Bend Road, Cincinnati OH 45224-1462
County: Hamilton FICE Identification: 010906
Unit ID: 201867
Telephone: (513) 761-2020 Carnegie Class: Spec-4-yr-Other
FAX Number: (513) 761-3333 Calendar System: Semester
URL: www.ccms.edu
Established: 1882 Annual Undergrad Tuition & Fees: N/A
Enrollment: 85 Coed
Affiliation or Control: Independent Non-Profit IRS Status: 501(c)3
Highest Offering: Baccalaureate
Accreditation: NH, FUSER

01 President .... Mr. Jack E. LECHNER, JR.
11 Vice President & COO .... Mr. Mark D. IVEY
07 Admissions Director .... Mr. Kevin BRINKMAN
37 Financial Aid Director .... Mr. Russ ROMANDINI
04 Administrative Asst to President .... Mrs. Beth WILLIAMS
05 Chief Academic Officer .... Ms. Teresa DUTKO
08 Director Library/IT .... Ms. Molly JONES
88 Office Manager .... Mr. Randy ANDERSON
06 Registrar .... Ms. Brooke BOLTON
30 Director of Development .... Ms. Ginny HIZER

Cincinnati State Technical and Community College (K)

3520 Central Parkway, Cincinnati OH 45223-2690
County: Hamilton FICE Identification: 010345
Unit ID: 201928
Telephone: (513) 569-1500 Carnegie Class: Assoc/HVT-Mix Trad/Non
FAX Number: (513) 569-1495 Calendar System: Other
URL: www.cincinnatistate.edu
Established: 1966 Annual Undergrad Tuition & Fees (In-State): $4,126
Enrollment: 8,807 Coed
Affiliation or Control: State IRS Status: 501(c)3
Highest Offering: Associate Degree
Accreditation: NH, ACFEI, ADNUR, CAHIIM, COARC, CONST, DIETT, DMS, EMT, MAC, MLTAD, OTA, SURGT

01 President .... Dr. Monica POSEY
05 Provost .... Mr. Robbin HOOPES
13 Vice President for Technology .... Mr. Frankie BAKER
103 Vice Pres Workforce Development .... Ms. Amy WALDBILLIG
84 VP Enrollment/Student Development .... Dr. Soni HILL
72 Dean of Innovative Technology .... Mr. Doug BOWLING
50 Dean of Business Technologies .... Ms. Yvonne BAKER
76 Interim Dean Health/Public Safety .... Ms. Denise ROHR
81 Dean Humanities/Sciences .... Ms. Angela HAENSEL
06 Registrar .... Mr. Jason A. MOORE
08 Library Director .... Mrs. Cindy SEFTON
35 Director Student Activities .... Ms. Andrea MILANI
15 Director of Human Resources .... Ms. Lawra BAUMANN
102 Executive Director CS Foundation .... Mr. Elliot RUTHER
04 Executive Administrative Associate .... Mrs. Lachanna JACKSON
19 Director of Public Safety .... Mr. Michael WYLIE
101 Secretary to the Board of Trustees .... Mrs. Nancy STUBBEMAN
88 Director Pathways to Employment .... Ms. Regina LIVERS
07 Director of Admissions .... Ms. Deborah POWELEIT
09 Director of Institutional Research .... Mr. Cody LOEW
10 Chief Financial/Business Officer .... Mr. Christopher CALVERT
37 Director Student Financial Aid .... Ms. Penny PARSONS

Clark State Community College (L)

570 E Leffel Lane, PO Box 570, Springfield OH 45501-0570
County: Clark FICE Identification: 004852
Unit ID: 201973
Telephone: (937) 325-0691 Carnegie Class: Assoc/MT-VT-Mix Trad/Non
FAX Number: (937) 328-6142 Calendar System: Semester
URL: www.clarkstate.edu
Established: 1966 Annual Undergrad Tuition & Fees (In-State): $3,728
Enrollment: 5,783 Coed
Affiliation or Control: State IRS Status: 501(c)3
Highest Offering: Baccalaureate
Accreditation: NH, ADNUR, EMT, MAC, MLTAD, PTAA

01 President .... Dr. Jo A. BLONDIN
05 Vice Pres Academic Affairs .... Dr. Tiffany HUNTER
10 VP for Business Affairs .... Larry WAKEFIELD
32 Senior VP of Student Success .... Dr. Theresa FELDER
102 Foundation Executive Director .... Toni OVERHOLSER
21 Controller .... Kathy NELSON
07 Dean Enrollment Services .... Ronald GORDON
124 Dean Student Engagemt/Support Svcs .... Nina WILEY
49 Dean Arts & Sciences .... Naomi LOUIS
50 Dean Business/Applied Technologies .... Aimee BELANGER-HAAS
76 Dean Health/Human/Public Services .... Rhoda SOMMERS
37 Financial Aid Director .... Suzanne HARMON
06 Registrar .... Diane SEAMAN
13 VP of Information Technology .... Dr. Matt FRANZ
15 Director of Human Resources .... Laura WHETSTONE
57 Exec Dir Performing Arts Center .... Adele ADKINS
08 Director Library Services .... Dr. Sterling J. COLEMAN, JR.
18 Dir Facilities/Oper/Maint .... Daniel AYARS
41 Dir Athletics and Student Life .... Justin MCCULLA
103 Dir Workforce & Business Solutions .... Leslie BEAVERS
88 Dir Commercial Trans Train Center .... Duane HODGE
106 Dir Center for Teaching & Learning .... Cindra PHILLIPS
26 Executive Director Marketing .... Laurie MEANS
04 Assistant to the President .... Mellanie TOLES
09 Institutional Research Technician .... Kelly NERIANI

Cleveland Institute of Art (M)

11610 Euclid Avenue, Cleveland OH 44106-1710
County: Cuyahoga FICE Identification: 003982
Unit ID: 202046
Telephone: (216) 421-7000 Carnegie Class: Spec-4-yr-Arts
FAX Number: (216) 421-7438 Calendar System: Semester
URL: www.cia.edu
Established: 1882 Annual Undergrad Tuition & Fees: $42,055
Enrollment: 636 Coed
Affiliation or Control: Independent Non-Profit IRS Status: 501(c)3
Highest Offering: Baccalaureate
Accreditation: NH, ART

01 President & CEO ... Mr. Grafton J. NUNES
04 Exec Assistant to CEO & VP IA ... Ms. Colleen SWEENEY
05 VP Academic/Dean Faculty Affairs ... Ms. Joyce KESSLER
84 VP Enrollment/Dean Admiss & Fin Aid ... Mr. Jonathan WEHNER
111 VP Institutional Advancement ... Ms. Malou MONAGO
26 VP Marketing & Communications ... Mr. Mark INGLIS
10 Sr VP Business Affairs & CFO ... Ms. Almut ZVOSEC
13 VP Support Service & CIO ... Mr. Mat FELTHOUSEN
15 VP Human Resources & Inclusion ... Mr. Raymond SCRAGG
32 Dean of Student Affairs ... Ms. Nancy NEVILLE
06 Registrar ... Ms. Marty MONDELLO-HENDREN
121 Director of Academic Services ... Ms. Elisaida MENDEZ
39 Director of Student Life & Housing ... Mr. Matthew SMITH
36 Director of Career Center ... Ms. Heather GOLDEN
08 Director of Library ... Ms. Laura PONIKVAR
31 Dir Continuing Ed & Community ... Ms. Gabrielle BURRAGE
07 Assoc Director of Admissions ... Mr. Tom GREEN
37 Director of Financial Aid ... Mr. Martin CARNEY
44 Dir of Annual Giving & Stewardship ... Ms. Alyssa CADY
102 Director of Foundation Relations ... Ms. Kate MACEK
88 Dir Leadership Giving/Corp Rels ... Mr. Michael DAGON
29 Director Alumni & Scholarships ... Ms. Alexandra BURRAGE
88 Art Director ... Mr. Richard SARIAN
27 Director of Communications ... Ms. Karen SANDSTROM
21 Assoc VP Business Ops & Reporting ... Ms. Julie MELVIN
19 Chief of Public Safety ... Mr. Steve HAMMETT
18 Director Facilities Mgmt & Safety ... Mr. Joe FERRITTO

Cleveland Institute of Music (A)

11021 East Boulevard, Cleveland OH 44106-1776
County: Cuyahoga FICE Identification: 003031
Unit ID: 202073
Telephone: (216) 791-5000 Carnegie Class: Spec-4-yr-Arts
FAX Number: (216) 791-3063 Calendar System: Semester
URL: www.cim.edu
Established: 1920 Annual Undergrad Tuition & Fees: $41,987
Enrollment: 393 Coed
Affiliation or Control: Independent Non-Profit IRS Status: 501(c)3
Highest Offering: Doctorate
Accreditation: NH, MUS

01 President/CEO ... Mr. Paul HOGLE
11 Senior Vice President ... Mr. Eric BOWER
05 Chief Academic Officer ... Dr. Judy BUNDRA
10 Controller ... Mr. Daniel HOUT-REILLY
05 Sr Assoc Dean ... Mr. Brian SWEIGART
13 Chief Technology Officer ... Mr. John MALCOLM
84 Assoc Dean of Enrollment Management ... Mr. Jerrod PRICE
32 Associate Dean of Student Affairs ... Mr. David GILSON
37 Director Financial Aid ... Ms. Kristine GRIPP
06 Assoc Dean Acad Affs/Registrar ... Mrs. Hallie MOORE
15 Sr Director Human Resources ... Mrs. Tammie BELTON
08 Director of the Library ... Dr. Kevin MCLAUGHLIN
04 Executive Admin Asst to President ... Ms. Nancy SNELL
09 Institutional Research Analyst ... Vacant

Cleveland State University (B)

2121 Euclid Avenue, Cleveland OH 44115-2214
County: Cuyahoga FICE Identification: 003032
Unit ID: 202134
Telephone: (216) 687-2000 Carnegie Class: DU-Higher
FAX Number: (216) 687-9366 Calendar System: Semester
URL: www.csuohio.edu
Established: 1964 Annual Undergrad Tuition & Fees (In-State): $10,457
Enrollment: 16,371 Coed
Affiliation or Control: State IRS Status: 501(c)3
Highest Offering: Doctorate
Accreditation: NH, CACREP, CAEP, CAMPEP, CEA, COPSY, IPSY, LAW, MUS, NURSE, OT, PH, PLNG, PTA, SP, SPAA, SW

01 President ... Mr. Harlan M. SANDS
05 Provost/Sr VP Academic Affairs ... Dr. Jianping ZHU
10 VP Business Affairs/Finance ... Vacant
84 Interim VP Enrollment Services ... Mr. Rob SPADEMAN
46 VP Research ... Dr. Jerzy SAWICKI
111 VP Univ Advanc/Exec Dir Foundation ... Ms. Berinthia LEVINE
32 Int Vice Provost/Dean of Students ... Dr. Shannon GREYBAR MILLIKEN
28 Int Chief Diversity/Inclusion Ofcr ... Dr. Ronnie DUNN
20 Vice Provost for Academic Planning ... Dr. Teresa LAGRANGE
20 Vice Provost Academic Programs ... Dr. Peter MEIKSINS
26 Assoc VP University Mktg ... Mr. Robert SPADEMAN
15 Chief Human Resources Ofcr ... Ms. Jeanell HUGHES
35 Assoc VP Student Affairs ... Vacant
21 Controller/Asst VP Finance ... Ms. Kathleen MURPHY
100 Chief of Staff/AVP Administration ... Ms. Heather LINK
49 Dean Col Liberal Arts/Soc Sci ... Dr. Gregory M. SADLEK
81 Dean College of Science ... Dr. Meredith R. BOND
50 Dean College of Business ... Dr. Sanjay PUTREVU
53 Dean College Education & Human Svcs ... Dr. Sajit ZACHARIAH
54 Dean Washkewicz Col Engineering ... Dr. Anette KARLSSON
58 Dean College Graduate Studies ... Dr. Nigamanth SRIDHAR
61 Dean of College of Law ... Mr. Lee FISHER
80 Dean College Urban Affairs ... Dr. Roland ANGLIN
92 Dean Honors College ... Dr. Elizabeth LEHFELDT
43 General Counsel ... Ms. Sonali B. WILSON
08 Int Director of Libraries ... Mr. David LODWICK
22 Dir Office of Institutional Equity ... Ms. Rachel LUTNER
07 Director Undergraduate Admissions ... Vacant
09 Director Institutional Research ... Mr. Tom GEAGHAN

85 Director International Programs ... Mr. Ali SOLTANSHAHI
38 Director Counseling Center ... Dr. Katharine HAHN
37 Director Student Financial Aid ... Ms. Rachel SCHMIDT
06 Asst Vice President/Registrar ... Ms. Janet STIMPLE
41 Director of Athletics ... Mr. Scott GARRETT
29 Asst VP Alumni Relations ... Mr. Brian BREITHOLZ
18 Int Exec Dir Facilities Services ... Mr. Bruce FERGUSON
96 Assoc Director Purchasing ... Ms. Laurie WOLOHAN
04 Director Office of the President ... Ms. Shane CONNOR
114 Sr Dir Budget & Operations ... Mr. William WILSON
106 Director Center for E-learning ... Ms. Caryn LANZO
13 Chief Info Technology Ofcr (CIO) ... Mr. David BRUCE
39 Dir Resident Life/Student Housing ... Ms. Lynn ELLISON
86 Pres Advisor Government Relations ... Dr. William J. NAPIER
19 Director Security/Safety ... Mr. Anthony TRASKA

The College of Wooster (C)

1189 Beall Avenue, Wooster OH 44691-2363
County: Wayne FICE Identification: 003037
Unit ID: 206589
Telephone: (330) 263-2000 Carnegie Class: Bac-A&S
FAX Number: (330) 263-2427 Calendar System: Semester
URL: www.wooster.edu
Established: 1866 Annual Undergrad Tuition & Fees: $50,250
Enrollment: 1,980 Coed
Affiliation or Control: Independent Non-Profit IRS Status: 501(c)3
Highest Offering: Baccalaureate
Accreditation: NH, CAEP, MUS

01 President ... Dr. Sarah BOLTON
05 Provost ... Dr. Lisa PERFETTI
10 Vice Pres Finance/Bus/Treasurer ... Mr. James PRINCE
111 Vice President for Advancement ... Mr. Wayne WEBSTER
84 Vice Pres Enrollment/College Rels ... Dr. Scott FRIEDHOFF
32 VP Stdnt Affairs/Dean of Students ... Mr. Scott C. BROWN
04 Administrative Asst to President ... Ms. Sally WHITMAN
18 Assoc VP Facilities Mgmt & Planning ... Mr. Mike TAYLOR
109 Assoc VP Facilities & Auxiliaries ... Ms. Jacqueline MIDDLETON
20 Dean Curriculum/Academic Engagement ... Bryan KARAZSIA
20 Dean for Faculty Development ... Dr. Christa CRAVEN
07 Dean of Admissions ... Ms. Jennifer D. WINGE
28 Chief Div/Equity/Inclusion Ofcr ... Ms. Ivonne M. GARCIA
13 Chief Information Planning Officer ... Dr. Ellen FALDUTO
06 Interim Registrar ... Ms. Kristine JAMIESON
08 Librarian of the College ... Dr. Irene HEROLD
37 Director of Financial Aid ... Ms. Dana KENNEDY
27 Director Communications ... Mr. Hugh HOWARD
29 Dir of Alumni Rels & Wooster Fund ... Mr. Thomas MCARTHUR
36 Director Career Services ... Ms. Lisa KASTOR
19 Director Security/Protective Svcs ... Mr. Steven GLICK
101 Secretary of College/Chief Staff ... Ms. Angela JOHNSTON

Columbus College of Art & Design (D)

60 Cleveland Avenue, Columbus OH 43215-1758
County: Franklin FICE Identification: 003039
Unit ID: 202170
Telephone: (614) 224-9101 Carnegie Class: Spec-4-yr-Arts
FAX Number: (614) 222-4040 Calendar System: Semester
URL: www.ccad.edu
Established: 1879 Annual Undergrad Tuition & Fees: $35,420
Enrollment: 1,075 Coed
Affiliation or Control: Independent Non-Profit IRS Status: 501(c)3
Highest Offering: Master's
Accreditation: NH, ART

01 President ... Dr. Melanie CORN
04 Exec Assistant to the President ... Ms. Sheri LUCAS
05 Provost ... Ms. Dona LANTZ
10 AVP Finance & Administration ... Mr. Tom DOTSON
11 VP Administration & Operations ... Ms. Lisa STONEMAN
30 Vice President for Advancement ... Ms. Lindsey DUNLEAVY
84 VP for Enrollment Management ... Ms. D. Jean HESTER
32 VP Student Affairs ... Mr. Chris MUNDELL
60 Dean School of Design Arts ... Mr. Tom GATTIS
57 Dean School of Studio Arts ... Ms. Julie TAGGART
26 VP Marketing & Communications ... Ms. Jill MOORHEAD
58 Dean of Graduate Studies ... Ms. Jennifer SCHLUETER
06 Registrar/Dir of Student Central ... Ms. Michele KIBLER
13 Chief Information Officer ... Mr. Matt GARDZINA
15 Director of Human Resources ... Ms. Beverly THOMAS
08 Director of Library Services ... Ms. Leslie JANKOWSKI NIEMCZURA
19 Director of Safety & Security ... Mr. Wallace TANKSLEY
18 Director of Facilities ... Vacant
38 Director of Counseling & Wellness ... Ms. Erin VLACH
37 Director Financial Aid ... Mr. Chad FOUST
36 Director Career Resources ... Ms. Tiffany SPERRING
21 Controller ... Mr. Roger ESCOLAS
35 Dir of Student Engagement ... Ms. Maria CLARK
51 Dir of Continuing Educ/Prof Studies ... Ms. Christine HILL
39 Director of Residence Life ... Ms. Liz GORDON-CANLAS
88 Assoc VP of Operations ... Mr. Dave STOCKWELL
40 Supply Store Manager ... Mr. Danny HINTY
35 Dean of Students ... Ms. Athena SANDERS

Columbus State Community College (E)

Box 1609, Columbus OH 43216-1609
County: Franklin FICE Identification: 006867
Unit ID: 202222
Telephone: (614) 287-5353 Carnegie Class: Assoc/MT-VT-High Non
FAX Number: (614) 287-5113 Calendar System: Semester
URL: www.cscc.edu
Established: 1963 Annual Undergrad Tuition & Fees (In-State): $4,284
Enrollment: 27,204 Coed
Affiliation or Control: State IRS Status: 501(c)3
Highest Offering: Associate Degree
Accreditation: NH, ACBSP, ACFEI, ADNUR, CAHIIM, COARC, CONST, CSHSE, DH, DIETT, EMT, MAC, MLTAD, RAD, SURGT

01 President ... Dr. David T. HARRISON
05 Senior VP Academic Affairs ... Dr. Kelly SIMONS
10 VP Business Svcs/CFO/Treasurer ... Ms. Aletha SHIPLEY
26 VP Enrollment Svcs & Marketing ... Mr. Allen KRAUS
13 VP Information Technology ... Dr. Michael BABB
11 VP Administration ... Mr. Richard HATCHER
03 Executive Vice President ... Dr. Rebecca BUTLER
12 Dean of Delaware Campus ... Dr. Tina DIGGS
49 Dean of Arts & Sciences ... Dr. Allysen TODD
76 Dean Health and Human Services ... Mr. Curt LAIRD
50 Dean Business & Engineering Tech ... Mr. Angelo FROLE
32 Administrator II EMSS/Student Life ... Ms. Renee HILL
102 Executive Director Foundation ... Ms. Andrea DENNING
91 Director IT Budget/Planning ... Mr. Etienne MARTIN
21 Director II Controller ... Ms. Jan ELLIS
06 Director Office of the Registrar ... Dr. Regina RANDALL
37 Director Financial Aid ... Mr. Jerry WADE
19 Chief of Police ... Chief Sean ASBURY
18 Director II Facilities Management ... Mr. Mark FRENCH
28 Dir of Global Diversity/Inclusion ... Mr. Brett WELSH
09 Director II Inst Effectiveness ... Dr. Jennifer ANDERSON
08 Director Library ... Mr. Bruce MASSIS
07 Director of Admissions ... Mr. Justin GROTE
40 Director Operations/Bookstore ... Ms. Stacey MULINEX
96 Director Procurement/College Svcs ... Mr. Bradley FARMER
20 Associate VP Academic Affairs ... Dr. Martin MALIWESKY
35 Exec Dean Advise & Student Support ... Ms. Desiree POLK-BLAND

Columbus State Community College-Delaware (F)

5100 Cornerstone Drive, Delaware OH 43015
Telephone: (740) 203-8345 Identification: 770353
Accreditation: &NH

Cuyahoga Community College (G)

700 Carnegie Avenue, Cleveland OH 44115-2878
County: Cuyahoga FICE Identification: 003040
Unit ID: 202356
Telephone: (216) 987-4000 Carnegie Class: Assoc/MT-VT-Mix Trad/Non
FAX Number: (216) 566-5977 Calendar System: Semester
URL: www.tri-c.edu
Established: 1963 Annual Undergrad Tuition & Fees (In-District): $3,436
Enrollment: 23,900 Coed
Affiliation or Control: State/Local IRS Status: 501(c)3
Highest Offering: Associate Degree
Accreditation: NH, ACFEI, ADNUR, CAHIIM, COARC, DH, DIETT, DMS, EMT, MAC, MLTAD, NDT, NMT, OTA, PTAA, RAD, SURGT

01 President ... Dr. Alex JOHNSON
05 Exec VP & Provost ... Dr. Karen MILLER
10 Exec VP Administration & Finance ... Mr. David KUNTZ
103 Exec VP Workforce/Comm & Econ Dev ... Mr. William GARY
12 Campus President East Campus ... Dr. Lisa WILLIAMS
12 President/CEO Corporate College ... Mr. Robert PETERSON
12 Campus President Metro Campus ... Dr. Michael SCHOOP
12 Campus President Westshore Campus ... Dr. Terri POPE
12 Campus President West Campus ... Dr. Donna IMHOFF
21 Vice Pres Finance & Business Svcs ... Ms. Jennifer DEMMERLE
15 Vice Pres/Chief Human Res Officer ... Ms. Lillian WELCH
30 Vice Pres Development/Foundation ... Ms. Megan O'BRYAN
27 Vice Pres/Chief Information Officer ... Mr. Gerard HOURIGAN
86 Vice Pres Govt Affs/Comm Outreach ... Ms. Claire ROSACCO
84 VP Inst Research/Enrollment Mgmt ... Ms. Angela JOHNSON
26 Vice Pres Integrated Communications ... Ms. Jenny FEBBO
43 Vice Pres Legal Services ... Ms. Renee RICHARD
20 Vice Pres Learning Engagement ... Ms. Lindsay ENGLISH
88 VP Accreditation/Health Initiatives ... Vacant
88 VP & Dean Public Safety & Crim Just ... Chief Clayton HARRIS
88 Vice Pres Manufacturing ... Ms. Alicia BOOKER
32 Assoc VP Access & Cmty Engagement ... Dr. JaNice MARSHALL
88 Exec Dir Access Learning & Success ... Dr. Sandra MCKNIGHT
88 Deputy Gen Counsel & Exec Dir ... Mr. Marvin RICHARDS
88 Exec Director Media Engineering ... Mr. Robert (Bob) BRYAN
13 Exec Director EIS ... Mr. Jon DOLINAR
88 Exec Director Plant Operations ... Mr. Shehadeh ABDELKARIM
88 Exec Dir Veteran Services/Programs ... Mr. Richard DE CHANT
88 Exec Dir College Services & Retail ... Mr. Chris MOIR
88 Exec Dir Supplier Managed Services ... Mr. Stephen HILBERT
96 VP Capital Const & Supply Mgmt ... Ms. Cynthia LEITSON
88 Dean GM Hospitality Management ... Mr. Michael HUFF
88 Exec Director Talent Management ... Mr. Barry ROYKO
20 Dean Learning & Engagement East ... Ms. Denise MCCORY
20 Dean Learning & Engagement West ... Dr. Janice TAYLOR HEARD
20 Dean Learning & Engagement Metro ... Ms. Delia BOBER
20 Dean Lrng & Engagement Westshore ... Mr. Robert SEARSON
35 Int Dean Access & Completion Metro ... Ms. Ralonda ELLIS-HILL
35 Dean Access & Completion West ... Dr. Tim DORSEY
35 Dean Access & Completion East ... Mr. Andrew CRAWFORD
35 Dean Access & Completion Westshore ... Dr. Ann PROUDFIT
66 Dean Nursing ... Dr. Vivian YATES
76 Program Director Dietary Technology ... Ms. Judith KAPLAN

76 Assoc Dean Health Careers & Science .... Mr. Gregory MALONE
81 Assoc Dean STEM West .... Mr. Ormond BRATHWAITE
83 Assoc Dean Social Sciences West .... Ms. Courtney CLARKE
49 Assoc Dean Liberal Arts East .... Dr. William CUNION
49 Assoc Dean Creative Arts ....Ms. Amy PARKS
49 Assoc Dean Liberal Arts West ....Dr. Felisa EAFFORD
50 Assoc Dean Bus/Math & Tech East ....Dr. Ann CONRAD
72 Assoc Dean Bus IT Applied Tech West .... Ms. Pamela GRANT
54 Dean Manufacturing Engineer .... Mr. Lam WONG
88 Assoc Dean Hospitality Management .... Ms. Karen MONATH
66 Assoc Dean Nursing ....Ms. Ebony DRUMMER
100 Chief of Staff/Exec Asst to Pres .... Ms. Ronna MCNAIR
23 Assoc Dean Public Safety & EMT ....Dr. James PLOSKONKA
28 Director of Diversity & Inclusion .... Ms. Magda GOMEZ
110 Exec Director Development ....Ms. Sharon COON
09 Exec Director Evidence Inquiry .... Mr. G. Rob STUART
38 Dean Access Completion .... Mrs. Ralonda ELLIS-HILL
38 Assistant Dean Counseling-East .... Ms. Kate VODICKA
38 Assistant Dean Counseling-West .... Mr. Christopher JOHNSTON
04 Executive Admin Associate .... Ms. Barbara BELL
102 Exec Director Development Office .... Ms. Kate MCDADE
41 Athletic Director West ....Mr. Mark RODRIGUEZ
88 Mgr Transfer Res Ctr Metro Campus ..... Ms. Melissa SWAFFORD
41 Dir Student Life/Athletics/Rec .... Ms. Jennifer DAVIS
88 Dean Creative Arts .... Dr. G. Paul COX
14 Int VP Workforce Innov/Dean IT .... Ms. Standish STEWART
88 Director Network Services .... Mr. Peter ANDERSON

Cuyahoga Community College Eastern Campus (A)

4250 Richmond Road, Highland Hills OH 44122
Telephone: (216) 987-6000 Identification: 770355
Accreditation: &NH

Cuyahoga Community College Metropolitan Campus (B)

2900 Community College Avenue, Cleveland OH 44115
Telephone: (800) 954-8742 Identification: 770354
Accreditation: &NH

Cuyahoga Community College Western Campus (C)

11000 Pleasant Valley Road, Parma OH 44130
Telephone: (800) 954-8742 Identification: 770356
Accreditation: &NH

Cuyahoga Community College Westshore (D)

31001 Clemens Road, Westlake OH 44145
Telephone: (800) 954-8742 Identification: 770357
Accreditation: &NH

Davis College (E)

4747 Monroe Street, Toledo OH 43623-4389
County: Lucas FICE Identification: 004855
Unit ID: 202435
Telephone: (419) 473-2700 Carnegie Class: Assoc/HVT-High Trad
FAX Number: (419) 473-2472 Calendar System: Quarter
URL: www.daviscollege.edu
Established: 1858 Annual Undergrad Tuition & Fees: $14,130
Enrollment: 91 Coed
Affiliation or Control: Proprietary IRS Status: Proprietary
Highest Offering: Associate Degree
Accreditation: NH

01 President .... Diane BRUNNER
05 Dean of Faculty .... Mary DELOE
32 VP of Student & Academic Services ....Mary RYAN BULONE
111 VP of Institutional Advancement .... Tim BRUNNER
37 Director Student Financial Aid .... Terry DIPPMAN
07 Director of Admissions ....Timothy BRUNNER
10 Bursar ....Barb HELMLINGER
36 Career Services Director ....Nick NIGRO
08 Librarian ....Peggy PETERSON-SENIUK
18 Facilities Manager .... Greg RIPPKE

The Defiance College (F)

701 N Clinton Street, Defiance OH 43512-1695
County: Defiance FICE Identification: 003041
Unit ID: 202514
Telephone: (419) 784-4010 Carnegie Class: Bac-Diverse
FAX Number: (419) 784-4101 Calendar System: Semester
URL: www.defiance.edu
Established: 1850 Annual Undergrad Tuition & Fees: $32,700
Enrollment: 614 Coed
Affiliation or Control: United Church Of Christ IRS Status: 501(c)3
Highest Offering: Master's
Accreditation: NH, IACBE, NURSE, SW

01 President .... Dr. Richanne C. MANKEY
05 VP for Academic Affairs .... Dr. Agnes CALDWELL
10 Vice Pres for Finance & Management ....Mr. Timothy PRUETT
32 VP Student Affs/Dean of Students ....Mrs. Lisa MARSALEK
84 Vice President for Enrollment Mgmt ....Mrs. Tracey D. FORD
88 Dean McMaster Sch Adv Hum .... Mrs. Mary Ann STUDER
07 Director of Admissions & Fin Aid .... Mrs. Brenda AVERESCH
15 Director of Human Resources ....Mrs. Mary E. BURKHOLDER
08 Dir of Library and Instr Resource ..Mrs. Lisa CRUMIT-HANCOCK
26 Director Public Relations/Marketing ....Vacant
13 Director of Computer Services .... Mr. Ryan NUNN
06 Registrar .... Dr. Robert DETWILER
37 Director of Financial Aid .... Mrs. Amy FRANCIS
41 Athletic Director .... Mr. Derek WOODLEY
28 Director Intercultural Relations .... Ms. Mercedes CLAY
39 Director of Residence Life .... Ms. Jennifer WALTON
18 Director of Physical Plant .... Mr. Cliff BRADY
21 Director of Accounting ....Mrs. Kristine BOLAND
04 Administrative Asst to President .... Mrs. Judy LYMANSTALL
103 Dir Workforce/Career Development .... Ms. Sally BISSELL
50 Dean of Business ....Mr. William SHOLL
53 Dean of Education .... Dr. Carla HIGGINS
38 Director Student Counseling ....Ms. Lynn BRAUN
44 Director of Annual Giving .... Mrs. Carol WHETSTONE

Denison University (G)

100 W College Street, Granville OH 43023-1359
County: Licking FICE Identification: 003042
Unit ID: 202523
Telephone: (740) 587-0810 Carnegie Class: Bac-A&S
FAX Number: (740) 587-6417 Calendar System: Semester
URL: www.denison.edu
Established: 1831 Annual Undergrad Tuition & Fees: $51,960
Enrollment: 2,341 Coed
Affiliation or Control: Independent Non-Profit IRS Status: 501(c)3
Highest Offering: Baccalaureate
Accreditation: NH

01 President .... Dr. Adam S. WEINBERG
05 Provost .... Dr. Kimberly A. COPLIN
100 Chief of Staff .... Dr. Rajesh BELLANI
10 VP Finance & Management ....Mr. David A. ENGLISH
111 VP Institutional Advancement .... Ms. Julia BEYER HOUPT
32 VP Student Development ....Dr. Laurel B. KENNEDY
84 VP Enrollment Management .... Mr. Gregory W. SNEED
89 Dean of First-Year Students .... Dr. Mark MOLLER
88 Special Asst to Pres & Provost .... Dr. Joyce MEREDITH
41 Assoc VP of Athletics .... Ms. Nan CARNEY-DEBORD
115 Chief Investment Officer .... Ms. Kathleen BROWNE
04 Executive Asst to President .... Ms. Nancy BERG

Eastern Gateway Community College - Jefferson County Campus (H)

110 John Scott Hwy, Steubenville OH 43952
County: Jefferson FICE Identification: 007275
Unit ID: 203331
Telephone: (740) 264-5591 Carnegie Class: Assoc/MT-VT-High Non
FAX Number: N/A Calendar System: Semester
URL: www.egcc.edu
Established: 1966 Annual Undergrad Tuition & Fees (In-District): $4,076
Enrollment: 8,526 Coed
Affiliation or Control: State/Local IRS Status: 501(c)3
Highest Offering: Associate Degree
Accreditation: NH, CAHIIM, COARC, DA, EMT, MAC, RAD

01 President .... Dr. Jimmie D. BRUCE
05 Vice President of Academic Affairs ....Vacant
43 VP of Admin Services/Legal Affairs .... Mr. James D. MILLER
32 VP of Online & Student Services .... Ms. Christina WANAT
12 Vice President of Youngstown Campus .... Mr. Arthur DALY
09 Interim VP Institutional Research .... Mr. Christopher BIRD
10 Chief Financial Officer .... Mr. Michael GEOGHEGAN
13 Chief Information Officer .... Mr. Robert ROESCHENTHALER
103 Exec Director of Workforce & Aspire .... Ms. Karla MARTIN
26 Exec Dir Marketing/Alumni/PR .... Mr. Keith MURDOCK
20 Interim Dean of Academics .... Dr. Thomas GRAHAM
111 Dir of Institutional Advancement .... Dr. James BABER
37 Interim Director of Financial Aid .... Mr. Kurt PAWLAK
15 Director of Human Resources .... Mr. Joshua MARTIN
21 Controller .... Mr. Robert SEMICH
76 Dean Health Science & Public Safety .... Dr. David KESLER
18 Director Building & Grounds ....Mr. Julius J. DZIEWATKOSKI
06 Registrar ....Ms. Marlise SIPES
114 Senior Budget Analyst .... Ms. Jennifer REED
41 Athletic Director .... Mr. John ZIZZO
106 Dean of Online Learning .... Ms. Vanessa BIRNEY
04 Executive Asst to President & BOT .... Ms. Georgenne KAMARADOS

Eastern Gateway Community College - Youngstown Campus (I)

101 East Federal Street, Youngstown OH 44503
Telephone: (800) 682-6553 Identification: 770987
Accreditation: &NH

† Branch campus of Eastern Gateway Community College in Steubenville, OH.

Edison State Community College (J)

1973 Edison Drive, Piqua OH 45356-9239
County: Miami FICE Identification: 012750
Unit ID: 202648
Telephone: (937) 778-8600 Carnegie Class: Assoc/MT-VT-High Non
FAX Number: (937) 778-1920 Calendar System: Semester
URL: www.edisonohio.edu
Established: 1973 Annual Undergrad Tuition & Fees (In-State): $4,698
Enrollment: 3,261 Coed
Affiliation or Control: State IRS Status: 501(c)3
Highest Offering: Associate Degree
Accreditation: NH, ADNUR, MLTAD, PTAA

01 President .... Dr. Doreen LARSON
04 Executive Asst to the President .... Ms. Heather LANHAM
05 Provost .... Mr. Chris SPRADLIN
10 VP of Administration & Finance .... Mr. John W. SHISHOFF
111 VP for Institutional Advancement ....Vacant
32 Dean of Student Affairs ....Ms. Jessica CHAMBERS
31 VP Business/Cmty Partnerships ....Mr. Rick HANES
13 Chief Information Officer ....Ms. Amy CROW
15 Exec Director Human Resources .... Mrs. Linda M. PELTIER
35 Director of Student Services ....Ms. Loleta COLLINS
49 Dean of Arts and Science ....Ms. Naomi LOUIS
50 Dean of Business/IT & Engineering ....Ms. Shirley MOORE
66 Dean of Nursing & Health Sciences ....Ms. Gwendolyn A. STEVENSON
09 Assoc Prov Planning/Effectiveness .... Ms. Mona WALTERS
88 Director of Student Success ....Ms. Pamela GIBELLINO
21 Controller ....Mr. James LEHMKUHL
41 Director Athletics .... Mr. Nathan COLE
37 Director of Financial Aid .... Ms. Chris CUMMINGS
26 Dir of Marketing & Communications ....Mr. Bruce MCKENZIE
84 Enrollment Manager .... Ms. Stacey BEAN
06 Registrar ....Ms. Mary BORNHORST
08 Director of Library/Learning Center ....Ms. Lisa HOOPS
18 Dir of Physical Plant/Facilities ....Mr. Douglas RIEHLE

ETI Technical College of Niles (K)

2076-86 Youngstown-Warren Road, Niles OH 44446-4398
County: Trumbull FICE Identification: 030790
Unit ID: 200590
Telephone: (330) 652-9919 Carnegie Class: Assoc/HVT-Mix Trad/Non
FAX Number: (330) 652-4399 Calendar System: Semester
URL: www.eticollege.edu
Established: 1989 Annual Undergrad Tuition & Fees: $10,272
Enrollment: 175 Coed
Affiliation or Control: Proprietary IRS Status: Proprietary
Highest Offering: Associate Degree
Accreditation: ACCSC

01 Director ....Mrs. Renee ZUZOLO
07 Director of Admissions .... Mrs. Diane MARSTELLER
37 Director Financial Aid ....Ms. Kay MADIGAN

Felbry College School of Nursing (L)

6055 Cleveland Avenue, Columbus OH 43231
County: Franklin FICE Identification: 042350
Unit ID: 487861
Telephone: (614) 781-1085 Carnegie Class: Not Classified
FAX Number: (614) 917-1010 Calendar System: Semester
URL: felbrycollege.edu
Established: Annual Undergrad Tuition & Fees: N/A
Enrollment: 160 Coed
Affiliation or Control: Proprietary IRS Status: Proprietary
Highest Offering: Associate Degree
Accreditation: ABHES

00 CEO .... Ms. Feyi TOLANI
01 Campus Director .... Ms. Lisa NUCCI
05 Dean/Dir of Nursing .... Dr. C. PRICE

Fortis College (M)

555 E Alex-Bell Road, Centerville OH 45459-6120
County: Montgomery FICE Identification: 021907
Unit ID: 205179
Telephone: (937) 433-3410 Carnegie Class: Assoc/HVT-High Trad
FAX Number: (937) 435-6516 Calendar System: Semester
URL: www.fortiscollege.edu
Established: 1970 Annual Undergrad Tuition & Fees: $14,060
Enrollment: 690 Coed
Affiliation or Control: Proprietary IRS Status: Proprietary
Highest Offering: Baccalaureate
Accreditation: ACCSC, ADNUR

01 President ....Gregory J. SHIELDS
05 VP/Chief Academic Officer .... Lisa MAYS
09 Dir Inst Effectiveness/Compliance ....LaRee PINGATORE
20 Director Education .... Lisa NAYS
07 Director Admissions ....Angela COOPER
37 Director Financial Aid ....Rachel KARMON

Fortis College (N)

2545 Bailey Road, Cuyahoga Falls OH 44221-2949
County: Summit FICE Identification: 009412
Unit ID: 204307
Telephone: (330) 923-9959 Carnegie Class: Spec 2-yr-Health
FAX Number: (330) 923-0886 Calendar System: Other
URL: www.fortis.edu
Established: 1922 Annual Undergrad Tuition & Fees: N/A
Enrollment: N/A Coed
Affiliation or Control: Proprietary IRS Status: Proprietary
Highest Offering: Associate Degree
Accreditation: ACCSC

01 Interim President .... Mr. Peter MARTINELLO

Fortis College (A)

4151 Executive Parkway, Suite 120,
Westerville OH 43081-3860
County: Franklin | Identification: 666602
Unit ID: 450058
Telephone: (614) 882-2551 | Carnegie Class: Spec 2-yr-Health
FAX Number: (614) 882-2914 | Calendar System: Quarter
URL: www.fortis.edu
Established: 2010 | Annual Undergrad Tuition & Fees: $15,200
Enrollment: 774 | Coed
Affiliation or Control: Proprietary | IRS Status: Proprietary
Highest Offering: Associate Degree
Accreditation: ABHES, RAD, SURGT

01 President ... Mr. Peter MARTINELLO
05 Dean of Education ... Ms. Nikki PAPPAS
06 Registrar ... Ms. Eva REDA
07 Director of Admissions ... Ms. Jackie CRANDELL
32 Chief Student Affairs/Student Life ... Mr. Michael TRAINA
36 Director Career/Student Svcs ... Mr. Kaiser JONES
37 Director Student Financial Aid ... Ms. Deidre VANCE

Franciscan University of Steubenville (B)

1235 University Boulevard, Steubenville OH 43952-1763
County: Jefferson | FICE Identification: 003036
Unit ID: 205957
Telephone: (740) 283-3771 | Carnegie Class: Masters/M
FAX Number: (740) 283-6472 | Calendar System: Semester
URL: www.franciscan.edu
Established: 1946 | Annual Undergrad Tuition & Fees: $27,630
Enrollment: 2,929 | Coed
Affiliation or Control: Roman Catholic | IRS Status: 501(c)3
Highest Offering: Master's
Accreditation: NH, CACREP, CAEP, NURSE, SW

01 President ... Rev. Dave PIVONKA, TOR
88 Chief Evangelization Officer ... Rev. Nathan MALAVOLTI, TOR
11 Chief Operating Officer ... Mr. William W. GORMAN
10 VP of Finance ... Mr. Richard ROLLINO
05 Chief Academic Officer ... Dr. Daniel KEMPTON
31 Exec Dir of Community Relations ... Mr. Mike FLORAK
45 Exec Dir of Institutional Effect ... Dr. James MELLO
15 Vice Pres of Human Resources ... Mr. Brenan PERGI
32 Vice President of Student Life ... Mr. David A. SCHMIESING
84 Vice Pres of Enrollment Management ... Mr. Joel S. RECZNIK
88 VP for Strategic Alliances ... Ms. Heather ULREY
35 Asst Vice Pres of Student Life ... Ms. Catherine J. HECK
88 Local Minister ... Rev. Luke ROBERTSON, TOR
42 University Chaplain ... Rev. Shawn ROBERSON, TOR
79 Dean of Humanities & Soc Sciences ... Dr. Regina BOERIO
107 Dean of Professional Programs ... Dr. Christin JUNGERS
81 Dean of Natural & Applied Science ... Dr. Daniel KUEBLER
73 Dean of Philosophy and Theology ... Dr. Paul SYMINGTON
13 Dir Information Technology Services ... Ms. Nancy OLIVER
121 Dir of Advising & Acad Operations ... Ms. Ann DULANY
105 Director Infrastructure Services ... Mr. Dennis BREEN
08 Director of Library ... Ms. Amy LEONI
88 Exec Director Christian Outreach ... Mr. Mark JOSEPH
112 Director of Planned Giving ... Dr. Mark E. RECZNIK
30 VP of Development ... Mr. Tom PAPPALARDO
29 Dir of Alumni & Constituent Rels ... Mr. Timothy J. DELANEY
26 Dir Marketing & Communications ... Ms. Lisa M. FERGUSON
07 Director of Admissions ... Mr. Christopher KRIVONIAK
36 Career Counselor/Internship Dev Dir ... Mr. Mark T. MCGUIRE
06 Registrar ... Mr. Cody SCHMITZ
84 Exec Dir of Enrollment Services ... Mr. John L. HERRMANN
09 Director of Institutional Research ... Dcn. Mark A. ERSTE, SR.
21 Controller ... Mr. Timothy HEFFRON
96 Director of Business Services ... Ms. Marlene K. TERPENNING
40 Director of Bookstore ... Ms. Dreama THOMPSON
91 Dir Enterprise Application Services ... Mrs. Pam SHANE
18 Director Physical Plant Services ... Mr. Joseph P. MCGURN
88 Director of Missionary Outreach ... Mr. Rhett YOUNG
88 Director of Chapel Ministries ... Mr. Robert PALLADINO
35 Dir Student Activities/Programming ... Mrs. Kathy L. MATTIOLI
104 Dir Student Success/Austrian Enroll ... Vacant
38 Director of Wellness Center ... Mr. Matthew BURRISS
41 Director of Athletics ... Vacant
36 Dir Career Planning & Services ... Mrs. Nancy S. RONEVICH
58 Director Graduate Education ... Dr. Mark FURDA
90 Coord Online Student Experience ... Ms. Sandi M. RADVANSKY
19 Director Campus Security ... Mr. Michael CONN
106 Dean of Online Programming ... Dr. Cory MALONEY
108 Director Institutional Assessment ... Vacant
04 Project Manager to President ... Mr. Daniel MILES
37 Director Student Financial Aid ... Mr. Jody PEELER
26 Exec Dir Marketing & Communications ... Ms. Kimberly SPONSELLER
101 Corporate Secretary of University ... Ms. Janine MURDOCK
19 Dir of Campus Safety & Compliance ... Mr. John PIZZUTI
112 Director of Major Gifts ... Mr. Scott GREVE
35 Dir of Student Development ... Mr. Matthew SCHAEFER
88 Director of Academic Effectiveness ... Dr. David BURTON
44 Director Annual Giving ... Mr. Benjamin GESSLER

Franklin University (C)

201 S Grant Avenue, Columbus OH 43215-5399
County: Franklin | FICE Identification: 003046
Unit ID: 202806
Telephone: (614) 797-4700 | Carnegie Class: Spec-4-yr-Bus
FAX Number: N/A | Calendar System: Trimester
URL: www.franklin.edu
Established: 1902 | Annual Undergrad Tuition & Fees: $12,649
Enrollment: 4,753 | Coed
Affiliation or Control: Independent Non-Profit | IRS Status: 501(c)3
Highest Offering: Doctorate
Accreditation: NH, CAHIIM, IACBE, NURSE

01 President ... Dr. David R. DECKER
11 Sr VP Administration/Chief of Staff ... Ms. Christi L. CABUNGCAL
05 SVP Academic Affairs ... Dr. Wendell SEABORNE
12 Exec VP Urbana Campus ... Dr. Christopher L. WASHINGTON
26 VP Marketing ... Ms. Linda M. STEELE
111 VP University Advancement ... Vacant
32 VP Student Affs & Enrollment Mgmt ... Dr. Lynne HULL
108 Exec Director Accreditation & Auth ... Ms. Danielle BUCKIUS
10 SVP/Chief Financial Officer ... Dr. Marvin BRISKEY
45 VP Planning & University Services ... Vacant
04 Executive Assistant to President ... Ms. Bonnie MCCANN
35 Dean of Students ... Dr. Blake RENNER
13 Chief Information Officer ... Mr. Rick SUNDERMAN
88 Dir of Accreditation & Inst Effect ... Ms. Susanne SMITH
09 Director Inst Effectiveness ... Mr. Kristopher COBLE
06 Registrar ... Mr. Frank YANCHAK
08 Director of Library Services ... Ms. Alyssa DARDEN
37 Director of Financial Aid ... Ms. Goldie LANGLEY
121 Exec Dir Student Affairs ... Ms. Wendi ROBINSON
88 VP Institute & Global Operations ... Mr. Patrick BENNETT
88 Exec Dir Domestic Partnership Dev ... Mr. Bill CHAN
18 Director of Facilities ... Mr. Carl BROWN
26 Director of Public Relations ... Ms. Sherry MERCURIO
29 Director of Alumni Engagement & Dev ... Vacant
96 Director of Purchasing ... Mr. Bob DONAHUE
118 Director of Benefits ... Ms. Brenda LISTON
88 Director Teaching Excellence ... Dr. Meghan RAEHLL
49 Dean Arts/Science & Technology ... Dr. Kody KUEHNL
50 Dean College of Business ... Dr. Andy IGONOR
69 Dean College of Health & Public Adm ... Dr. Jonathan MCCOMBS
53 Dean College of Education ... Dr. Craig MEREDITH
88 SVP Global Programs ... Dr. Godfrey MENDES
15 Director of Human Resources ... Ms. Molly MILLER
88 Director of Accounting ... Mr. Sean HUNTER
88 Exec Dir of Financial Services ... Mr. Randolph SNYDER
19 Director Security/Safety ... Mr. Clifton SPINNER

Galen College of Nursing (D)

100 E Business Way, Suite 200, Cincinnati OH 45241
Telephone: (513) 475-3600 | Identification: 770537
Accreditation: &SC, ADNUR, NURSE

† Branch campus of Galen College of Nursing, Louisville, KY

Global Tech College (E)

4346 Secor Rd, Toledo OH 43623
County: Lucas | Identification: 667346
Telephone: (567) 377-7010 | Carnegie Class: Not Classified
FAX Number: (567) 377-7173 | Calendar System: Quarter
URL: www.globaltech.edu
Established: 2012 | Annual Undergrad Tuition & Fees: N/A
Enrollment: N/A | Coed
Affiliation or Control: Proprietary | IRS Status: Proprietary
Highest Offering: Associate Degree
Accreditation: CNCE

01 President ... Dr. Joseph G. HOSNY
11 Dir Admin & Financial Affs ... Persilla ZERVOS
05 Dir Academic Affs & Student Svcs ... Dr. Farhang AKBAR-KHANZDEH
07 Dir of Admissions & Marketing ... Joanne HOSNY

God's Bible School and College (F)

1810 Young Street, Cincinnati OH 45202-6838
County: Hamilton | FICE Identification: 022205
Unit ID: 202903
Telephone: (513) 721-7944 | Carnegie Class: Spec-4-yr-Faith
FAX Number: (513) 763-6649 | Calendar System: Semester
URL: www.gbs.edu
Established: 1900 | Annual Undergrad Tuition & Fees: $7,040
Enrollment: 306 | Coed
Affiliation or Control: Interdenominational | IRS Status: 501(c)3
Highest Offering: Master's
Accreditation: NH, BI

01 President ... Rodney S. LOPER
05 Vice President for Academic Affairs ... Aaron PROFITT
32 Vice President for Student Affairs ... Richard MILES
30 Vice President for Donor Relations ... Marc SANKEY
06 Registrar ... Kent STETLER
08 Head Librarian ... Stephanie OWENS
10 Vice President for Finance ... David FREDERICK
13 Dir of UX and Digital Strategies ... Jason WEED
84 Vice Pres for Enrollment Services ... Matt HALLAM
37 Financial Aid Coordinator ... Sharree POUZAR

Good Samaritan College of Nursing and Health Science (G)

375 Dixmyth Avenue, Cincinnati OH 45220-2489
County: Hamilton | FICE Identification: 006494
Unit ID: 202912
Telephone: (513) 862-2743 | Carnegie Class: Spec-4-yr-Other Health
FAX Number: (513) 862-3572 | Calendar System: Semester
URL: www.gscollege.edu
Established: 2001 | Annual Undergrad Tuition & Fees: $15,470
Enrollment: 413 | Coed
Affiliation or Control: Independent Non-Profit | IRS Status: 501(c)3
Highest Offering: Baccalaureate
Accreditation: NH, ADNUR, NUR

01 Interim President ... Dr. Judy KRONENBERGER
05 Dean Academic Affairs/Allied Health ... Dr. Pryze SMITH
10 College Business Administator ... Vacant
11 Associate Dean of Campus Operations ... Dr. Beth MOORE
09 Dir of Inst Assessment/Educ Tech ... Dr. Terri PULLEN
84 Director of Enrollment Management ... Dr. Trent HAYES
06 Registrar ... Ms. Leah BOERGER

Heidelberg University (H)

310 E Market Street, Tiffin OH 44883-2462
County: Seneca | FICE Identification: 003048
Unit ID: 203085
Telephone: (419) 448-2000 | Carnegie Class: Bac-Diverse
FAX Number: (419) 448-2124 | Calendar System: Semester
URL: www.heidelberg.edu
Established: 1850 | Annual Undergrad Tuition & Fees: $31,000
Enrollment: 1,201 | Coed
Affiliation or Control: United Church Of Christ | IRS Status: 501(c)3
Highest Offering: Master's
Accreditation: NH, ACBSP, CAATE, CACREP, #CAEP, MUS

01 President ... Dr. Robert HUNTINGTON
05 VP for Academic Affairs & Provost ... Dr. Beth SCHWARTZ
10 VP for Admin & Business Affairs ... Mr. Hoa NGUYEN
84 VP for Enrollment Mgmt ... Mr. Doug KELLAR
111 VP Univ Advancement & Marketing ... Mr. Phil NESS
29 Exec Dir of Alumni Eng & Major Gift ... Ms. Ashley HELMSTETTER
13 Assoc VP for Information Resources ... Mr. Kurt HUENEMANN
18 Assoc VP for Facilities & Engr ... Mr. Rodney MORRISON
06 Registrar ... Ms. Cindy SUTER
50 Dean of Business & Technology ... Dr. Scott JOHNSON
79 Dean of Humanities/Educ & Arts ... Dr. Julie O'REILLY
81 Dean of Sciences ... Dr. Bryan SMITH
108 Dir of Academic Planning/Assessmen ... Dr. Sarah LUCZYK
104 Director Intl Affairs & Studies ... Ms. Julie ARNOLD
26 Dir of Marketing & Communications ... Mr. Rick SHERLOCK
36 Dir of Career Develop & Placement ... Mr. Mark MCKEE
121 Exec Dir of Student Acad Support ... Dr. Ellen NAGY
08 Director of Library ... Ms. Laurie REPP
41 Athletic Director ... Mr. Matt PALM
21 Business Officer ... Ms. Barb GABEL
37 Director Student Financial Aid ... Mrs. Juli WEININGER
30 Exec Dir for Development ... Mr. James MINEHART
32 Dean of Student Affairs ... Dr. Chris ABRAMS
39 Asst Dn Stdnt Affs for Campus Life ... Mr. Mark ZENO
124 Dir Student Engagement ... Ms. Jacqueline SIRONEN
15 Chief Human Resources Officer ... Ms. Margaret RUDOLPH
21 Controller ... Mr. Joel WILKINS
04 Exec Asst to President & Provost ... Ms. Monica VERHOFF
42 Director of Campus Ministry ... Rev. Paul STARK
19 Director Security/Safety ... Mr. Jeff RHOADES
07 Director of Admission ... Mr. Tom ALEXANDER

Herzing University-Akron (I)

1600 S Arlington Street, 100, Akron OH 44306-3958
Telephone: (330) 724-1600 | FICE Identification: 020695
Accreditation: &NH, ADNUR, MAC, NURSE

† Regional accreditation is carried under the parent institution in Madison, WI.

Hiram College (J)

Box 67, Hiram OH 44234-0067
County: Portage | FICE Identification: 003049
Unit ID: 203128
Telephone: (330) 569-3211 | Carnegie Class: Bac-Diverse
FAX Number: (330) 569-5494 | Calendar System: Other
URL: www.hiram.edu
Established: 1850 | Annual Undergrad Tuition & Fees: $36,358
Enrollment: 1,221 | Coed
Affiliation or Control: Independent Non-Profit | IRS Status: 501(c)3
Highest Offering: Master's
Accreditation: NH, CAEP, MUS, NURSE

01 President ... Dr. Lori E. VARLOTTA
05 VP Academic Affairs/Dean of College ... Dr. Judy MUYSKENS
10 CFO/VP Business and Finance ... Ms. Nancy RUBIN
30 VP Development & Alumni Relations ... Ms. Jennifer SCHULLER
32 Vice President & Dean of Students ... Dr. Elizabeth M. OKUMA
84 VP of Enrollment Management ... Mr. Daniel SUMMERS
20 Associate Dean of the College ... Dr. Ella KIRK
107 Director Professional/Grad Studies ... Dr. Amber CHENOWETH
06 Registrar ... Ms. Theresa FULLER
08 Head Librarian ... Vacant
29 Director Alumni Relations ... Ms. Jackie CRANDALL
37 Director Financial Services ... Ms. Linda SHIREY NELSON
36 Director of Career Services ... Ms. Bethani BURKHART
13 Executive Director IT ... Mr. Matthew MCKENNA
09 Director of Institutional Research ... Dr. Laura VAN WORMER
41 Director of Athletics ... Mr. Todd HIBBS

15 Executive Director Human Resources ... Ms. Lisa DURKIN
18 Director of the Physical Plant ... Mr. Rudy BRAYDICH
21 Controller ... Mr. Brett RIEBAU
35 Int Director of Campus Involvement ... Ms. Sarah DOWD
38 Director Student Counseling ... Dr. Kevin P. FEISTHAMEL
28 Director Ethnic Diversity Affairs ... Ms. Detra E. WEST
96 Director of Purchasing ... Mr. Shane KARDOS
26 Exec Dir Marketing/Communications ... Ms. Kim HOLM
04 Executive Asst to President ... Mr. Phil J. EAVES
25 Dir Institutional Grants ... Dr. Michael BENEDICT
104 Study Away Coordinator ... Ms. Brittany JACKSON
19 Director Security/Safety ... Mr. Daniel FYNES
39 Interim Director Student Housing ... Mr. Ed FRATO-SWEENEY
44 Exec Dir Annual Giving ... Ms. Aimee BELL

Hocking College (A)

3301 Hocking Parkway, Nelsonville OH 45764-9704
County: Athens FICE Identification: 007598
Unit ID: 203155
Telephone: (740) 753-3591 Carnegie Class: Assoc/MT-VT-Mix Trad/Non
FAX Number: (740) 753-7005 Calendar System: Semester
URL: www.hocking.edu
Established: 1968 Annual Undergrad Tuition & Fees (In-State): $4,540
Enrollment: 3,375 Coed
Affiliation or Control: State IRS Status: 501(c)3
Highest Offering: Associate Degree
Accreditation: NH, ACBSP, ACFEI, ADNUR, DH, EMT, MAC, PNUR, #PTAA

01 President ... Dr. Betty YOUNG
10 Exec Director Finance/Treasurer ... Mr. Mark FULLER
05 VP Academic/Workforce Development ... Dr. Myriah DAVIS
32 VP Administration/Student Affairs ... Ms. Jacqueline HAGEROTT
15 Director Human Resources ... Ms. Elizabeth DENNIS
04 Executive Assistant to President ... Ms. Sheree CUNNINGHAM
37 Exec Director Financial Aid ... Ms. Deneene MERCHANT
08 Dir Learning Resource Ctr/Librarian ... Mr. Jeff GRAFFIUS
26 Exec Dir Mktg/Public & Cmty Rels ... Mr. Tim BRUNICARDI
19 Chief Hocking College Police ... Ms. Tiffany TIMS
06 Registrar ... Ms. Kensey LOVE
18 Exec Dir Facilities/Skill Trades ... Mr. Bryan LUTZ
102 Director Foundation ... Mr. Douglas WELLS
21 Controller/Assistant Treasurer ... Mrs. Anna JOHNSON
100 Chief of Staff ... Mr. Jeff DAUBENMIRE

Hocking College Perry Campus (B)

5454 State Route 37, New Lexington OH 43764
Telephone: (740) 342-3337 Identification: 770359
Accreditation: &NH

Hondros College of Nursing (C)

1810 Successful Drive, Fairborn OH 45324
Telephone: (937) 879-1940 Identification: 770751
Accreditation: ABHES

Hondros College of Nursing (D)

5005 Rockside Road, Suite 130, Independence OH 44131
Telephone: (216) 524-1143 Identification: 770750
Accreditation: ABHES

Hondros College of Nursing (E)

7600 Tyler's Place Boulevard, West Chester OH 45069
Telephone: (513) 508-3005 Identification: 770749
Accreditation: ABHES

Hondros College of Nursing (F)

4140 Executive Parkway, Westerville OH 43081-3855
County: Franklin FICE Identification: 040743
Unit ID: 203386
Telephone: (614) 508-7277 Carnegie Class: Spec-4-yr-Other Health
FAX Number: (614) 508-7280 Calendar System: Quarter
URL: www.hondros.edu
Established: 1981 Annual Undergrad Tuition & Fees: $18,270
Enrollment: 2,093 Coed
Affiliation or Control: Proprietary IRS Status: Proprietary
Highest Offering: Baccalaureate
Accreditation: ABHES, NURSE

01 CEO ... Mr. Harry T. WILKINS
12 Campus Executive Director ... Ms. Kelly CAVANAGH
66 Asst Director of Nursing ... Ms. Debra PIZZUTI
07 Director of Admission ... Mr. Robert MINTO
06 Registrar ... Ms. Michelle HARDEN

International College of Broadcasting (G)

6 S Smithville Road, Dayton OH 45431-1898
County: Montgomery FICE Identification: 013132
Unit ID: 203289
Telephone: (937) 258-8251 Carnegie Class: Spec 2-yr-A&S
FAX Number: (937) 258-8714 Calendar System: Semester
URL: www.icb.edu
Established: 1968 Annual Undergrad Tuition & Fees: $12,569
Enrollment: 54 Coed
Affiliation or Control: Proprietary IRS Status: Proprietary
Highest Offering: Associate Degree
Accreditation: ACCSC

01 President ... J. Michael LEMASTER
05 School Director ... Ronda DOSTER
07 Director of Admissions ... John CHAFFIN

James A. Rhodes State College (H)

4240 Campus Drive, Lima OH 45804-3597
County: Allen FICE Identification: 010027
Unit ID: 203678
Telephone: (419) 995-8200 Carnegie Class: Assoc/HVT-High Non
FAX Number: (419) 221-0450 Calendar System: Semester
URL: www.rhodesstate.edu
Established: 1971 Annual Undergrad Tuition & Fees (In-State): $4,085
Enrollment: 3,760 Coed
Affiliation or Control: State IRS Status: 501(c)3
Highest Offering: Associate Degree
Accreditation: NH, ACBSP, ADNUR, COARC, COARCP, CSHSE, DH, EMT, MAC, OTA, PTAA, RAD

01 Interim President ... Dr. Cynthia E. SPIERS
10 Vice President Business & Finance ... Mr. Russ LITKE
05 Vice President for Academic Affairs ... Dr. Vicki DEKETELAERE
32 Vice President for Student Affairs ... Dr. Rose REINHART
45 VP Institutional Effect/Planning ... Vacant
30 Executive Director of Development ... Mr. Kevin L. REEKS
20 Associate VP for Academic Affairs ... Dr. Chris BOYETT
21 Controller/Asst Treasurer ... Mr. David BRUNS
37 Director Financial Aid ... Ms. Pamela HUGHES
09 Director Institutional Research ... Mr. Eric SPONSELLER
36 Director of Career Development ... Ms. Krista RICHARDSON
08 Head Librarian ... Ms. Tina SCHNEIDER
15 Director Human Resources ... Vacant
50 Dean Business/Tech & Public Svcs ... Dr. Antoinette BALDIN
49 Dean Div of Arts & Sciences ... Dr. Fernando ARZOLA
76 Dean of Health Sciences ... Dr. Paula BOLEY
18 Chief Facilities/Physical Plant ... Vacant
26 Asst Dir Mktg & College Relations ... Ms. Melissa SPONSELLER
38 Director Advising & Counseling ... Ms. Kendra BERMOSK

John Carroll University (I)

1 John Carroll Boulevard, Cleveland OH 44118
County: Cuyahoga FICE Identification: 003050
Unit ID: 203368
Telephone: (216) 397-1886 Carnegie Class: Masters/M
FAX Number: (216) 397-4256 Calendar System: Semester
URL: www.jcu.edu
Established: 1886 Annual Undergrad Tuition & Fees: $41,340
Enrollment: 3,545 Coed
Affiliation or Control: Roman Catholic IRS Status: 501(c)3
Highest Offering: Beyond Master's But Less Than Doctorate
Accreditation: NH, CACREP, CAEP, CAEPN

01 President ... Dr. Michael JOHNSON
88 Interim Title IX Coordinator ... Dr. Sherri CRAHEN
04 Assistant to the President ... Bridget RINI
88 VP for Univ Mission & Identity ... Dr. Edward PECK
43 General Counsel ... Colleen TREML
05 Provost & Academic Vice President ... Dr. Steven HERBERT
10 Executive VP & CFO ... Dennis HAREZA
32 Vice President for Student Affairs ... Dr. Mark MCCARTHY
111 VP for University Advancement ... Doreen RILEY
84 VP for Enrollment Management ... Stephanie LEVENSON
26 VP for Integrated Marketing & Comm ... Vacant
18 Associate VP for Facilities ... Carol DIETZ
20 Assoc Academic Vice President ... Dr. James KRUKONES
35 Assoc VP & Dean of Students ... Dr. Sherri CRAHEN
108 Asst Provost Assessment & IE ... Dr. R. Todd BRUCE
121 Asst Provost Academic Advising ... Dr. Maryclaire MORONEY
36 AVP & Exec Dir of Career Services ... Patrick MULLANE
37 Asst VP Enrollment/Financial Svcs ... Claudia WENZEL
30 AVP for Development ... Richard DAY
15 AVP Human Resources ... Jennifer RICK
84 AVP Enrollment Operations ... Steve VITATOE
08 Director of the Library ... Michelle MILLET
13 Chief Information Officer ... James BURKE
50 Dean Boler College of Business ... Dr. Alan MICIAK
49 Dean College of Arts & Sciences ... Dr. Margaret FARRAR
58 Assoc Dean Grad & Prof Studies ... Dr. Anne KUGLER
83 Assoc Dean Humanities & Soc Sci ... Dr. Rodney HESSINGER
81 Assoc Dean Sciences & Mathematics ... Dr. Graciela LACUEVA
113 Finance Manager ... John BRAUTIGAN
109 Director of Auxiliary Services ... Rory HILL
21 Controller ... John CLIFFORD
25 Director of Sponsored Research ... Erica KENNEDY
114 Dir of Budget & Financial Analysis ... Jennifer DILLON
96 Director of Purchasing ... Lou GENOVESE
112 Senior Director of Major Gifts ... Mary RYCYNA
29 Exec Dir of Alumni Rel & Annual Giv ... David VITATOE
112 Sr Dir Philanthropic Relations ... Peter BERNARDO
31 Dir Ctr for Service & Social Action ... Katherine FEELY, SND
102 Dir Foundation Rels & Grant Writing ... Pamela GEORGE-MERRILL
86 Manager of Govt & Comm Relations ... Kate MALONE
19 Director & Chief of JCUPD ... Brian HURD
09 Director of Institutional Research ... Maria O'CONNOR
117 Dir Regulatory Affairs & Risk Mgmt ... Garry HOMANY
22 Affirm Action Officer for faculty ... Dr. James KRUKONES
91 Director Enterprise Applications ... John SULLY
24 Center Digital Media Fac Liaison ... Dr. Jay TARBY
119 Data Security Engineer ... James SPITZNAGEL

105 Director of Web & Digital Media ... Jason LEE
104 Asst Dir of International Services ... Megan MCBRIDE
93 Dir Ctr for Student Div & Inclusion ... Salomon RODEZNO
23 Dir of Student Health & Wellness ... Janet KREVH
92 Director Honors Program ... Dr. Angela JONES
06 Registrar ... Michelle REYNARD
38 Director Univ Counseling Services ... Dr. Mark ONUSKO
39 Director of Residence Life ... Lisa BROWN CORNELIUS
41 Sr Director Athletics & Recreation ... Michelle MORGAN
42 Director of Campus Ministry ... John SCARANO

Kent State University Kent Campus (J)

PO Box 5190, Kent OH 44242-0001
County: Portage FICE Identification: 003051
Unit ID: 203517
Telephone: (330) 672-3000 Carnegie Class: DU-Higher
FAX Number: (330) 672-2190 Calendar System: Semester
URL: www.kent.edu
Established: 1910 Annual Undergrad Tuition & Fees (In-State): $10,312
Enrollment: 28,972 Coed
Affiliation or Control: State IRS Status: 501(c)3
Highest Offering: Doctorate
Accreditation: CONST, NH, AAB, ART, AUD, CAATE, CACREP, CAEPN, CIDA, CLPSY, DANCE, DIETD, DIETI, EXSC, JOUR, LIB, LSAR, MUS, NAIT, NRPA, NURSE, PH, POD, SCPSY, SP, SPAA, THEA

01 President ... Dr. Todd DIACON
05 Interim Sr Vice President/Provost ... Dr. Melody TANKERSLEY
10 Senior Vice Pres Finance & Admin ... Dr. Mark M. POLATAJKO
15 Vice Pres Human Resources ... Mr. Jack WITT
111 Vice Pres Institutional Advancement ... Mr. Stephen SOKANY
32 Vice Pres Student Affairs ... Dr. Janie D. LITTLE
84 Vice Pres Enrollment Management ... Dr. Mary G. PARKER
26 Senior VP Strategic Communications ... Ms. Karen CLARKE
46 Vice President Research ... Dr. Paul E. DICORLETO
13 Vice Pres Information Services/CIO ... Mr. John M. RATHJE
28 VP Diversity/Equity/Inclusion ... Dr. Alfreda BROWN
20 Dean Undergraduate Studies ... Dr. Eboni PRINGLE
35 Student Ombuds ... Ms. Amy QUILLIN
20 Int Assoc Prov for Academic Affairs ... Dr. Melody MUNRO-STASIUK
20 Assoc Provost Faculty Affairs ... Ms. Sue AVERILL
29 Asst Vice Pres Alumni Affairs ... Mrs. Lori RANDORF
07 Director of Admissions ... Ms. Laurre DONLEY
16 Human Resources Director-CPM ... Mr. David DIXON
06 Registrar ... Ms. Gail REBETA
43 Vice Pres General Counsel ... Mr. Willis WALKER
100 VP and University Secretary ... Ms. Charlene K. REED
41 Director Intercollegiate Athletics ... Mr. Joel NIELSEN
118 Director of Compliance & Benefits ... Vacant
37 Exec Director Student Financial Aid ... Mr. Mark EVANS
19 Director of Public Safety ... Mr. Dean TONDIGLIA
12 Dean Trumbull Campus ... Dr. Lance GRAHN
96 Director of Procurement ... Mr. Timothy J. KONCZAL
49 Dean Arts & Sciences ... Dr. James BLANK
50 Dean of Business Administration ... Dr. Deborah F. SPAKE
53 Interim Dean EHHS ... Dr. James HANNON
57 Dean of the Arts ... Dr. John R. CRAWFORD-SPINELLI
66 Dean College of Nursing ... Dr. Barbara BROOME
51 Interim Asst VP Cont & Dist Educ ... Ms. Valerie I. KELLY
92 Dean Honors College ... Dr. Alison SMITH
08 Dean of University Libraries ... Mr. Kenneth BURHANNA
48 Dean Architecture/Environ Design ... Mr. Mark MISTUR
60 Dean Col of Comm & Information ... Dr. Amy REYNOLDS
54 Dean Aeronautics & Engineering ... Dr. Christina BLOEBAUM
88 Dean College of Podiatric Medicine ... Dr. Allan BOIKE
20 Sr Assoc Dean-CPM ... Dr. Vincent J. HETHERINGTON
21 Director Business Admin Svcs ... Mr. Mark M. MATEJCIK
08 Library Director-CPM ... Mrs. Donna M. PERZESKI
18 Dir Opers Satellite Facilities CPM ... Mr. Dan RIDGWAY
04 Admin Assistant to the President ... Ms. Diana BOLDON
101 Secretary of the Institution/Board ... Ms. Charlene NICHOL
86 Director Government Relations ... Mr. Nicholas GATTOZZI

Kent State University at Ashtabula (K)

3300 Lake Road W, Ashtabula OH 44004-2299
Telephone: (440) 964-3322 FICE Identification: 003052
Accreditation: &NH, ADNUR, COARC, OTA, PTAA, RAD

† Regional accreditation is carried under the parent institution in Kent, OH.

Kent State University East Liverpool Campus (L)

400 E Fourth Street, East Liverpool OH 43920-3497
Telephone: (330) 385-3805 FICE Identification: 003056
Accreditation: &NH, ADNUR, OTA, PTAA

† Regional accreditation is carried under the parent institution in Kent, OH.

Kent State University Geauga Campus (M)

14111 Claridon-Troy Road,
Burton Township OH 44021-9500
Telephone: (440) 834-4187 FICE Identification: 003059
Accreditation: &NH, ADNUR

† Regional accreditation is carried under the parent institution in Kent, OH.

Kent State University Salem Campus (A)

2491 State Route 45 South, Salem OH 44460-9412
Telephone: (330) 332-0361 FICE Identification: 003061
Accreditation: &NH, RAD, RTT

† Regional accreditation is carried under the parent institution in Kent, OH.

Kent State University Stark Campus (B)

6000 Frank Avenue NW, North Canton OH 44720-9988
Telephone: (330) 499-9600 FICE Identification: 003054
Accreditation: &NH

† Regional accreditation is carried under the parent institution in Kent, OH.

Kent State University Trumbull Campus (C)

4314 Mahoning Avenue, NW, Warren OH 44483-1998
Telephone: (330) 847-0571 FICE Identification: 003064
Accreditation: &NH

† Regional accreditation is carried under the parent institution in Kent, OH.

Kent State University Tuscarawas Campus (D)

330 University Drive, NE,
New Philadelphia OH 44663-9403
Telephone: (330) 339-3391 FICE Identification: 003062
Accreditation: &NH, ADNUR

† Regional accreditation is carried under the parent institution in Kent, OH.

Kenyon College (E)

106 College-Park Street, Gambier OH 43022-9623
County: Knox FICE Identification: 003065
Unit ID: 203535
Telephone: (740) 427-5000 Carnegie Class: Bac-A&S
FAX Number: (740) 427-3077 Calendar System: Semester
URL: www.kenyon.edu
Established: 1824 Annual Undergrad Tuition & Fees: $55,930
Enrollment: 1,677 Coed
Affiliation or Control: Independent Non-Profit IRS Status: 501(c)3
Highest Offering: Baccalaureate
Accreditation: NH

01 President .... Dr. Sean DECATUR
05 Provost .... Dr. Joe L. KLESNER
111 Vice President Advancement .... Ms. Colleen GARLAND
10 Vice President for Finance .... Mr. Todd E. BURSON
08 Vice Pres Library & Info Svcs .... Mr. Ronald K. GRIGGS
100 Chief of Staff .... Ms. Susan MORSE
21 Assoc Vice President for Finance .... Vacant
112 Assoc VP for Planned Giving .... Mr. Kyle W. HENDERSON
32 Dean of Students .... Ms. Robin HART RUTHENBECK
07 Dean of Admissions/Fin Aid .... Ms. Diane ANCI
20 Associate Provost .... Dr. Sheryl HEMKIN
20 Associate Provost .... Dr. Jeff BOWMAN
06 Registrar/Dean Academic Support .... Ms. Ellen K. HARBOURT
26 Vice President for Communications .... Ms. Janet MARSDEN
29 Dir Alumni/Parent Rels .... Mr. Scott R. BAKER
37 Director of Financial Aid .... Mr. Craig SLAUGHTER
38 Director of Counseling Services .... Mr. Christopher SMITH
15 Director of Human Resources .... Ms. Jennifer G. CABRAL
42 Director of Religious/Spiritual .... Rabbi Marc BRAGIN
21 Chief Business Officer .... Mr. Mark KOHLMAN
22 Civil Rights/Title IX Coordinator .... Ms. Samantha HUGHES
19 Director of Campus Safety .... Mr. Robert D. HOOPER
09 Director of Institutional Research .... Ms. Erika M. FARFAN
21 Manager of Business Services .... Mr. Frederick S. LINGER
28 Director of Multicultural Affairs .... Mr. A. Chris KENNERLY
101 Director of Board Relations .... Ms. Kathryn LAKE
04 Executive Asst to President .... Ms. Mary Ellen O'MEARA
41 Athletic Director .... Ms. Jill MCCARTNEY

Kettering College (F)

3737 Southern Boulevard, Kettering OH 45429-1299
County: Montgomery FICE Identification: 007035
Unit ID: 203544
Telephone: (937) 395-8601 Carnegie Class: Spec-4-yr-Other Health
FAX Number: (937) 395-8106 Calendar System: Semester
URL: www.kc.edu
Established: 1967 Annual Undergrad Tuition & Fees: $12,960
Enrollment: 824 Coed
Affiliation or Control: Seventh-day Adventist IRS Status: 501(c)3
Highest Offering: Doctorate
Accreditation: NH, ARCPA, COARC, DMS, NUR, OT, PAST, RAD

00 Chairman of the Board .... Mr. Walter SACKETT
01 President .... Dr. Nate BRANDSTATER
15 Vice President Human Resources .... Mr. Timothy DUTTON
05 Dean for Academic Affairs .... Dr. Rafael CANIZALES
32 Dean of Student Success .... Mr. Adam BROWN
102 President of Foundation .... Mr. Rick THIE, II
84 Assoc Dean Enrollment Mgmt .... Mrs. Jessica BEANS
10 Chief Business Officer .... Mr. Brent DAVIS
21 Director of Finance/Administration .... Mr. Nicholas HENSON
06 Registrar .... Mrs. Robin VANDERBILT
37 Director Student Financial Aid .... Mrs. Kim RAWLINS
40 Manager Bookstore .... Mrs. Jessica OLDFIELD
42 Chaplain Director Campus Ministry .... Mr. Steve CARLSON
32 Director Student Life .... Mr. Kris HARTER
26 Public Relations Officer .... Ms. Lauren BROOKS
08 Director of Library .... Ms. Pamela STEVENS
07 Director of Admissions .... Mrs. Katrina HILL
29 Director Alumni Relations .... Mr. Ben HOTELLING
13 Senior Information Officer .... Mr. Jim NESBIT

Lake Erie College (G)

391 W Washington Street, Painesville OH 44077-3389
County: Lake FICE Identification: 003066
Unit ID: 203580
Telephone: (440) 375-7000 Carnegie Class: Masters/M
FAX Number: (440) 375-7005 Calendar System: Semester
URL: www.lec.edu
Established: 1856 Annual Undergrad Tuition & Fees: $31,422
Enrollment: 1,177 Coed
Affiliation or Control: Independent Non-Profit IRS Status: 501(c)3
Highest Offering: Master's
Accreditation: NH, ARCPA, CAEPT, IACBE

01 President .... Dr. Brian POSLER
05 Vice Pres for Academic Affairs/CAO .... Bryan DEPOY
10 Vice Pres Administration & Finance .... Brian DIRK
30 VP for Institutional Advancement .... Tony FULGENZIO
32 VP Student Affairs .... Billie DUNN
07 VP Admission .... Mike BROWN
53 Dean School of Educ & Prof Studies .... Dr. Katharine DELAVAN
50 Dean School of Business .... Dr. Jennifer KINNAIRD
88 Dean School of Equine Studies .... Dr. Pam HESS
79 Dean School of Arts/Human & SS .... Dr. Jennifer SWARTZ-LEVINE
81 Dean School of Nat Sci & Math .... Dr. Jonathan TEDESCO
06 Registrar .... Barbara HELMS
107 Director Prof Development .... Lisa STRAUSBAUGH
88 Director Physician Assistant Pgm .... Sean KRAMER
36 Dir Career Dev/Experiential Lrng .... Eric EVANS
13 Director of Information Technology .... Brad LUHTA
38 Director Student Success Center .... Dr. John SPIESMAN
15 Director Human Resources .... Andrea MYERS
18 Director Physical Plant .... Herb DILL
29 Director Alumni Relations .... Debra REMINGTON
41 Director Athletics .... Kelly KISH
08 Director Lincoln Library .... Jeanna PURSES
19 Director Security .... Richard KLINE
40 Bookstore Manager .... Natalie SCALA
04 Executive Asst to President & BOD .... Julie HERBERT
31 Director College Events .... Leah JACKSON
44 Director of Development .... Pamela PALERMO
37 Director Student Financial Aid .... Tricia PANGONIS
26 Exec Dir Public Relations/Marketing .... Michelle ROWLEY

Lakeland Community College (H)

7700 Clocktower Drive, Kirtland OH 44094-5198
County: Lake FICE Identification: 006804
Unit ID: 203599
Telephone: (440) 525-7000 Carnegie Class: Assoc/HT-High Non
FAX Number: (440) 525-7651 Calendar System: Semester
URL: www.lakelandcc.edu
Established: 1967 Annual Undergrad Tuition & Fees (In-District): $3,863
Enrollment: 7,581 Coed
Affiliation or Control: State/Local IRS Status: 501(c)3
Highest Offering: Associate Degree
Accreditation: NH, ADNUR, CAHIIM, COARC, DH, EMT, HT, IFSAC, MAC, MLTAD, RAD, SURGT

01 President .... Dr. Morris W. BEVERAGE, JR.
05 Exec VP & Provost .... Dr. Laura BARNARD
10 Exec Vice Pres/Treasurer .... Mr. Michael E. MAYHER
100 Chief of Staff/Sr VP Inst Effectiv .... Ms. Catherine BUSH
26 Chief Commun Ofcr/VP College Rels .... Ms. Dawn M. PLANTE
20 Assoc Provost Teach & Learn .... Dr. Deborah L. HARDY
84 Assoc Provost for Enrollment Mgmt .... Vacant
32 Assoc VP Student Dev/Dean of Stdnts .... Mr. Richard J. NOVOTNY
81 Dean of Arts and Sciences .... Mr. Adam CLOUTIER
76 Dean of Health Technologies .... Dr. Deborah L. HARDY
88 Interim Dean of Applied Studies .... Dr. Laura BARNARD
21 VP/Chief Fiscal Officer .... Ms. Andrea AUSPERK
13 CIO Administrative Technologies .... Mr. Rick PENNY
21 Controller .... Mr. Michael GRAFF
15 Director Human Resources .... Ms. Cathy BUSH
18 Director for Facilities Management .... Mr. Bert DIEHL
19 Chief of Police/Director of Safety .... Mr. Ronald MORENZ
07 Director for Admissions/Registrar .... Ms. Tracey L. COOPER
37 Dir Financial Aid/Enroll Support .... Ms. Melissa A. AMSPAUGH
35 Director of Student Activities .... Mr. Mario PETITTI
30 Dir Development/Alumni Relations .... Mr. Gregory SANDERS
96 Director of Purchasing .... Mr. Tom A. KIRCHNER
09 Dir Institutional Research .... Mr. Joshua TERCHEK
43 General Legal Counsel .... Mr. Michael FISHER
86 Director Government Relations .... Ms. Amy SABATH

Lakewood College (I)

2231 North Taylor Road, Cleveland Heights OH 44112
County: Cuyahoga Identification: 666715
Telephone: (800) 517-0857 Carnegie Class: Not Classified
FAX Number: (216) 803-9899 Calendar System: Other
URL: www.lakewoodcollege.edu
Established: 1998 Annual Undergrad Tuition & Fees: N/A
Enrollment: N/A Coed
Affiliation or Control: Independent Non-Profit IRS Status: 501(c)3
Highest Offering: Associate Degree
Accreditation: DEAC

01 CEO and Founder .... Ms. Tanya HAGGINS
05 Academic Dean .... Mr. James GEPPERTH
30 Vice President of Business Develop .... Mr. Isaac HAGGINS
11 Vice President of Operations .... Mr. Anthony NATHAL

Lorain County Community College (J)

1005 N Abbe Road, Elyria OH 44035-1691
County: Lorain FICE Identification: 003068
Unit ID: 203748
Telephone: (440) 365-5222 Carnegie Class: Assoc/HT-Mix Trad/Non
FAX Number: (440) 365-6519 Calendar System: Semester
URL: www.lorainccc.edu
Established: 1963 Annual Undergrad Tuition & Fees (In-District): $3,485
Enrollment: 11,042 Coed
Affiliation or Control: State/Local IRS Status: 501(c)3
Highest Offering: Baccalaureate
Accreditation: NH, ADNUR, ART, DH, DMS, EMT, MAC, MLTAD, OTA, PNUR, PTAA, RAD, SURGT

01 President .... Dr. Marcia J. BALLINGER
46 VP Strategic & Institutional Devel .... Ms. Tracy A. GREEN
05 Provost/VP Acad & Learner Svcs .... Dr. Jonathan N. DRYDEN
10 Vice President Admin Svcs/Treasurer .... Mr. Jonathan VOLPE
88 Assoc Prov University Partnership .... Dr. John R. CROOKS
08 Dean Library/Instruction Media .... Ms. Karla ALEMAN
84 Assoc Prov Enroll/Fin Career Svcs .... Ms. Marissa VERNON WHITE
13 Chief Information Tech Officer .... Mr. Donald HUFFMAN
15 Director Human Resources .... Mr. Keith BROWN
88 Dir Talent and Business Innovation .... Ms. Terri B. SANDU
18 Director of Physical Plant .... Mr. Leo MAHONEY
57 Dir Stocker Humanit/Fine Arts Ctr .... Ms. Janet HERMAN-BARLOW
54 Dean Engr/Business & Info Tech .... Ms. Kelly ZELESNIK
76 Int Dean Allied Health & Wellness .... Dr. Hope MOON
79 Int Dean Arts/Humanities .... Dr. Karin HOOKS
81 Dean Science/Mathematics .... Mr. Aaron WEISS
83 Int Dean Social Science/Human Svc .... Dr. Steven HUBBARD
06 Registrar .... Ms. Sun Kyong JAMERSON
101 Executive Assoc Board Liaison .... Ms. Jocelyn WIESER
19 Director of Campus Security .... Mr. Ken COLLINS
26 Dir School & Community Partnership .... Ms. Cynthia KUSHNER
102 LCC Foundation Exec Director .... Ms. Lisa BROWN
31 Director Strategic Cmty Engagement .... Ms. Alison MUSSER

Lourdes University (K)

6832 Convent Boulevard, Sylvania OH 43560-2898
County: Lucas FICE Identification: 003069
Unit ID: 203757
Telephone: (419) 885-3211 Carnegie Class: Masters/S
FAX Number: (419) 882-3987 Calendar System: Semester
URL: www.lourdes.edu
Established: 1958 Annual Undergrad Tuition & Fees: $22,480
Enrollment: 1,352 Coed
Affiliation or Control: Roman Catholic IRS Status: 501(c)3
Highest Offering: Doctorate
Accreditation: NH, ANEST, CAEPT, IACBE, NURSE, SW

01 President .... Dr. Mary Ann GAWELEK
00 President Emerita .... Sr. Ann Francis KLIMKOWSKI
05 Vice President of Academic Affairs .... Dr. Terry KELLER
10 Vice Pres Finance & Administration .... Mr. Jeffrey WILLIAMS
42 Vice Pres for Mission & Ministry .... Sr. Ann Carmen BARONE, OSF
111 Vice President for Inst Advancement .... Ms. Vicki STOUFFER
49 Dean College of Arts & Sciences .... Dr. Kate BEUTEL
53 Dean College of Social Services .... Dr. Joyce LITTEN
66 Dean College of Nursing .... Vacant
50 Dean Col Business & Leadership .... Dr. David BURKITT
32 VP Student Affairs/Dean of Students .... Mr. Greg KNESER
39 Asst Dean of Residence Life .... Mr. T. Todd MASMAN
37 Director of Financial Aid .... Mr. Todd CHIARELOTT
26 Director of University Relations .... Ms. Helene SHEETS
08 Director of Library Services .... Sr. Sandra RUTKOWSKI
06 Registrar .... Ms. Brianna LIEVENS PILBEAM
13 Chief Information Officer .... Vacant
15 Director of Human Resources .... Ms. Beverly SANDERS
36 Director of Career Counseling .... Ms. Andrea DOMACHOWSKI
21 Asst Vice Pres for Finance .... Ms. Kimberly MCGILL
30 Director of Donor Relations .... Ms. Brittany TELANDER
18 Director of Facilities & Grounds .... Mr. Michael CRAVENS
19 Title IX Coord & Dir Public Safety .... Ms. Michelle MCDEVITT
07 Associate Director of Admissions .... Ms. Erin GIBSON
123 Director of Graduate Admissions .... Ms. Tara HANNA
88 Dir Campus Ministry/Svc Learning .... Sr. Barbara VANO, OSF
40 Manager of Bookstore .... Ms. Ann MORRIS
121 Director of Student Success .... Ms. Alisa SMITH

Malone University (L)

2600 Cleveland Avenue NW, Canton OH 44709-3308
County: Stark FICE Identification: 003072
Unit ID: 203775
Telephone: (330) 471-8100 Carnegie Class: Masters/M
FAX Number: (330) 471-8478 Calendar System: Semester
URL: www.malone.edu
Established: 1892 Annual Undergrad Tuition & Fees: $30,860
Enrollment: 1,705 Coed
Affiliation or Control: Friends IRS Status: 501(c)3
Highest Offering: Master's
Accreditation: NH, ACBSP, CACREP, CAEP, MUS, NURSE, SW

01 President ... Dr. David A. KING
10 Vice Pres for Finance/CFO ... Mrs. Katie A. ROBBINS
05 Interim Provost ... Dr. Gregory J. MILLER
32 Chief Student Development Officer ... Ms. Melody K. SCOTT
111 Vice Pres for Advancement ... Mrs. Barbara A. BEUSCHER
26 Vice Pres for Marketing & Comm ... Mr. Timothy A. BRYAN
84 Vice Pres for Enrollment Management ... Mr. S. Mark SEYMOUR
66 Dean Sch of Nursing & Health Sci ... Dr. Debra A. LEE
21 Controller ... Vacant
06 Registrar ... Mr. Gary L. PHELPS
07 Director of Admissions ... Mrs. Linda A. KURTZ HOFFMAN
29 Int Dir of Alumni/Parent Relations ... Ms. Megan J. MAUCK
110 Dir of Adv Rsrch/Foundation Grants ... Mrs. Paula M. CALHOUN
108 Director of Assessment ... Dr. Matthew P. PHELPS
37 Director of Financial Aid ... Mrs. Pamela S. PUSTAY
41 Athletic Director ... Mr. Charles R. GRIMES
08 Director of Library ... Ms. Rebecca L. FORT
106 Dir Online Education/E-learning ... Mr. John W. KOSHMIDER, III
93 Director of Multicultural Services ... Mrs. Brenda D. STEVENS
104 Dir Ctr Cross-Cultural Engagement ... Dr. John (Jack) P. HARRIS, II
19 Director Security/Safety ... Mr. David W. BURNIP
13 Chief Information Officer ... Mr. M. Adam KLEMANN
90 Senior Network Engineer ... Mr. James M. SHAFFER
42 Director of Spiritual Formation ... Rev Dr. Linda J. LEON
105 Content Mgr for Publications/Web ... Vacant
40 Bookstore Manager ... Mrs. Kathy L. SECREST
04 Exec Asst to Pres/Asst to Board ... Mrs. Teresa L. PITTINGER
88 Assistant to the Provost ... Ms. Karen R. WARNER
92 Director of Honors Program ... Dr. Steven M. JENSEN
89 Dir of the College Experience Pgm ... Dr. Marcia K. EVERETT
38 Director of Counseling Center ... Mr. Timothy T. MORBER
23 Health Center Director ... Ms. Rebecca K. RODAK

Marietta College (A)

215 Fifth Street, Marietta OH 45750-4033
County: Washington FICE Identification: 003073
Unit ID: 203845
Telephone: (740) 376-4000 Carnegie Class: Bac-Diverse
FAX Number: (800) 331-7896 Calendar System: Semester
URL: www.marietta.edu
Established: 1835 Annual Undergrad Tuition & Fees: $36,040
Enrollment: 1,145 Coed
Affiliation or Control: Independent Non-Profit IRS Status: 501(c)3
Highest Offering: Master's
Accreditation: NH, ARCPA, CAATE, CAEP, MUS

01 President ... Dr. William N. RUUD
05 Provost/Dean of Faculty ... Dr. Janet L. BLAND
10 VP for Administration & Finance ... Ms. Michele L. MARRA
111 Interim VP for Advancement ... Ms. Jenni CUSHMAN
32 VP Student Life/Chf Diversity Ofcr ... Dr. Richard K. DANFORD
84 VP for Enrollment Mgmt ... Mr. Scot SCHAEFER
88 Dean McDonough Ctr for Leadership ... Dr. Gamaliel (Gama) PERRUCI
101 Secretary to the Board of Trustees ... Dr. Mark MILLER
08 Director of Library ... Dr. N. Douglas ANDERSON
07 Assistant VP for Enrollment Mgmt ... Ms. Kelli BARNETTE
18 Director of Physical Plant ... Mr. Fred R. SMITH
06 Registrar ... Ms. Tina K. PERDUE
15 Director of Human Resources ... Ms. Debra C. WAYLAND
19 Chief of Campus Police ... Mr. James S. WEAVER
26 Exec Dir of Strategic Comm & Mktg ... Mr. Thomas D. PERRY
09 Institutional Researcher ... Mr. William (Bill) CLARK
36 Career Center Director ... Vacant
41 Director of Athletics ... Mr. Larry R. HISER
13 Director of Information Technology ... Mr. Aaron COWDERY
63 PA Program Director ... Ms. Miranda COLLINS
104 Director of Education Abroad ... Ms. Christy BURKE
25 Grants Officer ... Ms. Chantal CENTOFANTI-FIELDS
51 Continuing Education ... Ms. Tina K. HICKMAN
35 Associate Dean of Students ... Ms. Nkenge FRIDAY
04 Executive Coordinator to President ... Ms. Paula LEWIS
29 Director Alumni Relations ... Ms. Dawn WERRY
28 Director of Diversity and Inclusion ... Dr. Nkenge FRIDAY
30 Director of Development ... Mr. Tom PERRY
37 Assistant VP for Student Enrollment ... Ms. Emily SCHUCK
44 Senior Director Annual Giving ... Ms. Kathryn GLOOR

Marion Technical College (B)

1467 Mount Vernon Avenue, Marion OH 43302-5694
County: Marion FICE Identification: 010736
Unit ID: 203881
Telephone: (740) 389-4636 Carnegie Class: Assoc/HVT-High Non
FAX Number: (740) 389-6136 Calendar System: Semester
URL: www.mtc.edu
Established: 1971 Annual Undergrad Tuition & Fees (In-State): $4,902
Enrollment: 2,524 Coed
Affiliation or Control: State IRS Status: 501(c)3
Highest Offering: Associate Degree
Accreditation: NH, ADNUR, CAHIIM, DMS, MAC, MLTAD, OTA, PTAA, RAD

01 President ... Dr. Ryan MCCALL
05 VP Academic Affairs & Student Svcs . Dr. Richard PRYSTOWSKY
111 Vice Pres Planning & Advancement ... Dr. Amy ADAMS
10 Interim Chief Financial Officer ... Mr. Jim NARGANG
45 Chief Strategy Officer ... Dr. Bob HAAS
15 Director Human Resources ... Ms. Brenda FEASEL
13 Executive Director IT Operations ... Mr. Steve DUVALL
26 Director of Marketing ... Mr. Justin DEAN
06 Registrar ... Ms. Kristy TAYLOR
37 Director Student Financial Aid ... Ms. Deb LANGDON
07 Director of Admissions ... Mr. Tony BOX
102 Director of Foundation ... Mr. Mike STUCKEY
121 Director of Student Advising ... Ms. Laura EMERICK
103 Director Ctr Workforce Development ... Ms. Tami GALLOWAY
88 Director College Credit Plus Pgm ... Ms. Tiffany WADE
88 Director Student Support Programs ... Ms. Kathy RICE
49 Dean of Arts and Sciences ... Ms. Jamilah TUCKER
72 Dean Tech & Professional Programs ... Ms. Debbie STARK
54 Director of Engineering Technology ... Ms. Eve FABRIZIO
66 Director of Nursing Technology ... Ms. Cynthia HARTMAN
88 Dir Physical Therapist Asst Pgm ... Mr. Chad HENSEL
88 Dir Occupational Therapy ... Mr. Josh LINE
04 Executive Assistant ... Ms. Laura WOUGHTER
18 Coord Facil Improvements/Operations ... Ms. Leeann GRAU

Mercy College of Ohio (C)

2221 Madison Avenue, Toledo OH 43604
County: Lucas FICE Identification: 030970
Unit ID: 203960
Telephone: (419) 251-1313 Carnegie Class: Spec-4-yr-Other Health
FAX Number: N/A Calendar System: Semester
URL: www.mercycollege.edu
Established: 1992 Annual Undergrad Tuition & Fees: $15,240
Enrollment: 1,416 Coed
Affiliation or Control: Roman Catholic IRS Status: 501(c)3
Highest Offering: Master's
Accreditation: NH, ADNUR, CAHIIM, EMT, NURSE, POLYT, RAD

01 President ... Dr. Susan WAJERT
05 VP Acad Affs/Dean of Faculty ... Dr. Trevor BATES
32 VP Student Affs/Dean of Student ... Mr. Marc ADKINS
66 Dean Nursing and Allied Hlth ... Dr. Elizabeth SPRUNK
76 Dean of Arts and Sciences ... Dr. Barbara STOOS
58 Dean of Graduate Studies ... Dr. Kim WATSON
117 Dir of Compliance/Risk Mgmt ... Ms. Leslie ERWIN
13 Dir of College Info Tech Services ... Mr. David BURGIN
10 Chief Financial Officer ... Ms. Andrea FLEMING
111 Int Director College Advancement ... Ms. Sandy SNYDER
84 VP of Strategic Plng & Enroll Mgmt ... Ms. Lori EDGEWORTH
08 Director Library/Resource Services ... Ms. Deborah JOHNSON
09 Dir Inst Research/Registrar ... Mr. Mark MCKELLIP
37 Financial Aid Director ... Ms. Julie LESLIE
26 Director of Communication ... Ms. Denise HUDGIN
42 Dir Campus Ministry & Svcs Learning ... Ms. Annie DEVINE
21 Business Manager ... Ms. Diane RAHN
18 Manager of Operations ... Ms. Sherri BOGGS
29 Director Alumni Relations ... Vacant
121 Assistant Dean of Student Success ... Ms. Lisa SANCRANT
36 Dir of Career/Prof Dev & Retention ... Ms. Kristen PORTER
106 Dir of Distance Education ... Dr. Dan FRENCH
28 Dir of Diversity & Inclusion ... Mr. Christopher MITCHELL
04 Administrative Asst to President ... Ms. Andrea RAFTERY
07 Director of Admissions ... Ms. Amy MERGEN

Methodist Theological School in Ohio (D)

3081 Columbus Pike, Delaware OH 43015-3211
County: Delaware FICE Identification: 003075
Unit ID: 203997
Telephone: (740) 363-1146 Carnegie Class: Spec-4-yr-Faith
FAX Number: (740) 362-3135 Calendar System: 4/1/4
URL: www.mtso.edu
Established: 1958 Annual Graduate Tuition & Fees: N/A
Enrollment: 138 Coed
Affiliation or Control: United Methodist IRS Status: 501(c)3
Highest Offering: Doctorate; No Undergraduates
Accreditation: NH, THEOL

01 President ... Rev. Jay A. RUNDELL
05 Dean and VP for Academic Affairs ... Dr. Valerie BRIDGEMAN
20 Associate Dean ... Dr. Yvonne ZIMMERMAN
04 Executive Asst to the President ... Ms. Leigh PRECISE
10 Controller ... Ms. Sarah MOUCH
26 Director of Communications ... Mr. Danny RUSSELL
84 Director of Enrollment Management ... Rev. Benjamin HALL
30 Director of Development ... Rev. Claudine LEARY
08 Director of the Library ... Mr. Paul BURNAM
06 Registrar ... Mr. Lee RICHARDS
37 Director of Financial Aid ... Ms. Molly HOFFMAN
32 Director of Student Services ... Ms. Kristin LOFRUMENTO
13 Director Information Technology ... Mr. Matthew REHM
18 Facilities Manager ... Mr. Keith HUFFMAN
15 Coordinator of Human Resources ... Ms. Erin WIGGINS

Miami University (E)

501 E High Street, Oxford OH 45056-1846
County: Butler FICE Identification: 003077
Unit ID: 204024
Telephone: (513) 529-1809 Carnegie Class: DU-Higher
FAX Number: (513) 529-3841 Calendar System: Semester
URL: www.miamioh.edu
Established: 1809 Annual Undergrad Tuition & Fees (In-State): $15,380
Enrollment: 19,700 Coed
Affiliation or Control: State IRS Status: 501(c)3
Highest Offering: Doctorate
Accreditation: NH, ART, CAATE, CAEP, CIDA, CLPSY, DIETD, @DIETI, IPSY, MUS, NURSE, SP, SW, THEA

01 President ... Dr. Gregory CRAWFORD
05 Provost/Exec Vice President ... Dr. Phyllis CALLAHAN
10 Sr VP Finance & Bus Svcs/Treasurer ... Dr. David CREAMER
32 Vice President Student Affairs ... Dr. Jayne E. BROWNELL
111 VP University Advancement ... Mr. Tom HERBERT
13 VP Information Technology/CIO ... Mr. David SEIDL
15 Asst Prov Acad Personnel ... Ms. Ruth GROOM
20 Assoc Provost for Undergrad Studies ... Dr. Carolyn A. HAYNES
35 Dean of Students ... Dr. Kimberly MOORE
26 Assoc VP Comm/Marketing ... Ms. Michele G. SPARKS
18 Assoc VP Facilities Planning & Op ... Mr. Cody J. POWELL
84 Sr VP Enroll Mgmt & Student Success ... Mr. Michael S. KABBAZ
28 VP Inst Diversity ... Dr. Ronald B. SCOTT
09 Asst VP Institutional Research ... Dr. William E. KNIGHT
29 Assoc Vice Pres Alumni Relations ... Mrs. Kim TAVARES
88 Director Institutional Relations ... Mr. Randi Malcolm THOMAS
27 Dir Univ Communications ... Ms. Claire M. WAGNER
100 Secy Board/Exec Asst to President ... Mr. Ted O. PICKERILL
49 Dean College Arts & Science ... Dr. Christopher A. MAKAROFF, JR.
53 Dean Education/Health & Society ... Dr. Michael DANTLEY
50 Dean Farmer Sch of Business ... Dr. Marc A. RUBIN
57 Dean College of Creative Arts ... Dr. Elizabeth R. MULLENIX
54 Dean College of Engr & Computing ... Dr. Marek DOLLAR
08 Dean University Libraries ... Mr. Jerome CONLEY
58 Dean Graduate School ... Dr. James T. ORIS
49 Dean Col of Lib Arts & Applied Sci ... Dr. Catherine U. BISHOP-CLARK
07 Assoc VP Strat Enroll Mgt/Mrkting ... Ms. Susan SCHAURER
51 Asst Provost Global Init & Cont Ed ... Ms. Cheryl D. YOUNG
108 Univ Dir Ctr for Teaching Excellenc ... Dr. Ellen J. YEZIERSKI
88 Univ Dir Liberal Educ/ Assessment ... Dr. Shelly JARRETT BROMBERG
92 Univ Dir Honors & Scholars Program ... Dr. Zeb BAKER
16 Assoc VP Human Resources ... Ms. Dawn FAHNER
23 Medical Director Student Health Svc ... Vacant
104 Dir Intl Student & Scholar ... Ms. Molly HEIDEMANN
06 University Registrar ... Ms. Mandy L. EUEN
36 Asst VP Career Exploration/Success ... Ms. Jen FRANCHAK
38 Director Student Counseling Service ... Dr. John A. WARD
19 Chief of Police/Dir Public Safety ... Mr. John MCCANDLESS
96 Chief Procurement Officer ... Mr. Mark TAYLOR
43 University General Counsel ... Ms. Robin L. PARKER
22 Director Equity & Equal Opportunity ... Ms. Kenya D. ASH
41 Director Intercollegiate Athletics ... Mr. David A. SAYLER
17 Director Student Wellness ... Ms. Rebecca BAUDRY YOUNG
04 Assistant to the President ... Ms. Dawn TSIRELIS
37 Assoc VP Student Enroll Svcs ... Mr. Brent L. SHOCK
102 Asst Dir Corporate/Foundation Rels ... Mr. Ryan GILLEY
109 Assoc VP Auxiliaries ... Vacant
44 Asst VP Dev Ind/Annual Giving ... Ms. Emily BERRY
114 Assoc VP Budgeting & Analysis ... Dr. David A. ELLIS
105 Univ Web Content Manager ... Ms. Jeri MOORE
25 Dir Research & Sponsored Pgms ... Ms. Anne P. SCHAUER
39 Director of Residence Life ... Dr. Vicka BELL-ROBINSON

Miami University Hamilton Campus (F)

1601 University Boulevard, Hamilton OH 45011-3399
Telephone: (513) 785-3000 FICE Identification: 003079
Accreditation: &NH

† Regional accreditation is carried under the parent institution in Oxford, OH.

Miami University Middletown (G)

4200 N University Boulevard, Middletown OH 45042-3497
Telephone: (513) 727-3200 FICE Identification: 003080
Accreditation: &NH

† Regional accreditation is carried under the parent institution in Oxford, OH.

The Modern College of Design (H)

1725 E David Road, Dayton OH 45440-1612
County: Montgomery FICE Identification: 025530
Unit ID: 205391
Telephone: (877) 300-9866 Carnegie Class: Spec 2-yr-A&S
FAX Number: (937) 294-5869 Calendar System: Semester
URL: www.themoderncollegeofdesign.com
Established: 1983 Annual Undergrad Tuition & Fees: $28,278
Enrollment: 211 Coed
Affiliation or Control: Proprietary IRS Status: Proprietary
Highest Offering: Baccalaureate
Accreditation: ACCSC

01 Owner/President/Creative Director ... Ms. Jessica BARRY
05 Vice President of Education ... Mr. Matt FLICK
32 Vice President of Student Affairs ... Ms. Melissa FERGUSON
36 Director of Career Services ... Mr. Brian PETRO
37 Director of Financial Aid ... Ms. Tracy GARDNER
07 Director of Admissions ... Ms. Mariesa BREWSTER

Mount Carmel College of Nursing (I)

127 S Davis Avenue, Columbus OH 43222-1504
County: Franklin FICE Identification: 030719
Unit ID: 204176
Telephone: (614) 234-5800 Carnegie Class: Spec-4-yr-Other Health
FAX Number: (614) 234-2875 Calendar System: Semester
URL: www.mccn.edu
Established: 1990 Annual Undergrad Tuition & Fees: $13,907
Enrollment: 1,069 Coed

Affiliation or Control: Roman Catholic IRS Status: 501(c)3
Highest Offering: Doctorate
Accreditation: NH, NURSE

01 Interim President Dr. Ann Marie BROOKS
05 Academic Dean Dr. Kathleen WILLIAMSON
58 Interim Assoc Dean Graduate Pgms Dr. Jami NININGER
66 Assoc Dean Undergrad Pgms Dr. Scott DOLAN
106 Asst Dean Distance Education Dr. Jami NININGER
06 Director Records & Registration Ms. Karen GREENE
10 Director Business Affairs Ms. Kathy SMITH
07 Director Admissions Dr. Kim CAMPBELL
37 Director Financial Aid Dr. Todd EVERETT
32 Director Student Life Ms. Colleen CIPRIANI
29 Director Alumni Relations Ms. Debbie BOGGS
26 Dir Marketing & College Relations Ms. Robin HUTCHINSON-BELL
108 Dir Institutional Effectiveness Ms. Susannah TOWNSEND
30 Director of Development Ms. Alyssa FRY
28 Director Diversity & Inclusion Dr. Hannah CLAYBORNE
117 Director Compliance Mr. Robert VAUGHN
08 Regional Director Library Services Mr. Stevo ROKSANDIC
04 Executive Assistant to President Vacant
12 Director Lancaster Campus Ms. Cora ARLEDGE

Mount St. Joseph University (A)

5701 Delhi Road, Cincinnati OH 45233-1670
County: Hamilton FICE Identification: 003033
Unit ID: 204200
Telephone: (513) 244-4200 Carnegie Class: Masters/L
FAX Number: (513) 244-4654 Calendar System: Semester
URL: www.msj.edu
Established: 1920 Annual Undergrad Tuition & Fees: $30,100
Enrollment: 2,010 Coed
Affiliation or Control: Roman Catholic IRS Status: 501(c)3
Highest Offering: Doctorate
Accreditation: NH, #ARCPA, CAATE, CAEP, NURSE, PTA, SW

01 President Dr. H. James WILLIAMS
111 VP of Institutional Advancement Ms. Raye ALLEN
26 Interim VP of Univ Communications Mr. Gregg GREENE
05 Provost Dr. Diana DAVIS
10 Chief Financial Officer Mr. Jeffrey C. BRIGGS
43 VP Compliance Risk/General Counsel Ms. Paige L. ELLERMAN
20 Assoc Provost for Academic Support Ms. Heather CRABBE
20 Associate Provost Academic Affairs Dr. Christa CURRY
13 AVP Campus Technology Mr. Alex NAKONECHNYI
15 Director of Human Resources Ms. Lisa KOBMAN
32 Dean of Students Ms. Janet COX
06 Registrar Ms. Irene RICHARDSON
29 Exec Director of Alumni Engagement Mr. Kelby SILER
37 Director Student Admin Services Ms. Kathy KELLY
36 Director Career/Exper Educ Ms. Linda POHLGEERS
102 Director Corporate & Found Rels Ms. Linda B. LIEBAU
18 Director Buildings & Grounds Mr. Michael DITTMER
09 Director Institutional Research Ms. Whitney KESSINGER
07 Director of Admission Ms. Peggy MINNICH
21 Controller Ms. Kristi BENGEL
38 Director Wellness Center Ms. Patsy SCHWAIGER
08 Director Library Mr. Scott LLOYD
13 Director Instructional Technology Ms. Kim HUNTER
19 Director of Campus Police Mr. John KRAFT
41 Director of Athletics Mr. Steve RADCLIFFE
88 Director Learning Center Ms. Meghann LITTRELL
42 Director of Mission Integration Sr. Karen ELLIOTT, CPPS
30 Director of Development Ms. Michelle OLMSTED
40 Manager of Bookstore Vacant
76 Dean of Health Sciences Dr. Darla VALE
79 Dean of Arts & Humanities Dr. Michael SONTAG
50 Dean of Business Dr. Jamal RASHED
53 Dean of Education Dr. Laura SAYLOR
83 Dean Behavioral & Natural Sciences Dr. Gene KRITSKY
27 Director of Marketing Vacant
91 Director Administrative Computing Mr. Dan LUKAC
105 Webmaster Ms. Carolyn BOLAND
44 Dir Individual & Campaign Giving Mr. Joe CORNELY
23 Coordinator Health Services Ms. Amy DEMKO
39 Coordinator of Residence Life Mr. Jeff HURLEY
04 Admin Asst to the President Ms. Tina MERSMANN
28 Chief Diversity & Inclusion Officer Vacant
121 Director Academic Advising Ms. Mary E. MAZUK

Mount Vernon Nazarene University (B)

800 Martinsburg Road, Mount Vernon OH 43050-9500
County: Knox FICE Identification: 007085
Unit ID: 204194
Telephone: (740) 392-6868 Carnegie Class: Masters/M
FAX Number: (740) 397-2769 Calendar System: Semester
URL: www.mvnu.edu
Established: 1968 Annual Undergrad Tuition & Fees: $29,244
Enrollment: 2,222 Coed
Affiliation or Control: Church Of The Nazarene IRS Status: 501(c)3
Highest Offering: Master's
Accreditation: NH, ACBSP, CAEPN, MUS, NURSE, SW

01 President/CEO Dr. Henry W. SPAULDING, II
10 Vice Pres for Finance/CFO Mr. Scott L. CAMPBELL
05 Vice Pres for Academic Affairs/CAO Dr. B. Barnett COCHRAN
32 Vice President Student Life Rev. Tracy WAAL
42 Campus Pastor Rev. Stephanie LOBDELL
26 VP for University Relations Rev. James SMITH
58 VP for Graduate and Prof Studies Rev. Eric STETLER
21 Director of Business Services Mr. Steven JENKINS
84 Assoc VP Enroll Mgmt/Marketing Ms. Beth DALONZO
88 Director of Faculty Services GPS Mr. Kevin CHANEY
06 University Registrar Mr. Mel SEVERNS
15 Director of Human Resources Mr. Alan SHAFFER
38 Director Counseling and Wellness Dr. Eric BROWNING
13 Director of Information Tech Mr. John WALCHLE
29 Director of Alumni Relations Mr. Travis KELLER
40 Director of the Bookstore Mrs. Gina A. BLANCHARD
27 Coord Communications & Pub Rels Ms. Samantha SCOLES
53 Dir Teacher Education/Certification Dr. Sharon METCALFE
37 Dir of Student Fin Services Mr. Jared SPONSELLER
18 Director of Facilities Operations Mr. Tony EDWARDS
21 Controller Ms. Debra DEVORE
35 Director of Campus Life Ms. Rochel FURNISS
28 Director Intercultural Affairs Mr. James M. SINGLETARY
108 Director University Assessment Vacant
04 Assistant to President Mrs. Pamela K. SNOW
08 Director of the Library Mr. Timothy RADCLIFFE
105 Director Web Services Mr. Carlos SERRAO
106 Dir Online Education/E-learning Vacant
50 Dean of the School of Business Dr. Melanie TIMMERMAN
81 Dean School of Natural & Social Sci Dr. LeeAnn COUTS
09 Director of Institutional Research Dr. Randie L. TIMPE
07 Director of Admissions Mr. Robert STANLEY
104 Director Study Abroad Ms. Krissta HADSELL
41 Athletic Director Mr. Chip WILSON
54 Dept Chair Engineering Dr. Jose OOMMEN
30 Director of Development Mr. Justin NOWICKI
39 Dir Resident Life/Student Housing Mr. Joshua KUSCH

Muskingum University (C)

163 Stormont Street, New Concord OH 43762-1199
County: Muskingum FICE Identification: 003084
Unit ID: 204264
Telephone: (740) 826-8211 Carnegie Class: Masters/S
FAX Number: (740) 826-8404 Calendar System: Semester
URL: www.muskingum.edu
Established: 1837 Annual Undergrad Tuition & Fees: $28,266
Enrollment: 2,369 Coed
Affiliation or Control: Presbyterian Church (U.S.A.) IRS Status: 501(c)3
Highest Offering: Beyond Master's But Less Than Doctorate
Accreditation: NH, CAATE, CAEP, CAEPN, MUS, NURSE

01 President Dr. Susan SCHNEIDER HASSELER
05 Provost Dr. Nancy J. EVANGELISTA
10 VP Business/Finance & Treasurer Mr. Philip LAUBE
30 Vice Pres of Inst Advancement Mr. Shea MCGREW
84 Vice Pres of Enrollment/Marketing Mr. Steve SOBA
32 Assoc VP for Student Affairs Mr. Michael MALONE
08 Director of Library Dr. Nainsi HOUSTON
06 Registrar Mr. Daniel B. WILSON
36 Assistant Director Career Services Mrs. Jacquelyn L. VASCURA
13 Director of Computer Services Mr. Ryan D. HARVEY
26 Dir Communications/Media Relations Mr. Aaron MARTIN
29 Director Alumni Relations Ms. Jennifer L. BRONNER
07 Director of Admissions Mrs. Marcy RITZERT
19 Director of Public Safety Mr. Danny E. VINCENT
42 College Minister Rev. William E. MULLINS
18 Supt of Building & Grounds Mr. Kevin J. WAGNER
41 Director of Athletics Mr. Steve BROCKELBANK
21 Associate Business Officer Mr. Timothy CROSS
37 Director of Student Financial Aid Mrs. Amber GUMP
38 Director of Student Counseling Mrs. Tracy F. BUGGLIN
40 Manager of Bookstore Mrs. Amber RODLAND
15 Human Resources Manager Ms. Kathy J. MOORE

MyComputerCareer (D)

380 Polaris Pkwy Suite 110, Westerville OH 43082
County: Delaware FICE Identification: 041245
Telephone: (614) 891-3200 Carnegie Class: Not Classified
FAX Number: N/A Calendar System: Quarter
URL: mycomputercareer.edu
Established: 2007 Annual Undergrad Tuition & Fees: N/A
Enrollment: N/A Coed
Affiliation or Control: Proprietary IRS Status: Proprietary
Highest Offering: Associate Degree
Accreditation: CNCE

01 Campus Director Curtis HEMMELER
07 Admissions Director Michael BROWN
37 Financial Aid Director Jennifer PRICE
36 Career Services Director Tricia MOSHER

North Central State College (E)

2441 Kenwood Circle, Mansfield OH 44906
County: Richland FICE Identification: 005313
Unit ID: 204422
Telephone: (419) 755-4800 Carnegie Class: Assoc/HVT-High Non
FAX Number: (419) 755-4750 Calendar System: Semester
URL: www.ncstatecollege.edu
Established: 1961 Annual Undergrad Tuition & Fees (In-State): $3,998
Enrollment: 3,050 Coed
Affiliation or Control: State IRS Status: 501(c)3
Highest Offering: Associate Degree
Accreditation: NH, ACBSP, ADNUR, COARC, EMT, OTA, PTAA, RAD

01 President Dr. Dorey DIAB
04 Exec Assistant to the President Mr. Stephen R. WILLIAMS
05 Vice President Academic Services Dr. Karen A. REED
32 Vice President Student Svcs & IE Mr. Thomas PRENDERGAST
10 VP/CFO of Business Services Ms. Lori L. MCKEE
26 Exec Dir Marketing & Public Rels Mr. Keith STONER
07 Director of Admissions Mr. Thomas MANSPERGER
15 Director of Human Resources Mr. R. Douglas HANUSCIN
37 Director of Financial Aid Mr. James PHINNEY
08 Head Librarian Ms. Vanessa KRAPS
22 Coord Disability Services Mr. Doug HESTAND
49 Dean of Liberal Arts Ms. Deborah HYSELL
50 Dean of Business Ind & Technology Dr. Gregory TIMBERLAKE
76 Dean Health Sciences Dr. Kelly GRAY
66 Asst Dean Health Sci/Dir Nursing Ms. Melinda ROEPKE
13 Director of IT Mr. Major PRICE, JR.
06 Registrar Mr. Mark J. MONNES
18 Manager of Facilities Mr. Kevin KLINE
96 Purchasing Specialist Ms. Renee NUSSBAUM
102 Exec Dir College Foundation Ms. Christine COPPER
09 Exec Dir Inst Effectiveness Mr. Thomas M. PRENDERGAST
121 Dir of Student Success & Transition Ms. Monica DURHAM
88 Director of Title III Ms. Beverly WALKER
88 Phi Theta Kappa Advisor Ms. Barb KEENER
40 Campus Bookstore Manager Ms. Carla BUTDORFF
21 Controller Ms. Lori L. MCKEE
105 Web Master Vacant
35 Coordinator of Student Engagement Mr. Andy SOKOLICH
41 Athletics & Student Engagement Ms. Jennifer RACER
29 Coord of Alumni/Employer Relations Mr. Randy BLANKENSHIP
36 Career Development Counselor Ms. Paula WALDRUFF
108 Director Institutional Assessment Dr. Gina KAMWITHI
19 Director Security/Safety Sgt. Jeffrey HOFFER
28 Director of Diversity Ms. Cheryl CATES

The North Coast College (F)

11724 Detroit Avenue, Lakewood OH 44107-3002
County: Cuyahoga FICE Identification: 012896
Unit ID: 206394
Telephone: (216) 221-8584 Carnegie Class: Bac/Assoc-Assoc Dom
FAX Number: (216) 221-2311 Calendar System: Semester
URL: www.thencc.edu
Established: 1966 Annual Undergrad Tuition & Fees: $20,439
Enrollment: 133 Coed
Affiliation or Control: Proprietary IRS Status: Proprietary
Highest Offering: Baccalaureate
Accreditation: ACCSC

01 President Dr. Milan MILASINOVIC
05 Dean of Academic Affairs Mr. Patrick MELNICK
37 Financial Aid Administrator Ms. Martha SNODGRASS

Northeast Ohio Medical University (G)

4209 State Route 44, PO Box 95,
Rootstown OH 44272-0095
County: Portage FICE Identification: 024544
Unit ID: 204477
Telephone: (330) 325-2511 Carnegie Class: Spec-4-yr-Med
FAX Number: (330) 325-7943 Calendar System: Other
URL: www.neomed.edu
Established: 1973 Annual Graduate Tuition & Fees: N/A
Enrollment: 930 Coed
Affiliation or Control: State IRS Status: 501(c)3
Highest Offering: First Professional Degree; No Undergraduates
Accreditation: NH, MED, PH, PHAR

01 President Dr. Jay A. GERSHEN
100 Chief of Staff/Secretary to BOT Ms. Michelle M. MULHERN
26 VP Govt & External Affairs Mr. John J. STILLIANA
46 VP Research Dr. Steven P. SCHMIDT
05 VP Academic Affairs Dr. Richard J. KASMER
17 VP Health Affairs Dr. Elisabeth H. YOUNG
10 VP Administration/Finance Mr. John W. WRAY
111 VP Advancement Mr. Daniel S. BLAIN
63 Dean College of Medicine Dr. Elisabeth H. YOUNG
58 Dean College of Graduate Studies Dr. Steven P. SCHMIDT
67 Dean College of Pharmacy Dr. Richard J. KASMER
43 General Counsel Ms. Maria R. SCHIMER
04 Special Asst to the President Ms. Christine R. CURRY
32 Sr Exec Dir Acad Affs & Stdnt Svcs Dr. Sandra M. EMERICK
88 Sr Ex Dir Wasson Ctr & Interprof Ed Dr. Holly A. GERZINA
88 Exec Dir Research Ms. Rebecca L. HAYES
09 Exec Dir Institutional Research Dr. Margarita D. KOKINOVA
84 Sr Exec Dir Strategic Enroll Init Mr. James F. BARRETT
88 Dir Comparative Medicine Unit Dr. Stanley D. DANNEMILLER
29 Dir Alumni Rels & Annual Giving Mr. Craig S. EYNON
38 Dir Counseling Services Dr. Jennifer L. DOUGALL
13 Sr Ex Dir Information Technology Mr. Ronald L. MCGRADY
15 Dir Human Resources Ms. Charity DAVIS
18 Dir Campus Operations Mr. Dale A. HLUCH
24 Dir Academic Technology Services Mr. Michael G. WRIGHT
26 Chief Marketing Officer Mr. Roderick L. INGRAM, SR.
08 Dir Learning Center Mr. Craig R. THEISSEN
19 Dir Public Safety/Police Chief Ms. Kali A. MEONSKE
124 Dir Academic Services Dr. Terri E. ROBINSON
96 Asst Dir of Accounting Ms. Jacalyn E. KOVACH
40 Supervisor Bookstore Ms. Christine L. KOVACICH
06 Registrar Ms. Katherine M. MIRANDA
37 Dir Financial Aid Mr. Michael A. KEMPE
28 VP HR & Diversity Mr. Andre L. BURTON

Northwest State Community College (A)

22-600 State Route 34, Archbold OH 43502-9542
County: Henry FICE Identification: 008677
Unit ID: 204440
Telephone: (419) 267-5511 Carnegie Class: Assoc/HVT-High Non
FAX Number: (419) 267-3688 Calendar System: Semester
URL: www.northweststate.edu
Established: 1968 Annual Undergrad Tuition & Fees (In-State): $4,098
Enrollment: 3,620 Coed
Affiliation or Control: State IRS Status: 501(c)3
Highest Offering: Associate Degree
Accreditation: NH, ACBSP, ADNUR, MAC

01 President .... Dr. Michael L. THOMSON
05 VP for Academics .... Ms. Lori ROBISON
03 Executive Vice President .... Mr. Todd HERNANDEZ
86 Assoc VP for Strategic Initiatives .... Mr. James HOOPS
32 VP Inst Effective/Student Success .... Dr. Cindy KRUEGER
49 Dean of Arts & Sciences .... Ms. Lana SNIDER
66 Dean of Nursing & Allied Health .... Ms. Kathy KEISTER
06 Registrar .... Ms. Connie KLINGSHIRN
18 Director of Plant Operations .... Mr. Kevin GERKEN
15 VP Human Resources .... Ms. Kathryn MCKELVEY
21 Director of Accounting & Finance .... Ms. Lynn SPEISER
21 Director Accounting & Business Svcs .... Ms. Jennifer THOME
07 Director of Admissions .... Ms. Terri LAVIN
10 Chief Fiscal & Admin Officer .... Ms. Kathy SOARDS
102 Executive Director Foundation .... Ms. Robbin WILCOX
37 Director Student Financial Aid .... Ms. Amber YOCOM
36 Career & Activities Coordinator .... Mr. Michael JACOBS
26 Marketing & Communications Coord .... Mr. James BELLAMY
40 Bookstore Manager .... Mr. Kemp STAPLETON
08 Director Library .... Ms. Kristi ROTROFF
20 Associate VP for Academics .... Dr. Daniel BURKLO
121 Director of Advising .... Ms. Cassie RICKENBERG
103 Director Workforce Development .... Mr. James DREWES
13 Dir Network Systems/Tech Support .... Mr. Robert DUNCAN
14 Director Data Systems .... Mr. Terry KING
88 Director CTS/AMTC .... Mr. David CONOVER
04 Executive Assistant .... Ms. Megan BATT

Notre Dame College (B)

4545 College Road, South Euclid OH 44121-4293
County: Cuyahoga FICE Identification: 003085
Unit ID: 204468
Telephone: (216) 381-1680 Carnegie Class: Masters/S
FAX Number: (216) 381-3802 Calendar System: Semester
URL: www.notredamecollege.edu
Established: 1922 Annual Undergrad Tuition & Fees: $30,160
Enrollment: 1,901 Coed
Affiliation or Control: Roman Catholic IRS Status: 501(c)3
Highest Offering: Master's
Accreditation: NH, CAEP, CAEPN, NURSE

01 Interim President .... Mr. John GALOVIC
05 Vice Pres Academic/Student Affs .... Dr. Vincent PALOMBO
10 Vice Pres Finance and CFO .... Ms. Cheryl NOVISKI
111 Vice Pres College Advancement .... Ms. Shawna WHITLOCK
26 Vice Pres for Board/Community Rels .... Ms. Karen L. POELKING
09 Vice Pres Inst Effectiveness .... Dr. Deborah SHEREN
88 Chief Mission Officer .... Sr. Carol ZIEGLER, SND
20 Dean of Academic Programs .... Dr. Ronald E. MATTHEWS
66 Nursing Division Chair .... Dr. David FOLEY
53 Education Division Chair .... Dr. Sue CORBIN
81 Math & Science Division Chair .... Dr. Sharon BALCHAK
50 Business Division Chair .... Ms. Natalie STROUSE
79 Arts and Humanities Division Chair .... Mr. Kenneth PALKO
84 Vice Pres for Enrollment .... Ms. Beth FORD
07 Asst Dean for Enrollment .... Mr. David HILBORN
06 Registrar .... Ms. Tracy SABRANSKY
37 Director of Financial Aid .... Ms. Allison MCBRADY
113 Director of Student Accounts .... Ms. Annette SZALAY
19 Director of Security/Safety .... Mr. Joseph GRECOL
18 Director of Physical Plant .... Mr. Tom MEEKS
13 Director of Information Technology .... Mr. Michael KIEC
15 Director of Human Resources .... Ms. Susan ANDERSON
08 Director of Library .... Ms. Karen ZOLLER
42 Director of Campus Ministry .... Mr. Ted STEINER
36 Director of Career Services .... Mr. George PHILLIPS
38 Director of Counseling Center .... Mr. Jerry HAYES
32 Dean of Students .... Ms. Tera JOHNSON
39 Director of Residence Life .... Ms. Carrie PITCAIRN
29 Director Alumni Relations .... Mr. Nick FORMICA
04 Assistant to the President .... Sr. Donna PALUF, SND
27 Chief Communications Officer .... Mr. Brian JOHNSTON
106 Dean Adult/Online/Graduate Educ .... Dr. Florentine HOELKER
41 Athletic Director .... Mr. Scott SWAIN

Oberlin College (C)

173 West Lorain Street, Oberlin OH 44074-1057
County: Lorain FICE Identification: 003086
Unit ID: 204501
Telephone: (440) 775-8121 Carnegie Class: Bac-A&S
FAX Number: (440) 775-8886 Calendar System: 4/1/4
URL: www.oberlin.edu
Established: 1833 Annual Undergrad Tuition & Fees: $55,052
Enrollment: 2,853 Coed
Affiliation or Control: Independent Non-Profit IRS Status: 501(c)3
Highest Offering: Master's
Accreditation: NH

01 President .... Ms. Carmen T. AMBAR
10 VP for Finance & Admin .... Ms. Rebecca VASQUEZ-SKILLINGS
30 Int VP Development/Alumni Affairs .... Ms. Rachel SMITH SILVER
26 Vice President College Relations .... Mr. Ben JONES
49 Acting Dean of Arts & Sciences .... Dr. David KAMITSUKA
64 Acting Dean Conservatory Music .... Dr. William QUILLEN
32 VP and Dean of Students .... Dr. Meredith RAIMONDO
07 Dean Admissions/Financial Aid .... Dr. Manuel CARBALLO
43 Vice President/GC and Secretary .... Ms. Donica VARNER
21 Asst Vice President Finance .... Vacant
29 Exec Director Alumni Assoc .... Ms. Danielle YOUNG
88 Assoc Dean of College of Arts & Sci .... Dr. Daphne JOHN
13 Chief Information Tech Officer .... Mr. Ben HOCKENHULL
08 Azariah Smith Root Dir of Libraries .... Dr. Alexia HUDSON-WARD
07 Director Admissions Conservatory .... Mr. Michael C. MANDEREN
38 Director of Counseling Center .... Dr. John HARSHBARGER
57 Director of Allen Art Museums .... Dr. Andria DERSTINE
06 Registrar .... Ms. Elizabeth CLERKIN
37 Director of Financial Aid .... Ms. Michele KOSBOTH
09 Director of Institutional Research .... Mr. Ross PEACOCK
18 Assistant VP of Facility Operations .... Mr. James S. KLAIBER
36 Interim Dir Career Devel/Placement .... Ms. Dana HAMDEN
42 Director Religious and Spiritual Li .... Rev. David F. DORSEY
39 Asst VP/Strategic Initiatives .... Mr. Adrian BATISTA
41 Director of Physical Educ/Athletics .... Ms. Natalie WINKELFOOS
19 Director of Safety & Security .... Mr. Michael MARTINSEN
28 Director Multicultural Affairs .... Ms. Zahida SHERMAN
96 Institutional Buyer .... Mr. Rick SNODGRASS
15 Chief Human Resources Officer .... Mr. Joseph VITALE, JR.
04 Assistant to President .... Mrs. Jennifer S. BRADFIELD
100 Chief of Staff .... Mr. Ferdinand PROTZMAN
102 Exec Dir Office of Foundations .... Ms. Pamela SNYDER
44 Sr Philanthropic Advisor .... Ms. Catherine GLETHEROW

Ohio Business College (D)

5202 Timber Commons Drive, Sandusky OH 44870-5894
Telephone: (419) 627-8345 Identification: 666467
Accreditation: COE

† Branch campus of Ohio Business College, Sheffield Village, OH.

Ohio Business College (E)

5095 Waterford Drive, Sheffield Village OH 44035-0701
County: Lorain FICE Identification: 021585
Unit ID: 203720
Telephone: (440) 934-3101 Carnegie Class: Assoc/HVT-High Trad
FAX Number: (440) 934-3105 Calendar System: Quarter
URL: www.ohiobusinesscollege.edu
Established: 1903 Annual Undergrad Tuition & Fees: $9,360
Enrollment: 228 Coed
Affiliation or Control: Proprietary IRS Status: Proprietary
Highest Offering: Associate Degree
Accreditation: COE, MAC

01 School Director .... Ms. Carson BURKE
05 Director of Education .... Ms. Diane HAGAN
07 Master Admissions Rep .... Ms. Nicole SMITH
37 Lead Financial Aid Administrator .... Mrs. Victoria DONLEY
36 Career Services Director .... Ms. Tanya FOOSE

Ohio Christian University (F)

1476 Lancaster Pike, Circleville OH 43113-0458
County: Pickaway FICE Identification: 003030
Unit ID: 201964
Telephone: (740) 474-8896 Carnegie Class: Masters/M
FAX Number: (740) 477-7755 Calendar System: Semester
URL: www.ohiochristian.edu
Established: 1948 Annual Undergrad Tuition & Fees: $20,806
Enrollment: 4,483 Coed
Affiliation or Control: Other Protestant IRS Status: 501(c)3
Highest Offering: Master's
Accreditation: NH, CAEPT

01 President .... Dr. Jon KULAGA
05 Provost .... Dr. Hank KELLY
10 Vice President of Finance .... Mr. Ted PERRY
111 Vice President for Advancement .... Vacant
84 AVP for Enrollment .... Mr. Kevin JONES
32 AVP Student Development .... Mr. Joseph WUEST
13 AVP for IT .... Mr. John BOCOOK
09 AVP for Institutional Research .... Dr. Cynthia TWEEDELL
88 Chief Relationship Officer .... Mr. Craig BROWN
06 Registrar .... Mr. Dustin EPPERLY
55 VP College of Adult & Graduate Stds .... Dr. Bradford SAMPLE
84 AVP of AGS Enrollment Mgmt .... Ms. Nicole DAVIS
08 Director of Library Services .... Mr. Paul ROBERTS
37 Director Student Financial Services .... Mr. Brandon RITCHEY
41 Athletic Director .... Mr. David BIRELINE
35 AVP of Student Services .... Ms. Robin PATRICK
15 AVP for Human Resources .... Ms. Ronda BALDWIN
50 Dean/Director of Business .... Mr. Monty LOBB
53 Director of Education .... Ms. Valerie JONES
04 Administrative Asst to President .... Mrs. Lois TAYLOR
07 Director of Admissions .... Vacant
106 PSEO Director .... Mrs. Beth ASH
19 Director of Security .... Vacant
26 Marketing Content Manager .... Mr. Dave HIRSHLER
16 Director of Human Resources .... Mr. Zach STEPHENS
39 Dir Resident Life/Student Housing .... Ms. Kelsey CUTRIGHT

Ohio Dominican University (G)

1216 Sunbury Road, Columbus OH 43219-2099
County: Franklin FICE Identification: 003035
Unit ID: 204617
Telephone: (614) 251-4500 Carnegie Class: Masters/L
FAX Number: (614) 251-4634 Calendar System: Semester
URL: www.ohiodominican.edu
Established: 1911 Annual Undergrad Tuition & Fees: $31,080
Enrollment: 1,714 Coed
Affiliation or Control: Roman Catholic IRS Status: 501(c)3
Highest Offering: Doctorate
Accreditation: NH, ACBSP, ARCPA, CAEPN, SW

01 President .... Dr. Robert GERVASI
05 Vice President Academic Affairs .... Dr. Manuel MARTINEZ
10 Vice Pres Finance & Admin/CFO .... Mr. Alvin RODACK
84 Vice Pres Enrollment Management .... Vacant
111 VP for Advancement & External Rels .... Mr. Mark COOPER
04 Executive Asst to the President .... Ms. Heather MORRIS
32 Assoc Vice Pres Student Success .... Ms. Sharon REED
20 Assoc Vice Pres Academic Affairs .... Dr. Linda WOLF
121 Dir of Advising & Student Success .... Mr. Adam HIRSCHFELD
07 Assoc VP Undergraduate Admissions .... Mr. Michael HALLIGAN
123 Assoc VP of Grad & Adult Admissions .... Mr. John NAUGHTON
114 Controller .... Ms. Vicki STEELE
13 Chief Information Officer .... Ms. Christine KURTH
37 Director of Financial Aid .... Ms. Tara SCHNEIDER
08 Director of the Library .... Ms. Michelle SARFF
36 Director Career Services .... Ms. Jessica HALL
15 Director of Human Resources .... Ms. Amy THOMAS
42 Director of Campus Ministry .... Fr. Paul COLLOTON
110 Assoc VP for Advancement .... Ms. Christie FLOOD-WEINER
39 Director of Resident Life .... Ms. Lara CONRAD
41 Athletic Director .... Mr. Jeff BLAIR
92 Director of Honors Program .... Mr. John MARAZITA
19 Director of Safety .... Mr. Robin OLSON
25 Dir of Sponsored Research .... Ms. Sarah ELVEY
06 Registrar .... Ms. Happiness MAPIRA

Ohio Northern University (H)

525 S Main Street, Ada OH 45810-1599
County: Hardin FICE Identification: 003089
Unit ID: 204635
Telephone: (419) 772-2000 Carnegie Class: Bac-Diverse
FAX Number: (419) 772-1932 Calendar System: Semester
URL: www.onu.edu
Established: 1871 Annual Undergrad Tuition & Fees: $32,260
Enrollment: 3,088 Coed
Affiliation or Control: United Methodist IRS Status: 501(c)3
Highest Offering: First Professional Degree
Accreditation: NH, CAATE, CAEPN, CEA, EXSC, LAW, MT, MUS, NAIT, NURSE, PHAR

01 President .... Dr. Daniel A. DIBIASIO
05 Provost/Vice Pres Academic Affairs .... Dr. Maria L. CRONLEY
10 Vice President Financial Affairs .... Mr. William H. BALLARD
111 Vice Pres of University Advancement . Ms. Shannon M. SPENCER
84 Vice Pres Enrollment Management .... Dr. William T. EIOLA
32 VP Student Affairs/Dean of Students .... Dr. Adriane L. THOMPSON-BRADSHAW
49 Dean of Arts & Sciences .... Dr. Holly L. BAUMGARTNER
54 Dean of Engineering .... Dr. John-David S. YODER
67 Dean of Pharmacy .... Dr. Steven J. MARTIN
50 Dean Business Administration .... Dr. John C. NAVIN
61 Dean of the College of Law .... Dr. Charles H. ROSE, III
110 Assistant VP for Advancement .... Mr. Scott D. WILLS
08 Director of Heterick Library .... Ms. Kathleen T. BARIL
39 Dir of Res Life/Int Dir Career Svcs .... Mr. Justin F. COURTNEY
38 Mental Health Counselor .... Ms. Marcia R. KOSTOFF
29 Director of Alumni Relations .... Mrs. Barbara A. MEEK
08 Director of the Law Library .... Dr. Nancy A. ARMSTRONG
42 University Chaplain .... Rev Dr. David E. MACDONALD
18 Director of Facilities .... Mr. Marc E. STALEY
13 Director of Technology .... Mr. Jeff A. RIEMAN
09 Director of Institutional Research .... Mr. Omer I. MINHAS
15 Director of Human Resources .... Ms. Tonya D. PAUL
20 Associate VP of Academic Affairs .... Dr. Juliet K. HURTIG
37 Asst VP for Enroll Mgt/Dir Fin Aid .... Mrs. Melanie K. WEAVER
21 University Controller .... Mr. Mark A. RUSSELL
26 Exec Dir Communications & Marketing .... Mrs. Amy M. PRIGGE
07 Director of Admissions .... Ms. Deborah L. MILLER
06 University Registrar .... Ms. Melanie J. HOUGH
28 Director Multicultural Development .... Ms. LaShonda E. GURLEY
41 Director of Athletics .... Mr. Thomas E. SIMMONS
44 Dir Annual Pgm & Donor Relations .... Ms. Ellie F. MCMANUS
96 Director of Business Services .... Ms. Vicki J. NIESE
101 Secretary to the Board .... Ms. Jennifer L. ROBY
19 Director of Public Safety .... Mr. Greg R. HORNE

The Ohio State University Main Campus (I)

281 W. Lane Ave., Columbus OH 43210-1358
County: Franklin FICE Identification: 003090
Unit ID: 204796
Telephone: (614) 292-6446 Carnegie Class: DU-Highest
FAX Number: (614) 292-9180 Calendar System: Semester
URL: www.osu.edu
Established: 1870 Annual Undergrad Tuition & Fees (In-State): $10,726
Enrollment: 59,837 Coed
Affiliation or Control: State IRS Status: 501(c)3

Highest Offering: Doctorate
Accreditation: NH, AAB, ACAE, ART, AUD, CAATE, CACREP, CAEP, CAHIIM, CIDA, CLPSY, COARC, CONST, DANCE, DENT, DH, DIETC, DIETD, DIETI, DMS, HSA, IPSY, LAW, LSAR, MED, MFCD, MIDWF, MT, MUS, NMT, NURSE, OPT, OPTR, OT, PCSAS, PH, PHAR, PLNG, PTA, RAD, RTT, SCPSY, SP, SPAA, SW, THEA, VET

01 President ... Dr. Michael V. DRAKE
05 Executive Vice Pres/Provost ... Dr. Bruce MCPHERON
10 Sr VP Business & Finance/CFO ... Mr. Michael PAPADAKIS
43 Sr VP & General Counsel ... Mr. Christopher M. CULLEY
32 Sr Vice President for Student Life . Dr. Javaune ADAMS-GASTON
20 Vice Provost for Academic Programs ... Mr. W. Randy SMITH
26 VP University Communications ... Ms. Ann HAMILTON
46 Sr Vice Pres for Research ... Dr. Morley O. STONE
86 Vice Pres of Govt Affairs ... Mr. Blake THOMPSON
23 Exec VP/Chancellor Health Affairs ... Dr. Harold L. PAZ
47 Vice Pres Ag Admin & Dean FAES ... Dr. Cathann KRESS
111 Sr VP for Advance/Pres OSU Found ... Mr. Michael EICHER
28 Vice Prov Diversity & Inclusion ... Dr. James L. MOORE
58 Vice Provost/Dean Grad School ... Dr. Alicia L. BERTONE
41 Sr VP/Athletics Director ... Mr. Gene D. SMITH
18 Assoc VP Facilities Op/Dev ... Mr. Mark E. CONSELYEA
84 Assoc VP Strategic Enroll Planning ... Ms. Stephanie R. SANDERS
13 Vice President and CIO ... Mr. Michael HOFHERR
08 Vice Provost/Director of Libraries ... Mr. Damon E. JAGGARS
100 Chief of Staff ... Ms. Katie HALL
101 Actg Secretary Board of Trustees ... Ms. Jessica A. EVELAND
17 COO Medical Center ... Mr. David P. MCQUAID
85 Vice Prov Glob Strat/Intl Affs ... Dr. Gil I. LATZ, II
90 Exec Dir Ohio Supercomp Ctr ... Mr. David HUDAK
29 SVP Alumni Rels/CEO Alumni Assoc ... Mr. James E. SMITH
12 Exec Dean of Reg Campuses ... Dr. William L. MACDONALD
49 Int Vice Prov/Exec Dean Arts & Sci ... Dr. Janet M. BOX-STEFFENSMEIER
50 Dean Fisher Col of Business ... Dr. Anil K. MAKHIJA
52 Dean College of Dentistry ... Dr. Patrick M. LLOYD
53 Dean College of Educ & Hum Ecology ... Dr. Donald L. POPE-DAVIS
54 Dean College of Engineering ... Dr. David B. WILLIAMS
61 Dean College of Law ... Dr. Alan C. MICHAELS
63 Dean College of Medicine ... Dr. K. Craig KENT
88 Dean College of Optometry ... Dr. Karla S. ZADNIK
67 Dean College of Pharmacy ... Dr. Henry J. MANN
69 Dean College of Public Health ... Dr. William J. MARTIN
70 Dean College of Social Work ... Dr. Tom GREGOIRE
74 Dean Col Veterinary Medicine ... Dr. Rustin MOORE
66 Dean College of Nursing ... Dr. Bernadette MELNYK
09 Asst VP Inst Research/Planning ... Ms. Julie CARPENTER-HUBIN
37 Exec Dir Student Financial Aid ... Vacant
06 University Registrar ... Mr. Jack MINER
88 Director OES Analysis & Reporting ... Ms. Gail C. STEPHENOFF
35 Sr Assoc VP Student Life ... Dr. Gretchen METZELAARS
96 Sr Director of Purchasing ... Mr. Nathan ANDRIDGE
11 Sr Vice Pres Admin & Planning ... Mr. Jay D. KASEY
19 Director of Public Safety ... Ms. Monica MOLL
39 Director Housing Administration . Ms. Toni GREENSLADE-SMITH
88 Dean JG College of Public Affairs ... Dr. Trevor L. BROWN
15 Sr VP Talent/Culture and HR ... Ms. Susan M. BASSO

The Ohio State University Agricultural Technical Institute (A)

1328 Dover Road, Wooster OH 44691-4000
Telephone: (330) 264-3911 FICE Identification: 010687
Accreditation: &NH

† Regional accreditation is carried under the parent institution in Columbus, OH.

The Ohio State University at Lima Campus (B)

4240 Campus Drive, Lima OH 45804-3597
Telephone: (419) 995-8600 FICE Identification: 003092
Accreditation: &NH

† Regional accreditation is carried under the parent institution in Columbus, OH.

The Ohio State University Mansfield Campus (C)

1760 University Drive, Mansfield OH 44906-1599
Telephone: (419) 755-4011 FICE Identification: 003093
Accreditation: &NH

† Regional accreditation is carried under the parent institution in Columbus, OH.

The Ohio State University at Marion (D)

1465 Mount Vernon Avenue, Marion OH 43302-5628
Telephone: (740) 389-6786 FICE Identification: 003094
Accreditation: &NH

† Regional accreditation is carried under the parent institution in Columbus, OH.

The Ohio State University Newark Campus (E)

1179 University Drive, Newark OH 43055-9990
Telephone: (740) 366-3321 FICE Identification: 003095
Accreditation: &NH

† Regional accreditation is carried under the parent institution in Columbus, OH.

Ohio Technical College (F)

1374 E 51st Street, Cleveland OH 44103-1269
County: Cuyahoga FICE Identification: 011745
Unit ID: 204608
Telephone: (216) 881-1700 Carnegie Class: Spec 2-yr-Tech
FAX Number: (216) 881-9145 Calendar System: Quarter
URL: www.ohiotech.edu
Established: 1969 Annual Undergrad Tuition & Fees: N/A
Enrollment: 883 Coed
Affiliation or Control: Proprietary IRS Status: Proprietary
Highest Offering: Associate Degree
Accreditation: ACCSC

01 President ... Mr. Bill HANTL
32 Director of Student Outcomes ... Mr. Peter PERKOWSKI
10 Chief Financial/Business Officer ... Mr. H. Charles KESSLER
11 Chief of Operations/Administration ... Mr. George VOINOVICH
19 Director Security/Safety ... Mr. Patrick WILSON
37 Director Student Financial Aid ... Mr. Michael CAMPBELL
03 Executive Vice President ... Mr. George VOINOVICH
06 Registrar ... Ms. Sarah MANCINI

Ohio University Main Campus (G)

1 Ohio University, Athens OH 45701-2979
County: Athens FICE Identification: 003100
Unit ID: 204857
Telephone: (740) 593-1000 Carnegie Class: DU-Higher
FAX Number: N/A Calendar System: Semester
URL: www.ohio.edu
Established: 1804 Annual Undergrad Tuition & Fees (In-State): $12,192
Enrollment: 29,369 Coed
Affiliation or Control: State IRS Status: 501(c)3
Highest Offering: Doctorate
Accreditation: NH, AAFCS, ADNUR, ARCPA, AUD, CAATE, CACREP, CAEPN, CEA, CIDA, CLPSY, COSMA, DANCE, DIETD, DIETI, FEPAC, IPSY, JOUR, MUS, NAIT, NRPA, NURSE, OSTEO, PH, PTA, SP, SW, THEA

01 President ... Dr. Duane NELLIS
100 Chief of Staff ... Ms. Jennifer KIRKSEY
05 Executive VP & Provost ... Dr. Chaden DJALALI
10 SVP for Finance & Administration ... Ms. Deborah SHAFFER
32 VP for Student Affairs ... Dr. Jason PINA
111 VP for University Advancement ... Mr. Nico KARAGOSIAN
13 Interim Chief Information Officer ... Mr. Christopher AMENT
46 VP Research & Dean Grad College ... Dr. Joseph SHIELDS
84 Vice Provost Enrollment Management ... Mr. Craig CORNELL
102 CEO University Foundation ... Mr. Nico KARAGOSIAN
43 Interim General Counsel ... Ms. Barbara NALAZEK
26 VP Univ Communications/Marketing ... Ms. Robin OLIVER
88 Dean University College ... Dr. Elizabeth SAYRS
49 Dean College of Arts & Sciences ... Dr. Florenz PLASSMANN
50 Dean College of Business ... Dr. Hugh SHERMAN
60 Dean Scripps Col Communication ... Dr. Scott TITSWORTH
53 Dean Patton College of Education ... Dr. Renee A. MIDDLETON
54 Dean Russ Col Engineering/Tech ... Dr. Mei WEI
57 Dean College of Fine Arts ... Dr. Matthew SHAFTEL
69 Dean Col Health/Human Services ... Dr. Randy LEITE
92 Dean Honors Tutorial College ... Dr. Donal SKINNER
63 Dean Heritage Col Osteopathic Med ... Dr. Kenneth JOHNSON
62 Interim Dean University Libraries ... Ms. Janet HULM
35 Dean of Students ... Dr. Jenny HALL-JONES
12 Int Exec Dean Regional Higher Educ ... Dr. Nicole PENNINGTON
12 Interim Dean Eastern Campus ... Dr. Jeremy WEBSTER
12 Dean Southern Campus ... Dr. Nicole PENNINGTON
12 Interim Dean Chillicothe Campus ... Dr. Dywayne NICELY
12 Dean Lancaster Campus ... Dr. James SMITH
12 Dean Zanesville Campus ... Dr. Jeremy WEBSTER
20 Associate Provost Academic Affairs ... Dr. Howard DEWALD
58 Asst Dean Graduate College ... Dr. Katherine TADLOCK
88 Vice Provost Global Affairs ... Dr. Lorna Jean EDMONDS
09 Int Assoc Prov Inst Rsrch/Effective ... Dr. Loralyn TAYLOR
41 Interim Director of Athletics ... Ms. Amy DEAN
06 University Registrar ... Mrs. Debra M. BENTON
15 Chief Human Resources Officer ... Ms. Colleen BENDEL
29 Asst Vice Pres Alumni Relations ... Ms. Erin ESSAK KOPP
36 Exec Dir Career/Leadership Dev Ctr ... Mr. Imants JAUNARAJS
07 Asst Vice Provost/Dir Ungrad Admiss .. Ms. Candace BOENINGER
38 Dir Counseling/Psychological Svcs ... Dr. Paul CASTELINO
112 Exec Director of Gift Planning ... Ms. Kelli KOTOWSKI
37 Dir Student Fin Aid/Scholarships ... Ms. Valerie MILLER
106 Chief Strategy/Innovation Officer ... Dr. Brad COHEN
19 Chief of Police ... Chief Andrew POWERS
85 Dir International Svcs/Operations ... Dr. Diane CAHILL
39 Exec Director Residential Housing ... Mr. Peter TRENTACOSTE
28 VP for Diversity & Inclusion ... Dr. Gigi SECUBAN
24 Media Library Manager ... Ms. Robin WOOTEN
113 Bursar ... Ms. Sherry ROSSITER
101 Secretary to Board of Trustees ... Dr. David MOORE
86 Director of Government Relations ... Mr. Eric BURCHARD
88 Ombudsman ... Mr. Mac STRICKLEN
04 Presidential Assistant ... Ms. Joanna STOLTZFUS

Ohio University Chillicothe Campus (H)

101 University Drive, Chillicothe OH 45601-0629
Telephone: (740) 774-7200 FICE Identification: 003102
Accreditation: &NH

† Regional accreditation is carried under the parent institution in Athens, OH.

Ohio University Eastern Campus (I)

45425 National Road, Saint Clairsville OH 43950-9724
Telephone: (740) 695-1720 FICE Identification: 003101
Accreditation: &NH

† Regional accreditation is carried under the parent institution in Athens, OH.

Ohio University Lancaster Campus (J)

1570 Granville Pike, Lancaster OH 43130-1097
Telephone: (740) 654-6711 FICE Identification: 003104
Accreditation: &NH, MAC

† Regional accreditation is carried under the parent institution in Athens, OH.

Ohio University Southern Campus (K)

1804 Liberty Avenue, Ironton OH 45638-2279
Telephone: (740) 533-4600 Identification: 666000
Accreditation: &NH

† Regional accreditation is carried under the parent institution in Athens, OH.

Ohio University Zanesville Branch (L)

1425 Newark Road, Zanesville OH 43701-2695
Telephone: (740) 453-0762 FICE Identification: 003108
Accreditation: &NH

† Regional accreditation is carried under the parent institution in Athens, OH.

Ohio Valley College of Technology (M)

15258 State Route 170, East Liverpool OH 43920
County: Columbiana FICE Identification: 023014
Unit ID: 204884
Telephone: (330) 385-1070 Carnegie Class: Spec 2-yr-Health
FAX Number: (330) 385-4606 Calendar System: Semester
URL: www.ovct.edu
Established: 1886 Annual Undergrad Tuition & Fees: $12,969
Enrollment: 162 Coed
Affiliation or Control: Proprietary IRS Status: Proprietary
Highest Offering: Associate Degree
Accreditation: ABHES

01 President ... Mr. Scott S. ROGERS
37 Director of Financial Aid ... Ms. Rebecca STECKMAN

Ohio Wesleyan University (N)

61 S Sandusky Street, Delaware OH 43015-2398
County: Delaware FICE Identification: 003109
Unit ID: 204909
Telephone: (740) 368-2000 Carnegie Class: Bac-A&S
FAX Number: (740) 368-3299 Calendar System: Semester
URL: www.owu.edu
Established: 1842 Annual Undergrad Tuition & Fees: $45,760
Enrollment: 1,560 Coed
Affiliation or Control: United Methodist IRS Status: 501(c)3
Highest Offering: Baccalaureate
Accreditation: NH, CAEP, MUS

01 President ... Dr. Rockwell F. JONES
05 Provost ... Dr. Charles L. STINEMETZ
10 VP for Finance/Admin/Treasurer ... Ms. Lauri STRIMKOVSKY
111 VP for University Advancement ... Ms. Natalie MILBURN DOAN
84 Vice President for Enrollment ... Dr. Stefanie NILES
32 Vice President for Student Affairs ... Dr. Dwayne K. TODD
26 Chief Communications Officer ... Mr. Will E. KOPP
09 Assoc Provost for Inst Research ... Dr. Dale E. SWARTZENTRUBER
108 Asst Provost Assmt/Accreditation ... Dr. Barbara S. ANDERECK
28 Chief Diversity Ofcr/Dn Div/ Inclus ... Dr. Juan Armando ROJAS JOO
37 Director Student Financial Aid ... Mr. Kevin F. PASKVAN
36 Director of Career Services ... Ms. Leslie J. MELTON
06 Registrar ... Ms. Shelly A. MCMAHON
13 Chief Information Officer ... Dr. Brian RELLINGER
19 Director of Public Safety ... Mr. Robert A. WOOD
29 Director Alumni Relations ... Ms. Katie P. WEBSTER
85 Director International Student Svcs ... Mr. Darrell J. ALBON
18 Director Physical Plant ... Mr. Peter K. SCHANTZ
15 Director Human Resources ... Mr. Scott L. SIMON
31 Director Community Svc Learning ... Ms. Sally S. LEBER
04 Asst to President/Board Secy ... Ms. Janet L. LEWIS
23 Director Wellness Center ... Ms. Marsha A. TILDEN
35 Dean of Students ... Dr. Dwayne K. TODD
39 Director Residential Life ... Mr. Brian J. EMERICK
41 Director of Athletics ... Mr. Doug W. ZIPP
42 Chaplain ... Rev. Jon R. POWERS
89 Director First Year Experience ... Mr. Brad T. PULCINI
92 Honors Program Director ... Dr. Amy MCCLURE
102 Foundation Relations Manager ... Ms. Sue E. HAIDLE
07 Director of Admissions ... Mr. Joshua STEVENS
40 Bookstore Manager ... Ms. Lisa K. TACKETT
38 Coord Counseling/Mental Health Svcs ... Dr. Doug L. BENNETT
96 Director of Purchasing ... Ms. Melanie T. KALB

Otterbein University (A)

1 South Grove Street, Westerville OH 43081-2006
County: Franklin FICE Identification: 003110
Unit ID: 204936
Telephone: (614) 890-3000 Carnegie Class: Masters/M
FAX Number: (614) 823-3114 Calendar System: Semester
URL: www.otterbein.edu
Established: 1847 Annual Undergrad Tuition & Fees: $31,874
Enrollment: 2,936 Coed
Affiliation or Control: United Methodist IRS Status: 501(c)3
Highest Offering: Doctorate
Accreditation: **NH**, ANEST, CAATE, CAEPN, MUS, NURSE, THEA

01 President ..... Dr. John L. COMERFORD
100 Chief of Staff ..... Ms. Kristine ROBBINS
05 Provost/VPAA ..... Dr. Wendy R. SHERMAN-HECKLER
32 Int Vice President Student Affairs ..... Ms. Dawn STEWART
10 Vice President for Business Affairs ..... Ms. Susan BOLT
111 VP Institutional Advancement ..... Mr. Michael MCGREEVEY
84 Vice President for Enrollment ..... Mr. Jefferson BLACKBURN-SMITH
91 Exec Director of Information Tech ..... Mr. Dave BENDER
08 Director of the Library ..... Ms. Tiffany LIPSTREU
06 Registrar ..... Mr. David SCHNEIDER
26 Exec Dir Marketing/Communications ..... Mr. Roberto C. PONCE
36 Director Career Planning/Placement ..... Mr. Ryan BRECHBILL
37 Director of Financial Aid ..... Mr. Thomas V. YARNELL
41 Athletic Director ..... Ms. Dawn STEWART
42 Chaplain ..... Dr. Judy GUION-UTSLER
107 Dean School of Prof Studies ..... Dr. Barbara H. SCHAFFNER
49 Dean School of Arts/Sciences ..... Dr. Paul EISENSTEIN
07 Director of Admissions ..... Mr. Mark MOFFETT
15 Director Human Resources ..... Mr. Scott FITZGERALD
18 Director/Physical Plant ..... Mr. Troy A. BONTE
29 Director Alumni Relations ..... Mr. Steve CRAWFORD
28 Director of Diversity ..... Mr. James PRYSOCK
21 Assistant Controller ..... Mr. Christopher A. HAYTER
09 Director of Institutional Research ..... Dr. Sean M. MCLAUGHLIN
19 Director of Security ..... Mr. Larry BANASZAK
04 Executive Assistant to President ..... Ms. Caroline VIEBRANZ
39 Director Student Housing ..... Ms. Tracy BENNER
38 Director Student Counseling ..... Dr. Kathleen RYAN
44 Director Annual Giving ..... Vacant

Owens Community College (B)

30335 Oregon, PO Box 10000, Toledo OH 43699-1947
County: Wood FICE Identification: 005753
Unit ID: 204945
Telephone: (567) 661-7000 Carnegie Class: Assoc/HVT-High Non
FAX Number: N/A Calendar System: Semester
URL: www.owens.edu
Established: 1965 Annual Undergrad Tuition & Fees (In-State): $5,150
Enrollment: 10,038 Coed
Affiliation or Control: State IRS Status: 501(c)3
Highest Offering: Associate Degree
Accreditation: **NH**, ACBSP, ACFEI, ADNUR, CAHIIM, DH, DIETT, DMS, EMT, MAC, NAIT, OTA, PTAA, RAD, RADMAG, SURGT

01 President ..... Dr. Steve ROBINSON
101 Secretary to the Board of Trustees ..... Ms. Patricia JEZAK
04 Executive Assistant to President ..... Ms. Kristine HOLLAND
05 VP Academic Affairs/Provost ..... Ms. Denise SMITH
10 Treasurer ..... Mr. Jeff GANUES
15 VP Human Resources ..... Ms. Lisa NAGEL
84 VP Enrollment Mgmt/Student Svcs ..... Ms. Amy GIORDANO
20 Assoc VP Academic Services ..... Vacant
103 Exec Dir Workforce/Comm Service ..... Mr. Robert KRAUS
12 Executive Director Findlay Campus ..... Ms. Julie BAKER
21 Controller ..... Ms. Katie FEHER
13 Chief Information Officer ..... Ms. Laurie ORZECHOWSKI
19 Chief of Police ..... Chief Steven HARRISON
37 Director Financial Aid ..... Ms. Andrea MORROW
26 Director Mktg & Communications ..... Mr. Jason GRIFFIN
18 Executive Director Operations ..... Ms. Danielle TRACY
09 Director Inst Research ..... Ms. Anne FULKERSON
81 Dean School of STEM ..... Mr. Glenn RETTIG
66 Dean School of Nursing/Health Prof ..... Ms. Cathy FORD
50 Dean Sch Business/Info/Public Svc ..... Vacant
57 Int Dean School of Liberal Arts ..... Mr. Michael SANDER
08 Director Library Services ..... Mr. Tom SINK
106 Director eLearning ..... Mr. Mark KARAMOL
43 Legal Services Coordinator ..... Ms. Linda WIRICK
06 Exec Dir Student Services/Registrar ..... Mr. David SHAFFER
86 Exec Dir Govt/Comm Relations ..... Ms. Jennifer FEHNRICH
29 Director Alumni Affairs ..... Ms. Jennifer FEHNRICH
32 Director Student Life/Stdnt Conduct ..... Ms. Danielle FILIPCHUK
109 Director Business Operations ..... Mr. David WAHR
85 Manager Intl Stdnt Services ..... Ms. Annette SWANSON
41 Director Athletics ..... Mr. JD ETTORE

Owens Community College Findlay Campus (C)

3200 Bright Road, Findlay OH 45840
Telephone: (567) 429-3500 Identification: 770360
Accreditation: **&NH**

Payne Theological Seminary (D)

PO Box 474, Wilberforce OH 45384-0474
County: Greene FICE Identification: 010017
Unit ID: 204990
Telephone: (937) 376-2946 Carnegie Class: Spec-4-yr-Faith
FAX Number: (937) 376-3330 Calendar System: 4/1/4
URL: www.payne.edu
Established: 1844 Annual Graduate Tuition & Fees: N/A
Enrollment: 187 Coed
Affiliation or Control: African Methodist Episcopal IRS Status: 501(c)3
Highest Offering: Doctorate; No Undergraduates
Accreditation: **THEOL**

01 President ..... Dr. Michael BROWN
05 Academic Dean ..... Dr. Michael MILLER
04 Executive Assistant to President ..... Mr. Kim KING
20 Associate Dean ..... Dr. Michael MILLER
30 Director of Development ..... Rev. Jules DUNHAM HOWIE
10 Director of Finance ..... Ms. Elise PEYROUX
37 Financial Aid Officer ..... Ms. Pat COPELY
06 Registrar ..... Ms. Maryjo LEWIS
07 Admissions Officer ..... Ms. Althea SMOOT

Pontifical College Josephinum (E)

7625 N High Street, Columbus OH 43235-1498
County: Franklin FICE Identification: 003113
Unit ID: 205027
Telephone: (614) 885-5585 Carnegie Class: Spec-4-yr-Faith
FAX Number: (614) 885-2307 Calendar System: Semester
URL: www.pcj.edu
Established: 1888 Annual Undergrad Tuition & Fees: $22,300
Enrollment: 150 Male
Affiliation or Control: Roman Catholic IRS Status: 501(c)3
Highest Offering: Beyond Master's But Less Than Doctorate
Accreditation: **NH**, THEOL

01 Rector/President ..... V.Rev. Steven P. BESEAU
10 VP for Administration/Treasurer ..... Mr. John O. ERWIN
05 Vice Rec Sch Theology/Dn Cmty Life ..... Rev. Ervens MENGELLE
30 Vice President for Advancement ..... Rev. John A. ALLEN
49 Vice Rector College Liberal Arts ..... Rev. Mike LUMPE
73 Academic Dean School of Theology ..... Dr. Perry J. CAHALL
49 Academic Dean College Liberal Arts ..... Dr. David J. DE LEONARDIS
06 Registrar ..... Mr. Samuel J. DEAN
08 Director Library Services ..... Mr. Peter G. VERACKA
37 Director Financial Aid ..... Mrs. Marky LEICHTNAM
108 Dir of Inst Plng/Assessment/Accred ..... Mr. Eric S. GRAFF
26 Director of Communications ..... Ms. Carolyn DINOVO
07 Admissions Coordinator ..... Ms. Arminda CRAWFORD
105 Web Developer ..... Ms. Tracy BROCKMAN

Professional Skills Institute (F)

1505 Holland Road, Maumee OH 43537
County: Lucas FICE Identification: 023377
Unit ID: 205054
Telephone: (419) 720-6670 Carnegie Class: Spec 2-yr-Health
FAX Number: (419) 720-6674 Calendar System: Quarter
URL: www.proskills.edu
Established: 1984 Annual Undergrad Tuition & Fees: $16,017
Enrollment: 415 Coed
Affiliation or Control: Proprietary IRS Status: Proprietary
Highest Offering: Associate Degree
Accreditation: **ABHES**, PTAA

00 CEO ..... Michael MARINO
01 Campus President ..... Michael SEIFERT
05 Dean of Education ..... Susan LIPPENS
07 Director of Admissions ..... Amanda BOYD

Rabbinical College of Telshe (G)

28400 Euclid Avenue, Wickliffe OH 44092-2584
County: Lake FICE Identification: 003115
Unit ID: 205124
Telephone: (440) 943-5300 Carnegie Class: Spec-4-yr-Faith
FAX Number: (440) 943-5303 Calendar System: Quarter
Established: 1941 Annual Undergrad Tuition & Fees: $13,100
Enrollment: 56 Male
Affiliation or Control: Independent Non-Profit IRS Status: 501(c)3
Highest Offering: Doctorate
Accreditation: **RABN**

01 President ..... Rabbi Shmuel Y. LEVIN
06 Registrar ..... Rabbi Abraham MATITIA

Remington College Cleveland Campus (H)

14445 Broadway Avenue, Cleveland OH 44125-1900
County: Cuyahoga FICE Identification: 007777
Unit ID: 375416
Telephone: (216) 475-7520 Carnegie Class: Assoc/HVT-Mix Trad/Non
FAX Number: (216) 475-6055 Calendar System: Other
URL: www.remingtoncollege.edu
Established: 1990 Annual Undergrad Tuition & Fees: $15,678
Enrollment: 670 Coed
Affiliation or Control: Independent Non-Profit IRS Status: 501(c)3
Highest Offering: Associate Degree
Accreditation: **ACCSC**, PTAA

01 Director of Campus Administration ..... Mr. Terhan FREEMAN

Rosedale Bible College (I)

2270 Rosedale Road, Irwin OH 43029-9517
County: Madison FICE Identification: 034253
Unit ID: 439899
Telephone: (740) 857-1311 Carnegie Class: Spec 2-yr-Other
FAX Number: (877) 857-1312 Calendar System: Semester
URL: www.rosedale.edu
Established: 1952 Annual Undergrad Tuition & Fees: $8,756
Enrollment: 48 Coed
Affiliation or Control: Mennonite Church IRS Status: 501(c)3
Highest Offering: Associate Degree
Accreditation: **BI**

01 President ..... Mr. Jeremy MILLER
05 Academic Dean ..... Mr. Phil WEBER
32 Dean of Students ..... Mr. Matthew SHOWALTER
84 Director of Enrollment Services ..... Mr. Hans SHENK
08 Director of Library Services ..... Mr. Reuben SAIRS
06 Registrar ..... Ms. Bethany PEACHEY
10 Chief Financial Officer ..... Mr. Lynford SCHROCK
26 Chief Public Relations Officer ..... Mr. Kenneth MILLER
04 Administrative Asst to President ..... Mrs. Twila WEBER
18 Chief Facilities/Physical Plant ..... Mr. Darnell BRENNEMAN

Saint Mary Seminary and Graduate School of Theology (J)

28700 Euclid Avenue, Wickliffe OH 44092-2585
County: Lake FICE Identification: 004061
Telephone: (440) 943-7600 Carnegie Class: Not Classified
FAX Number: (440) 943-7577 Calendar System: Semester
URL: www.stmarysem.edu
Established: 1848 Annual Graduate Tuition & Fees: N/A
Enrollment: N/A Coed
Affiliation or Control: Roman Catholic IRS Status: 501(c)3
Highest Offering: Doctorate; No Undergraduates
Accreditation: **NH**, THEOL

01 President/Rector ..... Rev. Mark A. LATCOVICH
03 Vice President/Vice Rector ..... Rev. Gerald J. BEDNAR
05 Academic Dean ..... Sr. Mary MCCORMICK, OSU
32 Student Dean ..... Rev. Michael G. WOOST
42 Spiritual Director ..... Rev. Mark HOLLIS
06 Registrar/Assistant Dean ..... Sr. Brendon ZAJAC, SND
08 Librarian ..... Mr. Alan K. ROME
10 CFO/Treasurer ..... Mr. Philip GUBAN
04 Administrative Asst to President ..... Mrs. Angie PAVLIK
90 Director Academic Computing ..... Sr. Brendon ZAJAC
18 Chief Facilities/Physical Plant ..... Mr. Philip GUBAN
108 Director Institutional Assessment ..... Dr. Edward KACZUK
13 Chief Info Technology Officer (CIO) ..... Mr. Alan K. ROME
19 Director Security/Safety ..... Mr. Philip GUBAN

Shawnee State University (K)

940 Second Street, Portsmouth OH 45662-4344
County: Scioto FICE Identification: 009942
Unit ID: 205443
Telephone: (740) 351-3205 Carnegie Class: Masters/S
FAX Number: (740) 351-3470 Calendar System: Semester
URL: www.shawnee.edu
Established: 1975 Annual Undergrad Tuition & Fees (In-State): $8,556
Enrollment: 3,582 Coed
Affiliation or Control: State IRS Status: 501(c)3
Highest Offering: Master's
Accreditation: **NH**, ADNUR, #CAATE, CAEPN, COARC, DH, EMT, MLTAD, NUR, OT, OTA, PTAA, RAD

01 President ..... Dr. Jeffrey BAUER
05 Provost/VP Academic & Student Affs ..... Dr. Becky THIEL
10 Vice President for Finance & Admin ..... Dr. Elinda BOYLES
111 VP for Advancement & Inst Rels ..... Mr. Eric BRAUN
43 General Counsel ..... Mr. Michael MCPHILLIPS
26 Director Communications ..... Ms. Elizabeth BLEVINS
107 Dean College Professional Studies ..... Dr. Paul MADDEN
49 Dean College Arts & Sciences ..... Dr. Roberta MILLIKEN
62 Dean Library Services ..... Ms. Janet STEWART
13 Director Univ Information Systems ..... Mr. Charles WARNER
30 Executive Director of Development ..... Mr. Eric BRAUN
07 Director of Admission ..... Ms. Amanda MEANS
06 Registrar ..... Ms. Tamara SHEETS
32 Dean of Students ..... Ms. Marcie SIMMS
15 Director of Human Resources ..... Ms. Malonda JOHNSON
41 Athletic Director ..... Mr. Jeff HAMILTON
37 Director of Financial Aid ..... Ms. Nicole NEAL
36 Director Career Svcs & Workforce ..... Ms. Angie DUDUIT
38 Director of Counseling & Psych Svcs ..... Dr. Linda KOENIG
88 Dean University College ..... Dr. Chris KACIR
85 Director for International Pgms ..... Mr. Ryan WARNER
18 Director of Facilities ..... Mr. Butch KOTCAMP
97 Director General Education Program ..... Dr. Michael BARNHART
09 Dir Inst Research/Spec Proj ..... Mr. Christopher SHAFFER
21 Controller ..... Mr. Greg BALLENGEE
19 Chief of Police ..... Mr. David THOROUGHMAN
04 Executive Asst to President ..... Ms. Pamela OTWORTH
39 Director Housing & Residence Life ..... Mr. Bill ROCKWELL
25 Chief Grants Administrator ..... Ms. Susie RATCLIFF

Sinclair Community College (A)

444 W Third Street, Dayton OH 45402-1460
County: Montgomery FICE Identification: 003119
Unit ID: 205470
Telephone: (937) 512-3000 Carnegie Class: Assoc/MT-VT-Mix Trad/Non
FAX Number: (937) 512-4596 Calendar System: Semester
URL: www.sinclair.edu
Established: 1887 Annual Undergrad Tuition & Fees (In-District): $2,870
Enrollment: 18,448 Coed
Affiliation or Control: State/Local IRS Status: 501(c)3
Highest Offering: Baccalaureate
Accreditation: **NH**, ACBSP, ACFEI, ADNUR, ART, CAHIIM, COARC, CSHSE, DH, DIETT, EMT, MAC, MLTAD, MUS, OTA, PTAA, RAD, SURGT, THEA

01 President .... Dr. Steven L. JOHNSON
00 President Emeritus .... Dr. Ned J. SIFFERLEN
05 Provost .... Dr. Dave COLLINS
10 Sr VP and CFO .... Mr. Jeff BOUDOURIS
103 SVP for Workforce Development .... Dr. Dave COLLINS
15 Director of Human Resources .... Mr. Nathaniel NEWMAN
84 VP Enroll Mgmt & Student Affairs .... Dr. Scott MARKLAND
12 VP for Regional Centers .... Ms. Madeline ISELI
100 VP for Advancement .... Mr. Adam MURKA
13 Chief Information Officer .... Mr. Scott MCCOLLUM
88 Chief School Partnership Officer .... Ms. Melissa TOLLE
106 Dean of eLearning .... Ms. Christina AMATO
20 Assoc Provost Student Completion .... Dr. Kathleen CLEARY
20 Associate Provost .... Ms. Jennifer KOSTIC
81 Dean of Science/Math/Engineering .... Mr. Anthony PONDER
76 Dean Health Sciences .... Ms. Rena SHUCHAT
50 Dean Business & Public Services .... Ms. Elizabeth ORLANDO
83 Dean Arts/Commun & Social Science .... Ms. Shari RETHMAN
43 General Counsel .... Ms. Lauren ROSS
06 Registrar .... Ms. Tina HUMMONS
37 Director Financial Aid/Enrollment .... Mr. Matthew MOORE
104 Director International Education .... Ms. Deborah GAVLIK
121 Director Academic Advising .... Ms. Karla KNEPPER

Southern State Community College (B)

100 Hobart Drive, Hillsboro OH 45133-9488
County: Highland FICE Identification: 012870
Unit ID: 205966
Telephone: (937) 393-3431 Carnegie Class: Assoc/MT-VT-High Non
FAX Number: (937) 393-9370 Calendar System: Semester
URL: www.sscc.edu
Established: 1975 Annual Undergrad Tuition & Fees (In-State): $5,012
Enrollment: 2,719 Coed
Affiliation or Control: State IRS Status: 501(c)3
Highest Offering: Associate Degree
Accreditation: **NH**, ADNUR, MAC

01 President .... Dr. Kevin S. BOYS
05 Vice President Academic Affairs .... Dr. Nicole ROADES
10 Vice President Business & Finance .... Mr. James E. BUCK
32 Vice Pres Student Svcs/Enroll Mgmt .... Mr. James BLAND
12 Director of Fayette Campus .... Dr. Jessica WISE
12 Director of Central Campus .... Mr. Jeff MONTGOMERY
103 Dean Workforce Dev/Community Svcs .... Ms. Amy MCCLELLAN
15 Director of Human Resources .... Ms. Mindy MARKEY-GRABILL
88 Dean of Adult Opportunity Center .... Ms. Karyn EVANS
91 Computer System/Communication Mgr .... Ms. Shirley A. CORNWELL
06 Registrar .... Ms. Amanda THOMPSON
66 Director of Nursing .... Dr. Julianne KREBS
08 Librarian .... Ms. Angel MOOTISPAW
37 Director Financial Aid .... Ms. Linda MYERS
07 Director of Admissions .... Ms. Lisa HORD
41 Athletic Director .... Mr. Matt WELLS
13 Executive Director of IT Services .... Mr. Brian RICE
04 Executive Asst to President .... Ms. Robin THOLEN

† Enrollment figure emcompasses all 4 campuses.

Southern State Community College Brown County Campus (C)

351 Brooks-Malott Rd, Mt Orab OH 45154
Telephone: (937) 444-7722 Identification: 770361
Accreditation: **&NH**

Southern State Community College Fayette Campus (D)

1270 US Route 62 SW,
Washington Court House OH 43160
Telephone: (740) 333-5115 Identification: 770362
Accreditation: **&NH**, COARC

Southern State Community College North Campus (E)

1850 Davids Drive, Wilmington OH 45177
Telephone: (937) 382-6645 Identification: 770363
Accreditation: **&NH**

Stark State College (F)

6200 Frank Avenue, NW, North Canton OH 44720-7299
County: Stark FICE Identification: 010881
Unit ID: 205841
Telephone: (330) 494-6170 Carnegie Class: Assoc/HVT-Mix Trad/Non
FAX Number: (330) 497-6313 Calendar System: Semester
URL: www.starkstate.edu
Established: 1960 Annual Undergrad Tuition & Fees (In-District): $4,070
Enrollment: 11,613 Coed
Affiliation or Control: State/Local IRS Status: 501(c)3
Highest Offering: Associate Degree
Accreditation: **NH**, ACBSP, ACFEI, ADNUR, CAHIIM, COARC, DH, DIETT, EMT, MAC, MLTAD, OTA, PTAA, SURGA, SURGT

01 President .... Dr. Para M. JONES
05 Provost and Chief Academic Officer .... Dr. Lada GIBSON-SHREVE
10 VP for Business and Finance .... Mr. Thomas A. CHIAPPINI
84 VP for Enrollment Management .... Dr. Stephanie SUTTON
15 Director of Human Resources .... Ms. Melissa A. GLANZ
53 Dean Ed/Liberal Arts/Math/Science .... Mr. Andrew STEPHAN
76 Dean Health and Human Services .... Dr. Kathleen SOMMERS
21 Controller .... Mr. Scott ANDREANI
37 Exec Dir Fin Aid & Registration .... Ms. Amy WELTY
18 Director of Physical Plant and Cons .... Mr. Steve SPRADLING
40 Bookstore Manager .... Ms. Kathryn FEICHTER
06 Registrar .... Ms. Pam ARRINGTON
111 Exec Dir Advance & SSC Foundation .... Ms. Marisa ROHN
114 Director of Budget .... Mr. Bruce WYDER
09 Director of Institutional Research .... Mr. Peter TRUMPOWER
54 Dean Engineering Technologies .... Dr. Don BALL
106 Director eStarkState .... Ms. Linda MOROSKO
08 Head Librarian .... Ms. Marcia ADDISON
04 Exec Admin Asst to President .... Ms. Catherine D. SPINO
07 Exec Director of Admissions .... Mr. J.P COONEY
50 Dean Business and IT .... Dr. James FALTER
26 Director of Marketing .... Ms. Robyn STEINMETZ
19 Director Security/Safety .... Mr. Gregory BOUDREAUX

Stautzenberger College (G)

8001 Katherine Boulevard, Brecksville OH 44141
Telephone: (440) 838-1999 Identification: 770760
Accreditation: **ACCSC**, DMS, SURTEC

Stautzenberger College (H)

1796 Indian Wood Circle, Maumee OH 43537-4007
County: Lucas FICE Identification: 004866
Unit ID: 205887
Telephone: (419) 866-0261 Carnegie Class: Assoc/HVT-Mix Trad/Non
FAX Number: (419) 867-9821 Calendar System: Other
URL: www.sctoday.edu
Established: 1926 Annual Undergrad Tuition & Fees: $14,843
Enrollment: 624 Coed
Affiliation or Control: Proprietary IRS Status: Proprietary
Highest Offering: Associate Degree
Accreditation: **ACCSC**, MLTAB

01 Campus President .... Ms. Amy BEAUREGARD
09 Compliance Officer .... Mr. Brian E. NIEDZWIECKI
07 Director of Admissions .... Mr. Ivan V. BAUBLITZ
05 Dean of Academics .... Vacant
37 Financial Aid Director .... Mrs. Mari L. HUFFMAN
36 Career Services Director .... Mr. Robert A. GARVER
06 Registrar .... Ms. Terri KINDER
08 Head Librarian .... Ms. Lori VAN LIERE
32 Dean of Students .... Ms. Britney WOODS

Terra State Community College (I)

2830 Napoleon Road, Fremont OH 43420-9670
County: Sandusky FICE Identification: 008278
Unit ID: 206011
Telephone: (419) 334-8400 Carnegie Class: Assoc/HVT-High Non
FAX Number: (419) 334-3719 Calendar System: Semester
URL: www.terra.edu
Established: 1968 Annual Undergrad Tuition & Fees (In-State): $4,652
Enrollment: 2,243 Coed
Affiliation or Control: State IRS Status: 501(c)3
Highest Offering: Associate Degree
Accreditation: **NH**, ADNUR, CAHIIM, MAC, PTAA

01 President .... Dr. Ron SCHUMACHER
111 VP Institutional Advancement .... Dr. Cory STINE
10 Co-Interim VP of Financial Affairs .... Ms. Jacque FOOS
10 Co-Interim VP of Financial Affairs .... Mr. Jerry BUCCILLA
05 Vice Pres Academic Affairs .... Mr. William TAYLOR
84 VP Student Affairs/Enrollment Svcs .... Dr. Kristen LINDSAY
50 Dean Business/Comm/Industrial Tech .... Ms. Ann SERGENT
76 Dean Allied Hlth/Nursing/Human Svcs .... Ms. Amy ANWAY
15 Director of Human Services .... Mr. Jeremy MCLANEY
09 Dir Planning/Inst Effectiveness .... Ms. Ellen WARDZALA
06 Registrar .... Mr. Eric STEINBERGER
13 Manager Information Technology .... Mr. Wayne YERDON
08 Librarian .... Ms. Amy KREILICK
04 Executive Assistant to President .... Ms. Jessica HUFFMAN
106 Instructional Technologist .... Ms. Melinda YERDON
32 Associate Dean of Students .... Mr. Todd LONG
38 Director ASC & Student Counseling .... Ms. Dori DALTON

Tiffin University (J)

155 Miami Street, Tiffin OH 44883-2161
County: Seneca FICE Identification: 003121
Unit ID: 206048
Telephone: (419) 447-6442 Carnegie Class: Masters/L
FAX Number: N/A Calendar System: Semester
URL: www.tiffin.edu
Established: 1888 Annual Undergrad Tuition & Fees: $25,000
Enrollment: 3,149 Coed
Affiliation or Control: Independent Non-Profit IRS Status: 501(c)3
Highest Offering: Doctorate
Accreditation: **NH**, ACBSP

01 President .... Dr. Lillian SCHUMACHER
05 Provost .... Dr. Peter HOLBROOK
84 VP Enrollment Management .... Dr. Amy WOOD
111 VP University Advancement .... Mr. Mitchell BLONDE
10 VP Finance/Administration .... Ms. Donna FRANK
15 AVP Human Resources .... Ms. Nadia LEWIS
108 VP Inst Planning & Effectiveness .... Dr. Teresa SHAFER
26 Marketing/Communications Coord .... Ms. Deborah ROSZMAN
04 Exec Assistant to the President .... Ms. Nancy GILBERT
32 Dean of Students .... Mr. Mike HERDLICK
13 Chief Information Officer .... Mr. Jason MARSON
07 Director Undergrad Admissions .... Ms. Sarah JOHNSON
27 Exec Dir Media Rels/Publications .... Ms. Lisa WILLIAMS
06 Registrar & Dean of Student Support .... Ms. Melissa WEININGER
41 Director Athletics .... Mr. Lonny ALLEN
21 Controller .... Ms. Jean THOMAS
08 Head Librarian .... Ms. Catherine CARLSON
29 Director Alumni Relations .... Ms. Vickie WILKINS
36 Exec Director of Career Services .... Ms. Amanda HUMMEL
18 Director of Physical Plant .... Mr. Mike HERDLICK
39 Director of Residence Life .... Mr. Jacob SIMON
44 Director of Annual Fund .... Ms. Mikki KING
28 AVP Equity/Access/Opp/Title IX .... Dr. Sharon PERRY-FANTINI
37 Director Student Financial Aid .... Ms. Andrea FABER
49 Dean of Arts & Sciences .... Dr. Joyce HALL-YATES
50 Dean of Business .... Dr. Terry SULLIVAN
83 Dean Criminal Justice/Social Sci .... Mr. David SELNICK
09 Director of Institutional Research .... Vacant
104 Director Study Abroad .... Mr. Jonathan BEARD
19 Director Security/Safety .... Mr. Sean DUROCHER
106 Vice Provost/Online & Extended Lrng .... Dr. Daniel CLARK

Tri-State Bible College (K)

506 Margaret Street, PO Box 445,
South Point OH 45680-8402
County: Lawrence FICE Identification: 034754
Unit ID: 206154
Telephone: (740) 377-2520 Carnegie Class: Spec-4-yr-Faith
FAX Number: (740) 377-0001 Calendar System: Semester
URL: www.tsbc.edu
Established: 1970 Annual Undergrad Tuition & Fees: $9,100
Enrollment: 39 Coed
Affiliation or Control: Independent Non-Profit IRS Status: 501(c)3
Highest Offering: Baccalaureate
Accreditation: **BI**

01 President .... Vacant
05 Vice President Academic Affairs .... Vacant
10 Vice President Finance .... Vacant
11 Vice Pres Administrative Affairs .... Ms. Roberta (Bobby) MERCER
32 Vice Pres Student Affairs .... Vacant
18 Vice President Operations .... Mr. Manfred LANGER
20 Academic Dean Online Programs .... Mr. David LAMBERT

Union Institute & University (L)

440 E McMillan Street, Cincinnati OH 45206-1947
County: Hamilton FICE Identification: 010923
Unit ID: 206279
Telephone: (513) 861-6400 Carnegie Class: DU-Mod
FAX Number: (513) 861-0779 Calendar System: Semester
URL: www.myunion.edu
Established: 1964 Annual Undergrad Tuition & Fees: $13,256
Enrollment: 1,085 Coed
Affiliation or Control: Independent Non-Profit IRS Status: 501(c)3
Highest Offering: Doctorate
Accreditation: **NH**, CACREP, LC, SW

01 President .... Dr. Karen SCHUSTER-WEBB
05 Vice President Academic Affairs .... Dr. Nelson SOTO
04 Executive Assistant to President .... Ms. Carolyn KRAUSE
10 Chief Financial Officer .... Mr. Kenneth CARROLL
15 Vice President Human Resources .... Ms. Patty BURKE
84 VP Enrollment Management .... Vacant
111 Vice President Advancement .... Ms. Carolyn KRAUSE
20 Associate VP of Academic Affairs .... Dr. Arlene SACKS
06 Registrar .... Ms. Lew Rita MOORE
13 Director Information Technology .... Mr. Shawn MCCOLLUM
18 Director Facilities Management .... Mr. Ken LAMB
12 Executive Director Florida Center .... Dr. Jay KEEHN
12 Executive Director LA Center .... Dr. Rhonda BRINKLEY-KENNEDY
12 National Dean Undergrad Programs .... Dr. Peter CACCAVERI
12 Executive Director Sacramento Ctr .... Ms. Julie CRANDALL
08 Director Library Services .... Mr. Matthew PAPPATHAN
37 Director Financial Aid .... Ms. Jean POHLMAN
29 Director Alumni Relations .... Dr. Rand OLIVER
32 Director Student Success .... Dr. Eric MAST
106 Dir Center for Teaching & Learning .... Dr. Bob COTTER

United Theological Seminary (A)

4501 Denlinger Road, Dayton OH 45426-2308
County: Montgomery FICE Identification: 003122
Unit ID: 206288
Telephone: (937) 529-2201 Carnegie Class: Spec-4-yr-Faith
FAX Number: (866) 433-8235 Calendar System: Semester
URL: www.united.edu
Established: 1871 Annual Graduate Tuition & Fees: N/A
Enrollment: 421 Coed
Affiliation or Control: United Methodist IRS Status: 501(c)3
Highest Offering: Doctorate; No Undergraduates
Accreditation: NH, THEOL

01 President .... Dr. Kent MILLARD
05 Vice Pres Academic Affairs & Dean .... Dr. David WATSON
10 Vice Pres Finance/Treasurer .... Mr. Steven SWALLOW
84 Vice Pres for Enrollment .... Dr. Bridget WEATHERSPOON
30 Vice Pres Development .... Ms. Callie PICARDO
101 Exec Asst to President/Corp Secy .... Ms. Laura WEBER
20 Assoc Dean Academic Affairs .... Dr. Vivian JOHNSON
06 Registrar .... Ms. Karen CLARK
13 Director of Information Technology .... Vacant
106 Assoc Dean Distance Learning .... Ms. Phyllis ENNIST
08 Librarian .... Ms. Sarah D. BROOKS BLAIR
42 Dean of the Chapel .... Dr. Rosario PICARDO
26 Director of Communications .... Ms. Rachel HURLEY
37 Director Financial Aid .... Ms. Marcia BYRD
29 Coordinator of Alumni/ae Relations .... Ms. Dawn GREENWALT
18 Facility Manager .... Mr. Ryan LEHMAN
108 Chf Strategy/Admin/Assessment Ofcr .... Ms. Karen E. PAYNE
07 Senior Dir Admissions .... Dr. Bridget WEATHERSPOON
32 Director of Student Services .... Rev. Chad CLARK

The University of Akron, Main Campus (B)

302 Buchtel Common, Akron OH 44325
County: Summit FICE Identification: 003123
Unit ID: 200800
Telephone: (330) 972-7111 Carnegie Class: DU-Higher
FAX Number: (330) 972-6990 Calendar System: Semester
URL: www.uakron.edu
Established: 1870 Annual Undergrad Tuition & Fees (In-State): $11,463
Enrollment: 20,169 Coed
Affiliation or Control: State IRS Status: 501(c)3
Highest Offering: Doctorate
Accreditation: NH, ACBSP, ANEST, ART, AUD, #CAATE, CACREP, CAEP, CAEPN, CIDA, COARC, COPSY, DANCE, DIETC, DIETD, IFSAC, IPSY, LAW, MAC, MFCD, MUS, NURSE, PH, SP, SW

01 Interim President .... Dr. John C. GREEN
11 Executive VP/Chief Admin Officer .... Dr. Rex RAMSIER
05 Int Exec VP/Chief Academic Officer .... Dr. Chand MIDHA
45 VP Innovation & Economic Dev .... Vacant
10 VP Finance & Administration/CFO .... Mr. Nathan J. MORTIMER
43 Vice President & General Counsel .... Ms. M. Celeste COOK
13 Chief Information Officer .... Mr. John T. CORBY
32 Dean of Students .... Mr. Mike STRONG
30 Vice President of Development .... Mrs. Kimberly M. COLE
18 Int Chief Planning & Facilities .... Mr. Stephen MYERS
88 Dir of Presidential Communication .... Mr. David NYPAVER
21 Assc VP Treasury/Financial Planning .... Mr. Brian E. DAVIS
46 Assoc Vice President for Research .... Mr. Kenneth G. PRESTON
22 VP Inclusion and Equity .... Ms. Jolene A. LANE
15 Assoc VP Talent Dev/Human Resources .... Mrs. Sarah J. KELLY
26 VP/Chief Comm and Marketing Officer .... Mr. Wayne R. HILL
35 VP for Student Affairs .... Dr. John A. MESSINA
19 Asst VP Camp Safety/Chief of Police .... Major Jim P. WEBER
43 Assoc VP & Assoc General Counsel .... Mr. John J. REILLY
06 Registrar .... Mr. Ronald L. BOWMAN, JR.
07 Director of Admissions .... Ms. Kim GENTILE
09 Asst Dir Institutional Research .... Ms. Lynn LUCAS
14 Director Technology Transfer .... Mr. Kenneth G. PRESTON
08 Dean University Libraries .... Dr. Aimee L. DECHAMBEAU
49 Int Dean Buchtel College Arts & Sci .... Dr. Linda M. SUBICH
54 Int Dean College of Engineering .... Dr. Craig MENZEMER
53 Interim Dean College of Education .... Dr. Jarrod TUDOR
50 Int Dean College of Business Admin .... Dr. Susan HANLON
76 Int Dean College Health Professions .... Dr. Elizabeth A. KENNEDY
72 Dean Col of Appl Sci & Technology .... Dr. Elizabeth A. KENNEDY
61 Dean School of Law .... Mr. Christopher PETERS
58 Exec Dean of Graduate School .... Dr. Chand MIDHA
54 Int Dean of Polymer Sci/Engineer .... Dr. Ali DHINOJWALA
12 Dean Wayne College .... Dr. Jarrod TUDOR
37 Director Student Financial Aid .... Mrs. Jennifer E. HARPHAM
29 Asst VP Alumni Relations .... Mr. Willy KOLLMAN
96 Director of Purchasing .... Ms. Luba CRAMER
88 Senior Director Integrated Comm .... Mr. Robert KROPFF
105 Director of Web Services .... Mr. Anthony W. SERPETTE
92 Int Dean Honors College .... Dr. John HUSS
88 Director UA Adult Focus .... Mrs. Laura H. CONLEY
41 Director Athletics .... Mr. Lawrence R. WILLIAMS
36 Ex Dir Counseling/Test/Career Ctr .... Dr. Juanita K. MARTIN
39 Dir of Residence Life and Housing .... Dr. Melinda GROVE
25 Asst VP Office Research Admin .... Ms. Katie WATKINS-WENDELL
85 Exec Dir Center for Intl Stds & Sch .... Ms. Nicola KILLE
23 Director Health Services .... Ms. Alma E. OLSON
86 Public Liaison/Asst Director RCBIAP .... Dr. Matthew P. AKERS
88 Director IT Support Services .... Mr. Neal L'AMOREAUX
88 Director of Media Relations .... Ms. Cristine BOYD
102 Asst VP Corp Fund Relations .... Mrs. Ellen PERDUYN
84 Assoc Prov Enrollment Management .... Mr. William KRAUS
100 Chief of Staff .... Vacant
104 Director Study Abroad .... Mr. Anthony P. COLUCCI, III
28 Chief Diversity Officer .... Ms. Jolene A. LANE

The University of Akron-Wayne College (C)

1901 Smucker Road, Orrville OH 44667-9758
Telephone: (330) 683-2010 FICE Identification: 010818
Accreditation: &NH

† Regional accreditation is carried under the parent institution in Akron, OH.

University of Cincinnati Main Campus (D)

2624 Clifton Avenue, Cincinnati OH 45221-0001
County: Hamilton FICE Identification: 003125
Unit ID: 201885
Telephone: (513) 556-6000 Carnegie Class: DU-Highest
FAX Number: (513) 556-3237 Calendar System: Semester
URL: www.uc.edu
Established: 1819 Annual Undergrad Tuition & Fees (In-State): $11,000
Enrollment: 37,155 Coed
Affiliation or Control: State IRS Status: 501(c)3
Highest Offering: Doctorate
Accreditation: NH, ANEST, ART, AUD, CAATE, CACREP, CAEP, CAEPN, CAHIIM, CAMPEP, CIDA, CLPSY, CONST, DANCE, DENT, DIETC, DIETD, LAW, MED, MIDWF, MT, MUS, NMT, NURSE, PH, PHAR, PLNG, PTA, RADMAG, SCPSY, SP, SW, THEA

01 President .... Dr. Neville G. PINTO
05 Exec VP/Provost Academic Affairs .... Dr. Kristi A. NELSON
11 Sr VP for Administration & Finance .... Mr. Robert AMBACH
03 Executive VP .... Dr. Ryan HAYS
46 Vice President for Research .... Dr. Patrick A. LIMBACH
63 Int Dean Med/Sr VP Health Affairs .... Dr. Andrew FILAK
30 VP Development/Alumni Rels .... Mr. Peter LANDGREN
86 Chief Marketing Officer .... Ms. Nicola ZIADY
32 Vice Pres Student Affairs & Svcs .... Ms. Debra S. MERCHANT
10 Vice President for Finance .... Mr. Patrick A. KOWALSKI
13 VP & CIO for Information Technology .... Dr. Nelson C. VINCENT
43 General Counsel .... Ms. Lori A. ROSS
15 Sr Assoc VP/Chief HR Officer .... Ms. Tamie L. GRUNOW
84 Sr Assoc Vice President Enrollment .... Dr. Caroline B. MILLER
31 Int Director Community Development .... Mr. Enrique David AVERION
26 Director Media Relations .... Ms. MB REILLY
07 Asst Vice Prov Admissions .... Ms. Tamara C. BYLAND
110 Vice Pres for Development .... Mr. Stephen ROSFELD
76 Dean Allied Health Sciences .... Dr. Tina WHALEN
49 Dean Arts & Sciences .... Dr. Valerio C. FERME
50 Dean Business .... Dr. Marianne W. LEWIS
64 Dean Col Conservatory of Music .... Dr. Stanley E. ROMANSTEIN
48 Dean Design/Architecture/Art & Plng .... Dr. Timothy J. JACHNA
53 Dean Education/Crim Justice & HS .... Dr. Lawrence J. JOHNSON
54 Dean Engineering & Applied Sci .... Dr. John W. WEIDNER
61 Dean Law .... Ms. Verna L. WILLIAMS
66 Dean Nursing .... Dr. Greer L. GLAZER
67 Dean Pharmacy .... Dr. Neil J. MACKINNON
70 Director School Social Work .... Dr. Ruth Anne VAN LOON
08 Dean Library .... Mr. Xuemao WANG
29 VP Alumni Affairs .... Ms. Jennifer HEISEY
28 VP Equity/Inclusion/Cmty Impact .... Dr. Bleuzette MARSHALL
41 Director Athletics .... Mr. Michael BOHN
40 Int Director Bookstore .... Mr. Shane ZALESKI
36 Int Dean Career Education .... Dr. Gisela ESCOE
38 Director Counseling Center .... Dr. Tara H. SCARBOROUGH
22 Exec Dir Equal Opportunity/Access .... Mr. Matthew J. OLOVSON
39 Sr Assoc VP Campus Services .... Mr. Todd DUNCAN
37 Director Student Financial Aid .... Mr. Randy ULSES
09 Director Institutional Research .... Mrs. Suzana H. LUZURIAGA
19 Director Public Safety .... Mr. James L. WHALEN
06 Registrar .... Dr. Douglas BURGESS
96 Assoc VP Purchasing .... Mr. Thomas B. GUERIN
45 Co-Dir Institute for Policy Rsrch .... Dr. Eric RADEMACHER
45 Co-Dir Institute for Policy Rsrch .... Dr. Kimberly DOWNING
104 Vice Provost International Programs .... Dr. Raj MEHTA
18 Chief Facilities/Physical Plant .... Mr. Joseph H. HARRELL
101 Exec Director Board of Trustees .... Ms. Nicole BLOUNT
88 Chief Innovation Officer .... Mr. David J. ADAMS
25 Assoc VP Sponsored Research .... Mr. Patrick E. CLARK
106 Asst VP eLearning .... Mr. Paul C. FOSTER
04 Administrative Asst to President .... Mr. Lawrence P. LAMPE
100 Chief of Staff .... Dr. Ryan HAYS
106 Vice Prov Dean Cincinnati Online .... Dr. Jason E. LEMON
108 Vice Prov Institutional Assessment .... Dr. Gigi ESCOE
102 Dir Foundation/Corporate Relations .... Mr. Danny FERRELL
105 Director Web Services .... Mr. Jeremy A. MARTIN
44 Exec Director Annual Giving .... Mr. James BARNARD

University of Cincinnati Blue Ash College (E)

9555 Plainfield Road, Blue Ash OH 45236-1096
County: Hamilton FICE Identification: 004868
Unit ID: 201955
Telephone: (513) 745-5600 Carnegie Class: Bac/Assoc-Assoc Dom
FAX Number: (513) 745-5780 Calendar System: Semester
URL: www.ucblueash.edu
Established: 1967 Annual Undergrad Tuition & Fees (In-State): $6,010
Enrollment: 4,779 Coed
Affiliation or Control: State IRS Status: 501(c)3
Highest Offering: Baccalaureate
Accreditation: NH, ADNUR, ART, DH, MAC, RAD

01 Dean .... Dr. Robin LIGHTNER
05 Assoc Dean Academic Affairs .... Dr. Tracy HERRMANN
10 Director Business Affairs & HR .... Mr. Marc WATSON
20 Asst Dean Academic Affairs .... Dr. Gregory METZ
18 Director Facilities & Campus Plan .... Mr. Rob KNARR
13 Director Information Technology .... Mr. Dale HOFSTETTER
07 Director Admissions .... Mr. Brad TATE
09 Director Institutional Research .... Mr. Steve MILLER
30 Director Development .... Ms. Jennifer BERIGAN
08 Library Director .... Ms. Heather MALONEY
26 Director Mktg/Communication .... Mr. Pete GEMMER
32 Director Student Engagement .... Ms. Sarah WOLFE
121 Interim Director Academic Advising .... Ms. Laurie MALONE
35 Director One Stop Student Services .... Ms. Martha GEIGER
15 HR Manager .... Ms. Amy SMITH
22 Director Accessibility Resources .... Ms. Pamela GOINES

University of Cincinnati-Clermont College (F)

4200 Clermont College Drive, Batavia OH 45103-1785
County: Clermont FICE Identification: 010805
Unit ID: 201946
Telephone: (513) 732-5200 Carnegie Class: Bac/Assoc-Mixed
FAX Number: (513) 732-5275 Calendar System: Quarter
URL: www.ucclermont.edu
Established: 1972 Annual Undergrad Tuition & Fees (In-State): $5,316
Enrollment: 2,799 Coed
Affiliation or Control: State IRS Status: 501(c)3
Highest Offering: Baccalaureate
Accreditation: NH, CAHIIM, PTAA, SURGA, SURGT

01 Dean .... Dr. Jeffrey C. BAUER
05 Assoc Dean Academic Affairs .... Dr. Mona SEDRAK
20 Assistant Dean Academic Affairs .... Mr. Richard STACKPOLE
18 Asst Dean Facilities & Tech Svcs .... Mr. Stephen W. YOUNG
26 Sr Asst Dean Student Services .... Ms. Mae HANNA
08 Director Library .... Vacant
24 Director Learning Center .... Dr. Eric MAST
09 Dir Institutional Effectiveness .... Ms. Susan RILEY
10 Director Business Affairs .... Mr. Daniel SOLAZZO
32 Sr Dir Retention & Student Success .... Ms. Jennifer RADT
07 Assoc Director Recruitment .... Mr. Blaine KELLY
06 Asst Dir Registration & Records .... Ms. Kristine LOUGHRAN
88 Director Disability Services .... Ms. Jennifer RADT
35 Director of Student Life .... Vacant
41 Athletic Director .... Mr. Brian SULLIVAN
30 Director of Development .... Ms. Dana PARKER

University of Dayton (G)

300 College Park, Dayton OH 45469-0001
County: Montgomery FICE Identification: 003127
Unit ID: 202480
Telephone: (937) 229-1000 Carnegie Class: DU-Higher
FAX Number: (937) 229-4000 Calendar System: Semester
URL: www.udayton.edu
Established: 1850 Annual Undergrad Tuition & Fees: $42,900
Enrollment: 10,882 Coed
Affiliation or Control: Roman Catholic IRS Status: 501(c)3
Highest Offering: Doctorate
Accreditation: NH, #ARCPA, ART, CACREP, CAEP, CEA, DIETD, LAW, MUS, PTA, SPAA

01 President .... Dr. Eric F. SPINA
05 Provost .... Dr. Paul H. BENSON
32 VP Student Development .... Mr. William M. FISCHER
10 EVP Finance & Admin Services .... Mr. Andrew E. HORNER
111 VP Univ Advancement .... Ms. Jennifer L. HOWE
41 VP/Director of Athletics .... Mr. Neil G. SULLIVAN
15 VP Human Resources .... Mr. Troy W. WASHINGTON
84 VP for Strategic Enrollment Mgmt .... Dr. Jason K. REINOEHL
46 VP of Research/Exec Dir UDRI .... Dr. John E. LELAND
30 Sr Dir Development/Principal Gifts .... Mr. James F. BROTHERS
42 Exec Director Campus Ministry .... Ms. Crystal C. SULLIVAN
88 VP for Mission and Rector .... Rev. James F. FITZ, SM
31 Dir Ctr for Ldrshp in Cmty .... Ms. Hunter P. GOODMAN
20 Assoc Provost Faculty & Admin Affs .... Dr. Carolyn ROECKER-PHELPS
88 Asc Prov Lrng Spprt/Dir Rch Tch Ctr .... Dr. Deborah J. BICKFORD
06 Registrar .... Ms. Jennifer M. CREECH
07 Asst VP/Dean of Admission & Fin Aid .... Mr. Robert F. DURKLE
19 Exec Director/Chief of Police .... Mr. Rodney CHATMAN
09 Director Institutional Studies .... Ms. Susan K. SEXTON
21 Comptroller .... Ms. Angela K. BUECHELE
35 Assoc VP/Dean of Students .... Ms. Christine M. SCHRAMM
36 Director Career Services .... Mr. Jason C. ECKERT
38 Asst VP Student Dev/Dir Counseling .... Vacant
18 VP for Facilities/Management/Plng .... Mr. Richard KRYSIAK, JR.
23 Medical Director Univ Health Ctr .... Dr. Mary P. BUCHWALDER
08 Dean University Libraries .... Ms. Kathleen M. WEBB
49 Dean College A&S .... Dr. Jason L. PIERCE
61 Dean School of Law .... Mr. Andrew L. STRAUSS
50 Dean Sch of Business Admin .... Dr. John MITTELSTAEDT
58 Assoc Prov Graduate Acad Affairs .... Dr. Paul M. VANDERBURGH
13 Assoc Provost & Chief Info Officer .... Dr. Thomas D. SKILL
53 Dean School of Educ & Health Sci .... Dr. Kevin R. KELLY
54 Dean School of Engineering .... Dr. Eddy M. ROJAS

29 Sr Development Officer .... Mr. Todd W. IMWALLE
35 Dir Student Life & Kennedy Union .... Ms. Amy L. LOPEZ-MATTHEWS
37 Exec Dir Flyers First/Dir Fin Aid .... Ms. Catherine MIX
39 Asst Dean Students & Dir Res Life .... Mr. Steven T. HERNDON
40 Manager UD Bookstore .... Ms. Julie M. BANKS
43 Univ Counsel/Dir Legal Affairs .... Ms. Mary A. RECKER
96 Dir Univ Purchases/Business Service .... Ms. Sara HARRISON
92 Dir University Honors/Scholars Pgm .... Dr. John P. MCCOMBE
94 Chair Women's/Gender Studies .... Dr. Corinne DEPRANO
22 Dir Affirmative Action & Compliance .... Ms. Patricia BERNAL-OLSON
86 Exec Dir Govt/Regional Relations .... Mr. S. Ted BUCARO
28 VP Diversity & Inclusion .... Dr. Lawrence A. BURNLEY
26 Dir Marketing & Creative Services .... Ms. Kim B. LALLY
04 Asst to President .... Ms. Annette MITCHELL
100 Executive Director .... Mr. Thomas U. WECKESSER
101 Secretary of the Board of Trustees .... Ms. Lisa S. RISMILLER

The University of Findlay (A)

1000 North Main Street, Findlay OH 45840-3653

County: Hancock — FICE Identification: 003045 — Unit ID: 202763

Telephone: (419) 422-8313 — Carnegie Class: DU-Mod

FAX Number: (419) 434-4822 — Calendar System: Semester

URL: www.findlay.edu

Established: 1882 — Annual Undergrad Tuition & Fees: $34,360

Enrollment: 4,888 — Coed

Affiliation or Control: Church Of God — IRS Status: 501(c)3

Highest Offering: Doctorate

Accreditation: NH, ACBSP, ARCPA, CAATE, CAEPN, CEA, DMS, NMT, NURSE, OT, PHAR, PTA, SW

01 President .... Dr. Katherine R. FELL
05 Vice President for Academic Affairs .... Dr. Darin FIELDS
10 VP Business Affairs/CFO/Treasurer .... Mr. Thomas LAUSE
84 VP Enrollment Mgmt .... Mr. Jeremy PITTMAN
111 Vice Pres University Advancement .... Dr. Marcia SLOAN LATTA
32 Vice President for Student Affairs .... Mr. David W. EMSWELLER
20 Assoc VP Academic Affairs .... Dr. C. Damon OSBORNE
04 Assistant to the President .... Ms. Liz DITTO
81 Dean College of Sciences .... Dr. Jeffrey FRYE
50 Interim Dean College of Business .... Dr. C. Damon OSBORNE
49 Dean Col of Arts/Hum & Social Sci .... Dr. Ronald TULLEY
76 Dean College Health Professions .... Dr. Richard STATES
67 Dean College of Pharmacy .... Dr. Debra PARKER
53 Dean College of Education .... Dr. Julie MCINTOSH
18 Director of Physical Plant .... Mr. Orion JONES
06 Registrar/Dir of Inst Research .... Mr. Tony G. GOEDDE
41 Athletic Director .... Ms. Brandi LAURITA
08 Director of Shafer Library .... Mr. Andrew WHITIS
37 Director of Financial Aid .... Mr. Joseph F. SPENCER
13 VP of Information Tech Services .... Dr. Raymond MCCANDLESS
29 Director of Alumni Affairs .... Vacant
26 Dir Public Relations/Media Rels .... Ms. Rebecca JENKINS
36 Director of Career/Prof Development .... Mr. Bradley C. HAMMER
15 Director of Human Resources .... Mr. Robert LINK
23 Director of Health Services .... Ms. Julie R. YINGLING
38 Director Counseling Services .... Ms. Karyn J. WESTRICK
40 Manager of Bookstore .... Mr. Jay CANTERBURY
42 Director Christian Ministries .... Mr. Matthew GINTER
19 Chief of Police/Dir of Security .... Mr. William SPRAW
104 Asst VP Intl/Intercult/Svc Engage .... Mr. Christopher SIPPEL
101 Secretary to the Board of Trustees .... Ms. Liz DITTO
25 Grants Manager .... Ms. Tricia VALASEK
85 Dir Intl Admiss/Stdnt Immigr Svcs .... Ms. Megan PRETTYMAN
21 Controller .... Ms. Megan SCHULTE
39 Asst Director of Housing .... Ms. Shari HELLMAN
35 Assistant Dean of Students .... Mr. Johnathan FERRARO
44 Director Annual Giving .... Ms. Kelly M. WARNER
30 Asst VP for Development .... Mr. Tyson PINION

University of Mount Union (B)

1972 Clark Avenue, Alliance OH 44601-3993

County: Stark — FICE Identification: 003083 — Unit ID: 204185

Telephone: (330) 821-5320 — Carnegie Class: Bac-Diverse

FAX Number: (330) 829-2811 — Calendar System: Semester

URL: www.mountunion.edu

Established: 1846 — Annual Undergrad Tuition & Fees: $30,860

Enrollment: 2,257 — Coed

Affiliation or Control: Independent Non-Profit — IRS Status: 501(c)3

Highest Offering: Doctorate

Accreditation: NH, ACBSP, ARCPA, #CAATE, CAEP, COSMA, MUS, NURSE, PTA

01 President .... Dr. W. R. MERRIMAN, JR.
05 Vice Pres Acad Affs/Dean of Univ .... Dr. Jeffrey R. BREESE
10 Vice Pres Business Affs/Treasurer .... Mr. Patrick D. HEDDLESTON
111 Vice President Univ Advancement .... Mr. Gregory KING
32 Vice Pres Student Affs/Dean Stdnts .... Mr. John FRAZIER
84 Vice President for Enrollment Mgmt .... Ms. Lindajean WESTERN
26 Vice President for Marketing .... Ms. Melissa GARDNER
08 Librarian .... Mr. Robert R. GARLAND
06 University Registrar .... Dr. Bryan BOATRIGHT
07 Director of Admission .... Mr. Eric YOUNG
112 Director of Planned Giving .... Ms. Sherrie WALLACE
13 Director of Information Technology .... Ms. Tina STUCHELL
110 Director of Advancement .... Mr. Joseph D. MONTGOMERY
29 Director Alumni/College Activities .... Ms. Audra YOUNGEN
85 Director Center for Global Educ .... Dr. Jennifer HALL
18 Director of Physical Plant .... Mr. Blaine D. LEWIS
15 Director of Human Resources .... Mr. Charles STUPPY
39 Director of Residence Life .... Ms. Sara SHERER
42 University Chaplain .... Rev. Kyle WOODROW
36 Exec Director of Career Services .... Ms. Jessica CUNION
40 Manager of University Store .... Ms. Aimee SCHULLER
41 Athletic Director .... Mr. Larry T. KEHRES
04 Exec Assistant to the President .... Ms. Caitlin CLARK
45 Assoc VP Planning Implementation .... Mr. Ronald CROWL
35 Associate Dean of Students .... Ms. Michelle GAFFNEY
96 Purchasing and Risk Manager .... Mr. Shawn BAGLEY
19 Director Security/Safety .... Mr. William KETJEN
28 Director of Diversity & Inclusion .... Mr. Ronald HOLDEN
38 Director of Counseling Services .... Ms. Francine PACKARD
44 Director of the Mount Union Fund .... Ms. Bethany LESLIE
37 Director Student Financial Aid .... Ms. Kathleen THOMAS

University of Northwestern Ohio (C)

1441 N Cable Road, Lima OH 45805-1498

County: Allen — FICE Identification: 004861 — Unit ID: 204486

Telephone: (419) 227-3141 — Carnegie Class: Bac/Assoc-Mixed

FAX Number: (419) 229-6926 — Calendar System: Quarter

URL: www.unoh.edu

Established: 1920 — Annual Undergrad Tuition & Fees: $11,350

Enrollment: 3,741 — Coed

Affiliation or Control: Independent Non-Profit — IRS Status: 501(c)3

Highest Offering: Master's

Accreditation: NH, ACBSP, CAHIIM, MAC

01 President .... Dr. Jeffrey A. JARVIS
05 Vice Pres Academic Affairs/Provost .... Dr. Dean HOBLER
10 Vice President Finance .... Mrs. Marcia EICKHOLT
07 Dir of Admissions-Coll of Business .... Mr. Tony AZZARELLO
18 Vice Pres of Property Management .... Vacant
26 VP Public Rels/Mktg/Special Events .... Mrs. Stephanie MALLOY
30 Vice President Development .... Mr. Steve FARMER
15 Exec Director of Human Resources .... Ms. Geri MORRIS
21 Controller .... Mr. James S. BRONDER
37 Director of Financial Aid .... Mr. Wendell SCHICK
04 Executive Assistant to President .... Mrs. Jennifer BENDELE
72 Dean College of Technologies .... Mr. Kevin MEAGER

University of Rio Grande (D)

218 N College Avenue, PO BOX 500, Rio Grande OH 45674-3100

County: Gallia — FICE Identification: 003116 — Unit ID: 205203

Telephone: (740) 245-5353 — Carnegie Class: Bac/Assoc-Mixed

FAX Number: (740) 245-5266 — Calendar System: Semester

URL: www.rio.edu

Established: 1876 — Annual Undergrad Tuition & Fees: $27,481

Enrollment: 1,812 — Coed

Affiliation or Control: Independent Non-Profit — IRS Status: 501(c)3

Highest Offering: Master's

Accreditation: NH, ADNUR, CAEP, CAEPN, COARC, DMS, IACBE, NUR, RAD, SW

01 Interim President .... Dr. Catherine M. CLARK-EICH
05 Provost/VP of Academic Affairs .... Dr. Richard SAX
10 Interim CFO/VP Finance .... Mr. Russell HENCHEY
32 COO/VP Student & Admin Affairs .... Mrs. Rebecca LONG
45 Associate Provost Inst Effective .... Dr. David A. LAWRENCE
15 Director of Human Resources .... Mr. Chris NOURSE
49 Dean College of Arts & Science .... Vacant
107 Dean College Prof/Tech Studies .... Dr. Donna MITCHELL
06 Registrar .... Vacant
07 Director of Recruitment .... Ms. Kristie RUSSELL
88 Dir Cmty Ptnrshp/Admission Process .... Mrs. Amanda EHMAN
111 Exec Dir Institutional Advancement .... Mrs. Kara WILLIS
35 Dean of Students .... Ms. Dena WARREN
41 Athletic Director .... Mr. Jeff LANHAM
08 Director of Davis Library .... Ms. Amy R. WILSON
13 Chief Information Officer .... Mr. Kingsley MEYER
14 Management Information Systems Adm .... Mr. Eric LOLLATHIN
29 Director of Alumni Relations .... Mrs. Delyssa EDWARDS
04 Exec to Pres/Board Professional .... Ms. Annette WARD
88 Chief Financial Officer RGCC .... Mr. Kent HALEY
19 Campus Police Chief .... Mr. Scott BORDEN
37 Director Financial Aid .... Mrs. Meghann FRALEY
89 Dir New Student Adv/Testing/Career .... Mrs. Susan HAFT
121 Director of Student Success .... Dr. Stephanie ALEXANDER

University of Toledo (E)

2801 W Bancroft, Toledo OH 43606-3390

County: Lucas — FICE Identification: 003131 — Unit ID: 206084

Telephone: (419) 530-4636 — Carnegie Class: DU-Higher

FAX Number: (419) 530-4984 — Calendar System: Semester

URL: www.utoledo.edu

Established: 1872 — Annual Undergrad Tuition & Fees (In-State): $10,293

Enrollment: 20,579 — Coed

Affiliation or Control: State — IRS Status: 501(c)3

Highest Offering: Doctorate

Accreditation: NH, #ARCPA, ART, CAATE, CACREP, CAEP, CAHIIM, CAMPEP, CEA, CLPSY, COARC, DENT, EMT, LAW, MED, MT, MUS, NRPA, NURSE, OT, PA, PH, PHAR, PTA, SP, SW, THEA

01 President .... Dr. Sharon L. GABER
100 Interim Chief of Staff .... Ms. Diane MILLER
05 Int EVP Academic Affairs/Provost .... Dr. Karen BJORKMAN
63 EVP for Clin Affs/Dean COMLS .... Dr. Christopher COOPER
10 Int EVP Finance & Admin/CFO .... Mr. Matt SCHROEDER
43 Vice President/General Counsel .... Mr. Peter J. PAPADIMOS
32 VP for Student Affairs .... Dr. Phillip COCKRELL
111 AVP for Advancement .... Ms. Cheryl ZWYER
84 VP Enrollment Management .... Mr. Jim ANDERSON
46 Vice President Research .... Dr. Frank J. CALZONETTI
13 Vice President CIO/CTO .... Mr. William MCCREARY
41 Vice Pres and Director of Athletics .... Mr. Michael E. O'BRIEN
28 VP for Diversity and Inclusion .... Dr. Willie MCKETHER
17 CEO Univ Toledo Med Ctr .... Mr. Daniel BARBEE
86 AVP Government Relations .... Ms. Diane MILLER
26 AVP Marketing/Communications .... Dr. Adrienne KING
06 University Registrar .... Ms. Julie R. QUINONEZ
58 Dean College of Graduate Studies .... Dr. Amanda BRYANT-FRIEDRICH
50 Dean Business & Innovation .... Dr. Anne BALASZ
53 Dean J Herb College of Educ .... Dr. Raymond WITTE
54 Dean Engineering .... Dr. Michael TOOLE
76 Dean Health & Human Services .... Dr. Christopher INGERSOLL
83 Dean Arts & Letters .... Dr. Charlene GILBERT
61 Dean Law .... Mr. Ben BARROSS
81 Interim Dean NSM .... Dr. John PLENEFISCH
66 Dean Nursing .... Dr. Linda LEWANDOWSKI
67 Dean Pharmacy & Pharm Sciences .... Vacant
92 Dean Jesup Scott Honors College .... Dr. Heidi APPEL
88 Dean University College .... Dr. Barbara KOPP-MILLER
35 AVP & Int Dean of Students .... Dr. Sammy SPANN
39 AVP Residence Life .... Ms. Valerie WALSTON
37 AVP Financial Aid/Enrollment Svcs .... Mr. Gina ROBERTS
15 Sr Director Faculty Labor Relations .... Mr. Kevin WEST
102 President Foundation .... Ms. Brenda LEE
29 Assoc Vice Pres Alumni Relations .... Mr. Daniel J. SAEVIG
36 Dir Exp Lrng and Career Svcs .... Ms. Shelly DROUILLARD
85 Director Ctr for Intl Studies .... Ms. Sara CLARK
21 Director Internal Audit .... Mr. David CUTRI
19 Chief of Police .... Mr. Jeff NEWTON
40 General Manager Bookstore SU .... Ms. Colleen STRAYER
18 AVP Facilities/Physical Plant .... Mr. Jason TOTH
08 Director University Libraries .... Dr. Beau CASE
04 Sr Dir of Admin Operations .... Ms. Katie DEBENEDICTIS
07 Director of Admissions .... Mr. Billie PIERCE
101 Secretary of the Institution/Board .... Ms. Joan STASA
96 Director of Supply Chain Management .... Ms. Jennifer PASTOREK

Urbana University (F)

579 College Way, Urbana OH 43078-2091

Telephone: (937) 772-9200 — FICE Identification: 003133

Accreditation: &NH

† Branch campus of Franklin University, Columbus, OH

Ursuline College (G)

2550 Lander Road, Cleveland OH 44124-4398

County: Cuyahoga — FICE Identification: 003134 — Unit ID: 206349

Telephone: (440) 449-4200 — Carnegie Class: Masters/M

FAX Number: (440) 646-8318 — Calendar System: Semester

URL: www.ursuline.edu

Established: 1871 — Annual Undergrad Tuition & Fees: $32,390

Enrollment: 1,123 — Female

Affiliation or Control: Roman Catholic — IRS Status: 501(c)3

Highest Offering: Doctorate

Accreditation: NH, CACREP, CAEP, CAEPN, IACBE, NURSE, SW

01 President .... Sr. Christine DEVINNE
05 Vice President Academic Affairs .... Dr. Kathryn LAFONTANA
10 Vice Pres & Chief Financial Officer .... Vacant
111 Vice Pres Institutional Advancement .... Mr. Richard KONISIEWICZ
32 Vice President of Student Affairs .... Ms. Deanne HURLEY
84 Vice Pres of Enrollment Management .... Ms. Susan DILENO
58 Interim Dean of Graduate Studies .... Dr. James CONNELL
49 Dean Arts & Sciences .... Dr. Elizabeth KAVRAN
66 Dean College of Nursing .... Dr. Patricia SHARPNACK
88 Exec Director Accelerated Program .... Ms. Brooke SCHARLOTT
08 Director of Library .... Ms. Suzanna SCHROEDER-GREEN
06 Registrar .... Ms. Leah SULLIVAN
21 Accounting Manager .... Ms. Susan VALITSKY
30 Director of Development .... Ms. Erin GAY MIYOSHI
37 Director of Financial Aid .... Ms. Mary Lynn PERRI
29 Dir Alumnae Relations/Annual Fund .... Ms. Lynne DEWYRE
26 Dir of Marketing/Communications .... Ms. Ann MCGUIRE
38 Director Counseling & Career Svcs .... Ms. Geraldine M. JENKINS
15 Director of Personnel .... Ms. Kelli KNAUS
13 Dir of Information Technology .... Mr. Richard MCCOURT
09 Director of Institutional Research .... Vacant
102 Dir of Corp & Foundation Relations .... Vacant
39 Director of Residence Life .... Ms. Gina DEMART-KRAUS
42 Director Campus Ministry .... Ms. Paula FITZGERALD
28 Asst Dean of Diversity .... Ms. Yolanda KING
106 Director Online Education/E-learnin .... Ms. Krystina ZEIT
93 Director of Wellness Program .... Vacant
24 Library Circulation Coordinator .... Ms. Marylouise DEEHR
40 Manager Bookstore .... Ms. Kendra CORENO
41 Athletic Director .... Ms. Cynthia MCKNIGHT
43 Dir Legal Services/General Counsel .... Mr. Terry BILLUPS
09 Institutional Research Analyst .... Ms. Marilyn VALENCIA
04 Sr Executive Asst to President .... Ms. Victoria SLONAKER

108 Interim Director Inst Assessment .... Dr. Mary Jo CHERRY
19 Director Security/Safety .... Mr. James KRZYWICKI
22 Dir Compliance/Title IX/Disability .... Ms. Deborah KAMAT

Valor Christian College (A)

PO Box 800, Columbus OH 43216

County: Franklin Identification: 667093
Unit ID: 486257
Telephone: (614) 837-4088 Carnegie Class: Spec 2-yr-Other
FAX Number: (614) 837-6904 Calendar System: Semester
URL: www.valorcollege.com
Established: 1990 Annual Undergrad Tuition & Fees: $6,220
Enrollment: 267 Coed
Affiliation or Control: Independent Non-Profit IRS Status: 501(c)3
Highest Offering: Associate Degree
Accreditation: BI

01 President .... Ken GRUNDEN
05 Vice Pres Academic Affairs .... Laquetta CORTNER
32 Dean of Students .... Cherisse CONLEY
35 Director of Student Life .... Ashton PARSLEY
04 Admin Asst to Pres/Office Mgr .... Nicki KUE
37 Director of Financial Aid .... Norm STOPPENBRINK

Walsh University (B)

2020 East Maple Street, North Canton OH 44720

County: Stark FICE Identification: 003135
Unit ID: 206437
Telephone: (330) 490-7090 Carnegie Class: Masters/M
FAX Number: (330) 499-7165 Calendar System: Semester
URL: www.walsh.edu
Established: 1958 Annual Undergrad Tuition & Fees: $29,980
Enrollment: 2,759 Coed
Affiliation or Control: Roman Catholic IRS Status: 501(c)3
Highest Offering: Doctorate
Accreditation: NH, CACREP, CAEPN, NURSE, OT, PTA

01 President .... Mr. Richard JUSSEAUME
10 Vice Pres Finance/Business Affairs .... Ms. Laurel LUSK
05 Provost/Vice Pres Academic Affairs .... Dr. Douglas PALMER
111 Vice Pres of Advancement .... Mr. Eric BELDEN
41 Vice Pres for Athletics .... Mr. Dale S. HOWARD
26 VP for Marketing/Communications .... Ms. Teresa FOX
13 VP of Administration/CIO .... Dr. Brian GREENWELL
45 VP for Strategy & Planning .... Mr. Derrick WYMAN
07 Vice Pres for Undergrad Admissions .... Ms. Rebecca CONEGLIO
88 Assoc VP for Mission Implementation .... Mr. Miguel CHAVEZ
20 Assoc VP & Dean of Academic Admin ...... Ms. Edna MCCULLOH
09 Dean Inst Effectiveness .... Dr. Ute LAHAIE
32 Dean of Students .... Mr. Bryan BADAR
18 Director of Facilities & Grounds .... Mr. John SCHISSLER
91 Database Administrator .... Ms. Hope STANCIU
22 Director of Compliance .... Mr. Jason FAUTAS
36 Dir of Career & Experiential Educ .... Ms. Abigail POESKE
42 Senior Chaplain .... Fr. Thomas CEBULA
38 Director Counseling Services .... Ms. Frances MORROW
42 Director of Campus Ministry .... Mr. Ben WALTHER
31 Dir Campus & Community Programs .... Ms. Jacqueline M. MANSER
37 Director Financial Aid .... Mrs. Holly VAN GILDER
15 Director of Human Resources .... Mr. Frank MCKNIGHT
29 Director of Alumni Relations .... Ms. Stephanie KOONTZ
25 Director of Grants .... Dr. Rachel HAMMEL
19 Chief of Campus Police .... Mr. Louis DARROW
08 Director of Library Services .... Ms. LuAnn BORIS
83 Dean School of Behav/Health Science .... Dr. Pamela RITZLINE
49 Dean School of Arts & Sciences .... Dr. Michael DUNPHY
66 Dean Byers School of Nursing .... Ms. Judy KREYE
79 Chair Div of Humanities .... Dr. Bradley BEACH
81 Chair Division of Math & Sciences .... Dr. Jackie NOVAK
92 Director Honors Program .... Dr. Hawkins TY
04 Administrative Asst to President .... Ms. Christine SCHEETZ
06 Registrar .... Ms. Stacie HERMAN
50 Dean DeVille School of Business .... Dr. Rajshekhar JAVALGI
53 Chair Div of Education .... Dr. Jeannie DEFAZIO
101 Secretary of the Institution/Board .... Dr. Douglas PALMER
104 Director Study Abroad .... Mr. Michael CINSON
39 Asst Dean of Students .... Ms. Tiffany KINNARD-PAYTON
96 Director of Purchasing .... Ms. Rebecca MIMA
88 Academic Projects .... Ms. Nancy BLACKFORD
28 Chief Diversity Officer .... Vacant

Washington State Community College (C)

710 Colegate Drive, Marietta OH 45750-9225

County: Washington FICE Identification: 010453
Unit ID: 206446
Telephone: (740) 374-8716 Carnegie Class: Assoc/HVT-High Non
FAX Number: (740) 374-9562 Calendar System: Semester
URL: www.wscc.edu
Established: 1971 Annual Undergrad Tuition & Fees (In-State): $3,888
Enrollment: 1,821 Coed
Affiliation or Control: State IRS Status: 501(c)3
Highest Offering: Associate Degree
Accreditation: NH, COARC, MLTAD, PTAA

01 President .... Dr. Vicky WOOD
10 VP of Finance & Admin/Treas .... Mr. Jess N. RAINES
111 VP of Institutional Advancement .... Ms. Amanda K. HERB
05 VP for Academic Affairs .... Ms. Sarah PARKER-CLEVER
13 Chief Information Officer .... Mr. Terry RATAICZAK
15 Executive Director Human Resources .... Mr. Jess N. RAINES
102 Exec Dir Foundation & Grants Dev .... Vacant
76 Dean of Health Sciences/Sciences .... Dr. Heather KINCAID
72 Dean of Technology and Transfer .... Vacant
06 Registrar .... Ms. Dustin TAYLOR
07 Director of Admissions .... Ms. Carrie THRASH
26 Dir of Marketing & Communications .... Ms. Elizabeth GODFREY
37 Director of Financial Aid .... Ms. Reba BARTRUG
08 Director Library Services .... Vacant
88 Director of College Access and ETS .... Ms. Donna MUNTZ

Wilberforce University (D)

PO Box 1001, Wilberforce OH 45384-1001

County: Greene FICE Identification: 003141
Unit ID: 206491
Telephone: (937) 376-2911 Carnegie Class: Bac-Diverse
FAX Number: (937) 376-2627 Calendar System: Semester
URL: www.wilberforce.edu
Established: 1856 Annual Undergrad Tuition & Fees: $13,250
Enrollment: 627 Coed
Affiliation or Control: African Methodist Episcopal IRS Status: 501(c)3
Highest Offering: Master's
Accreditation: #NH, CACREP

01 President .... Dr. Elfred A. PINKARD
03 EVP/CIO/VP Student Engagement .... Dr. Tashia BRADLEY
10 Sr VP of Administration & Finance .... Mr. William WOODSON
15 VP of Administration and HR . Mrs. Anita R. JEFFERSON-GOMEZ
05 Vice President of Academic Affairs .... Dr. Edward HILL
111 Int Dir Institutional Advancement .... Ms. Jocelyn NEELY
49 Interim Dean of Arts & Sciences .... Dr. Michael ROBINSON
107 Int Dean of Professional Studies .... Dr. Anuradha VENKATESWARAN
07 Interim Director of Admissions .... Ms. Krystal TONEY
06 Registrar .... Mrs. Rudell MOORE
113 Assistant Bursar .... Ms. Debra OLIVER
41 Athletic Director .... Mr. Dereck WILLIAMS
51 Director of CLIMB Program .... Mrs. Anna CARTER
25 Director Title III/Sponsored Pgms .... Mrs. Jacqueline WATERS
19 Chief of Campus Police & Safety .... Mr. Jon CROSS
04 Executive Asst to the President .... Mrs. Danita PEARL
18 Chief Facilities/Physical Plant Ofc .... Mr. Kevin FRYE
37 Director Student Financial Aid .... Mrs. Andrea SANDERS
08 Director of Library Services .... Ms. Stephanie ROSTRON
13 Interim Director of IT .... Mr. Andrew MONCE
29 Director Alumni Affairs .... Ms. Jocelyn NEELY
21 Controller .... Ms. Mary MORALE

Wilmington College (E)

1870 Quaker Way, Wilmington OH 45177-2499

County: Clinton FICE Identification: 003142
Unit ID: 206507
Telephone: (937) 382-6661 Carnegie Class: Bac-Diverse
FAX Number: (937) 383-8574 Calendar System: Semester
URL: www.wilmington.edu
Established: 1870 Annual Undergrad Tuition & Fees: $25,675
Enrollment: 1,169 Coed
Affiliation or Control: Friends IRS Status: 501(c)3
Highest Offering: Master's
Accreditation: NH, CAATE, CAEP

01 President .... Dr. James M. REYNOLDS
04 Assistant to the President .... Mrs. Leslie A. NICHOLS
05 Int Vice President Academic Affairs .... Dr. Steve SZEGHI
10 Vice President Business/Finance .... Mr. Bradley J. MITCHELL
30 Vice President College Advancement .... Mr. Matt WAHRHAFTIG
88 Vice President External Programs .... Ms. Sylvia STEVENS
88 VP Academic Affairs & Faculty Dean .... Dr. Erica A. GOODWIN
32 Vice Pres Student Affs/Stdnt Life .... Ms. Sigrid B. SOLOMON
41 Vice President Athletic Admin .... Dr. Terry A. RUPERT
84 Chief Enrollment Officer/Admissions .... Mr. Dennis KELLY
20 Assoc Vice Pres Academic Affairs .... Dr. Cole DAWSON
09 Dir Institutional Effectiveness .... Mr. Daniel MCCAMISH
26 Sr Dir of Pub Relations/Admissions .... Mr. Randall F. SARVIS
06 Registrar/Academic Records .... Ms. Sue HUTCHENS
08 Director of Watson Library .... Ms. Lucinda CHANDLER
15 Director of Human Resources .... Ms. Libby HAYES
36 Director of Career Services .... Dr. Nina TALLEY
18 Director of Physical Plant .... Mr. Terry L. JOHNSON
29 Dir Alumni/Parent Rels/Advancement .... Ms. Monica GINNEY
37 Dir Financial Aid/One Stop Center .... Ms. Cheryl LOUALLEN
07 Director of Admission .... Mr. Adam LOHREY
21 Controller .... Ms. Kelly DUFFY

Wilmington College Blue Ash Branch (F)

9987 Carver Road, Blue Ash OH 45242

Telephone: (513) 793-1337 Identification: 770364
Accreditation: &NH

Winebrenner Theological Seminary (G)

950 N Main Street, Findlay OH 45840-3652

County: Hancock FICE Identification: 004060
Unit ID: 206516
Telephone: (419) 434-4200 Carnegie Class: Spec-4-yr-Faith
FAX Number: (419) 434-4267 Calendar System: Trimester
URL: www.winebrenner.edu
Established: 1942 Annual Graduate Tuition & Fees: N/A
Enrollment: 62 Coed
Affiliation or Control: Independent Non-Profit IRS Status: 501(c)3
Highest Offering: Doctorate; No Undergraduates
Accreditation: NH, CACREP, THEOL

01 President/CEO .... Dr. Brent C. SLEASMAN
05 VP of Academic Advancement .... Dr. Bruce COATS
10 Director of Finance .... Mr. Tom WEAVER
08 College Librarian .... Mrs. Margaret HIRSCHY
06 Registrar .... Vacant
04 Assistant to the President .... Vacant
108 Director Institutional Assessment .... Dr. Kathryn HELLEMAN
07 Director of Admissions .... Ms. Amy J. KINNEY

Wittenberg University (H)

PO Box 720, Springfield OH 45501-0720

County: Clark FICE Identification: 003143
Unit ID: 206525
Telephone: (937) 327-6231 Carnegie Class: Bac-A&S
FAX Number: (937) 327-6340 Calendar System: Semester
URL: www.wittenberg.edu
Established: 1845 Annual Undergrad Tuition & Fees: $39,500
Enrollment: 1,884 Coed
Affiliation or Control: Evangelical Lutheran Church In America
IRS Status: 501(c)3
Highest Offering: Master's
Accreditation: NH, CAEPN, MUS, NURSE

01 President .... Dr. Michael FRANDSEN
05 Provost .... Dr. Michelle MATTSON
10 Vice Pres Finance/Administration .... Mr. Rob YOUNG
84 Vice Pres Enrollment Management .... Ms. Carola THORSON
111 Vice Pres Advancement .... Ms. Rebecca KOCHER
26 Vice Pres Marketing/Communications .... Ms. Karen GERBOTH
20 Asst Provost Academic Services .... Dr. Mary Jo ZEMBAR
09 Asst Prov Acad Affs/Inst Research .Dr. Darby L. HILLER-FREUND
107 Dean Graduate/Professional Studies .... Dr. Barbara RANDAZZO
35 Dean of Students .... Ms. Casey GILL
124 Sr Assoc Dean Stdnt Success/Retent .... Mr. Jonathan DURAJ
85 Director International Education .... Ms. JoAnn BENNETT
42 Pastor to the University .... Rev. Rachel SANDUM TUNE
08 Director of the Library .... Mr. Douglas K. LEHMAN
13 Chief Information Officer .... Mr. Richard MICKOOL
31 Director Community Service .... Ms. Kristen L. COLLIER
06 Registrar .... Ms. Debra LOVELESS
41 VP/Director Athletics/Recreation .... Dr. Gary WILLIAMS
58 Director Graduate Studies in Educ .... Dr. Amy MCGUFFEY
94 Director of Women's Studies .... Dr. Heather H. WRIGHT
29 Dir of Alumni/Lifelong Engagement .... Ms. Holly GERSBACHER
27 Sports Information Director .... Mr. AJ MEYER
105 Sr Writer/Web Communications Spec .... Mr. Ryan MAURER
39 Associate Dean for Residence Life .... Ms. Sherri SADOWSKI
38 Director Student Counseling .... Ms. Amanda JONES
88 Director Student Involvement .... Ms. Carol NICKOSON
28 Assoc Dean Diversity & Inclusion .... Mr. Joshua MOORE
37 Exec Director of Financial Aid .... Ms. Amy BARNHART
15 Director Human Resources .... Ms. Mary Beth WALTER
19 Chief of Police .... Mr. Jim HUTCHINS
40 Manager of Bookstore .... Ms. Amy GARNER

Wright State University Main Campus (I)

3640 Colonel Glenn Highway, Dayton OH 45435-0001

County: Greene FICE Identification: 003078
Unit ID: 206604
Telephone: (937) 775-3333 Carnegie Class: DU-Higher
FAX Number: (937) 775-3301 Calendar System: Semester
URL: www.wright.edu
Established: 1964 Annual Undergrad Tuition & Fees (In-State): $9,254
Enrollment: 15,957 Coed
Affiliation or Control: State IRS Status: 501(c)3
Highest Offering: Doctorate
Accreditation: NH, CAATE, CACREP, CAEPN, CEA, CLPSY, EXSC, IPSY, MED, MT, MUS, NURSE, PH, SPAA, SW

01 President .... Dr. Cheryl B. SCHRADER
05 EVP Academic Affairs/Provost .... Dr. Susan EDWARDS
10 Vice Pres Finance and Operations .... Mr. Walter J. BRANSON
32 Int Vice Provost Student Affairs .... Dr. Gary DICKSTEIN
46 Int VProv Research/Graduate Studies .... Ms. Ellen REINSCH FRIESE
111 Int Vice Pres Univ Advancement .... Mr. Bill BIGHAM
84 Vice Provost Student Success .... Dr. Paul B. CARNEY
58 Interim Dean Sch Graduate Studies .... Dr. Barry MILLIGAN
08 University Librarian .... Ms. Sue POLANKA
15 Assoc Vice Pres for Human Resources .... Ms. Shari MICKEY-BOGGS
50 Int Dean Raj Soin Col of Business .... Dr. Thomas L. TRAYNOR
53 Dean Education/Human Services .... Dr. Joseph E. KEFERL
54 Interim Dean Engr/Computer Science .... Dr. Brian RIGLING
12 Interim Dean WSU Lake Campus .... Vacant
49 Dean Liberal Arts .... Dr. Linda CARON
66 Int Dean College Nursing & Health .... Dr. Deborah L. ULRICH
63 Dean Boonshaft School of Medicine .... Dr. Margaret DUNN
83 Dean Sch of Prof Psychology .... Dr. LaPearl Logan WINFREY
81 Dean Science/Mathematics .... Dr. Douglas W. LEAMAN
06 Registrar .... Ms. Amanda STEELE-MIDDLETON
13 Chief Information Officer .... Mr. Craig WOOLLEY

36 Director Career Services ... Ms. Cheryl STUART
37 Director of Financial Aid ... Vacant
38 Director Counsel/Wellness Svcs ... Dr. Robert A. RANDO
29 Exec Director Alumni Relations ... Mr. Gregory SCHARER
28 Chief Diversity Officer ... Ms. Lindsay MILLER
22 Director Disability Services ... Mr. Tom WEBB
86 Assoc VP Public Affairs ... Mr. Robert E. HICKEY, JR.
41 Director of Athletics ... Mr. Bob GRANT
43 General Counsel ... Mr. Larry CHAN
40 Store Manager ... Ms. Jennifer L. GEBHART
85 Director Intl Student/Scholar Svcs ... Mr. Steven J. LYONS
39 Director Residence Services ... Mr. Daniel BERTSOS
19 Chief Police Department ... Mr. David A. FINNIE
92 Director Honors Program ... Dr. Susan CARRAFIELLO
94 Director Womens Studies Program ... Dr. Hope JENNINGS
09 Asst VP Institutional Research ... Mr. Craig THIS
04 Executive Asst to President ... Ms. Teresa M. BEDWELL
102 CFO WSU Foundation ... Mr. Robert BATSON
44 Director Annual Giving ... Ms. Amy N. SHOPE JONES
101 Secretary of the Board ... Mr. Larry CHAN
26 Director Communications ... Mr. Seth BAUGUESS
18 Chief Real Estate & Facilities Ofc ... Mr. Greg SAMPLE
26 Director Marketing ... Mr. Mark D. ANDERSON

Wright State University Lake Campus (A)

7600 Lake Campus Drive, Celina OH 45822-2952
Telephone: (419) 586-0300 FICE Identification: 009169
Accreditation: &NH

† Regional accreditation is carried under the parent institution in Dayton, OH.

Xavier University (B)

3800 Victory Parkway, Cincinnati OH 45207-1096
County: Hamilton FICE Identification: 003144
Unit ID: 206622
Telephone: (513) 745-3000 Carnegie Class: Masters/L
FAX Number: (513) 745-4223 Calendar System: Semester
URL: www.xavier.edu
Established: 1831 Annual Undergrad Tuition & Fees: $38,530
Enrollment: 6,786 Coed
Affiliation or Control: Roman Catholic IRS Status: 501(c)3
Highest Offering: Doctorate
Accreditation: NH, CAATE, CACREP, CAEPT, CEA, CLPSY, HSA, MACTE, MUS, NURSE, OT, RAD, SW

01 President ... Rev. Michael J. GRAHAM, SJ
88 Vice President Emeritus ... Dr. John F. KUCIA
05 Provost/Chief Academic Officer ... Dr. Melissa J. BAUMANN
10 VP Financial Admin/CBO ... Mr. Phil CHICK
26 Vice Pres for University Relations ... Mr. Gary R. MASSA
88 Vice Pres Mission & Identity/CMO ... Dr. Debra MOONEY
13 Exec Dir Information Technologies ... Mr. Mark BROCKMAN
28 VP Inst Diversity/Inclusion & CDIO ... Dr. Janice B. WALKER
27 Director Strategic Communications ... Vacant
30 Assoc VP for University Relations ... Ms. Susan ABEL
32 Assoc Prov/Chief Student Affs Ofcr ... Dr. David J. JOHNSON
20 Associate Provost & CIO ... Mr. Jeff EDWARDS
18 Vice President for Facilities ... Mr. Robert M. SHEERAN
11 VP for Admin/Director Athletics ... Mr. Greg CHRISTOPHER
15 Assoc Vice Pres for Human Resources ... Mrs. Connie PERME
84 Vice Pres Enrollment Management ... Mr. Aaron MEIS
44 Exec Dir Gifts & Estate Planning ... Mr. Mark MCLAUGHLIN
42 Dir Center for Mission/Identity ... Mr. Joseph P. SHADLE
06 Registrar ... Dr. Andrea WAWRZUSIN
121 Exec Dir of Student Support Svcs ... Ms. Lea MINNITI
27 Assoc VP Marketing & Communications .. Mr. Doug RUSCHMAN
39 Sr Dir Student Affairs/Ofc Res Life ... Ms. Lori A. LAMBERT
40 Director of Bookstore ... Mr. Steve EAGLE
86 Director of Government Relations ... Mr. Sean COMER
83 Interim Dean College Prof Sciences ... Dr. Linda SCHOENSTEDT
07 Dir Enr Prospect Mgmt/Parent Rels ... Vacant
35 Sr Dir Student Affairs/ Involvement ... Ms. Leah BUSAM KLENOWSKI
49 Dean College Arts & Sciences ... Dr. David MENGEL
66 Interim Dean College of Nursing ... Dr. Judith LEWIS
19 Dir Public Safety/Chief of Police ... Chief Robert WARFEL
37 Director of Financial Aid ... Ms. Donna SALAK
43 General Counsel/Sec of the Board ... Mr. Joseph H. FELDHAUS
29 Dir Alumni Rels/Ex Dir Athletic Dev ... Mr. Brian MALEY
09 Dir Office Institutional Research ... Mrs. Emily SHIPLEY
50 Dean Williams College of Business ... Dr. Thomas HAYES
51 Dir Adult & Prof Educ at Xavier ... Ms. Patricia MEYER
96 Dir Purchasing & Supply Management ... Mr. John MERCER
88 Dir TRIO Student Support Services ... Dr. Daniel L. MCSPADDEN

Youngstown State University (C)

One University Plaza, Youngstown OH 44555-0001
County: Mahoning FICE Identification: 003145
Unit ID: 206695
Telephone: (330) 941-3001 Carnegie Class: Masters/L
FAX Number: (330) 941-7169 Calendar System: Semester
URL: www.ysu.edu
Established: 1908 Annual Undergrad Tuition & Fees (In-State): $8,967
Enrollment: 12,521 Coed
Affiliation or Control: State IRS Status: 501(c)3
Highest Offering: Doctorate
Accreditation: NH, ANEST, ART, CAATE, CACREP, CAEP, COARC, DH, DIETC, DIETD, DIETT, EMT, EXSC, MAC, MLTAD, MUS, NUR, NURSE, PH, PTA, SW

01 President ... Mr. James P. TRESSEL
05 Provost/VP Academic Affairs ... Dr. Brien N. SMITH
10 Vice Pres Finance & Business Op ... Mr. Neal P. MCNALLY
09 Vice Pres for Institutional Effect ... Dr. Mike SHERMAN
32 Vice Pres for Student Affairs ... Dr. Eddie HOWARD, JR.
43 Vice President and General Counsel ... Ms. Holly A. JACOBS
26 Assoc VP for University Relations ... Mrs. Shannon TIRONE
13 AVP/Chief Information Officer ... Mr. James YUKECH
86 Assoc VP Government Relations ... Mr. Michael HRIPKO
49 Int Dean Liberal Arts/Soc Science ... Dr. Martha PALLANTE
50 Dean of Business Administration ... Dr. Betty Jo LICATA
53 Dean of Education ... Dr. Charles HOWELL
81 Dean of Science/Tech/Eng/Math ... Dr. Wim F. STEELANT
57 Dean Creative Arts & Communication ... Dr. Phyllis M. PAUL
76 Int Dean Health & Human Services ... Dr. Tammy A. KING
58 Dean College of Graduate Studies ... Dr. Salvatore A. SANDERS
20 Assoc Provost Acad Pgms/Planning ... Dr. Kevin BALL
41 Exec Director of Athletics ... Mr. Ronald A. STROLLO
08 Manager Library Operations ... Ms. Anna TORRES
29 Dir University Events & Protocol ... Ms. Jacquelyn LEVISEUR
07 Director Undergrad Recruit/Admiss ... Ms. Sue E. DAVIS
06 Registrar ... Ms. Jeanne HERMAN
19 Chief of University Police ... Mr. Shawn V. VARSO
18 Associate Vice President Facilities ... Mr. John P. HYDEN
23 Dir Environ/Occup Health & Safety ... Mr. Daniel SAHLI
37 Director Financial/Scholarships ... Ms. Elaine RUSE
21 Director General Accounting ... Ms. Katrena J. DAVIDSON
21 Cash Management Officer ... Mr. David EDWARDS
39 Int Director Housing Services ... Ms. Kelly BEERS
88 Director Support Services ... Mr. Danny J. O'CONNELL
90 Director Media/Acad Computing ... Mr. Michael S. HRISHENKO
35 Dir Campus Rec/Intramural Sports ... Ms. Joy POLKABLA-BYERS
88 Director WYSU-FM ... Mr. Gary SEXTON
04 Exec Assistant to President ... Ms. Cynthia M. BELL
106 Dir Online Education/E-learning ... Ms. Jessica CHILL
104 Assoc Provost Intl Programs ... Dr. Nathan MYERS
108 Director Institutional Assessment ... Ms. Hillary FUHRMAN
22 Dir Affirmative Action/EEO ... Mr. Mark WEIR
38 Director Student Counseling ... Dr. Ann JARANSKI
15 Chief Human Resources Officer ... Ms. Cynthia KRAVITZ

Zane State College (D)

9900 Brick Church Road, Cambridge OH 43725
Telephone: (740) 432-6568 Identification: 770365
Accreditation: &NH

Zane State College (E)

1555 Newark Road, Zanesville OH 43701-2626
County: Muskingum FICE Identification: 008133
Unit ID: 204255
Telephone: (740) 454-2501 Carnegie Class: Assoc/MT-VT-High Non
FAX Number: (740) 454-0035 Calendar System: Semester
URL: www.zanestate.edu
Established: 1969 Annual Undergrad Tuition & Fees (In-State): $5,156
Enrollment: 2,514 Coed
Affiliation or Control: State IRS Status: 501(c)3
Highest Offering: Associate Degree
Accreditation: NH, ACBSP, ACFEI, CAHIIM, MAC, MLTAD, OTA, PTAA, RAD

01 President ... Dr. Chad M. BROWN
100 Chief of Staff/Exec Dir of Found ... Mr. Anthony ADORNETTO
05 Provost/Chief Academic Officer ... Dr. Richard WOODFIELD
10 Chief Financial Officer ... Ms. Terri M. BALDWIN
84 Enrollment/Dir of Outreach Recruit ... Ms. Molly DUNN
50 Dean of Bus & Engineering ... Mrs. Marcie MOORE
103 Dean Workforce Development ... Ms. Tracey HOOPER-PORTER
15 Chief Human Resources Officer ... Dr. James KEMPER
13 Exec Dir of IT/IR ... Mr. Joseph KEATING
09 Dir of Institutional Research ... Mr. Andrew MORRISON
25 Director of Grants & Contracts ... Vacant
26 Director of Marketing ... Mrs. Jenn FOLDEN
32 Director of Student Services ... Mr. Konrad AKENS
21 Comptroller ... Ms. Tammy S. HUFFMAN
40 Director of Bookstore Operations ... Ms. Vicki MITCHELL
76 Dean Health/Liberal Arts/Public Svc ... Dr. Barbara SHELBY
06 Asst Dean Curriculum/Registrar ... Ms. Theresa KOLK-CONNER
18 Director of Facilities ... Mr. Andy FREEMAN
04 Exec Asst to Pres/Coord Annual Giv ... Mrs. Julie A. MACLAINE
106 Dir Online Education/E-learning ... Mr. Phil WENTWORTH

OKLAHOMA

Bacone College (F)

2299 Old Bacone Road, Muskogee OK 74403-1568
County: Muskogee FICE Identification: 003147
Unit ID: 206817
Telephone: (918) 683-4581 Carnegie Class: Bac-Diverse
FAX Number: (918) 781-7422 Calendar System: Semester
URL: www.bacone.edu
Established: 1880 Annual Undergrad Tuition & Fees: $17,700
Enrollment: 934 Coed
Affiliation or Control: American Baptist IRS Status: 501(c)3
Highest Offering: Baccalaureate
Accreditation: #NH, IACBE, NURSE, RAD

01 President ... Dr. Ferlin CLARK
05 VP of Academic Affairs ... Dr. Leroy THOMPSON
32 VP of Student Affairs ... Ms. Kaila HARJO
30 VP of Development ... Ms. Mindi KEE
10 VP of Finance/CFO ... Mr. Jerome STEELE
88 Chair Indigenous Online Teaching ... Mr. Kyle E. TAYLOR
42 Chair Christian Ministry ... Rev Dr. Leroy THOMPSON
06 Registrar ... Mrs. Linda MILAM
40 Bookstore Manager ... Ms. Dawn OSBORNE
41 Interim Athletic Director ... Mr. Carl COWAN
37 Director of Financial Aid ... Mr. Josh CHAPMAN
15 Director Human Resources ... Ms. Alta CROCKETT
07 Director of Admissions ... Vacant
08 Dir Betts Library/Head Librarian ... Mr. David MCMILLIAN
13 Director of Network Systems ... Mr. Chris EHLERS
04 Assistant to President ... Ms. Marcia TAYLOR
19 Chief of Campus Police ... Mr. Gerlad BAKER

Cameron University (G)

2800 W Gore Boulevard, Lawton OK 73505-6377
County: Comanche FICE Identification: 003150
Unit ID: 206914
Telephone: (580) 581-2200 Carnegie Class: Masters/M
FAX Number: (580) 581-2867 Calendar System: Semester
URL: www.cameron.edu
Established: 1908 Annual Undergrad Tuition & Fees (In-State): $6,450
Enrollment: 4,524 Coed
Affiliation or Control: State IRS Status: 501(c)3
Highest Offering: Master's
Accreditation: NH, ACBSP, CAEPN, COARC, MUS, RAD

01 President ... Dr. John M. MCARTHUR
05 Vice President for Academic Affairs .. Dr. Ronna J. VANDERSLICE
10 Vice Pres for Business & Finance ... Ms. Ninette CARTER
111 Vice Pres University Advancement ... Mr. Albert D. JOHNSON, JR.
84 VP for Enroll Mgmt & Stdnt Success ... Mr. Jerrett PHILLIPS
20 Assoc Vice Pres Academic Affairs ... Dr. Margery KINGSLEY
20 Asst Vice Pres Academic Affairs ... Ms. Susan CAMP
49 Dean School of Arts and Sciences ... Dr. Von E. UNDERWOOD
58 Dean School of Grad & Prof Studies ... Dr. Jennifer DENNIS
21 Controller ... Ms. Lindsey BILLEN
26 Senior Director of Public Affairs ... Mr. Keith MITCHELL
30 Director of Development ... Ms. Lorie GARRISON
29 Director of Alumni Relations ... Vacant
41 Director Athletic Administration ... Mr. Jim C. JACKSON
07 Director of Admissions ... Ms. Brenda DALLY
06 Registrar ... Mrs. Linda PHILLIPS
09 Dir Inst Rsrch/Assess/Accountabilty ... Dr. Karla OTY
37 Director of Financial Assistance ... Mr. Justin STREATER
13 Director Information Tech Services ... Mr. Kelly MCCLURE
15 Director of Human Resources ... Ms. Jamie SMITH
36 Director of Student Development ... Dr. Jennifer PRUCHNICKI
32 Dean of Students ... Dr. Zeak NAIFEH
19 Director Public Safety ... Mr. John DEBOARD
18 Director Physical Facilities ... Mr. Robert HANEFIELD
96 Purchasing Agent ... Ms. Laura KANE
22 EEO Officer/Title IX Coordinator ... Mr. Thomas RUSSELL

Carl Albert State College (H)

1507 S McKenna, Poteau OK 74953-5208
County: Le Flore FICE Identification: 003176
Unit ID: 206923
Telephone: (918) 647-1200 Carnegie Class: Assoc/HT-High Trad
FAX Number: (918) 647-1201 Calendar System: Semester
URL: www.carlalbert.edu
Established: 1933 Annual Undergrad Tuition & Fees (In-State): N/A
Enrollment: N/A Coed
Affiliation or Control: State IRS Status: 501(c)3
Highest Offering: Associate Degree
Accreditation: NH, ADNUR, PTAA

01 President ... Mr. Jay FALKNER
32 VP for Student Affairs/Athletic Dir ... Mr. Randy GRAVES
05 Vice President of Academic Affairs ... Mr. Marc WILLIS
10 Chief Financial Officer ... Mr. Brian ROBERTS
84 VP of Enrollment Management ... Mr. Bill NOWLIN
13 Director Information Technology ... Mr. Michael MARTIN
101 Secy of the Board/Exec Asst to Pres ... Ms. Jean Ann BARLOW
26 Dir Marketing/Community Relations ... Ms. Shannen MCCROSKEY
06 Registrar/VA Coordinator ... Ms. Dee Ann DICKERSON
37 Director of Financial Aid ... Ms. Suzanne PRUITT
88 TRIO Director ... Ms. Michelle WHITE
08 Interim Director of Libraries ... Mr. James HARRIS
18 Director of Physical Plant ... Mr. Chuck LEWIS
15 Human Resources Dir/Title IX Coord ... Ms. Vicki SULLIVAN
21 Business Office Manager ... Ms. Amanda WILSON
108 Inst Effect/Assessment Officer ... Ms. Kelly KELLOGG
102 Exec Dir of CASC Dev Foundation ... Ms. Mandy ROBERTS
106 Coord for Virtual Campus/English ... Ms. Sarah BROWN
19 Instructor/Campus Police Coord ... Mr. Chad BROWN

Carl Albert State College Sequoyah County Campus (I)

1601 S. Opdyke St, Sallisaw OK 74955
Telephone: (918) 775-6977 Identification: 770366
Accreditation: &NH

College of the Muscogee Nation (J)

PO Box 917, 2170 Raven Circle, Okmulgee OK 74447
County: Okmulgee Identification: 667122
Unit ID: 480967
Telephone: (918) 549-2800 Carnegie Class: Tribal
FAX Number: (918) 759-6930 Calendar System: Trimester

URL: www.CMN.edu
Established: 1994 Annual Undergrad Tuition & Fees: $6,600
Enrollment: 227 Coed
Affiliation or Control: Tribal Control IRS Status: 501(c)3
Highest Offering: Associate Degree
Accreditation: NH

01 President ... Mr. Robert BIBLE
05 Dean of Academic Affairs ... Dr. Monte RANDALL

Community Care College (A)

4242 S Sheridan Road, Tulsa OK 74145-1119
County: Tulsa FICE Identification: 033674
Unit ID: 439570
Telephone: (918) 610-0027 Carnegie Class: Spec 2-yr-Health
FAX Number: (918) 610-0029 Calendar System: Other
URL: www.communitycarecollege.edu
Established: 1995 Annual Undergrad Tuition & Fees: N/A
Enrollment: 581 Coed
Affiliation or Control: Independent Non-Profit IRS Status: 501(c)3
Highest Offering: Associate Degree
Accreditation: ACCSC, MAAB, SURGT

01 President ... Dr. Raye MAHLBERG
04 Admin Assistant to the President ... Brandi PACKARD
06 Registrar ... Brigitte KURR
07 Director of Admissions ... Tawni EDWARDS
10 Chief Financial/Business Officer ... Vacant
15 Chief Human Resources Officer ... Vacant
36 Director Career Services ... Linda DEWITT
37 Director Student Financial Aid ... Karissa MARCANGELI

Connors State College (B)

700 College Road, Warner OK 74469-9700
County: Muskogee FICE Identification: 003153
Unit ID: 206996
Telephone: (918) 463-2931 Carnegie Class: Assoc/HT-High Trad
FAX Number: (918) 463-2233 Calendar System: Semester
URL: www.connorsstate.edu
Established: 1908 Annual Undergrad Tuition & Fees (In-State): $3,600
Enrollment: 2,295 Coed
Affiliation or Control: State IRS Status: 501(c)3
Highest Offering: Associate Degree
Accreditation: NH, ADNUR, OTA, PTAA

01 President ... Dr. Ronald S. RAMMING
05 VP for Academic Affairs ... Dr. Janet WANSICK
10 VP for Fiscal Services ... Mr. Mike LEWIS
26 Assoc VP for External Affairs ... Vacant
37 Director of Financial Aid ... Ms. Mattie KEYS
08 Director of Learning Center ... Ms. Ona BRITTON-SPEARS
13 Director of Information Technology ... Vacant
06 Registrar ... Vacant
07 Director of Recruitment ... Ms. Logan NERO
15 Director of Human Resources ... Mr. Bart HOWELL
09 Director of Institutional Research ... Vacant
41 Athletic Director ... Mr. Bill MUSE
32 Dean of Students ... Mr. Mike JACKSON
35 Asst Dean of Students ... Mr. Jacob LAWSON
19 Chief of Police ... Mr. James MENDENHALL
04 Executive Asst to the President ... Ms. Cindy ANDERSON
20 Asst VP Acad/Stdt Affs/Acad Support ... Ms. Robin O'QUINN

East Central University (C)

1100 E 14th Street, Ada OK 74820-6899
County: Pontotoc FICE Identification: 003154
Unit ID: 207041
Telephone: (580) 332-8000 Carnegie Class: Masters/L
FAX Number: (580) 332-1623 Calendar System: Semester
URL: www.ecok.edu
Established: 1909 Annual Undergrad Tuition & Fees (In-State): $6,810
Enrollment: 3,719 Coed
Affiliation or Control: State IRS Status: 501(c)3
Highest Offering: Master's
Accreditation: NH, ACBSP, CACREP, CAEPN, MUS, NUR, SW

01 President ... Dr. Katricia PIERSON
05 Acting Provost/VP Academic Affairs ... Dr. Brenda SHERBOURNE
20 Associate Provost ... Dr. Adrianna LANCASTER
32 VP Student Development ... Dr. Gerald FORBES
10 Exec VP Administration/Finance ... Ms. Jessica KILBY
111 VP Institutional Advancement ... Ms. Amy FORD
53 Int Dean College of Educ & Psych ... Dr. Phyllis ISAACS
50 Dean School of Business ... Mr. Wendell GODWIN
81 Dean College of Health & Sciences ... Dr. Kenneth ANDREWS
49 Dean College of Lib Arts & Soc Sci ... Dr. Katherine LANG
58 Dean College of Grad Studies ... Dr. Adrianna LANCASTER
06 Registrar ... Ms. ADeidra SIMMONS
13 Director Information Technology ... Mr. Jeremy BENNETT
09 Director Inst Effectiveness ... Ms. Meredith JONES
26 Director Mktg & Communication ... Ms. Amy FORD
41 Director Athletics ... Dr. Jeff WILLIAMS
18 Director Facilities Mgmt ... Mr. Darryl OVERSTREET
15 Director Employment Services ... Mr. Ty ANDERSON
29 Director Alumni Relations ... Ms. Ashia HILLMAN
07 Director Admissions ... Mr. Sheppard MCCONNELL
96 Director Purchasing ... Ms. Chandra MILLER
37 Director Financial Aid ... Ms. Becky ISAACS
08 Director Library ... Ms. Dana BELCHER
23 Director Stdnt Health Services ... Ms. Lisa LETELLIER
39 Director Housing & Resid Life ... Ms. Debbie CHALMERS
38 Director Stdnt Counseling Ctr ... Ms. Jennifer COX
85 Director Intl Student Pgms & Svcs ... Ms. Jessika BAILEY
108 Director Assessment ... Dr. Robin ROBERSON
25 Director Grants & Research ... Ms. Leah LYON
20 Director Academic Services ... Ms. Holly SEWELL
22 Dir Testing/Accessibility Services ... Ms. Kim ROGERS
21 Controller ... Ms. Kelly DICKEY
113 Bursar ... Mr. Brian HAMPTON
19 Chief of University Police ... Mr. Bert MILLER

Eastern Oklahoma State College (D)

1301 W Main Street, Wilburton OK 74578-4999
County: Latimer FICE Identification: 003155
Unit ID: 207050
Telephone: (918) 465-2361 Carnegie Class: Assoc/HT-High Trad
FAX Number: (918) 465-2431 Calendar System: Semester
URL: www.eosc.edu
Established: 1909 Annual Undergrad Tuition & Fees (In-State): $4,572
Enrollment: 1,319 Coed
Affiliation or Control: State IRS Status: 501(c)3
Highest Offering: Associate Degree
Accreditation: NH, ADNUR, #COARC

01 President ... Dr. Stephen E. SMITH
05 Interim VP of Academic Affairs ... Dr. Karen HARRISON
32 VP for Student/External Affairs ... Dr. Trish MCBEATH
12 Dean of McAlester Campus ... Ms. Anne BROOKS
35 Director of Student Life ... Mr. Bryan DENNY
41 Athletic Director ... Mr. Matt HARPER
26 Dir Marketing/Communications ... Mrs. Trish MCBEATH
13 Chief Technical Officer ... Mr. Jeff WEEMS
08 Director Library & Media Services ... Ms. Maria MARTINEZ
15 VP for Administrative Services/HR ... Mrs. Amy ARMSTRONG
06 Registrar/Admissions ... Mrs. Jennifer LABOR
18 Director Physical Plant Operations ... Mr. Alan MOSS
37 Financial Aid Director ... Ms. Mimi KELLEY
19 Campus Police Chief ... Mr. Alton JONES

Family of Faith Christian University (E)

PO Box 1805, Shawnee OK 74802-1805
County: Pottawatomie FICE Identification: 036763
Unit ID: 443058
Telephone: (405) 695-5533 Carnegie Class: Spec-4-yr-Faith
FAX Number: (405) 273-8535 Calendar System: Semester
URL: www.familyoffaith.edu
Established: 1992 Annual Undergrad Tuition & Fees: $6,570
Enrollment: 90 Coed
Affiliation or Control: Independent Non-Profit IRS Status: 501(c)3
Highest Offering: Baccalaureate
Accreditation: BI

01 President ... Dr. Samuel W. MATTHEWS
05 Provost ... Mrs. Elaine W. PHILLIPS
10 Vice Pres Operations/Finance ... Mr. Daniel MATTHEWS
32 Vice Pres Student Affairs ... Mrs. Dara GILLIAM
20 Vice President Academic Affairs ... Ms. Bonnie CARRERA
42 Director of Spiritual Life ... Mr. Daniel J. MATTHEWS
108 Dir of Accreditation/Assessment ... Mrs. Elaine W. PHILLIPS
104 Director of International Studies ... Mrs. Dara GILLIAM

Langston University (F)

PO Box 1500, Langston OK 73050
County: Logan FICE Identification: 003157
Unit ID: 207209
Telephone: (405) 466-2231 Carnegie Class: Masters/S
FAX Number: N/A Calendar System: Semester
URL: www.langston.edu
Established: 1897 Annual Undergrad Tuition & Fees (In-State): $6,226
Enrollment: 2,219 Coed
Affiliation or Control: State IRS Status: 501(c)3
Highest Offering: Doctorate
Accreditation: NH, ACBSP, CACREP, CAEPN, NUR, PTA

01 President ... Dr. Kent J. SMITH, JR.
05 Vice President Academic Affairs ... Dr. Ruth JACKSON
10 VP Fiscal/Admin Affairs ... Vacant
30 VP Inst Development/External Affs ... Mrs. Mautra JONES
100 Chief of Staff ... Mrs. Theresa D. GRAVES
13 Chief Information Officer ... Mr. Pritchard MONCRIFFE
111 Assoc VP Institutional Advancement ... Mrs. Marla MAYBERRY
21 Comptroller ... Vacant
32 Dean of Students ... Mr. Joshua BUSBY
29 Director Alumni Affairs ... Mrs. Vonnie WARE-ROBERTS
26 Director Public Relations ... Mrs. Mautra JONES
07 Director of Admissions ... Mr. Carlos ROBINSON
37 Director Financial Aid ... Ms. Shelia R. MCGILL
15 Director of Human Resources ... Mrs. Cynthia S. BUCKLEY
09 Director Inst Research & Planning ... Dr. Carol S. CAWYER
06 Registrar ... Ms. Deleanor A. KIRKPATRICK
41 Athletic Director ... Mrs. Donnita ROGERS
19 Chief of Police ... Mr. Mario HOLLAND
96 Purchasing Manager ... Ms. Chaste COPPAGE
49 Dean School of Arts & Sciences ... Dr. Alonzo F. PETERSON
50 Dean School of Business ... Dr. Joshua M. SNAVELY
47 Dean School Agric/Applied Science ... Dr. Wesley L. WHITTAKER
66 Dean School of Nursing/Hlth Profess ... Dr. Teressa HUNTER
53 Dean School of Education/Behav Sci ... Dr. Ruth R. JACKSON
88 Dean School of Physical Therapy ... Dr. Elicia L. POLLARD
84 Exec Director Enrollment Mgmt ... Dr. Jason JOHNSON
04 Executive Asst to President ... Ms. Elaine C. PRESTON
39 Director Student Housing ... Dr. Carolyn EASTLIN
44 Annual Giving Officer ... Ms. Jillian B. WHITAKER

Mid-America Christian University (G)

3500 SW 119th Street, Oklahoma City OK 73170-4500
County: Cleveland FICE Identification: 006942
Unit ID: 245953
Telephone: (405) 691-3800 Carnegie Class: Masters/M
FAX Number: (405) 692-3165 Calendar System: Semester
URL: www.macu.edu
Established: 1953 Annual Undergrad Tuition & Fees: $19,604
Enrollment: 2,093 Coed
Affiliation or Control: Church Of God IRS Status: 501(c)3
Highest Offering: Master's
Accreditation: NH

01 President ... Dr. John D. FOZARD
03 VP College of Adult & Grad Studies ... Dr. Bobbie SPURGEON-HARRIS
05 Vice Pres for Academic Affairs ... Dr. Sharon LEASE
32 VP Student Engagement/Success ... Vacant
45 VP for University Advancement ... Mr. Steve SEATON
13 Chief Information Officer ... Mr. Jody ALLEN
15 Director of Human Resources ... Mrs. Darwina MARSHALL
108 Dir Institutional Effectiveness ... Mr. Ray DILLMAN
42 Exec Director of Church Relations ... Rev. Morgan ALSIP
06 Registrar ... Ms. Stephanie DAVIDSON
37 Director Office of Financial Aid ... Ms. Deaun MAAS-STEED
07 Asst VP of Enrollment Services ... Mr. Mike WILKINSON
18 Director of Facilities ... Ms. Connie GALL
29 Director Alumni Relations ... Vacant
04 Executive Asst to President ... Mrs. Alecia SHANNON
08 Director of Library Services ... Ms. Marsha KENDRICK
10 Chief Financial Officer ... Mrs. Mici SARTIN
19 Director of Public Safety ... Mr. Tim GIBSON
41 Athletic Director ... Mr. Marcus MOELLER

Murray State College (H)

One Murray Campus, Tishomingo OK 73460-3130
County: Johnston FICE Identification: 003158
Unit ID: 207236
Telephone: (580) 387-7000 Carnegie Class: Assoc/HT-High Trad
FAX Number: (580) 371-9844 Calendar System: Semester
URL: www.mscok.edu
Established: 1908 Annual Undergrad Tuition & Fees (In-State): $6,010
Enrollment: 2,292 Coed
Affiliation or Control: State IRS Status: 501(c)3
Highest Offering: Associate Degree
Accreditation: NH, ADNUR, OTA, PTAA

01 President ... Ms. Joy MCDANIEL
05 VP Acad Affs/Institutional Effect ... Ms. Becky HENTHORN
04 Exec Assistant to President/Board ... Mrs. Amy CASKEY
10 VP Finance/Administration/CFO ... Mr. Dennis WESTMAN
32 Vice Pres for Student Affairs ... Ms. Michaelle GRAY
20 Dean of Instruction ... Ms. Ginger COTHRAN
18 AVP Facilities/Safety ... Mr. Sam HOLT
102 Exec Director MSC Foundation ... Vacant
37 Dir Financial Aid ... Ms. Traci FRANKS
08 Director of Library ... Ms. Mary RIXEN
74 Veterinary Tech Program Director ... Ms. Debbie REED
66 Director of Nursing ... Ms. Robin COPPEDGE
07 Registrar ... Ms. Liesl PAYNE
15 Director of Human Resources ... Ms. Michaelle GRAY
35 Director Student Support Services ... Ms. Linda TAYLOR
21 Comptroller ... Ms. Sherry GRAY-DEVINE

Northeastern Oklahoma Agricultural and Mechanical College (I)

200 I Street, NE, Miami OK 74354-6434
County: Ottawa FICE Identification: 003160
Unit ID: 207290
Telephone: (918) 542-8441 Carnegie Class: Assoc/MT-VT-High Trad
FAX Number: (918) 542-9759 Calendar System: Semester
URL: www.neo.edu
Established: 1919 Annual Undergrad Tuition & Fees (In-State): $4,758
Enrollment: 2,055 Coed
Affiliation or Control: State IRS Status: 501(c)3
Highest Offering: Associate Degree
Accreditation: NH, ADNUR, MLTAD, PTAA

01 Interim President ... Dr. Mark RASOR
05 Vice President Academic Affairs ... Dr. Bethene FAHNESTOCK
10 Vice President for Fiscal Affairs ... Mr. Mark RASOR
32 VP Student Affairs/Enrollment Svcs ... Mrs. Amy ISHMAEL
20 Asst VP for Academic Affairs ... Mr. Dustin GROVER
37 Director of Financial Aid ... Mr. David FISHER
26 Chief Public Relations Officer ... Mr. Jordan ADAMS
15 Director Human Resources ... Vacant
18 Director Facilities/Physical Plant ... Mr. Steve GRIMES
13 Coord Instructional Technology ... Mr. Matt WESTPHAL
30 Exec Dir Development Foundation ... Ms. Jennifer WALKER

121 Director Academic Advising Center ... Mrs. Rachel LLOYD
41 Athletic Director ... Mr. Joe RENFRO
105 Webmaster ... Mr. David FRAZIER
06 Registrar ... Mrs. Shay CLAPP
21 AVP for Fiscal Affairs/Controller ... Mr. Michael ALLGOOD
40 Bookstore Manager ... Mrs. Kathryn VANOVER
08 Director Library Services ... Ms. Sloane ARANA
47 Department Chair Agriculture ... Dr. Mary BOOTH
83 Department Chair Social Science ... Dr. Jeff BIRDSONG
57 Dept Chair Commun/Performing Arts ... Dr. Jeff BIRDSONG
81 Dept Chair Mathematics/Science ... Mr. Steve DIXON
66 Dept Chr Nurs/Allied Hlth/Phys Educ ... Mrs. Deborah MORGAN
50 Dept Chair Business and Technology ... Mrs. Joy BAUER
04 Executive Asst to President ... Mrs. Kendra CUMMINS
19 Director Security/Safety ... Mr. Mark WALL
39 Director Student Housing ... Mr. Jim ROWLAND
90 Coordinator IT/Technical Services ... Mr. Matt WESTPHAL
96 Coordinator of Purchasing ... Mrs. Gina RENTFROW

Northeastern State University (A)

600 N Grand Avenue, Tahlequah OK 74464-2399

County: Cherokee
FICE Identification: 003161
Unit ID: 207263
Telephone: (918) 456-5511
Carnegie Class: Masters/L
FAX Number: (918) 458-2015
Calendar System: Semester
URL: www.nsuok.edu
Established: 1909
Annual Undergrad Tuition & Fees (In-State): $6,650
Enrollment: 7,909
Coed
Affiliation or Control: State
IRS Status: 501(c)3
Highest Offering: First Professional Degree
Accreditation: NH, ACBSP, CACREP, CAEP, DIETD, MT, MUS, NUR, OPT, OPTR, SP, SW

01 President ... Dr. Steve TURNER
05 Provost & VP Academic Affairs ... Dr. Debborah LANDRY
11 VP for Administration/Finance ... Ms. Christy LANDSAW
86 Dir Community/Government Relations ... Vacant
26 VP University Relations ... Mr. Dan MABERY
32 Vice President Student Affairs ... Dr. Jerrid FREEMAN
20 Asst VP Academic Affairs Admin ... Dr. Sophia SWEENEY
20 Asst VP Academic Affairs Admin ... Dr. Pam FLY
12 Dean Broken Arrow Campus ... Dr. Roy WOOD
12 Dean Muskogee Campus ... Dr. Kimberly WILLIAMS
49 Dean College of Liberal Arts ... Dr. Mike CHANSLOR
50 Dean College of Business/Technology ... Dr. Janet BUZZARD
53 Dean College of Education ... Dr. Vanessa ANTON
81 Dean Science & Health Professions ... Dr. Pamela HATHORN
88 Dean Optometry ... Dr. Douglas PENISTEN
08 Exec Director of NSU Libraries ... Vacant
108 Exec Director Inst Effectiveness ... Dr. Julia SAWYER
30 Director of Development ... Ms. Peggy GLENN-SUMMITT
15 Director of Human Resources ... Ms. Monica BARNETT
37 Director Student Financial Services ... Dr. Teri COCHRAN
06 Registrar ... Ms. Janet KELLEY
07 Director Admissions/Recruitment ... Ms. Chenoa WORTHINGTON
84 Asst VP Enrollment Management ... Mr. Dan MABERY
18 Assistant VP Facilities ... Mr. Jonathan ASBILL
41 Director of Athletics ... Mr. Tony DUCKWORTH
19 Director of Campus Police ... Ms. Patti BUHL
29 Director Alumni Services ... Mr. Daniel JOHNSON
07 Asst Director of Admission/Rec ... Ms. Damita CUNNINGHAM
109 Director of Auxiliary Services ... Mr. Chris ADNEY
39 Director of Housing ... Mr. Craig REINEHR
35 Asst VP Student Affairs Admin ... Ms. Sheila SELF
96 Director Purchasing Contr Payments ... Mr. Austin ROSENTHAL
44 Stewards/Annual Giving Coordinator ... Ms. Cami HIGHERS
04 Administrative Asst to President ... Ms. Robin HUTCHINS
13 Chief Info Tech Officer/Director IT ... Dr. Richard REIF

Northeastern State University (B)

3100 East New Orleans St, Broken Arrow OK 74014

Telephone: (918) 449-6000
Identification: 770372
Accreditation: &NH

Northeastern State University at Muskogee (C)

2400 W Shawnee, Muskogee OK 74401

Telephone: (918) 683-0040
Identification: 770373
Accreditation: &NH, OT

Northern Oklahoma College (D)

1220 E Grand Avenue, PO Box 310,
Tonkawa OK 74653-0310

County: Kay
FICE Identification: 003162
Unit ID: 207281
Telephone: (580) 628-6200
Carnegie Class: Assoc/MT-VT-High Non
FAX Number: (580) 628-6209
Calendar System: Semester
URL: www.noc.edu
Established: 1901
Annual Undergrad Tuition & Fees (In-State): $4,170
Enrollment: 4,276
Coed
Affiliation or Control: State
IRS Status: 501(c)3
Highest Offering: Associate Degree
Accreditation: NH, ACBSP, ADNUR, COARC

01 President ... Dr. Cheryl EVANS
05 Vice President for Academic Affairs ... Dr. Pam STINSON
10 Vice President Financial Affairs ... Mrs. Anita SIMPSON
12 Vice President for NOC Enid ... Vacant
12 Vice President for NOC Stillwater ... Ms. Diana WATKINS
32 Vice President for Student Affairs ... Mr. Jason JOHNSON
30 Vice President for Devel/Cmty Rels ... Mrs. Sheri SNYDER
13 Director Information Technology ... Mr. Michael MACHIA
15 Director Human Resources ... Ms. Shannon CRANFORD
84 Vice Pres Enroll Mgmt/Registrar ... Dr. Rick EDGINGTON
08 Director of Library Services ... Mr. Benjamin HAINLINE
18 Assoc Vice Pres of Physical Plant ... Mr. Larry DYE
41 Athletic Director ... Mr. Jeremy HISE
37 Director Student Financial Aid ... Ms. Holly LEE
40 Manager Student Bookstore ... Mrs. Jimilea JANSSON

Northwestern Oklahoma State University (E)

709 Oklahoma Boulevard, Alva OK 73717-2799

County: Woods
FICE Identification: 003163
Unit ID: 207306
Telephone: (580) 327-1700
Carnegie Class: Masters/S
FAX Number: (580) 327-1881
Calendar System: Semester
URL: www.nwosu.edu
Established: 1897
Annual Undergrad Tuition & Fees (In-State): $7,471
Enrollment: 2,096
Coed
Affiliation or Control: State
IRS Status: 501(c)3
Highest Offering: Doctorate
Accreditation: NH, ACBSP, CAEPN, NUR, SW

01 President ... Dr. Janet L. CUNNINGHAM
11 Vice President for Administration ... Dr. David M. PECHA
05 Vice President for Academics ... Dr. Bo S. HANNAFORD
20 Assoc VP for Academics ... Dr. James L. BELL
26 Assoc VP for University Relations ... Mr. Steven J. VALENCIA
32 Dean of Student Affairs ... Mr. Calleb N. MOSBURG
41 Athletic Director ... Mr. Brad FRANZ
06 Registrar ... Ms. Sheri K. LAHR
37 Director Financial Aid ... Ms. Tara HANNAFORD
113 Bursar ... Ms. Paige FISCHER
07 Asst Dean of Students & Recruitment ... Mr. Matt ADAIR
18 Chief Facilities/Physical Plant ... Mr. Jim DETGEN
15 Human Resource Director ... Ms. Cheryl ELLIS
29 Director Alumni Relations ... Mr. John W. ALLEN
58 Assoc Dean of Graduate Studies ... Dr. Shawn P. HOLLIDAY
08 Director of Libraries ... Mrs. Shannon LEAPER
09 Institutional Research Specialist ... Ms. Kylea C. AMERIN

Oklahoma Baptist University (F)

500 W University, Shawnee OK 74804-2590

County: Pottawatomie
FICE Identification: 003164
Unit ID: 207403
Telephone: (405) 585-4000
Carnegie Class: Bac-Diverse
FAX Number: N/A
Calendar System: Semester
URL: www.okbu.edu
Established: 1910
Annual Undergrad Tuition & Fees: $28,258
Enrollment: 2,093
Coed
Affiliation or Control: Southern Baptist
IRS Status: 501(c)3
Highest Offering: Master's
Accreditation: NH, ACBSP, CAEP, MUS, NURSE

01 President ... Dr. Pat TAYLOR
05 Provost ... Dr. Susan DEWOODY
10 Exec VP Business Affs/Admin Svcs ... Mr. Randy L. SMITH
111 Sr VP for Advancement & Univ Rels ... Dr. Will SMALLWOOD
26 Assoc VP Marketing & Communication ... Mrs. Paula GOWER
79 Director of Teacher Education ... Dr. Pam ROBINSON
11 Director of Executive Offices ... Mrs. Tonia KELLOGG
37 Director Student Financial Services ... Mrs. Jonna G. RANEY
88 Dir of Events/Conf & Camps ... Ms. Cynthia K. GATES
06 Dir Academic Records/Registrar ... Ms. Marcia MCQUERRY
21 Asst VP Finance/Admin Svcs ... Mrs. Lauri A. FLUKE
21 Controller ... Mr. Steven FLOYD
15 Director of Human Resources ... Mr. Mike JOHNSON
35 Director of Campus Services ... Mr. Larry A. WALKER
19 Chief of University Police ... Mr. David SHANNON
41 Athletic Director ... Mr. Robert DAVENPORT
18 Mgr of Facility Services ... Mr. Robert MARQUARDT
84 Assoc VP for Enrollment Management ... Mr. Bruce PERKINS
36 Dir of Career Services & Alumni Eng ... Ms. Lori R. HAGANS
57 Dean College of Fine Arts ... Dr. Chris MATHEWS
81 Dean College of Math and Science ... Dr. Chris JONES
50 Dean College of Business ... Dr. David C. HOUGHTON
66 Dean College of Nursing ... Dr. Lepaine MCHENRY
108 AVP of Institutional Effectiveness ... Vacant
07 Director of Admissions ... Mr. Will BRANTLEY
04 Exec Secretary to the President ... Mrs. Angela WILLIAMS
39 Director Student Housing ... Vacant

Oklahoma Christian University (G)

PO Box 11000, Oklahoma City OK 73136-1100

County: Oklahoma
FICE Identification: 003165
Unit ID: 207324
Telephone: (405) 425-5000
Carnegie Class: Masters/L
FAX Number: (405) 425-5090
Calendar System: Semester
URL: www.oc.edu
Established: 1950
Annual Undergrad Tuition & Fees: $22,760
Enrollment: 2,458
Coed
Affiliation or Control: Independent Non-Profit
IRS Status: 501(c)3
Highest Offering: Master's
Accreditation: NH, ACBSP, CAEPN, CIDA, MT, MUS, NURSE

01 President ... Mr. John DESTEIGUER
11 Chief Operations Officer ... Mr. Jeff DIMICK
05 Chief Academic Officer ... Dr. Scott LAMASCUS
26 Chief Communications Officer ... Mrs. Risa FORRESTER
111 Chief Advancement Officer ... Mr. Alan PHILLIPS
43 Chief Legal Officer ... Mr. Stephen ECK
32 Chief Student Life Officer & Dean ... Mr. Neil ARTER
07 Chief Admissions Officer ... Mr. Will BLANCHARD
13 Chief Tech and Campus Op Officer ... Mr. John HERMES
112 Chief Gifts Officer ... Mr. Kent ALLEN
50 Dean Col of Business Administration ... Dr. Jeff SIMMONS
73 Dean College of Biblical Studies ... Dr. Charles RIX
49 Dean College of Liberal Arts ... Dr. Tina WINN
54 Dean Col of Engineering & Comp Sci ... Dr. Byron NEWBERRY
81 Dean Col of Nat & Health Sciences ... Dr. Jeff MCCORMACK
06 Assoc Dean for Academics/Registrar ... Dr. Stephanie BAIRD
08 Library Director ... Mrs. Tamie L. WILLIS
19 Chief of Police Dept ... Mr. Greg GILTNER
41 Athletic Director ... Mr. David LYNN
18 Director of Physical Plant Services ... Mr. Cary FALLING
37 Exec Dir Financial Svcs & Budgets ... Mr. Clint LARUE
104 Director of International Programs ... Mr. John OSBORNE
15 Chief Human Resources Officer ... Mr. Terry WINN
42 Dean for Spiritual Life ... Mr. Jeff MCMILLON
89 Dir of Freshman Experience ... Mr. Trent DOBBS
88 Director of Creative Services ... Mrs. Tessa WRIGHT
36 Dir of Calling and Career Services ... Mrs. Susan HOOVER
85 International Student Advisor ... Mrs. Joslyn HILL
38 Director of Counseling Services ... Mr. Sheldon ADKINS
121 Director of Student Success ... Mrs. Amy JANZEN
35 Assistant Dean of Students ... Mr. Gary JONES
04 Executive Assistant to President ... Mrs. Teri MUELLER
09 Institutional Effectiveness Analyst ... Mr. Phil DREW
39 Director Student Housing ... Mrs. Candace BASS
10 Chief Financial Officer ... Mrs. Jennifer RAY

Oklahoma City Community College (H)

7777 S May Avenue, Oklahoma City OK 73159-4444

County: Oklahoma
FICE Identification: 010391
Unit ID: 207449
Telephone: (405) 682-1611
Carnegie Class: Assoc/HT-High Trad
FAX Number: (405) 682-7585
Calendar System: Other
URL: www.occc.edu
Established: 1972
Annual Undergrad Tuition & Fees (In-District): $4,059
Enrollment: 12,342
Coed
Affiliation or Control: State/Local
IRS Status: 501(c)3
Highest Offering: Associate Degree
Accreditation: NH, ACBSP, ADNUR, EMT, OTA, PTAA

01 President ... Dr. Jerry L. STEWARD
100 Chief of Staff ... Dr. Donald HACKLER
04 Exec Assistant to the President ... Ms. Roshell ROBERTS
101 Exec Asst to the Board of Regents ... Ms. Roshell ROBERTS
03 Executive Vice President ... Dr. Marlene LANDINI
05 VP for Academic Affairs ... Mr. Greg GARDNER
32 VP Student Affairs ... Dr. Jeremy THOMAS
10 Acting Chief Financial Officer ... Ms. Cynthia GARY
103 VP Community Development ... Mr. Lemuel BARDEGUEZ
15 Vice Pres Human Resources ... Dr. Regina SWITZER
13 Acting VP of IT Infrastructure ... Mr. Tim WHISENHUNT
20 Associate VP Academic Affairs ... Ms. Kim JAMESON
18 Exec Dir of Facilities Management ... Mr. Chris SNOW
79 Dean of Arts English/Humanities ... Dr. Thomas HARRISON
76 Dean of Health Professions ... Dr. Vincent BRIDGES
81 Dean Math/Engineering/Phys Science ... Dr. Max SIMMONS
83 Acting Dean of Social Sciences ... Ms. Kim JAMESON
50 Dean of Bus & Information Tech ... Mr. John CLAYBON
30 Chief Development Officer ... Mr. Von ALLEN
26 Exec Director of Marketing & PR ... Ms. Jennifer MCCOLLUM
25 Director of Grants & Contracts ... Mr. Von ALLEN
09 Dir Institutional Effectiveness ... Dr. Janet PERRY
37 Director of Student Financial Aid ... Ms. Sonya GORE
32 Dir of Student Engagement and Alum ... Mr. Randy CASSIMUS
21 Director of Financial Accounting ... Ms. Brenda CARPENTER
114 Dir of Budgeting/Fiscal Planning ... Mr. David CHURCHILL
19 Chief of Police ... Mr. Daniel PIAZZA
113 Bursar ... Ms. Cynthia GARY
40 Director of Bookstore ... Ms. Brenda REINKE
117 Emergency Manager ... Mr. Patrick SOLINSKI
96 Director of Purchasing ... Mr. Craig SISCO
88 Director of Cultural Programs ... Ms. Leila LENORE
88 Dir Recreation and Fitness ... Mr. Michael SHUGART
103 Director Career Transitions Program ... Ms. Lisa BROWN
16 Dir of Human Resources Services ... Dr. Regina SWITZER
22 Director of Equal Opportunity ... Dr. Cary PIRRONG
14 Dir Enterprise Resource Planning ... Ms. Connie DRUMMOND
14 Dir Info Technology Infrastructure ... Mr. Rob GREGGS
14 Dir of Info Systems and Services ... Mr. Tim WHISENHUNT
08 Director of Library Services ... Ms. Ann RAIA
88 Dir of Ctr for Learning/Teaching ... Dr. Glenne WHISENHUNT
07 Acting Dir of Recruitment & Admiss ... Mr. Kevin EDDINGS
121 Director of Academic Advising ... Ms. Stephanie MILLER
06 Acting Registrar ... Ms. Amanda WILLIAMS-MIZE

Oklahoma City University (I)

2501 N Blackwelder, Oklahoma City OK 73106-1493

County: Oklahoma
FICE Identification: 003166
Unit ID: 207458
Telephone: (405) 208-5000
Carnegie Class: DU-Mod
FAX Number: (405) 208-5916
Calendar System: Semester
URL: www.okcu.edu
Established: 1904
Annual Undergrad Tuition & Fees: $31,026

Enrollment: 2,845 Coed
Affiliation or Control: United Methodist IRS Status: 501(c)3
Highest Offering: First Professional Degree
Accreditation: NH, #ARCPA, CAEPN, LAW, MACTE, MUS, NUR

01 President Ms. Martha BURGER
05 Interim Provost/VPAA Dr. George SIMS
111 VP University Advancement Ms. Lynnann STERK-BROOKS
10 CFO/VP Finance & Business Opers Mr. Dave MCCONNELL
32 VP Student Affairs/Dean of Students Dr. Amy AYRES
84 Asst VP/Dean Enrollment Services Mr. Kevin WINDHOLZ
06 Registrar Mr. Charles MONNOT
09 Director of Institutional Research Dr. Kelly WILLIAMS
08 Director Dulaney-Browne Library Dr. Victoria SWINNEY
37 Director of Student Financial Svcs Mr. Kurt GRAU
27 Director of Communications Ms. Leslie BERGER
15 VP for Human Resources Ms. Joey CROSLIN
92 Director of Honors Program Dr. Karen YOUMANS
07 Director of Undergrad Admissions Ms. Tasha CASEY-LOVELESS
18 Chief Facilities/Physical Plant Mr. Mark CLOUSE
29 Director Alumni Engagement Ms. Megan HORNBEEK ALLEN
36 Director of Career Services Ms. Tiffany SMITH
49 Dean of Arts & Sciences Dr. Amy E. CATALDI
50 Dean School of Business Dr. Steve AGEE
61 Dean School of Law Mr. James ROTH
64 Dean School of Music Mr. Mark PARKER
66 Dean of School of Nursing Dr. Lois SALMERON
73 Director School of Religion Dr. Sharon BETSWORTH
88 Dean School of Amer Dance/Arts Mgt Mr. John BEDFORD
88 Associate Dean School of Theatre Vacant
104 Director Study Abroad Vacant
108 Director Institutional Assessment Vacant
13 Chief Info Officer (CIO) Mr. Gerry HUNT
19 Chief of Police Mr. Rusty PYLE
38 Director of Counseling Services Ms. Mindy WINDHOLZ
39 Director University Housing Mr. Casey KREGER
41 Director of Athletics Mr. Jim ABBOTT
43 University General Counsel Ms. Casey ROSS
44 Director Annual Giving Ms. Carrie SAUER
04 Administrative Asst to President Ms. Sarah POWERS
28 Dir Stdnt Engage/Incl/Multicult Pgm Mr. Russ TALL CHIEF
105 Web Services Manager Mr. Brian BYRNE

Oklahoma Panhandle State University (A)

Box 430, Goodwell OK 73939-0430
County: Texas FICE Identification: 003174
Unit ID: 207351
Telephone: (580) 349-2611 Carnegie Class: Bac-Diverse
FAX Number: (580) 349-2302 Calendar System: Semester
URL: www.opsu.edu
Established: 1909 Annual Undergrad Tuition & Fees (In-State): $7,930
Enrollment: 1,138 Coed
Affiliation or Control: State IRS Status: 501(c)3
Highest Offering: Baccalaureate
Accreditation: NH, CAEP, NUR

01 President Dr. Tim FALTYN
05 Vice Pres Academic Affairs Dr. Julie DINGER
10 Vice Pres Business & Fiscal Affairs Mr. Benny DAIN
111 Vice President of Outreach Dr. Ryan BLANTON
47 Dean Agriculture/Science/Nursing Ms. Shawna TUCKER
50 Dean Business & Technology Mr. Davin WINGER
57 Dean Arts & Education Dr. Brad DUREN
32 Dean of Student Services Mr. Michael HARRIS
06 Registrar/Director of Admissions Ms. Amber GLASS
37 Director Student Financial Aid Ms. Erin MOORE
09 Director Institutional Research Mr. Dillon SCHOENHALS
13 Director of Technology Mr. Howard HENDERSON
15 Director Personnel Services Ms. Dana COLLINS
08 Director of Library Ms. Alton (Tony) HARDMAN
21 Comptroller Ms. Elizabeth MCMURPHY
38 Director Counseling/Career Services Ms. Deanna Rene RAMON
26 Campus Communications Director Ms. Alyssa LAROCQUE
41 Athletic Officer Ms. Meghan MULCAHY
40 Bookstore Manager Ms. Ariana HOOKS
18 Director Physical Plant Ms. Laura DURAN
29 Director Alumni Relations Mr. Nick TUTTLE
96 Director of Purchasing Ms. Carol HILL
04 Administrative Asst to President Ms. Laura TORRES
07 Director of Recruitment Ms. Jade SINGLETON-REICH

Oklahoma State University (B)

Stillwater OK 74078
County: Payne FICE Identification: 003170
Unit ID: 207388
Telephone: (405) 744-5000 Carnegie Class: DU-Highest
FAX Number: N/A Calendar System: Semester
URL: osu.okstate.edu/
Established: 1890 Annual Undergrad Tuition & Fees (In-State): $9,019
Enrollment: 25,295 Coed
Affiliation or Control: State IRS Status: 501(c)3
Highest Offering: Doctorate
Accreditation: NH, AAB, CAATE, CACREP, CAEPN, CARTE, CIDA, CLPSY, COPSY, DIETD, DIETI, JOUR, LSAR, MFCD, MUS, NURSE, PCSAS, SCPSY, SP, THEA, #VET

01 President Dr. V. Burns HARGIS
04 Exec Assistant to the President Ms. Deborah LANE
102 President & CEO OSU Foundation Mr. Kirk JEWELL
03 Sr Vice President & General Counsel Mr. Gary C. CLARK
05 Provost & Sr Vice President Dr. Gary SANDEFUR
10 Sr Vice Pres Admin & Finance Mr. Joseph B. WEAVER, JR.
47 VP/Dean/Director Ag Sci & Nat Res Dr. Thomas COON
41 Vice President Athletic Programs Mr. Mike HOLDER
26 Vice Pres Enroll Mgmt/Univ Mktg Mr. Kyle WRAY
46 Vice President for Research Dr. Kenneth SEWELL
32 Vice President Student Affairs Dr. Lee E. BIRD
09 Assoc VP/Dir Inst Res/Info Mgmt Dr. Christie HAWKINS
20 Prov/Sr VP Academic Affairs Dr. Pamela FRY
58 Assoc Provost/Dean Graduate College Dr. Sheryl TUCKER
21 Assoc Vice President & Controller Ms. Tammy ECK
28 Assoc VP Institutional Diversity Dr. Jason KIRKSEY
24 Asst Prov/Dir Inst Tch/Lrng Excel Dr. Christine ORMSBEE
13 Chief Information Officer Ms. Darlene HIGHTOWER
18 Chief Facilities Officer Mr. Ron TARBUTTON
96 Chief Procurement Officer Mr. Scott SCHLOTTHAUER
19 Chief Public Safety Officer Mr. Michael ROBINSON
36 Director Career Services Dr. Pam EHLERS
27 Director Communication Services Mr. Gary SHUTT
25 Dir Grants/Contracts/Financial Admn Dr. Robert DIXON
37 Director Scholarships/Financial Aid Mr. Chad BLEW
39 Director of University Housing Dr. Leon MCCLINTON
108 Director Univ Assessment & Testing Mr. James KNECHT
38 Director University Counseling Svcs Dr. Trevor RICHARDSON
23 Director University Health Services Mr. Christopher BARLOW
88 Assoc Dir Institutional Research Mr. Doug REED
40 Dir Student Union Bookstore Mr. Lance HINKLE
39 Asst Director Resident Life Ms. Tanya MASSEY
85 Asst Dir Intl Students & Scholars Mr. Tim T. HUFF
53 Dean College of Education Dr. John ROMANS
54 Dean Engineering Dr. Paul J. TIKALSKY
92 Dean Honors College Dr. Keith GARBUTT
59 Dean Human Sciences Dr. Stephan M. WILSON
08 Dean Library Dr. Sheila G. JOHNSON
50 Dean Spears School of Business Dr. Ken EASTMAN
74 Dean Veterinary Medicine Dr. Christopher R. ROSS
43 Board of Regents General Counsel Mr. Steve STEPHENS
06 Registrar Ms. Rita PEASTER

Oklahoma State University Center for Health Sciences College of Osteopathic Medicine (C)

1111 W 17th Street, Tulsa OK 74107-1898
Telephone: (918) 582-1972 FICE Identification: 011282
Accreditation: &NH, FEPAC, OSTEO

† Regional accreditation is carried under the parent institution in Stillwater, OK.

Oklahoma State University Institute of Technology-Okmulgee (D)

1801 E Fourth Street, Okmulgee OK 74447-3901
County: Okmulgee FICE Identification: 003172
Unit ID: 207564
Telephone: (918) 293-4678 Carnegie Class: Bac/Assoc-Mixed
FAX Number: (918) 293-4644 Calendar System: Trimester
URL: www.osuit.edu
Established: 1946 Annual Undergrad Tuition & Fees (In-State): $5,550
Enrollment: 2,496 Coed
Affiliation or Control: State IRS Status: 501(c)3
Highest Offering: Baccalaureate
Accreditation: NH, ADNUR

01 President Dr. Bill PATH
10 VP Fiscal Services Mr. Jim SMITH
05 VP Academic Affairs Dr. Scott NEWMAN
32 VP Student Services Dr. Ina AGNEW
20 Associate VP Academic Affairs Ms. Jody GRAMMER
103 Assoc VP Workforce & Econ Dev Mr. Charles HARRISON
66 Dean Nursing & Health Sciences Ms. Jana MARTIN
49 Dean Arts & Sciences Dr. Mark ALLEN
72 Int Dean Automotive Technologies Mr. Terryl LINDSEY
72 Dean Construction Technologies Mr. Steve OLMSTEAD
88 Dean Culinary Arts Mr. Gene LEITERMAN
54 Dean Engineering Technologies Dr. Abul HASAN
88 Dean Diesel & Heavy Equipment Tech Mr. Terryl LINDSEY
88 Int Dean Energy Technologies Dr. Abul HASAN
77 Int Dean Information Technologies Mr. Gene LEITERMAN
57 Dean Visual Communications Mr. James MCCULLOUGH
37 Dir Student Financial Services Mr. Matt SHORT
13 Associate VP Technology Services Mr. Kevin HULETT
06 Registrar Ms. Crystal BOWLES
07 Director of Admissions Ms. Crystal BOWLES
106 Int Director of Distance Learning Ms. Jenny DUNCAN
15 Director of Human Resources Ms. Paula NORTH
09 Director of Institutional Research Ms. Michelle CANAN
18 Dir Physical Plant Services Mr. Mark PITCHER
35 Dean of Students Mr. Devin DEBOCK
109 Dir Student Union & Auxiliary Svcs Mr. James BYRD
35 Director of Student Life Ms. Kamie RASH
39 Director of Residential Life Mr. Bo HUDSON
08 Director of Library Ms. Jenny DUNCAN
96 Director of Purchasing Ms. Jalynda BAILEY
38 Counselor Ms. Kathy AVERY
40 Manager Bookstore Ms. Alison WARD
26 Director of Marketing Ms. Shari ERWIN
19 Campus Police Chief Mr. Matt WOOLIVER
04 Admin Asst to President Ms. Claudette BUTCHER
88 Dir Tutoring Ctr/Acad Accommodation Mr. Chad SPURLOCK
29 Director Alumni Relations Vacant
30 Director Development Ms. Mae BARTEL

Oklahoma State University - Oklahoma City (E)

900 N Portland Ave, Oklahoma City OK 73107-6195
County: Oklahoma FICE Identification: 009647
Unit ID: 207397
Telephone: (405) 947-4421 Carnegie Class: Bac/Assoc-Assoc Dom
FAX Number: (405) 945-3289 Calendar System: Semester
URL: www.osuokc.edu
Established: 1961 Annual Undergrad Tuition & Fees (In-State): $4,498
Enrollment: 5,839 Coed
Affiliation or Control: State IRS Status: 501(c)3
Highest Offering: Baccalaureate
Accreditation: NH, ADNUR, DIETT, DMS, EMT, IFSAC

01 President Dr. Brad WILLIAMS
05 Vice President Academic Affairs Dr. Joey FRONHEISER
10 Vice President Budget & Finance Ms. Ronda REECE
20 Associate VP Academic Affairs Mr. Tracy EDWARDS
32 Vice Pres of Student Experience Mr. Darioush YASSERI
30 Associate Dir Development Mr. Donovan WOODS
11 Vice Pres of Operations Mr. Mike WIDELL
08 Director Library Services Ms. Elaine REGIER
37 Director Financial Aid Ms. Bessie CARTER
15 Director Human Resources Ms. Melissa HERREN
18 Dir of Building Maint/Energy Mgr Mr. Mickey FULLER
26 Sr Dir Marketing/Communications Mr. Nick TROUGAKOS
84 Sr Dir of Enrollment Management Mr. Kyle WILLIAMS
96 Director of Purchasing Ms. Sharon FITZPATRICK
06 Registrar Mr. Kyle BROWN
25 Sr Dir Institutional Grants Ms. Jackie WESTON
19 Director Security/Safety Mr. Darvin GORE
108 Sr Dir Institutional Effectiveness Ms. Virginia SMITH

Oklahoma State University - Tulsa (F)

700 N Greenwood Avenue, Tulsa OK 74106-0702
Telephone: (918) 594-8000 Identification: 666053
Accreditation: &NH

† Regional accreditation is carried under the parent institution in Stillwater, OK.

Oklahoma Wesleyan University (G)

2201 Silver Lake Road, Bartlesville OK 74006-6299
County: Washington FICE Identification: 003151
Unit ID: 206835
Telephone: (918) 333-6151 Carnegie Class: Masters/M
FAX Number: (918) 335-6228 Calendar System: Semester
URL: www.okwu.edu
Established: 1910 Annual Undergrad Tuition & Fees: $27,136
Enrollment: 1,204 Coed
Affiliation or Control: Wesleyan Church IRS Status: 501(c)3
Highest Offering: Master's
Accreditation: NH, CAEPN, IACBE, NURSE

01 President Dr. Jim DUNN
05 Provost/VP for Academic Affairs Dr. Mark WEETER
10 Vice President for Business Affairs Mrs. Andrea ZEPEDA
32 Vice Pres for Student Development Mr. Kyle WHITE
84 Vice President for Enrollment Svcs Mrs. Samantha PETERSON
35 Assoc VP for Student Dev Rev. Ben ROTZ
53 Dean School of Educ & Exercise Sci Dr. Jeffrey KEENEY
73 Dean Sch of Ministry/Christ Theol Dr. Jerome VAN KUIKEN
49 Dean of School of Arts & Sciences Dr. Dalene FISHER
50 Dean of School of Business Dr. Wendel WEAVER
66 Dean of School of Nursing Dr. Jessica JOHNSON
106 Dean of Online Learning Dr. Devon SMITH
21 Director of Accounting Mrs. Tabitha BENBROOK
06 Registrar Mr. Jeff LEBERT
13 Director of Information Technology Mr. Eric GOINGS
08 Head Librarian Mrs. Cheryl SALERNO
37 Director of Financial Aid Mrs. Kandi MOLDER
15 Director of Human Resources Mrs. Rachel GLASS-SHOWLER
41 Athletic Director Mr. Kirk KELLEY
04 Executive Assistant to President Ms. Leeann LITTLE
39 Director of Residential Life Ms. Megan BREID
89 Dir of First & Second Year Exper Mr. Aaron BUNKER
23 Director of Student Health Exper Mrs. Debra COOK
18 Director of Buildings and Grounds Mr. Dalton HIGGINS
19 Director of Campus Safety Mr. Stevan DJUKIC
101 Secretary of the Institution/Board Mr. Trevor SHAKIBA

Oklahoma Wesleyan University Tulsa Campus (H)

10810 E 45th Street, Tulsa OK 74146
Telephone: (918) 728-6143 Identification: 770378
Accreditation: &NH

Oral Roberts University (I)

7777 S Lewis Avenue, Tulsa OK 74171-0003
County: Tulsa FICE Identification: 003985
Unit ID: 207582
Telephone: (918) 495-6161 Carnegie Class: Bac-Diverse
FAX Number: (918) 495-6033 Calendar System: Semester
URL: www.oru.edu
Established: 1965 Annual Undergrad Tuition & Fees: $27,728
Enrollment: 3,919 Coed
Affiliation or Control: Independent Non-Profit IRS Status: 501(c)3
Highest Offering: Doctorate

Accreditation: **NH**, ACBSP, CAEPN, MUS, NURSE, SW, THEOL

01 President ... Dr. William M. WILSON
05 Provost ... Dr. Kathaleen REID-MARTINEZ
10 Chief Financial Officer ... Mr. Neal STENZEL
11 Chief Operations Officer ... Mr. Tim PHILLEY
111 VP for Advancement ... Mrs. Laura BISHOP
84 VP for Enrollment Management ... Dr. Nancy BRAINARD
43 University Counsel ... Mr. Terry KOLLMORGEN
32 Vice President Student Life ... Dr. Clarence BOYD
13 AVP of Technology & Innovation ... Mr. Michael MATHEWS
21 Controller ... Ms. Michelle MCMILLAN
08 Dean of the University Library ... Dr. Mark ROBERTS
54 Dean Col of Science & Engineering ... Dr. Kenneth WEED
49 Dean Col of Arts & Cultural Studies ... Dr. Mark HALL
73 Dean College Theology/Ministry ... Dr. Wonsuk MA
50 Dean College of Business ... Dr. Julie HUNTLEY
66 Dean & Chairman College of Nursing ... Dr. Kenda JEZEK
53 Dean College of Education ... Dr. Kim BOYD
32 Dean of Student Development ... Ms. Lori COOK
88 Assoc Vice Pres of Student Services ... Dr. Sergio MATVIUK
09 Dir of Institutional Effectiveness ... Dr. Connie SJOBERG
41 Director for Athletics ... Mr. Mike CARTER
25 Grants Facilitator ... Ms. Andrea STOGUE
38 Director of Student Counseling ... Ms. Staley FRENCH
92 Director of Honors Program ... Dr. John KORSTAD
88 Director Student Accounts ... Ms. Karen BAUER
96 Director of Purchasing ... Mr. Mark PEPIN
06 Interim Registrar ... Mr. Lee TARRANT
07 Director of Admissions ... Mrs. Alison VUJNOVIC
84 Coord International Enrollment ... Ms. Wendy MORTON
88 Director of Online Enrollment ... Mr. Nathan CARSON
37 Director of Financial Aid ... Ms. Emily ATKERSON
19 Director of Security/Safety ... Mr. Bill (William) HUNT
15 Human Resources Director ... Dr. Matt OLSEN
04 Executive Asst to President ... Mrs. Lisa BOWMAN
101 Secretary of the Institution/BOT ... Ms. Adreanne CATES

Phillips Theological Seminary (A)

901 N Mingo Road, Tulsa OK 74116-5612
County: Tulsa — FICE Identification: 025602
Unit ID: 414966
Telephone: (918) 610-8303 — Carnegie Class: Spec-4-yr-Faith
FAX Number: (918) 610-8404 — Calendar System: Semester
URL: www.ptstulsa.edu
Established: 1906 — Annual Graduate Tuition & Fees: N/A
Enrollment: 112 — Coed
Affiliation or Control: Christian Church (Disciples Of Christ) — IRS Status: 501(c)3
Highest Offering: Doctorate; No Undergraduates
Accreditation: **THEOL**

01 President ... Gary PELUSO-VERDEND
05 Vice Pres Academic Affairs & Dean ... Nancy Claire PITTMAN
10 Vice Pres Finance & Admin ... Karen MCMILLAN
108 Assoc Dean Assessment & Faculty Dev ... Joseph A. BESSLER
20 Assoc Dn Contextual Ed/Church Rels ... John THOMAS, JR.
73 Director Doctor of Ministry Program ... Kathleen D. MCCALLIE
37 Financial Aid Officer ... John FOREST
08 Library Director ... Sandy SHAPOVAL
29 Sr Director Stewardship ... Geoffrey BREWSTER
44 Stewardship Director ... Malisa PIERCE
26 Sr Director Seminary Relations ... Kurt GWARTNEY
06 Registrar ... Toni WINE IMBLER
07 Dir Admissions/Student Services ... Mary Ann MORRIS
15 Human Resources Manager ... Gwen DERRICK
04 Executive Assistant to President ... Ashley M. GIBSON

Platt College (B)

201 N Eastern Avenue, Moore OK 73160
Telephone: (405) 445-6329 — Identification: 770585
Accreditation: **ACCSC**, #COARC

Platt College (C)

3801 S Sheridan, Tulsa OK 74145-1132
County: Tulsa — FICE Identification: 023068
Unit ID: 245962
Telephone: (918) 663-9000 — Carnegie Class: Spec 2-yr-Health
FAX Number: (918) 622-1240 — Calendar System: Other
URL: www.plattcolleges.edu
Established: 1979 — Annual Undergrad Tuition & Fees: N/A
Enrollment: 329 — Coed
Affiliation or Control: Proprietary — IRS Status: Proprietary
Highest Offering: Associate Degree
Accreditation: **ACCSC**

01 Executive Director of Campus ... Cheryl BEESE
07 Director of Admission & Marketing ... Vacant

Randall University (D)

3701 S. I-35 Service Road, Moore OK 73160
County: Cleveland — FICE Identification: 010266
Unit ID: 207157
Telephone: (405) 912-9000 — Carnegie Class: Bac-A&S
FAX Number: (405) 912-9050 — Calendar System: Semester
URL: www.ru.edu
Established: 1959 — Annual Undergrad Tuition & Fees: $15,108
Enrollment: 322 — Coed
Affiliation or Control: Free Will Baptist — IRS Status: 501(c)3
Highest Offering: Master's
Accreditation: **TRACS**

01 President ... Dr. Timothy W. EATON
03 Executive Vice President ... Dr. Mark H. BRAISHER
05 Chief Academic Officer ... Dr. Brent SYKES
10 Chief Business Officer ... Ms. Pat MILLER
32 Dean of Students ... Ms. Jody BLACKWELL
111 VP Institutional Advancement ... Mr. Bob THOMPSON
07 Admissions Coordinator ... Mr. Bobby THOMPSON
37 Financial Aid Coordinator ... Mr. Cliff BRISTOW
08 LRC Director ... Ms. Nancy J. DRAPER
13 Director of MIS ... Mr. Quentin C. LOOP
06 Registrar ... Ms. Patti ASHBY
58 Dean of Graduate Studies ... Dr. Mark H. BRAISHER
39 Resident Life Coordinator ... Ms. Jody BLACKWELL
41 Athletic Director ... Mr. Mark BEROKOFF
40 Bookstore Manager ... Ms. Traci MORRIS
106 Director of Online Learning ... Dr. Michelle COFFMAN

Redlands Community College (E)

1300 S Country Club Road, El Reno OK 73036-5304
County: Canadian — FICE Identification: 003156
Unit ID: 207069
Telephone: (405) 262-2552 — Carnegie Class: Assoc/HT-High Non
FAX Number: (405) 422-1200 — Calendar System: Semester
URL: www.redlandscc.edu
Established: 1938 — Annual Undergrad Tuition & Fees (In-District): $5,300
Enrollment: 2,023 — Coed
Affiliation or Control: State/Local — IRS Status: 501(c)3
Highest Offering: Associate Degree
Accreditation: **NH**, ADNUR

01 President ... Mr. Jack BRYANT
05 Chief Academic Officer ... Ms. Rose Marie MOORE
10 Exec Vice Pres of Admin & Finance ... Ms. Jena MARR
47 Dept Head of Agriculture ... Ms. Annie PEARSON
18 Director Physical Plant ... Mr. Richard BUCHHOLZ
08 Director Learning Resource Center ... Mrs. Rebecca RATTERMAN
06 Registrar/Director Student Records ... Ms. Holly AVILA
37 Director Financial Aid ... Ms. Paris PRZEKURAT
41 Athletic Director ... Mr. Eli ZUCKSWORTH
13 Director of Information Technology ... Mr. David SOOTER
22 Director of Upward Bound ... Mrs. Kacey DANIELS
09 Coord of Institutional Research ... Mr. Troy MILLIGAN
32 Director Student Services ... Ms. Amy GRAHAM
21 Business Office Supervisor ... Mrs. Brenda HARKINS
15 Coordinator Personnel/Payroll ... Mrs. Kim ANDRADE
26 Director of Communication/Marketing ... Mrs. Dayna ROWE
39 Coordinator of Resident Life ... Ms. Tina JACOBS

Rogers State University (F)

1701 W Will Rogers Boulevard,
Claremore OK 74017-3252
County: Rogers — FICE Identification: 003168
Unit ID: 207661
Telephone: (918) 343-7777 — Carnegie Class: Bac-Diverse
FAX Number: (918) 343-7898 — Calendar System: Semester
URL: www.rsu.edu
Established: 1909 — Annual Undergrad Tuition & Fees (In-State): $7,200
Enrollment: 3,728 — Coed
Affiliation or Control: State — IRS Status: 501(c)3
Highest Offering: Master's
Accreditation: **NH**, ADNUR, EMT, NUR

01 President ... Dr. Larry RICE
05 Vice President for Academic Affairs ... Dr. Richard BECK
10 Exec VP for Admin & Finance ... Vacant
30 Vice President for Development ... Vacant
32 Vice Pres for Student Affairs ... Dr. Brent MARSH
84 Vice President Enrollment Mgmt ... Dr. Heidi HOSKINSON
12 Assoc VP Bartlesville Campus ... Vacant
20 Assoc VP for Academic Affairs ... Dr. Mary MILLIKIN
21 Comptroller/Asst Vice Pres Bus Affs ... Mr. Mark MEADORS
12 Director Pryor Campus ... Ms. Faith GATES
107 Dean School of Professional Studies ... Dr. Susan WILLIS
49 Dean School of Arts and Sciences ... Dr. Keith MARTIN
35 Director of Student Development ... Mr. Paul EICHER
08 Director of the Library ... Mr. J. Alan LAWLESS
07 Director of Admissions ... Ms. Joy Lin HALL
29 Director of Alumni ... Ms. Tanya SMITH
04 Exec Assistant to the President ... Ms. Rhonda SPURLOCK
18 Director Physical Plant ... Mr. Karl REYNOLDS
19 Director Campus Police ... Mr. Gary BOERGERMANN
26 Director Public Relations ... Mr. David HAMBY
37 Director of Financial Aid ... Ms. Lori DEARDORFF
91 Director Administrative Computing ... Ms. Cathy BURNS
13 Director Information Technology ... Mr. Brian REEVES
15 Director of Human Resources ... Ms. Jamil HAYNES
41 Director of Athletics ... Mr. Chris RATCLIFF
39 Director Residential Life ... Ms. Kyla SHORT
23 Director Student Health Clinic ... Ms. Lisa MARTIN

Rogers State University-Bartlesville (G)

401 South Dewey Avenue, Bartlesville OK 74003
Telephone: (918) 338-8000 — Identification: 770379
Accreditation: **&NH**

Rogers State University-Pryor (H)

2155 Highway 69A, Pryor Creek OK 74361
Telephone: (918) 825-6117 — Identification: 770380
Accreditation: **&NH**

Rose State College (I)

6420 SE 15th, Midwest City OK 73110-2799
County: Oklahoma — FICE Identification: 009185
Unit ID: 207670
Telephone: (405) 733-7311 — Carnegie Class: Assoc/HT-Mix Trad/Non
FAX Number: (405) 733-7399 — Calendar System: Semester
URL: www.rose.edu
Established: 1970 — Annual Undergrad Tuition & Fees (In-District): $4,319
Enrollment: 7,452 — Coed
Affiliation or Control: State/Local — IRS Status: 501(c)3
Highest Offering: Associate Degree
Accreditation: **NH**, ADNUR, CAHIIM, COARC, DA, DH, MLTAD, RAD

01 President ... Dr. Jeanie WEBB
10 Exec Vice President and CFO ... Dr. Kent LASHLEY
05 Vice President for Academic Affairs ... Dr. Jeff CALDWELL
32 Vice President for Student Affairs ... Mr. Lance NEWBOLD
26 VP for External Affairs ... Ms. Tamara PRATT
13 Vice President for Info Technology ... Mr. John PRIMO
86 Vice Pres for Military/Govt Rels ... Mr. Stan GREIL
41 Exec Dir Athletic Programs ... Mr. Coty COOPER
102 Exec Dir Foundation & Resource Dev ... Ms. Cindy MIKEMAN
20 AVP Acad Affs & Inst Effectiveness ... Ms. Isabelle BILLEN
27 Assoc VP External Affairs ... Dr. Bret WOOD
21 Sr Dir Fiscal Operations ... Mr. Raymond BLANKE
15 Sr Dir Human Res/Affirm Act Ofcr ... Ms. Alberta NUTTER
109 Assoc VP for Campus Operations ... Mr. Richard ANDREWS
84 Assoc VP Enrollment Mgmt/ Registrar ... Ms. Mechelle AITSON-ROESSLER
37 Director Financial Aid ... Mr. Steve DAFFER
26 Director Marketing ... Mr. Daniel BECK
18 Director Operations ... Mr. Ardie RODGERS
41 Dir Health & Wellness Activities ... Mr. Chris LELAND
88 Director Special Services ... Dr. Joanne STAFFORD
08 Dean Learning Resources Center ... Mr. Chris MEYER
50 Dean Business & Info Tech Division ... Dr. Mark TIPPIN
54 Dean Engineering & Science Division ... Dr. Wayne JONES
79 Dean Humanities Division ... Ms. Toni CASTILLO
76 Dean Health Sciences Division ... Ms. Barbara BAUMEISTER
83 Dean Social Sciences Division ... Dr. Juanita ORTIZ
101 Exec Asst to the President & Board ... Ms. Michelle NUTTER
19 Coord of Safety/Security/Risk Mgmt ... Mr. Joedon HUGHES
39 Director of Residence Life ... Ms. Alyssa LOVELESS
28 Director of Diversity ... Dr. Monique BRUNER

Seminole State College (J)

PO Box 351, Seminole OK 74818-0351
County: Seminole — FICE Identification: 003178
Unit ID: 207740
Telephone: (405) 382-9950 — Carnegie Class: Assoc/HT-High Trad
FAX Number: (405) 382-3122 — Calendar System: Semester
URL: www.sscok.edu
Established: 1931 — Annual Undergrad Tuition & Fees (In-District): $5,040
Enrollment: 1,633 — Coed
Affiliation or Control: State/Local — IRS Status: 501(c)3
Highest Offering: Associate Degree
Accreditation: **NH**, ADNUR, MLTAD, PTAA

01 President ... Ms. Lana REYNOLDS
05 Vice President Academic Affairs ... Dr. Larry GUERRERO
10 Vice President Fiscal Affairs ... Mr. Tony CROUCH
32 Vice President of Student Affairs ... Mr. Bill KNOWLES
13 Director Mgmt Information Systems ... Mr. Marc HUNTER
66 Director of Nursing ... Ms. Valarie WATTS
06 Registrar ... Mrs. Sheila MORRIS
15 Director Human Resources ... Mrs. Courtney JONES
26 Director of Public Relations ... Ms. Kristin DUNN
04 Administrative Asst to President ... Ms. Mechell DOWNEY
37 Director Student Financial Aid ... Ms. Melanie RINEHART
39 Director Student Housing ... Ms. Melinda SIMS
41 Athletic Director ... Mr. Mike ST. JOHN

Southeastern Oklahoma State University (K)

425 W University Blvd, Durant OK 74701-3330
County: Bryan — FICE Identification: 003179
Unit ID: 207847
Telephone: (580) 745-2000 — Carnegie Class: Masters/L
FAX Number: N/A — Calendar System: Semester
URL: www.se.edu
Established: 1909 — Annual Undergrad Tuition & Fees (In-State): $6,750
Enrollment: 4,006 — Coed
Affiliation or Control: State — IRS Status: 501(c)3
Highest Offering: Master's
Accreditation: **NH**, AAB, CACREP, CAEP, MUS

01 President ... Mr. Sean BURRAGE
05 Vice Pres Acad Affairs ... Dr. Bryon CLARK
10 Vice President Business Affairs ... Mr. Dennis WESTMAN
32 Vice President of Student Affairs ... Ms. Liz MCCRAW
07 Assoc Dean Admissions/Registrar ... Ms. Kristie LUKE
58 Dean Graduate School ... Mr. Tim BOATMUN

Code	Title	Name
111	Vice President of Univ Advancement	Mr. Kyle STAFFORD
37	Director Student Financial Aid	Mr. Tony LEHRLING
08	Library Director	Ms. Sandra THOMAS
41	Director of Athletics	Mr. Keith BAXTER
26	Dir Univ Comm/Spec Asst Pres	Mr. Alan BURTON
21	Director Finance/Controller	Ms. Crystal CHEEK
18	Director Facilities/Physical Plant	Mr. Dan SIMMONS
28	Director of Compliance and Safety	Mr. Mike DAVIS
96	Purchasing Agent	Ms. Dana BELL
40	Book Store Manager	Ms. Jackie CODNER
29	Director Alumni Relations	Mr. Mark WEBB
106	Dir Online Education/E-learning	Ms. Christala SMITH
19	Chief of Police	Mr. Durwood COOK
39	Director Student Housing	Dr. Kelly D'ARCY
04	Exec Asst to President	Ms. Terri ROGERS

Southern Nazarene University (A)

6729 NW 39 Expressway, Bethany OK 73008-2694

County: Oklahoma FICE Identification: 003149

Unit ID: 206862

Telephone: (405) 789-6400 Carnegie Class: Masters/L

FAX Number: (405) 491-6381 Calendar System: Semester

URL: www.snu.edu

Established: 1899 Annual Undergrad Tuition & Fees: $25,234

Enrollment: 2,165 Coed

Affiliation or Control: Church Of The Nazarene IRS Status: 501(c)3

Highest Offering: Doctorate

Accreditation: NH, ACBSP, CAEP, CAEPN, MUS, NURSE

Code	Title	Name
01	President	Dr. J. Keith NEWMAN
05	Provost & VP Academic Affairs	Dr. Timothy EADES
03	Executive Vice President	Dr. Mike REDWINE
10	Vice President Financial Affairs	Dr. Scott STRAWN
88	VP of Church Relations	Dr. Terry TOLER
88	VP Intercultural Lrng/Engagement	Dr. Lena CROUSO
26	VP University Relations	Mr. Brent LAVIGNE
42	Univ Pastor/Dean of the Chapel	Dr. Blair SPINDLE
84	Assoc VP for Enrollment Management	Mr. Chris PETERSON
79	Dean College of Humanities	Dr. Steve BETTS
81	Dean College of Sci & Health	Dr. Mark WINSLOW
06	Registrar	Mr. Charles CHITWOOD
37	Director Student Financial Aid/PGS	Mr. Perry DIEHM
37	Dir of Financial Aid/Traditional	Mrs. Jamie SALAZAR
32	Assoc VP for Student Life	Mrs. Marian REDWINE
38	Director Student Counseling	Mrs. Kimberly CAMPBELL
36	Director Career Planning/Placement	Mrs. Michelle MULLENS
08	Director Learning Resources Center	Mrs. Konstance CROWNOVER
29	Director Alumni Relations	Mrs. Amy SHIROLA
13	Director Information Technology	Mr. Keith CUMMINGS
121	Assoc VP for Student Success	Mrs. Misty JAGGERS
09	Director Institutional Research	Dr. Elizabeth HOCKER
58	Dean Col of Grad & Prof Study	Vacant
66	Director of Nursing	Dr. Susan BARNES
15	Director Human Resources	Mrs. Gail COLLIER
18	Director of Physical Plant	Mr. Ron LESTER
24	Director Network	Mrs. Chichi FREELANDER
88	Director Creative Development	Mrs. Colleen BROWN
40	Bookstore Manager	Mr. Keith PIERCE
41	Athletic Director	Mr. Bobby MARTIN
53	Vice Prov/Dean Col Teach/Learn	Dr. Dennis WILLIAMS
04	Executive Asst to President	Mrs. Tollya SPINDLE
19	Director Security/Safety	Mr. Glen HOLCOMB
25	Chief Contracts/Grants Admin	Dr. Gwen HACKLER
39	Director Student Housing	Mrs. Katy BRADLEY
28	Director of Diversity	Dr. Lena CROUSO

Southwestern Christian University (B)

PO Box 340, 7210 NW 39th Expressway,
Bethany OK 73008-0340

County: Oklahoma FICE Identification: 003180

Unit ID: 207856

Telephone: (405) 789-7661 Carnegie Class: Bac-Diverse

FAX Number: (405) 495-0078 Calendar System: Semester

URL: www.swcu.edu

Established: 1946 Annual Undergrad Tuition & Fees: $15,080

Enrollment: 670 Coed

Affiliation or Control: Pentecostal Holiness Church IRS Status: 501(c)3

Highest Offering: Master's

Accreditation: NH

Code	Title	Name
01	President	Dr. Tom L. MURRAY
05	VP Academic Affairs	Dr. Adrian HINKLE
32	Vice President for Student Services	Mr. Brad DAVIS
41	Vice President of Athletics	Mr. Mark ARTHUR
11	Associate VP Operations & Athletics	Mr. Joe BLACKWELL
10	Controller	Ms. Teresa THORNTON
37	Director of Financial Aid	Mrs. Kellye JOHNSON
07	Director of Admissions	Mrs. Jessie BURPO
08	Director of Library Services	Mr. Michael LOWDER
06	Registrar	Mr. Mason PINION
58	Director of Graduate Studies	Dr. Matt BENNETT
20	Dean of Academics	Dr. Gayle KEARNS
18	Director of Plant/Property Mgmt	Mr. Robert PALMER
26	Director of Sports Information/PR	Mr. Matthew STEPHENS
13	Director of Information Technology	Mr. Scott KLEPPER
106	Dean of Online Education	Vacant
15	Director of Human Resources	Ms. Rita PALMER
30	Chief Development Officer	Ms. April BLACK
84	Dean of Enrollment Management	Mr. Robert LENK

Code	Title	Name
04	Executive Asst to President	Ms. Erin BROWN
19	Director Security/Safety	Mr. Darin DAVIS
39	Director of Housing	Mr. Zach SHERRILL
39	Director Student Life/Resident Dir	Ms. Kaylee BISHOP

Southwestern Oklahoma State University (C)

100 Campus Drive, Weatherford OK 73096-3098

County: Custer FICE Identification: 003181

Unit ID: 207865

Telephone: (580) 772-6611 Carnegie Class: Masters/L

FAX Number: (580) 774-3795 Calendar System: Semester

URL: www.swosu.edu

Established: 1901 Annual Undergrad Tuition & Fees (In-State): $7,335

Enrollment: 5,448 Coed

Affiliation or Control: State IRS Status: 501(c)3

Highest Offering: First Professional Degree

Accreditation: NH, CAEPN, CAHIIM, IACBE, MLTAB, MUS, NAIT, NUR, OTA, PHAR, PTAA, #RAD

Code	Title	Name
01	President	Dr. Randy L. BEUTLER
10	VP Business and Finance	Ms. Brenda K. BURGESS
05	VP for Academic Affairs/Provost	Dr. James D. SOUTH
32	VP Student Affairs	Dr. Ruth BOYD
20	Assoc Provost Acad Affairs	Dr. Joel KENDALL
26	VP for Marketing/Public Relations	Mr. Brian D. ADLER
111	Asst to Pres/Dir Inst Advancement	Mr. Garrett KING
96	Dir Business Affairs/Comptroller	Ms. Patricia GARCIA
35	Dean of Students/Dir Student Act	Vacant
13	Dir Information Technology Services	Ms. Karen KLEIN
06	Registrar	Mr. Shamus MOORE
08	Library Director	Mr. Jason M. DUPREE
37	Director Student Financial Services	Mr. Jerome L. WICHERT
15	VP Human Resources/Affirm Action	Mr. David MISAK
84	Dir Enrollment Mgmt/Career Svcs	Mr. Todd BOYD
41	Athletic Director	Mr. Todd THURMAN
06	Registrar Sayre Campus	Ms. Terry BILLEY
38	Director Counseling Services	Ms. Laci STRICKLER
18	Director Physical Plant	Mr. James SKINNER
57	Director of Facilities FAC & PCEC	Mr. Nate DOWNS
36	Career Services Coordinator	Ms. Heather HUMMEL
58	Dean College of Prof/Grad Studies	Dr. Chad L. KINDER
49	Dean College of Arts/Sciences	Dr. Jason JOHNSON
67	Dean College of Pharmacy	Dr. David RALPH
12	Dean College of Assoc/Applied Prog	Mr. Bill SWARTWOOD
53	Assoc Dean Sch of Behavioral Sci	Dr. Randy BARNETT
50	Assoc Dean School of Business/Tech	Dr. Patsy PARKER
66	Assoc Dn Sch Nursing/Allied Health	Dr. Darryl BARNETT
04	Exec Assistant to the President	Ms. Misty ZINK
105	Director Web Services	Ms. Karen WILSON
106	Director of CETL	Ms. Lisa FRIESSEN
108	Director Assessment & Testing	Ms. Jan KLIEWER
19	Director Public Safety	Ms. Kendra BROWN
25	Director of Sponsored Programs	Dr. Lori GWYN
39	Director Residence Life & Housing	Mr. Chad MARTIN

† Campus at Sayre offers a two-year degree and is regionally accredited (NH) under parent institution.

Spartan College of Aeronautics and Technology (D)

8820 E Pine Street, Tulsa OK 74115

County: Tulsa FICE Identification: 007678

Unit ID: 207254

Telephone: (918) 836-6886 Carnegie Class: Spec-4-yr-Other Tech

FAX Number: (918) 831-5287 Calendar System: Other

URL: www.spartan.edu

Established: 1928 Annual Undergrad Tuition & Fees: $17,702

Enrollment: 1,127 Coed

Affiliation or Control: Proprietary IRS Status: Proprietary

Highest Offering: Baccalaureate

Accreditation: ACCSC

Code	Title	Name
00	CEO	Mr. Rob POLSTON
01	President	Ms. Kari PAHNO
11	Chief Academic & Operations Ofcr	Dr. Todd CELLINI
10	CFO	Mr. Michael O'CONNOR
05	Dean of Academic Affairs	Mr. Reggie NAIR
32	Dean of Student Affairs	Ms. Jeana WILEY
18	Dean of Operations	Mr. Damon BOWLING
04	Executive Asst to President	Ms. Catherine LOEPER
07	Director of Admissions	Mr. Claude BECKLES
37	Director Student Financial Aid	Ms. Megan COKER
06	Registrar	Ms. Rachel WINKLE

Tulsa Community College (E)

6111 E Skelly Drive, Tulsa OK 74135-6198

County: Tulsa FICE Identification: 009763

Unit ID: 207935

Telephone: (918) 595-7000 Carnegie Class: Assoc/MT-VT-High Trad

FAX Number: (918) 595-7092 Calendar System: Semester

URL: www.tulsacc.edu

Established: 1968 Annual Undergrad Tuition & Fees (In-State): $3,349

Enrollment: 16,897 Coed

Affiliation or Control: State IRS Status: 501(c)3

Highest Offering: Associate Degree

Accreditation: NH, ADNUR, CAHIIM, COARC, CVT, DH, MLTAD, OTA, PTAA, RAD

Code	Title	Name
01	President/CEO	Dr. Leigh GOODSON
05	Sr VP and Chief Academic Officer	Dr. Cynthia HESS
32	Sr Student Affairs Officer	Dr. Jan L. CLAYTON
111	VP Advancement & Foundation Pres	Vacant
11	VP Administration	Mr. Sean A. WEINS
103	VP Workforce Development	Mr. Peter SELDEN
43	General Counsel	Ms. MacKenzie WILFONG
100	Sr Strat Advisor to the President	Ms. Lindsay WHITE
12	Provost Southeast Campus	Dr. Greg STONE
12	Provost Metro Campus	Dr. Angela SIVADON
12	Provost Northeast Campus & Asst VP	Dr. Eunice TARVER
12	Provost West Campus	Dr. Kristopher COPELAND
10	Chief Financial Officer	Mr. Mark MCMULLEN
13	Chief Technology Officer	Mr. Michael SIFTAR
15	Chief Human Resources Officer	Ms. Sandy COOPER
84	Asst VP Enrollment Mgmt	Ms. Eileen KENNEY
26	Sr Dir Marketing/Communications	Ms. Kari SHULTS
12	Dean Community Campuses	Dr. Paula WILLYARD
08	Dean Libraries	Ms. Paula SETTOON
49	Dean Arts and Sciences	Ms. Tracy SKOPEK
54	Dean Engr/Aviation/Public Svcs	Dr. Patrick GREEN
57	Dean Visual & Performing Arts	Ms. Kelly CLARK
66	Dean Nursing	Vacant
76	Dean Allied Health	Ms. Deborah BATSON
81	Dean Science & Mathematics	Ms. Lyn KENT
88	Dean Center for Creativity	Ms. Annina COLLIER
89	Dean Engaged Learning	Ms. Cindy SHANKS
50	Dean Business & IT	Mr. David POTH
28	Dean Diversity/Inclusion	Vacant
18	Dir Physical Facilities	Mr. Steven COX
88	Dir Emergency Ops/Title IX	Ms. Heather HANCOCK
37	Dir Financial Aid	Ms. Karen JEFFERS
96	Dir Purch & Inventory Control	Mr. Bill CREECH
108	Dir Institutional Rsrch/Assessment	Dr. Jennifer IVIE
19	Dir Campus Public Safety	Mr. Melvin MURDOCK
25	Dir Sponsored Programs	Dr. Barbara WAXMAN
104	Dir Global Learning	Dr. Douglas PRICE
106	Dir Online Learning	Mr. Randy G. DOMINGUEZ
51	Dir Continuing Education	Ms. Beth WILD
06	Dir Compl Reporting/Col Registrar	Ms. Traci HECK
07	Dir Admissions/Prosp Stdnt Svcs	Ms. Rachael ACHIVARE-HILL
36	Dir Career and Retention Svcs	Ms. Laura MCNEESE
30	Dir of Development	Ms. Rachel HUTCHINGS
112	Dir of Major Gifts	Ms. Monica CHAMP
105	Web Manager	Ms. Melissa CLOUD
92	Honors Program Coord	Ms. Susan ONEAL
04	Exec Asst to President	Ms. Carrie BATESON

Tulsa Community College Metro Campus (F)

909 South Boston Avenue, Tulsa OK 74119

Telephone: (918) 595-7224 Identification: 770383

Accreditation: &NH, DMS

Tulsa Community College Northeast Campus (G)

3727 East Apache Street, Tulsa OK 74115

Telephone: (918) 595-7524 Identification: 770384

Accreditation: &NH

Tulsa Community College Southeast Campus (H)

10300 East 81st Street, Tulsa OK 74133

Telephone: (918) 595-7724 Identification: 770385

Accreditation: &NH

Tulsa Community College West Campus (I)

7505 W 41st Street, Tulsa OK 74107-8633

Telephone: (918) 595-8060 Identification: 770386

Accreditation: &NH

Tulsa Welding School (J)

2545 E 11th Street, Tulsa OK 74104-3909

County: Tulsa FICE Identification: 009618

Unit ID: 207962

Telephone: (918) 587-6789 Carnegie Class: Spec 2-yr-Tech

FAX Number: (918) 587-8170 Calendar System: Other

URL: www.weldingschool.com

Established: 1949 Annual Undergrad Tuition & Fees: N/A

Enrollment: 926 Coed

Affiliation or Control: Proprietary IRS Status: Proprietary

Highest Offering: Associate Degree

Accreditation: ACCSC

Code	Title	Name
01	Campus President	Ms. Frances HESTON
05	Academic Dean	Vacant
07	Director of Adult Admissions	Vacant
37	Director of Financial Aid	Ms. Tiffany TYRRELL
36	Director of Career Services	Ms. Veronica HIBBERT

University of Central Oklahoma (K)

100 N University Drive, Edmond OK 73034-5209

County: Oklahoma FICE Identification: 003152

Unit ID: 206941

Telephone: (405) 974-2000 Carnegie Class: Masters/L

FAX Number: (405) 359-5841 Calendar System: Semester

URL: www.uco.edu

Established: 1890 Annual Undergrad Tuition & Fees (In-State): $7,489

Enrollment: 15,979 Coed
Affiliation or Control: State IRS Status: 501(c)3
Highest Offering: Master's
Accreditation: NH, ART, CAATE, CAEPN, CIDA, DIETD, DIETI, EXSC, FEPAC, FUSER, MUS, NURSE, SP

01 President ... Ms. Patti NEUHOLD-RAVIKUMAR
05 Provost/Vice Pres Academic Affairs ... Dr. John BARTHELL
11 Vice Pres for Operations ... Mr. Kevin FREEMAN
32 Vice President Student Affairs ... Dr. Myron POPE
13 Chief Information Officer ... Ms. Sonya WATKINS
26 Vice Pres University Relations ... Mr. Charlie JOHNSON
86 Vice Pres Public Affairs ... Dr. Mark KINDERS
30 Vice Pres Development ... Mrs. Anne HOLZBERLEIN
06 Associate Vice President/Registrar ... Dr. Adam JOHNSON
20 Assoc VP Academic Affairs ... Dr. Charlotte SIMMONS
108 Assoc VP Inst Effectiveness ... Dr. Gary STEWARD
21 Asst VP Financial Operations ... Ms. Lisa HARPER
18 Asst Vice Pres Facilities Mgt ... Mr. Mark RODOLF
35 Asst Vice Pres Student Affairs ... Mr. Cole STANLEY
88 Asst Vice Pres Operations ... Mr. Benjamin HASTINGS
41 Athletic Director ... Mr. Eddie GRIFFIN
09 Exec Dir Institutional Research ... Ms. Cindy BOLING
08 Exec Director University Libraries ... Dr. Habib TABATABAI
37 Director Student Financial Services ... Ms. Deanna BRANDT
29 Director Alumni Relations ... Ms. Lauri MONETTI
85 Exec Dir Global Affairs ... Dr. Dennis DUNHAM
19 Exec Dir Public Safety/Trans ... Mr. Jeff HARP
15 Asst VP Human Resources ... Ms. Diane FEINBERG
88 Exec Director Leadership Central ... Dr. Jarrett JOBE
07 Dir of Undergraduate Admissions ... Mr. Dallas CALDWELL
28 Director of Diversity & Inclusion ... Ms. MeShawn CONLEY
96 Director of Purchasing ... Mr. David YOUNG
50 Dean of Business Administration ... Dr. Monica LAM
53 Dean College Education ... Dr. James MACHELL
49 Dean College of Liberal Arts ... Dr. Catherine WEBSTER
81 Dean College Math/Science ... Dr. Wei CHEN
58 Dean Graduate Studies ... Dr. Jeanetta SIMS
57 Dean College Fine Arts & Design ... Dr. Steven HANSEN

University of Oklahoma Health Sciences Center (A)

1100 N. Lindsay, Oklahoma City OK 73104
Telephone: (405) 271-4000 FICE Identification: 005889
Accreditation: &NH, ARCPA, AUD, CAMPEP, DENT, DH, DIETC, DIETI, DMS, HSA, IPSY, MED, NMT, NURSE, OT, PDPSY, PH, PHAR, PTA, RAD, RADDOS, RTT, SP

† Regional accreditation is carried under the parent institution in Norman, OK.

University of Oklahoma Norman Campus (B)

660 Parrington Oval, Norman OK 73019-3070
County: Cleveland FICE Identification: 003184
Unit ID: 207500
Telephone: (405) 325-0311 Carnegie Class: DU-Highest
FAX Number: (405) 325-7605 Calendar System: Semester
URL: www.ou.edu
Established: 1890 Annual Undergrad Tuition & Fees (In-State): $11,538
Enrollment: 28,527 Coed
Affiliation or Control: State IRS Status: 501(c)3
Highest Offering: Doctorate
Accreditation: NH, AAB, CAEPN, CIDA, CONST, COPSY, JOUR, LAW, LIB, LSAR, MUS, PLNG, SPAA, SW

01 Interim President ... Mr. Joseph HARROZ, JR.
10 SVP & Chief Financial Officer ... Mr. Kenneth D. ROWE
11 VP Operations ... Mr. Eric W. CONRAD
05 Senior Vice President/Provost ... Dr. J. Kyle HARPER
43 VP of Univ/General Counsel ... Mr. Anil V. GOLLAHALLI
32 VP Student Affairs/Dean of Students ... Dr. David SURRATT
101 VP Univ Governance/Exec Sec ... Dr. Chris A. PURCELL
30 Interim VP University Development ... Ms. Jill HUGHES
88 Interim Sr Assoc VP Univ Outreach ... Dr. Belinda P. BISCOE
58 Dean Graduate College ... Dr. Randy S. HEWES
46 Vice Pres for Research ... Vacant
26 VP for Marketing & Communication ... Ms. Lauren BROOKEY
13 Associate VP and CIO ... Mr. David HORTON
86 Exec Dir of Governmental Affairs ... Mr. John P. WOODS
20 Assoc Provost/Dir of Acad Integrity ... Dr. Gregory M. HEISER
121 Assoc Prov for Acad Advising ... Dr. Kathleen S. SMITH
09 Assoc Provost/Dir Inst Research ... Ms. Susannah B. LIVINGOOD
18 Director Facilities Management ... Mr. Brian F. ELLIS
109 Director of Food Services ... Mr. Frank M. HENRY
41 VP for Intercollegiate Athletics ... Mr. Joseph R. CASTIGLIONE
21 Assistant VP & Controller ... Ms. Karen SMITH
23 Assoc VP for Stdnt Affs/Health Svs ... Dr. William R. WAYNE
36 Director Career Services ... Ms. Robin E. HUSTON
19 Chief of Police ... Ms. Elizabeth G. WOOLLEN
15 Sr VP & Chief Human Resources Ofcr ... Dr. Jacqueline H. WOLF
22 Equal Opportunity Officer ... Mr. Bobby J. MASON
84 Sr Assoc VP for Enrollment ... Mr. Jeffrey J. BLAHNIK
25 Assoc VP for Research Services ... Ms. Andrea D. DEATON
85 Dir International Student Services ... Ms. Robyn D. ROJAS
104 Director Education Abroad ... Ms. Whitney R. FRANCA
37 Dir of Financial Aid & Scholarships ... Mr. Bradley T. BURNETT
51 Assoc Provost/Interim Dean for PACS ... Dr. Martha L. BANZ
48 Dean Col of Architecture ... Mr. Hans W. BUTZER
49 Dean Col of Arts & Sciences ... Dr. David R. WROBEL
53 Dean Jeannine Rainbolt Col of Educ ... Dr. Gregg A. GARN
54 Dean Gallogly Col of Engineering ... Vacant
57 Dean Weitzenhoffer Col Fine Arts ... Ms. Mary Margaret HOLT
61 Interim Dean College of Law ... Ms. Katheleen GUZMAN
08 Interim Dean Univ Libraries ... Mr. Carl GRANT
65 Dean Col Atmospheric/Geographic Sc ... Dr. Berrien MOORE, III
50 Interim Dean Price Col of Business ... Dr. Wayne B. THOMAS
92 Interim Dean Honors College ... Dr. Douglas D. GAFFIN
60 Dean Gaylord Col Journ/Mass Comm ... Mr. Ed KELLEY
89 Dean University College ... Dr. Nicole J. CAMPBELL
65 Dean Mewborne Col of Earth & Energy ... Dr. J. Michael STICE
82 VP/Interim Dean Col Intl Studies ... Dr. Jill IRVINE
28 Interim VP of Diversity & Inclusion ... Dr. Jane N. IRUNGU
04 Administrative Asst to President ... Ms. Sherry L. EVANS
102 Dir Foundation/Corporate Relations ... Mr. Guy L. PATTON
105 Assoc VP/Director Web Services ... Ms. Erin A. YARBROUGH
96 Director of Purchasing ... Vacant
112 Exec Dir Planned Giving/Development ... Mr. Eric E. MELTON
116 Chief Audit Executive ... Mr. Charles D. WRIGHT
88 Assoc Provost Fac & Student Affairs ... Mr. Christopher O. WALKER
88 Exec Dir of Technology Advancement ... Mr. Aaron A. BIGGS
88 Assoc Provost Academic Engagement ... Ms. Michelle A. EODICE
88 Assoc Prov/Dir Acad Financial Plng ... Mr. Stewart M. BERKINSHAW

† Tuition is based on 30 credit hour per year.

University of Oklahoma Schusterman Center (C)

4502 E 41st Street, Tulsa OK 74135-2512
Telephone: (918) 660-3000 Identification: 770387
Accreditation: &NH, ARCPA, OT

University of Science and Arts of Oklahoma (D)

1727 W Alabama, Chickasha OK 73018-5322
County: Grady FICE Identification: 003167
Unit ID: 207722
Telephone: (405) 224-3140 Carnegie Class: Bac-A&S
FAX Number: (405) 574-1220 Calendar System: Trimester
URL: www.usao.edu
Established: 1908 Annual Undergrad Tuition & Fees (In-State): $7,200
Enrollment: 882 Coed
Affiliation or Control: State IRS Status: 501(c)3
Highest Offering: Baccalaureate
Accreditation: NH, CAEP, MUS

01 President ... Dr. John H. FEAVER
05 VP for Academic Affairs ... Dr. Krista MAXSON
10 Vice Pres for Business & Finance ... Mr. Mike D. COPONITI
84 Vice Pres for Enrollment Management ... Ms. Monica TREVINO
30 Vice Pres University Advancement ... Mr. Sid HUDSON
08 VP for Library/Information Services ... Ms. Nicole MCMONAGLE
06 Registrar/Dir of Enrollment/Records ... Ms. Chelsea PHILLIPS
26 Dir of Communications/Marketing ... Ms. Amy GODDARD
37 Director of Financial Aid ... Ms. Laura I. COPONITI
32 Dean of Students/Dir Student Svcs ... Ms. Nancy HUGHES
29 Director of Alumni Development ... Ms. Misti MCCLELLAN
18 Director of Physical Plant ... Mr. Mike COPONITI
09 Director of Institutional Research ... Ms. Kristi JOHN
15 Director Personnel Services ... Mr. Mike COPONITI
07 Director of Admissions ... Ms. Laura COPONITI
38 Director Student Counseling ... Ms. Misty STEELE
49 Chair Div of Arts & Humanities ... Dr. Stephen WEBER
50 Chair Div of Business & Social Sci ... Dr. James VAUGHN
53 Chair Division of Education ... Dr. Donna GOWER
81 Chair Div of Science/Physical Educ ... Dr. J.C SANDERS
88 Chair Interdisciplinary Studies ... Dr. Jennifer LONG
19 Director Security/Safety ... Vacant
41 Athletic Director ... Mr. Brisco MCPHERSON

University of Tulsa (E)

800 S Tucker, Tulsa OK 74104
County: Tulsa FICE Identification: 003185
Unit ID: 207971
Telephone: (918) 631-2000 Carnegie Class: DU-Higher
FAX Number: (918) 631-2033 Calendar System: Semester
URL: www.utulsa.edu
Established: 1894 Annual Undergrad Tuition & Fees: $41,509
Enrollment: 4,433 Coed
Affiliation or Control: Independent Non-Profit IRS Status: 501(c)3
Highest Offering: Doctorate
Accreditation: NH, CAATE, CEA, CLPSY, LAW, MUS, NUR, SP

01 President ... Dr. Gerard CLANCY
10 Exec Vice President & Treasurer ... Mr. Kevan C. BUCK
05 Provost/Exec VP Academic Affairs ... Ms. Janet LEVIT
111 Vice Pres Institutional Advancement ... Dr. Kayla HALE
84 VP Enrollment Mgmt/Student Services ... Mr. Earl JOHNSON
41 VP & Athletic Director ... Dr. Derrick GRAGG
13 VP Info Services & CIO ... Mr. Richard KEARNS
28 VP Diversity & Engagement ... Ms. Jacqueline H. CALDWELL
86 VP Public Affairs/COO Gilcrease ... Ms. Susan NEAL
20 Sr Vice Provost ... Dr. Richard REDNER
46 Vice Prov Research/Dean Grad School ... Dr. Janet A. HAGGERTY
104 Vice Provost Global Education ... Dr. Jane KUCKO
121 Sr Vice Prov Oper & Student Success ... Mr. John BURY
42 University Chaplain ... Dr. Jeffrey FRANCIS
49 Dean Arts & Sciences ... Dr. Kalpana MISRA
50 Dean Business Administration ... Dr. A. Gale SULLENBERGER
54 Dean Engineering/Natural Sciences ... Dr. James R. SOREM, JR.
61 Dean Law ... Ms. Lyn ENTZEROTH
08 RM & Ida McFarlin Dean of Library ... Mr. Adrian W. ALEXANDER
110 Assoc VP Institutional Advancement ... Ms. Amy ENGLAND
06 Registrar ... Ms. Ginna V. LANGSTON
15 Executive Dir of Human Resources ... Ms. Sherry ESKEW
22 Dir Acad Support/504 Coordinator ... Dr. Tawny RIGSBY
18 Assoc VP Operations/Physical Plant ... Mr. Robert SHIPLEY
21 Assoc VP & Controller ... Mr. Michael D. THESENVITZ
07 Assoc VP Enrollment Dean Admission ... Ms. Casey REED
32 Assoc VP Enrollment Dean Students ... Mr. Michael MILLS
39 Assoc VP Director Housing ... Ms. Melissa H. FRANCE
85 Dean International Students ... Ms. Pamela A. SMITH
51 Dean Lifelong Learning ... Dr. J. Phillip APPLEGATE
62 Assoc Dean McFarlin Library ... Ms. Francine J. FISK
88 Director Helmerich Center ... Ms. Susan NEAL
38 Director Counseling & Psych Svcs ... Dr. Michael MCCLENDON
19 Director Campus Security ... Mr. Joseph F. TIMMONS
29 Exec Director Alumni Relations ... Ms. Amy M. FREIBERGER
36 Director Career Services ... Ms. Shelly HOLLY
37 Director Student Financial Svcs ... Ms. Vicki A. HENDRICKSON
96 Director Purchasing ... Mr. Jerry R. HOLLOWAY
90 Dir Academic Tech Services ... Ms. Janet CAIRNS
91 Dir ERP Operations ... Mr. Martin PAGE
31 Dir True Blue Neighbors/Public Aff ... Ms. Danielle HOVENGA
26 Dir Marketing & Communications ... Ms. Mona CHAMBERLIN
105 Exec Dir Digital Communication ... Mr. Matt CASTEEL
101 Secretary Board of Trustees ... Ms. June E. BROWN
04 Sr Admin Associate to President ... Ms. Susan LAYMAN

Western Oklahoma State College (F)

2801 N Main Street, Altus OK 73521-1397
County: Jackson FICE Identification: 003146
Unit ID: 208035
Telephone: (580) 477-2000 Carnegie Class: Assoc/MT-VT-High Trad
FAX Number: (580) 477-7777 Calendar System: Semester
URL: www.wosc.edu
Established: 1926 Annual Undergrad Tuition & Fees (In-State): $4,662
Enrollment: 1,346 Coed
Affiliation or Control: State IRS Status: 501(c)3
Highest Offering: Associate Degree
Accreditation: NH

01 President ... Dr. Chad WIGINTON
05 VP for Academic Affairs ... Ms. Chrystal OVERTON
10 Vice President for Business Affairs ... Ms. Melissa MCMAHON
32 Vice Pres Student Support Services ... Ms. Terri PEARSON
09 Dir of Institutional Effectiveness ... Mr. Justin SMITH
26 Director of Public Relations ... Ms. Zadie CURRY
07 Director of Admissions & Registrar ... Ms. Lana SCOTT
37 Director of Financial Aid ... SaVana DENTON
30 Dir Development/Alumni Relations ... Ms. Whitney GRAHAM
41 Director Athletics ... Vacant
08 Director of Learning Resources ... Ms. Suzanne ROOKER
15 Director Personnel Services ... Ms. April NELSON
18 Director Physical Plant ... Mr. Doyle JENCKS
40 Bookstore Manager ... Ms. Kass DEWEESE
38 Counselor ... Ms. Cheryl ORR

OREGON

American College of Healthcare Sciences (G)

5005 SW Macadam, Portland OR 97239
County: Multnomah FICE Identification: 041944
Unit ID: 443599
Telephone: (503) 244-0726 Carnegie Class: Spec-4-yr-Other Health
FAX Number: (503) 244-0727 Calendar System: Semester
URL: www.achs.edu
Established: 1978 Annual Undergrad Tuition & Fees: $10,800
Enrollment: 663 Coed
Affiliation or Control: Proprietary IRS Status: Proprietary
Highest Offering: Master's
Accreditation: DEAC

01 President/CEO ... Dorene PETERSEN
11 Chief Operating Officer ... Tracey ABELL
32 Dean of Students ... Heather BALEY
07 Dean of Admissions ... Amy SWINEHART
06 Registrar ... Jennifer MORRISON
26 Chief Marketing Officer ... Kate HARMON
37 Director of Financial Aid ... Stephanie NORTH
08 Director of Library Services ... Ashley EHMIG

Birthingway College of Midwifery (H)

12113 SE Foster Road, Portland OR 97266-4042
County: Multnomah FICE Identification: 036683
Unit ID: 442949
Telephone: (503) 760-3131 Carnegie Class: Spec-4-yr-Other Health
FAX Number: (503) 760-3332 Calendar System: Quarter
URL: www.birthingway.edu
Established: 1993 Annual Undergrad Tuition & Fees: N/A
Enrollment: 58 Coed
Affiliation or Control: Independent Non-Profit IRS Status: 501(c)3
Highest Offering: Baccalaureate
Accreditation: MEAC

01 President ... Ms. Holly SCHOLLES
05 Academic Coordinator ... Ms. Nichole REDING
10 Finance Coordinator ... Ms. Elizabeth BRAGG
20 Faculty Coordinator ... Ms. Natalie HUTCHINSON
37 Financial Aid Officer ... Ms. Stace MAURER
06 Registrar ... Ms. Claire HOFFMAN
88 Midwifery Program Coordinator ... Ms. Heather HACK-SULLIVAN
08 Head Librarian ... Ms. Nora BARNETT

Blue Mountain Community College (A)

PO Box 100, Pendleton OR 97801-0100

County: Umatilla/Morrow/Baker — FICE Identification: 003186
Unit ID: 208275
Telephone: (541) 276-1260 — Carnegie Class: Assoc/HT-High Non
FAX Number: (541) 278-5886 — Calendar System: Quarter
URL: www.bluecc.edu
Established: 1962 — Annual Undergrad Tuition & Fees (In-District): $5,810
Enrollment: 1,417 — Coed
Affiliation or Control: State/Local — IRS Status: 501(c)3
Highest Offering: Associate Degree
Accreditation: NW, DA

01 President ... Mr. Dennis BAILEY-FOUGNIER
05 Vice President of Instruction ... Mr. John FIELDS
32 Vice Pres Student Affairs ... Ms. Diane DREBIN
11 Vice Pres Admin Services ... Ms. Tammie PARKER
08 Director of Library & Media Svcs ... Vacant
102 Executive Director Foundation ... Ms. Margaret GIANOTTI
37 Director of Student Financial Aid ... Ms. Yadira GONZALEZ
04 Administrative Asst to President ... Ms. Shannon FRANKLIN
10 AVP Finance & Business Operations ... Ms. Celeste TATE
106 Dir Online Education/E-learning ... Mr. Bruce KAUSS
13 Chief Info Technology Officer (CIO) ... Mr. Brad HOLDEN
38 Director Student Counseling ... Vacant
15 Director Human Resources ... Vacant
41 Athletic Director ... Ms. Dawn MCCLENDON
26 Chief Public Relations/Marketing ... Ms. Casey WHITE-ZOLLMAN
75 Dean CTE/Community Educ ... Mr. Wade MULLER
121 Dean Student Success & Retention ... Ms. Brenna HINES
84 Director Enrollment Svcs/Registrar ... Ms. Theresa BOSWORTH
18 Chief Facilities/Physical Plant ... Mr. Dwayne WILLIAMS
49 Dean Instruction Arts & Letters ... Mr. Daniel G. ANDERSON

Central Oregon Community College (B)

2600 NW College Way, Bend OR 97703

County: Deschutes — FICE Identification: 003188
Unit ID: 208318
Telephone: (541) 383-7700 — Carnegie Class: Assoc/HT-High Trad
FAX Number: (541) 383-7506 — Calendar System: Quarter
URL: www.cocc.edu
Established: 1949 — Annual Undergrad Tuition & Fees (In-District): $3,951
Enrollment: 5,205 — Coed
Affiliation or Control: Local — IRS Status: 501(c)3
Highest Offering: Associate Degree
Accreditation: NW, ACFEI, CAHIIM, COMTA, DA, EMT, IFSAC, MAC

01 President ... Dr. Laurie CHESLEY
05 Vice President for Instruction ... Dr. Betsy JULIAN
11 Vice Pres for Administration ... Mr. Matthew J. MCCOY
10 Chief Financial Officer ... Mr. David DONA
56 Dean of Extended Learning ... Mr. Jerry SCHULZ
20 Instructional Dean ... Dr. Michael FISHER
20 Instructional Dean ... Dr. Jennifer NEWBY
84 Dean of Student/Enrollment Svcs ... Dr. Alicia MOORE
07 Director of Admissions & Records ... Mr. Tyler HAYES
08 Director of Library Services ... Dr. Tina HOVEKAMP
26 Director College Relations ... Mr. Ronald S. PARADIS
13 Director Information Technology ... Mr. Dan CECCHINI
18 Director Campus Services ... Mr. Joe VIOLA
15 Director Human Resources ... Ms. Laura BOEHME
32 Director of Student and Campus Life ... Mr. Andrew DAVIS
09 Dir Institutional Effectiveness ... Ms. Brynn PIERCE
38 Director Student Counseling ... Ms. Seana BARRY
40 Director Bookstore/Auxiliary Svcs ... Ms. Lori BENEFIEL
108 Director Curriculum & Assessment ... Ms. Vickery VILES
19 Director Security/Safety ... Mr. Peter OSTROVSKY
25 Director Contracts/Risk Management ... Ms. Sharla ANDRESEN
102 Director Foundation ... Mr. Zak BOONE
51 Director of Continuing Education ... Ms. Glenda LANTIS

Chemeketa Community College (C)

PO Box 14007, Salem OR 97309-7070

County: Marion — FICE Identification: 003218
Unit ID: 208390
Telephone: (503) 399-5000 — Carnegie Class: Assoc/HT-Mix Trad/Non
FAX Number: (503) 399-5214 — Calendar System: Quarter
URL: www.chemeketa.edu
Established: 1962 — Annual Undergrad Tuition & Fees (In-District): $4,725
Enrollment: 10,279 — Coed
Affiliation or Control: Local — IRS Status: 501(c)3
Highest Offering: Associate Degree
Accreditation: NW, ADNUR, CAHIIM, DA, EMT, IFSAC

01 President/Chief Executive Officer ... Dr. Jessica HOWARD
05 VP/Chief Academic Officer ... Mr. Jim EUSTROM
03 VP Governance & Administration ... Mr. David HALLETT
12 Campus President Yamhill Valley ... Mr. Jim EUSTROM
26 Assoc VP/Chief Information Officer ... Mr. JD WOLFE
107 Exec Dean Gen Educ/Transfer Studies ... Mr. Don BRASE
20 Exec Dean Career/Tech Education ... Mr. Johnny MACK
32 Exec Dean Student Dev/Learning Res ... Mr. Manuel GUERRA
88 Exec Dean Acad Progress/Reg Ed Svcs ... Ms. Holly NELSON
88 Dean Emergency Services ... Mr. Marshall ROACHE
83 Dean Liberal Arts & Social Sciences ... Mr. Keith RUSSELL
76 Dean Health Services ... Ms. Sandra KELLOGG
37 Director Financial Aid ... Mr. Ryan WEST
38 Dean Counseling/Career Services ... Vacant
72 Dean Applied Technologies ... Mr. Larry CHEYNE
81 Dean Science/Eng/Math/Comp Science ... Vacant
50 Dn Bus/Tech/Early Chld Ed/Vis Comm ... Ms. R. TAYLOR
27 Dir Marketing/Public Relations ... Ms. Marie HULETT
53 Dean Curriculum Inst/Accreditation ... Ms. Jess STAHL
47 Dir Agric Sciences/Wine Studies ... Ms. Jessica SANDROCK
08 Director Library/Learning Resources ... Ms. Natalie BEACH
88 Director Northwest Innovations ... Mr. Brian RADER
10 Assoc VP Financial Management ... Ms. Miriam SCHARER
18 Dir Capital Projects/Facilities ... Mr. Rory ALVAREZ
15 Director Human Resources ... Ms. Alice SPRAGUE
19 Director Public Safety ... Mr. Bill KOHLMEYER
109 Director Auxiliary/Contracted Svcs ... Ms. Meredith SCHREIBER
41 Dean Health/Human Perf/Athletics ... Ms. Cassie BELMODIS
50 Exec Dir Chemeketa Ctr Bus/Industry ... Ms. Diane MCLARAN
88 Coordinator Prof Tech Educ ... Mr. Ed WOODS
28 Diversity & Equity Officer ... Ms. Vivi CALEFFI-PRICHARD
35 Dean Student Retention/College Life ... Mr. Mike EVANS
84 Registrar/Dir Enrollment Services ... Ms. Melissa FREY
102 Executive Director Foundation ... Mr. Phillip HUDSPETH
25 Grants Coordinator ... Vacant
09 Director of Institutional Research ... Mr. Fauzi NAAS
43 General Counsel/Legal Resources ... Ms. Rebecca HILLYER
12 Dean Woodburn Center ... Mr. Elias VILLEGAS
12 Director Polk Center ... Mr. Glen MILLER
12 Director Yamhill Valley Campus ... Ms. Danielle HOFFMAN

Clackamas Community College (D)

19600 Molalla Avenue, Oregon City OR 97045-7998

County: Clackamas — FICE Identification: 004878
Unit ID: 208406
Telephone: (503) 594-6000 — Carnegie Class: Assoc/HT-High Non
FAX Number: N/A — Calendar System: Quarter
URL: www.clackamas.edu
Established: 1966 — Annual Undergrad Tuition & Fees (In-District): $4,944
Enrollment: 6,326 — Coed
Affiliation or Control: Local — IRS Status: 501(c)3
Highest Offering: Associate Degree
Accreditation: NW, MAC

01 President ... Dr. Tim COOK
05 VP Instruct & Stdnt Svcs/Provost ... Dr. David PLOTKIN
11 Vice Pres College Services ... Ms. Alissa MAHAR
04 Executive Asst to the President ... Ms. Denice BAILEY
102 Executive Director Foundation ... Vacant
26 Public Information Officer ... Ms. Lori HALL
06 Registrar/Enrol Svcs/Operations Mgr ... Mr. Chris SWEET
32 Assoc Dean Acad Found/Connect Div ... Ms. Darlene GEIGER
13 Dean/CIO Information Technology ... Mr. Dion BAIRD
49 Dean Arts & Sciences ... Ms. Sue GOFF
46 Dean Inst Effectiveness & Planning ... Mr. Jason KOVAC
72 Assoc Dn Tech/Hlth Occup/Wrkfc Div ... Mr. Jarett GILBERT
15 Dean Human Resources ... Ms. Melissa RICHARDSON
88 Dir Office Education Partnerships ... Ms. Jaime CLARKE
10 Dean Business Services ... Mr. Jeff SHAFFER
11 Dean Campus Services ... Mr. Bob COCHRAN
18 Director Campus Services ... Mr. Lloyd HELM
41 Director Health/PE/Athletics ... Mr. Jim MARTINEAU
13 Director IT Operations ... Mr. David GATES
09 Director of Institutional Research ... Ms. Lisa Anh NGUYEN
37 Director Student Financial Aid ... Ms. Karen ASH

Clatsop Community College (E)

1651 Lexington Avenue, Astoria OR 97103

County: Clatsop — FICE Identification: 003189
Unit ID: 208415
Telephone: (503) 325-0910 — Carnegie Class: Assoc/HVT-High Non
FAX Number: (503) 325-5738 — Calendar System: Quarter
URL: www.clatsopcc.edu
Established: 1958 — Annual Undergrad Tuition & Fees (In-District): $4,122
Enrollment: 819 — Coed
Affiliation or Control: State/Local — IRS Status: 501(c)3
Highest Offering: Associate Degree
Accreditation: NW

01 President ... Mr. Chris BREITMEYER
05 VP Academic & Student Affairs ... Dr. Margaret R. FRIMOTH
10 Vice President Finance & Operations ... Ms. JoAnn ZAHN
32 Vice President of Student Success ... Mr. Jerad SORBER
06 Registrar ... Ms. Siv Serene BARNUM
26 Director Marketing & Communication ... Ms. Julie KOVATCH
13 Director Computer Services ... Mr. Greg RIEHL
15 Interim Director Human Resources ... Ms. Naomi GARBUTT
37 Director Student Financial Aid ... Mr. Lloyd MUELLER
09 Director of Institutional Research ... Vacant
18 Director Physical Plant ... Mr. Greg DORCHEUS
21 Director Accounting Services ... Ms. Margaret ANTILLA
102 Director College Foundation ... Ms. Sunny KLEVER
04 Executive Coordinator to President ... Ms. Patricia SCHULTE
51 Distance Education Coordinator ... Mrs. Kirsten HORNING

College of Emergency Services (F)

12438 SE Capps Road, Clackamas OR 97015

County: Clackamas — Identification: 667128
Telephone: (971) 236-9231 — Carnegie Class: Not Classified
FAX Number: (971) 653-9239 — Calendar System: Semester
URL: www.collegeofems.com
Established: 1995 — Annual Undergrad Tuition & Fees: N/A
Enrollment: N/A — Coed
Affiliation or Control: Proprietary — IRS Status: Proprietary
Highest Offering: Associate Degree
Accreditation: ABHES, EMT

01 Program Medical Director ... Dr. David LEHRFELD

Columbia Gorge Community College (G)

400 East Scenic Drive, The Dalles OR 97058

County: Wasco — FICE Identification: 041519
Unit ID: 420556
Telephone: (541) 506-6000 — Carnegie Class: Assoc/HT-High Non
FAX Number: N/A — Calendar System: Quarter
URL: www.cgcc.edu
Established: 1977 — Annual Undergrad Tuition & Fees (In-District): $4,392
Enrollment: 791 — Coed
Affiliation or Control: State/Local — IRS Status: 501(c)3
Highest Offering: Associate Degree
Accreditation: NW, MAC

01 President ... Dr. Marta CRONIN
05 VP of Instructional Services ... Lori UFFORD
10 VP of Financial Services ... Michael MALLERY
32 Chief Student Services Officer ... Vacant
26 Manager Marketing & Cmty Outreach ... Dan SPATZ
13 Exec Director of Infrastructure ... Danny DEHAZE
06 Registrar ... Dawn SALLEE-JUSTESEN
07 Director of Admissions ... Vacant
08 Director of Library Services ... Vacant
108 Dir Curriculum & Assessment ... Susan LEWIS
15 Director Human Resources ... Courtney JUDAH
18 Director of Facilities Services ... Jacob TODA
37 Director Financial Aid ... Mike JOHNSON
102 Foundation Director ... Stephanie HOPPE
04 Exec Assistant to the President ... Tiffany PRINCE

Concorde Career College (H)

1425 NE Irving Street, Suite 300, Portland OR 97232

County: Multnomah — FICE Identification: 008887
Unit ID: 208479
Telephone: (503) 281-4181 — Carnegie Class: Spec 2-yr-Health
FAX Number: (503) 281-6739 — Calendar System: Other
URL: www.concorde.edu/campus/portland
Established: 1996 — Annual Undergrad Tuition & Fees: N/A
Enrollment: 448 — Coed
Affiliation or Control: Proprietary — IRS Status: Proprietary
Highest Offering: Associate Degree
Accreditation: ACCSC, COARC, MAC, POLYT, SURGT

01 Campus President ... Kim IERIEN

Concordia University (I)

2811 NE Holman Avenue, Portland OR 97211-6099

County: Multnomah — FICE Identification: 003191
Unit ID: 208488
Telephone: (503) 288-9371 — Carnegie Class: DU-Mod
FAX Number: (503) 280-8518 — Calendar System: Semester
URL: www.cu-portland.edu
Established: 1905 — Annual Undergrad Tuition & Fees: $31,158
Enrollment: 5,125 — Coed
Affiliation or Control: Lutheran Church - Missouri Synod
IRS Status: 501(c)3
Highest Offering: Doctorate
Accreditation: NW, ACBSP, LAW, NURSE, SW

01 Interim President ... Mr. Johnnie DRIESSNER
26 Exec Vice Pres External Affairs ... Dr. Gary WITHERS
102 Exec Vice Pres Strategic Planning ... Mr. Johnnie DRIESSNER
05 Interim Chief Academic Officer ... Ms. Michelle COWING
10 Chief Financial Officer ... Vacant
11 Chf Operating Ofcr/Chf Gen Counsel ... Vacant
32 Vice Pres Student Affairs ... Ms. Megan BOUSLAUGH
84 Vice President Enrollment ... Ms. Bobi SWAN
15 Vice President of Human Resources ... Ms. Heyke KIRKENDALL-BAKER
41 Director Athletics ... Mr. Brian JAMROS
13 VP Info Systems/Chief Info Officer ... Mr. Jason NAIRN
04 Executive Administrator ... Ms. Brenna HUGHEY
30 Chief Development Officer ... Mr. Kevin MATHENY
06 Registrar ... Ms. Heather SKOCILICH
09 Director of Institutional Research ... Vacant
18 Chief Facilities/Physical Plant ... Mr. Doug MEYER
27 Chief Public Relations Officer ... Ms. Madeline TURNOCK
29 Director Alumni & Parent Engagement ... Ms. Becky SPRECHER
35 Dean of Students ... Mr. Steve DEKLOTZ
08 Librarian ... Mr. Brent MAI
37 Asst Vice Pres of Financial Aid ... Ms. Mary MCGLOTHLAN
19 Director of Campus Safety ... Mr. John HROMCO
38 Director Student Counseling ... Mr. Greg PETERSON

85 Director of International Studies .... Ms. Linda ROUNTREE
42 Director of Campus Ministries .... Rev. Bo BAUMEISTER
50 Dean School of Management .... Dr. Michelle COWING
53 Dean College of Education .... Dr. Sheryl REINISCH
49 Dean College of Arts & Sciences .... Dr. David KLUTH
76 Int Dean Col Health/Human Services .... Dr. Julie DODGE
61 Dean School of Law .... Ms. Cathy SILAK

Corban University (A)

5000 Deer Park Drive SE, Salem OR 97317
County: Marion FICE Identification: 001339
Unit ID: 210331
Telephone: (503) 581-8600 Carnegie Class: Bac-Diverse
FAX Number: (503) 585-4316 Calendar System: Semester
URL: www.corban.edu
Established: 1935 Annual Undergrad Tuition & Fees: $33,040
Enrollment: 1,187 Coed
Affiliation or Control: Independent Non-Profit IRS Status: 501(c)3
Highest Offering: Master's
Accreditation: NW, CACREP

01 President .... Dr. Sheldon NORD
05 Provost/Executive Vice President .... Dr. Thomas CORNMAN
10 Controller/Assoc VP for Finance .... Ms. Dee WENDLER
32 Vice President For Student Life .... Dr. Brenda ROTH
26 Vice Pres for Strategic Initiatives .... Mr. Steve SAMMONS
111 Chief Advancement Officer .... Mr. Terry CHANEY
35 Dean of Students .... Mr. Nathan GEER
88 Director of DMin Program .... Dr. Leroy GOERTZEN
88 Associate Provost Global Engagement .... Dr. Janine ALLEN
49 Dean of Arts and Sciences .... Dr. Felicia SQUIRES
50 Dean Hoff School of Business .... Mr. Shawn HUSSEY
53 Dean of Education and Counseling .... Dr. Kristin DIXON
13 Chief Information Officer .... Mr. Brian SCHMIDT
18 Campus Care Project Manager .... Mr. Troy CROFF
84 Vice Provost for Enrollment .... Dr. Chris VETTER
08 Librarian .... Mr. Garrett TROTT
06 University Registrar .... Dr. Chris VETTER
42 Assoc Dir of Spiritual Formation .... Mr. Eugene EDWARDS
73 Dean School of Ministry .... Dr. Gregory TRULL
41 Athletic Director .... Mr. Twiggs REED
26 Director of Marketing/Comm .... Mr. Chris HOLDREN
121 Director of Student Support .... Mr. Daren MILIONIS
21 Sr Director of Accounting .... Mrs. Ellen ZARFAS
37 Director of Financial Aid .... Ms. Mary MCGLOTHLAN
40 Bookstore Manager .... Mr. Larry HULTBERG
123 Asst Dir Grad/Online Admissions .... Ms. Allison SMALL
04 Executive Asst to President .... Ms. Kathy MARTENS
104 Director Study Abroad .... Mr. Sam PEARSON
106 Director of Academic Services .... Mr. Dan CHRISTENSEN
15 Director of Human Resources .... Vacant
118 Payroll & Benefits Manager .... Ms. Kathy GALLAGHER
19 Chief of Security .... Mr. Mike ROTH
38 Clinical Director .... Dr. Mary AGUILERA
07 Director of TUG Admissions .... Mr. Jordan LINDSEY

Eastern Oregon University (B)

One University Boulevard, La Grande OR 97850-2807
County: Union FICE Identification: 003193
Unit ID: 208646
Telephone: (541) 962-3672 Carnegie Class: Masters/M
FAX Number: (541) 962-3493 Calendar System: Quarter
URL: www.eou.edu
Established: 1929 Annual Undergrad Tuition & Fees (In-State): $8,679
Enrollment: 3,016 Coed
Affiliation or Control: State IRS Status: 501(c)3
Highest Offering: Master's
Accreditation: NW, IACBE

01 President .... Mr. Thomas INSKO
05 Provost/Sr VP Academic Affairs .... Dr. Sarah WITTE
32 Vice President for Student Affairs .... Dr. Lacy KARPILO
10 Vice President Finance & Admin .... Ms. Lara MOORE
30 Vice Pres UA .... Mr. Tim SEYDEL
49 Dean Col Arts/Humanities/Social Sci .... Mr. Nathan LOWE
50 Dean Colleges of Business .... Dr. Matt SEIMEARS
53 Dean Colleges of Education .... Dr. Ed HENNINGER
37 Director of Financial Aid .... Ms. Sandy HENRY
08 Director of Pierce Library .... Ms. Karen CLAY
07 Director of Admissions .... Ms. Gina GALAVIZ
06 Registrar .... Ms. Emily SHARRATT
15 Director of Human Resources .... Mr. Chris MCLAUGHLIN
29 Dir of Alumni Relations .... Ms. Jessie BOWMAN
41 Director of Athletics .... Ms. Anji WEISSENFLUH
39 Director of Residence Life .... Mr. Jeremy JONES
18 Director of Facilities & Planning .... Mr. John GARLITZ
38 Director Counseling Center .... Dr. Marianne WEAVER
04 Exec Assistant to the President .... Ms. Katelyn WINKLER
21 Director of Business Affairs .... Ms. Cora BEACH
20 Int Vice Provost Academic Affairs .... Dr. Donald WOLFF
88 Learning Center Operations Manager .... Ms. Kathryn SHORTS
35 Dir of Student Relations/Title IX ...... Ms. Colleen DUNNE-CASCIO
19 Campus Security/Public Safety Ofcr .... Mr. Bill BENSON

George Fox University (C)

414 N Meridian, Newberg OR 97132-2697
County: Yamhill FICE Identification: 003194
Unit ID: 208822
Telephone: (503) 538-8383 Carnegie Class: DU-Mod
FAX Number: (503) 554-3880 Calendar System: Semester
URL: www.georgefox.edu
Established: 1891 Annual Undergrad Tuition & Fees: $36,020
Enrollment: 4,076 Coed
Affiliation or Control: Friends IRS Status: 501(c)3
Highest Offering: Doctorate
Accreditation: NW, ACBSP, CAATE, CACREP, CAEPN, CLPSY, IPSY, MUS, NURSE, PTA, SW, THEOL

01 President .... Dr. Robin E. BAKER
05 Provost .... Dr. Linda SAMEK
10 Exec VP Finance/Business Operations .... Ms. Vicki PIERSALL
111 Vice President of Advancement .... Mr. Michael REZA
32 Vice President Student Life .... Dr. Bradley A. LAU
84 VP Enrollment & Marketing .... Mr. Ryan DOUGHERTY
45 Chief Strategy Officer .... Mr. Rob WESTERVELT
28 AVP Intercultural Engagement .... Dr. Rebecca HERNANDEZ
21 Asst VP of Finance/Controller .... Ms. Cris BANTON
100 Chief of Staff .... Ms. Melissa D. TERRY
08 Dean of Libraries .... Mr. Ryan INGERSOLL
07 Director of Undergrad Admissions .... Ms. Lindsay KNOX
06 Registrar .... Ms. Melissa THOMAS
36 Dir of Career Services/IDEA Center .... Ms. Wendy FLINT
18 Director of Plant Services .... Mr. Jeremiah HORTON
37 Director of Financial Aid .... Ms. Johanna KAYE
96 Director Purchasing/Admin Services .... Mr. Matt HAMMAR
41 Director of Athletics .... Mr. Adam PUCKETT
105 Director of Web Development .... Mr. Peter CRACKENBERG
15 Executive Director Human Resources .... Ms. Nichole DREW
42 Univ Pastor/Dean of Spiritual Life .... Ms. Jamie NOLING-AUTH
26 Director of Executive Communication .... Mr. Rob FELTON
13 Chief Information Officer .... Mr. Tim GOODFELLOW
19 Director Security Services .... Mr. Ed GIEROK
35 Dean Stdnt Svcs/Dir Hlth/Counseling ...... Dr. William C. BUHROW
73 Dean of Portland Seminary .... Dr. Roger NAM
49 Dean School of Arts & Sciences .... Ms. Laura HARTLEY
83 Dean Sch Behavioral/Health Sci .... Dr. James D. FOSTER
53 Dean School of Education .... Mr. Marc SHELTON
50 Dean School of Business .... Dr. Jekabs BIKIS
54 Dean of Engineering .... Dr. Robert HARDER
09 Chief Data Officer .... Mr. Tyler SUSMILCH
04 Executive Asst to the President .... Ms. Jennifer MCCOLLUM
101 Secretary of the Institution/Board .... Ms. Melissa TERRY
103 Recruiting and Training Manager .... Ms. Kara HOLCOMBE
104 Director Study Abroad .... Mr. Paul CHAMBERLAIN
108 Director Institutional Assessment .... Mr. Rob BOHALL
25 Chief Contract/Grants Administrator .... Ms. Tai HARDEN-MOORE
29 Director Alumni Affairs .... Ms. Sara REAMY
30 Executive Director of Development .... Mr. Kyle DICKINSON
39 Director University Housing .... Ms. Kayin GRIFFITH
44 Director Annual Giving .... Mr. Gene CHRISTIAN
90 Director Academic Computing .... Mr. Josh NAUMAN

Gutenberg College (D)

1883 University Street, Eugene OR 97403-1368
County: Lane FICE Identification: 039324
Telephone: (541) 683-5141 Carnegie Class: Not Classified
FAX Number: (541) 683-6997 Calendar System: Quarter
URL: www.gutenberg.edu
Established: 1994 Annual Undergrad Tuition & Fees: N/A
Enrollment: N/A Coed
Affiliation or Control: Independent Non-Profit IRS Status: 501(c)3
Highest Offering: Baccalaureate
Accreditation: TRACS

01 President .... Chris SWANSON
10 Vice President Finance .... Moctar ZIBARE
05 Dean .... Thomas DEWBERRY
07 Admissions Director .... Eliot GRASSO
06 Registrar .... Chris SWANSON
39 Dir Resident Life/Student Housing .... Gil GRECO

Klamath Community College (E)

7390 S 6th Street, Klamath Falls OR 97603-7121
County: Klamath FICE Identification: 034283
Unit ID: 428392
Telephone: (541) 882-3521 Carnegie Class: Assoc/MT-VT-High Non
FAX Number: (541) 885-7758 Calendar System: Quarter
URL: www.klamathcc.edu
Established: 1996 Annual Undergrad Tuition & Fees (In-District): $4,404
Enrollment: 1,683 Coed
Affiliation or Control: State/Local IRS Status: 501(c)3
Highest Offering: Associate Degree
Accreditation: NW

01 President .... Dr. Roberto GUTIERREZ
11 Vice Pres Administrative Svcs .... Ms. Tricia FISCUS
05 Vice Pres Academic Affairs .... Ms. Jamie JENNINGS
32 Vice Pres Student Affairs .... Ms. Allison BRYSON
88 Exec Director External Programs .... Mr. Charles MASSIE
15 Exec Dir Legal & Human Resources .... Mr. Michael BLADE
20 Dean of Instruction .... Dr. Jeanne LAHAIE
20 Dean of Instruction .... Mr. Christopher STICKLES
103 Director of Workforce .... Vacant
13 Director Information Services .... Mr. Paul BREEDLOVE
06 Registrar .... Mr. M. SHABBIR
26 Director of Communications .... Ms. Lacey JARRELL
18 Facilities Director .... Mr. Mike HOMFELDT
10 Director Business Services .... Vacant
37 Financial Aid Director .... Ms. Robin SUNDSETH
04 Executive Admin Asst to President .... Ms. Shannon CHILDS
09 Institutional Researcher .... Mr. Bill JENNINGS
25 Grants Program Manager .... Mr. Peter LAWSON

Lane Community College (F)

4000 E 30th Avenue, Eugene OR 97405-0640
County: Lane FICE Identification: 003196
Unit ID: 209038
Telephone: (541) 463-3000 Carnegie Class: Assoc/HT-High Trad
FAX Number: (541) 463-5201 Calendar System: Quarter
URL: www.lanecc.edu
Established: 1964 Annual Undergrad Tuition & Fees (In-District): $4,812
Enrollment: 7,637 Coed
Affiliation or Control: Local IRS Status: 501(c)3
Highest Offering: Associate Degree
Accreditation: NW, ACFEI, DA, DH, EMT, MAC, PTAA

01 President .... Dr. Margaret HAMILTON
05 Chief Academic Officer .... Dr. Paul JARRELL
11 Vice President College Operations .... Mr. Brian KELLY
49 Assoc VP Academic/Student Affairs .... Dr. Jennifer FREI
68 Dean Health/PE/Athletics .... Mr. Grant MATTHEWS
28 AVP Diversity/Equity/Inclusion .... Mr. Greg EVANS
13 Chief Information Officer .... Dr. Bill SCHUETZ
10 Chief Financial Officer .... Mr. Greg HOLMES
15 Chief Human Resources Officer .... Mr. Dennis CARR
18 Director Facilities & PM .... Ms. Jennifer HAYWARD
19 Interim Director Public Safety .... Ms. Lisa RUPP
08 Library Dean .... Dr. Rick STODDART
121 Dean Student Success .... Ms. Lida HERBURGER
88 Dean of New Student Transitions .... Ms. Helen FAITH
26 Public Information Officer .... Ms. Joan ASCHIM
102 Foundation Director .... Ms. Wendy JETT
04 Executive Asst to President/Board .... Ms. Donna ZMOLEK
30 Development Director .... Ms. Tiana MARRONE-CREECH
44 Annual Gifts Officer .... Mr. Philip HUDSPETH
104 Director International Programs .... Ms. Jennifer FALZERANO
06 Registrar .... Ms. Dawn WHITING
37 Director Student Financial Aid .... Mr. Elijah HERR
113 Director Student Financial Services .... Mr. Matt FADICH

Lewis and Clark College (G)

0615 SW Palatine Hill, Portland OR 97219-7899
County: Multnomah FICE Identification: 003197
Unit ID: 209056
Telephone: (503) 768-7000 Carnegie Class: Bac-A&S
FAX Number: (503) 768-7055 Calendar System: Semester
URL: www.lclark.edu
Established: 1867 Annual Undergrad Tuition & Fees: $50,934
Enrollment: 3,339 Coed
Affiliation or Control: Independent Non-Profit IRS Status: 501(c)3
Highest Offering: Doctorate
Accreditation: NW, CACREP, CAEPN, LAW, MFCD

01 President .... Dr. Wim WIEWAL
03 VP/Secretary and General Counsel .... Mr. David REESE
49 Dean of Arts & Sciences .... Dr. Bruce SUTTMEIER
58 Dean Grad Sch Education/Counseling .... Dr. Scott FLETCHER
61 Dean of the Law School .... Ms. Jennifer JOHNSON
28 Dean of Diversity and Inclusion .... Mr. Mark FIGUEROA
10 Vice Pres Business/Finance/Treas .... Mr. Alan FINN
111 Vice Pres Institutional Advancement .... Mr. Josh WALTER
32 Vice President of Student Life .... Ms. Robin HOLMES-SULLIVAN
09 Assoc VP Research & Planning .... Dr. Mark FIGUEROA
26 Exec Dir of Public Affairs & Comm .... Mr. Joe BECKER
07 VP for Enrollment .... Ms. Lisa MEYER
13 Assoc VP & Chief Information Ofcr .... Mr. Adam BUCHWALD
15 Assoc VP/Director Human Resources .... Mrs. Heyke KIRKENDALL-BAKER
18 Assoc Vice Pres Facilities .... Mr. Michel GEORGE
06 Registrar College of Arts/Sciences .... Ms. Judy FINCH
06 Registrar Law School .... Mr. Seneca GRAY
06 Registrar Graduate School .... Ms. Courtney WHETSTINE
37 Director of Financial Aid .... Ms. Anastacia DILLON
08 Director of Watzek Library .... Mr. Mark DAHL
85 Assoc Dean Intl Stdnts & Scholars .... Mr. Brian WHITE
30 Assoc VP & Director of Development ...... Mr. Aaron WHITEFORD
29 Senior Director Alumni/Parent Pgms ... Mr. Andrew MCPHEETERS
19 Director of Campus Safety .... Ms. Donna HENDERSON
42 Dean of Religious & Spiritual Life .... Dr. Mark DUNTLEY
41 Interim Director of Athletics .... Mr. Mark PIETROK
39 Director of Housing & Orientation .... Ms. Sandi BOTTEMILLER
14 Director of IT Operations .... Mr. Patrick RYALL
23 Assoc Dean Stdnt Health & Wellness .... Dr. John HANCOCK
101 Executive Asst Board Relations .... Ms. Moira DOMANN
04 Executive Asst to the President .... Ms. Annette LANIER
102 Director Corp/Foundation Relations .... Vacant
104 Director Overseas & Off Campus Pgms .... Ms. Blythe KNOTT

Linfield College (H)

900 SE Baker Street, McMinnville OR 97128-6894
County: Yamhill FICE Identification: 003198
Unit ID: 209065
Telephone: (503) 883-2200 Carnegie Class: Bac-A&S
FAX Number: (503) 883-2472 Calendar System: 4/1/4
URL: www.linfield.edu
Established: 1858 Annual Undergrad Tuition & Fees: $43,302
Enrollment: 1,535 Coed
Affiliation or Control: American Baptist IRS Status: 501(c)3
Highest Offering: Baccalaureate
Accreditation: NW, #CAATE, MUS, NURSE

01 President .... Dr. Miles DAVIS

05	Vice Pres Academic Affairs/ Provost	Ms. Susan AGRE-KIPPENHAN
10	Vice Pres Finance/Admin/CFO	Ms. Mary Ann RODRIGUEZ
111	VP Inst Advancement/General Counsel	Mr. John MCKEEGAN
84	Vice Pres for Enrollment Management	Dr. Miles DAVIS
32	VP Student Affairs/Dean of Students	Ms. Susan HOPP
66	Dean of Nursing	Dr. Kim DUPREE JONES
20	Associate Dean of Faculty	Dr. Jackson MILLER
35	Associate Dean of Students	Mr. Jeff MACKAY
15	Director of Human Resources	Ms. Heidi NELSON
18	Director Facilities & Auxiliary Svc	Ms. Allison HORN
28	Director Multicultural Programs	Vacant
06	Registrar	Ms. Diane CRABTREE
07	Director of Admission	Ms. Lisa KNODLE-BRAGIEL
08	Library Director	Ms. Susan BARNES WHYTE
09	Director of Institutional Research	Ms. Jennifer BALLARD
37	Director of Financial Aid	Ms. Keri BURKE
13	Chief Technology Officer	Ms. Virginia TOMLINSON
105	Webmaster	Mr. Jonathan PIERCE
85	Director of International Programs	Dr. Shaik ISMAIL
51	Director of Continuing Education	Dr. Laura BRENER
19	Director of Security	Mr. Dennis MARKS
38	Director of Counseling Services	Ms. Patricia HADDELAND
26	Director Communications/Marketing	Mr. Scott Bernard NELSON
44	Director of Annual Giving	Ms. Lisa GOODWIN
30	Director of Development	Mr. Craig HAISCH
102	Dir Corp & Foundation Relations	Ms. Catherine JARMIN MILLER
29	Director of Constituent Engagement	Ms. Joni CLAYPOOL
36	Director of Careers	Mr. Michael HAMPTON
42	Chaplain	Dr. David MASSEY
41	Athletic Director	Mr. Garry KILLGORE
40	Bookstore Manager	Ms. Katlyn ADAMS
04	Exec Assistant to the President	Ms. Kathy COOK

Linn-Benton Community College (A)

6500 Pacific Boulevard, SW, Albany OR 97321-3774
County: Linn FICE Identification: 006938
Unit ID: 209074
Telephone: (541) 917-4999 Carnegie Class: Assoc/MT-VT-Mix Trad/Non
FAX Number: (541) 917-4445 Calendar System: Quarter
URL: www.linnbenton.edu
Established: 1966 Annual Undergrad Tuition & Fees (In-District): $4,922
Enrollment: 5,830 Coed
Affiliation or Control: State/Local IRS Status: 501(c)3
Highest Offering: Associate Degree
Accreditation: NW, DA, MAC, OTA, POLYT, SURGT

01	President	Dr. Gregory J. HAMANN
05	Vice Pres Academic Affs/Wrkfce Dev	Dr. Ann BUCHELE
10	Vice Pres Finance & Operations	Mr. Dave HENDERSON
12	Regional Director Benton County	Mr. Jeff DAVIS
15	Dir Human Resources/Affirm Act Ofcr	Mr. Scott ROLEN
41	Director of Athletics	Mr. Mark MAJESKY
81	Dean Science/Engr & Tech	Ms. Kristina HOLTON
49	Dean Arts/Soc Sci/Humanities Div	Ms. Katie WINDER
20	Dean Instruction	Mr. Richard FEATHERSTONE
111	Exec Dir Institutional Advancement	Ms. Jennifer BOEHMER
04	Executive Asst to President	Ms. Amanda KLIEVER
06	Registrar	Mr. Danny AYNES
13	Chief Info Technology Officer (CIO)	Mr. Michael QUINER
18	Chief Facilities/Physical Plant	Mr. Terrell LANGLEN
19	Director Security/Safety	Ms. Marcene OLSON
28	Director of Diversity	Mr. Javier CERVANTES
09	Director of Institutional Research	Mr. Justin SMITH
37	Dir Financial Aid/Veterans Affairs	Ms. Elaine ROBINSON

Mount Angel Seminary (B)

1 Abbey Drive, Saint Benedict OR 97373-0505
County: Marion FICE Identification: 003203
Unit ID: 209241
Telephone: (503) 845-3951 Carnegie Class: Spec-4-yr-Faith
FAX Number: (503) 845-3128 Calendar System: Semester
URL: www.mountangelabbey.org
Established: 1889 Annual Undergrad Tuition & Fees: $22,046
Enrollment: 175 Coed
Affiliation or Control: Roman Catholic IRS Status: 501(c)3
Highest Offering: Doctorate
Accreditation: NW, THEOL

01	President-Rector	Msgr. Joseph V. BETSCHART
05	Academic Dean	Dr. Shawn KEOUGH
11	VP of Admin/Dir Pastoral Formation	Rev. Stephen CLOVIS
20	Associate Dean	Dr. Andrew CUMMINGS
73	Associate Academic Dean Theology	Vacant
06	Registrar/Director of Financial Aid	Mr. Terence MERRITT
07	Director of Admissions	Fr. Teresio CALDWELL, OSB
04	Admin Asst to the President-Rector	Mrs. Carol MARTIN
37	Student Financial Aid	Ms. Marina KEYS
10	Procurator	Fr. Martin GRASSEL, OSB
30	Director of Development	Ms. Jodi KILCUP
26	Communications Manager	Ms. Theresa MYERS
08	Librarian	Ms. Victoria ERTELT
29	Alumni Relations	Ms. Maurissa FISHER
112	Director of Planned Giving	Ms. Susan GALLAGHER
44	Director of Annual Giving	Ms. Melissa EDDINGS

Mt. Hood Community College (C)

26000 SE Stark, Gresham OR 97030-3300
County: Multnomah FICE Identification: 003204
Unit ID: 209250
Telephone: (503) 491-6422 Carnegie Class: Assoc/HT-Mix Trad/Non
FAX Number: (503) 491-7389 Calendar System: Quarter
URL: www.mhcc.edu
Established: 1965 Annual Undergrad Tuition & Fees (In-District): $5,441
Enrollment: 8,680 Coed
Affiliation or Control: Local IRS Status: 501(c)3
Highest Offering: Associate Degree
Accreditation: NW, COARC, DH, FUSER, PTAA, SURGT

01	President	Dr. Lisa SKARI
05	Vice President of Instruction	Mr. Alfred MCQUARTERS
15	Director Human Resources	Mr. Travis BROWN
88	Dir Child Dev/Family Support Pgms	Ms. Jean WAGNER
10	Chief Operations Officer	Ms. Jennifer DEMENT
09	Director of Institutional Research	Mr. Sergey SHEPELOV
88	Dir Student Development Tech	Ms. Christi HART
32	Executive Dean of Student Services	Mr. John HAMBLIN
13	Chief Information Officer	Ms. Linda VIGESAA
29	Exec Dir Foundation/Alumni Rels	Mr. Al SIGALA
76	Dean Allied Health & Nursing	Ms. Sheryl CADDY
81	Dean Visual Arts/Integ Media/Sci	Ms. Elise HUGGINS
79	Dean Humanities/Math/Social Science	Ms. Sara RIVARA
50	Dean Business and Info Systems	Vacant
103	Int Exec Dean Workforce/CTE/Partner	Vacant
04	Executive Asst to the President	Ms. Felisha BREWER
101	Executive Asst to the Board	Ms. Laurie POPP
106	Director Online Learning	Ms. Cat SCHLEICHERT
41	Athletic Director	Dr. Kim HYATT

Multnomah University (D)

8435 NE Glisan Street, Portland OR 97220-5898
County: Multnomah FICE Identification: 003206
Unit ID: 209287
Telephone: (503) 255-0332 Carnegie Class: Spec-4-yr-Faith
FAX Number: (503) 254-1268 Calendar System: Semester
URL: www.multnomah.edu
Established: 1936 Annual Undergrad Tuition & Fees: $25,900
Enrollment: 654 Coed
Affiliation or Control: Independent Non-Profit IRS Status: 501(c)3
Highest Offering: Doctorate
Accreditation: NW, THEOL

01	President	Dr. G. Craig WILLIFORD
84	VP Enrollment Management/IT	Ms. Gina BERQUIST
10	CFO and VP Administration	Mr. W. Chandler WILSON
111	Vice President of Advancement	Dr. Robert LARSON
49	Dean School of Arts and Sciences	Dr. Daniel SCALBERG
73	Dean School of Bible & Theology	Dr. Derek CHINN
106	Academic Dean for Online Learning	Mr. Alin VRANCILA
32	Interim Director/Dean of Students	Mr. Shane MEYER
42	Assoc Dean Spiritual Life/Pastor	Mr. Richard WARD
35	Associate Dean of Student Success	Mrs. Christy MARTIN
12	Executive Director of MU Reno	Mr. John MCKENDRICKS
108	Dir of Institutional Effectiveness	Dr. David FUNK
06	Registrar	Ms. Amy M. STEPHENS
21	Controller	Mrs. Debbie WHITEHEAD
08	Librarian	Dr. Philip M. JOHNSON
37	Director Student Financial Aid	Mrs. Naomi PERRY
36	Seminary Director of Placement	Vacant
13	Director Information Technology	Mrs. Brenda GIBSON
15	Director of Human Resources	Ms. Tracy L. MORESCHI
41	Athletic Director	Ms. Lois VOS
26	Dir of Marketing/Communications	Mrs. Alyssa TRULEN
84	Director of Enrollment Services	Mrs. Mindy-Kate HASENKAMP
18	Executive Director of Operations	Mr. Eric LINMAN
29	Director Alumni & Parent Relations	Ms. Cynthia MATHAI
04	Assistant to the President	Mrs. Denise STONE
19	Director of Campus Safety	Mr. Josh HARPER
38	Director Student Counseling	Mrs. Rebecca JONES
121	Associate Dean of Student Success	Mrs. Christy MARTIN
106	Dir Online Education/E-learning	Mr. Levi MARTIN
50	Dean of Business	Vacant
53	Dean of Education	Vacant
28	Director of Cultural Integration	Dr. Jessica L. TAYLOR

National University of Natural Medicine (E)

049 SW Porter Street, Portland OR 97201-4878
County: Multnomah FICE Identification: 025340
Unit ID: 209296
Telephone: (503) 552-1555 Carnegie Class: Spec-4-yr-Other Health
FAX Number: (503) 499-0022 Calendar System: Quarter
URL: nunm.edu
Established: 1956 Annual Undergrad Tuition & Fees: N/A
Enrollment: 597 Coed
Affiliation or Control: Independent Non-Profit IRS Status: 501(c)3
Highest Offering: Doctorate
Accreditation: NW, ACUP, NATUR

01	President	Dr. Christine GIRARD
05	Provost/VP Academic Affairs	Dr. Glenn C. SMITH
10	EVP/Chief Finance Officer	Mr. Gerald BORES
09	VP of Inst Effectiveness	Ms. Cheryl MILLER
15	VP of Human Resources	Ms. Kathy STANFORD
84	VP of Enrollment Management	Mrs. Beth WOODWARD
04	Executive Asst to the President	Ms. Mary ADNEY
63	Dean of Naturopathic Medicine	Dr. Shehab EL-HASHEMY
63	Dean Classical Chinese Medicine	Dr. Laurie REGAN
58	Dean of Graduate Studies	Dr. Charles KUNERT
20	Dean of Undergraduate Studies	Dr. Tim IRVING

17	Interim Chief Medical Officer	Dr. Melanie HENDRICKSEN
06	Registrar	Ms. Kelly GAREY
07	Director of Admissions	Mr. Ryan HOLLISTER
37	Associate Director of Financial Aid	Ms. Sally KALSTROM
13	Manager of IT	Mr. Steve FONG
08	College Librarian	Ms. Noelle STELLO
19	Director of Campus Security	Mr. Spencer BRAZES
36	Manager of Career Services	Ms. Tafflyn WILLIAMS-THOMAS
51	Manager of Continuing Education	Mr. Jeremy SLOAN
38	Director Student Counseling	Dr. Adrienne WOLMARK
28	Director of Equity & Inclusion	Ms. Ayasha SHAMSUD-DIN
120	Director Instructional Design/Tech	Mr. Justin FOWLER
46	Director Helfgott Research Inst	Dr. Ryan BRADLEY
18	Manager of Facilities	Mr. Dave MCALLISTER
121	Director of Student Success	Ms. Morgan CHICARELLI
23	VP Health Centers & Aux Ops	Ms. Nora SANDE
32	Dean of Students	Ms. Rachael ALLEN

New Hope Christian College (F)

2155 Bailey Hill Road, Eugene OR 97405-1194
County: Lane FICE Identification: 021597
Unit ID: 208725
Telephone: (541) 485-1780 Carnegie Class: Spec-4-yr-Faith
FAX Number: (541) 343-5801 Calendar System: Semester
URL: www.newhope.edu
Established: 1925 Annual Undergrad Tuition & Fees: $14,830
Enrollment: 93 Coed
Affiliation or Control: Other IRS Status: 501(c)3
Highest Offering: Baccalaureate
Accreditation: BI

01	President	Dr. Wayne CORDEIRO
05	Academic Dean	Mr. Donald GRAFTON
11	Vice President of Operations	Mr. Tristan J. KELLEY
04	Executive Assistant to President	Mrs. Lori HIGASHI
13	Chief Technology Officer	Mr. Peter THOURSON
32	Dean of Student Services	Mr. Aaron CORDEIRO
35	Director of Student Life	Mr. Paul WRIGHT
29	Director of Alumni Relations	Vacant
84	Enrollment Management	Mr. Christopher KIRIAKOS
37	Director of Financial Aid	Ms. Sayaka MEARIG
06	Assistant to the Registrar	Ms. Floria GRAFTON
10	Financial Services	Ms. Elaine NAULU
08	Head Librarian	Ms. Uilani CORDEIRO

Northwest Christian University (G)

828 E. 11th Ave., Eugene OR 97401-3745
County: Lane FICE Identification: 003208
Unit ID: 209409
Telephone: (541) 343-1641 Carnegie Class: Masters/M
FAX Number: (541) 343-9159 Calendar System: Semester
URL: www.nwcu.edu
Established: 1895 Annual Undergrad Tuition & Fees: $30,050
Enrollment: 798 Coed
Affiliation or Control: Christian Church (Disciples Of Christ)
IRS Status: 501(c)3
Highest Offering: Master's
Accreditation: NW, CACREP, IACBE, NURSE

01	President	Dr. Joseph WOMACK
04	Exec Admin Asst to President	Ms. Jennifer BOX
05	VP Academic Affairs/Dean of Faculty	Dr. Dennis LINDSAY
10	VP Finance & Administration	Mr. Gene DE YOUNG
32	VP Student Development/Enrollment	Mr. Michael FULLER
111	VP Advancement	Dr. Keith POTTER
26	Director Marketing & Communication	Mr. Patrick WALSH
07	Dean of Admission	Ms. Kacie GERDRUM
37	Director Financial Aid	Ms. Jocelyn HUBBS
41	Athletic Director	Mr. Corey ANDERSON
42	Campus Pastor	Mr. Troy DEAN
39	Dir Res Life/Dean of Students	Mr. Greg BROCK
35	Director Student Programs	Ms. Princess FOX
36	Dir Academic Svc & Career Develop	Ms. Angela DOTY
06	Registrar	Ms. Gillian HEINE
108	Director of Assessment	Mr. Brian MILLS
44	Director of Annual Fund	Ms. Camile OGDEN
29	Director of Alumni Relations	Ms. Corynn GILBERT
107	Assoc Dean of Professional Studies	Vacant
50	Dean of Business	Mr. Dave WALSH
83	Assistant Dean of CMHC	Dr. Ryan MELTON
53	Asst Dean of Teacher Education	Ms. Kathy DITOMMASO OWEN
66	Associate Dean of Nursing	Dr. Linda VELTRI
13	Director of Information Technology	Mr. Stead HALSTEAD
08	Director Kellenberger Library	Mr. Steve SILVER
18	Plant Manager	Mr. Oskar BUCHER

Oregon College of Oriental Medicine (H)

75 NW Couch Street, Portland OR 97209-4018
County: Multnomah FICE Identification: 026037
Unit ID: 369659
Telephone: (503) 253-3443 Carnegie Class: Spec-4-yr-Other Health
FAX Number: (503) 253-2701 Calendar System: Quarter
URL: www.ocom.edu
Established: 1983 Annual Graduate Tuition & Fees: N/A
Enrollment: 260 Coed
Affiliation or Control: Independent Non-Profit IRS Status: 501(c)3
Highest Offering: Doctorate; No Undergraduates
Accreditation: ACUP

01 President/CEO .... Dr. Sherri GREEN
10 Chief Finance Officer .... Vacant
11 Vice Pres Planning & Operations .... Dr. Phil LUNDBERG
05 Vice Pres Comm & Academic Services .... Dr. Beth HOWLETT
58 Dean of Master's Studies .... Dr. Martin KIDWELL
63 Dean of Doctoral Studies .... Dr. Beth BURCH
88 Associate Dean of Doctoral Studies .... Dr. Zhaoxue LU
88 Assoc Dean of Clinical Education .... Dr. Debra MULROONEY
46 Interim Director of Research .... Ben MARX
15 Director of Human Resources .... Amber APPLETON
06 Registrar .... Carol ACHESON
07 Director of Admissions .... Carolyn DENNIS
37 Director Student Financial Aid .... Tracy REISINGER
44 Director of Annual Giving .... Mike PAULSEN
08 Director of Library Services .... Candise BRANUM
13 Director of Facilities and IT .... Chris LANGFORD
88 Director of Doctoral Services .... Anna GRACE
38 Director Student Counseling .... Elizabeth MILES
32 Dir of Student and Alumni Affairs .... Mike LAW

Oregon Culinary Institute (A)

1701 SW Jefferson Street, Portland OR 97201-2571
Telephone: (503) 961-6200 Identification: 666177
Accreditation: ACICS

† Branch campus of Pioneer Pacific College, Wilsonville, OR.

Oregon Health & Science University (B)

3181 SW Sam Jackson Park Road,
Portland OR 97239-3098
County: Multnomah FICE Identification: 004882
Unit ID: 209490
Telephone: (503) 494-8311 Carnegie Class: Spec-4-yr-Med
FAX Number: (503) 494-5738 Calendar System: Quarter
URL: www.ohsu.edu
Established: 1887 Annual Undergrad Tuition & Fees (In-State): N/A
Enrollment: 2,895 Coed
Affiliation or Control: State IRS Status: 501(c)3
Highest Offering: Doctorate
Accreditation: NW, ANEST, ARCPA, CAHIIM, CAMPEP, DENT, DIETI, EMT, IPSY, MED, MIDWF, MT, NURSE, PH, RTT

01 President .... Dr. Danny O. JACOBS
03 Executive Vice Provost .... Dr. David W. ROBINSON
05 Provost Education & Research .... Dr. Elena ANDRESEN
18 Assoc VP Facilities/Physical Plant .... Mr. Scott PAGE
84 Vice Prov Enroll & Academic Program .... Ms. Cherie HONNELL
46 Chief Research Officer .... Dr. Peter BARR-GILLESPIE
63 Dean School of Medicine .... Dr. Sharon ANDERSON
52 Dean School of Dentistry .... Dr. Phillip T. MARUCHA
69 Dean Joint School of Public Health .... Dr. David BANGSBERG
66 Dean School of Nursing .... Dr. Susan BAKEWELL-SACHS
06 Registrar .... Mrs. Mickie BUSH
17 Director University Hospital .... Mr. Peter RAPP
88 Director Vollum Inst Adv Biomed Res .. Dr. Richard H. GOODMAN
15 Vice Provost of Human Resources .... Mr. Dan FORBES
08 University Librarian .... Ms. Kristine ALPI
26 VP and Chief Marketing Officer .... Ms. Kimberly OVITT
88 Director Child Devel/Rehab Center .... Dr. Brian ROGERS
37 Director Student Financial Aid .... Ms. Rachel DURBIN
28 Vice Pres for Equity & Inclusion .... Dr. Brian GIBBS
108 Vice Provost Educ Improve/Innovat .... Dr. Constance TUCKER

Oregon Institute of Technology (C)

3201 Campus Drive, Klamath Falls OR 97601-8801
County: Klamath FICE Identification: 003211
Unit ID: 209506
Telephone: (541) 885-1000 Carnegie Class: Bac-Diverse
FAX Number: (541) 885-1101 Calendar System: Quarter
URL: www.oit.edu
Established: 1947 Annual Undergrad Tuition & Fees (In-State): $10,118
Enrollment: 5,486 Coed
Affiliation or Control: State IRS Status: 501(c)3
Highest Offering: Master's
Accreditation: NW, COARC, DH, DMS, IACBE, MT, POLYT

01 President .... Dr. Nagi G. NAGANATHAN
05 Provost/Vice Pres Academic Affairs .... Vacant
10 VP Finance/Administration .... Mr. Brian FOX
32 VP Student Affairs/Dean of Students .... Dr. Erin FOLEY
37 Director of Financial Aid .... Ms. Tracey A. LEHMAN
15 Director of Human Resources .... Vacant
07 Director of Admissions .... Mr. Erik JOHNSON
06 Registrar .... Ms. Wendy IVIE
21 Assistant VP Financial Operations .... Ms. Stephanie POPE
13 Assoc VP/Chief Information Officer .... Ms. Connie ATCHLEY
26 Associate VP of Communications .... Ms. Di SAUNDERS
23 Director Student Health Services .... Mrs. Gaylyn MAURER
18 Director Facilities Svcs .... Mr. Thom DARRAH
41 Athletic Director .... Mr. John VANDYKE
35 Director Campus Life .... Ms. Holly ANDERSON
88 Assoc Director Campus Life .... Ms. Josie HUDSPETH
36 Director of Career Services .... Ms. Jennifer KASS
09 Institutional Research Analyst .... Mr. Farooq SULTAN
30 Assoc VP Devel/Alumni Relations .... Mrs. Tracy RICKETTS
04 Sr Exec Assistant to the President .... Mrs. Adria D. PASCHAL
101 Secretary of the Institution/Board .... Ms. Sandra FOX
19 Director Security/Safety .... Mr. Edward DANIELS
39 Dir Resident Life/Student Housing .... Ms. Mandi CLARK
43 Director of Legal Services .... Mr. David GROFF
84 Assoc VP Strategic Enrollment .... Ms. Erika VETH
96 Director of Procurement Contracts .... Ms. Vivian CHEN

Oregon State University (D)

1500 SW Jefferson Avenue, Corvallis OR 97331-8507
County: Benton FICE Identification: 003210
Unit ID: 209542
Telephone: (541) 737-0123 Carnegie Class: DU-Highest
FAX Number: N/A Calendar System: Quarter
URL: www.oregonstate.edu
Established: 1868 Annual Undergrad Tuition & Fees (In-State): $11,166
Enrollment: 30,896 Coed
Affiliation or Control: State IRS Status: 501(c)3
Highest Offering: Doctorate
Accreditation: NW, CAATE, CACREP, CAEPN, CAMPEP, CEA, CONST, DIETD, DIETI, IPSY, PH, PHAR, SPAA, VET

01 President .... Dr. Edward J. RAY
05 Provost/Exec Vice President .... Dr. Ed FESER
10 Int Vice Pres Finance/Admin .... Mr. Mike GREEN
111 Vice Pres University Advancement .... Mr. Steve CLARK
46 Vice President for Research .... Ms. Cynthia SAGERS
20 Vice Prov Academic Affs/Intl Pgms .... Ms. Susan CAPALBO
32 Int Vice Prov for Student Affairs .... Mr. Dan LARSON
12 V Prov/Campus Ex Ofcr OSU-Cascades .... Dr. Rebecca JOHNSON
102 President & CEO OSU Foundation .... Mr. Mike GOODWIN
47 Dean of Agricultural Sciences .... Dr. Dan ARP
50 Dean of Business .... Dr. Mitzi MONTOYA
54 Dean of Engineering .... Dr. Scott ASHFORD
65 Dean of Forestry .... Dr. Thomas MANESS
68 Dean of Health & Human Sciences .... Dr. Javier NIETO
65 Dean of Earth/Ocean & Atmos Science .... Dr. Roberta MARINELLI
67 Dean of Pharmacy .... Dr. Mark ZABRISKIE
81 Dean of Science .... Dr. Roy HAGGERTY
74 Interim Dean of Veterinary Medicine .... Dr. Susan TORNQUIST
51 Assoc Provost Extended Campus .... Dr. David A. KING
35 Interim Dean of Student Life .... Mr. Dan LARSON
92 Dean University Honors College .... Dr. Toni DOOLEN
53 Dean of Education .... Dr. Toni DOOLEN
08 University Librarian .... Ms. Faye CHADWELL
22 Director Equity and Inclusion .... Dr. Allison DAVIS-WHITE EYES
43 General Counsel .... Ms. Becca GOSE
41 Director Intercollegiate Athletics .... Mr. Scott BARNES
37 Dir of Financial Aid/Scholarship .... Mr. Doug SEVERS
23 Dir Student Health Services .... Ms. Jenny HAUBENREISER
38 Dir Univ Counseling/Psych Svcs .... Dr. Jackie ALVAREZ
39 Director Univ Housing/Dining Svcs .... Mr. Dan LARSON
06 Registrar .... Ms. Rebecca MATHERN
07 Director of Admissions .... Mr. Noah BUCKLEY
24 Director Media & Outreach Services .... Mr. John GREYDANUS
14 Dir of Enterprise Computing Service .... Mr. Kent KUO
21 AVP Finance & Administration .... Mr. Mike GREEN
15 Director of Human Resources .... Ms. Donna CHASTAIN
19 Director Public Safety .... Ms. Suzy TANNENBAUM
29 Exec Dir of Alumni Association .... Ms. Kathy BICKEL
86 Director Government Relations .... Mr. Jock S. MILLS
27 Dir News/Comm Svcs/Asst Vice Pres .... Ms. Annie HECK
26 Director of University Marketing .... Ms. Melody K. OLDFIELD
105 Asst Director Web Communications .... Mr. David A. BAKER
28 Chief Diversity Officer .... Ms. Charlene ALEXANDER
09 Director of Institutional Research .... Mr. Salvador CASTILLO
40 General Mgr & CEO OSU Bookstores .... Mr. Steve E. ECKRICH
96 Manager Procurement/Contract Svcs .... Ms. Kelly L. KOZISEK
101 Secretary of the Institution/Board .... Ms. Debbie COLBERT

Pacific Bible College (E)

28 S. Fir St., Suite 212, Medford OR 97501
County: Jackson Identification: 667252
Unit ID: 407610
Telephone: (541) 776-9942 Carnegie Class: Spec 2-yr-Other
FAX Number: (541) 770-9065 Calendar System: Semester
URL: www.pacficbible.edu
Established: 1991 Annual Undergrad Tuition & Fees: $3,650
Enrollment: 34 Coed
Affiliation or Control: Non-denominational IRS Status: 501(c)3
Highest Offering: Associate Degree
Accreditation: BI

01 President .... Mr. Mike ROBINSON
05 Chief Academic Officer .... Mr. Stuart BOYER

Pacific Northwest College of Art (F)

511 NW Broadway, Portland OR 97209-3023
County: Multnomah FICE Identification: 003207
Unit ID: 209603
Telephone: (503) 226-4391 Carnegie Class: Spec-4-yr-Arts
FAX Number: (503) 226-3587 Calendar System: Semester
URL: www.pnca.edu
Established: 1909 Annual Undergrad Tuition & Fees: $38,250
Enrollment: 512 Coed
Affiliation or Control: Independent Non-Profit IRS Status: 501(c)3
Highest Offering: Master's
Accreditation: NW, ART

01 Interim President .... Dr. Christopher MAPLES
05 Chief Academic Officer .... Ms. Kate COPELAND
111 Vice President for Advancement .... Ms. Candace HORTER
11 Vice President for Administration .... Darby KNOX
37 Director Financial Aid .... Ms. Ingrid BAKER
32 Asst Director of Student Life .... Mr. Jackson SEEMAYER
43 Dir Legal Services/General Counsel .... Ms. Cordelia DANIELS
19 Director Security/Safety .... Mr. Manuel GUERRA

Pacific University (G)

2043 College Way, Forest Grove OR 97116-1797
County: Washington FICE Identification: 003212
Unit ID: 209612
Telephone: (503) 357-6151 Carnegie Class: DU-Mod
FAX Number: (503) 352-2242 Calendar System: Semester
URL: www.pacificu.edu
Established: 1849 Annual Undergrad Tuition & Fees: $44,298
Enrollment: 3,893 Coed
Affiliation or Control: Independent Non-Profit IRS Status: 501(c)3
Highest Offering: Doctorate
Accreditation: NW, #ARCPA, AUD, CAATE, CAEPN, CLPSY, DH, IPSY, MUS, OPT, OPTR, OT, PHAR, PTA, SP, SW

01 President .... Dr. Lesley M. HALLICK
05 Vice Pres Academic Affairs/Provost .... Dr. John MILLER
10 Vice Pres Finance & Administration .... Mr. Jim LANGSTRAAT
111 Vice Pres University Advancement .... Ms. Cassie WARMAN
32 Vice Pres Enrollment/Student Affs .... Dr. Mark ANKENY
35 Assoc Vice Pres Student Affairs .... Mr. Will PERKINS
26 Assoc VP of Marketing/Comm .... Ms. Jenni LUCKETT
110 Assoc VP for University Advancement .... Ms. Jan STRICKLIN
21 Assistant Vice Pres for Finance .... Mr. William RAY
20 Vice Provost Academic Affairs .... Dr. Lisa CARSTENS
18 Director of Facilities .... Ms. Cindy SCHUPPERT
07 Executive Director of Admissions .... Ms. Karen DUNSTON
06 Registrar .... Ms. Anne HERMAN
37 Director Financial Aid .... Ms. Leslie LIMPER
13 Interim Chief Information Officer .... Mr. Ted KRUPICKA
88 Director of Conference Services .... Ms. Jill THORNTON
88 Director University Events .... Ms. Paula THATCHER
76 Exec Dean Col of Health Professions .. Dr. Ann BARR-GILLESPIE
49 Dean of Arts & Sciences .... Dr. Sarah PHILLIPS
63 Dean College of Optometry .... Dr. Jennifer COYLE
67 Dean School of Pharmacy .... Dr. Reza KARIMIGEVARI
53 Dean College of Education .... Dr. Leif GUSTAVSON
83 Dean School of Grad Psych .... Dr. Joaquin BORREGO
41 Athletic Director .... Mr. Kenneth SCHUMANN
76 Director School Physical Therapy .... Dr. Kevin CHUI
76 Dir School Occupational Therapy .... Dr. Kevin CHUI
15 Dir Human Resources/Legal Affairs .... Ms. Jennifer YRUEGAS
23 Director of Health Services .... Ms. Victoria KEYTON
123 Exec Director of Grad/Prof Admiss .... Mr. Jon-Erik LARSEN
76 Director Physician Asst Studies .... Dr. Mary VON
29 Director Alumni Relations .... Ms. Martha CALUS-MCLAIN
08 Dean of University Libraries .... Mr. Isaac GILMAN
32 Dir Univ Center/Student Activities .... Mr. Steve KLEIN
52 Director Dental Hygiene Studies .... Ms. Amy COPLEN
40 Manager Bookstore .... Ms. Stacie BLANKENHORN
38 Interim Director Counseling Center .... Ms. Laura STALLINGS
09 Director of Institutional Research .... Mr. William O'SHEA
04 Executive Asst to President .... Ms. Sue WEINBENDER
100 Chief of Staff .... Ms. Mic HOWE
112 Major Gift Ofcr Found/Corp Rels .... Ms. Amy CALLAHAN
104 Director International Programs .... Dr. Stephen PRAG
28 Director Equity/Diversity/Inclusion .... Ms. Narcedalia RODRIGUEZ
50 Dean of College of Business .... Dr. James GOODRICH

Pioneer Pacific College (H)

27375 SW Parkway Avenue, Wilsonville OR 97070-9296
County: Clackamas FICE Identification: 023301
Unit ID: 210076
Telephone: (503) 682-3903 Carnegie Class: Bac/Assoc-Assoc Dom
FAX Number: (503) 682-1514 Calendar System: Other
URL: www.pioneerpacific.edu
Established: 1981 Annual Undergrad Tuition & Fees: $13,338
Enrollment: 1,036 Coed
Affiliation or Control: Proprietary IRS Status: Proprietary
Highest Offering: Baccalaureate
Accreditation: ACICS, RAD

01 President .... Mr. Don MOUTOS
05 Vice President of Academic Affairs .... Mr. Fred OSBORN
10 Vice Pres of Accounting/Controller .... Ms. Wendy HUTCHINSON

Pioneer Pacific College-Springfield (I)

3800 Sports way, Springfield OR 97477
Telephone: (541) 684-4644 Identification: 770764
Accreditation: ACICS

Portland Community College (J)

PO Box 19000, Portland OR 97280-0990
County: Multnomah FICE Identification: 003213
Unit ID: 209746
Telephone: (971) 722-6111 Carnegie Class: Assoc/HT-Mix Trad/Non
FAX Number: (971) 722-4960 Calendar System: Quarter
URL: www.pcc.edu/
Established: 1961 Annual Undergrad Tuition & Fees (In-District): $4,340
Enrollment: 28,005 Coed
Affiliation or Control: Local IRS Status: 501(c)3
Highest Offering: Associate Degree

Accreditation: NW, ADNUR, CAHIIM, DA, DH, DT, EMT, IFSAC, MAC, MLTAD, RAD

01 College President ... Mr. Mark MITSUI
03 Executive Vice President ... Ms. Sylvia KELLEY
100 Program Administrator ... Dr. Traci FORDHAM
05 Vice President of Academic Affairs ... Ms. Katy W. HO
32 Interim Vice Pres Student Affairs ... Dr. Heather LANG
10 Vice Pres Finance/Administration ... Mr. Eric BLUMENTHAL
21 Acting Assoc VP Financial Services ... Ms. Dina FARRELL
13 Chief Information Officer ... Mr. Michael NORTHOVER
12 Campus President Sylvania ... Dr. Lisa AVERY
12 Campus President Cascade ... Dr. Karin EDWARDS
12 Campus President Rock Creek ... Dr. Chris VILLA
12 Interim Campus President Southeast ... Ms. Jen PIPER
20 Dean Instruction Sylvania ... Dr. Karen PAEZ
20 Dean Instruction Cascade Campus ... Mr. Kurt SIMONDS
20 Dean Instruction Rock Creek Campus ... Dr. Cheryl SCOTT
20 Int Dean Instruct Southeast Campus ... Ms. Sarah TILLERY
32 Int Dn Student Dev Sylvania Campus ... Ms. Pam BLUMENTHAL
32 Dean Stdnt Dev Rock Creek Campus ... Mr. Ryan A. AIELLO
121 Dean of Student Success ... Vacant
32 Dean Student Dev Cascade Campus ... Ms. Michele CRUSE
84 Dean of Enrollment Management ... Ms. Tammy N. BILLICK
15 Associate VP Human Resources ... Ms. Lisa BLEDSOE
18 Director Facilities Management ... Mr. Tony ICHSAN
08 Dean Library Services ... Ms. Michelle M. BAGLEY
09 Dir Institutional Effectiveness ... Ms. Laura MASSEY
19 Director Public Safety ... Mr. Derrick FOXWORTH
37 Director Financial Aid ... Mr. Peter GOSS
22 Chief Diversity Officer ... Ms. Tricia BRAND
30 Director of Development ... Ms. Ann PRATER
07 Manager of Registration Services ... Ms. Darilis GARCIA-MCMILLIAN
06 Registrar ... Mr. Ryan CLARK
31 Director of Community Engagement ... Ms. Kate CHESTER
96 Manager Purchasing ... Mr. Mike MATHEWS

Portland State University (A)

PO Box 751, Portland OR 97207-0751
County: Multnomah FICE Identification: 003216
Unit ID: 209807
Telephone: (503) 725-3000 Carnegie Class: DU-Higher
FAX Number: (503) 725-4882 Calendar System: Quarter
URL: www.pdx.edu
Established: 1946 Annual Undergrad Tuition & Fees (In-State): $9,105
Enrollment: 26,693 Coed
Affiliation or Control: State IRS Status: 501(c)3
Highest Offering: Doctorate
Accreditation: NW, CACREP, CAEP, CEA, HSA, LC, MUS, PH, PLNG, SP, SPAA, SW, THEA

01 Interim President ... Dr. Stephen PERCY
43 General Counsel ... Ms. Cindy STARKE
05 Provost & VP Academic Affairs ... Dr. Susan JEFFORDS
10 Vice President Finance/Admin ... Dr. Kevin REYNOLDS
102 CEO PSU Foundation ... Mr. Bill BOLDT
100 Chief of Staff & VP Public Affairs ... Vacant
84 Vice Pres Enrollment Mgmt ... Mr. Chuck KNEPFLE
46 Vice Pres Research & Grad Studies ... Dr. Mark MCLELLAN
22 Int VP Global Diversity & Inclusion ... Ms. Julie CARON
45 Vice Prov Academic/Fiscal Planning ... Vacant
20 Vice Provost Acad Pers Ldrshp & Dev ... Dr. Shelly CHABON
26 Assoc VP Communications ... Mr. Christopher BRODERICK
09 Director Inst Research/Planning ... Dr. Kathi A. KETCHESON
19 Int Director Campus Public Safety ... Mr. Joe SCHILLING
13 AVP/Chief Information Officer ... Mr. Kirk KELLY
86 AVP Government Relations ... Mr. Kevin NEELY
08 Dean University Librarian ... Mr. Thomas BIELAVITZ
41 Athletics Director ... Ms. Valerie CLEARY
49 Interim Dean of CLAS ... Dr. Matt CARLSON
50 Dean of SBA ... Mr. Clifford ALLEN
53 Dean Graduate Sch of Education ... Dr. Marvin LYNN
54 Dean Col Engr/Computer Science ... Dr. Richard CORSI
57 Dean College of the Arts ... Dr. Leroy BYNUM
70 Dean School of Social Work ... Dr. Laura NISSEN
80 Int Dean Col Urban/Public Affairs ... Dr. Sy ADLER
35 Dean Student Life ... Ms. Michele TOPPE
85 Dir Diversity & Mult Student Svcs ... Vacant
06 AVP & University Registrar ... Ms. Cindy BACCAR
23 Exec Dir Stdnt Health & Counseling ... Dr. Dana TASSON
58 Dean Graduate Studies ... Ms. Rossitza WOOSTER

Process Work Institute (B)

2049 NW Hoyt Street, Portland OR 97209
County: Multnomah Identification: 667297
Telephone: (503) 223-8188 Carnegie Class: Not Classified
FAX Number: (503) 227-7003 Calendar System: Quarter
URL: www.processwork.edu
Established: 1989 Annual Graduate Tuition & Fees: N/A
Enrollment: N/A Coed
Affiliation or Control: Independent Non-Profit IRS Status: 501(c)3
Highest Offering: Master's; No Undergraduates
Accreditation: ACICS

01 Executive Director/Dean ... Dr. Hellene GRONDA

Reed College (C)

3203 SE Woodstock Boulevard, Portland OR 97202-8199
County: Multnomah FICE Identification: 003217
Unit ID: 209922
Telephone: (503) 771-1112 Carnegie Class: Bac-A&S
FAX Number: (503) 777-7769 Calendar System: Semester
URL: www.reed.edu
Established: 1908 Annual Undergrad Tuition & Fees: $56,340
Enrollment: 1,470 Coed
Affiliation or Control: Independent Non-Profit IRS Status: 501(c)3
Highest Offering: Master's
Accreditation: NW

01 President ... Dr. Audrey BILGER
111 Vice President College Relations ... Mr. Hugh E. PORTER
05 Dean of the Faculty ... Dr. Nigel J. NICHOLSON
10 Vice President & Treasurer ... Dr. Lorraine ARVIN
32 Vice President for Student Life ... Dr. Michael BRODY
04 Exec Asst to the President ... Ms. Dawn G. THOMPSON
28 Dean for Institutional Diversity ... Dr. Mary B. JAMES
35 Dean of Students ... Vacant
23 Director Health & Counseling ... Vacant
07 Vice Pres/Dean Admission & Fin Aid ... Mr. Milyon TRULOVE
06 Registrar ... Ms. Nora MCLAUGHLIN
08 College Librarian ... Ms. Dena HUTTO
30 Executive Director of Development ... Ms. Sarah PANETTA
37 Director of Financial Aid ... Ms. Sandy SUNDSTROM
09 Director of Institutional Research ... Mr. Mike TAMADA
26 Exec Dir Comm & Public Affairs ... Ms. Mandy HEATON
29 Director of Alumni Programs ... Ms. Katie RAMSEY
13 Chief Information Officer ... Dr. Martin D. RINGLE
105 Director of Web Support Services ... Ms. Marianne M. COLGROVE
91 Director Administrative Computing ... Mr. Gabriel LEAVITT
21 Associate Treasurer & Controller ... Mr. Rob TUST
15 Director of Human Resources ... Ms. Michelle VALINTIS
29 Sr Dir Alumni Pgms & Annual Fund ... Ms. Mary M. ASKELSON
102 Dir Corporate/Foundation Support ... Vacant
104 Director International Programs ... Dr. Paul D. DEYOUNG
36 Dean of Stdnts/Dir Life Beyond Reed ... Ms. Alice HARRA
88 Director of Special Programs ... Ms. Barbara A. AMEN
18 Director Facilities Operations ... Mr. Townsend ANGELL
19 Director Community Safety ... Mr. Gary GRANGER
41 Director of Athletics/Fitness ... Mr. Michael LOMBARDO
40 Director Bookstore & Auxiliary Svcs ... Ms. Jessica VALESKE
39 Asst Dean of Students for Res Life ... Ms. Amy SCHUCKMAN

Rogue Community College (D)

3345 Redwood Highway, Grants Pass OR 97527-9298
County: Josephine FICE Identification: 010182
Unit ID: 209940
Telephone: (541) 956-7500 Carnegie Class: Assoc/HT-Mix Trad/Non
FAX Number: (541) 471-3591 Calendar System: Quarter
URL: www.roguecc.edu
Established: 1970 Annual Undergrad Tuition & Fees (In-District): $4,524
Enrollment: 4,610 Coed
Affiliation or Control: Local IRS Status: 501(c)3
Highest Offering: Associate Degree
Accreditation: NW, EMT

01 College President ... Dr. Cathy KEMPER-PELLE
05 Interim VP Instruction ... Ms. Juliet LONG
13 VP College Svcs/CIO ... Mr. Curtis SOMMERFELD
117 Director Risk Mgmt/Title IX ... Mr. Sean TAGGART
32 VP Student Svcs/CSSO/ADA ... Ms. Kori EBENHACK
72 Dean Health & Public Service ... Ms. Teri SMITH
88 Director Small Bus Dev Center ... Mr. Ronald GOSS
81 Dean Sch of Science/Tech ... Vacant
08 Head Librarian ... Mr. Robert FELTHOUSEN
102 Executive Director Foundation ... Ms. Judy BASKER
15 Director HR ... Ms. Jamee HARRINGTON
24 Director Instructional Media ... Mr. Josh OGLE
109 Director Bookstore and Shipping/Rec ... Ms. Laura HAGA-DUFFY
26 Dir Marketing/Public Info Officer ... Mr. Grant WALKER
37 Dir Student Financial Aid ... Ms. Frankie EVERETT
14 Director IT Network & User Support ... Mr. Mike MCCLURE
88 Director TRiO-EOC ... Ms. Janet BASNEY
88 Director TRiO-SSS ... Ms. Colletta YOUNG
09 Director of Institutional Research ... Ms. Laurie ROE
88 Apprenticeship Coordinator ... Ms. Cathy PIERSON
96 Contract and Procurement Manager ... Ms. Jodie FULTON
91 Director of IT Programming ... Mr. Al SHELDON
18 Director of Facilities/Operations ... Mr. Grant LAGORIO
20 Data Mgmt Specialist Curriculum/Sch ... Ms. Marita WILDER
88 Director of Student Programs ... Ms. Rene MCKENZIE
07 Director Enrollment Services ... Ms. Dani CROUCH
88 Asst Director Admissions & Recruit ... Ms. Nicole SAKRAIDA
04 Assistant to the President/Gov ... Vacant
04 Assistant to the President/Opers ... Ms. Rosalyn MENDOZA
35 Dean of Student Success ... Ms. August FARNSWORTH
88 Coord Student Conduct/Title IX ... Mr. Chauncey KIELEY
10 Chief Financial Officer ... Ms. Lisa STANTON
108 Outcomes & Assessment Strategist ... Vacant
28 Diversity Programming Coordinator ... Ms. Sally SNYDER
38 Faculty/Chair Student Counseling ... Ms. Michelle GRAY
50 Faculty/Dept Chair Bus Tech ... Ms. Melissa POLEN
06 Registrar ... Ms. Dani CROUCH
88 Director Educational Partnerships ... Mr. Daye STONE
51 Director of Continuing Educ ... Ms. Diane HOOVER
88 Director Adult Basic Skills ... Ms. Julie ROSSI
76 Chair Allied Health Occupations ... Mr. Sam BATTRICK
88 SOHOPE Director ... Ms. Lisa PARKS
41 Athletic Director ... Mr. Darren VAN LEHN

Southern Oregon University (E)

1250 Siskiyou Boulevard, Ashland OR 97520-5001
County: Jackson FICE Identification: 003219
Unit ID: 210146
Telephone: (541) 552-7672 Carnegie Class: Masters/L
FAX Number: (541) 552-6329 Calendar System: Quarter
URL: www.sou.edu
Established: 1872 Annual Undergrad Tuition & Fees (In-State): $9,615
Enrollment: 6,191 Coed
Affiliation or Control: State IRS Status: 501(c)3
Highest Offering: Master's
Accreditation: NW, ACBSP, CACREP, MUS

01 President ... Dr. Linda SCHOTT
05 Prov/VP Acad & Student Affairs ... Dr. Susan WALSH
10 VP for Finance & Administration ... Mr. Greg PERKINSON
30 Vice President Development ... Ms. Janet FRATELLA
15 Director for Human Resource Svcs ... Ms. Alana LARDIZABAL
84 VP Enrollment Mgmt & Student Affs ... Vacant
26 Ex Dir Interactive Mktg/Media Rels ... Ms. Nicolle ALEMAN
18 Dir for Facilities Mgmt & Planning ... Mr. Drew GILLILAND
21 Director of Business Services ... Mr. Steve LARVICK
08 University Librarian ... Mr. Jeffrey GAYTON
51 Exec Dir Division of Continuing Edu ... Ms. Jeanne STALLMAN
19 Director of Campus Public Safety ... Vacant
29 Director of Alumni Affairs ... Mr. Mike BEAGLE
88 Director of Schneider Museum of Art ... Mr. Scott MALBAURN
28 Director of Diversity and Inclusion ... Vacant
57 Director Performing Arts ... Dr. David HUMPHREY
83 Director Social Sciences ... Dr. Dan DENEUI
97 Director Undergraduate Studies ... Dr. Lee AYERS
81 Director STEM ... Dr. Sherry ETTLICH
50 Dir Business Comm & Environment ... Ms. Katie PITTMAN
79 Director Humanities & Culture ... Dr. Scott REX
88 Director Educ Health & Leadership ... Dr. John KING
06 Registrar ... Dr. Matt STILLMAN
07 Director of Admissions ... Ms. Kelly MOUTSATSON
09 Director of Institutional Research ... Mr. Chris STANEK
41 Athletic Director ... Mr. Matt SAYRE
101 University Board Secretary ... Ms. Sabrina PRUD'HOMME
39 Director Student Housing ... Ms. Staci BUCHWALD
38 Director Student Support & Interven ... Ms. Taylor BURKE
86 Director Government Relations ... Ms. Jeanne STALLMAN

Southwestern Oregon Community College (F)

1988 Newmark Avenue, Coos Bay OR 97420-2911
County: Coos FICE Identification: 003220
Unit ID: 210155
Telephone: (541) 888-2525 Carnegie Class: Assoc/MT-VT-High Trad
FAX Number: (541) 888-7285 Calendar System: Quarter
URL: www.socc.edu
Established: 1961 Annual Undergrad Tuition & Fees (In-District): $6,077
Enrollment: 2,099 Coed
Affiliation or Control: Local IRS Status: 501(c)3
Highest Offering: Associate Degree
Accreditation: NW, ACFEI, EMT, MAAB

01 President ... Dr. Patty SCOTT
11 VP Administrative Services ... Mr. Jeff WHITEY
05 VP Instructional Services ... Dr. Ali MAGEEHON
32 VP Enrollment & Student Services ... Mr. Tim DAILEY
12 Executive Dean Curry County ... Mr. Doug BUNN
72 Dean of Career and Technical Educ ... Mr. Daniel KOOPMAN
20 Dean of LDC ... Mr. Rod KELLER
84 Dean of Enrollment Services ... Mr. Tom NICHOLLS
111 Dean of Advancement/Alumni Rels ... Ms. Elise HAMNER
13 Exec Director Integrated Technology ... Mr. Carl GERISCH
88 Exec Director OCCI (Culinary) ... Mr. Randy TORRES
41 Director Athletics ... Dr. Mike HERBERT
07 Director of Admissions ... Mr. Tom NICHOLLS
19 Director Campus Safety ... Mr. Joe THOMAS
18 Director Facilities Services ... Ms. Emerald BRUNETT
06 Registrar ... Vacant
37 Director Financial Aid ... Ms. Avena SINGH
15 Chief Human Resources Officer ... Ms. Rachele LYON
10 Chief Business Officer ... Ms. Kathy DIXON
66 Director Nursing ... Ms. Joannie MILLER
39 Director Residence Life ... Mr. Joe BELTER
88 Director SOCC Business Dev Center ... Mr. John BACON
38 Director Student Support Services ... Ms. Michele BENOIT
40 Manager Bookstore ... Ms. Clarissa RICKELS
09 Institutional Researcher ... Ms. Robin BUNNELL
35 Coordinator Student Life and Events ... Mr. Kyle CROY
04 Exec Asst to the Pres/Board of Educ ... Ms. Dina LASKEY
26 Chief Public Relations/Marketing ... Ms. Anne MATTHEWS

Sumner College (G)

8338 NE Alderwood Road, Ste 100, Portland OR 97220
County: Multnomah FICE Identification: 021049
Unit ID: 208512
Telephone: (503) 972-6230 Carnegie Class: Spec 2-yr-Health
FAX Number: (503) 952-0010 Calendar System: Other
URL: www.sumnercollege.edu
Established: 1974 Annual Undergrad Tuition & Fees: N/A
Enrollment: 322 Coed
Affiliation or Control: Proprietary IRS Status: Proprietary
Highest Offering: Associate Degree
Accreditation: ABHES, ACICS

01 President ... Joanna S. RUSSELL

Tillamook Bay Community College (A)

4301 3rd Street, Tillamook OR 97141
County: Tillamook Identification: 666647
Unit ID: 420723
Telephone: (503) 842-8222 Carnegie Class: Assoc/HT-High Non
FAX Number: (503) 842-8336 Calendar System: Quarter
URL: www.tillamookbaycc.edu
Established: 1981 Annual Undergrad Tuition & Fees (In-District): $3,888
Enrollment: 227 Coed
Affiliation or Control: State/Local IRS Status: 501(c)3
Highest Offering: Associate Degree
Accreditation: NW

01 President .... Dr. Ross L. TOMLIN
05 Chief Academic Officer .... Dr. Teresa RIVENES
10 Comptroller/Budget Officer .... Ms. Kyra WILLIAMS
30 Dir Development & Marketing .... Mrs. Heidi LUQUETTE
32 Dir Student Services & Registrar .... Mrs. Rhoda HANSON
15 Dir Human Resources/Facilities .... Mr. Pat RYAN
09 Dir of Institutional Effectiveness .... Ms. Erin MCCARLEY

Treasure Valley Community College (B)

650 College Boulevard, Ontario OR 97914-3423
County: Malheur FICE Identification: 003221
Unit ID: 210234
Telephone: (541) 881-8822 Carnegie Class: Assoc/HT-Mix Trad/Non
FAX Number: (541) 881-2753 Calendar System: Quarter
URL: www.tvcc.cc
Established: 1961 Annual Undergrad Tuition & Fees (In-District): $5,445
Enrollment: 1,793 Coed
Affiliation or Control: Local IRS Status: 501(c)3
Highest Offering: Associate Degree
Accreditation: NW, ADNUR

01 President .... Dr. Dana YOUNG
05 Vice President of Academic Affairs .... Mr. Eddie ALVES
11 Vice Pres Admin Services .... Ms. Shirley HAIDLE
32 Vice President of Student Services .... Mr. Brad HAMMOND
08 Librarian .... Mr. Dennis GILL
26 Assoc VP College/Public Relations .... Ms. Abby LEE
10 Comptroller .... Ms. Shirley HAIDLE
37 Financial Aid Director .... Ms. Diahann DERRICK
13 Director Information Technology .... Mr. Scott CARPENTER
07 Director of Admissions .... Ms. Stephanie OESTER
15 Director of Human Resources .... Ms. Anne-Marie KELSO
51 Director of Continuing Education .... Ms. Andrea TESTI
18 Dir of Housing/Building & Grounds .... Ms. Michelle POTTER
41 Athletic Director .... Mr. Andy WARD
06 Registrar .... Vacant
09 Director of Institutional Effective .... Mr. Miguel LOPEZ
102 TVCC Foundation Exec Dir .... Ms. Cathy YASUDA
40 Bookstore Manager .... Mr. Kjetil ROM
04 Executive Asst to President .... Ms. Gina ROPER
19 Director Security/Safety .... Ms. Michelle POTTER
39 Director Student Housing .... Ms. Tasha WIXOM
07 Director Admissions/Student Success .... Mr. Travis MCFETRIDGE

Umpqua Community College (C)

1140 Umpqua College Road, Roseburg OR 97470
County: Douglas FICE Identification: 003222
Unit ID: 210270
Telephone: (541) 440-4600 Carnegie Class: Assoc/MT-VT-High Non
FAX Number: (541) 440-4637 Calendar System: Quarter
URL: www.umpqua.edu
Established: 1964 Annual Undergrad Tuition & Fees (In-District): $5,001
Enrollment: 1,909 Coed
Affiliation or Control: Local IRS Status: 501(c)3
Highest Offering: Associate Degree
Accreditation: NW, DA, EMT

01 President .... Dr. Debra THATCHER
05 Provost .... Dr. Kacy CRABTREE
10 CFO .... Ms. Natalya BROWN
37 Director of Financial Aid .... Ms. Michelle BERGMANN
13 Director Informational Technology .... Ms. Kathy THOMASON
08 Director of Library Services .... Ms. Carol MCGEEHON
103 Director of Community/Workforce .... Ms. Robin VAN WINKLE
09 Director Institutional Research .... Mr. Steve ROGERS
15 Director of Human Resources .... Ms. Lynn JOHNSON
04 Executive Asst to President & Board .... Ms. Robynne WILGUS
06 Director of Registration & Records .... Ms. Brenna HOBBS
111 Director of Advancement .... Vacant
18 Director of Facilities & Security .... Mr. Jess MILLER
26 Director of Communications & Market .... Ms. Tiffany COLEMAN
41 Athletic Director .... Mr. Craig JACKSON
96 Purchasing Manager .... Mr. Jules DEGIULIO

University of Oregon (D)

1585 E. 13th Avenue, Eugene OR 97403
County: Lane FICE Identification: 003223
Unit ID: 209551
Telephone: (541) 346-1000 Carnegie Class: DU-Highest
FAX Number: N/A Calendar System: Quarter
URL: www.uoregon.edu
Established: 1876 Annual Undergrad Tuition & Fees (In-State): $11,898
Enrollment: 22,887 Coed
Affiliation or Control: State IRS Status: 501(c)3
Highest Offering: Doctorate
Accreditation: NW, ART, CEA, CIDA, CLPSY, COPSY, IPSY, JOUR, LAW, LSAR, MFCD, MUS, PCSAS, PLNG, SCPSY, SP, SPAA

01 President .... Mr. Michael H. SCHILL
100 Sr Advisor/Chief of Staff to Pres .... Mr. Greg J. STRIPP
05 Provost & Senior Vice President .... Dr. Patrick PHILLIPS
10 VP Finance & Admin & CFO .... Ms. Jamie H. MOFFITT
32 VP Student Life .... Dr. Kevin MARBURY
111 VP University Advancement .... Mr. Michael C. ANDREASEN
46 VP Research & Innovation .... Dr. David CONOVER
26 VP University Communications .... Mr. Kyle HENLEY
43 Vice President and General Counsel .... Mr. Kevin REED
20 VProv Undergrad Educ/Stdnt Success .... Dr. Doneka SCOTT
28 VP Equity & Inclusion .... Dr. Yvette M. ALEX-ASSENSOH
84 VP Student Svcs & Enrollment Mgmt ....Dr. Roger J. THOMPSON
13 Vice Prov Information Services/CIO .... Ms. Jessie MINTON
85 Dean/Vice Provost Global Engagement .... Dr. Dennis C. GALVAN
86 Assoc Vice Pres Federal Affairs .... Ms. Betsy A. BOYD
86 Assoc VP State & Community Affairs .... Ms. Libby BATLAN
29 AVP Alumni Affairs/Exec Dir UOAA .... Mr. Raphe BECK
102 Chief Investment Officer Foundation .... Mr. Jay NAMYET
06 University Registrar .... Ms. Julia POMERENK
07 Director of Admissions .... Mr. Jim H. RAWLINS
08 Interim Dean of Libraries .... Mr. Mark WATSON
21 Dir Business Affairs and Controller .... Mr. Kelly B. WOLF
37 Director Student Financial Aid .... Mr. Jim J. BROOKS
36 Director of Career Center .... Mr. Paul TIMMINS
15 Chief Human Resources Officer .... Mr. Mark SCHMELZ
18 Assoc VP Planning & Facilities Mgmt .... Mr. Mike HARWOOD
22 Assoc VP AAEO & Title IX .... Ms. Darci HEROY
41 Director Intercollegiate Athletics .... Mr. Rob A. MULLENS
56 Executive Dir UO Academic Extension .... Ms. Sandra K. GLADNEY
49 Interim Dean College Arts & Science .... Dr. Bruce BLONIGEN
48 Interim Dean College of Design .... Ms. Laura VANDENBURGH
50 Dean College of Business .... Dr. Sarah NUTTER
53 Dean College of Education .... Dr. Randy W. KAMPHAUS
60 Dean School of Journ & Comm .... Dr. Juan-Carlos MOLLEDA
58 Dean of Graduate School .... Dr. Janet WOODRUFF-BORDEN
61 Dean School of Law .... Ms. Marcilynn BURKE
64 Dean School of Music & Dance .... Dr. Sabrina MADISON-CANNON
92 Dean Clark Honors College .... Dr. Gabe PAQUETTE
09 Director of Institutional Research .... Dr. JP MONROE
38 Dir Counseling & Testing Center .... Dr. Shelly K. KERR
96 Chief Procurement Officer .... Mr. Greg SHABRAM
101 Secretary of the University/Board .... Ms. Angela WILHELMS
19 Chief of Police .... Mr. Matthew CARMICHAEL
39 Director Student Housing .... Mr. Michael M. GRIFFEL
114 Vice Provost Budget & Planning .... Dr. Brad SHELTON
90 Director Academic Technology .... Ms. Helen Y. CHU
04 Senior Assistant to the President .... Ms. Kristyn ELTON
106 Assoc VP Online & Distance Educ .... Ms. Carol GERING
30 Senior Assoc VP for Development .... Mr. Paul ELSTONE

University of Portland (E)

5000 N Willamette Boulevard, Portland OR 97203-5798
County: Multnomah FICE Identification: 003224
Unit ID: 209825
Telephone: (503) 943-8000 Carnegie Class: Masters/M
FAX Number: (503) 943-7491 Calendar System: Semester
URL: www.up.edu
Established: 1901 Annual Undergrad Tuition & Fees: $45,904
Enrollment: 4,396 Coed
Affiliation or Control: Independent Non-Profit IRS Status: 501(c)3
Highest Offering: Doctorate
Accreditation: NW, CAEPN, MUS, NURSE, SW, THEA

01 President .... Rev. Mark L. POORMAN, CSC
05 Provost .... Dr. Thomas G. GREENE
111 Vice Pres for Univ Relations .... Mr. Bryce STRANG
11 Vice Pres for University Operations .... Mr. James B. RAVELLI
10 Vice Pres for Financial Affairs .... Mr. Alan P. TIMMINS
32 Vice President for Student Affairs ...... Rev. John J. DONATO, CSC
43 Vice President and Gen Counsel .... Ms. Andrea M. BARTON
15 Vice President for Human Resources .... Ms. Sandy S. CHUNG
26 Vice Pres for Mktg & Communications ... Mr. Michael LEWELLEN
41 Vice President for Athletics .... Mr. Scott R. LEYKAM
07 Dean of Admissions .... Mr. Jason S. MCDONALD
30 Assoc VP for Development .... Ms. Amy EATON
21 Assoc Vice Pres & Controller .... Mr. Eric C. BARGER
20 Associate Provost .... Ms. Elise MOENTMANN
06 Registrar .... Ms. Roberta D. LINDAHL
08 Dean of Library .... Ms. Xan ARCH
36 Director Career Services .... Ms. Amy E. CAVANAUGH
37 Director Student Financial Aid .... Ms. Janet K. TURNER
27 Director Marketing and Comm ...... Ms. Rachel E. BARRY-ARQUIT
49 Dean of Arts & Sciences .... Dr. Herbert A. MEDINA
50 Dean of Business .... Dr. Robin D. ANDERSON
66 Dean of Nursing .... Dr. Casey R. SHILLAM
54 Interim Dean of Engineering .... Dr. Matthew B. KUHN
53 Dean of Education .... Dr. John L. WATZKE
23 Director University Health Center .... Ms. Carol A. DELL'OLIVER
19 Director Public Safety .... Ms. Sara WESTBROOK
29 Director Alumni Relations .... Mr. Craig A. SWINYARD
39 Director Residence Life .... Mr. Andrew WEINGARTEN
42 Director Campus Ministry .... Rev. James T. GALLAGHER, CSC
25 Associate Director of Grants .... Ms. Annie M. KAFFEN
18 Director Facilities Planning Constr .... Mr. Paul J. LUTY
18 Asst Director Physical Plant .... Mr. Joe CATES
40 Director Bookstore .... Ms. Erin L. CAVE
88 Director University Events .... Mr. Joe D. KALEEL
09 Director Institutional Research .... Ms. Elizabeth LEE
35 Director Student Activities .... Mr. Jeromy A. KOFFLER
04 Administrative Asst to President .... Ms. Kathy M. SIMEK
85 Asst Provost Intl Educ/Diver/Inclus . Mr. Eduardo R. CONTRERAS
13 Chief Info Technology Officer .... Mr. Curtis R. PEDERSON
112 Dir Gift Planning & Major Gifts .... Ms. Sharon K. HOGAN
04 Admin Asst to Office of President .... Ms. Kristin S. NIELSEN
104 Director of Studies Abroad .... Ms. Kallan PICHA
88 Special Asst to President .... Mr. Evan LEADEM

University of Western States (F)

2900 NE 132nd Avenue, Portland OR 97230-3099
County: Multnomah FICE Identification: 012309
Unit ID: 210438
Telephone: (503) 256-3180 Carnegie Class: Spec-4-yr-Other Health
FAX Number: (503) 251-5723 Calendar System: Quarter
URL: www.uws.edu
Established: 1904 Annual Undergrad Tuition & Fees: N/A
Enrollment: 1,050 Coed
Affiliation or Control: Independent Non-Profit IRS Status: 501(c)3
Highest Offering: Doctorate
Accreditation: NW, CHIRO

01 President .... Dr. Joseph BRIMHALL
03 Executive Vice President .... Dr. Rosalia MESSINA
45 Sr VP of Finance and Administration .... Mr. Glenn FORD
100 Chief of Staff .... Ms. Elena HOWELLS
10 Chief Business Officer .... Ms. Lisa LOPEZ
05 Provost/VP Academic Affairs .... Dr. Dana SIMS-BARBARICK
88 Special Assistant to the President .... Dr. Patrick BROWNE
23 Chief Clinical Excellence Officer .... Dr. Joseph PFEIFER
11 VP for Operations & Campus Planning .... Dr. Sara MATHOV
88 Associate Dean Clinical Internship .... Dr. Stanley EWALD
13 Director of Information Technology .... Vacant
84 VP of Enrollment & Student Services .... Dr. Colman JOYCE
20 Dean of Teaching and Learning .... Dr. Denise DALLMANN
32 Dean of Student Affairs .... Dr. Peter SZUCS
26 AVP University Comm & Marketing .... Ms. Megan NUGENT
15 Director Human Resources .... Ms. Kathleen CANNON
06 Registrar .... Ms. Michelle DODGE
08 Dean of Library Services .... Ms. Janet TAPPER
88 Dean College of Chiropractic .... Dr. Kathleen GALLIGAN
58 Dean College of Graduate Studies ....Dr. Dana SIMS-BARBARICK
108 Director Academic Assessment .... Dr. Cecelia MARTIN
07 Executive Director of Admissions .... Mr. Joshua CIVIELLO
18 Director Campus Facilities .... Mr. Terry COWDIN
37 Director Financial Aid .... Ms. Kim LAMBORN
31 Director Community Engagement .... Ms. Alisa FAIRWEATHER
21 Controller .... Mr. Tim GWYNN
30 Development Officer .... Ms. Amy LODHOLZ
29 Alumni Relations Manager .... Ms. Julie STUTZMAN
09 AVP Institutional Effectiveness .... Dr. Rachael PANDZIK
108 Dir Inst Appraisal and Accred .... Dr. Susan DONOFF
38 Dir Clinical Mental Hlth Counseling .... Dr. Michelle COX
04 Exec Assistant Office of the Pres .... Ms. Miranda HOLTMANN
25 Research/Inst Review Board Admin .... Ms. Leslie TAKAKI

Warner Pacific College (G)

2219 SE 68th Avenue, Portland OR 97215
County: Multnomah FICE Identification: 003225
Unit ID: 210304
Telephone: (503) 517-1020 Carnegie Class: Bac-Diverse
FAX Number: (503) 517-1350 Calendar System: Semester
URL: www.warnerpacific.edu
Established: 1937 Annual Undergrad Tuition & Fees: $18,660
Enrollment: 409 Coed
Affiliation or Control: Church Of God IRS Status: 501(c)3
Highest Offering: Master's
Accreditation: NW, SW

01 President .... Dr. Andrea P. COOK
05 Vice Pres Acad Affs/Dean of Faculty .... Dr. Reginald NICHOLS
10 VP Finance/Chief Financial Officer .... Mr. Doug WADE
111 VP Inst Advancement/External Rels .... Ms. Robin BEAVERS
32 VP Student Life/Dean of Students .... Mr. Jon SAMPSON
84 VP for Enrollment and Marketing .... Mr. Dale SEIPP
20 Assoc VP for Academic Affairs .... Dr. Lori K. JASS
37 Ex Dir Stdnt Financial Svcs/Fin Aid .... Mrs. Cindy POLLARD
07 Director of Admissions .... Mr. Dan WORKMAN
41 Athletics Director .... Mr. Michael WILSON
08 Director of Library Services .... Dr. Lishi KWASITSU
06 Registrar .... Dr. Marlo WATERS
13 Director Information Technology .... Ms. Linda RUDAWITZ
29 Dir Alumni Relations/Annual Giving .... Ms. Stephanie HARVEY
88 Dir of Contextualized Ministries .... Dr. Jess BIELMAN
42 Campus Pastor .... Ms. Michelle LANG
35 Director of Student Life .... Mr. Jared VALENTINE
18 Director of Facilities .... Mr. Dean JENKS
15 Director of Human Resources .... Mrs. Bev FITTS
09 Dir of Assessment/Inst Research .... Ms. Aundrea SNITKER
26 Dir Marketing/Communications .... Ms. Melody BURTON
38 Director Student Counseling .... Mr. Gene HALL
21 Associate Business Officer .... Vacant
36 Director of Academic Support .... Mr. Rod JOHANSON

Western Oregon University (H)

345 N Monmouth Avenue, Monmouth OR 97361-1394
County: Polk FICE Identification: 003209
Unit ID: 210429
Telephone: (503) 838-8000 Carnegie Class: Masters/L
FAX Number: (503) 838-8474 Calendar System: Quarter
URL: www.wou.edu

Established: 1856 Annual Undergrad Tuition & Fees (In-State): $10,197
Enrollment: 5,336 Coed
Affiliation or Control: State IRS Status: 501(c)3
Highest Offering: Beyond Master's But Less Than Doctorate
Accreditation: NW, CACREP, CAEPN, MUS

01 President ... Dr. Rex FULLER
03 Vice President & General Counsel ... Mr. Ryan HAGEMANN
05 Provost ... Dr. Rob WINNINGHAM
32 Vice President Student Affairs ... Dr. Gary DUKES
10 VP Finance & Administration ... Dr. Ana KARAMAN
35 Dean of Students ... Ms. Tina M. FUCHS
49 Dean Col Liberal Arts & Sciences ... Dr. Kathy CASSITY
53 Dean College of Education ... Dr. Mark GIROD
20 Interim Assoc VP Academic Programs .. Dr. Erin BAUMGARTNER
43 Deputy General Counsel ... Mr. Carson CAMPBELL
06 Registrar ... Ms. Amy CLARK
111 Executive Director of Advancement ... Ms. Erin MCDONOUGH
08 Dean Hamersly Library ... Chelle BATCHELOR
13 Director University Computing Svcs ... Mr. William KERNAN
15 Associate VP Human Resources ... Ms. Judy J. VANDERBURG
18 Director Facilities Services ... Mr. Michael SMITH
19 Director University Public Safety ... Ms. Rebecca CHILES
23 Dir Student Health/Counseling Ctr ... Ms. Beth SCROGGINS
26 Dir Public Relations/Communications ... Ms. Denise VISUANO
32 Dir Student Engagement ... Mr. Patrick MOSER
37 Director Financial Aid ... Ms. Kella HELYER
41 Athletic Director ... Mr. Curtis CAMPBELL
46 Dir of Teaching Research Institute ... Vacant
85 Dir Intl Students/Scholars Affairs ... Mr. Neng YANG
28 Dir Multicultural Student Svcs/Pgms ... Ms. Anna HERNANDEZ-HUNTER
22 Director AAEO ... Ms. Judy J. VANDERBURG
29 Dir Leadership Giving/Athletic Dev ... Mr. Michael FEULING
04 Executive Asst to President ... Mrs. LouAnn VICKERS
21 Director of Business Services ... Vacant
07 Director of Admissions ... Mr. Rob FINDTNER
09 Director of Institutional Research ... Mr. Abdus SHAHID
108 Assoc Provost Program Development ... Ms. Sue MONAHAN
86 Associate VP for Public Affairs ... Mr. Dave MCDONALD

Western Seminary (A)

5511 SE Hawthorne Boulevard, Portland OR 97215-3399
County: Multnomah FICE Identification: 007178
Unit ID: 210368
Telephone: (503) 517-1800 Carnegie Class: Spec-4-yr-Faith
FAX Number: (503) 517-1801 Calendar System: Semester
Established: 1927 Annual Graduate Tuition & Fees: N/A
Enrollment: 736 Coed
Affiliation or Control: Independent Non-Profit IRS Status: 501(c)3
Highest Offering: Doctorate; No Undergraduates
Accreditation: NW, CACREP, THEOL

01 President ... Dr. Randal R. ROBERTS
10 Administrative Vice President/CFO ... Mr. Wing-Kit CHUNG
05 VP Academic Affairs/Dean of Faculty ... Dr. Charles CONNIRY
32 VP Student Services ... Dr. Reid KISLING
88 VP Educ Innovation/Global Outreach ... Dr. Andy PETERSON
111 VP of Advancement ... Mr. Robert JONES
20 Associate Academic Dean ... Ms. Julia MAYO
06 Registrar/Dir Inst Effectiveness ... Ms. Sandra FOSTER
21 Controller ... Mr. Jonathan GIBSON
35 Dean of Students ... Mr. Andy PELOQUIN
36 Director of Student Placement ... Mr. Greg MOON
13 Director of Information Services ... Mr. Doug MABRY
37 Financial Aid Director ... Mr. Luke TODD
106 Asst Director of Distance Education ... Mr. Jon RAIBLEY
15 Assistant Human Resources Director ... Ms. Ashley MITCHELL
08 Library Director ... Mr. Matthew THIESEN
26 Director of Marketing ... Ms. Rebekah BUCHTERKIRCHEN
18 Chief Facilities/Physical Plant ... Mr. Cliff STEIN
106 Director of Distance Education ... Mr. James STEWART
07 Director of Admissions ... Ms. Allison MURPHY

Willamette University (B)

900 State Street, Salem OR 97301-3930
County: Marion FICE Identification: 003227
Unit ID: 210401
Telephone: (503) 370-6300 Carnegie Class: Bac-A&S
FAX Number: (503) 370-6148 Calendar System: Semester
URL: www.willamette.edu
Established: 1842 Annual Undergrad Tuition & Fees: $50,279
Enrollment: 2,498 Coed
Affiliation or Control: Independent Non-Profit IRS Status: 501(c)3
Highest Offering: Doctorate
Accreditation: NW, CEA, LAW, MUS, SPAA

01 President ... Dr. Stephen THORSETT
05 Sr VP for Academic/Student Affairs ... Dr. Carol LONG
10 VP for Finance and Treasurer ... Mr. Dan VALLES
111 Vice President for Advancement ... Ms. Shelby RADCLIFFE
07 VP & Dean of Admission ... Mr. Jeremy BOGAN
13 Vice President and CIO ... Ms. Jacqueline BARRETTA
32 VP Student Affairs/Dean of Students ... Dr. Edward G. WHIPPLE
49 Dean of the College Liberal Arts ... Dr. Ruth P. FEINGOLD
61 Dean of the College of Law ... Mr. Curtis BRIDGEMAN
50 Dean Graduate School Management ... Dr. Mike HAND
42 Chaplain ... Dr. Karen WOOD
23 Director of Bishop Wellness Center ... Mr. Donald A. THOMSON
88 Director Center Dispute Resolution ... Dr. Aaron SIMOWITZ
91 Director Administrative Computing .. Mr. Harvey J. PRUDHOMME
37 Director Student Financial Aid ... Ms. Patricia K. HOBAN
09 Director of Institutional Research ... Dr. Michael J. MOON
06 University Registrar ... Ms. Laura JACOBS ANDERSON
08 University Librarian ... Mr. Craig MILBERG
21 Controller ... Mr. Kenneth PIFER
40 Bookstore Manager ... Mr. Dan C. VALLES
104 Director of International Education ... Mr. Kris LOU
41 Athletic Director ... Mr. Rob PASSAGE
29 Assoc VP Alumni & Parent Relations ... Mr. Tyler REICH
112 Assoc Dir of Dev for Gift Planning ... Ms. Cathy M. GASKIN
15 VP Human Resources/Risk Management ... Ms. Shana SECHRIST
35 Assoc Dean Stdnts/Stdnt Activities ... Ms. Lisa C. HOLLIDAY
36 Director Career Development ... Ms. Mandy DEVEREUX
28 Director of Multicultural Affairs ... Mr. Gordon K. TOYAMA
18 Director Facilities Management ... Mr. Gary GRIMM
26 Chief Communications Officer ... Mr. Tim COBB
19 Director Security/Safety ... Mr. Ross STOUT
04 Executive Assistant to President ... Ms. Elizabeth GARLAND
100 Director Office of the President ... Ms. Colleen KAWAHARA
22 VP Equity/Diver/Incl/Title IX Coord ... Ms. Jade AGUILAR
39 Director of Housing & Conferences ... Mr. Scott ETHERTON
43 General Counsel ... Ms. Yvonne TAMAYO

PENNSYLVANIA

Albright College (C)

13th & Bern Streets, PO Box 15234,
Reading PA 19612-5234
County: Berks FICE Identification: 003229
Unit ID: 210571
Telephone: (610) 921-2381 Carnegie Class: Bac-A&S
FAX Number: (610) 921-7530 Calendar System: 4/1/4
URL: www.albright.edu
Established: 1856 Annual Undergrad Tuition & Fees: $45,306
Enrollment: 2,036 Coed
Affiliation or Control: United Methodist IRS Status: 501(c)3
Highest Offering: Master's
Accreditation: M

01 President ... Dr. Jacquelyn S. FETROW
05 Acting Provost/VP Academic Affairs ... Dr. Karen CAMPBELL
10 Vice President Finance & Admin ... Mr. Gregory L. FULMER
111 Vice President Advancement ... Ms. Christy AGNESE
84 Interim VP Enrollment Mgmt ... Ms. Kathy BONAVIST
32 VP Student & Campus Life/CHO ... Ms. Samantha WESNER
26 Vice President for Communications ... Ms. Jennifer STOUDT
13 VP DSI & Chief Information Officer ... Ms. Rashmi RADHAKRISHNAN
89 Assoc Dean First Yr Exp/Acad Affs ... Dr. Robert SEESENGOOD
08 Interim Director Library Services ... Ms. Sandy STUMP
102 Dir The Fund for Albright ... Ms. Caitlin KAMERER
14 Deputy Chief Information Officer ... Mr. Jason HOERR
21 Associate VP & Controller ... Mr. Rick W. MELCHER
88 Asst to Vice Pres Fin/Admin Svcs ... Mrs. Margie PRATT
37 Director of Financial Aid ... Mr. Chris HANLON
107 Interim Dir School of Prof Studies ... Ms. Tracy GRAY HAYES
35 Asst Dean of Stdnts/Dir Cmty Stand ... Ms. Amanda HANINCIK
06 Registrar ... Ms. Dawn RENTA
36 Acting Dir Career Development ... Ms. Laura KLINE
39 Director of Residential Life ... Ms. Amanda HIGGINBOTHAM
38 Director of Counseling ... Dr. Brenda J. INGRAM-WALLACE
18 Director Facilities/Svcs/Ops ... Vacant
41 Co-Athletic Director ... Mr. Richard E. FERRY
41 Co-Athletic Director ... Ms. Janice J. LUCK
19 Director of Public Safety ... Mr. Michael L. GROSS
40 Book Store Manager ... Ms. Heather SHERMAN
42 Interim Chaplain ... Rev. Melvin SENSENIG
42 Interim Chaplain ... Rev. Ibrahim BANGURA
15 Director of Human Resources ... Ms. Kimberly A. HUBRIC
85 Dir OSIL Coord Multicultural ... Ms. Tiffany CLAYTON
09 Director of Institutional Research ... Mr. Jack LAFAYETTE
25 Dir of Grants & Sponsored Programs ... Vacant
92 Director Honors Program ... Dr. Julia F. HEBERLE
07 Director of Admission ... Ms. Jennifer WILLIAMSON
88 Director of Conferences ... Ms. Lois A. KUBINAK
100 Chief of Staff ... Ms. Kathy L. CAFONCELLI
121 Associate Dean Academic Success ... Ms. Julia MATTHEWS
88 Director of Schumo Center ... Ms. Alison BURKE
22 Director of Student Accessibility ... Vacant
109 General Manager Dining Services ... Mr. Heath MCCORMICK
106 Dir Digital Learning & Innovation ... Ms. Michele MISLEVY
112 Sr Dir Prospect Research & Mgmt ... Mrs. Jessica MORRIS
108 Assessment Coordinator ... Mrs. Maria QUEERY

Allegheny College (D)

520 N Main Street, Meadville PA 16335-3902
County: Crawford FICE Identification: 003230
Unit ID: 210669
Telephone: (814) 332-3100 Carnegie Class: Bac-A&S
FAX Number: (814) 332-2796 Calendar System: Semester
URL: www.allegheny.edu
Established: 1815 Annual Undergrad Tuition & Fees: $47,540
Enrollment: 1,802 Coed
Affiliation or Control: United Methodist IRS Status: 501(c)3
Highest Offering: Baccalaureate
Accreditation: M

01 President ... Dr. Hilary L. LINK
03 Exec Vice President and COO ... Ms. Eileen E. PETULA
30 SVP Development & Alumni Affairs ... Ms. Marjorie S. KLEIN
84 Senior VP for Enrollment ... Mr. Cornell LESANE, II
32 VP Student Life/Dean of Students ... Ms. April THOMPSON
04 Assistant to the President ... Ms. Pamela S. HIGHAM
110 AVP Development & Alumni Affairs ... Mr. Philip R. FOXMAN
26 Vice President College Relations ... Ms. Susan SALTON
05 Provost & Dean of the College ... Dr. Ronald B. COLE
28 Assoc Dean Students Cmty/Involvemnt ... Mr. Justin ADKINS
20 Associate Provost ... Dr. Terry BENSEL
37 Senior Assoc Dir Financial Aid ... Ms. Natasha ECKART
108 VP for Info Svcs & Assessment ... Dr. Richard A. HOLMGREN
06 Registrar ... Dr. Ian BINNINGTON
08 Director of the Library ... Dr. Richard A. HOLMGREN
15 Director of Human Resources ... Ms. Jennifer MANGUS
19 Interim Director of Public Safety ... Mr. Doug MERCHBAKER
44 Director of Annual Giving ... Ms. Sara PINEO
18 Director Physical Plant ... Vacant
13 Director of Enterprise Services ... Mr. Jason M. RAMSEY
41 Director of Athletics ... Mr. William ROSS
31 Director of Civic Engagement ... Dr. David RONCOLATO
38 Director of Counseling Center ... Dr. Trae YECKLEY
09 Director of Institutional Research ... Vacant
36 Director Career Education ... Mr. James FITCH
88 Associate Dean for Wellness Educ ... Ms. Gretchen BECK
10 CFO & Treasurer ... Ms. Linda S. WETSELL
42 Chaplain ... Dr. Jane Ellen NICKELL
88 Dir Center Political Participation ... Dr. Brian HARWARD
22 Director of Disability Services ... Mr. John J. MANGINE
57 Director of Art & Publications ... Ms. Penny M. DREXEL
27 Assoc Dir Marketing & Communication ... Mr. Jason ANDRACKI
40 Manager of Bookstore ... Vacant
96 Purchasing & Student Services Coord ... Ms. Kathleen M. CONAWAY

Allegany College of Maryland Bedford County Campus (E)

18 North River Lane, Everett PA 15537-1410
Telephone: (814) 652-9528 Identification: 770124
Accreditation: &M

† Branch campus of Allegany College of Maryland, Cumberland, MD

Alvernia University (F)

400 Saint Bernardine Street, Reading PA 19607-1799
County: Berks FICE Identification: 003233
Unit ID: 210775
Telephone: (610) 796-8200 Carnegie Class: Masters/M
FAX Number: (610) 777-6632 Calendar System: Semester
URL: www.alvernia.edu
Established: 1958 Annual Undergrad Tuition & Fees: $34,900
Enrollment: 2,838 Coed
Affiliation or Control: Roman Catholic IRS Status: 501(c)3
Highest Offering: Doctorate
Accreditation: M, ACBSP, CAATE, CACREP, NURSE, OT, #PTA, SW

01 President ... Dr. John R. LOYACK
05 Provost ... Dr. Glynis FITZGERALD
10 VP for Finance & Administration ... Mr. Douglas F. SMITH
111 Vice Pres for Advancement ... Mr. Tony DEMARCO
32 Vice Pres Univ Life/Dean of Stdnts ... Vacant
84 Vice Pres for Enrollment Management ... Dr. John R. MCCLOSKEY, JR.
42 Asst to the President for Mission ... Ms. Julianne WALLACE
26 VP Mktg & Comms/Chief PR Ofcr ... Dr. Deidra HILL
35 Director of Student Activities ... Ms. Abby SWATCHICK
39 Director Residence Life ... Ms. Karolina DREHER
06 Registrar ... Ms. Beki STEIN
21 Controller ... Mr. Larry SHAUB
110 Assoc VP of Advancement ... Mr. Thomas MINICK
92 Director Honors Program ... Dr. Victoria WILLIAMS
41 Director Athletics & Recreation ... Mr. Bill STILES
07 Dean of UG Admissions ... Ms. Rebecca FINNKENNEY
09 Director of Institutional Research ... Dr. Evelina PANAYOTOVA
15 Director Human Resources ... Ms. Laurel CLINE
18 Dir of Facilities Planning ... Mr. David REPPERT
36 Director of Career Services ... Mrs. Megan ADUKAITIS
37 Dir of Student Financial Planning ... Ms. Christine SAADI
96 Procurement Manager ... Ms. Ann NAWROCKI
28 Dir of Multicultural Initiatives ... Ms. Wanda COPELAND
113 Director of Student Billing ... Ms. Gwynne KOLODZIEJSKI
31 Dir Ctr for Community Engagement ... Mr. Jay WORRALL
58 Dean of Graduate & Cont Studies ... Ms. Daria LATORRE
49 Dean of Arts & Sciences ... Dr. Beth ROTH
107 Dean of Professional Programs ... Ms. Karen S. THACKER
04 Assistant to the President ... Ms. Karen SCHRODER
13 CIO ... Mr. Carl MARKS
19 Director of Public Safety ... Mr. Edward HEIM
08 Director of Library ... Ms. Sharon NEAL
25 Director of Grants ... Ms. Mary CHOWN

The American College of Financial Services (G)

630 Allendale Rd, King of Prussia PA 19406
County: Montgomery FICE Identification: 033173
Unit ID: 210809
Telephone: (610) 526-1000 Carnegie Class: Spec-4-yr-Bus
FAX Number: (610) 526-1310 Calendar System: Other
URL: www.theamericancollege.edu
Established: 1927 Annual Undergrad Tuition & Fees: N/A
Enrollment: 8,864 Coed
Affiliation or Control: Independent Non-Profit IRS Status: 501(c)3

Highest Offering: Doctorate
Accreditation: M

01 President & CEO .... Mr. George NICHOLS, III
05 Executive Vice President & Provost .... Dr. Chad PATRIZI
20 Dean of Academics .... Ms. Sophia DUFFY
111 VP Advancement/Alumni Rel .... Mr. Stephen J. GROURKE
15 VP Admin & Chief HR Officer .... Ms. Deborah GLENN
45 VP Organizational Effectiveness .... Mr. Bryan JOHNSON
32 VP Student Experience .... Mr. Brian KAIN
04 Assistant to the President .... Ms. Jean C. MEYER
117 Chief Financial and Risk Officer .... Mr. Gary TANG
26 Chief Marketing Officer .... Mr. James KATSAOUNIS
13 Chief Technology Officer .... Mr. Ed M. MCEVOY
108 AVP Institutional Assessment .... Mr. Thomas ARMINGTON
06 Registrar .... Ms. Antoinette CHRISTALDI
08 Head of Library Services .... Mr. John H. WHITHAM
88 Director Exam Systems .... Ms. Diane M. HAMMONDS
88 Chief Product & Innovation Officer .... Mr. David EURICH

Arcadia University (A)

450 S Easton Road, Glenside PA 19038-3295
County: Montgomery   FICE Identification: 003235
Unit ID: 211088
Telephone: (215) 572-2900   Carnegie Class: Masters/L
FAX Number: (215) 572-0240   Calendar System: Semester
URL: www.arcadia.edu
Established: 1853   Annual Undergrad Tuition & Fees: $43,580
Enrollment: 3,811   Coed
Affiliation or Control: Independent Non-Profit   IRS Status: 501(c)3
Highest Offering: Doctorate
Accreditation: M, ACBSP, ARCPA, ART, FEPAC, PH, PTA

01 President .... Dr. Ajay NAIR
05 Provost & VP Academic Affairs .... Dr. Jeff RUTENBECK
84 VP Enrollment Management .... Mr. Mark LAPREZIOSA
10 Interim VP Finance & Treasurer .... Ms. Julie ROSNER-LENGELE
43 General Counsel .... Ms. Margaret CALLAHAN
13 Interim Chief Information Officer .... Ms. Leslie MARGOLIS
111 VP University Advancement .... Ms. Brigette BRYANT
32 Dean of Students .... Mr. Andrew GORETSKY
18 Assoc VP Facilities/Capital Plng .... Mr. Thomas J. MACCHI
88 VP/Exec Dir Col of Global Studies .... Ms. Lorna STERN
21 Assoc VP Finance & COO TCGS .... Ms. Colleen BURKE
15 Interim Assoc VP Human Resources .... Mr. Brian FRENCH
20 Deputy Provost .... Dr. Thomas EGAN
06 Registrar .... Mr. William ELNICK
06 Associate Registrar .... Mrs. Nicole M. ZUCKER
49 Dean College Arts & Sciences .... Dr. Rebecca KOHN
76 Dean College of Health Sciences .... Dr. Rebecca L. CRAIK
51 Coord Office of Continuing Studies .... Ms. Kathryn PHILLIPS
50 Dean School of Global Business .... Mr. Thomas M. BRINKER, JR.
58 Dean Graduate & Undergrad Studies .... Dr. Nancy ROSOFF
82 Dean International Affairs .... Dr. Warren HAFFAR
53 Interim Dean of Education .... Dr. John GROVES
28 Assoc Dean Institutional Diversity .... Ms. Judith DALTON
35 Dean of Students .... Dr. Andrew GORETZKY
20 Assoc Dean Undergraduate Studies .... Mr. Bruce KELLER
88 Asst Dean Graduate Studies .... Ms. Mary Kate MCNULTY
109 Director Auxiliary Services .... Ms. Mimi BASSETTI
29 Director Alumni Relations .... Mr. Jeffery SPENCE
88 Director University Art Gallery .... Mr. Richard TORCHIA
41 Director Athletics & Recreation .... Mr. Brian GRANATA
88 Director Campus Visits and EM .... Ms. Kathleen BEARDSLEY
36 Director Career Education .... Ms. Marissa DEITCH
38 Director Counseling Services .... Ms. Amy HENNING
37 Exec Dir Financial Aid & Enroll Mgt .... Ms. Holly R. KIRKPATRICK
25 Director Sponsored Research .... Ms. Nataliia SHABLIA
88 Director of Academic Administration .... Ms. Kristin O. JUDGE
96 Purchasing Coordinator .... Ms. Jennifer SUDLOW
88 Payroll Manager .... Ms. Sharon ANTHONY
19 Interim Director of Public Safety .... Ms. Eileen GILLEECCE
88 Title IX Coordinator .... Ms. Nora NELLE
101 Executive Dir Board of Trustees .... Mr. Kevin MULDOON
88 Assoc Dean International Affairs .... Ms. Janice FINN
45 Director of Strategic Initiatives .... Mr. Joseph S. SUN
07 Director of Admissions .... Ms. Collene PERNICELLO
26 Chief Public Relations/Marketing .... Ms. Laura BALDWIN

Berks Technical Institute (B)

2205 Ridgewood Road, Wyomissing PA 19610-1168
County: Berks   FICE Identification: 022539
Unit ID: 213534
Telephone: (610) 372-1722   Carnegie Class: Assoc/HVT-Mix Trad/Non
FAX Number: (610) 376-4684   Calendar System: Other
URL: www.berks.edu
Established: 1974   Annual Undergrad Tuition & Fees: N/A
Enrollment: 724   Coed
Affiliation or Control: Proprietary   IRS Status: Proprietary
Highest Offering: Associate Degree
Accreditation: ACCSC, MAC

01 Campus Director .... Ms. Elizabeth VLASTOS
05 Dean .... Mr. James REECE

Bidwell Training Center (C)

1815 Metropolitan Street, Pittsburgh PA 15233-2200
County: Allegheny   FICE Identification: 031015
Unit ID: 211149
Telephone: (412) 323-4000   Carnegie Class: Spec 2-yr-Tech
FAX Number: (412) 325-7378   Calendar System: Quarter
URL: bidwelltraining.edu
Established: 1968   Annual Undergrad Tuition & Fees: N/A
Enrollment: 141   Coed
Affiliation or Control: Independent Non-Profit   IRS Status: 501(c)3
Highest Offering: Associate Degree
Accreditation: ACCSC, MAC

01 Executive Director .... Dr. Kimberly RASSAU
11 Senior Director/Operations .... Mr. Ken HUSELTON
05 Program Coordinator .... Dr. Susan COOPER

Bryn Athyn College of the New Church (D)

PO Box 717, Bryn Athyn PA 19009-0717
County: Montgomery   FICE Identification: 003228
Unit ID: 210492
Telephone: (267) 502-2400   Carnegie Class: Bac-A&S
FAX Number: (215) 938-2658   Calendar System: Trimester
URL: www.brynathyn.edu
Established: 1876   Annual Undergrad Tuition & Fees: $22,860
Enrollment: 335   Coed
Affiliation or Control: Church of New Jerusalem   IRS Status: 501(c)3
Highest Offering: Master's
Accreditation: M

01 President .... Mr. Brian BLAIR
10 Chief Finance Officer .... Mr. Daniel T. ALLEN
05 Dean of Academic Affairs .... Dr. Wendy CLOSTERMAN
73 Dean of Theological School .... Rev. Andrew M T. DIBB
32 Dean of Student Affairs .... Dr. Suzanne NELSON
07 Asst VP of Admissions/Fin Aid .... Mr. Brian KEISTER
08 Director of Swedenborg Library .... Mrs. Carol TRAVENY
41 Director of Athletics .... Mr. David LEACH
13 Chief Information Officer .... Ms. Lelia HOWARD
15 Director of Human Resources .... Ms. Renee ROSENFELD
19 Director of Public Safety .... Mr. James KALAVIK
42 Chaplain .... Rev. Grant SCHNARR
04 Executive Asst to President .... Ms. Melodie GREER
14 Director Information Technology .... Mr. Richard DAUM

Bryn Mawr College (E)

101 N Merion Avenue, Bryn Mawr PA 19010-2899
County: Montgomery   FICE Identification: 003237
Unit ID: 211273
Telephone: (610) 526-5000   Carnegie Class: Bac-A&S
FAX Number: (610) 526-7450   Calendar System: Semester
URL: www.brynmawr.edu
Established: 1885   Annual Undergrad Tuition & Fees: $52,360
Enrollment: 1,640   Female
Affiliation or Control: Independent Non-Profit   IRS Status: 501(c)3
Highest Offering: Doctorate
Accreditation: M, SW

01 President .... Kimberly CASSIDY
05 Provost .... Mary J. OSIRIM
49 Dean Undergraduate College .... Jennifer WALTERS
10 Chief Financial Officer .... Kari FAZIO
30 Chief Development Officer .... Bob MILLER
84 Chief Enrollment Officer .... Cheryl HORSEY
26 Chief Communications Officer .... Jesse GALE
08 Director Libraries/Chief Info Ofcr .... Gina SIESING
58 Dean of Graduate Studies .... Sharon BURGMAYER
28 Asst Dean Col of Access/Cmty Devel .... Vanessa CHRISTMAN
06 Registrar .... Kirsten O'BEIRNE
37 Director of Financial Aid .... Susan CHADWICK
19 Director of Public Safety .... Tom KING
41 Dir Athletics & Physical Education .... Kathleen TIERNEY
21 Controller .... Tijana STEFANOVIC
09 Director of Institutional Research .... Richard BARRY
18 Director of Facilities .... Nina BISBEE
07 Director of Admissions .... Marissa TURCHI
15 Director of Human Resources .... Martin MASTASCUSA
29 Director of Alumnae Relations .... Millie BOND
101 Secretary of the Institution/Board .... Ruth LINDEBORG

Bucknell University (F)

1 Dent Drive, Lewisburg PA 17837
County: Union   FICE Identification: 003238
Unit ID: 211291
Telephone: (570) 577-2000   Carnegie Class: Bac-A&S
FAX Number: (570) 577-3760   Calendar System: Semester
URL: www.bucknell.edu
Established: 1846   Annual Undergrad Tuition & Fees: $56,092
Enrollment: 3,678   Coed
Affiliation or Control: Independent Non-Profit   IRS Status: 501(c)3
Highest Offering: Master's
Accreditation: M, MUS

01 President .... Dr. John C. BRAVMAN
100 Chief of Staff .... Vacant
04 Executive Director President Office .... Ms. Carol M. KENNEDY
101 University Secretary .... Ms. Carol M. KENNEDY
41 Director Athletics & Recreation .... Mr. Jermaine M. TRUAX
05 Provost .... Dr. Elisabeth MERMANN-JOZWIAK
20 Vice Provost .... Dr. Robert MIDKIFF
20 Assoc Provost .... Dr. Karen M. MORIN
49 Dean of Arts & Sciences .... Dr. Karl VOSS
50 Dean Freemen College of Management .... Dr. Raquel M. ALEXANDER
54 Dean of Engineering .... Dr. Patrick MATHER
92 Honors Council Chair .... Dr. Robert W. JACOB
88 Dir Provost Business Operations .... Ms. Pamela A. BENFER
88 Dir Small Business Development Ctr .... Mr. Steven V. STUMBRIS
88 Exec Dir Weis Center Perform Arts .... Ms. Kathryn L. MAGUET
111 VP University Advancement .... Dr. Scott G. ROSEVEAR
30 Assoc VP University Advancement .... Mr. Joshua L. GRILL
30 Assoc VP University Advancement .... Ms. Kathleen GRAHAM
110 Executive Dir Leadership Gifts .... Mr. Mark SHARER
88 Senior Development Adviser .... Mr. Mark ELLIOTT
110 Exec Dir Adv Strategy Integration .... Ms. Lucille TARIN
110 Dir Parents Fund & Family Programs .... Ms. Ann L. DISTEFANO
110 Sr Adviser University Advancement .... Mr. Patrick FLANNERY
110 Dir Prospect Research & Mgmt .... Ms. Cynthia D. JANESCH
110 Dir Adv Marketing/Research/Strategy .... Ms. Jamie JORDAN
110 Dir Stewardship & Donor Relations .... Ms. Rhonda K. MILLER
29 Senior Associate Director .... Ms. Kristin STETLER
44 Dir Annual Fund Individual Giving .... Ms. Abbey SCHECKTER
112 Director of Gift Planning .... Ms. Melissa M. DIEHL
102 Dir Corporate & Foundation Rels .... Mr. Edmond CLARKE
26 Interim Chief Communication Officer .... Ms. Heather JOHNS
27 Director of Media Relations .... Mr. Mike FERLAZZO
88 Senior Director Creative Services .... Ms. Lisa D. SCOTT
10 VP Finance & Administration .... Mr. David J. SURGALA
21 Assoc VP/Treasurer and Controller .... Ms. Elizabeth D. STEWART
45 Director Business Planning .... Vacant
115 Dir of Investments .... Mr. John R. LUTHI
25 Executive Dir Sponsored Projects .... Mr. Robert GUTIERREZ
88 Assoc Controller Financial Services .... Mr. Ronald E. STAUFFER, II
109 Director of Business Services .... Ms. Lori J. WILSON
114 Dir of Budget & Financial Modeling .... Ms. Andrea FEATHERSTONE
88 Asst Controller .... Ms. Michelle M. HENDRICKS
88 Assoc Controller Accounting Svcs .... Mr. William D. GEORGE
88 Dir Financial Information Systems .... Ms. Pamela K. NOONE
88 Director of Disbursement Services .... Mr. Jody D. GRAYBILL
113 Bursar Services Manager .... Ms. Carol YOST
96 Director of Procurement Services .... Vacant
88 Exec Dir Events Management Office .... Ms. Dana M. MIMS
116 Director of Internal Audit .... Mr. Robert L. HOSTER
117 Dir Risk Management & Insurance .... Mr. Clint D. WEVODAU
15 VP Human Resources .... Mr. Pierre D. JOANIS
16 Dir of Recruitment & Compensation .... Ms. Marcia J. COONEY
118 Director of HRIS & Benefits .... Ms. Cindy L. BILGER
09 Asst Prov Inst Research/Assessment .... Mr. Kevork T. HORISSIAN
28 Interim Assoc Provost Diversity .... Dr. Thelathia N. YOUNG
43 General Counsel .... Vacant
19 Chief of Public Safety .... Mr. Stephen J. BARILAR
18 AVP Facilities & Sustainability .... Mr. Kenneth OGAWA
88 Dir of Construction & Design .... Ms. Kathy MONTEIRO
13 VP Library & Information Technology .... Mr. Param S. BEDI
14 Exec Dir Enterprise Technologies .... Mr. Kevin WILLEY
105 Director of Web Services .... Vacant
119 Chief Info Sec Officer .... Vacant
32 Dean of Students .... Ms. Amy A. BADAL
35 Associate Dean of Students .... Mr. Jeffrey VAN LONE
35 Associate Dean of Students .... Ms. Denelle BROWN
35 Associate Dean of Students .... Ms. Kari M. CONRAD
84 VP Enrollment Management .... Mr. William T. CONLEY
07 Dean of Admissions .... Mr. Kevin MATHES
37 Director Financial Aid .... Ms. Andrea C. LEITHNER STAUFFER
39 Dir of Housing Services .... Mr. Stephen J. APANEL
88 Dir Card Svcs & Student Transit .... Mr. Glenn R. FISHER
36 Exec Director Career Services .... Ms. Pamela G. KEISER
38 Dir Counseling & Stdnt Dev Ctr .... Dr. Kelly KETTLEWELL
22 Dir of Disability Services .... Ms. Heather L. FOWLER
42 University Chaplain .... Rev. Kurt D. NELSON
85 Dir International Student Services .... Ms. Jennifer E. FIGUEROA
104 Dir Global & Off-Campus Education .... Mr. Stephen K. APPIAH-PADI
88 Title IX Coord Clery Act Comp .... Ms. Kathleen GRIMES
88 Dir of Civic Engagement .... Vacant
88 Director Women's Resource Center .... Ms. Kelsey HICKS
88 Director Office of LGBTQ Resources .... Mr. William K. MCCOY
88 Director of Writing Center .... Ms. Deirdre M. O'CONNOR

Bucks County Community College (G)

275 Swamp Road, Newtown PA 18940-4106
County: Bucks   FICE Identification: 003239
Unit ID: 211307
Telephone: (215) 968-8000   Carnegie Class: Assoc/HT-Mix Trad/Non
FAX Number: (215) 968-8129   Calendar System: Semester
URL: www.bucks.edu
Established: 1964   Annual Undergrad Tuition & Fees (In-District): $4,513
Enrollment: 7,784   Coed
Affiliation or Control: Local   IRS Status: 501(c)3
Highest Offering: Associate Degree
Accreditation: M, ACBSP, ADNUR, ART, MLTAD, MUS, RAD

01 President .... Dr. Stephanie SHANBLATT
05 Provost .... Ms. Lisa ANGELO
10 VP for Administrative Affairs & CFO .... Mr. Dennis W. MATTHEWS
111 Vice Pres Advancement .... Dr. Tobias BRUHN
20 Assoc Provost Academic Affairs .... Dr. Kelly KELLEWAY
14 Assoc VP Tech & Innovation/CIO .... Mr. Brant STEEN
21 Controller .... Mr. David JERDAN
114 Exec Dir Budget & Internal Audit .... Ms. Loren HERBERT
09 Exec Dir Inst Research & Assessment .... Vacant
103 Exec Dir Workforce Development .... Ms. Susan HERRING
18 Exec Director Physical Plant .... Mr. Martin SNYDER

26 Exec Dir Marketing/Public Relations ... Ms. Megan SMITH
04 Exec Assistant to President & Board ... Ms. Kathleen C. FEDORKO
15 Exec Director Human Resources ... Dr. Patricia BRINING
96 Director of Purchasing ... Mr. James F. LOUGHERY
106 Associate Dean Bucks Online ... Ms. Georglyn L. DAVIDSON
37 Director Financial Aid ... Ms. Donna M. WILKOSKI
36 Director Career Services ... Ms. Sharon STEPHENS
32 Director Student Life & Athletics ... Mr. Matt J. CIPRIANO
19 Exec Dir Security & Safety ... Mr. Dennis MCCAULEY
08 Director Library Services ... Ms. Monica KUNA
07 Director of Admissions ... Ms. Marlene T. BARLOW
06 Registrar ... Ms. Rebecca BREUNINGER
29 Alumni Relations Manager ... Ms. Christina MCGINLEY
68 Dean Kinesiology & Sport Studies ... Dr. Priscilla RICE
81 Dean STEM ... Dr. Shawn WILD
50 Dean Business Studies ... Ms. Tracy TIMBY
57 Dean Arts ... Mr. John MATHEWS
83 Dean Social & Behavioral Sci ... Dr. Lynn DELLAPIETRA
76 Dean Health Sciences ... Dr. Constance CORRIGAN
88 Dean Lang & Literature ... Ms. Nicole TRACEY
102 Dir Foundation/Alumni ... Ms. Jennifer SALISBURY
88 Dean Learning Resources ... Mr. Bill HEMMIG

Butler County Community College (A)

107 College Drive, Butler PA 16002
County: Butler FICE Identification: 003240
Unit ID: 211343
Telephone: (724) 287-8711 Carnegie Class: Assoc/MT-VT-High Trad
FAX Number: (724) 285-6047 Calendar System: Semester
URL: www.bc3.edu
Established: 1965 Annual Undergrad Tuition & Fees (In-District): $4,950
Enrollment: 3,338 Coed
Affiliation or Control: Local IRS Status: 501(c)3
Highest Offering: Associate Degree
Accreditation: M, ACBSP, ADNUR, MAC, PTAA

01 President ... Dr. Nicholas C. NEUPAUER
05 VP for Academic Affairs ... Dr. Belinda M. RICHARDSON
11 VP for Administration & Finance ... Mr. James A. HRABOSKY
32 VP Student Affairs/Enrollment Mgt ... Dr. G. Case WILLOUGHBY
10 Chief Business Officer ... Mr. Wm. Jake FRIEL
50 Interim Dean of Business ... Ms. Sherri MACK
83 Dean Social Science/Humanities ... Mr. Stephen M. JOSEPH
66 Dean of Nursing/Allied Health ... Ms. Patricia T. ANNEAR
72 Dean of Nat Science/Tech ... Mr. Matt KOVAC
106 Dean of Education Technology ... Ms. Ann MCCANDLESS
08 Dean of Library Services ... Mr. Martin J. MILLER
35 Dean of Students ... Dr. Joshua NOVAK
103 Dean of Workforce Development ... Ms. Lisa M. CAMPBELL
15 Int Exec Director Human Resources ... Ms. Christina M. FLEEGER
26 Exec Director of Comm & Marketing .. Ms. Jessica M. MATONAK
51 Director of Lifelong Learning ... Mr. Paul M. LUCAS
07 Dean of Admissions ... Ms. Amy DOUBLE PIGNATORE
13 Director of Information Technology ... Vacant
32 Director of Student Life ... Mr. Rob A. SNYDER
09 Dean of Institutional Research ... Ms. Sharla M. ANKE
18 Exec Director of Operations ... Mr. Brian R. OPITZ
12 Director of BC3 @ Armstrong ... Ms. Karen ZAPP
12 Director of BC3 @ Lawrence Crossing ... Mr. Sean M. CARROLL
12 Director of BC3 @ Cranberry ... Ms. Lauren A. BUCHANAN
12 Director of BC3 @ LindenPointe ... Mr. John P. SUESSER
12 Director of BC3 @ Brockway ... Ms. Jill MARTIN-REND
37 Director of Financial Aid ... Ms. Julianne E. LOUTTIT
41 Athletic Director ... Mr. Rob A. SNYDER
75 Coord of Business/Industry Trng ... Ms. Kathy STROBEL
102 Exec Director of the Foundation ... Ms. Ruth PURCELL
19 Director of Campus Police/Security ... Mr. K. Scott RICHARDSON
88 Director of Cultural Center ... Mr. Lawrence E. STOCK
88 Director of Children's Center ... Ms. Judith A. ZUZACK
88 Associate Director Admissions ... Ms. Morgan M. RIZZARDI
40 Bookstore Manager ... Mr. Richard A. BENKO
96 College Services/Purchasing Agent ... Ms. Nicole BARNES
105 Web Manager ... Mr. R. Dennis BIRKES
30 Assoc Dir of the Foundation ... Ms. Michelle E. JAMIESON
04 Administrative Asst to President ... Ms. Juliann SHEPTAK
22 Dir Affirmative Action/EEO ... Ms. Christina M. FLEEGER
06 Registrar ... Ms. Amy DOUBLE PIGNATORE
29 Director Alumni Affairs ... Ms. Michelle E. JAMIESOON

Byzantine Catholic Seminary of Ss. Cyril and Methodius (B)

3605 Perrysville Avenue, Pittsburgh PA 15214-2229
County: Allegheny FICE Identification: 041180
Unit ID: 444103
Telephone: (412) 321-8383 Carnegie Class: Spec-4-yr-Faith
FAX Number: (412) 321-9936 Calendar System: Semester
URL: www.bcs.edu
Established: 1950 Annual Graduate Tuition & Fees: N/A
Enrollment: 24 Coed
Affiliation or Control: Other IRS Status: 501(c)3
Highest Offering: Master's; No Undergraduates
Accreditation: THEOL

01 Rector ... V.Rev. Robert M. PIPTA
32 Director of Human Formation ... Rev. Joel BARSTAD
05 Academic Dean ... Rev. Christiaan KAPPES
06 Registrar/Dir of Seminary Opers ... Ms. Carol PRYZBOROKI
10 Chief Financial Officer ... Dcn. Robert SHALHOUB

Cabrini University (C)

610 King of Prussia Road, Radnor PA 19087-3698
County: Delaware FICE Identification: 003241
Unit ID: 211352
Telephone: (610) 902-8200 Carnegie Class: Masters/L
FAX Number: (610) 902-8204 Calendar System: Semester
URL: www.cabrini.edu
Established: 1957 Annual Undergrad Tuition & Fees: $31,920
Enrollment: 2,305 Coed
Affiliation or Control: Roman Catholic IRS Status: 501(c)3
Highest Offering: Doctorate
Accreditation: M, SW

01 President ... Dr. Donald TAYLOR
05 Provost/VP Academic Affairs ... Dr. Chioma UGOCHUKWU
10 VP Finance & Treasurer ... Mr. Eric OLSON
111 VP Institutional Advancement ... Mr. Stephen HIGHSMITH
32 VP of Student Life ... Dr. Christine LYSIONEK
84 Interim VP of Enrollment Management ... Ms. Barbara ELLIOTT
26 Exec Dir Marketing & Communication ... Ms. Lori IANNELLA
35 Dean of Students ... Dr. Stephen RUPPRECHT
50 Dean School Bus/Arts & Media ... Dr. Tim MANTZ
53 Dean School of Education ... Dr. Beverly BRYDE
76 Dean Sch Nat Sciences & Allied Hlth ... Dr. Richard THOMPSON
04 Executive Asst to the President ... Ms. Joan KLECKNER
06 Registrar ... Mr. Gerard DONAHUE
08 Library Director ... Ms. Anne SCHWELM
91 Director Administrative Computing ... Mr. Rob GETZ
19 Director Public Safety ... Mr. Joseph FUSCO
18 Director of Facilities ... Ms. Dawn BARNETT
29 Dir Alumni Engagement/Annual Giving ... Ms. Jackie MARCIANO
37 Director of Financial Aid ... Ms. Susan WENDLING
36 Dir of Career & Professional Dev ... Ms. Erin GABRIELE
41 Director of Athletics & Recreation ... Mr. Bradley KOCH
15 Director Human Resources ... Ms. Denise JOHNSTON
21 Controller ... Ms. Diane SCUTTI
24 Coord of Education Resources Center ... Ms. Mary BUDZILOWICZ
40 Bookstore Manager ... Mr. Bill BRIDDES
105 Director of Content Marketing ... Ms. Linda BOYK
09 Asst Provost Instl Effectiveness ... Dr. Maliha ZAMAN
35 Exec Dir Student Engage/Leadership ... Ms. Anne FILIPPONE
92 Director of the Honors Program ... Dr. Jennifer BULCOCK
28 Dir Student Diversity Initiatives ... Mr. Jose RODRIGUEZ
38 Director Counseling/Psych Service ... Dr. Sara MAGGITTI
39 Director of Residence Life ... Mr. Brett BUCKRIDGE
07 Director UG Admissions ... Vacant
101 Exec Governance Admin Sec Board ... Mrs. Nancy OLLINGER
102 Dir Grants & Foundation Relations ... Vacant
88 Creative Director ... Mr. Kevin HAUGH
86 Chief of Staff/VP External Rels ... Mr. Brian EURY
96 Procurement Manager ... Ms. Elizabeth KANARAS

Cairn University (D)

200 Manor Avenue, Langhorne Manor PA 19047-2990
County: Bucks FICE Identification: 003351
Unit ID: 215114
Telephone: (215) 752-5800 Carnegie Class: Masters/S
FAX Number: (215) 702-4341 Calendar System: Semester
URL: www.cairn.edu
Established: 1913 Annual Undergrad Tuition & Fees: $27,279
Enrollment: 1,060 Coed
Affiliation or Control: Independent Non-Profit IRS Status: 501(c)3
Highest Offering: Master's
Accreditation: M, BI, IACBE, MUS, SW

01 President ... Dr. Todd J. WILLIAMS
05 Sr VP & Provost ... Dr. Jason VANBILLIARD
32 Sr VP Student Affairs & Admin ... Mr. J. Scott CAWOOD
111 Sr VP Advancement & Communications ... Mr. Paul NEAL
10 Sr VP Finance ... Mr. Yunn KANG
15 VP Human Resources ... Ms. Mary BOYER
88 Special Assistant to President ... Dr. Timothy HUI
07 Assistant VP Admissions ... Mr. Thomas SHERF
06 Registrar ... Dr. Steven SCHLENKER
35 Dean Student Life ... Mr. Adam PORCELLA
73 Dean School of Divinity ... Dr. Jonathan L. MASTER
49 Dean School of Liberal Arts & Sci ... Dr. Brenda MELLON
50 Dean School of Business ... Mr. Evan CURRY
53 Dean School of Education ... Dr. Dianne ALEXANDER
64 Dean School of Music ... Dr. Benjamin HARDING
70 Dean School of Social Work ... Dr. Lloyd GESTOSO
88 Director Center Urban Engagement ... Dr. Coz L. CROSSCOMBE
108 Asst Prov Assessment/Accreditation ... Ms. Rebecca LIPPERT
29 Vice President Alumni/Cmty Affairs ... Mr. Nathan WAMBOLD
30 Vice President Philanthropy ... Ms. Tammy BUTLER
41 Director Athletics ... Mr. Jay BUTLER
18 Director Campus Services ... Mr. Andrew NORTON
36 Director Career Center ... Ms. Teri T. CANTANIO
39 Director Community Life ... Mr. Russell SCHNEIDER
38 Director Counseling Services ... Dr. Jeffrey S. BLACK
37 Director Financial Aid ... Mr. Stephen CASSEL
23 Director Health Services ... Ms. Alison KIKENDALL
08 Director Library ... Ms. Stephanie KACELI
106 Dir Educ Tech & Distance Learning ... Mr. Sali KACELI
09 Director Research & Analytics ... Ms. Cheryl STUM
19 Director Safety & Security ... Mr. Chris LLOYD
13 Director Tech Svcs/Data Governance ... Mr. David HUI
14 Director information Systems ... Mr. Vimul ROS
21 Director Business Services ... Mr. Andrew HUI
04 Administrative Asst to President ... Ms. Lori MILLER
26 Director Marketing ... Mr. John MULVANEY

Carlow University (E)

3333 Fifth Avenue, Pittsburgh PA 15213-3165
County: Allegheny FICE Identification: 003303
Unit ID: 211431
Telephone: (800) 333-2275 Carnegie Class: Masters/L
FAX Number: (412) 578-6668 Calendar System: Semester
URL: www.carlow.edu
Established: 1929 Annual Undergrad Tuition & Fees: $29,454
Enrollment: 2,248 Coed
Affiliation or Control: Roman Catholic IRS Status: 501(c)3
Highest Offering: Doctorate
Accreditation: M, #COARC, COPSY, NURSE, SW

01 President ... Dr. Suzanne K. MELLON
05 Provost/VP Academic Affairs ... Dr. Sibdas GHOSH
10 CFO/VP Finance & Admin Services ... Mr. David J. MEADOWS
111 VP Advancement ... Ms. Kimberley A. HAMMER
88 Special Asst to Pres/Mercy Heritage ... Sr. Sheila A. CARNEY, RSM
32 VP Student Affairs/Dean of Students ... Mr. Timothy P. PHILLIPS
66 Dean Health and Wellness ... Dr. Lynn E. GEORGE
83 Dean Leadership & Social Change ... Dr. Stephanie A. WILSEY
49 Dean Learning & Innovation ... Dr. Matthew E. GORDLEY
106 Dean Online/Digital Learning ... Dr. Michael JONES
107 Dean College of Prof Studies ... Dr. James W. ICE
13 Chief Information Officer ... Mr. Gregory L. DUMONT
04 Exec Asst to the President ... Ms. Juliet A. CREEHAN
09 Sr Dir Inst Research/Effect/Plng ... Dr. Edith L. COOK
15 Director Human Resources ... Ms. Bridgette N. COFIELD
06 Registrar ... Ms. Elizabeth A. MCCLINTOCK
88 Head of Campus Laboratory School ... Ms. Jessica WEBSTER
84 Dir Enrollment Mgmt/Operations ... Mr. Joel W. MULLNER
123 Director Graduate Admissions ... Ms. Wendy S. PHILLIPS
36 Director Career Development ... Ms. Jennifer A. O'TOOLE
88 Dir Student Accounts ... Mr. James V. SHANKEL
08 Exec Dir Library & Lrng Commons ... Dr. Michael JONES
35 Asst Dean of Students ... Ms. Erin I. BOYLES
39 Director Campus Life ... Mr. Keith CERRONI
23 Director Health Services ... Ms. Carla R. BERGAMASCO
41 Director Athletics ... Mr. George S. SLIMAN
88 Director Wellness & Fitness Svcs ... Ms. Julie M. GAUL
21 Controller ... Ms. Deanna J. SIEBERKROB
18 Director Facilities ... Mr. Bert GARCIA
19 Chief of Police ... Ms. Corrin M. CULHANE
37 Director Financial Aid ... Ms. Natalie L. WILSON
112 Director of Major Gifts ... Ms. Nicole DEMARTINO
29 Director Alumni Engagement ... Ms. Lachelle N. BINION
102 Director of Corp & Found Relations ... Ms. Patricia L. BEAUMONT
27 Director Media & Public Rels ... Mr. Andrew G. WILSON
108 Director of Assessment ... Vacant
42 Campus Minister ... Ms. Siobhan K. DEWITT
100 Spec Asst to Pres Cmty/Govt Rel/Bd ... Ms. Shawn K. NELSON

Carnegie Mellon University (F)

5000 Forbes Avenue, Pittsburgh PA 15213-3890
County: Allegheny FICE Identification: 003242
Unit ID: 211440
Telephone: (412) 268-2000 Carnegie Class: DU-Highest
FAX Number: (412) 268-2330 Calendar System: Semester
URL: www.cmu.edu
Established: 1900 Annual Undergrad Tuition & Fees: $55,465
Enrollment: 13,869 Coed
Affiliation or Control: Independent Non-Profit IRS Status: 501(c)3
Highest Offering: Doctorate
Accreditation: M, MUS, SPAA

01 President ... Dr. Farnam JAHANIAN
05 Provost/Chief Academic Officer ... Dr. James H. GARRETT, JR.
10 Vice President and CFO ... Ms. Angela BLANTON
111 VP for University Advancement ... Mr. Scott MORY
46 VP for Research ... Dr. Michael MCQUADE
43 Vice President/General Counsel ... Ms. Mary Jo DIVELY
26 Int VP Marketing & Communications ... Mr. Scott MORY
101 Secretary of the Corporation ... Ms. Cathy A. LIGHT
04 Exec Asst to President/Office Mgr ... Ms. Kelly ELDER
20 Vice Provost for Education ... Dr. Amy L. BURKERT
11 Vice President for Operations ... Dr. Rodney P. MCCLENDON
100 Chief of Staff/VP Strategic Init ... Mr. Daryl WEINERT
32 VP Student Affairs/Dean of Students ... Ms. Gina CASALEGNO
13 Chief Information Officer ... Mr. Stan M. WADDELL
15 AVP & Chief Human Resources Officer ... Mrs. Michelle PIEKUTOWSKI
29 Asst VP Alumni Relations ... Ms. Nancy MERRITT
18 Asc VP Campus Design/Facility Devel ... Mr. Ralph R. HORGAN
27 Exec Dir For Media Relations ... Mr. Kenneth WALTERS
28 Asst Vice Pres for Diversity & EOS ... Mr. Everett L. TADAMY
41 Dir Athletics & Physical Education ... Mr. Josh CENTOR
19 Director Security/Chief Univ Police ... Mr. Thomas A. OGDEN
84 AVP & Dir of Enrollment Services ... Ms. Lisa M. KRIEG
14 Director Software Engr Inst ... Dr. Paul D. NIELSEN
07 Dean of Admissions ... Mr. Michael STEIDEL
08 Dean of University Libraries ... Mr. Keith WEBSTER
06 Registrar ... Mr. John R. PAPINCHAK
09 Director of Institutional Research ... Ms. Janel SUTKUS
36 Assoc Dean for Career/Prof Dev ... Mr. Kevin MONAHAN
38 Dir Counseling & Psychological Svcs ... Dr. Kurt KUMLER
54 Dean Carnegie Inst of Technology ... Vacant
57 Dean College Fine Arts ... Dr. Dan J. MARTIN
49 Dean Dietrich College ... Dr. Richard SCHEINES
50 Dean Tepper School of Business ... Dr. Robert DAMMON
81 Dean Mellon College of Science ... Dr. Rebecca W. DOERGE

80 Dean Heinz Sch Publ Policy/Mgmt .... Dr. Ramayya KRISHNAN
77 Dean School of Computer Sciences .... Vacant
35 Asst Dean of Student Affairs .... Ms. Renee CAMERLENGO
102 Dir Foundation Relations .... Ms. Jennifer SOBOL
104 Director of International Education .... Ms. Linda GENTILE
25 Chief Contracts/Grants Admin .... Mr. Matthew D'EMILIO
37 Director Student Financial Aid .... Mr. Brian HILL
39 Director Housing Services .... Mr. Thomas COOLEY
30 Sr Assoc Vice Pres for Development .... Ms. Pamela EAGER
86 Assoc VP Government Relations .... Mr. Timothy MCNULTY
96 Director University Procurement .... Vacant

Cedar Crest College (A)

100 College Drive, Allentown PA 18104-6196
County: Lehigh FICE Identification: 003243
Unit ID: 211468
Telephone: (610) 437-4471 Carnegie Class: Masters/S
FAX Number: (610) 437-5955 Calendar System: Semester
URL: www.cedarcrest.edu
Established: 1867 Annual Undergrad Tuition & Fees: $39,216
Enrollment: 1,664 Female
Affiliation or Control: Non-denominational IRS Status: 501(c)3
Highest Offering: Doctorate
Accreditation: M, ACBSP, ANEST, DIETD, DIETI, FEPAC, NUR, NURSE, SW

01 President .... Dr. Elizabeth MEADE
05 Provost .... Dr. Robert A. WILSON
10 Chief Financial Officer/Treasurer .... Ms. Audra J. KAHR
111 VP Institutional Advancement .... Ms. Valerie DOWNING
84 VP Enrollment Mgmt/Student Affairs . Ms. Mary-Alice OZECHOSKI
06 Registrar .... Ms. Janet BAKER
29 Exec Director for Alumnae Affairs .... Ms. Lori GALLAGHER
19 Chief of Campus Safety and Security .... Mr. Mark VITALOS
18 Director of Facilities .... Ms. Kimberly SHERR
08 Library Director .... Ms. Mary Beth FREEH
13 Director Information Technology .... Mr. Bruce SARTE
09 Dir of Institutional Research .... Ms. Lyn WILLIAMS
04 Assistant to the President .... Ms. Meghan GRADY
37 Dir Student Financial Services .... Ms. Valerie KREISER
22 Director Health/Counseling Services .... Ms. Nancy ROBERTS
26 Dir Marketing/Communication .... Ms. Allison GOODIN
40 Manager Bookstore .... Ms. Maureen YOACHIM

Central Penn College (B)

600 Valley Road, Summerdale PA 17093-0309
County: Cumberland FICE Identification: 004890
Unit ID: 211477
Telephone: (800) 759-2727 Carnegie Class: Bac-Diverse
FAX Number: (717) 732-5254 Calendar System: Quarter
URL: www.centralpenn.edu
Established: 1881 Annual Undergrad Tuition & Fees: $18,714
Enrollment: 1,224 Coed
Affiliation or Control: Proprietary IRS Status: Proprietary
Highest Offering: Master's
Accreditation: M, MAC, OTA, PTAA

01 President .... Dr. Linda FEDRIZZI-WILLIAMS
05 VPAA/Provost .... Dr. Eric ZEGLEN
84 VP Enrollment Mgmt & Marketing .... Dr. Stacey OBI
10 Chief Financial Officer .... Mr. Shawn FARR
06 Director Records & Registration .... Mr. Jen CORRELL
108 Institutional Effectiveness Officer .... Dr. Shawn HUMPHREY
18 Facilities Director .... Mr. Robert WHITCOMB, III
26 Director of Marketing & Comm .... Mrs. Mary E. WETZEL
37 Financial Aid Director .... Ms. Kathy J. SHEPARD
41 Athletic Director .... Mr. Michael KNILL
36 Career Services Director .... Mr. Steven HASSINGER
15 Exec Director of Human Resources .... Ms. Maggie LEBO
39 Residence Life Director .... Ms. Lindsay GARBER

Chatham University (C)

Woodland Road, Pittsburgh PA 15232-2826
County: Allegheny FICE Identification: 003244
Unit ID: 211556
Telephone: (412) 365-1100 Carnegie Class: DU-Mod
FAX Number: (412) 365-1505 Calendar System: Other
URL: www.chatham.edu
Established: 1869 Annual Undergrad Tuition & Fees: $37,611
Enrollment: 2,269 Coed
Affiliation or Control: Independent Non-Profit IRS Status: 501(c)3
Highest Offering: Doctorate
Accreditation: M, ARCPA, CIDA, COPSY, IACBE, NURSE, OT, PTA, SW

01 President .... Dr. David FINEGOLD
10 Vice Pres Finance/Administration .... Mr. Walter B. FOWLER
05 Vice President Academic Affairs .... Dr. Jenna TEMPLETON
84 Vice Pres Enrollment Management .... Ms. Amy BECHER
32 VP Student Affairs/Dean of Stdnts .... Dr. Zauyah WAITE
26 Vice Pres for Mktg & Communications .... Mr. Bill CAMPBELL
111 Vice Pres University Advancement .... Ms. Carey MILLER
106 Director Chatham Online .... Mr. Mark KASSEL
88 Dn Falk Sch Sustainability/Environ .... Dr. Peter WALKER
21 Assoc VP Finance/Admin .... Ms. Jennifer HOERSTER
45 VP of Planning/Sec to the Board .... Mr. Sean COLEMAN
09 Director of IR & Effectiveness .... Mr. Giovanni GAROFALO
06 Registrar .... Ms. Maria KRONISER
37 Asst Vice Pres Financial Aid .... Ms. Jennifer A. BURNS
08 Director of Library .... Ms. Jill AUSEL
29 Director of Alumni Engagement .... Ms. Dana DEPASQUALE

44 Director of Annual Giving .... Vacant
30 Executive Director of Development .... Ms. Amanda KILE
15 Asst VP of Human Resources .... Mr. Frank M. GRECO
18 Director of Facilities Management .... Mr. Robert R. DUBRAY
19 Chief of Police .... Ms. Valerie TOWNSEND
41 Director of Athletics .... Mr. Leonard TREVINO
36 Asst Dean of Students .... Ms. Mary UTTER
38 Director of Student Counseling .... Dr. Elsa M. ARCE
35 Asst Dean of Students .... Ms. Heather BLACK
49 Dean School Arts/Science/Business .... Dr. Darlene MOTLEY
76 Dean School of Health Sciences .... Dr. Patricia DOWNEY
04 Exec Assistant to the President .... Ms. Brittany TYLER
13 CIO/Director of Info Technology .... Mr. Paul STEINHAUS
39 Director Residence Life .... Mr. Shawn A. MCQUILLAN
88 Dir University Sustainability .... Ms. Mary WHITNEY
102 Grants Manager .... Mr. Thomas MCGEE
104 Study Abroad Coordinator .... Ms. Karin CHIPMAN
28 Director of Multicultural Affairs .... Dr. Randi CONGLETON
50 Interim Chair/Director Business .... Mr. James PIERSON
53 Director of Education .... Dr. Kristin HARTY
105 Web Content Manager .... Ms. Sara POLETTI

Chestnut Hill College (D)

9601 Germantown Avenue, Philadelphia PA 19118-2693
County: Philadelphia FICE Identification: 003245
Unit ID: 211583
Telephone: (215) 248-7000 Carnegie Class: Masters/M
FAX Number: (215) 248-7155 Calendar System: Semester
URL: www.chc.edu
Established: 1924 Annual Undergrad Tuition & Fees: $36,180
Enrollment: 1,846 Coed
Affiliation or Control: Roman Catholic IRS Status: 501(c)3
Highest Offering: Doctorate
Accreditation: M, CLPSY, IPSY, MACTE

01 President .... Sr. Carol Jean VALE, SSJ
05 Vice Pres for Academic Affairs .... Dr. Christopher DOUGHERTY
10 Vice Pres for Financial Affairs/COS .... Mr. David WOODFORD
30 Vice President for Inst Advancement ..... Ms. Susannah COLEMAN
32 Vice President for Student Life .... Dr. Lynn ORTALE
07 Vice President for Admissions .... Mr. Kevin HEARN
11 Asst to Pres for Administration .... Sr. Kathryn MILLER, SSJ
42 Asst to Pres for Mission & Ministry .... Ms. Cara MCMAHON
58 Dean School of Graduate Studies .... Dr. William CUNNINGHAM
97 Dean School of Undergrad Studies .... Sr. Cecelia CAVANAUGH, SSJ
51 Dean Continuing/Professional Stds .... Dr. Elaine GREEN
08 Dean Library/Information Resources .... Sr. Mary Josephine LARKIN, SSJ
20 Director Student Success .... Ms. Clare DOYLE
06 Registrar .... Mr. Michael REIG
35 Dean of Student Life .... Dr. Krista BAILEY MURPHY
38 Director Counseling Center .... Sr. Sheila KENNEDY, SSJ
85 Director of Global Education .... Ms. Ann LIBERONA
28 Dir Cultural Diversity Initiatives .... Dr. Juliana MOSLEY
23 Director Health Services .... Ms. Deirdre HORAN
36 Director of Career Development .... Ms. Nancy DACHILLE
07 Dir Admission/Sch Graduate Studies .... Ms. Ariel EDWARDS
07 Director Accelerated Admissions .... Ms. April FOWLKES
21 Controller .... Mr. Mitch BILKER
37 Int Director Financial Aid .... Ms. Yolanda COLE
09 Director of Institutional Research .... Sr. Patricia O'DONNELL, SSJ
102 Dir Corporate/Found/Govt Relations .... Ms. Rebecca POWERS
29 Director of Alumnae/i Affairs .... Ms. Maureen MCLAUGHLIN
41 Director of Athletics .... Mr. Jesse BALCER
15 Director Human Resources .... Ms. Sharon DOUGHERTY
19 Dir Security/Safety/Bldgs/Grounds .... Ms. Polly TETI
18 Director of Physical Plant .... Mr. Mark MCGRATH
88 Financial Systems Analyst .... Ms. Meg O'BRIEN
26 Director of Communications .... Mr. James BARRY
39 Director Residence Life .... Ms. Jenn THORPE
04 Administrative Asst to President .... Ms. Regina BERNHARDT
40 Manager of Campus Store .... Ms. Jennifer WARING

Clarks Summit University (E)

538 Venard Road, S. Abington Twp. PA 18411-1297
County: Lackawanna FICE Identification: 002670
Unit ID: 211024
Telephone: (570) 586-2400 Carnegie Class: Spec-4-yr-Faith
FAX Number: (570) 585-9226 Calendar System: Semester
URL: www.clarkssummitu.edu
Established: 1932 Annual Undergrad Tuition & Fees: $23,890
Enrollment: 741 Coed
Affiliation or Control: Baptist IRS Status: 501(c)3
Highest Offering: Doctorate
Accreditation: M, BI

01 President .... Dr. James R. LYTLE
05 VP of Academics .... Dr. William J. HIGLEY
10 VP of Business and Finance .... Vacant
32 Vice Pres Student Services .... Mr. Frank JUDSON
35 Dean of Students .... Mr. Ted BOYKIN
34 Associate Dean of Women .... Mrs. Faye MOORE
04 Exec Dir of President's Office .... Mr. Paul GOLDEN
11 Exec Dir of Administrative Svcs .... Mr. Allen R. DREYER
37 Director of Financial Aid .... Mr. Larry ELLIS
84 Director Enrollment Management .... Ms. Kati RAVEN
13 Director of Information Technology .... Mr. David BOSKET
06 Registrar .... Mr. Chris WELMAN
09 Director of Institutional Research .... Mr. Robert PLANTZ
29 Director of Alumni Services .... Mr. Paul GOLDEN

73 Dean of School of Theology .... Dr. David A. LACKEY
53 Dean of School of Education .... Dr. Ritch KELLEY
49 Dean of School of Arts & Sciences .... Dr. Janet K. HICKS

Commonwealth Technical Institute at the Hiram G. Andrews Center (F)

727 Goucher Street, Johnstown PA 15905-3092
County: Cambria FICE Identification: 025366
Unit ID: 212975
Telephone: (814) 255-8200 Carnegie Class: Assoc/HVT-High Non
FAX Number: (814) 255-5709 Calendar System: Semester
URL: www.dli.pa.gov/Individuals/Disability-Services/hgac/
Established: 1959 Annual Undergrad Tuition & Fees: $12,594
Enrollment: 183 Coed
Affiliation or Control: Proprietary IRS Status: Proprietary
Highest Offering: Associate Degree
Accreditation: ACCSC

01 Center Director .... Jill MORICONI
11 Center Deputy Director .... James MARKER
05 Director of Education .... Karen BILCHAK
07 Director of Admissions .... Jason GIES
32 Chief Student Life Officer .... Stacie ANDREWS
37 Director Student Financial Aid .... Chris ZAKRAYSEK

Community College of Allegheny County (G)

800 Allegheny Avenue, Pittsburgh PA 15233-1895
County: Allegheny FICE Identification: 003231
Unit ID: 210605
Telephone: (412) 323-2323 Carnegie Class: Assoc/MT-VT-Mix Trad/Non
FAX Number: (412) 237-4420 Calendar System: Semester
URL: www.ccac.edu
Established: 1966 Annual Undergrad Tuition & Fees (In-District): $4,315
Enrollment: 16,147 Coed
Affiliation or Control: State/Local IRS Status: 501(c)3
Highest Offering: Associate Degree
Accreditation: M, ADNUR, CAHIIM, COARC, DIETT, DMS, EMT, MAC, MLTAD, NMT, OTA, PTAA, RTT, SURGT

01 President .... Dr. Quintin B. BULLOCK
05 Provost/Exec Vice Pres Acad Affairs .... Dr. Stuart BLACKLAW
10 Vice President Finance .... Ms. Joyce BRECKENRIDGE
43 Vice President and General Counsel ...... Mr. Anthony DITOMMSO
12 Campus President Allegheny .... Dr. Evon WALTERS
12 Interim Campus President Boyce .... Dr. Evon WALTERS
12 Interim Campus President North .... Ms. Charlene NEWKIRK
12 Campus President South .... Ms. Charlene NEWKIRK
103 Interim VP Workforce Development .... Ms. Deborah KILLMYER
15 VP Human Resources .... Ms. Kimberly MANIGAULT
102 CEO Educational Foundation .... Vacant
13 Interim Chief Information Officer .... Mr. Chuck GRAHAM
06 Registrar .... Dr. Diane JACOBS
18 Director of Facilities Management .... Mr. James MESSER
21 Controller .... Mr. James FLYNN
25 Executive Director Grants .... Dr. Michael AYEWHO
96 Director Purchasing/Contracts Admin .... Mr. Mike CVETIC
28 Special Asst to Pres for Diversity .... Mr. Andrew HUGHEY
26 Executive Director Public Relations .... Ms. Elizabeth JOHNSTON
04 Assistant to the President & BOT ...... Ms. Bonita L RICHARDSON
100 Chief of Staff .... Dr. Frank SARGENT
19 Director Security/Safety .... Mr. Andre HENDERSON

Community College of Allegheny County Boyce Campus (H)

595 Beatty Road, Monroeville PA 15146-1396
Telephone: (724) 327-1327 Identification: 770150
Accreditation: &M

Community College of Allegheny County North Campus (I)

8701 Perry Highway, Pittsburgh PA 15237-5353
Telephone: (412) 366-7000 Identification: 770151
Accreditation: &M

Community College of Allegheny County, South Campus (J)

1750 Clairton Road, West Mifflin PA 15122-3029
Telephone: (412) 469-1100 Identification: 770152
Accreditation: &M

Community College of Beaver County (K)

1 Campus Drive, Monaca PA 15061-2588
County: Beaver FICE Identification: 006807
Unit ID: 211079
Telephone: (724) 480-2222 Carnegie Class: Assoc/HVT-Mix Trad/Non
FAX Number: (724) 480-3573 Calendar System: Semester
URL: www.ccbc.edu
Established: 1966 Annual Undergrad Tuition & Fees (In-District): $5,970
Enrollment: 2,506 Coed
Affiliation or Control: State/Local IRS Status: 501(c)3
Highest Offering: Associate Degree

Accreditation: M, ADNUR

01 President .... Dr. Roger W. DAVIS
05 Executive Vice President & Provost .... Dr. Shelly MOORE
10 VP Finance/Operations and IT .... Mr. Glenn NATALI
15 VP Human Resources .... Ms. Sally MERCER
32 VP Student Affairs & Enrollment .... Ms. Janice M. KAMINSKI
18 Assoc VP & Dir Facilities & Ground .... Mr. Scott MONIT
13 AVP of IT .... Mr. Brandon BERG
26 Exec Dir Public Relations & Mktg .... Ms. Leslie A. TENNANT
84 Director Enrollment Services .... Ms. Angela M. HAMILTON
103 Dean Workforce & Continuing Educ .... Mr. John S. GOBERISH
37 Director Student Financial Services .... Ms. Janet DAVIDSON
04 Assistant to the President & Board .... Ms. Roni GILES
76 Dean Nursing & Allied Health .... Ms. Elaine STROUSS
49 Senior Dean .... Dr. John HIGGS
88 Dean Aviation Sciences .... Vacant
88 Dean HS Academies & Dual Enroll .... Ms. Joyce CIRELLI
111 Exec Dir Advance & Sponsored Pgms .... Mr. Kolton CODNER
35 Director of Student Life .... Mr. Colin SISK
88 Associate Dean .... Dr. Katie THOMAS
88 Associate Dean .... Dr. Chet THOMPSON

Community College of Philadelphia (A)

1700 Spring Garden Street, Philadelphia PA 19130-3991
County: Philadelphia FICE Identification: 003249
Unit ID: 215239
Telephone: (215) 751-8000 Carnegie Class: Assoc/HT-High Trad
FAX Number: (215) 751-8762 Calendar System: Semester
URL: www.ccp.edu
Established: 1965 Annual Undergrad Tuition & Fees (In-District): $5,142
Enrollment: 17,296 Coed
Affiliation or Control: State/Local IRS Status: 501(c)3
Highest Offering: Associate Degree
Accreditation: M, ACFEI, ADNUR, COARC, DH, MLTAD, RAD

01 President .... Dr. Donald GENERALS
10 Vice President Business & Finance .... Mr. Jacob EAPEN
45 VP Strategic Initiatives and COS .... Dr. Judith GAY
111 Vice Pres Institutional Advancement .... Vacant
05 VP Academic and Student Success .... Dr. Samuel HIRSCH
86 Vice Pres Marketing/Government Rels .... Vacant
103 VP Workforce Dev & Economic Innova .... Ms. Carol DE FRIES
43 General Counsel .... Ms. Victoria ZELLERS
13 Chief Information Officer .... Ms. Jody BAUER
32 Dean of Students .... Dr. David ASENCIO
84 Dean of Enrollment Services .... Dr. Donna RICHEMOND
49 Dean Liberal Studies .... Dr. Chae SWEET
51 Dean Div Adult/Community Education .... Dr. David E. THOMAS
72 Div Dean of Business/Technology .... Dr. Pam CARTER
09 Director Institutional Research .... Dr. Dawn SINNOT
06 Director Stdnt Records/Registration .... Ms. Bonnie HARRINGTON
18 Chief Facilities/Physical Plant .... Mr. Michael FOHNER
28 Affirmative Action Director .... Mr. Simon BROWN
07 Director of Recruitment/Admissions .... Mr. Jason HAND
37 Director Financial Aid .... Vacant
96 Director of Purchasing .... Ms. Marsia HENLEY
38 Dept Head Student Counseling .... Ms. Carmen COLON
36 Coord Career Info/Placement Svcs .... Ms. Tracy HANTON
29 Coord Alumni Rels/Annual Giving .... Ms. Lyvette BROOKS
25 Coord Grants/Prospect Research .... Ms. Anne GRECO

Curtis Institute of Music (B)

1726 Locust Street, Philadelphia PA 19103-6187
County: Philadelphia FICE Identification: 003251
Unit ID: 211893
Telephone: (215) 893-5252 Carnegie Class: Spec-4-yr-Arts
FAX Number: (215) 893-9065 Calendar System: Semester
URL: www.curtis.edu
Established: 1924 Annual Undergrad Tuition & Fees: $2,900
Enrollment: 172 Coed
Affiliation or Control: Independent Non-Profit IRS Status: 501(c)3
Highest Offering: Master's
Accreditation: M, MUS

01 President & Chief Executive Officer .... Mr. Roberto DIAZ
11 Sr Vice Pres Administration .... Mr. Larry BOMBACK
111 Vice President Inst Advancement .... Mr. Christopher MOSSEY
05 Dean of Academics/Students .... Mr. Paul BRYAN
13 Chief Technology Officer .... Mr. Matt MORGAN
06 Registrar .... Mr. Darin KELLY
07 Admissions Officer .... Mr. Christopher HODGES
08 Library Director .... Ms. Michelle OSWELL

Delaware County Community College (C)

901 S Media Line Road, Media PA 19063-1094
County: Delaware FICE Identification: 007110
Unit ID: 211927
Telephone: (610) 359-5000 Carnegie Class: Assoc/MT-VT-High Trad
FAX Number: (610) 359-5343 Calendar System: Semester
URL: www.dccc.edu
Established: 1967 Annual Undergrad Tuition & Fees (In-District): $5,520
Enrollment: 11,030 Coed
Affiliation or Control: State/Local IRS Status: 501(c)3
Highest Offering: Associate Degree
Accreditation: M, ADNUR, ART, COARC, EMT, MAC, SURGT

01 President .... Dr. L. Joy GATES BLACK
10 Vice Pres Administration/Treasurer .... Dr. Patricia BENSON
05 Provost .... Dr. Monica PARRISH TRENT
111 Vice President for Advancement .... Ms. Rachael HUNSINGER PATTEN
12 Vice Provost & Vice Pres Chester Co .... Dr. Mary Jo BOYER
84 Vice President of Enrollment Mgmt .... Dr. Paula R. PITCHER
13 CIO Information Technology .... Ms. Bianca VALENTE
32 Vice Provost Student/Instr Support .... Dr. Grant S. SNYDER
88 Director Municipal Police Academy .... Mr. William DAVIS
106 Dean Distance Learning Services .... Mr. Alexander PLUCHUTA
37 Director of Financial Aid .... Mr. Raymond L. TOOLE
07 Asst VP Enrollment Svcs & Registrar .... Ms. Hope L. DIEHL
36 Dean Career/Counseling Center .... Dr. Mitchell MURTHA
108 Assoc Vice Prov Inst Effectiveness .... Dr. Christopher TOKPAH
21 Associate VP Finance .... Ms. Lori COLGAN
103 Director Workforce Entry Center .... Ms. Susan E. BOND
15 Director Human Resources .... Ms. Sara EVANS
91 Director Admin Computing .... Mr. Bob HARDCASTLE
29 Director Alumni Programs .... Mr. Douglas J. FERGUSON
89 Director of First Year Experience .... Dr. Kendrick MICKENS
25 Director Grants Management .... Ms. Susan M. SHISLER-RAPP
31 Director Community Education .... Ms. Patricia S. SCEPANSKY
35 Director Campus Life .... Ms. Allyson GLEESON
19 Director Safety & Security .... Mr. Matthew BRENNER
88 Dir Dual Enrollment HS Initiatives .... Ms. Patricia SHANNON
12 Director Southeast & UD Centers .... Ms. Jane SCHURMAN
88 Director Assessment Center .... Vacant
96 Director Purchasing .... Ms. Genine FEDELE
18 Dir Facilities & Construction Svcs .... Mr. Mark LEFKOF
103 Dean Workforce Dev & Cmty Educ .... Ms. Karen KOZACHYN
81 Dean STEM .... Dr. Mark SCHWARTZ
88 Dean Educational Support Svcs .... Vacant
50 Dean Business & Social Science .... Dr. Marian MCGORRY
79 Dean Comm/Arts & Humanities .... Dr. Nicholas WERNICKI
76 Dean Health/Nursing/EMS .... Dr. Faye A. MELOY
40 Manager Bookstore .... Mr. Jamar ABDULLAH
04 Executive Assistant to President .... Ms. Diane FOSTER
26 Executive Dir of Marketing & Comm .... Mr. Daniel KANAK
100 Chief of Staff .... Mr. Harry COSTIGAN
88 Asst to President for Communication .... Mr. Anthony TWYMAN

Delaware Valley University (D)

700 E Butler Avenue, Doylestown PA 18901-2697
County: Bucks FICE Identification: 003252
Unit ID: 211981
Telephone: (215) 345-1500 Carnegie Class: Masters/S
FAX Number: (215) 345-5277 Calendar System: Semester
URL: www.delval.edu
Established: 1896 Annual Undergrad Tuition & Fees: $39,440
Enrollment: 2,422 Coed
Affiliation or Control: Independent Non-Profit IRS Status: 501(c)3
Highest Offering: Doctorate
Accreditation: M, ACBSP, LSAR

01 President .... Dr. Maria GALLO
04 Executive Asst to the President .... Ms. Kristen OLSZEWSKI
100 Chief of Staff .... Dr. Terry JACKSON
05 VP Academic Affairs/Dean of Faculty .... Dr. Benjamin RUSILOSKI
32 VP Campus Life & Inclusive Excel .... Dr. April VARI
10 Int VP for Finance & Administration .... Ms. Cheryl MOYER
30 VP for Development & Alumni Affairs .... Mr. Keith RICHARDSON
09 Exec Dir of Institutional Research .... Ms. Regina BALL
84 VP for Enrollment Management .... Mr. Dwayne WALKER
81 Dean of Life & Physical Sciences .... Dr. Jean SMOLEN
47 Dean Agriculture & Environ Science .... Dr. Broc SANDELIN
50 Dean Business & Humanities .... Dr. Tanya CASAS
58 Dean of Graduate & Prof Studies .... Dr. James MORYAN
06 Registrar .... Mr. James SLIZEWSKI
41 Athletic Director .... Mr. David DUDA
26 Assoc VP Marketing & Communications .... Mr. Tom DURSO
21 Asst VP Finance & Administration .... Ms. Cheryl MOYER
07 Director of Admissions .... Mr. Dwayne WALKER
13 Exec Director Technology Services .... Mr. Mike DAVIS
36 Exec Dir Ctr for Student Prof Dev .... Dr. Benjamin RUSILOSKI
08 Librarian .... Mr. Peter A. KUPERSMITH
37 Director Student Financial Aid .... Mrs. Joan HOCK
58 Dir Graduate & Professional Studies .... Ms. Yolonda UDVARDY
38 Director Counseling/Learn Support .... Ms. Sharon DONNELLY
23 Director Health Services .... Ms. Miriam TORRES
14 Assoc Dir of Help Desk Operations .... Mr. Darren MOSES
35 Asst Dean of Stdnts/Dir Stdnt Inv .... Mr. Andrew MOYER
19 Director Security/Public Safety .... Ms. Cynthia TRANSUE
15 Director of Human Resources .... Ms. Jill BLANCO
18 Director of Facilities & Grounds .... Mr. Pat CALLAHAN
44 Director Annual Giving & Adv Svcs .... Mr. Kevin LADDEN
96 Director of Purchasing .... Mr. William LYLE
102 Dir Foundation/Corporate Relations .... Ms. Wendy CONNUCK
88 Experiential Learning Advisor .... Ms. Darrah MUGRAUER
104 Director Study Abroad .... Ms. Stephanie WOBENSMITH
106 Dir Online Education/E-learning .... Ms. Cynthia RENNER
29 Director Alumni Engagement .... Ms. Christina RISO

DeSales University (E)

2755 Station Avenue, Center Valley PA 18034-9568
County: Lehigh FICE Identification: 003986
Unit ID: 210739
Telephone: (610) 282-1100 Carnegie Class: Masters/L
FAX Number: (610) 282-2254 Calendar System: Semester
URL: www.desales.edu
Established: 1965 Annual Undergrad Tuition & Fees: $37,400
Enrollment: 3,315 Coed
Affiliation or Control: Roman Catholic IRS Status: 501(c)3
Highest Offering: Doctorate
Accreditation: M, ACBSP, ARCPA, NURSE, PTA

01 President .... V.Rev. James J. GREENFIELD, OSFS
04 Executive Admin Asst to President .... Ms. Mary A. GOTZON
03 Executive Vice President .... Dr. Gerard JOYCE
88 Vice President for Mission .... Rev. Kevin NADOLSKI, OSFS
88 VP for Marketing & Strat Planning .... Dr. David GILFOIL
05 Provost .... Bro. Daniel WISNIEWSKI, OSFS
06 Registrar .... Mr. Thomas MANTONI
84 Assoc VP for Enrollment Management .... Ms. Mary BIRKHEAD
08 Librarian .... Ms. Deborah MALONE
51 Assistant Dean of Lifelong Learning .... Ms. Joann HAWS
20 Assoc Provost of Academic Pgm .... Dr. Robert BLUMENSTEIN
36 Exec Dir of Career Development .... Ms. Kristin EICHOLTZ
111 Vice Pres Institutional Advancement .... Mr. Thomas L. CAMPBELL
86 Director of Government Relations .... Vacant
102 Director Corp/Foundation Relations .... Mrs. Kathy DIAMANDOPOULOS
26 Executive Director of Communication .... Mr. Thomas MCNAMARA
44 Assoc VP for Annual Giving .... Ms. Lina BARBIERI
29 Director of Alumni Relations .... Mr. Michael RITCHIE
10 VP for Admin & Finance .... Mr. Robert J. SNYDER
45 Assoc VP for Admin & Planning .... Mr. Peter RAUTZHAN
21 Director of Finance/Treasurer .... Mr. Michael SWEETANA
19 Chief of Police .... Chief Steven MARSHALL
09 Dir of Institutional Rsrch/Analysis .... Ms. Lisa PLUMMER
88 VP of Campus Environment .... Mr. Marc ALBANESE
18 Director of Facilities .... Mr. Jim MOLCHANY
40 Campus Store Manager .... Mr. Joseph JUDGE
15 Exec Dir of Human Resources .... Ms. Margie GRANDINETTI
16 HR Generalist .... Ms. Lisa LIGHTCAP
13 Director of Information Technology .... Mr. James MAZUROWSKI
32 Vice President for Student Life .... Mrs. Linda ZERBE
84 Dean of Enrollment Mgmt .... Mr. Derrick WETZEL
35 Dean of Students .... Rev. Edward OGDEN
39 Director of Residence Life .... Ms. Melinda QUINONES
07 Director of Admissions .... Ms. Kate MCNALLY
37 Director of Student Financial Aid .... Mrs. Joyce FARMER
42 Chaplain .... Rev. Dan LANNEN
38 Asst Dean of Students for Wellness .... Ms. Wendy KRISAK
41 Athletic Director .... Mr. Scott COVAL
28 Director Multicultural/Intl Affairs .... Vacant
58 Dean of Graduate Education .... Mr. Ron NORDONE
96 Director of Campus Environment .... Mr. Jeffrey RICHTER
104 Director of International Learning .... Mr. Brian MACDONALD
50 Division Head of Business .... Mr. Christopher R. COCOZZA
53 Dean of Education .... Dr. Judith RANCE-RONEY
105 Director Web Communications .... Ms. Kristin LAUDENSLAGER
106 Dir Distance Educ/Instruction Tech .... Dr. Eric HAGAN

Dickinson College (F)

Box 1773, College & Louther Street,
Carlisle PA 17013-2896
County: Cumberland FICE Identification: 003253
Unit ID: 212009
Telephone: (717) 243-5121 Carnegie Class: Bac-A&S
FAX Number: N/A Calendar System: Semester
URL: www.dickinson.edu
Established: 1783 Annual Undergrad Tuition & Fees: $54,661
Enrollment: 2,382 Coed
Affiliation or Control: Independent Non-Profit IRS Status: 501(c)3
Highest Offering: Baccalaureate
Accreditation: M

01 President .... Dr. Margee M. ENSIGN
05 Provost/Dean of the College .... Dr. Neil B. WEISSMAN
84 VP Enrollment Management .... Ms. Catherine M. DAVENPORT
10 VP Finance & Administration .... Dr. Bronté BURLEIGH-JONES
111 VP College Advancement .... Mr. Kirk I. SWENSON
32 VP Student Life .... Dr. George H. STROUD
13 VP & Chief Information Officer .... Mr. Robert E. RENAUD
09 VP Inst Effectiveness/Inclusivity .... Dr. Brenda K. BRETZ
07 Dean of Admissions .... Vacant
15 Assoc VP Human Resource Services .... Ms. Debra HARGROVE
43 General Counsel/Chief Legal Officer .... Mr. Kendall ISAAC
100 Chief of Staff/Secretary of College .... Ms. Karen N. FARYNIAK
18 Assoc VP Sustain & Facilities Plng .... Mr. Kenneth E. SHULTES
20 Sr Assoc Provost Academic Affairs .... Dr. John H. HENSON
20 Asst Provost for Curriculum .... Ms. Deb L. BOLEN
110 Assoc VP College Advancement .... Mr. Brian G. FALCK
109 Assoc VP Auxil Svcs & Budget Mgmt .... Vacant
26 VP Marketing & Communications .... Ms. Connie MCNAMARA
06 Registrar .... Ms. Mary Ann LEIDIGH
41 Athletic Director .... Mr. Joel M. QUATTRONE
09 Dir Institutional Effectiveness .... Mr. Lester D. KO
37 Director of Financial Aid .... Ms. Leah YOUNG
104 Assoc Provost/Exec Dir Global Stdy .... Ms. Samantha C. BRANDAUER
31 Ex Dir Ctr Civic Learning & Action .... Dr. Gary R. KIRK
88 Assoc Provost/Dir Ctr Sustbility Ed .... Dr. Neil A. LEARY
36 Asst Provost/Dir Career Development .... Mr. Philip JONES
88 Interim Exec Dir Wellness Center .... Dr. Don J. DOMENICI
35 Assoc VP Stdnt Ldrshp/Campus Engmnt .... Ms. Rebecca J. HAMMELL
21 Assoc VP Fin Ops & Controller .... Mr. Sean WITTE
90 Director Academic Computing .... Ms. Patricia A. PEHLMAN
27 Director of Media Relations .... Ms. Christine BAKSI
29 Director of Alumni Relations .... Ms. Liz TOTH
114 Director Planning & Budget .... Ms. Margaret STAFFORD
08 Director Library Services .... Ms. Eleanor MITCHELL
40 Int Dir Col Bookstore/Central Svcs .... Ms. Lori COLEMAN

19 Asst VP Compliance/Campus Safety .... Ms. Dolores A. DANSER
91 Assoc VP Enterprise Systems .... Ms. Jill M. FORRESTER
102 Dir Academic & Foundation Relations .... Ms. Cheryl E. KREMER
39 Assoc Dean Stdnts/Dir Res Life .... Ms. Angie HARRIS
88 Executive Director Donor Relations .... Ms. Tara C. RENAULT
113 Bursar Financial Operations .... Ms. Sally HECKENDORN
105 Director Online Marketing .... Ms. Sarah M. SHERIFF
42 Director Cmty Svcs/Religious Life .... Rev. Donna D. HUGHES
88 Title IX Coordinator .... Ms. Katharina MATIC

Douglas Education Center (A)

130 Seventh Street, Monessen PA 15062-1097
County: Westmoreland FICE Identification: 020683
Unit ID: 212045
Telephone: (724) 684-3684 Carnegie Class: Spec 2-yr-A&S
FAX Number: (724) 684-7463 Calendar System: Semester
URL: www.dec.edu
Established: 1904 Annual Undergrad Tuition & Fees: $18,980
Enrollment: 229 Coed
Affiliation or Control: Proprietary IRS Status: Proprietary
Highest Offering: Associate Degree
Accreditation: ACCSC

01 President .... Mr. Jeffrey D. IMBRESCIA
05 Vice President of Academic Affairs .... Mr. Julian IMBRESCIA
10 Director of Financial Services .... Mr. Debra B. WISE
20 Senior Academic Affairs Coordinator ... Ms. N. Renee MCDOWELL
07 Executive Director of Admissions .... Mr. Tony BAEZ MILAN
11 Executive Director of Operations .... Ms. Amanda PHILLIPS
26 Chief Marketing Officer .... Mr. Kevin G. FEAR
88 Supervisor of Cosmetology .... Ms. Karen NELSON
36 Director of Career Services .... Ms. Dana MELVIN
32 Student Life/Social Media .... Ms. Janelle IMBRESCIA
13 Exec Dir of Information Technology .... Mr. John SECHRIST

Drexel University (B)

3141 Chestnut Street, Philadelphia PA 19104-2875
County: Philadelphia FICE Identification: 003256
Unit ID: 212054
Telephone: (215) 895-2000 Carnegie Class: DU-Highest
FAX Number: (215) 895-1414 Calendar System: Quarter
URL: www.drexel.edu
Established: 1891 Annual Undergrad Tuition & Fees: $53,244
Enrollment: 24,190 Coed
Affiliation or Control: Independent Non-Profit IRS Status: 501(c)3
Highest Offering: Doctorate
Accreditation: M, ANEST, ARCPA, ART, CAHIIM, CEA, CIDA, CLPSY, CONST, DENT, DIETD, HT, IPSY, LAW, LC, LIB, MED, MFCD, NURSE, PA, PH, PTA

01 President .... Mr. John A. FRY
05 Provost/Executive Vice President .... Dr. Brian BLAKE
111 SVP Inst Advancement .... Vacant
11 Exec Vice Pres/Treasurer/COO .... Mrs. Helen Y. BOWMAN
84 SVP Enrollment Mgmt/Student Success .... Vacant
26 Sr VP University Communications .... Ms. Lori N. DOYLE
43 Sr VP & General Counsel .... Mr. Michael J. EXLER
86 Sr VP Govt & Community Relations .... Mr. Brian T. KEECH
20 Interim Vice Provost .... Dr. Shivanthi ANANDAN
13 Vice Pres IRT & CIO .... Mr. Thomas DECHIARO
88 Exec Dir & Vice Prov Cultural Partn .... Dr. Rosalind REMER
07 Sr Vice Pres/Dean of Admissions .... Ms. Evelyn THIMBA
102 Sr VP Corp Relations & Economic Dev .... Mr. Keith A. ORRIS
46 Sr Vice Provost for Research .... Dr. Aleister SAUNDERS
32 Sr Vice Pres/Dean of Student Life .... Dr. Subir SAHU
09 Vice Provost Institutional Research .... Dr. Mark FREEMAN
100 VP & Exec Dir Office of President .. Mr. Gregory P. MONTANARO
108 Exec Dir Compliance/Privacy & IA .... Mr. Jason R. CONNELL
115 Vice President Investments .... Ms. Catherine B. ULOZAS
88 Sr Vice Provost Partnerships .... Dr. Lucy E. KERMAN
15 Vice Pres Human Resources & PMOE .... Ms. Megan E. WEYLER
49 Dean College Arts & Sciences .... Dr. Donna MURASKO
50 Int Dean LeBow College of Business .... Dr. Paul E. JENSEN
54 Int Dean College of Engineering .... Dr. Giuseppe R. PALMESE
77 Dean Col of Computing & Informatics .... Dr. Yi DENG
92 Dean of Pennoni Honors College .... Dr. Paula COHEN
88 Dean Grad Sch of Biomed Science .... Dr. Elisabeth VANBOCKSTAELE
62 Dean of Libraries .... Dr. Danuta A. NITECKI
88 Dean of Close School .... Dr. Donna M. DECAROLIS
61 Dean Kline School of Law .... Mr. Roger J. DENNIS
60 Dean Col of Media Arts & Design .... Mr. Allen C. SABINSON
53 Dean School of Education .... Dr. Nancy B. SONGER
63 Sr VP & Dean College of Medicine .... Dr. Daniel V. SCHIDLOW
66 Int Dean Col Nursing/Health Prof .... Dr. Susan S. SMITH
69 Dean Urban Health Collaborative .... Dr. Ana V. DIEZ ROUX
88 Dean School Biomed Engineering .... Dr. Paul BRANDT-RAUF
19 Vice President Public Safety .... Ms. Eileen W. BEHR
41 Athletic Director .... Dr. Eric A. ZILLMER
36 Vice Prov Career Development Ctr .... Vacant
22 Assoc VP Equality & Diversity .... Ms. Michele M. ROVINSKY-MAYER
106 SVP of Drexel & President of DEL .... Dr. Susan C. ALDRIDGE
85 Assoc Vice Provost Intl Programs .... Ms. Daniela E. ASCARELLI
88 Vice Chair Faculty Senate .... Dr. Michael KENNEDY
88 Director AJ Drexel Autism Institute ... Dr. Craig J. NEWSCHAFFER

Duquesne University (C)

600 Forbes Avenue, Pittsburgh PA 15282-0001
County: Allegheny FICE Identification: 003258
Unit ID: 212106
Telephone: (412) 396-6000 Carnegie Class: DU-Higher
FAX Number: (412) 396-4186 Calendar System: Semester
URL: www.duq.edu
Established: 1878 Annual Undergrad Tuition & Fees: $38,178
Enrollment: 9,190 Coed
Affiliation or Control: Roman Catholic IRS Status: 501(c)3
Highest Offering: Doctorate
Accreditation: M, #ARCPA, CAATE, CACREP, CAEPN, CEA, CLPSY, FEPAC, LAW, MUS, NURSE, OT, PHAR, PTA, SCPSY, SP

01 President .... Mr. Kenneth G. GORMLEY
04 Assistant to the President .... Ms. Margaret EISEMAN
05 Provost/Academic Vice President .... Dr. David J. DAUSEY
10 Vice Pres for Finance & Business .... Dr. Matthew J. FRIST
32 Vice Pres for Student Life .... Dr. Douglas FRIZZELL
111 VP for University Advancement .... Mr. John J. PLANTE
88 Vice President Mission & Identity .... Rev. Raymond FRENCH, CSSP
43 VP Legal Affairs & General Counsel .... Ms. Madelyn REILLY
26 VP Marketing and Communications .... Mr. Gabriel WELSCH
20 Assoc Academic Vice Pres Research .... Dr. Alan W. SEADLER
20 Assoc Academic Vice President .... Dr. Jeffrey A. MILLER
13 Vice President/CIO .... Dr. Charles R. BARTEL
109 Director Auxiliary Services .... Mr. Scott RICHARDS
85 Exec Dir International Programs .... Dr. Joseph DECROSTRA
84 Vice Pres Enrollment Management .... Mr. Paul-James CUKANNA
06 Registrar .... Ms. Kim HOERITZ
08 Librarian .... Dr. Sara BARON
29 Asst Vice Pres Alumni Relations .... Ms. Sarah SPERRY
09 Director of Institutional Research .... Mr. Matthew NORTH
37 Director Financial Aid .... Mr. Richard C. ESPOSITO
15 Asst Vice Pres/CHRO .... Mr. John G. GREENO
19 Director of Security .... Mr. Thomas HART
88 Dir Environmental Health/Safety .... Ms. Paula D. SWEITZER
18 Asst VP/Chief Facilities Officer .... Mr. Rodney W. DOBISH
36 Director of Career Services .... Ms. Nicole FELDHUES
41 Director of Athletics .... Mr. David HARPER
22 Dir Anti-discrimination/Risk Mgmt .... Mr. Sean F. WEAVER
23 Director Health Service .... Ms. Dessa MRVOS
38 Dir University Counseling Center .... Dr. Ian C. EDWARDS
39 Director Residence Life .... Mrs. Sharon G. OELSCHLAGER
42 Director Campus Ministry .... Rev. William CHRISTY
28 AVP Diversity/Inclus/Stdnt Advance .... Mr. Jeff MALLORY
50 Dean Business & Administration .... Dr. Dean B. MCFARLIN
66 Dean of Nursing .... Dr. Mary Ellen S. GLASGOW
67 Dean of Pharmacy .... Dr. J. Douglas BRICKER
64 Interim Dean of Music .... Dr. David Allen WEHR
53 Dean of Education .... Dr. Cindy M. WALKER
76 Dean of Health Sciences .... Dr. Fevzi AKINCI
61 Dean of Law .... Ms. April BARTON
49 Dean of Liberal Arts/Graduate .... Dr. Kristine BLAIR
65 Dean of Natural/Environment Sci .... Dr. Philip P. REEDER
40 Bookstore Manager .... Mr. John KACHUR
07 Director of Admissions .... Ms. Debra A. ZUGATES
100 Chief of Staff/AVP Ofc of President .... Ms. Mary Ellen SOLOMON
30 Asst VP for External Relations .... Ms. Mary Beth FORD
106 Dir Online Education/E-learning .... Dr. Michael W. BRIDGES

Eastern University (D)

1300 Eagle Road, Saint Davids PA 19087-3696
County: Delaware FICE Identification: 003259
Unit ID: 212133
Telephone: (610) 341-5800 Carnegie Class: Masters/L
FAX Number: (610) 341-1377 Calendar System: Semester
URL: www.eastern.edu
Established: 1925 Annual Undergrad Tuition & Fees: $32,947
Enrollment: 3,291 Coed
Affiliation or Control: American Baptist IRS Status: 501(c)3
Highest Offering: Doctorate
Accreditation: M, CAATE, EXSC, NURSE, SW, THEOL

01 President .... Dr. Ronald A. MATTHEWS
10 Vice Pres for Finance/Operations .... Mr. J. Pernell JONES
05 Provost .... Dr. Kenton SPARKS
06 Registrar .... Ms. Sarah ROCHE
32 Vice Prov Student Development .... Ms. Jacqueline IRVING
45 Vice Pres Inst Plng/Research/Assess .... Dr. Christine P. MAHAN
111 Vice President Advancement .... Ms. Kathy MEZA
110 Associate VP Advancement .... Ms. Natissa KULTAN-PFAUTZ
07 Exec Director Enrollment .... Mr. Michael DZIEDZIAK
15 Chief Human Resources Officer .... Ms. Kacey BERNARD
118 Benefits/Training Administrator .... Ms. Patti MCHUGH
04 Exec Asst to the President .... Ms. Heather NORCINI
12 Executive Dean Esperanza College .... Ms. Marilyn MARSH
76 Dean College of Health and Sciences .... Dr. Patricia REGER
73 Dean Palmer Theological Seminary .... Dr. F. David BRONKEMA
50 Int Dean Col of Business Leadership .... Dr. Al SOCCI
92 Dean College Arts/Humanities/Honors .... Dr. Brian WILLIAMS
53 Dean College of Education .... Dr. Susan EDGAR-SMITH
18 Exec Dir Facilities/Campus Svcs .... Mr. Jeffrey GROMIS
105 Senior Web Manager .... Ms. Allison MARSHALECK
09 Asst VP/Dir Institutional Research ... Mr. Thomas A. DAHLSTROM
26 Assoc VP Marketing/Enroll & Comm .... Mr. Michael THOMAS
113 Senior Director Student Accounts .... Ms. Lisa WELLER
08 Director of University Library .... Ms. Joy DLUGOSZ
42 University Chaplain .... Rev Dr. Joseph B. MODICA
37 Director of Financial Aid .... Ms. Andrea RUTH
13 Chief Information Officer .... Mr. Eric MCCLOY
24 Media Services Supervisor .... Mr. Paul THORPE
36 Director of Talent & Career Dev .... Ms. Sarah TODD
102 Dir Foundations/Grants/Govt Rel .... Ms. Ingrid COOPER
41 Director of Athletics .... Mr. Eric MCNELLEY
19 Director of Public Safety .... Mr. Michael BICKING
88 Exec Dir Conferences/Spec Events .... Ms. Meggin CAPERS
38 Dir Counseling/Academic Support .... Dr. Lisa M. HEMLICK
85 Dir Intl Student & Scholar Services .... Ms. Augusta ALLEN
39 Housing Coordinator .... Ms. Courtney JOHNSON
40 Follett Bookstore Manager .... Mr. Christopher HOAGLAND
93 Int Dir Multicultural Student Init .... Ms. Theresa NOYE
109 Director Auxiliary Services .... Mr. Byron MCMILLAN
120 Mgr Instruct Design & Lrng Tech .... Ms. Susan YAVOR
44 Exec Dir Annual Giving/Alumni .... Ms. Elizabeth LOCHNER
104 Sr Assoc Registrar/Crd Off Camp Pgm .... Ms. Lori BRISTOL
106 Dir Center Teach/Learn/Tech .... Dr. Rebecca GIDJUNIS

† Parent institution of Palmer Theological Seminary.

Elizabethtown College (E)

1 Alpha Drive, Elizabethtown PA 17022-2298
County: Lancaster FICE Identification: 003262
Unit ID: 212197
Telephone: (717) 361-1000 Carnegie Class: Bac-A&S
FAX Number: (717) 361-1207 Calendar System: Semester
URL: www.etown.edu
Established: 1899 Annual Undergrad Tuition & Fees: $46,940
Enrollment: 1,735 Coed
Affiliation or Control: Church Of The Brethren IRS Status: 501(c)3
Highest Offering: Doctorate
Accreditation: M, ACBSP, MUS, OT, SW

01 President .... Ms. Cecilia M. MCCORMICK
05 Sr Vice Pres Acad Affs/Dn Faculty .... Dr. Elizabeth (Betty) RIDER
10 Vice Pres Finance/Strategy .... Mr. Gerald SILBERMAN
111 VP Advancement/Cmty Relations .... Mr. David C. BEIDLEMAN
84 Vice Pres Enrollment Management .... Mr. John F. CHAMPOLI
32 Vice Pres Student Life .... Mr. Celestino LIMAS
51 Dean of SCPS/Prof of Edu .... Dr. Rachel E. FINLEY-BOWMAN
07 Director Admissions .... Ms. Lauren C. DEIBLER
35 Asst Dean of Students & Dir of CSS .... Ms. Stephanie A. RANKIN
26 Exec Dir Marketing/ Communications .... Ms. Elizabeth (Liz) A. BRAUNGARD
102 Exec Dir Foundation/Govt Relations .... Ms. Lesley M. FINNEY
09 Director Institutional Research .... Ms. Debra K. SHEESLEY
37 Director of Financial Aid .... Ms. Melodie R. JACKSON
08 Director The High Library .... Ms. Sarah PENNIMAN
29 Exec Director Alumni Devel/Programs .... Mr. Mark A. CLAPPER
19 Director of Campus Security .... Mr. Andrew L. POWELL
41 Director of Athletics .... Mr. Chris MORGAN
42 Chaplain/Director Religious Life .... Dr. Tracy SADD

Erie Institute of Technology (F)

940 Millcreek Mall, Erie PA 16565-1002
County: Erie FICE Identification: 022039
Unit ID: 212434
Telephone: (814) 868-9900 Carnegie Class: Spec 2-yr-Tech
FAX Number: (814) 868-9977 Calendar System: Semester
URL: www.erieit.edu
Established: 1958 Annual Undergrad Tuition & Fees: $14,990
Enrollment: 295 Coed
Affiliation or Control: Proprietary IRS Status: Proprietary
Highest Offering: Associate Degree
Accreditation: ACCSC

01 Director .... Mr. Paul FITZGERALD
05 Director of Education .... Ms. Kate HUSHON
37 Financial Aid Officer .... Ms. Erin POULLIOT
07 Admissions Director .... Ms. Barb BOLT
36 Career Services Director .... Ms. Amy ROWE

Esperanza College (G)

4261 North 5th Street, Philadelphia PA 19140
Telephone: (215) 324-0746 Identification: 770153
Accreditation: &M

† Branch campus of Eastern University, Saint Davids, PA

Evangelical Theological Seminary (H)

121 S College Street, Myerstown PA 17067-1299
County: Lebanon FICE Identification: 003263
Unit ID: 212443
Telephone: (717) 866-5775 Carnegie Class: Spec-4-yr-Faith
FAX Number: (717) 866-4667 Calendar System: 4/1/4
URL: www.evangelical.edu
Established: 1953 Annual Graduate Tuition & Fees: N/A
Enrollment: 111 Coed
Affiliation or Control: Evangelical Congregational Church
IRS Status: 501(c)3
Highest Offering: Doctorate; No Undergraduates
Accreditation: M, MFCD, THEOL

01 President .... Dr. Anthony L. BLAIR
111 Exec Dir Institutional Advancement .... Rev. Ann E. STEEL
10 Vice President Finance & Operations .... Mr. Kevin C. HENRY
26 Director of Marketing .... Mr. Mike DONGHIA
05 EVP/Dean of Academic Services .... Mr. James E. EHRMAN
08 Exec Dir Pense Learning Ctr .... Dr. Mark DRAPER
18 Director of Buildings & Grounds .... Mr. William J. ROBERTSON
88 Database Manager .... Mrs. Marsha A. CONLEY
84 Director of Enrollment Mgmt .... Ms. Gwen SCHEIRER
04 Executive Asst to President .... Mrs. Jayne SENSENIG

Fortis Institute (A)

5757 West Ridge Road, Erie PA 16506-1013
County: Erie FICE Identification: 030108
Unit ID: 216418
Telephone: (814) 838-7673 Carnegie Class: Assoc/HVT-High Trad
FAX Number: (814) 838-8642 Calendar System: Quarter
URL: www.fortis.edu
Established: 1984 Annual Undergrad Tuition & Fees: $13,157
Enrollment: 391 Coed
Affiliation or Control: Proprietary IRS Status: Proprietary
Highest Offering: Associate Degree
Accreditation: ACICS

† In teach-out.

Fortis Institute (B)

166 Slocum Street, Forty Fort PA 18704-2347
County: Luzerne FICE Identification: 030115
Unit ID: 249609
Telephone: (570) 288-8400 Carnegie Class: Spec 2-yr-Health
FAX Number: (570) 287-7936 Calendar System: Other
URL: www.fortis.edu
Established: 1984 Annual Undergrad Tuition & Fees: $13,369
Enrollment: 159 Coed
Affiliation or Control: Proprietary IRS Status: Proprietary
Highest Offering: Associate Degree
Accreditation: ACCSC

01 Campus President ... Madeline LEVY CRUZ
05 Director of Education ... Christopher JONES
07 Director of Admissions ... Jane AUSTIN
37 Director Financial Aid ... Ruth BRUMAGIN

Fortis Institute (C)

517 Ash Street, Scranton PA 18509
County: Lackawanna FICE Identification: 030116
Unit ID: 385503
Telephone: (570) 558-1818 Carnegie Class: Spec 2-yr-Health
FAX Number: (570) 342-4537 Calendar System: Other
URL: www.fortis.edu/scranton-pennsylvania.php
Established: 1986 Annual Undergrad Tuition & Fees: $28,802
Enrollment: 287 Coed
Affiliation or Control: Proprietary IRS Status: Proprietary
Highest Offering: Associate Degree
Accreditation: ACCSC, DH

01 Campus President ... Ms. Madeline LEVY CRUZ
06 Registrar ... Mr. Art BOBBOUINE
07 Director of Admissions ... Mr. Timothy PARSONS
36 Director Student Placement ... Ms. Heather CONTARDI
37 Director Student Financial Aid ... Ms. Stacie TAROLI

† Tuition varies by degree program.

Franklin & Marshall College (D)

PO Box 3003, Lancaster PA 17604-3003
County: Lancaster FICE Identification: 003265
Unit ID: 212577
Telephone: (717) 358-3971 Carnegie Class: Bac-A&S
FAX Number: (717) 358-4183 Calendar System: Semester
URL: www.fandm.edu
Established: 1787 Annual Undergrad Tuition & Fees: $56,550
Enrollment: 2,283 Coed
Affiliation or Control: Independent Non-Profit IRS Status: 501(c)3
Highest Offering: Baccalaureate
Accreditation: M

01 President ... Dr. Barbara K. ALTMANN
10 Vice Pres for Finance and Treasurer ... Mr. Paul MUTONE
111 Vice Pres for College Advancement ... Mr. Matthew EYNON
84 VP/Dean of Admission/Financial Aid ... Mr. Don SALEH
26 Vice Pres for College Communication . Ms. Barbara STAMBAUGH
05 Provost/Dean of Faculty ... Dr. Cameron WESSON
32 VP and Dean of Student Affairs ... Ms. Margaret HAZLETT
88 Assoc Dean of Col & Dir Klehr Ctr ... Dr. Ralph TABER
11 Associate VP for Administration ... Mr. Barry BOSLEY
45 VP for Planning ... Dr. Alan S. CANIGLIA
100 Chief of Staff ... Ms. Robyn PIGGOTT
08 College Librarian ... Mr. Scott VINE
85 Assoc Dean International Programs ... Ms. Sue MENNICKE
20 Associate Dean of Faculty ... Dr. Marcus W. THOMSEN
20 Associate Dean of Faculty ... Dr. Kimberly ARMSTRONG
28 Assoc Dean of Multicultural Affairs ... Dr. Marion A. COLEMAN
88 Assistant Dean/College House Dean ... Ms. Chelsea B. BROWN
88 Assistant Dean/College House Dean ... Ms. Courtnee N. JORDAN-COX
88 Assistant Dean/College House Dean ... Dr. Beth PROFFITT
88 Assistant Dean/College House Dean ... Mr. Todd DEKAY
88 Assistant Dean/College House Dean ... Dr. Brian W. SAMBLE
21 Controller ... Mr. Sean GALLOWAY
15 Assistant VP Human Resources ... Ms. Melanie A. DESANTIS
18 Associate VP/Facilities Management ... Mr. Mike WETZEL
19 Assoc VP Public Safety ... Mr. William MCHALE, JR.
23 Managing Physician Student Wellness ... Dr. Amy A. MYERS
13 VP and Chief Information Officer ... Ms. Carrie RAMPP
37 Director Financial Aid ... Mr. Clarke C. PAINE
38 Head of Counseling Services ... Dr. Lauren A. FIRESTONE
90 Dir Instruct/Emerging Technology ... Mr. Teb LOCKE
06 Registrar & Assoc Director Inst Res ... Ms. Christine D. ALEXANDER
29 Asst VP/Alumni Engagement ... Ms. Amy T. LAYMAN
07 Director of Admission ... Ms. Julie A. KERICH
41 Athletic Director ... Ms. Patricia EPPS
43 General Counsel ... Mr. Pierce BULLER
101 Secretary of the Institution/Board ... Ms. Robyn PIGGOTT
102 Sr Dir Col Grants/Found & Corp ... Mr. Ryan SAUDER
44 Director Annual Giving ... Mr. Ramy RAHAL
39 Dir Resident Life/Student Housing ... Ms. Lori N. FOUST

Gannon University (E)

University Square, Erie PA 16541-0001
County: Erie FICE Identification: 003266
Unit ID: 212601
Telephone: (814) 871-7000 Carnegie Class: DU-Mod
FAX Number: (814) 871-7338 Calendar System: Other
URL: www.gannon.edu
Established: 1925 Annual Undergrad Tuition & Fees: $32,136
Enrollment: 4,149 Coed
Affiliation or Control: Roman Catholic IRS Status: 501(c)3
Highest Offering: Doctorate
Accreditation: M, ACBSP, ANEST, ARCPA, CAATE, CACREP, CEA, COARC, COARCP, NURSE, OT, PTA, RAD, SW

01 President ... Dr. Keith TAYLOR
05 VP Academic Affairs ... Dr. Walter IWANENKO, JR.
10 Vice Pres Planning and Finance ... Ms. Valerie BACIK
30 Vice Pres University Advancement ... Mr. R. Scott RASH
88 Assoc Vice President for Mission ... Rev. Michael KESICKI
84 Vice President for Enrollment ... Mr. William EDMONDSON
32 VP Student Development & Engagement ... Mr. Brian NICHOLS
20 VP Academic Administration ... Dr. Steven A. MAURO
04 Assistant to the President ... Ms. Darlene A. MCMICHAEL
79 Dean Col Humanities/Educ/Soc Sci ... Dr. Lori LINDLEY
54 Dean Col Engineering/Business ... Dr. Karinna VERNAZA
76 Dean Morosky Col Health Prof/Sci ... Dr. Sarah EWING
49 Director of Liberal Studies ... Rev. Shawn CLERKIN
08 Director Nash Library ... Mr. Ken BRUNDAGE
37 Director of Financial Aid ... Ms. Sharon A. KRAHE
06 Registrar ... Ms. Kara A. MORGAN
36 Dir Career Devel/Employment Svcs ... Mr. Brian COLLINGWOOD
39 Director of Residence Life ... Ms. Denise GOLDEN
23 Head Nurse ... Vacant
88 Dir Student Organiz/Leadership Dev ... Ms. Beth Ann SCHICK
44 Director Development ... Ms. Cathy FRESCH
26 Chief Marketing/Communications Ofcr ... Mr. Douglas OATHOUT
102 Dir of Research/Foundation Rels ... Vacant
21 Controller ... Mr. David NIEMIRA
114 Assoc Vice President Budget ... Ms. Mary Kathleen LEONARD
15 Exec Director of Human Resources ... Mr. Robin WILLIAMS
41 Director of Athletics ... Ms. Lisa GODDARD MCGUIRK
19 Director Campus Police & Safety ... Mr. Les FETTERMAN
13 Director of Computing/Telecomm ... Mr. Mark JORDANO
42 University Chaplain ... Vacant
07 Director of Admissions ... Mr. Thomas P. CAMILLO
09 Director of Institutional Research ... Mr. Dana BAGWELL
18 Chief Facilities/Physical Plant ... Mr. Josh EBERLE
27 Chief Media Relations Officer ... Vacant
38 Director Student Counseling ... Mr. Brian COLLINGWOOD
86 Dir Community/Government Relations ... Ms. Erika A. RAMALHO
96 Director of Purchasing ... Mr. Andrew TEETS
40 Bookstore Manager ... Ms. Amber COOK

Geisinger Commonwealth School of Medicine (F)

525 Pine Street, Scranton PA 18509
County: Lackawanna FICE Identification: 041672
Unit ID: 456542
Telephone: (570) 504-7000 Carnegie Class: Spec-4-yr-Med
FAX Number: (570) 504-9660 Calendar System: Semester
URL: https://www.geisinger.edu/education
Established: 2009 Annual Graduate Tuition & Fees: N/A
Enrollment: 520 Coed
Affiliation or Control: Independent Non-Profit IRS Status: 501(c)3
Highest Offering: Doctorate; No Undergraduates
Accreditation: M, MED

01 President and Dean ... Dr. Steven J. SCHEINMAN
10 VP for Finance & Admin/CFO ... Ms. Anna ARVAY
28 VP Cmty Engage/Chf Diversity Ofcr ... Dr. Ida L. CASTRO
05 VP Acad Affairs/Vice Dean Med Ed ... Dr. William JEFFRIES
45 VP Strat Plng Com/Vice Dean Grad Ed .. Dr. Venard S. KOERWER
32 Assoc Dean Student Affairs ... Dr. Tanja ADONIZIO
20 Assoc Dean Educ Admin ... Dr. Andrea DIMATTIA
07 Assoc Dean Admission/Enrol/Fin Aid ... Dr. Michelle SCHMUDE
21 Senior Dir Opers/Acad Affairs ... Mr. Sam DIAZ
35 Asst Dean of Students ... Ms. Jacquelyn GHORMOZ
06 Registrar ... Mr. Edward LAHART
37 Director of Financial Aid ... Ms. Sue MCNAMARA
29 Director Alumni Relations ... Mr. Christopher BOLAND

Geneva College (G)

3200 College Avenue, Beaver Falls PA 15010-3557
County: Beaver FICE Identification: 003267
Unit ID: 212656
Telephone: (724) 846-5100 Carnegie Class: Masters/M
FAX Number: (724) 847-6687 Calendar System: Semester
URL: www.geneva.edu
Established: 1848 Annual Undergrad Tuition & Fees: $27,230
Enrollment: 1,598 Coed
Affiliation or Control: Reformed Presbyterian Church IRS Status: 501(c)3
Highest Offering: Master's
Accreditation: M, ACBSP, CACREP

01 President ... Dr. Calvin L. TROUP
05 Provost ... Dr. Melinda R. STEPHENS
111 Vice Pres of Advancement ... Dr. Marvin L. DEWEY
10 VP Bus/Finance/Int Title IX Coord ... Mr. Timothy R. BAIRD
84 VP Enrollment & Marketing ... Mr. Anthony TURNER
13 CIO & VP Information Technology ... Mr. Scott F. BARNES
21 Controller ... Mrs. Kami S. GREENE
07 Assoc VP for Enrollment ... Mr. David B. LAYTON
32 Dean of Student Development ... Ms. Jamie R. SWANK
35 Director of Student Engagement ... Mr. Randon T. WILLARD
58 Dean Grad/Adult & Online Programs ... Mr. John D. GALLO
06 Registrar ... Mr. William M. STARKE
37 Director of Student Financial Svcs ... Ms. Allyson D. GRUBB
08 Librarian ... Vacant
26 Director Public Relations ... Mrs. Cheryl L. JOHNSTON
29 Alumni Relations Coordinator ... Ms. Kelly J. SANZARI
41 Director of Athletics ... Mr. Van G. ZANIC
18 Director of Physical Plant ... Mr. Robert M. SKOFF
36 Director of Career Development ... Ms. Cara E. FULTON
85 International Admissions Counselor ... Vacant
40 Campus Store Manager ... Ms. Rachael E. VAN DERVEER
19 Director of Security ... Mr. Dennis E. DAMAZO
28 Interim Coordinator of Diversity ... Mrs. Kristie A. MARTEL
92 Director of Honors Program ... Dr. Eric MILLER
39 Director of Residence Life ... Mrs. Kelsey L. MURPHY
23 Health Services Director ... Mrs. Beth L. CARLSON
96 Director of Purchasing ... Mr. Daniel A. BEILSTEIN
88 Accounting and Payroll Manager ... Mr. William NICHOLS
88 ACCESS Director ... Mr. Thomas C. PYLE
04 Executive Asst to President ... Mrs. Andrea KAMICKER
09 Director of Institutional Research ... Mr. Jordan BOUSCHER
50 Business Dept Chair ... Ms. Christen S. ADELS
53 Education Dept Chair ... Mrs. Adel G. AIKEN
54 Engineering Dept Chair ... Dr. Anthony C. COMER
90 Director of Technology Services ... Mr. Jeremy T. YERSE
07 Associate Dir of Recruitment ... Mr. Dana M. PHELGAR
104 Dir Crossroads/Ctr Special Programs ... Dr. Jeffrey S. COLE
105 Online Marketing/Webmaster ... Mr. Michael W. DUNCAN
106 Dean Grad/Adult/Online Programs ... Mr. John D. GALLO
15 Chief Human Resources Officer ... Mrs. Sue THOMPSON
30 Director of Development ... Ms. Kelli J. MCKEE

Gettysburg College (H)

300 N Washington Street, Gettysburg PA 17325-1486
County: Adams FICE Identification: 003268
Unit ID: 212674
Telephone: (717) 337-6000 Carnegie Class: Bac-A&S
FAX Number: (717) 337-6008 Calendar System: Semester
URL: www.gettysburg.edu
Established: 1832 Annual Undergrad Tuition & Fees: $54,480
Enrollment: 2,411 Coed
Affiliation or Control: Evangelical Lutheran Church In America
IRS Status: 501(c)3
Highest Offering: Baccalaureate
Accreditation: M, MUS

01 President ... Mr. Robert IULIANO
03 Executive Vice President ... Ms. Jane D. NORTH
05 Provost ... Dr. Christopher ZAPPE
30 Vice Pres Dev & Alumni/Parent Rels ... Ms. Elizabeth DIEHL
10 Vice President Finance/Treasurer ... Mr. Daniel T. KONSTALID
32 Vice President for College Life ... Dr. Julie L. RAMSEY
84 Vice Pres Enrollment/Education Svcs ... Ms. Barbara B. FRITZE
13 Vice President Information Tech ... Dr. Rod TOSTEN
45 Assoc Provost for Plng/Fac & Tech ... Ms. Rhonda GOOD
28 Chief Diversity Officer ... Ms. Jeanne ARNOLD
21 Associate Vice President/Treasurer ... Mr. Christopher DELANEY
26 Exec Dir Communications/Marketing ... Ms. Jamie YATES
35 Associate Dean of College Life ... Mr. James P. DUFFY
110 Associate Vice Pres for Development ... Vacant
85 Dir International Student Services ... Mr. Brad LANCASTER
06 Registrar ... Mr. Brian REESE
37 Exec Director of Financial Aid ... Ms. Christina L. GORMLEY
07 Dean of Admissions ... Ms. Gail M. SWEEZEY
42 Chaplain ... Rev. Kristin LARGEN
09 Director for Institutional Analysis ... Ms. Suhua DONG
38 Exec Dir of Health & Counseling ... Ms. Kathy BRADLEY
08 Dean of the Library ... Ms. Robin WAGNER
29 Exec Director of Alumni Relations ... Mr. Joe LYNCH
41 Exec Director for Athletics ... Mr. Mike M. MATTIA
19 Asst VP Col Life/Exec Dir Safety ... Mr. William J. LAFFERTY
18 Exec Dir Facilities Plng & Mgmt ... Mr. James BIESECKER
21 Sr Dir of Financial Svcs/Controller ... Ms. Sharon S. DAYHOFF
80 Director Center for Public Service ... Ms. Gretchen NATTER
39 Dir Res Life & First Yr Programs ... Ms. Danielle PHILLIPS
20 Dean of Academic Advising ... Ms. Anne LANE
23 Director Health Services ... Ms. Judith WILLIAMS
122 Dir Student Activities & Greek Life ... Mr. Jonathan ALLEN
40 Director of College Bookstore ... Mr. Michael J. KOTLINSKI
94 Dir Women's Center ... Ms. Valentina CUCUZZA
96 Asst Director of Procurement ... Ms. Patricia K. VERDEROSA
15 Co-Director Human Resources ... Ms. Jennifer R. LUCAS
15 Co-Director Human Resources ... Ms. Regina Z. CAMPO
102 Dir Foundation/Govt & FAC Grants ... Ms. Laura RUNYAN
27 Dir Comm Content/Comm & Marketing ... Ms. Carina SITKUS
104 Dir Global Init/Ctr Global Educ ... Ms. Rebecca A. BERGREN

04 Administrative Asst to President ... Ms. Pamela EISENHART
109 Exec Dir Aux Svcs/Life Safety Mgr ... Mr. Peter C. NORTH
36 Exec Dir Ctr for Career Engagement ... Mr. Marc GOLDMAN

Gratz College (A)

7605 Old York Road, Melrose Park PA 19027-3010
County: Montgomery FICE Identification: 004058
Unit ID: 212771
Telephone: (215) 635-7300 Carnegie Class: Spec-4-yr-Faith
FAX Number: (215) 635-1046 Calendar System: Trimester
URL: www.gratz.edu
Established: 1895 Annual Undergrad Tuition & Fees: N/A
Enrollment: 247 Coed
Affiliation or Control: Independent Non-Profit IRS Status: 501(c)3
Highest Offering: Doctorate
Accreditation: M

01 President ... Dr. Paul FINKELMAN
05 Dean ... Dr. Honour MOORE
26 Chief Public Relations Officer ... Ms. Dodi KLIMOFF
08 Librarian ... Ms. Donna GUERIN
84 Director of Enrollment Management ... Ms. Kim REILLY
06 Student Records ... Ms. Lovisa WOODSON
15 Personnel Services ... Ms. Yaffa HOWARD
30 Dir Institutional Advancement ... Ms. Naomi HOUSMAN
07 Assistant Director of Admissions ... Ms. Mindy BLECHMAN
88 Dir Jewish Community High Sch ... Ms. Dina MAIBEN
37 Student Financial Services Advisor ... Ms. Jeanne CAVALIERI-GROVER
105 Director Web Services ... Ms. Suzette MARTINEZ-QUILES
106 Online Education/E-learning ... Ms. Vickie BRACE
13 Chief Info Technology Officer ... Ms. Suzette MARTINEZ-QUILES
53 Director of MA Education Pgm ... Mr. Dave MALTER
18 Chief Facilities/Physical Plant ... Mr. Ernest COLLINS
04 Administrative Asst to President ... Ms. Dodi KLIMOFF
10 Mgr Business Operations/Facilities ... Mr. Thomas CIPRIANO, JR.

Great Lakes Institute of Technology (B)

5100 Peach Street, Erie PA 16509
County: Erie FICE Identification: 021122
Unit ID: 213181
Telephone: (814) 864-6666 Carnegie Class: Spec 2-yr-Health
FAX Number: (814) 868-1717 Calendar System: Other
URL: www.glit.edu
Established: 1965 Annual Undergrad Tuition & Fees: N/A
Enrollment: 396 Coed
Affiliation or Control: Proprietary IRS Status: Proprietary
Highest Offering: Associate Degree
Accreditation: ACCSC, DMS, SURGT

01 Director/CEO ... Eric BERRIOS
07 Director of Admissions ... Barbara BOLT
37 Director Student Financial Aid ... Andrew DICK
05 Director of Education ... Vickie CLEMENTS

Grove City College (C)

100 Campus Drive, Grove City PA 16127-2104
County: Mercer FICE Identification: 003269
Unit ID: 212805
Telephone: (724) 458-2000 Carnegie Class: Bac-A&S
FAX Number: (724) 458-2190 Calendar System: Semester
URL: www.gcc.edu
Established: 1876 Annual Undergrad Tuition & Fees: $17,930
Enrollment: 2,373 Coed
Affiliation or Control: Non-denominational IRS Status: 501(c)3
Highest Offering: Baccalaureate
Accreditation: M, ACBSP, EXSC, @SW

01 President ... Mr. Paul J. MCNULTY
05 Interim Provost/VP Academic Affairs ... Dr. David J. AYERS
10 Vice Pres for Business & Finance ... Mr. Michael R. BUCKMAN
32 Vice Pres For Student Life/Learning ... Mr. Larry E. HARDESTY
111 Vice President for Inst Advancement .. Mr. Jeffrey D. PROKOVICH
11 Vice President for Operations ... Mr. James M. LOPRESTI
13 Vice Pres/Chief Information Officer ... Dr. Vincent F. DISTASI
84 VP of Enrollment Svcs & Registrar ... Dr. John G. INMAN
88 Vice Pres for Student Recruitment ... Mr. Lee S. WISHING, III
100 Assistant to the President ... Ms. Betty L. TALLERICO
49 Interim Dean Sch of Arts/Letters ... Dr. Paul C. KEMENY
81 Dean Sch of Sci/Engr/Math ... Dr. Richard N. SAVAGE
21 Director of Financial Services ... Mrs. Michelle M. WILLIAMS
15 Director of Human Resources ... Mrs. Marci K. WAGNER
35 Assistant Dean of Students ... Dr. John M. COYNE
07 Director of Admissions ... Vacant
36 Director of Career Services ... Ms. Amanda L. SPOSATO
08 Librarian ... Mrs. Barbra M. MUNNELL
37 Director of Financial Aid ... Mr. Thomas G. BALL
88 Dir Std Rec/Club Sports/Frat Life ... Mr. Andrew A. TONCIC, JR.
35 Director Stdnt Activities/Programs ... Mr. T. Scott GORDON
19 Director of Campus Safety ... Mr. Seth J. VAN TIL
23 Director of Health & Wellness Ctr ... Mrs. Amy E. PAGANO
40 Bookstore Manager ... Mrs. Carrie J. ROSE
41 Athletic Director ... Mr. Todd D. GIBSON
42 Interim Chaplain ... Rev Dr. D. Dean WEAVER
29 Sr Dir Alumni & College Relations ... Ms. Melissa A. MACLEOD
30 Sr Director of Development ... Mr. Brian M. POWELL
26 Sr Director of Communications ... Mrs. Jacquelyn P. MULLER
38 Director of College Counseling ... Dr. Suzanne N. HOUK
39 Director of Residence Life ... Mr. Jonathan J. DIBENEDETTO

Gwynedd Mercy University (D)

1325 Sumneytown Pike, PO Box 901,
Gwynedd Valley PA 19437-0901
County: Montgomery FICE Identification: 003270
Unit ID: 212832
Telephone: (215) 646-7300 Carnegie Class: Masters/M
FAX Number: (215) 641-5596 Calendar System: Semester
URL: www.gmercyu.edu
Established: 1948 Annual Undergrad Tuition & Fees: $33,600
Enrollment: 2,808 Coed
Affiliation or Control: Roman Catholic IRS Status: 501(c)3
Highest Offering: Doctorate
Accreditation: M, COARC, IACBE, NURSE, RTT, SW

01 President ... Ms. Deanne H. D'EMILIO
05 VP Academic Affairs ... Dr. Mary H. VAN BRUNT
10 Vice President Finance & Admin ... Mr. Kevin O'FLAHERTY
111 Vice Pres Institutional Advancement ... Mr. Gerald MCLAUGHLIN
32 VP Stdnt Svcs/Dean of Students ... Mr. Joshua STERN
42 VP Mission & Ministry ... Sr. Catherine MCMAHON, RSM
84 VP for Mktg & Enroll Mgmt ... Ms. Kelly STATMORE
101 Secretary of the Institution/Board ... Ms. Barbara MCHALE
108 AVP for Assessment & Compliance ... Dr. Dawn HAYWARD
06 Registrar ... Ms. Joanna RAUDENBUSH
08 Director of Library ... Mr. Daniel SCHABERT
37 Director of Student Financial Aid ... Ms. Elizabeth HOWARD
13 Chief Information Officer ... Mr. Joseph PUPO
29 Director Alumni Relations ... Ms. Gianna QUINN
09 Director of Institutional Research ... Dr. Jing GAO
15 Director Human Resources ... Ms. Rosina DEVER
21 Controller ... Ms. Jennifer GINNETTI
38 Director Counseling ... Ms. Pamela MOORE
07 Director of Undergrad Admissions ... Ms. Michele DIEHL
96 Director of Procurement ... Mr. Frank PETKA
102 Dir Foundation/Corporate Relations ... Ms. Josephina BANNER
19 Director Campus Safety/Security ... Ms. Joanna GALLAGHER
41 Athletic Dir/Head Women's Bsktbl ... Mr. Keith MONDILLO
39 Director Student Housing ... Mr. Bryan DUNPHY-CULP

HACC, Central Pennsylvania's Community College (E)

1 HACC Drive, Harrisburg PA 17110-2999
County: Dauphin FICE Identification: 003273
Unit ID: 212878
Telephone: (800) 222-4222 Carnegie Class: Assoc/MT-VT-High Trad
FAX Number: (717) 909-1491 Calendar System: Semester
URL: www.hacc.edu
Established: 1964 Annual Undergrad Tuition & Fees (In-District): $6,683
Enrollment: 18,681 Coed
Affiliation or Control: State/Local IRS Status: 501(c)3
Highest Offering: Associate Degree
Accreditation: M, ACBSP, ACFEI, ADNUR, ART, COARC, CSHSE, CVT, DA, DH, DMS, EMT, MAC, MLTAD, PNUR, RAD, SURGT

01 President/CEO ... Dr. John J. SYGIELSKI
05 Provost/VP Academic Affairs ... Dr. Cynthia A. DOHERTY
32 VP Student Affairs/Enrollment Mgmt ... Dr. Clarresa MORTON
10 Vice Pres Finance/CFO ... Mr. Timothy SANDOE
111 VP College Advancement ... Dr. Linnie S. CARTER
20 Assoc Provost Academic Affairs ... Dr. Kathleen T. DOHERTY
103 Assoc Provost Workforce Development ... Mr. Victor RODGERS
15 Chief HR Officer ... Ms. Aimee B. BROUGH
28 Chief Inclusion/Diversity Officer ... Dr. Warren R. ANDERSON
12 Campus VP Harrisburg Campus ... Mr. Noah J. ROUFOS-ABBEY
12 Campus VP Lancaster/Lebanon ... Vacant
12 Exec Dir Lebanon Campus ... Ms. Laurie A. BOWERSOX
12 Campus VP Gettysburg ... Ms. Shannon S. HARVEY
12 Campus VP York ... Dr. Darryl E. JONES
106 Associate Provost Virtual Learning ... Ms. Doreen FISHER-BAMMER
08 Executive Director HACC Libraries ... Ms. Beth A. EVITTS
121 Dean Student/Acad Success ... Vacant
06 Registrar ... Dr. Genita D. MANGUM
26 VP Information Technology/CIO ... Mr. Robert H. MESSNER
96 Director Procurement and Contracts ... Mr. Lee W. HAYES
19 Director Safety and Security ... Mr. Ivan A. QUINONES
40 Director College Bookstores ... Mr. Kyle J. DIBRITO
21 Controller ... Vacant
09 Exec Dir Inst Effectiveness ... Mr. Lynold K. MCGHEE
37 Director Financial Aid ... Mr. Andrew E. MARAH
84 Dean Enrollment Management ... Vacant
102 Executive Director HACC Foundation ... Dr. Linnie S. CARTER
04 Executive Asst to the President ... Mrs. Kristin GRAESER

HACC Gettysburg Campus (F)

731 Old Harrisburg Road, Gettysburg PA 17325
Telephone: (717) 337-3855 Identification: 770156
Accreditation: &M

Harcum College (G)

750 Montgomery Avenue, Bryn Mawr PA 19010-3476
County: Montgomery FICE Identification: 003272
Unit ID: 212869
Telephone: (610) 525-4100 Carnegie Class: Assoc/HVT-High Trad
FAX Number: (610) 526-6009 Calendar System: Semester
URL: www.harcum.edu
Established: 1915 Annual Undergrad Tuition & Fees: $24,200
Enrollment: 1,481 Coed
Affiliation or Control: Independent Non-Profit IRS Status: 501(c)3
Highest Offering: Associate Degree
Accreditation: M, ADNUR, DA, DH, HT, MLTAD, OTA, PTAA, RAD

01 President ... Dr. Jon Jay DETEMPLE
05 EVP/VP of Academic & Legal Affairs ... Dr. Julia INGERSOLL
10 Vice Pres of Finance & Operations ... Dr. Patricia BENSON
32 Dean of Student Life ... Mr. Edward KOVACS
84 Exec Dir Enrollment Management ... Ms. Rachel BOWEN
111 VP of College Advancement ... Mr. John HAYDEN
20 Asst VP Academic Support Services ... Ms. Koyuki YIP
51 Exec Dir of Partnership Sites ... Ms. Evelyn SANTANA
18 Facilities Manager ... Mr. Nikolay KARPALO
15 Exec Dir of HR & Compliance Officer ... Mr. Hunt BARDINE
06 Registrar ... Ms. Karen JOHNSON
08 Director of Library Services ... Ms. Katie MCGOWAN
85 Director of International Programs ... Ms. Michelle STANZIANO
26 Dir of Communications & Marketing ... Ms. Gale MARTIN
29 Director of Alumni Relations ... Ms. Melissa SAMANGO
38 Director of Counseling Services ... Ms. Kathy ANTHONY
36 Dir of Career & Transfer Services ... Ms. Danyele DOVE
37 Director of Financial Aid ... Ms. Melissa WALSH
39 Assistant Dean of Students ... Mr. Jameel TUCKER
35 Director of Campus Activities ... Ms. Laurie PLAZA
21 Director of Business Services ... Mr. Stephen KLEPONIS
19 Director of Campus Safety ... Mr. Rick SANFILIPPO
41 Director of Athletics ... Mr. Drew KELLY
04 Dir President's Office Operations ... Ms. Tricia FLEMING
13 IT Executive Director ... Mr. John SUPPLEE
09 Director of Institutional Research ... Mr. Tim ELY
106 Dir Online Education/E-learning ... Mr. Stephen PIPITONE
108 Director Institutional Assessment ... Mr. Tim ELY
50 Director of Business Mgmt Program ... Mr. Mike PRUSHAN
86 External Affairs ... Dr. Jon Jay DETEMPLE

Harrisburg Area Community College Lancaster Campus (H)

1641 Old Philadelphia Pike, Lancaster PA 17602
Telephone: (717) 293-5000 Identification: 770157
Accreditation: &M

Harrisburg Area Community College Lebanon Campus (I)

735 Cumberland Street, Lebanon PA 17042
Telephone: (717) 270-4222 Identification: 770158
Accreditation: &M

Harrisburg Area Community College York Campus (J)

2010 Pennsylvania Avenue, York PA 17404
Telephone: (717) 718-0328 Identification: 770159
Accreditation: &M

Harrisburg University of Science and Technology (K)

326 Market Street, Harrisburg PA 17101-2116
County: Dauphin FICE Identification: 039483
Unit ID: 446640
Telephone: (717) 901-5100 Carnegie Class: Masters/L
FAX Number: (717) 901-3152 Calendar System: Trimester
URL: www.harrisburgu.edu
Established: 2001 Annual Undergrad Tuition & Fees: $23,900
Enrollment: 3,997 Coed
Affiliation or Control: Independent Non-Profit IRS Status: 501(c)3
Highest Offering: Doctorate
Accreditation: M

01 President/CEO ... Dr. Eric D. DARR
05 Provost/Chief Academic Officer ... Dr. Bilita S. MATTES
10 COO/Chief Financial Officer ... Mr. Duane F. MAUN
103 VP Strategic Workforce Development . Ms. Kelly POWELL LOGAN
26 Assoc VP Comm/Marketing/Alum Rels ... Mr. Steven M. INFANTI
88 Assoc VP for University Centers ... Ms. Kelly POWELL LOGAN
13 Assoc VP/Chief Technology Officer ... Mr. Alex C. PITZNER
108 Director of Assessment ... Ms. Penny L. WEIDNER
100 Chief of Staff ... Mr. Douglas FIRESTONE
37 Director Financial Aid ... Mr. Vincent P. FRANK
06 Registrar ... Ms. Sandra NELSON
07 Director of Admissions ... Ms. Laurie BARROW
08 University Librarian ... Mr. David RUNYON
32 Director of Student Services ... Ms. Melissa MORGAN

Haverford College (L)

370 Lancaster Avenue, Haverford PA 19041-1392
County: Delaware & Montgomery FICE Identification: 003274
Unit ID: 212911
Telephone: (610) 896-1000 Carnegie Class: Bac-A&S
FAX Number: (610) 896-4202 Calendar System: Semester
URL: www.haverford.edu
Established: 1833 Annual Undergrad Tuition & Fees: $54,838
Enrollment: 1,296 Coed
Affiliation or Control: Independent Non-Profit IRS Status: 501(c)3
Highest Offering: Master's
Accreditation: M

01 President ... Dr. Wendy E. RAYMOND
05 Provost ... Dr. Frances R. BLASE
10 SVP Finance/Chief Admin Officer ... Mitchell L. WEIN
30 VP for Institutional Advancement ... Ann W. FIGUEREDO
20 Dean of the College ... Dr. Martha DENNEY
07 VP & Dean of Admission ... Jess LORD
104 Director of Intl Academic Programs ... Rebecca AVERY
89 Dean of First Year Students ... Katrina GLANZER
115 Chief Investment Officer ... Michael CASEL
88 Asst VP Institutional Advancement ... Diane WILDER
100 VP & Chief of Staff ... Dr. Jesse LYTLE
41 Director of Athletics ... Wendall SMITH
26 Asst VP College Communications ... Chris MILLS
09 Director of Institutional Research ... Catherine FENNELL
08 Librarian ... Dr. Terry SNYDER
15 Director of Human Resources ... T. Muriel BRISBON
21 Assoc VP & Controller ... Deborah FULLAM
96 Director of Purchasing ... Nikoletta MILLAS
18 Director of Physical Plant ... Donald CAMPBELL
19 Director of Safety & Security ... Thomas KING
88 Director Conferences/Dir Campus Ctr ... Geoffey LABE
109 Assoc Director of Dining Services ... Vacant
40 Bookstore Manager ... Lydia WHITELAW
39 Director of Student Housing ... Nathan DIEHL
34 Director of Women's Center ... Vacant
23 Director of Health Services ... Catherine SHARBAUGH
38 Director Counseling/Disability Svcs ... Dr. Philip ROSENBAUM
36 Dean of Career/Prof Advising ... Amy FEIFER
06 Registrar ... James KEANE
37 Director of Financial Aid ... Michael COLAHAN
29 Director of Alumni & Parent Rels ... Lauren PORTNOY
44 Director of Gift Planning ... Olga BRIKER
20 Director for Academic Resources ... Alex MOLOT
28 Assoc Dean Diversity/Access/Engage ... Dr. Theresa TENSUAN
32 Asst Dean of Student Activities ... Michael ELIAS
13 Chief Information Officer ... Megan FITCH
04 Administrative Asst to President ... Joan WANKMILLER

Holy Family University (A)

9801 Frankford Avenue, Philadelphia PA 19114-2009

County: Philadelphia FICE Identification: 003275
Unit ID: 212984
Telephone: (215) 637-7700 Carnegie Class: Masters/L
FAX Number: (215) 637-3787 Calendar System: Semester
URL: www.holyfamily.edu
Established: 1954 Annual Undergrad Tuition & Fees: $30,346
Enrollment: 3,081 Coed
Affiliation or Control: Roman Catholic IRS Status: 501(c)3
Highest Offering: Doctorate
Accreditation: M, ACBSP, IFSAC, NURSE, RAD

01 President ... Sr. Maureen MCGARRITY
10 VP for Finance & Administration ... Mr. Eric NELSON
05 VP for Academic Affairs ... Dr. Michael MARKOWITZ
42 VP for Mission ... Ms. Margaret S. KELLY
13 VP for Information Technology ... Mr. Eugene KOVALCHICK
32 Dean of Students ... Vacant
111 VP for University Advancement ... Dr. James GARVEY
32 VP for Student Affairs ... Dr. Abigail WERNICKI
06 Assoc VP Academic Svcs/Registrar ... Dr. Ann Marie VICKERY
58 Dean for Graduate and Prof Studies ... Dr. Karen GALARDI
35 Assoc VP of Student Life ... Mr. Michael MCNULTY
28 Assoc VP Inst Effective/Diversity ... Dr. Nicole STOKES-DUPASS
37 Director Student Financial Aid ... Ms. Janice HETRICK
21 Assoc VP/Controller and Treasurer ... Ms. Anne MCMAHON
15 Assoc VP for Human Resources ... Ms. Jennifer LULING
30 Asst VP for Development ... Mr. Joshua LISS
102 AVP Corp Foundation & Govt Rels ... Ms. Kim CAULFIELD
08 Exec Director Library Services ... Ms. Shannon BROWN
26 Exec Dir Marketing/Communications ... Vacant
38 Director Counseling Center ... Mr. John WATSON
42 Director of Campus Ministry ... Rev. James MACNEW
07 Director Undergraduate Admissions ... Ms. Lauren CAMPBELL
41 Director of Athletics ... Mr. Timothy HAMILL
53 Dean of the School of Education ... Dr. Kevin ZOOK
66 Dean Nursing/Allied Health Prof ... Dr. Cynthia RUSSELL
49 Dean of School of Arts & Sciences ... Dr. Rochelle ROBBINS
50 Dean of School of Business Admin ... Dr. J. Barry DICKINSON
29 Asst Dir Alumni & Parent Relations ... Ms. Julie REMPFER
09 Director of Institutional Research ... Vacant
18 Director Campus Operations ... Mr. Ralph CARP
39 Assoc Director Residence Life ... Ms. Kim MAGUIRE
100 Special Asst to the President ... Ms. Kate BRESLIN
105 Web Specialist ... Mr. Robert TOEPPNER
19 Director Security/Safety-Allied ... Mr. Dave NEUMAN
85 Dir International Student Affairs ... Sr. Josita CHURLA
23 Director of Health Services ... Ms. Julie HUMMER
108 Dir Inst Assessment/Accreditation ... Mr. John ANDELFINGER
44 Director Annual Giving ... Ms. Christina BENDER

Hussian College (B)

1500 Spring Garden Street, Philadelphia PA 19130

County: Philadelphia FICE Identification: 007469
Unit ID: 212993
Telephone: (215) 574-9600 Carnegie Class: Spec-4-yr-Arts
FAX Number: (215) 574-9800 Calendar System: Semester
URL: www.hussiancollege.edu
Established: 1946 Annual Undergrad Tuition & Fees: $21,990
Enrollment: 52 Coed
Affiliation or Control: Proprietary IRS Status: Proprietary
Highest Offering: Baccalaureate
Accreditation: ACCSC

01 President ... Dr. Jeremiah STAROPOLI
05 Chief Academic Officer (Provost) ... Sylvia MCCRAY
06 Registrar ... Maureen FLANAGAN

Immaculata University (C)

1145 King Road, Immaculata PA 19345-0654

County: Chester FICE Identification: 003276
Unit ID: 213011
Telephone: (610) 647-4400 Carnegie Class: DU-Mod
FAX Number: (610) 251-1668 Calendar System: Semester
URL: www.immaculata.edu
Established: 1920 Annual Undergrad Tuition & Fees: $27,350
Enrollment: 2,481 Coed
Affiliation or Control: Roman Catholic IRS Status: 501(c)3
Highest Offering: Doctorate
Accreditation: M, ACBSP, CACREP, CLPSY, DIETD, DIETI, IPSY, MUS, NURSE

01 President ... Ms. Barbara LETTIERE
05 VP Academic Affairs & Provost ... Dr. Angela TEKELY
10 Vice Pres Finance/Administration ... Mr. Bruce FRIEDMAN
111 Vice Pres Advancement ... Ms. Susan ARNOLD
32 VP Student Development & UG Admiss ... Ms. Patti CANTERINO
42 Vice Pres of Mission and Ministry ... Sr. Mary HENRICH, IHM
06 Registrar ... Ms. Collette DELANEY
26 Exec Director of Communications ... Ms. Melissa KUSHNER
15 Exec Director of Human Res/Title IX ... Ms. Geri LARSEN
08 Executive Director of Library ... Dr. Jeffrey ROLLISON
13 Exec Director of Info Tech Services ... Mr. Bryan STEINBURG
07 Director of Admissions ... Ms. Christine ESBENSEN
90 Director Academic Technology ... Mr. Ron COSTELLO
14 Director of Technical Services ... Mr. Craig NESSON
37 Director Student Financial Aid ... Mr. Robert FOREST
88 Director Curriculum & Instruction ... Ms. Dorothy (Darcy) DOYLE
112 Director Annual & Leadership Giving ... Ms. Mary RAVENFELD
91 Director Administrative Computing ... Mr. Grant DAVIS
29 Director Alumni Relations ... Ms. Karen MATWEYCHUK
36 Director Career & Prof Development ... Ms. Heidi HARRISON
41 Athletic Director ... Ms. Janelle CRONMILLER
104 Director Study Abroad ... Sr. Elaine GLANZ, IHM
85 International Student Services ... Sr. Janet WALTERS, IHM
42 Chaplain ... Fr. Kevin MCCABE
20 Dean of Academic Affairs ... Ms. Mary Kate BOLAND
58 Dean College of Graduate Studies ... Dr. Thomas O'BRIEN
34 Dean College of Undergrad Studies ... Dr. Jean SHINGLE
107 Dean College of Adult Prof Studies ... Dr. Jean SHINGLE
21 Director of Finance/Controller ... Ms. Joanne CRISTINZIO
19 Director Campus Safety & Protection ... Mr. Dennis DOUGHERTY
88 Dir of Business Systems Analysis ... Ms. June GORMAN
38 Director Counseling Services ... Ms. Jessica GILPERT
18 Director of Facilities ... Vacant
25 Director of Sponsored Research ... Mr. Michael SCHUTZ
45 Director of Strategic Initiatives ... Sr. M. Carroll ISSELMANN, IHM
110 Director of Advancement Services ... Ms. Martha BORRACCINI
39 Director Res Life & Student Housing ... Ms. Jenny LUCAS
108 Assoc Director Academic Assessment ... Ms. Bobbijo PINNELLI
09 Office Inst Research/Effectiveness ... Ms. Cecelia OSWALD
04 Administrative Asst to President ... Ms. Leslie BOKOSKI
106 Online Education/E-learning ... Dr. Angela TEKELY
121 Exec Director of Academic Success ... Sr. Joseph Marie CARTER, IHM
28 Director of Diversity & Inclusion ... Ms. Marisa KINSEY

Institute of Medical and Business Careers (D)

133 Jefferson Rd, Ste 101, Pittsburgh PA 15235

County: Allegheny FICE Identification: 041551
Telephone: (412) 244-3240 Carnegie Class: Not Classified
FAX Number: (412) 244-3241 Calendar System: Other
URL: www.imbc.edu
Established: Annual Undergrad Tuition & Fees: N/A
Enrollment: N/A Coed
Affiliation or Control: Proprietary IRS Status: Proprietary
Highest Offering: Associate Degree
Accreditation: ABHES

01 Director ... Ms. Jennifer SMITH

International Institute for Restorative Practices (E)

531 Main Street, Bethlehem PA 18018

County: Northampton FICE Identification: 042061
Unit ID: 448691
Telephone: (610) 807-9221 Carnegie Class: Spec-4-yr-Other
FAX Number: (610) 807-0423 Calendar System: Trimester
URL: www.iirp.edu
Established: 2005 Annual Graduate Tuition & Fees: N/A
Enrollment: 98 Coed
Affiliation or Control: Independent Non-Profit IRS Status: 501(c)3
Highest Offering: Master's; No Undergraduates
Accreditation: M

01 President ... Dr. John BAILIE
05 Provost ... Dr. Craig ADAMSON
11 Vice President for Administration ... Ms. Linda B. KLIGMAN

JNA Institute of Culinary Arts (F)

1212 S Broad Street, Philadelphia PA 19146-3119

County: Philadelphia FICE Identification: 031033
Unit ID: 419341
Telephone: (215) 468-8800 Carnegie Class: Spec 2-yr-A&S
FAX Number: (215) 468-8838 Calendar System: Quarter
URL: www.culinaryarts.edu
Established: 1988 Annual Undergrad Tuition & Fees: $14,575
Enrollment: 46 Coed
Affiliation or Control: Proprietary IRS Status: Proprietary
Highest Offering: Associate Degree
Accreditation: ACCSC

01 Director ... Mr. Joseph DIGIRONIMO

Johnson College (G)

3427 North Main Avenue, Scranton PA 18508-1495

County: Lackawanna FICE Identification: 021142
Unit ID: 213233
Telephone: (570) 702-8900 Carnegie Class: Assoc/HVT-High Trad
FAX Number: (570) 348-2181 Calendar System: Semester
URL: www.johnson.edu
Established: 1912 Annual Undergrad Tuition & Fees: $18,991
Enrollment: 451 Coed
Affiliation or Control: Independent Non-Profit IRS Status: 501(c)3
Highest Offering: Associate Degree
Accreditation: @M, ACCSC, PTAA, RAD

01 President & CEO ... Dr. Katie LEONARD
10 Chief Financial Officer ... Ms. Liz RENDA
05 Chief Academic Officer ... Dr. Kellyn NOLAN
09 Director of Inst Effectiveness ... Ms. Laura LITTLE
04 Assistant to the President ... Ms. Julia JACIEN
08 Resource Officer ... Ms. Ashley HASSENBEIN
32 Director of Student Engagement ... Mr. Nolan RENZ
38 Counselor/Manager Disability Svcs ... Ms. Emily HOLMES
06 Assistant Registrar ... Ms. Aubree ARMEZZANI
11 Chief Administrative Officer ... Mr. Mike NOVAK
13 Director of Information Technology ... Mr. Jerry MARSH
15 VP of Human Resources & Sr Advisor ... Ms. Stephenie VERGNETTI
18 Director of Facilities ... Mr. Joseph MUSHENO
26 Assoc Director of Communications ... Ms. Sean Ann KELLY
30 Manager of Development ... Ms. Tracey PRATT
36 Career Services Manager ... Ms. Dana HEALEY
37 Director of Financial Aid ... Ms. Jess FARRELL
07 Assoc VP of Enrollment Services ... Mr. William BURKE

Juniata College (H)

1700 Moore Street, Huntingdon PA 16652-2119

County: Huntingdon FICE Identification: 003279
Unit ID: 213251
Telephone: (814) 641-3000 Carnegie Class: Bac-A&S
FAX Number: (814) 641-3199 Calendar System: Semester
URL: www.juniata.edu
Established: 1876 Annual Undergrad Tuition & Fees: $45,597
Enrollment: 1,495 Coed
Affiliation or Control: Independent Non-Profit IRS Status: 501(c)3
Highest Offering: Master's
Accreditation: M, IACBE, SW

01 President ... Dr. James A. TROHA
05 Provost ... Dr. Lauren BOWEN
84 VP Enrollment ... Mr. Jason E. MORAN
32 VP Student Life & Dean of Students ... Dr. Matthew DAMSCHRODER
111 VP for Advancement ... Mr. James R. WATT
13 Asst VP/Chief Information Officer ... Ms. Anne WOOD
10 Controller/Chief Financial Officer ... Ms. Karla D. WISER
28 Dean Inst Equity & Inclusive Excel ... Ms. Marita GILBERT
85 Dean of International Education ... Ms. Kati R. CSOMAN
06 Registrar ... Ms. Lucille CONDRON
27 Exec Director of Marketing ... Ms. Rosann BROWN
37 Dir Student Financial Plng ... Ms. Tracie M. PATRICK
08 Dean of the Library ... Ms. Lisa MCDANIELS
15 Director of Human Resources ... Ms. Tracy L. GRAJEWSKI
09 Dir Institutional Planning/Research ... Ms. Carlee K. RANALLI
18 Director of Facilities Services ... Mr. Tristan S. DEL GIUDICE
19 Director Public Safety ... Mr. Jesse W. LEONARD
41 Athletic Director ... Mr. Greg M. CURLEY
90 Dir Technology Solutions Center ... Mr. Joel C. PHEASANT
113 Bursar ... Ms. Lauren A. PEROW
114 Budget Director ... Ms. Susan F. SHONTZ
112 Senior Director of Major Gifts ... Mr. Joel DIAMOND
124 Asst Dean of Students Campus Life ... Ms. Erin PASCHAL
88 Director of Conferences & Events ... Ms. Lorri P. SHIDELER
07 Senior Associate Dean of Admission ... Ms. Terri L. BOLLMAN-DALANSKY
29 Director Alumni Relations ... Mr. David D. MEADOWS
39 Director of Residential Life ... Ms. Tasia Y. WHITE
04 Executive Asst to President ... Mrs. Bethany D. SHEFFIELD
43 College Counsel ... Mr. David P. ANDREWS

Keystone College (I)

One College Green, P.O. Box 50,
La Plume PA 18440-0200

County: Lackawanna FICE Identification: 003280
Unit ID: 213303
Telephone: (570) 945-8000 Carnegie Class: Bac-Diverse

FAX Number: (570) 945-8962　Calendar System: Semester
URL: www.keystone.edu
Established: 1868　Annual Undergrad Tuition & Fees: $26,720
Enrollment: 1,523　Coed
Affiliation or Control: Independent Non-Profit　IRS Status: 501(c)3
Highest Offering: Master's
Accreditation: M, IACBE

01 President .... Dr. Tracy BRUNDAGE
05 Provost & VP Academic Affairs .... Vacant
10 Vice Pres Finance & Administration .... Mr. Stuart RENDA
111 Vice President for Advancement .... Ms. Frances LANGAN
84 Vice Pres Enrollment & Marketing .... Dr. Janine BECKER
32 Dean of Student Life .... Ms. Nicole LANGAN
08 Associate Dean of Miller Library .... Ms. Mari FLYNN
07 Director of Admissions .... Ms. Jennifer SEKOL
06 Registrar .... Ms. Kate OWENS
37 Associate Dean/Financial Aid Dir .... Ms. Delaina JAYNE
13 Chief Information Officer .... Mr. Charles L. PROTHERO
15 Director of Human Resources .... Vacant
26 Senior Director College Relations .... Mr. Fran CALPIN
29 Director of Alumni Engagement .... Ms. Ehrin CLARK
09 Director Institutional Research .... Ms. Robyn DICKINSON
41 Director of Athletics .... Dr. Matthew GRIMALDI

King's College (A)

133 N River Street, Wilkes-Barre PA 18711-0801
County: Luzerne　FICE Identification: 003282
Unit ID: 213321
Telephone: (570) 208-5900　Carnegie Class: Masters/M
FAX Number: (570) 825-9049　Calendar System: Semester
URL: www.kings.edu
Established: 1946　Annual Undergrad Tuition & Fees: $37,226
Enrollment: 2,469　Coed
Affiliation or Control: Roman Catholic　IRS Status: 501(c)3
Highest Offering: Master's
Accreditation: M, ARCPA, CAATE

01 President .... Rev. John RYAN, CSC
05 Provost & VP for Academic Affairs .... Dr. Joseph EVAN
10 Int Exec VP for Business Affairs .... Ms. Allison SAMANAS
111 Vice President for Inst Advancement .... Mr. Frederick PETTIT
32 Vice President for Student Affairs .. Ms. Janet E. MERCINCAVAGE
84 Vice President for Enrollment Mgmt .... Mr. Robert REESE
04 Exec Assistant to the President .... Mrs. Anne NOONE
13 Associate VP/Chief Info Officer .... Mr. Paul J. MORAN
08 Director of Library .... Mr. David SCHAPPERT
35 Assoc Vice Pres Student Affairs .... Mr. Robert B. MCGONIGLE
50 Dean Wm G McGowan Sch Business .... Dr. Barry WILLIAMS
06 Registrar .... Mr. Daniel T. CEBRICK
37 Director of Financial Aid .... Mr. Jared MENGHINI
42 Chaplain/Director Campus Ministry ... Rev. Thomas LOONEY, CSC
36 Director Career Planning & Placemnt .... Mr. Christopher SUTZKO
15 Associate VP Human Resources .... Vacant
26 Director of Public Relations .... Mr. John MCANDREW
29 Senior Director of Engagement .... Ms. Patrice PERSICO
18 Executive Director of Facilities .... Mr. Thomas BUTCHKO
19 Director of Security/Safety .... Mr. James GILGALLON
41 Dir of Intercollegiate Athletics .... Ms. Cheryl J. ISH
21 Controller and Chief Risk Officer .... Ms. Holly KULP
39 Assoc Dean of Students Res Life .... Ms. Megan SELLICK
09 Director of Institutional Research .... Ms. Marian K. PALMERI
28 Director of College Diversity .... Ms. Jasmine TABRON-GIDDINGS
90 Managing Dir of User Services .... Mr. Raymond G. PRYOR
91 Managing Director for MIS .... Mr. William M. CORCORAN
112 Major Gifts Officer .... Mr. Richard LANAHAN
104 Director Study Abroad .... Ms. Margaret KOWALSKY
25 Dir of Inst and Academic Grants .... Ms. Michelle GIOVAGNOLI
44 Director Annual Giving .... Ms. Desiree VOITEK

La Roche University (B)

9000 Babcock Boulevard, Pittsburgh PA 15237-5898
County: Allegheny　FICE Identification: 003987
Unit ID: 213358
Telephone: (412) 367-9300　Carnegie Class: Masters/S
FAX Number: (412) 536-1062　Calendar System: Semester
URL: www.laroche.edu
Established: 1963　Annual Undergrad Tuition & Fees: $28,564
Enrollment: 1,535　Coed
Affiliation or Control: Roman Catholic　IRS Status: 501(c)3
Highest Offering: Doctorate
Accreditation: M, ACBSP, ADNUR, ANEST, ART, CIDA, NUR

01 President .... Sr. Candace INTROCASO, CDP
04 Exec Asst to the President .... Ms. Karen P. WILLOUGHBY
05 VP for Acad Affairs & Acad Dean .... Dr. Howard J. ISHIYAMA
84 VP for Enrollment Mgmt .... Dr. James (Chip) E. WEISGERBER
10 VP for Business & Finance .... Mr. Robert VOGEL
32 VP for Student Life/Dean Stdnts .... Ms. Colleen RUEFLE
111 VP for University Advancement .... Mr. Michael ANDREOLA
20 Assoc VP Academic Affairs .... Dr. Rosemary MCCARTHY
20 Assoc VP Academic Affairs .... Dr. Thomas G. SCHAEFER
121 Assoc Dean Academic/Student Support .... Ms. Marie DEEM
35 Director of Student Development .... Mr. David DAY
83 Div Chair Natural & Behavioral Sci .... Dr. Rebecca BOZYM
79 Div Chair Humanities .... Dr. Jeff RITTER
50 Div Co-Chair Business .... Dr. Lynn ARCHER
50 Div Co-Chair Business .... Ms. Shelia MUELLER
57 Div Chair Design .... Ms. Lisa KAMPHAUS
53 Div Co-Chair Education & Nursing .... Dr. Kathryn SILVIS
53 Div Co-Chair Education & Nursing .... Dr. Terri LIBERTO
06 Registrar .... Ms. Joan CUTONE
08 Director Library/Learning Center .... Ms. Alecia KERR
07 Executive Director for Enrollment .... Ms. Hope SCHIFFGENS
26 Assoc VP Mktg & Media Relations .... Mr. Brady BUTLER
37 Director of Financial Aid .... Ms. Sharon PLATT
41 Director of Athletics .... Mr. Jim TINKEY
42 Director of Mission & Ministry .... Sr. Elena ALMENDAREZ
39 Director Residence Life .... Ms. Ashley TESTA
13 Director Information Technology .... Ms. Terri BALLARD
85 Director International Student Svcs .... Dr. Natasha GARRETT
29 Director Alumni Relations .... Ms. Gina MILLER
21 Director of Finance .... Ms. Cathleen JACOBS
09 Director of Institutional Research .... Ms. Patricia A. CONNOLLY
18 Assoc VP of Facilities Management .... Mr. J.R YOUNG
38 Director Counseling Services .... Ms. Lori AREND
19 Director Public Safety .... Mr. Mark WILCOX
15 Assoc VP of Human Resources .... Ms. Eileen PETRONE
40 Bookstore Manager .... Ms. Michelle JAMES
113 Director of Student Accounts .... Ms. Danya TINKEY
101 Secretary of the Institution/Board .... Ms. Kathy KOZDEMBA
104 Coordinator Study Abroad .... Ms. Nicole GABLE
44 Dir Annual Giving/Advancement Srvs .... Mr. Craig BRUNO
86 Director Government Relations .... Mr. Michael ANDREOLA
102 Dir Foundation/Corporate Relations .... Ms. Janet DENNIS
28 Director of Diversity and Inclusion .... Ms. Candace OKELLO
105 Director Web Services .... Mr. David SIROKI

La Salle University (C)

1900 W Olney Avenue, Philadelphia PA 19141-1199
County: Philadelphia　FICE Identification: 003287
Unit ID: 213367
Telephone: (215) 951-1000　Carnegie Class: Masters/L
FAX Number: N/A　Calendar System: Semester
URL: www.lasalle.edu
Established: 1863　Annual Undergrad Tuition & Fees: $30,710
Enrollment: 5,197　Coed
Affiliation or Control: Roman Catholic　IRS Status: 501(c)3
Highest Offering: Doctorate
Accreditation: M, ANEST, CACREP, CLPSY, DIETC, DIETD, MFCD, NURSE, PH, SP, SW

01 President .... Dr. Colleen M. HANYCZ
05 Provost/VP Academic Affairs .... Dr. Brian A. GOLDSTEIN
04 Exec Admin Asst to the President .... Ms. Maryanne TAYLOR
111 VP University Advancement .... Ms. Cathleen PARSONS-NIKOLIC
10 VP Finance and Administration .... Mrs. Stephanie PRICKEN
32 VP Student Affairs & Enrollment Mgt .... Dr. Dawn M. SOUFLERIS
43 Vice President and General Counsel .... Mr. Kevin DOLAN
20 Assistant Provost .... Bro. John MCGOLDRICK
07 Asst VP Enrollment Services .... Ms. Kathryn PAYNE
30 Asst VP Development .... Mr. Daniel JOYCE
49 Dean School of Arts & Sciences .... Dr. Lynn A. TEXTER
50 Dean School of Business Admin . Ms. MarySheila A. MCDONALD
66 Dean School of Nursing/Health Sci .... Dr. Kathleen CZEKANSKI
22 Affirmative Action Officer/Title IX .... Ms. Rose Lee PAULINE
26 AVP Marketing and Communication .... Dr. Angela M. POLEC
29 AVP Alumni Relations .... Mr. Trey P. ULRICH
30 Exec Dir Advancement Operations .... Mr. Melissa SLY
58 Dir Grad Ctr/East European Studies .... Vacant
77 Director MS/CIS .... Ms. Margaret MCCOEY
53 Director Grad Education Program .... Dr. Greer RICHARDSON
83 Dir Grad Counseling & Family Therap .... Dr. Donna A. TONREY
73 Director Grad Pgms of Theology .... Fr. Francis J. BERNA
60 Dir Grad Communication .... Dr. Michael SMITH
66 Director Undergraduate Nursing .... Vacant
66 Dir Grad Nursing RN-MSN Pgm .... Dr. Patricia DILLON
69 Dir Master Public Health Program .... Dr. Candace ROBERTSON-JAMES
88 Dir Grad Econ Crime Forensics .... Ms. Margaret MCCOEY
88 Dir Grad Pgm Human Capital Develop .... Ms. Lynnette CLEMENT
58 Dir Grad Pgm Nonprofit Leadership .... Dr. Laura OTTEN
39 Asst VP Res Life Community Dev .... Mr. Alan B. WENDELL
35 Asst VP for Campus Life .... Ms. Anna M. ALLEN
42 Director Univ Ministry & Service .... Bro. Robert J. KINZLER
92 Dir University Honors Program .... Bro. Michael MCGINNISS
13 Chief Information Officer .... Mr. Karl HORVATH
08 Director of the Library .... Ms. Sarah CLARK
18 Asst VP Facilities Mgmt .... Mr. Dennis SHORES, JR.
19 Asst VP Public Safety .... Ms. Amanda GUTHORN
15 Asst VP Human Resources .... Ms. Kristin HEASLEY
41 Dir Intercollegiate Athletics .... Mr. Brian BAPTISTE
112 Director of Major Gifts .... Ms. Theresa MALANDRA
102 Director of The La Salle Fund .... Mr. Brian FRANKOWSKI
45 Dir Prospect Research/Strategy .... Ms. Karen MCNAMARA
07 Executive Director of Admission .... Mr. James C. PLUNKETT
37 Director Financial Aid .... Ms. Jennifer HOUSEMAN
06 Registrar .... Ms. Jean W. LANDIS
88 Dir Doctorate in Psych Program .... Dr. Megan SPOKAS
88 Dir Academic Partnerships .... Dr. Elizabeth LANGEMAK
72 Graduate Director Instruct Tech Mgt .... Ms. Margaret MCCOEY
88 Director Part-time MBA Program .... Mr. John FARRELL
88 Director Full-time MBA Program .... Ms. Elizabeth SCOFIELD
40 Manager Campus Store .... Mr. James PALLANTE
28 Multicultural Education Coordinator .... Ms. Cherylyn L. RUSH
105 Director of Web Communication .... Mr. Gregory FALA
66 Dir Doctor of Nursing Practice Pgm .... Dr. Patricia BICKNELL
88 Director Graduate History .... Dr. George B. STOW
58 Associate Provost .... Dr. Holly HARNER
88 Dir Clinical Counseling Psych .... Dr. Donna TONREY
88 Director of Athletic Development .... Mr. Brian QUINN
88 Sr Dir of Brand Marketing .... Ms. Amy CRANSTON
100 Chief of Staff/Dir of Gov Affairs .... Mr. Joseph MEADE
104 Director Study Abroad Program .... Ms. Melinda INGERSOLL
96 Director of Procurement .... Mr. Christopher KANE
09 Director of Institutional Research .... Dr. Danielle BROWN
101 Secretary of the Institution/Board .... Ms. Lisa WILLIE
106 Director Online/Hybrid Learning .... Mr. David LEES
25 Chief Contract/Grants Administrator .... Ms. Wendy ARDAGNA
38 Director Student Counseling .... Ms. Jessica BRANNAN
44 Director Annual Giving .... Mr. Brian FRANKOWSKI
90 Director Academic Computing .... Mr. Gabe RADI

Lackawanna College (D)

501 Vine Street, Scranton PA 18509-3206
County: Lackawanna　FICE Identification: 003283
Unit ID: 213376
Telephone: (570) 961-7810　Carnegie Class: Bac/Assoc-Assoc Dom
FAX Number: (570) 961-7858　Calendar System: 4/1/4
URL: www.lackawanna.edu
Established: 1894　Annual Undergrad Tuition & Fees: $15,660
Enrollment: 1,604　Coed
Affiliation or Control: Independent Non-Profit　IRS Status: 501(c)3
Highest Offering: Baccalaureate
Accreditation: M, DMS, OTA, PTAA, SURGT

01 President .... Mr. Mark VOLK
03 Exec Vice Pres/Chief Innovation Ofc .... Dr. Jill MURRAY
10 Vice Pres Finance/Administration .... Mr. John RISBOSKIN
05 Vice President Academic Affairs .... Dr. Erica PRICCI
32 VP for Student Affairs .... Mrs. Suellen MUSEWICZ
84 VP for Enrollment Management .... Mr. T.J ELTRINGHAM
111 Vice Pres for College Advancement .... Mr. Brian COSTANZO
15 VP for Human Resources .... Ms. Renee MUNDY
35 Dean of Students .... Mr. Dan LAMAGNA
20 Dean of Faculty .... Mrs. Suzanne CERCONE
29 Director Alumni Relations .... Ms. Michelle NEWBERRY
88 Dir Programming & Special Events .... Mr. Jim CULLEN
26 Director of External Relations .... Ms. Sharon LYNETT
41 Director of Athletics .... Ms. Joya WHITTINGTON
88 Director of Advising & Transfer Svc . Mrs. Barbara NOWOGORSKI
06 Registrar .... Mrs. Theresa SCOPELLITI
19 Director of Public Safety .... Mr. Gary SHOENER
12 Director of Hazleton Center .... Mrs. April HARRIS-SNYDER
07 Director of Admissions .... Mr. Jeffery GREGORY
88 Program Director School of PNGT .... Mrs. Jeannine MCKNIGHT
08 Library Director .... Mrs. Mary Beth ROCHE
25 Grant Admin/AssessmentCoord .... Ms. Michelle MCGLOIN
39 Director Housing & Residence Life .... Vacant
18 Director of Facilities .... Mr. Derek GREGORY
37 Director of Financial Aid .... Mr. Matthew PETERS
12 Director Towanda Center .... Ms. Kim MAPES
13 Director of MIS .... Mrs. Melanie KOWALSKI
35 Director of Student Life .... Ms. Karen LEGGE
07 Assistant Director of Admissions .... Vacant
88 Service Learning Coordinator .... Vacant
04 Executive Asst to President .... Ms. Mary A. OLIVERI
106 Dir Online Education/E-learning .... Mr. Gopu KIRON
101 Secy of the Institution/Board .... Ms. Mary A. OLIVERI
86 Director Government Relations .... Mrs. Cathy WECHSLER

Lafayette College (E)

730 High Street, Markle Hall Suite, Easton PA 18042-1798
County: Northampton　FICE Identification: 003284
Unit ID: 213385
Telephone: (610) 330-5000　Carnegie Class: Bac-A&S
FAX Number: (610) 330-5127　Calendar System: Semester
URL: www.lafayette.edu
Established: 1826　Annual Undergrad Tuition & Fees: $53,630
Enrollment: 2,594　Coed
Affiliation or Control: Independent Non-Profit　IRS Status: 501(c)3
Highest Offering: Baccalaureate
Accreditation: M

01 President .... Dr. Alison R. BYERLY
05 Provost .... Dr. John MEIER
30 Vice Pres Dev/College Relations .... Ms. Kimberly SPANG
32 VP Campus Life .... Dr. Annette DIORIO
15 Vice President Human Resources .... Ms. Leslie F. MUHLFELDER
26 VP Marketing/Communications .... Mr. Mark EYERLY
13 VP and Chief Information Officer .... Mr. John L. O'KEEFE
10 VP Finance & Administration .... Mr. Roger DEMARESKI
54 Director of Engineering .... Dr. Scott R. HUMMEL
100 VP & Liaison to Board of Trustees .... Dr. Melissa STARACE
84 Vice Pres for Enrollment Management .... Mr. Gregory MACDONALD
121 Dean Advising & Co-Curricular Pgms .... Dr. Mike OLIN
08 Dean of Libraries .... Ms. Anne HOUSTON
35 Dean of Students .... Dr. Chris HUNT
07 Dean of Admissions .... Mr. Matthew HYDE
37 Assoc VP of Financial Aid .... Dr. Forrest STUART
09 Director of Institutional Research .... Dr. Simon T. TONEV
06 Registrar .... Mr. Francis A. BENGINIA
41 Director of Athletics .... Ms. Sherryta FREEMAN
36 Asst VP of Career Services .... Mr. Mike SUMMERS
23 Director Health Services .... Dr. Jeffrey E. GOLDSTEIN
38 Director Counseling Center .... Dr. Melissa GARRISON
19 Director of Public Safety .... Mr. Jeffrey E. TROXELL
18 Dir Physical Planning & Plant Oper .... Mr. Bruce S. FERRETTI
29 Executive Director Alumni Relations .... Ms. Rachel NELSON MOELLER
16 Director of HR/Employment .... Ms. Lisa Youngkin REX
96 Manager of Procurement .... Ms. Patricia REICH

88 Title IX Coordinator .... Ms. Jessica BROWN
20 Dean of Faculty .... Dr. Jamila BOOKWALA
115 Chief Investment Officer .... Mr. Joseph S. BOHRER
04 Executive Assistant to President .... Ms. Katherine D. KANEPS

Lake Erie College of Osteopathic Medicine (A)

1858 W Grandview Boulevard, Erie PA 16509-1025
County: Erie FICE Identification: 030908
Unit ID: 407629
Telephone: (814) 866-6641 Carnegie Class: Spec-4-yr-Med
FAX Number: (814) 866-8123 Calendar System: Semester
URL: www.lecom.edu
Established: 1992 Annual Graduate Tuition & Fees: N/A
Enrollment: 4,163 Coed
Affiliation or Control: Independent Non-Profit IRS Status: 501(c)3
Highest Offering: First Professional Degree; No Undergraduates
Accreditation: M, DENT, OSTEO, PHAR

01 President/CEO .... Dr. John M. FERRETTI
05 Provost/Sr Vice Pres/Dean Acad Affs .... Dr. Silvia M. FERRETTI
10 Vice Pres of Fiscal Affairs/CFO .... Mr. Steve G. INMAN
67 VP Acad Affs/Dn LECOM Sch Pharmacy .... Dr. Hershey BELL
12 Vice Pres for LECOM at Seton Hill .... Dr. Irving FREEMAN
52 Dean School of Dental Medicine .... Dr. Mathew BATEMAN
20 Assoc Dean Acad Affairs Bradenton .... Dr. Mark KAUFFMAN
63 Assoc Dean Clinical Educ Bradenton .... Dr. Anthony J. FERRETTI
88 Assoc Dean Preclinical Ed Emeritus .... Dr. Christine KELL
63 Assoc Dean of Clinical Education .... Dr. Michael ROWANE
63 Asst Dean of Clinical Education .... Dr. Regan SHABLOSKI
63 Asst Dean Preclinical Ed Bradenton .... Dr. Mark COTY
63 Assoc Dean Preclinical Educ Erie .... Dr. Jon KALMEY
63 Assoc Dean Biomedical Sciences .... Dr. Randy KULESZA
58 Dean Graduate Studies .... Dr. Timothy NOVAK
67 Assoc Dean of Accelerated Pathway .... Dr. Rachel OGDEN
67 Assoc Dean Florida .... Dr. Katherine TROMP
52 Asst Dean of Education Dental .... Dr. Marc OTTENGA
31 Director of External Affairs .... Msgr. David RUBINO
32 Director of Student Affairs .... Dr. David FRIED
35 Asst Dir of Student Affairs .... Mr. Jamie MURPHY
09 Inst Dir Plng/Assess/Accred/Rsrch .... Dr. Mathew BATEMAN
43 Dir Legal Services/General Counsel .... Mr. Richard FERRETTI
27 Acting Inst Dir Comm/Marketing .... Mr. Eric NICASTRO
08 Inst Dir of Learning Resources .... Mr. Dan WELCH
88 Director of Behavioral Health .... Dr. Melanie DUNBAR
13 Director of Information Technology .... Mr. Randy HARRIS
46 Asst Dean of Research .... Dr. Bertalan DUDAS
88 Director of Research Medical Col .... Dr. Diana SPEELMAN
15 Inst Dir of Human Resources .... Mr. Aaron SUSMARSKI
28 Inst Director of Diversity .... Dr. Sonia DILLION
19 Inst Dir of Police & Security .... Mr. Kevin GOODE
88 Asst Dean Med Educ/Fac Dev .... Dr. Mark TERRELL
18 Facilities Director .... Mr. Brian KING
37 Inst Director of Financial Aid .... Ms. Bonnie CRILLEY
06 Institutional Registrar .... Mr. Jeremy SIVILLO
96 Inst Director of Purchasing .... Ms. Naz KROL
30 Inst Director of Public Development .... Mr. Sean WILEY
04 Admin Assistant to the President .... Ms. Helen R. MCKENZIE

Lancaster Bible College (B)

901 Eden Road, Lancaster PA 17601-5036
County: Lancaster FICE Identification: 003285
Unit ID: 213400
Telephone: (717) 569-7071 Carnegie Class: Masters/S
FAX Number: (717) 560-8260 Calendar System: Semester
URL: www.lbc.edu
Established: 1933 Annual Undergrad Tuition & Fees: $25,270
Enrollment: 2,207 Coed
Affiliation or Control: Independent Non-Profit IRS Status: 501(c)3
Highest Offering: Doctorate
Accreditation: M, BI, COSMA, MUS, SW

01 President .... Dr. Ben GUTIERREZ
04 Assistant to the President .... Mrs. Judith M. HECKAMAN
03 Executive Vice President .... Mr. John ZESWITZ
05 Provost .... Dr. Philip E. DEARBORN
32 VP for Student Experience .... Mr. Josh BEERS
111 VP of Advancement .... Vacant

Lancaster County Career and Technology Center (C)

1730 Hans Herr Drive, P.O. Box 527,
Willow Street PA 17584
County: Lancaster FICE Identification: 023108
Unit ID: 418533
Telephone: (717) 464-7050 Carnegie Class: Spec 2-yr-Health
FAX Number: (717) 464-9518 Calendar System: Semester
URL: www.lancasterctc.edu
Established: 1970 Annual Undergrad Tuition & Fees (In-District): N/A
Enrollment: 422 Coed
Affiliation or Control: State/Local IRS Status: 501(c)3
Highest Offering: Associate Degree
Accreditation: COE

01 Superintendent of Record .... Dr. Michael LEICHLITER
11 Administrative Director .... Dr. Stuart SAVIN

Lancaster Theological Seminary (D)

555 W James Street, Lancaster PA 17603-2812
County: Lancaster FICE Identification: 003286
Unit ID: 213446
Telephone: (717) 393-0654 Carnegie Class: Spec-4-yr-Faith
FAX Number: (717) 393-4254 Calendar System: Trimester
URL: www.lancasterseminary.edu
Established: 1825 Annual Graduate Tuition & Fees: N/A
Enrollment: 96 Coed
Affiliation or Control: United Church Of Christ IRS Status: 501(c)3
Highest Offering: Doctorate; No Undergraduates
Accreditation: M, THEOL

01 President .... Dr. Carol E. LYTCH
10 Vice President Business & Finance .... Ms. Elizabeth P. BENNETT
05 Vice Pres Academic Affairs & Dean .... Dr. Vanessa LOVELACE
07 Dir of Admissions & Financial Aid .... Rev. Stephen J. WOLMA
08 Seminary Librarian .... Mrs. Myka K. STEPHENS
06 Registrar .... Mrs. Teresa BENNEIAN
30 Exec Dir of Development & Comm .... Vacant
13 Director Computing/Information Mgmt .... Mr. Augustine APPREY
04 Exec Assistant to the President .... Ms. Rachel GOODRICH

Lansdale School of Business (E)

290 Wissahickon Ave, North Wales PA 19454-4114
County: Montgomery FICE Identification: 007779
Unit ID: 213473
Telephone: (215) 699-5700 Carnegie Class: Assoc/HVT-High Trad
FAX Number: (215) 699-8770 Calendar System: Semester
URL: www.LSB.edu
Established: 1918 Annual Undergrad Tuition & Fees: $11,100
Enrollment: 163 Coed
Affiliation or Control: Proprietary IRS Status: Proprietary
Highest Offering: Associate Degree
Accreditation: ACCSC

01 President .... Mr. Marlon D. KELLER
03 Executive Director .... Mrs. Marianne H. JOHNSON
32 Student Services Coordinator .... Ms. Jacklyn G. WHEELER
08 Librarian .... Mrs. Marie B. WALCROFT
37 Financial Aid Coordinator .... Mr. David E. SOUZA
36 Career Services Coordinator .... Ms. Kellyann R. GERIA

Laurel Business Institute (F)

11 East Penn Street, Uniontown PA 15401-3453
County: Fayette FICE Identification: 025462
Unit ID: 250027
Telephone: (724) 439-4900 Carnegie Class: Assoc/HVT-Mix Trad/Non
FAX Number: (724) 439-3607 Calendar System: Semester
URL: www.laurel.edu
Established: 1985 Annual Undergrad Tuition & Fees: $10,104
Enrollment: 238 Coed
Affiliation or Control: Proprietary IRS Status: Proprietary
Highest Offering: Associate Degree
Accreditation: ACCSC, COARC

01 President .... Mrs. Nancy M. DECKER
11 Executive Director .... Mrs. Bonnie MARSH
10 Vice President of Finance .... Ms. Vicki M. JOLLIFFE
15 Vice President of Human Resources .... Mr. Chuck SANTORE, JR.
13 Director of IT .... Mr. Ken LAPIKAS
37 Vice President of Financial Aid .... Ms. Stephanie M. MIGYANKO
07 Director of Admission .... Mr. Douglas S. DECKER

Laurel Technical Institute (G)

200 Sterling Avenue, Sharon PA 16146
County: Mercer FICE Identification: 020925
Unit ID: 215992
Telephone: (724) 983-0700 Carnegie Class: Assoc/HVT-Mix Trad/Non
FAX Number: (724) 983-8355 Calendar System: Semester
URL: www.laurel.edu
Established: 1925 Annual Undergrad Tuition & Fees: $10,104
Enrollment: 177 Coed
Affiliation or Control: Proprietary IRS Status: Proprietary
Highest Offering: Associate Degree
Accreditation: ACCSC, COARC

01 President .... Ms. Nancy DECKER
05 Director/Exec VP of Operations .... Mr. Douglas DECKER
07 Director of Admission .... Mr. Douglas DECKER

Lebanon Valley College (H)

101 N College Avenue, Annville PA 17003-1400
County: Lebanon FICE Identification: 003288
Unit ID: 213507
Telephone: (717) 867-6161 Carnegie Class: Masters/S
FAX Number: (717) 867-6124 Calendar System: Semester
URL: www.lvc.edu
Established: 1866 Annual Undergrad Tuition & Fees: $43,650
Enrollment: 1,910 Coed
Affiliation or Control: United Methodist IRS Status: 501(c)3
Highest Offering: Doctorate
Accreditation: M, ACBSP, MUS, PTA, @SP

01 President .... Dr. Lewis E. THAYNE
05 Vice Pres Academic Affairs .... Dr. Monica R. COWART
111 Int Vice President of Advancement .... Mr. Matthew WEAVER
10 Vice Pres Finance/Administration .... Mr. Shawn P. CURTIN
84 Vice President of Enrollment .... Mr. Edwin R. WRIGHT
32 VP Student Affairs/Dean of Students . Mr. Gregory H. KRIKORIAN
26 Chief Communications Officer .... Mrs. Molly O'BRIEN-FOELSCH
13 Senior Director of Information Tech .... Mr. David W. SHAPIRO
15 Director of HR/Title IX Coordinator .... Mrs. Ann C. HAYES
20 Dean of Faculty .... Dr. Marc HARRIS
09 Director of Institutional Research .... Vacant
58 Assoc Dean of Grad Stds/Cont Educ .... Vacant
06 Assistant Dean and Registrar .... Mr. Jeremy A. MAISTO
41 Director of Athletics .... Mr. Richard L. BEARD
114 Director of Finance and Budget .... Ms. Wendy ALBERT
21 Controller .... Mr. Gabriel PAZ
37 Director of Financial Aid .... Mrs. Kendra M. FEIGERT
36 Director of Career Development .... Mr. Matthew RANDALL
28 Director of Intercultural Affairs .... Mrs. Renata WILLIAMS
19 Director of Public Safety .... Mr. Brent OBERHOLTZER
104 Director of Global Education .... Mrs. Jill T. RUSSELL
39 Director of Residential Life .... Ms. Caitlin LENKER
22 Director of Accessibility Resources .... Mrs. Erin E. HANNAFORD
50 Director of the MBA Program .... Dr. David M. SETLEY
107 Director of Professional Studies .... Vacant
08 Int Director of the Bishop Library .... Mrs. Maureen A. BENTZ
105 Director of Communications .... Vacant
30 Interim Director of Development .... Mr. Joseph MARTELLARO
18 Director of Facilities Management .... Mr. Michael MUMPER
35 Assoc Dean Student Affairs .... Dr. Robert L. MIKUS
42 Chaplain .... Mr. Daniel LEBO
27 Director Campus Communications .... Dr. Thomas M. HANRAHAN
91 Dir Enterprise Information Systems .... Mr. Robert J. DILLANE
90 Director of Client Services .... Mr. Michael C. ZEIGLER
24 Director of Audiovisual Technology .... Mr. Andrew S. GREENE
38 Director of Counseling .... Dr. Stephanie A. FALK
88 Director of Student Activities .... Mrs. Jennifer M. EVANS
88 Assistant Controller .... Mr. Todd M. LATSHAW
29 Director Alumni & Parent Engagement .... Mrs. Susan SARISKY JONES

Lehigh Carbon Community College (I)

4525 Education Park Drive, Schnecksville PA 18078-2598
County: Lehigh FICE Identification: 006810
Unit ID: 213525
Telephone: (610) 799-2121 Carnegie Class: Assoc/MT-VT-Mix Trad/Non
FAX Number: (610) 799-1527 Calendar System: Semester
URL: www.lccc.edu
Established: 1966 Annual Undergrad Tuition & Fees (In-District): $4,080
Enrollment: 6,956 Coed
Affiliation or Control: Local IRS Status: 501(c)3
Highest Offering: Associate Degree
Accreditation: M, ACBSP, ADNUR, CAHIIM, CSHSE, OTA, PNUR, PTAA

01 President .... Dr. Ann D. BIEBER
05 Interim VP Academic/Student Dev .... Ms. Larissa M. VERTA
10 VP Finance & Admin Svcs .... Ms. Stefanie E. NESTER
84 VP Enrollment Management .... Ms. Cindy M. HANEY
04 Exec Asst to President and Board .... Mrs. Cindy L. BROOKS
32 Dean of Student Development .... Ms. Peggy M. HEIM
106 Dean Regional & Distance Educ .... Ms. Kelly TRAHAN
81 Interim Dean Science/Engr/Math .... Mr. Erik CSIKOS
13 Chief Information Officer .... Vacant
79 Int Dean Humanities/Social Sciences .... Ms. Melanie TURRANO
76 Dean Healthcare Sciences .... Mr. Craig A. KOLLER
103 Dean Employer Engage & Cmty Educ .... Ms. Terri K. KEEFE
26 Exec Dir College Relations .... Ms. Linda BAKER
09 Exec Dir Inst Research & Effectiv .... Mr. Fawad RAFI
50 Dean Bus/Educ/Legal/Soc Svc .... Dr. Cecelia A. CONNELLY-WEIDA
114 Dir Budgets & Purchasing .... Ms. Shannon HELMER
102 Executive Director Foundation .... Ms. Silvia VARGAS
07 Exec Director of Enrollment .... Ms. Ellia SABLAN-ZEBEDY
36 Dir Career Development .... Ms. Christina L. MOYER
88 Assoc Dean Prof Accred/Curriculum .... Mr. Scott W. AQUILA
88 Dir High School Connections .... Ms. Jennifer K. AQUILA
15 Dir HR/Title IX/Equity Coord .... Ms. Donna M. WILLIAMS
88 Dir Org & Faculty Development .... Ms. Cheryl A. DOLL
66 Director Nursing Programs .... Ms. Tina VANBUREN
35 Dir Student Life .... Ms. Gene F. EDEN
14 Asst Dir Technical Architect .... Mr. Ervin J. MEASE
18 Dir Facilities Management .... Mr. George CALABA
37 Exec Dir Fin Aid & Scholarship .... Ms. Tracey RICHARDS
88 Dir Academic Grants .... Ms. Linda L. MESICS
41 Director Athletics .... Mr. Andrew JOHNSON
88 Dir Early Learning Center .... Ms. Elizabeth D. LIPMAN
88 Grant Writer .... Ms. Mary KOVALCHICK
25 Asst Dir Literacy .... Ms. Allison J. LUDLOW
74 Dir Veterinary Tech Program .... Ms. Lisa A. MARTINI-JOHNSON
27 Marketing/Publications Specialist .... Ms. Leanne R. RECLA
06 Dir Registration/Student Records .... Mr. Gregory J. GOLETZ, JR.
40 Bookstore Manager .... Mr. Zachary POTTER
38 Dir Counseling & Cmty Standards .... Mr. Brian C. DELONG
19 Dir Public Safety .... Mr. James W. SURGEONER
113 Dir Student Accounts .... Ms. Stacey A. BETZ
121 Assoc Dean Student Success .... Ms. Dorothy COLLINS

Lehigh University (J)

27 Memorial Drive W, Bethlehem PA 18015-3094
County: Northampton FICE Identification: 003289
Unit ID: 213543
Telephone: (610) 758-3000 Carnegie Class: DU-Higher
FAX Number: (610) 691-5420 Calendar System: Semester
URL: www.lehigh.edu

Established: 1865 Annual Undergrad Tuition & Fees: $52,930
Enrollment: 7,017 Coed
Affiliation or Control: Independent Non-Profit IRS Status: 501(c)3
Highest Offering: Doctorate
Accreditation: M, COPSY, IPSY, SCPSY, THEA

01 President Dr. John D. SIMON
05 Provost & VP for Academic Affairs Dr. Patrick V. FARRELL
10 Vice Pres Finance & Administration Ms. Patricia A. JOHNSON
88 VP for International Affairs Dr. Cheryl A. MATHERLY
30 VP Development and Alumni Relations Mr. Joseph E. BUCK
46 VP/Assoc Prov Research/Grad Studies Dr. Alan J. SNYDER
26 VP Communications & Public Affairs Mr. Frederick J. MCGRAIL
28 VP Diversity/Inclusion & Equity Dr. Donald A. OUTING
115 Chief Investment Officer Ms. Kristin AGATONE
09 Vice Provost Institutional Research Dr. Yenny ANDERSON
32 Vice Provost Student Affairs Dr. Ricardo HALL
13 Vice Provost Library & Tech Svcs Dr. Bruce M. TAGGART
88 Vice Provost for Academic Diversity Mr. Henry U. ODI
86 Assoc VP for Govt Relations Mr. Christopher C. CARTER
21 Assoc VP Finance/Asst Secy Board Ms. Denise M. BLEW
15 Assoc VP for Human Resource Mr. Chris HALLADAY
18 Assoc VP Facilities Svcs/Architect Mr. Brent STRINGFELLOW
20 Deputy Provost Academic Affairs Ms. Jennifer M. JENSEN
35 Dean of Students Ms. Katherine W. LAVINDER
29 Asst VP of Alumni Engagement Ms. Jennifer L. CUNNINGHAM
31 Asst VP Community & Regional Affs Ms. Adrienne J. WASHINGTON
54 Dean Engr & Applied Science Dr. Stephen P. DEWEERTH
49 Interim Dean Arts & Sciences Dr. Cameron E. WESSON
50 Dean of Business/Economics Dr. Georgette C. PHILLIPS
53 Dean of Education Dr. William GAUDELLI
69 Inaugural Dean College of Health Dr. Whitney WITT
07 Vice Provost Admiss/Financial Aid Mr. Dan WARNER
41 Murray H Goodman Dean of Athletics Mr. Joseph D. STERRETT
06 Registrar Mr. Steven H. WILSON
37 Director Financial Aid Ms. Jennifer L. MERTZ
106 Director Distance Education Ms. Margaret A. PORTZ
36 Director Career Services Ms. Lori B. KENNEDY
23 Inaugural Exec Dir Health Center Mr. David RUBENSTEIN
39 Director Residential Services Mr. Ozzie BREINER
40 Director Bookstore Mr. Brian ADLER
19 Chief University Police Mr. Jason D. SCHIFFER
38 Director of Counseling Services Dr. Ian T. BIRKY
42 Chaplain Rev. Lloyd H. STEFFEN
43 General Counsel Mr. Frank A. ROTH
114 Director of Budget Mr. Stephen J. GUTTMAN
96 Manager Strategic Sourcing Ms. Jane ALTEMOSE
84 Director Enrollment Management Ms. Jennifer E. O'BRIEN-KNOTTS
100 Chief of Staff Mr. Erik J. WALKER
04 Executive Asst to the President Ms. Donna L. FEIST
104 Director Study Abroad Ms. Katie W. RADANDE

Lincoln Technical Institute (A)

5151 Tilghman Street, Allentown PA 18104-3298
County: Lehigh FICE Identification: 007759
Unit ID: 213570
Telephone: (610) 398-5300 Carnegie Class: Assoc/HVT-High Trad
FAX Number: (610) 395-2706 Calendar System: Semester
URL: www.lincolntech.edu
Established: 1946 Annual Undergrad Tuition & Fees: N/A
Enrollment: 444 Coed
Affiliation or Control: Proprietary IRS Status: Proprietary
Highest Offering: Associate Degree
Accreditation: ACCSC

01 Campus President Mrs. Angela REPPERT
05 Director of Education Ms. Anne CONNELY
66 Director of Nursing Mrs. Michelle DAVIS
11 Director of Administrative Services Mrs. Rebecca DRAYTON
07 Director of Admissions Mr. Vincent SALVATORIELLO
36 Director of Career Services Mrs. Charmain BRODY
37 Financial Aid Manager Ms. Erica BRANDI

Lincoln Technical Institute (B)

9191 Torresdale Avenue, Philadelphia PA 19136-1595
County: Philadelphia FICE Identification: 007832
Unit ID: 213589
Telephone: (215) 335-0800 Carnegie Class: Spec 2-yr-Tech
FAX Number: (215) 335-1443 Calendar System: Other
URL: www.lincolntech.com
Established: 1946 Annual Undergrad Tuition & Fees: N/A
Enrollment: 246 Coed
Affiliation or Control: Proprietary IRS Status: Proprietary
Highest Offering: Associate Degree
Accreditation: ACCSC

01 Campus President Mr. Jim KUNTZ
07 Dir Admiss High School/Adult Educ Mr. Alfred JACKSON
32 Student Services Coordinator Ms. Mijana KONA
05 Director of Education Mrs. Jennifer MCLAUGHLIN
11 Director Administration Ms. Gina ALTSHULER
36 Director of Career Services Ms. Emily MATTHEWS

Lincoln University (C)

1570 Baltimore Pike, Lincoln University PA 19352-0999
County: Chester FICE Identification: 003290
Unit ID: 213598
Telephone: (484) 365-8000 Carnegie Class: Masters/M
FAX Number: (484) 365-7316 Calendar System: Semester
URL: www.lincoln.edu
Established: 1854 Annual Undergrad Tuition & Fees (In-State): $11,036
Enrollment: 2,266 Coed
Affiliation or Control: State Related IRS Status: 501(c)3
Highest Offering: Master's
Accreditation: M, NURSE

01 President Dr. Brenda A. ALLEN
111 VP for Institutional Advancement Dr. Mellissia ZANJANI
100 Chief of Staff/Mgr Board Trustees Ms. Diane M. BROWN
05 Provost and VP for Academic Affairs Dr. Patricia RAMSEY
10 Vice Pres Fiscal Affairs/Treasurer Mr. Charles GRADOWSKI
32 Dean of College/VP Student Success Dr. Lenetta LEE
15 Vice President Human Resources Mr. Jake TANKSLEY
13 Chief Information Officer Mr. Justin MCKENZIE
42 Chaplain Rev Dr. Frederick FAISON
09 Dir of Inst Effectiv/Research/Plng Ms. Tiffany LEE
08 Director of Library Science Ms. Carla SARRATT
35 Assoc Dean of College/Students Rev Dr. Frederick FAISON
84 Assoc Provost Enrollment Management Dr. Kimberly TAYLOR-BENNS
26 Director of Comm & Public Relations Ms. Shelby MIX
29 Director of Alumni Relations Ms. Deborah JOHNSON
06 Registrar Ms. Catherine RUTLEDGE
36 Director Career Development Mr. Ralph SIMPSON
41 Director of Athletics Mr. Harry STINSON
21 Controller Mr. Jay SIMMONS
85 Director of International Services Ms. Dafina BLACKSHER DIABATE
23 Director Health Services Ms. Velva GREENE-RAINEY
123 Dir Graduate Student Svcs/Admission Ms. Jernice LEA
37 Director Financial Aid Ms. Kim ANDERSON
96 Director of Purchasing Ms. Sue REED
83 Dean of the Faculty Dr. Patricia JOSEPH
121 Assoc VP Academic Support Ms. Evelyn POE
07 Director of Admissions Mrs. Nokoia FORDE
19 Director Security/Safety Mr. Marc PARTEE
25 Interim Contract/Grants Admin Ms. Marion BERNARD-AMOS
38 Director Student Counseling Ms. Rachel MANSON
39 Executive Director Residence Life Mr. Brian DUBENION
44 Director Annual Giving Mr. Rich LANCASTER
90 Proj Manager Academic Computing Ms. Nancy EVANS

Luzerne County Community College (D)

1333 S Prospect Street, Nanticoke PA 18634-3899
County: Luzerne FICE Identification: 006811
Unit ID: 213659
Telephone: (570) 740-0200 Carnegie Class: Assoc/HVT-High Trad
FAX Number: (570) 740-0750 Calendar System: Semester
URL: www.luzerne.edu
Established: 1966 Annual Undergrad Tuition & Fees (In-District): $5,430
Enrollment: 5,360 Coed
Affiliation or Control: Local IRS Status: 501(c)3
Highest Offering: Associate Degree
Accreditation: M, ACBSP, ADNUR, COARC, DH, EMT, SURGT

01 President Mr. Thomas P. LEARY
101 Executive Asst to President/BOT Ms. Paula LABENSKI
05 Vice Pres Academic Affairs Dr. Cheryl LESSER
32 VP of Enrollment Mgmt/Student Dev Ms. Rosana REYES
103 VP of Applied Tech/Workforce Devel Ms. Susan SPRY
15 Dean Human Resources Mr. John SEDLAK
66 Dean of Nursing/Health Sciences Ms. Deborah VILEGI PAYNE
13 Vice President of Operations & CTO Mr. Don NELSON
10 VP of Finance Ms. Cheryl BAUR
07 Assistant Director Admissions Mr. Ed HENNIGAN
37 Director of Student Financial Aid Mr. Mark CARPENTIER
08 Director of Library Mrs. Mia W. BASSHAM
38 Dir Counseling/Stdnt Support Svcs Mrs. Janine KELLEY
35 Dir Student Life/Athletics Ms. Mary SULLIVAN
09 Director Inst Research/Planning Ms. Graceann PLATUKUS
18 Director of Physical Plant Mr. Keith GRAHAM
30 Exec Dir of Institutional Advance Ms. Sandra NICHOLAS
84 Director Enrollment Management Mr. Jim DOMZALSKI
26 Director of College Relations Ms. Lisa NELSON
29 Director Alumni Relations Ms. Bonnie LAUER
28 Diversity Coordinator Ms. Judi MYERS
19 Director of Public Safety/Security Mr. William BARRETT

Lycoming College (E)

700 College Place, Williamsport PA 17701-5192
County: Lycoming FICE Identification: 003293
Unit ID: 213668
Telephone: (570) 321-4000 Carnegie Class: Bac-A&S
FAX Number: (570) 321-4337 Calendar System: Semester
URL: www.lycoming.edu
Established: 1812 Annual Undergrad Tuition & Fees: $40,315
Enrollment: 1,217 Coed
Affiliation or Control: United Methodist IRS Status: 501(c)3
Highest Offering: Baccalaureate
Accreditation: M

01 President Dr. Kent C. TRACHTE
05 Provost and Dean of the College Dr. Philip W. SPRUNGER
10 VP for Finance and Admin/Treasurer Mr. Jeffrey L. BENNETT
111 Executive Vice President Mr. Charles W. EDMONDS
84 VP for Enrollment Management Mr. Michael J. KONOPSKI
21 Controller Ms. Dawn HENDRICKS
32 Vice President for Student Life Dr. Daniel P. MILLER
20 Assoc Provost for Experiential Lrng Dr. Susan ROSS
89 Dean for First Year Students Mr. Andrew W. KILPATRICK
08 Director of Snowden Library Ms. Paige S. FLANAGAN
06 Registrar Ms. Whitney A. MERINAR
37 Director of Financial Aid Mr. James LAKIS
13 Chief Information Officer Mr. Robert L. DUNKLEBERGER
29 Director Alumni Relations Ms. Amy S. REYES
112 Sr Dir for Major Planned Gifts Mr. Robb DIETRICH
39 Assoc Dean of Students Ms. Kate HUMMEL
41 Director of Athletics Mr. Michael CLARK
110 Assoc Dir of Major Gifts Mr. Gregory J. BELL
44 Director of Annual Giving Ms. Lesley LARSON
88 Dir Civic Engagement & Pers Dev Ms. Mallory L. WEYMER
15 Director of Human Resources Ms. Kacy HAGAN
18 Chief Facilities/Physical Plant Mr. F. Douglas KUNTZ
23 Director of Health Services Ms. Sondra L. STIPCAK
38 Director Student Counseling Mr. Townsend VELKOFF
40 Campus Store Manager Ms. Patricia E. BAUSINGER
92 Lycoming Scholars Dr. Cullen CHANDLER
94 Women's Studies Dr. Kerry RICHMOND
118 Human Resources Benefits Coord Ms. Cathleen A. LUTZ
04 Assistant to the President Ms. Diane CARL
09 Director of Institutional Research Dr. Chiaki KOTORI
108 Associate Provost Dr. Eileen PELUSO
90 Dir of IT Core Services Ms. Nicole KUNTZ
91 Director Administrative Computing Ms. Janet PAYNE
07 Director of Admissions Ms. Jessica A. QUINTANA HESS
102 Foundations Relations Officer Ms. Melanie TAORMINA
104 Coordinator of Study Abroad Ms. Allison HOLLADAY
105 Director Web Services Mr. Robert BROWN
19 Director Security/Safety Mr. Eric A. TALLMAN
26 Sr Dir of Marketing & Comm Ms. Marla KRAMER

Manor College (F)

700 Fox Chase Road, Jenkintown PA 19046-3399
County: Montgomery FICE Identification: 003294
Unit ID: 213774
Telephone: (215) 885-2360 Carnegie Class: Assoc/MT-VT-High Trad
FAX Number: (215) 576-6564 Calendar System: Semester
URL: www.manor.edu
Established: 1947 Annual Undergrad Tuition & Fees: $17,179
Enrollment: 632 Coed
Affiliation or Control: Independent Non-Profit IRS Status: 501(c)3
Highest Offering: Baccalaureate
Accreditation: M, ACBSP, DA, DH

01 President Dr. Jonathan PERI
05 Provost and VPAA Dr. Calandra D. LOCKHART
06 Registrar Ms. Dianne I. SARIDAKIS
13 Information Technology Manager Mr. Brian WHELAN
15 Director of Human Resources Ms. Christine COLELLA
10 VP of Finance & Facilities Ms. Janice SALERNO
19 Chief of Public Safety Mr. Edward SALAMON
111 VP for Institutional Advancement Ms. Kimberly HAMM
26 VP of Marketing/Communications Ms. Heather G. DOTCHEL
32 VP and Dean of Student Affairs Ms. Allison C. MOOTZ
84 VP of Enrollment Ms. Stephanie WALKER
37 Director Financial Aid Mr. Chris T. HARTMAN
38 Director Counseling Ms. Christine B. PRINCE
39 Assistant Director Residence Life Ms. Lynn WALES
41 Director Athletics Mr. John DEMPSTER
79 Humanities and Social Science Chair Dr. Matthew SMALARZ
08 Head Librarian Vacant
09 Director of Institutional Research Mr. John T. KREBS
04 Exec Assistant to the President Mrs. Katharina M. KILMER
50 Sr Dean Business/Technology Dr. Marc MINNICK
53 Dean/Dir Instruct Learning Init Dr. Cherie CROSBY
103 Director Workforce Development Mr. Nick RUDNYTZKY
105 Director Web Services Mrs. Heather DOTCHEL
108 Director Institutional Assessment Mr. John KREBS
96 Director of Purchasing Mrs. Janice SALERNO

Marywood University (G)

2300 Adams Avenue, Scranton PA 18509-1598
County: Lackawanna FICE Identification: 003296
Unit ID: 213826
Telephone: (570) 348-6211 Carnegie Class: Masters/L
FAX Number: (570) 961-4769 Calendar System: Semester
URL: www.marywood.edu
Established: 1915 Annual Undergrad Tuition & Fees: $34,910
Enrollment: 2,945 Coed
Affiliation or Control: Roman Catholic IRS Status: 501(c)3
Highest Offering: Doctorate
Accreditation: M, ACBSP, ARCPA, ART, CAATE, CACREP, CAEPN, CLPSY, DIETD, DIETI, MUS, NURSE, SP, SW

01 President Sr. Mary PERSICO, IHM
05 Provost/Vice Pres Academic Affairs Dr. Susan C. TURELL
10 VP Business Affairs/Treasurer Ms. Tammy J. MCHALE
111 Vice Pres University Advancement Dr. Renee G. ZEHEL
84 VP Enrollment Svcs/Student Success Ms. Ann BOLAND-CHASE
101 Secretary Univ & General Counsel Ms. Mary T. GARDIER PATERSON
15 Director of Human Resources Vacant
26 Director Marketing/Communication Mr. James M. BROWN
18 Asst VP for Buildings & Grounds Mrs. Wendy YANKELITIS
49 Dean College of Arts/Science Dr. Frances M. ZAUHAR
76 Interim Dean Col Hlth/Human Svcs Dr. Lori E. SWANCHAK
107 Dean Col of Prof Studies Mr. James J. SULLIVAN
90 Director User Support Services Dr. Michael MIRABITO

70 Director School of Social Work .... Dr. Stephen BURKE
08 Director of Library Services .... Mr. Zhong M. GENG
06 Registrar .... Ms. Rosemary BURGER
07 Sr Dir of University Admissions .... Mr. Matthew F. HERR
21 Controller/Asst Treasurer .... Mr. Patrick E. CASTELLANI
37 Director of Financial Aid .... Ms. Barbara L. SCHMITT
44 Annual Giving Officer .... Ms. Patricia H. ROSETTI
112 Director of Planned Giving .... Ms. Elizabeth A. CONNERY
27 Public Relations Director .... Ms. Juneann GRECO
42 Chaplain/Asst Dir Campus Ministry .... Rev. Joseph P. ELSTON
32 Dean of Students .... Mr. Ross NOVAK
41 Director Athletics/Recreation .... Dr. Mary Jo GUNNING
36 Asst Dir of Advising & Career Dev .... Ms. Christina BRUNDAGE
42 Dir of Mission & Campus Ministry .... Sr. Catherine LUXNER
88 Dir of Dining Services .... Mr. Mark DEVLIN
13 Director of Information Officer .... Mr. Thomas E. STEFFES
19 Chief Campus Safety .... Mr. Michael C. PASQUALICCHIO
23 Director of Student Health Services .... Ms. Maura K. SMITH
38 Director Counseling & Student Devel .... Dr. Robert S. SHAW
40 Bookstore Manager .... Ms. Joan DIEHL
104 Assoc Dir Intl & Multicultl Affairs .... Ms. Anne O. MALONEY
110 Dir Advancement Services .... Ms. Elizabeth M. STIRES
29 Director of Alumni Engagement .... Ms. Cara GREEN
35 Dir of Student Act/Leadership Devel .... Ms. Kimberly E. COLEMAN
22 Dir of Student Equity/Inclusion .... Dr. Lia Richards PALMITER
09 Asst Dir for Research & Spons Pgms .... Dr. Diane KELLER
45 Assistant Provost .... Ms. Leslie W. CHRISTIANSON
04 Exec Secretary to the President .... Ms. Robyn M. KRUKOVITZ

McCann School of Business & Technology (A)

2200 North Irving Street, Allentown PA 18109
Telephone: (484) 223-4600 Identification: 770768
Accreditation: ACCSC, MAC, MLTAD

† Branch campus of Platt College, Tulsa, OK.

McCann School of Business & Technology (B)

7495 Westbranch Highway, Lewisburg PA 17837
Telephone: (570) 497-8014 Identification: 666485
Accreditation: ACCSC, #SURGT

† Branch campus of Platt College, Tulsa, OK.

Mercyhurst University (C)

501 E 38th Street, Erie PA 16546-0001
County: Erie FICE Identification: 003297
Unit ID: 213987
Telephone: (814) 824-2000 Carnegie Class: Masters/M
FAX Number: (814) 824-2438 Calendar System: Semester
URL: www.mercyhurst.edu
Established: 1926 Annual Undergrad Tuition & Fees: $37,170
Enrollment: 2,759 Coed
Affiliation or Control: Roman Catholic IRS Status: 501(c)3
Highest Offering: Doctorate
Accreditation: M, #ARCPA, CAATE, DANCE, IACBE, MUS, NUR, PTAA, SW

01 President .... Mr. Michael T. VICTOR
05 Provost & VP Academic Affairs .... Dr. Leanne M. ROBERTS
10 Vice Pres Finance & Administration .... Mr. David P. MYRON
12 Exec VP Mercyhurst - NE .... Dr. Clinton D. JONES
30 Vice Pres University Development .... Mr. Caleb M. PIFER
32 Vice Pres of Student Life .... Dr. Laura ZIRKEL
84 VP for Enrollment .... Mr. Joe HOWARD
13 Chief Information Officer .... Ms. Jeanette BRITT
18 Director Facilities/Physical Plant .... Mr. David MYRON
38 Director Student Counseling Service .... Ms. Judy SMITH
07 Director Undergraduate Admissions .... Mr. Christian BEYER
06 Registrar .... Ms. Michele WHEATON
08 Dir Univ Libraries/Online Learning .... Ms. Darci JONES
39 Dir Residential Life/Stdnt Conduct .... Ms. Megan MCKENNA
19 Director of Public Safety Programs .... Mr. Donald J. FUHRMANN
29 Dir Alumni Rels & Annual Giving .... Ms. Courtney OLEVNIK
42 Director of Campus Ministry .... Fr. James PISZKER
37 Director of Student Financial Svcs .... Ms. Carrie NEWMAN
41 Director of Athletics .... Mr. Bradley DAVIS
09 Director of Institutional Research .... Mrs. Sheila W. RICHTER
15 Director Human Resources .... Mrs. Jamie BRENEMAN
93 Coordinator Multicultural Affairs .... Mr. Tyler BRENTLEY
04 Administrative Asst to President .... Ms. Stacey WILEY
104 Director Study Abroad .... Dr. Heidi HOSEY
26 Chief Public Relations/Marketing .... Mrs. Dionne VEITCH
43 Dir Legal Services/General Counsel .... Mrs. Meredith BOLLHEIMER

Mercyhurst University Northeast (D)

16 W Division Street, North East PA 16428
Telephone: (814) 725-6100 Identification: 770161
Accreditation: &M, ADNUR, COARC, MLTAD, OTA

Messiah College (E)

One College Avenue, Mechanicsburg PA 17055
County: Cumberland FICE Identification: 003298
Unit ID: 213996
Telephone: (717) 766-2511 Carnegie Class: Masters/M
FAX Number: (717) 691-6025 Calendar System: Semester
URL: www.messiah.edu
Established: 1909 Annual Undergrad Tuition & Fees: $35,160
Enrollment: 3,331 Coed
Affiliation or Control: Interdenominational IRS Status: 501(c)3
Highest Offering: Doctorate
Accreditation: M, ACBSP, ART, CAATE, CACREP, DIETD, DIETI, MUS, NURSE, OT, @PTA, SW, THEA

01 President .... Dr. Kim S. PHIPPS
05 Provost .... Dr. Randall G. BASINGER
10 Vice Pres for Finance & Planning .... Mr. David S. WALKER
11 Vice President for Operations .... Mrs. Kathrynne G. SHAFER
111 Vice President for Advancement .... Mr. Barry G. GOODLING
84 Vice Pres for Enrollment Management .... Mr. John A. CHOPKA
15 VP for Human Res & Compliance .... Ms. Amanda A. COFFEY
13 VP Info Technology/Assoc Provost .... Dr. William G. STRAUSBAUGH
32 Vice Provost & Dean of Students .... Dr. Kristin M. HANSEN-KIEFFER
58 Asst Provost/Dean of Grad Studies .... Dr. Robert PEPPER
57 Dean School of the Arts .... Dr. Richard E. ROBERSON
53 Dean School of Bus/Educ/Soc Sci .... Dr. Caroline MAURER
79 Dean School of Humanities .... Dr. Peter K. POWERS
81 Dean School of Science/Engr/Health .... Dr. Angela HARE
35 Associate Dean of Students .... Mr. Douglas M. WOOD
30 Exec Director of Development .... Dr. Jon C. STUCKEY
93 Dir of Intercultural Office .... Vacant
07 Director of Admissions .... Mrs. Dana J. BRITTON
37 Director of Financial Aid .... Mr. Gregory L. GEARHART
39 Asst Dir of Residence Life/Housing .... Mr. Bryce WATKINS
21 Dir Financial Operations/Controller .... Mrs. Christine HARTMAN
06 Registrar .... Mrs. Carrie WIDDOWSON
08 Director of the Murray Library .... Ms. Linda POSTON
91 Director Information Services .... Mr. John P. LUFT
90 Dir Learning Technology Services .... Mrs. Susan K. SHANNON
09 Director of Institutional Research .... Ms. Laura M. MILLER
42 College Pastor .... Dr. Donald OPITZ
26 Exec Director Communications .... Mrs. Carla E. GROSS
29 Director Alumni & Parent Relations .... Mr. Jay W. MCCLYMONT
38 Director of the Engle Center .... Ms. Eleanor MUIR
41 Exec Dir of Athletics/Fundraising .... Mr. Jack T. COLE
92 Dir of the College Honors Program .... Dr. James LAGRAND
18 Director of Facility Services .... Mr. Bradley A. MARKLEY
36 Dir Career/Profess Development .... Mrs. Christina R. HANSON
40 Campus Store Manager .... Ms. Candice TRITLE
19 Director Safety/Dispatch Services .... Ms. Cindy L. BURGER
04 Executive Coordinator for President .... Mrs. Karin BISBEE
96 Purchasing Manager .... Mrs. Daisy ANDERSON
23 Coordinator of Health Services .... Mrs. Michelle LUCAS
105 Web Services Manager .... Ms. Ramona FRITSCHI
108 Director of Assessment .... Ms. Kate WILKINS
28 Special Asst to Pres for Diversity .... Dr. Todd ALLEN

Missio Seminary (F)

200 N Main Street, Hatfield PA 19440-2499
County: Montgomery FICE Identification: 023230
Unit ID: 211130
Telephone: (215) 368-5000 Carnegie Class: Spec-4-yr-Faith
FAX Number: (215) 368-2301 Calendar System: Semester
URL: www.missio.edu
Established: 1971 Annual Graduate Tuition & Fees: N/A
Enrollment: 227 Coed
Affiliation or Control: Independent Non-Profit IRS Status: 501(c)3
Highest Offering: Doctorate; No Undergraduates
Accreditation: M, THEOL

01 President .... Dr. Frank JAMES, III
84 VP of Enrollment Mgmt & Mktg .... Mr. Ryan EGLI
05 Dean of the Faculty .... Dr. David LAMB
04 Executive Assistant to the Pres .... Mrs. Beatrice L. BARKLEY
88 Director of DMin Program .... Dr. Kyuboem LEE
20 Director of Academic Services .... Mr. Rick HOUSEKNECHT
13 Director of Information Technology .... Mr. Gregg ALDERFER
18 Director of Physical Plant .... Mr. Anthony W. PLETSCHER
101 Secretary of the Institution/Board .... Mrs. Rebecca CAMPBELL
37 Director Student Financial Aid .... Ms. Kim BILLUPS
08 Director of Library Services .... Ms. Lydia PUTNAM
15 HR Manager .... Ms. Kim BALTIMORE
29 Director Alumni Relations .... Mr. Paul ZAZZO
30 Director of Development .... Mr. Charles BLACHFORD

Misericordia University (G)

301 Lake Street, Dallas PA 18612-1098
County: Luzerne FICE Identification: 003247
Unit ID: 214069
Telephone: (570) 674-6400 Carnegie Class: DU-Mod
FAX Number: (570) 675-2441 Calendar System: Semester
URL: www.misericordia.edu
Established: 1924 Annual Undergrad Tuition & Fees: $33,240
Enrollment: 2,708 Coed
Affiliation or Control: Roman Catholic IRS Status: 501(c)3
Highest Offering: Doctorate
Accreditation: M, #ARCPA, DMS, IACBE, NURSE, OT, PTA, RAD, SP, SW

01 President .... Dr. Thomas J. BOTZMAN
10 Vice Pres Finance & Administration .... Mr. Mark VAN ETTEN, JR.
05 Vice President Academic Affairs .... Dr. David REHM
111 VP of Institutional Advancement .... Ms. Susan M. HELWIG
88 Vice Pres of Mission Integration .... Sr. Jean MESSAROS
45 Sec to BOT/VP Plng/External Rels .... Dr. Barbara SAMUEL
32 Vice President of Student Life .... Ms. Kathleen FOLEY
84 Vice President of Enrollment Mgmt .... Mr. Glenn BOZINSKI
21 Controller .... Mr. Ronald S. HROMISIN
06 Registrar .... Mr. Joseph REDINGTON
35 Dean of Students .... Ms. Amy LAHART
29 Director Alumni Relations .... Ms. Lailani AUGUSTINE
08 Librarian .... Ms. Jennifer LUKSA
04 Exec Assistant to the President .... Ms. Lisa BORCHERT
96 Director of Purchasing .... Mr. Thomas F. KANE
121 Director of Student Success Center .... Ms. Jessica RANDALL
42 Director Campus Ministry .... Ms. Christine SOMERS
41 Director of Athletics .... Mr. Charles EDKINS
39 Director of Residents .... Mr. Angelo NUDO
14 Manager Applications Development .... Mr. Matt MIHAL
13 Director of Information Technology .... Mr. Val APANOVICH
88 Director of Student Activities .... Ms. Darcy BRODMERKEL
36 Dir Insalaco Ctr Career Development .... Ms. Bernadette RUSHMER
102 Dir Foundation/Government Relations .... Mr. Larry PELLEGRINI
51 Director of Adult Education/CACE .... Mr. Paul NARDONE
15 Director of Human Resources .... Ms. Pamela PARSNIK
04 Special Assistant to President .... Mr. James ROBERTS
37 Director of Financial Aid .... Ms. Susan FRONZONI
19 Assoc Director Security/Safety .... Mr. Robert ZAVADA
18 Director of Facilities .... Mr. Taras MIHALKO
09 Asst Dir of Institutional Research .... Ms. Sharon HUDAK
90 Manager of User Services .... Mr. David A. JOHNDROW
07 Director of Admissions .... Ms. Donna CERZA
104 Director Study Abroad .... Mr. Michael SIMONS
110 Director of Advancement Services .... Ms. Roxanne JOHNSTON

Montgomery County Community College (H)

340 Dekalb Pike, Blue Bell PA 19422-1400
County: Montgomery FICE Identification: 004452
Unit ID: 214111
Telephone: (215) 641-6300 Carnegie Class: Assoc/MT-VT-Mix Trad/Non
FAX Number: (215) 461-1460 Calendar System: Semester
URL: www.mc3.edu
Established: 1964 Annual Undergrad Tuition & Fees (In-District): $5,730
Enrollment: 10,392 Coed
Affiliation or Control: State/Local IRS Status: 501(c)3
Highest Offering: Associate Degree
Accreditation: M, ADNUR, CSHSE, DH, IFSAC, MAC, MLTAD, PTAA, RAD, SURGT

01 Interim President .... Dr. Victoria BASTECKI-PEREZ
04 Exec Assistant to the President .... Ms. Elaine CARON
101 Exec Asst to the Board of Trustees .... Ms. Deborah A. ROGERS
05 VP for Academic Affairs & Provost .... Dr. Victoria BASTECKI-PEREZ
103 VP of Workforce Development .... Vacant
13 VP for Information Technology .... Ms. Celeste M. SCHWARTZ
10 VP for Finance & Administration .... Mr. Charles SOMERS
111 Vice Pres for Advancement .... Mr. Jay BROWNING
32 VP of Student Services .... Mr. Philip NEEDLES
06 Registrar .... Ms. Sherry PHILLIPS
15 Executive Director Human Resources .... Ms. Diane O'CONNOR
21 Controller .... Ms. Heather MEIER
110 Director of Development .... Vacant
19 Director of Campus Safety .... Vacant
37 Director of Financial Aid .... Ms. Christal CHATMAN
09 Exec Dir of Inst Research .... Mr. David KOWALSKI
28 Dir Equity & Diversity Initiatives .... Ms. Rose MAKOFSKE
29 Dir of Alumni Rel & Major Gifts .... Vacant
26 Director of Strategic Communication .... Ms. Diane VANDYKE
07 Exec Dir of Enrollment Services .... Ms. Maureen CARVER
08 Dean of Libraries & Acad Support .... Vacant
18 Director of Facilities Mgmt .... Vacant
102 Dir of Corp & Found Rels & Grants .... Vacant
35 Dean of Student Affairs .... Ms. Nicole HENDERSON
96 Director of Procurement .... Ms. Jenny RARIG
88 Executive Director of Workforce Dev .... Mr. Gregory SKELLEY
50 Dean of Business/Entrepreneurship .... Mr. Gaetan GIANNINI
86 Director Government Relations .... Mr. Michael BETTINGER
41 Dir Athletics & Campus Recreation .... Ms. Kelly DUNBAR
84 Exec Director Enrollment Management .... Ms. Michelle BROWN
90 Director Academic Computing .... Vacant

Montgomery County Community College West Campus (I)

101 College Drive, Pottstown PA 19464
Telephone: (610) 718-1800 Identification: 770162
Accreditation: &M

Moore College of Art and Design (J)

1916 Race Street, Philadelphia PA 19103-1179
County: Philadelphia FICE Identification: 003300
Unit ID: 214148
Telephone: (215) 965-4000 Carnegie Class: Spec-4-yr-Arts
FAX Number: (215) 568-8017 Calendar System: Semester
URL: www.moore.edu
Established: 1848 Annual Undergrad Tuition & Fees: $41,424
Enrollment: 404 Female
Affiliation or Control: Independent Non-Profit IRS Status: 501(c)3
Highest Offering: Master's
Accreditation: M, ART, CIDA

01 President .... Ms. Cecelia FITZGIBBON
10 SVP Finance & Administration .... Mr. William L. HILL, II
05 Academic Dean .... Ms. Patti PHILLIPS
32 Dean of Students .... Mr. Joshua WILKIN
20 Assoc Dean Educational Support Svcs .... Ms. Claudine THOMAS
39 Director Residence Life/Housing .... Ms. Kimberley FOX
88 Director of Galleries .... Ms. Gabrielle LAVIN

51 Assoc Dean Cont Educ/Grad Studies .... Dr. Joanna JENKINS
26 Chief Mktg & Communications Ofcr .... Ms. Nicole STEINBERG
30 Director of Development .... Ms. Elizabeth CAHILL
110 Assoc Director of Development .... Ms. Patricia MA
29 Dir Alumnae Affairs/Annual Fund .... Ms. Claire WILSON
08 Library Director .... Ms. Kimberly LESLEY
07 Dean of Admissions ....Mr. Jonathan SQUIRE
37 Director of Financial Aid .... Ms. Devon WEAVER
06 Registrar .... Ms. Brooke TOBEY
18 Director of Operations ....Mr. Kenneth M. FERRETTI
15 Director Human Resources ....Ms. Rachel PHILLIPS
36 Director Career Center .... Ms. Belena CHAPP
38 Director Student Counseling .... Ms. Ruth R. GAYLE
90 Academic Computing Manager .... Mr. Dennis DAWTON
04 Executive Asst to President .... Ms. Alysson CWYK
28 Director of Student Life/Diversity ..... Ms. Shannon DOBROVOLNY

Moravian College (A)

1200 Main St., Bethlehem PA 18018-6650
County: Northampton FICE Identification: 003301
Unit ID: 214157
Telephone: (610) 861-1300 Carnegie Class: Bac-A&S
FAX Number: (610) 625-7918 Calendar System: Semester
URL: www.moravian.edu
Established: 1742 Annual Undergrad Tuition & Fees: $43,636
Enrollment: 2,446 Coed
Affiliation or Control: Moravian Church IRS Status: 501(c)3
Highest Offering: Doctorate
Accreditation: M, ACBSP, CAATE, MUS, NURSE, @SP, THEOL

01 President .... Dr. Bryon L. GRIGSBY
05 Provost .... Dr. Cynthia KOSSO
10 Vice President Finance & Admin ....Mr. Mark F. REED
30 VP Development and Alumni ....Ms. Jill C. ANDERSON
32 VP Student Affairs Dean of Students .... Dr. Nicole L. LOYD
73 Vice Pres/Dean of the Seminary .... Dr. Frank CROUCH
13 Chief Information Officer .... Mr. David BRANDES
09 VP Planning and Research ....Ms. Carole A. REESE
15 VP Human Resources ....Mr. Jon B. CONRAD
35 Asst VP Student Affairs .... Ms. Amy SAUL
20 Assoc Provost ....Dr. Carol TRAUPMAN-CARR
21 Assoc VP for Finance ....Ms. Anne M. REID
84 Dean of Enrollment ....Mr. William SLIWA
39 Assoc Dean of Students ....Ms. Liz YATES SEAMAN
113 Director of Student Accounts .... Ms. Dawn SNOOK
06 Institutional Registrar ....Ms. Monique DAVIS
21 Dir Business/Financial Operations .... Ms. Rachel LYALL
18 Dir Facilities Mgt Plng/Construct .... Mr. Douglas J. PLOTTS
19 Chief of Police .... Mr. George BOKSAN
26 Dir of Marketing & Communications ....Mr. Michael CORR
08 Library Director .... Ms. Janet OHLES
37 Director of Financial Aid Services ....Dr. Dennis P. LEVY
40 Bookstore Manager ....Mr. Robert RUSH, III
41 Director of Athletics ....Ms. Mary Beth SPIRK
42 Chaplain ....Rev. Jennika BORGER
88 Director of the Payne Gallery ....Dr. David LEIDICH
101 Asst to President/Board of Trustees ....Mrs. Elaine C. DEITCH
23 Nurse Coordinator ....Mrs. Stephanie C. DILLMAN
123 Dean of Grad & Adult Enrollment ....Mr. Scott DAMS
29 Asst Dir Career & Alumni Relations .... Ms. Patricia HANNA
105 Webmaster .... Ms. Christie JACOBSEN

Mount Aloysius College (B)

7373 Admiral Peary Highway, Cresson PA 16630-1999
County: Cambria FICE Identification: 003302
Unit ID: 214166
Telephone: (814) 886-6383 Carnegie Class: Bac-Diverse
FAX Number: (814) 886-2978 Calendar System: Semester
URL: www.mtaloy.edu
Established: 1853 Annual Undergrad Tuition & Fees: $23,110
Enrollment: 1,740 Coed
Affiliation or Control: Independent Non-Profit IRS Status: 501(c)3
Highest Offering: Master's
Accreditation: M, ACBSP, ADNUR, DMS, MLTAD, NUR, PTAA, SURGT

01 President .... Dr. John MILLS
05 Sr VP Academic Affs/Dean of Faculty .... Dr. Patricia IRELAND
32 VP Student Affs/Dean Students .... Vacant
84 VP Enrollment Mgmt/Dean Admissions ....Mr. Francis C. CROUSE, JR.
07 Director of Freshman Admissions .... Mr. Andrew D. CLOUSE
07 Director of Transfer Admissions ....Mr. Richard MISHLER
111 VP Institutional Advancement .... Vacant
10 VP Finance & Administration .... Mr. Michael BAKER
06 Registrar .... Dr. Christopher M. LOVETT
08 Director of Library .... Vacant
37 Director of Financial Aid .... Ms. Stacy L. SCHENK
15 Director of Human Resources .... Ms. Tonia J. GORDON
26 Director of Communications .... Mr. Sam WAGNER
13 Director of Information Technology .... Mr. Rich J. SHEA
23 Director of Health Services ....Ms. Shannon D. GROVE
40 Director of Bookstore .... Ms. Christine M. CLINTON
41 Director of Athletics .... Mr. Kevin KIME
19 Director of Safety & Security .... Mr. William H. TREXLER
18 Director of Physical Plant .... Mr. Gerald RUBRITZ
09 Institutional Researcher ....Mr. Bryan J. PEARSON
36 Career Development Coordinator .... Vacant
38 Dir Student Counseling/Disabilities ....Ms. Marisa L. EVANS
39 Director of Residence Life .... Mr. Matthew LOVELL
42 Director Campus Ministry .... Ms. Amy KANICH
44 Manager of Annual Giving .... Ms. Sally GORDON
04 Administrative Asst to President .... Ms. Carla NELEN

Muhlenberg College (C)

2400 West Chew Street, Allentown PA 18104-5586
County: Lehigh FICE Identification: 003304
Unit ID: 214175
Telephone: (484) 664-3100 Carnegie Class: Bac-A&S
FAX Number: (484) 664-3234 Calendar System: Semester
URL: www.muhlenberg.edu
Established: 1848 Annual Undergrad Tuition & Fees: $52,595
Enrollment: 2,367 Coed
Affiliation or Control: Evangelical Lutheran Church In America
IRS Status: 501(c)3
Highest Offering: Baccalaureate
Accreditation: M

01 Interim President ....Dr. Kathleen HARRING
05 Provost ....Dr. Kathleen HARRING
10 Treasurer & Chief Finance Officer ....Mr. Kent DYER
26 Vice President Communications ....Mr. Brian SPEER
111 Vice President of Advancement ....Ms. Rebekkah L. BROWN
15 Vice President for Human Resources .... Ms. Anne SPECK
32 Vice President of Student Affairs ....Ms. Allison GULATI
51 VP/Exec Director Wescoe School .... Dr. A.J LEMHENEY
04 Exec Asst to the President & BoT ....Ms. Sonya CONRAD
30 Senior Assoc VP for Development .... Ms. Deborah J. KIPP
35 Dean of Students ....Ms. Allison GULATI
20 Dean of Academic Life ....Dr. Bruce ANDERSON
104 Dean of Global Education .... Dr. Donna M. KISH-GOODLING
37 Assoc Dean Admission/Dir Finan Aid ...... Mr. Gregory S. MITTON
22 Asst Dean Acad Res/Disability Svcs .... Mr. David HALLOWELL
29 Asst VP Alumni Affairs/Career Svc .... Ms. Natalie HAND
88 Dean Wescoe Sch of Continuing Educ ....Ms. Jane E. HUDAK
84 VP of Enrollment Management .... Mr. Robert SPRINGALL
08 Director of Trexler Library ....Ms. Tina L. HERTEL
06 Registrar .... Ms. Deborah TAMTE-HORAN
13 Chief Information Officer ....Mr. Allan CHEN
19 Dir/Chief of Campus Safety/Security ....Mr. Brian FIDATI
124 Assoc Dean Stdnts/Dir Stdnt Engage .Ms. Janette SCHUMACHER
36 Executive Director Career Svcs .... Mr. Tom DOWD
114 Chief Budget/Accting Ofcr ....Mr. Jason FEIERTAG
23 Exec Dir Health/Counseling Svcs .... Ms. Brynnmarie DORSEY
38 Director Counseling Services .... Dr. Timothy SILVESTRI
42 Chaplain ....Rev. Kristen GLASS PEREZ
09 Dir Institutional Research/Records ....Ms. Nicole HAMMEL
18 Director Plant Operations ....Mr. James BOLTON
96 Director of Business Svcs .... Mr. Brian BLENIS
40 Bookstore Manager .... Ms. Karen R. NORMANN

Neumann University (D)

One Neumann Drive, Aston PA 19014-1298
County: Delaware FICE Identification: 003988
Unit ID: 214272
Telephone: (610) 459-0905 Carnegie Class: Masters/L
FAX Number: (610) 459-1370 Calendar System: Semester
URL: www.neumann.edu
Established: 1965 Annual Undergrad Tuition & Fees: $31,400
Enrollment: 2,715 Coed
Affiliation or Control: Roman Catholic IRS Status: 501(c)3
Highest Offering: Doctorate
Accreditation: M, ACBSP, CAATE, CACREP, MT, NUR, PTA, SW

01 President ....Dr. Chris E. DOMES
05 Vice President Academic Affairs .... Dr. Lawrence DIPAOLO
43 General Counsel .... Ms. Danielle MCNICHOL
10 Vice Pres Finance/Administration ....Mr. Gene MCWILLIAMS
42 Vice President Mission/Ministry ....Sr. Marguerite O'BEIRNE, OSF
111 Vice Pres Inst Advance/Univ Rels .... Ms. Carrie SNYDER
32 Vice Pres Student Affairs & Enroll .... Dr. Christopher HAUG
15 Vice President HR & Risk Management ....Mr. David W. BROWNLEE
49 Dean Division of Arts & Science .... Dr. Alfred G. MUELLER, II
50 Dean Div of Business/Info Mgmt .... Dr. Eric R. WELLINGTON
53 Dean Div of Educ/Human Svcs ....Dr. Barbara HANES
51 Dean Cont Adult/Prof Studies .... Dr. Jilian DONNELLY
66 Dean Div Nursing/Health Sciences .... Dr. Kathleen HOOVER
04 Asst to President/Board Liaison .... Ms. Patricia KLUSMAN
06 Registrar .... Mr. Joel A. NATALE
18 Facilities Director .... Mr. William LEONARD
19 Director Safety & Security ....Mr. Leon FRANCIS
08 Director Library .... Ms. Tiffany MCGREGOR
26 Exec Director Mktg/Communications .... Mr. Stephen BELL
09 Dir of IR and Assessment .... Ms. Melissa THORPE
42 Chaplain .... Fr. Suresh RAJ, OFM CAP
44 Director Annual Giving/Prospect Mgt .... Vacant
29 Dir Alumni Rels/Special Programs .... Ms. Judi STANAITIS
38 Director Counseling .... Vacant
39 Director Housing & Residence Life .... Vacant
13 Exec Director University Computing .... Vacant
24 Director Academic Resource Center ....Ms. Theresa HUKE
41 Director Athletics .... Mr. Chuck SACK
36 Dir Career & Personal Development ....Ms. Preeti SINGH
121 Dean Academic Support Services ....Mr. Michael MULLEN
88 Director Child Development Center ....Ms. Mary Ann MELISI
21 Controller .... Mr. John YOUHOUSE
37 Director Financial Assistance ....Ms. Eileen TUCKER
23 Director Health Services .... Ms. Janet GEDDIS
96 Coordinator for Purchasing .... Ms. Elena BARRAR
88 Director Physical Therapy Program ....Dr. Robert POST
07 Dir of Undergraduate Admissions ....Mr. Edward WRIGHT
88 Dir Ctr for Sprt/Spir/Char Dev .... Ms. Lee M. DELLEMONACHE
90 Director Instructional Technology .... Vacant
88 Director Conference/Scheduling Svcs .... Ms. Melissa HAINES

40 Director University Bookstore ....Ms. Natalie VAN WYK
88 Director Developmental Education .... Ms. Lori BLOUNT
104 Asst Dir International Studies Educ ....Ms. Jen MINTZER
121 Director of Student Success .... Ms. Coleen NEDBALSKI
105 Director Web Services .... Vacant
106 Dir Online Education/E-learning .... Dr. Jilian DONNELLY
84 Dean of Enrollment Management .... Ms. Susan P. KASSAB
88 Program Director Athletic Training ....Dr. Hubert LEE
123 Dir of Adult & Graduate Admissions .... Dr. Erika DAVIS

New Castle School of Trades (E)

4117 Pulaski Road, New Castle PA 16101
County: Lawrence FICE Identification: 007780
Unit ID: 214290
Telephone: (724) 964-8811 Carnegie Class: Assoc/HVT-High Trad
FAX Number: (724) 202-6147 Calendar System: Other
URL: www.ncstrades.edu
Established: 1945 Annual Undergrad Tuition & Fees: N/A
Enrollment: 763 Coed
Affiliation or Control: Proprietary IRS Status: Proprietary
Highest Offering: Associate Degree
Accreditation: ACCSC

01 Director .... Mr. Jim BUTTERMORE
05 Director of Education .... Mr. Tony GIOVANNELLI
07 Director of Admissions .... Mr. Joe BLAZAK
88 Veteran Affairs Director .... Mr. Jim CATHELINE
10 Fiscal Director .... Mrs. Donna DAVIS
36 Director Student Placement ....Mrs. Carrie KRAYNAK
37 Director Student Financial Aid ....Mrs. Trudy SOTTER

Northampton Community College (F)

3835 Green Pond Road, Bethlehem PA 18020-7599
County: Northampton FICE Identification: 007191
Unit ID: 214379
Telephone: (610) 861-5300 Carnegie Class: Assoc/MT-VT-High Trad
FAX Number: (610) 861-5070 Calendar System: Semester
URL: www.northampton.edu
Established: 1967 Annual Undergrad Tuition & Fees (In-District): $4,380
Enrollment: 9,921 Coed
Affiliation or Control: State/Local IRS Status: 170(c)1
Highest Offering: Associate Degree
Accreditation: M, ACBSP, ADNUR, DH, DMS, FUSER, PNUR, RAD

01 President .... Dr. Mark H. ERICKSON
05 Vice President Academic Affairs .... Dr. Carolyn BORTZ
100 Chief of Staff .... Dr. David RUTH
10 Vice President Finance & Operations .... Mr. James F. DUNLEAVY
30 Vice Pres Institutional Advancement ....Ms. Sharon BEALES
32 Vice Pres Enroll/Student Affairs .... Mr. Sedwick HARRIS
31 Vice President Community Education .... Ms. Lauren LOEFFLER
12 Dean Monroe Campus ....Dr. Matthew J. CONNELL
79 Dean Humanities & Social Sciences .... Dr. Christine PENSE
53 Dean Education/Academic Success ....Dr. Elizabeth BUGAIGHIS
50 Dean Business & Technology .... Dr. Denise FRANCOIS-SEENY
76 Dean Allied Health & Sciences ....Dr. Judith REX
13 Assoc VP/Chief Information Officer .... Dr. Deborah BURAK
26 Exec Dir Marketing & Communications .... Mr. Brad DREXLER
06 Interim Registrar ....Ms. Ginger YAVORSKI
07 Director Admissions ....Mr. James MCCARTHY
37 Director Financial Aid ....Ms. Cynthia L. KING
108 Dir of Institutional Effectiveness ....Ms. Dorothy SCHRAMM
15 Exec Dir Human Resources/Title IX .... Vacant
09 Director of Institutional Research .... Ms. Kathy KAPCSOS
18 Director Buildings & Grounds .... Mr. Mark K. CULP
29 Dir Alumni Engagement/Annual Fund .... Ms. Karen GLOSE
36 Director Career Services .... Ms. Karen VERES
35 Dean of Students .... Mr. Eric ROSENTHAL
84 Senior Assoc Dir of Enrollment Svcs ....Ms. Mary S. MANCINO

Northampton Community College Monroe County Branch Campus (G)

205 Old Mill Road, Tannersville PA 18372
Telephone: (570) 620-9221 Identification: 770164
Accreditation: &M

Peirce College (H)

1420 Pine Street, Philadelphia PA 19102-4699
County: Philadelphia FICE Identification: 003309
Unit ID: 214883
Telephone: (215) 545-6400 Carnegie Class: Bac-Diverse
FAX Number: (215) 670-9366 Calendar System: Semester
URL: www.peirce.edu
Established: 1865 Annual Undergrad Tuition & Fees: $15,060
Enrollment: 1,478 Coed
Affiliation or Control: Independent Non-Profit IRS Status: 501(c)3
Highest Offering: Master's
Accreditation: M, ACBSP, CAHIIM

01 President & CEO ....Ms. Mary Ellen CARO
10 VP Finance/Administration .... Ms. Elizabeth M. KRAPP
05 VP Academic Advancement .... Dr. Rita J. TOLIVER-ROBERTS
111 VP Institutional Advancement .... Ms. Uva C. COLES
26 Vice President Integrated Marketing ....Mr. Joseph GUZZARDO
32 VP Student Services/Retention Mgmt ....Mr. Brad K. HODGE
15 VP Human Res/Chief Diversity Ofcr ....Ms. Harriet S. GOLEN
108 Asst VP Institutional Assessment ....Ms. Debra S. SCHRAMMEL

13 Chief Information Officer ... Mr. James T. BURNS
109 Chief Auxiliary Services Officer ... Mr. Vito R. CHIMENTI
20 Assoc Dean Academic Ops/Faculty Sup ... Mr. Jon LENROW
04 Administrative Asst to President ... Ms. Tara E. MCBRIDE
06 Registrar ... Dr. Shannon BEGLEY

Penn Commercial Business/ Technical School (A)

242 Oak Spring Road, Washington PA 15301-6822

County: Washington FICE Identification: 004902
Unit ID: 214892
Telephone: (724) 222-5330 Carnegie Class: Assoc/HVT-High Trad
FAX Number: (724) 222-4722 Calendar System: Quarter
URL: www.penncommercial.edu
Established: 1929 Annual Undergrad Tuition & Fees: $19,129
Enrollment: 225 Coed
Affiliation or Control: Proprietary IRS Status: Proprietary
Highest Offering: Associate Degree
Accreditation: ACCSC

01 Director ... Mr. Robert S. BAZANT
11 Vice President of Operations ... Ms. Marianne ALBERT
04 Assistant to the President ... Ms. Barbara KENNEDY
07 Director of Admissions ... Mr. Ron ZUBATY
32 Director of Student Services ... Ms. Kristine GORBY
37 Director of Financial Aid ... Ms. Jayme TUITE
88 Director of Education ... Ms. Pat DECONCILLIS
05 Director of Academic Affairs ... Ms. Anita ROSELL
09 Director of Reports & Statistics ... Mrs. Melissa PAPSON
36 Director of Career Services ... Ms. Ashley SUBACIS

Penn State University Park (B)

201 Old Main, University Park PA 16802-1503

County: Centre FICE Identification: 003329
Unit ID: 214777
Telephone: (814) 865-4700 Carnegie Class: DU-Highest
FAX Number: (814) 863-7590 Calendar System: Semester
URL: www.psu.edu
Established: 1855 Annual Undergrad Tuition & Fees (In-State): $18,454
Enrollment: 47,119 Coed
Affiliation or Control: State Related IRS Status: 501(c)3
Highest Offering: Doctorate
Accreditation: M, ART, CAATE, CACREP, CAEPN, CEA, CLPSY, COPSY, DIETD, FEPAC, HSA, IPSY, JOUR, LAW, LSAR, MUS, NURSE, PCSAS, SCPSY, SP, THEA

01 President ... Dr. Eric J. BARRON
05 Executive Vice President & Provost ... Dr. Nicholas P. JONES
46 Vice President for Research ... Dr. Lora G. WEISS
32 Vice President for Student Affairs ... Dr. Damon R. SIMS
26 Vice Pres Strategic Communications ... Mr. Lawrence H. LOKMAN
30 Vice Pres Devel/Alumni Relations ... Mr. O. Richard BUNDY, III
10 Sr Vice Pres Finance & Bus/Treas ... Mr. David J. GRAY
106 Vice President for Outreach ... Ms. Tracey D. HUSTON
11 Vice President for Administration ... Mr. Frank GUADAGNINO
104 Int Vice Provost Global Programs ... Dr. Robert G. CRANE
43 Vice President & General Counsel ... Dr. Stephen S. DUNHAM
49 Vice Pres & Dean Undergrad Educ ... Dr. Robert N. PANGBORN
20 Vice Provost Faculty Affairs ... Dr. Kathleen BIESCHKE
28 Vice Provost Educational Equity ... Dr. Marcus A. WHITEHURST
12 Vice Pres Commonwealth Campuses ... Dr. Madlyn L. HANES
13 Interim Vice Pres Info Tech/CIO ... Mr. Donald J. WELCH
45 Vice Provost Plng and Assessment ... Dr. Lance C. KENNEDY-PHILLIPS
09 Asst VP Institutional Research ... Dr. Karen VANCE
108 Asst VP Lrng Outcomes Assessment .. Dr. Suzanne E. WEINSTEIN
45 Asst VP for Strategic Planning ... Dr. Daniel NEWHART
22 Assoc Vice Pres Affirmative Action ... Dr. Suzanne C. ADAIR
114 University Budget Officer ... Ms. Mary Lou D. ORTIZ
21 Assoc Vice Pres Finance/Corp Cont ... Mr. Joseph J. DONCSECZ
21 Assoc Vice Pres Finance & Business ... Mr. Kurt A. KISSINGER
15 Vice Pres Human Resources ... Ms. Lorraine GOFFE
18 Assoc Vice President Physical Plant ... Mr. William E. SITZABEE, JR.
109 Assoc VP Auxiliary & Business Svcs ... Mr. John PAPAZOGLOU
106 Interim Vice Prov Online Education ... Dr. Renata S. ENGEL
27 Director News/Media Relations ... Ms. Lisa M. POWERS
39 Asst VP for Housing & Food Svcs ... Ms. Cheryl FABRIZI
37 Asst VP UG Ed/Exec Dir Stdnt Aid ... Ms. Melissa J. KUNES
29 AVP Alumni Rels/CEO PS Alum Assoc ... Mr. Paul J. CLIFFORD
115 Exec Director Office of Investment ... Mr. David E. BRANIGAN
07 Interim Exec Dir UG Admissions ... Mr. Vince TIMBERS
38 Director Counseling/Psych Services ... Dr. Benjamin D. LOCKE
41 Athletic Director ... Ms. A. Sandy BARBOUR
86 Vice Pres for Govt & Cmty Rels ... Mr. Zachery MOORE
06 University Registrar ... Mr. Robert A. KUBAT
36 Senior Director Career Services ... Dr. Robert M. ORNDORFF
17 CEO Penn State Health ... Mr. Stephen M. MASSINI
08 Dean Univ Libraries/Scholar Comm ... Ms. Barbara I. DEWEY
47 Dean Agricultural Sciences ... Dr. Richard T. ROUSH
48 Dean Arts & Architecture ... Dr. Barbara O. KORNER
50 Dean Business ... Dr. Charles H. WHITEMAN
60 Dean Communications ... Dr. Marie HARDIN
65 Dean Earth & Mineral Sciences ... Dr. Lee KUMP
53 Dean Education ... Dr. Kimberly LAWLESS
54 Dean Engineering ... Dr. Justin SCHWARTZ
58 V Prov Grad Educ/Dean Grad School ... Dr. Regina VASILATOS-YOUNKEN
76 Dean Health & Human Dev ... Mr. Dennis G. SHEA
66 Dean School of Nursing ... Ms. Laurie A. BADZEK
56 Assoc Dean/Dir Coop Extension ... Dr. Dennis D. CALVIN
49 Assoc Dean Liberal Arts ... Mr. David S. BENNETT, JR.
81 Dean Science ... Dr. Douglas R. CAVENER
72 Dean Info Sciences and Technology ... Dr. Andrew L. SEARS
92 Dean Honors College ... Dr. Peggy A. JOHNSON
61 Dean Penn State Law ... Dr. Hari M. OSOFSKY
63 Dean College of Medicine ... Dr. Kevin BLACK
75 Chief Penn College of Technology ... Dr. Davie J. GILMOUR
44 Executive Director Annual Giving ... Ms. Jennifer D. BENOIT
88 Assoc Vice President for Research ... Dr. John W. HANOLD
19 Asst VP Univ Police/Public Safety ... Mr. Joseph MILEK
23 Director University Health Services ... Dr. Robin E. OLIVER-VERONESI
96 Director Procurement Services ... Mr. R. Duane ELMORE
31 Director Campus & Cmty Events ... Ms. Barbara ETTARO
102 Exec Dir Corp/Foundation Relations ... Mr. Mark S. ARMAGOST
04 Exec Admin Assistant to President ... Ms. Carmella MULROY-DEGENHART
40 General Manager Bookstore ... Ms. Jennifer L. GUYER
25 Contract Coordinator ... Ms. Cristene N. BOOB
16 Senior Director Employee Relations ... Ms. Susan M. RUTAN
116 Director of Internal Audit ... Mr. Daniel P. HEIST
119 Chief Information Security Officer ... Mr. Donald J. WELCH, JR.

† The legal name of Penn State and all its campuses is The Pennsylvania State University. For communication purposes, the name is shortened to Penn State followed by the name of the campus.

Penn State Abington (C)

1600 Woodland Road, Abington PA 19001-3918
Telephone: (215) 881-7300 FICE Identification: 003342
Accreditation: &M, ART

† Regional accreditation is carried under the parent institution in University Park, PA.

Penn State Altoona (D)

3000 Ivyside Park, Altoona PA 16601-3777
Telephone: (814) 949-5000 FICE Identification: 003331
Accreditation: &M, ART

† Regional accreditation is carried under the parent institution in University Park, PA.

Penn State Beaver (E)

100 University Drive, Monaca PA 15061-2764
Telephone: (724) 773-3800 FICE Identification: 003332
Accreditation: &M

† Regional accreditation is carried under the parent institution in University Park, PA.

Penn State Berks (F)

Tulpehocken Road, PO Box 7009,
Reading PA 19610-1016
Telephone: (610) 396-6000 FICE Identification: 003334
Accreditation: &M, OTA

† Regional accreditation is carried under the parent institution in University Park, PA.

Penn State Brandywine (G)

25 Yearsley Mill Road, Media PA 19063-5522
Telephone: (610) 892-1200 FICE Identification: 006922
Accreditation: &M

† Regional accreditation is carried under the parent institution in University Park, PA.

Penn State Dickinson Law (H)

150 South College Street, Carlisle PA 17013-2861
Telephone: (717) 240-5000 FICE Identification: 003254
Accreditation: &M, LAW

† Part of Penn State University. Regional accreditation is carried under the parent institution in University Park, PA.

Penn State DuBois (I)

One College Place, DuBois PA 15801-2549
Telephone: (814) 375-4700 FICE Identification: 003335
Accreditation: &M, OTA, PTAA

† Regional accreditation is carried under the parent institution in University Park, PA.

Penn State Erie, The Behrend College (J)

4701 College Drive, Erie PA 16563-0001
Telephone: (814) 898-6000 FICE Identification: 003333
Accreditation: &M

† Regional accreditation is carried under the parent institution in University Park, PA.

Penn State Fayette, The Eberly Campus (K)

2201 University Drive, Lemont Furnace PA 15456-1025
Telephone: (724) 430-4100 FICE Identification: 003336
Accreditation: &M, EMT, PTAA

† Regional accreditation is carried under the parent institution in University Park, PA.

Penn State Great Valley School of Graduate Professional Studies (L)

30 E Swedesford Road, Malvern PA 19355-1488
Telephone: (610) 648-3200 FICE Identification: 003348
Accreditation: &M

† Regional accreditation is carried under the parent institution in University Park, PA.

Penn State Greater Allegheny (M)

4000 University Drive, McKeesport PA 15132-7644
Telephone: (412) 675-9000 FICE Identification: 003339
Accreditation: &M

† Regional accreditation is carried under the parent institution in University Park, PA.

Penn State Harrisburg (N)

777 West Harrisburg Pike, Middletown PA 17057-4846
Telephone: (717) 948-6250 FICE Identification: 006814
Accreditation: &M, CAEPN, SPAA

† Regional accreditation is carried under the parent institution in University Park, PA.

Penn State Hazleton (O)

76 University Drive, Hazleton PA 18202-8025
Telephone: (570) 450-3000 FICE Identification: 003338
Accreditation: &M, MLTAD, PTAA

† Regional accreditation is carried under the parent institution in University Park, PA.

Penn State Lehigh Valley (P)

2809 Saucon Valley Road, Center Valley PA 18034-8447
Telephone: (610) 285-5000 FICE Identification: 003330
Accreditation: &M

† Regional accreditation is carried under the parent institution in University Park, PA.

Penn State Milton S. Hershey Medical Center College of Medicine (Q)

500 University Drive, Hershey PA 17033-2360
Telephone: (717) 531-8563 FICE Identification: 006813
Accreditation: &M, ARCPA, IPSY, MED, PAST, PH

† Regional accreditation is carried under the parent institution in University Park, PA.

Penn State Mont Alto (R)

One Campus Drive, Mont Alto PA 17237-9700
Telephone: (717) 749-6000 FICE Identification: 003340
Accreditation: &M, OTA, PTAA

† Regional accreditation is carried under the parent institution in University Park, PA.

Penn State New Kensington (S)

3550 Seventh Street Road, Route 780,
New Kensington PA 15068-1765
Telephone: (724) 334-5466 FICE Identification: 003341
Accreditation: &M, RAD

† Regional accreditation is carried under the parent institution in University Park, PA.

Penn State Schuylkill (T)

200 University Drive, Schuylkill Haven PA 17972-2202
Telephone: (570) 385-6000 FICE Identification: 003343
Accreditation: &M, RAD

† Regional accreditation is carried under the parent institution in University Park, PA.

Penn State Scranton (U)

120 Ridge View Drive, Dunmore PA 18512-1602
Telephone: (570) 963-2500 FICE Identification: 003344
Accreditation: &M

† Regional accreditation is carried under the parent institution in University Park, PA.

Penn State Shenango (V)

147 Shenango Avenue, Sharon PA 16146-1537
Telephone: (724) 983-2803 FICE Identification: 003345
Accreditation: &M, OTA, PTAA

† Regional accreditation is carried under the parent institution in University Park, PA.

Penn State Wilkes-Barre (A)

Old Route 115, PO Box PSU, Lehman PA 18627-0217
Telephone: (570) 675-2171 FICE Identification: 003346
Accreditation: &M

† Regional accreditation is carried under the parent institution in University Park, PA.

Penn State York (B)

1031 Edgecomb Avenue, York PA 17403-3326
Telephone: (717) 771-4000 FICE Identification: 003347
Accreditation: &M

† Regional accreditation is carried under the parent institution in University Park, PA.

Pennco Tech (C)

3815 Otter Street, Bristol PA 19007-3696
County: Bucks FICE Identification: 009449
Unit ID: 214944
Telephone: (215) 785-0111 Carnegie Class: Spec 2-yr-Tech
FAX Number: (215) 785-1945 Calendar System: Other
URL: www.penncotech.edu
Established: 1973 Annual Undergrad Tuition & Fees: N/A
Enrollment: 315 Coed
Affiliation or Control: Proprietary IRS Status: Proprietary
Highest Offering: Associate Degree
Accreditation: ACCSC

01 CEO ... Michael S. HOBYAK
05 Director of Education/School Dir ... Fred PARCELLS
07 Director of Admissions ... Glen SLATER
06 Registrar ... Sondra KOOB
32 Director Student Services ... Hakien COLES
37 Director Student Financial Aid ... Keena FITZHUGH
36 Director Career Services ... Teresa SCHEERER

Pennsylvania Academy of the Fine Arts (D)

128 N Broad Street, Philadelphia PA 19102-1424
County: Philadelphia FICE Identification: 021073
Unit ID: 214971
Telephone: (215) 972-7600 Carnegie Class: Spec-4-yr-Arts
FAX Number: (215) 569-0153 Calendar System: Semester
URL: www.pafa.edu
Established: 1805 Annual Undergrad Tuition & Fees: $38,878
Enrollment: 268 Coed
Affiliation or Control: Independent Non-Profit IRS Status: 501(c)3
Highest Offering: Master's
Accreditation: M, ART

01 President & CEO ... Dr. David R. BRIGHAM
26 Chief Marketing Officer ... Ms. Malini DODDAMANI
10 Chief Financial Officer ... Mr. Anthony DECOCINIS
07 Dean of Enrollment ... Ms. Casey TURNER
57 Dean of the School of Fine Arts ... Mr. Clint A. JUKKALA
32 Dean of Students ... Ms. Anne K. STASSEN
35 Director of Student Services ... Ms. Morgan HOBBS
37 Director of Financial Aid ... Ms. Celeste FRANKLIN
36 Director of Career Services ... Mr. Gregory MARTINO
08 Director of Library Services ... Mr. Brian DUFFY
06 Registrar ... Mr. Peter MEDWICK
18 Director of Facilities Management ... Mr. Ed POLETTI
19 Director of Security and Safety ... Mr. Jimmie GREENO
13 Director of Information Technology ... Mr. Kevin MARTIN
04 Exec Assistant to President and CEO ... Ms. Sheryl KESSLER
58 Director of Grad Program Services ... Mr. Steven CONNELL
20 Academic Services Coordinator ... Mr. C.J STAHL
38 Student Care Coordinator ... Ms. Juliana FOMENKO
88 Executive Assistant to the Dean ... Ms. Katharine S. PEPPLE
15 Chief Human Resources Officer ... Ms. Lisa BIAGAS

Pennsylvania College of Art & Design (E)

204 N Prince Street, Box 59, Lancaster PA 17608-0059
County: Lancaster FICE Identification: 022699
Unit ID: 215053
Telephone: (717) 396-7833 Carnegie Class: Spec-4-yr-Arts
FAX Number: (717) 396-1339 Calendar System: Semester
URL: www.pcad.edu
Established: 1982 Annual Undergrad Tuition & Fees: $25,850
Enrollment: 260 Coed
Affiliation or Control: Independent Non-Profit IRS Status: 501(c)3
Highest Offering: Master's
Accreditation: M, ART

01 President ... Mr. Michael MOLLA
84 Dean of Enrollment ... Ms. Debbie BAZARSKY
26 Dir Strategic Communications ... Ms. Daina SAVAGE
10 VP for Finance ... Ms. Jonelle MATTHEWS
05 Provost ... Vacant
07 Director of Admissions ... Ms. Jenn RENKO
32 Dean of Student Services ... Ms. Jessica EDONICK
37 Dir Financial Aid/Registrar ... Mr. J. David HERSHEY
13 Director of Information Technology ... Mr. Derrick GUTIERREZ
51 Director of Continuing Education ... Ms. Natalie LASCEK
30 Director of Development ... Vacant
35 Director Student Life ... Mr. Jeff BINGEMAN
113 Bursar ... Ms. Lisa GOOD
18 Director of Facilities ... Mr. Dan FREILER
04 Exec Asst to the President ... Ms. Amy GASTON
90 Director Academic Computing ... Mr. Hylon PLUMB
08 Library Director ... Ms. Karen HUTCHISON

Pennsylvania College of Health Sciences (F)

850 Greenfield Road, Lancaster PA 17601
County: Lancaster FICE Identification: 009863
Unit ID: 442356
Telephone: (800) 622-5443 Carnegie Class: Spec-4-yr-Other Health
FAX Number: (717) 947-6250 Calendar System: Semester
URL: www.pacollege.edu
Established: 1903 Annual Undergrad Tuition & Fees: $28,412
Enrollment: 1,793 Coed
Affiliation or Control: Independent Non-Profit IRS Status: 501(c)3
Highest Offering: Doctorate
Accreditation: M, ADNUR, COARC, CVT, DMS, MT, NMT, NURSE, RAD, SURGT

01 President ... Dr. Mary Grace SIMCOX
05 VP Academic Affairs & Enrollment ... Dr. Kim JOHNSTON
108 VP Institutional Effectiveness ... Dr. Penni LONGENECKER
10 VP Finance & Administration ... Mr. Thomas HULSTINE
111 VP Advancement ... Ms. Ellen WILEY
15 VP Human Resources ... Ms. Nancy FLOREY
13 AVP Information Technology ... Mr. Kevin BALSBAUGH
32 AVP Student Affairs ... Mr. Matthew SWATCHICK
04 Administrative Asst to President ... Ms. Susan GARDINA
06 Registrar ... Mr. Edwin ADDIS
19 Director Security/Safety ... Mr. Scott LOKEY
66 AVP Nursing ... Dr. Jean HERSHEY

Pennsylvania College of Technology (G)

One College Avenue, Williamsport PA 17701-5799
County: Lycoming FICE Identification: 003395
Unit ID: 366252
Telephone: (570) 326-3761 Carnegie Class: Bac/Assoc-Mixed
FAX Number: (570) 327-4503 Calendar System: Semester
URL: www.pct.edu
Established: 1989 Annual Undergrad Tuition & Fees (In-State): $16,740
Enrollment: 5,457 Coed
Affiliation or Control: State IRS Status: 501(c)3
Highest Offering: Master's
Accreditation: M, ACBSP, ACFEI, ADNUR, ARCPA, CAHIIM, CONST, DH, EMT, NAIT, NUR, OTA, PNUR, PTAA, RAD, SURGT

01 President ... Dr. Davie Jane GILMOUR
05 VP for Academic Affairs/Provost ... Dr. Michael J. REED
10 Senior VP for Finance/CFO ... Ms. Suzanne T. STOPPER
111 Vice Pres Institutional Advancement ... Ms. Loni N. KLINE
13 Vice Pres for Info Tech/CIO ... Mr. A.J LACOMBA
84 VP Enrollment Mgmt & Assoc Provost ... Dr. Carolyn R. STRICKLAND
32 VP for Student Affairs ... Mr. Elliott STRICKLAND, JR.
103 VP for Workforce Development ... Ms. Shannon M. MUNRO
15 VP for Human Resources ... Ms. Hillary E. HOFSTROM
20 Associate VP for Instruction ... Mr. Tom F. GREGORY
04 Administrative Asst to President ... Mrs. Valerie A. BAIER
66 Dean of Nursing & Health Sciences ... Dr. Sandra L. RICHMOND
88 Dean Construction & Design Tech ... Dr. Carol A. LUGG
54 Dean Industrial/Comp/Engineering ... Mr. Dave R. COTNER
81 Dean of Sciences/Human/Visual Comm ... Dr. Sue A. KELLEY
65 Dean Transportation/Natl Resources ... Mr. Brett A. REASNER
50 Dean of Business/Hospitality ... Dr. Lisa M. ANDRUS
102 Exec Dir of Penn College Foundation ... Mr. Kyle A. SMITH
103 Exec Dir General Services ... Mr. Timothy O. RISSEL
08 Director of the Madigan Library ... Ms. Tracey AMEY
14 Director Instructional Technology ... Mr. Walter J. SHULTZ, JR.
18 Director of Facilities Operations ... Mr. Don J. LUKE
09 Exec Dir Assessment/Research/Plng ... Dr. Brian L. CYGAN
06 Assistant Registrar ... Ms. Maria N. PISELLI
35 Associate Dean of Student Affairs ... Dr. Jennifer MCLEAN
39 Dir Residence Life/Student Conduct ... Mr. Jon D. WESCOTT
19 Chief of Police ... Mr. Chris E. MILLER
26 Assoc VP Public Rels & Marketing ... Mr. Joseph S. YODER
29 Director Alumni Relations ... Ms. Kimberly R. CASSEL
88 Director of Corporate Relations ... Ms. Elizabeth A. BIDDLE
88 Director Children Learning Center ... Ms. Barbara J. ALBERT
40 Director of College Store ... Ms. Jennifer L. MCCRACKEN
41 Director of Athletics ... Mr. John D. VANDEVERE
91 Director Administrative Info Sys ... Ms. Kathleen A. KELSEY
23 Director College Health Services ... Mr. Carl L. SHANER
124 Director of Student Engagement ... Mr. Anthony J. PACE
22 Director of Disability Services ... Ms. Kay E. DUNKLEBERGER
85 Coord International Programs ... Ms. Shanin L. DOUGHERTY
96 Director/Procurement Services ... Ms. Karen P. FESSLER
07 Director of Admissions ... Ms. Audriana L. EMPET
89 Director of College Transitions ... Ms. Kathleen V. MCNAUL
38 Director Student Counseling ... Dr. Kathy W. ZAKARIAN
100 Chief of Staff ... Mr. Patrick MARTY
30 Director of Development ... Ms. Heather M. SHUEY
44 Director Annual Giving ... Ms. Angie E. MYERS

† Affiliate of Pennsylvania State University.

Pennsylvania Highlands Community College (H)

101 Community College Way, Johnstown PA 15904-2949
County: Cambria FICE Identification: 031804
Unit ID: 414911
Telephone: (814) 262-6400 Carnegie Class: Assoc/MT-VT-High Non
FAX Number: (814) 269-9700 Calendar System: Semester
URL: www.pennhighlands.edu
Established: 1994 Annual Undergrad Tuition & Fees (In-District): $5,820
Enrollment: 2,814 Coed
Affiliation or Control: State/Local IRS Status: 501(c)3
Highest Offering: Associate Degree
Accreditation: M, MAC

01 Acting Chairperson ... Lorraine DONAHUE
32 VP of Student Services ... Trish CORLE
10 VP of Finance/Administration ... Lorraine DONAHUE
05 Interim VP of Academic Affairs ... Dr. Barbara ZABOROWSKI
15 Assistant VP of Human Resources ... Susan FISHER
09 Assistant VP of IR/Assessment ... Gary BOAST
13 Chief Information Officer ... Matthew HOFFMAN
12 Director Blair Center ... Chris FARRELL
12 Director Huntingdon Center ... Marissa DAVIS
12 Director Somerset Center ... Adam BOWSER
12 Director Ebensburg Center ... Robert SEKERAK
06 Dean Enrollment Services/Registrar ... Michelle STUMPF
88 Dean of Faculty ... Erica REIGHARD
88 Dean of Curriculum ... Cynthia MCCABE
103 Dean of Career Svcs/Workforce Dev ... Larry BRUGH
18 Director of Facilities Operation ... Reb BROWNLEE
21 Director of Finance/Administration ... Christopher PRIBULSKY
37 Director of Student Financial Svcs ... Judy EBBERTS
26 Director of Marketing/Communication ... Raymond WEIBLE, JR.
19 Director of Security and Safety ... Cregg DIBERT
35 Dir of Student Activities/Athletics ... Suzanne BRUGH
121 Director of Student Success Center ... Mindy NITCH
91 Dir Tech Support & Systems Admin ... Ron RHOADES
04 Assistant to the President ... Nicole ROBSON

Pennsylvania Institute of Health and Technology (I)

PO Box 278 1015 Mount Braddock Road, Mount Braddock PA 15465-0278
Telephone: (724) 437-4600 Identification: 666035
Accreditation: ABHES

† Branch campus of West Virginia Junior College, Morgantown, WV.

Pennsylvania Institute of Technology (J)

800 Manchester Avenue, Media PA 19063-4098
County: Delaware FICE Identification: 010998
Unit ID: 214582
Telephone: (610) 892-1500 Carnegie Class: Spec 2-yr-Health
FAX Number: (610) 892-1510 Calendar System: Semester
URL: www.pit.edu
Established: 1953 Annual Undergrad Tuition & Fees: $13,365
Enrollment: 447 Coed
Affiliation or Control: Independent Non-Profit IRS Status: 501(c)3
Highest Offering: Associate Degree
Accreditation: M, PTAA

01 President/CEO ... Mr. William B. ROBINSON
11 Vice President/COO ... Mr. Jack BACON
05 Provost ... Dr. Robert E. HANCOX
10 Chief Financial Officer ... Ms. Annamarie CASSIDY
32 Director of Student Services ... Ms. Kamira EVANS
06 Dir of Inst Research/Registrar ... Mr. Craig M. JACOBS
07 Director of Admissions ... Mr. Matthew MEYERS
37 Financial Aid Director ... Ms. Laura BLOMGREN
18 Director of Facilities ... Mr. Frederick FIVECOAT
13 Dir of Information Technology ... Mr. Michael TESTA
08 Director of the Library ... Ms. Lynea ANDERMAN
20 Asst Dean of Academic Affairs ... Ms. Rachelle CHAYKIN
04 Executive Asst to President ... Ms. Kathryn DIGIORGIO

*Pennsylvania's State System of Higher Education, Office of the Chancellor (K)

Dixon University Ctr, 2986 N 2nd St, Harrisburg PA 17110-1201
County: Dauphin FICE Identification: 029371
Unit ID: 214661
Telephone: (717) 720-4000 Carnegie Class: N/A
FAX Number: (717) 720-4011
URL: www.passhe.edu

01 Chancellor ... Dr. Daniel GREENSTEIN
03 Deputy Chancellor ... Mr. Randy GOIN, JR.
10 Vice Chancellor Admin/Finance ... Ms. Sharon MINNICH
05 Vice Chancellor/CAO ... Vacant
88 Chief Transformation Officer ... Ms. Sarah BAUDER
26 Chief Strategic Relations Officer ... Mr. Cody JONES
43 Chief Legal Counsel ... Mr. Andrew LEHMAN
88 System Redesign Project Manager ... Ms. Rosa LARA

*Bloomsburg University of Pennsylvania (A)

400 E Second Street, Bloomsburg PA 17815-1399
County: Columbia FICE Identification: 003315
Unit ID: 211158
Telephone: (570) 389-4000 Carnegie Class: Masters/L
FAX Number: (570) 389-3700 Calendar System: Semester
URL: www.bloomu.edu
Established: 1839 Annual Undergrad Tuition & Fees (In-State): $10,958
Enrollment: 9,260 Coed
Affiliation or Control: State IRS Status: 501(c)3
Highest Offering: Doctorate
Accreditation: M, ANEST, ART, AUD, #CAATE, CAEPN, EXSC, MUS, NURSE, SP, SW, THEA

02 President .... Dr. Bashar W. HANNA
05 Sr VP & Provost Acad Affairs .... Dr. Diana ROGERS-ADKINSON
10 Vice Pres Finance/Administration .... Mr. John F. LOONAN
32 Vice Pres Student Affairs .... Dr. Dionne D. SOMERVILLE
111 Vice Pres University Advancement .... Mr. Erik EVANS
84 Vice Pres Strategic Enroll Mgmt .... Mr. Thomas FLETCHER
86 Director External & Govt Relations .... Mr. Dan KNORR
100 Chief of Staff .... Dr. Peter T. KELLY
20 Interim Vice Provost/Dean UG Educ .... Dr. Mark BAUMAN
58 Int Assoc Vice Prov/Dean Grad Stds .... Dr. Heather FELDHAUS
13 Assoc VP Technology & Library Svcs .... Mr. Wayne C. MOHR
108 Asst VP Planning & Assessment .... Vacant
18 Asst VP for Facilities Management .... Mr. Eric NESS
21 Asst VP Finance/Budget & Bus Svcs .... Ms. Claudia THRUSH
35 Asst VP Student Affairs .... Mr. James MCCORMACK
26 AVP Marketing/Communications .... Ms. Jennifer UMBERGER
29 AVP Alumni/Professional Engagement .... Ms. Lynda MICHAELS
07 AVP for Undergraduate Admissions .... Mr. Christopher LAPOS
121 AVP Student Success .... Ms. Marty WYGMANS
49 Dean College of Liberal Arts .... Dr. James BROWN
50 Dean Zeigler College of Business .... Dr. Todd SHAWVER
81 Dean College of Science/Tech .... Dr. Robert S. ARONSTAM
53 Interim Dean College of Education .... Dr. Darlene PERNER
15 Director Human Resources/Labor Rel .... Mr. Jerry REED
46 Dir Research Programs .... Ms. Sadie HAUCK
06 Registrar/Dir Enroll Services .... Mr. Joseph KISSELL
09 Director of Institutional Research .... Ms. Karen L. SLUSSER
104 Director Global & Multicultural Ed .... Vacant
37 Director Financial Aid .... Ms. Amanda KISHBAUGH
36 Dir Career/Professional Development .... Dr. Wren FRITSKY
90 Manager Technology Support Services .... Mr. David S. CELLI
40 Manager University Store .... Ms. Laura HEGER
41 Director of Athletics .... Mr. Michael S. MCFARLAND
42 Director Protestant Campus Ministry .... Rev. Jill YOUNG
42 Director Catholic Campus Ministry .... Fr. Richard MOWERY
19 Dir Bloomsburg University Police .... Mr. Leo SOKOLOSKI
92 Director Univ Honors Pgm .... Dr. Julie VANDIVERE
96 Director Procurement & Operations .... Mr. Jeffrey MANDEL
08 Director Library Services .... Ms. Charlotte DROLL
91 Dir Applications Development .... Ms. Frances DONAHOE
102 Exec Dir BU Foundation .... Mr. Jerome DVORAK

*California University of Pennsylvania (B)

250 University Avenue, California PA 15419-1394
County: Washington FICE Identification: 003316
Unit ID: 211361
Telephone: (724) 938-4000 Carnegie Class: Masters/L
FAX Number: (724) 938-4138 Calendar System: Semester
URL: www.calu.edu
Established: 1852 Annual Undergrad Tuition & Fees (In-State): $11,108
Enrollment: 7,788 Coed
Affiliation or Control: State IRS Status: 501(c)3
Highest Offering: Doctorate
Accreditation: M, ACBSP, ART, #CAATE, CACREP, CAEPN, NRPA, NURSE, PTAA, SP, SW, THEA

02 President .... Ms. Geraldine JONES
100 Chief of Staff to the President .... Ms. Kelly MORAN
05 Provost/Sr VP for Acad Affairs .... Dr. Bruce BARNHART
10 VP Administration & Finance .... Mr. Robert THORN
84 VP for Enrollment Management .... Mr. T. David GARCIA
09 Int Director of Inst Research .... Ms. Donna WRIGHT
58 Acting Dean of Graduate Studies .... Dr. Yugo IKACH
124 Assoc Prov/Student Retention Ofcr .... Dr. Dan M. ENGSTROM
30 VP for Development & Alumni .... Mr. Anthony F. MAURO
32 Assoc VP Student Affairs .... Dr. Timothy SUSICK
13 Assoc VP for University Technology .... Mr. Paul ALLISON
72 Dean of Science/Technology .... Dr. Brenda L. FREDETTE
49 Dean of Liberal Arts .... Dr. Kristen MAJOCHA
53 Dean Col Education/Human Svcs .... Dr. Kevin A. KOURY
62 Dean of Library Services .... Mr. Douglas HOOVER
07 Dean of Admissions .... Ms. Tracey SHEETZ
106 Exec Dir Global Online .... Vacant
37 Director of Financial Aid .... Mr. Jeff DERUBBO
06 Registrar .... Ms. Heidi WILLIAMS
36 Director of Career Services .... Ms. Rhonda GIFFORD
92 Director Honors Program .... Mr. Mark AUNE
29 Director of Alumni Relations .... Mr. Ryan BARNHART
39 Assoc Dir of OnCampus Living .... Mrs. Shelata CAMARDA-WEBB
94 Director Women's Studies .... Dr. Marta MCCLINTOCK
85 International Student Advisor .... Mr. John WATKINS
41 Athletic Director .... Dr. Karen HJERPE
15 Director of Personnel .... Mr. Eric GUISER
22 Director of Social Equity .... Dr. John BURNETT
19 Chief of Police .... Mr. Ed MCSHEFFERY
18 Director of Facilities Mgmt .... Mr. Mike KANALIS
26 VP for Communications & Marketing .... Mrs. Christine KINDL
27 Director of Marketing .... Ms. Keli HENDERSON
88 Director of Creative Services .... Mr. Greg SOFRANKO
40 Book Store Manager .... Ms. Amy NASH
96 Director of Purchasing .... Ms. Joyce SHEPPICK
108 Director Institutional Assessment .... Dr. Leonard COLELLI

*Cheyney University of Pennsylvania (C)

1837 University Circle PO Box 200,
Cheyney PA 19319-0200
County: Delaware FICE Identification: 003317
Unit ID: 211608
Telephone: (610) 399-2000 Carnegie Class: Bac-A&S
FAX Number: (610) 399-2415 Calendar System: Semester
URL: www.cheyney.edu
Established: 1837 Annual Undergrad Tuition & Fees (In-State): $10,533
Enrollment: 755 Coed
Affiliation or Control: State IRS Status: 501(c)3
Highest Offering: Master's
Accreditation: M

02 President .... Mr. Aaron A. WALTON
05 Provost .... Ms. Kizzy MORRIS
10 Exec Dir Finance & Admin .... Ms. Cynthia MOULTRIE
21 Interim Controller/AVP Finance .... Ms. Layna HOLMES-BUTLER
38 Chairperson Guidance & Counseling .... Ms. Jolly RAMAKRISHNAN
06 Dir Enrollment Services/Registrar .... Ms. Margaret OMWENGA
37 Director Student Financial Services .... Ms. Suzanne SPARROW
09 Director Institutional Research .... Dr. Erika SHEHATA
18 Exec Director of Operations .... Mr. James LEWIS
19 Director of Campus & Public Safety .... Mr. Lawrence RICHARDS
41 Interim Athletic Director .... Vacant
17 College Physician .... Dr. Pamela HADLEY
43 University Legal Counsel .... Ms. Cathleen MCCORMICK
32 Exec Dir Campus Life & Student Affs .... Ms. Elisabeth BURTON
39 Dir Residence Life & Housing .... Ms. Lauren SEALY
103 Dir Title III/Grants Administration .... Ms. Mamie STEPHENS
113 Bursar .... Ms. Lauronda FLETCHER
92 Director of Keystone Honors Academy .... Mr. Julani GHANA
84 Exec Dir Enrollment Management .... Mr. Jeffrey JONES
25 Grant and Contract Accountant .... Ms. Flavia STOVALL
04 Executive Associate to President .... Ms. Ramona DIXON
15 Director of Human Resources .... Mr. John GRUENWALD

*Clarion University of Pennsylvania (D)

840 Wood Street, Clarion PA 16214-1232
County: Clarion FICE Identification: 003318
Unit ID: 211644
Telephone: (814) 393-2000 Carnegie Class: Masters/L
FAX Number: (814) 393-1826 Calendar System: Semester
URL: www.clarion.edu
Established: 1867 Annual Undergrad Tuition & Fees (In-State): $11,175
Enrollment: 5,225 Coed
Affiliation or Control: State IRS Status: 501(c)3
Highest Offering: Doctorate
Accreditation: M, ART, CAEPN, CSHSE, LIB, NURSE, SP

02 President .... Dr. Dale-Elizabeth PEHRSSON
05 Provost/AVP .... Dr. Pamela GENT
32 Vice Pres Student & University Affs .... Dr. Susanne FENSKE
10 Vice Pres Finance/Administration .... Mr. Leonard CULLO
102 Chief Exec Officer Foundation .... Mr. Michael R. KEEFER
111 Vice President Univ Advancement .... Mr. James GEIGER
11 Assoc VP for Administration .... Mr. Timothy P. FOGARTY
22 Director of Social Equity .... Ms. Amy SALSGIVER
84 AVP of Enrollment Management .... Mr. David DOLLINS
08 Dean of Libraries .... Dr. Terry S. LATOUR
49 Dean of Arts & Sciences .... Dr. Laura DELBRUGGE
50 Dean of Business Administration .... Dr. Philip FRESE
06 Registrar .... Ms. Lisa L. HEPLER
21 Assoc VP for Finance .... Ms. Tamara B. VARSEK
13 Assoc VP for Information Technology .... Mr. Samuel T. PULEIO
46 Director Faculty Research .... Dr. Amy ESTERHUIZEN
26 Dir of Marketing & Communications .... Ms. Tina HORNER
37 Director of Student Financial Svcs .... Ms. Sue BLOOM
18 Assoc Director of Facilities Mgmt .... Mr. Chad THOMAS
29 Director of Alumni Relations .... Ms. Ann THOMPSON
36 Dir Career/Professional Development .... Mr. William BAILEY
39 Director of Residence Life .... Ms. Jennifer GRAHAM
19 Director of Public Safety .... Mr. Jason HENDERSHOT
41 Athletic Director .... Ms. Wendy SNODGRASS
96 Director of Purchasing .... Mr. Rein A. POLD
09 Inst Research Business Analyst .... Mr. Robert GATESMAN
112 Director of Planned Giving .... Mr. Larry W. JAMISON

*East Stroudsburg University of Pennsylvania (E)

200 Prospect Street, East Stroudsburg PA 18301-2999
County: Monroe FICE Identification: 003320
Unit ID: 212115
Telephone: (570) 422-3211 Carnegie Class: Masters/L
FAX Number: (570) 422-3777 Calendar System: Semester
URL: www.esu.edu
Established: 1893 Annual Undergrad Tuition & Fees (In-State): $11,502
Enrollment: 6,742 Coed
Affiliation or Control: State IRS Status: 501(c)3
Highest Offering: Doctorate
Accreditation: M, CAATE, CAEPN, EXSC, NRPA, NUR, PH, SP, SW

02 President .... Dr. Marcia G. WELSH
05 Provost/Vice Pres Academic Affairs .... Ms. Joanne Z. BRUNO
32 Vice President Student Affairs .... Vacant
10 Vice Pres Administration & Finance .... Mr. Kenneth A. LONG
46 VP Economic Devel/ Entrepreneurship .... Ms. Mary Frances POSTUPACK
84 Vice Pres Enrollment Management .... Mr. David BOUSQUET
58 Director Graduate/Extended Studies .... Dr. William BAJOR
49 Dean of Arts & Sciences .... Dr. Andra BASU
76 Dean of Health Sciences .... Dr. Denise SEIGART
53 Dean of Education .... Dr. Terry BARRY
50 Dean of Business & Management .... Dr. Sylvester WILLIAMS
08 Dean of Library & Univ Collections .... Dr. Jingfeng XIA
20 Assoc Provost .... Dr. Jeffrey WEBER
35 Dean of Student Life .... Vacant
100 Chief of Staff .... Mr. Miguel BARBOSA
07 Director of Admissions .... Vacant
06 Registrar/Dir Enrollment Services .... Vacant
37 Sr Assoc Director Financial Aid .... Vacant
36 Dir Career/WF & Econ Dev/Entrepren .... Ms. Sharone JONES
38 Director Counseling Center .... Dr. Linda L. VAN METER
41 Director of Athletics .... Dr. Gary GRAY
39 Dir Residential/Dining Services .... Mr. Curtis DUGAR
88 Dir of Student Activity Association .... Mr. Joe AKOB
21 Controller .... Ms. Donna R. BULZONI
13 Chief Information Officer .... Mr. Robert D'AVERSA
15 Director of Human Resources .... Ms. Teresa FRITSCHE
18 Int Director Facilities Management .... Mr. John BLOSHINSKI
96 Asst Dir of Procurement/Contracting .... Ms. Denise AYLWARD
29 Director of Alumni Engagement .... Mr. Leon S. JOHN, JR.
26 Director University Relations .... Dr. Brenda FRIDAY
09 Dir Inst Effect/Planning/Assessment .... Dr. Robert SMITH
28 Director of Multicultural Affairs .... Ms. Juanita M. JENKINS

*Edinboro University (F)

219 Meadville Street, Edinboro PA 16444-0001
County: Erie FICE Identification: 003321
Unit ID: 212160
Telephone: (814) 732-2000 Carnegie Class: Masters/L
FAX Number: (814) 732-2880 Calendar System: Semester
URL: www.edinboro.edu
Established: 1857 Annual Undergrad Tuition & Fees (In-State): $10,574
Enrollment: 5,574 Coed
Affiliation or Control: State IRS Status: 501(c)3
Highest Offering: Doctorate
Accreditation: M, ART, ACBSP, CACREP, CAEPN, NUR, NURSE, SP, SW

02 President .... Dr. Guiyou HUANG
05 Provost/VP Acad/Student Affairs .... Dr. Michael HANNAN
30 Assistant VP University Advancement .... Ms. Marilyn GOELLNER
15 Director of Human Resources/Faculty .... Mr. Wayne PATTERSON
84 VP for Enrollment Management .... Mr. William EDMONDS
09 Dir Inst Research & Assessment .... Mr. Matthew CETTIN
20 Sr Exec Associate to the Provost .... Ms. Judy KUBEJA
18 Dir Facilities Management/Planning .... Vacant
26 Director of Marketing .... Mr. William BERGER
37 Director of Student Financial Aid .... Ms. Kelly VITELLI
92 Director Honors Program .... Dr. Roger SOLBERG
22 Dir of Social Equity/Title IX Coord .... Mr. Ronald O. WILSON
79 Int Dn Col Arts/Humanities/Soc Sci .... Dr. Scott MILLER
81 Interim Dean Col Science & Health .... Dr. Denise OHLER
58 Exec Director of Graduate Studies .... Dr. Erinn LAKE
53 Interim Dean School of Education .... Dr. Erinn LAKE
50 Dean School of Business .... Dr. Scott MILLER
06 Registrar .... Mr. Tim W. PILEWSKI
36 Dir Office of Career Development .... Ms. Monica CLEM
29 Dir Alumni Relations/Fund Devel .... Mr. Jon PULICE
41 Athletic Director .... Mr. Bruce BAUMGARTNER
19 Chief of Police .... Ms. Angela VINCENT
23 Medical Dir Student Health Services .... Dr. Thomas MITCHELL
109 Director Auxiliary Operations .... Vacant
85 Dir Global Education Office .... Ms. Linda KIGHTLINGER
25 Dir Grant & Sponsored Programs .... Ms. Rosmari GRAHAM
14 Dir Networks & Telecommunications .... Ms. Karen MURDZAK
90 Director Client Support Services .... Mr. Dennis J. BRADLEY
13 Director of Information Services .... Ms. Sallie A. TERPACK
96 Director Purchasing & Contracts .... Ms. Darla SPAID
30 Director of Development .... Ms. Julie A. CHACONA
44 Assistant VP for Advancement .... Ms. Marilyn GOELLNER
114 Director of Budget and Payroll .... Ms. Theresa VILLELLA
07 Director of Admissions .... Ms. Diane RAYBUCK
113 Bursar .... Ms. Shari GOULD
17 Director of Health & Wellness Ctr .... Ms. Darla ELDER
106 Manager of Online Programs .... Dr. James BOULDER
24 Learning Technology Specialist .... Ms. Jill LINTON
88 Coordinator Non-Credit Programs .... Ms. Beth ZEWE
35 Associate Student Affairs Officer .... Ms. Stacie WALBERT

*Indiana University of Pennsylvania (G)

1011 South Drive, Indiana PA 15705-0001
County: Indiana FICE Identification: 003277
Unit ID: 213020
Telephone: (724) 357-2100 Carnegie Class: DU-Mod
FAX Number: (724) 357-6213 Calendar System: Semester
URL: www.iup.edu
Established: 1875 Annual Undergrad Tuition & Fees (In-State): $12,979
Enrollment: 12,431 Coed
Affiliation or Control: State IRS Status: 501(c)3
Highest Offering: Doctorate

Accreditation: M, ACFEI, ART, #CAATE, CACREP, CAEP, CLPSY, COARC, DIETD, DIETI, EXSC, MUS, NURSE, PLNG, SP, THEA

02 President ... Dr. Michael A. DRISCOLL
05 Provost & Sr. VP Academic Affairs ... Dr. Timothy S. MOERLAND
11 Vice Pres Administration/Finance ... Mrs. Susanna C. SINK
32 Vice President Student Affairs ... Dr. Thomas SEGAR
84 VP Enrollment Management ... Ms. Patricia MCCARTHY
111 Vice Pres University Advancement ... Dr. Khatmeh OSSEIRAN-HANNA
10 Assoc Vice President for Finance ... Mr. Richard WHITE
20 Assoc VP Academic Administration ... Dr. John N. KILMARX
58 Dean Graduate Studies & Research ... Dr. Randy L. MARTIN
15 Assoc Vice Pres Human Resources ... Mr. Craig BICKLEY
31 Assoc VP for Univ & Cmty Engagement ... Vacant
79 Dean College Humanities & Soc Sci ... Dr. Yaw A. ASAMOAH
50 Dean Eberly Col Bus/Inform Tech ... Dr. Robert C. CAMP
53 Dean College Educ/Educ Tech ... Dr. Lara M. LUETKEHANS
81 Dean Col Natural Science & Math ... Dr. Deanne SNAVELY
57 Dean College of Fine Arts ... Dr. Curt SCHEIB
66 Dean College Health & Human Svcs ... Dr. Sylvia GAIKO
08 Dean of Libraries ... Dr. Erik NORDBERG
06 Registrar ... Mrs. Lisa BRAY
13 Chief Information Officer ... Mr. William S. BALINT
45 Exec Dir of Planning & Assessment ... Mrs. Barbara MOORE
14 Exec Dir of Technology Services Ctr . Mr. Todd D. CUNNINGHAM
26 Exec Dir of Marketing/Communication ... Dr. Michael POWERS
28 Asst to the Pres for Social Equity ... Vacant
19 Director of Public Safety & Police ... Mr. Kevin THELEN
36 Director Career Development Ctr ... Dr. Tammy P. MANKO
29 Director Alumni Relations ... Mrs. Mary MORGAN
44 Director Annual Giving ... Ms. Stephanie SELL
85 Asst VP Intl Education & Global ... Dr. Michele L. PETRUCCI
46 Assistant Dean for Research ... Dr. Hilliary E. CREELY
39 Exec Director Housing/Resid Living ... Dr. Sondra R. DENNISON
40 Co-op Store Director ... Mr. Tim L. SHARBAUGH
41 Athletic Director ... Mr. Todd GARZARELLI
23 Nurse Director ... Ms. Melissa L. DICK
12 Director of Regional Campuses ... Mr. Richard J. MUTH
43 Staff Attorney ... Mr. Jeff HAWKINS
27 Exec Director of Media Relations ... Ms. Michelle S. FRYLING
96 Procurement Srvs & Central Store ... Mr. Terry BRESLAWSKI
86 Exec Asst to Pres for Govt Relation ... Ms. Robin A. GORMAN
37 Director of Financial Aid ... Ms. Ragan K. GRIFFIN
35 Assoc VP Student Affairs/Well-Being ... Vacant
88 Dir Admin Services Culinary Arts ... Ms. Enid E. RESENIC
07 Executive Director of UG Admissions ... Ms. Stacy HOPKINS
26 Chief Marketing Officer ... Mr. Chris NOAH
18 Assoc VP for Facilities Management ... Mr. R. Michael BROWN
28 Diversity/Inclusion/Title IX Coord ... Ms. Elise GLENN

*Kutztown University of Pennsylvania (A)

15200 Kutztown Road, Kutztown PA 19530-0730

County: Berks | FICE Identification: 003322
Unit ID: 213349
Telephone: (610) 683-4000 | Carnegie Class: Masters/L
FAX Number: (610) 683-4693 | Calendar System: Semester
URL: www.kutztown.edu
Established: 1866 | Annual Undergrad Tuition & Fees (In-State): $10,802
Enrollment: 8,329 | Coed
Affiliation or Control: State | IRS Status: 501(c)3
Highest Offering: Doctorate
Accreditation: M, ART, CACREP, CAEPN, COSMA, MUS, SW

02 President ... Dr. Kenneth S. HAWKINSON
05 Provost/VP Academic Affairs ... Dr. Anne ZAYAITZ
10 VP Administration & Finance ... Mr. Gerald L. SILBERMAN
84 VP Enrollment Management ... Dr. Warren HILTON
22 VP Compliance/Equity ... Mr. Jesus PENA
102 Executive Director KU Foundation ... Mr. Alex OGEKA
26 VP University Relations & Athletics ... Mr. Matt SANTOS
20 Vice Prov Acad Affs/Dean Grad Stds ... Dr. Carole WELLS
21 Asst VP Finance & Business Services ... Mr. Matthew DELANEY
32 Asst VP/Dean of Students ... Dr. Donavan MCCARGO
13 Asst Vice Pres/Info Technology ... Mr. Troy VINGOM
15 Asst VP for Human Resources ... Ms. Sharon M. PICUS
18 Asst Vice President for Facilities ... Mr. Terry BROWN
57 Dean College Visual/Perf Arts ... Dr. Michele KIEC
49 Dean College Liberal Arts/Sci ... Dr. David BEOUGHER
50 Dean College of Business ... Dr. Anne CARROLL
53 Dean College Education ... Dr. John WARD
62 Director of Library Services ... Ms. Martha STEVENSON
09 Director Institutional Research ... Ms. Natalie CARTWRIGHT
06 Registrar ... Mr. Ted WITRYK
37 Director of Financial Aid ... Mr. Bernard L. MCCREE
39 Director Housing/Residential Svcs ... Mr. Kent R. DAHLQUIST
41 Director of Athletics ... Mr. Gregory BAMBERGER
38 Director Counseling & Psych Svcs ... Dr. Lisa COULTER
96 Purchasing Manager ... Vacant
07 Spec Asst Enrl Mgmt/Div Recr Admis ... Vacant
19 Chief of Police ... Mr. John DILLON
36 Director Career/Community Services ... Ms. Kerri GARDI
04 Sr Executive Assoc to President ... Ms. Toyia HEYWARD
108 Assoc Prov Accreditation/Acad Affs ... Dr. Karen RAUCH
106 Dir Online Education/E-learning ... Mr. Douglas SCOTT

*Lock Haven University (B)

401 N Fairview Street, Lock Haven PA 17745-2390

County: Clinton | FICE Identification: 003323
Unit ID: 213613
Telephone: (570) 484-2011 | Carnegie Class: Masters/M
FAX Number: (570) 484-2432 | Calendar System: Semester
URL: www.lockhaven.edu
Established: 1870 | Annual Undergrad Tuition & Fees (In-State): $10,878
Enrollment: 3,827 | Coed
Affiliation or Control: State | IRS Status: 170(c)1
Highest Offering: Master's
Accreditation: M, ACBSP, ADNUR, ARCPA, CAATE, CACREP, CAEPN, NRPA, NUR, SW

02 President ... Dr. Robert PIGNATELLO
05 Provost & Executive Vice President ... Dr. Donna WILSON
11 COO & Senior Vice President ... Mr. William HANELLY
32 Dean of Student Affairs ... Dr. Dwayne ALLISON
84 Vice President for Enrollment Mgmt ... Dr. Tyana LANGE
111 VP for University Advancement ... Mr. Joseph FIOCHETTA
49 Dean of Liberal Arts & Education ... Dr. Koyoko AMANO
83 Dean Natural/Behavioral/Health Sci ... Dr. Jonathan LINDZEY
50 Dean Business/Info Sys/Human Svcs ... Dr. John NAURIGHT
12 Director Clearfield Branch Campus ... Vacant
85 Director of International Studies ... Ms. Rosana CAMPBELL
09 Director Institutional Research ... Mr. John (Mike) ABPLANALP
15 Associate VP of Human Resources ... Ms. Deana HILL
07 Director of Admissions ... Ms. Angelic HARDY
06 Registrar ... Ms. Jill MITCHLEY
22 Dir Affirm Action/Equal Opportunity ... Mr. Lucas FANNING
37 Director of Financial Aid ... Ms. Aristalia BENITEZ
36 Director of Career Services ... Ms. Maryjo CAMPANA
26 Exec Director of Communications ... Ms. Elizabeth ARNOLD
19 Director of Public Safety ... Vacant
18 Director of Facilities ... Mr. Scott MCCALL
41 Director of Athletics ... Dr. Tom GIOGLIO
66 Director of Nursing Program ... Dr. Darlene ARDARY
38 Director of Counseling ... Dr. Dan TESS
90 Dir Computing/Instructional Tech ... Mr. Boise MILLER
88 Director of Physician Asst Program ... Mr. Walt EISENHAUER
92 Director Honors Program ... Dr. Elizabeth GRUBER
94 Director Women's Studies ... Dr. Holle CANATELLA
93 Director Minority Students ... Mr. Kenneth HALL
40 Manager University Bookstore ... Vacant
29 Director Alumni Relations ... Ms. Ashley KOSER
103 Workforce Development Manager ... Ms. Shannon WALKER
101 Secretary of the Board of Trustees ... Ms. Gwen BECHDEL

*Mansfield University of Pennsylvania (C)

Academy Street, Mansfield PA 16933-1697

County: Tioga | FICE Identification: 003324
Unit ID: 213783
Telephone: (570) 662-4000 | Carnegie Class: Bac-A&S
FAX Number: (570) 662-4995 | Calendar System: Semester
URL: www.mansfield.edu
Established: 1857 | Annual Undergrad Tuition & Fees (In-State): $12,330
Enrollment: 1,882 | Coed
Affiliation or Control: State | IRS Status: 501(c)3
Highest Offering: Master's
Accreditation: M, ACBSP, COARC, DIETD, MUS, NUR, RAD, SW

02 President ... Mr. Charles PATTERSON
10 Int VP Finance/Administration ... Ms. Kathryn CROSSIN
05 Provost/VP Academic Affairs ... Mr. John ULRICH
08 Director Library/Info Resource Svcs ... Mr. Scott R. DIMARCO
18 Director of Facilities Management ... Mr. Kenneth B. LAWTON
26 Dir of Marketing and Communications ... Mr. Ryan MCNAMARA
32 Interim Dean of Students ... Ms. Dusty ZEYN
37 Director of Student Financial Aid ... Ms. Pamela KATHCART
19 Dir University Police & Safety ... Mr. Scott HENRY
41 Associate Director of Athletics ... Ms. Kristen DECKER
09 Dir Institutional Rsrch/Assess Data ... Dr. John COSGROVE
29 Director of Alumni/Govt Relations ... Ms. Casey WOOD
06 Registrar ... Ms. Lori CASS
38 Director Counseling Services ... Ms. Jolene MEISNER
07 Dir of Admissions Tactical/Enroll ... Ms. Rachel GREEN
13 Director of Campus Technologies ... Mr. Nicholas ANDRE

*Millersville University of Pennsylvania (D)

PO Box 1002, Millersville PA 17551-0302

County: Lancaster | FICE Identification: 003325
Unit ID: 214041
Telephone: (717) 871-4636 | Carnegie Class: Masters/L
FAX Number: (717) 871-7930 | Calendar System: 4/1/4
URL: www.millersville.edu
Established: 1855 | Annual Undergrad Tuition & Fees (In-State): $12,226
Enrollment: 7,720 | Coed
Affiliation or Control: State | IRS Status: 501(c)3
Highest Offering: Doctorate
Accreditation: M, ACBSP, ART, CAEPN, COARC, MUS, NAIT, NURSE, SW

02 President ... Dr. Daniel A. WUBAH
05 Vice Pres Academic Affs/Provost ... Dr. Vilas A. PRABHU
10 Interim VP Finance & Administration ... Mr. Guilbert BROWN
111 Interim Vice Pres for Advancement ... Ms. Alice R. MCMURRY
32 VP Student Affs & Enrollment Mgmt ... Mr. Brian HAZLETT
28 Chief Diversity Officer ... Vacant
20 Associate Provost Academic Admin ... Dr. James A. DELLE
108 Asst VP Inst Assessment & Planning ... Dr. Lisa R. SHIBLEY
13 Associate VP for Info Tech/CIO ... Mr. Stephen J. DIFILIPO, JR.
15 Exec Director of Human Resources .. Ms. Diane L. COPENHAVER
37 Assoc VP Student Financial Aid ... Mr. Dwight G. HORSEY
35 Assoc VP SA and Enrollment Mgmt ... Mr. Renardo A. HALL
35 AVP Stdnt Affairs/Enrollment Mgmt ... Mr. Thomas J. RICHARDSON
26 Asst VP Communications/Marketing . Mr. Gregory E. FREEDLAND
18 Asst VP Facilities ... Mr. Thomas A. WALTZ, JR.
53 Dean Education & Human Services ... Dr. George P. DRAKE, JR.
79 Dean Arts/Human & Social Sci ... Dr. Ieva ZAKE
81 Dean Science & Technology ... Dr. Mike JACKSON
100 Interim Chief of Staff ... Dr. Victor S. DESANTIS
06 Registrar ... Ms. Alison M. HUTCHINSON
07 Director of Admissions ... Ms. Katy A. CHARLES
121 Interim Director Student Success ... Ms. Darlene R. NEWMAN
36 Assoc Director Career Management ... Ms. Margo J. SASSAMAN
38 Director Counseling/Human Devel ... Dr. Kelsey K. BACKELS
19 Chief of University Police ... Mr. Peter J. ANDERS
41 Director of Intercollegiate Ath ... Mr. Miles P. GALLAGHER
40 University Store Manager ... Ms. Audrey HERR
42 Campus Minister ... Ms. Yvonne L. DEBLOIS
30 AVP Advancement & Dir Ext Rels ... Mr. Steven A. DIGUISEPPE
110 Assoc VP for Advancement ... Ms. Alice R. MCMURRY
09 Director Institutional Research ... Dr. Kyle W. VERBOSH
112 Major Gift Officer ... Ms. Amy C. SPELLMAN
102 Dir Sponsored Pgms & Research Admin ... Dr. Rene MUNOZ
96 Director Purchasing/Campus Svcs ... Vacant
57 Director Visual & Performing Arts ... Ms. Robin D. ZAREMSKI
27 Director of Communications ... Ms. Janet E. KACSKOS
106 Director of Online Programs ... Ms. Janice R. MOORE
29 Director Alumni Engagement ... Ms. Denise D. BERG
43 Dir Legal Services/General Counsel ... Mr. Jeffrey HAWKINS
101 Executive Secretary ... Ms. Jennifer L. HART

*Shippensburg University of Pennsylvania (E)

1871 Old Main Drive, Shippensburg PA 17257-2200

County: Cumberland | FICE Identification: 003326
Unit ID: 216010
Telephone: (717) 477-7447 | Carnegie Class: Masters/L
FAX Number: (717) 477-1273 | Calendar System: Semester
URL: www.ship.edu
Established: 1871 | Annual Undergrad Tuition & Fees (In-State): $12,718
Enrollment: 6,570 | Coed
Affiliation or Control: State | IRS Status: 501(c)3
Highest Offering: Doctorate
Accreditation: M, CACREP, CAEPN, JOUR, SW

02 President ... Dr. Laurie A. CARTER
05 Provost & VP Academic Affairs ... Dr. Tom ORMOND
45 Chief Strategy Officer ... Dr. Sue MUKHERJEE
84 Sr VP Enr Mgmt/Stdnt Affs/Stdnt Svc ... Dr. B. Donta TRUSS
10 Sr VP Administration & Finance ... Mr. Scott BARTON
26 Assoc VP External Relations ... Dr. Kim GARRIS
15 Assoc VP for A&F/CHRO ... Dr. David TOPPER
102 Pres Shippensburg Univ Foundation ... Dr. Leslie CLINTON
21 Assoc VP for A&F/CFO ... Ms. Melinda D. FAWKS
13 AVP Technology/CITO ... Ms. Amy DIEHL
14 Deputy CITO/Exec Dir Ac Tech & User ... Dr. Justin SENTZ
20 Assoc Provost ... Dr. Tracy SCHOOLCRAFT
51 Dean Prof/Cont Distance Education ... Dr. Carolyn CALLAGHAN
121 Sr Assoc VP for Student Success ... Vacant
35 Dean of Students ... Ms. Donna GROSS
06 Registrar ... Ms. Cathy J. SPRENGER
36 Dir Career & Community Engagement . Ms. Victoria BUCHBAUER
37 Director Financial Aid ... Ms. Trina SNYDER
29 Dir Alumni Outreach & Data Mgmt ... Ms. Lori SMITH
27 Interim Communications & Marketing ... Vacant
39 Executive Director of Campus Life ... Mr. Barry MCCLANAHAN
08 Dean of Libraries ... Ms. Michelle FOREMAN
22 Executive Director Social Equity ... Ms. Carlesha HALKIAS
88 Director Womens Center ... Ms. Stephanie ERDICE
09 Int Dir Inst Research & Assessment ... Mr. Korey J. PAUL
25 Dir Institute for Public Service ... Mr. Christopher WONDERS
38 Int Director Counseling Services ... Dr. Christopher CARLTON
88 Director of Conference Services ... Ms. Elizabeth KNOUSE
53 Dean College Education & Human Svcs ... Dr. Nicole R. HILL
49 Dean College Arts & Science ... Dr. James MIKE
50 Dean College of Business ... Dr. John KOOTI
121 AVP & Dean for Student Success ... Ms. Denise YARWOOD
18 Chief Facilities/Physical Plant ... Mr. Adam ROTH
96 Director of Purchasing/Contracting ... Mr. Wesley LIGHT
07 AVP for Enrollment Management ... Dr. Jennifer A. HAUGHIE
19 Director Public Safety ... Vacant
41 Athletic Director ... Mr. Jeff A. MICHAELS
04 Int Special Asst to the President ... Mr. Samual FRUSHOUR
101 Secretary of the Institution/Board ... Vacant
104 Assoc Dean Stdnts/Dir Intl Programs ... Ms. Mary BURNETT
100 Chief of Staff ... Vacant

*Slippery Rock University of Pennsylvania (F)

1 Morrow Way, Slippery Rock PA 16057-1326

County: Butler | FICE Identification: 003327
Unit ID: 216038
Telephone: (724) 738-9000 | Carnegie Class: Masters/L
FAX Number: (724) 738-2169 | Calendar System: Semester
URL: www.sru.edu
Established: 1889 | Annual Undergrad Tuition & Fees (In-State): $10,757
Enrollment: 8,866 | Coed
Affiliation or Control: State | IRS Status: 501(c)3
Highest Offering: Doctorate
Accreditation: M, ART, ACBSP, #ARCPA, CAATE, CAEPN, CARTE, COSMA, DANCE, EXSC, MUS, NUR, PTA, SW, THEA

02 President .... Dr. William BEHRE
05 Int Provost/VP Acad & Student Affs .... Dr. Jerry CHMIELEWSKI
11 Sr VP for Admin & Economic Devel .... Dr. Amir MOHAMMADI
111 Int Vice Pres for Univ Advancement .... Dr. Amir MOHAMMADI
10 Chief Financial Officer .... Ms. Molly MERCER
18 Asst Vice Pres for Facilities/Plng .... Mr. Scott ALBERT
15 Chief Human Resources Officer .... Ms. Lynne M. MOTYL
28 Asst VP Div & Compliance/Title IX .... Ms. Holly M. MCCOY
100 Chief of Staff .... Ms. Tina L. MOSER
84 Chief Enrollment Mgmt Officer .... Dr. Amanda A. YALE
13 Assoc Provost Info Technology .... Dr. John ZIEGLER
102 Exec Director SRU Foundation Inc .... Dr. Edward BUCHA
26 Chief Comm/Public Affairs Officer .... Ms. Rita E. ABENT
37 Director Student Financial Aid .... Ms. Alyssa DOBSON
19 Director Public Safety .... Mr. Paul NOVAK
19 Interim Director University Police .... Mr. Kevin SHARKEY
09 Chief Data Officer .... Ms. Carrie J. BIRCKBICHLER
08 Manager of Library Operations .... Ms. Jennifer J. BARTEK
14 Director of Info & Adm Tech Svcs .... Mr. Henry MAGUSIAK
06 Director Acad Records & Registrar .... Ms. Connie EDWARDS
07 Director Undergraduate Admissions .... Mr. Michael MAY
23 Director Health Services .... Ms. Kristina BENKESER
36 Assistant Director Career Services .... Ms. Renee COYNE
29 Director Alumni Affairs .... Ms. Kelly BAILEY
81 Interim Dean Col Health/Engr/Sci .... Dr. Michael ZIEG
123 Director Graduate Admissions ... Ms. Brandi WEBER-MORTIMER
41 Athletic Director .... Mr. Paul A. LUEKEN
39 Director of Residence Life .... Mr. Patrick T. BESWICK
25 Director Grants & Sponsored Rsrch . Ms. Nancy L. CRUIKSHANK
38 Director of Student Counseling .... Dr. Chris CUBERO
93 Director of Inclusive Excellence .... Ms. Corinne J. GIBSON
96 Director of Contracts & Purchasing .... Mr. James REVESZ
88 Assoc Provost Trans Exper .... Dr. Bradley WILSON
49 Dean College Liberal Arts .... Dr. Danny BAUER
50 Dean College of Business .... Dr. Lawrence SHAO
53 Dean College of Education .... Dr. Keith DILS
121 Assoc Provost Student Success .... Mr. David WILMES

*West Chester University of Pennsylvania (A)

University & High Street, West Chester PA 19383-0001
County: Chester FICE Identification: 003328
Unit ID: 216764
Telephone: (610) 436-1000 Carnegie Class: Masters/L
FAX Number: (610) 436-3115 Calendar System: Semester
URL: www.wcupa.edu
Established: 1871 Annual Undergrad Tuition & Fees (In-State): $10,412
Enrollment: 17,306 Coed
Affiliation or Control: State IRS Status: 501(c)3
Highest Offering: Doctorate
Accreditation: M, ART, CAATE, CACREP, CAEPN, CLPSY, COARC, DIETD, @DIETI, EXSC, FEPAC, MUS, NURSE, PH, SP, SPAA, SW, THEA

02 President .... Dr. Chris FIORENTINO
100 Vice President University Affairs .... Dr. John VILLELLA
04 Sr Assoc to the President .... Ms. Rachel SHEARER
22 Chief Diversity & Inclusion Officer .... Dr. Tracey RAY
05 Executive VP & Provost .... Dr. R. Lorraine BERNOTSKY
10 Vice President Admin/Finance .... Mr. Todd MURPHY
13 Vice President IS&T .... Dr. Dikran KASSABIAN
119 Information Security Officer .... Mr. Frank PISCITELLO
32 Vice President Student Affairs .... Dr. Zebulun DAVENPORT
88 Asst VP for Student Development .... Ms. Judy KAWAMOTO
88 AVP for Identity/Health/Wellness .... Mr. Antonio DELGADO
49 Dean College Arts & Humanities .... Dr. Jen BACON
20 Vice Provost .... Vacant
58 Senior Vice Provost .... Dr. Jeffery OSGOOD
07 Asst VP Admissions .... Ms. Sarah FREED
53 Dean College of Education .... Dr. Cheryl D. NEALE-MCFALL
50 Interim Dean College of BPM .... Dr. Evan LEACH
81 Dean College Science & Math .... Dr. Radha PYATI
76 Dean College Health Science .... Dr. Scott HEINERICHS
64 Dean School of Music .... Dr. Chris HANNING
25 Assoc VP Sponsored Research .... Dr. Nicole BENNETT
23 Director Student Health Center .... Vacant
15 Interim AVP Human Resources .... Ms. Kate BOVE
35 AVP for Admin Svcs/Spec Projects .... Ms. Sara HINKLE
35 AVP Student Life/Dean of Students .... Mr. Gerald MARTIN
21 AVP Finance/Business Svcs .... Vacant
84 Asst Prov & Asst VP Enrollment Mgmt . Mr. Joseph SANTIVASCI
85 Interim Dir International Programs .... Dr. Vishal SHAH
102 Chief Exec Officer WCU Foundation ... Mr. Christopher MOMINEY
18 Interim Assoc VP for Facilities .... Mr. Gary BIXBY
88 Dir Facilities Finance/Support Svcs .... Ms. Susan MILLER
21 Controller .... Ms. Brenda SMALL
09 AVP Institutional Research .... Ms. Lisa YANNICK
113 Bursar/Director Student Finan Svcs .... Ms. Colleen CORRADO
114 Director Budget .... Ms. Ilene MATES
26 Asst VP Communications & Marketing .... Ms. Nancy GAINER
88 Director Publications/Printing Svcs .... Mr. Matthew BORN
31 Director Cultural/Community Affairs .... Mr. John RHEIN
88 Director Conference Services .... Ms. Mary Beth KURIMAY
08 University Librarian .... Ms. Mary PAGE
88 Director Teacher Education Center .... Dr. James B. PRICE
36 Director Career Devel Center .... Ms. Jennifer ROSSI-LONG
88 Dir Acad Development Pgm .... Dr. John CRAIG
88 Dir Learning Asst/Resource .... Dr. Jocelyn MANIGO
37 Director Financial Aid .... Mr. Brandon VINSON
38 Director Counseling Center .... Dr. Rachel DALTRY
29 Director Alumni Relations .... Ms. Jenna BIRCH
41 Director Athletics .... Dr. Terry BEATTIE
88 Director Sports Information .... Mr. James ZUHLKE
28 Dir Multicultural Affairs .... Dr. Dametraus JAGGERS
88 Sr Director Women & Gender Equity .... Ms. Sendy ALCIDONIS
19 Interim Dir Public Safety .... Mr. Jon BRILL
96 Director Business Services .... Mr. Jeff BAUN
88 Dir Environmental Health/Safety .... Vacant
14 Exec Dir IT/Infastructure Svcs .... Mr. Joseph SINCAVAGE
91 AVP & Deputy CIO/EdTech & User Svc .... Mr. JT SINGH
88 Asst Dir Sourcing/Planning/Project .... Ms. Chaw-ye CHANG
105 Exec Dir Enterprise Services .... Vacant
89 Director New Student Programs .... Mr. Jared BROWN
88 Asst Dean of Students .... Mr. Peter GALLOWAY
39 Senior Director Residence Life .... Ms. Marion MCKINNEY
88 Asst Dean of Student Conduct .... Ms. Christina BRENNER
88 Dir Student Leadership/Involve .... Mr. Charles WARNER
109 Senior Director Sykes Student Union .... Mr. David TIMMANN
122 Senior Dir Fraternity & Sorority .... Ms. Cara JENKINS
88 Dir Service Lrng & Volunteer Pgm .... Vacant
121 Sr Vice Provost Student Success .... Ms. Kathleen HOWLEY
88 Dir Pre-major Academic Advising .... Dr. Ann COLGAN
92 Director Honors College .... Dr. Kevin DEAN
104 Asst VP for International Programs .... Vacant
106 Exec Director Distance Educ Svcs .... Dr. Rui LI
88 Exec Dir Student Service Inc .... Ms. Donna SNYDER
40 Student Svcs Inc Bookstore Manager ..... Mr. Stephen MANNELLA
06 Registrar .... Ms. Megan JERABEK

*Clarion University - Venango (B)

1801 W First Street, Oil City PA 16301-3297
Telephone: (814) 676-6591 FICE Identification: 003319
Accreditation: &M, ADNUR, COARC, NAIT, NUR

*Lock Haven University Clearfield Branch Campus (C)

201 University Drive, Clearfield PA 16830
Telephone: (814) 768-3405 Identification: 770186
Accreditation: &M

Philadelphia College of Osteopathic Medicine (D)

4170 City Avenue, Philadelphia PA 19131-1694
County: Philadelphia FICE Identification: 003352
Unit ID: 215123
Telephone: (215) 871-6100 Carnegie Class: Spec-4-yr-Med
FAX Number: (215) 871-6719 Calendar System: Trimester
URL: www.pcom.edu
Established: 1899 Annual Graduate Tuition & Fees: N/A
Enrollment: 2,860 Coed
Affiliation or Control: Independent Non-Profit IRS Status: 501(c)3
Highest Offering: Doctorate; No Undergraduates
Accreditation: M, ARCPA, CLPSY, IPSY, OSTEO

01 President & CEO .... Dr. Jay S. FELDSTEIN
05 Provost/Sr VP Academic Affairs/Dean .... Dr. Kenneth J. VEIT
10 Vice Pres Finance/Treasurer/CFO .... Mr. Peter DOULIS
17 Chief Acad Ofcr-PCOM Mednet-Opti .... Dr. David KUO
43 Chief Legal Affairs Officer .... Mr. David F. SIMON
63 Dean Osteopathic Med Pgm-GA Campus .... Dr. William CRAVER, III
67 Dean School of Pharmacy .... Dr. Shawn SPENCER
20 Assoc Dean Graduate Medical Educ .... Dr. David KUO
20 Assoc Dean Clinical Education .... Dr. Joseph KACZMARCZYK
20 Assoc Dean Curriculum .... Dr. Kerin FRESA
20 Assoc Dean Curriculum .... Dr. Bonnie BUXTON
12 Chief Campus Officer-Georgia Campus .... Mr. Bryan GINN
46 Chief Science Officer .... Dr. Mindy GEORGE-WEINSTEIN
32 Chief Student Affairs Officer .... Ms. Patience MASON
26 Chief Marketing/Communications Ofcr ... Ms. Wendy W. ROMANO
37 Chief Student Financial Aid Officer .... Mr. Samuel MATHENY
15 Chief Human Resources Officer .... Ms. Christina MAZZELLA
07 Chief Admissions Officer .... Ms. Deborah A. BENVENGER
28 Chief Diversity Officer .... Dr. Marcine PICKRON-DAVIS
13 Chief Technology Officer .... Mr. Richard SMITH
88 Chief Compliance Officer .... Ms. Margaret MCKEON
117 Risk Manager .... Mr. Isiah LOPEZ
18 Chief Facilities/Plant Operations .... Mr. Frank H. WINDLE
111 Chief Advancement Officer .... Ms. Carrie COLLINS
08 Chair of Library/Exec Director .... Ms. Stephanie FERRETTI
06 Interim Registrar .... Mr. Samuel MATHENY
96 Purchasing Manager .... Ms. LaVerne MAYES
19 Director Security/Safety .... Mr. Richard KRALLE

Pittsburgh Career Institute (E)

421 Seventh Avenue, Pittsburgh PA 15219-1907
County: Allegheny FICE Identification: 022023
Unit ID: 216782
Telephone: (412) 281-2600 Carnegie Class: Spec 2-yr-Health
FAX Number: (412) 227-0807 Calendar System: Other
URL: www.pci.edu
Established: 2014 Annual Undergrad Tuition & Fees: $25,964
Enrollment: 237 Coed
Affiliation or Control: Proprietary IRS Status: Proprietary
Highest Offering: Associate Degree
Accreditation: ACICS, COARC, DMS

01 Campus President .... Patti L. YAKSHE

Pittsburgh Institute of Aeronautics (F)

5 Allegheny County Airport, West Mifflin PA 15122-2674
County: Allegheny FICE Identification: 005310
Unit ID: 215381
Telephone: (412) 346-2100 Carnegie Class: Spec 2-yr-Tech
FAX Number: (412) 466-0513 Calendar System: Quarter
URL: www.pia.edu
Established: 1929 Annual Undergrad Tuition & Fees: $21,589
Enrollment: 409 Coed
Affiliation or Control: Independent Non-Profit IRS Status: 501(c)3
Highest Offering: Associate Degree
Accreditation: ACCSC

01 President/CEO .... Ms. Suzanne L. MARKLE
05 Director of Education .... Mr. Jason S. MONGAN
37 Director of Financial Aid .... Mr. Jonathan S. VUKMANIC
26 Director of Marketing/IT .... Mr. Steven D. SABOLD
07 Director of Admissions .... Ms. Roxanne OBER
18 Director of Campus Operations .... Mr. Gary E. HOYLE

Pittsburgh Institute of Mortuary Science (G)

5808 Baum Boulevard, Pittsburgh PA 15206-3706
County: Allegheny FICE Identification: 010814
Unit ID: 215390
Telephone: (412) 362-8500 Carnegie Class: Spec 2-yr-A&S
FAX Number: (412) 362-1684 Calendar System: Trimester
URL: www.pims.edu
Established: 1939 Annual Undergrad Tuition & Fees: N/A
Enrollment: 209 Coed
Affiliation or Control: Independent Non-Profit IRS Status: 501(c)3
Highest Offering: Associate Degree
Accreditation: FUSER

01 President & CEO .... Mr. Eugene C. OGRODNIK
05 Program Director .... Dr. Barry T. LEASE
11 Chief of Operations/ Administration .... Dr. Joseph A. MARSAGLIA, JR.
06 Registrar .... Ms. Karen S. ROCCO
07 Director of Admissions .... Mr. Jessca T. MILLER
08 Chief Library Officer .... Ms. Gretchen BARRETT

Pittsburgh Technical College (H)

1111 McKee Road, Oakdale PA 15071-3205
County: Allegheny FICE Identification: 007437
Unit ID: 215415
Telephone: (412) 809-5100 Carnegie Class: Bac/Assoc-Assoc Dom
FAX Number: (412) 809-5320 Calendar System: Quarter
URL: www.ptcollege.edu
Established: 1946 Annual Undergrad Tuition & Fees: $16,801
Enrollment: 1,835 Coed
Affiliation or Control: Independent Non-Profit IRS Status: 501(c)3
Highest Offering: Baccalaureate
Accreditation: M, ACFEI, MAC, PNUR, SURGT

01 President .... Dr. Alicia HARVEY-SMITH
03 Executive Vice President .... Mr. George PRY
10 Interim CFO .... Mr. Jay CLAYTON
20 Vice President Education .... Mrs. Eileen STEFFAN
26 Vice Pres Marketing/Communication .... Mr. Barry SHEPARD
13 CIO .... Mr. Bill SHOWERS
32 Vice President Student Services .... Mr. Keith MERLINO
21 Vice President Financial Services .... Mrs. Connie VANCAMP
101 Secretary of Board of Trustees .... Mrs. Ruth DELACH
43 General Counsel .... Mr. William KIEFER
06 Registrar .... Ms. Samantha BYCURA
36 Interim Director of Career Services .... Mrs. Kristy SWEGMAN
27 Director of Enrollment Marketing .... Mrs. Jennifer DONOVAN
15 Director of Human Resources .... Mrs. Nancy STARR
19 Director of Security .... Mr. Gary RUPERT
39 Director of Resident Life .... Ms. Gloria RITCHIE
18 Director of Facilities Services .... Mr. Tom VUCELICH
37 Director Student Financial Aid .... Ms. Teresa BARGER
88 Manager of Compliance .... Ms. Melissa BROWN
40 Campus Store Manager .... Mrs. Cynthia KLEIN
29 Alumni Coordinator .... Mrs. Christine IOLI

Pittsburgh Theological Seminary (I)

616 N. Highland Avenue, Pittsburgh PA 15206-2596
County: Allegheny FICE Identification: 003356
Unit ID: 215424
Telephone: (412) 362-5610 Carnegie Class: Spec-4-yr-Faith
FAX Number: N/A Calendar System: Semester
URL: www.pts.edu
Established: 1794 Annual Graduate Tuition & Fees: N/A
Enrollment: 213 Coed
Affiliation or Control: Presbyterian Church (U.S.A.) IRS Status: 501(c)3
Highest Offering: Doctorate; No Undergraduates
Accreditation: M, THEOL

01 President .... Dr. David V. ESTERLINE
05 VP Academic Affs/Dean of Faculty .... Dr. Heather H. VACEK
111 VP Seminary Advancement .... Vacant
32 VP Student Svcs/Dean of Students .... Mr. John WELCH
45 VP Planning/Inst Effectiveness .... Dr. James DOWNEY
10 Vice Pres Finance & Administration .... Mr. Thomas HINDS
06 Registrar .... Ms. Anne B. MALONE

08 Director of the Library ... Ms. Michelle SPOMER
88 Director of Field Education ... Dr. Catherine M. BRALL
29 Director of Alumni/ae Services ... Rev. Carolyn CRANSTON
88 Director Doctor of Ministry Program ... Dr. Brian WELLS
51 Director Continuing Education ... Dr. Helen BLIER
37 Director of Financial Aid ... Ms. Cheryl DEPAOLIS
84 Director of Enrollment Management ... Ms. Tracy RIGGLE YOUNG
04 Administrative Asst to President ... Rev. Andrew GREENHOW
13 Director of Information Technology ... Mr. David MIDDLETON
15 Human Resources Manager ... Ms. Karen MCMANON
18 Facilities Director ... Mr. Tom FULTON
30 Director of Development ... Mr. Dominick OLIVER

Point Park University (A)

201 Wood Street, Pittsburgh PA 15222-1984
County: Allegheny FICE Identification: 003357
Unit ID: 215442
Telephone: (412) 391-4100 Carnegie Class: Masters/L
FAX Number: (412) 392-3998 Calendar System: Semester
URL: www.pointpark.edu
Established: 1960 Annual Undergrad Tuition & Fees: $31,450
Enrollment: 4,224 Coed
Affiliation or Control: Independent Non-Profit IRS Status: 501(c)3
Highest Offering: Doctorate
Accreditation: M, CLPSY, DANCE, IACBE

01 President ... Dr. Paul HENNIGAN
05 Provost ... Dr. John PEARSON
20 Assistant Provost ... Dr. Jonas PRIDA
10 Sr VP Finance and Operations ... Ms. Bridget MANCOSH
43 Sr VP and General Counsel ... Vacant
26 VP of External Affairs ... Ms. Mariann K. GEYER
84 VP Enrollment Management ... Ms. Trudy WILLIAMS
30 Asst VP Development/Alumni Rels ... Ms. Stephanie ADAMCZYK
32 VP of Student Affairs ... Mr. Keith PAYLO
15 VP of Human Resources ... Ms. Lisa STEFANKO
07 Asst Vice Pres for Admissions ... Vacant
96 Asst VP Procurement/Business Svcs ... Ms. Ruth RAULUK
18 Vice President of Operations ... Mr. Christopher J. HILL
19 AVP Public Safety/Chief Police ... Mr. Jeffrey D. BESONG
09 AVP Institutional Research ... Mr. Christopher E. CHONCEK
21 AVP of Finance ... Mr. Jim HARDT
20 Asst VP Academic Affairs ... Mr. Nelson CHIPMAN
13 Asst Vice Pres Info Technology ... Mr. Tim WILSON
50 Dean Rowand School of Business ... Dr. Steve TANZILLI
53 Chair Education ... Dr. Darlene MARNICH
79 Chair Psychology ... Dr. Brent ROBBINS
54 Chair Natural Science/Engr Tech ... Dr. Gregg JOHNSON
88 Chair Criminal Justice/Intell Stds ... Mr. Michael BOTTA
88 Chair Business Management ... Mr. Patrick MULVIHILL
88 Chair Acctg Econ & Fin/IT ... Ms. Margaret GILFILLAN
88 Chair Theatre ... Mr. Aaron BOLLINGER
88 Chair Dance ... Mr. Garfield LEMONIUS
88 Chair Cinema ... Ms. Cara FRIEZ-LEWINTER
88 Chair Literary Arts ... Dr. Sarah PERRIER
60 Chair School of Communication ... Dr. Thom BAGGERMAN
88 Chair Sport Art Entertain Mgmt ... Mr. Bob DERDA
83 Chair Humanities/Social Science ... Dr. Channa NEWMAN
88 Chair Community Engagement ... Dr. Heather STARR FIEDLER
04 Exec Assistant to the President ... Ms. Margaret SMITH
06 University Registrar ... Mr. Scott SPENCER
08 Director/Librarian/Academic Svcs ... Ms. Liz EVANS
27 Mng Dir Marketing/Public Relations ... Mr. Louis CORSARO
39 Director of Campus Life ... Ms. Janet D. EVANS
07 Director of Admissions ... Ms. Joell MINFORD
41 Director of Athletics ... Mr. John ASHAOLU
88 Dir Conference & Event Services ... Ms. Christina MORTON
38 Director of Counseling Services ... Dr. Kurt KUMLER
106 Dir Online Education/E-learning ... Mr. Nelson CHIPMAN
29 Director Alumni Relations ... Vacant
37 Director Student Financial Aid ... Mr. George SANTUCCI
44 Director Annual Fund Pgms/Indiv Giv ... Vacant
88 Dir Center for Media Innovation ... Mr. Andrew CONTE
28 Director of Title IX and Diversity ... Ms. Vanessa LOVE

Reading Area Community College (B)

PO Box 1706, Reading PA 19603-1706
County: Berks FICE Identification: 010388
Unit ID: 215585
Telephone: (610) 372-4721 Carnegie Class: Assoc/MT-VT-Mix Trad/Non
FAX Number: (610) 372-4264 Calendar System: Semester
URL: www.racc.edu
Established: 1971 Annual Undergrad Tuition & Fees (In-District): $5,580
Enrollment: 4,207 Coed
Affiliation or Control: State/Local IRS Status: 501(c)3
Highest Offering: Associate Degree
Accreditation: M, ADNUR, COARC, MLTAD, PNUR

01 President ... Dr. Susan D. LOONEY
05 SVP Academic Affairs/Provost ... Ms. Cynthia SEAMAN
10 Sr VP Fin & Admin Svcs/Treasurer ... Mr. Kenneth DEARSTYNE
30 VP External Aff/Exec Dir Foundation ... Mr. Michael NAGEL
32 Dean of Student Affairs ... Ms. Maria MITCHELL
21 Assoc VP for Bus Svcs/Controller ... Ms. Dolores PETERSON
84 Dean of Enrollment Management ... Ms. Kay LITMAN
09 Dean Assessment/Research/Planning ... Dr. Maria HINOJOSA
81 Interim Assoc Dean STEM/Health Prof ... Ms. Patricia MEJABI
62 Asst Dean Library Svcs/Learning Res ... Ms. Mary Ellen HECKMAN
50 Assoc Dean of Business Division ... Ms. Linda BELL
79 Assoc Dean Foundational Studies ... Mr. Jeremy CROWE
83 Assoc Dean Social Sci/Human Svc/CAH ... Dr. Robin ECKERT
15 Director Human Resources ... Ms. Dolores PETERSON
103 Exec Dir Workforce Dev/Cmty Educ ... Ms. Bonnie SPAYD
26 Director Marketing/Communications ... Mr. David HESSEN
13 Director Information Technology ... Mr. Anderson FORREST
37 Director Financial Aid/Registrar ... Mr. Benjamin ROSENBERGER
57 Dir of Miller Center for the Arts ... Ms. Cathleen STEPHEN
96 Director of Purchasing ... Mr. Michael HODOWANEC
18 Director of Facilities ... Mr. Kevin MACKLEN
04 Exec Admin Asst to the President ... Ms. Sandra STRAUSE
20 Dean of Instruction ... Mr. Kevin COOTS
07 Dir Admiss & Enrollment Svcs ... Ms. Kathy CUNNINGHAM
35 Coordinator of Student Life ... Vacant

Reconstructionist Rabbinical College (C)

1299 Church Road, Wyncote PA 19095-1898
County: Montgomery FICE Identification: 022734
Unit ID: 215619
Telephone: (215) 576-0800 Carnegie Class: Spec-4-yr-Faith
FAX Number: (215) 576-6143 Calendar System: Semester
URL: www.rrc.edu
Established: 1968 Annual Graduate Tuition & Fees: N/A
Enrollment: 40 Coed
Affiliation or Control: Jewish IRS Status: 501(c)3
Highest Offering: Doctorate; No Undergraduates
Accreditation: M

01 President ... Rabbi Deborah WAXMAN
05 Vice Pres Academic Affairs ... Dr. Elsie STERN
45 VP Strategic Advancement ... Mr. Joel WEISS
03 Executive Vice President ... Rabbi Amber POWERS
26 Asst Vice Pres Communications ... Mr. Robert BERSHAD
11 Director of Operations ... Mr. Robert CHAVEZ
08 Library Director ... Rabbi Alan LAPAYOVER

Reformed Episcopal Seminary (D)

826 Second Avenue, Blue Bell PA 19422-1257
County: Montgomery Identification: 667050
Unit ID: 216348
Telephone: (610) 292-9852 Carnegie Class: Spec-4-yr-Faith
FAX Number: (610) 292-9853 Calendar System: Quarter
URL: www.reseminary.edu
Established: 1887 Annual Graduate Tuition & Fees: N/A
Enrollment: 13 Coed
Affiliation or Control: Reformed Episcopal Church IRS Status: 501(c)3
Highest Offering: Master's; No Undergraduates
Accreditation: THEOL

01 President and Dean ... Rev Dr. Jonathan S. RICHES
111 Associate Dean of External Affairs ... Rev Dr. Derek COOPER
08 Librarian ... Rev. Russell BUCHANAN
07 Director of Admissions & Recruiting ... Dr. Robert ARNER
30 Director of Development ... Dr. Manny HOWARD
13 Dir Information Technology/Web Dev ... Rev. Vic BROBERG
21 Bookkeeper ... Rev. Shawn D. RILEY

Reformed Presbyterian Theological Seminary (E)

7418 Penn Avenue, Pittsburgh PA 15208-2594
County: Allegheny FICE Identification: 003358
Unit ID: 215628
Telephone: (412) 731-6000 Carnegie Class: Spec-4-yr-Faith
FAX Number: (412) 731-4834 Calendar System: Quarter
URL: www.rpts.edu
Established: 1810 Annual Graduate Tuition & Fees: N/A
Enrollment: 101 Coed
Affiliation or Control: Reformed Presbyterian Church IRS Status: 501(c)3
Highest Offering: Doctorate; No Undergraduates
Accreditation: THEOL

01 President ... Dr. Barry J. YORK
08 Head Librarian ... Mr. Thomas G. REID, JR.
10 Treasurer ... Mr. James MCFARLAND
06 Registrar/Dir Admiss & Stdnt Svcs ... Mr. Edwin BLACKWOOD
37 Director of Financial Aid ... Mrs. Sharon SAMPSON
111 Dir of Development & Inst Advance ... Mr. Mark SAMPSON
18 Director of Support Services ... Rev. Andrew JACKSON

The Restaurant School at Walnut Hill College (F)

4207 Walnut Street, Philadelphia PA 19104-3518
County: Philadelphia FICE Identification: 021928
Unit ID: 215637
Telephone: (215) 222-4200 Carnegie Class: Spec-4-yr-Other
FAX Number: (215) 222-4219 Calendar System: Other
URL: www.walnuthillcollege.edu
Established: 1974 Annual Undergrad Tuition & Fees: $23,550
Enrollment: 334 Coed
Affiliation or Control: Proprietary IRS Status: Proprietary
Highest Offering: Baccalaureate
Accreditation: ACCSC

01 President ... Mr. Daniel LIBERATOSCIOLI
03 Executive Vice President ... Mr. Karl D. BECKER
11 Vice President Administrative Svcs ... Ms. Peggy LIBERATOSCIOLI
10 Vice President of Operations ... Mr. Dennis LIBERATI
88 Vice President of Culinary Arts ... Chef Gary TREVISANI
05 Chief Academic Officer ... Mr. David MORROW
20 Assoc Dean Teaching/Learning ... Dr. Joshua SEERY
07 Director of Admissions ... Mr. Karl BECKER
21 Controller ... Mr. Chris MOLZ
32 Dir Student/Community Engagement ... Ms. Meghan BLOOME
37 Director Financial Aid ... Ms. Peggy LIBERATOSCIOLI
50 Director School of Management ... Mr. David MORROW
26 Director of Marketing ... Ms. Valery SNISARENKO

Robert Morris University (G)

6001 University Boulevard,
Moon Township PA 15108-1189
County: Allegheny FICE Identification: 003359
Unit ID: 215655
Telephone: (412) 397-6400 Carnegie Class: DU-Mod
FAX Number: (412) 397-5958 Calendar System: Semester
URL: www.rmu.edu
Established: 1921 Annual Undergrad Tuition & Fees: $30,300
Enrollment: 5,076 Coed
Affiliation or Control: Independent Non-Profit IRS Status: 501(c)3
Highest Offering: Doctorate
Accreditation: M, CAEPT, NMT, NURSE

01 President ... Dr. Christopher HOWARD
10 SVP Business Affairs/Treasurer ... Mr. Jeffrey A. LISTWAK
05 Provost & Sr VP Academic Affairs ... Dr. Mary Ann A. RAFOTH
43 General Counsel & VP Legal Affairs ... Ms. Renee T. CAVALOVITCH
45 VP Corporate Rels & Strategic Plng ... Dr. Derya A. JACOBS
84 VP Enrollment Management ... Ms. Wendy C. BECKEMEYER
32 Vice President for Student Life ... Mr. John A. MICHALENKO
30 Vice President for Development ... Mr. Matthew B. MILLET
18 Vice Pres for Facilities ... Mr. Perry F. ROOFNER
26 Vice Pres Public Rels/Marketing ... Mr. Jonathan E. POTTS
09 VP Planning & Administration ... Dr. David R. MAJKA
41 VP & Director of Athletics ... Mr. Chris KING
50 Dean School of Business ... Dr. Michelle PATRICK
54 Dean School of Engr/Math/Science ... Dr. Maria V. KALEVITCH
79 Int Dean Sch Informatics/Humanities ... Mr. Jon RADERMACHER
66 Int Dean School of Nursing/Educ ... Mr. George SEMICH
88 Dir Univ/Athletic Sponsorship ... Mr. Matt F. O'BRIEN
84 Assoc VP Enrollment Management ... Ms. Kellie L. LAURENZI
31 AVP Cmty Engage/Leadership Devel ... Ms. Peggy M. OUTON
46 Assoc Provost Research/Graduate ... Dr. Sushil ACHARYA
35 Assistant Dean of Students ... Mrs. Maureen H. KEEFER
08 Director University Library ... Dr. Timothy M. SCHLAK
21 Chief Acctg/Financial Planning Ofcr ... Ms. Melissa A. MICCO
06 University Registrar ... Ms. Daniell C. MATTHEWS
19 Director Public Safety ... Mr. Randy L. MINK
36 Director Career Center ... Ms. Kishma P. DECASTRO-SALLIS
39 Director Residence Life ... Mrs. Anne L. LAHODA
28 Chief Diversity/Inclusion Officer ... Dr. Anthony G. ROBINS
27 Sr Dir Marketing & Public Relations ... Mr. Brian J. EDWARDS
109 Sr Director Financial Planning ... Ms. Anita NILKANT
37 Sr Director Financial Aid ... Ms. Stephanie N. HENDERSHOT
44 Director Annual Giving ... Ms. Jen YOUNG
04 Exec Assistant to the President ... Ms. Ronita GILES
101 Board Liaison & Asst Secretary ... Ms. Jill KRIEGER

Rosedale Technical College (H)

215 Beecham Drive, Suite 2, Pittsburgh PA 15205-9791
County: Allegheny FICE Identification: 012050
Unit ID: 215682
Telephone: (412) 521-6200 Carnegie Class: Spec 2-yr-Tech
FAX Number: (412) 521-2520 Calendar System: Semester
URL: www.rosedaletech.org
Established: 1949 Annual Undergrad Tuition & Fees: $14,530
Enrollment: 372 Coed
Affiliation or Control: Independent Non-Profit IRS Status: 501(c)3
Highest Offering: Associate Degree
Accreditation: ACCSC

01 President ... Dennis F. WILKE
05 Director of Education ... Kara CHAN
30 VP College Development/Comm ... Debbie BIER
84 Director of Student Enrollment ... Dave DETAR

Rosemont College (I)

1400 Montgomery Avenue, Rosemont PA 19010-1699
County: Montgomery FICE Identification: 003360
Unit ID: 215691
Telephone: (610) 527-0200 Carnegie Class: Masters/M
FAX Number: (610) 527-0341 Calendar System: Semester
URL: www.rosemont.edu
Established: 1921 Annual Undergrad Tuition & Fees: $19,900
Enrollment: 1,008 Coed
Affiliation or Control: Roman Catholic IRS Status: 501(c)3
Highest Offering: Master's
Accreditation: M

01 President ... Dr. Sharon LATCHAW HIRSH
05 Provost/VP Academic/Student Affairs ... Dr. Lisa DOLLING
10 VP for Finance & Administration ... Dr. Randy ELDRIDGE
37 Dir Enrollment Svcs/Fin Compliance ... Vacant
30 Vice Pres College Relations ... Ms. Christyn MORAN
32 Dean of Students ... Mr. Troy CHIDDICK
88 Vice President for Mission ... Sr. Jeanne Marie HATCH, SHCJ
08 Exec Director of Library Services ... Mrs. Catherine FENNELL

58	Dean Schools Graduate/Prof Studies	Vacant
20	Academic Dean Undergrad College	Mrs. Paulette HUTCHINSON
29	Director of Alumni Relations	Mr. Joseph DARRAH
26	Managing Director of Communications	Ms. Kathleen SMYSER
41	Director of Athletics	Mr. Joseph PAVLOW
15	Asst VP Human Resources	Ms. Jane FEDEROWICZ
42	Director of Campus Ministry	Ms. Regina INGIOSI
18	Director of Operations	Mr. Raymond A. BROWN
38	Director of Counseling Cntr	Ms. Kruti QUAZI
39	Director of Residence Life	Mr. Benjamin HUELSKAMP
19	Director of Public Safety	Mr. Matthew BAKER
21	Controller	Ms. Faith BYRNE
07	Director of Admissions	Ms. Catarina MOREIRA

Saint Charles Borromeo Seminary (A)

100 E Wynnewood Road, Wynnewood PA 19096-3099

County: Montgomery — FICE Identification: 003364
Unit ID: 216047
Telephone: (610) 667-3394 — Carnegie Class: Spec-4-yr-Faith
FAX Number: (610) 667-7635 — Calendar System: Semester
URL: www.scs.edu
Established: 1832 — Annual Undergrad Tuition & Fees: $20,655
Enrollment: 222 — Male
Affiliation or Control: Roman Catholic — IRS Status: 501(c)3
Highest Offering: Master's
Accreditation: M, THEOL

01	Rector & President	M.Rev. Timothy C. SENIOR
05	Vice President for Academic Affairs	Rev. Robert A. PESARCHICK
03	Vice Rector	Rev. Joseph SHENOSKY
10	Chief Financial Officer	Mr. Mark MCLAUGHLIN
108	VP Info Services & Assessment	Mrs. Cait KOKOLUS
33	Dean of Men Theology	Rev. Brian KANE
33	Dean of Men College	Rev. George SZPARAGOWSKI
08	Director of Library Services	Mr. James HUMBLE
06	Registrar	Mr. Todd CHIARAVALLOTI
42	Dir Spiritual Formation Theology	Fr. Herb SPERGER
42	Dir Spiritual Formation College	Fr. Dennis CARBONARO
88	Director Pastoral/Apostolic Form	Rev. Augustine ESPOSITO
73	Dean School of Theological Studies	Rev. Patrick BRADY
21	Director of Financial Services	Ms. Barbara COADY
37	Director Student Financial Aid	Ms. Nora DOWNEY

Saint Francis University (B)

PO Box 600, Loretto PA 15940-0600

County: Cambria — FICE Identification: 003366
Unit ID: 215743
Telephone: (814) 472-3000 — Carnegie Class: Masters/L
FAX Number: (814) 472-3003 — Calendar System: Semester
URL: www.francis.edu
Established: 1847 — Annual Undergrad Tuition & Fees: $36,410
Enrollment: 2,680 — Coed
Affiliation or Control: Roman Catholic — IRS Status: 501(c)3
Highest Offering: Doctorate
Accreditation: M, ARCPA, EXSC, IACBE, NURSE, OT, PTA, SW

01	President	Rev. Malachi VAN TASSELL, TOR
05	Vice President for Academic Affairs	Dr. Karan POWELL
10	Vice President for Finance	Mr. Jeffrey SAVINO
32	Vice Pres for Student Development	Dr. Frank MONTECALVO
42	Director of Mission Integration	Vacant
111	Vice President for Advancement	Mr. Robert CRUSCIEL
84	Vice Pres for Enrollment Management	Ms. Cynthia SISSON
86	Asst VP Govt Rels/Grants/Found	Mr. Robert YOUNG
08	Dean of Library Services	Ms. Sandra A. BALOUGH
97	Dean of General Education	Dr. Jessica CAMMARATA
06	Registrar	Vacant
09	Director of Institutional Research	Ms. Kate DEATER
37	Financial Aid Director	Mr. Shane HIMES
26	Director Marketing & Public Affairs	Ms. Marie YOUNG
30	Director of Development	Ms. Marie B. MELUSKY
38	Director of Counseling Center	Vacant
13	Director Computer Services	Vacant
29	Director of Alumni Relations	Mr. Eric HORELL
51	Dean Francis Worldwide	Dr. Karen SRBA
18	Director of Physical Plant	Mr. David WILLIAMS
21	Controller	Mr. Thomas R. FRITZ
41	Director of Athletics	Ms. Susan ROBINSON-FRUCHTL
88	Dir Small Business Devel Center	Mr. Barry SURMA
19	University Police	Capt. Eric ALLEN
39	Director of Residence Life	Mr. Donald MILES
42	Director of Campus Ministry	Rev. James PUGLIS
121	Dir Center for Academic Success	Ms. Renee BERNARD
35	Dir of Student Engagement	Mr. Bobby ANDERSON
15	Director of Human Resources	Ms. Marian BENDER
28	Director of Multicultural Affairs	Ms. Lynne BANKS
96	Director of Purchasing	Mr. Caleb DRENNING
20	Associate Provost	Dr. Peter R. SKONER
40	Manager of Bookstore	Ms. Barbara SHINGLE
04	Admin Assistant to the President	Ms. Vickie SOYKA

Saint Joseph's University (C)

5600 City Avenue, Philadelphia PA 19131-1376

County: Philadelphia — FICE Identification: 003367
Unit ID: 215770
Telephone: (610) 660-1000 — Carnegie Class: Masters/L
FAX Number: (610) 660-1201 — Calendar System: Semester
URL: www.sju.edu
Established: 1851 — Annual Undergrad Tuition & Fees: $44,974
Enrollment: 8,085 — Coed
Affiliation or Control: Roman Catholic — IRS Status: 501(c)3
Highest Offering: Doctorate
Accreditation: M

01	President	Dr. Mark C. REED
05	Provost	Dr. Cheryl A. MCCONNELL
10	VP Financial Affairs	Mr. David R. BEAUPRE
26	VP University Relations	Mr. Joseph P. KENDER
88	Executive Director of Mission	Rev. Dan JOYCE, SJ
49	Dean College of Arts & Sciences	Dr. Shaily A. MENON
50	Dean Haub School of Business	Dr. Joseph A. DIANGELO, JR.
32	VP Student Life	Dr. Cary M. ANDERSON
41	VP Director of Athletics	Ms. Jill R. BODENSTEINER
84	VP Enrollment Management	Ms. Karen PELLEGRINO
27	Chief Marketing/Communications	Ms. Marie E. WILLIAMS
11	AVP Administrative Services	Mr. Timothy MCGURIMAN
43	General Counsel	Ms. Marianne SCHIMELFINIG
100	AVP Chief of Staff	Ms. Sarah F. QUINN
84	AVP Enrollment Management	Mr. Robert J. MCBRIDE
13	Chief Information Officer	Mr. Francis J. DISANTI

St. Tikhon's Orthodox Theological Seminary (D)

PO Box 130, South Canaan PA 18459-0130

County: Wayne — FICE Identification: 039193
Telephone: (570) 561-1818 — Carnegie Class: Not Classified
FAX Number: N/A — Calendar System: Semester
URL: www.stots.edu
Established: 1938 — Annual Undergrad Tuition & Fees: N/A
Enrollment: N/A — Coed
Affiliation or Control: Other — IRS Status: 501(c)3
Highest Offering: First Professional Degree
Accreditation: THEOL

01	President	Metr. Tikhon MOLLARD
03	Rector/CEO	Abp. Michael DAHULICH
05	Seminary Dean/COO	V.Rev. Steven A. VOYTOVICH
10	Chief Financial Officer	V.Rev. Dennis SWENCKI
04	Administrative Asst to Dean/COO	Mr. Marshall M. GOODGE
08	Librarian	Prof. Sergei D. ARHIPOV
06	Registrar/Director Academic Affairs	Dr. Paul J. WITEK
30	Dir Office of Mission Development	Dr. David FOX
32	Director Student Life	Fr. Ignatius GAUVAIN

Saint Vincent College (E)

300 Fraser Purchase Road, Latrobe PA 15650-2690

County: Westmoreland — FICE Identification: 003368
Unit ID: 215798
Telephone: (724) 805-2500 — Carnegie Class: Bac-A&S
FAX Number: (724) 805-2019 — Calendar System: Semester
URL: www.stvincent.edu
Established: 1846 — Annual Undergrad Tuition & Fees: $35,462
Enrollment: 1,865 — Coed
Affiliation or Control: Roman Catholic — IRS Status: 501(c)3
Highest Offering: Doctorate
Accreditation: M, ACBSP, ANEST

01	President	Fr. Paul TAYLOR, OSB
05	VP Academic Affairs	Dr. John SMETANKA
10	VP/Chief Finance/Admin Officer	Mr. Richard WILLIAMS
32	VP Student Affairs	Ms. Mary COLLINS
07	Dean of Admissions	Ms. Heather KABALA
13	Chief Information Officer	Mr. Peter E. MAHONEY
50	Dean McKenna Sch Bus/Econ/Govt	Dr. Gary QUINLIVAN
81	Dean Science/Math & Computing	Dr. Stephen M. JODIS
49	Dean Arts/Humanities/Social Science	Dr. Margaret WATKINS
06	Registrar	Ms. Celine R. BRUDNOK
08	Librarian	Bro. David KELLY, OSB
29	Director of Alumni Affairs	Mr. Shawn GOUCH
36	Director Career Services	Ms. Courtney BAUM
15	Director of Human Resources	Ms. Judith MAHER
42	Director of Campus Ministry	Rev. Killian LOCH, OSB
23	Director Wellness Center	Ms. Gretchen FLOCK
19	Director Public Safety	Ms. Stephanie FAGO
41	Athletic Director	Rev. Myron KIRSCH, OSB
35	Dean of Students	Mr. Robert BAUM
96	Director of Purchasing	Mr. Terry NOEL
18	Director of Facility Management	Mr. Douglas EPPLEY
40	Manager Book Center	Rev. Anthony GROSSI, OSB
58	Coord of Graduate Studies	Ms. Amanda GUNTHER
04	Administrative Asst to President	Ms. Lisa POOLE
104	Director Study Abroad	Ms. Sara HART
37	Director Student Financial Aid	Ms. Mary GAZAL
102	Dir Foundation/Govt/Corporate Rels	Ms. Christine FOSCHIA
43	Dir Legal Services/General Counsel	Mr. Bruce ANTKOWIAK
108	Director Assessment & IR	Ms. Julia CAVALLO

Saint Vincent Seminary (F)

300 Fraser Purchase Road, Latrobe PA 15650-2690

County: Westmoreland — Identification: 666018
Unit ID: 215813
Telephone: (724) 805-2592 — Carnegie Class: Spec-4-yr-Faith
FAX Number: (724) 532-5052 — Calendar System: Semester
URL: www.saintvincentseminary.edu
Established: 1846 — Annual Undergrad Tuition & Fees: N/A
Enrollment: 47 — Coed
Affiliation or Control: Roman Catholic — IRS Status: 501(c)3
Highest Offering: Master's
Accreditation: THEOL

01	Rector	V.Rev. Edward M. MAZICH, OSB
88	Director of Spiritual Formation	Rev. Boniface N. HICKS, OSB
05	Academic Dean	Rev. Patrick T. CRONAUER, OSB
03	Vice-Rector	Rev. John-Mary TOMPKINS, OSB
42	Director of Liturgy	Rev. Cyprian G. CONSTANTINE, OSB
88	Director of Pastoral Formation	Rev. Nathan MUNSCH, OSB
32	Dean of Students	Rev. Emmanuel O. AFUNUGO
38	Dir of Pre-Theologian Formation	Dr. Lawrence SUTTON
04	Administrative Asst to President	Ms. Lisa POOLE
06	Registrar	Ms. Celine BRUDNOK
07	Dean of Admissions	Ms. Heather KABALA
08	Director of Libraries	Br. David KELLY, OSB
09	Director of Institutional Research	Ms. Julia CAVALLO
10	Chief Business Officer	Mr. Richard WILLIAMS
101	Secretary of the Institution/Board	Rev. Jeffrey S. NYARDY, OSB
105	Director of Web Services	Ms. Cindy HOFFMAN
11	Chief of Administration	Rt Rev. Douglas R. NOWICKI, OSB
13	Chief Info Technology Officer (CIO)	Mr. Peter MAHONEY
15	Director Personnel Services	Mrs. Judith MAHER
18	Chief Facilities/Physical Plant	Mr. Douglas EPPLEY
19	Director Security/Safety	Sgt. Stephanie FAGO
22	Dir Affirmative Action/EEO	Miss Eileen FLINN
25	Chief Contracts/Grants Admin	Ms. Christine L. FOSCHIA
26	Assoc Dir Marketing & Comm	Mr. James BURGER
28	Director of Diversity	Dr. Nancy ROTTLER
29	Director Alumni Relations	Mr. Shawn GOUCH
30	Chief Development/Advancement	Mr. Shannon JORDAN
37	Director Student Financial Aid	Ms. Mary GAZAL
41	Athletic Director	Rev. Myron KIRSCH, OSB
43	Dir Legal Services/General Counsel	Mr. Bruce ANTKOWIAK
44	Director Annual or Planned Giving	Mr. David HOLLENBAUGH
96	Director of Purchasing	Mr. Terry NOEL
108	Director Institutional Assessment	Mr. Joshua W. SHRUM
26	Dir of PR - Archabbey & Seminary	Ms. Kim METZGAR
104	Director Study Abroad	Ms. Sara HART
106	Director Online Education	Mr. Roberto WISNESCKI
36	Director Student Placement	Ms. Courtney BAUM
39	Director Resident Life	Ms. Jenna CHURILLA
45	Chief Institutional Planning Office	Mrs. Gina NALEVANKO
50	Dean of School of Business	Dr. Gary M. QUINLIVAN
53	Dean of Arts/Humanitie or Education	Dr. Margaret WATKINS
86	Assistant to President/Mission	Rev. Thomas HART, OSB
90	Director Academic Computing	Mr. Justin FABIN
91	Director Administrative Computing	Mr. Joshua SEEVERS

Salus University (G)

8360 Old York Road, Elkins Park PA 19027-1516

County: Philadelphia — FICE Identification: 003311
Unit ID: 214564
Telephone: (215) 780-1400 — Carnegie Class: Spec-4-yr-Other Health
FAX Number: (215) 780-1325 — Calendar System: Quarter
URL: www.salus.edu
Established: 1919 — Annual Undergrad Tuition & Fees: N/A
Enrollment: 1,141 — Coed
Affiliation or Control: Independent Non-Profit — IRS Status: 501(c)3
Highest Offering: Doctorate
Accreditation: M, ARCPA, AUD, OPT, OPTR, OT, SP

01	President	Dr. Michael H. MITTLEMAN
05	Vice President Faculty Affairs	Dr. Barry ECKERT
10	Vice Pres Finance/Business Affairs	Mr. Donald KATES
17	Vice Pres Clinical Services	Dr. John GAAL
45	Vice President for Inst Planning	Mr. Brian ZUCKERMAN
32	Dean Student Affairs	Dr. James CALDWELL
09	Asst Dir Research Admin	Ms. Lydia PARKE
06	Registrar	Ms. Shannon BOSS
13	Chief Information Officer	Mr. William BRICHTA
38	Director Personal/Prof Development	Dr. James CALDWELL
37	Assoc Dean Student Financial Affs	Ms. Jamie SCHLANG
18	Director Physical Plant	Mr. Richard ECHEVARRI
30	Director of Development	Ms. Jackie PATTERSON
26	Director Publications/Communication	Ms. Alexis ABATE
29	Director Alumni Relations/Giving	Ms. Kate BREMER
51	Coord Continuing/Post-Graduate Educ	Mrs. Melissa VITEK
58	Chairperson Graduate Studies	Vacant
40	Bookstore Manager	Mr. Joe NOCE
24	Director Instructional Media	Mr. Glenn ROEDEL
36	Dir Student Placement/Student Affs	Mr. Ryan HOLLISTER
84	Director Enrollment Management	Dr. Jim CALDWELL
88	Exec Dir Inst Visually Impaired	Dr. Brooke KRUEMMLING
08	Head Librarian	Ms. Marietta DOOLEY
19	Director of Security	Vacant
15	Dir Human Res/Affirm Action/Facil	Ms. Maura KEENAN
96	Director of Purchasing	Ms. Lydia FRIEL

Seton Hill University (H)

1 Seton Hill Drive, Greensburg PA 15601-1599

County: Westmoreland — FICE Identification: 003362
Unit ID: 215947
Telephone: (724) 834-2200 — Carnegie Class: Masters/M
FAX Number: N/A — Calendar System: Semester
URL: www.setonhill.edu
Established: 1883 — Annual Undergrad Tuition & Fees: $35,748
Enrollment: 2,470 — Coed
Affiliation or Control: Roman Catholic — IRS Status: 501(c)3
Highest Offering: Master's
Accreditation: M, ARCPA, DENT, DIETC, EXSC, IACBE, MFCD, MUS, SW

01	President	Dr. Mary FINGER
32	VP Mission	Sr. Vivien LINKHAUER, SC
05	Provost	Sr. Susan YOCHUM, SC

10	Vice Pres Finance & Business	Ms. Jennifer LUNDY
111	Vice Pres Institutional Advancement	Ms. Molly ROBB SHIMKO
13	Chief Information Officer	Ms. Melissa ALSING
84	Vice Pres Enrollment Management	Mr. Brett FRESHOUR
21	Controller	Vacant
35	Vice President for Student Affairs	Dr. Rosalie CARPENTER
07	Director Undergraduate Admissions	Ms. Allison SASSO
08	Director of Library	Mr. David STANLEY
29	Director of Alumni Relations	Ms. Ashley ZWIERZELEWSKI
37	Director of Financial Aid	Ms. Tracey DE BAEZ SNYDER
36	Director of Career Development	Ms. Renee STAREK
15	Director of Human Resources	Mrs. Darlene SAUERS
18	Director Facilities	Mr. Bill VOKES
41	Executive Athletic Director	Mr. Chris SNYDER
42	Director Campus Ministry	Sr. Maureen O'BRIEN
06	Registrar	Ms. Constance BECKEL
38	Director Student Counseling	Ms. Teresa BASSI-COOK
09	Director of Institutional Research	Dr. Jason DRAPER
26	Chief Public Relations Officer	Ms. Jennifer REEGER
96	Director of Purchasing	Mr. Charles O'NEILL
19	Director Public Safety/Police Chief	Ms. Michele PROCTOR
22	Dir Affirmative Action/EEO	Ms. Darlene SAUERS
25	Dir Grants & Government Support	Ms. Cynthia FERRARI
39	Director Student Housing	Mr. Cory CAMPBELL
04	Exec Asst to the President/Provost	Ms. Jennifer ZEMBA
100	Chief of Staff	Ms. Carol BILLMAN
43	General Counsel	Ms. Imogene CATHEY

South Hills School of Business and Technology (A)

541 58th Street, Altoona PA 16602

Telephone: (814) 944-6134 Identification: 770772

Accreditation: ACCSC, CAHIIM, MAAB

South Hills School of Business and Technology (B)

480 Waupelani Drive, State College PA 16801-4516

County: Centre FICE Identification: 013263

Unit ID: 216083

Telephone: (814) 234-7755 Carnegie Class: Assoc/HT-High Trad

FAX Number: (814) 234-0926 Calendar System: Quarter

URL: www.southhills.edu

Established: 1970 Annual Undergrad Tuition & Fees: $16,865

Enrollment: 423 Coed

Affiliation or Control: Proprietary IRS Status: Proprietary

Highest Offering: Associate Degree

Accreditation: ACCSC, CAHIIM, DMS, MAAB

00	Owner	Mrs. Maralyn MAZZA
01	President	Mr. S. Paul MAZZA, III
05	Director	Mr. Mark MAGGS
06	Registrar	Ms. Ingrid THOMPSON
07	Director of Admissions	Ms. Holly EMERICK
26	Chief Public Relations/Marketing	Ms. Misty FREDERICK-RITZ
37	Director Student Financial Aid	Mr. LeRoy SPICER
20	Director of Education	Ms. Susan VIDMAR

Susquehanna University (C)

514 University Avenue, Selinsgrove PA 17870-1025

County: Snyder FICE Identification: 003369

Unit ID: 216278

Telephone: (570) 374-0101 Carnegie Class: Bac-A&S

FAX Number: (570) 372-4040 Calendar System: Semester

URL: www.susqu.edu

Established: 1858 Annual Undergrad Tuition & Fees: $47,290

Enrollment: 2,351 Coed

Affiliation or Control: Evangelical Lutheran Church In America

IRS Status: 501(c)3

Highest Offering: Baccalaureate

Accreditation: M, MUS

01	President	Dr. Jonathan GREEN
100	VP & Chief of Staff	Dr. Philip E. WINGER
05	Interim Provost/Dean of Faculty	Dr. Dave RAMSARAN
10	Executive VP for Finance & Admin	Mr. Michael COYNE
111	Vice President for Advancement	Ms. Melissa KOMORA
84	VP for Enrollment & Student Fin Svc	Ms. Madeleine E. RHYNEER
32	VP Student Engagement & Success	Dr. Susan LANTZ
20	Assoc Provost/Dean A&S	Dr. Valerie G. MARTIN
50	Dean Weis School of Business	Dr. Matthew ROUSU
26	VP for Marketing & Communications	Mr. Aaron MARTIN
112	Asst VP Adv/Major & Planned Giving	Ms. Kim ANDRETTA
04	Senior Admin Asst to the President	Ms. Sharon POPE
38	Dean Health & Wellness	Dr. Stacey PEARSON-WHARTON
89	Director of First Year Experience	Ms. Samantha PROFFITT
28	Asst Dean Student Div & Inclusion	Ms. Dena SALERNO
07	Director of Admission	Mr. Philip BETZ
08	Interim Director of the Library	Mr. Robert SIECZKIEWICZ
37	Director of Student Financial Svcs	Mr. Justin RUMMEL
06	Registrar	Ms. Alison A. RICHARD
42	University Chaplain	Rev. Scott M. KERSHNER
13	Chief Information Officer	Vacant
41	Director of Athletics	Vacant
18	Director of Facilities Management	Mr. Chris C. BAILEY
36	Asst Provost/Dir Career Development	Ms. Michaeline SHUMAN
88	Director of Event Management	Ms. Michelle HARMAN
29	Asst VP Alumni/Parent & Donor	Ms. Becky DEITRICK
108	Dir Institutional Effectiveness	Dr. Dave RAMSARAN
25	Grants Coordinator	Mr. Malcolm DERK
104	Dean of Global Programs	Dr. Scott MANNING
15	VP of Human Resources	Ms. Jennifer BUCHER
19	Director Public Safety	Mr. Angelo MARTIN
92	Director of Honors Program	Dr. Marcos KRIEGER
22	Dir of Workforce Div & Inclusion	Vacant

Swarthmore College (D)

500 College Avenue, Swarthmore PA 19081-1390

County: Delaware FICE Identification: 003370

Unit ID: 216287

Telephone: (610) 328-8000 Carnegie Class: Bac-A&S

FAX Number: (610) 328-8000 Calendar System: Semester

URL: www.swarthmore.edu

Established: 1864 Annual Undergrad Tuition & Fees: $52,588

Enrollment: 1,577 Coed

Affiliation or Control: Independent Non-Profit IRS Status: 501(c)3

Highest Offering: Baccalaureate

Accreditation: M

01	President	Valerie A. SMITH
05	Provost	Sarah WILLIE LEBRETON
10	Vice President Finance & Admin	Gregory N. BROWN
111	Vice President for Advancement	Karl CLAUSS
15	Vice Pres for Human Resources	Pamela PRESCOD-CAESAR
26	VP Communications	Andy HIRSCH
07	Vice Pres & Dean of Admissions	Jim BOCK
18	Assoc VP Sustainable Fac Op/Cap Pln	Andrew FEICK
21	Asst Vice Pres Finance & Controller	Alice TURBIVILLE
32	Vice President and Dean of Students	James TERHUNE
28	Assoc Dean of Diversity/Inclusion	Shá DUNCAN SMITH
06	Registrar	Martin O. WARNER
08	College Librarian	Peggy SEIDEN
09	Director Institutional Research	Robin H. SHORES
29	Director Alumni & Parent Engagement	Lisa SHAFER
37	Director of Financial Aid	Varo L. DUFFINS
36	Director Career Services	Nancy BURKETT
19	Director of Public Safety	Michael HILL
43	General Counsel	Sharmaine LAMAR
23	Director Worth Health Center	Alice HOLLAND
38	Director Psychological Services	David RAMIREZ
41	Director Physical Educ/Athletics	Adam HERTZ
13	Chief Info Technology Officer	Joel COOPER
35	Director Student Engagement	Rachel HEAD
104	Director Off-Campus Study	Pat MARTIN
39	Director of Residential Communities	Isaiah THOMÁS
105	Web Developer	Les LEACH
22	Dir Equal Opportunity & Engagement	Vacant
96	Director of Purchasing	Vacant
100	Chief of Staff	Edward P. ROWE

Talmudical Yeshiva of Philadelphia (E)

6063 Drexel Road, Philadelphia PA 19131-1296

County: Philadelphia FICE Identification: 012523

Unit ID: 216311

Telephone: (215) 477-1000 Carnegie Class: Spec-4-yr-Faith

FAX Number: (215) 477-5065 Calendar System: Semester

Established: 1953 Annual Undergrad Tuition & Fees: $9,175

Enrollment: 114 Male

Affiliation or Control: Independent Non-Profit IRS Status: 501(c)3

Highest Offering: First Talmudic Degree

Accreditation: RABN

01	Chief Executive Officer (President)	Mr. Alexander TAUB
05	Dean	Rabbi Shmuel KAMENETSKY
05	Dean	Rabbi Yehuda SVEI
05	Dean	Rabbi Sholom KAMENETSKY

Temple University (F)

1330 Polett Walk, 200 Sullivan Hall,
Philadelphia PA 19122-6072

County: Philadelphia FICE Identification: 003371

Unit ID: 216339

Telephone: (215) 204-7405 Carnegie Class: DU-Highest

FAX Number: (215) 204-5600 Calendar System: Semester

URL: www.temple.edu

Established: 1884 Annual Undergrad Tuition & Fees (In-State): $16,970

Enrollment: 39,967 Coed

Affiliation or Control: State Related IRS Status: 501(c)3

Highest Offering: Doctorate

Accreditation: M, #ARCPA, ART, CAATE, CAHIIM, CARTE, CLPSY, DANCE, DENT, HSA, IPSY, JOUR, LAW, LSAR, MED, MUS, NRPA, NURSE, OT, PCSAS, PH, PHAR, PLNG, POD, PTA, SCPSY, SP, SW, THEA

01	President	Dr. Richard M. ENGLERT
03	VP for Public Affairs	Mr. William T. BERGMAN, JR.
05	Exec VP and Provost	Ms. JoAnne A. EPPS
11	Exec VP & COO	Mr. Kevin G. CLARK
43	VP & University Counsel	Mr. Michael B. GEBHARDT
32	VP for Student Affairs	Dr. Theresa A. POWELL
13	VP Computer/CIO	Ms. Cindy LEAVITT
17	Sr EVP for Health Affairs	Dr. Larry R. KAISER
26	Sr Vice Provost Strategic Comm	Dr. Elizabeth LEEBRON TUTELMAN
10	VP/CFO & Treasurer	Mr. Kenneth H. KAISER
88	VP International Affairs	Dr. Hai-Lung DAI
35	Assoc VP/Dean of Students	Dr. Stephanie IVES
111	VP Institutional Advancement	Mr. James F. CAWLEY
46	VP for Research Administration	Dr. Michele M. MASUCCI
18	VP Planning & Capital Projects	Mr. Gennaro J. LEVA
21	Sr Assoc VP Finance	Mr. William J. WILKINSON
88	Assoc VP Business Services	Mr. Michael D. SCALES
15	Assoc VP Human Resources	Ms. Sharon I. BOYLE
21	Assoc VP/Controller	Mr. David MARINO
22	Asst VP Inst Diversity	Dr. Tiffenia D. ARCHIE
21	Asst VP Fin/Admin & Treasurer	Ms. Kathryn P. D'ANGELO
88	Vice Provost for Faculty Affairs	Dr. Kevin J. DELANEY
20	Vice Provost Undergrad Studies	Dr. Daniel BERMAN
108	Vice Provost Assessment	Dr. Jodi LEVINE LAUFGRABEN
08	Dean for University Libraries	Mr. Joseph P. LUCIA
06	Registrar	Mr. Bhavesh BAMBHROLIA
41	Director of Athletics	Mr. Patrick KRAFT
38	Director Tuttleman Counseling Svcs	Dr. John L. DIMINO
36	Director Career Services	Ms. Shannon CONKLIN
88	Chief Compliance Officer	Mr. Alejandro J. DIAZ
09	Director IR/Assessment	Ms. Sally M. FRAZEE
104	AVP Intl Affairs for Educ Abroad	Dr. Alistair HOWARD
23	Sr Admin Student & Employee Health	Dr. Mark DENYS
37	Director Student Financial Svcs	Ms. Emilie VANTRIESTE
88	Vice Provost University College	Dr. Vicki Lewis MCGARVEY
96	Director Purchasing	Ms. Donna L. SCHWEIBENZ
113	Dir Financial Accouting/Bursar	Mr. Conrad MUTH
97	Assoc Vice Provost Undergrad	Ms. Michele O'CONNOR
12	Director TU Center City	Mr. William PARSHALL
84	Vice Provost Enroll Mgmt	Mr. Shawn L. ABBOTT
40	Bookstore General Manager	Mr. James HANLEY
49	Dean College of Liberal Arts	Dr. Richard DEEG
53	Dean College of Education	Dr. Greg ANDERSON
61	Dean Beasley School of Law	Mr. Gregory M. MANDEL
64	Dean Boyer College of Music	Dr. Robert T. STROKER
57	Dean Tyler School of Art	Ms. Susan CAHAN
50	Dean Fox Sch of Business & Mgmt	Dr. Ronald ANDERSON
52	Dean Kornberg School of Dentistry	Dr. Amid ISMAIL
63	Dean Lewis Katz School of Medicine	Dr. Larry KAISER
67	Int Dean School of Pharmacy	Dr. Michael R. BORENSTEIN
54	Dean College of Engineering	Dr. Keya SADEGHIPOUR
88	Dean School of Podiatric Medicine	Dr. John A. MATTIACCI
72	Dean College of Science & Tech	Dr. Michael KLEIN
60	Dean Klein College of Media & Comm	Mr. David BOARDMAN
69	Dean College of Public Health	Dr. Laura SIMINOFF
88	Dean Sch Sports/Tour & Hosp Mgmt	Dr. Ronald ANDERSON
12	Dean Temple Japan Campus	Dr. Bruce STRONACH
12	Int Dir & Acting Dean Temple Rome	Ms. Fay R. TRACHTENBERG
07	Director of Admissions	Ms. Karin W. MORMANDO
101	VP & Secretary of Board of Trustees	Ms. Anne K. NADOL
19	Executive Director Public Safety	Mr. Charles LEONE

Thaddeus Stevens College of Technology (G)

750 E King Street, Lancaster PA 17602-3198

County: Lancaster FICE Identification: 007912

Unit ID: 216296

Telephone: (717) 299-7731 Carnegie Class: Assoc/HVT-High Trad

FAX Number: (717) 299-7748 Calendar System: Semester

URL: www.stevenscollege.edu

Established: 1905 Annual Undergrad Tuition & Fees (In-State): $8,030

Enrollment: 1,142 Coed

Affiliation or Control: State IRS Status: 501(c)3

Highest Offering: Associate Degree

Accreditation: M

01	President	Dr. William E. GRISCOM
05	Interim VP Academic Affairs	Dr. Timothy BIANCHI
10	Vice President Finance and Admin	Mrs. Betty TOMPOS
32	Director of Student Services	Dr. Christopher METZLER
84	Dean of Enrollment Svcs/Admissions	Mr. Michael DEGROFT
08	Learning Resources Center Director	Ms. Jennifer LANDIS
108	Director Assessment/Accountability	Ms. Cheryl LUTZ
15	Human Resource Specialist	Ms. Heather BURKY
26	Director of Marketing	Ms. Ann VALUCH
29	Alumni Foundation Exec Director	Mr. Alex MUNRO
37	Director Financial Aid/Registrar	Ms. Melissa WISNIEWSKI
41	Dir Student Srvs/Athletic Director	Dr. Christopher METZLER
30	Director of Development	Mr. Allen TATE
36	Director of Career Services	Ms. Laurie GROVE
38	Coordinator of Student Counseling	Ms. Debra SCHUCH
39	Director Residence Life/Registrar	Mr. Jason KUNTZ
18	Facilities Maintenance Manager	Mr. Darryl NUNN, JR.

† Qualified individuals are eligible for full scholarships based on family/financial status.

Thiel College (H)

75 College Avenue, Greenville PA 16125-2181

County: Mercer FICE Identification: 003376

Unit ID: 216357

Telephone: (724) 589-2000 Carnegie Class: Bac-Diverse

FAX Number: (724) 589-2850 Calendar System: Semester

URL: www.thiel.edu

Established: 1866 Annual Undergrad Tuition & Fees: $31,700

Enrollment: 766 Coed

Affiliation or Control: Evangelical Lutheran Church In America

IRS Status: 501(c)3

Highest Offering: Master's

Accreditation: M, @SP

01 President ....Dr. Susan TRAVERSO
05 VP Academic Affairs/Dean of College .... Dr. Elizabeth FROMBGEN
30 Vice Pres for College Advancement .... Ms. Roberta LEONARD
10 Senior VP Finance/Management .... Mr. Robert SCHMOLL
13 Director IT Services ....Mr. Homer BLOOM
04 Executive Asst to President .... Mrs. Amy TACZANOWSKY
32 VP of Student Life .... Mr. Michael MCKINNEY
84 VP Enrollment Management ....Mrs. Ashley ZULLO
20 Assoc Academic Dean .... Dr. Greg BUTCHER
26 Exec Dir Communications/Marketing ....Mr. Richard ORR
41 Director of Athletics .... Ms. Amy SCHAFER
44 Dir of Special & Planned Giving ....Mr. Mario MARINI
29 Director of Alumni Relations .... Mr. David HUMMEL
18 Director of Facilities ....Mr. Andrew M. HOUPT
08 Director Library ....Mr. Allen MORRILL
15 Director Human Resources .... Mrs. Jennifer CLARK
36 Director of Career Development .... Ms. Clarissa S. ARBUCKLE
19 Chief of Police/Dir Public Safety ....Mr. Dennis BISH
06 Registrar ....Ms. Denise UREY
42 Campus Pastor ....Rev. Brian T. RIDDLE
07 Director of Admissions ....Mrs. Sonya L. LAPIKAS
37 Exec Director Financial Aid ....Ms. Cynthia H. FARRELL
23 Director Student Health Services ....Vacant
28 Assoc Dean for Diversity .... Mr. Anthony E. JONES
38 Director Counseling Center .... Ms. Melanie R. BROADWATER

Thomas Jefferson University (A)

925 Chestnut Street, Suite #110, Philadelphia PA 19107
County: Philadelphia FICE Identification: 012393
Unit ID: 216366
Telephone: (215) 955-6000 Carnegie Class: DU-Higher
FAX Number: (215) 955-1122 Calendar System: Quarter
URL: www.jefferson.edu
Established: 1824 Annual Undergrad Tuition & Fees: $40,651
Enrollment: 4,028 Coed
Affiliation or Control: Independent Non-Profit IRS Status: 501(c)3
Highest Offering: Doctorate
Accreditation: M, ACBSP, ANEST, ARCPA, ART, CAATE, CAMPEP, CYTO, DENT, DMS, EMT, MED, MFCD, MIDWF, MT, NMT, NURSE, OT, OTA, PAST, PERF, PH, PHAR, PTA, RAD, RADDOS, RADMAG, RTT

01 President/CEO Jefferson Health .... Dr. Stephen K. KLASKO
11 EVP & Chief Operating Officer .... Ms. Kathleen GALLAGHER
100 EVP/Chief of Staff ....Mr. John EKARIUS
05 VC & Provost/EVP Academic Affairs .... Dr. Mark L. TYKOCINSKI
26 EVP Univ Marketing/Relations ....Mr. Charles LEWIS
10 Exec VP/Chief Financial Officer ....Mr. Peter L. DEANGELIS, JR.
111 EVP Institutional Advancement ....Dr. Elizabeth DALE
43 EVP & Chief Legal Counsel .... Ms. Cristina G. CAVALIERI
46 Assoc Provost Clinical Research ....Dr. David WHELLAN
18 Sr Vice Pres for Facilities Mgmt ....Mr. Clayton MITCHELL
15 EVP/Chief Human Resources Ofcr ....Mr. Jeffrey STEVENS
28 SVP/Chief Diversity/Inclusion Ofcr .... Mr. Joseph HILL
58 Dean Jeff College of Life Sciences .... Dr. Gerald GRUNWALD
63 Dean Sidney Kimmel Medical College .. Dr. Mark L. TYKOCINSKI
66 Dean Jeff Col of Nursing .... Dr. Marie MARINO
67 Dean Jefferson College of Pharmacy ....Dr. Rebecca FINLEY
76 Dean Jeff Col Health Professions .... Dr. Michael DRYER
69 Dean Jefferson Sch of Pop Health .... Dr. David NASH
32 Dean of Student & Admissions SKMC ....Dr. Clara A. CALLAHAN
07 Director of Admissions ....Ms. Erin FINN
06 University Registrar .... Mr. Kris PELUSZAK
29 Exec Director of Alumni Assoc SKMC .... Ms. Cristina GESO
08 University Librarian ....Mr. Anthony FRISBY
23 Medical Director Univ Health Svcs .... Dr. Ellen M. O'CONNOR
24 Director Medical Media Services ....Mr. Pejman MAKARECHI
35 Assoc VP Student Affairs ....Ms. Jennifer FOGERTY
39 Manager Housing/Residence Life ....Ms. Laurie YUNKE
37 Univ Director Student Financial Aid ....Ms. Susan MCFADDEN
40 Director Bookstore .... Mr. Travis HARLEY
13 Chief Information Officer ....Mr. Nassar NIZAMI
19 Director of Security .... Mr. Joseph BYHAM
85 Dir International Exchange Services ....Ms. Janice M. BOGEN
07 Dir Admission/Recruitment/Grad Stds .... Mr. Marc STEARNS
22 Assoc Dean Diversity/Minority Affs .... Dr. Bernard LOPEZ
96 Director of Purchasing ....Mr. Robert C. BURKHOLDER
35 Associate Provost Student Affairs ....Dr. Charles A. POHL
04 Executive Associate to President ....Ms. Grace L. HARDESKI
09 Interim Dir of Inst Research ....Dr. Raelynn COOTER
101 Secretary of the Institution/Board ....Ms. Michele R. DOUGHERTY
102 Dir Foundation/Corporate Relations .... Ms. Molly GERBER
103 Dir Workforce/Career Development ....Ms. Jennifer M. GRONSKY
105 Director Web Services ....Ms. Chris MCNAMEE-SMITH
25 Chief Contracts/Grants Admin .... Mr. Timothy SHAILEY
36 Director Student Placement .... Ms. Jennifer GRONSKY
38 Director Student Counseling ....Dr. Deanna NOBLEZA
44 Director Annual or Planned Giving .... Ms. Lisa REPKO
45 Chief Institutional Planning ....Vacant
84 Director Enrollment Management ....Ms. Erin M. FINN
86 Director Government Relations ....Mr. Hugh J. LAVERY
90 Director Academic Computing .... Mr. Michael DEVENNEY
104 Director Study Abroad .... Ms. Madeleine WILCOX
106 Dean Online Education/E-learning .... Dr. Anthony FRISBY
41 Athletic Director .... Mr. Thomas SHIRLEY
50 Dean of Business Administration ....Dr. Philip RUSSEL
53 Dean School of Education .... Dr. Matt D. BAKER
54 Dean School of Engineering ....Dr. Ron KANDER
79 Dean Col of Humanities and Science ....Dr. Barbara KIMMELMAN
48 Dean Architecture/Built Environment .... Dr. Barbara KLINKHAMMER

Triangle Tech (B)

191 Performance Road, Sunbury PA 17801
Telephone: (570) 988-0700 Identification: 770586
Accreditation: ACCSC

Triangle Tech, Bethlehem (C)

3184 Airport Road, Bethlehem PA 18017
Telephone: (610) 266-2910 Identification: 770587
Accreditation: ACCSC

Triangle Tech, Dubois (D)

225 Tannery Row Rd, Falls Creek PA 15840
County: Clearfield FICE Identification: 021744
Unit ID: 216454
Telephone: (814) 371-2090 Carnegie Class: Assoc/HVT-High Trad
FAX Number: (814) 371-9227 Calendar System: Semester
URL: www.triangle-tech.edu
Established: 1982 Annual Undergrad Tuition & Fees: $17,294
Enrollment: 143 Coed
Affiliation or Control: Proprietary IRS Status: Proprietary
Highest Offering: Associate Degree
Accreditation: ACCSC

01 Director ....Mr. Steve CURLL
03 Assistant Director ....Mr. Brad GEER
05 Academic Affairs Advisor .... Mrs. Joan HOCKMAN
07 Admiss/Recruiting/Training Coord ....Mrs. Joy BURKE
36 Career Advisor ....Ms. Erica BUZARD
37 Financial Aid Administrator ....Ms. Michelle L. JASHINSKI

Triangle Tech, Erie (E)

2000 Liberty Street, Erie PA 16502-2594
County: Erie FICE Identification: 020902
Unit ID: 216427
Telephone: (814) 453-6016 Carnegie Class: Spec 2-yr-Tech
FAX Number: (814) 454-2818 Calendar System: Semester
URL: www.triangle-tech.edu
Established: 1976 Annual Undergrad Tuition & Fees: $17,056
Enrollment: 61 Coed
Affiliation or Control: Proprietary IRS Status: Proprietary
Highest Offering: Associate Degree
Accreditation: ACCSC

00 CEO .... Mr. James R. AGRAS
01 Campus Director ....Mrs. Deborah HEPBURN
07 Executive Director of Admissions ....Mrs. Terry KUCIC

Triangle Tech, Greensburg (F)

222 E Pittsburgh Street, Suite A,
Greensburg PA 15601-3304
County: Westmoreland FICE Identification: 021290
Unit ID: 216445
Telephone: (724) 832-1050 Carnegie Class: Spec 2-yr-Tech
FAX Number: (724) 834-0325 Calendar System: Semester
URL: www.triangle-tech.edu
Established: 1944 Annual Undergrad Tuition & Fees: $17,252
Enrollment: 121 Coed
Affiliation or Control: Proprietary IRS Status: Proprietary
Highest Offering: Associate Degree
Accreditation: ACCSC

00 Chairman/CEO .... James R. AGRAS
01 President ....Timothy J. MCMAHON
05 Exec Dir of Compliance & Education .... Deborah G. HEPBURN
12 Director of Branch Campus/CEO .... John GOLOFSKI

Triangle Tech, Pittsburgh (G)

1940 Perrysville Avenue, Pittsburgh PA 15214-3897
County: Allegheny FICE Identification: 007839
Unit ID: 216436
Telephone: (412) 359-1000 Carnegie Class: Assoc/HVT-Mix Trad/Non
FAX Number: (412) 359-1012 Calendar System: Semester
URL: www.triangle-tech.edu
Established: 1944 Annual Undergrad Tuition & Fees: $17,288
Enrollment: 144 Coed
Affiliation or Control: Proprietary IRS Status: Proprietary
Highest Offering: Associate Degree
Accreditation: ACCSC

00 Chairman/CEO .... James R. AGRAS
01 President ....Timothy J. MCMAHON
03 Executive Vice President ....Rudy J. AGRAS
15 Vice President of Human Resources .... Sofia A. JANIS
05 Exec Dir of Compliance & Education .... Deborah G. HEPBURN
07 Exec Director of Admissions .... Terry KUCIC
21 Controller .... Sharon GRASWICK
32 Dir School Oper & Student Affairs ....Stephanie CRAIG
12 School Director .... John KIMPAN

Trinity Episcopal School for Ministry (H)

311 11th Street, Ambridge PA 15003-2397
County: Beaver FICE Identification: 022993
Unit ID: 216463
Telephone: (724) 266-3838 Carnegie Class: Spec-4-yr-Faith
FAX Number: (724) 266-4617 Calendar System: Semester
URL: www.tsm.edu
Established: 1976 Annual Graduate Tuition & Fees: N/A
Enrollment: 180 Coed
Affiliation or Control: Protestant Episcopal IRS Status: 501(c)3
Highest Offering: Doctorate; No Undergraduates
Accreditation: THEOL

01 Dean/President .... Rev. Henry L. THOMPSON
05 Academic Dean .... Dr. Erika MOORE
111 Dean of Advancement ....Vacant
32 Dean of Students/Director of Alumni .... Mr. Geoffrey MACKEY
06 Registrar/Financial Aid Director .... Ms. Stacey WILLIARD
07 Director of Admissions/Recruitment ....Ms. Janessa FISK
11 Dean of Administration ....Mrs. Karen GETZ
30 Director of Development ....Mr. Jerry MOTE
04 Administrative Asst to President .... Ms. Lee-Anna UPPERMAN
26 Director of Communications .... Ms. Mary Lou HARJU
15 Human Resources Administrator ....Ms. Elaine LUCCI
13 Information Technology Manager ....Mr. Steve SIMS

United Lutheran Seminary (I)

61 Seminary Ridge, Gettysburg PA 17325-1795
County: Adams FICE Identification: 003291
Unit ID: 213631
Telephone: (717) 338-3000 Carnegie Class: Spec-4-yr-Faith
FAX Number: N/A Calendar System: 4/1/4
URL: www.unitedlutheranseminary.edu
Established: 1826 Annual Graduate Tuition & Fees: N/A
Enrollment: 285 Coed
Affiliation or Control: Evangelical Lutheran Church In America
IRS Status: 501(c)3
Highest Offering: Doctorate; No Undergraduates
Accreditation: M, THEOL

01 Interim President ....Dr. Richard GREEN
111 Vice Pres Advancement .... Ms. Angela ZIMMANN
32 VP Student Svcs/Enrollment ....Vacant
05 Dean of the Seminary ....Dr. J. Jayakiran SEBASTIAN
10 Chief Financial Officer/CFO ....Vacant
26 Chief Communications Officer ....Vacant
08 Library Director and Archivist ....Mr. Evan E. BOYD
37 Director of Financial Aid .... Ms. Kimberley CLARK
06 Registrar ....Ms. Julie RITTER
13 Director of Info Systems/Ed Tech ....Mr. Donald L. REDMAN
15 Human Resources Director ....Mr. Edwell HENRY, II

The University of the Arts (J)

320 S Broad Street, Philadelphia PA 19102-4944
County: Philadelphia FICE Identification: 003350
Unit ID: 215105
Telephone: (215) 717-6030 Carnegie Class: Spec-4-yr-Arts
FAX Number: (215) 717-6045 Calendar System: Semester
URL: www.uarts.edu
Established: 1876 Annual Undergrad Tuition & Fees: $44,930
Enrollment: 1,860 Coed
Affiliation or Control: Independent Non-Profit IRS Status: 501(c)3
Highest Offering: Master's
Accreditation: M, ART, MUS

01 President .... Mr. David YAGER
05 VP for Academic Affairs .... Ms. Carol GRANEY
100 Assistant to the President ....Ms. Susannah AYSCUE
10 Vice Pres Finance/Administration .... Mr. Stephen LIGHTCAP
13 Vice Pres Technology & Info Svcs ....Vacant
32 VP Enroll Mgmt & Student Affairs .... Mr. Rick LONGO
111 Vice Pres Advancement/Devel .... Mr. Andrew PACK
06 Registrar .... Mr. Jeffrey KISLER
04 Senior Administrative Assistant .... Ms. Carley JOHNSON
28 Title IX Coord & Diversity Admin ....Ms. Lexi MORRISON
07 AVP of Admissions ....Ms. Heeseung LEE
15 AVP for Human Resources ....Ms. Christine SCHAEFFER
26 AVP Enrollment Marketing .... Ms. Maria RAHA
37 AVP for Student Financial Aid .... Ms. Mariann CARDONICK
09 Dir of Inst Rsrch & Effectiveness ....Dr. Deborah DUFFY

University of Pennsylvania (K)

1 College Hall, Room 100, Philadelphia PA 19104-6830
County: Philadelphia FICE Identification: 003378
Unit ID: 215062
Telephone: (215) 898-5000 Carnegie Class: DU-Highest
FAX Number: (215) 898-5756 Calendar System: Semester
URL: www.upenn.edu
Established: 1740 Annual Undergrad Tuition & Fees: $55,584
Enrollment: 25,367 Coed
Affiliation or Control: Independent Non-Profit IRS Status: 501(c)3
Highest Offering: Doctorate
Accreditation: M, ANEST, CAMPEP, CEA, CLPSY, DENT, IPSY, LAW, LSAR, MED, MIDWF, NURSE, PAST, PCSAS, PH, PLNG, SW, #VET

01 President .... Dr. Amy GUTMANN
03 Executive Vice President .... Mr. Craig CARNAROLI
05 Provost ....Dr. Wendell E. PRITCHETT
06 Registrar .... Ms. Margaret KIP
07 Dean of Admissions .... Mr. Eric J. FURDA
32 Vice Provost University Life .... Dr. Valarie S. MCCOULLUM
10 Vice Pres Finance & Treasurer .... Ms. MaryFrances MCCOURT

18 Vice Pres Facil/Real Est Svcs ... Ms. Anne PAPAGEORGE
17 CEO Univ of PA Health System ... Mr. Kevin B. MAHONEY
08 Vice Provost/Dir of Libraries ... Ms. Constantia CONSTANTINOU
13 Vice Pres Info Technology/CIO ... Mr. Thomas H. MURPHY
100 Vice Pres & Chief of Staff ... Mr. Gregory S. ROST
09 Sr VP Inst Rsrch/Chf Diversity Ofc ... Ms. Joann MITCHELL
30 Vice Pres Dev/Alumni Relations ... Mr. John H. ZELLER
15 Vice Pres Human Resources ... Dr. John J. HEUER
86 Vice Pres Govt & Cmty Relations ... Mr. Jeffrey COOPER
19 Vice President Public Safety ... Ms. Maureen RUSH
26 Vice Pres for Univ Communications ... Mr. Stephen J. MACCARTHY
21 Vice Pres Business Services ... Ms. Marie D. WITT
114 Vice Pres Budget Mgmt Analysis ... Mr. Trevor C. LEWIS
43 Senior Vice Pres/General Counsel ... Ms. Wendy S. WHITE
101 VP & University Secretary ... Ms. Leslie L. KRUHLY
20 Vice Provost for Education ... Dr. Beth A. WINKELSTEIN
20 Vice Provost Faculty Affairs ... Dr. Anita L. ALLEN
29 Asst Vice Pres Alumni Relations ... Mr. Fredrick H. WAMPLER
46 Vice Provost for Research ... Dr. Dawn A. BONNELL
88 Assoc Vice Pres Rsrch Svcs ... Ms. Elizabeth D. PELOSO
116 Assoc VP Audit Compl & Privacy ... Mr. Gregory J. PELLICANO
31 Assoc VP/Dir Ctr Cmty Partnerships ... Dr. Ira HARKAVY
28 Assoc Vice Prov Equity & Access ... Rev. William GIPSON
21 Comptroller ... Mr. John F. HORN
63 Exec Vice Pres/Dean Sch of Medicine ... Dr. J. L. JAMESON
49 Dean School Arts & Sciences ... Dr. Steven J. FLUHARTY
54 Dean School of Engr/Applied Science ... Dr. Vijay KUMAR
66 Dean School of Nursing ... Dr. Antonia VILLARRUEL
50 Dean Wharton School ... Dr. Geoffrey GARRETT
60 Dean Annenberg Sch Communications ... Dr. John L. JACKSON, JR.
52 Dean School of Dental Medicine ... Dr. Mark S. WOLFF
48 Dean School of Design ... Dr. Frederick STEINER
53 Dean Graduate School Education ... Dr. Pam GROSSMAN
61 Dean School of Law ... Dr. Theodore W. RUGER
70 Dean School Social Policy/Practice ... Dr. Sara BACHMAN
74 Dean School of Veterinary Medicine ... Dr. Joan C. HENDRICKS
107 Vice Dean Liberal & Prof Studies ... Ms. Nora E. LEWIS
88 Assoc VP Inst Rsrch/Sr Adv to Pres ... Dr. Stacey J. LOPEZ
85 Dir Intl Student & Scholar Svcs ... Dr. Rodolfo R. ALTAMIRANO
36 Exec Dir of Career Services ... Dr. Barbara HEWITT
37 Dir Student Financial Aid ... Ms. Elaine P. VARAS
35 Assoc Vice Prov for Student Affairs ... Ms. Tamara KING
38 Dir Counseling/Psych Services ... Dr. Gregory EELLS
102 Exec Dir Corp & Found Rels ... Dr. Diana B. ALTEGOER
22 Exec Dir Affirm Action & Equal Op ... Mr. Sam B. STARKS
23 Exec Dir Student Health Services ... Dr. Giang T. NGUYEN
88 Exec Art Dir Annenberg Ctr Per Arts ... Mr. Christopher A. GRUITS
88 Exec Dir Morris Arboretum ... Mr. Paul W. MEYER
88 Dir Institute of Contemporary Art ... Ms. Amy SADAO
88 Dir Museum of Archlgy/Anthrplgy ... Mr. Julian F. SIGGERS
41 Dir Intercollegiate Athletics ... Ms. M. Grace CALHOUN
14 IT Director ... Mr. James F. JOHNSON
91 IT Exec Dir Admin Info Tech ... Ms. Jeanne F. CURTIS
39 Exec Dir Col Houses & Acad Svcs ... Mr. Martin REDMAN
42 University Chaplain ... Rev. Charles L. HOWARD
104 Director Study Abroad ... Mr. Nigel COSSAR
106 Exec Director Online Learning Init ... Dr. Rebecca STEIN
04 Executive Asst to President ... Ms. Jodi SARKISIAN
105 Dir Web Strategy & Visual Comm ... Mr. Steven MINICOLA
44 Exec Dir Gift Plng/Assoc Gen Couns ... Ms. Marcie L. MERZ
96 Director of Purchasing ... Mr. Mark MILLS

University of Phoenix Philadelphia Campus (A)

30 South 17th Street, Philadelphia PA 19103-4001
Telephone: (267) 234-2000 Identification: 770933
Accreditation: &NH, ACBSP

† No longer accepting campus-based students.

University of Pittsburgh (B)

4200 Fifth Avenue, Pittsburgh PA 15260-3583
County: Allegheny FICE Identification: 003379
Unit ID: 215293
Telephone: (412) 624-4141 Carnegie Class: DU-Highest
FAX Number: N/A Calendar System: Semester
URL: www.pitt.edu
Established: 1787 Annual Undergrad Tuition & Fees (In-State): $19,080
Enrollment: 28,642 Coed
Affiliation or Control: State Related IRS Status: 501(c)3
Highest Offering: Doctorate
Accreditation: M, ANEST, ARCPA, AUD, CAATE, CACREP, CAHIIM, CEA, CLPSY, DENT, DH, DIETC, DIETD, EMT, HSA, HT, IPSY, LAW, LIB, MED, @MIDWF, NURSE, OPE, OT, PCSAS, PH, PHAR, PTA, SP, SPAA, SW, THEA

01 Chancellor and Chief Exec Officer ... Dr. Patrick GALLAGHER
05 Sr Vice Chancellor & Provost ... Dr. Ann E. CUDD
63 Sr VC Health Sci/Dean Sch of Med ... Dr. Arthur S. LEVINE
101 Sr VC Engagement/Secy BOT ... Dr. Kathy W. HUMPHREY
88 Dep Sec & Sr Assoc Gen Counsel ... Ms. Cynthia C. MOORE
10 Senior Vice Chancellor and CFO ... Mr. Hari SASTRY
21 Controller ... Mr. Thurman D. WINGROVE
88 Treasurer ... Mr. Paul LAWRENCE
115 Chief Investment Officer ... Mr. Gregory G. SCHULER
46 Sr Vice Chancellor for Research ... Dr. Rob A. RUTENBAR
111 VC Advancement/Alumni Relations ... Ms. Kristin DAVITT
43 Sr Vice Chanc & Chief Legal Officer ... Ms. Geovette E. WASHINGTON
26 Vice Chanc for Communications ... Ms. Ellen L. MORAN
100 Chief of Staff ... Mr. Kevin WASHO
11 Sr VC Business and Operations ... Mr. Gregory A. SCOTT
86 Vice Chanc Community & Govt Rels ... Mr. Paul A. SUPOWITZ
15 Vice Chanc Human Resources ... Ms. Cheryl L. JOHNSON
20 Vice Provost Undergraduate Studies ... Dr. Joseph J. MCCARTHY
58 Vice Provost Graduate Studies ... Dr. Nathan N. URBAN
45 Executive Vice Provost ... Dr. David N. DEJONG
88 Vice Prov Fac Affairs Dev/Diversity ... Ms. Laurie J. KIRSCH
88 Vice Provost Data & Information ... Mr. Stephen R. WISNIEWSKI
21 VC Business and Real Estate ... Mr. Eli SHORAK
102 VC Corporate & Foundation Relations ... Mr. Thomas P. CRAWFORD
109 Assoc VC Business & Aux Services ... Mr. James V. EARLE
88 Director Sustainability ... Ms. Aurora SHARRARD
11 Director Administration ... Ms. Laura W. ZULLO
19 Assoc VC Public Safety & Emer Mgmt ... Mr. Ted P. FRITZ
18 Assoc VC Facilities Mgmt ... Mr. Scott C. BERNOTAS
16 Asst VC Human Resources ... Mr. Derek SMITH
27 Dir Media Rel & Univ Spokesperson ... Mr. Joseph T. MIKSCH
06 University Registrar ... Ms. Patti J. MATHAY
41 Director of Athletics ... Ms. Heather R. LYKE
07 Chief Enrollment Officer ... Mr. Marc L. HARDING
32 Vice Prov & Dean of Students ... Mr. Kenyon R. BONNER
49 Dean Deitrich Sch Arts & Sci/CGS ... Dr. Kathleen M. BLEE
92 Acting Dean Honors College ... Dr. Audrey J. MURRELL
50 Dean Jos M Katz Gr Sch Bus ... Dr. Arjang A. ASSAD
53 Dean School of Education ... Dr. Valerie KINLOCH
54 Dean Swanson School of Engineering ... Mr. James R. MARTIN, II
61 Dean School of Law ... Ms. Amy J. WILDERMUTH
80 Dean Grad Sch Public/Intl Affs ... Dr. John T. KEELER
70 Dean School of Social Work ... Ms. Elizabeth M. FARMER
62 Dean School of Computing and Inform ... Dr. Paul R. COHEN
52 Dean School of Dental Medicine ... Dr. Bernard J. COSTELLO
66 Dean School of Nursing ... Dr. Jacqueline DUNBAR-JACOB
67 Dean School of Pharmacy ... Dr. Patricia D. KROBOTH
69 Dean Grad School Public Health ... Dr. Donald S. BURKE
76 Dean Sch of Health & Rehabilitation ... Dr. Anthony DELITTO
12 President Johnstown Campus ... Dr. Jem M. SPECTAR
12 President Greensburg Campus ... Dr. Sharon P. SMITH
12 Interim Pres Bradford & Titusville ... Dr. Lawrence F. FEICK
104 Vice Provost Global Affairs ... Dr. Ariel ARMONY
40 Director University Stores ... Ms. Monica D. RATTIGAN
24 Dir Univ Ctr for Teach & Learning ... Ms. Cynthia GOLDEN
13 Chief Info Officer and Dir CSSD ... Vacant
09 Director Institutional Research ... Mr. Robert D. GOGA
116 Director Internal Audit ... Mr. John P. ELLIOTT
36 Assoc Dean & Dir Career Dev ... Ms. Cheryl S. FINLAY
39 Assoc Dean and Dir Residence Life ... Mr. Steven L. ANDERSON
35 Assoc Dean & Dir Student Life ... Ms. Linda WILLIAMS-MOORE
08 Dir Univ Library System ... Ms. Kornelia TANCHEVA
19 Chief University Police ... Mr. James K. LOFTUS
23 Director Student Health Svcs ... Ms. Marian S. VANEK
96 Manager Purchasing Services ... Mr. Thomas E. YOUNGS, JR.
112 Charitable Rel Mgr Planned Giving ... Vacant
04 Exec Asst to the Chancellor ... Ms. Mary Jo RACE
106 Dir Online Programs ... Ms. Lorna R. KEARNS
37 Director Financial Aid ... Dr. Randall MCCREADY
38 Interim Director Counseling Center ... Ms. Marian S. VANEK
28 Vice Chanc Diversity & Inclusion ... Ms. Pamela W. CONNELLY
88 Director University Press ... Mr. Peter KRACHT
88 Int Dir Univ Ctr Soc & Urban Res ... Mr. Scott R. BEACH
88 Dir Ctr for Philosophy of Science ... Mr. Edouard MACHERY
88 Dir Learning Research & Dev Center ... Mr. Charles A. PERFETTI

University of Pittsburgh at Bradford (C)

300 Campus Drive, Bradford PA 16701-2812
Telephone: (814) 362-7500 FICE Identification: 003380
Accreditation: &M, ADNUR, #CAATE, NUR

† Regional accreditation is carried under the parent institution in Pittsburgh, PA.

University of Pittsburgh at Greensburg (D)

150 Finoli Drive, Greensburg PA 15601-5898
Telephone: (724) 837-7040 FICE Identification: 003381
Accreditation: &M

† Regional accreditation is carried under the parent institution in Pittsburgh, PA.

University of Pittsburgh at Johnstown (E)

450 Schoolhouse Road, Johnstown PA 15904-2990
Telephone: (814) 269-7000 FICE Identification: 003382
Accreditation: &M, COARC

† Regional accreditation is carried under the parent institution in Pittsburgh, PA.

University of Pittsburgh at Titusville (F)

504 E Main, Titusville PA 16354-2097
Telephone: (814) 827-4400 FICE Identification: 003383
Accreditation: &M, ADNUR, #PTAA

† Regional accreditation is carried under the parent institution in Pittsburgh, PA.

University of the Sciences in Philadelphia (G)

600 S 43rd Street, Philadelphia PA 19104-4495
County: Philadelphia FICE Identification: 003353
Unit ID: 215132
Telephone: (215) 596-8800 Carnegie Class: Spec-4-yr-Other Health
FAX Number: (215) 895-1100 Calendar System: Semester
URL: www.usciences.edu
Established: 1821 Annual Undergrad Tuition & Fees: $25,000
Enrollment: 2,359 Coed
Affiliation or Control: Independent Non-Profit IRS Status: 501(c)3
Highest Offering: Doctorate
Accreditation: M, ACBSP, OT, PHAR, PTA

01 President ... Dr. Paul KATZ
05 Provost ... Dr. Peter J. MILLER
10 Chief Financial/Operating Officer ... Dr. Valerie WEIL
102 Dir of Corporate & Foundation Rels ... Ms. Rebecca POWERS
13 Associate VP & CIO ... Dr. Mark NESTOR
14 Exec Dir Information Technology ... Mr. John MASCIANTONIO
37 Director of Financial Aid ... Ms. Pamela RAMANATHAN
06 Registrar ... Ms. Therese ANDERSON
29 Director of Alumni Relations ... Mr. Casey RYAN
32 Dean of Students ... Mr. Ross RADISH
49 Dean Misher College Arts & Sci ... Dr. Suzanne K. MURPHY
76 Dean Samson College of Health Sci ... Dr. Michelle E. COHEN
15 Director Human Resources ... Dr. Ruth ROBERTS
19 Director Public Safety/Security ... Mr. Michael STITLEY
41 Athletic Director ... Dr. Mark CASERIO
21 Controller/Asst VP Finance ... Ms. Brigid K. ISACKMAN
96 Director Purchasing/Auxiliary Svcs ... Mr. Vincent HORN
20 Associate Provost Academic Affairs ... Dr. John CONNORS
04 Executive Asst to President ... Ms. Beth PILIPZECK
104 Director Study Abroad ... Mr. James YARRISH
106 Exec Director Academic Technology ... Dr. Rodney B. MURRAY
07 Executive Director of Admissions ... Mr. Augustine DISTEFANO
30 Senior Director of Development ... Ms. Kim BARKHAMER

The University of Scranton (H)

800 Linden St, Scranton PA 18510-4622
County: Lackawanna FICE Identification: 003384
Unit ID: 215929
Telephone: (570) 941-7400 Carnegie Class: Masters/L
FAX Number: (570) 941-6369 Calendar System: Semester
URL: www.scranton.edu
Established: 1888 Annual Undergrad Tuition & Fees: $44,532
Enrollment: 5,373 Coed
Affiliation or Control: Roman Catholic IRS Status: 501(c)3
Highest Offering: Doctorate
Accreditation: M, ANEST, CACREP, CSHSE, EXSC, HSA, NURSE, OT, PTA

01 President ... Rev. Scott R. PILARZ, SJ
05 Sr VP Academic Affairs & Provost ... Dr. Jeff GINGERICH
10 Sr VP Finance & Administration ... Mr. Edward J. STEINMETZ, JR.
111 VP for University Advancement ... Mr. Thomas MACKINNON
84 VP Enroll Mgmt/External Affairs ... Mr. Gerald C. ZABOSKI
114 Asst VP Budget/Financial Planning ... Mr. Patrick R. DONOHUE
13 CIO ... Ms. Susan G. BOWEN
15 Assoc Vice Pres Human Resources ... Ms. Patricia L. TETREAULT
42 Exec Dir of the Jesuit Center ... Rev. Patrick ROGERS, SJ
43 General Counsel ... Mr. Robert B. FARRELL
100 Chief of Staff ... Mr. Francis LOVECCHIO
49 Dean Arts & Sciences ... Dr. Brian P. CONNIFF
50 Int Dean Kania School Management ... Dr. Murli RAJAN
107 Dean Panuska Col of Prof Studies ... Dr. Debra A. PELLEGRINO
08 Dean of the Library/Info Fluency ... Mr. Charles E. KRATZ, JR.
51 Asst Dir for OL/Off Campus-Programs ... Mrs. Lisa M. LOBASSO
32 Vice President for Student Life ... Dr. Robert W. DAVIS, JR.
20 Assoc Provost Academic Affairs ... Dr. Sunil AHUJA
07 Assoc VP Admiss & Undergrad Enroll ... Mr. Joseph M. ROBACK
07 Asst VP Admissions & Enrollment ... Ms. Mary Kay ASTON
18 Assoc VP Facilities Operations ... Mr. James L. CAFFREY
29 Exec Dir Alumni/Donor Engagement ... Ms. Ashley ALT
06 Registrar ... Ms. Julie FERGUSON
37 Director of Financial Aid ... Mr. William R. BURKE
36 Director of Career Services ... Ms. Chris WHITNEY
28 Director of Equity/Diversity Office ... Ms. Christine BLACK
38 Director of Counseling Center ... Mr. Thomas P. SMITH
96 Director of Purchasing ... Mr. Gary S. ZAMPANO
04 Admin Assistant to the President ... Ms. Maribeth A. SMITH
101 Secretary of the Institution/Board ... Mrs. Tara M. SEELY
104 Director Study Abroad ... Rev. John SIVALON
108 Director Institutional Assessment ... Dr. Mary Jane K. DIMATTIO
19 Director Security/Safety ... Mr. Donald J. BERGMANN
41 Athletic Director ... Mr. David L. MARTIN

University of Valley Forge (I)

1401 Charlestown Road, Phoenixville PA 19460-2373
County: Chester FICE Identification: 003306
Unit ID: 216542
Telephone: (610) 935-0450 Carnegie Class: Bac-Diverse
FAX Number: (610) 935-9353 Calendar System: Semester
URL: www.valleyforge.edu
Established: 1939 Annual Undergrad Tuition & Fees: $21,341
Enrollment: 764 Coed
Affiliation or Control: Assemblies Of God Church IRS Status: 501(c)3
Highest Offering: Master's
Accreditation: #M, SW

01 President ... Rev. David S. KIM
32 VP of Student Life ... Rev. Jennifer D. GALE
05 VP of Academic Affairs ... Dr. Jerome N. DOUGLAS
09 VP of Institutional Effectiveness ... Dr. Todd G. GUEVIN
43 University Counsel ... Rev. Shahan G. TEBERIAN
10 VP of Finance ... Mr. Frank VIOLA, JR.
13 Director of Information Technology ... Mr. Paul VAN RIJN

21 Controller Mr. Valen P. CIANCI
18 Director of Facilities Operations Vacant
07 Director of Admissions Ms. Claire M. EILER
30 Director of Development Mrs. Tyra R. TEBERIAN
41 Director of Athletics Ms. Gretchen L. LEVAN
37 Director of Financial Aid Vacant
19 Director of Security Mr. John YOUNT
15 Director Human Resources Mrs. Veronica A. BIRD
96 Director of Purchasing Vacant
08 Librarian/Dir Storms Research Ctr Ms. Laura V. O'REILLY
121 Director of Student Success Mrs. Sarah PEPPEL
11 Director of Operations Mrs. Julia G. PATTON
12 Director of Virginia Campus Dr. William J. BAKER
26 Director of Marketing Mr. Dominick GARCIA
06 Registrar Mr. Chris J. ADDICKS
23 Director of Health Services Mrs. Lauren BORN
39 Director of Housing Mr. Yung Won S. PARK
04 Administrative Asst to President Mrs. Lauren B. PERDAN

Ursinus College (A)

PO Box 1000, 601 East Main Street,
Collegeville PA 19426-1000

County: Montgomery FICE Identification: 003385
Unit ID: 216524
Telephone: (610) 409-3000 Carnegie Class: Bac-A&S
FAX Number: (610) 489-0627 Calendar System: Semester
URL: www.ursinus.edu
Established: 1869 Annual Undergrad Tuition & Fees: $52,050
Enrollment: 1,507 Coed
Affiliation or Control: Independent Non-Profit IRS Status: 501(c)3
Highest Offering: Baccalaureate
Accreditation: M

01 President Dr. Brock BLOMBERG
05 Vice Pres Academic Affairs/Dean Dr. Mark SCHNEIDER
10 Vice Pres Finance & Administration Ms. Annette PARKER
111 Senior Vice Pres for Advancement Ms. Jill A. MARSTELLER
84 Vice President for Enrollment Ms. Shannon ZOTTOLA
32 VP for College & Comm Engagement Dr. Heather LOBBAN-VIRAVONG
21 Associate Vice President Ms. Mary CORRELL
112 Exec Director of Planned Giving Mr. Mark P. GADSON
08 Special Library Collections Mr. Charles JAMISON
36 Director of Career & Post-Grad Dev Ms. Sharon HANSEN
18 Director of Facilities Mr. Steve GEHRINGER
41 Director of Athletics Mrs. Laura MOLIKEN
26 Chief Communications Officer Mr. Thomas YENCHO
37 Director Student Financial Services Mrs. Ellen CURCIO
06 Registrar Ms. Barbara A. BORIS
29 Director of Alumni Relations Ms. Pamela PANARELLA
15 Director Human Resources Ms. Kelley WILLIAMS
09 Director of Institutional Research Vacant
102 Dir Foundation/Corporate Relations Ms. Ava WILLIS-BARKSDALE
13 Chief Info Technology Officer (CIO) Mr. Gene SPENCER
28 Dir of Institute for Incl & Equity Mr. Terrence WILLIAMS
88 Business Coord Conf & Spec Events Ms. Teri A. LOBO

Valley Forge Military College (B)

1001 Eagle Road, Wayne PA 19087-3695

County: Delaware FICE Identification: 003386
Unit ID: 216551
Telephone: (610) 989-1200 Carnegie Class: Assoc/HT-High Trad
FAX Number: (610) 975-9642 Calendar System: Semester
URL: www.vfmac.edu
Established: 1935 Annual Undergrad Tuition & Fees: $29,975
Enrollment: 265 Coed
Affiliation or Control: Independent Non-Profit IRS Status: 501(c)3
Highest Offering: Associate Degree
Accreditation: M

01 Superintendent/COO Col. Stu HELGESON
05 Dean of College Ms. Maureen MALONE
00 Chairman of the Board Mr. John ENGLISH
10 Chief Financial Officer Mr. Vincent VUONO
30 Vice Pres of Development Mr. Greg BRINN
18 Director of Facilities Mr. George ELSE
23 Director of Health Services Ms. Debbie HAMMER
07 Senior Director College Admissions Ms. Dawn DREESE
08 Director of Library Services Ms. Dana KERRIGAN
13 Director Information Technology Mr. Michael G. BROCK
41 Director of Athletics Mr. Richard CASEY
32 Commandant of Cadets Col. Keneth DETREUX
35 Coordinator of Student Services Mr. Mike PACHELLA
121 Academic Advisor Ms. Marney VANDEMARK
06 Registrar Mr. Dylan HILEMAN
37 Director of Financial Aid Ms. Elizabeth SIERRA
103 Director of Human Resources Ms. Kate SMITH
26 Chief Public Relations/Marketing Ms. Mary HELLER
29 Director Alumni Relations Mr. Tom GOLDBLUM
09 Director of Institutional Research Ms. Deepa RAMAKRISHNAN
108 Director Institutional Assessment Ms. Sukulpa BASU

Vet Tech Institute (C)

125 Seventh Street, Pittsburgh PA 15222-3400

County: Allegheny FICE Identification: 008568
Unit ID: 213914
Telephone: (412) 391-7021 Carnegie Class: Spec 2-yr-Health
FAX Number: (412) 232-4348 Calendar System: Semester
URL: www.vti.edu
Established: 1958 Annual Undergrad Tuition & Fees: $15,020
Enrollment: 343 Coed
Affiliation or Control: Proprietary IRS Status: Proprietary
Highest Offering: Associate Degree
Accreditation: ACCSC

01 Director Mrs. Jackie FLYNN

Villanova University (D)

800 Lancaster Avenue, Villanova PA 19085-1699

County: Delaware FICE Identification: 003388
Unit ID: 216597
Telephone: (610) 519-4500 Carnegie Class: DU-Higher
FAX Number: (610) 519-5000 Calendar System: Semester
URL: www.villanova.edu
Established: 1842 Annual Undergrad Tuition & Fees: $53,308
Enrollment: 10,967 Coed
Affiliation or Control: Roman Catholic IRS Status: 501(c)3
Highest Offering: Doctorate
Accreditation: M, ANEST, CACREP, LAW, NURSE, SPAA

01 President Rev. Peter M. DONOHUE, OSA
43 Vice President & General Counsel Mr. E. Michael ZUBEY, JR.
05 Provost Dr. Patrick G. MAGGITTI
111 Sr Vice Pres University Advancement Mr. Michael O'NEILL
03 Exec Vice President Mr. Kenneth G. VALOSKY
13 Vice Pres/Chief Information Officer Mr. Stephen FUGALE
32 Vice President for Student Life Rev. John P. STACK, OSA
26 Vice Pres University Communication Ms. Ann DIEBOLD
42 Vice Pres for Mission & Ministry Dr. Barbara E. WALL
10 Vice President for Finance Mr. Neil J. HORGAN
20 Vice Provost for Academics Dr. Craig WHEELAND
35 Assoc Vice Pres for Student Life Ms. Kathleen J. BYRNES
15 AVP Human Res/Affirm Action Ofcr Ms. Ellen KRUTZ
109 Assoc Vice Pres for Auxiliary Svcs Mr. Anthony ALFANO
29 Assoc Vice Pres Alumni Relations Mr. George R. KOLB
46 Assoc Vice Provost for Research Dr. Amanda GRANNAS
28 Assoc Vice Prov Diversity/Inclusion Dr. Teresa A. NANCE
84 Dean Enrollment Management Mr. J. Leon WASHINGTON
09 Exec Dir Planning/Inst Research Dr. James F. TRAINER
18 Vice Pres Facilities Management Mr. Robert MORRO
07 Director University Admission Mr. Michael M. GAYNOR
08 Librarian & Dir of Falvey Library Ms. Millicent GASKELL
35 Asst Vice Pres & Dean of Students Mr. Tom DEMARCO
49 Dean Liberal Arts & Sciences Dr. Adele LINDENMEYR
50 Dean Villanova Sch of Business Dr. Joyce RUSSELL
58 Dean Graduate Studies LA&S Dr. Emory WOODARD
61 Dean Widger School of Law Mr. Mark ALEXANDER
66 Dean of Nursing Dr. Donna HAVENS
54 Interim Dean of Engineering Dr. Randy D. WEINSTEIN
88 Dir Ctr Worship/Spirituality Ms. Linda JACZYNSKI
88 Dir Ctr Service/Social Justice Ms. Kate GIANCATARINO
88 Dir Ctr Grad Pastoral Ministry Educ Dr. John P. EDWARDS
107 Dean Col of Professional Studies Dr. Christine PALUS
85 Dir Intl Students & Human Services Mr. Stephen T. MCWILLIAMS
37 Director Financial Assistance Ms. Bonnie Lee BEHM
19 Director of Public Safety Mr. David TEDJESKE
36 Executive Director Career Services Mr. Kevin GRUBB
92 Director of the Honors Program Dr. Thomas W. SMITH
38 Director of Univ Counseling Center Dr. Joan G. WHITNEY
94 Dir Gender & Women's Studies Dr. Shauna M. MACDONALD
39 Director for Housing Services Ms. Marie SCHAUDER
96 Director of Procurement Mr. John R. DURHAM
27 Director of Media Relations Mr. Jonathan GUST
41 Director of Athletics Mr. Mark JACKSON
23 Director Student Health Center Dr. Mary MCGONIGLE
23 Medical Director Student Health Ctr Dr. Brian BULLOCK
06 Registrar Ms. Pamela BRAXTON
88 University Compliance Officer Ms. Leyda L. BENITEZ
100 Executive Assistant to President Ms. Erin BUCKLEY
106 Exec Dir Online Programs Ms. Kristy IRWIN
53 Assoc Vice Prov Teach/Learning Dr. Matthew KERBEL
86 AVP Government Relations Mr. Chris KOVOLSKI

Washington & Jefferson College (E)

60 S Lincoln Street, Washington PA 15301-4801

County: Washington FICE Identification: 003389
Unit ID: 216667
Telephone: (724) 503-1001 Carnegie Class: Bac-A&S
FAX Number: (724) 223-6534 Calendar System: 4/1/4
URL: www.washjeff.edu
Established: 1781 Annual Undergrad Tuition & Fees: $47,964
Enrollment: 1,412 Coed
Affiliation or Control: Independent Non-Profit IRS Status: 501(c)3
Highest Offering: Master's
Accreditation: M

01 President Dr. John KNAPP
05 VP Academic Affairs/Dean of College Dr. Jeffrey FRICK
10 CFO/VP Business/Finance Mr. Jim IRWIN
30 VP Development/Alumni Relations Mr. Michael P. GRZESIAK
84 VP for Enrollment Ms. Nicole FOCARETO
21 Assoc VP for Business & Finance Mr. Thomas SZEJKO
32 VP and Dean of Student Life Ms. Eva CHATTERJEE-SUTTON
111 Dir of Campaigns & Advancement Ops Ms. Lori WEAVER
20 Associate Dean for Academic Affairs Dr. Dana SHILLER
28 Asst Dean Stdnt Life/Dir Diver Pgm Vacant
20 Associate Dean for Academic Affairs Dr. Steven MALINAK
18 Dir of Campus Operations & Planning Mr. Jim MILLER
26 VP Marketing/Communications Ms. Kelly KIMBERLAND
06 Registrar Ms. Leslie MAXIN
29 Assoc VP Alumni Relations & Dev Ms. Michele HUFNAGEL
07 Dean of Admission Mr. Robert ADKINS
37 Director of Financial Aid Ms. Charlene BEDILLION
13 Dir of Information/Technology Svcs Mr. Daniel FAULK
15 Director Human Resources Vacant
19 Director Protection Services Mr. Robert COCCO
36 Director Career Services Ms. Roberta CROSS
40 Bookstore Manager Ms. Cynthia BRICELAND
41 Director of Athletics Mr. Scott MCGUINNESS
08 Director of Library Services Ms. Ronalee CIOCCO
102 Foundation & Corp Relations Officer Ms. Marian CHAMBERS
91 Director for Admin Computing Mr. Michael A. TIMKO
104 Director of Study Abroad Ms. Sara KOCHUBA
108 Dir of Assessment & Inst Research Ms. Lindsey GUINN
121 Director of Academic Advising Mr. Richard BARBER
88 Director Conferences and Events Ms. Maureen VALENTINE
38 Director of Counseling Services Ms. Shelly LEAR
39 Director of Residence Life Mr. Justin SWANK
88 Ethics & Compliance Officer Ms. Angela COLORITO

Waynesburg University (F)

51 W College Street, Waynesburg PA 15370-1222

County: Greene FICE Identification: 003391
Unit ID: 216694
Telephone: (724) 627-8191 Carnegie Class: Masters/M
FAX Number: N/A Calendar System: Semester
URL: www.waynesburg.edu
Established: 1849 Annual Undergrad Tuition & Fees: $24,820
Enrollment: 1,736 Coed
Affiliation or Control: Presbyterian Church (U.S.A.) IRS Status: 501(c)3
Highest Offering: Doctorate
Accreditation: M, #CAATE, CACREP, IACBE, NURSE

00 Chancellor Dr. Timothy R. THYREEN
01 President Mr. Doug LEE
05 Provost Dr. Dana BAER
10 Chief Financial Officer Vacant
32 VP of Student Services Rev. James TINNEMEYER
06 Registrar Mrs. Vicki WILSON
41 Athletic Director Mr. Larry MARSHALL
13 VP Information Technology Services Mr. William DUMIRE
08 Director Eberly Library Mr. Rea REDD
26 Communication Specialist Ms. Ashley WISE
36 Director of Placement Mrs. Marie E. COFFMAN
38 Student Counselor Mrs. Jane S. OWEN
21 Business Ofc Supervisor/Controller Mrs. Laura COSS
23 Director of Health Services Ms. Jennifer SHIRING
15 Director Human Resources Mr. Tom HELMICK
37 Director Student Financial Aid Mr. Matthew STOKAN

Westminster College (G)

319 South Market Street, New Wilmington PA 16172-0001

County: Lawrence FICE Identification: 003392
Unit ID: 216807
Telephone: (724) 946-8761 Carnegie Class: Bac-A&S
FAX Number: (724) 946-7132 Calendar System: Semester
URL: www.westminster.edu
Established: 1852 Annual Undergrad Tuition & Fees: $36,806
Enrollment: 1,263 Coed
Affiliation or Control: Presbyterian Church (U.S.A.) IRS Status: 501(c)3
Highest Offering: Master's
Accreditation: M, MUS

01 President Dr. Kathy B. RICHARDSON
05 Vice Pres Academic Affairs Dr. Jeffrey S. COKER
111 VP Institutional Advancement Mr. Matthew P. STINSON
10 Vice Pres Finance/Mgmt Services Mr. Kenneth J. ROMIG
84 Vice President for Enrollment Dr. Jeffrey S. COKER
32 VP Student Affs/Dean Student Affs Dr. Carllos D. LASSITER
42 College Chaplain Rev. James R. MOHR
35 Assoc Dean of Student Affairs Ms. Gina M. VANCE
08 CIO/Assoc Dean Library/Info Service Ms. Erin T. SMITH
20 Assoc Dean Acad Affs/Asst to Pres Dr. Jamie G. MCMINN
37 Director Student Financial Aid Ms. Cheryl GERBER
06 Registrar Mr. Scott D. WIGNALL
36 Director of Professional Dev Center Dr. Jamie G. MCMINN
29 Sr Director of Alumni Engagement Ms. Kara H. MONTGOMERY
58 Director of Graduate School Dr. Alison L. DUBOIS
41 Athletic Director Mr. James E. DAFLER
18 Director of Physical Plant Vacant
21 Business Manager Ms. Janet M. SMITH
19 Director of Public Safety Vacant
23 Director of the Wellness Center Ms. Melissa M. BARON
40 Bookstore Manager Ms. Kay A. GALANSKI
21 Controller Vacant
15 Director of Human Resources Ms. Kimberlee K. CHRISTOFFERSON
38 Counselor Ms. Sarah M. GELLMAN
28 Director of Diversity Services Ms. Jeannette HUBBARD

Westminster Theological Seminary (H)

2960 Church Road, Glenside PA 19038

County: Montgomery FICE Identification: 003393
Unit ID: 216816
Telephone: (215) 887-5511 Carnegie Class: Spec-4-yr-Faith
FAX Number: (215) 887-5404 Calendar System: Semester
URL: www.wts.edu
Established: 1929 Annual Graduate Tuition & Fees: N/A
Enrollment: 673 Coed
Affiliation or Control: Independent Non-Profit IRS Status: 501(c)3
Highest Offering: Doctorate; No Undergraduates

Accreditation: M, THEOL

01 President .... Dr. Peter A. LILLBACK
05 Dean of Faculty .... Dr. David B. GARNER
43 General Counsel .... Mr. James M. SWEET
32 VP for Campus Life/Dean of Students .... Mr. Steven J. CARTER
111 Vice Pres Advancement .... Vacant
11 Vice President of Operations .... Mr. Chun LAI
106 Dean of Online Learning .... Mr. Iain DUGUID
07 Admissions Coord & Fin Aid Officer .... Mrs. Cyndi MYERS
84 Director of Enrollment .... Mr. Jonathan M. BRACK
08 Director of Library Services ... Mr. Alexander (Sandy) FINLAYSON
73 Director DMin .... Dr. John CURRIE
13 Associated Director of Technology .... Mr. Sam IM
18 Physical Plant Manager .... Mr. Richard W. MAIENSHEIN
04 Executive Asst to President .... Ms. Gospel G. PORQUEZ

Westmoreland County Community College (A)

145 Pavilion Lane, Youngwood PA 15697-1895
County: Westmoreland FICE Identification: 010176
Unit ID: 216825
Telephone: (724) 925-4000 Carnegie Class: Assoc/HVT-Mix Trad/Non
FAX Number: (724) 925-1150 Calendar System: Semester
URL: www.westmoreland.edu
Established: 1970 Annual Undergrad Tuition & Fees (In-District): $5,214
Enrollment: 5,084 Coed
Affiliation or Control: Local IRS Status: 501(c)3
Highest Offering: Associate Degree
Accreditation: M, ACFEI, ADNUR, DA, DH, #DMS, MAC

01 President .... Dr. Tuesday STANLEY
05 Vice Pres Acad Affs/Stdnt Svcs .... Dr. Kristy BISHOP
11 Vice Pres Administrative Services .... Mr. Steve LIPPIELLO
103 VP Workforce & Cmty Devel/Cont Educ .... Mr. David PISTNER
25 Director of Grants .... Ms. Debra J. WILLIAMS
15 Director Human Resources .... Ms. Lauren M. FARRELL
106 Dean Dist Educ/Learning Resources .... Ms. Annette BOYER
50 Dean Business/Math/Science/Engineer .... Ms. Cynthia PROCTOR
76 Dean Health Profess/Culinary Arts .... Mr. Bruce WASSUNG
72 Dean Technology .... Dr. Byron KOHUT
79 Dean Public Svc/Human/Soc Science .... Dr. Andrew BARNETTE
84 Vice Pres Enrollment Mgmt .... Ms. Sydney BEELER
102 Exec Director Education Foundation .... Ms. Debra D. WOODS
37 Director Financial Aid .... Ms. Darylann THOMAS
18 Director Facilities .... Mr. Jeff MARTINEC
13 Director Information Technology .... Mr. Steve BUDNY
26 Exec Dir Marketing/ Communications .... Ms. Janet K. CORRINNE-HARVEY
07 Director Admissions/Registrar .... Ms. Janice T. GRABOWSKI
41 Director Student Life/Athletics .... Mr. Brian K. ROSE
45 Dean Planning/Assessment & IE .... Ms. Lindsay HERROD
96 Director of Purchasing .... Ms. Jill BUDNY

Widener University (B)

One University Place, Chester PA 19013-5792
County: Delaware FICE Identification: 003313
Unit ID: 216852
Telephone: (610) 499-4000 Carnegie Class: DU-Mod
FAX Number: N/A Calendar System: Semester
URL: www.widener.edu
Established: 1821 Annual Undergrad Tuition & Fees: $45,948
Enrollment: 6,518 Coed
Affiliation or Control: Independent Non-Profit IRS Status: 501(c)3
Highest Offering: Doctorate
Accreditation: M, CAEPN, CLPSY, HSA, IPSY, LAW, NURSE, PTA, SW

01 President .... Dr. Julie E. WOLLMAN
05 Provost .... Dr. Andrew A. WORKMAN
10 Sr Vice Pres Administration/Finance .... Mr. Joseph J. BAKER
111 Vice Pres University Advancement .... Ms. Theresa TRAVIS
13 Chief Information Officer .... Mr. Eric BEHRENS
21 Associate VP & Controller .... Ms. Catherine MCGEEHAN
11 Associate VP of Administration .... Mr. George E. HASSEL
15 Assoc VP for Human Resources ... Ms. Alison KISS DOUGHERTY
18 Director of Operations .... Vacant
58 Assoc Provost Grad Studies .... Dr. Kimberly C. O'HALLORAN
20 Associate Provost Undergraduate .... Dr. Geraldine A. BLOEMKER
32 Dean of Students .... Dr. John P. DOWNEY
54 Dean School of Engineering .... Dr. Fred A. AKL
49 Dean College Arts & Sciences .... Dr. David E. LEAMN
50 Dean School of Business Admin .... Dr. Jayati GHOSH
66 Dean School of Nursing .... Dr. Anne M. KROUSE
88 Dean Sch Human Svc Professions .... Dr. Robin L. DOLE
113 Bursar .... Ms. Diana BARRACLOUGH
08 Director Wolfgram Library .... Ms. Deborah G. MORLEY
84 Assoc VP for Enrollment Services .... Mr. Thomas K. MALLOY
06 Director of Records/Registration .... Ms. Kristen CHANDO
09 Dir of Inst Res & Effectiveness .... Dr. Stephen W. THORPE
36 Placement Director .... Ms. Janet R. LONG
41 Director of Athletics .... Mr. Jack L. SHAFER
85 Director International Student Svcs .... Ms. Kandy TURNER
19 Director of Campus Safety .... Mr. Patrick SULLIVAN
40 Manager Campus Bookstore .... Vacant
91 Director Information Systems .... Mrs. Linda TAYLOR
88 Director Technical Resources .... Mr. Perry M. DRAYFAHL
96 Director of Purchasing .... Ms. Michelle SHELTON
121 Dir Student Success/Retention .... Mr. Timothy J. CAIRY
92 Dir Honors Program in General Educ .... Dr. Ilene LIEBERMAN
94 Director of Women's Studies .... Dr. Annalisa CASTALDO
86 Director Government Relations .... Vacant
100 Chief of Staff .... Dr. Kathryn J. HERSCHEDE
26 Director of Communications .... Ms. Mary ALLEN
39 Dir Resident Life/Student Housing ... Ms. Catherine A. FEMINELLA

† See Delaware listing of Widener University School of Law.

Widener University Commonwealth Law School (C)

3800 Vartan Way, PO Box 69380,
Harrisburg PA 17106-9380
Telephone: (717) 541-3900 Identification: 667244
Accreditation: &M, LAW

† Branch campus of Widener University, Chester, PA.

Wilkes University (D)

84 W South Street, Wilkes-Barre PA 18766-0001
County: Luzerne FICE Identification: 003394
Unit ID: 216931
Telephone: (570) 408-5000 Carnegie Class: DU-Mod
FAX Number: (570) 408-2934 Calendar System: Semester
URL: www.wilkes.edu
Established: 1933 Annual Undergrad Tuition & Fees: $36,194
Enrollment: 5,545 Coed
Affiliation or Control: Independent Non-Profit IRS Status: 501(c)3
Highest Offering: Doctorate
Accreditation: M, ACBSP, CEA, NURSE, PHAR

01 President .... Dr. Paul S. ADAMS
05 Provost & Sr Vice President .... Dr. Terese WIGNOT
10 Vice Pres Finance & General Counsel ... Mr. Loren D. PRESCOTT
30 Chief Development Officer .... Mrs. Margaret A. STEELE
21 Controller .... Ms. Janet KOBYLSKI
84 VP for Enrollment Mgmt & Marketing .... Ms. Kishan ZUBER
20 Associate Provost for Academics .... Dr. Jonathan D. FERENCE
32 Vice President Student Affairs .... Dr. Mark R. ALLEN
15 Chief Human Resource Officer .... Mr. Joseph HOUSENICK
35 Dean of Students .... Mr. Mark R. ALLEN
54 Dean of Science & Engineering .... Dr. Prahlad MURTHY
49 Dean College Arts & Humanities .... Dr. Paul RIGGS
67 Dean Nesbitt School of Pharmacy .... Dr. Scott STOLTE
53 Dean School of Education .... Dr. Rhonda RABBITT
86 Asst to Pres External Affairs .... Mr. Michael WOOD
50 Dean Sidhu School of Business .... Dr. Abel ADEKOLA
62 Dean Library .... Mr. John STACHACZ
09 Exec Director Info/Analysis/Plng .... Mr. Brian BOGERT
29 Director of Alumni Affairs .... Ms. Leigh Ann JACOBSON
41 Director of Athletics .... Ms. Addy MALATESTA
23 Director Health Services .... Ms. Diane E. O'BRIEN
36 Director Career Services .... Mrs. Carol A. BOSACK-KOSEK
39 Director Residence Life .... Ms. Deborah L. SCHEIBLER
58 Director Graduate Teacher Education .... Ms. Grace SURDOVEL
06 Registrar .... Mrs. Susan A. HRITZAK
37 Executive Director of Financial Aid .... Mrs. Jane F. DESSOYE
26 Executive Director of Marketing ... Ms. Kimberly BOWER SPENCE
18 Director Facilities Services .... Mr. Charles CARY
07 Exec Dir Undergraduate Enrollment .... Ms. Amy M. TERKOWSKI
28 Exec Director of Diversity .... Ms. Georgia COSTALAS
96 Dir Procurement & Financial Svcs .... Ms. Alicia BOND
25 Director of Sponsored Programs .... Ms. Amanda MODROVSKY
27 Director of Communications .... Ms. Gabrielle D'AMICO
04 Executive Assistant to President .... Ms. Bridget GIUNTA

Williamson College of the Trades (E)

106 S New Middletown Road, Media PA 19063-5299
County: Delaware FICE Identification: 041238
Unit ID: 216940
Telephone: (610) 566-1776 Carnegie Class: Not Classified
FAX Number: (610) 566-6502 Calendar System: Semester
URL: www.williamson.edu
Established: 1888 Annual Undergrad Tuition & Fees: $27,571
Enrollment: N/A Male
Affiliation or Control: Independent Non-Profit IRS Status: 501(c)3
Highest Offering: Associate Degree
Accreditation: ACCSC

01 President .... Mr. Michael J. ROUNDS
03 Senior VP/Chief of Staff .... Dr. Todd M. ZACHARY
05 VP and Dean of Education/ CAO .... Dr. Samuel H. WRIGHTSON, JR.
10 VP Resource Management/CFO .... Ms. Nancy M. CATANIA
111 VP Institutional Advancement .... Ms. Arlene A. SNYDER
11 VP Plans and Operations .... Mr. Corey A. JACKSON
108 VP Research and Assessment .... Mr. Thomas E. WISNESKI
32 Dean of Students .... Mr. Thomas J. MOFFITT
84 VP Enrollment Management .... Mr. Jason C. MERILLAT
41 Athletic Director/Sports Center Mgr .... Mr. Dale H. PLUMMER
38 Chaplain/Counselor .... Rev. Mark A. SPECHT
06 Registrar .... Ms. Stephanie C. BOON
04 Admin Assistant to the President .... Ms. Joan E. BERRY
36 Director Student Placement .... Ms. Margret T. KINGHAM
39 Director Residence Life .... Mr. John J. TULLY

Wilson College (F)

1015 Philadelphia Avenue, Chambersburg PA 17201-1285
County: Franklin FICE Identification: 003396
Unit ID: 217013
Telephone: (717) 264-4141 Carnegie Class: Masters/S
FAX Number: (717) 264-1578 Calendar System: 4/1/4
URL: www.wilson.edu
Established: 1869 Annual Undergrad Tuition & Fees: $24,595
Enrollment: 1,216 Coed
Affiliation or Control: Presbyterian Church (U.S.A.) IRS Status: 501(c)3
Highest Offering: Master's
Accreditation: M

01 President .... Dr. Barbara K. MISTICK
05 VP for Academic Affairs/Dean of Fac .... Dr. Elissa HEIL
111 VP for Institutional Advancement .... Ms. Camilla B. RAWLEIGH
10 Vice Pres Finance & Administration .... Mr. Brian ECKER
84 Interim VP for Enrollment .... Mr. David BOISVERT
32 Vice President for Student Dev/Dean .... Dr. Mary Beth WILLIAMS
100 Chief of Staff .... Ms. Melissa J. IMES
06 Registrar .... Ms. Jean B. HOOVER
37 Dean of Financial Aid .... Ms. Linda D. BRITTAIN
09 Director of Institutional Effective .... Ms. Cynthia M. EMORY
08 AVP for Technology and Library Svcs .... Mr. Jose DIEUDONNE
18 Director of Physical Plant .... Mr. Jason WARRENFELTZ
26 Manager of Media Relations .... Ms. Cathy MENTZER
40 College Store Coordinator .... Ms. Robin HERRING
41 Athletic Director .... Ms. Lori FREY
88 Director of Conferences .... Ms. Emily MULBAY
29 Director of Alumnae Programs .... Ms. Marybeth FAMULARE
15 Director Human Resources .... Vacant
121 Assoc Dean of Academic Advising .... Dr. Deborah AUSTIN
21 Assoc VP for Finance/Admin .... Ms. Lori TOSTEN
36 Director of Career Development .... Ms. Linda A. BOECKMAN
38 Director of Student Counseling .... Ms. Megan CAVANAUGH
88 Dir of Single Parent Scholars Pgm .... Ms. Katherine KOUGH
37 Coordinator of Financial Aid .... Ms. Christine KNOUSE
28 Coordinator of Diversity .... Vacant
42 Chaplain .... Rev. Derek WADLINGTON
39 Director of Residence Life .... Mr. Ryan COLL
102 Dir Foundation/Corporate Relations .... Ms. Margaret LIGHT
07 Director of Admissions .... Mr. Michael MONTANA

Won Institute of Graduate Studies (G)

137 S Easton Road, Glenside PA 19038
County: Montgomery FICE Identification: 039493
Unit ID: 442064
Telephone: (215) 884-8942 Carnegie Class: Spec-4-yr-Other Health
FAX Number: (215) 884-9002 Calendar System: Trimester
URL: www.woninstitute.edu
Established: 2002 Annual Graduate Tuition & Fees: N/A
Enrollment: 74 Coed
Affiliation or Control: Independent Non-Profit IRS Status: 501(c)3
Highest Offering: Doctorate; No Undergraduates
Accreditation: M, ACUP

01 President .... Dr. Bokin KIM
11 Chief Administrative Officer .... Ms. Colleen O'CONNELL
10 Chief Financial Officer .... Ms. Maria PERRY
05 Chief Academic Officer .... Dr. Gerry O'SULLIVAN
06 Registrar .... Mr. Max FINKEL
08 Librarian .... Vacant
85 International Student Advisor .... Dr. Hojin PARK
13 Chief Info Technology Officer (CIO) .... Ms. Elizabeth REED
04 Admin Assistant to the President .... Mr. Frederick RANALLO-HIGGINS
18 Chief Facilities/Phys Plant Ofcr .... Mr. Youngbin KIM

The Workforce Institute's City College (H)

1231 North Broad Street, Philadelphia PA 19122
County: Philadelphia FICE Identification: 031091
Unit ID: 214023
Telephone: (215) 568-9215 Carnegie Class: Spec 2-yr-Tech
FAX Number: (215) 568-3511 Calendar System: Semester
URL: www.citycollege-careers.org
Established: 1974 Annual Undergrad Tuition & Fees: $12,097
Enrollment: 23 Coed
Affiliation or Control: Independent Non-Profit IRS Status: 501(c)3
Highest Offering: Associate Degree
Accreditation: ACCSC

01 President .... Dr. Richard COHEN
11 Executive Director .... Ms. Wendy-Anne ROBERTS-JOHNSON
10 Controller .... Ms. Mary DURSO
05 Director of Education .... Mr. Robert PHILLIPS
37 Financial Aid Director .... Ms. Madeline SARGENT
07 Admissions Representative .... Mr. Eric MAISTER
36 Career Manager .... Mr. Eric MAISTER

Yeshiva Beth Moshe (I)

930 Hickory Street, Scranton PA 18505-2196
County: Lackawanna FICE Identification: 013134
Unit ID: 217040
Telephone: (570) 346-1747 Carnegie Class: Spec-4-yr-Faith
FAX Number: (570) 346-2251 Calendar System: Semester
Established: 1965 Annual Undergrad Tuition & Fees: $9,400
Enrollment: 35 Male
Affiliation or Control: Independent Non-Profit IRS Status: 501(c)3
Highest Offering: Second Talmudic Degree
Accreditation: RABN

01 Chief Executive Officer .... Rabbi Yaakov SCHNAIDMAN
03 Executive Director .... Rabbi Avrohom PRESSMAN

York College of Pennsylvania (A)

Country Club Road, York PA 17403-3651
County: York FICE Identification: 003399
Unit ID: 217059
Telephone: (717) 846-7788 Carnegie Class: Masters/S
FAX Number: (717) 849-1607 Calendar System: Semester
URL: www.ycp.edu
Established: 1787 Annual Undergrad Tuition & Fees: $20,100
Enrollment: 4,415 Coed
Affiliation or Control: Independent Non-Profit IRS Status: 501(c)3
Highest Offering: Doctorate
Accreditation: M, ACBSP, ANEST, COARC, COSMA, MUS, NRPA, NURSE

01 President .... Dr. Pamela J. GUNTER-SMITH
05 Provost & Dean Academic Affairs .... Dr. Laura NIESEN DE ABRUNA
10 Chief Financial Officer .... Mr. Matthew SMITH
20 Assoc Dean Academic Affairs .... Dr. Carl SEAQUIST
121 Associate Provost .... Dr. Joshua LANDAU
32 Dean of Student Affairs .... Mr. Joseph F. MERKLE
18 Dean of Campus Operations .... Dr. Kenneth M. MARTIN
111 VP of Development .... Mr. Troy MILLER
50 Associate Dean Business .... Dr. James NORRIE
41 Asst Dean Athletics & Recreation .... Mr. Paul SAIKIA
84 Dean of Enrollment Management .... Dr. Danny GREEN
26 Chief Communication & Mktg Officer ... Ms. Mary E. DOLHEIMER
07 Director of Admissions .... Mr. Michael THORP
06 Registrar .... Mr. William BENTON
08 Librarian .... Mr. Jim KAPOUN
37 Director of Financial Aid .... Mr. Eric DINSMORE
13 CIO .... Dr. Ilya YAKOVLEV
29 Director Alumni Relations .... Mrs. Kristin SCHAB
36 Asst Dean Career Development .... Ms. Beverly A. EVANS
06 Assistant Registrar .... Mr. Matthew ROSS
19 Director of Public Safety .... Mr. Edward C. BRUDER
39 Director of Residence Life .... Mr. Robbie BACON
15 Director Human Resources .... Mrs. Vicki L. STEWART
38 Director Counseling Services .... Mr. Darrell WILT
91 Dir Administrative Computer Center .... Mr. Brian K. SMELTZER
23 Director Health Services .... Mrs. Amy DOWNS
40 Director Bookstore .... Mrs. Lynn P. FERRO
88 Director Campus & Special Events .... Ms. Sherry HEFLIN
102 Dir Corporate/Foundation/Govt Rels .... Mr. Jeffrey VERMEULEN
27 College Editor .... Mrs. Gail HUGANIR
42 Coordinator Religious Activities .... Mrs. Louise WORLEY
31 Dean Ctr for Community Engagement .... Dr. Dominic F. DELLICARPINI
09 Director of Institutional Research .... Dr. Sarah GALLIMORE
24 Dir Center for Teaching & Learning .... Mrs. Cindy CRIMMINS
112 Sr Dir Principal & Planned Gifts .... Ms. Robin BRENTON
04 Executive Asst to President .... Mrs. Cynthia E. REISINGER

YTI Career Institute (B)

2900 Fairway Drive, Altoona PA 16602
County: Blair FICE Identification: 030819
Unit ID: 375939
Telephone: (814) 944-5643 Carnegie Class: Assoc/HVT-High Trad
FAX Number: (959) 282-5093 Calendar System: Quarter
URL: www.yti.edu
Established: 2006 Annual Undergrad Tuition & Fees: N/A
Enrollment: 172 Coed
Affiliation or Control: Proprietary IRS Status: Proprietary
Highest Offering: Associate Degree
Accreditation: ACCSC, #COARC, MAC

01 Campus President .... Ms. Danielle STALTER
05 Director of Education .... Mr. Carl KENYON

† Effective February 12, 2018, Altoona Campus has ceased recruiting new students

YTI Career Institute (C)

3050 Hempland Road, Lancaster PA 17601
Telephone: (717) 295-1100 Identification: 770588
Accreditation: ACCSC, CAHIIM, MAC

YTI Career Institute (D)

1405 Williams Road, York PA 17402-9017
County: York FICE Identification: 021274
Unit ID: 217077
Telephone: (717) 757-1100 Carnegie Class: Assoc/HVT-High Trad
FAX Number: (717) 757-4964 Calendar System: Quarter
URL: www.yti.edu
Established: 1967 Annual Undergrad Tuition & Fees: N/A
Enrollment: 1,165 Coed
Affiliation or Control: Proprietary IRS Status: Proprietary
Highest Offering: Associate Degree
Accreditation: ACCSC, ACFEI, MAC

01 Chairman and CEO .... Mr. Timothy FOSTER
12 President - York .... Ms. Adrienne SCOTT
12 VP Operations/Educ - Lancaster .... Ms. Adrienne SCOTT
12 President - Altoona .... Ms. Vicki KANE
12 Assoc Director - MTC .... Mr. Juddson HILL
05 Director of Education .... Mr. James VERGOS

RHODE ISLAND

Brown University (E)

One Prospect Street, Providence RI 02912
County: Providence FICE Identification: 003401
Unit ID: 217156
Telephone: (401) 863-1000 Carnegie Class: DU-Highest
FAX Number: (401) 863-3700 Calendar System: Semester
URL: www.brown.edu
Established: 1764 Annual Undergrad Tuition & Fees: $55,466
Enrollment: 10,095 Coed
Affiliation or Control: Independent Non-Profit IRS Status: 501(c)3
Highest Offering: Doctorate
Accreditation: EH, IPSY, MED, PDPSY, PH

01 President .... Christina H. PAXSON
05 Provost .... Richard M. LOCKE
45 Exec Vice Pres Planning & Policy .... Russell C. CAREY
43 Vice President/General Counsel .... Eileen GOLDGEIER
10 Exec VP Finance/Administration .... Barbara D. CHERNOW
21 VP for Finance & CFO .... Jay CALHOUN
26 VP for Communications .... Cass CLIATT
15 Vice Pres for Human Resources .... Amanda BAILEY
111 Senior VP for Advancement .... Sergio GONZALEZ
32 Vice Pres Campus Life/Student Svcs .... Eric S. ESTES
28 VP Institutional Equity & Diversity .... Shontay DELALUE
30 Vice Pres for Development .... Patricia JACKSON
13 Chief Digital/Information Officer .... William THIRSK
100 Assistant to the President .... Kimberly O. ROSKIEWICZ
20 Dean of the Faculty .... Kevin MCLAUGHLIN
63 Dean Medicine & Biological Sciences .... Jack ELIAS
58 Dean of Graduate School .... Andrew G. CAMPBELL
20 Dean of the College .... Rashid ZIA
54 Dean of the School of Engineering .... Lawrence E. LARSON
69 Dean School of Public Health .... Bess MARCUS
107 Dean School Professional Studies .... Karen H. SIBLEY
46 Vice President for Research .... Jill PIPHER
20 Deputy Provost .... Elizabeth DOHERTY
08 University Librarian .... Joseph MEISEL
07 Dean of Admission .... Logan POWELL
37 Dean of Financial Aid .... James TILTON
06 University Registrar .... Robert F. FITZGERALD
41 Director of Athletics .... Jack HAYES
18 VP for Facilities Management .... Michael GUGLIELMO, JR.
86 Asst VP Govt & Community Relations .... Albert A. DAHLBERG
21 University Controller .... Charlene M. SWEENEY
29 Vice President Alumni Relations .... Andrew B. SHAINDLIN
23 Exec Dir of Health & Wellness .... Vanessa M. BRITTO
38 Dir Counseling & Psychological Svcs .... William D. MEEK
19 Exec Dir & Chief of Public Safety .... Mark J. PORTER
09 Director of Institutional Research .... Katharine T. BARNES

Bryant University (F)

1150 Douglas Pike, Smithfield RI 02917-1291
County: Providence FICE Identification: 003402
Unit ID: 217165
Telephone: (401) 232-6000 Carnegie Class: Masters/M
FAX Number: (401) 232-6319 Calendar System: Semester
URL: www.bryant.edu
Established: 1863 Annual Undergrad Tuition & Fees: $43,973
Enrollment: 3,751 Coed
Affiliation or Control: Independent Non-Profit IRS Status: 501(c)3
Highest Offering: Beyond Master's But Less Than Doctorate
Accreditation: EH, ARCPA

00 Chairman Board of Trustees .... Mr. William CONATY
01 President .... Mr. Ronald K. MACHTLEY
04 Exec Asst to the President .... Dr. Roger ANDERSON
05 Provost .... Mr. Glenn SULMASY
32 VP Student Affairs/Dean of Students .... Vacant
82 VP International Affairs .... Dr. Hong YANG
10 VP Business Affairs .... Mr. Barry F. MORRISON
111 VP University Advancement .... Mr. David WEGRZYN
13 VP Information Services/CIO .... Mr. Chuck LOCURTO
84 VP Enrollment Management .... Ms. Michelle CLOUTIER
15 VP Human Resources .... Mr. Timothy PAIGE
18 Exec Director Facilities Mgmt .... Mr. James VECCHIONE
26 Assoc VP University Relations .... Ms. Elizabeth O'NEILL
21 Assoc VP Business & Controller .... Mr. Farokh BHADA
20 Associate Provost .... Dr. Carol DEMORANVILLE
49 Dean College of Arts & Sciences .... Dr. Bradford MARTIN
50 Dean College of Business .... Dr. Madan ANNAVARJULA
51 Dir Exec Development Center .... Ms. Annette CERILLI
88 Exec Dir Hassenfeld Institute .... Mr. Gary SASSE
88 Dir RI Export Assistance Center .... Vacant
89 Dir Academic Center for Excellence .... Dr. Laurie L. HAZARD
20 Dir Faculty Dev and Innovation .... Dr. Edward KAIRISS
06 Registrar .... Ms. Susan MCLACKEN
35 Asst VP for Student Affairs .... Mr. John DENIO
39 Assoc Dean of Students .... Mr. Robert SLOSS
88 Dir Bryant Center Operations .... Mr. Richard DANKEL
36 Dir Career Services .... Dr. Kevin GAW
42 Chaplain Campus Ministry .... Rev. Philip DEVENS
38 Dir Counseling Services .... Mr. William PHILLIPS
28 Asst VP Student Engagement .... Dr. Mailee KUE
19 Dir Public Safety .... Mr. Stephen BANNON
88 Asst Dir Women's Center .... Ms. Kelly BOUTIN
37 Dir Financial Aid .... Mr. John B. CANNING
88 Dir Conferences & Special Events .... Ms. Sheila GUAY
30 Exec Dir Development .... Mr. Edward MAGRO
29 Dir Alumni Relations .... Ms. Robin T. WARDE
90 Dir Acad Computing & Media Svcs .... Mr. Phillip LOMBARDI
91 Dir Admin Systems .... Ms. Christine BIGWOOD
14 Dir Computer & Telecomm Svcs .... Mr. Richard SIEDZIK
16 Assoc Dir Human Resources .... Ms. Catherine CURRIE
41 Dir Athletics .... Mr. Bill SMITH
09 Dir Planning & Inst Research .... Mr. Robert JONES
88 Exec Dir US-China Institute .... Dr. Hong YANG
40 Manager Bookstore .... Mr. Stanley STOWIK
104 Director Study Abroad .... Ms. Cindi LEWIS
102 Dir Foundation/Corporate Relations .... Ms. Robin RICHARDSON
105 Chief Library Officer .... Ms. Laura KOHL

College Unbound (G)

325 Public Street, Providence RI 02905
County: Providence Identification: 667355
Telephone: (401) 752-2640 Carnegie Class: Not Classified
FAX Number: N/A Calendar System: Semester
URL: www.collegeunbound.org
Established: 2009 Annual Undergrad Tuition & Fees: N/A
Enrollment: N/A Coed
Affiliation or Control: Independent Non-Profit IRS Status: 501(c)3
Highest Offering: Baccalaureate
Accreditation: @EH

01 President .... Dennis LITTKY

Community College of Rhode Island (H)

400 East Avenue, Warwick RI 02886-1807
County: Kent FICE Identification: 003408
Unit ID: 217475
Telephone: (401) 825-1000 Carnegie Class: Assoc/MT-VT-High Trad
FAX Number: (401) 825-2166 Calendar System: Semester
URL: www.ccri.edu
Established: 1964 Annual Undergrad Tuition & Fees (In-State): $4,564
Enrollment: 14,758 Coed
Affiliation or Control: State IRS Status: 501(c)3
Highest Offering: Associate Degree
Accreditation: EH, ACBSP, ADNUR, ART, COARC, COMTA, DA, DH, DMS, HT, MLTAD, MUS, OTA, PNUR, PTAA, RAD

01 President .... Dr. Meghan HUGHES
05 Vice President for Academic Affairs .... Dr. Rosemary COSTIGAN
10 Vice President Finance/Strategy .... Ms. Kristen ALBRITTON
32 VP Stdnt Affs & Chf Outcomes Ofcr .... Ms. Sara ENRIGHT
111 AVP Institutional Advancement/Col .... Mr. Robert (Bobby) G. GONDOLA, JR.
32 Assoc VP for Student Services .... Vacant
18 Director of Physical Plant .... Mr. Kenneth F. MCCABE
79 Dean for Arts/Humanities/Social Sci .... Dr. Bryan BROPHY-BAERMANN
76 Interim Dean Health & Rehab Service .... Dr. Suzanne M. CARR
50 Interim Dean Bus/Sci/Tech & Math .... Dr. Lauren A. WEBB
103 Vice President of Workforce Develop .... Mr. Julian ALSSID
08 Interim Dean of Learning Resources .... Ms. Catherine M. POIRIER
35 Dean of Students .... Mr. Michael J. CUNNINGHAM, II
21 Controller .... Mr. David J. RAWLINSON
35 Assoc Dean Student Life/Svc Lrng .... Dr. Rebecca H. YOUNT
15 Director of Human Resources .... Ms. Sheri L. NORTON
13 Chief Information Officer .... Mr. Peter D. SHOUDY
19 Acting Dir of Safety & Security .... Mr. Sean COLLINS
26 Director Marketing & Communications .... Ms. Amy P. KEMPE
41 Interim Director of Athletics .... Mr. Kevin S. SALISBURY
09 Director Inst Research/Planning .... Mr. Rajiv R. MALHOTRA
113 Bursar .... Vacant
88 Director Access to Opportunity .... Ms. Tracy KARASINSKI
109 Auxiliary Svcs Business Director .... Dr. Raymond N. KARASEK, III
29 Director of Alumni Affairs .... Vacant
22 Dir AA/EEO/Div/Incl/Title IX Coord .... Ms. Elizabeth CANNING
96 Director of Purchasing .... Ms. Lisa M. CONSIDINE-FONTES
21 Business Manager .... Ms. Ruth A. BARRINGTON
36 Coordinator Career Services .... Ms. Camille NUMRICH
37 Director of Financial Aid .... Ms. Kelly A. MORRISSEY
04 Assistant to the President .... Ms. Deborah M. ZIELINSKI
06 Registrar .... Ms. Cathy L. PICARD-TESSIER
07 Director of Admissions .... Ms. Teresa M. KLESS
100 AVP for Administration .... Ms. Alix R. OGDEN
11 Director of Operations (IS) .... Mr. William R. FERLAND
38 Dean Student Dev/Assessment .... Mr. Robert D. CIPOLLA
43 Dir Legal Services/General Counsel .... Mr. Ronald A. CAVALLARO

Johnson & Wales University (I)

8 Abbott Park Place, Providence RI 02903-3703
County: Providence FICE Identification: 003404
Unit ID: 217235
Telephone: (401) 598-1000 Carnegie Class: Masters/L
FAX Number: (401) 598-2880 Calendar System: Quarter
URL: https://www.jwu.edu/
Established: 1914 Annual Undergrad Tuition & Fees: $32,441
Enrollment: 8,563 Coed
Affiliation or Control: Independent Non-Profit IRS Status: 501(c)3
Highest Offering: Doctorate
Accreditation: EH, #ARCPA, DIETD

01 Chancellor .... Ms. Mim L. RUNEY
05 Provost .... Ms. Billye AUCLAIR
12 Providence Campus President .... Ms. Marie BERNARDO-SOUSA

11 SVP of Admin & Enrollment Mgmt .... Vacant
26 SVP of Communication .... Mr. Doug WHITING
00 Chairman of the Board .... Mr. James H. HANCE, JR.
08 Dean of Libraries .... Ms. Rosita HOPPER
76 Int Dean Col of Health & Wellness .... Ms. Laura GALLIGAN
49 Dean of Arts & Sciences .... Mr. Michael R. FEIN
50 Dean of College of Business .... Mr. Lou D'ABROSCA
106 Dean College of Online Education .... Mr. David CARTWRIGHT
88 Interim Dean Col of Culinary Arts .... Ms. Susan MARSHALL
54 Dean of College of Engr & Design .... Mr. Frank TWEEDIE
88 Dean College of Hospitality Mgmt .... Mr. Paul J. MCVETY
106 Vice President of Online Education .... Ms. Cindy PARKER
111 VP of Advancement & Univ Relations .... Ms. Maureen DUMAS
112 Exec Dir of Major Gifts .... Vacant
10 Vice Chancellor of Finance & Admin .... Mr. Joseph J. GREENE
21 Vice President of Finance .... Ms. Danielle SANTAMARIA
27 Dir of Mktg Development/ Fulfillment .... Ms. Kristine E. MCNAMARA
109 Vice President of Auxiliary Service .... Mr. Michael DOWNING
114 University Budget Director .... Ms. Eileen T. HASKINS
21 Director of Accounting Services .... Ms. Laurie O'KEEFE
116 Dir of Financial Plng & Analysis .... Ms. Michele VON HEIN
121 Dir Center for Academic Support .... Vacant
15 Vice President of Human Resources .... Ms. Diane D'AMBRA
16 Director of Human Resources .... Ms. Rebecca TONDREAU
88 Director of Payroll .... Ms. Christine WOOD
118 Director of Benefits .... Ms. Christine OLIVER
09 Director of Institutional Research .... Mr. George REZENDES
108 Dir Institutional Effectiveness .... Ms. Eileen DEMAGISTRIS
29 Dir of Alumni Relations .... Ms. Lori ZABATTA
43 General Counsel .... Ms. Luba SHUR
19 Dir of Campus Safety & Security .... Mr. LeRoy ROSE, JR.
18 Exec Dir Facilities/Design & Const .... Mr. Jason WITHAM
86 VP Comm/Government Relations .... Ms. Lisa PELOSI
13 Chief Information Officer .... Mr. Akhi GUPTA
119 Director of Information Security .... Mr. Nicholas TELLA
120 Director Online Education .... Ms. Amy RICCI
32 VP of Stdnt Affairs/Dean of Stdnts .... Mr. Ronald MARTEL
38 Assoc Dean Counsel/Health/Wellness .... Mr. Joseph BARRESI, JR.
41 Assoc Dean of Students Athletics .... Ms. Mel GRAF
35 Assoc Dean of Student Services .... Mr. Dameian SLOCUM
101 University Secretary .... Ms. Emily GILCREAST
07 Dir of Undergraduate Admissions .... Ms. Amy OCONNELL
123 Dir Continuing Ed & Grad Admissions .... Ms. Teresa MAUK
06 University Registrar .... Ms. Tammy HARRIGAN
37 VP Student Academic Financial Svcs .... Ms. Lynn ROBINSON
39 Director of Residential Life .... Mr. Nev KRAGULJEVIC
36 VP of Experiential Educ/Career Svcs .... Vacant
88 Dean Experiential Educ/Career Svcs .... Ms. Sheri YOUNG
85 Dir International Student Services .... Mr. Wesley ROY
104 Dir Study Abroad Programs .... Ms. Lisa MCADAM DONEGAN

New England Institute of Technology (A)

One New England Tech Blvd., East Greenwich RI 02818
County: Kent FICE Identification: 007845
Unit ID: 217305
Telephone: (800) 736-7744 Carnegie Class: Bac/Assoc-Mixed
FAX Number: (401) 886-0859 Calendar System: Quarter
URL: www.neit.edu
Established: 1940 Annual Undergrad Tuition & Fees: $29,856
Enrollment: 2,793 Coed
Affiliation or Control: Independent Non-Profit IRS Status: 501(c)3
Highest Offering: Doctorate
Accreditation: EH, ADNUR, COARC, MLTAD, NUR, OT, OTA, PTAA, SURGT

01 President .... Mr. Richard I. GOUSE
03 Executive Vice President .... Mr. Scott FREUND
05 Senior Vice President and Provost .... Dr. Douglas H. SHERMAN
10 Sr VP Financial Affs & Endowment .... Ms. Cheryl C. CONNORS
32 Vice Pres Student Support Services .... Ms. Catherine B. KENNEDY
21 VP of Finance & Business Admin .... Mr. Kenneth JALBERT
20 Associate Provost .... Dr. Henry YOUNG
07 Director of Admissions .... Ms. Lynn FAWTHROP
37 Director Financial Aid .... Ms. Anna KELLY
08 Director Library .... Ms. Sharon CHARETTE
36 Director of Career Services .... Ms. Patricia BLAKEMORE
109 Director Auxiliary Services .... Mr. Patrick TRACEY
06 Registrar .... Ms. Sarah BOSWORTH
35 Director Student Affairs .... Ms. Lee PEEBLES
13 Chief Info Technology Officer (CIO) .... Mr. Jacques LAFLAMME
18 Chief Facilities/Physical Plant .... Mr. Patrick TRACEY
26 Chief Public Relations/Marketing .... Mr. Steven H. KITCHIN
84 Director Enrollment Management .... Ms. Lynn FAWTHROP
103 Dir Workforce/Career Development .... Mr. Steven H. KITCHIN
19 Director Security/Safety .... Ms. Pamela MOFFATT-LIMOGES
43 Dir Legal Services/General Counsel .... Mr. Philip PARSONS
96 Director of Purchasing .... Mr. William MENARD
108 Director Institutional Assessment .... Dr. Douglas SHERMAN
39 Director Student Housing .... Ms. Danielly JAMOUS

Providence College (B)

1 Cunningham Square, Providence RI 02918-0001
County: Providence FICE Identification: 003406
Unit ID: 217402
Telephone: (401) 865-1000 Carnegie Class: Masters/L
FAX Number: (401) 865-2057 Calendar System: Semester
URL: www.providence.edu
Established: 1917 Annual Undergrad Tuition & Fees: $50,528
Enrollment: 4,646 Coed
Affiliation or Control: Roman Catholic IRS Status: 501(c)3
Highest Offering: Master's
Accreditation: EH, SW

01 President .... Rev. Brian J. SHANLEY, OP
03 Executive Vice President/Treasurer .... Rev. Kenneth R. SICARD, OP
04 Asst to Pres & Exec Vice President .... Ms. Ann MANCHESTER-MOLAK
05 Sr VP Academic Affairs/Provost .... Dr. Hugh F. LENA, III
10 Sr VP for Finance & Business/CFO .... Mr. John M. SWEENEY
30 Sr VP for Institutional Advancement .... Mr. Gregory T. WALDRON
32 Vice Pres Student Affairs .... Ms. Kristine C. GOODWIN
43 Vice President/General Counsel .... Ms. Marifrances MCGINN
42 Vice Pres for Mission & Ministry .... Rev. R. Gabriel PIVARNIK, OP
21 Assoc VP for Finance/Asst Treasurer .... Ms. Jacqueline M. WHITE
35 Assoc VP for Student Affairs .... Dr. Steven A. SEARS
20 Assoc VP for Academic Affairs .... Dr. Brian J. BARTOLINI
41 Assoc VP for Athletics/Athletic Dir .... Mr. Robert G. DRISCOLL
15 Assoc Vice Pres for Human Resources .... Ms. Kathleen M. ALVINO
28 Assoc VP/Chief Diversity Officer .... Vacant
26 Assoc VP Public Affairs/Cmty Rels .... Mr. Steven J. MAURANO
20 Asst Vice Pres for Academic Affairs .... Mr. Charles J. HABERLE
21 Asst Vice Pres for Business Svcs .... Vacant
29 Asst Vice Pres for Alumni Relations .... Mr. Robert FERREIRA
44 Asst Vice Pres for Development .... Ms. Lynne FRASER
45 Asst VP Capital Projects & Fac Plng .... Mr. Mark F. RAPOZA
58 Dean of Undergrad & Grad Studies .... Rev. Mark D. NOWEL, OP
49 Dean School of Arts & Sciences .... Dr. Sheila A. LIOTTA
107 Dean School of Professional Studies .... Dr. Brian M. MCCADDEN
07 Assoc VP Admissions/Financial Aid .... Mr. Raul A. FONTS
50 Dean School of Business .... Dr. Sylvia MAXFIELD
51 Actg Dean Sch Continuing Education .... Ms. Madeleine METZLER
35 AVP Stdnt Affs/Asst Dean of Stdnts .... Ms. Tiffany D. GAFFNEY
06 Registrar .... Ms. Yvonne D. ARRUDA
104 Dean of International Studies .... Vacant
35 Director of Student Activities .... Ms. Sharon L. HAY
84 Associate Dean of Enrollment Svcs .... Ms. Lucille A. CALORE
37 Exec Director of Financial Aid .... Ms. Sandra J. OLIVEIRA
19 Exec Director Safety & Security .... Vacant
88 Asst VP Integrated Learning & Admin .... Ms. Patricia A. GOFF
18 Exec Director of Physical Plant .... Vacant
08 Director of Library .... Dr. Donald R. BAILEY
09 Director of Institutional Research .... Ms. Melanie R. SULLIVAN
90 Dir Enterprise Infrastructure & Ops .... Mr. Carmine R. PISCOPO
92 Director Liberal Arts Honors .... Dr. Stephen J. LYNCH
96 Exec Director of Business Services .... Mr. Gene R. ROBBINS
88 Director of Academic Svcs/Wrt Ctr .... Mr. Bryan D. MARINELLI
38 VP Student Development & Compliance .... Dr. James F. CAMPBELL
13 Chief Info Technology Officer (CIO) .... Mr. Paul V. FONTAINE

Rhode Island College (C)

600 Mount Pleasant Avenue, Providence RI 02908-1991
County: Providence FICE Identification: 003407
Unit ID: 217420
Telephone: (401) 456-8000 Carnegie Class: Masters/L
FAX Number: (401) 456-8379 Calendar System: Semester
URL: www.ric.edu
Established: 1854 Annual Undergrad Tuition & Fees (In-State): $8,929
Enrollment: 8,171 Coed
Affiliation or Control: State IRS Status: 501(c)3
Highest Offering: Doctorate
Accreditation: EH, ANEST, ART, CACREP, MUS, NURSE, SW

01 President .... Dr. Frank A. SANCHEZ
05 Int Provost/VP Academic Affairs .... Dr. Roberta S. PEARLMUTTER
10 VP Administration/Finance .... Mr. Stephen NEDDER
32 Int VP for Student Success .... Mr. Eric M. RIVERA
111 VP College Advance & Ext Rels .... Ms. Kimberly C. DUMPSON
45 Exec Dir Strategic Initiative .... Mr. Clark M. GREENE
107 Assoc VP Prof Studies & Cont Educ .... Ms. Jenifer GIROUX
28 Assoc VP Comm/Equity & Diversity .... Ms. Anna M. CANO-MORALES
102 Executive Director RIC Foundation .... Mr. Edwin R. PACHECO
20 Vice Prov Undergraduate Affairs .... Dr. Holly L. SHADOIAN
32 Assoc VP Student Success .... Dr. Ducha HANG
35 Asst VP Stdnt Success/Dean of Stdnt .... Dr. Tamika WORDLOW-WILLIAMS
13 Asst VP Information Services/CIO .... Mr. Jon BARTELSON
84 Dean of Enrollment Management .... Mr. James TWEED
11 Asst VP Administration .... Mr. Jeffrey L. MARTIN
58 Int Dean of Graduate Studies .... Dr. Leslie SCHUSTER
49 Dean Faculty Arts & Sciences .... Dr. Earl L. SIMSON
53 Dean Sch Education & Human Dev .... Dr. Jeannine DINGUS-EASON
50 Dean School of Business .... Dr. Jeffrey MELLO
66 Int Dean School of Nursing .... Dr. Debra SERVELLO
70 Int Dean School of Social Work .... Dr. Jayashree NIMMAGADDA
15 Director of Human Resources .... Ms. Maggie SULLIVAN
22 Dir Institutional Equity .... Ms. Margaret A. LYNCH GADALETA
19 Director of Security & Safety .... Mr. James MENDONCA
09 Dir Inst Research & Planning .... Dr. Christopher P. HOURIGAN
114 Director of Budget .... Mr. Robert EATON
18 Director Facilities & Operations .... Mr. James M. JERUE
18 Director Capital Projects .... Mr. Kevin J. FITTA
96 Director of Purchasing .... Ms. Jessica L. SILVA
08 Director of the Library .... Ms. Carissa DELIZIO
07 Director of Admissions .... Mr. Jason S. ANTHONY
06 Director of Records .... Ms. Tamecka C. HARDMON
37 Director Student Financial Aid .... Mr. Kenneth S. FERUS
41 Dir of Athletics .... Mr. Donald E. TENCHER
90 Director User Support Services .... Mr. David E. TOMS
91 Director Management Info Sys .... Dr. Bin YU
119 Director of Information Security .... Mr. Henk E. SONDER
39 Int Director Res Life/Housing .... Ms. Darcy DUBOIS
36 Director Career Dev Center .... Ms. Demetria MORAN
23 Int Dir College Health Services .... Ms. Christie RISHWORTH
38 Int Director Counseling Center .... Dr. Ryan PORELL
29 Director Alumni Affairs .... Ms. Suzanna ALBA
104 Director of Study Abroad .... Ms. Gersende CHANFRAU
28 Director of Unity Center .... Ms. Pegah RAHMANIAN
113 Bursar .... Ms. Charlene L. SZCZEPANEK
105 Director Web Services .... Ms. Karen M. RUBINO
26 Dir of College Comm & Marketing .... Mr. Chad A. MINNICH

Rhode Island School of Design (D)

2 College Street, Providence RI 02903-2784
County: Providence FICE Identification: 003409
Unit ID: 217493
Telephone: (401) 454-6100 Carnegie Class: Spec-4-yr-Arts
FAX Number: (401) 454-6320 Calendar System: 4/1/4
URL: www.risd.edu
Established: 1877 Annual Undergrad Tuition & Fees: $50,960
Enrollment: 2,440 Coed
Affiliation or Control: Independent Non-Profit IRS Status: 501(c)3
Highest Offering: Master's
Accreditation: EH, ART, LSAR

01 President .... Ms. Rosanne SOMERSON
100 Chief of Staff and Communications .... Ms. Taylor SCOTT
05 Provost .... Dr. Kent KLEINMAN
10 Sr VP Finance and Administration .... Mr. Dave PROULX
84 VP Enrollment .... Mr. Jamie O'HARA
88 Director RISD Museum of Art .... Mr. John W. SMITH
111 VP Institutional Engagement .... Mr. O'Neil OUTAR
26 Chief Marketing/Communcation Ofcr .... Ms. Kerci M. STROUD
20 Vice Provost .... Dr. Dan CAVICCHI
28 Assoc Prov Social Equity/Inclusion .... Mr. Matthew SHENODA
20 Assoc Prov Rsrch/Strtgic Prtnrships .... Ms. Sarah CUNNINGHAM
45 VP Integrated Planning .... Ms. Mara HERMANO
15 VP Human Resources .... Ms. Candace BAER
18 VP Campus Services .... Mr. Jack SILVA
43 General Counsel .... Mr. Steven MCDONALD
32 Dean Student Affairs .... Vacant
20 Interim Dean of Faculty .... Dr. Patricia BARBEITO
48 Dean Architecture & Design .... Ms. Scheri FULTINEER
57 Dean of Fine Arts .... Mr. Robert BRINKERHOFF
88 Dean Experimntal/Foundation Studies .... Ms. Joanne STRYKER
49 Dean of Liberal Arts .... Dr. Damian WHITE
08 Dean of Libraries .... Ms. Margot NISHIMURA
07 Assoc VP Enrollment .... Mr. Edward NEWHALL, JR.
37 Asst VP for Enrollment Services .... Mr. Anthony GALLONIO
13 CIO .... Mr. Rick MICKOOL
06 Registrar .... Ms. Alison SHERMAN

Roger Williams University (E)

One Old Ferry Road, Bristol RI 02809-2921
County: Bristol FICE Identification: 003410
Unit ID: 217518
Telephone: (401) 253-1040 Carnegie Class: Masters/M
FAX Number: N/A Calendar System: Semester
URL: www.rwu.edu
Established: 1956 Annual Undergrad Tuition & Fees: $34,522
Enrollment: 5,024 Coed
Affiliation or Control: Independent Non-Profit IRS Status: 501(c)3
Highest Offering: First Professional Degree
Accreditation: EH, CONST, LAW

01 President .... Dr. Ioannis MIAOULIS
05 Acting Provost .... Dr. Ioannis MIAOULIS
10 EVP Finance/Administration/Int COO .... Mr. Jerome WILLIAMS
84 VP Enrollment Mgmt & Marketing .... Mr. Brian WILLIAMS
21 VP for Accounting/Treasury Mgmt .... Mr. Marc LEONETTI
32 Vice President for Student Life .... Mr. John J. KING
111 VP Institutional Advancement .... Ms. Lisa RAIOLA
28 Vice President/Chief Diversity Ofcr .... Dr. Ame LAMBERT
88 Vice President University College .... Ms. Jamie SCURRY
08 Dean University Library .... Ms. Betsy P. LEARNED
35 Asst VP & Dean of Student Life .... Ms. Lisa LANDREMAN
88 Assoc VP Enrollment Mgmt/Marketing .... Ms. Tracy M. DACOSTA
88 Assoc VP Enrollment Mgmt/Marketing .... Ms. Amy TIBERIO
15 Asst Vice Pres of Human Resources .... Mr. Thomas MCDONOUGH
09 AVP for Institutional Research .... Ms. Jennifer DUNSEATH
51 Dean of University College .... Ms. Gena BIANCO
26 AVP of Marketing/Communications .... Ms. Lynne MELLO
44 AVP of Annual Giving .... Ms. Neuvia WALLACE-DAVIS
88 AVP of Institutional Advancement .... Ms. Christine PARKER
28 Dir Inst Diversity/Equity/Inclusion .... Ms. Zolla QUEZADA
61 Dean RWU School of Law .... Mr. Michael J. YELNOSKY
48 Dean Sch Arch/Art & Hist Preserv .... Mr. Stephen E. WHITE
50 Dean Gabelli School of Business .... Dr. Susan MCTIERNAN
54 Dean Sch Engrng/Comput/Constr Mgmt .... Dr. Robert A. POTTER
61 Dean School of Justice Studies .... Dr. Eric BRONSON
20 Vice Provost Academic Affairs .... Dr. Robert SHEA
07 Director Graduate Admissions .... Mr. Marcus HANSCOM
49 Dean Sch Social/Natural Sciences .... Dr. Benjamin GREENSTEIN
13 Chief Information Officer .... Mr. Daryl FORD
07 Dir Admissions Operations/Outreach .... Ms. Amanda MARSILI
37 Director Student Financial Aid .... Ms. Diane USHER
96 Director of Purchasing .... Ms. Kathy KANTERMAN
88 Director of Special Events .... Ms. Heidi DAGWAN
06 Registrar .... Mr. Daniel O'DRISCOLL
19 Director of Public Safety .... Mr. Steven MELARAGNO
41 Director of Athletics .... Ms. Kristen JACOBS
18 Asst Vice President Facilities Mgmt .... Mr. John TAMEO
36 Assoc Dean/Dir Ctr Career/Prof Dev .... Mr. Stephen CANTINE

38 Int Dir Counseling/Student Devel .... Mr. Christopher BAILEY
23 Director Health Services .... Ms. Anne M. MITCHELL
39 Director of Residence Life/Housing .... Mr. Abbas S. HILL
88 Director of Prospect Research .... Ms. Nancy L. RAMOS
39 Title IX Coord/Dir Gndr & Sxlty Ctr .... Ms. Jennifer STANLEY
40 Manager Bookstore .... Vacant

Salve Regina University (A)

100 Ochre Point Avenue, Newport RI 02840-4192
County: Newport FICE Identification: 003411
Unit ID: 217536
Telephone: (401) 847-6650 Carnegie Class: Masters/L
FAX Number: (401) 341-2925 Calendar System: Semester
URL: www.salve.edu
Established: 1947 Annual Undergrad Tuition & Fees: $40,150
Enrollment: 2,823 Coed
Affiliation or Control: Roman Catholic IRS Status: 501(c)3
Highest Offering: Doctorate
Accreditation: EH, ART, CACREP, IACBE, NURSE, SW

01 President .... Dr. Kelli ARMSTRONG
05 Vice Pres Academic Affairs/Provost .... Dr. Nancy SCHREIBER
32 Vice President Student Affairs .... Mr. J. Malcolm SMITH
111 VP University Rels/Advancement .... Mr. Michael L. SEMENZA
10 Vice President Administration & CFO .... Mr. William B. HALL
84 Vice Pres Enrollment Management .... Mr. James R. FOWLER
88 Vice Pres for Mission
Integration .... Dr. Theresa LADRIGAN-WHELPLEY
26 Assoc Vice Pres Univ Rels/CCO ...... Ms. Kristine HENDRICKSON
21 Assoc Vice Pres Finance/
Controller .... Mr. Michael N. GRANDCHAMP
13 Assoc VP Info Technology/CIO .... Mr. Irving BRUCKSTEIN
15 Interim Director Human Resources .... Ms. Nancy ESCHER
20 Associate Provost .... Dr. Donna M. COOK
09 Dir Inst Research/Effectiveness .... Ms. Annemarie BARTLETT
07 Dean of Undergraduate Admissions .... Ms. Colleen EMERSON
35 Assoc VP and Dean of Students .... Mr. J. Malcolm SMITH
06 Registrar .... Ms. Alissa BERTRAM
37 Director of Financial Aid .... Ms. Anne MCDERMOTT
29 Director Alumni & Parent Pgms .... Dr. Gerry WILLIS
41 Athletic Director .... Ms. Jody MOORADIAN
08 Director of Library Services .... Ms. Dawn EMSELLEM
39 Director of Residence Life .... Dr. Jim MOURNIGHAN
90 Director Academic Computing .... Mr. Brian A. MCDONNELL
18 Director of Facilities .... Mr. Eric MILNER
19 Director of Security/Safety .... Mr. Michael CARUOLO
40 Director of Bookstore .... Mr. Michael LEDDY
44 Sr Dir Advancement Operations/
Pgms .... Ms. Victoria DUCLOS-BARRETT
23 Director Health Services .... Ms. Sharon Q. CAPUANO
35 Director of Student Activities .... Ms. Chiquita BAYLOR
36 Director of Career Development .... Mr. Michael WISNEWSKI
96 Director of Purchasing .... Ms. Patrice COLEMAN
104 Director of International Programs .... Ms. Erin FITZGERALD
38 Dir of Student Counseling
Services .... Ms. Meghan M. DECARVALHO

University of Rhode Island (B)

45 Upper College Road, Kingston RI 02881
County: Washington FICE Identification: 003414
Unit ID: 217484
Telephone: (401) 874-1000 Carnegie Class: DU-Higher
FAX Number: (401) 874-7149 Calendar System: Semester
URL: www.uri.edu
Established: 1892 Annual Undergrad Tuition & Fees (In-State): $14,138
Enrollment: 18,089 Coed
Affiliation or Control: State IRS Status: 501(c)3
Highest Offering: Doctorate
Accreditation: EH, CAEPN, CAMPEP, CLPSY, CYTO, DIETD, DIETI, EXSC, LIB, LSAR, MFCD, MUS, NURSE, PHAR, PTA, SCPSY, SP

01 President .... Dr. David M. DOOLEY
100 Chief of Staff .... Ms. Michelle CURRERI
05 Provost/Vice Pres Academic Affairs .... Dr. Donald H. DEHAYES
46 Vice Pres Research/Economic Devel .... Dr. Peter SNYDER
10 Vice Pres for Admin & Finance .... Ms. Abigail RIDER
88 Assoc VP Res/Int Prop Mgmt/Comm .... Mr. Michael KATZ
88 Dir Univ Res External Relations .... Ms. Melissa MCCARTHY
88 Dir Research Development .... Ms. Karen MARKIN
25 Director Sponsored Projects .... Ms. Winifred NWANGWU
29 Exec Dir Alumni Relations/Secy Assn .... Ms. Michele NOTA
26 Exec Dir Ext Rels & Communications .... Ms. Kelly MAHONEY
27 Exec Dir Communications & Mktg .... Ms. Linda A. ACCIARDO
88 Dir Publications and Creative Svcs .... Vacant
114 Dir Budget & Financial Planning .... Ms. Linda BARRETT
21 Controller .... Ms. Tricia CASEY
15 Asst Vice Pres Human Resource
Admin .... Ms. Anne Marie COLEMAN
16 Director Personnel Services .... Ms. Laura KENERSON
18 Asst Vice Pres Business Services .... Vacant
19 Director Public Safety .... Mr. Stephen N. BAKER
12 Dir W.A. Jones Campus .... Ms. Maria DISANO
88 Assoc Dean Business Administration .... Dr. Shaw CHEN
88 Dir Capital Projects .... Mr. Paul DEPACE
88 Dir Planning & Real Estate Dev .... Mr. Ryan CARILLO
88 Dir Property & Support Svc .... Mrs. Vicki DUBE
96 Director Purchasing & Univ Stores .... Ms. Tracey ANGELL
28 Int Chief Diversity Officer .... Ms. Mary Grace ALMANDREZ
43 General Counsel .... Mr. Louis J. SACCOCCIO
32 Vice President Student Affairs .... Ms. Kathy M. COLLINS
109 Dir Dining Services .... Mr. Pierre ST-GERMAIN
41 Director of Athletics .... Mr. Thorr D. BJORN
103 Dir Career and Experiential Edu .... Ms. Kim STACK
38 Director Counseling Center .... Dr. Robert SAMUELS
88 Dir Recreational Services .... Ms. Jodi HAWKINS
35 Dean of Students .... Mr. Daniel GRANEY
88 Dir Special Pgms/Talent Devel .... Mr. Gerald WILLIAMS
88 Int Mgr Conf & Spec Pgm .... Ms. Sheri DAVIS
35 Asst VP Student Affs & Dir HRL .... Mr. Frankie MINOR
39 Assoc Dir Housing & Res Life .... Dr. Jeffrey PLOUFFE
23 Director Health Services .... Ms. Ellen REYNOLDS
40 Administrator Bookstore .... Mr. Paul WHITNEY
88 Spec Asst to the Prov for Acad Plng .... Ms. Ann M. MORRISSEY
88 Int Vice Prov Acad Finan/Personnel .... Dr. Matthew H. BODAH
84 Vice Provost Enrollment Management .... Mr. Dean LIBUTTI
07 Dean of Admissions .... Ms. Cynthia L. BONN
06 Dir Enrollment Services .... Dr. Carnell JONES
20 Vice Provost for Acad & Fac Init .... Dr. Anne VEEGER
13 Int Chief Information Officer .... Mr. Karlis KAUGARS
90 Dir Media & Technology Services .... Mr. David S. PORTER
91 Dir University Computing Systems .... Ms. Donna BELDEN
51 A S Feinstein Col Educ & Prof Stds .... Dr. Anthony ROLLE
49 Dean of Arts & Sciences .... Dr. Jeanette E. RILEY
50 Dean Business Administration .... Dr. Maling EBRAHIMPOUR
54 Dean of Engineering .... Dr. Raymond M. WRIGHT
88 Dean Univ Col & Spec Acad Pgms .... Dr. Jayne E. RICHMOND
58 Dean of Graduate School .... Dr. Nasser H. ZAWIA
66 Dean of Nursing .... Dr. Barbara E. WOLFE
67 Dean of Pharmacy .... Dr. Paul LARRAT
69 Dean Col of Health Sciences .... Dr. Gary LIGUORI
53 Director School of Education .... Dr. David BYRD
88 Dean Grad School Oceanography .... Dr. Bruce CORLISS
88 Dean of Environment & Life Sciences .... Dr. John KIRBY
08 Dean University Libraries .... Mr. Karim B. BOUGHIDA
22 Director Affirm Act/Equal Oppty/Div .... Ms. Roxanne GOMES
37 Sr Assoc Dir Enrol Svcs/Fin Aid .... Mr. Paul LANGHAMMER
92 Director Honors Program .... Dr. Lynne DERBYSHIRE
102 President URI Foundation .... Ms. Elizabeth O'ROURKE
85 Vice Provost for Global Initiatives .... Ms. Gifty AKO-ADOUNVO
106 Dir Learning/Assessment & Online .... Dr. Diane GOLDSMITH
94 Dir Gender and Women Studies .... Dr. Rosaria PISA
105 Manager Web Services .... Ms. Lisa CHEN
30 Manager Advancement Services .... Mr. John PELTIER
44 Dir of Annual & Parent Giving .... Ms. Nicole PETERS

University of Rhode Island Feinstein Providence Campus (C)

80 Washington Street, Providence RI 02903
Telephone: (401) 277-5000 Identification: 770118
Accreditation: &EH

University of Rhode Island Narragansett Bay Campus (D)

215 South Ferry Road, Narragansett RI 02882-1197
Telephone: (401) 874-6222 Identification: 770129
Accreditation: &EH

SOUTH CAROLINA

Aiken Technical College (E)

PO Drawer 696, Aiken SC 29802-0696
County: Aiken FICE Identification: 010056
Unit ID: 217615
Telephone: (803) 508-7263 Carnegie Class: Assoc/MT-VT-High Trad
FAX Number: N/A Calendar System: Semester
URL: www.atc.edu
Established: 1972 Annual Undergrad Tuition & Fees (In-District): $4,656
Enrollment: 2,399 Coed
Affiliation or Control: State/Local IRS Status: 501(c)3
Highest Offering: Associate Degree
Accreditation: SC, ACBSP, ADNUR, DA, MAC, PNUR, RAD, SURGT

01 President .... Dr. Forest E. MAHAN
04 Executive Assistant to President .... Ms. Jill UHLER
30 Director Foundation & Alumni .... Ms. Mary COMMONS
05 VP Academic & Student Affairs .... Dr. Vinson BURDETTE
108 VP Inst Effectiveness/Accreditation .... Vacant
76 Dean of Health Sciences .... Dr. Keith BRAMMELL
72 Dean of Technical Education .... Vacant
97 Dean of General Education .... Fr. Frederick ROGERS
51 Dean Business/Computer Technology .... Dr. Steven SIMMONS
10 Vice Pres Administrative Services .... Mr. Andy JORDAN
37 Director of Financial Aid .... Ms. Sue SIMS
13 Director of Info Systems Mgmt .... Mr. Walter BUSBEE
15 Director of Human Resources .... Ms. Sylvia BYRD
21 Controller .... Ms. Betsy CLINE
96 Director of Purchasing .... Ms. Toni MARSHALL
18 Director Facilities & Operations .... Vacant
06 Registrar .... Mrs. Dawn BUTTS
38 Director Counseling/Disabilities .... Mr. Rich WELDON
26 Director Marketing & PR .... Ms. Nikasha DICKS

Allen University (F)

1530 Harden Street, Columbia SC 29204-1085
County: Richland FICE Identification: 003417
Unit ID: 217624
Telephone: (803) 376-5700 Carnegie Class: Bac-A&S
FAX Number: N/A Calendar System: Semester
URL: www.allenuniversity.edu
Established: 1870 Annual Undergrad Tuition & Fees: $12,940
Enrollment: 590 Coed
Affiliation or Control: African Methodist Episcopal IRS Status: 501(c)3
Highest Offering: Master's
Accreditation: SC

01 President .... Dr. Ernest MCNEALEY
05 VP Academic Affairs .... Dr. Charlene SPEAREN
81 Dean Mathematics/Natural Sciences .... Dr. Steffani DRIGGINS
79 Dean Arts and Humanities .... Dr. Kevin TRUMPETER
73 Dean Seminary .... Dr. Jamal HOPKINS
50 Dean Business/Soc Sci & Education ..... Dr. Kareem MUHAMMAD
32 VP Student Affairs .... Dr. Cynthia SELLERS-SIMON
10 VP Fiscal Affairs .... Ms. Ruby FIELDING
111 VP Institutional Advancement .... Mr. Dub TAYLOR
30 Director of Development .... Dr. Teesa BRUNSON
26 Dir Marketing &
Communications .... Ms. Elizabeth MOSELY-HAWKINS
15 Chief Human Resources Officer .... Ms. Andraea HERRIN
41 Athletic Director .... Mr. Gregory THOMPSON
09 Director Institutional Research .... Vacant
08 Library Director .... Ms. Carol BOWERS
90 Director of IT Services .... Mr. Samuel PASCHAL
36 Director Counseling/Placement .... Dr. Flavia ELDEMIRE
39 Director Residential Life & Health .... Ms. Oveta GLOVER
35 Director of Student Activities .... Ms. Lisa REEVES
19 Chief of Police .... Chief Kelvin DAVIS
84 Dean Enrollment Mgmt/Registrar .... Ms. Marilyn DEBERRY
07 Director of Admissions .... Mr. Charles SINGLEY
37 Director of Financial Aid .... Ms. Lola KENNEDY
21 Comptroller .... Mr. John SAMPSON
113 Bursar .... Ms. Sharon DAVIS
18 Director of Operations .... Mr. Vincent NORTHINGTON
29 Director of Alumni Affairs .... Vacant
25 Director of Sponsored Programs .... Ms. Deitra BRIGGMAN
88 Director of Bands .... Mr. Eddie ELLIS
04 Executive Assistant .... Ms. Violet HARRISON

Anderson University (G)

316 Boulevard, Anderson SC 29621-4035
County: Anderson FICE Identification: 003418
Unit ID: 217633
Telephone: (864) 231-2000 Carnegie Class: Masters/M
FAX Number: (864) 231-2004 Calendar System: Semester
URL: www.andersonuniversity.edu
Established: 1911 Annual Undergrad Tuition & Fees: $28,000
Enrollment: 3,494 Coed
Affiliation or Control: Other IRS Status: 501(c)3
Highest Offering: Doctorate
Accreditation: SC, ACBSP, ART, CAEPN, MUS, NURSE, @PTA, THEA

01 President .... Dr. Evans P. WHITAKER
05 Exec Vice Pres/Provost & CFO .... Dr. Danny PARKER
10 Sr VP Administration & Brand .... Mr. David RASHED
20 Sr VP Inst Eff/Vice Provost .... Mrs. Susan WOOTEN
30 SVP Development/Pres Affairs .... Mr. James LANDRITH
32 Sr VP Student Development .... Dr. James FEREIRA
13 VP Information Technology .... Mr. Peter HARVIN
28 VP Diversity and Inclusion .... Mr. Beverly MCADAMS
42 VP Church Rel/Sr Campus Pastor .... Dr. James CLINE
42 VP Christian Life/Campus Min .... Rev. Samuel BRASHIER
84 VP Enrollment Management .... Ms. Pam ROSS
26 Dir Marketing & Communications .... Mr. Barry RAY
27 Assoc VP Mktg/Comm/Post-Tr .... Mr. James DUGUID
20 Asst Provost .... Mr. Nathan COX
20 Asst Provost .... Dr. Ryan NEAL
29 Assoc VP for Alumni and Parent Rel .... Mr. Jason RUTLAND
73 Dean COCS & Clamp Div Sch .... Mr. James DUDUIT
66 Dean School of Nursing .... Dr. Carol ARCHULETA
49 Dean College of Arts/Sciences .... Dr. Wayne COX
57 Dean SC School of the Arts .... Dr. David LARSON
88 Dean School Int Design .... Ms. Emily MARTIN
50 Dean College of Business .... Mr. Steven NAIL
76 Dean College of Health Professions .... Dr. Donald PEACE
82 Dean School Pub Svc/Admin .... Dr. Timothy TURNER
53 Dean College of Education .... Dr. Mark BUTLER
88 Assoc Dean College of Business .... Dr. John DUNCAN
121 Dean Student Success .... Dr. Linda KING
06 Dean Enroll Svcs & Univ Registrar .... Mrs. Carol PARKER
14 Dean Ctr for Innovation/Digi .... Dr. Benjamin DEATON
88 Dean Student Life .... Mr. Jonathan GROPP
88 Dean Student Development .... Ms. Robyn SANDERSON
41 Dir Athletics .... Mr. William D'ANDREA
88 Exec Dir Conf Svcs/Univ Events .... Mrs. Jody BRYANT
39 Assoc Dean of Residence Life .... Ms. Melissa JONES
07 Dir Admission .... Mr. Jacob QUEEN
08 Dir Thrift Library .... Mr. Kent MILLWOOD
09 Dir External Reporting .... Mr. Daryl A. IVERSON
15 Dir Human Resources .... Ms. Martha MCMINN
18 Dir Facilities .... Mr. Charles DICKERSON
19 Dir Campus Safety .... Mr. James KINES
21 Controller .... Ms. Kristie COLE
88 Dir Sports Med/Asst Dir Ath .... Mr. William DUVALL
23 Dir Health Services/Nurse .... Mrs. Debbie TAYLOR
35 Dir Student Activities .... Ms. Bethany TURNER
36 Dir Career Services .... Ms. Kelly BELL
37 Dir Financial Services .... Mrs. Nancy TATE
38 Dir Counseling .... Ms. Erin MAURER
104 Dir International
Programs .... Dr. Ann-Margaret THEMISTOCLEOUS
04 Exec Assistant to the President .... Mrs. Diane SUTHERLAND

Benedict College (A)

1600 Harden Street, Columbia SC 29204-1086

County: Richland FICE Identification: 003420
Unit ID: 217721
Telephone: (803) 253-5000 Carnegie Class: Bac-Diverse
FAX Number: (803) 253-5059 Calendar System: Semester
URL: www.benedict.edu
Established: 1870 Annual Undergrad Tuition & Fees: $16,600
Enrollment: 2,090 Coed
Affiliation or Control: Independent Non-Profit IRS Status: 501(c)3
Highest Offering: Baccalaureate
Accreditation: SC, ACBSP, ART, CAEPN, SW

01 President Dr. Roslyn C. ARTIS
05 Vice Pres for Academic Affairs Dr. Janeen WITTY
100 Chief of Staff Dr. Ceeon D. SMITH
10 Vice President Business/Finance Mr. Chris THOMPSON
108 Assoc VP for Academic Assessment Dr. Kimberly HAYNES STEPHENS
32 Vice President Student Affairs Mr. Gary E. KNIGHT
111 Vice Pres Institutional Advancement Mrs. Leandra H. BURGESS
20 Assoc Vice Pres Academic Affairs Dr. George A. DEVLIN
21 Asst VP for Business & Finance Ms. Jackie BROWN
26 Asst VP for Comm & Marketing Ms. Kymm HUNTER
07 Director of Admissions Ms. Keisha MONTGOMERY
29 Assistant VP for Alumni Relations Mrs. Ada A. BELTON
13 System Administrator Mr. Darren CLINTON
84 VP for Enrollment Management Dr. Emmanuel LALANDE
15 Interim Director of Human Resources Ms. Elaine BROWN
06 Registrar/Director Student Records Mrs. Wanda A. SCOTT-KINNEY
41 Athletics Director Mr. Willie WASHINGTON
38 Exec Dir Career Pathways Initiative Ms. Tondaleya JACKSON
42 Campus Minister Rev. Thomas DAVIS
19 Director Campus Safety Mr. Kevin PORTEE
36 Career Development Coordinator Ms. Sonya JOHNSON
37 Director Financial Aid Ms. Monique RICKENBAKER
19 Director Physical Plant Mr. Todd FOSTER
08 Director of Library Mrs. Darlene ZINNERMAN-BETHEA
09 Research Coordinator Dr. Dawn MILLS CAMPBELL
88 Assessment Coordinator Dr. Chasisity SPRINGS
25 Coordinator Title III Ms. Deborah MCKENZIE
49 Dean Sch Human/Arts/Soc Sci Vacant
50 Interim Dean School of Bus/Econ Dr. Tracy DUNN
53 Interim Dean Educ/Health Human Svcs Dr. Tracy MIDDLETON
72 Dean Sch Science/Tech/Engrng/Math Dr. Fouzi ARAMMASH
92 Dean School of Honors Dr. Warren ROBINSON
57 Chair Communications and Arts Ms. Gina MOORE
50 Chair Business Admin/Mgmt/Mktg Mr. Melvin MILLER
88 Chair Education and Family Studies Dr. Tracy MIDDLETON
70 Chair Social Work Dr. John MILLER
88 Chair Bio/Chem/Enviroment Hlth Sci Dr. Larry LOWE
68 Chair Health/Physical Ed/Recreation Dr. Paula SHELBY
54 Chair Comp Science/Physics/Engr Dr. Fouzi H. ARAMMASH
88 Int Chair Economics/Finance/Acctg Dr. Victor OYINBO

Bob Jones University (B)

1700 Wade Hampton Boulevard,
Greenville SC 29614-0001

County: Greenville FICE Identification: 003421
Unit ID: 217749
Telephone: (864) 242-5100 Carnegie Class: Masters/S
FAX Number: (864) 235-6661 Calendar System: Semester
URL: www.bju.edu
Established: 1927 Annual Undergrad Tuition & Fees: $18,150
Enrollment: 2,916 Coed
Affiliation or Control: Independent Non-Profit IRS Status: 501(c)3
Highest Offering: Doctorate
Accreditation: SC, TRACS

00 Chancellor Dr. Bob JONES, III
01 President Dr. Stephen D. PETTIT
05 Exec Vice Pres for Academic Affairs Dr. Gary M. WEIER
88 Exec VP for Enrollment & Min Advanc Dr. Samuel E. HORN
111 VP Advancement & Alumni Relations Mr. John D. MATTHEWS
26 Chief Communication Officer Ms. Carol A. KEIRSTEAD
11 Vice Provost/Chief Admin Officer Dr. David A. FISHER
45 Vice Provost Strategic Initiatives Dr. Beverly CORMICAN
10 Chief Financial Officer Mr. Steve DICKINSON
32 VP Student Develop & Discipleship Rev. Alan T. BENSON
84 Chief Enrollment Officer Dr. Bobby WOOD
15 Chief Human Resources Officer Mr. Kevin L. TAYLOR
13 Chief Information Officer Mr. Marvin P. REEM
49 Dean College of Arts and Science Dr. Renae WENTWORTH
73 Dean School of Religion & Seminary Dr. Samuel E. HORN
57 Dean Sch Fine Arts & Communication Dr. Darren P. LAWSON
53 Dean School of Education Dr. Brian A. CARRUTHERS
50 Dean School of Business Mr. Mike BUITER
76 Interim Dean Sch of Health Sciences Dr. Jessica MINOR
06 Registrar Dr. Daniel SMITH
33 Dean of Men Mr. Jonathan G. DAULTON
34 Dean of Women Ms. Deneen LAWSON
07 Director of Admission Mr. Gary A. DEEDRICK
88 Director of Ministry Training Dr. Nathan G. CROCKETT
41 Athletic Director Dr. Neal RING
37 Director of Financial Aid Mrs. Susan YOUNG
08 Dean of Libraries Vacant
09 Sr Dir Planning/Rsrch/Assessment Rev. Phil GERARD
100 Chief of Staff Mr. Randy PAGE

Central Carolina Technical College (C)

506 N Guignard Drive, Sumter SC 29150-2499

County: Sumter FICE Identification: 003995
Unit ID: 218858
Telephone: (803) 778-1961 Carnegie Class: Assoc/MT-VT-High Trad
FAX Number: (803) 778-7880 Calendar System: Semester
URL: www.cctech.edu
Established: 1962 Annual Undergrad Tuition & Fees (In-State): $5,166
Enrollment: 3,720 Coed
Affiliation or Control: State IRS Status: 501(c)3
Highest Offering: Associate Degree
Accreditation: SC, ADNUR, MAC, SURGT

01 President Dr. Michael MIKOTA
05 Vice President for Academic Affairs Mr. Myles WILLIAMS
10 Vice President for Business Affairs Ms. Terry L. BOOTH
32 Vice President for Student Affairs Ms. Lisa BRACKEN
04 Assistant to the President Ms. Diana REARDON
51 Dean Cont Educ/Workforce Devel Ms. Elizabeth WILLIAMS
08 Dean of Learning Resources Ms. Nancy BISHOP
30 Director of Development and Alumni Ms. Misty HATFIELD
26 Director Public Relations Ms. Catherine FRYE
15 Director of Personnel Mrs. Ronalda S. STOVER
13 Director Information Systems Mr. Brian DAVIS
06 Registrar Ms. Jennifer SZUPKA
37 Director Student Financial Aid Mr. Ken BERNARD
09 Dir Research/Institutional Effect Mr. Bryan MAY
07 Director of Student Engagement Mrs. Barbara WRIGHT
54 Dean of Industrial and Engineering Mr. Brent RUSSELL
76 Dean of Health Sciences Ms. Mary Jo ARDIS
97 Dean of General Education Mr. Jason TISDEL

Charleston School of Law (D)

81 Mary Street, PO Box 535, Charleston SC 29402

County: Charleston FICE Identification: 040963
Unit ID: 451510
Telephone: (843) 329-1000 Carnegie Class: Spec-4-yr-Law
FAX Number: (843) 720-7899 Calendar System: Semester
URL: www.charlestonlaw.edu
Established: 2003 Annual Graduate Tuition & Fees: N/A
Enrollment: 564 Coed
Affiliation or Control: Proprietary IRS Status: Proprietary
Highest Offering: First Professional Degree; No Undergraduates
Accreditation: LAW

01 President Mr. J. Edward BELL, III
05 Dean & Provost Mr. Andrew L. ABRAMS
20 Associate Dean Academic Affairs Ms. Margaret M. LAWTON
07 Assoc Dean Admission/Financial Aid Ms. Jacqueline B. BELL
32 Assoc Dean of Students Mr. Brett BARKER
13 Assoc Dean of Info Services Ms. Lisa SMITH-BUTLER
36 Asst Dean Career Services Mr. Mark S. MOORE
10 Chief Financial Officer Ms. Wende WOOD
06 Registrar Ms. Jennifer SUMMERS
15 Director Human Resources Ms. Shera L. SILVIS
08 Director of Library Ms. Katie BROWN

Charleston Southern University (E)

PO Box 118087, Charleston SC 29423-8087

County: Charleston FICE Identification: 003419
Unit ID: 217688
Telephone: (843) 863-7000 Carnegie Class: Masters/M
FAX Number: (843) 863-8074 Calendar System: Semester
URL: www.csuniv.edu
Established: 1964 Annual Undergrad Tuition & Fees: $25,540
Enrollment: 3,492 Coed
Affiliation or Control: Southern Baptist IRS Status: 501(c)3
Highest Offering: Doctorate
Accreditation: SC, #ARCPA, CAATE, CAEPN, IACBE, MUS, NUR

01 President Dr. Dondi E. COSTIN
03 Executive Vice President Dr. Michael BRYANT
05 Vice President Academic Affairs Dr. Jacqueline FISH
10 VP for Business Affairs & Athletics Mr. Luke BLACKMON
04 Exec Assistant to the President Mrs. Faye WOOD
07 Director of Admissions Mrs. Kimberly FORD
84 Vice Pres Enrollment Management Mr. Jim RHOTON
30 Vice Pres Development Mr. David BAGGS
20 Asst VP for Academic Affairs Dr. Scott YARBROUGH
110 VP for Development & Planned Giving Mr. Bill WARD
32 Dean of Students Mr. Clark CARTER
13 Chief Information Officer Mr. Shannon PHILLIPS
08 Director of the Library Mr. Eric KISTLER
06 Registrar Mrs. Amanda SISSON
29 Director of BUC Club Mr. Tyler DAVIS
21 VP for Finance Mrs. Janet MIMS
26 Director of Integrated Marketing Mr. Richard ESPOSITO
09 Dir of Institutional Effectiveness Mr. Jeffrey BABETZ
58 Dir of Graduate Business Program Dr. Maxwell ROLLINS
41 Athletic Director Mr. Jeff BARBER
42 Asst Dean Campus Ministries Mr. Jon DAVIS
19 Director of Security Mr. John WILSON
90 Director of Computer Science Dr. Valerie SESSIONS
18 Director of Facility Services Mr. Nick CIMORELLI
29 Dir of Alumni & Parent Engagement Mr. Christian HANLEY
07 Director of Enrollment Services Mr. Nick BALLENGER
15 Director of Human Resources Mrs. Lindsey WALKE
36 Assistant Dean for Career Center Dr. Nina GRANT
38 Director of Student Counseling Mrs. Kimberly PERKINS
96 Director of Purchasing Mrs. Lisa OROZCO
37 Director Student Financial Aid Mrs. Teri KARGES
39 Assistant Dean of Residence Life Ms. Julie ALIMPICH
50 Dean College of Business Dr. David PALMER
83 Dean Humanities/Social Sciences Dr. Dan FULTZ
81 Dean Science & Mathematics Dr. Todd ASHBY
66 Dean of Nursing/Health Sciences Dr. Andreea MEIER
53 Dean College of Education Dr. George METZ
20 Assistant VP Academic Affairs Dr. Marc EMBLER
104 Director International Programs Mrs. Stephanie LEVAN
108 Director Institutional Assessment Mr. Jeff BABETZ

The Citadel, The Military College of South Carolina (F)

171 Moultrie Street, Charleston SC 29409-0001

County: Charleston FICE Identification: 003423
Unit ID: 217864
Telephone: (843) 225-3294 Carnegie Class: Masters/L
FAX Number: (843) 953-5287 Calendar System: Semester
URL: www.citadel.edu
Established: 1842 Annual Undergrad Tuition & Fees (In-State): $12,516
Enrollment: 3,717 Coed
Affiliation or Control: State IRS Status: 501(c)3
Highest Offering: Beyond Master's But Less Than Doctorate
Accreditation: SC, CACREP, CAEP, CAEPN, NURSE

01 President Gen. Glenn M. WALTERS, RET.
00 Chairman of the Board Col. Fred L. PRICE
05 Provost/Dean BGen. Sally SELDEN
11 Senior Vice Pres for Operations Col. Thomas G. PHILIPKOSKY
10 Vice President of Finance Col. Charles CANSLER
32 Commandant of Cadets Capt. Eugene PALUSO
26 Vice President for Comm & Marketing Col. John DORRIAN
41 Dir Intercollegiate Athletics Mr. Mike CAPACCIO
102 Chief Exec Officer of Foundation Dr. Jay DOWD
04 Executive Assistant to President Cdr. William LIND
18 Vice Pres Facilities/Engineering Cdr. Jeffrey LAMBERSON
43 General Counsel Mr. Mark C. BRANDENBURG
20 Assoc Provost Academic Affairs Col. David ALLEN
108 Dir Accreditation and Assessment Ms. Karin ROOF
07 Director of Admissions LtCol. John W. POWELL, JR.
06 Registrar Maj. Lisa M. BLAKE
113 Treasurer Ms. Lindsey M. NETTLES
29 Exec Dir Alumni Affairs Mr. McAlister TOM
08 Director of Library Vacant
13 Chief Information Officer Maj. Kyle HERRON
109 Asst VP Auxiliary Services Maj. Kevin REID
37 Director Financial Aid/ Scholarships LtCol. Henry M. FULLER, JR.
15 Chief Human Resources Officer Maj. Leah S. SCHONFELD
36 Director of Career Services Ms. Page TISDALE
38 Director of Citadel Counseling Ctr Dr. Suzanne BUFANO
84 Assoc Provost for Enrollment Mgmt Vacant
09 Director of Institutional Research Ms. Lisa L. PACE
19 Director of Public Safety Chief Michael TURNER
23 College Physician Dr. Carey M. CAPELL
40 Director of the Cadet Store Ms. Linda MATTINGLY
42 Chaplain/Dir Religious Activities Cdr. Joe MOLINA
92 Director Honors Program Dr. Deirdre RAGAN
86 Director Govt & Community Affairs Col. Cardon B. CRAWFORD
96 Director of Purchasing LtCol. James P. DE LUCA
22 Dir Affirmative Action/Equal Oppty Ms. Shawn EDWARDS
50 Dean of the School of Business Col. Michael WEEKS
53 Int Dean of the School of Education Col. Renee JEFFERSON
54 Dean of the School of Engineering Col. Ronald W. WELCH
81 Dean School of Science/Math Col. Darin T. ZIMMERMAN
79 Dean Sch Humanities/Social Sciences Col. Winifred B. MOORE
101 Spec Asst to President/Brd Matters Ms. Lori HEDSTROM
93 Director Multicultural Affairs LtCol. Robert P. PICKERING
16 Deputy Director of Human Resources Mr. Wesley S. SAMS
114 Chief Budget Administrator Maj. Michael S. KEENEY
121 Director of Student Success LtCol. Jane WARNER
116 Audit Officer Mr. Gary MALLOY
28 Asst Provost for Diversity Maj. Jaye SMITH
21 Controller LtCol. Frank LOGAN
105 College Web Designer Mr. Morgan SPENCER
119 IT Security Manager Mr. Justin CONSOLVO
58 Asst Dean of Graduate College Ms. Emily THOMAS
44 Sr Director of Legacy Giving Mr. Bill YAEGER
112 VP Legacy/Annual Reunion Giving Mr. Jonathan KRESKEN
27 Director of Marketing Ms. Kara KLEIN
104 Director Study Abroad Maj. Zane SEGLE
120 Director Teaching Innovation Dr. Diana CHESHIRE

Claflin University (G)

400 Magnolia Street, Orangeburg SC 29115-4477

County: Orangeburg FICE Identification: 003424
Unit ID: 217873
Telephone: (800) 922-1276 Carnegie Class: Bac-Diverse
FAX Number: (803) 531-2860 Calendar System: Semester
URL: www.claflin.edu
Established: 1869 Annual Undergrad Tuition & Fees: $16,854
Enrollment: 2,129 Coed
Affiliation or Control: United Methodist IRS Status: 501(c)3
Highest Offering: Master's
Accreditation: SC, ACBSP, CAEPN, MUS, NURSE

01 President Dr. Dwaun B. WARMACK
11 Vice President for Administration Mr. Drexel B. BALL
05 Provost/Chief Academic Officer Dr. Karl S. WRIGHT

10 Vice President for Fiscal Affairs ....Mrs. Tijuana R. HUDSON
111 Vice Pres Institutional Advancement ....Rev. Whittaker V. MIDDLETON
32 Vice Pres Student Devel & Services ....Dr. Leroy A. DURANT
45 VP Plng/Assessment/Information Svcs ....Dr. Zia HASAN
20 Vice Provost for Academic Programs ....Dr. Angela W. PETERS
26 AVP Communications & Marketing ....Mr. George W. JOHNSON
39 Exec Dir Housing & Res Life ....Mr. Dillon BECKFORD
108 AVP Institutional Effectiveness ....Dr. Bridget P. DEWEES
112 AVP of Major & Planned Gifts ....Mr. Marcus BURGESS
07 Director of Admissions ....Mr. Michael ZEIGLER
79 Dean Sch Humanities & Soc Science ....Dr. Isaiah R. MCGEE
50 Dean School of Business ....Dr. Nicholas HILL
53 Dean School of Education ....Dr. Anthony PITTMAN
81 Dean Sch Natural Sciences & Math ....Dr. Verlie A. TISDALE
13 Asst VP Information Tech Svcs ....Mr. James E. BRENN
51 Int Exec Dir for Prof/Cont Studies ....Mr. Mark A. ROBERTS
08 Library Director ....Mrs. Marilyn GIBBS DRAYTON
37 Director of Financial Aid ....Ms. Terria C. WILLIAMS
36 Director of Career Development ....Mrs. Carolyn R. SNELL
41 Athletic Director ....Dr. Jerome H. FITCH
15 Senior Director of Human Resources ....Ms. Shirley A. BIGGS
06 Registrar ....Mrs. Tanika L. BEARD
29 Director Alumni Affairs/Annual Fund ....Mrs. Zelda LEE
19 Chief of Campus Public Safety ....Mr. Steven A. PEARSON
109 Director of Auxiliary Services ....Vacant
46 Asst Vice Provost for Research ....Vacant
04 Executive Admin Asst to President ....Ms. Melvenia WILLIAMS
09 Director of Institutional Research ....Dr. Corey R. AMAKER
84 Director Enrollment Management ....Dr. Leroy A. DURANT
104 Director Study Abroad ....Dr. Jacqueline JACKSON

Clemson University (A)

201 Sikes Hall, Clemson SC 29634-0001
County: Pickens FICE Identification: 003425
Unit ID: 217882
Telephone: (864) 656-3311 Carnegie Class: DU-Highest
FAX Number: (864) 656-4040 Calendar System: Semester
URL: www.clemson.edu
Established: 1889 Annual Undergrad Tuition & Fees (In-State): $15,374
Enrollment: 24,387 Coed
Affiliation or Control: State IRS Status: 501(c)3
Highest Offering: Doctorate
Accreditation: SC, ART, CACREP, CAEPN, CARTE, CONST, CVT, DIETD, IPSY, LSAR, NRPA, NURSE, PH, PLNG

01 President ....Dr. James P. CLEMENTS
05 Provost ....Dr. Robert H. JONES
43 General Counsel ....Mr. W.C. (Chip) HOOD
10 Exec VP for Finance & Operations ....Mr. Anthony E. WAGNER
32 VP Student Affairs ....Dr. Almeda JACKS
101 Executive Secretary to the Board ....Ms. Angie LEIDINGER
111 Vice President for Advancement ....Mr. A. Neill CAMERON, JR.
103 Vice Pres Public Svc ....Dr. George R. ASKEW
46 Vice President for Research ....Dr. Tanju KARANFIL
88 Vice Pres for Economic Development ....Dr. John M. BALLATO
13 Vice Prov Computer/Info Technology ....Mr. Russell KAURLOTO
88 Vice Provost for International Affs ....Ms. Sharon NAGY
100 Chief of Staff ....Mr. Max ALLEN
29 Chief Alumni Officer ....Mr. Brian J. O'ROURKE
18 Chief Facilities Officer ....Mr. Todd BARNETTE
35 Associate VP/Dean of Students ....Dr. Joy S. SMITH
88 Assoc Provost Faculty Development .Ms. Amy L. LAWTON-RAUH
26 Chief Public Affairs Officer ....Mr. Mark D. LAND
08 Dean of Libraries ....Mr. Christopher N. COX
07 Director of Admissions ....Mr. David KUSKOWSKI
06 Registrar ....Mrs. Debra SPARACINO
37 Director of Financial Aid ....Mrs. Elizabeth MILAM
36 Director of Career Center ....Mr. Burton O'NEIL
38 Director Counseling/Psych Services ....Dr. Raquel J. CONTRERAS
47 Dean Col Agric/Forestry/Life Sci ....Dr. Keith L. BELLI
58 Dean Graduate School/Vice Provost ....Vacant
48 Dean Col Arch/Arts/Humanities ....Vacant
54 Dean Col Engr/Sciences ....Dr. Anand GRAMOPADHYE
83 Dean Col of Behavioral/Social Sci ....Dr. Leslie HOSSFELD
50 Dean College of Business ....Ms. Wendy YORK
53 Dean College of Education ....Dr. George J. PETERSON
81 Dean of Science ....Dr. Cynthia YOUNG
09 Director Institutional Research ....Dr. Juan XU
39 Executive Director of Housing ....Ms. Kathy B. HOBGOOD
41 Director of Athletics ....Mr. Dan RADAKOVICH
112 Director of Estate & Planned Giving ....Ms. Jovanna J. KING
22 Director Access & Equity ....Mr. Lewis J. KNIGHTON, JR.
28 Director of Diversity ....Mr. Lee A. GILL
23 Director Student Health Services ....Mr. George W. CLAY
15 Chief Human Resources Officer ....Ms. Emily WATROUS
91 Executive Director Enterprise Appl ....Mr. Barrett KENDJORIA
25 Director Sponsored Programs ....Ms. Sheila T. LISCHWE
19 Director Law Enforcement & Safety ....Chief Greg MULLEN
96 Director of Purchasing ....Mr. Michael NEBESKY
04 Int Asst to the President/Vice Prov ....Dr. Jeremy R. KING
88 Dir Teaching Effectiveness & Innova ....Ms. Taimi OLSEN
121 Director of Academic Success Center ....Ms. Susan WHORTON
104 Director Study Abroad ....Mr. Paul PAPARELLA

Clinton College (B)

1029 Crawford Road, Rock Hill SC 29730-5152
County: York FICE Identification: 004923
Unit ID: 217891
Telephone: (803) 327-7402 Carnegie Class: Bac/Assoc-Mixed
FAX Number: (803) 327-3261 Calendar System: Semester
URL: www.clintoncollege.edu
Established: 1894 Annual Undergrad Tuition & Fees: $10,020
Enrollment: 170 Coed
Affiliation or Control: African Methodist Episcopal Zion Church
IRS Status: 501(c)3
Highest Offering: Baccalaureate
Accreditation: TRACS

01 President ....Dr. Lester A. MCCORN
04 Exec Assistant to the President ....Ms. Cheryl J. MCCULLOUGH
05 VP Academic Affairs/Dean ....Dr. Alvin MCLAMB
111 VP Institutional Advancement ....Vacant
32 VP for Student Affairs ....Dr. Angelyne BROWN
10 VP for Business & Finance ....Ms. Archinya INGRAM
06 Registrar ....Ms. Laveria WYNN
37 Financial Aid ....Ms. Pamela WHITE
08 Director Library Services ....Vacant
41 Athletic Director ....Mr. Alfonzo DUNCAN
18 Superintendent Buildings/Grounds ....Mr. Donnie INGRAM
07 Director of Admissions ....Mr. Sedrick SINGLETARY
35 Director Student Support Services ....Ms. Judith COWAN

Coastal Carolina University (C)

PO Box 261954, Conway SC 29528-6054
County: Horry FICE Identification: 003451
Unit ID: 218724
Telephone: (843) 347-3161 Carnegie Class: Masters/L
FAX Number: (843) 349-2990 Calendar System: Semester
URL: www.coastal.edu
Established: 1954 Annual Undergrad Tuition & Fees (In-State): $11,716
Enrollment: 10,663 Coed
Affiliation or Control: State IRS Status: 501(c)3
Highest Offering: Doctorate
Accreditation: SC, ART, CAEPN, MUS, NUR, PH, THEA

01 President ....Dr. David A. DECENZO
05 Provost and VP Academic Affairs ....Dr. Daniel J. ENNIS
10 Vice President Finance/CFO ....Mr. David FROST
30 Interim Vice Pres Philanthropy ....Mr. Bryan STEROS
32 Vice President Student Affairs ....Dr. Deborah CONNER
26 Vice Pres Univ Communications ....Vacant
15 Vice Pres Human Resources ....Ms. Beverly J. LANDRUM
50 Dean Business Administration ....Dr. Barbara RITTER
53 Dean of Education ....Dr. Edward JADALLAH
79 Dean of Humanities & Fine Arts ....Dr. Claudia BORNHOLDT
81 Dean of Science ....Dr. Michael H. ROBERTS
97 Dean of University College ....Dr. Sara HOTTINGER
13 Chief Information & Technology Ofcr ....Mr. Abdallah HADDAD
20 Assoc Provost Operations ....Ms. Sallie CLARKSON
108 Assoc Prov Assessment/Accreditation ....Dr. James SOLAZZO
58 Interim Dean Graduate Studies ....Dr. Robert F. YOUNG
104 Assoc Provost Global Initiatives .Dr. Darla J. DOMKE-DAMONTE
09 Exec Dir of Planning and Research ....Ms. Christine L. MEE
06 University Registrar ....Mr. Daniel M. LAWLESS
19 Director Public Safety ....Mr. David ROPER
21 Controller ....Mr. Gregory T. THOMPSON
28 VP for Diversity/Equity & Inclusion ....Dr. Atiya STOKES-BROWN
41 Director of Athletics ....Mr. Matthew L. HOGUE
35 Asst VP Student Affairs ....Dr. Jennie M. CASSIDY
85 Director of International Programs ....Vacant
39 Sr Dir of Housing ....Ms. Kathy A. DALEY
37 Dir Financial Aid & Scholarship ....Ms. Wendy WATTS
92 Director Honors Program ....Dr. Louis E. KEINER
36 Director Career Services ....Dr. Verne W. WALKER
96 Dir Procurement/Business Services ....Mr. Dean P. HUDSON
18 Director of Facilities Planning ....Mr. T. Rein MUNGO
27 Assoc VP for Univ Communications ....Ms. Martha S. HUNN
29 Executive Director Alumni Relations ....Ms. Diane F. SANDERS
07 Assoc Provost Admiss & Merit Awards ....Ms. Amanda E. CRADDOCK
22 Assoc VP Human Resources/EEO ....Ms. Kimberly B. SHERFESEE
43 Sr VP/University Counsel ....Mr. Carlos JOHNSON
90 Sr Dir Enterprise System Support ....Mr. Fadi N. BAROODY
08 University Librarian ....Dr. Melvin D. DAVIS
100 Chief of Staff/VP Exec Initiatives ....Mr. Travis E. OVERTON

Coker University (D)

300 E College Avenue, Hartsville SC 29550-3797
County: Darlington FICE Identification: 003427
Unit ID: 217907
Telephone: (843) 383-8000 Carnegie Class: Masters/S
FAX Number: (843) 383-8319 Calendar System: Semester
URL: www.coker.edu
Established: 1908 Annual Undergrad Tuition & Fees: $29,548
Enrollment: 1,109 Coed
Affiliation or Control: Independent Non-Profit IRS Status: 501(c)3
Highest Offering: Master's
Accreditation: SC, ART, CAEPN, DANCE, MUS

01 President ....Vacant
05 Provost & Dean of Faculty ....Dr. Susan HENDERSON
03 Executive Vice President ....Dr. Tracy PARKINSON
28 Dir of Diversity/Interfaith/Inclus ....Ms. Darlene SMALL
13 Director of IT ....Dr. Cathy CUPPETT
41 VP Athletics & Athletic Facilities ....Dr. Lynn GRIFFIN
58 VP Graduate & Professional Programs ....Dr. Kathryn FLAHERTY
84 VP for Enrollment Management ....Mr. Adam CONNOLLY
11 VP for Student Affairs ....Ms. Brianna DOUGLAS
09 Dir of Institutional Research ....Ms. Lynn RAWLS
10 Chief Financial Officer ....Ms. Robin A. PERDUE
37 Dir of Student Financial Planning ....Mrs. Betty B. WILLIAMS
111 VP for External Relations ....Dr. William CARSWELL
29 Director of Alumni Engagement ....Ms. Shelli WILSON
07 Director of Admissions ....Vacant
08 Director of the Library ....Mr. Todd RIX
19 Director of Campus Safety ....Mr. George MITCHELL
04 Executive Asst to President ....Ms. Heather NORMENT
15 Director of Human Resources ....Ms. Ella MARSHALL
39 Dir Resident Life/Student Housing ....Mr. Evan VAUGHN
44 Director of Philanthropy ....Ms. Peggy SMITH
53 Dean of Education ....Dr. Karen CARPENTER

College of Charleston (E)

66 George Street, Charleston SC 29424-0100
County: Charleston FICE Identification: 003428
Unit ID: 217819
Telephone: (843) 953-5507 Carnegie Class: Masters/L
FAX Number: (843) 953-5811 Calendar System: Semester
URL: www.cofc.edu
Established: 1770 Annual Undergrad Tuition & Fees (In-State): $12,838
Enrollment: 10,863 Coed
Affiliation or Control: State IRS Status: 501(c)3
Highest Offering: Master's
Accreditation: SC, CAATE, CAEPN, MUS, SPAA, THEA

01 President ....Dr. Andrew T. HSU
05 Interim Provost & Exec Vice Pres ....Dr. Frances C. WELCH
100 Chief of Staff ....Mr. Paul D. PATRICK
101 Vice Pres Col Events/Exec Sec BOT ....Ms. Elizabeth W. KASSEBAUM
04 Sr Exec Admin for the President ....Ms. Debbie HAMMOND
10 Interim EVP for Business Affairs ....Mr. Edward POPE
21 Interim Chief Financial Officer ....Ms. Dawn E. WILLAN
18 VP for Facilities Management ....Mr. John P. MORRIS
26 VP Mktg/Comm/Chief Mktg Officer ....Mr. Mark E. BERRY
111 Exec VP Institutional Advancement ....Mr. Chris TOBIN
32 Exec Vice President Student Affairs ....Ms. Alicia D. CAUDILL
35 Dean of Students ....Dr. Jeri O. CABOT
43 General Counsel Legal Affairs ....Ms. Angela B. MULHOLLAND
19 Chief of Police/Dir Public Safety ....Chief Robert S. REESE
20 Associate Provost ....Dr. Deanna M. CAVENY
20 Associate Vice Pres ....Dr. Lynne E. FORD
104 Assoc Provost International Educ ....Dr. Andrew M. SOBIESUO
13 Senior VP/Chief Information Officer ....Mr. Mark STAPLES
21 Dir of Financial Services ....Ms. Debye B. ALDERMAN
109 Dir Business & Auxiliary Services ....Ms. Amy K. ORR
96 Chief Procurement Officer ....Ms. Wendy E. WILLIAMS
30 Vice President Development ....Ms. Cathryn A. MAHON
15 VP of Human Resources ....Mr. Edward POPE
22 Dir Equal Opportunity Programs ....Ms. Kimberly A. GERTNER
21 Interim Sr VP of Fiscal Services ....Ms. Dawn E. WILLAN
84 Vice Pres Enrollment Planning ....Mr. Jimmie A. FOSTER
09 Director of Institutional Research ....Ms. Michelle L. SMITH
28 Associate VP Diversity ....Dr. Renard HARRIS
88 Asst VP New Student Programs ....Ms. Melinda MILEY
06 Registrar ....Ms. Mary C. BERGSTROM
21 Controller ....Ms. Dawn E. WILLAN
21 Treasurer ....Mr. David G. KATZ
58 Interim Dean of the Graduate School ....Dr. Godfrey GIBBISON
57 Dean School of the Arts ....Ms. Valerie B. MORRIS
50 Dean School of Business ....Dr. Alan T. SHAO
53 Acting Dean School of Education ....Dr. Courtney A. HOWARD
88 Dean School of Languages ....Dr. Timothy JOHNSON
81 Interim Dean School Science & Math ....Dr. Sebastian VAN DELDEN
79 Interim Dean Sch of Human/Soc Sci ....Dr. Gibbs KNOTTS
107 Dean College of Charleston North ....Dr. Godfrey GIBBISON
62 Dean of Libraries ....Dr. John WHITE
51 Director CCEPD ....Dr. Alice M. HAMILTON
92 Dean Honors College ....Dr. Trisha H. FOLDS-BENNETT
41 Director Athletics ....Mr. Matt ROBERTS
25 Director Research and Grants ....Ms. Susan A. RIVALEAU
37 Interim Dir Fin Asst/Vet Affairs ....Mr. Robert N. KERSEY
07 Exec Dir of Admissions ....Ms. Suzette STILLE
29 Vice President Alumni Affairs ....Ms. Ann PRYOR
121 Dir Center for Academic Advising ....Ms. Karen HAUSCHILD
88 Dir Center for Student Learning ....Ms. Melinda L. COLEMAN
108 AVP Inst Effectiveness ....Dr. Divya BHATI
22 Dir Ctr for Disabilities Services ....Ms. Deborah F. MIHAL
35 Dir Student Life & Stern Center ....Ms. Christine WORKMAN
36 Director Career Services ....Mr. Jim ALLISON, JR.
38 Dir Counseling & Substance Abuse ....Ms. Leslie F. ARMENIOX
23 Director Health Services ....Ms. Bridget MCLERNON-SYKES
39 Director Residence Life ....Ms. Melantha ARDREY
88 Dir Environmental Health and Safety ....Mr. Randy L. BEAVER
88 Director of ECDC ....Ms. Katie HOUSER
35 AVP Student Affairs/Dir HSLC ....Mr. K. Michael DUNCAN
18 Director of Sustainability ....Mr. P. Brian FISHER
31 Exec Dir Cmty Rels/Ombudsperson ....Ms. Evelyn H. NADEL
20 Dir Undergrad Academic Services ....Ms. Michelle G. FUTRELL

Columbia College (F)

1301 Columbia College Drive, Columbia SC 29203-5998
County: Richland FICE Identification: 003430
Unit ID: 217934
Telephone: (803) 786-3012 Carnegie Class: Masters/S
FAX Number: (803) 786-3752 Calendar System: Semester
URL: www.columbiasc.edu
Established: 1854 Annual Undergrad Tuition & Fees: $19,500
Enrollment: 1,514 Female
Affiliation or Control: United Methodist IRS Status: 501(c)3
Highest Offering: Master's
Accreditation: SC, ART, CAEPN, DANCE, MUS, NURSE, SW

01	President	Dr. Carol A. MOORE
05	Interim Provost	Dr. Madeleine SCHEP
10	Vice President for Finance	Ms. Wilma ALLEN
84	Vice Pres for Enrollment Management	Vacant
111	VP for Advancement	Mr. Francis G. SCHODOWSKI
32	VP for Student Affairs	Ms. LaNae R. BUDDEN
29	Exec Director of Alumnae Relations	Ms. Julie KING
09	Director Institutional Research	Dr. Scott A. SMITH
08	Director of Library	Ms. Jane TUTTLE
19	Chief of Police	Chief Wayne JAMISON
37	Director of Financial Aid	Mr. Justin PICHEY
36	Director of Ctr for Career Coaching	Mr. Nigel SMITH
13	Dir of Info Technology Services	Vacant
18	Director of Facilities Management	Ms. Gaby HICKMAN
26	Exec Director Mktg & Communications	Vacant
41	Director of Athletics	Ms. Debra STROMAN
40	Director Bookstore	Ms. Cory CORP
38	Director Counseling Services	Ms. Mimi MERIWETHER
04	Executive Assistant to President	Ms. Joye G. HIPP
07	Director of Admissions	Mr. Ryan LONGE
92	Director Honors Program/Faculty Dev	Dr. John ZUBIZARRETA
06	Registrar	Ms. Sharon HOFFMAN
15	Chief Human Resources Officer	Ms. Beverly JAMES
28	Director of Diversity	Ms. Melissia BRANNEN
39	Director Residence Life	Ms. Shade' HOLMES
44	Director Annual Giving	Mr. Vinnie MALONEY

Columbia International University (A)

7435 Monticello Road, Columbia SC 29203

County: Richland — FICE Identification: 003429 — Unit ID: 217925

Telephone: (803) 754-4100 — Carnegie Class: Masters/S
FAX Number: (803) 786-4209 — Calendar System: Semester
URL: www.ciu.edu
Established: 1923 — Annual Undergrad Tuition & Fees: $23,690
Enrollment: 966 — Coed
Affiliation or Control: Independent Non-Profit — IRS Status: 501(c)3
Highest Offering: Doctorate
Accreditation: SC, BI, CACREP, THEOL

01	President	Dr. Mark A. SMITH
00	Chancellor	Dr. Bill H. JONES
05	Senior Vice President/Provost	Dr. Jim LANPHER
112	Senior Vice President	Mr. D. Keith MARION
111	VP of Institutional Advancement	Mrs. Diane MULL
32	VP Student Svcs & Online Studies	Dr. Rick CHRISTMAN
73	Dean Seminary & School of Ministry	Dr. John HARVEY
49	Dean College of Arts & Sciences	Dr. Bryan BEYER
53	Dean College of Education	Dr. Connie MITCHELL
104	Dean College Intercultural Studies	Dr. Edward SMITHER
50	Dean Sch of Business & Prof Studies	Dr. Scott ADAMS
09	Dir Institutional Research/Assessmt	Dr. Roxianne SNODGRASS
101	Assoc Provost Online Studies	Dr. Brian SIMMONS
08	Director of Library	Mrs. Cynthia SNELL
06	University Registrar	Mrs. Jennifer BOOTH
15	Director Human Resources	Mr. Donald E. JONES
32	Dean of Students	Mr. Rick SWIFT
07	VP Enrollment & Marketing	Mrs. Silvia LUCASCHI-DECKER
13	VP Information Technology	Mrs. Michele BRANCH-FRAPPIER
18	Director Physical Plant	Mr. Phil MILLER
10	Chief Financial Officer	Mr. Rob HARTMAN
37	Director Financial Aid	Mrs. Patty HIX
04	Administrative Asst to President	Mrs. Debbie GERMANY
19	Director Security/Safety	Mr. Scott DEAL
41	Athletic Director	Mr. James WHITAKER

Converse College (B)

580 E Main, Spartanburg SC 29302-0006

County: Spartanburg — FICE Identification: 003431 — Unit ID: 217961

Telephone: (864) 596-9000 — Carnegie Class: Masters/S
FAX Number: (864) 596-9158 — Calendar System: 4/1/4
URL: www.converse.edu
Established: 1889 — Annual Undergrad Tuition & Fees: $18,340
Enrollment: 1,478 — Female
Affiliation or Control: Independent Non-Profit — IRS Status: 501(c)3
Highest Offering: Doctorate
Accreditation: SC, ART, CAEPN, CIDA, MFCD, MUS

01	President	Ms. Krista L. NEWKIRK
05	Provost	Dr. Jeffrey H. BARKER
10	Vice Pres Finance/Administration	Mr. Wayde DAWSON
111	VP Institutional Advancement	Mrs. Krista BOFILL
79	Dean Humanities/Sciences/Business	Dr. Erin TEMPLETON
57	Dean School of the Arts	Dr. Boone HOPKINS
53	Dean of Education/Grad Studies	Dr. Lienne MEDFORD
32	Dean of Students	Ms. Rhonda MINGO
08	Librarian	Mr. Wade WOODWARD
37	Director of Financial Planning	Mr. James KELLAM
06	Registrar	Ms. Gee SIGMAN
15	Human Resources Director	Dr. Keshia GILLIAM
13	Chief Information Officer	Mr. Zach CORBITT
26	Director of Media/Communications	Ms. Holly DUNCAN
04	Assistant to the President	Mrs. Pamela GREENWAY
38	Director of Counseling Services	Ms. Bethany GARR
09	Director Institutional Research	Dr. Yongmei LI
84	Vice Pres of Enrollment Management	Ms. Jamie GRANT
18	Chief Facilities/Physical Plant	Mr. Gladden SMOKE

Denmark Technical College (C)

PO Box 327, Denmark SC 29042-0327

County: Bamberg — FICE Identification: 005363 — Unit ID: 217989

Telephone: (803) 793-5176 — Carnegie Class: Assoc/HVT-Mix Trad/Non
FAX Number: (803) 793-5942 — Calendar System: Semester
URL: www.denmarktech.edu
Established: 1948 — Annual Undergrad Tuition & Fees (In-State): $5,568
Enrollment: 523 — Coed
Affiliation or Control: State — IRS Status: 501(c)3
Highest Offering: Associate Degree
Accreditation: SC, ACBSP

01	Interim President	Dr. Christopher HALL
09	VP for Inst Research/Plng/Dev	Vacant
05	VP for Academic Affairs	Vacant
10	VP for Fiscal Affairs	Vacant
84	VP for Enrollment Management	Mr. Marcus CORBETT
15	Director of Human Resources	Mr. Thomas MAYER
32	Associate VP for Student Services	Ms. Avis GATHERS
08	Dean of Learning Resources Ctr	Ms. Carolyn FORTSON
13	Director of Information Technology	Vacant
19	Chief of Public Safety	Mr. Dustin JOHNSON
36	Director Career Plng/Placement	Mrs. Leslie HOLMAN-BROOKS
37	Director of Financial Aid	Vacant
88	Dean of Public Service	Mrs. Rosaland KENNER
49	Dean of Arts & Sciences	Dr. Danny SWILLEY
66	Dean of Nursing	Ms. Teneane FOSTER
54	Dean of Industrial/Related Tech	Mr. Stephen MANSON
50	Dean Business/Computer/Related Tech	Mrs. Tia WRIGHT-RICHARDS
07	Director of Recruitment	Ms. Crystal BRAILEY
103	AVP Economic/Workforce Development	Mr. Stephen MASON
39	Director Student Housing	Vacant
06	Registrar	Ms. Carolyn GRIMES
04	Administrative Asst to President	Mrs. Gwendolyn BAMBERG

ECPI University-Charleston (D)

7410 Northside Drive, Ste 100,
North Charleston SC 29420

Telephone: (843) 606-5902 — Identification: 770955
Accreditation: &SC, MAAB

† Branch campus of ECPI University, Virginia Beach, VA

ECPI University-Columbia (E)

250 Berryhill Road, Ste 300, Columbia SC 29210-6467

Telephone: (803) 772-3333 — Identification: 770956
Accreditation: &SC, MAAB

† Branch campus of ECPI University, Virginia Beach, VA

ECPI University-Greenville (F)

1001 Keys Drive, Ste 100, Greenville SC 29615

Telephone: (864) 288-2828 — Identification: 770954
Accreditation: &SC, MAAB

† Branch campus of ECPI University, Virginia Beach, VA

Edward Via College of Osteopathic Medicine-Carolinas Campus (G)

350 Howard Street, Sparntanburg SC 29303

Telephone: (864) 327-9800 — Identification: 770941
Accreditation: OSTEO

† Branch campus of Edward Via College of Osteopathic Medicine, Blacksburg, VA.

Erskine College (H)

PO Box 338, 2 Washington Street,
Due West SC 29639-0338

County: Abbeville — FICE Identification: 003432 — Unit ID: 217998

Telephone: (864) 379-2131 — Carnegie Class: Bac-Diverse
FAX Number: (864) 379-2167 — Calendar System: Semester
URL: www.erskine.edu
Established: 1837 — Annual Undergrad Tuition & Fees: $36,150
Enrollment: 694 — Coed
Affiliation or Control: Other — IRS Status: 501(c)3
Highest Offering: Doctorate
Accreditation: SC, #CAATE, CAEPN, THEOL

01	President	Dr. Robert E. GUSTAFSON
05	Provost Erskine College	Dr. J. T. HELLAMS
10	VP for Finance & Operations	Mr. Christian HABEGER
111	VP for Advancement	Mr. Mike IRVIN
41	Athletic Director	Mr. Mark L. PEELER
73	Provost Theological Seminary	Dr. Leslie HOLMES
32	VP for Student Success	Dr. Wendi SANTEE
08	Assoc Dean of Library & Inst Effect	Mr. John F. KENNERLY, JR.
06	Registrar	Mrs. Tracy M. SPIRES
26	Director Marketing & Creative Svcs	Mrs. Kayli HIBBARD
37	Director of Student Financial Aid	Mrs. Amanda TAYLOR
13	Director of Information Technology	Ms. Stephanie HUDSON
09	Director of Institutional Research	Mr. Buck F. BROWN, JR.
42	Chaplain	Mr. Paul G. PATRICK
21	Accounting Manager	Mrs. Kelly MCALHANEY
15	Director Human Resources	Mrs. Barbara PECK
19	Chief of Erskine Police	Mr. Matthew BUSBY
29	Director of Alumni Affairs	Mr. Paul BELL
04	Administrative Asst to President	Vacant
07	Director of Admissions	Ms. Kassi CHOU
27	Director Communications/Media Rels	Mrs. Joyce GUYETTE
36	Coordinator for Student Transitions	Mr. Trent D. PAYNE
84	Dean of Enrollment	Mr. Tim REES

Florence - Darlington Technical College (I)

PO Box 100548, Florence SC 29502-0548

County: Florence — FICE Identification: 003990 — Unit ID: 218025

Telephone: (843) 661-8324 — Carnegie Class: Assoc/HVT-High Trad
FAX Number: (843) 661-8011 — Calendar System: Semester
URL: www.fdtc.edu
Established: 1964 — Annual Undergrad Tuition & Fees (In-District): $4,462
Enrollment: 5,439 — Coed
Affiliation or Control: State/Local — IRS Status: 501(c)3
Highest Offering: Associate Degree
Accreditation: SC, ADNUR, CAHIIM, COARC, CSHSE, DA, DH, MLTAD, RAD, SURGT

01	President	Mr. Edward E. BETHEA
05	Vice President Academic Affairs	Dr. Marc DAVID
10	Vice Pres Business Affairs	Mr. Douglas LANGE
111	Director Institutional Advancement	Ms. Lauren DORTON
26	VP Marketing/Public Affs/Info Tech	Mr. Tyron JONES
10	Assoc Vice Pres Business Office	Ms. Connie MORRIS
76	Assoc VP Allied Health	Dr. Dan AVERETTE
15	Assoc VP Internal Relations/EEO	Mr. Terry DINGLE
09	Director Institutional Research	Mr. Gary ANCHETA
06	Registrar	Ms. Genell GAUSE
37	Director Financial Aid	Ms. Monica STARR
96	Director of Purchasing	Ms. Toni RICHARDSON
07	Director of Admissions	Ms. Paula MCLAUGHLIN
18	Director of Facilities	Mr. Christopher TAYLOR
04	Admin Assistant to the President	Ms. Kimberley LUTZ

Forrest College (J)

601 E River Street, Anderson SC 29624-2405

County: Anderson — FICE Identification: 004924 — Unit ID: 218043

Telephone: (864) 225-7653 — Carnegie Class: Assoc/HVT-High Trad
FAX Number: (864) 261-7471 — Calendar System: 4/1/4
URL: www.forrestcollege.edu
Established: 1946 — Annual Undergrad Tuition & Fees: $10,525
Enrollment: 72 — Coed
Affiliation or Control: Proprietary — IRS Status: Proprietary
Highest Offering: Associate Degree
Accreditation: ACICS, MAC

01	President/Chief Academic Officer	Dr. C. John RE
00	Chairman Board of Directors	Dr. C. John RE
05	Academic Dean	Jesse HARRIS
11	Administrative Dean	Kathy CHILDRESS
101	Secy/Treasurer Board of Directors	Charles PALMER
06	Registrar	June PETERSON
08	Librarian	Brandy ROSCOE
76	Medical Assisting Program Coord	Celina CHASTAIN
07	Admissions Rep	Jennifer ROGERS
07	Admissions Rep	Stephanie GARRETT
37	Financial Aid Clerk	Sharon ALEWINE

Francis Marion University (K)

PO Box 100547, Florence SC 29501-0547

County: Florence — FICE Identification: 009226 — Unit ID: 218061

Telephone: (843) 661-1362 — Carnegie Class: Masters/S
FAX Number: (843) 661-1202 — Calendar System: Semester
URL: www.fmarion.edu
Established: 1970 — Annual Undergrad Tuition & Fees (In-State): $11,976
Enrollment: 3,786 — Coed
Affiliation or Control: State — IRS Status: Exempt
Highest Offering: Doctorate
Accreditation: SC, #ARCPA, ART, CAEPN, NUR, @SP, THEA

01	President	Dr. Luther F. CARTER
05	Provost/Dean Col of Liberal Arts	Dr. Peter D. KING
10	Vice President Business Affairs	Mr. John J. KISPERT
11	Vice President Administration	Dr. Charlene WAGES
30	Vice President Devel/Exec Dir	Mr. Darryl BRIDGES
26	VP Public & Community Affairs	Mr. Tucker MITCHELL
32	Vice President for Student Affairs	Mrs. Teresa RAMEY
41	Athletic Director	Mr. Murray G. HARTZLER
20	Assoc Provost For Academic Affairs	Dr. Christopher KENNEDY
84	Assoc Provost of Enrollment Mgmt	Dr. Alissa WARTERS
121	Assoc Provost for Advising	Dr. Jennifer KUNKA
21	Asst Vice Pres for Accounting	Mrs. Cathy SWARTZ
88	Asst Vice Pres Financial Services	Mr. Thomas WELCH
50	Dean School of Business	Dr. Hari K. RAJAGOPALAN
53	Dean School of Education	Dr. Tracy MEETZE-HOLCOMBE
76	Dean School of Health Sciences	Dr. Ruth A. WITTMANN-PRICE
08	Dean of the Library	Mrs. Joyce M. DURANT
37	Financial Assistance Director	Ms. Kimberly M. ELLISOR

06 Registrar Ms. Ann WILLIAMS
38 Director Counseling and Testing Dr. Rebecca L. LAWSON
18 Director of Facilities Management Mr. Ralph U. DAVIS
36 Director Career Development Dr. Ronald E. MILLER, JR.
07 Director of Admissions Mrs. Jamie HUNT
35 Asst Dean of Students Ms. R. Daphne CARTER
29 Director of Alumni Affairs Mr. David L. DAUGHERTY
92 Director of Purchasing Mr. Paul MACDONALD
92 Director of Honors Program Dr. Jon W. TUTTLE
13 Chief Information Officer Mr. John DIXON
04 Administrative Asst to President Mrs. Kim DAVIS
105 Director of Multimedia Services Mr. Larry B. FALCK
19 Chief of Campus Police Mr. Donald R. TARBELL
39 Director Student Housing Mrs. Cheryl R. TUTTLE
43 General Counsel Mr. Jonathan P. EDWARDS
96 AVP of Purchasing/Contractual Svcs Mr. Eric GARRIS

Furman University (A)

3300 Poinsett Highway, Greenville SC 29613-0001
County: Greenville FICE Identification: 003434
Unit ID: 218070
Telephone: (864) 294-2000 Carnegie Class: Bac-A&S
FAX Number: (864) 294-3001 Calendar System: Semester
URL: www.furman.edu
Established: 1826 Annual Undergrad Tuition & Fees: $49,532
Enrollment: 2,949 Coed
Affiliation or Control: Independent Non-Profit IRS Status: 501(c)3
Highest Offering: Master's
Accreditation: SC, CAEPN, MUS

01 President Dr. Elizabeth DAVIS
05 VP Academic Affairs & Provost Dr. Ken PETERSON
10 VP for Finance & Administration Ms. Susan MADDUX
07 Vice President for Enrollment Dr. Michael HENDRICKS
32 Vice President for Student Life Ms. Connie L. CARSON
30 Vice President for Development Ms. Heidi H. MCCRORY
26 VP University Communications Mr. Tom EVELYN
20 Associate Academic Dean Dr. Beth PONTARI
100 Chief of Staff Ms. Elizabeth SEMAN
06 University Registrar Ms. Kendra WOODSON
58 Director Graduate Studies Dr. Troy M. TERRY
08 Director Libraries Vacant
19 Chief of Police Mr. John MILBY
108 Asst Vice President Assessment Dr. David EUBANKS
37 Assoc Vice Pres of Financial Aid Vacant
29 Director of Alumni Association Ms. Allsion FOY
07 Assoc Vice President of Admissions Mr. Brad POCHARD
44 Director of Annual Giving Vacant
112 Director of Planned & Major Gifts Mr. John KEMP
25 Grants Administrator Ms. Judith J. ROMANO
94 Dir Women's/Gender/Sexuality Study Dr. Gretchen BRAUN
15 Asst VP Human Resources/AAO Mr. Robert BIERLY
13 Chief Information Officer Mr. David STEINOUR
36 Director Career Services Dr. John D. BARKER
109 Auxiliary Services Director Ms. Rebecca VUKSTA
18 Asst VP for Facilities Services Mr. Jeff P. REDDERSON
51 Director Continuing Education Vacant
41 Director of Athletics Mr. Jason DONNELLEY
46 Director UG Research Dr. Erik CHING
88 Director CTL Dr. Min-Ken LIAO
17 Director Student Health Services Dr. Ann KNOWLES
38 Director Counseling Center Dr. Thomas BAEZ
39 Director University Housing Mr. Ronald C. THOMPSON
88 Director Accessibility Resources Ms. Judy BAGLEY
42 Chaplain Dr. Vaughn CROWETIPTON
40 Director Bookstore Ms. Crystal JARROUGE
04 Executive Asst to President Ms. Cindy ALEXANDER
114 Assoc VP Finance Budget Director Ms. Amy BLACKWELL
96 Director of Purchasing Ms. Jannie CHOICE
35 Director Student Activities Ms. Jessica BERKEY
104 Director Study Abroad Ms. Nancy GEORGIEV
43 Dir Legal Services/General Counsel Ms. Meredith GREEN
28 Director of Diversity Dr. Michael E. JENNINGS

Greenville Technical College (B)

PO Box 5616, Greenville SC 29606-5616
County: Greenville FICE Identification: 003991
Unit ID: 218113
Telephone: (864) 250-8000 Carnegie Class: Assoc/MT-VT-High Trad
FAX Number: N/A Calendar System: Semester
URL: www.gvltec.edu
Established: 1962 Annual Undergrad Tuition & Fees (In-State): $4,566
Enrollment: 11,745 Coed
Affiliation or Control: State IRS Status: 501(c)3
Highest Offering: Baccalaureate
Accreditation: SC, ACBSP, ACFEI, ADNUR, CAHIIM, COARC, DA, DH, DMS, EMT, MAC, MLTAD, OTA, PTAA, RAD, SURGT

01 President Dr. Keith MILLER
05 VP Learning/Workforce Dev Dr. Jermaine WHIRL
10 Vice President Finance Mrs. Jacqueline DIMAGGIO
32 Vice President Student Services Dr. Matteel JONES
111 VP Advancement Ms. Ann WRIGHT
51 AVP Econ Dev/Corp Training Mrs. Jennifer MOOREFIELD
45 VP Institutional Effectiveness Mrs. Lauren SIMER
04 Administrative Asst to President Ms. Rita SNYDER
06 Registrar Mrs. Gloria CARDEN
07 Director Enrollment Services Ms. Tanisha LATIMER
15 VP Human Resources Ms. Susan M. JONES
18 Director Facilities Mr. Scott WILBANKS
19 Chief of Police Mr. Terence BROOKS
25 Director Research and Grants Ms. Elizabeth VARGA
26 Director Marketing/Communications Mr. Joshua FRIESEN
28 AVP Executive Affairs Ms. Wendy WALDEN
37 Director Financial Aid Mr. D.J WETZEL
50 Dean Business and Technology Ms. Michelle E. BYRD
13 Chief Information Technology Office Mr. Lee TENNENT
86 Director Government Relations Mr. Eric BEDINGFIELD
21 AVP Finance Ms. Lisa MANGIONE
09 Director of Institutional Research Dr. Larry MILLER
104 Director International Education Dr. Bonnie SMITH
108 Director Institutional Assessment Ms. Christin CORRELL
96 Procurement Manager Mr. Brian HARVEY

Horry-Georgetown Technical College (C)

2050 Highway 501 E, Conway SC 29526-9521
County: Horry FICE Identification: 004925
Unit ID: 218140
Telephone: (843) 347-3186 Carnegie Class: Assoc/MT-VT-High Trad
FAX Number: (843) 347-4207 Calendar System: Semester
URL: www.hgtc.edu
Established: 1966 Annual Undergrad Tuition & Fees (In-District): $4,252
Enrollment: 7,079 Coed
Affiliation or Control: State/Local IRS Status: 501(c)3
Highest Offering: Associate Degree
Accreditation: SC, ACFEI, ADNUR, #COARC, DA, DH, DMS, EMT, PNUR, PTAA, RAD, SURGT

01 President Dr. Marilyn J. FORE
05 VP for Academic Affairs Dr. Jennifer WILBANKS
10 VP Business Affairs/Administration Mr. Harold HAWLEY
13 VP for Technology Mr. John DOVE
103 VP Wrkfc Dev/Prov GS/Georgetwn Camp . Mr. Gregory MITCHELL
84 Registrar Mrs. Heather HOPPE
32 VP for Student Affairs Dr. Melissa BATTEN
20 AVP for Institutional Support Dr. Becky BOONE
49 AVP Acad Affs Arts/Science/Bus Dr. Candace HOWELL
66 AVP Acad Affs Nursing/Health Sci Dr. Christy BAILEY
15 VP Human Res/Employee Rels Mrs. Jacquelyne SNYDER
08 Director of Library Services Mr. Richard MONIZ
21 AVP/Controller Ms. Ellen BLACK
84 AVP Student Enrollment Services Ms. Cynthia JOHNSTON
18 Superintendent Buildings & Grounds Mr. Kevin BROWN
37 Dir of Financial Aid/Veterans Affs Ms. Susan THOMPSON
36 Career Resource Ctr Coordinator Ms. April GARNER
09 AVP Inst Planning/Research/Grant Ms. Lori HEAFNER
96 Procurement Manager Ms. Dianna CECALA
105 Web Services Coordinator Mr. Kevin ENGELMAN
19 Director Security/Safety Mr. Barry MARSH
106 Director of Distance Learning Mr. Daniel HOPPE
26 Director of Public Relations Ms. Nicole HYMAN
27 Director of Marketing Ms. Lari ROPER

Lander University (D)

320 Stanley Avenue, Greenwood SC 29649-2099
County: Greenwood FICE Identification: 003435
Unit ID: 218229
Telephone: (864) 388-8000 Carnegie Class: Bac-Diverse
FAX Number: (864) 388-8890 Calendar System: Semester
URL: www.lander.edu
Established: 1872 Annual Undergrad Tuition & Fees (In-State): $11,700
Enrollment: 2,849 Coed
Affiliation or Control: State IRS Status: 501(c)3
Highest Offering: Master's
Accreditation: SC, ART, CAEPN, MACTE, MUS, NURSE

01 President Dr. Richard E. COSENTINO
05 Provost/Vice Pres Academic Affairs Dr. Scott JONES
10 Vice Pres Business/Administration Dr. Stacie BOWIE
32 Vice President for Student Affairs Mr. Boyd YARBROUGH
111 Vice President for Univ Advancement Mr. Mike WORLEY
86 VP for Governmental Relations Mr. Adam TAYLOR
84 VP for Enrollment & Access Mgmt Mr. Andy BENOIT
08 Librarian Ms. Lisa WIECKI
38 Director Counseling Ms. Debra J. FRANKS
41 Vice President/Athletic Director Mr. Brian REESE
15 Director Human Resources Ms. London THOMAS
19 Director University Police Mr. Greg ALLEN
26 Director of Public Information Mrs. Megan PRICE
37 Director of Financial Aid Mrs. Michelle LODATO
36 Director of Career Services Mrs. Amanda MORGAN
21 Controller Mr. Tom COVAR
40 Dir Bookstore/Procurement/Print Svc Mrs. Mary W. MCDANIEL
13 Dir Office Info Tech Services Mrs. Robin P. LAWRENCE
07 Director of Admissions Mrs. Jennifer M. MATHIS
18 Director Physical Plant/Engr Svcs Mr. Jeff S. BEAVER
06 Registrar Ms. Kelly PROCTOR
29 Director Alumni Relations Ms. Denise MANLEY
09 Director of Institutional Research Mr. Mac KIRKPATRICK

Limestone College (E)

1115 College Drive, Gaffney SC 29340-3799
County: Cherokee FICE Identification: 003436
Unit ID: 218238
Telephone: (864) 489-7151 Carnegie Class: Bac-Diverse
FAX Number: (864) 487-8706 Calendar System: Semester
URL: www.limestone.edu
Established: 1845 Annual Undergrad Tuition & Fees: $25,025
Enrollment: 2,661 Coed
Affiliation or Control: Independent Non-Profit IRS Status: 501(c)3
Highest Offering: Master's
Accreditation: SC, ACBSP, CAATE, CAEPN, MUS, SW

01 President Dr. Darrell PARKER
05 Provost Dr. Karen W. GAINEY
10 VP Finance & Administration Mr. Reggie BROWNING
111 VP Institutional Advancement Ms. Kelly T. CURTIS
84 Vice President Enrollment Services Mr. Christopher N. PHENICIE
32 Dean of Student Life Mr. Robert A. OVERTON
13 Chief Information Officer Mr. Jim LONG
41 Vice Pres Intercollegiate Athletics Mr. Michael H. CERINO
108 Dean of Accreditation Dr. Shelly MEYERS
121 Dean of Student Success Mrs. Stacey W. MASON
04 Executive Asst to the President Mrs. Brandi P. HARTMAN
35 Dir of Recruitment & Student Svcs Mr. Kip ALTMAN
06 Registrar Ms. Pennie D. HUGHES
37 Director Financial Aid Ms. Summer NANCE
08 Director Library Ms. Lizah ISMAIL
26 Vice Pres Communications/Marketing Mr. Charles W. WYATT
36 Dir Center for Professional Dev Ms. Lindsay BATHOLOMEW
18 Director Physical Plant Mr. Hayden HUTCHINGS
92 Director Academic Honors Program Dr. Jonathan SARNOFF
70 Director & Chair of Social Work Mr. Henry HIOTT
19 Chief Campus Security Mr. William J. PETTY
21 Controller Mr. Jeremy C. WHITAKER
23 Campus Nurse Mrs. Sandy B. GREEN
110 Director Advancement Services Ms. Andrea B. DAVIS
88 Director Academic Advising Ms. Pennie D. HUGHES
30 Assoc VP for Development Ms. Candace R. WATERS
109 Director Food Services Mr. Joe FIELDS
42 College Chaplain Rev. J. Ron SINGLETON
53 Dir of Teacher Education Dr. Jimmie HALE
88 Dir Accessibility Services/PALS Ms. Andrea L. ALLISON
15 Dir Human Resources/AAEEO Officer Ms. Janie CORRY
58 Dir Grad Studies/Admiss & Enroll Ms. Adair HUDSON
88 Sr Assoc Athletics Dir Compliance Mr. Dennis L. BLOOMER
07 Director Admissions Mr. Travis W. MCDOWELL
40 Campus Store Manager Mrs. Patti H. MCCRAW
38 College Counselor Mrs. Mary B. CAMPBELL
50 Dean Business & Prof Studies Dr. Paul R. LEFRANCOIS
81 Dean Natural & Health Sciences Mr. Brian F. AMELING
79 Dean Arts & Humanities Dr. Gena E. POOVEY
53 Dean Educ & Behavioral Sciences Dr. Betsy A. WITT
22 Dir Affirm Action/Equal Opportunity Ms. Janie CORRY
39 Director Residential Life & Housing Ms. Jessica D. GOINS
09 Director of Institutional Research Dr. Keith KEPPLEY
101 Secretary of the Institution/Board Mrs. Brandi P. HARTMAN

Medical University of South Carolina (F)

179 Ashley Avenue, Charleston SC 29425
County: Charleston FICE Identification: 003438
Unit ID: 218335
Telephone: (843) 792-2300 Carnegie Class: Spec-4-yr-Med
FAX Number: N/A Calendar System: Semester
URL: www.musc.edu
Established: 1824 Annual Undergrad Tuition & Fees (In-State): N/A
Enrollment: 2,985 Coed
Affiliation or Control: State IRS Status: Exempt
Highest Offering: Doctorate
Accreditation: SC, ANEST, ARCPA, CAMPEP, DENT, DIETI, HSA, IPSY, MED, NURSE, OT, PERF, PHAR, PTA

01 President Dr. David J. COLE
05 EVP Academic Affairs & Provost Dr. Lisa SALADIN
17 Dean Col of Medicine Dr. Raymond DUBOIS
10 Exec Vice President Finance & Admin Ms. Lisa P. MONTGOMERY
30 Interim Vice President Development Ms. Linda COX
17 VP Clinical Affairs Dr. Patrick J. CAWLEY
13 VP Information Technology/CIO Mr. Michael P. CAPUTO
20 Assoc Prov Education/Student Life Dr. Darlene L. SHAW
46 VP Research Dr. Kathleen T. BRADY
108 Assoc Provost Institutional Effect Dr. Suzanne THOMAS
52 Dean of Dental Medicine Dr. Sarandeep HUJA
76 Dean of Health Professions Dr. Zoher F. KAPASI
58 Dean of Graduate Studies Dr. Paula TRAKTMAN
66 Dean of Nursing Dr. Linda WEGLICKI
67 Dean of Pharmacy Dr. Philip D. HALL
08 Director of Libraries Ms. Shannon JONES
84 Director Enrollment Management Mr. George W. OHLANDT
28 Director Student Programs Mr. Kevin SMUNIEWSKI
43 General Counsel Ms. Annette R. DRACHMAN
26 Chief Communication & Marketing Ofc Ms. Sheila CHAMPLIN
22 Dir Affirm Act/Equal Opportunity Mr. Michael VANDERHURST
07 Director of Admissions Ms. Lyla HUDSON
18 Chief Facilities/Physical Plant Mr. Greg WEIGLE
06 Registrar Ms. Melissa A. FREELAND
15 Director Personnel Services Ms. Susan H. CARULLO
38 Director Student Counseling Dr. Alice Q. LIBET
29 Director Alumni Affairs Ms. Linda COX
37 Director Student Financial Aid Mr. Joseph M. DURANT
96 Director of Purchasing Ms. Velma STAMP

† Tuition varies by degree program.

Midlands Technical College (G)

PO Box 2408, Columbia SC 29202-2408
County: Richland FICE Identification: 003993
Unit ID: 218353
Telephone: (803) 738-8324 Carnegie Class: Assoc/MT-VT-High Trad
FAX Number: (803) 738-7784 Calendar System: Semester

URL: www.midlandstech.edu
Established: 1974 Annual Undergrad Tuition & Fees (In-District): $4,530
Enrollment: 10,625 Coed
Affiliation or Control: State/Local IRS Status: 501(c)3
Highest Offering: Associate Degree
Accreditation: SC, ACBSP, ADNUR, CAHIIM, COARC, CSHSE, DA, DH, MAC, MLTAD, NMT, PNUR, PTAA, RAD, SURGT

01 President ... Dr. Ronald RHAMES
03 Provost ... Dr. Barrie KIRK
05 Vice Provost Academics ... Dr. Diane CARR
51 Vice Provost Corp & Continuing Ed ... Ms. Amy SCULLY
10 Vice President for Business Affairs ... Ms. Debbie WALKER
32 Vice Pres Student Development Svcs ... Dr. Mary HOLLOWAY
30 VP for Institutional Support ... Ms. Starnell BATES
26 Assoc Vice President for Marketing ... Ms. Stefanie GOEBELER
43 General Counsel ... Vacant
102 Associate VP for Philanthropy ... Ms. Nancy MCKINNEY
06 Registrar ... Ms. Carla KAISER
13 Director Information Resource Mgmt ... Mr. Tony HOUGH
37 Director of Student Financial Aid ... Ms. Angela WILLIAMS
84 AVP Enrollment Management Services ... Ms. Sylvia LITTLEJOHN
26 Director of Public Affairs ... Mr. Todd GAVIN
15 Human Resource Director ... Ms. Faye GOWANS
07 Director of Admissions ... Mr. Derrah CASSIDY
124 Director of Student Retention ... Mr. Shickre SABBAGHA
04 Executive Asst to the President ... Ms. Kim BOATWRIGHT
08 Chief Library Officer ... Ms. Florence MAYS
09 Director of Institutional Research ... Ms. Dorcas KITCHINGS
101 Secretary of the Institution/Board ... Ms. Bridget SALLEY
106 Director of Distance Learning ... Ms. Mary Helen HENDRIX
108 Director Institutional Assessment ... Ms. Dorcas KITCHINGS
18 Chief Facilities/Physical Plant Ofc ... Ms. Teresa COOK
19 Director Security/Safety ... Mr. Myron CHAMBLISS
22 Director Affirmative Action/Equal O ... Mr. Ian MACLEAN
25 Chief Contract/Grants Administrator ... Ms. Alice APPLEBY
29 Director Alumni Affairs ... Mr. Allen SHARPE
96 Director of Purchasing ... Ms. Latitia TREZEVANT
121 Director Academic & Career Advising ... Mr. Andrew NEWTON

Miller-Motte Technical College (A)

2451 Highway 501, Conway SC 29526
Telephone: (843) 614-3638 Identification: 770778
Accreditation: ACCSC, MAC

† Branch campus of Platt College, Tulsa, OK.

Miller-Motte Technical College (B)

8085 Rivers Avenue, North Charleston SC 29406
Telephone: (843) 733-3073 Identification: 666256
Accreditation: ACCSC, #SURGT

† Branch campus of Platt College, Tulsa, OK.

Morris College (C)

100 W College Street, Sumter SC 29150-3599
County: Sumter FICE Identification: 003439
Unit ID: 218399
Telephone: (803) 934-3200 Carnegie Class: Bac-Diverse
FAX Number: (803) 773-3687 Calendar System: Semester
URL: www.morris.edu
Established: 1908 Annual Undergrad Tuition & Fees: $13,886
Enrollment: 747 Coed
Affiliation or Control: Baptist IRS Status: 501(c)3
Highest Offering: Baccalaureate
Accreditation: SC, ACBSP, CAEP

01 President ... Dr. Leroy STAGGERS
04 Management Specialist ... Vacant
05 Interim Academic Dean ... Dr. Jacob BUTLER
10 Director of Business Affairs ... Mr. Robert EAVES
45 Dir Planning/Govt Relations/IR ... Ms. Dorothy S. CHEAGLE
32 Dean Student Affairs ... Dr. Juana DAVIS-FREEMAN
15 Dir Human Resources ... Mrs. Abby LAWSON
111 Director Inst Advanc/Church Rels ... Rev. Melvin MACK
42 College Minister ... Dr. Charles M. PEE
84 Dir Enrollment Mgmt & Records ... Dr. Wanda RAMSEY
37 Director of Financial Aid ... Mrs. Sandra S. GIBSON
108 Director of Assessment ... Dr. Lewis P. GRAHAM, JR.
13 Director MIS/Computer Center ... Vacant
21 Chief Accountant ... Mrs. Bernice IRBY
29 Director Alumni Affairs ... Mrs. Altoya A. FELDER-DEAS
26 Director Public Relations ... Ms. Andrea BUTLER
88 Director Learning Resources Ctr ... Ms. Janet S. CLAYTON
08 Head Librarian ... Ms. Margaret N. MUKOOZA
36 Director Career Services ... Vacant
20 Dir Academic Administrative Svcs ... Dr. Kay M. RHOADS
38 Director Counseling ... Ms. Quanda D. SIMS
39 Director Residential Life ... Mrs. Tonia F. WASHINGTON
41 Director of Athletics ... Mr. Clarence M. HOUCK
23 Director of Health Services ... Mrs. Johnell ROGERS
89 Director of Freshmen Studies ... Vacant
40 Bookstore Manager ... Ms. Jeanette MOSES-HOLMES
35 Coordinator Student Activities ... Mr. Alston FREEMAN
19 Coordinator Campus Safety Services ... Ms. Lucille W. WILLIAMS
18 Chief Facilities/Physical Plant Off ... Mr. Lenn RAMSEY

Newberry College (D)

2100 College, Newberry SC 29108-2126
County: Newberry FICE Identification: 003440
Unit ID: 218414
Telephone: (800) 845-4955 Carnegie Class: Bac-Diverse
FAX Number: (803) 321-5627 Calendar System: Semester
URL: www.newberry.edu
Established: 1856 Annual Undergrad Tuition & Fees: $26,424
Enrollment: 1,181 Coed
Affiliation or Control: Evangelical Lutheran Church In America
IRS Status: 501(c)3
Highest Offering: Baccalaureate
Accreditation: SC, CAEPN, MUS, NURSE

01 President ... Dr. Maurice W. SCHERRENS
05 Interim VP for Acad Affairs ... Dr. Sid PARRISH
10 VP for Admin Affairs & CFO ... Ms. Kathy WORSTER
111 VP for Institutional Advancement ... Mr. Scott JOYNER
20 Assoc VP Academic Affairs ... Dr. Timothy G. ELSTON
84 Dean of Enrollment Management ... Mr. Chris HARRIS
32 Dean of Student Affairs ... Dr. Sandra ROUSE
41 Director of Athletics ... Mr. Ralph PATTERSON
15 Director of Human Resources ... Mrs. Peggy SHULER
06 Registrar ... Ms. Carol BICKLEY
29 Assoc Dir of Alumni Relations ... Mr. Jeff WICKER
08 Librarian ... Mr. Austin REID
18 Director of Facilities ... Mr. Fred ERRIGO
42 Chaplain ... Rev. Ernie WORMAN
21 Director of Accounting ... Ms. Landee BUZHARDT
38 Dir Health & Counselling Services ... Mrs. Martha DORRELL
37 Assoc Dir of Financial Aid ... Mrs. Danielle BELL
26 Director of Marketing & PR ... Vacant
19 Director Security/Safety ... Mr. Paul WHITMAN
37 Director of Financial Aid ... Vacant
100 Chief of Staff ... Ms. Bobbie SIDES

North Greenville University (E)

PO Box 1892, Tigerville SC 29688-1892
County: Greenville FICE Identification: 003441
Unit ID: 218441
Telephone: (864) 977-7000 Carnegie Class: Masters/S
FAX Number: (864) 977-7021 Calendar System: Semester
URL: www.ngu.edu
Established: 1892 Annual Undergrad Tuition & Fees: $19,750
Enrollment: 2,565 Coed
Affiliation or Control: Southern Baptist IRS Status: 501(c)3
Highest Offering: Doctorate
Accreditation: SC, #ARCPA, CAEP, COSMA, MUS

01 President/CEO ... Dr. Gene C. FANT, JR.
04 Admin Assistant for President ... Ms. Angie WATSON
03 Executive Vice President ... Mr. Rich GRIMM
05 Provost & Dean of Univ Faculty ... Dr. Nathan FINN
32 Vice President Student Services ... Ms. Rachael RUSSIAKY
20 Assoc Provost for Undergrad Studies ... Dr. Linwood HAGIN
10 Senior Vice President for Finance ... Ms. Michelle L. SABOU
07 Senior Director of NGU Central ... Ms. Keli SEWELL
111 Vice President for Advancement ... Mr. Marty O'GWYNN
88 Senior Dir for Church Engagement ... Rev. Mayson EASTERLING
42 Senior Campus Pastor ... Dr. Steve CROUSE
102 Director of Dev & Foundation Giving ... Dr. Phil GARDNER
13 VP Information Technology Services ... Mr. Tim HUGGINS
109 Senior AVP Tigerville Operations ... Mr. Billy WATSON
09 Director of Institutional Research ... Dr. George A. HOPSON, JR.
06 Registrar ... Ms. Pam FARMER
18 VP Campus Enhancement Service ... Mr. Mick DANIEL
41 Athletic Director ... Ms. Jan MCDONALD
34 Assoc Dir for Women's Housing ... Ms. Lorry GREEN
33 Director for Res Life & Housing ... Mr. Dillon KEY
08 Director of Hester Library ... Ms. Carla MCMAHAN
19 Director Campus Security ... Mr. Rick MORRIS
58 AVP for Adult & Grad Acad Svcs ... Dr. Tawana SCOTT
35 VP Campus Ministries/Student Engage ... Mr. Jody JENNINGS
26 Director of Communications ... Mr. LaVerne B. HOWELL
112 Dir of Resource Dev & Planned Gifts ... Mrs. Julie STYLES
15 Human Resource Manager ... Mrs. Beth HOUCK
40 Bookstore Manager ... Mrs. Cindy COWAN
38 Personal Counselor Men ... Mr. Steve BIELBY
38 Personal Counselor Women ... Miss Sara BLACK
36 Director of Career Planning ... Mr. Stuart FLOYD
23 Director Health Services ... Vacant
102 Dir of Dev & Corporate Relations ... Mr. Jason ROSS
14 Asst VP Information Tech Services ... Mr. Paul GARRETT
37 Director Financial Planning ... Vacant
53 Dean Education ... Dr. Constance WRIGHT
79 Dean Humanities & Sciences ... Dr. H. Paul THOMPSON
57 Dean Communication & Fine Arts ... Dr. Web DRAKE
73 Dean Christian Studies ... Dr. Walter JOHNSON
50 Dean Business & Entrepreneurship ... Dr. John DUNCAN
68 Dean Wellness & Sport Professions ... Dr. Jeff BRIGGS
106 Assoc VP of NGU Online ... Dr. Lena MASLENNIKOVA
35 Assoc VP for Student Engagement ... Dr. Jared THOMAS
12 Asst VP of Greer Campus Operations ... Mr. Justin PITTS
29 Director of Alumni Engagement ... Mr. Lamont SULLIVAN
31 Sr Dir of Church & Cmty Engagement ... Dr. Tony BEAM

Northeastern Technical College (F)

1201 Chesterfield Hwy, Cheraw SC 29520
County: Chesterfield FICE Identification: 007602
Unit ID: 217837
Telephone: (843) 921-6900 Carnegie Class: Assoc/HVT-Mix Trad/Non
FAX Number: (843) 537-6148 Calendar System: Semester
URL: www.netc.edu
Established: 1969 Annual Undergrad Tuition & Fees (In-State): $4,398
Enrollment: 1,063 Coed
Affiliation or Control: State IRS Status: 501(c)3
Highest Offering: Associate Degree
Accreditation: SC

01 President ... Dr. Kyle WAGNER
05 Vice President of Instruction ... Dr. Edwin DELGADO
10 Director of Finance ... Mr. Robert CHARLES
111 Asst VP for Inst Advancement ... Mrs. Erin FANN
15 Director for Human Resources ... Mrs. Christi MEGGS
06 Registrar ... Ms. Anne JONES
26 Coordinator for Public Relations ... Ms. Shannon JUSTICE
84 Dean of Student Engagement ... Mr. Darin COLEMAN
08 Head Librarian ... Mr. Ronnie STAFFORD
09 Director of Institutional Research ... Vacant
04 Executive Assistant ... Ms. Sharekka BRIDGES
101 Secretary of the Board ... Ms. Lib NORTON
13 Information Technology Manager ... Mr. Josh BRITT
32 Dean of Students ... Ms. Danielle PACE
37 Director Student Financial Aid ... Ms. Sheryll MARSHALL

Orangeburg-Calhoun Technical College (G)

3250 Saint Matthews Road, Orangeburg SC 29118-8299
County: Orangeburg FICE Identification: 006815
Unit ID: 218487
Telephone: (803) 536-0311 Carnegie Class: Assoc/HVT-Mix Trad/Non
FAX Number: (803) 535-1388 Calendar System: Semester
URL: www.octech.edu
Established: 1966 Annual Undergrad Tuition & Fees (In-State): $4,466
Enrollment: 2,479 Coed
Affiliation or Control: State IRS Status: 501(c)3
Highest Offering: Associate Degree
Accreditation: SC, ACBSP, ADNUR, COARC, MAC, PNUR, PTAA, RAD

01 President ... Dr. Walt TOBIN
05 Vice Pres Academic Affairs ... Mrs. Donna ELMORE
10 Vice President Business Affairs ... Mr. Kim HUFF
32 Vice President of Student Services ... Dr. Sandra S. DAVIS
11 Dean of Administration ... Mr. Mike HAMMOND
36 Training/Econ Development Director ... Mrs. Sandra MOORE
06 Registrar ... Ms. Amy OTT
30 Dean Development/Marketing ... Ms. Faith MCCURRY
46 Dean Planning/Research/Development ... Ms. Faith MCCURRY
13 Director Information Technology ... Mr. John MCCASKILL
08 Dean Learning Resource Ctr/Library ... Mr. Haley HALL
18 Physical Plant Director ... Mr. James S. BRYANT, III
37 Director Student Financial Aid ... Ms. Bichevia GREEN
07 Director of Admissions ... Vacant
19 Chief of Safety/Security ... Mr. Douglas STOKES
09 Dir Acad Support/Inst Effectiveness ... Mr. Cleveland WILSON
15 Human Resource Director ... Ms. Marie HOWELL
96 Procurement Manager ... Mrs. Scarlet GEDDINGS
84 Enrollment/Records Mgmt Specialist ... Ms. Phyllis STOUDENMIRE

Piedmont Technical College (H)

620 N. Emerald Road, Greenwood SC 29646
County: Greenwood FICE Identification: 003992
Unit ID: 218520
Telephone: (864) 941-8324 Carnegie Class: Assoc/HVT-High Trad
FAX Number: (864) 941-8555 Calendar System: Semester
URL: www.ptc.edu
Established: 1966 Annual Undergrad Tuition & Fees (In-District): $4,421
Enrollment: 4,596 Coed
Affiliation or Control: State/Local IRS Status: 501(c)3
Highest Offering: Associate Degree
Accreditation: SC, ADNUR, COARC, CVT, #FUSER, MAC, OTA, RAD, SURGT

01 President ... Dr. L. Rayburn BROOKS
10 Vice Pres Business & Finance ... Ms. K. Paige CHILDS
05 Vice President Academic Affairs ... Dr. Jack BAGWELL
32 Vice Pres Student Affairs ... Mr. Joshua BLACK
102 Asst VP Development/PTC Foundation ... Ms. Fran K. WILEY
51 Assoc Vice Pres Cont Educ/Econ Dev ... Mr. Rusty DENNING
108 Assoc VP Assessment/Compliance ... Dr. Donna FOSTER
84 Assoc VP Enrollment/Communications ... Mr. Joshua BLACK
20 Assoc Vice Pres Academic Affairs ... Dr. Darrin CAMPEN
15 Assoc VP Human Resources ... Ms. Alesia BROWN
13 Asst Vice Pres Information Tech ... Mr. Joel GRIFFIN
49 Dean Arts & Science ... Dr. Brad GRIGGS
76 Dean Health Care ... Ms. Tara GONCE
54 Dean Engr/Industrial Technology ... Mr. Hadi HAMID
66 Dean Nursing ... Ms. Tara GONCE
35 Dean of Student Services ... Ms. Tamatha SELLS
07 Dean of Admissions ... Ms. Renae FRAZIER
09 Director Institutional Reporting ... Ms. Zeolean F. KINARD
26 Director Marketing/Public Relations ... Mr. Russell MARTIN
88 Director Genesis Initiatives ... Mr. Steve B. COLEMAN
18 Director Facilities Management ... Mr. J. Chad TEAGUE
08 Head Librarian ... Ms. Meredith DANIEL
19 Director Campus Police/Security ... Mr. Terry LEDFORD
37 Director of Financial Aid ... Ms. Missy PERRY
06 Registrar ... Ms. Tameika WIDEMAN
21 Controller ... Ms. Wendy HUGHES
21 Sr Accountant ... Ms. Crystal PITTMAN

Presbyterian College (I)

503 S Broad Street, Clinton SC 29325-2865
County: Laurens FICE Identification: 003445
Unit ID: 218539
Telephone: (864) 833-2820 Carnegie Class: Bac-A&S
FAX Number: (864) 833-8481 Calendar System: Semester

URL: www.presby.edu
Established: 1880 Annual Undergrad Tuition & Fees: $38,660
Enrollment: 1,280 Coed
Affiliation or Control: Presbyterian Church (U.S.A.) IRS Status: 501(c)3
Highest Offering: Doctorate
Accreditation: SC, CAEPN, MUS, PHAR

01 President ... Mr. Robert E. STATON
04 Executive Asst to the President ... Mrs. Jenny G. BOGAN
05 Provost ... Dr. Donald R. RABER, II
84 Dean of Enrollment Management ... Mr. Brian J. FORTMAN
07 Director of Admissions ... Mr. Mark O. FOX, II
20 Dean of Academic Programs ... Dr. J. Alicia ASKEW
37 VP for Enrollment & Financial Aid .. Mrs. Suzanne M. PETRUSCH
09 Director of Institutional Research ... Dr. Norman B. BRYAN, JR.
08 Director of Thomason Library ... Mr. David W. CHATHAM
24 Director of Media Services ... Mr. Douglas J. WALLACE
104 Director of International Programs ... Mr. Viet X. HA
85 Asst Dir of International Programs ... Ms. Adriana K. SMITH
06 Registrar & Director of Records ... Mrs. Vicky W. WILSON
67 Interim Dean School of Pharmacy ... Dr. Dick STULL
07 Dir of Admissions Pharmacy School ... Ms. Katherine J. KANE
10 VP Finance/Administration ... Mr. Jeff P. SCACCIA
21 Controller ... Ms. Dawn W. DURHAM
18 Exec Director of Campus Services ... Mr. Michael D. CRISP
37 Director of Financial Aid ... Mr. Brian J. FORTMAN
13 Director of Information Technology ... Mr. H. William ROACH
90 Academic Computing Services Coord ... Dr. Robert W. HOWILER
91 Desktop Support/Aux Systems Sr Tech ... Ms. Nellie R. SHELTON
109 Manager of Auxiliary Services ... Mr. Jason T. KOENIG
32 VP for Campus Life/Dean of Students ... Dr. Joy S. SMITH
39 Assoc Dean Students/Residence Life ... Mr. Andrew T. PETERSON
36 Assoc Dean Students/Career Dev ... Ms. Kimberly A. LANE
42 Director of Campus Ministries .. Ms. Rachel E. PARSONS-WELLS
19 Director of Safety & Risk Mgmt ... Mr. Lawrence P. MULHALL
38 Director Counseling Services ... Ms. Susan C. GENTRY-WRIGHT
111 VP for Advancement ... Ms. Jacki BERKSHIRE
88 Asst Athletic Dir for Development ... Mr. Harold E. NICHOLS, JR.
29 Director Alumni Relations ... Ms. Leni N. PATTERSON
41 Interim Director of Athletics ... Mrs. Dee A. NICHOLS
15 VP of Human Resources ... Ms. Barbara H. FAYAD

Professional Golfers Career College (A)

4454 Bluffton Pk Crescent, Ste 200, Bluffton SC 29910
Telephone: (843) 757-9611 Identification: 770779
Accreditation: CNCE

† Branch campus of Professional Golfers Career College, Temecula, CA

Sherman College of Chiropractic (B)

PO Box 1452, Spartanburg SC 29304-1452
County: Spartanburg FICE Identification: 020637
Unit ID: 218751
Telephone: (864) 578-8770 Carnegie Class: Spec-4-yr-Other Health
FAX Number: (864) 599-4860 Calendar System: Quarter
URL: www.sherman.edu
Established: 1973 Annual Graduate Tuition & Fees: N/A
Enrollment: 397 Coed
Affiliation or Control: Independent Non-Profit IRS Status: 501(c)3
Highest Offering: Doctorate; No Undergraduates
Accreditation: SC, CHIRO

01 President ... Dr. Edwin CORDERO
03 Exec Asst to President/Sr VP ... Ms. Roberta THOMAS-WOOD
11 Senior Vice President ... Dr. Neil COHEN
05 Provost ... Dr. Robert IRWIN
20 Vice Pres of Academic Affairs ... Dr. Joseph DONOFRIO
10 Vice Pres for Business & Finance ... Mrs. Karen CANUP
32 Vice Pres for Student Affairs ... Mrs. LaShanda HUTTO-HARRIS
07 Sr Director of Enrollment Services ... Ms. Kendra STRANGE
06 Registrar ... Ms. Melody SABIN
08 Director of Learning Resouces ... Mrs. Chandra PLACER
37 Director of Financial Aid ... Mr. Chris ROBERSON
45 Dir Institutional Effectiveness ... Mrs. Crissy LEWIS
26 Director of Public Relations ... Ms. Karen RHODES
09 Director of Institutional Research ... Dr. Pengju George LUO
106 Dir Online Education/E-learning ... Dr. Billie HARRINGTON
15 Director Personnel Services ... Mrs. Mandy SMITH
19 Director Security/Safety ... Mr. Patrick LAUSIER

South Carolina State University (C)

300 College Street, NE, Orangeburg SC 29117-0001
County: Orangeburg FICE Identification: 003446
Unit ID: 218733
Telephone: (803) 536-7000 Carnegie Class: Masters/S
FAX Number: (803) 533-3622 Calendar System: Semester
URL: www.scsu.edu
Established: 1896 Annual Undergrad Tuition & Fees (In-State): $11,060
Enrollment: 2,942 Coed
Affiliation or Control: State IRS Status: 501(c)3
Highest Offering: Doctorate
Accreditation: SC, AAFCS, ART, CACREP, CAEPN, DIETD, MUS, SP, SW

01 President ... Mr. James E. CLARK
100 Chief of Staff ... Ms. Shondra F. ABRAHAM
05 Provost ... Dr. Learie B. LUKE
10 Vice Pres for Finance/Mgmt ... Mrs. Teare BREWINGTON
32 Vice Pres for Student Affairs ... Dr. Tamara JEFFRIES-JACKSON
88 Executive Dir 1890 Programs ... Dr. Louis D. WHITESIDES
43 General Counsel ... Ms. Mercedes P. PINCKNEY
20 Acting Associate Provost ... Dr. Matthew GUAH
111 VP Inst Advancement/External Rels ... Ms. Sonja A. BELLAMY-BENNETT
46 Assoc Provost/Sponsored Program ... Mr. Elbert R. MALONE
07 Director of Admissions ... Ms. Stacey SOWELL
81 Dean Col Sci/Math/Engineering Tech . Dr. Stanley N. IHEKWEAZU
53 Actg Dean Col Educ/Human & Soc Sci ... Dr. Janice B. OWENS
58 Dean Col of Graduate Studies ... Dr. Frederick M G. EVANS
50 Dean School of Business ... Dr. Barbara L. ADAMS
08 Acting Dean Library Services ... Dr. Ruth A. HODGES
124 Manager Student Success Retention ... Dr. Diane S. BRUCE
06 Acting Registrar ... Ms. Felicia L. MCMILLAN
13 Interim Director UCITS ... Mr. Curtis L. BRADLEY
37 Director of Financial Aid ... Ms. Tangar YOUNG
38 Director Counseling/Student Dev ... Dr. Cherilyn Y. TAYLOR-MINNIEFIELD
27 Dir of Marketing/Public Relations ... Ms. Kay E. SNIDER
36 Director of Career Placement ... Mr. Joseph THOMAS
15 Director Human Resource Mgmt ... Mr. Ronald S. YORK
41 Director Athletics ... Mr. Stacy L. DANLEY
18 Director of Facilities Mgmt ... Mr. Ken DAVIS
96 Director Procurement Services ... Ms. Jessica FAVOR
39 Director of Residential Life ... Ms. Cammy GRATE
19 Chief of Campus Police ... Mr. Joseph B. NELSON
92 Dean Honors College ... Dr. Harriet A. ROLAND
88 Director Sports Information ... Mr. Kendrick D. LEWIS
25 Dir Grants & Contract ... Ms. Gwendolyn F. MITCHELL
88 Director of Title III ... Ms. Gloria D. PYLES
28 Director of Multicultural Affairs ... Ms. Carolyn G. FREE
88 Station Manager WSSB-FM ... Mr. Carlito D. A'SEE
88 Athletics Compliance Coordinator ... Ms. Monique M. CARROLL
101 Secretary/Board of Trustees ... Ms. Eartha J. MOSLEY
104 Dir International/National Exchange ... Ms. Dominique ROLLE
105 Web Services ... Mr. Jason BARR
29 Director Alumni Relations ... Ms. Iva L. GARDNER
108 Dir of Institutional Effectiveness ... Ms. Valerie GOODWIN
88 Director IP Stanback Museum/Planet ... Dr. Frank C. MARTIN
106 Exe Dir Teach/Learning/Ext Studies ... Dr. Diane M. BURNETTE
09 Director Institutional Research ... Mrs. Cammie S. BERRY
30 Development Officer ... Mr. Davion L. PETTY
44 Director Annual Giving ... Ms. Iva L. GARDNER
84 Director Enrollment Management ... Ms. Betty R. BOATWRIGHT
26 Public Relations Coordinator ... Ms. Chaundra J. MIKELL

South University Columbia Campus (D)

9 Science Court, Columbia SC 29203-6400
Telephone: (803) 799-9082 FICE Identification: 004922
Accreditation: &SC, ACBSP, CACREP, MAC, NURSE, OTA, PHAR, PTAA

† Regional accreditation is carried under the parent institution in Savannah, GA.

Southern Wesleyan University (E)

907 Wesleyan Drive, PO Box 1020,
Central SC 29630-1020
County: Pickens FICE Identification: 003422
Unit ID: 217776
Telephone: (864) 644-5556 Carnegie Class: Masters/L
FAX Number: N/A Calendar System: Semester
URL: www.swu.edu
Established: 1906 Annual Undergrad Tuition & Fees: $25,476
Enrollment: 1,688 Coed
Affiliation or Control: Wesleyan Church IRS Status: 501(c)3
Highest Offering: Doctorate
Accreditation: SC, CAEPN, MUS

01 President ... Dr. Todd S. VOSS
05 Provost ... Dr. April WHITE PUGH
10 VP for Finance & Auxiliary Services ... Mr. Mark T. REEVES
32 Vice President for Student Life ... Dr. Chris CONFER
111 Vice President for Advancement ... Mr. Scott DRURY
108 Dean of Institutional Effectiveness ... Mr. Robert HUDSON
49 Dean College of Arts & Sciences ... Dr. Randolph JOHNSON
41 Athletic Director ... Mr. Chris WILLIAMS
50 Dean of the School of Business ... Dr. Stephen PREACHER
53 Dean of the School of Education ... Dr. Sandra MCLENDON
106 Dir Center for Teaching Excellence ... Dr. Karen LEE
37 Director of Financial Aid ... Mrs. Melanie GILLESPIE
15 Director of Human Resources ... Mrs. Dana L. FROST
08 Director of Library Services ... Mrs. Shannon BROOKS
06 Registrar ... Ms. Janice HARTSOE
29 Exec Dir of Alumni/Constituent Rels ... Vacant
38 Director Student Counseling ... Ms. Monica PEREZ
07 Director of Online Admissions ... Mr. Brice BICKEL
07 Director of On Campus Admissions ... Mr. David SLABAUGH
19 Director Security/Safety ... Mr. Brad BOWEN
26 Director of Communications ... Mr. Ed WELCH
39 Director of Residence Life ... Mr. Jason TEGAN
36 Director of Career Services ... Mrs. Ellen PATE
42 AVP Spiritual Life/Univ Chaplain ... Rev. Ken DILL
04 Administrative Asst to President ... Ms. Amy JARRETT

Spartanburg Community College (F)

107 Community College Drive, Spartanburg SC 29303
County: Spartanburg FICE Identification: 003994
Unit ID: 218830
Telephone: (864) 592-4600 Carnegie Class: Assoc/MT-VT-Mix Trad/Non
FAX Number: (864) 592-4642 Calendar System: Semester
URL: www.sccsc.edu
Established: 1963 Annual Undergrad Tuition & Fees (In-State): $4,662
Enrollment: 4,635 Coed
Affiliation or Control: State IRS Status: 501(c)3
Highest Offering: Associate Degree
Accreditation: SC, ACFEI, ADNUR, COARC, DA, EMT, MAC, MLTAD, RAD, SURGT

01 President ... Mr. Henry C. GILES, JR.
05 Sr Vice President Academic Affairs ... Dr. Cheryl COX
10 Vice Pres for Business Affairs ... Mr. Ray SWITZER
111 Exec Dir Advancement/SCC Foundation ... Mrs. Bea SMITH
32 Vice President for Student Affairs ... Mr. Ron JACKSON
84 Assc Vice Pres Enroll Mgt/Retention ... Mrs. Lynn F. DALE
20 Assoc Vice Pres of Instruction ... Mr. Michael BECK
88 Vice Pres for Economic Development ... Mr. Michael P. FORRESTER
12 Executive Director Cherokee Campus ... Mr. Daryl SMITH
12 Exec Director Tyger River Campus ... Dr. Anya SEBASTIEN
12 Exec Director Downtown Campus ... Ms. Witney FISHER
12 Site Coord Union County Campus ... Mr. Issac MCKISSICK
108 Director Eval/Accreditation/Plng ... Mr. Jay JACKSON
88 Dean of CCE ... Ms. Rhonda JOHNS
08 Dean of Learning Resources ... Mr. Mark ROSEVEARE
76 Dean Health & Human Services ... Dr. Benita YOWE
49 Dean of Arts & Sciences ... Mrs. Kem HARVEY
07 Director Recruiting/Admissions Svcs ... Ms. Quiana REED
15 Assoc Vice Pres of Human Resources ... Mr. Rick TEAL
13 Director Information Technologies ... Mr. Peter C. GALLEN
09 Director of Institutional Research ... Mr. Jack R. BOURGEOIS
26 Director Marketing/Public Relations ... Mrs. Cheri ANDERSON-HUCKS
29 Alumni Relations Coordinator ... Ms. Charm LOWE
38 Director Advising/Early Alert Svcs ... Mr. Michael HARVEY
14 Director Computer Center ... Mrs. Tina S. REID
18 Director Campus Operations ... Mr. Winston ANDERSON
19 Director Security/Safety ... Mr. Scott KELLEY
06 Registrar ... Ms. Celia N. BAUSS
96 Director Purchasing Office ... Vacant
21 Director of Finance ... Vacant
37 Director of Financial Aid ... Mr. Jeffery BOYLE
106 Dir Online Education/E-learning ... Mr. Neil GRIFFIN
25 Director of Contracts & Grants ... Ms. Caroline SEXTON
72 Dean of Technologies ... Mr. Jeff HUNT
04 Administrative Asst to President ... Mrs. Donna WALKER
36 Director Student Placement ... Ms. Jennifer LITTLE
90 Director Academic Computing ... Mr. Roy SMITH
103 Director Workforce Development ... Mrs. Latokia TRIGG

Spartanburg Methodist College (G)

1000 Powell Mill Road, Spartanburg SC 29301-5899
County: Spartanburg FICE Identification: 003447
Unit ID: 218821
Telephone: (864) 587-4000 Carnegie Class: Assoc/HT-High Trad
FAX Number: (864) 587-4355 Calendar System: Semester
URL: www.smcsc.edu
Established: 1911 Annual Undergrad Tuition & Fees: $17,035
Enrollment: 790 Coed
Affiliation or Control: United Methodist IRS Status: 501(c)3
Highest Offering: Baccalaureate
Accreditation: SC

01 President ... Mr. W. Scott COCHRAN
05 Exec VP Acad Affairs/Student Dev ... Dr. Mark G. GIBBS
10 Executive VP for Business Affairs ... Mr. Eric MCDONALD
111 Vice Pres Institutional Advancement ... Mrs. Jennifer DILLENGER
84 Vice Pres Enrollment Management ... Mr. Ben MAXWELL
26 Vice President for Marketing ... Mrs. Lisa WARE
88 Vice President for Prof Development ... Ms. Courtney SHELTON
13 Vice Pres for Operations Info Tech ... Mr. Trey ARRINGTON
32 Dean of Students ... Ms. Teresa FERGUSON
06 Registrar ... Ms. Jill R. JOHNSON
08 Library Director ... Ms. Lori HETRICK
04 Admin Assistant to the President ... Mrs. Cheryl SOMERSET
44 Director of Planned Giving ... Mr. Don TATE
37 Director of Financial Aid ... Vacant
38 Director of Student Counseling ... Ms. Alesia LOWE-JENKINS
42 Chaplain/Director Church Relations ... Rev. Tim DRUM
41 Director of Athletics ... Ms. Megan AIELLO
18 Director Facilities Management ... Mr. Marty WOODS
29 Director of Alumni Relations ... Mrs. Leah L. PRUITT
15 Exec Director of Human Resources ... Mrs. Jenny R. DUNN
44 Director of Church Funding ... Vacant
19 Chief of Campus Public Safety ... Ms. Teresa D. FERGUSON
09 Exec Dir Analytics & Improvement ... Mr. Jason WOMICK
39 Director Student Housing ... Ms. Trina GILLIAM
108 Director Institutional Assessment ... Ms. Jessica HARWOOD

Technical College of the Lowcountry (H)

921 S Ribaut Road, PO Box 1288,
Beaufort SC 29901-1288
County: Beaufort FICE Identification: 009910
Unit ID: 217712
Telephone: (843) 525-8211 Carnegie Class: Assoc/HVT-High Trad
FAX Number: (843) 525-8330 Calendar System: Semester
URL: www.tcl.edu
Established: 1969 Annual Undergrad Tuition & Fees (In-State): $4,684
Enrollment: 2,314 Coed
Affiliation or Control: State IRS Status: 501(c)3
Highest Offering: Associate Degree
Accreditation: SC, ADNUR, COMTA, PNUR, PTAA, RAD, SURGT

01 President ... Dr. Richard J. GOUGH
11 Vice Pres Administrative Services ... Mr. Andrew SMITH
05 Vice President for Academic Affairs ... Ms. Nancy WEBER
32 Vice President for Student Affairs ... Ms. Nancy WEBER
35 AVP for Student Affairs ... Mr. Rodney ADAMS
09 Director for Research/Planning ... Ms. Camille MYERS
15 Human Resources Director ... Ms. Sharon O'NEAL
20 Director for Learning Resources ... Ms. Sasha BISHOP
50 Div Dean Business Technologies ... Ms. Kelli BONIECKI
49 Div Dean Arts & Sciences ... Dr. Gayle TREMBLE
76 Dean Health Sciences ... Dr. Glenn LEVICKI
13 Director of Information Technology ... Mr. Hayes WISER
37 Director Financial Aid ... Ms. Georgeann WILLIAMS
111 VP for Inst Advancement ... Ms. Mary Lee CARNS
26 AVP for Public Relations ... Ms. Leigh COPELAND
40 Bookstore Director ... Ms. Louise RENNIX
18 Director of Facility Management ... Mr. Larry BECKLER
96 Director of Purchasing ... Ms. Carol MACK
06 Registrar ... Ms. Allison CANNING
103 Director for Workforce Solutions ... Ms. Melanie GALLION
04 Administrative Asst to President ... Ms. Ann CULLEN

Tri-County Technical College (A)

PO Box 587, Pendleton SC 29670-0587

County: Anderson   FICE Identification: 004926
Unit ID: 218885
Telephone: (864) 646-8361   Carnegie Class: Assoc/MT-VT-High Trad
FAX Number: (864) 646-1889   Calendar System: Semester
URL: www.tctc.edu
Established: 1962   Annual Undergrad Tuition & Fees (In-District): $4,326
Enrollment: 6,069   Coed
Affiliation or Control: State/Local   IRS Status: 501(c)3
Highest Offering: Associate Degree
Accreditation: SC, ACBSP, ADNUR, DA, MAC, MLTAD, PNUR, SURGT

01 President ... Dr. Galen DEHAY
05 Senior Vice President ... Vacant
10 Vice Pres Business Affairs ... Ms. Cara HAMILTON
102 Executive Director TCTC Foundation ... Mr. Grayson KELLY
15 Asst VP Human Resources ... Mrs. Marci LEAKE
32 Asst VP Student Support/Engagement ... Ms. Linda JAMEISON
51 Dean of Continuing Education ... Mr. Rick COTHRAN
84 Dean College Transitions ... Ms. Jenni CREAMER
35 Dean of Student Development ... Mr. Mark DOUGHERTY
49 Dean Arts & Sciences Division ... Mr. Tom LAWRENCE
72 Dean Engineering Technology Div ... Ms. Amanda ORZECHOWSKI
50 Dean Business/Human Services Div ... Mrs. Jackie BLAKLEY
76 Dean Health Education Division ... Mr. Ahmad CHAUDHRY
37 Student Financial Aid Director ... Mr. Adam GHILONI
13 CIO/Information Technology Dir ... Mr. Luke VANWINGERDEN
26 Dir Public Relations/Communication ... Mrs. Rebecca W. EIDSON
30 Director of Development ... Mrs. Courtney WHITE
07 Director of Admissions ... Ms. Tiffiny BLACKWELL
06 Registrar ... Mr. Scott HARVEY
09 Director of Institutional Research ... Mr. Chris MARINO
18 Chief Facilities/Physical Plant ... Mr. Ken KOPERA
21 Director of Fiscal Affairs ... Ms. Tracy WACTOR
96 Director of Purchasing ... Ms. Kristal DOHERTY
38 Director of Student Life/Counseling ... Ms. Croslena JOHNSON
04 Admin Assistant to the President ... Ms. Kathleen C. BRAND
100 Chief of Staff ... Mr. Dan COOPER

Trident Technical College (B)

PO Box 118067, Charleston SC 29423-8067

County: Charleston   FICE Identification: 004920
Unit ID: 218894
Telephone: (843) 574-6111   Carnegie Class: Assoc/MT-VT-High Trad
FAX Number: (843) 574-6541   Calendar System: Semester
URL: www.tridenttech.edu
Established: 1964   Annual Undergrad Tuition & Fees (In-District): $4,551
Enrollment: 13,271   Coed
Affiliation or Control: State/Local   IRS Status: 501(c)3
Highest Offering: Associate Degree
Accreditation: SC, ACBSP, ACFEI, ADNUR, CAHIIM, COARC, CSHSE, DA, DH, EMT, MAC, MLTAD, OTA, PNUR, PTAA, RAD

01 President ... Dr. Mary THORNLEY
10 Vice Pres Finance & Administration ... Mr. Scott POELKER
05 Vice President Academic Affairs ... Dr. Cathy ALMQUIST
32 Vice President Student Services ... Dr. Patrice DAVIS
111 Vice President Advancement ... Ms. Meg HOWLE
51 Vice Pres Continuing Educ/Econ Dev ... Mr. Robert WALKER
13 Vice Pres Information Technology ... Mr. M.G MITCHUM
45 Assoc VP Planning/Accreditation ... Mr. James "Dub" GREEN
20 Asst Vice Pres Instruction ... Mr. David HARRIS
35 Asst VP for Student Development ... Ms. Pam BROWN
15 Associate VP Human Resources ... Ms. DeVetta HUGHES
96 Dir Procurement/Risk Management ... Ms. Carol BELCHER
109 Dir Auxiliary Enterprises/Bookstore ... Ms. Jloundia PINCKNEY
18 Director Facilities ... Mr. Eric HAMILTON
21 Director Finance ... Ms. Melody TAYLOR
26 Director Marketing ... Ms. Tina AHLEMANN
27 Director Public Info ... Mr. David HANSEN
88 Assistant VP Community Partnerships ... Ms. Melissa STOWASSER
30 Vice President Development ... Ms. Lisa PICCOLO
14 Dir Information Technology Training ... Mr. Joseph GIBSON
124 Dean of Student Engagement ... Mr. Brian ALMQUIST
81 Dean Science & Mathematics ... Vacant
79 Dean Humanities & Social Sciences ... Dr. Tim BROWN
106 Asst VP Educ Tech/Online College ... Ms. Connie JOLLY
54 Dean Engineering & Construction ... Mr. Tim FULFORD
76 Dean Health Sciences ... Ms. Krista HARRINGTON
57 Dean Film Media and Visual Arts ... Mr. Glenn SEALE
88 Dean Manufacturing & Maintenance ... Mr. Robert ELLIOTT
88 Dean Culinary Inst of Charleston ... Mr. Mike SABOE
107 Dean Public/Profess & Legal Studies ... Ms. Jan UTSEY
66 Dean Nursing ... Ms. Nancy HILBURN
75 Dean Aeronautical Studies ... Dr. Barry FRANCO
12 Dean Berkeley Campus ... Dr. Karen WRIGHTEN
12 Dean Mount Pleasant Campus ... Dr. Darren FELTY
12 Dean Palmer Campus ... Dr. Louester ROBINSON
19 Director Public Safety ... Mr. Mario EVANS
06 Registrar ... Mr. Evan REICH
07 Director of Admissions ... Ms. Clara MARTIN
09 Director of Institutional Research ... Ms. Samantha RICHARDS
37 Director Student Financial Aid ... Ms. Sarah DOWD
04 Executive Asst to President ... Ms. Helen SUGHRUE

University of South Carolina Columbia (C)

Columbia SC 29208-0001

County: Richland   FICE Identification: 003448
Unit ID: 218663
Telephone: (803) 777-7000   Carnegie Class: DU-Highest
FAX Number: (803) 777-0101   Calendar System: Semester
URL: www.sc.edu
Established: 1801   Annual Undergrad Tuition & Fees (In-State): $12,616
Enrollment: 34,731   Coed
Affiliation or Control: State   IRS Status: 501(c)3
Highest Offering: Doctorate
Accreditation: SC, ANEST, #ARCPA, ART, CAATE, CACREP, CAEP, CAHIIM, CEA, CLPSY, DANCE, HSA, IPSY, JOUR, LAW, LIB, MED, MUS, NURSE, PH, PHAR, PTA, SCPSY, SP, SPAA, SW, THEA

01 President ... Dr. Robert CASLEN
13 Vice President for IT & CIO ... Mr. Doug FOSTER
88 University Treasurer ... Mr. Patrick LARDNER
116 Exec Dir of Audit & Advisory Svcs ... Ms. Pam DORAN
05 Interim Provost ... Dr. Tayloe HARDING
20 V Prov & Dean for U Grad Studies ... Dr. Sandra KELLY
11 Sr VP for Administration & COO ... Mr. Edward I. WALTON
10 CFO & VP for Finance ... Vacant
32 V Prov Acad Supp & Dean of Students ... Dr. Dennis A. PRUITT
15 Vice President Human Resources ... Mr. Christopher D. BYRD
30 VP Development & Alumni Relations ... Ms. Jancy HOUCK
46 Vice President for Research ... Dr. Prakash NAGARKATTI
26 Int Dir of Comm & Public Affs ... Ms. Sally MCKAY
101 Univ Secretary and Sec to Board ... Mr. Cantey HEATH
58 Vice Prov & Dean Grad School ... Dr. Cheryl ADDY
85 Vice Provost & Dir Global Carolina ... Dr. Allen MILLER
84 Asst V Prov Enrl Mgmt & Dean UG Adm ... Mr. Scott VERZYL
63 Exec Dean School of Medicine ... Dr. Les HALL
08 Dean of University Libraries ... Dr. Tom MCNALLY
43 Gen Counsel & Exec Dir Compliance ... Mr. Walter H. PARHAM
09 Exec Dir Inst Rsch/Assess/Analytics ... Ms. Sabrina ANDREWS
18 VP for Facilities & Transportation ... Mr. Derrick E. HUGGINS
19 Assoc VP Law Enfr & Chief of Police ... Mr. Christopher L. WUCHENICH
37 Dir Student Fin Aid & Scholarship ... Mr. Joey DERRICK
36 Director Career Center ... Ms. Helen POWERS
06 University Registrar ... Mr. Aaron C. MARTERER
22 Exec Asst to Pres Equal Oppty Pgm ... Mr. Clifford SCOTT
88 NCAA Compliance Coord ... Mr. Christopher ROGERS
07 Director of Admissions ... Dr. Mary WAGNER
39 Director Housing ... Ms. Kristen KENNEDY
23 Exec Director Student Health Svcs ... Dr. Deborah C. BECK
41 Athletic Director ... Mr. Ray TANNER
35 Assoc VP for Student Life ... Mr. Jerry T. BREWER
27 Director News & Internal Relations ... Mr. Wesley T. HICKMAN
96 Director of Purchasing ... Mrs. Venis MANIGO
29 Exec Director Alumni Association ... Mr. Jack CLAYPOOLE
88 VP for System Planning ... Dr. Mary Anne FITZPATRICK
12 Chancellor Palmetto College ... Dr. Susan ELKINS
88 Dean Hospitality/Retail/Sport HMgt ... Dr. Haemoon OH
50 Dean Moore School of Business ... Dr. Peter J. BREWS
53 Dean College of Education ... Dr. Jon E. PEDERSEN
54 Dean Col Engineering & Computing ... Dr. Hossein HAJ-HARIRI
69 Dean Arnold School of Public Health ... Dr. G. Thomas CHANDLER
60 Dean Col of Info & Communications ... Mr. Charles BIERBAUER
61 Dean School of Law ... Dr. Robert M. WILCOX
88 Sr Assoc Dean School of Medicine ... Dr. Caughman TAYLOR
63 Dean Greenville School of Medicine ... Dr. Jerry R. YOUKEY
67 Dean College of Pharmacy ... Dr. Stephen J. CUTLER
49 Dean Col of Arts & Sciences ... Dr. Lacy FORD
64 Dean School of Music ... Dr. Tayloe HARDING
92 Dean SC Honors College ... Dr. Steve LYNN
66 Dean College of Nursing ... Dr. Jeannette ANDREWS
70 Dean College of Social Work ... Dr. Sarah GEHLERT
92 Dir Fellowships & Scholar Programs ... Ms. Novella BESKID
88 Asst Provost Academic Programs ... Dr. Tena CREWS
88 Executive Director USC Connect ... Dr. Irma J. VANSCOY
28 Sr Assc Prov & Chief Diversity Ofcr ... Mr. John DOZIER
86 Director Govt & Community Relations ... Ms. Shirley D. MILLS
88 Director of Economic Engagement ... Mr. William B. KIRKLAND
86 Director of State Govt Relations ... Mr. Derrick MEGGIE

University of South Carolina Aiken (D)

471 University Parkway, Aiken SC 29801-6399

County: Aiken   FICE Identification: 003449
Unit ID: 218645
Telephone: (803) 648-6851   Carnegie Class: Bac-Diverse
FAX Number: (803) 641-3362   Calendar System: Semester
URL: www.usca.edu
Established: 1961   Annual Undergrad Tuition & Fees (In-State): $10,760
Enrollment: 3,506   Coed
Affiliation or Control: State   IRS Status: 501(c)3
Highest Offering: Master's
Accreditation: SC, CAEPN, MUS, NURSE

01 Chancellor ... Dr. Sandra JORDAN
111 Vice Chanc Advance & External Rels ... Ms. Mary DRISCOLL
32 Vice Chancellor Student Life & Svcs ... Vacant
13 Vice Chancellor Information Tech ... Mr. Ernest PRINGLE
10 VC for Admin and Finance/CFO ... Mr. Cam REAGIN
20 Asst Vice Chanc Academic Affairs ... Dr. Tim LINTNER
84 Assoc Vice Chanc Enrollment Mgmt ... Mr. Daniel J. ROBB
50 Dean School of Business Admin ... Dr. Michael FEKULA
53 Dean of the School of Education ... Dr. Judy BECK
66 Dean of the School of Nursing ... Dr. Thayer MCGAHEE
09 Dir Inst Effect/Research/Compliance ... Ms. Nicole SPENSLEY
08 Library Director ... Rodney LIPPARD
25 Director Sponsored Research ... Dr. Bill PIRKLE
40 Purchasing Manager ... Ms. Heidi DIFRANCO
109 Dir Campus Auxil & Support Services ... Mr. Jeff JENIK
88 Director Children's Center ... Ms. Lynn WILLIAMS
88 Dir USCA Convocation Center ... Mr. Josh SMALL
12 Exec Dir of Etherredge Center ... Mr. Jack BENJAMIN
21 Controller ... Mr. Kevin CRAWFORD
15 Dir Human Resources & Affirm Action ... Ms. Maria CHANDLER
88 Dir Campus Recreation & Wellness ... Ms. Mila PADGETT
07 Director of Admissions ... Mr. Andrew HENDRIX
36 Director of Career Services ... Mr. Corey FERALDI
37 Director Financial Aid ... Linda A. HIGGINS
06 Registrar ... Mr. Brock GILLIAM
14 Director of Client Services ... Mr. Chris SPIRES
105 Dir Network Systems/Arch & Infra ... Ms. Joann WILLIAMSON
41 Director of Athletics ... Mr. Jim HERLIHY
38 Director Counseling & Disabilities ... Ms. Cynthia B. GELINAS
23 Director Student Health Center ... Ms. Cynthia B. GELINAS
39 Director of Housing ... Mr. Deri WILLS
28 Dir Global Stds/Multicult Engagemnt ... Mr. Mutombo KABASELE
35 Asst Vice Chanc Student Life ... Mr. Ahmed SAMAHA
19 Chief of Police ... Mr. Kevin LILES
29 Dir Alumni Rels/Cmty Partnerships ... Mr. Randy DUCKETT
51 Dir Office of Ext Pgms & Life Lrng ... Vacant
112 Director of Major Gifts ... Ms. Robin CALLICOTT
26 Dir Marketing & Community Relations ... Mr. James RABY
88 Director Instructional Services ... Mr. Keith PIERCE

University of South Carolina Beaufort (E)

1 University Boulevard, Bluffton SC 29909-6085

County: Beaufort   FICE Identification: 003450
Unit ID: 218654
Telephone: (843) 208-8000   Carnegie Class: Bac-A&S
FAX Number: (843) 208-8299   Calendar System: Semester
URL: www.uscb.edu
Established: 1959   Annual Undergrad Tuition & Fees (In-State): $10,730
Enrollment: 2,077   Coed
Affiliation or Control: State   IRS Status: 501(c)3
Highest Offering: Baccalaureate
Accreditation: SC, CAEPN, CSHSE, NURSE

01 Chancellor ... Dr. Al M. PANU
05 Provost & Exec VC for Acad Affairs ... Dr. Eric SKIPPER
111 Vice Chanc Advancement & Ext Rels ... Dr. Anna PONDER
84 Vice Chanc for Enrollment Mgmt ... Mr. Mack PALMOUR
10 Vice Chanc Finance/Operations ... Mr. Earle HOLLEY
32 Vice Chanc Student Development ... Dr. Douglas OBLANDER
41 Athletic Director ... Mr. Quin MONAHAN
13 Chief Information Officer ... Vacant
20 Assoc Vice Chanc for Acad Affairs ... Dr. Martha MORIARTY
08 Interim Director of Libraries ... Ms. Melanie HANES-RAMOS
15 Director of Human Resources ... Dr. Sue GOLABEK
37 Director of Financial Aid ... Ms. Patricia GREENE
09 Dir Inst Effectiveness/Research ... Mr. Brian MALLORY
18 Director of Facilities ... Mr. Mike PARROTT
36 Director of Career Services ... Ms. Leta SALAZAR
06 Registrar ... Mr. Gary SUTTON
35 Director of Student Life ... Ms. Alison MATHE
39 Director Housing and Judicial ... Ms. Deonne YEAGER
88 Director of Military Program ... Mr. Michael WEISS
114 Budget Director ... Ms. Mary CORDRAY

University of South Carolina Lancaster (F)

PO Box 889, Lancaster SC 29721-0889

Telephone: (803) 313-7000   FICE Identification: 003453
Accreditation: &SC, ACBSP, ADNUR, PNUR

† Regional accreditation is carried under University of South Carolina - Columbia.

University of South Carolina Salkehatchie (G)

PO Box 617, Allendale SC 29810-0617

County: Allendale   FICE Identification: 003454
Unit ID: 218681
Telephone: (803) 584-3446   Carnegie Class: Assoc/HT-Mix Trad/Non
FAX Number: (803) 584-5038   Calendar System: Semester
URL: uscsalkehatchie.sc.edu
Established: 1965   Annual Undergrad Tuition & Fees (In-State): $7,558

Enrollment: 1,011 Coed
Affiliation or Control: State IRS Status: 501(c)3
Highest Offering: Associate Degree
Accreditation: &SC

01 Dean .... Dr. Chris NESMITH
32 Asc Dean Student Svcs/Dir Athletics .... Ms. Jane T. BREWER
08 Head Librarian .... Mr. Daniel JOHNSON
11 Director of Finance .... Ms. Jessica ALL
37 Director Financial Aid .... Ms. Julie HADWIN
18 Dir Facilities/Safety/HR Director .... Dr. William A. SANDIFER
40 Bookstore Manager .... Mr. Lamar HEWETT
07 Director of Admissions/Registrar .... Ms. Carmen BROWN
30 Chief Development .... Dr. Ann C. CARMICHAEL
84 Exec Director Enrollment Mgmt Svcs .... Mr. Tony JACKSON
88 Director Leadership Institute .... Mr. Greg FENNESSY
88 Sports Information Director .... Mr. Trent KINARD

† Regional accreditation is carried under University of South Carolina - Columbia.

University of South Carolina School of Medicine Greenville (A)

607 Grove Road, Greenville SC 29605
County: Greenville Identification: 667114
Telephone: (864) 455-7992 Carnegie Class: Not Classified
FAX Number: (864) 455-8404 Calendar System: Semester
URL: greenvillemed.sc.edu
Established: 2010 Annual Graduate Tuition & Fees: N/A
Enrollment: N/A Coed
Affiliation or Control: State IRS Status: 501(c)3
Highest Offering: Doctorate; No Undergraduates
Accreditation: MED

01 Dean .... Dr. Jerry R. YOUKEY
05 Associate Dean for Faculty Affairs .... Dr. Robert BEST
32 Associate Dean for Student Affairs .... Dr. Paul CATALANA
20 Asst Dean Academic Affairs .... Dr. April BUCHANAN
10 Exec Dir Business Opers & Finance .... Kristin LACEY
30 Sr Director of Development .... Susan WARD
13 Director of IT and Facilities .... Ron KNAPPENBERGER
15 Director of HR and Faculty Affairs .... Claire GREGG
06 Registrar & Financial Aid Director .... Casey WILEY

University of South Carolina Sumter (B)

200 Miller Road, Sumter SC 29150-2498
County: Sumter FICE Identification: 003426
Unit ID: 218690
Telephone: (803) 775-8727 Carnegie Class: Assoc/HT-High Non
FAX Number: (803) 775-2180 Calendar System: Semester
URL: www.uscsumter.edu
Established: 1966 Annual Undergrad Tuition & Fees (In-State): $7,558
Enrollment: 1,002 Coed
Affiliation or Control: State IRS Status: 501(c)3
Highest Offering: Associate Degree
Accreditation: &SC

01 Regional Campus Dean .... Mr. Michael SONNTAG
05 Exec Assoc Dean Acad/Stdnt Affairs .... Mr. Eric REISENAUER
32 Dir of Student Life and eSports ... Mr. Kristopher E. WEISSMANN
10 Assoc Dean for Admin/Financial Svcs ... Mr. Bruce K. BLUMBERG
09 Institutional Research Analyst .... Mr. Chuck W. WRIGHT
08 Head Librarian .... Ms. Sharon H. CHAPMAN
07 Director of Admissions Services .... Mr. Keith E. BRITTON
51 Dir of Educational Partnerships .... Ms. Lara K. RICHARDSON
26 Dir of Public Relations/Marketing .... Ms. Misty HATFIELD
40 Bookstore Manager .... Ms. Julie MCCOY
15 Human Resources Officer .... Ms. Marchetta L. WILLIAMS
88 Program Dir Opportunity Scholars .... Ms. Lisa ROSDAIL
87 Director Shaw AFB Programs .... Mr. Rick BOYD
41 Athletic Director .... Ms. Adrienne CATALDO
13 Director of Info Technology .... Mr. Brian SMITH
37 Dir of Fin Aid & Veterans Affairs .... Ms. Lisa JEFFORDS
84 Exec Dir Enrollment Mgmt Svcs .... Mr. Joseph MEWS

† Regional accreditation is carried under University of South Carolina - Columbia.

University of South Carolina Union (C)

PO Drawer 729, Union SC 29379-0729
County: Union FICE Identification: 004927
Unit ID: 218706
Telephone: (864) 429-8728 Carnegie Class: Assoc/HT-High Non
FAX Number: (864) 427-3682 Calendar System: Semester
URL: uscunion.sc.edu
Established: 1965 Annual Undergrad Tuition & Fees (In-State): $7,558
Enrollment: 903 Coed
Affiliation or Control: State IRS Status: 501(c)3
Highest Offering: Associate Degree
Accreditation: &SC

01 Dean/Distinguished Prof Emeritus .... Dr. John CATALANO
05 Associate Dean Acad Affairs .... Dr. Randy LOWELL
84 Enrollment Director .... Mr. Bradley GREER
37 Director Financial Aid .... Mr. Robert HOLCOMBE
15 Human Resources .... Ms. Susan P. JETT
40 Bookstore Manager .... Ms. Tanja BLACK
13 Director of Information Technology .... Mr. Keith CAMP
30 Director of Marketing & Development .... Ms. Annie SMITH
08 Library Manager .... Ms. Sharon L. RUPP
121 Coord Academic Success Center .... Ms. Tammy WARR
10 Director of Budget and Business Ops .... Ms. Michele LEE
12 USC Laurens Location Director .... Mr. Matt DEAN
19 Health and Safety/Security Director .... Mr. Tony GREGORY
18 Maintenance Director .... Mr. Donald LAWSON
06 Registrar .... Mr. Blake WILSON

† Regional accreditation is carried under University of South Carolina - Columbia.

University of South Carolina Upstate (D)

800 University Way, Spartanburg SC 29303-4996
County: Spartanburg FICE Identification: 006951
Unit ID: 218742
Telephone: (864) 503-5000 Carnegie Class: Bac-Diverse
FAX Number: (864) 503-5375 Calendar System: Semester
URL: www.uscupstate.edu
Established: 1967 Annual Undergrad Tuition & Fees (In-State): $11,852
Enrollment: 5,990 Coed
Affiliation or Control: State IRS Status: 501(c)3
Highest Offering: Master's
Accreditation: SC, ART, CAEP, CAHIIM, NURSE

01 Chancellor .... Dr. Brendan KELLY
05 Prov/Sr Vice Chanc Academic Affairs .... Dr. Clif FLYNN
13 Int Vice Chanc Information Tech .... Mr. Luke VANWINGERDEN
10 Vice Chanc for Finance and Admin . Ms. Sheryl TURNER-WATTS
111 VC Advance/Upstate Foundation .... Dr. Meredith BRUNEN
45 VC Cmty-Based Rsrch/Engagement/Plng ...... Ms. Kathleen BRADY
12 Dir Acad Engagement Greenville Ctr .... Dr. Judith PRINCE
20 Assoc VC Academic Affairs .... Dr. Warren CARSON
32 VC Student Affs/Dean of Students .... Ms. Laura PUCKETT-BOLER
06 Registrar .... Ms. Mary David FOX
84 Vice Chanc Enrollment Services .... Ms. Donette STEWART
38 Director Counseling Services .... Dr. Elizabeth JODOIN
28 Chief Diversity Officer .... Mr. Alphonso ATKINS, JR.
08 Dean Library .... Ms. Frieda M. DAVISON
37 Director Financial Aid .... Ms. Bonnie C. CARSON
49 Dean Arts & Sciences .... Dr. Dirk SCHLINGMANN
50 Dean Johnson Col Business & Econ .... Dr. Frank RUDISILL
53 Interim Dean Education .... Dr. Charles LOVE
66 Dean Nursing .... Dr. Katharine GIBB
58 Director Graduate Education .... Dr. Tina HERZBERG
29 Director of Alumni Relations .... Mr. Joshua JONES
102 Director Dev & Found Scholarships .... Vacant
40 Director Bookstore .... Mr. Jerry CARROLL
41 Interim Athletic Director .... Mr. Jeff CRANE
18 Director Custodial Services .... Mr. Paul SCHMIDT
19 Dir Public Safety & Chief of Police .... Mr. Klay PETERSON
35 Asst Dean/Director Student Life .... Ms. Khrystal SMITH
39 Dir Housing Residential Life .... Ms. Mandy WHITTEN
23 Director Health Services .... Ms. Mary BUCHER
26 Exec Dir Univ Boards & Public Affs .... Mr. John F. PERRY
09 Dir Inst Research and Bus Intel .... Mr. Adam LONG
88 Dir for Fitness and Campus Rec .... Mr. Mark RITTER
22 Dir Disability Services .... Ms. Wendy WOODSBY
51 Dir Continuing Education .... Dr. Faruk TANYEL
114 Budget Manager .... Ms. Vintress BROWN
22 Dir Equal Opp & Employee Relations .... Ms. Sharon WOODS
104 Dir Intl Studies & Language Svcs .... Dr. Deryle HOPE
25 Dir Sponsored Awards .... Ms. Elaine MARSHALL
106 Dir Distance Education .... Dr. David MCCURRY
92 Director Honors Program .... Dr. Cathy CANINO
88 Dir Ctr Teaching Excellence .... Dr. June CARTER

Voorhees College (E)

PO Box 678, Denmark SC 29042-0678
County: Bamberg FICE Identification: 003455
Unit ID: 218919
Telephone: (803) 780-1234 Carnegie Class: Bac-Diverse
FAX Number: (803) 780-1015 Calendar System: Semester
URL: www.voorhees.edu
Established: 1897 Annual Undergrad Tuition & Fees: $12,630
Enrollment: 475 Coed
Affiliation or Control: Protestant Episcopal IRS Status: 501(c)3
Highest Offering: Baccalaureate
Accreditation: SC, ACBSP

01 President .... Dr. W. Franklin EVANS
05 Provost/VP Academic Affairs .... Dr. Ronnie HOPKINS
10 VP Fiscal/Business Affairs .... Mrs. V. Diane O'BERRY
30 VP Inst Advancement & Development .... Dr. Gwynth NELSON
84 VP Enrollment Mgmt/Student Affairs .... Ms. Charlene JOHNSON
06 Registrar .... Ms. Felicia MASON-GARNER
32 Dean of Students .... Mr. Adrian WEST
21 Director of Financial Aid .... Mr. Augusta KITCHEN
35 Director Student Support Services .... Ms. Lynda JEFFERSON
08 Director of Library Services .... Mr. Herman MASON, JR.
18 Director of Physical Plant .... Mr. Willie JEFFERSON
29 Director Alumni Affairs .... Ms. Stephanie RIVERS-KLUTTZ
36 Director Career Pathways Initiative .... Mr. Kimoni HICKMAN
42 Chaplain .... Rev. James YARSIAH
31 Director External Affairs .... Mr. Willie JEFFERSON
19 Director of Safety/Security .... Mr. Marquez CLAXTON
23 Director of Health Services .... Ms. Suzanne WILLIAMS
07 Director of Admissions/Recruitment .... Ms. Phyllis THOMPSON
15 Director of Human Resources .... Mrs. Constance COLTER-BRABHAM
13 Chief Technology Officer .... Mr. Monterrio JONES
40 College Store Manager .... Mrs. Shanda RUFFIN
100 Chief of Staff/Dir Title III .... Mr. Shemrico STANLEY

Williamsburg Technical College (F)

601 Martin Luther King, Jr. Avenue,
Kingstree SC 29556-4103
County: Williamsburg FICE Identification: 009322
Unit ID: 218955
Telephone: (843) 355-4110 Carnegie Class: Assoc/MT-VT-High Non
FAX Number: (843) 355-4296 Calendar System: Semester
URL: www.wiltech.edu
Established: 1969 Annual Undergrad Tuition & Fees (In-District): $4,368
Enrollment: 732 Coed
Affiliation or Control: State/Local IRS Status: 501(c)3
Highest Offering: Associate Degree
Accreditation: SC

01 President .... Dr. Patricia A. LEE
10 VP Administration & Finance .... Ms. Melissa A. COKER
05 VP for Academic/Student Affairs .... Dr. Clifton R. ELLIOTT
30 Assoc VP for Inst Advancement .... Mr. Andrew MULLER
18 Assoc VP for Facilities Management .... Mr. Tyrone THOMAS
32 Assoc VP for Student Affairs .... Dr. Alexis W. DUBOSE
20 Assoc VP for Academic Affairs .... Mrs. Margaret CHANDLER
103 Dir of Workforce Dev/Cont Education .... Vacant
08 Library Director .... Dr. Brandolyn LOVE
37 Director of Financial Aid .... Mrs. Jean BOOS
13 Director MIS .... Mr. Strong ROBERT
07 Director of Admissions/Advisement .... Ms. Cheryl DUBOSE
26 Director of Public Relations .... Ms. Rebecca BRADFORD
21 Comptroller .... Ms. Suzanna PUSHIA
15 Human Resources Manager .... Ms. Jennifer STRONG
40 Bookstore Manager/Purchasing Agent .... Mrs. Monica ELLIOTT

Winthrop University (G)

Oakland Avenue, Rock Hill SC 29733-0001
County: York FICE Identification: 003456
Unit ID: 218964
Telephone: (803) 323-2211 Carnegie Class: Masters/L
FAX Number: (803) 323-3001 Calendar System: Semester
URL: www.winthrop.edu
Established: 1886 Annual Undergrad Tuition & Fees (In-State): $15,730
Enrollment: 6,073 Coed
Affiliation or Control: State IRS Status: 501(c)3
Highest Offering: Beyond Master's But Less Than Doctorate
Accreditation: SC, ART, #CAATE, CACREP, CAEPN, CIDA, COSMA, DANCE, DIETD, DIETI, EXSC, JOUR, MUS, SW, THEA

01 President .... Dr. Daniel F. MAHONY
05 Provost/Exec VP Academic Affairs .... Dr. Adrienne MCCORMICK
10 Vice President Finance & Business .... Mr. Justin T. OATES
111 Vice Pres Institutional Advancement .... Mr. Evan BOHNEN
32 Vice President of Student Affairs .... Mrs. Sheila BURKHALTER
84 VP Access & Enrollment Management .... Mr. Eduardo PRIETO
100 Chief of Staff .... Dr. Kimberly A. FAUST
26 Vice President University Relations .... Vacant
19 Asst VP/Chief Campus Police .... Chief Kenneth R. SCOGGINS
20 Vice Prov Acad Quality/Innovation .... Dr. Meg WEBBER
88 Asst VP Curriculum/Program Support .... Mr. Tim DRUEKE
13 Asst Vice Pres Comp & Info Tech .... Mr. Patrice BRUNEAU
21 Associate VP Finance/Business .... Ms. Amanda F. MAGHSOUD
18 Assoc VP Facilities Management .... Vacant
15 VP Human Res/Empl Div & Wellness .... Ms. Lisa COWART
11 Vice Provost for Administration .... Ms. Karen JONES
27 Assoc VP/Exec Dir University Rels .. Ms. Ellen M. WILDER-BYRD
58 Dean of Graduate School .... Dr. Jack DEROCHI
49 Dean College Arts & Science .... Dr. Takita SUMTER
50 Dean Col of Business Administration .... Dr. P.N SAKSENA
53 Dean College of Education .... Dr. Jennie RAKESTRAW
64 Dean College of Visual/Perf .... Dr. Jeffrey BELLANTONI
08 Dean Library Services .... Dr. Mark Y. HERRING
97 Dean University College .... Dr. Gloria JONES
35 Dean of Students .... Vacant
41 Athletic Director .... Mr. Ken HALPIN
06 Registrar .... Ms. Gina G. JONES
07 Director of Admissions .... Mr. David ROLLINGS
37 Director of Financial Aid .... Ms. Michelle HARE
39 Interim Director of Resident Life .... Mr. Howard SEIDLER
36 Director Career Development/Svcs .... Ms. Ellin MCDONOUGH
96 Director Procurement/Risk Mgmt .... Vacant
53 Director Teaching/Learning Ctr .... Vacant
23 Dir Health/Counseling Services .... Ms. Jackie CONCODORA
85 Director International Center .... Dr. Leigh POOLE
29 Exec Dir Alumni Rels/Annual Giving .... Ms. Lori TUTTLE
88 Advancement Services Manager .... Ms. Katherine LANGER
105 Director Web Development .... Mr. James U. RAY
106 Director of Online Learning .... Dr. Kimarie WHETSTONE
104 Study Abroad Coordinator .... Ms. Chelsi COLLETON
108 Director of Assessment .... Dr. Noreen GAUBATZ
28 Assoc VP HR & Director of Diversity .... Ms. Zantrell Y. JONES
04 Administrative Asst to President .... Ms. Tammie C. PHILLIPS
102 Dir Foundation/Corporate Relations .... Ms. Robin EMBRY

Wofford College (H)

429 N Church Street, Spartanburg SC 29303-3663
County: Spartanburg FICE Identification: 003457
Unit ID: 218973
Telephone: (864) 597-4000 Carnegie Class: Bac-A&S

FAX Number: (864) 597-4018 Calendar System: 4/1/4
URL: www.wofford.edu
Established: 1854 Annual Undergrad Tuition & Fees: $43,985
Enrollment: 1,678 Coed
Affiliation or Control: United Methodist IRS Status: 501(c)3
Highest Offering: Baccalaureate
Accreditation: SC

01 President .... Dr. Nayef H. SAMHAT
10 Chief Financial Officer .... Mr. Christopher L. GARDNER
05 Provost .... Dr. Michael J. SOSULSKI
111 Sr Vice Pres for Advancement .... Dr. David S. WOOD
11 Sr Vice Pres for Administration .... Mr. David M. BEACHAM
32 Vice President for Student Affairs .... Ms. Roberta H. BIGGER
13 CIO/Assoc VP Information Services .... Mr. Fredrick M. MILLER
84 Vice President for Enrollment .... Mr. Brand R. STILLE
26 VP for Marketing and Communications ... Ms. Annie S. MITCHELL
18 Assoc VP Facilities/Cap Projects .... Mr. Jason H. BURR
21 Assoc VP for Finance and Controller .... Mr. Chris L. GARDNER
08 Dean of Library .... Mr. Kevin REYNOLDS
82 Dean of International Programs .... Ms. Amy E. LANCASTER
23 Assoc Dean Students/Dir Health Svcs .... Ms. Beth D. WALLACE
20 Associate Academic Officer .... Dr. Stacey R. HETTES
04 Exec Admin Asst to President .... Ms. Tonya K. BRYSON
41 Director of Athletics .... Mr. Richard A. JOHNSON
06 College Registrar .... Ms. Jennifer R. ALLISON
42 Chaplain .... Rev.Dr. Ronald R. ROBINSON
15 Director of Human Resources .... Ms. Chee J. LEE
07 Director of Admissions .... Mr. John W. BIRNEY
09 Director of Institutional Research .... Mr. Raymond H. RUFF, III
101 Secretary to the Board of Trustees .... Mr. David M. BEACHAM
108 Dir Institutional Effectiveness .... Dr. John D. MILES
38 Director Student Counseling .... Ms. Perry V. HENSON
19 Director Campus Safety .... Col. James R. HALL
28 Director of Diversity/Inclusion .... Vacant
29 Director Alumni & Parents .... Mr. Thomas M. HENSON, JR.
36 Exec Director The Space .... Mr. P. Curtis MCPHAIL
37 Director Financial Aid .... Ms. Carolyn B. SPARKS
39 Asst Dean of Students for Res Life .... Mr. Brian J. LEMERE
44 Director Gift Planning .... Ms. Lisa H. DE FREITAS
96 Director Business Srvs/Risk Mgmt .... Mr. Daniel P. DEETER

York Technical College (A)

452 S Anderson Road, Rock Hill SC 29730-3395
County: York FICE Identification: 003996
Unit ID: 218991
Telephone: (803) 327-8000 Carnegie Class: Assoc/MT-VT-High Trad
FAX Number: (803) 327-8059 Calendar System: Semester
URL: www.yorktech.edu
Established: 1964 Annual Undergrad Tuition & Fees (In-State): $4,817
Enrollment: 4,538 Coed
Affiliation or Control: State IRS Status: 501(c)3
Highest Offering: Associate Degree
Accreditation: SC, ACBSP, ADNUR, DA, DH, MLTAD, PNUR, RAD, SURGT

01 President .... Dr. Greg F. RUTHERFORD
05 Exec Vice Pres Acad/Student Affs .... Dr. Stacey MOORE
10 VP Business Services .... Dr. Marc TARPLEE
111 Vice President for Advancement .... Ms. Melanie E. JONES
32 Assoc VP Academic/Student Affairs .... Vacant
50 Assoc VP Business/Computer/AA/AS .... Dr. Yolanda WILSON
76 Assoc VP Health & Human Services .... Ms. Linda WEAVER-GRIGGS
54 Assoc Dean Industry/Engineer Tech .... Mr. Michael MCCLAIN
103 Asst VP Economic/Workforce Dev .... Ms. Sonia YOUNG
15 Asst Vice Pres of Human Resources .... Ms. Edwina ROSEBORO-BARNES
08 Librarian .... Ms. Erinnae BAKER
84 Dean of Enrollment Services .... Dr. Monique PERRY
35 Dean for Student Engagement .... Mr. James ROBSON
88 Dean Center for Teaching/Learning .... Ms. Kathy L. HOELLEN
09 Director of Institutional Research .... Dr. Mary Beth SCHWARTZ
37 Director Compliance/Financial Aid .... Vacant
13 Information Services Director .... Mr. Richard PARTRIDGE
19 Chief Campus Security .... Mr. Bryan L. MCDOUGALD
18 Facilities Management Director .... Mr. Robert L. BROWN
06 Registrar .... Vacant
26 Director of Strategic Communication .... Vacant
07 Director Admissions .... Ms. Lydia HALL
04 Administrative Asst to President .... Mrs. Jennifer GAMMON

SOUTH DAKOTA

Augustana University (B)

2001 S Summit, Sioux Falls SD 57197-0001
County: Minnehaha FICE Identification: 003458
Unit ID: 219000
Telephone: (605) 274-0770 Carnegie Class: Masters/S
FAX Number: (605) 274-5299 Calendar System: 4/1/4
URL: www.augie.edu
Established: 1860 Annual Undergrad Tuition & Fees: $33,018
Enrollment: 2,080 Coed
Affiliation or Control: Evangelical Lutheran Church In America
IRS Status: 501(c)3
Highest Offering: Master's
Accreditation: NH, CAATE, MUS, NURSE

01 President .... Ms. Stephanie HERSETH SANDLIN
05 Sr VP Academic Affairs .... Dr. Colin IRVINE
32 Vice President Student Services .... Vacant
10 Vice Pres Finance/Administration .... Mr. Shannan NELSON
111 Vice President for Advancement .... Dr. Pamela HOMAN
84 Vice President for Enrollment .... Ms. Nancy DAVIDSON
11 Assoc VP Admin/Chief Info Officer .... Mr. Daniel D. DRENKOW
21 Assoc Vice President for Finance .... Ms. Carol SPILLUM
20 Assoc VP for Academic Affairs .... Dr. Mitchell G. KINSINGER
51 Assoc VP of Grad and Cont Educ .... Dr. Jerry JORGENSEN
35 Acting Dean of Students .... Mr. Mark BLACKBURN
15 Vice President of Human Resources .... Ms. Deanna VERSTEEG
37 Director of Financial Aid .... Ms. Tresse EVENSON
08 Director of Library .... Ms. Ronelle THOMPSON
13 Director Mgmt Information Systems .... Ms. Debra FREDERICK
18 Assoc VP for University Services .... Mr. Rick TUPPER
29 Asst VP for Alumni Relations .... Vacant
41 Athletic Director .... Mr. Josh MORTON
06 Registrar/Asst Dean of Instr Data .... Ms. Joni KRUEGER
36 Exec Director of Career/Success Ctr .... Ms. Billie STREUFERT
121 Dir of Student Acad Support Service .... Ms. Susan BIES
104 Director of International Programs .... Mr. Ben IVERSON
19 Director of Campus Safety .... Mr. Galen SMIDT
09 Dir Inst Research/Effect/Assessment .... Mr. Jay KAHL
28 Director of Diversity .... Ms. Willette CAPERS
44 Director Annual Giving .... Ms. Kiana OVERBY

Dakota Wesleyan University (C)

1200 W University, Mitchell SD 57301-4398
County: Davison FICE Identification: 003461
Unit ID: 219091
Telephone: (605) 995-2600 Carnegie Class: Bac-Diverse
FAX Number: (605) 995-2699 Calendar System: Semester
URL: www.dwu.edu
Established: 1885 Annual Undergrad Tuition & Fees: $27,640
Enrollment: 908 Coed
Affiliation or Control: United Methodist IRS Status: 501(c)3
Highest Offering: Master's
Accreditation: NH, CAATE, IACBE, NURSE

01 President .... Dr. Amy C. NOVAK
10 Executive Vice President .... Ms. Theresa KRIESE
05 Provost .... Dr. Joseph ROIDT
07 VP Admissions/Mktg/Communications .... Ms. Fredel THOMAS
111 VP for Institutional Advancement .... Ms. Kitty ALLEN
26 Dir of Marketing & Communications .... Ms. Jan LARSON
06 Registrar .... Ms. Jerry LUCKETT
88 Dir Kelley Ctr for Entrepreneurship .... Dr. Ryan VAN ZEE
88 Executive Director McGovern Center .... Dr. John LANG
08 Chief Info Ofcr/Dir Lrng Resources .... Mr. Kevin KENKEL
29 Director of Alumni Relations .... Mr. Jory HANSEN
37 Director of Financial Aid .... Ms. Mary ALEXANDER
15 Director of Human Resources .... Ms. Janet HAYEN
42 Campus Pastor .... Rev. Eric VAN METER
41 Athletic Director .... Mr. Jon HART
18 Director of Physical Plant .... Mr. Louis SCHOENFELDER
32 Director of Student Life .... Mr. John KIPPES
35 Director Student Support Services .... Ms. Laurie JOHNSON
40 Director of University Services .... Ms. Lori SOLBERG
88 Dean Col Ldrshp & Pub Service .... Dr. Anne KELLY
51 Dean Col Adult and Prof Studies .... Dr. Derek DRIEDGER
79 Dean College Arts & Humanities .... Dr. Vince REDDER
88 Dean Col Health/Fitness & Science .... Dr. Bethany MELROE LEHRMAN
04 Exec Admin Asst to President .... Ms. Emily GEORGE
50 Chair of Business .... Ms. Christine MAUSZYCKI
53 Chair of Education .... Dr. Ashley DIGMANN
13 Chief Info Technology Officer (CIO) .... Mr. Chad HARVEY
50 Director of Business Grad Program .... Dr. Monty BOHRER
53 Coord of Master of Arts in Educ .... Ms. Melissa WEBER
88 Dir of Master of Athletic Training .... Dr. Dan WAGNER

Institute of Lutheran Theology (D)

PO Box 833, Brookings SD 57006
County: Brookings Identification: 667318
Telephone: (605) 692-9337 Carnegie Class: Not Classified
FAX Number: N/A Calendar System: Semester
URL: www.ilt.edu
Established: 2009 Annual Graduate Tuition & Fees: N/A
Enrollment: N/A Coed
Affiliation or Control: Independent Non-Profit IRS Status: 501(c)3
Highest Offering: Doctorate; No Undergraduates
Accreditation: BI

01 President .... Dr. Dennis BIELFELDT
05 Dean of Academic Affairs .... Dr. Jonathan SORUM
03 Executive Vice President .... Mr. Leon MILES
07 Admissions Coordinator .... Ms. Threasa HOPKINS
06 Registrar .... Ms. Kelli ANAWSKI
111 Director of Donor Services .... Rev. Eric SWENSSON
08 Librarian .... Rev. David PATTERSON

John Witherspoon College (E)

4024 Sheridan Lake Road, Rapid City SD 57702
County: Pennington Identification: 667246
Telephone: (605) 342-0317 Carnegie Class: Not Classified
FAX Number: N/A Calendar System: Semester
URL: www.jwc.edu
Established: 2004 Annual Undergrad Tuition & Fees: N/A
Enrollment: N/A Coed
Affiliation or Control: Independent Non-Profit IRS Status: 501(c)3
Highest Offering: Baccalaureate
Accreditation: TRACS

01 President .... Dr. Ronald J. LEWIS
05 Chief Academic Officer .... Mr. Edwin C. EGBERT
00 Chairman of the Board .... Rev. Arthur G. SARTORIUS
10 Chief Financial Officer .... Mrs. Carol B. HARRIS
08 Coordinator of Learning Resources .... Ms. Michelle C. PORTER
32 Dean of Students .... Mrs. Alesha F. LIMBO
07 Director of Admissions .... Mrs. Rebecca E. PONTIOUS
06 Registrar .... Mrs. Pamela S. RIDER
125 President Emeritus/Chancellor .... Dr. C. Richard WELLS

Lake Area Technical Institute (F)

1201 Arrow Avenue, PO Box 730,
Watertown SD 57201-2869
County: Codington FICE Identification: 005309
Unit ID: 219143
Telephone: (605) 882-5284 Carnegie Class: Assoc/HVT-High Trad
FAX Number: (605) 882-6299 Calendar System: Semester
URL: www.lakeareatech.edu
Established: 1965 Annual Undergrad Tuition & Fees (In-District): $5,332
Enrollment: 2,055 Coed
Affiliation or Control: Local IRS Status: 501(c)3
Highest Offering: Associate Degree
Accreditation: NH, DA, EMT, MAC, MLTAD, OTA, PNUR, PTAA

01 President .... Mr. Michael D. CARTNEY
03 Executive Vice President .... Ms. Diane STILES
84 Director of Enrollment .... Mr. Eric SCHULTZ
05 Dean of Academics .... Ms. Kim BELLUM
32 Director of Student Services .... Ms. LuAnn STRAIT
88 Corporate Education Coordinator .... Mr. Steven HAUCK
35 Director of Support Services .... Mr. Shane ORTMEIER
37 Director of Financial Aid .... Ms. Marlene SEEKLANDER
13 Director of Information Technology .... Mr. Dennis HELLER
88 Director of Outreach .... Mr. Shane SWENSON
06 Registrar .... Ms. Jodi MESSERLI
08 Librarian .... Ms. Nicki YACKLEY-FRANKEN
108 Assessment Coordinator .... Ms. Gina GRANT
25 Grant Writer .... Ms. Terri CORDREY
102 Foundation Development Officer .... Ms. Morgan JOHNSON

Mitchell Technical Institute (G)

1800 E Spruce, Mitchell SD 57301-2002
County: Davison FICE Identification: 008284
Unit ID: 219189
Telephone: (605) 995-3025 Carnegie Class: Assoc/HVT-High Trad
FAX Number: (605) 995-3083 Calendar System: Semester
URL: www.mitchelltech.edu
Established: 1968 Annual Undergrad Tuition & Fees (In-District): $6,720
Enrollment: 1,187 Coed
Affiliation or Control: Local IRS Status: 501(c)3
Highest Offering: Associate Degree
Accreditation: NH, ACFEI, MAC, MLTAD, RAD, RTT

01 President .... Mr. Mark WILSON
03 Vice President .... Mr. John HEEMSTRA
04 Associate to the President .... Ms. Julie BROOKBANK
05 Vice President for Academics .... Dr. Carol GRODE-HANKS
84 Dean of Enrollment Services .... Mr. Clayton DEUTER
13 Director of Technology .... Mr. David BOOS
10 Financial Comptroller .... Mr. Jared HOFER
121 Dean of Student Success .... Mr. Scott FOSSUM
09 Accred & Inst Effectiveness Dir .... Ms. Marla SMITH
103 Director of Advanced Technical Educ .... Mr. Doug GREENWAY
18 Buildings & Grounds Director .... Mr. John SIEVERDING
15 Human Resources Manager .... Ms. Elizabeth KITCHENS
102 Foundation Director .... Ms. Heather LENTZ
36 Career Svcs & Advising Dir .... Ms. Janet GREENWAY
06 Registrar .... Ms. Jill GREENWAY
37 Director Student Financial Aid .... Ms. Morgan HUBER
105 Marketing Director .... Mr. Bob KOBERNUSZ

Mount Marty College (H)

1105 W 8th, Yankton SD 57078-3724
County: Yankton FICE Identification: 003465
Unit ID: 219198
Telephone: (605) 668-1011 Carnegie Class: Masters/S
FAX Number: (605) 668-1607 Calendar System: Semester
URL: www.mtmc.edu
Established: 1936 Annual Undergrad Tuition & Fees: $27,276
Enrollment: 1,048 Coed
Affiliation or Control: Roman Catholic IRS Status: 501(c)3
Highest Offering: Master's
Accreditation: NH, ANEST, NURSE

01 President .... Dr. Marcus LONG
101 Assistant to the President .... Ms. Joanna MUELLER
05 Interim VP Academic Affairs & Dean .... Sr. Candy CHRYSTAL
10 VP for Finance & Administration .... Ms. Tabitha LIKNESS
111 VP for Advancement .... Ms. Barb REZAC
32 Dean of Students .... Dr. Katie HARRELL
09 Director of Inst Effectiveness .... Ms. Kristen WELKER
66 Dean of Nursing & Health Sciences .... Dr. Kathy MAGORIAN
42 Director of Campus Ministry .... Mr. Jordan FOOS
12 Director of Watertown Location .... Dr. Cristina GORDON
37 Director Student Financial Aid .... Mr. Ken KOCER
06 Registrar .... Ms. Jonna SUPURGECI
13 Chief Information Officer .... Mr. Christian HUNHOFF

08 Director of Library Ms. Sandra BROWN
40 Dir Bookstore/Central Scheduling Ms. Mary ABBOTT
36 Dir Career Planning Ms. Keley SMITH-KELLER
41 Athletic Director Mr. Chris KASSIN
15 Director of Human Resources Ms. Julie DATHER
26 Exec Dir of Marketing & Comm Ms. Kelsey FREIDEL NELSON
44 Director of Annual/Planned Giving Ms. Shannon VIERECK
29 Director Alumni Relations Ms. Ashley GULLIKSON
07 Dean of Enrollment Ms. Stephanie MOSER
18 Director of Facilities & Operations Mr. Chad ALTWINE
39 Dir of Res Life/Campus Security Mr. Tim CHAMBERS

National American University (A)

5301 Mt. Rushmore Road, Rapid City SD 57701-8932
County: Pennington FICE Identification: 004057
Unit ID: 219204
Telephone: (605) 721-5200 Carnegie Class: Bac-Diverse
FAX Number: (605) 721-5241 Calendar System: Quarter
URL: www.national.edu
Established: 1941 Annual Undergrad Tuition & Fees: $15,000
Enrollment: 1,346 Coed
Affiliation or Control: Proprietary IRS Status: Proprietary
Highest Offering: Doctorate
Accreditation: NH, CAHIIM, IACBE, MAC, NURSE

01 Chief Executive Officer/President Dr. Ronald SHAPE
05 Provost & Chief Academic Officer Dr. Lynn PRIDDY
10 Chief Financial Officer Dr. David HEFLIN
84 Vice Pres Enrollment/Marketing Mr. David CASTLE

Oglala Lakota College (B)

Box 490, Kyle SD 57752-0490
County: Oglala Lakota FICE Identification: 014659
Unit ID: 219277
Telephone: (605) 455-6000 Carnegie Class: Tribal
FAX Number: (605) 455-2787 Calendar System: Semester
URL: www.olc.edu
Established: 1971 Annual Undergrad Tuition & Fees: $2,684
Enrollment: 1,246 Coed
Affiliation or Control: Tribal Control IRS Status: 501(c)3
Highest Offering: Master's
Accreditation: NH, SW

01 President Mr. Thomas H. SHORTBULL
05 Vice President for Instruction Dr. Dawn FRANK
10 Vice President for Business Ms. Julie JOHNSON
06 Registrar Ms. Leslie MESTETH
08 Director Learning Resources Ms. Michelle MAY
15 Personnel Director Ms. Faith RICHARDS
37 Financial Aid Director Ms. Cheryce GULLIKSON
84 Director Enrollment Management Ms. Lynn CUNY
07 Director of Admissions Ms. Leslie MESTETH
09 Director of Institutional Research Ms. Susanne AUER
96 Assoc Business Ofcr/Dir Purchasing Ms. Arlis POURIER
29 Director Alumni Relations Ms. Marilyn POURIER
89 Director of Freshman Studies Ms. Susanne AUER
13 MIS Director Mr. Cliff DELONG
32 Director Student Affairs Mr. Don GIAGO
30 Inst Development Coordinator Ms. Marilyn POURIER
51 Community/Cont Education Coord Ms. Kateri MONTILEAUX
88 Applied Science Department Chair Mr. David WHITE BULL
81 Math & Science Department Chair Ms. Karla WITT
49 Art & History Department Chair Ms. Kim BETTELYOUN
53 Education Department Chair Ms. Shannon AMIOTTE
66 Nursing Department Chair Ms. Michelle BRUNS
83 Social Work Department Chair Ms. Monique APPLE
88 LAKOTA Studies Department Chair Ms. Karen LONE HILL
18 Chief Facilities/Physical Plant Mr. Tony WARD

Presentation College (C)

1500 N Main Street, Aberdeen SD 57401-1280
County: Brown FICE Identification: 003467
Unit ID: 219295
Telephone: (605) 225-1634 Carnegie Class: Spec-4-yr-Other Health
FAX Number: (605) 229-8330 Calendar System: Semester
URL: www.presentation.edu
Established: 1951 Annual Undergrad Tuition & Fees: $20,375
Enrollment: 761 Coed
Affiliation or Control: Roman Catholic IRS Status: 501(c)3
Highest Offering: Master's
Accreditation: NH, #CAATE, IACBE, NURSE, RAD

01 President Dr. Margaret HUBER
05 Vice Pres for Academics Dr. Diane DUIN
10 Vice Pres for Finance Dr. Christopher STOCKLIN
84 Vice Pres for Enrollment/Marketing Mr. Marcus GARSTECKI
32 Vice Pres for Student Services Mr. Bob SCHUCHARDT
111 Vice President for Advancement Vacant
88 Executive Director for Mission Sr. Pam DONELAN
06 Registrar Ms. Maureen SCHUCHARDT
37 Director Student Financial Aid Ms. Amber BROCKEL
108 Assessment Coordinator Dr. Nancy VANDER HOEK
15 Director of Human Resources Dr. Jason PETTIGREW
04 Administrative Asst to President Ms. Stacy BAUER
26 Dir of Marketing/Public Relations Mr. Tim BECKHAM
07 Director of Admissions Vacant
09 Director of Institutional Research Vacant
29 Director Alumni Relations Ms. Teresa GAROFALO
39 Director Student Housing Mr. DJ MOUNGA
41 Athletic Director Vacant

Sinte Gleska University (D)

PO Box 105, Mission SD 57555-0105
County: Todd FICE Identification: 021437
Unit ID: 219374
Telephone: (605) 856-5880 Carnegie Class: Tribal
FAX Number: (605) 856-5401 Calendar System: Semester
URL: www.sintegleska.edu
Established: 1970 Annual Undergrad Tuition & Fees: $3,154
Enrollment: 581 Coed
Affiliation or Control: Independent Non-Profit IRS Status: 501(c)3
Highest Offering: Master's
Accreditation: NH

01 President Mr. Lionel BORDEAUX
05 Provost/COO Mr. Phil BAIRD
32 Vice Pres Student Services Ms. Debra BORDEAUX
31 VP Community Education Ms. Sherry RED OWL NEISS
20 Vice Pres Academic Affairs Ms. Cheryl MEDEARIS
10 CFO/VP Finance Ms. Ieshia POIGNEE
06 Registrar Mr. Jack HERMAN
08 Int Library Director Ms. Diana DILLON
37 Director Financial Aid Mr. Midas GUNHAMMER
55 Director Adult Education Mr. Sherman MARSHALL, II
15 Interim Personnel Director Ms. Stephanie WHITE EYES

Sioux Falls Seminary (E)

2100 S Summit Avenue, Sioux Falls SD 57105-2729
County: Minnehaha FICE Identification: 004056
Unit ID: 219240
Telephone: (605) 336-6588 Carnegie Class: Spec-4-yr-Faith
FAX Number: (605) 335-9090 Calendar System: 4/1/4
URL: www.sfseminary.edu
Established: 1858 Annual Graduate Tuition & Fees: N/A
Enrollment: 229 Coed
Affiliation or Control: North American Baptist IRS Status: 501(c)3
Highest Offering: Doctorate; No Undergraduates
Accreditation: NH, THEOL

01 President Mr. Gregory J. HENSON
05 Chief Academic Officer & Dean Dr. Larry W. CALDWELL
10 CFO and VP of Operations Mr. Nathan M. HELLING
26 Chief Creative Ofcr/VP Proj Design Ms. Shanda L. STRICHERZ
23 Director of Clinical Services Dr. Douglas ANDERSON
21 Office Manager Ms. LaNeil R. BARTELL
38 Director of Counseling Programs Dr. Gretchen L. HARTMANN
88 Dir of Luther House of Study Dr. Chris M. CROGHAN
88 Dir of Wesley House of Study Dr. Steve A. TREFZ

Sisseton-Wahpeton College (F)

PO Box 689, Sisseton SD 57262-0689
County: Roberts FICE Identification: 022773
Unit ID: 219408
Telephone: (605) 698-3966 Carnegie Class: Tribal
FAX Number: (605) 698-3132 Calendar System: Semester
URL: www.swc.tc
Established: 1979 Annual Undergrad Tuition & Fees (In-District): $4,410
Enrollment: 197 Coed
Affiliation or Control: Local IRS Status: 501(c)3
Highest Offering: Associate Degree
Accreditation: NH

01 President Dr. Randy SMITH
05 Vice President of Academic Affairs Dr. Jeanette GRAVDAHL
10 Chief Financial Officer Vacant
37 Financial Aid Director Mr. Sylvan FLUTE
07 Registrar Mrs. Darlene REDDAY
66 Director Nursing Ms. Nola RAGAN
29 Alumni Director Mr. Vince OWEN
13 Director Information Technology Mr. Derrick LAWRENCE
18 Facilities Manager Mr. Russell EBERHARDT
06 Registrar Ms. Darlene REDDAY

*South Dakota State Board of Regents System Office (G)

306 E Capitol Avenue, Suite 200, Pierre SD 57501-2545
County: Hughes FICE Identification: 033438
Telephone: (605) 773-3455 Carnegie Class: N/A
FAX Number: (605) 773-5320
URL: www.sdbor.edu

01 Executive Director & CEO Dr. Paul B. BERAN
00 Board President Mr. Bob SUTTON
10 System VP Finance & Administration Heather FORNEY
05 System VP Academic Affairs Dr. Jay PERRY
46 System Asst VP Research & Econ Dev Mr. Nathan LUKKES
43 General Counsel Mr. Nathan LUKKES
15 System Director of Human Resources Ms. Kayla BASTIAN
26 System Director of Communications Dr. Janelle TOMAN
32 System Director of Student Affairs Ms. Molly WEISGRAM
09 System Dir Institutional Research Vacant
13 System CIO Mr. David HANSEN
20 System Assoc VP of Academic Affairs Dr. Joelle MALEY
116 System Internal Auditor Ms. Shelly ANDERSON

*The University of South Dakota (H)

414 E Clark, Vermillion SD 57069-2390
County: Clay FICE Identification: 003474
Unit ID: 219471
Telephone: (605) 677-5011 Carnegie Class: DU-Higher
FAX Number: (605) 677-5073 Calendar System: Semester
URL: www.usd.edu
Established: 1862 Annual Undergrad Tuition & Fees (In-State): $9,061
Enrollment: 10,261 Coed
Affiliation or Control: State IRS Status: 501(c)3
Highest Offering: Doctorate
Accreditation: NH, ARCPA, ART, AUD, CACREP, CAEPN, CLPSY, DH, EMT, JOUR, LAW, MED, MUS, NURSE, OT, PTA, SP, SPAA, SW, THEA

02 President Ms. Sheila K. GESTRING
05 Provost/VP Academic Affairs Dr. Kurt HACKEMER
17 VP Health Affairs/Dean Med School Dr. Mary DEKKER NETTLEMAN
10 Vice Pres Administration/Finance Mr. Adam ROSHEIM
46 VP Research/Sponsored Programs Dr. Mary BERRY
26 VP Marketing/Enroll Svcs/Univ Rels Mr. Scott POHLSON
32 VP Student Svcs & Dean of Students Dr. Kimberly GRIEVE
15 Assistant VP Human Resources Mr. Emery WASLEY
13 Chief Information Officer Ms. Cheryl TIAHRT
102 President/CEO Univ Foundation Mr. Steve BROWN
28 Associate VP of Diversity Mr. Lamont SELLERS
18 Asst VP Facilities Management Mr. Brian LIMOGES
09 AVP Inst Research/Plng/Assessment Mr. Daniel PALMER
51 Assoc Provost Cont & Distance Educ Dr. Michael CARD
12 Exec Dir University Ctr Sioux Falls Dr. Carmen SIMONE
100 Chief of Staff Ms. Laura MCNAUGHTON
43 General Counsel Mr. AJ FRANKEN
96 Director of Auxiliary Services Mr. Darby GANSCHOW
08 Dean of Libraries Mr. Daniel R. DAILY
36 Dir Ctr for Academic & Career Plng Mr. Steve WARD
37 Director of Financial Aid Ms. Julie H. PIER
41 Director Athletics Mr. David HERBSTER
19 Dir University Police Department Mr. Peter E. JENSEN
06 Registrar Ms. Jennifer M. THOMPSON
84 Dean of Enrollment Mr. Mark PETTY
49 Dean College Arts & Sciences Dr. Michael KRUGER
50 Dean School of Business Dr. Venky VENKATACHALAM
53 Interim Dean School of Education Dr. Amy SCHWEINLE
57 Dean College Fine Arts Dr. Larry SCHOU
61 Dean School of Law Mr. Neil FULTON
58 Dean Graduate School Dr. Ranjit KOODALI
76 Dean School of Health Sciences Dr. Haifa ABOUSAMRA
04 Asst to the President Ms. Niki SMIDT

*Black Hills State University (I)

1200 University Street #9501, Spearfish SD 57799-9500
County: Lawrence FICE Identification: 003459
Unit ID: 219046
Telephone: (605) 642-6111 Carnegie Class: Masters/S
FAX Number: (605) 642-6763 Calendar System: Semester
URL: www.bhsu.edu
Established: 1883 Annual Undergrad Tuition & Fees (In-State): $8,733
Enrollment: 4,178 Coed
Affiliation or Control: State IRS Status: 501(c)3
Highest Offering: Master's
Accreditation: NH, CAEP, CAEPN, MUS

02 Interim President Dr. Laurie NICHOLS
05 Provost/Vice Pres Academic Affairs Dr. Chris CRAWFORD
10 Vice President Finance/Admin Ms. Kathy J. JOHNSON
111 Vice Pres University Advancement Mr. Steve L. MEEKER
32 VP for Enrollment & Student Affairs Dr. Lois FLAGSTAD
26 Director Univ & Community Relations Ms. Corinne HANSEN
13 Data Processing Supervisor Ms. Roxy SCHMIT
37 Director Student Financial Aid Ms. Deb HENRIKSEN
38 Director Counseling Center Dr. Lois FLAGSTAD
22 Title IX Coordinator Dr. Michael L. ISAACSON
35 Dean of Students Dr. Jane KLUG
15 Director of Human Resources Ms. Melissa CHRISTENSEN
06 Registrar Ms. April M. MEEKER
07 Interim Director of Admissions Ms. Barbara O'MALLEY
21 Director of Business Services Mr. Brandon BENTLEY
18 Director Facilities/Physical Plant Mr. Randy CULVER
29 Director Alumni Relations Mr. Tom WHEATON
09 Director of Institutional Research Mr. Rich LOOSE
08 Director Library Operations Mr. Scott AHOLA
104 Director International Studies Mr. Eric LEISE
30 Director of Development Ms. Shauna JUNEK
19 Director Security/Safety Mr. Philip PESHECK
40 Director University Bookstore Mr. Michael JASTORFF
41 Director of Athletics Mr. Jhett ALBERS
14 Director Network & Computer Svcs Mr. Fred NELSON
49 Dean College of Liberal Arts Dr. Amy FUQUA
50 Dean Col of Business & Natural Sci Dr. Gregory FARLEY
53 Dean Col of Educ & Behavioral Sci Dr. Sharman ADAMS
04 Administrative Asst to President Vacant
25 Chief Contracts/Grants Admin Mr. William KELLY

*Dakota State University (J)

820 N Washington Avenue, Madison SD 57042-1799
County: Lake FICE Identification: 003463
Unit ID: 219082
Telephone: (888) 378-9988 Carnegie Class: Masters/S
FAX Number: N/A Calendar System: Semester
URL: www.dsu.edu
Established: 1881 Annual Undergrad Tuition & Fees (In-State): $9,276
Enrollment: 3,307 Coed
Affiliation or Control: State IRS Status: 501(c)3
Highest Offering: Doctorate
Accreditation: NH, ACBSP, CAEP, CAHIIM, COARC

02 President ... Dr. José -Marie GRIFFITHS
04 Senior Secretary President's Ofc ... Mrs. Megan BOUSQUET
05 Provost & VP Academic Affairs ... Dr. Jim MORAN
10 Vice Pres for Business & Admin Svcs ... Mr. Stacy L. KRUSEMARK
32 Int Vice Pres Student Affairs ... Mr. James JACOBSEN
13 VP for Technology/CIO ... Mr. David B. OVERBY
111 VP Inst Advancement/Communications ... Mr. Mark MILLAGE
15 Vice Pres Human Resources/Title IX ... Ms. Angi KAPPENMAN
41 Director of Athletics ... Mr. Jeff L. DITTMAN
26 Dir Communications & Marketing ... Ms. Kelli KOEPSELL
49 Int Dean Col of Arts and Sciences ... Dr. Judy DITTMAN
50 Dean Col Business/Info Systems ... Dr. Dorine BENNETT
77 Dean Beacom College ... Dr. Richard HANSON
53 Dean College of Education ... Dr. Crystal PAULI
58 Dean of Graduate Studies/Research ... Dr. Mark HAWKES
108 Director of Assessment ... Dr. Jeanette MCGREEVY
09 Int Dir Institutional Research ... Ms. Laura OSBORN
08 Director of Library ... Ms. Jan Brue ENRIGHT
106 Director Online Education ... Ms. Sarah RASMUSSEN
25 Director of Sponsored Programs ... Vacant
06 Registrar ... Ms. Kathryn CALLIES
21 Controller ... Ms. Amy L. DOCKENDORF
18 Director Facilities Management ... Mr. Corey BRASKAMP
25 Director of Budget & Grants Admin ... Ms. Sara HARE
25 Director CAHIT ... Mr. Dan FRIEDRICH
36 Director Career Services ... Ms. Deb ROACH
84 Assoc VP of Enrollment/Marketing ... Ms. Amy S. CRISSINGER
35 Asst Dean for Student Affairs ... Mr. Steven J. BARTEL
121 Asst Director Student Success ... Ms. Nicole BOWEN
40 Director of Bookstore ... Ms. Patti WEBER
28 Coordinator Diversity & Inclusion ... Vacant
37 Director Financial Aid ... Ms. Denise R. GRAYSON
07 Asst Director of Admissions ... Ms. Amber SCHMIDT
104 Dir International Programs ... Ms. Nicole CLAUSSEN
14 Dir Technical Ops & Development ... Mr. Brent VAN AARTSEN
91 Dir Admin Computing Services ... Mrs. Stephanie BAATZ
119 Security Engineer ... Mr. David MILLER
24 Multimedia Specialist ... Vacant
112 Director of Major/Planned Gifts ... Ms. Jona M. SCHMIDT
30 Development Officer ... Ms. Jill RUHD
44 Annual Fund Manager ... Ms. Carrie SLAATHAUG

*Northern State University (A)

1200 S Jay Street, Aberdeen SD 57401-7198
County: Brown FICE Identification: 003466
Unit ID: 219259
Telephone: (605) 626-3011 Carnegie Class: Masters/S
FAX Number: (605) 626-3022 Calendar System: Semester
URL: www.northern.edu
Established: 1901 Annual Undergrad Tuition & Fees (In-State): $8,497
Enrollment: 3,611 Coed
Affiliation or Control: State IRS Status: 501(c)3
Highest Offering: Master's
Accreditation: NH, ACBSP, ART, CACREP, CAEPN, MUS

02 President ... Dr. Timothy DOWNS
05 Provost/VP Academic Affairs ... Dr. Michael WANOUS
10 VP for Finance/Administration ... Ms. Veronica PAULSON
32 VP for Student Affairs/Enroll Mgmt ... Dr. Jeremy REED
20 Asst VP Academic Affairs ... Vacant
35 Associate VP for Student Affairs ... Dr. Checka LEINWALL
13 VP for Information Technologies ... Dr. Debbi BUMPOUS
30 VP of Development ... Mr. Jon OLSON
102 President/CEO of Foundation ... Mr. Todd JORDRE
06 Registrar ... Ms. Peggy HALLSTROM
08 Director of Library ... Mr. Robert RUSSELL
38 Director of Counseling Center ... Ms. Heather ALDENTALER
09 Dir Institutional Research/Assmnt ... Dr. Brenda MAMMENGA
25 Director Sponsored Projects ... Ms. Karen MARCHANT
37 Director of Financial Aid ... Ms. Sharon KIENOW
39 Director of Residence Life ... Mr. Martin SABOLO
21 Controller ... Ms. Kay FREDRICK
15 Director of Human Resources ... Ms. Susan BOSTIAN
26 Director of Communications/Mrktg ... Mr. Justin FRAASE
18 Director of Facilities Management ... Mr. Monte MEHLHOFF
49 Dean College of Arts & Science ... Dr. Joshua HAGEN
50 Interim Dean School of Business ... Dr. Douglas OHMER
53 Interim Dean School of Education ... Dr. Jeffrey HOWARD
57 Dean School of Fine Arts ... Dr. Kenneth BOULTON
58 Director Graduate Studies ... Vacant
41 Director of Athletics ... Mr. Joshua MOON
40 Director of Bookstore ... Ms. Beth RASMUSSON
96 Director of Purchasing ... Mr. Earl WEISENBURGER
92 Director of Honors Program ... Dr. Erin FOUBERG
88 Director of International Programs ... Dr. Leigh NEYS
28 Interim Multicultural Advisor ... Mr. Layton COOPER
04 Administrative Asst to President ... Ms. Lisa GROTE
104 Study Abroad Coordinator ... Ms. Dominika BLUM
106 Director Online Education ... Mr. Ronald BROWNIE
88 Director University College ... Mr. Steve RASMUSSEN
36 Director Student Placement ... Ms. Britt LORENZ
29 Coordinator of Alumni Operations ... Ms. Lauren BITTNER
110 Director Development ... Ms. Kelli FRITZ

*South Dakota School of Mines and Technology (B)

501 E Saint Joseph, Rapid City SD 57701-3995
County: Pennington FICE Identification: 003470
Unit ID: 219347
Telephone: (605) 394-2511 Carnegie Class: Spec-4-yr-Eng
FAX Number: (605) 394-3388 Calendar System: Semester
URL: www.sdsmt.edu
Established: 1885 Annual Undergrad Tuition & Fees (In-State): $10,560
Enrollment: 2,778 Coed
Affiliation or Control: State IRS Status: 501(c)3
Highest Offering: Doctorate
Accreditation: NH

02 President ... Dr. James RANKIN
05 Interim Provost/VP Academic Affairs ... Dr. Lance ROBERTS
10 Vice Pres Finance/Administration ... Ms. Heather FORNEY
46 Vice President of Research ... Dr. Ralph DAVIS
32 VP Student Affs/Dean of Students ... Dr. Patricia G. MAHON
15 Vice President Human Resources ... Ms. Kelli R. SHUMAN
20 Associate Provost Academic Affairs ... Dr. Kathryn E. ALLEY
88 Assoc Provost Acad Administration ... Ms. Molly MOORE
96 Director of Business Services ... Ms. Barbara MUSTARD
26 Dir of Marketing & Communications ... Ms. Ann M. BRENTLINGER
29 Interim Dir of Alumni Association ... Mr. Shane LEE
13 Director of Information Tech Svcs ... Mr. Bryan J. SCHUMACHER
08 Director of Devereaux Library ... Ms. Patricia M. ANDERSEN
36 Assistant VP for Student Dev ... Vacant
37 Director of Financial Aid ... Mr. David W. MARTIN
41 Director of Athletics ... Mr. Joel LUEKEN
102 President SDSM&T Foundation ... Mr. Joel KINCART
18 Director of Facilities & Risk Mgmt ... Ms. Jerilyn C. ROBERTS
21 Director of Finance/Controller ... Ms. Heather FORNEY
39 Asst Dean of Students/Dir of Res ... Dr. Daniel SEPION
85 Director Ivanhoe International Ctr ... Ms. Susan R. AADLAND
58 Dean of Graduate Education ... Dr. Maribeth H. PRICE
38 Director Counseling/ADA Svcs ... Ms. Megan REDER-SCHOPP
06 Registrar ... Mr. Philip HUNT
40 Director of University Bookstore ... Mr. Marlin L. KINZER
35 Dir of Student Act/Leadership Ctr ... Mr. Cory L. HEADLEY
28 Director of Multicultural Affairs ... Mr. Jesse HERRERA

*South Dakota State University (C)

Campanile Avenue, Brookings SD 57007-2298
County: Brookings FICE Identification: 003471
Unit ID: 219356
Telephone: (605) 688-4151 Carnegie Class: DU-Higher
FAX Number: (605) 688-5822 Calendar System: Semester
URL: www.sdstate.edu
Established: 1881 Annual Undergrad Tuition & Fees (In-State): $8,764
Enrollment: 12,516 Coed
Affiliation or Control: State IRS Status: 501(c)3
Highest Offering: Doctorate
Accreditation: NH, AAB, CAATE, CACREP, CAEPN, CIDA, CONST, DIETD, DIETI, EXSC, JOUR, MT, MUS, NURSE, PHAR

02 President ... Dr. Barry H. DUNN
05 Provost/Vice Pres Acad Affairs ... Dr. Dennis HEDGE
32 Vice President Student Affairs ... Dr. Michaela WILLIS
46 VP for Research/Economic Dev ... Dr. Daniel SCHOLL
13 VP for Tech/Security ... Dr. Michael ADELAINE
10 Vice Pres Finance & Admin/CFO ... Dr. Robert KOHRMAN
20 Assoc Vice Pres for Academic Affs ... Dr. Mary Kay HELLING
18 Asst Vice Pres Facilities Services ... Mr. Dean KATTELMANN
88 Asst VP AA Intl Affairs/Outreach ... Vacant
15 Asst Vice Pres Human Resources ... Mr. Marc SERRETT
100 Chief of Staff ... Ms. Karyn WEBER
08 Dean of the Library ... Dr. Kristi TORNQUIST
07 Director of Admissions ... Mr. Shawn HELMBOLT
06 Registrar ... Ms. Joyce KEPFORD
38 Director Wellness ... Ms. Tammy LUNDAY
37 Financial Aid Officer ... Ms. Beth VOLLAN
102 President & CEO of Foundation ... Mr. Steve ERPENBACH
29 President & CEO Alumni Affairs ... Ms. Andi FOUBERG
19 Chief Security/Safety ... Mr. Tim HEATON
39 Director of Residential Life ... Ms. Rebecca PETERSON
40 Director of Bookstore ... Mr. Derek PETERSON
41 Director of Athletics ... Mr. Justin SELL
28 Dir of Diver/Equity/Inclus/Access ... Ms. Kas WILLIAMS
56 Interim Director of Extension ... Dr. Karla TRAUTMAN
26 Dir Marketing & Communications ... Mr. Michael LOCKREM
96 Purchasing Director ... Ms. Vicki SOREN
43 General Counsel ... Dr. Tracy GREENE
25 Director of Grants/Contracts ... Ms. Jill O'NEIL
24 Mgr Instructional Design Services ... Dr. Shouhong ZHANG
85 Mgr International Students/Scholars ... Mr. Greg WYMER
47 Dean Col of Agric/Food & Envr Sci ... Dr. John KILLEFER
49 Dean Col of Arts/Hum & SS ... Dr. Lynn SARGEANT
54 Dean of Engineering ... Dr. Bruce BERDANIER
53 Dean Education & Human Science ... Dr. Jill THORNGREN
66 Dean of Nursing ... Dr. Mary Anne KROGH
67 Dean of Pharmacy ... Dr. Jane MORT
58 Dean of Graduate School ... Dr. Kinchel DOERNER
92 Dean Honors College ... Dr. Rebecca BOTT
81 Dean Col of Natural Science ... Dr. Charlene WOLF-HALL
51 Dir Continuing & Distance Educ ... Ms. Lindsey HAMLIN
09 Coordinator Institutional Research ... Ms. Jennifer VANDER WAL
104 Director Study Abroad ... Ms. Sally GILLMAN
108 Director Institutional Assessment ... Dr. Janna HANSON
22 Title IX Coord/EEO ... Ms. Michelle JOHNSON
90 Asst Vice Pres for Technology ... Mr. Ryan KNUTSON
04 Admin Assistant to the President ... Ms. Linda SCHUMACHER
84 Director Enrollment Management ... Dr. Michaela WILLIS

Southeast Technical Institute (D)

2320 N Career Avenue, Sioux Falls SD 57107-1302
County: Minnehaha FICE Identification: 007764
Unit ID: 219426
Telephone: (605) 367-7624 Carnegie Class: Assoc/HVT-High Trad
FAX Number: (605) 367-8305 Calendar System: Semester
URL: www.southeasttech.edu
Established: 1968 Annual Undergrad Tuition & Fees (In-District): $6,240
Enrollment: 2,244 Coed
Affiliation or Control: Local IRS Status: 501(c)3
Highest Offering: Associate Degree
Accreditation: NH, ADNUR, CVT, DMS, NDT, NMT, SURGT

01 President ... Mr. Robert J. GRIGGS
05 Vice President of Academics ... Mr. Benjamin VALDEZ
10 Vice President Finance & Operations ... Mr. Richard KLUIN
84 VP for Enrollment Management ... Ms. Megan FISCHER
32 Exec Dir Stdnt Affs/Inst Effectiv ... Mr. Tracy NOLDNER
06 Director Student Success/Registrar ... Ms. Kristie VORTHERMS
13 Director Info Tech/CIO ... Mr. Erik VANLAECKEN
15 Human Resources Director ... Ms. Kathy STRUCK
121 Director of Academic Support ... Dr. Craig PETERS
20 Director of Curriculum/Instruction ... Ms. Kristin POSSEHL
26 Marketing/Communications Coord ... Ms. Jennifer LAMBLEY
37 Financial Aid Director ... Mr. Micah HANSEN
102 Foundation Director ... Mr. Stephen WILLIAMSON
21 Business Manager ... Mr. James WESTCOTT
38 Student Personal Counselor ... Ms. Nicole MCMILLIN
04 Admin Assistant to the President ... Ms. Vicki OSWALD

University of Sioux Falls (E)

1101 W 22nd Street, Sioux Falls SD 57105-1699
County: Minnehaha FICE Identification: 003469
Unit ID: 219383
Telephone: (605) 331-5000 Carnegie Class: Masters/M
FAX Number: (605) 331-6615 Calendar System: 4/1/4
URL: www.usiouxfalls.edu
Established: 1883 Annual Undergrad Tuition & Fees: $18,280
Enrollment: 1,453 Coed
Affiliation or Control: American Baptist IRS Status: 501(c)3
Highest Offering: Beyond Master's But Less Than Doctorate
Accreditation: NH, CAEP, IACBE, NURSE, SW

01 President ... Dr. Brett BRADFIELD
100 Dir Presidential and Bd Operations ... Ms. Karen BANGASSER
05 VP for Academic Affairs ... Ms. Joy LIND
50 Chair School of Business ... Dr. Tricia COLE
53 Chair School of Education ... Ms. Michelle HANSON
57 Chair Visual & Performing Arts ... Mr. Jonathan NEIDERHISER
65 Chair of Natural Sciences ... Dr. William SOEFFING
79 Chair of Humanities ... Ms. Jenny BANGSUND
83 Chair of Social Sciences ... Ms. Beth O'TOOLE
66 Director School of Nursing ... Ms. Jessica CHERENEGAR
88 Director of Degree Comp Program ... Ms. LuAnn GROSSMAN
06 Registrar ... Ms. Anna HECKENLAIBLE
10 VP for Business and Finance ... Ms. Marsha DENNISTON
21 Senior Accountant ... Ms. Molly HOFFMAN
111 VP for Institutional Advancement ... Mr. Todd KNUTSON
112 VP for Principal Gifts ... Mr. Jon HIATT
30 Dir of Institutional Advancement ... Ms. Julie IVERSON
26 Dir of Marketing and Communications ... Ms. Sarah STRASBURG
84 VP for Enrollment Management ... Ms. Aimee VANDER FEEN
07 Director of Enrollment Management ... Mr. Ben WEINS
37 Director of Financial Aid ... Ms. Karrie MORGAN
15 VP of Human Resources ... Ms. Julie GEDNALSKE
09 AVP of Institutional Research ... Dr. Jason DOUMA
32 VP Student Dev/Dean of Students ... Mr. Corey ROSS
39 Asst Dean of Stdnts/Dir Res Life ... Ms. Ashley MATURAN
42 Dean of the Chapel ... Rev. Dennis L. THUM
38 University Counselor ... Ms. Michelle DEHOOGH-KLIEWER
104 Director of International Education ... Mr. Randy NELSON
13 VP Info Technology and CIO ... Mr. William BARTELL
91 Dir Administrative Applications ... Ms. Brenda THOMAS
106 Director of Online Education ... Ms. Veda IVERSON
08 Librarian ... Ms. Annie STERNBURG
41 Director of Athletics ... Ms. Pam GOHL
18 Director of Facilities ... Mr. Brad FLAYTON
19 Director of Campus Safety ... Mr. Kevin GREBIN
40 Dir of Cougar Central Bookstore ... Ms. Jennifer KNUTSON

Western Dakota Technical Institute (F)

800 Mickelson Drive, Rapid City SD 57703-4018
County: Pennington FICE Identification: 010170
Unit ID: 219480
Telephone: (605) 394-4034 Carnegie Class: Assoc/HVT-Mix Trad/Non
FAX Number: (605) 394-1789 Calendar System: Semester
URL: www.wdt.edu
Established: 1968 Annual Undergrad Tuition & Fees (In-District): $7,710
Enrollment: 1,050 Coed
Affiliation or Control: Local IRS Status: 501(c)3
Highest Offering: Associate Degree
Accreditation: NH, EMT, MLTAD, SURGT

01 President ... Dr. Ann BOLMAN
05 VP for Teaching and Learning ... Ms. Tiffany HOWE
10 VP for Finance and Operations ... Mr. Brian WATLAND
108 VP for Institutional Effectiveness ... Ms. Kelly OEHLERKING
15 Human Resources Director ... Ms. Theresa SCHARN
07 Admissions & Financial Aid Director ... Ms. Jill ELDER
06 Registrar/Student Success Director ... Ms. Debbie TOMS
18 Facilities Director ... Mr. Daryl LEMME
26 Marketing Coordinator ... Ms. Pam STILLMAN-ROKUSEK
111 Associate Dean of Advancement ... Ms. Chandra CALVERT
04 Executive Assistant to President ... Ms. Kathi MAXSON
09 Reporting & Analysis Director ... Mr. Mark MCGRATH
102 Foundation Director ... Ms. Danita SIMONS
13 Information Systems Director ... Mr. Matthew GREENE

TENNESSEE

American Baptist College (A)

1800 Baptist World Center Drive, Nashville TN 37207
County: Davidson FICE Identification: 010460
Unit ID: 219505
Telephone: (615) 256-1463 Carnegie Class: Spec-4-yr-Faith
FAX Number: (615) 226-7855 Calendar System: Semester
URL: www.abcnash.edu
Established: 1924 Annual Undergrad Tuition & Fees: $10,074
Enrollment: 115 Coed
Affiliation or Control: Baptist IRS Status: 501(c)3
Highest Offering: Baccalaureate
Accreditation: BI

01 President ... Dr. Forrest E. HARRIS, SR.
05 Vice Pres Academic Affairs ... Dr. LaShante WALKER
10 VP Administration/Finance ... Atty. Richard JACKSON
32 Vice Pres Campus Life ... Mr. Martin ESPINOSA
06 Registrar ... Mr. Cedric AARON
21 Controller ... Ms. Brooke BELL
08 Director Library Services ... Ms. Nicole WHITE
04 Executive Assistant to President ... Ms. Mary CARPENTER
25 Dir Proposal/Grant Research Devel ... Dr. Regina PRUDE
07 Dir Admissions/Public Relations ... Ms. Dee BOMER

American National University (B)

1328 Highway 11 W, Bristol TN 37620-8530
Telephone: (423) 878-4440 Identification: 666500
Accreditation: DEAC

† Branch campus of American National University, Salem, VA

Aquinas College (C)

4210 Harding Pike, Nashville TN 37205-2005
County: Davidson FICE Identification: 003477
Unit ID: 219578
Telephone: (615) 297-7545 Carnegie Class: Spec-4-yr-Other Health
FAX Number: N/A Calendar System: Semester
URL: www.aquinascollege.edu
Established: 1961 Annual Undergrad Tuition & Fees: N/A
Enrollment: N/A Coed
Affiliation or Control: Roman Catholic IRS Status: 501(c)3
Highest Offering: Master's
Accreditation: SC

01 President ... Sr. Mary Agnes GREIFFENDORF, OP
10 Vice Pres of Finance ... Vacant
05 Provost and Vice Pres for Academics ... Sr. Thomas More STEPNOWSKI, OP
32 Director of Student Activities ... Vacant
20 Associate Provost ... Dr. William SMART
26 Dir of Communications/ Marketing ... Sr. Marie Bernadette THOMPSON, OP
07 Dir of Admiss & Registrar ... Sr. Gianna JUNKER, OP
08 Librarian ... Sr. Mary Esther POTTS, OP
30 Director of Development ... Vacant
53 Dean School of Education ... Sr. Mary Rachel CAPETS, OP
21 Business Manager ... Mrs. Monica WARREN
09 Director of Institutional Research ... Dr. William SMART
29 Director of Alumni Relations ... Vacant
18 Chief of Facilities/Physical Plant ... Mr. John WALL
121 Director of Student Learning Svcs ... Sr. Mary Edith HUMPHRIES, OP
88 Director of Catechetics ... Mr. Jason GALE
88 Dir Center for Catholic Education ... Sr. Elizabeth Anne ALLEN, OP
19 Director Security/Safety ... Mr. Anthony ATWOOD
04 Administrative Asst to President ... Mrs. Brenda L. KINCAID
101 Secretary of the Institution/Board ... Sr. John Mary FLEMING, OP
13 Chief Info Technology Officer (CIO) ... Mrs. Joyce WALL
15 Chief Human Resources Officer ... Ms. Anne TARWATER
37 Director Student Financial Aid ... Mrs. Cynthia PIANA

Austin Peay State University (D)

601 College Street, Clarksville TN 37044-0002
County: Montgomery FICE Identification: 003478
Unit ID: 219602
Telephone: (931) 221-7011 Carnegie Class: Masters/L
FAX Number: (931) 221-7475 Calendar System: Semester
URL: www.apsu.edu
Established: 1927 Annual Undergrad Tuition & Fees (In-State): $8,159
Enrollment: 10,463 Coed
Affiliation or Control: State IRS Status: 501(c)3
Highest Offering: Doctorate
Accreditation: SC, ART, CACREP, CAEPN, MT, MUS, NURSE, RAD, RTT, SW

02 President ... Dr. Alisa WHITE
05 Provost/VP Academic Affairs ... Dr. Rex GANDY
10 Vice President for Finance & Admin ... Mr. Mitch ROBINSON
43 VP Legal Affairs & Sec to Board ... Ms. Dannelle WHITESIDE
32 VP for Student Affairs ... Dr. Eric NORMAN
111 VP External Affairs ... LtGen. Ron BAILEY
21 Assoc VP for Finance ... Mr. Benjamin HARMON
20 Vice Provost/Assoc VP Acad Affairs ... Dr. Lynne CROSBY
84 Assoc Provost for Enrollment Mgmt ... Dr. Beverly BOGGS
110 Asst VP Univ Advancement ... Mr. Kristopher PHILLIPS
86 Asst VP Cmty & Govt Relations ... Ms. Carol D. CLARK
26 Exec Dir Marketing/Public Rels ... Mr. Bill PERSINGER
12 Exec Dir APSU Fort Campbell ... Dr. Kristine NAKUTIS
29 Director of Alumni Relations ... Ms. Nicole PETERSON
114 Director Budgets ... Ms. Sonja STEWART
08 Director Library ... Mr. Joe WEBER
13 Assoc VP & Chief Info Officer ... Ms. Judith MOLNAR
09 Dir Decision Support/Inst Effective ... Dr. Andrew LUNA
07 Director of Admissions ... Ms. Amy CORLEW
06 Registrar ... Ms. Telaina WRIGLEY
18 Director of Plant Administration ... Mr. Thomas HUTCHINS
45 Dir University Design/Construction ... Mr. Marc BRUNNER
41 Athletic Director ... Mr. Gerald HARRISON
88 Athletics Communication Manager ... Mr. Cody BUSH
37 Director of Student Financial Aid ... Ms. Donna PRICE
121 AVP Student Success/Strategic Init ... Dr. Loretta GRIFFY
38 Dir of Student Counseling Services ... Dr. Jeff RUTTER
35 Assoc Vice Pres & Dean of Students ... Mr. Gregory SINGLETON
88 Dir African Amer Cultural Ctr ... Vacant
15 Exec Director Human Resources ... Ms. Sheraine GILLIAM-HOLMES
16 Director of Human Resources ... Ms. Fonda FIELDS
19 Director Public Safety ... Mr. Michael KASITZ
39 Asst Vice President Student Affairs ... Mr. F. Joe MILLS
116 Director Internal Audit ... Mr. Blayne CLEMENTS
25 Int Dir Research & Sponsored Pgms ... Dr. Raja DAKSHINAMURTHY
96 Director of Purchasing ... Ms. Judy BLAIN
22 Dir Equal Opportunity/Affirm Action ... Ms. Sheila M. BRYANT
36 Director of Career Services ... Ms. Amanda WALKER
49 Dean College Arts & Letters ... Mr. Barry JONES
81 Interim Dean College Science & Math ... Dr. Karen MEISCH
83 Dean Col Behav Health Science ... Dr. Tucker BROWN
58 Assoc Provost/Dean Col Grad Stds ... Dr. Chad BROOKS
56 Exec Dir Extend/Intl Educ ... Dr. Tim HUDSON
106 Int Director of Distance Education ... Ms. Lady MORAN
104 Dir Study Abroad/Intl Exchange ... Dr. Marissa CHANDLER
50 Dean College of Business ... Dr. Mickey HEPNER
53 Dean College of Education ... Dr. Prentice CHANDLER

Baptist College of Health Sciences (E)

1003 Monroe Avenue, Memphis TN 38104-3199
County: Shelby FICE Identification: 034403
Unit ID: 219639
Telephone: (901) 575-2247 Carnegie Class: Spec-4-yr-Other Health
FAX Number: (901) 572-2461 Calendar System: Trimester
URL: www.bchs.edu
Established: 1994 Annual Undergrad Tuition & Fees: $11,900
Enrollment: 1,075 Coed
Affiliation or Control: Independent Non-Profit IRS Status: 501(c)3
Highest Offering: Doctorate
Accreditation: SC, COARC, DMS, MT, NMT, NURSE, RAD, RTT

01 President ... Dr. Betty S. MCGARVEY
04 Administrative Asst to President ... Ms. Dina BACHOR
05 Provost/VP Academic Affairs ... Dr. Loredana C. HAEGER
84 VP Enrollment Mgmt & Student Affs ... Dr. Tammy FOWLER
10 Vice President Financial & Business ... Ms. Leanne SMITH
11 Vice President Admin Svcs/HR ... Dr. Adonna CALDWELL
97 Dean General Educ & Health Studies ... Dr. Barry SCHULTZ
66 Dean Nursing ... Dr. Anne M. PLUMB
76 Dean Allied Health ... Dr. Carol WARREN
32 Dean Student Services ... Ms. Nancy REED
06 Registrar ... Mrs. Erica CHANDLER
07 Director of Admissions ... Ms. Lissa MORGAN
09 Dir of Institutional Effectiveness ... Dr. Cameron A. CONN
29 Director Alumni Relations/Marketing ... Ms. Megan M. BURSI
35 Director Student Services & Housing ... Mr. Jeremy WILKES
37 Director Financial Aid ... Ms. Joanna DARDEN

Belmont University (F)

1900 Belmont Boulevard, Nashville TN 37212-3757
County: Davidson FICE Identification: 003479
Unit ID: 219709
Telephone: (615) 460-6000 Carnegie Class: DU-Mod
FAX Number: (615) 460-6446 Calendar System: Semester
URL: www.belmont.edu
Established: 1890 Annual Undergrad Tuition & Fees: $34,310
Enrollment: 8,012 Coed
Affiliation or Control: Christian Churches And Churches of Christ
IRS Status: 501(c)3
Highest Offering: Doctorate
Accreditation: SC, ART, CAEPN, CIDA, LAW, MUS, NURSE, OT, PHAR, PTA, SW, THEA

01 President ... Dr. Robert C. FISHER
05 Provost ... Dr. Thomas D. BURNS
100 Vice President/Chief of Staff ... Dr. Susan H. WEST
43 Vice Pres for Admin & Univ Counsel ... Dr. Jason ROGERS
108 VP for Institutional Effectiveness ... Dr. Paula GILL
30 VP Development/External Relations ... Dr. Perry MOULDS
10 Vice President Finance & Operations ... Mr. Steven T. LASLEY
42 VP Spiritual Development ... Dr. Todd LAKE
26 VP Marketing & Public Relations ... Mr. John CARNEY
13 Assoc VP/Chief Information Officer ... Mr. William INGRAM
32 Assoc Provost/Dean of Students ... Dr. John DELONY
20 Assoc Provost for Academic Affairs ... Vacant
84 Assoc Provost/Dean Enrollment Svcs ... Dr. David MEE
09 Assoc Provost/Assess/Inst Research ... Vacant
88 Assoc Provost ISGE ... Dr. Mimi BARNARD
50 Dean College of Business ... Dr. Patrick RAINES
57 Dean College Visual/Performing Arts ... Dr. Stephen EAVES
88 Dean College of Ent & Music Bus ... Mr. Doug HOWARD
49 Dean Col of Lib Arts & Soc Sci ... Dr. Bryce SULLIVAN
81 Dean Col of Sciences & Mathematics ... Dr. Thomas SPENCE
76 Dean Col Health Sciences/Nursing ... Dr. Cathy TAYLOR
73 Dean of Col Theol & Christian Min ... Dr. Darrell GWALTNEY
61 Dean College of Law ... Dr. Alberto GONZALES
67 Dean College of Pharmacy ... Dr. Phil JOHNSTON
06 University Registrar ... Mr. Steven REED
35 Asst Dean of Student Support Svcs ... Ms. Angie BRYANT
39 Assistant Dean of Student Housing ... Mr. Anthony DONOVAN
07 Director of University Admissions ... Vacant
15 Sr Director of Human Resources ... Mrs. Leslie A. LENSER
37 Director of Financial Aid ... Mrs. Patricia SMEDLEY
29 Director of Alumni Relations ... Mr. Mike CORTESE
18 Director of Facilities Management ... Mr. Robert CHAVEZ
19 Chief of Campus Security ... Mr. Pat CUNNINGHAM
90 Director Technology Services ... Mr. Randall REYNOLDS
08 Director of Library Services ... Ms. Sue MASZAROS
41 Athletics Director ... Mr. Scott CORLEY
40 Manager Bookstore ... Mrs. Catherine MURPHY
36 Dir Career & Professional Develop ... Ms. Mary Claire DISMUKES
38 Director Student Counseling ... Ms. Katherine CORNELIUS
104 Director Study Abroad ... Ms. Shelley JEWELL
85 Director of International Education ... Ms. Katherine SKINNER

Bethel University (G)

325 Cherry Avenue, McKenzie TN 38201-1705
County: Carroll FICE Identification: 003480
Unit ID: 219718
Telephone: (731) 352-4000 Carnegie Class: Masters/L
FAX Number: (731) 352-4069 Calendar System: Semester
URL: www.bethelu.edu
Established: 1842 Annual Undergrad Tuition & Fees: $16,552
Enrollment: 5,779 Coed
Affiliation or Control: Cumberland Presbyterian IRS Status: 501(c)3
Highest Offering: Master's
Accreditation: SC, ARCPA, #CAATE, NURSE

01 President ... Dr. Walter BUTLER
05 Chief Academic Officer ... Dr. Phyllis CAMPBELL
49 VP College of Arts and Sciences ... Ms. Cindy MALLARD
107 VP College of Professional Studies ... Mrs. Kimberly MARTIN
76 VP College of Health Sciences ... Dr. Joe HAMES
10 VP of Finance ... Mr. David HUSS
30 Vice President for Development ... Dr. Dale HENRY
06 University Registrar ... Dr. Becky HAMES
84 Director of Recruitment & Admission ... Mr. John NORWOOD
07 Admissions Coordinator ... Mrs. Tina HODGES
32 Dean of Student Affairs ... Mr. James STEWART
26 Director of Public Relations ... Ms. Michelle MITCHELL
88 Director of College Orientation ... Mrs. Sandy LOUDEN
42 Chaplain ... Rev. Anne HAMES
08 Library Director ... Ms. Jill WHITFILL
15 Human Resource Director ... Ms. Carolyn DOTSON
41 Athletic Director ... Mr. Dale KELLEY
09 Dir of Institutional Effectiveness ... Ms. Janie AMBURGEY
29 Director Alumni Relations ... Mrs. Myra CARLOCK
18 Chief Facilities/Physical Plant ... Mr. Randy TANAKA
04 Administrative Asst to President ... Ms. Vicky WILLIAMS
105 Director Web Services ... Mr. Sean HINES
13 Chief Info Technology Officer (CIO) ... Mr. Jimmy BOMAR
19 Director Security/Safety ... Mr. Daniel THOMAS
39 Director Student Housing ... Ms. Peggy CARTER

Bryan College (H)

721 Bryan Drive, Dayton TN 37321-6275
County: Rhea FICE Identification: 003536
Unit ID: 219790
Telephone: (423) 775-2041 Carnegie Class: Masters/S
FAX Number: (423) 775-7330 Calendar System: Semester
URL: www.bryan.edu
Established: 1930 Annual Undergrad Tuition & Fees: $26,800
Enrollment: 1,397 Coed
Affiliation or Control: Independent Non-Profit IRS Status: 501(c)3
Highest Offering: Master's
Accreditation: SC, IACBE

01 President ... Dr. Stephen D. LIVESAY
04 Exec Assistant to the President ... Ms. Margaret A. LEGG
05 Provost/VP of Academics ... Dr. Doug MANN
10 VP of Finance and Enrollment ... Mr. Rick J. TAPHORN
30 Vice Pres of College Advancement ... Mr. Chuck S. BAKER
32 VP Student Services/Ministries ... Mr. Timothy J. HOSTETLER
13 Vice Pres Information Systems ... Vacant
58 Dean Sch of Adult & Graduate Stds ... Dr. Adina SCRUGGS
54 Dean School of Engineering ... Dr. Thomas H. MARSHALL
35 Dean of Students ... Mr. Bruce A. MORGAN
37 Director of Financial Aid ... Mr. David L. HAGGARD
14 Director of Information Systems ... Mr. James SULLIVAN
06 Registrar ... Ms. Janet M. PIATT
08 Director of Library Sciences ... Dr. Gary N. FITSIMMONS
15 Director Personnel Services ... Mrs. Angie C. PRICE
41 Athletic Director ... Mr. Mike KEEN
18 Director of Physical Plant ... Mr. David A. MORGAN
29 Director of Alumni Affairs ... Mrs. Paulakay HALL
07 Director of Admissions ... Mr. Joshua D. HOOD
88 Accreditation Liaison ... Mr. Samuel J. YOUNGS

Carson-Newman University (A)

1646 Russell Avenue, PO Box 557,
Jefferson City TN 37760-2204
County: Jefferson | FICE Identification: 003481
Unit ID: 219806
Telephone: (865) 471-2000 | Carnegie Class: DU-Mod
FAX Number: (865) 471-3502 | Calendar System: Semester
URL: www.cn.edu
Established: 1851 | Annual Undergrad Tuition & Fees: $27,900
Enrollment: 2,514 | Coed
Affiliation or Control: Southern Baptist | IRS Status: 501(c)3
Highest Offering: Doctorate
Accreditation: SC, AAFCS, ART, CACREP, CAEPN, DIETD, MUS, NURSE

01 President .... Mr. Charles FOWLER
05 EVP/Provost .... Dr. Paul PERCY
20 Associate Provost .... Dr. Jeremy BUCKNER
111 Vice President for Advancement .... Mr. Scott FAULKENBERRY
32 Vice President Student Affairs .... Dr. Ross BRUMMETT
10 Vice President for Finance/Business .... Mrs. Martha CHAMBERS
35 Asst Vice Pres of Student Affairs .... Mrs. Shelley BALL
08 Dean of Library Services .... Mr. Bruce KOCOUR
26 Exec Dir University Relations .... Mr. Charles KEY
37 Director Financial Aid .... Mrs. Danette SEALE
38 Director Counseling Services .... Mrs. Jennifer CATLETT
13 Chief Information Officer .... Mr. David TUELL
18 Chief Facilities/Physical Plant .... Mr. Ondes WEBSTER
84 Asst Vice Pres of Enrollment Mgmt .... Mr. Aaron PORTER
92 Director of Honors Program .... Dr. Andrew SMITH
21 Asst Vice Pres Finance/Business .... Mrs. Elaine SMITH
41 Athletic Director .... Mr. Matthew POPE
85 Dean of Global Education .... Vacant
06 Registrar .... Mrs. Sheryl GRAY

Chattanooga College (B)

5600 Brainerd Road #B-38, Chattanooga TN 37411
County: Hamilton | FICE Identification: 022042
Unit ID: 220118
Telephone: (423) 305-7783 | Carnegie Class: Spec 2-yr-Health
FAX Number: (423) 624-1575 | Calendar System: Quarter
URL: www.chattanoogacollege.edu
Established: 1968 | Annual Undergrad Tuition & Fees: $10,690
Enrollment: 273 | Coed
Affiliation or Control: Proprietary | IRS Status: Proprietary
Highest Offering: Associate Degree
Accreditation: ACCSC

01 President .... Mr. William G. FAOUR
03 Vice President .... Mr. Toney C. MCFADDEN
37 Director Financial Aid .... Ms. Beth GASS

Christian Brothers University (C)

650 East Parkway S, Memphis TN 38104-5581
County: Shelby | FICE Identification: 003482
Unit ID: 219833
Telephone: (901) 321-3000 | Carnegie Class: Masters/L
FAX Number: (901) 321-3494 | Calendar System: Semester
URL: www.cbu.edu
Established: 1871 | Annual Undergrad Tuition & Fees: $32,820
Enrollment: 2,157 | Coed
Affiliation or Control: Roman Catholic | IRS Status: 501(c)3
Highest Offering: Master's
Accreditation: SC, #ARCPA, CAEPN, NURSE

01 President .... Mr. John T. SHANNON, JR.
05 VP Academics & Student Life .... Dr. Paul HAUGHT
11 Chief Operating Officer .... Mr. Chris KOCH
10 CFO & VP Administration .... Mr. Ronald BRANDON
111 Vice Pres Institutional Advancement .... Mr. Mark BILLINGSLEY
84 VP for Enrollment Management .... Dr. Anne KENWORTHY
26 VP for Communications & Marketing .. Ms. Deborah BLANCHARD
20 Assoc VP of Acad & Strategic Init .... Dr. Jack HARGETT
32 Dean of Students .... Ms. Karen CONWAY
13 Associate VP for ITS .... Mr. Brett DOTY
06 Registrar .... Mr. Scott SUMMERS
36 Director Career Center .... Mrs. Amy WARE
08 Director of Plough Library .... Ms. Kay CUNNINGHAM
07 Director of Admissions .... Ms. Kristi FORMAN
38 Director of Counseling .... Ms. Beverly WORD
37 Director Financial Resources .... Ms. Elizabeth ROMAGNI
09 Dir Inst Research/Effectiveness .... Ms. Melissa S. ANDREWS
39 Director Residence Life .... Mr. Alton WADE
35 Associate VP for Student Life .... Dr. Timothy DOYLE
42 Director of Ministry and Mission .....Br. Dominic EHRMANTRAUT
92 Director Honors Program .... Dr. Tracie L. BURKE
41 Athletic Director .... Mr. Brian SUMMERS
112 Major Gift Officer .... Dr. Leslie GRAFF
29 Director Alumni/Annual Giving .... Ms. Bettye DURHAM
21 Cash Management Manager .... Mr. Thomas COCHRAN
15 Director of Personnel .... Ms. Theresa JACQUES
18 Chief Facility/Physical Plant .... Mr. Bill HECHT
19 Director of Security .... Mr. John D. LOTRIONTE
40 Director Bookstore .... Ms. Shannon DAVIS
50 Dean School of Business .... Dr. Joseph TUREK
54 Dean School of Engineering .... Dr. Pong MALASRI
49 Dean School of Arts .... Dr. Scott GEIS
81 Dean School of Science .... Dr. James MCGUFFEE
107 Dir Graduate/Professional Stds Pgms .... Ms. Toni BENNETT
58 Director Graduate Education Program .... Dr. Samantha ALPERIN
58 Director MBA Program .... Dr. Scott LAWYER
66 Director Nursing Program .... Dr. Jennifer HITT
88 Director Physician Assistant Stds .... Ms. Teresa PRESTON
04 Senior Executive Asst to President .... Mrs. Donna M. FREEMAN
104 Director Study Abroad .... Vacant
25 Chief Contracts/Grants Admin .... Ms. Kathleen TERRY-SHARP

Concorde Career College (D)

5100 Poplar Avenue, Suite 132, Memphis TN 38137-0132
County: Shelby | FICE Identification: 021571
Unit ID: 219903
Telephone: (901) 761-9494 | Carnegie Class: Spec 2-yr-Health
FAX Number: (901) 761-3293 | Calendar System: Semester
URL: www.concorde.edu
Established: 1967 | Annual Undergrad Tuition & Fees: N/A
Enrollment: 1,420 | Coed
Affiliation or Control: Proprietary | IRS Status: Proprietary
Highest Offering: Associate Degree
Accreditation: #COE, CAHIIM, CAHIIM, #COARC, DH, MLTAD, OTA, POLYT, #PTAA, RAD

01 Campus President .... Mrs. Lori SPENCER
11 Regional Vice President Operations .... Mr. Tommy STEWART

The Crown College of the Bible (E)

2307 W. Beaver Creek Drive, Powell TN 37849
County: Knox | Identification: 667141
Telephone: (865) 938-8186 | Carnegie Class: Not Classified
FAX Number: (865) 938-8188 | Calendar System: Semester
URL: thecrowncollege.edu
Established: 1991 | Annual Undergrad Tuition & Fees: N/A
Enrollment: N/A | Coed
Affiliation or Control: Baptist | IRS Status: 501(c)3
Highest Offering: Master's
Accreditation: TRACS

01 Founder & President .... Mr. Clarence SEXTON
05 Vice President of Academics .... Mr. Tim TOMLINSON
11 Vice President of Operations .... Mr. M. Shannon SEXTON
10 Chief Financial Officer .... Mr. Charles PRESCOTT

Cumberland University (F)

1 Cumberland Square, Lebanon TN 37087-3554
County: Wilson | FICE Identification: 003485
Unit ID: 219949
Telephone: (615) 444-2562 | Carnegie Class: Masters/M
FAX Number: (615) 444-2569 | Calendar System: Semester
URL: www.cumberland.edu
Established: 1842 | Annual Undergrad Tuition & Fees: $22,890
Enrollment: 2,314 | Coed
Affiliation or Control: Independent Non-Profit | IRS Status: 501(c)3
Highest Offering: Master's
Accreditation: SC, ACBSP, CAATE, NURSE

01 President .... Dr. Paul STUMB
05 Provost/Vice Pres Academic Affairs .... Dr. William MCKEE
10 Vice President of Finance .... Ms. Judy G. JORDAN
111 Vice President of Advancement .... Mr. Stewart "Scott" LAWRENCE
13 Vice Pres IT/Campus Services .... Mr. Joe GRAY
45 Vice President/Chief Strategy Ofcr .... Mr. William WILLIAMS, JR.
32 AVP/Dean of Students .... Ms. Stephanie DAVIS
66 Dean Nursing and Health Sciences .... Dr. Mary GRIFFITH
100 Executive Coordinator to President .... Ms. Leslie STEELE
08 Director Library Services .... Ms. Bettina WARKENTIN
84 Exec Director Enrollment Services .... Mr. Eddie LOVIN
41 Director of Athletics .... Mr. Ron PAVAN
06 Registrar .... Ms. Tammi PAVAN
15 Human Resources Generalist .... Ms. Tammy MARSHALL
14 Director of Information Technology .... Mr. Jerry ENGLAND
09 Director of Institutional Research .... Mr. Larry F. VAUGHAN
26 Exec Dir Communications/Marketing .... Ms. Caitlin VAUGHN
36 Dir of Career Services/Internships .... Ms. Courtney VICK
37 Director Student Financial Aid .... Ms. Beatrice LACHANCE
39 Director Student Housing .... Ms. Catie STRAUBE
50 Dean Labry School of Business .... Dr. Chris FULLER
53 Dean of Humanities/Education & Art .... Dr. Eric CUMMINGS
27 Exec Dir Public Relations .... Mr. William "Rusty" RICHARDSON

Daymar College (G)

2691 Trenton Road, Clarksville TN 37040-6718
Telephone: (931) 552-7600 | Identification: 666492
Accreditation: ACCSC, PTAA

† Branch campus of Daymar College, Nashville, TN.

Daymar College (H)

415 Golden Bear Court, Murfreesboro TN 37128-5508
Telephone: (615) 217-9347 | Identification: 666392
Accreditation: ACCSC

† Branch campus of Daymar College, Nashville, TN.

Daymar College (I)

560 Royal Parkway, Nashville TN 37214
County: Davidson | FICE Identification: 004934
Unit ID: 220002
Telephone: (615) 361-7555 | Carnegie Class: Bac/Assoc-Mixed
FAX Number: (615) 367-2736 | Calendar System: Quarter
URL: www.daymarcollege.edu
Established: 1884 | Annual Undergrad Tuition & Fees: $15,000
Enrollment: 237 | Coed
Affiliation or Control: Proprietary | IRS Status: Proprietary
Highest Offering: Baccalaureate
Accreditation: ACCSC

01 Campus President .... Dr. Barry BROOKS
05 Campus Dean .... Ms. Laurna TAYLOR
10 Senior Financial Services Officer .... Ms. Laura BEATTY
32 Director Student Services .... Ms. LaTonya EMORY
36 Career Services Coordinator .... Ms. Krystan MASON

East Tennessee State University (J)

1276 Gilbreath Drive, Johnson City TN 37614-1700
County: Washington | FICE Identification: 003487
Unit ID: 220075
Telephone: (423) 439-1000 | Carnegie Class: DU-Higher
FAX Number: (423) 439-5770 | Calendar System: Semester
URL: www.etsu.edu
Established: 1911 | Annual Undergrad Tuition & Fees (In-State): $8,935
Enrollment: 14,353 | Coed
Affiliation or Control: State | IRS Status: 501(c)3
Highest Offering: Doctorate
Accreditation: SC, ART, AUD, CACREP, CAEPN, CIDA, CLPSY, COARC, CSHSE, DH, DIETD, DIETI, MED, MUS, NUR, NURSE, PH, PHAR, PTA, RAD, SP, SW, THEA

02 President .... Dr. Brian E. NOLAND
100 Chief of Staff .... Dr. Adam S. GREEN
11 Chief Operating Officer .... Mr. Jeremy B. ROSS
10 Chief Financial Officer .... Dr. B. J. KING
05 Sr VP for Academics/Interim Provost .... Dr. Wilsie S. BISHOP
111 VP University Advancement .... Ms. Pamela S. RITTER
32 VP for Student Life and Enrollment .... Dr. Joe H. SHERLIN
41 Director of Athletics .... Mr. Scott N. CARTER
28 Int Spec Asst to Pres Equity/Incl .... Dr. Keith V. JOHNSON
116 Director of Internal Audit .... Ms. Rebecca B. LEWIS
43 University Counsel .... Dr. Mark A. FULKS
26 Exec Director of Univ Relations/CCO .... Mr. Joseph E. SMITH
35 Assoc VP Student Life & Enrollment .... Dr. Jeffery S. HOWARD
84 Asst VP Student Life & Enrollment .... Dr. Sam MAYHEW
35 Dean of Students .... Dr. T. Michelle BYRD
51 Dean Cont Studies & Acad Outreach .... Dr. Richard E. OSBORN
46 Vice Prov Research/Sponsored Pgms .... Dr. William R. DUNCAN
20 Vice Provost Academic Affairs .... Dr. M. Marshall GRUBE
20 Vice Provost Undergraduate Ed .... Dr. William G. KIRKWOOD
18 Assoc VP for Facilities Management .... Mr. Jay S. NELSON
13 CIO/Sr Vice Provost for ITS .... Dr. Karen D. KING
11 Assoc VP Administrative Services .... Dr. Katherine M. KELLEY
112 Exec Director for Planned Giving .... Vacant
29 Assoc VP Univ Adv/Exec Dir Alumni .... Dr. Robert M. PLUMMER
86 Assoc VP for Comm & Gov Relations .... Ms. Bridget R. BAIRD
49 Dean College Arts & Science .... Dr. Gordon K. ANDERSON
50 Dean College of Business/Technology .... Dr. Dennis R. DEPEW
76 Dean College of Clin/Rehab Sci .... Dr. Donald A. SAMPLES
53 Interim Dean College of Education .Dr. Janna L. SCARBOROUGH
92 Dean Honors College .... Dr. Chris KELLER
63 Dean College of Medicine .... Dr. William A. BLOCK
67 Dean College of Pharmacy .... Dr. Debbie C. BYRD
66 Dean College of Nursing .... Dr. Wendy M. NEHRING
69 Dean College of Public Health .... Dr. Randolph F. WYKOFF
58 Dean School of Graduate Studies .... Dr. Sharon J. MCGEE
08 Dean of Libraries .... Mr. David P. ATKINS
06 Interim University Registrar .... Dr. Evelyn N. ROACH
36 Director University Career Services .... Dr. Jeffrey L. ALSTON
38 Director Counseling Center .... Dr. Dan L. JONES
37 Director of Financial Aid .... Ms. Catherine A. MORGAN
92 Director University Honors Program ... Dr. Karen R. KORNWEIBEL
39 Director Student Housing .... Dr. Bonnie L. BURCHETT
85 Dir International Programs/Services .... Dr. Maria D. COSTA
93 Multicultural Director .... Ms. Laura C. TERRY
19 Asst VP Pub Safety/Chief of Police .... Ms. Nicole N. COLLINS
25 Director of Sponsored Programs .... Ms. Wendy ECKERT
94 Director of Women's Studies .... Dr. Phyllis A. THOMPSON
105 Web Manager .... Ms. Michaele D. LAWS
15 Exec Director Human Resources .... Ms. Lori ERICKSON
108 Dir Institutional Effectiveness .... Dr. Cheri CLAVIER
45 Assoc VP/Chief Planning Officer .... Dr. Michael B. HOFF

Fisk University (K)

1000 17th Avenue N, Nashville TN 37208-3051
County: Davidson | FICE Identification: 003490
Unit ID: 220181
Telephone: (615) 329-8500 | Carnegie Class: Bac-A&S
FAX Number: N/A | Calendar System: Semester
URL: www.fisk.edu
Established: 1866 | Annual Undergrad Tuition & Fees: $21,480
Enrollment: 701 | Coed
Affiliation or Control: Independent Non-Profit | IRS Status: 501(c)3
Highest Offering: Master's
Accreditation: #SC, MUS

01 President .... Dr. Kevin D. ROME
05 Provost/VP of Academic Affairs .... Dr. Vann R. NEWKIRK
10 Vice President for Finance and CFO .... Ms. Willie R. HUGHEY
04 Exec Assistant to the President .... Mrs. Sherri B. RUCKER
111 Vice President of Inst Advancement .... Dr. Jens FREDERIKSEN
09 Assoc VP Inst Effectiveness/Accred .... Dr. Jason R. CURRY

32 VP of Student Affairs .... Mr. Willie L. JUDE
20 Vice Provost Academic Initiatives .... Dr. Arnold BURGER
121 Vice Provost Student Success/AESP .... Dr. Kenneth E. JONES
13 Director of Information Technology .... Mr. Kenneth SESSIONS
29 Exec Director of Alumni Affairs .... Mrs. Adrienne LATHAM
07 Dean of Recruitment & Admission .... Vacant
37 Director of Financial Aid .... Ms. Irene MOORE
06 Registrar .... Ms. Lisa DIXON
08 University Librarian .... Dr. Jessie C. SMITH
81 Dean Sch Natural Science/Math/Bus .... Dr. Cathy MARTIN
79 Dean School Humanities/Social Sci .... Dr. Reavis MITCHELL
41 Dir of Athletics & Intramural Pgms .... Dr. Larry GLOVER
42 Dean of the Chapel .... RevDr. Jason CURRY
25 Dir Sponsored Research & Programs .... Dr. Marcia MILLET
112 Director of Planned Giving .... Ms. Sheila SMITH
18 Director of Facilities .... Mr. David COBB
19 Chief/Director of Campus Safety .... Mr. Mickey WEST
96 Director of Purchasing .... Mr. David COBB
36 Exec Director Career Development .... Ms. Latreace WELLS
38 Coordinator of Student Counseling .... Dr. Sheila PETERS
15 Director of Human Resources .... Ms. Merdis BUCKLEY
102 AVP Foundation/Corporate Relations .... Vacant
105 Webmaster .... Vacant
39 Director Student Housing .... Dr. Christopher DUKE
43 Dir Legal Services/General Counsel . Ms. Stacey GARRETT-KOJU
106 Dir Online Education/E-learning .... Dr. Shirley BROWN
86 Director Government Relations .... Vacant
26 Director Marketing & Communication .... Ms. Madeline GUINEE
35 Asst VP/Dean of Student Engagement .... Dr. Natara GARVIN
100 Chief of Staff .... Mr. Joseph P. WATKINS
104 Director Study Abroad .... Mr. Duwon CLARK

Fortis Institute (A)

1025 Highway 111, Cookeville TN 38501-4305

County: Putnam FICE Identification: 023263
Unit ID: 418870
Telephone: (931) 526-3660 Carnegie Class: Spec 2-yr-Health
FAX Number: (931) 372-2603 Calendar System: Quarter
URL: www.fortis.edu/cookeville-tennessee.php
Established: 1970 Annual Undergrad Tuition & Fees: $15,201
Enrollment: 175 Coed
Affiliation or Control: Proprietary IRS Status: Proprietary
Highest Offering: Associate Degree
Accreditation: ACCSC, MLTAD, RAD, SURGT

01 Campus President .... Mr. James WILLIAMSON
06 Registrar .... Ms. Wendy BANDY
07 Director of Admissions .... Mr. David HANEY
10 Chief Business Officer .... Ms. Melissa LEWIS
36 Director Student Placement .... Ms. Cindy GARRISON
37 Director Student Financial Aid .... Ms. Lisa WALLING

Fortis Institute-Nashville (B)

3354 Perimeter Hill Drive Ste 105, Nashville TN 37211

Telephone: (615) 320-5917 Identification: 770509
Accreditation: ABHES, CVT, MLTAD, RAD, SURGT, SURTEC

† Branch campus of Fortis Institute, Baton Rouge, LA.

Freed-Hardeman University (C)

158 E Main, Henderson TN 38340-2398

County: Chester FICE Identification: 003492
Unit ID: 220215
Telephone: (731) 989-6000 Carnegie Class: Masters/S
FAX Number: N/A Calendar System: Semester
URL: www.fhu.edu
Established: 1869 Annual Undergrad Tuition & Fees: $21,950
Enrollment: 1,972 Coed
Affiliation or Control: Churches Of Christ IRS Status: 501(c)3
Highest Offering: Doctorate
Accreditation: SC, ACBSP, CAEPN, NURSE, SW, THEOL

01 President .... Mr. David R. SHANNON
04 Executive Assistant to President .... Mrs. Donna STEELE
05 Provost and VP Academics .... Dr. Charles VIRES
10 VP for Financial Services and CFO .... Mr. Jeff LOYD
111 VP for Community Engagement .... Mr. Dave CLOUSE
32 VP Student Services .... Dr. Wayne SCOTT
20 Associate VP for Academics .... Dr. Vicki JOHNSON
110 Associate VP for Advancement .... Mr. Kyle LAMB
84 Associate VP Enrollment Management .... Mr. Joseph ASKEW
115 Associate VP of Finance .... Mr. Jay SATTERFIELD
41 Director of Athletics .... Mr. Michael MCCUTCHEN
110 Associate VP Community Engagement .... Mr. Ryan MALECHA
07 Director of Admissions .... Mrs. Kaylan STEWART
29 Director of Alumni Engagement .... Mr. Chris RAMEY
35 Dean of Students .... Mr. Stuart VARNER
35 Dean of Student Life .... Mr. Tony ALLEN
06 Registrar .... Mr. Jared GOTT
37 Director Student Financial Services .... Mrs. Summer JUDD
08 Library Director .... Mr. Wade OSBURN
70 Director of Social Work Program .... Mrs. Nadine MCNEAL
24 A-V Supervisor .... Mrs. Gail NASH
21 Controller .... Mrs. Courtney INSELL
108 Dir Institutional Effectiveness .... Mr. A.B WHITE
09 Director of Institutional Research .... Mr. Micah SMITH
18 Director of Facilities and Grounds .... Mr. Shannon SEWELL
73 Dean College of Biblical Studies ...... Dr. Mark A. BLACKWELDER
50 Dean College of Business .... Dr. Jason BRASHIER
53 Dean College of Educ & Behav Sci .... Dr. Sharen CYPRESS
49 Dean College of Arts & Sciences .... Dr. LeAnn SELF-DAVIS
92 Dean of Honors College .... Dr. Jenny JOHNSON
104 Dir of International Studies .... Dr. Jenny JOHNSON
36 Director of Univ Career Center .... Mr. Jonathan HARRISON
96 Purchasing Coordinator .... Mrs. Mallory WHITE
40 University Book Store Manager .... Ms. Katie NIXON
19 Director of Campus Safety/Security .... Mr. Stewart BRACKIN

Harding School of Theology (D)

1000 Cherry Road, Memphis TN 38117-5499

Telephone: (901) 761-1350 FICE Identification: 004081
Accreditation: &NH, THEOL

† Regional accreditation is carried under Harding University, Searcy, AR.

Huntington University of Health Sciences (E)

118 Legacy View Way, Knoxville TN 37918

County: Knox Identification: 666971
Unit ID: 488068
Telephone: (865) 524-8079 Carnegie Class: Bac-A&S
FAX Number: (865) 524-8339 Calendar System: Semester
URL: www.huhs.edu
Established: 1985 Annual Undergrad Tuition & Fees: $6,685
Enrollment: 166 Coed
Affiliation or Control: Proprietary IRS Status: Proprietary
Highest Offering: Doctorate
Accreditation: DEAC

01 Chief Executive Officer/President .... Dr. Art PRESSER
05 Provost .... Mr. Gene BRUNO
10 Chief Financial Officer .... Mr. Robert SCHMAEF
11 Sr VP Admin & Academic Affairs .... Ms. Jennifer GREEN
20 Assoc Director of Academic Affairs .... Mr. John LABIG
07 Director of Admissions .... Mr. Gregory SCOTT
21 Director of Finance .... Ms. Jeannette MINIX
37 Director of Financial Aid .... Ms. Heather MORRISON-MONGER
06 Registrar .... Ms. Brittany LONGNECKER
08 Head Librarian .... Ms. Pam WREN
58 Dean of Graduate Studies .... Dr. Denise WOOD

John A. Gupton College (F)

1616 Church Street, Nashville TN 37203-2920

County: Davidson FICE Identification: 008859
Unit ID: 220464
Telephone: (615) 327-3927 Carnegie Class: Spec 2-yr-A&S
FAX Number: (615) 321-4518 Calendar System: Semester
URL: www.guptoncollege.edu
Established: 1946 Annual Undergrad Tuition & Fees: $11,158
Enrollment: 110 Coed
Affiliation or Control: Independent Non-Profit IRS Status: 501(c)3
Highest Offering: Associate Degree
Accreditation: SC, FUSER

01 President .... Mr. B. Steven SPANN
08 Library Director .... Mr. William P. BRUCE
06 Registrar .... Ms. Lisa MOFFITT

Johnson University (G)

7900 Johnson Drive, Knoxville TN 37998-0001

County: Knox FICE Identification: 003495
Unit ID: 220473
Telephone: (865) 573-4517 Carnegie Class: Spec-4-yr-Faith
FAX Number: (865) 251-2337 Calendar System: Semester
URL: www.johnsonu.edu
Established: 1893 Annual Undergrad Tuition & Fees: $16,060
Enrollment: 1,153 Coed
Affiliation or Control: Christian Churches And Churches of Christ
IRS Status: 501(c)3
Highest Offering: Doctorate
Accreditation: #SC, BI, CACREP

01 President .... Dr. Thomas SMITH
05 VP for Academic Affairs/Provost .... Dr. Jon WEATHERLY
111 VP for External Relations .... Richard CLARK
32 VP for Student Services .... David LEGG
10 VP for Finance .... Cindy BARNARD
11 VP for Administration .... Cliff MCCARTNEY
125 President Emeritus .... Dr. Gary WEEDMAN
49 Dean Arts & Sciences .... Dr. Gary STRATTON
60 Dean Communication & Creative Arts .... Dr. Matthew BROADDUS
73 Dean Congregational Ministry .... Dr. Daniel OVERDORF
82 Dean Intercultural Studies .... Dr. Linda WHITMER
83 Dean Social & Behavioral Sciences .... Dr. Sean RIDGE
53 Dean Templar School of Education .... Dr. Roy MILLER
42 Dean of the Chapel .... Dr. Bill WOLF
20 Director of Program Administration .... Joy WINGFIELD
20 Vice Provost for Academic Services .... Dr. Greg LINTON
13 Director of IT .... Glenn FEASTER
41 Athletic Director .... Ken UNDERWOOD
07 Director of Admissions .... Lisa TARWATER
20 Assoc Provost for Online Education .... Dr. John KETCHEN
15 Director Human Resources .... Leslie BEAN
18 Director of Plant Services .... Ben LUTZ, JR.
08 Library Director .... Carrie Beth LOWE
09 Director of IE & Accreditation .... Emili WILLIAMS
37 Director of Financial Aid .... Vacant
06 Registrar .... Andrew FRAZIER
121 Director of Academic Support .... Kelly ESTES
35 Assoc Dean of Students .... Deborah LANE

King University (H)

1350 King College Road, Bristol TN 37620-2699

County: Sullivan FICE Identification: 003496
Unit ID: 220516
Telephone: (423) 968-4861 Carnegie Class: Masters/L
FAX Number: (423) 968-4456 Calendar System: Other
URL: www.king.edu
Established: 1867 Annual Undergrad Tuition & Fees: $29,714
Enrollment: 2,162 Coed
Affiliation or Control: Presbyterian Church (U.S.A.) IRS Status: 501(c)3
Highest Offering: Doctorate
Accreditation: SC, #CAATE, NURSE, SW

01 President .... Mr. Alexander W. WHITAKER, IV
05 Provost .... Dr. Matthew ROBERTS
10 Vice President for Admin & Finance .... Mr. James P. DONAHUE
32 Vice President for Student Affairs .... Dr. Robert A. LITTLETON
84 Int Vice Pres of Enrollment Mgmt .... Dr. Jon HARR
111 Vice President for Advancement .... Mr. Brent DAVISON
100 Chief of Staff .... Mrs. Rebecca J. THOMAS
08 Dean of Library Services .... Ms. Erika BRAMMER
35 Assoc VP/Dean of Student Success .... Mr. Matthew S. PELTIER
04 Executive Assistant to President .... Ms. Holly L. STEVENS
06 Registrar/Dir Regist & Records .... Mrs. Jessica SWINEY
110 Associate Director of Development .... Mr. Logan JENNINGS
42 Chaplain .... Dr. Brian ALDERMAN
21 Director of Business Operations .... Mr. Thomas R. LARSON
41 Athletic Director .... Mr. J. David HICKS
38 Director of Counseling .... Ms. Heather C. BRADDOCK
88 Sports Information Director .... Mr. Travis L. CHELL
40 Bookstore Manager .... Ms. Susan D. MARSHALL
37 Director Student Financial Aid .... Mr. Richard BRAND
18 Chief Facilities/Physical Plant .... Mr. Todd THOMAS
92 Director of Honors Program .... Dr. Craig STREETMAN
27 Asst VP Marketing & Communications .... Ms. Kalonn GENTRY
27 Assoc Director of Communication .... Vacant
36 Director of Career Services .... Ms. Finley GREEN
29 Director Alumni & Cmty Engagement ..... Mrs. Jenna M. CHRISTIE
13 Chief Information Officer .... Mr. Joel ROBERTSON
19 Director Safety & Security .... Mr. Benny BERRY
39 Dir Resident Life/Student Housing .... Mr. Chase ARNDT

Lane College (I)

545 Lane Avenue, Jackson TN 38301-4598

County: Madison FICE Identification: 003499
Unit ID: 220598
Telephone: (731) 426-7500 Carnegie Class: Bac-A&S
FAX Number: (731) 427-3987 Calendar System: Semester
URL: www.lanecollege.edu
Established: 1882 Annual Undergrad Tuition & Fees: $11,500
Enrollment: 1,420 Coed
Affiliation or Control: Christian Methodist Episcopal IRS Status: 501(c)3
Highest Offering: Baccalaureate
Accreditation: SC

01 President .... Dr. Logan C. HAMPTON
03 Executive Vice President/Chaplain .... Dr. Moses GOLDMON
11 Exec Vice Pres Administration .... Ms. Sherrill B. SCOTT
32 Vice President Student Affairs .... Mr. Darryl MCGEE
111 Vice Pres Inst Advance/Dir Alum Aff .... Ms. Tori HALIBURTON
13 Assoc VP Information Technology ... Mr. Earnest L. MITCHELL, III
100 Chief of Staff/VP Inst Advancement ...... Ms. Darlette C. SAMUELS
09 Director of Financial Aid .... Ms. Regina ANDERSON
08 Librarian .... Ms. Lan WANG
06 Registrar .... Mr. Terry W. BLACKMON
20 Director Academic Assessment .... Vacant
19 Director of Safety/Security .... Mr. Steaven JOY
29 Director Alumni Relations .... Ms. Tori HALIBURTON
27 Chief Information Officer .... Vacant
86 Dir Gov Relations/Sr Adv to Pres .... Mr. Richard DONNELL

Lee University (J)

1120 N Ocoee Street, Cleveland TN 37320-3450

County: Bradley FICE Identification: 003500
Unit ID: 220613
Telephone: (423) 614-8000 Carnegie Class: Masters/M
FAX Number: (423) 614-8083 Calendar System: Semester
URL: www.leeuniversity.edu
Established: 1918 Annual Undergrad Tuition & Fees: $17,690
Enrollment: 5,370 Coed
Affiliation or Control: Church Of God IRS Status: 501(c)3
Highest Offering: Doctorate
Accreditation: SC, ACBSP, CAATE, CAEP, CAEPN, MFCD, MUS, NURSE

01 President .... Dr. C. Paul CONN
04 Executive Assistant to President .... Mrs. Stephanie TAYLOR
10 Vice President Business & Finance .... Mr. Chris CONINE
05 Vice President for Academic Affairs .... Dr. Deborah MURRAY
84 Vice President for Enrollment .... Mr. Phil COOK
26 VP for University Relations .... Dr. Jerome HAMMOND
32 VP for Student Development .... Dr. Mike HAYES
13 VP for Information & Marketing .... Dr. Jayson VANHOOK
11 VP for Operations .... Mr. Cole STRONG
21 Comptroller .... Mr. Duane PACE
37 Director of Financial Aid .... Mrs. Marian DILL

35 Dean of Students Mr. Alan MCCLUNG
15 Director of Human Resources Mrs. Amy BALLARD
14 Director of IT Operations Mr. Chris GOLDEN
14 Director of IT Systems Mr. Nate TUCKER
29 Director of Alumni Relations Vacant
39 Director of Residential Life Mr. Jarad RUSSELL
06 Registrar Mrs. Erin LOONEY
113 Bursar Ms. Kristy HARNER
08 Librarian Dr. Louis MORGAN
42 Director of Campus Ministries Dr. Rob FULTZ
25 Director of Grants Mrs. Vanessa HAMMOND
19 Director of Campus Safety Mr. Matt BRINKMAN
23 Director of Health Services Ms. Rachel COFFEY
27 Director of Public Information Mr. Brian CONN
73 Dean School of Religion Dr. Terry CROSS
49 Dean College of Arts & Sciences Dr. Matthew MELTON
53 Dean College of Education Dr. William ESTES
64 Dean School of Music Dr. William GREEN
66 Dean School of Nursing Dr. Sara CAMPBELL
51 Exec Dir of Div of Adult Learning Dr. Joshua BLACK
123 Director of Graduate Enrollment Dr. Jeffery MCGIRT
38 Director of Counseling Center Dr. David QUAGLIANA
18 Director of Physical Plant Mr. Larry BERRY
41 Athletic Director Mr. Larry CARPENTER
104 Director of Global Perspectives Mrs. Angeline MCMULLIN
36 Director of Calling and Career Dr. Sheila CORNEA
07 Director of Admissions Mr. Darren ECHOLS
09 Director of Institutional Research Mrs. Shannon ROWLAND

LeMoyne-Owen College (A)

807 Walker Avenue, Memphis TN 38126-6595
County: Shelby FICE Identification: 003501
Unit ID: 220604
Telephone: (901) 435-1000 Carnegie Class: Bac-Diverse
FAX Number: (901) 435-1699 Calendar System: Semester
URL: www.loc.edu
Established: 1862 Annual Undergrad Tuition & Fees: $11,196
Enrollment: 863 Coed
Affiliation or Control: Multiple Protestant Denominations
IRS Status: 501(c)3
Highest Offering: Baccalaureate
Accreditation: SC, ACBSP, CAEPN

01 Interim President Dr. Carol JOHNSON-DEAN
05 VP Academic and Student Affairs Dr. Terrell STRAYHORN
10 VP Finance and Administration Ms. Loretta STUBBS
88 Director Title III Administration Ms. Shirley HILL
32 Dean of Students Mr. Kenneth QUINN
111 VP Institutional Advancement Ms. Brenda GAINES-OLLIE
13 VP Information Technology Mr. Dwayne CABLE
84 Exec Dir Strategic Enrollment Mgmt Dr. Delphia HARRIS
15 Director of Human Resources Ms. Neva BURKE
08 Librarian Ms. Annette BERHE
37 Director Student Financial Services Ms. Phyllis TORRY
06 Registrar Ms. Mona WASHINGTON
100 Chief of Staff Vacant
29 Director of Alumni Relations Ms. Frankie JEFFRIES
21 Executive Finance Director Ms. Yolanda EMODOGO
09 Director Institutional Research Mr. Reoungeneria MCFARLAND
92 Director Du Bois Honors Program Mr. Dorsey PATTERSON
50 Chair Div Business & Econ Devel Dr. Katherine CAUSEY
53 Chair Education Division Dr. Ralph CALHOUN
57 Chair Div Fine Arts & Humanities Mr. Claybourne FOSTER
65 Chair Div Natural & Math Science Dr. Sherry PAINTER
83 Chair Div Social & Behavioral Sci Mr. Michael ROBINSON
38 Director Student Counseling Mr. Tony WHITSON
26 Dir Public Relations & Marketing Vacant
41 Director of Athletics Mr. Clint JACKSON
11 Director Administrative Services Mr. Jesse CHATMAN
88 Exec Director Engaged Student Learn Dr. Linda WHITE
07 Director of Admissions Mr. Samuel KING
04 Administrative Asst to President Ms. Velma GRAY
18 Chief Facilities/Physical Plant Mr. Anthony COWAN
39 Director of Campus Living and Learn Mr. Shawn RUCKER
25 Grant Writer Ms. Michelle COWAN
35 Director of Student Development Ms. Jean SAULSBERRY
88 Director Freshmen Seminar Ms. Meridith RUCKER

Lincoln College of Technology Nashville (B)

1524 Gallatin Avenue, Nashville TN 37206-3298
County: Davidson FICE Identification: 007440
Unit ID: 221148
Telephone: (615) 226-3990 Carnegie Class: Spec 2-yr-Tech
FAX Number: (615) 262-8466 Calendar System: Other
URL: www.lincolncollegeoftechnology.com
Established: 1919 Annual Undergrad Tuition & Fees: N/A
Enrollment: 1,495 Coed
Affiliation or Control: Proprietary IRS Status: Proprietary
Highest Offering: Associate Degree
Accreditation: ACCSC

01 President Mr. Jim COAKLEY
05 Academic Dean Ms. Jackie RODDY
07 Vice President of Admissions Mr. Shayne PULVER
37 Director of Financial Aid Mr. Chris BIDDLE
06 Registrar Mr. Gary WHITE

Lincoln Memorial University (C)

6965 Cumberland Gap Parkway,
Harrogate TN 37752-1901
County: Claiborne FICE Identification: 003502
Unit ID: 220631
Telephone: (423) 869-3611 Carnegie Class: DU-Mod
FAX Number: (423) 869-6250 Calendar System: Semester
URL: www.lmunet.edu
Established: 1897 Annual Undergrad Tuition & Fees: $22,010
Enrollment: 4,770 Coed
Affiliation or Control: Independent Non-Profit IRS Status: 501(c)3
Highest Offering: Doctorate
Accreditation: SC, ACBSP, ADNUR, ANEST, ARCPA, CAATE, CACREP, CAEPN, LAW, MT, NUR, OSTEO, SW, VET

01 President Dr. E. Clayton HESS
30 VP University Advancement Ms. Cynthia L. WHITT
05 VP Academic Affairs Dr. Jay STUBBLEFIELD
10 VP Finance & Administration Ms. Christy GRAHAM
20 Vice Dean Academic Affairs LMU-DCOM Dr. Jonathan LEO
61 VP/Dean School of Law Judge Gary WADE
84 VP/Dean Enrollment & Student Affs Dr. Jody GOINS
74 VP & Dean College of Veterinary Med Dr. Jason JOHNSON
88 VP/Dean College of Osteopathic Med Dr. Brian KESSLER
76 Dean Allied Health Sciences Dr. Elizabeth THOMPSON
35 Associate Dean of Students Ms. Elise SYOEN
53 Dean of School of Education Dr. Sylvia LYNCH
81 Dean of Mathematics & Sciences Dr. Adam ROLLINS
66 VP & Dean School of Nursing Dr. Mary Anne MODRCIN
50 Dean School of Business Dr. James MAXWELL
04 Exec Assistant to the President Mrs. Janet SMITH
37 Exec Dir Student Financial Services Ms. Tammy TOMFOHRDE
88 AVP Planning/Inst Effectiveness Ms. Kala PERKINS-HOLTSCLAW
09 Director of Institutional Research Vacant
41 Athletic Director Mr. Brian HUTCHINSON
18 Director Infrastructure Management Mr. David LAWS
15 Interim Director of Human Resources Ms. Amy EADS-ARNOLD
96 Director Purchasing Ms. Aprile MASON
06 Registrar Ms. Helen BAILEY
42 University Chaplain Vacant
43 General Counsel Ms. Jennifer (Nikki) PRICE
13 Chief Information Officer Mr. Jason MCCONNELL
26 Sr Dir Marketing/Public Relations Mrs. Katherine M. REAGAN
29 Sr Director Alumni Services Ms. Sheliah COSBY
40 Bookstore Manager (Barnes & Noble) Ms. Tammy GILBERT
49 Dean of Arts/Humanities/Social Sci Dr. Martin SELLERS
121 VP Acad Svcs/Institutional Effect Dr. Travis WRIGHT
88 Advisor to the President Dr. Evelyn SMITH
63 VP/Dean School of Medical Sciences Dr. Mark MORAN

Lipscomb University (D)

One University Park Dr., Nashville TN 37204-3951
County: Davidson FICE Identification: 003486
Unit ID: 219976
Telephone: (615) 966-1000 Carnegie Class: DU-Mod
FAX Number: (615) 966-1798 Calendar System: Semester
URL: www.lipscomb.edu
Established: 1891 Annual Undergrad Tuition & Fees: $32,144
Enrollment: 4,642 Coed
Affiliation or Control: Churches Of Christ IRS Status: 501(c)3
Highest Offering: Doctorate
Accreditation: SC, ACBSP, #ARCPA, CACREP, CAEPN, DIETD, DIETI, MFCD, MUS, NUR, PHAR, SW, THEOL

01 President Dr. L. Randolph LOWRY, III
05 Provost Dr. W. Craig BLEDSOE
45 SVP for Strategy Dr. Susan C. GALBREATH
13 SVP & CIO Mr. Mike GREEN
111 SVP Advancement Dr. John LOWRY
32 SVP Enroll Mgmt/Student Engagement Dr. Matt PADEN
10 Senior VP Finance & Administration Mr. Danny H. TAYLOR
43 General Counsel Dr. David WILSON
26 VP Marketing Mr. Dave BRUNO
29 VP Alumni Relations Mr. Phil ELLENBURG
15 VP Human Resources Ms. Christy HOOPER
41 Director of Athletics Mr. Philip HUTCHESON
26 VP University Relations Mr. Walt LEAVER
84 VP Enrollment Management Mr. Byron LEWIS
42 VP Church Services Dr. Scott SAGER
32 VP of Student Life Mr. Al STURGEON
28 Spec Counsel for Diversity/Inclus Dr. William L. TURNER
88 VP Corporate Relations Mr. Michael WINEGEART
73 Dean College of Bible & Ministry Dr. C. Leonard ALLEN
53 Dean Col of Education Dr. Deborah BOYD
49 Int Dean Col of Liberal Arts & Sci Dr. Randy BOULDIN
67 Dean College of Pharmacy Dr. Roger DAVIS
50 Dean College of Business Dr. Ray ELDRIDGE
54 Dean College of Engineering Mr. David ELROD
57 Dean Shinn Col Ent & Arts Mr. Mike FERNANDEZ
80 Dean Col Leadership & Public Svc Dr. Steve JOINER
55 Dean School of Computing/Technology Dr. Fortune MHLANGA
107 Dean Col Professional Studies Dr. Nina MOREL
08 Dean & Director of Library Services Ms. Sandra PARHAM
58 Vice Provost for Grad Studies Dr. Randy BOULDIN
28 Assoc Prov Diversity & Inclusion Dr. Norma BURGESS
88 Vice Provost for Inst Effectiveness Dr. Elaine GRIFFIN
88 Director Academic Finance Ms. Carol LUSK
121 Senior Director of Student Success Dr. Brian MAST
103 Director of Career Development Ctr Ms. Monica WENTWORTH
20 Associate Provost Academic Support Mr. Steve PREWITT
88 Assoc Provost Inst Effectiveness Dr. Catherine TERRY
06 Registrar Ms. Teresa WILLIAMS
07 Asst VP of Undergrad Admissions Mr. Johnathan AKIN
28 Asst Dean Intercultural Development Mr. Prentice ASHFORD
73 Assoc Dir Hazelip Sch of Theology Dr. Mark BLACK
88 Senior Campus Minister Mr. Steve DAVIDSON
88 Found Dir Inst for Sustain Practice Mr. Dodd GALBREATH
88 Dir Inst for Christian Spirituality Dr. Kris MILLER
106 Dean Online Education Dr. Nina MOREL
83 Chair Grad Studies in Psychology Dr. Shanna RAY
09 Director of Institutional Research Mr. Matt REHBEIN
38 Director Counseling Center Dr. Frank SCOTT
88 Dir Inst for Law Justice & Society Dr. Randy SPIVEY
88 Dir Inst for Civic Leadership Dr. Michelle STEELE
19 ED of Campus Security & Safety Mr. Kyle DICKERSON
86 Director Community & Govt Relations Mr. Brent CULBERSON
21 Assoc VP Finance Mr. Darrell DUNCAN
102 AVP Donor Relations & Stewardship Mr. David ENGLAND
39 Dean of Housing and Residence Life Ms. Laurie SAIN
37 Director of Financial Aid Ms. Tiffany SUMMERS
44 Asst VP Annual Giving & Advanc Svcs Ms. Carrie THOMPSON
14 Assistant CIO Mr. Dave WAGNER
18 Director of Service Operations Mr. Jeff WILSON
04 Admin Assistant to the President Ms. Leslie LANDISS
104 Director Study Abroad Vacant

Martin Methodist College (E)

433 W Madison Street, Pulaski TN 38478-2799
County: Giles FICE Identification: 003504
Unit ID: 220701
Telephone: (931) 363-9800 Carnegie Class: Bac-Diverse
FAX Number: (931) 363-9818 Calendar System: Semester
URL: www.martinmethodist.edu
Established: 1870 Annual Undergrad Tuition & Fees: $24,246
Enrollment: 988 Coed
Affiliation or Control: United Methodist IRS Status: 501(c)3
Highest Offering: Master's
Accreditation: SC, NURSE

01 President Dr. Mark D. LA BRANCHE
05 Vice President of Academic Affairs Dr. Judy B. CHEATHAM
10 VP for Finance & Administration Ms. Rhonda CLINARD
111 Vice Pres for College Advancement Vacant
06 Registrar Dr. Chris MATTINGLY
41 Athletic Director Mr. Jeff N. BAIN
42 Chaplain Rev. Laura KIRKPATRICK
08 Librarian Mr. Richard MADDEN
40 Director of Bookstore Mrs. Margaret W. JACKSON
29 Alumni Affairs Director Mrs. Jaymi RAY
04 Assistant to the President Mrs. Kim W. HARRISON
07 Director of Admissions Mrs. Abby STANTON
15 Director Personnel Services Mr. James R. HLUBB
37 Director Student Financial Aid Mrs. Emma HLUBB
18 Chief Facilities/Physical Plant Mr. Melvin EARLS
26 Director of Public Relations Mrs. Susan CARLISLE
38 Dir Student Counseling/Career/Svcs Mrs. Julie SHELTON
85 Director Foreign Students Mrs. Robin HOOD
13 Director of Technology Mr. Cedric NKULU
09 Director of Institutional Research Vacant
19 Director Security/Safety Dr. Daniel MCMASTERS

Maryville College (F)

502 E Lamar Alexander Parkway,
Maryville TN 37804-5907
County: Blount FICE Identification: 003505
Unit ID: 220710
Telephone: (865) 981-8000 Carnegie Class: Bac-Diverse
FAX Number: (865) 981-8010 Calendar System: Semester
URL: www.maryvillecollege.edu
Established: 1819 Annual Undergrad Tuition & Fees: $34,880
Enrollment: 1,181 Coed
Affiliation or Control: Independent Non-Profit IRS Status: 501(c)3
Highest Offering: Baccalaureate
Accreditation: SC, MUS

01 President Dr. William T. BOGART
04 Assistant to President Ms. Suzette DONOVAN
00 Chairman of the Board Dr. Mary Kay SULLIVAN
05 Interim Vice Pres & Dean of College Dr. Dan KLINGENSMITH
10 VP of Finance & Administration Mr. Jeffery S. INGLE
32 Vice President & Dean of Students Dr. Melanie V. TUCKER
111 VP for Institutional Advancement Ms. Suzy BOOKER
07 VP for Admissions & Financial Aid Ms. Alayne BOWMAN
26 Exec Dir for Mktg & Communications Ms. Karen ELDRIDGE
20 Associate Dean & Director of IR Dr. Jerilyn SWANN
121 Asst Dean of Academic Success Ms. Jan TAYLOR
06 Registrar Ms. Kathi WILSON
21 Controller Ms. Julie RAMSEY
35 Assistant Dean of Students Ms. Kristin GOURLEY
104 Director of International Education Ms. Kirsten SHEPPARD
13 Director of Information Technology Mr. John BERRY
121 Director Academic Support Center Ms. Kim D. OCHSENBEIN
36 Director of the Career Center Ms. Christy MCDONALD
37 Director of Financial Aid Ms. Erin JOHNSON
41 Athletic Director Ms. Kandis SCHRAM
08 Director of the Library Ms. Angela QUICK
18 Director of Physical Plant Mr. Reggie DAILEY
42 Campus Minister Rev. Anne MCKEE
15 Director of Human Resources Ms. Keni LANAGAN

38 Director of Counseling .... Mr. Bruce HOLT
30 Director of Development .... Mr. Eric BELLAH
88 Asst Director of Maryville Fund .... Ms. Meghan FAGG
29 Director of Alumni Affairs .... Ms. Angie HARRIS
112 Director of Major Gifts .... Ms. Diana CANACARIS
28 Director of Multicultural Affairs .... Mr. Larry ERVIN
40 Bookstore Manager .... Mr. Ryan LILLY
88 Gen Mgr Clayton Center for the Arts .... Mr. Blake SMITH
19 Director of Safety & Security .... Mr. John MCMURTRIE
39 Housing Coordinator .... Mrs. Raeann REIHL

Meharry Medical College (A)

1005 Dr. D. B. Todd Jr. Boulevard,
Nashville TN 37208-3501
County: Davidson FICE Identification: 003506
Unit ID: 220792
Telephone: (615) 327-6111 Carnegie Class: Spec-4-yr-Med
FAX Number: (615) 327-6540 Calendar System: Semester
URL: www.mmc.edu
Established: 1876 Annual Graduate Tuition & Fees: N/A
Enrollment: 826 Coed
Affiliation or Control: Independent Non-Profit IRS Status: 501(c)3
Highest Offering: Doctorate; No Undergraduates
Accreditation: SC, DENT, MED, PH

01 President/Chief Executive Ofcr .... Dr. James E.K HILDRETH
03 EVP for Administration .... Dr. Peter E. MILLET
63 Sr VP Health/Dean Sch of Medicine ..... Dr. Veronica T. MALLETT
11 Sr Vice Pres for BOT Relations .... Dr. Saletta HOLLOWAY
26 VP Marketing/Communications .... Vacant
10 Sr Vice President Finance/CFO .... Mrs. LaMel BANDY-NEAL
32 Sr Vice Pres Student Affairs .... Dr. A. Dexter SAMUELS
46 SVP Research/Innovation .... Dr. Maria DE FATIMA LIMA
88 SVP Development/Faculty Affairs .... Dr. Patricia MATTHEWS-JUAREZ
13 CIO/Ellucian Contract .... Mr. Scott FERGUSON
15 Assoc Vice Pres Human Resources .... Mr. Mark SMITH
21 Assoc Vice Pres Financial Systems .... Mr. Larry HOLDEN
111 SVP Institutional Advancement .... Mr. Patrick H. JOHNSON
25 Asst Controller Grants/Contracts .... Ms. Zulfat A. SUARA
43 SVP/General Counsel/Corp Sec ... Mrs. Ivanetta DAVIS-SAMUELS
58 Dean Graduate Studies and Research .... Dr. Maria DE FATIMA LIMA
51 Director Lifelong Learning .... Dr. Allyson FLEMING
76 Dean Allied Health Professions .... Vacant
52 SVP & Dean School of Dentistry ...... Dr. Cherae FARMER-DIXON
29 Executive Director Alumni Affairs .... Dr. Henry MOSES
07 Dir Admissions & Recruitment .... Ms. April E. CURRY-ROBERTS
08 Director of Library .... Vacant
19 Director Campus Safety & Security .... Ms. Theresa MCKINNON
37 Director Student Financial Aid .... Ms. Barbara THARPE
09 Director Institutional Research .... Dr. Chau-Kuang CHEN
100 Chief of Staff/Dir Title III Adm .... Mrs. Sandra ANDERSON-WILLIAMS
18 Director Facilities .... Mr. George N. KELLY
38 Director Counseling Center .... Ms. Sharda D. MISHRA
06 Registrar .... Ms. Miacia PORTER
04 Executive Assistant to the Pres .... Ms. Kimberly STEVENSON

Memphis College of Art (B)

1930 Poplar Avenue, Memphis TN 38104
County: Shelby FICE Identification: 003507
Unit ID: 220808
Telephone: (901) 272-5100 Carnegie Class: Spec-4-yr-Arts
FAX Number: (901) 272-5104 Calendar System: Semester
URL: www.mca.edu
Established: 1936 Annual Undergrad Tuition & Fees: N/A
Enrollment: 303 Coed
Affiliation or Control: Independent Non-Profit IRS Status: 501(c)3
Highest Offering: Master's
Accreditation: SC, ART

01 President .... Ms. Laura HINE
05 Acting VP Academic Affairs .... Ms. Haley MORRIS-CAFIERO
10 VP Operations/Chief Financial Ofcr .... Ms. Lisa ZYRIEK
111 Vice President Advancement .... Vacant
32 VP Student Affairs/Dean of Students .... Mr. Bud RICHEY
26 Vice Pres Communications/Mrktng .... Vacant
21 Assoc Vice Pres for Operations .... Vacant
08 Librarian .... Ms. Katie SCHWEHR
04 Assistant to President .... Vacant
07 Dean of Admissions .... Ms. Annette JAMES-MOORE
35 Director Student Life .... Ms. Nicholous DARMSTAEDTER
37 Director Financial Aid .... Ms. Erica SIMPSON
06 Registrar .... Ms. Erica SIMPSON
36 Director Career Development .... Ms. Carrie Allison BROOKS
19 Director Campus Security .... Vacant
109 Business Office Manager .... Vacant
31 Director Community Education .... Ms. Cecelia PALAZOLA

† In teach-out mode.

Memphis Theological Seminary (C)

168 East Parkway S at Union, Memphis TN 38104-4395
County: Shelby FICE Identification: 010529
Unit ID: 220871
Telephone: (901) 458-8232 Carnegie Class: Spec-4-yr-Faith
FAX Number: (901) 452-4051 Calendar System: Semester
URL: www.memphisseminary.edu
Established: 1852 Annual Graduate Tuition & Fees: N/A
Enrollment: 228 Coed
Affiliation or Control: Cumberland Presbyterian IRS Status: 501(c)3
Highest Offering: Doctorate; No Undergraduates
Accreditation: SC, THEOL

01 Interim President .... Dr. Susan PARKER
05 Vice President Academic Affs & Dean .... Dr. Peter GATHJE
10 Vice President of Operations/ CFO .... Mrs. Cassandra F. PRICE-PERRY
108 Assoc Dean Inst Effectiveness .... Dr. Gail ROBINSON
08 Director of Library Services .... Dr. Deborah TAYLOR
32 Exec Director of Student Services .... Dr. Barry L. ANDERSON
06 Dir Acad Rec/Regist & Accreditation .... Dr. Gail D. ROBINSON

Meridian Institute of Surgical Assisting (D)

1507 County Hospital Road, Nashville TN 37218
County: Davidson FICE Identification: 041650
Unit ID: 461324
Telephone: (877) 954-1500 Carnegie Class: Spec 2-yr-Health
FAX Number: (615) 746-6765 Calendar System: Semester
URL: www.meridian-institute.edu
Established: 1999 Annual Undergrad Tuition & Fees: N/A
Enrollment: 576 Coed
Affiliation or Control: Proprietary IRS Status: Proprietary
Highest Offering: Associate Degree
Accreditation: ABHES, SURGA, SURTEC

01 President .... Mr. Dennis STOVER

Mid-America Baptist Theological Seminary (E)

2095 Appling Road, Cordova TN 38016-4911
County: Shelby FICE Identification: 029172
Telephone: (901) 751-8453 Carnegie Class: Not Classified
FAX Number: (901) 751-8454 Calendar System: Semester
URL: www.mabts.edu
Established: 1972 Annual Undergrad Tuition & Fees: N/A
Enrollment: N/A Coed
Affiliation or Control: Independent Non-Profit IRS Status: 501(c)3
Highest Offering: Doctorate
Accreditation: SC

01 President .... Dr. Michael R. SPRADLIN
03 Executive Vice President .... Dr. Bradley THOMPSON
05 Academic Vice President .... Dr. Timothy SEAL
10 Vice Pres for Finance & Operations .... Mr. Randy REDD
30 VP of Institutional Advancement .... Mr. Nathan COLE
12 Director NE Branch .... Dr. Michael HAGGARD
06 Registrar .... Mrs. Rose MINK
08 Director of Library Services .... Mr. Terrence BROWN
07 Director of Admissions .... Dr. Tanner HICKMAN
04 Admin Assistant to the President .... Mrs. Maria WOOTEN
18 Supt of Buildings & Grounds .... Mr. Gene APPLEBURY
40 Manager Bookstore .... Mr. David FOUST

Mid-South Christian College (F)

PO Box 181056, Memphis TN 38181
County: Shelby Identification: 667046
Unit ID: 481225
Telephone: (901) 375-4400 Carnegie Class: Spec-4-yr-Faith
FAX Number: (901) 375-4085 Calendar System: Semester
URL: www.midsouthchristian.edu
Established: 1959 Annual Undergrad Tuition & Fees: $7,902
Enrollment: 19 Coed
Affiliation or Control: Independent Non-Profit IRS Status: 501(c)3
Highest Offering: Baccalaureate
Accreditation: BI

01 President .... Mr. Larry GRIFFIN
05 Academic Dean .... Dr. Robert GRIFFIN
04 Executive Assistant .... Mrs. Jane GIBSON
06 Registrar .... Mr. Keith GRAHAM
08 Head Librarian .... Mrs. Judi HOMAN
10 Business Manager .... Mrs. Renae MASK
37 Director Student Financial Aid .... Mrs. Mary JACKSON

Middle Tennessee School of Anesthesia (G)

PO Box 417, 315 Hospital Drive, Madison TN 37116-6414
County: Davidson FICE Identification: 007783
Unit ID: 220996
Telephone: (615) 868-6503 Carnegie Class: Spec-4-yr-Other Health
FAX Number: (615) 868-9885 Calendar System: Quarter
URL: www.mtsa.edu
Established: 1950 Annual Graduate Tuition & Fees: N/A
Enrollment: 249 Coed
Affiliation or Control: Independent Non-Profit IRS Status: 501(c)3
Highest Offering: Doctorate; No Undergraduates
Accreditation: SC, ANEST

01 President .... Dr. Christopher P. HULIN
05 Dean .... Dr. Mana OVERSTREET
10 VP for Finance & Administration .... Sam L. MINTEN
30 VP for Advancement & Alumni .... James B. CLOSSER
20 Program Administrator .... Dr. Rusty GENTRY
09 Dir of Inst Effectiveness & LR .... Dr. Amy C. GIDEON
07 Coord Admissions/Recruitment .... Pam NIMMO
13 Director Information Technology .... Aaron HASTINGS
37 Director Financial Aid .... Debbie ROSE

Middle Tennessee State University (H)

1301 E Main Street, Murfreesboro TN 37132-0001
County: Rutherford FICE Identification: 003510
Unit ID: 220978
Telephone: (615) 898-2300 Carnegie Class: DU-Mod
FAX Number: N/A Calendar System: Semester
URL: www.mtsu.edu
Established: 1911 Annual Undergrad Tuition & Fees (In-State): $8,858
Enrollment: 21,913 Coed
Affiliation or Control: State IRS Status: 501(c)3
Highest Offering: Doctorate
Accreditation: SC, AAB, AAFCS, ART, CAATE, CACREP, CAEPN, CIDA, DIETD, JOUR, MUS, NAIT, NRPA, NURSE, SW, THEA

02 President .... Dr. Sidney A. MCPHEE
05 University Provost .... Dr. Mark E. BYRNES
10 VP Business & Finance .... Mr. Alan R. THOMAS
111 Vice President Univ Advancement .... Mr. William J. BALES
32 VP Student Affairs .... Dr. Debra K. SELLS
13 VP Info Tech/Chief Info Officer .... Mr. Bruce PETRYSHAK
58 Vice Provost Rsrch/Dean Grad Stds .... Dr. David L. BUTLER
121 Vice Provost for Student Success .... Dr. Richard D. SLUDER
43 Univ Counsel & Asst to the Pres ...... Ms. Heidi M. ZIMMERMAN
04 Exec Assistant to the President .... Ms. Kimberly S. EDGAR
22 Asst to the President for Equity .... Dr. Marian V. WILSON
07 Assoc Vice Prov UG Recruitment .... Dr. Laurie B. WITHEROW
14 Assoc Vice Pres Info Technology .... Mr. Tom WALLACE
21 Assoc Vice Pres Business Office .... Ms. Kathy THURMAN
35 Assoc Vice Pres/Dean Student Life .... Ms. Sarah SUDAK
15 Asst Vice Pres Human Resource Svcs .... Ms. Kathy I. MUSSELMAN
18 Asst Vice Pres Facilities Services .... Mr. Joe WHITEFIELD
11 Asst Vice Pres Admin/Business Svcs ..... Ms. Kimberly WILLIAMS
91 Senior Associate VP for ITD .... Mrs. Lisa C. ROGERS
90 Asst Vice Pres Acad & Instruct Tech .... Ms. Barbara J. DRAUDE
81 Dean Col Basic/Applied Science .... Dr. Robert U. FISCHER, JR.
83 Dean College Behavioral & Hlth Sci .... Dr. Harold D. WHITESIDE
60 Dean College Media & Entertain .... Dr. Ken A. PAULSON
50 Dean College of Business .... Dr. David J. URBAN
53 Dean College of Education .... Dr. Lana C. SEIVERS
49 Dean Col of Liberal Arts .... Dr. Karen K. PETERSEN
51 Assoc Dean University College .... Dr. Phillip PHILLIPS
92 Dean University Honors College .... Dr. John R. VILE
08 Dean University Library .... Dr. Jason MARTIN
09 Asst Vice Provost for IEPR .... Mr. Chris BREWER
36 Dir Career & Development Center .... Mr. Dusty DODDRIDGE
88 Assoc Vice Prov Student Success .... Mr. Vincent L. WINDROW
37 Dir of Financial Aid & Scholarship .... Mr. Stephen F. WHITE
25 Dir Research & Sponsored Programs .... Mr. Jeffry B. PORTER
29 Director Alumni Relations .... Ms. Ginger C. FREEMAN
40 General Manager Bookstore .... Mr. Jeff WHITWELL
24 Manager Center for Educational Med .... Mr. Anthony TATE
38 Director Counseling Services .... Dr. MaryKaye ANDERSON
30 Director Development Office .... Ms. Patricia BRANAM
84 Director Enrollment Technical Sys .... Ms. Teresa W. THOMAS
27 Director News & Media Relations .... Mr. Jimmy W. HART
41 Director of Athletics .... Mr. Chris J. MASSARO
23 Director of Student Health Services .... Mr. Richard L. CHAPMAN
06 Registrars Office .... Ms. Susan FIELDHOUSE
19 Chief of Police/Dir Public Safety .... Mr. Carl S. PEASTER
39 Dir Resident Life/Student Housing ..... Ms. Michelle SAFEWRIGHT
96 Executive Director of Procurement .... Mr. Shirman THOMAS
104 Director Education Abroad .... Ms. Katrine KOVAR

Miller-Motte Technical College (I)

6397 Lee Highway, Suite 100, Chattanooga TN 37421
Telephone: (423) 414-3247 Identification: 770781
Accreditation: ACCSC, SURGT

† Branch campus of Platt College, Tulsa, OK.

Milligan College (J)

2010 Milligan College PO Box 500,
Milligan College TN 37682-4000
County: Carter FICE Identification: 003511
Unit ID: 486901
Telephone: (423) 461-8700 Carnegie Class: Masters/M
FAX Number: (423) 461-8755 Calendar System: Semester
URL: www.milligan.edu
Established: 1866 Annual Undergrad Tuition & Fees: $33,700
Enrollment: 1,171 Coed
Affiliation or Control: Independent Non-Profit IRS Status: 501(c)3
Highest Offering: Doctorate
Accreditation: SC, #ARCPA, CACREP, CAEPN, NURSE, OT, THEOL

01 President .... Dr. William B. GREER
05 Vice Pres Academic Affairs/Dean .... Dr. Garland YOUNG
32 Vice Pres Student Devel & Athletics .... Mr. Mark FOX
111 Vice Pres Institutional Advancement .... Mrs. Rhajon SMITH
84 Vice Pres Enrollment Management .... Dr. Lee HARRISON
10 Vice Pres Business & Finance .... Mrs. Jacqui STEADMAN
06 Registrar .... Mrs. Stacy DAHLMAN
07 Director of Admissions .... Ms. Kristin WRIGHT
08 Director of Library Services .... Mr. Gary DAUGHT
35 Director of Student Activities .... Mr. Jason ONKS

29 Director of Alumni Relations ... Ms. Theresa GARBE
15 Director Personnel Services ... Ms. Robbyn MAYLOTT
09 Director of Institutional Research ... Ms. Brenda BOURN
37 Coordinator of Financial Aid ... Ms. Diane KEASLING
26 Director of Church Relations ... Mr. Kit DOTSON
36 Director Student Placement ... Ms. Beth ANDERSON
18 Service Manager Facilities ... Mr. Ken BROYLES
28 Director Multicultural Engagement ... Ms. Gwen ELLIS
27 Dir of Public Relations/Marketing ... Ms. Chandrea SHELL
19 Director Property & Risk Management ... Mr. Brent NIPPER
44 Director Annual Giving ... Mrs. Theresa GARBE
90 Director of Information Technology ... Mrs. Amanda BRISTOL
04 Admin Assistant to the President ... Ms. Kathy BARNES
30 Director of Development ... Theresa GARBE
38 Director Student Counseling ... Dr. Rebecca SAPP

National College (A)

5760 Stage Road, Bartlett TN 38134
Telephone: (901) 213-1681 Identification: 770783
Accreditation: ABHES

National College (B)

2576 Thousand Oaks Cove, Memphis TN 38118
Telephone: (901) 363-9046 Identification: 770785
Accreditation: ABHES, CAHIIM

National College (C)

1638 Bell Road, Nashville TN 37211
County: Davidson FICE Identification: 004617
Unit ID: 388043
Telephone: (615) 333-3344 Carnegie Class: Assoc/HVT-High Trad
FAX Number: (615) 333-3429 Calendar System: Quarter
URL: www.national-college.edu
Established: 1991 Annual Undergrad Tuition & Fees: $17,361
Enrollment: 207 Coed
Affiliation or Control: Proprietary IRS Status: Proprietary
Highest Offering: Associate Degree
Accreditation: ABHES

01 Director ... Mr. Jerry KAVALIERATOS

North Central Institute (D)

168 Jack Miller Boulevard, Clarksville TN 37042-4810
County: Montgomery FICE Identification: 030791
Unit ID: 418889
Telephone: (931) 431-9700 Carnegie Class: Spec 2-yr-Tech
FAX Number: (931) 431-9771 Calendar System: Semester
URL: www.nci.edu
Established: 1988 Annual Undergrad Tuition & Fees: N/A
Enrollment: 93 Coed
Affiliation or Control: Proprietary IRS Status: Proprietary
Highest Offering: Associate Degree
Accreditation: COE

01 President ... Tamela K. TALIENTO
06 Registrar ... Michelle HARTSON
07 Dean of Admissions ... Dale WOOD
37 Director of Financial Aid ... Michelle HARTSON
13 Director of Information Technology ... Leo JORDAN
10 Comptroller ... Patricia BELL

Nossi College of Art (E)

590 Creative Way, Nashville TN 37115
County: Davidson FICE Identification: 025782
Unit ID: 368452
Telephone: (615) 514-2787 Carnegie Class: Spec-4-yr-Arts
FAX Number: (615) 514-2788 Calendar System: Trimester
URL: www.nossi.edu
Established: 1973 Annual Undergrad Tuition & Fees: $17,800
Enrollment: 253 Coed
Affiliation or Control: Proprietary IRS Status: Proprietary
Highest Offering: Baccalaureate
Accreditation: ACCSC

01 President ... Ms. Nossi VATANDOOST
03 Executive Vice President ... Mr. Cyrus VATANDOOST
05 Vice President for Academic Affairs ... Dr. Byron EDWARDS
07 Admissions Director ... Mrs. Mitzi HATFIELD
06 Registrar ... Mrs. Mindy GILBERT
08 Head Librarian ... Mrs. Kolleen LONGMIRE
26 Chief Public Relations/Marketing ... Mrs. Libby LUFF
10 Business Office Manager ... Mrs. Kristi BINKLEY
32 Chief Student Affairs/Student Life ... Mr. Kendall WHITESIDE
36 Director Student Placement ... Mr. Barry HOWARD

Omega Graduate School (F)

500 Oxford Drive, Dayton TN 37321-6736
County: Rhea FICE Identification: 038403
Unit ID: 461120
Telephone: (423) 775-6596 Carnegie Class: Spec-4-yr-Other
FAX Number: (423) 775-6599 Calendar System: Semester
URL: www.ogs.edu
Established: 1981 Annual Graduate Tuition & Fees: N/A
Enrollment: 90 Coed
Affiliation or Control: Independent Non-Profit IRS Status: 501(c)3
Highest Offering: Doctorate; No Undergraduates
Accreditation: TRACS

01 President ... Dr. Kimberly GEIGER
00 Chancellor ... Dr. David ANDERSON
05 Dean of Faculty ... Dr. Robert ANDREWS
11 Vice President of Administration ... Dr. Paul LAWHORN
07 Director of Admissions & Phys Opers ... Dr. Curtis MCCLANE
108 Director of Assessment ... Dr. Joshua REICHARD
10 Business Officer ... Ms. Sharlene DANIEL
29 Director Alumni Relations ... Dr. Bonnie LIBHART
62 Director of Library Science ... Dr. David WARD
06 Registrar ... Dr. Paul LAWHORN
08 Librarian ... Ms. Sarah LAMBERT
26 Dir Public Relations/Marketing ... Dr. Cathie HUGHES

Pentecostal Theological Seminary (G)

900 Walker Street, NE, Cleveland TN 37311
County: Bradley FICE Identification: 021883
Unit ID: 219842
Telephone: (423) 478-1131 Carnegie Class: Spec-4-yr-Faith
FAX Number: (423) 478-7711 Calendar System: 4/1/4
URL: www.ptseminary.edu
Established: 1975 Annual Graduate Tuition & Fees: N/A
Enrollment: 474 Coed
Affiliation or Control: Church Of God IRS Status: 501(c)3
Highest Offering: Doctorate; No Undergraduates
Accreditation: SC, THEOL

01 President ... Dr. Michael L. BAKER
05 Dean of Faculty/VP for Academics ... Dr. David S. HAN
108 VP for Inst Effect/Accreditation ... Dr. Oliver L. MCMAHAN
10 Director of Finance ... Mr. Caleb PEACOCK
04 Exec Assistant to the President ... Mrs. Teresa GILBERT
06 Director of Acad Records/Registrar ... Ms. Anita F. BLEVINS
15 Director of Human Resources ... Mrs. Joylita W. TERPSTRA
18 Dir of Facilities/Support Services ... Mr. Phillip WOODS
32 Sr Dir of Student Svcs & Cmty Life ... Dr. Welton WRISTON
37 Director of Financial Aid ... Mrs. Robin SLUDER
07 Director of Admissions ... Mr. Lee SEALS
106 Director Online Learning ... Dr. Robert BLACKABY
29 Director of Alumni Relations ... Mrs. Sharon BAKER
13 Director of Information Technology ... Mr. Ken L. SMITH
36 Director Student Placement ... Dr. Daniel D. TOMBERLIN

Remington College (H)

2710 Nonconnah Boulevard, Memphis TN 38132-2110
Telephone: (901) 345-1000 Identification: 666062
Accreditation: ACCSC

† Branch campus of Remington College, Mobile, AL.

Remington College (I)

441 Donelson Pike, Suite 150, Nashville TN 37214-3558
Telephone: (615) 889-5520 Identification: 666307
Accreditation: ACCSC, DH

† Branch campus of Remington College, Mobile, AL.

Rhodes College (J)

2000 North Parkway, Memphis TN 38112-1690
County: Shelby FICE Identification: 003519
Unit ID: 221351
Telephone: (901) 843-3000 Carnegie Class: Bac-A&S
FAX Number: N/A Calendar System: Semester
URL: www.rhodes.edu
Established: 1848 Annual Undergrad Tuition & Fees: $47,890
Enrollment: 2,010 Coed
Affiliation or Control: Presbyterian Church (U.S.A.) IRS Status: 501(c)3
Highest Offering: Master's
Accreditation: SC, MUS

01 President ... Dr. Marjorie HASS
100 Exec Assistant to the President ... Ms. Melody H. RICHEY
05 Provost ... Dr. Milton MORELAND
32 VP for Student Life ... Dr. Russ WIGGINTON
10 VP for Finance & Business Affairs ... Mr. Kyle WEBB
30 Vice President for Development ... Ms. Jennifer G. WADE
84 Vice Pres Enrollment/Communications ... Mr. Carey THOMPSON
88 Vice Pres of Strategic Initiatives ... Dr. Sherry TURNER
13 Chief Information Officer ... Mr. Jose RODRIGUEZ
35 Associate Dean of Students ... Dr. Jamia STOKES
35 Associate Dean of Students ... Dr. Meredith DAVIS
35 Associate Dean of Students ... Dr. Alicia GOLSTON
20 Assoc Dean of Academic Affairs ... Dr. Brian W. SHAFFER
06 Registrar ... Ms. DeAnna ADAMS
37 Director of Financial Aid ... Mr. Michael MORGAN
08 Director of Info Services ... Ms. Darlene D. BROOKS
29 Director of Alumni Relations ... Ms. Tracy PATTERSON
15 Director of Human Resources ... Ms. Claire R. SHAPIRO
14 Director of Info Services ... Mr. Richard TRENTHEM
19 Director of Campus Safety ... Mr. Ike SLOAS
41 Director of Athletics ... Mr. Matt DEAN
36 Director of Career Services ... Ms. Sandra G. TRACY
38 Director of Counseling Services ... Ms. Pam DETRIE
18 Director of Physical Plant ... Mr. Brian E. FOSHEE
88 Director of Athletic Giving ... Mr. Jim DUNCAN
26 Chief of Communications ... Mr. Matt GERIEN
09 Director of Inst Effectiveness ... Ms. Dawn CLEMENT
07 Director of Admission ... Mr. Jeffery NORRIS

108 Director of Assessment ... Mr. Brian BRASKICH
31 Director of Community Relations ... Ms. Kerri CAMPBELL
44 Director of Annual Giving ... Ms. Kerry CONNORS
110 Senior Director of Development ... Ms. Amanda TAMBURRINO
112 Director of Golden Lynx Program ... Dr. Nichole SOULE
21 Senior Associate Comptroller ... Ms. Wanda JONES
25 Director of Grants ... Ms. Shantih SMYTHE

Richmont Graduate University (K)

1815 McCallie Avenue, Chattanooga TN 37404
County: Hamilton FICE Identification: 033554
Unit ID: 441104
Telephone: (423) 266-4574 Carnegie Class: Spec-4-yr-Other Health
FAX Number: (423) 265-7375 Calendar System: Semester
URL: www.richmont.edu
Established: 1933 Annual Graduate Tuition & Fees: N/A
Enrollment: 254 Coed
Affiliation or Control: Independent Non-Profit IRS Status: 501(c)3
Highest Offering: Master's; No Undergraduates
Accreditation: SC, CACREP

01 President ... Dr. Timothy QUINNAN
05 Dean School of Counseling ... Dr. Stephen BRADSHAW
10 VP of Finance ... Mr. Tim MCPHERSON
13 VP of Information Technology ... Mr. Darwin BLANDON
84 VP of Enrollment Management ... Ms. Roxanne SHELLABARGER
88 VP of Integration ... Dr. Dan SARTOR
32 Dean of Students ... Dr. Amanda BLACKBURN
73 Dean School of Ministry ... Dr. Josh RICE
88 Dean of Clinical Affairs ... Dr. Vanessa SNYDER
100 Chief of Staff ... Mr. Philip BURNS
08 Director of Libraries ... Mr. Ron BUNGER
09 Director of Institutional Research ... Dr. Mary PLISCO
108 Dean of Assessment/Planning/Accred ... Dr. Sonja SUTHERLAND
18 Facilities Manager ... Mr. Neil ANDERSON
26 Director of Communications ... Mr. Scottie BLACKBURN
29 Director Alumni Relations ... Ms. Martha BUSBY
30 Director of Development ... Ms. Amy ESTES
37 Director of Financial Aid ... Mr. Morris LUTES
07 Director of Admissions ... Mr. Tyson FANT

SAE Institute Nashville (L)

7 Music Circle North, Nashville TN 37203
County: Davidson FICE Identification: 038303
Unit ID: 446525
Telephone: (615) 244-5848 Carnegie Class: Spec 2-yr-Tech
FAX Number: (615) 244-3192 Calendar System: Semester
URL: nashville.sae.edu
Established: 1976 Annual Undergrad Tuition & Fees: $31,415
Enrollment: 192 Coed
Affiliation or Control: Proprietary IRS Status: Proprietary
Highest Offering: Associate Degree
Accreditation: ACCSC

01 Director of Education ... Mr. Ty LANDERS

Sewanee: The University of the South (M)

735 University Avenue, Sewanee TN 37383-1000
County: Franklin FICE Identification: 003534
Unit ID: 221519
Telephone: (931) 598-1000 Carnegie Class: Bac-A&S
FAX Number: (931) 598-1145 Calendar System: Semester
URL: www.sewanee.edu
Established: 1857 Annual Undergrad Tuition & Fees: $45,120
Enrollment: 1,778 Coed
Affiliation or Control: Protestant Episcopal IRS Status: 501(c)3
Highest Offering: Doctorate
Accreditation: SC, THEOL

01 Vice Chancellor & President ... Dr. John M. MCCARDELL, JR.
05 Provost ... Dr. Nancy BERNER
111 Vice President for Univ Relations ... Mr. Jay FISHER
88 Special Assistant to the VC ... Mr. Frank GLADU
117 Vice President Risk Management ... Mr. Eric HARTMAN
13 Assoc Provost Info Tech/Librarian ... Dr. Vicki G. SELLS
49 VP/Dean College of Arts & Sciences ... Dr. Terry L. PAPILLON
73 VP/Dean of the School of Theology .. Rt Rev. J. Neil ALEXANDER
32 VP/Dean of Students ... Mr. Marichal GENTRY
09 Asst Prov Academic Svcs/Inst Rsrch ... Dr. Paul G. WILEY
07 Dean of Admission & Financial Aid . Ms. Lee Ann M. BACKLUND
37 Assoc Dean Student Financial Aid ... Ms. Beth CRAGAR
20 Associate Dean for Academic Affairs ... Dr. Alex M. BRUCE
26 Assoc VP Marketing/Communications ... Mr. Parker OLIVER
15 Director of Human Resources ... Ms. Mary WILSON
41 Director of Athletics ... Mr. Mark F. WEBB
29 Director of Alumni Relations ... Ms. Susan S. ASKEW
36 Director of Career Services ... Ms. Kim D. HEITZENRATER
38 Director of Wellness Center ... Dr. Nicole NOFFSINGER-FRAZIER
93 Dir of Multicultural Student Affs ... Mr. Eric V. BENJAMIN
18 AVP Facilities Planning/Operations ... Mr. Austin OAKES
43 University Legal Counsel ... Ms. Lucy A. SINGER
19 Chief of Police ... Ms. Marie FERGUSON
10 VP for Finance and Treasurer ... Dr. Douglass WILLIAMS
23 Director of Univ Health Services ... Ms. Karen THARP
24 Director of Media Services ... Mr. Michael OSTROWSKI
42 University Chaplain & Dean ... VRev. Thomas E. MACFIE, JR.
28 Assoc Dean Faculty Dev & Inclusion ... Dr. Betsy SANDLIN

104 Assoc Dean of Global Education ....Dr. Scott WILSON
04 Admin Assistant to the President ....Ms. Rene WORLEY
39 Dir Resident Life/Student Housing ....Ms. Kate REED
44 Director Sewanee Fund ....Ms. Whitney FRANKLIN

South College (A)

3904 Lonas Drive, Knoxville TN 37909-3323
County: Knox FICE Identification: 004938
Unit ID: 220552
Telephone: (865) 251-1800 Carnegie Class: Spec-4-yr-Other Health
FAX Number: (865) 584-7335 Calendar System: Quarter
URL: www.south.edu
Established: 1882 Annual Undergrad Tuition & Fees: $16,575
Enrollment: 2,146 Coed
Affiliation or Control: Proprietary IRS Status: Proprietary
Highest Offering: Doctorate
Accreditation: SC, ARCPA, DMS, MAC, NMT, NURSE, OTA, PHAR, PTA, PTAA, RAD

01 Chancellor ....Mr. Stephen A. SOUTH
111 Vice Chancellor Inst Adv & Effect ....Dr. Kim B. HALL
10 Chief Financial Officer ....Mr. Brad ADAMS
05 Chief Academic Officer ....Mr. Jeremy WELLS
84 Vice Chancellor Online Op ....Mr. Steven READ
12 Campus President Atlanta ....Mr. Joshua HUFFAKER
12 Campus President Nashville ....Mr. Nick SOUTH
12 Campus President Asheville ....Dr. Lisa SATTERFIELD
15 VP Talent Mgmt & HR ....Mr. Randall CARR
37 VP Financial Aid ....Dr. Carol COLVIN
26 VP Marketing ....Ms. Suzanne GAMBLE
11 Director of Administrative Support ....Mr. Ron HALL
84 VP Enrollment Management ....Ms. Carrie MAJOR
20 VP Student Success/Acad Dean Lonas ....Dr. A.J CHASE
37 Sr Director of Financial Aid ....Mr. Larry BROADWATER
13 Director Instructional Technology ....Dr. Stephen JAMES
08 Head Librarian ....Ms. Anya MCKINNEY
06 Inst Registrar ....Ms. Kristi MORGAN
36 Career Services Coordinator ....Mr. Gary TAYLOR

Southern Adventist University (B)

Box 370, 5010 University Drive,
Collegedale TN 37315-0370
County: Hamilton FICE Identification: 003518
Unit ID: 221661
Telephone: (423) 236-2000 Carnegie Class: Masters/M
FAX Number: (423) 236-1777 Calendar System: Semester
URL: www.southern.edu
Established: 1892 Annual Undergrad Tuition & Fees: $21,950
Enrollment: 3,035 Coed
Affiliation or Control: Seventh-day Adventist IRS Status: 501(c)3
Highest Offering: Doctorate
Accreditation: SC, ADNUR, CACREP, CAEP, IACBE, MUS, NUR, @PTAA, SW

01 President ....Dr. David C. SMITH
05 Sr Vice Pres Academic Admin ....Dr. Robert YOUNG
10 Sr Vice Pres Financial Admin ....Mr. Tom VERRILL
32 Vice Pres Student Development ....Mr. Dennis NEGRÓN
111 Vice Pres Advancement ....Mrs. Carolyn HAMILTON
84 Vice Pres Enrollment Management ....Mr. Glenn CARTER
26 Vice Pres Marketing/University Rels ....Ms. Ingrid SKANTZ
20 Assoc VP Academic Admin ....Dr. Dionne FELIX
21 Assoc VP Financial Admin ....Mr. Marty HAMILTON
13 Assoc VP Information Systems ....Mr. Gary SEWELL
15 Assoc VP Human Resources ....Mrs. Brenda FLORES-LOPEZ
96 Assoc VP of Retail/Auxiliary Ops ....Mr. Russell ORRISON
39 Dean of Students/Dir Residence Life ....Dr. Lisa HALL
50 Dean School of Business/Mgmt ....Dr. Stephanie SHEEHAN
53 Dean School of Education/Psych ....Dr. Tammie OVERSTREET
57 Dean School of Visual Art/Design ....Mr. Randy CRAVEN
60 Dean School of Journalism/Comm ....Dr. Rachel WILLIAMS-SMITH
64 Dean School of Music ....Dr. Peter COOPER
66 Dean School of Nursing ....Dr. Holly GADD
68 Dean Sch of Phys Ed/Health/Wellness ....Dr. Robert BENGE
73 Dean School of Religion ....Dr. Greg KING
77 Dean School of Computing ....Dr. Rick HALTERMAN
70 Dean Social Work/Family Studies ....Dr. Kristie WILDER
72 Chair Technology ....Mr. Dale WALTERS
88 Chair Phys Therapist Asst Program ....Dr. Chris STEWART
81 Chair Mathematics ....Dr. Kevin BROWN
76 Chair Biology/Allied Health ....Dr. Keith SNYDER
88 Chair Chemistry ....Dr. Brent HAMSTRA
88 Chair English ....Dr. Keely TARY
88 Chair History & Political Studies ....Dr. Lisa DILLER
88 Chair Physics/Engineering ....Dr. Ken CAVINESS
18 Director Plant Services ....Mr. Eric SCHOONARD
35 Director Student Life/Activities ....Ms. Kari SHULTZ
37 Director Student Finance ....Mrs. Paula WALTERS
09 Director Inst Research/Planning ....Dr. Chris HANSEN
45 Director Strategic Initiatives ....Mrs. Barb EDENS
07 Director of Admissions ....Mr. Rick ANDERSON
08 Director of Libraries ....Mrs. Deyse BRAVO
06 Director Records & Advisement ....Mrs. Joni I. ZIER
29 Director Alumni Relations ....Ms. Evonne CROOK
38 Director Student Success Center ....Dr. Jim WAMPLER
04 Administrative Asst to President ....Mrs. Joylynn SCOTT

Southern College of Optometry (C)

1245 Madison Avenue, Memphis TN 38104-2222
County: Shelby FICE Identification: 003517
Unit ID: 221670
Telephone: (901) 722-3200 Carnegie Class: Spec-4-yr-Other Health
FAX Number: (901) 722-3279 Calendar System: Trimester
URL: www.sco.edu
Established: 1932 Annual Graduate Tuition & Fees: N/A
Enrollment: 534 Coed
Affiliation or Control: Independent Non-Profit IRS Status: 501(c)3
Highest Offering: Doctorate; No Undergraduates
Accreditation: SC, OPT, OPTR

01 President ....Dr. Lewis REICH
04 Executive Admin Assistant to Pres ....Ms. Sandra S. STEPHENS
05 VP for Academic Affairs ....Dr. John B. CAMPBELL
111 Vice President for Inst Advancement ....Vacant
102 Int Dir of Corp/Foundation Rels ....Ms. Kate BUCKO
10 Vice President for Finance & Admin ....Mr. David L. WEST
13 Exec Dir of Information Services ....Mr. Dean SWICK
18 Physical Plant Manager ....Mr. Trey ADAMS
17 Vice Pres for Clinical Programs ....Dr. James E. VENABLE
23 Director of Clinic Operations ....Mr. Gary SNUFFIN
84 Vice President for Student Services ....Mr. Joseph H. HAUSER
123 Dir of Admissions/Enrollment Svcs ....Mr. Michael N. ROBERTSON
88 Director of Student Recruitment ....Ms. Sunnie EWING
08 Director of Library ....Ms. Leslie HOLLAND
26 Dir of Strategic Communication/Mktg ....Mr. Jim HOLLIFIELD
15 Executive Director Human Resources ....Ms. Tracy LINDOW
37 Director of Financial Aid ....Ms. Cindy GARNER
09 Director of Institutional Research ....Dr. Michael CHRISTENSEN
108 Director Institutional Assessment ....Ms. Pamela MOSS
19 Manager of Security/Safety ....Mr. Don HENSON
101 Secretary to the Institution/Board ....Ms. Sandra STEPHENS
29 Director of Alumni & Spec Events ....Ms. Beth FISHER
30 Senior Dir of Development ....Ms. Cecily FREEMAN
20 Dir of Academic Programs ....Dr. Lindsay ELKINS
21 Controller ....Ms. Carolyn WARREN
36 Director of Hayes Center ....Dr. Lisa WADE
121 Dir of Academic Support Services ....Dr. Carrie LEBOWITZ

*Tennessee Board of Regents Office (D)

1 Bridgestone Park, Nashville TN 37214
County: Davidson FICE Identification: 029031
Unit ID: 409379
Telephone: (615) 366-4400 Carnegie Class: N/A
FAX Number: (615) 366-3922
URL: www.tbr.edu

01 Chancellor ....Dr. Flora TYDINGS
05 Vice Chancellor Academic Affairs ....Mr. Randy SCHULTE
03 Executive Vice Chancellor ....Mr. James KING
10 Vice Chanc Business & Finance ....Mr. Danny GIBBS
11 Vice Chanc Admin & Fac Mgmt ....Mr. David B. GREGORY
12 EVC TN Colleges of Applied Tech ....Mr. James KING
13 Chief Information Officer ....Mr. Stephen VIEIRA
103 Vice Chanc for Economic/Cmty Devel ....Ms. Carol PURYEAR
43 General Counsel ....Ms. Mary MOODY
09 Asst Vice Chanc Research/Assessment ....Mr. Chris TINGLE
32 Assoc Vice Chanc Student Success ....Ms. Heidi LEMING
15 Asst Vice Chanc for Human Resources ....Ms. April PRESTON
21 Asst Vice Chanc Business/Finance ....Ms. Renee STEWART
26 Communications Director ....Mr. Rick LOCKER

*Chattanooga State Community College (E)

4501 Amnicola Highway, Chattanooga TN 37406-1097
County: Hamilton FICE Identification: 003998
Unit ID: 219824
Telephone: (423) 697-4400 Carnegie Class: Assoc/MT-VT-High Trad
FAX Number: N/A Calendar System: Semester
URL: www.chattanoogastate.edu
Established: 1965 Annual Undergrad Tuition & Fees (In-State): $4,063
Enrollment: 8,152 Coed
Affiliation or Control: State IRS Status: 501(c)3
Highest Offering: Associate Degree
Accreditation: SC, ACBSP, ADNUR, CAHIIM, COARC, DA, DH, DMS, EMT, MAC, NMT, PTAA, RAD, RTT, SURGT

02 President ....Dr. Rebecca ASHFORD
05 Interim Vice Pres Academic Affairs ....Dr. Roy SOFIELD
10 Exec Vice Pres Business & Finance ....Ms. Tammy SWENSON
32 Vice President Student Affairs ....Ms. Debbie ADAMS
72 Exec VP Technical College ....Dr. James BARROTT
13 Vice Pres Information Technology ....Dr. Gardner LONG
111 Vice President College Adv & PR ....Ms. Nancy PATTERSON
21 Asst Vice Pres Business & Finance ....Ms. Susan JOSEPH
35 Asst Vice Pres Student Affairs ....Mr. Brad MCCORMICK
45 Exec Director Inst Eff/Rsrch/Plng ....Dr. Traci WILLIAMS
18 Executive Director Plant Operations ....Mr. Guy DAVIS
20 Asst VP Academic Resources ....Ms. Judy LOWE
09 Director Institutional Research ....Ms. Bonnie RIGGS
26 Director Marketing ....Ms. Patty BROWN
37 Director Student Financial Aid ....Mr. Reed ALLISON
07 Director of Admissions ....Ms. Gail CAMPBELL
28 Director Multicultural Services ....Ms. Mary KNAFF
41 Athletic Director ....Ms. Tammy SWENSON
88 Dean Acad Assessment/Accred/Compl ....Mr. John HAWORTH
08 Dean Library Services ....Ms. Susan JENNINGS
76 Dean Allied Health & Nursing ....Dr. Mark KNUTSEN
79 Dean Humanities & Fine Arts ....Mr. Darrin HASSEVOORT
83 Assc VP Acad Aff/Dean Soc/Behav Sci ....Dr. Mosunmola GEORGE-TAYLOR

81 Interim Dean Math & Sciences ....Dr. Karen EASTMAN
50 Dean Business ....Mr. Barry JENNISON
35 Dean Student Engag/Support Svcs ....Ms. Sandy RUTTER
75 Dean Technical College ....Dr. Mike RICKETTS
54 Dean Engineering & Info Technology ....Dr. Tremaine POWELL
84 Dir Welcome Center/Recruiting ....Ms. Kisha CALDWELL
06 Director of Records ....Vacant
15 Exec Dir HR/Affirm Action/Title I ....Mr. Brian EVANS
103 Director Economic & Workforce Dev ....Mr. Bo DRAKE
19 Interim Chief Security/Safety ....Mr. Donald COLEMAN
36 Director Student Placement ....Ms. Stephanie HOLLIS
124 Dir Educ Outreach Program/Retention ....Ms. Michelle OLSON-KILGORE
110 Director College Advancement ....Ms. Tamberly SAWYERS
96 Director of Purchasing ....Ms. Kristie FARRIS

*Cleveland State Community College (F)

PO Box 3570, Cleveland TN 37320-3570
County: Bradley FICE Identification: 003999
Unit ID: 219879
Telephone: (423) 472-7141 Carnegie Class: Assoc/HT-Mix Trad/Non
FAX Number: (423) 478-6255 Calendar System: Semester
URL: www.clevelandstatecc.edu
Established: 1967 Annual Undergrad Tuition & Fees (In-State): $4,235
Enrollment: 3,005 Coed
Affiliation or Control: State IRS Status: 501(c)3
Highest Offering: Associate Degree
Accreditation: SC, ACBSP, ADNUR, EMT, MAC, NAIT

02 President ....Dr. William SEYMOUR
05 Vice President for Academic Affairs ....Dr. Denise KING
32 Vice President for Student Services ....Dr. Michael STOKES
10 VP Finance & Operations ....Mrs. Alisha FOX
09 Director of Institutional Research ....Mr. David KNOPP
37 Director of Financial Aid ....Mrs. Jamie HAMBY
26 Director of Marketing ....Vacant
06 Registrar ....Mrs. Gail GREENWOOD
15 Director of Human Resources ....Mrs. Joan BATES
08 Director of the Library ....Ms. Maud MUNDAVA
13 Director of Information Technology ....Mr. Chris MOWERY
19 Chief of Campus Police ....Mrs. Jennifer BLEDSOE
50 Dean of Business & Healthcare ....Ms. Susan WEBB-CURTIS
66 Director of Nursing ....Mrs. Nancy THOMAS
79 Dean of Arts/Hum/Social Sci/Ed ....Dr. Barsha PICKELL
81 Dean of STEM & Advanced Technology ....Mrs. Karen WYRICK
38 Dir Student Development/ACCESS Ctr ....Mr. Mark WILSON
103 Dir Workforce Development ....Vacant
07 Director of Admissions ....Ms. Suzanne BAYNE
41 Athletic Director ....Mr. Mike POLICASTRO

*Columbia State Community College (G)

1665 Hampshire Pike, Columbia TN 38401-5653
County: Maury FICE Identification: 003483
Unit ID: 219888
Telephone: (931) 540-2722 Carnegie Class: Assoc/HT-High Trad
FAX Number: (931) 540-2535 Calendar System: Semester
URL: www.columbiastate.edu
Established: 1966 Annual Undergrad Tuition & Fees (In-State): $4,269
Enrollment: 5,938 Coed
Affiliation or Control: State IRS Status: 501(c)3
Highest Offering: Associate Degree
Accreditation: SC, ACBSP, ADNUR, COARC, EMT, MLTAD, NAIT, RAD

02 President ....Dr. Janet F. SMITH
05 VP for Academic Affairs ....Dr. Mary Lou D'ALLEGRO
10 VP for Finance & Administration ....Ms. Elaine CURTIS
111 VP for Advancement ....Ms. Bethany LAY
20 Assoc VP Faculty/Curric & Programs ....Ms. Joni L. LENIG
32 VP for Student Affairs ....Ms. Ruth Ann HOLT
13 Assoc VP for Info Technology ....Dr. Emily SICIENSKY
21 Assoc VP for Business Services ....Mr. Keith ISBELL
26 Director of Communications ....Ms. Amy SPEARS-BOYD
28 Asst to Pres for Access & Diversity ....Dr. Christa S. MARTIN
06 Director Records ....Ms. Sharon G. BOWEN
15 Director Human Resources ....Ms. Christie MILLER
08 Director Library ....Mr. Aaron WIMER
45 Assoc VP for Plng/Effect & Reten ....Ms. Tammy BORREN
37 Director of Financial Aid ....Vacant
41 Director Athletics ....Mr. Johnny LITTRELL
18 Director Facility Services & Safety ....Mr. Tim HALLMARK
12 VP for Williamson Campus & Ext Svcs ....Dr. Dearl LAMPLEY
96 Coordinator Purchasing ....Mr. Jon ARNOLD
84 Chief Enrollment Svcs Officer ....Ms. Jill RILEY
103 Dir Workforce/Career Development ....Ms. LK BROWNING
104 Director Study Abroad ....Mr. Wes DULANEY
106 Dir Academic Engagement/Innovation ....Ms. Marla CARTWRIGHT
108 Director Institutional Assessment ....Mr. Harry DJUNAIDI
19 Director Security/Safety ....Mr. Randy CARROLL
04 Admin Assistant to the President ....Ms. Betty YATES
07 Director of Admissions ....Ms. Jill RILEY
25 Chief Contract/Grants Administrator ....Mr. Brett SEYBERT
29 Director Alumni Affairs ....Ms. Molly COCHRAN
44 Director Annual Giving ....Mr. Chris HENSON
91 Director Administrative Computing ....Dr. Emily SICIENSKY

*Dyersburg State Community College (A)

1510 Lake Road, Dyersburg TN 38024-2450
County: Dyer FICE Identification: 006835
Unit ID: 220057
Telephone: (731) 286-3200 Carnegie Class: Assoc/HT-Mix Trad/Non
FAX Number: (731) 286-3333 Calendar System: Semester
URL: www.dscc.edu
Established: 1967 Annual Undergrad Tuition & Fees (In-State): $4,235
Enrollment: 2,843 Coed
Affiliation or Control: State IRS Status: 501(c)3
Highest Offering: Associate Degree
Accreditation: SC, ACBSP, ADNUR, CAHIIM, EMT

02 President ....Dr. Karen A. BOWYER
05 Vice President for the College ....Vacant
10 Vice President Finance/Admin Svcs ....Dr. Charlene WHITE
111 VP Inst Advancement/Cont Education ....Vacant
13 Vice President of Technology ....Mr. Josh DUGGIN
32 Dean of Student Services ....Ms. Larenda FULTZ
08 Dean of Learning Resources Center ....Ms. Susan CHARLEY
37 Director of Financial Aid ....Mrs. Kacee HARDY
09 Director of Institutional Research ....Ms. Mary RICKS
15 Director of Human Resources ....Ms. Sheila GILLAHAN
103 Exec Director of Workforce Services ....Ms. Connie STEWART
29 Director of Alumni Relations ....Ms. Amy FINCH
121 Academic/Career Counselor ....Ms. Sherry BAKER
41 Director of Athletics ....Vacant
18 Director of Physical Plant ....Mr. Kent JETTON
07 Director of Admissions & Records ....Ms. Heather GANN
26 Director of Public Information ....Ms. Amy FINCH
96 Director of Administrative Services ....Ms. Beth MULLINS
21 Business & Student Fin Svcs Manager ....Ms. Donna MEALER
49 Dean of Arts & Sciences ....Mr. James BARHAM
72 Dean of Business/Tech/Allied Health ....Ms. Julie FRAZIER
66 Dean of Nursing ....Ms. Amy JOHNSON
04 Administrative Asst to President ....Ms. Edith CARLTON

*Jackson State Community College (B)

2046 North Parkway, Jackson TN 38301-3797
County: Madison FICE Identification: 004937
Unit ID: 220400
Telephone: (731) 424-3520 Carnegie Class: Assoc/HT-Mix Trad/Non
FAX Number: (731) 425-2647 Calendar System: Semester
URL: www.jscc.edu
Established: 1965 Annual Undergrad Tuition & Fees (In-State): $4,221
Enrollment: 4,746 Coed
Affiliation or Control: State IRS Status: 501(c)3
Highest Offering: Associate Degree
Accreditation: SC, ACBSP, ADNUR, #COARC, EMT, MLTAD, NAIT, OTA, PTAA, RAD

02 President ....Dr. Allana HAMILTON
05 VP of Academic Affairs ....Dr. Larry BAILEY
10 Vice Pres of Finance & Admin Affs ....Mr. Tim DELLINGER
30 Director of Development ....Ms. Lindsey TRITT
32 VP of Student Services ....Mr. Brian GANN
111 VP of Institutional Advancement ....Mr. Bobby SMITH
116 Internal Auditor ....Ms. Chrystal PITTMAN
15 Dir Human Resources/Affirm Action ....Ms. Amy WEST
09 Dir Inst Research & Accountability ....Mrs. Sara VONDERHEIDE
13 Director of Information Technology ....Ms. Dana NAILS
21 Director of Business Services ....Mr. Adina KERFOOT
18 Director of Physical Plant ....Mr. Preston TURNER
96 Director of Purchasing ....Mr. Robert D. HEMRICK
12 Director Lexington Campus ....Ms. Sandy STANFILL
12 Director Savannah Campus ....Mrs. Meda FALLS
12 Director Humboldt Campus ....Ms. Lisa ROJAS
26 Director of PR and Marketing ....Mr. John MCCOMMON
37 Director Student Financial Aid ....Mr. John BRANDT
07 Director of Admissions and Records ....Ms. Robin MAREK
08 Head Librarian ....Mr. Scott COHEN
19 Director Security/Safety ....Mr. Shane YOUNG
41 Athletic Director ....Mr. Steve CORNELISON
04 Admin Assistant to the President ....Ms. Heather FREEMAN
22 Dir Affirmative Action/Equal Opp ....Ms. Amy WEST

*Motlow State Community College (C)

PO Box 8500, Lynchburg TN 37352-8500
County: Moore FICE Identification: 006836
Unit ID: 221096
Telephone: (931) 393-1500 Carnegie Class: Assoc/HT-High Trad
FAX Number: (931) 393-1681 Calendar System: Semester
URL: www.mscc.edu
Established: 1969 Annual Undergrad Tuition & Fees (In-State): $4,241
Enrollment: 6,594 Coed
Affiliation or Control: State IRS Status: 501(c)3
Highest Offering: Associate Degree
Accreditation: SC, ACBSP, ADNUR, EMT, NAIT

02 President ....Dr. Michael TORRENCE
05 Executive VP for Academic Affairs ....Dr. Jeffrey HORNER
10 Vice Pres for Finance & Admin ....Ms. Hilda TUNSTILL
26 VP External Affairs ....Ms. Terri BRYSON
13 Chief Information Officer ....Ms. Cynthia LOGAN
32 Asst VP for Student Affairs ....Dr. Mika'il PETIN
72 Dean Career & Tech Programs ....Mr. Fred RASCOE
35 Interim Dean of Students ....Ms. Debra SMITH
76 Dean Allied Health ....Ms. Pat HENDRIX
12 Dean of McMinnville Campus ....Ms. Misty MAZZIE
12 Dean of Moore County Campus ....Mr. Sidney HILL
12 Asst Dean Fayetteville Campus ....Ms. Lisa SMITH
12 Dean of Smyrna Campus ....Dr. Gregory KILLOUGH
18 Director of Facilities ....Mr. Brian GAFFORD
88 Exec Dir of Community Relations ....Ms. Brenda CANNON
08 Director of Libraries ....Mr. Chris BRYANT
102 Exec Dir of the Foundation ....Ms. Lane YODER
37 Exec Dir of Financial Aid ....Mr. Joe MYERS, JR.
38 Director of Disability & Testing ....Ms. Belinda CHAMPION
07 Director of Admissions & Records ....Ms. Mae SANDERS
19 Director of Public Safety ....Mr. Ray HIGGINBOTHAM
41 Dean of Athletics ....Dr. John CHANDLER
91 Director Admin Computing ....Ms. Rexann BUMPUS
84 Director of Recruitment ....Vacant
15 Exec Dir of Human Resources ....Ms. Laura JENT
21 Director of Fiscal Services ....Ms. Sandy SCHAFFER
121 Director of Student Success ....Mr. Sidney MCPHEE
04 Executive Administrator ....Ms. Shelley SMITH
88 Director of Adult Initiatives ....Ms. Allison BARTON
27 Dir of Communications & Media Rels ....Vacant
90 Dean of Academic Technology ....Mr. Terry DURHAM
66 Director of Nursing ....Ms. Amy HOLDER
14 Director of Tech Operations ....Mr. Jeffery SHORT
88 Director of TN Promise ....Mr. Jonathan GRAHAM
09 Dir of Inst Effect & Assessment ....Ms. Amanda BOWERS
25 Director of Grants ....Ms. Tammy O'DELL

*Nashville State Community College (D)

120 White Bridge Road, Nashville TN 37209-4515
County: Davidson FICE Identification: 008145
Unit ID: 221184
Telephone: (615) 353-3333 Carnegie Class: Assoc/HT-High Trad
FAX Number: (615) 353-3713 Calendar System: Semester
URL: www.nscc.edu
Established: 1969 Annual Undergrad Tuition & Fees (In-State): $4,191
Enrollment: 8,197 Coed
Affiliation or Control: State IRS Status: 501(c)3
Highest Offering: Associate Degree
Accreditation: SC, ACBSP, ACFEI, ADNUR, NAIT, OTA, SURGT

02 President ....Dr. Shanna L. JACKSON
05 Vice Pres of Academic Affairs ....Dr. William T. BROWN
10 Vice Pres Finance & Administration ....Mrs. Mary M. CROSS
103 VP Economic and Community Dev ....Ms. Ginger HAUSSER
45 Assoc VP Planning/Research ....Vacant
30 Exec Dir of Devel/Dir Public Affs ....Mrs. Lauren P. BELL
32 Interim VP Student Affairs & Enroll ....Dr. Carol J. MARTIN-OSORIO
116 Director Internal Auditor ....Mr. Andrew L. MCARTHUR
12 Director Clarksville Campus ....Ms. Kathleen AKERS
06 Director of Records & Registration ....Ms. Melissa PAULEY
84 Interim Chief Enrollment Officer ....Mrs. Laura P. MORAN
13 Director Technology Services ....Mr. Paul A. KAMINSKY
19 Director of Safety and Security ....Mr. Derrek G. SHEUCRAFT
37 Director of Financial Aid ....Ms. Jennifer D. BYRD
15 Director of Human Resources ....Mrs. Sheryl R. GOSSARD
18 Executive Director of Operations ....Mr. Christopher SAUNDERS
26 Director of Creative Services ....Ms. Ellen L. ZINK
106 Director of Online Learning ....Ms. Shelley J. GROSS-GRAY
83 Dean of Social and Life Sciences ....Dr. Julie E. WILLIAMS
81 Dean Science/Tech/Eng/Math (STEM) ....Dr. Sarah E. ROBERTS
79 Dean English/Humanities & Arts ....Dr. Patricia J. ARMSTRONG
62 Dean Lrng Resources & Online Learn ....Dr. Faye M. JONES
50 Dean Business/Mgmt & Hospitality ....Ms. Karen L. STEVENSON
96 Director of Purchasing ....Ms. Jo SMITH
76 Director of Healthcare Professions ....Dr. Cynthia G. WALLER
22 Compliance & Diversity Officer ....Ms. Mia SNEED

*Northeast State Community College (E)

PO Box 246, 2425 Highway 75, Blountville TN 37617-0246
County: Sullivan FICE Identification: 005378
Unit ID: 221908
Telephone: (423) 323-3191 Carnegie Class: Assoc/MT-VT-High Trad
FAX Number: (423) 279-7636 Calendar System: Semester
URL: www.northeaststate.edu
Established: 1965 Annual Undergrad Tuition & Fees (In-State): $4,248
Enrollment: 6,088 Coed
Affiliation or Control: State IRS Status: 501(c)3
Highest Offering: Associate Degree
Accreditation: SC, ACBSP, ADNUR, CVT, DA, EMT, MLTAD, NAIT, SURGT

02 President ....Dr. Bethany FLORA
04 Exec Assistant to the President ....Ms. Hali COX
05 Int Vice Pres Academic Affairs ....Dr. Connie MARSHALL
10 VP Finance & Admin ....Dr. Allen BOTTORFF
32 Vice President Student Success ....Dr. Susan GRAYBEAL
103 VP Economic & Workforce Development ....Dr. Sam ROWELL
56 Asst VP Multi-Campus Programs ....Dr. Pashia HOGAN
111 Chief Advancement Officer ....Vacant
06 Registrar ....Ms. Deidra CLOSE
15 Director Human Resources ....Ms. Megan JONES
31 Director Community Relations ....Mr. Robert CARPENTER
26 Director of Marketing ....Ms. Amanda ADAMS
45 Director Planning & Assessment ....Mr. John GRUBB
08 Dean Library ....Mr. Christopher DEMAS
79 Dean Humanities ....Mr. William WILSON
81 Dean Mathematics ....Ms. Malissa TRENT
76 Dean Health Professions ....Ms. Connie MARSHALL
72 Int Asst Dean Advance Technologies ....Mr. Keith TITTLE
83 Dean Behavior/Social Sciences ....Dr. Xiaoping WANG
81 Dean Science Division ....Dr. Carolyn MCCRACKEN
50 Dean Business Technologies ....Mr. Danny L. LAWSON
66 Director of Nursing ....Dr. Johanna NEUBRANDER
84 Dean of Enrollment Management ....Ms. Jennifer STARLING
88 Veterans Affairs Tech Clerk ....Mr. John ADCOX
09 Institutional Effectiveness Officer ....Ms. Kim GANT
18 Director of Plant Operations ....Mr. Pete MILLER
28 Chief Diversity Officer ....Ms. Linda CALVERT
37 Director of Financial Aid ....Ms. Mary CHAMBLISS
96 Purchasing Coordinator ....Ms. Bernice HAGAMAN

*Pellissippi State Community College (F)

PO Box 22990, Knoxville TN 37933-0990
County: Knox FICE Identification: 012693
Unit ID: 221643
Telephone: (865) 694-6400 Carnegie Class: Assoc/HT-Mix Trad/Non
FAX Number: (865) 539-7240 Calendar System: Semester
URL: www.pstcc.edu
Established: 1974 Annual Undergrad Tuition & Fees (In-State): $4,276
Enrollment: 11,168 Coed
Affiliation or Control: State IRS Status: 501(c)3
Highest Offering: Associate Degree
Accreditation: SC, ACBSP, ACFEI, ADNUR, NAIT

02 President ....Dr. L. Anthony WISE, JR.
125 President Emeritus ....Vacant
05 Interim VP of Academic Affairs ....Ms. Katheryn BYRD
13 Vice President Information Services ....Ms. Audrey J. WILLIAMS
10 Vice President Business & Finance ....Mr. Ronald L. KESTERSON
21 Asst VP Business Services ....Ms. Renee MOORE
102 Exec Director of Foundation ....Ms. Aneisa L. ROLEN
32 Vice President of Student Affairs ....Dr. Rushton JOHNSON, JR.
103 Exec Dir Business/Workforce Dev ....Ms. Teri T. BRAHAMS
12 Campus Dean Blount County Programs ....Ms. Holly L. BURKETT
12 Campus Dean Strawberry Pl Program ....Dr. Mike NORTH
12 Campus Dean Magnolia Ave Programs ..Ms. Rosalyn P. TILLMAN
12 Campus Dean Division Street Program ....Ms. Esther L. DYER
35 Dean of Students ....Mr. Travis C. LOVEDAY
35 Asst VP of Student Services ....Dr. Elizabeth E. FIRESTONE
88 Manager Accounts Payable ....Ms. Debra CLARK
20 Asst VP of Academic Affairs ....Dr. Beth NORTON
84 Asst VP Enrollment Services ....Ms. Leigh A. TOUZEAU
22 Exec Director Equity & Compliance ....Ms. Annazette HOUSTON
35 Dir of Student Life & Recreation ....Vacant
36 Director of Placement ....Ms. Cynthia ATCHLEY
28 Director of Disability Services ....Ms. Ann E. SATKOWIAK
26 Director Marketing & Communications ....Ms. Julia H. WOOD
07 Dir of Admiss & Records/Registrar ....Ms. Melanie M. PARADISE
08 Director of Library Services ....Dr. Mary Ellen SPENCER
24 Dir Educ Technology Svcs ....Ms. Kristy M. CONGER
37 Director of Financial Aid ....Mr. Dick W. SMELSER
108 Dir Inst Effective/Assessment/Plng ....Ms. Nancy A. RAMSEY
88 Asst Director Inst Effectiveness ....Ms. Olga EBERT-HOLBERG
18 Director of Facilities ....Ms. Regina MCNEW
19 Interim Chief of Police ....Mr. Terry M. CROWE, JR.
114 Director Budget & Payroll ....Ms. Nancy DONAHUE
96 Director of Purchasing ....Mr. John S. CLARK
15 Director Human Resources ....Ms. Carole GARY
25 Director Grant Development ....Ms. Danette Johnson HENNEKE
104 Exec Dir TnCIS/International Educ ....Ms. Tracey BRADLEY
112 Director Major Gift Development ....Ms. Marilyn RODDY
44 Dir Annual Giving & Scholarships ....Mr. David L. HARRELL
29 Director Alumni & Donor Engagement ....Vacant
91 Dir Applications Programming Sup ....Mr. James (Dean) COPPLE
88 Dir of Network & Technical Services ....Mr. Larry BATES
28 Director of Access & Diversity ....Ms. Gayle E. WOOD
88 Director of Academic Testing ....Ms. Joan NEWMAN
88 Dir Curriculum & New Programs ....Ms. Judy GOSCH
121 Director of Advising ....Ms. Rachael C. CRAGLE
88 Dir Academic Support Programs ....Ms. Jan T. SHARP
113 Bursar ....Ms. Mandy BENTZ
116 Director of Internal Audit ....Ms. Suzanne WALKER
88 Director of PACE ....Ms. Kellie TOON
89 Director of New Student Orientation ....Ms. Rebecca MILAM
88 Director TRIO Student Support Svcs . Ms. Venetia C. WILLLIAMS
88 Director Veteran Services ....Mr. Trevor A. HARVEY
103 Director of Sales/Bus & Comm Svcs ....Mr. Tim WILSON
88 Dir of Solution Mgmt/Bus & Comm Svc ....Mr. Todd EVANS

*Roane State Community College (G)

276 Patton Lane, Harriman TN 37748-5011
County: Roane FICE Identification: 009914
Unit ID: 221397
Telephone: (865) 354-3000 Carnegie Class: Assoc/HT-High Trad
FAX Number: (865) 882-4585 Calendar System: Semester
URL: www.roanestate.edu
Established: 1971 Annual Undergrad Tuition & Fees (In-State): $4,443
Enrollment: 5,626 Coed
Affiliation or Control: State IRS Status: 501(c)3
Highest Offering: Associate Degree
Accreditation: SC, ACBSP, ADNUR, CAHIIM, COARC, COMTA, DH, EMT, OPD, OTA, POLYT, PTAA, RAD, SURGT

02 President ....Dr. Chris WHALEY
05 Vice Pres for Student Learning/CAO ....Dr. Diane WARD

10 Vice Pres Business & Finance ... Ms. Marsha MATHEWS
103 VP Workforce Development/Athletics ... Ms. Teresa S. DUNCAN
84 VP Enrollment Mgt/Student Services ... Dr. Jamie STRINGER
12 Exec Dir of Oak Ridge & Cmty Rel ... Dr. Owen DRISKILL
32 Dean of Students ... Vacant
108 VP Inst Effectiveness & Planning ... Ms. Karen L. BRUNNER
21 Director of Accounting Services ... Ms. Michelle PATTERSON
17 Dean Health Sciences ... Dr. Patricia JENKINS
13 Interim Computer Info Officer ... Ms. Keri PHILLIPS
09 Director Institutional Research ... Mr. Jeffrey J. TINLEY
22 Coordinator Affirmative Action ... Mr. Odell FEARN
08 Director of Library Services ... Mr. Robert M. BENSON
06 Director of Records & Registration ... Vacant
18 Director Physical Plant & Expo Ctr ... Mr. Stan R. STARKEY
29 Director Alumni Relations ... Mr. Scott K. NIERMANN
96 Director of Purchasing & Contracts ... Ms. Dana WEST
36 Workforce Placement & Job Placement ... Ms. Kim HARRIS
04 Executive Assistant to President ... Vacant
19 Director Safety/Chief of Police ... Mr. William KAIN
88 Special Assistant to President ... Ms. Tamsin MILLER
41 Athletic Director ... Mr. Randy NESBIT
104 Interim Director Study Abroad ... Mr. Charlie COBB
79 Dean Humanities ... Dr. Myra PEAVYHOUSE
83 Dean Social/Behavioral Sciences ... Dr. Donald LANZA
81 Interim Dean Math & Science ... Mr. Bruce CANTRELL
121 Dean of Student Academic Services ... Ms. Kathryn L. RHODES
121 Director of Student Success ... Ms. Kathryn R. BAKER
116 Director of Internal Audit ... Ms. Cynthia CORTESIO
119 Director IT Computing ... Mr. Peter SOUZA
20 Director Curriculum/Program Plng ... Ms. Amy KEELING
118 Manager Employee Benefits ... Ms. Joyce MARSALIS
07 Director of Admissions ... Vacant
102 Executive Director Foundation ... Mr. Scott K. NIERMANN
106 Director Online Education/E-learnin ... Dr. Susan R. SUTTON
15 Director Human Resources ... Mr. Odell FEARN
26 Executive Dir ORBC/Community Rels ... Dr. Owen DRISKILL
37 Director Student Financial Aid ... Ms. Robin TOWNSON
38 Director Student Counseling ... Ms. Tracey WATSON
91 Director Administrative Computing ... Mr. Chris PANKRATZ

*Southwest Tennessee Community College (A)

PO Box 780, Memphis TN 38101-0780

County: Shelby | FICE Identification: 010439 | Unit ID: 221485
Telephone: (901) 333-5000 | Carnegie Class: Assoc/HT-High Trad
FAX Number: (901) 333-4645 | Calendar System: Semester
URL: www.southwest.tn.edu
Established: 2000 | Annual Undergrad Tuition & Fees (In-State): $4,255
Enrollment: 9,099 | Coed
Affiliation or Control: State | IRS Status: 501(c)3
Highest Offering: Associate Degree
Accreditation: SC, ACBSP, ACFEI, ADNUR, EMT, MLTAD, PTAA, RAD

02 President ... Dr. Tracy D. HALL
04 Assistant to the President ... Ms. Aquila PHILLIPS
05 Vice President of Academic Affairs ... Vacant
86 Exec Asst to Pres Govt Rels/Dir Ath ... Mr. Sherman D. GREER
111 Vice Pres Institutional Advancement ... Vacant
10 Vice Pres Finance & Admin Services ... Mr. Michael NEAL
32 Vice Pres Student Affairs ... Mrs. Jacqueline A. FAULKNER
84 Assoc VP of Enrollment Services ... Ms. Shanita L. BROWN
15 Assoc Vice Pres Human Resources ... Ms. Iliana RICELLI
103 Assoc Vice Pres of Workforce Dev ... Ms. Anita BRACKIN
26 Exec Director of Comm & Marketing ... Ms. Daphne THOMAS
13 Exec Dir Information Systems (CIO) ... Mr. Michael D. BOYD
22 Exec Dir Equity and Compliance ... Mrs. Monika L. JOHNSON
06 Registrar ... Ms. Veda TAYLOR
18 Director Physical Plant ... Mr. Jonathan A. WELDON
37 Director of Financial Aid ... Ms. Maureen R. PHILLIPS
09 Institutional Research Analyst ... Mr. Stephan JUMA
19 Director Public Safety ... Mrs. Lezley A. WEBB

*Volunteer State Community College (B)

1480 Nashville Pike, Gallatin TN 37066-3188

County: Sumner | FICE Identification: 009912 | Unit ID: 222053
Telephone: (615) 452-8600 | Carnegie Class: Assoc/HT-High Trad
FAX Number: (615) 230-3577 | Calendar System: Semester
URL: www.volstate.edu
Established: 1970 | Annual Undergrad Tuition & Fees (In-State): $4,522
Enrollment: 8,838 | Coed
Affiliation or Control: State | IRS Status: 501(c)3
Highest Offering: Associate Degree
Accreditation: SC, ACBSP, CAHIIM, COARC, DA, DMS, EMT, MLTAD, POLYT, PTAA, RAD

02 President ... Dr. Jerry FAULKNER
05 Vice President Academic Affairs ... Dr. George PIMENTEL
10 Vice President Business & Finance ... Ms. Beth CARPENTER
32 Vice President Student Services ... Dr. Emily SHORT
30 Vice Pres for Resource Development ... Ms. Karen MITCHELL
45 Vice Pres Inst Planning/Research ... Ms. Colette CATANIA
20 Asst VP of Academic Affairs ... Vacant
21 Asst Vice Pres Business & Finance ... Ms. Renee AUSTIN
51 Asst VP for Economic & Cmty Devel ... Mrs. Hilary B. MARABETI
76 Dean of Health ... Mr. Elvis BRANDON
79 Dean Humanities ... Dr. Tonya DANIELS
53 Dean Social Science/Education ... Mr. James BROWN
81 Dean Math & Science ... Dr. Tom EKMAN
50 Dean of Business ... Dr. Andy WHITE
15 Dir Personnel/Affirm Act/Human Res ... Ms. Lori CUTRELL
08 Director Library Services ... Ms. Sarah SMITH
07 Dir Admissions & College Registrar ... Mr. Tim AMYX
13 Director Information Technology ... Mr. Kevin BLANKENSHIP
37 Director Student Financial Aid ... Ms. Donna H. DUNAWAY
26 Director Public Relations ... Mrs. Tami WALLACE
18 Senior Director Physical Plant ... Mr. William NEWMAN
19 Chief Security & Safety ... Ms. Angela LAWSON
41 Director of Athletics ... Mr. Bobby HUDSON
106 Director Distance Learning ... Ms. Rhonda GREGORY
88 Special Adult Programs/ADA Director ... Ms. Leslie SMITH
09 Director of Institutional Research ... Mrs. Ann Marie CALDERON
96 Director Purchasing ... Vacant
24 Director Media Services ... Vacant
124 Director Retention Support Services ... Ms. Heather HARPER
36 Admin of Work-Based Learning ... Dr. Rick PARRENT
38 Director Counseling & Testing ... Mr. Terry BUBB
28 Manager of Diversity & Inclusion ... Mr. Jeff KING
88 Dir Health Sciences Ctr of Emphasis ... Ms. Terri CRUTCHER
06 Registrar ... Mr. Tim AMYX
04 Executive Administrative Associate ... Ms. Karen WALLER
102 Foundation Development Officer ... Ms. Alison MUNCY
35 Mgr of Student Engagement & Support ... Ms. Heather HARPER

*Walters State Community College (C)

500 S Davy Crockett Parkway, Morristown TN 37813-6899

County: Hamblen | FICE Identification: 008863 | Unit ID: 222062
Telephone: (423) 585-2600 | Carnegie Class: Assoc/HT-High Trad
FAX Number: (423) 585-6853 | Calendar System: Semester
URL: www.ws.edu
Established: 1969 | Annual Undergrad Tuition & Fees (In-State): $4,224
Enrollment: 6,075 | Coed
Affiliation or Control: State | IRS Status: 501(c)3
Highest Offering: Associate Degree
Accreditation: SC, ACBSP, ACFEI, ADNUR, CAHIIM, COARC, EMT, NAIT, OTA, PTAA, SURGT

02 President ... Dr. Anthony R. MIKSA
04 Exec Director to the President ... Ms. Leann LONG
05 Vice President Academic Affairs ... Dr. Donna SEAGLE
10 Vice President Business Affairs ... Dr. Mark HURST
32 Vice President Student Affairs ... Ms. Angi SMITH
111 Asst Vice Pres College Advancement ... Mr. Chris CATES
45 VP for Planning/Research/Assessment . Dr. Debbie L. MCCARTER
20 VP for Educational Outreach ... Dr. John LAPRISE
35 Asst Vice Pres Student Affairs ... Mr. Michael A. CAMPBELL
18 Asst Vice Pres Facilities Mgmt ... Vacant
21 Asst Vice Pres Business Affairs ... Ms. Heather CARRIER
08 Dean of Library ... Dr. Jamie POSEY
31 Dean of Workforce Training ... Dr. Joseph L. COMBS
19 Dean of Public Safety Division ... Vacant
17 Dean Health Programs ... Ms. Marty K. RUCKER
12 Dean Greenville/Greene Co Center ... Mr. Mark WILLS
12 Dean Sevier County Campus ... Dr. Jama SUTTON
83 Dean of Behavioral/Social Sciences ... Mr. Darrel MCGHEE
50 Dean of Business ... Mr. Darrel MCGHEE
79 Dean of Humanities ... Mr. Chippy MCLAIN
81 Dean of Mathematics ... Mr. John C. KNIGHT
49 Interim Dean of Natural Science ... Dr. Matthew SMITH
75 Dean of Technical Education ... Mr. Thomas R. SEWELL
06 Dean Student Info System/Records ... Ms. Linda MASON
103 Dean Ctr for Workforce Development ... Vacant
37 Director of Financial Aid ... Ms. Laura RODRIGUEZ
38 Exec Director Counseling/Testing ... Dr. Andy HALL
15 Exec Director of Human Resources ... Mr. Jarvis JENNINGS
26 Vice President Public Information ... Mr. James B. PECTOL
13 Interim Chief Information Officer ... Mr. Stephen ANNIS
41 Director of Athletics ... Mr. Derek CREECH
07 Director of Admissions ... Ms. Avery SWINSON
19 Chief of Campus Police ... Ms. Sarah ROSE
89 Director Freshmen Studies ... Vacant
36 Director Student Placement ... Dr. Andy HALL
92 Director Honors Program ... Ms. Janice M. DONAHUE
96 Asst Director of Purchasing ... Ms. Renee JARNIGAN
105 Director of Network Services ... Mr. Bill R. MOREFIELD
84 Director Enrollment Development ... Ms. Avery SWINSON
93 Coord Minority Student Recruit ... Ms. Roxanne BOWEN
108 Exec Dir of Planning & Assessment ... Dr. Deanna GARMAN

Tennessee State University (D)

3500 John A Merritt Boulevard, Nashville TN 37209-1561

County: Davidson | FICE Identification: 003522 | Unit ID: 221838
Telephone: (615) 963-5000 | Carnegie Class: DU-Higher
FAX Number: (615) 963-7412 | Calendar System: Semester
URL: www.tnstate.edu
Established: 1912 | Annual Undergrad Tuition & Fees (In-State): $8,792
Enrollment: 8,177 | Coed
Affiliation or Control: State | IRS Status: 501(c)3
Highest Offering: Doctorate
Accreditation: #SC, AAFCS, ADNUR, ART, CAEP, CAHIIM, COARC, COPSY, DH, DIETD, MUS, NAIT, NUR, OT, PH, PTA, SP, SPAA, SW

02 President ... Dr. Glenda GLOVER
05 Int Vice President Academic Affairs ... Dr. Alisa MOSLEY
04 Senior Office Assistant ... Ms. Zanetta GOOCH
10 VP Business & Finance ... Mr. Horace CHASE
11 VP Administrative Affairs ... Ms. Jane JACKSON
32 Vice Pres Student Affairs ... Ms. Tracey FORD
30 VP Institutional Advancement ... Vacant
41 Athletic Director ... Mrs. Teresa LAWRENCE-PHILLIPS
43 University Legal Counsel ... Mr. Laurence PENDLETON
84 Assoc Provost Enrollment Mgmt ... Dr. John CADE
20 Assoc VP Academic Affairs ... Dr. Patricia CROOK
20 AVP Academic Affairs/Extended Educ ... Dr. Evelyn NETTLES
15 Assoc VP/Dir Human Resources ... Ms. Linda C. SPEARS
21 Assoc VP Financial Services ... Mr. Bradley WHITE
37 Asst VP Financial Aid ... Ms. Amy B. WOOD
26 Asst VP Public Rels/Communication ... Ms. Kelli SHARPE
09 Asst VP Inst Effectiveness/Research ... Ms. Eloise ALEXIS
18 Director Facilities/Physical Plant ... Mr. Daniel WOOTEN
28 Dir Equity Diversity & Compliance ... Ms. Tiffa COX
06 Registrar ... Mrs. Thelria HARDAWAY
19 Chief TSU Police Department ... Mr. Richard BRIGGANCE
08 Dean Libraries & Media Centers ... Dr. Murle KENERSON
49 Dean College of Liberal Arts ... Dr. Gloria C. JOHNSON
50 Dean College of Business ... Dr. Millicent LOWNES-JACKSON
53 Int Dean College of Education ... Dr. Heraldo RICHARDS
54 Dean College of Engr/Tech/Comp Sci ... Dr. S. Keith HARGROVE
47 Dn Agriculture/Human & Natural Sci ... Dr. Carter CATLIN
76 Int Dean College of Health Sciences ... Dr. Ronald BARREDO

Tennessee Technological University (E)

1 William L. Jones Drive, Cookeville TN 38505

County: Putnam | FICE Identification: 003523 | Unit ID: 221847
Telephone: (931) 372-3101 | Carnegie Class: DU-Higher
FAX Number: (931) 372-3898 | Calendar System: Semester
URL: www.tntech.edu
Established: 1915 | Annual Undergrad Tuition & Fees (In-State): $8,731
Enrollment: 10,504 | Coed
Affiliation or Control: State | IRS Status: 501(c)3
Highest Offering: Doctorate
Accreditation: SC, AAFCS, ART, CACREP, CAEP, CAEPN, DIETD, MUS, NURSE

02 President ... Dr. Philip B. OLDHAM
05 Provost/Vice President ... Dr. Lori M. BRUCE
10 Vice Pres Planning & Finance ... Dr. Claire STINSON
32 Vice President Student Affairs ... Mr. Marc BURNETT
35 Asst VP Multicultural Affairs ... Mr. Robert OWENS
46 Int VP Research/Econ Development ... Dr. Francis OTUONYE
86 Chief Government Affairs Officer ... Dr. Terry SALTSMAN
88 Assoc VP for Research ... Dr. Francis O. OTUONYE
111 Vice President Univ Advancement ... Dr. Kevin BRASWELL
20 Sr Assoc VP Academic Affairs ... Dr. Mark STEPHENS
20 Assoc Provost/Vice Pres Acad Affs ... Dr. Xiaoming (Sharon) HUO
13 Chief Information Officer ... Ms. Yvette CLARK
37 Director Financial Aid ... Ms. Mary BENEDICT
08 Dean Library & Learning Asst ... Dr. Doug BATES
09 Interim Director Inst Research ... Dr. Mark STEPHENS
45 Director of Strategic Planning ... Mr. Michael AIKENS
15 Assoc VP Human Resources ... Dr. Leslie CRICKENBERGER
19 Director of University Police ... Mr. Tony NELSON
39 Interim Director of Housing ... Mr. Joshua EDMONDS
41 Director of Athletics ... Mr. Mark WILSON
18 Assoc VP Physical Plant ... Mr. Craig SHORT
38 Director Counseling Center ... Ms. Patricia SMITH
23 Director of Health Svcs ... Ms. Leigh A. RAY
36 Director Career Development ... Mr. Russ COUGHENOUR
26 Chief Communication Officer ... Ms. Karen LYKINS
85 Director International Education ... Mr. Charles WILKERSON
06 Registrar ... Ms. Brandi HILL
92 Director Honors Program ... Dr. Rita BARNES
93 Director Multicultural Affairs ... Ms. Charria CAMPBELL
96 Director of Purchasing ... Ms. Judy M. HULL
21 Associate VP Business ... Ms. Emily WHEELER
43 Director University Counsel ... Ms. Kae CARPENTER
29 Dir Alumni Engagement & Annual Giv ... Mr. Brandon BOYD
116 Director of Internal Audit ... Ms. Deanna METTS
22 Dir of AA & Employee Relations ... Ms. Elizabeth GAYS
07 Director of Admissions ... Dr. Stephen KELLER
19 Dir Capital Project Administration ... Mr. James COBB
84 VP of Enrollment Management ... Dr. Brandon JOHNSON
49 Dean of Arts & Sciences ... Dr. Paul SEMMES
54 Dean of Engineering ... Dr. Joseph SLATER
47 Dean Agric & Human Ecology ... Dr. Darron SMITH
50 Dean of Business Admin ... Dr. Thomas PAYNE
53 Dean College of Education ... Dr. Lisa ZAGUMNY
57 Dean of College of Fine Arts ... Dr. Jennifer SHANK
66 Dean School of Nursing ... Dr. Kim HANNA
88 Dean Interdisciplinary Studies ... Dr. Mike GOTCHER
58 Assoc Dean of Graduate Studies ... Dr. Alice CAMUTI
04 Administrative Asst to President ... Ms. Diane SMITH
105 Director Web Services ... Mr. Cody BRYANT
108 Director Institutional Assessment ... Dr. Theresa ENNIS
90 Director Academic Computing ... Mr. Jason HOFFERT
91 Dir Enterprise Application System ... Ms. Lisa MAAS
110 Director of Advancement ... Ms. Michelle ARBOGAST
104 Director Study Abroad ... Ms. Amy MILLER
100 Chief of Staff ... Mr. Lee WRAY

Tennessee Wesleyan University (F)

204 East College St., Athens TN 37303

County: McMinn | FICE Identification: 003525 | Unit ID: 221731
Telephone: (423) 745-7504 | Carnegie Class: Bac-Diverse
FAX Number: (423) 744-9968 | Calendar System: Semester
URL: www.tnwesleyan.edu

Established: 1857 Annual Undergrad Tuition & Fees: $24,300
Enrollment: 951 Coed
Affiliation or Control: United Methodist IRS Status: 501(c)3
Highest Offering: Master's
Accreditation: SC, DH, NURSE, SW

01 President .... Dr. Harley KNOWLES
05 Vice President for Academic Affairs .... Dr. Grant WILLHITE
10 Vice Pres Financial/Business Affs .... Mrs. Gail HARRIS
32 Vice President for Student Life .... Dr. Scott MASHBURN
111 Vice President of Advancement .... Vacant
37 Assoc VP Financial Aid .... Mrs. Lacey WEESE
108 Assoc VP for Inst Effectiveness .... Dr. Stephanie SMALLEN
07 Asst VP of Admissions .... Ms. Ginger MURPHY
04 Executive Assistant to President .... Mrs. Gail ROGERS
08 Dir of Library & Info Svcs .... Ms. Julie ADAMS
06 Registrar .... Mrs. Julie MCCASLIN
41 Athletic Director .... Mr. Donny MAYFIELD
15 Human Resources Director .... Mr. Kyle FULBRIGHT
18 Chief of Facilities/Physical Plant .... Mr. Mike INGRAM
26 Dir of Marketing/Communications .... Ms. Katherine DAVIS
13 Exec Dir of Information Tech/CIO .... Mr. Brandon LAMBDIN

Trevecca Nazarene University (A)

333 Murfreesboro Road, Nashville TN 37210-2877
County: Davidson FICE Identification: 003526
Unit ID: 221892
Telephone: (615) 248-1200 Carnegie Class: DU-Mod
FAX Number: (615) 248-7728 Calendar System: Semester
URL: www.trevecca.edu
Established: 1901 Annual Undergrad Tuition & Fees: $25,598
Enrollment: 3,620 Coed
Affiliation or Control: Church Of The Nazarene IRS Status: 501(c)3
Highest Offering: Doctorate
Accreditation: SC, ARCPA, CACREP, CAEPN, MUS, NURSE, SW

01 President .... Dr. Dan BOONE
04 Assistant to the President .... Ms. Anne TWINING
05 University Provost/Senior VP .... Dr. Tom MIDDENDORF
26 Vice President External Relations .... Mrs. Peggy J. COONING
20 Assoc Vice Pres Academic Programs .... Dr. Jim HIATT
88 Assoc VP Accred/State Authorization .... Dr. Jonathan BARTLING
27 Assoc Vice Pres Marketing & Comm .... Mr. Matthew TOY
32 Assoc Provost/Dean of Student Dev .... Vacant
84 Assoc Provost/Dean of Enroll Mgmt .... Ms. Holly WHITBY
73 Dean School of Theol/Christian Min .... Dr. Timothy M. GREEN
88 Assoc Dean Doctoral Programs .... Dr. Heidi VENTURA
35 Asc Dean Student Community Life .... Mr. Matt SPRAKER
39 Asc Dean Students Residential Life .... Mrs. Ronda LILIENTHAL
53 Dean of the School of Education .... Dr. Suzann HARRIS
49 Dean of School of Arts & Science .... Dr. Lena WELCH
64 Dean School of Music & Worship Arts .... Dr. David DIEHL
13 Chief Information Officer/ITS .... Mr. John EBERLE
06 Registrar .... Ms. Katrina CHAPMAN
19 Director of Security .... Mr. Greg DAWSON
07 Director of Admissions .... Ms. Melinda MILLER
41 Athletic Director .... Mr. Mark ELLIOTT
88 Director Ctr/Ldrshp Calling Service .... Ms. Michelle GAERTNER
38 Director Counseling Services .... Dr. Sara HOPKINS
28 Coord Student Engagement/Diversity .... Mr. Brodrick THOMAS
106 Director Online Learning .... Ms. LaMetrius DANIELS
21 Director of Financial Services .... Mr. Chuck SEAMAN
15 Director Human Resources .... Mr. Steve SEXTON
76 Director Physician Asst Pgm .... Mr. Bret REEVES
18 Director Plant Operations .... Mr. Glen LINTHICUM
29 Director Alumni/Church Engagement .... Mr. Michael JOHNSON
30 Director of Development Operations .... Ms. Christy GRANT
27 Mgr of Content & Media Relations .... Ms. Mandy CROW
89 Coordinator Freshman Year Exper .... Ms. Megan MCGHEE
124 Coordinator of Assessment/Retention .... Mr. Jeffrey SWINK

Tusculum University (B)

60 Shiloh Road, Greeneville TN 37743-9997
County: Greene FICE Identification: 003527
Unit ID: 221953
Telephone: (423) 636-7300 Carnegie Class: Masters/M
FAX Number: (423) 638-7166 Calendar System: Semester
URL: https://home.tusculum.edu/
Established: 1794 Annual Undergrad Tuition & Fees: $24,860
Enrollment: 1,767 Coed
Affiliation or Control: Presbyterian Church (U.S.A.) IRS Status: 501(c)3
Highest Offering: Master's
Accreditation: #SC, ACBSP, NURSE

01 President .... Dr. James HURLEY
05 VP Academic Affairs .... Dr. Madison SOWELL
111 VP Institutional Advancement .... Ms. Jill SAYLERS
10 Vice Pres/Chief Financial Officer .... Mr. John WILKINSON
84 VP for Enrollment Management .... Dr. Ramona WILLIAMS
32 VP of Student Success & Athletics .... Mr. Doug JONES
20 Associate VP for Academic Affairs .... Dr. Lisa JOHNSON
20 Asst VP for Academic Affairs .... Dr. Jo LOBERTINI
35 Dean of Students .... Dr. David SMITH
06 Registrar .... Ms. Laura GIANFRANCESCO
21 Controller .... Ms. Tammy CHILDS
07 Director of Operations/Admissions .... Ms. Melissa RIPLEY
20 Asst VP for Academic Affairs .... Dr. Carl LARSEN
15 Director Human Resources .... Ms. Danelle SELLS
36 Director Career Counseling .... Ms. Robin LAY
08 Librarian .... Ms. Kathy HICKS
37 Director of Financial Aid .... Ms. Ashley EDENS
26 Director of Communications .... Ms. Suzanne RICHEY
13 Director of Information Systems .... Dr. Blair HENLEY
18 Director Facilities Management .... Mr. David MARTIN
92 Director of Honors Program .... Dr. Mary COOPER
40 Bookstore Manager .... Mr. Cliff HOY
19 Director of Campus Safety .... Mr. Jonathan GRESHAM
76 EVP of College of Health Sciences .... Dr. Andrew BUZZELLI
49 Dean Col of Civic & Liberal Arts .... Mr. Wayne THOMAS
50 Dean College of Business .... Dr. Jacob FAIT
53 Dean College of Education .... Dr. Tricia HUNSADER
66 Dean of School of Nursing .... Dr. Lori ANDERSON
09 Director of Institutional Research .... Ms. Christy COLE

Union University (C)

1050 Union University Drive, Jackson TN 38305-3697
County: Madison FICE Identification: 003528
Unit ID: 221971
Telephone: (731) 668-1818 Carnegie Class: DU-Mod
FAX Number: (731) 661-5175 Calendar System: 4/1/4
URL: www.uu.edu
Established: 1823 Annual Undergrad Tuition & Fees: $32,610
Enrollment: 3,377 Coed
Affiliation or Control: Southern Baptist IRS Status: 501(c)3
Highest Offering: Doctorate
Accreditation: SC, ANEST, ART, CAATE, CAEPN, MUS, NURSE, PHAR, SW

01 President .... Dr. Samuel (Dub) W. OLIVER
05 Provost/VP Academic Affairs .... Dr. John T. NETLAND
10 Sr Vice Pres Business Services .... Mr. Gary L. CARTER
111 Vice Pres Institutional Advancement .Mrs. Catherine KWASIGROH
84 Vice Pres Enrollment Management .... Mr. Dan GRIFFIN
32 Dean of Students .... Dr. Bryan CARRIER
42 Vice Pres for University Ministries .... Dr. Todd BRADY
108 Asst Provost Accred & Research .... Dr. Michele ATKINS
04 Exec Assistant to the President .... Mrs. Gaye CHRISTY
21 Assoc Vice Pres Business Svcs .... Mr. Robert SIMPSON
08 Director of the Library Services .... Mrs. Melissa MOORE
26 Assoc VP University Communications .... Mr. Tim ELLSWORTH
13 Assoc VP Information Technology .... Mr. James AVERY
15 Assoc VP Business Svcs/Human Res .... Dr. John CARBONELL
07 Asst VP for Undergraduate Admiss .... Mr. Robbie GRAVES
37 Director Student Financial Planning .... Mr. John WINDHAM
49 Dean College Arts & Sciences .... Dr. Hunter BAKER
50 Dean School of Business .... Dr. Jason GARRETT
66 Dean School of Nursing .... Dr. Kelly HARDEN
53 Dean College of Education .... Dr. John FOUBERT
88 Dean Sch of Theology & Missions .... Dr. Ray VANNESTE
67 Dean School of Pharmacy .... Dr. Sheila MITCHELL
91 Assoc Dir Information Technology .... Miss Karen MCWHERTER
36 Dir Vocation Ctr/Life Call/Career .... Mr. Alex HUGUENARD
14 Director of Data Management .... Mr. David PORTER
06 Registrar .... Mrs. Susan HOPPER
19 Director of Security/Safety .... Mr. Yancey PETTIGREW
41 Director of Athletics .... Mr. Tommy SADLER
18 Chief Facilities/Physical Plant .... Mr. Stephen HOPPER
70 Dean School of Social Work .... Mrs. Mary Anne POE
51 Dean School Adult & Prof Studies .... Dr. Beverly ABSHER

The University of Memphis (D)

Southern Avenue, Memphis TN 38152
County: Shelby FICE Identification: 003509
Unit ID: 220862
Telephone: (901) 678-2000 Carnegie Class: DU-Higher
FAX Number: N/A Calendar System: Semester
URL: www.memphis.edu
Established: 1912 Annual Undergrad Tuition & Fees (In-State): $9,317
Enrollment: 21,521 Coed
Affiliation or Control: State IRS Status: 501(c)3
Highest Offering: Doctorate
Accreditation: SC, ART, AUD, CACREP, CAEPN, CIDA, CLPSY, COPSY, DIETD, DIETI, HSA, IPSY, JOUR, LAW, MUS, NURSE, PH, PLNG, SCPSY, SP, SPAA, SW, THEA

02 President .... Dr. M. David RUDD
05 Provost .... Dr. Tom NENON
20 Vice Provost Academic Innovation .... Dr. Richard IRWIN
10 Chief Financial Officer .... Mr. Raaj KURAPATI
88 Asst VP Campus Planning Design .... Mr. Tony POTEET
18 Asst VP Physical Plant .... Mr. Ron BROOKS
19 Chief of Police .... Ms. Mary BALEE
116 Chief Audit Executive .... Ms. Vicki DEATON
111 Chief Advancement Officer .... Ms. Joanna CURTIS
32 Vice Pres Student Academic Success .. Dr. Karen WEDDLE-WEST
35 Asst VP Student Aff/Dev .... Dr. Daniel A. BUREAU
26 VP External Relations .... Ms. Tammy HEDGES
46 Exec VP Research & Innovation .... Dr. Jasbir DHALIWAL
41 Interim Director of Athletics .... Mr. Allie PRESCOTT
43 University Counsel .... Ms. Melanie MURRY
22 Dir of Institutional Equity .... Mr. Kenneth ANDERSON
13 CIO/Vice Provost for Info Tech .... Dr. Robert JACKSON
84 Vice Provost Enrollment Services .... Dr. William AKEY
58 Dean Graduate School .... Dr. Robin POSTON
21 Asst Vice Pres Business & Finance .... Vacant
15 Asst Vice Pres Human Resources .... Ms. Maria ALAM
08 Assoc Dean U of M Libraries .... Mr. John EVANS
09 Director Institutional Research .... Ms. Bridgette DECENT
36 Director Career & Employment Svcs .... Ms. Alisha D. ROSE
06 Registrar .... Ms. Darla KEEL
37 Director of Student Aid .... Ms. Karen SMITH
96 Director of Purchasing .... Mr. Stuart THOMAS
29 Director of Alumni Relations .... Ms. Kristie GOLDSMITH
92 Director University Honors Program .... Dr. Melinda L. JONES
07 Director of Admissions .... Dr. William AKEY
28 Director of Diversity Initiatives .... Dr. Karen WEDDLE-WEST
88 Dean Comm Sciences/Disorders .... Dr. Linda D. JARMULOWICZ
49 Dean of Arts & Sciences .... Dr. Abby PARRILL-BAKER
50 Dean Business & Economics .... Dr. Damon FLEMING
53 Dean of Education .... Dr. Kandi HILL-CLARKE
54 Dean of Engineering .... Dr. Richard J. SWEIGARD
88 Dean University College .... Dr. Richard IRWIN
57 Dean Communication & Fine Arts .... Dr. Anne HOGAN
61 Int Dean School of Law .... Ms. Kate SCHAFFZIN
66 Dean School of Nursing .... Dr. Lin ZHAN
69 Dean School of Public Health .... Dr. James G. GURNEY
76 Dir School of Health Studies .... Dr. Richard J. BLOOMER
104 Director Study Abroad .... Ms. Rebecca DYCK-LAUMANN
108 Director Institutional Assessment .... Dr. Colton COCKRUM
38 Director Student Counseling .... Dr. Jane CLEMENT
112 Director of Planned Giving .... Mr. Dan MURRELL
102 Dir Foundation/Corporate Relations .... Vacant
106 Exe Dean Global/Academic Innovation .... Dr. Richard L. IRWIN
11 Chief of Operations/Administration .... Mr. Bruce HARBER
44 Director Annual Giving .... Ms. Rachel BROWN
86 Director Government Relations .... Mr. Ted TOWNSEND
04 Sr Director Office of the President .... Ms. Stephanie BEASLEY
39 Director of Residence Life .... Mr. Steve LOGAN

University of Phoenix Memphis Campus (E)

65 Germantown Court, Cordova TN 38018-7290
Telephone: (901) 751-1086 Identification: 770224
Accreditation: &NH

† No longer accepting campus-based students.

*University of Tennessee System Office (F)

800 Andy Holt Tower, Knoxville TN 37996-0180
County: Knox FICE Identification: 008051
Telephone: (865) 974-1000 Carnegie Class: N/A
FAX Number: (865) 974-3753
URL: www.tennessee.edu

01 Interim President .... Mr. Randy BOYD
11 Exec VP/Chief Operating Officer .... Dr. Tonjanita JOHNSON
05 VP Academic Affairs/Student Success .... Dr. Linda C. MARTIN
30 Int CEO Foundation/VP Devel/Alumni .... Mr. Kerry WITCHER
86 VP for Government Rels/Advocacy .... Mr. Anthony HAYNES
45 VP Research/Outreach/Economic Dev .... Dr. Stacey PATTERSON
10 CFO .... Mr. David L. MILLER
43 General Counsel/Secretary .... Mr. Matthew SCOGGINS
15 Vice President for Human Resources .... Vacant
86 Vice Pres Institute for Public Svc .... Dr. Herb BYRD
26 Assoc VP Communications/Marketing .... Ms. Tiffany CARPENTER
13 Chief Information Officer .... Mr. Les MATHEWS
21 Exec Dir Auditing/Consulting Svcs .... Mr. Brian DANIELS
29 Asst VP UTN Alumni Affairs .... Mr. Kerry WITCHER

*University of Tennessee, Knoxville (G)

1331 Circle Park, Andy Holt Tower,
Knoxville TN 37996-0184
County: Knox FICE Identification: 003530
Unit ID: 221759
Telephone: (865) 974-1000 Carnegie Class: DU-Highest
FAX Number: (865) 974-1182 Calendar System: Semester
URL: www.utk.edu
Established: 1794 Annual Undergrad Tuition & Fees (In-State): $13,006
Enrollment: 28,321 Coed
Affiliation or Control: State IRS Status: 501(c)3
Highest Offering: Doctorate
Accreditation: SC, ANEST, ART, CACREP, CAEPN, CIDA, CLPSY, COPSY, DENT, DIETD, DIETI, IPSY, JOUR, LAW, LIB, LSAR, MUS, NRPA, NURSE, PAST, PH, RAD, SCPSY, SW, THEA, VET

02 Chancellor .... Dr. Donde L. PLOWMAN
100 Chancellor's Executive Assistant .... Dr. Rachel J. RUI
05 Provost/Senior Vice Chancellor .... Dr. David MANDERSHEID
32 Vice Chancellor for Student Life .... Dr. Vincent CARILLI
46 Int Vice Chancellor for Research .... Dr. Robert NOBLES, II
10 Senior VC Finance & Administration .... Mr. Chris CIMINO
28 Int VC for Diversity and Engagement .... Mr. Tyvi SMALL
26 Vice Chancellor for Communications .... Mrs. Tisha BENTON
30 Vice Chancellor for Development .... Mr. Chip BRYANT
20 Vice Provost for Faculty Affairs .... Dr. John ZOMCHICK
20 Vice Provost for Academic Affairs .... Dr. RJ HINDE
58 Vice Provost/Dean Graduate School .... Dr. Dixie THOMPSON
35 AVC Student Life/Dean of Students .... Dr. Shea K. HOUZE
39 Asst VC Student Life .... Dr. Frank CUEVAS
51 Asst Provost Univ Outrch/Cont Educ .... Dr. Norvel BURKETT
84 Vice Provost Enrollment Svcs .... Ms. Kari ALLDREDGE
18 Assoc Vice Chanc Facilities Svcs .... Mr. Dave IRVIN
41 Vice Chancellor/Dir Athletics .... Mr. Phillip FULMER
28 Assoc Vice Chanc Equity & Diversity .... Ms. Jennifer RICHTER
37 Director of Financial Aid .... Mr. Jeffrey G. GERKIN
09 Dir Inst Research/Assessment .... Ms. Denise GARDNER
38 Director of Student Counseling .... Dr. Victor BARR
06 Registrar .... Ms. Monique W. ANDERSON
47 Dean Ag Sciences/Natural Resources .... Dr. Caula BEYL
48 Dean of Architecture and Design .... Dr. Scott POOLE
50 Dean Business Administration .... Dr. Steve MANGUM

60 Dean Communication/Information ... Dr. Michael WIRTH
53 Dean Educ/Health/Human Sciences ... Dr. Robert RIDER
54 Interim Dean of Engineering ... Dr. Lynne PARKER
61 Dean of Law ... Prof. Melanie WILSON
49 Dean of Arts & Sciences ... Dr. Theresa LEE
66 Dean of Nursing ... Dr. Victoria NIEDERHAUSER
70 Interim Dean of Social Work ... Dr. David DUPPER
74 Dean of Veterinary Medicine ... Dr. James P. THOMPSON
12 Chancellor of UTIA ... Dr. Tim L. CROSS
08 Dean of Libraries ... Dr. Steve SMITH
12 Executive Director of UTSI ... Dr. Mark WHORTON
07 Director of Undergrad Admissions ... Mr. Fabrizio D'ALOISIO
13 Associate VC & CIO ... Mr. Joel REEVES
29 Associate VC of Alumni Affairs ... Mr. Lee PATOUILLET

*University of Tennessee at Chattanooga (A)

615 McCallie Avenue, Chattanooga TN 37403-2504
County: Hamilton | FICE Identification: 003529
Unit ID: 221740
Telephone: (423) 425-4111 | Carnegie Class: DU-Mod
FAX Number: (423) 425-2200 | Calendar System: Semester
URL: www.utc.edu
Established: 1886 | Annual Undergrad Tuition & Fees (In-State): $8,664
Enrollment: 11,587 | Coed
Affiliation or Control: State | IRS Status: 501(c)3
Highest Offering: Doctorate
Accreditation: SC, ANEST, ART, CAATE, CACREP, CAEPN, CIDA, DIETD, JOUR, MUS, NURSE, OT, PTA, SPAA, SW, THEA

02 Chancellor ... Dr. Steven R. ANGLE
05 Provost & Sr VC Academic Affs ... Dr. Jerold HALE
20 Int Vice Prov for Academic Affairs ... Dr. Matt MATTHEWS
111 Vice Chanc University Advancement ... Dr. Bryan ROWLAND
10 Exec Vice Chanc Fin/Operations & IT ... Dr. Richard BROWN
46 Vice Chancellor for Research ... Dr. Joanne ROMAGNI
32 Vice Chanc Student Dev ... Vacant
21 Assoc Vice Chanc Business/Fin Affs .. Ms. Vanasia Conley PARKS
26 Vice Chanc Comm & Mktg ... Mr. George HEDDLESTON
41 Vice Chanc & AD ... Mr. Mark WHARTON
26 Asst VC University Relations ... Ms. Gina STAFFORD
18 Asst VC Operations/Fac Plng & Mgt ... Mr. Tom M. ELLIS
13 CIO ... Mr. Dennis GENDRON
100 Chief of Staff ... Ms. Terry DENNISTON
08 Dean of UTC Library ... Ms. Theresa LIEDTKA
35 Assoc Dean of Student Life ... Mr. Jim HICKS
84 Vice Chanc Enrollment Mgmt ... Dr. Yancy FREEMAN
06 Director Records & Registrar ... Mr. Joel WELLS
13 Manager Client Solutions/IT ... Vacant
09 Dir of Planning/Eval/Inst Research ... Ms. Eva LEWIS
36 Asst Dir Placemt/Student Employment ... Mrs. Donna COOPER
15 Exec Director of Human Resources ... Ms. Laure POU
38 Executive Director of Counseling ... Dr. Elizabeth O'BRIEN
37 Director of Financial Aid ... Ms. Jennifer BUCKLES
58 Dean of the Graduate School ... Dr. Joanne ROMAGNI
49 Interim Dean of Arts & Sciences ... Dr. Joe WILFERTH
50 Dean of Business Administration ... Dr. Robert DOOLEY
53 Dean of Health/Educ/Prof Studies ... Dr. Valerie RUTLEDGE
54 Dean Engineering/Comp Science ... Dr. Daniel PACK
66 Director of Nursing ... Dr. Chris SMITH
22 Int Director of Equity & Inclusion ... Ms. Rosite DELGADO
25 Director of Sponsored Programs ... Ms. Meredith PERRY
29 Director of Alumni Affairs ... Ms. Jayne HOLDER
96 Procurement & Contract (Purchasing) ... Ms. Melissa HAYS
19 Chief of Police ... Mr. Robert RATCHFORD
39 Director Student Housing ... Ms. Valara SAMPLE
92 Dean Honors College ... Dr. Linda FROST
88 Director of Civic Engagement ... Mr. David STEELE
104 Exec Director International Program ... Mr. Takeo SUZUKI
43 Dir Legal Services/General Counsel ... Mr. Yousef A. HAMADEH

*University of Tennessee at Martin (B)

554 University Street, Martin TN 38238-0001
County: Weakley | FICE Identification: 003531
Unit ID: 221768
Telephone: (731) 881-7000 | Carnegie Class: Masters/S
FAX Number: (731) 881-7019 | Calendar System: Semester
URL: www.utm.edu
Established: 1900 | Annual Undergrad Tuition & Fees (In-State): $9,512
Enrollment: 6,772 | Coed
Affiliation or Control: State | IRS Status: 501(c)3
Highest Offering: Master's
Accreditation: SC, AAFCS, CAEP, CEA, DIETD, DIETI, JOUR, MUS, NUR, SW

02 Chancellor ... Dr. Keith S. CARVER, JR.
05 Provost & VC for Academic Affairs ... Dr. Philip A. CAVALIER
10 Vice Chanc for Finance & Admin ... Ms. Petra R. MCPHEARSON
32 Vice Chanc for Student Affairs ... Dr. John A. LEWTER
111 Vice Chancellor Univ Advancement ... Mr. Andrew A. WILSON
20 Assoc Provost for Academic Affs ... Dr. Victoria S. SENG
13 Chief Information Officer ... Ms. Amy C. BELEW
114 Int Dir Budget & Mgmt Report ... Ms. Carol WILLIAMS
35 Asst Vice Chanc for Student Affairs ... Mr. John C. ABEL
30 Asst VChanc Devel & Planned Giving . Ms. Jeanna C. SWAFFORD
04 Exec Assistant to the Chancellor ... Ms. Edie B. GIBSON
29 Int Dir for Alumni Relations ... Ms. Jacqueline JOHNSON
06 Dir of Acad Records & Registrar ... Ms. Martha BARNETT
28 Equity & Diversity Ofcr AA/EEO ... Mr. Joe T. HENDERSON
15 Director of Human Resources ... Mr. Michael WASHINGTON
09 Director Institutional Research ... Dr. Desiree A. MCCULLOUGH
41 Dir Intercollegiate Athletics ... Mr. Kurt MCGUFFIN
08 Director of Library ... Dr. John BURCH
18 Director of Physical Plant Opers ... Dr. Tim J. NIPP
19 Director of Public Safety ... Mr. Scott D. ROBBINS
96 Purchasing Agent ... Ms. Lori A. DONAVANT
23 Dir Student Health & Counseling Svc ... Ms. Shannon DEAL
39 Asst VC Student/Residential Life ... Ms. Gina MCCLURE
26 Chief Communications Officer ... Mr. Robert (Bud) D. GRIMES
85 Dir Tenn Intensive English Pgm ... Ms. Amy E. FENNING
47 Dean Col Agri & App Sciences ... Dr. Todd A. WINTERS
50 Int Dean Col Business & Global Affs ... Dr. Katherine N. HIGH
53 Dean Col Educ/Health/Behav Sci ... Ms. Cynthia L. WEST
79 Dean Col Humanities/Fine Arts ... Dr. Lynn M. ALEXANDER
54 Dean Col Engr & Natural Sci ... Dr. Shadow ROBINSON
105 Director Web Services ... Mr. Brian C. INGRAM
25 Exec Dir Res Outreach/Econ Dev ... Dr. Charles T. DEAL
84 Exec Dir Enr Svcs/Stdnt Engagement ... Dr. James D. MANTOOTH
07 Director of Admissions ... Ms. Destin TUCKER
37 Asst Dir Financial Aid/Scholarship ... Ms. Amy MISTRIC

*University of Tennessee Health Science Center (C)

910 Madison Avenue, Memphis TN 38163
Telephone: (901) 448-5500 | FICE Identification: 006725
Accreditation: SC, ANEST, #ARCPA, AUD, CAHIIM, CYTO, DENT, DH, HT, IPSY, MED, MT, NURSE, OT, PHAR, PTA, SP

Vanderbilt University (D)

2305 West End Avenue, Nashville TN 37203
County: Davidson | FICE Identification: 003535
Unit ID: 221999
Telephone: (615) 322-7311 | Carnegie Class: DU-Highest
FAX Number: (615) 343-7765 | Calendar System: Semester
URL: www.vanderbilt.edu
Established: 1873 | Annual Undergrad Tuition & Fees: $49,816
Enrollment: 12,592 | Coed
Affiliation or Control: Independent Non-Profit | IRS Status: 501(c)3
Highest Offering: Doctorate
Accreditation: SC, AUD, CACREP, CAEP, CAMPEP, CLPSY, DENT, DIETI, DMS, IPSY, LAW, MED, MIDWF, MT, MUS, NDT, #NMT, NURSE, PCSAS, PERF, PH, SP, THEOL

01 Chancellor ... Dr. Nicholas ZEPPOS
05 Provost/Vice Chancellor ... Dr. Susan R. WENTE
63 Dean School of Medicine ... Dr. Jeffrey R. BALSER
10 Vice Chancellor Finance/CFO ... Mr. Brett SWEET
11 Vice Chanc Administration ... Mr. Eric KOPSTAIN
30 Vice Chanc Dev & Alumni Relations ... Ms. Susie STALCUP
46 Vice Provost for Research ... Dr. Padma RAGHAVAN
115 Vice Chanc for Investments ... Mr. Anders W. HALL
28 VC Equity/Diversity/Inclusion ... Mr. James E. PAGE, JR.
15 Chief Human Resources Ofcr ... Ms. Barbara CARROLL
41 Vice Chanc & Athletics Director ... Dr. Malcolm TURNER
88 Dir Trust and Estate Admin ... Ms. Susan HART
26 Vice Chancellor for Communications ... Mr. Steve ERTEL
13 Vice Chancellor Information Tech ... Mr. John M. LUTZ
86 Vice Chancellor Public Affairs ... Mr. Nathan GREEN
43 Vice Chancellor/General Counsel ... Ms. Ruby Z. SHELLAWAY
09 Asst Provost/Exec Dir Inst Research ... Ms. Olivia KEW-FICKUS
20 Vice Provost Learning & Res Affairs ... Ms. Cynthia J. CYRUS
58 Dean of the Graduate School ... Dr. Mark T. WALLACE
08 University Librarian ... Dr. Valerie HOTCHKISS
27 Dean of Student Publicats/Comm ... Mr. F. Clark WILLIAMS
21 Asst V Chanc for Finance/Controller ... Ms. Dalana ROBERTSON
06 Registrar ... Mr. Bart P. QUINET
84 Vice Provost Univ Enrollment Affs ... Dr. Douglas CHRISTIANSEN
07 Dir Undergraduate Admissions ... Mr. John GAINES
37 Director Student Financial Aid ... Mr. Brent B. TENER
38 Director Univ Counseling Center ... Dr. Todd WEINMAN
36 Exec Dir Career Center ... Dr. Katharine S. BROOKS
25 Director Sponsored Programs ... Mr. Andrew BUDELL
32 Dean of Students/Assoc Provost ... Mr. Mark BANDAS
106 Assoc Provost for Educ Tech & Dev ... Dr. John M. SLOOP
49 Dean College of Arts & Science ... Dr. John G. GEER
54 Dean School of Engineering ... Dr. Philippe M. FAUCHET
66 Dean School of Nursing ... Dr. Linda NORMAN
53 Dean Education & Human Development ... Dr. Camilla P. BENBOW
64 Dean Blair School of Music ... Dr. Mark WAIT
73 Dean of the Divinity School ... Dr. Emilie M. TOWNES
61 Dean of the School of Law ... Dr. Chris GUTHRIE
50 Dean Owen Grad School of Mgmt ... Dr. M. Eric JOHNSON
45 Int Vice Prov Strategic Initiatives ... Dr. William H. ROBINSON
20 Vice Prov Acad Affairs/Dean of Fac ... Dr. Vanessa BEASLEY
88 Vice Prov for Faculty Affairs ... Dr. Tracey GEORGE
42 Associate Chaplain ... Rev. Gretchen PERSON
19 AVC/Chief of Public Safety ... Mr. August J. WASHINGTON
22 Dir EO/AA & Disability Svcs ... Ms. Anita JENIOUS
41 Dir Sport Operations/Asst Vice Chan ... Mr. Brockton WILLIAMS
39 Sr Director Housing Operations ... Mr. James S. KRAMKA
44 Asst Vice Chancellor Annual Giving ... Mr. Kyle D. MCGOWAN
86 Asst Vice Chanc Federal Relations ... Ms. Christina D. WEST

Visible Music College (E)

200 Madison Avenue, Memphis TN 38103
County: Shelby | FICE Identification: 039823
Unit ID: 449764
Telephone: (901) 381-3939 | Carnegie Class: Spec-4-yr-Arts
FAX Number: (901) 377-0544 | Calendar System: Semester
URL: www.visible.edu
Established: 2000 | Annual Undergrad Tuition & Fees: $19,500
Enrollment: 124 | Coed
Affiliation or Control: Independent Non-Profit | IRS Status: 501(c)3
Highest Offering: Master's
Accreditation: TRACS

01 President ... Dr. Ken STEORTS
05 Vice President of Academics ... Dr. Cameron HARVEY
111 Vice President of Advancement ... Geordy WELLS
10 Vice President of Business ... Ben RAWLEY
32 Vice President of Students ... JD WILSON
07 Director of Admissions ... Steve STEELE
06 Registrar ... Sunethra GUY
37 Financial Aid Manager ... Tonya WILLIAMS
15 Human Resources Coordinator ... Toni MELTON
18 Operations/IT Manager ... Heath BENSON
84 Enrollment Manager ... LaToya CHAVERS

Watkins College of Art (F)

2298 Rosa L. Parks Boulevard, Nashville TN 37228-1306
County: Davidson | FICE Identification: 030888
Unit ID: 392840
Telephone: (615) 383-4848 | Carnegie Class: Spec-4-yr-Arts
FAX Number: (615) 383-4849 | Calendar System: Semester
URL: www.watkins.edu
Established: 1885 | Annual Undergrad Tuition & Fees: $24,450
Enrollment: 210 | Coed
Affiliation or Control: Independent Non-Profit | IRS Status: 501(c)3
Highest Offering: Master's
Accreditation: SC, ART

01 President ... Dr. J. KLINE
111 Vice Pres Institutional Advancement ... Ms. Autumn PARROT
05 Int Vice President Academic Affairs ... Ms. Cary Beth MILLER
10 Vice Pres Finance and Operations ... Mr. Dwayne BREEDING
84 Vice Pres Strategic Enrollment Mgmt ... Ms. Alison MIYAUCHI
26 Director of Communications ... Mr. Brendan TAPLEY
06 Registrar ... Ms. Tracie JOHNSON
37 Director Financial Aid ... Ms. Regina GILBERT
08 Library Director ... Ms. Amy KAMMERMAN
13 Director Information Technology ... Mr. Shawn MAGGARD
18 Director of Facilities ... Mr. Martin DILLINGHAM
88 Chair Film School ... Mr. Richard GERSHMAN
57 Chair Fine Art Department ... Ms. Kristi HARGROVE
88 Chair Graphic Design Department ... Mr. Dan BRAWNER
88 Chair Interior Design Department ... Mr. Stefan BRUCE
88 Chair Photography Department ... Ms. Kristy HARGROVE
97 Director General Education ... Ms. Cary Beth MILLER
51 Director Community Education ... Ms. Maggie FANSHER
32 Director Student Life ... Ms. Roshaunda ROSS

Welch College (G)

1045 Bison Trail, Gallatin TN 37066
County: Sumner | FICE Identification: 030018
Unit ID: 220206
Telephone: (615) 675-5255 | Carnegie Class: Bac-Diverse
FAX Number: (615) 296-0400 | Calendar System: Semester
URL: www.welch.edu
Established: 1942 | Annual Undergrad Tuition & Fees: $19,012
Enrollment: 366 | Coed
Affiliation or Control: Free Will Baptist | IRS Status: 501(c)3
Highest Offering: Master's
Accreditation: SC, BI

01 President ... Dr. J. Matthew PINSON
05 Provost ... Dr. Matthew J. MCAFFEE
45 Vice Pres for Strategic Initiatives ... Dr. P. Greg KETTEMAN
10 Vice President Financial Affairs ... Mr. Craig MAHLER
32 VP Student Svcs/Dean of Students ... Dr. Jon FORLINES
111 Vice Pres Institutional Advancement ... Mr. David WILLIFORD
108 Vice Pres for Inst Effectiveness ... Dr. Kevin HESTER
20 Vice Provost for Academic Admin ... Mr. Matthew BRACEY
34 Dean of Women ... Mrs. Susan FORLINES
55 Dean of Enriched Adult Studies ... Mr. William SLATER
08 Librarian ... Mrs. Krista THORNSBURY
09 Director of Institutional Research ... Mr. Wayne SPRUILL
84 Dir of Enrollment Services ... Mr. Daniel WEBSTER
26 Chief Public Relations/Marketing ... Mr. Josh OWENS
106 Dir of Online and Adult Studies ... Mr. Allan CROWSON
44 Director of the Annual Fund ... Mr. Mike EDWARDS
18 Director of Plant Operations ... Mr. Sandy GOODFELLOW
41 Athletic Director ... Mr. Greg FAWBUSH
37 Student Financial Aid Coordinator ... Mrs. Angie EDGMON
06 Registrar ... Dr. Sharon RODGERS
04 Exec Assistant to the President ... Mrs. Martha FLETCHER

William Moore College of Technology (H)

1200 Poplar Avenue, Memphis TN 38104
County: Shelby | FICE Identification: 011553
Unit ID: 222105
Telephone: (901) 726-1977 | Carnegie Class: Not Classified
FAX Number: (901) 726-1978 | Calendar System: Trimester
URL: www.williammoore.org
Established: 1909 | Annual Undergrad Tuition & Fees: $7,305
Enrollment: N/A | Coed
Affiliation or Control: Independent Non-Profit | IRS Status: 501(c)3
Highest Offering: Associate Degree
Accreditation: COE

Williamson College (A)

274 Mallory Station Road, Franklin TN 37067
County: Williamson | FICE Identification: 035135
Unit ID: 443340
Telephone: (615) 771-7821 | Carnegie Class: Spec-4-yr-Bus
FAX Number: (615) 771-7810 | Calendar System: Other
URL: www.williamsoncc.edu
Established: 1996 | Annual Undergrad Tuition & Fees: $13,525
Enrollment: 58 | Coed
Affiliation or Control: Non-denominational | IRS Status: 501(c)3
Highest Offering: Master's
Accreditation: BI

01 President ... Dr. Ed SMITH
11 Vice President for Operations ... Ms. Susan MAYS
32 Director of Student Services ... Robyn WOLLAS
06 Registrar/Dir Instl Effectiveness ... Ms. Karen HUDSON
37 Dir Financial Aid/Veteran Affairs ... Ms. Cristina MAJORS
07 Admissions Department Manager ... Ms. Laura FLOWERS

TEXAS

Abilene Christian University (B)

ACU Box 29100, Abilene TX 79699-9100
County: Taylor | FICE Identification: 003537
Unit ID: 222178
Telephone: (325) 674-2000 | Carnegie Class: Masters/L
FAX Number: (325) 674-2202 | Calendar System: Semester
URL: www.acu.edu
Established: 1906 | Annual Undergrad Tuition & Fees: $34,850
Enrollment: 5,145 | Coed
Affiliation or Control: Churches Of Christ | IRS Status: 501(c)3
Highest Offering: Doctorate
Accreditation: SC, CIDA, DIETD, DIETI, JOUR, MFCD, MUS, NURSE, OT, SP, SW, THEOL

01 President ... Dr. Phil SCHUBERT
100 Senior Advisor to the President ... Ms. Suzanne ALLMON
88 VP Center for Building Community ... Dr. Gary D. MCCALEB
05 Provost ... Dr. Robert RHODES
111 VP for Advancement ... Mr. Jim ORR
84 VP Enrollment & Student Engagement ... Mrs. Tamara LONG
10 VP & Chief Business Officer ... Vacant
12 VP/Administative Officer ACU Dallas ... Dr. Stephen JOHNSON
115 Chief Investment Ofcr/Pres ACIMCO ... Mr. Jack W. RICH
43 Vice President & General Counsel ... Mr. Slade SULLIVAN
00 Chancellor ... Dr. Royce MONEY
88 Assistant to the Chancellor ... Mr. Jim HOLMANS
102 ACU Foundation President ... Mr. Brad T. BENHAM
20 Vice Provost ... Dr. Susan LEWIS
84 Asst VP Enrollment Dallas ... Ms. Jessica MANNING
49 Dean College of Arts & Sciences ... Dr. Greg STRAUGHN
73 Dean College of Biblical Studies ... Dr. Ken R. CUKROWSKI
50 Dean College of Business Admin ... Dr. Brad CRISP
53 Dean College of Educ & Human Svcs ... Dr. Jennifer SHEWMAKER
92 Dean Honors College ... Dr. Jason MORRIS
58 Dean Graduate & Professional Stds ... Dr. Joey COPE
66 Dean School of Nursing ... Dr. Marcia STRAUGHN
08 Dean Library/Educational Technology ... Dr. John WEAVER
104 Director of the Ctr Intl Educ ... Dr. Stephen SHEWMAKER
32 Dean of Students ... Mr. Mark LEWIS
36 Director Career Center ... Mrs. Jill FORTSON
06 Registrar/Dir of Academic Dev ... Dr. Eric GUMM
11 Senior VP of Operations ... Mr. Kevin CAMPBELL
26 Chief Marketing Officer ... Mr. Jason GROVES
39 Dir Residence Life/Stdnt Advocacy ... Ms. Shannon KACZMAREK
38 Director Univ Counseling Center ... Mr. Tyson ALEXANDER
18 Associate VP of Operations ... Mr. Corey RUFF
24 Exec Dir/Assoc Dean Teaching & Lrng ... Dr. Laura CARROLL
29 Asst VP Alumni & Univ Relations ... Mr. Craig FISHER
19 Chief of Police ... Mr. Jimmy ELLISON
112 Dir Endowment Strategy/Sr Adv Ofcr ... Mr. Don GARRETT
41 Director of Athletics ... Mr. Allen WARD
15 Chief HR Officer/Title IX Coord ... Mrs. Wendy JONES
88 Director of Faculty Development ... Dr. Cliff BARBARICK
09 Asst Provost for Inst Effectiveness ... Dr. Chris RILEY
96 Director of Purchasing/Procurement ... Ms. Sandy HALL
101 Secretary to the Board of Trustees ... Mr. Slade SULLIVAN
04 Exec Assistant Office of President ... Mrs. Stephanie A. WOODLEE
46 Dir Research/Sponsored Programs ... Dr. Megan ROTH
07 Director of Enrollment Operations ... Mr. Garrett SUBLETTE
88 Director of Compliance ... Mrs. Sherita NICKERSON

*Alamo Community College District Central Office (C)

201 W. Sheridan, San Antonio TX 78204-1429
County: Bexar | FICE Identification: 003607
Unit ID: 222497
Telephone: (210) 485-0020 | Carnegie Class: N/A
FAX Number: (210) 486-9166
URL: www.alamo.edu

01 Chancellor ... Dr. Mike FLORES
05 Vice Chanc for Academic Success ... Dr. George RAILEY, JR.
11 Vice Chanc for Finance & Admin ... Dr. Diane E. SNYDER
32 Vice Chancellor for Student Success ... Dr. Adelina SILVA
103 Vice Chanc Economic/Workforce Devel ... Mr. Robert MCKINLEY
13 VC Plng/Performance/Info Systems ... Dr. Thomas CLEARY
15 Assoc Vice Chanc Human Resources . Ms. Linda BOYER-OWENS
18 Assoc Vice Chanc Facilities ... Mr. John STRYBOS
10 Assoc VC Finance & Fiscal Services ... Ms. Pamela ANSBOURY
04 Deputy to the Chancellor ... Ms. Michelle PERALES
111 Int Exec Director Inst Advancement ... Dr. Marie KANE
116 Director of Internal Audit ... Mr. Bill WULLENJOHN
96 Director Acquisitions & Admin Svcs ... Mr. Gary O'BAR
19 Chief Department of Public Safety ... Mr. Don ADAMS
21 Comptroller ... Ms. Gettie MORENO
12 President Northwest Vista College ... Dr. Ric BASER
12 President San Antonio College ... Dr. Robert VELA
12 President St Philip's College ... Dr. Adena WILLIAMS LOSTON
12 President Palo Alto College ... Dr. Robert GARZA
12 Pres Northeast Lakeview College ... Dr. Veronica GARCIA
37 Director Student Financial Aid ... Mr. Harold WHITIS
43 Dir Legal Services/General Counsel ... Mr. Ross LAUGHEAD
09 Dist Dir Inst Rsch/Effect/Planning ... Mr. Velda VILLARREAL

*Northeast Lakeview College (D)

1201 Kitty Hawk Road, Universal City TX 78148
County: Bexar | Identification: 667278
Unit ID: 488730
Telephone: (210) 486-5000 | Carnegie Class: Assoc/HT-Mix Trad/Non
FAX Number: N/A | Calendar System: Semester
URL: www.alamo.edu/nlc
Established: 2007 | Annual Undergrad Tuition & Fees (In-District): $2,820
Enrollment: 3,860 | Coed
Affiliation or Control: Local | IRS Status: 501(c)3
Highest Offering: Associate Degree
Accreditation: SC

02 President ... Dr. Veronica GARCIA
05 Int VP Academic Success ... Dr. Laura SANCHEZ
11 Vice Pres of College Services ... Mr. Shayne WEST
32 Vice Pres Student Success ... Dr. Tangila DOVE

*Northwest Vista College (E)

3535 N Ellison Drive, San Antonio TX 78251-4217
County: Bexar | FICE Identification: 033723
Unit ID: 420398
Telephone: (210) 486-4000 | Carnegie Class: Assoc/HT-High Non
FAX Number: (210) 486-9105 | Calendar System: Semester
URL: www.alamo.edu/nvc
Established: 1995 | Annual Undergrad Tuition & Fees (In-District): $2,820
Enrollment: 16,752 | Coed
Affiliation or Control: Local | IRS Status: 501(c)3
Highest Offering: Associate Degree
Accreditation: SC

02 President ... Dr. Ric N. BASER
03 Vice President for College Services ... Mrs. Erin L. SHERMAN
05 Vice President for Academic Success ... Dr. Daniel POWELL
32 Vice President for Student Success ... Mrs. Deborah GAITAN
04 Executive Assistant to President ... Dr. Lisa MCGOLDRICK
111 Director Institutional Advancement ... Mrs. Lynne DEAN
08 Director Learning Resources Center ... Mrs. Norma VELEZ-VENDRELL
38 Dean for Student Success ... Mrs. Jennifer COMEDY-HOLMES
26 Dir of Public Relations & Marketing ... Mrs. Renata SERAFIN
13 Director Info/Communications Tech ... Mr. Felix SALINAS
37 Associate Director of Financial Aid ... Mrs. Rosalinda ENCINA
113 Assistant Bursar ... Mrs. Patricia SANCHEZ
15 Sr Human Resources Generalist ... Mrs. Stacey L. BLUM
45 Director of Resources & College Dev ... Ms. Judy V. CAMARGO
18 Superintendent NVC ... Mr. Bernie ZERTUCHE
88 Dean for Academic Success/Support ... Mr. Patrick FONTENOT
49 Dean for Academic Success ... Dr. Russell FROHARDT
50 Dean for Academic Success ... Dr. Charles HINKLEY
09 Director of Institutional Research ... Dr. Eliza HERNANDEZ
84 Director of Enrollment Management ... Mrs. Yolanda REYES-GUEVARA
07 Associate Director of Admissions ... Mrs. Yvonne GUERRA
121 Dean for Student Success-Academic ... Mrs. Robin LUND

*Palo Alto College (F)

1400 W Villaret Boulevard, San Antonio TX 78224-2499
County: Bexar | FICE Identification: 023413
Unit ID: 246354
Telephone: (210) 486-3000 | Carnegie Class: Assoc/HT-High Non
FAX Number: (210) 921-5005 | Calendar System: Semester
URL: www.alamo.edu
Established: 1985 | Annual Undergrad Tuition & Fees (In-District): $2,820
Enrollment: 9,368 | Coed
Affiliation or Control: Local | IRS Status: 501(c)3
Highest Offering: Associate Degree
Accreditation: SC

02 President ... Dr. Robert GARZA
05 Vice President for Academic Success ... Ms. Elizabeth TANNER
10 Int Vice Pres of College Services ... Ms. Katherine BEAUMONT DOSS
32 Vice President for Student Success ... Mr. Gilberto BECERRA
49 Dean Academic Success ... Mr. Patrick LEE
50 Dean Academic Success ... Dr. Raymond PFANG
08 Dean of Learning Resources ... Ms. Tina MESA
35 Int Dean of Student Success ... Mr. Carlos CRUZ
26 Director of Public Relations ... Mr. Jerry ARELLANO
113 Assistant Bursar ... Mr. Edward SANCHEZ
37 Assc Dir Student Financial Services ... Ms. Shirley LEIJA
41 Athletic Director ... Miss Shanea ALLEN
18 Facilities Superintendnt/Phys Plant ... Mr. Sergio RIVERA
29 Coordinator Alumni Relations ... Ms. Leticia INOCENCIO
09 Dir Inst Rsrch/Plng/Effectiveness ... Mr. George GUAJARDO
25 Director of Advancement & Grants ... Ms. Stephanie VASQUEZ
04 Administrative Asst to President ... Mrs. Connie ACOVIO
13 Chief Info Technology Director ... Mr. Nicolas BLAKENEY

*St. Philip's College (G)

1801 Martin Luther King, San Antonio TX 78203-2098
County: Bexar | FICE Identification: 003608
Unit ID: 227854
Telephone: (210) 486-2000 | Carnegie Class: Assoc/HVT-High Non
FAX Number: N/A | Calendar System: Semester
URL: www.alamo.edu/spc/
Established: 1898 | Annual Undergrad Tuition & Fees (In-District): $2,820
Enrollment: 12,050 | Coed
Affiliation or Control: Local | IRS Status: 501(c)3
Highest Offering: Associate Degree
Accreditation: SC, ACFEI, CAHIIM, COARC, CVT, DMS, HT, MLTAD, OTA, PTAA, RAD, SURGT

02 President ... Dr. Adena WILLIAMS LOSTON
05 Vice Pres of Academic Success ... Dr. Randall DAWSON
32 Vice Pres of Student Success ... Dr. Mordecai BROWNLEE
11 Vice President for College Svcs ... Mr. Lacy HAMPTON
35 Dean for Student Success ... Dr. Paul MACHEN
35 Dean for Student Success ... Ms. Christina CORTEZ
88 Dean for Acad Success Interdisc Pgm ... Mr. Luis LOPEZ
75 Dean Acad Success Applied Sci/Tech ... Mr. Christopher BEARDSALL
49 Dean for Acad Success Arts & Sci ... Mr. George JOHNSON
76 Dean for Acad Success Health Sci ... Ms. Jessica COOPER
37 Asst Director of Financial Aid ... Ms. Grace ZAPATA
45 Director Planning & Research ... Dr. Maria HINOJOSA
113 Assistant Bursar ... Ms. Sophia GONZALEZ
26 Director of Public Relations ... Ms. Adrian JACKSON
72 Director Instructional Technology ... Mr. John ORONA
18 Chief Facilities/Physical Plant ... Ms. Bertha NORWOOD
111 Director Institutional Advancement ... Dr. Sharon CROCKETT-RAY
114 Campus Budget Officer ... Mr. Jorge FLORES

*San Antonio College (H)

1819 N Main, San Antonio TX 78212-4299
County: Bexar | FICE Identification: 009163
Unit ID: 227924
Telephone: (210) 486-0000 | Carnegie Class: Assoc/HT-High Non
FAX Number: N/A | Calendar System: Semester
URL: www.alamo.edu/sac
Established: 1925 | Annual Undergrad Tuition & Fees (In-District): $2,820
Enrollment: 19,385 | Coed
Affiliation or Control: Local | IRS Status: 501(c)3
Highest Offering: Associate Degree
Accreditation: SC, ADNUR, CEA, DA, EMT, FUSER, MAC

02 President ... Dr. Robert H. VELA
32 Vice President of Student Success ... Dr. Lisa ALCORTA
11 Vice President of College Services ... Dr. Stella LOVATO
05 Vice President of Academic Success ... Dr. Johnny BLACKWOOD
35 Dean of Student Success ... Dr. Tiffany COX HERNANDEZ
72 Dean of Academic Success Prof/Tech ... Ms. Vernell E. WALKER
106 Dean of Academic Success Online DC ... Dr. Sobia KHAN
49 Dean of Academic Success Art & Sci ... Dr. Conrad KRUEGER
88 Dean of Performance Excellence ... Dr. Francisco SOLIS
35 Dean of Student Success ... Dr. Maria DE LOS REYES
26 Director of Public Relations ... Ms. Vanessa TORRES
08 Director of Library Services ... Mr. LeBlanc LEE
07 Director of Admissions ... Ms. Amy PENA
84 Director of Enrollment Services ... Mr. J. Martin ORTEGA
85 Coordinator International Students ... Ms. Patrice BALLARD

Alvin Community College (I)

3110 Mustang Road, Alvin TX 77511-4898
County: Brazoria | FICE Identification: 003539
Unit ID: 222567
Telephone: (281) 756-3500 | Carnegie Class: Assoc/MT-VT-High Non
FAX Number: (281) 756-3854 | Calendar System: Semester
URL: www.alvincollege.edu
Established: 1948 | Annual Undergrad Tuition & Fees (In-District): $1,680
Enrollment: 5,785 | Coed
Affiliation or Control: Local | IRS Status: 501(c)3
Highest Offering: Associate Degree
Accreditation: SC, ADNUR, COARC, DMS, EMT, NDT, POLYT

01 President ... Dr. Christal M. ALBRECHT
05 Vice President Instruction ... Dr. Cynthia GRIFFITH
10 VP Administrative Services ... Mr. Karl STAGER
32 VP Student Services ... Dr. Jade BORNE
49 Dean of Arts & Sciences ... Vacant
76 Dean Legal and Health Sciences ... Dr. Stacy EBERT
51 Dean/Exec Dir Cont Ed/Wkforce Devel ... Mr. Jim SIMPSON
97 Dean General Educ/Academic Support ... Dr. Nadezhda (Nadia) NAZARENKO
88 Dean Prof/Tech/Human Performance ... Dr. Linda AUSTIN
06 Registrar ... Ms. Irene M. ROBINSON
08 Director Library Services ... Ms. Rebecca MCCLAIN
21 Director Fiscal Affairs/Controller ... Ms. Deborah KRAFT
13 Director Information Technology ... Mr. Kelly KLIMPT

37 Dir Student Financial Aid Placement ... Ms. Gabriela LEON
15 Exec Director Human Resources ... Ms. Karen EDWARDS
18 Director Physical Plant ... Ms. Hameedah MAJEED
29 Director Alumni Relations ... Ms. Wendy DEL BELLO
07 Director Advising Services ... Ms. Regan METOYER
09 Exec Dir of Inst Effective/Research ... Ms. Pamelyn SHEFMAN
30 Chief Development ... Ms. Wendy DEL BELLO
26 Chief Public Relations Officer ... Ms. Wendy DEL BELLO
88 Assistant Director Fiscal Affairs ... Ms. Laurel JOSEPH
35 Coordinator Student Activities ... Vacant
04 Administrative Asst to President ... Ms. Tammy GIFFROW
19 Director Security/Safety ... Mr. Mark (Jeff) EARLE

Amarillo College (A)

PO Box 447, Amarillo TX 79178-0001

County: Potter FICE Identification: 003540
Unit ID: 222576
Telephone: (806) 371-5000 Carnegie Class: Assoc/MT-VT-High Trad
FAX Number: (806) 371-5370 Calendar System: Semester
URL: www.actx.edu
Established: 1929 Annual Undergrad Tuition & Fees (In-District): $2,136
Enrollment: 10,259 Coed
Affiliation or Control: State/Local IRS Status: 501(c)3
Highest Offering: Associate Degree
Accreditation: SC, ADNUR, COARC, DA, DH, EMT, FUSER, MLTAD, MUS, NMT, OTA, PTAA, RAD, RTT, SURGT

01 President ... Dr. Russell D. LOWERY-HART
03 Executive Vice President ... Mr. Mark D. WHITE
05 VP of Academic Affairs ... Dr. Tamara T. CLUNIS
10 VP of Business Affairs ... Mr. Steve G. SMITH
26 VP Communications & Marketing ... Mr. Kevin J. BALL
84 VP of Enrollment Management ... Mr. Bob C. AUSTIN
32 VP of Student Affairs ... Ms. Denese SKINNER
15 VP for Human Resources ... Ms. Cheryl JONES
20 Assoc VP Academic Affairs ... Mr. Frank E. SOBEY
102 Dir AC Foundation/Development ... Mrs. Kathleen B. DOWDY
51 Dean of Continuing Education ... Ms. Toni B. GRAY
76 Dean of Health Sciences ... Mrs. Kimberly A. CROWLEY
18 Manager Physical Plant ... Mr. Jim BACA
37 Director Financial Aid ... Ms. Kelly PRATER
08 Director AC Library Network ... Ms. Emily R. GILBERT
06 Registrar ... Mrs. Diane BRICE
19 Chief of Police ... Ms. Stephanie N. BIRKENFELD
27 Dir Foundation Mktg/Special Events .. Mrs. Tracy D. DOUGHERTY
09 Exec Dir Decision Analytics & IR .. Mr. Collin C. WITHERSPOON
121 Director of Advising ... Mr. Ernesto F. OLMOS
88 Director Amarillo Museum of Art ... Mrs. Kim B. MAHAN
88 Director Criminal Justice Program ... Mr. Eric C. WALLACE
96 Director of Purchasing/Records Ret ... Ms. Kimberly L. CARLILE
81 Dean of STEM ... Dr. Carol BUSE
72 Interim Dean of Technical Education ... Ms. Linda MUNOZ
49 Dean of Liberal Arts ... Ms. Rebecca EASTON
88 Dean Academic Success ... Ms. Edythe L. CARTER
88 Vice Pres Strategic Initiatives ... Ms. Cara J. CROWLEY
07 Recruitment Coordinator ... Mr. Richie GARZA
13 Chief Information Officer ... Mr. Shane E. HEPLER
04 Administrative Asst to President ... Ms. Joy D. BRENNEMAN
106 Dir Online Education/E-learning ... Ms. Heather L. VORAN
108 Director Inst Effectiveness ... Ms. Tina M. BABB
25 Chief Contracts/Grants Admin ... Ms. Teresa G. CLEMONS
35 Director of Student Life ... Ms. Amber HAMILTON
88 Director of Outreach Services ... Ms. Cassie MONTGOMERY
12 Dean of Campus Ops Moore County ... Ms. Renee VINCENT
12 Dean of Campus Ops Hereford ... Mr. Daniel ESQUIVEL

Amberton University (B)

1700 Eastgate Drive, Garland TX 75041

County: Dallas FICE Identification: 022594
Unit ID: 222628
Telephone: (972) 279-6511 Carnegie Class: Masters/L
FAX Number: (972) 279-9773 Calendar System: Semester
URL: www.amberton.edu
Established: 1971 Annual Undergrad Tuition & Fees: N/A
Enrollment: 1,257 Coed
Affiliation or Control: Independent Non-Profit IRS Status: 501(c)3
Highest Offering: Master's
Accreditation: SC

01 President ... Dr. Melinda REAGAN
05 Academic Dean ... Dr. Deborah HILL
111 Dean Univ Advance/VP Strategic Svcs ... Dr. Jo Lynn LOYD
10 Chief Business Officer ... Mr. Brent BRADSHAW
06 Registrar ... Ms. Hannah GRAY
32 Dean for Student Services ... Dr. Robert RUPE
84 Director for Recruiting ... Mr. Glenn SORRELLS
08 Head Librarian ... Ms. Jaimie QUINN
29 Dir Alumni Relations & Inst Rsrch ... Dr. Jo Lynn LOYD
07 Director of Admissions ... Dr. Deborah HILL

American College of Acupuncture and Oriental Medicine (C)

9100 Park West Drive, Houston TX 77063-4104

County: Harris FICE Identification: 031533
Unit ID: 429085
Telephone: (713) 780-9777 Carnegie Class: Spec-4-yr-Other Health
FAX Number: (713) 781-5781 Calendar System: Trimester
URL: www.acaom.edu
Established: 1991 Annual Graduate Tuition & Fees: N/A
Enrollment: 120 Coed
Affiliation or Control: Proprietary IRS Status: Proprietary
Highest Offering: Doctorate; No Undergraduates
Accreditation: SC, ACUP

01 President ... Dr. John Paul LIANG
11 Vice President of Operations ... Ms. Angel GUINARA
05 Dean of Academic Affairs ... Dr. Wen HUANG
20 Dean of Clinical Training ... Dr. Baisong ZHONG
06 Registrar ... Ms. Vicki ROSSMAN
09 Dir Inst Research/Effectiveness ... Mr. Michael Dale STAFFORD
37 Financial Aid Ofcr/Inst Compliance ... Ms. Theresa LIGON

American InterContinental University - Houston (D)

9999 Richmond Avenue, Houston TX 77042-4516

Telephone: (832) 201-3600 Identification: 666335
Accreditation: &NH, ACBSP

† Regional accreditation is carried under the parent institution in Schaumburg, IL.

Ana G. Mendez University Dallas Campus (E)

3010 N. Stemmons Fwy, Dallas TX 75247

Telephone: (469) 341-7300 Identification: 770947
Accreditation: &M

† Branch campus of Universidad Ana G. Mendez, Rio Piedras, PR

Angelina College (F)

PO Box 1768, Lufkin TX 75902-1768

County: Angelina FICE Identification: 006661
Unit ID: 222822
Telephone: (936) 639-1301 Carnegie Class: Assoc/HVT-Mix Trad/Non
FAX Number: (936) 639-4299 Calendar System: Semester
URL: www.angelina.edu
Established: 1966 Annual Undergrad Tuition & Fees (In-District): $2,640
Enrollment: 5,215 Coed
Affiliation or Control: State/Local IRS Status: 501(c)3
Highest Offering: Associate Degree
Accreditation: SC, COARC, DMS, EMT, RAD, SURGT

01 President ... Dr. Michael SIMON
05 Vice Pres Academic Affairs ... Dr. Cynthia CASPARIS
10 Vice President Business Services ... Mr. Chris SULLIVAN
31 Dean of Community Services ... Mr. Tim DITORO
32 Dean of Student Affairs ... Mr. Steve HUDMAN
13 Dir Management Information Systems ... Mr. Kenneth STREET
37 Interim Dir Student Financial Aid ... Mr. Glen GOFORTH
18 Chief Facilities/Physical Plant ... Mr. Steve CAPPS
15 Director Human Resources ... Mrs. Tifini WHIDDON
07 Dir Enrollment Services/Registrar ... Mrs. Sandra COX
106 Director Distance Education ... Mrs. Judy WRIGHT
21 Controller ... Mrs. Melissa GOINS
04 Administrative Asst to President ... Ms. Tracy NEAL

AOMA Graduate School of Integrative Medicine (G)

4701 West Gate Boulevard, Austin TX 78745

County: Travis FICE Identification: 031564
Unit ID: 429094
Telephone: (512) 454-1188 Carnegie Class: Spec-4-yr-Other Health
FAX Number: (512) 454-7001 Calendar System: Quarter
URL: www.aoma.edu
Established: 1993 Annual Graduate Tuition & Fees: N/A
Enrollment: 160 Coed
Affiliation or Control: Proprietary IRS Status: Proprietary
Highest Offering: Doctorate; No Undergraduates
Accreditation: SC, ACUP

01 President ... Dr. Mary FARIA
05 Vice President of Faculty ... Dr. Qianzhi (Jamie) WU
88 VP of Academics & Accreditation ... Dr. Lesley HAMILTON
32 Dean of Students ... Mr. Robert LAGUNA
10 Acting CFO ... Ms. Linda FONTAINE
88 Director of Clinical Education ... Dr. Jing FAN
11 Director of Operations ... Ms. Inge BOTHMA
08 Head Librarian ... Mr. David YORK
07 Director of Admissions ... Mr. Brian BECKER
06 Registrar ... Ms. Ashley LOYD
58 Dean of Academics ... Dr. Yuxin HE
88 Director of Herbal Studies ... Dr. Violet SONG
88 Director Acupuncture ... Dr. Yuxing LIU
23 Clinic Business Director ... Ms. Stephanee OWENBY
121 Academic Advisor ... Mr. Robert LAGUNA
26 Dir of Marketing and Outreach ... Vacant
37 Director Student Financial Aid ... Ms. Estella SEARS
81 Director of Biomedical Sciences ... Dr. Raja MANDYAM
09 Dir Inst Effectiveness/Cont Educ ... Ms. Cara EDMOND

Arlington Baptist University (H)

3001 W Division, Arlington TX 76012-3497

County: Tarrant FICE Identification: 020814
Unit ID: 222877
Telephone: (817) 461-8741 Carnegie Class: Spec-4-yr-Faith
FAX Number: (817) 274-1138 Calendar System: Semester
URL: www.ABU.edu
Established: 1939 Annual Undergrad Tuition & Fees: $13,690
Enrollment: 173 Coed
Affiliation or Control: Baptist IRS Status: 501(c)3
Highest Offering: Master's
Accreditation: BI

01 President ... Vacant
05 Vice Pres Academic Affairs ... Ms. Janie TAYLOR
32 Dean of Students ... Mr. John BROWN
10 Business Manager/Dir Financial Aid ... Mr. David INGRAM
06 Registrar ... Ms. Janie TAYLOR
08 Head Librarian ... Ms. Amy SCHAEFFER
18 Director Physical Plant ... Mr. Scott RITCHEY
40 Director Bookstore ... Mrs. Vickie BRYANT
111 Director Institutional Advancement ... Vacant
41 Athletic Director ... Mr. Cliff MCDANIEL
106 Dir Online Education/E-learning ... Dr. Carl JOHNSON
37 Director Student Financial Aid ... Mrs. Cindy TREAT
13 Chief Info Technology Officer (CIO) ... Mr. Gary POOL

The Art Institute of Austin (I)

101 W. Louis Henna Blvd, Ste 100, Austin TX 78728

Telephone: (512) 691-1707 Identification: 770973
Accreditation: &SC, CIDA

Art Institute of Dallas (J)

8080 Park Lane, Suite 100, Dallas TX 75231-5993

Telephone: (214) 692-8080 FICE Identification: 025396
Accreditation: &SC, ACFEI, CIDA

† Regional accreditation is carried under the parent institution, Miami International University, Miami, FL.

The Art Institute of Houston (K)

4140 Southwest Freeway, Houston TX 77027

County: Harris FICE Identification: 021171
Unit ID: 222938
Telephone: (713) 623-2040 Carnegie Class: Spec-4-yr-Arts
FAX Number: (713) 966-2700 Calendar System: Quarter
URL: www.aih.aii.edu
Established: 1978 Annual Undergrad Tuition & Fees: $17,568
Enrollment: 1,096 Coed
Affiliation or Control: Proprietary IRS Status: Proprietary
Highest Offering: Baccalaureate
Accreditation: SC, ACFEI, CIDA

01 President ... Susanne BEHRENS
05 Provost ... Dr. Gary EATON
32 Dean of Student Affairs ... LaToya NORTHINGTON
07 Senior Director of Admissions ... Jane CHASTANT
15 Human Resources Generalist ... Elizabeth WHITTINGTON
37 Dir of Student Financial Services ... Kelly GARRETT
06 Registrar ... Grace JACKSON
04 Administrative Asst to President ... Teresa SMITH

The Art Institute of San Antonio (L)

10000 IH-10 W, Ste 200, San Antonio TX 78230

Telephone: (210) 338-7320 Identification: 770974
Accreditation: &SC, CIDA

Auguste Escoffier School of Culinary Arts (M)

6020-B Dilliard Circle, Austin TX 78752-4438

County: Travis FICE Identification: 037276
Unit ID: 444556
Telephone: (512) 451-5743 Carnegie Class: Spec 2-yr-A&S
FAX Number: (512) 467-9120 Calendar System: Quarter
URL: www.escoffier.edu
Established: 1997 Annual Undergrad Tuition & Fees: N/A
Enrollment: 490 Coed
Affiliation or Control: Proprietary IRS Status: Proprietary
Highest Offering: Associate Degree
Accreditation: COE, ACFEI

01 Campus President ... Mr. Marcus MCMELLON
07 Director of Admissions ... Mr. David R. NORRIS
37 Director Student Financial Aid ... Ms. Larresia WHITTEN
36 Director of Career Services ... Ms. Ann DERRICK
10 Director Business Operations ... Ms. Mary REARDON

Austin College (N)

900 N Grand Avenue, Sherman TX 75090-4400

County: Grayson FICE Identification: 003543
Unit ID: 222983
Telephone: (903) 813-2000 Carnegie Class: Bac-A&S
FAX Number: (903) 813-3199 Calendar System: 4/1/4
URL: www.austincollege.edu
Established: 1849 Annual Undergrad Tuition & Fees: $39,960
Enrollment: 1,228 Coed
Affiliation or Control: Presbyterian Church (U.S.A.) IRS Status: 501(c)3
Highest Offering: Master's
Accreditation: SC

01 President ... Mr. Steven P. O'DAY
05 VP Acad Aff & Dean of the Faculty ... Dr. Beth GILL
32 Vice Pres Student Affairs/Athletics ... Mr. Timothy P. MILLERICK
111 Int VP Institutional Advancement ... Ms. Gillian LOCKE

10 Vice President for Business Affairs .... Ms. Heidi B. ELLIS
84 Vice President for Inst Enrollment .... Ms. Baylee L. KOWERT
21 Assoc VP Business Affairs .... Ms. Karen JOHNSON
110 Assoc VP for Inst Advancement .... Ms. Cary E. WACKER
29 Exec Dir Alumni Engagement .... Ms. Kate SHELLEY
37 AVP/Exec Director Financial Aid .... Ms. Laurie COULTER
07 AVP Enrollment/Dean of Admission .... Mr. Alan RAMIREZ
42 Chaplain/Dir of Church Relations .... Dr. John D. WILLIAMS
35 Dean of Students .... Mr. Michael DEEN
06 Exec Dir Inst Research/Registrar .... Dr. Eugenia HARRIS
08 College Librarian/Library Director .... Ms. Barbara CORNELIUS
79 Dean of Humanities .... Dr. Max GROBER
81 Dean of Sciences .... Dr. Steve GOLDSMITH
83 Dean of Social Sciences .... Dr. Lisa M. BROWN
15 Director of Human Resources .... Mr. Keith L. LAREY
36 Director Career Services .... Ms. Margie A. NORMAN
13 Director IT .... Mr. Garrett HUBBARD
53 Chair of Education Dept .... Dr. Julia SHAHID
104 International Education Coordinator .... Ms. Cheryl MARCELO
26 Director of Public Affairs .... Dr. Lynn Z. WOMBLE
19 Chief of Police .... Mr. James PERRY
40 Manager of Campus Bookstore .... Ms. Helen BERGMAN
27 Exec Dir Editorial Communications .... Ms. Vickie S. KIRBY
18 Exec Director of Facilities .... Mr. David TURK
96 Purchasing Representative .... Ms. Geni KELSO
102 Dir Corp/Foundation/Gov Relations .... Ms. Lisa SIMPSON
41 Director of Athletics .... Mr. David NORMAN
101 Asst to Pres/Asst Sec of Board .... Ms. Genna BETHEL
38 Coordinator of Counseling .... Ms. Tracy POWERS
39 Director of Residence Life .... Mr. Patrick MILLER

Austin Community College District (A)

5930 Middle Fiskville Road, Austin TX 78752-4390

County: Travis FICE Identification: 012015
Unit ID: 222992
Telephone: (512) 223-7598 Carnegie Class: Assoc/MT-VT-Mix Trad/Non
FAX Number: (512) 223-7185 Calendar System: Semester
URL: www.austincc.edu
Established: 1972 Annual Undergrad Tuition & Fees (In-District): $2,550
Enrollment: 40,803 Coed
Affiliation or Control: State/Local IRS Status: 501(c)3
Highest Offering: Baccalaureate
Accreditation: SC, ACBSP, ACFEI, ADNUR, CAHIIM, DH, DMS, EMT, MLTAD, OTA, PNUR, PTAA, RAD, SURGT

01 President/CEO .... Dr. Richard M. RHODES
03 Provost/Exec Vice Pres .... Dr. Charles COOK
10 EVP Finance & Administration .... Mr. Neil W. VICKERS
11 EVP Campus Operation & Public Affs .. Dr. Molly Beth MALCOLM
05 VP Instruction .... Mr. Michael T. MIDGLEY
32 Interim VP Student Services .... Dr. Guillermo MARTINEZ
15 VP Human Resources .... Ms. Geraldine TUCKER
09 VP Effectiveness & Accountability .... Ms. Soon O. FLYNN
21 VP Business Services .... Ms. Angela HODGE
13 VP Information Technology .... Mr. Imad CONSTANTINI
45 VP Inst Planning/Develop & Eval .... Dr. Mary E. HARRIS
18 VP Facilities & Construction .... Mr. William S. MULLANE
26 VP Communications & Marketing .... Ms. Brette E. LEA
06 Registrar .... Ms. Glynis MILLER
07 Executive Director of Admissions .... Ms. Linda TERRY
08 Dean Library Services .... Dr. Julie TODARO
19 Chief of Police .... Mr. Lynn DIXON
37 Executive Director Financial Aid .... Mr. Jason BRISENO
96 Director Procure to Pay .... Mr. Robert HALL
29 Director Alumni Relations .... Ms. Mary Ann CICALA
04 Special Assistant to the President .... Ms. Pamela SUTTON

Austin Graduate School of Theology (B)

7640 Guadalupe Street, Austin TX 78752

County: Travis FICE Identification: 023628
Unit ID: 247825
Telephone: (512) 476-2772 Carnegie Class: Spec-4-yr-Faith
FAX Number: (512) 476-3919 Calendar System: Semester
URL: www.austingrad.edu
Established: 1976 Annual Undergrad Tuition & Fees: N/A
Enrollment: 36 Coed
Affiliation or Control: Independent Non-Profit IRS Status: 501(c)3
Highest Offering: Master's
Accreditation: SC

01 President .... Dr. Stanley G. REID
37 Vice President/Dir Financial Aid .... Mr. Dave ARTHUR
07 Dir Recruiting & Admiss/Registrar .... Ms. Lindi PARSHALL

Austin Presbyterian Theological Seminary (C)

100 E 27th Street, Austin TX 78705-5797

County: Travis FICE Identification: 003544
Unit ID: 223001
Telephone: (512) 472-6736 Carnegie Class: Spec-4-yr-Faith
FAX Number: (512) 479-0738 Calendar System: Semester
URL: www.austinseminary.edu
Established: 1902 Annual Graduate Tuition & Fees: N/A
Enrollment: 158 Coed
Affiliation or Control: Presbyterian Church (U.S.A.) IRS Status: 501(c)3
Highest Offering: Doctorate; No Undergraduates
Accreditation: SC, THEOL

01 President .... Rev. Theodore J. WARDLAW
05 Academic Dean .... Dr. David H. JENSEN
10 Vice Pres Finance/Administration .... Ms. Heather ZDANCEWICZ
111 Vice Pres Institutional Advancement .... Ms. Donna SCOTT
32 Dean of Students .... Rev. Sarah GAVENTA
84 Vice Pres for Enrollment Management .... Rev. Jorge D. HERRERA
51 VP Education Beyond the Walls .... Ms. Melissa WIGINTON
08 Director of the Stitt Library .... Dr. Timothy LINCOLN
06 Asst Dean Academic Affs/Registrar .... Ms. Jacqueline D. HEFLEY
26 Director of Communications .... Ms. Randal WHITTINGTON
100 Chief of Staff/President's Office .... Ms. Mona SANTANDREA
13 Senior Director of Info Technology .... Ms. Julie NEWTON
37 Director of Financial Aid .... Ms. Glenna BALCH
18 Chief Facilities/Physical Plant .... Mr. John EVERETT
30 Director of Development .... Rev. Alan KRUMMENACHER
110 Director of Advancement Services .... Mr. JR BARDEN
29 Director Alumni & Church Relations .... Mr. Gary MATHEWS

Bakke Graduate University (D)

8515 Greenville Ave, S206, Dallas TX 75243-7039

County: Dallas FICE Identification: 031108
Unit ID: 420705
Telephone: (214) 329-4447 Carnegie Class: Spec-4-yr-Faith
FAX Number: (214) 347-9367 Calendar System: Semester
URL: www.bgu.edu
Established: 1990 Annual Graduate Tuition & Fees: N/A
Enrollment: 67 Coed
Affiliation or Control: Independent Non-Profit IRS Status: 501(c)3
Highest Offering: Doctorate; No Undergraduates
Accreditation: TRACS

01 President .... Dr. Brad SMITH
05 Academic Dean .... Dr. Bryan MCCABE
10 Chief Operations/Financial Ofcr .... Ms. Carolyn COCHRAN
06 Registrar .... Dr. Martine AUDEOUD
07 Admissions Coordinator .... Ms. Kafi CARRASCO
08 Head Librarian .... Ms. Jennifer ROMAN
106 Dir Online Education/E-learning .... Ms. Nathalia BURROWES
37 Director Student Financial Aid .... Ms. Carolyn COCHRAN
09 Dir Institutional Effectiveness .... Dr. Judi MELTON

Baptist Health System School of Health Professions (E)

8400 Datapoint Drive, San Antonio TX 78229

County: Bexar FICE Identification: 006606
Unit ID: 223083
Telephone: (210) 297-9636 Carnegie Class: Spec-4-yr-Other Health
FAX Number: (210) 297-0075 Calendar System: Semester
URL: www.bshp.edu
Established: 1903 Annual Undergrad Tuition & Fees: N/A
Enrollment: 665 Coed
Affiliation or Control: Proprietary IRS Status: Proprietary
Highest Offering: Master's
Accreditation: ABHES, ADNUR, NUR, RAD, SURGT, SURTEC

01 President and Dean .... Dr. Bill DREES
05 Chief Academic Officer .... Steve KOLAR
04 Administrative Asst to President .... Diane TYLER
07 Director of Admissions .... Jillian DENMAN
08 Director of Library .... Anita SHAW
106 Director of Gen Educ and Online .... Lucinda FLORES
10 Director of Finance .... Priti LAXMI
37 Director of Student Financial Aid .... Patrick REYNA
13 Director of Information Systems .... Nancy ORTIZ
06 Registrar .... Rebecca WATTS
06 Registrar .... Laura GOMEZ

† Tuition varies by degree program.

Baptist Hospitals of Southeast Texas School of Radiologic Technology (F)

3030 Fannin Ste A, Beaumont TX 77704

County: Jefferson Identification: 667153
Telephone: (409) 212-5724 Carnegie Class: Not Classified
FAX Number: N/A Calendar System: Semester
URL: www.bhset.net
Established: 1952 Annual Undergrad Tuition & Fees: N/A
Enrollment: N/A Coed
Affiliation or Control: Independent Non-Profit IRS Status: 501(c)3
Highest Offering: Associate Degree
Accreditation: RAD

01 Program Director .... Deborah SMITH
11 Chief of Administration .... David PARMER

Baptist Missionary Association Theological Seminary (G)

P.O. Box 670/1530 East Pine Street, Jacksonville TX 75766-5407

County: Cherokee FICE Identification: 023312
Unit ID: 223117
Telephone: (903) 586-2501 Carnegie Class: Spec-4-yr-Faith
FAX Number: (903) 586-0378 Calendar System: Semester
URL: www.bmats.edu
Established: 1957 Annual Undergrad Tuition & Fees: $6,900
Enrollment: 161 Coed
Affiliation or Control: Baptist IRS Status: 501(c)3
Highest Offering: Master's
Accreditation: SC, THEOL

01 President .... Dr. Charley HOLMES
05 Dean/Registrar .... Dr. Philip ATTEBERY
04 Assistant to the President .... Keri SOUTHERN
32 Director of Student Services .... Dr. Ronnie J. JOHNSON
08 Library Director .... Jacob GUCKER
10 Chief Business Officer .... Chris PROCTOR

Baptist University of the Americas (H)

7838 Barlite Blvd., San Antonio TX 78224-1336

County: Bexar FICE Identification: 037333
Unit ID: 444398
Telephone: (210) 924-4338 Carnegie Class: Spec-4-yr-Faith
FAX Number: (210) 924-0888 Calendar System: Semester
URL: www.bua.edu
Established: 1947 Annual Undergrad Tuition & Fees: $6,240
Enrollment: 177 Coed
Affiliation or Control: Baptist IRS Status: 501(c)3
Highest Offering: Baccalaureate
Accreditation: BI

01 President .... Dr. Abraham JAQUEZ
100 Chief of Staff .... Dr. Gabriel CORTES
05 Interim Dean Academic Affairs .... Dr. Mario RAMOS
10 Director for Admin and Finance .... Mr. Daniel CANCINO, JR.
37 Financial Aid Administrator .... Mrs. Araceli ACOSTA

Baylor College of Medicine (I)

One Baylor Plaza, Houston TX 77030-3411

County: Harris FICE Identification: 004949
Unit ID: 223223
Telephone: (713) 798-4951 Carnegie Class: Spec-4-yr-Med
FAX Number: (713) 798-3692 Calendar System: Quarter
URL: www.bcm.edu
Established: 1900 Annual Graduate Tuition & Fees: N/A
Enrollment: 1,585 Coed
Affiliation or Control: Independent Non-Profit IRS Status: 501(c)3
Highest Offering: Doctorate; No Undergraduates
Accreditation: SC, ANEST, ARCPA, IPSY, MED, OPE

00 Chancellor .... Dr. Bert O'MALLEY
01 President and CEO .... Dr. Paul KLOTMAN
05 Provost/SVP Acad & Faculty Affairs .... Dr. Alicia MONROE
17 Vice Pres/Chief Medical Officer .... Dr. Steve SIGWORTH
10 Sr VP/Chief Business Officer .... Mrs. Kimberly C. DAVID
30 Vice Pres Philanthropy .... Mr. James DIGAN
43 Sr Vice Pres/General Counsel .... Mr. Robert F. CORRIGAN, JR.
26 VP Commun/Community Outreach .... Ms. Claire M. BASSETT
15 Vice President Human Resources .... Mr. Dane FRIEND
46 Sr Vice President/Dean Research .... Dr. Adam KUSPA
13 VP Information Technology .... Mr. Lee LEIBER
86 Vice Pres Government Relations .... Mr. Tom KLEINWORTH
88 Dean Natl Sch Tropical Medicine .... Dr. Peter J. HOTEZ
21 VP Finance/CFO .... Ms. Julie NICKELL
63 Dean School of Medicine .... Dr. Jennifer CHRISTNER
58 Int Dean Grad Sch Biomed Sciences .... Dr. Adam KUSPA
76 Dean School of Health Professions .... Dr. Robert MCLAUGHLIN
28 Sr Assoc Dean Diversity .... Vacant
51 Sr Assoc Dean Cont Medical Educ ... Dr. C. Michael FORDIS, JR.
07 Assoc Dean Admission .... Dr. Karen JOHNSON
07 Assistant Dean for Admissions .... Dr. Jesus G. VALLEJO
35 Assistant Dean Student Affairs .... Dr. Andrea G. STOLAR
21 Controller .... Mr. Douglas R. SPADE
20 Assoc Provost Academic Affairs .... Ms. Lily SHIH
37 Director Student Financial Planning .... Ms. Hilda DELEON
32 Assoc Dean of Student Affairs .... Mr. Joseph KASS
88 Exec Director Environmental Safety .... Mr. Paul MURACA
75 Director Occupational Medicine .... Dr. James E. KELAHER
29 Director Alumni Affairs .... Mr. Alexander M. HOPKINS
96 Director Supply Chain Management .... Mr. Miguel MACHADO
06 Registrar .... Ms. Latoya R. WHITAKER
88 Asst Dean Graduate Medical Educ .... Dr. Nana E. COLEMAN
88 Associate Dean Curriculum .... Dr. Nadia ISMAIL
88 Associate Provost Faculty Affairs .... Dr. William THOMSON
09 Assoc Provost Fac Dev/Inst Research .... Dr. Nancy MORENO
28 Assoc Prov Inst Diversity/Stdnt Svc .... Dr. Toi HARRIS
04 Admin Assistant to the President .... Ms. Julie WOLKEN
100 Chief of Staff .... Ms. Lorie TABAK
101 Exec Dir Inst Gov/Board Rels .... Ms. Carolyn COCANOUGHER
88 Asst Dean Curriculum .... Dr. Stacy ROSE

Baylor University (J)

One Bear Place #97096, Waco TX 76798-7096

County: McLennan FICE Identification: 003545
Unit ID: 223232
Telephone: (254) 710-3555 Carnegie Class: DU-Higher
FAX Number: (254) 710-3557 Calendar System: Semester
URL: www.baylor.edu
Established: 1845 Annual Undergrad Tuition & Fees: $45,542
Enrollment: 17,059 Coed
Affiliation or Control: Baptist IRS Status: 501(c)3
Highest Offering: Doctorate
Accreditation: SC, CAATE, CIDA, CLPSY, DIETD, DIETI, HSA, IPSY, JOUR, LAW, MIDWF, MUS, NURSE, PH, @PTA, SP, SW, THEA, THEOL

01 President .... Dr. Linda A. LIVINGSTONE

05 Provost ... Dr. Nancy W. BRICKHOUSE
100 Chief of Staff to the President ... Dr. Robyn L. DRISKELL
10 Chief Business Officer ... Mr. Brett DALTON
117 Chief Compliance and Risk Officer ... Mr. Blake ABBE
111 VP for Advancement ... Mr. David ROSSELLI
32 Vice President Student Life ... Dr. Kevin P. JACKSON
26 VP Marketing & Comm/CMO ... Mr. Jason D. COOK
29 Vice Pres Constituent Engagement ... Vacant
43 Gen Counsel/CLO & Corp Sec ... Mr. Christopher W. HOLMES
41 VP & Director of Athletics ... Mr. Mack RHOADES, IV
09 Director Inst Research/Testing ... Dr. Kathleen MORLEY
21 VP of Financial Operations ... Mrs. Susan D. ANZ
114 AVP of Budget & Planning ... Mr. Brian S. DENMAN
18 VP for Facilities & Oper Mgmt ... Vacant
15 VP & Chief Human Resource Officer ... Mrs. Cheryl GOCHIS
13 Int VP Information Tech/Deputy CIO ... Mr. Jon ALLEN
08 Interim Dean of Libraries ... Mr. John WILSON
35 Associate Vice Pres Student Life ... Dr. Martha Lou SCOTT
06 Registrar ... Mr. Jonathan C. HELM
45 Assoc VP for Strategic Initiatives ... Mr. Chris KRAUSE
90 Assoc Vice Pres Electronic Library ... Mr. Timothy M. LOGAN
108 Dir of Inst Planning & Assessment ... Dr. J. Ben COX
97 Vice Provost Undergrad Education ... Dr. Wesley NULL
20 Vice Prov/Academic Affs & Policy ... Dr. James BENNIGHOFF
46 Int Vice Provost Research ... Dr. Kevin CHAMBLISS
84 Assoc VP of Enrollment Mgmt ... Ms. Jennifer CARRON
115 VP & Chief Investment Officer ... Mr. R. Brian WEBB
19 Chief of Police ... Mr. Brad WIGTIL
93 Director Multiculture Affairs ... Mrs. Pearlie BEVERLY
121 Director Academic Support Programs ... Ms. Sally FIRMIN
23 Medical Director Health Center ... Dr. Sharon STERN
36 Exec Dr Career & Professional Dev ... Vacant
25 Asst Vice Prov Res & Dir Spons Prog ... Ms. Lisa H. MCKETHAN
38 Exec Director Counseling Svcs ... Dr. James G. MARSH
40 Director Baylor Bookstore ... Ms. Pam STANDERFER
86 Director Governmental Relations ... Ms. Rochonda FARMER-NEAL
96 Asst VP for Procurement Services ... Mr. Tom HOFFMEYER
51 Dir of Continuing Education ... Ms. Gabriela COLMAN
49 Dean College of Arts/Sciences ... Dr. Lee C. NORDT
50 Dean School of Business ... Dr. Terry S. MANESS
53 Interim Dean School of Education ... Dr. Terrell F. SAXON
61 Dean School of Law ... Mr. Bradley TOBEN
64 Dean School of Music ... Dr. Gary MORTENSON
66 Dean School of Nursing ... Dr. Shelley F. CONROY
58 Vice Provost & Dean Graduate School ... Dr. Larry LYON
73 Dean Truett Theological Sem ... Dr. Todd D. STILL
54 Dean Engineering & Computer Science ... Dr. Dennis L. O'NEAL
92 Dean Honors College/Dir BU in DC ... Dr. Thomas S. HIBBS
85 Vice Provost for Global Engagement ... Dr. Jeffrey S. HAMILTON
35 Dean Student Development ... Dr. Elizabeth PALACIOS
35 Dean Student Learning & Engagement ... Dr. Jeff DOYLE
42 University Chaplain ... Dr. Burt BURLESON
88 Assoc Dean Student Conduct Admin ... Ms. Bethany J. MCCRAW
37 Sr Dir of Student Financial Aid ... Ms. Lisa MARTIN
88 Assoc VP Public Safety & Security ... Mr. Mark CHILDERS
04 Exec Assistant to the President ... Ms. Mia CASEY
101 Secretary of the Institution/Board ... Ms. Kristy ORR
104 Director Study Abroad ... Mr. Bo WHITE
28 Manager of EEO & Inclusion ... Ms. Shirl BROWN
39 Director Campus Living & Learning ... Ms. Tiffany P. LOWE
44 Director Annual Giving ... Ms. Laura KRAMER-LUCAS

B.H. Carroll Theological Institute (A)

6500 N Belt Line Road, Suite 100, Irving TX 75063-6056
County: Tarrant Identification: 667089
Telephone: (972) 580-7600 Carnegie Class: Not Classified
FAX Number: (972) 756-0600 Calendar System: Semester
URL: www.bhcarroll.edu
Established: 2004 Annual Graduate Tuition & Fees: N/A
Enrollment: N/A Coed
Affiliation or Control: Southern Baptist IRS Status: 501(c)3
Highest Offering: Doctorate; No Undergraduates
Accreditation: BI, THEOL

01 President ... Dr. C. Gene WILKES
10 CFO/Director Business Affairs ... Ms. Debra HOLDER
06 Registrar ... Dr. Stan MOORE
07 Director of Admissions ... Ms. Michelle MARTIN
13 Director Information Technology ... Mr. Carl HEATH
09 Dir of Institutional Effectiveness ... Ms. Amanda CRANE

The Bible Seminary (B)

2655 South Mason Rd, Katy TX 77450
County: Harris Identification: 667371
Telephone: (281) 646-1109 Carnegie Class: Not Classified
FAX Number: (281) 646-1110 Calendar System: Semester
URL: thebibleseminary.org
Established: 2008 Annual Graduate Tuition & Fees: N/A
Enrollment: N/A Coed
Affiliation or Control: Non-denominational IRS Status: 501(c)3
Highest Offering: Master's; No Undergraduates
Accreditation: @TRACS

01 President ... Dr. K. Lynn LEWIS
05 Provost ... Dr. Scott STRIPLING
10 Vice Pres Finance & Administration ... Mr. Rick MCCALIP

Blinn College (C)

902 College Avenue, Brenham TX 77833-4098
County: Washington FICE Identification: 003549
Unit ID: 223427
Telephone: (979) 830-4000 Carnegie Class: Assoc/HT-High Trad
FAX Number: (979) 830-4030 Calendar System: Semester
URL: www.blinn.edu
Established: 1883 Annual Undergrad Tuition & Fees (In-District): $2,832
Enrollment: 19,476 Coed
Affiliation or Control: State/Local IRS Status: 501(c)3
Highest Offering: Associate Degree
Accreditation: SC, ADNUR, CAHIIM, DH, EMT, IFSAC, PTAA, RAD

01 Chancellor ... Dr. Mary HENSLEY
43 Exec Vice Chanc/General Counsel ... Mr. Leighton SCHUBERT
101 Special Asst to Chancellor/BOT ... Ms. Laurie CLARK
05 Vice Chancellor Academic Affairs ... Dr. Marcelo BUSSIKI
32 Vice Chancellor Student Svcs/Admin ... Ms. Karen BUCK
10 Vice Chanc Business/Finance/CFO ... Mr. Richard CERVANTES
15 Asst Vice Chanc Human Resources ... Ms. Marie KIRBY
32 Asst Vice Chanc Student Services ... Dr. John TURNER
12 Executive Dean Bryan Campus ... Dr. Jimmy BYRD
12 Executive Dean RELLIS Campus ... Mr. Chris MARRS
18 AVC Facilities/Planning/Constr ... Mr. Richard O'MALLEY
09 Dean Inst Research/Effectiveness ... Vacant
06 Dean Admissions/Records/Registrar ... Ms. Christy JOHANSON
88 Judicial Officer ... Ms. Sigrid WOODS
102 Exec Dir Foundation/Alumni Affairs ... Ms. Susan MYERS
12 Exec Dean Schulenburg Campus ... Ms. Rebecca GARLICK
12 Exec Dean Sealy Campus ... Ms. Lisa CATON
72 Dean Technical/Prof Programs ... Mr. Jon (Jay) ANDERSON
35 Dean Student Engagement ... Dr. Becky MCBRIDE
13 Dir Administrative Computing Svcs ... Ms. Christine WIED
37 Dean Financial Aid/Scholarships ... Mr. Brent WILLIFORD
41 Athletic Dir/Mens Head Bsktbl Coach ... Mr. Scott SCHUMACHER
19 Chief College Police Department ... Mr. John CHANCELLOR
96 Director Purchasing/Transportation ... Mr. Ross SCHROEDER
07 Director Admissions & Records ... Ms. Kristi URBAN
26 Dir Marketing/Communications ... Mr. Rich BRAY
39 Dir Housing/Residential Life ... Mr. Ryan MILLER
04 Admin Assistant to the President ... Ms. Sharon JOHNSTON
121 Exec Dir Academic Success ... Ms. Joyce LANGENEGGER
54 Dean Business/Engineering ... Mr. Max HIBBS
90 Director Academic Computing ... Mr. Michael WELCH

Brazosport College (D)

500 College Drive, Lake Jackson TX 77566-3199
County: Brazoria FICE Identification: 007287
Unit ID: 223506
Telephone: (979) 230-3000 Carnegie Class: Bac/Assoc-Mixed
FAX Number: (979) 230-3443 Calendar System: Semester
URL: www.brazosport.edu
Established: 1968 Annual Undergrad Tuition & Fees (In-District): $2,715
Enrollment: 4,245 Coed
Affiliation or Control: Local IRS Status: 501(c)3
Highest Offering: Baccalaureate
Accreditation: SC, EMT

01 President ... Dr. Millicent M. VALEK
05 Provost Academic & Student Affairs ... Dr. Lynda VILLANUEVA
103 VP Industry & Community Resources ... Ms. Anne BARTLETT
111 VP College Advancement ... Ms. Tracee WATTS
15 VP Human Resources ... Mr. Marshall CAMPBELL
10 VP Financial Services & CFO ... Mr. David MARSHALL
32 Dean of Student Services ... Ms. Jo GREATHOUSE
20 Dean of Instruction ... Mr. Jeffrey DETRICK
45 Dean Plng/Inst Effectiv/Research ... Dr. Douglas WALCERZ
07 Director Admissions/Registrar ... Ms. Priscilla SANCHEZ
38 Director Counseling and Testing ... Mr. Arnold RAMIREZ
26 Director Marketing & Communications ... Mr. Kyle SMITH
13 Director Information Technology ... Mr. Ron PARKER
37 Director of Financial Aid ... Ms. Kay WRIGHT
08 Director Library & Learning Service ... Ms. Cassie BRUNER
18 Director Facility Services ... Mr. John DITTO
88 Director Small Business Dev Center ... Dr. Janice GOINES
31 Director Community Education ... Ms. Deborah EWING
88 Director Children's Center ... Ms. Christine WEBSTER
109 Director Business Services ... Ms. Ginger WOOSTER
116 Internal Auditor ... Ms. Evelyn CRUZ
09 Dir Planning/Inst Effectiv/Research ... Ms. Cindy ULLRICH
04 Admin Assistant to the President ... Ms. Kasie GUTHRIE
19 Director Security/Safety ... Mr. Chad LEVERITT

Brite Divinity School (E)

2925 Princeton Street, Fort Worth TX 76129-0001
County: Tarrant Identification: 666228
Unit ID: 450304
Telephone: (817) 257-7575 Carnegie Class: Spec-4-yr-Faith
FAX Number: (817) 257-6932 Calendar System: Semester
URL: www.brite.tcu.edu
Established: 1873 Annual Graduate Tuition & Fees: N/A
Enrollment: 224 Coed
Affiliation or Control: Independent Non-Profit IRS Status: 501(c)3
Highest Offering: Doctorate; No Undergraduates
Accreditation: SC, THEOL

01 President & Chief Executive Officer ... Dr. D. Newell WILLIAMS
05 Exec Vice President/Dean ... Dr. Michael MILLER
10 Vice President Business/Finance ... Ms. Michele G. SMITH
32 Associate Dean for Common Life ... Dr. Valerie FORSTMAN

Carrington College - Mesquite (F)

3733 West Emporium Circle, Mesquite TX 75150
Telephone: (972) 682-2800 Identification: 770967
Accreditation: &WJ

† Branch campus of Carrington College - Sacramento, Sacramento, CA

Center for Advanced Legal Studies (G)

800 W Sam Houston Pkwy, S Suite 100, Houston TX 77042
County: Harris FICE Identification: 026047
Unit ID: 379782
Telephone: (713) 529-2778 Carnegie Class: Spec 2-yr-Other
FAX Number: (855) 422-4466 Calendar System: Other
URL: www.paralegal.edu
Established: 1987 Annual Undergrad Tuition & Fees: N/A
Enrollment: 219 Coed
Affiliation or Control: Proprietary IRS Status: Proprietary
Highest Offering: Associate Degree
Accreditation: COE

01 School Director/Co-Founder ... Mr. Doyle HAPPE
05 Dean ... Mr. Thomas SWANSON
07 Director of Admissions ... Mr. James SCHEFFER

Central Texas College (H)

PO Box 1800, Killeen TX 76540-9990
County: Bell FICE Identification: 004003
Unit ID: 223816
Telephone: (254) 526-7161 Carnegie Class: Assoc/HT-High Non
FAX Number: (254) 526-0817 Calendar System: Semester
URL: www.ctcd.edu
Established: 1965 Annual Undergrad Tuition & Fees (In-District): $2,700
Enrollment: 15,672 Coed
Affiliation or Control: Local IRS Status: 501(c)3
Highest Offering: Associate Degree
Accreditation: SC, ADNUR, EMT, MLTAD

01 Chancellor ... Mr. Jim YEONOPOLUS
03 Deputy Chanc US Campus Operations ... Dr. Tina ADY
11 Deputy Chanc Finance & Admin ... Dr. Michele CARTER
05 Deputy Chanc Acad & Student Success ... Dr. Robin GARRETT
12 Dean Continental & Ft Hood Campuses ... Mr. Raul GARCIA
12 Dean Central Campus ... Ms. Janice ANDERSON
32 Dean Student Services ... Dr. Johnelle WELSH
08 Dean Library Services ... Ms. Lori PURSER
38 Associate Dean Guidance/Counseling ... Ms. Eva HUTCHENS
06 Associate Dean Admin/Reg/Records ... Mr. Stephen O'DONOVAN
10 Comptroller ... Mr. Bob LIBERTY
15 Director Human Resource Mgmt ... Ms. Holly JORDAN
106 Director Distance Education/Ed Tech ... Ms. Sharon DAVIS
18 Director Facilities Management ... Mr. Mark HARMSEN
21 Director Business Services ... Mr. Ted GONZALEZ
30 Director College Development ... Ms. Marcine CHAMBERS
09 Dir Institutional Effectiveness ... Dr. Jennifer CAMERON
13 Director Information Technology ... Mr. Cliff GAINES
07 Director Admissions/Recruitment ... Ms. Shannon BRALLEY
88 Director Testing ... Mr. Victor GATES
85 Director International Student Svcs ... Ms. Rebecca LOPEZ
22 Director Disability Support Svcs ... Dr. Christy SHANK
88 Director Substance Abuse Resource . Dr. Gerald MAHONE-LEIWS
36 Director Career Planning/Placement ... Ms. Keisha HOLMAN
26 Dir Community Relations/Marketing ... Ms. Barbara MERLO
88 Liaison Military Programs ... Ms. Diana CASTILLO
19 Chief Police/Security Services ... Chief Joseph BARRAGAN
40 Manager Bookstore ... Ms. Regina MARTINEZ-WOODRUFF
37 Director Student Financial Aid ... Ms. Annabelle SMITH
96 Director of Purchasing ... Mr. Ted GONZALEZ
04 Administrative Asst to President ... Ms. Debra HAVENS
43 Dir Legal Services/General Counsel ... Ms. Deborah SHIBLEY
86 Director Government Relations ... Mr. Rudy SANDOVAL
25 Chief Contract and Grants Administr ... Vacant

Chamberlain University-Houston (I)

11025 Equity Drive, Houston TX 77041
Telephone: (713) 277-9800 Identification: 770500
Accreditation: &NH, NURSE

† Branch campus of Chamberlain University-Addison, Addison, IL

Chamberlain University-Irving (J)

4800 Regent Boulevard, Irving TX 75063
Telephone: (469) 706-6705 Identification: 770853
Accreditation: &NH, NURSE

† Branch campus of Chamberlain University-Addison, Addison, IL

Chamberlain University-Pearland (K)

12000 Shadow Creek Pkwy, Pearland TX 77584
Telephone: (832) 664-7000 Identification: 770934
Accreditation: &NH, NURSE

† Branch campus of Chamberlain College of Nursing-Addison, Addison, IL.

Christ Mission College (L)

10822 FM 1560, San Antonio TX 78254
County: Bexar Identification: 667320
Telephone: (210) 688-3101 Carnegie Class: Not Classified
FAX Number: N/A Calendar System: Semester

URL: www.cmctx.org
Established: 1926 Annual Undergrad Tuition & Fees: N/A
Enrollment: N/A Coed
Affiliation or Control: Independent Non-Profit IRS Status: 501(c)3
Highest Offering: Baccalaureate
Accreditation: @BI

01 President .... Dr. Monte MADSEN
05 VP of Academics .... Rev. Alicia CARRASCO
32 VP of Student Services .... Rev. Reva MADSEN
10 VP of Finance .... Ms. Nancy CAVE
84 Enrollment Manager/Registrar .... Ms. Evelyn ARIAS

Cisco College (A)

101 College Heights, Cisco TX 76437-1900
County: Eastland FICE Identification: 003553
Unit ID: 223898
Telephone: (254) 442-5000 Carnegie Class: Assoc/MT-VT-High Trad
FAX Number: (254) 442-5100 Calendar System: Semester
URL: www.cisco.edu
Established: 1940 Annual Undergrad Tuition & Fees (In-State): $3,810
Enrollment: 3,279 Coed
Affiliation or Control: State IRS Status: 501(c)3
Highest Offering: Associate Degree
Accreditation: SC, COARC, MAC, SURGT

01 President .... Dr. Thad ANGLIN
05 Chief Instruction Officer .... Dr. Carol DUPREE
32 Vice President for Student Services .... Dr. Jerry DODSON
13 Exec Dir of Information Technology .... Mr. Steve POWELL
30 Director of Development .... Ms. Martha MONTGOMERY
37 Director of Financial Aid .... Ms. Linda SELLERS
15 Director of Human Resources .... Ms. Shelli GARRETT
08 Director of Library Services .... Ms. Donna CLARK
19 Director Campus Safety .... Mr. Roger TIGHE
07 Director of Enrollment Services .... Ms. Shirley DOVE
04 Executive Asst to President .... Ms. Sydni RABB
103 Dean Workforce/Economic Development .... Dr. Kam ZINSSER
106 Dir Online Education/E-learning .... Ms. Sheron CATON
35 Dean of Student Services .... Mr. Bryan COTTRELL
10 Dean of Business Svcs/CFO .... Ms. Audra TAYLOR
96 Director of Purchasing .... Ms. Beverly MASSEY

Clarendon College (B)

PO Box 968, Clarendon TX 79226-0968
County: Donley FICE Identification: 003554
Unit ID: 223922
Telephone: (806) 874-3571 Carnegie Class: Assoc/HVT-Mix Trad/Non
FAX Number: (806) 874-3201 Calendar System: Semester
URL: www.clarendoncollege.edu
Established: 1898 Annual Undergrad Tuition & Fees (In-District): $2,712
Enrollment: 1,648 Coed
Affiliation or Control: State/Local IRS Status: 501(c)3
Highest Offering: Associate Degree
Accreditation: SC

01 President .... Dr. Robert RIZA
05 Exec VP Academic/Student Affairs .... Mr. Tex BUCKHAULTS
100 Chief of Staff .... Vacant
41 Athletic Director .... Mr. Mark JAMES
10 Vice Pres Administrative Services .... Mr. Rit CHRISTIAN
37 Director of Financial Aid .... Mrs. Amanda SMITH
32 Director of Student Life .... Mr. Joey MULDER
84 Assoc Dean of Enrollment Services .... Mrs. Becky GREEN
13 Director of Information Technology .... Mr. Will THOMPSON
09 Director of Institutional Research .... Dr. Robert TAYLOR
08 Librarian .... Ms. Pamela REED
81 Division Chair Science/Health .... Mrs. Scarlet ESTLACK
49 Division Chair Liberal Arts .... Mrs. Kim JEFFREY

Coastal Bend College (C)

3800 Charco Road, Beeville TX 78102-2197
County: Bee FICE Identification: 003546
Unit ID: 223320
Telephone: (361) 358-2838 Carnegie Class: Assoc/HVT-High Non
FAX Number: (361) 354-2333 Calendar System: Semester
URL: www.coastalbend.edu
Established: 1965 Annual Undergrad Tuition & Fees (In-District): $2,646
Enrollment: 4,463 Coed
Affiliation or Control: State/Local IRS Status: 501(c)3
Highest Offering: Associate Degree
Accreditation: SC, DH, RAD

01 Interim President .... Dr. Carry DEATLEY
05 VP of Instruction/Econ Development .... Dr. Carry DEATLEY
20 Dean of Academics .... Mr. Zachary SUAREZ
20 Assistant Dean of Academics .... Ms. Kayla JONES
32 Exec Dean of Student Services .... Ms. Lupe GANCERES
07 Director of Admissions/Registrar .... Ms. Candy FULLER
26 Director of Marketing & PR .... Mr. Bernard SAENZ
37 Director of Financial Aid .... Ms. Nora MORALES
12 Director of Alice Campus .... Mr. David SULLIVAN
12 Director of Kingsville Campus .... Mr. Joseph HAYEN
45 VP of Strategic Planning and Admin .... Vacant
10 Exec Director of Business Services .... Vacant
08 Director Library Services .... Ms. Sarah MILNARICH
15 Human Resources Office Manager .... Mrs. Audrey RAMIREZ
13 Director of IT Services/Webmaster .... Mr. Amador RAMIREZ
18 Director of Physical Plant .... Mr. Jacinto (JC) COLMENERO

04 Executive Asst to President .... Ms. Anna GARCIA
103 Dean of Workforce Training .... Ms. Julia GARCIA
39 Disability/Student Life and Housing .... Vacant
09 Dir of Institutional Effectiveness .... Vacant
102 Exec Dir CBC Foundation .... Ms. Madeline MADDEN
19 Director Security/Safety .... Dr. Kevin BEHR
41 Athletic Director .... Mr. Paul CANTRELL
76 Assistant Dean of Allied Health .... Ms. Loana HERNANDEZ
88 Director of Dual Enrollment .... Ms. Susie GAITAN
103 Asst Dean of Workforce Training .... Ms. Noemi AGUILAR

College of Biblical Studies-Houston (D)

7000 Regency Square Boulevard, Houston TX 77036-3298
County: Harris FICE Identification: 034224
Unit ID: 388520
Telephone: (713) 785-5995 Carnegie Class: Spec-4-yr-Faith
FAX Number: (713) 785-5998 Calendar System: Semester
URL: www.cbshouston.edu
Established: 1976 Annual Undergrad Tuition & Fees: $6,955
Enrollment: 428 Coed
Affiliation or Control: Independent Non-Profit IRS Status: 501(c)3
Highest Offering: Baccalaureate
Accreditation: SC, BI

01 President .... Dr. Bill BLOCKER
04 Executive Assistant .... Mrs. Vicki PATTERSON
05 Provost/Academic Dean .... Dr. Joseph D. PARLE
11 VP Administration/COO .... Mr. Paul KEITH
10 Chief Financial Officer/Controller .... Mrs. Jan WHITEHEAD
84 Assoc VP Enrollment Services .... Dr. Lisa STEWART
26 Exec Director of Marketing and PR .... Vacant
88 Dean of Operations .... Mr. Shane BOOTHE
09 Dean Institutional Effectiveness .... Dr. Joel BADAL
18 Dir Real Estate Operations .... Mr. Terry BRYAN
15 Director of Human Resources .... Mr. Paul KEITH
06 Registrar .... Vacant
08 Director of Library Services .... Mr. Artis LOVELADY, III
07 Director of Admissions .... Dr. Lisa STEWART
106 Assoc Dean Dist Educ Operations .... Mr. Shane BOOTHE
20 Assoc Dean Faculty and Curr Dev .... Dr. Brittany BURNETTE
37 Senior Financial Aid Officer .... Vacant

College of Biomedical Equipment Technology (E)

11550 IH 10 West Suite 190, San Antonio TX 78230
County: Bexar Identification: 667323
Telephone: (210) 233-1102 Carnegie Class: Not Classified
FAX Number: N/A Calendar System: Other
URL: www.cbet.edu
Established: 2010 Annual Undergrad Tuition & Fees: N/A
Enrollment: N/A Coed
Affiliation or Control: Proprietary IRS Status: Proprietary
Highest Offering: Associate Degree
Accreditation: CNCE

01 President & CEO .... Mr. Bill BASSUK

The College of Health Care Professions (F)

6330 East Highway 290, Suite 180, Austin TX 78723
County: Travis FICE Identification: 034263
Unit ID: 437635
Telephone: (512) 617-5700 Carnegie Class: Spec 2-yr-Health
FAX Number: (512) 892-6643 Calendar System: Other
URL: www.chcp.edu
Established: 1988 Annual Undergrad Tuition & Fees: N/A
Enrollment: 372 Coed
Affiliation or Control: Proprietary IRS Status: Proprietary
Highest Offering: Associate Degree
Accreditation: ABHES

01 President .... Ms. Sara RAMBIKUR

The College of Health Care Professions (G)

240 Northwest Mall Boulevard, Houston TX 77092
County: Harris FICE Identification: 031281
Unit ID: 392257
Telephone: (713) 425-3100 Carnegie Class: Spec-4-yr-Other Health
FAX Number: (713) 425-3192 Calendar System: Other
URL: www.chcp.edu
Established: 1988 Annual Undergrad Tuition & Fees: N/A
Enrollment: 1,402 Coed
Affiliation or Control: Proprietary IRS Status: Proprietary
Highest Offering: Associate Degree
Accreditation: ABHES, SURGT, SURTEC

01 Campus President .... Dr. Himesh LAKHLANI

The College of Health Care Professions-Dallas (H)

8585 N Stemmons Freeway, Ste N-300, Dallas TX 75247
Telephone: (214) 420-3400 Identification: 770531
Accreditation: ABHES

The College of Health Care Professions-Fort Worth (I)

4248 North Freeway, Fort Worth TX 76137
Telephone: (817) 632-5900 Identification: 770532
Accreditation: ABHES

The College of Health Care Professions-McAllen (J)

1917 Nolana Avenue, Ste 100, McAllen TX 78504
Telephone: (956) 800-1500 Identification: 770963
Accreditation: ABHES

The College of Health Care Professions-San Antonio (K)

4738 Northwest Loop 410, San Antonio TX 78229
Telephone: (210) 298-3600 Identification: 770964
Accreditation: ABHES, SURTEC

College of the Mainland (L)

1200 Amburn Road, Texas City TX 77591-2499
County: Galveston FICE Identification: 007096
Unit ID: 226408
Telephone: (409) 938-1211 Carnegie Class: Assoc/HVT-Mix Trad/Non
FAX Number: (409) 933-8010 Calendar System: Semester
URL: www.com.edu
Established: 1966 Annual Undergrad Tuition & Fees (In-District): $1,773
Enrollment: 4,328 Coed
Affiliation or Control: Local IRS Status: 501(c)3
Highest Offering: Associate Degree
Accreditation: SC, ADNUR, CAHIIM, EMT, MAC

01 President .... Dr. Warren NICHOLS
05 Vice President for Instruction .... Dr. Jerry FLIGER
10 Vice President for Fiscal Affairs .... Dr. Clen BURTON
32 Vice President for Student Services .... Dr. Vicki STANFIELD
35 Assoc VP Student Success & Conduct .... Ms. Kris KIMBARK
07 Assoc VP for Enrollment/Registrar .... Mrs. Kelly MUSICK
18 Assoc VP Facility Services .... Mr. Charles KING
08 Director Library Services .... Ms. Kathryn PARK
102 Director of Foundation .... Dr. Lisa WATSON
28 Director of Institutional Equity .... Ms. Lonica BUSH
96 Director of Purchasing .... Ms. Sonja BLINKA
09 Research Specialist .... Ms. Lauren HARPER
04 Admin Assistant to the President .... Ms. Michelle GERAMI

Collin County Community College District (M)

3452 Spur 399, McKinney TX 75069
County: Collin FICE Identification: 023614
Unit ID: 247834
Telephone: (972) 758-3805 Carnegie Class: Assoc/HT-Mix Trad/Non
FAX Number: (972) 758-3807 Calendar System: Semester
URL: www.collin.edu
Established: 1985 Annual Undergrad Tuition & Fees (In-District): $1,504
Enrollment: 31,609 Coed
Affiliation or Control: State/Local IRS Status: 501(c)3
Highest Offering: Associate Degree
Accreditation: SC, ACFEI, ADNUR, CAHIIM, COARC, DH, EMT, POLYT, SURGT

01 District President .... Dr. H. Neil MATKIN
04 Exec Asst to Pres/Board Secy .... Ms. Kristy HORKMAN
100 Chief of Staff .... Ms. Kimberly K. DAVISON
03 Executive VP .... Dr. Sherry L. SCHUMANN
11 Sr VP Campus Operations .... Dr. Toni P. JENKINS
10 Chief Financial Officer .... Mr. Steven BASSETT
26 Interim Chief PR Officer .... Ms. Marisela CADENA-SMITH
13 Chief Innovation Officer .... Mr. Michael DICKSON
15 Chief Talent Officer (HR) .... Mr. Floyd W. NICKERSON
111 VP Advancement .... Ms. Lisa R. VASQUEZ
05 VP Academic Affairs .... Dr. Jon H. HARDESTY
12 VP/Provost-Frisco .... Dr. Don L. WEASENFORTH
12 VP/Provost-McKinney .... Vacant
12 VP/Provost-Plano .... Dr. Abe JOHNSON
12 VP/Provost-Allen .... Dr. Bill L. KING
12 VP/Provost-Wylie .... Dr. Mary S. MCRAE
32 Chief Student Success Officer .... Vacant
09 VP Institutional Research .... Dr. Thomas K. MARTIN
21 Assoc VP Financial Svcs & Rprtng .... Ms. Barbara A. JOHNSTON
21 Assoc VP/Controller .... Ms. Julie M. BRADLEY
35 VP Student & Enrollment Services .... Dr. Albert TEZENO
88 Assoc VP P-12 Partnerships .... Mr. Raul J. MARTINEZ
14 Assoc VP/Chief Info Officer (IT) .... Mr. David R. HOYT
76 Dean Health Sci/Emergency Svcs .... Ms. Michelle L. MILLEN
66 Dean Nursing .... Dr. Jane L. LEACH
103 Dean Workforce Educ-Frisco .... Ms. Karen MUSA
97 Dean Academic Affairs-Frisco .... Ms. Wendy A. GUNDERSON
97 Dean Academic Affairs-McKinney .... Ms. Brenda C. CARTER
79 Dean Comm & Humanities-Plano .... Dr. Meredith L. WANG
57 Dean Fine Arts & Educ-Plano .... Dr. Garry W. EVANS
81 Dean Math & Sciences-Plano .... Dr. Mary E. BARNES-TILLEY
97 Dean Academic Affairs-Allen .... Dr. Amy T. GAINER
103 Dean Workforce Educ-Allen .... Mr. Michael COFFMAN
20 Dean Academic & Workforce-Wylie .... Mr. S. Craig LEVERETTE
55 Dean Evening & Weekend College .... Ms. Gaye M. COOKSEY
106 Dean Strategic Initiatives .... Mr. Mark S. GARCIA
06 Dean Admissions/District Registrar .... Mr. Todd E. FIELDS

35 District Dean Students ....Mr. Terrence P. BRENNAN
84 Dean Student & Enrol Svcs-Frisco ....Dr. Alicia L. HUPPE
84 Dean Student & Enrol Svcs-McKinney ....Mr. James N. BARKO
84 Dean Student & Enrol Svcs-Plano ....Mr. Douglas G. WILLIS
18 Executive Director Facilities ....Mr. Jason PARRY
19 Chief of Police ....Mr. William F. TAYLOR
08 Exec Dir Library-Frisco ....Ms. Vidya KRISHNASWAMY
08 Exec Dir Library-McKinney ....Ms. Faye M. DAVIS
08 Exec Dir Library-Plano ....Ms. Linda A. KYPRIOS
37 Dir Financial Aid & Vet Affairs ....Mr. Alan D. PIXLEY
41 Director Athletics ....Dr. Albert TEZENO
96 Director Purchasing ....Ms. Cynthia L. WHITE
25 Dir Workforce & Econ Dev (Grants) ..Ms. Natalie G. GREENWELL

Commonwealth Institute of Funeral Service (A)

415 Barren Springs Drive, Houston TX 77090-5913

County: Harris FICE Identification: 003556
Unit ID: 366261
Telephone: (281) 873-0262 Carnegie Class: Spec 2-yr-A&S
FAX Number: (281) 873-5232 Calendar System: Quarter
URL: www.commonwealth.edu
Established: 1936 Annual Undergrad Tuition & Fees: $13,363
Enrollment: 215 Coed
Affiliation or Control: Independent Non-Profit IRS Status: 501(c)3
Highest Offering: Associate Degree
Accreditation: FUSER

01 President ....Mr. Glenn A. BOWER
10 Vice President/Treasurer ....Mr. W. Blair WALTRIP
05 Dean of Academic Affairs ....Mr. Stuart MOEN
32 Dean of Students ....Mr. Christopher LAYTON
37 Director Student Financial Aid ....Ms. Marlene PERRY
06 Registrar ....Ms. Patricia MORENO
08 Head Librarian ....Ms. Melissa DAVIS

Concorde Career College (B)

12606 Greenville Avenue, Suite 130, Dallas TX 75243

Telephone: (469) 221-3400 Identification: 770593
Accreditation: ACCSC, COARC, DH, PTAA, SURGT

† Branch campus of Concorde Career College, Aurora, CO

Concorde Career College (C)

4803 NW Loop 410, Suite 200, San Antonio TX 78229

Telephone: (210) 428-2000 Identification: 770594
Accreditation: ACCSC, COARC, DH, PTAA, SURGT

† Branch campus of Concorde Career College, Kansas City, MO

Concorde Career Institute (D)

3015 West I-20, Grand Prairie TX 75052

County: Tarrant FICE Identification: 035423
Unit ID: 441742
Telephone: (469) 348-2500 Carnegie Class: Spec 2-yr-Health
FAX Number: (469) 348-2580 Calendar System: Semester
URL: www.concorde.edu
Established: 1991 Annual Undergrad Tuition & Fees: N/A
Enrollment: 768 Coed
Affiliation or Control: Proprietary IRS Status: Proprietary
Highest Offering: Associate Degree
Accreditation: ACCSC, NDT, POLYT, SURGT

01 Campus President ....Mr. Mike LOVEJOY

Concordia University Texas (E)

11400 Concordia University Drive, Austin TX 78726

County: Travis FICE Identification: 003557
Unit ID: 224004
Telephone: (512) 313-3000 Carnegie Class: Masters/L
FAX Number: (512) 313-3999 Calendar System: Semester
URL: www.concordia.edu
Established: 1926 Annual Undergrad Tuition & Fees: $31,810
Enrollment: 2,620 Coed
Affiliation or Control: Lutheran Church - Missouri Synod
IRS Status: 501(c)3
Highest Offering: Doctorate
Accreditation: SC, IACBE, NURSE

01 President/CEO ....Dr. Donald CHRISTIAN
04 Executive Asst to Pres/CEO ....Ms. Dana KORNFUEHRER
05 Provost & Executive VP ....Dr. Kristi KIRK
11 VP Administration & COO ....Ms. Beth ATHERTON
10 Chief Financial Officer ....Ms. Sarah LOGHIN
45 VP Strategic Planning & QI/CSO ....Dr. Shane SOKOLL
42 Campus Pastor ....Rev. Steve FICK
20 Associate Provost ....Dr. Lynette GILLIS
07 AVP Admissions/Chief Enroll Ofc ....Ms. Jennielle STROTHER
30 VP of Philanthropy ....Mr. James CANDIDO
26 AVP Marketing/Communications ....Ms. Lisa KESSLER
18 AVP Building Operations ....Mr. Dan GREGORY
21 Controller ....Ms. Maria ANAYA
49 Dean College of Arts & Sciences ....Vacant
106 Sr Dir Online & Digital Learning ....Dr. Alex HERRON
66 Dean College of Nursing ....Dr. Kathy LAUCHNER
53 Dean College of Education ....Dr. James MCCONNELL
50 Dean College of Business/Comm ....Dr. Randolph WILT
57 Dir School of Fine Arts ....Dr. Kelly GORDON
81 Dir School of Nat/Applied Sciences ....Dr. Philip SCHIELKE
79 Dir School of Humanities ....Dr. Ann SCHWARTZ
06 Dir Student Registration & Records ....Ms. Lerla MCGRUDER
37 Director Student Financial Services ....Mr. Russell JEFFREY
41 Athletic Director ....Ms. Ronda SEAGRAVES
121 Director Student Success Center ....Ms. Ruth COOPER
36 Dir Vocation & Prof Development ....Ms. Randa SCOTT
32 AVP Student Life/Dean of Students ....Dr. Elizabeth MEDINA
39 Director of Residential Life ....Mr. Jakob ADAM
08 Director of Library Services ....Ms. Mikail MCINTOSH-DOTY
58 Director MBA Graduate Program ....Dr. Elise BRAZIER
19 Chief of Police ....Mr. Shane SEXTON
29 Dir Donor & Alumni Relations ....Mr. Jeff FROSCH
102 Dir Found/Corp & Govt Relations ....Ms. Meghann BOLTON
44 Dir Donor Relations ....Ms. Tina HAMILTON
09 Dir Inst Research & Effectiveness ....Dr. Trey BUCHANAN
96 Director Support Services ....Mr. Eric SILBER
105 Web Administrator ....Mr. Bryan GILBERT

Criswell College (F)

4010 Gaston Avenue, Dallas TX 75246-1537

County: Dallas FICE Identification: 041218
Unit ID: 475608
Telephone: (214) 821-5433 Carnegie Class: Spec-4-yr-Faith
FAX Number: (214) 370-0497 Calendar System: Semester
URL: www.criswell.edu
Established: 1970 Annual Undergrad Tuition & Fees: $10,710
Enrollment: 264 Coed
Affiliation or Control: Independent Non-Profit IRS Status: 501(c)3
Highest Offering: Master's
Accreditation: SC

01 President ....Barry CREAMER
05 VP of Academic Affairs ....Christopher GRAHAM
10 Chief Business Officer/VP Finance ....Kevin STILLEY
32 VP of Student Affairs ....Russell MARRIOTT
111 VP of Advancement ....Joseph WOODDELL
100 Chief of Staff ....Daisy REYNOLDS

Culinary Institute LeNotre (G)

7070 Allensby Street, Houston TX 77022-4322

County: Harris FICE Identification: 037233
Unit ID: 444565
Telephone: (713) 692-0077 Carnegie Class: Spec 2-yr-A&S
FAX Number: (713) 692-7399 Calendar System: Other
URL: www.culinaryinstitute.edu
Established: 1998 Annual Undergrad Tuition & Fees: $15,938
Enrollment: 368 Coed
Affiliation or Control: Proprietary IRS Status: Proprietary
Highest Offering: Associate Degree
Accreditation: ACCSC, ACFEI

05 VP Academic Affairs-Provost ....Mr. Pablo FUENTES

Culinary Institute of America San Antonio (H)

312 Pearl Parkway, Bldg 3,Ste 2102,
San Antonio TX 78215

Telephone: (210) 554-6400 Identification: 770131
Accreditation: &M

† Branch campus of The Culinary Institute of America, Hyde Park, NY

Dallas Baptist University (I)

3000 Mountain Creek Parkway, Dallas TX 75211-9299

County: Dallas FICE Identification: 003560
Unit ID: 224226
Telephone: (214) 333-7100 Carnegie Class: DU-Mod
FAX Number: (214) 333-5447 Calendar System: 4/1/4
URL: www.dbu.edu
Established: 1898 Annual Undergrad Tuition & Fees: $28,870
Enrollment: 5,067 Coed
Affiliation or Control: Baptist IRS Status: 501(c)3
Highest Offering: Doctorate
Accreditation: SC, ACBSP, CAEP, CEA, MUS

00 Chancellor ....Dr. Gary COOK
01 President ....Dr. Adam WRIGHT
100 Chief of Staff ....Mr. Dan GIBSON
04 Executive Asst to the President ....Mrs. Alyssa FURR
05 Provost ....Dr. Norma HEDIN
10 Vice Pres for Financial Affairs ....Dr. Matt MURRAH
11 VP of Administration and Enrollment ....Mr. Jonathan TEAT
32 Vice President for Student Affairs ....Dr. Jay HARLEY
85 Vice Pres for International Affairs ....Mr. Randy BYERS
88 Sr Advisor to Pres for Acad Affs ....Dr. Denny DOWD
20 Associate Provost ....Mrs. Deemie NAUGLE
20 Asst Provost/Director Hybrid Educ ....Dr. Mark HALE
20 Acad Dean/Accreditation Liaison ....Dr. Gail LINAM
06 Registrar ....Ms. Linda RONEY
35 Dean of Students ....Mrs. Tempress ASAGBA
84 Associate VP for Enrollment ....Mr. Jason WILLIAMS
07 Asst VP for UG Enrollment ....Dr. John BORUM
07 Director of Admissions ....Mr. Richard NASSAR
58 Dean Cook School of Leadership ....Dr. Jack GOODYEAR
104 Dean Global Studies/Pre-Prof Pgms ....Dr. David COOK
50 Dean College of Business ....Dr. Jeff JOHNSON
81 Dean College Natural Science & Math ....Dr. Dionisio FLEITAS
53 Dean College of Education ....Dr. Neil DUGGER
57 Dean College of Fine Arts ....Dr. Ron BOWLES
73 Dean College of Christian Faith ....Dr. Wayne DAVIS
79 Dean Col Humanities/Social Sciences ....Dr. Rob SULLIVAN
106 Assoc VP for IT & Dean Online Educ ....Dr. Matt WINN
114 Asst VP for Financial Affairs ....Mr. Danny HASSETT
21 Controller ....Mrs. Mendi MCMAHAN
37 Director of Financial Aid ....Mrs. Shermain REED
113 Dir of Student Account Services ....Mr. Max BUSSE
13 Asst VP for Information Tech Svcs ....Mr. Michael STEWART
105 Director of Web Services ....Mrs. Anu CHIVUKULA
29 Director of Alumni Affairs ....Mrs. Kathryn ROBNETT
08 Director of the Library ....Mr. Scott JEFFRIES
15 Director of Human Resources ....Mrs. Tamy ROGERS
43 General Counsel ....Ms. Christa POWERS
88 Dir Intl Admissions & Immigration ....Mr. Timothy WATTS
85 Director of Intl Student Services ....Mrs. Susie CASSEL
41 Director of Athletics ....Mr. Connor SMITH
122 Director of Student Life ....Mr. David REYES
121 Director of Student Success ....Mrs. Molly TAYLOR
36 Director of Career Services ....Mrs. Marion HILL-HUBBARD
38 Dir Counseling & Spiritual Care ....Dr. Jordan DAVIS
27 Assistant VP for Communications ....Mrs. Layna EVANS
27 Director of Marketing ....Mr. Caleb LONG
39 Director of University Housing ....Ms. Allyson MILLER
24 Director of Media Services ....Mr. Rob LEWIS
19 Chief of Police ....Mr. John SHAW
19 Director of Campus Security ....Mr. Donald KABETZKE
108 Coord Institutional Effectiveness ....Mrs. Carol REID
09 Coord of Institutional Research ....Mr. John EDWARDS
88 Academic Projects Administrator ....Ms. Lou ESPARZA
40 Manager Bookstore ....Mr. Cole MARTIN
26 Vice President for Communications .. Dr. Blake KILLINGSWORTH
111 Vice President for Advancement ....Mr. Ryan HEFTON

Dallas Christian College (J)

2700 Christian Parkway, Dallas TX 75234-7299

County: Dallas FICE Identification: 006941
Unit ID: 224244
Telephone: (972) 241-3371 Carnegie Class: Spec-4-yr-Faith
FAX Number: (972) 241-8021 Calendar System: 4/1/4
URL: www.dallas.edu
Established: 1950 Annual Undergrad Tuition & Fees: $18,734
Enrollment: 231 Coed
Affiliation or Control: Christian Churches And Churches of Christ
IRS Status: 501(c)3
Highest Offering: Baccalaureate
Accreditation: BI

01 President ....Dr. Brian D. SMITH
05 Interim VP for Academic Affairs ....Mr. Bruce LONG
84 VP for Enrollment Management ....Mr. Ken FAFFLER
111 VP for Institutional Advancement ....Mr. Mark WORLEY
10 VP of Finance & Operations ....Ms. Andrea SHORT
108 Dir Institutional Effectiveness ....Mr. Bruce LONG
06 Registrar ....Mrs. Crystal LAIDACKER
37 Dir of Student Financial Svcs ....Ms. Breanda WILLIAMS
18 Director of Facilities ....Mr. David LAGUNEZ
04 Exec Admin Assistant to the Pres ....Ms. Annette ESCLAVON
08 Director of Library Services ....Ms. Jane REYNOLDS

*Dallas County Community College District (K)

1601 South Lamar Street, Dallas TX 75215

County: Dallas FICE Identification: 009331
Unit ID: 224253
Telephone: (214) 378-1601 Carnegie Class: N/A
FAX Number: (214) 378-1810
URL: www.dcccd.edu

01 Chancellor ....Dr. Joe D. MAY
86 EVC Public/Govt Affairs ....Dr. Justin LONON
100 Chief of Staff ....Dr. Iris A. FREEMON
43 District General Counsel ....Mr. Robert WENDLAND
86 Chief Legislative Counsel ....Mr. Isaac FAZ
45 Chief Strategy Officer ....Ms. Mary BRUMBACH
10 Chief Financial Officer ....Mr. John ROBERTSON
13 Chief Innovation Officer (CIO) ....Mr. Tim MARSHALL
101 Board Relations Executive ....Mrs. Perla MOLINA
102 Chief Advance Officer/Dir of Fndn ....Dr. Pyeper WILKINS

*Brookhaven College (L)

3939 Valley View, Dallas TX 75244-4997

County: Dallas FICE Identification: 021002
Unit ID: 223524
Telephone: (972) 860-4700 Carnegie Class: Assoc/MT-VT-High Non
FAX Number: (972) 860-4897 Calendar System: Semester
URL: www.brookhavencollege.edu
Established: 1978 Annual Undergrad Tuition & Fees (In-District): $1,770
Enrollment: 13,286 Coed
Affiliation or Control: State/Local IRS Status: 501(c)3
Highest Offering: Associate Degree
Accreditation: SC, ADNUR, ART, EMT, RAD

02 Interim President ....Dr. Justin LONON
05 Interim VP of Academic Affairs ....Dr. Giraud POLITE
10 Vice President of Business Services ....Mr. George HERRING
32 Vice Pres Student Dev/Enroll Mgmt ....Mr. Oscar LOPEZ

04 Exec Asst to College President ... Ms. Edna LOVE
103 Assoc VP Workforce/Continuing Educ ... Mr. Vernon L. HAWKINS
30 Assoc Vice Pres Development ... Ms. Marilyn K. LYNCH
50 Exec Dean Business Studies ... Dr. Giraud POLITE
45 Exec Dean Educational Resources ... Ms. Sarah FERGUSON
57 Exec Dean Fine Arts/Physical Educ ... Mr. Rick MAXWELL
81 Exec Dean Science/Math ... Dr. Kathryn WETZEL
23 Exec Dean of Health/Human Svcs ... Dr. Juanita FLINT
09 Exec Dir Plng/Rsrch/Inst Effective ... Dr. Michael DENNEHY
13 Director Information Technology ... Mr. Michael DEASON
83 Exec Dean Social Sci/Distance Lrng ... Mr. Sam GOVEA
26 Executive Dean Communications ... Mrs. Kendra VAGLIENTI
84 Exec Dean Stdnt Success/Enroll Svcs ... Ms. Brenda DALTON
27 Dir Marketing/Public Information ... Ms. Meridith DANFORTH
07 Director of Admissions/Registrar ... Ms. Thoa Hoang VO
41 Director of Athletics ... Mr. Kevin HURST
21 Director of Business Operations ... Ms. Willadean MARTIN
36 Director Career Services ... Ms. Dominica MCCARTHY
18 Director of Facilities ... Vacant
15 Exec Dir of Human Resources ... Ms. Terri EDRICH
35 Admin Office of Student Life ... Mr. Brian BORSKI
19 Captain of College Police ... Mr. Mark LOPEZ
88 Director of Sustainability ... Ms. Carrie SCHWEITZER

*Cedar Valley College (A)

3030 N Dallas Avenue, Lancaster TX 75134-3799
County: Dallas FICE Identification: 003561
Unit ID: 223773
Telephone: (972) 860-8201 Carnegie Class: Assoc/MT-VT-High Non
FAX Number: (972) 682-7075 Calendar System: Semester
URL: www.cedarvalleycollege.edu
Established: 1974 Annual Undergrad Tuition & Fees (In-District): $1,770
Enrollment: 7,443 Coed
Affiliation or Control: State/Local IRS Status: 501(c)3
Highest Offering: Associate Degree
Accreditation: SC

02 President ... Dr. Joseph SEABROOKS
05 Vice President for Instruction ... Ms. Audra BARRETT
32 VP Student Services/Enrollment Mgmt ... Dr. Lisa COPPRUE
10 Vice Pres Business/Admin Services ... Mr. Huan LUONG
81 Exec Dean Science/Tech/Engr/Math ... Mr. Eddy RAWLINSON
50 Exec Dean Bus/Wrkfce/Skilled Trades ... Dr. Ruben JOHNSON
49 Exec Dean Liberal Arts/Gen Ed Trans ... Dr. Solomon CROSS
51 Assoc Dean Open Enroll/Cont Educ ... Mr. Raymond RIVERA
88 Dir Sustainability/Advance Projects ... Dr. Maria BOCCALANDRO
35 Dean Student Support Services ... Ms. Grenna ROLLINGS
84 Sr Exec Dean Enrollment Mgmt ... Ms. Jarlene DECAY
08 Director Library Services ... Ms. Vidya KRISHNASWAMY
09 Dir Plng/Rsrch/Inst Effectiveness ... Ms. Nicole HAAN
18 Director Facilities Management ... Mrs. Cindy A. ROGERS
26 College Chief Marketing Officer ... Mr. Henry MARTINEZ
15 Exec Director of Human Resources ... Mr. Warren DAVIS
13 Director Information Technology ... Mr. Michael WHITE
111 Exec Director of Advancement ... Ms. Patricia DAVIS
21 Assoc Director of Business Office ... Mr. Jim JONES

*Eastfield College (B)

3737 Motley Drive, Mesquite TX 75150-2099
County: Dallas FICE Identification: 008510
Unit ID: 224572
Telephone: (972) 860-7100 Carnegie Class: Assoc/HT-High Non
FAX Number: (972) 860-8373 Calendar System: Semester
URL: www.eastfieldcollege.edu
Established: 1970 Annual Undergrad Tuition & Fees (In-District): $1,770
Enrollment: 16,196 Coed
Affiliation or Control: State/Local IRS Status: 170(c)1
Highest Offering: Associate Degree
Accreditation: SC

02 President ... Dr. Eddie TEALER
05 Exec VP Academic Affairs ... Dr. Mike J. WALKER
10 VP Business Services ... Mr. Jose C. RODRIGUEZ
45 Vice President Planning & Research . Dr. Kimberly K. CHANDLER
15 Exec Administrator Human Resources ... Mr. Larry L. WILSON
32 Assoc VP Student Svcs Admin ... Dr. Jose DELA CRUIZ
111 AVP Advancement & Communication ... Ms. Sharon L. COOK
84 Exec Dean Access and Enrollment ... Dr. Patty R. YOUNG
12 Exec Dir Pleasant Grove Campus ... Mr. Javier E. OLGUIN
20 Assoc VP Academic Affairs ... Ms. Rachel B. WOLF
72 Executive Dean of Career Tech ... Ms. Johnnie O. BELLAMY
81 Executive Dean STEM ... Dr. Jess P. KELLY
83 Exec Dean Social Sciences ... Ms. Courtney CARTER-HARBOUR
103 Director Workforce Devel ... Mrs. Christa K. JONES
08 Executive Dean Library ... Ms. Karla J. GREER
57 Exec Dean Arts and Communications ... Ms. Courtney CARTER-HARBOUR
21 Exec Admin of Financial Affairs ... Ms. Heidi M. BASSETT
18 Director Facilities Management ... Mr. Michael BRANTLEY
124 Dean Ofc Stdnt Engagement/Retention . Ms. Tania WITTGENFELD
46 Dean Resource Development ... Dr. Tricia THOMAS-ANDERSON
51 Exec Dean Continuing Education ... Vacant
26 Director of Marketing ... Ms. Donielle R. JOHNSON
106 Dean Inst Support & Distance Educ ... Mr. Abuzafar M. BASHET
88 Assoc Dean Educational Resources ... Ms. Lucinda A. GONZALES

*El Centro College (C)

801 Main Street, Dallas TX 75202-3604
County: Dallas FICE Identification: 004453
Unit ID: 224615
Telephone: (214) 860-2000 Carnegie Class: Assoc/HVT-High Non
FAX Number: (214) 860-2335 Calendar System: Semester
URL: www.elcentrocollege.edu
Established: 1966 Annual Undergrad Tuition & Fees (In-District): $1,770
Enrollment: 10,797 Coed
Affiliation or Control: State/Local IRS Status: 501(c)3
Highest Offering: Associate Degree
Accreditation: SC, ACFEI, ADNUR, COARC, CVT, DH, DMS, EMT, MAC, MLTAD, PNUR, RAD, SURGT

02 President ... Dr. Jose ADAMES
05 Exec VP Academic Affairs ... Dr. Greg MORRIS
32 VP Student Svcs & Enrollment ... Ms. Karen STILLS
10 VP Business Services ... Ms. Lenora REECE
30 Manager of Development ... Vacant
76 Int Exec Dean Health Sciences ... Dr. Greg MORRIS
97 Exec Dean Academic Transfer ... Dr. Anthony MANSUETO
81 Exec Dean STEM ... Ms. Beth STALL
50 Exec Dean Business/Design/Pub Svc ... Dr. Sherry JONES
103 Dean of Instruct/CE/Workforce Educ ... Ms. Elizabeth GUERRA
106 Dean Instruct Innov/Acad Support ... Ms. Karla DAMRON
20 Assoc Instructional Dean ... Ms. Joselyn GONZALEZ
09 Dean Institutional Effectiveness ... Vacant
35 Dean Student Support Services ... Dr. Tracy JOHNSON
121 Dean Student Success ... Mr. Cornelius JOHNSON
89 Director College Programs ... Mr. Patrick VASQUEZ
08 Lead Librarian ... Dr. Norman HOWDEN
07 Assoc Dean Enroll Services ... Ms. Rebecca J. GARZA
12 Exec Director West Campus ... Ms. Kathy ACOSTA
15 Interim Exec Dir Human Resources ... Dr. Alfredo SANJUAN
19 Int Director College Police ... Mr. James SMITH
26 Dir Marketing/Communications ... Ms. Priscilla A. STALEY
18 Col Director Facilities Services ... Mr. Jeremy MCCLELLAND
21 Dir Business Operations ... Ms. Keisha FARRINGTON
37 Dir Student Financial Aid ... Ms. Pam A. LUCAS
13 Director Information Technology ... Mr. Michael C. JOHNSON
85 Dir Col Pgms/International Center ... Mr. Robert G. REYES
36 Pgm Svcs Coord Career Services ... Ms. Christol JOHNSON
38 Licensed Psychologist ... Mr. David THOMPSON
23 Senior Manager Health Center ... Ms. LaJoyya JOHNSON
04 Executive Asst to President ... Ms. Ida KELLER
40 Manager Bookstore ... Ms. Venus MCGUIRE

*Mountain View College (D)

4849 W Illinois Avenue, Dallas TX 75211-6599
County: Dallas FICE Identification: 008503
Unit ID: 226930
Telephone: (214) 860-8680 Carnegie Class: Assoc/HT-High Non
FAX Number: (214) 860-8521 Calendar System: Semester
URL: www.mountainviewcollege.edu
Established: 1970 Annual Undergrad Tuition & Fees (In-District): $1,770
Enrollment: 10,220 Coed
Affiliation or Control: State/Local IRS Status: 501(c)3
Highest Offering: Associate Degree
Accreditation: SC

02 Interim President ... Dr. Sharon DAVIS
05 Vice President of Instruction ... Dr. Lori DODDY
32 VP Student Svcs/Enrollment Mgmt ... Dr. Leonard GARRETT
10 Int Vice Pres of Business Services ... Dr. Elsy CARRANZA
84 Exec Dean Student Support Svcs ... Mr. Matthew SANCHEZ
90 Exec Dean Curriculum & Instruction ... Dr. Karen VALENCIA
06 Assoc Dean Admission/Enrollment ... Ms. Glenda GARRETT
18 Director Facilities Services ... Mr. Allan KNOTT
09 Dir of Planning/Research & IE ... Ms. Iva BERGERON
88 Administrator of Special Programs ... Ms. Cathy EDWARDS
103 Exec Dean of Workforce/Cont Educ ... Ms. Pat WEBB
26 Director Public Info/Marketing ... Ms. Jill LAIN
21 Director of Business Operations ... Mr. Jose RODRIGUEZ
15 Exec Director Human Resources ... Mr. Jarred DAVIS
36 Director Career Development ... Ms. Regina GARNER
45 Dean Resource Development ... Ms. Heather A. MARSH
04 Administrative Asst to President ... Mr. Michael ARREDONDO
08 Head Librarian ... Ms. Jean BAKER
41 Athletic Director ... Mr. Manuel MANTRANA

*North Lake College (E)

5001 N MacArthur Boulevard, Irving TX 75038-3899
County: Dallas FICE Identification: 020774
Unit ID: 227191
Telephone: (972) 273-3000 Carnegie Class: Assoc/HT-High Non
FAX Number: (972) 273-3014 Calendar System: Semester
URL: www.dcccd.edu
Established: 1977 Annual Undergrad Tuition & Fees (In-District): $1,770
Enrollment: 10,953 Coed
Affiliation or Control: State/Local IRS Status: 501(c)3
Highest Offering: Associate Degree
Accreditation: SC, CONST

02 President ... Dr. Christa SLEJKO
05 Vice President Academic Affairs ... Dr. Shawnda FLOYD
10 Vice Pres Business Services ... Vacant
32 VP Stdnt Svcs/Enrollment Mgmt ... Dr. Marisa PIERCE
84 Dean of Enrollment Mgmt/Stdnt Svcs ... Ms. Anabel JUAREZ
124 Dean of Student Engagement ... Ms. Francyenne MAYNARD
26 Director Marketing & Public Info ... Ms. Gina FEDERER
12 Exec Director North & South Campus ... Mr. Arthur JAMES
12 Exec Dean West Campus ... Dr. Paul KELEMEN
09 Exec Dir Institutional Research ... Dr. Karen MONGO
18 Director Facilities Services ... Mr. John WATSON
19 Director Campus Police ... Mr. Randy REED
111 Dean of Advancement ... Dr. Kristine MASSEY
15 Director Human Resources ... Mr. Willie NEAL
21 Director Business Operations ... Ms. Elsy CARRANZA
35 Dir Student Programs/Resources ... Ms. Beth NIKOPOULOS
103 Director Workforce Dev/CE ... Mr. Tim SAMUELS
49 Executive Dean Liberal Arts ... Dr. Kristopher COPELAND
81 Exec Dean Math/Science ... Dr. Matthew DEMPSEY
50 Exec Dean Arts/Bus/Sports Sci Tech ... Dr. David EVANS
04 Administrative Asst to President ... Ms. Kari ANDREWS
41 Athletic Director ... Mr. Greg SOMMERS

*Richland College (F)

12800 Abrams Road, Dallas TX 75243-2199
County: Dallas FICE Identification: 008504
Unit ID: 227766
Telephone: (972) 238-6100 Carnegie Class: Assoc/HT-High Non
FAX Number: (972) 238-6957 Calendar System: Semester
URL: www.rlc.dcccd.edu
Established: 1972 Annual Undergrad Tuition & Fees (In-District): $1,770
Enrollment: 18,794 Coed
Affiliation or Control: State/Local IRS Status: 501(c)3
Highest Offering: Associate Degree
Accreditation: SC, MAC, MUS

02 President ... Dr. Kathryn K. EGGLESTON
04 Dean/Exec Assistant to President ... Ms. Janet C. JAMES
05 Exec VP Acad Affs & Stdnt Success ... Dr. Shannon K. CUNNINGHAM
10 VP for Business Services ... Mr. Ron M. CLARK
10 VP for Business Services ... Mr. Finney VARGHESE
84 Assoc VP Enrollment/Supt RCHS ... Ms. Donna WALKER
54 Exec Dean Sch of Engr & Technology . Dr. Raghunath KANAKALA
79 Exec Dean Human/Fine & Perf Arts ... Ms. Diane HILBERT
81 Exec Dean of Science & Health Prof ... Dr. Dwight RANDLE
09 Exec Dean Plng/Rsrch/Inst Effect ... Ms. Fonda L. VERA
60 Exec Dean School of Communications ... Ms. Susan E. BARKLEY
81 Exec Dean School of Mathematics ... Mr. Thales GEORGIOU
83 Exec Dean Soc Sciences & Wellness ... Dr. LaQueta WRIGHT
88 Exec Dean World Langs & Cultures ... Ms. Diana URRUTIA
06 Registrar ... Vacant
41 Director Athletic Programs ... Mr. Guy SIMMONS
32 Director of Student Life ... Ms. Erin LEWIS
08 Dean Educational Services ... Ms. Laura MCKINNON
26 Dir College Comm and Marketing ... Ms. Whitney ROSENBALM
18 Director of Facilities Services ... Mr. Kenneth DUNSON
15 Executive Director Human Resources ... Vacant
19 Chief of College Police ... Mr. Robert D. BAKER
88 Principal Richland Collegiate HS ... Mr. Craig HINKLE

Dallas Institute of Funeral Service (G)

3909 S Buckner Boulevard, Dallas TX 75227-4314
County: Dallas FICE Identification: 010761
Unit ID: 224271
Telephone: (214) 388-5466 Carnegie Class: Spec 2-yr-A&S
FAX Number: (214) 388-0316 Calendar System: Quarter
URL: www.dallasinstitute.edu
Established: 1945 Annual Undergrad Tuition & Fees: $11,870
Enrollment: 111 Coed
Affiliation or Control: Independent Non-Profit IRS Status: 501(c)3
Highest Offering: Associate Degree
Accreditation: FUSER

01 President ... Mr. Wayne CAVENDER
07 Admissions Rep ... Ms. Olga RETANA
37 Director Financial Aid ... Ms. DeDe WILLIS
06 Registrar ... Ms. Tammy LEONARD

Dallas International University (H)

7500 W Camp Wisdom Road, Dallas TX 75236-5629
County: Dallas FICE Identification: 038513
Telephone: (972) 708-7340 Carnegie Class: Not Classified
FAX Number: (972) 708-7292 Calendar System: Other
URL: www.diu.edu
Established: 1999 Annual Undergrad Tuition & Fees: N/A
Enrollment: N/A Coed
Affiliation or Control: Independent Non-Profit IRS Status: 501(c)3
Highest Offering: Doctorate
Accreditation: SC

01 President ... Dr. Doug TIFFIN
11 Vice President of Operations ... Mr. Jeff MINARD
15 Chief Human Resources Officer ... Vacant
10 Vice President of Finance ... Mr. Rod JENKINS
32 Dean of Students ... Mrs. Meg TRIHUS
05 Dean of Academic Affairs ... Dr. Scott BERTHIAUME
42 Chaplain ... Mrs. Christine HARLAN
101 Secretary to the Board of Trustees ... Mr. David HARRELL
30 Director of Development ... Vacant
04 Administrative Asst to President ... Mrs. Gail DYKSTRA
09 Director of Inst Research/Svcs ... Mr. Richard LYNCH
21 Business Manager ... Mr. Paul SETTER
96 Lead Accountant ... Mr. Dan WALTON
35 Assistant Dean of Students ... Ms. Caiti PLANTE
20 Academic Dean Assistant ... Mr. Dan BOERGER
08 Library Director ... Ms. Ferne WEIMER
84 Director of Recruiting ... Ms. Sheri MCMILLAN
07 Director of Admissions ... Mr. Stephen NASH
104 International Student Coordinator ... Mrs. Maggie JOHNSON
06 Registrar ... Mrs. Lynne LAMIMAN

37 Financial Aid Administrator ... Mr. Ken PRETTOL
29 Alumni Relations Coordinator ... Ms. Debbie MANTER
13 Director of Information Services ... Mr. Matt LONG
24 Director of Media Services ... Mr. Bill HARRIS
44 Development Assistant ... Mrs. Tricia REIMAN
26 Director of External Relationships ... Mr. John OH
125 President Emeritus ... Dr. David ROSS

† (f.k.a. Graduate Institute of Applied Linguistics)

Dallas Nursing Institute (A)

2101 Waterview Pkwy, Suite 100, Richardson TX 75080

County: Dallas
FICE Identification: 034165
Unit ID: 437732
Telephone: (469) 941-8300
Carnegie Class: Spec-4-yr-Other Health
FAX Number: (214) 575-9090
Calendar System: Semester
URL: www.dni.edu
Established: 1991
Annual Undergrad Tuition & Fees: N/A
Enrollment: 175
Coed
Affiliation or Control: Proprietary
IRS Status: Proprietary
Highest Offering: Baccalaureate
Accreditation: ABHES

01 Dean of Nursing/Executive Director ... Ms. Gwen GASTON
32 Director of Student Affairs/Admin ... Ms. Brigit MATTIX

Dallas Theological Seminary (B)

3909 Swiss Avenue, Dallas TX 75204-6493

County: Dallas
FICE Identification: 003562
Unit ID: 224305
Telephone: (214) 887-5000
Carnegie Class: Spec-4-yr-Faith
FAX Number: (214) 887-5532
Calendar System: Semester
URL: www.dts.edu
Established: 1924
Annual Graduate Tuition & Fees: N/A
Enrollment: 2,369
Coed
Affiliation or Control: Independent Non-Profit
IRS Status: 501(c)3
Highest Offering: Doctorate; No Undergraduates
Accreditation: SC, THEOL

01 President ... Dr. Mark L. BAILEY
05 Vice Pres Academic Affairs ... Dr. Mark M. YARBROUGH
32 VP of Student Life & Dean of Stdnt ... Dr. George HILLMAN
10 VP for Business & Finance ... Mr. Dale C. LARSON
111 Vice President for Advancement ... Ms. Kimberly B. TILL
11 Vice President Campus Operations ... Mr. Robert F. RIGGS
26 Exec Dir of Mktg and Communications ... Mr. Edward HERRELKO
102 Exec Dir Dallas Seminary Found ... Mr. Scott TALBOT
20 Academic Dean/Dean of Acad Admin ... Dr. James H. THAMES
12 Dean of DTS Houston ... Dr. Bruce W. FONG
12 Dean DTS Washington DC ... Dr. Rodney ORR
58 Director of PhD Studies ... Dr. Vic A. ANDERSON
58 Director of DMin Studies ... Dr. D. Scott BARFOOT
09 Dir Inst Research & Effectiveness ... Mr. David HIONIDES
06 Registrar ... Ms. Sabrina HOPSON
88 Exec Dir of Leadership Center ... Dr. Bill HENDRICKS
88 Exec Dir of Cultural Engagement ... Dr. Darrell L. BOCK
07 Director of Admissions ... Mr. Luke BRYANT
08 Library Director ... Mr. Marvin T. HUNN, II
84 Dean of Enrollment Svcs and Ed Tech ... Mr. John DYER
29 Director of Alumni Services ... Dr. Greg A. HATTEBERG
36 Director of Placement ... Dr. Paul E. PETTIT
24 Director of Media Support ... Mr. James W. HOOVER
42 Campus Pastor ... Dr. Joe M. ALLEN, JR.
35 Assistant Dean of Students ... Ms. Lynn Etta G. MANNING
35 Assistant Dean of Students ... Dr. Terrance S. WOODSON
88 Associate Dean of Academic Admin ... Mr. Nate MCKANNA
13 Director of Information Technology ... Mr. Kevin COX
19 Chief of Campus Police ... Mr. John S. BLOOM
39 Director of Housing ... Mr. Drew H. WILLIAMS
106 Dir Online and Distance Education ... Mr. Robert M. ABEGG
88 Director of Chinese Studies ... Dr. Samuel CHIA
88 Director of DTS en Espanol ... Dr. Gerardo ALFARO
38 Director of Counseling Services ... Dr. Kelly CHEATHAM
21 Controller ... Ms. Patricia MAYABB
40 Director of Book Center ... Mr. Kevin D. STERN
85 Dir for Intl Stdnt Svcs/Disabilitiy ... Ms. Carisa ASH
04 Administrative Asst to President ... Ms. Michelle B. SCHIWIETZ
15 Director Human Resources ... Mr. Wes WADA
88 Dir of Maintenance Operations ... Mr. Brian GERBERICH
18 Director of Facilities Coord ... Mr. Glenn MONRO
88 Campus Operations Administrator ... Mrs. Dee LITTLEJOHN
110 Executive Dir for Advancement ... Mr. Donnie SNYDER
112 Director of Donor Management ... Mr. Jacob BECK
101 Admin Coord for Board Mtgs ... Ms. Margaret TOLLIVER
37 Director Student Financial Aid ... Mr. Cody JACOBS
96 Director of Purchasing ... Ms. Lisa REEVES

Del Mar College (C)

101 Baldwin Blvd., Corpus Christi TX 78404-3897

County: Nueces
FICE Identification: 003563
Unit ID: 224350
Telephone: (361) 698-1200
Carnegie Class: Assoc/HVT-High Trad
FAX Number: (361) 698-1559
Calendar System: Semester
URL: www.delmar.edu
Established: 1935
Annual Undergrad Tuition & Fees (In-District): $2,729
Enrollment: 11,476
Coed
Affiliation or Control: Local
IRS Status: 501(c)3
Highest Offering: Associate Degree
Accreditation: SC, ACFEI, ADNUR, ART, CAHIIM, COARC, DA, DH, DMS, EMT, MLTAD, MUS, OTA, PTAA, RAD, SURGT, THEA

01 President & CEO ... Dr. Mark ESCAMILLA
43 General Counsel ... Mr. Augustin RIVERA, JR.
05 Exec VP & Chief Academic Officer ... Dr. Beth LEWIS
10 VP & Chief Financial Officer ... Mr. Raul GARCIA
103 VP Workforce Dev/Strategic Init ... Ms. Lenora KEAS
13 CIO & VP Facilities & Operations ... Mr. August ALFONSO
18 Vice Pres Facilities & Operations ... Mr. August ALFONSO
11 VP Administration & HR ... Ms. Tammy MCDONALD
32 Vice President for Student Affairs ... Dr. Rito SILVA
19 Chief of Security ... Ms. Lauren WHITE
26 Exec Dir Strategic Comm/Govt Rels ... Mr. Jay KNIOUM
30 Exec Director of Development ... Ms. Mary MCQUEEN
07 Dean Student Outreach/Enroll Svcs ... Ms. Patricia BENAVIDES-DOMINGUEZ
124 Dean Student Engagement & Retention ... Ms. Cheryl SANDERS
49 Dean Division Arts & Sciences ... Dr. Jonda HALCOMB
17 Int Dean Health Sciences & Prof ... Ms. Jennifer SRAMEK
75 Dean Bus/Ind/Public Safety ... Mr. Charles MCKINNY
51 Dean CE & Off Campus Programs ... Dr. Leonard RIVERA
88 Dean Workforce Pgms/Corporate Svcs ... Mr. Daniel KORUS
108 Dean Institutional Effect/Assess ... Dr. Kristina WILSON
08 Dean of Learning Resources ... Mr. Cody GREGG
21 Comptroller/Revenue Budget Admin ... Mr. John J. JOHNSON
114 Dir Accounting/Budget Officer ... Dr. Cathy WEST
96 Director of Purchasing/Business Svc ... Mr. David DAVILA
88 Dir Environmental/Health/Safety ... Mr. Chris TWEDDLE
37 Director of Financial Aid ... Mr. Joseph RUIZ
06 Registrar ... Ms. Elizabeth ADAMSON
32 Dir Student Leadership/Campus Life ... Ms. Beverly CAGE
09 Director of Institutional Research ... Mr. Sushil PALLEMONI
15 Director of Human Resources ... Mr. Jerry W. HENRY
88 Director of Payroll ... Ms. Katrina GARCIA

East Texas Baptist University (D)

One Tiger Drive, Marshall TX 75670-1498

County: Harrison
FICE Identification: 003564
Unit ID: 224527
Telephone: (903) 935-7963
Carnegie Class: Bac-Diverse
FAX Number: (903) 938-7798
Calendar System: Semester
URL: www.etbu.edu
Established: 1912
Annual Undergrad Tuition & Fees: $26,370
Enrollment: 1,533
Coed
Affiliation or Control: Baptist
IRS Status: 501(c)3
Highest Offering: Master's
Accreditation: SC, #CAATE, MUS, NURSE

01 President ... Dr. J. Blair BLACKBURN
05 Provost & Vice Pres Acad Affairs ... Dr. Thomas SANDERS
10 Vice Pres Financial Affairs ... Mr. Lee FERGUSON
84 Vice Pres Enrollment/Admin Affairs ... Mr. Kevin CAFFEY
111 Vice Pres University Advancement ... Dr. Scott BRYANT
32 Vice President for Student Affairs ... Dr. Heather HADLOCK
41 Vice President for Athletics ... Mr. Ryan ERWIN
20 Assistant Provost for Acad Affairs ... Dr. Emily PREVOST
110 Asst Vice Pres Univ Advancement ... Mrs. Allison PETEET
35 Asst Vice Pres for Student Affairs ... Mrs. Tara BACHTEL
09 Dean Acad Services & Inst Research ... Dr. Marty WARREN
107 Dean School of Professional Studies ... Dr. Joseph BROWN
53 Dean School of Education ... Dr. John SARGENT
88 Dean School of Christian Studies ... Dr. John HARRIS
83 Dean Sch of Natural/Social Sci ... Dr. Laurie SMITH
50 Dean School of Business ... Dr. Barry EVANS
79 Dean School of Humanities ... Dr. Jerry SUMMERS
57 Dean School of Comm & Perf Arts ... Dr. Tom WEBSTER
106 Dean of Online Education ... Dr. Colleen HALUPA
66 Dean School of Nursing ... Dr. Rebekah GRIGSBY
55 Director for Adult Education ... Mr. Vince BLANKENSHIP
35 Dean of Students ... Mr. Blair PREVOST
07 Asst Vice President for Enrollment ... Dr. Jeremy JOHNSTON
13 Director of Inst Technology ... Mr. Barry HALE
08 Dean of Library Services ... Mrs. Elizabeth PONDER
26 Asst Vice Pres for Mktg/Comm ... Ms. Becky DAVIS
37 Director of Financial Aid ... Mr. Nathan FLORY
88 Director Baptist Student Ministry ... Mr. David GRIFFIN
40 Bookstore Manager ... Mr. Jamie DOWDY
18 Director of Physical Operations ... Mr. Stephen RATCLIFF
85 Dir Global Educ/Grt Commission Ctr ... Dr. Lisa SEELEY
121 Director of Academic Success ... Mrs. Kelley PAUL
11 Asst Vice Pres for Univ Operations ... Mr. Chris CRAWFORD
19 Director of Security & Compliance ... Mr. Larry NORTHCUTT
123 Director of Graduate Admissions ... Mr. Den MURLEY
39 Director of Res Life/Student Hsg ... Ms. Lauren MOORE
88 Director of Student Activities ... Ms. Laura COURSEY
06 University Registrar ... Mr. Troy WHITE
42 Dean of Spiritual Life ... Dr. Scott STEVENS
29 Dir Alumni Rels/Advancement Comm ... Ms. Emily ROBERSON

El Paso Community College (E)

P.O. Box 20500, El Paso TX 79998

County: El Paso
FICE Identification: 010387
Unit ID: 224642
Telephone: (915) 831-2000
Carnegie Class: Assoc/HT-High Trad
FAX Number: N/A
Calendar System: Semester
URL: www.epcc.edu
Established: 1969
Annual Undergrad Tuition & Fees (In-District): $3,010
Enrollment: 28,750
Coed
Affiliation or Control: Local
IRS Status: 501(c)3
Highest Offering: Associate Degree
Accreditation: SC, ADNUR, CAHIIM, COARC, DA, DH, DMS, EMT, MAC, MLTAD, PTAA, RAD, SURGT

01 President ... Dr. William SERRATA
05 Vice Pres Instruction & WF Educ ... Mr. Steve SMITH
11 Vice Pres Financial and Admin Ops ... Ms. Josette SHAUGHNESSY
13 Vice Pres Information Tech/CIO ... Dr. Jenny GIRON
32 Vice Pres Student & Enroll Svcs ... Dr. Kenneth GONZALEZ
108 Vice Pres Rsrch/Accred & Planning ... Dr. Julie PENLEY
114 AVP Budget and Financial Svcs ... Mr. Fernando FLORES
26 AVP External Rel Comm and Dev ... Ms. Keri L. MOE
121 AVP Instruction & Student Success ... Dr. Paula MITCHELL
103 AVP Workforce and CE ... Dr. Jaime FARIAS
12 Dean Instruct Programs-MDP Campus ... Mr. Joshua I. VILLALOBOS
76 Dean Health Career/TechEd/Math/Sci ... Vacant
60 Dean Arts/Comm/Career/TechEd/SoSc ... Dr. Eileen G. CONKLIN
83 Dean Arts/Comm & Soc Sci ... Ms. Janet L. EVELER
49 Dean Arch/Arts/Math/Science ... Dr. Carlos C. AMAYA
79 Dean ESL Reading/Social Science ... Ms. Susana RODARTE
57 Dean Comm/Performing Arts ... Mr. Blayne J. PRIMOZICH
53 Dean Education/Career/Tech Pgms ... Dr. Myshie M. PAGEL
66 Dean Nursing ... Ms. Paula G. MEAGHER
88 Dean ATC ... Dr. Olga L. VALERIO
12 Dean Instructional Pgms NW Campus ... Dr. Lydia TENA
81 Dean Math/Sci/Career Tech Educ ... Mr. Ernest R. WEBB, II
88 Dean Dual Credit & Early Col ... Ms. Maria Antonieta BADILLO
15 Exec Dir Human Resources ... Dr. Andrew M. PENA
14 Exec Dir Net Sys & Support Svcs ... Mr. Marco A. FERNANDEZ
14 Exec Dir IT Soft A Analytics ... Mr. Abraham A. HUBAIL
37 Exec Dir Student Financial Aid ... Ms. Ines LOPEZ
18 Exec Director Physical Plant ... Mr. Richard L. LOBATO
07 Exec Director Admissions/Registrar ... Dr. Cassandra M. LACHICA-CHAVEZ
102 Exec Dir Resource Dev/Foundation ... Dr. Dolores GROSS
41 Athletic Director ... Mr. Felix HINOJOSA
45 Dir Institutional Effectiveness ... Dr. James Ron STROUD
88 Dir Recruitment Services ... Mr. Edgar PALACIOS
88 Dir WF Strategic Initiatives ... Dr. Carmen AGUILERA-GOERNER
88 Dir Contract Opportunity Center ... Mr. Pablo ARMENDARIZ
23 Dir CE Health ... Ms. Marta A. DE LA FUENTE
88 Dir EPCC TV ... Mr. Ebert M. PATRICK
88 Dir Small Business Dev Center ... Mr. Joseph C. FERGUSON
109 Dir Auxiliary Services ... Mr. Juan S. FLORES
45 Dir Institutional Planning ... Ms. Christina C. FRESCAS
88 Dir College Accred Compliance ... Ms. Mary Beth HAAN
88 Dir Curriculum Instruction Dev ... Ms. Yvette V. HUERTA
56 Dir Community Education Program ... Mr. Andres MURO
55 Dir Senior Adult Programs ... Ms. Mary A. YANEZ
88 Dir Quality Enhancement Plan Assess ... Dr. Ondrea M. QUIROS
35 Dir Stdnt Ldrshp Campus Life ... Ms. Arvis C. JONES
36 Dir Career & Transfer Services ... Ms. Carla CARDOZA
96 Dir Purchasing & Contract Mgmt ... Mr. Ruben C. GALLARDO
09 Director Institutional Research ... Dr. Carol KAY
28 Dir of Diversity & Inclusion Pgrm ... Ms. Olga CHAVEZ
16 Dir Human Resources Development ... Mr. Alex HERNANDEZ
114 Director Budget ... Ms. Laura TELLEZ
88 Dir College Access/Development Ctr ... Vacant
22 Dir Ctr for Students w/Disabilities ... Ms. Maria LOPEZ
25 Director Grants Management ... Vacant
103 Director Workforce Development ... Ms. Luz E. TABOADA
88 Director Student Success ... Ms. Lucia M. RODRIGUEZ
88 Dir Law Enforcement Trng Academy ... Mr. Barry J. BOGLE
88 Project Dir Stemgrow Artic Program ... Dr. Mozella GARCIA
19 Chief of Police ... Mr. Jose L. RAMIREZ
21 Comptroller ... Ms. Ana ZUNIGA
04 Exec Asst to the President & BOT ... Ms. Pamela PAYNE

Fortis College (F)

1201 West Oaks Mall, Houston TX 77082

County: Harris
FICE Identification: 034244
Unit ID: 392415
Telephone: (713) 266-6594
Carnegie Class: Spec 2-yr-Health
FAX Number: (713) 782-5873
Calendar System: Quarter
URL: fortiscollege.edu
Established:
Annual Undergrad Tuition & Fees: N/A
Enrollment: 251
Coed
Affiliation or Control: Proprietary
IRS Status: Proprietary
Highest Offering: Associate Degree
Accreditation: ACCSC, SURGT

01 Campus President ... Justin POND

Frank Phillips College (G)

PO Box 5118, Borger TX 79008-5118

County: Hutchinson
FICE Identification: 003568
Unit ID: 224891
Telephone: (806) 457-4200
Carnegie Class: Assoc/HT-High Non
FAX Number: (806) 457-4224
Calendar System: Semester
URL: www.fpctx.edu
Established: 1948
Annual Undergrad Tuition & Fees (In-District): $3,308
Enrollment: 1,491
Coed
Affiliation or Control: Local
IRS Status: 501(c)3
Highest Offering: Associate Degree
Accreditation: SC

01 President ... Dr. Jud HICKS
05 Vice President of Academic Affairs ... Dr. Shannon CARROLL
103 Dean of Career & Technical Educ ... Ms. Taryn FRALEY
08 Director of the Library ... Mr. Jason PRICE
18 Director Physical Plant ... Ms. Regina HANEY
111 Director Advancement ... Ms. Jackie BRAND
37 Dir Student Financial Services ... Ms. Beverly FIELDS
38 Director Student Counseling/Testing ... Ms. Deborah JOHNSON

07 Director Admissions & Records ... Ms. Michele STEVENS
10 Director of Accounting ... Ms. Teri LANGWELL
26 Director of Marketing ... Ms. Arielle BOONE

Galen College of Nursing (A)

7411 John Smith Drive, Suite 1400,
San Antonio TX 78229
Telephone: (210) 733-3056 Identification: 770538
Accreditation: &SC, ADNUR, NURSE

† Branch campus of Galen College of Nursing, Louisville, KY

Galveston College (B)

4015 Avenue Q, Galveston TX 77550-7496
County: Galveston FICE Identification: 004972
Unit ID: 224961
Telephone: (409) 944-4242 Carnegie Class: Assoc/MT-VT-Mix Trad/Non
FAX Number: (409) 944-1500 Calendar System: Semester
URL: www.gc.edu
Established: 1966 Annual Undergrad Tuition & Fees (In-District): $2,050
Enrollment: 2,208 Coed
Affiliation or Control: State/Local IRS Status: 501(c)3
Highest Offering: Baccalaureate
Accreditation: SC, ADNUR, EMT, NMT, #RAD, RTT, SURGT

01 President ... Dr. Myles SHELTON
05 Vice President of Instruction ... Dr. Cissy MATTHEWS
11 VP for Admin/Student Services ... Dr. Van PATTERSON
32 Associate VP of Student Services ... Mr. Ron C. CRUMEDY
75 Dean of Tech & Prof Education ... Ms. Vera LEWIS-JASPER
30 Dir of Development/GC Foundation ... Ms. Maria TRIPOVICH
10 Comptroller/CFO ... Mr. M. Jeff ENGBROCK
13 Director of Info Technology ... Mr. Jason SMITH
26 Director of Public Affairs ... Ms. Carol LANGSTON
15 Dir Human Resources/Risk Management ... Dr. Mary Jan LANTZ
41 Athletic Director/Head Coach ... Ms. Christa HARTNETT
07 Director Admissions/Registrar ... Mr. Scott BRANUM
66 Director of Nursing ... Ms. Donna CARLIN
09 Director Inst Effectiveness/Rsrch ... Vacant
18 Director of Facilities/Security ... Mr. Tim W. SETZER
08 Dir of Library/Learning Resources ... Ms. Telishia MICKENS
37 Director of Financial Aid ... Ms. Meghann NASH
04 Executive Assistant ... Ms. Carla D. BIGGERS

Grace School of Theology (C)

3705 College Park Drive, The Woodlands TX 77384
County: Montgomery Identification: 667100
Unit ID: 481401
Telephone: (877) 476-8674 Carnegie Class: Spec-4-yr-Faith
FAX Number: (877) 735-2867 Calendar System: Semester
URL: www.gsot.edu
Established: 2002 Annual Undergrad Tuition & Fees: $5,280
Enrollment: 397 Coed
Affiliation or Control: Independent Non-Profit IRS Status: 501(c)3
Highest Offering: Doctorate
Accreditation: THEOL, TRACS

01 President ... Dr. Dave ANDERSON
43 Exec Vice President/General Counsel ... Mr. Tom KRUPPSTADT
05 Vice Pres Academic Affairs ... Dr. Al LETTING, III
30 Vice Pres Advancement ... Mr. Daniel LABRY
32 Vice Pres Student Services ... Mr. Mark HAYWOOD

Grayson College (D)

6101 Grayson Drive, Denison TX 75020-8299
County: Grayson FICE Identification: 003570
Unit ID: 225070
Telephone: (903) 465-6030 Carnegie Class: Assoc/MT-VT-Mix Trad/Non
FAX Number: (903) 463-5284 Calendar System: Semester
URL: www.grayson.edu
Established: 1963 Annual Undergrad Tuition & Fees (In-District): $2,040
Enrollment: 4,389 Coed
Affiliation or Control: State/Local IRS Status: 501(c)3
Highest Offering: Baccalaureate
Accreditation: SC, ACFEI, ADNUR, DA, EMT, MLTAD

01 President ... Dr. Jeremy P. MCMILLEN
05 Vice President of Instruction ... Dr. Dava WASHBURN
32 Vice President of Student Affairs ... Dr. Regina ORGAN
10 Vice President for Business Svcs ... Mr. Giles BROWN
13 VP for Information Technology ... Mr. Gary PAIKOWSKI
04 Assistant to the President ... Dr. Molly HARRIS
102 Exec Dir Grayson College Foundation ... Mr. Randy TRUXAL
07 Director of Admissions/Registrar ... Ms. Brandi FURR
37 Director of Financial Aid ... Ms. Amanda HOWELL
14 Director of Network Services ... Mr. Mike BROWN
19 Chief of Campus Police ... Mr. Kevin NUGENT
26 Marketing & Public Relations Coord ... Ms. Rhea BERMEL
21 Director of Fiscal Services ... Mr. Danny HYATT
41 Athletic Director ... Mr. Mike MCBRAYER
40 Bookstore Manager ... Ms. Venus MCGUIRE
08 Chief Library Officer ... Mrs. Lisa HEBERT
09 Director of Institutional Research ... Dr. Debbie SMARR
103 Director Workforce Development ... Mrs. Djuna FORRESTER
15 Chief Human Resources Officer ... Mrs. Jennifer BECHERER
39 Dir Resident Life/Student Housing ... Mrs. Barbara MALONE
20 Dean of Academic Studies ... Dr. Chase MACHEN

Hallmark University (E)

10401 IH-10 W, San Antonio TX 78230-1737
County: Bexar FICE Identification: 010509
Unit ID: 225201
Telephone: (210) 690-9000 Carnegie Class: Bac/Assoc-Mixed
FAX Number: (210) 697-8225 Calendar System: Semester
URL: www.hallmarkuniversity.edu
Established: 1969 Annual Undergrad Tuition & Fees: N/A
Enrollment: 883 Coed
Affiliation or Control: Independent Non-Profit IRS Status: 501(c)3
Highest Offering: Master's
Accreditation: ACCSC

01 President/CEO ... Mr. Joseph B. FISHER
09 Chief Advancement/Inst Effect Ofcr ... Mr. Brent FESSLER
05 University Provost ... Dr. Michael PHILLIPS
11 Chief Operations Officer ... Mr. Samuel (Lee) BEAUMONT
13 Chief Info Technology Officer (CIO) ... Mr. Taylor MERCIER
111 Vice President of Advancement . Mr. Clarence (Reggie) WILLIAMS

Hardin-Simmons University (F)

2200 Hickory, Abilene TX 79698-0001
County: Taylor FICE Identification: 003571
Unit ID: 225247
Telephone: (325) 670-1000 Carnegie Class: Masters/M
FAX Number: (325) 670-1267 Calendar System: Semester
URL: www.hsutx.edu
Established: 1891 Annual Undergrad Tuition & Fees: $28,990
Enrollment: 2,252 Coed
Affiliation or Control: Baptist IRS Status: 501(c)3
Highest Offering: Doctorate
Accreditation: SC, ACBSP, #ARCPA, CAATE, CACREP, MUS, NURSE, PTA, SW, THEOL

01 President ... Dr. Eric I. BRUNTMYER
05 Provost & Chief Academic Officer ... Dr. Christopher L. MCNAIR
10 Vice President for Finance ... Dr. Jodie MCGAUGHEY
30 VP for Institutional Advancement ... Mr. Mike HAMMACK
84 VP for Enrollment Management ... Mrs. Vicki HOUSE
07 Assoc VP for Enrollment Svcs ... Mr. Jim JONES
49 Dean College of Liberal Arts ... Dr. Stephen COOK
50 Dean Kelley College of Business ... Mr. Michael MONHOLLON
64 Dean College of Fine Arts ... Dr. Robert TUCKER
73 Assoc Dean Logsdon Sch of Theology ... Dr. Larry MCGRAW
58 Dean of Graduate Studies ... Dr. Nancy KUCINSKI
13 Assoc Vice Pres Technical Services ... Mr. Travis P. SEEKINS
21 Controller - Financial Reporting ... Mrs. Katie PARNELL
38 Assoc VP Academic Advising/Retent ... Mrs. Gracie CARROLL
08 Dean/Dir of University Libraries ... Mrs. Elizabeth J. NORMAN
06 Registrar ... Mrs. Kacey HIGGINS
35 Dean of Students ... Mrs. Stacey MARTIN
29 Director of Alumni Relations ... Mrs. Jenn WALDMANN
42 Chaplain ... Dr. Kelly PIGOTT
39 Director of Residence Life ... Ms. Hollly EDWARDS
15 Director of Human Resources ... Ms. Tera GIBSON
27 Dir of Univ Marketing ... Mr. Grey HOFF
37 Dir Student Fin Aid & Scholarships ... Mrs. Landri OGNOWSKI
18 Facilities Services Director ... Mr. Tim MCCARRY
41 Athletic Director ... Mr. John M. NEESE
85 Director of International Studies ... Dr. Allan J. LANDWER
28 Coord of Student Diversity Programs ... Dr. Kelvin J. KELLEY

Hill College (G)

112 Lamar Drive, Hillsboro TX 76645-2711
County: Hill FICE Identification: 003573
Unit ID: 225371
Telephone: (254) 659-7500 Carnegie Class: Assoc/MT-VT-High Non
FAX Number: (254) 582-7591 Calendar System: Semester
URL: www.hillcollege.edu
Established: 1923 Annual Undergrad Tuition & Fees (In-District): $2,382
Enrollment: 4,236 Coed
Affiliation or Control: Local IRS Status: 501(c)3
Highest Offering: Associate Degree
Accreditation: SC, CVT, EMT

01 President ... Dr. Pamela BOEHM
04 Executive Asst to the President ... Ms. Vonnie MORPHEW
05 Vice President Instruction ... Dr. Kerry SCHINDLER
25 Vice President External Affairs ... Ms. Jessyca BROWN
10 Vice Pres Administrative Services ... Mr. Billy D. CURBO
32 Vice President Student Services ... Ms. Lizza TRENKLE
13 Vice Pres Information Technology ... Mrs. Jessie WHITE
21 Dean Financial Services ... Mrs. Debbie GERIK
08 Librarian - Hill Campus ... Mr. Joseph SHAUGHNESSY
08 Librarian - Cleburne Campus ... Vacant
15 Director Human Resources ... Mrs. Jamie JASKA
12 Exec Dir JCC/Dean of Students ... Vacant
41 Athletic Director ... Mr. Paul BROWN
26 Director of Marketing & Public Rels ... Mrs. Robin DEMOTT
09 Dir of Institutional Effectiveness ... Ms. Sherry DAVIS
37 Director of Financial Aid ... Ms. Kathleen PUSTEJOVSKY
18 Director Physical Plant ... Mr. Frank WILLIAMS
29 Director Alumni Relations ... Mr. Preston MCREYNOLDS

Houston Baptist University (H)

7502 Fondren Road, Houston TX 77074-3298
County: Harris FICE Identification: 003576
Unit ID: 225399
Telephone: (281) 649-3000 Carnegie Class: Masters/L
FAX Number: (281) 649-3012 Calendar System: Semester
URL: www.hbu.edu
Established: 1960 Annual Undergrad Tuition & Fees: $32,530
Enrollment: 3,325 Coed
Affiliation or Control: Southern Baptist IRS Status: 501(c)3
Highest Offering: Doctorate
Accreditation: SC, NUR

01 President ... Dr. Robert SLOAN
05 Provost/Vice Pres Academic Affairs ... Dr. Michael ROSATO
10 CFO/COO ... Ms. Sandra MOONEY
111 Vice Pres Advancement & Univ Rels ... Mrs. Sharon SAUNDERS
84 Vice Pres Enrollment Management ... Mr. James STEEN
26 VP for Innovation & Strategic Mktg ... Dr. Jerome JOHNSTON
112 VP of Major Gifts ... Mr. Charles BACARISSE
20 Associate Provost ... Dr. Crystal LEE
20 Associate Provost ... Ms. Ritamarie TAUER
20 Associate Provost ... Dr. Jeffrey GREEN
18 Assoc VP for Facilities & Operation ... Mr. John HOLMES
114 Planning & Budget Director ... Mr. Michael DEI
79 Dean School of Humanities ... Dr. Jodey HINZE
50 Dean School of Business ... Dr. Kenneth HOLT
81 Dean Col of Science & Engineering ... Dr. Stan NAPPER
92 Director Honors College ... Dr. Gary HARTENBURG
53 Dean College of Education ... Dr. Julie FERNANDEZ
57 Dean School of Fine Arts ... Dr. Jayme MCGHAN
66 Dean Sch Nursing & Allied Hlth ... Dr. Renae SCHUMANN
41 Athletic Director ... Mr. Steve MONIACI
06 University Registrar ... Ms. Erinn HUGHES
08 Director of Libraries ... Mr. Dean RILEY
42 Assoc University Minister ... Mr. Saleim KAHLEH
21 Assoc VP Financial Operations ... Ms. Loree WATSON
39 Director Residence Life ... Ms. Ashley HANEY
13 Chief Information Officer (IT) ... Ms. Rosa BEAUGENE
09 Dir Inst Research & Effectiveness ... Mr. Todd COCKRELL
32 Assoc Provost Student Life ... Mr. Whittington GOODWIN
88 SACS Liaison ... Ms. Ritamarie TAUER
04 Admin Asst to the President ... Ms. Karen FRANCIES
15 Director of Human Resources ... Vacant
36 Dir of Career & Calling ... Mr. Aaron SWARTS
37 Sr Dir Financial Aid & Scholarships ... Ms. Veronica GABBARD
96 Cost Control Analyst ... Ms. Jody WILDING
88 Asst VP for Recruitment & Mktg ... Mr. Cary DELMARK
07 Director of Admissions ... Mr. Clint STRICKLAND
106 Assoc Provost E-Learning & Cont Edu ... Dr. Paulita BROOKER
108 Director Assessment and Compliance ... Ms. Lisa COVINGTON
11 Chief of Operations/Administration ... Mr. John HOLMES
19 Director Security/Safety ... Chief John KARSHNER
29 Asst VP Univ Relations/Events ... Ms. Candace DESROSIERS
30 Director of Development ... Dr. Tommy BAMBRICK
43 General Counsel ... Mr. Tyler BOYD
44 Director Annual Giving ... Ms. Page HERNANDEZ
90 Academic Technology Support Manager ... Ms. Alison STONE
91 Dir Enterprise Applications/ITS ... Ms. Linda PEREZ

Houston Community College (I)

3100 Main Street, Houston TX 77002
County: Harris FICE Identification: 010633
Unit ID: 225423
Telephone: (713) 718-2000 Carnegie Class: Assoc/HT-High Trad
FAX Number: N/A Calendar System: Semester
URL: www.hccs.edu
Established: 1971 Annual Undergrad Tuition & Fees (In-State): $1,632
Enrollment: 57,120 Coed
Affiliation or Control: State IRS Status: 501(c)3
Highest Offering: Associate Degree
Accreditation: SC, ACBSP, ACFEI, ART, CAHIIM, COARC, DA, DH, DMS, EMT, HT, MAC, MLTAD, NMT, OTA, PTAA, RAD, SURGT

01 Chancellor ... Dr. Cesar MALDONADO
100 Chief of Staff ... Vacant
04 Sr Exec Assistant to the Chancellor ... Ms. Keiana BLAKE
10 VC Finance & Administration/CFO ... Dr. Janet WORMACK
43 General Counsel ... Mr. E. Ashley SMITH
05 VC Instructional Services/CAO ... Dr. Norma PEREZ
32 Interim VC Student Services ... Dr. Shantay GRAYS
13 VC Information Technology ... Dr. William E. CARTER
45 VC Planning and Inst Effectiveness ... Dr. Kurt EWEN
20 Interim AVC Instructional Services ... Dr. Jerome DRAIN
21 AVC Finance & Accounting ... Ms. Carin HUTCHINS
88 AVC College Readiness ... Dr. Catherine O'BRIEN
20 AVC Curriculum & Learning ... Ms. Sandra FULTON
84 Interim AVC Enrollment Services ... Ms. Indra PELAEZ
35 Int AVC Student Engagement/Success ... Ms. Susan GOLL
86 AVC Government & External Relations ... Mr. Remmele YOUNG
18 Chief Facilities Officer ... Mr. Marshall HEINS
15 Chief Human Resource Officer ... Ms. Janet MAY
22 Director EEO/Compliance ... Mr. David CROSS
114 Exec Director Budget & Treasury Ops ... Dr. Karla BENDER
26 AVC Communications & Marketing ... Dr. Megan PALSA
66 Dean Nursing ... Dr. Donna SPIVEY
07 Director of Admissions & Registrar ... Ms. Mary LEMBURG
09 Exec Dir of Inst Research & Innov ... Dr. Martha OBURN
46 Director of Resource Development ... Vacant
102 Executive Director Foundation ... Ms. Karen SCHMIDT
12 President Northeast College ... Dr. Monique UMPHREY
12 President Southwest College ... Dr. Madeline BURILLO
12 President Central College ... Dr. Muddassir SIDDIQI
12 President Southeast College ... Dr. Melissa GONZALEZ
12 President Northwest College ... Dr. Zachary HODGES
12 President Coleman College ... Dr. Phillip NICOTERA
106 President Online College ... Dr. Margaret FORD FISHER

29 Alumni Relations Specialist .... Vacant
96 Exec Dir Procurement Operations .... Mr. Rogelio ANASAGASTI
113 Int Director Student Financial Svcs .... Ms. Oanh NGUYEN
37 Exec Director Student Financial Aid .... Ms. JoEllen SOUCIER
116 Director Internal Auditing .... Mr. Terrance CORRINGAN
50 COE Dean Business/Logistics .... Ms. Connie PORTER
88 Dean English .... Ms. Amy TAN
46 Dean Construction .... Mr. Kris ASPER
59 Int COE Dean Consumer Arts & Sci .... Ms. Suzette BRIMMER
72 COE Dean Digital & Info Tech .... Mr. Sean OTMISHI
65 Dean Earth Life Natural Science .... Dr. Manhal SCHBAT
54 COE Dean Engineering .... Mr. John VASSELLI
88 COE Dean Global Energy .... Mr. Morteza SAMEEI
76 COE Dean Health Science .... Mr. Jeff GRICAR
49 Dean Liberal Arts & Humanities .... Mr. Theodore HANLEY
88 Int COE Dean Advanced Manufacturing .... Dr. Ritu RAJU
88 COE Dean Material Science .... Vacant
81 Dean Mathematics .... Mr. Timor SEVER
72 COE Dean Media Arts & Tech .... Mr. Jimmy ADAMS
88 COE Dean Public Safety .... Mr. Alvin COLLINS
83 Dean Social & Behavioral Science .... Mr. J. Aaron KNIGHT
57 COE Dean Visual & Performing Arts .... Ms. Colleen REILLY
88 COE Dean Automotive Technology .... Mr. David VOGEL
106 Dean Online College/Instruct Tech .... Dr. Timothy SNYDER
88 Exec Director Accounting .... Mr. Nandy BALDONADO
08 Exec Director Library Resources .... Mr. Michael STAFFORD
101 Director Board Services .... Ms. Sharon WRIGHT

Houston Graduate School of Theology (A)

4300-C West Bellfort, Houston TX 77035
County: Harris FICE Identification: 023202
Unit ID: 246345
Telephone: (713) 942-9505 Carnegie Class: Spec-4-yr-Faith
FAX Number: (713) 942-9506 Calendar System: Semester
URL: www.hgst.edu
Established: 1983 Annual Graduate Tuition & Fees: N/A
Enrollment: 145 Coed
Affiliation or Control: Independent Non-Profit IRS Status: 501(c)3
Highest Offering: Doctorate; No Undergraduates
Accreditation: THEOL

01 President .... Dr. James H. FURR
05 Academic Dean .... Dr. Becky L. TOWNE
10 Chief Operating/Financial Officer .... Ms. Tracee FLETCHER
07 Dir of Admissions/Recruiting .... Vacant
06 Registrar .... Ms. Laura HAMILTON
08 Director of Library Services .... Ms. Janet KENNARD

Houston International College-Cardiotech Ultrasound School (B)

12135 Bissonnet, Ste E, Houston TX 77099
County: Harris FICE Identification: 041385
Unit ID: 458034
Telephone: (281) 495-0078 Carnegie Class: Spec 2-yr-Health
FAX Number: (281) 495-5618 Calendar System: Semester
URL: www.cardiotech.org
Established: 2003 Annual Undergrad Tuition & Fees: $11,200
Enrollment: 71 Coed
Affiliation or Control: Proprietary IRS Status: Proprietary
Highest Offering: Associate Degree
Accreditation: ABHES

01 Director .... Ms. Joan DOUGLAS

Howard College (C)

1001 Birdwell Lane, Big Spring TX 79720-3799
County: Howard FICE Identification: 003574
Unit ID: 225520
Telephone: (432) 264-5000 Carnegie Class: Assoc/HT-High Non
FAX Number: (432) 264-5082 Calendar System: Semester
URL: www.howardcollege.edu
Established: 1945 Annual Undergrad Tuition & Fees (In-District): $2,560
Enrollment: 4,264 Coed
Affiliation or Control: State/Local IRS Status: 501(c)3
Highest Offering: Associate Degree
Accreditation: SC, ADNUR, COARC, DH, EMT, RAD, SURGT

01 President .... Dr. Cheryl T. SPARKS
05 Vice President Academic Affairs .... Dr. Amy BURCHETT
20 Admin Dean Instruction SWCD .... Mr. Danny CAMPBELL
32 Admin Dean Student Services SWCD .... Ms. Nancy BONURA
103 Workforce & Cmty Dev Officer-SA .... Ms. Jamie RAINEY
12 Admin Dean Big Spring Area .... Mrs. Erin MACKENZIE
10 Chief Business Officer .... Mr. Steve SMITH
18 Chief Ops/Safety/Security Officer .... Mr. Fabian SERRANO
10 Chief Fiscal Officer/Controller .... Ms. Brenda CLAXTON
08 Dean of Libraries .... Mrs. Mavour BRASWELL
13 Dean Information Technology .... Mr. Eric HANSEN
106 Director eLearning Services .... Ms. Kym CLARK
37 Dean Financial Aid .... Mrs. Candice MALDONADO
26 Director Information/Marketing .... Ms. Cindy SMITH
41 Chief Athletic/Spec Projects Ofcr .... Mr. Terry HANSEN
15 Director Human Resources/Payroll .... Ms. Rhonda KERNICK
12 Admin Dean-San Angelo .... Ms. Pam CALLAN
06 District Registrar .... Mrs. TaNeal RICHARDSON
21 Director Student Accounting .... Ms. Laura FITZPATRICK
30 Director Institutional Advancement .... Mrs. Julie BAILEY

76 Dean Health Professions .... Ms. Luci GABEHART
09 Research and Reporting Officer .... Ms. Rebecca VILLANUEVA
21 Director Financial Accounting .... Ms. Jeannie CARROLL
108 Director Institutional Assessment .... Mr. Bryan STOKES
121 Director Student Support .... Ms. Tara LISLE
04 Executive Asst to the President .... Ms. Emma GARCIA

Howard Payne University (D)

1000 Fisk Street, Brownwood TX 76801-2794
County: Brown FICE Identification: 003575
Unit ID: 225548
Telephone: (325) 646-2502 Carnegie Class: Bac-Diverse
FAX Number: (325) 649-8975 Calendar System: Semester
URL: www.hputx.edu
Established: 1889 Annual Undergrad Tuition & Fees: $28,090
Enrollment: 1,072 Coed
Affiliation or Control: Baptist IRS Status: 501(c)3
Highest Offering: Master's
Accreditation: SC, #CAATE, MUS, SW

01 President .... Dr. Cory HINES
05 Acting Provost .... Dr. Celeste CHURCH
10 Int Chief Financial Officer .... Mr. Mike RODGERS
32 Vice Pres Stdnt Life/Dean Stdnts .... Dr. Magen BUNYARD
30 Vice President Development .... Dr. Dale MEINECKE
84 Assoc VP for Enrollment Management .... Vacant
15 Asst VP for Bus & Hum Resources .... Mr. Bill FISHBACK
18 AVP Facilities/Planning .... Mr. Roger DEWELL
13 Asst VP Information Technology .... Dr. Jodi GOODE
06 Asst VP of University Records .... Dr. Wendy MCNEELEY
37 Director Financial Aid .... Mrs. Karen LAQUEY
07 Director of Admission .... Mrs. P.J GRAMLING
36 Dir Academic Testing/Career Svcs .... Ms. Wendy MCNEELEY
26 Director of Publications .... Mr. Kyle C. MIZE
09 Director Institutional Research .... Dr. Celeste CHURCH
41 Athletic Director .... Mr. Hunter SIMS
91 Database Administrator .... Mr. Tyler CHRISTIANSEN
90 Computer Network Administrator .... Mr. Russell EZZELL
29 Director of Alumni Relations .... Mrs. Laura BENOIT
88 Special Events Coordinator .... Ms. Kathy JAMES
04 Executive Assistant to President .... Ms. Tammy LOWREY
38 PT University Counselor .... Mr. Jerry LESLIE
56 Dean Extended Education .... Vacant
08 Director of Libraries .... Mrs. Deborah DILL
81 Dean School of Science & Math .... Dr. Pam BRYANT
50 Dean School of Business .... Dr. Brad LEMLER
53 Dean School of Education .... Dr. Kylah CLARK-GOFF
64 Dean School of Music & Fine Arts .... Dr. Richard FIESE
73 Dean School of Christian Studies .... Dr. Donnie AUVENSHINE
79 Dean School of Humanities .... Dr. Millard KIMERY
104 Director International Study .... Dr. Jennifer MCNIECE
19 Chief of Police .... Lt. Bob PACATTE
102 Director of Corp/Cmty/Found Rels .... Mrs. Karina DANIEL

Huston-Tillotson University (E)

900 Chicon Street, Austin TX 78702-2795
County: Travis FICE Identification: 003577
Unit ID: 225575
Telephone: (512) 505-3000 Carnegie Class: Bac-Diverse
FAX Number: (512) 505-3190 Calendar System: Semester
URL: www.htu.edu
Established: 1875 Annual Undergrad Tuition & Fees: $14,346
Enrollment: 1,102 Coed
Affiliation or Control: Multiple Protestant Denominations
IRS Status: 501(c)3
Highest Offering: Master's
Accreditation: SC, ACBSP

01 President & CEO .... Dr. Colette PIERCE BURNETTE
04 Executive Assistant to President .... Ms. Janice GOLD
11 VP/COO/Clerk to Board .... Mr. Wayne KNOX
10 VP for Administration & Finance .... Mr. Damon JOHNSON
111 Vice Pres Institutional Advancement .... Ms. Valerie MELTON
05 Provost/VP Academic Affairs ...... Dr. Archibald W. VANDERPUYE
20 Associate Provost .... Dr. Beverly L. DOWNING
32 Dean of Student Affairs .... Ms. Ericka JONES
84 Dean of Enrollment Management .... Dr. Rhonda M. MOSES
08 Director of Library and Media Svcs .... Ms. Danielle MCGHEE
36 Director Career & Grad Development .... Mr. Steven HATCHETT
41 Director of Athletics .... Mr. Charles H. DUBRA
06 University Registrar .... Mrs. Earnestine J. STRICKLAND
13 Int Director Information Technology .... Mr. Malcolm HARAWAY
26 Int Director of Public Relations .... Ms. Valerie MELTON
18 Director of Facilities Operations .... Mr. Thomas GANCHUK
30 Civic Engagement/Community Outreach .... Ms. Linda Y. JACKSON
29 Interim Director of Alumni Affairs .... Ms. Valerie MELTON
35 Coordinator of Campus Life .... Mr. Delton PIERCE
88 Dir of Ctr for Academic Excellence .... Ms. Jenifer MILES
15 Interim Director of Human Resources .... Ms. Brenda KELLEY
38 Dir Counseling & Consultation Ctr .... Rev. Donald E. BREWINGTON
42 University Chaplain .... Rev. Donald E. BREWINGTON
07 Director of Admission .... Ms. Asia HANEY
49 Dean College of Arts & Sciences .... Dr. Michael HIRSCH
50 Dean School of Business/Technology .... Dr. Steven EDMOND
37 Asst Director of Financial Aid .... Mr. Ambrose PRICE
22 Coord Counseling/Disability Svcs .... Ms. Sarah GAINES

Interactive College of Technology (F)

213 West Southmore, Ste 101, Pasadena TX 77502
County: Harris FICE Identification: 023313
Unit ID: 440776
Telephone: (713) 920-1120 Carnegie Class: Spec 2-yr-Other
FAX Number: (713) 477-0348 Calendar System: Semester
URL: www.ict.edu
Established: Annual Undergrad Tuition & Fees: $9,530
Enrollment: 17 Coed
Affiliation or Control: Proprietary IRS Status: Proprietary
Highest Offering: Associate Degree
Accreditation: COE

01 Campus Director .... Bill MCGUIRE

Jacksonville College (G)

105 B. J. Albritton Drive, Jacksonville TX 75766-4759
County: Cherokee FICE Identification: 003579
Unit ID: 225876
Telephone: (903) 586-2518 Carnegie Class: Assoc/HT-High Non
FAX Number: (903) 586-0743 Calendar System: Semester
URL: www.jacksonville-college.edu
Established: 1899 Annual Undergrad Tuition & Fees: $8,000
Enrollment: 546 Coed
Affiliation or Control: Baptist IRS Status: 501(c)3
Highest Offering: Associate Degree
Accreditation: SC

01 President .... Dr. Mike SMITH
03 Vice President Executive Affairs .... Dr. Blanton FEASTER
05 VP Academic Affairs/Academic Dean .... Mrs. Marolyn WELCH
32 Acting Dean of Students .... Dr. Blanton FEASTER
10 Business Manager .... Ms. Jennifer HUGHES
41 Athletic Director .... Mr. Ken HAMILTON
06 Registrar .... Ms. Jodye JAY
08 Director of Library Services .... Ms. Linda THOMAS
07 Director of Admissions .... Mr. Will CUMBEE
18 Director of Maintenance .... Mr. Martin MCRAE
26 Director Public Relations .... Dr. David HEFLIN
29 Director of Alumni Relations .... Mr. Randy DECKER
37 Director of Financial Aid .... Mr. Paul GALYEAN
39 Director of Housing .... Mr. David WHITE
19 Chief of Security .... Mr. Micael MORSE
13 Chief Info Officer/Dir Distance Edu .... Mr. Michael CREECH

Jarvis Christian College (H)

Highway 80 E., PR 7631, Hawkins TX 75765-1470
County: Wood FICE Identification: 003637
Unit ID: 225885
Telephone: (903) 730-4890 Carnegie Class: Bac-Diverse
FAX Number: (903) 769-4842 Calendar System: Semester
URL: www.jarvis.edu
Established: 1912 Annual Undergrad Tuition & Fees: $11,720
Enrollment: 909 Coed
Affiliation or Control: Christian Church (Disciples Of Christ)
IRS Status: 501(c)3
Highest Offering: Baccalaureate
Accreditation: SC, ACBSP, SW

01 President .... Dr. Lester C. NEWMAN
05 Provost/Vice Pres Academic Affairs .... Dr. Glenell PRUITT
10 Vice Pres Administration & Finance .... Ms. Paula LOVE
111 VP Institutional Advancement/Devel .... Dr. Kenoye EKE
32 Vice Pres Student Services .... Dr. Tessie BRADFORD
09 Dir Inst Research & Effectiveness .... Dr. Charlise ANDERSON
13 Int Director Information Technology .... Mr. Stan FRIDIE
06 Registrar .... Ms. Laura LANDER
39 Director Student Facilities/Housing .... Mr. Keyun SWINNEY
84 Exec Director Enrollment Management .. Mr. Christopher WOOTEN
26 Director of Communications .... Mr. Eric STRINGFELLOW
100 Chief of Staff/Director Title III .... Mrs. Cynthia STANCIL
08 Head Librarian .... Mr. Rodney ATKINS
38 Director Career Services .... Mr. Chestley TALLEY
37 Director of Financial Aid .... Ms. Cecelia JONES
41 Athletic Director .... Mr. Bobby LADNER
42 Chaplain/Director of Religious Life .... Vacant
15 Director Human Resources .... Vacant
18 Chief Facilities/Physical Plant .... Mr. Willie SANDIFER
04 Admin Assistant to the President .... Ms. Crystal HUDSON
19 Director Security/Safety .... Mr. Dean RIVARD
28 Coordinator of Diversity .... Mrs. Linda HERNANDEZ
29 Executive Director Alumni Affairs .... Mr. William HAMPTON
50 Dean of Business .... Dr. Benson KARIUKI
53 Dean of Education .... Dr. DeMesia STARLING
51 Dean Adult & Continuing Education .... Dr. Dorothy LANGLEY
96 Purchasing Clerk .... Ms. Brandy GRAY

KD Conservatory College of Film and Dramatic Arts (I)

2600 N Stemmons Fwy, Suite 117, Dallas TX 75207-2111
County: Dallas FICE Identification: 023182
Unit ID: 225991
Telephone: (214) 638-0484 Carnegie Class: Spec 2-yr-A&S
FAX Number: (214) 630-5140 Calendar System: Semester
URL: www.kdstudio.com
Established: 1979 Annual Undergrad Tuition & Fees: $16,993
Enrollment: 142 Coed
Affiliation or Control: Proprietary IRS Status: Proprietary

Highest Offering: Associate Degree
Accreditation: THEA

01 President/CEO ... Ms. Kathy TYNER
05 Director/CAO ... Mr. Michael SCHRAEDER
64 Program Chair - MT ... Mr. Michael SERRECCHIA
88 Program Chair - Film Program ... Mr. Dennis BISHOP
11 Head of Operations ... Ms. Becky HARRIS
32 Head of Student Services ... Ms. Ashlyn NICHOLS
37 Student Financial Aid ... Ms. Linda CRAFT
08 Chief Library Officer ... Ms. Judith HEAD

Kilgore College (A)

1100 Broadway, Kilgore TX 75662-3299
County: Gregg | FICE Identification: 003580
Unit ID: 226019
Telephone: (903) 984-8531 | Carnegie Class: Assoc/HVT-High Trad
FAX Number: (903) 983-8600 | Calendar System: Semester
URL: www.kilgore.edu
Established: 1935 | Annual Undergrad Tuition & Fees (In-District): $1,896
Enrollment: 5,684 | Coed
Affiliation or Control: Local | IRS Status: 501(c)3
Highest Offering: Associate Degree
Accreditation: SC, ADNUR, EMT, PTAA

01 President ... Dr. Brenda S. KAYS
05 Vice President of Instruction ... Dr. Michael H. TURPIN
11 Vice Pres Administrative Services ... Vacant
32 EVP & Chief Student Affairs Ofcr ... Dr. Mike JENKINS
09 Vice Pres Institutional Planning ... Mrs. Staci MARTIN
57 Div Dean Liberal & Fine Arts ... Mrs. Becky JOHNSON
81 Div Dean Science/Math/Health Sci ... Dr. Sandra CARROLL
50 Div Dean Public Services/Technology ... Mr. D'Wayne SHAW
50 Div Dean Business/Info Tech ... Mr. Richard CRUTCHER
75 Dir of Adult Voc Educ ... Ms. Martha WOODRUFF
06 Registrar ... Mr. Chris GORE
15 Director of Human Resources ... Mr. Tony JOHNSON
13 Director of Information Technology ... Mr. John COLVILLE
08 Director Library ... Vacant
40 Manager of Bookstore ... Vacant
19 Chief of Police ... Chief Heath CARIKER
84 Dir of Marketing & Enrollment Mgmt ... Mr. Manny ALMANZA
04 Assistant to the President ... Mrs. Nancy LAW
30 Chief Development Officer ... Mr. Michael HAGELOH
37 Financial Aid Officer ... Mr. Reggie BRAZZLE
85 Admissions/International Specialist ... Ms. Chrissy PATTERSON
26 Asst Dir of Marketing & Public Info ... Mr. Chris CRADDOCK
09 Coord of Institutional Research ... Vacant
38 Coordinator of Counseling ... Mrs. Pam GATTON
39 Coordinator of Residential Life ... Mrs. Ashley MASON
07 Director of Admissions ... Mr. Chris GORE
106 Distance Learning Specialist ... Mr. William STOWE
18 Chief Facilities/Physical Plant ... Mr. Jeff WILLIAMS
41 Athletic Director ... Mr. Jimmy RIEVES
10 Chief Financial/Business Officer ... Mrs. Nancy WYLIE
101 Secretary of the Institution/Board ... Mrs. Nancy LAW
102 Dir of Fndn/Community Relations ... Mrs. Merlyn HOLMES

The King's University (B)

2121 E. Southlake Boulevard, South Lake TX 76092-6507
County: Tarrant | FICE Identification: 035163
Unit ID: 439701
Telephone: (817) 722-1700 | Carnegie Class: Spec-4-yr-Faith
FAX Number: N/A | Calendar System: Quarter
URL: tku.edu/
Established: 1997 | Annual Undergrad Tuition & Fees: $15,000
Enrollment: 662 | Coed
Affiliation or Control: Independent Non-Profit | IRS Status: 501(c)3
Highest Offering: Doctorate
Accreditation: BI, TRACS

01 President ... Dr. Jon CHASTEEN
05 Provost/CAO ... Dr. David COLE
09 Vice Pres Institutional Effective ... Dr. Linda RINN
11 Vice Pres Business Admin/CFO ... Ms. Ashley GREEN
84 VP Enrollment Mgmt/Student Dev ... Dr. Rhonda DAVIS
20 Exec Dean Academic Affairs ... Dr. Daniel DAVIS
10 Director of Finance ... Mr. Lyle WEBER
15 Director Human Resources ... Ms. Tiffany BRITTAIN
32 Director Student Success ... Ms. Tonya MAJOR
07 Director of Admissions ... Ms. Angela PRUIS
06 Registrar ... Mrs. Megan GRONDIN
37 Director Student Financial Services ... Mr. Travis TERMIN
08 Director of Library Services ... Mr. Tracey R. LANE
111 Exec Director of Advancement ... Mr. Bryan CHAMBERS
13 Director Information Management ... Ms. Esther KUHN
113 Coordinator Student Accounts ... Ms. Lynn FREDERICK
90 Dir Acad Computing/Dir Student Affs ... Prof. Donald C. BRUBAKER
29 Director Alumni Relations ... Ms. Maureen A. BRODERSON
96 Director of Purchasing ... Mr. Bob CARON
28 Director of Diversity ... Dr. Michael J. GREGG
102 Dir Foundation/Corporate Relations ... Mr. Lee S. MIMMS
26 Dir of Marketing/Communications ... Mr. Michael KEITH
18 Director Buildings/Operations ... Mr. David REYES
106 Distance Education Coordinator ... Ms. Stephanie STRIDER

Laredo College (C)

West End Washington Street, Laredo TX 78040-4395
County: Webb | FICE Identification: 003582
Unit ID: 226134
Telephone: (956) 722-0521 | Carnegie Class: Assoc/MT-VT-High Trad
FAX Number: (956) 721-5381 | Calendar System: Semester
URL: www.laredo.edu
Established: 1946 | Annual Undergrad Tuition & Fees (In-District): $3,300
Enrollment: 9,881 | Coed
Affiliation or Control: Local | IRS Status: 501(c)3
Highest Offering: Baccalaureate
Accreditation: SC, ADNUR, EMT, OTA, PTAA, RAD

01 President ... Dr. Ricardo SOLIS
05 Provost/VP of Academic Affairs ... Dr. Marisela RODRIGUEZ
84 VP of Student Success & Enrollment ... Dr. Federico SOLIS
25 VP for Resource Development ... Dr. Nora R. GARZA
10 Chief Financial Officer ... Mr. Cesar VELA
26 Exec Dir Strategic & External Init ... Dr. Rodney RODRIGUEZ
09 Exec Dir Inst Effectiveness & Rsrch ... Dr. David ARREAZOLA
32 Associate VP of Student Services ... Mr. Robert OCHOA
103 Dean of Workforce Educ ... Mr. Heriberto HERNANDEZ
76 Dean of Health Sciences ... Dr. Dianna MILLER
51 Dean of Community Education ... Ms. Sandra CORTEZ
49 Interim Dean of Arts & Sciences ... Dr. Horacio SALINAS

Lee College (D)

511 S Whiting, PO Box 818, Baytown TX 77522-0818
County: Harris | FICE Identification: 003583
Unit ID: 226204
Telephone: (281) 427-5611 | Carnegie Class: Assoc/HVT-High Trad
FAX Number: (281) 425-6555 | Calendar System: Semester
URL: www.lee.edu
Established: 1934 | Annual Undergrad Tuition & Fees (In-District): $2,043
Enrollment: 7,717 | Coed
Affiliation or Control: State/Local | IRS Status: 501(c)3
Highest Offering: Associate Degree
Accreditation: SC, ADNUR, CAHIIM

01 President ... Dr. Dennis BROWN
04 Executive Assistant to President ... Ms. Leslie D. GALLAGHER
03 Executive Vice President ... Vacant
10 VP Finance & Administration ... Ms. Annette FERGUSON
103 VP Workforce/Community Development ... Dr. Angela ORIANO
05 VP Instruction ... Dr. Veronique TRAN
32 VP Student Affairs ... Dr. Donnetta SUCHON
12 Dean of Huntsville Center at TDCJ ... Ms. Donna P. ZUNIGA
108 Exec Dir Assessment & Accreditation ... Dr. Brandon COMBS
13 Chief Information Officer ... Dr. Carolyn A. LIGHTFOOT
84 Exec Dir Enrollment/Registrar ... Mr. Scott BENNETT
15 Director Human Resources ... Ms. Amanda SUMMERS
26 Director Marketing & Public Affairs ... Ms. Susan SMEDLEY
37 Director Financial Aid ... Mr. Felipe LEAL
102 Exec Dir Foundation & Resource Dev ... Ms. Pam WARFORD
96 Director Purchasing ... Mr. Mike SPARKES
124 Exec Dir Retention/Transition Svcs ... Ms. Victoria MARRON

LeTourneau University (E)

PO Box 7001, 2100 S Mobberly Ave,
Longview TX 75607-7001
County: Gregg | FICE Identification: 003584
Unit ID: 226231
Telephone: (903) 233-3000 | Carnegie Class: Masters/M
FAX Number: (903) 233-3101 | Calendar System: Semester
URL: www.letu.edu
Established: 1946 | Annual Undergrad Tuition & Fees: $30,210
Enrollment: 3,003 | Coed
Affiliation or Control: Independent Non-Profit | IRS Status: 501(c)3
Highest Offering: Master's
Accreditation: NURSE

01 President ... Dr. Dale A. LUNSFORD
05 Provost & VP for Academic Affairs ... Dr. Steven D. MASON
30 Vice President for Development ... Dr. Terry ZEITLOW
10 VP Finance/Administration ... Mr. Mike HOOD
32 VP for Student Affairs ... Ms. Kristy MORGAN
84 VP Residential Enrollment Services ... Mr. Carl ARNOLD
26 VP Marketing & Communications ... Mr. Don EGLE
88 Assoc Prov for Residential Admin ... Dr. Benjamin CALDWELL
88 VP for Global Operations ... Dr. Melanie ROUDKOVSKI
18 Asst VP of Facilities Services ... Mr. Chris CHAPMAN
53 Dean School of Education ... Dr. Larry FRAZIER
50 Dean School of Business ... Dr. Van GRAHAM
54 Dean Sch Engineering & Engr Tech ... Dr. Steve STARRETT
49 Dean School of Arts & Sciences ... Dr. Larry FRAZIER
88 Dean School of Aeronautical Science ... Mr. Fred L. RITCHEY
35 Dean of Students ... Mr. Steve CONN
08 Director Learning Resource Center ... Ms. Shelby WARE
41 Director of Athletics ... Ms. Terri DEIKE
25 Director Office of Sponsored Pgms ... Mr. Paul R. BOGGS
13 Chief Information Officer ... Mr. Ken JOHNSON
15 Director of Human Resources ... Mrs. Phyllis TURNER
23 Director Health Services ... Ms. Julie MOORE
19 Chief of Police ... Mr. Michael SCHULTZ
36 Director of Career Services ... Ms. Rachel OLSHINE
06 University Registrar ... Mr. Texas RUEGG
84 Director of Enrollment Services ... Ms. Kristine SLATE
29 Director of Alumni & Parent Rels ... Vacant
27 Director of University Relations ... Ms. Janet RAGLAND
27 Director Marketing & Communication ... Ms. Kate GRONEWALD
21 Controller ... Ms. Vikki KEILERS
09 Asst VP for Accreditation & QA ... Dr. Karl PAYTON
88 Executive Dir Ctr for Faith & Work ... Mr. Bill PEEL
04 Administrative Asst to President ... Mrs. Denise BAILEY
106 Assoc VP for Global Student Success ... Mr. Carlton MITCHELL
37 Director Student Financial Aid ... Ms. Tracy WATKINS
38 Director Center for Counseling ... Mrs. Treva BARHAM
104 Chief Global Initiatives Officer ... Mr. Alan CLIPPERTON
73 Dean School of Theology & Vocation ... Dr. Kelly LIEBENGOOD
66 Dean School of Nursing ... Dr. Kimberly QUIETT
101 Secretary of the Institution/Board ... Mr. Bud MCGUIRE
105 Director Web Services ... Mr. Mark ROEDEL
39 Director Student Housing ... Mr. Tony ZAPPASODI

Lincoln College of Technology (F)

2915 Alouette Drive, Grand Prairie TX 75052
County: Tarrant | FICE Identification: 008353
Unit ID: 226277
Telephone: (972) 660-5701 | Carnegie Class: Spec 2-yr-Tech
FAX Number: (972) 660-6148 | Calendar System: Other
URL: www.lincolntech.com
Established: | Annual Undergrad Tuition & Fees: N/A
Enrollment: 898 | Coed
Affiliation or Control: Proprietary | IRS Status: Proprietary
Highest Offering: Associate Degree
Accreditation: ACCSC

01 Campus President ... Mr. Mike COULING

Lone Star College System (G)

5000 Research Forest Drive,
The Woodlands TX 77381-4356
County: Harris | FICE Identification: 011145
Unit ID: 227182
Telephone: (832) 813-6500 | Carnegie Class: Assoc/HT-Mix Trad/Non
FAX Number: N/A | Calendar System: Semester
URL: www.lonestar.edu
Established: 1972 | Annual Undergrad Tuition & Fees (In-District): $1,600
Enrollment: 72,336 | Coed
Affiliation or Control: State/Local | IRS Status: 501(c)3
Highest Offering: Associate Degree
Accreditation: SC, ADNUR, CAHIIM, CEA, COARC, DH, DMS, EMT, MAC, MUS, OTA, PTAA, RAD, SURGT

01 Chancellor ... Dr. Stephen HEAD
12 President of LSC-CyFair ... Dr. Seelpa KESHVALA
12 President of LSC-Houston North ... Dr. Quentin WRIGHT
12 President of LSC-Kingwood ... Dr. Katherine PERSSON
12 President of LSC-Montgomery ... Dr. Rebecca RILEY
12 President of LSC-North Harris ... Dr. Gerald NAPOLES
12 President of LSC-Tomball ... Dr. Lee Ann NUTT
12 President of LSC-University Park ... Dr. Shah ARDALAN
13 Vice Chanc College Services/CIO ... Mr. Link ALANDER
32 Vice Chancellor Student Success ... Dr. Archie BLANSON
43 Chief Operating Officer/Gen Counsel ... Mr. Mario CASTILLO
100 VC/Chief of Staff/Board Liaison ... Ms. Helen CLOUGHERTY
10 Chief Financial Officer ... Ms. Jennifer MOTT
05 Vice Chancellor Academic Success ... Dr. Dwight SMITH, III
37 Sr Assoc Vice Chanc Financial Aid ... Ms. Johanna BOLEY
31 Senior AVC External & Employer Rel ... Ms. Linda HEAD
15 Senior Assoc VC Human Resources ... Ms. Margaret KERSTENS
19 Senior Assoc VC & Chief of Police ... Mr. Paul WILLINGHAM
86 Associate VC Governmental Relations ... Mr. Jesse AYALA
09 Assoc VC Analytics & Inst Reporting ... Ms. Marian CHANEY
114 Associate VC Budget & Treasury ... Ms. Tammy CORTES
21 AVC Fin Reporting & Ops/Controller ... Ms. Lorena FACCINI-VITO
105 Assoc VC Enterprise Applications ... Mr. Longin GOGU
106 Assoc Vice Chancellor LSC-Online ... Dr. Robert GREENE
88 AVC Governance/Audit & Compliance ... Ms. Sandra GREGERSON
20 Associate VC Academic Affairs ... Dr. Valerie JONES
14 Assoc Vice Chanc Campus Services ... Mr. Earl JUELG
88 AVC Real Estate & Strategic Plng ... Mr. Randal KEY
18 Assoc VC Facilities & Construction ... Ms. Denise NEU
35 AVC Student Success & Completion ... Ms. Jamie POSEY
109 Associate VC Supply Management ... Vacant
26 AVC Marketing & Communications ... Ms. Poornima SWAMINATHAN
96 Executive Director Procurement ... Ms. Cynthia BRIGHT
116 Exec Dir Audit & Consulting Svcs ... Ms. Leticia CHARBONNEAU
96 Exe Dir Facilities/Cons Procurement ... Mr. William DODD
88 Exec Dir Organizational Development ... Dr. Alicia FRIDAY
06 Exec Dir Records/Enroll & Registrar ... Ms. Connie GARRICK
07 Exec Dir Admissions & Prosp Student ... Dr. Laura ISDELL
102 Executive Director LSC Foundation ... Ms. Nicole ROBINSON GAUTHIER
25 Exec Director Resource Dev & Admin ... Ms. Elizabeth THOMPSON
45 Exec Dir Strategic Plng/Assessment ... Dr. Christopher TKACH
14 Exec Director Technical Services ... Ms. Sherry WATSON
08 Director Library Technical Services ... Ms. Carol STEINMETZ
08 Director Library LSC-CyFair ... Ms. Susan GREEN
08 Director Library LSC-Houston North ... Vacant
08 Dir Academic Success LSC-Kingwood ... Ms. Kaleigh VONDERVOR
08 Dean Acad Sup/Lib LSC-Montgomery ... Ms. Sarah PALACIOS-WILHELM
08 Director Library LSC-North Harris ... Ms. Christine RAMSEY
08 Director Library LSC-Tomball ... Ms. Bobbye SILVA
08 Dir Student Lrng Ctr LSC-Univ Park ... Ms. Shannon HAUSINGER
30 Director Constituent Engagement ... Ms. Susan SUMMERS
04 Executive Assistant to Chancellor ... Ms. Fatima BARNETT

Lubbock Christian University (H)

5601 19th Street, Lubbock TX 79407-2099
County: Lubbock | FICE Identification: 003586
Unit ID: 226383
Telephone: (806) 796-8800 | Carnegie Class: Masters/M
FAX Number: (806) 720-7255 | Calendar System: Semester

URL: www.lcu.edu
Established: 1957 Annual Undergrad Tuition & Fees: $22,440
Enrollment: 1,883 Coed
Affiliation or Control: Churches Of Christ IRS Status: 501(c)3
Highest Offering: Master's
Accreditation: SC, NUR, SW, @THEOL

01 Interim CEO .... Mr. Al ROBERTS
03 Executive Vice President .... Dr. Brian STARR
05 Provost & Chief Academic Officer .... Dr. Foy MILLS
43 General Counsel .... Dr. Bart PRUITT
111 Vice Pres University Advancement .... Mr. Raymond RICHARDSON
10 Chief Financial Officer .... Mr. Brandon GOEN
13 Vice President for Technology .... Dr. Karl MAHAN
26 Sr Vice Pres University Relations .... Mr. John KING
32 Vice Pres Student Affairs .... Mr. Randal DEMENT
84 Vice Pres Enrollment Management .... Dr. Mondy BREWER
107 Dean Col of Professional Studies .... Dr. Toby ROGERS
49 Dean College Liberal Arts/Education .... Dr. Susan BLASSINGAME
73 Dean Col Biblical Stds/Behavior Sci .... Dr. Jesse LONG
50 Dean School of Business .... Mr. Tracy MACK
09 Asst VP for Instl Effectiveness .... Mr. Randy SELLERS
29 AVP Alumni/Community Relations .... Mrs. Sheila DYE
41 Athletic Director .... Mr. Paul HISE
06 Registrar .... Ms. Sonja DIXON
37 Director of Financial Assistance .... Mrs. Amy HARDESTY
35 Dean of Students .... Mr. Josh STEPHENS
08 Director of Library Services .... Mr. Mark GOTTSCHALK
18 Director of Campus Facilities .... Mr. Mike SELLECK
38 Director Student Counseling .... Mr. John MAPLES
92 Director of Honors College .... Dr. Stacy PATTY
23 Director of Medical Clinic .... Dr. Jeff SMITH
14 Sr Director of Technology Services .... Mr. Robert SMITH
22 Disability Services Coordinator .... Mr. Justin ARCHER
39 Director of Residential Life .... Mrs. Sunny PARK
07 Director of Admissions .... Mr. Chris HAYES
15 Human Resources Director .... Mrs. Brenda LOWE
19 Dir Public Safety/Chief Police .... Mr. Michael SMITH
40 Bookstore Manager .... Mrs. Denise MCNEILL
04 Assistant to the President .... Dr. David FRAZE

McLennan Community College (A)

1400 College Drive, Waco TX 76708-1498
County: McLennan FICE Identification: 003590
Unit ID: 226578
Telephone: (254) 299-8000 Carnegie Class: Assoc/HT-Mix Trad/Non
FAX Number: (254) 299-8654 Calendar System: Semester
URL: www.mclennan.edu
Established: 1965 Annual Undergrad Tuition & Fees (In-District): $3,450
Enrollment: 8,880 Coed
Affiliation or Control: State/Local IRS Status: 501(c)3
Highest Offering: Associate Degree
Accreditation: SC, ADNUR, CAHIIM, #COARC, EMT, MAC, MLTAD, OTA, PTAA, RAD, SURGT

01 President .... Dr. Johnette MCKOWN
10 Vice Pres Finance & Administration .... Dr. Stephen BENSON
05 Vice President Instruction .... Dr. Fred HILLS
22 Equal Employment Opportunity Ofcr .... Mr. Al POLLARD
32 Vice President Student Success .... Dr. Drew CANHAM
09 Vice Pres Research/Effectiveness .... Dr. Phil RHODES
102 Exec Director MCC Foundation .... Ms. Kim PATTERSON
96 Director Purchasing & Auxil Svcs .... Ms. Jodi TINDELL
37 Director Financial Aid .... Mr. James KUBACAK
26 Director Marketing & Communication .... Ms. Lisa ELLIOTT
41 Director Athletics .... Mrs. Shawn TROCHIM
06 Director Records & Registration .... Mr. Herman V. TUCKER
07 Director Admissions & Recruitment .... Mrs. Karen CLARK
08 Director Library Services .... Mr. Daniel MARTINSEN
15 Director Human Resources .... Ms. Missy KITTNER
18 Director Physical Plant .... Mrs. Dianne E. FEYERHERM
21 Director Financial Services .... Mrs. Terry LECHLER
76 Dean Health Professions .... Ms. Glynnis GAINES
49 Dean Arts & Sciences .... Dr. Chad EGGLESTON
51 Dean Continuing Education .... Dr. Frank GRAVES

McMurry University (B)

1400 Sayles Boulevard, Abilene TX 79697
County: Taylor FICE Identification: 003591
Unit ID: 226587
Telephone: (325) 793-3800 Carnegie Class: Bac-Diverse
FAX Number: (325) 793-4805 Calendar System: Semester
URL: www.mcm.edu
Established: 1923 Annual Undergrad Tuition & Fees: $27,419
Enrollment: 1,108 Coed
Affiliation or Control: United Methodist IRS Status: 501(c)3
Highest Offering: Master's
Accreditation: SC, NURSE

01 President .... Dr. Sandra HARPER
05 Vice Pres Academic Affairs .... Dr. James HUNT
10 Vice Pres Finance & Administration .... Mrs. Lisa L. WILLIAMS
111 Vice Pres Institutional Advancement .... Ms. Debra HULSE
26 Vice Pres Marketing/Communication .... Ms. Robin DANIELS
105 Webmaster .... Mr. Jim QUINNETT
14 Director of Customer Services .... Mr. Freddie FAMBLE, JR.
13 Director of Administrative Systems .... Ms. Kathy DENSLOW
06 Registrar .... Mrs. Carolyn A. CALVERT
08 Director Jay-Rollins Library .... Ms. Terry YOUNG
32 Dean of Students & Campus Life .... Mr. Allen WITHERS
66 Dean School of Nursing .... Dr. Donalyn ALEXANDER
35 Director of Student Activities .... Ms. Erica MEDINA
37 Director of Financial Aid .... Mr. Tim SECHRIST
21 Controller .... Ms. Tina SCHUELLER
15 Director of Human Resources .... Ms. Lecia HUGHES
108 Dir of Institutional Effectiveness .... Dr. Jori SECHRIST
09 Director of Institutional Research .... Ms. Terry NIXON
29 Director Alumni Relations .... Ms. Suzann COUTS
36 Director Counseling & Career Svcs .... Mr. James GREER
41 Director of Athletics .... Dr. Sam FERGUSON
42 Dir of Religious Life/Univ Chaplain .... Rev. Marty CASHBURLESS
19 Director of Campus Security .... Mr. Mark R. ODOM
23 Director of Health Services .... Ms. Ronda HOELSCHER
39 Director of Residence Life .... Ms. Jessica NGUYEN
102 Executive Director Donor Relations .... Ms. Nancy SMITH
92 Director Honors Program .... Dr. Philip LE MASTERS
106 Director of Online Education .... Dr. Alicia WYATT
04 Executive Asst to President .... Ms. Jerri GAZAILLE
50 Dean School of Business .... Dr. Paul MASON
18 Dir Facilities & Campus Projects .... Mr. Carl SCOTT

Messenger College (C)

2705 Brown Trail Ste 408, Bedford TX 76021
County: Tarrant FICE Identification: 030926
Unit ID: 417752
Telephone: (817) 554-5950 Carnegie Class: Spec-4-yr-Faith
FAX Number: (817) 391-4003 Calendar System: Semester
URL: www.messengercollege.edu
Established: 1987 Annual Undergrad Tuition & Fees: $9,180
Enrollment: 51 Coed
Affiliation or Control: Pentecostal Church of God IRS Status: 501(c)3
Highest Offering: Baccalaureate
Accreditation: TRACS

01 President .... Rev. Randall K. LAWRENCE
05 VP of Academic Affairs .... Dr. Candace RAYBURN
08 Head Librarian .... Mary THOMASON
10 VP of Business Affairs .... Angela HEPPNER
32 VP of Student Development .... Fiona PARKER
37 Dir Student Financial Aid/Registrar .... Carolyn R. DOWD

MIAT College of Technology (D)

533 Northpark Central Drive, Houston TX 77073
Telephone: (713) 401-3399 Identification: 770972
Accreditation: ACCSC

† Branch campus of MIAT College of Technology, Canton, MI

Midland College (E)

3600 N Garfield, Midland TX 79705-6397
County: Midland FICE Identification: 009797
Unit ID: 226806
Telephone: (432) 685-4500 Carnegie Class: Bac/Assoc-Assoc Dom
FAX Number: (432) 685-4714 Calendar System: Semester
URL: www.midland.edu
Established: 1969 Annual Undergrad Tuition & Fees (In-District): $2,670
Enrollment: 5,564 Coed
Affiliation or Control: Local IRS Status: 501(c)3
Highest Offering: Baccalaureate
Accreditation: SC, CAHIIM, COARC, DMS, EMT

01 President .... Dr. Steve THOMAS
03 Vice President Instructional Svcs .... Dr. Damon KENNEDY
88 Special Advisor to President .... Dr. Deana SAVAGE
10 Vice Pres Administrative Services .... Mr. Rick BENDER
32 Vice President Student Services .... Mrs. Julia VICKERY
13 Vice Pres Info Tech/Facilities .... Vacant
101 Asst to President/Sec to Board .... Mrs. Bahola EDWARDS
106 Dean of Distance Learning/Cont Educ .... Mr. Dale BEIKIRCH
57 Dean of Fine Arts/Communication .... Dr. William FEELER
72 Dean of Applied Technology .... Mr. Curt PERVIER
76 Dean of Health Sciences .... Ms. Carmen EDWARDS
81 Dean of Math/Natural Sciences .... Dr. Margaret WADE
83 Associate Dean/Adult Education .... Mrs. Lynda WEBB
111 Exec Dir Inst Advancement/Col Found .... Ms. Rebecca BELL
06 Registrar .... Mrs. Angela BALCH
08 Head Librarian .... Mr. Howard MARKS
15 Director of Human Resources/Payroll .... Mrs. Natasha MORGAN
18 Director Physical Plant .... Vacant
19 Chief of Police .... Mr. Richard MCKEE
35 Student Life Director .... Mr. Ty SOLIZ
41 Athletic Director .... Mr. Forrest ALLEN
09 Dir Institutional Effect/Planning .... Vacant
37 Director Student Financial Aid .... Ms. Yolanda RAMOS
96 Director Purchasing .... Ms. Barbara FENNELL
84 Dean of Enrollment Management .... Dr. Formon THOMPSON
30 Director Devel & Alumni Relations .... Mrs. Taylor SHORB
26 Director Marketing & Communication .... Ms. Travis WOODWARD
108 Director Institution Effectiveness ... Mrs. Kathryn ZIMMERHANZEL
97 Dean Instructional Support Services .... Mr. Michael DIXON

Midwestern State University (F)

3410 Taft Boulevard, Wichita Falls TX 76308-2095
County: Wichita FICE Identification: 003592
Unit ID: 226833
Telephone: (940) 397-4000 Carnegie Class: Masters/L
FAX Number: (940) 397-4042 Calendar System: Semester
URL: www.msutexas.edu
Established: 1922 Annual Undergrad Tuition & Fees (In-State): $9,233
Enrollment: 6,080 Coed
Affiliation or Control: State IRS Status: 501(c)3
Highest Offering: Master's
Accreditation: SC, ART, #CAATE, CAEP, CAEPN, COARC, DH, MUS, NURSE, RAD, SW, THEA

01 President .... Dr. Suzanne SHIPLEY
05 Provost .... Dr. James JOHNSTON
10 VP Business Affairs & Finance .... Vacant
111 VP Univ Advancement & Student Affs .... Mr. Anthony VIDMAR
32 VP Student Affairs .... Dr. Keith LAMB
84 VP Enrollment Management .... Mr. Fred DIETZ
18 Assoc VP Facilities Services .... Mr. Kyle OWEN
35 Assoc VP Student Affairs .... Mr. Matthew PARK
13 Chief Information Systems .... Dr. David SANCHEZ
06 Registrar .... Ms. Darla INGLISH
08 University Librarian .... Dr. Clara LATHAM
37 Director of Student Financial Aid .... Ms. Kathy PENNARTZ-BROWNING
38 Director of Counseling Center .... Dr. Pam MIDGETT
51 Director of Extended Education .... Dr. Pamela MORGAN DAVIS
07 Director of Admissions .... Ms. Gayonne BEAVERS
19 Chief of Police .... Mr. Patrick COGGINS
26 Director Public Info/Marketing .... Ms. Julie GAYNOR
88 Dir Donor Services and Scholarships .... Ms. Laura PETERSON
36 Director Career Management Center .... Mr. Dirk WELCH
41 Director of Athletics .... Mr. Kyle WILLIAMS
15 Director of Human Resources .... Ms. Dawn FISHER
09 Director of Inst Effectiveness .... Mr. Mark MCCLENDON
21 Controller .... Mr. Chris STOVALL
23 Director Vinson Health Center .... Dr. Keith WILLIAMSON
20 Associate VP Academic Affairs .... Dr. Kristen GARRISON
50 Dean College Business Admin .... Dr. Jeff STAMBAUGH
53 Dean College of Education .... Dr. Matthew CAPPS
57 Dean College of Fine Arts .... Dr. Martin CAMACHO
76 Dean Col Health Sci/Human Svcs .... Dr. Jeffrey KILLION
79 Dean College Humanities/Social Sci .. Dr. Samuel E. WATSON, III
81 Dean College of Science/Math & Engr .... Dr. Margaret BROWN MARSDEN
86 Director Board & Govt Relations .... Ms. Deborah L. BARROW
29 Director of Alumni Relations .... Ms. Leslee PONDER
121 Director of Academic Success Center .... Ms. Ashley HURST
105 Webmaster .... Mr. Jonathan SHIREY
96 Director of Purchasing .... Mr. Stephen SHELLEY
22 Dir Disability Support Services .... Ms. Debra HIGGINBOTHAM
39 Director Housing & Residence Life .... Ms. Kristi SCHULTE
30 Director University Development .... Mr. Steve SHIPP
104 Director of International Education .... Dr. Michael MILLS
88 Assoc Dir of Career Mgmt & Testing .... Ms. Lynn DUCIOAME
85 Director International Services .... Dr. Randy GLEAN
114 Director Budget & Management .... Ms. Valarie MAXWELL
88 Director Museum .... Ms. Tracee ROBERTSON
88 Director Student Support Services .... Ms. Lisa ESTRADA-HAMBY
88 Campus Postal Supervisor .... Mr. Jon LANE
92 Coordinator Honors Program .... Mr. Cody PARISH
43 Dir Legal Services/General Counsel .... Mr. Barry MACHA
28 Dir Eqty/Inclusion/Multi-Cult Affs .... Dr. Syreeta GREENE

Navarro College (G)

3200 W Seventh Avenue, Corsicana TX 75110-4899
County: Navarro FICE Identification: 003593
Unit ID: 227146
Telephone: (903) 874-6501 Carnegie Class: Assoc/MT-VT-High Trad
FAX Number: (903) 874-4636 Calendar System: Semester
URL: www.navarrocollege.edu
Established: 1946 Annual Undergrad Tuition & Fees (In-District): $2,430
Enrollment: 8,968 Coed
Affiliation or Control: Local IRS Status: 501(c)3
Highest Offering: Associate Degree
Accreditation: SC, ADNUR, EMT, MLTAD, OTA, PTAA

01 District President .... Dr. Kevin G. FEGAN
05 Vice Pres Academic Affairs .... Dr. Carol HANES
10 Vice President Finance & Admin .... Ms. Teresa THOMAS
111 VP Oper/Institutional Advancement .... Dr. Harold HOUSLEY
32 Vice President Student Services .... Ms. Maryann HAILEY
84 VP Enroll Mgmt/Inst Effect .... Ms. Sina RUIZ
15 VP Human Resources .... Ms. Marcy BALLEW
26 Director of Mktg/Public Relations .... Ms. Stacie SIPES
41 Athletic Director .... Mr. Michael LANDERS
20 Executive Dean of Acad Studies .... Dr. Jeanetta GROCE
103 Exec Dean Wrkfc/Career & Tech Educ .... Ms. Tammy GALLOWAY
106 Dean of Online Instruction .... Mr. Matthew MILLER
76 Dean Midlothian Campus/Health Prof .... Mr. Guy FEATHERSTON
12 Dean of Mexia Campus .... Ms. Christina MIMS
51 Dean of Continuing Education .... Dr. Micaela HERNDON
08 Dean of Libraries .... Mr. Tim KEVIL
07 Dir of Admissions/Registrar .... Ms. Tammy ADAMS
18 Exec Director of Facilities .... Mr. Karl HUMPHRIES
13 Director of IT .... Mr. Barry SULLIVAN
37 Director Student Financial Aid .... Ms. Kristal NICHOLSON
39 Director of Residence Life .... Mr. Charles BETTS
104 Director of International Programs .... Ms. Elizabeth PILLANS
88 Academic Dean of Ellis County .... Ms. Terry GIBSON
81 Dean Science/Kinesiology/Dev Stds .... Dr. Richard PHILLIPS
04 Exec Asst to District President .... Ms. Leslie SMITH

North American University (H)

11929 W. Airport Boulevard, Stafford TX 77477
County: Fort Bend FICE Identification: 041795
Unit ID: 461795
Telephone: (832) 230-5555 Carnegie Class: Masters/M
FAX Number: N/A Calendar System: Semester
URL: www.na.edu

Established: 2010 Annual Undergrad Tuition & Fees: $9,900
Enrollment: 568 Coed
Affiliation or Control: Non-denominational IRS Status: 501(c)3
Highest Offering: Master's
Accreditation: ACCSC

01 President ... Dr. Serif A. TEKALAN
05 Provost/Vice Pres Academic Affairs ... Dr. Faruk TABAN
11 VP Admin Affairs/Assoc Prof ... Dr. Kadir ALMUS
04 Administrative Asst to President ... Jill SELTZER
06 Registrar ... Edra EDWARDS
07 Senior Admissions Officer ... Anthony SORIANO
08 Head Librarian ... Gary CHAUFFEE
106 Dir Online Education/E-learning ... Mustafa MALDAR
13 Chief Info Technology Officer (CIO) ... Khudoyor S. ORTIKOV
32 Dean Student Affairs/Student Life ... Dr. Osman KANLIOGLU
37 Assoc Dir Student Financial Aid ... Tia SIMON
10 Chief Financial Ofcr/Dir Bus Affs ... Dovran OVEZOV

North Central Texas College (A)

1525 W. California Street, Gainesville TX 76240-4699
County: Cooke FICE Identification: 003558
Unit ID: 224110
Telephone: (940) 668-7731 Carnegie Class: Assoc/MT-VT-High Trad
FAX Number: (940) 668-6049 Calendar System: Semester
URL: www.nctc.edu
Established: 1924 Annual Undergrad Tuition & Fees (In-District): $2,184
Enrollment: 10,327 Coed
Affiliation or Control: State/Local IRS Status: 501(c)3
Highest Offering: Associate Degree
Accreditation: SC, ADNUR, EMT, SURGT

01 President ... Dr. G. Brent WALLACE
05 Provost/Chief Fiscal Officer ... Dr. Andrew FISHER
32 Vice President of Student Services ... Dr. O. John MADUKO
10 Vice Chanc Fiscal Affairs ... Dr. Van MILLER
11 Vice Chanc Administrative Affairs ... Mr. Robbie BAUGH
30 Vice Chanc External Affairs ... Ms. Debbie SHARP
103 Assoc VC Academic Partnerships ... Dr. Emily KLEMENT
108 Assoc VC Strategic Planning/IR ... Mr. David BROWN
13 AVC Information Technology ... Ms. Denise CASON
08 Dean of Libraries ... Ms. Diane ROETHER
15 Director Human Resources ... Ms. Kay SCHROEDER
37 Director Financial Aid ... Ms. Ashley TATUM
06 Registrar/Director of Admissions ... Ms. Melinda CARROLL
38 Sr Director Advising/Counseling ... Ms. Tracey FLENIKEN
26 Dir Marketing and Public Relations ... Mrs. Dianne WALTERSCHEID
41 Athletic Director ... Mr. Van HEDRICK
35 Director of Student Life ... Ms. Daisy GARCIA
76 Dean of Health Science ... Dr. Bonita VINSON
81 Dean of Instruction Gainesville ... Ms. Sara FLUSCHE
49 Dean of Instruction Corinth ... Dr. Larry GILBERT
49 Dean of Instruction Flower Mound ... Mrs. Sara ALFORD
19 Police Chief ... Mr. James FITCH
35 Dean of Student Affairs ... Dr. Roxanne DEL RIO
12 Dean of Denton County Campuses ... Mr. Roy CULBERSON
12 Director of Flower Mound Campus ... Ms. Jessica DEROCHE
12 Director of Bowie Campus ... Dr. Jose DASILVA
12 Director of Graham Campus ... Ms. Kim BIRDWELL

Northeast Texas Community College (B)

PO Box 1307, Mount Pleasant TX 75456-1307
County: Titus FICE Identification: 023154
Unit ID: 227225
Telephone: (903) 434-8100 Carnegie Class: Assoc/MT-VT-High Non
FAX Number: (903) 434-4402 Calendar System: Semester
URL: www.ntcc.edu
Established: 1984 Annual Undergrad Tuition & Fees (In-District): $2,849
Enrollment: 3,110 Coed
Affiliation or Control: Local IRS Status: 501(c)3
Highest Offering: Associate Degree
Accreditation: SC, EMT, FUSER, MAC, MLTAD, PTAA

01 President ... Dr. Ron CLINTON
04 Executive Asst to the President ... Ms. Pat L. TALLANT
05 Vice Pres for Instruction ... Dr. Kevin ROSE
11 Vice Pres Administrative Services ... Mr. Jeffrey CHAMBERS
111 Executive Vice Pres Advancement ... Dr. Jonathan W. MCCULLOUGH
32 VP for Student & Outreach Services ... Dr. Josh STEWART
103 Assoc VP for Workforce Development ... Vacant
37 Dean Enroll/Dir Student Fin Assist ... Ms. Kim IRVIN
76 Interim Dean of Health Sciences ... Mr. Gaylon BARRETT
56 Associate Dean of Outreach Services ... Ms. Melody HENRY
18 Director of Plant Services ... Mr. Tom RAMLER
08 Director Learning Commons ... Mr. Ron BOWDEN
13 Director of Computer Services ... Mr. Sebastian BARRON
26 Director Marketing/Public Relations ... Ms. Jodi PACK
06 Registrar ... Ms. Betsy GOODING
15 Director Human Resources ... Ms. Amy ADKINS
10 Controller ... Ms. Brandi M. CAVE
09 Dir Institutional Effectiveness ... Ms. Toni LABEFF
07 Admissions Coordinator ... Mr. Nick JACKSON
36 Career Development/Advisor ... Ms. Lynda WATSON
84 Dean of Enrollment Management ... Ms. Kim IRVIN
28 Director of Diversity ... Mr. Rico WILLIS
30 Director of Development ... Ms. Nita MAY
121 Advising Team Lead ... Ms. Katherine BELEW

Oblate School of Theology (C)

285 Oblate Drive, San Antonio TX 78216-6693
County: Bexar FICE Identification: 003595
Unit ID: 227289
Telephone: (210) 341-1366 Carnegie Class: Spec-4-yr-Faith
FAX Number: (210) 341-4519 Calendar System: Semester
URL: www.ost.edu
Established: 1903 Annual Graduate Tuition & Fees: N/A
Enrollment: 146 Coed
Affiliation or Control: Roman Catholic IRS Status: 501(c)3
Highest Offering: Doctorate; No Undergraduates
Accreditation: PAST, THEOL

01 President ... Rev. Ronald ROLHEISER
05 Vice Pres Academic Affairs/Dean ... Dr. Scott WOODWARD
10 Vice Pres Finance/Human Resources ... Mr. Rene ESPINOSA
111 Vice Pres Institutional Advancement ... Mrs. Lea KOCHANEK
20 Associate Dean ... Sr. Linda GIBLER
51 Assoc Dean of Continuing Education ... Mrs. Rose MARDEN
88 Director Oblate Renewal Center ... Mrs. K.T COCKERELL
18 Director of Physical Plant ... Mr. Edward BERRIGAN
08 Director of the Library ... Ms. Maria GARCIA
06 Registrar & Director of Admissions ... Mr. Mario PORTER
88 Director Theological Field Edu ... Mrs. Bonnie ABADIE
88 Director Ministry to Ministers Pgm ... Rev. James MYERS
88 Director DMin Program ... Rev. Wayne CAVALIER
88 Director PhD Program ... Rev. John MARKEY
26 Director of Communications ... Mr. Michael PARKER

Odessa College (D)

201 W University Boulevard, Odessa TX 79764-7127
County: Ector FICE Identification: 003596
Unit ID: 227304
Telephone: (432) 335-6400 Carnegie Class: Assoc/MT-VT-Mix Trad/Non
FAX Number: (432) 335-6860 Calendar System: Semester
URL: www.odessa.edu
Established: 1946 Annual Undergrad Tuition & Fees (In-District): $2,778
Enrollment: 6,282 Coed
Affiliation or Control: Local IRS Status: 501(c)3
Highest Offering: Baccalaureate
Accreditation: SC, ADNUR, EMT, MUS, PTAA, RAD, SURGT

01 President ... Dr. Gregory D. WILLIAMS
05 Vice President for Instruction ... Ms. Aimee CALLAHAN
32 VP Student Svcs/Enrollment Mgmt ... Ms. Kimberly MCKAY
13 Vice President for Information Tech ... Mr. Shawn SHREVES
09 VP for Institutional Effectiveness ... Dr. Donald WOOD
100 Chief of Staff ... Mr. Robert RIVAS
11 Vice President for Administration ... Mr. Ken ZARTNER
10 Chief Financial Officer ... Ms. Brandy HAM
49 Sr Dean School Liberal Arts & Educ ... Dr. Eric YEAGER
81 Sr Dean School of STEM ... Dr. Diane CARRASCO-JACQUEZ
50 Dean School of Business & Industry ... Dr. Jennifer MYERS
76 Int Dean School of Health Sciences ... Ms. Nicole HAYS
111 Exec Director for Advancement ... Ms. Jacqui GORE
84 Exec Director Enrollment Services ... Mr. Timothy CLARK
88 Exec Dean of Academic Partnerships ... Dr. Jonathan FUENTES
06 Registrar ... Ms. Karen DOUGHTY
41 Director Intercollegiate Athletics ... Mr. Wayne BAKER
37 Director Student Financial Svcs ... Ms. Ashley WARREN
18 Director Facilities & Construction ... Mr. Bryan HEIFNER
26 Exec Director of Marketing ... Mr. Frank RICH
121 Exec Director Student Completion ... Ms. Kristi CLEMMER
96 Dir of Purchasing/Business Services ... Ms. Cindy CURNUTT
04 Admin Assistant to the President ... Mr. Gene AGNEW

Our Lady of the Lake University (E)

411 SW 24th Street, San Antonio TX 78207-4689
County: Bexar FICE Identification: 003598
Unit ID: 227331
Telephone: (210) 434-6711 Carnegie Class: DU-Mod
FAX Number: (210) 431-3928 Calendar System: Semester
URL: www.ollusa.edu
Established: 1895 Annual Undergrad Tuition & Fees: $28,740
Enrollment: 3,212 Coed
Affiliation or Control: Roman Catholic IRS Status: 501(c)3
Highest Offering: Doctorate
Accreditation: SC, ACBSP, COPSY, MFCD, SP, SW

01 President ... Dr. Diane MELBY
10 Vice President Finance & Facilities ... Mr. Anthony TURRIETTA
11 Vice President Administration ... Ms. Rosalinda GARCIA
111 Vice President of Inst Advancement ... Ms. Georgina SCHMAL
13 Vice President of Mission and Minis ... Ms. Gloria URRABAZO
05 Vice President for Academic Affairs ... Dr. Lourdes ALVAREZ
32 Int Vice President of Student Life ... Dr. George A. WILLIAMS, JR.
13 Chief Technology Officer ... Mr. Curtis L. SPEARS
26 Chief Communication Officer ... Ms. Anne GOMEZ
84 Chief Enrollment Officer ... Mr. Nelson DELGADO
108 Exec Director of Inst Effectiveness ... Vacant
09 Director of Institutional Research ... Mr. Humberto ESPINOZA-MOLINA
14 Director of Infrastructure Services ... Mr. Jeffrey ALLEN
37 Director of Financial Aid ... Ms. Esmarelda FLORES
18 Director Physical Plant ... Mr. Darrell R. GLASSCOCK
15 Director Human Resources ... Mr. Phillip VARGAS
19 Chief of Police/Dir Campus Safety ... Mr. Ramon ZERTUCHE
06 Registrar ... Ms. Betty GALVAN
42 University Chaplain ... Fr. Kevin FAUSZ

39 Director Residence Life ... Ms. Victor G. SALAZAR
36 Director Career Counsel/Placement ... Mr. Andres JAIME
23 Director of Health Services ... Ms. Julie STUCKEY
40 Director Bookstore ... Ms. Jennifer WOLFF
102 Corporate Relations Officer ... Ms. Roxanne SANCHEZ
44 Dir Advancement Svcs/Annual Giving ... Mr. John SANCHEZ
29 Dir Alumni/Stewardship Relations ... Ms. Debora GUZMAN

Panola College (F)

1109 West Panola Street, Carthage TX 75633-2397
County: Panola FICE Identification: 003600
Unit ID: 227386
Telephone: (903) 693-2000 Carnegie Class: Assoc/MT-VT-Mix Trad/Non
FAX Number: (903) 693-1167 Calendar System: Semester
URL: www.panola.edu
Established: 1947 Annual Undergrad Tuition & Fees (In-District): $1,920
Enrollment: 2,465 Coed
Affiliation or Control: Local IRS Status: 501(c)3
Highest Offering: Associate Degree
Accreditation: SC, ADNUR, CAHIIM, EMT, MLTAD, OTA

01 President ... Dr. Gregory S. POWELL
05 Vice President of Instruction ... Dr. Billy W. ADAMS
32 Vice President of Student Services ... Mr. Don CLINTON
10 Vice President of Fiscal Services ... Vacant
49 Dean of Arts/Sciences/Technology ... Mrs. Natalie OSWALT
106 Dean of Distance/Digital Learning ... Mrs. Teresa BROOKS
76 Dean of Health Sciences ... Mrs. Kelly REED-HIRSCH
15 Director of Human Resources ... Mr. Mike EDENS
07 Director of Admissions/Registrar ... Mr. Jeremy DORMAN
111 Dir Institutional Advancement ... Mrs. Jessica PACE
08 Director of Library ... Mrs. Cristie FERGUSON
103 Dir of Workforce & Economic Devel ... Mrs. Whitney MCBEE
09 Director of Institutional Research ... Mrs. Tryphena WALKER
12 Director of Shelby County Operation ... Mrs. Cancee LESTER
12 Director of Marshall Operations ... Mrs. Laura WOOD
13 Director of IT Service ... Mr. Allen WEST
19 Campus Police Chief ... Mr. Scott BURKHALTER
37 Director Student Financial Aid ... Mrs. Denise WELCH
26 Marketing Coordinator ... Vacant
18 Dir of Facilities/Physical Plant ... Mr. Alan MOON

Paris Junior College (G)

2400 Clarksville Street, Paris TX 75460-6298
County: Lamar FICE Identification: 003601
Unit ID: 227401
Telephone: (903) 785-7661 Carnegie Class: Assoc/MT-VT-High Non
FAX Number: (903) 782-0370 Calendar System: Semester
URL: www.parisjc.edu
Established: 1924 Annual Undergrad Tuition & Fees (In-District): $2,400
Enrollment: 4,835 Coed
Affiliation or Control: State/Local IRS Status: 501(c)3
Highest Offering: Associate Degree
Accreditation: SC, ADNUR, EMT, RAD, SURGT

01 President ... Dr. Pamela D. ANGLIN
05 Vice President of Academic Studies ... Vacant
103 Vice President Workforce Education ... Mr. John SPRADLING
32 VP Student Access/Success ... Mrs. Sheila REECE
60 Dean Communications/Arts ... Vacant
76 Dean Health Occupations ... Dr. Greg FERENCHAK
06 Registrar ... Mrs. Amie CATO
10 Controller ... Mrs. Keitha CARLTON
37 Director Student Financial Aid ... Mrs. Linda SLAWSON
09 Director Institutional Research ... Vacant
111 Director Institutional Advancement ... Mr. Derald BULLS
35 Director Student Life ... Mr. Kenneth WEBB
13 Director Information Technology ... Mr. Eddie MAHAR
26 Chief Public Relations Officer ... Ms. Margaret RUFF
18 Manager Plant Operations ... Vacant
15 Director Personnel Services ... Vacant

Parker University (H)

2540 Walnut Hill Lane, Dallas TX 75229-5609
County: Dallas FICE Identification: 023053
Unit ID: 243823
Telephone: (972) 438-6932 Carnegie Class: Spec-4-yr-Other Health
FAX Number: (214) 902-2496 Calendar System: Trimester
URL: www.parker.edu
Established: 1982 Annual Undergrad Tuition & Fees: $15,564
Enrollment: 1,263 Coed
Affiliation or Control: Independent Non-Profit IRS Status: 501(c)3
Highest Offering: Doctorate
Accreditation: SC, CAHIIM, CHIRO, COMTA, OTA

01 President ... Dr. William E. MORGAN
05 Provost ... Dr. Jayne MOSCHELLA
63 Vice Pres College of Chiropractic ... Dr. Patrick BODNAR
20 Associate Provost Academics ... Janell E. GIBSON
10 Chief Financial/Business Officer ... Theresa GUERRA
15 Chief Human Resources Officer ... Sandra MCLEAN

Paul Quinn College (I)

3837 Simpson Stuart Road, Dallas TX 75241-4398
County: Dallas FICE Identification: 003602
Unit ID: 227429
Telephone: (214) 376-1000 Carnegie Class: Bac-Diverse
FAX Number: (214) 379-5559 Calendar System: Semester
URL: www.pqc.edu

Established: 1872 Annual Undergrad Tuition & Fees: $8,920
Enrollment: 519 Coed
Affiliation or Control: African Methodist Episcopal IRS Status: 501(c)3
Highest Offering: Baccalaureate
Accreditation: TRACS

01 President ... Dr. Michael J. SORRELL
05 Vice Pres Academic Affairs ... Dr. Chris DOWDY
10 Chief Financial Officer ... Mr. Bruce BRINSON
09 VP Institutional Programs ... Dr. Kizuwanda GRANT
100 Chief of Staff/Dir Inst Effective ... Dr. Chris DOWDY
06 Registrar ... Ms. Twyla GILLS
08 Director Library Services ... Ms. Clarice MEDLEY-WEEKS
13 Director of Technology ... Vacant
41 Dir Athletics/External Affairs ... Ms. Kelsel THOMPSON
37 Director of Financial Aid ... Ms. Mildred MARTINEZ
35 Dean Student Support Services ... Vacant
18 Director of Facilities ... Vacant
30 Dir Development/Special Events ... Mr. Dennis COLEMAN
23 Campus Nurse ... Ms. Glenda DAVIS
07 Director of Recruiting ... Mrs. Jessika LARA
29 Director of Alumni Affairs ... Mr. Dexter EVANS

Peloton College (A)

8150 N. Central Expy, Ste M-2240, Dallas TX 75206
County: Dallas FICE Identification: 041687
Unit ID: 459514
Telephone: (214) 777-6433 Carnegie Class: Not Classified
FAX Number: (214) 777-6477 Calendar System: Quarter
URL: pelotoncollege.edu
Established: 2005 Annual Undergrad Tuition & Fees: $13,225
Enrollment: N/A Coed
Affiliation or Control: Proprietary IRS Status: Proprietary
Highest Offering: Associate Degree
Accreditation: COE

01 Campus President ... Valerie JOHNSON HOLSINGER

Pima Medical Institute-El Paso (B)

6926 Gateway Blvd., E., El Paso TX 79915
Telephone: (915) 633-1133 Identification: 770962
Accreditation: ABHES, OTA, RAD

† Branch campus of Pima Medical Institute-Tucson, Tucson, AZ

Pima Medical Institute-Houston (C)

10201-C Katy Freeway, Houston TX 77024
Telephone: (713) 778-0778 Identification: 770510
Accreditation: ABHES, COARC, DH, DMS, OTA, PTAA, RAD

† Branch campus of Pima Medical Institute-Tucson, Tucson, AZ

Quest College (D)

5430 Fredericksburg Road, Ste 310,
San Antonio TX 78229
County: Bexar FICE Identification: 034003
Unit ID: 439507
Telephone: (210) 366-2701 Carnegie Class: Not Classified
FAX Number: (210) 366-0738 Calendar System: Semester
URL: www.questcollege.edu
Established: 1995 Annual Undergrad Tuition & Fees: N/A
Enrollment: 54 Coed
Affiliation or Control: Proprietary IRS Status: Proprietary
Highest Offering: Associate Degree
Accreditation: COE

00 Owner/Administrator ... Ms. Jeanne MARTIN
01 School Director ... Ms. Sandy CLAUSS

Ranger College (E)

1100 College Circle, Ranger TX 76470-3298
County: Eastland FICE Identification: 003603
Unit ID: 227687
Telephone: (254) 647-3234 Carnegie Class: Assoc/HT-High Trad
FAX Number: (254) 647-1656 Calendar System: Semester
URL: www.rangercollege.edu
Established: 1926 Annual Undergrad Tuition & Fees (In-District): $3,065
Enrollment: 2,412 Coed
Affiliation or Control: Local IRS Status: 501(c)3
Highest Offering: Associate Degree
Accreditation: SC

01 President ... Dr. William J. CAMPION
12 Vice President Brown County ... Dr. Gordon WARREN
05 Vice President ... Dr. Jennifer KENT
10 Vice President Business Service/CFO ... Mrs. Gaylyn MENDOZA
103 Vice President Workforce Devel ... Mr. Dixon BAILEY
32 Vice President of Student Services ... Mr. Derrick WORRELS
108 Vice President of Accreditation ... Mr. Matt CARDIN
09 Director of Institutional Research ... Mr. John SLAUGHTER
84 Dean of Enrollment Management ... Mr. Robert CULVERHOUSE
18 Director of Physical Plant ... Mr. Chuck LEMASTER
37 Director of Financial Aid ... Mr. Don HILTON
38 Director of Counseling ... Mr. Gabe LEWIS
15 Human Resources ... Mr. Brad KELLER
113 Bursar ... Ms. Evonne CHERRY
41 Athletic Director ... Mr. Billy GILLISPIE
40 Director Bookstore ... Miss Cindy STRINGER
08 Director of Library Services ... Mr. Kevin HENARD
04 Admin Assistant to the President ... Miss Raime J. PRESTON
13 Information Technology Admin ... Mr. Glenn PAUL

Reformed Theological Seminary (F)

1202 Dragon Street, Suite 104, Dallas TX 75207
Telephone: (214) 295-8599 Identification: 667055
Accreditation: &SC, THEOL

† Branch campus of Reformed Theological Seminary, Jackson, MS

Remington College-Dallas Campus (G)

1800 Eastgate Drive, Garland TX 75041-5513
County: Dallas FICE Identification: 030265
Unit ID: 223463
Telephone: (972) 686-7878 Carnegie Class: Bac/Assoc-Mixed
FAX Number: (972) 686-5116 Calendar System: Quarter
URL: www.remingtoncollege.edu
Established: 1987 Annual Undergrad Tuition & Fees: $15,898
Enrollment: 971 Coed
Affiliation or Control: Independent Non-Profit IRS Status: 501(c)3
Highest Offering: Baccalaureate
Accreditation: ACCSC

01 Campus President ... Dr. Rose VAN ALSTINE
05 Academic Dean ... Dr. Rose VAN ALSTINE

Remington College-Fort Worth Campus (H)

300 E Loop 820, Fort Worth TX 76112-1225
Telephone: (817) 451-0017 Identification: 666063
Accreditation: ACCSC

Remington College-Houston Southeast Campus (I)

20985 Interstate 45 South, Webster TX 77598
Telephone: (281) 554-1700 Identification: 770601
Accreditation: ACCSC

Remington College-North Houston Campus (J)

11310 Greens Crossing, Suite 300, Houston TX 77067
Telephone: (281) 885-4450 Identification: 770600
Accreditation: ACCSC

Rice University (K)

PO Box 1892, Houston TX 77251-1892
County: Harris FICE Identification: 003604
Unit ID: 227757
Telephone: (713) 348-0000 Carnegie Class: DU-Highest
FAX Number: N/A Calendar System: Semester
URL: www.rice.edu
Established: 1891 Annual Undergrad Tuition & Fees: $47,350
Enrollment: 7,022 Coed
Affiliation or Control: Independent Non-Profit IRS Status: 501(c)3
Highest Offering: Doctorate
Accreditation: SC

01 President ... Mr. David W. LEEBRON
101 Deputy Sec to Board of Trustees ... Ms. Cynthia L. WILSON
05 Provost ... Vacant
11 Vice President Administration ... Dr. Kevin KIRBY
10 Vice President Finance ... Ms. Kathy COLLINS
30 Vice Pres Development/Alumni Rels ... Ms. Kathi D. WARREN
115 Vice Pres Investments/Treasurer ... Ms. Allison THACKER
84 Vice President for Enrollment ... Ms. Yvonne DASILVA
26 Vice President for Public Affairs ... Ms. Linda THRANE
13 Vice President IT & CIO ... Ms. Klara JELINKOVA
46 Vice Provost Research ... Dr. Yousif SHAMOO
20 Vice Provost for Academic Affairs ... Dr. Fred HIGGS
08 Vice Provost/University Librarian ... Ms. Sara LOWMAN
45 Vice President Strategic Inits ... Dr. Caroline LEVANDER
15 Associate Vice Pres Human Resources ... Ms. Joan NELSON
91 Assoc Vice Pres for Admin Systems ... Mr. Randy CASTIGLIONI
43 VP & General Counsel ... Mr. Richard A. ZANSITIS
06 Registrar ... Mr. David TENNEY
29 Asst VP for Alumni Relations ... Ms. Marthe GOLDEN
37 Director Student Financial Services ... Ms. Anne E. WALKER
25 AVP Sponsored Proj/Res Compliance ... Ms. Krystal TOUPS
41 Director of Athletics ... Dr. Joseph KARLGAARD
85 Assoc Vice Provost Intl Education ... Dr. Adria BAKER
39 Assoc Vice Pres Housing & Dining ... Mr. Mark DITMAN
23 Director Student Health Services ... Dr. Stacy WARE
09 Assoc VP Institutional Research ... Dr. John M. CORNWELL
21 University Controller ... Mr. Bradley FRALIC
116 Director of Internal Audit ... Ms. Janet COVINGTON
19 Chief of Campus Police ... Mr. James TATE
22 Director of Affirmative Action ... Dr. Richard BAKER
27 Dir of News & Media Relations ... Mr. Doug MILLER
21 Director Administrative Services ... Mr. Eugen RADULESCU
28 Director of Diversity ... Dr. Roland B. SMITH
38 Director of Student Counseling ... Dr. Timothy K. BAUMGARTNER
36 Dir Center for Career Development ... Ms. Nicole VAN DEN HEUVEL
96 Director of Procurement ... Mr. Brian SOIKA
79 Dean of School of Humanities ... Dr. Kathleen CANNING
58 Dean Graduate/Postdoctoral Stds ... Dr. Seiichi MATSUDA
97 Dean of Undergraduate Education ... Dr. Bridget GORMAN
48 Dean of Architecture ... Vacant
64 Dean of Shepherd School of Music ... Dr. Robert YEKOVICH
54 Dean GR Brown School Engineering ... Dr. Reginald DESROCHES
50 Dean JH Jones Graduate Sch Business ... Dr. Peter RODRIGUEZ
83 Dean of Social Sciences ... Vacant
81 Dean of Wiess Sch Natural Science ... Dr. Peter ROSSKY
51 Dean Glasscock Sch Continuing Stds ... Dr. Robert BRUCE
22 Director of Compliance ... Mr. Ken LIDDLE
18 Chief Facilities/Physical Plant ... Ms. Kathy JONES
04 Admin Assistant to the President ... Ms. Hope GATLIFF
102 Dir Foundation/Corporate Relations ... Ms. Katie CERVENKA

Rio Grande Bible Institute (L)

4300 South US Highway 281, Edinburg TX 78539-9650
County: Hidalgo Identification: 666395
Unit ID: 475185
Telephone: (956) 380-8100 Carnegie Class: Spec-4-yr-Faith
FAX Number: (956) 380-8256 Calendar System: Semester
URL: www.riogrande.edu
Established: 1946 Annual Undergrad Tuition & Fees: N/A
Enrollment: N/A Coed
Affiliation or Control: Independent Non-Profit IRS Status: 501(c)3
Highest Offering: Baccalaureate
Accreditation: BI

01 President ... Dr. Lawrence B. WINDLE
04 Admin Assistant to President ... Mr. Eduardo CALLEJA
05 Vice Pres of Academic Division ... Mr. John LOTZGESELL
26 Vice Pres Ministerial Advancement ... Mr. Bob ALLEN
32 Dean of Students ... Mr. Nelson MATUS
21 Comptroller ... Mr. Jonathan WHITE
08 Librarian ... Mrs. Donna ANTONIUK
06 Registrar ... Mr. Keith SWARTZBAUGH

St. Edward's University (M)

3001 S Congress Avenue, Austin TX 78704-6489
County: Travis FICE Identification: 003621
Unit ID: 227845
Telephone: (512) 448-8400 Carnegie Class: Masters/L
FAX Number: (512) 448-8492 Calendar System: Semester
URL: www.stedwards.edu
Established: 1885 Annual Undergrad Tuition & Fees: $45,428
Enrollment: 4,447 Coed
Affiliation or Control: Independent Non-Profit IRS Status: 501(c)3
Highest Offering: Doctorate
Accreditation: SC, CACREP, SW

00 Board Chair ... Mr. Martin E. ROSE
01 President ... Dr. George E. MARTIN
05 Provost ... Dr. Andrew PRALL
10 Vice Pres for Finance & Admin ... Ms. Kimberly KVAAL
111 Vice President for Advancement ... Mr. Joe DEMEDEIROS
26 Vice Pres Marketing & Communication ... Ms. Christie CAMPBELL
84 Vice Pres for Enrollment Management ... Ms. Tracy L. MANIER
32 Vice President for Student Affairs ... Dr. Lisa L. KIRKPATRICK
13 Vice President Information Tech ... Mr. David E. WALDRON
45 VP Inst Effectiveness & Planning ... Mr. Justin M. SLOAN
42 Director of Campus Ministry ... Fr. Peter J. WALSH
108 Assoc VP Inst Research/Assessment ... Dr. David A. BLAIR
21 Assoc VP for Finance ... Ms. Kelli L. GREEN
20 Assoc VP for Academic Affairs ... Dr. Molly E. MINUS
35 Dean of Students/Title IX Deputy ... Mr. Steven J. PINKENBURG
124 Assoc VP Stdnt Acad Support Svcs ... Dr. Nicole G. TREVINO
30 Assoc VP for Development ... Mr. Gregory PERRIN
18 Director Facilities Operations ... Mr. James H. MORRIS
91 Assoc VP Digital Effectiveness ... Ms. Angela M. SVOBODA
88 AVP Global Initiatives ... Dr. Caroline MORRIS
109 Sr Director for Business Services ... Ms. Rebekah DESAI
88 Director for Capital Projects ... Mr. Steve D. RAMIREZ
15 Director of Human Resources ... Vacant
11 Assoc VP University Operations ... Vacant
100 Chief of Staff/Sustainability Coord ... Ms. Cristina L. BORDIN
83 Dean Behavioral & Social Sciences ... Dr. Brenda J. VALLANCE
50 Dean Munday Sch of Business . Dr. Marianne WARD-PERADOZA
53 Dean Sch of Human Development & Edu ... Dr. Glenda BALLARD
79 Dean School of Arts & Humanities ... Dr. Sharon D. NELL
81 Dean School of Natural Sciences ... Dr. Gary MORRIS
97 Assoc VP of General Education ... Dr. Cory LOCK
89 Director of Freshman LC ... Dr. Alexandra L. BARRON
08 Dean of Munday Library ... Mr. Pongracz SENNYEY
07 Dean of Admissions ... Mr. Drew NICHOLS
06 Registrar ... Mr. Patrick W. FIELDS
110 Director of Development ... Ms. Anne E. WESTDYKE
36 Dir Career & Prof Development ... Mr. Raymond C. ROGERS
29 Director of Alumni & Parent Pgms ... Ms. Karin DICKS
104 Director of Study Abroad . Ms. Emily E. SPANDIKOW WESCOTT
24 IT Strategist & Enterprise Solution ... Mr. Antonio T. CHAVEZ
90 Dir Instructional & Emerging Tech ... Ms. Rebecca F. DAVIS
105 Midware/User Experience Architect ... Mr. Tim TASHJIAN
27 Sr Director of Communications ... Ms. Mischelle R. DIAZ
38 Dean of Student Development ... Dr. Calvin A. KELLY
102 Director Foundation Relations ... Ms. Allison M. RASP
44 Director Annual Giving ... Ms. Sarah B. DICKENS
37 Director Student Financial Aid ... Ms. Jennifer M. BECK
85 Dir International Student Services ... Ms. Kathy JACKSON
41 Associate VP Athletics ... Ms. Debora W. TAYLOR
113 Director of Student Accounts ... Mr. Peter J. BEILHARZ
35 Dean of Student Engagement ... Mr. Thomas B. SULLIVAN

123 Dir Graduate and Transfer Admission .... Mr. David C. BRALOWER
39 Director for Housing Operations .... Mr. James S. LOVE
04 Admin Assistant to President .... Ms. Lorraine M. PAGAN
86 Dir Govt & Community Relations .... Ms. Liz JOHNSON
19 Chief/Director of Police Services .... Mr. Homer J. HUERTA
09 Director of Institutional Research .... Ms. Danica D. FRAMPTON
108 Director Institutional Assessment .... Mr. Matthew DESANTIS
121 Director of Academic Success .... Ms. Mary E. CULKIN
96 Director Procurement Services .... Mr. Scott H. FLETCHER
28 Director of Diversity & Inclusion .... Ms. Joi T. TORRES
40 Campus Stores Manager .... Ms. Jessica BRIGHT
16 Assoc Dir Human Resources .... Ms. Jennifer CHARLES
16 Assoc Dir Human Resources .... Dr. Melissa G. ESQUEDA

St. Mary's University (A)

One Camino Santa Maria, San Antonio TX 78228-8572
County: Bexar | FICE Identification: 003623
Unit ID: 228149
Telephone: (210) 436-3011 | Carnegie Class: Masters/L
FAX Number: (210) 436-3500 | Calendar System: Semester
URL: www.stmarytx.edu
Established: 1852 | Annual Undergrad Tuition & Fees: $30,650
Enrollment: 3,649 | Coed
Affiliation or Control: Roman Catholic | IRS Status: 501(c)3
Highest Offering: Doctorate
Accreditation: **SC**, CACREP, LAW, MFCD, MUS

01 President .... Mr. Thomas M. MENGLER
05 Provost/VP Academic Affairs .... Dr. Aaron TYLER
10 Int Vice Pres for Admin & Finance .... Mr. Aaron HANNA
84 Vice Prov Enrollment Management .... Dr. Rosalind ALDERMAN
32 Vice Prov Stdnt Dev/Dean of Stdnts .... Mr. Timothy BESSLER
111 Vice Pres University Advancement .... Mr. Richard (Rick) KIMBROUGH, II
88 Vice President Mission & Rector .... Rev. Tim EDEN, SM
50 Dean Bill Greehey Sch Business .... Dr. Tanuja SINGH
79 Dean Humanities & Social Science .... Dr. Leona PALLANSCH
54 Dean Science/Engrng/Technology .... Dr. Winston EREVELLES
61 Interim Dean of Law .... Mr. Vincent JOHNSON
39 Director Residence Life .... Mr. James VILLARREAL
100 Chief of Staff/Office of President .... Ms. Dianne L. PIPES
06 Registrar .... Ms. Christina VILLANUEVA
07 Director Undergraduate Admission .... Mr. Ryan KONKRIGHT
08 Exec Director Louis J Blume Library .... Ms. Caroline BYRD
37 Dir Financial Aid/Enrollment Ops .... Ms. Marivel OJEDA
38 Assoc Dir Student Counseling Ctr .... Ms. Deidra COLEMAN
90 Exec Dir/Instructor Acad Tech .... Mr. Jeff SCHOMBURG
15 Exec Dir Human Res/Title IX Coord .... Ms. Janet GUADARRAMA
13 Vice Pres Information Services .... Mr. Curtis WHITE
119 Dir Network Security Administration .... Mr. Robert STOOKSBERRY
14 Director Systems Support Services .... Mr. Frank NIEWIERSKI
42 Exec Director University Ministry .... Mr. Jose MATOS AUFFANT
29 Executive Director Alumni Relations .... Mr. Peter HANSEN
21 Director of Finance .... Vacant
21 Director of Accounting Operations .... Ms. Sheila NIX
26 Senior Director Communications .... Mrs. Gina FARRELL

*San Jacinto College District (B)

4624 Fairmont Parkway, Pasadena TX 77504-3323
County: Harris | FICE Identification: 029137
Telephone: (281) 998-6150 | Carnegie Class: N/A
FAX Number: N/A
URL: www.sanjac.edu

01 Chancellor .... Dr. Brenda HELLYER
03 Deputy Chancellor and President .... Dr. Laurel WILLIAMSON
05 Chief Academic Officer (Provost) .... Mr. Van WIGGINTON
10 Vice Chancellor Fiscal Affairs .... Mrs. Teri ZAMORA
15 Vice Chanc Human Resources .... Mrs. Sandra RAMIREZ
13 CIO .... Mr. Rob STANICIC
26 Vice Chanc Marketing/Govt Rels .... Mrs. Teri CRAWFORD
45 Vice Chanc Strategic Initiatives .... Dr. Allatia HARRIS
84 Dean Enroll Mgmt/College Registrar .... Ms. Wanda MUNSON
09 Director of Research .... Mr. George GONZALEZ
37 Dean Financial Aid Services .... Mr. Robert MERINO
96 Director Contracts & Purchasing .... Ms. Ann KOKX-TEMPLET
04 Administrative Asst to President .... Ms. Mandi REILAND
19 Manager SHERM .... Mrs. Susana GONZALEZ
25 Chief Contracts/Grants Admin .... Mr. Michael MOORE
29 Director Alumni Relations .... Ms. Ruth KEENAN
32 Chief Student Affairs/Student Life .... Ms. Joanna ZIMMERMANN
43 Dir Legal Services/General Counsel .... Ms. Clare IANNELLI
06 College Registrar .... Mr. Kevin MCKISSON

*San Jacinto College Central (C)

8060 Spencer Highway, Pasadena TX 77505-5903
County: Harris | FICE Identification: 003609
Unit ID: 227979
Telephone: (281) 998-6150 | Carnegie Class: Assoc/MT-VT-Mix Trad/Non
FAX Number: (281) 476-1892 | Calendar System: Semester
URL: www.sanjac.edu
Established: 1960 | Annual Undergrad Tuition & Fees (In-District): $1,548
Enrollment: 30,509 | Coed
Affiliation or Control: Local | IRS Status: 501(c)3
Highest Offering: Associate Degree
Accreditation: **&SC**, ACFEI, ADNUR, COARC, DMS, MLTAD, RAD, SURGT

02 Deputy Chancellor and President .... Dr. Laurel WILLIAMSON
05 Provost .... Mr. Van A. WIGGINTON
32 Associate VC Student Services .... Ms. Joanna ZIMMERMANN
06 College Registrar .... Mr. Kevin MCKISSON
49 Dean of Liberal Arts .... Dr. DeRhonda MCWAINE
50 Dean Business & Technology .... Dr. James RAGAISIS
88 Assc VC/Sr VP Ctr Petro/Energy/Tech .... Mr. James GRIFFIN
76 Dean Natural and Health Sciences .... Ms. Rhonda BELL
11 Dean of Administration .... Mr. Scott R. GERNANDER
35 Dean Student Development .... Ms. Shelley RINEHART
37 Dean Financial Aid Services .... Mr. Robert MERINO
88 Dean Compliance & Judicial Affairs .... Ms. Clare IANNELLI
92 Director Honors Program .... Dr. Eddie WELLER
88 Director Dual Credit .... Ms. Nicole BARNES
08 Director Library .... Ms. Karen BLANKENSHIP
88 Director Campus Services .... Mr. Christopher CRUMLEY
121 Director Student Success .... Ms. Dawn SHEDD
88 Dir Educ Planning/Couns/Completion .... Ms. Christine TORRES

† Regional accreditation is carried under the parent institution (district office) in Pasadena, TX.

*San Jacinto College North (D)

5800 Uvalde Road, Houston TX 77049-4599
County: Harris | Identification: 666747
Unit ID: 22797901
Telephone: (281) 458-4050 | Carnegie Class: Not Classified
FAX Number: (281) 459-7125 | Calendar System: Semester
URL: www.sanjac.edu
Established: 1974 | Annual Undergrad Tuition & Fees (In-District): N/A
Enrollment: N/A | Coed
Affiliation or Control: Local | IRS Status: 501(c)3
Highest Offering: Associate Degree
Accreditation: **&SC**, ACFEI, CAHIIM, EMT, MAC

02 Deputy Chancellor and President .... Dr. Laurel WILLIAMSON
05 Provost .... Dr. William RAFFETTO
32 Associate VC Student Services .... Ms. Joanna ZIMMERMAN
07 College Registrar/Dean of Enroll .... Mr. Kevin MCKISSON
11 Dean Administration .... Ms. Minelia IZAGUIRRE
76 Dean Natural and Health Sciences .... Dr. Teddy FARIAS
50 Dean Business and Technology .... Ms. Heather RHODES
88 Dean Comp & Judicial Affairs .... Ms. Clare IANNELLI
62 Director Library .... Ms. Lyn GARNER
49 Dean Liberal Arts .... Mr. Shawn SILMAN
41 Athletic Director .... Mr. Tom ARRINGTON
92 Director Honors Program .... Dr. Eddie WELLER
88 Dual Credit Director .... Dr. Anne DICKENS
55 Director Evening/Weekend Services .... Mr. Don SPIES
121 Director Student Success Center .... Ms. Erika HERNANDEZ
37 Dean Financial Aid Services .... Mr. Robert MERINO
32 Dean Student Development .... Ms. Tami KELLY
88 Dir Educational Planning & Counsel .... Ms. Sonia TOWNSEND

† Regional accreditation is carried under the parent institution (district office) in Pasadena, TX.

*San Jacinto College South (E)

13735 Beamer Road, Houston TX 77089-6099
County: Harris | Identification: 666748
Unit ID: 22797902
Telephone: (281) 484-1900 | Carnegie Class: Not Classified
FAX Number: (281) 922-3401 | Calendar System: Semester
URL: www.sanjac.edu
Established: 1979 | Annual Undergrad Tuition & Fees (In-District): N/A
Enrollment: N/A | Coed
Affiliation or Control: Local | IRS Status: 501(c)3
Highest Offering: Associate Degree
Accreditation: **&SC**, ADNUR, PTAA

02 Deputy Chancellor and President .... Dr. Laurel WILLIAMSON
05 Provost .... Dr. Brenda JONES
32 Associate VC Student Services .... Ms. Joanna ZIMMERMANN
49 Dean of Liberal Arts & College Prep .... Ms. Ann TATE
50 Dean Business & Technology .... Mr. Kevin MORRIS
76 Dean Health and Natural Sciences .... Dr. Alexander OKWONNA
11 Dean Administration .... Mr. Joseph HEBERT
84 Dean Enrollment Services .... Mr. Kevin MCKISSON
88 Dean Comp & Judicial Affairs .... Ms. Clare IANNELLI
92 Director Honors Program .... Dr. Eddie WELLER
55 Director Evening Division .... Mr. Ross KELSEY
62 Director Library .... Mr. Richard MCKAY
41 Director Athletics .... Ms. Kelly SAENZ
88 Dual Credit Director .... Ms. Kristen ROSS
06 College Registrar .... Mr. Kevin MCKISSON
32 Dean Student Development .... Ms. Debbie SMITH
88 Director Education Planning .... Ms. Tanesha ANTOINE
88 Director Student Success Center .... Ms. Diana SHOKRALLA
37 Dean Financial Aid Services .... Mr. Robert MERINO

† Regional accreditation is carried under the parent institution (district office) in Pasadena, TX.

School of Automotive Machinists & Technology (F)

1911 Antoine Drive, Houston TX 77055
County: Harris | FICE Identification: 030323
Unit ID: 377218
Telephone: (713) 683-3817 | Carnegie Class: Spec 2-yr-Tech
FAX Number: (713) 683-7077 | Calendar System: Semester
URL: www.samtech.edu
Established: 1985 | Annual Undergrad Tuition & Fees: N/A
Enrollment: 163 | Coed
Affiliation or Control: Proprietary | IRS Status: Proprietary
Highest Offering: Associate Degree
Accreditation: **ACCSC**

01 President/Dir of Education .... Judson MASSINGILL
11 CEO/Sch Exec Director/Administrator .... Linda MASSINGILL
07 Director of Admissions .... Scott MORRIS
37 Financial Aid Director .... Susie FAERMAN

Schreiner University (G)

2100 Memorial Boulevard, Kerrville TX 78028-5611
County: Kerr | FICE Identification: 003610
Unit ID: 228042
Telephone: (830) 896-5411 | Carnegie Class: Bac-Diverse
FAX Number: (830) 896-3232 | Calendar System: Semester
URL: www.schreiner.edu
Established: 1923 | Annual Undergrad Tuition & Fees: $27,960
Enrollment: 1,312 | Coed
Affiliation or Control: Presbyterian Church (U.S.A.) | IRS Status: 501(c)3
Highest Offering: Master's
Accreditation: **SC**, NURSE

00 Chancellor .... Dr. Timothy SUMMERLIN
01 President .... Dr. Charlie MCCORMICK
05 Provost/Vice Pres Academic Affairs .... Dr. Travis FRAMPTON
10 Vice Pres Administration & Finance .... Mr. Bill MUSE
84 VP Stdnt Recruit/Ext Rels/Mktg/Comm .... Mr. Mark TUSCHAK
13 AVP Information Technology Services .... Mr. Rex QUICK
09 AVP Inst Planning Financial Svcs .... Dr. Lucien COSTLEY
30 Director of Development .... Ms. Marta DIFFEN
07 Interim Director of Admissions .... Ms. Danielle JENSCHKE
37 Director of Financial Services .... Ms. Natalie SANDOVAL
06 Assistant Provost & Registrar .... Ms. Darlene BANNISTER
121 Dean Acad Support/Student Outcomes .... Dr. William WOODS
20 Dean of Faculty .... Dr. William DAVIS
21 Assistant Controller .... Ms. Elizabeth OEHLER
42 Campus Minister .... Vacant
32 Dean of Students .... Dr. Charlie HUEBER
27 Director of Mktg & Communications .... Dr. David SMITH
41 Athletic Director .... Mr. Bill RALEIGH
15 Director of Human Resource Services .... Ms. Wendy BLAETTNER
18 Director Campus Operations .... Mr. Ed WINGARD
29 Director Alumni Relations .... Ms. Tammi BINGHAM
38 Director Student Counseling .... Ms. Kimberly J. WOODS
36 Director Advising & Career Devel .... Ms. Cristina MARTINEZ
04 Admin Assistant to the President .... Ms. Deborah SCOTT
08 Interim Director Library .... Ms. Lisa MCCORMICK
19 Chief of Security .... Mr. Ken JACOBS
39 Director Residence Life .... Ms. Norma CASTANON

Seminary of the Southwest (H)

501 E. 32nd St., Austin TX 78705
County: Travis | FICE Identification: 003566
Unit ID: 224712
Telephone: (512) 472-4133 | Carnegie Class: Spec-4-yr-Faith
FAX Number: (512) 472-3098 | Calendar System: 4/1/4
URL: www.ssw.edu
Established: 1952 | Annual Graduate Tuition & Fees: N/A
Enrollment: 116 | Coed
Affiliation or Control: Protestant Episcopal | IRS Status: 501(c)3
Highest Offering: Master's; No Undergraduates
Accreditation: **SC**, CACREP, THEOL

01 Dean & President .... V.Rev. Cynthia Briggs KITTREDGE
05 Academic Dean .... Dr. Scott BADER-SAYE
03 Executive Vice President .... Mr. Fred CLEMENT
111 VP of Institutional Advancement .... Mr. Wally MOORE
07 Director of Admissions .... Rev. Hope BENKO
26 Director of Communications .... Mr. Eric SCOTT
10 Accounting Director .... Vacant
06 Registrar/Director of Assessment .... Ms. Madelyn SNODGRASS
08 Director of the Booher Library .... Ms. Alison POAGE
18 Director of Facilities Management .... Mr. Tigh WALTERS
13 Director Information Technology .... Mr. Erik MORROW
100 Chief of Staff to Dean/President .... Ms. Lesley WILDER
44 Director of Annual Giving .... Ms. Katherine BAILEY BROWN

South Plains College (I)

1401 College Avenue, Levelland TX 79336-6595
County: Hockley | FICE Identification: 003611
Unit ID: 228158
Telephone: (806) 894-9611 | Carnegie Class: Assoc/MT-VT-Mix Trad/Non
FAX Number: (806) 894-5274 | Calendar System: Semester
URL: www.southplainscollege.edu
Established: 1957 | Annual Undergrad Tuition & Fees (In-State): $2,240
Enrollment: 9,329 | Coed
Affiliation or Control: State | IRS Status: 501(c)3
Highest Offering: Associate Degree
Accreditation: **SC**, ADNUR, COARC, EMT, PTAA, SURGT

01 President .... Dr. Robin SATTERWHITE
05 Vice President Academic Affairs .... Dr. Ryan GIBBS
10 Vice Pres Business Affairs .... Ms. Teresa GREEN
32 Vice President of Student Affairs .... Dr. Stan DEMERRITT
111 Vice Pres Institutional Advancement .... Mr. Stephen S. JOHN
49 Dean of Arts & Sciences .... Mr. Alan WORLEY
76 Dean of Health Occupations .... Mr. Jerry FINLEY
75 Dean of Technical Education .... Mr. Robbie M. BLAIR
51 Dean Continuing & Distance Educ .... Mr. Ryan FITZGERALD

11 Dean Administrative Services .... Mr. Ronnie WATKINS
07 Dean of Admissions & Records .... Ms. Kathryn PEREZ
12 Dean of Reese Center .... Ms. Kara MARTINEZ
09 Assoc Dean of Research & Reports .... Vacant
26 Assoc Dean of College Relations .... Mr. Dane DEWBRE
13 Assoc Dean Information Technology .... Mr. James HOWELL
103 Assoc Dean Workforce Development .... Vacant
35 Assoc Dean of Students .... Mr. Shane HILL
121 Director of Advising and Testing .... Mrs. Lola HERNANDEZ
37 Director of Financial Aid .... Ms. Susan NAZWORTH
08 Director of Libraries .... Mr. Mark GOTTSCHALK
30 Director of Development .... Ms. Julie GERSTENBERGER
15 Director of Human Resources .... Mrs. Jeri Ann DEWBRE
41 Director of Athletics .... Mr. Roger REDING
06 Registrar .... Mr. Andrew RUIZ
18 Director of Physical Plant .... Mr. Cary MARROW
40 Bookstore Manager .... Mr. Roger SHULL
28 Diversity Coord/Career Counselor .... Ms. Maria LOPEZ-STRONG

South Texas College (A)

3201 W Pecan, McAllen TX 78501
County: Hidalgo FICE Identification: 031034
Unit ID: 409315
Telephone: (956) 872-5051 Carnegie Class: Bac/Assoc-Assoc Dom
FAX Number: (956) 971-3739 Calendar System: Semester
URL: www.southtexascollege.edu
Established: 1993 Annual Undergrad Tuition & Fees (In-District): $3,780
Enrollment: 31,321 Coed
Affiliation or Control: State/Local IRS Status: 501(c)3
Highest Offering: Baccalaureate
Accreditation: SC, ACBSP, CAHIIM, COARC, EMT, OTA, PTAA

01 President .... Dr. Shirley A. REED
05 Int Vice Pres Academic Affs/CAO .... Dr. Anahid PETROSIAN
10 VP Finance/Administrative Svcs .... Ms. Maria G. ELIZONDO
32 VP Student Affairs/Enroll Mgmt .... Mr. Matthew HEBBARD
13 VP Info Services/Planning .... Dr. David PLUMMER
111 Vice Pres Institutional Advancement .... Vacant
88 Associate Dean for Industry & Econ .... Mr. Carlos MARGO
83 Dean Liberal Arts/Soc Sci .... Dr. Margaretha BISCHOFF
50 Dean Business/Technology .... Mr. Mario REYNA
76 Int Dean Nursing/Allied Health .... Mr. Jayson VALERIO
81 Dean Math/Science/BA Programs .... Dr. Ali ESMAEILI
37 Assoc Dean Student Financial Svcs .... Mr. Mike CARRANZA
21 Comptroller .... Ms. Myriam LOPEZ
15 Director Human Resources .... Ms. Brenda Jo BALDERAZ
51 Dir Cont/Prof & Workforce Education .. Mr. Juan Carlos AGUIRRE
96 Director Purchasing .... Ms. Rebecca CAVAZOS
09 Dir Research/Analytical Svcs .... Mr. Serkan CELTEK
121 Dean Student Support Svcs .... Mr. Pablo HERNANDEZ, JR.
18 Director Operations/Maintenance .... Mr. George MCCALEB
18 Director Facilities Plan/Construct .... Mr. Ricardo DE LA GARZA
25 Grants/Contracts Compliance Officer .... Ms. Samantha URIEGAS
12 Campus Administrator Starr Cty .... Dr. Arthuro MONTIEL
12 Campus Administrator Mid-Valley .... Mr. Daniel MONTEZ
88 Employee Relations Officer .... Ms. Laura REQUENA
106 Dean Distance Learning .... Vacant
26 Director Public Rels/Marketing .... Mr. Daniel RAMIREZ
88 Dir of Student Activ & Wellness .... Mr. Elibariki NGUMA
84 Dean Enrollment Services/Registrar .... Mr. Matthew HEBBARD
20 Asst to VP Instructional Svcs .... Dr. Anahid PETROSIAN
19 Director Security .... Mr. Paul VARVILLE
13 Chief Information Officer .... Ms. Alicia GOMEZ
08 Director Library Technical Services .... Mr. Jesus CAMPOS
88 Dir Centers for Lrg Excellence .... Ms. Teresa GARCIA
88 Administrator High School Programs .... Mr. Nicolas GONZALEZ
90 Dir Info Commons Open Labs .... Dr. Lelia SALINAS
35 Dean Student Affairs .... Mr. Pablo HERNANDEZ, JR.
119 Chief Information Security Officer .... Mr. Victor GONZALEZ

South Texas College of Law Houston (B)

1303 San Jacinto Street, Houston TX 77002-7000
County: Harris FICE Identification: 004977
Unit ID: 228194
Telephone: (713) 659-8040 Carnegie Class: Spec-4-yr-Law
FAX Number: (713) 646-2909 Calendar System: Semester
URL: www.stcl.edu
Established: 1923 Annual Graduate Tuition & Fees: N/A
Enrollment: 936 Coed
Affiliation or Control: Independent Non-Profit IRS Status: 501(c)3
Highest Offering: First Professional Degree; No Undergraduates
Accreditation: LAW

01 President and Dean .... Mr. Michael F. BARRY
111 VP of Philanthropy/Alumni Relations .... Ms. Mindy GUTHRIE
05 Vice President & Associate Dean .... Mr. John WORLEY
20 Vice President and Associate Dean .... Ms. Vanessa BROWNE-BARBOUR
04 Sr Exec Assistant to President/Dean .... Ms. Jennifer M. HUDSON
10 Vice President and CFO .... Mr. Gregory A. BROTHERS
09 Vice Pres Strategic Plng/Inst Rsrch .. Mr. Jeffrey L. RENSBERGER
08 Director Library Svcs .... Ms. Colleen MANNING
20 Vice President & Associate Dean .... Mr. T. Gerald TREECE
20 Vice President & Associate Dean .... Ms. Catherine G. BURNETT
13 Vice President Technology .... Mr. Randy MARAK
15 VP for HR and General Counsel .... Mr. Steve ALDERMAN
26 VP & Dir Marketing/Communications .... Ms. Diane SUMMERS
20 Asst Dean Academic Affairs .... Ms. Gena L. SINGLETON
06 Registrar .... Ms. Mandi GIBSON
36 Director of Career Resources .... Ms. Nazleen JIWANI
07 Assistant Dean for Admissions .... Ms. Alicia CRAMER
21 Controller .... Ms. Paula STAPLETON
37 Director of Financial Aid .... Ms. Emily SILLCOCKS
19 Director Security .... Mr. Kent BRAZELTON
24 Dir Instructional Technology Svcs .... Mr. Terry SMITH
14 Director Information Services .... Mr. George MILZ
43 General Counsel .... Mr. Steve ALDERMAN
44 Director of Annual Giving .... Ms. Kia WISSMILLER
29 Director of Alumni Relations .... Vacant
102 Dir of Foundations & Corp Relations .... Ms. Julie BLAIR
18 Chief Facilities/Physical Plant .... Mr. William HILL
96 Sr Manager of Office Services .... Ms. Dorrie RUSHING
26 Director of Public Relations .... Ms. Claire CATON
101 Secretary of the Institution/Board .... Ms. Jennifer M. HUDSON
104 Assistant Dean & Dir Study Abroad .... Ms. Wanda MORROW
108 Director Institutional Assessment .... Ms. Francesca BONADUCE DE NIGRIS
121 Asst Dean Academic Success .... Ms. Lisa YARROW

South University-Austin (C)

1220 W. Louis Henna Boulevard, Round Rock TX 78681
Telephone: (512) 516-8800 Identification: 770917
Accreditation: &SC, ACBSP, NURSE, PTAA

† Branch campus of South University, Savannah, GA

Southern Bible Institute and College (D)

PO Box 763609, Dallas TX 75376
County: Dallas Identification: 667365
Telephone: (972) 224-5481 Carnegie Class: Not Classified
FAX Number: (972) 224-9517 Calendar System: Semester
URL: www.southernbible.org
Established: Annual Undergrad Tuition & Fees: N/A
Enrollment: N/A Coed
Affiliation or Control: Non-denominational IRS Status: 501(c)3
Highest Offering: Baccalaureate
Accreditation: @BI

01 President .... Dr. Martin E. HAWKINS

Southern Methodist University (E)

6425 Boaz Lane, Dallas TX 75205-0100
County: Dallas FICE Identification: 003613
Unit ID: 228246
Telephone: (214) 768-2000 Carnegie Class: DU-Higher
FAX Number: (214) 768-1001 Calendar System: Semester
URL: www.smu.edu
Established: 1911 Annual Undergrad Tuition & Fees: $54,492
Enrollment: 11,789 Coed
Affiliation or Control: United Methodist IRS Status: 501(c)3
Highest Offering: Doctorate
Accreditation: SC, ART, CACREP, CLPSY, DANCE, LAW, MUS, THEA, THEOL

01 President .... Dr. R. Gerald TURNER
11 VP Executive Affairs .... Dr. Harold W. STANLEY
05 Interim Provost/VP Academic Affairs .... Dr. Peter K. MOORE
10 VP Business & Finance .... Ms. Chris C. REGIS
30 VP Devel & External Affairs .... Mr. Brad E. CHEVES
43 Gen Counsel/VP Leg Affs/Govt Rels .... Mr. Paul J. WARD
32 VP Student Affairs .... Dr. Kenechukwu (K.C.) MMEJE
41 Director of Athletics .... Mr. Richard L. HART
21 Treasurer/Chief Investment Officer .... Mr. Rakesh DAHIYA
13 Chief Information Officer .... Dr. Michael H. HITES
20 Assoc Provost for Faculty Affairs .... Dr. Douglas A. REINELT
20 Int Assoc Provost/Cur Innov/Policy .... Dr. David Y. SON
121 Assoc Provost Stdnt Acad Success .... Dr. Sheri KUNOVICH
108 Assoc Provost Inst Planning/Effct .... Dr. Patricia ALVEY
51 Assoc Provost Continuing Education .... Ms. Larenda MIELKE
46 Assoc VP Research/Dean Grad Studies .... Dr. James E. QUICK
84 Assoc VP Enroll Management .... Mr. Wes K. WAGGONER
15 Assoc VP/Chief Human Res Officer .... Ms. Sheri STARKEY
117 Assoc VP/Chief Risk Officer .... Mr. Warren RICKS
114 Assoc VP Budgets .... Mr. Ernie BARRY
35 Assoc VP & Dean of Students .... Dr. Melinda SUTTON NOSS
109 Assoc VP of Campus Services .... Ms. Alison TWEEDY
18 Assoc VP Facilities Plng/Management .... Mr. Michael S. MOLINA
100 Asst Provost/Chief of Staff .... Mr. Daniel P. EADY
49 Dean Dedman College .... Dr. Thomas DIPIERO
50 Dean Cox School of Business .... Dr. Matthew B. MYERS
54 Dean Lyle School of Engr .... Dr. Marc CHRISTENSEN
57 Dean Meadows Sch of the Arts .... Dr. Sam HOLLAND
53 Dean Sch of Educ/Human Dev .... Dr. Stephanie L. KNIGHT
61 Dean Dedman School of Law .... Ms. Jennifer M. COLLINS
73 Dean Perkins School of Theology .... Dr. Craig C. HILL
08 Dean of SMU Libraries .... Ms. Holly JEFFCOAT
07 Dean of Undergraduate Admissions .... Ms. Elena D. HICKS
26 Asst VP for Public Affairs .... Ms. Regina MOLDOVAN
112 Asst VP for Principal & Major Gifts .... Mr. Blake DAVIS
19 Chief of Police .... Mr. Jim L. WALTERS
06 Registrar .... Mr. John A. HALL
113 University Bursar .... Mr. Albert JABOUR
42 University Chaplain .... Dr. Stephen RANKIN
37 Exec Director Financial Aid .... Mr. Marc PETERSON
12 Executive Director SMU-in-Taos .... Dr. Michael ADLER
27 Exec Dir of Creative Marketing .... Vacant
88 Exec Dir Program Services/Donor Rel .... Ms. Dana AYRES
44 Exec Dir Annual Giving/Alumni Rel .... Ms. Astria SMITH
23 Assoc Dean of Health Services .... Dr. Randy P. JONES
04 Ex Ast to Pres/Ex Dir Inst Acc/Eqt .... Ms. Samantha THOMAS
119 Chief Security Officer .... Mr. George FINNEY
116 Chief of Compliance/Audit Services .... Mr. Dexter E. BURGER
58 Asst Dean of Graduate Studies .... Dr. Alan ITKIN
104 Director Study Abroad .... Dr. Catherine WINNIE
96 Director of Procurement .... Ms. Shannon BROWN
25 Director of Sponsored Projects .... Ms. Ruth V. LOZANO
38 Director of Counseling Services .... Dr. Cathey SOUTTER
102 Dir Corp & Foundation Relations .... Mr. Rob STRAUSS
29 Int Dir Alumni Relations/ Engagement .... Ms. Mary Margaret RANGEL
91 Director of Application Support .... Mr. Curt HERRIDGE
90 Director of Academic Technology .... Mr. Jason WARNER
09 Director of Institutional Research .... Dr. Michael D. TUMEO
39 Asst VP/Dean Res Life/Stdnt Housing .... Ms. Melinda CARLSON

Southern Reformed College and Seminary (F)

4740 Dacoma Street, Ste H, Houston TX 77092
County: Harris Identification: 667364
Telephone: (713) 467-4501 Carnegie Class: Not Classified
FAX Number: N/A Calendar System: Semester
URL: srsem.net
Established: Annual Undergrad Tuition & Fees: N/A
Enrollment: N/A Coed
Affiliation or Control: Independent Non-Profit IRS Status: 501(c)3
Highest Offering: Master's
Accreditation: @BI

01 President/CEO .... Dr. James A. LEE

Southwest Texas Junior College (G)

2401 Garner Field Road, Uvalde TX 78801-6221
County: Uvalde FICE Identification: 003614
Unit ID: 228316
Telephone: (830) 278-4401 Carnegie Class: Assoc/HT-Mix Trad/Non
FAX Number: (830) 591-7354 Calendar System: Semester
URL: www.swtjc.edu
Established: 1946 Annual Undergrad Tuition & Fees (In-District): $2,382
Enrollment: 6,660 Coed
Affiliation or Control: Local IRS Status: 501(c)3
Highest Offering: Associate Degree
Accreditation: SC

01 President .... Dr. Hector GONZALES
11 Vice President Administrative Svcs .... Mr. Derek SANDOVAL
32 Vice President Student Services .... Mrs. Margot MATA
10 Vice President Finance .... Dr. Anne TARSKI
05 Vice President Academic Services .... Dr. Mark UNDERWOOD
12 Vice President Del Rio .... Mrs. Connie BUCHANAN
12 Vice President Eagle Pass .... Mr. Gilbert S. BERMEA
103 Dean of Workforce Education .... Mr. Juan (Johnny) C. GUZMAN
49 Dean of College of Liberal Arts .... Dr. Cheryl L. SANCHEZ
121 Director of Academic Advising .... Vacant
37 Director of Financial Aid .... Ms. Yvette HERNANDEZ
13 Co-Director of Information Tech .... Ms. Denise ODEN
13 Co-Director of Information Tech .... Mr. Frankie PANNELL
18 Physical Plant Director .... Mr. Kirk M. PALERMO
35 Director Student Success .... Dr. Randa SCHELL
15 Human Resources Coordinator .... Mr. Oscar S. GARCIA
09 Director of Institutional Research .... Dr. Renee ZIMMERMAN
06 Registrar .... Mr. Steve MARTINEZ
08 Head Librarian .... Ms. Brenda CANTU
19 Director Security/Safety .... Mr. Johnny FIELD
96 Purchasing Manager .... Mr. Santos DIAZ

Southwest University at El Paso (H)

1414 Geronimo Drive, El Paso TX 79925
County: El Paso FICE Identification: 041317
Unit ID: 451556
Telephone: (915) 778-4001 Carnegie Class: Bac/Assoc-Mixed
FAX Number: (915) 778-1575 Calendar System: Other
URL: www.southwestuniversity.edu
Established: 2001 Annual Undergrad Tuition & Fees: $15,500
Enrollment: 1,527 Coed
Affiliation or Control: Proprietary IRS Status: Proprietary
Highest Offering: Baccalaureate
Accreditation: ABHES, NURSE, RAD

01 President .... Ms. Yolanda ARRIOLA
05 School Director .... Ms. Marisol GUTIERREZ

Southwestern Adventist University (I)

100 W Hillcrest Street, Keene TX 76059-0567
County: Johnson FICE Identification: 003619
Unit ID: 228468
Telephone: (817) 645-3921 Carnegie Class: Bac-Diverse
FAX Number: (817) 202-6744 Calendar System: Semester
URL: www.swau.edu
Established: 1893 Annual Undergrad Tuition & Fees: $21,564
Enrollment: 817 Coed
Affiliation or Control: Seventh-day Adventist IRS Status: 501(c)3
Highest Offering: Master's
Accreditation: SC, IACBE, NURSE

01 President .... Dr. Ken SHAW

05 VP for Academic Administration ....Dr. Donna BERKNER
10 VP for Financial Administration ....Mr. Joel WALLACE
84 VP for Enrollment ....Ms. Enga ALMEIDA
32 VP for Student Services ....Mr. James THE
42 VP for Spiritual Development ....Mr. Russ LAUGHLIN
20 Asst VP for Academic Admin ....Dr. Marcel SARGEANT
37 Asst VP for Student Finance ....Mr. Duane VALENCIA
21 Asst VP Financial Administration ....Mr. Greg A. WICKLUND
06 Registrar ....Mr. Jason KOWARSCH
08 Librarian ....Ms. Cristina M. THOMSEN
34 Dean of Women ....Mrs. Janelle D. WILLIAMS
33 Dean of Men ....Mr. William IVERSON
13 Dir Information Technology Svcs ....Mr. E. Charles LEWIS
18 Plant Engineer ....Mr. Dale E. HAINEY
26 Director of Marketing ....Mr. Timothy KOSAKA
29 Director of Alumni Relations ....Mrs. Vonda SEALS
38 Director of Counseling & Testing ....Dr. R. Mark ALDRIDGE
22 Director of Disability Services ....Ms. Lillian LOPEZ
121 Dir Ctr for Acad Success/Advising ....Mrs. Renata OCAMPO
07 Director of Admissions ....Ms. Rahneeka HAZELTON
15 Director of Human Resources ....Ms. Genelle ROGERS
19 Assoc Director of Security ....Mr. Matthew AGEE
25 Grant Writer ....Dr. Tom BUNCH
41 Athletic Director ....Mr. Tyler WOOLDRIDGE
44 Senior Director for Development ....Ms. Kisha NORRIS
50 Chair Business Dept ....Mr. Joshua MICHALSKI
53 Chair Education Dept ....Dr. Donna BERKNER

Southwestern Assemblies of God University (A)

1200 Sycamore, Waxahachie TX 75165-2397

County: Ellis — FICE Identification: 003616 — Unit ID: 228325
Telephone: (972) 937-4010 — Carnegie Class: Masters/S
FAX Number: (972) 923-0488 — Calendar System: Semester
URL: www.sagu.edu
Established: 1927 — Annual Undergrad Tuition & Fees: $19,582
Enrollment: 2,162 — Coed
Affiliation or Control: Assemblies Of God Church — IRS Status: 501(c)3
Highest Offering: Doctorate
Accreditation: SC, IACBE, @SW

01 President ....Dr. Kermit S. BRIDGES
05 Vice President for Academics ....Dr. Paul BROOKS
32 Vice President for Student Develop ....Rev. Terry PHIPPS
10 Vice Pres for Business & Finance ....Dr. Fred GORE
111 Vice President for Univ Advancement ....Rev. Rick BOWLES
84 Vice Pres Enrollment & Retention ....Vacant
20 Dean of Academic Services ....Rev. Donny LUTRICK
58 Dean of Graduate Studies ....Dr. Dennis ROBINSON
73 Dean Col Bible & Church Ministries ....Dr. Michael CLARENSAU
50 Dean Col of Business & Education ....Dr. Sue TAYLOR
64 Dean Col of Music & Comm Arts ....Mr. Del GUYNES
09 Vice Pres for Inst Effectiveness ....Dr. Kim BERNECKER
106 Dean for Dist Educ & Ext Sites ....Rev. Joseph HARTMAN
06 Registrar ....Ms. Heather FRANCIS
35 Dean of Students ....Rev. Lance MECHE
88 Director of Learning Centers ....Mr. Nolan JONES
13 Sr Dir Information Technology ....Mr. Kirk PASCHALL
29 Director of Alumni Relations ....Vacant
08 Director of Learning Resources ....Ms. Radonna HOLMES
14 Director of Campus Software ....Mr. Mark WALKER
21 Dir of Business Services ....Ms. Katie WHITE
88 Senior Director of Accounting ....Mr. Paul SMITH
37 Sr Director of Financial Aid ....Mr. Jeff FRANCIS
19 Director of Security ....Mr. Ron CRANE
07 Assistant Dean of Admissions ....Mr. Joshua MARTIN
24 Director of Media Services ....Mr. John COOKMAN
88 Director of Accounts Receivable ....Mr. Chris BACA
36 Director of Career Development ....Ms. Beverly ROBINSON
41 Athletic Director ....Dr. Jesse GODDING
26 Director of University Marketing ....Mr. Ryan MCELHANY
15 Director of Human Resources ....Mrs. Ruth ROBERTS
38 Counselor ....Vacant
07 Director of On Campus Admissions ....Mr. Joshua DUNN
88 Director of Admissions Info Systems ....Mr. Jarrod PACE
04 Executive Asst to President ....Ms. Patricia BROOKS
108 Director Institutional Assessment ....Rev. Jerry ROBERTS

Southwestern Baptist Theological Seminary (B)

PO Box 22370, Fort Worth TX 76122

County: Tarrant — FICE Identification: 003617
Telephone: (817) 923-1921 — Carnegie Class: Not Classified
FAX Number: (817) 921-8766 — Calendar System: Semester
URL: www.swbts.edu
Established: 1908 — Annual Undergrad Tuition & Fees: N/A
Enrollment: N/A — Coed
Affiliation or Control: Southern Baptist — IRS Status: 501(c)3
Highest Offering: Doctorate
Accreditation: SC, MUS, THEOL

01 President ....Dr. Adam W. GREENWAY
05 Provost/VP for Academic Admin ....Dr. Randy L. STINSON
26 Vice Pres for Strategic Initiatives ....Mr. Colby ADAMS
10 Vice Pres Business Administration ....Mr. Kevin ENSLEY
111 Vice Pres Institutional Advancement ....Mr. Travis TRAWICK
108 AVP Institutional Effectiveness ....Dr. Mark LEEDS
73 Dean of the School of Theology ....Dr. Jeffrey BINGHAM
53 Int Dean Sch of Educ Ministries ....Dr. Michael WILDER
64 Int Dean Sch of Ch Music/Worship ....Dr. Joseph CRIDER
73 Int Dean Sch of Evangelism/Missions ....Dr. John MASSEY
49 Dean L.R. Scarborough College ....Dr. Mike WILKINSON
34 Dean of Women ....Dr. Terri STOVALL
88 Dean of the School of Preaching ....Dr. David ALLEN

Southwestern Christian College (C)

Box 10, Terrell TX 75160-9002

County: Kaufman — FICE Identification: 003618 — Unit ID: 228486
Telephone: (972) 524-3341 — Carnegie Class: Bac/Assoc-Mixed
FAX Number: (972) 563-7133 — Calendar System: Semester
URL: www.swcc.edu
Established: 1949 — Annual Undergrad Tuition & Fees: $8,131
Enrollment: 159 — Coed
Affiliation or Control: Churches Of Christ — IRS Status: 501(c)3
Highest Offering: Baccalaureate
Accreditation: SC

01 President/CEO ....Dr. Ervin SEAMSTER, JR.
30 Vice President for Instl Expansion ....Dr. James MAXWELL
05 Vice President Academic Affairs ....Ms. Sylvia THOMAS
10 Vice President Fiscal Affairs ....Mr. Douglas HOWIE
32 Vice President Student Affairs ....Mr. Ben FOSTER
26 Vice President Public Relations ....Vacant
08 Librarian ....Mrs. Doris JOHNSON
07 Director Admissions/Retention Coord ....Mr. Warren ROBERTS
37 Director of Financial Aid ....Ms. Tonya DEAN
44 Director of Development ....Vacant

Southwestern University (D)

1001 E University Avenue, Georgetown TX 78626-6144

County: Williamson — FICE Identification: 003620 — Unit ID: 228343
Telephone: (512) 863-6511 — Carnegie Class: Bac-A&S
FAX Number: (512) 863-5788 — Calendar System: Semester
URL: www.southwestern.edu
Established: 1840 — Annual Undergrad Tuition & Fees: $42,000
Enrollment: 1,396 — Coed
Affiliation or Control: United Methodist — IRS Status: 501(c)3
Highest Offering: Baccalaureate
Accreditation: SC, MUS

01 President ....Dr. Edward B. BURGER
42 University Chaplain ....Vacant
04 Exec Asst for Pres/Board Liaison ....Ms. Patricia WITT
05 Dean of Faculty ....Dr. Alisa GAUNDER
32 Vice President for Student Life ....Ms. Jaime WOODY
13 Assoc VP Information Technology ....Mr. Todd WATSON
10 VP for Finance and Administration ....Mr. Craig ERWIN
30 Vice Pres for University Relations ....Mr. Paul SECORD
20 Assoc VP for Academic Affairs ....Ms. Julie A. COWLEY
26 VP Integrated Communications/CMO ....Vacant
15 Assoc VP for Human Resources ....Ms. Elma F. BENAVIDES
35 Dean of Students ....Ms. Shelley STORY
29 Assoc VP for Alumni & Parents ....Ms. Megan FRISQUE
44 Director of Annual Giving ....Mr. Wesley CLARK
41 Assoc VP Intercollegiate Athletics ....Dr. Glada C. MUNT
21 Assoc VP Finance Acct/Controller ....Ms. Brenda THOMPSON
19 Chief of Police ....Mr. Brad DUNN
84 Dean of Enrollment Services ....Ms. Christine BOWMAN
36 Dir Ctr Career & Prof Development ....Mr. Daniel OROZCO
121 Dir of Academic Success ....Mr. David SEILER
88 Dir Paideia Program/Assoc Professor ....Dr. Sergio COSTOLA
85 Director Intercultural Learning ....Ms. Tisha KORKUS
09 Dir Inst Research & Effectiveness ....Ms. Natasha WILLIAMS
28 Asst Dean Multicultural Affairs ....Ms. Terri JOHNSON
31 Sr Dir Community Engaged Learning ....Dr. Sarah BRACKMANN
08 Dir of Library Resources ....Ms. Amy ANDERSON
84 VP Recruitment & Enrollment ....Mr. Tom F. DELAHUNT
91 Director Administrative Computing ....Ms. Jennifer O'DANIEL
102 Senior Dir of Foundation Relations ....Ms. Sonya ROBINSON
105 Webmaster ....Mr. Ed HILLIS
18 Assoc VP Facilities Mgmt ....Vacant
39 Director of Residence Life ....Ms. Lisa DELA CRUZ

Stark College & Seminary (E)

7000 Ocean Drive, Corpus Christi TX 78412

County: Nueces — Identification: 667345
Telephone: (361) 991-9403 — Carnegie Class: Not Classified
FAX Number: N/A — Calendar System: Semester
URL: www.stark.edu
Established: 1947 — Annual Undergrad Tuition & Fees: N/A
Enrollment: N/A — Coed
Affiliation or Control: Independent Non-Profit — IRS Status: 501(c)3
Highest Offering: Master's
Accreditation: BI

01 President ....Dr. Anthony CELELLI
05 Provost ....Dr. Jena DUNN

Stephen F. Austin State University (F)

2008 Alumni Drive, Rusk 206,
Nacogdoches TX 75961-3940

County: Nacogdoches — FICE Identification: 003624 — Unit ID: 228431
Telephone: (936) 468-2011 — Carnegie Class: DU-Mod
FAX Number: (936) 468-2202 — Calendar System: Semester
URL: www.sfasu.edu
Established: 1921 — Annual Undergrad Tuition & Fees (In-State): $8,316
Enrollment: 12,614 — Coed
Affiliation or Control: State — IRS Status: 501(c)3
Highest Offering: Doctorate
Accreditation: SC, AAFCS, ART, CAATE, CACREP, CAEPN, CIDA, DIETD, DIETI, IPSY, MUS, NUR, SP, SW, THEA

01 Interim President ....Dr. Steven B. WESTBROOK
05 Provost/VP Academic Affairs ....Dr. Steven H. BULLARD
10 Vice Pres Finance/Administration ....Dr. Danny R. GALLANT
32 Interim VP for University Affairs ....Dr. Adam PECK
111 Vice Pres University Advancement ....Ms. Jill STILL
29 Exec Director Alumni ....Mr. Craig A. TURNAGE
20 Assoc Provost/VP Academic Affairs ....Dr. Marc GUIDRY
84 Exec Dir of Enrollment Mgmt ....Ms. Erma BRECHT
26 Exec Dir Univ Mktg Comm ....Dr. Shirley A. LUNA
43 General Counsel ....Mr. Damon DERRICK
06 Registrar ....Ms. Lynda LANGHAM
09 Director Institutional Research ....Ms. Karyn HALL
08 Library Director ....Ms. Shirley DICKERSON
39 Director of Residence Life ....Mr. Winston BAKER
18 Director of Physical Plant ....Mr. Ron WATSON
37 Director of Financial Aid ....Ms. Rachele GARRETT
22 Director Affirmative Action ....Vacant
13 Chief Information Officer ....Mr. Anthony ESPINOZA
15 Director of Human Resources ....Ms. Loretta C. DOTY
19 Chief of University Police ....Mr. John FIELDS
23 Director Health Services ....Dr. Janice LEDET
41 Director of Intercol Athletics ....Mr. Ryan IVEY
35 Interim Dean Student Affairs ....Dr. Hollie GAMMEL-SMITH
38 Director of Counseling ....Ms. Jill MILEM
96 Director of Procurement ....Ms. Kay JOHNSON
46 Dir Research/Sponsored Programs ....Vacant
58 Dean Research & Graduate Studies ....Dr. Pauline SAMPSON
49 Dean College Liberal/Applied Arts ....Dr. Brian MURPHY
47 Dean College Forestry/Agriculture ....Dr. Hans M. WILLIAMS
53 Dean of College of Education ....Dr. Judy A. ABBOTT
57 Dean College Fine Arts ....Dr. A.C. (Buddy) HIMES
50 Dean College of Business ....Dr. Timothy BISPING
81 Dean College Sciences & Math ....Dr. Kimberly M. CHILDS
04 Special Asst to President ....Ms. Susan H. WILLLIAMS
101 Coordinator of Board Affairs ....Ms. Judith P. BUCKINGHAM
30 Exec Director of Development ....Dr. Joel L. TURNER, III
104 Director International Programs ....Ms. Heather CATTON
105 University Webmaster ....Mr. Jason L. JOHNSTONE
106 Int Dir Instructional Technology ....Ms. Mary D. SMITH
108 Dir Institutional Effectiveness ....Mr. John CALAHAN
121 Asst Dean Stdnt Affairs Support ....Dr. Michael E. WALKER
07 Associate Director of Admissions ....Mr. Kevin L. DAVIS

Tarrant County College District (G)

1500 Houston Street, Fort Worth TX 76102-6599

County: Tarrant — FICE Identification: 003626 — Unit ID: 228547
Telephone: (817) 515-5100 — Carnegie Class: Assoc/HT-Mix Trad/Non
FAX Number: (817) 515-5350 — Calendar System: Semester
URL: www.tccd.edu
Established: 1965 — Annual Undergrad Tuition & Fees (In-District): $1,661
Enrollment: 52,957 — Coed
Affiliation or Control: State/Local — IRS Status: 501(c)3
Highest Offering: Associate Degree
Accreditation: SC, ACFEI, ADNUR, CAHIIM, COARC, CONST, DH, DIETT, DMS, EMT, PTAA, RAD, SURGT

01 Chancellor ....Dr. Eugene V. GIOVANNINI
11 Chief Operating Officer ....Ms. Susan ALANIS
13 Chief Technology Officer ....Mr. Robert PACHECO
05 Exec Vice Chancellor & Provost ....Dr. Elva C. LEBLANC
88 EVP Corp Solutions/Economic Dev ....Vacant
26 VC Communications/External Affairs ....Mr. Reginald GATES
20 VP Academic Affairs SO ....Dr. Shannon YDOYAGA
20 VP Academic Affairs NE ....Dr. Linda S. BRADDY
20 VP Academic Affairs NW ....Dr. Judith GALLAGHER
20 VP Academic Affairs SE ....Dr. Zena JACKSON
20 VP Academic Affairs TR ....Dr. Thomas MILLS
20 VP Academic Affairs TCC Connect ....Dr. Marcel KERR
32 VP Student Dev Services NE ....Dr. Mayra OLIVARES-URUETA
32 VP Student Dev Services SE ....Dr. Michael DUPONT
32 VP Student Dev Services SO ....Dr. Stephanie HILL
32 VP Student Dev Services TR ....Dr. Julie AMON
32 VP Student Dev Services NW ....Dr. Joe RODE
88 VP Acad Outreach & SS TCC Connect ....Dr. Aubra J. GANNT
12 President South Campus ....Dr. Peter JORDAN
12 President Northwest Campus ....Dr. Zarina BLANKENBAKER
12 President Northeast Campus ....Dr. Kenya AYERS
12 President Southeast Campus ....Dr. William COPPOLA
12 President Trinity River Campus ....Dr. Stephen S. MADISON
12 President TCC Connect Campus ....Dr. Carlos MORALES
84 Assoc Vice Chanc Enrol/Acad Support ....Mr. David XIMENEZ
15 Chief Human Resources Officer ....Dr. Ricardo CORONADO
25 District Exec Dir Grants Dev/Compl ....Ms. Kim MOSS-LINNEAR
21 Assoc Vice Chancellor Finance ....Mrs. Nancy H. CHANG
20 Assoc VChanc Acad Affs/Stdnt Dev ....Dr. Nancy CURE
102 Executive Director TCC Foundation ....Dr. Joe MCINTOSH
09 Exec Dir Inst Intell & Research ....Dr. Rosemary REYNOLDS
27 Exec Dir Comm/PR/Marketing ....Ms. Suzanne GROVES
88 Assoc Vice Chanc Real Estate/Facs ....Mr. Gary PREATHER
19 Chief of Police ....Mr. Shaun WILLIAMS
20 Dist Reg & Dir Academic Supp Svcs ....Mr. John D. SPENCER
08 Director Library Services NE ....Mr. Mark DOLIVE
08 Director Library Services SO ....Vacant
08 Director Library Services NW ....Ms. Alex POTEMKIN

08 Director Library Services SE .... Ms. Jotisa KLEMM
08 Director Library Services TR .... Ms. Susan SMITH
06 Registrar South Campus .... Ms. Vanessa WALKER
06 Registrar Northeast Campus .... Mr. Brian D. BARRETT
06 Registrar Northwest Campus .... Ms. Christy KLEMIUK
06 Registrar Southeast Campus .... Mr. Kenne EVANS
06 Registrar Trinity Campus .... Mr. Vikas RAJPUROHIT
38 Director of Counseling SO .... Ms. Ticily MEDLEY
38 Director of Counseling NE .... Dr. Condoa PARRENT
38 Director of Counseling NW .... Ms. Lilia COVIO-CALZADA
38 Director of Counseling SE .... Ms. Renetta WRIGHT
38 Director of Counseling TR .... Dr. Deidra TURNER
37 District Director Financial Aid .... Ms. Samantha STALNAKER
37 Director of Financial Aid SO .... Ms. JoLynn H. SPROLE
37 Director of Financial Aid NE .... Ms. Mary BLEDSOE
37 Director of Financial Aid NW .... Ms. Trina SMITH-PATTERSON
37 Director of Financial Aid SE .... Ms. Elizabeth LANDWERMEYER
37 Director of Financial Aid TR .... Mr. William MCMULLEN
35 Dir Student Development Svcs NE .... Mr. Victor BALLESTEROS
35 Dir Student Development Svcs SO .... Dr. Jared M. COBB
35 Dir Student Development Svcs NW .... Dr. Vesta M. MARTINEZ
35 Dir Student Development Svcs SE .... Mr. Douglas C. PEAK
35 Dir Student Development Svcs TR .... Mr. Carter BEDFORD
88 Director of Business Services .... Mrs. Kathy M. CRUSTO-WAY
96 Exec Dir of Procurement .... Mr. Michael (Mike) HERNDON
18 Exec Dir Inst Strategic Development .... Ms. Margaret K. LUTTON
07 Dist Dir of Admiss & Records .... Ms. Rebecca (Becki) GRIFFITH
28 Dir of Equity & Inclusion .... Mr. Andrew DUFFIELD
29 Alumni and Comm Specialist .... Ms. Gloria FISHER
43 Associate General Counsel .... Ms. Carol BRACKEN
100 Chief of Staff .... Dr. Kelley MILLS

Temple College (A)

2600 S First Street, Temple TX 76504-7435
County: Bell FICE Identification: 003627
Unit ID: 228608
Telephone: (254) 298-8282 Carnegie Class: Assoc/MT-VT-High Trad
FAX Number: (254) 298-8266 Calendar System: Semester
URL: www.templejc.edu
Established: 1926 Annual Undergrad Tuition & Fees (In-District): $2,376
Enrollment: 4,999 Coed
Affiliation or Control: Local IRS Status: 501(c)3
Highest Offering: Associate Degree
Accreditation: SC, ADNUR, COARC, DH, DMS, EMT, SURGT

01 President .... Dr. Christina PONCE
05 Vice Pres Academic Affairs .... Mr. Mark SMITH
10 Vice Pres Administrative Svcs/CFO .... Mr. Brandon BOZON
21 AVP of Finance .... Mr. Gary JACKSON
31 AVP Acad Outreach & Ext Programs .... Vacant
15 Assoc VP Resource Management .... Dr. Randy BACA
106 Dir Web Applications & System .... Vacant
84 Div Dir Student & Enrollment Svcs .... Ms. Carey ROSE
08 Div Director of Learning Resources .... Mr. Kevin HENARD
30 Exec Dir Institutional Advancement .... Mrs. Jennifer GRAHAM
38 Director Student Advising .... Ms. Danya BAILEY
04 Assistant to the President & Board .... Mrs. Judith DOHNALIK
37 Director of Financial Aid .... Vacant
26 Director Marketing/Public Relations .... Ms. Ellen DAVIS
18 Dir Facilities/Physical Plant .... Mr. Al KENT
96 Director of Purchasing .... Mr. Brian SUPAK
32 Director Student Life .... Mrs. Ruth BRIDGES
06 Registrar .... Mrs. Toni CUELLAR
41 Athletic Director .... Mr. Craig MCMURTRY
19 Chief of Police .... Mr. Michael MARKUM

Texarkana College (B)

2500 N Robison Road, Texarkana TX 75599
County: Bowie FICE Identification: 003628
Unit ID: 228699
Telephone: (903) 823-3456 Carnegie Class: Assoc/HVT-High Non
FAX Number: (903) 823-3451 Calendar System: Semester
URL: www.texarkanacollege.edu
Established: 1927 Annual Undergrad Tuition & Fees (In-District): $2,236
Enrollment: 4,250 Coed
Affiliation or Control: Local IRS Status: 501(c)3
Highest Offering: Associate Degree
Accreditation: SC, ADNUR, EMT

01 President .... Dr. Loyd J. SMITH
05 Vice President of Instruction .... Dr. Donna MCDANIEL
10 Chief Finance Officer .... Mrs. Kim JONES
32 Dean of Students .... Mr. Robert JONES
13 Chief Info Technology Officer .... Mr. Mike DUMDEI
30 Director Foundation/Development .... Mrs. Katie ANDRUS
09 Director Inst Rsrch & Effectiveness .... Mrs. Phyllis DEESE
18 Director Facilities Services .... Mr. Rick BOYETTE
26 Director Inst Adv/Public Relations .... Mrs. Suzy IRWIN
88 Director KTXK Radio .... Mr. Steve MITCHELL
15 Director Human Resources .... Mrs. Phyllis DEESE
103 Dean Workforce & Cont Education .... Mr. Brandon WASHINGTON
81 Dean STEM .... Dr. Catherine HOWARD
76 Dean Health Sciences .... Mrs. Courtney SHOALMIRE
49 Dean Liberal & Performing Arts .... Mrs. Mary E. YOUNG
50 Dean Business & Social Sciences .... Dr. John Dixon BOYLES
08 Director Library/Student Support .... Dr. Tonja MACKEY
84 Enrollment Management/Registrar .... Mr. Brandon HIGGINS
07 Director of Admissions .... Mr. Lee WILLIAMS
37 Director Student Financial Aid .... Mrs. Susan JOHNSTON
04 Presidential Events Coordinator .... Mrs. Mindy PRESTON

*The Texas A & M University System Office (C)

301 Tarrow Street, 7th Floor, College Station TX 77840
County: Brazos FICE Identification: 003629
Unit ID: 228732
Telephone: (979) 458-6000 Carnegie Class: N/A
FAX Number: (979) 458-6044
URL: www.tamus.edu

01 Chancellor .... Mr. John SHARP
05 Vice Chanc for Academic Affairs .... Dr. James HALLMARK
10 Deputy Chancellor & CFO .... Mr. Billy HAMILTON
26 Vice Chanc for Marketing & Comm .... Mr. Laylan COPELIN
116 Chief Auditor .... Ms. Charlie HRNCIR
43 General Counsel .... Mr. Ray BONILLA
46 Vice Chancellor for Research .... Dr. Jon MOGFORD
21 Vice Chanc for Business Affairs .... Mr. Phillip RAY
13 Chief Information Officer .... Mr. Mark STONE
115 Chief Investment Ofcr/Treasurer .... Ms. Maria ROBINSON
100 Exec Assistant to the Chancellor .... Ms. Stephanie BJUNE
12 Director RELLIS Campus .... Ms. Kellly TEMPLIN

*Prairie View A & M University (D)

P.O. Box 519, Prairie View TX 77446-0519
County: Waller FICE Identification: 003630
Unit ID: 227526
Telephone: (936) 261-3311 Carnegie Class: Masters/L
FAX Number: (936) 261-2115 Calendar System: Semester
URL: www.pvamu.edu
Established: 1876 Annual Undergrad Tuition & Fees (In-State): $10,533
Enrollment: 9,219 Coed
Affiliation or Control: State IRS Status: 501(c)3
Highest Offering: Doctorate
Accreditation: #SC, DIETD, DIETI, MUS, NUR, NURSE, SW

02 President .... Dr. Ruth J. SIMMONS
05 Int Provost/Sr VP Academic Affairs .... Dr. James M. PALMER
20 Assoc Prov & Assoc VP Acad Affairs .... Dr. James J. WILSON, JR.
10 Sr Vice President Business Affairs .... Dr. Corey S. BRADFORD, SR.
32 Vice Pres of Student Affairs .... Dr. Timothy SAMS
46 Int VP Research/Innov/Spons Pgms .... Dr. Ali FARES
41 Vice Pres/Director of Athletics .... Mr. Fred WASHINGTON
11 Vice President for Administration .... Dr. Michael L. MCFRAZIER
30 Vice Pres of Development .... Ms. Carme WILLIAMS
100 Chief of Staff .... Ms. Yolanda BEVILL
84 Vice President Enrollment Mgmt .... Dr. Sarina PHILLIPS
21 Asst VP for Financial Accounting .... Mr. Rod MIRELES
92 Director of Honors Program .... Dr. James J. WILSON, JR.
109 Asst VP Auxiliary Enterprises .... Ms. Tressey D. WILSON
09 Director Institutional Research .... Mr. Dean WILLIAMSON
07 Int Dir of Undergraduate Admissions .... Ms. Lenice BROWN
18 Int Assistant VP of Physical Plant .... Mr. Charles MUSE
15 Asst VP of Human Resources .... Ms. Radhika AYYAR
63 Director Undergrad Med Acad .... Dr. Dennis E. DANIELS
13 Interim Chief Information Officer .... Mr. Midhat ASGHAR
58 Interim Dean Graduate Studies .... Dr. Tamara L. BROWN
50 Dean College of Business .... Dr. Munir QUDDUS
47 Dean Col Agriculture/Human Sciences .... Dr. Gerard D'SOUZA
66 Dean College of Nursing .... Dr. Betty ADAMS
49 Dean College of Arts & Sciences .... Dr. Danny R. KELLEY
48 Dean School of Architecture .... Dr. Ikhlas SABOUNI
83 Int Dean Col of Juv Justice/Psych .... Dr. Camille GIBSON
53 Interim Dean College of Education .... Dr. Michael L. MCFRAZIER
54 Dean College of Engineering .... Dr. Pamela OBIOMON
21 Director of Treasury Services .... Ms. Equilla JACKSON
56 Administrator Coop Extension .... Dr. Carolyn J. WILLIAMS
19 Chief of Police .... Dr. Keith JEMISON
29 Director Alumni Affairs .... Ms. Carol CAMPBELL
06 Registrar/Records .... Ms. Deborah J. DUNGEY
85 Director of International Students .... Ms. Elma D. GONZALEZ
88 Immigration Services Coord .... Mrs. Evelyn J. MCGINTY
96 Procurement Sup/HUB Coordinator .... Mr. Jim A. NELMS

*Tarleton State University (E)

1333 W Washington, Box T-0001,
Stephenville TX 76402-0001
County: Erath FICE Identification: 003631
Unit ID: 228529
Telephone: (254) 968-9000 Carnegie Class: Masters/L
FAX Number: (254) 968-9920 Calendar System: Semester
URL: www.tarleton.edu
Established: 1899 Annual Undergrad Tuition & Fees (In-State): $7,292
Enrollment: 13,019 Coed
Affiliation or Control: State IRS Status: 501(c)3
Highest Offering: Doctorate
Accreditation: SC, ACBSP, CAATE, CACREP, DMOLS, HT, MLTAD, MT, MUS, NURSE, SW

02 President .... Dr. F. Dominic DOTTAVIO
100 Chief of Staff .... Dr. Kimberly MCCUISTION
05 Provost/Exec VPAA .... Dr. Karen MURRAY
30 Vice Pres Inst Advancement .... Dr. Kyle W. MCGREGOR
10 VP Finance/Administration .... Dr. Rick RICHARDSON
32 VP Student Affairs .... Dr. Kelli C. STYRON
84 VP Enrollment Mgmt .... Dr. Javier GARZA
26 VP Marketing & Communications .... Ms. Cecilia JACOBS
20 AVP Outreach & Off Campus Programs .... Dr. Rusty FREED
20 Assoc VP Academic Administration .... Dr. Mark MORVANT
20 Assoc Provost & Senior VP CAFA .... Dr. Diane TAYLOR
36 Director of Career Services .... Ms. Alana HEFNER
18 Dir of Facilities & Construction .... Mr. Perry HENDERSON
35 Exec Director Student Services .... Ms. Donna STROHMEYER
21 Asst VP Finance/Controller .... Ms. Lori BEATY
121 AVP Strategic Student Success .... Mr. Gabriel BERMEA
30 Asst VP Development .... Ms. Janice HORAK
84 Asst VP Strategic Recruitment Init .... Ms. Amanda NICKERSON
76 Int Dean Col Health Sci & Hum Svcs .... Dr. Sally LEWIS
81 Dean College Science & Technology .... Dr. James PIERCE
50 Dean Col of Business Administration .... Dr. Chris SHAO
47 Dean Col Agricultural/Environ Sci .... Dr. Steve DAMRON
53 Dean College of Education .... Dr. Jordan BARKLEY
49 Int Dean College Liberal/Fine Arts .... Dr. Eric MORROW
58 Dean College of Graduate Studies .... Dr. Barry LAMBERT
07 Director Undergraduate Admissions .... Ms. Cynthia HESS
22 Dir Student Disability Services .... Ms. Trina GEYE
08 University Librarian .... Mrs. Donna SAVAGE
92 Exec Dir of Honors College .... Dr. Craig CLIFFORD
37 Director Student Financial Aid .... Ms. Kathy PURVIS
09 Director Institutional Research .... Dr. Mike HAYNES
13 CIO/Exec Dir Information Tech Svcs .... Ms. Rebecca GRAY
15 Int Director of Employee Services .... Ms. Wendy HAYNES
35 Asst VP for Student Affairs .... Dr. ShaRhonda MACKLIN
41 Athletic Director .... Mr. Lonn REISMAN
23 Director Student Health Center .... Ms. Bridgette BEDNARZ
38 Director Student Counseling .... Dr. Brenda FAULKNER
19 University Police Chief .... Mr. Matt WELCH
88 Exec Dir of Student Engagement .... Mr. Darrell BROWN
24 Dir Center for Instr Innovation .... Dr. Kelli SHAFFER
44 Asst VP Advancement & Ext Relations .... Ms. Sabra GUERRA
104 Dir International Academic Programs .... Dr. Marilyn ROBITAILLE
06 Registrar .... Mr. David SUTTON
96 Mgr Purchasing/HUB .... Ms. Cori LUTTRELL
25 Contract Specialist .... Ms. Kim MEDFORD
40 Manager Campus Store .... Ms. Carrie MCCANN
105 Web Administrator .... Ms. Daphne HUNT
04 Administrative Asst to President .... Ms. Tauna BERTSCH
29 Director Alumni Relations .... Ms. Jessica EVANS
117 Dir & Univ Compliance Officer .... Mr. Kent STYRON
39 Dir Resident Life/Student Housing .... Ms. Shelly BROWN
54 Assoc Dean Engineering .... Dr. Denise MARTINEZ

*Texas A & M International University (F)

5201 University Boulevard, Laredo TX 78041-1900
County: Webb FICE Identification: 009651
Unit ID: 226152
Telephone: (956) 326-2001 Carnegie Class: Masters/L
FAX Number: (956) 326-2348 Calendar System: Semester
URL: www.tamiu.edu
Established: 1969 Annual Undergrad Tuition & Fees (In-State): $7,176
Enrollment: 7,640 Coed
Affiliation or Control: State IRS Status: 501(c)3
Highest Offering: Doctorate
Accreditation: SC, NUR, SPAA

02 President .... Dr. Pablo ARENAZ
05 Provost .... Dr. Thomas R. MITCHELL
10 Vice Pres Finance & Administration .... Mr. Juan J. CASTILLO, JR.
111 Vice Pres Institutional Advancement .... Ms. Rosanne PALACIOS
32 Vice Pres for Student Success .... Dr. Minita RAMIREZ
11 Assoc Vice Pres for Administration .... Vacant
88 Dir of Compliance .... Mrs. Lorissa M. CORTEZ
13 Assoc VP Information Technology/CIO .... Dr. Leebrian E. GASKINS
20 Associate Provost .... Dr. Stephen M. DUFFY
49 Dean College Arts & Sciences .... Dr. Claudia E. SAN MIGUEL
50 Dean AR Sanchez Jr Sch of Business .... Dr. Steve R. SEARS
66 Dean Canseco School of Nursing .... Dr. Glenda C. WALKER
08 Dir Sue & Radcliffe Killam Library .... Mr. Douglas M. FERRIER
07 Director Admissions .... Mrs. Rosie A. DICKINSON
06 Associate VP/Univ Registrar .... Mr. Juan G. GARCIA, JR.
15 Director of Human Resources .... Ms. Jan ASPELUND
26 Director Public Rels Mktg/Info Svcs .... Mr. Steve K. HARMON
37 Director Financial Aid .... Mrs. Laura M. ELIZONDO
41 Director of Athletics .... Mr. Gilbert G. ZIMMERMANN
18 Director Physical Plant .... Mr. Roberto A. GARZA
29 Director Alumni Relations .... Mrs. Yelitza M. HOWARD
36 Director Career Services .... Mrs. Cassandra L. WHEELER
39 Director of Residence Life/Housing .... Mr. Manuel VELA, III
38 Dir Student Couns/Disb Svcs .... Ms. Aracely C. HERNANDEZ
96 Dir Purchasing & Support Services .... Ms. Ann E. GUTIERREZ
92 Assoc Prof Director Honors Pgm .... Dr. Deborah L. BLACKWELL
21 Comptroller .... Ms. Elena M. MARTINEZ
35 Associate VP Student Success .... Ms. Gina D. GONZALEZ
88 Dir Recruitment/School Relations .... Mr. Guillermo F. GONZALEZ, JR.
108 Assoc VP Institutional Assessment .... Dr. David E. ALLEN
54 Dean of University College .... Dr. Catheryn J. WEITMAN
09 Director of Institutional Research .... Mr. Sheng Chien R. LEE

*Texas A & M University (G)

1246 TAMU, College Station TX 77843-1246
County: Brazos FICE Identification: 003632
Unit ID: 228723
Telephone: (979) 845-2217 Carnegie Class: DU-Highest
FAX Number: (979) 845-5027 Calendar System: Semester
URL: www.tamu.edu
Established: 1876 Annual Undergrad Tuition & Fees (In-State): $11,870
Enrollment: 67,929 Coed
Affiliation or Control: State IRS Status: 501(c)3
Highest Offering: Doctorate

Accreditation: SC, CAATE, CLPSY, CONST, COPSY, DENT, DH, DIETD, DIETI, FEPAC, HSA, IPSY, LAW, LSAR, MED, NRPA, NURSE, PH, PLNG, SCPSY, SPAA, VET

02 President .... Mr. Michael K. YOUNG
05 Provost/Exec Vice President .... Dr. Carol A. FIERKE
03 SVP Health Science Center .... Dr. Carrie L. BYINGTON
10 EVP Finance & Operations/CFO .... Dr. Jerry STRAWSER
26 Sr VP Marketing/Communications .... Ms. Amy B. SMITH
13 Vice President IT & CIO .... Ms. M. Dee CHILDS
15 VP HR & Org Effectiveness .... Dr. Jeff RISINGER
32 Vice President Student Affairs .... Dr. Daniel J. PUGH, SR.
46 VP Research .... Dr. Mark A. BARTEAU
86 VP Govt Rels/Strategic Initiatives .... Mr. Michael O'QUINN
88 Dean/VP Innovation/Econ Development .. Dr. Andrew P. MORRISS
88 VP Brand & Business Dev .... Mr. Shane HINCKLEY
12 COO TAMU Galveston Campus .... Col. Michael E. FOSSUM
28 VP/Assoc Prov Diversity .... Dr. Robin R. MEANS COLEMAN
20 Vice Prov & Chief Intl Officer .... Dr. Michael BENEDIK
20 Vice Prov Acad Affairs & Strat Init .... Dr. Michael STEPHENSON
84 VP Enrollment & Acad Svcs .... Mr. Joseph P. PETTIBON, II
43 Deputy General Counsel .... Mr. Brooks MOORE
47 Dean Agriculture & Life Science .... Dr. Patrick J. STOVER
48 Dean Architecture .... Dr. Jorge VANEGAS
50 Dean Business .... Dr. Eli JONES
52 Dean Dentistry .... Dr. Lawrence E. WOLINSKY
53 Dean Education & Human Development .... Dr. Joyce M. ALEXANDER
54 Dean Engineering .... Dr. M. Katherine BANKS
65 Dean Geosciences .... Dr. Debbie THOMAS
80 Dean Govt & Public Service .... Gen. Mark A. WELSH, III
61 Dean Law .... Mr. Robert B. AHDIEH
49 Dean Liberal Arts .... Dr. Pamela R. MATTHEWS
63 Dean Medicine .... Dr. Carrie L. BYINGTON
66 Dean Nursing .... Dr. Nancy FAHRENWALD
67 Dean Pharmacy .... Dr. Indra K. REDDY
69 Interim Dean Public Health .... Dr. John AUGUST
81 Dean Science .... Dr. Valen E. JOHNSON
74 Dean Vet Med & Biomed Sciences .... Dr. Eleanor M. GREEN
08 Dean/Director Libraries .... Mr. David H. CARLSON
88 Dir Inst Biosciences & Tech .... Dr. Kenneth RAMOS
12 Dean & COO TAMU Qatar Campus .... Dr. Cesar MALAVE
20 Dean of Faculties/Assoc Prov .... Dr. Blanca LUPIANI
20 Assoc Prov Undergrad Studies .... Dr. Ann KENIMER
107 Assoc Prov Grad/Prof Studies .... Dr. Karen BUTLER-PURRY
84 Assoc VP Enrollment Management .... Mr. Lynn BARNES
37 Asst VP Scholarships & Fin Aid .... Ms. Delisa F. FALKS
06 Registrar .... Ms. Venesa A. HEIDICK
36 Exec Dir Career Center .... Ms. Samantha WILSON
14 Exec Dir Division of IT .... Mr. Pete MARCHBANKS
23 Director Student Health Center .... Dr. Martha C. DANNENBAUM
38 Exec Dir Student Counseling Svcs .... Dr. Mary Ann COVEY
39 Director Residence Life/Housing .... Ms. Chareny L. RYDL
92 Assistant Provost Honors Programs .... Dr. Sumana DATTA
104 Executive Director Study Abroad .... Dr. Holly HUDSON
09 Exec Dir Data & Research Svcs .... Dr. David J. MARTIN
102 President Texas A&M Foundation .... Mr. Tyson VOELKEL
29 Pres Assoc of Former Students .... Mr. Porter GARNER
19 Chief University Police .... Mr. J. Michael E. REAGAN
41 Athletic Director .... Mr. Ross BJORK
106 Asst Prov Academic Innovation .... Dr. Jocelyn WIDMER
20 Assoc Prov Acad Affs/Stdnt Success .... Dr. Timothy P. SCOTT

*Texas A & M University-Central Texas (A)

1001 Leadership Place, Killeen TX 76549
County: Bell Identification: 667086
Unit ID: 483036
Telephone: (245) 519-5400 Carnegie Class: Masters/M
FAX Number: (245) 519-5482 Calendar System: Semester
URL: www.tamuct.edu
Established: 1999 Annual Undergrad Tuition & Fees (In-State): N/A
Enrollment: 2,575 Coed
Affiliation or Control: State IRS Status: 501(c)3
Highest Offering: Master's
Accreditation: SC, ACBSP, CACREP, NURSE, SW

02 President .... Dr. Marc A. NIGLIAZZO
46 VP for Research and Economic Dev .... Dr. Russell PORTER
04 Administrative Asst to President .... Ms. Vicky FERGUSON
05 Chief Academic Officer .... Dr. Peg GRAY-VICKREY
07 Director Recruitment & Admissions .... Mr. Joshua SMITH
08 Head Librarian .... Ms. Bridgit MCCAFFERTY
09 Director of Institutional Research .... Mr. Paul TURCOTTE
10 Chief Business Officer .... Dr. Cynthia A. CARTER-HORN
13 Chief Info Technology Officer (CIO) .... Mr. Todd LUTZ
15 Director Human Resources .... Ms. Tina FLOREZ-NEVAREZ
22 Chief Compliance Officer .... Ms. Deserie MENSCH
111 Exec Dir Univ Comm/Advancement .... Dr. Karen CLOS
32 Chief Student Affairs/Student Life .... Dr. Brandon GRIGGS
36 Director Student Placement .... Ms. Heather WHEELER
37 Dir Student Financial Assistance .... Ms. Irene MONTALVO
50 Interim Dean of Business .... Dr. Lucas LOAFMAN
53 Dean of Education .... Dr. Edward HILL
49 Dean of Arts & Science .... Dr. Jerry JONES
06 Registrar .... Ms. Hannah MCDONALD
106 Dir Online Education/E-learning .... Dr. Richard SCHILKE
108 Director Institutional Assessment .... Mr. Paul TURCOTTE
19 Chief of Police .... Mr. Charles RODRIGUEZ
28 Director of Diversity .... Mr. Larry DAVIS
84 Director Enrollment Management .... Mr. Clifton JONES
96 Director of Purchasing .... Mr. Johnathan FUSELIER
38 Director Student Counseling .... Dr. Carmelia AMUNA
104 Chief Study Abroad Officer .... Dr. DeEadra ALBERT GREEN
90 Director Academic Computing .... Dr. Richard SCHILKE

*Texas A & M University - Commerce (B)

PO Box 3011, Commerce TX 75429-3011
County: Hunt FICE Identification: 003565
Unit ID: 224554
Telephone: (903) 886-5000 Carnegie Class: DU-Mod
FAX Number: (903) 886-5888 Calendar System: Semester
URL: www.tamuc.edu
Established: 1889 Annual Undergrad Tuition & Fees (In-State): $8,748
Enrollment: 13,244 Coed
Affiliation or Control: State IRS Status: 501(c)3
Highest Offering: Doctorate
Accreditation: SC, ART, CACREP, MUS, NURSE, SW

02 President & CEO .... Dr. Mark J. RUDIN
125 President Emeritus .... Dr. Ray M. KECK, III
125 President Emeritus .... Dr. Keith MCFARLAND
05 Provost & VP Academic Affairs .... Dr. John HUMPHREYS
10 VP Business & Administration .... Ms. Alicia CURRIN
111 VP Institutional Advancement .... Ms. Keturi DELONG
46 VP Research & Economic Development .... Ms. Cece GASSNER
100 Chief of Staff .... Ms. Linda KING
88 Chief Compliance Officer .... Ms. Heidi R. RICHARDS
41 Athletic Director .... Mr. Tim MCMURRAY
26 Exec Director Marketing & Comm .... Mr. Michael JOHNSON
20 Assoc Provost Academic Foundations .... Dr. Ricky DOBBS
21 Assoc VP Business Admin/Comptroller .... Ms. Paula HANSON
114 Assoc VP and Chief Budget Officer .... Ms. Tina LIVINGSTON
113 Bursar & Director Student Accounts .... Mr. Charles ROBNETT
06 Registrar .... Ms. Paige BUSSELL
88 Dir of Acct & Financial Reporting .... Ms. Sarah BAKER
08 Dean of Libraries .... Ms. Lanee DUNLAP
13 Chief Information Officer .... Mr. Tim MURPHY
37 Interim Dir Fin Aid & Scholarships .... Mr. Lester MCKENZIE
58 Dean Graduate School .... Dr. Jennifer SCHROEDER
53 Interim Dean Educ & Human Services .... Dr. Madeline JUSTICE
79 Dean Humanities/Social Sci & Art .... Dr. William KURACINA
54 Dean Science & Engineering .... Dr. Brent DONHAM
50 Dean Business .... Dr. Shanan GIBSON
47 Dean Agric & Natural Resources .... Dr. Randy HARP
92 Dean Honors College .... Dr. Ray GREEN
106 Dean College of Innovation & Design .... Dr. Yvonne VILLANUEVA-RUSSELL
09 Exec Dir Inst Effective & Research .... Dr. Dan SU
07 Director of Undergrad Admissions .... Mr. Jody TODHUNTER
88 Director of Academic Testing .... Dr. Hattie POWELL
32 Dean of Students .... Dr. Thomas NEWSOM
35 Assoc Dean Campus Life & Stdnt Dev .... Mr. Steve HIRST
29 Director of Alumni Relations .... Mr. Derryle PEACE
19 Chief of Police .... Mr. Bryan VAUGHN
12 Director Dallas and Frisco Campuses .... Ms. Araceli HILL
12 Director Metroplex Center .... Mr. Russell BLANCHETT
12 Director Navarro Partnership .... Ms. Virginia MONK
38 Director Counseling Center .... Dr. Nick PATRAS
39 Dir Residential Living & Learning .... Mr. Michael STARK
117 Dir of Campus Operations & Safety .... Mr. Ethan D. PREAS
23 Director Student Health Center ... Ms. Maxine MENDOZA-WELCH
85 Director International Programs .... Dr. Titilola ADEWALE
96 Chief Procurement Ofcr & HUB Coord .... Mr. Travis BALL
105 Web Application Developer .... Mr. Rick BARR
120 LMS Coordinator .... Mr. Brett MURREY
15 Chief Human Resources Officer .... Dr. Edward W. ROMERO
16 Assoc Director Human Resources .... Ms. Tammi THOMPSON
118 Sr Employee Benefits Rep .... Ms. Cindy TODHUNTER
18 Exec Dir Facilities Support Svcs .... Mr. Tony BRANDT
22 Title IX Coordinator .... Vacant
110 Assoc VP for Advancement .... Mr. Wyman WILLIAMS
30 Director Donor Relations .... Ms. Amber COUNTIS
44 Director Annual & Spons Programs .... Ms. Iris BEARE
110 Restricted Funds & Exec Gifts Admin .... Ms. Brenda MORRIS
109 Auxiliary Services Manager .... Ms. Jennifer PERRY
84 Interim VP Enrollment Management .... Dr. Lee YOUNG
36 Director Career Development .... Ms. Lacey HENDERSON
89 Dir First Year & Transition Program .... Ms. Kristen NEELEY
28 Dir Student Diversity & Inclusion .... Dr. Fred FUENTES
122 Director Fraternity & Sorority Life .... Ms. Amanda HORNE

*Texas A & M University - Corpus Christi (C)

6300 Ocean Drive, Corpus Christi TX 78412
County: Nueces FICE Identification: 011161
Unit ID: 224147
Telephone: (361) 825-5700 Carnegie Class: DU-Higher
FAX Number: (361) 825-5887 Calendar System: Semester
URL: www.tamucc.edu
Established: 1947 Annual Undergrad Tuition & Fees (In-State): $9,055
Enrollment: 12,232 Coed
Affiliation or Control: State IRS Status: 501(c)3
Highest Offering: Doctorate
Accreditation: SC, CAATE, CACREP, MT, MUS, NURSE

02 President/CEO .... Dr. Kelly M. QUINTANILLA
05 Provost & VP for Acad Affairs .... Dr. Clarenda PHILLIPS
10 Exec VP for Finance/Admin .... Ms. Jaclyn MAHLMANN
111 Acting VP Institutional Advancement .... Ms. Jaime NODARSE BARRERA
32 VP Student Engagement & Success .... Dr. Don ALBRECHT
46 VP for Research & Innovation .... Dr. Ahmed MAHDY
20 Assoc Provost .... Dr. Amy ALDRIDGE SANFORD
88 Project Manager IV .... Ms. Claire SNYDER
13 Sr Assoc VP for Technology/CIO .... Mr. Edward EVANS
84 VP Enrollment Management .... Mr. Andy BENOIT
35 Assoc VP Student Engagement .... Ms. Ann DEGAISH
08 Dean of University Libraries .... Dr. Catherine RUDOWSKY
09 Sr AVP Planning & Inst Research .... Dr. Katie BONTRAGER
26 Director of Marketing .... Ms. Ashley LARRABEE
30 Asst VP Development .... Ms. Kimberly BECERRA
20 Asst VP for Academic Affairs .... Mr. Michael RENDON
07 Exec Director of Admissions .... Mr. Oscar REYNA
37 Director of Financial Assistance .... Ms. Jeannie GAGE
31 Director Community Outreach .... Mr. Joseph MILLER
15 Director of Human Resources .... Ms. Debra CORTINAS
36 Director Career Services .... Ms. Terri HOWE
38 Exec Director Student Engagement .... Dr. Amanda DRUM
22 Dir Equal Opportunity Employee .... Mr. Sam RAMIREZ
11 Exec Dir Administrative Services .... Ms. Judy HARRAL
96 Dir Procurement & Disbursements .... Mr. Will HOBART
113 Bursar .... Ms. Christina HOLZHEUSER
58 Dean College of Grad Studies .... Dr. Karen MCCALEB
49 Dean College of Liberal Arts .... Dr. Mark HARTLAUB
50 Dean College of Business .... Dr. John E. GAMBLE
53 Dean College of Education .... Dr. Dean SCOTT
54 Dean College of Science & Engr .... Dr. Frank PEZOLD
66 Dean College of Nursing/Health Sci .... Dr. Julie HOFF
04 Admin Assistant to the President .... Ms. Peggy GAFFNEY
19 Director Environ Health & Safety .... Mr. Roy COONS
25 Manager Contracts .... Ms. Deborah ZENTMIRE
29 Exec Director of Alumni Relations .... Mr. Russell WAGNER
39 Manager Housing Business Operations .... Ms. Stephanie BOX
41 Athletic Director .... Mr. Jonathan PALUMBO

*Texas A & M University - Kingsville (D)

700 University Boulevard, Kingsville TX 78363-8202
County: Kleberg FICE Identification: 003639
Unit ID: 228705
Telephone: (361) 593-2111 Carnegie Class: DU-Higher
FAX Number: (361) 593-3107 Calendar System: Semester
URL: www.tamuk.edu
Established: 1925 Annual Undergrad Tuition & Fees (In-State): $8,922
Enrollment: 8,674 Coed
Affiliation or Control: State IRS Status: 501(c)3
Highest Offering: Doctorate
Accreditation: SC, DIETD, DIETI, MUS, NAIT, PHAR, SP, SW

02 President .... Dr. Mark A. HUSSEY
100 Chief of Staff II .... Mr. Randy HUGHES
43 Director of Risk & Compliance .... Ms. Karen B. ROYAL
05 Provost & Vice Pres Acad Affs .... Dr. George A. RASMUSSEN
32 Acting Director of Student Affairs .... Ms. Antonia ALVAREZ
10 VP Finance/Chief Financial Officer .... Mr. Jacob FLOURNOY
111 VP Institutional Advancement .... Mr. Bradley WALKER
21 Exec Director Financial Reporting .... Ms. Joanne MACIAS
117 Exec Director Risk Management .... Dr. Shane CREEL
36 Interim Director of Career Services .... Ms. Christina RODRIGUEZ-GONZALEZ
109 Director of Auxiliary Services .... Mr. Crispin TREVINO
88 Director of Recreational Sports .... Mr. Ian BROWN
84 VP Enrollment Management .... Dr. Maureen CROFT
13 Chief Information Officer .... Mr. Robert PAULSON
14 Assoc CIO .... Mr. Lonnie NAGEL
88 Dir Enterprise Applications .... Vacant
35 Assistant VP Student Affairs .... Ms. Kirsten COMPARY
20 Associate VP Academic Affairs .... Dr. Jaya S. GOSWAMI
85 Dir International Student Services .... Mr. Peter LI
58 Assoc VP Research & Grad Studies .... Dr. Allen RASMUSSEN
88 Associate VP Student Access .... Dr. Maria MARTINEZ
47 Dean College Agriculture .... Dr. Shad NELSON
49 Dean Arts & Sciences .... Dr. Dolores GUERRERO
50 Dean Business Administration .... Dr. Natalya DELCOURE
53 Interim Dean College of Education .... Dr. Steve BAIN
54 Dean Engineering .... Dr. Mohammad ALAM
121 Int Assoc VP for Student Success .... Dr. Shannon BAKER
26 Director Communications .... Ms. Adriana GARZA
08 Library Director .... Mr. Bruce R. SCHUENAMAN
09 Institutional Research Director .... Ms. Miao ZHUANG
88 Exec Director Citrus Center .... Dr. John DA GRACA
88 Director King Ranch Institute .... Dr. Clay P. MATHIS
88 Exec Dir Wildlife Research CKWRI .... Dr. David HEWITT
06 Registrar .... Ms. Mildred SLAUGHTER
07 Exec Director of Admissions .... Ms. Shelly KEY
29 Director Development and Alumni Rel .... Vacant
41 Exec Dir Athletics & Campus Rec .... Mr. Stephen ROACH
106 Int Exec Dir Distance Learning .... Mr. Rolando GARZA
110 Advancement Services Director .... Ms. Lori RUSSEK
23 Director Student Health Services .... Ms. Jo Elda CASTILLO-ALANIZ
88 Director John E Conner Museum .... Mr. Jonathan PLANT
15 Exec Dir Human Resources .... Mr. Henry BURGOS
18 Exec Director Physical Plant .... Mr. Andy GONZALEZ
96 Assoc VP Support Services .... Mr. Ralph STEPHENS
39 Exec Director Residence Life .... Mr. Tom MARTIN
46 Exec Dir Strategic Sourcing .... Ms. Maricelda ZARATE
35 Director Student Activities .... Ms. Erin MCCLURE
19 Chief of Police .... Mr. Felipe GARZA
37 Director Student Financial Aid .... Mr. Raul CAVAZOS
113 Exec Dir Student Accts & Bursar .... Mr. Carlos MARTINEZ
88 Bible Chair Baptist .... Mr. Mike CERVANTES

88 Bible Chair Catholic ..... Ms. Nina JOINER
04 Sr Exec Asst to President ..... Ms. Margarita M. GALVAN
104 Director Study Abroad ..... Mr. Peter LI
25 Exec Dir Research & Spons Programs ..... Vacant
86 Director Government Relations ..... Mr. Luis GONZALEZ

*Texas A & M University-San Antonio (A)

One University Way, San Antonio TX 78224
County: Bexar — Identification: 666689
Unit ID: 459949
Telephone: (210) 784-1000 — Carnegie Class: Masters/L
FAX Number: (210) 784-6219 — Calendar System: Semester
URL: www.tamusa.edu
Established: 2009 — Annual Undergrad Tuition & Fees (In-District): $8,656
Enrollment: 6,337 — Coed
Affiliation or Control: State/Local — IRS Status: 501(c)3
Highest Offering: Master's
Accreditation: SC

02 President ..... Dr. Cynthia TENIENTE-MATSON
05 Provost/VP Academic Affairs ..... Dr. Michael O'BRIEN
10 Vice Pres Finance/Administration ..... Dr. William SPINDLE
32 Vice President for Student Affairs ..... Dr. Melissa MAHAN
111 VP for University Advancement ..... Dr. Jeanette DEDIEMAR
84 VP for Enrollment Management ..... Dr. Brandy MCLELLAND
09 AVP of Institutional Effectiveness ..... Ms. Jane MIMS
50 Acting Dean College of Business ..... Dr. Kathleen VOGES
49 Dean College of Arts & Sciences ..... Dr. Mirley BALASUBRAMANYA
53 Dean College of Education & Devel ..... Dr. Carl SHEPERIS
100 Chief of Staff/Dir Pres Operation ..... Ms. Jessica LOUDERMILK
29 Director Alumni Affairs ..... Dr. Mary Kay COOPER
26 Exec Dir of Mktg/Communications ..... Mr. Cristian SANDOVAL
13 Chief Information Officer ..... Mr. William GRIFFENBERG
07 Director of Admissions ..... Ms. Melinda THOMAS
37 Dir of Financial Aid & Scholarships ..... Mr. Phillip RODGERS
06 Registrar ..... Ms. Rachel MONTEJANO
15 Chief Human Resources Officer ..... Ms. Martha GONZALEZ
18 Director of Facilities ..... Mr. Todd MOCABEE
38 Director of Counseling ..... Dr. Mary BUZZETTA
96 Dir Procurement/Auxiliary Services ..... Mr. Dan GARZA

*Texas A & M University - Texarkana (B)

7101 University Avenue, Texarkana TX 75503
County: Bowie — FICE Identification: 031703
Unit ID: 224545
Telephone: (903) 223-3000 — Carnegie Class: Masters/M
FAX Number: (903) 832-8890 — Calendar System: Semester
URL: www.tamut.edu
Established: 1971 — Annual Undergrad Tuition & Fees (In-State): $7,363
Enrollment: 2,066 — Coed
Affiliation or Control: State — IRS Status: 501(c)3
Highest Offering: Doctorate
Accreditation: SC, CACREP, NURSE

02 President ..... Dr. Emily FOURMY CUTRER
05 Provost/Vice Pres Academic Affairs ..... Dr. David YELLS
10 VP Finance & Administration ..... Mr. Jeff HINTON
30 Assoc VP University Advancement ..... Mrs. LeAnne WRIGHT
84 VP Student Engagement/Enrol/Success ..... Ms. Kathy WILLIAMS
100 Chief of Staff President's Office ..... Ms. Vicki MELDE
13 Chief Information Technology ..... Mr. Robert LEITGEB
32 Assistant VP of Student Affairs ..... Mr. Carl GREIG
121 Asst Vice Pres for Student Success ..... Mrs. Elizabeth PATTERSON
20 Assoc Provost/SACSCOC Liaison ..... Vacant
49 Dean Col Arts & Sciences/Education ..... Dr. Delbert DOUGHTY
50 Dean Col of Bus/Engineering/Tech ..... Dr. Gary STADING
114 Director of Budgets ..... Mrs. Ramona GREEN
21 Controller ..... Mrs. Jackie ELDER
37 Dir Financial Aid & Veteran Svcs ..... Mr. Michael FULLER
15 Director Human Resources & EEO ..... Ms. Charlotte BANKS
08 Director Library ..... Mrs. Teri STOVER
18 Director Physical Plant ..... Mr. Alan BEATTY
18 Police Chief/Director Security ..... Mr. Alex SERRANO
96 Director Purchasing ..... Mrs. Cynthia HENDERSON
07 Director of Admissions ..... Mr. Toney FAVORS
26 Director Communications ..... Mr. John BUNCH
104 Director of International Studies ..... Dr. Jennifer DAVIS
41 Director of Athletics ..... Mr. Michael GALVAN
04 Exec Admin Assistant to President ..... Ms. Loren LOFTIN
06 Registrar ..... Mrs. Jana BOATRIGHT
38 Director Student Counseling ..... Vacant
29 Alumni Relations Coordinator ..... Mr. Mark MISSILDINE

*West Texas A & M University (C)

2403 Russell C. Long Blvd., Canyon TX 79015
County: Randall — FICE Identification: 003665
Unit ID: 229814
Telephone: (806) 651-0000 — Carnegie Class: Masters/L
FAX Number: (806) 651-2126 — Calendar System: Semester
URL: www.wtamu.edu
Established: 1910 — Annual Undergrad Tuition & Fees (In-State): $7,935
Enrollment: 10,060 — Coed
Affiliation or Control: State — IRS Status: 501(c)3
Highest Offering: Doctorate
Accreditation: SC, MUS, NURSE, SP, SW, THEA

02 President ..... Dr. Walter V. WENDLER
05 Provost/Vice Pres Acad Affairs ..... Dr. Wade SHAFFER
10 Vice Pres for Business and Finance ..... Mr. Randy RIKEL
32 Vice Pres Student Enroll Eng & Succ ..... Mr. Michael J. KNOX
111 VP Philanthropy & Alumni Relations ..... Dr. Todd W. RASBERRY
28 Chief Diversity/Inclusion Officer ..... Ms. Angela ALLEN
100 Chief of Staff/Asst VP Strat Plng ..... Ms. Tracee POST
06 Registrar ..... Ms. Tana J. MILLER
07 Director of Admissions ..... Mr. Jeff S. BAYLOR
08 Dir Information/Library Resources ..... Ms. Shawna J. KENNEDY-WITTHAR
36 Dir Career Planning/Placement ..... Ms. Amber BLACK
37 Director Student Financial Aid ..... Ms. Marian K. GIESECKE
51 Dir Education on Demand ..... Ms. Andrea PORTER
23 Director Medical Service ..... Dr. Jim GIBBS
19 Police Chief ..... Chief Shawn G. BURNS
26 Exec Dir Comm Mktg & Events ..... Ms. Ann UNDERWOOD
29 Director of Alumni Relations ..... Ms. Becky STOGNER
38 Director Counseling Services ..... Ms. Dayna SCHERTLER
41 Director of Athletics ..... Mr. Michael MCBROOM
09 AVP Inst Research & Effectiveness ..... Mr. Jarvis D. HAMPTON
13 Chief Information Officer ..... Mr. James D. WEBB
96 Director of Purchasing ..... Vacant
40 Manager Bookstore ..... Mr. Terry S. NEPPER
15 Director Personnel Services ..... Ms. Nancy HAMPTON
47 Dean Col Agri/Natural Sciences ..... Dr. Kevin POND
50 Dean College of Business ..... Dr. Neil W. TERRY
53 Dean Col Education/Social Sciences ..... Dr. Eddie W. HENDERSON
57 Dean College Fine Arts/Humanities ..... Dr. Jessica MALLARD
54 Dean Col Eng/Comp Sci/Mathematics ..... Dr. Emily HUNT
46 VP for Research & Compliance ..... Dr. Angela SPAULDING
66 Dean College of Nursing/Health Sci ..... Dr. Dirk NELSON
104 Director Study Abroad ..... Ms. Carolina GALLOWAY

*Texas A & M University at Galveston (D)

PO Box 1675, Galveston TX 77553-1675
Telephone: (409) 740-4414 — FICE Identification: 010298
Accreditation: &SC

† Regional accreditation is carried under the parent institution Texas A & M University, College Station, TX.

Texas Baptist Institute and Seminary (E)

1300 Longview Drive, Henderson TX 75652
County: Rusk — Identification: 667363
Telephone: (903) 657-6543 — Carnegie Class: Not Classified
FAX Number: N/A — Calendar System: Quarter
URL: tbi.edu
Established: — Annual Undergrad Tuition & Fees: N/A
Enrollment: N/A — Coed
Affiliation or Control: Independent Non-Profit — IRS Status: 501(c)3
Highest Offering: Master's
Accreditation: @BI

01 President ..... Ray O. BROOKS

Texas Chiropractic College (F)

5912 Spencer Highway, Pasadena TX 77505-1699
County: Harris — FICE Identification: 003635
Unit ID: 228866
Telephone: (281) 487-1170 — Carnegie Class: Spec-4-yr-Other Health
FAX Number: (281) 487-2009 — Calendar System: Trimester
URL: www.txchiro.edu
Established: 1908 — Annual Undergrad Tuition & Fees: N/A
Enrollment: 263 — Coed
Affiliation or Control: Independent Non-Profit — IRS Status: 501(c)3
Highest Offering: Doctorate
Accreditation: SC, CHIRO

01 President ..... Dr. Stephen FOSTER
05 VP for Academic Affairs ..... Dr. John MROZEK
10 Chief Financial Officer ..... Vacant
11 VP of Administrative Services ..... Dr. Sandra HUGHES
111 Exec Dir of Institution Advancement ..... Ms. Monique LEWIS
32 Exec Director of Student Services ..... Ms. Kristina HANSON
63 Assoc VP of Clinics ..... Vacant
06 Registrar ..... Ms. Sarah TROTMAN
15 Director of Human Resources ..... Mrs. Sue ARNOLD
26 Director of Communications ..... Ms. Chelsea GRUNDEN
08 Director of Library Services ..... Ms. Carol WEBB
37 Director of Financial Aid ..... Mr. Arthur GOUDEAU
29 Development & Alumni Relations Coor ..... Ms. Toui NGO
07 Assistant Director of Admissions ..... Ms. Emery CARTER
101 Secretary of the Institution/Board ..... Mrs. Sue ARNOLD

Texas Christian University (G)

2800 S University Drive, Fort Worth TX 76129-2800
County: Tarrant — FICE Identification: 003636
Unit ID: 228875
Telephone: (817) 257-7000 — Carnegie Class: DU-Higher
FAX Number: (817) 257-7333 — Calendar System: Semester
URL: www.tcu.edu
Established: 1873 — Annual Undergrad Tuition & Fees: $46,950
Enrollment: 10,489 — Coed
Affiliation or Control: Christian Church (Disciples Of Christ) — IRS Status: 501(c)3
Highest Offering: Doctorate
Accreditation: SC, ANEST, ART, CAATE, CIDA, DANCE, DIETC, DIETD, JOUR, #MED, MUS, NURSE, SP, SW

01 Chancellor ..... Dr. Victor J. BOSCHINI, JR.
05 Provost/Vice Chanc Academic Affairs ..... Dr. Teresa ABI-NADER DAHLBERG
10 Vice Chanc Finance & Administration ..... Mr. Brian G. GUTIERREZ
111 Vice Chanc University Advancement ..... Mr. Donald J. WHELAN, JR.
32 Vice Chancellor Student Affairs ..... Dr. Kathryn CAVINS-TULL
26 Vice Chanc Mktg & Communication ..... Ms. Tracy SYLER-JONES
15 Vice Chancellor Human Resources ..... Ms. Yohna CHAMBERS
20 Vice Provost for Academic Affairs ..... Dr. Susan M. WEEKS
41 Director Athletics ..... Mr. Jeremiah DONATI
115 Chief Investment Officer ..... Mr. Jim HILLE
13 Chief Technology Officer ..... Mr. Bryan LUCAS
88 Chief University Compliance Officer ..... Ms. Andrea NORDMANN
100 Chief of Staff/Sec of the Board ..... Ms. Jean MRASEK
86 Chancellor's Intern/Govt Affairs ..... Ms. Lauren NIXON
29 Assoc Vice Chanc Alumni Relations ..... Ms. Amanda STALLINGS
110 Assoc Vice Chanc Advancement Ops ..... Mr. Travis SOYER
35 Assoc VC/Dean Student Development ..... Dr. Barbara B. HERMAN
35 Assoc Vice Chanc/Dean Campus Life ..... Dr. Michael RUSSEL
21 Interim Assoc VC & Controller ..... Ms. Kim ADAMS
16 Asst VC for Human Resources ..... Ms. Rachelle BLACKWELL
18 Assoc Vice Chanc for Facilities ..... Mr. Todd S. WALDVOGEL
44 Assoc VC Donor Relations ..... Ms. Julie WHITT
28 Sr Adv/Chief Incl Ofcr/Title IX ..... Mr. Darron TURNER
30 Assoc VC University Development ..... Mr. David NOLAN
88 Asst VC School & College Dev ..... Mr. Adam BAGGS
09 Assoc Provost Research/Dean Grad ..... Dr. Floyd L. WORMLEY, JR.
20 Assoc Provost Academic Plng/Budget ..... Ms. Megan M. SOYER
94 AVProvost/Dean Interdisc Stds ..... Dr. Karen STEELE
108 Asst Dir Inst Effectiveness ..... Dr. Christopher HIGHTOWER
49 Dean Addran College of Liberal Arts ..... Dr. Andrew SCHOOLMASTER
50 Dean Neeley School of Business ..... Mr. Daniel W. PULLIN
60 Dn Bob Schieffer Col Communication ..... Dr. Kristie BUNTON
53 Interim Dean College of Education ..... Dr. Jan LACINA
57 Interim Dean College of Fine Arts ..... Dr. Richard GIPSON
66 Dean Harris College of Nursing ..... Dr. Christopher WATTS
54 Dean Col of Science & Engineering ..... Dr. Phil HARTMAN
63 Dean School of Medicine ..... Dr. Stuart FLYNN
92 Dn John V Roach Honors College ..... Dr. Diane SNOW
08 Dean of the Library ..... Dr. June KOELKER
07 Dean of Admission ..... Mr. Heath A. EINSTEIN
22 Affirmative Action Officer ..... Dr. Cheryl TAYLOR
06 Registrar ..... Ms. Mary KINCANNON
19 Chief TCU Police ..... Mr. Steve G. MCGEE
42 Minister to the University ..... Rev. Angela KAUFMAN
110 Assoc VC Strategy/Advance Admin ..... Ms. Michelle CLARK
106 Asst Provost of Educ Tech/Fac Dev ..... Ms. Romana HUGHES
104 Dir Ctr Intl Studies/Study Abroad ..... Dr. Sandra CALLAGHAN
25 Director Contract Administration ..... Mr. Matthew WALLIS
16 Director Employee Relations ..... Ms. Kristen TAYLOR
51 Director Extended Education ..... Mr. David A. GREBEL
07 Director of Undergraduate Admission ..... Ms. Mandy CASTRO
88 Assoc Director Transfer Admission ..... Ms. April YANDELL
23 Director Health Services ..... Dr. Jane TORGERSON
09 Director Institutional Research ..... Dr. Cathan COGHLAN
24 Int Dir Instructional Services ..... Ms. Deana RAY
85 Director International Student Svcs ..... Mr. John L. SINGLETON
38 Director Mental Health Services ..... Dr. Eric WOOD
96 Asst Dir/Purchasing Agent ..... Mr. Roger D. FULLER
39 Director Housing & Residential Life ..... Mr. Craig ALLEN
37 Dir Scholarships & Financial Aid ..... Ms. Victoria CHEN
105 Dir Website Social Media Management ..... Mr. Corey REED
25 Director Sponsored Programs ..... Ms. LeAnn FORSBERG
36 Exec Dir Career Services ..... Mr. Mike CALDWELL
102 Sr Dir Corporate/Found Relations ..... Mr. Jason BYRNE
19 Asst Vice Chan Public Safety ..... Mr. Adrian ANDREWS
93 Asst Vice Chan Multicult/Intl ..... Dr. Mark KAMIMURA-JIMENEZ
43 General Counsel ..... Mr. Lee TYNER
84 Assoc Provost of Enrollment Manage ..... Mr. Mike SCOTT

Texas College (H)

2404 N Grand Avenue, Tyler TX 75702-1962
County: Smith — FICE Identification: 003638
Unit ID: 228884
Telephone: (903) 593-8311 — Carnegie Class: Bac-Diverse
FAX Number: (903) 593-0588 — Calendar System: Semester
URL: www.texascollege.edu
Established: 1894 — Annual Undergrad Tuition & Fees: $10,008
Enrollment: 992 — Coed
Affiliation or Control: Christian Methodist Episcopal — IRS Status: 501(c)3
Highest Offering: Baccalaureate
Accreditation: SC

01 President ..... Dr. Dwight FENNELL
05 Vice President Academic Affairs ..... Dr. Lisa TAYLOR
10 Vice Pres Business & Finance ..... Mr. James HARRIS
32 Vice Pres Student Affairs ..... Dr. Cynthia MARSHALL BIGGINS
84 Dean Enrollment Services ..... Mr. John ROBERTS
30 Development Officer ..... Vacant
42 Dean of Chapel/Campus Ministry ..... Dr. Jamie CAPERS
09 Dir Inst Research/Effectiveness ..... Dr. Cynthia MARSHALL-BIGGINS
08 Director of Library Services ..... Mrs. Linda SIMMONS-HENRY
13 Asst Dir Information Technology ..... Mr. Ocie FISHER
15 Director Human Resources ..... Ms. Lois BOWIE
41 Athletic Director ..... Ms. Elissia BURWELL
37 Director Financial Aid ..... Ms. Angela SPEECH
18 Director Physical Plant ..... Mr. Anthony PARKER

19 Director Security/Safety ..... Mr. Derrick BROWN
26 Coordinator Public Relations ..... Vacant
29 Coordinator Alumni Affairs ..... Vacant
04 Exec Asst to the President ..... Mrs. Angelia FENNELL
06 Registrar ..... Mr. John ROBERTS

Texas Health and Science University (A)

4005 Manchaca Road, Austin TX 78704-6737
County: Travis FICE Identification: 031795
Unit ID: 430704
Telephone: (512) 444-8082 Carnegie Class: Spec-4-yr-Other Health
FAX Number: (512) 444-6345 Calendar System: Trimester
URL: www.thsu.edu
Established: 1990 Annual Undergrad Tuition & Fees: N/A
Enrollment: 111 Coed
Affiliation or Control: Proprietary IRS Status: Proprietary
Highest Offering: Master's; No Lower Division
Accreditation: ACICS, ACUP

01 President ..... Dr. Louis AGNESE
88 VP of International ..... Mr. Wen Huei CHEN
58 VP/MBA Director ..... Dr. Shu-Chiang LIN
05 Academic Dean/Biomed Dir ..... Dr. Maoyi CAI
108 Assessment Dir/Assoc Dir DAOM ..... Ms. Marty CALLIHAM
37 Financial Aid/Intl Student Advisor ..... Mr. Antonio HOLLOWAY
32 Senior Admin/Dean of Students ..... Mrs. Wai Lan KUO
08 Administrative Coordinator ..... Mrs. Iris GONG
06 Registrar/Administrator ..... Ms. Priscilla ELIZONDO
20 Academic Dean/Dean of Students SA ..... Dr. Kai-Chang CHAN
08 Librarian ..... Mr. David SYLVIA
88 Clinic Director ..... Dr. Hai Tao CAO
88 Director of Herbal Department ..... Ms. Allison YU
88 Director of Acupuncture ..... Dr. Sung Wook HONG

† Granted candidacy at the Doctorate level by ACAOM.

Texas Lutheran University (B)

1000 W Court Street, Seguin TX 78155-5999
County: Guadalupe FICE Identification: 003641
Unit ID: 228981
Telephone: (830) 372-8000 Carnegie Class: Bac-Diverse
FAX Number: (830) 372-8096 Calendar System: Semester
URL: www.tlu.edu
Established: 1891 Annual Undergrad Tuition & Fees: $29,960
Enrollment: 1,394 Coed
Affiliation or Control: Evangelical Lutheran Church In America
IRS Status: 501(c)3
Highest Offering: Master's
Accreditation: SC, ACBSP, CAATE, MUS, NURSE

01 President ..... Dr. Debbie COTTRELL
05 Interim VP for Academic Affairs ..... Dr. Annette CITZLER
10 Vice President Finance ..... Mr. Andrew NELSON
84 VP for Enrollment and Marketing ..... Ms. Sarah STORY
30 VP for Development/Alumni Relations ..... Ms. Renee REHFELD
32 VP/Dean of Student Life & Learning ..... Ms. Kristi QUIROS
06 Director of Records & Registration ..... Mr. Glenn YOCKEY
08 Library Director ..... Ms. Martha RINN
113 Dir of Student Financial Services ..... Ms. Cathleen WRIGHT
42 Campus Pastor ..... Vacant
38 Director Counseling & Disabilities ..... Dr. Marlene MORIARITY
07 Director of Admissions ..... Ms. ALecia MCCAIN
15 Director of Human Resources ..... Ms. Toi TURNER
41 Director of Athletics ..... Mr. Bill MILLER
09 Director of Institutional Research ..... Ms. Jean CONSTABLE
04 Exec Assistant to the President ..... Ms. Susan RINN
101 Secretary of the Institution/Board ..... Ms. Susan RINN
102 Dir Foundation/Corporate Relations ..... Mr. Sam EHRLICH
104 Director Study Abroad ..... Ms. Charla BAILEY
26 Director of Marketing ..... Ms. Ashlie FORD
108 Director of Academic Assessment ..... Dr. Michael CZUCHRY
13 Chief Info Technology Officer (CIO) ..... Mr. William SENTER
18 Chief Facilities/Physical Plant ..... Mr. Kirk HERBOLD
19 University Police Chief ..... Chief Irene GARCIA
29 Director Alumni Relations ..... Ms. Taylor CARLETON
39 Director of Residence Life ..... Mr. Eric BOOTH
44 Director Annual Giving ..... Ms. Taylor CARLETON
22 Dir Affirm Action/EEO/Diversity ..... Ms. Toi TURNER
43 Dir Legal Services/General Counsel ..... Mr. James FROST
28 Chair Diversity Committee ..... Dr. Corinne CASTRO
50 Chair Business & Econ Department ..... Dr. Fernando GARZA
53 Chair Education Department ..... Dr. Jeannette JONES

Texas Southern University (C)

3100 Cleburne Street, Houston TX 77004-4584
County: Harris FICE Identification: 003642
Unit ID: 229063
Telephone: (713) 313-7011 Carnegie Class: DU-Higher
FAX Number: (713) 313-1092 Calendar System: Semester
URL: www.tsu.edu
Established: 1927 Annual Undergrad Tuition & Fees (In-State): $9,173
Enrollment: 10,237 Coed
Affiliation or Control: State IRS Status: 170(c)1
Highest Offering: Doctorate
Accreditation: SC, CAEPN, CAHIIM, COARC, #DIETD, LAW, MT, NAIT, PHAR, PLNG, SPAA, SW

01 President ..... Dr. Austin A. LANE
05 Provost/VP Academic Affairs ..... Dr. Kendall HARRIS
10 Vice President for Admin & Finance ..... Mr. Kenneth HUEWITT
111 Vice Pres University Advancement ..... Ms. Melinda SPAULDING
100 Chief of Staff ..... Ms. Heidi SMITH
43 General Counsel ..... Mr. Hao LE
41 VP Intercollegiate Athletics ..... Mr. Kevin GRANGER
32 VP Student Svcs/Dean of Students ..... Vacant
09 Int Assoc Provost/Assoc VP Research ..... Dr. Adebayo O. OYEKAN
88 Dir Title III & Ofc of Sponsored Pr ..... Ms. Demetria JOHNSON-WEEKS
15 Sr Assoc VP of Human Resources ..... Ms. Yolanda EDMOND
26 Assoc VP of Communications ..... Mr. Steve SCHEFFLER
84 Assoc VP Enrollment Management ..... Mr. Wendell WILLIAMS
06 University Registrar ..... Ms. Marilyn C. SQUARE
08 Exec Director Libraries/Museums ..... Dr. Janice L. PEYTON
50 Int Dean School of Business ..... Dr. John H. WILLIAMS
51 Int Dir Office of Cont Education ..... Dr. Melanie LAWSON
53 Dean College of Education ..... Dr. Lillian B. POATS
80 Dean School of Public Affairs ..... Dr. Theophilus HERRINGTON
61 Acting Dean School of Law ..... Dr. Gary L. BLEDSOE
67 Int Dean Col Pharmacy & Health Sci ..... Dr. Shirlette MILTON
72 Int Dean College of Science/Tech ..... Dr. John B. SAPP
60 Dean School of Communications ..... Dr. Maurice ODINE
19 Chief of Police ..... Chief Mary YOUNG
39 Director of Student Housing ..... Ms. Yvette BARKER
92 Dean Freeman Honors College ..... Dr. Dianne JEMISON-POLLARD
96 Exec Dir Procurement Services ..... Mr. Gregory G. WILLIAMS
18 Exec Director Facilities & Maint ..... Vacant
13 Chief Information Officer ..... Mr. Mario BERRY
58 Dean Graduate School ..... Dr. Gregory H. MADDOX
21 Exec Dir of Business Svcs ..... Mr. Charles E. HENRY
21 Controller ..... Ms. Christina ORDONEZ-CAMPOS
124 Dir Acad Ret Svcs Spec Asst/Provost ..... Ms. Lori A. LABRIE
114 Exec Director Budget ..... Mr. Elias HAILU
108 Exec Dir Inst Assess/Plng/Effect ..... Dr. Rajanel CROCKEM
29 Exec Dir Alumni Rels/Spec Events ..... Ms. Connie L. COCHRAN
88 Director of Scholarships ..... Ms. Cynthia LEE
20 Associate Dean for Academic Affairs ..... Dr. Bernnell PELZIER-GLAZE
90 Senior Academic Technology Officer ..... Mr. Darnell JOSEPH
88 Associate Director of QEP Office ..... Dr. Arbolina L. JENNINGS
106 Dir Online Education/E-learning ..... Vacant
37 Director Student Financial Aid ..... Ms. Linda BALLARD
86 Director of Governmental Relations ..... Mr. Dominique CALHOUN
04 Administrative Asst to President ..... Ms. Regina WILLIAMS

Texas Southmost College (D)

80 Fort Brown, Brownsville TX 78520-4993
County: Cameron FICE Identification: 003643
Unit ID: 227377
Telephone: (956) 295-3600 Carnegie Class: Assoc/MT-VT-High Non
FAX Number: (956) 295-3384 Calendar System: Semester
URL: www.tsc.edu
Established: 1926 Annual Undergrad Tuition & Fees (In-District): $3,198
Enrollment: 6,216 Coed
Affiliation or Control: State/Local IRS Status: 501(c)3
Highest Offering: Associate Degree
Accreditation: SC, DMS, EMT, MLTAD

01 President ..... Dr. Jesus R. RODRIGUEZ
05 Vice President of Instruction ..... Dr. Joanna KILE
10 Vice Pres of Finance/Administration ..... Dr. Gisela FIGUEROA
111 Vice Pres of Inst Advancement ..... Vacant
20 Assoc VP of Instruction/Acad Svcs ..... Dr. Angelica M. FUENTES
81 Dean of STEM and CTE ..... Dr. Murad ABUSALIM
79 Dean of Humanities ..... Dr. Brian MCCORMACK
76 Dean of Health Professions ..... Dr. Jaime TUCKER
07 Exec Dir of Admissions & Records ..... Ms. Vanessa VASQUEZ
09 Exec Director of IR & Compliance ..... Mr. Oscar O. HERNANDEZ
106 Dir Educ Technology & Online Lrng ..... Ms. Antonia SALDIVAR
13 Vice President of Information Tech ..... Mr. Luis VILLARREAL
15 Chief Human Resources Officer ..... Ms. Lissa FRAUSTO
25 Coord Sponsored Pgms/Grants Ctr ..... Dr. Leonor BARRERA
32 Exec Director of Student Life ..... Mr. Armando PONCE
18 Exec Dir Facilities/Physical Plant ..... Mr. Ariel DE LA FUENTE
36 Coord Transfer/Career & Employ Svcs ..... Mr. Rene VALDEZ
37 Director Student Financial Aid ..... Vacant
96 Coordinator of Purchasing ..... Ms. Patricia SALDIVAR
04 Administrative Asst to the Pres ..... Ms. Maria HERNANDEZ

Texas State Technical College Waco (E)

3801 Campus Drive, Waco TX 76705-1695
County: McLennan FICE Identification: 003634
Unit ID: 487320
Telephone: (254) 867-4893 Carnegie Class: Assoc/HVT-Mix Trad/Non
FAX Number: (254) 867-3973 Calendar System: Semester
URL: www.tstc.edu
Established: 1965 Annual Undergrad Tuition & Fees (In-State): $5,570
Enrollment: 12,717 Coed
Affiliation or Control: State IRS Status: 501(c)3
Highest Offering: Associate Degree
Accreditation: SC, CAHIIM, DH, EMT, SURGT

01 Chancellor ..... Mr. Mike REESER
05 Provost Waco ..... Mr. Adam C. HUTCHISON
11 VC/Chief Academic Officer ..... Mr. Jeff KILGORE
86 VC/Chief Govt Affairs Officer ..... Mr. Roger MILLER
10 VC/Chief Financial Officer ..... Mr. Jonathan HOEKSTRA
100 VC/Chief of Staff to the Chancellor ..... Mrs. Gail LAWERENCE
32 VC/Chief Student Services Officer ..... Mr. Rick HERRERA
43 VC/Chief Legal Officer ..... Mr. Ray RUSHING
88 VC/Chief Policy Officer ..... Mr. Michael A. BETTERSWORTH
12 Provost Fort Bend County ..... Mr. Randall WOOTEN
12 Provost Harlingen ..... Ms. Cledia HERNANDEZ
12 Provost Marshall ..... Mr. Barton DAY
12 Provost West Texas ..... Mr. Rick DENBOW
12 Provost North Texas ..... Mr. Marcus BALCH
12 Provost Williamson County ..... Mr. Edgar PADILLA
04 Exec Assistant to the Chancellor ..... Ms. Jennifer TINDELL
06 Registrar ..... Ms. Maria ARREDONDO
15 Associate VC Human Resources ..... Ms. Pamela MAYFIELD
18 Chief Facilities/Physical Plant Ofc ..... Mr. Ray FRIED
102 CEO TSTC Foundation ..... Ms. Beth WOOTEN
101 Secretary of the Institution/Board ..... Mr. Ray RUSHING
19 Police & Safety Commissioner ..... Mr. Aurelio TORRES
36 Exec Director Student Placement ..... Ms. Kacey DARNELL
37 Director Student Financial Aid ..... Ms. Jackie ADLER
96 Senior Exec Director of Purchasing ..... Ms. Melinda BOYKIN

*The Texas State University System (F)

601 Colorado Street, Austin TX 78701-2904
County: Travis FICE Identification: 033442
Telephone: (512) 463-1808 Carnegie Class: N/A
FAX Number: N/A
URL: www.tsus.edu

01 Chancellor ..... Brian MCCALL
05 Vice Chanc Academic & Health Affs ..... John HAYEK
43 Vice Chanc & General Counsel ..... Fernando C. GOMEZ
10 Vice Chancellor and CFO ..... Daniel HARPER
86 Vice Chanc Government Relations ..... Sean CUNNINGHAM
26 Deputy Vice Chanc Mktg & Comm ..... Mike WINTEMUTE
116 Chief Audit Executive ..... Carole M. FOX
11 Director of Administration ..... Laura TIBBITTS

*Lamar Institute of Technology (G)

PO Box 10043, Beaumont TX 77710-0043
County: Jefferson FICE Identification: 036273
Unit ID: 441760
Telephone: (409) 880-8321 Carnegie Class: Assoc/HVT-High Trad
FAX Number: (409) 813-1844 Calendar System: Semester
URL: www.lit.edu
Established: 1995 Annual Undergrad Tuition & Fees (In-State): $4,743
Enrollment: 2,983 Coed
Affiliation or Control: State IRS Status: 501(c)3
Highest Offering: Associate Degree
Accreditation: SC, CAHIIM, COARC, DH, DMS, EMT, RAD

02 President ..... Dr. Lonnie HOWARD
05 Executive Vice President/Provost ..... Dr. Kerry MIX
10 Chief Business and Financial Office ..... Ms. Bonnie ALBRIGHT
15 Vice President for Human Resources ..... Mrs. Catherine BLANCHARD
45 Vice Pres Strategic Initiative ..... Mr. David MOSLEY
103 Dean Strategic & Workforce Init ..... Ms. Miranda PHILLIPS
37 Director of Financial Aid ..... Ms. Linda KORNS
13 Int Director Information Technology ..... Mr. Samuel DOCKENS
30 Exec Dir Devel/Dir LIT Foundation ..... Mr. Pat CALHOUN
26 Dir Marketing & Communication ..... Mr. Chris ELLIOTT
18 Interim Maintenance Coordinator ..... Ms. Dawna WHITMIRE
04 Exec Assistant to the President ..... Ms. Judy HOFFPAUIR
06 Registrar ..... Mr. David SHORT

*Lamar University (H)

PO Box 10001, Beaumont TX 77710-0009
County: Jefferson FICE Identification: 003581
Unit ID: 226091
Telephone: (409) 880-7011 Carnegie Class: DU-Mod
FAX Number: (409) 880-8404 Calendar System: Semester
URL: www.lamar.edu
Established: 1923 Annual Undergrad Tuition & Fees (In-State): $8,373
Enrollment: 14,506 Coed
Affiliation or Control: State IRS Status: 501(c)3
Highest Offering: Doctorate
Accreditation: SC, ACFEI, ART, AUD, CACREP, CAEPN, CONST, DIETD, DIETI, MUS, NUR, SP, SW

02 President ..... Dr. Kenneth R. EVANS
05 Provost/Vice Pres Academic Affairs ..... Dr. James W. MARQUART
10 Vice Pres Finance/Operations ..... Mr. Edward Craig NESS
111 Vice Pres University Advancement ..... Mr. Juan ZABALA
13 Vice Pres Information Technology ..... Ms. Priscilla PARSONS
20 Acting Associate Provost ..... Dr. Joseph E. NORDGREN
106 Vice Provost for Digital Learning ..... Dr. Brenda NICHOLS
15 Assoc Vice Pres Human Resources ..... Ms. Catherine BENSON
18 Interim AVP Facilities Mgmt ..... Mr. David MARTIN
21 Assoc Vice Pres Finance/Controller ..... Ms. Jamie LARSON
58 Dean of Graduate Studies ..... Dr. William HARN
49 Dean College Arts & Sciences ..... Dr. Lynn MAURER
50 Dean College of Business ..... Dr. Dan FRENCH
53 Dean College of Educ & Human Devel ..... Dr. Robert SPINA
54 Dean College of Engineering ..... Dr. Brian CRAIG
57 Dean College of Fine Arts & Comm ..... Dr. Derina HOLTZHAUSEN
08 Interim VP Library Sciences ..... Dr. Arne ALMQUIST
06 Registrar ..... Mr. David SHORT, JR.
88 Assoc Provost of Distance Learning ..... Dr. Paula NICHOLS
20 Director Strategic Implementation ..... Vacant

30 Director of Development ... Vacant
09 Director Institutional Research ... Dr. Gregory MARSH
36 Assoc Dir Career Services ... Ms. Angela THOMAS
23 Director Health Services ... Ms. Shawn GRAY
19 Chief University Police ... Mr. Hector FLORES
26 Director of Public Affairs ... Ms. Shelly VITANZA
29 Director Alumni Relations ... Ms. Shannon FIGUEROA
37 Exec Director Student Financial Aid ... Ms. Carly BROUSSARD
96 Director of Purchasing ... Ms. Stacy CARTER-ELIZONDO
07 Director of Admissions ... Vacant
100 Chief of Staff ... Mr. Dean M. TERREBONNE

*Lamar State College-Orange (A)

410 Front Street, Orange TX 77630-5802
County: Orange FICE Identification: 023582
Unit ID: 226107
Telephone: (409) 883-7750 Carnegie Class: Assoc/HVT-Mix Trad/Non
FAX Number: (409) 882-3374 Calendar System: Semester
URL: www.lsco.edu
Established: 1969 Annual Undergrad Tuition & Fees (In-State): $4,370
Enrollment: 2,293 Coed
Affiliation or Control: State IRS Status: 501(c)3
Highest Offering: Associate Degree
Accreditation: SC

02 President ... Dr. Thomas A. JOHNSON
05 Executive VP/Provost ... Dr. Al BARRINGER
10 CFO ... Mrs. Mary WICKLAND
32 VP Student Svcs & Auxiliary Ent ... Mr. Brian HULL
08 Director of Library Services ... Ms. Mary MCCOY
06 Registrar ... Mrs. Becky J. MCANELLEY
37 Director Student Financial Aid ... Mr. Kerry J. OLSON
15 Human Resources Director ... Ms. Sherrie WILLOUGHBY
18 Director of Physical Plant ... Mr. Charles MITCHELL
13 Coord Information Resources ... Ms. Linda G. BURNETT
09 Coordinator Institutional Research ... Dr. Hunter KEENEY
25 Contracts/Grants Administrator ... Mrs. Mary WICKLAND
72 Dean of Technical Studies ... Ms. Gina A. SIMAR
20 Associate Dean of Academic Studies ... Dr. Suzonne CROCKETT
49 Dean of Liberal Arts ... Dr. Gwen WHITEHEAD
96 Director of Purchasing ... Ms. Maria GARCIA

*Lamar State College-Port Arthur (B)

1500 Procter Street, Port Arthur TX 77640-6604
County: Jefferson FICE Identification: 023485
Unit ID: 226116
Telephone: (409) 983-4921 Carnegie Class: Assoc/HVT-High Trad
FAX Number: (409) 984-6032 Calendar System: Semester
URL: www.lamarpa.edu
Established: 1909 Annual Undergrad Tuition & Fees (In-State): $6,013
Enrollment: 2,293 Coed
Affiliation or Control: State IRS Status: 501(c)3
Highest Offering: Associate Degree
Accreditation: SC, SURGT

02 President ... Dr. Betty REYNARD
05 Vice President Academic Affairs ... Dr. Pamela MILLSAP
10 Vice President Finance & Operations ... Ms. Mary WICKLAND
32 Dean of Student Services ... Dr. Deborrah HEBERT
04 Admin Assistant to the President ... Mrs. Donna SCHION
08 Dean Library Services ... Ms. Helena GAWU
06 Registrar ... Ms. Robin HUMPHREY
37 Director Financial Aid ... Ms. Sharon THIBODEAUX
45 Director Inst Effectiveness ... Mr. James M. KNOWLES
18 Director of Physical Plant ... Mr. Warren S. ODOM
26 Public Information Officer ... Mr. Gerry DICKERT
56 Dir External Learning Experiences ... Dr. Gary STRETCHER
13 Dir Information Technology Services ... Mr. Samir GHORAYEB
15 Director Human Resources ... Ms. Tammy RILEY
09 Director of Institutional Research ... Mrs. Petra UZORUO
103 Dean Workforce/Continuing Educ Pgms ... Dr. Ben STAFFORD
72 Dean Technical Programs ... Ms. Shelia TRAHAN
97 Dept Head Gen Ed & Developmental ... Dr. Michelle DAVIS
50 Dept Head Business & Technology ... Mrs. Sheila GUILLOT
39 Director Student Housing ... Dr. Deborrah HEBERT
41 Athletic Director ... Mr. Scott STREET
96 Director of Purchasing/Contracts ... Mrs. Maria GARCIA
76 Dept Head Allied Health ... Ms. Shirley MACNEILL
64 Dept Head Commercial Music ... Mr. John FREYERMUTH
84 Director Enrollment Services ... Mr. David MORALES

*Sam Houston State University (C)

1806 Avenue J, Suite 303, Huntsville TX 77340-0001
County: Walker FICE Identification: 003606
Unit ID: 227881
Telephone: (936) 294-1111 Carnegie Class: DU-Mod
FAX Number: (936) 294-1465 Calendar System: Semester
URL: www.shsu.edu
Established: 1879 Annual Undergrad Tuition & Fees (In-State): $8,296
Enrollment: 20,938 Coed
Affiliation or Control: State IRS Status: Exempt
Highest Offering: Doctorate
Accreditation: SC, ART, CAATE, CACREP, CAEPN, CIDA, CLPSY, DIETD, DIETI, FEPAC, MUS, NURSE, THEA

02 President ... Dr. Dana G. HOYT
05 Provost/VPAA ... Dr. Richard EGLSAER
10 VP for Finance & Operations ... Dr. Carlos HERNANDEZ
111 VP for University Advancement ... Mr. Frank HOLMES
84 VP for Enrollment Management ... Dr. Heather THIELEMANN
32 VP for Student Affairs ... Mr. Frank PARKER
13 VP for Information Technology ... Mr. Mark ADAMS
41 Athletic Director ... Mr. Bobby WILLIAMS
100 Chief of Staff ... Ms. Kathy GILCREASE
20 Vice Provost ... Dr. Chris MAYNARD
58 Dean Graduate Studies ... Dr. Ken HENDRICKSON
25 Assoc VP Research/Sponsored Program ... Dr. Chad HARGRAVE
106 Assoc VP Distance Learning ... Dr. William ANGROVE
21 Asst VP Finance & Operations ... Ms. Sylvia RAPPE
18 Assoc VP Facilities Management ... Mr. Juan NUNEZ
15 Assoc VP for HR & Risk Management ... Mr. David HAMMONDS
26 Assoc VP Marketing & Comm ... Ms. Kris KASKEL-RUIZ
30 Assoc VP for Development ... Ms. Thelma MOONEY
88 Assoc VP Enrollment Management ... Vacant
35 Assoc VP Student Affairs/Rec Sports ... Dr. Keith JENKINS
14 Assoc VP Infrustructure/Support Svc ... Mr. Terrance HARRIS
105 Assoc VP Enterprise Services ... Dr. Judith LEWIS
09 Asst VP Institutional Effectiveness ... Ms. Donna ARTHO
50 Dean of Business Administration ... Dr. Mitchell MUEHSAM
61 Dean of Criminal Justice ... Dr. Phillip LYONS
53 Dean of Education ... Dr. Stacey EDMONSON
57 Dean of Arts & Media ... Dr. Ronald SHIELDS
83 Dean of Humanities/Social Sciences ... Dr. Abbey ZINK
81 Dean of Sciences ... Dr. John PASCARELLA
76 Dean of Health Sciences ... Dr. Rodney RUNYAN
63 Dean of Osteopathic Medicine ... Dr. Charles HENLEY
08 Executive Director Library Services ... Mr. Eric OWEN
19 Director Public Safety Services ... Mr. Kevin MORRIS
06 Registrar ... Ms. Teresa RINGO
07 Director Undergraduate Admissions ... Ms. Angie TAYLOR
37 Director Financial Aid ... Ms. Lydia HALL
39 Director Residence Life ... Ms. Joellen TIPTON
17 AVP SA/Student Hlth & Couns Center ... Dr. Drew MILLER
29 Director Alumni Relations ... Mr. Charlie VIENNE
35 Dean of Students ... Mr. John YARABECK
108 Assoc VP Planning & Assessment ... Dr. Somer FRANKLIN
43 Dir Legal Services/General Counsel ... Ms. Rhonda BEASSIE
21 Controller ... Ms. Amanda WITHERS
88 Treasurer ... Vacant
114 Director of University Budget ... Mr. Edgar SMITH
110 Director Advancement Services ... Ms. Patricia LEWIS
88 Museum Director ... Mr. Mac WOODWARD
88 Asst VP Enrollment Management ... Ms. Leah MULLIGAN
35 Asst VP Student Affairs ... Dr. Kristy VIENNE
35 Director of Student Activities ... Mr. Brandon COOPER
88 Dir Stdnt Affairs Finance & Budget ... Ms. Lynn CLOPTON
28 Dir Equity & Inclusion & Title IX ... Ms. Jeanine BIAS
88 Dir of Leadership Initiatives ... Ms. Meredith CONREY
90 Assoc VP Client Services ... Mr. Terry BLAYLOCK
88 Director IT Project Management ... Ms. Linda MCINTOSH
119 Director Information Security ... Mr. Steven FREY
88 Director IT Finance & Budget ... Ms. Deborah MCKERALL

*Sul Ross State University (D)

PO Box C-100, Alpine TX 79832-0001
County: Brewster FICE Identification: 003625
Unit ID: 228501
Telephone: (432) 837-8011 Carnegie Class: Masters/L
FAX Number: (432) 837-8334 Calendar System: Semester
URL: www.sulross.edu
Established: 1917 Annual Undergrad Tuition & Fees (In-State): $6,816
Enrollment: 2,946 Coed
Affiliation or Control: State IRS Status: 501(c)3
Highest Offering: Master's
Accreditation: SC, NURSE

02 President ... Dr. Bill KIBLER
05 Exec VP Academic/Provost ... Dr. Jim CASE
10 Vice Pres for Finance & Operations ... Mr. Cesario E. VALENZUELA
84 Vice Pres Enrollment Management ... Dr. Allison HARRIS
30 Assoc Vice Pres University Services ... Mr. Leo G. DOMINGUEZ
12 Rio Grande College Dean ... Dr. Veronica MENDEZ MAQUEO
11 Director of Administration ... Ms. Yvonne REALIVASQUEZ
06 Director Records & Registration ... Ms. Pamela S. PIPES
08 Dean Library & Info Technology ... Ms. April AULTMAN BECKER
32 Dean of Students ... Mr. Leo DOMINGUEZ
92 Dir Honors Prog/Acad Ctr Excellence ... Dr. Kathy STEIN
26 Director News & Publications ... Mr. Stephen W. LANG
37 Dir Financial Assistance ... Mr. Mickey CORBETT
49 Dean Arts & Science ... Dr. Jay DOWNING
107 Dean Education & Professional Stds ... Vacant
47 Dean Agricult/Natural Resource Sci ... Dr. Robert J. KINUCAN
15 Director of Human Resources ... Mrs. Karlin DEVOLL
18 Asst Director of Physical Plant ... Mr. Edmundo NATERA
19 Director Dept of Public Safety ... Mr. Kent DUNEGAN
21 Director of Accounting Services ... Mr. Santiago CASTILLO
39 Director Residential Living ... Mr. Bradley GWATNEY
41 Director of Athletics ... Mr. Bobby S. MESKER
38 Director of Counseling Ctr ... Ms. Mary SCHWARTZE
13 Chief Information Officer ... Mr. David W. GIBSON
96 Director of Purchasing ... Mr. Noe HERNANDEZ
88 Dir Center for Big Bend Studies ... Mr. Andy CLOUD
29 Director Alumni Relations ... Ms. Aida LUEVANOS
88 Director of Upward Bound ... Ms. Barbara VEGA
88 Director of University Archives ... Ms. Melleta BELL
88 Director Small Business Devel Ctr ... Ms. Patricia K. LONG
88 Law Enforcement Academy Coord ... Ms. Clariza PINA
07 Director Admissions & Records ... Ms. Claudia WRIGHT
88 Mail Service Supervisor ... Ms. Leticia GONZALES
116 Internal Auditor ... Mr. Scott A. CUPP
36 Coord Career Services & Testing ... Ms. Jan L. RUEB
09 Dir of Institutional Effectiveness ... Dr. Jeanne QVARNSTROM

*Texas State University (E)

601 University Drive, San Marcos TX 78666-4615
County: Hays FICE Identification: 003615
Unit ID: 228459
Telephone: (512) 245-2111 Carnegie Class: DU-Higher
FAX Number: (512) 245-3040 Calendar System: Semester
URL: www.txstate.edu
Established: 1899 Annual Undergrad Tuition & Fees (In-State): $10,280
Enrollment: 38,666 Coed
Affiliation or Control: State IRS Status: 170(c)1
Highest Offering: Doctorate
Accreditation: SC, CAATE, CACREP, CAEPT, CAHIIM, CEA, CIDA, COARC, CONST, DIETD, DIETI, HSA, IPSY, JOUR, MT, MUS, NRPA, NURSE, PTA, RTT, SP, SPAA, SW

02 President ... Dr. Denise M. TRAUTH
05 Provost/Vice Pres Academic Affairs ... Dr. Gene BOURGEOIS
100 Special Assistant to the President ... Dr. Lisa LLOYD
32 Vice President Student Affairs ... Dr. Joanne H. SMITH
10 Vice Pres Finance/Support Services ... Mr. Eric ALGOE
111 Vice Pres University Advancement ... Dr. Barbara BREIER
13 Vice Pres Information Technology ... Mr. Kenneth PIERCE
83 Dean College of Applied Arts ... Dr. T. Jaime CHAHIN
50 Dean McCoy Col of Business Admin ... Dr. Denise T. SMART
57 Dean College Fine Arts & Comm ... Dr. John FLEMING
53 Dean College of Education ... Dr. Michael O'MALLEY
76 Dean College Health Professions ... Dr. Ruth B. WELBORN
83 Dean College Liberal Arts ... Dr. Mary BRENNAN
81 Dean College of Science & Engr ... Dr. Christine HAILEY
58 Dean The Graduate College ... Dr. Andrea GOLATO
97 Dean Univ Col & Dir PACE Center ... Dr. Daniel BROWN
92 Dean Honors College ... Dr. Heather GALLOWAY
20 Assoc Vice Pres Academic Affairs ... Dr. Vedaraman SRIRAMAN
15 Asst VP of Human Resources ... Mr. John E. MCBRIDE
20 Associate Provost ... Dr. Debbie M. THORNE
18 Associate VP of Facilities ... Mr. Thomas F. SHEWAN
46 Assoc VP Research & Dir of Fed Rels ... Dr. Walter E. HORTON
35 Assoc VP Stdnt Affs/Dean of Stdnt ... Dr. Margarita M. ARELLANO
20 Assoc Vice Pres for Inst Effective ... Dr. Beth E. WUEST
21 Assoc VP Financial Services ... Mr. Darryl BORGONAH
84 Assoc VP Enroll Mgmt/Marketing ... Mr. Gary T. RAY
08 Associate VP University Library ... Ms. Joan L. HEATH
20 Assistant VP for Academic Services ... Dr. Mary Ellen CAVITT
38 Interim Director Counseling Center ... Dr. Heather A. AIDALA
07 AVP Enroll Mgmt/Dir Undergrad Admis ... Ms. Stephanie ANDERSON
28 AVP/Dir Student Diversity/Inclusion ... Dr. Sherri BENN
110 Asst VP University Advancement ... Mr. Dan PERRY
115 Asst VP UA Business Operations ... Vacant
88 Assoc VP Finance/Support Svcs Plng ... Ms. Nancy NUSBAUM
14 Assoc VP for Technology Resources ... Mr. Mark HUGHES
90 Assoc VP Technology Innovation ... Dr. Carlos SOLIS
106 Asst VP Distance & Extended Learn ... Mr. Dana WILLETT
06 University Registrar ... Mr. Louis E. JIMENEZ
91 Director Enterprise Systems ... Mr. Martin MILLS
37 Director of Fin Aid & Scholarships ... Dr. Christopher MURR
36 Interim Director Career Services ... Mr. Ralph LEAL
41 Director of Athletics ... Dr. Lawrence B. TEIS
29 Director of Alumni Affairs ... Ms. Kim GANNON
27 Director Univ News Services ... Mr. Jayme L. BLASCHKE
20 Asst VP Academic Affairs ... Dr. Edna REHBEIN
25 Director of Sponsored Programs ... Vacant
19 Director University Police ... Ms. Laurie CLOUSE
23 Director Student Health Center ... Dr. Emilio CARRANCO
39 Director Housing & Residential Life ... Dr. Rosanne PROITE
40 Manager University Bookstore ... Mr. John ROOT
09 Asst VP for Institutional Research ... Mr. Joseph M. MEYER
22 Chief Diversity/Dir Equity & Inclus ... Ms. Ameerah MCBRIDE
96 Director Purchasing ... Mr. Dan ALDEN
88 Director of University Marketing ... Mr. Daniel W. EGGERS
116 Director of Audit & Analysis ... Mr. Steve R. MCGEE
88 Director Campus Recreation ... Dr. Christy NOLAN
88 Director LBJ Student Center ... Mr. Jack RAHMANN
124 Director Retention Mgmt & Planning ... Dr. Jen BECK
22 Int Director Disability Services ... Dr. Skyller WALKES
108 Dir Univ Planning & Assessment ... Dr. Ana Lisa GARZA
104 Asst VP for International Affairs ... Vacant
88 Director Learning Spaces ... Mr. Brian SHANKS
119 Chief Information Security Officer ... Mr. Daniel C. OWEN
90 Asst VP IT Assistance Center ... Mr. Benjamin ROGERS

*Texas Tech University System (F)

1508 Knoxville Ave, Lubbock TX 79409-2013
County: Lubbock Identification: 667242
Telephone: (806) 742-0012 Carnegie Class: N/A
FAX Number: N/A
URL: www.texastech.edu

01 Chancellor ... Dr. Tedd L. MITCHELL
05 Vice Chancellor Academic Affairs ... Dr. John OPPERMAN
10 Vice Chancellor & CFO ... Mr. Gary BARNES
111 Vice Chancellor Inst Advancement ... Mr. Patrick KRAMER
86 Vice Chanc Governmental Relations ... Ms. Martha BROWN
18 Vice Chanc Facil Plng/Construction ... Mr. Billy BREEDLOVE
43 Vice Chancellor & General Counsel ... Mr. Eric D. BENTLEY
116 Vice Chancellor Audit ... Mrs. Kim TURNER

*Angelo State University (A)

2601 West Avenue N, San Angelo TX 76909-0001
County: Tom Green FICE Identification: 003541
Unit ID: 222831
Telephone: (325) 942-2555 Carnegie Class: Masters/L
FAX Number: N/A Calendar System: Semester
URL: www.angelo.edu
Established: 1928 Annual Undergrad Tuition & Fees (In-State): $7,436
Enrollment: 10,417 Coed
Affiliation or Control: State IRS Status: 501(c)3
Highest Offering: Doctorate
Accreditation: SC, ACBSP, CAEP, MUS, NURSE, PTA, SW

02 President ....Dr. Brian J. MAY
05 Provost/Vice Pres Academic Affairs ....Dr. Donald R. TOPLIFF
30 VP for Development & Alumni Rels ....Ms. Jamie AKIN
10 VP for Finance and Administration ....Ms. Angelina WRIGHT
32 VP for Student Affs & Enroll Mgmt ....Dr. Javier FLORES
58 Dean Col of Grad Studies & Research ....Dr. Micheal SALISBURY
54 Dean of College of Sci & Engr ....Dr. Paul SWETS
50 Dean College of Business ....Dr. Clifton JONES
53 Dean College of Education ....Dr. Scarlet CLOUSE
66 Dean College Health & Human Service ....Dr. Leslie MAYRAND
79 Dean College of Arts & Humanities ....Dr. John KLINGEMANN
06 Director of Registrar Services ....Ms. Rosalinda CASTRO
89 Dean Freshman College ....Dr. John WEGNER
09 Director of Accountability ....Ms. Brandy HAWKINS
08 Exec Director of Library ....Vacant
36 Director Career Development ....Ms. Julie J. RUTHENBECK
15 Director of Human Resources ....Mr. Kurtis R. NEAL
37 Director of Student Financial Aid ....Mr. Charles E. KERESTLY
26 Director of Communications & Mktg ....Ms. Rebekah BRACKIN
29 Director Development & Alumni Svcs ....Ms. Kimberly ADAMS
35 Exec Director of Student Affairs ....Dr. Bradley PETTY
18 Director of Facilities Management ....Mr. Jay HALBERT
39 Dir of Housing & Residential Pgm ....Ms. Tracy W. BAKER
40 Manager Bookstore ....Ms. Michaela REYNOLDS
41 Athletic Director ....Mr. James REID
19 Chief of University Police ....Mr. James E. ADAMS
13 Assoc VP Information Technology/CIO ....Mr. Douglas FOX
21 Director of Business Services ....Ms. Jessica MANNING
96 Director Purchasing and Travel ....Vacant
92 Director of Honors Program ....Dr. Shirley EOFF
04 Executive Asst to the President ....Ms. Adelina C. MORALES
104 Director of International Studies ....Ms. Meghan PACE
07 Director of Admissions ....Ms. Sharla ADAM
38 Director of Counseling Services ....Mr. Mark REHM
84 Director Enrollment Management ....Mr. Jeffrey SEFCIK
43 Sr Exec Asst to Pres/Gen Counsel ....Mr. Joe MUNOZ

† Affiliated with Texas Tech University in Lubbock, TX

*Texas Tech University (B)

2500 Broadway, Lubbock TX 79401
County: Lubbock FICE Identification: 003644
Unit ID: 229115
Telephone: (806) 742-2121 Carnegie Class: DU-Highest
FAX Number: (806) 742-2138 Calendar System: Semester
URL: www.ttu.edu
Established: 1923 Annual Undergrad Tuition & Fees (In-State): $9,080
Enrollment: 36,996 Coed
Affiliation or Control: State IRS Status: 170(c)1
Highest Offering: Doctorate
Accreditation: SC, ARCPA, ART, CACREP, CAEPN, CIDA, CLPSY, COPSY, DANCE, DIETD, DIETI, IPSY, LAW, LSAR, MFCD, MIDWF, MUS, SPAA, SW, THEA

00 Chancellor ....Dr. Tedd L. MITCHELL
02 President ....Dr. Lawrence SCHOVANEC
101 Sec Board Regents/Ex Asst to Chanc ....Ms. Christina MARTINEZ
05 Provost and Senior Vice President ....Dr. Michael GALYEAN
10 Chief Operating Ofcr/SVP Admin/Fin ....Ms. Noel SLOAN
111 Vice Chanc Inst Advancement ....Mr. Patrick KRAMER
86 Vice Chancellor Govt Relations ....Ms. Martha BROWN
43 Vice Chanc & General Counsel ....Mr. Eric D. BENTLEY
18 VC Facilities Planning Construction ....Mr. Billy BREEDLOVE
20 Sr Vice Provost Academic Affairs ....Dr. Rob STEWART
100 President's Chief of Staff ....Ms. Grace HERNANDEZ
29 EVP & CEO Texas Tech Alumni Assoc ....Mr. Curt LANGFORD
46 Vice President for Research ....Dr. Joseph HEPPERT
28 Vice Pres Institutional Diversity ....Dr. Carol A. SUMNER
84 Assoc VP Enrollment Management ....Dr. Ethan LOGAN
20 Vice Provost Academic Affairs ....Ms. Genevieve DURHAM DECESARO
21 Asst Vice Pres & Controller ....Ms. Sharon WILLIAMSON
82 Vice Provost International Affairs ....Dr. Sukant MISRA
08 Dean of Libraries ....Dr. Bella GERLICH
60 Dean Media & Communications ....Dr. David PERLMUTTER
32 Asst Dean of Students ....Ms. Denise TIJERINA
37 Executive Director Fin Aid ....Vacant
13 Chief Information Officer ....Mr. Sam SEGRAN
06 Registrar ....Ms. Bobbie BROWN
07 Executive Director of Admissions ....Ms. Jamie HANSARD
27 Managing Dir Commun & Marketing ....Mr. Chris COOK
04 Executive Asst to President ....Ms. Mikki ROSS
31 Director Community Engagment ....Vacant
44 Managing Director Annual Giving ....Mr. Daniel BURGNER
23 Managing Dir Student Health Serv ....Ms. Evelyn MCPHERSON
39 Managing Dir Student Housing ....Mr. Sean DUGGAN
36 Director Career Center ....Mr. Jay KILLOUGH
15 Managing Director of HR Management ....Ms. Jodie BILLINGSLEY
22 Asst Vice Chanc Admin/Mng Dir EEO ....Ms. Charlotte BINGHAM
38 Director Student Counseling ....Dr. Richard LENOX
41 Director of Athletics ....Mr. Kirby HOCUTT
47 Dean Agricultural Sci/Natural Res ....Dr. William F. BROWN
49 Dean of Arts & Sciences ....Dr. Brent LINDQUIST
48 Dean of Architecture ....Dr. James P. WILLIAMSON
50 Dean Business Administration ....Dr. Margaret L. WILLIAMSON
53 Interim Dean of Education ....Dr. Robin LOCK
54 Dean of Engineering ....Dr. Albert SACCO, JR.
88 Dean of Human Sciences ....Dr. Linda HOOVER
61 Dean School of Law ....Dr. Jack NOWLIN
58 Dean of Graduate School ....Dr. Mark SHERIDAN
92 Dean Honors College ....Dr. Michael SAN FRANCISCO
57 Dean Visual & Performing Arts ....Dr. Noel ZAHLER
19 Chief of Police ....Mr. Kyle K. BONATH
09 Managing Dir Institutional Research ....Ms. Vicki WEST
96 Chief Procurement Officer ....Ms. Jennifer ADLING

*Texas Tech University Health Sciences Center (C)

3601 4th Street, Lubbock TX 79430-0001
County: Lubbock FICE Identification: 010674
Unit ID: 229337
Telephone: (806) 743-1000 Carnegie Class: Spec-4-yr-Med
FAX Number: N/A Calendar System: Semester
URL: www.ttuhsc.edu
Established: 1969 Annual Undergrad Tuition & Fees (In-State): N/A
Enrollment: 5,453 Coed
Affiliation or Control: State IRS Status: 501(c)3
Highest Offering: Doctorate
Accreditation: SC, AUD, CAATE, CACREP, DMOLS, MED, MT, NURSE, OT, PH, PHAR, PTA, SP

02 President ....Dr. Tedd L. MITCHELL
10 Vice Pres & Chief Financial Officer ....Ms. Penny HARKEY
05 Exec Vice Pres Academic Affairs ....Dr. Rial D. ROLFE
26 Vice Pres External Relations ....Ms. Kendra BURRIS
17 Exec Vice Pres Rural/Community Hlth ....Dr. Billy U. PHILIPS, JR.
46 Senior Vice President for Research ....Dr. Quentin SMITH
13 Vice Pres Info Tech/Chief Info Ofcr ....Dr. Chip SHAW
86 VP Federal and State Relations ....Mr. Ryan HENRY
88 Vice President of Health Policy ....Dr. Cynthia JUMPER
28 VP of Diversity & Inclusion ....Dr. Kim PECK
100 Chief of Staff ....Ms. Didit MARTINEZ
43 Senior Assoc General Counsel ....Mr. Jon MCGOUGH
21 Assoc Vice Pres Business Affairs ....Mr. Mike CROWDER
15 Int AVP of Human Resources ....Dr. Janet L. COQUELIN
108 Asst VP Academic Affairs ....Dr. Kari DICKSON
30 Asst VC Institutional Advancement ....Ms. Kendra BURRIS
32 AVP Student Services ....Ms. Margret DURAN
22 Asst Vice Pres Compliance ....Ms. Sonya CASTRO-QUIRINO
18 Int AVP of Physical Plant ....Mr. Greg LOVETT
63 Dean of Medical School ....Dr. Steven L. BERK
58 Dean Grad Sch Biomed Sciences ....Dr. Brandt L. SCHNEIDER
66 Dean of Nursing School ....Dr. Michael L. EVANS
76 Dean of Allied Health Sciences Sch ....Dr. Lori RICE-SPEARMAN
67 Dean of Pharmacy School ....Dr. Quentin R. SMITH
63 Reg Dean Medicine Amarillo Campus ....Dr. Richard JORDAN
63 Reg Dean Medicine Odessa Campus ....Dr. Gary VENTOLINI
66 Reg Dean Nursing Abilene ....Ms. Pearl E. MERRITT
66 Reg Dean Nursing Odessa Campus ....Dr. Sharon CANNON
76 Reg Dean Allied Health Amarillo ....Dr. Michael HOOTEN
76 Reg Dean Allied Health Odessa ....Dr. Neeraj KUMAR
67 Reg Dean Pharmacy Abilene ....Dr. Cindy RAEHL
67 Reg Dean Pharmacy Amarillo ....Dr. Thomas THEKKUMKARA
67 Reg Dean Pharmacy Dallas ....Dr. Roland PATRY
67 Reg Dean Pharmacy Lubbock ....Dr. Charles E. SEIFERT
06 Registrar ....Ms. Tamara N. KRAUSER
08 Exec Director of HSC Libraries ....Dr. Richard NOLLAN
21 Managing Dir Accounting Services ....Ms. Melody OLIPHINT
22 Director of Equal Employment ....Ms. Charlotte BINGHAM
25 Director of Sponsored Programs ....Ms. Erin WOODS
37 Director of Financial Aid ....Mr. Marcus WILSON
25 Sr Director of Contracting ....Mr. Jim LEWIS
19 Information Security Officer ....Mr. Andrew HOWARD
96 Managing Director of Purchasing ....Mr. John G. HAYNES
09 Chief Analyst Inst Research ....Mr. Kevin MCINTYRE
29 Director of Alumni Relations ....Ms. Julie DOSS
88 Sr Director Office of Global Health ....Ms. Michelle ENSMINGER

*Texas Tech University Health Sciences Center at El Paso (D)

5001 El Paso Drive, El Paso TX 79905
County: El Paso Identification: 667243
Telephone: (915) 215-4300 Carnegie Class: Not Classified
FAX Number: N/A Calendar System: Semester
URL: www.elpaso.ttuhsc.edu
Established: 2014 Annual Undergrad Tuition & Fees (In-State): N/A
Enrollment: N/A Coed
Affiliation or Control: State IRS Status: 170(c)1
Highest Offering: Doctorate
Accreditation: SC, MED, NURSE

01 President ....Dr. Richard LANGE
05 Provost ....Dr. Paul OGDEN
111 Assoc Vice Chanc Inst Advancement ....Dr. Andrea TAWNEY
10 Vice Pres Finance & Administration ....Ms. Sue FUCIARELLI
11 Vice President for Operations ....Vacant
26 Vice Pres Outreach/Cmty Engagement ....Dr. Jose Manuel DE LA ROSA
13 Assoc VP Information Technology ....Mr. Jerry RODRIGUEZ
32 Interim Asst VP Student Services ....Dr. Valerie PATON
63 Dean School of Medicine ....Dr. Richard LANGE
66 Dean School of Nursing ....Dr. Stephanie WOODS
88 Dean Graduate School of Biomedical ....Dr. Rajkumar LAKSHMANASWAMY
52 Dean School of Dental Medicine ....Dr. Richard BLACK
04 Assistant to President ....Ms. Vanessa SOLIS
06 Registrar ....Ms. Diana ANDRADE
15 Chief Human Resources Officer ....Ms. Rebecca SALCIDO
18 Chief Facilities/Physical Plant Ofc ....Mr. Leo PEREYRA

Texas Wesleyan University (E)

1201 Wesleyan, Fort Worth TX 76105-1536
County: Tarrant FICE Identification: 003645
Unit ID: 229160
Telephone: (817) 531-4444 Carnegie Class: DU-Mod
FAX Number: (817) 531-4425 Calendar System: Semester
URL: www.txwes.edu
Established: 1890 Annual Undergrad Tuition & Fees: $30,300
Enrollment: 2,396 Coed
Affiliation or Control: United Methodist IRS Status: 501(c)3
Highest Offering: Doctorate
Accreditation: SC, ANEST, CAATE, MFCD, MUS

01 President ....Mr. Frederick G. SLABACH
05 Provost/Sr Vice President ....Dr. Allen HENDERSON
10 VP Finance & Administration ....Mrs. Donna NANCE
100 Chief of Staff and General Counsel ....Ms. Patti GEARHART TURNER
32 VP Student Affairs/Dean of Students ....Mr. Dennis HALL
30 VP University Advancement ....Mr. Jim LEWIS
84 VP Enroll/Marketing/Communications ....Mr. John VEILLEUX
26 Assoc VP Marketing/ Communications ....Ms. Shannon LAMBERSON
15 AVP of Human Resources ....Ms. Angela DAMPEER
20 Assoc Provost Academic Affairs ....Dr. Steven DANIELL
20 Associate Provost ....Dr. Helena BUSSELL
41 Athletic Director ....Mr. Ricky DOTSON
53 Dean School of Education ....Dr. Carlos MARTINEZ
50 Dean of School of Business ....Dr. Hector QUINTANILLA
79 Int Dean School Arts & Letters ....Dr. Gladys CHILDS
83 Dean School of Natural & Social Sci ....Dr. Ricardo RODRIGUEZ
39 Asst Dn Stdnts/Dir Residence Life ....Dr. Dennis HALL
06 Registrar ....Mr. Sloan WHITE
08 Library Science Assoc Professor ....Ms. Elizabeth HOWARD
21 Controller ....Ms. Jacqueline RUTLEDGE
07 Assoc Vice Pres Enrollment ....Ms. Djuana YOUNG
37 Director Financial Aid ....Ms. Aarika RAMON
42 Chaplain ....Ms. Gladys CHILDS
38 Director of Counseling ....Dr. Linda METCALF
29 Director Alumni Relations ....Ms. DeAwna WOOD
96 Director of Purchasing ....Ms. Deborah CAVITT
36 Director Career Services/Counselor ....Dr. Gary STOUT
18 Exec Dir of Facil/Opers/Emr Svcs ....Mr. Brian FRANKS
04 Executive Assistant to the Pres ....Mrs. Sherry SANDLES
09 Director Institutional Research ....Vacant
19 Director Campus Safety/Security ....Mr. Chris BECKRICH

Texas Woman's University (F)

P.O. Box 425587, Denton TX 76204-5587
County: Denton FICE Identification: 003646
Unit ID: 229179
Telephone: (940) 898-2000 Carnegie Class: DU-Mod
FAX Number: (940) 898-3198 Calendar System: Semester
URL: www.twu.edu
Established: 1901 Annual Undergrad Tuition & Fees (In-State): $7,796
Enrollment: 15,473 Coed
Affiliation or Control: State IRS Status: 501(c)3
Highest Offering: Doctorate
Accreditation: SC, ACBSP, CACREP, COPSY, DANCE, DH, DIETD, DIETI, HSA, IPSY, LIB, MFCD, MUS, NURSE, OT, PTA, SCPSY, SP, SW

01 Chancellor & President ....Dr. Carine FEYTEN
05 Interim Provost/VP Acad Affairs ....Dr. Carolyn KAPINUS
10 VP Finance/Administration ....Mr. Jason TOMLINSON
32 VP Student Life ....Dr. Monica MENDEZ-GRANT
111 VP University Advancement ....Dr. Kimberly RUSSELL
84 VP Enrollment Services ....Dr. Randall LANGSTON
20 Executive Vice Provost ....Dr. Jennifer MARTIN
09 Vice Prov Inst Research/Improvement ....Dr. Mark S. HAMNER
15 Sr Assoc VP Human Resources ....Mr. Lewis BENAVIDES
13 Assoc VP Technology/CIO ....Ms. Raechelle CLEMMONS
21 Assoc VP Finance ....Ms. Rana ASKINS
18 Assoc VP Facilities ....Mr. Robert RAMIREZ
26 Assoc VP Marketing/Communication ....Ms. Cindy POLLARD
96 Asst VP Procurement Services ....Ms. Vanna PARR
69 Dean College Health Sciences ....Dr. Christopher T. RAY
107 Dean College Prof Education ....Dr. Lisa HUFFMAN
58 Interim Dean Graduate School ....Dr. Claire SAHLIN
50 Dean College of Business ....Dr. James LUMPKIN
66 Dean College Nursing ....Dr. Anita HUFFT
49 Dean College Arts & Sciences ....Dr. Abigail TILTON
08 Dean of Libraries ....Ms. Suzanne SEARS
06 Registrar ....Mr. Bobby LOTHRINGER
113 Bursar ....Mr. Glen RAY
19 Executive Dir of Public Safety ....Mr. Samuel GARRISON
38 Dir Counseling Center ....Dr. Denise LUCERO-MILLER
41 Athletic Director ....Ms. Chalese CONNORS
23 Dir Student Health Services ....Dr. Connie MENARD
39 Director University Housing ....Ms. Jill ECKARDT

29 Exec Dir Alumni Engagement ... Ms. Jasmine CARTER
37 Interim Dir Student Fin Aid ... Ms. Joyce SONENBERG
04 Executive Asst to Chancellor/Pres ... Ms. Lorie HUSLIG
100 Chief of Staff ... Mr. Christopher JOHNSON
04 Coord Events/Outreach & Comm ... Ms. Amelia BRIZICKY
104 Director Study Abroad ... Ms. Annie PHILLIPS
106 Dir Teach & Learn w/Technology ... Dr. Lynda MURPHY
108 Dir Academic Assessment ... Dr. Terry SENNE
07 Interim Dir of Admissions ... Ms. Nikki YOUNG
86 Dir Governmental & Legis Affairs ... Mr. Kevin CRUSER
43 General Counsel ... Ms. Katherine GREEN
36 Director Career Connections Center ... Ms. Laura SHACKELFORD
28 Exec Dir Diversity/Incl & Outreach ... Ms. Becky RODRIGUEZ

Trinity University (A)

One Trinity Place, San Antonio TX 78212-7200
County: Bexar FICE Identification: 003647
Unit ID: 229267
Telephone: (210) 999-7011 Carnegie Class: Masters/S
FAX Number: (210) 999-7696 Calendar System: Semester
URL: www.trinity.edu
Established: 1869 Annual Undergrad Tuition & Fees: $42,976
Enrollment: 2,571 Coed
Affiliation or Control: Independent Non-Profit IRS Status: 501(c)3
Highest Offering: Master's
Accreditation: SC, CAEPN, HSA

01 President ... Dr. Danny ANDERSON
05 Vice Pres Academic Affairs ... Dr. Deneese JONES
10 VP Finance and Administration ... Mr. Gary LOGAN
111 VP Alumni Relations & Development ... Mr. Michael BACON
13 VP Info Resources ... Mr. Jim BRADLEY
84 VP Enrollment/Student Retention ... Mr. Eric MALOOF
32 Vice Pres Student Life ... Dr. Sheryl R. TYNES
20 Assoc VP Faculty Recruitment & Dev ... Dr. Duane COLTHARP
114 Assoc VP Budget & Research ... Dr. Michael SOTO
21 Assoc VP for Finance ... Ms. Diana HEEREN
35 Assoc VP Stdnt Affs/Dean of Stdnt ... Mr. David M. TUTTLE
09 Assoc VP/Dir Institutional Research ... Ms. Kara LARKAN
88 AVP Conferences/Special Pgms ... Mr. Bruce BRAVO
37 Asst VP Student Financial Svcs ... Ms. Christina PIKLA
19 Asst VP Public Safety/Ent Risk Mgmt ... Mr. Paul CHAPA
15 Assistant VP Human Resources ... Ms. Barbara BARAN-CENTENO
06 Registrar ... Mr. Alfred RODRIGUEZ
07 Director Admissions/Operations ... Ms. Valerie SCHWEERS
38 Director Counseling/Health Svcs ... Dr. Gary W. NEAL
88 Director Student Involvement ... Ms. Jamie THOMPSON
36 Director of Career Services ... Ms. Katie RAMIREZ
13 Dir/Chief Info Technology Officer ... Mr. Fred ZAPATA
44 Sr Director of Annual Giving Pgms ... Ms. Kathy MCNEILL
29 Senior Director of Alumni Relations ... Mr. Ryan FINNELLY
04 Assistant to the President ... Ms. Claire SMITH
18 Director Facility Services ... Mr. James BAKER
42 Chaplain ... Rev. Alex SERNA-WALLENDER
96 Director of Purchasing ... Vacant
28 Director Diversity ... Ms. Jamie THOMPSON
41 Athletic Director ... Mr. Bob KING
40 Manager of Bookstore ... Ms. Susie JUVERA

Trinity Valley Community College (B)

100 Cardinal Drive, Athens TX 75751-2734
County: Henderson FICE Identification: 003572
Unit ID: 225308
Telephone: (903) 677-8822 Carnegie Class: Assoc/MT-VT-High Non
FAX Number: (903) 675-6316 Calendar System: Semester
URL: www.tvcc.edu
Established: 1946 Annual Undergrad Tuition & Fees (In-District): $2,640
Enrollment: 4,449 Coed
Affiliation or Control: State/Local IRS Status: 501(c)3
Highest Offering: Associate Degree
Accreditation: SC, ADNUR, EMT, SURGT

01 President ... Dr. Jerry KING
05 Vice President for Instruction ... Dr. Wendy ELMORE
111 VP of Institutional Advancement ... Ms. Kristen BENNETT
32 Vice President Student Services ... Dr. Jay KINZER
13 VP of Information Technology ... Mr. Brett DANIEL
10 Vice Pres Administrative Services ... Mr. David HOPKINS
20 Assoc VP Instruction Academic Educ ... Mrs. Kristin SPIZZIRRI
103 Associate VP of Workforce Education ... Ms. Kristin WALKER
14 Assoc VP of Information Technology ... Vacant
21 Dir of Acct Services & Controller ... Ms. Courtney WALKER
12 Assoc VP of TDCJ Programs ... Dr. Sam HURLEY
18 Asst VP of Facilities Management ... Mr. David GRAEM
76 Provost Health Occupations ... Dr. Helen REID
12 Provost Kaufman County Campus ... Dr. Algia ALLEN
12 Provost Anderson County Campus ... Dr. Jeff WATSON
84 AVP of Enrollment Mgmt/Registrar ... Ms. Tammy DENNEY
09 Dir Strategic Planning/SACS ... Ms. Tina RUMMEL
08 Director Learning Resource Center ... Ms. Karla BRYAN
06 Assistant Registrar ... Ms. Caroline WHITAKER
26 Director Marketing/Communications ... Ms. Marlo BITTER
07 Director School Relations ... Ms. Audrey HAWKINS
37 Dir Student Fin Aid/Veteran Svcs ... Ms. Tonya RICHARDSON-DEAN
41 Athletic Director ... Mr. Jay KINZER
19 Director of Campus Police ... Mr. Stewart NEWBY
36 Placement Officer ... Vacant
40 Bookstore Manager ... Mrs. Beth Ann KIDD
35 Director of Housing/Judicial Ofc ... Mr. Harold JONES
51 Dir Adult/Continuing Education ... Ms. Chris HICKS

15 Director of Human Resources ... Ms. Janene DOTTS
96 Purchasing/Contracts/Ins Coord ... Ms. Lawanna SEWALT
04 Executive Asst to the President ... Ms. Norma SHERAM
106 Director of Distance Learning ... Ms. Holley COLLIER
36 Director of Student Pathways ... Ms. Janet GREEN

Tyler Junior College (C)

PO Box 9020, Tyler TX 75711-9020
County: Smith FICE Identification: 003648
Unit ID: 229355
Telephone: (903) 510-2200 Carnegie Class: Bac/Assoc-Assoc Dom
FAX Number: (903) 510-2632 Calendar System: Semester
URL: www.tjc.edu
Established: 1926 Annual Undergrad Tuition & Fees (In-District): $2,962
Enrollment: 11,649 Coed
Affiliation or Control: State/Local IRS Status: 170(c)1
Highest Offering: Baccalaureate
Accreditation: SC, CAHIIM, COARC, #COARCP, DA, DH, DMS, EMT, MLTAD, OTA, PTAA, RAD, SURGT

01 President/Chief Executive Officer ... Dr. Juan E. MEJIA
04 Exec Asst to President ... Ms. Debra HOLCOMB
10 VP Finance & Admin Affairs/CFO ... Ms. Sarah E. VAN CLEEF
05 VP Stdnt & Acad Affairs/Provost ... Vacant
111 VP Inst Advance/Exec Dir Foundation ... Mr. D. Mitch ANDREWS
51 Dean Continuing Studies ... Dr. Aubrey D. SHARPE
15 Exec Dir Human Resources ... Mr. S. Kevin FOWLER
18 Dir Facilities & Construction ... Mr. Mark GARTMAN
26 VP Mktg Media Enroll Mgt/CCO ... Mrs. Kimberly LESSNER
13 Chief Information Officer ... Mr. Jeffrey HASSETT
35 Dean of Students ... Ms. Tampa J. NANNEN
32 Assoc Vice Prov Student Affairs ... Dr. Timothy S. DRAIN
81 Dean Engineering Math and Sciences ... Dr. J. Cliff BOUCHER
76 Dean Nursing Health Sciences ... Vacant
79 Dean Humanities Comm Fine Arts ... Ms. Linda GARY
107 Int Dean Professional Tech Programs ... Ms. Lorretta SWAN
103 Assoc Vice Prov Acad & Wrkfc Affs ... Mr. Bryan RENFRO
20 Dean Academic Success ... Mr. Dometrius HILL
21 Controller ... Mr. Hunter THROCKMORTON
88 Exec Dir Business Services ... Ms. Carol HUTSON
88 Dir Academic Svcs/Inst Effective ... Mr. Thomas ELDER
07 Director Admissions ... Mrs. Claire MIZELL
06 Registrar ... Ms. Britt SABOTA
27 Dir Public Affairs Media Relations ... Mrs. Rebecca SANDERS
09 Dir Institutional Research ... Dr. Afton BARBER
37 Director Financial Aid ... Ms. Devon WIGGINS
08 Director Learning Resource Center ... Ms. Marian D. JACKSON
96 Director Campus Services ... Ms. Dana BALLARD
35 Director Student Life ... Mrs. Lauren TYLER
39 Director Residential Life ... Ms. Diana KAROL
88 Director Testing ... Mr. Roger GRIMM
121 Director Academic Advising ... Mr. Chris FONTAINE
29 Director Alumni Relations ... Ms. Susan FARRINGTON
88 Director SBDC ... Mr. Donald W. PROUDFOOT
44 Director Annual Giving ... Ms. Whitney PATTERSON
106 Director Distance Education ... Mr. Ken CRAVER
19 Director Campus Police ... Mr. Michael SEALE
92 Director Honors Program ... Mr. David FUNK
112 Director Major Gifts ... Ms. Barabara KING
119 Director Information Security ... Vacant
16 Assistant Director Human Resources ... Mrs. Connie J. RUSSELL
16 Assistant Dir Human Res Title IX ... Mr. Andrew CANTEY
118 Manager Benefits Compensation ... Ms. DeVonne CAGLE
38 Counselor Learning Specialist ... Mrs. Tracey WILLIAMS
36 Specialist Career Planning ... Ms. Tracey MAPLES
108 Dir Institutional Effectiveness ... Dr. Belinda PRIHODA
101 Secretary of the Institution/Board ... Ms. Ellen MATTHEWS

University of Dallas (D)

1845 E Northgate Drive, Irving TX 75062-4736
County: Dallas FICE Identification: 003651
Unit ID: 224323
Telephone: (972) 721-5000 Carnegie Class: Masters/L
FAX Number: (972) 721-5017 Calendar System: Semester
URL: www.udallas.edu
Established: 1956 Annual Undergrad Tuition & Fees: $40,652
Enrollment: 2,510 Coed
Affiliation or Control: Roman Catholic IRS Status: 501(c)3
Highest Offering: Doctorate
Accreditation: SC

01 President ... Dr. Thomas S. HIBBS
04 Exec Admin Asst to the President ... Mrs. Shannon BRUSH
84 Assistant VP Enrollment ... Mrs. Elizabeth GRIFFIN-SMITH
10 Associate VP Finance & Admin ... Mr. Leonard ROBERTSON
05 Provost ... Dr. Jonathan J. SANFORD
111 VP Advancement ... Ms. Joan CANTY
43 VP Legal & Board Services ... Ms. Karin RILLEY
13 Assistant VP Information Systems ... Mrs. Ruchi SHETH
32 Dean of Students ... Ms. Julia L. CARRANO
50 Dean College of Business ... Dr. Brett LANDRY
49 Interim Dean of Constantin College ... Dr. Sally J. HICKS
58 Dean Grad School of Liberal Arts ... Dr. Joshua S. PARENS
73 Dean School of Ministry ... Dr. Ted WHAPHAM
08 Dean of Libraries and Research ... Ms. Cherie L. HOHERTZ
06 Registrar ... Mrs. Kathy MCGRAW
19 Police Chief ... Mr. Russell GREENE
13 Director Information Technology ... Mr. Richard HAYTER
14 Director of IT User Support Service ... Mr. Sabyasachi SANYAL
41 Director of Athletics ... Mr. Richard STROCKBINE

42 Director of Campus Ministry ... Mr. Nicolas LOPEZ
18 Director of Facilities ... Mr. Jerry HABA
21 Associate VP Finance/CFO ... Mr. Leonard A. ROBERTSON
15 Asst Vice President for HR ... Dr. Richard HUNTLEY
09 Dir of Institutional Effectiveness ... Ms. Vicky MORRIS-DUEER
26 Exec Dir of Marketing & Comm ... Mr. Clifford SMITH
96 Manager of Purchasing ... Mr. Ron CARVALHO
104 Director for Rome & Summer Programs ... Mrs. Becky DAVIES
23 Director of Health Center ... Dr. Lora RODRIGUEZ
36 Director of Career Services ... Ms. Amy YOUNG
37 Director Financial Aid ... Mrs. Taryn ANDERSON
07 Director of UG Admission ... Mr. Michael J. PROBUS
123 Director COB Graduate Admissions ... Ms. Breanna COLLINS
35 Director Student Affairs ... Mr. Seth OLDHAM
39 Director Housing Operations ... Mrs. Betty PERRETTA

*University of Houston System (E)

4302 University Dr., 212 E. Cullen,
Houston TX 77204-2018
County: Harris FICE Identification: 011721
Unit ID: 229407
Telephone: (713) 743-1000 Carnegie Class: N/A
FAX Number: N/A
URL: www.uhsa.uh.edu

01 Chancellor ... Dr. Renu KHATOR
05 Sr VC for Academic Affairs/Provost ... Dr. Paula M. SHORT
43 Vice Chancellor/General Counsel ... Ms. Dona H. CORNELL
10 VC Administration/Finance ... Mr. Jim MCSHAN
32 Vice Chanc Student Affs/Enrol Mgmt ... Dr. Richard WALKER
111 VC University Advancement ... Ms. Eloise D. BRICE
26 Vice Chanc Marketing/Comm/Media ... Ms. Lisa K. HOLDEMAN
13 Assoc VC CIO/Information Technology ... Dr. Dennis FOUTY
21 Sr Assoc Vice Chancellor Finance ... Mr. Raymond BARTLETT
11 Assoc VC Administration ... Dr. Emily MESSA
86 Vice Chanc Govt Relations ... Mr. Jason S. SMITH
15 Exec Director Human Resources ... Ms. Connie KEMP
116 Director Internal Auditing ... Mr. Don GUYTON
88 Treasurer ... Ms. Roberta (Robbi) PURYEAR
100 Chief of Staff ... Mr. Michael JOHNSON

*University of Houston (F)

4302 University Dr., 212 E. Cullen,
Houston TX 77204-2018
County: Harris FICE Identification: 003652
Unit ID: 225511
Telephone: (713) 743-1000 Carnegie Class: DU-Highest
FAX Number: N/A Calendar System: Semester
URL: www.uh.edu
Established: 1927 Annual Undergrad Tuition & Fees (In-State): $8,913
Enrollment: 45,364 Coed
Affiliation or Control: State IRS Status: Exempt
Highest Offering: Doctorate
Accreditation: SC, AAFCS, CAATE, CAEP, CEA, CLPSY, CONST, COPSY, DIETD, DIETI, IPSY, LAW, MUS, NAIT, NURSE, OPT, OPTR, PHAR, SCPSY, SP, SW

02 President ... Dr. Renu KHATOR
05 SVP Academic Affairs/Provost ... Dr. Paula M. SHORT
10 Sr Vice Pres Administration/Finance ... Mr. Jim MCSHAN
111 VP University Advancement ... Ms. Eloise D. BRICE
32 VP Student Affairs/Enrollment Svcs ... Dr. Richard WALKER
26 VP for Mktg/Communications ... Ms. Lisa K. HOLDEMAN
86 VP Govt & Community Relations ... Mr. Jason S. SMITH
43 VP Legal Affairs & Gen Counsel ... Ms. Dona H. CORNELL
46 VP Research/Tech Transfer ... Dr. Amr ELNASHAI
100 Chief of Staff ... Mr. Mike JOHNSON
31 VP for Community Rels & Inst Access ... Dr. Elwyn C. LEE
88 Vice Provost Global Strategies ... Dr. Jaime ORTIZ
29 Assoc VP Alumni Association ... Mr. Mike PEDE
13 Assoc VP Information Tech/CIO ... Dr. Dennis FOUTY
15 Assoc VP Human Resources ... Mr. Gaston REINOSO
27 Executive Director Media Relations ... Mr. Mike S. ROSEN
20 Vice Provost & Dean UG Stdnts ... Dr. Teri E. LONGACRE
58 Vice Provost & Dean Grad School ... Dr. Sarah LARSEN
88 Assoc Provost Fac Dev/Affairs ... Dr. Mark CLARKE
21 Assoc Provost Finance & Admin ... Dr. Sabrina HASSUMANI
35 Assoc VC/VP Student Affairs ... Dr. Daniel MAXWELL
88 Assoc VP Stdnt Affs/Dean of Stdnts ... Dr. William MUNSON
91 Asst VP Enterprise Sys Adm ... Mr. Keith MARTIN
21 Associate VC/VP Finance ... Mr. Raymond BARTLETT
88 Assoc Prov Educ Innov & Tech ... Dr. Jeff MORGAN
22 Int Asst VC/VP Equal Opportunity ... Ms. Toni J. BENOIT
45 Director Inst Plng/Analysis ... Mr. Miquel RAMOS
41 VP Intercollegiate Athletics ... Mr. Chris PEZMAN
37 Exec Dir Scholarships & Fin Aid ... Ms. Briget JANS
15 Exec Dir Human Resources ... Ms. Connie KEMP
06 University Registrar ... Mr. Scott SAWYER
07 Executive Director of Admissions ... Mr. Mardell MAXWELL
19 Asst VC/VP Public Safety/Security ... Mr. Malcolm DAVIS
96 Director of Purchasing ... Mr. Jack TENNER
49 Dean Col Liberal Arts/Soc Sci ... Dr. Antonio TILLIS
81 Dean Col Natural Sci & Math ... Dr. Dan WELLS
88 Dean College of Optometry ... Dr. Michael D. TWA
72 Dean College of Technology ... Dr. Anthony P. AMBLER
66 Dean School of Nursing ... Dr. Kathryn M. TART
54 Dean Cullen College of Engineering ... Dr. Joseph W. TEDESCO
48 Dean College of Architecture ... Ms. Patricia Belton OLIVER
70 Dean Graduate Col of Social Work ... Dr. Alan DETLAFF
63 Dean Col Medicine/VP Medical Affs ... Dr. Stephen J. SPANN
67 Dean College of Pharmacy ... Dr. Lamar PRITCHARD

53 Dean College of Education ... Dr. Robert MCPHERSON
50 Dean Bauer Col Business Admin ... Mr. Paul A. PAVLOU
88 Dean Hilton Col Htl/Restaurant Mgt ... Dr. Dennis REYNOLDS
08 Dean University Libraries ... Ms. Lisa A. GERMAN
92 Dean Honors College ... Dr. William MONROE
61 Dean UH Law Center ... Mr. Leonard M. BAYNES
11 Assoc VC/VP Administration ... Dr. Emily MESSA
88 Chief Energy Officer ... Dr. Ramanan KRISHNAMOORTI
57 Dean McGovern College of the Arts ... Dr. Andrew DAVIS
04 Sr Exec Assistant to the President ... Ms. Carmen HERNANDEZ
101 Exec Administrator to Board ... Ms. Germaine MATHISEN
25 Exec Dir Contract and Grants ... Ms. Beverly RYMER
39 Exec Dir Res Life/Student Housing ... Mr. Don YACKLEY

*University of Houston - Clear Lake (A)

2700 Bay Area Boulevard, Houston TX 77058
County: Harris FICE Identification: 011711
Unit ID: 225414
Telephone: (281) 283-7600 Carnegie Class: Masters/L
FAX Number: (281) 283-2219 Calendar System: Semester
URL: www.uhcl.edu
Established: 1971 Annual Undergrad Tuition & Fees (In-State): $7,002
Enrollment: 8,542 Coed
Affiliation or Control: State IRS Status: 501(c)3
Highest Offering: Doctorate
Accreditation: SC, CAEPN, IPSY, MFCD, NUR, PSPSY, SW

02 President ... Dr. Ira K. BLAKE
05 Sr Vice Pres for Acad Affairs ... Dr. Steven BERBERICH
10 Int VP Administration & Finance ... Ms. Usha MATHEW
04 Executive Asst to the President ... Ms. Berenice WEBSTER
20 Int Assoc VP Academic Affairs ... Dr. Kathryn MATTHEW
111 Acting VP University Advancement ... Mr. Mark D. LINDEMOOD
32 Vice President of Student Affairs ... Mr. Aaron J. HART
21 Associate Vice President Finance ... Ms. Usha MATHEW
84 Assoc Vice Pres Enrollment Mgmt ... Dr. Yvette BENDECK
50 Dean College Business ... Dr. Edward WALLER
79 Dean College Human Sci/Humanities ... Dr. Rick SHORT
35 Dean of Students ... Mr. David A. RACHITA
28 Asst Dean Student Diversity ... Vacant
88 Exec Dir Strategic Partnerships ... Mr. Dwayne BUSBY
85 Exec Dir Intl Admissions/Programs ... Vacant
45 Exec Dir Planning and Assessment ... Ms. Pat CUCHENS
15 Executive Director Human Resources ... Dr. William B. MCGONAGLE
13 Int Exec Dir University Computing ... Mr. Mike LIVINGSTON
96 Exec Dir of Procurement & Payables ... Ms. Debra CARPENTER
25 Exec Dir Sponsored Programs ... Dr. Nancy DEVINO
37 Int Exec Director Financial Aid ... Ms. Holly NOLAN
88 Exec Dir Environment Inst Houston ... Dr. George GUILLEN
106 Director Distance/Off-Campus Educ ... Ms. Lisa GABRIEL
26 Exec Dir University Communications ... Vacant
30 Dir Development & Alumni Relations ... Vacant
36 Ex Dir Counseling/Hlth/Career Svcs ... Dr. Cindy COOK
12 Dir Camp Operat/UHCL Pearland Camp ... Dr. Kathy DUPREE
23 Dir Health & Disability Services ... Ms. Regina PICKETT
07 Exec Director of Admissions ... Vacant

*University of Houston - Downtown (B)

One Main Street, Houston TX 77002-1014
County: Harris FICE Identification: 003612
Unit ID: 225432
Telephone: (713) 221-8001 Carnegie Class: Masters/L
FAX Number: (713) 221-8075 Calendar System: Semester
URL: www.uhd.edu
Established: 1974 Annual Undergrad Tuition & Fees (In-State): $6,500
Enrollment: 13,919 Coed
Affiliation or Control: State IRS Status: Exempt
Highest Offering: Master's
Accreditation: SC, SW

02 President ... Dr. Juan S. MUNOZ
04 Executive Asst to President ... Ms. Vanessa PIGEON
22 Title IX/Equity & Diversity Ofcr ... Ms. Erika HARRISON
05 Provost/SVP Acad & Stdnt Affairs ... Dr. Edward CARL LINK
20 Assoc VP for Academic Affairs ... Dr. Faiza KHOJA
84 VP Enrollment Management ... Dr. Jimmy JUNG
50 Dean Davies College of Business ... Dr. Charles E. GENGLER
79 Dean Col Humanities/Social Sci ... Dr. DoVeanna FULTON
80 Dean College of Public Service ... Dr. Jonathan SCHWARTZ
72 Dean Col Sciences & Tech ... Dr. Akif UZMAN
49 Dean University College ... Dr. T. Scott MARZILLI
88 Dir QEP & CCESL ... Dr. Poonam SALHOTRA
08 Executive Director WI Dykes Library ... Ms. Pat ENSOR
106 Exec Dir Off Campus/OL Coordinator ... Mr. Louis D. EVANS, III
46 Asst VP Research/Sponsored Pgms ... Dr. Jerry JOHNSON
09 Director of Institutional Research ... Ms. Carol M. TUCKER
108 Dir Institutional Assessment ... Dr. Lea CAMPBELL
109 Dir Institutional Data Analyst ... Dr. Nazly DYER
88 Director O'Kane Gallery ... Mr. Mark CERVENKA
88 Exec Director of Scholars Academy ... Dr. Mary Jo PARKER
88 Dir Teaching & Learning Excel ... Dr. Gregory DEMENT
124 Dir Gator Success Center ... Dr. Jemma SYLVESTER-CAESAR
88 Director of Advising Services ... Ms. Reyna ROMERO
121 Director of Academic Support Center ... Dr. Isidro GRAU
88 Exec Dir Academic Admin & Ops ... Ms. Chris RODNEY
88 Dir Strategic Initiatives & Project ... Ms. Lucy BOWEN
92 Director Honors Program ... Dr. Mari NICHOLSON-PREUSS
88 Dir Applied Business/Technology Ctr ... Mr. G. V. KRISHNAN
88 Dir Criminal Justice Center ... Mr. Steven BRACKEN
88 Dir Ctr Public Svc & Com Res ... Mr. Steven VILLANO
88 Dir Center for Entrepreneurship ... Mr. William DUDLEY
117 Dir Insurance & Risk Management Ctr ... Ms. Priscilla OEHLERT
36 Dir Davies COB Career Dev Center ... Mr. Brett HOBBY
88 Exec Dir Inst & Faculty ... Dr. Sedef SMITH
88 Dir Business Analytics & Dec ... Ms. Emily LEFFLER
38 Dir Student & Advising Services ... Mr. Ben ROBLES
88 Dir DCOB Admin & Operations ... Ms. Berna MCELYEA
88 Dir of Retail Mgmt Center ... Mr. Tracy DAVIS
10 VP Administration & Finance ... Mr. David M. BRADLEY
111 VP Advancement & External Rels ... Ms. Johanna WOLFE
13 Assoc VP Information Technology ... Mr. Hossein SHAHROKHI
91 Director Enterprise Systems ... Mr. Kong YIN
88 Dir Technology Learning Services ... Mr. John LANE
14 Director Technical Services ... Ms. Grace DAVILA
88 Dir IT Infrastructure & Comm Svcs ... Mr. Miguel RUIZ
90 Exec Dir Information Technology ... Mr. Said FATTOUH
88 Dir IT Business Services ... Ms. Jacqueline SMITH
88 Dir IT Project Management Office ... Ms. Kimberly SOLOMON
88 Dir User Support Services ... Ms. Cheryl ROBERTSON
88 Dir University Business Services ... Ms. Mary TORRES
88 Dir Admin Ops & Compliance ... Ms. Stefany RECORDS
105 Dir Web & Digital Marketing ... Ms. Laura WAITS
114 Exec Dir Budget/Proc & Contr Proc ... Ms. Theresa MENELEY
21 Asst VP Business Affairs ... Mr. George W. ANDERSON
88 Dir Financial Reporting ... Ms. Delethia MURRAY
18 Asst VP Facilities Management ... Mr. Timothy RYCHLEC
88 Dir Building Maintenance ... Mr. Abraham FLORES
88 Dir MEP ... Mr. Kris ZIMMERMAN
19 Ex Dir Public Safety/Chf of Police ... Mr. Michael BENFORD
117 Director Emergency Management ... Ms. Carol MANOUSOS
88 Dir Environmental Health & Safety ... Mr. Edward ARIAS
113 Dir Student Financials ... Ms. Lauren BELLENGER
88 Dir Accounts Payable ... Ms. Cynthia CONNER
15 VP Employment Svcs & Operations ... Ms. Ivonne MONTALBANO
118 Dir Benefits & Compensation ... Ms. Erica MORALES
88 Dir Talent Acquisition & Management ... Ms. Chetiqua M. HERRON
16 Director Payroll & Records ... Ms. April FRANK
32 AVP Stdnt Success/Dean of Students ... Vacant
06 Assoc VP Enrollment Mgmt/ Registrar ... Mr. Daniel VILLANUEVA, JR.
88 Director Student Activities ... Mr. Tremaine KWASIKPUI
28 Dir Ctr Stdnt Diversity Equ & Incl ... Dr. John HUDSON
07 Int Exec Dir Admiss & Financial Aid ... Ms. Ceshia LOVE
37 Director Financial Aid ... Ms. LaTasha GOUDEAU
41 Director Sports & Fitness ... Mr. Richard SEBASTIANI
36 Dir Career Development Center ... Ms. Katherine KNAPP
88 Director Disability Services ... Dr. Hope PAMPLIN
88 Director Veterans Services ... Mr. Richard SELVERA
88 Dir Minority Male Recruitment ... Dr. Pierre BANKS
88 Director Testing Services ... Mr. Robert ALONZO
88 Dir Campus Solution Services ... Ms. Rocio BEIZA
88 Exec Dir Student Comm & Trans Pgm ... Ms. Jenna TABAKMAN
88 Dir Enrollment Communication & CRM ... Mrs. Courtney SCHROEDER
88 Dir Student Transition Programs ... Mr. Eugene BERNARD
88 Director Talent Search ... Mr. Brian FLORES
88 Director Upward Bound ... Ms. Dawanna LEWIS
26 Exec Dir of University Relations ... Ms. Elisa OLSEN
102 Director Corporate Relations ... Mr. Jacob LIPP
88 Dir Advancement Services & Bus Ops ... Mr. Brian DRAKE
29 Director Events & Alumni Relations ... Dr. Liza ALONZO
27 Director Communications ... Mr. P. Michael EMERY
27 Director Marketing ... Ms. Toye SIMMONS

*University of Houston - Victoria (C)

3007 N Ben Wilson, Victoria TX 77901-4450
County: Victoria FICE Identification: 013231
Unit ID: 225502
Telephone: (361) 570-4848 Carnegie Class: Masters/L
FAX Number: (361) 580-5534 Calendar System: Semester
URL: www.uhv.edu
Established: 1973 Annual Undergrad Tuition & Fees (In-State): $6,491
Enrollment: 4,353 Coed
Affiliation or Control: State IRS Status: 501(c)3
Highest Offering: Master's
Accreditation: SC, CACREP, NURSE

02 President ... Dr. Robert K. GLENN
11 Vice Pres Administration & Finance ... Mr. Wayne B. BERAN
05 Provost/VP Acad Affairs ... Dr. Chance M. GLENN, SR.
32 Vice President Student Affairs ... Dr. Jay LAMBERT
49 Dean Arts & Sciences ... Dr. Jeffrey DI LEO
50 Dean Business Admin ... Dr. Ken COLWELL
53 Dean Education & Human Development ... Dr. Fred LITTON
111 VP Advancement & External Relations ... Mr. Jesse D. PISORS
08 Interim Director of Library ... Ms. Karen LOCHER
13 Sr Dir of Instructional Technology ... Mr. Randy FAULK
15 Dir Human Res/Deputy EO/Title IX ... Ms. Laura L. SMITH
84 Asst VP for Enrollment Mgmt ... Dr. Denee THOMAS
88 Dir Small Business Development Ctr ... Ms. Lindsay YOUNG
06 Registrar ... Ms. Trudy WORTHAM
37 Director Financial Aid ... Ms. Lashon WILLIAMS
18 Director Facilities ... Mr. John BURKE
10 Director Business Services ... Mr. Tim MICHALSKI
21 Comptroller ... Ms. Valerie WALDEN
41 Director Athletics ... Mr. Ashley WALYUCHOW
26 Director Marketing & Communications ... Ms. Paula COBLER
38 Director of Counseling Center ... Vacant
35 Dir Student Svcs & Judicial Affs ... Dr. Michael WILKINSON
114 Director of Budget ... Ms. Karen SANDERS
39 Director Residence Life & Univ Comm ... Mr. Brandon W. LEE
88 Director Capital Projects ... Mr. Matt ALEXANDER
04 Executive Adm Asst to President ... Ms. Kathy WALTON
25 Dir Grants & Contracts ... Ms. Angela HARTMANN
108 Dir Inst Research/Effectiveness ... Dr. Sharon M. BAILEY
102 Sr Dir Corp/Foundation Relations ... Ms. Courtney M. SIDES
29 Dir Alumni/Annual Giving ... Ms. Kira MUDD
20 Assoc Prov University College ... Dr. Beverly TOMEK
85 Director International Programs ... Ms. Ludmi HERATH
88 Sr Dir Enroll Mgmt/External Rels ... Ms. Karla DECUIR
88 Coordinator Title IX ... Ms. Rebecca LAKE
07 Director Admissions/Recruitment ... Mr. Billy LAGAL
19 Campus Security & Safety ... Mr. Travis GUNDELACH

University of the Incarnate Word (D)

4301 Broadway, San Antonio TX 78209-6397
County: Bexar FICE Identification: 003578
Unit ID: 225627
Telephone: (210) 829-6000 Carnegie Class: DU-Mod
FAX Number: (210) 829-1220 Calendar System: Semester
URL: www.uiw.edu
Established: 1881 Annual Undergrad Tuition & Fees: $31,484
Enrollment: 8,603 Coed
Affiliation or Control: Roman Catholic IRS Status: 501(c)3
Highest Offering: Doctorate
Accreditation: SC, ACBSP, CAATE, CIDA, DIETD, DIETI, HSA, MUS, NMT, NURSE, OPT, OPTR, @OSTEO, #OTA, PHAR, PTA, THEA

01 President ... Dr. Thomas M. EVANS
88 Senior Advisor to the President ... Dr. Denise DOYLE
88 Senior Advisor to the President ... Sr. Kathleen COUGHLIN
88 Vice President Mission and Ministry ... Sr. Walter MAHER
04 Executive Assistant to President ... Ms. Christine LUNA
43 VP Legal Affairs/General Counsel ... Ms. Cindy ESCAMILLA
05 Provost ... Dr. Barbara ARANDA-NARANJO
18 VP Campus Life/Facilities Mgmt ... Dr. David M. JURENOVICH
111 VP Development/Univ Relations ... Mr. Christopher M. GALLEGOS
10 Vice Pres for Business & Finance ... Mr. Douglas ENDSLEY
104 Vice Pres International Programs ... Mr. Marcos FRAGOSO
107 Dean School of Professional Studies ... Mr. Vincent C. PORTER
13 Vice Pres Information Resources ... Ms. Lisa BAZLEY
84 Vice Pres for Enrollment Services ... Dr. Cyndi WILSON-PORTER
20 Assoc Provost Academic Support ... Ms. Sandy MCMAKIN
76 Assoc Provost for Health Profes ... Vacant
46 Assoc Provost for Research/Grad Edu ... Dr. Ana HAGENDORF
108 Assoc Provost Acad Affairs/IE ... Dr. Glenn JAMES
21 Comptroller ... Ms. Edith COGDELL
50 Dean H-E-B Sch Business & Admin ... Dr. Forrest F. AVEN
57 Dean Humanities Arts & Social Sci ... Dr. Kevin VICHCALES
66 Dean Nursing & Health Professions ... Vacant
53 Dean Dreeben School of Education ... Dr. Denise STAUDT
54 Dean Math Science Engineering ... Dr. Carlos GARCIA
88 Dean Interactive Media & Design ... Dr. Sharon WELKEY
67 Dean Feik School of Pharmacy ... Dr. David MAIZE
88 Dean School of Optometry ... Dr. Timothy WINGERT
58 Director of Graduate Studies ... Dr. Trinidad MACIAS
62 Dean of Library Services ... Ms. Tracey MENDOZA
88 Dean School Physical Therapy ... Dr. Caroline GOULET
32 Associate Dean Campus Engagement ... Dr. Paul AYALA
88 Assoc Dean Military/Veteran Affairs ... Mr. Jon LOVEJOY
29 Director of Alumni/Parent Relations ... Dr. Lisa MCNARY
26 Director of Comm/Marketing ... Ms. Margaret L. GARCIA
07 Dean of Enrollment ... Ms. Heather RODRIGUEZ
38 Director of Counseling ... Dr. Christie MELONSON
121 Director of Academic Advising ... Dr. Sonia JASSO
88 Director Learning Assistance Center ... Ms. Cristina ARIZA
06 Registrar ... Ms. Marisol M. SCHEER
37 Director of Financial Aid ... Ms. Amy CARCANAGUES
39 Director of Residence Life ... Ms. Diane SANCHEZ
35 Director of Campus Engagement ... Ms. Nataly LOPEZ
23 Associate Dean Health Services ... Dr. Corinne JEDYNAK-BELL
42 Chaplain ... Fr. Tom DYMOWSKI
42 Director of Campus Ministry ... Ms. Elisabeth VILLARREAL
15 Director of Human Resources ... Ms. Annette THOMPSON
96 Director of Purchasing ... Mr. Sam WAGES
18 Director Facilities Mgmt & Services ... Mr. Steve HEYING
41 Director of Athletics ... Mr. Brian WICKSTROM
88 Sr Director Infrastructure Svcs ... Mr. Neil SCHROEDER
88 Director of Enterprise Applications ... Vacant
90 Director Instructional Technology ... Ms. Kathy BOTTARO
88 Director of Technology Support ... Mr. Anthony RAMOS
09 Director of Institutional Research ... Vacant
36 Director of Career Services ... Ms. Jessica L. WILSON
100 Chief of Staff ... Mr. Michael LARKIN
102 Dir Foundation/Corporate Relations ... Mr. Jon GILLESPIE
19 Chief of Police ... Mr. Robert CHAVEZ
112 Dir of Major Gifts/Planned Giving ... Mr. Alex CASTANEDA
63 Dean School of Osteopathic Medicine ... Dr. Robyn PHILLIPS-MADSON
30 Director of Development ... Ms. Rosie GARCIA
88 Director Print Svcs/Graphic Design ... Mr. Michael HOOD
88 Special Assistant for Projects ... Dr. Bobbye FRY

University of Mary Hardin-Baylor (E)

900 College Street, Belton TX 76513-2578
County: Bell FICE Identification: 003588
Unit ID: 226471
Telephone: (254) 295-8642 Carnegie Class: Masters/L
FAX Number: (254) 295-4535 Calendar System: Semester
URL: www.umhb.edu
Established: 1845 Annual Undergrad Tuition & Fees: $28,650
Enrollment: 3,914 Coed
Affiliation or Control: Southern Baptist IRS Status: 501(c)3
Highest Offering: Doctorate

Accreditation: SC, ACBSP, ART, CACREP, MUS, NURSE, PTA, SW

01 President/CEO .... Dr. Randy G. O'REAR
03 Sr Vice Pres Admin/COO .... Dr. Steve THEODORE
05 Provost/Sr VP Academic Affs .... Dr. John VASSAR
108 Vice Prov for Institutional Effect .... Dr. Danny MYNATT
45 VP Campus Planning & Support .... Mr. Marvin EE
30 Vice Pres for Development .... Dr. Rebecca O'BANION
26 VP Communication/Special Projects .... Dr. Paula TANNER
32 Vice Pres for Student Life .... Dr. Brandon SKAGGS
41 Vice Pres Athletics .... Mr. Randy MANN
10 Vice Pres Business/Finance/CFO .... Mrs. Jennifer RAMM
15 Vice Pres Human Resources .... Mrs. Susan OWENS
13 Int Vice Pres Info Tech .... Mr. Shawn KUNG
84 Vice Pres Enrollment Mgmt .... Dr. Gary LAMM
18 Assoc Vice Pres for Campus Planning .... Mr. Bob PATTEE
21 Controller .... Mrs. Charla KAHLIG
50 Dean McLane College of Business .... Dr. Ken SMITH
79 Int Dean of Humanities & Sciences .... Dr. Jacky DUMAS
66 Dean of Nursing .... Dr. Michele HACKNEY
53 Dean of Education .... Dr. Joan BERRY
76 Executive Dean Health Sciences .... Dr. Colin WILBORN
88 Dean of Christian Studies .... Dr. Tim CRAWFORD
57 Dean Visual/Performing Arts .... Dr. Kathryn FOUSE
35 Dean of Students .... Dr. Michael BURNS
39 Director of Residence Life .... Dr. Kyle SMITH
04 Special Asst to President .... Mrs. Candace WILLIAMS
06 Registrar .... Mrs. Amy MCGILVRAY
88 Director Strategic Engagement .... Ms. Melissa WILLIAMS
07 Director of Admissions & Recruiting .... Dr. Brent BURKS
08 Interim Director Learning Resources .... Ms. Teresa BUCK
27 Director Marketing/Public Relations .... Mr. James STAFFORD
09 Director Institutional Research .... Ms. Jen JONES
37 Director Financial Aid .... Mr. Ron BROWN
92 Director Honors Program .... Dr. David HOLCOMB
19 Director Campus Police .... Mr. Gary SARGENT
96 Purchasing Manager .... Mrs. Jennifer WEBB
29 Director Alumni Relations .... Mr. Jeff SUTTON
42 University Chaplain .... Dr. George LOUTHERBACK
36 Director Career Services .... Mr. Don OWENS
38 Director Couns Testing & Health .... Mr. Nate WILLIAMS
85 Dir International Student Services .... Mrs. Elizabeth TANAKA
110 Senior Director of Development .... Mr. Michael BALL
40 Bookstore Manager .... Ms. Debbie COTTRELL
104 Director Study Abroad .... Dr. Michelle REINA

University of North Texas (A)

1155 Union Circle #311277, Denton TX 76203-5013
County: Denton FICE Identification: 003594
Unit ID: 227216
Telephone: (940) 565-2000 Carnegie Class: DU-Highest
FAX Number: (940) 565-7600 Calendar System: Semester
URL: www.unt.edu
Established: 1890 Annual Undergrad Tuition & Fees (In-State): $10,852
Enrollment: 38,276 Coed
Affiliation or Control: State IRS Status: 501(c)3
Highest Offering: Doctorate
Accreditation: SC, ART, AUD, CACREP, CAEP, CEA, CIDA, CLPSY, COPSY, FEPAC, JOUR, LIB, MUS, SP, SPAA, SW

01 President .... Dr. Neal SMATRESK
00 Chancellor .... Ms. Lesa ROE
05 Provost/Vice Pres Academic Affairs .... Dr. Jennifer COWLEY
10 Sr VP Finance/Administration .... Mr. Bob BROWN
46 VP Research/Innovation .... Dr. Narendra DAHOTRE
32 Vice President Student Affairs .... Dr. Elizabeth WITH
43 Vice Chancellor/General Counsel .... Ms. Nancy S. FOOTER
26 VP for Marketing/Communications .... Mr. Jim BERSCHEIDT
30 Associate VP for Development .... Ms. Eileen P. MORAN
84 VP for Enrollment .... Mr. Shannon M. GOODMAN
13 Assoc VP for Univ Info Svcs .... Dr. V. Allen A. CLARK
20 Vice Provost for Academic Affairs .... Dr. Michael MCPHERSON
20 Vice Provost for Academic Resources .... Mr. Robert A. WATLING
20 Vice Provost for Faculty Success .... Vacant
88 Vice Provost for Academic Admin .... Vacant
100 VP for Planning/Chief of Staff .... Dr. Debbie ROHWER
41 VP & Director of Athletics .... Mr. Wren BAKER
35 Asst VP and Dean of Students .... Dr. Maureen MCGUINNESS
13 Chief Technology Officer .... Vacant
114 Budget Director .... Ms. Brenda CATES
121 Exec Dir Lrng Technologies .... Dr. Patrick PLUSCHT
28 VP Institutional Equity & Diversity .... Dr. Joanne WOODARD
31 Vice Prov for Community Engagement .... Vacant
18 Assoc Vice President for Facilities .... Mr. David REYNOLDS
08 Dean of Libraries .... Ms. Diane BRUXVOORT
37 Exec Dir Fin Aid/Univ Admissions .... Ms. Zelma DELEON
49 Dean College of Liberal Arts & SSci .... Dr. Tamara BROWN
81 Dean College of Science .... Dr. Su GAO
50 Dean College Business .... Dr. Marilyn WILEY
53 Dean College of Education .... Dr. Randy BOMER
57 Dean College of CVAD .... Mr. Greg WATTS
69 Dean Health & Public Service .... Dr. Neale CHUMBLER
64 Dean College of Music .... Dr. John W. RICHMOND
59 Dean Col of Merch/Hosp & Tourism .... Dr. Jana HAWLEY
77 Dean College of Information .... Dr. KINSHUK
58 Dean Toulouse Grad School .... Dr. Victor PRYBUTOK
92 Dean of TAMS/Honors College .... Dr. Glenisson DE OLIVEIRA
60 Dean Mayborn Sch of Journalism .... Dr. Andrea MILLER
54 Dean College of Engineering .... Dr. Hanchen HUANG
88 Dean New College at Frisco .... Dr. Wesley RANDALL
90 Director Acad Computing/User Svcs .... Dr. Philip C. BACZEWSKI
09 Director Institutional Research .... Dr. Mary BARTON
108 Associate Vice President DAIR .... Dr. Jason F. SIMON
88 Director of Accreditation .... Ms. Elizabeth VOGT
07 Assoc VP Enrollment/Univ Admissions .... Dr. Rebecca LOTHRINGER
51 Director Lifelng Learning .... Dr. Stephanie REINKE
06 AVP Enrollment & Registrar .... Ms. Lynn MCCREARY
15 Chief Human Capital Officer .... Dr. Barbara ABERCROMBIE
36 Exec Dir Career & Leadership .... Mr. Dan NAEGELI
19 Director/Chief of Police .... Mr. Ed REYNOLDS
39 Exec Director Housing .... Ms. Gina VANACORE
85 Vice Provost & Dean Intl Affairs .... Dr. Pia WOOD
23 Exec Dir Stdnt Health/Wellness .... Dr. Herschel VOORHEES
111 Vice President for Advancement .... Dr. David WOLF
04 Executive Asst to President .... Ms. Ruby RAINES
101 Secretary of the Institution/Board .... Dr. Rosemary R. HAGGETT
104 Director Study Abroad .... Ms. Amy SHENBERGER
88 VP Digital Strategy/Innovation .... Dr. Adam FEIN
88 Chief Compliance Officer .... Mr. Clay SIMMONS
22 AVP/Director Equal Opportunity .... Ms. Eve BELL
25 Director Pre-Awards/Contracts .... Ms. Carla MCGUIRE
29 Exec Director Alumni Relations .... Mr. Rob MCINTURF
38 AVP Student Counseling/Testing .... Dr. Teresa MCKINNEY
86 Director Government Relations .... Mr. Jack MORTON

University of North Texas at Dallas (B)

7300 University Hills Blvd, Dallas TX 75241
County: Dallas Identification: 667124
Unit ID: 484905
Telephone: (972) 780-3600 Carnegie Class: Masters/M
FAX Number: (972) 780-3606 Calendar System: Semester
URL: www.untdallas.edu
Established: 2000 Annual Undergrad Tuition & Fees (In-State): $9,139
Enrollment: 3,509 Coed
Affiliation or Control: State IRS Status: 501(c)3
Highest Offering: Doctorate
Accreditation: SC, #LAW

01 President .... Mr. Robert MONG
10 Exec Vice Pres Administration & CFO .... Mr. James E. MAIN
05 Provost/EVP Academic Affairs .... Dr. Betty STEWART

University of North Texas Health Science Center at Fort Worth (C)

3500 Camp Bowie Boulevard, Fort Worth TX 76107-2699
County: Tarrant FICE Identification: 009768
Unit ID: 228909
Telephone: (817) 735-2000 Carnegie Class: Spec-4-yr-Med
FAX Number: N/A Calendar System: Semester
URL: www.unthsc.edu
Established: 1966 Annual Graduate Tuition & Fees: N/A
Enrollment: 2,285 Coed
Affiliation or Control: State IRS Status: 501(c)3
Highest Offering: Doctorate; No Undergraduates
Accreditation: SC, ARCPA, HSA, #MED, OSTEO, PH, PHAR, PTA

01 President .... Dr. Michael R. WILLIAMS
10 EVP for Finance and Operations .... Mr. Gregory R. ANDERSON
05 Provost/Exec VP Academic Affairs .... Dr. Charles TAYLOR
86 Vice President Governmental Affairs .... Mr. Dan JENSEN
63 Dean Texas Col of Osteopathic Med .... Dr. Frank FILIPETTO
45 VP Research .... Vacant
58 Dean Grad Sch Biomed Sciences .... Dr. Michael MATHIS
76 Dean School of Health Professions .... Dr. J. Glenn FORISTER
69 Dean of School of Public Health .... Dr. Dennis THOMBS
37 Director Student Financial Aid .... Mr. Joseph SANCHEZ
32 Vice Provost Student Affairs .... Ms. Trisha VANDUSER
19 Chief of Police .... Mr. Jeff ARRINGTON
111 VP Institutional Advancement .... Mr. Doug WHITE
09 VP for Strategic Alignment .... Ms. Jeanie FOSTER
21 Vice President Finance & Planning .... Mr. Geoff SCARPELLI
15 Director Human Resources .... Ms. Angela BROWN
06 Registrar .... Mrs. Elizabeth MEDDERS
08 Director of Lewis Library .... Mr. Daniel BURGARD
88 Chief Compliance Officer .... Mrs. Desiree RAMIREZ
04 Executive Assistant President Ofc .... Ms. Joanna BAKSH
26 Sr Director Brand & Communication .... Ms. Amy BURESH
100 Chief of Staff .... Ms. Susan ROSS

University of Phoenix Dallas Campus (D)

12400 Coit Road, Dallas TX 75251-2004
Telephone: (972) 385-1055 Identification: 770227
Accreditation: &NH, ACBSP

† Branch campus of University of Phoenix, Phoenix, AZ

University of Phoenix Houston Campus (E)

11451 Katy Freeway, Houston TX 77079-2004
Telephone: (713) 465-9966 Identification: 770229
Accreditation: &NH, ACBSP

† Branch campus of University of Phoenix, Phoenix, AZ

University of Phoenix San Antonio Campus (F)

8200 IH-10 West, Suite 1000, San Antonio TX 78230-3876
Telephone: (210) 524-2100 Identification: 770231
Accreditation: &NH, ACBSP

† Branch campus of University of Phoenix, Phoenix, AZ

University of St. Augustine for Health Sciences (G)

5401 La Crosse Ave, Austin TX 78739
Telephone: (512) 394-9766 Identification: 770940
Accreditation: &WC, OT, #PTA, @SP

† Branch campus of University of St. Augustine for Health Sciences, San Marcos, CA.

University of St. Thomas (H)

3800 Montrose Boulevard, Houston TX 77006-4696
County: Harris FICE Identification: 003654
Unit ID: 227863
Telephone: (713) 522-7911 Carnegie Class: Masters/L
FAX Number: (713) 525-2125 Calendar System: Semester
URL: www.stthom.edu
Established: 1947 Annual Undergrad Tuition & Fees: $33,580
Enrollment: 3,168 Coed
Affiliation or Control: Roman Catholic IRS Status: 501(c)3
Highest Offering: Doctorate
Accreditation: SC, CAEPT, NURSE, THEOL

01 President .... Dr. Richard LUDWICK
04 Special Assistant to the President .... Ms. Cindy VIAUD
04 Exec Assistant to the President .... Ms. Anne LAMBERT
05 Vice Pres Academic Affairs .... Dr. Chris P. EVANS
10 Vice President for Finance .... Mr. Spencer CONROY
30 Vice Pres for Inst Advancement .... Vacant
32 Vice Pres Student Affairs .... Ms. Patricia MCKINLEY
13 Chief Information Officer .... Mr. Roger PARKS
84 Vice Pres Enrollment Management .... Mr. Arthur ORTIZ
26 VP Marketing/Communication .... Mr. Jeff OLSEN
11 Assoc VP of Human Resources .... Mr. Randy GRAHAM
35 Asst VP Student Affs/Dean Students .... Ms. Lindsey MCPHERSON
66 Dean School of Nursing .... Dr. Poldi TSCHIRCH
49 Interim Dean Arts & Sciences .... Dr. John STARNER
73 Dean School of Theology .... Dr. Sandra C. MAGIE, CM
50 Dean Cameron School of Business .... Dr. Beena GEORGE
53 Dean School of Education .... Dr. Paul PAESE
08 Dean of Libraries .... Mr. James PICCININNI
37 Dean of Scholarships/Financial Aid .... Ms. Lynda MCKENDREE
58 Dir Center for Thomistic Studies .... Dr. Steve JENSEN
82 Director Center for Intl Studies .... Dr. Hans STOCKTON
88 Director Center for Irish Studies .... Ms. Lori GALLAGHER
88 Director Center for Faith & Culture .... Fr. Binh QUACH
06 Registrar .... Mr. Nathan DUGAT
90 Director of Technical Svcs .... Mr. Al DESHOTEL
91 Director of Application Svcs .... Ms. Kelly KLITZ
38 Exec Dir Counseling & Disability .... Dr. Rose SIGNORELLO
42 Director of Campus Ministry .... Fr. Chris VALKA
39 Director Residence Life .... Ms. Ana Alicia LOPEZ
88 Asst Dir of Recreational Sports .... Mr. Scott LATHAM
18 Asst VP Facilities Operations .... Mr. Howard A. ROSE
21 Controller .... Mr. Keith SCHEFFLER
113 Bursar .... Mr. Richard SHUMAN
88 Director of Veteran Services .... Ms. Trisha RUIZ
26 Director of Communications .... Ms. Sandra SOLIZ
88 Director of Creative Services .... Ms. Marionette MITCHELL
108 Dir Assessment/Inst Effectiveness .... Dr. Dominic AQUILA
19 Chief of Police .... Mr. H. E JENKINS
41 Athletic Director .... Mr. Todd SMITH
104 Director Study Abroad .... Dr. Hans STOCKTON
29 Sr Dir Donor & Alumni Relations .... Dr. Carla ALSANDOR
88 Director of Program Marketing .... Mr. Chris ZEGLIN

*University of Texas System Administration (I)

210 West 7th Street, Austin TX 78701-2982
County: Travis FICE Identification: 003655
Unit ID: 229090
Telephone: (512) 499-4201 Carnegie Class: N/A
FAX Number: (512) 499-4215
URL: www.utsystem.edu

01 Chancellor .... Mr. James B. MILLIKEN
88 Sr Adv to the Chanc/Chief T&I Ofcr .... Ms. Julie GOONEWARDENE
100 Chief of Staff Office of Chanc .... Mr. Art MARTINEZ
05 Exec VC Academic Affairs .... Dr. Steve LESLIE
17 Int Exec VC Health Affairs .... Ms. Amy SHAW THOMAS
10 Exec Vice Chanc Business Affairs .... Dr. Scott C. KELLEY
43 Vice Chanc & General Counsel .... Mr. Dan SHARPHORN
86 Vice Chanc for Govt Relations .... Ms. Stacey NAPIER
26 Vice Chanc for Ext Rels/Comm & Adv .... Dr. Randa S. SAFADY
45 VC for Inst Research & Analysis .... Dr. Stephanie A. HUIE
18 AVC Facilities Plng/Construction .... Mr. Michael O'DONNELL
13 Assoc VC & Chief Info Officer .... Mr. David CRAIN
21 Assoc VC and Controller .... Ms. Veronica HINOJOSA-SEGURA
27 Dir of Media Rel & Comm Pgm .... Ms. Karen ADLER
88 Executive Director of Real Estate .... Mr. Kirk TAMES
30 AVC for Dev & Gift Planning Svcs .... Ms. Julia LYNCH
19 Director of Police .... Mr. Michael J. HEIDINGSFIELD
88 Asst VC for Capital Projects .... Mr. Stephen HARRIS
04 Administrative Asst to Chancellor .... Ms. Katherine IANNESSA

*The University of Texas at Arlington (J)

701 S Nedderman Drive, Arlington TX 76013
County: Tarrant FICE Identification: 003656
Unit ID: 228769
Telephone: (817) 272-2101 Carnegie Class: DU-Highest

FAX Number: (817) 272-5656 Calendar System: Semester
URL: www.uta.edu
Established: 1895 Annual Undergrad Tuition & Fees (In-State): $10,496
Enrollment: 46,497 Coed
Affiliation or Control: State IRS Status: 170(c)1
Highest Offering: Doctorate
Accreditation: SC, ART, CAATE, CAEPN, CEA, CIDA, LSAR, MUS, NURSE, PLNG, SPAA, SW

02 President Dr. Vistasp M. KARBHARI
05 Provost & VP Acad Affairs Dr. Teik LIM
10 Chief Financial Officer and VP Ms. Kelly DAVIS
32 VP Student Affairs Ms. Lisa NAGY
46 Vice President Research Dr. Duane DIMOS
13 Chief Information Officer Mr. Jeffery NEYLAND
11 Vice Pres Admin & Campus Operations Mr. John D. HALL
15 Vice President for Human Resources Ms. Jean HOOD
84 VP for Enrollment Management Dr. Troy JOHNSON
111 VP for Institutional Advancement Vacant
45 Asst V Provost Inst Eff/Report Dr. Rebecca LEWIS
16 Asst Vice Pres Human Resources Ms. Eunice M. CURRIE
18 Asst VP Campus Operation/Facilities Mr. Bill POOLE
121 Assoc V Prov Div of Stdnt Success Dr. Ashley PURGASON
100 Chief of Staff and Assoc VP Ms. Salma ADEM
58 Assoc Dean of Graduate Studies Mr. Raymond L. JACKSON
48 Dean College Arch/Urban/Pub Affairs Dr. Adrian PARR
50 Dean College of Business Mr. Harry DOMBROSKI
54 Dean of Engineering Dr. Peter CROUCH
49 Dean of Liberal Arts Dr. Elisabeth CAWTHON
66 Dean of Nursing Dr. Elizabeth MERWIN
81 Dean of Science Dr. Morteza KHALEDI
70 Dean School of Social Work Dr. Scott RYAN
53 Dean College of Education Dr. Teresa TABER DOUGHTY
92 Interim Dean Honors College Dr. Tim HENRY
08 Dean of Libraries Dr. Rebecca BICHEL
12 Exec Dir of UTA Ft Worth Center Vacant
37 Director of Financial Aid Dr. Karen KRAUSE
23 Director Student Health Center Mr. Robert BLUM
22 Director Equal Opportunity Services Mr. Eddie FREEMAN
41 Athletic Director Mr. Jim BAKER
19 Dir Environmental Health Safety Ms. Leah HOY
85 Executive Director Intl Education Mr. Jay HORN
88 Director Multicultural Outreach Mr. Casey GONZALES
93 Director Multicultural Affairs Ms. Melanie JOHNSON
86 VP Government Relations Mr. Jeff JETER
43 Dir Legal Services/General Counsel Mr. Shelby BOSEMAN
96 Director of Purchasing Ms. Julia CORNWELL
29 Exec Dir for Alumni & Donor Rels Ms. Julie BARFIELD
04 Executive Assoc to President Ms. Elsa CORRAL

*University of Texas at Austin (A)

110 Inner Campus Drive, Austin TX 78705
County: Travis FICE Identification: 003658
Unit ID: 228778
Telephone: (512) 471-3434 Carnegie Class: DU-Highest
FAX Number: (512) 471-2942 Calendar System: Semester
URL: www.utexas.edu
Established: 1883 Annual Undergrad Tuition & Fees (In-State): $10,610
Enrollment: 51,525 Coed
Affiliation or Control: State IRS Status: 170(c)1
Highest Offering: Doctorate
Accreditation: SC, ART, AUD, CAATE, CEA, CIDA, CLPSY, COPSY, DANCE, DIETC, DIETD, IPSY, JOUR, LAW, LIB, LSAR, #MED, MUS, NURSE, PHAR, PLNG, SCPSY, SP, SPAA, SW

02 President Dr. Gregory L. FENVES
05 Executive VP & Provost Dr. Maurie MCINNIS
10 SVP & Chief Financial Officer Mr. Darrell BAZZELL
28 VP for Diversity & Cmty Engagement Mr. Leonard MOORE
11 Associate Vice President Dr. Marla MARTINEZ
46 Vice President for Research Dr. Daniel JAFFE
63 Vice President for Medical Affairs Dr. S. Claiborne JOHNSTON
30 Vice Pres for Development Mr. Scott RABENOLD
32 VP Stdnt Affairs & Dean of Students Dr. Soncia R. REAGINS-LILLY
41 Vice President & Athletics Director Mr. Christopher DEL CONTE
13 VP & Chief Information Officer Mr. Chris SEDORE
27 Chief Communications Officer Mr. Gary SUSSWEIN
43 Vice President Legal Affairs Mr. James DAVIS
88 Deputy to the Pres Strategy/Policy Dr. Harrison A. KELLER
100 Deputy to the President Ms. Nancy A. BRAZZIL
04 Executive Assistant to President Ms. Rebecca L. BAUGHMAN
88 Sr Vice Prov Resource Management Dr. Daniel T. SLESNICK
20 VP Advocacy & Dispute Resolution Dr. Janet M. DUKERICH
88 Vice Provost for Biomed Sciences Vacant
46 Asst VP Res/Dir Sponsored Projects Ms. Renee K. GONZALES
08 Vice Provost/Director UT Libraries Dr. Lorraine J. HARICOMBE
104 Dir of Intl Student & Scholar Svcs Dr. Teri ALBRECHT
88 Assoc VP Strat Acad Initiatives Dr. Linda N. DICKENS
100 Chief of Staff Mr. Carlos E. MARTINEZ
86 Assoc VP for Governmental Relations Vacant
114 Budget Office Director Ms. Elvia H. ROSALES
105 Web and Mobile Applications Manager Ms. Tracy H. BROWN
88 Assoc Vice Prov Acad Business Affs Ms. Kathryn V. FOSTER
07 Assoc Vice Prov for Enrollment Ms. Carolyn K. CONNERAT
88 Workday Implementation Advisor Ms. Renee L. WALLACE
18 Associate VP Utilities/Energy Mgmt Mr. Juan ONTIVEROS
15 Associate VP Human Resources Ms. Adrienne HOWARTH-MOORE
22 Exec Dir Org Culture & Inclusion Dr. Yulanda MCCARTY-HARRIS
37 Exec Dir Office of Financial Aid Ms. Diane C. TODD SPRAGUE
39 Director Housing & Food Service Mr. Rene RODRIGUEZ
100 Chief of Staff & Exec Sr Assoc AD Ms. Christine A. PLONSKY
19 Asst VP Campus Sec/Chief of Police Mr. David CARTER
48 Dean of Architecture Dr. Michelle ADDINGTON
50 Dean McCombs School of Business Dr. Jay C. HARTZELL
60 Dean of Communication Dr. Jay M. BERNHARDT
53 Dean of Education Dr. Charles MARTINEZ
54 Dean of Engineering Dr. Sharon L. WOOD
57 Dean of Fine Arts Dr. Douglas J. DEMPSTER
62 Dean School of Information Dr. Eric MEYER
65 Dean Jackson School of Geosciences Dr. Sharon MOSHER
61 Dean School of Law Mr. Ward FARNSWORTH
49 Dean of Liberal Arts Dr. Randy L. DIEHL
81 Dean College of Natural Sciences Dr. Paul GOLDBART
66 Dean of Nursing Dr. Alexa M. STUIFBERGEN
67 Dean of Pharmacy Dr. M. Lynn CRISMON
80 Dean LBJ School Public Affs Dr. Angela EVANS
70 Dean Social Work Dr. Luis H. ZAYAS
97 Dean of Undergrad Studies Dr. Brent L. IVERSON
26 Director of Communications Mr. Joey WILLIAMS
88 Executive Director for Univ Unions Mr. Mulugeta FEREDE
27 Director Univ of Texas Press Mr. David S. HAMRICK

*The University of Texas at Dallas (B)

800 West Campbell Road, Richardson TX 75080
County: Collin FICE Identification: 009741
Unit ID: 228787
Telephone: (972) 883-2111 Carnegie Class: DU-Highest
FAX Number: (972) 883-2237 Calendar System: Semester
URL: www.utdallas.edu
Established: 1969 Annual Undergrad Tuition & Fees (In-State): $13,034
Enrollment: 27,642 Coed
Affiliation or Control: State IRS Status: 501(c)3
Highest Offering: Doctorate
Accreditation: SC, ACAE, AUD, IPSY, SP, SPAA

02 President Dr. Richard BENSON
03 Executive Vice President Dr. B. Hobson WILDENTHAL
05 VP Academic Affairs and Provost Dr. Inga MUSSELMAN
10 Vice President for Business Affairs Dr. Calvin D. JAMISON
32 Vice President Student Affairs Dr. Gene FITCH
46 VP for Research Dr. Joseph J. PANCRAZIO
20 Vice Provost Dr. John WIORKOWSKI
30 Vice President for Development Dr. Kyle EDGINGTON
13 VP Info Technology and CIO Mr. Frank FEAGANS
28 Vice President of Diversity Dr. George W. FAIR
114 Asst VP and Chief Budget Officer Mr. Orkun TOROS
21 VP Finance & Controller Mr. Terry PANKRATZ
26 VP Public Affairs Ms. Amanda O. ROCKOW
45 Exec Director Strategic Planning Dr. Lawrence J. REDLINGER
35 Dean of Students Dr. Amanda SMITH
58 Dean Graduate Studies Dr. Juan E. GONZALEZ
53 Dean Undergraduate Education Dr. Jessica C. MURPHY
79 Dean School Arts & Humanities Dr. Dennis KRATZ
50 Dean School of Management Dr. Hasan PIRKUL
81 Dean Sch of Natural Science/Math Dr. Bruce NOVAK
82 Int Dean Sch Econ/Political/PoliSci Dr. Jennifer HOLMES
76 Dean Sch Behavioral/Brain Science Dr. Steven L. SMALL
97 Dean School General Studies Dr. George W. FAIR
54 Dean EJ Sch of Engr/Computer Sci Dr. Mark W. SPONG
88 Dean Sch Arts/Tech & Emerg Media Dr. Anne BALSAMO
92 Dean Honors College Dr. Edward HARPHAM
08 Dean of Libraries Dr. Ellen SAFLEY
06 Registrar Ms. Jennifer MCDOWELL
12 Exec Director of Callier Center Dr. Thomas F. CAMPBELL
18 Assoc VP Facilities Management Mr. Doug TOMLINSON
15 Assoc VP Human Resources Ms. Colleen DUTTON
96 Exec Dir Procurement Management Dr. Reda BERNOUSSI
19 Chief of Police Mr. Larry ZACHARIAS
36 Director Career Services Ms. Keri BURNS
38 Director Student Counseling Mr. James P. CANNICI
116 Institutional Chief Audit Executive Ms. Toni STEPHENS
41 Director Intercollegiate Athletics Mr. Bill PETITT
78 Assoc Dir Co-operative Education Mr. Michael J. CHOATE
90 Assoc VP/Chief Tech Officer Mr. Brian DOURTY
29 Senior Director of Alumni Relations Ms. Jill ARREDONDO
04 Executive Associate to President Ms. Kimberly GOODFRIEND
105 Director Web Services Mr. Joe WILSON
106 Asst Provost Learning Tech Mr. Darren CRONE
39 Asst VP Residential Life Mr. Ryan WHITE
104 Director Study Abroad Ms. Lisabeth LASSITER
37 Director Student Financial Aid Ms. Beth TOLAN
43 University Attorney Mr. Timothy SHAW
84 Asst Provost Enrollment Management Mr. Wray WELDON
05 Interim Provost Dr. John WIEBE
03 Executive Vice President Mr. Ricardo ADAUTO, III
10 VP Business Affairs Mr. Mark MCGURK
46 Vice President for Research Dr. Roberto OSEGUEDA
13 Vice Pres Info Resources & Planning Dr. Steve RITER
32 Vice President Student Affairs Dr. Gary EDENS
30 VP Asset Mgmt/Development Mr. Benjamin GONZALEZ
58 Dean of Graduate School Dr. Stephen L. CRITES
50 Dean of Business Administration Dr. James E. PAYNE
53 Dean of Education Dr. Clifton TANABE
54 Dean of Engineering Dr. Theresa MALDONADO
49 Dean of Liberal Arts Dr. Denis O'HEARN
76 Dean of Health Sciences Dr. Shafik DHARAMSI
81 Dean of Science Dr. Robert KIRKEN
66 Interim Dean of School of Nursing Dr. Patricia T. CASTIGLIA
26 Assoc VP External Relations & Comm Ms. Estrella ESCOBAR
18 Assoc VP Business Affs/Facilities Mr. Greg L. MCNICOL
08 Assoc Vice President Library Mr. Robert L. STAKES
111 Asst Vice Pres University Relations Mr. Beto LOPEZ
22 Assoc VP Human Resources Ms. Sandy VASQUEZ
29 Asst VP Alumni Relations Ms. Maribel VILLALVA
84 Asst VP Enrollment Services Dr. Amanda VASQUEZ
19 Chief Campus Police Mr. Clifton WALSH
37 Asst VP for Financial Services Dr. Heidi GRANGER
23 Director of Student Health Center Ms. Louise P. CASTRO
36 Director of Career Services Ms. Betsy CASTRO-DUARTE
35 Associate VP/Dean of Students Dr. Catherine M. MCCORRY-ANDALIS
108 Assoc VP Inst Eval/Rsrch & Planning Dr. Roy MATHEW
39 Executive Dir of Housing Services Ms. Victoria SUTTMILLER
40 Director of University Bookstore Mr. Matt CULBERSON
41 Athletics Director Mr. Jim SENTER
38 Director Counseling Services Ms. Brian SNEED
96 Assoc VP Purchasing/General Svcs Dr. Diane N. DEHOYOS

*University of Texas at El Paso (C)

500 W University Avenue, El Paso TX 79968-8900
County: El Paso FICE Identification: 003661
Unit ID: 228796
Telephone: (915) 747-5000 Carnegie Class: DU-Highest
FAX Number: (915) 747-5111 Calendar System: Semester
URL: www.utep.edu
Established: 1914 Annual Undergrad Tuition & Fees (In-State): $8,198
Enrollment: 25,078 Coed
Affiliation or Control: State IRS Status: 501(c)3
Highest Offering: Doctorate
Accreditation: SC, CACREP, MT, MUS, NURSE, OT, PH, @PHAR, PTA, SP, SPAA, SW

02 President Dr. Diana S. NATALICIO

*The University of Texas Rio Grande Valley (D)

1201 W University Drive, Edinburg TX 78539-2999
County: Hidalgo FICE Identification: 003599
Unit ID: 227368
Telephone: (888) 882-8201 Carnegie Class: DU-Higher
FAX Number: (956) 665-2150 Calendar System: Semester
URL: www.utrgv.edu
Established: 2015 Annual Undergrad Tuition & Fees (In-State): $7,813
Enrollment: 27,809 Coed
Affiliation or Control: State IRS Status: 501(c)3
Highest Offering: Doctorate
Accreditation: SC, ARCPA, CACREP, #MED, MT, MUS, NURSE, OT, SP, SW, THEA

02 President Dr. Guy BAILEY
03 Deputy President Dr. Janna ARNEY
05 EVP Academic Affairs Dr. Patricia MCHATTON
10 EVP for Finance and Administration Mr. Rick ANDERSON
46 EVP Research/Graduate Studies Dr. Parwinder GREWAL
111 VP for Institutional Advancement Dr. Kelly SCRIVNER
86 VP for Governmental & Community Rel Ms. Veronica GONZALES
32 Sr Assoc VP for Student Success Dr. Luzelma CANALES
84 VP for Strategic Enrollment Dr. Maggie HINOJOSA
20 AVP Faculty Affairs Dr. Shawn SALADIN
21 Assoc VP Financial Services Ms. Karla LOYA
28 Sr AVP Faculty Success & Diversity Dr. Selina MIRELES
11 VP for Admin Support Services Mr. Doug ARNEY
45 Assoc VP for Planning & Analysis Mr. Juan C. GONZALEZ
18 Assoc VP for Facilities Ms. Marta SALINAS-HOVAR
110 Assoc VP for Advancement Services Vacant
88 Assoc VP for Governmental Relations Mr. Richard P. SANCHEZ
26 Assoc VP for University Marketing Mr. Patrick GONZALES
109 Assoc VP for Campus Auxiliary Svcs Ms. Letty BENAVIDES
31 Assoc VP for Community Engagement Ms. Cristina TREJO
09 AVP Strategic Analysis and Inst Res Ms. Susan BROWN
88 Assoc VP Inst Accreditation Dr. Christine SHUPALA
88 Assoc VP Academic & Inst Excellence Dr. Laura SAENZ
53 Dean College of Educ & P-16 Dr. Alma RODRIGUEZ
50 Int Dean Business Entrepreneurship Dr. Wesley BALDA
81 Interim Dean College of Sciences Dr. Mohammed FAROOQUI
54 Dean College Engr/Comp Sci Dr. Ala QUBBAJ
76 Dean College of Health Professions Dr. Michael LEHKER
49 Dean College of Fine Arts Dr. Steven BLOCK
83 Dean College of Liberal Arts Dr. Walter DIAZ
63 EVP Health Affairs Dr. John KROUSE
66 Dean School of Nursing Dr. Sharon RADZYMINSKI
43 Chief Legal Officer Ms. Karen ADAMS
15 Chief Human Resources Officer Mr. Mike JAMES
06 Registrar Ms. Sofia MONTES
22 Chief Compliance Officer Ms. Diane SHEPPARD
13 Chief Information Officer Dr. Jeffrey GRAHAM
119 Chief Info Security Officer Mr. Thomas OWEN
29 Exec Dir of Alumni Relations Mrs. Marisa CAMPIRANO
41 Athletics Director Vacant
46 Exec Dir Research Administration Ms. Rosalinda SALAZAR
04 Assistant to the President Ms. Maria CONDE
08 Dean of Libraries Mr. Paul SHARPE
37 Director of Financial Aid Mr. Elias OZUNA
92 Dean Honors College Dr. Mark ANDERSEN
88 Exec Dir B3 Institute Dr. Francisco GUAJARDO

*The University of Texas at San Antonio (E)

One UTSA Circle, San Antonio TX 78249-0169
County: Bexar FICE Identification: 010115
Unit ID: 229027

Telephone: (210) 458-4011 Carnegie Class: DU-Higher
FAX Number: (210) 458-4187 Calendar System: Semester
URL: www.utsa.edu
Established: 1969 Annual Undergrad Tuition & Fees (In-State): $8,049
Enrollment: 30,768 Coed
Affiliation or Control: State IRS Status: 501(c)3
Highest Offering: Doctorate
Accreditation: SC, ART, CACREP, CEA, CIDA, CONST, MUS, SPAA, SW

02 President .... Dr. Taylor EIGHMY
05 Provost/Vice Pres Academic Affs .. Dr. Kimberly ANDREWS ESPY
10 Vice Pres for Business Affairs .... Ms. Kathryn FUNK-BAXTER
46 Int Vice President for Research .... Dr. Bernard ARULANANDAM
32 Vice President for Student Affairs .... Mr. Samuel GONZALES
20 AVP/AV Provost Inst Initiatives .... Dr. Howard GRIMES
13 VP Information Mgmt/Technology .... Ms. Kendra KETCHUM
28 Vice President Inclusive Excellence .... Dr. Myron ANDERSON
09 AVP Acad Compl/Inst Effectiveness ...... Mr. Steve L. WILKERSON
12 Vice Provost for Downtown Campus .... Dr. Jesse T. ZAPATA
100 Chief of Staff .... Ms. Mary DIAZ
20 Int Vice Prov/Dean Univ College .... Dr. Heather J. SHIPLEY
21 Associate VP Financial Affairs .... Ms. Sheri HARDISON
27 AVP Comm & Special Projects Officer .... Ms. Anne C. PETERS
08 Dean of Libraries .... Dr. Dean D. HENDRIX
92 Dean of Honors College .... Dr. Sean KELLY
58 Int Vice Prov/Dean Graduate School .... Dr. Can SAYGIN
50 Dean College of Business .... Dr. Wm Gerard (Gerry) Y. SANDERS
57 Dean College of Liberal & Fine Arts .... Dr. Daniel J. GELO
54 Dean College of Engineering .... Dr. Joann BROWNING
83 Interim Dean College of Sciences .... Dr. Howard GRIMES
48 Dean School of Architecture .... Prof. John MURPHY
53 Dean College Educ/Human Development .... Dr. Margo DELLI CARPINI
80 Dean College of Public Policy .... Dr. Rogelio SAENZ
19 AVP Public Safety/Chief of Police .... Mr. Gerald LEWIS
41 VP ICA and Athletics Director .... Dr. Lisa D. CAMPOS
43 Interim Chief Legal Officer .... Mr. John P. DANNER
117 Dir Inst Compliance & Risk Services .... Mr. James R. WEAVER
116 Chief Audit Executive .... Paul A. TYLER
26 Associate VP for Comm/Marketing .... Mr. Joe IZBRAND
86 AVP Government Relations & Policy .. Mr. Albert A. CARRISALEZ
04 Exec Assistant Office of President .... Ms. Yvonne DE LEON
07 Director of Admissions .... Ms. Beverly WOODSON DAY
88 Asst VP Strategic Initiatives .... Ms. Elvira E. LEAL
105 Associate Director of Web/Portal .... Mr. Shashi B. PINHEIRO
106 Director of Online Learning .... Ms. Marcela V. RAMIREZ
108 Assistant Vice Provost Assessment .... Dr. Kasey NEECE-FIELDER
18 Int Senior AVP for Business Affairs .... Mr. David J. RIKER
25 Dir Grants/Contracts/Financial Svcs .... Mr. Daniel ANZAK
28 Associate Provost .... Col. Lisa C. FIRMIN, RET.
37 Director of Student Financial Aid .... Ms. Diana S. MARTINEZ
38 Director Counseling Services .... Dr. Melissa HERNANDEZ
39 Director Student Housing/Residence .... Mr. Daniel L. GOCKLEY
30 Asst VP Operations/Talent Mgmt .... Ms. Rebecca ANDERSON
37 Interim Director Financial Aid .... Ms. Erika M. COX
90 Director of Academic Computing .... Mr. John P. SOUDAH
96 Director Business Contracts .... Mr. Robert L. DICKENS

*University of Texas at Tyler (A)

3900 University Boulevard, Tyler TX 75799-6699
County: Smith FICE Identification: 011163
Unit ID: 228802
Telephone: (903) 566-7000 Carnegie Class: DU-Mod
FAX Number: (903) 566-7068 Calendar System: Semester
URL: www.uttyler.edu
Established: 1971 Annual Undergrad Tuition & Fees (In-State): $8,292
Enrollment: 10,402 Coed
Affiliation or Control: State IRS Status: 501(c)3
Highest Offering: Doctorate
Accreditation: SC, CACREP, MUS, NAIT, NURSE, PHAR

02 President .... Dr. Michael TIDWELL
05 Provost/VP Academic Affairs .... Dr. Amir MIRMIRAN
30 Vice President Univ Advancement .... Mr. Orrie COVERT
32 Vice Pres for Student Success .... Ms. Ona TOLLIVER
13 Vice President & CIO IT .... Dr. Sherri WHATLEY
20 Vice Provost AA/Grad Studies .... Dr. William GEIGER
46 Exec Director Research .... Dr. Kouider MOKHTARI
10 VP for Budget and CFO .... Dr. Kimberly LAIRD
15 Director of Human Resources .... Ms. Gracy BUENTELLO
21 Assoc VP for Business Affairs .... Vacant
86 AVP Gov & Community Relations .... Dr. Laura JACKSON
84 AVP for Enrollment Management .... Ms. Sarah BOWDIN
108 Asst Vice Pres for Assessment/IE .... Dr. Lou Ann BERMAN
49 Dean College of Arts & Sciences .... Dr. Neil GRAY
50 Dean College Business & Technology .... Dr. Robert BEATTY
53 Dean College Educ & Psych .... Dr. Wesley HICKEY
54 Dean College of Engineering .... Dr. Javier KYPUROS
66 Dean College Nursing & Health Sci .... Dr. Yong TAI WANG
67 Dean College of Pharmacy .... Dr. Lane BRUNNER
08 Exec Director of the Library .... Ms. Rebecca MCKAY JOHNSON
21 Director of Financial Services .... Ms. Cindy TROYER
18 AVP for Facilities Management .... Mr. Jerry STUFF
29 Exec Dir Career Success & Alumni .... Dr. Rosemary COOPER
26 Exec Dir Marketing & Communication .... Ms. Beverley GOLDEN
121 Associate Dean of Student Success .... Ms. Kim HARVEY-LIVINGSTON
39 Director of Residence Life .... Dr. Jennifer WATERS
06 Registrar .... Ms. Sarah BOWDIN
09 Director Institutional Analysis .... Ms. Cindy STRAWN
19 Chief University Police .... Mr. Mike W. MEDDERS
04 Executive Asst to President .... Ms. Janet ROBERTSON
07 Asst Director of Admissions .... Ms. Whitney RAINS
37 Director of Student Financial Aid .... Mr. Scott LAPINSKI
43 Chief Legal Officer .... Mr. Michael DONLEY
106 Assoc Provost UG Adm & On-line Educ .... Dr. Colleen SWAIN
41 Athletic Director .... Dr. Howard PATTERSON
44 Director of Annual Giving .... Mr. Daniel ONDERKO

*The University of Texas Health Science Center at Houston (UTHealth) (B)

PO Box 20036, Houston TX 77225-0036
County: Harris FICE Identification: 004951
Unit ID: 229300
Telephone: (713) 500-4472 Carnegie Class: Spec-4-yr-Med
FAX Number: (713) 500-3026 Calendar System: Semester
URL: www.uth.edu
Established: 1972 Annual Undergrad Tuition & Fees (In-State): N/A
Enrollment: 5,242 Coed
Affiliation or Control: State IRS Status: 501(c)3
Highest Offering: Doctorate
Accreditation: SC, ANEST, CAHIIM, #CAMPEP, DENT, DH, DIETI, HSA, IPSY, MED, NURSE, PERF, PH

02 President .... Dr. Giuseppe N. COLASURDO
11 Exec VP & COO .... Mr. T. Kevin DILLON
03 Senior VP & COO UT Physicians .... Mr. Andrew CASAS
63 Dean McGovern Medical School .... Dr. Barbara J. STOLL
69 Dean School of Public Health .... Dr. Eric BOERWINKLE
52 Dean School of Dentistry .... Dr. John A. VALENZA
58 Dean Grad Sch Biomedical Sciences ..... Dr. Michael BLACKBURN
58 Dean Grad Sch Biomedical Sciences .... Dr. Michelle C. BARTON
66 Interim Dean Cizik Sch of Nursing ... Dr. Diane M. SANTA MARIA
88 Dean Sch of Biomed Informatics .... Dr. Jiajie W. ZHANG
05 Exec VP & Chief Academic Officer ... Dr. Michael R. BLACKBURN
117 Vice President Enterprise Risk Mgmt .... Ms. Karen K. SPILLAR
10 Sr VP Finance & Business Svcs & CFO .... Mr. Michael TRAMONTE
46 Vice Dn Rsrch/Dir Molecular Med .... Dr. John HANCOCK
30 Vice Pres Development .... Mr. Kevin J. FOYLE
15 VP/Chief Human Resources Officer .... Mr. Eric FERNETTE
43 VP/Chief Legal Officer .... Mr. Melissa K. PIFKO
88 Asst VP & Chief Compliance Officer .... Mr. William S. LEMAISRE
43 VP/Chief Legal Officer .... Mr. Daniel J. REAT
86 VP Govt Relations .... Mr. Scott FORBES
88 VP Research & Technology .... Dr. Bruce D. BUTLER
109 VP Auxiliary Enterprises .... Mr. Charles A. FIGARI
13 VP/Chief Information Officer .... Mr. Amar YOUSIF
18 VP Facilities Planning & Engr .... Mr. Richard L. MCDERMOTT
90 Asst VP Academic Technology .... Dr. William A. WEEMS
116 Asst VP & Chief Audit Officer .... Mr. Daniel SHERMAN
09 Asst VP Institutional Research .... Ms. Deanne HERNANDEZ
06 Registrar .... Mr. Robert JENKINS
19 Assoc VP/Chief of Police .... Mr. William ADCOX
40 Executive Director HCPC .... Dr. Jair C. SOARES
41 Director Recreation/Intramural Pgms .... Ms. Pauline M. HABETZ
85 Director International Affairs .... Ms. Rose Mary VALENCIA
39 Director University Housing .... Mr. Billy C. HINTON
26 Executive Director Public Affairs .... Ms. Meredith RAINE
37 Director Student Financial Svcs .... Ms. Araceli ALVAREZ
25 Assoc VP Sponsored Projects Admin ...... Ms. Kathleen KREIDLER
14 Exec Director & Chief Tech Ofcr .... Mr. Kevin B. GRANHOLD
88 Director Educational Tech Nursing .... Ms. Linda L. CRAYS
88 Director Interactive Video Medical .... Dr. Stephen J. FATH
100 Chief of Staff Office of the Pres .... Ms. Rose HOCHNER
105 Executive Director Univ Web Svcs .... Ms. Jennifer L. CANUP
22 AVP Diversity & Equal Opportunity .... Ms. Deana K. MOYLAN
28 VP Diversity & Assoc Dean Med .... Dr. Latonya J. LOVE

*University of Texas Health Science Center at San Antonio (C)

7703 Floyd Curl Drive, San Antonio TX 78229-3900
County: Bexar FICE Identification: 003659
Unit ID: 228644
Telephone: (210) 567-7000 Carnegie Class: Spec-4-yr-Med
FAX Number: N/A Calendar System: Other
URL: www.uthscsa.edu
Established: 1959 Annual Undergrad Tuition & Fees (In-State): N/A
Enrollment: 3,277 Coed
Affiliation or Control: State IRS Status: 501(c)3
Highest Offering: Doctorate
Accreditation: SC, ARCPA, CAMPEP, COARC, DENT, DH, DIETC, EMT, HT, IPSY, MED, MT, NURSE, OT, PTA, RADDOS, @SP

02 President .... Dr. William L. HENRICH
03 Sr Exec Vice President & COO .... Mr. Michael E. BLACK
11 Exec VP for Facility Planning/Admin .... Mr. James D. KAZEN
10 Vice President & CFO .... Ms. Andrea M. MARKS
05 VP Acad/Fac & Student Affairs .... Dr. Jacqueline L. MOK
13 Vice Pres & Chief Information Ofcr .... Mr. Yeman COLLIER
46 Vice President for Research .... Dr. Andrea GIUFFRIDA
86 VP for Governmental Relations .... Mr. Armando DIAZ
30 VP Inst Advancement/Chief Dev Ofcr ... Ms. Deborah H. MORRILL
26 VP & Chief Marketing/Comm Officer .... Ms. Heather ADKINS
15 Vice Pres of Human Resources .... Mr. J. Michael TESH
100 VP & Chief of Staff .... Ms. Mary G. DELAY
21 Asst Vice Pres for Business Affairs .... Mr. Gerard E. LONG
09 Asst VP Research .... Dr. Mark J. NIJLAND
43 Asst VP/Chief Legal Officer .... Mr. Jack C. PARK
63 Dean School of Medicine .... Dr. Robert HROMAS
52 Dean School of Dentistry .... Dr. William W. DODGE
58 Dean Graduate Biomed Science .... Dr. David WEISS
76 Dean School Health Professions .... Dr. David C. SHELLEDY
66 Dean School of Nursing .... Dr. Eileen T. BRESLIN
32 Director for Student Life .... Ms. Le Keisha JOHNSON
06 Registrar .... Ms. Blanca GUERRA
08 Senior Director of Libraries .... Mr. Owen H. ELLARD
19 Chief of Police .... Mr. Michael PARKS
88 Exec Dir Acad/Fac/Studnt Ombudspers .... Dr. Bonnie L. BLANKMEYER
37 Director of Financial Aid .... Ms. Ellen NYSTROM
38 Director of Student Counseling .... Dr. Mia VEVE
96 Sr Dir Supply Chain Mngmt/HUB Coord .... Mr. Eric R. WALLS
07 Director of Admissions .... Vacant
102 Development Officer .... Ms. Leslie M. PAYNE
44 Interim Director Planned Giving .... Ms. Jennifer M. CLARK

*The University of Texas Health Science Center at Tyler (D)

11937 US Hwy 271, Tyler TX 75708-3154
County: Smith Identification: 667206
Unit ID: 485537
Telephone: (903) 877-7777 Carnegie Class: Spec-4-yr-Other Health
FAX Number: N/A Calendar System: Semester
URL: www.uthct.edu
Established: 1977 Annual Graduate Tuition & Fees: N/A
Enrollment: 35 Coed
Affiliation or Control: State IRS Status: 501(c)3
Highest Offering: Master's; No Undergraduates
Accreditation: SC, IPSY

02 President and CEO .... Dr. Kirk A. CALHOUN
11 Exec VP/Chief Operating Officer .... Joseph F. WOELKERS
05 Sr VP Academic Affairs/Provost .... Dr. Jeffrey L. LEVIN
46 Sr VP Research & Graduate Studies .... Dr. Steven IDELL
23 Sr VP/CMO & Physician in Chief .... Dr. Steven W. COX
88 Sr VP Population Health .... Dr. David L. LAKEY
17 Sr VP/CAO Hospital & Clinics .... Timothy G. OCHRAN
10 VP/Chief Financial Officer .... Kris KAVASCH
15 VP Human Resources/CHRO .... Cynthia SCOTT-LUNAU
43 VP Legal Affs/Chief Legal Officer .... Carl BARANOWSKI
45 VP Planning & Public Policy .... Daniel DESLATTE
13 VP Information Technology (CIO) .... John YODER
30 VP Institutional Advancement .... Marilyn GLASS
18 Assoc VP Physical Plant .... Kenny HUFFMAN
20 Assoc VP Academic Affairs ..... Dr. Pierre F. NEUENSCHWANDER
32 Director of Student Affairs .... Dr. Mickey SLIMP
08 Director of Library Services .... Thomas CRAIG
09 Director of Institutional Research .... Anna KURDOWSKA
86 Exec Dir University/Community Affs .... Kimberly ASHLEY
96 Director of Purchasing .... Crystal SMITH
37 Director Student Financial Aid .... Araceli ALVAREZ
06 Registrar .... Robert JENKINS
04 Admin Assistant to President .... Mitzi HARRIS
19 Chief of Police .... Chief Robert CROMLEY
26 Chief Public Affairs/Market Exec .... Rachel ROBERTS

*The University of Texas MD Anderson Cancer Center (E)

1515 Holcombe Boulevard, Houston TX 77030-4000
County: Harris FICE Identification: 025554
Unit ID: 416801
Telephone: (713) 792-6161 Carnegie Class: Spec-4-yr-Other Health
FAX Number: N/A Calendar System: Semester
URL: www.mdanderson.org
Established: 1941 Annual Undergrad Tuition & Fees (In-District): N/A
Enrollment: 357 Coed
Affiliation or Control: State/Local IRS Status: 501(c)3
Highest Offering: Doctorate
Accreditation: SC, CAMPEP, CGTECH, CYTO, DENT, DMOLS, HT, MT, PAST, RAD, RADDOS, RADMAG, RTT

02 President .... Dr. Peter PISTERS
10 Sr Vice President/CFO .... Mr. Ben MELSON
17 Chief Medical Officer .... Dr. Stephen HAHN

*The University of Texas Medical Branch (F)

301 University Boulevard, Galveston TX 77555-0100
County: Galveston FICE Identification: 004952
Unit ID: 228653
Telephone: (409) 772-1011 Carnegie Class: Spec-4-yr-Med
FAX Number: N/A Calendar System: Semester
URL: www.utmb.edu
Established: 1891 Annual Undergrad Tuition & Fees (In-State): N/A
Enrollment: 3,302 Coed
Affiliation or Control: State IRS Status: 170(c)1
Highest Offering: Doctorate
Accreditation: SC, #ARCPA, BBT, COARC, DENT, DIETI, MED, MT, NURSE, OT, PH, PTA

02 President .... Dr. David L. CALLENDER
04 Associate Chief of Staff .... Ms. Mary Ann PEDRAZA
05 Exec VP/Provost/Dean Sch of Med .... Dr. Charles P. MOUTON
23 Exec VP & CEO Health System .... Dr. Tim HARLIN
10 Chief Financial Officer .... Ms. Cheryl SADRO
86 Sr VP Health Policy & Legis Affairs .... Dr. Ben G. RAIMER

88 VP & Chief Physician Executive .... Dr. Rex M. MCCALLUM
17 Chief Medical Officer .... Dr. Gulshan SHARMA
66 Sr VP & Dean of Nursing .... Dr. Deborah J. JONES
76 SVP & Dean Sch Health Professions .... Dr. David A. BROWN
58 VP & Dean Grad Sch of Biomed Sci .... Dr. David W. NIESEL
15 VP and Chief HR Officer .... Dr. Vivian D. KARDOW
13 VP Information Services & CIO .... Mr. Todd A. LEACH
21 VP Finance Academic Enterprise .... Ms. Frances HUTCHISON
18 VP Business Ops & Facilities .... Mr. Michael B. SHRINER
11 VP/Chief Admin Officer AE .... Mr. Loren SKINNER
21 Assoc VP Finance CMC .... Mr. David M. CONNAUGHTON
45 Sr VP for Strategic & Business Plan .... Dr. Rebecca KORENEK
43 Sr VP General Counsel .... Ms. Carolee KING
26 VP Marketing & Communications .... Mr. Stephen CAMPBELL
07 Asst Dean Admissions & Recruitment .... Dr. Richard CARROLL
32 Assoc Dean Student Affairs/Adm SON .... Dr. Diana PRESSLEY
46 Assoc VP Research Admin .... Ms. Toni J. D'AGOSTINO
08 Assoc VP Academic Res/Library .... Ms. Patricia A. CIEJKA
09 Assoc VP Inst Effectiveness .... Dr. John C. MCKEE
27 Assoc VP Public Affairs .... Ms. Mary G. HAVARD
21 AVP Financial Capital Planning .... Mr. Matthew FURLONG
114 VP Finance Institution Support .... Ms. Celia BAILEY-OCHOA
116 VP Audit Services .... Ms. Kimberly K. ROGERS
30 Assoc VP Chief Develop Officer .... Ms. Betsy B. CLARDY
88 VP & Chief Compliance Officer .... Mr. Tobin R. BOENIG
06 AVP Univ Student Svcs & Registrar .... Mr. William S. BOEH
19 Chief of University Police .... Mr. Kenith ADCOX
96 Assoc VP Supply Chain Management .... Mr. Frank REIGHARD
38 Director Student Wellness Services ... Dr. Olawunmi A. AKINPELU
100 Chief of Staff .... Ms. Sheila LIDSTONE
16 Assoc VP HR Talent Manager .... Vacant
105 Director Digital Communications .... Mr. Eduardo VALDES
108 Asst Director Inst Effectiveness .... Mr. Jason FRY
37 Director Student Financial Service .... Ms. Carol CROMIE
117 Assoc VP Operations Risk Management ..... Mr. Steve J. LEBLANC
88 Field House Facilities Ops Manager .... Ms. Leslie BLACKETER
53 VP Education IE & HEC .... Dr. Janet H. SOUTHERLAND

*University of Texas Permian Basin (A)

4901 E University Boulevard, Odessa TX 79762-0001
County: Ector FICE Identification: 009930
Unit ID: 229018
Telephone: (432) 552-2020 Carnegie Class: Masters/L
FAX Number: (432) 552-2374 Calendar System: Semester
URL: www.utpb.edu
Established: 1969 Annual Undergrad Tuition & Fees (In-State): $6,260
Enrollment: 7,022 Coed
Affiliation or Control: State IRS Status: 501(c)3
Highest Offering: Master's
Accreditation: SC, ART, #CAATE, CAEPN, MUS, NURSE, SW

02 President .... Dr. Sandra WOODLEY
05 Provost/Vice Pres Academic Affairs .... Dr. Dan HEIMMERMANN
32 Sr AVP Academic & Student Services ..... Dr. Rebecca SPURLOCK
49 Dean College of Arts & Science .... Dr. Scott MCKAY
50 Dean School of Business .... Dr. Steven BEACH
53 Dean College of Education .... Dr. Larry DANIEL
66 Dean College of Nursing .... Dr. Donna BEUK
54 Dean College of Engineering .... Dr. George NNANNA
07 Director Admissions .... Mr. Scott SMILEY
06 Registrar .... Mr. Joe SANDERS
18 Chief Facilities/Physical Plant .... Mr. David WAYLAND
36 Dir Student Placement/Counseling .... Vacant
29 Alumni Relations .... Mr. Jeff MEYERS
39 Director Student Housing .... Ms. Chermae PEEL
10 Chief Financial/Business Officer .... Mr. Cesar VALENZUELA
15 Chief Human Resources Officer .... Mr. Jasen WITT
20 Associate Academic Officer .... Dr. Steve WILSON
26 Chief Public Relations Officer .... Ms. Tatum GUINN
35 Associate Student Affairs Officer .... Mr. Corey BENSON
04 Admin Asst to the President .... Ms. CC SERRATO
41 Athletic Director .... Mr. Scott FARMER
08 Chief Library Officer .... Dr. Sophia KAANE
111 Dir of Institutional Advancement .... Mr. Wendell SNODGRASS
37 Director Student Financial Aid .... Mr. Omar LIVINGSTON
84 Director Enrollment Management .... Ms. MJ HUEBNER
100 Chief of Staff .... Ms. Tatum HUBBARD
21 Assoc Financial/Business Officer .... Ms. Felecia BURNS
114 Chief Budget Administrator .... Ms. Griselda MEDING

*University of Texas Southwestern Medical Center (B)

5323 Harry Hines Boulevard, Dallas TX 75390-9002
County: Dallas FICE Identification: 010019
Unit ID: 228635
Telephone: (214) 648-3111 Carnegie Class: Spec-4-yr-Med
FAX Number: N/A Calendar System: Semester
URL: www.utsouthwestern.edu
Established: 1943 Annual Undergrad Tuition & Fees (In-State): N/A
Enrollment: 2,238 Coed
Affiliation or Control: State IRS Status: 501(c)3
Highest Offering: Doctorate
Accreditation: SC, ARCPA, CACREP, CAMPEP, CLPSY, DIETC, IPSY, MED, OPE, PAST, PTA, RTT

02 President .... Dr. Daniel K. PODOLSKY
100 Vice President & Chief of Staff .... Dr. Robin M. JACOBY
05 EVP/Provost/Dean SMS .... Dr. W. P. Andrew LEE
20 Vice Provost Sr Assoc Dean Ed .... Dr. Charles M. GINSBURG
20 Vice Provost Sr Assoc Dean Faculty .... Dr. Dwain L. THIELE
03 Exec VP Health System Affairs .... Dr. John WARNER
10 Exec Vice Pres Business Affairs .... Mr. Arnim DONTES
111 Exec VP Institutional Advancement .... Dr. Marc A. NIVET
46 Vice Provost/Dean of Basic Research .... Dr. David W. RUSSELL
23 Vice President Clinical Operations ...... Dr. John D. RUTHERFORD
88 Vice President/CEO University Hosp .... Dr. John WARNER
88 VP & Chief Quality Officer .... Dr. William DANIEL
21 Vice President Financial Affairs .... Mr. Michael SERBER
86 Vice Pres Govt Affairs & Policy .... Ms. Angelica MARIN-HILL
26 Vice Pres & Exec Global Advancement ... Dr. Cheyenne CURRALL
17 Vice President Health System Opers .... Vacant
15 Vice President Human Resources .... Ms. Janelle BROWNE
43 Vice President Legal Affairs .... Ms. Leah A. HURLEY
88 Vice Pres Technology Development .... Vacant
30 Vice President Development .... Ms. Amanda BILLINGS
102 Vice Pres Community and Corp Rels ...... Mr. Ruben E. ESQUIVEL
13 Vice Pres Information Resources .... Mr. Marc MILSTEIN
18 Vice President Facilities Mgmt .... Mr. Juan M. GUERRA, JR.
09 Vice President Research Admin .... Vacant
20 Vice Pres Academic Affairs/CAO .... Mr. Cameron SLOCUM
88 Assoc Vice Pres Ambulatory Care .... Vacant
11 Assoc VP/Chief Operating Officer .... Ms. Becky MCCULLEY
88 Assoc Vice Pres Chief Nursing Ofcr .... Ms. Susan HERNANDEZ
96 Asst Vice Pres Materials Mgmt .... Mr. Charles COBB
88 Assoc Vice Pres & Clinical Exec Neu .... Dr. Christopher MADDEN
88 Assoc Vice Pres Parkland HHS Aff .... Dr. Carlos GIROD
108 Asst Vice Pres Academic Plng Assmnt .... Mr. James DRAKE
27 Asst Vice Pres Marketing .... Ms. Dorothea BONDS
21 Asst Vice Pres Acctg Fiscal Svcs .... Ms. Sharon LEARY
08 Asst Vice Pres Library Services .... Ms. Kelly GONZALEZ
58 Dean Grad School Biomedical Science .... Dr. Andrew ZINN
76 Dean School of Health Professions .... Dr. Jon WILLIAMSON
28 Assoc Dean Faculty Diversity & Dev .... Dr. Byron L. CRYER
88 Assoc Dean Global Health .... Dr. Fiemu E. NWARIAKU
63 Assoc Dean Grad Medical Education .... Dr. Bradley MARPLE
63 Assoc Dean Undergrad Medical Educ .... Dr. Robert REGE
32 Assoc Dean Student Affairs .... Dr. Angela MIHALIC
88 Assoc Dean Credentialing Ed Outcome .... Dr. James M. WAGNER
32 Assoc Dean Student Affairs .... Dr. Blake BARKER
93 Assoc Dean Student Diversity & Incl .... Dr. Shawna NESBITT
06 Associate Registrar .... Vacant
07 Assoc Director of Admissions .... Vacant
37 Director Student Financial Aid .... Ms. Melet LEAFGREEN
84 Director Enrollment Services .... Ms. Shannon WILLIAMS

Vernon College (C)

4400 College Drive, Vernon TX 76384-4092
County: Wilbarger FICE Identification: 010060
Unit ID: 229504
Telephone: (940) 552-6291 Carnegie Class: Assoc/MT-VT-High Non
FAX Number: (940) 553-3902 Calendar System: Semester
URL: www.vernoncollege.edu
Established: 1970 Annual Undergrad Tuition & Fees (In-District): $3,080
Enrollment: 3,005 Coed
Affiliation or Control: State/Local IRS Status: 501(c)3
Highest Offering: Associate Degree
Accreditation: SC, CAHIIM, SURGT

01 President .... Dr. Dusty R. JOHNSTON
04 Admin Secretary to the President .... Ms. Mary KING
05 Vice Pres of Instructional Services .... Dr. Elizabeth CRANDALL
10 Vice Pres Administrative Services .... Mr. Garry DAVID
32 Vice President of Student Services .... Dr. James NORDONE, JR.
103 Dean of Instructional Services .... Ms. Shana DRURY
111 Dir Inst Advance/VC Foundation .... Ms. Michelle ALEXANDER
88 Director of Quality Enhancement .... Dr. Donnie KIRK
09 Dir of Institutional Effectiveness .... Mrs. Betsy HARKEY
37 Director Financial Aid .... Mrs. Melissa J. ELLIOTT
08 Director of Library Services .... Ms. Marion GRONA
18 Director Physical Plant .... Mr. Lyle BONNER
15 Director of Human Resources .... Mrs. Haven DAVID
39 Director of Housing .... Mr. Jesse DOMINQUEZ
35 Dean of Student Services .... Mrs. Kristin HARRIS
84 Dir of Enrollment Mgmt & Registrar .... Mrs. Amanda RAINES
66 Dir Associate Degree in Nursing .... Dr. Mary RIVARD
19 Director of Campus Police .... Mr. Kevin HOLLAND

Vet Tech Institute of Houston (D)

4669 Southwest Freeway, Suite 100, Houston TX 77027
County: Harris FICE Identification: 021448
Unit ID: 223472
Telephone: (713) 629-8940 Carnegie Class: Spec 2-yr-Health
FAX Number: (713) 629-0059 Calendar System: Semester
URL: www.vettechinstitute.edu/houston
Established: 2007 Annual Undergrad Tuition & Fees: $14,700
Enrollment: 191 Coed
Affiliation or Control: Proprietary IRS Status: Proprietary
Highest Offering: Associate Degree
Accreditation: ACCSC

01 Director/Chief Academic Officer .... Mr. Elbert HAMILTON, JR.

Victoria College (E)

2200 E Red River, Victoria TX 77901-4494
County: Victoria FICE Identification: 003662
Unit ID: 229540
Telephone: (361) 573-3291 Carnegie Class: Assoc/MT-VT-High Trad
FAX Number: (361) 572-3850 Calendar System: Semester
URL: www.victoriacollege.edu
Established: 1925 Annual Undergrad Tuition & Fees (In-District): $2,232
Enrollment: 3,962 Coed
Affiliation or Control: Local IRS Status: 501(c)3
Highest Offering: Associate Degree
Accreditation: SC, ADNUR, COARC, EMT, PTAA

01 President .... Dr. David HINDS
05 Vice President of Instruction .... Ms. Cindy BUCHHOLZ
10 Vice Pres Administrative Svcs .... Mr. Keith BLUNDELL
32 Dean of Student Services .... Dr. Edrel STONEHAM
111 VP College Advance/External Affairs .... Ms. Jennifer L. YANCEY
09 Dir Inst Effect/Research/Assess .... Mr. Matt WILEY
07 Registrar .... Ms. Madelyne TOLLIVER
18 Director Physical Plant .... Mr. Marty DECKARD
37 Director Financial Aid .... Ms. Kim OBSTA
15 Director Human Resources .... Ms. Terri KURTZ
26 Dir Marketing & Communications .... Mr. Darin KAZMIR
38 Director Advising/Counseling .... Mr. Robert CUBRIEL, III
96 Director of Purchasing .... Ms. Lydia HUBER
21 Director of Finance .... Ms. Tracey BERGSTROM
35 Director of Student Life .... Ms. Elaine EVERETT-HENSLEY
13 Director Technology Services .... Mr. Andy FARRIOR
04 Exec Admin Asst to President .... Ms. Mary Ann RODRIGUEZ
102 Exec Dir of College Advance & Found .... Ms. Amy MUNDY

Vista College (F)

6101 Montana Avenue, El Paso TX 79925-2021
County: El Paso FICE Identification: 025720
Unit ID: 365204
Telephone: (915) 779-8031 Carnegie Class: Assoc/HVT-High Trad
FAX Number: (915) 779-8097 Calendar System: Semester
URL: www.vistacollege.edu
Established: 1987 Annual Undergrad Tuition & Fees: $15,680
Enrollment: 4,701 Coed
Affiliation or Control: Proprietary IRS Status: Proprietary
Highest Offering: Associate Degree
Accreditation: COE

01 Campus Director .... Mr. Antonio RICO
06 Registrar .... Ms. Valerie PARKS
07 Assoc Director of Admissions .... Mr. Andre RAYOS
37 Director Student Financial Aid .... Ms. Adrianna DURAN
63 Program Director Allied Health .... Ms. Juana CERVANTES
36 Sr Career Services Coordinator .... Ms. Lorraine ESTRADA

Vista College (G)

4620 50th Street, Lubbock TX 79414
Telephone: (806) 785-2100 Identification: 770549
Accreditation: COE

Vista College-Online (H)

300 N. Coit Road, Suite 300, Richardson TX 75080
County: Davis FICE Identification: 025728
Unit ID: 377342
Telephone: (972) 707-8600 Carnegie Class: Bac/Assoc-Mixed
FAX Number: (972) 707-8575 Calendar System: Other
URL: www.vistacollege.edu/online/
Established: Annual Undergrad Tuition & Fees: N/A
Enrollment: 565 Coed
Affiliation or Control: Proprietary IRS Status: Proprietary
Highest Offering: Baccalaureate
Accreditation: ACCSC

01 Director .... Mr. Art WALLER

Wade College (I)

1950 Stemmons Fwy, Ste 4080, LB 562, Dallas TX 75207
County: Dallas FICE Identification: 010130
Unit ID: 226879
Telephone: (214) 637-3530 Carnegie Class: Bac/Assoc-Mixed
FAX Number: (214) 637-0827 Calendar System: Trimester
URL: www.wadecollege.edu
Established: 1962 Annual Undergrad Tuition & Fees: $13,989
Enrollment: 151 Coed
Affiliation or Control: Proprietary IRS Status: Proprietary
Highest Offering: Baccalaureate
Accreditation: SC, CIDA

01 President .... Dr. Harry DAVROS
03 Executive Vice President .... Mr. John CONTE
05 Dean of Academic Affairs .... Ms. Elizabeth JOHNSTON
37 Director Compliance & Finance .... Ms. Lisa HOOVER
07 Director of Admissions .... Mr. James SCHROEDER
36 Director of Career Services .... Mrs. Jennifer MAGEE
08 Director Learning Resources .... Mrs. April LUYCKX

Wayland Baptist University (J)

1900 West Seventh Street, Plainview TX 79072-6998
County: Hale FICE Identification: 003663
Unit ID: 229780
Telephone: (806) 291-1000 Carnegie Class: Masters/L
FAX Number: (806) 291-1975 Calendar System: Semester
URL: www.wbu.edu
Established: 1908 Annual Undergrad Tuition & Fees: $20,070
Enrollment: 4,847 Coed
Affiliation or Control: Southern Baptist IRS Status: 501(c)3
Highest Offering: Doctorate
Accreditation: SC, MUS, NUR

Code	Title	Name
01	President	Dr. Bobby L. HALL
05	Vice Pres of Academic Affairs	Dr. Cindy M. MCCLENAGAN
84	Vice Pres Enrollment Management	Dr. D. Claude LUSK
20	Vice Pres of External Campuses	Dr. Elane SEEBO
111	Vice Pres of Institutional Advance	Dr. Kevin LUDLUM
10	Chief Financial Officer	Mrs. Lezlie HUKILL
45	Exec Dir of Strategic Initiatives	Dr. Daniel BROWN
26	Exec Dir of Marketing	Mr. Gary VAUGHN
12	Exec Dir/Campus Dean Albuquerque	Dr. Tom FISHER
12	Exec Dir/Campus Dean Wichita Falls	Dr. Jerry FAUGHT
12	Exec Dir/Campus Dean Amarillo	Dr. J. B BOREN
12	Exec Dir/Campus Dean Anchorage	Dr. Eric ASH
12	Exec Dir/Campus Dean Clovis	Dr. Gary MITCHELL
12	Exec Dir/Campus Dean Fairbanks	Dr. Beth DURBIN
12	Exec Dir/Campus Dean Hawaii	Dr. Dan JACOBSON
12	Exec Dir/Campus Dean Lubbock	Dr. David BISHOP
12	Exec Dir/Campus Dean Sierra Vista	Dr. D. Glenn SIMMONS
12	Exec Dir/Campus Dean San Antonio	Dr. James ANTENEN
12	Exec Dir/Campus Dean Phoenix	Dr. Andrew MARQUEZ
83	Acad Dean School Behav & Soc Sci	Dr. Peter BOWEN
50	Academic Dean School of Business	Dr. Kelly WARREN
53	Academic Dean School of Education	Dr. Gene WHITFILL
57	Academic Dean School of Fine Arts	Dr. Candace KELLER
79	Int Acad Dean Sch of Lang & Lit	Dr. Joshua MORA
81	Academic Dean School Math/Sciences	Dr. Adam REINHART
64	Academic Dean School of Music	Dr. Ann B. STUTES
66	Academic Dean School of Nursing	Dr. Diane FRAZOR
73	Academic Dean School Rel & Phil	Dr. Stephen STOOKEY
06	University Registrar	Mrs. Julie BOWEN
32	Exec Dir Student Services	Mr. Brad MILES
41	Dir of Intercollegiate Athletics	Mr. Rick COOPER
07	Director of Admissions	Mrs. Debbie STENNETT
29	Director Alumni Relations	Mrs. Teresa YOUNG
88	Dir Denominational Rel/Mission Ctr	Mr. Donnie BROWN
44	Director of Annual Giving	Mr. Gary ZACHER
30	Dir of Donor Relations/Stewardship	Mrs. Amber MCCLOUD
37	Director of Financial Aid	Vacant
58	Director of Graduate Studies	Ms. Amanda STANTON
15	Director of HR & Wellness Mgr	Mr. Ron APPLING
13	Director Information Technology	Mrs. Katrina SMITH
09	Dir Inst Research/Effectiveness	Dr. Morris THOMPSON
08	Director of Libraries	Dr. Polly R. LACKEY
88	Exec Director Property Management	Mr. Trevor MORRIS
27	Director of Communications	Mr. Jonathan PETTY
23	Director of Health Services	Mrs. Coralyn DILLARD
39	Coordinator of Student Housing	Mr. Glynn BOYDSTON
38	Dir Counseling/Career/Disability	Ms. Teresa MOORE
40	Director of University Store	Mr. Brad HENDERSON
106	Director of WBUonline	Dr. Trish RITSCHEL-TRIFILO
105	Director of Web Services	Mrs. Charlotte SCHUMACHER
88	Dir BAS/BCM & Assoc Registrar	Ms. Caitlin ODOM
19	WBU Chief of Police	Vacant
18	Chief Facilities/Physical Plant	Mr. David MURPHREE
04	Exec Asst to President	Mrs. Cynthia TREVINO
110	Director of Advancement Services	Mrs. Amber SMITH
112	Senior Major Gift Officer	Mr. Mike MELCHER

Weatherford College (A)

225 College Park Drive, Weatherford TX 76086-5699

County: Parker | FICE Identification: 003664 | Unit ID: 229799

Telephone: (817) 594-5471 | Carnegie Class: Assoc/MT-VT-High Trad

FAX Number: (817) 598-6210 | Calendar System: Semester

URL: www.wc.edu

Established: 1869 | Annual Undergrad Tuition & Fees (In-District): $2,550

Enrollment: 6,357 | Coed

Affiliation or Control: Local | IRS Status: 501(c)3

Highest Offering: Associate Degree

Accreditation: SC, ADNUR, COARC, DMS, EMT, OTA, PTAA, RAD

Code	Title	Name
01	President	Dr. Tod Allen FARMER
04	Exec Asst to the President	Mrs. Theresa R. HUTCHISON
05	VP of Instruction & Student Svcs	Mr. Michael ENDY
10	Exec VP Financial/Admin Affairs	Mrs. Andra R. CANTRELL
111	Vice Pres Institutional Advancement	Mr. Brent BAKER
76	Dean of Health & Human Sciences	Ms. Katherine BOSWELL
20	Dean Educational/Instructional Sppt	Ms. Rhonda TORRES
32	Executive Dean of Student Services	Mr. Adam FINLEY
103	Assoc Dean Workforce/Economic Devel	Mrs. Janetta KRUSE
26	Dir Communications/Public Relations	Mrs. Crystal WOERLY
31	Dean of Community Programs	Mr. Duane DURRETT
88	Director Transportation Programs	Mr. Terry PILGRIM
09	Dir Inst Research and Assessment	Mr. Lee BUTLER
35	Assoc Dean Student Development	Mr. Doug JEFFERSON
36	Dir of Career Svcs/Transfer Center	Mr. John TURNTINE
109	Director Food Services	Ms. Erin DAVIDSON
37	Director Student Financial Aid	Mr. Donnie PURVIS
21	Controller	Mrs. Rebecca DEPUY
15	Director Human Resources	Ms. Ralinda STONE
07	Director of Admissions/Veterans	Mr. Ralph WILLINGHAM
13	Director Technology Services	Mr. Greg SHRADER
08	Director of Library Services	Mrs. Valorie STARR
18	Director of Facilities	Ms. Rhonda SWAN
96	Director of Purchasing	Mrs. Jeanie HOBBS
19	Chief of Campus Police	Mr. Paul STONE
38	Student Counseling	Ms. Phyllis TIFFIN
88	Director Upward Bound	Mr. Jeff KHALDEN
29	Director Alumni Relations	Mr. Brent BAKER
53	Director of Teacher Education	Dr. Joyce MELTON PAGES
06	Registrar	Mrs. Vicki TRAWEEK
88	Director of Testing	Ms. Gwen CRABTREE
121	Dir of Outreach/Student Success	Ms. Kay LANDRUM
88	Director Special Populations	Mrs. Dawn KAHLDEN
39	Director Student Housing	Miss Faith STIFFLER
41	Athletic Director	Mr. Bob MCKINLEY

West Coast University (B)

8435 N Stemmons Freeway, Dallas TX 75247-3900

Telephone: (214) 453-4533 | Identification: 770485

Accreditation: &WC

† Branch campus of West Coast University, North Hollywood, CA

Western Technical College (C)

9624 Plaza Circle, El Paso TX 79927-2105

County: El Paso | FICE Identification: 020983 | Unit ID: 224679

Telephone: (915) 532-3737 | Carnegie Class: Spec 2-yr-Tech

FAX Number: (915) 532-6946 | Calendar System: Other

URL: www.westerntech.edu

Established: 1969 | Annual Undergrad Tuition & Fees: N/A

Enrollment: 1,042 | Coed

Affiliation or Control: Proprietary | IRS Status: Proprietary

Highest Offering: Associate Degree

Accreditation: ACCSC, PTAA

Code	Title	Name
01	Plaza Main Campus President	Ms. Mary CANO
03	Chief Executive Officer	Mr. Brad KUYKENDALL
11	Chief Administrative Officer	Mr. Bill TERRELL
12	Executive VP/Campus School Director	Ms. Mary CANO
07	VP Admissions/Marketing	Ms. Lynda CERVANTES
05	Diana Branch Campus President	Ms. Margie AGUILAR
10	Accounting Controller	Ms. Laura PLUMMER
37	Student Financial Services Director	Ms. Danielle PICCHI
36	Director Career Services	Ms. Helen GARCIA
13	Information Technology Director	Mr. Jose PEREZ
18	Facilities Maintenance Director	Mr. Jose PEREZ

Western Technical College (D)

9451 Diana Drive, El Paso TX 79924-6936

Telephone: (915) 566-9621 | Identification: 666103

Accreditation: ACCSC, COMTA

Western Texas College (E)

6200 College Avenue, Snyder TX 79549-6189

County: Scurry | FICE Identification: 009549 | Unit ID: 229832

Telephone: (325) 573-8511 | Carnegie Class: Assoc/HT-High Non

FAX Number: (325) 573-9321 | Calendar System: Semester

URL: www.wtc.edu

Established: 1969 | Annual Undergrad Tuition & Fees (In-District): $2,790

Enrollment: 2,250 | Coed

Affiliation or Control: State/Local | IRS Status: 501(c)3

Highest Offering: Associate Degree

Accreditation: SC

Code	Title	Name
01	President	Dr. Barbara R. BEEBE
04	Assistant to the President	Ms. Melanie SCHWERTNER
10	Chief Financial Officer	Ms. Patricia CLAXTON
09	Dean Inst Research & Effectiveness	Mr. Britt CANADA
05	Dean of Instructional Affairs	Ms. Stephanie DUCHENEAUX
32	Dean of Student Services	Mr. Ralph RAMON
72	Dean of Technology/Info Security	Ms. Emily POWELL
103	Dean Workforce Development	Vacant
41	Athletic Director	Ms. Tammy DAVIS
06	Registrar	Ms. Donna MORRIS
37	Director Financial Aid	Ms. Tevian SIDES
21	Controller	Ms. Marjann MORROW
15	Director of Human Resources	Ms. Sheila WILLIAMSON
85	Dir International Student Services	Ms. Melissa DOUCETTE
96	Director of Purchasing & Compliance	Mr. Mitch CALHOUN

Wharton County Junior College (F)

911 Boling Highway, Wharton TX 77488-3298

County: Wharton | FICE Identification: 003668 | Unit ID: 229841

Telephone: (979) 532-4560 | Carnegie Class: Assoc/MT-VT-High Trad

FAX Number: (979) 532-6526 | Calendar System: Semester

URL: www.wcjc.edu

Established: 1946 | Annual Undergrad Tuition & Fees (In-District): $2,352

Enrollment: 7,050 | Coed

Affiliation or Control: Local | IRS Status: 501(c)3

Highest Offering: Associate Degree

Accreditation: SC, CAHIIM, #CSHSE, DH, EMT, PTAA, RAD

Code	Title	Name
01	President	Ms. Betty A. MCCROHAN
05	Vice President of Instruction	Ms. Leigh Ann COLLINS
11	Vice President Administrative Svcs	Mr. Bryce KOCIAN
13	Vice President of Technology & IR	Ms. Pamela YOUNGBLOOD
32	Vice President of Student Services	Vacant
09	VP of Planning/Inst Effectiveness	Dr. Amanda ALLEN
21	Dean of Financial & Business Svcs	Mr. Gus WESSELS
26	Director of Marketing & Comm	Ms. Zina CARTER
06	Registrar	Ms. Karen PREISLER
37	Director of Financial Aid	Ms. Leslie KOLOJACO
08	Director Library Info/Tech Services	Ms. Kwei HSU
18	Director of Facilities Management	Mr. Mike FEYEN
15	Director of Human Resources	Ms. Judy JONES
09	Director of Inst Effectiveness	Vacant
96	Director of Purchasing	Mr. Philip WUTHRICH
101	Secretary of the Institution/Board	Mrs. Deanna FEYEN
19	Director Security/Safety	Mr. Danny TERRONEZ
41	Athletic Director	Mr. Keith CASE

Wiley College (G)

711 Wiley Avenue, Marshall TX 75670-5199

County: Harrison | FICE Identification: 003669 | Unit ID: 229887

Telephone: (903) 927-3300 | Carnegie Class: Bac-Diverse

FAX Number: (903) 938-8100 | Calendar System: Semester

URL: www.wileyc.edu

Established: 1873 | Annual Undergrad Tuition & Fees: $12,306

Enrollment: 1,323 | Coed

Affiliation or Control: United Methodist | IRS Status: 501(c)3

Highest Offering: Baccalaureate

Accreditation: SC, ACBSP

Code	Title	Name
01	President and CEO	Dr. Herman J. FELTON, JR.
10	Vice Pres for Business & Finance	Mr. George STIELL
05	Int Provost/VP Academic Affairs	Dr. Cynthia Lemelle HESTER
32	Vice President Student Affairs	Mr. Brandon DUMAS
111	Vice Pres Institutional Advancement	Mr. Marcel R. MCGEE
84	Vice Pres for Enrollment Services	Dr. Vaneshette HENDERSON
13	Director of Information Technology	Mr. Chris WATSON
21	Senior Staff Accountant	Ms. Shae BOGUE
53	Interim Dean Sch of Education	Dr. Kristi YOUNG
42	Dean of Chapel	Rev. Dominique A. ROBINSON
04	Special Assistant to the President	Mrs. Karen HELTON
50	Interim Dean Sch of Business & Tech	Dr. Cha HYUNGJU
49	Dean School of Sciences	Dr. Brooke WOODARD
79	Interim Dean Sch of Social Sci/Hum	Dr. Devissi MUHAMMAD
26	Dir of Marketing and Communications	Ms. Tammy TAYLOR
08	Director of Library Services	Dr. Martha Lopez COLEMAN
06	Interim Registrar	Ms. Gloria MITCHELL
07	Director of Admissions	Mr. Maurice OSBORNE
15	Vice Pres of Human Resources	Mrs. Krystal MOODY
18	Superintendent of Facilities	Mr. Percy MURRAY
37	Director of Financial Aid	Mr. Thomas D. HASKINS
29	Director of Alumni Relations	Vacant
09	Director of Institutional Research	Dr. Emmanuel NGWANG
11	Director Administrative Svcs	Mr. O. Ivan WHITE
23	College Nurse	Ms. Lakeita WIGGINS
41	Director of Athletics	Mr. Brandon K. DUMAS
96	Purchasing Manager	Mr. Johnny JOHNSON
35	Director of Student Development	Ms. Darby SMITH
101	Secretary of the Institution/Board	Mrs. Cassandra M. JOHNSON
106	Dir Online Education/E-learning	Vacant
19	Interim Director Security/Safety	Mr. Jason BRATTON
39	Director of Residence Life	Mr. Howard FISHER
43	Dir Legal Services/General Counsel	Ms. Kemisha R. ROSTON
112	Director Major Gifts/Planned Giving	Mr. Charles CORNISH
90	Director Academic Computing	Vacant
100	Executive Asst to the President	Mrs. Cassandra M. JOHNSON

UTAH

Brigham Young University (H)

Provo UT 84602-0002

County: Utah | FICE Identification: 003670 | Unit ID: 230038

Telephone: (801) 422-4000 | Carnegie Class: DU-Higher

FAX Number: N/A | Calendar System: Semester

URL: www.byu.edu

Established: 1875 | Annual Undergrad Tuition & Fees: $5,620

Enrollment: 34,334 | Coed

Affiliation or Control: Latter-day Saints | IRS Status: 501(c)3

Highest Offering: Doctorate

Accreditation: NW, ART, CAATE, #CAEP, CAEPT, CLPSY, COPSY, DANCE, DIETD, DIETI, IPSY, JOUR, LAW, MFCD, MT, MUS, NRPA, NURSE, PH, SP, SPAA, SW, THEA

Code	Title	Name
01	President	Mr. Kevin J. WORTHEN
05	Academic Vice President	Dr. C. Shane REESE
10	VP Finance/Administration/CFO	Mr. Brian K. EVANS
111	Advancement Vice President	Dr. Matthew O. RICHARDSON
13	Vice Pres Info Tech/Chief Info Ofcr	Dr. J. Kelly FLANAGAN
88	International Vice President	Dr. Sandra ROGERS
32	Student Life Vice President	Mrs. Julie FRANKLIN
43	Asst to President/General Counsel	Mr. Steven M. SANDBERG
45	Asst to Pres Planning/Assessment	Dr. Rosemary THACKERAY
26	Asst to Pres Univ Communications	Mrs. Carri P. JENKINS
20	Assoc Academic VP Faculty Dev	Dr. Laura BRIDGEWATER
20	Assoc Academic VP Faculty Rels	Dr. Brad L. NEIGER
20	Assoc Acad VP Undergraduate Stds	Dr. John R. ROSENBERG
46	Assoc Acad VP Research/Grad Stds	Dr. Larry L. HOWELL
35	Assoc Student Life Vice Pres/Dean	Dr. Sarah WESTERBERG
18	Asst Admin VP Physical Facilities	Mr. Ole M. SMITH
15	Asst Admin VP Human Resource Svcs	Mr. David TUELLER
35	Asst Admin VP/Stdnt Auxiliary Svc	Mr. Carr KRUEGER
29	Managing Dir Alumni/Ext Rels	Mr. Steven J. HAFEN
30	Managing Dir LDS Philanthropies	Dr. Tanise CHUNG-HOON
84	Exec Dir Enrollment Services	Mr. Christian FAULCONER
37	Director Financial Aid/Scholarships	Mr. Stephen E. HILL
88	Dean Undergraduate Education	Dr. Susan RUGH
08	University Librarian	Ms. Jennifer PAUSTENBAUGH
58	Dean Graduate Studies	Dr. John S. KAUWE
51	Dean Continuing Education	Dr. Lee GLINES
47	Dean Life Sciences	Dr. James P. PORTER

54 Dean Engineering & Technology .... Dr. Michael A. JENSEN
83 Dean Family Home & Social Science .... Dr. Benjamin M. OGLES
57 Dean Fine Arts & Communications .... Dr. Edward E. ADAMS
79 Dean Humanities .... Dr. J. Scott MILLER
61 Dean Law School .... Dr. D. Gordon SMITH
50 Dean Marriott School Management .... Dr. Brigitte MADRIAN
53 Dean McKay School of Education .... Dr. Mary Anne PRATER
81 Dean Physical & Math Science .... Dr. Gus L. HART
66 Dean Nursing .... Dr. Patricia K. RAVERT
73 Dean Religious Education .... Dr. Daniel JUDD
38 Director Counseling & Career Ctr .... Dr. Steven A. SMITH
09 Dir Institutional Assess/Analysis .... Dr. Danny R. OLSEN
06 University Registrar .... Mr. Barry ALLRED
07 Director Admission Services .... Ms. Lori GARDINER
96 Director of Purchasing .... Mr. W. Timothy HILL
88 Dir University Accessibility Center .... Dr. Gerilynn VORKINK
19 Managing Dir/Chief Univ Police .... Mr. James C. AUTRY
39 Director Student Housing .... Vacant
41 Athletic Director .... Mr. Tom HOLMOE
88 Director BYU Broadcasting .... Mr. Michael DUNN
88 University Treasurer .... Mr. David W. PAUL
14 Assistant VP Technology .... Mr. Nathan HATCH
119 Chief Information Security Officer .... Mr. Tracy FLINDERS
28 Asst to Pres for Stdnt Succ & Incl .... Dr. Vernon L. HEPERI
43 Deputy General Counsel .... Mr. Christian A. FOX

Broadview University (A)

1902 W 7800 S, West Jordan UT 84088-4021
County: Salt Lake FICE Identification: 011166
Unit ID: 230056
Telephone: (801) 542-7600 Carnegie Class: Bac/Assoc-Mixed
FAX Number: (801) 542-7601 Calendar System: Quarter
URL: www.broadviewuniversity.edu
Established: 1971 Annual Undergrad Tuition & Fees: $15,900
Enrollment: 172 Coed
Affiliation or Control: Proprietary IRS Status: Proprietary
Highest Offering: Master's
Accreditation: ACICS

01 President .... Mr. Terry MYHRE
05 Director .... Mr. Mark GLUTZ

Eagle Gate College (B)

915 North 400 West, Layton UT 84041
Telephone: (801) 546-7500 Identification: 770812
Accreditation: ABHES

Eagle Gate College (C)

5588 S Green Street, Suite 150, Murray UT 84123-6965
County: Salt Lake FICE Identification: 021785
Unit ID: 230366
Telephone: (801) 333-8100 Carnegie Class: Bac/Assoc-Mixed
FAX Number: (801) 263-6520 Calendar System: Other
URL: www.eaglegatecollege.edu
Established: 1979 Annual Undergrad Tuition & Fees: $10,975
Enrollment: 329 Coed
Affiliation or Control: Proprietary IRS Status: Proprietary
Highest Offering: Baccalaureate
Accreditation: ABHES, NURSE

01 Campus Director .... Mickie MILLER

Fortis College (D)

3949 South 700 East, Suite 150, Salt Lake City UT 84107
Telephone: (801) 713-0915 Identification: 666762
Accreditation: ACCSC, ADNUR, DH

† Tuition varies by degree program.

Independence University (E)

4021 South 700 East, Suite 400,
Salt Lake City UT 84107-2453
County: Salt Lake FICE Identification: 022061
Unit ID: 465812
Telephone: (801) 290-3240 Carnegie Class: Masters/M
FAX Number: (801) 263-0345 Calendar System: Other
URL: www.independence.edu
Established: 1978 Annual Undergrad Tuition & Fees: $16,972
Enrollment: 8,605 Coed
Affiliation or Control: Independent Non-Profit IRS Status: 501(c)3
Highest Offering: Master's
Accreditation: ACCSC, NURSE

01 President .... Vacant
03 Executive Vice President .... Mr. Alan HANSEN
05 Chief Academic Officer (Provost) .... Ms. Marilee HALL
07 Director of Admissions .... Ms. Elisha ANDERSON
11 Chief of Operations/Administration .... Mr. Kody LARSEN
36 Director Student Placement .... Ms. Ericka MARSHALL
08 Chief Library Officer .... Ms. Alana HOWELL

LDS Business College (F)

95 North 300 West, Salt Lake City UT 84101-3500
County: Salt Lake FICE Identification: 003672
Unit ID: 230418
Telephone: (801) 524-8100 Carnegie Class: Assoc/MT-VT-High Trad
FAX Number: (801) 524-1900 Calendar System: Semester
URL: www.ldsbc.edu
Established: 1886 Annual Undergrad Tuition & Fees: $3,440
Enrollment: 2,045 Coed
Affiliation or Control: Latter-day Saints IRS Status: 501(c)3
Highest Offering: Associate Degree
Accreditation: NW, MAC

01 President .... Dr. Bruce C. KUSCH
04 Executive Admin Asst .... Ms. Kristen WILLIAMS
05 Vice Pres of Academics .... Vacant
32 Vice Pres Student Services .... Dr. Guy M. HOLLINGSWORTH
11 Vice Pres of Administration .... Mr. Vince A. VAUGHN
13 Chief Information Officer .... Ms. Christina BAUM
10 Director Financial Svcs/Controller .... Mr. Chris REITZ
50 Dir Strat Initiatives/Instl Assess .... Mr. Robert O. SALMON
20 Dir Curriculum/Academic Programs .... Ms. Cathy T. CAREY
84 Director Enrollment Management .... Ms. Kristen WHITTAKER
15 Director of Human Resources .... Mr. Brady J. KIMBER
26 Manager of Public Affairs .... Mr. C. Royce HINTON
36 Director of Career Services .... Mr. Rob BAGLEY
06 Registrar .... Ms. Maren LYTHGOE
08 Dir of Library/Inform Resources .... Vacant
37 Student Financial Services Manager .... Ms. Melanie CONOVER
40 Bookstore Manager .... Mr. Kent CHRISTENSEN

Midwives College of Utah (G)

1174 E Graystone Way Suite 2,
Salt Lake City UT 84106-2671
County: Salt Lake City Identification: 666281
Unit ID: 480985
Telephone: (866) 680-2756 Carnegie Class: Spec-4-yr-Other Health
FAX Number: (866) 207-2024 Calendar System: Semester
URL: www.midwifery.edu
Established: 1980 Annual Undergrad Tuition & Fees: $6,945
Enrollment: 247 Coed
Affiliation or Control: Independent Non-Profit IRS Status: 501(c)3
Highest Offering: Master's
Accreditation: MEAC

01 President .... Ms. Kristi RIDD-YOUNG
05 Academic Dean .... Ms. Kaylee RIDD
17 Clinical Director .... Ms. Maria CRANFORD
06 Registrar .... Ms. Laura PARK
07 Admissions .... Ms. Allyson JUNEAU-BUTLER
13 Chief Info Technology Officer (CIO) .... Mr. Alan BELLOWS
37 Financial Aid Director .... Ms. Whitney MESYEF
58 Graduate Dean .... Ms. Megan KOONTZ
10 Chief Business Officer .... Ms. Julie DELONG
101 Secretary of the Institution/Board .... Ms. Rebecca PORTER
26 Chief Public Relations/Marketing .... Ms. Masha MESYEF
32 Chief Student Affairs/Student Life .... Ms. Cheryl FURER
38 Director Of Student Counseling .... Ms. Tamara TAIT
113 Bursar .... Ms. Kimberloy MUELLER
44 Director Annual Giving .... Ms. Jennifer BERTAGNOLE

Neumont University (H)

143 South Main, Salt Lake City UT 84111
County: Salt Lake FICE Identification: 010098
Unit ID: 445692
Telephone: (801) 302-2800 Carnegie Class: Spec-4-yr-Other Tech
FAX Number: (801) 302-2811 Calendar System: Quarter
URL: www.neumont.edu
Established: 2003 Annual Undergrad Tuition & Fees: $24,750
Enrollment: 484 Coed
Affiliation or Control: Proprietary IRS Status: Proprietary
Highest Offering: Baccalaureate
Accreditation: ACCSC

01 President/Campus Director Utah .... Aaron REED
05 VP Academic Operations .... Tim CLARK
10 VP/Chief Financial Officer .... Andrew FULLER
32 Director of Student Affairs .... Corrine PADILLA
06 Registrar .... Alice NGUYEN
37 Director Financial Aid .... Nate BLANCHARD

New Charter University (I)

50 W. Broadway, Suite 300, Salt Lake City UT 84101
County: Salt Lake FICE Identification: 041292
Telephone: (801) 883-8336 Carnegie Class: Not Classified
FAX Number: (801) 855-5922 Calendar System: Trimester
URL: www.new.edu
Established: 1994 Annual Undergrad Tuition & Fees: N/A
Enrollment: N/A Coed
Affiliation or Control: Proprietary IRS Status: Proprietary
Highest Offering: Master's
Accreditation: DEAC

01 President .... Ms. Diane JOHNSON
11 Vice President of Operations .... Ms. Amie ADER-BEELER
05 Academic Dean .... Ms. Mary Beth FINN
06 Senior Registrar .... Mr. Adam CHRISTIAN
10 Operations Manager .... Ms. Kristina ARCUTT

Nightingale College (J)

175 South Main Street, Suite 400,
Salt Lake City UT 84405
County: Salt Lake FICE Identification: 038383
Unit ID: 444787
Telephone: (801) 689-2160 Carnegie Class: Spec-4-yr-Other Health
FAX Number: (801) 689-3114 Calendar System: Semester
URL: www.nightingale.edu
Established: 2010 Annual Undergrad Tuition & Fees: N/A
Enrollment: 326 Coed
Affiliation or Control: Proprietary IRS Status: Proprietary
Highest Offering: Baccalaureate
Accreditation: ABHES, ADNUR, NURSE

01 President/CEO .... Mr. Mikhail SHNEYDER
10 Vice Pres Operations/Controller .... Ms. Kara HARMON
26 VP Partnerships & Business Devel .... Mr. Jonathan TANNER
06 Registrar .... Ms. Rachel OUTEIRO
07 Director of Admissions .... Ms. Jeana REECE
37 Director Student Financial Aid .... Ms. Jennifer MORRIS

Provo College (K)

1450 W 820 N, Provo UT 84601-1305
County: Utah FICE Identification: 023608
Unit ID: 380438
Telephone: (801) 818-8900 Carnegie Class: Bac/Assoc-Mixed
FAX Number: (801) 375-9728 Calendar System: Other
URL: www.provocollege.edu
Established: 1984 Annual Undergrad Tuition & Fees: $12,955
Enrollment: 502 Coed
Affiliation or Control: Proprietary IRS Status: Proprietary
Highest Offering: Associate Degree
Accreditation: ABHES, NURSE, PTAA

01 Campus President .... Mr. Todd SMITH
05 Academic Dean .... Mrs. Jana COLYAR
10 Business Manager .... Ms. Julie BRADFORD
37 Financial Services Assoc Director .... Ms. Lena CLARK
06 Registrar .... Mrs. April ACUNA
32 Dir of Placement/Student Services .... Ms. Christine ANDERSON

Rocky Mountain University of Health Professions (L)

122 East 1700 South, Building C, Provo UT 84606-7379
County: Utah FICE Identification: 041932
Unit ID: 475495
Telephone: (801) 375-5125 Carnegie Class: Spec-4-yr-Other Health
FAX Number: (801) 375-2125 Calendar System: Trimester
URL: www.rm.edu
Established: 1998 Annual Graduate Tuition & Fees: N/A
Enrollment: 856 Coed
Affiliation or Control: Proprietary IRS Status: Proprietary
Highest Offering: Doctorate; No Undergraduates
Accreditation: NW, ARCPA, NURSE, PTA, @SP

01 President/CEO .... Dr. Richard P. NIELSEN
05 Exec VP Academic Affairs/Provost .... Dr. Mark HORACEK
11 Exec VP Operations/CFO .... Mr. Jeff B. BATE
45 EVP Strategy & Engagement .... Dr. Jessica D. EGBERT
84 AVP Enrollment Management .... Mr. Bryce GREENBERG
20 AVP Academic Administration .... Mr. Richard PETERSON
46 Director ORSP .... Dr. Robert PETTITT
51 Director Continuing Education .... Vacant
32 Director Student & Alumni Affairs .... Ms. Lori SISK
100 Chief of Staff & ALO .... Dr. Sandra PENNINGTON
13 Chief Info Technology Officer/CIO .... Mr. David PAYNE

Stevens-Henager College (M)

755 South Main Street, Logan UT 84321
Telephone: (435) 752-0903 Identification: 770603
Accreditation: ACCSC, MAC

Stevens-Henager College (N)

1890 South 1350 West, Ogden UT 84401
County: Weber FICE Identification: 003674
Unit ID: 230621
Telephone: (801) 622-1567 Carnegie Class: Spec-4-yr-Other Health
FAX Number: (801) 621-0853 Calendar System: Quarter
URL: www.stevenshenager.edu
Established: 1891 Annual Undergrad Tuition & Fees: $16,972
Enrollment: 205 Coed
Affiliation or Control: Independent Non-Profit IRS Status: 501(c)3
Highest Offering: Baccalaureate
Accreditation: ACCSC, MAC, SURGT

01 Pres of Ogden Campus/Regional Dir .... Ms. Vicky DEWSNUP
07 Director of Admissions .... Mr. Eric SIMPSON
32 Director of Student Services .... Mr. Doug BURCH
05 Chief Academic Officer .... Dr. Wayne HUNSAKER
10 Chief Business Officer .... Mr. Leland NEIL
36 Director Career Services .... Ms. Allison MURPHY

Stevens-Henager College (O)

1476 S Sandhill Road, Orem UT 84058-7310
Telephone: (801) 418-1450 FICE Identification: 030030
Accreditation: ACCSC, MAC

Stevens-Henager College, St. George Campus (P)

1568 South River Road Suite 200, St. George UT 84790
Telephone: (435) 628-9902 Identification: 770604

Accreditation: ACCSC

Stevens-Henager College (A)

383 W Vine Street, Salt Lake City UT 84123
Telephone: (801) 281-7620 Identification: 666038
Accreditation: ACCSC, COARC

† Branch campus of Stevens-Henager College, Ogden, UT.

University of Phoenix Utah Campus (B)

5373 South Green Street, Salt Lake City UT 84123-4642
Telephone: (801) 263-1444 Identification: 770232
Accreditation: &NH, ACBSP, CACREP, CAEPN

† No longer accepting campus-based students.

The Utah College of Dental Hygiene at Careers Unlimited (C)

1176 S 1480 W, Orem UT 84058-4905
County: Utah FICE Identification: 034633
Unit ID: 448239
Telephone: (801) 426-8234 Carnegie Class: Spec-4-yr-Other Health
FAX Number: (801) 224-5437 Calendar System: Other
URL: www.ucdh.edu
Established: 2006 Annual Undergrad Tuition & Fees: N/A
Enrollment: 116 Coed
Affiliation or Control: Proprietary IRS Status: Proprietary
Highest Offering: Baccalaureate
Accreditation: ACCSC, DH

01 College President ... Mr. Brent MOLEN
10 College VP/CFO/Director Compliance ... Ms. Krista MCCLURE
00 Director Emeritus/CEO ... Mr. Kenneth MOLEN

*Utah System of Higher Education (D)

The Gateway, 60 S 400 W, Salt Lake City UT 84101-1284
County: Salt Lake FICE Identification: 009339
Telephone: (801) 321-7101 Carnegie Class: N/A
FAX Number: (801) 321-7199
URL: www.higheredutah.org

01 Exec Ofcr/Int Comm of Higher Educ ... Dr. David WOOLSTENHULME
05 Assoc Commissioner Academic Affairs ... Dr. Elizabeth J. HITCH
10 Int Assoc Comm Finance/Facilities ... Dr. Richard AMON
37 Exec Director Student Financial Aid ... Mr. David A. FEITZ
88 UESP Executive Director ... Ms. Lynne WARD

*The University of Utah (E)

201 South 1460 East, Salt Lake City UT 84112-1107
County: Salt Lake FICE Identification: 003675
Unit ID: 230764
Telephone: (801) 581-7200 Carnegie Class: DU-Highest
FAX Number: (801) 581-3007 Calendar System: Semester
URL: www.utah.edu
Established: 1850 Annual Undergrad Tuition & Fees (In-State): $9,222
Enrollment: 32,800 Coed
Affiliation or Control: State IRS Status: 501(c)3
Highest Offering: Doctorate
Accreditation: NW, ARCPA, AUD, CAATE, CAEP, CAMPEP, CEA, CLPSY, COPSY, DANCE, DENT, DIETC, HSA, IPSY, LAW, MED, MIDWF, MT, MUS, NDT, NMT, NRPA, NURSE, OT, PH, PHAR, PLNG, PTA, SCPSY, SP, SPAA, SW

02 President ... Dr. Ruth V. WATKINS
05 Sr Vice Pres Academic Affairs ... Dr. Barbara H. SNYDER
43 Chief General Counsel ... Ms. Phyllis J. VETTER
11 Vice Pres Administrative Services ... Mr. John E. NIXON
32 Vice President Student Affairs ... Ms. Lori K. MCDONALD
111 Vice Pres Institutional Advancement ... Ms. Heidi D. WOODBURY
86 Vice President Government Relations ... Mr. Jason P. PERRY
15 Assoc Vice Pres for Human Resources ... Ms. Joan GINES
46 Vice President Research ... Dr. Andrew S. WEYRICH
04 Exec Asst to the President ... Ms. Julia A. JONES
13 Chief Information Officer ... Mr. Stephen H. HESS
21 Chief Strategy Officer ... Ms. Patricia A. ROSS
88 Chief Global Officer ... Dr. Chris M. IRELAND
16 Chief Human Resources Officer ... Mr. Jeff C. HERRING
26 Chief Mktg & Communications Officer ... Mr. William J. WARREN
20 Sr AVP AA & Dean Undergrad Studies ... Dr. Martha S. BRADLEY
84 Sr Assoc VP for Enrollment Mgmt ... Mr. Steve ROBINSON
10 Chief Financial Officer Main Campus ... Ms. Cathy ANDERSON
18 Chief Design & Construction Officer ... Ms. Robin BURR
21 Assoc VP Admin/Finance & Bus Svcs ... Vacant
22 Assoc VP Equity/Diversity ... Dr. Kathryn B. STOCKTON
88 Associate Vice President Research ... Dr. Diane E. PATAKI
88 Assoc VP Acad Affairs/Faculty ... Dr. Sarah PROJANSKY
35 AVP Student Affs/Bus/Auxil Svcs ... Dr. Jerry L. BASFORD
109 Assoc VP Admin Svc/Auxiliary Svc ... Mr. Gordon N. WILSON
48 Dean Architecture & Planning ... Dr. Keith D. MOORE
50 Dean David Eccles Sch of Business ... Dr. Taylor R. RANDALL
52 Dean School of Dentistry ... Dr. Wyatt R. HUME
53 Dean College of Education ... Dr. Elaine CLARK
54 Dean College of Engineering ... Dr. Richard B. BROWN
57 Dean Col of Fine Arts/AVP the Arts ... Dr. John W. SCHEIB
68 Dean College of Health ... Dr. David H. PERRIN
92 Dean Honors College ... Dr. Sylvia D. TORTI
79 Dean College of Humanities ... Dr. Stuart K. CULVER
61 Dean S J Quinney College of Law ... Dr. Robert W. ADLER
65 Dean Coll of Mines & Earth Science ... Dr. Darryl P. BUTT
63 Dean School of Medicine ... Dr. Michael L. GOOD
66 Dean College of Nursing ... Dr. Barbara L. WILSON
67 Dean College of Pharmacy ... Dr. Randall T. PETERSON
81 Dean College of Science ... Dr. Henry WHITE
83 Dean Col Social/Behav Science ... Dr. Cynthia BERG
70 Dean College of Social Work ... Dr. Martell L. TEASLEY
35 Dean of Students ... Dr. Lori MCDONALD
06 University Registrar ... Mr. Timothy J. EBNER
17 CEO Univ Hospitals & Clinics ... Mr. Gordon L. CRABTREE
96 Director Procurement ... Mr. Glendon G. MITCHELL
94 Chair Gender Studies ... Dr. Susie S. PORTER
77 Director School of Computing ... Mr. Ross T. WHITAKER
88 Dir Dental Clinic/Gen Residence ... Dr. Craig PROCTOR
88 Asst Dean Clinical Affairs/Care ... Vacant
07 Interim Director Admissions ... Mr. Steve ROBINSON
29 Exec Director Alumni Association ... Mr. Todd ANDREWS
112 Director Planned Giving ... Ms. Jessica NELSON
37 Dir Financial Aid & Scholarships ... Ms. Brenda BURKE
08 Dean MLIB/University Librarian ... Ms. Alberta D. COMER
08 Interim Dir Eccles Health Sci Lib ... Ms. Melissa L. RETHLEFSEN
08 Dir S J Quinney Col of Law/Lib ... Ms. Melissa BERNSTEIN
36 Director of Career Services ... Mr. Stan D. INMAN
38 Director Counseling Center ... Dr. Lauren WEITZMAN
39 Director Housing & Res Education ... Ms. Barbara REMSBURG
39 Director Univ Student Apartments ... Ms. Jennifer G. REED
88 Dir Natural History Museum of Utah ... Dr. Sarah B. GEORGE
19 Chief of Police ... Mr. Dale G. BROPHY
40 Director Campus Bookstore ... Mr. Daniel L. ARCHER
85 Director Intl Student/Scholar Svcs ... Ms. Chelsea WELLS
25 Dir Office of Sponsored Projects ... Mr. Brent K. BROWN
31 Dir Univ Neighborhood Partners . Ms. Jennifer A. MAYOR-GLENN
09 Director Institutional Analysis ... Dr. Michael D. MARTINEAU
41 Athletics Director ... Mr. Mark M. HARLAN

*Southern Utah University (F)

351 W University Blvd, Cedar City UT 84720-2470
County: Iron FICE Identification: 003678
Unit ID: 230603
Telephone: (435) 586-7700 Carnegie Class: Masters/L
FAX Number: (435) 586-5475 Calendar System: Semester
URL: www.suu.edu
Established: 1897 Annual Undergrad Tuition & Fees (In-State): $6,770
Enrollment: 9,468 Coed
Affiliation or Control: State IRS Status: 501(c)3
Highest Offering: Master's
Accreditation: NW, ART, CAATE, CAEP, DANCE, IPSY, MUS, NURSE, SPAA

02 President ... Mr. Scott L. WYATT
05 Interim Provost ... Dr. Robert EVES
10 Vice Pres of Finance & Admin ... Mr. Marvin DODGE
32 Asst VP/Dean Student Services ... Mr. Jason RAMIREZ
111 Vice Pres Advance/Enrollment Mgmt ... Mr. Stuart JONES
58 Assoc Provost ... Dr. James SAGE
29 Vice Pres Alumni/Community Rels ... Ms. Mindy BENSON
28 Asst to Pres Diversity/Inclusion ... Dr. Schvalla RIVERA
07 Exec Director of Admissions ... Mr. Brandon WRIGHT
18 AVP of Facilities Management ... Mr. Tiger FUNK
84 AVP for Enrollment Management ... Mr. Brandon WRIGHT
26 Exec Director Brand Strategy ... Ms. Nikki KOONTZ
08 Dean/Director Library/Univ Studies ... Vacant
51 Dean of Continuing/Profess Studies ... Vacant
114 Director of Budget and Planning ... Ms. Mary Jo ANDERSON
75 Director CTE ... Vacant
06 Registrar ... Mr. John ALLRED
15 Director Human Resources ... Mr. David T. MCGUIRE
88 Dean Integrative/Engaged Learning ... Dr. Patrick CLARKE
37 Director of Financial Aid ... Mr. David HUGHES
41 Athletic Director ... Ms. Debbie CORUM
43 Legal Counsel ... Ms. Ann Marie ALLEN
79 Dean Col Humanities/Soc Sci ... Ms. Jean BOREEN
50 Dean School of Business ... Ms. Mary PEARSON
53 Dean College of Education ... Dr. Shawn L. CHRISTIANSEN
81 Dean College of Sci and Engineering ... Dr. Robert EVES
57 Dean College Performing/Visual Arts ... Mrs. Shauna MENDINI
96 Director of Purchasing ... Mr. Bradley BROWN
09 Exec Dir Inst Research/Assessment ... Mr. Christian REINER
38 Director Student Counseling ... Dr. Curtis HILL
04 Exec Assistant to the President ... Ms. Jennifer OBERHELMAN
13 Chief Information Technology Office ... Mr. Matt ZUFELT
86 Director Government Relations ... Ms. Donna LAW
19 Chief of Police ... Mr. Rick BROWN
45 Chief Institutional Planning Ofcr ... Dr. Steve MEREDITH

*Dixie State University (G)

225 S University Avenue, Saint George UT 84770-3876
County: Washington FICE Identification: 003671
Unit ID: 230171
Telephone: (435) 652-7500 Carnegie Class: Bac/Assoc-Mixed
FAX Number: (435) 656-4001 Calendar System: Semester
URL: www.dixie.edu
Established: 1911 Annual Undergrad Tuition & Fees (In-State): $5,253
Enrollment: 9,673 Coed
Affiliation or Control: State IRS Status: 501(c)3
Highest Offering: Master's
Accreditation: NW, ACBSP, ADNUR, CAEPT, COARC, DH, EMT, MT, MUS, NUR, PTAA, RAD, SURGT

02 President ... Dr. Richard B. WILLIAMS
11 Vice Pres Administrative Services ... Mr. Paul MORRIS
05 Provost/VP Academic Affairs ... Dr. Michael LACOURSE
32 Vice Pres Student Affairs ... Dr. Peter GITAU
111 Vice Pres Advancement ... Mr. Brad LAST
86 Asst to Pres for Govt/Comm Rels ... Mr. Henrie WALTON
79 Dean College Humanities/Social Sci ... Dr. Stephen LEE
66 Dean College Health Sciences ... Dr. Eliezer BERMUDEZ
50 Dean College of Business ... Dr. Kyle WELLS
81 Dean College Science & Technology ... Dr. Eric PEDERSEN
53 Dean College Education ... Dr. Brenda SABEY
51 Assoc Prov Cmty Global Outreach ... Dr. Nancy HAUCK
35 Dean of Students ... Mr. Del BEATTY
13 Chief Information Officer ... Mr. Gary J. KOEVEN
10 AVP Admin Svcs Spec Proj ... Mr. A. Scott TALBOT
15 Exec Director of Human Resources ... Mr. Travis ROSENBERG
18 Exec Dir Facilities Management ... Ms. Sherry RUESCH
08 Dean of Library & Learning Svcs ... Ms. Kelly PETERSEN-FAIRCHILD
109 Executive Director Auxiliaries ... Mr. Don STECK
37 Exec Director Financial Aid ... Mr. J. D ROBERTSON
84 Asst VP Enrollment Services ... Ms. Darlene DILLEY
06 Registrar ... Ms. Julie STENDER
121 Director of Advisement ... Mr. Mike OLSEN
26 VP of Mktg & Communication ... Dr. Jordan SHARP
18 Director Facilities Operation ... Mr. Doug WHITEHEAD
19 Dir Public Safety/Chief of Police ... Mr. Blair BARFUSS
41 Exec Director of Athletics ... Dr. Jason BOOTHE
39 Director Housing & Residential Life ... Mr. Seth GUBLER
09 Director of Institutional Research ... Ms. Andrea BROWN
04 Assistant to the President ... Ms. Theresa BONDAD
35 Dir Student Involvement & Ldrshp ... Mr. Luke KEROUAC
96 Director of Purchasing ... Ms. Jackie FREEMAN
29 Director of Alumni Relations ... Mr. John BOWLER
36 Exec Director of Career Services ... Ms. Ali THREET
105 Director of Network Services ... Mr. Allen FOX
25 Director of Payroll & Grants ... Ms. Krystal THOMPSON
28 Assoc VP for Campus Diversity ... Dr. Tasha TOY
43 General Counsel ... Mr. Doajo HICKS
91 Director Administrative Computing ... Mr. James MILLER
100 Chief of Staff ... Mr. Courtney WHITE
104 Director of Global Education ... Dr. Luis AREVALO
88 Exec Dir Acad Innovation & Ldrshp ... Mr. Bruce HARRIS
108 Director of Assessment ... Dr. Laura SNELSON
07 Director of Admissions ... Mr. Brett SCHWARTZ
106 Dir of Distance & Digital Learning ... Mr. Ryan HOBBS
20 Assoc Provost Acad & Budget Plng ... Dr. Pamela CANTRELL
21 Exec Dir Business Services ... Mr. Scott JENSEN
30 Director of Development ... Mr. Ken BEAZER
38 Director of Health & Counseling ... Dr. Dylan MATSUMORI
121 Assoc Prov for Acad Success ... Dr. Sarah VANDERMARK

*Utah State University (H)

Logan UT 84322-0001
County: Cache FICE Identification: 003677
Unit ID: 230728
Telephone: (435) 797-1000 Carnegie Class: DU-Higher
FAX Number: (435) 797-3880 Calendar System: Semester
URL: www.usu.edu
Established: 1888 Annual Undergrad Tuition & Fees (In-State): $8,138
Enrollment: 27,679 Coed
Affiliation or Control: State IRS Status: 501(c)3
Highest Offering: Doctorate
Accreditation: NW, ART, AUD, CACREP, CEA, CIDA, DIETC, DIETD, DIETI, IPSY, LSAR, MFCD, MUS, NUR, PSPSY, SP, SW

02 President ... Dr. Noelle E. COCKETT
05 Provost ... Dr. Frank GALEY
43 General Counsel ... Ms. Mica MCKINNEY
10 Vice President Business & Finance ... Mr. Dave COWLEY
32 Vice President Student Services ... Mr. James MORALES
56 Vice Pres Extension & Agriculture ... Dr. Kenneth L. WHITE
58 Vice Provost of Graduate Stds ... Mr. Richard INOUYE
13 CIO/Assoc VP Information Technology ... Dr. Eric HAWLEY
18 Associate VP for Facilities ... Mr. Charles DARNELL
07 Asst VP Recruitment/Enrollment Svcs ... Mr. John MORTENSEN
20 VP for Academic/Instructional Svcs ... Dr. Robert WAGNER
08 Dean Libraries ... Mr. Brad COLE
26 Associate VP of Communications ... Mr. Tim VITALE
09 Dir Analysis Assess/Accreditation ... Mr. Michael TORRENS
22 Exec Director Affirmative Action ... Ms. Alison ADAMS-PERLAC
41 Athletic Director ... Mr. John HARTWELL
25 Exec Director Sponsored Programs ... Mr. Kevin PETERSON
86 VP Government Relations ... Mr. Neil N. ABERCROMBIE
15 Exec Director of Human Resources ... Mr. Doug BULLOCK
19 Exec Director Univ Police Dept ... Mr. Earl MORRIS
06 Registrar ... Mr. Fran HOPKIN
36 Exec Dir Career Services/Coop Educ ... Ms. Donna E. CROW
37 Director of Financial Aid ... Mr. Art YOUNG
38 Interim Director Counseling Center ... Dr. LuAnn HELMS
40 Director of Campus Store ... Mr. John BOSTOCK
92 Director of Honors ... Ms. Kristine MILLER
96 Director of Purchasing ... Mr. Jeff CROSBIE
47 Dean of Agriculture ... Dr. Kenneth L. WHITE
57 Dean of Arts ... Dr. Craig JESSOP
50 Dean of Business ... Mr. Douglas D. ANDERSON
53 Dean of Education ... Dr. Beth FOLEY
54 Dean of Engineering ... Dr. Jagath KALUARACHCHI
79 Dean Humanities/Social Science ... Dr. Joseph WARD
65 Dean of Natural Resources ... Dr. Chris LUECKE
81 Dean of Science ... Dr. Maura HAGAN

*Utah Valley University (A)

800 W University Parkway, Orem UT 84058-5999
County: Utah FICE Identification: 004027
Unit ID: 230737
Telephone: (801) 863-8000 Carnegie Class: Masters/S
FAX Number: (801) 226-5207 Calendar System: Semester
URL: www.uvu.edu
Established: 1941 Annual Undergrad Tuition & Fees (In-State): $5,726
Enrollment: 37,282 Coed
Affiliation or Control: State IRS Status: 501(c)3
Highest Offering: Master's
Accreditation: NW, ADNUR, CAEP, CEA, #COARC, DH, EMT, IFSAC, IPSY, MUS, NUR, SW

02 President .... Dr. Astrid TUMINEZ
05 Provost/VP Academic Affairs .... Dr. Wayne VAUGHT
11 VP Finance & Administration .... Dr. Val L. PETERSON
32 VP Student Affairs .... Dr. Kyle REYES
30 VP Development/Alumni .... Mr. Scott COOKSEY
26 VP University Relations .... Dr. Cameron K. MARTIN
45 VP Planning/Budgets & HR .... Ms. Linda MAKIN
10 Assoc VP Finance .... Mr. Jacob ATKIN
20 Assoc VP Engaged Learning .... Mrs. Cheryl A. HANEWICZ
18 Assoc VP Facilities Planning .... Mr. Frank YOUNG
20 Assoc VP Academic Programs .... Mr. David CONNELLY
27 Assoc VP College Mktg/Communication ..... Mr. Stephen L. WHITE
20 Assoc VP Academic Affairs/Admin .... Dr. Kathren BROWN
124 Assoc VP Student Success/Retention .... Ms. Michelle KEARNS
100 Chief of Staff .... Mr. Justin D. JONES
31 Assoc VP Community Outreach .... Ms. Jessica GILMORE
21 Asst VP/Controller Business Svcs .... Mr. Kedric BLACK
07 Sr Director Admissions .... Mr. Kris COLES
84 Assoc VP Enrollment Management .... Mr. Andrew STONE
72 Dean Computing/Technology .... Dr. Saeed MOAVENI
57 Dean School of the Arts .... Dr. Stephen PULLEN
81 Dean College of Science .... Dr. Daniel FAIRBANKS
50 Dean School of Business .... Dr. Norman WRIGHT
97 Dean University College .... Dr. Forrest G. WILLIAMS
76 Dean Health and Public Services .... Dr. David MCENTIRE
53 Dean School of Education .... Dr. Vessela K. ILIEVA
79 Dean Humanities & Social Sciences .... Dr. Steven C. CLARK
15 AVP Human Resources/Equity Officer .... Ms. Marilyn S. MEYER
37 Director Financial Aid/Scholarship .... Mr. John D. CURL
19 Dir Public Safety/Chief of Police .... Mr. Matthew D. PEDERSEN
112 Director of Planned Giving .... Ms. Cristina PIANEZZOLA
09 Director Institutional Research .... Mr. Timothy STANLEY
41 Director of Athletics .... Mr. Jared M. SUMSION
24 Director Studios & Engineering .... Mr. Will MCKINNON
40 Director Bookstore .... Ms. Louise BRIDGE
06 Registrar .... Ms. LuAnn SMITH
28 Dir Multicultural Student Services .... Ms. Darah M. SNOW
29 Director Alumni Relations .... Mr. Kevin R. WALKENHORST
121 Director Academic Counseling Center .... Mr. Adam BLACK
96 Director of Purchasing .... Mr. Ryan LINDSTROM
04 Executive Asst to President .... Mrs. Gail L. SCHWANITZ
08 Director Library .... Ms. Lesli BAKER
102 Director UVU Foundation .... Ms. Julie S. ANDERSON
36 Director Career Development .... Mr. Michael J. SNAPP
104 Director Study Abroad .... Mr. Baldomero LAGO
105 Director Web Services .... Mr. Nathan GERBER
108 Institutional Review Board Chair .... Ms. Michaela A. GAZDIK-STOFER
13 Assoc VP Info Technology/CIO .... Mr. Ray WALKER
90 Director Academic IT & Analytics .... Ms. Laura BUSBY
22 Dir Affirmative Action/Equal Oppty .... Ms. Laura CARLSON
43 Director Legal Services .... Ms. Karen M. CLEMES
110 Assoc VP Development .... Mr. Jerry D. HENLEY
44 Director Annual Giving .... Mr. Justin L. FERRELL
83 Int Dean Social/Behavioral Sciences .... Dr. Julie RICH
79 Dean of Arts & Humanities .... Dr. Scott SPRENGER
81 Dean of Science .... Dr. Andrea EASTER-PILCHER
54 Dean Engr/Applied Science & Tech .... Dr. David FERRO
35 Dean of Students .... Dr. Jeffrey J. HURST
06 Registrar .... Mr. Casey D. BULLOCK
19 Director Public Safety .... Mr. Dane LEBLANC
29 Exec Director Alumni Association .... Ms. Nancy COLLINWOOD
38 Dir Counseling & Psycholog Services .... Dr. Dianna K. ABEL
36 Director of Career Services .... Dr. Winn STANGER
37 Director of Financial Aid .... Mr. Jed SPENCER
27 Director of Media Relations .... Mr. John L. KOWALEWSKI
07 Director of Admissions .... Mr. Scott TEICHERT
08 University Librarian .... Ms. Wendy HOLLIDAY
22 Dir Equal Opportunity/Affirm Action .... Dr. Barry G. GOMBERG
41 Dir of Intercollegiate Athletics .... Mr. Tim CROMPTON
40 Bookstore Director .... Mr. Tim ECK
25 Director Sponsored Projects .... Mr. James TAYLOR
85 Director Services Intl Students .... Dr. Mary A. MACHIRA
23 Director Student Health Center .... Dr. Shawn D. MCQUILKIN
26 Director Public Relations .... Ms. Allison B. HESS
43 University Counsel .... Dr. G. Richard HILL
39 Int Dir Housing & Residence Life .... Ms. Angie BETANCOURT
96 Director of Purchasing .... Ms. Nancy E. EMENGER
92 Director of Honors Program .... Dr. Dan BEDFORD
114 Dir of Financial Rep & Investments .... Mr. Wendall RICH
94 Director Women's Center .... Ms. Stephanie MCCLURE
04 Executive Asst to the President .... Ms. Sherri COX
09 Director of Institutional Research .... Mr. Clayton ANDERSON
104 Director Study Abroad .... Ms. Rebecca SCHWARTZ
108 Dir of Institutional Effectiveness .... Dr. Gail NIKLASON
90 Director Academic Computing .... Mr. Carey ANSON
45 Director of Strategic Initiatives .... Dr. Steven RICHARDSON
88 Director of Economic Development .... Mr. Guy LETENDRE
105 Director Web Services .... Mr. Peter WAITE
44 Director Annual Giving .... Ms. Nancy COLLINWOOD
86 Director Government Relations .... Ms. Christina MILLARD

*Weber State University (B)

3850 Dixon Parkway, Ogden UT 84408
County: Weber FICE Identification: 003680
Unit ID: 230782
Telephone: (801) 626-6000 Carnegie Class: Masters/L
FAX Number: (801) 626-7922 Calendar System: Semester
URL: www.weber.edu
Established: 1889 Annual Undergrad Tuition & Fees (In-State): $5,859
Enrollment: 27,949 Coed
Affiliation or Control: State IRS Status: 501(c)3
Highest Offering: Master's
Accreditation: NW, ADNUR, ART, CAATE, CAHIIM, CEA, CIDA, COARC, CONST, DH, EMT, HSA, MLTAD, MT, MUS, NUR, SW

02 President .... Dr. Brad L. MORTENSEN
05 Provost .... Dr. Madonne MINER
10 Vice Pres Administrative Services .... Dr. Norm TARBOX
111 Vice Pres for Univ Advancement .... Dr. Betsy MENNELL
32 Vice Pres Student Affairs .... Dr. Brett PEROZZI
13 VP for Information Technology .... Dr. Bret ELLIS
20 Vice Provost & Dean Online/Cont Edu .... Dr. Bruce DAVIS
28 AVP Diversity/Chief Diversity Ofcr .... Dr. Adrienne G. GILLESPIE
21 Asst VP for Financial Services .... Mr. Steven E. NABOR
15 Interim Asst VP for Human Resources .... Dr. Jessica OYLER
18 Assoc VP for Facilities Management .... Mr. Mark HALVERSON
84 Asst Prov for Enrollment Services .... Dr. Bruce BOWEN
20 Asst Prov & Dean of Undergraduates .... Dr. Brenda MARSTELLER-KOWALEWSKI
76 Dean Health Professions .... Dr. Yasmen SIMONIAN
50 Interim Dean Business/Economics .... Dr. Matthew MOURITSEN
53 Dean of Education .... Dr. Kristin HADLEY
20 Assoc Provost Learning Advancement .... Dr. David HUBERT
88 Exec Dir Bus Dev Resources .... Ms. Beth COLOSIMO
103 Assoc VP Workforce & Econ Dev .... Mr. Rick BOUILLON
114 Asst VP Budget Services & Fin Plng .... Mr. Darren MARSHALL
21 Asst VP/Controller .... Ms. Debra GLENN
18 Assoc VP of Facilities Services .... Mr. Robert ASKERLUND
13 Chief Information/Security Officer .... Mr. Bill ZOUMADAKIS
116 Director Internal Audit .... Mr. Travis LANSING
121 Int Sr Dir Planning & Implementatn .... Ms. Candida DARLING
19 Executive Director Public Safety .... Mr. Shane CRABTREE
41 Director Athletics .... Mr. Kevin M. DUSTIN
35 Dean of Students/Asst Vice Pres .... Dr. Kenneth STONEBROOK
84 Assoc VP Enrollment Mgmt .... Mr. Ryan FARLEY
39 Asst VP Student Services .... Mr. Curt LARSEN
121 Asst VP Student Development .... Dr. Kathryn COQUEMONT
15 Asst Vice Pres of Human Resources .... Mr. Craig GARDNER
108 Asst VP Strategy and Analysis .... Dr. Lauralea EDWARDS
88 Asst Provost Curriculum & Acad Sys .... Ms. Rachel LEWIS
09 Strategic Analysis & Accred Dir .... Dr. Jessie WINITZKY-STEPHENS
30 Exec Dir Development/Foundation .... Ms. Nancy MICHALKO
26 Asst VP Inst Mktg/Communications .... Mr. Michael NAVARRE
31 Director Community Relations .... Ms. Jennifer SELTZER-STITT
43 Gen Counsel & Risk Management .... Mr. Chris LACOMBE
86 Director Local Gov Relations .... Mr. Scott E. BROWN
25 Director Sponsored Projects .... Ms. Nicole OMER
88 Assoc VP People & Workplace Culture .... Dr. Sara REED
60 Dean Arts/Communication/Media .... Mr. Richard SCOTT
50 Dean School of Business .... Dr. Dennis BROMLEY
88 Dean SAT/Technical Specialties .... Dr. Eric HEISER
76 Dean School of Health Sciences .... Dr. Erica WIGHT
79 Dean Humanities/Social Sciences .... Dr. Roderic LAND
81 Dean Science/Math & Engineering .... Dr. Craig CALDWELL
07 Director of Admissions .... Ms. Kate GILDEA-BRODERICK
37 Dir Financial Aid & Scholarships .... Ms. Cristi MILLARD
36 Asst Dir Career Services .... Ms. Wendy POTTER
121 Director Academic Advising .... Ms. Ashley SOKIA
06 Registrar & Academic Records .... Ms. MaryEtta CHASE
117 Director Risk Management .... Ms. Mikel BIRCH
88 Director Special Events .... Ms. Marilee DUNN
96 Director Purchasing & AP .... Mr. Brandon THOMAS
88 Director Testing Services .... Ms. Lakiesha FEHOKO
04 Exec Asst to President & Board Sec .... Ms. Sandra LEHMAN
88 Director Concurrent Enrollment .... Mr. Brandon KOWALLIS
88 Learning Outcomes Assessment Coord .... Dr. Tom ZANE

*Snow College (C)

150 College Avenue, Ephraim UT 84627-1299
County: Sanpete FICE Identification: 003679
Unit ID: 230597
Telephone: (435) 283-7000 Carnegie Class: Bac/Assoc-Assoc Dom
FAX Number: (435) 283-6879 Calendar System: Semester
URL: www.snow.edu
Established: 1888 Annual Undergrad Tuition & Fees (In-State): $3,742
Enrollment: 5,563 Coed
Affiliation or Control: State IRS Status: 501(c)3
Highest Offering: Baccalaureate
Accreditation: NW, ACBSP, ADNUR, MUS, PNUR, THEA

02 President .... Dr. Gary L. CARLSTON
05 Vice President for Academic Affairs .... Dr. Steven HOOD
10 VP Finance/Administrative Services .... Mr. Jacob DETTINGER
32 Vice President Student Success .... Mr. Craig MATHIE
13 Chief Info Technology Officer (CIO) .... Mr. Phil ALLRED
35 Director Student Life/Leadership .... Ms. Michelle BROWN
75 Dean Business & Applied Tech .... Mr. Mike MEDLEY
36 Director of Student Support Svcs .... Mr. Michael ANDERSON
08 Director of Libraries .... Mr. Jon OSTLER
09 Dir Institutional Planning/Research .... Ms. Beckie HERMANSEN
15 Director Human Resources .... Mr. Randy BRABY
18 Director Campus Services Ephraim .... Ms. Leslee COOK
24 Director TTC .... Mr. Chase MITCHELL
39 Director Residential Life .... Ms. Jessica SIEGFRIED
41 Athletic Director .... Mr. Robert NIELSON
06 Registrar .... Mr. Micah STRAIT
07 Director Admissions .... Mr. Jeffrey SAVAGE
21 Budget Director .... Ms. Sherri HANSEN
26 Marketing/Communications Director .... Mr. John STEVENS
35 Director Student Affairs .... Mr. Mike ANDERSON
37 Director Student Financial Svcs .... Mr. Jack DALENE
38 Dir Student Counseling/Wellness Ctr .... Mr. Allen RIGGS
96 Director of Purchasing .... Mr. Michael JORGENSEN
111 Dir Advancement/Govt Relations .... Ms. Rosie CONNOR
27 Director of Campus Relations .... Ms. Heidi STRINGHAM
04 Administrative Asst to President .... Ms. Marci LARSEN

*Salt Lake Community College (D)

4600 S Redwood Road, Salt Lake City UT 84123-3197
County: Salt Lake FICE Identification: 005220
Unit ID: 230746
Telephone: (801) 957-4111 Carnegie Class: Assoc/HT-Mix Trad/Non
FAX Number: (801) 957-4444 Calendar System: Semester
URL: www.slcc.edu
Established: 1948 Annual Undergrad Tuition & Fees (In-State): $3,843
Enrollment: 29,620 Coed
Affiliation or Control: State IRS Status: 501(c)3
Highest Offering: Associate Degree
Accreditation: NW, ACFEI, ADNUR, #COARC, DH, FUSER, MAC, OTA, PTAA, RAD, SURGT

02 President .... Dr. Deneece HUFTALIN
05 Provost for Academic Affairs .... Dr. Clifton SANDERS
10 Vice Pres Business Services .... Mr. Jeff WEST
32 VP Student Affairs & Enrollment Mgt .... Dr. Charles LEPPER
111 Vice Pres Institutional Advancement .... Ms. Alison MCFARLANE
86 VP Govt & Community Relations .... Mr. Tim SHEEHAN
108 Vice Pres Inst Effectiveness .... Mr. Jeffrey AIRD
28 Spec Asst to President & CDO .... Dr. Lea Lani KINIKINI

* Utah State University Eastern (E)

451 E 400 N, Price UT 84501-2699
Telephone: (435) 613-5000 FICE Identification: 003676
Accreditation: &NW, ADNUR, PNUR

† Regional accreditation is carried under the parent institution in Logan, UT.

Western Governors University (F)

4001 S 700 E, Suite 700, Salt Lake City UT 84107-2533
County: Salt Lake FICE Identification: 033394
Unit ID: 433387
Telephone: (801) 274-3280 Carnegie Class: Masters/L
FAX Number: (801) 274-3305 Calendar System: Other
URL: www.wgu.edu
Established: 1996 Annual Undergrad Tuition & Fees: $6,670
Enrollment: 98,627 Coed
Affiliation or Control: Independent Non-Profit IRS Status: 501(c)3
Highest Offering: Master's
Accreditation: NW, ACBSP, CAEPN, CAHIIM, NURSE

01 President .... Scott D. PULSIPHER
05 Provost/Chief Academic Officer .... Dr. Marni B. STEIN
30 Sr VP University Development .... Matt SANDERS
10 Vice Pres Finance/Administration .... David GROW
09 Vice Pres Quality/Inst Research .... Jason LEVIN
26 Vice President of Marketing .... Carey HILDERBRAND
15 Vice President of Human Resources .... Bonnie PATTEE
37 Vice Pres of Financial Aid .... Bob COLLINS
27 Vice President of Public Relations .... Joan MITCHELL
86 Director Government Relations .... Chris BONNELL
100 Chief of Staff .... Gilbert ROJAS
13 Chief Information Officer .... David MORALES

Westminster College (G)

1840 S 1300 E, Salt Lake City UT 84105-3697
County: Salt Lake FICE Identification: 003681
Unit ID: 230807
Telephone: (801) 484-7651 Carnegie Class: Masters/L
FAX Number: (801) 466-6916 Calendar System: Semester
URL: www.westminstercollege.edu
Established: 1875 Annual Undergrad Tuition & Fees: $34,000
Enrollment: 2,570 Coed
Affiliation or Control: Independent Non-Profit IRS Status: 501(c)3
Highest Offering: Master's
Accreditation: NW, AAB, ACBSP, ANEST, CACREP, MACTE, NURSE, PH

01 President .... Dr. Bethami DOBKIN
05 Provost .... Dr. Debbie TAHMASSEBI
10 Vice Pres Finance & Administration .... Mr. Curtis W. RYAN
111 Vice Pres Institutional Advancement .... Mr. Daniel LEWIS
84 Vice President Enrollment Mgmt .... Ms. Erica JOHNSON
28 Int VP Diversity/Equity/Inclusion .... Dr. Tamara STEVENSON
26 Chief Marketing Officer .... Ms. Sheila YORKIN

49 Dean School of Arts & Sciences .... Dr. Lance NEWMAN
66 Dean School of Nursing/Hlth Science .... Dr. Sheryl STEADMAN
50 Dean School of Business .... Dr. Orn B. BODVARSSON
53 Dean School of Education .... Dr. Melanie AGNEW
32 VP of Student Affairs & DOS .... Mr. Karnell MCCONNELL-BLACK
29 Director Alumni Relations .... Vacant
09 Director of Inst Research/Assess .... Ms. Nichole GREENWOOD
45 Chief Strategy Officer .... Vacant
13 VP and Chief Information Officer .... Mr. Peter GRECO
43 General Counsel/Chief Risk Officer .... Ms. Kathryn HOLMES
21 Director of Accounting Services .... Ms. Jennifer MEDRANO
15 Director of Human Resources .... Ms. Julie FREESTONE
06 Registrar .... Mr. Michael SANTAROSA
37 Director of Financial Aid .... Mr. Joshua MONTAVON
07 Director Undergraduate Admissions .... Ms. Quincey OTUAFI
18 Director Plant/Facilities .... Mr. Richard A. BROCKMYER
36 Director of Career Resource Center .... Ms. Brianna MIDGLEY
08 Director Giovale Library .... Ms. Emily SWANSON
35 Dean of Students .... Mr. Karnell BLACK
39 Director of Student Involvement .... Mr. Oliver ANDERSON
88 Director of Conference Services .... Mr. Jeff BROWN
19 Director of Campus Safety .... Ms. Bri BUCKLEY
41 Director of Athletics .... Mr. Shay WYATT
42 Director of Spiritual Life .... Ms. Jan SAAED
38 Director of Campus Counseling .... Ms. Trisha JENSEN
92 Dean of Honors College .... Dr. Richard BADENHAUSEN
91 Database Administrator .... Ms. Roksana REZAEI
04 Exec Asst to Pres/Dir Board Rels .... Ms. Emmalee SZWEDKO
22 Title IX Coordinator/EEO Compliance .... Ms. Katherine THOMAS
102 Dir Foundation/Corporate Relations .... Mr. Jeff DRIGGS
30 Executive Director of Development .... Ms. Nancy BROWN

† Granted candidacy at the Doctorate level.

VERMONT

Bennington College (A)

One College Drive, Bennington VT 05201-6003
County: Bennington FICE Identification: 003682
Unit ID: 230816
Telephone: (802) 442-5401 Carnegie Class: Bac-A&S
FAX Number: (802) 447-4269 Calendar System: Semester
URL: www.bennington.edu
Established: 1932 Annual Undergrad Tuition & Fees: $53,860
Enrollment: 851 Coed
Affiliation or Control: Independent Non-Profit IRS Status: 501(c)3
Highest Offering: Master's
Accreditation: EH

01 President .... Dr. Isabel ROCHE
05 Acting Provost .... Mr. John BULLOCK
20 Acting Dean of the College .... Ms. Oceana WILSON
10 VP for Finance & Administration .... Mr. Brian MURPHY
45 Sr VP for Institutional Initiatives .... Vacant
88 Sr VP for Strategic Partnerships .... Ms. Paige BARTELS
111 VP for Institutional Advancement .... Mr. Matt RIZZO
84 VP for Enrollment .... Mr. Tony CABASCO
28 VP for Inst Inclusion/Equity .... Ms. Delia SAENZ
18 AVP for Facilities Mgmt & Planning .... Mr. Andy SCHLATTER
26 Chief Communications Officer .... Mr. Duncan DOBBELMANN
32 Dean of Students .... Ms. Natalie BASIL
09 Dean of Research/Plng/Assessment .... Mr. Zeke BERNSTEIN
08 Dean of the Library .... Ms. Oceana WILSON
15 Director of Human Resources .... Ms. Heather FALEY
37 Director of Financial Aid .... Ms. Heather CLIFFORD
13 Director of IT .... Mr. Jude HIGDON
04 Senior Exec Asst to the Pres .... Ms. Shannon HOWLETT
19 Director Security/Safety .... Mr. Ken COLLAMORE

Champlain College (B)

163 S Willard Street, Burlington VT 05402-0670
County: Chittenden FICE Identification: 003684
Unit ID: 230852
Telephone: (802) 860-2700 Carnegie Class: Masters/L
FAX Number: (802) 860-2750 Calendar System: Semester
URL: www.champlain.edu
Established: 1956 Annual Undergrad Tuition & Fees: $41,010
Enrollment: 4,749 Coed
Affiliation or Control: Independent Non-Profit IRS Status: 501(c)3
Highest Offering: Master's
Accreditation: EH, ACBSP, ART, SW

01 Interim President .... Dr. Laurie QUINN
05 Acting Provost .... Dr. Catherine L MORGAN
10 Vice President Finance and Planning .... Shelley NAVARI
84 Vice President Enrollment .... Dr. Lisa BLUNDERS
111 Vice President Advancement .... Robert M. CALDWELL
32 Vice President of Student Affairs .... Dr. Angela BATISTA
21 Director Finance & Asst Treasurer .... April O'DELL
13 Vice Pres Technology & CIO .... Jeff BROWN
36 Director Career Collaborative .... Dr. Tanja HINTERSTOISSER
53 Dean Education/Human Stds Div .... Dr. Laurel BONGIORNO
88 Dean Comm/Creative Media Div .... Dr. Paula WILLOQUET-MARICONDI
50 Dean Stiller School of Business .... Dr. Scott BAKER
77 Dean Information Tech/Science .... Dr. Scott STEVENS
106 Asst Provost for Online Education .... Dr. Johnna HERRICK-PHELPS
07 Director of Admissions .... Diane SOBOSKI
06 Registrar .... Tara ARNESON
37 Director of Financial Aid .... Gregory DAVIS
38 Director of Counseling Center .... Skip HARRIS
18 Director of Physical Plant .... Vacant
19 Director of Security & Safety .... Bruce BOVAT
23 Director Health Services .... Annika HAWKINS-HILKE
88 Senior Dir Learning & Teaching .... Rebecca MILLS
15 Vice Pres of Human Capital .... Jennifer ARCHAMBAULT
39 Director of Residential Life .... Vacant
85 Senior Director Intl Education .... Dr. Noah GOLDBLATT
26 External Relations & Comm Director .... Sandy YUSEN
08 Interim Director Library .... Emily CRIST
103 Assoc Dir Talent & Engagement .... Sara QUINTANA
110 Asst VP of Advancement .... Sarah ANDRIANO
40 Campus Store Manager .... Kevin MCCANN
108 Director Learning Assessment .... Ellen ZEMAN
105 Director Web Services .... Brian ANDREWS
25 Chief Contracts/Grants Admin .... Ted WINOKUR
09 Director of Institutional Research .... Gabrielle SEALY
100 Chief of Staff .... Katherine BIRROW
44 Director Annual Giving .... Regina FARRELL
29 Director of Engagement .... Nariah BROADUS

Goddard College (C)

123 Pitkin Road, Plainfield VT 05667-9432
County: Washington FICE Identification: 003686
Unit ID: 230889
Telephone: (800) 468-4888 Carnegie Class: Masters/M
FAX Number: (802) 454-1029 Calendar System: Semester
URL: www.goddard.edu
Established: 1863 Annual Undergrad Tuition & Fees: $16,586
Enrollment: 496 Coed
Affiliation or Control: Independent Non-Profit IRS Status: 501(c)3
Highest Offering: Master's
Accreditation: #EH

01 President .... Dr. Bernard BULL
05 Chief Academic Officer .... Dr. Steven JAMES
10 Chief Financial and Admin Officer .... Ms. Leesa STEWART
30 Director of Development .... Ms. Meg HAMMOND
26 Director of Marketing .... Mr. Joshua AUERBACH
13 Director of IT .... Mr. Ron MARION
07 Director of Admissions .... Vacant
06 Registrar .... Ms. Annette FITZGERALD
37 Director of Financial Aid .... Ms. Beverly JENE
08 Director of Information Access .... Ms. Clara BRUNS
18 Director of Facilities Operations .... Mr. J.C MYERS
32 Director of Student Services .... Ms. Deborah BLOOM
88 Director of WGDR/WGDH Radio .... Mr. Kris GRUEN
04 Executive Assistant to President .... Ms. Lisa LARIVEE

Landmark College (D)

19 River Road South, Putney VT 05346
County: Windham FICE Identification: 025326
Unit ID: 247649
Telephone: (802) 387-4767 Carnegie Class: Bac/Assoc-Mixed
FAX Number: (802) 387-6868 Calendar System: Semester
URL: www.landmark.edu
Established: 1985 Annual Undergrad Tuition & Fees: $56,800
Enrollment: 461 Coed
Affiliation or Control: Independent Non-Profit IRS Status: 501(c)3
Highest Offering: Baccalaureate
Accreditation: EH

01 President .... Dr. Peter A. EDEN
03 Executive Vice President .... Mr. Jon A. MACCLAREN
05 VP Academic Affairs .... Dr. Gail GIBSON SHEFFIELD
111 VP Institutional Advancement .... Ms. Ellen SMITH
32 VP Student Affairs/Dean Campus Life .... Mr. Michael LUCIANI
84 VP Enrollment Management .... Mr. Kevin MAYNE
88 VP Educational Research/Innovation .... Ms. Manju BANERJEE
04 Assistant to the President .... Ms. Tiffany KERYLOW
13 Chief Technology Officer .... Ms. Corinne BELL
10 Chief Financial Officer .... Mr. Jon MACCLAREN
36 Director Career Connections .... Ms. Jan COPLAN
26 Director Marketing & Communications .... Mr. Mark DIPIETRO
18 Director of Facilities .... Mr. Kyle SKROCKI
08 Director Library Services .... Ms. Jennifer LANN
06 Registrar .... Ms. Nichole NIETSCHE
41 Director Athletics .... Ms. Kari POST
37 Director Financial Aid .... Mr. Michael MERTES
38 Director of Counseling/Wellness .... Ms. Jacala MILLS
23 Director of Health Services .... Mr. Jeff HUYETT
15 Director Human Resources .... Ms. Janie JENKINS-EVANS
21 Controller .... Mr. Mark HIGGINS
35 Dean of Students .... Ms. Kelly O'RYAN
07 Director of Admissions .... Ms. Sydney RUFF
19 Director Campus Safety .... Mr. Orlando ALVAREZ
29 Associate Director Alumni Affairs .... Ms. Tricia STANLEY
30 Sr Dir Institutional Advancement .... Ms. Carol NARDINO
104 Director International Education .... Ms. Peg ALDEN
106 Director Online Learning .... Ms. Denise JAFFE
40 Bookstore Manager .... Ms. Kimberly KEMPF

Marlboro College (E)

PO Box A, Marlboro VT 05344-9999
County: Windham FICE Identification: 003690
Unit ID: 230940
Telephone: (802) 257-4333 Carnegie Class: Bac-A&S
FAX Number: (802) 257-4154 Calendar System: Semester
URL: www.marlboro.edu
Established: 1946 Annual Undergrad Tuition & Fees: $40,840
Enrollment: 185 Coed
Affiliation or Control: Independent Non-Profit IRS Status: 501(c)3
Highest Offering: Master's
Accreditation: EH

01 President .... Mr. Kevin F. QUIGLEY
11 Chief Operating Officer .... Ms. Rebecca CATARELLI
114 Chief Planning & Budget Officer .... Mr. Robert WEBBER
05 Dean of Faculty/Chief Academic Ofcr .... Mr. Richard GLEJZER
07 Dean of Admissions .... Mr. Fumio SUGIHARA
32 Dean of Students .... Mr. Patrick CONNELLY
58 Assoc Dean Graduate/Profess Stds .... Mr. Tristan TOLENO
111 Director of Advancement .... Ms. Rennie WASHBURN
08 Library Director .... Ms. Beth RUANE
06 Registrar .... Ms. Cathy FULLER
102 Dir Corp & Foundation Relations .... Ms. Hillary TWINING
26 Dir of Marketing/Communications .... Vacant
18 Director of Plant Operations .... Mr. Dan J. COTTER
82 World Studies Director .... Ms. Jaime TANNER
04 Asst to President .... Ms. Tracy WHEELER
29 Director Alumni Relations .... Ms. Maia SEGURA
104 Director Study Abroad .... Ms. Maggie PATARI
13 Chief Info Technology Officer (CIO) .... Mr. John BAKER
41 Athletic Director .... Mr. Adam KATRICK

Marlboro College Graduate School (F)

PO Box A, Marlboro VT 05344
Telephone: (802) 258-9200 Identification: 770120
Accreditation: &EH

Middlebury Bread Loaf School of English (G)

75 Franklin Street, Middlebury VT 05753
Telephone: (802) 443-5418 Identification: 770119
Accreditation: &EH

† Bread Loaf School of English is a summer graduate program and the enrollment figure is for the summer term.

Middlebury College (H)

Old Chapel, Middlebury VT 05753-6200
County: Addison FICE Identification: 003691
Unit ID: 230959
Telephone: (802) 443-5000 Carnegie Class: Bac-A&S
FAX Number: (802) 443-2071 Calendar System: 4/1/4
URL: www.middlebury.edu
Established: 1800 Annual Undergrad Tuition & Fees: $54,450
Enrollment: 2,591 Coed
Affiliation or Control: Independent Non-Profit IRS Status: 501(c)3
Highest Offering: Doctorate
Accreditation: EH

01 President .... Dr. Laurie L. PATTON
05 Exec VP and Provost .... Dr. Jeff CASON
10 Exec VP Finance & Administration .... Mr. David J. PROVOST
15 VP for HR/Chief Risk Officer .... Ms. Karen MILLER
111 VP for Advancement .... Ms. Colleen FITZPATRICK
03 Sr Vice Pres/Philanthropic Advisor .... Mr. Michael SCHOENFELD
20 VP Academic Affairs/Dean of Faculty .... Dr. Sujata MOORTI
26 VP for Communications & Marketing .... Mr. David J. GIBSON
32 VP for Student Affairs .... Dr. Baishakhi TAYLOR
43 General Counsel/Chief of Staff .... Ms. Hannah ROSS
28 Chief Diversity Officer .... Dr. Miguel FERNANDEZ
58 VP Acad Affs/Dean of the Institute .... Dr. Jeffrey DAYTON-JOHNSON
07 Dean of Admissions .... Ms. Nicole CURVIN
104 Dean of International Programs .... Dr. Carlos VELEZ
45 Assoc Provost for Planning .... Mr. LeRoy GRAHAM
08 Dean of the Library .... Mr. Michael D. ROY
37 Assoc VP Student Financial Services ... Ms. Kim DOWNS-BURNS
13 Associate VP/CIO for ITS .... Mr. Vijay MENTA
79 VP for AA/Dean of Language Schs .... Dr. Stephen SNYDER
20 Dean of Curriculum .... Dr. Suzanne GURLAND
09 Dean for Faculty Dev & Research .... Dr. James RALPH
21 Director of Business Services .... Mr. Matt CURRAN
29 Assoc VP Alumni & Parent Programs .... Ms. Margaret STOREY GROVES
23 Exec Dir Health & Counseling Svcs .... Dr. Augustus JORDAN
42 Dean of Spiritual/Religious Life .... Mr. Mark ORTEN
41 Director of Athletics .... Mr. Erin QUINN
35 Assoc Dn of the Col/Dir Pub Safety . Ms. Elizabeth B. BURCHARD
06 Registrar .... Ms. Jennifer THOMPSON
15 Director of Human Resources .... Ms. Cheryl MULLINS
40 Bookstore Manager .... Ms. Erin JONES-POPPE
108 Dir Assessment & Inst Rsch .... Ms. Adela LANGROCK
25 Director of Grants & Sponsored Pgm .... Mr. Chuck MASON

† Tuition figure is a comprehensive fees figure.

New England Culinary Institute (I)

7 School Street, Montpelier VT 05602-9720
County: Washington FICE Identification: 022540
Unit ID: 230977
Telephone: (802) 225-3200 Carnegie Class: Spec-4-yr-Other
FAX Number: (802) 225-3280 Calendar System: Semester
URL: www.neci.edu
Established: 1980 Annual Undergrad Tuition & Fees: $22,200
Enrollment: 144 Coed
Affiliation or Control: Proprietary IRS Status: Proprietary
Highest Offering: Baccalaureate

Accreditation: ACCSC

01 CEO/President .... Dr. Milan MILASINOVIC
05 Dean of Education/Dept Chr Cul Arts .... Mr. Lyndon VIRKLER
88 Chair Baking & Pastry Programs .... Chef Kathleen KESSLER
106 Chair Online Programs .... Chef Peg CHECCI
06 Registrar .... Ms. Gail MACDONALD
07 Director of Admissions .... Mr. Dwight CROSS
15 Director Human Resources .... Ms. Karen MADIGAN
18 Director of Facilities .... Mr. William COLGAN
36 Career Services Manager .... Ms. Eunice JORDAN
20 Sr Dir Operations & Education .... Chef David MILES
37 Director Financial Aid .... Ms. Jessica CHAPPEL

Norwich University (A)

158 Harmon Drive, Northfield VT 05663-1000

County: Washington
FICE Identification: 003692
Unit ID: 230995
Telephone: (802) 485-2000
Carnegie Class: Masters/L
FAX Number: (802) 485-2032
Calendar System: Semester
URL: www.norwich.edu
Established: 1819
Annual Undergrad Tuition & Fees: $40,014
Enrollment: 4,100
Coed
Affiliation or Control: Independent Non-Profit
IRS Status: 501(c)3
Highest Offering: Master's
Accreditation: EH, ACBSP, CAATE, NURSE

01 President .... Dr. Richard W. SCHNEIDER
05 Provost & Dean of Faculty .... Dr. Sandra AFFENITO
58 VP & Dean Col of Grad/Cont Studies .... Dr. William CLEMENTS
32 VP Student Affairs & Technology .... Dr. Frank VANECEK
30 VP Alumni & Development Relations .... Mr. David J. WHALEY
88 VP Strategic Partnership .... Mr. Phillip SUSMANN
84 VP of Enrollment Management .... Mr. Greg MATTHEWS
26 VP of Communications .... Ms. Kathy MURPHY-MORIARITY
10 Chief Financial Officer .... Ms. Lauren WOBBY
11 Chief Administrative Officer .... Mr. David MAGIDA
107 Dean Col of Professional Schools .... Mr. Aron TEMKIN
83 Dean College of Liberal Arts .... Dr. Edward KOHN
81 Dean College of Science/Mathematics .... Dr. Michael MCGINNIS
88 Dean College of National Services .... Col. Jeremy MILLER
29 Assoc VP Alumni Relations .... Ms. Diane SCOLARO
20 Assoc VP Academic Affairs .... Dr. Natalia BLANK
04 Exec Assistant to President .... Ms. Laura AMELL
35 Dean of Students .... Ms. Martha MATHIS
08 Interim Head Librarian .... Mr. Greg SAUER
41 Athletic Director .... Mr. Anthony A. MARIANO
18 Director Facilities/Operations .... Mr. Bizhan YAHYAZADEH
37 Director of Student Financial Aid .... Ms. Meaghan DRUMM
38 Dir Student Counseling/Wellness .... Ms. Nicole KROTINGER
07 Director of Admissions .... Mr. Tim REARDON
06 Int Registrar & Inst Research Dir .... Mr. Dan CARROLL
102 Dir Foundation/Corporate Relations .... Ms. Lindsay BUDNIK
103 Director Career Development .... Ms. Kathryn PROVOST
19 Director Security/Safety .... Mr. Larry ROONEY
15 Director of Human Resources .... Mr. Dana MOSS

Saint Michael's College (B)

One Winooski Park, Colchester VT 05439-0001

County: Chittenden
FICE Identification: 003694
Unit ID: 231059
Telephone: (802) 654-2000
Carnegie Class: Bac-A&S
FAX Number: (802) 654-2297
Calendar System: Semester
URL: www.smcvt.edu
Established: 1904
Annual Undergrad Tuition & Fees: $45,375
Enrollment: 2,077
Coed
Affiliation or Control: Roman Catholic
IRS Status: 501(c)3
Highest Offering: Master's
Accreditation: EH, CEA

01 President .... Dr. D. E. Lorraine M. STERRITT
04 Assistant to the President .... Mrs. Ellen M. DEORSEY
05 Interim VP for Academic Affairs .... Dr. Jeffrey TRUMBOWER
10 Vice President for Finance .... Mr. Robert ROBINSON
32 Vice President for Student Affairs .... Dr. Dawn M. ELLINWOOD
84 Vice Pres Enrollment/Marketing .... Vacant
15 Vice President for Human Resources .... Ms. Eileen O'ROURKE
111 Vice Pres for Inst Advancement .... Ms. Krystyna DAVENPORT BROWN
42 Director Edmundite Campus Ministry .... Rev. Brian J. CUMMINGS, SSE
07 Director of Admission .... Mr. Michael STEFANOWICZ
13 Chief Information Officer .... Mr. William O. ANDERSON
41 Director of Athletics .... Dr. Christopher KENNEY
26 Dir Marketing/Communications .... Mr. Alex BERTONI

School for International Training (SIT) (C)

1 Kipling Road, Brattleboro VT 05302-0676

County: Windham
FICE Identification: 008860
Unit ID: 231068
Telephone: (802) 257-7751
Carnegie Class: Masters/M
FAX Number: (802) 258-3110
Calendar System: Other
URL: www.sit.edu
Established: 1964
Annual Undergrad Tuition & Fees: N/A
Enrollment: 257
Coed
Affiliation or Control: Independent Non-Profit
IRS Status: 501(c)3
Highest Offering: Master's
Accreditation: EH

01 President .... Dr. Sophia HOWLETT
05 Academic Dean .... Mr. Said GRAIOUID
05 Academic Dean .... Ms. Aynn SETRIGHT
05 Academic Dean .... Mr. Brian HAMMER
05 Academic Dean .... Ms. Katy DE LA GARZA
10 CFO .... Mr. Kote LOMIDZE
13 Director of IT .... Mr. Roger BOYLE
43 General Counsel .... Ms. Lisa RAE
58 Dean SIT Graduate Institute .... Dr. Kenneth WILLIAMS
15 Senior HR Manager .... Ms. Gretchen MAGNUSON
07 Assoc Dean of Admissions .... Mr. Eric WIRTH
06 Registrar .... Ms. Ginny NELLIS
04 Executive Asst to SIT President .... Ms. Adelee AUSTIN
108 Assoc Dean for Assessment .... Dr. Kathryn INSKEEP
29 Director of Alumni Engagement .... Ms. Carla LINEBACK
08 Head Librarian .... Mr. Patrick SPURLOCK

Sterling College (D)

PO Box 72, Craftsbury Common VT 05827-0072

County: Orleans
FICE Identification: 021435
Unit ID: 231095
Telephone: (802) 586-7711
Carnegie Class: Bac-A&S
FAX Number: (802) 586-2596
Calendar System: Semester
URL: www.sterlingcollege.edu
Established: 1958
Annual Undergrad Tuition & Fees: $38,300
Enrollment: 154
Coed
Affiliation or Control: Independent Non-Profit
IRS Status: 501(c)3
Highest Offering: Baccalaureate
Accreditation: EH

01 President .... Mr. Matthew A. DERR
05 Dean of Academics .... Dr. Laura SPENCE
07 Dean of Admission Services .... Ms. Amalia HARRIS
111 Dean of Advancement and Alumni Rels .... Ms. Christina GOODWIIN
10 Vice President and COO .... Mr. Peter MERRILL
08 Librarian .... Ms. Petra VOGEL
18 Director of Facilities .... Mr. Kelly JONES
32 Director of Community .... Mr. Julian SHARP
06 Asst Dean of Academics & Registrar .... Ms. Laura Lea BERRY
26 Director of Marketing .... Ms. Lou LEPPING
37 Director of Financial Aid .... Ms. Barbara STUART

University of Vermont (E)

South Prospect Street, Burlington VT 05405-0160

County: Chittenden
FICE Identification: 003696
Unit ID: 231174
Telephone: (802) 656-3131
Carnegie Class: DU-Higher
FAX Number: N/A
Calendar System: Semester
URL: www.uvm.edu
Established: 1791
Annual Undergrad Tuition & Fees (In-State): $18,276
Enrollment: 13,340
Coed
Affiliation or Control: State
IRS Status: 501(c)3
Highest Offering: Doctorate
Accreditation: EH, CAATE, CACREP, CAEP, CLPSY, DENT, DIETC, DIETD, IPSY, MED, MT, NURSE, PTA, RTT, SP, SPAA, SW

01 President .... Dr. Suresh GARIMELLA
05 Interim Provost and Sr VP .... Dr. Patricia A. PRELOCK
10 VP for Finance & Treasurer .... Mr. Richard H. CATE
86 VP University Relations & Admin .... Dr. Thomas J. GUSTAFSON
46 VP Research .... Dr. Richard A. GALBRAITH
30 CEO & President The UVM Foundation .... Mr. Shane JACOBSON
43 VP Legal Affairs & General Counsel .... Ms. Sharon REICH PAULSEN
84 VP Enrollment Management .... Ms. Stacey R. KOSTELL
13 Chief Information Officier .... Dr. T. Simeon ANANOU
20 Assoc Prov Faculty Affairs .... Dr. Jim VIGOREAUX
20 Assoc Provost Academic Affairs .... Dr. Jennifer DICKINSON
32 Vice Provost for Student Affairs .... Dr. Annie STEVENS
15 VP for Human Resources & Diversity .... Dr. Wanda R. HEADING-GRANT
100 VP for Executive Operations .... Dr. Gary L. DERR
118 Assoc Chief Human Resource Officer .... Mr. Jes KRAUS
35 Dean of Students .... Dr. David A. NESTOR
29 VP for Alumni Relations .... Mr. Alan E. RYEA
63 Dean College of Medicine .... Dr. Richard L. PAGE
66 Interim Dean Nursing & Health Sci .... Dr. Scott THOMAS
49 Dean Arts & Sciences .... Dr. William A. FALLS
47 Dean Agriculture & Life Sciences .... Dr. Thomas C. VOGELMANN
54 Dean Engineering & Math Sciences .... Dr. Linda SCHADLER
53 Dean Education & Social Svcs .... Dr. Scott THOMAS
50 Dean Business Administration .... Dr. Sanjay SHARMA
92 Dean Honors College .... Dr. David JENEMANN
65 Dean Environment & Natural Resource .... Dr. Nancy E. MATHEWS
56 Director Extension .... Mr. Chuck ROSS
58 Dean Graduate College .... Dr. Cynthia J. FOREHAND
51 Dean Continuing & Distance Educ .... Ms. Cynthia L. BELLIVEAU
08 Dean Libraries & Learning Res .... Dr. Bryn GEFFERT
06 Registrar .... Ms. Veronika CARTER
09 Director Institutional Research .... Dr. Alexander C. YIN
26 Director University Communications .... Mr. Enrique CORREDERA
14 Assoc Chief Information Officer .... Ms. Julia H. RUSSELL
25 Executive Director Research Admin .... Mr. Brian PRINDLE
114 University Budget Director .... Vacant
19 Chief of Police Services .... Ms. Lianne M. TUOMEY
41 Director of Athletics .... Mr. Jeffrey L. SCHULMAN
36 Director Career Services .... Ms. Pamela K. GARDNER
23 Director Ctr for Health & Wellbeing .... Dr. Harry CHEN
38 Counsel/Psych Services Program Dir .... Dr. Todd N. WEINMAN
39 Director Residential Life .... Mr. Rafael RODRIGUEZ
40 Director University Bookstore .... Mr. Jay E. MENNINGER
85 Director Intl Education Services .... Ms. Kimberly A. HOWARD
112 VP for Principal Gifts .... Mr. Mark W. DORGAN
44 Asst VP Development & Gift Planning .... Ms. Amy PALMER-ELLIS
123 Director Graduate Admissions .... Ms. Kimberly L. HESS
07 Dir Undergraduate Admissions .... Mr. Ryan HARGRAVES
37 Director Student Financial Services .... Ms. Marie D. JOHNSON
96 Director Purchasing Services .... Ms. Natalie L. GUILLETTE
94 Director Women's Center .... Ms. Melissa MURRAY
24 Access/Media Services Librarian .... Mr. Aaron F. NICHOLS
101 Board of Trustees Coordinator .... Ms. Corinne B. THOMPSON
04 Admin Assistant to the President .... Ms. Janis AUDET-KRANS

Vermont College of Fine Arts (F)

36 College Street, Montpelier VT 05602-3145

County: Washington
FICE Identification: 003697
Unit ID: 455992
Telephone: (802) 828-8600
Carnegie Class: Spec-4-yr-Other
FAX Number: (802) 828-8649
Calendar System: Semester
URL: www.vcfa.edu
Established: 2008
Annual Graduate Tuition & Fees: N/A
Enrollment: 388
Coed
Affiliation or Control: Independent Non-Profit
IRS Status: 501(c)3
Highest Offering: Master's; No Undergraduates
Accreditation: EH, ART

01 Interim President .... Ms. Leslie Colis WARD
05 Academic Dean .... Mr. Matthew MONK
10 VP for Finance & Admin .... Ms. Katie GUSTAFSON
32 VP Student Services .... Mr. David MARKOW
04 Assistant to President .... Ms. Kerry MACDONALD
26 Exec Dir Marketing/Communications .... Mr. Alastair HAYES
06 Registrar .... Ms. Jody MAUNSELL
08 Head Librarian .... Mr. Jim NOLTE
13 Director of IT .... Mr. Peter TIMPONE
18 Dir Facilities/Operations .... Mr. Matthew COYNE
07 Dir Admissions & Financial Aid .... Ms. Lucy BOURGEAULT

† Carnegie Graduate Instructional Program classification is Postbac-A&S

Vermont Law School (G)

164 Chelsea Street, PO Box 96, South Royalton VT 05068-0096

County: Windsor
FICE Identification: 011934
Unit ID: 231147
Telephone: (802) 831-1000
Carnegie Class: Spec-4-yr-Law
FAX Number: (802) 831-1163
Calendar System: Semester
URL: www.vermontlaw.edu
Established: 1972
Annual Graduate Tuition & Fees: N/A
Enrollment: 632
Coed
Affiliation or Control: Independent Non-Profit
IRS Status: 501(c)3
Highest Offering: First Professional Degree; No Undergraduates
Accreditation: EH, LAW

01 President and Dean .... Mr. Thomas MCHENRY
05 Vice Dean for Faculty .... Ms. Cynthia LEWIS
32 Vice Dean for Students .... Ms. Beth MCCORMACK
10 Vice President for Finance .... Ms. Lorraine ATWOOD
07 Vice President for Enrollment .... Mr. John MILLER
111 Vice President of Advancement .... Vacant
88 Director Environmental Law Ctr .... Ms. Jennifer RUSHLOW
35 Assoc Dean Student Affs & Diversity .... Ms. Shirley JEFFERSON
20 Assoc Dean for Academic Affs .... Ms. Laurie BEYRANEVAND
106 Director of Distance Learning .... Ms. Sarah REITER
15 Human Resources Director .... Ms. Kimberly HARRIS
08 Library Director .... Ms. Jane WOLDOW
21 Comptroller .... Mr. Robert WEBBER
06 Registrar .... Ms. Maureen MORIARTY
37 Director of Financial Aid .... Ms. Melody DEFLORIO
18 Facilities Manager .... Mr. Jeffrey KNUDSEN
26 Director of Communications .... Ms. Angela CAMPBELL
13 Technology Operations Manager .... Mr. Oscar TREVINO
04 Exec Asst to the President/Dean .... Ms. Susan FOLGER
40 Bookstore Manager .... Ms. Amy MCDOWELL
29 Director of Alumni Affairs .... Ms. Melissa HARWOOD
102 Director Foundation/Corporate Rels .... Mr. David THURLOW

*Vermont State Colleges Office of the Chancellor (H)

PO Box 7, Montpelier VT 05601

County: Washington
FICE Identification: 029162
Unit ID: 231156
Telephone: (802) 224-3000
Carnegie Class: N/A
FAX Number: (802) 224-3035
URL: www.vsc.edu

01 Chancellor .... Mr. Jeb SPAULDING
43 Vice President/General Counsel .... Ms. Sophie ZDATNY
10 Vice Pres/Chief Financial Officer .... Mr. Stephen WISLOSKI
05 Chief Academic/Tech Officer .... Dr. Yasmine ZIESLER
11 Administrative Director .... Ms. Jennifer PORRIER
86 Dir External/Governmental Affairs .... Ms. Tricia COATES
26 Chief Information Officer .... Mr. Kevin CONROY
18 Director of Facilities .... Mr. Richard ETHIER
13 Director of Information Technology .... Mr. Doug EASTMAN
15 Director of Human Resources .... Ms. Nancy SHAW
09 Director of Institutional Research .... Mr. Patroklos KARANTINOS
88 Director of Payroll/Benefits .... Ms. Tracy SWEET
25 Grants Compliance Officer .... Ms. Betsy WARD

*Castleton University (A)

62 Alumni Drive, Castleton VT 05735-4454
County: Rutland FICE Identification: 003683
Unit ID: 230834
Telephone: (802) 468-5611 Carnegie Class: Bac-Diverse
FAX Number: (802) 468-6470 Calendar System: Semester
URL: www.castleton.edu
Established: 1787 Annual Undergrad Tuition & Fees (In-State): $12,314
Enrollment: 2,141 Coed
Affiliation or Control: State IRS Status: 501(c)3
Highest Offering: Master's
Accreditation: EH, CAATE, NURSE, SW

02 President .... Ms. Karen SCOLFORO
04 Exec Assistant to the President .... Ms. Rita B. GENO
05 Academic Dean .... Dr. Jonathan SPIRO
20 Associate Academic Dean .... Mr. Peter KIMMEL
10 Director of Finance .... Ms. Laura JAKUBOWSKI
32 Dean of Students .... Mr. Dennis PROULX
84 Dean of Enrollment .... Mr. Maurice OUIMET
15 Director of Human Resources .... Ms. Janet HAZELTON
35 Associate Dean of Students .... Ms. Victoria ANGIS
06 Registrar .... Ms. Lori ARNER
37 Director Student Financial Aid .... Ms. Kathy O'MEARA
53 Director of Education .... Dr. Richard REARDON
18 Director of Physical Plant .... Mr. Chuck LAVOIE
36 Dir of Career Development .... Ms. Renee BEAUPREWHITE
23 Wellness Center Director .... Ms. Martha COULTER
13 Chief Technology Officer .... Ms. Gayle MALINOWSKI

*Community College of Vermont (B)

PO Box 489, Montpelier VT 05601
County: Washington FICE Identification: 011167
Unit ID: 230861
Telephone: (802) 828-2800 Carnegie Class: Assoc/MT-VT-Mix Trad/Non
FAX Number: (802) 828-2805 Calendar System: Semester
URL: www.ccv.edu
Established: 1970 Annual Undergrad Tuition & Fees (In-State): $7,120
Enrollment: 5,504 Coed
Affiliation or Control: State IRS Status: 501(c)3
Highest Offering: Associate Degree
Accreditation: EH

02 President .... Ms. Joyce M. JUDY
11 Dean of Administration .... Mr. Andrew PALLITO
05 Dean of Academic Services .... Ms. Deborah STEWART
32 Dean of Student Services .... Ms. Heather WEINSTEIN
20 Associate Academic Dean .... Ms. Diane HERMANN-ARTIM
35 Associate Dean of Students .... Ms. Angela ALBECK
12 Exec Director of Academic Center .... Mr. Eric SAKAI
84 Dean of Enrollment & Cmty Relations .... Ms. Katie MOBLEY
88 Dean of Academic Center Admin .... Ms. Tapp BARNHILL
15 Director Human Resources .... Mr. Robert FINNEGAN
06 Registrar .... Mr. John Paul REES
07 Director of Admissions .... Mr. Adam WARRINGTON
37 Director of Financial Aid .... Mr. Ryan DULUDE
09 Dir Institutional Research/Planning .... Ms. Laura MASSELL
26 Director of Communications .... Ms. Katherine POWERS
88 Director of Secondary Initiatives .... Ms. Natalie SEARLE
36 Director of Career Training Program .... Vacant
27 Dir of Marketing Operations .... Ms. Danielle BRESETTE
10 Chief Financial/Business Officer .... Mr. Nathan HOCK
30 Director of Resource Development .... Ms. Aimee STEPHENSON
106 Dir of Online Teaching & Learning .... Ms. Jennifer ALBERICO
13 Director of IT Infrastructure .... Mr. Charles BOMBARD
90 Director of Academic Technology .... Mr. Anthony HARRIS
91 Dir of Administrative Technology .... Ms. Megan TUCKER

*Northern Vermont University-Johnson (C)

337 College Hill, Johnson VT 05656
County: Lamoille FICE Identification: 003688
Unit ID: 230913
Telephone: (802) 635-1240 Carnegie Class: Masters/S
FAX Number: (802) 635-1230 Calendar System: Semester
URL: www.northernvermont.edu
Established: 1828 Annual Undergrad Tuition & Fees (In-State): $12,074
Enrollment: 1,552 Coed
Affiliation or Control: State IRS Status: 501(c)3
Highest Offering: Master's
Accreditation: EH

02 President .... Dr. Elaine C. COLLINS
05 Provost .... Dr. Nolan T. ATKINS
11 Dean of Administration .... Ms. Sharron R. SCOTT
32 Dean of Students .... Mr. Jonathan M. DAVIS
13 Chief Info Technology Officer (CIO) .... Vacant
84 Dean of Enrollment/Marketing .... Mr. Michael FOX
35 Associate Dean of Students .... Ms. Michele WHITMORE
06 Registrar .... Mr. Douglas EASTMAN
106 Assoc Dean of Distance Education .... Ms. Bobbi Jo CARTER
18 Director of Physical Plant .... Vacant
41 Assoc Dean Athletics/Recreation .... Mr. Jamey VENTURA
38 Director of Counseling Services .... Ms. Kate MCCARTHY
30 Univ Development/External Rels Ofcr .... Ms. Leah HOLLENBERGER
36 Director of Advising .... Ms. Sara KINERSON
89 Director of First-Year Experience .... Ms. Margo WARDEN
19 Director of Public Safety .... Mr. Michael PALAGONIA
26 Director Marketing/Communications .... Ms. Sylvia PLUMB
07 Director of Admissions .... Mr. Patrick ROGERS
79 Chair Humanities .... Dr. Lisa CLINE
53 Chair Education .... Dr. Rob SCHULZE
65 Chair Environ/Health Sciences .... Dr. Elizabeth DOLCI
88 Chair Performing Arts .... Ms. Bethany PLISSEY
57 Chair Fine Arts .... Mr. Ken LESLIE
50 Chair Business/Economics .... Mr. James BLACK
60 Chair Writing/Literature .... Dr. Sharon TWIGG
81 Chair Mathematics .... Dr. Julie THEORET
83 Chair Behavioral Sciences .... Dr. Susan GREEN

*Northern Vermont University-Lyndon (D)

1001 College Road, PO Box 919,
Lyndonville VT 05851-0919
Telephone: (802) 626-6200 FICE Identification: 003689
Accreditation: &EH, EXSC

*Vermont Technical College (E)

124 Admin Drive, PO Box 500,
Randolph Center VT 05061-0500
County: Orange FICE Identification: 003698
Unit ID: 231165
Telephone: (802) 728-1000 Carnegie Class: Bac/Assoc-Mixed
FAX Number: (802) 728-1508 Calendar System: Semester
URL: www.vtc.edu
Established: 1866 Annual Undergrad Tuition & Fees (In-State): $15,108
Enrollment: 1,616 Coed
Affiliation or Control: State IRS Status: 501(c)3
Highest Offering: Master's
Accreditation: EH, ADNUR, COARC, DH, EMT, NUR, PNUR

02 President .... Ms. Patricia L. MOULTON
05 Dean of Academic Affairs .... Dr. Ana GAILLAT
32 Dean of Students .... Mr. Jason ENSER
20 Dean Academic Pgm Development .... Mr. Brent SARGENT
11 Dean of Administration .... Mr. Littleton TYLER
13 Chief Technology Officer .... Ms. Kellie B. CAMPBELL
30 Assoc Dean Inst Advancement .... Vacant
66 Assoc Dean of Nursing .... Ms. Sarah BILLINGS-BERG
07 Asst Dean of Admissions .... Ms. Jessica VAN DEREN
06 Registrar .... Ms. Shelly RUSS
10 Controller .... Ms. Brenda FLINT
37 Exec Director of Student Services .... Ms. Catherine MCCULLOUGH
19 Director Public Safety .... Mr. Emile FREDETTE
18 Director Facilities .... Mr. Theodore MANAZIR
36 Director Career Development .... Ms. Karry BOOSKA
15 Director of Human Resources .... Ms. Kelly-Rue RISO
26 Dir Marketing/Communications .... Ms. Amanda CHAULK
08 Director of Library .... Ms. Jane KEARNS

VIRGINIA

Advanced Technology Institute (F)

5700 Southern Boulevard, Virginia Beach VA 23462-2409
County: City of Virginia Beach FICE Identification: 031275
Unit ID: 231411
Telephone: (757) 490-1241 Carnegie Class: Spec 2-yr-Tech
FAX Number: (757) 499-5929 Calendar System: Semester
URL: www.auto.edu
Established: 1993 Annual Undergrad Tuition & Fees: $13,200
Enrollment: 464 Coed
Affiliation or Control: Proprietary IRS Status: Proprietary
Highest Offering: Associate Degree
Accreditation: ACCSC

01 Campus Director .... Mr. Cenek PICKA
05 Director of Education .... Mr. Cenek PICKA
07 Director of Admissions .... Mr. Mike AMBROSE
32 Director of Student Services .... Mr. Kirk CLAYTON
37 Director Student Financial Aid .... Mr. Chad MARTS
06 Registrar .... Mrs. Shannon VOIGT
13 Director of Information Technology .... Mr. Rey LIZAN
36 Director Student Placement .... Mr. Kirk CLAYTON
39 Director Student Housing .... Mr. Kirk MANGHAM

American National University (G)

1813 E Main Street, Salem VA 24153-4598
County: Roanoke FICE Identification: 003726
Unit ID: 232797
Telephone: (540) 986-1800 Carnegie Class: Bac/Assoc-Mixed
FAX Number: (540) 444-4198 Calendar System: Quarter
URL: www.an.edu
Established: 1886 Annual Undergrad Tuition & Fees: $17,361
Enrollment: 980 Coed
Affiliation or Control: Proprietary IRS Status: Proprietary
Highest Offering: Master's
Accreditation: DEAC, CEA, MAC, NURSE

01 President .... Mr. Frank E. LONGAKER
11 Sr Exec VP of Campus Operations .... Mr. Joel MUSGROVE
10 Vice President of Financial Svcs .... Ms. April HOWARD
12 Campus Director .... Mr. Ramon FLORES

American National University (H)

3926 Seminole Trail, Charlottesville VA 22911-8397
Telephone: (434) 220-7960 Identification: 666501
Accreditation: DEAC

American National University (I)

1515 Country Club Road, Harrisonburg VA 22802
Telephone: (540) 432-0943 Identification: 666503
Accreditation: DEAC

American National University (J)

104 Candlewood Court, Lynchburg VA 24502-2653
Telephone: (434) 239-3500 Identification: 666504
Accreditation: DEAC

Appalachian College of Pharmacy (K)

1060 Dragon Road, Oakwood VA 24631
County: Buchanan FICE Identification: 041806
Unit ID: 449922
Telephone: (276) 498-4190 Carnegie Class: Spec-4-yr-Other Health
FAX Number: (276) 498-4193 Calendar System: Semester
URL: www.acpharm.org
Established: 2003 Annual Graduate Tuition & Fees: N/A
Enrollment: 210 Coed
Affiliation or Control: Independent Non-Profit IRS Status: 501(c)3
Highest Offering: Doctorate; No Undergraduates
Accreditation: SC, PHAR

01 President .... Mr. Michael G. MCGLOTHLIN
05 Dean .... Dr. Susan L. MAYHEW
10 Chief Financial Officer .... Ms. Holli HARMAN
07 Dir of Admissions/Fin Aid/Registrar .... Ms. Vickie KEENE
103 Dir of Institutional Development .... Mr. Terry KILGORE
32 Dir Student Services/Alumni Affairs .... Mr. Jason MCGLOTHLIN
13 Dir Safety/Information Technology .... Mr. David DEEL
08 Library Director .... Ms. Melissa SPEED

Appalachian School of Law (L)

1169 Riverside Drive, Grundy VA 24614-2825
County: Buchanan FICE Identification: 035593
Unit ID: 432348
Telephone: (800) 895-7411 Carnegie Class: Spec-4-yr-Law
FAX Number: (276) 935-8261 Calendar System: Semester
URL: www.asl.edu
Established: 1995 Annual Undergrad Tuition & Fees: N/A
Enrollment: 128 Coed
Affiliation or Control: Independent Non-Profit IRS Status: 501(c)3
Highest Offering: First Professional Degree
Accreditation: LAW

01 Dean and COO .... Ms. Sandra K. MCGLOTHLIN
05 Assoc Dean of Academic Affairs .... Mr. Mason HEIDT
08 Director of Library .... Mr. Chris KING
36 Director of Career Services .... Ms. Lucy MCGEE
13 Director of Information Services .... Mr. Brian PRESLEY
15 Director Cmty Service & Personnel .... Ms. Jina M. SAULS
07 Director of Admissions .... Ms. Kelsea WAGNER
06 Registrar .... Ms. Beth STANLEY
37 Financial Aid Officer .... Mr. David BROOKSHIRE
09 Director of Institutional Research .... Ms. Rebecca ENGLAND
10 Director of the Business Office .... Ms. Peggy STREET
32 Student Services Coordinator .... Ms. Glenna OWENS

The Art Institute of Virginia Beach (M)

4500 Main Street, Ste 100, Virginia Beach VA 23462
Telephone: (757) 493-6700 Identification: 770977
Accreditation: &SC, ACFEI

† Branch campus of The Art Institute of Atlanta, Atlanta, GA

Atlantic University (N)

215 67th Street, Virginia Beach VA 23451-8101
County: Virginia Beach Identification: 666653
Telephone: (757) 631-8101 Carnegie Class: Not Classified
FAX Number: (757) 631-8096 Calendar System: Trimester
URL: www.atlanticuniv.edu
Established: 1930 Annual Graduate Tuition & Fees: N/A
Enrollment: N/A Coed
Affiliation or Control: Independent Non-Profit IRS Status: 501(c)3
Highest Offering: Master's; No Undergraduates
Accreditation: DEAC

01 CEO .... Kevin TODESCHI
05 Vice Pres Academic Affairs .... James VAN AUKEN
84 Assoc VP Enrollment Management .... Rachel VINCITORE

Averett University (O)

420 W Main Street, Danville VA 24541-3692
County: Independent City FICE Identification: 003702
Unit ID: 231420
Telephone: (434) 791-5600 Carnegie Class: Bac-Diverse
FAX Number: (434) 791-7181 Calendar System: Semester
URL: www.averett.edu
Established: 1859 Annual Undergrad Tuition & Fees: $34,520

Enrollment: 927 Coed
Affiliation or Control: Independent Non-Profit IRS Status: 501(c)3
Highest Offering: Master's
Accreditation: SC, NURSE

01 President .... Dr. Tiffany M. FRANKS
32 Executive Vice President .... Mr. Charles S. HARRIS
05 Vice Pres for Academic Affairs .... Dr. Timothy FULOP
10 Vice President Business & Finance .... Mr. Aaron HOWELL
30 Vice Pres Institutional Advancement .... Mr. Albert RAWLEY
15 Director of Human Resources .... Mrs. Kathie TUNE
84 Vice Pres Enrollment Management .... Ms. Stacy GATO
37 Director Student Financial Services .... Mr. Carl BRADSHER
21 Controller .... Ms. Lisa STEWART
08 Director of Library .... Vacant
36 Director of Career Development .... Ms. Angie MCADAMS
06 Registrar .... Mrs. Janet ROBERSON
26 Dir of Marketing/Communications .... Ms. Cassie JONES
29 Director Alumni Relations .... Mr. Dan HAYES
09 Dir Institutional Research/Effect .... Ms. Pam MCKIRDY
07 Director of Admissions .... Mr. Joel NESTER
18 Chief Facilities/Physical Plant .... Vacant
35 Director of Student Affairs .... Ms. Lesley VILLAROSE
38 Director of Student Counseling .... Mrs. Joan KAHWAJY-ANDERSON
04 Exec Assistant to the President .... Ms. Cyndie BASINGER
102 Dir Dev/Corporations & Foundations .... Ms. Emma LUGAR
104 Director Study Abroad .... Dr. Catherine CLARK
13 Chief Information Tech Officer .... Mr. Kevin LIPSCOMB
19 Chief of Campus Safety & Security .... Mr. Jamie WALKER
41 Athletic Director .... Ms. Meg STEVENS

Bethel College (A)

1705 Todds Lane, Hampton VA 23666
County: Hampton City FICE Identification: 041538
Unit ID: 458113
Telephone: (757) 826-1883 Carnegie Class: Spec-4-yr-Faith
FAX Number: (757) 826-5436 Calendar System: Semester
URL: www.bcva.edu
Established: 2004 Annual Undergrad Tuition & Fees: $8,420
Enrollment: 39 Coed
Affiliation or Control: Assemblies Of God Church IRS Status: 501(c)3
Highest Offering: Baccalaureate
Accreditation: BI

01 President .... Dr. Mark WOOTTON
05 Academic Dean/Exec Vice President .... Dr. Ron DEBERRY
32 Student Affairs .... Vacant
06 Registrar .... Vacant
08 Librarian .... Ms. Jenell SANFORD

Bluefield College (B)

3000 College Avenue, Bluefield VA 24605-1799
County: Tazewell FICE Identification: 003703
Unit ID: 231554
Telephone: (276) 326-3682 Carnegie Class: Bac-Diverse
FAX Number: (276) 326-4288 Calendar System: Semester
URL: www.bluefield.edu
Established: 1922 Annual Undergrad Tuition & Fees: $26,060
Enrollment: 997 Coed
Affiliation or Control: Baptist IRS Status: 501(c)3
Highest Offering: Master's
Accreditation: SC, CAEPT, NURSE

01 President .... Dr. David W. OLIVE
04 Assistant to the President .... Mrs. Jordan P. DILLON
05 VP for Academic Affairs & Athletics .... Dr. Marshall FLOWERS
10 VP Finance/Administration .... Mrs. Ruth BLANKENSHIP
84 VP for Enrollment Mgmt/Student Dev .... Mr. Michael J. WHITE
06 Registrar .... Ms. Jennifer LAMB
08 Co-Director of Library Services .... Ms. Paula BEASLEY
08 Co-Director of Library Services .... Mr. Werner LIND
111 Associate VP of Advancement/Alumni .... Mr. Josh CLINE
32 Associate VP Student Development .... Mr. Joshua ARNOLD
06 Dean of Registration Services .... Mr. Bryan FRAZIER
37 Director of Financial Aid .... Ms. Cary WRIGHT
42 Campus Minister .... Dr. Henry CLARY
41 Athletic Director .... Mrs. Tonia WALKER
40 Campus Store Manager .... Ms. Beth KINSER
18 Director of Maintenance .... Mr. Brandon DUNFORD
19 Coordinator of Campus Safety .... Mr. Gary RUTH
15 Human Resources Director .... Ms. Judy PEDNEAU
13 Chief Info Technology Officer .... Mr. Chip LAMBERT
53 Dean School of Education .... Dr. Tom BREWSTER
07 Director of Admissions .... Mr. Matthew HAMILTON
106 Dean of Online & Distance Educ .... Mrs. Patricia NEELY
26 Director Marketing/Public Relations .... Mrs. Lindsey AKERS
110 Asst Dir of Advancement & Alumni .... Mrs. Nicole KAKLIS
39 Dir Resident Life/Student Housing .... Mrs. Jessica SMITH
112 Dir Planned Giving/Major Gifts .... Mr. Vincent KEENE

Bon Secours Memorial College of Nursing (C)

8550 Magellan Parkway, Ste 1100, Richmond VA 23227
County: Henrico FICE Identification: 010043
Unit ID: 233356
Telephone: (804) 627-5300 Carnegie Class: Spec-4-yr-Other Health
FAX Number: (804) 627-5330 Calendar System: Semester
URL: www.bsmcon.edu
Established: 1961 Annual Undergrad Tuition & Fees: N/A
Enrollment: 477 Coed
Affiliation or Control: Independent Non-Profit IRS Status: 501(c)3
Highest Offering: Baccalaureate
Accreditation: ABHES, NURSE

05 Vice Pres Academic Affairs/Provost .... Dr. Melanie H. GREEN
66 Dean of Nursing .... Dr. Barbara C. SORBELLO
11 Dean of Administration .... Dr. Benji DJEUKENG
32 Dean of Student Services .... Ms. Leslie WINSTON
88 Dean of Clinical Simulation Center .... Ms. Holly PUGH
10 Dean of Finance .... Ms. Amy POZZA
88 Associate Dean of Nursing .... Dr. Chris-Tenna M. PERKINS
32 Associate Dean of Student Services .... Ms. Carrie NEWCOMB
06 Registrar Specialist .... Mr. Shawn RUPPERT
08 Librarian .... Ms. Tina METZGER
29 Director Alumni Relations .... Ms. Jennifer GOINS
36 Director of Student Success .... Ms. Lydia LISNER
37 Director Student Financial Aid .... Ms. Kelley FLORIAN

Bridgewater College (D)

402 E College Street, Bridgewater VA 22812-1599
County: Rockingham FICE Identification: 003704
Unit ID: 231581
Telephone: (540) 828-8000 Carnegie Class: Bac-A&S
FAX Number: (540) 828-5479 Calendar System: Semester
URL: www.bridgewater.edu
Established: 1880 Annual Undergrad Tuition & Fees: $35,160
Enrollment: 1,889 Coed
Affiliation or Control: Church Of The Brethren IRS Status: 501(c)3
Highest Offering: Master's
Accreditation: SC, CAATE

01 President .... Dr. David W. BUSHMAN
03 Executive Vice President .... Mr. Roy W. FERGUSON, JR.
05 Provost/VP for Academic Affairs .... Dr. Leona SEVICK
10 Vice Pres for Finance & Treasurer .... Ms. Anne B. KEELER
111 Vice Pres for Institutional Advance .... Dr. Maureen SILVA
26 Assoc VP Marketing & Communications .... Ms. Abbie PARKHURST
84 Vice President for Enrollment Mgmt .... Mr. Michael A. POST
18 Director of Sustainability .... Mr. Teshome H. MOLALENGE
40 Bookstore Manager .... Ms. Sarah LANDIS
20 Associate Dean of Academic Affairs .... Dr. Robert B. ANDERSEN
32 VP for Student Life/Dean of Student .... Dr. Leslie FRERE
36 Director of Career Services .... Ms. Sherry TALBOTT
121 Director of Academic Support Svcs .... Dr. Raymond W. STUDWELL, II
42 Chaplain .... Rev. Robert R. MILLER
07 Director of Admissions .... Mr. Jarret L. SMITH
37 Director of Financial Aid .... Mr. Scott D. MORRISON
113 Director of Finance & Budget .... Ms. Penny E. REARDON
13 Director of Info Tech Center .... Ms. Kristy K. RHEA
41 Director of Athletics .... Mr. Curtis L. KENDALL
38 Director of Counseling Services .... Dr. J. N. RITTENHOUSE
29 Dir of Alumni Rels & Annual Giving .... Mr. Colby HORNE
09 Director of Institutional Research .... Ms. Dawn S. DALBOW
15 Director of Human Resources .... Mrs. Kimberly P. HARPER
08 Library Director .... Mr. Andrew L. PEARSON
06 Registrar .... Ms. Cynthia K. HOWDYSHELL
21 Controller .... Ms. Mary S. SCHWAB
27 Editor/Dir of Media Relations .... Ms. Jessica E. LUCK
18 Director of Facilities .... Mr. David R. VANDEVANDER
19 Campus Police Chief .... Mr. Milton S. FRANKLIN
23 Director of Student Health Services .... Ms. Paige FRENCH
28 Director of Multicultural Services .... Dr. Robert G. BRYANT
109 Director of Dining Services .... Ms. Mary DAVIS
04 Administrative Asst to President .... Mrs. Elaine C. DELLINGER
39 Director Student Housing .... Ms. Suzanne MULLINS
104 Director International Education .... Mrs. Anne MARSH
30 Director of Development .... Ms. Meg RINER

Bryant & Stratton College (E)

8141 Hull Street Road, North Chesterfield VA 23235-6411
Telephone: (804) 745-2444 Identification: 666496
Accreditation: &M, ADNUR, MAC, NURSE, PNUR

† Regional accreditation is carried under the parent institution (corporate office) in Buffalo, NY.

Bryant & Stratton College (F)

301 Centre Pointe Drive, Virginia Beach VA 23462-4417
Telephone: (757) 499-7900 FICE Identification: 010061
Accreditation: &M, MAC

† Regional accreditation is carried under the parent institution (corporate office) in Buffalo, NY.

California University of Management and Sciences Virginia (G)

12801 Fair Lakes Pkwy., Fairfax VA 22033
Telephone: (703) 663-8088 Identification: 666734
Accreditation: ACICS

† Branch campus of California University of Management and Sciences, Anaheim, CA.

Centra College of Nursing (H)

905 Lakeside Drive, Suite A, Lynchburg VA 24501
County: Independent City FICE Identification: 021758
Unit ID: 232618
Telephone: (434) 200-3070 Carnegie Class: Spec-4-yr-Other Health
FAX Number: (434) 200-5505 Calendar System: Semester
URL: www.centracollege.edu
Established: 2011 Annual Undergrad Tuition & Fees: $12,301
Enrollment: 302 Coed
Affiliation or Control: Independent Non-Profit IRS Status: 501(c)3
Highest Offering: Baccalaureate
Accreditation: ABHES

01 Dean .... Dr. Melody SHARP
66 Assoc Director ADN Program .... Dr. Jim EMERSON
66 Assoc Director PN Program .... Ms. Dana GRANT
108 Accreditation Specialist .... Ms. Holly PUCKETT
37 Financial Aid/Enrollment Manager .... Mr. Aaron ELLENBURG

Centura College (I)

932 Ventures Way, Chesapeake VA 23320
Telephone: (757) 549-2121 Identification: 770608
Accreditation: ACCSC

Centura College (J)

616 Denbigh Boulevard, Newport News VA 23608
Telephone: (757) 874-2121 Identification: 770606
Accreditation: ACCSC

Centura College (K)

7020 N Military Highway, Norfolk VA 23518-4202
Telephone: (757) 853-2121 Identification: 770605
Accreditation: ACCSC

Centura College (L)

7914 Midlothian Turnpike, North Chesterfield VA 23235
County: Chesterfield FICE Identification: 031264
Unit ID: 427982
Telephone: (804) 330-0111 Carnegie Class: Spec 2-yr-Health
FAX Number: (804) 330-3809 Calendar System: Semester
URL: www.centuracollege.edu
Established: 1992 Annual Undergrad Tuition & Fees: $16,337
Enrollment: 98 Coed
Affiliation or Control: Proprietary IRS Status: Proprietary
Highest Offering: Associate Degree
Accreditation: ACCSC

01 Campus Executive Director .... Robert JONES, III

Centura College (M)

2697 Dean Drive, Suite 100, Virginia Beach VA 23452-7431
County: City of Virginia Beach FICE Identification: 023344
Unit ID: 232016
Telephone: (757) 340-2121 Carnegie Class: Bac/Assoc-Mixed
FAX Number: (757) 340-9704 Calendar System: Semester
URL: www.centuracollege.edu
Established: 1969 Annual Undergrad Tuition & Fees: $15,887
Enrollment: 150 Coed
Affiliation or Control: Proprietary IRS Status: Proprietary
Highest Offering: Baccalaureate
Accreditation: ACCSC

01 Campus Executive Director .... Wendy DAVIDSON
11 Assistant Campus Executive Director .... Dennis RYAN
05 Director of Education .... Emily SIMMONS
07 Director of Admissions .... Charade CLARK
06 Registrar .... Deanna MERCIER
37 Financial Aid Officer .... Vanessa MONTOYA
10 Bursar .... Sarah TROUT
32 Student Services Coordinator .... Leteesha RODRIGUEZ
36 Career Services Coordinator .... Alexis PALMER
08 Librarian .... Jeffery BARBOUR

Chamberlain University-Arlington (N)

2450 Crystal Drive, Arlington VA 22202
Telephone: (703) 416-7300 Identification: 770497
Accreditation: &NH, NURSE

† Branch campus of Chamberlain University-Addison, Addison, IL

Chester Career College (O)

751 West Hundred Road, Chester VA 23836-2516
County: Chesterfield FICE Identification: 034095
Unit ID: 437769
Telephone: (804) 751-9191 Carnegie Class: Spec 2-yr-Health
FAX Number: (804) 751-2599 Calendar System: Semester
URL: www.chestercareercollege.edu
Established: 1997 Annual Undergrad Tuition & Fees: N/A
Enrollment: 181 Coed
Affiliation or Control: Proprietary IRS Status: Proprietary
Highest Offering: Associate Degree
Accreditation: COE

01 Campus Director .... Ms. Debbie HARRIS
05 Academic Dean/Dir Allied Health .... Ms. Sandra KERRICK
06 Registrar .... Ms. Annette WHITE

08 Head Librarian ... Ms. Kathy PHILO
36 Director Job Placement ... Mrs. Tamara KNIGHT
37 Director Student Financial Aid ... Ms. Jennifer GLOVER

Christendom College (A)

134 Christendom Drive, Front Royal VA 22630-6534
County: Warren FICE Identification: 036653
Telephone: (540) 636-2900 Carnegie Class: Not Classified
FAX Number: (540) 636-1655 Calendar System: Semester
URL: www.christendom.edu
Established: 1977 Annual Undergrad Tuition & Fees: N/A
Enrollment: N/A Coed
Affiliation or Control: Roman Catholic IRS Status: 501(c)3
Highest Offering: Master's
Accreditation: SC

01 President ... Dr. Timothy T. O'DONNELL
03 Executive Vice President ... Mr. Mark ROHLENA
10 Vice President of Finance ... Mr. Kenneth FERGUSON
05 Vice President Academic Affairs ... Dr. Gregory TOWNSEND
111 Vice President for Advancement ... Mr. Paul JALSEVAC
18 Vice President of Operations ... Mr. Michael S. FOECKLER
84 Vice Pres Enrollment & Marketing ... Mr. Thomas MCFADDEN
21 Controller ... Mr. Luke FIER
32 Director of Student Affairs ... Ms. Amanda GRAF
20 Academic Dean ... Mr. Ben REINHARD
06 Registrar ... Mr. Walter A. JANARO
07 Director of Admissions ... Mr. Sam PHILLIPS
08 Director of Christendom Library ... Mr. Andrew V. ARMSTRONG
37 Financial Aid Officer ... Mrs. Alisa L. POLK
29 Asst Dir Alumni/Donor Relations ... Mr. Vince CRISTE
13 Director of Computer Services ... Mr. Douglas S. BRIGGS
06 Registrar/Business Officer NDGS ... Miss Maura MCMAHON
41 Athletic Director ... Mr. Patrick QUEST
04 Exec Assistant to the President ... Mrs. Brenda SEELBACH
58 Dean of the Graduate School ... Dr. Robert J. MATAVA

Christopher Newport University (B)

1 Avenue of the Arts, Newport News VA 23606-3072
County: Independent City FICE Identification: 003706
Unit ID: 231712
Telephone: (757) 594-7000 Carnegie Class: Masters/S
FAX Number: N/A Calendar System: Semester
URL: www.cnu.edu
Established: 1960 Annual Undergrad Tuition & Fees (In-State): $14,754
Enrollment: 5,081 Coed
Affiliation or Control: State IRS Status: 501(c)3
Highest Offering: Master's
Accreditation: SC, CAEP, MUS, SW, THEA

01 President ... Hon. Paul S. TRIBLE, JR.
100 Chief of Staff ... Mrs. Cynthia R. PERRY
05 Provost ... Dr. David C. DOUGHTY
03 Executive Vice President ... Mr. William L. BRAUER
43 University Counsel ... Ms. Maureen MATSEN
111 Vice Pres for Univ Advancement ... Mrs. Adelia P. THOMPSON
45 Vice Pres for Strategy & Planning ... Mrs. Jennifer B. LATOUR
26 Chief Communications Officer ... Mr. James HANCHETT
15 Director of Human Resources ... Ms. Ashleigh ANDREWS
04 Exec Assistant to President/Board ... Mrs. Beverley D. MUELLER
07 Dean of Admission ... Mr. Robert J. LANGE
84 VP for Enroll/Student Success ... Dr. Lisa DUNCAN RAINES
32 Vice President of Student Affairs ... Dr. Kevin M. HUGHES
49 Dean College Arts & Humanities ... Dr. Lori J. UNDERWOOD
83 Dean College of Social Sciences ... Dr. Quentin KIDD
83 Dean College Nat/Behav Science ... Dr. Nicole R. GUAJARDO
50 Dean Luter School of Business ... Dr. George H. EBBS
41 Director of Athletics ... Mr. Kyle S. MCMULLIN
21 University Comptroller ... Mrs. Diane REED
06 University Registrar ... Mrs. Julianna M. WAIT
37 Director of Financial Aid ... Ms. Christina L. RUSSELL
39 Director of Housing ... Mr. Andrew H. KOERNERT
09 Director of Institutional Research ... Ms. Donna A. VARNER
13 Chief Information Officer ... Mr. Andrew B. CRAWFORD
114 Director of Planning & Budget ... Ms. Patricia L. MCDERMOTT
116 Director of University Audit ... Ms. Faith D. BELOTE
108 Director of Assessment & Evaluation ... Mr. Jason C. LYONS
96 Director of Materiels Management ... Mrs. Elizabeth M. WARDROP
08 University Librarian ... Ms. Mary K. SELLEN
19 University Police Chief ... Mr. Daniel WOLOSZYNOWSKI
18 Director of Facilities Mgmt ... Mr. Scott GESELE
110 Asst VP for University Advancement ... Mr. Keith D. ROOTS
26 Exec Dir of University Relations ... Mrs. Amie G. DALE
27 Director of External Relations ... Mr. Thomas E. KRAMER
29 Director of Alumni Relations ... Mr. Baxter VENDRICK
22 Director of Title IX and EO ... Ms. Michelle L. MOODY
38 Exec Dir Counseling/Health Services ... Dr. William V. RITCHEY
36 Director Center of Career Planning ... Ms. Elizabeth K. WESTLEY
104 Director of Study Abroad ... Ms. Amanda K. PIERCE

College of William & Mary (C)

PO Box 8795, Williamsburg VA 23187-8795
County: Independent City FICE Identification: 003705
Unit ID: 231624
Telephone: (757) 221-4000 Carnegie Class: DU-Higher
FAX Number: (757) 221-1259 Calendar System: Semester
URL: www.wm.edu
Established: 1693 Annual Undergrad Tuition & Fees (In-State): $23,400
Enrollment: 8,740 Coed
Affiliation or Control: State IRS Status: 501(c)3
Highest Offering: Doctorate
Accreditation: SC, CACREP, CAEPN, IPSY, LAW

01 President ... Dr. Katherine A. ROWE
05 Provost ... Dr. Michael HALLERAN
11 Sr VP for Finance & Administration ... Mr. Samuel E. JONES
111 VP for University Advancement ... Dr. Matthew T. LAMBERT
45 VP Strategic Initiatives ... Mr. Henry R. BROADDUS
32 VP Student Affairs ... Dr. Virginia M. AMBLER
41 Director of Athletics ... Ms. Samantha HUGE
29 Ex Dir Alumni Engagement ... Ms. Marilyn W. MIDYETTE
49 Dean Faculty of Arts & Sciences ... Dr. Katharine CONLEY
50 Dean Mason School of Business ... Mr. Lawrence B. PULLEY
53 Dean School of Education ... Dr. Spencer NILES
61 Dean William & Mary Law School ... Mr. Davison M. DOUGLAS
88 Dean and Director of VIMS ... Dr. John T. WELLS
08 Dean University Libraries ... Ms. Carrie COOPER
43 University Counsel ... Ms. Carrie NEE
20 Vice Prov Academic & Faculty Affs ... Ms. Ann Marie STOCK
82 Vice Prov Intl Affairs/Reves Ctr ... Dr. Stephen E. HANSON
46 Vice Provost Rsch & Grad Prof Stds ... Dr. Dennis M. MANOS
14 Deputy CIO ... Ms. Bernadette KENNEY
108 Assoc Provost Inst Accred ... Dr. Susan L. BOSWORTH
07 Dean of Admission/Assoc Prov Enroll ... Mr. Tim A. WOLFE
06 Assoc Provost & Univ Registrar ... Ms. Sara L. MARCHELLO
09 Assoc Provost Inst Research ... Dr. Jeremy P. MARTIN
106 Acting Dir eLearning Initiatives ... Mr. Adam P. BARGER
88 Dean for Educational Policy ... Dr. John DONAHUE
58 Dean Graduate Studies & Research ... Dr. Virginia J. TORCZON
92 Dean Honors/Interdisciplinary Stds ... Dr. Teresa V. LONGO
88 Dean of Undergraduate Studies ... Dr. Janice L. ZEMAN
104 Director of Global Education ... Ms. Sylvia M. MITTERNDORFER
86 Government Relations ... Mr. Colin SMOLINSKY
26 Chief Com Officer Univ Web/Design ... Mr. Brian W. WHITSON
88 Assoc VP Development/Campaign Dir ... Mr. Mark L. BEGLY
30 Assoc VP University Development ... Mr. Earl T. GRANGER, III
18 Assoc Vice Pres Facilities Mgmt ... Mr. Van DOBSON
35 Dean of Students ... Ms. Marjorie S. THOMAS
25 Director of Sponsored Programs ... Ms. Jane A. LOPEZ
22 Asst Dir Diversity & Inclusion ... Ms. Sharron GATLING
37 Director Student Financial Aid ... Mr. Joseph DOBROTA
15 Chief Human Resources Officer ... Mr. Christopher D. LEE
36 Director Career Development ... Ms. Kathleen I. POWELL
19 AVP Public Safety/Chief of Police ... Dr. Deborah CHEESEBRO
10 Chief Financial Officer ... Ms. Amy S. SEBRING
39 Assoc VP Stdnt Affs/Dir of Res Life ... Ms. Maggie EVANS
96 Director of Procurement ... Ms. Erma BAKER
100 Asst to President/Chief of Staff ... Mr. Michael J. FOX
101 Secretary to the Board of Visitors ... Mr. Michael J. FOX
04 Executive Asst to President ... Ms. Cynthia A. BRAUER
105 Director of University Web & Design ... Ms. Tina L. COLEMAN
88 Assoc VP for Health & Wellness ... Dr. Robert K. CRACE
28 Chief Diversity Officer ... Dr. Fanchon GLOVER
44 Director Annual Giving ... Mr. Daniel H. FREZZA
90 Director Academic Computing ... Mr. Michael T. MURPHY

Columbia College (D)

8620 Westwood Center Drive, Vienna VA 22182
County: Fairfax FICE Identification: 041273
Unit ID: 455983
Telephone: (703) 206-0508 Carnegie Class: Assoc/HT-High Trad
FAX Number: (703) 206-0488 Calendar System: Other
URL: www.ccdc.edu
Established: 1999 Annual Undergrad Tuition & Fees: N/A
Enrollment: 357 Coed
Affiliation or Control: Proprietary IRS Status: Proprietary
Highest Offering: Associate Degree
Accreditation: COE

01 President/Founder ... Dr. Richard K. KIM
05 Academic Director ... Dr. James CHO

Culinary Institute of Virginia (E)

2428 Almeda Avenue, Ste 106, Norfolk VA 23513-2448
Telephone: (757) 858-2433 Identification: 770960
Accreditation: &SC

Divine Mercy University (F)

45154 Underwood Ln, Sterling VA 20166
County: Loudoun FICE Identification: 038724
Unit ID: 445869
Telephone: (703) 416-1441 Carnegie Class: Spec-4-yr-Other Health
FAX Number: (703) 416-8588 Calendar System: Semester
URL: www.divinemercy.edu
Established: 1998 Annual Graduate Tuition & Fees: N/A
Enrollment: 241 Coed
Affiliation or Control: Independent Non-Profit IRS Status: 501(c)3
Highest Offering: Doctorate; No Undergraduates
Accreditation: SC, CLPSY

01 President ... Fr. Charles SIKORSKY
05 VP Academic Affairs ... Vacant
10 VP Finance and Operations ... Mr. Antonio MAZA
84 VP Enrollment and Marketing ... Mr. Tom BROOKS
121 VP Academic & Student Support ... Ms. Laura TUCKER
83 Dean IPS ... Dr. Suzanne N. HOLLMAN
83 Dean School of Counseling ... Dr. Harvey PAYNE
106 Associate VP Program Development ... Dr. Stephen GRUNDMAN
32 Dean of Students ... Ms. Jennifer KARNS
08 Director of Library Services ... Mr. Jeffrey ELLIOTT
06 Registrar ... Ms. Catherine ROSASCHI
21 Director of Student Accounts ... Ms. Mabel IMALA
26 Director of Marketing ... Ms. Rose GEBKEN
37 Director Financial Aid ... Ms. Antoinette WORMLEY
26 Director of Communications ... Vacant
07 Associate VP Admissions ... Ms. Tambi SPITZ KILHEFNER
101 Secretary of the Board ... Ms. Becci SHEPTOCK
11 Director of Operations ... Ms. Helen TRUPPO

Eastern Mennonite University (G)

1200 Park Road, Harrisonburg VA 22802-2462
County: Independent City FICE Identification: 003708
Unit ID: 232043
Telephone: (540) 432-4000 Carnegie Class: Masters/M
FAX Number: (540) 432-4444 Calendar System: Semester
URL: www.emu.edu
Established: 1917 Annual Undergrad Tuition & Fees: $37,110
Enrollment: 1,530 Coed
Affiliation or Control: Mennonite Church IRS Status: 501(c)3
Highest Offering: Doctorate
Accreditation: SC, CACREP, CAEPN, NURSE, PAST, SW, THEOL

01 President ... Dr. Susan SCHULTZ-HUXMAN
05 Provost ... Dr. Fred L. KNISS
111 Vice President for Advancement ... Mr. Kirk L. SHISLER
10 Interim CFO ... Mr. Timothy W. STUTZMAN
09 Vice Pres of Inst Effectiveness ... Dr. Scott BARGE
58 Graduate and Seminary Dean ... Dr. Suzanne K. COCKLEY
06 University Registrar ... Mr. David A. DETROW
07 Director Undergraduate Admissions ... Mr. Matthew RUTH
08 Director of Libraries ... Dr. G. Marcille H. FREDERICK
37 Director of Financial Assistance ... Ms. Michele R. HENSLEY
36 Director Career Services/Testing ... Ms. Kimberly PHILLIPS
29 Director of Alumni/Parent Relations ... Mr. Jeffrey A. SHANK
04 Assistant to the President ... Ms. Laura J. DAILY
41 Athletic Director ... Mr. David A. KING
42 Campus Pastor ... Mr. Brian M. BURKHOLDER
18 Director of Physical Plant ... Mr. Ed LEHMAN
15 Director Human Resources ... Ms. Marybeth SHOWALTER
21 Controller ... Mr. Timothy STUTZMAN
38 Director Student Counseling ... Ms. Tempest D. ANDERSON
35 Assoc Dean of Students ... Ms. Rachel R. SAWATZKY
35 Assoc Dean of Students ... Mr. Jonathan SWARTZ

Eastern Virginia Career College (H)

10304 Spotsylvania Avenue, Ste. 400,
Fredericksburg VA 22408-8605
County: Spotsylvania FICE Identification: 036543
Unit ID: 441858
Telephone: (540) 373-2200 Carnegie Class: Spec 2-yr-Health
FAX Number: (540) 373-4465 Calendar System: Other
URL: www.evcc.edu
Established: 2000 Annual Undergrad Tuition & Fees: N/A
Enrollment: 195 Coed
Affiliation or Control: Proprietary IRS Status: Proprietary
Highest Offering: Associate Degree
Accreditation: COE, OTA

01 Chief Executive Officer/President ... Ms. Christine CARROLL
03 Executive Vice President ... Ms. Dorie MILFORD
05 Academic Director ... Mr. Brian TERRILL
07 Campus Director & Dir of Admissions ... Mr. Abdullah JOHNSON
11 Director of Operations ... Vacant
108 Director Compliance ... Ms. Heather BURNHAM
37 Financial Aid Administrator ... Ms. Nicole JENKINS
36 Director of Career Services ... Ms. Cynthia ROTHELL
06 Registrar ... Mr. Mark PLAUGHER
113 Bursar ... Mr. Dillon KRESS

Eastern Virginia Medical School (I)

Box 1980, Norfolk VA 23501-1980
County: Independent City FICE Identification: 010338
Unit ID: 231970
Telephone: (757) 446-5600 Carnegie Class: Spec-4-yr-Med
FAX Number: (757) 446-5135 Calendar System: Other
URL: www.evms.edu
Established: 1973 Annual Graduate Tuition & Fees: N/A
Enrollment: 1,256 Coed
Affiliation or Control: Independent Non-Profit IRS Status: 501(c)3
Highest Offering: Doctorate; No Undergraduates
Accreditation: SC, ARCPA, CLPSY, IPSY, MED, PA, PH, SURGA

01 President/Provost/Dean ... Dr. Richard V. HOMAN
04 Sr Exec Assistant to the President ... Ms. Tracy L. MORTON
116 Director Internal Audit ... Mr. Robert B. WOOD
11 VP and Chief Operating Officer ... Mr. Brant M. COX
17 Vice Pres/Dean Sch of Health Prof ... Dr. Charles D. COMBS
88 Assoc Dean for Health Professions ... Dr. Jeffrey A. JOHNSON
10 Vice Pres Administration/Finance ... Mr. Mark R. BABASHANIAN
19 Chief of Police ... Mr. Andrew J. MITCHELL
18 Director Facilities/Physical Plant ... Mr. Doug MARTIN
28 Vice President for Diversity ... Mr. Mekbib L. GEMEDA
88 Vice Provost for Faculty Affairs ... Dr. Elza MYLONA
88 Vice Dean Clinical Affairs ... Dr. Alfred Z. ABUHAMAD
23 CEO EVMS Medical Group ... Mr. James F. LIND
05 Vice Dean Academic Affairs ... Dr. Ronald W. FLENNER
43 Vice President and General Counsel ... Ms. Stacy R. PURCELL
58 Vice Dean Grad Medical Education ... Dr. Linda R. ARCHER
09 Vice Dean for Research ... Dr. William J. WASILENKO
88 Asst Dean Hum Sub Protection/IRB ... Dr. Harry J. TILLMAN

50 Assoc Dean Business/Admin Affairs ... Mr. David E. HUBAND
84 Assoc Dean Admissions and Enroll ... Dr. Thomas D. KIMBLE
32 Assoc Dean for Student Affairs ... Dr. Allison P. KNIGHT
88 Assoc Dean Clinical Education ... Dr. Brooke HOOPER
20 Assoc Dean for Academic Affairs ... Dr. Senthil K. RAJASEKARAN
88 Assoc Dean Translational Research ... Dr. John SEMMES
88 Assoc Dean Clinical Research ... Dr. Elias SIRAJ
88 Assoc Dean Clinical Integration ... Dr. Mily KANNARKAT
08 Director of Library Services ... Ms. Kerrie S. SHAW
35 Director of Student Affairs ... Ms. Joann BAUTTI
93 Asst Dean for Diversity ... Ms. Gail C. WILLIAMS
06 Registrar ... Mr. David R. GOLAY
15 Director Human Resources ... Mr. Matthew R. SCHENK
21 Assoc VP for Financial Services ... Ms. Helen S. HESELIUS
88 Director for Technology Transfer ... Mr. Paul B. DIMARCO
37 Director Student Financial Aid ... Ms. Deborah R. BROWN
21 Director for Business Management ... Ms. Tammy A. CHRISMAN
96 Director of Materials Management ... Mr. Steven LEE
13 Chief Information Officer ... Ms. Deborah A. TAYLOR
26 Asst VP Marketing/Communication ... Dr. Vincent A. RHODES
29 Exec Dir Alumni and Donor Relations ... Ms. Ashley GENTRY
30 Sr Assoc VP Development and Alumni . Ms. Connie L. MCKENZIE
88 Director of the Brock Institute ... Dr. Cynthia ROMERO
51 Director for Continuing Med Educ ... Ms. Drucie A. PAPAFIL
88 Director Occupational Health ... Ms. Heather SINGLETON
25 Director Sponsored Programs ... Ms. Yolanda F. DEMORY
88 Director Rad Safety Env Health ... Mr. Courtney A. KERR
117 Director Risk Management ... Ms. Donita M. LAMARAND
118 Director Health Analytics ... Dr. Sunita DODANI
88 Director Bus Intel & Analytics ... Mr. Stephen RICHARD
108 Director Institutional Assessment ... Dr. Molly O'KEEFE

† Member of Virginia Consortium for Professional Psychology.

ECPI University (A)

5555 Greenwich Road, Virginia Beach VA 23462-6554
County: Independent City — FICE Identification: 010198
Unit ID: 248934
Telephone: (757) 671-7171 — Carnegie Class: Masters/M
FAX Number: (757) 671-8661 — Calendar System: Semester
URL: www.ecpi.edu
Established: 1966 — Annual Undergrad Tuition & Fees: $16,039
Enrollment: 11,972 — Coed
Affiliation or Control: Proprietary — IRS Status: Proprietary
Highest Offering: Master's
Accreditation: SC, ACFEI, MAAB, NUR, NURSE

01 President ... Mr. Mark B. DREYFUS
12 Campus President ... Mr. Michael HECK
05 Campus Dir of Academic Affairs ... Patricia OÆKEEFE

ECPI University-Northern Virginia (B)

10021 Balls Ford Road, Ste 100, Manassas VA 20109
Telephone: (703) 330-5300 — Identification: 770957
Accreditation: &SC, MAAB, RAD, SURTEC

ECPI University-Richmond/Innsbrook (C)

4305 Cox Road, Glen Allen VA 23060
Telephone: (804) 894-9150 — Identification: 770961
Accreditation: &SC

ECPI University-Richmond/Moorefield (D)

800 Moorefield Park Drive, Richmond VA 23236
Telephone: (804) 330-5533 — Identification: 770958
Accreditation: &SC, CAHIIM, MAAB, SURTEC

ECPI University-Roanoke (E)

5234 Airport Road, Ste 200, Roanoke VA 24012
Telephone: (540) 563-8000 — Identification: 770959
Accreditation: &SC, MAAB

Edward Via College of Osteopathic Medicine (F)

2265 Kraft Drive, Blacksburg VA 24060
County: Montgomery — FICE Identification: 037093
Unit ID: 442806
Telephone: (540) 231-4000 — Carnegie Class: Spec-4-yr-Med
FAX Number: (540) 231-5252 — Calendar System: Semester
URL: www.vcom.edu
Established: 2002 — Annual Graduate Tuition & Fees: N/A
Enrollment: 1,969 — Coed
Affiliation or Control: Independent Non-Profit — IRS Status: 501(c)3
Highest Offering: Doctorate; No Undergraduates
Accreditation: OSTEO

01 President ... Dr. Dixie TOOKE-RAWLINS
05 Provost/EVP & Founding Dean ... Dr. Dixie TOOKE-RAWLINS
10 Vice President Finance/CFO ... Mr. Chuck SWAHA
32 Vice Pres Student Services ... Mr. William KING
26 VP Communication/Marketing ... Ms. Cindy SHEPARD RAWLINS
11 Vice President Operations ... Mr. Bill PRICE
30 VP College Development/Alumni Rels ... Mr. Thim CORVIN
46 Vice Provost for Research ... Dr. Gunnar BROLINSON
12 Dean Carolinas Campus ... Dr. Timothy J. KOWALSKI
12 Dean Virginia Campus ... Dr. Jan M. WILLCOX
63 Dean Grad Cert/Pre-Med Program ... Dr. Brian W. HILL
21 Sr Exec Dir Administrative Svcs ... Ms. Patty SMITH

Emory & Henry College (G)

PO Box 947, 30461 Garnand Drive, Emory VA 24327-0947
County: Washington — FICE Identification: 003709
Unit ID: 232025
Telephone: (276) 944-4121 — Carnegie Class: Bac-A&S
FAX Number: (276) 944-6934 — Calendar System: Semester
URL: www.ehc.edu
Established: 1836 — Annual Undergrad Tuition & Fees: $35,100
Enrollment: 1,226 — Coed
Affiliation or Control: United Methodist — IRS Status: 501(c)3
Highest Offering: Doctorate
Accreditation: SC, #ARCPA, CAATE, CAEPT, OT, PTA

01 President ... Dr. John W. WELLS
43 Exec Asst to Pres/General Counsel ... Mr. Mark R. GRAHAM
05 Provost ... Dr. Michael J. PUGLISI
10 Int VP for Business and Finance ... Ms. Benita BARE
32 VP Student Life/Student Success ... Mr. John HOLLOWAY
111 VP for Institutional Advancement ... Mr. Joseph P. TAYLOR
84 AVP Enrollment Management ... Mr. Anthony GRAHAM
09 Dir Institutional Research/Effect ... Mr. Gregory G. STEINER
29 Director of Alumni Affairs ... Ms. Monica S. HOEL
37 Director of Financial Aid ... Ms. Scarlett BLEVINS
06 Registrar ... Ms. Tammy SHEETS
36 Director of Career Services ... Ms. Amanda GARDNER
38 Director Student Counseling ... Mr. Todd STANLEY
26 VP of Marketing Communications ... Ms. Jennifer PEARCE
13 Chief Information Officer/Librarian ... Ms. Ruth CASTILLO
18 Dir of Facilities Plng/Management ... Mr. Scott E. WILLIAMS
40 Bookstore Manager ... Mr. Terry RICHARDSON
42 Chaplain ... Rev. Mary K. BRIGGS
15 Director Human Resources ... Ms. Kim STEINER
35 Dean of Students ... Mr. James BOWYER
21 Associate VP Business/Finance ... Ms. Benita BARE
39 Director of Housing ... Ms. Lacey SOUTHWICK
41 Interim Director of Athletics ... Ms. Anne CRUTCHFIELD
19 Chief of Campus Police ... Mr. Scott POORE
102 Director Foundation Relations ... Ms. Ginger WILLIAMS
104 Director Study Abroad ... Dr. Celeste GAIA
105 Digital Marketing Manager ... Ms. Rachael WILBUR
44 Director Annual Giving ... Ms. Ronan KING
04 Admin Assistant to the President ... Ms. Faye STEVENS
88 Director of Life Long Learning ... Mr. Joseph BOTANA
28 Director of Diversity ... Ms. Patricia GONZALEZ

Faith Bible College (H)

6330 Newtown Road, Suite 211, Norfolk VA 23502
County: Independent City — Identification: 667285
Telephone: (757) 423-2095 — Carnegie Class: Not Classified
FAX Number: (757) 222-1341 — Calendar System: Semester
URL: www.faithbiblecollege.com
Established: 1995 — Annual Undergrad Tuition & Fees: N/A
Enrollment: N/A — Coed
Affiliation or Control: Independent Non-Profit — IRS Status: 501(c)3
Highest Offering: Associate Degree
Accreditation: @BI

01 President ... Rev. Shannon TERHUNE
05 Vice Pres Academic Affairs ... Dr. Kevin NEWMAN
31 VP Community/Church Relations ... Capt. Dale PARKER
06 Registrar ... Ms. Brenda BODNAR

Ferrum College (I)

PO Box 1000, 215 Ferrum Mtn Road, Ferrum VA 24088-9001
County: Franklin — FICE Identification: 003711
Unit ID: 232089
Telephone: (540) 365-2121 — Carnegie Class: Bac-Diverse
FAX Number: (540) 365-4269 — Calendar System: Semester
URL: www.ferrum.edu
Established: 1913 — Annual Undergrad Tuition & Fees: $34,175
Enrollment: 1,137 — Coed
Affiliation or Control: United Methodist — IRS Status: 501(c)3
Highest Offering: Baccalaureate
Accreditation: SC, SW

01 President ... Dr. David L. JOHNS
05 Provost ... Dr. Aime SPOSATO
10 VP for Administration and Finance ... Mr. Chris BURNLEY
111 Vice Pres Institutional Advancement ... Mr. Wilson PAINE
84 VP for Enrollment Management ... Mr. James A. PENNIX
32 Dean of Student Life ... Ms. Nicole LENEZ
42 Dean of Chapel ... Dr. Jan C. NICHOLSON ANGLE
04 Special Asst to the President ... Ms. Courtney L. BROWN
06 Registrar ... Mrs. Yvonne S. WALKER
07 Dean of Admissions ... Mr. Jason D. BYRD
09 Director of Inst Research ... Mrs. Ursa JOHNSON
08 Director Stanley Library ... Dr. Eric RECTOR
37 Director of Financial Aid ... Ms. Heather HOLLANDSWORTH
29 Director Alumni & Family Programs ... Mrs. Tracy S. HOLLEY
26 Director of Public Relations ... Vacant
41 Director of Athletics ... Mr. J. Abraham NAFF
18 Director of Physical Plant ... Mr. Brad BISHOP
35 Dir Student Leadership & Engagement ... Mr. Justin MUSE
13 Dir of Network Services ... Mr. Eugene HACKER
15 Dir of Human Resources ... Mr. Chris CHANDLER
40 Bookstore Manager ... Vacant
19 Chief of Ferrum College Police Dept ... Chief J. F. OWENS
36 Dir of Career Services ... Mrs. Leslie HOLDEN
88 Director of Academic Accessibility ... Ms. Nancy S. BEACH
91 Dir Administrative Computing ... Mr. Shawn SHIRLEY
58 Dir School of Graduate/Online Stds ... Dr. Sandra VIA
49 Dean Sch Arts/Sciences & Business ... Dr. Jason POWELL
83 Dean Sch Health Prof/Social Science ... Dr. Angie DAHL

Fortis College (J)

6300 Center Drive, Building 22, Norfolk VA 23502
County: Independent City — FICE Identification: 023427
Unit ID: 233329
Telephone: (757) 499-5447 — Carnegie Class: Spec 2-yr-Health
FAX Number: N/A — Calendar System: Quarter
URL: www.fortis.edu/campuses
Established: — Annual Undergrad Tuition & Fees: $16,019
Enrollment: 229 — Coed
Affiliation or Control: Proprietary — IRS Status: Proprietary
Highest Offering: Associate Degree
Accreditation: ACICS

01 President ... Mr. Matthew BANO

Fortis College (K)

2000 Westmoreland Street, Suite A, Richmond VA 23230
Telephone: (804) 323-1020 — Identification: 770815
Accreditation: ACICS, DA, SURGT

George Mason University (L)

4400 University Drive - MSN 3A1, Fairfax VA 22030-4444
County: Fairfax — FICE Identification: 003749
Unit ID: 232186
Telephone: (703) 993-1000 — Carnegie Class: DU-Highest
FAX Number: N/A — Calendar System: Semester
URL: www.gmu.edu
Established: 1957 — Annual Undergrad Tuition & Fees (In-State): $12,462
Enrollment: 35,984 — Coed
Affiliation or Control: State — IRS Status: 501(c)3
Highest Offering: Doctorate
Accreditation: SC, ART, CAATE, CAEP, CAEPN, CAHIIM, CEA, CLPSY, EXSC, HSA, IPSY, LAW, MUS, NRPA, NURSE, PH, SPAA, SW

01 Interim President ... Ms. Anne HOLTON
05 Provost & Executive Vice President ... Dr. S. David WU
10 Senior VP of Administration/Finance ... Ms. Carol D. KISSAL
100 Chief of Staff ... Dr. Dietra Y. TRENT
84 Vice Pres Enrollment Management ... Mr. David BURGE
18 Vice Pres for Facilities ... Mr. Frank STRIKE
86 VP Government & Community Relations ... Mr. Paul LIBERTY
111 VP Univ Advancement & Alumni Rels ... Ms. Trishana BOWDEN
13 VP Information Technology/CIO ... Ms. Marilyn SMITH
32 Vice President for University Life ... Ms. Rose PASCARELL
46 Vice President for Research ... Dr. Deborah CRAWFORD
28 VP Compliance/Diversity & Ethics ... Mr. Julian WILLIAMS
15 VP for HR/Payroll & Fac/Staff Life ... Mr. Lester ARNOLD
43 University Counsel ... Mr. Brian WALTHER
45 Assoc VP for Business Services ... Mr. Bill DRACOS
21 Assoc VP/Controller Fiscal Services ... Ms. Deb DICKENSON
20 VP Acad Innovation & New Ventures ... Dr. Michelle MARKS
20 Assoc Prov Acad Initiatives & Svcs ... Dr. Janette MUIR
88 Assoc Prov for Academic Admin ... Ms. Renate H. GUILFORD
88 Assoc Prov for a Sustainable Earth ... Dr. Cody EDWARDS
35 Exec Dir Office Student Involvement ... Ms. Lauren LONG
35 Assistant Vice Pres University Life ... Dr. Kahan SABLO
06 University Registrar ... Mr. Doug MCKENNA
37 Director Student Financial Aid ... Dr. Sandra TARBOX
36 Assoc Dir Univ Career Services ... Ms. Saskia CAMPBELL
08 Dean of Libraries/Univ Librarian ... Mr. John G. ZENELIS
23 Int Exec Dir Student Health Svcs ... Dr. Lisa PARK
29 Assoc VP Alumni Relations ... Ms. Christine CLARK-TALLEY
41 Asst VP/Dir Intercolleg Athletics ... Mr. Brad EDWARDS
20 Associate Provost Academic Affairs ... Ms. Gesele DURHAM
19 Chief of Police ... Mr. Carl ROWAN
79 Dean Col Humanities/Social Sciences ... Ms. Ann ARDIS
61 Dean School of Law ... Dr. Henry BUTLER
80 Dean Schar School of Policy & Govt ... Dr. Mark ROZELL
50 Dean School of Business ... Dr. Maury PEIPERL
53 Dean College of Educ & Human Devel ... Dr. Mark R. GINSBERG
54 Dean Volgenau School of Engineering ... Dr. Kenneth BALL
66 Dean College of Health & Human Svcs ... Dr. Germaine LOUIS
81 Interim Dean College of Science ... Mr. Ali ANDALIBI
88 Dean Sch Conflict Analysis & Resol ... Dr. Alpaslan OZERDEM
88 Dean CVPA/Exec Dir HPAC ... Dr. Rick DAVIS
38 Assoc Dean/Chief Mental Health Ofcr ... Dr. Rachel WERNICKE
09 Asst Provost Institutional Research ... Ms. Angela DETLEV
96 Chief Procurement Officer ... Mr. Cliff SHORE
04 Director of Presidential Admin ... Ms. Sharon CULLEN
101 Sec Pro Tem to Board of Visitors ... Ms. Kathy CAGLE
21 Assoc Director Finance & Business ... Ms. Maria FIORE
108 Asst Prov Inst Effectiveness ... Ms. Shannon NIX
25 Asc VP Rsrch Ops Ofc Sponsored Pgms ... Mr. Mike LASKOFSKI
44 Director Annual Giving/Ofc Advance ... Mr. William AYREA
102 Dir Corporate/Foundation Relations ... Ms. Mercedes PRICE
26 Assoc Vice President for Marketing ... Mr. Eric WOODALL
106 Director Digital Learning ... Mr. Stephen NODINE
90 Exec Dir Learning Support Svcs ... Ms. Joy TAYLOR
07 Dean of Admissions ... Ms. Amy TAKAYAMA-PEREZ

88 Director of Strategic Real Estate .... Mr. Steve GOLDIN
114 AVP Strategic Planning & Budgeting .... Ms. Rene STEWART O'NEAL

Hampden-Sydney College (A)

PO Box 128, Hampden-Sydney VA 23943-0667
County: Prince Edward FICE Identification: 003713
Unit ID: 232256
Telephone: (434) 223-6000 Carnegie Class: Bac-A&S
FAX Number: N/A Calendar System: Semester
URL: www.hsc.edu
Established: 1775 Annual Undergrad Tuition & Fees: $45,746
Enrollment: 1,046 Male
Affiliation or Control: Presbyterian Church (U.S.A.) IRS Status: 501(c)3
Highest Offering: Baccalaureate
Accreditation: SC

01 President .... Dr. John L. STIMPERT
05 Dean of the Faculty .... Dr. Walter M. MCDERMOTT
10 VP Business Affairs & Finance ... Mr. P. Kenneth COPELAND, JR.
111 VP for College Advancement .... Vacant
07 Dean of Admissions .... Ms. Anita H. GARLAND
32 Dean of Students .... Dr. Robert P. SABBATINI
121 Associate Dean Academic Success .... Ms. Lisa A. BURNS
41 Director of Athletics .... Mr. Chad E. EISELE
08 Director of the Library & Computing .... Ms. Shaunna E. HUNTER-MCKINNEY
06 Registrar .... Ms. Dawn L. CONGLETON
37 Director of Financial Aid .... Ms. Zita M. BARREE
29 Director of Alumni Relations .... Mr. Cameron MARSHALL
18 Director of Physical Plant .... Mr. John C. PRENGAMAN
36 Dir Career Ed/Vocational Reflection ...... Ms. Stephanie N. JOYNES
15 Director of Human Resources .... Ms. Sue V. CARTER
19 Dir Public Safety/Chief of Police .... Mr. T. Mark FOWLER
40 Bookstore Manager .... Ms. Kimberly S. MICHAUX
09 Assoc Dean Inst Effectiveness .... Dr. Christine C. ROSS
26 Director Communications & Marketing .... Mr. Gordon W. NEAL
21 Controller .... Mr. Michael A. SMITH
35 Dir of Student Affairs Operations .... Ms. Sandy P. COOKE
39 Director of Residence Life .... Mr. John HOLLEMON
25 Director of College Grants .... Vacant
104 Dir Global Education & Study Abroad ...... Dr. Daniella WIDDOWS

Hampton University (B)

200 William R. Harvey Way, Hampton VA 23668
County: Independent City FICE Identification: 003714
Unit ID: 232265
Telephone: (757) 727-5000 Carnegie Class: DU-Higher
FAX Number: (757) 727-5085 Calendar System: Semester
URL: www.hamptonu.edu
Established: 1868 Annual Undergrad Tuition & Fees: $26,702
Enrollment: 4,618 Coed
Affiliation or Control: Independent Non-Profit IRS Status: 501(c)3
Highest Offering: Doctorate
Accreditation: SC, AAB, CACREP, CAEP, CAEPN, IACBE, JOUR, MUS, NURSE, #PHAR, PTA, SP

01 President .... Dr. William R. HARVEY
03 Senior Vice President .... Mr. Paul C. HARRIS
05 Chancellor & Provost .... Dr. JoAnn W. HAYSBERT
10 Vice Pres Business Affs/Treasurer .... Mrs. Doretha J. SPELLS
11 Vice Pres for Administrative Svcs .... Dr. Barbara L. INMAN
43 Vice President/General Counsel .... Atty. Faye HARDY-LUCAS
30 Interim VP for Development .... Mrs. Evelyn GRAHAM
100 Chief of Staff .... Dr. Charrita D. QUIMBY
21 Asst VP Business Affs/Comptroller .... Mrs. Denise NICHOLS
25 Asst Vice Pres Grants Management .... Mrs. Lillie F. GREEN
20 Asst Provost Academic Affairs .... Dr. Pollie MURPHY
26 Asst VP for Marketing .... Ms. B. DaVida PLUMMER
45 Asst Prov Research & Grantsmanship .... Dr. Michelle PENN-MARSHALL
88 Dean of Judicial Affairs .... Mr. Woodson H. HOPEWELL, JR.
39 Dean of Residential Life .... Miss Jewel B. LONG
07 Dean of Admissions .... Mrs. Angela BOYD
06 Registrar .... Mrs. Jorsene COOPER
36 Dir Career Counsel/Planning Ctr .... Mrs. Bessie WILLIS
38 Interim Director Counseling Center .... Dr. Richard MASON
08 Administrator University Libraries .... Mrs. Tina ROLLINS
29 Director of Alumni Affairs .... Ms. Brint MARTIN
15 Director of Human Resources .... Ms. Rikki THOMAS
14 Director Computer Center .... Mr. Darien HAWKINS
37 Financial Aid Officer .... Mr. Martin MILES
27 Director of University Relations .... Mr. Matthew WHITE
09 Director Institutional Research .... Dr. Michelle CLAWSON
23 Director Student Health Services .... Dr. Karen WILLIAMS
42 University Chaplain .... Dr. Debra L. HAGGINS
18 Director Buildings & Grounds .... Mr. Randall HARDY
87 Director of Summer Sessions .... Dr. Pollie MURPHY
19 Chief of Campus Police .... Mr. David GLOVER
86 Director Government Relations .... Mr. Wilbert L. THOMAS
96 Asst Director of Purchasing .... Ms. Debra HARDEN
40 University Bookstore Manager .... Ms. Michelle R. MILLER
53 Dean School of Liberal Arts & Educ . Dr. Linda MALONE-COLON
66 Dean School of Nursing .... Dr. Shevallanie LOTT
81 Dean School of Science .... Dr. Calvin LOWE
50 Dean School of Business .... Dr. Ziette H. HAYES
54 Dean Sch of Engineering/Technology .... Dr. Joyce SHIRAZI
67 Dean School of Pharmacy .... Dr. Anand IYER
58 Dean the Graduate College .... Dr. Michelle PENN-MARSHALL
60 Dean Scripps Howard Sch Journ/Comm ... Ms. DaVida PLUMMER
88 Dean University College .... Dr. Kim LUCKES

Hollins University (C)

PO Box 9707, Roanoke VA 24020-1688
County: Roanoke FICE Identification: 003715
Unit ID: 232308
Telephone: (540) 362-6000 Carnegie Class: Bac-A&S
FAX Number: (540) 362-6642 Calendar System: 4/1/4
URL: www.hollins.edu
Established: 1842 Annual Undergrad Tuition & Fees: $39,035
Enrollment: 790 Female
Affiliation or Control: Independent Non-Profit IRS Status: 501(c)3
Highest Offering: Master's
Accreditation: SC, CAEPT

01 President .... Ms. Nancy O. GRAY
10 Executive VP and COO .... Ms. Kerry EDMONDS
05 Interim VP for Academic Affairs .... Dr. Daniel DERRINGER
111 Vice Pres for External Relations .... Ms. Suzy MINK
84 Vice Pres Enrollment and Marketing .... Ms. Ashley BROWNING
20 Chair of the Faculty .... Ms. Darla SCHUMM
32 Dean of Students .... Ms. Patty O'TOOLE
20 Interim VP for Academic Programs .... Dr. Alison RIDLEY
58 Dean of Graduate Studies .... Dr. Julie DELOIA
28 Associate Dean Intercultural Pgms .... Ms. Jeri L. SUAREZ
04 Executive Assistant to President .... Ms. Brook E. DICKSON
06 Registrar .... Ms. Patricia BROKKEN
08 Director of the Library .... Mr. Luke VILELLE
15 Director of Human Resources .... Ms. Alicia GODZWA
26 Director of Public Relations .... Mr. Jeff HODGES
29 Director of Alumnae Relations .... Ms. Lauren WALKER
36 Exec Director Career Center .... Ms. Karen CARDOZO
37 Director Financial Aid .... Ms. Mary Jean CORRISS
41 Director of Athletics .... Ms. Myra SIMS
18 Director Plant Operations/Services .... Ms. Mae RAMSEY
104 Director International Programs .... Vacant
13 Chief Info Technology Officer .... Vacant
19 Director Security/Safety .... Mr. David CARLSON
39 Dir Housing & Residential Life .... Ms. Melissa HINE
07 Director of Admissions .... Ms. Cailin ASIP

iGlobal University (D)

8133 Leesburg Pike, #230, Vienna VA 22182
County: Fairfax Identification: 667105
Unit ID: 483780
Telephone: (703) 941-2020 Carnegie Class: Spec-4-yr-Bus
FAX Number: (703) 941-2025 Calendar System: Quarter
URL: www.igu.edu
Established: 2008 Annual Undergrad Tuition & Fees: $13,820
Enrollment: 255 Coed
Affiliation or Control: Proprietary IRS Status: Proprietary
Highest Offering: Master's
Accreditation: ACCSC

01 President & CEO .... Dr. David Y. SOHN
05 Director of Education .... Dr. Yohannes ABATE

Ivy Christian College (E)

9401 Mathy Drive, Suite 380, Fairfax VA 22031
County: Fairfax Identification: 667213
Telephone: (703) 425-4143 Carnegie Class: Not Classified
FAX Number: (703) 425-4148 Calendar System: Quarter
URL: www.ivy.edu
Established: 2006 Annual Undergrad Tuition & Fees: N/A
Enrollment: N/A Coed
Affiliation or Control: Independent Non-Profit IRS Status: 501(c)3
Highest Offering: Baccalaureate
Accreditation: TRACS

01 President .... Dr. David Y. PAK
05 Academic Dean .... Mr. Paul CLAY-ROOLS
11 Chief Operating Officer .... Mr. John YOO
32 Director of Student Affairs .... Mr. Byung KIM
07 Director of Admissions .... Ms. Nicole ARDELEAN
10 Director of Finance & Registrar .... Yoomin KIM
09 Librarian .... Mr. Steven KROMPF

James Madison University (F)

800 S Main Street, Harrisonburg VA 22807-0001
County: Independent City FICE Identification: 003721
Unit ID: 232423
Telephone: (540) 568-6211 Carnegie Class: Masters/L
FAX Number: N/A Calendar System: Semester
URL: www.jmu.edu
Established: 1908 Annual Undergrad Tuition & Fees (In-State): $12,016
Enrollment: 21,836 Coed
Affiliation or Control: State IRS Status: 501(c)3
Highest Offering: Doctorate
Accreditation: SC, ARCPA, ART, AUD, CAATE, CACREP, CAEP, CAEPN, DANCE, DIETD, IPSY, MUS, NURSE, OT, PSPSY, SP, SPAA, SW, THEA

01 President .... Mr. Jonathan R. ALGER
05 Provost/Senior VP Academic Affairs .... Dr. Heather COLTMAN
10 Sr Vice Pres Administration/Finance .... Mr. Charles W. KING
32 VP Student Affairs .... Dr. Timothy M. MILLER
111 Vice Pres University Advancement .... Dr. Nick LANGRIDGE
84 VP Access and Enrollment Mgmt .... Ms. Donna L. HARPER
13 AVP Information Technology .... Mr. Dale B. HULVEY
81 Dean College Science/Math .... Dr. Cynthia BAUERLE
49 Dean College Arts/Letters .... Dr. Robert AGUIRRE
76 Dean Col of Health & Behav Studies .... Dr. Sharon LOVELL
50 Dean College of Business .... Dr. Michael BUSING
57 Dean College Visual Performing Arts .... Dr. George E. SPARKS
53 Dean College of Education .... Dr. Mark L'ESPERANCE
72 Dean College of Int Science & Engr .... Dr. Robert KOLVOORD
58 Interim Dean Graduate School .... Dr. John BURGESS
97 Dean University Studies .... Dr. Linda C. HALPERN
08 Dean Libraries .... Dr. Bethany NOWVISKIE
43 University Counsel .... Mr. Jack KNIGHT
114 Asst Vice Pres Budget Management .... Ms. Diane L. STAMP
07 Dean of Admissions .... Mr. Michael D. WALSH
37 Dir Financial Aid & Scholarships .... Mr. Brad BARNETT
15 Director Human Resources .... Mr. Chuch FLICK
09 Director Institutional Research .... Dr. Christopher D. OREM
41 Director of Athletics .... Mr. Jeffrey T. BOURNE
26 Dir Comm & Univ Spokesperson .... Mr. Bill J. WYATT
06 University Registrar .... Ms. Michele M. WHITE
19 Interim Chief of Police .... Mr. Kevin LANOUE
22 Dir of EEO .... Mr. James R. ROBINSON
29 Director Alumni Relations .... Ms. Carrie COMBS
27 Senior Advancement Marketing Dir .... Mr. David R. TAYLOR

The John Leland Center for Theological Studies (G)

1306 N Highland Street, Arlington VA 22201
County: Arlington Identification: 666340
Telephone: (703) 812-4757 Carnegie Class: Not Classified
FAX Number: (703) 812-4764 Calendar System: Other
URL: www.leland.edu
Established: 1998 Annual Graduate Tuition & Fees: N/A
Enrollment: N/A Coed
Affiliation or Control: Baptist IRS Status: 501(c)3
Highest Offering: Master's; No Undergraduates
Accreditation: THEOL

01 Interim President .... Rev. J. Brent WALKER
05 Academic Dean .... Dr. John LEE
04 Assistant to the President .... Ms. Shana WRIGHT
08 Librarian .... Ms. Monica LEAK
06 Registrar .... Ms. Andrea BAKKE
84 Director of Enrollment .... Ms. Jacqueline COKER
10 Director of Finance .... Mr. Mel HARRIS
26 Chief Public Relations Officer .... Ms. Vicki BOHANNON

Liberty University (H)

1971 University Boulevard, Lynchburg VA 24515
County: Independent City FICE Identification: 020530
Unit ID: 232557
Telephone: (434) 582-2000 Carnegie Class: DU-Mod
FAX Number: N/A Calendar System: Semester
URL: www.liberty.edu
Established: 1971 Annual Undergrad Tuition & Fees: $22,584
Enrollment: 75,044 Coed
Affiliation or Control: Other IRS Status: 501(c)3
Highest Offering: Doctorate
Accreditation: SC, ACBSP, CAATE, CACREP, CAEPN, COARC, COSMA, EXSC, FEPAC, LAW, MUS, NURSE, OSTEO, SW

01 President .... Mr. Jerry FALWELL, JR.
03 Executive Vice President & COO .... Mr. Randy SMITH
05 Provost .... Dr. Scott HICKS
106 Provost for Online Programs .... Mr. Shawn D. AKERS
20 Vice Provost .... Dr. Ronald E. HAWKINS
32 Sr Vice President Student Affairs .... Dr. Mark L. HINE
10 Exec VP Finance .... Dr. Robert L. RITZ
84 Exec VP of Enrollment Mgmt & Mktg .... Mr. Ron KENNEDY
15 Exec VP Human Resources .... Mrs. Laura J. WALLACE
21 Sr Vice Pres Finance & Invest Mgmt .... Mr. Don MOON
88 Sr VP for Spiritual Development .... Mr. David NASSER
37 VP of Student Financial Services .... Mrs. Ashley REICH
26 VP of Marketing & Communication .... Ms. Kristin CONRAD
45 AVP for Institutional Effectiveness .... Mr. H. Skip KASTROLL
13 Chief Information Officer .... Mr. John GAUGER
06 University Registrar .... Mrs. Helene VANCE
43 General Counsel .... Mr. David M. CORRY
08 Dean Jerry Falwell Library .... Mrs. Angela RICE
80 Interim Dean School of Govt .... Mr. Ron MILLER
18 Sr VP Campus Facilities & Transport .... Mr. Charles SPENCE
88 VP of Major Construction .... Mr. Daniel DETER
30 VP of Development .... Mr. Chris CARROLL
41 Director of Athletics .... Mr. Ian MCCAW
49 Dean College of Arts & Sciences .... Dr. Roger D. SCHULTZ
83 Dean School of Behavioral Sciences .... Dr. Kenyon KNAPP
50 Dean School of Business .... Dr. Dave BRAT
60 Dean School of Comm & Digital Cont .... Dr. Bruce KIRK
57 Dean School of Visual & Perf Arts .... Mr. Scott HAYES
97 Dean CASAS .... Dr. Brian YATES
73 Dean School of Divinity .... Dr. Ed HINDSON
53 Dean School of Education .... Dr. Heather SCHOFFSTALL
88 VP of Campus Recreation .... Mr. Chris MISIANO
88 VP Designated Campus Facilities .... Mr. Scott STARNES
19 Chief of Police LUPD .... Col. Richard HINKLEY
54 Dean School of Engineering .... Mr. Mark HORSTEMEYER
97 Dean College of General Studies .... Dr. Ester WARREN
28 VP for Equity & Inclusion/CDO .... Mr. Greg DOWELL
61 Dean School of Law .... Mr. Keith FAULKNER
88 Dean School of Aeronautics .... Mr. Jim MOLLOY
88 Dir Center for Teaching Excellence .... Mr. Shawn BIELICKI
58 Admin Dean for Grad Education .... Dr. David CALLAND

76 Dean School of Health Sciences .... Dr. Ralph LINSTRA
63 Dean College of Osteopathic Med ....Dr. Peter BELL
64 Dean School of Music .... Dr. Vernon WHALEY
35 Dean of Students ....Mr. Robert MULLEN
66 Dean School of Nursing .... Dr. Shanna AKERS
04 Exec Assistant to the President ....Ms. Amanda STANLEY

Longwood University (A)

201 High Street, Farmville VA 23909-1801
County: Prince Edward FICE Identification: 003719
Unit ID: 232566
Telephone: (434) 395-2000 Carnegie Class: Masters/M
FAX Number: (434) 395-2635 Calendar System: Semester
URL: www.longwood.edu
Established: 1839 Annual Undergrad Tuition & Fees (In-State): $13,340
Enrollment: 5,074 Coed
Affiliation or Control: State IRS Status: 501(c)3
Highest Offering: Master's
Accreditation: SC, CAATE, CAEP, EXSC, MUS, NRPA, NURSE, SP, SW, THEA

01 President .... Mr. W. Taylor REVELEY, IV
05 Provost/Vice Pres Academic Affairs .... Dr. Larissa FERGESON
10 Vice Pres Administration & Finance .... Ms. Louise WALLER
32 Vice President for Student Affairs ....Dr. Tim J. PIERSON
111 VP for Institutional Advancement .... Ms. Courtney HODGES
45 VP for Strategic Operations ....Ms. Victoria KINDON
13 Chief Information Officer ....Ms. Victoria KINDON
84 Assoc VP Enrollment Management ....Dr. Jennifer K. GREEN
26 Asst VP Marketing/Communications ....Ms. Sabrina BROWN
96 Assoc VP for Admin & Finance ....Ms. Cathryn B. MOBLEY
29 AVP for Alumni & Career Services .... Mr. Ryan CATHERWOOD
09 Director Assessment/Inst Research ....Dr. David LEHR
06 Registrar ....Mrs. Susan HINES
07 Dean of Admissions ....Mr. Jason C. FAULK
08 Dean of Library ....Mr. Brent ROBERTS
28 Dir Citizen Ldrshp/Soc Justice Educ .... Mr. Jonathan E. PAGE
38 Director Student Counseling .... Dr. Maureen J. WALLS-MCKAY
36 Asst Dir Campus Career Engagement ....Ms. Kyle HODGES
37 Director Financial Aid ....Ms. Sarah DOHENY
15 Chief Human Resources Officer ....Ms. Lisa MOONEY
18 Dir Facilities Operations Services ....Mr. Alvin B. MYERS
100 Chief of Staff/Vice President ....Mr. Justin POPE
41 Director of Athletics ....Ms. Michelle MEADOWS

Mary Baldwin University (B)

318 Prospect Street, Staunton VA 24401
County: Augusta FICE Identification: 003723
Unit ID: 232672
Telephone: (540) 887-7000 Carnegie Class: DU-Mod
FAX Number: (540) 886-5561 Calendar System: Other
URL: www.marybaldwin.edu
Established: 1842 Annual Undergrad Tuition & Fees: $31,110
Enrollment: 1,654 Coed
Affiliation or Control: Presbyterian Church (U.S.A.) IRS Status: 501(c)3
Highest Offering: Doctorate
Accreditation: SC, #ARCPA, CAEPT, NURSE, OT, PTA, SW

01 President ....Dr. Pamela FOX
05 Provost/VP for Academic Affairs ....Dr. Ty BUCKMAN
10 Vice President Business/Finance ....Ms. Jennifer M. SAUER
84 VP Enrollment Mgmt .... Dr. Jim MCCOY
111 VP University Advancement ....Mr. Charles E. DAVIS, III
26 VP External Affairs ....Ms. Aimee ROSE
76 VP MDCHS ....Dr. Deb GREUBEL
32 VP for Student Engagement ....Dr. Ernest E. JEFFRIES
28 Assoc VP for Inclusive Excellence ....Rev. Andrea CORNELL-SCOTT
88 Commandant VWIL/Sr Advisor to Pres ...BGen. Teresa A. DJURIC
09 Institutional Report/Research Coord .... Ms. Carrie BOYD
13 Dir of Enterprise Systems Mgmt ....Mr. Lee REID
06 Registrar ....Ms. Kimberlely D. ROBINSON
08 Director of Library ....Ms. Carol CREAGER
49 Dean of College of Arts & Sciences ....Dr. Martha J. WALKER
50 Dean of Col Business & Prof Stds ....Dr. Joseph R. SPRANGEL, JR.
53 Dean of College of Education ....Dr. Rachel POTTER
57 Dean of Visual & Perform Arts ....Dr. Paul MENZER
15 Director of Human Resources ....Ms. Shelly IRVINE
18 AVP of Facilities & Capital Plng ....Mr. Keith CALLAHAN
114 Dir of Budgets/Business Operation .... Mr. Rick CZERWINSKI
29 Director of Alumni Engagement ....Vacant
36 Director Career to Career Center ....Ms. Nell DESMOND
37 Director of Financial Aid ....Ms. Robin DIETRICH
04 Executive Presidential Assistant .... Ms. Sharon S. BOSSERMAN
41 Athletic Director ....Vacant
123 AVP of Online & Graduate Enrollment ....Vacant
19 Director Security/Safety .... Mr. Thomas L. BYERLY

Marymount University (C)

2807 N Glebe Road, Arlington VA 22207-4299
County: Arlington FICE Identification: 003724
Unit ID: 232706
Telephone: (703) 522-5600 Carnegie Class: Masters/L
FAX Number: (703) 284-1637 Calendar System: Semester
URL: www.marymount.edu
Established: 1950 Annual Undergrad Tuition & Fees: $31,926
Enrollment: 3,375 Coed
Affiliation or Control: Roman Catholic IRS Status: 501(c)3
Highest Offering: Doctorate
Accreditation: SC, ACBSP, CACREP, CAEP, CAEPN, CIDA, HSA, NURSE, PTA

00 Chair Board of Trustees .... Dr. Edward BERSOFF
01 President .... Dr. Irma BECERRA
05 Provost & Vice Pres Acad Affairs ....Dr. Hesham EL-REWINI
10 Vice Pres Financial Affairs .... Mr. Alphonso DIAZ
111 Vice Pres University Advancement .... Mr. Joseph FOSTER
32 Vice Pres Student Affairs .... Dr. Linda MCMURDOCK
26 Int VP Marketing & Enrollment Mgmt .... Dr. Irma BECERRA
20 Assoc VP Academic Affairs ....Dr. Susanne NINASSI
84 Assoc VP Mktg & Enrollment Mgmt .... Mrs. Francesca REED
58 Assoc Provost Research & Grad Ed ....Dr. Rita WONG
09 AVP Planning & Inst Effectiveness .... Mr. Michael SCHUCHERT
109 Asst VP Campus Planning & Mgmt ....Mr. Upendra MALANI
21 Asst VP Fin Affairs & Controller ....Mr. Ronald SOMERVELL
15 Asst VP Human Resources ....Ms. Kendra GILLESPIE
45 Asst VP Strategic Initiatives ....Dr. Christina RAJMAIRA
06 Interim University Registrar ....Ms. Rachel POLETO
08 University Librarian ....Ms. Alison GREGORY
13 Chief Information Officer .... Mr. Steve MUNSON
35 Dean Student Life ....Vacant
79 Dean Sch Design/Arts & Humanities ....Dr. Christina CLARK
50 Int Dean Sch Business & Technology ..... Mr. Jonathan ABERMAN
81 Dean Sch Sciences/Mathematics/Educ . Dr. Catherine WEHLBURG
76 Dean Malek Sch Health Professions ....Dr. Jeanne MATTHEWS
121 Dean Student Success .... Dr. Demetrius JOHNSON
124 Asst Dean Student Engagement .... Dr. Vernon WILLIAMS
04 Executive Asst to President ....Vacant
104 Exec Director Center Global Studies ....Mr. Victor BETANCOURT SANTIAGO
88 Exec Dir Center Teaching & Learning ....Ms. Michelle STEINER
07 Director Admissions ....Vacant
19 Dir Campus Safety & Transportation ....Mr. Eric HOLS
23 Director Student Health Center ....Vacant
25 Dir Office of Sponsored Programs ....Vacant
31 Director Saints Center for Service ....Dr. Kelly DALTON
36 Director Career Services ....Vacant
37 Director Financial Aid ....Mrs. Deborah RAINES
38 Director Counseling Center ....Dr. Laura FINKELSTEIN
39 Asst Dir Res Life/Learning Cmties .... Ms. Tina HOPP
41 Director Athletics ....Ms. Jamie REYNOLDS
42 Director Campus Ministry ....Fr. Joseph RAMPINO
85 Dir International Student Services ....Mrs. Aline ORFALI
89 Int Dir Academic Advising Center .... Dr. Jennifer SPAFFORD
91 Int Dir Admin Information Systems .... Mr. Steve MUNSON
92 Director Honors Program .... Dr. Stacy LOPRESTI-GOODMAN
108 Director Institutional Assessment ....Ms. Ann BOUDINOT
114 Director Budget & Risk Management ..... Mrs. Margaret AXELROD
119 Director Infrastructure & Security ....Mr. David LUTES
120 Dir Fac Dev Teaching & Instr Design ..Dr. Joseph PROVENZANO
88 Dir Enrollment Information Systems .... Mrs. Sara MEEHAN
88 Director IT Support Services ...... Mr. Oscar VENTURA-MENDOZA
88 Dir Planning & Service Quality Init .... Mrs. Anne STANCIL
88 Director Student Access Services .... Mr. Sven JONES
88 Dir Student Conduct/Acad Integrity ..... Mr. Christopher FIORELLO
40 Manager Marymount Univ Bookstore .... Mr. Troy KELLY
96 Coordinator of Purchasing ....Vacant
105 Senior Web Application Manager ....Mr. Yong SHIN
113 Bursar ....Mr. Anantha GORTI
118 Senior Manager Total Rewards ....Mrs. Paula POLSON
88 Title IX Coordinator .... Ms. Angela NASTASE

Medical Careers Institute (D)

1001 Omni Boulevard Suite 200,
Newport News VA 23606-4388
Telephone: (757) 873-2423 FICE Identification: 022472
Accreditation: &SC, CAHIIM, MAAB, PTAA, RAD

† Regional accreditation is carried under the parent institution, ECPI College of Technology, in Virginia Beach, VA.

Medical Careers Institute (E)

2809 Emerywood Parkway, Suite 400,
Richmond VA 23294
Telephone: (804) 521-5999 Identification: 667038
Accreditation: &SC, MAAB, PTAA

† Regional accreditation is carried under the parent institution ECPI College of Technology, Virginia Beach, VA.

Norfolk State University (F)

700 Park Avenue, Norfolk VA 23504-8000
County: Independent City FICE Identification: 003765
Unit ID: 232937
Telephone: (757) 823-8600 Carnegie Class: Masters/M
FAX Number: (757) 823-2067 Calendar System: Semester
URL: www.nsu.edu
Established: 1935 Annual Undergrad Tuition & Fees (In-State): $9,490
Enrollment: 5,303 Coed
Affiliation or Control: State IRS Status: 501(c)3
Highest Offering: Doctorate
Accreditation: SC, CAEPN, CLPSY, DIETD, JOUR, KIN, MUS, NAIT, NUR, SW

01 President .... Dr. Javaune ADAMS-GASTON
05 Provost/Vice Pres Academic Affs ....Dr. Leroy HAMILTON, JR.
10 Vice Pres Finance and Admin ....Mr. Gerald E. HUNTER
111 Vice Pres Univ Advancement .... Dr. Deborah C. FONTAINE
32 Vice Pres Student Affs/Enroll Mgmt ....Dr. Michael M. SHACKLEFORD
20 Interim Vice Provost ....Dr. Leroy HAMILTON, JR.
21 AVP/University Controller ....Mrs. Karla J. AMAYA GORDON
43 University Counsel ....Ms. Pamela F. BOSTON
07 Exec Director of Admissions ....Dr. Juan M. ALEXANDER
38 Director of Counseling ....Ms. Vanessa C. JENKINS
06 Registrar ....Mr. Michael CARPENTER
08 Interim Dean of Library Services ....Mr. Tommy L. BOGGER
37 Director of Financial Aid ....Dr. Melissa BARNES
36 Director of Career Services ....Ms. Alisha BAZEMORE
15 Assoc VP Human Resources ....Vacant
29 Dir Alumni Relations/Annual Giving ....Ms. Michelle D. HILL
49 Interim Dean of Liberal Arts .... Dr. Cassandra NEWBY-ALEXANDER
50 Interim Dean of Business ....Mr. Glenn R. CARRINGTON
76 Act Dean of Science/Eng/Technology ....Dr. Joseph C. HALL
70 Dean of Social Work .... Dr. Rowena G. WILSON
92 Dean of Honors College ....Dr. Page LAWS
58 Dean of Graduate Studies & Research . Dr. George E. MILLER, III
86 Legislative Liaison ....Mr. Robert L. TURNER
26 Exec Dir Communications & Marketing .Ms. Stevalynn R. ADAMS
09 Dir Institutional Research ....Mr. Ephraim BENNETT
39 Exec Dir Housing & Residence Life ...Mrs. Faith M. FITZGERALD
41 Athletics Director ....Vacant
18 Assoc Vice Pres Facilities Mgmt .... Mr. Anton KASHIRI
85 Dir International Student Services ....Mrs. Beverly HARRIS
35 Dean of Students ....Ms. Marable D. MICHELLE
35 Assoc Vice Pres for Student Affairs .... Mrs. Julia WINGARD

† Member of Virginia Consortium for Professional Psychology.

Old Dominion University (G)

5115 Hampton Boulevard, Norfolk VA 23529-0001
County: Independent City FICE Identification: 003728
Unit ID: 232982
Telephone: (757) 683-3000 Carnegie Class: DU-Higher
FAX Number: (757) 683-4505 Calendar System: Semester
URL: www.odu.edu
Established: 1930 Annual Undergrad Tuition & Fees (In-State): $10,560
Enrollment: 24,375 Coed
Affiliation or Control: State IRS Status: 501(c)3
Highest Offering: Doctorate
Accreditation: SC, ANEST, ART, CACREP, CAEPN, CLPSY, CSHSE, CYTO, DH, EXSC, MT, MUS, NAIT, NMT, NRPA, NURSE, PH, PTA, SP, SPAA

01 President ....Mr. John R. BRODERICK
05 Provost/VP Academic Affairs ....Dr. Austin O. AGHO
10 Vice President Admin & Finance ....Mr. Gregory E. DUBOIS
46 Vice President for Research ....Dr. Morris W. FOSTER
15 Vice Pres for Human Resources ... Ms. September C. SANDERLIN
30 Vice Pres University Advancement ....Mr. Alonzo C. BRANDON
88 Vice Prov Faculty Affs/Strat Init .... Dr. Katherine W. HAWKINS
88 Vice Prov Academic Programs ....Dr. Brian K. PAYNE
20 Assoc Vice Pres Academic Affairs .... Ms. Elaine M. PEARSON
21 Assoc VP for Financial Services ...... Ms. Deborah L. SWIECINSKI
88 Asst VP Regional/Higher Educ Ctrs ....Ms. Renee E. OLANDER
56 Assoc VP Distance Learning ....Mr. Andrew R. CASIELLO
84 Assoc Vice Pres Enrollment Mgmt ....Ms. Jane H. DANE
44 Assoc Vice Pres for Advancement .... Mr. Daniel J. GENARD
88 Assoc VP Student Engagement ....Dr. Johnny W. YOUNG
109 Asst Vice Pres Auxiliary Services ....Mr. Todd K. JOHNSON
21 Asst VP Finance/Univ Controller ....Ms. Mary C. DENEEN
13 Assoc Vice Pres University Svcs/ CIO ....Mr. James R. WATERFIELD
31 Asst Vice Pres Community Engagement ....Ms. Karen F. MEIER
35 Int VP Student Engage/Enroll Svcs . Dr. Donald M. STANSBERRY
20 Asst VP Undergraduate Studies .... Ms. Judith M. BOWMAN
29 Assoc Vice Pres of Alumni Rels .... Ms. Joy L. JEFFERSON
26 AVP Strategic Comm/Marketing .... Ms. Giovanna M. GENARD
22 Asst VP Inst Equity & Diversity ....Ms. ReNee S. DUNMAN
58 Dean The Graduate School ....Dr. Robert WOJTOWICZ
49 Dean College Arts & Letters ....Dr. Kent L. SANDSTROM
81 Dean College of Sciences ....Dr. Gail DODGE
76 Dean College Health Sciences ....Dr. Bonnie VAN LUNEN
50 Dean Strome College of Business ....Dr. Jeff F. TANNER
53 Dean Darden College of Education ....Dr. Jane S. BRAY
54 Int Dean College Engineering/Tech ....Dr. Ben STUART
92 Dean Honors College ....Dr. David D. METZGER
20 Exec Dir Ctr High Impact Practices ....Ms. Lisa MAYES
36 Int Exec Dir Career Management Ctr .... Ms. Beverly FORBES
93 Exec Dir of Intercultural Relations ....Ms. Lesa C. CLARK
43 Asst Atty Gen/Assoc Univ Counsel ....Mr. Richard E. NANCE
85 Senior International Officer .... Dr. Paul CURRANT
08 University Librarian ....Mr. George J. FOWLER
06 University Registrar ....Mr. Humberto PORTELLEZ
07 Exec Director of Admissions .... Dr. J. Christopher FLEMING
41 Director of Athletics ....Dr. C. Wood SELIG
37 Director Student Financial Aid .... Ms. Vera E. RIDDICK
31 Director of Community Relations ....Ms. Cecelia T. TUCKER
88 Director Military Affairs ....Mr. Robert E. CLARK
38 Sr Exec Director Counseling Svcs .... Dr. Nancy BADGER
23 Director Student Health Center ....Ms. Jennifer J. FOSS
85 Director Intl Students/Scholar Svcs .... Ms. Robbin S. FULMORE
39 Int Assoc Dean of Student Housing .... Ms. Bridget K. WEIKEL
18 Director Facilities Management .... Mr. Michael J. BRADY
19 AVP for Public Safety/Chief Police ....Ms. Rhonda L. HARRIS
28 Int Dir Inst Equity/Diversity/EO/AA .... Ms. Ariana WRIGHT
109 Director of Procurement Services .... Ms. Etta A. HENRY
94 Director Women's Studies ....Dr. Jennifer N. FISH
16 Dir of HR Employee Rels/Strat Init .... Ms. JaRenae WHITEHEAD
35 Dir Leadership/Student Involvement .... Ms. Nicole C. KIGER
40 University Bookstore Manager ....Ms. Rhyannon POTTER
04 Asst to the President ....Ms. Velvet L. GRANT
86 Director of Governmental Relations .... Ms. Annie K. MORRIS

† Member of Virginia Consortium for Professional Psychology.

Patrick Henry College (A)

Ten Patrick Henry Circle, Purcellville VA 20132

County: Loudoun FICE Identification: 039513
Telephone: (540) 338-1776 Carnegie Class: Bac-A&S
FAX Number: (540) 441-8709 Calendar System: Semester
URL: www.phc.edu
Established: 2000 Annual Undergrad Tuition & Fees: N/A
Enrollment: N/A Coed
Affiliation or Control: Independent Non-Profit IRS Status: 501(c)3
Highest Offering: Baccalaureate
Accreditation: TRACS

01 President ... Mr. Jack HAYE
125 Chancellor Emeritus ... Dr. Michael P. FARRIS
03 Executive Vice President ... Mr. Howard SCHMIDT
10 VP for Administration & Finance ... Mr. Daryl WOLKING
09 VP for Institutional Effectiveness ... Mr. Rodney J. SHOWALTER
111 Vice President for Advancement ... Mr. Tom ZIEMNICK
05 Dean of Academic Affairs ... Dr. Mark MITCHELL
32 Dean of Student Affairs ... Ms. Sandra K. CORBITT
08 Director of the Library ... Ms. Sara E. PENSGARD
07 Director of Student Recruitment ... Mr. Stephen C. PIERCE
26 Director of Communications ... Mr. Stephen C. ALLEN

Protestant Episcopal Theological Seminary in Virginia (B)

3737 Seminary Road, Alexandria VA 22304-5201

County: Independent City FICE Identification: 003731
Unit ID: 233259
Telephone: (703) 370-6600 Carnegie Class: Not Classified
FAX Number: N/A Calendar System: Semester
URL: www.vts.edu
Established: 1823 Annual Graduate Tuition & Fees: N/A
Enrollment: N/A Coed
Affiliation or Control: Protestant Episcopal IRS Status: 501(c)3
Highest Offering: Doctorate; No Undergraduates
Accreditation: THEOL

01 Dean and President ... Rev. Ian S. MARKHAM
05 VP of Academic Affairs ... Rev. Melody D. KNOWLES
111 VP of Institutional Advancement ... Mrs. Linda DIENNO
10 VP for Finance and Operations ... Ms. Jacqueline BALLOU
11 VP for Admin and Inst Effectiveness ... Ms. Katie GLOVER
32 Assoc Dean of Students ... Rt Rev. Jim MATHES
21 Comptroller ... Ms. Olivine PILLING
06 Registrar ... Mrs. Rachel HOLM
08 Head Librarian ... Dr. Mitzi J. BUDDE
26 Director of Communications ... Mr. Curtis PRATHER
07 Director of Admissions ... Mr. Derek GRETEN-HARRISON

Radford University (C)

801 East Main Street, Radford VA 24142

County: Radford City FICE Identification: 003732
Unit ID: 233277
Telephone: (540) 831-5000 Carnegie Class: Masters/L
FAX Number: N/A Calendar System: Semester
URL: www.radford.edu
Established: 1910 Annual Undergrad Tuition & Fees (In-State): $11,210
Enrollment: 9,418 Coed
Affiliation or Control: State IRS Status: 170(c)1
Highest Offering: Doctorate
Accreditation: SC, ART, CAATE, CACREP, CAEPN, CIDA, COPSY, DANCE, DIETD, MUS, NRPA, NURSE, OT, PTA, SP, SW, THEA

01 President ... Dr. Brian O. HEMPHILL
05 Int Provost/VP Academic Affairs ... Dr. Kenna COLLEY
10 VP Finance and Administration/CFO ... Mr. Chad REED
13 VP Information Technology/CIO ... Mr. Danny KEMP
32 VP Student Affairs ... Dr. Susan TRAGESER
26 VP University Relations ... Ms. Ashley SCHUMAKER
111 VP University Advancement ... Ms. Wendy LOWERY
84 VP Enrollment Mgmt ... Ms. Katherine MCCARTHY
50 Dean Davis Col Business & Econ ... Dr. Joy BHADURY
53 Int Dean Col Education & Human Dev ... Dr. Tamara WALLACE
76 Dean Waldron Col Health & Hum Serv ... Dr. Kenneth COX
83 Int Dean Col Humanities/Behav Sci ... Dr. Matthew SMITH
81 Dean Artis College Science & Tech ... Dr. J. Orion ROGERS
57 Dean Col Visual & Performing Arts ... Ms. Margaret DEVANEY
58 Dean Graduate Studies/Research ... Dr. Benjamin D. CALDWELL
07 Dean of Admissions ... Vacant
08 Dean of the Library ... Mr. Steven HELM
06 Registrar ... Mr. Matthew BRUNNER
37 Director of Financial Aid ... Ms. Barbara PORTER
29 Executive Dir of Alumni Relations ... Ms. Laura TURK
41 Director Intercollegiate Athletics ... Mr. Robert LINEBURG
15 Asst VP for Human Resources ... Vacant
35 AVP Student Affs/Dean of Student ... Ms. Angela MITCHELL
19 Chief of Police ... Mr. David UNDERWOOD
09 Director of Institutional Research ... Dr. Eric LOVIK
101 Secretary of the Board of Visitors ... Ms. Karen CASTEELE
100 Chief of Staff ... Ms. Ashley SCHUMAKER
102 Dir Foundation/Corporate Relations ... Mr. Benjamin HILL
28 Director of Institutional Equity ... Dr. Andrea ZUSCHIN
44 Director Annual Giving ... Vacant
86 Exec Director of Govt Relations ... Ms. Lisa GHIDOTTI
96 Exec Director of Strategic Sourcing ... Ms. Kimberly DULANEY

Radford University Carilion (D)

101 Elm Avenue SE, Roanoke VA 24013

Telephone: (540) 985-8483 FICE Identification: 006622
Accreditation: &SC, ARCPA, COARC, EMT, MT, NURSE, OT, OTA, PTAA, SURGT

Randolph College (E)

2500 Rivermont Avenue, Lynchburg VA 24503-1555

County: Independent City FICE Identification: 003734
Unit ID: 233301
Telephone: (434) 947-8000 Carnegie Class: Bac-A&S
FAX Number: (434) 947-8139 Calendar System: Semester
URL: www.randolphcollege.edu
Established: 1891 Annual Undergrad Tuition & Fees: $39,585
Enrollment: 684 Coed
Affiliation or Control: United Methodist IRS Status: 501(c)3
Highest Offering: Master's
Accreditation: SC, CAEP

01 President ... Dr. Bradley W. BATEMAN
05 VP Academic Affs & Dean of College ... Dr. Carl A. GIRELLI
111 Vice Pres Institutional Advancement ... Ms. Farah MARKS
10 Vice Pres Finance & Administration ... Vacant
32 VP Student Affs & Dean of Students ... Dr. Wesley FUGATE
100 Special Assistant to the President ... Mr. Steve WILLIS
20 Associate Dean of the College ... Ms. Bunny GOODJOHN
29 Director Alumnae & Alumni Pgm ... Ms. Phebe WESCOTT
09 Dir IR/Planning & Assessment ... Dr. John F. KEENER
15 Director Human Resources ... Ms. Sharon SAUNDERS
18 Chief Facilities/Physical Plant ... Mr. John LEARY
21 Director of Finance ... Mr. Jonathan TYREE
38 Director Student Counseling ... Ms. Jennifer BONDURANT
08 Librarian ... Ms. Lisa BROUGHMAN
06 Registrar ... Ms. Jeanette RORK
37 Dir Student Financial Services ... Mr. Ryan MCNAMARA
36 Director of Career Development ... Ms. Christine HARRIGER
13 Director of Information Technology ... Mr. Victor GOSNELL
04 Administrative Asst to President ... Ms. Cindy LYONS
07 Director of Admissions ... Vacant
19 Director Security/Safety ... Mr. Kris IRWIN
41 Athletic Director ... Mr. Anthony BERICH
26 Chief Public Relations/Marketing ... Ms. Brenda EDSON

Randolph-Macon College (F)

204 Henry Street, PO Box 5005, Ashland VA 23005-5505

County: Hanover FICE Identification: 003733
Unit ID: 233295
Telephone: (804) 752-7200 Carnegie Class: Bac-A&S
FAX Number: (804) 752-7231 Calendar System: Other
URL: www.rmc.edu
Established: 1830 Annual Undergrad Tuition & Fees: $41,300
Enrollment: 1,453 Coed
Affiliation or Control: United Methodist IRS Status: 501(c)3
Highest Offering: Baccalaureate
Accreditation: SC, #CAEP

01 President ... Mr. Robert R. LINDGREN
05 Provost/VP for Academic Affairs ... Dr. Alisa J. ROSENTHAL
10 Vice Pres of Admin & Finance ... Mr. Paul DAVIES
111 Vice Pres for College Advancement ... Ms. Diane M. LOWDER
84 Vice Pres for Enroll/Admiss/Fin Aid ... Dr. David L. LESESNE
32 Vice President for Student Affairs ... Dr. Grant L. AZDELL
04 Executive Assistant to the Pres ... Ms. Jennifer L. THOMPSON
07 Director of Admissions ... Ms. Erin SLATER
45 Exec Dir Strategic Planning ... Dr. Katherine M. RUEFF
29 Exec Director Alumni Relations ... Ms. Alice D. LYNCH
26 Dir of Marketing & Communications ... Mrs. Anne Marie LAURANZON
37 Director of Financial Aid ... Mrs. Mary Y. NEAL
13 CIO and ITS Director ... Mr. Kirk BAUMBACH
06 Registrar ... Mrs. Alana DAVIS
38 Director of Counseling Services ... Dr. D. Craig ANDERSON
09 Director of Institutional Research ... Dr. Katherine D. WALKER
18 Dir of Operations & Physical Plant ... Mr. Thomas P. DWYER
42 Chaplain ... Rev. Kendra S. GRIMES
19 Director of Campus Safety ... Mr. Maurice J. KIELY
41 Athletic Director ... Mr. Jeffrey S. BURNS
15 Director Human Resources ... Mrs. Sharon S. JACKSON
21 Controller ... Ms. Barbara A. DAUBERMAN
20 Associate Dean of the College ... Dr. Lauren C. BELL
36 Director of Professional Develop ... Ms. Catherine A. ROLLMAN
35 Asst Dean of Students ... Mr. James D. MCGHEE, JR.
40 Bookstore Manager ... Mrs. Barclay F. DUPRIEST
114 Director of Budget/Financial Analys ... Mrs. Caroline C. BUSCH
08 Head Librarian ... Ms. Nancy K. FALCIANI-WHITE
102 Dir Foundation/Corporate Relations ... Mr. Robert H. PATTERSON
104 Director Study Abroad ... Ms. Tammi L. REICHEL
28 Director of Diversity ... Ms. Alicia C. ELMS
39 Director Student Housing ... Ms. Melissa LEECY
44 Dir Annual Giving & Alumni Rel ... Mr. Richard M. GOLEMBESKI

Reformed Theological Seminary (G)

8227 Old Courthouse Rd, Vienna VA 22182

Telephone: (703) 448-3393 Identification: 666079
Accreditation: &SC, THEOL

† Regional accreditation is carried under the parent institution in Jackson, MS.

Regent University (H)

1000 Regent University Drive, Virginia Beach VA 23464-9800

County: Independent City FICE Identification: 030913
Unit ID: 231651
Telephone: (757) 352-4127 Carnegie Class: DU-Mod
FAX Number: (757) 352-4381 Calendar System: Semester
URL: www.regent.edu
Established: 1977 Annual Undergrad Tuition & Fees: $18,380
Enrollment: 9,488 Coed
Affiliation or Control: Independent Non-Profit IRS Status: 501(c)3
Highest Offering: Doctorate
Accreditation: SC, ACBSP, CACREP, CAEPT, CLPSY, LAW, NURSE, THEOL

01 Chancellor & CEO ... Dr. M.G. (Pat) ROBERTSON
05 Executive VP for Academic Affairs ... Dr. Gerson MORENO-RIANO
32 Executive VP for Student Life ... Dr. Joseph UMIDI
43 Senior VP & General Counsel ... Mr. Louis A. ISAKOFF
29 Vice President for Alumni Relations ... Mrs. Ann LEBLANC
26 VP for Marketing & Public Relations ... Mrs. Sherri MILLER
10 VP for Business Administration ... Mr. Steve BRUCE
15 VP for Human Resources & Admin ... Mrs. Martha J. SMITH
20 Associate VP for Academic Affairs ... Mr. Douglas COOK
88 Associate VP for Teaching/Learning ... Vacant
61 Dean School of Law ... Hon. Mark MARTIN
49 Int Dean College of Arts & Sciences ... Dr. Joshua MCMULLEN
08 Dean of University Library ... Dr. Esther GILLIE
50 Dean School of Business/Leadership ... Dr. Doris GOMEZ
80 Int Dean School of Government ... Dr. Steve PERRY
53 Dean School of Education ... Dr. Kurt KREASSIG
83 Dean Psychology & Counseling ... Dr. William HATHAWAY
73 Dean School of Divinity ... Dr. Corne BEKKER
06 Registrar ... Dr. Donna HOLCOMB
84 Associate VP of Enrollment Mgmt ... Mrs. Heidi CECE
35 Director of Student Activities ... Ms. Amber STEELE
106 Director of CTL ... Vacant
37 Director of Financial Aid ... Ms. Rachael MOSER
09 Director of Institutional Research ... Dr. Amanda WYNN
18 Director of Facility Management ... Mr. Kim HEGWER
88 Exec Director of Alumni Relations ... Ms. Lyn KAISER
42 Director of Campus Ministries ... Mr. Mark LAWRENCE
108 Director of Assessment ... Dr. Ryan MURNANE
123 Sr Dir Military & Veterans Affairs ... Mr. Bob HABIB
39 Assistant VP for Student Life ... Mr. Adam WILLIAMS
96 Manager of Purchasing ... Mrs. Pauline CARRAWAY
04 Assistant to the Chancellor ... Ms. Laurie Ann FINN
13 Asst Vice Pres of Info Technology ... Mr. Jonathan HARRELL
41 Athletic Director ... Dr. Samuel BOTTA

Richard Bland College (I)

11301 Johnson Road, South Prince George VA 23805-7100

County: South Prince George FICE Identification: 003707
Unit ID: 233338
Telephone: (804) 862-6100 Carnegie Class: Assoc/HT-High Trad
FAX Number: (804) 862-6207 Calendar System: Semester
URL: www.rbc.edu
Established: 1960 Annual Undergrad Tuition & Fees (In-State): $8,100
Enrollment: 2,487 Coed
Affiliation or Control: State IRS Status: 501(c)3
Highest Offering: Associate Degree
Accreditation: SC

01 President ... Dr. Debbie L. SYDOW
05 Provost ... Dr. Maria DEZENBERG
10 Chief Business Officer ... Mr. Paul EDWARDS
100 Chief of Staff ... Ms. Lashrecse AIRD
18 Director Capital Assets/Operations ... Mr. Eric KONDZIELAWA
04 Executive Assistant to President ... Ms. Lisa L. POND
26 Director of Communications ... Ms. Joanne WILLIAMS
30 Chief Development Officer ... Dr. James T. HART
15 Director of Human Resources ... Ms. Cassandra STANDBERRY
19 Chief Campus Safety/Police ... Mr. Jeffrey BROWN
43 College Counsel ... Ms. Ramona TAYLOR
121 Director of Student Success ... Ms. Celia BROCKWAY
41 Director Athletics & Recreation ... Mr. Scott NEWTON
39 Director of Housing ... Ms. Lisa MABRY
37 Director of Financial Aid ... Ms. Lisa JOHNSON
06 Director of Records & Registration ... Ms. Giovanka OBERMULLER
07 Director of Admissions ... Mr. Ryan CHISHOLM
38 Dir of Counseling/Student Support ... Dr. Evanda WATTS-MARTINEZ
88 Director Athletic Communications ... Mr. Greg PROUTY
35 Director of Student Activities ... Mr. Michael ROGERS
109 Assoc Director Aux Enterprises ... Ms. Jamie CAMP
27 Asst Director Communications ... Mr. Robin J. DEUTSCH
21 Controller ... Ms. Melissa MAHONEY
113 Bursar ... Ms. Melissa MAHONEY
96 Procurement Manager ... Mr. Greg JOHNSON
119 Information Security Officer ... Ms. Deborah JAMES
14 Manager Projects & Telecom ... Mr. George JELLERSON
14 Technology Support Manager ... Mr. Clifton YOUNG
16 HR Specialist ... Ms. Alice JABBOUR
08 Head Librarian ... Ms. Carly BASKERVILLE
88 Director of Account & Finance ... Mr. Mark JACOBSON
88 Program Mgr Strategic Initiatives ... Ms. Stacey SOKOL
25 Director of Grants/Partnerships ... Ms. Jamie CAMP
88 Business Manager ... Mr. Preston BOUSMAN
13 Chief Info/Strategy & Innovation ... Dr. Kenneth LATESSA

Riverside College of Health Careers (A)

316 Main Street, Newport News VA 23601
County: Independent City FICE Identification: 021400
Unit ID: 233408
Telephone: (757) 240-2200 Carnegie Class: Spec 2-yr-Health
FAX Number: (757) 240-2225 Calendar System: Semester
URL: www.riverside.edu
Established: 1916 Annual Undergrad Tuition & Fees: $17,610
Enrollment: 336 Coed
Affiliation or Control: Independent Non-Profit IRS Status: 501(c)3
Highest Offering: Associate Degree
Accreditation: ABHES, ADNUR, PNUR, PTAA, RAD, SURGT, SURTEC

01 System Director of Education .... Robin M. NELHUEBEL
06 Registrar .... Lori ARNDER
08 Head Librarian .... Cassandra MOORE
10 Director of Campus Resources .... Michael HAMILTON
07 Recruitment Coordinator .... Cynthia REDDINGTON

Roanoke College (B)

221 College Lane, Salem VA 24153-3747
County: Independent City FICE Identification: 003736
Unit ID: 233426
Telephone: (540) 375-2500 Carnegie Class: Bac-A&S
FAX Number: (540) 375-2205 Calendar System: Semester
URL: www.roanoke.edu
Established: 1842 Annual Undergrad Tuition & Fees: $44,155
Enrollment: 2,035 Coed
Affiliation or Control: Evangelical Lutheran Church In America
IRS Status: 501(c)3
Highest Offering: Baccalaureate
Accreditation: SC, ACBSP, #CAATE, CAEPT

01 President .... Mr. Michael C. MAXEY
05 Vice President/Dean of the College .... Dr. Richard A. SMITH
84 VP of Enroll Svcs/Dean Adm/Fin Aid .... Dr. Brenda P. POGGENDORF
32 Vice President Student Affairs .... Dr. Richard A. SMITH
10 Vice President Business Affairs .... Mr. David MOWEN
30 Vice President Resource Development .... Mr. Aaron L. FETROW
26 Exec Dir/Marketing Communications .... Ms. Melanie W. TOLAN
13 Chief Information Officer .... Mr. Mark D. POORE
09 Dir Institutional Research .... Dr. Jack K. STEEHLER
20 Assoc Dean Academic Affairs .... Dr. Gail A. STEEHLER
06 Assoc Dean Acad Affairs/Registrar .... Ms. Leah L. RUSSELL
07 Director of Recruitment .... Mr. Courtney PENN
35 AVP/Dean of Students/Student Affs .... Dr. Brian T. CHISOM
39 Director of Residence Life/Housing .... Mr. Jimmy R. WHITED
92 Director of Honors Programs .... Dr. Chad T. MORRIS
08 Director of the Library .... Ms. Elizabeth MCCLENNEY
36 Director of Career Services .... Ms. Toni D. MCLAWHORN
24 Media Technology Director .... Vacant
31 Dir of Community Programs .... Ms. Tanya RIDPATH
26 Director of Public Relations .... Ms. Teresa T. GEREAUX
44 Director of Gift Planning .... Mr. Richard J. POGGENDORF
29 Dir of Alumni/Family Relations .... Mrs. Sally WALKER
114 Director of Finance & Budget .... Mr. Adam NEAL
91 Database Director .... Ms. Mitzi B. STEELE
15 Director Human Resources .... Mrs. Kathy MARTIN
40 Bookstore Coordinator/Buyer .... Ms. Melissa B. RUTLEDGE
19 Director Campus Safety .... Mr. Thomas A. RAMBO
23 Dir Student Health/Counseling Svcs .... Ms. Sandra W. MCGHEE
41 Athletic Director .... Mr. M. Scott ALLISON
42 Chaplain/Dean of the Chapel .... Rev. Christopher M. BOWEN
104 Director International Education .... Dr. Pamela A. SEROTA COTE
28 Director of Multicultural Affairs .... Vacant
04 Executive Assistant to President .... Mrs. Whitney C. ALDRIDGE

Saint Michael College of Allied Health (C)

8305 Richmond Hwy, Ste 10A, Alexandria VA 22309
County: Independent City Identification: 667226
Unit ID: 486424
Telephone: (703) 746-8708 Carnegie Class: Spec 2-yr-Health
FAX Number: (703) 746-8709 Calendar System: Other
URL: www.stmichaelcollegeva.us
Established: 2007 Annual Undergrad Tuition & Fees: $16,300
Enrollment: 47 Coed
Affiliation or Control: Proprietary IRS Status: Proprietary
Highest Offering: Associate Degree
Accreditation: COE, PNUR

01 Director .... Dr. Michael ADEDOKUN

Sentara College of Health Sciences (D)

1441 Crossways Boulevard, Ste 105,
Chesapeake VA 23320
County: Chesapeake City FICE Identification: 031065
Unit ID: 232885
Telephone: (757) 388-2900 Carnegie Class: Spec-4-yr-Other Health
FAX Number: (757) 222-7694 Calendar System: Semester
URL: www.sentara.edu
Established: 1892 Annual Undergrad Tuition & Fees: N/A
Enrollment: 440 Coed
Affiliation or Control: Independent Non-Profit IRS Status: 501(c)3
Highest Offering: Master's
Accreditation: ABHES, CVT, NURSE, SURGT, SURTEC

01 Executive Director & Dean .... Mrs. Angela TAYLOR
05 Dean Academic Affairs .... Dr. Cynthia BANKS
45 Asst Dean Institutional Effective .... Ms. Metta ALSOBROOK
10 Asst Dean Administration & Finance .... Mr. Christopher NELSON
84 Director of Enrollment Management .... Mr. Joseph HOWE
08 Manager Library Services .... Ms. Suzanne DUNCAN
37 Financial Aid Advisor .... Ms. Mary Ann RIVERA
07 Admissions Recruiter .... Mr. Jeremy BROFFT
07 Admissions Recruiter .... Mr. Kevin LAWRENCE

Shenandoah University (E)

1460 University Drive, Winchester VA 22601-5195
County: Independent City FICE Identification: 003737
Unit ID: 233541
Telephone: (540) 665-4500 Carnegie Class: DU-Mod
FAX Number: N/A Calendar System: Semester
URL: www.su.edu
Established: 1875 Annual Undergrad Tuition & Fees: $32,530
Enrollment: 3,844 Coed
Affiliation or Control: United Methodist IRS Status: 501(c)3
Highest Offering: Doctorate
Accreditation: SC, ARCPA, CAATE, CAEP, COARC, MIDWF, NURSE, OT, PHAR, PTA

01 President .... Dr. Tracy FITZSIMMONS
05 Provost .... Dr. Adrienne G. BLOSS
10 Vice Pres Administration & Finance .... Mr. Robert L. KEASLER
32 Vice President for Student Life .... Rev Dr. Rhonda VANDYKE
111 Senior VP for Advancement .... Mr. Mitchell L. MOORE
84 VP for Student Success .... Dr. Yolanda BARBIER GIBSON
35 Dean of Students .... Dr. Sue O'DRISCOLL
26 Director of Media Relations .... Dr. Cathy LORANGER
49 Dean of College of Arts & Sciences .... Dr. Jeffrey COKER
50 Dean of Byrd School of Business .... Dr. Astrid SHEIL
64 Dean of Shenandoah Conservatory .... Dr. Michael J. STEPNIAK
67 Dean of Dunn School of Pharmacy .... Dr. Robert DICENZO
07 Exec of Recruitment & Admissions .... Mr. Andy WOODALL
124 Dir of Student Engagement .... Vacant
08 Director of Library Services .... Mr. Christopher A. BEAN
06 Registrar .... Ms. Emily HOLLINS
21 Asst VP for Admin & Finance .... Ms. Courtney JARRETT
37 Student Financial Services Dir .... Dr. Karen H. BUCHER
36 Director of Career/Prof Development .... Ms. Jennifer A. SPATARO-WILSON
18 Director of Physical Plant .... Mr. Barry SCHNOOR
23 Interim Director of Wellness Center .... Mrs. Lisa DARSCH
15 Director of Human Resources .... Mr. Christopher GRANT
41 Athletic Director .... Dr. Bridget LYONS
91 Database & System Administrator .... Mr. Seth BURKE
13 Director of Institutional Computing .... Mr. Quaiser ABSAR
66 Dean Custer School of Nursing .... Dr. Kathleen LASALA
88 Director Div of Athletic Training .... Dr. Rose A. SCHMIEG
88 Dir Div of Occupational Therapy .... Dr. Cathy SHANHOLTZ
88 Dir Div of Physical Therapy .... Dr. Sheri HALE
112 Director of Planned Gifts .... Ms. Ann BRANDER
19 Director of Public Safety .... Mr. Ricky FRYE
102 Dir of Grant Supp & Foundation Rels .... Ms. Marguerite LANDENBURGER
109 Director Auxiliary Services .... Ms. Pamela B. BURKE
88 Dir Div of Physician Asst Studies .... Dr. Anthony MILLER
20 Director Learning Services .... Ms. Holli PHILLIPS
42 Dean of Spiritual Life .... Rev Dr. Justin ALLEN
88 Dir Division of Respiratory Care .... Dr. Melissa CARROLL
09 Director Institutional Research .... Mr. Howard BALLENTINE
40 Bookstore Manager .... Ms. Kimberly OTYENOH
96 Purchasing/Accounts Payable Manager .... Ms. Susan LANDIS
24 Coordinator Media Services .... Vacant
38 Director of Counseling Center .... Ms. Allison COLLAZO
04 Executive Asst to President .... Ms. Kim KECKLEY
101 Secretary of the Board of Trustees .... Ms. Laura CLAWSON
53 Director School of Education .... Dr. Jill LINDSEY
104 Director International Programs .... Dr. Bethany GALIPEAU-KONATE
44 Director Annual Giving .... Vacant
43 General Counsel .... Mr. Philip EVANS
28 Director of Inclusion & Diversity .... Ms. Margaret MCCAMPBELL LIEN
29 Executive Director Alumni Affairs .... Ms. Emily BURNER

South University (F)

2151 Old Brick Road, Glen Allen VA 23060
Telephone: (888) 422-5076 Identification: 770919
Accreditation: &SC, ACBSP, #ARCPA, CACREP, NURSE, OTA, PTAA

† Branch campus of South University, Savannah, GA

South University (G)

301 Bendix Road, Suite 100, Virginia Beach VA 23452
Telephone: (877) 206-1845 Identification: 770920
Accreditation: &SC, ACBSP, CACREP, NURSE, OTA, PTAA

† Branch campus of South University, Savannah, GA

Southern Virginia University (H)

1 University Hill Drive, Buena Vista VA 24416-3097
County: Rockbridge FICE Identification: 003738
Unit ID: 233611
Telephone: (540) 261-8400 Carnegie Class: Bac-A&S
FAX Number: (540) 266-3859 Calendar System: Semester
URL: www.svu.edu
Established: 1867 Annual Undergrad Tuition & Fees: $16,495
Enrollment: 911 Coed
Affiliation or Control: Independent Non-Profit IRS Status: 501(c)3
Highest Offering: Baccalaureate
Accreditation: SC

01 President .... Dr. Reed N. WILCOX
100 Executive VP/Chief of Staff .... Mr. Brett GARCIA
05 Provost .... Dr. Jeremiah JOHN
10 VP Finance .... Mr. Robert E. HUCH
32 VP Student Life .... Mr. Cameron CROWTHER
84 VP Enrollment & Marketing .... Mr. Christopher PENDLETON
111 VP Institutional Advancement .... Mr. Dana OAKS
46 VP Educational Research & Dev .... Dr. Karen M. WALKER
11 Exec Dir of Campus Operations .... Mr. Arthur FURLER
04 Administrative Asst to President .... Mrs. Kristie GIBBONS
06 University Registrar .... Ms. Whitney M. LARSEN
08 Director of Library Services .... Mrs. Stephanie K. HARDY
20 Associate Provost .... Dr. Samuel HIRT
20 Associate Provost .... Dr. Timothy KNUDSON
57 Division Chair Fine & Perf Arts .... Dr. Eric HANSON
79 Division Chair Humanities .... Dr. James LAMBERT
81 Div Chair Science & Mathematics .... Dr. Roger JOHNSON
83 Div Chair Social & Behavioral Sci .... Dr. Iana KONSTANTINOVA
83 Div Chair Business/Family Dev/Psych .... Dr. Jeffrey BATIS
53 Director of Teacher Education .... Ms. Kimberly KEARNEY
09 Dir of Institutional Effectiveness .... Dr. Jon WALLIN
37 Director of Financial Aid .... Mr. Tyson COOPER
15 Human Resources Manager .... Mr. Robbie BAILEY
88 Title IX/Sr Women's Athletic Admin .... Ms. Deidra DRYDEN
96 Senior Accountant .... Mr. Trenton DESPAIN
41 Athletic Director .... Mr. Jason LAMB
29 Alumni Relations Coordinator .... Mr. Cameron CROWTHER
38 Director of Student Support .... Dr. Chad KELLAND
36 Director Career Development Center .... Mr. Cameron T. CROWTHER
85 Foreign Students PDSO .... Ms. Whitney M. LARSEN
19 Director Security/Safety .... Mr. Zachary ELLIOTT
109 Director of Food Services .... Mrs. Effie WALLACE
18 Asst Dir Facilities/Physical Plant .... Mr. Byron PORTER
101 Secretary of the Institution/Board .... Mr. James SKEEN
13 Chief Information Technology Office .... Mr. David JONES
50 Program Coordinator Business .... Dr. John CHAPMAN

Southside College of Health Sciences (I)

430 Clairmont Court, Suite 200,
Colonial Heights VA 23834
County: Independent City FICE Identification: 012744
Unit ID: 233082
Telephone: (804) 765-5800 Carnegie Class: Spec 2-yr-Health
FAX Number: (804) 765-5944 Calendar System: Semester
URL: www.srmconline.com
Established: 1895 Annual Undergrad Tuition & Fees: $14,708
Enrollment: 110 Coed
Affiliation or Control: Proprietary IRS Status: Proprietary
Highest Offering: Associate Degree
Accreditation: ABHES, ADNUR, DMS, RAD

03 Vice President .... Mrs. Cynthia SWINEFORD

Sovah School of Health Professions (J)

142 South Main Street, Danville VA 24541
County: Independent City FICE Identification: 021116
Unit ID: 232724
Telephone: (434) 799-2271 Carnegie Class: Spec 2-yr-Health
FAX Number: (434) 799-3718 Calendar System: Semester
URL: www.danvilleregional.com
Established: 1898 Annual Undergrad Tuition & Fees: N/A
Enrollment: 20 Coed
Affiliation or Control: Proprietary IRS Status: Proprietary
Highest Offering: Associate Degree
Accreditation: ABHES, RAD

01 Director Radiology Pgms/Tech .... Mr. Kevin MURRAY

Standard Healthcare Services College of Nursing (K)

7704 Leesburg Pike, Suite 1000, Falls Church VA 22043
County: Fairfax Identification: 667129
Unit ID: 483814
Telephone: (703) 891-1787 Carnegie Class: Spec 2-yr-Health
FAX Number: (703) 891-1789 Calendar System: Other
URL: www.standardcollege.edu
Established: 2004 Annual Undergrad Tuition & Fees: N/A
Enrollment: 351 Coed
Affiliation or Control: Proprietary IRS Status: Proprietary
Highest Offering: Associate Degree
Accreditation: ABHES

01 Executive Director .... Ms. Isibor J. NOSEGBE
06 Registrar .... Ms. Lisley M. ANCO
05 Director of Education .... Mr. Sakpa S. AMARA
32 Dean of Student Services .... Mrs. Sondra BROWN
37 Financial Aid .... Mrs. Brenda GARCES

07 Admissions .... Mrs. Candice SAVICE
10 Business Office .... Mrs. Nganya M. NANYARO

Stratford University (A)

7777 Leesburg Pike, Suite 1LN, Falls Church VA 22043
County: Fairfax FICE Identification: 025412
Unit ID: 438498
Telephone: (703) 821-8570 Carnegie Class: Masters/L
FAX Number: N/A Calendar System: Quarter
URL: www.stratford.edu
Established: 1976 Annual Undergrad Tuition & Fees: $15,135
Enrollment: 2,282 Coed
Affiliation or Control: Proprietary IRS Status: Proprietary
Highest Offering: Master's
Accreditation: ACICS, CEA, MAAB, NURSE

01 President .... Dr. Richard SHURTZ
12 EVP/Main Campus Director .... Ms. Mary Ann SHURTZ
05 VP Faculty and Academic Affairs .... Dr. Lee SMITH
88 VP Accreditation/State Licensure .... Dr. James FLAGGERT
88 VP International Programs .... Mr. Feroze KHAN
13 Chief Information Officer (CIO) .... Mr. Kevin COUGHENOUR
26 EVP Marketing .... Ms. Mary Ann SHURTZ

† University administration building is located at 3201 Jermantown Rd, Ste 500 Fairfax, VA 22030.

Stratford University Alexandria Campus (B)

2900 Eisenhower Avenue, Alexandria VA 22314
Telephone: (571) 777-0130 Identification: 770856
Accreditation: ACICS, ACFEI, MAAB

Stratford University Woodbridge Campus (C)

14349 Gideon Drive, Woodbridge VA 22192
Telephone: (703) 810-3254 Identification: 770817
Accreditation: ACICS, ACFEI

Sweet Briar College (D)

134 Chapel Road, Sweet Briar VA 24595-9998
County: Amherst FICE Identification: 003742
Unit ID: 233718
Telephone: (434) 381-6100 Carnegie Class: Bac-A&S
FAX Number: (434) 381-6173 Calendar System: Semester
URL: www.sbc.edu
Established: 1901 Annual Undergrad Tuition & Fees: $21,000
Enrollment: 323 Female
Affiliation or Control: Independent Non-Profit IRS Status: 501(c)3
Highest Offering: Master's
Accreditation: SC

01 President .... Dr. Meredith WOO
11 VP Finance/Operations & Auxiliary .... Mr. Luther T. GRIFFITH
04 Exec Asst Office of the President .... Mrs. Dawn GATEWOOD
30 Vice Pres Alumnae Relations/Devel .... Ms. Mary Pope M. HUTSON
09 Dir of Institutional Effectiveness .... Ms. Kim SINHA
05 Dean of Academic Affairs .... Dr. Teresa GARRETT
08 Dir Integrated Information Systems .... Mr. Hooshang FOROUDASTAN
41 Athletics Director .... Ms. Jodi CANFIELD
32 Dean of Student Life/Academic Supp .... Mrs. Marcia THOM-KALEY
15 Director of Human Resources .... Ms. Nickcole MAYNARD-ERRAMI
18 Director Physical Plant .... Vacant
19 Director of Campus Safety .... Mr. Brian MARKER
37 Director Financial Aid .... Ms. Wanda SPRADLEY
40 Book Shop Manager .... Ms. Dottie BOONE
96 Director Purchasing .... Ms. Karen L. THORP
88 Director of Hospitality .... Ms. Cathy MAYS
38 Mental Health Counselor/Health Svcs .... Vacant
36 Director Career Services .... Ms. Barbara WATTS
39 Director Residence Life & Housing .... Mr. Victor LINDSEY
26 Director of Media/Marketing & Comm .... Ms. Melissa RICHARDS
06 Registrar .... Ms. Kim WOOD
07 Director of Admissions Operations .... Ms. Melanie CAMPBELL
13 Chief Info Technology Officer (CIO) .... Mr. Hooshang FOROUDASTAN
25 Chief Contracts/Grants Admin .... Ms. Kathleen PLACIDI
29 Director Alumnae Relations .... Ms. Claire GRIFFITH
54 Chair Engineering/Computer Sci/Phys .... Mr. Henry YOCHUM
47 Director of Agriculture .... Mr. Nathan KLUGER

Union Presbyterian Seminary (E)

3401 Brook Road, Richmond VA 23227-4597
County: Independent City FICE Identification: 003743
Unit ID: 233842
Telephone: (804) 355-0671 Carnegie Class: Spec-4-yr-Faith
FAX Number: (804) 355-3919 Calendar System: Semester
URL: www.upsem.edu
Established: 1812 Annual Graduate Tuition & Fees: N/A
Enrollment: 160 Coed
Affiliation or Control: Presbyterian Church (U.S.A.) IRS Status: 501(c)3
Highest Offering: Doctorate; No Undergraduates
Accreditation: SC, THEOL

01 President .... Dr. Brian K. BLOUNT
10 Vice Pres Finance & Administration .... Mr. Michael B. CASHWELL
30 Vice President Advancement .... Mr. Richard WONG
84 VP Student Life/Enrollment Mgmt .... Ms. Michelle WALKER
05 Dean Union Presby Sem (Richmond) .... Dr. Kenneth J. MCFAYDEN
12 Dean Union Presby Sem (Charlotte) .... Dr. Richard N. BOYCE
20 Associate Dean Academic Programs .... Dr. E. Carson BRISSON
07 Director of Admissions .... Ms. Mairi RENWICK
06 Registrar .... Mr. J. Stanley HARGRAVES
08 Seminary Librarian .... Dr. Christopher RICHARDSON
13 Director Technology Services .... Mr. John R. WILSON
36 Director Student Placement .... Dr. Susan E. FOX
37 Director of Financial Aid .... Ms. Michelle WALKER

University of Fairfax (F)

1813 E. Main Street, Salem VA 24153
County: Independent City Identification: 667094
Telephone: (888) 980-9151 Carnegie Class: Not Classified
FAX Number: N/A Calendar System: Other
URL: www.ufairfax.edu
Established: 2002 Annual Undergrad Tuition & Fees: N/A
Enrollment: N/A Coed
Affiliation or Control: Other IRS Status: Proprietary
Highest Offering: Doctorate
Accreditation: DEAC

01 President .... Mr. Frank LONGAKER
05 Dean/Chief Academic Officer .... Dr. Paula CHERRY
11 Vice President Operations .... Mr. Joel MUSGROVE
26 VP Marketing & Communications .... Mr. Chuck STEENBURGH

† Tuition is $895 per semester credit.

University of Lynchburg (G)

1501 Lakeside Drive, Lynchburg VA 24501-3199
County: Independent City FICE Identification: 003720
Unit ID: 232609
Telephone: (434) 544-8100 Carnegie Class: Masters/M
FAX Number: (434) 544-8539 Calendar System: Semester
URL: www.lynchburg.edu
Established: 1903 Annual Undergrad Tuition & Fees: $39,530
Enrollment: 2,810 Coed
Affiliation or Control: Christian Church (Disciples Of Christ)
IRS Status: 501(c)3
Highest Offering: Doctorate
Accreditation: SC, ACBSP, ARCPA, CAATE, CACREP, EXSC, MUS, NURSE, PTA

01 President .... Dr. Kenneth R. GARREN
05 Provost & VP for Academic Affs .... Dr. Allison JABLONSKI
10 Vice President Business & Finance .... Mr. Steve BRIGHT
111 Sr Vice President Advancement .... Dr. J. Michael BONNETTE
84 Vice Pres Enrollment Management .... Mrs. Rita DETWILER
32 Interim VP & Dean of Student Devel .... Dr. Aaron SMITH
45 VP Inst Planning/Effectiveness .... Dr. Debbie DRISCOLL
26 Assoc VP Communications & Marketing .... Mr. Mike JONES
50 Dean College of Business .... Dr. Nancy HUBBARD
53 Dean Col of Educ/Ldrship Stds/Couns .... Dr. Roger JONES
20 Assoc Provost .... Dr. Charles WALTON
49 Assoc Dean LC Arts & Sciences .... Dr. Oeida HATCHER
81 Assoc Dean School of Sciences .... Dr. William LOKAR
76 Dean College of Health Sciences .... Dr. Rusty SMITH
06 Int Registrar/Academic/Student Info .... Mrs. Susan KENNON
08 Director of the Library .... Mrs. Jennifer HORTON
37 Director of Financial Aid .... Ms. Elayne PELOQUIN
07 Director of Admissions .... Ms. Sharon WALTERS-BOWER
102 Director of Grants Management .... Ms. Carol HARDIN
13 Director Information and Technology .... Mrs. Jackie ALMOND
15 Human Resource Director .... Ms. Linda HALL
19 Director Security/Safety .... Mr. Bob DRISKILL
28 Diversity and Inclusion Officer .... Vacant
29 Director Alumni Relations .... Ms. Heather GARNETT
39 Director Residence Life .... Ms. Kristen COOPER
41 Athletic Director .... Mr. Jon WATERS
96 Purchasing and Logistics Coord .... Mrs. Cynthia PONTON
04 Admin Assistant to the President .... Mrs. Debra WYLAND
09 Director of Institutional Research .... Dr. Debbie DRISCOLL

University of Management & Technology (H)

1901 Fort Myer Drive, Suite 700, Arlington VA 22209-1609
County: Arlington FICE Identification: 041103
Unit ID: 437097
Telephone: (703) 516-0035 Carnegie Class: DU-Mod
FAX Number: (703) 516-0985 Calendar System: Semester
URL: www.umtweb.edu
Established: 1998 Annual Undergrad Tuition & Fees: $9,450
Enrollment: 1,176 Coed
Affiliation or Control: Proprietary IRS Status: Proprietary
Highest Offering: Doctorate
Accreditation: DEAC

01 President .... Dr. Yanping CHEN
05 Academic Dean .... Dr. J. Davidson FRAME

University of Mary Washington (I)

1301 College Avenue, Fredericksburg VA 22401-5300
County: Independent City FICE Identification: 003746
Unit ID: 232681
Telephone: (540) 654-1000 Carnegie Class: Masters/M
FAX Number: (540) 654-1073 Calendar System: Semester
URL: www.umw.edu
Established: 1908 Annual Undergrad Tuition & Fees (In-State): $12,714
Enrollment: 4,808 Coed
Affiliation or Control: State IRS Status: 501(c)3
Highest Offering: Master's
Accreditation: SC, NURSE

01 President .... Dr. Troy PAINO
05 Provost .... Dr. Nina MIKHALEVSKY
100 Chief of Staff .... Dr. Jeffrey MCCLURKEN
10 VP for Admin & Finance .... Mr. Paul MESSPLAY
32 Vice President Student Affairs .... Dr. Juliette LANDPHAIR
111 Vice Pres for Advance & Univ Rels .... Ms. Lisa BOWLING
102 CEO of UMW Foundation .... Mr. Jeffrey W. ROUNTREE
13 Chief Information Officer .... Mr. Hall CHESHIRE
88 Exec Dir Ctr Economic Development .... Mr. Brian J. BAKER
22 VP Equity & Access/Chief Div Ofcr .... Ms. Sabrina C. JOHNSON
15 Executive Director Human Resources .... Ms. Beth WILLIAMS
105 Director of Digital Communication .... Dr. Anand RAO
21 Director of Business Svcs .... Ms. Kathy SANDOR
20 Assoc Provost for Academic Affairs .... Dr. John T. MORELLO
18 Assoc Vice Pres Facilities Services .... Mr. John P. WILTENMUTH
84 Vice Pres for Enrollment Mgmt .... Ms. Kimberley BUSTER-WILLIAMS
111 Assoc VP Univ Advance/Alumni Rel .... Mr. Kenneth L. STEEN
53 Dean of College of Education .... Dr. Peter KELLY
50 Dean College of Business .... Dr. Lynne RICHARDSON
49 Dean College of Arts & Sciences .... Dr. Keith MELLINGER
35 Assoc VP & Dean of Student Life .... Mr. Cedric B. RUCKER
37 Director of Financial Aid .... Mr. Timothy SAULNIER
09 Director of Institutional Research .... Mr. Mathew C. WILKERSON
116 Director of Internal Audit .... Mr. Davis MCCRORY
39 Asst Dean for Res Life & Housing .... Mr. David FLEMING
06 Registrar .... Ms. Rita DUNSTON
41 Interim Athletic Director .... Mr. Patrick CATULLO
08 University Librarian .... Ms. Rosemary ARNESON
88 Director of Publications .... Ms. Neva S. TRENIS
88 Director of Dodd Auditorium .... Mr. Doug NOBLE
121 Assoc Provost Academic Engagement .... Dr. Timothy O'DONNELL
19 Chief of Police .... Mr. Michael W. HALL
29 Exec Director Alumni Relations .... Mr. Mark THADEN
107 Ex Dir Continuing/Professional Stds .... Ms. Kimberly YOUNG
38 Director of Talley Center .... Mr. Tevya ZUKOR
28 Director of Disability Resources .... Ms. Jessica MACHADO
23 University Physician/Health Center .... Ms. Nancy WANG
96 Director of Procurement Services .... Ms. Melva KISHPAUGH
09 Assoc Provost for Inst Analysis/Eff .... Dr. Debra SCHLEEF
26 Assoc VP University Relations .... Ms. Anna B. BILLINGSLEY
27 Director Media & Public Relations .... Ms. Marty G. MORRISON
27 Director of University Marketing .... Mr. Malcolm HOLMES
88 Director of Design Services .... Ms. AJ NEWELL
04 Executive Office Manager .... Ms. Paula ZERO
101 Clerk of Board of Visitors .... Dr. Jeff MCCLURKEN
104 Dir Ctr for International Education .... Dr. Jose SAINZ
30 Director of Development .... Mr. Zachary HATCHER
44 Director Annual Giving .... Mrs. Elizabeth HUNSINGER

University of North America (J)

12750 Fair Lakes Circle, Fairfax VA 22033
County: Fairfax Identification: 667241
Telephone: (571) 633-9651 Carnegie Class: Not Classified
FAX Number: (703) 890-3372 Calendar System: Semester
URL: www.uona.edu
Established: Annual Undergrad Tuition & Fees: N/A
Enrollment: N/A Coed
Affiliation or Control: Independent Non-Profit IRS Status: 501(c)3
Highest Offering: Master's
Accreditation: ACICS

00 CEO .... Marty MARTIN
01 President .... Jill MARTIN
05 VP of Academic Affairs .... Peter WEST
20 VP of Educational Operations .... Jason KOO
37 Director Financial Affairs .... Vacant

University of the Potomac (K)

7799 Leesburg Pike, Suite 200, Falls Church VA 22043
Telephone: (202) 521-1290 Identification: 666178
Accreditation: &M

† Regional accreditation is carried under the parent institution in Washington, DC.

University of Richmond (L)

28 Westhampton Way, Richmond VA 23173-1903
County: Independent City FICE Identification: 003744
Unit ID: 233374
Telephone: (804) 289-8000 Carnegie Class: Bac-A&S
FAX Number: (804) 287-6540 Calendar System: Semester
URL: www.richmond.edu
Established: 1830 Annual Undergrad Tuition & Fees: $52,610
Enrollment: 4,023 Coordinate
Affiliation or Control: Independent Non-Profit IRS Status: 501(c)3
Highest Offering: Doctorate
Accreditation: SC, CAEPT, LAW

01 President .... Dr. Ronald A. CRUTCHER
05 Executive VP & Provost .... Dr. Jeffrey LEGRO
10 EVP & COO Business & Finance .... Mr. David B. HALE
32 Vice President Student Affairs .... Dr. Stephen D. BISESE
111 Vice President Advancement .... Vacant
13 VP & Chief Information Officer .... Mr. Keith J. MCINTOSH

84 Vice Pres Enrollment Management ....Dr. Stephanie DUPAUL
45 Vice President Planning & Policy ....Dr. Lori G. SCHUYLER
101 VP & Secretary Board of Trustees ....Dr. Ann Lloyd BREEDEN
04 Assistant to President ....Ms. Ashleigh BROCK
88 President & CIO Spider Mgmt Company ....Mr. Rob BLANDFORD
15 Senior Assoc VP Human Resources ....Mr. Carl K. SORENSEN
18 AVP for Facilities & Univ Architect ....Mr. Andrew S. MCBRIDE
29 Asst VP Alumni & Career Services ....Ms. Denise D. SMITH
102 Asst VP Foundation/Corp/Govt Rels ...Ms. Michelle E. WAMSLEY
42 University Chaplain ....Rev. Craig T. KOCHER
07 Assoc VP and Dean of Admissions ....Mr. Gil VILLANUEVA
08 University Librarian ....Mr. Kevin BUTTERFIELD
09 Dir Institutional Effectiveness ....Ms. Melanie JENKINS
06 University Registrar ....Ms. Susan D. BREEDEN
37 AVP & Director ....Mr. William B. BRYAN
36 Dir Career Development Center ....Ms. Leslie W. STEVENSON
38 Director of CAPS ....Dr. Peter O. LEVINESS
96 Director Strategic Sourcing ....Ms. Jean C. HINES
35 Assoc VP Student Development ....Dr. Tina Q. CADE
41 Director of Athletics ....Mr. John HARDT
104 Director Study Abroad ....Ms. Michele D. COX
105 Director Web Services ....Mr. Eric F. PALMER
33 Dean of Richmond College ....Dr. Joseph R. BOEHMAN
34 Dean Westhampton College ....Dr. Mia R. GENONI
49 Dean School of Arts & Sciences ....Dr. Patrice D. RANKINE
50 Dean School of Business ....Dr. Mickey QUIÑONES
61 Dean School of Law ....Dr. Wendy C. PERDUE
51 Dean School Continuing Studies ....Dr. Jamelle WILSON
88 Dean Jepson School Leader Stds ....Dr. Sandra J. PEART
19 Assc VP Public Sfty/Chief of Police ....Mr. David M. MCCOY
23 Director Health Center ....Dr. Lynne P. DEANE
26 Asst VP for Communications ....Mr. John M. BARRY
40 Manager University Bookstore ....Ms. Liz ST. JOHN
28 Director Common Ground ....Dr. Glyn HUGHES
39 Director Student Housing ....Mr. Patrick B. BENNER
43 VP & General Counsel ....Ms. Shannon E. SINCLAIR
91 Dir Enterprise Application ....Mr. Lee PARKER, III
44 Director Annual Giving ....Ms. Kim LEBAR

University of Virginia (A)

1827 University Avenue, Charlottesville VA 22904

County: Independent City — FICE Identification: 003745
Unit ID: 234076
Telephone: (434) 924-0311 — Carnegie Class: DU-Highest
FAX Number: (434) 924-0938 — Calendar System: Semester
URL: www.virginia.edu
Established: 1819 — Annual Undergrad Tuition & Fees (In-State): $17,653
Enrollment: 24,360 — Coed
Affiliation or Control: State — IRS Status: 501(c)3
Highest Offering: Doctorate
Accreditation: SC, CAATE, CACREP, CAEP, CAEPT, CLPSY, DENT, DIETI, IPSY, LAW, LSAR, MED, NURSE, PAST, PCSAS, PH, PLNG, PSPSY, SP

01 President ....Mr. James E. RYAN
00 Rector ....Mr. Frank M. CONNER, III
101 Secretary Board of Visitors ....Ms. Susan G. HARRIS
05 Exec Vice President & Provost ....Ms. M. Elizabeth MAGILL
03 Exec Vice Pres/Chief Operating Ofcr ....Ms. Jennifer (J.J.) WAGNER DAVIS
43 University Counsel ....Mr. Timothy HEAPHY
116 Chief Audit Executive ....Ms. Carolyn SAINT
100 Asst VP & Chief of Staff ....Ms. Margaret S. GRUNDY
22 Assoc VP Equal Opp Pgms/Civ Rights ...Ms. Catherine C. SPEAR
17 Exec Vice Pres for Health Affairs ....Ms. Pamela M. SUTTON-WALLACE
23 CEO Medical Center ....Ms. Pamela M. SUTTON-WALLACE
88 Health System CFO ....Mr. Douglas E. LISCHKE
111 Sr Vice Pres for Advancement ....Mr. John C. JEFFRIES, JR.
10 Vice President for Finance ....Ms. Melody BIANCHETTO
115 Chief Investment Officer ....Mr. Robert DURDEN
88 Exec Director The Jefferson Trust ....Mr. Wayne COZART
32 Vice Pres/Chief Student Affs Ofcr ....Ms. Patricia M. LAMPKIN
35 Associate VP/Dean of Students ....Mr. Allen W. GROVES
36 Assoc VP Career & Prof Development ....Mr. Everette FORTNER
93 Dean African-American Affairs ....Dr. Maurice APPREY
23 Exec Director Student Health ....Dr. Christopher HOLSTEGE
39 Exec Dir Housing & Residence Life ....Ms. Gay PEREZ
35 Assoc VP for Student Affairs ....Ms. Susan M. DAVIS
40 Assistant Director of UVa Bookstore ....Mr. Roy CADOFF
46 Vice Pres for Research ....Mr. Melur RAMASUBRAMANIAN
25 Asst VP Research Admin ....Vacant
28 VP/Chief Officer Diversity/Equity ....Mr. Marcus L. MARTIN
41 Dir Intercollegiate Athletic Pgms ....Ms. Carla WILLIAMS
15 VP/Chief Human Resources Officer ....Ms. Kelley STUCK
26 VP Communication/Chief Mktg Officer ....Mr. David W. MARTEL
12 Chancellor UVA's College at Wise ....Ms. Donna P. HENRY
11 Sr Vice President for Operations ....Ms. Colette SHEEHY
21 Assoc VP Business Operations ....Mr. Richard A. KOVATCH
88 Architect for the University ....Ms. Alice J. RAUCHER
88 University Building Official ....Mr. Ben HAYS
18 Assoc VP & Chief Facilities Officer .....Mr. Donald E. SUNDGREN
37 Asst Vice Pres Student Finan Svcs ....Mr. Stephen A. KIMATA
96 Director of Procurement Services ....Mr. John MCHUGH
13 VP for Information Technology ....Mr. Ronald R. HUTCHINS
20 Vice Prov for Academic Affairs ....Mr. Archie L. HOLMES, JR.
108 Assoc Prov Inst Assess & Studies ....Ms. Christina MORELL
88 Vice Prov Faculty Affairs ....Ms. Manté BRANDT-PEARCE
100 Vice Prov for Admin/Chief of Staff ....Ms. Anda L. WEBB
88 Vice Prov for the Arts ....Mr. Jody K. KIELBASA
88 Vice Prov for Acad Outreach ....Mr. Louis NELSON
88 Vice Provost for Global Affairs ....Mr. Stephen D. MULL
06 Registrar ....Ms. Laura HAWTHORNE
07 Dean of Admission ....Mr. Gregory W. ROBERTS
61 Dean School of Law ....Ms. Risa L. GOLUBOFF
49 Dean School of Arts & Sciences ....Mr. Ian B. BAUCOM
63 Dean School of Medicine ....Dr. David S. WILKES
66 Dean School of Nursing ....Dr. Dorrie K. FONTAINE
54 Dean Schl Engr/Applied Science ....Mr. Craig H. BENSON
48 Dean School of Architecture ....Ms. Ila BERMAN
50 Dean School of Commerce ....Mr. Carl P. ZEITHAML
80 Dean Sch Leadership/Public Policy ....Mr. Allan C. STAM
53 Dean School of Education ....Mr. Robert C. PIANTA
50 Dean Grad School Business Admin ....Mr. Scott C. BEARDSLEY
51 Dean Cont/Professional Studies ....Mr. Alejandro HERNANDEZ
88 Director Applied Research Inst ....Ms. Joan M. BIENVENUE
88 Director Center for Politics ....Mr. Larry J. SABATO
88 Director Data Science Inst ....Mr. Philip E. BOURNE
08 Univ Librarian/Dean of Libraries ....Mr. John M. UNSWORTH
87 Dir Summer & Special Academic Pgms ....Mr. Dudley J. DOANE
104 Dir International Studies Office ....Mr. Dudley J. DOANE
19 Chief of Police ....Mr. Tommye S. SUTTON
94 Dir Study in Women Gender Sexuality ....Ms. Charlotte PATTERSON

The University of Virginia's College at Wise (B)

One College Avenue, Wise VA 24293-4412

County: Wise — FICE Identification: 003747
Unit ID: 233897
Telephone: (276) 328-0100 — Carnegie Class: Bac-A&S
FAX Number: (276) 376-1012 — Calendar System: Semester
URL: www.uvawise.edu
Established: 1954 — Annual Undergrad Tuition & Fees (In-State): $10,119
Enrollment: 2,095 — Coed
Affiliation or Control: State — IRS Status: 501(c)3
Highest Offering: Baccalaureate
Accreditation: SC, CAEP, NURSE

01 Chancellor ....Dr. Donna P. HENRY
05 Provost/Vice Chan for Acad Affairs ....Dr. Sanders HUGUENIN
111 Vice Chanc for Advancement ....Ms. Valerie S. LAWSON
10 Vice Chanc Finance/Administration ....Mr. Sim E. EWING
84 Vice Chancellor Enrollment Mgmt ....Mr. Chris DEARTH
20 Academic Dean ....Dr. Amelia J. HARRIS
32 Vice Chancellor for Student Affairs ....Mrs. Jewell B. WORLEY
21 Comptroller ....Mrs. Kristy ROBERTSON
06 Registrar ....Ms. Narda PORTER
08 Director of the Library ....Mr. Robin P. BENKE
15 Director of Human Resources ....Ms. Stephanie D. PERRY
88 Director of College Services ....Mr. Joseph B. KISER
26 Director of News & Media Relations ....Ms. Kathy STILL
29 Director of Alumni Relations ....Ms. Elizabeth BOYD
37 Director of Financial Aid ....Ms. Rebecca HUFFMAN
35 Asst Dir of Student Activities ....Mr. Nathan RASNAKE
36 Dir of Discovery & Planning ....Ms. Neva BRYAN
38 Personal Counselor/Health Services ....Ms. Sara SCHILL
19 Campus Police Chief ....Mr. Ronnie SHORTT
12 Site Director UVA-Wise Programs ....Ms. Courtney L. CONNER
27 Associate Vice Chancellor of Info ....Dr. P. Scott BEVINS
24 Director of Media Services ....Ms. Rosa BOTT
40 Bookstore Manager ....Mr. Scott LAWSON
39 Director of Residence Life ....Mr. Josh JUSTICE
108 Director Institutional Assessment ....Mr. David KLOCEK
100 Chief of Staff ....Ms. Huda ADEN

Virginia Beach Theological Seminary (C)

2221 Centerville Turnpike, Virginia Beach VA 23464-6847

County: Virginia Beach — FICE Identification: 039663
Unit ID: 449834
Telephone: (757) 479-3706 — Carnegie Class: Spec-4-yr-Faith
FAX Number: N/A — Calendar System: Semester
URL: www.vbts.edu
Established: 1995 — Annual Graduate Tuition & Fees: N/A
Enrollment: 34 — Coed
Affiliation or Control: Baptist — IRS Status: 501(c)3
Highest Offering: Doctorate; No Undergraduates
Accreditation: TRACS

01 President ....Dr. Daniel K. DAVEY
05 Chief Academic Officer ....Dr. Eric J. LEHNER
07 Director of Admissions/Registrar ....Mr. Edward R. ESTES, IV
10 Financial Officer ....Capt. Tony A. BRAZAS
08 Head Librarian ....Dr. Michael H. WINDSOR

Virginia Bible College (D)

1006 Williamstown Dr, Dumfries VA 22026

County: Prince William — Identification: 667327
Telephone: (703) 445-9056 — Carnegie Class: Not Classified
FAX Number: (703) 445-9057 — Calendar System: Quarter
URL: vabiblecollege.org
Established: 2011 — Annual Undergrad Tuition & Fees: N/A
Enrollment: N/A — Coed
Affiliation or Control: Independent Non-Profit — IRS Status: 501(c)3
Highest Offering: Doctorate
Accreditation: @TRACS

01 President ....Dr. Derek GRIER
05 VP of Academic & Student Affs ....Dr. Shennell JANUARY
58 Director of Graduate Studies ....Dr. James BOWERS
06 Registrar ....Ms. Monique MAXWELL
08 Librarian ....Ms. Donna MCDONALD

Virginia Christian University (E)

14012-F Sullyfield Circle, Chantilly VA 20151

County: Fairfax — Identification: 667352
Telephone: (703) 629-1281 — Carnegie Class: Not Classified
FAX Number: (703) 657-0690 — Calendar System: Semester
URL: vacuniv.org/
Established: 2005 — Annual Undergrad Tuition & Fees: N/A
Enrollment: N/A — Coed
Affiliation or Control: Presbyterian Church In America — IRS Status: 501(c)3
Highest Offering: Master's
Accreditation: @BI

01 President ....Dr. Thomas RHEE
05 Academic Dean & Dir Graduate Pgm ....Dr. Sunik HWANG
15 Vice Pres & Dir Human Resources ....Dr. Joshua PARK
32 Dean of Students ....Dr. Hyejoo LEE
10 Director of Finance ....Mr. Dae C. KIM
06 Director of Registration ....Ms. Sooyoung YIM
13 Director of Technology ....Mr. Junwhan KIM

Virginia Commonwealth University (F)

901 W Franklin Street, Box 842527,
Richmond VA 23284-2527

County: Independent City — FICE Identification: 003735
Unit ID: 234030
Telephone: (804) 828-0100 — Carnegie Class: DU-Highest
FAX Number: N/A — Calendar System: Semester
URL: www.vcu.edu
Established: 1838 — Annual Undergrad Tuition & Fees (In-State): $14,493
Enrollment: 30,675 — Coed
Affiliation or Control: State — IRS Status: 501(c)3
Highest Offering: Doctorate
Accreditation: SC, ANEST, ART, CACREP, CAEPN, CAMPEP, CEA, CIDA, CLPSY, COPSY, DANCE, DENT, DH, DIETI, EMT, FEPAC, HSA, IPSY, #JOUR, MED, MT, MUS, NMT, NURSE, OT, PAST, PDPSY, PH, PHAR, PLNG, PTA, RAD, RTT, SPAA, SW, THEA

01 President/Pres & Chair VCU Hlth Sys ....Dr. Michael RAO
05 Provost & VP for Academic Affairs ....Dr. Gail HACKETT
17 VP Health Sci/CEO VCU Health Sys ....Dr. Marsha RAPPLEY
17 VP Clinical Svcs/CEO VCU Hospital ....Ms. Deborah DAVIS
10 SVP & Chief Financial Officer ....Ms. Karol GRAY
46 Vice President for Research ....Dr. Francis L. MACRINA
111 VP Development/Alumni Relations ....Mr. Jay DAVENPORT
86 Exec Director Government Relations ....Ms. Karah L. GUNTHER
32 Sr Vice Prov Student Affairs ....Dr. Charles J. KLINK
88 Vice Prov for Life Sciences ....Dr. Robert M. TOMBES
09 Asst VProv Inst Rsrch & Decision Su ....Ms. Monal PATEL
84 VProv Strategic Enrollment Mgmt ....Dr. Tomika LEGRANDE
13 Chief Information Officer Tech Svcs .....Mr. Alexander L. HENSON
18 Assoc VP Facilities Management ....Mr. Richard F. SLIWOSKI
88 AVP Strategic Enrollment Svcs ....Ms. Anjour HARRIS
15 Asst Vice Pres for Human Resource ....Ms. Cathleen C. BURKE
08 University Librarian ....Mr. John E. ULMSCHNEIDER
43 Interim University Counsel ....Mr. Jake A. BELUE
41 Vice Pres & Director of Athletics ....Mr. Edward K. MCLAUGHLIN
21 Asst Vice Pres of Business Services ......Ms. Diane L. REYNOLDS
39 Asst VP/Exec Dir Res Life/Housing ....Mr. Curtis ERWIN
06 Univ Registrar & Dir Records/Regis ....Mr. Bernard C. HAMM
37 Executive Director of Financial Aid ....Mr. Marc VERNON
38 Dir of Counseling Services ....Dr. Jihad N. AZIZ
36 Int Dir University Career Center ....Ms. Haley SIMS
35 Assoc Vice Prov/Dean Student Affs ....Dr. Reuban B. RODRIGUEZ
29 Assoc VP Alumni Relations ....Mr. Jason DAVENPORT
88 Exec Dir Global Education Office ....Dr. R. McKenna BROWN
88 Dir Ctr for Environmental Studies ....Dr. Gregory C. GARMAN
25 Sr Assoc VP Rsrch Admin/Compliance ....Ms. Susan E. ROBB
19 Asst Vice Pres Campus Police ....Mr. John A. VENUTI
31 VProv/Div Community Engagement .....Dr. Catherine W. HOWARD
92 Dean Honors College ....Dr. Barry L. FALK
67 Dean of Pharmacy ....Dr. Joseph T. DIPIRO
66 Dean of School of Nursing ....Dr. Jean GIDDENS
63 Dean of School of Medicine ....Dr. Peter F. BUCKLEY
53 Dean School of Education ....Dr. Andrew P. DAIRE
52 Dean of Dentistry ....Dr. David C. SARRETT
50 Dean School of Business ....Mr. Ed GRIER
49 Dean Humanities & Sciences ....Dr. Monsterrat FUENTES
57 Dean School of Arts ....Mr. Shawn BRIXEY
70 Dean School of Social Work ....Dr. Beth ANGELL
76 Dean Allied Health Professions ....Dr. Cecil B. DRAIN
58 Dean Graduate School ....Dr. F. Douglas BOUDINOT
54 Dean of School of Engineering ....Dr. Barbara D. BOYAN
96 Director Procurement Svcs ....Ms. Brenda MOWEN
26 Vice President University Relations ....Ms. Pamela D. LEPLEY
104 Director Study Abroad ....Ms. Stephanie DAVENPORT TIGNOR
45 Sr Exec Dir Strategy & Pres Admin ....Dr. Kevin ALLISON
106 Exec Director Online @VCU ....Ms. Monica J. OROZCO
90 Director Academic Technologies ....Ms. Colleen BISHOP
108 Dir Academic Integrity & Assessment ....Dr. Scott F. OATES
22 VP Inclusive Excellence ....Dr. Aashir NASIM
105 Deputy Dir Application Services ....Mr. James B. YUCHA
30 Sr Assoc VP for Development ....Mr. Magnus H. JOHNSSON
44 Executive Director Annual Giving ....Mr. Michael P. ANDREWS

*Virginia Community College System Office (A)

300 Arboretum Place, Suite 200, Richmond VA 23236
County: Independent City FICE Identification: 008904
Telephone: (804) 819-4901 Carnegie Class: N/A
FAX Number: N/A
URL: www.vccs.edu

01 Chancellor ... Dr. Glenn DUBOIS
05 Sr Vice Chanc Acad/Workforce Pgms ... Dr. Sharon MORRISSEY
10 Sr Vice Chanc Admin/Finance/Tech ... Dr. Craig HERNDON
13 Chief Information Officer ... Dr. Michael RUSSELL
111 Vice Chanc Institutional Advance ... Dr. Jennifer SAGER GENTRY
15 Assoc Vice Chanc Human Resource Svc ... Dr. Christopher LEE
18 Assoc Vice Chanc/Facility Mgmt ... Mr. Bert JONES
43 General Counsel ... Ms. Greer SAUNDERS
116 Director of Internal Audit ... Mr. Whit MADERE
21 Controller ... Mr. Randall ELLIS
04 Exec Assistant to the Chancellor ... Ms. Rose Marie OWEN

*Blue Ridge Community College (B)

PO Box 80, Weyers Cave VA 24486-0080
County: Augusta FICE Identification: 006819
Unit ID: 231536
Telephone: (540) 234-9261 Carnegie Class: Assoc/HT-Mix Trad/Non
FAX Number: (540) 234-8189 Calendar System: Semester
URL: www.brcc.edu
Established: 1967 Annual Undergrad Tuition & Fees (In-State): $5,364
Enrollment: 4,200 Coed
Affiliation or Control: State IRS Status: 501(c)3
Highest Offering: Associate Degree
Accreditation: SC, ADNUR

02 President ... Dr. John A. DOWNEY
05 Vice Pres Instruction/Student Svcs ... Dr. Robert YOUNG
10 VP Finance/Administration ... Ms. Cynthia PAGE
15 Director of Human Resources ... Mr. Tim NICELY
30 Exec Dir Development/Foundation ... Ms. Amy L. KIGER
20 Dean of Academic Affairs ... Ms. Marlena JARBOE
20 Dean of Academic Affairs ... Dr. David URSO
51 Dean of Continuing Education ... Dr. Kevin B. RATLIFF
32 Dean Student Services ... Ms. Annette WILLIAMS
08 Head Librarian ... Mr. Kyle MCCARRELL
26 Chief Public Relations Officer ... Ms. Bridget BAYLOR
06 Registrar/Admissions ... Ms. Lisa ADKINS
21 Director of Finance & Facilities ... Ms. Franki HAMPTON
09 Director Institutional Research ... Dr. Susan E. CROSBY
37 Financial Aid Coordinator ... Ms. Megan HARTLESS
36 Career Services/Recruitment Coord ... Ms. Carmel MURPHY-NORRIS
84 Enrollment Services Assistant ... Ms. Karen WELCHER

*Central Virginia Community College (C)

3506 Wards Road, Lynchburg VA 24502-2498
County: Independent City FICE Identification: 004988
Unit ID: 231697
Telephone: (434) 832-7600 Carnegie Class: Assoc/HT-High Non
FAX Number: (434) 386-4700 Calendar System: Semester
URL: www.centralvirginia.edu
Established: 1966 Annual Undergrad Tuition & Fees (In-State): $4,838
Enrollment: 4,128 Coed
Affiliation or Control: State IRS Status: 501(c)3
Highest Offering: Associate Degree
Accreditation: SC, COARC, EMT, RAD

02 President ... Dr. John CAPPS
05 VP Student & Academic Services ... Dr. Muriel MICKLES
10 Vice President Finance & Admin Svcs ... Mr. Lewis BRYANT, III
111 VP Inst Advancement/Exec Dir Fndn ... Mr. Christopher BRYANT
13 Vice Pres of Information Technology ... Mr. David LIGHTFOOT
45 Dean Inst Effectiveness/Planning ... Ms. Kristen OGDEN
32 Dean of Student Services ... Ms. Patricia SAFFIOTI
09 Director of Strategic Initiatives ... Mr. William SANDIDGE
29 Director Alumni/Public Relations ... Mr. Kenneth BUNCH
06 College Registrar ... Ms. Karen ALEXANDER
84 Dean of Enrollment Management ... Mr. Michael FARRIS
15 Human Resource Director ... Mr. Randall FRANKLIN
56 Distance Education Supervisor ... Mr. Ed MCGEE
60 Coordinator of Library Services ... Mr. Michael T. FEIN
79 Dean Humanities/Social Science ... Dr. Muriel MICKLES
50 AVP of Business & Allied Health ... Dr. James LEMONS
81 Dean of Science/Math/Engineering ... Dr. Cynthia WALLIN
04 General Administration Coordinator ... Ms. Dianne SYKES

*Dabney S. Lancaster Community College (D)

1000 Dabney Drive, Clifton Forge VA 24422-1000
County: Alleghany FICE Identification: 004996
Unit ID: 231873
Telephone: (540) 863-2820 Carnegie Class: Assoc/HT-High Non
FAX Number: (540) 863-2915 Calendar System: Semester
URL: www.dslcc.edu
Established: 1962 Annual Undergrad Tuition & Fees (In-State): $4,725
Enrollment: 1,260 Coed
Affiliation or Control: State IRS Status: 501(c)3
Highest Offering: Associate Degree
Accreditation: SC, ACFEI, ADNUR

02 President ... Dr. John J. RAINONE
05 Vice President of Academic Affairs ... Dr. Benjamin WORTH
10 Vice President Finance/Admin Svcs ... Mrs. Angela GRAHAM
51 VP Continuing Educ/Workforce Svcs ... Mr. Gary S. KEENER
09 AVP of Institutional Effectiveness ... Dr. Matthew MCGRAW
32 Director of Student Services ... Mr. Joseph HAGY
111 Director of Inst Advancement ... Ms. Rachael G. THOMPSON
08 Director of Learning Resources ... Ms. Nova WRIGHT
13 Technical Services Manager ... Mr. Wayne RAUENZAHN
15 Director of Human Resources ... Ms. April TOLLEY
18 Buildings & Grounds Supervisor ... Mr. Steven N. RICHARDS
21 Business Manager ... Ms. Deidre WOLFE
07 Admissions Officer ... Ms. Suzanne OSTLING
37 Coord of Student Financial Aid ... Mrs. Coty LANFORD
30 Marketing & Development Coordinator ... Ms. Jodi BURGESS
04 Executive Asst to President ... Ms. Phyllis BARTLEY
06 Records Clerk ... Miss Rebecca STOVER

*Danville Community College (E)

1008 S Main Street, Danville VA 24541-4088
County: Independent City FICE Identification: 003758
Unit ID: 231882
Telephone: (434) 797-2222 Carnegie Class: Assoc/MT-VT-High Non
FAX Number: (434) 797-8514 Calendar System: Semester
URL: www.danville.edu
Established: 1967 Annual Undergrad Tuition & Fees (In-State): $4,710
Enrollment: 3,101 Coed
Affiliation or Control: State IRS Status: 501(c)3
Highest Offering: Associate Degree
Accreditation: SC

02 President ... Dr. Jacqueline GILL-POWELL
05 Vice Pres Academic/Student Services ... Dr. Debra HOLLEY
10 Vice Pres Financial/Admin Services ... Mr. Charles TOOTHMAN
30 Vice President of Development ... Mr. Shannon HAIR
09 Dir of Plng/Effectiveness/Research ... Mr. Cory POTTER
26 Public Relations/Marketing Manager ... Mr. Bobby ROACH
04 Admin Assistant to the President ... Ms. Connie P. WANN
08 Chief Library Officer ... Mr. Christopher FORD
103 Asst Vice Pres Workforce Services ... Mr. Jimmie TICKLE
15 Chief Human Resources Officer ... Ms. Ann TAYLOR
37 Director Student Financial Aid ... Ms. Angela TURNER

*Eastern Shore Community College (F)

29300 Lankford Highway, Melfa VA 23410-9755
County: Accomack FICE Identification: 003748
Unit ID: 232052
Telephone: (757) 789-1789 Carnegie Class: Assoc/MT-VT-Mix Trad/Non
FAX Number: (757) 789-1737 Calendar System: Semester
URL: www.es.vccs.edu
Established: 1971 Annual Undergrad Tuition & Fees (In-State): $4,800
Enrollment: 644 Coed
Affiliation or Control: State IRS Status: 501(c)3
Highest Offering: Associate Degree
Accreditation: SC

02 President ... Dr. James M. SHAEFFER
05 VP of Acad/Student Affs & WDS ... Vacant
11 Assoc VP Administration ... Ms. Eve BELOTE
32 Coordinator of Student Services ... Mrs. Cheryll MILLS
09 Director of Institutional Research ... Ms. Judith GRIER
26 Marketing and Development Officer ... Mr. William LECATO
06 Registrar ... Mrs. Artima TAYLOR-THORNTON
37 Financial Aid Coordinator ... Ms. Carole READ
15 Human Resource Officer ... Ms. Beth LUNDE
18 Chief Facilities/Physical Plant ... Vacant
04 Admin Assistant to the President ... Ms. Bette CORNELL
07 Admissions Officer ... Vacant
19 Director Security/Safety ... Mr. David BRANCH
30 Director of Development ... Vacant

*Germanna Community College (G)

2130 Germanna Highway, Locust Grove VA 22508-2102
County: Orange FICE Identification: 008660
Unit ID: 232195
Telephone: (540) 423-9030 Carnegie Class: Assoc/HT-Mix Trad/Non
FAX Number: (540) 727-3207 Calendar System: Semester
URL: www.germanna.edu
Established: 1970 Annual Undergrad Tuition & Fees (In-State): $4,913
Enrollment: 6,688 Coed
Affiliation or Control: State IRS Status: 501(c)3
Highest Offering: Associate Degree
Accreditation: SC, ADNUR, DA, PTAA

02 President ... Dr. Janet GULLICKSON
04 Exec Assistant to the President ... Ms. Pamela JACKSON
05 VP Academic Affairs & Workforce Dev ... Dr. Jeanne WESLEY
10 VP Finance & Administrative Svcs ... Dr. John M. DAVIS
32 Dean of Student Services ... Ms. Pam FREDERICK
45 Director Planning/Research/Effectiv ... Dr. Nicole MUNDAY
08 Head Librarian ... Ms. Tamara REMHOF
06 Registrar ... Ms. Cheri MAEA
72 Dean Professional & Technical Study ... Ms. Denise TALLEY
106 Dean Distance Educ & Lrng Resources ... Dr. Yanyan YONG
66 Dean of Nursing & Health Technology ... Dr. Patti LISK
15 Associate VP of Human Resources ... Mrs. Laurie BOURNE
18 Building & Ground Supervisor ... Mr. Garland FENWICK
26 Director of Marketing ... Mr. James SOLOMON
49 Dean of Arts & Sciences ... Dr. Shashuna GRAY
103 Dean of Workforce Prof Development ... Ms. Martha O'KEEFE
19 Chief of Police ... Mr. Craig BRANCH
37 Director Student Financial Aid ... Mr. Aaron WHITACRE

*J. Sargeant Reynolds Community College (H)

PO Box 85622, Richmond VA 23285-5622
County: Henrico FICE Identification: 003759
Unit ID: 232414
Telephone: (804) 371-3000 Carnegie Class: Assoc/MT-VT-Mix Trad/Non
FAX Number: (804) 371-3650 Calendar System: Semester
URL: www.reynolds.edu
Established: 1972 Annual Undergrad Tuition & Fees (In-State): $4,998
Enrollment: 9,334 Coed
Affiliation or Control: State IRS Status: 501(c)3
Highest Offering: Associate Degree
Accreditation: SC, ACFEI, ADNUR, COARC, DA, EMT, MLTAD, OPD

02 President ... Dr. Paula P. PANDO
05 Vice President Academic Affairs ... Dr. Kimbrly A. BRITT
111 Vice President Advancement ... Mrs. Elizabeth S. LITTLEFIELD
103 VP Comm Col Workforce Alliance ... Mr. Wesley SMITH
10 VP Finance and Administration ... Ms. Amelia M. BRADSHAW
32 VP Student Affairs/Title IX Coord ... Vacant
45 Assoc VP Policy/Inst Effectiveness ... Dr. Timothy MERRILL
79 Dean School of Humanities/Soc Sci ... Vacant
50 Dean School of Business ... Mr. David J. BARRISH
76 Dean School of Nursing/Allied Hlth ... Dr. Susan S. HUNTER
81 Dean School of Math Sci Engineering ... Mr. Raymond A. BURTON
20 Asst VP Academic Affairs ... Mr. Ty CORBIN
09 Director Office Inst Effectiveness ... Vacant
15 Assoc VP HR/Equal Emp Oppty Ofcr ... Ms. Corliss B. WOODSON
37 Director of Financial Aid ... Ms. Sherika CHARITY
07 Director of Admissions & Records ... Mrs. Karen M. PETTIS-WALDEN
88 Director Outreach and Recruitment ... Ms. Hilda M. BILLUPS
27 Director Communications ... Mr. Joseph SHILLING
26 Director of Marketing ... Ms. Kelly A. SMITH
08 Director of Info/Library Services ... Ms. Hong WU
88 Director of Learning Communities ... Mr. Charles PETERSON, JR.
18 Director Facilities Mgmt/Planning ... Mr. Michael VERDU
30 Director of Development ... Ms. Marianne S. MCGHEE
88 Director of Middle College ... Ms. Mary Jo WASHKO
84 Director of Enrollment Services ... Mr. Brian A. RICHARDSON
06 Registrar ... Ms. Denise S. TUNSTALL
19 Chief of Police ... Mr. Paul L. RONCA
04 Admin Assistant to the President ... Ms. Ann M. BUSHEY

*John Tyler Community College (I)

13101 Jefferson Davis Highway, Chester VA 23831-5316
County: Chesterfield FICE Identification: 004004
Unit ID: 232450
Telephone: (804) 796-4000 Carnegie Class: Assoc/HT-High Non
FAX Number: (804) 796-4163 Calendar System: Semester
URL: www.jtcc.edu
Established: 1965 Annual Undergrad Tuition & Fees (In-State): $4,800
Enrollment: 10,380 Coed
Affiliation or Control: State IRS Status: 501(c)3
Highest Offering: Associate Degree
Accreditation: SC, ADNUR, EMT, FUSER

02 President ... Dr. Edward (Ted) E. RASPILLER
04 Admin Assistant to the President ... Ms. Kara CARTER
05 VP Learning & Student Success ... Dr. William FIEGE
10 VP Administration ... Ms. Susan GRINNAN
111 VP Institutional Advancement ... Ms. Rachel BIUNDO
103 VP Workforce Dev/Credential Attain ... Ms. Elizabeth CREAMER
32 Assoc VP of Enrollment ... Dr. Julie RANSON
21 Assoc VP of Financial Services ... Ms. Natolyn QUASH
35 Dean of Students ... Ms. Sandra KIRKLAND
49 Dean Arts/Humanities/Soc Sciences ... Dr. Mikell BROWN
81 Assoc VP of Learning ... Dr. Johanna WEISS
09 Dir Institutional Effectiveness ... Dr. Keri-Beth PETTENGILL
08 Librarian ... Ms. Molli GONZALEZ
37 Director Financial Aid ... Mr. Tony JONES
19 Asst Dir College Safety & Security ... Ms. Tanya BROWN
26 Public Relations Manager ... Ms. Holly WALKER
36 Assoc Dean of Advising ... Ms. Altrice SMITH
18 Dir Facilities Operations/Safety ... Mr. Greg A. DUNAWAY
06 Dir Admissions & Records/Registrar ... Mr. Leigh BAXTER

*Lord Fairfax Community College (J)

173 Skirmisher Lane, Middletown VA 22645-1745
County: Frederick FICE Identification: 008659
Unit ID: 232575
Telephone: (540) 868-7000 Carnegie Class: Assoc/HT-High Non
FAX Number: (540) 868-7100 Calendar System: Semester
URL: www.lfcc.edu
Established: 1970 Annual Undergrad Tuition & Fees (In-State): $4,739
Enrollment: 6,891 Coed
Affiliation or Control: State IRS Status: 501(c)3
Highest Offering: Associate Degree
Accreditation: SC, ADNUR, CAHIIM, EMT, SURGT

02 President ... Dr. Kim BLOSSER
12 Provost Fauquier Campus ... Dr. Christopher COUTTS

05 VP Academic & Student Affairs .... Dr. Karen KELLISON
103 VP of Workforce & Prof Development .... Ms. Jeanian CLARK
111 Assoc VP of Inst Advance/Educ Fdn .... Ms. Liv HEGGOY
09 Dir Planning/Inst Effectiveness .... Dr. John MILAM
50 Dean Business/Technology/Education .... Ms. Brenda BYARD
81 Dean Science/Eng/Math & Health .... Dr. Ia GOMEZ
83 Dean Hum/Social Sciences/Stdnt Dev .... Dr. James GILLISPIE
32 Dean of Students .... Ms. Amber FOLTZ
88 Dean Fauquier Campus .... Dr. Carolline WOOD
88 Director Learning Resources Center .... Mr. David R. GRAY
37 Director of Financial Aid .... Mr. Steven WILSON
88 Librarian .... Ms. Kerry KILPATRICK
25 Dir Grants & Title IX Coord .... Ms. Lyda KISER
26 Dir Marketing & Outreach .... Ms. Brandy BOIES
35 Assoc Dean of Student Services .... Dr. Mia S. DEZURA
88 Coord Business/Industry Trng .... Mr. Bill PENCE
88 Coord Business/Industry Trng .... Mr. Larry BAKER
88 Dir Marketing/Business/Ind Trng .... Mr. Guy E. CURTIS, III
20 Associate Dean of Instruction .... Ms. Heather BURTON
88 Director Small Business Dev Center .... Ms. Christine KRIZ

*Mountain Empire Community College (A)

3441 Mountain Empire Road,
Big Stone Gap VA 24219-4634

County: Wise FICE Identification: 009629
Unit ID: 232788
Telephone: (276) 523-2400 Carnegie Class: Assoc/MT-VT-High Non
FAX Number: (276) 523-8297 Calendar System: Semester
URL: www.mecc.edu
Established: 1972 Annual Undergrad Tuition & Fees (In-State): $4,710
Enrollment: 2,684 Coed
Affiliation or Control: State IRS Status: 501(c)3
Highest Offering: Associate Degree
Accreditation: SC, ADNUR, COARC

02 President .... Dr. Kristen WESTOVER
05 VP Academic & Student Services .... Dr. Victoria RATLIFF
10 Vice Pres Finance & Admin Services .... Mr. Ron VICARS
111 Vice Pres Institutional Advancement .... Vacant
32 Dean of Student Services .... Ms. Lelia BRADSHAW
07 Dean Admission/Financial Aid .... Ms. Kristy HALL
08 Director of Library Services .... Dr. Michael GILLEY
76 Dean of Health Sciences .... Ms. Kim DORTON
13 Dir Ctr Computing & Info Technology .... Vacant
15 Director Personnel Services .... Ms. Pam GILES
18 Chief Facilities/Physical Plant .... Mr. Preston LAYNE
49 Dean Arts & Sciences .... Ms. Harriett ARRINGTON
72 Dean of Industrial Tech/Health Sci .... Mr. Tommy CLEMENTS
26 Chief Public Relations Officer .... Ms. Amy GREEAR
19 Chief of Police .... Mr. Russell CYPHERS
04 Admin Assistant to the President .... Ms. Peggy GIBSON

*New River Community College (B)

5251 College Drive, Dublin VA 24084

County: Pulaski FICE Identification: 005223
Unit ID: 232867
Telephone: (540) 674-3600 Carnegie Class: Assoc/HT-High Non
FAX Number: (540) 674-3642 Calendar System: Semester
URL: www.nr.edu
Established: 1969 Annual Undergrad Tuition & Fees (In-State): $4,697
Enrollment: 4,626 Coed
Affiliation or Control: State IRS Status: 501(c)3
Highest Offering: Associate Degree
Accreditation: SC

02 President .... Dr. Patricia B. HUBER
05 VP for Instruction/Student Services .... Dr. Peter T. ANDERSON
10 Vice Pres for Finance & Technology ... Mr. John L. VAN HEMERT
30 VP for WD and External Relations .... Dr. Mark C. ROWH
09 Dir Inst Effectiveness/Research .... Dr. Frederick M. STREFF
102 Executive Director of Foundation .... Ms. Angie E. COVEY
49 Dean of Arts & Sciences .... Ms. Sarah TOLBERT-HURYSZ
50 Dean of Business & Technologies .... Ms. Debra BOND
32 Dean of Student Services .... Dr. Deborah KENNEDY
15 Dir of Human Resources & Bus
Oper .... Ms. Melissa P. ANDERSON
06 Registrar .... Mrs. Tammy SMITH
37 Financial Aid Manager .... Mrs. Shauna CROSSCUP
88 Emergency Coordination Officer .... Mr. Joseph WILLIAMS
96 Inventory and Purchasing Technician ...... Ms. Monica W. CARDEN
106 Director Distance Education .... Mrs. Linda C. CLAUSSEN
08 Coordinator of Library Services .... Mrs. Sandra B. SMITH
07 Coord Admissions/Records/Stdnt Svcs .... Mrs. Tammy SMITH
18 Chief Facilities/Physical Plant .... Mr. Anthony J. NICOLO
88 Coordinator of WorkKeys Center .... Mr. Ross MATNEY
88 Enrollment Coordinator .... Mrs. Lori MITCHELL
26 Public Relations Specialist .... Mrs. Jill ROSS
22 Coord Ctr for Disability Services .... Ms. Lucy J. HOWLETT
04 Administrative Asst to President .... Mrs. Kathy T. RIDPATH

*Northern Virginia Community College (C)

4001 Wakefield Chapel Road, Annandale VA 22003-3796

County: Fairfax FICE Identification: 003727
Unit ID: 232946
Telephone: (703) 323-3000 Carnegie Class: Assoc/HT-Mix Trad/Non
FAX Number: (703) 323-3767 Calendar System: Semester
URL: www.nvcc.edu
Established: 1965 Annual Undergrad Tuition & Fees (In-State): $5,610
Enrollment: 51,190 Coed
Affiliation or Control: State IRS Status: 501(c)3
Highest Offering: Associate Degree
Accreditation: SC, ADNUR, CAHIIM, COARC, DA, DH, DMS, EMT, OTA, PTAA

02 Interim President .... Dr. Mel D. SCHIAVELLI
05 Exec VP/Chief Academic Officer .... Dr. Mel D. SCHIAVELLI
13 Vice Pres of Information Technology .... Dr. Steven G. SACHS
103 VP of Workforce Development .... Mr. Steve PARTRIDGE
20 Assoc VP Academic Services .... Dr. Sharon N. ROBERTSON
32 Vice President Student
Services .... Dr. Frances VILLAGRAN-GLOVER
84 Assoc VP Stdnt Svcs & Enroll Mgmt .... Dr. Elizabeth HARPER
12 Provost Alexandria Campus .... Dr. Annette HAGGRAY
12 Provost Loudoun Campus .... Dr. Julie LEIDIG
12 Provost Manassas Campus .... Dr. Molly LYNCH
102 Exec Dir NVCC Education Foundation .... Vacant
25 Director of Grants .... Dr. Syedur RAHMAN
15 AVP of Human Resources .... Ms. Charlotte M. CALOBRISI
96 Director of Purchasing .... Vacant
37 Dir Stdnt Financial Aid/Support Svc .... Ms. Joan A. ZANDERS
21 Associate VP for Administration .... Mr. Cory THOMPSON
18 Director of Facilities .... Mr. Steven PATTERSON
19 Director Security/Safety .... Chief Daniel DUSSEAU

*Patrick Henry Community College (D)

645 Patriot Avenue, Martinsville VA 24112

County: Henry FICE Identification: 003751
Unit ID: 233019
Telephone: (276) 638-8777 Carnegie Class: Assoc/HT-Mix Trad/Non
FAX Number: (276) 656-0320 Calendar System: Semester
URL: www.patrickhenry.edu
Established: 1962 Annual Undergrad Tuition & Fees (In-State): $4,720
Enrollment: 2,263 Coed
Affiliation or Control: State IRS Status: 501(c)3
Highest Offering: Associate Degree
Accreditation: SC, ADNUR, EMT

02 President .... Dr. Angeline D. GODWIN
05 VP Academic/Student Develop Svcs .... Dr. Greg HODGES
10 VP Finance & Admin Services .... Mr. John HANBURY
103 VP Workforce/Economic/Community Dev .... Mrs. Rhonda HODGES
30 Director of Development .... Mrs. Tiffani UNDERWOOD
121 Dean Academic Success/Col Transfer .... Mr. Terry YOUNG
81 Dean STEM/Health/Applied Programs .... Dr. Colin FERGUSON
66 Coordinator Nursing/Allied Health .... Ms. Amy WEBSTER
13 Dean of Technology .... Mr. David DEAL
15 Director of Human Resources .... Ms. Belinda STOCKTON
84 Dean Student Success/Enroll Svcs .... Dr. Virginia JONES
07 Coord Admiss & Accel Lrng .... Ms. Meghan EGGLESTON
26 Public Relations & Mktg Mgr .... Mr. Randy FERGUSON
06 Registrar .... Ms. Jessica CARTER
37 Financial Aid/Veterans Admin .... Mrs. Cindy KELLER
08 Asst Coord Library Services .... Ms. Marcia SEATON-MARTIN
25 Chief Contracts/Grants Admin .... Ms. Sarah B. MORRISON
41 Athletic Director .... Mr. Brian HENDERSON
09 Director Institutional Research .... Dr. Christopher WIKSTROM
18 Chief Facilities/Physical Plant .... Ms. Roberta WRIGHT
19 Director Security/Safety .... Mr. Gary DOVE
96 Director of Purchasing .... Ms. Lori CONNER
04 Administrative Asst to President .... Ms. Jencie GIBSON

*Paul D. Camp Community College (E)

100 N College Drive, Franklin VA 23851-0737

County: Independent City FICE Identification: 009159
Unit ID: 233037
Telephone: (757) 569-6700 Carnegie Class: Assoc/HT-High Non
FAX Number: (757) 569-6795 Calendar System: Semester
URL: www.pdc.edu
Established: 1970 Annual Undergrad Tuition & Fees (In-State): $4,730
Enrollment: 1,404 Coed
Affiliation or Control: State IRS Status: 501(c)3
Highest Offering: Associate Degree
Accreditation: SC, ADNUR

02 President .... Dr. Daniel W. LUFKIN
05 VP Academic/Student Development .... Dr. Tara ATKINS-BRADY
11 Operations Manager .... Mr. Phillip BRADSHAW
111 Dir of Institutional Advancement .... Mrs. Stacy PAULEY
32 Dean Student Services .... Ms. Trina JONES
20 Dean of Suffolk Academic Programs .... Dr. Justin OLIVER
08 Coordinator of Library Services .... Ms. Cirrus GUNDLACH
12 Academic Director-Smithfield .... Mrs. Antoinette JOHNSON
103 Dir of Workforce Development .... Mrs. Angela LAWHORNE
09 Coord Inst Research/Assessment .... Ms. Damay J. BULLOCK
15 Human Resources Manager .... Mrs. Rachel BEALE
26 Public Relations Specialist .... Ms. Wendy HARRISON
37 Financial Aid Coordinator .... Dr. Teresa HARRISON
04 Assistant to the President .... Ms. Cathy CUTCHINS
06 Registrar .... Mrs. Donna DOUGLAS-RUMBLE
07 Dean of Student Services .... Mrs. Trina JONES
41 Athletic Director .... Mrs. Carrie HOEFT

*Piedmont Virginia Community College (F)

501 College Drive, Charlottesville VA 22902-7589

County: Independent City FICE Identification: 009928
Unit ID: 233116
Telephone: (434) 977-5200 Carnegie Class: Assoc/HT-High Non
FAX Number: (434) 296-8395 Calendar System: Semester
URL: www.pvcc.edu
Established: 1972 Annual Undergrad Tuition & Fees (In-State): $4,790
Enrollment: 5,608 Coed
Affiliation or Control: State IRS Status: 501(c)3
Highest Offering: Associate Degree
Accreditation: SC, ADNUR, DMS, EMT, RAD, SURGT

02 President .... Dr. Frank FRIEDMAN
05 VP Instruction/Student Svcs .... Dr. John DONNELLY
10 Vice President Finance/Admin Svcs .... Mr. Kim MCMANUS
111 Vice Pres Advancement/Development ...... Mr. Harry STILLERMAN
79 Dean Humanities/Fine Arts/Soc Sci .... Dr. Leonda KENISTON
50 Dean of Student Srvs/Admissions .... Dr. Andrew RENSHAW
17 Dean Health & Life Sciences .... Dr. Jean CHAPPELL
103 Dean Workforce Services .... Ms. Valerie PALAMOUNTAIN
13 Chief Information Officer .... Ms. Sue HAAS
09 Dir Inst Research/Planning/Effect .... Dr. Jolene HAMM
06 Registrar .... Ms. Allyson REA
96 Business Manager .... Ms. Tracy CERSLEY
18 Facilities Manager .... Mr. Timothy WOODSON
15 Human Resources Director .... Mrs. Teresa WILLIS
26 Marketing/Media Relations Director .... Vacant
88 Outreach Manager .... Ms. Denise MCCLANAHAN
08 Director Library Services .... Ms. Crystal NEWELL
37 Director Financial Aid .... Ms. Crystal FILER-OGDEN
121 Director Advising & Transfer .... Mr. Kemper STEELE

*Rappahannock Community College (G)

12745 College Drive, Glenns VA 23149-0287

County: Gloucester FICE Identification: 009160
Unit ID: 233310
Telephone: (804) 758-6700 Carnegie Class: Assoc/HT-High Non
FAX Number: (804) 758-3852 Calendar System: Semester
URL: www.rappahannock.edu
Established: 1970 Annual Undergrad Tuition & Fees (In-State): $4,820
Enrollment: 3,229 Coed
Affiliation or Control: State IRS Status: 501(c)3
Highest Offering: Associate Degree
Accreditation: SC, ADNUR, EMT

02 President .... Dr. Shannon KENNEDY
32 VP Instruction/Student Development .... Dr. A. Donna ALEXANDER
10 Vice Pres Finance/Admin Services .... Mr. Bill DOYLE
103 Vice Pres Workforce/Cmty Devel .... Dr. Jason PERRY
05 Academic Dean .... Dr. Marty BROOKS
35 Dean Student Development .... Dr. Dave KEEL
30 VP of College Advancement .... Ms. Sarah POPE
108 Dean Research/Effectiveness/Plng .... Dr. Glenda D. HAYNIE
37 Financial Aid/Veteran Affairs Ofcr .... Ms. Vickisha HARRIS
15 Director Human Resources .... Mrs. Caroline W. STELTER
18 Facilities/Physical Plant Supv .... Mr. John LEONARD
10 Business Manager .... Ms. Alissa NASHWINTER
06 Student Records/Information Coord .... Ms. Felicia B. PACKETT
08 Library Coordinator .... Mr. Dan REAM

*Southside Virginia Community College (H)

109 Campus Drive, Alberta VA 23821-2930

County: Brunswick FICE Identification: 008661
Unit ID: 233639
Telephone: (434) 949-1000 Carnegie Class: Assoc/HT-High Non
FAX Number: (434) 949-7863 Calendar System: Semester
URL: www.southside.edu
Established: 1970 Annual Undergrad Tuition & Fees (In-State): $4,695
Enrollment: 3,611 Coed
Affiliation or Control: State IRS Status: 501(c)3
Highest Offering: Associate Degree
Accreditation: SC, ADNUR, EMT

02 President .... Dr. Quentin R. JOHNSON
05 Vice Pres Academics & Stdnt Affairs .... Vacant
103 Vice Pres Workforce Development .... Dr. Keith HARKINS
10 Vice Pres Finance & Administration .... Mrs. Shannon V. FEINMAN
111 Director Institutional Advancement .... Mrs. Mary Jane ELKINS
13 Chief Information Officer .... Mr. Chad WOLLENBERG
84 Dean Enrollment Management .... Ms. Dorothea KNOTT
79 Dean of Humanities/Social Sciences .... Dr. Dixie DALTON
75 Dean of Career & Occup Technology .... Dr. Chad PATTON
09 Dir Institutional Effectiveness .... Ms. Robin DANIEL
66 Dean of Nursing/Health Technology .... Dr. Michelle K. EDMONDS
102 Exec Director SVCC Foundation .... Mrs. Mary Jane ELKINS
08 College Librarian .... Ms. Marika PETERSON
26 Public Relations & Mktg Specialist .... Mrs. Christie C. HALES
37 Director of Financial Aid .... Mrs. Sally THARRINGTON
28 Director of Diversity .... Vacant
15 Human Resources Manager .... Ms. Bethany W. HARRIS
18 Buildings/Grounds Supt Christanna .... Mr. Roger WRAY
18 Buildings/Grounds Superintendent .... Mr. Eddie BENNETT
38 Dean of Student Success .... Mrs. Bernadette BATTLE
21 Business Manager .... Mrs. Toni LAMBERT
04 Admin Assistant to the President .... Ms. Angela JACKSON

*Southwest Virginia Community College (I)

Box SVCC, Richlands VA 24641-1101

County: Tazewell FICE Identification: 007260
Unit ID: 233648
Telephone: (276) 964-2555 Carnegie Class: Assoc/MT-VT-Mix Trad/Non
FAX Number: (276) 964-9307 Calendar System: Semester
URL: www.sw.edu

Established: 1967 Annual Undergrad Tuition & Fees (In-State): $4,703
Enrollment: 2,304 Coed
Affiliation or Control: State IRS Status: 501(c)3
Highest Offering: Associate Degree
Accreditation: SC, ADNUR, EMT, OTA, RAD

02 President ... Dr. Thomda F. WRIGHT
05 VP Acad & Student Services ... Dr. Robert BRANDON
10 Vice Pres Finance/Admin Svcs ... Mr. Chris LEWIS
04 General Admin Coordinator ... Mrs. Kristy ISRAEL
79 Dean Humanities/Soc Science ... Dr. Brian WRIGHT
81 Dean Math/Natural Sci/Health Tech ... Mr. Jereial FLETCHER
50 Dean Business/Engr & Indust Tech ... Mr. James DYE
103 Pgm Developer Workforce Solutions ... Vacant
32 Dean Student Success ... Mrs. Dyan E. LESTER
09 Institutional Research Officer ... Mrs. Cathy L. SMITH-COX
102 VP SWCC Educ Foundation & Dev ... Mrs. Susan L. LOWE
19 Campus Police Chief ... Mr. Jerry STINSON
21 Business Manager ... Mr. Michael BALES
18 Physical Plant Superintendent ... Mr. Tony MCGHEE
26 Public Relations Coordinator ... Mr. John DEZEMBER
08 Coordinator of Library Services ... Ms. Teresa A. YEAROUT
106 Distance Learning ... Mrs. Melissa STILTNER
25 Grants Administrator ... Ms. Phyllis ROBERTS
105 Director Web Services ... Ms. Teresa PRUETT
13 Chief Info Technology Officer (CIO) ... Mr. Charles MUSICK
37 Financial Aid Manager ... Mrs. Donna PRICE
41 Athletic Director ... Mr. Jason VENCILL
15 AVP Human Resources Officer ... Ms. Kimberly STEINER

*Thomas Nelson Community College (A)

99 Thomas Nelson Drive, Hampton VA 23666
County: Independent City FICE Identification: 006871
Unit ID: 233754
Telephone: (757) 825-2700 Carnegie Class: Assoc/MT-VT-Mix Trad/Non
FAX Number: (757) 825-2763 Calendar System: Semester
URL: www.tncc.edu
Established: 1967 Annual Undergrad Tuition & Fees (In-State): $4,806
Enrollment: 8,286 Coed
Affiliation or Control: State IRS Status: 501(c)3
Highest Offering: Associate Degree
Accreditation: SC, ADNUR, DH

02 President ... Dr. John T. DEVER
05 Vice Pres for Academic Affairs ... Dr. Susan ENGLISH
32 Int Vice Pres for Student Affairs ... Ms. Kris RARIG
11 Vice President for Admin/Finance ... Vacant
103 Int Vice Pres Workforce Development ... Dr. Susan ENGLISH
111 Vice Pres Institutional Advancement ... Ms. Cynthia CALLAWAY
20 Provost Historic Triangle Campus ... Dr. Patrick TOMPKINS
13 Int Director of Information Tech ... Ms. Debra HUDGINS
121 Dir Student Success/Advising ... Ms. Crystal ANDERSON
10 Assoc VP for Financial Services ... Ms. Teresa BAILEY
60 Int Dean Comm/Social Sciences ... Dr. Ursula BOCK
81 Dean Science/Engr/Technology ... Mr. Seyed AKHAVI
50 Dean Bus/Public Svcs/IT/Math ... Dr. Charles SWAIM
76 Interim Dean Health Professions ... Mr. Paul LONG
37 Dir Financial Aid/Veteran Affairs ... Ms. Tamika BYBEE
18 Mgr Facilities/Plng/Capital Outlay ... Mr. Mark KRAMER
30 Director of Development ... Ms. Tracy ASHLEY
08 Director of Learning Resources ... Dr. Richard HODGES
09 Dir Inst Research and Effectiveness ... Mr. Steven FELKER
15 Director of Human Resources ... Dr. Lynda BYRD-POLLER

*Tidewater Community College (B)

121 College Place, Norfolk VA 23510
County: Independent City FICE Identification: 003712
Unit ID: 233772
Telephone: (757) 822-1122 Carnegie Class: Assoc/HVT-High Trad
FAX Number: (757) 822-1060 Calendar System: Semester
URL: www.tcc.edu
Established: 1968 Annual Undergrad Tuition & Fees (In-State): $5,561
Enrollment: 22,776 Coed
Affiliation or Control: State IRS Status: 501(c)3
Highest Offering: Associate Degree
Accreditation: SC, ACFEI, ADNUR, CAHIIM, COARC, DMS, EMT, FUSER, MLTAD, OTA, PTAA, RAD

02 Interim President ... Dr. Gregory T. DECINQUE
05 Interim Exec VP Academic & CAO ... Dr. Corey L. MCCRAY
10 Vice President Finance ... Ms. Phyllis F. MILLOY
84 VP Communication & Enrollment Mgmt ... Ms. Marian ANDERFUREN
102 Exec Dir Ed Fndn/Dir Govt Cmty Rels ... Mr. Steven M. JONES
88 Exec Dir Real Estate Dev/COO Facil ... Mr. Matthew J. BAUMGARTEN
13 VP Info Systems/Inst Effectiveness ... Mr. Curtis K. AASEN
103 VP for Workforce Solutions ... Dr. Corey L. MCCRAY
32 Interim VP Student Affairs ... Dr. Karen CAMPBELL
12 Provost Portsmouth Campus ... Dr. Michelle W. WOODHOUSE
12 Interim Provost Norfolk Campus ... Mr. Emanuel CHESTNUT
12 Interim Provost Chesapeake Campus ... Dr. James EDWARDS
12 Provost Virginia Beach Campus ... Dr. Michael D. SUMMERS
15 Associate VP Human Resources/EEO ... Ms. Beth LUNDE
11 Chief Admin Officer Educ Foundation ... Ms. Susan M. JAMES
20 AVP Academic Affairs ... Dr. Kellie C. SOREY
106 AVP Distance Learning ... Mr. John MOREA
08 AVP for Libraries ... Mr. Steve E. LITHERLAND
36 AVP Academic & Career Planning ... Dr. Karen D. CAMPBELL
27 AVP Mktg & Enrollment Mgmt ... Mr. Curt J. WYNN
21 Associate VP for Finance ... Ms. Heather H. TAYLOR
79 Dean of Hum & Soc Sci Chesapeake ... Ms. Diane N. RYAN
81 Dean Sci/Tech/Eng/Math Chesapeake ... Mr. Thomas B. STOUT
35 Int Dean of Stdnt Svcs Chesapeake ... Mr. Kevin MCCARTHY
81 Dean Lang/Math/Science Norfolk ... Dr. Kerry S. RAGNO
50 Interim Pathway Dean of Bus Norfolk ... Ms. Nancy N. PRATHER-JOHNSON
35 Interim Dean of Stdnt Svcs Norfolk ... Ms. Kia HARDY
50 Interim Dean Bus/Pub Svcs/Tech PT ... Mr. Peter T. AGBAKPE
81 Dean Lang/Math/Science Portsmouth ... Ms. Jenefer D. SNYDER
35 Dean of Student Svcs Portsmouth ... Ms. Dana M. HATHORN
66 Dean School Nursing Portsmouth ... Vacant
54 Dean Math Eng & Ind Tech Va Beach ... Mr. David A. EKKER
76 Pathway Dean Health Prof VA Beach ... Mr. Thomas G. CALOGRIDES, JR.
77 Pathway Dean Comp Sc & IT Va Beach ... Mr. William CLEMENT
81 Dean Natural Sciences Va Beach ... Mr. Gregory P. FRANK
88 Pathway Dean Pub/Prof Svcs Va Beach ... Mr. Joseph J. FAIRCHILD
79 Dean Humanities Va Beach ... Ms. Marcanne ANDERSEN
35 Dean of Student Svcs Va Beach ... Dr. Marilyn R. HODGE
88 Dir Reg Automotive Ctr Chesapeake ... Mr. Beno RUBIN
14 Director of Information Technology ... Mr. Ken BALLARD
06 College Registrar ... Vacant
57 Interim Director Visual Arts Center ... Ms. Corrine LILYARD-MITCHELL
18 Director of Facilities ... Mr. Albert THOMPSON
19 Director of Public Safety ... Mr. Timothy L. MALLORY
88 Int Exec Dir Ctr Military Vet Educ ... Ms. Batanya M. GIPSON
88 Interim AVP Business Corp Solutions ... Ms. Karen MILLER
88 Associate VP Prof Dev Solutions ... Ms. Lisa L. PETERSON
88 Exec Dir Roper Performing Arts Ctr ... Mr. Paul H. LASAKOW
96 Assoc Dir Materiel Mgmt Proc Svcs ... Mr. Thom HUTCHINS
37 Dir Central Financial Aid ... Mr. Justin CRISTELLO
109 Director Auxiliary Services ... Ms. Bridgett M. PASSAUER
88 Dir Gen Educ Assess Trans Partnrshp ... Ms. Jennifer FERGUSON
45 Dir of Planning & Accountability ... Dr. Kimberly M. BOVEE
25 Director Grants/Sponsored Programs ... Ms. Laverne ELLERBE
88 Director of Intercultural Learning ... Dr. Jeanne B. NATALI
04 Exec Asst to President ... Ms. Latesha JOHNSON

*Virginia Highlands Community College (C)

PO Box 828, Abingdon VA 24212-0828
County: Washington FICE Identification: 007099
Unit ID: 233903
Telephone: (276) 739-2400 Carnegie Class: Assoc/HT-Mix Trad/Non
FAX Number: (276) 739-2590 Calendar System: Semester
URL: www.vhcc.edu
Established: 1967 Annual Undergrad Tuition & Fees (In-State): $4,710
Enrollment: 2,328 Coed
Affiliation or Control: State IRS Status: 501(c)3
Highest Offering: Associate Degree
Accreditation: SC, ADNUR

02 Interim President ... Dr. Charlie WHITE, JR.
05 VP Instruction & Student Services ... Dr. Stacy THOMAS
10 VP Financial/Administrative Svcs ... Ms. Christine FIELDS
111 VP Institutional Advancement ... Ms. Laura PENNINGTON
49 Dean of Arts & Sciences Div ... Ms. Barbara MANUEL
107 Dean Professional/Tech Studies Div ... Dr. Beth PAGE
09 Dir of Institutional Rsrch/Effectiv ... Mr. Robert E. MAY
66 Interim Coordinator of Nursing ... Ms. Deborah CLARKSTON
103 Workforce Development Coordinator ... Mr. Robert PHILLIPS
106 Dir Learning Resources/Online Lrng ... Mr. Ken FAIRBANKS
08 Coordinator of Library Services ... Vacant
121 Academic Counselor ... Mr. Michael MCBRIDE
37 Financial Aid Coordinator ... Ms. Nancy HOPE
07 Coordinator of Admissions & Records ... Ms. Paige KELLY
15 Human Resource Manager ... Ms. Laura MCCLELLAN
26 Coord Public Relations & Marketing ... Ms. Kellie CROWE
88 Director of EXCEL ... Ms. Karen CHEERS
21 Finance Manager ... Ms. Mary SNEAD
13 IT Coordinator ... Mr. Glen JOHNSON
18 Buildings & Grounds Superintendent ... Mr. Ernest L. NUNLEY
19 Campus Police Chief ... Mr. Blake ANDIS

*Virginia Western Community College (D)

3093 Colonial Avenue SW, Roanoke VA 24015-4705
County: Independent City FICE Identification: 003760
Unit ID: 233949
Telephone: (540) 857-8922 Carnegie Class: Assoc/MT-VT-High Non
FAX Number: (540) 857-6526 Calendar System: Semester
URL: www.virginiawestern.edu
Established: 1966 Annual Undergrad Tuition & Fees (In-State): $5,355
Enrollment: 7,271 Coed
Affiliation or Control: State IRS Status: 501(c)3
Highest Offering: Associate Degree
Accreditation: SC, ACBSP, ACFEI, DH, MLTAD, RAD, RTT

02 President ... Dr. Robert H. SANDEL
10 Vice Pres of Finance/Admin Services ... Ms. Lisa RIDPATH
05 Vice Pres Academic/Student Affs ... Dr. Elizabeth WILMER
111 Vice Pres Institutional Advancement ... Ms. Marilyn HERBERT-ASHTON
103 Vice Pres Workforce Development Svc ... Dr. Milian HAYWARD
45 Dean Institutional Effectiveness ... Ms. Rachelle KOUDELIK-JONES
49 Dean Liberal Arts/Social Sciences ... Ms. Amy ANGUIANO
76 Dean Health Professions ... Ms. Carole GRAHAM
81 Dean Science/Tech/Engineering/Math ... Ms. Amy WHITE
50 Dean Business/Trades/Technology ... Ms. Yvonne CAMPBELL
24 Dean Learning Resources ... Mr. Christopher PORTER
32 Dean of Student Services ... Ms. Lori BAKER
09 Director Institutional Research ... Ms. Carol ROWLETT
18 Director of Facilities Planning ... Mr. Kevin G. WITTER
26 Director Marketing/Strategic Comm ... Mr. Josh MEYER
06 Registrar ... Ms. Karin COLE
19 Campus Police Chief ... Mr. Craig HARRIS
37 Coord Financial Aid/Veterans Affs ... Mr. David BROD
103 Workforce Operations Supervisor ... Ms. Cassandra DOVE
13 Dir Information Educ Technology ... Mr. Shivaji SAMANTA
15 Assoc VP of Human Resources ... Ms. Jennifer PITTMAN
21 Business Manager ... Mrs. Fredona AARON
84 Coordinator for Enrollment Services ... Ms. Brooke FERGUSON
08 Coordinator of the Library ... Vacant
36 Coordinator Career Services ... Ms. Shonny COOKE
25 Coord Grants Dev & Special Projects ... Ms. Marilyn J. HERBERT-ASHTON
30 Coordinator of Development ... Ms. Carole TARRANT
04 Admin Assistant to the President ... Ms. Amy BALZER

*Wytheville Community College (E)

1000 E Main Street, Wytheville VA 24382-3308
County: Wythe FICE Identification: 003761
Unit ID: 234377
Telephone: (276) 223-4700 Carnegie Class: Assoc/HT-High Non
FAX Number: (276) 223-4778 Calendar System: Semester
URL: www.wcc.vccs.edu
Established: 1963 Annual Undergrad Tuition & Fees (In-State): $4,725
Enrollment: 2,676 Coed
Affiliation or Control: State IRS Status: 501(c)3
Highest Offering: Associate Degree
Accreditation: SC, ADNUR, DH, MLTAD, PTAA

02 President ... Dr. Dean SPRINKLE
05 Vice Pres Instruction/Student Devel ... Dr. Lorri HUFFARD
10 Vice Pres Finance & Admin Services ... Ms. Crystal Y. CREGGER
09 Director of Institutional Research ... Dr. Kent F. GLINDEMANN
30 Vice Pres of College Development ... Dr. Rhonda K. CATRON-WOOD
103 Vice Pres of Workforce Development ... Mr. Perry HUGHES
83 Dean of Transfer & Social Sciences ... Mr. Jacob SURRATT
76 Int Dean Health/Occupational Pgms ... Mr. Tommy ARNOLD
32 Dean of Student Services ... Ms. Renee THOMAS
13 Director of Technology/CIO ... Mr. Shawn MCREYNOLDS
06 Acting Registrar ... Ms. April MULLINS
15 Human Resources Manager ... Ms. Malinda EVERSOLE
26 Acting Public Relations Coordinator ... Mr. Kenneth AKERS
08 Coordinator of Library Services ... Mr. George E. MATTIS, JR.
96 Procurement Officer ... Vacant
106 Dir Distance/Distributive Learning ... Mr. Dave DICK
37 Coordinator Financial Aid ... Ms. Mary Beth GALLAGHER
04 Administrative Asst to President ... Ms. Denita BURNETT
29 Development Svcs/Alumni Coordinator ... Vacant
18 Chief Facilities/Physical Plant Ofc ... Mr. Jim VICARS
19 Director Security/Safety ... Mr. Steve BURNETTE
108 Director Institutional Assessment ... Dr. Kent GLINDEMANN

Virginia International University (F)

4401 Village Drive, Fairfax VA 22030
County: Fairfax FICE Identification: 041440
Unit ID: 460376
Telephone: (703) 591-7042 Carnegie Class: Spec-4-yr-Other Tech
FAX Number: (703) 591-7046 Calendar System: Semester
URL: www.viu.edu
Established: 1998 Annual Undergrad Tuition & Fees: $10,328
Enrollment: 445 Coed
Affiliation or Control: Independent Non-Profit IRS Status: 501(c)3
Highest Offering: Master's
Accreditation: ACICS, CEA

01 President ... Dr. Isa SARAC
10 Exec Vice Pres Finance & IT ... Mr. Prashish SHRESTHA
32 EVP Student/University Affairs ... Dr. Suleyman BAHCECI
05 Vice Pres of Academic Affairs ... Dr. Ronald KOVACH
09 Vice Pres Inst Effectiveness ... Ms. Christina KOONTS
06 Registrar ... Ms. Yoko ULCHIDA GURSEN
100 Assoc Vice Pres/Chief of Staff ... Ms. Camilla MEROS

Virginia Military Institute (G)

319 Letcher Avenue, Lexington VA 24450-0304
County: Independent City FICE Identification: 003753
Unit ID: 234085
Telephone: (540) 464-7230 Carnegie Class: Bac-A&S
FAX Number: (540) 464-7583 Calendar System: Semester
URL: www.vmi.edu
Established: 1839 Annual Undergrad Tuition & Fees (In-State): $18,862
Enrollment: 1,722 Coed
Affiliation or Control: State IRS Status: 501(c)3
Highest Offering: Baccalaureate
Accreditation: SC

01 Superintendent ... Gen. J. H. Binford PEAY
05 Dean of the Faculty ... BGen. Robert W. MORESCHI
10 Director Finance/Admin ... Col. Dallas B. CLARK
32 Commandant of Cadets ... Col. William J. WANOVICH
100 Chief of Staff ... Col. James P. INMAN

04 Exec Asst to the Superintendent ..... LtCol. Sean P. HARRINGTON
21 Assoc Business Exec/Treasurer ....Col. Jeffrey L. LAWHORNE
07 Director of Admissions .... Col. Vernon L. BEITZEL
88 Exec Director Museum Programs ....Col. Keith E. GIBSON
37 Director of Financial Aid .... Capt. Brian L. QUISENBERRY
35 Deputy Commandant ....Vacant
36 Director of Career Services ....LtCol. Ammand SHEIKH
41 Director Intercollegiate Athletics ....Mr. David L. DILES
26 Director Communications & Marketing .... Col. Stewart D. MACINNIS
29 Executive VP Alumni Association .....Mr. Thomas A. BRASHEARS
102 Exec VP VMI Foundation/Fund Raising ....Mr. Warren J. BRYAN
88 Exec VP Keydet Club/Athletic Fund ....Mr. Meade B. KING
06 Registrar .... Col. Janet M. BATTAGLIA
15 Director Human Resources ....LtCol. Richard A. PARELLA, JR.
18 Director Physical Plant ....LtCol. Michelle P. CARUTHERS
09 Director Institutional Research ....LtCol. Lee L. RAKES
109 Director Auxiliary Services ....Col. David P. WILLIAMS
40 Manager Bookstore .... Mr. Bradley N. MCDOUGAL
42 Institute Chaplain ....Col. Robert E. PHILLIPS, SR.
17 Institute Physician ....Dr. David L. COPELAND
88 Director of Athletic Communications ....Mr. Wade H. BRANNER
08 Head Librarian ....Col. Dorothy C. LOCKABY
38 Director of Cadet Counseling .... LtCol. Sarah L. JONES
13 Director Information Technology .... Col. Wesley L. ROBINSON
96 Director of Purchasing ....Maj. Kathy H. TOMLIN
30 CEO Alumni Agencies ....Cmdr. Stephen M. MACONI

† Tuition includes required room and board and quartermaster charges.

Virginia Polytechnic Institute and State University (A)

Blacksburg VA 24061-0202
County: Montgomery FICE Identification: 003754
Unit ID: 233921
Telephone: (540) 231-6000 Carnegie Class: DU-Highest
FAX Number: (540) 231-9263 Calendar System: Semester
URL: www.vt.edu
Established: 1872 Annual Undergrad Tuition & Fees (In-State): $13,620
Enrollment: 34,440 Coed
Affiliation or Control: State IRS Status: 501(c)3
Highest Offering: Doctorate
Accreditation: SC, ART, CACREP, CAEP, CAEPN, CEA, CIDA, CLPSY, CONST, DIETD, DIETI, IPSY, LSAR, MED, MFCD, MUS, PCSAS, PH, PLNG, SPAA, THEA, VET

01 President .... Timothy D. SANDS
05 Exec Vice President & Provost ....Cyril R. CLARKE
11 SVP Operations & Administration ....Dwayne PINKNEY
13 Vice Pres Information Tech & CIO ....Scott F. MIDKIFF
32 Vice President Student Affairs ....Patricia A. PERILLO
111 Vice Pres for Advancement ....Charles D. PHLEGAR
29 Sr Assoc Vice Pres Alumni Relations .Matthew M. WINSTON, JR.
28 VP Strat Affairs/Vice Prov Incl Div ....Menah PRATT-CLARKE
46 VP Research & Innovation ....Theresa MAYER
20 Vice Prov for Undergrad Acad Affs .... Rachel L. HOLLOWAY
58 Vice President and Dean Grad Educ ....Karen P. DEPAUW
56 VP Outreach/International Affs ....Guru GHOSH
10 Vice President for Finance and CFO .... M. Dwight SHELTON, JR.
15 Vice Pres for Human Resources ....Bryan GAREY
21 Vice Pres Business Affairs ....Lisa WILKES
07 AV Prov Enrol Mgt/Dir UG Admiss ....Juan P. ESPINOZA
35 Dean of Students ....Byron A. HUGHES, JR.
88 AV Prov Academic Decision Support ....R. Thulasi KUMAR
43 University Counsel ....Kay K. HEIDBREDER
84 Vice Prov for Enroll & Degree Mgmt ....Luisa HAVENS
37 Dir of Scholarships/Financial Aid .... Elizabeth ARMSTRONG
20 Vice Provost Faculty Affairs ....Jack FINNEY
45 Vice Provost Academic Resource Mgmt ....Kenneth SMITH
20 Vice Prov LSIE ....G. Don TAYLOR, JR.
23 Director Schiffert Health Center ....Kanitta CHAROENSIRI
18 Assoc Vice Pres/Chief Facilities ....Christopher KIWUS
109 Director of Dining Services ....Ted FAULKNER
39 Int Dir Housing and Res Life ....Frances KEENE
41 Athletic Director ....Whit BABCOCK
26 Sr Assoc Vice Pres Univ Relations ....Tracy VOSBURGH
38 Director Student Counseling ....Chris FLYNN
40 Executive Director Bookstore ....Donald J. WILLIAMS
62 Dean of University Libraries ....Tyler WALTERS
47 Dean of Agriculture/Life Sciences ....Alan GRANT
48 Dean of Architecture/Urban Studies ....Richard J. BLYTHE
49 Dean College of Science ....Sally C. MORTON
50 Dean of Business ....Robert T. SUMICHRAST
54 Dean of Engineering ....Julia ROSS
79 Dean Liberal Arts & Human Sciences ....Rosemary BLIESZNER
74 Int Dean of Veterinary Medicine ....Gregory B. DANIEL
65 Dean of Natural Resources & Environ ......Paul M. WINISTORFER
96 Director of Procurement ....Mary HELMICK
63 Dean of VTC School of Medicine ....Cynda Ann JOHNSON
91 Assoc Vice Pres for Enterprise Sys ....Deborah M. FULTON
12 VP for the National Capital Region ....Steven H. MCKNIGHT
102 CEO Virginia Tech Foundation ....John E. DOOLEY
04 Exec Dir to Office of the President ....Cheryl PETERSON
06 Assoc Vice Prov and Univ Registrar ....Rick SPARKS
100 VP for Policy and Gov/Sec to BOV ....Kim O'ROURKE
104 Director Global Education Office .... Theresa C. JOHANSSON
105 Director Web Communications ....John JACKSON
106 Exec Dir Tech-enhanced Learning .... Dale PIKE
88 Asst Provost Regional Accreditation ....Kristen BUSH
19 Chief of Police/Dir of Security ....Kevin FOUST
22 Asst VP Equity and Accessibility ....Kelly OAKS
25 Director of Contracts ....Frank FITZGERALD

44 Director Annual or Planned Giving ....Randy HOLDEN
86 Exec Director Government Relations ....Chris YIANILOS
76 VP for Health Sciences and Tech ....Michael J. FRIEDLANDER
108 Director Assessment and Evaluation ....Bethanny BODO

Virginia State University (B)

One Hayden Drive,
Virginia State University VA 23806-0001
County: Chesterfield FICE Identification: 003764
Unit ID: 234155
Telephone: (804) 524-5000 Carnegie Class: Masters/M
FAX Number: (804) 524-6506 Calendar System: Semester
URL: www.vsu.edu
Established: 1882 Annual Undergrad Tuition & Fees (In-State): $9,056
Enrollment: 4,713 Coed
Affiliation or Control: State IRS Status: 501(c)3
Highest Offering: Doctorate
Accreditation: SC, ART, CAEPN, DIETD, DIETI, MUS, NAIT, SW

01 President .... Dr. Makola M. ABDULLAH
10 Vice President for Finance .... Mr. Kevin DAVENPORT
05 Provost/VP for Academic Affairs ....Dr. Donald PALM
32 VP for Student Success & Engagement ....Vacant
111 VP for Institutional Advancement .... Ms. Reshunda MAHONE
11 Vice President for Administration ....Mr. Hubert D. HARRIS
20 Vice Provost ....Vacant
84 Asst VP/Student Enrollment Services ....Dr. Jame'l HODGES
21 Assoc Vice President for Finance .... Ms. Sheila MCNAIR
50 Dean Reginald F Lewis Col Business . Dr. Emmanuel OMOJOKUN
54 Dean College of Engineering & Tech .... Dr. Dawit HAILE
79 Dean Col of Humanities & Soc Sci .... Dr. Andrew KANU
47 Dean College of Agriculture ....Dr. Marion R. MCKINNEY
58 Dean Graduate Studies ....Vacant
62 Dean Library & Library Services .. Dr. Elsie S. WEATHERINGTON
76 Dean College of Natural Health Sci .... Dr. Larry BROWN
53 Dean College of Education .... Dr. Willis W. WALTER
06 Registrar .... Mrs. Debera BONNER
09 Director Inst Planning/Assessment .... Dr. Tia A. MINNIS
37 Director of Financial Aid ....Mrs. Myra PHILLIPS
19 Chief of Police and Public Safety ....Mr. David BRAGG
27 Media Specialist ....Mr. Jesse VAUGHAN
18 Director of Facilities .... Mr. Gilbert HANZLIK
07 Director for Enrollment Services ....Mr. Rodney HALL
26 Director for Communication .... Mrs. Pamela TURNER
15 HR Director .... Mrs. Tanya SIMMONS
39 Director Residence Facilities ....Dr. Kelvin RACHELL
36 Director Career Services .... Mr. Joseph LYONS
40 Bookstore Manager ....Mr. Kevin POWELL
92 Director Honors Program ....Mr. Daniel M. ROBERTS
41 Athletic Director .... Mrs. Peggy DAVIS
42 Minister .... Rev. Delano DOUGLAS
29 Director of Alumni Relations ....Ms. Charmica D. EPPS
13 Deputy Chief Information Officer ....Dr. Michael G. POWELL
23 Director of Student Health Services .... Dr. Darylnet LYTTLE
25 Contract Manager ....Ms. Linda SCOTT
87 Director Summer School Session .... Dr. Vykuntapathi THOTA
96 Director of Purchasing .... Mr. Ryan FEREBEE
38 Director University Counseling ....Vacant
88 Special Assistant to the President .... Mr. Osubi CRAIG
04 Executive Assistant to President .... Mrs. Danette JOHNSON
101 Special Asst to President & Board .... Dr. Annie REDD
43 General Counsel .... Ms. Ramona L. TAYLOR

Virginia Union University (C)

1500 N Lombardy Street, Richmond VA 23220-1784
County: Independent City FICE Identification: 003766
Unit ID: 234164
Telephone: (804) 257-5600 Carnegie Class: Bac-A&S
FAX Number: (804) 257-5818 Calendar System: Semester
URL: www.vuu.edu
Established: 1865 Annual Undergrad Tuition & Fees: $17,748
Enrollment: 1,674 Coed
Affiliation or Control: Baptist IRS Status: 501(c)3
Highest Offering: Doctorate
Accreditation: SC, ACBSP, CAEPN, SW, THEOL

01 President ....Dr. Hakim J. LUCAS
03 Executive Vice President ....Dr. Allia CARTER
05 Senior VP/Provost .... Dr. Joy P. GOODRICH
20 Associate Provost ....Dr. Lisa T. MOON
84 VP Enroll Mgmt & Student Affs ....Dr. Tierney J. BATES
32 AVP Student Affairs ....Vacant
07 Director of Admissions ....Ms. Toyarna Y. THOMAS
10 Sr VP Financial Affairs ....Mr. Gregory LEWIS
102 S VP Corporate & External Rels .... Mr. Maurice W. CAMPBELL
26 AVP Public Rel & Communications ....Ms. Pam H. COX
53 Dean Evelyn R Syphax Sch Educ .... Dr. Kimberly GAITERS
49 Dean Arts & Sciences ....Dr. Ted L. RITTER
50 Dean Sydn Lewis Sch of Business .... Dr. Robin DAVIS
100 Chief of Staff ....Vacant
103 Director Workforce Development .... Ms. Felicia COSBY
73 Int Dean School of Theology ....Dr. Gregory HOWARD
25 Director Sponsored Pgm/Title III .... Ms. Linda JACKSON
15 Director Human Resources ....Ms. Tamica S. EPPS
06 Registrar .... Ms. Marilyn A. BROOKS
38 Director Counseling ....Dr. Shanita BROWN
29 Director of Alumni Relations ....Mr. Dominique FOWLER
08 Library Director ....Ms. Pamela B. FOREMAN
37 Director Financial Aid ....Ms. Keisha L. POPE
13 Director Bus Intel & Technology .... Ms. Doreen O. DIXON

42 University Pastor ....Rev. Angelo V. CHATMON
41 Athletic Director ....Ms. Felicia JOHNSON
19 Chief University Police .... Ms. Meshia THOMAS
90 Academic Technology ....Mr. Tyler J. BAPTISTE
21 Asst VP Finan Affairs/Comptroller ....Ms. Stephanie M. WHITE
40 Bookstore Manager ....Ms. Terri WYATT
39 Dean of Students/Dir of Housing ....Ms. Brooke C. BERRY
31 Coordinator Student & Community Eng .... Ms. Claudia E. WALL
18 Director Facilities Management .... Mr. Freddie ROBINSON
96 Director of Purchasing ....Ms. Beverly R. SMITH
04 Executive Asst to President .... Ms. Renee W. JOLLEY
104 Dir Ctr for International Studies .... Dr. David A. ADEWUYI
106 Dir Life-long Learning/Exce Ed ....Vacant
108 Director Institutional Assessment ....Dr. Lisa T. MOON
44 AVP Institutional Giving ....Ms. Lisa D. WINN
101 Secretary of the Institution/Board .... Ms. Renee W. JOLLEY
105 Director Web Services ....Ms. Kiara MCGOWAN-POWELL

Virginia University of Integrative Medicine (D)

9401 Mathy Drive, Fairfax VA 22031
County: Fairfax Identification: 667208
Unit ID: 490106
Telephone: (703) 323-5690 Carnegie Class: Spec-4-yr-Other Health
FAX Number: (703) 323-5692 Calendar System: Quarter
URL: www.vuom.org
Established: Annual Undergrad Tuition & Fees: N/A
Enrollment: 187 Coed
Affiliation or Control: Independent Non-Profit IRS Status: 501(c)3
Highest Offering: Master's
Accreditation: ACUP

01 President ....John SHIN
05 Vice Pres Academic Affairs/CEO .... Tae CHEONG-CHOO
11 COO/Director of Admissions ....John YOO
26 Marketing Director/Student Affairs ....Yoomin KIM

Virginia University of Lynchburg (E)

2058 Garfield Avenue, Lynchburg VA 24501-6417
County: Independent City FICE Identification: 003762
Unit ID: 234137
Telephone: (434) 528-5276 Carnegie Class: Bac-A&S
FAX Number: (434) 528-4257 Calendar System: Semester
URL: www.vul.edu
Established: 1886 Annual Undergrad Tuition & Fees: $9,000
Enrollment: 304 Coed
Affiliation or Control: Independent Non-Profit IRS Status: 501(c)3
Highest Offering: Doctorate
Accreditation: TRACS

01 President .... Dr. Kathy C. FRANKLIN
05 Vice President of Academic Affairs ....Dr. Kathie CARWILE
10 Vice President of Finance ....Dr. Donald LESLIE
32 Director of Student Affairs .... Dr. Philip CAMPBELL
11 Chief Operating Officer .... Mr. Jason J. RANDOO
06 Head Registrar .... Mr. Robbie ADAMS
84 Director of Admissions ....Ms. Angelique CARTER
18 Dir of Facilities/Maintenance .... Mr. Vern DEBILZAN
106 Director of Distant Learning .... Ms. Katrina V. FRANKLIN
19 Director Security/Safety ....Mr. Robert CABLER, JR.
37 Director of Financial Aid ....Ms. Romena MORGAN
04 Special Assistant to the COO .... Mr. Ryan MICKLES
08 Head Librarian ....Ms. Lisa KRAJECKI
13 Director of IT/IE .... Mr. Haniel SINGH

Virginia Wesleyan University (F)

5817 Wesleyan Drive, Virginia Beach VA 23455
County: Independent City FICE Identification: 003767
Unit ID: 234173
Telephone: (757) 455-3200 Carnegie Class: Bac-A&S
FAX Number: (757) 461-4944 Calendar System: 4/1/4
URL: www.vwu.edu
Established: 1961 Annual Undergrad Tuition & Fees: $36,660
Enrollment: 1,470 Coed
Affiliation or Control: United Methodist IRS Status: 501(c)3
Highest Offering: Master's
Accreditation: SC, NRPA, SW

01 President ....Dr. Scott D. MILLER
03 Senior Vice President .... Dr. Mort GAMBLE
05 Vice President for Academic Affairs .... Dr. Maynard SCHAUS
10 Vice President for Finance & Admin ....Mr. James E. COOPER
32 VP for Student Affairs ....Dr. Keith E. MOORE
84 Vice President for Enrollment ....Mr. David WAGGONER
41 Executive Director of Athletics .... Ms. Tina HILL
21 Assistant VP for Finance ....Ms. Sylvia SCHELLY
35 Asst VP for Student Affairs ....Mr. Jason SEWARD
101 Exec Asst to President/Board Sec .... Ms. Kelly BARHAM
04 Admin Asst to President/Board Comm ....Mrs. Jodi L. CHALER
26 Asst VP for Marketing & Comm ....Ms. Stephanie SMAGLO
13 Chief Information Officer ....Dr. Chris DAVIS
88 Exec Dir Quality Enhancement Plan .... Dr. Sara SEWELL
20 Assoc VP for Academic Affairs ....Dr. Susan LARKIN
112 Asst VP for Advancement .... Ms. Sharon LADERBERG
20 Asst VP for Academic Affairs ....Dr. Loren L. MARQUEZ
39 Director of Residence Life ....Mr. David STUEBING
45 Exec Dir of College Rel/Strat Plng .... Ms. Laynee H. TIMLIN
55 Coordinator of Evening/Weekend Pgm ... Ms. Pamela PARAMORE

08 Library Director ... Mrs. Susan ERICKSON
15 Director of Human Resources ... Ms. Karla R. RASMUSSEN
06 Registrar ... Ms. Regina COTTER
37 Director of Financial Aid ... Ms. Teresa L. RHYNE
96 Director of Purchasing ... Ms. Midge ZIMMERMAN
31 Dir Center for Civic Leadership ... Dr. Brian KURISKY
36 Dir of Career Dev & Internships ... Vacant
19 Director of Security ... Mr. Victor DORSEY
18 Director of Physical Plant Opers ... Mr. Donald COBERLY
42 Chaplain ... Rev. Greg WEST
38 Director of Counseling Services ... Mr. Bill BROWN
29 Exec Dir of Annual Giv/Alumni Rel ... Ms. Lori HARRIS
92 Dean Batten Honors College ... Dr. Joyce B. EASTER
122 Director of Student Activities ... Ms. A. Kate COUCH
40 Bookstore Manager ... Ms. Kim S. BROWN
79 Dean Sch Arts & Humanities ... Dr. Travis MALONE
81 Dean Sch Math & Natural Sciences ... Dr. Victor TOWNSEND
83 Dean Sch of Social Science ... Dr. Leslie CAUGHELL
78 Dean of University College ... Dr. Paul EWELL
107 Dean of Professional Studies ... Dr. Ben DOBRIN
09 Director of Institutional Research ... Mr. Shane BOYD
104 Director of Study Away Programs ... Ms. Amanda REINIG
119 Info SecurityOfcr/Network Admin ... Ms. Marcia WILLIAMS
88 Dep Dir of The Lighthouse ... Ms. Amy RUSH
44 Asst Dir of Annual Giving & Alumni ... Ms. Kelly CORDOVA
88 Dir Innov Teach & Engaged Lrng ... Dr. Denise WILKINSON
07 Director for Enrollment ... Ms. Heather CAMPBELL
88 Dir for Enrollment Batten Honors ... Dr. Denise CUNNINGHAM
102 Director of Special Gifts ... Ms. Tiffany WILLIAMS

Washington and Lee University (A)

204 W Washington Street, Lexington VA 24450-2116
County: Independent City FICE Identification: 003768
Unit ID: 234207
Telephone: (540) 458-8400 Carnegie Class: Bac-A&S
FAX Number: (540) 458-8945 Calendar System: Other
URL: www.wlu.edu
Established: 1749 Annual Undergrad Tuition & Fees: $52,455
Enrollment: 2,220 Coed
Affiliation or Control: Independent Non-Profit IRS Status: 501(c)3
Highest Offering: Doctorate
Accreditation: SC, CAEP, JOUR, LAW

01 President ... Dr. William C. DUDLEY
05 Provost ... Dr. Marc CONNER
20 Associate Provost ... Dr. Paul YOUNGMAN
10 Vice Pres for Finance and Admin ... Mr. Steven G. MCALLISTER
111 Vice Pres University Advancement ... Mr. Dennis W. CROSS
32 VP Student Affs & Dean of Students ... Ms. Sidney S. EVANS
101 Sr Asst to Pres/Sec of University ... Mr. James D. FARRAR
43 General Counsel ... Ms. Jennifer KIRKLAND
49 Dean of the College ... Dr. Lena HILL
50 Dean of the Williams School ... Mr. Robert D. STRAUGHAN
61 Dean of the Law School ... Mr. Brant J. HELLWIG
26 Chief Communications Officer ... Ms. Jessica WILLETT
35 Dean of Student Life ... Mr. David M. LEONARD
35 Assoc Dean of Students ... Ms. Tammi R. SIMPSON
30 Exec Dir for University Development ... Mr. Tres MULLIS
41 Director of Athletics ... Ms. Janine M. HATHORN
89 Associate Dean of Students ... Mr. Jason L. RODOCKER
07 Dean of Admissions/Financial Aid ... Ms. Sally S. RICHMOND
09 Asst Provost for Inst Effectiveness ... Mr. Bryan PRICE
06 University Registrar ... Mr. Scott DITTMAN
08 University Librarian ... Mr. John TOMBARGE
85 Director International Education ... Dr. Mark E. RUSH
29 Exec Director of Alumni Affairs ... Mr. Waller T. DUDLEY
15 Exec Director of Human Resources ... Ms. Mary E. MAIN
37 Director of Financial Aid ... Mr. James D. KASTER
18 Exec Dir of University Facilities ... Mr. Tom KALASKY
21 Associate Treasurer & Controller ... Mrs. Deborah Z. CAYLOR
13 Chief Technology Officer ... Mr. David SAACKE
24 Senior Academic Technologist ... Mr. Brandon R. BUCY
36 Dean of Career and Prof Devel ... Mr. John A. JENSEN
23 Director Student Health/Counseling ... Dr. Jane T. HORTON
88 Director of Dining Services ... Ms. Jennifer HICKEY
109 Director of Administrative Services ... Mr. K. C SCHAEFER
04 Admin Assistant to the President ... Ms. Andrea VELASQUEZ
19 Director of Public Safety ... Mr. Ethan KIPNES
28 Dean Diversity/Inclusion/Stdnt Eng ... Ms. Tamara FUTRELL
122 Director of Greek Life ... Ms. Corey GANT
44 Director Annual Giving ... Ms. Missy WITHEROW
53 Director of Teacher Education ... Dr. Haley SIGLER

Washington University of Virginia (B)

4300 Evergreen Lane, Annandale VA 22003
County: Fairfax Identification: 666234
Telephone: (703) 333-5904 Carnegie Class: Not Classified
FAX Number: (703) 333-5906 Calendar System: Semester
URL: www.wuv.edu
Established: 1982 Annual Undergrad Tuition & Fees: N/A
Enrollment: N/A Coed
Affiliation or Control: Non-denominational IRS Status: 501(c)3
Highest Offering: Doctorate
Accreditation: BI, IACBE, THEOL

01 President ... Dr. Peter M. CHANG
03 Executive Vice President ... Mrs. Joyce Gunhee PARK
07 Dean of Enrollment ... Mr. David Y. LEE
08 Head Librarian ... Mr. Robert ROSE, JR.
50 Dean School of Business ... Mr. Won Eog KIM
05 Dean of Academics ... Dr. Wonho JUNG
06 Registrar ... Ms. Keoung Min KIM
38 Director Student Counseling ... Dr. Young C. YOO

Wave Leadership College (C)

1000 North Great Neck Road, Virginia Beach VA 23454
County: Independent City Identification: 667210
Unit ID: 486594
Telephone: (757) 481-5005 Carnegie Class: Spec 2-yr-Other
FAX Number: (757) 496-6697 Calendar System: Semester
URL: www.wavecollege.com
Established: 2000 Annual Undergrad Tuition & Fees: $7,145
Enrollment: 67 Coed
Affiliation or Control: Independent Non-Profit IRS Status: 501(c)3
Highest Offering: Associate Degree
Accreditation: BI

01 President ... Steve KELLY
03 Executive Vice President ... Derek P. HOLSER
05 Academic Dean ... Sarah HUMMEL
32 Dean of Students ... James KNARR
06 Registrar ... Jacquie EVANS
08 Librarian ... Sasha MATTHEWS
37 Financial Aid Director ... James KNARR
85 International Student Liaison ... Jimada ROBINSON

WASHINGTON

Bastyr University (D)

14500 Juanita Drive NE, Kenmore WA 98028-4966
County: King FICE Identification: 022425
Unit ID: 235547
Telephone: (425) 602-3000 Carnegie Class: Spec-4-yr-Other Health
FAX Number: (425) 823-6222 Calendar System: Quarter
URL: www.bastyr.edu
Established: 1978 Annual Undergrad Tuition & Fees: N/A
Enrollment: 1,195 Coed
Affiliation or Control: Independent Non-Profit IRS Status: 501(c)3
Highest Offering: Doctorate
Accreditation: NW, ACUP, DIETD, DIETI, MEAC, NATUR

01 President ... Mr. Harlan PATTERSON
05 Senior Vice President/Provost ... Dr. Dave RULE
111 Vice President Advancement ... Dr. Jeanne GALLOWAY
10 AVP Budget & Finance/CFO ... Ms. Amanda REINHARD
32 Vice President of Student Affairs ... Ms. Susan L. WEIDER

Bates Technical College (E)

1101 S Yakima Avenue, Tacoma WA 98405-4895
County: Pierce FICE Identification: 005306
Unit ID: 235671
Telephone: (253) 680-7000 Carnegie Class: Assoc/HVT-High Non
FAX Number: (253) 680-7101 Calendar System: Quarter
URL: www.batestech.edu
Established: 1940 Annual Undergrad Tuition & Fees (In-State): $5,391
Enrollment: 3,448 Coed
Affiliation or Control: State IRS Status: 501(c)3
Highest Offering: Associate Degree
Accreditation: NW, ACBSP, ACFEI, DA, DT, OTA

01 President ... Dr. Lin ZHOU
05 Exec VP of Instruction/Student Svcs ... Mr. Al GRISWOLD
04 Exec Asst to the President ... Ms. Becky WELCH
32 Vice President of Student Services ... Mr. Steve ASHPOLE
15 Director of Human Resources ... Ms. Christina NELSON
11 Vice Pres Administrative Services ... Ms. Rob'n LEWIS
18 Int Exec Dir Facilities/Operations ... Mr. Bob ROEHL
96 General Services Manager ... Vacant
37 Financial Aid Director ... Vacant
13 Exec Director of IT ... Ms. Agnes FIGUEROA
84 Dir of Enrollment Mgt/Admission ... Ms. Morenika JACOBS
09 Director of Institutional Research ... Vacant
19 Director Security/Safety ... Mr. Dee NELONS
08 Head Librarian ... Mr. Mike WOOD
30 Exec Dir of Resource Development ... Ms. Sarah ALLEN

Bellevue College (F)

3000 Landerholm Circle, SE, Bellevue WA 98007-6484
County: King FICE Identification: 003769
Unit ID: 234669
Telephone: (425) 564-1000 Carnegie Class: Bac/Assoc-Assoc Dom
FAX Number: (425) 564-4065 Calendar System: Quarter
URL: www.bellevuecollege.edu
Established: 1965 Annual Undergrad Tuition & Fees (In-State): $3,778
Enrollment: 13,322 Coed
Affiliation or Control: State IRS Status: 501(c)3
Highest Offering: Baccalaureate
Accreditation: NW, CIDA, DMS, NDT, NMT, NURSE, RADDOS, RTT

01 President ... Dr. Jerry WEBER
04 Exec Asst to the President ... Ms. Donna SULLIVAN
11 Vice Pres Administrative Services ... Mr. Dennis CURRAN
05 Provost Academic & Student Affairs ... Dr. Kristen JONES
15 Vice Pres of Human Resources ... Ms. Suzette YAEZENKO
111 Vice Pres Institutional Advancement ... Ms. Gayle BARGE
32 Vice President of Student Affairs ... Dr. Kirsten JONES
103 Vice Pres of Econ & Wkfrc Dev ... Mr. Albert LEWIS
28 Int Vice President of Diversity ... Dr. Gilbert VILLALPANDO
13 Vice Pres of Information Resources ... Mr. Rodger HARRISON
09 Int Assoc VP Effect & Strat Plng ... Mr. Alec CAMPBELL
51 Dean Continuing Education ... Vacant
79 Int Dean of Arts and Humanities ... Mr. Tuan DANG
76 Dean of HSEWI ... Ms. Leslie HEIZER NEWQUIST
83 Dean of Social Science ... Mr. Rob VIENS
88 Associate Dean of Student Programs ... Vacant
35 Dean of Student Life ... Michael KAPTIK
84 Dean of Enrollment & Registrar Svcs ... Ms. Rae Ellen REAS
85 Dean of Intl Educ & Global Init ... Mr. Jean D'ARC CAMPBELL
10 Int Exec Dir Finance/Auxiliary Svc ... Mr. James CRASWELL
08 Dean of Library Media Center ... Ms. Vivienne MCCLENDON
26 Director of Marketing ... Ms. Katherine HALL
37 Director Financial Aid ... Ms. Melanie RUIZ
19 Director of Public Safety ... Mr. My TRAN
13 Director Computing Services ... Vacant
91 Manager Networking Svcs & Security ... Mr. Gary FARRIS
41 Director of Athletics ... Mr. Jeremy EGGERS
38 Student Counseling ... Mr. Harlan LEE
40 Director Bellevue College Bookstore ... Ms. Kristen CONNELY
96 Int Exec Dir Physical Plant Ops ... Mr. William TRIBBLE

Bellingham Technical College (G)

3028 Lindebergh Avenue, Bellingham WA 98225-1599
County: Whatcom FICE Identification: 004999
Unit ID: 234696
Telephone: (360) 752-7000 Carnegie Class: Bac/Assoc-Assoc Dom
FAX Number: (360) 676-2798 Calendar System: Quarter
URL: www.btc.edu
Established: 1957 Annual Undergrad Tuition & Fees (In-District): $3,600
Enrollment: 2,392 Coed
Affiliation or Control: State/Local IRS Status: 501(c)3
Highest Offering: Baccalaureate
Accreditation: NW, ACFEI, ADNUR, DA, DH, SURGT

01 President ... Dr. Kimberly PERRY
04 Exec Assistant to the President ... Ms. Ronda LAUGHLIN
05 Vice President of Academic Affairs ... Mr. Walter HUDSICK
32 Vice President of Student Services ... Ms. Michele WALTZ
11 VP of Administrative Services ... Ms. Chad STITELER
72 Dean of Prof Technical Education ... Ms. Tonya MCCABE
72 Dean of Prof Technical Education ... Mr. Ray KUBISTA
102 Director Foundation ... Mr. Dean FULTON
15 Int Exec Director Human Resources ... Ms. Tami WILLETT
37 Exec Dir Stdnt Financial Resources ... Ms. Chantel MCMAHAN
06 Director Registration/Enrollment ... Ms. Joan KAMMERZELL
13 Dir Computer/Info Support Svcs ... Mr. Curtis PERERA
08 Director Library Svcs & eLearning ... Ms. Dawn HAWLEY
18 Chief Facilities/Physical Plant ... Mr. David JUNGKUNTZ
26 Director of Communications ... Ms. Marni SALING MAYER
07 Director of Admissions ... Vacant
36 Exec Dir Student Entry & Advising ... Mr. Matthew SANTOS
45 Exec Dir of Inst Planning & Advance ... Ms. RaeLyn AXLUND MCBRIDE
19 Director Security/Safety ... Mr. Al JENSEN
38 Interim Student Counselor ... Ms. Nyssa HOWELL

Big Bend Community College (H)

7662 Chanute Street NE, Moses Lake WA 98837-3299
County: Grant FICE Identification: 003770
Unit ID: 234711
Telephone: (509) 793-2222 Carnegie Class: Assoc/HT-High Trad
FAX Number: (509) 762-6329 Calendar System: Quarter
URL: www.bigbend.edu
Established: 1962 Annual Undergrad Tuition & Fees (In-State): $4,161
Enrollment: 1,975 Coed
Affiliation or Control: State IRS Status: 501(c)3
Highest Offering: Associate Degree
Accreditation: NW, ADNUR

01 President ... Dr. Terry LEAS
10 Vice Pres Administrative Services ... Ms. Linda SCHOONMAKER
05 VP Learning & Student Success ... Dr. Bryce HUMPHERYS
15 VP of Human Resources & Labor ... Mrs. Kim GARZA
103 Dean Workforce Education ... Ms. Daneen BERRY-GUERIN
88 Dean of Transitional Studies ... Ms. Faviola BARBOSA
32 Dean of Student Services ... Mr. Andre GUZMAN
49 Dean of Arts & Sciences ... Ms. Kathleen DUVALL
53 Dean Educ/Health/Language Skills ... Vacant
35 Director of Student Programs ... Ms. Kim JACKSON
37 Director of Financial Aid ... Ms. Rita RAMIREZ
06 Registrar ... Ms. Starr BERNHARDT
08 Director of Library Resources ... Mr. Tim FUHRMAN
41 Director of Athletics ... Mr. Mark POTH
102 Dir Inst Advancement/Exec Dir Found ... Mrs. LeAnne PARTON
26 Director of Communications ... Mr. Matt KILLEBREW
21 Exec Director of Business Services ... Ms. Charlene RIOS
40 Director of Bookstore ... Mrs. Caren COURTRIGHT
96 Director of Purchasing ... Mr. Joe AUVIL
39 Residence Hall Coordinator ... Mr. Luis ALVARADO
09 Dean of Institutional Research ... Ms. Valerie PARTON
13 Director of IT ... Vacant
19 Director Security/Safety ... Mr. Kyle FOREMAN
04 Executive Asst to President ... Ms. Melinda DOURTE
18 Chief Facilities/Physical Plant ... Ms. Char RIOS

Carrington College - Spokane (I)

10102 E Knox Avenue, Suite 200, Spokane WA 99206
Telephone: (509) 462-3722 Identification: 666385

Accreditation: &WJ, MAAB, RAD

† Regional accreditation is carried under the parent institution in Sacramento, CA.

Cascadia College (A)

18345 Campus Way, NE, Bothell WA 98011-8205
County: King FICE Identification: 034835
Unit ID: 439190
Telephone: (425) 352-8000 Carnegie Class: Bac/Assoc-Assoc Dom
FAX Number: (425) 352-8313 Calendar System: Quarter
URL: www.cascadia.edu
Established: 2000 Annual Undergrad Tuition & Fees (In-District): $3,931
Enrollment: 3,425 Coed
Affiliation or Control: State/Local IRS Status: Exempt
Highest Offering: Baccalaureate
Accreditation: NW

01 President ... Dr. Eric MURRAY
101 Exec Asst to the President ... Vicki NEWTON
11 VP for Administrative Services/HR ... Martin LOGAN
10 Dir of Finance ... Sharon WAYMIRE
13 Dir of Information Services ... Brian CULVER
88 Org Ch Mgmt/Project Manager ... Scott MCKEAN
18 Asst Director of Facilities ... Kimberlee CLARK
05 VP for Student Learning & Success ... Dr. Kerry LEVETT
20 Dean of Student Learning ... Dr. Erik TINGELSTAD
20 Dean of Student Learning ... Kristina YOUNG
32 Dean of Student Success Services ... Erin BLAKENEY
20 Dean of Student Learning ... Lyn EISENHOUR
45 Dir Institutional Effectiveness ... Glenn COLBY
84 Dir Enrollment Services ... Shawn MILLER
37 Dir Student Financial Services ... Deann HOLLIDAY
121 Dir Student Adv & Support Services ... Gordon DUTRISAC
35 Dir of Student Life ... Becky RIOPEL
111 VP for External Rels & Planning ... Meagan WALKER
85 Dir of International Programs ... Yukari ZEDNICK
30 Asst Dir of Development ... Mark COLLINS
27 Manager Recruitment & Outreach ... Sara GOMEZ-TAYLOR
118 Manager of Payroll ... Melissa STONER
88 Manager of Professional Development ... Samantha BROWN
16 Human Resources Generalist ... Haley GREEN
16 Human Resources Generalist ... Elizabeth ENGLUND

Central Washington University (B)

400 E University Way, Ellensburg WA 98926-7501
County: Kittitas FICE Identification: 003771
Unit ID: 234827
Telephone: (509) 963-2111 Carnegie Class: Masters/L
FAX Number: (509) 963-3206 Calendar System: Quarter
URL: www.cwu.edu
Established: 1890 Annual Undergrad Tuition & Fees (In-State): $8,072
Enrollment: 12,901 Coed
Affiliation or Control: State IRS Status: 501(c)3
Highest Offering: Master's
Accreditation: NW, CACREP, CONST, DIETD, DIETI, EMT, IPSY, MUS

01 President ... Dr. James L. GAUDINO
05 Provost/VP Academic & Student Life ... Dr. Katherine FRANK
10 VP Business & Financial Affairs ... Mr. Joel KLUCKING
100 Chief of Staff ... Ms. Linda SCHACTLER
20 Assoc Provost UG/Faculty Affairs ... Dr. Gail MACKIN
56 Assoc Provost Ext Learn & Outreach ... Dr. Gayla STONER
88 Assoc Provost Accreditation ... Dr. Bernadette JUNGBLUT
84 Vice Pres Enrollment Management ... Ms. Sharon O'HARE
32 Dean of Student Success ... Dr. Gregg HEINSELMAN
11 VP of Operations ... Mr. Andreas BOHMAN
58 Dean Graduate Studies/Research ... Dr. Kevin ARCHER
49 Dean College of Arts/Humanities ... Dr. Todd SHIVER
50 Dean College of Business ... Mr. Jeffrey L. STINSON
53 Dean College of Educ/Prof Studies ... Dr. Paul BALLARD
83 Dean College of the Sciences ... Dr. Tim ENGLUND
08 Dean of Library Services ... Dr. Rebecca LUBAS
111 Vice Pres University Advancement ... Mr. Scott WADE
07 Assoc VP of Admissions & Enrollment ... Mr. Josh HIBBARD
26 Vice Pres of Public Affairs ... Ms. Kremiere JACKSON
28 Vice Pres of Diversity ... Dr. Delores CLEARY

Centralia College (C)

600 Centralia College Boulevard,
Centralia WA 98531-4035
County: Lewis FICE Identification: 003772
Unit ID: 234845
Telephone: (360) 736-9391 Carnegie Class: Bac/Assoc-Assoc Dom
FAX Number: (360) 330-7108 Calendar System: Quarter
URL: www.centralia.edu
Established: 1925 Annual Undergrad Tuition & Fees (In-State): $4,437
Enrollment: 3,122 Coed
Affiliation or Control: State IRS Status: 501(c)3
Highest Offering: Baccalaureate
Accreditation: NW

01 President ... Dr. Robert MOHRBACHER
05 Vice President Instruction ... Dr. Joyce HAMMER
32 Vice President of Students ... Mr. Robert COX
10 Vice Pres Finance/Administration ... Mr. Steve WARD
15 VP Human Resources/Legal Affairs ... Ms. Julie HUSS
103 Dean Workforce Education ... Mr. Jake FAY
08 Dean of Library Services/E-Learning ... Vacant
88 Dean of Academic Transfer Programs ... Mr. Christian BRUHN
09 Director of Institutional Research ... Mr. Scott WAGEMANN
88 Dir WorkFirst & Worker Retraining ... Ms. Margret FRIEDLEY
84 Director of Enrollment Services ... Ms. Kimberly INGRAM
37 Director of Financial Aid ... Ms. Tracy DAHL
13 Director Information Technology ... Mr. Samuel SMALL
41 Director of Sports Programs ... Mr. Bob PETERS
29 Director Alumni Relations ... Ms. Christine FOSSETT
96 Director of Purchasing ... Ms. Bonnie MYER
26 Dir College Relations & Events ... Ms. Amanda HAINES
06 Registration Specialist ... Vacant
40 Bookstore Manager ... Ms. Tammy STRODEMIER
97 Program Coordinator ... Ms. Monica BRUMMER

Charter College (D)

17200 SE Mill Plain Blvd, Suite 100, Vancouver WA 98683
County: Clark FICE Identification: 025769
Unit ID: 102845
Telephone: (360) 448-2000 Carnegie Class: Not Classified
FAX Number: N/A Calendar System: Quarter
URL: www.chartercollege.edu
Established: 2010 Annual Undergrad Tuition & Fees: N/A
Enrollment: 2,664 Coed
Affiliation or Control: Proprietary IRS Status: Proprietary
Highest Offering: Baccalaureate
Accreditation: ABHES

02 Campus President ... Heather ALLEN

City University of Seattle (E)

521 Wall Street, Suite 100, Seattle WA 98121
County: King FICE Identification: 013022
Unit ID: 234915
Telephone: (206) 239-4500 Carnegie Class: Masters/L
FAX Number: (206) 239-4802 Calendar System: Quarter
URL: www.cityu.edu
Established: 1973 Annual Undergrad Tuition & Fees: $16,973
Enrollment: 2,199 Coed
Affiliation or Control: Independent Non-Profit IRS Status: 501(c)3
Highest Offering: Doctorate
Accreditation: NW, ACBSP, CACREP

01 President ... Mr. Randy C. FRISCH
101 Exec Asst Office of the President ... Ms. Nandi MOONFLOWER
32 Vice President Student Services ... Dr. Melissa E. MECHAM
05 Provost ... Dr. Scott CARNZ
10 Chief Financial Officer ... Mr. Christopher BRYAN
84 Vice Pres Enrollment Management ... Vacant
50 Dean School of Management ... Mr. Tom CARY
53 Dean Albright Sch of Education ... Dr. Vicki BUTLER
20 Dean/EVP Academic Affairs ... Ms. Mary MARA
15 Director of Human Resources ... Ms. Janet O'LEARY
08 Director Library Services ... Mr. Matthew LECHNER
37 Dir Student Financial Svcs ... Ms. Darcy KELLER
29 Alumni Relations Manager ... Mr. Alex WEBSTER
13 Director of Information Technology ... Mr. Kevin H. BROWN
07 Director of Enrollment & Advising ... Ms. Teresa D'AMBROSIO
85 Director Intl Student Office ... Ms. Sabine SAWAY
18 Facilities Manager ... Mr. Troy CRABREE
06 Registrar ... Ms. Kathleen YACKEY

Clark College (F)

1933 Fort Vancouver Way, Vancouver WA 98663-3598
County: Clark FICE Identification: 003773
Unit ID: 234933
Telephone: (360) 992-2000 Carnegie Class: Bac/Assoc-Assoc Dom
FAX Number: (360) 992-2871 Calendar System: Quarter
URL: www.clark.edu
Established: 1933 Annual Undergrad Tuition & Fees (In-State): $4,287
Enrollment: 10,000 Coed
Affiliation or Control: State IRS Status: 501(c)3
Highest Offering: Baccalaureate
Accreditation: NW, ADNUR, DH, MAC

01 President ... Mr. Robert KNIGHT
05 Vice President of Instruction ... Dr. Sachi HORBACK
32 Vice President of Student Affairs ... Mr. William BELDEN
11 Vice President of Admin Services ... Mr. Bob WILLIAMSON
15 Assoc Vice Pres of Human Resources ... Ms. Stefani COVERSON
45 Assoc VP Planning/Inst Effective ... Ms. Shanda HALUAPO
51 Assoc VP Corp & Continuing Educ ... Mr. Kevin WITTE
84 Dir of Enrollment/Registrar ... Ms. Mirranda SAARI
75 Dean of WF Professional Tech Ed ... Ms. Genevieve HOWARD
79 Dean Engl/Comm/Hum/Basic Educ ... Mr. Jim WILKINS-LUTON
76 Assoc Dean of Health Science ... Vacant
83 Dean Social Sciences/Fine Arts ... Mr. Miles JACKSON
52 Dean of Business & Health Sciences ... Ms. Brenda WALSTEAD
04 Exec Assistant to the President ... Ms. Leigh KENT
41 Interim Director of Athletics ... Ms. Laura LEMASTERS
16 Associate Director Human Resources ... Vacant
08 Int Dir of Library Services ... Ms. Korey MARQUEZ
18 Dir of Facility Services ... Mr. Tim PETTA
26 Chief Communications Officer ... Ms. Kelly LOVE
36 Director Career/Employment Services ... Ms. Edie BLAKELY
37 Director of Financial Aid ... Ms. Chippi BELLO
10 Director of Business Services ... Ms. Sabra SAND
35 Dir Stdnt Life/Multicult Stdnt Affs ... Ms. Sarah GRUHLER
121 Director of Advising Center ... Mr. John MADUTA
25 Director of Grant Development ... Vacant
28 Int AVP Diversity/Equity/Inclusion ... Ms. Rashida WILLARD
19 Director of Security & Safety ... Mr. Michael SEE
85 International Recruitment Manager ... Vacant
40 Bookstore Manager ... Ms. Monica KNOWLES
88 Mature Learning & Travel Stds Mgr ... Ms. Tracy REILLY-KELLY
96 Purchasing Manager ... Ms. Lisa HASART
102 Foundation CEO ... Ms. Lisa GIBERT
105 Information Technology Specialist ... Mr. Chris CONCANNON
29 Director Alumni Relations ... Ms. Vivian MANNING
13 Chief Information Technology Office ... Ms. Valerie MORENO
103 Director Workforce Development ... Mr. Kevin WITTE

Clover Park Technical College (G)

4500 Steilacoom Boulevard, SW,
Lakewood WA 98499-4004
County: Pierce FICE Identification: 005752
Unit ID: 234951
Telephone: (253) 589-5800 Carnegie Class: Bac/Assoc-Assoc Dom
FAX Number: (253) 589-5851 Calendar System: Quarter
URL: www.cptc.edu
Established: 1942 Annual Undergrad Tuition & Fees (In-State): $5,740
Enrollment: 3,883 Coed
Affiliation or Control: State IRS Status: 501(c)3
Highest Offering: Baccalaureate
Accreditation: NW, DA, HT, MAC, MLTAD, SURGT

01 President ... Dr. Joyce LOVEDAY
04 Executive Assistant ... Cherie STEELE
05 Vice President Instruction ... Mabel EDMONDS
10 Vice Pres Finance & Admin Svcs ... Larry CLARK
32 VP Student Success ... Scott LATIOLAIS
26 VP Strategic Development ... Dr. Tawny DOTSON
15 Human Resources Director ... Kirk WALKER
103 Dir of Workforce Development ... Cristeen CROUCHET
13 Dir Information Technology ... Pamela JETER
37 Director Financial Aid ... Celva BOON
18 Director Facilities Services ... John KANISS
12 Dir Northwest Career/Tech HS ... Loren DAVIS
84 Director of Enrollment Services ... Cynthia MOWRY
114 Dir Budget & Finance ... Lisa WOLCOTT
121 Dean Student Success ... Dean KELLY
88 Director Compliance ... Lisa BEACH
96 Purchasing & Supply Specialist ... Kimberly BILLS
27 Marketing/Outreach Coordinator ... Janet HOLM
09 Institutional Researcher ... Samantha DANA
40 Bookstore Coordinator ... Kariena MELLOR
06 Registrar/Associate Dean ... Cynthia MOWRY
88 Dean Division B ... Dr. Claire KORSCHINOWSKI
88 Dean Division C ... Michelle HILLESLAND
88 Interim Dean Division A ... Dr. Chris CHEN MAHONEY
28 Exec Dir Equity/Diversity/Inclusion ... Shareka FORTIER
105 Web Content Manager ... Jessica CAREY
85 Mgr Intl Education Programs ... Yuko CHARTRAW

Columbia Basin College (H)

2600 N 20th Avenue, Pasco WA 99301-3397
County: Franklin FICE Identification: 003774
Unit ID: 234979
Telephone: (509) 547-0511 Carnegie Class: Bac/Assoc-Mixed
FAX Number: (509) 546-0404 Calendar System: Quarter
URL: www.columbiabasin.edu
Established: 1955 Annual Undergrad Tuition & Fees (In-State): $5,288
Enrollment: 6,708 Coed
Affiliation or Control: State IRS Status: 170(c)1
Highest Offering: Baccalaureate
Accreditation: NW, ADNUR, DH, EMT, MAC, NURSE, SURGT

01 President ... Dr. Rebekah WOODS
05 Vice President Instruction ... Vacant
10 Vice Pres Administrative Services ... Mr. Tyrone BROOKS
32 Vice President of Student Services ... Ms. Cheryl HOLDEN
15 VP Human Resources/Legal Affairs ... Ms. Camilla GLATT
13 Asst VP Infrastructure Services ... Mr. Brian DEXTER
09 Dean for Organizational Learning ... Dr. Jason ENGLE
49 Dean Arts & Humanities ... Mr. Bill MCKAY
08 Assoc Dean Library Services ... Ms. Keri LOBDELL
102 Executive Director Foundation ... Mr. Kevin RUSCH
40 Bookstore Director ... Ms. Debra BRUCE
18 Director of Plant Operations ... Vacant
41 Athletic Director ... Mr. Scott ROGERS
26 Marketing/Communications Director ... Ms. Anna TENSMEYER
35 Director of Student Activities ... Ms. Alice SCHLEGEL
37 Director Student Financial Aid ... Mr. Ben BEUS
96 Director of Purchasing ... Vacant
06 Associate Registrar ... Ms. Donna KORSTAD
04 Admin Assistant to the President ... Ms. Darlene SCRIVNER
07 Director of Admissions ... Ms. Kelsey MYERS
39 Director Resident Life ... Mr. Dan QUOCK
50 Dean for Business & Computer Sci ... Mr. Hansen STEWART

*Community Colleges of Spokane District 17 (I)

501 N Riverpoint Boulevard, Ste 126,
Spokane WA 99217-6000
County: Spokane FICE Identification: 010784
Telephone: (509) 434-5107 Carnegie Class: N/A
FAX Number: (509) 434-5120
URL: www.ccs.spokane.edu

01 Chancellor ... Dr. Christine JOHNSON
12 Pres Spokane Community College ... Dr. Kevin BROCKBANK
12 Pres Spokane Falls Cmty College ... Dr. Kimberlee MESSINA
05 Vice Pres Instruction/Provost ... Ms. Jenni MARTIN
20 Vice President of Learning SCC ... Ms. Jenni MARTIN
20 Vice President of Learning SFCC ... Dr. Andrew FELDMAN
32 VP of Student Services SCC ... Dr. Glen COSBY
32 VP of Student Services SFCC ... Dr. Chrissy DAVIS JONES
10 Chief Financial Officer ... Ms. Lisa HJALTALIN
11 Chief Administration Officer ... Mr. Greg L. STEVENS
26 Public Information Officer ... Ms. Carolyn CASEY
41 Dist Director of Athletics PE/Rec ... Mr. Ken BURRUS
102 Executive Director CCS Foundation ... Ms. Heather BEEBE STEVENS
40 Director College Bookstores ... Ms. Shami R. RUGGLES
18 District Director of Facilities ... Mr. John GILLETTE
103 Exec Dir Ctr Wkforce/Cont Ed ... Mr. Nolan GRUVER
07 Dir Admissions/Registration ... Mr. Chantel BLACK
96 Purchasing Manager ... Ms. Laurel CAMPBELL
106 Dir Online Education/E-learning ... Mr. Patrick MCEACHERN

*Spokane Community College (A)

North 1810 Greene Street, Spokane WA 99217-5499
County: Spokane FICE Identification: 003793
Unit ID: 236692
Telephone: (509) 533-7000 Carnegie Class: Bac/Assoc-Assoc Dom
FAX Number: N/A Calendar System: Quarter
URL: www.scc.spokane.edu
Established: 1963 Annual Undergrad Tuition & Fees (In-State): $3,547
Enrollment: 10,014 Coed
Affiliation or Control: State IRS Status: 501(c)3
Highest Offering: Baccalaureate
Accreditation: NW, ACFEI, ADNUR, CAHIIM, COARC, CVT, DA, DMS, MAC, RAD, SURGT

00 District Chancellor ... Dr. Christine JOHNSON
02 President ... Dr. Kevin BROCKBANK
05 VP of Instruction ... Ms. Jenni MARTIN
32 Vice President of Student Services ... Dr. Glen COSBY
121 Director Student Success & Outreach ... Dr. Lori HUNT
07 Director Admissions & Registration ... Ms. Chantel BLACK
35 Associate Dean Student Development ... Mr. Connan CAMPBELL
51 Dean Adult Basic Education ... Dr. Sherri FUJITA
49 Dean Arts & Sciences ... Ms. Gwendolyn JAMES
50 Dean Business/Hospitality/Info Tech ... Mr. Jeff BROWN
88 Assoc Dean Corrections Education ... Mr. Kevin HOUSE
56 Dean Extended Learning ... Ms. Jaclyn JACOT
76 Dean Health & Environmental Science ... Dr. J.L HENRIKSEN
66 Associate Dean of Nursing ... Dr. Cheri OSLER
75 Dean for Technical Education ... Mr. Dave COX
41 Interim Director Athletics/PE ... Mr. Bobby LEE
09 Sr Dir Inst Effectiveness/Planning ... Ms. Charlie POTTER
88 Assistant Dean PACE Services ... Ms. Linda AMES
06 Registrar ... Ms. Chantel BLACK
37 Director Financial Aid ... Ms. Tammy ZIBELL
10 Chief Financial Officer ... Ms. Lisa HJALTALIN
40 Director of College Bookstores ... Ms. Shami RUGGLES
11 Chief Administration Officer ... Mr. Greg STEVENS
26 Chief Public Information Officer ... Ms. Carolyn CASEY
30 District Development Officer ... Ms. Heather BEEBE-STEVENS
20 District Provost ... Dr. Valerie SENATORE
38 Student Counseling Department Chair ... Ms. Rebecca GOSS
96 District Director of Purchasing ... Ms. Nanette SPEAR
04 Executive Asst to President ... Ms. Joanne ARSENAULT
13 Chief Info Technology Officer (CIO) ... Mr. Rick SPARKS

*Spokane Falls Community College (B)

3410 W Fort George Wright Drive,
Spokane WA 99224-5288
County: Spokane FICE Identification: 009544
Unit ID: 236708
Telephone: (509) 533-3500 Carnegie Class: Bac/Assoc-Assoc Dom
FAX Number: (509) 533-3237 Calendar System: Quarter
URL: www.spokanefalls.edu
Established: 1967 Annual Undergrad Tuition & Fees (In-State): $3,547
Enrollment: 5,589 Coed
Affiliation or Control: State IRS Status: Exempt
Highest Offering: Baccalaureate
Accreditation: NW, OTA, PTAA

02 President ... Dr. Kimberlee MESSINA
04 Exec Asst to the President ... Ms. Jan CARPENTER
05 Vice President of Learning ... Dr. Andrew FELDMAN
32 Int Vice President of Student Svcs ... Dr. Chrissy DAVIS
81 Dean Computing/Math & Science ... Mr. James BRADY
83 Dean Soc Sci/Acct/Econ/Hum Svcs ... Ms. Elodie GOODMAN
79 Dean Humanities ... Dr. Linda BEANE-BOOSE
57 Dean Visual & Performing Arts ... Dr. Bonnie BRUNT
50 Dean Bus/Prof Stds/Workforce ... Ms. Lora SENF
121 Int Dean Student Support Services ... Ms. Cynthia VIGIL
07 Dir Recruit/New Stdnt Entry Center ... Ms. Lori WILLIAMS
38 Counseling Department Chair ... Ms. Shawna SHELTON
37 Director of Financial Aid ... Ms. Marjorie DAVIS
06 Registrar ... Ms. Sindie HOWLAND
41 Athletic Director ... Vacant
19 Security & Safety Supervisor ... Mr. Kenneth DEMELLO
09 Dir Inst Effectiveness/Research ... Ms. Sally JACKSON
15 Chief Human Resources Officer ... Mr. Greg STEVENS
10 Chief Business Officer ... Ms. Lisa HJALTALIN
13 Chief Info Technology Officer (CIO) ... Mr. Rick SPARKS
102 Exec Director CCS Foundation ... Ms. Heather BEEBE-STEVENS
85 Dean for Global Education ... Ms. Hadda ESTRADA
08 District Director of Libraries ... Dr. Mary Ann GOODWIN
106 District Director of e-Learning ... Mr. Patrick MCEACHERN
103 Chief Workforce Development Officer ... Mr. Nolan GRUVER
26 Public Information Officer ... Ms. Carolyn CASEY
18 Director of Facilities ... Mr. John GILLETTE
96 Director of Purchasing ... Vacant

Cornish College of the Arts (C)

1000 Lenora Street, Seattle WA 98121-2707
County: King FICE Identification: 012315
Unit ID: 235024
Telephone: (206) 726-5151 Carnegie Class: Spec-4-yr-Arts
FAX Number: (206) 720-1011 Calendar System: Semester
URL: www.cornish.edu
Established: 1914 Annual Undergrad Tuition & Fees: $41,642
Enrollment: 658 Coed
Affiliation or Control: Independent Non-Profit IRS Status: 501(c)3
Highest Offering: Baccalaureate
Accreditation: NW, ART

01 President ... Dr. Raymond TYMAS-JONES
05 Provost ... Vacant
111 VP Institutional Advancement ... Ms. Anne DERIEUX
10 VP Finance & Administration ... Ms. Christene A. JAMES
84 VP of Enrollment Management ... Mr. Ryan O'MEALEY
18 VP of Operations ... Mr. Brandon BIRD
32 Dean of Student Life ... Ms. Brittany HENDERSON
06 Dean of Academic Services/Registrar ... Ms. Adrienne M. BOLYARD
15 Director of Human Resources ... Mr. Roy BROWN, III
13 Director of Information Technology ... Mr. Jon GRAEF
100 Chief of Staff ... Mr. Rick SMITH
21 Controller ... Ms. Tina CHAMBERLAIN
08 Director of Library Services ... Ms. Hollis NEAR
07 Director of Admissions ... Ms. Sharron STARLING
26 Dir of Marketing & Communications ... Ms. Natasha DWORKIN
38 Director Student Counseling ... Ms. Lori KOSHORK
37 Asst Director of Financial Aid ... Ms. Margaret MURRAY
19 Manager Security & Safety ... Mr. David GOMEZ
30 Director of Development ... Ms. Pat BAKO

DigiPen Institute of Technology (D)

9931 Willows Road, NE, Redmond WA 98052
County: King FICE Identification: 037243
Unit ID: 443410
Telephone: (425) 558-0299 Carnegie Class: Bac-Diverse
FAX Number: (425) 558-0378 Calendar System: Semester
URL: www.digipen.edu
Established: 1988 Annual Undergrad Tuition & Fees: $31,340
Enrollment: 1,102 Coed
Affiliation or Control: Proprietary IRS Status: Proprietary
Highest Offering: Master's
Accreditation: ACCSC

01 President ... Mr. Claude COMAIR
32 Sr VP Student & External Affairs ... Ms. Angela KUGLER
11 COO - International ... Mr. Jason CHU
35 Dean of Students ... Mr. Marshall TRAVERSE
07 Director of Admissions ... Ms. Danial POWERS

Eastern Washington University (E)

526 5th Street, Cheney WA 99004-1619
County: Spokane FICE Identification: 003775
Unit ID: 235097
Telephone: (509) 359-6200 Carnegie Class: Masters/L
FAX Number: (509) 359-6927 Calendar System: Quarter
URL: www.ewu.edu
Established: 1882 Annual Undergrad Tuition & Fees (In-State): $7,323
Enrollment: 12,607 Coed
Affiliation or Control: State IRS Status: 501(c)3
Highest Offering: Doctorate
Accreditation: NW, CAATE, CACREP, DH, MUS, NRPA, OT, PLNG, PTA, SP, SPAA, SW

01 President ... Dr. Mary CULLINAN
05 Provost/VP of Academic Affairs ... Dr. Scott GORDON
10 Vice President for Business/Finance ... Ms. Mary VOVES
32 Vice President for Student Affairs ... Ms. Angela JONES
111 Vice President of Advancement ... Ms. Barbara RICHEY
32 VP Diversity & Inclusion ... Ms. Shari CLARKE
13 VP Info Technology/CIO ... Mr. Brad CHRIST
20 Vice Prov Academic Admin ... Dr. David MAY
28 VP for Diversity & Inclusion ... Ms. Shari CLARKE
88 AVP Academic Planning ... Mr. Mark BALDWIN
78 Dean of University College ... Ms. Lynn BRIGGS
88 Associate Dean University College ... Dr. Chuck LOPEZ
08 Interim Dean of Libraries ... Dr. Justin OTTO
06 Interim Registrar ... Mr. Anthony SILECCHIA
41 AVP/Director of Athletics ... Ms. Lynn HICKEY
21 Assoc VP Finance/Chief Fin Officer ... Ms. Toni HABEGGER
18 Assoc Vice Pres for Facilities ... Mr. Shawn KING
84 Assoc VP Enrollment Management ... Dr. Jens LARSON
07 Assoc Dir of Admissions Operation ... Mr. Boubacar BOUARÉ
86 Asst Director of Government Affairs ... Mr. Nathan FITZGERALD
36 Asst VP Student Svcs/Dir Career Dev ... Ms. Virginia (Gini) HINCH
15 AVP of Human Resources ... Ms. Deborah DANNER
26 Asst VP Marketing/Communications ... Mr. Lance KISSLER
101 Exec Assistant to the President/BOT ... Ms. Chandalin BENNETT
100 Chief of Staff ... Ms. Sara SEXTON-JOHNSON
92 Spec Asst to Provost for Honors ... Dr. Naomi YAVNEH KLOS
88 Asst Dir International Admissions ... Ms. Jennifer NEHUS
37 Dir of Financial Aid & Scholarships ... Mr. Bruce DEFRATES
40 Bookstore Director ... Ms. Devon TINKER
51 Dir of Continuing Education & RS ... Ms. Brenda BLAZEKOVIC
06 Associate Registrar ... Ms. Debra FOCKLER
29 AVP of Philanthropy ... Ms. Lisa POPLAWSKI
39 Sr Director Housing/Residence Life ... Mr. Josh ASHCROFT
38 Director Counseling & Psych Svcs ... Dr. Robert QUACKENBUSH
19 Director Public Safety/Chief Police ... Chief Timothy L. WALTERS
27 Director of Media Relations ... Mr. David MEANY
22 Director Equal Opportunity ... Mr. Ray RECTOR
50 Dean Business & Public Admin ... Dr. Ahmad TOOTOONCHI
49 Dean College Arts/Letters/Education ... Dr. Roy SONNEMA
83 Dean Col Soc/Behav Sci/Soc Work ... Dr. Jonathan ANDERSON
81 Dean Col Science/Technology/Math ... Dr. David BOWMAN
66 Dean Health Science & Public Health ... Dr. Laureen O'HANLON
35 Assoc VP/Dean of Student Life ... Dr. Amy JOHNSON
09 Int Director Institutional Research ... Ms. Tara MOSES
44 Assistant Director of Annual Giving ... Ms. Kyndell WHITE
104 Int Manager of Global Initiatives ... Ms. Megan ABBEY
25 Exec Dir Grants & Research Dev ... Ms. Ruth GALM

Edmonds Community College (F)

20000 68th Avenue W, Lynnwood WA 98036-5999
County: Snohomish FICE Identification: 005001
Unit ID: 235103
Telephone: (425) 640-1459 Carnegie Class: Bac/Assoc-Assoc Dom
FAX Number: (425) 771-3366 Calendar System: Quarter
URL: www.edcc.edu
Established: 1967 Annual Undergrad Tuition & Fees (In-State): $4,136
Enrollment: 8,100 Coed
Affiliation or Control: State IRS Status: 501(c)3
Highest Offering: Associate Degree
Accreditation: NW, CONST

01 President ... Dr. Amit B. SINGH
05 Exec Vice President Instruction ... Dr. Charlie CRAWFORD
10 Vice Pres Finance & Operations ... Mr. Kevin MCKAY
15 Exec Director of Human Resources ... Ms. Mushka ROHANI
32 Vice President Student Services ... Ms. Christina CASTORENA
103 VP Workforce Development/Training ... Dr. Terry COX
84 Assoc Dean Student Enroll/Fin Aid ... Ms. Christina RUSS
35 Dean Student Life/Development ... Mr. Jorge DE LA TORRE
04 Interim Exec Asst to the President ... Ms. Emily BENALI
121 Dean Student Success/Retention ... Dr. Steve WOODARD
102 Exec Director College Foundation ... Mr. Brad THOMAS
88 Director Advising ... Ms. Olla IBRAHIM
25 Exec Director Grants & Research ... Ms. Cat CAROTHERS
26 Dir Marketing/Public Information ... Ms. Marisa PIERCE
13 Director Information Technology ... Ms. Eva SMITH
18 Dir Facilities/Planning/Operations ... Ms. Stephanie TEACHMAN
41 Athletic Director ... Mr. Spencer STARK
85 Dir International Student Services ... Ms. Lisa THOMPSON
09 Institutional Researcher ... Ms. Wenlan JING
28 VP Equity & Inclusion ... Dr. Yvonne TERRELL-POWELL
108 Exec Dir Inst Effect/Strategic Plng ... Mr. James MULIK
96 Director of Finance ... Ms. Janie BARNETT-PARKER
27 Marketing Manager ... Vacant
06 Dir Enrollment Svcs/Registrar ... Ms. Christina RUSS
21 Director of Accounting ... Ms. Geni TEAGUE
37 Director Financial Aid ... Ms. MiChelle THORSEN
38 Dir Counseling & Resource Center ... Ms. Jessica BURWELL
39 Housing Dir/Housing for Students ... Mr. Luke BOTZHEIM
50 Dean Business Division ... Mr. Andrew WILLIAMS
29 Director of Alumni Affairs ... Ms. Lisa CARROLL
36 Director Entry Services ... Mr. Mark DIVIRGILIO

† Granted candidacy at the Baccalaureate level.

Everett Community College (G)

2000 Tower Street, Everett WA 98201-1390
County: Snohomish FICE Identification: 003776
Unit ID: 235149
Telephone: (425) 388-9100 Carnegie Class: Assoc/HT-High Non
FAX Number: (425) 388-9129 Calendar System: Quarter
URL: www.everettcc.edu
Established: 1941 Annual Undergrad Tuition & Fees (In-State): $3,794
Enrollment: 7,740 Coed
Affiliation or Control: State IRS Status: 501(c)3
Highest Offering: Associate Degree
Accreditation: NW, ADNUR, MAC

01 President ... Dr. Daria WILLIS
04 Sr Exec Asst to President ... Ms. Kelly BERGER
04 Exec Asst to President ... Ms. Jeri POURCHOT
05 EVP Instruction/Student Svcs ... Mr. John BONNER
111 Vice Pres of College Advancement ... Dr. John OLSON
10 Vice Pres of Administrative Svcs ... Ms. Denise GREGORY WYATT
26 Vice Pres of College Services ... Mr. Patrick SISNEROS
60 Dean Communication/Social Sciences ... Mr. Eugene MCAVOY
32 Dean of Student Development ... Mr. Anthony WILLIAMS
81 Dean of Math & Science ... Mr. Al FRIEDMAN
62 Dean of Arts & Learning Resources ... Vacant
76 Dean Health Sciences/Public Safety ... Vacant
53 Dean of Basic & Adult Education ... Ms. Katie JENSEN
28 Chief Diversity & Equity Officer ... Ms. Maria PENA
51 Director Continuing Education ... Ms. Kristen MCCONAHA
84 Dean Enrollment/Student Finan Svcs ... Ms. Laurie FRANKLIN
50 Dean of Business & Applied Tech ... Mr. William STUFLICK

19 Dir of Campus Safety & Security Mr. Charles MACKLIN
88 Vice Pres of Corporate Training Mr. John BONNER
09 Director Institutional Research Ms. Stephanie CHADWICK
41 Director of Athletics Mr. Garet STUDER
40 Director of Bookstore Ms. Rachael WATSON
22 Dir Center for Disability Services Mr. Eric TREKELL
06 Registrar Mr. Karl RITTER SMITH
104 Assoc Vice Pres Intl Studies Mr. Visakan GANESON
13 Chief Information Technology Office Mr. Tim RAGER

The Evergreen State College (A)

2700 Evergreen Parkway, NW, Olympia WA 98505-0005
County: Thurston FICE Identification: 008155
Unit ID: 235167
Telephone: (360) 867-6000 Carnegie Class: Masters/S
FAX Number: N/A Calendar System: Quarter
URL: www.evergreen.edu
Established: 1967 Annual Undergrad Tuition & Fees (In-State): $7,746
Enrollment: 3,907 Coed
Affiliation or Control: State IRS Status: 501(c)3
Highest Offering: Master's
Accreditation: NW

01 President Dr. George S. BRIDGES
05 Provost/VP for Student & Acad Life Dr. Jennifer DRAKE
32 Vice Prov for Student & Acad Life Dr. Wendy ENDRESS
10 Vice President Finance/Operations Dr. John CARMICHAEL
111 Vice President College Advancement Ms. Amanda WALKER
26 Vice President College Relations Ms. Sandra KAISER
28 VP Incl Excellence & Stdnt Success Dr. Chassity HOLLIMAN-DOUGLAS
88 VP for Indigenous Arts & Education Ms. Tina KUCKKAHN-MILLER
84 Chief Enrollment Officer Mr. Eric PEDERSEN
15 Assoc Vice Pres for Human Resources Ms. Laurel UZNANSKI
21 Assoc Vice Pres Business Services Mr. Dave KOHLER
08 Dean of Library Services Mr. Greg MULLINS
121 Dir of Academic and Career Advising Vacant
101 Executive Assoc/Secretary to BOT Ms. Susan HARRIS
22 Affirm Action/Equal Opp Officer Ms. Lorie MASTIN
13 Director Computing/Communications Mr. Antonio ALFONSO
37 Director of Financial Aid Ms. Tracy HALL
06 Registrar Ms. Elaine HAYASHI-PETERSEN
09 Director of Institutional Research Vacant
18 Director of Facilities Mr. William WARD
38 Dir Counseling & Health Services Ms. Elizabeth MCHUGH
96 Purchasing and Contracts Manager Mr. Brant EDDY
07 Director of Admissions Mr. Wade ARAVE
88 Director of Sustainability Mr. Scott MORGAN

Faith International University (B)

3504 N Pearl Street, Tacoma WA 98407-2607
County: Pierce FICE Identification: 036894
Unit ID: 443049
Telephone: (253) 752-2020 Carnegie Class: Spec-4-yr-Faith
FAX Number: (253) 759-1790 Calendar System: Quarter
URL: www.faithseminary.edu
Established: 1969 Annual Undergrad Tuition & Fees: $7,875
Enrollment: 288 Coed
Affiliation or Control: Interdenominational IRS Status: 501(c)3
Highest Offering: Doctorate
Accreditation: TRACS

01 President Dr. Michael J. ADAMS
05 Vice Pres Academic Affs/Provost Dr. H. Wayne HOUSE
104 VP Intl Affs/Dean Korean Division Dr. Kyu H. LEE
11 VP Administrative/Student Affs Mr. John WHEELER
88 Admin Dean Korean Division Dr. Miae LEE
10 Chief Financial Officer Vacant
07 Director of Admissions Ms. Karen BURNWORTH
08 Director Library Services Dr. Timothy HYUN
04 Exec Administrative Assistant Ms. Kimberly ADAMS
06 Registrar Ms. Mary VELONI

Gather 4 Him Bible College (C)

3021 West Clearwater Avenue, Kennewick WA 99336
County: Benton Identification: 667359
Telephone: (509) 420-4545 Carnegie Class: Not Classified
FAX Number: N/A Calendar System: Semester
URL: college-gather4him.net
Established: 2008 Annual Undergrad Tuition & Fees: N/A
Enrollment: N/A Coed
Affiliation or Control: Independent Non-Profit IRS Status: 501(c)3
Highest Offering: Associate Degree
Accreditation: ●TRACS

01 President Bob NASH

Gonzaga University (D)

502 East Boone Avenue, Spokane WA 99258-0102
County: Spokane FICE Identification: 003778
Unit ID: 235316
Telephone: (509) 328-4220 Carnegie Class: DU-Mod
FAX Number: (509) 313-5718 Calendar System: Semester
URL: www.gonzaga.edu
Established: 1887 Annual Undergrad Tuition & Fees: $43,210
Enrollment: 7,506 Coed
Affiliation or Control: Roman Catholic IRS Status: 501(c)3
Highest Offering: Doctorate
Accreditation: NW, ANEST, CACREP, CEA, LAW, MUS, NURSE

01 President Dr. Thayne M. MCCULLOH
100 Chief of Staff Mr. John SKLUT
05 Provost Dr. Deena GONZALEZ
42 VP for Mission & Ministry Ms. Michelle WHEATLEY
45 Chief Strategy Officer Mr. Charles J. MURPHY
43 General Counsel Ms. Maureen MCGUIRE
41 Director of Athletics Mr. Michael L. ROTH
04 Executive Asst to President Ms. Julia BJORDAHL
101 Secretary to the Board Ms. Maureen MCGUIRE
100 Faculty Advisor to the President Dr. Ellen M. MACCARONE
17 Director Reg Health Partnership Dr. Courtney LAW
20 Assc Prov Educational Effectiveness Dr. Ron LARGE
84 Assoc Prov Enrollment Management Ms. Julie A. MCCULLOH
06 Assc Prov Academic Administration Dr. Jolanta A. WEBER
28 Assoc Prov/Chief Diversity Officer Dr. Raymond REYES
32 Assoc Prov Student Development Dr. Judith BIGGS GARBUIO
08 Dean of Library Services Dr. Paul J. BRACKE
49 Interim Dean of Arts & Sciences Dr. Matt BAHR
53 Dean of Education Dr. Yoli CARTER
50 Dean of Business Dr. Kenneth ANDERSON
54 Dean Engineering & Applied Sciences Dr. Karlene HOO
61 Dean of Law Dr. Jacob ROOKSBY
66 Dean of Nursing/Human Phys Dr. Vincent SALYERS
88 Dean of Leadership Studies Dr. Rosey HUNTER
106 Director of Virtual Campus Vacant
108 Faculty Director of Assessment Dr. Patrick T. MCCORMICK
110 Director University Advancement Ms. Stephanie ROCKWELL
112 Senior Director Planned Giving Ms. Judy ROGERS
88 Senior Director Donor Relations Ms. Laura GATEWOOD
27 Director of Community and PR Ms. Mary Joan HAHN
29 Director of Engagement & Alumni Ms. Kara HERTZ
26 Associate VP for Marketing/Comm Mr. Dave SONNTAG
21 Controller Ms. Deena PRESNELL
96 Director Purchasing Vacant
15 Assoc VP for Human Resources Mr. Thomas CHESTER
22 Asst Director Equity & Inclusion Ms. Chris PURVIANCE
09 Director of Institutional Research Dr. Maxwell KWENDA
88 Assistant VP for Mission & Ministry Vacant
13 Chief Information Officer Mr. Borre ULRICHSEN
19 Director Security/Safety Mr. Scott SNIDER
18 Director Plant Services Ken SAMMONS
07 Director of Undergraduate Admission Ms. Erin HAYS
36 Asst VP Career/Prof Development Mr. Ray ANGLE
39 Director Student Housing Mr. Dennis COLESTOCK
88 Asst VP Student Well Being/Healthy Mr. Eric BALDWIN
37 Dean of Student Finance Services Mr. James WHITE
35 Dean of Student Engagement Mr. Matt LAMSMA
38 Director of Counseling Services Dr. Fernando ORITZ
92 Director Honors Program Dr. Linda TREDENNICK
36 Director Career Center Dr. Mary HEITKEMPER
104 Dir Center for Global Engagement Mr. Richard O. MENARD
88 Asst AVP for Global Engagement Vacant
88 Director of Gonzaga-In-Florence Dr. Jason HOUSTON
88 Sr Publications Ed & Content Strat Ms. Kathryn VANSKIKE
111 VP for University Advancement Mr. Joe POSS
10 Chief Financial Officer Mr. Joe SMITH
11 VP for Administration Mr. James ANGELOSANTE

Grays Harbor College (E)

1620 Edward P. Smith Drive, Aberdeen WA 98520-7500
County: Grays Harbor FICE Identification: 003779
Unit ID: 235334
Telephone: (360) 532-9020 Carnegie Class: Bac/Assoc-Assoc Dom
FAX Number: (360) 538-4299 Calendar System: Quarter
URL: www.ghc.edu
Established: 1930 Annual Undergrad Tuition & Fees (In-District): $4,080
Enrollment: 1,971 Coed
Affiliation or Control: State/Local IRS Status: 501(c)3
Highest Offering: Baccalaureate
Accreditation: NW, ADNUR

01 President Dr. James MINKLER
04 Senior Admin Assistant to President Ms. Sandra ZELASKO
05 Vice President for Instruction Vacant
10 Chief Financial Officer Vacant
32 Vice President for Student Services Dr. Jennifer ALT
13 Chief Exec Information Technology Mr. Andrew GLASS
75 Dean Vocational Instruction Dr. Lucas RUCKS
35 Assoc Dean for Student Services Vacant
08 Assoc Dean Library/Media Services Mr. Stanley HORTON
07 Assoc Dean of Admissions Vacant
15 Chief Human Resources Officer Mr. Darin JONES
37 Director Student Financial Aid Ms. Stacey SAVINO
18 Dir Campus Operations/Sfty/Security Mr. Lance JAMES
38 Director of Counseling Vacant
30 Chief Development Officer Ms. Lisa SMITH
26 Director Public Relations Ms. Jane F. GOLDBERG
09 Chief Inst Effect/Research/Plng Ms. Kristy ANDERSON
06 Registrar Mr. Jerad SORBER
41 Athletic Director Mr. Tom SUTERA
106 Dir Online Education/E-Learning Mr. James UMPHRES

Green River College (F)

12401 SE 320th Street, Auburn WA 98092-3699
County: King FICE Identification: 003780
Unit ID: 235343
Telephone: (253) 288-3340 Carnegie Class: Bac/Assoc-Assoc Dom
FAX Number: N/A Calendar System: Quarter
URL: www.greenriver.edu
Established: 1965 Annual Undergrad Tuition & Fees (In-State): $4,053
Enrollment: 8,048 Coed
Affiliation or Control: State IRS Status: 501(c)3
Highest Offering: Baccalaureate
Accreditation: NW, OTA, PTAA

01 President Dr. Suzanne JOHNSON
05 Vice Pres of Instruction Dr. Rolita EZEONU
13 Exec Dir of Information Technology Camella MORGAN
10 VP of Business Affairs & HR Shirley BEAN
15 Senior Director of Human Resources Vacant
32 Vice President of Student Services Dr. Deborah CASEY POWELL
56 VP Intl Programs/Extended Learning Wendy STEWART
72 Dean Prof/Tech Ed/Trades & Tech Timm LOVITT
49 Dean Fine Arts/Math/Soc Sci/Library Christie GILLILAND
79 Dean English/Humanities Jamie FITZGERALD
84 Dean of Enrollment & Completion David LARSEN
06 Director of Enrollment Services Jenny WHEELER
37 Director of Financial Aid Teresa BUCHMANN
111 VP of College Advancement George FRASIER
114 Director of Budget Janee SOMMERFELD
21 Senior Director of Financial Svcs Janee SOMMERFELD
18 Director of Facilities Robert OLSON
26 Senior Director College Relations Philip DENMAN
12 Dean for Branch Campuses & A&P Dev Tsai-En CHENG
09 Dir Institutional Effectiveness Fia ELIASSON-CREEK
28 Dir Diversity/Equity & Inclusion Marwa ALMUSAWI
96 Director of Procurement Laura LOWE
19 Director of Campus Safety Derek RONNFELDT
41 Director Athletics Shannon PERCELL
04 Executive Assistant to President Suzanne MCCUDDEN
103 Director Workforce Education Cathy ALSTON

Heritage University (G)

3240 Fort Road, Toppenish WA 98948-9599
County: Yakima FICE Identification: 003777
Unit ID: 235422
Telephone: (509) 865-8600 Carnegie Class: Masters/L
FAX Number: (509) 865-7976 Calendar System: Semester
URL: www.heritage.edu
Established: 1982 Annual Undergrad Tuition & Fees: $17,914
Enrollment: 1,044 Coed
Affiliation or Control: Independent Non-Profit IRS Status: 501(c)3
Highest Offering: Master's
Accreditation: NW, #ARCPA, MT, NURSE, SW

01 President Dr. Andrew C. SUND
05 Provost/VP Academic Affairs Dr. Kazuhiro SONODA
32 VP Student Affairs & Enrollment Dr. Melissa HILL
10 Chief Financial Officer Mr. Taylor HALL
111 VP Advancement/Marketing/Comm Mr. David WISE
13 Director Information Technology Mr. Aaron KRANZ
84 Assoc VP Enrollment Management Vacant
53 Dean of Education & Psychology Vacant
49 Associate Dean Arts & Sciences Ms. Mary JAMES
06 Registrar Mr. Luis GUTIERREZ
18 Director Physical Plant/Maintenance Mr. Jeff BEEHLER
37 Director of Financial Aid Ilda MEZA
08 Library Dir/Reference Librarian Mr. Daniel LIESTMAN
07 Director of Admissions Mr. Gabriel PINON
26 Communications Officer Ms. Bonnie HUGHES
09 Inst Research Administrator Ms. Kandace NASH
15 Human Resource Manager Ms. Rosaelia ITURBIDE
21 Controller Mr. Mark MCNABB
04 Manager President's Office Ms. Betty J. SAMPSON
103 Director Workforce Development Mr. Martin VALADEZ
19 Director Security/Safety Mr. Joseph LAREZ

Highline College (H)

PO Box 98000, 2400 S 240th Street,
Des Moines WA 98198-9800
County: King FICE Identification: 003781
Unit ID: 235431
Telephone: (206) 878-3710 Carnegie Class: Bac/Assoc-Assoc Dom
FAX Number: (206) 870-3779 Calendar System: Quarter
URL: www.highline.edu
Established: 1961 Annual Undergrad Tuition & Fees (In-State): $4,026
Enrollment: 6,824 Coed
Affiliation or Control: State IRS Status: 501(c)3
Highest Offering: Baccalaureate
Accreditation: NW, ADNUR, COARC, MAC

01 President Dr. John MOSBY
11 Vice Pres Administrative Services Mr. Michael PHAM
05 Int Vice Pres for Academic Affairs Ms. Emily LARDNER
111 VP Inst Advancement/Cmty Rels Mr. Josh GERSTMAN
32 Int Vice Pres for Student Services Dr. Saovra EAR
20 Dean of Instruction-Vocational Vacant
20 Int Dean of Instruction Transfer Dr. Raegan COPELAND
35 Assoc Dean CLS/Engage/Assessment Mr. Jonathan BROWN
31 Exec Dir Community Education Ms. Judy PERRY
84 Assoc Dean Enroll Svcs/Registrar Ms. Lorraine ODOM
26 Dir Marketing/Design/Production Mr. Tony JOHNSON
15 Int Exec Dir of Human Resources Mr. Steve SLONIKER
10 Director Financial Services Ms. Cathy CARTWRIGHT
13 Executive Director and CIO Mr. Tim WRYE
18 Director Facilities & Operations Mr. Barry HOLLDORF
19 Dir Safety/Sec & Emergency Manager Mr. David MENKE
41 Director Athletics Mr. John DUNN
30 Director of Development Ms. Asha BHAGA
09 Director Institutional Research Ms. Emily COATES
40 Bookstore Manager Ms. Kristi DOPP
96 Manager of Purchasing Ms. Dianna THIELE

06 Registrar .... Vacant
07 Director of Admissions .... Ms. L. Michelle KUWASAKI
85 Dir International Student Program .... Ms. Mariko FUJIWARA

Lake Washington Institute of Technology (A)

11605 132nd Avenue NE, Kirkland WA 98034-8506
County: King FICE Identification: 005373
Unit ID: 235699
Telephone: (425) 739-8100 Carnegie Class: Bac/Assoc-Assoc Dom
FAX Number: (425) 739-8299 Calendar System: Quarter
URL: www.lwtech.edu
Established: 1949 Annual Undergrad Tuition & Fees (In-State): $4,251
Enrollment: 3,697 Coed
Affiliation or Control: State IRS Status: 170(c)1
Highest Offering: Baccalaureate
Accreditation: NW, ACFEI, ADNUR, DA, DH, FUSER, MAC, OTA, PTAA

01 President .... Dr. Amy MORRISON
88 Spec Asst to President .... Ms. Andrea I. OLSON
04 Sr Exec Asst to President and Board .... Ms. Heather DEGRAW
32 VP Student Services .... Dr. Ruby HAYDEN
05 VP of Instruction .... Dr. Suzanne AMES
10 VP Administrative Services .... Mr. Bill THOMAS
53 Dean of Instruction .... Mr. Douglas J. EMORY
76 Dean of Instruction .... Dr. Aparna SEN
72 Dean of Instruction .... Mr. Michael RICHMOND
72 Dean of Instruction .... Mr. Mike POTTER
106 Dean of Instruction .... Ms. Sally HEILSTEDT
88 Principal/Dean High School Programs .... Mr. Tuan DANG
104 Dean of Instruction International .... Dr. David RECTOR
30 Exec Director Development .... Ms. Elisabeth SORENSEN
15 Exec Director Human Resources .... Ms. Meena PARK
09 Director Research & Grants .... Ms. Cathy COPELAND
26 Director Communications/Marketing .... Ms. Leslie SHATTUCK
13 Chief Information Officer .... Mr. Chris MCLAIN
25 Dir of Research & Grant Development .... Ms. Cathy COPELAND
88 Associate Dean Funeral Services .... Ms. Lisa MEEHAN
66 Associate Dean Nursing Program .... Vacant
88 Director TRiO Projects .... Ms. Erin SMITH
08 Librarian .... Mr. Greg BEM
76 Director PTA Program .... Ms. Andrea WESTMAN
18 Director Facilities & Operations .... Mr. Casey HUEBNER
37 Director Financial Aid .... Ms. Kimberly GEER
84 Director Enrollment Services .... Ms. Larisa AKSELRUD
103 Director Workforce Development .... Ms. Demetra BIROS
21 Director of Financial Services .... Mr. Xieng LIM
93 Director Student Programs .... Ms. Sheila WALTON
96 Manager Purchasing Service .... Mr. Isaac ROBINSON
105 Website/Digital Content Specialist .... Ms. Alisa SHTROMBERG
40 Manager Bookstore .... Mr. Russ MERKOW
19 Director Security/Safety .... Mr. Anthony BOWERS
35 Director Student Development .... Ms. Katie VIOLA

Lower Columbia College (B)

PO Box 3010, Longview WA 98632-0310
County: Cowlitz FICE Identification: 003782
Unit ID: 235750
Telephone: (360) 442-2311 Carnegie Class: Assoc/MT-VT-High Non
FAX Number: (360) 442-2109 Calendar System: Quarter
URL: www.lowercolumbia.edu
Established: 1934 Annual Undergrad Tuition & Fees (In-State): $3,864
Enrollment: 2,935 Coed
Affiliation or Control: State IRS Status: 170(c)1
Highest Offering: Associate Degree
Accreditation: NW, ADNUR, MAC

01 President .... Mr. Christopher C. BAILEY
05 Vice President of Instruction .... Ms. Kristen FINNEL
11 Vice President Administrative Svcs .... Mr. Nolan WHEELER
32 Vice President of Student Services .... Ms. Sue ORCHARD
103 Dean Workforce/Continuing Educ .... Ms. Tamra BELL
20 Dean Instructional Programs .... Mr. Kyle HAMMON
76 Executive Dean Allied Health/Nurse .... Ms. Karen JOINER
09 Assoc VP Effectiveness & Col Rels .... Ms. Wendy HALL
18 Director of Campus Services .... Mr. Richard HAMILTON
102 VP Foundation/HR/Legal Affairs .... Ms. Kendra SPRAGUE
41 Athletic Director .... Mr. Kirc J. ROLAND
21 Controller .... Ms. Desiree GAMBLE
37 Financial Aid Officer .... Ms. Marisa GEIER
08 Associate Dean Resource Svcs .... Ms. Melinda HARBAUGH
13 Director of Information Technology .... Mr. Brandon RAY
40 Director of Bookstore .... Mr. Cliff HICKS
07 Director Admissions/Registrar .... Ms. Nichole SEROSHEK
96 Director of Purchasing .... Ms. Claudia SLABU
04 Executive Assistant .... Ms. Linda J. CLARK
06 Registrar .... Ms. Nichole SEROSHEK
106 Dir Online Education/E-learning .... Ms. Sarah GRIFFITH
19 Director Security/Safety .... Mr. Jason ARROWSMITH
29 Director Alumni Relations .... Ms. Serina GRAHAM

Northwest College of Art & Design (NCAD) (C)

1126 Pacific Avenue, Suite 101, Tacoma WA 98402
County: Pierce FICE Identification: 026021
Unit ID: 377546
Telephone: (253) 272-1126 Carnegie Class: Spec-4-yr-Arts
FAX Number: (253) 572-9058 Calendar System: Semester
URL: www.ncad.edu
Established: 1982 Annual Undergrad Tuition & Fees: $20,600
Enrollment: 85 Coed
Affiliation or Control: Proprietary IRS Status: Proprietary
Highest Offering: Baccalaureate
Accreditation: ACCSC

01 President .... Craig FREEMAN
05 Director of Education .... Susan OGILVIE
11 Director of Operations .... Kim PERIGARD
06 Registrar .... Ashley JONES
13 IT Admin .... Skye CARLSON
07 Admissions Representative .... Ashley MILLER
37 Financial Aid .... Julie PERIGARD
08 Head Librarian .... Dan ROTHROCK

Northwest Indian College (D)

2522 Kwina Road, Bellingham WA 98226-9217
County: Whatcom FICE Identification: 021800
Unit ID: 380377
Telephone: (360) 676-2772 Carnegie Class: Tribal
FAX Number: (360) 738-0136 Calendar System: Quarter
URL: www.nwic.edu
Established: 1978 Annual Undergrad Tuition & Fees: $4,437
Enrollment: 544 Coed
Affiliation or Control: Other IRS Status: 501(c)3
Highest Offering: Baccalaureate
Accreditation: NW

01 President .... Dr. Justin GUILLORY
10 Chief Financial Officer .... Ms. Billie KINLEY
05 Vice Pres Instruction/Student Svcs .... Ms. Carole RAVE
11 Vice Pres Campus Development .... Mr. David OREIRO
03 VP for Research/Sponsored Programs .... Ms. Barbara ROBERTS
25 Sponsored Programs Coordinator .... Ms. Debbie MELE MAI
04 Exec Assistant to the President .... Ms. Frances SELLARS
106 Dean of Academic/Distant Learning .... Mr. Rudy VENDIOLA
32 Dean of Student Life .... Ms. Victoria RETASKET
37 Asc Dn Students/Fin Aid Dir/Admiss .... Ms. Shayna NISHIYAMA
13 IS Director .... Mr. Cameron REVARD
08 Library Director .... Ms. Valerie MCBETH
06 Registrar .... Ms. Patricia CUEVA
09 Director of Institutional Research .... Ms. Carmen BLAND
15 Director Human Resources .... Ms. Darcilynn BOB
18 Director of Facilities Maintenance .... Mr. Jon DAVIS
19 Security Manager .... Ms. Lavonne BALLEW
102 Director of NWIC Foundation .... Mr. Greg MASTEN
41 Athletic Director .... Mr. Michael SCHJANG
96 Purchasing Manager .... Mr. Charlie ROBERTS
26 Chief Public Relations/Marketing .... Ms. Barbara LEWIS
111 Director Institutional Advancement .... Mr. John GLOVER
103 Director Workforce Development .... Mr. Robert DECOTEAU
39 Director Resident Life Center .... Mr. Keith TOM

Northwest School of Wooden Boatbuilding (E)

42 N Water Street, Port Hadlock WA 98339-8706
County: Jefferson FICE Identification: 041550
Unit ID: 458140
Telephone: (360) 385-4948 Carnegie Class: Spec 2-yr-Tech
FAX Number: (360) 385-5089 Calendar System: Other
URL: www.nwswb.edu
Established: 1981 Annual Undergrad Tuition & Fees: $14,450
Enrollment: 48 Coed
Affiliation or Control: Independent Non-Profit IRS Status: 501(c)3
Highest Offering: Associate Degree
Accreditation: ACCSC

01 Executive Director .... Ms. Betsy DAVIS

Northwest University (F)

PO Box 579, Kirkland WA 98083-0579
County: King FICE Identification: 003783
Unit ID: 236133
Telephone: (425) 822-8266 Carnegie Class: Masters/M
FAX Number: (425) 889-5224 Calendar System: Semester
URL: www.northwestu.edu
Established: 1934 Annual Undergrad Tuition & Fees: $31,540
Enrollment: 1,250 Coed
Affiliation or Control: Assemblies Of God Church IRS Status: 501(c)3
Highest Offering: Doctorate
Accreditation: NW, ACBSP, COPSY, NURSE

01 President .... Dr. Joseph CASTLEBERRY
05 Provost .... Dr. Jim HEUGEL
10 Chief Financial Officer .... Mr. John JORDAN
111 Senior VP of Advancement .... Mr. Ken CORNELL
42 Campus Pastor .... Rev. Christian DAWSON
06 Registrar .... Mrs. Sandy HENDRICKSON
07 Director of Admissions .... Mr. Andy HALL
37 Director of Financial Aid .... Mr. Roger WILSON
41 Athletic Director .... Mr. Gary MCINTOSH
08 College Librarian .... Mr. Adam EPP
38 Wellness Ctr Administrative Coord .... Ms. Denise JOHNSON
29 Dir of Alumni Svcs/Parent Rels .... Mr. Ronnie HASTIE, III
15 Director Human Resources .... Ms. Victoria CLARK
121 Director Academic Success/Advising .... Mrs. Traci GRANT
32 Dean of Students .... Mr. Rick ENGSTROM
26 Director of Marketing .... Mr. Steve BOSTROM
04 Administrative Asst to President .... Ms. Ashley MONROY

50 Dean College of Business .... Dr. Teresa GILLESPIE
53 Dean College of Education .... Dr. Molly QUICK
28 Director of Multicultural Life .... Mr. Blake SMALL
39 Director of Res Life and Housing .... Ms. Sarah JOBSON
13 Director of Information Technology .... Mr. David BAZAN
30 Executive Director of Development .... Mr. Justin KAWABORI

Olympic College (G)

1600 Chester Avenue, Bremerton WA 98337-1699
County: Kitsap FICE Identification: 003784
Unit ID: 236188
Telephone: (360) 792-6050 Carnegie Class: Bac/Assoc-Assoc Dom
FAX Number: (360) 475-7151 Calendar System: Quarter
URL: www.olympic.edu
Established: 1946 Annual Undergrad Tuition & Fees (In-State): $3,771
Enrollment: 6,476 Coed
Affiliation or Control: State IRS Status: 501(c)3
Highest Offering: Baccalaureate
Accreditation: NW, ACFEI, ADNUR, MAC, NURSE, PTAA

01 President .... Dr. Martin CAVALLUZZI
05 Vice President for Instruction .... Dr. Mary GARGUILE
10 Acting Vice Pres for Administration .... Ms. Ariel BIRTLEY
32 Vice President for Student Services .... Ms. Elaine WILLIAMS-BRYANT
22 Vice President Equity & Inclusion .... Ms. Cheryl NUÑEZ
15 Associate VP Human Resources .... Dr. Joan HANTEN
04 Exec Assistant to the President .... Mr. Adam MORRIS
37 Director Student Financial Services .... Ms. Heidi TOWNSEND
26 Director of Communications .... Mr. Shawn DEVINE
84 Dean of Enrollment Services .... Dr. Jennifer GLASIER
18 Mgr Capital Projects .... Ms. Ariel BIRTLEY
21 Director of Business Services .... Ms. Karen WIKLE
96 Procurement Officer .... Ms. Diana LAKE
36 Director Career Center .... Ms. Teresa MCDERMOTT
09 Exec Director Inst Effectiveness .... Dr. Allison PHAYRE
28 Supervisor Multicltrl/Student Pgms .... Ms. Jodie COLLINS
103 Dean Workforce Development .... Ms. Amy HATFIELD
08 Dean Library/Lrng Resources/eLrng .... Ms. Erica COE
50 Dean Business & Technology .... Dr. Norma WHITACRE
81 Dean Math/Engineer/Sci/Health .... Mr. John VAUGHAN
79 Dean Humanities/Social Science .... Dr. Rebecca SEAMAN
13 Exec Dir of Technical Services .... Ms. Evelyn HERNANDEZ
19 Director of Campus Safety .... Mr. Stephen DAVIS
25 Director of College Grant Devel .... Ms. Sarah BROWNGOETZ
29 Exec Dir of Foundation/Alumni Assn .... Mr. David EMMONS
41 Director of Athletics .... Mr. Barry JANUSCH

Pacific Lutheran University (H)

12180 Park Avenue S., Tacoma WA 98447-0003
County: Pierce FICE Identification: 003785
Unit ID: 236230
Telephone: (253) 531-6900 Carnegie Class: Masters/M
FAX Number: (253) 535-8320 Calendar System: 4/1/4
URL: www.plu.edu
Established: 1890 Annual Undergrad Tuition & Fees: $42,436
Enrollment: 3,122 Coed
Affiliation or Control: Evangelical Lutheran Church In America
IRS Status: 501(c)3
Highest Offering: Doctorate
Accreditation: NW, MFCD, MUS, NURSE, SW

01 President .... Mr. Allan BELTON
101 Director of Admin & Sec to Board .... Ms. Vicky L. WINTERS
04 Asst to the President .... Ms. Julie L. MIX
05 Provost .... Dr. Joanna GREGSON
20 Assoc Provost Undergrad Programs .... Dr. Jan P. LEWIS
51 Assoc Provost for Grad & Cont Educ .... Dr. Geoffrey E. FOY
88 Dean for Exclusive Excellence .... Dr. Jennifer A. SMITH
11 Senior VP & Chief Admin Officer .... Mr. Allan BELTON
111 Vice Pres for Univ Relations .... Mr. Daniel J. LEE
32 Vice Pres for Student Life .... Dr. Joanna C. ROYCE-DAVIS
84 Dean for Enrollment Management .... Mr. Michael T. FRECHETTE
121 Exec Dir Ctr for Student Success .... Ms. Kris H. PLAEHN
07 Director of Admissions .... Ms. Melody A. FERGUSON
26 Assoc VP Marketing & Comm .... Ms. Lace M. SMITH
10 Assoc VP for Finance .... Mr. Patrick D. GEHRING
42 University Pastor .... Rev. Jen RUDE
57 Dean School of Arts & Communication .... Dr. Cameron D. BENNETT
50 Dean School of Business .... Dr. Chung-Shing LEE
53 Dean School of Educ & Kinesiology .... Dr. Karen E. MCCONNELL
66 Dean School of Nursing .... Dr. Barbara HABERMANN
79 Dean Humanities .... Dr. Kevin J. O'BRIEN
81 Dean Natural Sciences .... Dr. Ann J. AUMAN
83 Dean Social Sciences .... Dr. Anna Y. LEON-GUERRERO
35 Dean of Students .... Dr. Eva R. FREY
88 Exec Dir Wang Ctr for Global Educ .... Dr. Tamara R. WILLIAMS
41 Director of Athletics & Recreation .... Ms. Laurie L. TURNER
06 Registrar .... Mr. Kevin A. BERG
39 Assoc VP for Campus Life .... Mr. Tom A. HUELSBECK
18 Assoc VP for Facilities Management .... Mr. Ray ORR
19 Director of Campus Safety & Info .... Ms. Tara SIMMELINK
36 Director Career Learning & Engage .... Mr. Kevin ANDREW
23 Director Health Services .... Ms. Elizabeth A. HOOPER
15 Assoc Vice Pres Human Resources .... Ms. Teri P. PHILLIPS
90 Dir of Enterprise Systems & Comm .... Mr. David P. ALLEN
13 Director Information Services .... Ms. Ardys E. CURTIS
40 Manager of Bookstore .... Mr. Josh C. GIRNUS
09 Dir Assessment/Accreditation/Rsrch .... Ms. Summer S. KENESSON

102 Corporate & Foundation Mgr .... Vacant
44 Director Annual Giving .... Ms. Andrea N. MICHELBACH
22 Dir Affirmative Action/EEO .... Ms. Teri P. PHILLIPS
28 Asst VP Diversity/Justice/Sustain .... Ms. Angie Z. HAMBRICK
29 Director Alumni Relations .... Ms. Jessica L. PAGEL
38 Director Counseling Center .... Dr. Kuldhir S. BHATI
08 Chief Library Officer .... Ms. Fran LANE RASMUS

Pacific Northwest University of Health Sciences (A)

111 University Parkway, Suite 202, Yakima WA 98901

County: Yakima FICE Identification: 041305
Unit ID: 455406
Telephone: (509) 452-5100 Carnegie Class: Spec-4-yr-Med
FAX Number: (509) 452-5101 Calendar System: Semester
URL: www.pnwu.edu
Established: 2005 Annual Graduate Tuition & Fees: N/A
Enrollment: 573 Coed
Affiliation or Control: Independent Non-Profit IRS Status: 501(c)3
Highest Offering: Doctorate; No Undergraduates
Accreditation: NW, OSTEO

01 President .... Dr. Michael J. LAWLER
05 Provost .... Dr. Edward BILSKY
10 Chief Financial Officer .... Ms. Ann HITTLE
11 Chief Operations Officer .... Mr. Frank D. ALVAREZ
30 Chief Development Officer .... Ms. Michele ERICKSON
63 Dean Col of Osteopathic Medicine .... Dr. Thomas SCANDALIS
08 Head Librarian .... Ms. Anita CLEARY
13 Chief Info Technology Officer (CIO) .... Mr. Jameson WATKINS
15 Director Personnel Services .... Ms. Erin MURPHY
18 Chief Facilities/Physical Plant .... Mr. Brent PERRIN
26 Chief Communications Officer .... Mr. Dean O'DRISCOLL
29 Director Alumni Relations .... Ms. Chanda ANDERSON
37 Director Student Financial Aid .... Ms. Laura PENDLETON
45 Chief Institutional Planning .... Ms. Angie GIRARD
04 Administrative Asst to President .... Ms. Vikki GORE
84 Dir Enrollment Services/Registrar .... Ms. LeAnn HUNTER
108 Dir Institutional Effectiveness .... Ms. Lori FULTON
32 Assoc Dean Student Affairs .... Dr. Stephen LAIRD
96 Asst Dir Procurement/Asset Mgmt .... Ms. Barbara ANDERSON
06 Registrar .... Ms. Le Anne RUSSELL

Peninsula College (B)

1502 East Lauridsen Boulevard,
Port Angeles WA 98362-6698

County: Clallam FICE Identification: 003786
Unit ID: 236258
Telephone: (360) 452-9277 Carnegie Class: Bac/Assoc-Assoc Dom
FAX Number: (360) 457-8100 Calendar System: Quarter
URL: www.pencol.edu
Established: 1961 Annual Undergrad Tuition & Fees (In-District): $4,453
Enrollment: 2,094 Coed
Affiliation or Control: State/Local IRS Status: 501(c)3
Highest Offering: Baccalaureate
Accreditation: NW, MAC

01 President .... Dr. Luke ROBINS
05 Vice President Instruction .... Dr. Sharon BUCK
11 Int Vice Pres Administrative Svcs .... Ms. Carie EDMISTON
32 Vice President Student Services .... Mr. Jack HULS
35 Assoc Dean of Student Success .... Ms. Cathy ENGLE
41 Assoc Dean Athletics/Student Prgms .... Mr. Rick ROSS
13 Int Director Information Technology .... Ms. Emma JANSSEN
04 Executive Asst to the President .... Ms. Kelly GRIFFITH
26 Public Information Officer .... Ms. Kari DESSER
15 Director of Human Resources .... Ms. Krista FRANCIS
85 Dir Intl Stdnt Pgm/Stdnt Recruit .. Ms. Sophia ILIAKIS-DOHERTY
102 Director College Foundation .... Ms. Getta ROGERS
09 Director of Institutional Research .... Ms. Katie MARKS
18 Director Physical Plant .... Mr. Rick CROOT
40 Bookstore Manager .... Mrs. Camilla RICO

Perry Technical Institute (C)

2011 W. Washington Avenue, Yakima WA 98903

County: Yakima FICE Identification: 009387
Unit ID: 236212
Telephone: (509) 453-0374 Carnegie Class: Spec 2-yr-Other
FAX Number: (509) 453-0375 Calendar System: Quarter
URL: www.perrytech.edu
Established: 1939 Annual Undergrad Tuition & Fees: N/A
Enrollment: 842 Coed
Affiliation or Control: Independent Non-Profit IRS Status: 501(c)3
Highest Offering: Associate Degree
Accreditation: ACCSC

01 President .... Christine COTE
04 Administrative Asst to President .... Renee KABRICH
06 Registrar .... Jill COPE
84 Director of Admissions & Marketing .... Nicole TRAMMELL
10 Chief Business Officer .... Cathy STERBENZ
102 Foundation Director .... Tressa SHOCKLEY
25 Grant Manager .... Trent HURLBUT
13 Chief Info Technology Officer (CIO) .... Josh PHILLIPS
15 Human Resource Manager .... Carol HELMS
19 Director of Facilities/Safety .... Kaila LOCKBEAM
07 Dir of Enrollment & Accreditation .... Magnus ALTMAYER
36 Director Student Placement .... Tressa SHOCKLEY

37 Director Student Financial Aid .... Mayra FERNANDEZ
05 Dean of Education .... Nathan HULL
20 Associate Dean .... Jason LAMIQUIZ
20 Associate Dean .... Garet GASSELING
96 Purchasing Manager .... Maria PULIDO
36 Assoc Director of Career Services .... Raul LUNA

Pierce College District (D)

1601 39th Avenue SE, Puyallup WA 98374

County: Pierce FICE Identification: 005000
Unit ID: 439145
Telephone: (253) 964-6500 Carnegie Class: Assoc/HT-Mix Trad/Non
FAX Number: N/A Calendar System: Quarter
URL: www.pierce.ctc.edu
Established: 1967 Annual Undergrad Tuition & Fees (In-State): $3,952
Enrollment: 4,590 Coed
Affiliation or Control: State IRS Status: 501(c)3
Highest Offering: Baccalaureate
Accreditation: NW, ADNUR, DH

01 District Chancellor .... Dr. Michele JOHNSON
12 President Pierce College Puyallup .... Dr. Darrell L. CAIN
12 President Fort Steilacoom .... Dr. Julie WHITE
05 VP Learning/Student Success-PY .... Dr. Matthew CAMPBELL
05 Vice Pres Learning/Stdnt Success-FS .... Dr. Debra GILCHRIST
10 Vice Pres Administrative Services .... Mr. Choi HALLADAY
111 VP Strategic Advancement .... Mr. Mike WARK
15 Vice President for Human Resources .... Ms. Holly GORSKI
103 VP Workforce/Economic/Prof Devel .... Ms. Jo Ann BARIA
13 Chief Information Officer .... Mr. Mike STOCKE
84 Dean Enroll Svcs/Fin Aid/Registrar .... Ms. Anne WHITE
08 Dean Libraries & Learning Resources .... Ms. Christie FLYNN
32 Dean of Student Success .... Ms. Agnes STEWARD
26 Dir Marketing and Communications .... Mr. Brian BENEDETTI
35 Dir Student Programs-Ft Steilacoom .... Mr. Cameron COX
41 Director District Athletics .... Mr. Duncan STEVENSON
18 Director of Facilities & Const Mgt .... Mr. Gregory RANDALL
35 Dir of Student Life-Puyallup .... Mr. Sean COOKE
85 Exec Dir of International Education .... Ms. Myung PARK
19 Campus Safety Officer .... Ms. Shelley MIELL
21 Director Fiscal Services .... Ms. Sylvia JAMES
37 District Director Financial Aid .... Ms. Trinity HUTTNER
84 Director Enrollment Services-Puy .... Ms. Els DEMING
96 Procurement Officer .... Mr. Curtis LEE
30 Director of Development .... Ms. Jennifer WOLBRECHT
09 Director Institutional Research .... Mr. Erik GIMNESS
49 Dean Arts & Humanities .... Dr. Holly SMITH
88 Dean Transitional Education .... Ms. Lori GRIFFIN
76 Dean Health & Technology .... Mr. Ronald MAY
81 Dean Natural Sciences .... Mr. Thomas BROXSON
83 Dean Business/Social Sciences .... Dr. Allison SIEVING
04 Admin Assistant to the President .... Ms. Christine BOITER
101 Secretary of the Institution/Board .... Ms. Marie HARRIS
28 Director of Diversity .... Mr. Charlie PARKER

Pima Medical Institute-Renton (E)

555 South Renton Village Place, Renton WA 98057

Telephone: (425) 228-9600 Identification: 770517
Accreditation: ABHES, COARC, OTA

† Branch campus of Pima Medical Institute-Tucson, Tucson, AZ

Pima Medical Institute-Seattle (F)

9709 3rd Avenue NE, Suite 400, Seattle WA 98115-2052

Telephone: (206) 322-6100 Identification: 666172
Accreditation: ABHES, DH, PTAA, RAD

† Branch campus of Pima Medical Institute-Tucson, Tucson, AZ

Renton Technical College (G)

3000 NE Fourth Street, Renton WA 98056-4123

County: King FICE Identification: 010434
Unit ID: 236382
Telephone: (425) 235-2352 Carnegie Class: Bac/Assoc-Assoc Dom
FAX Number: (425) 235-7832 Calendar System: Quarter
URL: www.rtc.edu
Established: 1942 Annual Undergrad Tuition & Fees (In-State): $5,466
Enrollment: 3,763 Coed
Affiliation or Control: State IRS Status: 501(c)3
Highest Offering: Baccalaureate
Accreditation: NW, ACFEI, DA, MAC, SURGT

01 President .... Dr. Kevin D. MCCARTHY
10 VP Finance/Administration .... Mr. Eduardo RODRIGUEZ
05 Vice President Instruction .... Vacant
32 VP Student Services .... Ms. Jessica GILMORE ENGLISH
97 Dean Basic Studies .... Ms. Jodi NOVOTNY
76 Dean Allied Health .... Mr. Christopher CARTER
103 Executive Dean Workforce/Econ Dev .... Mr. Jacob JACKSON
50 Dean Bus/Educ/Hum Svcs/Gen Educ .... Ms. Sarah WAKEFIELD
102 Foundation Executive Director .... Ms. Carrie SHAW
13 Chief Information Officer .... Mr. Paul CORRIGLIANO
07 Director Enrollment Services .... Vacant
111 Exec Dir Institutional Advancement .... Vacant
08 Director Library .... Ms. Cheyenne RODUIN
21 Budget/Accounting/Fin Svcs Mgr .... Ms. Raevel CHEA
15 Executive Director Human Resources .... Ms. Lesley HOGAN
37 Director Financial Aid .... Ms. Celva BOON
18 Facilities & Grounds Svcs Director .... Mr. Mark DANIELS

19 Safety & Security Manager .... Mr. Matthew VIELBIG
88 Dean Culinary Arts .... Mr. Doug MEDBURY
26 Dir College Relations/ Marketing .... Ms. Katherine HEDLAND HANSEN
38 Dean Student Success .... Mr. Aaron READER
35 Director Student Programs .... Ms. Jessica SUPINSKI
06 Registration Coordinator .... Ms. Ly CHANG
88 Director Outreach/Entry Services .... Mr. Anthony COVINGTON
04 Executive Asst to President .... Ms. Di BEERS
88 Capital Projects/Space Planning Dir .... Mr. Barry BAKER
09 Director of Institutional Research .... Mr. Jichul KIM
96 Purchasing Agent .... Mr. Kawika WAIAMAU-ARIOTA

Saint Martin's University (H)

5000 Abbey Way, SE, Lacey WA 98503-7500

County: Thurston FICE Identification: 003794
Unit ID: 236452
Telephone: (360) 491-4700 Carnegie Class: Masters/M
FAX Number: (360) 459-4124 Calendar System: Semester
URL: www.stmartin.edu
Established: 1895 Annual Undergrad Tuition & Fees: $37,356
Enrollment: 1,565 Coed
Affiliation or Control: Roman Catholic IRS Status: 501(c)3
Highest Offering: Master's
Accreditation: NW, ACBSP, CAEPT, NURSE, SW

00 Chancellor .... Abbot Neal G. ROTH, OSB
01 President .... Dr. Roy F. HEYNDERICKX
05 Provost & Vice President .... Dr. Kate BOYLE
10 Vice President of Finance .... Ms. Sara SAAVEDRA
111 Vice Pres Inst Advancement .... Ms. Cecelia LOVELESS
26 VP of Marketing/ Communications .... Ms. Genevieve CANCEKO CHAN
13 Associate Vice President/CIO .... Mr. Greg DAVIS
15 Associate VP of Human Resources .... Ms. Cynthia JOHNSON
49 Dean College of Arts & Sciences .... Dr. Jeff CRANE
53 Dean of Education .... Dr. Fumie HASHIMOTO
50 Dean of Business .... Vacant
54 Dean of Engineering .... Dr. David OLWELL
32 Dean Student Services .... Ms. Melanie RICHARDSON
84 Dean Enrollment Management .. Ms. Pamela HOLSINGER-FUCHS
104 Associate Dean Intl Programs .... Dr. Roger DOUGLAS
21 Controller .... Ms. Burcu BRYAN
37 Director Financial Aid .... Ms. Barbara CLOUTIER
29 Alumni Engagement Manager .... Ms. Kim NELSON
06 Assistant Registrar .... Ms. Ronda VANDERGIFF
18 Director Facilities Management .... Mr. Philip CHEEK
110 Asst Vice Pres Inst Advancement .... Ms. Katie WOJKE
36 Director of Career Placement .... Ms. Ann ADAMS
41 Athletic Director .... Mr. Bob GRISHAM
56 Director Extension Programs .... Mr. Cruz ARROYO
08 Dean of Library & Learning Resource .... Ms. Amy STEWART-MAILHIOT
42 Director Campus Ministry .... Ms. Colleen DUNNE
39 Assoc Dean of Students/Dir Housing .... Mr. Justin STERN
38 Dir Office of Counseling & Wellness .... Dr. Kelley SIMMONS
09 Director Institutional Grants/Rsrch .... Ms. Erin HOILAND
04 Admin Assistant to the President .... Ms. Brenda LUND
108 Dir of Assessment & Accreditation .... Ms. Sheila STEINER
19 Director Public Safety .... Mr. Will STAKELIN

*Seattle Colleges (I)

1500 Harvard Avenue, Seattle WA 98122-3803

County: King FICE Identification: 010106
Telephone: (206) 934-4100 Carnegie Class: N/A
FAX Number: (206) 934-3883
URL: www.seattlecolleges.edu

01 Chancellor .... Dr. Shouan PAN
05 VC Academic & Student Success .... Dr. Kurt BUTTLEMAN
13 Chief Information Officer .... Dr. Cindy RICHE
10 Interim VC of Finance & Operations .... Ms. Jennifer STROTHER
26 Assoc VC Comms & Strat Initiatives .... Dr. Earnest PHILLIPS
111 Assoc VC of Advancement .... Ms. Kerry HOWELL
12 President South Seattle College .... Dr. Rosie RIMANDO-CHAREUNSAP
12 President North Seattle College .... Dr. Warren BROWN
12 President Seattle Central College .... Dr. Sheila EDWARDS LANGE
103 Assoc VC of Workforce Education .... Dr. Malcolm GROTHE
15 Int VC of Human Resources .... Ms. Jennifer DIXON

*North Seattle College (J)

9600 College Way N, Seattle WA 98103-3599

County: King FICE Identification: 009704
Unit ID: 236072
Telephone: (206) 934-3600 Carnegie Class: Bac/Assoc-Assoc Dom
FAX Number: (206) 934-3606 Calendar System: Quarter
URL: www.northseattle.edu
Established: 1970 Annual Undergrad Tuition & Fees (In-State): $4,461
Enrollment: 6,259 Coed
Affiliation or Control: State IRS Status: 170(c)1
Highest Offering: Baccalaureate
Accreditation: NW, MAC

02 President .... Dr. Warren BROWN
05 Vice President for Instruction .... Mr. Peter LORTZ
32 Interim VP for Student Services .... Ms. Toni CASTRO
11 Vice President of Administration .... Ms. Andrea JOHNSON
36 Exec Dean Career/Workforce Educ .... Dr. John LEDERER

79 Dean Art/Humanities/Social Sciences .... Mr. Brian PALMER
81 Dean Math & Science .... Ms. Alissa AGNELLO
103 Dean Workforce Instruction .... Mr. Aaron KORNGIEBEL
08 Dean Library & Media Services .... Dr. Aryana BATES
121 Dean Student Success Svcs .... Ms. Alice MELLING
88 Dean Basic/Transitional Stds .... Mr. Curtis BONNEY
111 Executive Director of Advancement .... Ms. Traci RUSSELL
26 Dir Marketing & Communications .... Ms. Melissa MIXON
84 Dean Enrollment Svcs/Registrar .... Ms. Kathy RHODES
51 Director Continuing Education .... Ms. Christy ISAACSON
37 Director Financial Aid Services .... Ms. Brianne SANCHEZ
35 Dean of Student Life .... Dr. Mari ACOB-NASH
103 Director Workforce Retraining .... Ms. Jeanette MILLER
09 Exec Dir Inst Effectiveness .... Dr. Stephanie DYKES
104 Interim Exec Dir International Pgms .... Ms. Anne FORESTER
15 Interim Human Resources Director .... Ms. Sylvia JUAREZ
18 Dir Facilities & Plant Operations .... Ms. Odessa WOODLEE
38 Counselor .... Dr. Lydia MINATOYA
13 Chief Info Technology Officer .... Dr. Cindy RICHE
19 Director Security/Safety .... Mr. Jeff YOUNG
28 Assoc VP Equity/Diversity/Inclusion .... Mr. D'Andre FISHER
07 Admissions/Residency Specialist .... Mr. Fleetwood L. WILSON
04 Executive Asst to President .... Ms. Toni STANKOVIC
114 Interim Dir Budget & Business Ops .... Mr. Soroush MALEKI
25 Director of Grants .... Ms. Ann RICHARDSON
41 Athletic Director .... Ms. Carianya NAPOLI

*Seattle Central College (A)

1701 Broadway, Seattle WA 98122-2400
County: King FICE Identification: 003787
Unit ID: 236513
Telephone: (206) 587-3800 Carnegie Class: Bac/Assoc-Assoc Dom
FAX Number: (206) 344-4390 Calendar System: Quarter
URL: seattlecentral.edu
Established: 1966 Annual Undergrad Tuition & Fees (In-State): $3,669
Enrollment: 6,928 Coed
Affiliation or Control: State IRS Status: 170(c)1
Highest Offering: Baccalaureate
Accreditation: NW, ACFEI, ADNUR, COARC, DH, SURGT

02 President .... Dr. Sheila EDWARDS LANGE
05 Vice Pres of Instruction .... Dr. Bradley LANE
11 Vice Pres Administrative Services .... Dr. Bruce RIVELAND
32 Vice Pres Student Services .... Ms. Yoshiko HARDEN
103 Executive Dean Workforce Educ .... Mr. Chris SULLIVAN
09 Exec Dir Inst Effectiveness .... Ms. Naina ESHWAR
37 Director of Financial Aid .... Mr. Kyle DARLING
102 Executive Director Foundation .... Ms. Jessica NOROUZI
26 Director of Communications .... Mr. Roberto BONACCORSO
08 Dean of Library Svcs/E-learn .... Ms. Lynn KANNE
49 Dean Basic Studies .... Ms. Laura DIZAZZO
76 Dean of Allied Health .... Mr. Barry ROBINSON
81 Dean of STEM .... Dr. Wendy ROCKHILL
83 Dean Arts/Humanities/Social Science .... Ms. Laila ABDALLA
104 Assoc VP International Education .... Dr. Andrea INSLEY
35 Dean Student Development .... Mr. Ricardo LEYVA-PUEBLA
13 Director Information Technology .... Mr. Tim RAGER
12 Dean of Seattle Maritime Academy .... Ms. Sarah SCHERER
12 Assoc Dean Seattle Culinary Academy .... Ms. Katherine KEHRLI
84 Dean Enrollment Services/Registrar .... Ms. Diane COLEMAN
19 Director Public Safety .... Mr. Sean CHESTERFIELD
18 Dir Facilities/Plant Operations .... Mr. David ERNEVAD
04 Executive Admin Asst to President .... Ms. Erin LEWIS
10 Chief Business Officer .... Mr. Dennis YASUKOCHI
15 Director Human Resources .... Mr. Scott RIXON
28 Dir Diversity/Equity & Inclusion .... Dr. Valerie HUNT
20 Director of Instruction Operation .... Ms. Marilyn MCCAMEY
66 Dean of Nursing .... Ms. Vicky HERTIG

*South Seattle College (B)

6000 16th Avenue, SW, Seattle WA 98106-1499
County: King FICE Identification: 009706
Unit ID: 236504
Telephone: (206) 934-5300 Carnegie Class: Bac/Assoc-Assoc Dom
FAX Number: (206) 934-5393 Calendar System: Quarter
URL: www.southseattle.edu
Established: 1969 Annual Undergrad Tuition & Fees (In-State): $4,717
Enrollment: 6,716 Coed
Affiliation or Control: State IRS Status: 501(c)3
Highest Offering: Baccalaureate
Accreditation: NW

02 President .... Dr. Rosie RIMANDO-CHAREUNSAP
05 Vice Pres Instruction .... Dr. Sayumi IREY
10 Vice Pres Finance/Admin Services .... Vacant
32 Vice President Student Services .... Mr. Joe BARRIENTOS
30 Director Advancement .... Vacant
45 Dean Instructional Resources .... Ms. Mary Jo WHITE
12 Dean of Georgetown Campus .... Vacant
97 Dean Basic & Transitional Studies .... Mr. John BOWERS
20 Interim Dean of Academic Programs .... Mr. Johnny HU
35 Dean Student Life .... Mr. Daniel JOHNSON
103 Exec Dean Prof/Tech/Workforce Educ .... Ms. Veronica WADE
17 Dean Hosp/Service Occupations .... Mr. Brian SCHEESLER
72 Dean Multi-Trades/Info Tech/Bus .... Vacant
84 Dean Enrollment Services .... Ms. Joyce ALLEN
88 Dean of Aviation .... Ms. Kim ALEXANDER
20 Assoc Dean Academic Programs .... Vacant
20 Assoc Dean Academic Programs .... Vacant
06 Assistant Registrar .... Ms. Marilyn ANDERSON-BURT
104 Exec Dir Ctr for Intl Education .... Ms. Kathie KWILINSKI

51 Director Continuing Education .... Ms. Luisa MOTTEN
103 Dir Workforce Dev/Employment Svcs .... Ms. Stephanie GUY
37 Dir Student Financial Assistance .... Ms. Corinne SOLTIS
26 Director Communications .... Mr. Ty SWENSON
15 Director Human Resources .... Ms. Linda MANNING
108 Exec Director Inst Effectiveness .... Mr. Greg DEMPSEY
13 Director Business Operation .... Vacant
18 Dir Facilities & Plant Operations .... Mr. Eric STEEN
28 AVP Equity/Diversity/Inclusion .... Dr. Betsy HASEGAWA
19 Manager Safety/Security .... Mr. James E. LEWIS
40 Manager Bookstore .... Vacant

Seattle Institute of East Asian Medicine (C)

226 South Orcas Street, Seattle WA 98108
County: King FICE Identification: 032803
Unit ID: 439914
Telephone: (206) 517-4541 Carnegie Class: Spec-4-yr-Other Health
FAX Number: (206) 299-3538 Calendar System: Trimester
URL: www.sieam.edu
Established: 1994 Annual Graduate Tuition & Fees: N/A
Enrollment: 27 Coed
Affiliation or Control: Proprietary IRS Status: Proprietary
Highest Offering: Doctorate; No Undergraduates
Accreditation: ACUP

01 President .... Craig MITCHELL
05 Academic Dean .... Katherine TAROMINA
07 Dir Admissions/Student Services .... Iris CUTLER
06 Registrar .... Corey OJIMA

Seattle Pacific University (D)

3307 Third Avenue W, Seattle WA 98119-1997
County: King FICE Identification: 003788
Unit ID: 236577
Telephone: (206) 281-2111 Carnegie Class: DU-Mod
FAX Number: (206) 281-2115 Calendar System: Quarter
URL: www.spu.edu
Established: 1891 Annual Undergrad Tuition & Fees: $42,939
Enrollment: 3,783 Coed
Affiliation or Control: Free Methodist IRS Status: 501(c)3
Highest Offering: Doctorate
Accreditation: NW, CACREP, CLPSY, DIETD, DIETI, MFCD, MUS, NURSE, THEOL

01 President .... Dr. Daniel J. MARTIN
05 Interim Provost .... Dr. Bruce CONGDON
10 VP for Finance & Business Affairs .... Mr. Craig G. KISPERT
32 VP for Student Life .... Dr. Jeffrey C. JORDAN
111 VP for Advancement .... Mrs. Louise S. FURROW
84 VP for Enrollment Mgmt & Mktg .... Mr. Nate MOUTTET
28 VP for Diversity/Equity/Inclusion .... Dr. Sandra MAYO
20 Vice Provost Academic Affairs .... Dr. Cynthia J. PRICE
18 Asst VP Facility Management .... Mr. David B. CHURCH
43 Asst VP Risk Mgmt & Univ Counsel .... Mr. Nick GLANCY
21 Asst VP for Financial Affairs .... Ms. Cherry GILBERT
13 Asst VP Information Technology .... Mr. Micah SCHAAFSMA
37 Asst VP UG Enrollment Oper & SFS .... Mr. Jordan L. GRANT
50 Dean School of Business/Govt/Econ .... Dr. Ross STEWART
53 Dean School of Education .... Dr. Nyaradzo MVUDUDU
66 Dean School of Health Sciences .... Dr. Lorie WILD
81 Interim Dean CAS-Sciences Division .... Dr. Derek WOOD
79 Dean CAS - Arts & Humanities Div .... Dr. Debra SEQUEIRA
88 Dean School of Psych/Fam & Cmty .... Dr. Katy TANGENBERG
73 Dean School of Theology .... Dr. Douglas M. STRONG
35 Dean of Students for Cmty Life .... Mr. Chuck STRAWN
35 Assoc VP Student Life .... Dr. Jacqui S. SMITH-BATES
08 University Librarian .... Mr. Michael PAULUS
38 Director Student Counseling Center .... Ms. Sharon BARR-JEFFREY
07 Sr Dir Recruitment and Admissions .... Mr. Jobe S. KORB-NICE
07 Director Undergraduate Admissions .... Ms. Ineliz SOTO FULLER
09 Director Institutional Research .... Mr. Stan LAN
06 University Registrar .... Mrs. Kenda GATLIN
26 Sr Dir Univ Comm & Marketing .... Mrs. Alison ESTEP
27 News & Media Relations Manager .... Mrs. Tracy C. NORLEN
109 Director of University Services .... Ms. Alexis CRUIKSHANK
19 Director of Safety & Security .... Mr. Mark REID
110 Director of Advancement .... Ms. Maribeth MARTIN LOPIT
29 Director of Alumni/Parent Relations .... Ms. Amanda STUBBERT
41 Athletic Director .... Mr. Jackson STAVA
15 Director of Human Resources .... Mr. Gary E. WOMELSDUFF
39 Director of Residence Life .... Mr. Gabe JACOBSEN
88 Director Student Programs .... Ms. Whitney BROETJE
88 Director of Multi-Ethnic Programs .... Ms. Serena MANZO
104 Director of Global Engagement .... Vacant
04 Executive Asst to President .... Mrs. Ruth JACOBSEN
42 University Chaplain .... Rev. Lisa ISHIHARA

The Seattle School of Theology and Psychology (E)

2501 Elliot Avenue, Seattle WA 98121-1177
County: King FICE Identification: 034664
Unit ID: 441131
Telephone: (206) 876-6100 Carnegie Class: Spec-4-yr-Other Health
FAX Number: (206) 876-6195 Calendar System: Trimester
URL: www.theseattleschool.edu
Established: 2001 Annual Graduate Tuition & Fees: N/A
Enrollment: 275 Coed
Affiliation or Control: Independent Non-Profit IRS Status: 501(c)3
Highest Offering: Master's; No Undergraduates
Accreditation: ⊕NW, THEOL

01 Acting President & Provost .... Dr. J. Derek MCNEIL
05 Assoc Dean for Teaching/Learning .... Dr. Misty Anne WINZENREID
10 Chief Financial Officer .... Vacant
111 Director of Advancement .... Mr. Andrew GREENE
32 VP Students & Alumni/Dn of Students .... Mr. Paul STEINKE
08 Dir Library Svcs/Inst Assessment .... Ms. Cheryl GOODWIN
06 Dir Academic Services/Registrar .... Ms. Kristen HOUSTON
84 VP of Enrollment & Brand .... Ms. Nicole GREENWALD
13 Director Computer & Info Services .... Ms. Grace LA TORRA
15 Director of Human Resources .... Ms. Kartha HEINZ

Seattle University (F)

901 12th Avenue, Seattle WA 98122-1090
County: King FICE Identification: 003790
Unit ID: 236595
Telephone: (206) 296-6000 Carnegie Class: DU-Mod
FAX Number: N/A Calendar System: Quarter
URL: www.seattleu.edu
Established: 1891 Annual Undergrad Tuition & Fees: $44,610
Enrollment: 7,278 Coed
Affiliation or Control: Roman Catholic IRS Status: 501(c)3
Highest Offering: Doctorate
Accreditation: NW, CACREP, DMS, LAW, MFCD, MIDWF, NURSE, SPAA, SW, THEOL

01 President .... Rev. Stephen V. SUNDBORG, SJ
05 Provost .... Dr. Shane MARTIN
20 Vice Provost .... Dr. Robert DULLEA
11 Executive Vice President Admin .... Dr. Timothy LEARY
10 Chief Financial Officer .... Ms. Connie KANTER
43 Vice Pres and University Counsel .... Ms. Mary S. PETERSEN
111 VP University Advancement .... Mr. Michael PODLIN
32 VP Student Development .... Dr. Michele MURRAY
88 Vice President Mission & Ministry .... Rev. Peter ELY, SJ
108 Assoc VP for Inst Effectiveness .... Dr. Robert DUNIWAY
84 Vice President for Enrollment Svcs .... Ms. Marilyn CRONE
26 Vice President for Communications .... Mr. Scott MCCLELLAN
28 Chief Diversity Officer .... Ms. Natasha MARTIN
15 VP Human Resources .... Ms. Michelle CLEMENTS
31 Executive Director Cmty Engagement .... Mr. Kent KOTH
49 Dean of Arts & Sciences .... Dr. David POWERS
50 Dean of Business & Economics .... Dr. Joseph M. PHILLIPS
53 Dean of Education .... Dr. Deanna SANDS
66 Dean of Nursing .... Dr. Kristen SWANSON
54 Dean of Science & Engineering .... Dr. Michael QUINN
61 Dean of Law .... Ms. Annette C. CLARK
73 Dean of Theology & Ministry .... Dr. Mark MARKULY
51 Dean Schl New & Continuing Studies .... Dr. Rick FEHRENBACHER
08 University Librarian .... Ms. Sara WATSTEIN
20 Assoc Provost Academic Achievement .... Dr. Charles LAWRENCE
87 Director Summer Programs .... Dr. Eva LASPROGATA
20 Assoc Provost Global Engagement .... Dr. Russell POWELL
123 Graduate Admissions .... Ms. Janet SHANDLEY
13 Chief Information Officer .... Mr. Chris VAN LIEW
21 Assoc VP of Finance .... Mr. Andrew O'BOYLE
18 Assoc VP Facilities Administration .... Mr. Robert SCHWARTZ
29 Asst VP Alumni Relations .... Ms. Susan VOSPER
14 Executive Director .... Mr. Dennis GENDRON
112 Sr Director of Planned Giving .... Ms. Sarah FINNEY
44 Director of Annual Giving .... Ms. Cathy REILLY
102 Dir of Foundation & Corporate Rels .... Ms. Jane SPALDING
35 Assoc Vice Pres Student Development .... Dr. Alvin STURDIVANT
06 University Registrar .... Mr. Andrew ANDERSON
07 Dean of Admissions .... Ms. Melore NIELSEN
09 Director of Institutional Research .... Dr. Irina VOLOSHIN
42 Director Campus Ministry .... Ms. Tammy LIDDELL
37 Director Student Financial Services .... Mr. Jeff SCOFIELD
41 Director of Athletics .... Mr. Bill HOGAN
19 Executive Director of Public Safety .... Mr. Timothy MARRON
35 Dean of Students .... Mr. Darrell GOODWIN
85 Director International Student Ctr .... Mr. Ryan GREENE
104 Director Education Abroad .... Ms. Gina LOPARDO
36 Executive Director Career Services .... Ms. Hilary FLANAGAN
38 Director Counseling Center .... Dr. Kimberly CALUZA
28 Director of Multicultural Affairs .... Ms. Tiffany GRAY
39 Dir Housing & Resid Life .... Ms. Kathleen BAKER
25 Director Research & Sponsored Proj .... Dr. Nalini IYER
96 Director of Purchasing .... Ms. Marie PETERSON
23 Director Student Health Center .... Ms. Maura O'CONNOR
04 Executive Secretary to President .... Ms. Liz PILATI
100 Assistant to the President .... Ms. Kathy YBARRA
105 Web Communications Manager .... Mr. Jason BEARD
22 Dir Professional Dev/EEO .... Ms. Helaina SOREY
86 Director of External Affairs .... Mr. Solynn MCCURDY
27 Associate Chief Information Officer .... Mr. Travis NATION

Shoreline Community College (G)

16101 Greenwood Avenue N, Shoreline WA 98133-5696
County: King FICE Identification: 003791
Unit ID: 236610
Telephone: (206) 546-4101 Carnegie Class: Assoc/MT-VT-High Non
FAX Number: (206) 546-4630 Calendar System: Quarter
URL: www.shoreline.edu
Established: 1964 Annual Undergrad Tuition & Fees (In-State): $3,873
Enrollment: 6,128 Coed
Affiliation or Control: State IRS Status: 170(c)1
Highest Offering: Associate Degree
Accreditation: NW, ADNUR, CAHIIM, DH, MLTAD

01 President ... Dr. Cheryl ROBERTS
05 VP Academic & Student Affs ... Mr. Phillip KING
15 VP Human Resources ... Vacant
111 VP Advancement ... Ms. Mary BRUEGGEMAN
26 Exec Dir Communication/Marketing ... Ms. Martha LYNN
114 Director Budget ... Ms. Satoko PRIGMORE
04 Exec Asst to the President ... Ms. Lori YONEMITSU
18 Director Facilities ... Mr. Jason FRANCOIS
19 Director Safety & Security ... Mr. Edwin LUCERO
66 Associate Dean Nursing ... Ms. Mary BURROUGHS
84 Director Enroll Svcs/Financial Aid ... Ms. Chris MELTON
38 Assoc Dean Counseling ... Vacant
109 Director Auxiliary Services ... Ms. Leah PEARCE
09 Dir Institutional Effectiveness ... Ms. Bayta MARING
08 Assoc Dean Library Services .. Ms. Leslie POTTER-HENDERSON
32 Dean of Students ... Vacant
103 Exec Dean Workforce & STEM ... Mr. Guy HAMILTON
79 Dean Humanities Division ... Ms. Nancy DICK
70 Actg Dean Social Science ... Mr. Tim WRIGHT
27 Exec Dir Communication/Marketing ... Ms. Martha LYNN
41 Athletic Director ... Mr. Steve ESKRIDGE
104 Manager Study Abroad ... Mr. Cory ANTHONY
105 Director Web Services ... Mr. Adam STAFFA
106 Executive Director E-learning ... Ms. Ann GARNSEY HARTER
13 Director Technology Support Svcs ... Mr. Gary KALBFLEISCH
29 Coordinator Alumni Affairs ... Ms. Ann FALK
39 Dir Stdnt Ldrshp/Residential Life ... Ms. Sundi MUSNICKI
96 Director of Financial Services ... Ms. Jennifer FENSKE

Skagit Valley College (A)

2405 College Way, Mount Vernon WA 98273-5899
County: Skagit FICE Identification: 003792
Unit ID: 236638
Telephone: (360) 416-7600 Carnegie Class: Bac/Assoc-Assoc Dom
FAX Number: (360) 416-7890 Calendar System: Quarter
URL: www.skagit.edu
Established: 1926 Annual Undergrad Tuition & Fees (In-State): $4,200
Enrollment: 4,670 Coed
Affiliation or Control: State IRS Status: 501(c)3
Highest Offering: Baccalaureate
Accreditation: NW, ACFEI, ADNUR, MAC

01 President ... Dr. Thomas KEEGAN
05 Vice President for Instruction ... Dr. Kenneth LAWSON
10 Vice Pres Administrative Services ... Mr. Ed JARAMILLO
12 Vice President of Whidbey Campus ... Dr. Laura CAILLOUX
104 Assoc VP International Education ... Ms. Mari ACOB-NASH
13 Dean of Information Technology ... Mr. Andy HEISER
103 Dean Workforce Education ... Mr. Darren GREENO
20 Dean Academic Education ... Dr. Gabriel MAST
84 Assoc Dean Enrollment Services ... Ms. Sinead PLAGGE
36 Assoc Dean Counseling ... Ms. Sandy JORDON
32 Director of Student Life ... Mr. Brian MURPHY
37 Director of Financial Aid ... Ms. Crystal ALLISON
15 Exec Director of Human Resources ... Ms. Carolyn TUCKER
18 Director of Facilities & Operations ... Mr. Dave SCOTT
26 Chief Public Information Officer ... Ms. Arden AINLEY
104 Director of International Programs ... Ms. Christa SCHULZ
40 Bookstore Manager ... Ms. Kim HALL
41 Athletic Director ... Mr. Steve EPPERSON
09 Director of Institutional Research ... Vacant

South Puget Sound Community College (B)

2011 Mottman Road, SW, Olympia WA 98512-6292
County: Thurston FICE Identification: 005372
Unit ID: 236656
Telephone: (360) 754-7711 Carnegie Class: Assoc/HT-Mix Trad/Non
FAX Number: (360) 664-0780 Calendar System: Quarter
URL: www.spscc.edu
Established: 1962 Annual Undergrad Tuition & Fees (In-State): $4,423
Enrollment: 4,951 Coed
Affiliation or Control: State IRS Status: 501(c)3
Highest Offering: Associate Degree
Accreditation: NW, ACFEI, DA, MAC

01 President ... Dr. Timothy STOKES
04 Special Assistant to the President ... Ms. Diana TOLEDO
05 Vice President for Instruction ... Dr. Michelle ANDREAS
32 Vice President for Student Services ... Dr. David PELKEY
11 Vice Pres Administrative Services ... Mr. Albert BROWN
07 Dean of Enrollment Services ... Mr. Steven ASHPOLE
18 Director of Facilities ... Mr. Marty MATTES
26 Chief Comm/Legislative Affairs Ofcr ... Ms. Kelly GREEN
35 Dean Student Engagement/Retention ... Ms. Jennifer MANLEY
37 Dean of Student Financial Services ... Ms. Johanna DWYER
15 Chief Human Resources Officer ... Ms. Samantha SOTO
102 Exec Director of College Foundation ... Ms. Tanya MOTE
28 Dir of Diversity/Equity/Inclusion ... Mr. Parfait BASSALE
09 Director of Institutional Research ... Ms. Jennifer TUIA
06 Director of Enrollment/Registrar ... Ms. Heidi DEARBORN
08 Dean of Academic Support Services ... Ms. Amy KELLY
19 Director of Safety & Security ... Mr. Robert SHAILOR
13 Interim Chief Information Officer ... Mr. Kennith HARDEN
72 Dean of Applied Technology ... Ms. Kathy HOOVER
76 Dean of Natural & Applied Sciences ... Dr. Kevin ASMAN
79 Dean of Humanities/Communications ... Dr. Melissa MEADE
83 Dean of Social Sciences & Business ... Dr. Valerie SUNDBY-THORP
96 Procurement & Supply Specialist 4 ... Ms. Vida SHERRARD-HANNON

Tacoma Community College (C)

6501 S 19th Street, Tacoma WA 98466-6100
County: Pierce FICE Identification: 003796
Unit ID: 236753
Telephone: (253) 566-5000 Carnegie Class: Bac/Assoc-Assoc Dom
FAX Number: N/A Calendar System: Quarter
URL: www.tacomacc.edu
Established: 1965 Annual Undergrad Tuition & Fees (In-State): $4,276
Enrollment: 6,496 Coed
Affiliation or Control: State IRS Status: 501(c)3
Highest Offering: Baccalaureate
Accreditation: NW, ADNUR, CAHIIM, COARC, DMS, EMT, RAD

01 President ... Dr. Ivan L. HARRELL, II
05 Provost/VP for Academic Affairs ... Dr. Marissa SCHLESINGER
11 Vice Pres Administrative Services ... Ms. Lon WHITAKER
32 Vice Pres Student Services ... Vacant
111 Vice Pres for College Advancement ... Mr. Bill RYBERG
28 VP Equity/Diversity/Inclusion ... Dr. Judy LOVELESS-MORRIS
15 Exec Director of Human Resources ... Mr. Stephen SMITH
88 Dir Conduct/Compliance ... Ms. Dolores HAUGEN
84 Dean for Enrollment & Student Suc ... Mr. Patrick BROWN
124 Dean of Retention & Student Success ... Ms. Jennifer FOUNTAIN
108 Dean Org Learning & Effectiveness ... Ms. Analea BRAUBURGER
18 Director Facilities/CapitalProjects ... Vacant
35 Director of Student Engagement ... Ms. Sonja MORGAN
37 Director Student Financial Aid ... Ms. Kim MATISON
04 Executive Asst Pres Office ... Ms. Angelique ODOM
09 Director of Institutional Research ... Ms. Kelley SADLER
41 Athletic Director ... Mr. Jason PRENEVOST
10 Director Financial Services ... Vacant
13 Director of IT ... Mr. Clay KRAUSS
106 Dir Online Education/E-learning ... Mr. Chris SORAN
19 Director Security/Safety ... Mr. Will HOWARD
26 Chief Public Relations/Marketing ... Ms. Tamyra HOWSER

University of Phoenix Western Washington Campus (D)

7100 Fort Dent Way, Suite 100, Tukwila WA 98188-8553
Telephone: (425) 572-1600 Identification: 770234
Accreditation: &NH, ACBSP

† No longer accepting campus-based students.

University of Puget Sound (E)

1500 N Warner St., Tacoma WA 98416-0002
County: Pierce FICE Identification: 003797
Unit ID: 236328
Telephone: (253) 879-3100 Carnegie Class: Bac-A&S
FAX Number: (253) 879-3500 Calendar System: Semester
URL: www.pugetsound.edu
Established: 1888 Annual Undergrad Tuition & Fees: $49,776
Enrollment: 2,701 Coed
Affiliation or Control: Independent Non-Profit IRS Status: 501(c)3
Highest Offering: Doctorate
Accreditation: NW, IPSY, MUS, OT, PTA

01 President ... Dr. Isiaah CRAWFORD
101 Board Secy/Dir Ofc of President ... Ms. Mary Elizabeth COLLINS
05 Provost ... Dr. Laura BEHLING
10 Executive Vice President/CFO ... Ms. Sherry B. MONDOU
26 Vice President University Relations ... Mr. David BEERS
84 Vice President Enrollment ... Ms. Laura E. MARTIN-FEDICH
32 VP Student Affairs/Dean of Students ... Dr. Uchenna BAKER
114 Assoc VP Accounting/Budget Svcs ... Ms. Janet S. HALLMAN
15 Assoc Vice Pres Human Resources ... Ms. Cindy MATERN
21 Assoc Vice Pres Business Services ... Mr. John M. HICKEY
18 Assoc Vice Pres Facilities Services ... Mr. Bob KIEF
37 Assoc VP for Student Financial Svcs ... Ms. Maggie A. MITTUCH
27 Executive Dir of Communications ... Ms. Gayle MCINTOSH
13 Chief Information Officer ... Mr. Jeremy L. CUCCO
28 Dean Diversity and Inclusion ... Dr. Michael BENITEZ
20 Associate Academic Dean ... Dr. Julie NELSON CHRISTOPH
20 Associate Academic Dean ... Dr. Sunil KUKREJA
20 Associate Academic Dean ... Dr. Renee HOUSTON
09 Dir Inst Research & Retention ... Ms. C. Ellen PETERS
06 Registrar ... Mr. Michael PASTORE
08 Library Director ... Ms. Jane CARLIN
41 Director of Athletics ... Ms. Amy E. HACKETT
29 Director Alumni & Parent Relations ... Ms. Allison CANNADY-SMITH
85 Director International Programs ... Mr. Roy ROBINSON
53 Dean School of Education ... Dr. Amy RYKEN
50 Dir School of Business/Leadership ... Vacant
64 Interim Director School of Music ... Dr. Gerard MORRIS
88 Director of Occupational Therapy ... Dr. Yvonne SWINTH
88 Director of Physical Therapy ... Dr. Robert BOYLES

University of Washington (F)

1400 NE Campus Parkway, Seattle WA 98195-0001
County: King FICE Identification: 003798
Unit ID: 236948
Telephone: (206) 543-2100 Carnegie Class: DU-Highest
FAX Number: (206) 543-9285 Calendar System: Quarter
URL: www.washington.edu
Established: 1861 Annual Undergrad Tuition & Fees (In-State): $11,207
Enrollment: 46,166 Coed
Affiliation or Control: State IRS Status: 501(c)3
Highest Offering: Doctorate
Accreditation: NW, ARCPA, AUD, CAHIIM, CEA, CLPSY, CONST, DENT, DIETC, EMT, HSA, IPSY, JOUR, LAW, LIB, LSAR, MED, MIDWF, MT, NURSE, OPE, OT, PAST, PCSAS, PDPSY, PH, PHAR, PLNG, PTA, SCPSY, SP, SPAA, SW

01 President ... Dr. Ana Mari CAUCE
05 Provost/Exec Vice Pres ... Dr. Mark RICHARDS
12 Chancellor Bothell Campus ... Dr. Bjong W. YEIGH
12 Chancellor Tacoma Campus ... Dr. Mark PAGANO
28 VP Minority Affs/Vice Prov Div ... Dr. Rickey HALL
17 Exec VP Med Affs/CEO UW Med/Dean ... Dr. Paul G. RAMSEY
111 Sr Vice Pres for Univ Advancement ... Vacant
15 Vice President Human Resources ... Ms. Mindy KORNBERG
13 Vice President for UW IT ... Mr. Aaron POWELL
21 Vice President for Finance ... Mr. Brian MCCARTAN
26 VP for Comm & Chief Marketing Ofcr ... Ms. Mary GRESCH
30 Vice President for Development ... Mr. Dan PETERSON
46 Vice Provost Research ... Dr. Mary E. LIDSTROM
51 Vice Provost UW Continuum College ... Dr. Rovy BRANON
45 Vice Provost Planning & Budgeting ... Ms. Sarah NORRIS HALL
20 Vice Prov/Dean Undergrad Acad Affs ... Dr. Ed TAYLOR
32 Vice President for Student Life ... Mr. Denzil SUITE
88 Vice Provost for Academic Personnel ... Dr. Cheryl A. CAMERON
86 Director Federal Relations ... Ms. Sarah CASTRO
100 Chief of Staff ... Ms. Margaret A. SHEPHERD
43 Division Chief Attorney General ... Ms. Sarah SCHULTE
06 University Registrar ... Ms. Helen GARRETT
29 VP Alumni & Stakeholder Engagement ... Mr. Paul RUCKER
17 Chief Operating Ofcr UW Medical Ctr ... Mr. Geoff P. AUSTIN
37 Asst VP Enroll/Exec Dir Fin Aid ... Ms. Kay LEWIS
84 Assoc VP Enrollment/Admissions ... Dr. Philip BALLINGER
09 Director Institutional Analysis ... Ms. Erin GUTHRIE
36 Director Career Center ... Ms. Susan TERRY
14 CFO/UW Information Technology ... Mr. Bill FERRIS
18 Assoc VP Capital Planning Devel ... Mr. Michael MCCORMICK
92 Director Honors Program ... Dr. Victoria LAWSON
41 Director Athletics ... Ms. Jennifer COHEN
08 VP for Digital Init/Dean Libraries ... Ms. Lizabeth A. WILSON
96 Executive Dir Procurement Services ... Mr. Mark CONLEY
58 Interim Dean Graduate School ... Dr. Rebecca AANERUD
49 Dean Arts & Sciences ... Dr. Robert STACEY
47 Dean Col of Built Environments ... Ms. Renee CHENG
22 Director of EOAA ... Mr. Torrey TIBURZI
50 Dean Business School ... Dr. Frank HODGE
54 Interim Dean of Engineering ... Dr. Gregory R. MILLER
61 Dean Law School ... Mr. Mario L. BARNES
70 Dean Social Work ... Dr. Edwina UEHARA
52 Interim Dean Dentistry ... Dr. Gary T. CHIODO
63 Dean Medicine ... Dr. Paul G. RAMSEY
66 Dean Nursing ... Dr. Azita EMAMI
67 Dean Pharmacy ... Dr. Sean SULLIVAN
69 Dean School of Public Health ... Dr. Hilary GODWIN
53 Dean College of Education ... Dr. Mia TUAN
80 Dean of Public Affairs ... Dr. Sandra O. ARCHIBALD
88 Dean Information School ... Dr. Anind DEY
88 Dean College of the Environment ... Dr. Lisa GRAUMLICH
04 Senior Executive Asst to President ... Ms. Lenina ARENAS-FUENTES
07 Director of Admissions ... Mr. Paul SEEGERT
104 Director Study Abroad ... Mr. Wolfram LATSCH
108 Director Educational Assessment ... Mr. Sean GEHRKE
19 Interim Chief of Police ... Mr. Randall WEST
38 Director Student Counseling ... Dr. Natacha F. KUNE
39 Asst Vice Pres of Student Life ... Ms. Pam SCHREIBER
101 Secretary to the Board of Regents ... Mr. Tyler LANGE
102 Asst Vice Pres Constituency Pgms ... Ms. Joanna GLICKLER
44 Sr Director Annual Philanthropy ... Ms. Jennifer MACCORMACK

Walla Walla Community College (G)

500 Tausick Way, Walla Walla WA 99362-9267
County: Walla Walla FICE Identification: 005006
Unit ID: 236887
Telephone: (509) 522-2500 Carnegie Class: Assoc/HVT-High Non
FAX Number: (509) 527-4480 Calendar System: Quarter
URL: www.wwcc.edu
Established: 1967 Annual Undergrad Tuition & Fees (In-State): $4,455
Enrollment: 4,253 Coed
Affiliation or Control: State IRS Status: 170(c)1
Highest Offering: Associate Degree
Accreditation: NW, ADNUR, MAC

01 President ... Dr. Derek R. BRANDES
05 Vice President of Instruction ... Dr. Chad HICKOX
76 Dean of Health Sciences Education ... Ms. Kathleen ADAMSKI
37 Financial Aid Director ... Ms. Danielle HODGEN
08 Director of Library Services ... Mrs. Stacy PREST
12 Dean Clarkston Campus ... Dr. Chad MILTENBERGER
41 Athletic Director ... Mr. Jeffrey E. REINLAND
15 Vice President of Human Resources .. Mrs. Sharon M. HARTFORD
18 Dir Facility Svcs/Capital Projects ... Mr. Shane LOPER
106 Director of eLearning ... Ms. Lisa CHAMBERLIN
88 Dean of Transitional Studies ... Ms. Darlene SNIDER
40 Bookstore Manager ... Ms. Alecia ANGELL
56 Director of Extended Learning ... Ms. Jodi WORDEN
26 Exec Dir Communications/Marketing ... Vacant
06 Registrar ... Mr. Carlos DELGADILLO
09 Exc Dir Institutional Effectiveness ... Dr. Nicholas VELLUZZI
103 Dean Workforce Education ... Mr. Jerry ANHORN, JR.
13 Director Technology Svcs ... Mr. Kevin COMBS

Walla Walla University (H)

204 S College Avenue, College Place WA 99324-1198
County: Walla Walla FICE Identification: 003799
Unit ID: 236896

Telephone: (509) 527-2615 Carnegie Class: Masters/S
FAX Number: (509) 527-2397 Calendar System: Quarter
URL: www.wallawalla.edu
Established: 1892 Annual Undergrad Tuition & Fees: $28,035
Enrollment: 1,825 Coed
Affiliation or Control: Seventh-day Adventist IRS Status: 501(c)3
Highest Offering: Master's
Accreditation: NW, ACBSP, ACFEI, MUS, NURSE, SW

01 President .... Dr. John MCVAY
05 Vice Pres Academic Administration .... Dr. Volker HENNING
10 Vice Pres Financial Administration .... Mr. Steve ROSE
32 Vice Pres Student Life and Mission .... Dr. Doug TILSTRA
111 VP Univ Relations/Advancement .... Ms. Jodi WAGNER
28 Asst to President for Diversity .... Dr. Pedrito MAYNARD-REID
04 Executive Asst Office of President .... Ms. Deirdre BENWELL
20 Associate Vice Pres Academic Admin .... Dr. Scott LIGMAN
21 Associate Vice Pres Financial Admin .... Mr. Ken VYHMEISTER
58 Assoc Vice Pres Graduate Programs .... Dr. Pam CRESS
35 Asst VP/Dean of Students .... Ms. Hilary CATLETT
08 Director of Libraries .... Ms. Carolyn GASKELL
06 Registrar .... Ms. Carolyn DENNEY
42 Chaplain .... Mr. Albert HANDEL
29 Director of Alumni Relations .... Mrs. Claudia SANTELLANO
13 Director Information Services .... Mr. Scott MCFADDEN
37 Assoc Director Financial Aid .... Ms. Nancy CALDERA
15 Director Human Resources .... Ms. Jennifer CARPENTER
18 Director of Facility Services .... Mr. George BENNETT
26 Dir Marketing/University Relations .. Ms. Emily MUTHERSBAUGH
07 Director of Admissions .... Mr. Dale MILAM
36 Director Career Development Center .... Mr. David LINDSTROM
38 Director Counseling/Testing .... Ms. Michelle NADEN
09 Director of Institutional Research .... Mr. Brian HARTMAN
41 Athletic Director .... Mr. Eric CANTRELL
19 Campus Security Director .... Ms. Courtney BRYANT
44 Director Gift Planning .... Ms. Dorita TESSIER
66 Dean of School of Nursing .... Dr. Lucille KRULL
73 Dean of School of Theology .... Dr. David THOMAS
54 Dean of School of Engineering .... Dr. Doug LOGAN
50 Dean of Business .... Vacant
53 Dean of Education .... Vacant
70 Dean of Social Work/Sociology .... Dr. Susan SMITH

Washington State University (A)

PO Box 645910, Pullman WA 99164-5910
County: Whitman FICE Identification: 003800
Unit ID: 236939
Telephone: (509) 335-3564 Carnegie Class: DU-Highest
FAX Number: N/A Calendar System: Semester
URL: www.wsu.edu
Established: 1890 Annual Undergrad Tuition & Fees (In-District): $11,584
Enrollment: 30,614 Coed
Affiliation or Control: State/Local IRS Status: 501(c)3
Highest Offering: Doctorate
Accreditation: NW, CAATE, CEA, CIDA, CLPSY, CONST, COPSY, DIETC, HSA, IPSY, LSAR, MUS, NURSE, PHAR, SP, SPAA, VET

01 President .... Dr. Kirk SCHULZ
05 Provost/Exec Vice President .... Dr. Mitzi MONTOYO
10 VP Finance/Administration .... Ms. Stacy PEARSON
111 VP Advancement/CEO WSU Foundation .... Ms. Lisa CALVERT
106 VP Academic Outreach/Innovation .... Dr. David CILLAY
32 VP Student Affairs .... Dr. Mary Jo GONZALES
13 VP Information Tech & CIO .... Mr. Sasi PILLAY
46 Vice President Research .... Dr. Christopher KEANE
86 VP External AffairsGovernment Rels .... Ms. Colleen KERR
26 Vice Pres Marketing/Communication .... Mr. Phil WEILER
20 Vice Provost for Faculty Affairs .... Vacant
12 Chancellor WSU Everett .... Dr. Paul PITRE
12 Chancellor WSU Spokane .... Dr. Daryll DEWALD
12 Chancellor WSU Tri-Cities .... Dr. Sandra HAYNES
12 Chancellor WSU Vancouver .... Dr. Mel NETZHAMMER
15 AVP/Chief Human Resources Ofcr .... Ms. Theresa ELLIOT-CHESLEK
37 AVP Financial Services .... Mr. Brian DIXON
35 AVP Student Affs/Dean of Students .... Ms. Jill CREIGHTON
43 Div Chief State Attorney Gen Office .... Ms. Danielle HESS
58 Dean of the Graduate School .... Dr. Lisa GLOSS
47 Dean Agric/Human Natl Res Sci .... Dr. Andre WRIGHT
50 Dean Carson College of Business .... Dr. Chip HUNTER
53 Dean College of Education .... Dr. Michael TREVISAN
54 Dean Engineering & Architecture .... Dr. Mary REZAK
66 Dean College of Nursing .... Vacant
67 Dean College of Pharmacy .... Dr. Gary POLLACK
60 Dean College of Communication .... Dr. Bruce PINKLETON
49 Dean College of Arts & Sciences .... Dr. Matthew JOCKERS
74 Dean College of Veterinary Medicine .... Dr. Bryan K. SLINKER
92 Dean Honors College .... Dr. M. Grant NORTON
114 Assoc VP & Chief Budget Officer .... Vacant
18 Assoc VP Facilities Services .... Ms. Olivia YANG
88 Dean University College .... Dr. Mary F. WACK
08 Dean Libraries .... Mr. Joseph STARRATT
06 University Registrar .... Mr. Matthew ZIMMERMAN
07 Director Admissions .... Ms. Wendy PETERSON
09 Assoc Dir Institutional Research .... Ms. Fran HERMANSTON
41 Director WSU Athletics .... Mr. Patrick CHUN
116 Director Internal Audit .... Ms. Heather LOPEZ
04 Administrative Asst to President .... Mrs. Ginger DRUFFEL

Washington State University-Spokane (B)

412 East Spokane Falls Blvd, Spokane WA 99207-9600
Telephone: (509) 358-7500 Identification: 770948
Accreditation: &NW, EXSC, #MED

Washington State University-Tri Cities (C)

2710 Crimson Way, Richland WA 99354-1671
Telephone: (509) 372-7000 Identification: 770949
Accreditation: &NW, CEA

Washington State University-Vancouver (D)

14204 NE Salmon Creek Ave, Vancouver WA 98686-9600
Telephone: (360) 549-9788 Identification: 770950
Accreditation: &NW

Wenatchee Valley College (E)

1300 Fifth Street, Wenatchee WA 98801-1799
County: Chelan FICE Identification: 003801
Unit ID: 236975
Telephone: (509) 682-6800 Carnegie Class: Bac/Assoc-Assoc Dom
FAX Number: (509) 682-6541 Calendar System: Quarter
URL: www.wvc.edu
Established: 1939 Annual Undergrad Tuition & Fees (In-State): $4,035
Enrollment: 3,556 Coed
Affiliation or Control: State IRS Status: 501(c)3
Highest Offering: Baccalaureate
Accreditation: NW, ADNUR, MAC, MLTAD, NURSE, RAD

01 President .... Mr. James RICHARDSON
04 Exec Assistant to President .... Mrs. Maria INIGUEZ
05 VP of Instruction .... Mr. Tod TREAT
11 VP of Administrative Services .... Mr. Brett RILEY
32 VP of Student Services & Enrollment .... Dr. Chio FLORES
49 Dean Lib Arts/Sciences/Basic Skills .... Ms. Holly BRINGHAM
12 Dean Omak Campus .... Vacant
103 Dean Workforce & Continuing Educ .... Mr. Joey WALTER
76 Dean Allied Health/Nursing .... Ms. Jenny CAPELO
15 Exec Director Human Resources .... Ms. Reagan BELLAMY
35 Associate Dean of Student Services .... Mr. Kevin BERG
18 Director of Facilities & Operations .... Mr. Rich PETERS
06 Dir of Enrollment Svcs/Registrar .... Mr. Jonathan BARNETT
08 Dn Libraries/Learning Technologies . Mr. Andrew HERSH-TUDOR
10 Director of Fiscal Services .... Ms. Janice FREDSON
26 Exec Dir of Communication Rels .... Ms. Libby SIEBENS
20 Coordinator of Transitional Studies .... Mr. Brent CARTER
27 Web Marketing/Graphic Design Spec .... Mr. Nick WINTERS
09 Exec Director of Inst Effectiveness .... Mr. Ty JONES
19 Safety/Security & Emergency Mgr .... Ms. Maria AGNEW
28 Asst Dean Campus Life/Equity & Inc .. Ms. Erin TOFTE-NORDVIK
102 Exec Director of WVC Foundation .... Ms. Rachel EVEY

Western Washington University (F)

516 High Street, Bellingham WA 98225-5950
County: Whatcom FICE Identification: 003802
Unit ID: 237011
Telephone: (360) 650-3000 Carnegie Class: Masters/L
FAX Number: (360) 650-3022 Calendar System: Quarter
URL: www.wwu.edu
Established: 1893 Annual Undergrad Tuition & Fees (In-State): $8,126
Enrollment: 15,915 Coed
Affiliation or Control: State IRS Status: 501(c)3
Highest Offering: Doctorate
Accreditation: NW, ART, @AUD, CACREP, CAEPN, CEA, MUS, NRPA, NURSE, PLNG, SP

01 President .... Dr. Sabah RANDHAWA
05 Vice Pres Academic Affairs/Provost .... Dr. Brent CARBAJAL
10 Vice Pres Business/Financial Affs .. Mr. Richard D. VAN DEN HUL
84 VP Enrollment/Student Services .... Dr. Melynda HUSKEY
26 Vice Pres for University Relations .... Mrs. Donna GIBBS
111 Vice Pres University Advancement .... Ms. Stephanie BOWERS
32 Asst VP Enrollment/Student Services .... Ms. Clara CAPRON
13 Vice Prov Info/Chief Info Officer .... Dr. Chuck LANHAM
58 Vice Prov Rsch/Dean Grad Sch .... Dr. Kathy KITTO
20 Vice Prov Undergraduate Education .... Dr. Steven L. VANDERSTAAY
22 Vice Prov Equal Oppty/Employmt Div .... Dr. Sue GUENTER-SCHLESINGER
51 Vice Prov Outreach Continuing Educ .... Dr. Earl F. GIBBONS
35 Dean of Students .... Mr. Theodore W. PRATT, JR.
15 Asst VP for Human Resources .... Ms. Chyerl WOLFE-LEE
06 Registrar .... Mr. David BRUNNEMER
07 Director of Admissions .... Mr. Cezar MESQUITA
36 Director Career Services Center .... Ms. Effie EISSES
37 Director Financial Aid .... Ms. Clara CAPRON
29 Executive Director Alumni Relations .... Ms. Deborah DEWEES
27 Director University Communications .... Mr. Paul COCKE
08 Dean of Libraries .... Dr. Mark GREENBERG
39 Director University Residences .... Mr. Leonard JONES
100 Chief of Staff/Secretary BOT .... Dr. Paul DUNN
09 Director of Institutional Research .... Dr. Ming ZHANG
18 Director of Facilities Management .... Mr. John A. FURMAN
19 Director of Public Safety .... Mr. Darin RASMUSSEN
41 Athletic Director .... Mr. Steven CARD
92 Director of Honors Program .... Dr. Scott LINNEMAN
96 Director of Business Services .... Mr. Pete HEILGEIST
79 Dean College of Humanities/Soc Sci .... Dr. Paqui PAREDES
72 Dean College of Science/Technology .... Dr. Brad JOHNSON
50 Dean College Business & Econ .... Dr. Scott YOUNG
65 Dean Huxley Col of the Environment . Dr. Steven HOLLENHORST
57 Dean College of Fine & Perf .... Dr. Christopher SPICER
53 Dean Woodring College of Education .... Dr. Horacio WALKER
12 Dean Fairhaven College .... Dr. Jack HERRING
04 Sr Executive Assistant to President .... Ms. Barbara A. SANDOVAL
104 Director Intl Student/Scholar Svcs .... Mr. Richard BRUCE
25 Contracts Assistant .... Ms. Andrea RODGER
38 Interim Director Counseling Center .... Dr. Anne Marie THEILER
43 AAG/Chief Legal Advisor .... Ms. Kerena HIGGINS
86 Director Government Relations .... Ms. Becca KENNA-SCHENK
108 Dir Institutional Effectiveness .... Dr. John KRIEG

Whatcom Community College (G)

237 W Kellogg Road, Bellingham WA 98226-8003
County: Whatcom FICE Identification: 010364
Unit ID: 237039
Telephone: (360) 383-3000 Carnegie Class: Bac/Assoc-Assoc Dom
FAX Number: (360) 383-4000 Calendar System: Quarter
URL: www.whatcom.edu
Established: 1970 Annual Undergrad Tuition & Fees (In-State): $4,551
Enrollment: 4,411 Coed
Affiliation or Control: State IRS Status: 501(c)3
Highest Offering: Baccalaureate
Accreditation: NW, ADNUR, MAC, PTAA

01 President .... Dr. Kathi HIYANE-BROWN
05 VP for Instruction .... Mr. Ed HARRI
11 VP for Administrative Services .... Mr. Nate LANGSTRAAT
32 VP for Student Services .... Dr. Luca LEWIS
20 Dean for Instruction .... Ms. Carla GELWICKS
08 Library Director .... Mr. Howard FULLER
10 Director for Business & Finance .... Mr. Ken BRONSTEIN
06 Registrar .... Mr. Michael SINGLETARY
37 Director of Financial Aid .... Mr. David KLAFFKE
85 Director of International Programs .... Mr. Kelly KESTER
40 Bookstore Manager .... Mr. Jon SPORES
18 Senior Facilities Director .... Mr. Brian KEELEY
04 Special Assistant to the President .... Ms. Rafeeka KLOKE
15 Executive Director Human Resources .... Ms. Becky RAWLINGS
09 Director for Assessment and IR .... Dr. Anne Marie KARLBERG

Whitman College (H)

345 Boyer Avenue, Walla Walla WA 99362-2083
County: Walla Walla FICE Identification: 003803
Unit ID: 237057
Telephone: (509) 527-5411 Carnegie Class: Bac-A&S
FAX Number: (509) 527-5859 Calendar System: Semester
URL: www.whitman.edu
Established: 1882 Annual Undergrad Tuition & Fees: $52,764
Enrollment: 1,510 Coed
Affiliation or Control: Independent Non-Profit IRS Status: 501(c)3
Highest Offering: Baccalaureate
Accreditation: NW

01 President .... Dr. Kathleen MURRAY
05 Provost/Dean of Faculty .... Dr. Alzada TIPTON
30 Vice President for Development .... Vacant
10 Treasurer/Chief Financial Officer .... Mr. Peter W. HARVEY
32 VP Student Affs/Dean Students .... Mr. Kazi JOSHUA
20 Associate Dean Faculty Development .... Dr. Helen KIM
07 Director of Admission .... Mr. Adam MILLER
13 Chief Information Officer .... Mr. Dan M. TERRIO
18 Director of the Physical Plant .... Mr. Daniel L. PARK
08 Director of Penrose Library .... Mrs. Dalia L. CORKRUM
91 Director of Enterprise Technology .... Mr. Michael OSTERMAN
09 Director of Institutional Research .... Dr. Neal J. CHRISTOPHERSON
20 Assoc Dean Academic Affairs .... Dr. Kendra J. GOLDEN
35 Associate Dean of Students .... Ms. Barbara A. MAXWELL
26 VP Enrollment & Communications .... Dr. Joshua JENSEN
38 Counseling Center Director .... Dr. Rae CHRESFIELD
39 Director Residence Life & Housing .... Ms. Nancy J. TAVELLI
29 Director Alumni Relations .... Ms. Nancy L. MITCHELL
104 Director of Off-Campus Studies .... Ms. Susan H. HOLME
15 Director Human Resources .... Mr. Shane WATKINS
06 Registrar .... Ms. Stacey J. GIUSTI
19 Director of Security .... Vacant
23 Director Health Services .... Ms. Claudia L. NESS
36 Director for Career Development .... Ms. Kim ROLFE
37 Director of Financial Aid Services .... Ms. Marilyn K. PONTI
41 Athletic Director .... Vacant
42 Coordinator of Spiritual Life .... Mr. Adam M. KIRTLEY
04 Senior Assistant to President .... Ms. Jennifer A. CASPER
44 Director of Annual Giving .... Ms. Lara MEYER

Whitworth University (I)

300 W Hawthorne Road, Spokane WA 99251-0001
County: Spokane FICE Identification: 003804
Unit ID: 237066
Telephone: (509) 777-1000 Carnegie Class: Masters/M
FAX Number: (509) 777-4763 Calendar System: 4/1/4
URL: www.whitworth.edu
Established: 1890 Annual Undergrad Tuition & Fees: $43,640
Enrollment: 2,627 Coed
Affiliation or Control: Presbyterian IRS Status: 501(c)3
Highest Offering: Master's
Accreditation: NW, CAATE, MFCD, MUS

01 President .... Dr. Beck A. TAYLOR
05 Provost & Executive Vice President .... Dr. Caroline SIMON
04 Exec Asst to President/Board Secy .... Ms. Ruth PELLS

10 VP Finance & Administration .... Mr. Larry PROBUS
32 VP for Student Life/Title IX .... Ms. Rhosetta RHODES
07 VP Admissions & Financial Aid .... Mr. Greg ORWIG
111 VP Institutional Advancement .... Dr. Scott MCQUILKIN
15 Assoc VP Human Resources .... Ms. JaCenda DAVIDSON
21 Assoc VP Finance & Administration .... Ms. Luz MERKEL
13 Chief Information Officer .... Mr. Kenneth BROWN
42 Dean Spiritual Life .... Dr. Forrest BUCKNER
41 Director of Athletics .... Mr. Timothy DEMANT
28 Chief Diversity Officer .... Dr. Lorna HERNANDEZ JARVIS
20 Associate Provost .... Dr. Brooke KIENER
110 Assoc VP Institutional Advancement .... Ms. Stacey SMITH
88 Asst VP Institutional Advancement .... Mr. Tad WISENOR
88 Assoc Athletics Director .... Ms. Jo WAGSTAFF
123 Int Dean Cont Studies/Grad Admiss .... Dr. Randy MICHAELIS
55 Assoc Dean Evening Business Pgm .... Ms. Christie ANDERSON
108 Dir of Assessment/Accreditation .... Dr. Deanna OJENNUS
25 Dir Sponsored Program/Grants .... Ms. Melinda STOOPS
88 Dir Office of Church Engagement .... Dr. Terry MCGONIGAL
53 Dean School of Education .... Dr. Ronald JACOBSON
50 Dean School of Business .... Dr. Timothy WILKINSON
49 Dean College of Arts & Sciences .... Dr. Noelle WIERSMA
06 Registrar .... Mr. Jose ORTIZ
88 Assoc Dean Grad Studies in Educ .... Ms. Roberta WILBURN
90 Dir Instructional Resources .... Mr. Kenneth PECKA
88 Assoc Dean Com Standards/Compliance ... Dr. Craig CHATRIAND
29 Dir Alumni/Parent Relations .... Mr. Dale HAMMOND
07 Director of Admissions .... Ms. Lara RAMSAY
18 Assoc VP of Facilities Services .... Mr. Christopher EICHORST
23 Director of Student Health Svcs .... Ms. Amy CUTLER
37 Director of Financial Aid .... Ms. Traci STENSLAND
93 Asst Dean Student DEI .... Mr. Shawn WASHINGTON
39 Asst Dean Student Life .... Mr. Timothy CALDWELL
68 Director of Athletic Training .... Dr. Cynthia WRIGHT
26 Dir Marketing & Communications .... Ms. Nancy HINES
38 Director Student Counseling Ctr .... Ms. Molly DEWALT
09 Director of Institutional Research .... Ms. Wendy OLSON
08 Dir Library/Assoc Dean Special Pgms .... Dr. Amanda CLARK
53 Director MIT .... Dr. David CHERRY
19 Director Security Services .... Mr. LeRoy MCCALL
73 Director MA Theology .... Dr. Jeremy WYNNE
104 Dir of International Education Ctr .... Mr. Nick VASILOFF
88 Dir US Cultural Studies .... Dr. Stacy KEOGH GEORGE
50 Dir Grad Studies Business .... Ms. Sinead VOORHEES
88 Dir Evening Teacher Certification .... Dr. Stacy HILL
102 Dir Foundation & Planned Gifts .... Ms. Holly NORTON
36 Director Career Services .... Ms. Tiffany RIDDLE
88 Director University Events .... Ms. Michelle DRENNEN

Yakima Valley College (A)

PO Box 22520, S 16th Ave & Nob Hill,
Yakima WA 98907-2520

County: Yakima — FICE Identification: 003805
Unit ID: 237109
Telephone: (509) 574-4600 — Carnegie Class: Bac/Assoc-Assoc Dom
FAX Number: (509) 574-6860 — Calendar System: Quarter
URL: www.yvcc.edu
Established: 1928 — Annual Undergrad Tuition & Fees (In-State): $5,163
Enrollment: 4,007 — Coed
Affiliation or Control: State — IRS Status: 170(c)1
Highest Offering: Baccalaureate
Accreditation: NW, ADNUR, DH, MAC, RAD, SURGT

01 President .... Dr. Linda KAMINSKI
05 Vice Pres Instruction/Student Svcs .... Mr. Tomas YBARRA
10 Vice Pres Administrative Services .... Dr. Teresa RICH
12 Dean Grandview Campus .... Mr. Marc COOMER
75 Dean College Career Readiness .... Mr. Marc COOMER
13 Director Tech Services .... Mr. Dilbar CHHOKAR
32 Dean Student Services .... Ms. Leslie BLACKABY
49 Dean Arts & Sciences .... Ms. Kerrie CAVANESS
103 Dean Workforce Education .... Ms. Paulette LOPEZ
08 Library Director .... Ms. Tammy SIEBENBERG
37 Director Student Financial Aid .... Mr. Oscar VERDUZCO
06 Registrar/Director of Admissions .... Ms. Lorena ALVARADO-VALDOVINOS
108 Dir Institutional Effectiveness .... Ms. Sheila DELQUADRI
29 Director Alumni Relations .... Ms. Deborah WILSON
26 Community Relations Coordinator .... Mr. Jay FRANK
15 Director Human Resources .... Mr. Steven SLONIKER
18 Director Facilities/Physical Plant .... Mr. Jeff MORROW
21 Director Accounting Services .... Ms. Clarissa WOLFE
35 Student Life Coordinator .... Ms. Laura YOLO
04 Executive Asst to President .... Ms. Megan JENSEN

WEST VIRGINIA

Alderson Broaddus University (B)

101 College Hill Drive, Philippi WV 26416-4600

County: Barbour — FICE Identification: 003806
Unit ID: 237118
Telephone: (800) 263-1549 — Carnegie Class: Bac-Diverse
FAX Number: (304) 457-6239 — Calendar System: Semester
URL: www.ab.edu
Established: 1871 — Annual Undergrad Tuition & Fees: $27,910
Enrollment: 1,020 — Coed
Affiliation or Control: American Baptist — IRS Status: 501(c)3
Highest Offering: Master's
Accreditation: #NH, ARCPA, CAEPT, NUR

01 President .... Dr. James (Tim) BARRY
05 Provost/Executive Vice President .... Dr. Joan L. PROPST
11 Vice Pres for Administration .... Mr. Bruce A. BLANKENSHIP
84 Vice Pres Enrollment Management .... Dr. Eric M. SHOR
10 Vice Pres for Finance/CFO .... Mr. Jeff A. ROGERS
32 Dean of Student Affairs .... Mr. Bruce A. BLANKENSHIP
20 Associate Provost .... Dr. Andrea J. BUCKLEW
56 Asst Provost Extended Learning .... Dr. James M. OWSTON
111 Assoc VP for Inst Advancement .... Mr. Joshua D. ALLEN
63 Dean College of Medical Science .... Mr. Thomas F. MOORE
53 Dean College of Education and Music .. Dr. Erin R. BRUMBAUGH
79 Dean Col of Humanities & Soc Sci .... Mrs. Kari M. SISK
81 Dean Col Health/Science/Tech/Math .... Dr. Michael J. BOEHKE
06 Registrar .... Dr. Saundra E. HOXIE
08 Director of Library Services .... Mr. David E. HOXIE
41 Athletic Director .... Mrs. Carrie BODKINS
42 Chaplain .... Dr. Carl W. GITTINGS
121 Dir Academic Ctr for Educ Success .... Dr. Amy MASON
21 Controller .... Mr. Chad A. MAYLE
29 Director of Alumni Relations .... Mr. Joshua D. ALLEN
44 Director of Annual Giving .... Mr. Steve M. DYE
40 Director of Campus Services .... Mr. Ed BURDA
36 Assoc Dean Students & Career Svcs .... Ms. Teresa D. VANALSBURG
38 Director of Counseling Services .... Mr. Chad HOSTETLER
37 Director of Financial Aid .... Ms. Lora R. BRYANT
18 Director of Facilities .... Mr. Lawrence J. TALLMAN
46 Dir of Information and Research .... Ms. Julia M. MORRIS
13 Director of Information Technology .... Ms. Carol WEAVER
26 Director of Mktg/Communications .... Ms. Dionne T. ALLEN
35 Dean of Students .... Mr. David A. FALLETA
19 Director Security/Safety .... Mr. Matthew SISK
04 Exec Asst to Pres/Sec to the Board .... Mrs. Karla R. HIVELY
105 Web Content Editor .... Vacant
07 Director of Admissions .... Ms. Molly L. HENDERSON
09 Director of Institutional Research .... Dr. Bob S. BUCKINGHAM
15 Director of Human Resources .... Ms. Jennifer R. PHILLIPS
39 Assoc Director of Housing .... Ms. Megan L. AVERY

American National University (C)

110 Park Center Drive, Parkersburg WV 26101

Telephone: (304) 699-3005 — Identification: 770787
Accreditation: DEAC

† Branch campus of American National University, Salem, VA

American National University (D)

421 Hilltop Drive, Princeton WV 24740

Telephone: (304) 431-1600 — Identification: 666499
Accreditation: DEAC

† Branch campus of American National University, Salem, VA

American Public University System (E)

111 W Congress Street, Charles Town WV 25414-1621

County: Jefferson — FICE Identification: 035393
Unit ID: 449339
Telephone: (304) 724-3700 — Carnegie Class: Masters/L
FAX Number: (304) 724-3780 — Calendar System: Other
URL: www.apus.edu
Established: 1991 — Annual Undergrad Tuition & Fees: $6,880
Enrollment: 46,420 — Coed
Affiliation or Control: Proprietary — IRS Status: Proprietary
Highest Offering: Doctorate
Accreditation: NH, ACBSP, IFSAC, NURSE, PH

01 President .... Dr. Wallace BOSTON
05 Provost .... Dr. Vernon SMITH
20 SVP/Vice Provost .... Dr. Gwen HALL
11 SVP/COO .... Mr. Bob GAY
10 VP Finance/CFO .... Ms. Claudine STUBBLEFIELD
43 VP/University Counsel .... Ms. J.J HERBERT
26 Sr VP/Chief Marketing Officer .....Ms. Beth LAGUARDIA COOPER
15 Sr VP Human Resources/Cmty Affairs ...... Ms. Amy PANZARELLA
88 Sr VP Special Projects .... Mr. Peter GIBBONS
13 Exec VP/Chief Technology Officer .... Mr. Patrik DYBERG
32 VP Student Services .... Ms. Caroline SIMPSON
06 Asst Provost/Registrar .... Ms. Michelle NEWMAN
53 Dean Academic Svcs/Sch of Education .... Dr. Conrad LOTZE
124 Dean Faculty & Student Success .... Dr. Grady BATCHELOR
90 VP Academic & Instructional Tech .... Ms. Karen V. SRBA
88 Sr VP/Chief Innovation Officer .... Ms. Amy BEVILACQUA
37 VP Financial Aid & Compliance .... Mr. Keith WELLINGS
84 VP Enrollment Mgt & Student Support .... Ms. Terry GRANT
21 Sr VP/Controller .... Ms. Melissa FREY
82 Dean Security & Global Studies .... Dr. Mark T. RICCARDI
76 Dean Health Sciences .... Dr. Brian FREELAND
81 Dean STEM .... Dr. Ahmed NAUMAAN
79 Dean Arts & Humanities .... Dr. Grace GLASS
50 Dean Business .... Dr. Chad PATRIZI

Appalachian Bible College (F)

161 College Drive, Mount Hope WV 25880

County: Raleigh — FICE Identification: 007544
Unit ID: 237136
Telephone: (304) 877-6428 — Carnegie Class: Spec-4-yr-Faith
FAX Number: (304) 877-5082 — Calendar System: Semester
URL: abc.edu
Established: 1950 — Annual Undergrad Tuition & Fees: $14,720
Enrollment: 277 — Coed
Affiliation or Control: Independent Non-Profit — IRS Status: 501(c)3
Highest Offering: Master's
Accreditation: NH, BI, CAEP

01 President .... Dr. Daniel L. ANDERSON
05 Interim VP for Academics .... Dr. John KING
10 Vice President for Business .... Vacant
30 Vice President for Development .... Dr. Jonathan A. RINKER
32 Vice President for Student Services .... Rev. David E. CHILDS
42 Vice Pres for Extension Ministries .... Mr. David J. HOLLOWAY
33 Dean of Men .... Mr. Kevin GULLION
34 Dean of Women .... Mrs. Linda J. CHILDS
06 Registrar .... Mr. Tim ROWE
07 Director of Admissions .... Mr. Benjamin CALE
08 Librarian .... Mr. David W. DUNKERTON
37 Director of Financial Aid .... Mrs. Laura MARTIN
04 Admin Assistant to the President .... Mrs. Aimee STILES
26 Director of Public Relations .... Miss Karisa A. CLARK

Bethany College (G)

31 E. Campus Drive, Bethany WV 26032-3002

County: Brooke — FICE Identification: 003808
Unit ID: 237181
Telephone: (304) 829-7000 — Carnegie Class: Bac-A&S
FAX Number: (304) 829-7700 — Calendar System: 4/1/4
URL: www.bethanywv.edu
Established: 1840 — Annual Undergrad Tuition & Fees: $29,773
Enrollment: 628 — Coed
Affiliation or Control: Christian Church (Disciples Of Christ) — IRS Status: 501(c)3
Highest Offering: Master's
Accreditation: NH, CAEPN, SW

01 President .... Dr. Tamara N. RODENBERG
05 Provost/Vice Pres Academic Affairs .... Dr. Joseph LANE
10 Vice President for Finance .... Mr. Dennis MCMASTER
111 Vice President for Advancement .... Mr. Chris LAMBERT
04 Asst to the President .... Ms. Stephanie GORDON
20 Associate Provost .... Ms. Katherine SHELEK-FURBEE
32 VIce President & Dean of Students .... Mr. Gerald STEBBINS
37 Director of Financial Aid .... Mrs. Jill FERNANDES
41 Director of Athletics & Recreation .... Mr. Stephen THOMPSON
09 Dir Institutional Research/Records .... Mr. Richard MILLER
88 Director of McCann Learning Center .... Ms. Heather TAYLOR
88 Dir Student Engag/Responsibility .... Ms. Amber SHIPLEY
89 Director First Year Experience .... Dr. Scott BROTHERS
104 Director of International Programs .... Dr. Harald MENZ
36 Director of Career Services .... Ms. Amy VANHORN
23 Director of the Byrd Health Center .... Mrs. Carol TYLER
26 Communications Manager .... Ms. Emily COWEN
29 Director of Alumni Engagement .... Mr. Mark PHILLIPS
30 Director of Advancement Services .... Ms. Shirley KEMP
88 Director of Sports Information .... Ms. Erikka SANSOM
88 Director of Church Relations .... Rev. Cherisna JEAN-MARIE
18 Director of Physical Plant .... Mr. Jay EISENHAUER
21 Director of Business Affairs .... Vacant
19 Int Director of Safety & Security .... Ms. Sara DENT
15 Director of Human Resources .... Vacant
39 Assistant Dean of Student Life .... Mr. Andrew LEWIS
35 Director of Student Activities .... Mr. Samuel GOODGE
42 Chaplain .... Rev. Cherisna JEAN-MARIE
08 Director of the Libraries .... Mrs. Heather MAY-RICCIUTI
06 Registrar .... Ms. Lisa CUCARESE
84 Vice Pres of Enrollment Management .... Mrs. Karen HUNT
109 Director of Dining Services .... Mr. John SHAFFER
40 Manager of the Bookstore .... Mr. Nicholas TROMBETTI
38 College Counselor .... Ms. Renee STOCK

Catholic Distance University (H)

115 West Congress Street, Charles Town WV 25414

County: Jefferson — FICE Identification: 041242
Unit ID: 475398
Telephone: (304) 724-5000 — Carnegie Class: Spec-4-yr-Faith
FAX Number: (304) 724-5017 — Calendar System: Other
URL: www.cdu.edu
Established: 1983 — Annual Undergrad Tuition & Fees: $10,175
Enrollment: 187 — Coed
Affiliation or Control: Independent Non-Profit — IRS Status: 501(c)3
Highest Offering: Master's
Accreditation: @NH, DEAC, @THEOL

01 President .... Dr. Marianne E. MOUNT
05 Academic Dean .... Dr. Peter BROWN
88 Dean of Catechetical Programs .... Sr. Mary Margaret SCHLATHER
06 Registrar .... Mrs. Theresa SNIDER
51 Continuing Education Support .... Mrs. Kathleen WOODDELL
26 Director of Communications .... Vacant
07 Director of Admissions .... Mrs. Carol CIULLO
37 Financial Aid Officer .... Mrs. Amy SHOUSE
13 Acting Director of Technology .... Mrs. Carol DALEY
111 Director Institutional Advancement .... Mrs. Annie HAGER
04 Admin Assistant to the President .... Ms. Mary Kate WHITE
08 Librarian .... Sr. Rebecca ABEL
10 Chief Financial/Business Officer .... Mrs. Angela RUDOLPH

Davis & Elkins College (I)

100 Campus Drive, Elkins WV 26241-3996

County: Randolph — FICE Identification: 003811
Unit ID: 237358
Telephone: (304) 637-1900 — Carnegie Class: Bac-Diverse

FAX Number: (304) 637-1413 Calendar System: Semester
URL: www.dewv.edu
Established: 1904 Annual Undergrad Tuition & Fees: $29,590
Enrollment: 837 Coed
Affiliation or Control: Presbyterian Church (U.S.A.) IRS Status: 501(c)3
Highest Offering: Baccalaureate
Accreditation: NH, ADNUR, CAEP, IACBE, THEA

01 President ....Mr. Chris A. WOOD
10 VP for Business & Administration ....Mr. Robert O. HARDMAN, II
05 Vice President for Academic Affairs ....Dr. Robert J. PHILLIPS
32 Vice President for Student Affairs ....Mr. Scott D. GODDARD
111 Vice Pres Institutional Advancement ....Dr. Rosemary M. THOMAS
15 Director Human Resources ....Ms. Jane COREY
06 Registrar ....Dr. Stephanie C. HAYNES
18 Director of Physical Plant ....Mr. Dan JUDY
37 Director Financial Planning ....Mr. Matthew A. SUMMERS
08 Assistant Director Booth Library ....Ms. Mary Jo DEJOICE
42 Chaplain ....Rev. Laura K. BREKKE WAGONER
41 Director of Athletics ....Mr. Jamie JOSS
19 Director of Public Safety ....Dr. Michael T. CURTIS
04 Executive Asst to the President ....Ms. Beth KING
13 Chief Information Officer ....Ms. Amy MATTINGLY
29 Director of Alumni Engagement ....Ms. Wendy MORGAN
84 Vice Pres for Enrollment Mgmt ....Dr. Rosemary M. THOMAS
09 Coordinator Institutional Research ....Mr. Nathaniel SAMS
26 Communications & Marketing ....Ms. Linda HOWELL SKIDMORE
07 Director of Admission ....Mr. Matthew K. SHIFLETT
22 Dir Affirm Action/Equal Opportunity ....Ms. Jane COREY
38 Director Student Counseling ....Ms. Margaret F. FALLETTA

Future Generations University (A)

400 Road Less Traveled, Franklin WV 26807-9201
County: Pendleton Identification: 666714
Unit ID: 481030
Telephone: (304) 358-2000 Carnegie Class: Spec-4-yr-Other
FAX Number: (304) 358-3008 Calendar System: Other
URL: www.future.edu
Established: 2003 Annual Graduate Tuition & Fees: N/A
Enrollment: 20 Coed
Affiliation or Control: Independent Non-Profit IRS Status: 501(c)3
Highest Offering: Master's; No Undergraduates
Accreditation: NH

01 President ....Dr. Daniel TAYLOR
11 Chief Operating Officer ....Stephanie HARTMAN
05 Chief Academic Officer ....Christie HAND
06 Registrar ....Jodie WIMER

Huntington Junior College (B)

900 Fifth Avenue, Huntington WV 25701-2004
County: Cabell FICE Identification: 009047
Unit ID: 237437
Telephone: (304) 697-7550 Carnegie Class: Spec 2-yr-Health
FAX Number: (304) 697-7554 Calendar System: Quarter
URL: www.huntingtonjuniorcollege.edu
Established: 1936 Annual Undergrad Tuition & Fees: $8,550
Enrollment: 368 Coed
Affiliation or Control: Proprietary IRS Status: Proprietary
Highest Offering: Associate Degree
Accreditation: NH, MAC

01 President ....Carolyn A. SMITH
03 Director ....Lake TACKETT
05 Academic Affairs Director ....Linda J. WEST
10 Chief Fiscal Officer ....Sharon SNODDY

Martinsburg College (C)

341 Aikens Center, Martinsburg WV 25404
County: Berkeley Identification: 667035
Unit ID: 487977
Telephone: (304) 945-0656 Carnegie Class: Assoc/HVT-High Non
FAX Number: (866) 703-6611 Calendar System: Other
URL: www.martinsburgcollege.edu
Established: 1980 Annual Undergrad Tuition & Fees: N/A
Enrollment: 879 Coed
Affiliation or Control: Proprietary IRS Status: Proprietary
Highest Offering: Associate Degree
Accreditation: DEAC

01 President ....Paul VIBOCH
05 Chief Academic Officer ....Rita CLAYPOLE
07 Director of Admissions ....Laurie MAURO
06 Registrar ....Debra HAYTAS

Mountain State College (D)

1508 Spring Street, Parkersburg WV 26101
County: Wood FICE Identification: 005008
Unit ID: 237598
Telephone: (304) 485-5487 Carnegie Class: Assoc/HVT-High Trad
FAX Number: (304) 485-3524 Calendar System: Quarter
URL: www.msc.edu
Established: 1888 Annual Undergrad Tuition & Fees: $8,215
Enrollment: 78 Coed
Affiliation or Control: Proprietary IRS Status: Proprietary
Highest Offering: Associate Degree
Accreditation: ACCSC

01 President ....Mrs. Judith SUTTON
11 Chief Operations Officer ....Mr. Kevin MERRITT

Ohio Valley University (E)

1 Campus View Drive, Vienna WV 26105-8000
County: Wood FICE Identification: 003819
Unit ID: 237640
Telephone: (304) 865-6000 Carnegie Class: Bac-Diverse
FAX Number: (304) 865-6001 Calendar System: Semester
URL: www.ovu.edu
Established: 1958 Annual Undergrad Tuition & Fees: $21,900
Enrollment: 560 Coed
Affiliation or Control: Churches Of Christ IRS Status: 501(c)3
Highest Offering: Master's
Accreditation: NH, CAEP, IACBE

01 President ....Mr. Michael ROSS
100 Chief of Staff ....Mr. Charles MORRIS
05 Provost ....Dr. Joy JONES
10 Vice President Finance/CFO ....Mrs. Lindsay COLE
11 Vice President of Support Services ....Ms. Cecelia GOFF
30 Director of Advancement ....Mr. Jack THORN
09 Director of OIE ....Vacant
18 Director of Campus Operations ....Vacant
36 Director of Career Services ....Vacant
32 Dean of Student Life ....Ms. Noelle HUNTER
08 Library Director ....Ms. Sonya HESCHT
06 Registrar ....Mr. Justin BOYCE
07 Director of Admissions Management ....Mr. Nathan GREENE
13 Chief Info Technology Officer ....Mr. Christopher LANG
26 Director of Marketing ....Mrs. Roxanne WILSON
19 Director Security/Safety ....Mr. Shawn COLLINS
37 Director Student Financial Aid ....Mrs. Lindsay COLE
53 Dean College of Education ....Mrs. Glenda J. PENNINGTON
50 Dean College of Business ....Dr. Dan BLAIR
49 Dean College of Arts & Sciences ....Dr. Wes CRUM
41 Athletic Director ....Mr. Chad PORTER

Salem University (F)

223 W Main Street, Box 500, Salem WV 26426-0500
County: Harrison FICE Identification: 003820
Unit ID: 237783
Telephone: (304) 326-1109 Carnegie Class: Masters/S
FAX Number: (304) 326-1306 Calendar System: Semester
URL: www.salemu.edu
Established: 1888 Annual Undergrad Tuition & Fees: $16,700
Enrollment: 1,126 Coed
Affiliation or Control: Proprietary IRS Status: Proprietary
Highest Offering: Master's
Accreditation: NH, ACBSP, CAEPN

01 CEO/President ....Mr. Danny D. FINUF
04 Executive Asst to President ....Mrs. Barbara L. MCCLAIN
03 Executive Vice President ....Dr. Cecil E. KIRKLAND
05 Provost ....Dr. Craig S. MCCLELLAN
37 Dir Financial Aid & Compliance ....Mr. Marty MEHRINGER
13 Director of Information Technology ....Mr. Scott CARR
07 Director of Admissions ....Ms. Iris ROBERTSON
10 Chief Financial Officer ....Mr. Dan NELANT
21 Controller ....Ms. Virginia RICHARDS
18 Facilities Director & Business Mgr ....Mrs. Stephanie ROBERTS
06 Registrar ....Mr. Joseph E. FERLIC
50 Dean of Business ....Dr. Marc D. GETTY
53 Dean of Education ....Dr. Craig S. MCCLELLAN
66 Director of Nursing Education ....Dr. Stephanie HOLADAY
08 Dean of Library Services ....Dr. Phyllis D. FREEDMAN
32 Dean of Student Affairs ....Dr. Dennis MCNABOE
19 Director of Campus Security ....Mr. Joseph E. SHAVER
41 Director of Athletics ....Mr. Steve POTTS
29 Director Alumni Relations ....Ms. Carolyn BACON
39 Director Student Housing ....Mr. Mark A. NESMITH

University of Charleston (G)

2300 Maccorkle Avenue, SE, Charleston WV 25304-1099
County: Kanawha FICE Identification: 003818
Unit ID: 237312
Telephone: (304) 357-4800 Carnegie Class: DU-Mod
FAX Number: (304) 357-4715 Calendar System: Semester
URL: www.ucwv.edu
Established: 1888 Annual Undergrad Tuition & Fees: $30,900
Enrollment: 2,481 Coed
Affiliation or Control: Independent Non-Profit IRS Status: 501(c)3
Highest Offering: Doctorate
Accreditation: NH, ADNUR, ARCPA, CAATE, CAEP, CIDA, NUR, OTA, PHAR, RAD

01 President ....Dr. Martin S. ROTH
05 Exec VP/Provost/Dean of Faculty ....Dr. Kim SPIEZIO
10 Exec VP Administration & Finance ....Mrs. Cleta M. HARLESS
30 Vice Pres for Development ....Ms. Deborah MORRIS
07 Exec VP/Chief Admissions/Mktg Ofcr ....Ms. Joan CLARK
32 Dean of Students ....Ms. Virginia MOORE
100 EVP Cont & Professional Educ/COO ....Dr. Jerry FORSTER
88 VP/Chief Innovation Executive ....Ms. Fonda HOLEHOUSE
06 Registrar ....Ms. Carol SPRADLING
26 Director of Marketing/Communication ....Mr. David TRAUBE
29 Director of Alumni Relations ....Ms. Molly BALLARD
21 Controller ....Ms. Terri UNDERHILL
13 Chief Information Officer ....Mr. Scott TERRY
08 Director of Library Services ....Mr. John ADKINS
85 Director International Student Pgms ....Ms. Violetta PETROSYAN
37 Associate Director Financial Aid ....Ms. Michelle MARLOWE
35 Dir of Student Involvement ....Ms. Skyler HUNT
40 Bookstore Manager ....Mr. Glenn JOHNSON
18 Director of Facilities Services ....Mr. Gary BOYD
41 Athletic Director ....Dr. Bren STEVENS
09 Director of Institutional Research ....Ms. Lisa DAWKINS
50 Dean Graduate School of Business ....Dr. Scott BELLAMY
67 Dean School of Pharmacy ....Dr. Michelle EASTON
49 Dean School of Arts & Sciences ....Dr. Barbara WRIGHT
76 Dean School of Health Sciences ....Dr. Pamela ALDERMAN
04 Administrative Asst to President ....Ms. Susan LEFEW
15 Director Human Resources ....Ms. Janice GWINN
19 Director Security/Safety ....Mr. Eric SMITH
38 Director Student Counseling ....Dr. Candace LAYNE
44 Director of Annual Fund ....Ms. Catherine ECKLEY

Valley College - Martinsburg Campus (H)

287 Aikens Center, Martinsburg WV 25404-6203
County: Berkeley FICE Identification: 026094
Unit ID: 377661
Telephone: (304) 263-0979 Carnegie Class: Spec 2-yr-Health
FAX Number: (304) 263-2413 Calendar System: Other
URL: www.valley.edu
Established: 1983 Annual Undergrad Tuition & Fees: N/A
Enrollment: 437 Coed
Affiliation or Control: Proprietary IRS Status: Proprietary
Highest Offering: Associate Degree
Accreditation: ACCSC

01 Campus Director ....Ms. Marianela ALBERTO
05 Dir Academic Affairs-Campus Pgms ....Ms. Judy BAUSERMAN

*West Virginia Council for Community & Technical College Education (I)

1018 Kanawha Boulevard E, Suite 700, Charleston WV 25301-2800
County: Kanawha Identification: 666993
Telephone: (304) 558-0265 Carnegie Class: N/A
FAX Number: (304) 558-1646
URL: www.wvctcs.org

01 Chancellor ....Sarah A. TUCKER

*Blue Ridge Community and Technical College (J)

13650 Apple Harvest Drive, Martinsburg WV 25403
County: Berkeley FICE Identification: 039573
Unit ID: 446774
Telephone: (304) 260-4380 Carnegie Class: Assoc/HT-High Non
FAX Number: (304) 260-1788 Calendar System: Semester
URL: www.blueridgectc.edu
Established: 1974 Annual Undergrad Tuition & Fees (In-State): $4,128
Enrollment: 5,708 Coed
Affiliation or Control: State IRS Status: 501(c)3
Highest Offering: Associate Degree
Accreditation: NH, ADNUR, CAHIIM, EMT, PTAA

02 President ....Dr. Peter G. CHECKOVICH
05 Vice President of Instruction ....Ms. Laura BUSEY
103 VP Engineer/Workforce Development ....Dr. Ann M. SHIPWAY
10 Chief Finance Officer ....Dr. Randall MILLER
84 VP of Enrollment Management ....Ms. Leslie C. SEE
11 VP of Administration ....Dr. Craig MILLER
13 Vice President of IT ....Mr. Michael BYERS
06 Registrar ....Dr. Angelic M. KINDER
121 Director of Access & Success ....Ms. Brenda NEAL
37 Director of Financial Aid ....Ms. Anna CRAWFORD
18 Director of Facilities ....Mr. Larry BICKETT

*BridgeValley Community & Technical College (K)

2001 Union Carbide Drive, South Charleston WV 25303
County: Kanawha FICE Identification: 040386
Unit ID: 484932
Telephone: (304) 205-6600 Carnegie Class: Assoc/HVT-High Trad
FAX Number: N/A Calendar System: Semester
URL: www.bridgevalley.edu
Established: 2014 Annual Undergrad Tuition & Fees (In-District): $4,820
Enrollment: 1,939 Coed
Affiliation or Control: State/Local IRS Status: Exempt
Highest Offering: Associate Degree
Accreditation: NH, ACBSP, ADNUR, COARC, DH, DMS, MLTAD

02 President ....Dr. Eunice BELLINGER
05 VP of Academic Affairs ....Dr. Peter SOSCIA
103 Vice Pres WF/Economic Develop ....Mr. Jeff WYCO
88 VP Community Education ....Ms. Laura MCCULLOUGH
32 VP Student Affairs/Col Advancement ....Vacant
11 VP of Operations ....Mr. Jason STARK
35 Dean of Students ....Mr. James MCDOUGLE
97 Dean of General Education ....Ms. Kristi ELLENBERG

20 Assoc VP Academic Affairs ... Ms. Suzette BREEDEN
06 Chief Records Officer/Registrar ... Mr. Roy SIMMONS
15 Chief Human Resources Officer ... Ms. Michelle BISSELL
10 Chief Financial Officer ... Ms. Cathy AQUINO
04 Special Asst to President ... Ms. Alicia SYNER
08 Director of Library Services ... Vacant
09 Chief Banner Officer ... Mr. James FAUVER
19 Chief of Police ... Mr. Bazra FAKHIR
26 Chief Marketing Officer ... Vacant
50 Dean Business/Legal/Human Svcs ... Ms. Kelly GROSE
72 Dean of Technology ... Mr. Norm MORTENSEN
37 Director of Financial Aid ... Ms. Mary BLIZZARD
36 Director of Student Placement ... Ms. Judy WHIPKEY
38 Director of Counseling Svcs ... Ms. Carla BLANKENBUEHLER
96 Chief Procurement Officer ... Mr. John POWELL
18 Chief Facilities/Physical Plant Ofc ... Mr. George BOSSIE

*Eastern West Virginia Community and Technical College (A)

316 Eastern Drive, Moorefield WV 26836-1155

County: Hardy FICE Identification: 041190
Unit ID: 438708
Telephone: (304) 434-8000 Carnegie Class: Assoc/HT-High Non
FAX Number: (304) 434-7000 Calendar System: Semester
URL: www.easternwv.edu
Established: 1999 Annual Undergrad Tuition & Fees (In-State): $3,552
Enrollment: 602 Coed
Affiliation or Control: State IRS Status: Exempt
Highest Offering: Associate Degree
Accreditation: NH, ADNUR

02 President ... Dr. Charles TERRELL
11 Exec Dean for Administrative Svcs ... Mr. John GALATIC
05 Dean for Teaching & Learning ... Mr. Curtis HAKALA
32 Dean of Student Access & Success ... Ms. Monica WILSON
04 President's Office Administrator ... Mr. Michael O'LEARY
13 Chief Information Technology Office ... Mr. Ronald HAMILTON
15 Chief Human Resources Officer ... Mr. Carlos GUTIERREZ

*Mountwest Community and Technical College (B)

One Mountwest Way, Huntington WV 25701

County: Cabell FICE Identification: 040414
Unit ID: 444954
Telephone: (304) 710-3140 Carnegie Class: Assoc/HVT-Mix Trad/Non
FAX Number: (304) 710-3187 Calendar System: Semester
URL: www.mctc.edu
Established: 1975 Annual Undergrad Tuition & Fees (In-District): $4,020
Enrollment: 1,914 Coed
Affiliation or Control: State/Local IRS Status: 501(c)3
Highest Offering: Associate Degree
Accreditation: NH, ACBSP, CAHIIM, COARC, EMT, MAC, PTAA

02 President ... Dr. Keith J. COTRONEO
10 Chief Financial Officer ... Mr. Derek ADKINS
32 Interim VP of Student Services ... Mr. James K. SKIDMORE
13 VP Operations and Info Technology ... Mrs. Terri L. TOMBLIN-BYRD
06 Associate Dean/Registrar ... Ms. Angela ROSS

*New River Community and Technical College (C)

280 University Drive, Beaver WV 25813

County: Raleigh FICE Identification: 039603
Unit ID: 447582
Telephone: (304) 929-5450 Carnegie Class: Assoc/HVT-Mix Trad/Non
FAX Number: (304) 929-5478 Calendar System: Semester
URL: www.newriver.edu
Established: 2003 Annual Undergrad Tuition & Fees (In-State): $4,286
Enrollment: 1,172 Coed
Affiliation or Control: State IRS Status: 501(c)3
Highest Offering: Associate Degree
Accreditation: NH, EMT, MLTAD

02 President ... Dr. Bonny COPENHAVER
04 Exec Secretary to the President ... Ms. Lori A. MIDKIFF
05 Vice Pres Academic/Student Affairs ... Dr. Richard B. PAGAN
13 VP Information Technology Services ... Dr. David J. AYERSMAN
15 Director Human Resources ... Ms. Amanda L. BAKER
26 Director of Communications ... Ms. Jenni CANTERBURY
12 Regional Director of Operations ... Mr. William POTTER
12 Regional Director of Operations ... Mr. Roger D. GRIFFITH
12 Regional Director of Operations ... Ms. Mary IGO
06 Registrar ... Ms. Janelle SCHOFIELD
08 Staff Librarian ... Mr. Robert H. COSTON
37 Director of Financial Aid ... Ms. Patricia HARMON
96 Director of Purchasing ... Ms. Twana JACKSON
10 Int VP of Finance/Administration ... Mr. Gerald SHIELDS
18 Director of Physical Plant ... Mr. Robert RUNION
84 Director of Enrollment Services ... Ms. Tracy L. EVANS
88 Dean of Transfer and Preprof ... Ms. Wendy PATRIQUIN

*Pierpont Community & Technical College (D)

1201 Locust Avenue, Fairmont WV 26554-2470

County: Marion FICE Identification: 040385
Unit ID: 443492
Telephone: (304) 367-4692 Carnegie Class: Assoc/HVT-Mix Trad/Non
FAX Number: (304) 367-4881 Calendar System: Semester
URL: www.pierpont.edu
Established: 1974 Annual Undergrad Tuition & Fees (In-State): $4,938
Enrollment: 1,855 Coed
Affiliation or Control: State IRS Status: 501(c)3
Highest Offering: Associate Degree
Accreditation: NH, ACFEI, CAHIIM, #COARC, @DIETT, EMT, MLTAD, NAIT, PTAA

01 President ... Dr. Johnny M. MOORE
04 Exec Assistant to the President ... Mrs. Cyndee K. SENSIBAUGH
05 Provost/VP for Academic Affairs ... Mr. Michael P. WAIDE
10 VP for Finance and Administration ... Mr. Dale R. BRADLEY
111 VP for Organization and Development ... Mr. Stephen E. LEACH
32 VP Student Services ... Mrs. Lyla D. GRANDSTAFF
50 Int Dean Sch of Bus/Aviation/Tech ... Dr. Kari COFFINDAFFER
76 Dean School of Health Sciences ... Mrs. Vickie FINDLEY
97 Dean School Gen Educ/Business Dev ... Mr. David BEIGHLEY
13 Int Exec Dir InfoTech/Elearning ... Ms. Robin STRADER
108 Director Institutional Assessment ... Ms. Nancy PARKS

*Southern West Virginia Community and Technical College (E)

P. O. Box 2900, Mount Gay WV 25637-2900

County: Logan FICE Identification: 003816
Unit ID: 237817
Telephone: (304) 792-7098 Carnegie Class: Assoc/MT-VT-High Trad
FAX Number: (304) 792-7046 Calendar System: Semester
URL: www.southernwv.edu
Established: 1971 Annual Undergrad Tuition & Fees (In-State): $3,892
Enrollment: 1,621 Coed
Affiliation or Control: State IRS Status: 501(c)3
Highest Offering: Associate Degree
Accreditation: NH, ADNUR, COARC, EMT, MLTAD, RAD, SURGT

02 President ... Dr. Robert E. GUNTER
10 VP for Finance & Administration ... Mr. Samuel M. LITTERAL
05 VP Academic Affairs ... Dr. Deanna M. ROMANO
103 VP Economic & Workforce Development ... Mr. Allyn S. BARKER
13 Chief Information Officer ... Mr. Tom COOK
111 VP for Institutional Advancement ... Ms. Rita G. ROBERSON
15 Human Resources Director ... Mr. James D. KENNEDY
04 Exec Asst to President & BOG ... Ms. Emma L. BAISDEN
09 Dir Institutional Effectiveness ... Vacant
12 Director Wyoming Campus Operations ... Mr. David LORD
12 Dir Williamson Campus Operations ... Mr. Perry JOBE
12 Director Logan Campus Operations ... Mr. Joe LINVILLE
06 Registrar ... Ms. Teri WELLS
37 Dir Student Financial Assistance ... Ms. Stella ESTEPP
08 Director of Libraries ... Ms. Kimberly L. MAYNARD
84 Dir Enroll Mgmt/Stdnt Engagement ... Mr. Darrell TAYLOR
22 Dir Affirmative Action/EEO ... Mr. James D. KENNEDY

*West Virginia Northern Community College (F)

1704 Market Street, Wheeling WV 26003-3643

County: Ohio FICE Identification: 009054
Unit ID: 238014
Telephone: (304) 233-5900 Carnegie Class: Assoc/HVT-High Non
FAX Number: (304) 232-4651 Calendar System: Semester
URL: www.wvncc.edu
Established: 1972 Annual Undergrad Tuition & Fees (In-State): $4,107
Enrollment: 1,650 Coed
Affiliation or Control: State IRS Status: 501(c)3
Highest Offering: Associate Degree
Accreditation: NH, ACFEI, ADNUR, CAHIIM, MAC, RAD, SURGT

02 Interim President ... Mr. Mike KOON
05 VP of Academic Affairs ... Dr. Jill LOVELESS
10 CFO & VP Administrative Services ... Mr. Jeff SAYRE
32 Vice President Student Services ... Mrs. Janet FIKE
26 Director of Marketing & PR ... Mr. David BARNHARDT
18 Director of Facilities ... Ms. Trish MARKER
15 Chief Human Resource Officer ... Mrs. Peggy CARMICHAEL
103 VP of Economic & Workforce Dev ... Mr. Larry TACKETT
04 Administrative Asst to President ... Ms. Stephanie KAPPEL

*New River Community and Technical College Greenbrier Valley Campus (G)

653 Church Street, Lewisburg WV 24901-1303

Telephone: (304) 647-6560 Identification: 770468
Accreditation: &NH

*New River Technical College Mercer County Campus (H)

1001 Mercer Street, Princeton WV 24740-8230

Telephone: (304) 425-5858 Identification: 770469
Accreditation: &NH

*New River Technical College Nicholas County Campus (I)

6101 Webster Road, Summersville WV 26651

Telephone: (304) 872-1236 Identification: 770470
Accreditation: &NH

*Southern West Virginia Community and Technical College-Boone/Lincoln Campus (J)

3505 Daniel Boone Parkway, Suite A, Foster WV 25081-8126

Telephone: (304) 369-2952 Identification: 770471
Accreditation: &NH

*Southern West Virginia Community and Technical College-Williamson Campus (K)

1601 Armory Drive, Williamson WV 25661

Telephone: (304) 235-6046 Identification: 770473
Accreditation: &NH, COARC

*Southern West Virginia Community and Technical College-Wyoming/McDowell Campus (L)

128 College Drive, Saulsville WV 25876

Telephone: (304) 294-8346 Identification: 770472
Accreditation: &NH

*West Virginia Northern Community College (M)

141 Main Street, New Martinsville WV 26155

Telephone: (304) 455-4684 Identification: 770474
Accreditation: &NH

*West Virginia Northern Community College (N)

150 Park Avenue, Weirton WV 26062

Telephone: (304) 723-2210 Identification: 770475
Accreditation: &NH

---

*West Virginia Higher Education Policy Commission (O)

1018 Kanawha Boulevard E, Ste 700, Charleston WV 25301-2887

County: Kanawha FICE Identification: 033440
Telephone: (304) 558-2101 Carnegie Class: N/A
FAX Number: (304) 558-5719
URL: www.wvhepc.edu

01 Interim Chancellor ... Dr. Sarah TUCKER
88 Chancellor WV Cmty/Tech Col System ... Dr. Sarah TUCKER
46 Director of Science and Research ... Dr. Jan TAYLOR
05 Vice Chancellor for Academic Affs ... Dr. Corley DENNISON
10 Vice Chancellor for Finance ... Dr. Edward MAGEE
32 Int Director of Student Services ... Ms. Elizabeth MANUEL
15 Vice Chancellor for Human Resources ... Ms. Trish HUMPHRIES
43 Interim General Counsel ... Ms. Candace KRAUS
11 Exec Vice Chancellor Administration ... Mr. Matt TURNER
45 Senior Director Policy & Planning ... Dr. Chris TREADWAY
37 Senior Director of Financial Aid ... Mr. Brian WEINGART
88 Director Administrative Services ... Ms. Cindy L. ANDERSON

*Bluefield State College (P)

219 Rock Street, Bluefield WV 24701-2198

County: Mercer FICE Identification: 003809
Unit ID: 237215
Telephone: (304) 327-4000 Carnegie Class: Bac-Diverse
FAX Number: (304) 325-7747 Calendar System: Semester
URL: www.bluefieldstate.edu
Established: 1895 Annual Undergrad Tuition & Fees (In-State): $7,056
Enrollment: 1,379 Coed
Affiliation or Control: State IRS Status: 501(c)3
Highest Offering: Baccalaureate
Accreditation: NH, ACBSP, ADNUR, CAEPN, NURSE, RAD

02 Interim President ... Dr. Robin CAPEHART
05 Vice Pres Academic Affairs/Provost ... Dr. Ted LEWIS
10 Vice Pres Financial/Admin Affairs ... Ms. Shelia JOHNSON
32 Vice President Student Affairs ... Dr. JoAnn ROBINSON
31 Int Vice Pres for Cmty Engagement ... Mr. Jim NELSON
88 Executive Dir Title III ... Dr. Guy SIMS
06 Registrar ... Ms. Terry THOMPSON
08 Director Library Services ... Ms. Joanna THOMPSON
13 Chief Technology Officer ... Mr. John SPENCER, JR.
07 Director of Admissions ... Vacant
37 Director of Financial Aid ... Vacant
15 Director of Human Resources ... Ms. Jonette AUGHENBAUGH
19 Director Public Safety ... Vacant
38 Director of Counseling ... Dr. Cravor JONES
29 Director Alumni Affairs ... Ms. Deirdre GUYTON
40 Manager Bookstore ... Ms. Susan PLUMLEY
41 Athletic Director ... Mr. John LEWIS
50 Dean School of Business ... Mr. Philip IMEL
49 Dean School of Arts and Sciences ... Dr. Martha EBORALL
54 Dean School of Eng Tech/Comp Sci ... Vacant
53 Dean School of Education ... Dr. Shelia SARGENT-MARTIN
66 Dean School Nursing/Allied Health ... Ms. Angela LAMBERT
66 ADN Program Director ... Ms. Sandra WYNN
66 BSN Program Director ... Ms. Carol COFER
88 Program Dir of Radiologic Tech ... Ms. Melissa HAYE
28 Asst to Pres Equity/Divers/Inclusn ... Dr. Guy SIMS
96 Director of Purchasing ... Mr. Paul RUTHERFORD

04	Admin Assistant to the President	Ms. Jeanne MORICLE
100	Chief of Staff	Mr. Terry WALLACE
18	Director of Physical Plant	Mr. Mike EARLS

*Concord University (A)

PO Box 1000, Athens WV 24712-1000
County: Mercer FICE Identification: 003810
Unit ID: 237330
Telephone: (304) 384-3115 Carnegie Class: Masters/M
FAX Number: (304) 384-9044 Calendar System: Semester
URL: www.concord.edu
Established: 1872 Annual Undergrad Tuition & Fees (In-State): $8,211
Enrollment: 2,194 Coed
Affiliation or Control: State IRS Status: 501(c)3
Highest Offering: Master's
Accreditation: NH, ACBSP, CAATE, CAEPN, SW

02	President & CEO	Dr. Kendra BOGGESS
05	VP & Academic Dean	Dr. Peter VISCUSI
111	VP for Advancement	Mrs. Alicia BESENYEI
20	Associate Dean	Dr. Kathy LIPTAK
32	VP Student Affairs	Dr. Sarah BEASLEY
10	VP for Business & Finance	Dr. Charles P. BECKER
11	VP of Administration	Mr. Rick DILLON
13	VP of Information Technology	Mr. Charles ELLIOTT
06	Registrar	Mrs. Susie LUSK
08	Director of Libraries	Mrs. Connie SHUMATE
37	Director of Student Financial Aid	Mrs. Tammy BROWN
29	Director Alumni & Donor Relations	Ms. Sarah TURNER
88	Director Bonner Scholars Program	Mrs. Kathy BALL
15	VP of Operations & HR Director	Mr. Daniel FITZPATRICK
18	Director Physical Plant	Mr. Gerry VON VILLE
19	Director of Public Safety	Chief Mark STELLA
36	Director of Career Services	Vacant
40	Bookstore Manager	Mrs. Sheila CONNER
41	Athletic Director	Mr. Kevin GARRETT
21	Financial Reporting Officer	Ms. Elizabeth J. CAHILL-MUSICK
24	Ctr for Academic Technologies	Mr. Steve MEADOWS
88	Graphic Art Designer	Mr. Foster SHEPPARD
25	Director of Grants and Contracts	Mrs. Melanie FARMER
12	Director of the Beckley Center	Dr. Susan WILLIAMS
96	Contract Specialist & Business Mgr	Ms. Andrea WEBB
124	Director of Retention	Vacant
04	Executive Assistant to President	Mrs. Lora WOOLWINE
88	Program Coordinator Advancement	Ms. Amy PITZER
110	Manager of University Advancement	Mr. Blake FARMER
39	Director Student Housing	Mr. Bill FRALEY

*Fairmont State University (B)

1201 Locust Avenue, Fairmont WV 26554-2470
County: Marion FICE Identification: 003812
Unit ID: 237367
Telephone: (304) 367-4000 Carnegie Class: Masters/S
FAX Number: (304) 367-4789 Calendar System: Semester
URL: www.fairmontstate.edu
Established: 1865 Annual Undergrad Tuition & Fees (In-State): $7,514
Enrollment: 3,886 Coed
Affiliation or Control: State IRS Status: 501(c)3
Highest Offering: Master's
Accreditation: NH, ACBSP, ADNUR, CAEP, CAEPN, NURSE

02	President FSU	Dr. Mirta M. MARTIN
05	Provost/VP Academic Affairs	Dr. Richard C. HARVEY
10	Vice Pres Admin/Fiscal Affairs	Ms. Christa KWIATKOWSKI
32	Vice Pres Student Services	Mr. Tim MCNEELY
15	VP for Human Resources	Mrs. Cynthia S. CURRY
13	VP IT & Chief Info Technology (CIO)	Dr. Joy A. HATCH
26	VP Univ Relations/Enroll/Marketing	Ms. Lyndsey DUGAN
108	Assc VP Institutional Effectiveness	Ms. Merri S. INCITTI
18	Asst Vice Pres for Facilities	Vacant
06	Registrar	Mrs. Cheri L. GONZALEZ
20	Executive Director Academic Program	Dr. Susan ROSS
49	Dean College of Liberal Arts	Vacant
72	Int Dean College of Science/Tech	Dr. Steven E. ROOF
50	Interim Dean School of Business	Dr. Timothy R. OXLEY
53	Int Assoc Dean Educ/Hlth/Hum Perf	Dr. Amanda METCALF
57	Dean School of Fine Arts	Vacant
66	Assoc Dean School of Nursing	Dr. Susan CLAYTON
119	Associate Information Tech Officer	Mr. Colton GRIFFIN
91	Manager IT Strategic Operations	Mr. George HERRICK
09	Director Institutional Research	Mr. Jacob R. ABRAMS
84	Dir Enrollment Strategic Operations	Mr. Corey HUNT
41	Director of Athletics	Mr. Chad FOWLER
19	Chief of Police	Mr. Matthew SWAIN
38	Dir of Counseling/Disability Svcs	Ms. Andrea M. PAMMER
37	Exec Dir Student Support Services	Ms. Tresa WEIMER
39	Exec Dir Res/Stdnt Life	Ms. Alicia KALKA
08	Interim Director Library Services	Ms. Sharon MAZURE
96	Director of Procurement	Ms. Monica J. COCHRAN
36	Director of Career Services	Dr. Ashley TASKER
14	Director IT Data Services	Ms. Joanie RAISOVICH
23	Director of Student Health Services	Vacant
121	Director of Academic Advising	Ms. Jennifer JONES
25	Director of Planning and Grants	Mrs. Amantha L. COLE
90	Sr Director Banner Administration	Dr. Senta CHMIEL
119	Manager Network Svcs & Security	Mr. Jon DODDS
07	Director of Recruitment	Mrs. Brittany STOUT
100	Chief of Staff	Mrs. Serena SCULLY
104	Director Study Abroad	Dr. Amanda K. STINEMETZ
88	Director Sponsored Awards Admin	Ms. Sandra SHRIVER
43	University General Counsel	Mrs. Jacqueline L. SIKORA

*Glenville State College (C)

200 High Street, Glenville WV 26351-1292
County: Gilmer FICE Identification: 003813
Unit ID: 237385
Telephone: (304) 462-7361 Carnegie Class: Bac-Diverse
FAX Number: (304) 462-7610 Calendar System: Semester
URL: www.glenville.edu
Established: 1872 Annual Undergrad Tuition & Fees (In-State): $6,919
Enrollment: 1,655 Coed
Affiliation or Control: State IRS Status: 501(c)3
Highest Offering: Baccalaureate
Accreditation: NH, CAEPN

02	Interim President	Dr. Kathleen L. NELSON
05	Provost/Vice Pres Academic Affairs	Dr. Victor VEGA
10	Vice Pres for Business & Finance	Mr. John BECKVOLD
41	Athletic Director	Mr. Jesse SKILES
111	Vice President for Advancement	Mr. David E. HUTCHISON
04	Executive Assistant to President	Ms. Teresa G. STERNS
53	Chair of Teacher Education	Dr. Jeff C. HUNTER
15	Chief Human Resources Officer	Ms. Krystal D. SMITH
37	Financial Aid Manager	Ms. Stephany HARPER
18	Exec Director of Facilities	Mr. Noah BALSER
39	Assoc Director of Residence Life	Mr. J. Trae SPRAGUE
23	Director Campus Health Services	Vacant
08	Director of Library	Ms. Gail L. WESTBROOK
21	Controller	Ms. Caren JENKINS
96	Director of Purchasing	Ms. Joyce E. RIDDLE
29	Dir of Alumni Affairs/Annual Giving	Mr. Conner FERGUSON
35	Dir Student Rights/Responsibilities	Ms. Jodi WALTERS
06	Registrar	Ms. Ann M. REED
13	Manager of Database Admin	Mr. Chuck SCHMIDT
121	Director of Academic Success Center	Ms. Stacy ADKINS
38	Professional Counselor	Mr. Timothy J. UNDERWOOD
84	VP for Enrollment Mgmt/Student Life	Mr. Charles M. CARVER
19	Associate Director of Public Safety	Mr. Ronald K. TAYLOR
20	Assoc VP for Academic Affairs	Dr. Gary Z. MORRIS

*Marshall University (D)

1 John Marshall Drive, Huntington WV 25755-0001
County: Cabell FICE Identification: 003815
Unit ID: 237525
Telephone: (304) 696-3170 Carnegie Class: DU-Higher
FAX Number: (304) 696-6565 Calendar System: Semester
URL: www.marshall.edu
Established: 1837 Annual Undergrad Tuition & Fees (In-State): $8,128
Enrollment: 13,246 Coed
Affiliation or Control: State IRS Status: 501(c)3
Highest Offering: Doctorate
Accreditation: NH, ADNUR, ANEST, CAATE, CACREP, CAEP, CAEPN, CAHIIM, CLPSY, COARC, CYTO, DIETD, DIETI, DMS, FEPAC, JOUR, MED, MLTAD, MT, MUS, NUR, PHAR, PTA, SP, SW

02	President	Dr. Jerome A. GILBERT
05	Provost/Sr VP Academic Affairs	Dr. Jaime TAYLOR
43	Sr VP Exec Affairs & Gen Counsel	Mr. F. Layton COTTRILL
10	Chief Financial Officer	Mr. Mark ROBINSON
26	Senior VP Communication/Marketing	Ms. Virginia R. PAINTER
63	Dean of Medicine	Dr. Joseph I. SHAPIRO
102	CEO MU Foundation Inc	Dr. Ron AREA
11	Sr VP for Administration	Ms. Brandi D. JACOBS
46	VP Research	Mr. John MAHER
53	Dean College of Education	Dr. Teresa EAGLE
29	Executive Director Alumni Relations	Mr. Matthew D. HAYES
30	Vice President Development	Mr. Lance WEST
28	Assoc VP Intercultural Affairs	Mr. Maurice R. COOLEY
13	Chief Technology Officer	Mr. Allen TAYLOR
07	Dean of Admissions	Dr. Tammy JOHNSON
32	Dean Student Affairs	Vacant
106	Asst VP Libraries & Online Learning	Dr. Monica BROOKS
58	Interim Dean Graduate College	Dr. David PITTENGER
49	Dean College Liberal Arts	Dr. Robert BOOKWALTER
50	Dean College of Business	Dr. Avinandan MUKHERJEE
57	Interim Dean College Arts & Media	Dr. Wendell DOBBS
67	Dean School of Pharmacy	Dr. Gayle A. BRAZEAU
66	Dean College of Health Prof	Dr. Michael PREWITT
54	Dean Col of Info Tech/Engr	Dr. Wael ZATAR
81	Dean College of Science	Dr. Charles SOMERVILLE
92	Dean Honors College	Dr. Nicola LOCASCIO
41	Director of Athletics	Mr. Mike HAMRICK
06	Registrar	Dr. Sonja G. CANTRELL
37	Dir Student Financial Aid	Ms. Pamela PALERMO
36	Director Career Services	Ms. Cristina C. MCDAVID
15	Director Human Resource Services	Mr. Bruce B. FELDER
19	Director of Public Safety	Mr. James E. TERRY
96	Director of Purchasing	Ms. Trace BROWN-DOLINSKI
18	Director Physical Plant	Mr. Travis BAILEY
39	Director Residence Services	Ms. Mistie BIBBEE
09	Asst to Pres/Sr VP Inst Rsch/Plng	Mr. Michael J. MCGUFFEY
22	Director Equity Programs	Ms. Debra HART
43	Assoc General Counsel	Ms. Jendonnae HOUDYSCHELL
86	Asst to Pres for External Liaison	Mr. William BURDETTE
114	Budget Director	Ms. Katrina ESKINS
04	Admin Assistant to the President	Ms. Cora PYLES

*Shepherd University (E)

PO Box 5000, Shepherdstown WV 25443-5000
County: Jefferson FICE Identification: 003822
Unit ID: 237792
Telephone: (304) 876-5000 Carnegie Class: Bac-A&S
FAX Number: (304) 876-3101 Calendar System: Semester
URL: www.shepherd.edu
Established: 1871 Annual Undergrad Tuition & Fees (In-State): $7,548
Enrollment: 3,736 Coed
Affiliation or Control: State IRS Status: 501(c)3
Highest Offering: Doctorate
Accreditation: NH, ART, CAEP, IACBE, MUS, NRPA, NURSE, SW

02	President	Dr. Mary HENDRIX
05	Provost	Dr. Scott BEARD
10	Vice President Finance	Ms. Pam STEVENS
32	Interim VP Student Affairs	Dr. John E. ADAMS
84	VPEM/Institution Compact Oversight	Mr. Bill SOMMERS
43	General Counsel	Mr. K. Alan PERDUE
11	Vice President Campus Services	Mr. Jack SHAW
81	Dean College of STEM	Dr. Robert WARBURTON
79	Dean Col Arts/Humanities/Social Sci	Dr. Robert TUDOR
50	Dean College of Business	Dr. Ben MARTZ
66	Dean College of Nursing/Ed/Hlth	Dr. Sharon MAILEY
88	Asst Provost Academic Cmty Outreach	Dr. Virginia HICKS
58	Dean School of Grad/Prof Studies	Dr. Richie STEVENS
121	Dean Teaching/Learning/Instruc Res	Dr. Laura RENNINGER
26	Exec Director Univ Communications	Ms. Valerie OWENS
09	Director Institutional Research	Ms. Sara MAENE
39	Director Residence Life	Dr. Elizabeth SECHLER
35	AVP Stndt Succ/Dir Cmty/Govt Rels	Ms. Holly FRYE
15	Director Human Resources	Dr. Marie DEWALT
13	Director Info Technology Services	Mr. Joey DAGG
06	Registrar	Ms. Tracy SEFFERS
07	Director of Admissions	Ms. Kristen LORENZ
37	Director of Financial Aid	Ms. Joyce CABRAL
19	Univ Police Chief	Mr. John MCAVOY
53	Director Teacher Education	Dr. Douglas KENNARD
18	Director of Facilities	Mr. James KING
41	Vice President for Athletics	Mr. Chauncey WINBUSH
96	Director of Procurement Services	Ms. Debra LANGFORD
38	Director of Counseling	Ms. Shanan SPENCER
29	Director of Alumni Affairs	Ms. Kim HUTTO
92	Director Honors Program	Dr. Mark CANTRELL
30	Executive Director of Development	Ms. Sherri JANELLE
104	Director Study Abroad	Ms. Yin STAR
25	Dir Grant Support/Corp/Found Rels	Ms. Jessica KUMP
08	Acting Dean Library	Dr. Laura RENNINGER
04	Executive Asst to the President	Mrs. Sonya SHOLLEY
44	Director of Annual Giving	Ms. Stacy MCFARLAND

*West Liberty University (F)

208 University Drive, West Liberty WV 26074
County: Ohio FICE Identification: 003823
Unit ID: 237932
Telephone: (304) 336-5000 Carnegie Class: Masters/S
FAX Number: (304) 336-8403 Calendar System: Semester
URL: www.westliberty.edu
Established: 1837 Annual Undergrad Tuition & Fees (In-State): $7,680
Enrollment: 2,443 Coed
Affiliation or Control: State IRS Status: 501(c)3
Highest Offering: Master's
Accreditation: NH, ARCPA, #CAATE, CAEPN, DH, IACBE, MT, MUS, NURSE, SW

02	President	Dr. Stephen G. GREINER
05	Provost	Dr. Brian L. CRAWFORD
32	VP of Student Services	Mr. Scott A. COOK
10	Executive Vice President & CFO	Ms. Roberta LINGER
81	Dean College of Sciences	Dr. Karen KETTLER
49	Dean College Liberal Arts	Dr. Gerard NECASTRO
57	Dean College Arts & Comm	Dr. Matthew HARDER
53	Interim Dean College of Education	Dr. Catherine MONTEROSO
66	Director of Nursing Programs	Dr. Rose M. KUTLENIOS
50	Interim Dean College of Business	Dr. Gregory CHASE
39	Exec Dir Housing & Student Life	Ms. Marcella T. SNYDER
15	Chief Human Resources Officer	Ms. Diana L. HARTO
13	Chief Technology Officer	Mr. Joseph RODELLA
09	Dir of Inst Research & Assessment	Ms. Paula J. TOMASIK
41	Director of Athletics	Mr. Lynn ULLOM
07	Exec Dir Admissions & Recruitment	Ms. Brenda M. KING
51	Director of Cont Educ/Special Pgm	Vacant
08	Director of Library	Ms. Cheryl R. HARSHMAN
29	Exec Dir of Alumni/Cmty Relations	Mr. Ron A. WITT
37	Director Financial Aid	Mrs. Katie R. COOPER
111	VP of Institutional Advancement	Mr. Jason W. KOEGLER
109	Director of Auxiliary Services	Vacant
38	Director of Counseling	Ms. Bridgette DAWSON
92	Director of the Honors Program	Dr. Shannon D. HALICKI
88	Director Dental Hygiene Programs	Ms. Stephanie MEREDITH
88	Dir Clinical Lab Science Program	Dr. William C. WAGENER
23	Director of Health Services	Ms. Cheryl C. BENNINGTON
88	Dir Physician Assistant Program	Dr. William A. CHILDERS, JR.
85	Coord International Student Rec	Ms. Mihaela SZABO
26	Executive Director of Marketing	Ms. Tammi SECRIST
101	Secretary of the Institution/Board	Ms. Mary A. EDWARDS
105	Director Creative/Web Master	Vacant
106	Dir Online Education/E-learning	Ms. Lucy KEFAUVER
18	Director of Physical Plant	Mr. Joe MILLS
19	Chief of Police/Dir Public Safety	Mr. Joseph MONTEMURRO
96	Director of Purchasing	Ms. Shawn E. TODD
06	Registrar	Mr. Scott A. COOK
102	Executive Director Foundation	Ms. Angela ZAMBITO-HILL
04	Admin Assistant to the President	Ms. Mary Ann EDWARDS
25	Chief Contract & Grants Admin	Ms. Laura MUSILLI

*West Virginia School of Osteopathic Medicine (A)

400 Lee Street North, Lewisburg WV 24901-1196
County: Greenbrier FICE Identification: 011245
Unit ID: 237880
Telephone: (304) 645-6270 Carnegie Class: Spec-4-yr-Med
FAX Number: (304) 645-4859 Calendar System: Semester
URL: www.wvsom.edu
Established: 1972 Annual Graduate Tuition & Fees: N/A
Enrollment: 849 Coed
Affiliation or Control: State IRS Status: 501(c)3
Highest Offering: First Professional Degree; No Undergraduates
Accreditation: NH, OSTEO

01	President	Dr. James W. NEMITZ
05	Vice Pres Academic Affairs & Dean	Dr. Craig BOISVERT
10	Vice Pres Finance & Facilities	Larry WARE
11	Vice Pres for Administration	Dr. Edward BRIDGES
43	Vice Pres Legal/Govt Affairs	Jeffrey SHAWVER
15	Vice Pres of Human Resources	Leslie BICKSLER
26	Vice Pres Communications	Marilea BUTCHER
20	Assoc Dean Osteopathic Medical Educ	Dr. Robert FOSTER
58	Assoc Dean Graduate Medical Educ	Dr. Victoria SHUMAN
20	Assoc Dean Preclinical Education	Dr. Roy RUSS
20	Assoc Dean Predoctoral Clin Educ	Dr. Robert PEPPER
20	Assoc Dean Research & Spons Pgms	Dr. Jandy HANNA
108	Assoc Dean Assessment/Educ Devel	Dr. Machelle LINSENMEYER
32	Assistant Dean Student Affairs	Dr. Rebecca MORROW
13	Chief Technology Officer	Kimberly RANSOM
16	Director of Human Resources	Tiffany BURNS
06	Registrar	Jennifer SEAMS
37	Director Financial Aid	Lisa SPENCER
30	Director Institutional Development	Heather ANTOLINI
29	Director of Alumni Relations	Shannon WARREN
07	Director of Admissions	Ronnie COLLINS
96	Director of Contracts	Betty BAKER
08	Director of Library	Mary ESSIG
24	Director of Media Services	Richard MCMAHAN
18	Director of Physical Plant II	William ALDER
35	Director of Student Life	Belinda EVANS
09	Coordinator Institutional Research	Lance RIDPATH
40	Business Manager/Bookstore	Cindi KNIGHT
114	Manager Payroll Senior	Stella DODRILL
125	President Emeritus	Dr. Michael ADELMAN

*West Virginia State University (B)

PO Box 1000, Institute WV 25112-1000
County: Kanawha FICE Identification: 003826
Unit ID: 237899
Telephone: (304) 766-3000 Carnegie Class: Bac-Diverse
FAX Number: (304) 720-2075 Calendar System: Semester
URL: www.wvstateu.edu
Established: 1891 Annual Undergrad Tuition & Fees (In-State): $8,212
Enrollment: 3,879 Coed
Affiliation or Control: State IRS Status: 501(c)3
Highest Offering: Master's
Accreditation: NH, ACBSP, CAEPN, SW

02	President	Dr. Anthony L. JENKINS
10	Interim VP for Business and Finance	Ms. Kristi WILLIAMS
05	Provost and VP for Academic Affairs	Vacant
84	VP Enroll Mgmt/Student Affairs	Dr. Yvette UNDERDUE MURPH
111	VP for University Advancement	Ms. Patricia J. SCHUMANN
20	Assoc Prov/AVP Academic Affairs	Dr. Scott WOODARD
100	Chief of Staff	Dr. DeNeia THOMAS
46	VP for Research & Public Service	Dr. Orlando F. MCMEANS
79	Int Dean Col of Arts & Humanities	Dr. Robert WALLACE
81	Dean Col of Natural Sci/Math	Dr. Naveed ZAMAN
107	Dean Col of Prof Studies	Dr. Paige CARNEY
50	Dean Col of Business Admin/Soc Sci	Vacant
26	Assistant VP of Comm & Marketing	Mr. Jack BAILEY
13	Director of Information Technology	Mr. Alan SKIDMORE
18	Int Director Physical Facilities	Mr. Dayton WILSON
06	Interim Dir Records & Registration	Ms. Traci WEST-MCCOMBS
19	Director of Public Safety	Chief Joseph SAUNDERS
15	Asst VP Human Resource	Mr. Justin CHERRY
08	Director of Drain-Jordan Library	Dr. Willette STINSON
37	Int Dir Student Financial Asst	Ms. Gwen BAUSLEY
29	Director of Alumni Relations	Ms. Belinda FULLER
36	Dir of Career Services & Coop Educ	Ms. Sandhya (Sandy) G. MAHARAJ
07	Director of Admissions	Ms. Jameelah MEANS
89	Coordinator of New Student Programs	Mrs. Sharon S. BANKS
96	Director of Purchasing	Vacant
106	Dir of Center for Online Learning	Dr. Thomas KIDDIE
41	Athletic Director	Mr. Nathan BURTON
39	Int Dir of Residence Life/Services	Mr. Derrien WILLIAMS
04	Admin Assistant to the President	Ms. Crystal WALKER
32	Chief Student Affairs/Student Life	Mr. Joe ODEN, JR.
86	Director Government Relations	Dr. DeNeia THOMAS

*West Virginia University (C)

1500 University Avenue, Morgantown WV 26506-0002
County: Monongalia FICE Identification: 003827
Unit ID: 238032
Telephone: (304) 293-0111 Carnegie Class: DU-Highest
FAX Number: (304) 293-5883 Calendar System: Semester
URL: www.wvu.edu
Established: 1867 Annual Undergrad Tuition & Fees (In-State): $8,856
Enrollment: 28,406 Coed
Affiliation or Control: State IRS Status: 501(c)3
Highest Offering: Doctorate
Accreditation: NH, ART, AUD, CAATE, CACREP, CAEPN, CEA, CLPSY, COPSY, DENT, DH, DIETD, DIETI, DMS, FEPAC, HT, IPSY, JOUR, LAW, LSAR, MED, MT, MUS, NMT, NURSE, OT, PA, PAST, PH, PHAR, PTA, RAD, RADMAG, RTT, SP, SPAA, SW, THEA

02	President/Chief Exec Officer	Mr. E. Gordon GEE
05	Provost & VP Acad Affairs	Ms. Mary Ann REED
10	VP & CFO	Ms. Paula CONGELIO
26	Vice Pres for University Relations	Ms. Sharon L. MARTIN
17	Vice Pres/Exec Dean Health Science	Dr. Clay B. MARSH
32	Vice President Student Affairs	Dr. William SCHAFER
46	Vice President for Research	Mr. Fred L. KING
102	President & CEO WVU Found	Ms. Cindi ROTH
15	VP for Talent & Culture	Mr. Cris DEBORD
20	Vice Provost Academic Affairs	Dr. Paul KREIDER
20	Assoc Provost Academic Personnel	Dr. Cecil B. WILSON
88	Director Research & Rural Health	Ms. Sandra Y. POPE
100	Senior Advisor to President	Mr. John J. COLE
28	Sr Advsr to Pres Diversity/Cmty OR	Mr. David M. FRYSON
88	Exec Officer for Policy Development	Dr. Jennifer L. FISHER
45	VP Strategic Initiatives	Mr. Rob ALSOP
28	VP Diversity Equity & Inclusion	Ms. Meshea L. POORE
21	Assoc Vice Pres for Finance	Ms. Anjali HALABE
56	Int Dean & Director Extension Svcs	Dr. Sue DAY-PERROOTS
13	Assoc Provost IT/CIO	Ms. Barbara E. DAWSON
18	Sr Assoc VP Facilities & Svcs	Mr. Jamie F. KOSIK
35	Assoc Vice Pres Student Affairs	Mr. Michael A. ELLINGTON
76	Asst VP Hlth Sci & Tech Academy	Ms. Ann L. CHESTER
84	Assoc VP Enroll Mgmt Svcs	Mr. Stephen LEE
88	Assoc VP Strategic Initiatives	Ms. Elizabeth P. REYNOLDS
88	Int Director Corporate Relations	Mr. Jack THOMPSON
25	Asst VP Office of Research Admin	Mr. Alan B. MARTIN
09	Director of Institutional Research	Ms. Donielle R. MAUST
39	Director Res Life/Dean of Students	Ms. Trish CENDANA
41	Dir & Assoc VP Intercoll Athletics	Mr. Shane LYONS
23	Director of Public Health	Dr. Cecil R. POLLARD
29	Exec Director Alumni Association	Mr. Sean FRISBEE
37	Asst VP Financial Aid	Ms. Sandra K. OERLY-BENNETT
06	University Registrar	Ms. Aimee D. PFEIFER
08	Dean of Library Services	Ms. Karen DIAZ
38	Asst VP Student Wellness	Dr. Catherine A. YURA
19	Chief of Police/Univ Police Dept	Capt. W. P. CHEDESTER
109	Sr Assoc VP Auxiliary Services	Mr. David BEAVER
88	VP Global Strategies	Dr. William BRUSTEIN
69	Assoc VP & Dean Public Health	Dr. Jeffrey COBEN
50	Dean & VP Business & Economics	Dr. Javier REYES
49	Dean of Arts & Sciences	Dr. Gregory DUNAWAY
57	Dean College of Creative Arts	Dr. Keith JACKSON
53	Interim Dean Educ & Human Resources	Dr. Tracy L. MORRIS
61	Dean of Law	Mr. Gregory W. BOWMAN
63	Executive Dean & VP of Medicine	Dr. Clay B. MARSH
52	Dean of Dentistry	Dr. Tom BORGIA
54	Int Dean of Engr/Mineral Resources	Dr. Earl SCIME
47	Interim Dean of Agric & Forestry	Dr. Keri BLEMINGS
67	Dean of Pharmacy	Dr. William P. PETROS
60	Dean of College of Media	Dr. Diana MARTINELLI
68	Interim Dean Physical Education	Dr. Jack WATSON
66	Dean of Nursing	Dr. Tara HULSEY
92	Dean of Honors College	Mr. Kenneth P. BLEMINGS
88	Dean Online Programs	Dr. Keith BAILEY
36	Director Career Services	Mr. David L. DURHAM
88	Assoc Provost Intl Acad Affairs	Dr. Michael LASTINGER
88	Campus Provost-WVUIT	Dr. Joan NEFF
88	Assoc Provost Grad Acad Affairs	Dr. Katherine A. KARRAKER
35	Assoc VP & Dean of Students	Mr. G. Corey FARRIS
105	Director Web Services	Ms. Cathy ORNDORFF
88	Asst VP Strategic/Academic Comm	Dr. Ann CLAYCOMB
88	Asst VP Entrepreneurship & Innov	Ms. Carrie WHITE
116	Director Internal Audit	Mr. Bryan D. SHAVER

*West Virginia University at Parkersburg (D)

300 Campus Drive, Parkersburg WV 26104-8647
County: Wood FICE Identification: 003828
Unit ID: 237686
Telephone: (304) 424-8000 Carnegie Class: Bac/Assoc-Mixed
FAX Number: (304) 424-8315 Calendar System: Semester
URL: www.wvup.edu
Established: 1961 Annual Undergrad Tuition & Fees (In-State): $3,722
Enrollment: 2,482 Coed
Affiliation or Control: State IRS Status: 501(c)3
Highest Offering: Baccalaureate
Accreditation: NH, ACBSP, ADNUR, CAEPN, NUR, SURGT

02	President	Dr. Christopher GILMER
03	VP & Chief of Staff	Mr. Brady WHIPKEY
05	Vice Pres of Academic Affairs	Dr. Chad CRUMBAKER
32	Executive Director Student Services	Mr. Kurt KLETTNER
20	Dean for Academic Affairs	Dr. Cynthia GISSY
103	Exec Dir Workforce/Economic Develop	Ms. Michele WILSON
10	Vice Pres Finance/Administration	Ms. Alice HARRIS
84	VP Enrollment Management	Dr. Steven SMITH
13	Chief Information Officer	Mr. Doug ANTHONY
22	Exec Dir Equity/Inclus/Compliance	Mrs. Debbie RICHARDS
111	VP Institutional Advancement	Dr. Torie JACKSON
15	Director Human Resources	Mr. Scott POE
09	Dir Inst Rsrch/Outcomes Assessment	Mr. Jeremy STARKEY
06	Registrar	Mrs. Leslie SIMS
37	Director of Financial Aid	Mrs. Heather SKIDMORE
21	Director of Business Services	Ms. Jeannine RATLIFFE
08	Director of Library	Mr. Stephen HUPP
50	Chair Business/Economics/Math Div	Mr. Jeff HOLLAND
53	Chair Education	Dr. David LANCASTER
81	Chair STEM Division	Dr. Jared GUMP

West Virginia Junior College (E)

1000 Virginia Street East, Charleston WV 25301-2817
County: Kanawha FICE Identification: 010573
Unit ID: 237987
Telephone: (304) 345-2820 Carnegie Class: Assoc/HVT-High Trad
FAX Number: (304) 345-1425 Calendar System: Quarter
URL: www.wvjc.edu
Established: 1892 Annual Undergrad Tuition & Fees: $12,818
Enrollment: 150 Coed
Affiliation or Control: Proprietary IRS Status: Proprietary
Highest Offering: Associate Degree
Accreditation: ABHES

01	Campus President	Ms. Michelle MILES
05	Academic Dean	Ms. Katie HARVEY

West Virginia Junior College (F)

148 Willey Street, Morgantown WV 26505-5596
County: Monongalia FICE Identification: 005007
Unit ID: 237996
Telephone: (304) 296-8282 Carnegie Class: Assoc/HVT-High Trad
FAX Number: (304) 581-6990 Calendar System: Quarter
URL: www.wvjc.edu
Established: 1922 Annual Undergrad Tuition & Fees: $13,210
Enrollment: 494 Coed
Affiliation or Control: Proprietary IRS Status: Proprietary
Highest Offering: Associate Degree
Accreditation: ABHES

01	President & CEO	Mr. Chad CALLEN
05	Academic Director	Ms. Brittany NUZZO
36	Career Services	Ms. Samantha ESPOSITO
37	Financial Aid Director	Ms. Patricia CALLEN

West Virginia Junior College-Bridgeport (G)

176 Thompson Drive, Bridgeport WV 26330
Telephone: (304) 842-4007 Identification: 770823
Accreditation: ABHES

West Virginia Wesleyan College (H)

59 College Avenue, Buckhannon WV 26201-2699
County: Upshur FICE Identification: 003830
Unit ID: 237969
Telephone: (304) 473-8000 Carnegie Class: Masters/S
FAX Number: N/A Calendar System: Semester
URL: www.wvwc.edu
Established: 1890 Annual Undergrad Tuition & Fees: $31,640
Enrollment: 1,449 Coed
Affiliation or Control: United Methodist IRS Status: 501(c)3
Highest Offering: Doctorate
Accreditation: NH, CAATE, CAEP, MUS, NURSE

01	President	Dr. Joel THIERSTEIN
05	Dean of Faculty/Chief Academic Ofcr	Dr. James MOORE
84	VP Enrollment Mgmt & Admissions	Mr. John WALTZ
111	VP Advancement	Mr. Robert SKINNER
10	Chief Financial Officer	Dr. Scott MCKINNEY
42	Dean of the Chapel	Rev. Lauren WEAVER
102	Director Foundation/Govt Relations	Ms. Nicki BENTLEY-COLTHART
11	Director of Administrative Services	Mr. Robert KIMBLE
37	Director Financial Aid	Ms. Susan GEORGE
29	Assoc VP Adv & Alumni Relations	Mr. William ARMISTEAD
08	Director of Library Services	Mr. Brett MILLER
06	Dir Acad & Career Svcs/Registrar	Ms. Tammy FREDERICK
39	Director Campus Life & Housing	Ms. Alisa LIVELY
09	Director of Institutional Research	Ms. Tammy CRITES
15	Director of Human Resources	Ms. Vickie CROWDER
18	Director of the Physical Plant	Mr. Vaughn HARTLEY
30	Director Advancement Operations	Ms. Rose Ellen LOUDIN
88	Director of Learning Center	Dr. Shawn KUBA
41	Director of Athletics	Mr. Randall TENNEY
10	Controller	Mr. Randall CRITES
40	Retail Store Manager	Ms. Jennifer FLETCHER
92	Director Honors Program	Ms. Jordana LAFANTASIE
93	Director Multicultural Programs	Mr. Robert QUARLES
112	Planned Giving Coordinator	Rev. David PETERS
38	Director of Counseling Services	Ms. Lori THOMPSON
31	Dir of Community Engagement	Ms. Katie LOUDIN
13	Director of Computing Services	Mr. Neil ROTH
04	Administrative Asst to President	Ms. Deborah K. MULLENS
19	Director of Security	Mr. David PARKS
43	Dir Legal Services/General Counsel	Mr. David W. MCCAULEY
101	Secretary of the Institution/Board	Ms. Deborah K. MULLENS
104	Director Study Abroad	Dr. Tamara BAILEY

Wheeling University (I)

316 Washington Avenue, Wheeling WV 26003-6295
County: Ohio FICE Identification: 003831
Unit ID: 238078
Telephone: (304) 243-2000 Carnegie Class: Masters/M
FAX Number: (304) 243-2243 Calendar System: Semester

URL: www.wju.edu
Established: 1954 Annual Undergrad Tuition & Fees: $29,290
Enrollment: 1,124 Coed
Affiliation or Control: Roman Catholic IRS Status: 501(c)3
Highest Offering: Doctorate
Accreditation: NH, ACBSP, CAATE, CAEPT, COARC, NURSE, PTA

01 President ... Ms. Ginny FAVEDE
10 Executive VP Operations & Finance ... Mr. Jeffrey STRADER
05 VP for Academic Affairs ... Ms. Laurie MCCULLOUGH
15 VP Human Resources & Compliance ... Mr. David HACKER
32 VP for Student Services ... Mr. Andrew LEWIS
07 Director of Admissions ... Ms. Jennifer BOARD
13 Director Information Technology ... Mr. Will ELMES
37 Director Financial Aid ... Ms. Christie L. TOMCZYK
06 Registrar ... Mr. Wilson TURNER
08 Librarian ... Ms. Kelly MUMMERT
42 Director of Campus Ministry ... Mr. Jamey BROGAN
41 Athletic Director ... Mr. Rudy YOVICH
18 Director of Facilities ... Mr. Bruce MCCOLLOCH
04 Executive Asst to President ... Ms. Melissa ROSE
106 Dir Online Education/E-learning ... Mr. D. Jason FRITZMAN
19 Director Public Safety ... Mr. Michael ANDERSON
29 Director Alumni Relations ... Ms. Kelly KLUBERT
38 Director of Counseling Center ... Ms. Tina TORDELLA

WISCONSIN

Alverno College (A)

3400 S 43rd Street, Box 343922,
Milwaukee WI 53234-3922
County: Milwaukee FICE Identification: 003832
Unit ID: 238193
Telephone: (414) 382-6000 Carnegie Class: Masters/M
FAX Number: (414) 382-6066 Calendar System: Semester
URL: www.alverno.edu
Established: 1887 Annual Undergrad Tuition & Fees: $28,302
Enrollment: 1,942 Female
Affiliation or Control: Independent Non-Profit IRS Status: 501(c)3
Highest Offering: Doctorate
Accreditation: NH, MUS, NURSE, @SW

01 President ... Dr. Andrea J. LEE, IHM
100 Chief of Staff ... Ms. Jill DESMOND
10 Vice Pres Finance/Administration ... Ms. Robin HANSEN
05 Interim VP for Academic Affairs ... Dr. Colleen HEGRANES
111 Vice President Advancement ... Ms. Andrea PETRIE
84 VP for Enrollment Services ... Ms. Kate LUNDEEN
32 VP of Student Affs/Dean of Students ... Dr. Wendy POWERS
07 Director of Admissions ... Ms. Janet STIKEL
121 Assoc Vice Pres for Student Success ... Sr. Marlene NEISES
06 Registrar ... Ms. Lori SZARZYNSKI
08 Director Library ... Mr. Larry DUERR
36 Director Career Studio ... Ms. Sandra SIIRA
13 Exec Dir Information Technology ... Ms. Anita EIKENS
37 Director of Financial Aid ... Ms. Amy CHRISTEN
30 Director of Development ... Ms. Kim MUENCH
29 Director Alumni Engagement ... Ms. Meghan WALSH
38 Director Advising ... Ms. Kate TISCH
15 Director Human Resources ... Ms. Mary CASEY
41 Director of Athletics ... Mr. Brad VANDEN BOOGAARD
42 Campus Minister ... Rev. Lisa CATHELYN
96 Purchasing Coordinator ... Ms. Anne MCCARRON
66 Dean School of Nursing ... Dr. Patti VARGA
107 Dean of Professional Studies ... Dr. Patricia LUEBKE
49 Dean School of Arts & Sciences ... Dr. Kevin CASEY
51 Dean School of Adult Learning ... Dr. Carole CHABRIES
88 Executive Office Manager ... Ms. Anna ARENS
18 Director Plant Operations ... Mr. John MARKS
19 Director Security/Safety ... Lt. Michelle ENGEL

Bellin College, Inc. (B)

3201 Eaton Road, Green Bay WI 54311
County: Brown FICE Identification: 006639
Unit ID: 238324
Telephone: (920) 433-6699 Carnegie Class: Spec-4-yr-Other Health
FAX Number: (920) 433-1923 Calendar System: Semester
URL: www.bellincollege.edu
Established: 1909 Annual Undergrad Tuition & Fees: $20,500
Enrollment: 440 Coed
Affiliation or Control: Independent Non-Profit IRS Status: 501(c)3
Highest Offering: Doctorate
Accreditation: NH, DMS, NURSE, RAD

01 President & CEO of the College ... Dr. Connie J. BOERST
10 VP of Business & Finance ... Mrs. Ginger B. KRUMMEN SCHRAVEN
66 Dean of Nursing ... Dr. Mary K. ROLLOFF
76 Dean of Allied Health Sciences ... Dr. Mark A. BAKE
32 Dean of Student Services ... Dr. Nancy M. BURRUSS
26 VP of Strategic Engagement & PR ... Mr. Matt G. RENTMEESTER
13 Director of Technology ... Mr. Travis A. SMITH
06 Registrar ... Mr. Russell J. LEARY
37 Director Financial Aid ... Mrs. Lena C. GOODMAN
04 Executive Assistant to President ... Ms. Jamie L. CAMPBELL
08 Head Librarian ... Ms. Cindy M. REINL
111 VP of Advancement ... Mr. Thomas J. SHEFCHIK

Beloit College (C)

700 College Street, Beloit WI 53511-5595
County: Rock FICE Identification: 003835
Unit ID: 238333
Telephone: (608) 363-2000 Carnegie Class: Bac-A&S
FAX Number: (608) 363-2717 Calendar System: Semester
URL: www.beloit.edu
Established: 1846 Annual Undergrad Tuition & Fees: $50,040
Enrollment: 1,402 Coed
Affiliation or Control: Independent Non-Profit IRS Status: 501(c)3
Highest Offering: Baccalaureate
Accreditation: NH

01 President ... Dr. Scott BIERMAN
05 Provost ... Dr. Eric BOYNTON
100 Chief of Staff ... Mr. Daniel J. SCHOOFF
45 VP Budget & Planning ... Ms. Stacie SCOTT
111 VP Development & Alumni Relations ... Ms. Amy WILSON
15 VP Human Resources and Operations ... Ms. Lori RHEAD
84 VP Enrollment ... Ms. Leslie DAVIDSON
32 Dean Equity/Cmty/Student Success ... Mr. Cecil YOUNGBLOOD
13 Chief Information Officer ... Dr. Pam MCQUESTEN
26 Chief Comm & Integ Mktg Officer ... Mr. Tim JONES
108 Dir Strategic Research & Assessment ... Ms. Ellie ANDERYRNE
09 Dir Inst Research/Assmt/Planning ... Ms. Ruth VATER
06 Registrar ... Ms. Mary BOROS-KAZAI
07 Director of Admissions ... Vacant
07 Director of Intl Admissions ... Ms. Erin GUTH
18 Director of Facilities ... Mr. Kerry SATTERWHITE
30 Exec Dir of Development ... Mr. Jon URISH
39 Director Resident Life/Conferences ... Dr. Ryan BOUCHARD
36 Director of Career Development ... Ms. Jessica FOX-WILSON
38 College Counselor ... Vacant
37 Director of Financial Aid ... Ms. Deb DEW
41 Athletic Director ... Mr. Tim SCHMIECHEN
40 Bookstore Director ... Mr. Peter FRONK

Cardinal Stritch University (D)

6801 N Yates Road, Milwaukee WI 53217-3985
County: Milwaukee FICE Identification: 003837
Unit ID: 238430
Telephone: (414) 410-4000 Carnegie Class: DU-Mod
FAX Number: (414) 410-4239 Calendar System: Semester
URL: www.stritch.edu
Established: 1937 Annual Undergrad Tuition & Fees: $29,998
Enrollment: 2,355 Coed
Affiliation or Control: Roman Catholic IRS Status: 501(c)3
Highest Offering: Doctorate
Accreditation: NH, ACBSP, NUR, NURSE

01 President ... Dr. Kathleen A. RINEHART
04 Exec Assistant to the President ... Ms. Barbara SCHROEDER
05 Vice Pres Academic Affairs ... Dr. Daniel J. SCHOLZ
111 Vice President for Univ Advancement ... Ms. Tonya M. MANTILLA
10 VP Finance/Administration ... Mr. Thomas J. CONGDON
84 VP Enrollment Management ... Ms. Tracy FISCHER
123 Vice President Graduate Enrollment ... Mr. Allan M. MITCHLER
32 Vice Pres Student Affairs ... Ms. Tracy A. FISCHER
88 Vice Pres Mission Engagement ... Mr. Sean T. LANSING
41 AVP/Director of Athletics ... Dr. Tim M. VAN ALSTINE
29 AVP Alumni Relations ... Ms. Corrine M. ANSHUS
13 Chief Information Officer ... Mr. David W. WEINBERG-KINSEY
66 Dean College Nursing/Health Science ... Dr. Kelly J. DRIES
50 Dean College of Business & Mgmt ... Dr. Janette M. BRAVERMAN
53 Dean College of Education & Ldrship ... Dr. Freda R. RUSSELL
49 Dean College of Arts & Sciences ... Dr. Daniel J. SCHOLZ
15 Director of Human Resources/Payroll ... Ms. Jackie L. SUKOWATY
06 University Registrar ... Ms. Christine GLYNN
113 Bursar ... Ms. Lisa M. LEWIN
37 Dir of Financial Aid ... Mr. Mark W. QUISTORF
117 Dir Treasury & Risk Management ... Mr. Scott A. HELLRUNG
20 Director of Academic Affairs ... Vacant
35 Dean of Students ... Ms. Donney MORONEY
36 Career Education ... Mr. Tom E. KIPP
38 Dir for Counseling/Mental Wellness ... Ms. Mary Beth WISNIEWSKI
104 Coord International Education ... Ms. Sarah R. SWEENEY
108 Dir of Institutional Effectiveness ... Mr. William L. MARCOU
91 Director of Enterprise Systems ... Ms. Susan L. INGLES
08 Director of University Library ... Ms. Laurie G. SWARTWOUT
102 Exec Dir Corporate & Foundation Rel ... Vacant
112 Director Major Gifts/Planned Giving ... Ms. Lisa M. HANDLER
26 Sr Dir Media Relations Adv Comm ... Ms. Kathleen M. HOHL
18 Sr Director of Facilities ... Mr. John B. GLYNN
19 Director of Security ... Mr. Andrew DE RUBERTIS

Carroll University (E)

100 N East Avenue, Waukesha WI 53186-5593
County: Waukesha FICE Identification: 003838
Unit ID: 238458
Telephone: (262) 547-1211 Carnegie Class: Masters/S
FAX Number: (262) 524-7646 Calendar System: Semester
URL: www.carrollu.edu
Established: 1846 Annual Undergrad Tuition & Fees: $31,918
Enrollment: 3,452 Coed
Affiliation or Control: Presbyterian Church (U.S.A.) IRS Status: 501(c)3
Highest Offering: Doctorate
Accreditation: NH, ARCPA, CAATE, MUS, NURSE, OT, PTA

01 President ... Dr. Cindy GNADINGER
05 Provost/Vice Pres Academic Affairs ... Dr. Mark BLEGEN
10 Vice Pres Finance/Administration ... Ms. Dana STUART
84 Vice President for Enrollment ... Mr. Teege METTILLE
111 Vice President for Advancement ... Mr. Stephen KUHN
32 Vice President Student Affairs ... Dr. Theresa BARRY
26 Vice Pres Marketing & Communication ... Ms. Jeannine SHERMAN
13 Chief Technology Officer (CIO) ... Ms. Sarah ALT
06 Registrar ... Ms. Ann HANDFORD
21 Assoc VP Finance & Administration ... Ms. Deidre ERWIN
37 Assoc VP Enroll/Dir Fin Aid ... Ms. Dawn M. SCOTT
15 Director of Human Resources ... Ms. Kim L. SHERROD
08 Library Director ... Mr. Joe HARDENBROOK
41 Athletic Director ... Mr. James HALL
107 Dir of Non-Trad Adult/Prof Studies ... Ms. Lynn NOVAK
28 Assoc Dean Multicult Affairs ... Ms. Vanessa PEREZ-TOPCZEWSKI
29 Sr Director Alumni Engagement ... Ms. Dolores M. BROWN
96 Business Mgr General Svcs ... Mr. Brian FULLER
07 Director of Trad & Intl Admissions ... Ms. Annie J. ASCHENBRENNER
18 Facilities Director ... Mr. Tom HEFFERNAN
38 Director Student Counseling ... Ms. Angie R. BRANNAN
04 Exec Assistant to the President ... Ms. Gina M. EHLER
123 Director Graduate Admissions ... Ms. Cindy HOLAHAN
121 Director of Student Success ... Mr. Jeff MCNAMARA
19 Director Security/Safety ... Mr. Kevin KOBER
22 Director of Compliance ... Ms. Suzanne LIDTKE
43 Director of Legal Services ... Ms. Cat JORGENS
50 Dean School of Business ... Mr. Steve BIALEK
49 Dean College of Arts & Sciences ... Dr. Charles BYLER
91 Director ITS ... Mr. Ryan CORCORAN

Carthage College (F)

2001 Alford Park Drive, Kenosha WI 53140-1994
County: Kenosha FICE Identification: 003839
Unit ID: 238476
Telephone: (262) 551-8500 Carnegie Class: Bac-Diverse
FAX Number: (262) 551-6208 Calendar System: 4/1/4
URL: www.carthage.edu
Established: 1847 Annual Undergrad Tuition & Fees: $43,550
Enrollment: 2,860 Coed
Affiliation or Control: Evangelical Lutheran Church In America
IRS Status: 501(c)3
Highest Offering: Master's
Accreditation: NH, CAATE, MUS, NURSE, SW

01 President/Chief Executive Officer ... Dr. John R. SWALLOW
04 Special Assistant to the President ... Ms. Dana KROLL
05 Provost/Chief Operating Officer ... Dr. David TIMMERMAN
10 VP Finance & Administration/CFO ... Mr. Dale MCCLAIN
111 VP for Institutional Advancement ... Dr. Thomas KLINE
26 Assoc VP Marketing/Communications ... Ms. Elizabeth YOUNG
84 VP for Enrollment ... Mr. Nick MULVEY
32 VP Student Affairs/Dean of Students ... Dr. Kimberlie GOLDSBERRY
101 Secretary of the Board of Trustees ... Mr. Dennis L. MONROE
108 VP Institutional Effectiveness ... Vacant
41 Director of Athletics ... Dr. Michelle MANNING
42 Campus Pastor ... Ms. Kara BAYLOR
06 Registrar ... Ms. Brigid PATTERSON
104 Director Study Abroad ... Dr. Erik KULKE
15 Director of Human Resources ... Ms. Marianne MARSHALL
19 Director of Public Safety ... Mr. Erin MORTENSEN
37 Assoc VP Student Financial Aid ... Mr. Vatistas VATISTAS

College of Menominee Nation (G)

PO Box 1179, Keshena WI 54135-1179
County: Menominee FICE Identification: 031251
Unit ID: 413617
Telephone: (800) 567-2344 Carnegie Class: Tribal
FAX Number: (715) 799-1336 Calendar System: Semester
URL: www.menominee.edu
Established: 1992 Annual Undergrad Tuition & Fees: $6,200
Enrollment: 285 Coed
Affiliation or Control: Tribal Control IRS Status: 501(c)3
Highest Offering: Baccalaureate
Accreditation: NH

01 President ... Dr. Paul F. TREBIAN
05 Chief Academic Officer ... Dr. Diana MORRIS
10 Chief Financial Officer ... Mr. David BETZIG
32 Dean of Student Services ... Vacant
51 Dean of Continuing Education ... Mr. Brian KOWALKOWSKI
20 Dean of Foundational Studies ... Ms. Jennifer MORRIS
100 Chief of Staff ... Ms. Melinda COOK
09 Director Institutional Research ... Ms. Geraldine SANAPAW
26 Director of Public Relations ... Ms. Irene KIEFER
13 IT Director ... Vacant
15 Human Resources Director ... Vacant
06 Registrar/Bursar ... Ms. Geraldine SANAPAW
37 Financial Aid Mgr ... Mr. Austin RETZLAFF
07 Dir of Advancement & Enrollment ... Ms. Tessa JAMES
88 Director of Vocational Rehab ... Ms. Myrna WARRINGTON
08 Director of Library Services ... Ms. Maria ESCALANTE

College of Menominee Nation Oneida Campus (H)

2733 S Ridge Road, Green Bay WI 54304
Telephone: (920) 965-0070 Identification: 770424
Accreditation: &NH

Columbia College of Nursing (A)

4425 N Port Washington Road, Glendale WI 53212
County: Milwaukee FICE Identification: 006640
Unit ID: 238573
Telephone: (414) 326-2330 Carnegie Class: Spec-4-yr-Other Health
FAX Number: (414) 236-2331 Calendar System: Semester
URL: www.ccon.edu
Established: 1901 Annual Undergrad Tuition & Fees: N/A
Enrollment: 122 Coed
Affiliation or Control: Independent Non-Profit IRS Status: 501(c)3
Highest Offering: Master's
Accreditation: NH, NURSE

01 President & Dean .... Dr. Heather VARTANIAN
10 Associate Dean of Finance .... Ms. Christina ITALIANO
05 Associate Dean of Academic Affairs ...... Dr. Tammy KASPROVICH
06 Registrar/Academic Advisor .... Mr. Ross BEATTIE
37 Director Student Financial Aid .... Ms. Danielle CARTER
24 Director Educational Media .... Mr. Keith JACKSON
07 Admissions Specialist .... Ms. Susan DONDERO

Concordia University Wisconsin (B)

12800 N Lake Shore Drive, Mequon WI 53097-2402
County: Ozaukee FICE Identification: 003842
Unit ID: 238616
Telephone: (262) 243-5700 Carnegie Class: DU-Mod
FAX Number: (262) 243-4351 Calendar System: 4/1/4
URL: www.cuw.edu
Established: 1881 Annual Undergrad Tuition & Fees: $29,450
Enrollment: 7,288 Coed
Affiliation or Control: Lutheran Church - Missouri Synod
IRS Status: 501(c)3
Highest Offering: Doctorate
Accreditation: NH, ARCPA, CAATE, DMS, IACBE, MAC, NURSE, OT, PHAR, PTA, @SP, SW

01 President .... Rev Dr. Patrick T. FERRY
11 Executive VP & Chief Oper Ofcr .... Mr. Allen J. PROCHNOW
05 Provost and Chief Academic Officer .... Dr. William R. CARIO
26 Senior VP University Affairs .... Ms. Gretchen M. JAMESON
111 Senior VP of Advancement .... Rev Dr. Roy PETERSON
102 VP of Foundation .... Mr. Dean D. RENNICKE
13 VP of Information Technology .... Mr. Thomas G. PHILLIP
32 VP of Student Life .... Mr. Steven P. TAYLOR
20 Vice Provost of Faculty Affairs .... Dr. Leah M. DVORAK
84 Vice Provost of Student Enrollment .... Dr. Michael D. UDEN
121 Asst VP Academics/Student Success .... Ms. Elizabeth A. POLZIN
07 Asst Vice President Admissions .... Mr. Robert J. NOWAK
27 Asst VP Strategic Communications .... Ms. Lisa LILJEGREN
85 Asst VP International Affairs .... Rev Dr. David C. BIRNER
42 Campus Pastor .... Rev. Steven N. SMITH
42 Campus Pastor .... Rev. Randall S. DUNCAN
88 Chair Faculty Senate .... Dr. Robert S. BURLAGE
49 Dean School Arts/Sciences .... Dr. Steven R. MONTREAL
50 Dean School of Business .... Dr. Daniel S. SEM
53 Dean School of Education .... Dr. James A. PINGEL
76 Dean School of Health Professions .... Dr. Linda M. SAMUEL
66 Dean School of Nursing .... Dr. Sharon L. CHAPPY
67 Dean School of Pharmacy .... Dr. Dean L. ARNESON
35 Dean of Students .... Dr. Steven W. GERNER
06 Registrar .... Mr. Carl R. BUTZ
29 Director of Alumni Relations .... Ms. Michelle L. WAGNER
41 Director of Athletics .... Dr. Rob M. BARNHILL
19 Director Campus Safety .... Mr. Mario VALDES
38 Director of Counseling .... Mr. David T. ENTERS
36 Director of Career Services .... Ms. Lisa K. JOHNSON
37 Director of Financial Aid .... Mr. William J. HENDERSON
15 Director Human Resources .... Ms. Kimberly R. MASENTHIN
09 Director of Institutional Research .... Dr. Tamara R. FERRY
24 Director Instructional Technology .... Mr. Sean B. YOUNG
08 Director of Library Services .... Mr. Christian R. HIMSEL
39 Director of Residence Life .... Ms. Beckie KRUSE
88 Exec Director Centers & Acceler .... Ms. Rochelle R. REGENAUER
88 Exec Director Cont & Dist Ed .... Ms. Sarah A. PECOR
18 Superintendent Buildings & Grounds ..... Mr. Stephen V. HIBBARD
40 Bookstore Manager .... Ms. Kia LOR

Edgewood College (C)

1000 Edgewood College Drive, Madison WI 53711-1997
County: Dane FICE Identification: 003848
Unit ID: 238661
Telephone: (608) 663-4861 Carnegie Class: DU-Mod
FAX Number: (608) 663-3291 Calendar System: Semester
URL: www.edgewood.edu
Established: 1927 Annual Undergrad Tuition & Fees: $29,500
Enrollment: 2,221 Coed
Affiliation or Control: Roman Catholic IRS Status: 501(c)3
Highest Offering: Doctorate
Accreditation: NH, ACBSP, MFCD, NURSE

01 President .... Dr. Scott FLANAGAN
05 VP Academic Affs/Academic Dean .... Dr. Dean PRIBBENOW
10 VP Business & Finance .... Mr. Michael GUNS
84 VP Enrollment Mgmt .... Dr. Amber SCHULTZ
88 Assoc VP Dominican Life & Mission .... Ms. Mary KLINK
111 VP Inst Advancement .... Mr. Gary KLEIN
20 Associate Academic Dean .... Dr. Kelley GRORUD
106 Assoc Acad Dean Online & Adult Lrng .... Dr. Karen FRANKER
49 Dean School of Arts & Sciences .... Dr. Melanie HERZOG
50 Interim Dean School of Business .... Dr. Victoria PALMISANO
53 Dean School of Education .... Dr. Timothy SLEKAR
88 Dean School of Integrative Studies .... Dr. Kristine MICKELSON
66 Dean School of Nursing .... Dr. Margaret NOREUIL
32 Dean of Students .... Dr. Heather HARBACH
07 Director Undergrad Admissions .... Vacant
13 Director Information Technology .... Mr. Patrick GUMIENY
09 Director Inst Assessment & Research .... Dr. Edward J. KEELEY
41 Director Athletics .... Mr. Al BRISACK
06 Registrar .... Ms. Michelle KELLEY
08 Library Director .... Dr. Nathan DOWD
36 Director Career Development .... Ms. Sara HANSON
29 Alumni Relations Director .... Ms. Abby PENTZ
26 Exec Dir of Mktg & Strat Comm .... Ms. Amy PIKALEK
27 Director Strategic Communication .... Mr. Edward TAYLOR
15 Director Human Resources .... Ms. Pamela LAVALLIERE
18 Director Facility Operations .... Ms. Susan VANDERSANDEN
38 Director Personal Counseling Svcs .. Dr. Megan COBB-SHEEHAN
21 Controller .... Ms. Jane WILHELM
28 Exec Dir Diversity & Inclusion .... Mr. Tony GARCIA
37 Director Student Financial Aid .... Ms. Kari GRIBBLE
39 Director Residence Life .... Ms. Claire MAND
23 Director Health Services .... Ms. Suzanne WALLACE

George Williams College of Aurora University (D)

350 Constance Boulevard, Williams Bay WI 53191
Telephone: (262) 245-5531 Identification: 770066
Accreditation: &NH

† Branch campus of Aurora University, Aurora, IL

Herzing University (E)

5218 E Terrace Drive, Madison WI 53718-8340
County: Dane FICE Identification: 009621
Unit ID: 240392
Telephone: (608) 249-6611 Carnegie Class: Masters/M
FAX Number: (608) 249-8593 Calendar System: Semester
URL: www.herzing.edu
Established: 1965 Annual Undergrad Tuition & Fees: $14,000
Enrollment: 2,156 Coed
Affiliation or Control: Independent Non-Profit IRS Status: 501(c)3
Highest Offering: Master's
Accreditation: NH, IACBE, NURSE

00 President .... Ms. Renee HERZING
01 Campus President .... Mr. William VINSON
10 CFO & Vice President of Finance .... Mr. Robert HERZOG
05 Interim Academic Dean .... Mr. William VINSON
37 Educational Funding Manager .... Mr. Clayton GROTH
32 Dir of Student Services/Registrar .... Ms. Amy HERFEL
07 Assoc Director of Admissions .... Ms. Danielle OEST
36 Career Development Specialist .... Ms. Marion DUREN

Herzing University Brookfield Campus (F)

555 South Executive Drive, Brookfield WI 53005
Telephone: (262) 649-1710 Identification: 770429
Accreditation: &NH, NURSE, PTAA

Herzing University Kenosha Campus (G)

4006 Washington Road, Kenosha WI 53144
Telephone: (262) 671-0675 Identification: 770430
Accreditation: &NH, NURSE

Herzing University Online (H)

W140N8917 Lilly Road, Menomonee Falls WI 53051
Telephone: (866) 508-0748 Identification: 770431
Accreditation: &NH, CAHIIM, MAAB, NURSE

Lac Courte Oreilles Ojibwa Community College (I)

13466 W Trepania Road, Hayward WI 54843-2181
County: Sawyer FICE Identification: 025322
Unit ID: 260372
Telephone: (715) 634-4790 Carnegie Class: Tribal
FAX Number: (715) 634-5049 Calendar System: Semester
URL: www.lco.edu
Established: 1982 Annual Undergrad Tuition & Fees: $4,590
Enrollment: 211 Coed
Affiliation or Control: Tribal Control IRS Status: 501(c)3
Highest Offering: Associate Degree
Accreditation: NH

01 President .... Dr. Russell SWAGGER
10 Chief Financial Officer .... Ms. Jill MATCHETT
05 Dean of Academic Affairs .... Ms. Lisa MUNIVE
51 Dean of Continuing Education .... Ms. Amber MARLOW
09 Dean of Institutional Research .... Dr. Annette ROBERTS
103 Chief Business Development .... Ms. Karen BREIT
32 Dean of Student Services .... Dr. Odawa WHITE
111 Dir Inst Advancement/
Development .... Ms. Jessica WAGNER-SCHULTZ
37 Financial Aid Director .... Ms. Jordan ST. GERMAINE
13 Director of Information Technology .... Mr. Kyle KORTENDICK
15 Human Resources Director .... Ms. Tamara THIMM
06 Registrar .... Dr. Annette ROBERTS
07 Admissions Recruiter .... Mr. James WHITE, JR.
08 Chief Library Officer .... Ms. Caryl PFAFF

Lakeland University (J)

W3718 South Dr, Plymouth WI 53073
County: Sheboygan FICE Identification: 003854
Unit ID: 238980
Telephone: (920) 565-1000 Carnegie Class: Masters/L
FAX Number: (920) 565-1060 Calendar System: Semester
URL: www.lakeland.edu
Established: 1862 Annual Undergrad Tuition & Fees: $28,870
Enrollment: 2,679 Coed
Affiliation or Control: United Church Of Christ IRS Status: 501(c)3
Highest Offering: Master's
Accreditation: NH

01 President .... Dr. David BLACK
04 Assistant to the President .... Ms. LaJill EDGE
05 Provost/Dean of College .... Dr. Margaret L. ALBRINCK
111 Vice President for Advancement .... Ms. Beth BORGEN
32 Vice President for Campus Life .... Mr. David SIMON
07 Director of Admissions .... Mr. Samuel POULETTE
10 Chief Financial Officer .... Ms. Amy WIRTZ
11 Chief Operating Officer .... Mr. Richard HAEN
06 Registrar .... Ms. Amanda HRUSKA
103 Director of Career Development .... Mrs. Jessica LAMBRECHT
09 Director of Institutional Research .... Mr. Paul WHITE
35 Dean of Students .... Ms. Leslie LASTER
08 Director of Library Services .... Ms. Ann K. PENKE
37 Director of Financial Aid .... Ms. Patty L. TAYLOR
26 Director of Communications .... Mr. David D. GALLIANETTI
29 Dir Alumni & Church Relations .... Ms. Linda BOSMAN
15 Manager of Human Resources .... Ms. Katrina KRUPSKI
41 Director of Athletics .... Ms. April ARVAN
18 Director of Facilities & Grounds .... Mr. Joe BENIGER
38 Director of Student Counselling .... Dr. Alexandra LIOSATOS
50 Dean School of Business & Enterpren ..... Dr. Scott NIEDERJOHN
81 Dean School of Science/Tech & Educ .... Dr. Brian FRINK
79 Dean Sch of Fine Arts & Humanities .... Dr. Joshua KUTNEY

Lawrence University (K)

711 E. Boldt Way, Appleton WI 54911
County: Outagamie FICE Identification: 003856
Unit ID: 239017
Telephone: (920) 832-7000 Carnegie Class: Bac-A&S
FAX Number: (920) 832-6978 Calendar System: Other
URL: www.lawrence.edu
Established: 1847 Annual Undergrad Tuition & Fees: $47,475
Enrollment: 1,467 Coed
Affiliation or Control: Independent Non-Profit IRS Status: 501(c)3
Highest Offering: Baccalaureate
Accreditation: NH, MUS

01 President .... Mr. Mark BURSTEIN
04 Executive Asst to the President .... Ms. Alice BOECKERS
05 Provost and Dean of the Faculty .... Ms. Catherine KODAT
10 VP Finance & Administration .... Mr. Christopher LEE
30 VP Development/Alumni Rels .... Mr. Calvin D. HUSMANN
32 VP for Student Life .... Mr. Christopher D. CARD
29 VP Alumni/Constituency Engagement ..... Mr. Mark D. BRESEMAN
28 VP for Diversity & Inclusion .... Dr. Kimberly BARRETT
26 Assoc Vice Pres Communications .... Ms. Megan J. SCOTT
44 Campaign Dir/Principal Gifts Ofcr .... Mr. Lucas A. BROWN
110 Assoc Vice Pres Development .... Ms. Stacy J. MARA
21 Controller .... Ms. Amy PRICE
64 Dean Conservatory of Music .... Mr. Brian G. PERTL
36 Dean of Career Services .... Mr. Mike K. O'CONNOR
121 Dean of Academic Success .... Ms. Monita M. GRAY
20 Associate Dean of the Faculty .... Dr. Peter A. BLITSTEIN
28 Asst Dean Students Multicul Affs .... Ms. Brittany M. BELL
09 Director of Research Administration ...... Ms. Kristin L. MCKINLEY
84 Vice Pres Enrollment/
Communications .... Mr. Kenneth L. ANSELMENT
37 Director of Financial Aid .... Mr. Ryan L. GEBLER
06 Registrar .... Vacant
08 Librarian .... Mr. Peter J. GILBERT
41 Athletic Director .... Ms. Christyn ABARAY
13 Director Information Tech Svcs .... Mr. Steven M. ARMSTRONG
15 Assoc Director of Human Resources .... Ms. Tina L. HARRIG
38 Assoc Dean Stdnts Health/Wellness ...... Mr. Rich L. JAZDZEWSKI

Maranatha Baptist University (L)

745 West Main Street, Watertown WI 53094-7600
County: Jefferson FICE Identification: 023172
Unit ID: 239071
Telephone: (920) 261-9300 Carnegie Class: Bac-Diverse
FAX Number: (920) 261-9109 Calendar System: Semester
URL: www.mbu.edu
Established: 1968 Annual Undergrad Tuition & Fees: $15,410
Enrollment: 1,139 Coed
Affiliation or Control: Independent Non-Profit IRS Status: 501(c)3
Highest Offering: Doctorate
Accreditation: NH, NURSE

01 President .... Dr. Martin MARRIOTT
43 Exec Vice President & Corp Counsel .... Dr. Matthew DAVIS
05 Vice President for Academic Affairs .... Dr. William LICHT
111 Vice President for Inst Advancement .... Dr. Jim H. HARRISON

10 Vice President for Business Affairs ... Mr. Donald DONOVAN
32 Dean of Students ... Dr. John DAVIS
06 Registrar ... Mr. Thomas CANNON
07 Director of Admissions ... Mr. Jonathan SHEELEY
30 Director of Development ... Mr. Steve BOARD
09 Director of Institutional Research ... Mr. Jonathan COLEMAN
15 Director Personnel Services ... Mr. Curt OBERHOLTZER
26 Chief Public Relations Officer ... Mr. Peter WRIGHT
41 Athletic Director ... Mr. Robert THOMPSON
08 Librarian ... Mr. Mark HANSON
35 Director Student Affairs ... Mr. Charles LEEDS
29 Director Alumni Relations ... Dr. John DAVIS
37 Director Student Financial Aid ... Mr. Bruce ROTH
13 Chief Info Technology Officer (CIO) ... Dr. Werner LUMM
19 Director Security/Safety ... Mr. Timothy JOHNS
106 Dir Online Education/E-learning ... Dr. Philip ALSUP
108 Director Institutional Assessment ... Mr. Jonathan COLEMAN
105 Director Web Services ... Mr. Peter WRIGHT
18 Chief Facilities/Physical Plant ... Dr. Werner LUMM
50 Dean School of Business ... Dr. Tracy FOSTER
53 Director School of Education ... Dr. David HANDYSIDE

Marian University (A)

45 S National Avenue, Fond Du Lac WI 54935-4699
County: Fond Du Lac FICE Identification: 003861
Unit ID: 239080
Telephone: (920) 923-7600 Carnegie Class: Masters/M
FAX Number: (920) 923-7154 Calendar System: Semester
URL: www.marianuniversity.edu
Established: 1936 Annual Undergrad Tuition & Fees: $27,400
Enrollment: 1,971 Coed
Affiliation or Control: Roman Catholic IRS Status: 501(c)3
Highest Offering: Doctorate
Accreditation: NH, NURSE, RAD, SW

01 President ... Dr. Andrew P. MANION
05 Provost & VP Academic Affairs ... Dr. Russell K. MAYER
10 VP Business & Finance ... Mr. David W. WONG
111 VP Advancement ... Ms. Stacey L. AKEY
32 VP for Student Engagement ... Ms. Kate CANDEE
84 VP Enrollment Management ... Mr. Jason M. HARMON
26 Senior VP for University Relations ... Dr. George E. KOONCE, JR.
04 Executive Assistant to President ... Ms. Carey C. GARDIN
21 Controller ... Ms. Dawn M. GUELL
107 Dean College of the Professions ... Vacant
49 Dean College Arts/Sciences/Letters ... Dr. Joseph J. FOY
35 Dean of Student Engagement ... Dr. Paul KRIKAU
08 Director of Libraries ... Ms. Kathryn A. JOHNSTON
18 Operations Manager/Facilities ... Vacant
90 Assoc VP Academic Administration ... Ms. Lynda K. SCHULTZ
114 Asst VP Budget/Systems/Analytics ... Mr. Thomas P. RICHTER
37 Director of Financial Aid ... Ms. Wendy A. HILVO
42 Director of Campus Ministry ... Sr. Edie A. CREWS, CSA
27 Asst VP Marketing & Communication ... Ms. Lisa L. KIDD
07 Dean of Admission ... Ms. Shannon S. LALUZERNE
15 Director of Human Resources ... Ms. Sabrina J. JOHNSON
41 Director of Athletics ... Mr. Jason BARTELT
121 Dean Advising/Academic Services ... Ms. Cathy M. MATHWEG
23 Director of Health Services ... Ms. Jodi S. SCHRAUTH
36 Director of Career Services ... Ms. Mary J. HATLEN
109 Director of Campus Dining Services ... Ms. Nikki A. KRAMER
40 Director of Bookstore ... Ms. Mary HALTER
38 Director of Counseling ... Ms. Robyn A. WILLIAMS
92 Director Honors Program ... Dr. Mathew P. SZROMBA
39 Director of Residence Life ... Ms. Severa KRUGER
104 Director of International Programs ... Dr. Cooper S. WAKEFIELD
19 Coordinator Security/Safety ... Vacant
106 Dean Adult & Online Studies ... Ms. Jennifer K. FARVOUR
28 Sr Asst to President Diversity ... Dr. Jeneise S. BRIGGS
06 Registrar ... Ms. Tarra M. BOURGEOIS

Marquette University (B)

PO Box 1881, Milwaukee WI 53201-1881
County: Milwaukee FICE Identification: 003863
Unit ID: 239105
Telephone: (414) 288-7700 Carnegie Class: DU-Higher
FAX Number: (414) 288-3300 Calendar System: Semester
URL: www.marquette.edu
Established: 1881 Annual Undergrad Tuition & Fees: $41,870
Enrollment: 11,426 Coed
Affiliation or Control: Roman Catholic IRS Status: 501(c)3
Highest Offering: Doctorate
Accreditation: NH, ANEST, ARCPA, CAATE, CACREP, CLPSY, COPSY, DENT, LAW, MIDWF, MT, NURSE, PTA, SP, THEA

01 President ... Dr. Michael R. LOVELL
05 Acting Provost ... Dr. Kimo AH YUN
10 Sr Vice President/COO/CFO ... Mr. Joel POGODZINSKI
31 Vice President Public Affairs ... Ms. Rana H. ALTENBURG
43 Vice President and General Counsel ... Ms. Cynthia M. BAUER
15 Vice President Human Resources ... Ms. Claudia PAETSCH
32 Vice President Student Affairs ... Dr. Xavier A. COLE
09 Vice Pres Research and Innovation ... Dr. Jeanne M. HOSSENLOPP
42 Acting Vice Pres Mission/ Ministry ... Rev. Frederick P. ZAGONE, S.J.
20 Senior Vice Prov Faculty Affairs ... Dr. Gary MEYER
26 Vice Pres Marketing & Communication ... Mr. David MURPHY
41 Vice Pres and Director of Athletics ... Mr. Bill SCHOLL
111 Vice Pres University Advancement ... Mr. Tim MCMAHON
28 Vice Pres Inclusive Excellence ... Dr. William WELBURN
88 Vice Pres Corporate Engagement ... Ms. Maura DONOVAN
84 Vice Pres Enrollment Management ... Dr. John BAWOROWSKY
20 Vice Provost Academic Affairs ... Dr. John J. SU
06 Registrar ... Ms. Georgia D. MCRAE
07 Dean of Admissions ... Mr. Brian TROYER
76 Dean of Health Sciences ... Dr. William CULLINAN
60 Acting Dean of Communication ... Dr. Sarah FELDNER
53 Dean of Education ... Dr. William A. HENK
49 Acting Dean of Arts & Sciences ... Dr. Heather HATHAWAY
61 Dean of the Law School ... Mr. Joseph D. KEARNEY
52 Dean of Dentistry ... Dr. William K. LOBB
66 Dean of Nursing ... Dr. Janet WESSEL KREJCI
54 Dean of Engineering ... Dr. Kristina ROPELLA
50 Acting Dean of Business Admin ... Dr. Joseph DANIELS
08 Dean of Libraries ... Ms. Janice WELBURN
58 VProv Grad/Prof Stds/Dn of Grad Sch ... Dr. Douglas WOODS
101 Sr Advisor to Pres/Corp Secretary ... Mr. Steven W. FRIEDER
13 Chief Information Officer ... Vacant
35 Dean of Students ... Dr. Stephanie QUADE
121 Assoc Vice Prov Acad Support Pgm ... Ms. Anne D. DEAHL
106 Chief of Digital Learning ... Dr. David SCHEJBAL
30 Senior Director of Development ... Mr. Timothy RIPPINGER
21 Senior Assoc Vice President Finance ... Ms. Theresa BLAZEI
45 VP Planning/Strategy ... Ms. Lora STRIGENS
35 Associate Vice Pres Student Affairs ... Dr. Jeff JANZ
39 Exec Dir Housing and Residence Life ... Ms. Mary JANZ
25 Exec Dir Research & Sponsored Prog ... Ms. Katherine DURBEN
23 Exec Dir University Medical Clinic ... Dr. Carolyn S. SMITH
36 Interim Dir Career Services Center ... Ms. Courtney HANSON
38 Director of Counseling Center ... Dr. Michael J. ZEBROWSKI
18 Dir Facilities & Campus Services ... Mr. Gregory ADAMS
37 Director of Financial Aid ... Ms. Susan M. TEERINK
104 Dir International Education Office ... Mr. Terence MILLER
40 Director Marquette Spirit Shop ... Mr. James K. GRAEBERT
29 Engagement Director ... Mr. Daniel DEWEERDT
19 Chief of Police ... Ms. Edith HUDSON
96 Director of Purchasing ... Ms. Jenny ALEXANDER
04 Executive Asst to President ... Mrs. Stacy ROMANT
106 Vice Provost Academic Planning ... Dr. Jennifer WATSON

Medical College of Wisconsin (C)

PO Box 26509, Milwaukee WI 53226-0509
County: Milwaukee FICE Identification: 024535
Unit ID: 239169
Telephone: (414) 955-8296 Carnegie Class: Spec-4-yr-Med
FAX Number: (414) 955-6560 Calendar System: Other
URL: www.mcw.edu
Established: 1893 Annual Graduate Tuition & Fees: N/A
Enrollment: 1,385 Coed
Affiliation or Control: Independent Non-Profit IRS Status: 501(c)3
Highest Offering: Doctorate; No Undergraduates
Accreditation: NH, AA, #CAMPEP, DENT, IPSY, MED, PDPSY, PH, @PHAR

01 President & CEO ... Dr. John R. RAYMOND, SR.
03 Provost/Exec VP/Dean ... Dr. Joseph E. KERSCHNER
04 Executive Asst to President ... Ms. Deborah CALVEY
05 Sr VP Strategic Acad Partnerships ... Dr. Cheryl A. MAURANA
10 Exec VP/COO/Finance ... Mr. Christopher KOPS
88 Dean Grad Sch Biomedical Science ... Dr. Ravi P. MISRA
30 Vice Pres of Development ... Vacant
15 Vice President Human Resources ... Ms. Sherri DUCHARME-WHITE
86 Vice Pres Government/Community Affs ... Ms. Kathryn A. KUHN
117 VP Corporate Compliance/Risk Mgmt ... Mr. Daniel WICKEHAM
26 VP Comm/Experience & Brand Strategy ... Ms. Mara LORD
13 VP Information Services ... Mr. David C. HOTCHKISS
27 Sr Assoc Vice Pres Communications ... Vacant
20 Assoc Provost/Sr Assoc Dean ... Dr. William J. HUESTON
20 Associate Provost Faculty Affairs ... Dr. Christina RUNGE
88 Assoc Provost Community Engagement ... Dr. Syed AHMED
28 Chief Diversity & Inclusion Officer ... Dr. C. Greer JORDAN
32 Assoc Dean Student Div & Inclusion ... Dr. Malika SIKER
63 Sr Assoc Dean Graduate Med Educ ... Dr. Kenneth B. SIMONS
88 Director Neuroscience Research Ctr ... Dr. Cecilia J. HILLARD
88 Associate Dean Curriculum ... Dr. Travis P. WEBB
114 Assoc Director Budget ... Ms. Lisa SCHEELE
13 Director Application Development ... Ms. Rebecca L. MORRISON
08 Director Medical Libraries ... Ms. Ellen N. SAYED
07 Director Admissions ... Ms. Alexis MEYER
06 Registrar ... Ms. Kerry J. GROSSE
18 VP Facilities & Operations ... Mr. Jeffrey BORNEMANN
37 Director Student Financial Services ... Ms. Kristin J. STUHR-MOOTZ
25 Director Grants & Contracts ... Ms. April HAVERTY
29 Exec Director Alumni Relations ... Vacant
96 Dir Purchasing & Payables ... Ms. Joan AGUADO WARE
40 Manager of Bookstore ... Ms. Cathy GRANFIELD
19 Director Public Safety ... Mr. David C. FELLER
43 Sr VP General Counsel ... Mr. John NEWSOME
10 Chief Financial Officer ... Mr. Barclay FERGUSON
67 Dean School of Pharmacy ... Dr. George MACKINNON
88 Managed Care Contract Mgr ... Mr. Jeffrey WOJNOWSKI
46 Assoc Provost for Research ... Dr. Ann NATTINGER
21 Assoc VP Financial Plng & Analysis ... Mr. Wayne STEMMER
101 Secretary of the Institution/Board ... Ms. Kristin NIEMIEC
44 Director Annual Giving ... Ms. Jyl BRENTANA

Midwest College of Oriental Medicine (D)

6232 Bankers Road, Racine WI 53403-9747
County: Racine FICE Identification: 030612
Unit ID: 383020
Telephone: (800) 593-2320 Carnegie Class: Spec-4-yr-Other Health
FAX Number: (262) 554-7475 Calendar System: Quarter
URL: www.acupuncture.edu
Established: 1979 Annual Undergrad Tuition & Fees: N/A
Enrollment: 55 Coed
Affiliation or Control: Proprietary IRS Status: Proprietary
Highest Offering: Master's; No Lower Division
Accreditation: ACUP

01 President ... Dr. William J. DUNBAR
05 Director of Academics ... Dr. Robert CHELNICK
12 Evanston Campus Director ... Dr. Kristine L. LA POINT
37 Director of Financial Aid ... Ms. Elizabeth M. HOJAN
07 Admissions Coord/Transfer Credit ... Ms. Liz WARKENTIN
06 Records Officer/Registrar ... Ms. Amy L. BENISH
08 Dean of Students/Librarian ... Mr. John BALLARINI
32 Dean of Students ... Ms. Olga GAJDOSIK
09 Research Director ... Vacant
85 Dean of Foreign Students ... Dr. Kris LA POINT
108 Clinic Tracking/Inst Evaluation ... Ms. Deirdre M. DUNBAR
91 Information Systems ... Mr. William H. LEHMAN
26 Marketing/Student Affairs ... Mr. Chris A. KRAJNIAK
88 Office Manager ... Ms. Stephanie M. PITTMAN

Milwaukee Career College (E)

3077 North Maryfair Road, Suite 300, Milwaukee WI 53222
County: Milwaukee FICE Identification: 041174
Unit ID: 449861
Telephone: (800) 754-1009 Carnegie Class: Spec 2-yr-Health
FAX Number: (414) 727-9557 Calendar System: Other
URL: www.mkecc.edu
Established: 2002 Annual Undergrad Tuition & Fees: N/A
Enrollment: 267 Coed
Affiliation or Control: Proprietary IRS Status: Proprietary
Highest Offering: Associate Degree
Accreditation: ABHES, SURTEC

01 President ... Jack TAKAHASHI

Milwaukee Institute of Art & Design (F)

273 E Erie Street, Milwaukee WI 53202-6003
County: Milwaukee FICE Identification: 020771
Unit ID: 239309
Telephone: (414) 847-3200 Carnegie Class: Spec-4-yr-Arts
FAX Number: (414) 291-8077 Calendar System: Semester
URL: www.miad.edu
Established: 1974 Annual Undergrad Tuition & Fees: $37,360
Enrollment: 660 Coed
Affiliation or Control: Independent Non-Profit IRS Status: 501(c)3
Highest Offering: Baccalaureate
Accreditation: NH, ART

01 President ... Mr. Jeff MORIN
05 VP of Academic Affairs ... Mr. David MARTIN
84 VP for Enrollment Management ... Ms. Mary C. SCHOPP
04 Executive Assistant to President ... Ms. Rachel FOSTER
09 Assoc VP Academic Plng/Assessment ... Ms. Cynthia LYNCH
10 VP for Financial Affairs ... Ms. Brenda JONES
26 VP of Development & Communications ... Ms. Vivian M. ROTHSCHILD
39 Director of Residential Living ... Ms. Marianne DI ULIO
32 Dean of Students ... Mr. Tony J. NOWAK
37 Executive Director of Financial Aid ... Ms. Carol MASSE
07 Director of Admissions ... Mr. David SIGMAN
88 Enroll Communications Specialist ... Ms. Stacey STEINBERG
08 Director of Library Services ... Ms. Cynthia D. LYNCH
36 Director of Career Services ... Mr. Duane P. SEIDENSTICKER
51 Dir Pre-College & Adult Learning ... Mr. Corbett TOOMSEN
19 Director Security/Safety ... Mr. Keith A. KOTOWICZ
06 Director of Registration Services ... Ms. Jean WEIMER
38 Director of Advising ... Ms. Alea CROSS
15 Director of Human Resources ... Mr. Dustin HOOT
20 Director of Academic Operations ... Ms. Marie COUTURE
18 Building Maintenance Manager ... Mr. Michael A. GOETZ
13 Director of Technology ... Mr. Matt OGDEN
88 Director of Emerging Technology ... Mr. Ben DEMBROSKI
88 Exec Director of Innovation Center ... Mr. Drew MAXWELL

Milwaukee School of Engineering (G)

1025 N Broadway, Milwaukee WI 53202-3109
County: Milwaukee FICE Identification: 003868
Unit ID: 239318
Telephone: (414) 277-7300 Carnegie Class: Masters/M
FAX Number: (414) 277-7454 Calendar System: Quarter
URL: www.msoe.edu
Established: 1903 Annual Undergrad Tuition & Fees: $40,749
Enrollment: 2,823 Coed
Affiliation or Control: Independent Non-Profit IRS Status: 501(c)3
Highest Offering: Master's
Accreditation: NH, CONST, NURSE, PERF

01 President ... Dr. John WALZ
05 Vice President Academics ... Dr. Eric BAUMGARTNER
10 Vice President of Finance and CFO ... Ms. Dawn THIBEDEAU
30 VP of Development/Alumni Rels ... Mr. Jeff SNOW
18 VP of Operations ... Mr. Kevin MORIN

84 VP of Enroll Mgmt & Dean of Student ... Dr. Timothy VALLEY
25 Dean Grants & Projects ... Mr. Sheku KAMARA
48 Chair Architectural Engr Dept ... Dr. Blake WENTZ
54 Chair Electrical Engr/CPU Sci Dept ... Dr. Stephen WILLIAMS
97 Chair General Studies Department ... Dr. Alicia DOMACK
81 Chair Physics/Chemistry/Mathematics ... Dr. Matey KALTCHEV
66 Chair Nursing Department ... Dr. Carol SABEL
06 Registrar ... Ms. Mary F. NIELSEN
13 Director of IT Services ... Mr. Rick THOMAS
26 VP Marketing & Community Engagement ... Mr. Sebastian THACHENKARY
27 Director Media Relations ... Ms. JoEllen BURDUE
15 Director of Human Resources ... Ms. Rebecca PLOECKELMAN
110 Director of Development ... Mr. Greg CASEY
32 Director Student Activities ... Mr. Nick SEIDLER
41 Director Athletics ... Mr. Brian MILLER
08 Director of Library & Info Services ... Mr. Gary S. SHIMEK
105 Director of Services/Webmaster ... Mr. Kent A. PETERSON
29 Director Alumni Affairs ... Ms. Cathy VAREBROOK
07 Director of Admissions ... Ms. Seandra MITCHELL
36 Director of Career Services ... Ms. Julie WAY
40 Bookstore Manager ... Mr. David P. ABRAHAMSON
04 Executive Admin to the President ... Ms. Kellyann M. REUTER
108 Asst VP Institutional Effectiveness ... Dr. Jill MEYER
19 Director Security/Safety ... Mr. Billy FYFE
37 Director Student Financial Aid ... Ms. Stephanie MEALY

Mount Mary University (A)

2900 N Menomonee River Parkway,
Milwaukee WI 53222-4597
County: Milwaukee | FICE Identification: 003869
Unit ID: 239390
Telephone: (414) 930-3000 | Carnegie Class: Masters/M
FAX Number: (414) 930-3712 | Calendar System: Semester
URL: www.mtmary.edu
Established: 1913 | Annual Undergrad Tuition & Fees: $30,100
Enrollment: 1,399 | Female
Affiliation or Control: Roman Catholic | IRS Status: 501(c)3
Highest Offering: Doctorate
Accreditation: NH, CACREP, CIDA, DIETC, DIETI, NURSE, OT, SW

01 President ... Dr. Christine PHARR
10 VP Finance & Admin Services ... Mr. Robert O'KEEFE
05 VP Academic Affairs ... Dr. Karen FRIEDLEN
84 Vice Pres Enrollment Services ... Mr. David WEGENER
30 Vice Pres Development ... Ms. Pamela OWENS
88 Vice President Mission/ Identity ... Sr. Joan PENZENSTADLER, SSND
32 Vice Pres Student Affairs ... Ms. Sarah OLEJNICZAK
81 Dean School Nat & Health Sci/Educ ... Dr. Cheryl BAILEY
50 Dean School Business/Arts & Design . Ms. Barbara ARMSTRONG
79 Dean Sch Hum/Social Sci/Interdisc ... Dr. Wendy WEAVER
35 Dean Student Affairs ... Vacant
58 Dean of Graduate Education ... Vacant
21 Sr Dir of Business Ofc/Controller ... Ms. Sharon ROOB
06 Registrar ... Dr. Mary KARR
110 Senior Development Officer ... Ms. Lisa BREITSPRECKER
26 Dir of Marketing & Communications ... Ms. Kathy VAN ZEELAND
29 Director of Alumnae Relations ... Vacant
123 Director of Graduate Admission ... Mr. Kirk HELLER DE MESSER
07 Director of Undergraduate Admission ... Mr. James WISEMAN
09 Director of Inst Effectiveness ... Vacant
08 Director of Library ... Mr. Daniel VINSON
13 Senior Director of IT ... Mr. Marc BELANGER
37 Director Financial Aid ... Ms. Debra DUFF
35 Director of Student Engagement ... Ms. Julie SCHNEITER
39 Director of Residence Life ... Vacant
36 Dir of Advising/Career Development ... Ms. Beth FELCH
104 Director of International Studies ... Ms. Nan METZGER
15 Senior Director of Human Resources ... Ms. Alisa BENDICKSON
41 Athletic Director ... Mr. Marc HEIDORF
42 Director of Campus Ministry ... Ms. Kathleen COFFEY
18 Director of Buildings & Grounds ... Mr. Gary KOENEN
19 Director of Public Safety ... Mr. Paul LESHOK
40 Mgr Barnes & Noble Bookstore ... Mr. Timothy STERNKE
04 Executive Assistant to President ... Mrs. Amy KNOX
102 Dir Fndn/Corp Rels & Int Dir of WLI ... Ms. Anne KAHL

Nashotah House (B)

2777 Mission Road, Nashotah WI 53058-9793
County: Waukesha | FICE Identification: 003874
Unit ID: 239424
Telephone: (262) 646-6500 | Carnegie Class: Spec-4-yr-Faith
FAX Number: (262) 646-6504 | Calendar System: Semester
URL: www.nashotah.edu
Established: 1842 | Annual Graduate Tuition & Fees: N/A
Enrollment: 73 | Coed
Affiliation or Control: Protestant Episcopal | IRS Status: 501(c)3
Highest Offering: Doctorate; No Undergraduates
Accreditation: THEOL

01 President/Dean ... Dr. Garwood P. ANDERSON
11 Chief Operating Officer ... Mr. Bill MONTEI
05 Provost ... Dr. Garwood P. ANDERSON
111 Exec VP Institutional Advancement ... Mr. Labin L. DUKE
13 IT/Database Administrator ... Mr. Matt BILLS
30 Senior Development Officer ... Rev. Jason TERHUNE
09 Asst Dean Institutional Research ... Rev. Esther KRAMER
32 Associate Dean of Students ... Vacant
101 Secretary of the Board of Trustees ... Rev. R. Brien KOEHLER
06 Registrar ... Ms. Carolee PUCHTER
08 Dir Francis Donaldson Library ... Dr. David G. SHERWOOD
26 Director Marketing/Communications ... Ms. Lisa SWAN
42 Director of Church Relations ... Ms. Carolyn BARTKUS
18 Maintenance Supervisor ... Mr. Ricco MEDINA
111 Manager Institutional Advancement ... Ms. Molly MCFADZEN

Northland College (C)

1411 Ellis Avenue, Ashland WI 54806-3999
County: Ashland | FICE Identification: 003875
Unit ID: 239512
Telephone: (715) 682-1699 | Carnegie Class: Bac-Diverse
FAX Number: (715) 682-1308 | Calendar System: Other
URL: www.northland.edu
Established: 1892 | Annual Undergrad Tuition & Fees: $36,183
Enrollment: 635 | Coed
Affiliation or Control: United Church Of Christ | IRS Status: 501(c)3
Highest Offering: Baccalaureate
Accreditation: NH

01 President ... Mr. Marvin SUOMI
100 Chief of Staff ... Ms. Dawn RIVARD
11 Chief Operating Officer ... Dr. Karl SOLIBAKKE
20 Associate Academic Dean ... Dr. Wendy GORMAN
32 Interim Dean of Students ... Ms. Melissa HARVEY
07 Dean of Admissions & Financial Aid ... Vacant
111 Exec Director of Advancement ... Vacant
26 Exec Director of Inst Marketing ... Ms. Demeri MULLIKIN
29 Director of Alumni Relations ... Ms. Jackie MOORE
41 Interim Athletic Director ... Mr. Seamus GREGORY
13 Information Services Director ... Mr. Todd PYDO
15 Interim Director Human Resources ... Ms. Sherri VENERO
08 Library Director ... Ms. Julia WAGGONER
39 Director of Residential Life ... Ms. Melissa HARVEY
25 Director of Sponsored Programs ... Ms. Lisa WILLIAMSON
37 Director of Student Financial Aid ... Ms. Kelly DUNN
38 Campus Counselor ... Mr. Scott JOHNSON
23 Interim Campus Nurse ... Ms. Jennifer NEWAGO
21 Controller ... Mr. Todd VYSKOCIL
28 Diversity and Inclusion Coordinator ... Ms. Ruth DE JESUS
09 Institutional Research Specialist ... Ms. Petra HOFSTEDT
06 Registrar ... Ms. Michelle BITZER
18 Director of Operations ... Mr. Paul WEBB
19 Campus Safety Director ... Mr. Dawayne LAMPSON

Ottawa University Wisconsin (D)

245 South Executive Drive, Brookfield WI 53005-4204
Telephone: (262) 879-0200 | Identification: 666084
Accreditation: &NH

† Regional accreditation is carried under the parent institution in Ottawa, KS.

Purdue University Global-Milwaukee (E)

201 West Wisconsin Ave, Milwaukee WI 53203
Telephone: (414) 223-2105 | Identification: 770986
Accreditation: &NH, ACBSP

† Regional accreditation is carried under Purdue University Global in Indianapolis, IN.

Rasmussen College - Green Bay (F)

904 South Taylor Street, Building 1, Green Bay WI 54303
Telephone: (920) 593-8400 | Identification: 667063
Accreditation: &NH, ADNUR, CAHIIM, MAAB, MLTAD

† Regional accreditation is carried under the parent institution in Saint Cloud, MN. The tuition figure is an average, actual tuition may vary.

Ripon College (G)

300 West Seward Street, PO Box 248,
Ripon WI 54971-0248
County: Fond du Lac | FICE Identification: 003884
Unit ID: 239628
Telephone: (920) 748-8115 | Carnegie Class: Bac-A&S
FAX Number: (920) 748-7243 | Calendar System: Semester
URL: www.ripon.edu
Established: 1851 | Annual Undergrad Tuition & Fees: $43,808
Enrollment: 756 | Coed
Affiliation or Control: Independent Non-Profit | IRS Status: 501(c)3
Highest Offering: Baccalaureate
Accreditation: NH

01 President ... Zachariah P. MESSITTE
04 Exec Sec to President & DOF ... Claudia M. LEISTIKOW
101 Special Assistant to the President ... Andrea N. YOUNG
05 VP & Dean of Faculty ... Ed WINGENBACH
111 VP for Advancement ... Shawn F. KARSTEN
10 Vice President for Finance ... Vacant
32 Vice President/Dean of Students ... Christophor M. OGLE
84 Vice President for Enrollment ... Jennifer L. MACHACEK
06 Assoc Dean of Faculty/Registrar ... Michele A. WITTLER
36 Asst Dean of Career & Prof Develop ... Lindsay A. BLUMER
07 Dean of Admissions ... Leigh D. MLODZIK
21 Associate VP for Finance ... Lori A. SCHULZE
08 Access Services Librarian ... Karlyn M. SCHUMACHER
35 Dir Student Activities/Orientation ... Sara VANSTEENBERGEN
121 Director Student Support Svcs ... Daniel J. KRHIN
39 Director of Residence Life ... Mark B. NICKLAUS
26 VP for Marketing & Communications ... Melissa K. ANDERSON
27 Dir of Creative & Social Media ... Richard T. DAMM
13 Exec Dir of Information Technology ... Tara A. LACHAPELL
109 General Manager Food Service ... Solon L. PIETILA
18 Director Physical Plant ... Brian SKAMRA
41 Director of Athletics ... Vacant
102 Dir Foundation & Govt Relations ... Terri L. HOLZMAN
29 Dir Constituent Engagement ... Amy L. GERRETSEN
15 Human Resource Administrator ... Jennifer FRANZ
38 Director of Counseling Services ... Cynthia S. VIERTEL
40 Bookstore Manager ... Noelle J. KORZENIEWSKI
37 Director Financial Aid ... Bryant K. ANDERSON
28 Dir of Multicultural Affairs ... Kyonna HENRY
44 Director Annual Giving ... Kelly A. NIELSEN
90 Director Academic Computing ... Andrew P. DESCH
91 Director Administrative Computing ... Gary S. RODMAN

Sacred Heart Seminary and School of Theology (H)

7335 S Highway 100, P.O. Box 429,
Hales Corners WI 53130-0429
County: Milwaukee | FICE Identification: 020780
Unit ID: 239637
Telephone: (414) 425-8300 | Carnegie Class: Spec-4-yr-Faith
FAX Number: (414) 529-6999 | Calendar System: Semester
URL: www.shsst.edu
Established: 1933 | Annual Graduate Tuition & Fees: N/A
Enrollment: 109 | Coed
Affiliation or Control: Roman Catholic | IRS Status: 501(c)3
Highest Offering: Master's; No Undergraduates
Accreditation: NH, THEOL

01 President-Rector ... V. Rev. Raúl L. GOMEZ, SDS
10 VP Finance & Business Svcs ... Mr. Christopher LAMBERT
05 VP Intellectual Formation ... Dr. Patrick J. RUSSELL
20 VP Pastoral Formation ... Dr. John OLESNAVAGE
42 VP Spiritual Formation ... Rev. Zbigniew MORAWIEC, SCJ
30 VP Inst Dev & External Affairs ... Dr. Christopher MCATEE
88 VP Intercultural Prep for Ministry ... Ms. Kelly KORNACKI
08 Director Library & Acad Supp Svcs ... Ms. Jennifer BARTHOLOMEW
88 Director Liturgy and Worship ... Rev. Brad KRAWCZYK
88 Director Lux Center ... Ms. Bonnie SHAFRIN
26 Director Marketing ... Ms. Monica MISEY
07 Director of Admissions ... Dr. Jeremy BLACKWOOD
18 Director Plant Operations ... Mr. Michael J. ERATO
88 Director Hispanic Studies ... Rev. James WALTERS, SCJ
88 Director Faculty Council ... Dr. Steven SHIPPEE
88 Asst to Rector Sponsor Relations ... Rev. Thomas KNOEBEL
06 Registrar ... Ms. Julie O'CONNOR
13 Information Systems Coordinator ... Ms. Mary GRIEGER
88 Design Project Manager ... Ms. Ruth MARKWORTH
04 Executive Asst to President-Rector ... Ms. Theresa M. ILLINGWORTH

Saint Norbert College (I)

100 Grant Street, De Pere WI 54115-2099
County: Brown | FICE Identification: 003892
Unit ID: 239716
Telephone: (920) 403-3181 | Carnegie Class: Bac-A&S
FAX Number: (920) 403-4008 | Calendar System: Semester
URL: www.snc.edu
Established: 1898 | Annual Undergrad Tuition & Fees: $38,129
Enrollment: 2,165 | Coed
Affiliation or Control: Roman Catholic | IRS Status: 501(c)3
Highest Offering: Master's
Accreditation: NH

01 President ... Dr. Brian BRUESS
05 Vice Pres Acad Affs/Dean of Col ... Dr. Jennifer BONDS-RAACKE
10 Vice President Business & Finance ... Ms. Autumn ANFANG
111 Vice Pres Institutional Advancement ... Mr. Jon ENSLIN
32 Int VP Mission & Student Affairs ... Ms. Julie MASSEY
84 Vice Pres Enrollment Mgmt/Comm ... Mr. Edward LAMM
110 Assoc Vice Pres Inst Advancement ... Ms. Lynette GREEN
09 AVP Institutional Effectiveness ... Dr. Ray ZURAWSKI
20 Associate Academic Dean ... Dr. Tynesha MEIDL
36 Director Career Services ... Ms. Mary Ellen OLSON
38 Dir Counseling/Career Programs ... Mr. Bruce ROBERTSON
07 Actg Exec Director of Admissions ... Mr. Mark SELIN
29 Director Alumni & Parent Relations ... Mr. William FALK
21 Director of Finance ... Ms. Elizabeth MILLER
37 Director of Financial Aid ... Ms. Jessica RAFELD
26 Int Dir Communications/Marketing ... Ms. Nina ROUSE
08 Director of Library ... Dr. Kristin D. VOGEL
15 Director Human Resources ... Ms. Sue BRINKMAN
41 Director Physical Educ/Athletics ... Mr. Tim BALD
06 Registrar ... Ms. Lauren GAECKE
13 Vice Pres & Chief Info Officer ... Mr. Lee REID
104 Assoc Academic Dir Global Affairs ... Mr. Dan STOLL
28 Dir Multicultural Student Services ... Ms. Bridgit MARTIN
18 Director Facilities/Physical Plant ... Mr. Patrick WRENN
40 Manager Bookstore Operations ... Mr. Ryan SILER
04 Executive Asst to President ... Ms. Jamie MCGUIRE
102 Dir Foundation/Corporate Relations ... Ms. Amy KUNDINGER
100 Chief of Staff ... Ms. Amy SORENSON
19 Director Security/Safety ... Mr. Eric DUNNING
39 Director Student Housing ... Mr. Michael PECKHAM

Silver Lake College of the Holy Family (A)

2406 S Alverno Road, Manitowoc WI 54220-9319
County: Manitowoc FICE Identification: 003850
Unit ID: 239743
Telephone: (920) 684-6691 Carnegie Class: Masters/S
FAX Number: (920) 684-7082 Calendar System: Semester
URL: www.sl.edu
Established: 1935 Annual Undergrad Tuition & Fees: $28,390
Enrollment: 475 Coed
Affiliation or Control: Roman Catholic IRS Status: 501(c)3
Highest Offering: Master's
Accreditation: NH, MUS, NURSE

Code	Title	Name
01	President	Dr. Robert CALLAHAN
04	Executive Asst to President	Ms. RK GREENING
42	VP for Mission Integration	Sr. Louise HEMBRECHT
10	Chief Financial Officer	Ms. Janeen MEIFERT
111	VP Advancement/External Relations	Ms. Tracy MILKOWSKI
32	Dean of Student Development	Dr. Rachel FISCHER
49	Dean School of Liberal Arts	Dr. Rachel WARE CARLTON
107	Dean School of Professional Studies	Ms. Brianna NEUSER
53	Dean School of Education	Dr. Michael DUNLAP
07	Director of Admissions	Mr. Ryan ROBERTS
07	Director of Admissions	Ms. Emily LENSMIRE
37	Director of Financial Aid	Ms. Erica PLOECKELMAN
41	Athletic Director	Mr. Brandt DANALS
88	Director of Strategic Partnerships	Mr. Matthew GOFF
06	Registrar/Dir of Academic Ops	Mr. Ronald JURGENS
29	Director of Alumni/Annual Giving	Ms. Libby RHODE
08	Assistant Librarian	Ms. Lisa KLIMENT
112	Planned Giving Officer	Ms. Cynthia ST. JOHN
39	Residence Hall Director	Ms. Kristin SORENSEN

*University of Wisconsin System (B)

1220 Linden Dr, 1720 Van Hise Hall,
Madison WI 53706-1559
County: Dane FICE Identification: 003894
Unit ID: 240435
Telephone: (608) 262-2321 Carnegie Class: N/A
FAX Number: (608) 262-3985
URL: www.wisconsin.edu

Code	Title	Name
01	President	Ray W. CROSS
100	Chief of Staff	Gary Allen BENNETT
05	VP Academic/Student Affairs	Karen SCHMITT
11	VP Administration	Robert CRAMER
10	VP Finance	Sean NELSON
30	Int VP Corp Rels & Econ Engagement	David BRUKARDT
15	Sr AVP Human Res/Workforce Dev	Shenita BROKENBURR
117	Assoc VP Administrative Services	Ruth ANDERSON
116	Assoc VP Cap Planning & Budget	Alexandria ROE
119	Int Assoc VP Info Security	Kathy MAYER
120	Assoc VP Learning/Info Tech	Steven HOPPER
88	Exec Dir Shared Services	Steve WILDECK
121	Associate VP Student Success	Christine NAVIA
20	Int AVP Acad Pgms/Educ Innovation	Carleen VANDE ZANDE
56	Sr AVP & Exec Dir Extended Campus	Aaron BROWER
09	Assoc VP Policy and Research	Ben PASSMORE
21	Sr Assoc VP Financial Admin	Julie GORDON
114	Asst VP Budget/Planning	Renee STEPHENSON
88	Director Trust Funds	Douglas HOERR
88	Exec Dir Business & Entrepreneur	Mark LANG
26	Exec Dir Public & Community Affairs	Jack JABLONSKI
27	Dir of Strategic Communications	Heather LAROI
86	Assoc VP Federal Relations	Kris ANDREWS
86	Sr Director State Relations	Jeff BUHRANDT
43	General Counsel	Quinn WILLIAMS
28	Dir Diversity and Inclusivity	Carl HAMPTON
101	ED & Corp Sec to Board of Regents	Jessica LATHROP
04	Admin Assistant to the President	Nicole SMENT

*University of Wisconsin-Madison (C)

500 Lincoln Drive, Madison WI 53706-1380
County: Dane FICE Identification: 003895
Unit ID: 240444
Telephone: (608) 262-1234 Carnegie Class: DU-Highest
FAX Number: (608) 262-0123 Calendar System: Semester
URL: www.wisc.edu
Established: 1848 Annual Undergrad Tuition & Fees (In-State): $10,555
Enrollment: 42,977 Coed
Affiliation or Control: State IRS Status: 501(c)3
Highest Offering: Doctorate
Accreditation: NH, ARCPA, ART, AUD, CAATE, CACREP, CAMPEP, CIDA, CLPSY, COPSY, CYTO, DANCE, DIETD, DMS, IPSY, LAW, LIB, LSAR, MED, MUS, NURSE, OT, PCSAS, PH, PHAR, PLNG, PTA, SCPSY, SP, SW, VET

Code	Title	Name
02	Chancellor	Dr. Rebecca BLANK
05	Provost Academic Affairs	Dr. Karl SCHOLZ
46	Int Chief Research Officer	Dr. Norman DRINKWATER
11	Vice Chancellor Administration	Mr. Laurent HELLER
100	Chancellor's Chief of Staff	Mr. Matt MAYRL
26	Vice Chanc University Relations	Mr. Charles HOSLET
32	Vice Chanc Student Affairs	Dr. Lori REESOR
84	Vice Provost Enrollment Management	Mr. Steven HAHN
13	CIO/Vice Prov Info Technology	Ms. Lois BROOKS
18	Assoc VC Facilities Plng/Mgmt	Mr. David DARLING
28	Vice Provost Diversity/Climate	Dr. Patrick SIMS
20	Vice Provost Faculty/Staff Pgms	Dr. Michael BERNARD-DONALS
20	Vice Provost Teaching/Learning	Dr. Steven M. CRAMER
10	Assoc Vice Chanc Finance/Admin	Mr. David MURPHY
21	Asst Vice Chanc Business Svcs	Mr. Dan LANGER
35	Int Dean of Students	Mr. Argyle WADE
58	Dean Graduate School	Dr. William J. KARPUS
49	Dean College Letters & Science	Dr. John K. SCHOLZ
63	Dean Medicine and Public Health	Dr. Robert N. GOLDEN
53	Dean School of Education	Dr. Diana HESS
50	Int Dean School of Business	Dr. Barry GERHART
67	Dean School of Pharmacy	Dr. Steven M. SWANSON
54	Dean of College of Engineering	Dr. Ian ROBERTSON
47	Dean of Agricultural/Life Sciences	Dr. Kathryn VANDENBOSCH
66	Dean of School of Nursing	Dr. Linda SCOTT
59	Dean of Human Ecology	Dr. Soyeon SHIM
74	Dean of Veterinary Medicine	Dr. Mark D. MARKEL
61	Dean of the Law School	Dr. Margaret RAYMOND
82	Dean International Studies	Dr. Guido PODESTÁ
43	Director of Admin Legal Services	Mr. Raymond P. TAFFORA
88	Dean Nelson Inst Environmental Stds	Dr. Paul ROBBINS
41	Director Intercollegiate Athletics	Mr. Barry L. ALVAREZ
88	Director of Physical Plant	Mr. Jay BIESZKE
88	Director of the Arboretum	Dr. Karen OBERHAUSER
88	Director State Lab of Hygiene	Dr. James SCHAUER
88	Director of Wisconsin Union	Mr. Mark C. GUTHIER
07	Director of Admissions	Mr. Andre PHILLIPS
08	Director of Libraries	Ms. Lisa CARTER
27	Director University Communications	Mr. John LUCAS
102	President UW Foundation	Dr. Michael M. KNETTER
37	Director Student Financial Aid	Mr. Derek KINDLE
38	Director Counseling Services	Ms. Andrea LAWSON
15	Int Chief Human Resources	Mr. Mark WALTERS
39	Director of University Housing	Dr. Jeffrey NOVAK
51	Dean Continuing Studies	Dr. Jeffrey RUSSELL
19	Chief of University Police	Ms. Kristen ROMAN
88	Director of Archives	Ms. Katie NASH
23	Int Director University Health Svcs	Dr. Bill KINSEY
88	Director of Space Management	Mr. Brent LLOYD
17	CEO Hospital & Clinics	Dr. Alan KAPLAN
109	Dir Auxiliary Operations Analysis	Ms. Donna HALLERAN
06	Registrar	Mr. Scott OWCZAREK
88	Secretary of the Faculty	Mr. Steven K. SMITH
88	Secretary of Academic Staff	Ms. Heather M. DANIELS
88	Director of Recreational Sports	Mr. John HORN
85	Dir International Student Services	Dr. Roopa RAWJEE
22	Dir Office of Equity & Diversity	Mr. Luis A. PINERO
96	Director of Purchasing	Ms. Lori VOSS
09	Dir Inst Rsrch/Acad Plng/Analysis	Dr. Jocelyn L. MILNER
88	Special Asst to Provost	Dr. Eden INOWAY-RONNIE
86	Sr Special Asst to Chanc Fed Rels	Mr. Michael LENN

*University of Wisconsin-Eau Claire (D)

105 Garfield Avenue, PO Box 4004,
Eau Claire WI 54702-4004
County: Eau Claire FICE Identification: 003917
Unit ID: 240268
Telephone: (715) 836-2637 Carnegie Class: Masters/M
FAX Number: (715) 836-2902 Calendar System: Semester
URL: www.uwec.edu
Established: 1916 Annual Undergrad Tuition & Fees (In-State): $8,820
Enrollment: 10,904 Coed
Affiliation or Control: State IRS Status: 501(c)3
Highest Offering: Doctorate
Accreditation: NH, CAATE, JOUR, MUS, NURSE, SP, SW

Code	Title	Name
02	Chancellor	Dr. James C. SCHMIDT
05	Prov/Vice Chanc Academic Affairs	Dr. Patricia A. KLEINE
100	Special Assistant to the Chancellor	Ms. Mary Jane BRUKARDT
84	Vice Chanc Enrollment Management	Mr. Albert COLOM
10	Vice Chanc Finance/Administration	Mr. John HAVEN, III
46	Asst VC Research/Sponsored Pgm	Dr. Karen G. HAVHOLM
18	Asst Chanc Facilities/Univ Rels	Mr. Michael J. RINDO
20	Assoc Vice Chanc Academic Affairs	Dr. Darrell NEWTON
20	Assoc Vice Chanc Academic Affairs	Dr. Michael J. CARNEY
26	Executive Director Mktg & Planning	Ms. Mary Jane BRUKARDT
22	Director of Affirmative Action	Ms. Teresa E. O'HALLORAN
111	Pres UWEC Found/Dir Univ Advance	Ms. Kimera K. WAY
32	Dean of Students	Dr. Joseph J. ABHOLD
08	Director of Libraries	Dr. Jill S. MARKGRAF
13	Chief Information Officer	Mr. Chip P. ECKARDT
14	Dir Learning & Technology Services	Mr. Craig A. MEY
15	Director of Human Resources	Mr. David J. MILLER
37	Director of Financial Aid	Ms. Nicole S. ANDREWS
38	Director of Counseling	Dr. Riley C. MCGRATH
06	Registrar	Ms. Kimberly B. O'KELLY
36	Assoc Director Career Services	Ms. Staci L. HEIDTKE
23	Director of Student Health Services	Ms. Laura G. CHELLMAN
39	Director of Housing & Res Life	Mr. J. Quincy CHAPMAN
41	Director of Athletics	Mr. Daniel J. SCHUMACHER
51	Director Continuing Education	Mr. Durwin LONG
85	Interim Lead Intl Education	Ms. Colleen C. MARCHWICK
102	Director Corporate Relations	Mr. John G. BACHMEIER
92	Interim Director of Honors Program	Dr. David JONES
26	Chief Public Relations Officer	Mr. Michael J. RINDO
27	Director of Integrated Marketing	Ms. Rebecca J. DIENGER
30	Chief Development/Alumni Relations	Ms. Kimera K. WAY
09	Institutional Planner	Mr. Andrew J. NELSON
108	Director of Assessment	Dr. Mary F. HOFFMAN
49	Interim Dean Col of Arts & Sciences	Dr. Rodd D. FREITAG
66	Dean Col of Nursing/Health Sciences	Dr. Linda K. YOUNG
53	Dean Col Education/Human Sciences	Dr. Carmen K. MANNING
50	Interim Dean College of Business	Dr. Timothy S. VAUGHAN
04	Interim Exec Asst to Chancellor	Ms. Corrynn MAHNKE

*University of Wisconsin-Green Bay (E)

2420 Nicolet Drive, Green Bay WI 54311-7001
County: Brown FICE Identification: 003899
Unit ID: 240277
Telephone: (920) 465-2000 Carnegie Class: Masters/M
FAX Number: (920) 465-2032 Calendar System: Semester
URL: www.uwgb.edu
Established: 1965 Annual Undergrad Tuition & Fees (In-State): $7,878
Enrollment: 7,174 Coed
Affiliation or Control: State IRS Status: 501(c)3
Highest Offering: Doctorate
Accreditation: NH, ART, CAHIIM, DIETD, DIETI, MUS, NURSE, SW

Code	Title	Name
02	Chancellor	Dr. Gary L. MILLER
05	Provost/Vice Chancellor	Dr. Michael ALEXANDER
12	CEO UW Manitowoc	Ms. Rachele BAKIC
12	CEO UW Marinette	Ms. Cindy BAILEY
12	CEO UW Sheboygan	Ms. Jennifer WILLIAMSON-MENDEZ
10	Vice Chanc Business & Finance	Ms. Sheryl VAN GRUENSVEN
111	Vice Chanc University Advancement	Mr. Tony WERNER
41	Athletic Director	Mr. Charles GUTHRIE
32	Vice Chancellor for Student Affairs	Dr. Eric ARNESON
20	Assoc Provost for Academic Affairs	Dr. Clifton GANYARD
53	Dean Health/Education/Social Well	Dr. Susan GALLAGHER-LEPAK
50	Dean Cofrin School of Business	Dr. Mathew DORNBUSH
49	Dean of Arts/Humanities	Dr. Chuck RYBAK
81	Dean of Science/Engr & Tech	Dr. John KATERS
07	Director of Admissions	Ms. Jennifer JONES
15	Asst VC Policy & Compliance	Mr. Christopher PAQUET
18	Dir Facilities Management/Planning	Mr. Paul PINKSTON
19	Director of Public Safety	Vacant
21	Controller	Ms. SuAnn DETAMPEL
84	Dean Enrollment	Ms. Jennifer JONES
46	Director of Institute for Research	Vacant
37	Director Financial Aid	Mr. James P. ROHAN
39	Director of Residence Life	Ms. Gail SIMS-AUBERT
24	Director Media Svcs/Telecomm	Vacant
23	Director Health Services	Ms. Amy HENNIGES
100	Chief of Staff	Mr. Ben JONIAUX
26	Director University Communications	Ms. Janet BONKOWSKI
36	Director Career Services	Ms. Linda G. PEACOCK-LANDRUM
29	Director Alumni Relations	Ms. Kari MOODY
35	Director Student Life	Ms. Claudia GUZMAN
06	Registrar	Mr. Daniel VANDE YACHT
04	Administrative Asst to President	Ms. Paula MARCEC
104	Director Study Abroad	Mr. Brent BLAHNIK
28	Diversity Director	Ms. Mai LO LEE
30	Director of Development	Mr. Jacob DEPAS
13	Asst Vice Chancellor for IT	Ms. Paula GANYARD
102	Director Foundation	Mr. Anthony WERNER
106	Executive Director of Continuing Ed	Ms. Joy RUZEK
54	Dean of Engineering	Dr. John KATERS
86	Director Government Relations	Mr. Ben JONIAUX
96	Procurement Specialist	Mr. Tory ORTSCHEID

*University of Wisconsin-La Crosse (F)

1725 State Street, La Crosse WI 54601-3788
County: La Crosse FICE Identification: 003919
Unit ID: 240329
Telephone: (608) 785-8000 Carnegie Class: Masters/L
FAX Number: (608) 785-8492 Calendar System: Semester
URL: www.uwlax.edu
Established: 1909 Annual Undergrad Tuition & Fees (In-State): $9,107
Enrollment: 10,548 Coed
Affiliation or Control: State IRS Status: 501(c)3
Highest Offering: Doctorate
Accreditation: NH, ANEST, ARCPA, CAATE, MUS, NMT, NRPA, OT, PH, PTA, RADDOS, RTT

Code	Title	Name
02	Chancellor	Dr. Joe GOW
05	Provost/Vice Chanc Acad Affairs	Dr. Betsy MORGAN
111	Vice Chancellor Advancement	Mr. Greg REICHERT
10	Vice Chancellor Admin & Finance	Dr. Bob HETZEL
50	Dean of Business Administration	Dr. Laura MILNER
53	Dean School of Education	Dr. Marcie WYCOFF-HORN
79	Dean of Liberal Studies	Dr. Karl KUNKEL
81	Dean Science/Health	Dr. Mark SANDHEINRICH
32	Vice Chancellor & Dean of Students	Dr. Vitaliano FIGUEROA
13	Chief Information Officer	Dr. Mohamed ELHINDI
51	Director Continuing Educ/Exten	Ms. Penny TIEDT
08	Director of Library	Mr. John JAX
85	Dir International Education & Engag	Ms. Emelee VOLDEN
07	Director ES/Admissions	Mr. Corey SJOQUIST
37	Director ES/Financial Aid	Ms. Louise L. JANKE
38	Director Counseling/Testing	Ms. Gretchen REINDERS
36	Director of Career Services	Ms. Becky VIANDEN
41	Athletic Director	Ms. Kim BLUM
26	Director News and Marketing	Mr. Brad R. QUARBERG
29	Director Alumni Relations	Ms. Janie M. MORGAN
23	Int Director Student Health Center	Dr. Christopher DURALL
09	Director Institutional Research	Ms. Natalie SOLVERSON
28	Vice Chancellor Diversity/Inclusion	Ms. Barbara E. STEWART
22	Director Affirmative Action	Dr. Nizam ARAIN
106	Dir Online Education/E-learning	Dr. Brian UDERMANN
39	Director Student Housing	Vacant

*University of Wisconsin-Milwaukee (A)

PO Box 413, Milwaukee WI 53201-0413
County: Milwaukee | FICE Identification: 003896
Unit ID: 240453
Telephone: (414) 229-1122 | Carnegie Class: DU-Highest
FAX Number: (414) 229-6329 | Calendar System: Semester
URL: www.uwm.edu
Established: 1885 | Annual Undergrad Tuition & Fees (In-State): $9,588
Enrollment: 24,988 | Coed
Affiliation or Control: State | IRS Status: 501(c)3
Highest Offering: Doctorate
Accreditation: NH, ART, CAATE, CEA, CLPSY, COPSY, DANCE, DMS, LIB, MT, MUS, NURSE, OT, PH, PLNG, PTA, RAD, SCPSY, SP, SW

02 Chancellor ... Dr. Mark A. MONE
05 Provost/Vice Chanc Academic Affairs ... Dr. Johannes BRITZ
10 Vice Chanc Finance & Admin Affs ... Ms. Robin L. VAN HARPEN
26 Vice Chanc Univ Relations/Comm ... Mr. Thomas L. LULJAK
46 Int Vice Provost of Research ... Dr. Mark T. HARRIS
30 Vice Chanc Development & Alumni Rel ... Dr. Patricia A. BORGER
88 Vice Chanc Global Inclusion & Engag ... Dr. Joan M. PRINCE
20 Assoc Vice Chanc Academic Affairs ... Dr. Devarajan VENUGOPALAN
20 Assoc Vice Chanc Academic Affairs ... Dr. Phyllis KING
84 Chief Enrollment Management ... Ms. Katie MIOTA
13 Assoc Vice Chanc/CIO ... Dr. Robert J. BECK
18 Assoc VC Facilities Planning/Mgmt ... Mr. Geoffrey HURTADO
102 President UWM Foundation ... Mr. David H. GILBERT
76 Dean College Health Sciences ... Dr. Timothy BEHRENS
48 Dean Architecture & Urban Planning ... Dr. Robert C. GREENSTREET
50 Dean School of Business ... Dr. Kaushal CHARI
53 Dean School of Education ... Dr. Alan R. SHOHO
54 Dean College Engr & Applied Science ... Dr. Brett PETERS
57 Dean Peck School of the Arts ... Dr. Scott EMMONS
65 Dean School of Freshwater Sciences ... Dr. J. Val KLUMP
69 Int Dean School Public Health ... Dr. Ronald PEREZ
58 Dean Graduate School ... Dr. Marija GAJDARDZISKA-JOSIFOVSKA
49 Dean College of Letters & Science ... Dr. Scott GRONERT
62 Dean School Information Studies ... Dr. Tomas LIPINSKI
66 Dean of College of Nursing ... Dr. Kim LITWACK
70 Dean School Social Welfare ... Dr. Stan STOJKOVIC
51 Dir School of Continuing Education ... Dr. Nancy NELSON
32 Dean of Students ... Mr. Adam JUSSEL
22 Dir Equity/Diversity Services ... Mr. Jamie CIMPL-WIEMER
08 Dean/Director of the Library ... Dr. Michael DOYLEN
43 Dir Legal Affairs ... Ms. Joely B. URDAN
06 Interim Registrar ... Ms. Kristin HIDEBRANDT
15 Assoc Vice Chanc Human Resources ... Mr. Timothy DANIELSON
19 Chief of University Police ... Mr. Joseph LEMIRE
88 Dir Office Sponsored Research ... Mr. Thomas MARCUSSEN
23 Dir Health Center ... Dr. Julia BONNER
108 Int Dir Assess/Institutional Rsrch ... Dr. Jonathan HANES
37 Director Financial Aid ... Mr. Timothy OPGENORTH
35 Senior Student Affairs Officer ... Ms. Kelly HAAG
41 Athletic Director ... Ms. Amanda BRAUN
88 Dir Restaurant Operations ... Mr. Scott HOFFLAND
36 Dir Career Planning & Resources ... Ms. Jean SALZER
27 Dir of Media Services ... Ms. Michelle JOHNSON
21 Assoc Vice Chanc Business & Finance ... Mr. Drew KNAB
29 Asst Vice Chanc Alumni Relations ... Ms. Amy LENSING TATE
96 Director of Procurement ... Mr. Tom SCRIVENER
114 Dir Budget & Planning ... Ms. Cindy KLUGE
105 Dir Web & Mobile Services ... Mr. Mark JACOBSON
106 Dir Online Education/E-Learning ... Ms. Laura PEDRICK
112 Dir of Gift Planning & Agreements ... Ms. Gretchen MILLER
97 Int Dean College of General Studies ... Dr. Stephen SCHMID
04 Admin Assistant to the Chancellor ... Ms. Christine ADAMS-MATT
07 Director of Admissions ... Mr. Patrick FAY
09 Director of Institutional Research ... Dr. Jonathan HANES
100 Chief of Staff ... Ms. Suzanne WESLOW
104 Director Study Abroad ... Mr. Mark ECKMAN
39 Director University Housing ... Ms. Arcetta KNAUTZ
44 Director Annual Giving ... Mr. Thomas BJORNSTAD

*University of Wisconsin-Oshkosh (B)

800 Algoma Boulevard, Oshkosh WI 54901
County: Winnebago | FICE Identification: 003920
Unit ID: 240365
Telephone: (920) 424-1234 | Carnegie Class: Masters/L
FAX Number: (920) 424-7317 | Calendar System: Semester
URL: www.uwosh.edu
Established: 1871 | Annual Undergrad Tuition & Fees (In-State): $7,621
Enrollment: 13,933 | Coed
Affiliation or Control: State | IRS Status: 501(c)3
Highest Offering: Doctorate
Accreditation: NH, ANEST, CAATE, CACREP, CSHSE, IFSAC, JOUR, MUS, NURSE, SW

02 Chancellor ... Dr. Andrew J. LEAVITT
05 Provost & Vice Chancellor ... Dr. John KOKER
20 Associate Vice Chancellor ... Ms. Carmen FAYMONVILLE
20 Asst Vice Chanc Acad Support ... Dr. Sylvia CAREY-BUTLER
121 AVC Curric Affs/Stdnt Acad Achvmt ... Dr. Charles HILL
32 Vice Chancellor Student Affairs ... Vacant
10 Vice Chanc Finance/Administration ... Dr. James FLETCHER
21 Associate Vice Chanc Admin Svcs ... Ms. Lori M. WORM
06 Registrar ... Ms. Lisa M. DANIELSON
22 Affirmative Action Officer ... Vacant
09 Director of Institutional Research ... Mr. Michael W. WATSON
38 Director of Counseling Center ... Dr. Sandy COX
13 CIO Director Info Technology ... Ms. Anne MILKOVICH
50 Dean Business ... Dr. Barbara L. RAU
66 Dean Nursing ... Dr. Judith WESTPHAL
53 Dean Education & Human Svcs ... Dr. Linda HALING
49 Interim Dean Letters & Sciences ... Dr. Colleen MCDERMOTT
102 Pres Univ of Wisc Oshkosh Foundatn ... Vacant
29 Director of Alumni Association ... Ms. Christine M. GANTNER
37 Director of Financial Aid ... Mr. Kim DONAT
26 Int Exec Dir Marketing/Comms ... Ms. Peggy BREISTER
35 Dean of Students ... Dr. Art MUNIN
58 Director Graduate Studies ... Mr. Gregory WYPISZYNSKI
07 Director of Admissions ... Mr. Paul GEDLINSKE
15 AVC Human Resources/Int Dir EO/AA ... Ms. Shawna KUETHER
18 Facilities/Physical Plant Director ... Mr. Chuck HERMES
36 Director of Career Services ... Ms. Jaime PAGE-STADLER
92 Director University Honors Program ... Dr. Laurence CARLIN
08 Interim Director Library ... Ms. Sarah NEISES
04 Administrative Asst to President ... Ms. Suzette THIBADEAU
104 Director Study Abroad ... Ms. Jennifer GRAFF
41 Athletic Director ... Mr. Darryl SIMS
90 Director Academic Computing ... Ms. Laura KNAAPEN

*University of Wisconsin-Parkside (C)

900 Wood Road, Box 2000, Kenosha WI 53141-2000
County: Kenosha | FICE Identification: 005015
Unit ID: 240374
Telephone: (262) 595-2345 | Carnegie Class: Bac-A&S
FAX Number: (262) 595-2202 | Calendar System: Semester
URL: www.uwp.edu
Established: 1968 | Annual Undergrad Tuition & Fees (In-State): $7,389
Enrollment: 4,277 | Coed
Affiliation or Control: State | IRS Status: 501(c)3
Highest Offering: Master's
Accreditation: NH, CAHIIM

02 Chancellor ... Deborah L. FORD
05 Provost/Vice Chancellor ... Robert DUCOFFE
111 Asst Chanc Univ Rels/Advancement ... Thomas KRIMMEL
20 Vice Provost Academic Affairs ... Gary WOOD
32 Vice Provost Student Affs & Enroll ... Tammy MCGUCKIN
10 Vice Pres Finance/Administration ... Scott MENKE
28 University Diversity & Inclusion ... Heather KIND-KEPPEL
35 Dean of Students ... Steve WALLNER
50 Dean Col of Bus Econ & Comput ... Dirk BALDWIN
49 Dean College of Arts & Humanities ... Lesley WALKER
81 Dean College of Nat & Hlth Sciences ... Emmanual OTU
83 Dean Social Sci & Prof Studies ... Peggy JAMES
51 Dir Continuing Educ & Cmty Engage ... Debra KARP
08 Director of the Library ... Anna STADICK
13 Interim Chief Information Officer ... Jordania LEON-JORDAN
35 Asst Dean of Students ... Damian EVANS
21 Dir Business Services/Controller ... Ann IVERSON
15 Asst Vice Chanc Human Resources ... Sheronda GLASS
19 Dir Campus Police/Public Safety ... James HELLER
37 Director Financial Aid ... Kristina KLEMENS
44 Annual Fund/Stewardship Coordinator ... Linnea BOOHER
06 Registrar ... Rhonda KIMMEL
36 Dir of Advising/Career Center ... Neil BAUMGARTNER
18 Director Facilities Management ... John BRUCH
94 Director of Women's Studies ... Linda CRAFTON
38 Dir Health/Counseling/Disability ... Renee KIRBY
40 Manager Bookstore ... Kim FLANNERY
07 Director Recruit & Admissions ... Troy MOLDENHAUER
04 Administrative Asst to Chancellor ... Franca CARLS
104 Admin Program Manager Intl Educ ... Elaine PHILIPPA
39 Asst Director Residence Life ... Adrienne BIRKHOLZ
41 Athletic Director ... Andrew GAVIN
105 Director Web Services ... Vacant
26 Chief Public Relations/Marketing ... John MIELKE

*University of Wisconsin-Platteville (D)

1 University Plaza, Platteville WI 53818-3099
County: Grant | FICE Identification: 003921
Unit ID: 240462
Telephone: (608) 342-1491 | Carnegie Class: Masters/L
FAX Number: (608) 342-1232 | Calendar System: Semester
URL: www.uwplatt.edu
Established: 1866 | Annual Undergrad Tuition & Fees (In-State): $7,796
Enrollment: 8,548 | Coed
Affiliation or Control: State | IRS Status: 501(c)3
Highest Offering: Master's
Accreditation: NH, MUS, NAIT

02 Chancellor ... Mr. Dennis J. SHIELDS
05 Act Provost/Vice Chanc Acad Affairs ... Dr. Joanne WILSON
26 Vice Chanc University Relations ... Ms. Rose M. SMYRSKI
10 Vice Chanc Admin Services ... Ms. Paige SMITH
30 Exec Dir Development/Alumni Rels ... Vacant
58 Director Graduate School ... Dr. Chanaka MENDIS
06 Registrar ... Mr. David S. KIECKHAFER
84 Vice Chanc Enroll/Student Support ... Ms. Angela M. UDELHOFEN
37 Director of Financial Aid ... Mr. John CAGE
38 Director Student Counseling ... Ms. Deirdre L. DALSING
26 Dir Univ Info/Comm/Public Rels ... Mr. Paul J. ERICKSON
41 Director Intercollegiate Athletics ... Mr. Shannon J. EALY
39 Director of Residence Life ... Mrs. Linda A. MULROY-BOWDEN
15 Director Human Resources/AA/EED ... Ms. Sarah VOSBERG
19 Director Security/Safety ... Chief Joseph M. HALLMAN
93 Dir Multicultural Educ Resource Ctr ... Ms. Angela M. MILLER
96 Director of Purchasing ... Mr. Lewis BETTINGER
08 Head Librarian ... Mr. James B. HIBBARD
18 Director of Facilities Management ... Mr. Pete D. DAVIS
36 Director of Career Center ... Mr. Trapper MITCHELL
51 Director Continuing Education ... Ms. Kerie WEDIGE
49 Int Dean Col Liberal Arts/Education ... Dr. Melissa E. GORMLEY
54 Dean Col of Engr/Math/Science ... Dr. Molly M. GRIBB
47 Dean Business Life Sci/Agric ... Dr. Wayne C. WEBER
28 Chief Diversity Officer ... Ms. Angela M. MILLER
20 Actg Asst Provost Academic Plng ... Dr. Chanaka MENDIS
13 Chief Information Officer ... Mr. Tony HAYES
51 Dean Distance/Cont & Grad Educ ... Dr. Craig WILSON
106 Asst Exec Director Alt Delivery Sys ... Mr. Michael GAU
21 Comptroller ... Ms. Cathy J. RIEDL-FARREY
35 Dean of Students ... Ms. Shanna E. CASPERSON
07 Director Admissions ... Ms. Heidi TUESCHER-GILLE
23 Admin Director Student Health Svcs ... Ms. Rachel HERMAN
88 Director PACCE ... Dr. Kevin J. BERNHARDT
121 Director Student Support Services ... Ms. Laura A. FRANKLIN
104 Director International Programs ... Ms. Donna L. ANDERSON
124 Director Retention Initiatives ... Ms. Karen MCLEER
09 Director of Institutional Research ... Dr. Debra HAGEN
108 Director of Academic Assessment ... Dr. Carolyn KELLER
25 Director Research & Sponsored Pgm ... Mr. William C. HOYER

*University of Wisconsin-River Falls (E)

410 S Third Street, River Falls WI 54022-5013
County: Pierce | FICE Identification: 003923
Unit ID: 240471
Telephone: (715) 425-3911 | Carnegie Class: Masters/M
FAX Number: (715) 425-4487 | Calendar System: Semester
URL: www.uwrf.edu
Established: 1874 | Annual Undergrad Tuition & Fees (In-State): $8,025
Enrollment: 6,105 | Coed
Affiliation or Control: State | IRS Status: 501(c)3
Highest Offering: Beyond Master's But Less Than Doctorate
Accreditation: NH, CACREP, MACTE, MUS, SP, SW

02 Chancellor ... Dr. Dean A. VAN GALEN
05 Vice Chancellor & Provost ... Dr. David TRAVIS
10 Assistant Chancellor Bus/Finance ... Ms. Elizabeth FRUEH
111 Asst Chancellor Advancement ... Mr. Richard FOY
85 Asst VC for International Programs ... Ms. Heidi SONESON
20 Associate VC Academic Affairs ... Dr. Wesley CHAPIN
32 Interim Asst VC Student Affairs ... Ms. Karla THOENNES
21 Controller ... Ms. Jody NICHOLS
47 Dean Agricult/Food/Environ Sci ... Dr. Dale GALLENBERG
53 Dean Education/Professional Studies ... Dr. Michael HARRIS
49 Dean of Arts & Sciences ... Dr. Dean YOHNK
50 Interim Dean Business & Economics ... Dr. Marina ONKEN
13 Chief Information Officer ... Mr. Joseph KMIECH
15 Human Resources Director ... Ms. Michelle DROST
18 Exec Dir Facilities/Planning/Mgmt ... Mr. Alan SYMICEK
22 Director Integrity & Compliance ... Ms. Jennifer LARIMORE
84 Director Enrollment/Student Success ... Mr. Mark R. MEYDAM
06 Registrar ... Mrs. Kelly BROWNING
07 Executive Director of Admissions ... Mrs. Sarah NELSON
46 Director Grants & Research ... Ms. Diane BENNETT
08 Director of Library ... Ms. Maureen OLLE-LAJOIE
41 Athletic Director ... Mrs. Crystal LANNING
37 Director Financial Assistance ... Mr. Robert BODE
45 Director Campus Planning ... Mr. Dale K. BRAUN
19 Director of Protective Services ... Mr. Karl FLEURY
96 Director of Purchasing Services ... Vacant
121 Dir Academic Success Center ... Ms. Kelly GRENZOW
29 Director Alumni Relations ... Mr. Pedro RENTA
09 Director of Institutional Research ... Ms. Stacy KARL
92 Director Honors Program ... Ms. Kathleen HUNZER
38 Director Student Counseling ... Ms. Alice REILLY-MYKLEBUST
56 Outreach Program Manager ... Ms. Pamela BOWEN
92 McNair Scholars Director ... Dr. Sierra HOWRY
26 Director Communications & Marketing ... Ms. Dina FASSINO
39 Director of Student Housing ... Ms. Karla THOENNES
40 Manager Bookstore ... Ms. Sherry REHNELT
04 Administrative Asst to Chancellor ... Vacant
86 Director Government Relations ... Ms. Beth SCHOMMER

*University of Wisconsin-Stevens Point (F)

2100 Main Street, Stevens Point WI 54481-3871
County: Portage | FICE Identification: 003924
Unit ID: 240480
Telephone: (715) 346-0123 | Carnegie Class: Masters/S
FAX Number: (715) 346-4841 | Calendar System: Semester
URL: www.uwsp.edu
Established: 1894 | Annual Undergrad Tuition & Fees (In-State): $8,239
Enrollment: 8,222 | Coed
Affiliation or Control: State | IRS Status: 501(c)3
Highest Offering: Doctorate
Accreditation: NH, ART, AUD, CAATE, CIDA, DANCE, DIETD, MT, MUS, NURSE, SP, SW, THEA

02 Chancellor ... Dr. Bernie PATTERSON
05 Provost & Vice Chancellor ... Dr. Greg SUMMERS
10 Vice Chancellor Business Affairs ... Ms. Kristen HENDRICKSON
32 Vice Chancellor Student Affairs ... Dr. Al THOMPSON
20 AVC for Tech/Learning/Acad Pgms ... Dr. Todd HUSPENI
100 Chief of Staff ... Dr. Robert MANZKE

15 AVC Person/Bdgt/Grants/Summer Pgms .... Dr. Katie JORE
51 Exec Dir UWSP Continuing Education ..... Mr. Wayne SORENSON
07 Director Admissions ....Vacant
37 Director of Financial Aid ....Ms. Mandy SLOWINSKI
19 Dir Safety & Loss Control ....Mr. Walter CLARK
111 Vice Chanc Univ Advancement ....Mr. Chris RICHARDS
29 Director of Alumni Affairs ....Ms. Laura GEHRMAN-ROTTIER
26 Dir Univ Relations/Comm ....Vacant
38 Director Counseling Center ....Dr. Stacey GERKEN
13 Dir of Information Technology ....Mr. Peter ZUGE
22 Director Equity/Affirmative Action ....Mr. Eric ROESLER
08 Director University Library ....Ms. Mindy KING
06 Registrar ....Mr. Ed LEE
18 Chief Facilities/Physical Plant ....Mr. Paul HASLER
36 Interim Director Career Services ....Ms. Sue KISSINGER
96 Purchasing Manager ....Ms. Heidi WALLNER
57 Dean Col Fine Arts/Commun ....Dr. Valerie CISLER
49 Interim Dean Col of Letters & Sci ....Dr. Eric YONKE
65 Dean Col of Natural Resources ....Dr. Christine L. THOMAS
107 Dean Col of Professional Studies ....Dr. Marty LOY
35 Director Student Affairs ....Dr. Al THOMPSON
04 Administrative Asst to President ....Ms. Sara BRANDL-REEVES
104 Director Study Abroad ....Dr. Eric YONKE
41 Athletic Director ....Mr. Brad DUCKWORTH
50 Dean of Business ....Dr. Kevin NEUMAN
84 Director Enrollment Management ....Ms. Carol SMITH
86 Director Government Relations ....Dr. Robert MANZKE
39 Director Student Housing ....Mr. Brian FAUST

*University of Wisconsin-Stout (A)

712 South Broadway, Menomonie WI 54751-2458
County: Dunn FICE Identification: 003915
Unit ID: 240417
Telephone: (715) 232-1122 Carnegie Class: Masters/L
FAX Number: (715) 232-1667 Calendar System: 4/1/4
URL: www.uwstout.edu
Established: 1891 Annual Undergrad Tuition & Fees (In-State): $9,457
Enrollment: 9,416 Coed
Affiliation or Control: State IRS Status: 501(c)3
Highest Offering: Beyond Master's But Less Than Doctorate
Accreditation: NH, ACBSP, ART, CACREP, CAEP, CEA, CIDA, CONST, DIETD, DIETI, MFCD

02 Chancellor ....Dr. Robert MEYER
05 Provost & Vice Chancellor ....Dr. Patrick GUILFOILE
10 Vice Chanc for Admin/Student Life ....Mr. Phil LYONS
20 Associate Vice Chancellor ....Dr. Glendali RODRIQUEZ
111 Vice Chanc Univ Advance/Alumni Rel ....Mr. Willie JOHNSON
45 Asst Chanc Plng/Assess/Rsrch/Qual ....Dr. Meridith WENTZ
49 Dean Col Arts/Humanities/Social Sci ....Dr. Maria ALM
53 Dean Col of Ed/Hosp/Hlth/Hum Sci ....Dr. Robert SALT
81 Dean Col of Science/Tech/Engr/Math ....Dr. Charles BOMAR
32 Dean of Students ....Ms. Sandi SCOTT
06 Registrar ....Mr. Josh LIND
84 Exec Dir Enrollment & Ret Svcs ....Mr. Aaron AURE
36 Director Career Services ....Mr. Bryan BARTS
08 Library Director ....Mr. Scott VRIEZE
15 Chief HR Officer & Sr Special Asst .... Ms. Kristi KRIMPELBEIN
37 Director Student Financial Aid ....Ms. Beth BOISEN
26 Director Univ Comm & External Rel ....Mr. Doug MELL
21 Director Business/Financial Svcs .. Ms. Kim SCHULTE-SHOBERG
13 Asst Chanc for Learning & IT/CIO ....Ms. Suzanne TRAXLER
38 Director Counseling Center ....Dr. Jeanne ROTHAUPT
23 Director Student Health Services ....Ms. Janice LAWRENCE-RAMAEKER
40 Director Bookstore ....Ms. Cathy CLOSE
44 Development Program Specialist ....Ms. Jennifer RUDIGER
85 Director International Educ ....Mr. Scott PIERSON
18 Director Facilities Management ....Mr. Justin UTPADEL
96 Director Purchasing ....Mr. Carley KUKUK
39 Dir University Housing ....Ms. Kathi BAKER
41 Director Athletics ....Mr. Duey NAATZ
29 Senior Alumni Relations Officer ....Ms. Mesa COVILL
117 Pgm Mgr/Dir of Safety & Risk Mgmt ....Mr. Jim UHLIR
19 Chief of Police/Director of Parking ....Mr. Jason SPETZ
106 Assoc Dir Stout Online ....Dr. Amy GULLIXSON
07 Director of Admissions ....Mr. Joel HELMS
35 Asst Director Student Life & Svcs .... Mr. Andrew CLEVELAND

*University of Wisconsin-Superior (B)

Belknap and Catlin, PO Box 2000,
Superior WI 54880-4500
County: Douglas FICE Identification: 003925
Unit ID: 240426
Telephone: (715) 394-8101 Carnegie Class: Bac-A&S
FAX Number: (715) 394-8454 Calendar System: Semester
URL: www.uwsuper.edu
Established: 1893 Annual Undergrad Tuition & Fees (In-State): $8,126
Enrollment: 2,595 Coed
Affiliation or Control: State IRS Status: 501(c)3
Highest Offering: Beyond Master's But Less Than Doctorate
Accreditation: NH, MUS, SW

02 Chancellor ....Dr. Renee WACHTER
05 Int Provost/Vice Chanc Acad Affairs ....Dr. Maria CUZZO
111 Vice Chanc University Advancement ... Ms. Jeanne E. THOMPSON
10 Vice Chanc Administration/Finance ....Mr. Jeff KAHLER
26 Dir Communications/Government Rels ....Ms. Jordan MILAN
84 Int Dir Enrollment Management ....Dr. Brenda HARMS
41 Athletic Director ....Mr. Nick BURSIK
32 Dean of Students ....Mr. Harry ANDERSON
15 Director Human Resources ....Mr. Cory KEMPF
22 Director of Diversity & Inclusion ....Dr. Jerel BENTON
06 Registrar ....Mr. Jeff KIRSHLING
07 Director of Admissions ....Mr. Jeremy NERE
21 Controller ....Mr. Robert B. WAKSDAHL
37 Director Student Financial Aid ....Ms. Donna R. DAHLVANG
51 Dir Center Cont Educ/Summer College .....Ms. Kathryn GUIMOND
106 Int Dir Library & Digital Strategy .... Mr. Michael BARTLETT
40 Director Bookstore ....Mr. Vaughn N. RUSSOM
29 Alumni Relations ....Ms. Heather THOMPSON
121 Dir Academic Advis/Career Svcs/ESC .Ms. Courtney ALEXANDER
18 Director Facilities Management ....Mr. Dustin JOHNSON
04 Executive Assistant to Chancellor ....Ms. Debbie SEGUIN
88 Executive Assistant to Provost ....Ms. Amy MISSINNE
09 Dir Institutional Research ....Ms. Emily NEUMANN
19 Director Public Safety/Parking Svc ....Mr. Gary GULBRANDSON
39 Director Residence Life ....Mr. Ryan KREUSER
13 Int Chief Informational Officer ....Mr. Thomas JANICKI
20 Dean of Academic Affairs ....Mr. Nick DANZ

*University of Wisconsin-Whitewater (C)

800 W Main, Whitewater WI 53190-1790
County: Walworth FICE Identification: 003926
Unit ID: 240189
Telephone: (262) 472-1918 Carnegie Class: Masters/L
FAX Number: (262) 472-1518 Calendar System: Semester
URL: www.uww.edu
Established: 1868 Annual Undergrad Tuition & Fees (In-State): $7,692
Enrollment: 12,434 Coed
Affiliation or Control: State IRS Status: 501(c)3
Highest Offering: Doctorate
Accreditation: NH, ART, CACREP, IPSY, MUS, SP, SW, THEA

02 Interim Chancellor ....Dr. Cheryl GREEN
05 Prov/Exec Vice Chanc Academic Affs ....Dr. Greg COOK
32 Int Vice Chancellor Student Affairs .... Dr. Artanya WESLEY
111 Int Vice Chanc Univ Advancement ....Mr. Tom STEVICK
11 Vice Chanc Administrative Affs ....Ms. Grace CRICKETTE
20 Assoc Vice Chanc Academic Affairs ....Vacant
13 Asst Vice Chanc Tech/Info Resource ....Dr. Elena POKOT
84 Asst Vice Chanc Enroll/Retention .... Mr. Matt ASCHENBRENER
09 Chief of Inst Research/Planning ....Ms. Lynsey SCHWABROW
37 Director of Financial Aid ....Mr. William TRIPPETT
26 AVC Marketing/Communications ....Ms. Sara KUHL
36 Dir of Career & Leadership Dev ....Mr. Ron BUCHHOLZ
15 Chief Human Resources Officer ....Ms. Janelle CROWLEY
85 Dir Center for Global Education ..... Ms. Candace A. CHENOWETH
44 Exec Dir University Development ....Ms. Kate LOFTUS
18 Director Facility Planning/Mgmt ....Ms. Tami MCCULLOUGH
28 Int AVC Diversity/Engagemnt/Success ....Dr. Ozalle TOMS
92 Director of Honors Program ....Dr. Elizabeth KIM
57 Dean Arts/Communication ....Dr. Eileen M. HAYES
50 Dean of Business & Economics ....Dr. John CHENOWETH
53 Int Dean Education/Prof Studies ....Dr. Robin FOX
49 Dean Letters & Sciences ....Dr. Franklin GOZA
58 Dean Grad Stds/Continuing Educ ....Dr. Seth MEISEL
04 Executive Asst to the Chancellor .... Mrs. Kari HEIDENREICH
41 Interim Athletic Director ....Mr. Ryan CALLAHAN

*University of Wisconsin-Platteville Baraboo Sauk County (D)

1006 Connie Road, Baraboo WI 53913
Telephone: (608) 355-5200 Identification: 770450
Accreditation: &NH

*University of Wisconsin-Eau Claire - Barron County (E)

1800 College Drive, Rice Lake WI 54868
Telephone: (715) 788-6244 Identification: 770457
Accreditation: &NH

*University of Wisconsin Fond du Lac (F)

400 University Drive, Fond du Lac WI 54935
Telephone: (920) 929-1100 Identification: 770451
Accreditation: &NH

*University of Wisconsin Fox Valley (G)

1478 Midway Road, Menasha WI 54952
Telephone: (920) 832-2600 Identification: 770456
Accreditation: &NH

*University of Wisconsin Marshfield/Wood County (H)

2000 West 5th Street, Marshfield WI 54449
Telephone: (715) 389-6530 Identification: 770455
Accreditation: &NH

*University of Wisconsin-Platteville Richland (I)

1200 Highway 14 West, Richland Center WI 53581-1316
Telephone: (608) 647-6186 Identification: 770458
Accreditation: &NH

*University of Wisconsin Rock County (J)

2909 Kellogg Avenue, Janesville WI 53546
Telephone: (608) 758-6565 Identification: 770452
Accreditation: &NH

*University of Wisconsin-Stevens Point at Wausau (K)

518 South 7th Avenue, Wausau WI 54401
Telephone: (715) 261-6100 Identification: 770461
Accreditation: &NH

*University of Wisconsin Washington County (L)

400 University Drive, West Bend WI 53095
Telephone: (262) 335-5200 Identification: 770462
Accreditation: &NH

*University of Wisconsin Waukesha (M)

1500 N University Drive, Waukesha WI 53188-2799
Telephone: (262) 521-5200 Identification: 770460
Accreditation: &NH

Viterbo University (N)

900 Viterbo Court, La Crosse WI 54601-8802
County: La Crosse FICE Identification: 003911
Unit ID: 240107
Telephone: (608) 796-3000 Carnegie Class: Masters/L
FAX Number: (608) 796-3050 Calendar System: Semester
URL: www.viterbo.edu
Established: 1890 Annual Undergrad Tuition & Fees: $27,970
Enrollment: 2,796 Coed
Affiliation or Control: Roman Catholic IRS Status: 501(c)3
Highest Offering: Doctorate
Accreditation: NH, ACBSP, CACREP, DIETC, DIETI, MUS, NURSE, SW

01 President ....Dr. Glena TEMPLE
05 Vice President for Academic Affairs ....Dr. Tracy STEWART
32 Vice Pres Student Affairs ....Mr. Rick TRIETLEY
84 Vice Pres Enrollment Management ....Ms. Michelle KRONFELD
10 Vice Pres Administration/Finance ....Mr. Todd M. ERICSON
111 VP Institutional Advance/Univ Rels ....Mr. Jim SALMO
21 Assistant Vice President Finance ....Mr. Eugene R. ALBERTS
07 Dean of Admission ....Vacant
42 University Chaplain ....Fr. Conrad A. TARGONSKI
66 Dean College of Nursing/Health ....Dr. Martha SCHECKEL
53 Dean Col of Education/Science/Math ....Dr. Sara COOK
49 Dean School Letters & Sciences ....Dr. Timothy SCHORR
57 Dean School of Fine Arts/Humanities ...... Dr. Timothy B. SCHORR
50 Dean Dahl School of Business ....Dr. Thomas E. KNOTHE
58 Dean Graduate/Prof/Adult Education ....Vacant
88 Director of Ethics in Leadership ....Dr. Richard L. KYTE
06 Registrar ....Ms. Kori SALASKI
08 Director of Library ....Ms. Kim OLSON-KOPP
13 Director Instruct/Info Technology .... Ms. Sarah BEARBOWER
41 Athletic Director ....Mr. Barry J. FRIED
37 Director of Financial Aid ....Ms. Terry W. NORMAN
26 Director of Marketing ....Ms. Audra NOE
29 Director Alumni Relations ....Ms. Kathleen A. DUERWACHTER
36 Director Career Planning/Placement . Ms. Beth D. DOLDER-ZIEKE
15 Director of Human Resources .... Ms. Heather BUTTERFIELD
09 Dir Assessment/Inst Research .... Ms. Naomi R. STENNES-SPIDAHL
18 Director Physical Plant ....Mr. Eugene M. MCCURDY
38 Dir Counseling/Student Development ... Ms. LeeAnn VAN VREEDE
39 Director of Residence Life .... Ms. Kirsten GABRIEL
53 Director Grad Studies in Education ..... Ms. Jeanette ARMSTRONG
19 Director Campus Safety ....Mr. Adam MALIN
07 Asst Director of Admissions ....Ms. Caitlin LOCY
04 Executive Admin Asst to President .... Ms. Sheila SEVERSON

Wisconsin Lutheran College (O)

8800 W Bluemound Road, Milwaukee WI 53226-4699
County: Milwaukee FICE Identification: 021366
Unit ID: 240338
Telephone: (414) 443-8800 Carnegie Class: Bac-Diverse
FAX Number: (414) 443-8514 Calendar System: Semester
URL: www.wlc.edu
Established: 1973 Annual Undergrad Tuition & Fees: $29,725
Enrollment: 1,114 Coed
Affiliation or Control: Independent Non-Profit IRS Status: 501(c)3
Highest Offering: Master's
Accreditation: NH, NURSE

01 President ....Dr. Daniel W. JOHNSON
05 Provost & VP of Academic Affairs ....Dr. John D. KOLANDER
32 Vice President Student Life ....Mr. Ryan OERTEL
10 Vice Pres Finance & Administration ....Mr. Gary SCHMID
26 Exec Dir Marketing & Communication ....Ms. Jennifer GARBO-SHAWHAN
30 Vice Pres Development ....Mr. Richard MANNISTO
15 Director of Human Resources ....Mr. Jon FLANAGAN
21 Asst Vice Pres Finance ....Mrs. Diane HOEHNKE
07 Vice President of Enrollment ....Mr. Lucas FAUST
06 Registrar ....Mr. Brett VALERIO
08 Director of Library Services ....Mrs. Starla C. SIEGMANN
37 Director Student Financial Aid ....Mrs. Linda L. LOEFFEL

42	Campus Pastor	Rev. Wayne SHEVEY
53	Director Teacher Education	Prof. James HOLMAN
39	Director Residential Life/Housing	Mr. Adam VOLBRECHT
41	Athletic Director	Mr. Edward NOON
88	Director of Arts Programming	Mrs. Loni BOYDL
13	Director of Information Technology	Mr. John MEYER
29	Director of Alumni Relations	Mrs. Lisa LEFFEL
88	Information Systems Analyst	Vacant
18	Chief Facilities/Physical Plant	Mr. Gary SCHMID
24	Media Services Coordinator	Mr. Tim SNYDER
04	Admin Assistant to the President	Mrs. Barb MATTEK
09	Director of Institutional Research	Mr. Rob HAHN
19	Director Security/Safety	Mr. Dan SMITH
49	Dean College of Arts & Sciences	Dr. Jarrod ERBE
107	Dean College Professional Studies	Mr. David BRIGHTSMAN
58	Dean Col Adult & Graduate Studies	Dr. Joyce NATZKE

Wisconsin School of Professional Psychology (A)

9120 W Hampton Avenue #212,
Milwaukee WI 53225-4960

County: Milwaukee — FICE Identification: 022713
Unit ID: 240213
Telephone: (414) 464-9777 — Carnegie Class: Spec-4-yr-Other Health
FAX Number: (414) 358-5590 — Calendar System: Semester
URL: www.wspp.edu
Established: 1979 — Annual Graduate Tuition & Fees: N/A
Enrollment: 78 — Coed
Affiliation or Control: Independent Non-Profit — IRS Status: 501(c)3
Highest Offering: Doctorate; No Undergraduates
Accreditation: NH, CLPSY

01	President	Dr. Kathleen M. RUSCH
05	Dean	Dr. Kristin A. JUERGENS
04	Assistant to the President	Ms. Veronica V. EGERSON
17	Director Clinical Training	Dr. Mary NEFF
08	Head Librarian	Ms. Rebecca DOUGHERTY
37	Director Student Financial Aid	Mr. Erik MOZOLIK
88	Practica/Internship Director	Dr. Susan DVORAK

*Wisconsin Technical College System (B)

PO Box 7874, Madison WI 53707-7874

County: Dane — Identification: 666185
Telephone: (608) 266-1207 — Carnegie Class: N/A
FAX Number: (608) 266-1285
URL: www.wtcsystem.edu

01	President	Dr. Morna K. FOY
03	Executive Vice President	Mr. James ZYLSTRA
05	Provost/Vice President	Dr. Colleen MCCABE
26	Dir Strategic Advancement	Mr. Conor SMYTH
04	Admin Assistant to the President	Ms. Julie DRAKE

*Blackhawk Technical College (C)

PO Box 5009, Janesville WI 53547-5009

County: Rock — FICE Identification: 005390
Unit ID: 238397
Telephone: (608) 758-6900 — Carnegie Class: Assoc/HVT-High Trad
FAX Number: (608) 757-7740 — Calendar System: Semester
URL: www.blackhawk.edu
Established: 1912 — Annual Undergrad Tuition & Fees (In-District): $4,364
Enrollment: 2,098 — Coed
Affiliation or Control: State/Local — IRS Status: 501(c)3
Highest Offering: Associate Degree
Accreditation: NH, ACFEI, ADNUR, DA, DMS, MAC, MLTAD, PTAA, RAD

02	President	Dr. Tracy P. PIERNER
05	Vice President Academic Affairs	Dr. Zahi ATALLAH
10	Vice President Admin Services	Ms. Renea L. RANGUETTE
15	Exec Director/Chief HR Officer	Mr. Brian B. GOHLKE
09	Exec Dir Institutional Research	Dr. Jon TYSSE
07	Exec Dir Student Services	Mr. Anthony LANDOWSKI
04	Asst to President/Board Liaison	Ms. Jacqueline J. PINS
13	Director IT Services	Mr. Mitch MILLER
26	Marketing & Communications Mgr	Ms. Jennifer THOMPSON
97	Dean General Education	Dr. Helen PROEBER
88	Learning Support Manager	Mr. Darian SNOW
76	Dean Health Sciences/Public Safety	Ms. Moira LAFAYETTE
19	Manager of Campus Safety & Security	Mr. Brad K. SMITH
88	EMS Fire Service & Paramedic Coord	Mr. Robert BALSAMO
72	Dean Advanced Mfg/Transport/Tech	Mr. Gary SAGANSKI
50	Dean Business	Dr. Helen PROEBER
21	Controller	Mr. Gerri DOWNING
25	Manager Grants Administration	Mr. Andrew S. MCGRATH
37	Director of Financial Aid	Vacant
06	Registrar	Ms. Brooke JOHNSON
18	Facilities Director	Mr. Steve KORMANAK
96	Purchasing Administrator	Vacant
08	Dir Teaching & Learning Resources	Ms. Lynn NEITZEL
102	Foundation Director	Mr. Tim MCKEARN
103	Director Workforce & Community Dev	Mr. Mark BOROWICZ

*Chippewa Valley Technical College (D)

620 W Clairemont Avenue, Eau Claire WI 54701-6162

County: Eau Claire — FICE Identification: 005304
Unit ID: 240116
Telephone: (715) 833-6200 — Carnegie Class: Assoc/HVT-High Non
FAX Number: (715) 833-6470 — Calendar System: Semester
URL: www.cvtc.edu
Established: 1912 — Annual Undergrad Tuition & Fees (In-District): $4,364
Enrollment: 7,134 — Coed
Affiliation or Control: Local — IRS Status: 501(c)3
Highest Offering: Associate Degree
Accreditation: NH, ACBSP, ADNUR, CAHIIM, COARC, DH, DMS, EMT, MAC, MLTAD, PTAA, RAD, SURGT

02	President	Bruce A. BARKER
05	Vice President Education	Julie FURST-BOWE
32	Vice President Student Services	Margo A. KEYS
10	Vice President Finance & Facilities	Kirk L. MOIST
13	Vice President IT/CIO	Tom J. LANGE
23	Exec Dean Health/Emgy Svcs & RF	Shelly OLSON
12	Chippewa Falls Campus Manager	Angela ECKMAN
12	Menomonie Campus Manager	Daniel LYTLE
75	Dean Skilled Trades & Engineering	Jeff SULLIVAN
06	Registrar	Jessica SCHWARTZ
84	Director of Enrollment Services	Jennifer ANDEREGG
26	Dir of Mktg/Comm & Recruitment	Joni GEROUX
88	Director of Curriculum & Prof Devel	Rachelle PHAKITTHONG
35	Student Central Manager	Laura ERICSON
35	Director of Student Life	Alisa S. SCHLEY
96	Purchasing Representative	Doug D. DEKAN
19	Public Safety Manager	Mark PROVOST
28	Diversity Manager	Mitch BARONI
88	Title IX Coordinator	Natalyn M. MARLAIRE
20	Dean Academic and Develop Services	Vacant
111	Exec Dir Institutional Advancement	Aliesha R. CROWE
108	Dir of College Effectiveness	Shana SCHMIDT
88	Intake Assessment Data Analyst	Philip V. PALSER
50	Exec Dean Bus/Arts/Science & Acad	Lynette LIVINGSTON
18	Director of Facilities	Rod BAGLEY
15	Director of Human Resources	Tam BURGAU
21	Director of Finance	Sara J. NICK
47	Dean Agric/Energy/Transportation	Adam WEHLING
88	Criminal Justice Director	Eric ANDERSON
88	Curr Spec/Instr Designer	Jodi RUST
76	Assoc Dean of Health	Amy OLSON
04	Executive Asst to President	Lauren SULLIVAN

*Fox Valley Technical College (E)

1825 N Bluemound Drive, Appleton WI 54914-1643

County: Outagamie — FICE Identification: 009744
Unit ID: 238722
Telephone: (920) 735-5600 — Carnegie Class: Assoc/HVT-High Non
FAX Number: (920) 735-2582 — Calendar System: Semester
URL: www.fvtc.edu
Established: 1967 — Annual Undergrad Tuition & Fees (In-District): $4,565
Enrollment: 11,660 — Coed
Affiliation or Control: State/Local — IRS Status: 501(c)3
Highest Offering: Associate Degree
Accreditation: NH, ACFEI, ADNUR, CAHIIM, DA, DH, EMT, IFSAC, MAC, OTA, PNUR

02	President	Dr. Susan A. MAY
03	Executive Vice President	Mr. Chris MATHENY
18	VP Facilities & Operations	Ms. Jill MCEWEN
32	Associate VP Student Services	Ms. Elizabeth BURNS
15	VP Human Resources	Ms. Deb GORMAN
10	VP Financial Services/CFO	Ms. Amy VAN STRATEN
13	VP Information Tech/CIO	Mr. Troy KOHL
97	Dean General Studies	Dr. Jennifer LANTER
47	Dean Mfg/Construction & Agric	Mr. Steve STRAUB
102	Exec Dir FVTC Foundation/Cmty Rels	Ms. Rebecca BOULANGER
12	Associate VP Regional Campuses	Ms. Deb HEATH
37	Director Student Financial Svcs	Ms. Stacy DORAN
06	Registrar	Mr. Brian BUSS
26	Director College Marketing	Ms. Barb DREGER
118	Director Compensation & Benefits	Ms. Barb KIEFFER
88	Director Venture Center	Ms. Amy PIETSCH
108	Director College Effectiveness	Dr. Patti FROHRIB

*Gateway Technical College (F)

3520 30th Avenue, Kenosha WI 53144-1690

County: Kenosha — FICE Identification: 005389
Unit ID: 238759
Telephone: (262) 564-2200 — Carnegie Class: Assoc/HVT-High Non
FAX Number: (262) 564-2201 — Calendar System: Semester
URL: www.gtc.edu
Established: 1911 — Annual Undergrad Tuition & Fees (In-District): $4,454
Enrollment: 9,166 — Coed
Affiliation or Control: State/Local — IRS Status: 501(c)3
Highest Offering: Associate Degree
Accreditation: NH, ACBSP, ADNUR, CAHIIM, DA, MAC, PTAA, SURGT

02	President	Dr. Bryan D. ALBRECHT
05	Exec VP/Prov/Chief Academic Officer	Ms. Zina HAYWOOD
11	Senior VP of Operations	Mr. Willaim WHYTE
12	Dean Racine Campus	Ms. Cyndean JENNINGS
12	Dean Elkhorn Campus	Mr. Michael O'DONNELL
12	Dean Kenosha Campus	Mr. Gary FLYNN
86	VP Government/Community Relations	Ms. Stephanie SKLBA
103	VP Workforce/Economic Develop Div	Dr. Matthew JANISIN
32	Vice Pres Student Svcs & Enroll Mgt	Ms. Stacy RILEY
108	Asst Provost/VP Inst Effectiveness	Dr. John THIBODEAU
121	Dean Learning Success	Dr. Tammi SUMMERS
06	Registrar	Ms. Chrystal MOEZ
09	Associate VP Institutional Research	Ms. Anne WHYNOTT
26	Director Marketing & Communications	Ms. Kristin GUNIA
07	Director of College Access	Ms. Amanda VIRZI
21	Controller	Ms. Sharon JOHNSON
37	Director Student Financial Aid	Ms. Pamela LOWREY
28	Director of Human Resources	Ms. Debbie MILLER
102	Foundation Executive Director	Dr. Jennifer CHARPENTIER
13	Chief Info Technology Officer (CIO)	Mr. Jeff ROBSHAW
04	Executive Assistant to President	Ms. Mary HARPE
19	Director Security/Safety	Mr. Thomas COUSINO
29	Director Alumni Affairs	Ms. Celeste HENKEN
50	Dean Sch of Business/Transportation	Mr. Joseph FULLINGTON
54	Dean Sch of Manufacturing/Engr/IT	Mr. Ray KOUKARI
08	District Library Manager	Mr. Gary FLYNN
15	VP of Human Resources	Ms. Jacqueline MORRIS

*Lakeshore Technical College (G)

1290 North Avenue, Cleveland WI 53015-1414

County: Manitowoc — FICE Identification: 009194
Unit ID: 239008
Telephone: (920) 693-1000 — Carnegie Class: Assoc/HVT-High Non
FAX Number: (920) 693-8078 — Calendar System: Semester
URL: www.gotoltc.edu
Established: 1913 — Annual Undergrad Tuition & Fees (In-District): $4,247
Enrollment: 2,734 — Coed
Affiliation or Control: State/Local — IRS Status: 501(c)3
Highest Offering: Associate Degree
Accreditation: NH, ACFEI, ADNUR, CAHIIM, EMT, PNUR, RAD

02	President	Dr. Paul CARLSEN
04	Executive Assistant	Ms. Heidi SOODSMA
05	Vice President of Instruction	Mr. James LEMEROND
32	Vice President of Student Success	Ms. Polly ABTS
15	Executive Dir of Human Resources	Ms. Shikara BEAUDOIN
10	Chief Financial Officer	Ms. Molly O'CONNELL
09	Quality/Continuous Improvement Mgr	Ms. Cheryl TERP
26	Vice President of Outreach	Ms. Julie MIRECKI
28	Multicultural Student Advocate	Ms. Nicole YANG
47	Dean of Agricultural and Manuf	Ms. Sheila SCHETTER
50	Dean Business & Technology	Mr. Doug HAMM
97	Dean General & Pre-College Educ	Ms. Meredith SAUER
84	Enrollment Services Manager	Mr. George HENZE
37	Financial Aid Manager	Ms. Jessica HEMENWAY
121	Director of Student Resources	Ms. Foua HANG
18	Physical Plant Supervisor	Mr. Bryan KOESER
08	Library Manager	Ms. Kelly CARPENTER
11	Vice President of Admin Services	Ms. Brenda RIESTERER
45	Vice President of Strategy	Ms. Tanya WASMER
111	Vice President of Advancement	Ms. Kristin LIPHART
76	Dean of Health & Human Services	Mr. Christopher SCHATZ
19	Dean of Public Safety & Energy	Mr. Ryan SKABROUD
66	Assoc Dean of Nursing & Nursing Ast	Ms. Lori HERTEL
88	Director of Student Outreach	Ms. Rhetta BAJCZYK
88	Dual Credit Manager	Ms. Courtney GAYNOR
88	Organizational Development Manager	Ms. Melissa BRAESCH
88	Accommodations Services Manager	Mr. Patrick NEUENFELDT
88	Testing Services Manager	Ms. Susan KINNESTON
88	Business/Mfg Assessment Svcs Mgr	Mr. William PERSINGER
25	Grant & Research Specialist	Ms. Shauna NISCHIK
121	Academic Advisor/Counselor	Ms. Kristi IRVING

*Madison Area Technical College (H)

1701 Wright Street, Madison WI 53704-2599

County: Dane — FICE Identification: 004007
Unit ID: 238263
Telephone: (608) 246-6100 — Carnegie Class: Bac/Assoc-Assoc Dom
FAX Number: (608) 246-6880 — Calendar System: Semester
URL: www.madisoncollege.edu
Established: 1912 — Annual Undergrad Tuition & Fees (In-District): $4,407
Enrollment: 15,410 — Coed
Affiliation or Control: State/Local — IRS Status: 501(c)3
Highest Offering: Associate Degree
Accreditation: NH, ACFEI, ADNUR, COARC, CSHSE, DH, EMT, MAC, MLTAD, OPTT, OTA, PTAA, RAD, SURGT

02	President	Dr. Jack E. DANIELS, III
04	Exec Asst to the President	Ms. Kristin ROLLING
05	Provost	Dr. Turina BAKKEN
32	Vice President Student Affairs	Dr. Howard SPEARMAN
26	Dir Commun/Strategic Marketing	Mr. Cary R. HEYER
45	VP Institutional Learning/Effect	Dr. Timothy L. CASPER
11	CFO/VP of Administrative Services	Mr. Mark THOMAS
15	Asst VP Human Resources	Ms. Rosemary BUSCHHAUS
13	Chief Information Officer	Mr. Shawn BELLING
103	Dean Workforce Education	Ms. Schauna RASMUSSEN
88	Dean Academic Advancement	Mr. Christopher P. VANDALL
54	Asst VP of Academic Operations	Ms. Denise REIMER
49	Dean Arts & Sciences	Dr. Todd H. STEBBINS
50	Dean Business & Applied Arts	Ms. Erin KOHL
76	Dean Health Education	Dr. Kendricks HOOKER
88	Asst VP for Strategic Prtnrshp Innv	Mr. Bryan M. WOODHOUSE
88	Dir of STEM Center	Mr. Kevin MIRUS
35	Asst VP/Dean of Students & SDS	Dr. Geraldo G. VILACRUZ
88	Asst VP Strat Academic Initiative	Dr. Shawna M. CARTER
35	Director Student Life	Ms. Renee M. ALFANO
12	Asst VP Regional Campuses	Mr. James FALCO
88	Dean of Faculty	Ms. Sarah FRITZ
36	Dir College & Career Transitions	Ms. Juanita COMEAU
06	Registrar	Mr. Bill W. DOUGHERTY
08	Director Library Services	Ms. Julie C. GORES

41 Athletic Director .... Mr. Stephen C. HAUSER
114 AVP Budget and Administration .... Ms. Sylvia RAMIREZ
22 Dir Disability Res and Testing .... Mr. Scott RITTER
10 Controller .... Ms. Lauralynn M. GRIGG
25 Director Grants & Special Projects .... Ms. Emily J. SANDERS
18 Director Facilities Services .... Mr. Michael M. STARK
102 Chief Exec Officer Foundation .... Ms. Tammy THAYER
09 Dir Inst Research & Effectiveness .... Mr. Ali R. ZARRINNAM
12 Dean Goodman South .... Ms. Valentina AHEDO
21 Assistant Controller .... Ms. Dorothy CONDUAH
37 Director Financial Aid .... Mr. Keyimani ALFORD
28 VP Equity/Diversity/Cmty Relations .... Ms. Lucia NUNEZ
19 Director Public Safety .... Mr. John FLANNERY

*Mid-State Technical College (A)

500 32nd Street N, Wisconsin Rapids WI 54494-5599
County: Wood FICE Identification: 005380
Unit ID: 239220
Telephone: (715) 422-5300 Carnegie Class: Assoc/HVT-Mix Trad/Non
FAX Number: (715) 422-5345 Calendar System: Semester
URL: www.mstc.edu
Established: 1967 Annual Undergrad Tuition & Fees (In-District): $4,432
Enrollment: 2,749 Coed
Affiliation or Control: State/Local IRS Status: 501(c)3
Highest Offering: Associate Degree
Accreditation: NH, ADNUR, CAHIIM, COARC, EMT, MAC, SURGT

02 President .... Dr. Shelly MONDEIK
05 Int Vice President of Academics .... Dr. Sandy KIDDOO
32 Vice President of Student Services .... Dr. Mandy LANG
10 Vice President Finance/Facilities .... Mr. Robb FISH
15 Vice President Human Resources .... Ms. Karen BRZEZINSKI
103 Vice President Workforce/Econ Dev .... Dr. Bobbi DAMROW
97 Dean Gen Educ & Learning Resource .... Ms. Beth SMITH
50 Dean Business & Technology .... Dr. Missy SKURZEWSKI-SERVANT
65 Dean Trans/Agric/Nat Res & Constr .... Mr. Ronald ZILLMER
88 Dean Health .... Ms. Colleen KANE
75 Dean Advanced Man & Engineering .... Mr. Alan JAVOROSKI
76 Dean Protective & Human Services .... Ms. Barb JASCOR
12 Dean Stevens Point Campus .... Mr. Volker GAUL
12 Dean Marshfield Campus .... Ms. Brenda DILLENBURG
84 Dean Enrollment Management .... Ms. Kerry FROEHLICH-MUELLER
35 Dean Student Support .... Ms. Christina LORGE-GROVER
26 Director Marketing & Communication .... Ms. Kolina STIEBER
102 Director Foundation and Alumni .... Ms. Jill STECKBAUER
18 Director Facilities/Procurement .... Mr. Matt SCHNEIDER
06 Registrar .... Ms. Denise BORLAND
04 Executive Administrative Assistant .... Ms. Angela SUSA
37 Manager Financial Aid .... Ms. Mary STRUTHERS

*Milwaukee Area Technical College (B)

700 W State Street, Milwaukee WI 53233-1443
County: Milwaukee FICE Identification: 003866
Unit ID: 239248
Telephone: (414) 297-6600 Carnegie Class: Assoc/HVT-High Trad
FAX Number: (414) 297-7990 Calendar System: Semester
URL: www.matc.edu
Established: 1912 Annual Undergrad Tuition & Fees (In-District): $4,589
Enrollment: 14,012 Coed
Affiliation or Control: Local IRS Status: 501(c)3
Highest Offering: Associate Degree
Accreditation: NH, ACFEI, ADNUR, AT, COARC, CVT, DH, DIETT, EMT, FUSER, MAC, MLTAD, OTA, PNUR, PTAA, RAD, SURGT

02 President .... Dr. Vicki J. MARTIN
05 Provost .... Dr. Mohammad DAKWAR
32 Vice Pres Student Services .... Vacant
10 Vice President of Finance .... Mr. Jeffrey HOLLOW
43 Vice President & Legal Counsel .... Ms. Janice FALKENBERG
13 Assoc VP Information Technology .... Mr. Thomas HAUSMANN
23 Dean Health Occupation .... Dr. Kelly DRIES
50 Int Dean Business & Graphic Arts .... Dr. Richard BUSALACCHI
24 General Manager Public Television .... Mr. Bohdan ZACHARY
35 Director Student Life .... Vacant
08 Director of Library .... Mr. Eguan BURROWS
37 Director Admissions/Financial Aid .... Vacant
90 Director Technical Services .... Mr. Michael GAVIN
21 Controller .... Ms. Eva KUETHER
19 Director Public Safety .... Ms. Aisha BARKOW
06 Registrar .... Ms. Sarah ADAMS
09 Director Institutional Research .... Dr. Yan WANG
84 Manager Recruitment .... Ms. Sophia WILLIAMS
29 Vice Pres Coll Advancement/Ext Comm .... Ms. Laura BRAY
38 Director Counseling & Advising Svcs .... Mr. Walter LANIER
26 Coord Design Center/Mktg & Comm .... Ms. Kathryn KAESERMANN
96 Procurement Manager .... Ms. Laura MOORE
41 Coordinator Athletics .... Mr. Randy CASEY

*Moraine Park Technical College (C)

235 N National Avenue, Fond Du Lac WI 54936-1940
County: Fond Du Lac FICE Identification: 009256
Unit ID: 239372
Telephone: (920) 922-8611 Carnegie Class: Assoc/HVT-High Non
FAX Number: (920) 929-2471 Calendar System: Semester
URL: www.morainepark.edu
Established: 1967 Annual Undergrad Tuition & Fees (In-District): $4,403
Enrollment: 5,012 Coed
Affiliation or Control: State/Local IRS Status: 501(c)3
Highest Offering: Associate Degree
Accreditation: NH, ADNUR, CAHIIM, COARC, EMT, MAC, MLTAD, RAD, SURGT

02 President .... Bonnie BAERWALD
05 Vice President Academic Affairs .... James R. EDEN
10 VP Finance and Administration .... Carrie KASUBASKI
32 Vice President Student Services .... James BARRETT
15 Vice President Human Resources .... Kathleen M. BROSKE
13 Chief Information Officer .... Jerry RICHARDS
20 Dean of Applied Technology & Trades .... Fred RICE
88 Dean of Health & Human Services .... Kristin M. FINNEL
97 Dean of General Education .... Lane HOLTE
103 Dean Economic & Workforce Devel .... JoAnn HALL
12 Dean of the West Bend Campus .... Peter J. RETTLER
35 Dean of Students .... Scott LIEBURN
06 Registrar .... Lane HOLTE
111 Director of College Advancement .... Dana BOURLAND
26 Dir Marketing/Communications .... Patricia LEHN
09 Director of Inst Effectiveness .... Bojan LJUBENKO
21 Director of Finance .... Tara WENDT
08 Library Services Coordinator .... Hans BAIERL
18 Facilities Operation Manager .... Benjamin HILL
96 Purchasing Manager .... Timothy KEENAN
19 Security Manager .... John FAEH

*Nicolet Area Technical College (D)

5364 College Drive, PO Box 518,
Rhinelander WI 54501-0518
County: Oneida FICE Identification: 005384
Unit ID: 239442
Telephone: (715) 365-4493 Carnegie Class: Assoc/HVT-High Non
FAX Number: (715) 365-4445 Calendar System: Semester
URL: www.nicoletcollege.edu
Established: 1967 Annual Undergrad Tuition & Fees (In-State): $4,404
Enrollment: 1,338 Coed
Affiliation or Control: State IRS Status: 501(c)3
Highest Offering: Associate Degree
Accreditation: NH, ADNUR, MAC

02 President .... Dr. Richard R. NELSON
05 Executive VP Acad & Student Affs .... Ms. Kathleen FERREL
10 Chief Financial Officer .... Mr. John VAN DE LOO
15 Director of Human Resources .... Dr. Dan GROLEAU
13 CIO .... Mr. Greg MILJEVICH
66 Dean of Health Occupations .... Ms. Candy DAILEY
103 Exec Dir Economic/Community Dev .... Ms. Sandy BISHOP
49 Dean of Univ Transfer/Liberal Arts .... Ms. Laura WIND-NORTON
88 Dean of Trade/Industry/Apprentice .... Mr. Jeff LABS
19 Assoc Dean/Dir Pub Safety/Security .... Mr. Jason GOELDNER
18 Director of Facilities .... Mr. Pete VANNEY
37 Director of Financial Aid .... Ms. Jill PRICE
102 Foundation Executive Director .... Ms. Heather SCHALLOCK
108 Dir Inst Effectiveness/Staff Dev .... Ms. Kelly HAVERKAMPF
45 Managing Dir Strategic Initiative .... Mr. Chuck KOMP
06 Registrar .... Ms. Leanne VIGUE-MIRANDA
04 Exec Asst to President/Board .... Ms. Anne E. BONACK
08 Manager of Library Services .... Ms. Nora CRAVEN
28 Diversity and Tribal Outreach Coord .... Ms. Susan CRAZY THUNDER

*Northcentral Technical College (E)

1000 W Campus Drive, Wausau WI 54401-1880
County: Marathon FICE Identification: 005387
Unit ID: 239460
Telephone: (715) 675-3331 Carnegie Class: Assoc/HVT-High Non
FAX Number: (715) 675-9776 Calendar System: Semester
URL: www.ntc.edu
Established: 1912 Annual Undergrad Tuition & Fees (In-District): $3,553
Enrollment: 5,167 Coed
Affiliation or Control: Local IRS Status: 501(c)3
Highest Offering: Associate Degree
Accreditation: NH, ADNUR, DH, EMT, MAC, MLTAD, RAD, SURGT

02 President .... Dr. Lori A. WEYERS
03 Executive Vice President .... Dr. Jeannie M. WORDEN
05 VP for Learning .... Dr. Darren ACKLEY
10 VP of Finance & General Counsel .... Ms. Roxanne LUTGEN
111 VP College Advance & Org Dev .... Dr. Vicki JEPPESEN
13 Chief Information Officer .... Dr. Chet A. STREBE
15 AVP of Human Resources .... Ms. Cher VINK
18 AVP of Facilities Management .... Mr. Rob ELLIOTT
26 AVP Mktg/PR & Leg Advoc .... Mrs. Katrina FELCH
107 Dean of Academic Excellence .... Dr. Emily STUCKENBRUCK
88 Dean Public Safety .... Ms. Sara GOSSFELD-BENZING
47 Dean Agricultural Sciences .... Dr. Vicky PIETZ
54 Dean Engineering and Technology .... Dr. Christopher SEVERSON
50 Dean Business and Virtual College .... Ms. Brandy BREUCKMAN
76 Dean of Health Sciences .... Ms. Marlene ROBERTS
22 Employment Coord/Affirm Action Ofcr .... Ms. Cindy THELEN
88 Dir Accred & Career Pathways .... Dr. Bonnie OSNESS
32 Director of Student Development .... Mr. Shawn P. SULLIVAN
19 Director of Security .... Mr. Jordan SCHULT
06 Registrar .... Mr. Nick BLANCHETTE
84 Dean of College Enrollment .... Dr. Sarah DILLON
121 Dean of Student Success .... Dr. Shannon LIVINGSTON
51 Dean Business & Industry/Cont Educ .... Dr. Brad GAST
04 Executive Asst to President .... Mrs. Nikki KOPP
09 Dean Acad and College Effectiveness .... Dr. Angela M. SERVI
37 Director Student Financial Aid .... Mr. Jeff CICHON
75 Dean Adv Manufacturing & Transport .... Dr. Greg CISEWSKI
97 Dean of General Studies .... Ms. Brooke SCHINDLER

*Northeast Wisconsin Technical College (F)

PO Box 19042, 2740 W Mason Street,
Green Bay WI 54307-9042
County: Brown FICE Identification: 005301
Unit ID: 239488
Telephone: (920) 498-5444 Carnegie Class: Assoc/HVT-Mix Trad/Non
FAX Number: (920) 498-6260 Calendar System: Semester
URL: www.nwtc.edu
Established: 1913 Annual Undergrad Tuition & Fees (In-District): $4,479
Enrollment: 11,488 Coed
Affiliation or Control: State/Local IRS Status: 501(c)3
Highest Offering: Associate Degree
Accreditation: NH, ACBSP, ADNUR, CAHIIM, COARC, DA, DH, DMS, EMT, MAC, MLTAD, PNUR, PTAA, RAD, SURGT

02 President .... Dr. H. Jeffrey RAFN
05 Vice President of Learning .... Dr. Kathryn ROGALSKI
32 Vice President of Student Services .... Dr. Colleen SIMPSON
111 Vice Pres of College Advancement .... Ms. Karen SMITS
15 Vice President of Human Resources .... Ms. Lisa MAAS
13 Chief Information Officer .... Mr. Daniel MINCHEFF
10 VP Business & Finance .... Mr. Robert MATHEWS
12 Dean Regional Learning .... Ms. Jan SCOVILLE
50 Dean College of Business .... Vacant
76 Dean Health Science .... Mr. Scott ANDERSON
72 Dean Trades & Engr Technologies .... Vacant
97 Dean General Education .... Ms. Michaeline SCHMIT
88 Dean Public Safety .... Mr. Randy SMITH
20 Dean Learning Solutions .... Ms. Anne KAMPS
103 Int Dean Corp Training/Economic Dev .... Ms. Meridith JAEGER
38 Dean of Student Success .... Ms. Vickie LOCK
07 Dean Enrollment Services/Registrar .... Mr. Mark FRANKS
37 Financial Aid Director .... Ms. Emily YSEBAERT
102 Foundation Director .... Ms. Crystal HARRISON
40 Director Bookstore .... Mr. Patrick SORELLE
26 Public Relations/Comm Specialist .... Ms. Kathleen FRYDA
18 Director of Facilities .... Mr. Chet LAMERS
08 Manager Library Services .... Ms. Kim LAPLANTE
104 Mgr Student Involvement/Intl Pgm .... Ms. Megan POPKEY
04 Administrative Asst to President .... Ms. Mary Jo TILOT
09 Institutional Researcher .... Mr. Jeff GREBINOSKI
105 Director Web Services .... Ms. Erica PLAZA
28 Director of Diversity .... Mr. Mohammed BEY
19 Director Security/Safety .... Mr. Randy SCHULTZ

*Southwest Wisconsin Technical College (G)

1800 Bronson Boulevard, Fennimore WI 53809-9778
County: Grant FICE Identification: 007669
Unit ID: 239910
Telephone: (608) 822-3262 Carnegie Class: Assoc/HVT-High Non
FAX Number: (608) 822-6019 Calendar System: Semester
URL: www.swtc.edu
Established: 1967 Annual Undergrad Tuition & Fees (In-District): $4,404
Enrollment: 2,367 Coed
Affiliation or Control: State/Local IRS Status: Exempt
Highest Offering: Associate Degree
Accreditation: NH, ADNUR, CAHIIM, MAC, MEAC, MLTAD, PTAA

02 President .... Dr. Jason S. WOOD
10 VP for Administrative Services .... Mr. Caleb WHITE
05 Chief Academic Officer .... Dr. Kathleen E. GARRITY
47 Dean of Industry/Trades/Agriculture .... Dr. Derek DACHELET
32 Chief Student Services Officer .... Dr. Kathleen E. GARRITY
15 Chief Human Resources Officer .... Ms. Krista WEBER
108 Manager of College Effectiveness .... Ms. Mandy HENKEL
111 Exec Dir of Advancement/Foundation .... Ms. Holly CLENDENEN
13 Director of IT Services .... Mr. Heath AHNEN
101 Executive Services Director .... Ms. Karen M. CAMPBELL
18 Director of Facilities .... Mr. Dan IMHOFF
37 Financial Aid Manager .... Ms. Corabeth HALVERSON
19 Director of Public Safety .... Ms. Kris WUBBEN
88 Dir of Business & Industry Services .... Ms. Amy CHARLES
20 Innovative/Alternative Learning Dir .... Ms. Kim MAIER
21 Controller .... Ms. Kelly KELLY
88 Director of Pre-College Programs .... Ms. Julie PLUEMER
06 Registrar .... Ms. Danielle SEIPPEL
88 Dining Services Manager .... Mr. Rex SMITH
76 Dean of Health Occupations/Service .... Ms. Cynde LARSEN

*Waukesha County Technical College (H)

800 Main Street, Pewaukee WI 53072-4696
County: Waukesha FICE Identification: 005294
Unit ID: 240125
Telephone: (262) 691-5566 Carnegie Class: Assoc/HVT-High Non
FAX Number: (262) 691-5593 Calendar System: Semester
URL: www.wctc.edu
Established: 1923 Annual Undergrad Tuition & Fees (In-District): $4,405
Enrollment: 7,696 Coed
Affiliation or Control: State/Local IRS Status: 501(c)3
Highest Offering: Associate Degree
Accreditation: NH, ACFEI, ADNUR, CAHIIM, DH, EMT, MAC, SURGT

02 President .... Ms. Kaylen A. BETZIG
05 VP Learning .... Dr. Bradley PIAZZA

32 VP Student Services ..... Ms. Nicole GAHAGAN
10 VP Finance ..... Dr. Jane KITTEL
15 VP Human Resource Svcs ..... Mr. David BROWN
26 VP Strat Mktg Innov & Effectiveness .. Dr. Ann KRAUSE-HANSON
13 Chief Information Officer ..... Mr. Rodney NOBLES
102 Dir Foundation/Corporate Relations ..... Ms. Ellen PHILLIPS
50 Dean Business Occupations ..... Ms. Kim EHLERT
75 Dean Industrial Occupations ..... Mr. Michael SHIELS
88 Dean Service Occupations ..... Dr. Greg WEST
97 Dean Acad Foundation & General Stds ..... Ms. Bethany LEONARD
76 Dean Health Occupations ..... Ms. Sandra STEARNS
27 Director PR/Marketing & Outreach ..... Mr. Andrew PALEN
18 Director Facilities Services ..... Mr. Jeffrey LEVERENZ
06 Registrar ..... Ms. Rachel BURLING
38 Dir Counslng/Advisng/Stdnt Access ..... Dr. Christopher DAOOD
36 Mgr Career Development Services ..... Ms. Debra WEBER
51 Exec Dir Corporate Training Ctr ..... Mr. Russ ROBERTS
07 Mgr Admissions/Testing Svcs ..... Ms. Kathleen KAZDA
88 Director Academic Excellence ..... Mr. Randall COOROUGH
25 Director of Grants & Contracts ..... Ms. Linda J. MILLER
37 Manager Financial Aid ..... Mr. Justin KEHRING
35 Coordinator Student Life ..... Mr. Jonathan N. PEDRAZA
08 Director of Library Services ..... Ms. Amy MANION
19 Environ Health & Safety Supervisor ..... Mr. Bruce NEUMANN
27 Specialist Public Relations ..... Ms. Michelle NELSON
96 Purchasing Specialist ..... Ms. Victoria NASH
28 Diversity Coordinator ..... Mr. Rolando DELEON
40 Bookstore Manager ..... Mr. James DRAEGER
22 Director Compliance & Equity ..... Ms. Sherry SIMMONS

*Western Technical College (A)

400 N Seventh Street, La Crosse WI 54601-3368
County: La Crosse FICE Identification: 003840
Unit ID: 240170
Telephone: (608) 785-9200 Carnegie Class: Assoc/HVT-High Trad
FAX Number: (608) 785-9205 Calendar System: Trimester
URL: www.westerntc.edu
Established: 1912 Annual Undergrad Tuition & Fees (In-District): $4,403
Enrollment: 4,108 Coed
Affiliation or Control: State/Local IRS Status: 501(c)3
Highest Offering: Associate Degree
Accreditation: NH, ADNUR, CAHIIM, COARC, DA, EMT, MAC, MLTAD, OTA, PTAA, RAD, SURGT

02 President ..... Dr. Roger STANFORD
10 Vice President Finance/Operations ..... Mr. Wade HACKBARTH
05 Vice President of Academic Affairs ..... Ms. Kathleen LINAKER
32 VP Student Service & Engagement ..... Ms. Amy THORNTON
12 Director of Regional Workforce Dev ..... Ms. Patti BALACEK
102 Executive Director Foundation ..... Mr. Michael SWENSON
37 Financial Aid Manager ..... Ms. Jerolyn R. GRANDALL
21 Controller ..... Ms. Amy SCHMIDT
103 Manager of Business & Industry Svcs ..... Ms. Angie MARTIN
07 Director Outreach & Admissions Svcs ..... Ms. Debra HETHER
36 Director Advising & Career Service ..... Ms. Barb KELSEY
124 Director of Counseling & Retention .. Ms. Ann BRANDAU-HYNEK
06 Registrar ..... Ms. Sandy PETERSON
35 Dean of Students ..... Ms. Shelley MCNEELY
72 Dean Integrated Technology ..... Mr. Josh GAMER
76 Dean Health & Public Safety ..... Mr. Kevin DEAN
97 Dean General Education ..... Ms. Diane NEEFE
50 Dean Business Education ..... Mr. Gary BROWN
13 Director Information Technology ..... Ms. Joan PIERCE
26 Director Marketing & Communications ..... Ms. Julie LEMON
29 Manager Alumni Relations ..... Ms. Sally EMERSON
40 Bookstore Manager ..... Mr. David R. WIGNES
15 Director Human Resources ..... Mr. John HEATH
09 Exec Dir Planning & Org Excellence ..... Ms. Tracy DRYDEN

*Wisconsin Indianhead Technical College (B)

505 Pine Ridge Drive, Shell Lake WI 54871-9300
County: Washburn FICE Identification: 011824
Unit ID: 240198
Telephone: (715) 468-2815 Carnegie Class: Assoc/HVT-Mix Trad/Non
FAX Number: (715) 468-2819 Calendar System: Semester
URL: www.witc.edu
Established: 1968 Annual Undergrad Tuition & Fees (In-State): $4,729
Enrollment: 3,021 Coed
Affiliation or Control: State IRS Status: Exempt
Highest Offering: Associate Degree
Accreditation: NH, ADNUR, CAHIIM, OTA

02 President ..... Mr. John WILL
10 VP Admin Svcs/Chief Financial Svcs ..... Mr. Steven DECKER
05 Vice President Academic Affairs ..... Ms. Stephanie ERDMANN
32 Vice President Student Affairs ..... Mr. Steve BITZER
103 VP Workforce Dev/Advancement ..... Mr. Craig FOWLER
09 VP Institutional Effectiveness ..... Ms. Susan YOHNK LOCKWOOD
13 Sr Director Technology Services ..... Mr. James DAHLBERG
37 Director Financial Aid ..... Mr. Terry KLEIN
06 Registrar ..... Mr. Shane EVENSON
84 Director of Enrollment Services ..... Vacant
26 Director Marketing/Communications ..... Ms. Jena VOGTMAN
15 Director Human Resources ..... Ms. Amanda GOHDE

*Chippewa Valley Technical College-Gateway (C)

2320 Alpine Road, Eau Claire WI 54703
Telephone: (715) 874-4600 Identification: 770420
Accreditation: &NH

*Chippewa Valley Technical College River Falls Campus (D)

500 South Wasson Lane, River Falls WI 54722
Telephone: (715) 425-3301 Identification: 770423
Accreditation: &NH

*Chippewa Valley Technical College-West (E)

4000 Campus Road, Eau Claire WI 54703
Telephone: (715) 852-1394 Identification: 770421
Accreditation: &NH

*Madison Area Technical College Commercial Avenue Education Center (F)

2125 Commercial Avenue, Madison WI 53704
Telephone: (608) 246-6100 Identification: 770436
Accreditation: &NH

*Madison Area Technical College Downtown Education Center (G)

211 North Carroll Street, Madison WI 53703
Telephone: (608) 246-6100 Identification: 770437
Accreditation: &NH

*Madison Area Technical College Fort Atkinson (H)

827 Banker Road, Fort Atkinson WI 53538
Telephone: (920) 568-7200 Identification: 770435
Accreditation: &NH

*Madison Area Technical College Portage (I)

330 West Collins Street, Portage WI 53901
Telephone: (608) 745-3100 Identification: 770438
Accreditation: &NH

*Madison Area Technical College Reedsburg (J)

300 Alexander Avenue, Reedsburg WI 53959
Telephone: (608) 524-7800 Identification: 770439
Accreditation: &NH

*Madison Area Technical College Watertown (K)

1300 West Main Street, Watertown WI 53098
Telephone: (920) 206-8000 Identification: 770440
Accreditation: &NH

*Moraine Park Technical College (L)

700 Gould Street, Beaver Dam WI 53916
Telephone: (920) 887-1428 Identification: 770446
Accreditation: &NH

*Moraine Park Technical College (M)

2151 North Main Street, West Bend WI 53090
Telephone: (262) 335-5713 Identification: 770447
Accreditation: &NH

*Northeast Wisconsin Technical College-Marinette Campus (N)

1601 University Drive, Marinette WI 54143
Telephone: (715) 735-9361 Identification: 770448
Accreditation: &NH

*Northeast Wisconsin Technical College-Sturgeon Bay Campus (O)

229 N 14th Avenue, Sturgeon Bay WI 54235
Telephone: (920) 746-4900 Identification: 770449
Accreditation: &NH

*Wisconsin Indianhead Technical College-Ashland Campus (P)

2100 Beaser Avenue, Ashland WI 54806
Telephone: (715) 682-8040 Identification: 770463
Accreditation: &NH

*Wisconsin Indianhead Technical College-New Richmond Campus (Q)

1019 S Knowles Avenue, New Richmond WI 54017
Telephone: (715) 246-6561 Identification: 770464
Accreditation: &NH, MAC

*Wisconsin Indianhead Technical College-Rice Lake Campus (R)

1900 College Drive, Rice Lake WI 54868
Telephone: (715) 234-7082 Identification: 770465
Accreditation: &NH, DA, EMT

*Wisconsin Indianhead Technical College-Superior Campus (S)

600 North 21st Street, Superior WI 54880
Telephone: (715) 394-6677 Identification: 770466
Accreditation: &NH, MAC

Wright Graduate University for the Realization of Human Potential (T)

N7698 County Highway H, Elkhorn WI 53121
County: Walworth Identification: 667224
Unit ID: 486460
Telephone: (262) 742-4444 Carnegie Class: Spec-4-yr-Other
FAX Number: (262) 721-0752 Calendar System: Quarter
URL: www.wrightgrad.edu
Established: 2006 Annual Graduate Tuition & Fees: N/A
Enrollment: 22 Coed
Affiliation or Control: Independent Non-Profit IRS Status: 501(c)3
Highest Offering: Doctorate; No Undergraduates
Accreditation: DEAC

00 CEO ..... Dr. Bob WRIGHT
01 Chancellor/Dir Career Svcs/CFO ..... Dr. Michael ZWELL
05 Chief Academic Officer ..... Dr. Judith WRIGHT
12 Campus Director ..... Ms. Kate HOLMQUEST

WYOMING

Casper College (U)

125 College Drive, Casper WY 82601-2458
County: Natrona FICE Identification: 003928
Unit ID: 240505
Telephone: (307) 268-2110 Carnegie Class: Assoc/MT-VT-Mix Trad/Non
FAX Number: (307) 268-2682 Calendar System: Semester
URL: www.caspercollege.edu
Established: 1945 Annual Undergrad Tuition & Fees (In-District): $3,072
Enrollment: 3,409 Coed
Affiliation or Control: Local IRS Status: 501(c)3
Highest Offering: Associate Degree
Accreditation: NH, ACBSP, ADNUR, ART, COARC, DANCE, EMT, MLTAD, MUS, OTA, RAD, THEA

01 President ..... Dr. Darren D. DIVINE
05 Vice President Academic Affairs ..... Dr. Brandon KOSINE
32 Vice President Student Services ..... Ms. Kim BYRD
10 Vice Pres Administrative Services ..... Ms. Lynnde COLLING
51 Exec Dean of Continuing Education ..... Dr. Laura DRISCOLL
15 Director Human Resources ..... Ms. Rhonda FRANZEN
07 Director Admissions/Student Success ..... Ms. Leanne LOYA
26 Director of Public Relations ..... Mr. Chris LORENZEN
18 Director Physical Plant ..... Mr. Eric RULOFSON
38 Director Student Counseling ..... Ms. Joanne THEOBALD
08 Director of the Library ..... Mr. Brad MATTHIES
13 Director Information Technology ..... Mr. Kent BROOKS
121 Director of Student Success Service ..... Ms. Leanne LOYA
39 Director of Housing ..... Vacant
41 Athletic Director ..... Ms. Angel SHARMAN
19 Director Campus Security ..... Ms. Lori ABRAMS
102 Exec Director Foundation ..... Ms. Denise BRESSLER
09 Institutional Researcher ..... Mr. Michael DEAL
37 Director of Student Financial Aid ..... Mrs. Shannon ESKAM
21 Dir Financial Services/Controller ..... Ms. Robyn LANDEN
96 Purchasing Coordinator ..... Mr. Paul CHRISTMAN
06 Registrar ..... Ms. Linda NICHOLS
29 Director Alumni Relations ..... Ms. Linda NIX
04 Executive Asst to President ..... Ms. Tina SILVA
108 Director Institutional Assessment ..... Dr. Melissa STAHLEY-CUMMINGS
25 Grant Coordinator ..... Ms. Katie MCMILLAN

Central Wyoming College (V)

2660 Peck Avenue, Riverton WY 82501-1520
County: Fremont FICE Identification: 007289
Unit ID: 240514
Telephone: (307) 855-2000 Carnegie Class: Assoc/MT-VT-High Non
FAX Number: (307) 855-2095 Calendar System: Semester
URL: www.cwc.edu
Established: 1966 Annual Undergrad Tuition & Fees (In-District): $3,120
Enrollment: 1,930 Coed
Affiliation or Control: Local IRS Status: 501(c)3
Highest Offering: Associate Degree
Accreditation: NH, ADNUR

01 President ..... Dr. Brad TYNDALL
04 Exec Asst to the President/Board ..... Ms. Linda BENDER
05 Vice Pres Academic Affairs ..... Dr. Katherine WELLS
10 Vice Pres Admin Svcs/CFO ..... Mr. Willie NOSEEP
32 Vice Pres Student Affairs ..... Ms. Cory DALY
13 Chief Information Officer ..... Mr. John WOOD
18 Chief Facilities/Physical Plant ..... Mr. Wayne ROBINSON
08 Director of Library Services ..... Ms. Kristy HARDTKE
26 Director of Marketing ..... Ms. Lori RIDGWAY
15 Dir for Human Resources ..... Mr. Scott MILLER
21 Finance Officer ..... Ms. Lindy PASKETT
19 Director of Campus Safety/Security ..... Mr. Chuck CARR
103 Dean Business/Technical & Workforce ..... Ms. Lynne MCAULIFFE
35 Dean of Students ..... Mr. Steve BARLOW

06 Registrar .... Ms. Connie NYBERG
49 Dean for Arts & Sciences .... Dr. Mark NORDEEN
102 Exec Director CWC Foundation .... Ms. Beth MONTEIRO
09 Director of Institutional Research ..... Ms. Louisa HUNKERSTORM

Eastern Wyoming College (A)

3200 W C Street, Torrington WY 82240-1699
County: Goshen FICE Identification: 003929
Unit ID: 240596
Telephone: (307) 532-8200 Carnegie Class: Assoc/MT-VT-High Non
FAX Number: (307) 532-8229 Calendar System: Semester
URL: ewc.wy.edu/
Established: 1948 Annual Undergrad Tuition & Fees (In-District): $2,928
Enrollment: 1,560 Coed
Affiliation or Control: State/Local IRS Status: 501(c)3
Highest Offering: Associate Degree
Accreditation: NH

01 President .... Dr. Lesley TRAVERS
04 Exec Asst to President/Board .... Ms. Sally WATSON
05 VP for Academic Services .... Dr. Heidi EDMUNDS
10 VP for Admin Services .... Mr. Kwin WILKES
32 VP for Student Services .... Mr. Roger HUMPHREY
12 VP for Douglas Campus .... Dr. Margaret FARLEY
30 Dir of Institutional Development .... Mr. John HANSEN
08 Director of Library Services .... Mrs. Casey DEBUS
41 Director of College Athletics .... Mr. Tom ANDERSEN
26 Director of College Relations .... Ms. Tami AFDAHL
18 Director of Physical Plant .... Mr. Keith JARVIS
39 Director of Residence Life .... Ms. Shannon JOLLEY
37 Director of Financial Aid .... Ms. Susan STEPHENSON
15 Director Human Resources .... Ms. Crystal SMITH
21 Business Office Director .... Ms. Karen PARRIOTT

Eastern Wyoming College-Douglas Campus (B)

800 South Wind River Drive, Douglas WY 82633
Telephone: (307) 624-7000 Identification: 770476
Accreditation: &NH, ADNUR

Gillette College (C)

300 West Sinclair, Gillette WY 82718
Telephone: (307) 681-6000 Identification: 770478
Accreditation: &NH

Laramie County Community College (D)

1400 E College Drive, Cheyenne WY 82007-3299
County: Laramie FICE Identification: 009259
Unit ID: 240620
Telephone: (307) 778-5222 Carnegie Class: Assoc/HVT-High Non
FAX Number: (307) 778-1399 Calendar System: Semester
URL: www.lccc.wy.edu
Established: 1968 Annual Undergrad Tuition & Fees (In-District): $3,426
Enrollment: 4,129 Coed
Affiliation or Control: State/Local IRS Status: 501(c)3
Highest Offering: Associate Degree
Accreditation: NH, ADNUR, DH, DMS, EMT, PTAA, RAD, SURGT

01 President .... Dr. Joe SCHAFFER
05 Vice President of Academic Affairs .... Dr. Clark HARRIS
10 Vice Pres of Administration/Finance .... Vacant
32 Vice President of Student Services .... Dr. Melissa STUTZ
13 Chief Technology Officer .... Mr. Chad MARLEY
15 Executive Director Human Resources .... Ms. Tammy MAAS
111 Assoc VP Institutional Advancement .... Ms. Lisa TRIMBLE
12 Assoc VP Albany County Campus .... Dr. Brady HAMMOND
45 Assc VP Institutional Effectiveness .... Dr. Kim BENDER
08 Assoc Dean Library/Learning Commons .... Ms. Maura HADAWAY
37 Director of Financial Aid .... Ms. Brandi PAYNE CERVERA
18 Director of Physical Plant .... Mr. Bill ZINK
21 Comptroller .... Ms. Nola ROCHA
29 Int Dir Alumni Affairs/Event Plans .... Ms. Lisa MURPHY
44 Dir Scholarships & Annual Giving .... Ms. Melissa DISHMAN
09 Director of Institutional Research .... Dr. Mark PERKINS
07 Dir of Admissions and Welcome Ctr .... Ms. Sarah HANNES
06 Registrar .... Ms. Stacy MAESTAS
49 Int Dean Sch of Arts & Humanities .... Dr. Jonathan CARRIER
50 Dean School of BATS .... Dr. Jill KOSLOSKY
76 Dean Sch of Health Sci & Wellness .... Ms. Starla MASON
81 Dean School Math & Science .... Mr. Bryan WILSON
103 Dean Sch of Outreach/Workforce Dev .... Ms. Maryellen TAST
19 Director Campus Safety & Security .... Mr. James CROSBY
41 Director of Athletics .... Mr. Clark RASMUSSEN
04 Executive Asst to President .... Ms. Vicki BOREING

Laramie County Community College Albany County Campus (E)

1125 Boulder Drive, Laramie WY 82070
Telephone: (307) 721-5138 Identification: 770477
Accreditation: &NH

Northern Wyoming Community College District (F)

1 Whitney Way, Sheridan WY 82801-1500
County: Sheridan FICE Identification: 003930
Unit ID: 240666
Telephone: (307) 675-0505 Carnegie Class: Assoc/HVT-High Non
FAX Number: (307) 675-0684 Calendar System: Semester
URL: www.sheridan.edu
Established: 1948 Annual Undergrad Tuition & Fees (In-District): $3,396
Enrollment: 4,133 Coed
Affiliation or Control: Local IRS Status: 501(c)3
Highest Offering: Associate Degree
Accreditation: NH, ADNUR, DH

01 President .... Dr. Paul R. YOUNG
05 VP Academic Affairs .... Dr. Estella CASTILLO-GARRISON
10 VP Admin & Finance/CFO .... Ms. Cheryl A. HEATH
12 VP Gillette College/CEO .... Dr. Mark G. ENGLERT
32 VP Student Affairs .... Dr. Leah BARRETT
75 Dean Career/Technical Education .... Mr. Jed JENSEN
15 Assistant Vice President for HR .... Ms. Jennifer MCARTHUR
26 AVP Strategic Comm/Public Rels .... Ms. Wendy M. SMITH
37 Director Financial Aid Services .... Ms. Heidi BALSTER
13 AVP for Info Tech Svcs/CIO .... Mr. Brady R. FACKRELL
09 AVP for Institutional Research .... Mr. Jason BROWNING
21 Director of Finance/Controller .... Ms. Gina KIDNEIGH
07 Executive Director of Admissions .... Mr. Joe B. MUELLER
39 Director Housing/Residential Educ .... Ms. Larissa B. BONNET
88 Director Veteran Services-Sheridan .... Mr. Tyler JENSEN
88 Director Veteran Services-Gillette .... Mr. Loren GROVES
18 AVP Facilities Management .... Mr. Kent A. ANDERSEN
18 Director Gillette Facilities .... Mr. Mark N. ANDERSEN
08 Librarian .... Ms. Katrina M. BROWN
19 Police Chief .... Mr. Jason VELA
41 Athletic Director .... Dr. Bubba HALL
100 Executive Office Manager .... Ms. Jana CLEMENTS
20 Assoc Academic Officer-Sheridan .... Ms. Martha DAVEY
20 Assoc Academic Officer-Gillette .... Dr. Matt EWERS
29 Alumni Relations .... Ms. Bobbi MITZEL
102 Dir Foundation/Corp Rels-Sheridan .... Ms. Jen CROUSE
102 Dir Foundation/Corp Rels-Gillette .... Ms. Heidi GROSS
38 Dir Student Svc/Counselor Gillette .... Ms. Susan SERGE
38 Coord Counseling ADA Svcs-Sheridan .... Ms. Amy BROWNING
84 Director Enrollment Management .... Mr. Micah OLSEN

Northwest College (G)

231 W 6th St, Powell WY 82435
County: Park FICE Identification: 003931
Unit ID: 240657
Telephone: (307) 754-6000 Carnegie Class: Assoc/MT-VT-Mix Trad/Non
FAX Number: (307) 754-6245 Calendar System: Semester
URL: www.nwc.edu
Established: 1946 Annual Undergrad Tuition & Fees (In-District): $3,447
Enrollment: 1,654 Coed
Affiliation or Control: State/Local IRS Status: 501(c)3
Highest Offering: Associate Degree
Accreditation: NH, ADNUR, ART, MUS

01 President .... Dr. Stefani HICSWA
05 Vice Pres Academic Affairs .... Dr. Gerald GIRAUD
32 Interim Vice Pres Student Affairs .... Mr. Dee HAVIG
11 Vice Pres Admin Services/Finance .... Ms. Lisa WATSON
26 Vice Pres College Relations .... Mr. Mark KITCHEN
102 Executive Director NWC Foundation .... Ms. Shelby WETZEL
20 Dean Student Learning .... Dr. Greg THOMAS
103 Dean Extended Campus/Workforce .... Mr. Dean BRUCE
08 Library Director .... Ms. Nancy MILLER
10 Finance Director .... Mr. Brad BOWEN
15 Human Resources Director .... Ms. Jill ANDERSON
13 Computing Services Director .... Mr. Casey DEARCORN
18 Facilities Director .... Mr. David PLUTE
06 Interim Registrar .... Mr. West HERNANDEZ
37 Financial Aid/Scholarships Director .... Mr. Shaman QUINN
39 Interim Residence Life Director .... Mr. Lee BLACKMORE
04 Exec Secretary to President & Board .... Ms. Diana GWYNN
07 Admissions Manager .... Mr. West HERNANDEZ
09 Institutional Research Manager .... Ms. Lisa SMITH
105 Marketing/Comm/Web Manager .... Ms. Carey MILLER
19 Campus Security Coordinator .... Mr. Lee BLACKMORE
41 Athletic Director .... Mr. Brian ERICKSON

University of Wyoming (H)

1000 E University Avenue, Dept 3434,
Laramie WY 82071-3434
County: Albany FICE Identification: 003932
Unit ID: 240727
Telephone: (307) 766-1121 Carnegie Class: DU-Higher
FAX Number: (307) 766-2271 Calendar System: Semester
URL: www.uwyo.edu
Established: 1886 Annual Undergrad Tuition & Fees (In-State): $5,400
Enrollment: 12,397 Coed
Affiliation or Control: State IRS Status: 501(c)3
Highest Offering: Doctorate
Accreditation: NH, CACREP, CAEPN, CLPSY, DIETD, LAW, MT, MUS, NURSE, PHAR, SP, SW

01 Acting President .... Dr. Neil THEOBALD
05 Provost/VP Academic Affairs .... Dr. Kate MILLER
11 Interim Vice President Admin .... Mr. Bill MAI
31 Interim Vice Pres Community Affairs .... Mr. Chris BOSWELL
46 Vice Pres Research & Economic Dev . Dr. Edmund SYNAKOWSKI
32 Vice President Student Affairs .... Mr. Sean BLACKBURN
13 Vice President Information Tech .... Mr. Robert R. AYLWARD
111 Vice Pres Institutional Advancement ...... Mr. W. Ben BLALOCK, III
43 Vice President & General Counsel .... Ms. Tara EVANS
41 Director Intercollegiate Athletics .... Mr. Tom BURMAN
20 Associate VP Academic Affairs .... Dr. Anne ALEXANDER
20 Associate VP Academic Affairs .... Dr. Tami BENHAM-DEAL
84 Associate VP Enrollment Management .... Mr. Kyle MOORE
14 Associate VP Budget and Inst Plan .... Mr. David JEWELL
35 Associate Dean of Students .... Dr. Nycole COURTNEY
110 Assoc VP Institutional Advancement .... Mr. John D. STARK
26 Assoc VP Communication/Marketing .... Mr. Chad BALDWIN
47 Dean of Agriculture/Natural Res .... Dr. Barbara RASCO
49 Dean of Arts & Sciences .... Dr. Paula LUTZ
50 Dean of Business .... Dr. David SPROTT
53 Dean of Education .... Dr. Ray REUTZEL
54 Dean of Engineering .... Dr. Michael PISHKO
76 Dean of Health Sciences .... Dr. David JONES
61 Dean of Law .... Dr. Klint ALEXANDER
12 Assoc Dean/Director UW at Casper .... Dr. Jeff EDGENS
08 Dean of Libraries .... Dr. Ivan GAETZ
65 Director Haub Sch Env/Nat Resources .... Dr. Melinda BENSON
07 Director of Admissions .... Ms. Shelley DODD
36 Director Advising/Career Services .... Ms. Evelyn J. CHYTKA
29 Exec Director Alumni Affairs .... Mr. Keener FRYE
88 Director American Heritage Center .... Ms. Bridgit BURKE
88 Director School of Energy Resources .... Dr. Mark NORTHAM
88 Director Art Museum .... Ms. Marianne WARDLE
88 Director Campus Recreation .... Mr. Patrick MORAN
15 Interim Director Human Resources .... Mr. Mark BERCHENI
18 Assoc Vice President UW Operations .... Mr. John DAVIS
92 Dean Honors College .... Mr. Peter PAROLIN
86 Director of Govt Relations .... Ms. Meredith ASAY
39 Exec Dir Res Life/Dining/Stdnt Un .... Mr. Eric WEBB
37 Int Director Student Financial Aid .... Ms. Carrie GOSE
06 Registrar .... Ms. Kwanna KING
23 Director Student Health Service .... Dr. Joanne E. STEANE
19 Chief University Police Dept .... Mr. Mike SAMP
38 Director Counseling Center .... Dr. Toi GEIL

Western Wyoming Community College (I)

2500 College Drive, Rock Springs WY 82901
County: Sweetwater FICE Identification: 003933
Unit ID: 240693
Telephone: (307) 382-1600 Carnegie Class: Assoc/HT-High Non
FAX Number: (307) 382-1636 Calendar System: Semester
URL: www.westernwyoming.edu
Established: 1959 Annual Undergrad Tuition & Fees (In-District): $2,953
Enrollment: 3,339 Coed
Affiliation or Control: State/Local IRS Status: 501(c)3
Highest Offering: Associate Degree
Accreditation: NH, ADNUR

01 President .... Dr. Kim K. DALE
05 VP for Student Learning .... Dr. Kim FARLEY
32 VP for Student Services .... Dr. Philip PARNELL
11 VP for Administrative Services .... Mr. Burt REYNOLDS
15 Assoc VP of Human Resources .... Ms. Joy ADAMS
10 Assoc VP of Finance .... Ms. Debbie BAKER
07 Director of Admissions .... Mr. Kurtis WILKINSON
06 Registrar .... Mr. Stuart MOORE
37 Director of Financial Aid .... Ms. Nicole CASTILLON
08 Director of Library Services .... Ms. Janice GROVER-ROOSA
18 Assoc VP of Physical Resources .... Mr. Michael BRADY
35 Dean of Students .... Mr. Dustin CONOVER
40 Bookstore Manager .... Ms. Natalie LANE
41 Athletic Director .... Dr. Lu SWEET
92 Director of Honors Program .... Mr. Richard KEMPA
09 Director of Planning & Improvement .... Mr. Mark REMBACZ
26 Coord of Marketing/Public Info .... Ms. Kimberly EMERSON
30 Dir Community College Relations .... Mr. David TATE
22 Dir Student Counseling/Disability .... Ms. Amy GALLEY
96 Director of Purchasing .... Ms. Tammy REGISTER
04 Executive Asst to President .... Ms. Kandy FRINK
19 Protective Services Supervisor .... Mr. Mark PADILLA
106 Director of Distance Learning .... Ms. Kasey DAMORI
13 Director of Information Technology .... Mr. Derek ROBINSON
20 Dean of Academics .... Dr. Clifford WITTSTRUCK

Wyoming Catholic College (J)

306 Main Street, Lander WY 82520
County: Fremont Identification: 667227
Telephone: (307) 332-2930 Carnegie Class: Not Classified
FAX Number: (307) 332-2918 Calendar System: Semester
URL: www.wyomingcatholic.edu
Established: 2005 Annual Undergrad Tuition & Fees: N/A
Enrollment: N/A Coed
Affiliation or Control: Roman Catholic IRS Status: 501(c)3
Highest Offering: Baccalaureate
Accreditation: NH

01 President .... Dr. Glen ARBERY
03 Executive Vice President .... Mr. Jonathan TONKOWICH
05 Interim Academic Dean .... Mr. Kyle WASHUT
10 Chief Financial Officer .... Mr. Paul MCCOWN
111 Vice Pres Advancement .... Mr. Joseph SUSANKA
06 Registrar .... Ms. Jennifer WESTMAN
32 Director of Student Services .... Ms. Hillary HALSMER
07 Director of Admissions .... Mr. Jonathan RENSCH

WyoTech (K)

1889 Venture Drive, Laramie WY 82070
County: Albany FICE Identification: 009157
Unit ID: 240718

Telephone: (307) 742-3776 Carnegie Class: Spec 2-yr-Tech
FAX Number: (307) 755-2484 Calendar System: Other
URL: www.wyotech.edu
Established: 1966 Annual Undergrad Tuition & Fees: N/A
Enrollment: 464 Coed
Affiliation or Control: Independent Non-Profit IRS Status: 501(c)3
Highest Offering: Associate Degree
Accreditation: ACCSC

01 President Mr. Caleb PERRITON
84 Director of Student Success Mr. Kyle MORRIS
36 Director of Career Services Mr. Martin AXLUND
88 Manager of Student Finance Ms. Brenda COSSITT
88 Enrollment Manager Mr. Glenn HALSEY
06 Registrar Ms. Revalee WEERHEIM
39 Housing Manager Mr. Gabe LUCERO

US SERVICE SCHOOLS

Air Force Institute of Technology (A)

2950 Hobson Way, Wright Patterson AFB OH 45433-7765
County: Greene FICE Identification: 003009
Unit ID: 200697
Telephone: (937) 255-6565 Carnegie Class: DU-Higher
FAX Number: (937) 656-7600 Calendar System: Quarter
URL: www.afit.edu
Established: 1919 Annual Graduate Tuition & Fees: N/A
Enrollment: 898 Coed
Affiliation or Control: Federal IRS Status: Exempt
Highest Offering: Doctorate; No Undergraduates
Accreditation: NH

01 Chancellor Dr. Todd I. STEWART
05 Provost/Vice Chancellor Dr. Sivaguru S. SRITHARAN
54 Dean Graduate School of Engr & Mgt Dr. Adedeji B. BADIRU
46 Dean for Research Dr. Heidi R. RIES
10 Chief Financial Officer Ms. Amber L. RICHEY
09 Director Institutional Research Dr. Nancy J. ROSZELL
07 Director Admissions/Registrar Ms. Kathleen K. BURDEN
32 Dean of Students Col. Adam REIMAN
20 Associate Dean for Academic Affairs Dr. Paul J. WOLF
13 Dir Communications & Information Major Jeremy MILLAR
08 Director D'Azzo Research Library Dr. Ellis BETECK
15 Director Personnel Services Ms. Leanne HEAGLE
18 Chief Facilities/Physical Plant Mr. Anthony KING
29 Manager Alumni Affairs Ms. Kathleen E. SCOTT
85 Director of Intl Student Affairs Vacant
40 Bookstore Supervisor Mr. Joseph SCOTT
106 Dir Online Education/E-learning Mr. John A. REISNER

Air University (B)

55 LeMay Plaza South, Maxwell AFB AL 36112-6335
County: Montgomery FICE Identification: 001001
Telephone: (334) 953-5613 Carnegie Class: Spec-4-yr-Other
FAX Number: (334) 953-2749 Calendar System: Other
URL: www.airuniversity.af.mil
Established: 1946 Annual Undergrad Tuition & Fees: N/A
Enrollment: N/A Coed
Affiliation or Control: Federal IRS Status: Exempt
Highest Offering: Doctorate
Accreditation: SC

01 Commander and President LtGen. Anthony J. COTTON
03 Vice Commander MajGen. Michael D. ROTHSTEIN
05 Chief Academic Officer Dr. Mark J. CONVERSINO
06 Registrar Dr. Michael J. MASTERSON
20 Deputy Director Academic Affairs Mr. Jay WARWICK
20 Director Academic Affairs Mr. John CARTER

† Parent institution of Community College of the Air Force, School of Advanced Air and Space Studies, and the Air Force Institute of Technology

Community College of the Air Force (C)

100 South Turner Blvd,
Maxwell AFB, Gunter Annex AL 36114-3011
Telephone: (334) 649-5000 FICE Identification: 012308
Accreditation: &SC

† Regional accreditation is carried under the parent institution, Air University, Maxwell AFB, AL.

Defense Language Institute (D)

1759 Lewis Road, Monterey CA 93944
County: Monterey FICE Identification: 001195
Unit ID: 428222
Telephone: (831) 242-5291 Carnegie Class: Spec 2-yr-Other
FAX Number: (831) 242-6495 Calendar System: Other
URL: www.dliflc.edu
Established: 1941 Annual Undergrad Tuition & Fees: N/A
Enrollment: N/A Coed
Affiliation or Control: Federal IRS Status: Exempt
Highest Offering: Associate Degree
Accreditation: WJ

01 Commandant Col. Gary M. HAUSMAN
11 Assistant Commandant Col. Stephanie R. KELLEY
05 Provost Dr. Robert SAVUKINAS
20 Associate Provost Dr. Hiam KANBAR
100 Chief of Staff Mr. Steven COLLINS
06 Registrar Vacant

† Associate Arts in Foreign Language authorized by US Congress in December 2001 and approved by ACCJC/WASC in June 2002.

59th Dental Training Squadron (E)

Bldg 3352, JBSA, Lackland AFB TX 78236
Telephone: (210) 292-8850 Identification: 770122
Accreditation: &M

† Branch campus of Uniformed Services University of the Health Sciences, Bethesda, MD

Joint Forces Staff College (F)

7800 Hampton Boulevard, Norfolk VA 23511-1702
Telephone: (757) 443-6124 Identification: 770121
Accreditation: &M

† Branch campus of National Defense University, Washington, DC

The Judge Advocate General's Legal Center & School (G)

600 Massie Road, Charlottesville VA 22903-1781
County: Albermarle Identification: 666974
Telephone: (434) 971-3300 Carnegie Class: Spec-4-yr-Other
FAX Number: (434) 971-3338 Calendar System: Quarter
URL: www.jagcnet.army.mil/tjaglcs
Established: 1951 Annual Graduate Tuition & Fees: N/A
Enrollment: N/A Coed
Affiliation or Control: Federal IRS Status: Exempt
Highest Offering: Master's; No Undergraduates
Accreditation: LAW

01 Commander/Commandant BGEN. Joseph B. BERGER
05 Dean COL. Jerrett W. DUNLAP
20 Associate Dean of Academics Mr. Maurice A. LESCAULT, JR.
32 Associate Dean of Students LTC. Temi ANDERSON

Marine Corps University (H)

2076 South Street, Quantico VA 22134-5068
County: Prince William Identification: 666745
Telephone: (703) 784-2105 Carnegie Class: Spec-4-yr-Other
FAX Number: (703) 784-1271 Calendar System: Semester
URL: www.mcu.usmc.mil
Established: 1989 Annual Graduate Tuition & Fees: N/A
Enrollment: N/A Coed
Affiliation or Control: Federal IRS Status: Exempt
Highest Offering: Master's; No Undergraduates
Accreditation: SC

01 President BGen. Jay BARGERON
05 Vice President for Academic Affairs Dr. Rebecca J. JOHNSON
11 VP for Operations & Planning Mr. Jay HATTON
10 VP Business Affairs Mr. Keil GENTRY
20 Director Academic Support Division Mr. Richard JAQUES
09 Director Institutional Research Vacant

National Defense University (I)

Fort Lesley J. McNair, Washington DC 20319-5066
FICE Identification: 031893
Unit ID: 423494
Telephone: (202) 685-3924 Carnegie Class: Spec-4-yr-Other
FAX Number: (202) 685-3920 Calendar System: Semester
URL: www.ndu.edu
Established: 1976 Annual Graduate Tuition & Fees: N/A
Enrollment: N/A Coed
Affiliation or Control: Federal IRS Status: Exempt
Highest Offering: Master's; No Undergraduates
Accreditation: M

01 President VADM. Fritz J. ROEGGE
03 Senior Vice President Amb. Arnold CHACON
05 Provost/Vice Pres Academic Affairs Dr. John W. YAEGER
11 Chief Operating Officer Mr. Robert C. KANE
43 General Counsel Ms. Mollie MURPHY
46 Sr Dir Research/Strategic Support Dr. Laura J. JUNOR
88 Chancellor CISA Dr. Charles B. CUSHMAN
88 Commandant ES BGen. Kyle W. ROBINSON
88 Commandant NWC RAdm. Cedrick PRINGLE
88 Chancellor CIC Mr. Thomas WINGFIELD
88 Commandant JFSC MGen. Lewis G. IRWIN
107 Deputy Director CAPSTONE Mr. Gerard M. MAUER, JR.
20 Deputy Vice Pres Academic Affairs Dr. Brian R. SHAW
32 Director of OIRPA Dr. B.J MILLER
06 University Registrar Mr. Larry JOHNSON
42 Chaplain COL. Ken WILLIAMS
26 Director of Strategic Communication Mr. Mark PHILLIPS
13 Chief Information Officer Ms. Diane E. WEBBER
105 Web/Social Media Manager Ms. Jennifer RUSSELL
10 Director Resource Management Ms. Ellen B. ROMINES
25 Director Contracting Ms. Kathryn GONZALES
23 Director Health Fitness Mr. Tony SPINOSA
15 Director Human Resources Ms. Leigh Ann MASSEY
08 Director Libraries Mr. David GANSZ
85 Dir International Student Mgmt Ofc Ms. Makila JAMES
18 Chief Facilities/Physical Plant Dr. Thomas J. KARNOWSKI
19 Director Security Mr. Tony BROWN
102 President/CEO NDU Foundation Vacant

National Intelligence University (J)

7400 Pentagon, Washington DC 20301
Identification: 666393
Telephone: (301) 243-2118 Carnegie Class: Not Classified
FAX Number: N/A Calendar System: Quarter
URL: www.ni-u.edu
Established: 1962 Annual Undergrad Tuition & Fees: N/A
Enrollment: N/A Coed
Affiliation or Control: Federal IRS Status: Exempt
Highest Offering: Master's
Accreditation: M

01 President Dr. J. Scott CAMERON
04 Executive Assistant to President Vacant
100 Exec VP Ops & Chief of Staff Col. Michael E. SENN
05 Exec VP & Provost Dr. Susan M. STUDDS
09 VP Research Dr. Terrence C. MARKIN
88 Executive Asst to Provost Mr. Jeffrey D. KIRKWOOD
46 Dir Ctr for Strategic Intel Rsrch Dr. Robert SMITH
108 Dir Institutional Effectiveness Ms. Ellen ROSENTHAL
10 VP Finance & Administration Mr. Stephen J. KERDA
18 Facilities Dr. Richard MESTAS
19 Security Officer Ms. Thelma FLAMER
06 Registrar/Dir Enrollment Services Mr. Eric H. STUPAR
08 Director Library Services Ms. Elizabeth E. VENTURA
58 Dean College Strategic Intel Dr. Frederick HAMMERSEN
12 Director NSA Campus Dr. Irene ZOPPI RODRIGUEZ
12 Director NGA Campus Dr. Mayur GOSAI
12 Director Reserve Monthly Pgm Lt Col. Andre LOBO
12 Director European Academic Ctr Mr. Kevin TALIAFERRO
12 Director Southern Academic Ctr Mr. Christopher MARSHALL
12 Director Quantico Academic Ctr Mr. William DAVIDSON
58 Dean School of Science & Tech Intel Dr. Brian HOLMES
26 VP Engagement Mr. Timothy LATTA
29 Dir Outreach & Alumni Affairs Mr. Thomas VAN WAGNER

Naval Postgraduate School (K)

1 University Circle, Room M10, Monterey CA 93943-5100
County: Monterey FICE Identification: 001310
Unit ID: 119678
Telephone: (831) 656-2441 Carnegie Class: Masters/L
FAX Number: (831) 656-2921 Calendar System: Quarter
URL: www.nps.edu
Established: 1909 Annual Undergrad Tuition & Fees: N/A
Enrollment: 2,704 Coed
Affiliation or Control: Federal IRS Status: Exempt
Highest Offering: Doctorate
Accreditation: WC, SPAA

01 President VAdm. Ann Elisabeth RONDEAU, RET.
05 Provost/Academic Dean Dr. Steven R. LERMAN
100 Chief of Staff CAPT. John M. WARD
20 Vice Provost for Academic Affairs Dr. Orrin Douglas MOSES
46 Dean of Research Dr. Jeffrey D. PADUAN
54 Dean Grad Sch Engr/Applied Sci Dr. Clyde SCANDRETT
58 Dean Sch of Intl Graduate Studies Dr. James J. WIRTZ
50 Dean Grad Sch Bus/Public Policy Dr. William R. GATES
72 Dean Grad Sch Oper & Info Sciences Dr. Gordon MCCORMICK
32 Dean of Students CAPT. Markus GUDMUNDSSON
10 Director Business Operations Mr. Les D. MARTIN
21 Comptroller Mr. Kevin K. LITTLE
13 Director Information Technology Mr. Joseph LOPICCOLO
08 University Librarian Ms. Eleanor S. UHLINGER
06 Registrar Mr. Mike ANDERSEN
15 Director Human Resources Ms. Ermelinda RODRIGUEZ-HEFFNER
56 Director of CED3 Mr. Tom M. MASTRE
07 Director of Admissions Ms. Sue DOOLEY
88 Director of Programs CDR. Yolanda KERN

Naval War College (L)

686 Cushing Road, Newport RI 02841-1207
County: Newport FICE Identification: 003413
Telephone: (401) 841-3089 Carnegie Class: Not Classified
FAX Number: (401) 841-1297 Calendar System: Trimester
URL: www.usnwc.edu
Established: 1884 Annual Graduate Tuition & Fees: N/A
Enrollment: N/A Coed
Affiliation or Control: Federal IRS Status: Exempt
Highest Offering: Master's; No Undergraduates
Accreditation: EH

01 President RADM. Shoshana CHATFIELD
04 Exec Assistant to the President LCDR. Jay BREWER
05 Provost Dr. Lewis M. DUNCAN
20 Deputy Provost Mr. Richard R. MENARD
20 Associate Provost Dr. James E. HICKEY
100 Vice Pres/Chief of Staff CAPT. Joseph C. GIRARD
20 Dean of Academic Affairs Dr. Phil HAUN
09 Dean Center for Warfare Studies Prof. Thomas CULORA
32 Dean of Students CAPT. Pat KEYES
08 Director H.E. Eccles Library Dr. Allen C. BENSON
106 Dean College of Distance Education Prof. Leonard Walter WILDEMANN
06 Assistant Registrar Ms. Michele BLACKBURN

46 Chairman Strategy & Policy ....Prof. David STONE
88 Chairman National Security Affairs ....Prof. Derek REVERON
88 Chairman Joint Military Operations . CAPT. Edmund HERNANDEZ
10 Chief Business Officer ....Mr. Robert SAMPSON
15 Director Military Personnel Svcs ....CDR. John ANDREW
15 Civilian Human Resources Officer ....Ms. Charlene HANSON
18 Chief Facilities/Physical Plant ....Mr. Shawn BOGDAN
26 Chief Public Relations Officer ....CDR. Gary ROSS
13 Chief Information Officer ....Mr. Joseph PANGBORN
19 Director of Security ....Mr. James HULL
29 Director Alumni Affairs ....Prof. Julia GAGE
104 Dean International Programs ....Prof. Thomas MANGOLD
88 Director of Events ....Ms. Karen SELLERS
88 Dean Maritime Operational Warfare ....Prof. Michael WHITE
88 Dean Leadership and Ethics ....Prof. Peg KLEIN

School of Advanced Air and Space Studies (A)

125 Chennault Circle, Maxwell AFB AL 36112-6424
Telephone: (334) 953-5155 Identification: 666746
Accreditation: &SC

† Regional accreditation is carried under the parent institution, Air University, Maxwell AFB, AL.

Uniformed Services University of the Health Sciences (B)

4301 Jones Bridge Road, Bethesda MD 20814-4799
County: Montgomery FICE Identification: 021610
Unit ID: 164137
Telephone: (301) 295-3013 Carnegie Class: Spec-4-yr-Med
FAX Number: (301) 295-3431 Calendar System: Quarter
URL: www.usuhs.edu
Established: 1972 Annual Undergrad Tuition & Fees: N/A
Enrollment: N/A Coed
Affiliation or Control: Federal IRS Status: Exempt
Highest Offering: Doctorate
Accreditation: M, ANEST, CLPSY, DENT, HSA, MED, NURSE, PH

01 President ....Dr. Richard W. THOMAS
05 Sr Vice Pres University Programs ....Dr. Thomas TRAVIS
05 Sr Vice Pres University Programs ....Dr. William ROBERTS
10 Vice Pres Finance & Admin ....Mr. Walter TINLING
26 Vice Pres External Affairs ....Dr. Jeffrey LONGACRE
46 Vice President for Research ....Dr. Yvonne MADDOX
04 Exec Assistant to the President ....Ms. Lorraine BREEN
21 AVP Resource Management ....Ms. Antoinette WHITMEYER
100 Chief of Staff ....Mr. Robert J. THOMPSON
63 Dean School of Medicine ....Dr. Arthur KELLERMANN
66 Dean Graduate School of Nursing ....Dr. Carol ROMANO
76 Dean School Allied Health Sci ....Dr. Mitchell SEAL
52 Dean Air Force Postgrad Dental Sch ....COL. Drew FALLIS
52 Executive Dean Postgrad Dental ....Dr. Thomas R. SCHNEID
58 Assoc Dean Graduate Education ....Dr. Saibal DEY
07 Assoc Dean Admiss & Recruiting SOM ....CDR. Robert LIOTTA
88 Assoc Dean Graduate Medical Educ ....CAPT. Jerri CURTIS
32 Assoc Dean Student Affairs ....COL. Lisa MOORES
20 Assoc Dean for Curriculum ....Dr. Arnyce POCK
88 Sr Assoc Dean for Faculty ....Dr. Brian REAMY
88 Assoc Dean for Medical Education ....COL. Catherine WITKOP
88 Assistant Dean Academic Support ....Dr. William WITTMAN
88 Assistant Dean Clinical Sciences ....CAPT. Pamela WILLIAMS
20 Assoc Dean Academic Affairs GSN ....Dr. Diane SEIBERT
13 Chief Information Officer ....Mr. Timothy RAPP
43 General Counsel ....Mr. Mark PETERSON
46 Director AFRRI ....CAPT. John GILSTAD
15 Director Civilian Human Res ....Mr. Darryl BROWN
08 Director University Librarian ....Ms. Alison ROLLINS
18 Director of Facilities ....Ms. Florence RICHARDSON
96 Director of Contracting ....Mr. Stephen DAVIS
29 Director Alumni Relations ....Ms. Sharon HOLLAND
19 Director Security/Safety ....Mr. Christopher MOTTLER

United States Air Force Academy (C)

2304 Cadet Drive, Suite 3800,
USAF Academy CO 80840-5002
County: El Paso FICE Identification: 001369
Unit ID: 128328
Telephone: (719) 333-9751 Carnegie Class: Bac-A&S
FAX Number: (719) 333-3647 Calendar System: Semester
URL: www.usafa.af.mil/
Established: 1954 Annual Undergrad Tuition & Fees: N/A
Enrollment: 4,276 Coed
Affiliation or Control: Federal IRS Status: Exempt
Highest Offering: Baccalaureate
Accreditation: NH, DENT

01 Superintendent ....LtGen. Jay B. SILVERIA
05 Chief Academic Officer ....BGen. Andrew ARMACOST
08 Head Librarian ....Mr. David A. SCHAFFER
09 Director of Institutional Research ....Col. John M. GARVER
10 Chief Business Officer ....Lt Col. Christopher D. CARROLL
100 Chief of Staff ....Ms. Gail B. COLVIN
101 Secretary of the Institution/Board ....Col. Huston R. CANTWELL
103 Dir Workforce/Career Development ....Dr. Steven K. JONES
104 Director Study Abroad ....Lt Col. Christopher S. KEAN
11 Chief of Administration ....SSgt. Khacy U. LAVA
13 Chief Info Technology Officer (CIO) ....Mr. Martin K. SCHLACTER
15 Director Personnel Services ....Mr. Dale A. HOGUE
18 Chief Facilities/Physical Plant ....Mr. Carlos R. CRUZ-GONZALEZ
19 Director Security/Safety ....Lt Col. Joseph R. VIGUERIA
22 Dir Affirmative Action/EO ....Mr. Bryan L. OSBORNE
26 Chief Public Affairs ....Lt Col. Tracy A. BUNKO
28 Director of Diversity ....Ms. Yvonne ROLAND
29 Director Alumni Relations ....Lt Col. Carla J. HUNSTAD
30 Chief Development/Advancement ....Mr. Tom R. MABRY
32 Chief Student Affairs/Student Life ....Col. Carrie J. BAUSANO
36 Director Student Placement ....MSgt. Laura A. ANGELES
37 Director Student Financial Aid ....LTC. Christopher D. CARROLL
39 Director Student Housing ....Mr. Dean S. MILLS
41 Athletic Director ....Mr. Nathan PINE
43 Dir Legal Services/General Counsel ....Col. Thomas A. ROGERS
45 Chief Institutional Planning ....Col. Tyler P. FRANDER
50 Head Dept of Management ....Col. Troy R. HARTING
54 Pgm Head Environmental Engineering ....Col. Joel A. SLOAN
84 Director Enrollment Management ....Col. Arthur W. PRIMAS, JR.
90 Director Academic Computing ....Mr. Eugene K. KAUPPILA
91 Director Administrative Computing ....Mr. Jason L. GUTIERREZ
96 Director of Purchasing ....Mr. James A. ANDERSON
06 Registrar ....Dr. Tom R. MABRY
07 Director of Admissions ....Col. Arthur W. PRIMUS, JR.
105 Director Web Services ....Mr. Andrew P. HAMILTON
108 Director Institutional Assessment ....Lt Col. Jennifer M. RUSSELL
44 Director Annual Giving ....Lt Col. Carla J. HUNSTAD
86 Director Government Relations ....Ms. Leslie Y. FORRESTER

United States Army Command and General Staff College (D)

100 Stimson Avenue, Fort Leavenworth KS 66027
County: Leavenworth FICE Identification: 001947
Unit ID: 156055
Telephone: (913) 684-3097 Carnegie Class: Spec-4-yr-Other
FAX Number: (913) 684-2906 Calendar System: Trimester
URL: usacac.army.mil/cac2/cgsc/
Established: 1881 Annual Graduate Tuition & Fees: N/A
Enrollment: N/A Coed
Affiliation or Control: Federal IRS Status: Exempt
Highest Offering: Master's; No Undergraduates
Accreditation: NH

01 Deputy Commandant ....BGen. Scott EFFLANDT
04 Assistant Deputy Commandant ....Col. Tom BOLEN
05 Dean of Academics ....Dr. James MARTIN
20 Deputy Provost ....Mr. Allen BORGARDTS
58 Director Graduate Degree Programs ....Dr. Robert BAUMANN
08 Director of Library ....Mrs. Beata MOORE
32 Director CGSS School ....Col. Robert AULT
06 Registrar ....Dr. Thomas E. CREVISTON
26 Chief Public Relations Officer ....Mr. Harry SARLES

United States Army War College (E)

122 Forbes Avenue, Carlisle PA 17013-5050
County: Cumberland Identification: 666235
Telephone: (717) 245-4711 Carnegie Class: Spec-4-yr-Other
FAX Number: (717) 245-4721 Calendar System: Other
URL: www.carlisle.army.mil
Established: 1901 Annual Graduate Tuition & Fees: N/A
Enrollment: N/A Coed
Affiliation or Control: Federal IRS Status: Exempt
Highest Offering: Master's; No Undergraduates
Accreditation: M

01 Commandant ....MajGen. John KEM
05 Provost ....Dr. Jim BRECKENRIDGE

United States Coast Guard Academy (F)

15 Mohegan Avenue, New London CT 06320-8100
County: New London FICE Identification: 001415
Unit ID: 130624
Telephone: (860) 444-8444 Carnegie Class: Bac-Diverse
FAX Number: (860) 444-8288 Calendar System: Semester
URL: www.cga.edu
Established: 1876 Annual Undergrad Tuition & Fees: N/A
Enrollment: 1,044 Coed
Affiliation or Control: Federal IRS Status: Exempt
Highest Offering: Baccalaureate
Accreditation: EH

01 Superintendent ....RADM. William G. KELLY
03 Assistant Superintendent ....CAPT. John C. VANN
45 Planning Officer ....CDR. Janine E. DONOVAN
05 Dean of Academics ....Dr. Kurt J. COLELLA
20 Associate Dean ....CAPT. Gregory HALL
45 Director of Academic Resources ....Dr. Eric J. PAGE
07 Director of Admissions ....CAPT. Michael C. FREDIE
32 Commandant of Cadets ....CAPT. Richard J. WESTER
06 Registrar ....Mr. Donald E. DYKES
08 Librarian ....Ms. Lucia MAZIAR
10 Comptroller ....CDR. Micheal FRIEND
26 Communication Director ....Mr. David M. SANTOS
09 Institutional Research ....Dr. Leonard M. GIAMBRA
13 Head of Information Services ....CDR. Christopher M. ARMSTRONG
16 Personnel Management Specialist ....Ms. Julie A. KELLY
15 Chief Personnel/Administration ....CAPT. William SMITH
18 Chief Facilities Engineer ....CDR. Cesar ACOSTA
22 Civil Rights Officer ....Mr. Roy P. ZIEGENGEIST
23 Clinic Director ....CAPT. Esan SIMON
38 Chief Cadet Counselor ....Dr. Daria PAPALIA
40 Bookstore Manager ....Ms. Lauri KERP
41 Director of Athletics ....Vacant
42 Command Chaplain ....CAPT. Ryan R. RUPE
43 Staff Legal Officer ....CDR. Ben G. KARPINSKI
85 International Cadet Advisor ....Dr. Kassim M. TARHINI
28 Instructor Inclusion and Diversity ....Dr. Aram DEKOVEN

United States Merchant Marine Academy (G)

300 Steamboat Road, Kings Point NY 11024-1634
County: Nassau FICE Identification: 002892
Unit ID: 197027
Telephone: (516) 773-5000 Carnegie Class: Bac-Diverse
FAX Number: (516) 773-5582 Calendar System: Trimester
URL: www.usmma.edu
Established: 1943 Annual Undergrad Tuition & Fees: $1,080
Enrollment: 975 Coed
Affiliation or Control: Federal IRS Status: Exempt
Highest Offering: Master's
Accreditation: M

01 Superintendent ....RADM. Jack BUONO
03 Deputy Superintendent ....RDML. Susan L. DUNLAP
05 Academic Dean & Provost ....Dr. John R. BALLARD
32 Commandant of Midshipmen ....CAPT. Mikel STROUD
20 Assistant Academic Dean ....Ms. Dianne TAHA
18 Asst Supt for Facilities ....CAPT. Theodore DOGONNIUCK
26 Director Office of External Affairs ....Mr. George RHYNEDANCE
07 Director of Admissions ....CDR. Michael BEDRYK
06 Registrar ....Ms. Lisa JERRY
13 Director Computer/Information Mgmt ....Vacant
15 Director Human Resources ....Vacant
10 Chief Financial Officer ....Mr. David SOCOLOF
29 Director Alumni Relations ....Mr. Jim TOBIN
36 Dir of Prof Develop/Career Services ....CAPT. Gene ALBERT
37 Director Student Financial Aid ....Mr. Joseph BECKER
96 Director of Purchasing ....Mr. Max DIAH
09 Director of Institutional Research ....Ms. Lori TOWNSEND
41 Athletic Director ....Ms. Maureen WHITE
108 Director Institutional Assessment ....Ms. Lori TOWNSEND
43 Dir Legal Services/General Counsel ....Ms. Ilene KREITZER
11 Chief of Administration ....Mr. John DEMERS
19 Director Security/Safety ....Mr. Jeffrey THOMAS
22 Director Affirmative Action/EEO ....Mr. Marvin WILLIAMS
04 Admin Assistant to the President ....Ms. Cynthia FLYNN
08 Chief Library Officer ....Ms. Donna SELVAGGIO

United States Military Academy (H)

West Point NY 10996-5000
County: Orange FICE Identification: 002893
Unit ID: 197036
Telephone: (845) 938-4041 Carnegie Class: Bac-A&S
FAX Number: (845) 938-3021 Calendar System: Semester
URL: www.westpoint.edu
Established: 1802 Annual Undergrad Tuition & Fees: N/A
Enrollment: 4,491 Coed
Affiliation or Control: Federal IRS Status: Exempt
Highest Offering: Baccalaureate
Accreditation: M

01 Superintendent/President ....LTG. Darryl A. WILLIAMS
05 Dean of Academic Board ....BG. Cindy JEBB
20 Vice Dean Academic Affairs ....Dr. Rachel SONDHEIMER
32 Commandant of Cadets ....BG. Curtis BUZZARD
100 Chief of Staff ....COL. Mark BIEGER
88 Garrison Commander ....COL. Harry MARSON
07 Director of Admissions ....COL. Deborah MCDONALD
06 Assoc Dean Operations/Registrar ....Dr. James DALTON
45 Associate Dean for Research ....Vacant
09 Institutional Research ....COL. Holly WEST
13 Chief Information Officer ....LTC. Edward TEAGUE
10 Director of Resource Management ....Ms. Melissa CARDONA
26 Public Affairs Officer ....LTC. Christopher OPHARDT
08 USMA Library ....Mr. Christopher BARTH
29 President Association of Graduates ....Mr. Todd BROWNE
38 Dir Center for Personal Development ....LTC. Darcy SCHNACK
41 Director Intercollegiate Athletics ....Mr. Mike BUDDIE
18 Chief Facilities/Physical Plant ....Mr. Matthew TALABER
15 Dir Center for Faculty Excellence ....Dr. Mark EVANS
35 Dir Ctr for Enhanced Performance ....LTC. Darcy SCHNACK
88 Director of Cadet Activities ....COL. Tom HANSBARGER
43 Chief Legal Assistance ....Mr. Micheal BARRETT
28 Director of Diversity ....Mr. Terry ALLBRITTEN
108 Director Institutional Assessment ....Mr. Gerald KOBYLSKI

United States Naval Academy (I)

121 Blake Road, Annapolis MD 21402-5000
County: Anne Arundel FICE Identification: 030430
Unit ID: 164155
Telephone: (410) 293-1000 Carnegie Class: Bac-A&S
FAX Number: (410) 293-3734 Calendar System: Semester
URL: www.usna.edu
Established: 1845 Annual Undergrad Tuition & Fees: N/A
Enrollment: 4,495 Coed
Affiliation or Control: Federal IRS Status: Exempt
Highest Offering: Baccalaureate
Accreditation: M

01 Superintendent VADM. Walter E. CARTER, JR.
32 Commandant of Midshipmen Capt. Thomas R. BUCHANAN
05 Academic Dean & Provost Dr. Andrew T. PHILLIPS
20 Vice Academic Dean Dr. Daniel W. O'SULLIVAN
07 Dean of Admissions Capt. Bruce J. LATTA
10 Associate Dean for Finances Capt. Peter A. NARDI
20 Assoc Dean for Academic Affairs Dr. Jennifer WATERS
08 Assoc Dean Information Svcs/Library Mr. James RETTIG
21 CFO/Deputy for Finance Mr. Joseph RUBINO
100 Chief of Staff Capt. Valerie R. OVERSTREET
11 CO Naval Support Activity Annapolis Capt. Homer DENIUS
06 Registrar Dr. Christopher A. DAVIS
26 Public Affairs Officer CDR. Alana GARAS
29 Senior Director of Engagement Mr. Craig WASHINGTON
21 Comptroller CDR. Todd W. HAUGE
13 Chief Information Officer CDR. Louis J. GIANNOTTI
88 Director Academic Center Dr. Bruce J. BUKOWSKI
09 Director Institutional Research Capt. Robert J. BRENNAN
18 Public Works Officer Capt. Nicholas MERRY
41 Athletic Director Mr. Chet GLADCHUK
42 Command Chaplain Capt. Francis P. FOLEY
30 Director Officer Development Capt. Mike MICHEL
15 Director Human Resources Mr. William COFFIN
28 Director of Diversity Capt. Timika LINDSAY

AMERICAN SAMOA

American Samoa Community College (A)

PO Box 2609, Pago Pago AS 96799-2609
County: American Samoa FICE Identification: 010010
Unit ID: 240736
Telephone: (684) 699-9155 Carnegie Class: Bac/Assoc-Assoc Dom
FAX Number: (684) 699-6259 Calendar System: Semester
URL: www.amsamoa.edu
Established: 1970 Annual Undergrad Tuition & Fees (In-State): $3,950
Enrollment: 1,095 Coed
Affiliation or Control: State IRS Status: 501(c)3
Highest Offering: Baccalaureate
Accreditation: WJ

01 President Dr. Rosevonne M. PATO
05 VP of Academic Affairs Mrs. Letupu MOANANU
88 Director of Samoan Studies Inst Mrs. Okenaisa FAUOLO-MANILA
88 Director of Land Grant/ACNR Mr. Ropeti ARETA
11 VP of Administration and Finance Mr. Sonny J. LEOMITI
108 Executive Director of IE Mr. Tauvela FALE
88 Executive Advisor Dr. Lina SCANLAN
88 Director of UCEDD Ms. Tafaimamao TUPUOLA
51 Director of Adult Education-LEL Vacant
88 Director of Small Business Dev Mr. Jason BETHAM
20 Dean of Academic Affairs Dr. Siamaua ROPETI
53 Teacher Educ Program Director Ms. Shirley DE LA ROSA
66 Nursing Program Director Ms. Lele V. AH MU
72 Trade and Tech Program Director Mr. Frederick R. SUISALA
32 Dean of Student Services Dr. Emilia LE'I
38 Program Director of Counseling Ms. Annie PANAMA
06 Registrar/Records Officer Mrs. Sifagatogo TUITASI
08 Program Director of Library Svcs Mr. Elvis ZODIACAL
37 Financial Aid Officer Mr. Peteru K. LAM YUEN
07 Admission Officer Mrs. Elizabeth LEUMA
10 Financial Officer Ms. Elsie LESA
13 Information Officer Vacant
18 Physical Facilities Maint Officer Mr. Lokeni LOKENI
15 Human Resources Officer Mrs. Sereima ASIFOA
96 Procurement Officer Mrs. Jessie SU'ESU'E
40 Bookstore Mgr/Dir Research Found Mrs. Alofia AFALAVA
04 Executive Secretary Mrs. Violina HUDSON
101 Board Secretary Mrs. Tiare TUPUA
19 Chief Security Officer Vacant

FEDERATED STATES OF MICRONESIA

College of Micronesia-FSM (B)

PO Box 159 Kolonia, Pohnpei FM 96941-0159
FICE Identification: 010343
Unit ID: 243638
Telephone: (691) 320-2480 Carnegie Class: Assoc/HT-High Trad
FAX Number: (691) 320-2479 Calendar System: Semester
URL: www.comfsm.fm
Established: 1963 Annual Undergrad Tuition & Fees (In-State): $4,750
Enrollment: 2,022 Coed
Affiliation or Control: State IRS Status: 501(c)3
Highest Offering: Associate Degree
Accreditation: WJ

01 President/CEO Dr. Joseph M. DAISY
09 Vice Pres for IEQA Vacant
05 Vice Pres for Instructional Affairs Mrs. Karen SIMION
84 Vice Pres Enroll Mgmt/Student Svcs Mr. Joey ODUCADO
11 Vice President Admin Services Mr. Joseph HABUCHMAI
56 Director of CRE (Land Grant) Vacant
12 Dean Chuuk Campus Mr. Kind KANTO
12 Dean Kosrae Campus Mr. Nena MIKE
12 Dean Yap Campus Ms. Lourdes ROBOMAN
10 Comptroller Mrs. Roselle TOGONON
12 Director FSM-FMI Campus Mr. Matthias EWARMAI
15 Director Human Resources Ms. Rencelly NELSON
20 Dean of Academic Programs Mrs. Maria DISION
08 Director Learning Resource Center Mrs. Jennifer HELIEISAR
75 Dir Career & Technical Education Mr. Grilly JACK
18 Director Physical Plant/Maintenance Mr. Francisco MENDIOLA
06 Registrar Mr. Doman DAOAS
21 Business Officer Manager Ms. Ritchie VALENCIA
37 Director of Financial Aid Mr. Faustino YAROFAISUG
38 Counselor Ms. Penselyn SAM
13 Director Information Technology Vacant
39 Director Residential/Campus Life Ms. Krystilyn M. ATKINSON
100 Chief of Staff Vacant
19 Supervisor Security/Safety Mr. Terry MARCUS
96 Director of Procurement Vacant

GUAM

Guam Community College (C)

PO Box 23069, Barrigada GU 96921-3069
County: Guam FICE Identification: 015361
Unit ID: 240745
Telephone: (671) 735-5531 Carnegie Class: Assoc/MT-VT-High Trad
FAX Number: (671) 734-5238 Calendar System: Semester
URL: www.guamcc.edu
Established: 1977 Annual Undergrad Tuition & Fees (In-District): $3,414
Enrollment: 2,055 Coed
Affiliation or Control: State/Local IRS Status: 501(c)3
Highest Offering: Associate Degree
Accreditation: WJ, ACFEI

01 President Dr. Mary Y. OKADA
05 Vice President Academic Affairs Dr. R. Ray D. SOMERA
10 Vice Pres Finance & Administration Ms. Carmen K. SANTOS
21 Controller Mr. Edwin E. LIMTUATCO
75 Dean Trades & Professional Services Dr. Virginia C. TUDELA
32 Dean Technology & Student Services Dr. Michael L. CHAN
26 Asst Dir Communications & Promo Mr. John DELA ROSA
04 Private Secretary Ms. Esther A. MUNA
101 Admin Secretary II BOT-Pres Ofc Ms. Bertha M. GUERRERO
07 Coordinator Admissions/Registration Ms. Tina M. QUINATA
45 Asst Dir Planning & Development Ms. Doris U. PEREZ
103 Asst Dir Cont Educ & Workforce Dev Ms. Rowena Ellen PEREZ
88 Assoc Dean Trade & Prof Svcs Ms. Pilar WILLIAMS
88 Assoc Dean Trade & Prof Svcs Vacant
35 Assoc Dean Tech & Student Svcs Mr. Ronald G. HARTZ
15 Administrator Human Resources Ms. Apolline SAN NICOLAS
18 Facilities Engineer Administrator Vacant
08 Librarian Ms. Christine B. MATSON
20 Admin Ofcr VP's Ofc-Academic Affs Ms. Ana Mari C. ATOIGUE
09 Asst Director AIER Ms. Marlena O. MONTAGUE
88 Pgm Spc Adult Basic Educ Ms. Ava M. GARCIA
88 Pgm Spc TRIO Programs Ms. Fermina A. SABLAN
35 Pgm Spc Ctr Student Involvement Ms. Latisha Ann N. LEON GUERRERO
23 LPN Health Services Center Ms. Eva Marie L. MUI
90 Program Specialist Acad Tech Mr. Wesley T. GIMA
37 Coordinator Student Financial Aid Ms. Esther A. RIOS
88 Program Spec Dean's Ofc TSS Dr. Julie ULLOA-HEATH
29 Pgm Specialist Alum & Fundraising Ms. Bonnie Mae M. DATUIN
29 Pgm Spc Alum & Fundraising Vacant
96 Supply Management Administrator Ms. Joleen M. EVANGELISTA
13 Data Processing Admin/MIS Mr. Francisco C. CAMACHO
51 Pgm Spc Continuing Educ Vacant
40 Bookstore Manager Mr. Daniel T. OKADA
55 Pgm Spc Night Administrator Mr. Huan HOSEI
19 Environmental Health/Safety Ofcr Mr. Gregorio T. MANGLONA
88 Pgm Spc Accomodative Svcs Mr. John F. PAYNE
88 Sustainability/Project Coordinator Mr. Francisco E. PALACIOS
45 Pgm Spec Planning & Development Vacant

Pacific Islands University (D)

172 Kinney's Road, Mangilao GU 96913
County: Guam FICE Identification: 034383
Unit ID: 439862
Telephone: (671) 734-1812 Carnegie Class: Bac-Diverse
FAX Number: (671) 734-1813 Calendar System: Semester
URL: www.piu.edu
Established: 1976 Annual Undergrad Tuition & Fees: $5,428
Enrollment: 55 Coed
Affiliation or Control: Independent Non-Profit IRS Status: 501(c)3
Highest Offering: Master's
Accreditation: TRACS

88 President/CEO Rev. Howard MERRELL
10 VP Finance/Administration Mr. Nino T. PATE
05 Vice President Academic Affairs Dr. Christel WOOD
20 Seminary Dean Vacant
49 Liberal Studies Chair Mrs. Dorothy HOUDE
73 Biblical Studies Chair Ms. Iotaka CHORAM
32 Vice President Student Development Mr. Alex TAVAREZ
21 Operations Director/Bookkeeper Ms. Celia ATOIGUE
04 Admin Assistant to the President Ms. Kathy MERRELL
08 Library Director Mr. Paul DRAKE
15 Human Resource Director Mr. Joshua COMBS
84 Int Enrollment Mgmt Dir/Registrar Mr. Joshua COMBS
37 Financial Aid Officer Ms. Delight SUDA

University of Guam (E)

UOG Station, Mangilao GU 96923-1800
County: Guam FICE Identification: 003935
Unit ID: 240754
Telephone: (671) 735-2990 Carnegie Class: Masters/M
FAX Number: (671) 734-2296 Calendar System: Semester
URL: www.uog.edu
Established: 1952 Annual Undergrad Tuition & Fees (In-State): $5,804
Enrollment: 3,917 Coed
Affiliation or Control: State IRS Status: 501(c)3
Highest Offering: Master's
Accreditation: WC, IACBE, NUR, SW

01 President Dr. Thomas W. KRISE
05 Sr VP Academic & Student Affairs Dr. Anita B. ENRIQUEZ
10 Vice Pres Administration & Finance Mr. Randall V. WIEGAND
46 Director Research & Sponsored Pgm Dr. Rachael T. LEON GUERRERO
43 University Legal Counsel Ms. Victorina M Y. RENACIA
13 Int Chief Information Officer Mr. Manuel B. HECHANOVA, JR.
22 Director EEO & Title IX/ADA Mr. Joseph B. GUMATAOTAO
100 Int Chief of Staff Mr. David S. OKADA
26 Director Integrated Mktg & Comm Mr. Jonas D. MACAPINLAC
45 Chief Planning Officer Mr. David S. OKADA
30 Dir Development & Alumni Affairs Mr. Norman ANALISTA
102 Exec Director Endowment Foundation Ms. Melanie MENDIOLA
108 AVP Institutional Effectiveness Ms. Deborah D. LEON GUERRERO
20 AVP Academic Excellence Mr. Troy MCVEY
49 Dean Col of Lib Arts & Social Sci Dr. James D. SELLMANN
47 Dean Col of Natural & Applied Sci Dr. Lee S. YUDIN
50 Dean Sch Business & Pub Admin Dr. Annette T. SANTOS
53 Dean School of Education Dr. Alicia AGUON
66 Dean of Nursing & Hlth Sci Dr. Margaret HATTORI-UCHIMA
54 Interim Dean School of Engineering Dr. Shahram KHOSROWPANAH
84 Dean Enroll Mgmt & Student Svcs Mr. Lawrence F. CAMACHO
06 Registrar Ms. Remy B. CRISTOBAL
37 Financial Aid Director Mr. Mark A. DUARTE
32 Student Life Officer Vacant
88 Director Guam CEDDERS Dr. Heidi E. SAN NICOLAS
08 Dean University Libraries Dr. Monique STORIE
88 Dir Micronesia Area Res Center Dr. Monique C. STORIE
88 Director Marine Laboratory Dr. Tom SCHILS
88 Dir Watr Env Rsrch Inst Wstrn Pac Dr. John JENSON
88 Dir Ctr for Island Sustainability Dr. Austin SHELTON
104 Director Prof/Intl Program Mr. Carlos TAITANO
88 Director TRIO Programs Vacant
15 Actg Chief Human Resources Officer Mr. Joseph B. GUMATAOTAO
18 Chief Plant Facilities Officer Mr. Sonny P. PEREZ
41 Field House/Athletics Director Mr. Doug PALMER
19 Safety Administrator Mr. Felix MANSAPIT
40 Director Bookstore & Auxiliary Svcs Ms. Ann S A. LEON GUERRERO
21 Comptroller Ms. Zeny ASUNCION-NACE
39 Int Director of Residence Halls Mr. Mark MENDIOLA
29 Director Alumni Affairs Mr. Norman ANALISTA

MARSHALL ISLANDS

College of the Marshall Islands (F)

PO Box 1258, Majuro MH 96960-1258
County: Marshalls FICE Identification: 030224
Unit ID: 376695
Telephone: (692) 625-3394 Carnegie Class: Assoc/HT-High Trad
FAX Number: (692) 625-7203 Calendar System: Semester
URL: www.cmi.edu
Established: 1989 Annual Undergrad Tuition & Fees (In-State): $4,885
Enrollment: 1,032 Coed
Affiliation or Control: State IRS Status: 501(c)3
Highest Offering: Associate Degree
Accreditation: WJ

01 President Dr. Theresa B. KOROIVULAONO
05 Vice Pres Academic/Student Affairs Dr. Elizabeth SWITAJ
10 Vice Pres Business & Admin Affairs Mr. Stevenson KOTTON
20 Dean of Academic Affairs Ms. Vasemaca SAVU
32 Dean of Student Success Vacant
06 Registrar Ms. Monica GORDON
07 Director of Admissions & Records Ms. Jomi CAPELLE
08 Director of Library Ms. Verenaisi BAVADRA
15 Human Resources Director Ms. Agnes KOTOISUVA
18 Director Physical Plant Mr. Emil DEBRUM
13 Director Information & Technology Mr. Bonifacio SANCHEZ
88 Director Nuclear Institute Ms. Mary L. SILK
37 Financial Aid Director Ms. Sali ANDRIKE
49 Chair Liberal Arts Ms. Oyinada OGUNMOKUN
50 Chair Business & IT Ms. Meitaka KENDALL-LEKKA
66 Chair Nursing Ms. Florence L. PETER
19 Director Security/Safety Mr. David DEBRUM
38 Dir Counseling/TRACC Ms. Demiana NAUSI KUMORU
09 Dir Inst Research/Assessment Ms. Cherly T. VILA
04 Admin Assistant to the President Ms. Takbar ISHIGURO
102 Director Foundation/Corporate Rels Ms. Jellesen RUBON
105 Director Web Services Mr. John VILLAFANIA

NORTHERN MARIANAS

Northern Marianas College (A)

PO Box 501250, Saipan MP 96950-1250

FICE Identification: 030330
Unit ID: 240790

Telephone: (670) 234-5498 Carnegie Class: Bac/Assoc-Mixed
FAX Number: (670) 234-1270 Calendar System: Semester
URL: www.marianas.edu
Established: 1976 Annual Undergrad Tuition & Fees (In-District): $4,038
Enrollment: 1,216 Coed
Affiliation or Control: State/Local IRS Status: 501(c)3
Highest Offering: Baccalaureate
Accreditation: WC

01 Interim President .... Mr. Frankie M. ELIPTICO
05 VP Learning & Student Success .... Ms. Cynthia I. DELEON
10 Chief Financial Officer .... Mr. Andrew REESE
04 Executive Secretary to President .... Ms. Becky SABLAN
20 Dean Learning & Student Success .... Ms. Charlotte CEPEDA
13 Dir Information Technology .... Mr. Adrian ATALIG
09 Dir Institutional Effectiveness .... Dr. Wesley WILSON
18 Director of Facilities .... Mr. Vincent MERFALEN
53 Director School of Education .... Mr. Roland MERAR
51 Director of Adult Basic Education .... Ms. Lorraine C. MAUI
37 Director of Financial Aid .... Ms. Daisy MANGLONA-PROPST
96 Procurement Manager .... Ms. Anita C. CAMACHO
106 Director of Distance Learning .... Mr. William HUNTER
06 Registrar .... Ms. Marji TAROPE
101 Executive Secretary to the Board .... Ms. Helen B. CAMACHO
84 Director Enrollment Services .... Mr. Manny CASTRO

PALAU

Palau Community College (B)

PO Box 9, Koror PW 96940-0009
County: Koror

FICE Identification: 011009
Unit ID: 243647

Telephone: (680) 488-2470 Carnegie Class: Assoc/HT-High Trad
FAX Number: (680) 488-2447 Calendar System: Semester
URL: www.palau.edu
Established: 1969 Annual Undergrad Tuition & Fees: $3,250
Enrollment: 532 Coed
Affiliation or Control: Federal IRS Status: Exempt
Highest Offering: Associate Degree
Accreditation: WJ

01 President .... Dr. Patrick U. TELLEI
05 Vice President Education & Training .... Vacant
11 Vice Pres Administration & Finance .... Mr. Jay OLEGERIIL
46 Vice Pres Cooperative Rsrch/Exten .... Mr. Thomas TARO
04 Exec Assistant to the President .... Mr. Todd NGIRAMENGIOR
32 Dean of Students .... Mr. Sherman DANIEL
20 Dean of Academic Affairs .... Mr. Robert RAMARUI
51 Dean of Continuing Education .... Mr. Jefferson THOMAS
30 Director of Development .... Mr. Tchuzie TADAO
37 Director of Financial Aid .... Mrs. Dahlia M. KATOSANG
07 Director of Admissions and Records .... Ms. Lesley B. ADACHI
15 Director of Human Resources .... Ms. Marie A. ANDERSON
18 Director of Physical Plant .... Mr. Clement KAZUMA
13 Director of Computer Systems .... Mr. Bruce RIMIRCH
35 Director of Student Life .... Ms. Hilda REKLAI
10 Director of Finance .... Ms. Uroi N. SALII
09 Director of Institutional Research .... Ms. Deikola OLIKONG
08 Interim Director Library Services .... Ms. Pioria ASITO
88 Accreditation Liaison Officer .... Ms. Deikola OLIKONG

PUERTO RICO

American University of Puerto Rico (C)

Box 2037, Bayamon PR 00960-2037
County: Bayamon

FICE Identification: 011941
Unit ID: 241100

Telephone: (787) 620-2040 Carnegie Class: Bac-Diverse
FAX Number: (787) 785-7377 Calendar System: Other
URL: www.aupr.edu
Established: 1963 Annual Undergrad Tuition & Fees: $6,221
Enrollment: 508 Coed
Affiliation or Control: Independent Non-Profit IRS Status: 501(c)3
Highest Offering: Master's
Accreditation: M

01 President .... Mr. Juan C. NAZARIO TORRES
03 Executive Vice President .... Mr. Jaime GONZALEZ
05 Vice President Acad/Student Affairs .... Dr. Jose RAMIREZ-FIGUEROA
10 Vice Pres Finance & Admin Affairs .... Mrs. Magda A. CANCEL-PEREZ
32 Dean Student Affairs .... Prof. Claribel RODRIGUEZ-VARGAS
06 Registrar .... Prof. Alex ROBLES MARRERO
07 Admissions Officer .... Ms. Keren LLANOS
08 Learning Resources Center Director .... Vacant
37 Coordinator Financial Aid .... Mrs. Nelly DUARTE
21 Director Accounting .... Mrs. Jeanette AVILES-FERRAN
38 Director Guidance Counseling .... Mrs. Luz S. HERNANDEZ
24 Director Educational Media .... Ms. Carol SANTIAGO
41 Athletic Director .... Mr. Manfredo VEGA
15 Director Human Resources .... Mr. Jorge ESCALERA MUÑOZ
12 Director Manati Campus .... Prof. Milagros RIVERA-OTERO
09 Dir Research/Institutional Planning .... Vacant
18 Chief Facilities/Physical Plant .... Mr. Efrain LUGO
36 Director of Student Placement .... Vacant
96 Director of Purchasing .... Mr. Pedro RENTAS
92 Director of Honors Program .... Prof. Claribel RODRIGUEZ
30 Chief Development .... Mr. Jaime GONZALEZ
20 Associate Academic Officer .... Prof. Zahira GARCIA
13 Director Computer Center .... Mr. Eric CHAPARRO
53 Dept Chair School of Education .... Dr. Jose RAMIREZ
50 Dept Chair Business Admin/Sec Sci .... Vacant
49 Department Chair Arts & Sciences .... Vacant
100 Chief of Staff .... Ms. Rosabel VAZQUEZ
102 Dir Foundation/Corporate Relations .... Dr. Adela VAZQUEZ
105 Director Web Services .... Vacant
19 Director Security/Safety .... Ms. Rosabel VAZQUEZ
45 Chief Institutional Planning .... Prof. Bolivar RAMIREZ-CARLO, III
04 Administrative Asst to President .... Mrs. Carmen ARROYO

Atenas College (D)

Paseo de las Atenas #101, Manati PR 00674

FICE Identification: 035443
Unit ID: 440651

Telephone: (787) 884-3838 Carnegie Class: Spec-4-yr-Other Health
FAX Number: (787) 854-4530 Calendar System: Semester
URL: www.atenascollege.edu
Established: 1996 Annual Undergrad Tuition & Fees: $7,370
Enrollment: 932 Coed
Affiliation or Control: Independent Non-Profit IRS Status: 501(c)3
Highest Offering: Baccalaureate
Accreditation: M, NURSE, PTAA

01 President .... Dra. Maria L. HERNANDEZ NUNEZ
04 Executive Assistant .... Mrs. Alba G. MORALES
05 Vice President Academic Affairs .... Prof. Widalys GONZALEZ
13 Vice Pres Tech Infrastructure .... Ms. Annette DAVILA
32 Vice President of Student Affairs .... Mrs. María C. MEDINA
45 VP Planning & Inst Development .... Mrs. Ingrid Y. COLON
10 VP Finance & Administrative Affairs ..... Mrs. Astrid Y. MELENDEZ
20 Associate VP of Academic Affairs .... Dra. Cenia K. ROMANO
36 Director of Recruitment & Cont Educ .... Mrs. Sally SANTA
15 Human Resources and Security Dir .... Mrs. Aurea FIGUEROA
21 Assoc VP of Finance & Admin Affs .... Mrs. Zulay SOTO
37 Financial Aid Administrator .... Mr. Manuel RÁMIREZ
06 Registrar .... Mrs. Walitza HERNÁNDEZ
08 Librarian .... Mrs. Karen ROSARIO
88 Coordinator Simulation Center .... Prof. Diana N. RAMOS
101 Admn Svcs Coordinator .... Mrs. Diana RODRIGUEZ
51 Recruiter & Continued Educ Link .... Mr. Ovidio SOTO

Atlantic University College (E)

PO Box 3918, Guaynabo PR 00970
County: Guaynabo

FICE Identification: 025054
Unit ID: 241216

Telephone: (787) 720-1022 Carnegie Class: Spec-4-yr-Other Tech
FAX Number: (787) 720-1092 Calendar System: Quarter
URL: www.atlanticu.edu
Established: 1983 Annual Undergrad Tuition & Fees: $7,425
Enrollment: 1,651 Coed
Affiliation or Control: Independent Non-Profit IRS Status: 501(c)3
Highest Offering: Master's
Accreditation: ACCSC, ACICS

01 President .... Dr. Teresa DE DIOS UNANUE
13 Exec Vice Pres/Dean Technology/ Mktg .... Prof. Heri MARTINEZ DE DIOS
05 Academic Dean .... Prof. Ivette CARBONELL
10 Asst Dean of Administration .... Prof. Viviana SANTIAGO
88 Dean of Digital Arts/Sciences .... Prof. Frances GRAU
06 Registrar .... Ms. Edna I. GUTIERREZ
38 Dir Student Counseling/ Placement .... Prof. Maria C. LOPEZ-CEPERO RAMOS
37 Director Financial Aid .... Mrs. Janice RIVERA
08 Head Librarian .... Ms. Awilda MORAN
07 Director of Admissions .... Mr. Joel MONTERO
21 Director Business Office .... Mrs. María del C MONTESINO
15 Officer of Human Resources .... Ms. Viviana SANTIAGO

Caribbean University (F)

Box 493, Bayamon PR 00960-0493
County: Bayamon

FICE Identification: 012525
Unit ID: 241377

Telephone: (787) 780-0070 Carnegie Class: Masters/S
FAX Number: (787) 785-0101 Calendar System: Semester
URL: www.caribbean.edu
Established: 1969 Annual Undergrad Tuition & Fees: $5,424
Enrollment: 1,470 Coed
Affiliation or Control: Independent Non-Profit IRS Status: 501(c)3
Highest Offering: Doctorate
Accreditation: M

01 President/CEO .... Dr. Ana E. CUCURELLA-ADORNO
03 Executive Director .... Mr. Victor T. ADORNO
05 Vice President of Academic Affairs .... Dr. Maritza DEL VALLE
45 Vice President of Planning and Info .... Mrs. Lillian MATOS
11 Dean Administration Affairs .... Mr. Hector GRACIA
32 Dean of Student Affairs .... Mr. Alex CLAUDIO
15 Int Director Human Resources .... Dr. Rebecca QUINTANA
37 Director Student Financial Aid .... Mrs. Denise ORTEGA
06 Registrar .... Ms. Rosalie MORALES
08 Librarian/Director Audio-Visual .... Mrs. Yanit DELGADO
12 Director of Carolina Campus .... Prof. Melba MARTINEZ
12 Director of Ponce Campus .... Prof. Sonia PACHECO
12 Director Vega Baja Campus .... Prof. Christian DE JESUS
26 Public Relations Director .... Mrs. Gricelie TORRES
58 Dean of Graduate Programs .... Dr. Zulma PENA
49 Director Department of Liberal Arts .... Prof. Lillian MERCADO
50 Director Dept Business Admin/Sec Sc .... Prof. Aida RIVERA
76 Director Dept Allied Sciences .... Dr. Ricardo MELGAREJO
54 Director Department Engineering/IT .... Dr. Hermes CALDERON
66 Coordinator Department of Nursing .... Prof. Noemi SANTOS
53 Dir Dept Education/Liberal Arts .... Prof. Arelis NEVAREZ
18 Chief Facilities/Physical Plant .... Mr. Ibrahim MESTRES
38 Director Counseling Center (CIOSE) .... Lic. Maria PEREZ
41 Athletic Director .... Mr. Rafael MARRERO PEREZ
22 Director of Compliance/Student Svcs .... Mrs. Elena GARCIA
12 Director of Bayamon Campus .... Prof. Alex CLAUDIO

Carlos Albizu University (G)

Box 9023711, San Juan PR 00902-3711
County: San Juan

FICE Identification: 010724
Unit ID: 241331

Telephone: (787) 725-6500 Carnegie Class: Spec-4-yr-Other Health
FAX Number: (787) 721-7187 Calendar System: Semester
URL: www.albizu.edu
Established: 1966 Annual Undergrad Tuition & Fees: $7,284
Enrollment: 1,319 Coed
Affiliation or Control: Independent Non-Profit IRS Status: 501(c)3
Highest Offering: Doctorate
Accreditation: M, CLPSY, IPSY, SP

01 President .... Dr. Jose PONS MADERA
00 Chair Board of Trustees ..... Mrs. Maria FELICIANO DE LA CRUZ
05 Provost .... Dr. Julio SANTANA MARINO
07 Director Admissions/Student Affs .... Vacant
32 Dean of Student Services .... Ms. Carmen RIVERA
10 Director of Finance .... Mr. Hector PENA
09 Dir of Planning/Inst Research .. Mr. Yoel A. VELAZQUEZ-OLIVER
46 Director Research/Training Program .... Dr. Lymaries PADILLA
51 Director Continuing Education .... Ms. Isabel HERNANDEZ
37 Director Financial Aid .... Mrs. Doris QUERO-MENDEZ
08 Director Library .... Ms. Yolanda ROSARIO-ROSARIO
06 Registrar .... Ms. Maria de Lourdes RIVERA-NIEVES
88 Dir Industrial/Org Psych Program .... Dr. Ramón RODRÍGUEZ MONTALBAN
13 Dir Information Technology Svcs .... Mr. Luis CAMACHO
88 Administrator Community Svcs Clinic .... Mr. Epifanio RIVERA
31 Director Community Services Clinic .... Dr. Luis CARABALLO
88 Dir PhD Clinical Psychology Program .... Mr. Marcos REYES
15 Exec Director of Human Resources .... Vacant
30 Director Development .... Vacant
97 Director Bachelor's Program .... Dra. Maria VELEZ
38 President Student Counseling .... Mr. Jose A. GARCIA
11 Director Administration .... Mr. Epifanio RIVERA
29 Director Alumni Relations .... Vacant
108 Dir Assessment and Accreditation .... Mr. Rafael MELENDEZ
58 Director of Graduate Education .... Dr. Luaida OYOLA

CEM College (H)

Calle Degetau #25, Bayamon PR 00961
Telephone: (787) 780-8900 Identification: 770590
Accreditation: ACCSC

CEM College (I)

Calle Dr. Vidal #8 y #53, Humacao PR 00791
Telephone: (787) 852-5505 Identification: 770589
Accreditation: ACCSC

CEM College (J)

Calle Cristy #56, Mayaguez PR 00680
Telephone: (787) 986-7440 Identification: 770591
Accreditation: ACCSC

CEM College (K)

Calle 13 #1206, Ext San Agustin, San Juan PR 00926
County: San Juan

FICE Identification: 021891
Unit ID: 241517

Telephone: (787) 765-4210 Carnegie Class: Spec-4-yr-Other Health
FAX Number: (787) 765-4277 Calendar System: Semester
URL: www.cemcollege.edu
Established: 1980 Annual Undergrad Tuition & Fees: $7,425
Enrollment: 442 Coed
Affiliation or Control: Independent Non-Profit IRS Status: 501(c)3
Highest Offering: Baccalaureate
Accreditation: ACCSC

01 President .... Mr. Juan C. PAGANI-SOTO
05 Academic Dean .... Dr. Aida MORA RIVERA
10 Dean of Administration/Finance .... Dr. Carlos RODRIGUEZ
06 Registrar .... Mrs. Margarita RIVERA
11 Campus Director .... Mrs. Brenda COLON
15 Human Resources Director ...... Mrs. Lilliana M. LOPEZ-MEDERO

Center for Advanced Studies On Puerto Rico and the Caribbean (A)

PO Box 902-3970, Old San Juan PR 00902-3970
County: San Juan FICE Identification: 021660
Unit ID: 241793
Telephone: (787) 723-4481 Carnegie Class: Spec-4-yr-Other
FAX Number: (787) 723-1023 Calendar System: Semester
URL: www.ceaprc.edu
Established: 1976 Annual Graduate Tuition & Fees: N/A
Enrollment: 514 Coed
Affiliation or Control: Independent Non-Profit IRS Status: 501(c)3
Highest Offering: Doctorate; No Undergraduates
Accreditation: M

01 Chancellor ... Dr. Amalia ALSINA-OROZCO
06 Registrar ... Mrs. Mayra I. RAMIREZ
08 Head Librarian ... Mr. Francis J. MOJICA
32 Students Affairs Dean ... Ms. Clarissa SANTIAGO-TORO
37 Financial Aid Officer ... Mrs. Lillian M. OLIVER
07 Admissions Director ... Mr. Jose F. PEREZ-RODRIGUEZ
38 Director Student Counseling ... Ms. Carmen B. ORTIZ

Colegio de Cinematografia, Artes y Television (B)

51 Calle Dr. Santiago Veve, Bayamon PR 00961
County: Bayamon FICE Identification: 031576
Unit ID: 430935
Telephone: (787) 779-2500 Carnegie Class: Assoc/MT-VT-High Trad
FAX Number: (787) 995-2525 Calendar System: Semester
URL: www.ccatpuertorico.com
Established: 1993 Annual Undergrad Tuition & Fees: $6,660
Enrollment: 778 Coed
Affiliation or Control: Proprietary IRS Status: Proprietary
Highest Offering: Associate Degree
Accreditation: ACCSC

01 President ... Ms. Carola GARCIA

Colegio Universitario de San Juan (C)

180 Jose R. Oliver Street, San Juan PR 00918
County: San Juan FICE Identification: 010567
Unit ID: 241720
Telephone: (787) 480-2400 Carnegie Class: Bac-Diverse
FAX Number: (787) 250-7395 Calendar System: Semester
URL: www.cunisanjuan.edu
Established: 1972 Annual Undergrad Tuition & Fees (In-District): $2,370
Enrollment: 1,480 Coed
Affiliation or Control: Local IRS Status: 501(c)3
Highest Offering: Baccalaureate
Accreditation: M, ADNUR, NURSE

01 Interim Chancellor ... Dr. Phaedra GELPI-RODRIGUEZ
45 Dir Planning/Inst Research/Ext Rels ... Dr. Haydee M. ZAYAS-HERNANDEZ
05 Interim Dean Academic Affairs . Prof. Nilda RODRIGUEZ-MOLINA
32 Dean Student Affairs ... Dr. Melvin VEGA-GONZALEZ
11 Dean Administrative Affairs ... Prof. Relon ACOSTA-TORO
51 Dir Continuing Educ/Extension Pgm ... Mrs. Annelis RIVERA-MARQUEZ
37 Manager Student Financial Aid .... Mrs. Kennia I. SANTOS-PEREZ
08 Head Librarian ... Mrs. Sheila VERA-MORALES
06 Registrar ... Mrs. Evelyn GUZMAN-LOPEZ
38 Counselor ... Mrs. Mara MALAVE-LASSO
36 Placement Officer ... Prof. Waleska Y. ROSA-NUNEZ
13 Administrator Info Systems/ Telecomm ... Mr. Zacarias POUERIET-DE LA CRUZ
72 Director Science & Technology Dept ... Prof. Marcus DROZ-RAMOS
76 Dir Health Related Science Dept ... Prof. Elizabeth ROSARIO-RODRIGUEZ
50 Dir Business Administration Dept ... Prof. Nilda E. RODRIGUEZ-MOLINA
97 Manager General Education Dept ... Prof. Carmen J. RODRIGUEZ-VINCENTY
88 Dir Behavioral Related Profess Dept ... Prof. Maria T. PEREZ-CASANOVA
04 Admin Assistant to the Chancellor ... Prof. Myrna CORTES-HUERTAS
15 Chief Human Resources Officer ... Ms. Isabel LOZADA-CRUZ

Columbia Central University (D)

PO Box 8517, Caguas PR 00726-8517
County: Caguas FICE Identification: 008902
Unit ID: 241304
Telephone: (787) 743-4041 Carnegie Class: Spec-4-yr-Other Health
FAX Number: (787) 746-5616 Calendar System: Semester
URL: www.columbiacentral.edu
Established: 1966 Annual Undergrad Tuition & Fees: $6,600
Enrollment: 1,410 Coed
Affiliation or Control: Proprietary IRS Status: Proprietary
Highest Offering: Master's
Accreditation: M, NUR

01 President ... Mrs. Daritza MULERO
05 VP Academic Affairs ... Mrs. Carmen J. LOPEZ
03 Senior VP of Operations ... Mrs. Carmen M. RIVERA
10 VP Finance and Administration ... Mrs. Yesenia CARRION
32 VP Student Affairs ... Mrs. Brendaliz ZAYAS
26 VP Marketing and Communication ... Mr. Angel QUIÑONES
12 Chancellor of Caguas Campus ... Mrs. Gladys SERRANO
12 Chancellor of Yauco Branch ... Dr. Jannette MENDEZ
20 Dean Academic Affairs ... Mr. Luis LOPEZ
08 Institutional Librarian ... Ms. Luz NEGRON
11 Director Administrative Support ... Ms. Carmen I. ROJAS
37 Financial Aid Director ... Mrs. Gloria MIRABAL
06 Registrar ... Ms. Wilmarie TORRES
38 Student Counselor ... Ms. Ingrid CARRION
15 Director Human Resources ... Ms. Elsie M. TORRES
36 Student Placement Director ... Ms. Iris TIZOL
18 Facilities & Development Director ... Mr. Jesus M. RIVERA

Columbia Centro Universitario (E)

Box 3062, Yauco PR 00698-3062
Telephone: (787) 856-0945 Identification: 666036
Accreditation: &M

† Regional accreditation is carried under the parent institution in Caguas, PR.

Conservatory of Music of Puerto Rico (F)

951 Ponce de Leon Ave. Miramar, Santurce PR 00907
County: San Juan FICE Identification: 010819
Unit ID: 241766
Telephone: (787) 751-0160 Carnegie Class: Spec-4-yr-Arts
FAX Number: (787) 766-1216 Calendar System: Semester
URL: www.cmpr.edu
Established: 1959 Annual Undergrad Tuition & Fees (In-State): $3,370
Enrollment: 466 Coed
Affiliation or Control: State IRS Status: 501(c)3
Highest Offering: Master's
Accreditation: M, MUS

01 Chancellor ... Dr. Pedro SEGARRA
05 Dean of Academic/Student Affairs ... Mr. Ariel GUZMAN
20 Assoc Dean of Academic/Student Affs ... Mr. Ernesto RAMOS
10 Dean of Finance/Administration ... Ms. Gloryber LABOY
37 Director Financial Aid ... Mr. Luis R. DIAZ
88 Director of Preparatory School ... Mr. Orlando MALDONADO
07 Admission Coordinator ... Mrs. Ana M. ARRAIZA
08 Librarian ... Mrs. Maria del Carmen MALDONADO
15 Human Resources Director ... Ms. Alba DAVILA
38 Counselor ... Ms. Mayra I. SIERRA
06 Registrar ... Mrs. Waleska MARTÍNEZ
09 Director of Institutional Research ... Mrs. Eutimia SANTIAGO
18 Chief Facilities/Physical Plant ... Mr. Jose MATOS
13 Information Technology Officer ... Mr. Luis A. CASTRO

Dewey University (G)

PO Box 19538, San Juan PR 00910-1538
County: San Juan FICE Identification: 031121
Unit ID: 431309
Telephone: (787) 753-0039 Carnegie Class: Not Classified
FAX Number: N/A Calendar System: Trimester
URL: www.dewey.edu
Established: 1992 Annual Undergrad Tuition & Fees: N/A
Enrollment: N/A Coed
Affiliation or Control: Independent Non-Profit IRS Status: 501(c)3
Highest Offering: Master's
Accreditation: ABHES

01 President/CEO ... Mr. Carlos A. QUINONES
03 Executive Vice President ... Ms. Yelitza FELICIANO
15 Chief Human Resources Officer ... Ms. Glenis VELEZ
19 Director Security/Safety ... Ms. Glorydeliz SOSA

Dewey University-Carolina (H)

Carr. #3, Km. 11, Lote 3-A, Carolina PR 00985
Telephone: (787) 769-1515 Identification: 770776
Accreditation: ABHES

Dewey University-Juana Diaz (I)

Rd 149, KM 55.9 Lomas Industrial PK, Juana Diaz PR 00795
Telephone: (787) 260-1023 Identification: 770774
Accreditation: ABHES

Dewey University-Manati (J)

Rd 604,Km 49.1 Tierra Nueva Salient, Manati PR 00674
Telephone: (789) 854-3800 Identification: 770807
Accreditation: ABHES

EDIC College (K)

PO Box 9120, Caguas PR 00726-9120
County: Caguas FICE Identification: 030219
Unit ID: 376321
Telephone: (787) 704-1020 Carnegie Class: Spec-4-yr-Other Health
FAX Number: (787) 746-0048 Calendar System: Semester
URL: ediccollege.edu
Established: 1987 Annual Undergrad Tuition & Fees: $7,100
Enrollment: 2,378 Coed
Affiliation or Control: Proprietary IRS Status: Proprietary
Highest Offering: Baccalaureate
Accreditation: ABHES

01 President/CEO ... Mr. Jose A. CORDOVA
11 Administrator ... Mrs. Milagros CARTAGENA
108 Licensing & Accreditation Director ... Vacant
12 Director of Branch Campus ... Mrs. Wilda VELEZ
12 Director of Branch Campus ... Mr. Ricardo FLORES
12 Director of Branch Campus ... Mrs. Bethzaida PINERO
05 Academic & Student Services Dean ... Mrs. Betsy VIDAL
10 Comptroller ... Mrs. Yazmin RIVERA
07 Admission & Marketing Director ... Ms. Tais LABORDE
15 Human Resource Director ... Ms. Norelis RODRIGUEZ
13 IT Director ... Mr. Wilfredo ROMERO
04 Admin Assistant to the President ... Mrs. Julie Ann WHITLOCK
06 Registrar ... Mrs. Iris LOPEZ
37 Director Student Financial Aid ... Mrs. Carmen FLORES

EDP University of Puerto Rico (L)

PO Box 192303, San Juan PR 00919-2303
County: San Juan FICE Identification: 021651
Unit ID: 243832
Telephone: (787) 765-3560 Carnegie Class: Masters/S
FAX Number: (787) 777-0025 Calendar System: Semester
URL: www.edpuniversity.edu
Established: 1968 Annual Undergrad Tuition & Fees: $6,200
Enrollment: 2,079 Coed
Affiliation or Control: Independent Non-Profit IRS Status: 501(c)3
Highest Offering: Master's
Accreditation: M, ADNUR

01 President ... Mrs. Gladys T. NIEVES
03 Institutional Vice President ... Dr. Marilyn PASTRANA
05 Dean of Academic Affairs ... Prof. María RIVERA
10 Vice President of Finance ... Mr. Luis RIVERA
26 AVP for Strategic Advancement ... Prof. Mayra RIVERA
108 AVP Institutional Compliance ... Dr. Alberto LOPEZ
13 AVP Administration and Technology ... Eng. Luis FUSTER
85 AVP Educational Innovation ... Prof. Sandra ARROYO
21 AVP for Financial Affairs ... Mrs. Marie Luz PASTRANA
09 AVP Assessment & Research ... Prof. Nydia RIVERA
14 Technology Affairs Dean ... Dr. Ramon MALLOL
06 Registrar ... Mrs. Marien DE JESÚS
08 Librarian ... Mrs. Igrí ENRIQUEZ
32 Dean of Student Affairs ... Prof. Alba FERRER
37 Director of Financial Aid ... Mr. Yaitzaenid GONZALEZ
07 Director of Admissions ... Mrs. Dendy VILA
15 Director Human Resources ... Mr. Héctor VAZQUEZ
36 Director Student Placement ... Ms. Tamara MORALES

EDP University of Puerto Rico (M)

PO Box 1674, 49 Betances Street, San Sebastian PR 00685-1674
Telephone: (787) 896-2252 Identification: 666488
Accreditation: &M

† Regional accreditation is carried under the parent institution in San Juan, PR.

Escuela de Artes Plasticas de Puerto Rico (N)

PO Box 9021112, San Juan PR 00902-1112
County: San Juan FICE Identification: 025694
Unit ID: 241951
Telephone: (787) 725-8120 Carnegie Class: Spec-4-yr-Arts
FAX Number: N/A Calendar System: Semester
URL: www.eap.edu
Established: 1966 Annual Undergrad Tuition & Fees (In-State): $3,462
Enrollment: 497 Coed
Affiliation or Control: State IRS Status: 501(c)3
Highest Offering: Baccalaureate
Accreditation: M, ART

01 Chancellor ... Prof. Ileana MUNOZ LANDRON
11 Dean of Administration . Prof. Maria del Carmen SANTOS RODRIGUEZ
05 Dean Academic Affairs ...... Prof. Luis J. BRIGANTTY GONZALEZ
06 Registrar ... Ms. Ileana MALDONADO
07 Officer of Admissions ... Ms. Kiara ALICEA DENIZARD
13 Chief Information Technology ... Ms. Limaris SOTO AQUINO
37 Director Student Financial Aid ... Ms. Lizbeth PARGAS
45 Director of Planning & Budget ... Mr. Carlos E. RIVERA
09 Institutional Research ... Dr. Shirley A. TAVARES
10 Chief Financial Officer ... Mr. Omar FALU MENDEZ
18 Coord Facilities/Physical Plant ... Mr. Edwin ALICEA
56 Coordinator Extension Program ... Prof. Keyshla DE JESUS
38 Counselor Stdnt Life/Counseling ... Ms. Susanne GOTAY
88 Coordinator Cultural Activities ... Mr. Adrian O. RIVERA NEGRON
105 Director Web Services ... Mr. Celso E. PORTELA IRIGOYEN
08 Library Director ... Ms. Estrella VAZQUEZ
20 Asst Dean Acad/Student Affairs ... Sr. Jesus OLIVERAS
15 Director Human Resources ... Mr. Alfredo AMY
57 Director Art Education ... Prof. Griselle SOTO VELEZ
97 Director General Studies ... Dr. Maria VAZQUEZ
88 Director Fashion Design ... Prof. Ana COLORADO
88 Director Industrial Design ... Prof. Vladimir GARCIA
88 Director Digital Art & Design ... Prof. Mauricio CONEJO
88 Director Painting ... Prof. Cacheila SOTO

88 Director Sculpture .... Prof. Linda SANCHEZ PINTOR
88 Director Printmaking .... Prof. Haydee LANDING

Evangelical Seminary of Puerto Rico (A)

Ponce De Leon Avenue 776, San Juan PR 00925-9907
County: San Juan FICE Identification: 006823
Unit ID: 243498
Telephone: (787) 763-6700 Carnegie Class: Spec-4-yr-Faith
FAX Number: (787) 751-0847 Calendar System: Semester
URL: www.se-pr.edu
Established: 1919 Annual Undergrad Tuition & Fees: N/A
Enrollment: 194 Coed
Affiliation or Control: Interdenominational IRS Status: 501(c)3
Highest Offering: Doctorate
Accreditation: M, THEOL

01 Acting President .... Dr. Juan R. MEJIAS-ORTIZ
05 Acting Academic Dean .... Dr. Palmira N. RIOS-GONZALEZ
10 Director Administration & Finances .. Ms. Myrna E. PEREZ-LOPEZ
06 Registrar .... Mrs. Keina TRONCOSO-FERNANDEZ
08 Head Librarian .... Mrs. Milka VIGO-VERESTIN
37 Student Financial Aid .... Ms. Damaris MERCADO-LÓPEZ
04 Administrative Asst to President . Mrs. Damaris TORRES-RIVERA
13 Chief Info Technology Officer ... Mr. Jesus RODRIGUEZ-CORTES
108 Director Institutional Assessment .... Dr. Juan R. MEJIAS-ORTIZ

Huertas College (B)

PO Box 8429, Caguas PR 00726-8429
County: Caguas FICE Identification: 022608
Unit ID: 242112
Telephone: (787) 746-1400 Carnegie Class: Spec-4-yr-Other Health
FAX Number: (787) 747-0170 Calendar System: Semester
URL: www.huertas.edu
Established: 1945 Annual Undergrad Tuition & Fees: $6,635
Enrollment: 727 Coed
Affiliation or Control: Proprietary IRS Status: Proprietary
Highest Offering: Baccalaureate
Accreditation: M, CAHIIM, OTA, PTAA

01 President .... Dr. Maria del Mar LOPEZ
03 Exec Vice President and Compliance .... Raul HERNANDEZ-RODRIGUEZ
05 Vice Pres Academic/Student Affairs ... Amarillys GARCIA-ACOSTA
10 Vice Pres Finance/Administrati .... Vacant
30 VP Planning and Development .... Ruth BONILLA
15 VP of Human Resources .... Leslie Ann GUZMAN
32 Associate VP of Student Success .... Maribel CONTRERAS
06 Registrar .... Krishna MARQUEZ
08 Head Librarian .... Maribel CONTRERAS
38 Director Student Counseling .... Evelyn COTTO
21 Director of Revenue .... Eva VEGA
22 Compliance Officer .... Vacant
04 Administrative Asst to President .... Iris COLON
07 Director of Admissions .... Hector MORALES
18 Chief Facilities/Physical Plant .... Ruben LOPEZ
26 Chief Public Relations/Marketing .... Amarilis LOPEZ
36 Director Student Placement .... Veronica RUIZ

Humacao Community College (C)

PO Box 9139, Humacao PR 00792-9139
County: Humacao FICE Identification: 023406
Unit ID: 242121
Telephone: (787) 852-1430 Carnegie Class: Bac/Assoc-Mixed
FAX Number: (787) 850-1577 Calendar System: Trimester
URL: www.hccpr.edu
Established: 1978 Annual Undergrad Tuition & Fees: $5,002
Enrollment: 468 Coed
Affiliation or Control: Independent Non-Profit IRS Status: 501(c)3
Highest Offering: Baccalaureate
Accreditation: ACICS

01 President .... Lic. Jorge E. MOJICA
03 Executive Vice President .... Prof. Aida E. RODRIGUEZ
05 Exec Director/Chief Academic Ofcr .... Dr. Brenda L. MORALES
55 Coordinator of Evening Session .... Prof. Ada BAEZ
88 Title V Project Director .... Mrs. Omayra RODRIGUEZ
81 STEM Project Director .... Mr. Jaime RIVERA
37 Director Student Financial Aid .... Mrs. Milagros CRUZ
36 Student Placement Officer .... Mrs. Ada BAEZ
36 Student Placement Officer .... Mrs. Nilkaliz DEL VALLE
07 Director Admissions .... Vacant
06 Registrar .... Mr. Israel LOPEZ
08 Head Librarian .... Mrs. Lourdes ELIZA
10 Treasury Officer (Finance) .... Mrs. Zuleika CABRERA
38 Student Counselor .... Mrs. Maria DELGADO
11 Chief College Administrator .... Mrs. Marianne BERRIOS
04 Admin Asst to Pres/Dir Personnel .... Mrs. Nilda E. RODRIGUEZ

ICPR Junior College (D)

558 Munoz Rivera Avenue, Hato Rey PR 00919-0304
County: San Juan FICE Identification: 011940
Unit ID: 243841
Telephone: (787) 753-6000 Carnegie Class: Spec 2-yr-Health
FAX Number: (787) 622-3416 Calendar System: Semester
URL: www.icprjc.edu
Established: 1946 Annual Undergrad Tuition & Fees: $7,010
Enrollment: 363 Coed
Affiliation or Control: Proprietary IRS Status: Proprietary
Highest Offering: Associate Degree
Accreditation: M

01 President/Chief Executive Officer .... Dr. Olga RIVERA
12 Hato Rey Campus Director .... Mrs. Awilda FONTANEZ
05 Academic Affairs Dean .... Mrs. Elsa RODRIGUEZ
07 Dir Admissions/Marketing Hato Rey .... Mrs. Beatriz FLORES
07 Dir Admissions/Marketing Mayaguez . Mrs. Lorraine CONTRERAS
07 Dir Admissions/Marketing Arecibo .... Vacant
07 Dir Admissions/Marketing Manati .... Mrs. Mariela CRUZ
10 Chief Financial Officer .... Mrs. Arelis DIAZ
37 Financial Aid Director .... Ms. Palmira ARROYO
12 Mayaguez Campus Director .... Dr. Sylvia RAMIREZ
12 Arecibo Campus Director .... Mr. Fernando GONZALEZ
12 Manati Campus Director .... Mr. Henberto RODRIGUEZ
06 Registrar Mayaguez .... Mrs. Olga NEGRON
06 Registrar Arecibo .... Mrs. Yaritza SANTIAGO
06 Registrar Manati .... Mrs. Vanessa TRINIDAD
26 Enrollment & Advertising Manager .... Ms. Vimarie ASENCIO
13 Chief Information Officer .... Mr. Nelson MEJIAS
08 Learning Res Librarian Hato Rey .... Mrs. Johanna MARTINEZ
08 Lrng Resources Librarian Mayaguez .... Mrs. Betania FELICIANO
08 Lrng Resources Librarian Arecibo .... Mrs. Irma JIMENEZ
08 Learning Resources Librarian .... Mr. Martin ROSADO
38 Professional Counselor Mayaguez .. Mrs. Maragnette CARABALLO
38 Professional Counselor Arecibo .... Mrs. Carol LUCIANO
38 Professional Counselor Manati .... Vacant
38 Professional Counselor Hato Rey .... Mrs. Nichole MALDONADO
15 Human Resources Director .... Mrs. Daisy CASTRO
43 Institutional Compliance Director .... Mrs. Lizzette VARGAS
56 Bayamon Extension Assoc Director .... Mrs. Lizzette VARGAS
20 Academic Coordinator Mayaguez .... Mrs. Eradina ROSAS
20 Academic Coordinator Arecibo .... Vacant
20 Academic Coordinator Manati .... Mrs. Maribel TORRES
20 Academic Coordinator Hato Rey .... Mrs. Lorna RAMOS

ICPR Junior College-Arecibo Campus (E)

20 Ave San Patricio, Arecibo PR 00614
Telephone: (787) 878-6000 Identification: 770166
Accreditation: &M

ICPR Junior College-Manati Branch Campus (F)

PO Box 49, Manati PR 00674-0049
Telephone: (787) 884-6000 Identification: 770168
Accreditation: &M

ICPR Junior College-Mayaguez Campus (G)

PO Box 1108, Mayaguez PR 00681-9913
Telephone: (787) 832-6000 Identification: 770167
Accreditation: &M

Instituto de Banca y Comercio (H)

709 Ferrocarril Street, Ponce PR 00717
Telephone: (787) 840-6119 Identification: 770773
Accreditation: &M, ACFEI

Instituto de Banca y Comercio (I)

61 Ponce de Leon Ave, San Juan PR 00917
Telephone: (787) 754-7120 Identification: 667107
Accreditation: &M, ACFEI

*Inter American University of Puerto Rico Central Office (J)

GPO Box 363255, San Juan PR 00936-3255
County: San Juan FICE Identification: 008242
Unit ID: 242671
Telephone: (787) 766-1912 Carnegie Class: N/A
FAX Number: (787) 751-3375
URL: www.inter.edu

01 President .... Mr. Manuel J. FERNOS
05 VP Academic & Student Affairs .... Mr. Juan F. MARTINEZ
10 VP Financial Affairs/Services .... Ms. Olga LUNA
42 Vice President Religious Affairs .... Rev. Norberto DOMINGUEZ
20 Associate VP Academic Affairs .... Dr. Rafael CABRERA
21 Assoc VP Financial Affairs/Services .... Ms. Marlene MANGUAL
32 Associate Vice Pres Student Affairs .... Dr. Patricia ALVAREZ
21 Assoc VP Accounting/Finance .... Mr. Orlando GONZALEZ
100 Exec Dir to Pres/Chief of Staff .... Mr. Dominique GILORMINI-DE GRACIA
26 Exec Dir Public Rels/Communications .... Mrs. Zaima NEGRON
84 Dir Inst Prom/Student Recruitment .... Mr. Antonio PANTOJA
09 Exec Director Inst Research .... Dr. Isaac SANTIAGO
13 Exec Dir Information/Telecom .... Mrs. Jossie SALGUERO
43 Exec Director Legal Services .... Mrs. Lorraine JUARBE
43 Exec Director Federal Legal Svcs .... Mr. Vladimir ROMAN
15 Exec Director Human Resources .... Ms. Maggie COLON
30 Exec Director Devel/Alumni Affairs . Dr. Nelida RIVERA-CLAUDIO

*Inter American University of Puerto Rico Aguadilla Campus (K)

Box 20000, Aguadilla PR 00605-9001
County: Aguadilla FICE Identification: 003939
Unit ID: 242626
Telephone: (787) 891-0925 Carnegie Class: Masters/S
FAX Number: (787) 882-3020 Calendar System: Other
URL: aguadilla.inter.edu
Established: 1957 Annual Undergrad Tuition & Fees: $5,902
Enrollment: 4,219 Coed
Affiliation or Control: Independent Non-Profit IRS Status: 501(c)3
Highest Offering: Master's
Accreditation: M, ADNUR, CAEPT, NUR, @SW

02 Chancellor .... Dr. Elie AGESILAS
05 Dean of Academic Affairs .... Dr. Evelyn CASTILLO
20 Associate Dean of Academic Affairs .... Dr. Sasha RUIZ
10 Dean of Administrative Affairs .... Mr. Israel AYALA
21 Asst Dean Administrative Affairs .... Mr. Irvin CANALES
32 Dean of Student Affairs .... Mrs. Ana C. LAUSELL
35 Asst Dean Student Affairs .... Mrs. Nayda SOTO
84 Enrollment Manager .... Prof. Myriam MARCIAL
30 Development and Alumni Director .... Mrs. Dolores SEPULVEDA
08 Library Director .... Mrs. Lizzie COLÓN
13 Director Information and Technology .... Mr. Asdrubal JIMENEZ
07 Admissions Director .... Mrs. Doris PEREZ
06 Registrar .... Mrs. Maria PEREZ
37 Financial Aid Director .... Mrs. Gloria CORTÉS
113 Bursar .... Mr. Hancy MUNIZ
15 Human Resources Director .... Mr. Jose R. AREIZAGA
96 Purchasing Officer .... Mrs. Lissette REILLO
121 Student Support Services Director .... Mrs. Ivonne ACEVEDO
81 Sciences and Technology Director .... Prof. Jose SOLORZANO
53 Education & Hum Studies Director .... Prof. Marylian RIVERA
50 Economic & Adm Sciences Director .... Prof. Raúl MENDOZA
83 Social Sciences & Behavior Director .... Prof. Janice LORENZO
42 Chaplain .... Rev. Manuel D. SILVA
88 Director of Upward Bound Program .... Ms. Mayra ROZADA
92 Honor Program Educational Director .... Ms. Yamilette PROSPER
18 Building Maintenance Director .... Mr. Jose CABAN
38 Counseling Office Director .... Ms. Dary ACEVEDO
41 Sports Director .... Ms. Yolanda PAGAN
19 Univ Security Guard Supervisor .... Mr. Efrain RAMOS
120 Distance Education Director .... Prof. Bernabe SOTO
88 Director Upward Bound Math/Sciences ...... Mrs. Nararly CLAUDIO
76 Health Sciences Director .... Dr. Lourdes OLAVARRIA
58 Graduate Studies Director .... Dr. Aris ROMAN

*Inter American University of Puerto Rico Arecibo Campus (L)

PO Box 4050, Arecibo PR 00614-4050
County: Arecibo FICE Identification: 005026
Unit ID: 242635
Telephone: (787) 878-5475 Carnegie Class: Masters/M
FAX Number: (787) 880-1624 Calendar System: Semester
URL: www.arecibo.inter.edu
Established: 1957 Annual Undergrad Tuition & Fees: $5,872
Enrollment: 4,320 Coed
Affiliation or Control: Independent Non-Profit IRS Status: 501(c)3
Highest Offering: Master's
Accreditation: M, ANEST, CAEPT, NUR, SW

02 Chancellor .... Dr. Rafael RAMIREZ-RIVERA
05 Dean of Academic Affairs .... Dr. Karen WOOLCOCK
11 Dean of Administrative Affairs .... Vacant
32 Dean of Student Affairs .... Mrs. Ilvis AGUIRRE
20 Assoc Dean of Academic Affairs .... Dr. Wanda I. BALSEIRO
08 Educational Resources Center Dir .... Mrs. Sara ABREU
113 Bursar .... Mr. Victor MALDONADO
37 Student Financial Aid Director .... Mr. Angel MENDEZ
06 Registrar .... Mrs. Carmen RODRIGUEZ
07 Director of Admissions .... Mrs. Provi MONTALVO
04 Executive Assistant to Chancellor .... Mrs. Enid ARBELO
56 Distance Learning Director .... Prof. Ebigaly OLIVER
45 Planning Director .... Mrs. Enid ARBELO
42 Religious Life Director .... Mr. Amilcar SOTO
15 Personnel Director .... Dr. Grisel CASTELLANOS
41 Athletic Department .... Ms. Ileana MORALES
50 Director Econ & Adms Sciences Dept .... Prof. Elba TORO
51 Continuing Education Director .... Mrs. Mariel LLERANDI
53 Director of Education Department .... Dr. Auris MARTINEZ
66 Director of Nursing Department .... Dr. Frances CORTES
79 Dir of Humanities Department .... Dr. Angel TRINIDAD
81 Director of Sciences & Tech Dept .... Dr. Lizbeth ROMERO
83 Director of Social Sciences Dept .... Dr. Lourdes CARRION
30 Development Director .... Vacant
38 Director Student Counseling .... Ms. Abigail TORRES
13 Director of Computing Center .... Mr. Jose SEGARRA
58 Director Graduate Program in Educ .... Dra. Ramonita DIAZ
18 Chief Facilities/Physical Plant .... Vacant
84 Director Enrollment Management .... Mrs. Carmen MONTALVO
88 Dir Graduate Program Anesthesia .... Prof. Ivan MOLINA
96 Purchasing Officer .... Mrs. Iris GONZALEZ
92 Coordinator Honor Program .... Ms. Vilmaris VAZQUEZ
108 Director Institutional Assessment .... Dr. Pedro RIVERA
26 Director of Marketing .... Mr. Juan RODRIGUEZ

*Inter American University of Puerto Rico Barranquitas Campus (M)

PO Box 517, Barranquitas PR 00794-0517
County: Barranquitas FICE Identification: 005027
Unit ID: 242644
Telephone: (787) 857-3600 Carnegie Class: Bac-Diverse
FAX Number: (787) 857-2244 Calendar System: Semester
URL: www.br.inter.edu
Established: 1957 Annual Undergrad Tuition & Fees: $5,902
Enrollment: 1,884 Coed

Affiliation or Control: Independent Non-Profit IRS Status: 501(c)3
Highest Offering: Master's
Accreditation: M, CAEPT, NURSE

02 Chancellor ... Dr. Juan A. NEGRON-BERRIOS
05 Dean Academic Affairs ... Dra. Filomena CINTRON-SERRANO
11 Dean Administrative Affairs ... Mr. Victor SANTIAGO-ROSADO
32 Dean Student Affairs ... Mrs. Aramilda CARTAGENA-SANTIAGO
84 Enrollment Manager ... Mrs. Lydia ARCE-RODRIGUEZ
15 Director Human Resources ... Mr. Jonathan ORTIZ-MORALES
113 Bursar Director ... Mr. Cristian J. RIOS-COLON
37 Financial Aid Director ... Mrs. Aixa SERRANO-FEBO
06 Registrar ... Mrs. Sandra M. MORALES-RODRIGUEZ
07 Director of Admissions ... Mr. Edgardo CINTRON-VEGA
53 Dir Education/Social Sci/ Humanities ... Mrs. Irma D. TORRES-SUAREZ
81 Dir Natural Sciences/ Technology ... Mrs. Maria M. MELENDEZ-ORTEGA
76 Dir Health Department ... Dra. Damaris COLON-RIVERA
50 Coord Business Administration ... Mr. Jose E. ORTIZ-ZAYAS
84 Director Recruitment/Promotion ... Mrs. Ana I. COLON-ALONSO
38 Director Upward Bound Program ... Mrs. Saraliz GONZALEZ-MELENDEZ
51 Director Continuing Education ... Vacant
88 Evaluation and Monitoring Officer ... Mrs. Carmen C. ROSADO-BERRIOS
29 Coord Alumni Relations ... Mrs. Aixa SERRANO-FEBO
08 Librarian ... Mrs. Maria del C RIVERA-ZAYAS
41 Athletic Director ... Mr. Israel RIVERA-MONTESINO
42 Chaplain ... Mr. Jose E. RODRIGUEZ-GARCIA
13 Director of Information Technology ... Mr. Carlos A. ROSARIO-CRUZ

*Inter American University of Puerto Rico Bayamon Campus (A)

500 Dr. John Will Harris Road, Bayamon PR 00957
County: Bayamon FICE Identification: 005028
Unit ID: 242705
Telephone: (787) 279-1912 Carnegie Class: Bac-Diverse
FAX Number: (787) 279-2205 Calendar System: Semester
URL: bayamon.inter.edu
Established: 1912 Annual Undergrad Tuition & Fees: $5,940
Enrollment: 4,612 Coed
Affiliation or Control: Independent Non-Profit IRS Status: 501(c)3
Highest Offering: Master's
Accreditation: M, AAB, OPTR

02 Acting Chancellor ... Dr. Carlos J. OLIVARES
04 Assistant to Chancellor ... Dr. Rafael R. CANALES
30 Chief Development ... Mr. Jaime COLON
05 Chief Academic Officer ... Dr. Anthony RIVERA
20 Associate Academic Officer ... Dra. Nydia I. FELICIANO
08 Head Librarian ... Mrs. Sandra ROSA
88 Internships and Exchanges Officer ... Mrs. Maritza ZAMBRANA
88 Acting Dean School of Aeronautics ... Prof. Luis E. ALCARAZ
54 Dean School of Engineering ... Dr. Javier QUINTANA
88 Director Electrical Engr Dept ... Prof. Miguel MUÑIZ
88 Director Industrial Engr Dept ... Prof. Catherine AGUILAR
88 Director Mechanical Engr Dept ... Dr. Eduardo PEREZ
81 Director Mathematics/Sciences ... Dra. Rosamil REY
50 Dir Business Administration Dept ... Prof. Edward VICENTE
60 Interim Dir Communications Dept ... Dra. Yadira G. NIEVES
77 Director Computer Sciences Dept ... Prof. Jose A. RODRIGUEZ
76 Director of Health Science ... Prof. Jose M. CRUZ
79 Director Humanities/Language Dept ... Dra. Gisela CARRERAS
75 Director Tech Institute ... Mrs. Liza FREYTES
32 Chief Students Life Officer ... Mrs. Gema C. TORRES
38 Director Student Counseling ... Vacant
41 Athletic Director ... Mr. Reynaldo ROLON
10 Chief Financial/Business Officer ... Mr. Serafin RIVERA
96 Purchasing Officer ... Mrs. Gladys ARROYO
21 Associate Business Officer ... Vacant
18 Chief Facilities/Physical Plant ... Eng. Jose A. FUENTES
15 Human Resources Director ... Mrs. Wilma FIGUEROA
84 Director Enrollment Services ... Miss Ivette NIEVES
35 Director of Students Services ... Mrs. Aurelis BAEZ
06 Registrar ... Mr. Eddie AYALA
13 Director Information Technology ... Mr. Edwin RIVERA
42 Director of Chaplaincy Office ... Rvda. Carmen I. PEREZ
106 Dir Online Education/E-learning ... Dr. Jose G. SANTIAGO
39 Housing Administrator ... Mr. Gerardo BURGOS
88 International Relations Director ... Mr. Luis ALCARAZ
108 Coordinator of Institutional Assess ... Dr. Jonathan VELAZQUEZ
113 Director Bursar Office ... Sr. Eduardo BERRIOS
26 Chief Pub Rels/Marketing/Comm Ofcr ... Sr. David LOPEZ

*Inter American University of Puerto Rico Fajardo Campus (B)

Call Box 70003, Fajardo PR 00738-7003
County: Fajardo FICE Identification: 022828
Unit ID: 242680
Telephone: (787) 863-2390 Carnegie Class: Masters/S
FAX Number: (787) 860-3470 Calendar System: Semester
URL: fajardo.inter.edu
Established: 1960 Annual Undergrad Tuition & Fees: $5,940
Enrollment: 2,113 Coed
Affiliation or Control: Independent Non-Profit IRS Status: 501(c)3
Highest Offering: Master's
Accreditation: M, CAEPT, SW

02 Chancellor ... Dr. Javier MARTINEZ-ORTIZ
05 Dean Academic Affairs ... Dr. Nedesha K. GONZALEZ
11 Dean Administrative Affairs ... Mr. Rafael E. MARIN
32 Dean for Student Affairs ... Mrs. Lyliana CRESPO
06 Registrar ... Mrs. Arlene PARRILLA
07 Director of Admissions ... Mrs. Ada CARABALLO
37 Director Student Financial Aid ... Mrs. Marilyn MARTINEZ
08 Librarian ... Ms. Angie COLON
15 Director of Personnel Office ... Mr. Angel J. RUIZ
09 Planning Director ... Ms. Hilda L. ORTIZ
41 Athletic Director ... Mr. Jose RUIZ
18 Physical Plant Supervisor ... Mr. Samuel GUERRIDO
42 Chaplain/Director Campus Ministry ... Rev. Rafael HIRALDO
50 Chairperson Business Department ... Prof. Wilfredo DEL VALLE
53 Chairperson Educ & Social Sci Dept ... Prof. Lorell RIVERA
79 Chairperson Humanities Dept ... Dr. Ilsa LOPEZ-VALLES
81 Chairperson Math/Science Dept ... Prof. Milagros DONATO
84 Director Enrollment Management ... Mrs. Glenda DIAZ

*Inter American University of Puerto Rico Guayama Campus (C)

Call Box 10004, Guayama PR 00785
County: Guayama FICE Identification: 022827
Unit ID: 242699
Telephone: (787) 864-2222 Carnegie Class: Bac-Diverse
FAX Number: (787) 866-5006 Calendar System: Semester
URL: www.guayama.inter.edu
Established: 1958 Annual Undergrad Tuition & Fees: $5,902
Enrollment: 1,922 Coed
Affiliation or Control: Independent Non-Profit IRS Status: 501(c)3
Highest Offering: Master's
Accreditation: M, CAEPT, NURSE

02 President ... Mr. Manuel J. FERNOS
00 Chancellor ... Dr. Angela DE JESUS-ALICEA
06 Registrar ... Mr. Luis A. SOTO
08 Librarian ... Mrs. Edny SANTIAGO
113 Bursar ... Ms. Teresa MANAUTOU
05 Dean of Academic Affairs ... Dr. Paula SAGARDIA
11 Dean of Administration ... Mr. Nestor A. LEBRON
32 Dean of Students ... Dr. Rosa J. MARTINEZ
07 Director Admissions ... Mrs. Laura FERRER
37 Director Financial Aid ... Mr. Jose A. VECHINI
29 Director Alumni Relations ... Dr. Jose ROMERO
51 Director Continuing Education ... Mrs. Leida VELAZQUEZ
15 Human Resources Officer ... Mrs. Maria MARES
18 Chief Facilities/Physical Plant ... Vacant
45 Dir Evaluation & Strategic Planning ... Vacant
30 Chief Devel/Dir Annual Plan Giving ... Vacant
42 Chaplain Director ... Rvdo. Arnaldo CINTRON
84 Director Enrollment Management ... Mrs. Eileen RIVERA
96 Director of Purchasing ... Mr. Rinaldo ROBLES
31 Dir of Community & New Student Rels ... Mrs. Luz ORTIZ
23 Director Health Services ... Mrs. Arcilia RIVERA
66 Director Nursing Program ... Dr. Marisol VELAZQUEZ
88 Dir Adult Higher Education Program ... Mrs. Carmen G. RIVERA
50 Dir Dept Business Admin/Econ Sci ... Dr. Rosalia MORALES
53 Dir Dept Education/Soc Sci/Hum Std ... Dr. Ray ROBLES
81 Dir Dept Natural & Applied Science ... Prof. Aida W. MIRANDA
09 Director of Institutional Research ... Dr. Isaac SANTIAGO

*Inter American University of Puerto Rico / Metropolitan Campus (D)

PO Box 191293, San Juan PR 00919-1293
County: San Juan FICE Identification: 003940
Unit ID: 242653
Telephone: (787) 250-1912 Carnegie Class: DU-Mod
FAX Number: (787) 250-0742 Calendar System: Trimester
URL: www.metro.inter.edu
Established: 1962 Annual Undergrad Tuition & Fees: $8,688
Enrollment: 8,607 Coed
Affiliation or Control: Independent Non-Profit IRS Status: 501(c)3
Highest Offering: Doctorate
Accreditation: M, ADNUR, CAEPT, MT, NUR, @SP, SW

02 Chancellor ... Prof. Marilina L. WAYLAND
05 Dean of Studies ... Prof. Migdalia TEXIDOR
32 Dean of Students ... Dr. Carmen OQUENDO
11 Dean of Faculty Cs Economics & Adm ... Prof. Fredrick VEGA
53 Dean of Education & Behavioral Sci ... Dr. Carmen COLLAZO
83 Director School of Psychology ... Dr. Jaime SANTIAGO
79 Dean Faculty of Humanities ... Dr. Oscar CRUZ
66 Director of Nursing ... Dr. Maria J. COLÓN
72 Director of Medical Technology ... Dr. Ida A. MEJIAS
81 Dean Faculty of Science & Tech ... Dr. Yogani GOVENDER
06 Registrar ... Ms. Lisette RIVERA
84 Enrollment Management ... Mr. Luis E. RUIZ
20 Associate Dean of Studies ... Vacant
08 Dir of Ctr for Access Info ... Ms. Maria de Lourdes RESTO
15 Human Resources Officer ... Mrs. Darlin TORRES
37 Director of Financial Aid ... Ms. Lillian CONCEPCION
18 Dir Conservation & General Services ... Vacant
38 Dir Student Placement/Guidanc/Couns ... Ms. Beatriz RIVERA
83 Director School of Social Work ... Dr. Jose CASTRO
53 Director School of Education ... Dr. Elizaida AYALA
85 Coord International Rels Office ... Prof. Ramon AYALA
73 Dir School of Theology ... Dr. Angel VELEZ
88 Dir School of Criminal Justice ... Prof. Luis SOTO

13 Director Informatic/Telecomm Center ... Mr. Eduardo ORTIZ
36 Director Student Placement ... Mrs. Adabel-Vanessa COLON
07 Dir of Recruit & Admission Office ... Mr. Reinaldo ROBLES
09 Dean of Research ... Dr. Carmen-Amalia MARRERO
30 Development & Fund Raising ... Mrs. Evelyn VEGA
96 Purchasing Officer ... Mrs. Patricia GONZALEZ
92 Coordinator of Honors Program ... Prof. Mariusz JACKO
113 Bursar ... Ms. Carmen RIVERA
106 Dir Online Education/E-learning ... Mr. Jairo PULIDO
19 Director Security/Safety ... Mr. George RIVERA
41 Athletic Director ... Mr. Jesus CORA

*Inter American University of Puerto Rico Ponce Campus (E)

104 Turpo Industrial Park Road, #1,
Mercedita PR 00715-1602
County: Ponce FICE Identification: 005029
Unit ID: 242662
Telephone: (787) 284-1912 Carnegie Class: Masters/S
FAX Number: (787) 841-0103 Calendar System: Semester
URL: ponce.inter.edu
Established: 1962 Annual Undergrad Tuition & Fees: $5,914
Enrollment: 5,205 Coed
Affiliation or Control: Independent Non-Profit IRS Status: 501(c)3
Highest Offering: Doctorate
Accreditation: M, CAEPT, PTAA, RAD

02 Chancellor ... Dr. Vilma E. COLON
05 Dean of Academic Affairs ... Dr. Jacqueline ALVAREZ
32 Dean of Students ... Mrs. Ana M. VILLANUEVA
10 Financial Officer ... Vacant
08 Director Education Resource Center ... Mrs. Maria SILVESTRINI
35 Director Student Services ... Mrs. Miriam MARTINEZ
113 Bursar ... Mr. Brian HERNANDEZ
06 Registrar ... Mrs. Maria del C PEREZ
30 Director of Development ... Mrs. Hilda V. STELLA
07 Director of Admissions ... Mr. Franco L. DIAZ
15 Human Resource Director ... Vacant
19 Supervisor of University Guard ... Mr. Reinaldo ROSADO
37 Director Student Financial Aid ... Ms. Karen CAQUIAS
41 Athletic Director ... Mr. Raul HERNANDEZ
58 Director of Graduate Programs ... Dr. Delma SANTIAGO
50 Director Business & Administration ... Mrs. Vivien MATTEI
79 Act Dir Humanistics/Pedagogical Std ... Dr. Jose CORDOVES
81 Director Mathematics/Sciences ... Dr. Hector W. COLON
83 Dir Social/Behavioral Science ... Ms. Lidis L. JUSINO
38 Dir Univ Integration Services Ofc ... Mr. Hector MARTINEZ
13 Director Computer Center ... Mr. Antonio RAMOS
26 Public Relations Officer ... Vacant
04 Chief Executive Assistant ... Mrs. Yinaira SANTIAGO
27 Dir Marketing & Student Promotion ... Vacant
106 Director Distance Education Program ... Dra. Alma RIOS
45 Director of Evaluation & Planning ... Vacant
18 Chief Facilities/Physical Plant ... Vacant
36 Director Student Placement ... Mr. Hector MARTINEZ
84 Enrollment Manager ... Mrs. Miriam MARTINEZ
42 Chaplain ... Rev. Lucy ROSARIO
51 Adult Education Director ... Mrs. Marilyn OLIVERAS
20 Assoc Dean Acad Affs/Distance Educ ... Dr. Omayra CARABALLO
11 Dean Administrative Affairs ... Mr. Julio MUNOZ
96 Purchasing Officer ... Mrs. Vivian ARMSTRONG

*Inter American University of Puerto Rico San German Campus (F)

PO Box 5100, San German PR 00683-9801
County: San German FICE Identification: 003938
Unit ID: 242617
Telephone: (787) 264-1912 Carnegie Class: DU-Mod
FAX Number: (787) 892-6350 Calendar System: Semester
URL: www.intersg.edu
Established: 1912 Annual Undergrad Tuition & Fees: $5,940
Enrollment: 4,759 Coed
Affiliation or Control: Independent Non-Profit IRS Status: 501(c)3
Highest Offering: Doctorate
Accreditation: M, CAEPT, IACBE, MT, NURSE, RAD

02 Chancellor ... Prof. Agnes MOJICA
05 Dean of Academic Affairs ... Dr. Nyvia ALVARADO
11 Dean of Administration ... Mrs. Frances CARABALLO
32 Dean of Students ... Mr. Raúl MEDINA
20 Associate Dean of Academic Affairs ... Prof. Vilma MARTÍNEZ
109 Auxiliary Dean of Administration ... Mrs. Marisol GONZÁLEZ
35 Associate Dean of Students ... Miss Idalmy RAMOS
15 Director of Human Resources ... Mrs. Evelyn TORRES
18 Acting Director Physical Plant ... Mr. José BERRÍOS
37 Director Financial Aid ... Mrs. Brunilda FERRER
06 Registrar ... Mrs. Arleen SANTANA
07 Director of Admissions ... Mrs. Mildred CAMACHO
08 Director of Library ... Mrs. Mayra RODRÍGUEZ
38 Director Student Counseling ... Mrs. Daisy PEREZ
09 Planning Evaluation & Development ... Dr. Caroline AYALA
19 Acting Director of Security ... Mr. Francisco BARBOSA
13 Director of Computer Center ... Mr. Rogelio TORO-ZAPATA
41 Athletic Director ... Prof. Francisco ACEVEDO
39 Director of Men Student Housing ... Mrs. Erlinda VEGA
39 Director of Women Student Housing ... Mrs. Hilda CRUZ
42 Dir Chaplaincy/Spiritual Well-being ... Rev. Pablo CARABALLO
04 Special Assistant of the Chancellor ... Mrs. Tary GARCÍA
04 Special Assistant of the Chancellor ... Mrs. Janine HADERTHAUER

51 Acting Director Continuing Educ ....Dr. Nyvia I. ALVARADO
58 Director Graduate Programs .... Dr. Zulma QUIÑONES
109 Manager of Food Services .... Mr. Orlando MOLINA
17 Health Services Officer .... Mrs. Gladys MEJIAS
30 Chief Development Officer ....Miss Leticia MARTINEZ
96 Director of Purchasing .... Mr. Israel CRUZ
113 Director Bursar's Office ....Mr. Carlos SEGARRA
53 Director of Education .... Dr. Miriam PADILLA
83 Dir Social Sciences & Liberal Arts .... Dr. Ingrid RODRIGUEZ
50 Director of Entrepreneurial & Mgmt .... Dr. Ailin PADILLA
88 Director of Biology & Environmental ....Prof. Iris SEDA
72 Director of Technical Studies ....Prof. Mildred ORTIZ
57 Director of Fine Arts .... Prof. Samuel ROSADO
76 Director of Health Sciences .... Dr. Ileana ORTIZ
88 Director of Language & Literature .... Dr. Marta VIADA
81 Director of Math & Applied Sciences ....Prof. Yvonne AVILES
92 Director of Honor Program ....Mrs. Sulmarie MORALES
26 Acting Coord External Resources .... Dr. Ramón FERNANDEZ
106 Dir Online Education/E-learning ....Prof. Luis ZORNOSA

*Inter American University of Puerto Rico School of Law (A)

PO Box 70351, San Juan PR 00936-8351

County: San Juan Identification: 666813
Unit ID: 242723
Telephone: (787) 751-1912 Carnegie Class: Spec-4-yr-Law
FAX Number: (787) 751-2975 Calendar System: Semester
URL: www.derecho.inter.edu
Established: 1961 Annual Graduate Tuition & Fees: N/A
Enrollment: 799 Coed
Affiliation or Control: Independent Non-Profit IRS Status: 501(c)3
Highest Offering: First Professional Degree; No Undergraduates
Accreditation: M, LAW

02 President ....Mr. Manuel J. FERNOS
61 Dean ....Dr. Julio E. FONTANET-MALDONADO
05 Dean for Academic Affairs ....Dr. Yanira REYES-GIL
32 Dean of Students .... Dr. Iris M. CAMACHO-MELENDEZ
11 Dean of Administration ...Mr. Juan C. HERNÁNDEZ-FERNÁNDEZ
06 Registrar ....Mrs. Sonia I. MONTALVO-COLÓN
08 Head Librarian ....Mr. Hector R. SANCHEZ-FERNANDEZ
61 Director of Legal Aid Clinic .. Mr. Rafael E. RODRÍGUEZ-RIVERA
37 Director of Financial Aid ....Mr. Ricardo CRESPO
07 Director of Admissions .... Mrs. Angela TORRES
18 Chief Facilities/Physical Plant ....Mr. Jose A. RIVERA
113 Director of Bursar Office ....Mrs. Ileana PIÑERO
45 Planning/Eval & Development Ofc .... Mrs. Edith C. PABON-RODRIGUEZ
121 Dir of Academic Support Program .. Mrs. Patricia OTÓN-OLIVIERI
88 Master Program Coordinator ....Dr. Luis E. ROMERO-NIEVES
04 Executive Asst to President .... Mr. Dominique GILORMINI
13 Chief Info Technology Officer ....Ms. Olga I. CRUZ-PABÓN
15 Director Personnel Services ....Mrs. Milagros AMALBERT
19 Director Security/Safety ....Mr. Victor RODRIGUEZ-CRUZ
30 Dir Development/Alumni Rels ....Mrs. Sheila GOMEZ
36 Director Student Placement/Counsel ....Mrs. Lin COLLAZO
51 Assoc Dean Acad Affs/Grad Pgm/ CLE ....Mr. Cesar ALVARADO-TORRES
35 Associate Dean for Student Affairs .... Mrs. Lin COLLAZO-CARRO
38 Director Student Counseling ....Vacant

*Inter American University of Puerto Rico School of Optometry (B)

500 John Will Harris Road, Bayamon PR 00957-6257

County: Bayamon Identification: 666601
Unit ID: 404222
Telephone: (787) 765-1915 Carnegie Class: Spec-4-yr-Other Health
FAX Number: (787) 767-3920 Calendar System: Semester
URL: www.optonet.inter.edu
Established: 1981 Annual Graduate Tuition & Fees: N/A
Enrollment: 233 Coed
Affiliation or Control: Independent Non-Profit IRS Status: 501(c)3
Highest Offering: First Professional Degree; No Undergraduates
Accreditation: M, OPT

02 Dean ....Dr. Andres PAGAN
05 Dean for Academic Affairs ....Dr. Angel F. ROMERO
11 Dean of Administration ....Mr. Francisco RIVERA
32 Dean of Student Affairs .... Dra. Iris R. CABELLO
42 Director Religious Life ....Dra. Ileana M. VARGAS
30 Director Development ....Mrs. Maria J. AULET
17 Dean of Clinical Affairs ....Dra. Damaris PAGAN
08 Library Director ....Mrs. Wilma MARRERO
15 Director Human Resources .... Mrs. Janice A. MARTINEZ
37 Financial Aid Officer .... Mrs. Sirimarie MARTINEZ
04 Executive Assistant of the Dean ....Mrs. Jackeline MEJIAS
06 Registrar ....Mrs. Luz OCASIO
26 Director Marketing/Promotion .... Mrs. Jaqueline PABON

Mech-Tech College (C)

PO Box 6118, Caguas PR 00726

County: Caguas FICE Identification: 030255
Unit ID: 414461
Telephone: (787) 744-1060 Carnegie Class: Assoc/HVT-High Trad
FAX Number: (787) 744-1035 Calendar System: Quarter
URL: www.mechtech.edu
Established: 1984 Annual Undergrad Tuition & Fees: $9,042
Enrollment: 2,448 Coed
Affiliation or Control: Proprietary IRS Status: Proprietary
Highest Offering: Associate Degree
Accreditation: CNCE

01 President .... Mr. Edwin J. COLON COSME

Monteclaro: Escuela de Hoteleria y Artes Culinarias (D)

PO Box 447 Palmer, Rio Grande PR 00721-0447

FICE Identification: 034143
Unit ID: 437705
Telephone: (787) 888-1135 Carnegie Class: Spec 2-yr-Other
FAX Number: (787) 888-1252 Calendar System: Semester
URL: www.monteclaro.edu
Established: 1996 Annual Undergrad Tuition & Fees: N/A
Enrollment: 16 Female
Affiliation or Control: Independent Non-Profit IRS Status: 501(c)3
Highest Offering: Associate Degree
Accreditation: ACCSC

01 President ....Ana T. GARCIA
05 Vice Pres Academic Affairs .... Wendy E. MALDONADO

National University College (E)

PMB452, PO Box 144035, Arecibo PR 00614-4035

Telephone: (787) 879-5044 Identification: 666489
Accreditation: &M

National University College (F)

P.O. Box 2036, Bayamon PR 00960

County: Puerto Rico FICE Identification: 022606
Unit ID: 242972
Telephone: (787) 780-5134 Carnegie Class: Spec-4-yr-Other Health
FAX Number: (787) 786-9093 Calendar System: Trimester
URL: www.nuc.edu
Established: 1982 Annual Undergrad Tuition & Fees: $6,675
Enrollment: 11,654 Coed
Affiliation or Control: Proprietary IRS Status: Proprietary
Highest Offering: Master's
Accreditation: M, ADNUR, CAEPT, NUR, PTAA

01 President ....Dr. Gloria E. BAQUERO
12 Campus Chancellor ....Ms. Daliana RIVERA
05 VP Academic Affairs .... Dr. Maria ESTRADA
32 Director Student Affairs ....Ms. Lisa ORTEGA
108 Institutional Dir of Assessment ....Ms. Lydia COLLAZO
46 Director Research & Development ....Mr. Angel AVILES
37 Director Financial Aid ....Ms. Sadi DEJESUS
06 Registrar .... Ms. Glorimar RODRIGUEZ

National University College (G)

190 Ave Gautier Benftez, Caguas PR 00725

Telephone: (787) 653-4733 Identification: 770928
Accreditation: &M

† Branch campus of National University College, Bayamon, PR.

National University College Ponce Campus (H)

PO Box 801243, Coto Laurel PR 00780-1243

Telephone: (787) 840-4474 Identification: 770169
Accreditation: &M

National University College Rio Grande Campus (I)

PO Box 3064, Rio Grande PR 00745

Telephone: (787) 809-5100 Identification: 770170
Accreditation: &M

Ponce Health Sciences University (J)

PO Box 7004, Ponce PR 00732-7004

County: Ponce FICE Identification: 024824
Unit ID: 243081
Telephone: (787) 840-2575 Carnegie Class: DU-Higher
FAX Number: (787) 840-9756 Calendar System: Semester
URL: www.psm.edu
Established: 1977 Annual Undergrad Tuition & Fees: $13,126
Enrollment: 1,004 Coed
Affiliation or Control: Independent Non-Profit IRS Status: 501(c)3
Highest Offering: Doctorate
Accreditation: M, CLPSY, IPSY, MED, PH

01 President/CEO .... Dr. David LENIHAN
05 Provost/VP Academic Affairs ....Dr. Jose TORRES-RUIZ
32 Vice Pres Student Affairs .... Dr. Elisandra RODRIGUEZ
45 VP of Strategic Planning ....Mr. Israel A. RUIZ
10 Chief Financial Officer ....Mr. Carlos ROJAS
04 Admin Assistant to the President .... Ms. Quetsy M. ROBLES
08 Chief Library Officer .... Ms. Carmen MALAVET
06 Registrar ....Vacant
07 Director of Admissions ....Mrs. Emsley VAZQUEZ
106 Dean of Online Learning .... Mr. Carlos SELLAS
13 Information Technology Officer .... Ms. Damaris TORRES
19 Director Security/Safety ....Mrs. Miriam PEREZ
37 Student Financial Aid Manager ....Mrs. Myrian GAUD
38 Student Counseling .... Mr. Jose A. SOTO-FRANCESCHINI
96 Director of Purchasing .... Mrs. Carmen A. ARROYO

The Pontifical Catholic University of Puerto Rico (K)

2250 Las Americas Avenue, Suite 564, Ponce PR 00717-9997

County: Ponce FICE Identification: 003936
Unit ID: 241410
Telephone: (787) 841-2000 Carnegie Class: DU-Mod
FAX Number: (787) 651-2034 Calendar System: Semester
URL: www.pucpr.edu
Established: 1948 Annual Undergrad Tuition & Fees: $5,490
Enrollment: 7,381 Coed
Affiliation or Control: Roman Catholic IRS Status: 501(c)3
Highest Offering: Doctorate
Accreditation: M, CACREP, CAEPT, LAW, MT, NUR, SW

00 Chancellor ....M.Rev. Ruben A. GONZALEZ MEDINA, CMF
01 President ....Dr. Jorge I. VELEZ AROCHO
04 Executive Assistant to President .... Lic. Liza RIESTRA
05 Vice President Academic Affairs .... Dr. Leandro COLON ALICEA
10 Vice President of Finance .... Lic. Jose A. FRONTERA AGENJO
32 Vice President for Student Affs ....Prof. Myriam D. LOPEZ
20 Assoc Vice Pres Academic Affairs .....Prof. Maria MUNIZ GARCIA
35 Assoc Vice Pres Student Affairs ....Vacant
09 Vice President Inst Rsrch/Dev Plng .... Dr. Felix CORTES
12 Rector Arecibo Branch .... Dr. Edwin HERNANDEZ
12 Rector Mayaguez Branch .... Dr. Olga HERNÁNDEZ
06 Registrar ....Prof. Ivan DAVILA
07 Interim Director of Admissions ....Prof. Carmen Z. TORRES
08 Director of the Library ....Prof. Magda VARGAS
37 Director of Student Aid ....Mrs. Maria NOLASCO
36 Director of Placement Services ....Mr. Enrique ARROYO
13 Director Computer Center ....Mr. Moises CABRERA
24 Director Educational Technology .... Dr. Edgar RODRIGUEZ
79 Dean of Arts & Humanities ...Rev. Juan Luis NEGRON DELGADO
81 Dean of Sciences .... Dra. Alma L. SANTIAGO
61 Interim Dean of the School of Law ....Lic. Fernando MORENO ORAMA
50 Dean Business Administration .... Dr. David ZAYAS
53 Dean of Education .... Dr. Myriam ZAYAS
58 Dean Institute of Graduate Studies .... Dr. Hernan VERA
48 Dean School of Architecture .... Mr. Luis V. BADILLO-LOZANO
51 Coord Continuing Education Inst ....Mrs. Karen G. MORALES
27 Communications ....Mrs. Jalibeth RODRIGUEZ
29 Alumni Relations Officer .... Mrs. Maria S. MASCARO
15 Director Human Resources ....Mr. Wilfredo CORNIER
40 Director Bookstore .... Mrs. Ashley VELEZ
41 Athletic Director ....Mr. Ramon HERNANDEZ
42 Chaplain .... Rev. Arnaldo ORTIZ
109 Director Auxiliary Enterprises ....Lic. Waddy MERCADO
26 Director Public Relations ....Mrs. Irem POVENTUD
38 Director Student Counseling ....Dr. Arvin BAEZ
18 Physical Plant/Safety & Security ....Mr. Julio PALMER
113 Treasurer Bursar's Office ....Mr. Juan E. ROMAN
96 Director of Purchasing ....Mr. Ruben CRUZ
88 Director of Biotechnology ....Dra. Cariluz SANTIAGO
88 Accreditation Liaison Officer .....Dr. Carmen J. ACOSTA-FUMERO
30 Infrastructure Director ....Ing. Armando RODRIGUEZ
84 Coord Institutional Recruitment ....Sr. Rene MARRERO
89 Director of Freshmen .... Dra. Elizabeth MARTINEZ
106 Dir Online Education/E-learning .... Dra. Ivette TORRES
19 Director Security/Safety ....Mr. Julio PALMER
43 Dir Legal Services/General Counsel .... Lic. Carolyn COSTAS
86 Director Government Relations ....Vacant
100 Chief of Staff .... Lic. Liza RIESTRA
108 Director Institutional Assessment .... Prof. Mishelle RIVERA
39 Director Student Housing ....Mr. Francisco LUGO
39 Director Student Housing .Hna. Gloria N. CARABALLO TURRELL
102 Dir Foundation/Corporate Relations ....Sra. Gladys M. DIAZ
104 Director Study Abroad ....Sr. Joel VELEZ
105 Webmaster II ....Mr. Francisco SUAREZ
88 Director of Compliance ....Lic. Waddy MERCADO

Pontifical Catholic University of Puerto Rico-Arecibo Campus (L)

Box 144045, Arecibo PR 00614-4045

Telephone: (787) 881-1212 Identification: 666603
Accreditation: &M

† Regional accreditation is carried under the parent institution in Ponce, PR.

Pontifical Catholic University of Puerto Rico-Mayaguez Campus (M)

Box 1326, Mayaguez PR 00681-1326

Telephone: (787) 834-5151 Identification: 666605
Accreditation: &M

† Branch campus of The Pontifical Catholic University of Puerto Rico, Ponce, PR.

Puerto Rico School of Nurse Anesthetists (N)

656 Ponce de Leon Avenue, Floor 1, Hato Rey PR 00918

County: San Juan Identification: 667341
Telephone: (787) 998-8997 Carnegie Class: Not Classified
FAX Number: (787) 998-8998 Calendar System: Semester
URL: www.eeapr.org
Established: Annual Undergrad Tuition & Fees: N/A
Enrollment: N/A Coed

Affiliation or Control: Proprietary IRS Status: Proprietary
Highest Offering: Master's
Accreditation: @M, ACICS

01 President .... Dr. Carlos J. BORRERO-RICE
05 Dean of Academic Affs & Accred .... Dr. Noraida DOMINGUEZ

San Juan Bautista School of Medicine (A)

PO Box 4968, Carretera 172, Caguas PR 00726-4968
County: San Juan FICE Identification: 031773
Unit ID: 430670
Telephone: (787) 743-3038 Carnegie Class: Spec-4-yr-Med
FAX Number: (787) 746-3093 Calendar System: Semester
URL: www.sanjuanbautista.edu
Established: 1978 Annual Undergrad Tuition & Fees: $9,172
Enrollment: 316 Coed
Affiliation or Control: Proprietary IRS Status: Proprietary
Highest Offering: First Professional Degree
Accreditation: M, MED

01 President/Dean .... Dr. Yocasta BRUGAL-MENA
11 Dean of Administration .... Mr. Carlos F. ABREU
05 Chief Academic Officer .... Dr. Irving MALDONADO-RIVERA
06 Registrar .... Ms. Aileen FIGUEROA
08 Head Librarian .... Mr. Carlos ALTAMIRANO
10 Chief Business Officer .... Mr. Juan C. CASTRO
32 Chief Student Affairs/Student Life .... Dr. Yolanda MIRANDA
37 Director Student Financial Aid .... Miss Beatriz DE LEON
07 Director of Admissions .... Ms. Jaymi SANCHEZ
108 Director Institutional Assessment .... Vacant
13 Chief Info Technology Officer (CIO) .... Mr. Jorge TORRES
38 Director Student Counseling .... Ms. Ilsa CENTENO

Seminario Teologico de Puerto Rico (B)

Urb Roosevelt 458 Jose Canals #301,
San Juan PR 00918
Telephone: (787) 274-1142 Identification: 770142
Accreditation: &M

† Branch campus of Nyack College, Nyack, NY

Trinity College of Puerto Rico (C)

PO Box 7313, Ponce PR 00732
FICE Identification: 031159
Unit ID: 431929
Telephone: (787) 848-5739 Carnegie Class: Spec 2-yr-Health
FAX Number: (787) 284-2537 Calendar System: Semester
URL: www.trinitypr.edu
Established: 1969 Annual Undergrad Tuition & Fees: $7,574
Enrollment: 149 Coed
Affiliation or Control: Independent Non-Profit IRS Status: 501(c)3
Highest Offering: Associate Degree
Accreditation: COE

01 Executive Director .... Maria DEL PILAR BONNIN OROZCO
05 Academic Dean .... Elizabeth PEREZ TOLEDO
10 Director of Finance Office .... Margarita PEREZ DE JESUS
06 Registrar .... Ana COLON SOTO

Universal Technology College of Puerto Rico (D)

111 Comercio Street, Aguadilla PR 00603
County: Aguadilla FICE Identification: 030297
Unit ID: 376385
Telephone: (787) 882-2065 Carnegie Class: Spec-4-yr-Other Health
FAX Number: (787) 891-2370 Calendar System: Semester
URL: www.unitecpr.edu
Established: 1987 Annual Undergrad Tuition & Fees: N/A
Enrollment: 285 Coed
Affiliation or Control: Independent Non-Profit IRS Status: 501(c)3
Highest Offering: Baccalaureate
Accreditation: ABHES

01 Chief Executive Officer .... Mrs. Keila LOPEZ
11 Administrative Manager .... Vacant
04 Executive Secretary .... Mrs. Marilyn GONZALEZ
05 Chief Academic Officer .... Vacant
06 Registrar .... Ms. Maria ALVAREZ
08 Director of Library .... Ms. Airlyn VAZQUEZ
10 Accountant .... Ms. Nancy MORALES
12 Director of Branch Campus .... Ms. Nelida CARDONA
13 Director Computer Center .... Mr. Zain CORDERO
15 Director Human Resources .... Ms. Yesenia NATAL
18 Chief Facilities/Physical Plant .... Mr. Danily NIEVES
32 Director Student Affairs .... Vacant
36 Student Placement Officer .... Mrs. Evelyn TORRES
45 Director Planning & Development .... Mrs. Evelyn TORRES
37 Director Student Financial Aid .... Mr. Samuel HERNANDEZ
38 Director Student Counsel .... Mrs. Dalia SANTIAGO
96 Purchasing Officer .... Mrs. Dolores MITJANS
23 Healthcare Services .... Mr. Silverio JIMENEZ
07 Coordinator of Admissions .... Mrs. Teresita RIVERA
50 Dir General Studies/Business Admin .... Mrs. Sandra GONZALEZ
72 Director of Industrial Technology .... Mr. Eduardo FIGUEROA

Universidad Adventista de las Antillas (E)

Box 118, Mayaguez PR 00681-0118
County: Mayaguez FICE Identification: 005019
Unit ID: 241191
Telephone: (787) 834-9595 Carnegie Class: Bac-Diverse
FAX Number: (787) 834-9597 Calendar System: Semester
URL: www.uaa.edu
Established: 1961 Annual Undergrad Tuition & Fees: $7,070
Enrollment: 1,271 Coed
Affiliation or Control: Seventh-day Adventist IRS Status: 501(c)3
Highest Offering: Master's
Accreditation: M, ANEST, #COARC, NUR, NURSE

01 President .... Dr. Obed JIMENEZ
10 Vice President Financial Affairs .... Mr. Misael JIMENEZ
32 Vice President for Students Affairs .... Mr. Jaime LOPEZ
30 VP Planning and Development .... Dr. Jose D. GOMEZ
20 Associate VP Academic Affairs .... Mrs. Yolanda PEREZ
21 Associate Financial Vice President .... Mrs. Madeline CRUZ
113 Director Student Finance Office .... Mrs. Gisselle RIVERA
66 Dean of the School of Nursing .... Dr. Maria ROSA
66 Director School of Nursing .... Mrs. Sylvia CARMENATTY
53 Dean of the School of Education .... Dr. Maritza LAMBOY
50 Director of Business Administration .... Dr. David L. RAMOS
81 Director Mathematics/Sciences/Comp .. Mrs. Alicia MORADILLOS
73 Director Theology Department .... Dr. Francisco VEGA
06 Registrar .... Mrs. Ana D. TORRES
07 Director of Admissions .... Mrs. Yolanda FERRER
37 Director of Student Financial Aid .... Mrs. Awilda MATOS
26 Dir Public Relations & Promotion .... Miss Lorell VARELA
108 Dir of Institutional Effectiveness .... Dr. Digna WILLIAMS
13 Director Computing and Information .... Mr. Heber VAZQUEZ
08 Librarian .... Mrs. Aixa VEGA
38 Counselor .... Mrs. Ivelisse PEREZ
88 Environmental Services Director .... Mr. Legna VARELA
18 Chief Facilities/Physical Plant .... Mr. Abel RODRIGUEZ
33 Dean of Men .... Mr. Hector MONTILLA

*Universidad Ana G. Mendez (F)

Apartado 21345, Rio Piedras PR 00928-1341
County: San Juan FICE Identification: 029078
Unit ID: 242060
Telephone: (787) 751-0178 Carnegie Class: N/A
FAX Number: (787) 766-1706
URL: www.suagm.edu

01 President .... Mr. Jose F. MENDEZ
05 Vice President for Academic Affairs .... Mr. Jorge L. CRESPO
10 Vice Pres Financial Affairs .... Mr. Carmelo TORRES
32 VP Student Affairs .... Dr. Mayra CRUZ
45 Vice President Planning & Research .... Mr. Jorge CRESPO
11 Executive & Operations Vice Pres .... Mr. Ricardo RODRIGUEZ
15 Vice President Human Resources .... Dr. Victoria DE JESUS
88 Acting Vice Pres International Affs .... Dr. Rafael NADAL
13 Chief Information Officer .... Sr. Kenneth MALDONADO
26 Associate Vice Pres for Public Rels .... Ms. Maria MARTINEZ
04 Exec Assistant to President .... Ms. Lydia I. MASSARI
06 Registrar .... Ms. Elisa QUILES
07 Director of Admissions .... Ms. Ramonita FUENTES

*Universidad Ana G. Mendez Carolina Campus (G)

Carr #190 Ave. Principal Sabana, Carolina PR 00983-2010
County: San Juan FICE Identification: 003941
Unit ID: 243346
Telephone: (787) 257-7373 Carnegie Class: Masters/L
FAX Number: (787) 776-1220 Calendar System: Semester
URL: www.suagm.edu/une
Established: 1949 Annual Undergrad Tuition & Fees: $5,820
Enrollment: 11,642 Coed
Affiliation or Control: Independent Non-Profit IRS Status: 501(c)3
Highest Offering: Master's
Accreditation: M, ACBSP, ACFEI, ADNUR, CAEPT, NUR, SW

01 President .... Mr. José F. MENDEZ
02 Chancellor .... Dr. Mildred HUERTAS SOLÁ
05 Vice Chancellor Academic Affairs .... Dr. Angel A. TOLEDO LÓPEZ
32 Vice Chancellor Student Affairs .... Dr. María G. VEAZ
84 Assoc VC Enrollment Management .... Mrs. Magda E. OSTOLAZA
15 Vice Pres Human Resources .... Dr. Victoria DE JESÚS
88 Dean Intl Sch Hosp/Culinary Arts .... Mrs. Terestella GONZÁLEZ
107 Dean Professional Studies .... Mrs. Mildred Y. RIVERA
06 Registrar .... Ms. Elisa QUILES
08 Director of Library .... Mrs. Elsa MARIANI
26 Director Public Relations .... Mrs. Ivonne D. ARROYO
83 Dean of Social and Human Sciences .... Dr. Evelyza CRESPO
50 Dean of Business Administration .... Dr. José E. BERRÍOS
72 Dean of Science and Technology .... Dr. Marielis E. RIVERA
76 Dean of Health Science .... Dr. Vanessa ORTIZ
19 Director Security/Safety .... Mr. José E. MACHUCA

*Universidad Ana G. Mendez Cupey Campus (H)

PO Box 21150, Rio Piedras PR 00928-1150
County: San Juan FICE Identification: 025875
Unit ID: 241739
Telephone: (787) 766-1717 Carnegie Class: Masters/L
FAX Number: (787) 759-7663 Calendar System: Semester
URL: umet.suagm.edu
Established: 1980 Annual Undergrad Tuition & Fees: $5,820
Enrollment: 13,003 Coed
Affiliation or Control: Independent Non-Profit IRS Status: 501(c)3
Highest Offering: Doctorate
Accreditation: M, ACBSP, ADNUR, CAEPT, NUR, @SW

02 SUAGM President .... Mr. José F. MENDEZ
00 Chancellor .... Dr. Carlos M. PADIN
03 Executive Vice President .... Mr. Ricardo RODRIGUEZ
05 Vice Chancellor Academic Affairs .... Dr. Juan OTERO
10 Vice President of Financial Affairs .... Mr. Carmelo TORRES
108 Asst Vice Chanc Inst Assessment .... Dr. Carmen M. LUNA
30 Asst Vice Chanc Inst Development .... Ms. Belissa AQUINO
32 Vice Chanc for Student Affairs .... Dr. Glenda BERMUDEZ
88 Executive Director Intl Affairs .... Dr. Zaida VEGA
26 Vice Chanc External Resources .... Dr. Gladys CORA
88 Assoc Vice Chanc Accred/Lic .... Mrs. Lina VEGA
11 Assoc Vice Chanc for Admin Affairs .... Dr. Gregorio VILLEGAS
15 Asst Vice Pres for Human Resources .... Mrs. Camile PEREZ
13 Director Information Resources .... Mr. Rafael I. GARCÍA
84 Int Assc Vice Chanc Student Recruit .... Mrs. Elizabeth CANCEL
114 Director Pres Analysis & Budget .... Mrs. Aixa ALDARONDO
45 Asst Vice President of Planning .... Dr. Mariela COLLAZO
124 Assoc Vice Chanc Retention/Develop .... Mrs. Awilda PEREZ
83 Dean Soc Scienc/Human & Comm .... Dr. Mariveliz CABAN
50 Dean of Business .... Dr. Belinda JUNQUERA
53 Dean of Education .... Dr. José R. CINTRON
76 Dean of Health Science .... Dr. Lourdes MALDONADO
81 Dean of Science/Technology & Envir .... Dr. Karen GONZALEZ
65 Assoc Dean of Environmental Affairs .... Dr. María C. ORTIZ
107 Assoc Dean of Professional Studies .... Ms. Melissa GUILLIANI
60 Assoc Dean of Communications .... Mrs. Sugelenia COTTO
79 Assoc Dean of Humanities .... Dr. Roxanna D. DOMENECH
75 Dean of Technical Studies .... Mrs. Laura E. APONTE
51 Exec Director Continuing Education .... Dr. Luis A. MARRERO
53 Assoc Dean of Education .... Dr. Janet RUÍZ
08 Head Librarian .... Mrs. Balbina J. ROJAS
18 Manager Operations & Facilities .... Eng. Carmencita TORRES
76 Director of Respiratory Therapy .... Mrs. Katherine GARCÍA
66 Director of Nursing .... Dr. Yanilda RODRIGUEZ
26 Director Public Relations .... Ms. Yvonne GUADALUPE
06 Registrar .... Mrs. Beatriz NIEVES
12 Additional Location Dir Bayamon .... Mr. Sixto BERMUDEZ
12 Additional Location Dir Aguadilla .... Mr. Luis A. RUIZ
12 Additional Location Dir Jayuya .... Dr. Irma del Pilar CRUZ
12 Additional Location Dir Comerío .... Mr. Sixto BERMUDEZ
07 Admissions Director .... Ms. Yadira RIVERA LUGO
41 Athletic Director .... Mr. Edgar I. DIAZ
19 Director Security/Safety .... Mr. Wilfredo RONDON
36 Director Student Placement .... Mrs. Lourdes E. MEDINA
37 Director Student Financial Aid .... Mr. Julio A. RODRÍGUEZ
38 Assoc Vice Chanc Student Wellness .... Mrs. Arelis VILLANUEVA

*Universidad Ana G. Mendez Gurabo Campus (I)

Estacion Universidad, Box 3030, Gurabo PR 00778-3030
County: Gurabo FICE Identification: 011719
Unit ID: 243601
Telephone: (787) 743-7979 Carnegie Class: DU-Mod
FAX Number: (787) 744-5394 Calendar System: Semester
URL: www.suagm.edu
Established: 1972 Annual Undergrad Tuition & Fees: $5,820
Enrollment: 17,034 Coed
Affiliation or Control: Independent Non-Profit IRS Status: 501(c)3
Highest Offering: Doctorate
Accreditation: M, CAEPT, COPSY, #DIETC, JOUR, LSAR, @NATUR, NURSE, #SP, SW

02 Chancellor .... Dr. David MENDEZ
11 Actg Vice Chancellor Admin Affairs .... Ms. Mari G. GONZALEZ
05 Vice Chancellor .... Dra. Nydia BOU
32 Vice Chancellor of Student Affairs .... Dra. Brunilda APONTE
08 Vice Chancellor Information Res .... Dr. Sarai LASTRA
92 Internship & Honors Program Coord .... Ms. Wanda I. GONZÁLEZ
88 Asst Vice Chanc Eval & Development .... Ms. Lizbeth RIVERA
21 Director of Admin Affairs .... Mrs. Belinda ROSA
53 Dean Education .... Dra. Elaine GUADALUPEZ
50 Dean Business and Entrepreneurship .... Dr. Juan Carlos SOSA
54 Dean Engineering .... Dr. Rolando GARCIA
72 Dean Natural Science & Technology .... Dr. Teresa LIPSETT
83 Dean Social Sciences/ Communications .... Dra. Maria del C. SANTOS
48 Dean Architecture/Design .... Ms. Aurorisa MATEO
76 Acting Dean Health Sciences .... Dra. Nydia BOU
88 Dean Technical Studies .... Ms. Maria E. FLORES
107 Dean Professional Stds & Cont Educ .... Ms. Mildred Y. RIVERA
58 Associate Dean of Graduate Studies .... Dr. Sharon CANTRELL
06 Registrar .... Mrs. Zoraida ORTIZ
97 Dean of Liberal Arts & Gen Studies .... Mr. Felix R. HUERTAS
26 Director of Marketing .... Ms. Melba G. SANCHEZ
37 Director Office of Financial Aid .... Mrs. Carmen J. RIVERA
26 Director Public Relations .... Ms. Iris SERRANO
18 Chief Facilities/Physical Plant .... Ms. Mayra RODRIGUEZ
29 Coordinator Alumni Relations .... Mr. Wilfredo HILLS
30 Chief Development Officer .... Mr. Rene S. RONDA
96 Director of Purchasing .... Ms. Norma C. DONEZ
07 Director of Admissions .... Mrs. Diriee Y. RODRIGUEZ
45 Aux Vice President of Planning .... Ms. Mari G. GONZALEZ
15 Aux Vice President Human Resources .... Mrs. Iris BERRIOS
36 Assoc Vice Chanc Student Placement .... Ms. Carmen PULLIZA

84 Asst Vice Chanc Enrollment Mgmt ....Ms. Maria V. FIGUEROA
114 Aux Vice President of Budget .... Ms. Camille LAMBOY
38 Assoc Vice Chanc Student Counseling ..... Ms. Samaris COLLAZO
106 Dir Online Education/E-learning .... Mr. Israel RODRIGUEZ
108 Asst Vice Chanc Assessment .... Mr. Ernesto ESPINOZA
41 Athletic Director .... Mr. Felix A. CARRASQUILLO

*Universidad Ana G. Mendez Online Campus (A)

PO Box 21345, San Juan PR 00928-1345

County: San Juan | Identification: 667292
Telephone: (787) 288-1118 | Carnegie Class: Not Classified
FAX Number: (787) 288-1141 | Calendar System: Semester
URL: agmonline.suagm.edu
Established: | Annual Graduate Tuition & Fees: N/A
Enrollment: N/A | Coed
Affiliation or Control: Independent Non-Profit | IRS Status: 501(c)3
Highest Offering: Master's; No Undergraduates
Accreditation: M

02 Chancellor .... Dr. Gino Q. NATALICCHIO
11 Vice Chanc Administrative Affairs .... Ms. Nilsa RODRÍGUEZ-MARTORELL
10 Acting Vice Chancellor .... Dr. Jose E. MALDONADO-ROJAS
06 Registrar ....Ms. Jessie PEREZ
07 Director of Admissions ....Ms. Marilys RIVERA
106 Director Online Education/E-learnin ....Ms. Denisse COLON
108 Director Institutional Assessment ....Ms. Dennise RIVERA
32 Chief Student Affairs .... Mr. Jose D. MARTINEZ
37 Director Student Financial Aid .... Mr. Eduardo VERA
38 Director Student Counseling ....Ms. Sharon CORREA

Universidad Central de Bayamon (B)

PO Box 1725, Bayamon PR 00960-1725

County: Bayamon | FICE Identification: 005022
Unit ID: 241225
Telephone: (787) 786-3030 | Carnegie Class: Masters/S
FAX Number: (787) 740-2200 | Calendar System: Semester
URL: www.ucb.edu.pr
Established: 1961 | Annual Undergrad Tuition & Fees: $6,260
Enrollment: 1,742 | Coed
Affiliation or Control: Roman Catholic | IRS Status: 501(c)3
Highest Offering: Master's
Accreditation: M, CACREP, NURSE, SW, THEOL

01 Interim President .... Prof. Angel VALENTIN
03 Executive Vice President ....Vacant
05 Academic Dean ....Ms. Cristina ALCARAZ
10 Dean Admin/Finance ....Mr. Juan J. GARCIA
32 Dean of Students .... Mrs. Niza ZAYAS
49 Dir Col Liberal Arts/Humanities/Ed ....Fray. Jose M. SANTIAGO
50 Dir Business Development & Tech ....Dr. Nidia COLON
08 Director Learning Resources ....Vacant
15 Director of Human Resources ....Mrs. Virna RIVERA
07 Director of Admissions .... Mrs. Wanda APONTE
37 Director Student Financial Aid .... Mrs. Edna ORTIZ
38 Dir Guidance/Counseling Center ....Mrs. Milagros M. RIVERA
06 Registrar ....Dr. Kendra M. ORTIZ
35 Coord Center Learning Stre (CFAEE) .... Mrs. Myrna PEREZ
13 Director of Information System ....Mr. Jose R. AVILES
18 Director Physical Facilities .... Mr. Eliezer GARCIA
26 Supt Marketing and Recruitment .... Ms. Magdalis LOPEZ
96 Purchase Officer .... Mrs. Jessica OJEDA
09 Institutional Research Officer .... Mrs. Luz M. PALACIOS
66 Nursing Program Coordinator ....Prof. Zaida RUIZ
20 Associate Academic Dean ....Mr. Pedro A. BERMUDEZ
29 Alumni Relations .... Mrs. Niza ZAYAS
81 Dir College Sciences/Health Prof .... Dr. Pedro ROBLES
04 Administrative Asst to President ....Mrs. Monica D. GONZALEZ
101 Secretary of the Institution/Board ....Prof. Wanda I. HERNANDEZ
105 Director Web Services ....Mr. Jose A. AVILES
106 Dir Online Education/E-learning ....Mr. Jorge L. DIAZ
108 Director Institutional Assessment ....Mrs. Vivian A. PADILLA
41 Athletic Director ....Mr. Juan A. FIGUEROA
88 Compliance Officer .... Ms. Elaine NUNEZ

Universidad Central Del Caribe (C)

PO Box 60-327, Bayamon PR 00960-6032

County: Bayamon | FICE Identification: 021633
Unit ID: 243568
Telephone: (787) 798-3001 | Carnegie Class: Spec-4-yr-Med
FAX Number: (787) 798-6836 | Calendar System: Semester
URL: www.uccaribe.edu
Established: 1976 | Annual Undergrad Tuition & Fees: $8,182
Enrollment: 466 | Coed
Affiliation or Control: Independent Non-Profit | IRS Status: 501(c)3
Highest Offering: Doctorate
Accreditation: M, #MED

01 President ....Dr. Waleska CRESPO-RIVERA
05 Dean for Academic Affairs .... Dr. Nereida DIAZ-RODRIGUEZ
20 Asst Dean of Curriculum Development ....Dr. Alvaro PEREZ
11 Dean Administrative Affairs ....Ms. Emilia SOTO
32 Dean Student Affairs ....Dr. Omar PEREZ
63 Dean of Medicine ....Dr. Jose Ginel RODRIGUEZ
88 Associate Dean of Medicine ....Mrs. Zilka RIOS
06 Registrar ....Ms. Nilda MONTANEZ-LOPEZ
07 Director of Admissions ....Ms. Irma L. CORDERO
37 Director Student Financial Aid .... Ms. Mayra SERRANO
10 Director of Finances ....Mrs. Iris J. FONT
08 Librarian ....Ms. Mildred RIVERA
51 Director of Continuing Medical Educ .... Dr. Frances GARCIA
38 Counselor ....Vacant
46 Dean of Research & Graduate Studies ..... Dr. Delia M. CAMACHO
20 Dean for Clinical & Faculty Affairs .... Dr. Harry MERCADO
30 Dean of Inst Devel & Strategic Plng .... Ms. Mildred RIVERA-MARRERO

Universidad Pentecostal Mizpa (D)

RR16 Box 4800, San Juan PR 00926

County: San Juan | FICE Identification: 031983
Unit ID: 441690
Telephone: (787) 720-4476 | Carnegie Class: Spec-4-yr-Faith
FAX Number: N/A | Calendar System: Semester
URL: www.mizpa.edu
Established: 1937 | Annual Undergrad Tuition & Fees: $4,220
Enrollment: 309 | Coed
Affiliation or Control: Pentecostal Church of God | IRS Status: 501(c)3
Highest Offering: Master's
Accreditation: BI

01 President .... Mrs. Naury Y. SANCHEZ CINTRON
05 Dean of Academic Affairs .Mr. Jose G. TORRACA MONDRIGUEZ
10 Dean Administration/Finance .Mrs. Maureen DE LEON MULLERT
32 Dean of Student Affairs ....Mr. Jorge A. BURGOS CARRION
42 Chaplain/Director Campus Ministry .....Mr. Harry MUNOZ COLON
35 Associate Student/Affairs Life ....Mrs. Daulan NIEVES GARCIA
06 Registrar ....Mr. Leonardo MELENDEZ LEON
08 Librarian ....Miss Melanie RODRIGUEZ MARTINEZ
37 Student Financial Aid Officer ....Mrs. Myriam JUARBE REY
26 Chief Public Relations Officer ....Mr. Rafael LABOY FUSTER
113 Bursar .... Geserie CRUZADO ROSADO
04 Administrative Asst to President ....Miss Jaydee A. GUZMAN QUILES

Universidad Politecnica de Puerto Rico (E)

Ponce de Leon 377, Box 192017, San Juan PR 00919-2017

County: San Juan | FICE Identification: 021000
Unit ID: 243577
Telephone: (787) 622-8000 | Carnegie Class: Spec-4-yr-Eng
FAX Number: (787) 754-8268 | Calendar System: Trimester
URL: www.pupr.edu
Established: 1966 | Annual Undergrad Tuition & Fees: $8,610
Enrollment: 4,315 | Coed
Affiliation or Control: Independent Non-Profit | IRS Status: 501(c)3
Highest Offering: Master's
Accreditation: M, LSAR

01 President .... Dr. Ernesto VAZQUEZ-BARQUET
03 Executive Vice President .... Eng. Ernesto VAZQUEZ-MARTINEZ
84 Vice Pres Enrollment Management ....Mr. Carlos PEREZ
05 Chief Academic Officer ....Dr. Miguel A. RIESTRA
06 Registrar .... Mrs. Mayra I. LOPEZ
07 Director Admissions .... Mrs. Teresa CARDONA
08 Head Librarian ....Mrs. Mirta COLON
37 Director Financial Aid ....Mr. Sergio VILLOLDO
15 Director Personnel Services ....Ms. Ana CASTELLANO
18 Chief Facilities/Physical Plant ....Mr. Herminio ROMERO
29 Alumni Relations .... Ms. Lourdes ALCRUDO
32 Director Student Affairs ....Mr. Carlos PEREZ
36 Director Student Placement .... Mrs. Angie ESCALANTE
38 Director Student Counseling .... Ms. Sheila VAZQUEZ
10 Associate Business Officer ....Vacant
96 Director of Purchasing ....Mr. Ramon RIVERA
19 Director Security/Safety .... Mr. Miguel ALBARRAN
41 Athletic Director ....Mr. Roberto MEDINA-ORTIZ
50 Dean of Business ....Vacant
49 Dean of Arts and Science/Education .... Dr. Catalina VICENS
54 Dean of Engineering ....Dr. Carlos J. GONZALEZ
106 Dir Online Education/E-learning .... Dr. Cuauhtemoc GODOY
108 Director Institutional Assessment .... Dr. Miguel A. RIESTRA-FERNANDEZ
91 Director Administrative Computing .... Mr. Pedro PEREZ-DORTA
09 Director of Institutional Research ....Dr. Miguel A. RIESTRA

Universidad Teologica Del Caribe (F)

PO Box 901, Saint Just PR 00978-0901

County: Trujillo Alto | FICE Identification: 023355
Unit ID: 241614
Telephone: (787) 761-0640 | Carnegie Class: Spec-4-yr-Faith
FAX Number: (787) 748-9220 | Calendar System: Semester
URL: www.utcpr.edu
Established: 1956 | Annual Undergrad Tuition & Fees: $4,342
Enrollment: 370 | Coed
Affiliation or Control: Church Of God | IRS Status: 501(c)3
Highest Offering: Master's
Accreditation: BI

01 President .... Francisco ORTIZ
05 Academic Dean .... Carmen AYALA
06 Registrar ....Awilda MORALES
10 Administration Dean .... Frankie NEGRON
32 Students Dean .... Wilfredo ADORNO
37 Financial Aid Director ....Claudia RODRIGUEZ
08 Librarian ....Graciela TORRES
45 Planning & Development Officer ....Ana CEPERO
106 Online Program Coordinator .... Raul MCCLIN
58 Graduate School Coordinator ....Samuel CARABALLO
12 North-Central (Dorado) Campus Coord ....Richard D'COSTA
04 Administrative Asst to the Pres ....Waleska VEGA
07 Admissions Officer ....Avianny PAULINO

*University of Puerto Rico-Central Administration (G)

1187 Flamboyan Street, San Juan PR 00926-1117

County: San Juan | FICE Identification: 003942
Unit ID: 243160
Telephone: (787) 250-0000 | Carnegie Class: N/A
FAX Number: (787) 759-6917
URL: www.upr.edu

01 President .... Dr. Jorge HADDOCK-ACEVEDO
03 Acting Executive Director ...... Mrs. Katherine MELÉNDEZ-MATEO
05 Vice President for Academic Affairs ....Dr. Ubaldo M. CORDOVA-FIGUEROA
09 Acting Director ....Dr. José R. RODRÍGUEZ-MEDINA
32 Acting Vice Pres - Student Affairs .....Dr. Aileen TORRES-MAYMÍ
12 Acting Chanc UPR-Rio Piedras Campus ....Dr. Luis A. FERRAO-DELGADO
12 Acting Chanc UPR-Mayaguez Campus .... Ms. Wilma SANTIAGO-GABRIELINI
12 Acting Chanc UPR-Medical SciencCam .... Dr. Segundo RODRÍGUEZ-QUILICHINI
12 Acting Chancellor UPR-Cayey Campus ....Dr. José A. MOLINA-COTTO
12 Acting Chanc UPR-Humacao Campus .... Dr. Héctor A. RÍOS-MAURY
12 Acting Chanc UPR-Bayamon Campus ...Dr. Miguel VELEZ-RUBIO
12 Acting Chancellor UPR-Ponce Campus ....Prof. Carmen BRACERO-LUGO
12 Acting Chanc UPR-Carolina Campus .... Prof. Jorge I. VALENTÍN-ASENCIO
12 Acting Chancellor UPR-Utuado Campus ....Dr. José L. HEREDIA-RODRÍGUEZ
12 Acting Chanc UPR-Aguadilla Campus ....Dr. Ivelice CARDONA-CORTÉS
12 Acting Chanc UPR-Arecibo Campus ....Dr. Carlos A. ANDÚJAR-ROJAS
30 Dir Devel & Alumni Affairs Office ....Vacant
88 Dir Ctrl Designer Construction ....Vacant
10 Acting Director Finance Office ..Mr. Antonio TEJERA-ROCAFORT
15 Acting Dir Human Resources Office ....Mr. Nelson RIVERA-VILLANUEVA
11 Director Administrative Service ....Vacant
13 Acting Dir Information Systems Ofc ....Mr. Heriberto LUNA-DE LOS SANTOS
37 Director Student Financial Aid ....Vacant
43 Acting Director Legal Affairs Ofc ....Ms. Soniemi RODRÍGUEZ-DÁVILA
88 Acting Admin Botanical Garden ....Mr. Carlos R. DÍAZ-PÉREZ
26 Acting Dir Press & Communications .... Ms. Joan M. HERNÁNDEZ-MARRERO
101 Acting Exec Sec University Board ....Dr. Divya C. COLÓN-ALCARAZ
114 Acting Director Budget Office .Mrs. Brunilda PEREIRA-VALENTÍN
18 Actg Dir Phys Dev/Infrastrcture Ofc ...... Mr. Adrián LOPEZ-NUNCI

*University of Puerto Rico-Aguadilla (H)

PO Box 6150, Aguadilla PR 00604-6150

County: Aguadilla | FICE Identification: 012123
Unit ID: 243106
Telephone: (787) 890-2681 | Carnegie Class: Bac-Diverse
FAX Number: (787) 891-3455 | Calendar System: Semester
URL: www.uprag.edu
Established: 1972 | Annual Undergrad Tuition & Fees (In-State): $4,654
Enrollment: 3,426 | Coed
Affiliation or Control: State | IRS Status: 501(c)3
Highest Offering: Baccalaureate
Accreditation: M, ACBSP, CAEPN

02 Acting Chancellor ....Dr. Ivelice CARDONA-CORTÉS
05 Acting Dean Academic Affairs .... Dr. Sonia RIVERA-GONZÁLEZ
11 Acting Dean Administrative Affairs ....Mr. Héctor M. VELEZ-RODRÍGUEZ
32 Acting Dean Student Affairs ....Prof. Pablo A. RAMÍREZ-MÉNDEZ
06 Registrar ....Mrs. Wanda FELICIANO-MÉNDEZ
07 Admissions Officer .... Mrs. Melba SERRANO
08 Head Librarian .... Prof. Elsa MATOS
13 Director of Computer Center .... Mr. Carlos JIMENEZ
15 Director of Personnel ....Mrs. Nilsa MORALES TORRES
19 Director of Security/Safety ....Mr. Edwin VAZQUEZ MEDINA
37 Director Student Financial Aid .... Mrs. Marta A. SOTO
51 Director Continuing Education ....Sr. Birilo SANTIAGO-VELÁZQUEZ
38 Director Student Counseling .... Dr. Gilberto HERRERA
45 Dir Planning/Inst Research Office ....Mr. Gerardo JAVARIZ
18 Chief Facilities/Physical Plant ....Vacant
29 Director Alumni Relations ....Mrs. Jeannette AQUINO
96 Purchasing Supervisor .... Mrs. Widylia MEDINA

*University of Puerto Rico at Arecibo (A)

Call Box 4010, Arecibo PR 00614-4010
County: Arecibo
FICE Identification: 007228
Unit ID: 243115
Telephone: (787) 815-0000
Carnegie Class: Bac-Diverse
FAX Number: (787) 880-2245
Calendar System: Semester
URL: www.upra.edu
Established: 1967
Annual Undergrad Tuition & Fees (In-State): $4,094
Enrollment: 3,799
Coed
Affiliation or Control: State
IRS Status: 501(c)3
Highest Offering: Baccalaureate
Accreditation: M, ACBSP, ADNUR, CAEPN, JOUR, NUR

02 Chancellor ... Dr. Carlos A. ANDÚJAR ROJAS
05 Dean of Academic Affairs ... Dr. Weyna M. QUIÑONES CASTILLO
11 Dean of Administrative Affairs ... Dr. Inocencio RODRÍGUEZ
32 Dean of Student Affairs ... Dr. José C. COLÓN
09 Dir Planning/Institutional Research ... Dr. Geissa TORRES
06 Registrar ... Mrs. Magaly MENDEZ
07 Director of Admissions ... Mrs. Magaly MENDEZ
08 Head Librarian ... Prof. Víctor MALDONADO
15 Director Human Resources ... Mrs. Sandra DE JESÚS
38 Director Student Counseling ... Prof. Niurka CARDONA
04 Assistant to the Chancellor ... Dr. José ALBERTY
37 Director Student Financial Aid ... Ms. Daliana FRESSE
41 Athletic Director ... Mr. Alexieyi RIVERA
13 Computing & Information Management ... Prof. Luis COLON
20 Assoc Dean of Academic Affairs ... Dra. Vanessa MONTALVO
92 Director Honors Program ... Dra. Jane ALBERDESTON
96 Director of Purchasing ... Mrs. Iris REYES

*University of Puerto Rico at Bayamon (B)

Carr. 174 #170 Industrial Minillas,
Bayamon PR 00959-1911
County: Bayamon
FICE Identification: 010975
Unit ID: 243133
Telephone: (787) 993-0000
Carnegie Class: Bac-Diverse
FAX Number: (787) 993-8900
Calendar System: Semester
URL: www.uprb.edu
Established: 1971
Annual Undergrad Tuition & Fees (In-State): $4,084
Enrollment: 4,531
Coed
Affiliation or Control: State
IRS Status: 501(c)3
Highest Offering: Baccalaureate
Accreditation: M, ACBSP, CAEPN

02 Chancellor ... Dr. Miguel VELEZ-RUBIO
05 Dean Academic Affairs ... Dr. Jorge ROVIRA-ALVAREZ
32 Dean Student Affairs ... Dr. Lenis TORRES-BERRIOS
06 Registrar ... Ms. Elizabeth ORTIZ-VARGAS
07 Director Admissions ... Ms. Minerva HERNÁNDEZ-BERNIER
08 Director Learning Resources ... Dr. Raúl PAGÁN-FALCÓN
11 Dean Administrative Affairs ... Mr. Luis MUÑOZ-ALVARADO
15 Director Human Resources . Ms. Carina FIGUEROA-RODRÍGUEZ
35 Director Student Activities ... Mrs. Maribelle PERGOLA-RIVERA
37 Director Student Financial Aid ... Mr. Marcos DE JESÚS
38 Director Student Counseling .. Dr. Irma J. SANTIAGO-SANTIAGO
81 Director Biology ... Dr. Darinel ORTIZ-PADILLAT
50 Director Business Administration ... Dr. Janet CABRERA-RIVERA
09 Director Planning & Inst Research ... Mr. Javier ZAVALA-QUIÑONES
53 Director Education ... Dr. José A. CRESPO-REYES
54 Director Engineering ... Prof. Jorge VELAR-PRIETO
68 Director Physical Education ... Prof. Carlos MARICHAL-LUGO
79 Director Humanities ... Dr. Luis PABÓN-BATLLE
83 Director Social Sciences ... Dr. Elizabeth CRESPO-KEBLER
77 Director Computer Science ... Dr. Nelliud TORRES-BATISTA
75 Director Secretarial Sciences ... Dr. Peggy SANTIAGO-LÓPEZ
72 Director Electronics ... Prof. Samuel LUGO-VÉLEZ
23 Director Health Services ... Dr. Kimberly RIVERA-SANTIAGO
96 Director Purchasing ... Ms. Allison M. BRACHE-MELLO
88 Director Special Services ... Ms. Shelciy COLLAZO-CASTRO
81 Director Physics ... Dr. Javier AVALOS-SÁNCHEZ
88 Director English ... Prof. Carmen SKERRETT-LLANOS
88 Director Spanish ... Dr. Raúl GUADALUPE-DE JESÚS
81 Director Mathematics ... Prof. Angel MORERA-GONZÁLEZ
88 Director Chemistry ... Dr. Marisol CORDERO-RIVERA
18 Coord Facilities/Physical Plant ... Mr. Carlos CLAUDIO-VILLAFAÑE
114 Director Budget ... Mr. Rafael L. GIERBOLINI-SANTIAGO
10 Director Finance ... Ms. Mayra NAVARRO-FIGUEROA
13 Director Information Systems .Ms. Barbara LANDRAU-ESPINOSA
105 Director Web Services ... Mr. Orlando ORENGO-ORTEGA
19 Director Security/Safety ... Mr. Victor RODRÍGUEZ-FIGUEROA
41 Athletic Director ... Mr. Gerardo BATISTA-SANTIAGO
43 Dir Legal Services/General Counsel ... Mr. Angel MARRERO-HERNÁNDEZ

*University of Puerto Rico-Carolina (C)

PO Box 4800, Carolina PR 00984-4800
County: San Juan
FICE Identification: 030160
Unit ID: 243142
Telephone: (787) 257-0000
Carnegie Class: Bac-Diverse
FAX Number: (787) 750-7940
Calendar System: Quarter
URL: www.uprc.edu
Established: 1974
Annual Undergrad Tuition & Fees (In-State): $6,121
Enrollment: 3,792
Coed
Affiliation or Control: State
IRS Status: 501(c)3
Highest Offering: Baccalaureate
Accreditation: M, ACBSP

02 Chancellor ... Dr. Jorge I. VALENTIN
05 Dean of Academic Affairs ... Dr. Jimmy TORRES
11 Dean Administrative Affairs ... Dr. José I. MEZA
32 Dean Student Affairs ... Dr. Gerardo PERFECTO
06 Registrar ... Mrs. Ana Y. RIVERA
15 Human Resources Director ... Mrs. Sheila D. SABAT
09 Director of Planning/Inst Research ... Dra. Cristina MARTINEZ
08 Director Learning Resources Center ... Prof. Stanley PORTELA
51 Director Continuing Education ... Prof. Miguel PERÉZ
07 Admissions Officer ... Mrs. Celia MENDEZ
13 Coord/Dir Computer Sys Center ... Mr. Juan CRUZ
37 Financial Aid Director ... Mr. Rafael RUIZ
22 Affirmative Action Officer ... Vacant
48 Director Graphic Arts/Advertising ... Prof. Orlando TORRES
50 Director Banking/Finance/Insurance ... Dr. George OTERO
81 Director Natural Sciences ... Dra. Karilys GONZALEZ
88 Director Secretarial Sciences ... Prof. Josefina RODRIGUEZ
83 Director Social Sciences ... Dr. Kathia WALKERS
68 Director Physical Education ... Prof. Walbert MARCANO
88 Director Auto Tech/Mech Engineering ... Dr. Jose MEZA
79 Director Humanities ... Dr. Bianca APONTE
88 Director Spanish ... Dra. Zulma PENCHI
88 Director English ... Prof. Wanda RODRIGUEZ
88 Dean Hotel Administration School ... Prof. Miguel E. PEREZ
23 Director Health Care ... Dr. Zaida DIAZ
18 Supt Operations & Maintenance ... Mr. Herman MUNIZ
41 Athletic Director ... Mr. Arcadio OCASIO
10 Chief Business Officer ... Mrs. Sarahi GUADALUPE

*University of Puerto Rico at Cayey (D)

PO BOX 372230, Cayey PR 00737-2230
County: Cayey
FICE Identification: 007206
Unit ID: 243151
Telephone: (787) 738-2161
Carnegie Class: Bac-A&S
FAX Number: N/A
Calendar System: Semester
URL: www.cayey.upr.edu
Established: 1967
Annual Undergrad Tuition & Fees (In-State): $4,089
Enrollment: 3,496
Coed
Affiliation or Control: State
IRS Status: 501(c)3
Highest Offering: Baccalaureate
Accreditation: M, ACBSP, CAEP

02 Chancellor ... Dr. Glorivee ROSARIO
05 Dean of Academic Affairs ... Prof. Irmannette TORRES-LUGO
11 Dean of Administration Affairs ... Prof. Isamel QUILES
32 Dean of Student Affairs ... Mr. Eleric RIVERA
08 Director Library ... Prof. Angel RIOS
06 Registrar ... Mrs. Daisy RAMOS
15 Director Human Resources ... Mrs. Enerida RODRIGUEZ
56 Head Extension Division ... Dr. Aurora GONZALEZ
37 Director Student Financial Aid ... Mrs. Pedro AYALA
38 Director Student Counseling ... Dr. Lino HERNANDEZ
13 Director Computer Center ... Mrs. Minerva DIAZ
45 Director Planning & Assessment ... Dr. Xiomara SANTIAGO
07 Director Admissions ... Mr. Jesus MARTINEZ
18 Director Facilities/Physical Plant ... Mr. Edwin MELENDEZ
23 Director Health Services ... Dr. Idellisse BALBES
19 Director Security/Safety ... Mr. Luis LOPEZ
92 Director Honor Program ... Dr. Olga COLON
41 Director Athletic Program ... Mr. Ismael RAMOS
96 Director Purchasing ... Mrs. Maria CORTES
43 Director Legal Services ... Mr. Francisco MORENO
88 Student Ombudsman ... Prof. Efrain COLON
53 Education ... Dr. Gabriel ROMAN
79 Humanities ... Dr. Walter MUCHER
83 Social Sciences ... Dr. Sarah MALAVE
88 Hispanic Studies ... Dr. Jose PEREZ
88 English ... Dr. Carmen GONZALEZ
81 Chemistry ... Dr. Wilfredo RESTO
65 Natural Science ... Dr. Olgary FIGUEROA
88 Biology ... Dr. Edwin VAZQUEZ
94 Women's Studies ... Dr. Irma LUGO
10 Chief Business Officer ... Ms. Glorimar ORTIZ
114 Director Budgeting ... Mrs. Maria SANTIAGO
81 Mathematics-Physics ... Dr. Jose ALONSO
50 Business Administration ... Prof. Edfel RIVERA
88 RISE Program ... Dr. Vibha BANSAL
88 Interdisciplinary Research Inst ... Ms. Vionex MARTI
88 Museum ... Mr. Jonathan BERRIOS
100 Chief of Staff ... Prof. Gladys RAMOS
101 Secretary of the Institution/Board ... Mrs. Iris LOPEZ
104 Director Study Abroad ... Ms. Elsandra RIVERA
105 Director Web Services ... Mr. William SANDOVAL
88 Director of Cultural Activities ... Vacant
88 Director of Preschool Develop ... Dr. Carmen BERRIOS
108 Director Institutional Assessment ... Dr. Xiomara SANTIAGO

*University of Puerto Rico-Humacao (E)

Call Box 860, Humacao PR 00792
County: Humacao
FICE Identification: 003943
Unit ID: 243179
Telephone: (787) 850-0000
Carnegie Class: Bac-Diverse
FAX Number: (787) 852-4638
Calendar System: Semester
URL: www.uprh.edu
Established: 1962
Annual Undergrad Tuition & Fees (In-State): $4,094
Enrollment: 3,723
Coed
Affiliation or Control: State
IRS Status: 501(c)3
Highest Offering: Baccalaureate
Accreditation: M, ACBSP, CAEPN, NUR, PTAA, SW

02 Interim Chancellor ... Dr. Hector RÍOS
05 Interim Dean of Academic Affairs ... Dr. Rosa REYES
11 Interim Dean Administrative Affairs ... Dr. Carlos O. FIGUEROA
04 Assistant to the Chancellor ... Mr. Juan C. CASTRO
04 Assistant to the Chancellor ... Mrs. Betty GARCÍA
32 Interim Dean of Student Affairs ... Prof. José A. BALDAGUEZ
20 Int Associate Dean Academic Affairs ... Prof. Ivelisse REYES
45 Interim Dir Planning Office ... Prof. Ivette IRIZARRY
06 Interim Registrar ... Mrs. Carmen B. RODRIGUEZ
07 Interim Director of Admissions ... Mrs. Carmen RIVERA
08 Director of the Library ... Vacant
13 Interim Dir System Info Ofc ... Mr. Efrain WILLIAMS
15 Interim Director Human Resources ... Mrs. Elsa SANTOS
10 Interim Director of Finance ... Mr. Nelson SANTOS
37 Interim Dir Financial Aid Officer ... Mr. Larry CRUZ
38 Director Counseling Office ... Vacant
51 Dir Continuing Education/Extension ... Dr. Moises CARTAGENA
23 Director Health Services ... Vacant
18 Chief Facilities/Physical Plant ... Mr. Pedro COTTO
19 Interim Director Security/Transit ... Mr. Juan C. CASTRO
88 Student Ombuds Person ... Mr. José R. JIMENEZ
41 Athletic Activities Director ... Mr. Elmer WILLIAMS
114 Interim Director of Budget Office ... Mrs. Daisy RIVERA
108 Office of Institutional Assessment ... Mrs. Elionexis VAZQUEZ
101 Sec of Academic Senate/Adm Board ... Prof. Amelia MALDONADO
26 Press Relations ... Mrs. Meiling VILLAFAÑE
50 Interim Dir Business Administration ... Prof. Aida KALIL
88 Interim Director of Biology Dept ... Dr. Hector AYALA
88 Interim Director of Chemistry Dept ... Dr. Fabio ALAPE
60 Interim Dir of Communication Dept ... Prof. Hector PIÑERO
53 Interim Director of Education Dept ... Dr. Ángel M. GIERBOLINI
88 Interim Director of English Dept ... Dr. Nilsa LUGO
79 Interim Director of Humanities Dept ... Dr. Rubén MOREIRA
81 Interim Dir of Mathematics Dept ... Prof. Bárbara SANTIAGO
66 Interim Director of Nursing Dept ... Dr. Alejandro BORRERO
75 Interim Dir Occup Therapy Dept ... Prof. Mayra LEBRON
88 Int Dir Office System Admin Dept ... Dr. Ana M. VAZQUEZ
76 Interim Dir Physical Therapy Dept ... Dr. Moises CARTAGENA
88 Interim Dir Physics & Elect Dept ... Dr. Rogerio FURLAN
83 Interim Dir Social Science Dept ... Dr. María de Lourdes LARA
70 Interim Dir of Social Work Dept ... Dr. Evelyn CRUZ
88 Interim Director of Spanish Dept ... Dr. Dalma G. GONZALEZ
88 Graphics Art Supervisor ... Mr. Carlos LAZU
22 Dir Affirmative Action/EEO ... Mrs. Mariolga ROTGER
46 Dir Subsidized Research & Programs ... Vacant
88 Director Day Care Center ... Mrs. Maggaly POMALAZA
88 Student Support Service Director ... Prof. Olga L. BERRÍOS
88 Upward Bound Director ... Mrs. Myriam CINTRÓN
88 Director of ExTgesis Journal ... Prof. Carlos R. GOMEZ
46 Int Assoc Dean Research & Tech ... Dr. Edgardo RIVERA
21 Interim Dir of Accounting Office ... Mr. Bernardino RODRÍGIEZ

*University of Puerto Rico-Mayaguez Campus (F)

Call Box 9000, Mayaguez PR 00681-9000
County: Mayaguez
FICE Identification: 003944
Unit ID: 243197
Telephone: (787) 832-4040
Carnegie Class: Masters/L
FAX Number: (787) 834-3031
Calendar System: Semester
URL: www.uprm.edu
Established: 1911
Annual Undergrad Tuition & Fees (In-State): $4,094
Enrollment: 13,481
Coed
Affiliation or Control: State
IRS Status: 501(c)3
Highest Offering: Doctorate
Accreditation: M, ACBSP, CAEP, NUR

02 Interim Chancellor ... Dr. Wilma SANTIAGO GABRIELINI
05 Dean of Academic Affairs ... Dr. Betsy MORALES
10 Interim Dean of Administration ... Carlos E. ROSAS MUÑIZ
32 Interim Dean of Students ... Dr. José L. PERDOMO
49 Interim Dean of Arts & Sciences ... Dr. Fernando GILBES SANTAELLA
54 Dean of Engineering ... Dr. Agustin RULLÁN TORO
47 Interim Dean Agricultural Sciences ... Dr. Elvin O. ROMÁN PAOLI
50 Int Dean Business Administration ... Prof. Mariel NIEVES HERNÁNDEZ

*University of Puerto Rico-Medical Sciences Campus (G)

PO Box 365067, San Juan PR 00936-5067
County: San Juan
FICE Identification: 024600
Unit ID: 243203
Telephone: (787) 758-2525
Carnegie Class: Spec-4-yr-Med
FAX Number: (787) 758-2556
Calendar System: Other
URL: www.rcm.upr.edu
Established: 1950
Annual Undergrad Tuition & Fees (In-State): N/A
Enrollment: 2,273
Coed
Affiliation or Control: State
IRS Status: 501(c)3
Highest Offering: Doctorate
Accreditation: M, ANEST, AUD, CAHIIM, CYTO, DA, DENT, DIETI, HSA, MED, MT, NMT, NURSE, OT, PH, PHAR, PTA, RAD, SP

02 Chancellor ... Dr. Segundo RODRIGUEZ
05 Dean Academic Affairs ... Dr. Jose HAWAYEK
32 Dean Students Affairs ... Dr. Maria M. HERNANDEZ
11 Dean of Administration ... Mr. Manuel COLON
63 Dean School of Medicine ... Dr. Agustin RODRIGUEZ
52 Dean School of Dental Medicine ... Dr. Jose MATOS

69 Dean Grad School Public Health .... Dr. Dharma VAZQUEZ
67 Dean School of Pharmacy .... Dr. Wanda MALDONADO
76 Dean School of Health Professions .... Dr. Barbara SEGARRA
66 Dean School of Nursing .... Dr. Suane SANCHEZ
100 Chief of Staff .... Dr. Ramon F. GONZALEZ
20 Associate Academic Officer .... Dr. Jose CAPRILES
13 Ctr Informatics/Technology Director .... Mr. Francisco PEREZ
43 Director Legal Services .... Ms. Cristina PARES
26 Chief Information Officer .... Ms. Vivian VAZQUEZ
06 Registrar .... Mr. Abelardo MARTINEZ
08 Library Director .... Dr. Carmen M. SANTOS
09 Director Inst & Academic Research .... Dr. Wanda BARRETO
24 Director Educational Media .... Vacant
35 Assoc Dean Student Affairs .... Dr. Blanca AMOROS
07 Director of Admissions .... Mrs. Maribel ORTIZ
38 Director of Student Counseling .... Prof. Blanca AMOROS
37 Director of Student Financial Aid .... Mrs. Yolanda RIVERA
10 Chief Financial Officer .... Ms. Yolanda QUINONES
15 Director Personnel Services .... Mr. Manuel CARDONA
18 Chief Facilities/Physical Plant .... Mr. Julio A. COLLAZO
96 Director of Purchasing .... Mr. Miguel BOBE
19 Director Security Office .... Mr. William FIGUEROA
108 Director Institutional Assessment .... Dr. Jose CAPRILES
25 Chief Contracts/Grants Admin .... Ms. Lysette BARRERAS

*University of Puerto Rico at Ponce (A)

PO Box 7186, Ponce PR 00732-7186

County: Ponce FICE Identification: 009652
Unit ID: 243212
Telephone: (787) 844-8181 Carnegie Class: Bac-A&S
FAX Number: N/A Calendar System: Semester
URL: www.uprp.edu
Established: 1970 Annual Undergrad Tuition & Fees (In-State): $4,089
Enrollment: 3,150 Coed
Affiliation or Control: State IRS Status: 501(c)3
Highest Offering: Baccalaureate
Accreditation: M, ACBSP, CAEPN, PTAA

02 Chancellor .... Dr. Tessie H. CRUZ
04 Assistant to the Chancellor .... Prof. Carmen A. BRACERO
05 Interim Dean Academic Affairs .... Dr. Federico IRIZARRY
11 Dean Administrative Affairs .... Mr. Isaac COLON
32 Dean Student Affairs .... Prof. Ivonne RODRÍGUEZ
20 Associate Academic Dean .... Dr. Joahana RAMOS
45 Dir Inst Research/Planning Officer .... Dr. Diana LOPEZ
08 Director Library .... Prof. José OLIVERAS
06 Registrar .... Mrs. Marya Z. SANTIAGO
38 Director of Student Counseling .... Dr. Efrain RIOS
07 Director of Admissions .... Mrs. Emily MATOS
37 Director of Financial Aid .... Mrs. Ada HERENCIA
15 Director of Personnel Services .... Dr. Ericka RODRÍGUEZ
88 Director of Cultural Activities .... Dr. Jose L. PONS
13 Director of Computer Center .... Mrs. Damarys HERNANDEZ
18 Chief Facilities/Physical Plant .... Mr. Alberto GARCIA
40 Director Bookstore .... Vacant
41 Athletic Director .... Mrs. Lesbia COLON
23 Director Health Services .... Dr. Yiselle LOPEZ
29 Director Alumni Relations .... Mr. Dámaso DE JESÚS
30 Chief Development .... Vacant
19 Director of Security/Traffic .... Mr. German PIMENTEL
88 Coordinator Security/Safety .... Mrs. Celia GONZÁLEZ
22 Coordinator Affirmative Action .... Dr. Yesenia QUIÑONES

*University of Puerto Rico-Rio Piedras Campus (B)

10 Ave Universidad, Ste 1001, San Juan PR 00925-2530

County: San Juan FICE Identification: 007108
Unit ID: 243221
Telephone: (787) 764-0000 Carnegie Class: DU-Higher
FAX Number: (787) 764-8799 Calendar System: Semester
URL: www.uprrp.edu
Established: 1903 Annual Undergrad Tuition & Fees (In-State): $4,094
Enrollment: 15,098 Coed
Affiliation or Control: State IRS Status: 501(c)3
Highest Offering: Doctorate
Accreditation: M, ACBSP, CACREP, CAEP, CAEPN, #DIETD, JOUR, LAW, LIB, PLNG, SPAA, SW

02 Interim President .... Dr. Jorge HADDOCK ACEVEDO
00 Interim Chancellor .... Dr. Luis A. FERRAO DELGADO
05 Dean Academic Affairs .... Dra. Leticia FERNANDEZ MORAL
11 Dean of Administration .... Dr. Aurora M. SOTOGRAS SALDANA
32 Dean of Students .... Dr. Gloria DÍAZ URBINA
20 Associate Dean Academic Affairs .... Dra. Clarisa CRUZ LUGO
50 Dean Business Administration .... Dr. Myrna LOPEZ GONZALEZ
48 Dean of Architecture .... Arq. Mayra JIMÉNEZ
81 Dean of Natural Sciences .... Dr. Rafael RIOS
83 Dean of Social Sciences .... Dr. Angelica VARELA LLAVONA
61 Dean of Law .... Ms. Vivian NEPTUNE
97 Dean of General Studies .... Dr. Aurelio GARCIA
79 Dean of Humanities .... Dr. Agnes BOSCH
58 Dean Graduate Studies/Research . Dr. Carmen MALDONA VLAAR
53 Dean of Education .... Dra. Mayra CHARRIEZ CORDERO
35 Asst Dean Student Affairs .... Ms. Marilu PEREZ HERNÁNDEZ
38 Director of Student Counseling .... Mrs. Maria JIMENEZ CHAFEY
30 Int Dir Devel & Alumni Relations .... Mrs. Elsa MARIN
06 Registrar .... Mr. Juan M. APONTE
08 Director of Library System .... Dr. Miguel SANTIAGO
15 Director of Human Resources .. Mrs. Terilyn M. SASTRE FUENTE
07 Director of Admissions .... Mr. Jessica A. MORALES TORRES
13 Director of Computer Center .... Mr. José PABÓN
62 Director Grad Sch Library/Info Sci .... Dr. José SANCHEZ
60 Director School of Communication .... Dr. Jorge SANTIAGO
58 Dir Graduate Sch of Planning .... Dr. Norma PENA RIVERA
51 Dir Continuing Educ/Extension .... Dr. Liza NIEVES
09 Director of Institutional Research .... Vacant
18 Chief Planning/Physical Devel Ofc .... Mr. Belkis FABREGAS
26 Chief Public Relations Officer .... Mrs. Lorna CASTRO
37 Director of Student Financial Aid .... Mr. Anibal ALVALLE
96 Director of Purchasing .... Mr. Ángel DÍAZ
114 Director of Budget .... Mr. Wilson CRESPO VALENTIN
19 Director Security/Safety .... Mr. Victor ROSARIO DELGADO

*University of Puerto Rico at Utuado (C)

PO Box 2500, Utuado PR 00641-2500

County: Utuado FICE Identification: 029384
Unit ID: 243188
Telephone: (787) 894-2828 Carnegie Class: Bac/Assoc-Mixed
FAX Number: (787) 894-1081 Calendar System: Semester
URL: www.uprutuado.edu
Established: 1979 Annual Undergrad Tuition & Fees (In-State): $4,094
Enrollment: 1,154 Coed
Affiliation or Control: State IRS Status: 501(c)3
Highest Offering: Baccalaureate
Accreditation: M, ACBSP, CAEPN

02 Chancellor .... Dr. Luis A. TAPIA
05 Academic Dean .... Dr. Wanda L. CAMARA
10 Chief Business Officer .... Dr. Luis E. ORTIZ
32 Chief Student Life Officer .... Dr. Enid RIVERA
08 Library Director .... Prof. Regina OQUENDO
09 Director Institutional Research .... Dr. Javier LUGO
06 Registrar .... Mrs. Marisol DIAZ
07 Director of Admission .... Prof. Amarilis CINTRON
15 Director Human Resources .... Ms. Gretchen COLLAZO
38 Director Student Counseling .... Vacant
37 Director Student Financial Aid .... Mrs. Eltie PEREZ
13 Director Information Systems .... Mr. Juan MARTINEZ
19 Director Security/Safety .... Vacant
41 Director of Athletics .... Mr. Miguel RODRIGUEZ
47 Director of Agriculture .... Dr. Olgaly RAMOS
50 Dir Office Systems/Business Admin .... Dr. Frank RIVAS
96 Director of Purchasing .... Ms. Luz E. MARTINEZ
51 Director Continuing Education .... Mrs. Livette REYES
53 Director Education .... Dr. Ferdinand ALVAREZ
65 Director Natural Sciences .... Dr. Carlos J. RODRÍGUEZ
79 Director Humanities/Spanish/English .... Dr. Ferdinand ALVAREZ

University of the Sacred Heart (D)

PO Box 12383, San Juan PR 00914-8505

County: San Juan FICE Identification: 003937
Unit ID: 243443
Telephone: (787) 728-1515 Carnegie Class: Masters/M
FAX Number: (787) 728-1692 Calendar System: Semester
URL: www.sagrado.edu
Established: 1935 Annual Undergrad Tuition & Fees: $6,000
Enrollment: 4,783 Coed
Affiliation or Control: Roman Catholic IRS Status: 501(c)3
Highest Offering: Master's
Accreditation: M, CAEPN, NURSE, SW

01 President .... Gilberto MARXUACH-TORROS
04 Admin Assistant to the President .... Gloriana YDRACH
05 Chief Academic Officer (Provost) .... María T. MARTÍNEZ
06 Registrar .... Eigna DE JESÚS
07 Director of Admissions .... Katherine CASTILLO
10 Chief Financial/Business Officer .... Guillermo NIGAGLIONI
13 Chief Information Technology Office .... Luis GOTELLI
15 Chief Human Resources Officer .... Marilyn FIGUEROA
32 Chief Student Affairs Officer .... Sara TOLOSA
37 Director Student Financial Aid .... Luis VELEZ
39 Dir Resident Life/Student Housing .... Carlos MOLL
41 Athletic Director .... Maria E. BATISTA
43 Director Legal Services .... Camelia FERNÁNDEZ
50 Dean of Business .... Javier HERNÁNDEZ

VIRGIN ISLANDS

University of the Virgin Islands (E)

#2 John Brewers Bay, Saint Thomas VI 00802-9990

FICE Identification: 003946
Unit ID: 243665
Telephone: (340) 776-9200 Carnegie Class: Bac-Diverse
FAX Number: (340) 693-1005 Calendar System: Semester
URL: www.uvi.edu
Established: 1962 Annual Undergrad Tuition & Fees (In-State): $5,235
Enrollment: 2,170 Coed
Affiliation or Control: State IRS Status: 501(c)3
Highest Offering: Doctorate
Accreditation: M, CAEPN, NUR

01 President .... Dr. David HALL
88 VP Business Development/Innovation .... Dr. Haldane DAVIES
04 Director of Presidential Operations .... Ms. Una DYER
101 Board Liaison .... Ms. Gail T. STEELE
05 Provost/VP of Academic Affairs .... Dr. Camille A. MCKAYLE
46 Interim Vice Provost/ECC/RPS .... Dr. Frank MILLS
53 Dean School of Education .... Dr. Linda V. THOMAS
81 Dean College of Sci & Math .... Dr. Sandra ROMANO
50 Dean School of Business .... Dr. Lucy J. REUBEN
49 Int Dean Col Liberal Arts/Soc Sci .... Dr. Kimarie ENGERMAN
66 Dean School of Nursing .... Ms. Beverley A. LANSIQUOT
104 Assoc Provost Grad/Global Acad Affs . Dr. James S. MADDIRALA
84 VP Access/Enroll Services .... Mr. David WUINEE
07 Coordinator Enrollment Services .... Ms. Charmaine I. SMITH
06 Registrar .... Ms. Monifa J. POTTER
37 Director of Financial Aid .... Ms. Cheryl A. ROBERTS
32 Dean of Students-STT Campus .... Ms. Verna J. RIVERS
36 Dir of Counseling/Career Services .... Ms. Patricia TOWAL
111 VP Institutional Advancement .... Mr. Mitchell NEAVES
44 Director of Annual Giving .... Ms. Linda SMITH
30 Capital Campaign Manager .... Mr. Jose Raul CARRILLO
10 VP Administration & Finance .... Ms. Shirley L. LAKE-KING
21 Acting Controller .... Ms. Stacey CHADOS
15 Director of HR/Org Development .... Mr. Charles Ronald MEEK
19 Acting Chief Campus Police/ Security .... Mr. Theodore E. GLASFORD
18 Director of Physical Plant .... Mr. Charles MARTIN
13 VP Info Services/Inst Assessment .... Ms. Sharlene J. HARRIS
08 Library Manager .... Mrs. Celia P. PRINCE-RICHARD
32 Dean of Students-STC Campus .. Ms. Hedda T. FINCH-SIMPSON

University of the Virgin Islands-St. Croix (F)

RR1, Box 10,000, Kingshill VI 00850-9781

Telephone: (340) 778-1620 Identification: 770173
Accreditation: &M

Index of Key Administrators

A

AABERG, Audun ... 701-654-1000.. 32 B

AABERGE, Nancy ... 406-874-6161 263 I aabergen@milescc.edu

AADLAND, Susan, R ... 605-394-6884 417 B susan.aadland@sdsmt.edu

AAMODT, Jennifer ... 701-777-3000 345 C jennifer.aamodt@und.edu

AAMOT, Chris ... 505-984-6000 287 J chris.aamot@sjc.edu

AANENSON, Erin ... 507-389-7342 241 C erin.aanenson@southcentral.edu

AANERUD, Rebecca ... 206-543-5139 485 F raan@uw.edu

AARON, Belinda ... 303-797-5711.. 76 I belinda.aaron@arapahoe.edu

AARON, Cedric ... 615-687-6896 418 A caaron@abcnash.edu

AARON, Charlene, S ... 217-525-5628 148 F charlene.aaron@sjcs.edu

AARON, Cheryl ... 617-989-4159 219 E aaronc@wit.edu

AARON, Fredona ... 540-857-6053 476 D faaron@virginiawestern.edu

AARON, Judith ... 718-636-3677 311 J jaaron@pratt.edu

AARON, Samantha, G ... 336-322-2280 336 G samantha.aaron@piedmontcc.edu

AARONBERG, Melissa .. 212-247-3434 305 G maaronberg@mandl.edu

AASEN, Curtis, K ... 757-822-1070 476 B caasen@tcc.edu

ABADIE, Bonnie ... 210-341-1366 441 C babadie@ost.edu

ABADINSKY, Alisa ... 301-405-9001 202 C aabadins@umd.edu

ABALOS, Victor ... 213-615-7270.. 36 F vabalos@thechicagoschool.edu

ABARAY, Christyn ... 920-832-6888 493 K christyn.abaray@lawrence.edu

ABATE, Alexis ... 215-780-1284 398 G aabate@salus.edu

ABATE, Yohannes ... 703-941-2020 468 D

ABAUNZA, George, E ... 201-559-6049 278 A abaunzag@felician.edu

ABAZI, Erlis ... 239-513-1122 101 C eabazi@hodges.edu

ABBA, Crystal ... 775-784-4901 270 K cabba@nshe.nevada.edu

ABBASSI, Pouria ... 310-825-8011.. 69 A pabbassi@asucla.ucla.edu

ABBATE, Anthony ... 505-438-8884 288 C abbate@acupuncturecollege.edu

ABBATE, Salavatore ... 707-864-7000.. 64 C salvatore.abbate@solano.edu

ABBATE, Skya ... 505-438-8884 288 C skya@acupuncturecollege.edu

ABBE, Blake ... 254-710-3945 431 J blake_abbe@baylor.edu

ABBEY, Craig, W ... 716-645-2791 316 F cwabbey@buffalo.edu

ABBEY, Megan ... 509-359-4858 480 E mabbey@ewu.edu

ABBOTT, Amy ... 850-478-8496 104 G info@pcci.edu

ABBOTT, Cameron ... 916-660-7110.. 63 I cabbott@sierracollege.edu

ABBOTT, Catherine ... 760-245-4271.. 73 D catherine.abbott@vvc.edu

ABBOTT, Charlene, R ... 337-475-5977 192 A cabbott@mcneese.edu

ABBOTT, Douglas, M ... 406-496-4127 265 A dabbott@mtech.edu

ABBOTT, Jenni ... 209-575-7795.. 75 J abbottj@mjc.edu

ABBOTT, Jill, M ... 218-299-3654 235 E jabbott@cord.edu

ABBOTT, Jim ... 405-208-5301 367 I jabbott@okcu.edu

ABBOTT, Judy, A ... 936-468-2901 445 F collegeofeducation@sfasu.edu

ABBOTT, Karen ... 978-998-7768 209 B kabbott@endicott.edu

ABBOTT, Larry ... 606-679-8501 182 C larry.abbott@kctcs.edu

ABBOTT, Linda ... 727-864-7840.. 97 J abbottlt@eckerd.edu

ABBOTT, Marilyn ... 636-949-4912 254 F mabbott@lindenwood.edu

ABBOTT, Mark, R ... 508-289-2500 220 D mabbott@whoi.edu

ABBOTT, Mary ... 605-668-1464 415 H mabbott@mtmc.edu

ABBOTT, Paula, J ... 308-254-7404 270 D abbottp@wncc.edu

ABBOTT, Shawn, L ... 215-204-4133 399 F shawn.abbott@temple.edu

ABBOUSHI, Fahmi ... 937-376-6398 350 D fabboushi@centralstate.edu

ABBY, Dean ... 617-332-3666 220 B dean_abby@williamjames.edu

ABD EL-FATAH, Samir Shahat ... 208-885-7208 131 G samir@uidaho.edu

ABD-EL-KHALICK, Fouad ... 919-966-1356 342 D fouad@unc.edu

ABDALA, Kami ... 609-586-4800 278 F abdalak@mccc.edu

ABDALLA, Laila ... 206-934-2926 484 A laila.abdalla@seattlecolleges.edu

ABDALLA, Stephanie ... 732-987-2541 278 B sabdalla@georgian.edu

ABDALLAH, Chaouki ... 404-894-8885 118 F ctabdallah@gatech.edu

ABDEL, Maria ... 305-474-6950 106 F mabdel@stu.edu

ABDELKARIM, Shehadeh ... 216-987-4899 351 G shehadeh.abdelkarim@tri-c.edu

ABDELLA, Stephen ... 716-338-1031 303 D steveabdella@mail.sunyjcc.edu

ABDELRAHMAN, Mohamed ... 719-549-2313.. 79 A mohamed.abdelrahman@csupueblo.edu

ABDOULAYE, Idriss ... 305-623-1405.. 99 D idriss.abdoulaye@fmuniv.edu

ABDOW, David ... 781-239-6015 205 E dabdow@babson.edu

ABDULLAH, Jamar ... 610-359-5310 382 C jabdullah@follett.com

ABDULLAH, Makola, M 804-524-5070 477 B president@vsu.edu

ABDULLAH, Shakeer ... 678-466-5433 116 E shakeerabdullah@clayton.edu

ABE, Christopher ... 805-437-3616.. 30 F christopher.abe@csuci.edu

ABE, Jennifer ... 310-338-7598.. 50 J jennifer.abe@lmu.edu

ABEAR, Lichele ... 631-687-5158 314 C labear@sjcny.edu

ABEBE, Daniel ... 773-702-7857 150 J dabebe@uchicago.edu

ABEGG, Robert, M ... 214-887-5321 436 B babegg@dts.edu

ABEL, Dianna, K ... 801-626-6406 461 B diannaabel@weber.edu

ABEL, Eileen ... 301-934-7846 198 A edabel@csmd.edu

ABEL, John, C ... 731-881-7526 428 B jabel@utm.edu

ABEL, Kevin ... 251-380-3024.... 6 H kabel@shc.edu

ABEL, Marc ... 847-578-3236 147 I marc.abel@rosalindfranklin.edu

ABEL, Rebecca ... 304-724-5000 487 H rabel@cdu.edu

ABEL, JR., Robert ... 213-252-5100.. 23 K rabeljr@alu.edu

ABEL, Susan ... 513-745-3334 365 B abel@xavier.edu

ABELA, Andrew, V ... 202-319-5290.. 91 B abela@cua.edu

ABELL, Anthony ... 727-376-6911 111 G anthony.abell@trinitycollege.edu

ABELL, Carol ... 320-363-5511 243 A abell@csbsju.edu

ABELL, Carol ... 320-363-5511 235 C cabell@csbsju.edu

ABELL, Debbie ... 618-453-6751 149 E kohley@siu.edu

ABELL, Donna ... 270-686-4575 182 B donna.abell@kctcs.edu

ABELL, Jane ... 760-366-5280.. 40 K jabell@cmccd.edu

ABELL, Jason ... 612-455-3420 234 D jason.abell@bcsmn.edu

ABELL, Russ ... 718-636-3684 311 J rabell@pratt.edu

ABELL, Tracey ... 503-244-0726 371 G traceyabell@achs.edu

ABELMANN, Ruth, E ... 603-862-2268 274 G ruth.abelmann@unh.edu

ABELS, Arnold ... 816-235-1218 261 C abelsa@umkc.edu

ABELS, Dianne ... 309-796-5394 132 G abelsd@bhc.edu

ABELSON, Clifford ... 978-681-0800 216 A abelson@mslaw.edu

ABENT, Rita, E ... 724-738-2919 395 F rita.abent@sru.edu

ABER, Suzanne ... 860-297-2525.. 88 C suzanne.aber@trincoll.edu

ABERCROMBIE, Barbara 214-752-5532 454 A barbara.abercrombie@untsystem.edu

ABERCROMBIE, Neil, N 435-797-0258 460 H neil.abercrombie@usu.edu

ABERLE-CANNATA, Denise ... 208-562-3218 130 F denisecannata@cwi.edu

ABERMAN, Jonathan ... 703-284-5910 469 C jonathan.aberman@marymount.edu

ABERNATHY, Allison ... 704-922-6486 334 F abernathy.allison@gaston.edu

ABERNATHY, Cammy ... 352-392-6000 109 F caber@ufl.edu

ABERNATHY, JaNan ... 870-733-6830.. 17 H jmabernathy@asumidsouth.edu

ABERNATHY, Jeff ... 989-463-7146 220 H abernathyj@alma.edu

ABERNATHY, Kat ... 719-549-2256.. 79 A kat.abernathy@csupueblo.edu

ABERNATHY, Robert ... 970-339-6363.. 76 G robert.abernathy@aims.edu

ABERNATHY, Sharon, A 573-875-7360 251 F saabernathy@ccis.edu

ABESAMIS, Naomi ... 714-992-7096.. 53 L nabesamis@fullcoll.edu

ABEYIE, Nana ... 212-650-6899 293 D nana@ccny.cuny.edu

ABEYTA, Aaron ... 719-587-7800.. 76 F aaabeyta@adams.edu

ABEZETIAN, Garrick ... 708-456-0300 150 I garrickabezetian@triton.edu

ABHOLD, Joseph, J ... 715-836-5992 496 D abholdjj@uwec.edu

ABI-NADER DAHLBERG, Teresa ... 817-257-4343 448 G t.dahlberg@tcu.edu

ABIKO, Geneva ... 805-756-2511.. 30 C greynaga@calpoly.edu

ABLESER, Judith ... 248-370-2455 229 G ableser@oakland.edu

ABO, Joel, C ... 386-312-4063 106 C joelabo@sjrstate.edu

ABORDONADO, Valentina ... 808-543-1143 127 H vabordonado@hpu.edu

ABORN, Kerrie ... 617-333-2294 208 E kaborn0315@curry.edu

ABOU-EL-KHEIR, Jasmine ... 773-896-2400 133 L yasmine.abou-el-kheir@ctschicago.edu

ABOUELENEIN, Baz ... 800-955-2527 173 F baz@grantham.edu

ABOUFADEL, Edward ... 616-331-2400 224 E aboufade@gvsu.edu

ABOUFADEL, Kathy ... 616-451-3511 223 B kaboufadel@davenport.edu

ABOUFARES, Moe ... 909-580-9661.. 34 E

ABOUSAMRA, Haifa ... 605-658-6500 416 H haifa.abousamra@usd.edu

ABPLANALP, John (Mike) ... 570-484-2525 395 B jabplana@lockhaven.edu

ABRAHAM, Alvin, V ... 651-962-5000 244 E abra1662@stthomas.edu

ABRAHAM, Angeles ... 310-287-4399.. 49 G abrahaa@wlac.edu

ABRAHAM, Diane ... 909-706-3548.. 74 I dabraham@westernu.edu

ABRAHAM, Doug ... 303-724-2000.. 83 C doug.abraham@ucdenver.edu

ABRAHAM, Edward ... 305-243-5677 112 E eabraham@med.miami.edu

ABRAHAM, Marc ... 303-753-6046.. 82 F mabraham@rmcad.edu

ABRAHAM, Margaret ... 516-463-5400 302 B margaret.abraham@hofstra.edu

ABRAHAM, Martin, A ... 309-298-1824 152 D ma-abraham@wiu.edu

ABRAHAM, Raymond ... 318-678-6000 187 A rabraham@bpcc.edu

ABRAHAM, Reed ... 662-246-6273 247 D rabraham@msdelta.edu

ABRAHAM, Sharon ... 734-487-1166 223 H sabraha1@emich.edu

ABRAHAM, Shondra, F . 803-536-7013 412 C sabraham@scsu.edu

ABRAHAM, Susan ... 510-849-8209.. 55 B sabraham@psr.edu

ABRAHAM, Thea ... 314-392-2231 256 C abrahamt@mobap.edu

ABRAHAM, Tracie, A ... 225-771-3590 190 H tracie_abraham@subr.edu

ABRAHAM, Tracie, A ... 225-771-3590 190 G tracie_abraham@subr.edu

ABRAHAMS, Faustina ... 417-625-9521 256 D abrahams-f@mssu.edu

ABRAHAMSON, April ... 701-228-5437 346 C april.abrahamson@dakotacollege.edu

ABRAHAMSON, David, P ... 414-277-7173 494 G abrahams@msoe.edu

ABRAJANO, Barbara ... 312-939-0111 136 D babrajano@eastwest.edu

ABRAM, Bobbi ... 626-585-7054.. 55 K blabram@pasadena.edu

ABRAMOVITZ, Todd ... 443-412-2291 199 A tabramovitz@harford.edu

ABRAMOVSKY, Aviva ... 716-645-2052 316 F aabramov@buffalo.edu

ABRAMS, Andrea, C ... 859-238-5267 179 F andrea.abrams@centre.edu

ABRAMS, Andrew, L ... 843-377-2145 407 D aabrams@charlestonlaw.edu

ABRAMS, Chris ... 419-448-2062 353 H cabrams@heidelberg.edu

ABRAMS, Eleanor ... 978-934-4355 211 G eleanor_abrams@uml.edu

ABRAMS, Elizabeth ... 831-459-2246.. 70 B esabrams@ucsc.edu

ABRAMS, Jacob, R ... 304-367-4798 490 B jabrams1@fairmontstate.edu

ABRAMS, Laura ... 718-997-5541 295 C laura.abrams@qc.cuny.edu

ABRAMS, Lori ... 307-268-2672 501 U lori.abrams@caspercollege.edu

ABRAMS, Nairobi ... 763-488-2426 238 B nairobi.abrams@hennepintech.edu

ABRAMSON, Alexis, R .. 603-646-2238 273 E alexis.r.abramson@dartmouth.edu
ABRAMSON, Jared .... 202-994-1000.. 91 F jabramson@gwu.edu
ABRAMSON, Nancy .... 212-678-8036 303 G naabramson@jtsa.edu
ABREGANO, Laurie .... 808-675-3487 127 E laurie.abregano@byuh.edu
ABREGO, Joshua .... 209-476-7840.. 66 G jabrego@clc.edu
ABRESCY, Chris .... 209-228-2586.. 69 B cabrescy@ucmerced.edu
ABREU, Carlos, F .... 787-743-3038 511 A cabreu@sanjuanbautista.edu
ABREU, Jonathan .... 212-752-1530 304 D jonathan.abreu@limcollege.edu
ABREU, Katie .... 410-334-2904 204 F kabreu@worwic.edu
ABREU, Sara .... 787-878-5475 508 L sabreu@arecibo.inter.edu
ABROMAITIS, James ..... 203-773-8578.. 84 F jabromaitis@albertus.edu
ABRON, Gisele .... 336-517-2160 327 B gabron@bennett.edu
ABSAR, Quaiser .... 540-665-4937 471 E qabsar@su.edu
ABSHER, Beverly .... 731-661-5363 427 C babsher@uu.edu
ABSHIRE, Aimee .... 337-482-6397 192 E aimee@louisiana.edu
ABSHIRE, Allen .... 606-218-5940 185 D allenabshire@upike.edu
ABSHIRE, Martha Ann .. 225-490-1685 186 F martha.abshire@franu.edu
ABSTON, Byron .... 205-391-2388.... 3 E babston@sheltonstate.edu
ABSTON, Kara .... 501-279-4332.. 19 D kabston@harding.edu
ABTS, Polly .... 920-693-1221 499 G polly.abts@gotoltc.edu
ABU-AGEEL, Nayef .... 301-369-2800 197 F nmabuageel@captechu.edu
ABU-AGEEL, Nayef .... 301-369-2468 197 F nmabuageel@captechu.edu
ABU-GHAZALEH, Nabil . 619-644-7100.. 44 I nabil.abu-ghazaleh@gcccd.edu
ABUHAMAD, Alfred, Z .. 757-446-5283 466 I abuhamaz@evms.edu
ABUSALIM, Murad .... 956-295-3568 449 D murad.abusalim@tsc.edu
ABUSHABAN, Sahar .... 619-660-4654.. 44 H sahar.abushaban@gcccd.edu
ABUTIN, Albert .... 714-992-7076.. 53 L aabutin@fullcoll.edu
ABUZNEID, Abdelshakour, A .... 203-576-4113.. 88 D abuzneid@bridgeport.edu
ACAMPORA, Christa, D 404-712-1238 117 F christa.d.acampora@emory.edu
ACARDO, John .... 630-637-5754 144 H jjacardo@noctrl.edu
ACCAPADI, Mamta, M .. 407-646-2185 105M maccapadi@rollins.edu
ACCARDI, Christen .... 315-279-5323 304 A caccardi@keuka.edu
ACCARDI, Michael .... 978-837-5062 216 D accardim@merrimack.edu
ACCIARDO, Linda, A ..... 401-874-2116 406 B lindaa@uri.edu
ACEVEDO, Beatriz .... 212-924-5900 322 B bursar@swedishinstitute.edu
ACEVEDO, Dary .... 787-891-0925 508 K dacevedo@aguadilla.inter.edu
ACEVEDO, Francisco ..... 787-892-5700 509 F facevedo@intersg.edu
ACEVEDO, Ivonne .... 787-891-0925 508 K iaecheva@ns.inter.edu
ACEVES, Salvador, D .... 303-458-4144.. 82 E saceves@regis.edu
ACEY, Denise .... 573-334-9181 255 A denise@metrobusinesscollege.edu
ACEY, Stacy .... 770-229-3226 124 G stacy.acey@sctech.edu
ACHAN, Jennifer .... 661-395-4482.. 46 L jennifer.achan@bakersfieldcollege.edu
ACHARYA, Raj .... 812-856-1079 156 B dean@soic.indiana.edu
ACHARYA, Raj .... 812-856-1079 156 A racharya@iu.edu
ACHARYA, Suresh .... 269-749-7666 229 H sacharya@olivetcollege.edu
ACHARYA, Sushil .... 412-397-6227 397 G acharya@rmu.edu
ACHENBACH, David ...... 508-793-3320 208 B dachenba@holycross.edu
ACHENBACH, USMS, Gerard .... 231-995-1203 228 G gachenbach@nmc.edu
ACHESON, Carol .... 503-253-3443 374 H cacheson@ocom.edu
ACHIVARE-HILL, Rachael .... 918-595-7941 370 E rachael.achivarehill@tulsacc.edu
ACHS, Carol .... 480-461-7742.. 13 D carol.achs@mesacc.edu
ACHTERMAN, Douglas .. 408-848-4809.. 43 J dachterman@gavilan.edu
ACIERNO, Lou .... 212-752-1530 304 D lou.acierno@limcollege.edu
ACKER, Lorraine .... 336-517-1374 327 B lorraine.acker@bennett.edu
ACKER, Lorraine .... 585-395-5871 318 B lacker@brockport.edu
ACKERLEY, Roseanne .... 513-487-3234 301 E rackerley@huc.edu
ACKERLY, David, D .... 510-642-7171.. 68 D dackerly@berkeley.edu
ACKERMAN, Debbie ...... 217-732-3155 141 I dackerman@lincolncollege.edu
ACKERMAN, Denise ...... 845-758-7625 290 G ackerman@bard.edu
ACKERMAN, Kathy .... 828-395-1522 335 D kackerman@isothermal.edu
ACKERMAN, Tom .... 352-271-2905 107 A thomas.ackerman@sfcollege.edu
ACKERMAN, Tom .... 618-664-6509 137 G tom.ackerman@greenville.edu
ACKERSON, Kelly .... 619-688-0800.. 40 E
ACKLAND, Terri .... 520-494-5227.. 11 K terri.ackland@centralaz.edu
ACKLEH, Azmy .... 337-482-6986 192 E asa5773@louisiana.edu
ACKLEY, Darren .... 715-675-3331 500 E ackley@ntc.edu
ACKLEY, Lavon .... 229-430-0415 113 I lackley@albanytech.edu
ACKMAN, Elizabeth, R .. 315-684-6043 321 D ackmaner@morrisville.edu
ACOB-NASH, Mari .... 206-934-3643 483 J maria.acob-nash@seattlecolleges.edu
ACOB-NASH, Mari .... 360-416-7786 485 A mari.acobnash@skaagit.edu
ACOLASTE, Ras .... 703-878-2800.. 92 G
ACOSTA, Anna Lisa .... 775-445-4265 271 G annalisa.acosta@wnc.edu
ACOSTA, Araceli .... 210-924-4338 431 H araceli.acosta@bua.edu
ACOSTA, Cesar .... 860-701-6727 504 F steven.c.acosta@uscg.mil
ACOSTA, Daniel .... 650-949-7514.. 43 B acostadaniel@fhda.edu
ACOSTA, Esmeralda, M . 623-845-3012.. 13 C esmeralda.acosta@gccaz.edu
ACOSTA, Kathy .... 214-860-1464 435 C kacosta@dcccd.edu
ACOSTA, Paul .... 209-954-5063.. 60 J pacosta@deltacollege.edu
ACOSTA, Pilar .... 407-708-2432 107 D acostap@seminolestate.edu
ACOSTA, Sara .... 708-524-6288 136 C sacosta@dom.edu
ACOSTA, Vanessa .... 714-966-8500.. 73 C vacosta@ves.edu
ACOSTA-FUMERO, Carmen, J .... 787-841-2000 510 K cacosta@pucpr.edu
ACOSTA-TORO, Relon ... 787-480-2463 507 C reacosta@sanjuanciudadpatria.com
ACOVIO, Connie .... 210-486-3960 429 F cacovio@alamo.edu
ACQUAAH, George .... 301-860-3610 203 C gacquaah@bowiestae.edu
ACQUAH, Ken .... 718-518-4369 294 B kacquah@hostos.cuny.edu
ACREE, Cheryl .... 229-333-2126 127 B cheryl.acree@wiregrass.edu
ACUFF, Keith .... 660-596-7301 260 D kacuff@sfccmo.edu
ACUNA, Angela .... 408-498-5133.. 38 F aacuna@cogswell.edu
ACUNA, April .... 801-818-8900 459 K april.acuna@provocollege.edu
ADACHI, Lesley, B .... 680-488-2471 506 B lbadachi@gmail.com
ADADE, Anthony .... 508-929-8714 213 E aadade@worcester.edu
ADAIR, Adam .... 870-512-7801.. 18 B adam_adair@asun.edu
ADAIR, Charles .... 631-420-2198 321 B charles.adair@farmingdale.edu
ADAIR, Kathy .... 906-248-3354 221 N kadair@bmcc.edu
ADAIR, Matt .... 952-829-2459 234 A matt.adair@bethfel.org
ADAIR, Matt .... 580-327-8418 367 E wmadair@nwosu.edu
ADAIR, Suzanne, C ...... 814-863-0471 392 B sca917@psu.edu
ADAM, Jakob .... 512-313-3000 434 E jakob.adam@concordia.edu
ADAM, Jamal .... 218-733-7600 238 F jamal.adam@lsc.edu
ADAM, Michelle .... 305-809-3279.. 99 C michelle.adam@fkcc.edu
ADAM, Sharla .... 325-942-2041 451 A sharla.adam@angelo.edu
ADAM, Terri .... 207-974-4691 194 H tadam@emcc.edu
ADAM, Wendy .... 413-597-2353 220 C ga1@williams.edu
ADAMCHAK, Andrea ...... 765-658-4440 154 F andreaadamchak@depauw.edu
ADAMCZUK, Agata .... 631-794-6250 321 B studyabroad@farmingdale.edu
ADAMCZYK, Julie, L ..... 989-837-4436 228 H adamczyk@northwood.edu
ADAMCZYK, Stephanie . 412-392-4205 397 A sadamczyk@pointpark.edu
ADAMES, Jose .... 214-860-2010 435 C jose.adames@dcccd.edu
ADAMO, Clare .... 860-632-3009.. 87 C cadamo@holyapostles.edu
ADAMO, Paul, J .... 607-436-2535 317 C paul.adamo@oneonta.edu
ADAMS, Adam .... 712-722-6006 164 K adam.adams@dordt.edu
ADAMS, Alex .... 559-325-5363.. 66 D alex.adams@cloviscollege.edu
ADAMS, Alexandra .... 816-501-2400 250 F alexandra.adams@avila.edu
ADAMS, Amanda .... 423-354-5143 425 E acadams@northeaststate.edu
ADAMS, Amy .... 740-389-4636 356 B adamsa@mtc.edu
ADAMS, Ann .... 312-491-2869 145 F a-adams@northwestern.edu
ADAMS, Ann .... 360-438-4382 483 H aadams@stmartin.edu
ADAMS, Ann Clay .... 404-687-4524 116 H adamsa@ctsnet.edu
ADAMS, Anthony, T ...... 334-229-5176.... 4 B atadams@alasu.edu
ADAMS, Barbara, L .... 803-536-8980 412 C badams@scsu.edu
ADAMS, Betty .... 713-797-7000 446 D bnadams@pvamu.edu
ADAMS, Billy, W .... 903-693-2028 441 F badams@panola.edu
ADAMS, Brad .... 865-251-1800 424 A badams@south.edu
ADAMS, Brenda .... 501-450-1226.. 19 F adams@hendrix.edu
ADAMS, Brett, C .... 443-352-4250 201 H bcadams@stevenson.edu
ADAMS, Brian .... 225-771-2520 190 H brian_adams@subr.edu
ADAMS, Bruce .... 504-286-5432 190 I badams@suno.edu
ADAMS, Bryan .... 617-353-3635 207 D bsadams@bu.edu
ADAMS, Carey .... 314-719-3609 253 C cadams@fontbonne.edu
ADAMS, Carol .... 678-717-2233 126 A carol.adams@ung.edu
ADAMS, Caroline .... 805-893-3285.. 70 A caroline.adams@ucsb.edu
ADAMS, Charles, H .... 813-974-3087 110 B chadams@honors.usf.edu
ADAMS, Chris .... 573-840-9666 260 I cadams@trcc.edu
ADAMS, Christopher, J . 631-451-4118 321 F adamsc@sunysuffolk.edu
ADAMS, Clint .... 303-373-2008.. 82 G president@rvu.edu
ADAMS, Colby .... 817-923-1921 445 B cadams@swbts.edu
ADAMS, Dania .... 305-348-3875 109 A dania.pearson_adams@fiu.edu
ADAMS, Darly .... 561-803-2000 104 C
ADAMS, David, J .... 513-556-5511 362 D davidj.adams@uc.edu
ADAMS, Dean .... 270-384-8036 183 C adamsd@lindsey.edu
ADAMS, DeAnna .... 901-843-3885 423 J registrar@rhodes.edu
ADAMS, Debbie .... 423-697-2493 424 E debbie.adams@chattanoogastate.edu
ADAMS, Denise .... 530-895-2329.. 27 F adamsde@butte.edu
ADAMS, Don .... 210-485-0088 429 C dadams@alamo.edu
ADAMS, Doug .... 217-443-8832 135 H dadams@dacc.edu
ADAMS, Edward .... 646-312-1190 292 L edward.adams@baruch.cuny.edu
ADAMS, Edward, E .... 801-422-8611 458 H ed_adams@byu.edu
ADAMS, Elizabeth .... 912-583-3242 115 E eadams@bpc.edu
ADAMS, Elizabeth, T ..... 818-677-2969.. 32 D elizabeth.t.adams@csun.edu
ADAMS, Ellen .... 718-631-6269 295 D eadams@qcc.cuny.edu
ADAMS, Eve .... 480-858-9100.. 16 A e.adams@scnm.edu
ADAMS, Grantley .... 860-738-6333.. 86 C gadams@nwcc.edu
ADAMS, Gregory .... 414-288-1492 494 B gregory.adams@marquette.edu
ADAMS, James, E .... 325-942-2071 451 A james.adams@angelo.edu
ADAMS, Jan .... 470-639-0556 122 D
ADAMS, Janieth .... 601-979-0928 246 E janieth.f.wilson_adams@jsums.edu
ADAMS, Jeff .... 479-788-7221.. 21 H jeff.adams@uafs.edu
ADAMS, Jeffrey, M .... 336-841-4581 329 G jeadams@highpoint.edu
ADAMS, Jennifer .... 315-792-7810 321 E jennifer.adams@sunypoly.edu
ADAMS, Jennifer .... 517-796-8482 225 C adamsjennifes@jccmi.edu
ADAMS, Jennifer .... 334-347-2623.... 2 A jadams@escc.edu
ADAMS, Jennifer .... 925-473-7302.. 40 J jadams@losmedanos.edu
ADAMS, Jennifer .... 614-236-6170 349 D jadams@capital.edu
ADAMS, Jim, J .... 909-599-5433.. 47 K jjadams@lifepacific.edu
ADAMS, Jimmy .... 713-718-2093 437 I jimmy.adams@hccs.edu
ADAMS, John .... 716-652-8900 292 I jadams@cks.edu
ADAMS, John, C .... 607-735-1802 299 D jadams@elmira.edu
ADAMS, John, E .... 828-262-6432 341 B adamsje2@appstate.edu
ADAMS, John, E .... 304-876-5214 490 E jadams@shepherd.edu
ADAMS, Johnnie .... 310-434-4302.. 62 E adams_johnnie@smc.edu
ADAMS, Jordan .... 918-540-6211 366 I jordan.m.adams@neo.edu
ADAMS, Josh .... 707-524-1731.. 62 F jadams2@santarosa.edu
ADAMS, Joshua .... 707-524-1731.. 62 F jadams2@santarosa.edu
ADAMS, Joy .... 307-382-1832 502 I jadams@westernwyoming.edu
ADAMS, Julie .... 423-746-5251 426 F jadams@tnwesleyan.edu
ADAMS, Julius, G .... 716-645-1971 316 F jgadams2@buffalo.edu
ADAMS, Karen .... 812-856-5596 156 B kadams@iu.edu
ADAMS, Karen .... 956-296-1416 455 D karen.adams@utrgv.edu
ADAMS, Karen, H .... 812-856-5596 156 A kadams@iu.edu
ADAMS, Kari .... 620-276-9638 173 E kari.adams@gcccks.edu
ADAMS, Kate .... 651-604-4101 236 J kadams@minneapolisbusinesscollege.edu
ADAMS, Kate .... 518-244-4594 313 D adamsk2@sage.edu
ADAMS, Katelyn, C .... 712-749-2103 163 D adamsk@bvu.edu
ADAMS, Katlyn .... 503-883-2505 373 H kadams@linfield.edu

AGDASI, Sam .... 909-274-4750.. 52 H
sagdasi@mtsac.edu
AGEE, Deborah, G .... 530-752-2396.. 68 E
dgagee@ucdavis.edu
AGEE, Doug, A .... 636-584-6714 252 J
doug.agee@eastcentral.edu
AGEE, Matthew .... 817-202-6788 444 I
matthewagee@swau.edu
AGEE, Patty, A .... 660-263-3900 251 A
pattyagee@cccb.edu
AGEE, Steve .... 405-208-5276 367 I
sagee@okcu.edu
AGESILAS, Elie .... 787-891-0925 508 K
eagesila@aguadilla.inter.edu
AGGARWAL, Reena .... 202-687-3784.. 92 A
aggarwal@georgetown.edu
AGHA, Farooq .... 919-497-3204 330 I
fagha@louisburg.edu
AGHO, Austin, O .... 757-683-3079 469 G
aagho@odu.edu
AGIDIUS, Erin .... 208-885-4285 131 G
erina@uidaho.edu
AGJMURATI, Nick .... 212-592-2002 315 H
nagjmurati@sva.edu
AGLAN, Heshmat .... 334-727-8355.... 7 D
aglan@tuskegee.edu
AGLIBOT, Rex .... 562-988-2278.. 25 R
AGNE, Anissa .... 904-620-2698 110 A
anissa.agne@unf.edu
AGNELLO, Alissa .... 206-934-3747 483 J
alissa.agnello@seattlecolleges.edu
AGNELLO-VELEY,
Josephine .... 860-906-5002.. 85 D
jagnello-veley@capitalcc.edu
AGNESE, Christy .... 610-921-7501 378 C
cagnese@albright.edu
AGNESE, Louis .... 512-444-8082 449 A
agnese@thsu.edu
AGNESI, Peter .... 954-201-5321.. 95 H
pagnesi@broward.edu
AGNEW, Brian .... 201-879-5355 275 H
bagnew@bergen.edu
AGNEW, F. Raymond .... 518-327-6317 311 G
ragnew@paulsmiths.edu
AGNEW, Gene .... 432-335-6411 441 D
gagnew@odessa.edu
AGNEW, Ina .... 918-293-4761 368 D
ina.agnew@okstate.edu
AGNEW, Maria .... 509-682-6659 486 E
magnew@wvc.edu
AGNEW, Melanie .... 801-832-2474 461 G
magnew@westminstercollege.edu
AGO, Emmanuel .... 718-862-7996 305 H
emmanuel.ago@manhattan.edu
AGOONS, Akwai .... 678-466-4000 116 E
akwaiagoons@clayton.edu
AGOSTA, Frank .... 212-592-2620 315 H
fagosta@sva.edu
AGOSTO, Efraín .... 212-870-1208 310 A
eagosto@nyts.edu
AGRAS, James, R .... 412-359-1000 400 E
jagras@triangle-tech.edu
AGRAS, James, R .... 412-359-1000 400 G
jagras@triangle-tech.edu
AGRAS, James, R .... 412-359-1000 400 F
jagras@triangle-tech.edu
AGRAS, Rudy, J .... 412-359-1000 400 G
ragras@triangle-tech.edu
AGRAWAL, C. Mauli ..... 816-235-1101 261 C
chancellor@umkc.edu
AGRAWAL, Devendra .... 909-469-7040.. 74 I
dagrawal@westernu.edu
AGRE-KIPPENHAN,
Susan .... 503-883-2409 373 H
sagreki@linfield.edu
AGRELA, Ramona .... 949-824-5962.. 68 G
ragrela@uci.edu
AGUADO WARE, Joan .. 414-955-8227 494 C
jaguado@mcw.edu
AGUAYO, Mary .... 909-593-3511.. 70 D
maguayo@laverne.edu
AGUE, Paul, E .... 619-201-8701.. 60 A
paul.ague@sdcc.edu
AGUERO-TROTTER,
Dianne .... 973-761-9500 283 B
AGUIAR, Aracely .... 310-287-4374.. 49 G
aguiara@wlac.edu
AGUILAR, Carmen .... 508-678-2811 213 G
carmen.aguilar@bristolcc.edu
AGUILAR, Catherine ...... 787-279-1912 509 A
caguilar@bayamon.inter.edu
AGUILAR, Cheryl, M ..... 909-607-1232.. 37 E
cheryl.aguilar@cmc.edu

AGUILAR, Elmer .... 559-925-3127.. 74 B
elmeraguilar@whccd.edu
AGUILAR, Jade .... 503-370-6195 378 B
aguilarj@willamette.edu
AGUILAR, Jose, A .... 951-827-3878.. 69 C
jose.aguilar@ucr.edu
AGUILAR, Kate .... 765-455-9203 156 D
kaguilar@iuk.edu
AGUILAR, Margie .... 915-566-9621 458 C
AGUILAR, Noemi .... 361-354-2306 433 C
aguilar@coastalbend.edu
AGUILERA, Mary .... 503-375-7113 373 A
maguilera@corban.edu
AGUILERA-GOERNER,
Carmen .... 915-831-7784 436 E
cagui205@epcc.edu
AGUINALDO, Estrella .... 310-834-3065.. 67 K
AGUINALDO, Teresa ..... 847-543-2288 135 B
com401@clcillinois.edu
AGUIRRE, Ilvis .... 787-878-5475 508 L
iaguirre@arecibo.inter.edu
AGUIRRE, Isaiah .... 951-343-5067.. 27 J
iaguirre@calbaptist.edu
AGUIRRE, Juan Carlos . 956-872-6782 444 A
jcaguirre@southtexascollege.edu
AGUIRRE, Katherine ..... 631-451-4022 321 G
aguirrk@sunysuffolk.edu
AGUIRRE, Maria .... 928-317-6180.. 10 J
maria.aguirre@azwestern.edu
AGUIRRE, Raymund .... 657-278-2515.. 31 E
raaguirre@fullerton.edu
AGUIRRE, Robert .... 540-568-7044 468 F
aguirrrd@jmu.edu
AGUIRRE, Tomas, A ..... 607-746-4440 320 G
aguirrta@delhi.edu
AGUIRRE BATTY,
Mercedes .... 973-300-2131 283 E
maguirrebatty@sussex.edu
AGUON, Alicia .... 671-735-2444 505 E
aliciaaguon@triton.uog.edu
AGVENT, Christina .... 203-596-8544.. 87 F
cagvent@post.edu
AGWUNOBI, Andrew ..... 860-679-2594.. 88 E
agwunobi@uchc.edu
AH MU, Lele, V .... 684-699-1586 505 A
leleahmu@ymail.com
AH YUN, Kimo .... 414-288-7133 494 B
james.ahyun@marquette.edu
AHA, Christian .... 856-225-6140 281 G
christian.aha@camden.rutgers.edu
AHDIEH, Robert, B .... 817-212-3838 446 G
dean@law.tamu.edu
AHEARN, Mary Colleen 815-836-5471 141 G
cahearn@lewisu.edu
AHEARN, Shawn .... 941-359-4200 110 D
sahearn@usf.edu
AHEDO, Valentina .... 608-246-6461 499 H
vahedo@madisoncollege.edu
AHERN, Catherine .... 585-785-1273 300 B
catherine.ahern@flcc.edu
AHERN, Joseph, F .... 845-758-7178 290 G
ahern@bard.edu
AHERN, Kathleen .... 203-285-2626.. 85 E
kahern@gwcc.commnet.edu
AHERN, Martin .... 617-984-1635 218 B
mahern@quincycollege.edu
AHLBAUM, Mitch .... 212-772-4946 294 C
mahlbaum@hunter.cuny.edu
AHLBERG, Tim .... 630-617-3309 136 G
ahlbergt@elmhurst.edu
AHLEMANN, Tina .... 843-574-6142 413 B
tina.ahlemann@tridenttech.edu
AHLQUIST, Michelle ..... 320-762-4918 237 B
michellea@alextech.edu
AHLSTRIN, Joseph .... 845-848-7900 298 D
joseph.ahlstrin@dc.edu
AHLUWALIA, Anoop ..... 732-224-1987 276 B
aahluwalia@brookdalecc.edu
AHMAD, Catherine .... 609-497-7804 280 D
AHMAD, Shahzad .... 320-308-4287 240 H
shah@stcloudstate.edu
AHMED, Andrea .... 520-383-8401.. 16 D
aahmed@tocc.edu
AHMED, Furquan .... 313-496-2674 232 C
fahmed1@wcccd.edu
AHMED, Haroon .... 212-752-1530 304 D
haroon.ahmed@limcollege.edu
AHMED, Ijaz .... 734-384-4103 227 G
iahmed@monroeccc.edu
AHMED, Juzar .... 812-465-7160 161 E
juzar@usi.edu
AHMED, M. Monir .... 909-537-3132.. 33 A
mahmed@csusb.edu

AHMED, Mustaq .... 419-358-3237 348 G
ahmedm@bluffton.edu
AHMED, Sadia .... 505-747-5429 287 G
sadia.ahmed@nnmc.edu
AHMED, Syed .... 414-955-7657 494 C
sahmed@mcw.edu
AHMEDNA, Mohamed ... 336-285-4794 341 F
ahmedna@ncat.edu
AHMIDOUCH, Abdellah 336-334-7567 341 F
abdellah@ncat.edu
AHN, Anne .... 714-533-1495.. 64 D
anneahn@southbaylo.edu
AHN, David .... 718-270-5118 295 A
dahn@mec.cuny.edu
AHN, Diane .... 916-577-2200.. 75 B
dahn@jessup.edu
AHN, Hee Young .... 323-731-2383.. 55 C
president@psuca.edu
AHN, Hongjun .... 714-533-3946.. 34 D
hjahn@calums.edu
AHNEN, Heath .... 608-822-2327 500 G
hahnen@swtc.edu
AHOLA, Scott .... 605-642-6359 416 I
scott.ahola@bhsu.edu
AHORRIO, Beatriz .... 212-694-1000 291 I
bahorrio@boricuacollege.edu
AHOUSE, Julie .... 828-726-2715 332 G
jahouse@cccti.edu
AHRENS, Emily .... 218-285-2203 240 D
emily.ahrens@rainyriver.edu
AHRENS, Joan .... 619-644-7155.. 44 I
joan.ahrens@gcccd.edu
AHRENS, Rebecca .... 417-873-7523 252 F
bahrens@drury.edu
AHUJA, Sima Saran ...... 845-575-3000 305 L
AHUJA, Sunil .... 570-941-7673 401 H
sunil.ahuja@scranton.edu
AIDALA, Heather, A ...... 512-245-2208 450 E
ha10@txstate.edu
AIELLO, Karen, M .... 973-655-4213 279 C
aiellok@mail.montclair.edu
AIELLO, Megan .... 864-587-4008 412 G
aiellom@smcsc.edu
AIELLO, Ryan, A .... 971-722-7390 375 J
ryan.aiello@pcc.edu
AIKEN, Adel, G .... 724-847-5002 384 G
aaiken@geneva.edu
AIKEN, Donn .... 518-464-8765 299 G
daiken@excelsior.edu
AIKEN, Irene .... 910-521-6271 343 B
irene.aiken@uncp.edu
AIKEN, Ryan .... 413-775-1309 214 C
aikenr@gcc.mass.edu
AIKENS, Fred, A .... 937-376-6668 350 D
faikens@centralstate.edu
AIKENS, Jane .... 641-472-1260 167 F
jaikens@mum.edu
AIKENS, Michael .... 931-372-3810 426 E
maikens@tntech.edu
AILSTOCK, M. Stephen . 410-777-2230 197 C
smailstock@aacc.edu
AIME, Marty .... 225-214-1953 186 F
morton.aime@franu.edu
AIMONE, Chris .... 812-877-8498 159 J
aimone@rose-hulman.edu
AINLEY, Arden .... 360-416-7716 485 A
arden.ainley@skagit.edu
AINSLEIGH, Susan .... 413-565-1000 205 G
sainsleigh@baypath.edu
AINSLEY, Sharon .... 908-852-1400 276 G
sharon.ainsley@centenaryuniversity.edu
AINSLIE, Andrew .... 585-275-3316 323 J
andrew.ainslie@simon.rochester.edu
AINSWORTH, Emma, L . 662-685-4771 245 D
eainsworth@bmc.edu
AINSWORTH, Stacy .... 318-345-9322 187 G
stacyainsworth@ladelta.edu
AIRD, Jeffrey .... 801-957-4090 461 D
jeffrey.aird@slcc.edu
AIRD, Lashrecse .... 804-862-6100 470 I
laird@rbc.edu
AIROZO, Paul .... 508-830-5051 213 B
pairozo@maritime.edu
AISTRUP, Joseph .... 334-844-4026.... 4 E
jaa0025@auburn.edu
AITKEN, Derek .... 510-885-3877.. 31 C
derek.aitken@csueastbay.edu
AITKEN, Meghan .... 973-290-4427 277 A
maitken@cse.edu
AITSON-ROESSLER,
Mechelle .... 405-733-7308 369 I
maitson-roessler@rose.edu

AIVARS, Paul .... 269-467-9945 224 A
paivars@glenoaks.edu
AIZAWA, Hatsue .... 620-241-0723 172 D
hatsue.aizawa@centralchristian.edu
AIZENSTAT, Stephen ..... 805-969-3626.. 55 E
saizenstat@pacifica.edu
AJE, John .... 609-984-1130 284 B
jaje@tesu.edu
AJIBADE, Victoria .... 718-270-3058 317 E
victora.ajibade@downstate.edu
AKAKPO, Koffi, C .... 859-246-6501 180 K
koffi.akakpo@kctcs.edu
AKANA, Brandyn .... 808-675-3677 127 E
brandyn.akana@byuh.edu
AKASSI, Monique .... 256-761-6211.... 7 B
makassi@tallafdega.edu
AKAU, Sherri .... 808-932-7407 128 E
akau714@hawaii.edu
AKBAR-KHANZDEH,
Farhang .... 567-377-7010 353 E
AKBARI, Hamid .... 507-457-5014 241 F
hakbari@winona.edu
AKCHIN, Lisa, G .... 410-455-2889 202 E
akchin@umbc.edu
AKE, Barb, L .... 407-582-1662 112 K
bake@valenciacollege.edu
AKENS, Cathy .... 336-334-5099 343 A
caakens@uncg.edu
AKENS, Konrad .... 740-588-1342 365 E
AKERMAN, Patricia .... 320-308-5966 241 A
pakerman@sctcc.edu
AKERS, Brandy .... 800-686-1883 222 E
bakers@cleary.edu
AKERS, Daniel .... 951-552-8579.. 27 J
dakers@calbaptist.edu
AKERS, Kathleen .... 931-472-3453 425 D
kathleen.akers@nscc.edu
AKERS, Kenneth .... 276-223-4118 476 E
kakers@wcc.vccs.edu
AKERS, Lex, A .... 309-677-2721 133 B
lakers@bradley.edu
AKERS, Lindsey .... 276-326-4212 465 B
lakers@bluefield.edu
AKERS, Mary Anne .... 443-885-3225 200 D
maryanne.akers@morgan.edu
AKERS, Matthew, P .... 330-972-7954 362 B
akers1@uakron.edu
AKERS, Shana .... 870-248-4000.. 18 F
shana.akers@blackrivertech.edu
AKERS, Shanna .... 434-592-3618 468 H
sakers@liberty.edu
AKERS, Shawn, D .... 434-592-4986 468 H
sdakers@liberty.edu
AKEY, Lynn .... 507-389-2419 239 C
lynn.akey@mnsu.edu
AKEY, Stacey, L .... 920-923-7652 494 A
sakey@marianuniversity.edu
AKEY, William .... 901-678-3993 427 D
wakey@memphis.edu
AKHATAR, Sumaira .... 510-356-4760.. 76 E
AKHAVI, Seyed .... 757-825-2898 476 A
akhavis@tncc.edu
AKHTAR, Shama .... 301-860-3402 203 C
sakhtar@bowiestate.edu
AKIN, Christopher, L .... 813-974-0898 110 B
cakin@usf.edu
AKIN, Daniel, L .... 919-761-2222 340 G
dakin@sebts.edu
AKIN, Jacob, J .... 507-933-7510 235 I
jakin@gustavus.edu
AKIN, Jamie .... 325-942-2116 451 A
jamie.akin@angelo.edu
AKIN, Johnathan .... 615-966-6150 421 D
johnathan.akin@lipscomb.edu
AKIN, Paul .... 502-897-4043 184 C
pakin@sbts.edu
AKIN, Renea .... 270-534-3461 182 F
renea.akin@kctcs.edu
AKINCI, Fevzi .... 412-396-5303 383 C
akincif@duq.edu
AKINLEYE, Johnson, O . 919-530-6104 342 A
johnson.akinleye@nccu.edu
AKINPELU,
Olawunmi, A .... 409-747-9508 456 F
oaakinpe@utmb.edu
AKINS, Ceciley .... 847-866-3971 137 E
ceciley.akins@garrett.edu
AKINS, Mike .... 904-596-2464 111 F
makins@tbc.edu
AKINS, Ralitsa .... 515-271-1400 164 I
AKINS, Renate .... 714-241-6146.. 38 C
rakins1@coastline.edu

AKINSANYA, Oluwafemi ... 718-289-5154 293 B
oluwafemi.akinsanya@bcc.cuny.edu
AKKAWI, Kayed ... 312-935-6025 147 D
kakkawi@robertmorris.edu
AKL, Fred, A ... 610-499-4036 403 B
faakl@widener.edu
AKL, Hatem ... 732-255-0400 280 A
hakl@ocean.edu
AKMAN, Jeffrey, S ... 202-741-2880.. 91 F
akman@gwu.edu
AKO-ADOUNVO, Gifty ... 401-874-2018 406 B
gako-adounvo@uri.edu
AKOB, Joe ... 570-422-3291 394 E
jakob@esu.edu
AKRIDGE, Jay ... 765-494-7420 159 E
akridge@purdue.edu
AKRIDGE, Travis ... 912-538-3125 124 F
takridge@southeasterntech.edu
AKRIGHT, Jan ... 217-228-5520 133 A
akrightj@brcn.edu
AKS, Richard ... 914-455-2650 306 F
raks@mercy.edu
AKSELRUD, Larisa ... 425-739-8515 482 A
larisa.akselrud@lwtech.edu
AKSU, Mert ... 313-994-6620 231 B
aksumn@udmercy.edu
AL-ASSAF, Yousef ... 585-475-2411 313 A
ymacad@rit.edu
AL-HAZZAM DAWASARI, Elizabeth ... 480-800-5457.. 15 P
edawsari@taliesin.edu
AL-MASRI, Ghada ... 510-659-6000.. 54 F
galmasri@ohlone.edu
ALAI, Meghan ... 732-906-2622 279 A
malai@middlesexcc.edu
ALAM, Maria ... 901-678-2867 427 D
malam@memphis.edu
ALAM, Mohammad ... 212-220-1299 293 A
malam@bmcc.cuny.edu
ALAM, Mohammad ... 361-593-2000 447 D
mohammad.alam@tamuk.edu
ALAMADARI, Jeanne ... 408-848-4802.. 43 J
jalamdari@gavilan.edu
ALAMEIDA, Marshall ... 415-485-9326.. 39 C
malameida@marin.edu
ALAMILLO, Laura ... 559-278-0240.. 31 D
lalamillo@csufresno.edu
ALAMO, Carlos ... 845-437-5601 324 C
ALANDER, Link ... 832-813-6832 439 G
link.s.alander@lonestar.edu
ALANIS, Jennifer ... 909-607-3470.. 45 A
j_alanis@hmc.edu
ALANIS, Susan ... 817-515-5203 445 G
susan.alanis@tccd.edu
ALAO, Solomon ... 443-885-3359 200 D
solomon.alao@morgan.edu
ALAPE, Fabio ... 787-850-9387 513 E
fabio.alape@upr.edu
ALASIO, Claire ... 732-571-3463 279 B
calasio@monmouth.edu
ALAVALAPATI, Janaki, R ... 334-844-1007.... 4 E
jra0024@auburn.edu
ALAVI, Maryam ... 404-894-2600 118 F
maryam.alavi@scheller.gatech.edu
ALBA, Suzanna ... 401-456-8086 405 C
salba@ric.edu
ALBAN, Elisa, C ... 909-621-8147.. 57 F
elisa.alban@pomona.edu
ALBANESE, Karli ... 909-599-5433.. 47 K
kalbanese@lifepacific.edu
ALBANESE, Linda ... 516-323-4025 307 F
lalbanese@molloy.edu
ALBANESE, Marc ... 610-282-1100 382 E
marc.albanese@desales.edu
ALBANO, John ... 209-386-6777.. 51 G
albano.j@mccd.edu
ALBANO, Ralph ... 202-319-5218.. 91 B
albano@cua.edu
ALBANO, Steve, D ... 609-984-1100 284 B
salbano@tesu.edu
ALBARRAN, Agustin ... 619-644-7161.. 44 I
agustin.albarran@gcccd.edu
ALBARRAN, Charo ... 707-256-7105.. 53 C
calbarran@napavalley.edu
ALBARRAN, Miguel ... 787-622-8000 512 E
malbarran@pupr.edu
ALBAWANEH, Mahmoud ... 562-985-5462.. 31 F
mahmoud.albawaneh@csulb.edu
ALBECK, Angela ... 802-654-0505 464 B
ara06040@ccv.vsc.edu
ALBENESE, David ... 857-701-1254 215 E
dalbenese@rcc.mass.edu
ALBER, Ivan ... 909-607-0119.. 37 G
ivan_alber@kgi.edu
ALBERDESTON, Jane ... 787-815-0000 513 A
jane.alberdeston@upr.edu
ALBERICO, Jennifer ... 802-254-6370 464 B
jaa05100@ccv.vsc.edu
ALBERS, Christopher ... 520-206-2692.. 15 D
calbers@pima.edu
ALBERS, Jhett ... 605-642-6885 416 I
jhett.albers@bhsu.edu
ALBERS, Nancy ... 318-797-5383 189 D
nancy.albers@lsus.edu
ALBERT, Barbara, J ... 570-326-3761 393 G
balbert@pct.edu
ALBERT, Eric ... 847-970-4861 152 A
ealbert@usml.edu
ALBERT, Gene ... 516-773-5000 504 G
albertg@usmma.edu
ALBERT, Juline ... 712-274-6400 170 E
juline.albert@witcc.edu
ALBERT, Marianne ... 724-222-5330 392 A
malbert@penncommercial.edu
ALBERT, Neil ... 315-228-7408 296 F
nalbert@colgate.edu
ALBERT, Patricia ... 336-272-7102 329 D
patricia.albert@greensboro.edu
ALBERT, OP, Peg ... 517-264-7000 230 E
palbert@sienaheights.edu
ALBERT, Rita ... 561-237-7231 102 V
ralbert@lynn.edu
ALBERT, Robert ... 606-783-2002 183 F
r.albert@moreheadstate.edu
ALBERT, Scott ... 724-738-4342 395 F
scott.albert@sru.edu
ALBERT, Sharon ... 831-755-6960.. 44 K
salbert@hartnell.edu
ALBERT, Shelly ... 618-650-3187 149 F
malbert@siue.edu
ALBERT, Wendy ... 717-867-6302 388 H
walbert@lvc.edu
ALBERT GREEN, DeEadra ... 254-519-5769 447 A
deeadra.albertgreen@tamuct.edu
ALBERT-KNOPP, Heather ... 207-801-5640 193 F
halbert-knopp@coa.edu
ALBERT LINK, Cindy ... 617-747-3096 206 E
clink@berklee.edu
ALBERTA, Vince ... 702-895-5165 271 E
vince.alberta@unlv.edu
ALBERTINI, Velmarie ... 561-868-3891 104 D
albertiv@palmbeachstate.edu
ALBERTO, Marianela ... 304-263-0979 488 H
ALBERTO, Paul, A ... 404-413-8100 119 E
palberto@gsu.edu
ALBERTS, Eugene, R ... 608-796-3849 498 N
eralberts@viterbo.edu
ALBERTS, J.J ... 508-541-1664 208 F
jalberts@dean.edu
ALBERTS, Kristin ... 904-256-7180 101 G
kalbert@ju.edu
ALBERTS, Trev ... 402-554-2305 270 B
talberts@unomaha.edu
ALBERTS, Vicki ... 701-255-3285 347 B
valberts@uttc.edu
ALBERTSON, Hattie ... 701-228-5454 346 C
hattie.c.albertson@dakotacollege.edu
ALBERTSON, Ronald, G 315-229-5962 314 F
ralbertson@stlawu.edu
ALBERTSON, Trevor ... 530-257-6181.. 47 F
talbertson@lassencollege.edu
ALBERTY, José ... 787-815-0000 513 A
jose.alberty@upr.edu
ALBIERI, Guilherme ... 212-938-5500 320 B
galbieri@sunyopt.edu
ALBILLAR, Karl ... 815-394-5058 147 G
kalbillar@rockford.edu
ALBIN-HILL, Jill ... 708-524-6980 136 C
jalbin@dom.edu
ALBITZ, Becky ... 845-575-3000 305 L
rebecca.albitz@marist.edu
ALBO-LOPEZ, Nicole ... 818-364-7635.. 49 B
albolonm@lamission.edu
ALBO-LOPEZ, Nicole ... 213-763-7025.. 49 E
albolonm@lattc.edu
ALBO-LOPEZ, Nicole, M ... 818-364-7635.. 49 B
albolonm@lamission.edu
ALBON, Darrell, J ... 740-368-3070 359 N
djalbon@owu.edu
ALBRECHT, Bryan, D ... 262-564-3000 499 F
albrechtb@gtc.edu
ALBRECHT, Christal, M . 281-756-3598 429 I
calbrecht@alvincollege.edu
ALBRECHT, Daniel ... 408-278-4343.. 75 B
dalbrecht@jessup.edu
ALBRECHT, Don ... 361-825-2612 447 C
don.albrecht@tamucc.edu
ALBRECHT, Jana ... 309-438-7018 139 E
jlalbre2@ilstu.edu
ALBRECHT, Janet ... 973-684-6136 280 B
aalbrecht@pccc.edu
ALBRECHT, John ... 775-673-7261 271 B
jalbrecht@tmcc.com
ALBRECHT, Teri ... 512-471-7885 455 A
teri@austin.utexas.edu
ALBRIGHT, Bonnie ... 409-880-7633 449 G
bsalbright@lit.edu
ALBRIGHT, Geri ... 205-929-6315.... 2 H
galbright@lawsonstate.edu
ALBRIGHT, Mike ... 845-341-4728 311 C
mike.albright@sunyorange.edu
ALBRIGHT, Polly ... 765-983-1858 154 G
albripo@earlham.edu
ALBRIGHT, Thomas ... 601-979-2580 246 E
thomas.e.albright@jsums.edu
ALBRIGHTY, Richard, C 773-508-3899 142 D
ralbright@luc.edu
ALBRINCK, Margaret, L 920-565-1021 493 J
albrinckm@lakeland.edu
ALBRITTON, Kristen ... 401-825-1000 404 H
kbalbritton@ccri.edu
ALBURCHER, Ronald ... 650-723-2300.. 65 J
ALBURN, Amelia ... 508-999-8658 211 F
amelia.alburn@umassd.edu
ALBURY, Gary ... 510-464-3536.. 56 G
galbury@peralta.edu
ALBURY, Wayne ... 402-872-2350 268 F
walbury@peru.edu
ALCAINO, Ricardo ... 805-893-4504.. 70 A
ricardo.alcaino@oeosh.ucsb.edu
ALCALA, Emma ... 719-549-3327.. 81 K
emma.alcala@pueblocc.edu
ALCALA-BURKHARDT, Celena ... 310-287-4290.. 49 G
alcalac@wlac.edu
ALCANTARA, Ryan ... 310-377-5501.. 51 B
ralcantara@marymountcalifornia.edu
ALCARAZ, Cristina ... 787-786-3030 512 B
calcaraz@ucb.edu.pr
ALCARAZ, Luis ... 787-279-1912 509 A
lalcaraz@bayamon.inter.edu
ALCARAZ, Luis, E ... 787-279-1912 509 A
lalcaraz@bayamon.inter.edu
ALCIDE, Tom ... 443-412-2489 199 A
talcide@harford.edu
ALCIDONIS, Sendy ... 610-436-2122 396 A
salcidonis@wcupa.edu
ALCINDOR, Frantz, L ... 212-217-3000 299 H
frantz_alcindor@fitnyc.edu
ALCOCER, Amy ... 252-335-0821 333 G
amy_alcocer68@albemarle.edu
ALCOCER, David ... 510-987-9112.. 68 C
david.alcocer@ucop.edu
ALCOCK, Sherry, B ... 563-387-1862 167 E
alcock@luther.edu
ALCOCK, Susan ... 810-762-3177 231 G
salcock@umich.edu
ALCON, Arnaa ... 508-531-6131 212 B
aalcon@bridgew.edu
ALCORN, Jill ... 916-660-7160.. 63 I
jalcorn1@sierracollege.edu
ALCORTA, Lisa ... 210-486-0953 429 H
lalcorta3@alamo.edu
ALCRUDO, Lourdes ... 787-622-8000 512 E
lalcrudo@pupr.edu
ALDAMA, Ben ... 479-986-6939.. 20 D
baldama@nwacc.edu
ALDAMA, Julie ... 562-907-4286.. 75 A
jaldama@whittier.edu
ALDARONDO, Aixa ... 787-766-1717 511 H
aialdarondo@suagm.edu
ALDAVA, Jesse ... 310-342-5200.. 72 D
ALDAY, Inaki ... 504-865-5000 191 B
ALDEN, Bernadette ... 413-662-5203 213 A
bernadette.alden@mcla.edu
ALDEN, Dan ... 512-245-2521 450 E
d_a29@txstate.edu
ALDEN, Kathy ... 770-533-6949 121 B
kalden@laniertech.edu
ALDEN, Peg ... 802-387-6821 462 D
palden@landmark.edu
ALDEN-RIVERS, Bethany ... 636-949-4737 254 F
balden-rivers@lindenwood.edu
ALDENTALER, Heather ... 605-626-2371 417 A
heather.aldentaler@northern.edu
ALDER, Kate ... 760-757-2121.. 52 E
kalder@miracosta.edu
ALDER, William ... 304-647-6203 491 A
walder@osteo.wvsom.edu
ALDERFER, Gregg ... 215-368-5000 390 F
galderfer@missio.edu
ALDERMAN, Brian ... 423-652-4708 420 H
bjalderman@king.edu
ALDERMAN, Debye, B .. 843-953-7458 408 E
aldermanda@cofc.edu
ALDERMAN, Norman (Mike), M ... 863-667-5129 107 K
nmalderman@seu.edu
ALDERMAN, Pamela ... 304-357-4875 488 G
pamelaalderman@ucwv.edu
ALDERMAN, Rosalind ... 210-436-3995 443 A
ralderman@stmarytx.edu
ALDERMAN, Steve ... 713-646-1812 444 B
salderman@stcl.edu
ALDOUS, Mary ... 518-743-2275 320 D
aldousm@sunyacc.edu
ALDRICH, Adrian, M ... 630-637-5201 144 H
amaldrich@noctrl.edu
ALDRICH, B.J ... 907-474-7043.. 10 A
bjaldrich@alaska.edu
ALDRICH, Christine ... 310-900-1600.. 40 A
caldrich@elcamino.edu
ALDRICH, Kimberly, J .. 269-337-7302 225 D
kim.aldrich@kzoo.edu
ALDRICH, Michael ... 808-675-3851 127 E
michael.aldrich@byuh.edu
ALDRIDGE, Doug ... 417-626-1234 257 F
aldridge.doug@occ.edu
ALDRIDGE, Mary ... 516-877-3843 289 C
aldridge@adelphi.edu
ALDRIDGE, R. Mark ... 817-202-6355 444 I
aldridge@swau.edu
ALDRIDGE, Susan, C ... 215-895-0528 383 B
susan.c.aldridge@drexel.edu
ALDRIDGE, Whitney, C . 540-375-2201 471 B
aldridge@roanoke.edu
ALDRIDGE, William, D . 202-885-8686.. 93 E
caldridge@wesleyseminary.edu
ALDRIDGE SANFORD, Amy ... 361-825-3996 447 C
amy.aldridge.sanford@tamucc.edu
ALEMAN, Karla ... 440-366-7278 355 J
ALEMAN, Nicolle ... 541-552-7246 376 E
alemann@sou.edu
ALEONG, Natasha ... 786-331-1000 103 G
naleong@maufl.edu
ALESSANDRELLO, Thomas ... 201-291-1111 291 D
tom@berkeleycollege.edu
ALESSANDRELLO, Thomas ... 201-291-1111 275 I
tom@berkeleycollege.edu
ALESSI, Mark ... 585-567-9456 302 D
mark.alessi@houghton.edu
ALEWINE, J. Alan ... 618-537-6524 143 B
jaalewine@mckendree.edu
ALEWINE, Sharon ... 864-225-7653 409 J
sharonalewine@forrestcollege.edu
ALEX, Elizabeth ... 816-654-7709 254 C
ealex@kcumb.edu
ALEX-ASSENSOH, Yvette, M ... 541-346-9170 377 D
yalex@uoregon.edu
ALEXANDER, A. Donna . 804-758-6703 475 G
dalexander@rappahannock.edu
ALEXANDER, Adrian, W 918-631-2356 371 E
adrian-alexander@utulsa.edu
ALEXANDER, Akeem ... 256-551-3130.... 2 E
akeem.alexander@drakestate.edu
ALEXANDER, Andrea ... 408-223-6796.. 61 L
andrea.alexander@evc.edu
ALEXANDER, Anne ... 307-766-4286 502 H
aalex@uwyo.edu
ALEXANDER, Ashley ... 202-885-3449.. 90 J
ashleya@american.edu
ALEXANDER, Beth, A ... 317-940-6378 153 F
balexand@butler.edu
ALEXANDER, Bishop ... 256-765-4201.... 8 E
jmalexander@una.edu
ALEXANDER, Bruce ... 315-786-2364 303 F
balexander@sunyjefferson.edu
ALEXANDER, Bryant, K . 310-338-7430.. 50 J
bryantkeithalexander@lmu.edu
ALEXANDER, Carol ... 701-349-5776 346 J
carolalexander@trinitybiblecollege.edu

ALEXANDER, Cassandra .... 229-430-4617 113 H
cassandra.alexander@asurams.edu
ALEXANDER, Charlene .. 541-737-5936 375 D
ALEXANDER, Chaz .... 907-563-7575.... 9 C
chaz.alesander@alaskacareercollege.edu
ALEXANDER, Christine, D .... 717-358-4168 384 D
christine.alexander@fandm.edu
ALEXANDER, Cindy ...... 864-294-3324 410 A
cindy.alexander@furman.edu
ALEXANDER, Courtney . 715-394-8305 498 B
calexan9@uwsuper.edu
ALEXANDER, Dannie ..... 269-488-4298 225 E
dalexander@kvcc.edu
ALEXANDER, David .... 919-546-8351 340 E
david.alexander@shawu.edu
ALEXANDER, Debra ...... 989-328-1276 228 A
debraj@montcalm.edu
ALEXANDER, Dianne ..... 215-702-4276 380 D
dalexander@cairn.edu
ALEXANDER, Donalyn ... 325-670-1198 440 B
donalyn.alexander@phssn.edu
ALEXANDER, F. King .... 225-578-2111 188 H
ALEXANDER, G. Rumay 919-966-7767 342 D
rumay@email.unc.edu
ALEXANDER, Gary .... 617-850-1322 210 D
galexander@hchc.edu
ALEXANDER, Ginny ...... 904-646-2205 100 B
ginny.alexander@fscj.edu
ALEXANDER, Herman ... 504-526-4745 189 H
hermana@nationsu.edu
ALEXANDER, Iwan .... 205-934-8400.... 8 A
ialex@uab.edu
ALEXANDER, J. Neil ..... 931-598-1288 423 M
jnalexan@sewanee.edu
ALEXANDER, Jeff .... 719-549-3253.. 81 K
jeff.alexander@pueblocc.edu
ALEXANDER, Jeffery ..... 805-546-3138.. 41 A
jeffery_alexander@cuesta.edu
ALEXANDER, Jenny ...... 414-288-7362 494 B
jenny.alexander@marquette.edu
ALEXANDER, John .... 205-391-2343.... 3 E
jalexander@sheltonstate.edu
ALEXANDER, John .... 530-642-5615.. 50 H
alexanj@flc.losrios.edu
ALEXANDER, Joyce, M . 979-845-5311 446 G
joycemalexander@tamu.edu
ALEXANDER, Juan, M .. 757-823-8396 469 F
jmalexander@nsu.edu
ALEXANDER, Karen .... 434-832-7623 474 C
alexanderk2@centralvirginia.edu
ALEXANDER, Katie .... 734-432-5837 227 A
ksalexander@madonna.edu
ALEXANDER, Keith .... 928-428-8279.. 12 E
keith.alexander@eac.edu
ALEXANDER, Kevin .... 970-943-0120.. 84 D
ALEXANDER, Kevin, L .. 714-449-7450.. 51 A
kalexander@ketchum.edu
ALEXANDER, Kim .... 206-934-6660 484 B
kim.alexander@seattlecolleges.edu
ALEXANDER, Kimberly .. 845-758-7516 290 G
kalexand@bard.edu
ALEXANDER, King .... 225-578-2111 188 I
alexander@lsu.edu
ALEXANDER, Klint .... 307-766-6416 502 H
klint.alexander@uwyo.edu
ALEXANDER, Laura .... 815-753-6565 145 C
lalexander@niu.edu
ALEXANDER, Laurence, B .... 870-575-8471.. 22 E
alexanderl@uapb.edu
ALEXANDER, Lea Ann .. 870-230-5305.. 19 E
alexande@hsu.edu
ALEXANDER, Lex .... 336-272-7102 329 D
lex.alexander@greensboro.edu
ALEXANDER, Lisa .... 315-464-4700 317 F
alexandl@upstate.edu
ALEXANDER, Lorraine ... 229-430-6624 113 I
lalexander@albanytech.edu
ALEXANDER, Lynn, M .. 731-881-7490 428 B
lalexand@utm.edu
ALEXANDER, Mark .... 662-243-2675 246 A
malexander@eastms.edu
ALEXANDER, Mark .... 610-519-7005 402 D
alexander@law.villanova.edu
ALEXANDER, Mary .... 605-995-2656 415 C
mary.alexander@dwu.edu
ALEXANDER, Matt .... 361-570-4823 453 C
alexanderm@uhv.edu
ALEXANDER, Michael ... 920-465-5161 496 E
alexandm@uwgb.edu
ALEXANDER, Michael, B .... 617-243-2221 210 G
malexander@lasell.edu
ALEXANDER, Michelle .. 940-552-6291 457 C
malexander@vernoncollege.edu
ALEXANDER, Missy ...... 203-837-8400.. 85 B
alexanderm@wcsu.edu
ALEXANDER, Nathan ..... 501-374-6305.. 21 A
nathan.alexander@shortercollege.edu
ALEXANDER, Otis .... 786-331-1000 103 G
oalexander@maufl.edu
ALEXANDER, Paul .... 508-362-2131 214 B
palexander@capecod.edu
ALEXANDER, Paul .... 701-349-5444 346 J
paulalexander@trinitybiblecollege.edu
ALEXANDER, Paul, H .... 714-879-3901.. 45 F
palexander@hiu.edu
ALEXANDER, Pearl .... 404-894-0300 118 F
pearl.alexander@ohr.gatech.edu
ALEXANDER, Raquel, M .... 570-577-1753 379 F
raquel.alexander@bucknell.edu
ALEXANDER, Rebecca .. 770-962-7580 120 E
ralexander@gwinnetttech.edu
ALEXANDER, Robert ..... 601-974-1062 247 B
robert.alexander@millsaps.edu
ALEXANDER, Ross .... 256-765-5950.... 8 E
ralexander3@una.edu
ALEXANDER, Sanquita .. 334-291-4996.... 1 H
sanquita.alexander@cv.edu
ALEXANDER, Scott .... 207-786-6000 193 B
salexan2@bates.edu
ALEXANDER, Seth .... 617-253-4900 215 G
ALEXANDER, State, W .. 704-216-6067 330 H
salexan@livingstone.edu
ALEXANDER, Stephanie 740-245-7366 363 D
alexandr@rio.edu
ALEXANDER, Taylor ...... 406-771-4314 264 G
taylor.alexander1@gfcmsu.edu
ALEXANDER, Tim .... 205-665-6155.... 8 D
talexand@montevallo.edu
ALEXANDER, Tom .... 419-448-2507 353 H
talexan1@heidelberg.edu
ALEXANDER, Tyson .... 325-674-2878 429 B
tma08a@acu.edu
ALEXANDER, Viola .... 706-507-8800 116 I
alexander_viola@columbusstate.edu
ALEXANDER, William .... 205-226-4736.... 5 A
walexand@bsc.edu
ALEXANDER-HERRIOTT, Vicki .... 641-472-1161 167 F
dof@mum.edu
ALEXANDER-WALLACE, Linda .... 718-518-4432 294 B
lalexander@hostos.cuny.edu
ALEXANDRE, Michele .... 727-562-7858 111 A
malexandrer@law.stetson.edu
ALEXANDROU, Cyprian 315-858-0450 302 C
cyprian@hts.edu
ALEXIS, Eloise .... 615-963-5504 426 D
ealexis@tnstate.edu
ALEXIS STEPHENS, Marnelle .... 312-922-1884 142 H
chancellor@maccormac.edu
ALEXO, JR., Kenneth .... 973-596-8293 279 F
kenneth.alexo@njit.edu
ALEXO, Michael .... 302-831-4573.. 90 F
malexo@udel.edu
ALEY, Danielle .... 828-395-1633 335 D
daley@isothermal.edu
ALFANO, Anthony .... 610-519-7730 402 D
anthony.alfano@villanova.edu
ALFANO, Cindy .... 309-268-8019 137 I
cindy.alfano@heartland.edu
ALFANO, Michael .... 203-365-7621.. 88 B
alfanom3@sacredheart.edu
ALFANO, Renee, M .... 608-243-4539 499 H
ralfano@madisoncollege.edu
ALFARO, Carolina .... 209-667-3982.. 33 C
calfaro@csustan.edu
ALFARO, Gerardo .... 214-887-5206 436 B
galfaro@dts.edu
ALFARO, Richard .... 408-855-5145.. 74 D
richard.alfaro@missioncollege.edu
ALFERNESS, Rod .... 805-893-3141.. 70 A
alferness@engineering.ucsb.edu
ALFIE, Rebeca .... 305-642-4104 105 D
ALFONSO, Antonio .... 360-867-6238 481 A
alfonsoa@evergreen.edu
ALFONSO, August .... 361-698-1300 436 C
aalfonso@delmar.edu
ALFONSO, Daniel .... 954-262-8835 103 M
djalfonso@nova.edu
ALFONSO, Jorge .... 305-821-3333.. 99 E
jalfonso@fnu.edu
ALFORD, Andrew .... 601-276-3704 249 B
aalford@smcc.edu
ALFORD, Brian .... 212-678-8195 322 G
ba2361@tc.columbia.edu
ALFORD, Cynthia .... 336-838-6111 339 B
clalford287@wilkescc.edu
ALFORD, Keith .... 315-443-4110 322 C
kalford@syr.edu
ALFORD, Keri .... 334-386-7179.... 5 D
kalford@faulkner.edu
ALFORD, Keyimani .... 608-246-6320 499 H
klalford@madisoncollege.edu
ALFORD, Michael .... 989-774-7161 222 C
alfor1wm@cmich.edu
ALFORD, Rodney .... 256-890-4733.... 1 F
rodney.alford@calhoun.edu
ALFORD, Sara .... 972-899-8414 441 A
salford@nctc.edu
ALFORD, Stephanie .... 410-337-6431 198 G
stephanie.bender@goucher.edu
ALFORQUE, Patrick .... 312-341-2277 147 H
palforque@roosevelt.edu
ALFRED, Reina .... 718-270-2611 317 E
reina.alfred@downstate.edu
ALFRED, Tangelia .... 323-241-5333.. 49 D
alfredtm@lasc.edu
ALFULTIS, Michael, A ... 718-409-7271 321 C
ALGATE, Jill .... 800-280-0307 152 H
jill.algate@ace.edu
ALGER, Jonathan, R ...... 540-568-6868 468 F
president@jmu.edu
ALGIER, Anne-Marie ..... 585-275-4085 323 J
anne-marie.algier@rochester.edu
ALGOE, Eric .... 512-245-2244 450 E
e_a231@txstate.edu
ALHANATI, Mark .... 310-954-4056.. 52 G
malhanati@msmu.edu
ALHONA, Steve .... 845-434-5750 322 A
salhona@sunysullivan.edu
ALI, Abe .... 909-274-4225.. 52 H
aali@mtsac.edu
ALI, Adel .... 320-308-3110 240 H
alali@stcloudstate.edu
ALI, Aneesah .... 219-980-6853 156 E
aneeali@iun.edu
ALI, Cheryl .... 609-497-7757 280 D
cheryl.ali@ptsem.edu
ALI, Hesham .... 402-554-2380 270 B
hali@unomaha.edu
ALI, Mahmood .... 641-472-1126 167 F
housing@mum.edu
ALI, Maisha .... 301-860-3416 203 C
mali@bowiestate.edu
ALI, Mansoor .... 401-225-2321 199 H
mali01@mica.edu
ALI, Mohammad .... 937-376-6235 350 D
mali@centralstate.edu
ALI, Omar .... 336-334-5538 343 A
ohali@uncg.edu
ALI, Rita .... 309-694-5561 138 C
rali@icc.edu
ALI, Yasmin .... 718-951-5000 293 C
yali@brooklyn.cuny.edu
ALIBERTI, Fred .... 518-629-7210 302 E
f.aliberti@hvcc.edu
ALIBRANDI, Cynthia, A 315-445-4462 304 C
alibraca@lemoyne.edu
ALICANDRO, Jean .... 860-832-1664.. 84 I
alicandro@ccsu.edu
ALICEA, Edwin .... 787-725-8120 507 N
ealicea@eap.edu
ALICEA, Victor, G .... 212-694-1000 291 I
valicea@boricuacollege.edu
ALICEA DENIZARD, Kiara .... 787-725-8120 507 N
kalicea@eap.edu
ALICEA-MALDONADO, Rafael .... 585-345-6820 301 A
ralicea-maldonado@genesee.edu
ALIMBOYOGUEN, Maribel .... 847-376-7053 145 G
malimboyoguen@oakton.edu
ALIMO, Craig .... 707-256-7364.. 53 C
calmio@napavalley.edu
ALIMPICH, Julie .... 843-863-7190 407 E
jalimpich@csuniv.edu
ALIPOE, Dovi .... 601-877-6543 244 H
alipoe@alcorn.edu
ALISE, Mark .... 504-865-5000 191 B
ALIVISATOS, Paul .... 510-642-1961.. 68 D
palivisatos@berkeley.edu
ALIX, Jeff .... 419-289-5093 348 A
jalix@ashland.edu
ALKIRE, Amy .... 612-330-1188 233 K
alkirea@augsburg.edu
ALKIRE, Laurie .... 308-635-6036 270 D
alkirel@wncc.edu
ALL, Jessica .... 803-812-7398 413 G
allj@mailbox.sc.edu
ALLAHBACHAYO, Salima .... 626-852-6439.. 36 K
sallahbachayo@citruscollege.edu
ALLAN, Carol .... 413-265-2289 208 C
allanc@elms.edu
ALLAN, Kevin .... 845-451-1460 298 A
kevin.allan@culinary.edu
ALLARD, Cathy .... 406-756-3900 263 F
callard@fvcc.edu
ALLARD, Dei .... 662-325-3555 247 F
da1112@msstate.edu
ALLARD, Ingrid, M .... 518-262-5919 289 F
allardi@amc.edu
ALLARD, Lee .... 505-454-3562 286 H
lallard@nmhu.edu
ALLBRITTEN, Jeffery ...... 239-489-9211 100 A
president@fsw.edu
ALLBRITTEN, Terry .... 845-938-7212 504 H
ALLCOCK, Melissa .... 270-534-3090 182 F
melissa.allcock@kctcs.edu
ALLCORN, Terry, A .... 417-268-6003 250 G
tallcorn@gobbc.edu
ALLCORN, Terry, L .... 407-582-1492 112 K
tallcorn@valenciacollege.edu
ALLDREDGE, Annita ...... 415-749-4560.. 60 G
aalldredge@sfai.edu
ALLDREDGE, Brian .... 415-514-0421.. 69 E
brian.alldredge@ucsf.edu
ALLDREDGE, Kari .... 865-974-1350 427 G
kalldre1@utk.edu
ALLEE, Kelly .... 217-234-5215 141 D
kallee@lakeland.cc.il.us
ALLEE, Rodney .... 317-632-5553 158 S
rallee@lincolntech.edu
ALLEGRETTA, Kerri .... 516-403-5392 324 G
kallegretta@webb.edu
ALLEGRETTO, Stephen, A .... 203-582-7962.. 87 G
stephen.allegretto@quinnipiac.edu
ALLEMAN, Vickie .... 415-257-1334.. 41 H
vickie.alleman@dominican.edu
ALLEMAN-BEYERS, Natalie .... 913-468-8500 174 D
nalleman@jccc.edu
ALLEN, Algia .... 972-563-9573 452 B
aallen@tvcc.edu
ALLEN, Aliquippa .... 205-652-3687.... 9 A
aallen@uwa.edu
ALLEN, Amanda .... 979-532-6468 458 F
allena@wcjc.edu
ALLEN, Amy .... 320-762-4591 237 B
amya@alextech.edu
ALLEN, Andrew .... 651-290-6463 242 G
andrew.allen@mitchellhamline.edu
ALLEN, Andrew .... 619-260-4816.. 71 J
andrewt@sandiego.edu
ALLEN, Angela .... 806-651-8482 448 C
aallen@wtamu.edu
ALLEN, Anita .... 478-825-6304 118 A
anita.allen@fvsu.edu
ALLEN, Anita, L .... 215-898-4032 400 K
aallen@law.upenn.edu
ALLEN, Ann Marie .... 435-586-7700 460 F
mciffallen@suu.edu
ALLEN, Anna .... 858-513-9240.. 26 G
anna.allen@ashford.edu
ALLEN, Anna, M .... 215-951-1374 387 C
aallen@lasalle.edu
ALLEN, Anthony .... 718-933-6700 307 G
aallen@monroecollege.edu
ALLEN, Anthony, W .... 573-629-3252 253 H
anthony.allen@hlg.edu
ALLEN, Augusta .... 610-341-5870 383 D
aallen6@eastern.edu
ALLEN, Bob .... 956-380-8125 442 L
ballen@riogrande.edu
ALLEN, Brenda .... 303-315-2104.. 83 C
brenda.j.allen@ucdenver.edu
ALLEN, Brenda, A .... 484-365-7400 389 C
ballen@lincoln.edu
ALLEN, Brian .... 815-939-5258 146 A
ballen@olivet.edu
ALLEN, Brian .... 919-546-8417 340 E
brian.allen@shawu.edu
ALLEN, C. Leonard .... 615-966-6064 421 D
leonard.allen@lipscomb.edu

ALMAGUER, Ben 559-651-2500 61 A
ben.almaguer@sjvc.edu
ALMANDREZ, Mary Grace 401-874-7077 406 B
mgalmandrez@uri.edu
ALMANZA, Manny 903-983-8218 439 A
malmanza@kilgore.edu
ALMANZAR, Karoline 909-469-5318 74 I
kalmanzar@westernu.edu
ALMAS, Emily, L 314-935-4893 262 A
emily.almas@wustl.edu
ALMEDA, Delilah 305-237-2951 103 D
dalmeda1@mdc.edu
ALMEIDA, Enga 817-202-6494 444 I
ealmeida@swau.edu
ALMEIDA, Paul, A 202-687-3883 92 A
almeidap@georgetown.edu
ALMENDAREZ, Elena 412-536-1053 387 B
elena.almendarez@laroche.edu
ALMON, Robert, C 212-346-1200 311 E
ralmon@pace.edu
ALMOND, Jackie 434-544-8457 472 G
almond.j@lynchburg.edu
ALMOND, James, S 765-494-9706 159 E
jsalmond@purdue.edu
ALMONTE, Loreto 305-821-3333 99 E
lalmonte@fnu.edu
ALMORADIE, Joel 718-522-9073 290 C
jalmoradie@asa.edu
ALMQUIST, Arne 409-880-8118 449 H
arne.almquist@lamar.edu
ALMQUIST, Brian 843-574-6011 413 B
brian.almquist@tridenttech.edu
ALMQUIST, Cathy 843-574-6057 413 B
cathy.almquist@tridenttech.edu
ALMQUIST, Jacqueline 531-622-2745 267 H
jalmquist@mccneb.edu
ALMUS, Kadir 832-230-5021 440 H
almus@na.edu
ALMUSAWI, Marwa 253-833-9111 481 F
malmusawi@greenriver.edu
ALMY, Marilynn 912-525-5000 123 G
malmy@scad.edu
ALNAJJAR, Hisham 860-768-4846 88 H
alnajjar@hartford.edu
ALNUTT, Mark, M 716-645-6811 316 F
ub-athleticdirector@buffalo.edu
ALO, Richard 850-412-5978 108 I
richard.alo@famu.edu
ALONGI, Manuela 718-982-2000 293 E
ALONSO, Carlos, J 212-854-6935 297 C
ca2201@columbia.edu
ALONSO, David 212-998-1077 310 B
david.alonso@nyu.edu
ALONSO, Jose 787-738-2161 513 D
jose.alonso@upr.edu
ALONZO, Jamie 408-741-2150 74 E
jamie.alonzo@westvalley.edu
ALONZO, Liza 713-221-8682 453 B
alonzol@uhd.edu
ALONZO, Mia 909-607-9192 37 C
mia.alonzo@claremont.edu
ALONZO, Patricia 989-317-4760 230 A
palonzo@sagchip.edu
ALONZO, Robert 713-221-8977 453 B
alonzor@uhd.edu
ALOYO, JR., Victor 609-688-1941 280 D
victor.aloyo@ptsem.edu
ALP, Nesli 812-237-3166 155 G
nesli.alp@indstate.edu
ALPERIN, Samantha 901-321-3116 419 C
salperin@cbu.edu
ALPERN, Robert, J 203-785-4672 89 D
robert.alpern@yale.edu
ALPI, Kristine 503-494-0455 375 B
alpi@ohsu.edu
ALPIN, Jolie 760-366-5210 40 K
jalpin@cmccd.edu
ALSABROOK, Meredith 205-226-4977 5 A
mwolfe@bsc.edu
ALSAFEER, Saif 904-735-5568 117 C
salsafeer@daltonstate.edu
ALSANDOR, Carla 713-525-3111 454 H
calsand@stthom.edu
ALSBERRY, Reis 850-412-7232 108 I
reis.alsberry@famu.edu
ALSHEIMER, Michael 315-792-7210 321 E
michael.alsheimer@sunypoly.edu
ALSINA-OROZCO, Amalia 787-723-4481 507 A
centro@ceaprc.edu
ALSING, Melissa 724-830-1850 398 H
malsing@setonhill.edu
ALSIP, Morgan 405-692-3244 366 G
ALSOBROOK, Joe 636-949-4164 254 F
jalsobrook@lindenwood.edu
ALSOBROOK, Metta 757-388-5733 471 D
malsobrook@sentara.edu
ALSOBROOKS, Scott 662-476-5050 246 A
salsobrooks@eastms.edu
ALSOP, Rob 304-293-5841 491 C
rob.alsop@mail.wvu.edu
ALSOP, Robert 641-585-8130 170 B
alsopb@waldorf.edu
ALSSID, Julian 401-825-2033 404 H
jalssid@ccri.edu
ALSTER, Samuel 732-765-9126 284 L
ygocb@yeshivanet.com
ALSTER, Shimon 732-765-9126 284 L
ygocb@yeshivanet.com
ALSTON, Carleta 312-850-7313 134 H
calston@ccc.edu
ALSTON, Cathy 253-833-9111 481 F
calston@greenriver.edu
ALSTON, Dawn 404-270-5077 125 B
dalston@spelman.edu
ALSTON, Jeffrey, L 423-439-6174 419 J
alstonj@etsu.edu
ALSTON, Kenyon 205-366-8980 7 A
kalston@stillman.edu
ALSTON, Micah, N 714-879-3901 45 F
mnalston@hiu.edu
ALSTON, Sharon 202-885-6053 90 J
salston@american.edu
ALSTON, Susan 860-512-2903 85 G
salston@manchestercc.edu
ALSTON, Vickie 479-979-1303 23 I
valston@ozarks.edu
ALSTON FORBES, Lakesha 252-328-6804 341 C
alstonl@ecu.edu
ALSTON-PINCKNEY, Elizabeth 704-216-6100 330 H
ealston-pinckney@livingstone.edu
ALSTROM, Mike 231-777-0307 228 D
mike.alstrom@muskegoncc.edu
ALSUP, Margaret 870-307-7474 20 A
margaret.alsup@lyon.edu
ALSUP, Philip 920-206-4081 493 L
philip.alsup@mbu.edu
ALT, Ashley 570-941-6497 401 H
ALT, Jason 914-674-7349 306 F
jalt@mercy.edu
ALT, Jennifer 360-538-4066 481 E
jennifer.alt@ghc.edu
ALT, Sarah 262-547-1211 492 E
salt@carrollu.edu
ALT, Susan 406-994-3344 264 D
salt@montana.edu
ALTAMIRANO, Carlos 787-743-3038 511 A
caltamirano@sanjuanbautista.edu
ALTAMIRANO, Rodolfo, R 215-573-6332 400 K
rudiea@pobox.upenn.edu
ALTARRIBA, Jeanette 518-442-5004 316 D
jaltarriba@albany.edu
ALTAYLI, Benek 719-255-3257 83 B
zaltayli@uccs.edu
ALTEGOER, Diana, B 215-898-8493 400 K
altegoer@upenn.edu
ALTEMOSE, Jane 610-758-4637 388 J
jca209@lehigh.edu
ALTENBURG, Rana, H 414-288-7430 494 B
rana.altenburg@marquette.edu
ALTERIO, Christopher 315-279-5483 304 A
calterio1@keuka.edu
ALTHAUS, Jon 217-234-5225 141 D
jalthaus@lakeland.cc.il.us
ALTIER, Jeffrey, P 386-822-8100 111 A
jaltier@stetson.edu
ALTIERE, Ralph 303-724-2887 83 C
ralph.altiere@ucdenver.edu
ALTIERI, Anthony 561-237-7275 102 V
aaltieri@lynn.edu
ALTIKULAC, John 770-426-2644 121 C
jaltikulac@life.edu
ALTMAN, Carolyn 912-486-1149 119 C
caltman@georgiasouthern.edu
ALTMAN, Don 480-219-6008 250 A
daltman@atsu.edu
ALTMAN, J.J 912-871-1648 122 I
jaltman@ogeecheetech.edu
ALTMAN, Joanne, D 336-841-9613 329 G
jaltman0@highpoint.edu
ALTMAN, Kip 864-488-4012 410 E
caltman@limestone.edu
ALTMAN, Miranda 410-778-7261 204 D
maltman2@washcoll.edu
ALTMANN, Barbara, K 717-358-3971 384 D
president@fandm.edu
ALTMAYER, Magnus 509-453-0374 483 C
magnus.altmayer@perrytech.edu
ALTOBELLO, Maria, R 603-647-3530 273 F
altobellom@franklinpierce.edu
ALTONGY-MAGEE, Kristy 508-373-5726 216 B
kristy.altongy-magee@mcphs.edu
ALTSCHULER, Glenn, C 607-255-7393 297 F
gca1@cornell.edu
ALTSHULER, Gina 215-335-0800 389 B
galtshuler@lincolntech.edu
ALTSHULER, Suzanne 732-224-2967 276 B
saltshuler@brookdalecc.edu
ALTUSKY, Shlomo Avidgor 718-868-2300 291 B
ALTWINE, Chad 605-668-1502 415 H
chad.altwine@mtmc.edu
ALVA, Sylvia, A 909-869-4382 30 D
saalva@cpp.edu
ALVALLE, Anibal 787-764-0000 514 B
anibal.alvalle@upr.edu
ALVARADO, Cecilia 951-222-8073 58 I
cecilia.alvarado@rcc.edu
ALVARADO, Christian 949-582-4340 64 G
calvarado@saddleback.edu
ALVARADO, Luis 509-793-2291 478 H
luisa@bigbend.edu
ALVARADO, Miguel 617-422-7423 217 C
malvarado@nesl.edu
ALVARADO, Nelly 310-900-1600 40 A
ALVARADO, Norman 718-779-1430 311 I
nalvarado@plazacollege.edu
ALVARADO, Nyvia 787-264-0409 509 F
nialvara@intersg.edu
ALVARADO, Nyvia, I 787-264-1912 509 F
nialvara@intersg.edu
ALVARADO-TORRES, Cesar 787-751-1912 510 A
calvarado@juris.inter.edu
ALVARADO-VALDOVINOS, Lorena 509-574-4702 487 A
lalvarado-valdovinos@yvcc.edu
ALVAREZ, Alex 323-466-6663 44 C
ALVAREZ, Alvin 415-338-6480 34 A
aalvarez@sfsu.edu
ALVAREZ, Ana 305-284-3584 112 E
aalvarez@miami.edu
ALVAREZ, Antonia 361-593-3612 447 D
antonia.alvarez@tamuk.edu
ALVAREZ, Araceli 713-500-3871 456 D
araceli.alvarez@uth.tmc.edu
ALVAREZ, Araceli 713-500-3871 456 B
araceli.alvarez@uth.tmc.edu
ALVAREZ, Arlene 909-558-4567 48 C
sm8026@bncollege.com
ALVAREZ, Barbara 650-508-3500 54 D
bgalvarez@ndnu.edu
ALVAREZ, Barbara 650-508-3512 54 D
bgalvarez@ndnu.edu
ALVAREZ, Barry, L 608-262-4312 496 C
bla@athletics.wisc.edu
ALVAREZ, Brian 516-364-0808 309 A
balvarez@nycollege.edu
ALVAREZ, Celso 718-429-6600 324 D
celso.alvarez@vaughn.edu
ALVAREZ, Christopher 760-845-3018 39 A
chalvarez@collegeofthedesert.edu
ALVAREZ, Cristina 909-537-5669 33 A
cristina.alvarez@csusb.edu
ALVAREZ, Ed 951-571-6186 58 G
ed.alvarez@mvc.edu
ALVAREZ, Elizabeth 785-227-3380 171 E
alvarezea@bethanylb.edu
ALVAREZ, Ferdinand 787-894-2828 514 C
ferdinand.alvarez1@upr.edu
ALVAREZ, Frank, D 509-452-5100 483 A
falvarez@pnwu.edu
ALVAREZ, Ivonne 619-388-2689 60 D
ialvarez@sdccd.edu
ALVAREZ, Jackie 541-737-2131 375 D
jackie.alvarez@oregonstate.edu
ALVAREZ, Jacqueline 413-542-2354 205 B
jalvarez@amherst.edu
ALVAREZ, Jacqueline 787-284-1912 509 E
jalvarez@ponce.inter.edu
ALVAREZ, Jon 617-253-1727 215 G
ALVAREZ, Linda 507-389-2986 239 C
linda.alvarez@mnsu.edu
ALVAREZ, Lourdes 210-434-6711 441 E
lalvarez@ollusa.edu
ALVAREZ, Maria 787-882-2065 511 D
registraduria@unitecpr.net
ALVAREZ, Maria, L 305-899-3085 95 C
malvarez@barry.edu
ALVAREZ, Melodie 808-853-1040 128 C
melodiealvarez@pacrim.edu
ALVAREZ, Orlando 802-387-1689 462 D
orlandoalvarez@landmark.edu
ALVAREZ, Patricia 787-766-1912 508 J
palvarez@inter.edu
ALVAREZ, Richard 718-997-5929 295 C
richard.alvarez@qc.cuny.edu
ALVAREZ, Rory 503-399-2594 372 C
rory.alvarez@chemeketa.edu
ALVAREZ, Timothy 719-384-6800 81 E
ALVAREZ, Veronica 661-291-3417 28 K
valvarez@calarts.edu
ALVAREZ-ORTIZ, Genette 516-572-7775 308 A
genette.ortiz@ncc.edu
ALVAREZ-ROBINSON, Sonia 404-385-3306 118 F
sonia@consulting.gatech.edu
ALVATER, Deborah 706-886-6831 125 D
dalvater@tfc.edu
ALVERO, Alicia 718-997-5903 295 C
alicia.alvero@qc.cuny.edu
ALVERSON, Amelia, J 212-851-7929 297 C
amelia.alverson@columbia.edu
ALVES, Antonio 203-773-8550 84 F
amalves@albertus.edu
ALVES, Eddie 541-881-5590 377 B
ealves@tvcc.cc
ALVES, Stephanie 925-969-2082 40 I
salves@dvc.edu
ALVEY, Patricia 214-768-4519 444 E
palvey@smu.edu
ALVINO, Kathleen, M 401-865-2430 405 B
kalvino@providence.edu
ALVIS, Robert 812-357-6543 160 D
ralvis@saintmeinrad.edu
ALVIS ROBINSON, Sierra 415-482-2463 41 H
sierra.alvisrobinson@dominican.edu
ALVITI, Eileen 617-747-2375 206 E
hroperations@berklee.edu
ALWAY, Tom 231-843-5967 232 J
talway@westshore.edu
AMACK, April 970-542-3187 81 A
april.amack@morgancc.edu
AMADI, Emmanual 662-254-3363 248 B
amadi@mvsu.edu
AMADOR, Carlos 646-768-5300 301 B
AMADOR, Lui 323-343-3200 32 A
lamador5@calstatela.edu
AMADOR, Tristen 303-458-4174 82 E
tamador@regis.edu
AMAKER, Corey, R 803-535-5075 407 G
camaker@claflin.edu
AMALBERT, Milagros 787-751-1912 510 A
mamalber@juris.inter.edu
AMALFITANO, Andrea 517-355-9616 227 D
amalfit1@msu.edu
AMAN, Rick 208-535-5366 130 C
rick.aman@cei.edu
AMANO, Koyoko 570-484-2073 395 B
kxa1026@lockhaven.edu
AMAR, Angela 702-895-3360 271 E
angela.amar@unlv.edu
AMAR, Harish 626-350-1500 28 J
AMAR, Salomon 914-594-4900 309 H
AMAR, Vikram 217-333-0931 151 D
amar@illinois.edu
AMARA, Sakpa, S 703-891-1787 471 K
samara@standardcollege.edu
AMARO, Jovana 336-322-2122 336 G
jovana.amaro@piedmontcc.edu
AMAROK, Barbara 907-443-8402 10 A
bjamarok@alaska.edu
AMARONE, Ben 203-787-8635 84 F
bamarone@albertus.edu
AMASON, Allen 912-478-2622 119 C
aamason@georgiasouthern.edu
AMASON, Amy 417-873-6968 252 F
aamason@drury.edu
AMATO, Christina 937-512-3703 361 A
AMATO, Christopher 863-298-6876 105 A
AMATO, John 515-271-2849 165 A
john.amato@drake.edu
AMATO, Leslie 530-541-4660 47 E
amato@ltcc.edu

ANDERSON, Bradford ... 805-756-5210.. 30 C bpanders@calpoly.edu
ANDERSON, Brian .... 907-561-1266.... 9 D
ANDERSON, Brian .... 662-329-7386 248 A banderson@muw.edu
ANDERSON, Bridgette ... 845-431-8655 298 E banderso@sunydutchess.edu
ANDERSON, Brooke ...... 617-627-4975 219 B brooke.anderson@tufts.edu
ANDERSON, Bruce .... 484-664-3130 391 C deanofacademiclife@muhlenberg.edu
ANDERSON, Bryant, K .. 920-748-8301 495 G andersonb@ripon.edu
ANDERSON, Carl, A ...... 202-526-3799.. 92 F canderson@johnpaulii.edu
ANDERSON, Carolyn ..... 815-280-2218 140 B caanders@jjc.edu
ANDERSON, Carrie .... 319-398-5500 167 C carrie.anderson@kirkwood.edu
ANDERSON, Cary, M .... 610-660-1045 398 C cander01@sju.edu
ANDERSON, Cathy .... 315-445-4300 304 C anderscr@lemoyne.edu
ANDERSON, Cathy .... 801-581-6940 460 E cathy.anderson@hsc.utah.edu
ANDERSON, Chanda ..... 509-452-5100 483 A cmanderson@pnwu.edu
ANDERSON, JR., Charles .... 606-487-3058 181 C chuck.anderson@kctcs.edu
ANDERSON, Charlise .... 903-730-4890 438 H canderson@jarvis.edu
ANDERSON, Chelsea .... 507-433-0829 240 F chelsea.anderson@riverland.edu
ANDERSON, Cheryl .... 406-656-9950 265 I canderson@yellowstonechristian.edu
ANDERSON, Chris .... 507-537-6272 241 D chris.anderson@smsu.edu
ANDERSON, Christie ..... 509-777-4218 486 I canderson@whitworth.edu
ANDERSON, Christina ... 218-855-8027 237 F canderson@clcmn.edu
ANDERSON, Christine ... 801-818-8900 459 K christine.anderson@provocollege.edu
ANDERSON, Christopher .... 716-375-2310 313 F canderso@sbu.edu
ANDERSON, Cindy .... 918-463-2931 366 B cindy.anderson@connorsstate.edu
ANDERSON, Cindy, L ... 304-558-4016 489 O cindy.anderson@wvhepc.edu
ANDERSON, Clayton ..... 801-626-6465 461 B canderson@weber.edu
ANDERSON, Cliff .... 763-433-1100 237 C clifford.anderson@anokaramsey.edu
ANDERSON, Clifford ..... 763-433-1100 237 D clifford.anderson@anokaramsey.edu
ANDERSON, Corey .... 541-684-7354 374 G canderson@nwcu.edu
ANDERSON, Countance 618-634-3360 149 A countancea@shawneecc.edu
ANDERSON, Crystal ...... 757-825-2810 476 A andersonc@tncc.edu
ANDERSON, Cynthia ..... 708-974-5347 144 C anderson@morainevalley.edu
ANDERSON, Cynthia ..... 828-398-7161 332 B cynthiaianderson@abtech.edu
ANDERSON, D. Craig ... 804-752-7270 470 F canderson@rmc.edu
ANDERSON, Daisy .... 717-796-1800 390 E anderson@messiah.edu
ANDERSON, Daniel, G .. 541-278-5743 372 A daanderson@bluecc.edu
ANDERSON, Daniel, J ... 336-278-7410 328 K andersd@elon.edu
ANDERSON, Daniel, L .. 304-877-6428 487 F president@abc.edu
ANDERSON, Danielle ..... 989-328-1217 228 A daniellea@montcalm.edu
ANDERSON, Danny .... 210-999-8401 452 A tupresident@trinity.edu
ANDERSON, Daphne ..... 312-225-1700 138 E danderson@ico.edu
ANDERSON, Darrel .... 913-971-3294 175 G dwanderson@mnu.edu
ANDERSON, Daryl .... 718-779-1430 311 I danderson1@mail.plazacollege.edu
ANDERSON, Dave .... 877-476-8674 437 C
ANDERSON, David .... 616-234-3638 224 D danderso@grcc.edu
ANDERSON, David .... 423-775-6596 423 F
ANDERSON, David, B ... 202-994-9120.. 91 F dbanderson@gwu.edu
ANDERSON, David, R ... 507-786-3000 243 C anderson@stolaf.edu
ANDERSON, Deborah, L .... 815-224-0406 139 F deborah_anderson@ivcc.edu
ANDERSON, Delia, C .... 617-732-2910 216 B delia.anderson@mcphs.edu
ANDERSON, Desiree ..... 925-631-8317.. 59 B dda3@stmarys-ca.edu
ANDERSON, Diane, K ... 269-387-2152 232 K diane.anderson@wmich.edu
ANDERSON, Diann .... 256-372-8094.... 1 A diann.anderson@aamu.edu
ANDERSON, Donald ...... 785-242-5200 176 D donald.anderson@ottawa.edu
ANDERSON, Donna .... 406-243-2288 264 A
ANDERSON, Donna, L .. 608-342-1739 497 D anderdon@uwplatt.edu
ANDERSON, Dorothy ..... 505-277-5824 288 G unmvphr@unm.edu
ANDERSON, Douglas .... 605-334-2696 416 E danderson@sfseminary.edu
ANDERSON, Douglas, D .... 435-797-2376 460 H douglas.anderson@usu.edu
ANDERSON, Duane .... 406-756-3818 263 F danderson@fvcc.edu
ANDERSON, Elisha .... 801-284-7531 459 E elisha.anderson@independence.edu
ANDERSON, Elizabeth ... 609-586-4800 278 F andersoe@mccc.edu
ANDERSON, Elizabeth ... 706-295-6846 119 A eanderson@gntc.edu
ANDERSON, Emily .... 773-481-8830 134 G afitzmaurice@ccc.edu
ANDERSON, Eric .... 712-707-7132 168 H eric.anderson@nwciowa.edu
ANDERSON, Eric .... 715-855-7512 499 D eanderson72@cvtc.edu
ANDERSON, Eric, R ...... 614-236-6606 349 D eanderson@capital.edu
ANDERSON, Erin .... 575-492-2676 286 J eanderson@nmjc.edu
ANDERSON, Erin .... 616-550-1760 224 C eanderson@gracechristian.edu
ANDERSON, Eugene ..... 315-443-9601 322 C genea@syr.edu
ANDERSON, Faith .... 912-443-5776 124 A fanderson@savannahtech.edu
ANDERSON, Garwood, P .... 262-646-6523 495 B ganderson@nashotah.edu
ANDERSON, Garwood, P .... 262-646-6500 495 B ganderson@nashotah.edu
ANDERSON, Gary .... 612-624-2424 243 E ander018@umn.edu
ANDERSON, George, W 713-221-8449 453 B andersong@uhd.edu
ANDERSON, Glenn .... 318-342-1600 192 F ganderson@ulm.edu
ANDERSON, Gordon, K 423-439-5671 419 J andersgk@etsu.edu
ANDERSON, Greg .... 215-204-8017 399 F gregory.anderson@temple.edu
ANDERSON, Gregory .... 951-222-8804.. 58 F gregory.anderson@rcc.edu
ANDERSON, Gregory .... 951-222-8000.. 58 I
ANDERSON, Gregory, R 817-735-7600 454 C gregory.anderson@unthsc.edu
ANDERSON, Harry .... 715-394-8241 498 B handerso@uwsuper.edu
ANDERSON, Heidi, M ... 410-651-6101 203 A hmanderson@umes.edu
ANDERSON, Holly .... 541-885-1389 375 C holly.anderson@oit.edu
ANDERSON, Ian .... 207-699-5033 194 D ianderson@meca.edu
ANDERSON, Jacqui .... 620-343-4600 173 A jaanderson@fhtc.edu
ANDERSON, James, A .. 910-672-1141 341 E janderson@uncfsu.edu
ANDERSON, James, A .. 719-333-2074 504 C james.anderson.72@usafa.edu
ANDERSON, James, D .. 217-333-7404 151 D janders@illinois.edu
ANDERSON, James, T .. 973-655-7022 279 C andersonja@mail.montclair.edu
ANDERSON, Janice .... 254-526-1116 432 H janice.anderson@ctcd.edu
ANDERSON, Jeanette .... 626-571-8811.. 72 C jeanettea@uwest.edu
ANDERSON, Jeff .... 808-245-8384 129 C jeffa@hawaii.edu
ANDERSON, Jeffrey, J .. 847-574-5210 141 C janderson@lfgsm.edu
ANDERSON, Jennifer .... 203-254-4000.. 86 I janderson@fairfield.edu
ANDERSON, Jennifer .... 614-287-5581 351 E jander02@cscc.edu
ANDERSON, Jeremy ...... 606-337-1533 179 G jeremy.anderson@ccbbc.edu
ANDERSON, Jeremy ...... 218-751-8670 242 J jeremyanderson@oakhills.edu
ANDERSON, Jerry .... 515-271-3985 165 A jerry.anderson@drake.edu
ANDERSON, Jill .... 307-754-6401 502 G jill.anderson@nwc.edu
ANDERSON, Jill, C .... 610-625-7910 391 A andersonj@moravian.edu
ANDERSON, Jillian .... 508-929-8072 213 E jillian.anderson@worcester.edu
ANDERSON, Jim .... 419-530-5731 363 E james.anderson7@utoledo.edu
ANDERSON, Joan, E ..... 508-793-3644 208 B janderso@holycross.edu
ANDERSON, Joanna ...... 660-596-7223 260 D janderson@sfccmo.edu
ANDERSON, Jody .... 706-778-3000 123 B jandersonl@piedmont.edu
ANDERSON, John .... 970-824-1110.. 78 G john.anderson@cncc.edu
ANDERSON, Jon .... 478-471-2700 121 F
ANDERSON, Jon (Jay) .. 979-209-7296 432 C jay.anderson@blinn.edu
ANDERSON, Jonathan .... 509-359-6081 480 E janderson@ewu.edu
ANDERSON, Jordan ...... 770-534-6126 115 D janderson6@brenau.edu
ANDERSON, Joshua ...... 602-429-4432.. 15 C janderson@ps.edu
ANDERSON, JP .... 585-594-6235 310 F andersonjp@roberts.edu
ANDERSON, Judith .... 507-538-0162 234 I anderson.judith@mayo.edu
ANDERSON, Julie .... 507-222-6824 234 F janderso@carleton.edu
ANDERSON, Julie .... 507-457-5122 241 F julie.anderson@winona.edu
ANDERSON, Julie .... 309-556-3780 139 G janders3@iwu.edu
ANDERSON, Julie, S ..... 801-863-5378 461 A julie.anderson@uvu.edu
ANDERSON, Justin .... 603-646-3661 273 E justin.anderson@dartmouth.edu
ANDERSON, Karen .... 256-726-7287.... 6 C kanderson@oakwood.edu
ANDERSON, Katherine, A .... 781-891-3441 206 D kanderson@bentley.edu
ANDERSON, Kathy .... 501-370-5306.. 20 G kanderson@philander.edu
ANDERSON, Kay .... 478-445-6286 118 C kay.anderson@gcsu.edu
ANDERSON, Keith .... 704-216-6248 330 H kanderson@livingstone.edu
ANDERSON, Kelsi .... 402-481-8602 265 K kelsi.anderson@bryanhealthcollege.edu
ANDERSON, Kenneth .... 509-313-3404 481 D anderson@gonzaga.edu
ANDERSON, Kenneth .... 901-678-2713 427 D kpndrsn1@memphis.edu
ANDERSON, Kevin .... 617-747-2359 206 E physicalplant@berklee.edu
ANDERSON, Kevin .... 251-380-3006.... 6 H jkanderson@shc.edu
ANDERSON, Kevin .... 239-432-6706 100 A kevin.anderson@fsw.edu
ANDERSON, Kevin, L .... 563-589-0211 170 D kanderson@wartburgseminary.edu
ANDERSON, Kim .... 218-935-0417 244 G kimberly.anderson@wetcc.edu
ANDERSON, Kim .... 484-365-7565 389 C kanderson@lincoln.edu
ANDERSON, Kirk, D ...... 309-794-7203 132 C kirkanderson@augustana.edu
ANDERSON, Kris .... 252-493-7348 336 H kanderson@email.pittcc.edu
ANDERSON, Kristine ..... 231-777-0447 228 D kristine.anderson@muskegoncc.edu
ANDERSON, Kristofer .... 501-420-1210.. 17 B kristofer.anderson@arkansasbaptist.edu
ANDERSON, Kristy .... 360-538-4151 481 E kanderso@ghc.edu
ANDERSON, OFM, Lawrence .... 518-783-2332 315 J landerson@siena.edu
ANDERSON, Layne .... 218-477-2447 239 D layne.anderson@mnstate.edu
ANDERSON, Leesa, P .... 706-778-3000 123 B landerson@piedmont.edu
ANDERSON, Leif, B ...... 612-330-1497 233 K andersol@augsburg.edu
ANDERSON, Leslie .... 870-733-6732.. 17 H landerson@asumidsouth.edu
ANDERSON, Leslie .... 888-488-4968.. 46 F landeson@itu.edu
ANDERSON, Linda .... 256-726-7095.... 6 C landerson@oakwood.edu
ANDERSON, Lisa .... 479-619-2227.. 20 D landerson7@nwacc.edu
ANDERSON, Lisa .... 718-270-5000 295 A lisa@mec.cuny.edu
ANDERSON, Lois .... 301-387-3042 198 F lois.anderson@garrettcollege.edu
ANDERSON, Lori .... 423-636-7300 427 B landerson@tusculum.edu
ANDERSON, Maria .... 973-655-5225 279 C andersonmar@mail.montclair.edu
ANDERSON, Marianne .. 410-386-8000 197 G manderson@carrollcc.edu
ANDERSON, Marie .... 909-469-5485.. 74 I manderson@westernu.edu
ANDERSON, Marie, A ... 680-488-2470 506 B mariea@palau.edu
ANDERSON, Mark .... 908-709-7010 284 C mark.anderson2@ucc.edu
ANDERSON, Mark, D .... 937-775-3570 364 I mark.anderson@wright.edu
ANDERSON, Marlene .... 701-224-5578 346 B marlene.anderson@bismarckstate.edu
ANDERSON, Mary Jo .... 435-865-8491 460 F andersonm@suu.edu
ANDERSON, MaryKaye . 615-898-2670 422 H marykaye.anderson@mtsu.edu
ANDERSON, Maureen ... 352-854-2322.. 96 O andersom@cf.edu
ANDERSON, Melinda, F 318-619-2916 188 J manderson@lsua.edu
ANDERSON, Melinda, R .... 252-335-3187 341 D mranderson@ecsu.edu
ANDERSON, Melissa, K 920-748-8365 495 G andersonmk@ripon.edu
ANDERSON, Melissa, L 336-841-9220 329 G manderson@highpoint.edu
ANDERSON, Melissa, P 540-674-3635 475 B manderson@nr.edu
ANDERSON, Michael .... 304-243-4453 491 I mdanderson@wju.edu
ANDERSON, Michael .... 318-345-9000 187 G michaelanderson19@ladelta.edu
ANDERSON, Michael .... 435-283-7000 461 C michael.anderson@snow.edu
ANDERSON, Michelle, J .... 718-951-5671 293 C bcpresident@brooklyn.cuny.edu
ANDERSON, Mike .... 435-283-7393 461 C mike.anderson@snow.edu
ANDERSON, Monique, W .... 865-974-2101 427 G manders3@utk.edu
ANDERSON, Myron .... 210-458-4011 455 E
ANDERSON, N. Douglas .... 740-376-4536 356 A doug.anderson@marietta.edu
ANDERSON, Neal .... 303-963-3463.. 77 G nanderson@ccu.edu
ANDERSON, Neil .... 423-648-2673 423 K nanderson@richmont.edu
ANDERSON, Nick .... 651-290-6358 242 G nick.anderson@mitchellhamline.edu
ANDERSON, Nickoel ..... 218-733-5990 238 F n.anderson@lsc.edu
ANDERSON, Nina .... 732-571-7551 279 B nanderso@monmouth.edu
ANDERSON, Oliver .... 801-832-2242 461 G oanderson@westminstercollege.edu
ANDERSON, Patricia ..... 775-753-2115 271 B pat.anderson@gbcnv.edu
ANDERSON, Paula .... 641-784-5148 165 H pkanders@graceland.edu
ANDERSON, Pauline ..... 850-729-6485 103 L ander113@nwfsc.edu
ANDERSON, Per, M ...... 218-299-3932 235 E anderson@cord.edu
ANDERSON, Peter .... 216-987-3538 351 G peter.anderson@tri-c.edu
ANDERSON, Peter, T .... 540-674-3631 475 B ptanderson@nr.edu

ANDÚJAR-ROJAS,
Carlos, A .... 787-815-0000 512 G
rectoria.arecibo@upr.edu
ANDÚJAR ROJAS,
Carlos, A .... 787-815-0000 513 A
rectoria.arecibo@upr.edu
ANFANG, Autumn .... 920-403-3251 495 I
autumn.anfang@snc.edu
ANG, Felix .... 831-459-2973.. 70 B
felix@ucsc.edu
ANGE, Nate .... 919-365-7711 340 H
ANGEL, Andrea, L .... 812-237-6155 155 G
andrea.angel@indstate.edu
ANGEL, David, P .... 508-793-7320 208 A
dangel@clarku.edu
ANGEL, Leigh .... 828-694-1729 332 E
ANGELE, Marie .... 402-399-2442 266 F
mangele@csm.edu
ANGELES, Laura, A .... 719-333-1042 504 C
laura.angeles@usafa.edu
ANGELIS, Peter .... 310-825-4941.. 69 A
pangelis@ha.ucla.edu
ANGELL, Alecia .... 509-527-3683 485 G
alecia.angell@wwcc.edu
ANGELL, Beth .... 804-827-1030 473 F
ANGELL, Townsend .... 503-777-7763 376 C
townsend.angell@reed.edu
ANGELL, Tracey .... 401-874-2326 406 B
tracey@uri.edu
ANGELO, Caroline .... 404-225-4545 114 H
cangelo@atlantatech.edu
ANGELO, Lisa .... 215-968-8048 379 G
lisa.angelo@bucks.edu
ANGELONE, Ida .... 973-353-5459 282 B
angelone@newark.rutgers.edu
ANGELONI, Lisa .... 609-771-3080 276 I
angeloni@tcnj.edu
ANGELOSANTE, James .. 509-313-6363 481 D
angelosante@gonzaga.edu
ANGELUCCI, Steve .... 859-233-8551 184 G
sangelucci@transy.edu
ANGEMI, Karen .... 909-621-8384.. 45 A
karen_angemi@hmc.edu
ANGEMI, Karen .... 909-621-8384.. 45 A
kangemi@hmc.edu
ANGER, Donna .... 907-474-6131.. 10 A
dmanger@alaska.edu
ANGER, Paul .... 928-428-6260.. 12 E
paul.anger@eac.edu
ANGION, Stanford .... 334-872-2533.... 6 F
stanfordangion@gmail.com
ANGIS, Victoria .... 802-468-1231 464 A
victoria.angis@castleton.edu
ANGLE, Ray .... 509-313-4100 481 D
angle@gonzaga.edu
ANGLE, Steven, R .... 423-425-4141 428 A
steven-angle@utc.edu
ANGLIM, Sean .... 315-568-3092 308 F
sanglim@nycc.edu
ANGLIN, Pamela, D ...... 903-785-7661 441 G
panglin@parisjc.edu
ANGLIN, Regina .... 910-678-8527 334 D
anglinr@faytechcc.edu
ANGLIN, Roland .... 216-687-5269 351 B
r.anglin@csuohio.edu
ANGLIN, Thad .... 254-442-5111 433 A
thad.anglin@cisco.edu
ANGOLA HARPER,
Tameka .... 334-727-8421.... 7 D
tharper@tuskegee.edu
ANGRISANI, Vincent ..... 718-997-5600 295 C
vincent.angrisani@qc.cuny.edu
ANGRIST, Michelle .... 518-388-6234 323 G
angristm@union.edu
ANGROVE, William .... 936-294-2774 450 C
wla002@shsu.edu
ANGSMAN, Rhonda ...... 317-921-4479 157 H
rangsman@ivytech.edu
ANGST, JR., Arthur, H .. 516-876-3094 319 A
angsta@oldwestbury.edu
ANGUEIRA, Annette, V . 240-895-3346 201 E
avangueira@smcm.edu
ANGUIANO, Amy .... 540-857-7254 476 D
aanguiano@virginiawestern.edu
ANGULO, Michael .... 609-652-4381 283 D
michael.angulo@stockton.edu
ANHORN, JR., Jerry ...... 509-527-4299 485 G
jerry.anhorn@wwcc.edu
ANICETTI, Rachel .... 925-473-7446.. 40 J
ranicetti@losmedanos.edu
ANICH, SVD, Kenneth ... 563-876-3353 164 J
kanich@dwci.edu

ANID, Nada .... 212-261-1572 309 F
nanid@nyit.edu
ANILOWSKI, Jennifer .... 860-253-3090.. 85 C
janilowski@asnuntuck.edu
ANISFELD, Sharon, C ... 617-559-8773 210 C
sanisfeld@hebrewcollege.edu
ANKE, Sharla, M .... 724-287-8711 380 A
sharla.anke@bc3.edu
ANKENY, Carrie .... 630-829-6028 132 E
croberts@ben.edu
ANKENY, Mark .... 503-352-2924 375 G
mankeny@pacificu.edu
ANKER, Laura, M .... 516-876-3460 319 A
ankerl@oldwestbury.edu
ANKER, Perryne .... 213-884-4133.. 24 A
panker@ajrca.edu
ANKERSON, Katherine .. 402-472-9216 269 J
kankerson1@unl.edu
ANNABLE, Ross .... 716-614-6407 310 C
rannable@niagaracc.suny.edu
ANNAN, Jack .... 970-521-6690.. 81 D
jack.annan@njc.edu
ANNARELLI, James, J ... 727-864-8243.. 97 J
annarejj@eckerd.edu
ANNAVARJULA, Madan 401-232-6227 404 F
mannavar@bryant.edu
ANNE, Kirk .... 585-245-5577 318 E
kma@geneseo.edu
ANNEAR, Patricia, T ..... 724-287-8711 380 A
patricia.annear@bc3.edu
ANNETT, JR., Bruce, J .. 248-204-2206 226 G
bannett@ltu.edu
ANNETTE, Harold .... 218-322-2353 238 E
harold.annette@itascacc.edu
ANNINO, Louis .... 203-932-7153.. 89 A
lannino@newhaven.edu
ANNIS, Stephen .... 423-318-2736 426 C
stephen.annis@ws.edu
ANNUNZIATA,
Margaret, H .... 336-249-8186 334 A
margaret_annunziata@davidsonccc.edu
ANOURO, Emmanuel .... 410-951-3444 203 D
eanouro@coppin.edu
ANSBOURY, Pamela ..... 210-485-0307 429 C
pansboury@alamo.edu
ANSBRO, Dawn .... 845-341-4337 311 C
dawn.ansbro@sunyorange.edu
ANSEL, Stuart .... 718-252-7800 322 J
ron.ansel@touro.edu
ANSELL, Charles .... 603-230-3509 272 I
cansell@ccsnh.edu
ANSELMENT,
Kenneth, L .... 920-832-6992 493 K
ken.anselment@lawrence.edu
ANSEVIN-ALLEN, Scott .. 603-899-4151 273 F
ansevis@franklinpierce.edu
ANSHUS, Corrine, M .... 414-410-4203 492 D
cmanshus@stritch.edu
ANSLEY, Kelly .... 706-880-8311 121 A
kansley@lagrange.edu
ANSON, Carey .... 801-626-7018 461 B
canson@weber.edu
ANSTOETTER, Don .... 314-792-6120 254 D
anstoetter@kenrick.edu
ANT, Susan .... 952-358-8906 239 F
susan.ant@normandale.edu
ANTCZAK, Frederick ...... 616-331-2495 224 E
antczakf@gvsu.edu
ANTEL, Lisa .... 203-596-4585.. 87 F
lantel@post.edu
ANTELMAN, Kristin .... 805-893-3256.. 70 A
kantelman@ucsb.edu
ANTENEN, James .... 210-826-7595 457 J
antenenj@wbu.edu
ANTER, David .... 805-378-1415.. 72 H
danter@vcccd.edu
ANTHONY, Cory .... 206-546-4627 484 G
canthony@shoreline.edu
ANTHONY, Cynthia .... 334-293-4504.... 1 C
cynthia.anthony@accs.edu
ANTHONY, Cynthia .... 205-929-3510.... 2 H
canthony@lawsonstate.edu
ANTHONY, David .... 315-464-8047 317 F
anthonyd@upstate.edu
ANTHONY, Doug .... 304-424-8280 491 D
doug.anthony@wvup.edu
ANTHONY, Jason, S ..... 401-456-8234 405 C
janthony@ric.edu
ANTHONY, Kathy .... 610-526-6045 385 G
kanthony@harcum.edu
ANTHONY, Linda .... 866-492-5336 244 F
linda.anthony@laureate.net
ANTHONY, Michael, D . 708-709-3501 146 D
manthony@prairiestate.edu

ANTHONY, Miriam .... 708-596-2000 149 B
manthony@ssc.edu
ANTHONY, Sharon .... 215-572-2850 379 A
anthony@arcadia.edu
ANTHONY, Yvonne, E ... 857-701-1230 215 E
yanthony@rcc.mass.edu
ANTHWAL, Sunny .... 845-398-4061 315 B
sunny@stac.edu
ANTIGUA, Diony .... 786-391-1167.. 94 I
ANTIGUA, Jose .... 786-391-1167.. 94 I
ANTILLA, Margaret .... 503-338-2428 372 E
mantilla@clatsopcc.edu
ANTKOWIAK, Alex .... 410-337-6061 198 G
alex.antkowiak@goucher.edu
ANTKOWIAK, Bruce ...... 724-805-2940 398 F
bruce.antkowiak@stvincent.edu
ANTKOWIAK, Bruce ...... 724-805-2940 398 E
bruce.antkowiak@stvincent.edu
ANTMAN, Karen, H .... 617-638-5300 207 D
kha4@bu.edu
ANTOINE, Linda .... 225-771-4580 190 G
linda_antoine@subr.edu
ANTOINE, Linda, B .... 225-771-4587 190 H
linda_antoine@subr.edu
ANTOINE, Tanesha .... 281-922-3453 443 E
tanesha.antoine@sjcd.edu
ANTOLINI, Heather .... 304-647-6374 491 A
hantolini@osteo.wvsom.edu
ANTON, Vanessa .... 918-444-3701 367 A
anton@nsuok.edu
ANTONAKAKIS, Helen ... 856-227-7200 276 E
hantonakakis@camdencc.edu
ANTONE, Blaine .... 520-383-0105.. 16 D
bantone@tocc.edu
ANTONELLI, Patricia ..... 603-897-8246 274 B
pantonelli@rivier.edu
ANTONELLI, Susan .... 617-521-2117 218 E
susan.antonelli@simmons.edu
ANTONELLO, Michael ... 561-237-7960 102 V
mantonello@lynn.edu
ANTONIO, Edward .... 218-299-3894 235 E
eantonio@cord.edu
ANTONIUK, Donna .... 956-380-8128 442 L
dantoniuk@riogrande.edu
ANTONOWICZ, Joseph . 908-737-3150 278 E
jantonow@kean.edu
ANTONS, Christopher ... 415-482-1932.. 41 H
christopher.antons@dominican.edu
ANTONUCCI, Carl .... 860 832 2099.. 84 I
antonucci@ccsu.edu
ANTROBUS, Barbara ..... 859-858-2285 178 H
ANTROP-GONZALEZ,
Rene .... 651-999-5959 238 H
rene.antropgonzalez@metrostate.edu
ANTUNES, Nancy .... 781-891-2686 206 D
nantunes@bentley.edu
ANTURKAR, Anjali, N ... 734-764-5132 231 E
anturkar@umich.edu
ANUMBA, Chimay .... 352-392-4836 109 F
anumba@ufl.edu
ANVINSON, Kimberly .... 701-231-7761 345 G
kimberley.anvinson@ndsu.edu
ANWAY, Amy .... 419-559-2371 361 I
aanway01@terra.edu
ANYANWU,
Fitzpatrick, U .... 337-421-6905 188 D
fitzpatrick.anyanwu@sowela.edu
ANZ, Susan, D .... 254-710-3731 431 J
susan_anz@baylor.edu
ANZAK, Daniel .... 210-458-5905 455 E
daniel.anzak@utsa.edu
ANZALDUA, Ricardo ..... 212-237-8316 294 D
ranzaldua@jjay.cuny.edu
ANZALONE, Alessandro 813-253-7960 101 A
aanzalone2@hccfl.edu
ANZALONE, Alex .... 813-253-7860 101 A
aanzalonegraci2@hccfl.edu
ANZINGER, John .... 240-629-7858 198 E
janzinger@frederick.edu
ANZUONI, Rebecca .... 617-373-7780 217 F
AOUN, Joseph, E .... 617-373-2101 217 F
AOYAMA, Yuko .... 508-793-7676 208 A
yaoyama@clarku.edu
APANEL, Stephen, J ..... 570-577-1195 379 F
stephen.apanel@bucknell.edu
APANOVICH, Val .... 570-674-6749 390 G
vapanovich@misericordia.edu
APAW, David .... 410-225-2464 199 H
dapaw@mica.edu
APEL, Scott .... 562-985-1658.. 31 F
scott.apel@csulb.edu
APEN, Lynette .... 408-270-6448.. 61 L
lynette.apen@evc.edu

APER, Jeffery, P .... 217-424-6220 143 H
japer@millikin.edu
APES, Chance .... 305-428-5700 103 E
capes@aii.edu
APFELBAUM, Randy ...... 646-592-4227 326 E
randy.apfelbaum@yu.edu
APFELTHALER, Gerhard . 805-493-3352.. 29 H
apfeltha@callutheran.edu
APGAR, Travis .... 518-276-6266 312 I
apgart@rpi.edu
APICERNO, Amy .... 727-864-8058.. 97 J
apiceral@eckerd.edu
APIGO, Mary-Jo .... 310-287-4410.. 49 G
apigomj@wlac.edu
APLIN, Greg .... 334-222-6591.... 2 I
jgaplin@lbwcc.edu
APODACA, John .... 505-428-1630 288 B
john.apodaca1@sfcc.edu
APODACA, Phillip, C .... 719-389-6613.. 77 H
papodaca@coloradocollege.edu
APOLLO, Richard, M .... 516-463-5405 302 B
richard.apollo@hofstra.edu
APONTE, Bianca .... 787-257-0000 513 C
bianca.aponte1@upr.edu
APONTE, Brunilda .... 787-743-7979 511 I
baponte@suagm.edu
APONTE, Juan, M .... 787-764-0000 514 B
juan.aponte6@upr.edu
APONTE, Laura, E .... 787-766-1717 511 H
um_laponte@suagm.edu
APONTE, Wanda .... 787-786-3030 512 B
waponte@ucb.edu.pr
APOSTOLAKOS,
Michael, J .... 585-275-4786 323 J
michael_apostolakos@urmc.rochester.edu
APPAVOO, Suresh .... 415-482-3598.. 41 H
suresh.appavoo@dominican.edu
APPEANING,
Vladimir, A .... 225-771-2705 190 H
appeaning@sus.edu
APPEL, Elizabeth, H ..... 410-777-7383 197 C
ehappel@aacc.edu
APPEL, Heidi .... 419-530-6031 363 E
heidi.appel@utoledo.edu
APPEL, Kellie .... 678-547-6397 121 E
appel_k@mercer.edu
APPEL, Steve .... 575-492-2187 289 A
sappel@usw.edu
APPELGET, Kristin .... 609-258-3018 280 E
appelget@princeton.edu
APPELT, Uschi .... 812-866-7221 155 C
appelt@hanover.edu
APPIAH-PADI,
Stephen, K .... 570-577-3796 379 F
s.appiahpadi@bucknell.edu
APPLE, Mark .... 317-955-6775 158 U
mapple@marian.edu
APPLE, Monique .... 605-455-6055 416 B
mapple@olc.edu
APPLE, Ryan .... 517-321-0242 224 F
rapple@glcc.edu
APPLEBEE, Paul .... 315-364-3240 325 B
papplebee@wells.edu
APPLEBURY, Gene .... 901-751-8453 422 E
gapplebury@mabts.edu
APPLEBY, Alice .... 803-822-3588 410 G
applebya@midlandstech.edu
APPLEBY, Leigh .... 860-723-0617.. 84 H
APPLEBY, Scott .... 574-631-6972 161 C
rappleby@nd.edu
APPLEGATE, J. Phillip .. 918-631-2070 371 E
phil-applegate@utulsa.edu
APPLEGATE, John .... 812-855-9198 156 A
jsapple@iu.edu
APPLEGATE, John, S .... 812-855-9198 156 B
jsapple@iu.edu
APPLEMAN, Boomer ...... 505-566-3318 288 A
applemanb@sanjuancollege.edu
APPLETON, Amber .... 503-253-3443 374 H
amber.appleton@ocom.edu
APPLETON, Lea .... 909-445-2590.. 37 F
lappleton@cst.edu
APPLIN, Mary Beth .... 601-857-3253 246 B
mary.applin@hindscc.edu
APPLING, Michele .... 229-317-6130 113 H
michelle.appling@asurams.edu
APPLING, Ron .... 806-291-3451 457 J
applingr@wbu.edu
APPREY, Augustine .... 717-290-8747 388 D
aapprey@lancasterseminary.edu
APPREY, Maurice .... 434-924-7923 473 A
ma9h@virginia.edu

APSEY, Curt ... 208-426-1826 129 I capsey@boisestate.edu
AQUILA, Dominic ... 713-525-6999 454 H aquilad@stthom.edu
AQUILA, Jennifer, K ... 610-799-1120 388 I jaquila@lccc.edu
AQUILA, Justin ... 260-399-7700 161 D jaquila@sf.edu
AQUILA, Scott, W ... 610-799-1550 388 I saquila@lccc.edu
AQUINO, Belissa ... 787-766-1717 511 H beaquino@suagm.edu
AQUINO, Carlos ... 251-626-3303 ... 7 E caquino@ussa.edu
AQUINO, Cathy ... 304-734-6611 488 K cathy.aquino@bridgevalley.edu
AQUINO, Jeannette ... 787-890-2681 512 H jeanette.aquino@upr.edu
ARABIE, Claire ... 337-482-1502 192 E claire@lousiana.edu
ARACENA, Dan ... 212-678-8231 322 G da2352@tc.columbia.edu
ARADINE, Bethany ... 585-345-6812 301 A baaradine@genesee.edu
ARAGON, Beverly ... 575-769-4001 285 K beverly.aragon@clovis.edu
ARAGON, Paul ... 575-769-4167 285 K paul.aragon@clovis.edu
ARAGON, Ruben ... 505-454-3332 286 H rubenaragon@nmhu.edu
ARAGON, Tammy ... 480-858-9100 .. 16 A t.aragon@scnm.edu
ARAGON-JOYCE, Karla .. 602-383-8228 .. 16 F karagon@uat.edu
ARAIMO, Angelo, G ... 718-390-3412 324 F aaraimo@wagner.edu
ARAIN, Nizam ... 608-785-8541 496 F narain@uwlax.edu
ARAKI, Fumiyo ... 661-253-7845 .. 28 K faraki@calarts.edu
ARAMBULA, Erika ... 308-367-5247 270 C earambula@unl.edu
ARAMMASH, Fouzi ... 803-705-4311 407 A fouzi.arammash@benedict.edu
ARAMMASH, Fouzi, H .. 803-705-4311 407 A fouzi.arammash@benedict.edu
ARANA, DeAnna ... 305-474-6074 106 F darana2@stu.edu
ARANA, Sloane ... 918-540-6393 366 I scbrown@neo.edu
ARANDA, Luis ... 319-385-8021 167 A luis.aranda@iw.edu
ARANDA-NARANJO, Barbara ... 210-829-3943 453 D naranjo@uiwtx.edu
ARANEO, Mary Lou ... 631-451-4611 321 F araneom@sunysuffolk.edu
ARANT, Alicia ... 406-243-5710 264 A alicia.arant@umontana.edu
ARANT, Mark ... 270-809-3744 183 G marant1@murraystate.edu
ARANT, T.J ... 678-407-5200 118 D tjarant@ggc.edu
ARAQUE, Teresa, M ... 239-513-1122 101 C taraque@hodges.edu
ARASIMOWICZ, George 937-376-6453 350 D garasimowicz@centralstate.edu
ARATA, Raquel ... 916-484-8364 .. 50 F aratar@arc.losrios.edu
ARAUJO, Nathan ... 909-447-2536 .. 37 F naraujo@cst.edu
ARAVE, Wade ... 360-867-6176 481 A aravew@evergreen.edu
ARAYA, Temesgen ... 413-597-2121 220 C
ARBALLO, Madelyn ... 909-274-7500 .. 52 H marballo@mtsac.edu
ARBELO, Enid ... 787-878-5475 508 L earbelo@arecibo.inter.edu
ARBERY, Glen ... 307-332-2930 502 J garbery@wyomingcatholic.edu
ARBIDE, Donna ... 202-994-1058 .. 91 F arbide@gwu.edu
ARBOGAST, Michelle ... 931-372-6091 426 E marbogast@tntech.edu
ARBONEAUX, Annette ... 225-216-8268 186 K arboneauxa@mybrcc.edu
ARBUCKLE, Clarissa, S . 724-589-2371 399 H carbuckle@thiel.edu
ARBUCKLE, Greg ... 270-745-4449 185 E greg.arbuckle@wku.edu
ARBUCKLE, Joanne ... 212-217-4000 299 H joanne_arbuckle@fitnyc.edu
ARBUTHNOT, Beth ... 706-864-1440 126 A beth.arbuthnot@ung.edu
ARCARESE, Chris ... 303-352-3032 .. 79 E chris.arcarese@ccd.edu
ARCARIO, Paul ... 718-482-5050 294 F arcariop@lagcc.cuny.edu
ARCE, Elsa, M ... 412-365-1282 381 C arce@chatham.edu
ARCE, Joshua ... 785-749-8482 173 G jarce@haskell.edu
ARCE, Katherine ... 310-338-2881 .. 50 J katherine.arce@lmu.edu
ARCE, Linda ... 617-243-2113 210 G larce@lasell.edu
ARCE-RODRIGUEZ, Lydia ... 787-857-3600 508 M larce@br.inter.edu
ARCELUS, Victor, J ... 860-439-2834 .. 86 H victor.arcelus@conncoll.edu
ARCENEAUX, Alex ... 985-448-4001 192 B alex.arceneaux@nicholls.edu
ARCH, Xan ... 503-943-7310 377 E arch@up.edu
ARCHAGA, Teresea ... 925-473-7552 .. 40 J tarchaga@losmedanos.edu
ARCHAMBAULT, Jennifer ... 802-865-5485 462 B jarchambault@champlain.edu
ARCHAMBAULT, Karen .. 856-222-9311 281 C karchambault@rcbc.edu
ARCHAMBAULT, Marc ... 386-226-7770 .. 98 A archamm1@erau.edu
ARCHAMBEAU, Jessica . 248-218-2038 229 J jarchambeau@rc.edu
ARCHBOLD, David, J ... 248-370-3358 229 G archbold@oakland.edu
ARCHER, Chris ... 603-623-0313 273 I chrisarcher@nhia.edu
ARCHER, Daniel, L ... 801-581-7028 460 E darcher@campusstore.utah.edu
ARCHER, Elizabeth ... 619-876-4250 .. 67 M earcher@usuniversity.edu
ARCHER, III, Frank ... 478-822-7593 118 A archerf@fvsu.edu
ARCHER, Justin ... 806-796-8800 439 H
ARCHER, Keith, A ... 641-269-9700 165 J archerke@grinnell.edu
ARCHER, Kevin ... 509-963-3101 479 B kevin.archer@cwu.edu
ARCHER, Len ... 407-303-5619 .. 94 D len.archer@ahu.edu
ARCHER, Linda, R ... 757-446-6190 466 I archerlr@evms.edu
ARCHER, Lynn ... 412-536-1182 387 B lynn.archer@laroche.edu
ARCHER, Marsi ... 417-625-9565 256 D archer-m@mssu.edu
ARCHER, Rebecca ... 321-674-7571 .. 99 B rarcher@fit.edu
ARCHER, Ron ... 714-879-3901 .. 45 F rarcher@hiu.edu
ARCHER-RIERSON, Abby ... 620-242-0439 175 F archera@mcpherson.edu
ARCHIBALD, Sandra, O 206-616-1648 485 F sarch@uw.edu
ARCHIE, Cephas ... 585-395-2504 318 B carchie@brockport.edu
ARCHIE, Tiffenia, D ... 215-204-9213 399 F tiffenia.archie@temple.edu
ARCHIE, Tracey ... 716-851-1118 299 F archie@ecc.edu
ARCHINAL, Ginette ... 336-278-7228 328 K garchinal@elon.edu
ARCHULETA, Carol ... 864-231-2000 406 G carchuleta@andersonuniversity.edu
ARCHULETA, Renee ... 303-914-6345 .. 82 C renee.archuleta@rrcc.edu
ARCHULETTA, Justin ... 907-745-3201 ... 9 B info@akbible.edu
ARCIERI, Michelle, C ... 202-994-5729 .. 91 F michelle@gwu.edu
ARCUINO, Cathy Lee ... 910-521-6000 343 B cathylee.arcuino@uncp.edu
ARCURI, Cody ... 718-817-4339 300 E carcuri@fordham.edu
ARCUTT, Kristina ... 801-883-8336 459 I karcutt@new.edu
ARDAGNA, Wendy ... 215-951-1049 387 C ardagnaw1@lasalle.edu
ARDALAN, Shah ... 281-290-2777 439 G shah.ardalan@lonestar.edu
ARDARY, Darlene ... 570-484-3427 395 B dardary@lockhaven.edu
ARDELEAN, Nicole ... 703-425-4143 468 E
ARDEN, Warwick, A ... 919-515-2195 342 B warwick_arden@ncsu.edu
ARDIS, Ann ... 703-993-8715 467 L aardis@gmu.edu
ARDIS, Mary Jo ... 803-778-7825 407 C ardismj@cctech.edu
ARDOVINI, Joanne ... 212-343-1234 306 J jardovini@mcny.edu
ARDREY, Melantha ... 843-953-3257 408 E ardreym@cofc.edu
AREA, Ron ... 304-696-2826 490 D area@marshall.edu
AREH, Julia ... 678-872-4201 118 E jareh@highlands.edu
AREIZAGA, Jose, R ... 787-891-0925 508 K jareizag@aguadilla.inter.edu
ARELLANO, Jerry ... 210-486-3884 429 F jarellano59@alamo.edu
ARELLANO, Margarita, M ... 512-245-2124 450 E ma33@txstate.edu
ARENA, Maryanne ... 585-345-6802 301 A mcarena@genesee.edu
ARENA, Meaghan ... 585-389-2525 308 B marena4@naz.edu
ARENARE, Debra ... 516-367-6890 296 D
ARENAS, Ruben ... 323-265-8641 .. 48 H arenasrj@elac.edu
ARENAS-FUENTES, Lenina ... 206-543-5010 485 F mlenina@uw.edu
ARENAZ, Pablo ... 956-326-2320 446 F president@tamiu.edu
AREND, Lori ... 412-536-2506 387 B lori.arend@laroche.edu
AREND, Matthew ... 517-629-0521 220 G marend@albion.edu
ARENDALE, Robert ... 832-377-1675 248 F rarendale@rts.edu
ARENDT, Thomas, K ... 562-902-3355 .. 65 C tomarendt@scuhs.edu
ARENIVAS, Marisol ... 575-492-2850 286 J marenivas@nmjc.edu
ARENS, Anna ... 414-382-6064 492 A anna.arens@alverno.edu
ARENS, Dave ... 712-279-1715 163 C dave.arens@briarcliff.edu
ARENS, Timothy, E ... 312-329-4191 144 B timothy.arens@moody.edu
ARENSDORF, Jill ... 785-628-4241 173 B jrarensdorf@fhsu.edu
ARENSMEYER, Lauri, D 208-496-1010 130 A arensmeyerl@byui.edu
ARENTSEN, Marc ... 508-541-1608 208 F marentsen@dean.edu
ARETA, Ropeti ... 684-699-1575 505 A a.areta@amsamoa.edu
AREVALO, Luis ... 435-652-7877 460 G arevalo@dixie.edu
AREY, Emily ... 704-669-4139 333 E areye@clevelandcc.edu
AREY, George, A ... 617-552-3060 207 B george.arey@bc.edu
AREY, Jason ... 207-216-4399 195 C jarey@yccc.edu
ARGENTIERI, Colleen ... 607-587-3932 320 C argentch@alfredstate.edu
ARGIRI, Elizabeth ... 586-445-7306 226 H argiril@macomb.edu
ARGO, Jennifer ... 256-782-5769 ... 5 J jlargo@jsu.edu
ARGO, Mike, A ... 870-235-4083 .. 21 D maargo@saumag.edu
ARGO, Steve ... 678-359-5073 119 F stephena@gordonstate.edu
ARGOV, Sharon ... 305-760-7500 102 U
ARGUELLES, Adrianna ... 718-939-5100 304 F aarguelles@libi.edu
ARHIN, Afua ... 910-672-1924 341 E aarhin@uncfsu.edu
ARHIPOV, Sergei, D ... 570-581-1818 398 D sergei.arhipov@stots.edu
ARIA, Dawn, J ... 518-580-5490 316 A daria@skidmore.edu
ARIA, Iyob ... 323-860-0789 .. 50 A
ARIANO, Patricia ... 630-829-6003 132 E pariano@ben.edu
ARIAS, Edward ... 713-221-8040 453 B ariase@uhd.edu
ARIAS, Evelyn ... 210-688-3101 432 L
ARIAS, Flerida ... 209-575-6060 .. 75 J ariasf@mjc.edu
ARIAS, Nuria, R ... 337-421-6903 188 D nuria.reyes-arias@sowela.edu
ARICK, Bruce, E ... 317-940-9481 153 F barick@butler.edu
ARIDA, Lisa, A ... 716-839-8218 298 B larida@daemen.edu
ARIOLA-SUKISAKI, Kainoa ... 808-932-7445 128 E kariola@hawaii.edu
ARIOVICH, Laura ... 301-546-7422 201 C
ARISTIZABAL, Humberto, X ... 410-543-6426 203 F hxarisitzabal@salisbury.edu
ARIZA, Cristina ... 210-829-3870 453 D mariza@uiwtx.edu
ARIZA, Diane ... 585-389-2025 308 B dariza3@naz.edu
ARLEDGE, Cora ... 740-689-4453 356 I carledge@mccn.edu
ARLINGTON, David, L .. 716-851-1987 299 F arlington@ecc.edu
ARLITSCH, Kenning ... 406-994-6978 264 D kenning.arlitsch@montana.edu
ARMACOST, Andrew ... 719-333-4270 504 C andrew.armacost@usafa.edu
ARMAGOST, Mark, S ... 814-863-4308 392 B msa17@psu.edu
ARMAS, Michelle ... 818-766-8151 .. 40 C marmas@concorde.edu
ARMBRISTER, Clarence (Clay), D ... 704-378-1000 330 D
ARMENDARIZ, John ... 617-373-2133 217 F
ARMENDARIZ, Pablo ... 915-831-7747 436 E parmend1@epcc.edu
ARMENIOX, Leslie, F ... 843-953-5640 408 E armenioxlf@cofc.edu
ARMENT, Susan ... 660-263-4100 257 B susana@macc.edu
ARMENTROUT, Janie ... 951-343-4210 .. 27 J jarmentrout@calbaptist.edu
ARMENTROUT, Renae ... 319-208-5015 169 F rarmentrout@scciowa.edu
ARMEZZANI, Aubree ... 570-702-8938 386 G aarmezzani@johnson.edu
ARMIJO, Danny ... 575-624-8250 287 A darmijo@nmmi.edu
ARMINGTON, Thomas .. 610-526-1391 378 G thomas.armington@theamericancollege.edu
ARMINI, Michael, A ... 617-373-5718 217 F
ARMINIAK, Anthony ... 734-374-3227 232 C aarmini1@wcccd.edu
ARMINIAK, Anthony ... 734-699-7008 232 C aarmini1@wcccd.edu
ARMISTEAD, Katya ... 805-893-8912 .. 70 A katya.armistead@sa.ucsb.edu
ARMISTEAD, Lisa, P ... 404-413-2091 119 E larmistead@gsu.edu
ARMISTEAD, Macon ... 334-833-4455 ... 5 H marmistead@hawks.huntingdon.edu
ARMISTEAD, William ... 304-473-8509 491 H armistead_w@wvwc.edu
ARMONY, Ariel ... 412-648-7374 401 B armony@pitt.edu
ARMOR, Thomas, W ... 317-738-8045 154 J tarmor@franklincollege.edu
ARMOUR, Janet ... 662-862-8383 246 D jyarmour@iccms.edu
ARMOUR, Lauren ... 770-533-7034 121 B larmour@laniertech.edu
ARMOUR, Lisa ... 352-381-3642 107 A lisa.armour@sfcollege.edu
ARMSTEAD, Cory ... 334-683-2333 ... 3 A carmstead@marionmilitary.edu
ARMSTEAD, Dori ... 704-233-8810 344 G armstead@wingate.edu
ARMSTEAD, Paula ... 510-748-5255 .. 56 F parmstead@peralta.edu
ARMSTRONG, Amy ... 918-465-1777 366 D aarmstrong@eosc.edu
ARMSTRONG, Andrew, V ... 540-636-2900 466 A armstrong@christendom.edu
ARMSTRONG, Barbara .. 414-930-3110 495 A armstrob@mtmary.edu
ARMSTRONG, Christopher, M ... 860-701-6194 504 F christopher.m.armstrong@uscg.mil
ARMSTRONG, Dana ... 508-213-2177 217 E dana.armstrong@nichols.edu
ARMSTRONG, David, A . 305-628-6663 106 F darmstrong@stu.edu
ARMSTRONG, David, M 816-501-2423 250 F david.armstrong@avila.edu

ARMSTRONG, Dayle ...... 909-469-5322.. 74 I
darmstrong@westernu.edu
ARMSTRONG, Elizabeth 540-231-7197 477 A
beth1@vt.edu
ARMSTRONG, Franca .... 315-334-7701 307 D
farmstrong@mvcc.edu
ARMSTRONG, Gary .... 816-415-7651 262 F
armstrongg@william.jewell.edu
ARMSTRONG, Greg .... 630-620-2175 145 D
grarmstrong@seminary.edu
ARMSTRONG, Jeanette .. 608-796-3395 498 N
jearmstrong@viterbo.edu
ARMSTRONG,
Jeffrey, D .... 805-756-1111.. 30 C
presidentsoffice@calpoly.edu
ARMSTRONG, Jennifer .. 909-607-9100.. 63 E
jarmstrong@kecksci.claremont.edu
ARMSTRONG, Jerry .... 303-373-2008.. 82 G
jarmstrong@rvu.edu
ARMSTRONG, Jon .... 785-628-4091 173 B
jdarmstrong@fhsu.edu
ARMSTRONG, Julie .... 810-989-5527 230 C
jarmstrong@sc4.edu
ARMSTRONG, Karla ...... 620-276-9577 173 E
karla.armstrong@gcccks.edu
ARMSTRONG, Keith ...... 719-590-6758.. 79 C
karmstrong@coloradotech.edu
ARMSTRONG, Kelli .... 401-341-2337 406 A
kelli.armstrong@salve.edu
ARMSTRONG, Kevin ...... 402-375-7510 268 G
kearmst1@wsc.edu
ARMSTRONG, Kim .... 501-337-5000.. 18 J
karmstrong@coto.edu
ARMSTRONG, Kim .... 309-694-5422 138 C
ARMSTRONG, Kimberly 717-358-3985 384 D
kim.armstrong@fandm.edu
ARMSTRONG, LaTonya . 773-291-6613 134 E
tarmstrong11@ccc.edu
ARMSTRONG, Lori .... 618-634-3313 149 A
loria@shawneecc.edu
ARMSTRONG, Lori, B ... 410-704-3570 204 A
larmstrong@towson.edu
ARMSTRONG,
Mary Beth .... 205-665-6015..... 8 D
armstrom@montevallo.edu
ARMSTRONG,
Mary Beth .... 205-665-6720..... 8 D
armstrom@montevallo.edu
ARMSTRONG, Myeshia . 323-265-8690.. 48 H
armstrmd@elac.edu
ARMSTRONG, Nancy, A 419-772-2251 358 H
n-armstrong@onu.edu
ARMSTRONG, Neal, R ... 520-621-3513.. 16 G
nra@email.arizona.edu
ARMSTRONG,
Patricia, J .... 615-353-3758 425 D
patricia.armstrong@nscc.edu
ARMSTRONG, Shirley ... 334-291-4964.... 1 H
shirley.armstrong@cv.edu
ARMSTRONG,
Steven, M .... 920-832-6769 493 K
steven.m.armstrong@lawrence.edu
ARMSTRONG, Tamara ... 916-568-3021.. 50 E
armstrt@losrios.edu
ARMSTRONG, Tonya ..... 919-572-1625 326 L
tarmstrong@apexsot.edu
ARMSTRONG, Tricia ...... 207-768-9533 196 E
patricia.armstrong@maine.edu
ARMSTRONG, Vivian ..... 787-284-1912 509 E
varmstro@ponce.inter.edu
ARMSTRONG, Wesley .... 828-262-2190 341 B
armstrongwr@appstate.edu
ARN, Diana .... 501-977-2001.. 23 A
arn@uaccm.edu
ARNADE, Peter .... 808-956-6460 128 F
parnade@hawaii.edu
ARNDER, Lori .... 757-240-2200 471 A
lori.arnder@rivhs.com
ARNDT, Chase .... 423-652-4341 420 H
chasevarndt@king.edu
ARNDT, Steven .... 910-678-8287 334 D
arndts@faytechcc.edu
ARNDT, Wayne .... 732-987-2237 278 B
warndt@georgian.edu
ARNER, Lori .... 802-468-1211 464 A
lori.arner@castleton.edu
ARNER, Robert .... 610-292-9852 397 D
robert.arner@reseminary.edu
ARNER, Timothy .... 641-269-4529 165 J
arnertim@grinnell.edu
ARNESON, Dean, L .... 262-243-5700 493 B
dean.arneson@cuw.edu
ARNESON, Eric .... 920-465-2511 496 E
arnesone@uwgb.edu
ARNESON, Rosemary .... 540-654-1147 472 I
rarneso3@umw.edu
ARNESON, Tara .... 802-865-5702 462 B
tarneson@champlain.edu
ARNETH, Tammy .... 585-343-0055 301 A
tlarneth@genesee.edu
ARNETT, Amy .... 207-509-7204 195 H
aarnett@unity.edu
ARNETT, David, J .... 978-478-3400 217 G
darnett@northpoint.edu
ARNETT, Donna .... 859-218-2247 185 B
donna.arnett@uky.edu
ARNETT, Jennifer .... 415-476-4998.. 69 E
jennifer.arnett@ucsf.edu
ARNETT, Katy, E .... 240-895-4451 201 E
kearnett@smcm.edu
ARNETT, Nathan .... 618-985-3741 139 I
nathanarnett@jalc.edu
ARNETTE, Drew .... 502-413-8801 184 E
darnette@sullivan.edu
ARNEY, Doug .... 956-882-7145 455 D
doug.arney@utrgv.edu
ARNEY, Janna .... 956-882-8833 455 D
janna.arney@utrgv.edu
ARNHOLT, JoAnn .... 848-932-7692 282 A
arnholt@echo.rutgers.edu
ARNITZ, Deborah .... 602-429-4927.. 15 C
darnitz@ps.edu
ARNN, Larry .... 517-607-2301 225 A
larnn@hillsdale.edu
ARNO, Marlene .... 716-851-1431 299 F
arno@ecc.edu
ARNOLD, Amelia .... 317-977-7778 259 H
amelia.arnold@slu.edu
ARNOLD, Angela .... 952-358-9045 239 F
angela.arnold@normandale.edu
ARNOLD,
Ariana Wright .... 202-806-1222.. 92 B
ARNOLD, Audrey .... 505-277-2511 288 G
aaronld5@unm.edu
ARNOLD, Benjamin .... 573-681-5079 254 E
arnoldb@lincolnu.edu
ARNOLD, Bill .... 989-463-7111 220 H
arnoldwh@alma.edu
ARNOLD, Brian .... 575-492-2104 289 A
barnold@usw.edu
ARNOLD, Brian .... 704-406-4732 329 A
barnold@gardner-webb.edu
ARNOLD, Carl .... 903-233-4310 439 E
carlarnold@letu.edu
ARNOLD, Claire .... 404-962-3024 126 F
claire.arnold@usg.edu
ARNOLD, Clinton, E ...... 562-903-4816.. 27 C
clinton.arnold@biola.edu
ARNOLD, David .... 575-492-2124 289 A
darnold@usw.edu
ARNOLD, Eli .... 404-364-8885 122 J
earnold@oglethorpe.edu
ARNOLD, Elizabeth .... 570-484-2293 395 B
earnold@lockhaven.edu
ARNOLD, Frances .... 413-559-6092 210 A
ARNOLD, Gerti .... 208-426-3236 129 I
gertiarnold@boisestate.edu
ARNOLD, Harvey .... 772-462-6210 101 E
harnold@irsc.edu
ARNOLD, James .... 573-875-7410 251 F
jarnold6@ccis.edu
ARNOLD, Jared .... 310-544-6419.. 59 E
jared.arnold@usw.salvationarmy.org
ARNOLD, Jeanne .... 717-337-6375 384 H
jarnold@gettysburg.edu
ARNOLD, Jill .... 573-629-3103 253 H
jarnold@hlg.edu
ARNOLD, Jon .... 714-895-8183.. 38 D
jarnold@gwc.cccd.edu
ARNOLD, Jon .... 931-540-2538 424 G
jarnold15@columbiastate.edu
ARNOLD, Joseph, E .... 202-885-8649.. 93 E
jearnold@wesleyseminary.edu
ARNOLD, Joshua .... 246-326-4206 465 B
jarnold@bluefield.edu
ARNOLD, Julie .... 419-448-2953 353 H
jarnold3@heidelberg.edu
ARNOLD, Justin .... 704-922-6448 334 F
arnold.justin@gaston.edu
ARNOLD, Kenneth, L ..... 707-256-3331.. 53 C
karnold@napavalley.edu
ARNOLD, Lester .... 703-993-2602 467 L
llarnold@gmu.edu
ARNOLD, Lorin Basden 845-257-3280 317 B
provost@newpaltz.edu
ARNOLD, Melinda .... 406-657-2367 264 E
melinda.arnold@msubillings.edu
ARNOLD, Richard .... 617-243-2217 210 G
rarnold@lasell.edu
ARNOLD, Rodney .... 870-743-3000.. 20 C
rarnold@northark.edu
ARNOLD, Sally .... 978-232-2041 209 B
sarnold@endicott.edu
ARNOLD, Shirley, E ...... 828-884-8329 327 C
arnoldse@brevard.edu
ARNOLD, Sue .... 281-998-6003 448 F
sarnold@txchiro.edu
ARNOLD, Susan .... 610-647-4400 386 C
sarnold@immaculata.edu
ARNOLD, Tai .... 518-587-2100 321 A
tai.arnold@esc.edu
ARNOLD, Timothy .... 716-338-1125 303 D
timothyarnold@mail.sunyjcc.edu
ARNOLD, Tommy .... 276-223-4829 476 E
tarnold@wcc.vccs.edu
ARNOLD, III, W. Ellis .. 501-450-1223.. 19 F
arnold@hendrix.edu
ARNOTT, Tamara .... 218-733-5923 238 F
tamara.arnott@lsc.edu
ARNOULD, Karen, A ..... 810-762-3344 231 G
karnould@umich.edu
ARNOVE, Theresa .... 410-532-5155 201 B
tarnove@ndm.edu
ARNQUIST, Lynn .... 320-762-4464 237 B
lynn.arnquist@alextech.edu
ARNST, Scott .... 810-762-3123 231 G
sarnst@umich.edu
ARNZEN, Diane .... 636-481-3282 254 A
darnzen@jeffco.edu
AROCHO, Ashley .... 212-650-6460 293 D
aarocho@ccny.cuny.edu
AROJO, Lisa .... 516-299-3522 304 G
lisa.arojo@liu.edu
AROMANDO, Drew, C .. 609-896-5367 281 B
aromando@rider.edu
ARON-SMITH, Lashun ... 317-543-3235 158 V
ARONIN, Heidi, J .... 718-270-1025 317 E
heidi.aronin@downstate.edu
ARONSON, Ann .... 612-624-6868 243 E
aronson@umn.edu
ARONSON, Hans-Erik ... 516-367-6890 296 D
ARONSON, Linda .... 508-849-3458 205 C
laronson@annamaria.edu
ARONSON, Stacey .... 320-589-6250 244 B
aronsosp@morris.umn.edu
ARONSON, Susan .... 213-624-1200.. 42 I
saronson@fidm.edu
ARONSTAM, Robert, S .. 570-389-5333 394 A
aronstam@bloomu.edu
ARONSTEIN, A-J .... 212-854-7758 290 J
aaronste@barnard.edu
ARORA, Deepa .... 478-934-6588 121 F
deepa.arora@mga.edu
ARORA SINGH, Alka ..... 623-845-3968.. 13 C
alka.arora.singh@gccaz.edu
AROZ, Susan, D .... 480-732-7075.. 12 P
sue.aroz@cgc.edu
ARP, Dan .... 541-737-2331 375 D
dan.arp@oregonstate.edu
ARP, Lauren .... 910-678-8201 334 D
arpl@faytechcc.edu
ARP, Robert .... 707-654-1037.. 32 B
rarp@csum.edu
ARPINO, Donald .... 617-879-7899 212 E
darpino@massart.edu
ARQUETTE, Toby .... 630-844-5614 132 D
tarquett@aurora.edu
ARRAIZA, Ana, M .... 787-751-0160 507 F
aarraiza@cmpr.pr.gov
ARREAZOLA, David .... 956-764-5950 439 C
darreazola@laredo.edu
ARREDONDO, Alice ...... 816-235-1208 261 C
arredondoal@umkc.edu
ARREDONDO, Jill .... 972-883-5380 455 B
jill.arredondo@utdallas.edu
ARREDONDO, Maria ..... 965-364-4322 449 E
paula.arredondo@tstc.edu
ARREDONDO, Marisol .. 714-628-7339.. 36 C
arredond@chapman.edu
ARREDONDO, Michael .. 214-860-8639 435 D
marredondo@dcccd.edu
ARRIA, Sal, A .... 800-650-4772.. 39 B
ARRIAZA, Cecilia .... 714-992-7087.. 53 L
carriaza@fullcoll.edu
ARRINGTON, Harriett .... 276-523-2400 475 A
harrington@mecc.edu
ARRINGTON, Jeff .... 817-735-2513 454 C
jeff.arrington@unthsc.edu
ARRINGTON, Jeffrey ..... 334-386-7105.... 5 D
jarrington@faulkner.edu
ARRINGTON, Pam .... 330-966-5460 361 F
parrington@starkstate.edu
ARRINGTON,
Stephanie, K .... 765-285-8304 153 C
skarrington@bsu.edu
ARRINGTON, Tom .... 281-459-7613 443 D
tom.arrington@sjcd.edu
ARRINGTON, Trey .... 864-587-4396 412 G
arringtont@smcsc.edu
ARRIOLA, Paul .... 630-617-3109 136 G
paula@elmhurst.edu
ARRIOLA, Susan .... 559-442-8237.. 66 E
susan.arriola@fresnocitycollege.edu
ARRIOLA, Yolanda .... 915-778-4001 444 H
ARROWOOD, Roarke ..... 828-835-4305 338 E
rarrowood@tricountycc.edu
ARROWSMITH, Jason ... 360-442-2270 482 B
jarrowsmith@lowercolumbia.edu
ARROYO, Carmen .... 787-620-2040 506 C
carroyo@aupr.edu
ARROYO, Carmen, A .... 787-840-2575 510 J
carroyo@psm.edu
ARROYO, Cheryl .... 219-989-2977 159 G
cheryla@pnw.edu
ARROYO, Cruz .... 253-964-4688 483 H
carroyo@stmartin.edu
ARROYO, Enrique .... 787-841-2000 510 K
earroyo@pucpr.edu
ARROYO, Erica .... 305-284-1724 112 E
earroyo@miami.edu
ARROYO, Gladys .... 787-279-1912 509 A
garroyo@bayamon.inter.edu
ARROYO, Ivonne, D ..... 787-257-7323 511 G
iarroyo@suagm.edu
ARROYO, Palmira .... 787-753-6335 508 D
ARROYO, Patti .... 303-404-5111.. 79 J
patti.arroyo@frontrange.edu
ARROYO, Rina .... 386-822-7773 111 A
rarroyo@stetson.edu
ARROYO, Sandra .... 787-765-3560 507 L
sandraarroyo@edpuniversity.edu
ARRUDA, Yvonne, D .... 401-865-2480 405 B
yarruda@providence.edu
ARRUTTI, Duane .... 505-277-8125 288 G
darruti@unm.edu
ARSENAULT, Joanne ..... 509-533-7042 480 A
joanne.arsenault@scc.spokane.edu
ARTALE, Maureen, P .... 607-436-3216 317 C
maureen.artale@oneonta.edu
ARTAMENKO, Dan .... 620-417-1550 176 K
dan.artamenko@sccc.edu
ARTAZ, Nancy .... 316-295-5514 173 D
artaz@friends.edu
ARTEAGA, Elizabeth ...... 714-628-4883.. 58 A
ARTEAGA-JOHNSON,
Craig .... 909-607-6643.. 57 F
craig.arteagajohnson@pomona.edu
ARTECONA, Sarah, N .... 305-284-5490 112 E
sartecona@miami.edu
ARTER, Neil .... 405-425-5906 367 G
neil.arter@oc.edu
ARTHO, Donna .... 936-294-3101 450 C
artho@shsu.edu
ARTHUR, Candis .... 859-985-3192 179 C
candis_arthur@berea.edu
ARTHUR, Christon .... 269-471-3404 221 B
christon@andrews.edu
ARTHUR, Dave .... 512-476-2772 431 B
finaid@austingrad.edu
ARTHUR, David .... 617-746-1990 210 E
david.arthur@hult.edu
ARTHUR, Gwendolynne 508-793-7384 208 A
garthur@clarku.edu
ARTHUR, Mark .... 405-789-7661 370 B
mark.arthur@swcu.edu
ARTHUR, Scott .... 303-724-8469.. 83 C
scott.arthur@ucdenver.edu
ARTHUR, Virginia .... 651-793-1900 238 H
ginny.arthur@metrostate.edu
ARTHURS, Jeffrey .... 978-468-7111 209 G
jarthurs@gordonconwell.edu
ARTIGUES, Jay .... 985-549-2253 192 D
jay.artigues@selu.edu
ARTIS, Christine .... 718-933-6700 307 G
cartis@monroecollege.edu
ARTIS, Lori .... 618-468-3000 141 F
lartis@lc.edu
ARTIS, Roslyn, C .... 803-705-4681 407 A
roslyn.artis@benedict.edu
ARTLEY, James .... 904-516-8745.. 98 P
jartley@fcsl.edu
ARTZE VEGA, Isis .... 407-582-3055 112 K
iartzevega@valenciacollege.edu

ARUK, Janette 585-785-1297 300 B janette.aruk@flcc.edu
ARULANANDAM, Bernard 210-458-6859 455 E bernard.arulanandam@utsa.edu
ARUM, Richard 949-824-8026 68 G richard.arum@uci.edu
ARVAN, April 920-565-2327 493 J arvanaa@lakeland.edu
ARVAY, Anna 570-504-9695 384 F aarvay@som.geisinger.edu
ARVIDSON, Susie 620-223-2700 173 C susiea@fortscott.edu
ARVIN, Lorraine 503-517-7625 376 C arvinl@reed.edu
ARVISO, Jason 505-786-4193 286 G jarviso@navajotech.edu
ARVIZU, Dan 575-646-2035 287 B chancellor.arvizu@nmsu.edu
ARVIZU, Primavera 559-791-2218 47 A parvizu@portervillecollege.edu
ARWOOD, Katie 989-328-1291 228 A katiea@montcalm.edu
ARZOLA, Fernando 419-995-8213 354 H arzola.f@rhodesstate.edu
ARZOLA, JR., Fernando 760-471-1316 71 I farzola@usk.edu
ARZROUNI-CHAHINIAN, Chaghig 510-925-4282 25 Q carzroun@aua.am
ASAAD, Diana 909-667-4423 37 H dasaad@claremontlincoln.edu
ASAGBA, Tempress 214-333-5340 434 I tempress@dbu.edu
ASAMOAH, Yaw, A 724-357-2280 394 G yaw.asamoah@iup.edu
ASANTE, Javonda 973-313-6211 283 B javonda.asante@shu.edu
ASANTE, Sylvia 859-985-3728 179 C asantes@berea.edu
ASARO, Linda 212-817-7490 293 F intstu@gc.cuny.edu
ASAWA, Archibald, E 949-480-4006 64 B asawa@soka.edu
ASAY, Meredith 307-766-2238 502 H masay@uwyo.edu
ASBILL, Jonathan 918-444-2400 367 A asbill01@nsuok.edu
ASBURY, Sean 614-287-2525 351 E sasbury@cscc.edu
ASCARELLI, Daniela, E 215-895-6280 383 B daniela.elena.ascarelli@drexel.edu
ASCENCIO, Jorge 714-895-8107 38 D jascencio@gwc.cccd.edu
ASCENCIO, Mario 626-396-2231 26 E mario.ascencio@artcenter.edu
ASCH, Emily 651-690-6650 242 R ejasch@stkate.edu
ASCHEMAN, SVD, Thomas 563-876-3353 164 J tascheman@dwci.edu
ASCHENBRENER, Matt 262-472-1570 498 C aschenbm@uww.edu
ASCHENBRENNER, Annie, J 262-524-7224 492 E aaschenb@carrollu.edu
ASCHER, Marie 914-594-4208 309 H marie_ascher@nymc.edu
ASCHER, Tom 815-939-5011 146 A tascher@olivet.edu
ASCHIM, Joan 541-463-5591 373 F aschimj@lanecc.edu
ASCHLIMAN, David, A 260-422-5561 155 H daaschliman@indianatech.edu
ASCIONE, Lou 619-388-7873 60 E lascione@sdccd.edu
ASDEL, Bryan 760-252-2411 26 I basdel@barstow.edu
ASEFAW, Kibrab 305-273-4499 96 L kibrab.asefaw@cbt.edu
ASELTYNE, Dennis 707-468-3131 51 E daseltyne@mendocino.edu
ASENCIO, David 215-751-8876 382 A dasencio@ccp.edu
ASENCIO, Vimarie 787-753-6000 508 D
ASENCIO-PINTO, Aida 708-209-3492 135 F aida.asencio-pinto@cuchicago.edu
ASETTA, Eric 617-824-3075 208 H eric_asetta@emerson.edu
ASGEIRSDOTTIR, Aslaug 207-786-6066 193 B aasgeirs@bates.edu
ASGHAR, Midhat 936-261-2156 446 D miasghar@pvamu.edu
ASH, Beth 740-474-8896 358 F bash@ohiochristian.edu
ASH, Carisa 214-887-5368 436 B cash@dts.edu
ASH, Carol 505-224-4000 285 J cash2@cnm.edu
ASH, David, E 989-774-3094 222 C ash1de@cmich.edu
ASH, Eric 907-375-4515 457 J ash@wbu.edu
ASH, Karen 503-594-3099 372 D karen.ash@clackamas.edu
ASH, Kenya, D 513-529-7157 356 E ashkd@miamioh.edu
ASH, Michael 402-559-3389 270 A michael.ash@unmc.edu
ASH, Michael 319-208-5050 169 F mash@scciowa.edu
ASH, Steven 352-854-2322 96 O ashs@cf.edu
ASHAOLU, John 412-392-3911 397 A jashaolu@pointpark.edu
ASHBURN, Beth, D 336-725-8344 339 F ashburnb@piedmontu.edu
ASHBURN, Maureen 617-735-9838 209 A ashburnm@emmanuel.edu
ASHBY, Brendan 651-846-1314 241 B brendan.ashby@saintpaul.edu
ASHBY, Deborah 910-898-9651 336 D ashbyd@montgomery.edu
ASHBY, Mae 407-708-2170 107 D kline@seminolestate.edu
ASHBY, Pamela 207-834-7516 196 C pam.ashby@maine.edu
ASHBY, Patti 405-912-9017 369 D pashby@ru.edu
ASHBY, Todd 843-863-7984 407 E tashby@csuniv.edu
ASHBY, Valerie 919-684-4510 328 G asdean@duke.edu
ASHCRAFT, Eric 859-846-5781 183 E ewashcraft@midway.edu
ASHCRAFT, Matthew 480-731-8121 12 O matthew.ashcraft@domail.maricopa.edu
ASHCROFT, Josh 509-359-2451 480 E jashcroft@ewu.edu
ASHDOWN, Jonathan 518-629-7149 302 E j.ashdown@hvcc.edu
ASHE, Susan 818-333-3558 53 G deanstudentsla@nyfa.edu
ASHER, Adam 815-928-5554 146 A adam@989group.com
ASHER, Curt 661-654-3042 30 E casher@csub.edu
ASHER, Joy 859-238-5284 179 F joy.asher@centre.edu
ASHER, Nancy 660-785-4143 260 J nasher@truman.edu
ASHERIAN, Armen 702-651-7481 271 A armen.asherian@csn.edu
ASHFORD, Bruce, R 919-761-2435 340 G bashford@sebts.edu
ASHFORD, Prentice 615-966-5210 421 D prentice.ashford@lipscomb.edu
ASHFORD, Rebecca 423-697-4455 424 E rebecca.ashford@chattanoogastate.edu
ASHFORD, Scott 541-737-1211 375 D scott.ashford@oregonstate.edu
ASHFORD, Will 815-921-4109 147 E w.ashford@rockvalleycollege.edu
ASHLEY, Annalee 912-478-5953 119 C aashley@georgiasouthern.edu
ASHLEY, Annalee 912-478-5331 119 C aashley@georgiasouthern.edu
ASHLEY, Donna 646-717-9706 300 G ashley@gts.edu
ASHLEY, Garrett, P 562-951-4625 30 B gashley@calstate.edu
ASHLEY, Kimberly 903-877-5739 456 D kimberly.ashley@uthct.edu
ASHLEY, Kurt 630-617-3262 136 G kurt.ashley@elmhurst.edu
ASHLEY, Lance 704-669-4092 333 E ashleyl@clevelandcc.edu
ASHLEY, Mark 909-621-8090 45 A mark_ashley@hmc.edu
ASHLEY, Richard 704-272-5463 337 I rashley@spcc.edu
ASHLEY, Tim, M 315-267-2222 319 D ashleytm@potsdam.edu
ASHLEY, Traci, D 919-209-2563 335 F tdashley@johnstoncc.edu
ASHLEY, Tracy 757-258-6674 476 A ashleyt@tncc.edu
ASHLEY, William, J 205-391-5880 3 E bashley@sheltonstate.edu
ASHMON, Scott 949-214-3201 40 F scott.ashmon@cui.edu
ASHMYAN, Ilya 201-360-4693 278 C iashmyan@hccc.edu
ASHOFF, Adam 661-362-2618 51 C aashoff@masters.edu
ASHOUR, Cheryl 780-744-1150 55 I cashour@palomar.edu
ASHPOLE, Steve 253-680-7005 478 E sashpole@batestech.edu
ASHPOLE, Steven 360-596-5240 485 B sashpole@spscc.edu
ASHRAF, Mitu 910-521-6464 343 B mohammed.ashraf@uncp.edu
ASHTON, Andrew 845-437-5787 324 C anashton@vassar.edu
ASHTON, Catherine 319-399-8623 164 A cashton@coe.edu
ASHTON, Loye 601-977-7944 249 C lashton@tougaloo.edu
ASHTON, Nadine 313-664-7673 222 F nashton@collegeforcreativestudies.edu
ASHTON-PRITTING, Randi, L 860-768-4268 88 H pritting@hartford.edu
ASHU, Benjamin 504-286-5279 190 I abenjamin@suno.edu
ASHWORTH, Dennis 706-355-5167 114 F dashworth@athenstech.edu
ASHWORTH, Ken 202-806-6100 92 B
ASIAMAH-ANDRADE, Akua 856-225-6322 281 G andradea@camden.rutgers.edu
ASIFOA, Sereima 684-699-9155 505 A s.asifoa@amsamoa.edu
ASIP, Cailin 540-362-6211 468 C adm@hollins.edu
ASITO, Pioria 680-488-3540 506 B pasito1149@gmail.com
ASKA, Aaron 201-200-3035 279 E aaska@njcu.edu
ASKELSON, Mary, M 503-788-6644 376 C askelsom@reed.edu
ASKERLUND, Robert 801-957-4101 461 D robert.askerlund@slcc.edu
ASKEW, Consuella, A 973-353-5222 282 B consuella.askew@rutgers.edu
ASKEW, George, R 864-656-3140 408 A gaskew@clemson.edu
ASKEW, J. Alicia 864-833-8215 411 I jaaskew@presby.edu
ASKEW, Joseph 731-989-6651 420 C jaskew@fhu.edu
ASKEW, Susan, S 931-598-1710 423 M saskew@sewanee.edu
ASKEW, Tara 706-649-1901 117 A taskew@columbustech.edu
ASKEW-ROBINSON, Jipaum 618-524-3003 149 A jipaumr@shawneecc.edu
ASKEY, Angela 520-494-5485 11 K angela.askey@centralaz.edu
ASKILDSON, Lance 808-735-4825 127 F lance.askildson@chaminade.edu
ASKINS, Rana 940-898-3505 451 F raskins@twu.edu
ASKREN, Mark 402-472-2311 269 J maskren1@unl.edu
ASLAM, Ersal 973-596-5303 279 F ersal.aslam@njit.edu
ASMAN, Kevin 360-596-5283 485 B kasman@spscc.edu
ASMUS, Colleen, M 850-474-2642 110 E casmus@uwf.edu
ASMUTH, Shawn 904-620-2730 110 A shawn.asmuth@unf.edu
ASOODEH, Mike, M 985-549-2314 192 D asoodeh@selu.edu
ASP, Martin 617-746-1990 210 E martin.asp@hult.edu
ASPEGREN, Eric 402-465-7734 268 H easpegre@nebrwesleyan.edu
ASPELUND, Jan 956-326-2361 446 F jan.aspelund@tamiu.edu
ASPER, Kris 713-718-6858 437 I kris.asper@hccs.edu
ASPERGER, Joseph 810-762-9749 225 H jasperge@kettering.edu
ASPINALL, David 910-221-2224 329 B daspinall@gcd.edu
ASPINWALL, Neil 337-421-6965 188 D neil.aspinwall@sowela.edu
ASSAD, Arjang, A 412-648-1556 401 B aassad@pitt.edu
ASSANIS, Dennis 302-831-2111 90 F president@udel.edu
ASSERSON, Elizabeth 406-994-4531 264 D basserson@montana.edu
ASTARITA, Susan 973-720-2201 284 I astaritas@wpunj.edu
ASTI, Tony 602-286-8000 13 B anthony.asti@gatewaycc.edu
ASTLEFORD, Matt 913-758-6253 177 F matt.astleford@stmary.edu
ASTOLFI, Amy 978-232-2001 209 B aastolfi@endicott.edu
ASTON, Mary Kay 570-941-5984 401 H marykay.aston@scranton.edu
ASTON, Rollah 575-624-7281 286 A rollah.aston@roswell.enmu.edu
ASTORGA, Juan Carlos 818-710-2248 49 C astorgjc@piercecollege.edu
ASUKILE, Imani, D 727-816-3192 104 F asukili@phsc.edu
ASUNCION-NACE, Zeny 671-735-2942 505 E znace@triton.uog.edu
ATALIG, Adrian 670-234-5498 506 A adrian.atalig@marianas.edu
ATALLAH, Zahi 608-757-7737 499 C zatallah@blackhawk.edu
ATANUS, Bernard 217-732-3155 141 I batanus@lincolncollege.edu
ATCHISON, Eric 501-660-1000 17 E eatchison@asusystem.edu
ATCHLEY, Connie 541-885-1720 375 C connie.atchley@oit.edu
ATCHLEY, Cynthia 865-694-6554 425 F catchley@pstcc.edu
ATCHLEY, Paul 813-974-4051 110 B patchley@usf.edu
ATCHLEY, Ruth Ann 813-974-7175 110 B ratchley@usf.edu
ATEKWANA, Estella 302-831-2841 90 F atekwana@udel.edu
ATENCIO, Elaine 619-260-4520 71 J atencio@sandiego.edu
ATENCIO, Wilma 719-846-5555 82 K wilma.atencio@trinidadstate.edu
ATES, Kerry, A 410-516-8068 199 D kates1@jhu.edu
ATEWOLOGUN, Adenuga 507-433-0607 240 F adenuga.atewologun@riverland.edu
ATHERTON, Beth 512-313-3000 434 E beth.atherton@concordia.edu
ATHERTON, Joe 707-467-3067 51 E jatherton@mendocino.edu
ATHMAN, Meredith, L 320-308-2102 240 H mlathman@stcloudstate.edu
ATIEH, Lute 816-279-7000 250 B lute@abtu.edu
ATIEH, Ramsey 816-279-7000 250 B ramsey@abtu.edu
ATIENZA, Johanna 626-529-8007 55 A
ATIENZA, Terri 847-947-5604 144 F tatienza@nl.edu
ATKERSON, Emily 918-495-7032 368 I eatkerson@oru.edu
ATKIN, Jacob 801-863-8576 461 A jacob.atkin@uvu.edu
ATKIN, Michael, B 818-947-2600 49 F atkinmb@lavc.edu
ATKINS, JR., Alphonso 864-503-5000 414 D
ATKINS, Angie, S 662-329-7126 248 A aatkins@muw.edu
ATKINS, Caroline 606-783-9381 183 F c.atkins@moreheadstate.edu
ATKINS, Christine 203-401-4071 84 F catkins@albertus.edu
ATKINS, Colette 319-398-5431 167 C colette.atkins@kirkwood.edu
ATKINS, Courtney, B 910-898-9602 336 D atkinsc@montgomery.edu
ATKINS, Darian 318-345-9265 187 G datkins@ladelta.edu
ATKINS, Darlenna, M 318-797-5237 189 D darlenna.atkins@lsus.edu
ATKINS, David, P 423-439-4337 419 J atkinsdp@etsu.edu
ATKINS, Deb 763-424-0993 239 G datkins@nhcc.edu
ATKINS, Elizabeth, A 856-225-2521 281 G atkins1@camden.rutgers.edu

ATKINS, Garry, L 205-726-2763 6 E glatkins@samford.edu
ATKINS, Kemal 603-358-2108 275 A kemal.atkins@keene.edu
ATKINS, Lisa 618-235-2700 149 H lisa.atkins@swic.edu
ATKINS, Michael 301-860-4362 203 C matkins@bowiestate.edu
ATKINS, Michele 731-661-5465 427 C matkins@uu.edu
ATKINS, Nolan, T 802-626-6406 464 C nolan.atkins@northernvermont.edu
ATKINS, Norman 212-228-1888 312 H
ATKINS, Paula 318-797-5116 189 D paula.atkins@lsus.edu
ATKINS, Rodney 903-730-4890 438 H ratkins@jarvis.edu
ATKINS-BRADY, Tara 757-569-6713 475 E tatkins-brady@pdc.edu
ATKINSON, Denese 606-886-3863 180 J denese.atkcinson@kctcs.edu
ATKINSON, Eva, G 270-686-4282 179 D eva.atkinson@brescia.edu
ATKINSON, Jeffrey 980-359-1039 344 G atkinson@wingate.edu
ATKINSON, Judith 856-415-2115 281 D jatkinson@rcgc.edu
ATKINSON, Justin 559-323-2100 60 I jatkinson@sjcl.edu
ATKINSON, Kent 208-882-1566 131 B katkinson@nsa.edu
ATKINSON, Krystilyn, M 691-320-2482 505 B
ATKINSON, Rose 406-768-6317 263 G ratkinson@fpcc.edu
ATKINSON, Sander 601-484-8707 247 A satkinso@meridiancc.edu
ATKINSON, Sheri 530-752-8787 68 E slatkinson@ucdavis.edu
ATKINSON, Simon 785-864-7298 177 D satkinson@ku.edu
ATKINSON, Susan 870-245-5581 20 E atkinsons@obu.edu
ATKINSON, Tyler 785-227-3380 171 E atkinsonts@bethanylb.edu
ATKINSON, Vicki 847-925-6346 137 H vatkinso@harpercollege.edu
ATKINSON-WILLOUGHBY, Brenda 202-687-5677 92 A ba3@georgetown.edu
ATOIGUE, Ana Mari, C 671-735-5527 505 C anamari.atoigue@guamcc.edu
ATOIGUE, Celia 671-734-1812 505 D catoigue@piu.edu
ATTALLA, Mohamed 217-300-7783 151 D mattalla@illinois.edu
ATTEBERRY, Mary, W 812-877-8449 159 J atteberr@rose-hulman.edu
ATTEBERY, Jani 520-494-5364 11 K jani.attebery@centralaz.edu
ATTEBERY, Philip 903-586-2501 431 G philip.attebery@bmats.edu
ATTEBURY, Kathy 406-994-4391 264 D attebury@montana.edu
ATTERBURY, G. Burnham 'Burnie' 209-932-2967 70 E batterbury@pacific.edu
ATTIPOE, Sherika 256-306-2560 1 F sherika.attipoe@calhoun.edu
ATTORD, DeNeen 813-663-0100 92 G
ATWATER, Caryn 336-272-7102 329 D caryn.atwater@greensboro.edu
ATWATER, Ken 813-253-7050 101 A katwater@hccfl.edu
ATWATER, Steve 907-474-6440 10 A satwater@alaska.edu
ATWATER, Steve 907-796-6050 10 B satwater@alaska.edu
ATWELL, Patrick 573-288-6424 252 E patwell@culver.edu
ATWOOD, Anthony 615-297-7545 418 C atwooda@aquinascollege.edu
ATWOOD, Lorraine 802-831-1204 463 G latwood@vermontlaw.edu
ATWOOD, Peter 617-585-0200 206 F peter.atwood@the-bac.edu
ATWOOD, Steve 573-840-9708 260 I satwood@trcc.edu
ATZERT, Andy 516-877-3424 289 C aatzert@adelphi.edu
AU, Gerard 909-537-5100 33 A gau@csusb.edu
AU, Mark 808-956-6423 128 F mgsau@hawaii.edu
AU, Mark, G 808-956-6423 128 D mgsau@hawaii.edu
AU, Peggy 510-628-8038 48 A peggyau@lincolnuca.edu
AU, Valerie 508-999-8826 211 F valerie.au@umassd.edu
AUBIN, Brendan 630-652-8500 136 B baubin@devry.edu
AUBIN, Mary Ann 314-792-6302 254 D aubin@kenrick.edu
AUBREY, Karen 706-880-8235 121 A kaubrey@lagrange.edu
AUBREY, Roxann 619-388-3428 60 C raubrey@sdccd.edu
AUBRY, Ann 309-556-3874 139 G aaubry@iwu.edu
AUBRY, Dawn, M 248-370-3228 229 G dmaubry@oakland.edu
AUBRY, Nadine 617-627-3310 219 B
AUCLAIR, Billye 401-598-5156 404 I bauclair@jwu.edu
AUCOIN, Brent 765-448-1986 154 H
AUDANT, Babette 718-518-4241 294 B baudant@hostos.cuny.edu
AUDEOUD, Martine 214-329-4447 431 D martine.audeoud@bgu.edu
AUDET, Charlotte 520-795-0787 10 H admissions@asaom.edu
AUDET, Shirley 860-465-5337 84 J audets@easternct.edu
AUDET, Suzanne 508-999-8076 211 F saudet@umassd.edu
AUDET-KRANS, Janis 802-656-7878 463 E janis.audet-krans@uvm.edu
AUDETTE, Bert 207-509-7277 195 H baudette@unity.edu
AUDUSSEAU, Loic 718-289-5168 293 B loic.audusseau@bcc.cuny.edu
AUDYATIS, Todd 508-531-2608 212 B taudyatis@bridgew.edu
AUER, Matthew, R 706-542-2059 125 G matthew.auer@uga.edu
AUER, Susanne 605-455-6049 416 B sauer@olc.edu
AUER, Susanne 605-455-6097 416 B sauer@olc.edu
AUERBACH, Joshua 802-322-1619 462 C joshua.auerbach@goddard.edu
AUERBACH, Steven 808-845-9143 129 B sauerbac@hawaii.edu
AUERNHEIMER, Brent 559-278-4373 31 D brent_auernheimer@csufresno.edu
AUGENSTEIN, Amee 260-459-4545 157 E aaugenstein@ibcfortwayne.edu
AUGENSTEIN, Heather 520-515-3649 11 M augensteinh@cochise.edu
AUGESTINE-COLLINS, Sandy 518-244-2274 313 D augsts@sage.edu
AUGHENBAUGH, Barbara 410-837-5719 204 B baughenbaugh@ubalt.edu
AUGHENBAUGH, Jonette 304-327-4049 489 P jaughenbaugh@bluefieldstate.edu
AUGHENBAUGH, Lisa 410-386-8494 197 G laughenbaugh@carrollcc.edu
AUGOSTINI, Christopher 404-712-6018 117 F christopher.l.augostini@emory.edu
AUGUST, Bonne 718-260-5560 295 B baugust@citytech.cuny.edu
AUGUST, John 979-436-9322 446 G august@tamhsc.edu
AUGUST, Michele 620-241-0723 172 D michele.august@centralchristian.edu
AUGUSTE, Wilkins 305-430-1167 99 D wilkins.auguste@fmuniv.edu
AUGUSTINE, Lailani 570-674-6248 390 G laugustine@misericordia.edu
AUGUSTINE, TJ 312-413-1454 151 B aaugustn@uic.edu
AUGUSTINE-CARREIRA, Jackie 760-245-4271 73 D jacqueline.augustine-carreira@vvc.edu
AUGUSTINE-PLAISANCE, LuAnn 718-409-7304 321 C laugustine@sunymaritime.edu
AULET, Maria, J 787-765-1915 510 B mjaulet@opto.inter.edu
AULGUR, Jeff 479-964-0583 18 C jaulgur@atu.edu
AULICINO, Christy, L 727-816-3443 104 F aulicic@phsc.edu
AULL, JR., Zeke 251-460-6609 8 F zaull@southalabama.edu
AULT, Jill 530-242-7689 63 H jault@shastacollege.edu
AULT, Kathy 308-635-6350 270 D aultk@wncc.edu
AULT, Robert 913-684-7316 504 D
AULTMAN BECKER, April 432-837-8124 450 D april.becker@sulross.edu
AUMAN, Ann, J 253-535-8485 482 H aumanaj@plu.edu
AUMAN, Timothy, L 336-758-5210 344 D aumantl@wfu.edu
AUMANN, Patricia 636-481-3552 254 A paumann@jeffco.edu
AUNAI, Samasoni 559-934-2000 74 A samaunai@whccd.edu
AUNE, Krystyna 808-956-7541 128 F krystyna@hawaii.edu
AUNE, Mark 724-938-4535 394 B aune@calu.edu
AUNE, Richard, S 507-933-7676 235 I raune@gustavus.edu
AUNE, Tami 507-933-6113 235 I taune@gustavus.edu
AUPPERLE, Jeff 765-998-4553 160 F jeffry_aupperle@taylor.edu
AURE, Aaron 715-232-1267 498 A aurea@uwstout.edu
AURICCHIO, Laura 212-636-6300 300 E lauricchio@fordham.edu
AURINGER, Melissa 303-458-3510 82 E mauringer@regis.edu
AURO, Fadi 314-792-6119 254 D auro@kenrick.edu
AURYAN, Mosen 609-771-2143 276 I auryanm@tcnj.edu
AUS, Andrea 406-756-3884 263 F aaus@fvcc.edu
AUSBAND, Avrohom 718-601-3523 326 D
AUSBORN, Dawn 910-630-7610 331 C dausborn@methodist.edu
AUSBURY, Brad 417-862-9533 253 D bausbury@globaluniversity.edu
AUSBURY, D. Bradley 417-862-9533 253 D bausbury@globaluniversity.edu
AUSEL, Jill 412-365-1244 381 C jausel@chatham.edu
AUSMUS, Ryan 620-227-9269 172 J rausmus@dc3.edu
AUSPERK, Andrea 440-525-7720 355 H aausperk1@lakelandcc.edu
AUSTAD, Janica 651-450-3521 238 D jaustad@inverhills.edu
AUSTEIN, Chad 908-737-7133 278 E caustein@kean.edu
AUSTER, Julie 646-592-4335 326 E julie.auster@yu.edu
AUSTIN, Adelee 802-258-3359 463 C adelee.austin@worldlearning.org
AUSTIN, Alton 352-854-2322 96 O austina@cf.edu
AUSTIN, Amber 502-863-7008 180 E amber_austin@georgetowncollege.edu
AUSTIN, Anne 870-612-2058 22 I anne.austin@uaccb.edu
AUSTIN, April 404-270-5153 125 B aprila@spelman.edu
AUSTIN, Bob, C 806-371-5024 430 A rcaustin@actx.edu
AUSTIN, Christine 479-880-4282 18 C caustin@atu.edu
AUSTIN, Christopher 225-578-2841 188 I ccaustin@lsu.edu
AUSTIN, Dale, F 616-395-7950 225 B austin@hope.edu
AUSTIN, Deborah 717-261-4381 403 F daustin@wilson.edu
AUSTIN, Elizabeth 508-854-2777 215 D eaustin@qcc.mass.edu
AUSTIN, Geoff, P 206-598-8318 485 F graustin@uw.edu
AUSTIN, Jane 570-288-8400 384 B janea@fortisinstitute.edu
AUSTIN, Jonathan 502-897-4121 184 C jaustin@sbts.edu
AUSTIN, L. Bruce 847-214-7366 136 F baustin@elgin.edu
AUSTIN, Laurie 718-960-8706 294 A laurie.austin@lehman.cuny.edu
AUSTIN, Linda 281-756-3631 429 I laustin@alvincollege.edu
AUSTIN, Marcia, M 727-816-3264 104 F austinm@phsc.edu
AUSTIN, Martha, F 603-646-8861 273 E martha.f.austin@dartmouth.edu
AUSTIN, Michael 812-488-1178 161 A ma352@evansville.edu
AUSTIN, Renee 615-230-3587 426 B renee.austin@volstate.edu
AUSTIN, Sheila 334-244-3425 4 F saustin1@aum.edu
AUSTIN, Suzanne, E 205-934-6290 8 A seaustin@uab.edu
AUSTIN, Tiffany 201-559-6000 278 A
AUSTIN, Tracey, M 603-526-3886 272 H taustin@colby-sawyer.edu
AUSTIN, William 908-689-7618 284 G will@warren.edu
AUSTIN-BRUNS, Emily 978-665-3025 212 C eaustinb@fitchburgstate.edu
AUSTIN-KETCH, Tammy 315-464-3900 317 F austinkt@upstate.edu
AUSTRIA, Rod, G 818-833-3333 49 B austrig@laccd.edu
AUTEN, Mike 402-844-7058 268 J mike@northeast.edu
AUTERO, Esa 954-545-4500 107 E academics@sfbc.edu
AUTIO, Wesley 413-545-2963 211 D autio@umass.edu
AUTRY, Dean 270-686-4464 182 B dean.autry@kctcs.edu
AUTRY, James, C 801-422-3928 458 H autry@byu.edu
AUVENSHINE, Donnie 325-649-8408 438 D dauvenshine@hputx.edu
AUVIL, Joe 509-793-2016 478 H joea@bigbend.edu
AVAKIAN, Satenik 510-925-4282 25 Q savakian@aua.am
AVALONE, Valarie, L 585-292-3021 307 H vavalone@monroecc.edu
AVALOS, Jesse 617-236-8827 209 D javalos@fisher.edu
AVALOS, Juan 949-582-4566 64 G javalos@saddleback.edu
AVALOS, Natalie 818-252-5107 75 C natalie.avalos@woodbury.edu
AVALOS-SÁNCHEZ, Javier 787-993-8863 513 B javier.avalos@upr.edu
AVALOS-THOMPSON, Marlena 708-656-8000 144 E m.avalos-thompson@morton.edu
AVANT, Robin 203-332-5984 85 F ravant@housatonic.edu
AVANT, Toni, D 662-915-7174 249 D tavant@olemiss.edu
AVEDESIAN, Starr 714-628-4862 58 A avedesian_starr@sccollege.edu
AVELINO, Melanie 336-633-0256 337 A mlavelino@randolph.edu
AVELLA, Christine 619-574-5803 43 E cavella@fst.edu
AVEN, Forrest, F 210-829-3190 453 D aven@uiwtx.edu
AVENDANO, John 904-646-2300 100 B
AVENIA, Bradford 303-273-3548 78 I bavenia@mines.edu
AVENT, Jenna 336-272-7102 329 D jenna.avent@greensboro.edu
AVENT, Randy, K 863-583-9050 109 B
AVENT, Sherri, M 336-334-7973 341 F avent@ncat.edu
AVERESCH, Brenda 419-783-2352 352 F baveresch@defiance.edu
AVERETT, Michael 252-399-6528 326 M maverett@barton.edu
AVERETTE, Dan 843-661-8161 409 I dan.averette@fdtc.edu
AVERILL, Sue 330-672-2220 354 J saveril2@kent.edu
AVERION, Enrique David 513-556-2861 362 D enrique.averion@uc.edu
AVERY, Alycia 603-626-9490 274 D a.avery@snhu.edu
AVERY, Brad 714-432-6420 38 E bavery@occ.cccd.edu
AVERY, Brandon 941-359-4331 110 D bavery@sar.usf.edu

B

BACCILE, Peter .... 734-973-3300 232 B
pbaccile@wccnet.edu
BACCOUS, Alesheia .... 919-833-3003 340 E
alesheia.baccous@shawu.edu
BACH, Alex .... 913-234-0610 172 E
alex.bach@cleveland.edu
BACH, Julie .... 708-714-9102 136 C
jbach@dom.edu
BACH, Larry, C .... 612-343-4703 242 H
lcbach@northcentral.edu
BACHAND, Donald, J ... 989-964-4041 230 B
dbachand@svsu.edu
BACHAS, Leonidas, G ... 305-284-4117 112 E
bachas@miami.edu
BACHHER, Jagdeep, S .. 510-987-0260.. 68 C
jagdeep.baccher@ucop.edu
BACHLE, Lori .... 402-552-6127 266 E
bachle@clarksoncollege.edu
BACHMAN, Katie .... 760-384-6150.. 46 M
katie.bachman@cerrocoso.edu
BACHMAN, Rob .... 303-762-6970.. 79 H
rob.bachman@denverseminary.edu
BACHMAN, Sara .... 215-898-5511 400 K
sbachman@upenn.edu
BACHMAYER, Carrie ..... 949-675-4451.. 46 D
carrie@idi.edu
BACHMEIER, James ...... 616-331-6805 224 E
bachmeij@gvsu.edu
BACHMEIER, John, G ... 715-836-5189 496 D
bachmejg@uwec.edu
BACHMEIER, Mark .... 828-262-6483 341 B
bachmeiermd@appstate.edu
BACHOR, Dina .... 901-572-2585 418 E
dina.bachor@bchs.edu
BACHRACH, Gavriel ...... 847-982-2500 138 A
bachrach@htc.edu
BACHRACH, Steven .... 732-571-3421 279 B
sbachrac@monmouth.edu
BACHRI, Abdel .... 870-235-4290.. 21 D
agbachri@saumag.edu
BACHTEL, Tara .... 903-923-2325 436 D
tbachtel@etbu.edu
BACHUS, Dan .... 602-639-7500.. 12 J
BACIGALUPI, Michael ... 606-218-5510 185 D
mbacigalupi@upike.edu
BACIK, Valerie .... 814-871-5571 384 E
bacik001@gannon.edu
BACK, Corey .... 317-921-4538 157 H
cback7@ivytech.edu
BACK, Tony .... 606-487-3302 181 C
tony.back@kctcs.edu
BACKELS, Kelsey, K ...... 717-871-7821 395 D
kelsey.backels@millersville.edu
BACKER, Joni .... 402-375-7200 268 G
jobacke1@wsc.edu
BACKHAUS, Kristin .... 845-257-2930 317 B
backhauk@newpaltz.edu
BACKLIN, William .... 785-833-4511 175 B
bill.backlin@kwu.edu
BACKLUND,
Lee Ann, M .... 931-598-1238 423 M
lafton@sewanee.edu
BACKMAN, Carey .... 585-389-2320 308 B
cbackma2@naz.edu
BACKOFEN, Susan .... 229-226-1621 125 C
sbackofen@thomasu.edu
BACKUS, Amy .... 216-368-2866 349 F
amy.backus@case.edu
BACKUS, Bruce, D .... 314-935-9882 262 A
backusb@wustl.edu
BACKUS, Robert, H .... 607-746-4677 320 G
backusrh@delhi.edu
BACON, Amy .... 417-447-2653 257 G
bacona@otc.edu
BACON, Carolyn .... 304-326-1242 488 F
carolyn.bacon@salemu.edu
BACON, Geoff .... 907-450-8200.... 9 G
gmbacon@alaska.edu
BACON, Gus .... 406-395-4875 265 G
gbacon@stonechild.edu
BACON, Jack .... 610-892-1501 393 J
jbacon@pit.edu
BACON, Jen .... 610-436-0045 396 A
jbacon@wcupa.edu
BACON, John .... 541-888-7001 376 F
john.bacon@socc.edu
BACON, John .... 252-493-7229 336 H
jbacon@email.pittcc.edu
BACON, Karen .... 646-592-4150 326 E
kbacon@yu.edu
BACON, Michael .... 210-999-7320 452 A
mbacon@trinity.edu
BACON, Robbie .... 717-815-6818 404 A
rbacon2@ycp.edu
BACON, Tiffany .... 954-486-7728 112 D
tbacon@ftl.edu
BACOTE-CHARLES, Terri 301-546-0409 201 C
bacotetk@pgcc.edu
BACOW, Lawrence, S ... 617-495-1502 210 B
president@harvard.edu
BACQUE, Heather .... 504-864-7225 189 F
heather.bacque@sodexo.com
BACZEWSKI, Philip, C .. 940-565-3886 454 A
baczewski@unt.edu
BADAL, Amy, A .... 570-577-1601 379 F
amy.badal@bucknell.edu
BADAL, Joel .... 832-252-4615 433 D
joel.badal@cbshouston.edu
BADALYAN, Anna .... 323-953-4000.. 48 I
badalya@lacitycollege.edu
BADAR, Bryan .... 330-490-7417 364 B
bbadar@walsh.edu
BADASZEWSKI, Philip .. 716-878-3000 318 C
badaszpd@buffalostate.edu
BADE, Michael .... 415-502-6460.. 69 E
michael.bade@ucsf.edu
BADE, Robert, E .... 727-816-3413 104 F
badeb@phsc.edu
BADE, William, D .... 217-786-2326 142 B
bill.bade@llcc.edu
BADEAU, Melissa .... 607-871-2698 289 H
badeau@alfred.edu
BADEAUX, Aimee .... 225-491-1624 186 F
aimee.badeaux@franu.edu
BADEN, Cory .... 407-646-2264 105 M
cbaden@rollins.edu
BADENES, José .... 310-338-7684.. 50 J
jose.badenes@lmu.edu
BADENHAUSEN,
Richard .... 801-832-2460 461 G
rbadenhausen@westminstercollege.edu
BADER, Irv .... 718-820-4880 322 J
irv.bader@touro.edu
BADER-SAYE, Scott .... 512-472-4133 443 H
scott.bader-saye@ssw.edu
BADGER, Nancy .... 757-683-4401 469 G
nbadger@odu.edu
BADILLO,
Maria Antonieta .... 919-831-6755 436 E
mbadill4@epcc.edu
BADILLO-LOZANO,
Luis, V .... 787-841-2000 510 K
luis_badillo@pucpr.edu
BADIRU, Adedeji, B ...... 937-255-3025 503 A
adedeji.badiru@afit.edu
BADMAN, Jodie, L .... 574-239-8404 155 D
jbadman@hcc-nd.edu
BADOLATO, Michael ...... 978-762-4000 215 B
mbadolat@northshore.edu
BADOVINAC, Amanda ... 406-496-4828 265 A
abadovinac@mtech.edu
BADOVINAC, Michele ... 209-468-9141.. 67 B
mbadovinac@sjcoe.net
BADOWSKA, Eva .... 718-817-4400 300 E
badowska@fordham.edu
BADOWSKI, Ryan .... 415-442-7833.. 44 D
rbadowski@ggu.edu
BADRY, Jay .... 909-687-1759.. 43 I
jaybadry@gs.edu
BADZEK, Laurie, A .... 814-863-9734 392 B
lzb340@psu.edu
BAENEN, Michael .... 617-627-3300 219 B
michael.baenen@tufts.edu
BAENNINGER,
MaryAnn .... 973-408-3100 277 C
president@drew.edu
BAER, Candace .... 401-454-6426 405 D
cbaer@risd.edu
BAER, Dana .... 724-852-3295 402 F
dbaer@waynesburg.edu
BAER, Danny .... 919-365-7711 340 H
BAER, Lori .... 816-802-3448 254 B
lbaer@kcai.edu
BAER, Natasha .... 763-433-1707 237 C
natasha.baer@anokaramsey.edu
BAERWALD, Bonnie ...... 920-929-2127 500 C
bbaerwald@morainepark.edu
BAEZ, Ada .... 787-285-5457 508 C
abaez4@hccpr.edu
BAEZ, Ada .... 787-852-1430 508 C
abaez4@hccpr.edu
BAEZ, Arvin .... 787-841-2000 510 K
arvin_baez@pucpr.edu
BAEZ, Aurelis .... 787-279-1912 509 A
abaez@bayamon.inter.edu
BAEZ, Juan .... 310-233-4427.. 49 A
baezrj@lahc.edu
BAEZ, Thomas .... 864-294-3031 410 A
thomas.baez@furman.edu
BAEZ MILAN, Tony .... 724-653-2183 383 A
tbaez@dec.edu
BAEZA, Marco .... 714-438-4707.. 38 B
mbaeza@mail.cccd.edu
BAEZA-ORTEGO, Gilda .. 575-538-6358 289 B
ortegog@wnmu.edu
BAFFA, Joe .... 714-556-3610.. 72 F
joe.baffa@vanguard.edu
BAGAYOKO, Diola .... 225-771-4845 190 H
diola_bagayoko@subr.edu
BAGBY, Sara .... 606-693-5000 182 G
srichardson@kmbc.edu
BAGDAZIAN, Robert, A . 805-525-4417.. 67 D
rbagdazian@thomasaquinas.edu
BAGEL, George .... 770-534-6265 115 D
gbagel@brenau.edu
BAGENTS, Bill .... 256-766-6610.... 5 F
bbagents@hcu.edu
BAGG, Eva .... 760-252-2411.. 26 I
ebagg@barstow.edu
BAGG, Mary Beth .... 317-788-3220 161 B
bagg@uindy.edu
BAGGERMAN, Thom ..... 412-392-4761 397 A
tbaggerman@pointpark.edu
BAGGETT, Cody .... 217-641-4300 140 A
cbaggett@jwcc.edu
BAGGISH, Mindy .... 909-593-3511.. 70 D
mbaggish@laverne.edu
BAGGOT, Joseph .... 507-222-4075 234 F
jbaggot@carleton.edu
BAGGS, Adam .... 817-257-6814 448 G
a.baggs@tcu.edu
BAGGS, David .... 843-863-7513 407 E
dbaggs@csuniv.edu
BAGGSON, Gulizar .... 479-619-2203.. 20 D
gbaggson@nwacc.edu
BAGILEO, Nick, J .... 202-526-3799.. 92 F
nbagileo@johnpaulii.edu
BAGLEY, Bob .... 706-233-7240 124 B
bbagley@shorter.edu
BAGLEY, Elizabeth .... 404-471-6339 113 G
ebagley@agnesscott.edu
BAGLEY, Judy .... 864-294-2320 410 A
judy.bagley@furman.edu
BAGLEY, Michael .... 530-741-5564.. 76 C
mbagley@yccd.edu
BAGLEY, Michelle, M ... 971-722-4497 375 J
michelle.bagley@pcc.edu
BAGLEY, Rob .... 801-524-1952 459 F
robbagley@ldsbc.edu
BAGLEY, Rod .... 715-833-6480 499 D
rbagley1@cvtc.edu
BAGLEY, Ryan .... 212-229-5662 308 C
bagleyr@newschool.edu
BAGLEY, Shawn .... 330-823-2280 363 B
bagleysp@mountunion.edu
BAGNALL, James .... 928-428-8414.. 12 E
jim.bagnall@eac.edu
BAGNELL, William .... 252-328-6858 341 C
bagnellw@ecu.edu
BAGNOLI, Joseph, P .... 641-269-3600 165 J
bagnolij@grinnell.edu
BAGSTAD, Kristi .... 563-588-6314 163 F
kristi.bagstad@clarke.edu
BAGWELL, Christopher . 228-896-2500 247 E
christopher.bagwell@mgccc.edu
BAGWELL, Dana .... 814-871-7238 384 E
bagwell002@gannon.edu
BAGWELL, Jack .... 864-941-8307 411 H
bagwell.j@ptc.edu
BAGWELL, Lydia .... 575-527-7766 287 E
lbagwell@nmsu.edu
BAH, Ibrahim .... 919-546-8565 340 E
ibrahim.bah@shawu.edu
BAHAMONDE, Rafael, E 317-274-2344 156 F
rbahamon@iupui.edu
BAHAN, Liz .... 415-420-8094.. 58 B
lbahan@reachinst.org
BAHAN, Rebecca .... 314-889-4509 253 C
rbahan@fontbonne.edu
BAHARANYI, Ntam .... 334-727-8659.... 7 D
nbaharanyi@tuskegee.edu
BAHCECI, Suleyman ...... 703-591-7042 476 F
BAHLS, Steven, C .... 309-794-7208 132 C
stevenbahls@augustana.edu
BAHR, Brett .... 218-755-2599 237 E
brett.bahr@bemidjistate.edu
BAHR, Christine, M ...... 618-537-6810 143 B
cmbahr@mckendree.edu
BAHR, Deb .... 319-399-8877 164 A
dbahr@coe.edu
BAHR, Jon .... 517-750-1200 230 H
jonathan.bahr@arbor.edu
BAHR, Matt .... 509-313-5952 481 D
bahr@gonzaga.edu
BAHU, Michelle .... 951-552-8967.. 27 J
mbahu@calbaptist.edu
BAI, Kang .... 815-836-5640 141 G
kbai@lewisu.edu
BAI, Lynn .... 516-739-1545 309 C
admissions@nyctcm.edu
BAI, Monica, S .... 928-523-6514.. 14 H
monica.bai@nau.edu
BAI, Yifeng .... 973-748-9000 276 A
yifeng_bai@bloomfield.edu
BAIA, Larissa .... 603-524-3207 272 K
lbaia@ccsnh.edu
BAIA, Patricia .... 518-445-2366 289 E
pbaia@albanylaw.edu
BAICHI, Jennifer .... 303-273-3280.. 78 I
jbaichi@mines.edu
BAICKER, Katherine ...... 773-702-0711 150 J
kbaicker@uchicago.edu
BAIDA, Ana .... 470-578-6555 120 L
abaida@kennesaw.edu
BAIDOO,
Christopher, E .... 619-239-0391.. 34 F
cbaidoo@cwsl.edu
BAIDWAN, Surjeet .... 410-951-6449 203 D
sbaidwan@coppin.edu
BAIER, Henry, D .... 734-764-3402 231 E
hbaier@umich.edu
BAIER, Valerie, A .... 570-326-3761 393 G
vbaier@pct.edu
BAIERL, Hans .... 920-924-3112 500 C
hbaierl@morainepark.edu
BAIERL, Kenneth, W ..... 574-520-4560 157 A
kbaierl@iusb.edu
BAIK, Sang .... 213-763-7007.. 49 E
baiks@lattc.edu
BAILARD, Rhiannon ...... 310-506-4702.. 56 C
rhiannon.bailard@pepperdine.edu
BAILARD, Rhiannon ...... 415-851-8858.. 68 F
bailardrhiannon@uchastings.edu
BAILER, Joseph .... 910-678-8585 334 D
bailerj@faytechcc.edu
BAILEY, Alison .... 309-438-2947 139 E
baileya@ilstu.edu
BAILEY, Amanda .... 401-863-6050 404 E
amanda_bailey@brown.edu
BAILEY, Angela, W .... 252-335-3513 341 D
awbailey@ecsu.edu
BAILEY, Anthony .... 213-740-2852.. 72 B
arbailey@usc.edu
BAILEY, Barbara .... 773-252-5311 147 B
barbara.bailey@resu.edu
BAILEY, Bliss, N .... 334-844-4511.... 4 E
bailebn@auburn.edu
BAILEY, Brian .... 312-567-6937 139 B
bbailey4@iit.edu
BAILEY, Cassy .... 785-594-8484 170 I
cassy.bailey@bakeru.edu
BAILEY, Charla .... 830-372-8098 449 B
cbailey@tlu.edu
BAILEY, Cheryl .... 414-930-3111 495 A
baileyc@mtmary.edu
BAILEY, Chris, C .... 570-372-4149 399 C
baileycj@susqu.edu
BAILEY, Christine .... 315-268-6578 296 A
cbailey@clarkson.edu
BAILEY, Christopher ..... 401-254-3124 405 E
cjbailey@rwu.edu
BAILEY, Christopher, C 360-442-2101 482 B
cbailey@lowercolumbia.edu
BAILEY, Christy .... 843-477-2166 410 C
christy.bailey@hgtc.edu
BAILEY, Cindy .... 715-735-4312 496 E
baileyc@uwgb.edu
BAILEY, Clint .... 252-328-2606 341 C
baileyrc@ecu.edu
BAILEY, Danya .... 254-298-8364 446 A
danya.bailey@templejc.edu
BAILEY, David, C .... 574-631-1097 161 C
bailey.77@nd.edu
BAILEY, Denice .... 503-594-3002 372 D
denice.bailey@clackamas.edu
BAILEY, Denise .... 903-233-3100 439 E
denisebailey@letu.edu
BAILEY, Dennis, A .... 850-644-8136 109 C
dbailey@fsu.edu
BAILEY, JR., Dexter, F . 626-395-6307.. 29 C

BAILEY, Dixon 254-647-3234 442 E
dbailey@rangercollege.edu
BAILEY, Donald, R 401-865-1188 405 B
drbailey@providence.edu
BAILEY, Ed 231-995-1215 228 G
ebailey@nmc.edu
BAILEY, Gary 616-538-2330 224 C
gbailey@gracechristian.edu
BAILEY, Guy 956-665-2100 455 D
president@utrgv.edu
BAILEY, Helen 423-869-6434 421 C
helen.bailey@lmunet.edu
BAILEY, Jack 304-766-4109 491 B
jbaile19@wvstateu.edu
BAILEY, Jalynda 918-293-5266 368 D
jalynda@okstate.edu
BAILEY, Jaye 408-924-1177 34 B
jaye.bailey@sjsu.edu
BAILEY, Jeannie 775-753-2317 271 B
jeannie.bailey@gbcnv.edu
BAILEY, Jeff 870-972-3077 17 G
jbailey@astate.edu
BAILEY, Jessica 252-246-1271 339 C
jbailey@wilsoncc.edu
BAILEY, Jessica, H 601-984-6300 249 E
jhbailey@umc.edu
BAILEY, Jessika 580-559-5252 366 C
jbailey@ecok.edu
BAILEY, Jodi 201-200-3507 279 E
jbailey2@njcu.edu
BAILEY, Joseph, A 585-345-6900 301 A
jabailey@genesee.edu
BAILEY, Julie 404-378-8821 116 H
baileyj@ctsnet.edu
BAILEY, Julie 432-264-5051 438 C
jbailey@howardcollege.edu
BAILEY, Julie, A 774-353-0661 206 B
julie.bailey@becker.edu
BAILEY, Keith 304-293-3733 491 C
keith.bailey@mail.wvu.edu
BAILEY, Kelly 724-738-4223 395 F
kelly.bailey@sru.edu
BAILEY, Kevin 704-687-2206 342 E
baileyk@uncc.edu
BAILEY, Kevin, S 573-882-1639 261 B
baileyks@missouri.edu
BAILEY, Kimberly 252-398-6260 328 D
ksbailey@chowan.edu
BAILEY, Larry 731-424-3520 425 B
lbailey@jscc.edu
BAILEY, Lena 517-371-5140 233 A
baileyl@cooley.edu
BAILEY, Lisa 909-652-6532 36 A
lisa.bailey@chaffey.edu
BAILEY, Mara 515-961-1684 169 D
mara.bailey@simpson.edu
BAILEY, Mark 205-853-1200 2 G
mbailey@jeffersonstate.edu
BAILEY, Mark 909-621-8219 56 J
mark_bailey@pitzer.edu
BAILEY, Mark, L 214-887-5001 436 B
mbailey@dts.edu
BAILEY, Mary 620-331-8332 174 C
mbailey@indycc.edu
BAILEY, Mary Kaye 702-651-7437 271 A
marykaye.bailey@csn.edu
BAILEY, Michael 352-588-8464 106 D
michael.bailey@saintleo.edu
BAILEY, Michael, A 202-687-6021 92 A
baileyma@georgetown.edu
BAILEY, Michelle 563-441-4152 165 E
mmbailey@eicc.edu
BAILEY, Mike 620-417-1044 176 K
mike.bailey@sccc.edu
BAILEY, Mike 309-341-5336 133 C
mbailey@sandburg.edu
BAILEY, Mitchell, A 650-574-6510 61 N
baileym@smccd.edu
BAILEY, Patrick 818-677-2393 32 D
patrick.bailey@csun.edu
BAILEY, Peter, A 302-295-1191 90 I
peter.a.bailey@wilmu.edu
BAILEY, Phillip 501-450-3262 23 H
phillipb@uca.edu
BAILEY, JR., Richard, J 505-747-2147 287 G
rick.bailey@nnmc.edu
BAILEY, JR., Richard, J 505-747-2140 287 G
rick.bailey@nnmc.edu
BAILEY, Rita 470-578-2364 120 L
rbaile62@kennesaw.edu
BAILEY, Robbie 540-261-8463 471 H
robbie.bailey@svu.edu
BAILEY, Robyn 847-635-1428 145 G
rbailey@oakton.edu
BAILEY, Ron 931-221-6206 418 D
baileyrl@apsu.edu
BAILEY, Sara 352-638-9814 95 D
sbailey@beaconcollege.edu
BAILEY, Sharon, M 361-570-4236 453 C
baileysm@uhv.edu
BAILEY, Shaun 559-934-2254 74 A
shaunbailey@whccd.edu
BAILEY, Tamara 304-473-8424 491 H
bailey_t@wvwc.edu
BAILEY, Tammy 252-789-0253 335 H
tammy.bailey@martincc.edu
BAILEY, Teresa 757-825-2770 476 A
baileyt@tncc.edu
BAILEY, Terry 706-272-2611 117 C
tbailey@daltonstate.edu
BAILEY, Thomas, R 212-678-3131 322 G
tb3@tc.columbia.edu
BAILEY, Tonya 517-483-1116 226 F
bailet20@lcc.edu
BAILEY, Travis 304-696-3032 490 D
bailey53@marshall.edu
BAILEY, William 814-393-2323 394 D
wbailey@clarion.edu
BAILEY BROWN, Katherine 512-472-4133 443 H
katherine.brown@ssw.edu
BAILEY-CHEN, Robin 213-252-5100 23 K
BAILEY FISCHER, Valerie 413-597-2483 220 C
vb7@williams.edu
BAILEY-FOUGNIER, Dennis 541-278-5950 372 A
BAILEY-HOFMANN, Holly 310-287-4547 49 G
baileyhh@wlac.edu
BAILEY HOGARTY, Sarah 415-703-9500 28 D
sbaileyhogarty@cca.edu
BAILEY-JONES, Jenny 662-472-9174 246 C
jbailey@holmescc.edu
BAILEY MURPHY, Krista 215-248-7142 381 D
murphyk@chc.edu
BAILEY-OCHOA, Celia 409-772-8909 456 F
cebailey@utmb.edu
BAILIE, John 267-246-5891 386 E
johnbailie@iirp.edu
BAILLARGEON, Betty 860-215-9207 86 F
bbaillargeon@trcc.commnet.edu
BAILLIE, Christopher 701-255-3285 347 B
cbaillie@uttc.edu
BAILO, Carole Anne 480-212-1704 15 Q
caroleanne@sessions.edu
BAILON, Kathy 213-624-1200 42 I
kbailon@fidm.edu
BAILY, Jessica 914-674-7611 306 F
jbaily@mercy.edu
BAILY, Scott 970-491-7655 78M
scott.baily@colostate.edu
BAIMA, Thomas, A 847-970-4866 152 A
tbaima@usml.edu
BAIN, Abbey 318-427-4468 188 J
BAIN, Brandi 520-494-5207 11 K
brandi.bain@centralaz.edu
BAIN, Jeff, N 931-363-9872 421 E
jbain@martinmethodist.edu
BAIN, Michael 404-669-2097 123 C
michael.bain@point.edu
BAIN, Steve 361-593-2802 447 D
steve.bain@tamuk.edu
BAIN-SELBO, Eric 765-455-9280 156 D
ebainsel@iu.edu
BAINE, Brad 870-759-4128 23 J
bbaine@williamsbu.edu
BAINES, Joel, D 225-578-9905 188 I
jbaines@lsu.edu
BAIR, Ava 719-336-1574 80 K
ava.bair@lamarcc.edu
BAIR, Ryan 309-677-2697 133 B
rbair@fsmail.bradley.edu
BAIRD, Bridget, R 423-439-8222 419 J
bairdb@etsu.edu
BAIRD, David 860-685-2119 89 C
dbaird@wesleyan.edu
BAIRD, Davis 508-793-7673 208 A
dbaird@clarku.edu
BAIRD, Denise 317-738-8270 154 J
dbaird@franklincollege.edu
BAIRD, Dion 503-594-0760 372 D
dion.baird@clackamas.edu
BAIRD, Phil 605-586-5880 416 D
phil.baird@sintegleska.edu
BAIRD, Rebecca 973-720-2713 284 I
bairdr3@wpunj.edu
BAIRD, Stephanie 405-425-5200 367 G
stephanie.baird@oc.edu
BAIRD, Tanya 719-549-2498 79 A
tanya.baird@csupueblo.edu
BAIRD, Thomas, A 734-647-6030 231 E
baird@umich.edu
BAIRD, Timothy, R 724-847-6490 384 G
trbaird@geneva.edu
BAIRD-JAMES, Allison 310-794-8686 69 A
abaird-james@finance.ucla.edu
BAISDEN, Emma, L 304-896-7402 489 E
emma.baisden@southernwv.edu
BAISEY, Michael 301-624-2892 198 E
mbaisey@frederick.edu
BAITMAN, Clay, L 618-235-2700 149 H
clay.baitman@swic.edu
BAJANDAS, Ivette 305-629-2929 106 H
ibajandas@sanignaciouniversity.edu
BAJCZYK, Rhetta 920-693-1159 499 G
rhetta.bajczyk@gotoltc.edu
BAJOR, William 570-422-3588 394 E
wbajor@esu.edu
BAJWA, Sreekala 406-994-3681 264 D
sreekala.bajwa@montana.edu
BAK, Doug 719-846-5513 82 K
doug.bak@trinidadstate.edu
BAKANE, Samir 973-655-7773 279 C
bakanes@mail.montclair.edu
BAKAR, Senem 202-885-3352 90 J
bakar@american.edu
BAKARI, Sentwali 719-255-3159 83 B
sbakari@uccs.edu
BAKE, Mark, A 920-433-6626 492 B
mark.bake@bellincollege.edu
BAKEMEIER, Emily, P 203-432-4444 89 D
emily.bakemeier@yale.edu
BAKER, Adria 713-348-6095 442 K
abaker@rice.edu
BAKER, Alvin 606-326-2422 180 I
alvin.baker@kctcs.edu
BAKER, Amanda 607-871-2164 289 H
bakera@alfred.edu
BAKER, Amanda, L 304-929-6717 489 C
abaker@newriver.edu
BAKER, Amy 573-288-6493 252 E
abaker@culver.edu
BAKER, Andrew, R 301-447-5295 200 E
baker@msmary.edu
BAKER, Ashley 504-520-7359 193 A
abaker12@xula.edu
BAKER, Barry 407-823-2564 109 E
barry.baker@ucf.edu
BAKER, Barry 425-235-2352 483 G
bbaker@rtc.edu
BAKER, Betty 304-793-6873 491 A
bbaker@osteo.wvsom.edu
BAKER, Bonnie 928-523-9413 14 H
bonnie.baker@nau.edu
BAKER, Brent 765-641-4138 153 B
babaker@anderson.edu
BAKER, Brent 817-598-6275 458 A
bbaker@wc.edu
BAKER, Brian 812-749-1212 159 C
bbaker@oak.edu
BAKER, Brian 336-278-7453 328 K
bbaker7@elon.edu
BAKER, Brian, J 540-654-1302 472 I
bbaker@umw.edu
BAKER, Carey 870-235-4042 21 D
clbaker@saumag.edu
BAKER, Caroline 410-455-8171 202 E
cbaker@umbc.edu
BAKER, Chuck, S 423-775-7136 418 H
cbaker0930@bryan.edu
BAKER, David, A 541-737-3871 375 D
david.baker@oregonstate.edu
BAKER, Deb 603-206-8152 272 L
dbaker@ccsnh.edu
BAKER, Debbie 307-382-1611 502 I
dbaker@westernwyoming.edu
BAKER, Deborah 413-565-1000 205 G
dbaker@baypath.edu
BAKER, Debra 662-246-6301 247 D
dbaker@msdelta.edu
BAKER, Diane 269-927-6287 226 D
baker@lakemichigancollege.edu
BAKER, Donna 816-584-6847 258 A
donna.baker@park.edu
BAKER, Elizabeth 252-222-6216 333 A
bakere@carteret.edu
BAKER, Elizabeth, A 312-942-2702 148 A
elizabeth_baker@rush.edu
BAKER, Emily 909-748-8047 71 G
emily_baker@redlands.edu
BAKER, Erinnae 803-981-7075 415 A
ebaker@yorktech.edu
BAKER, Erma 757-221-3954 466 C
eabaker01@wm.edu
BAKER, Frankie 513-569-1453 350 K
frankie.baker@cincinnatistate.edu
BAKER, Gail, F 619-260-4553 71 J
provost@sandiego.edu
BAKER, Gary 941-752-5431 108 G
bakerg@scf.edu
BAKER, Gerlad 918-781-7220 365 F
bakerg@bacone.edu
BAKER, Gisella 319-296-4465 166 B
gisella.baker@hawkeyecollege.edu
BAKER, Hilary 818-677-7750 32 D
hilary.baker@csun.edu
BAKER, Hunter 731-661-5519 427 C
hbaker@uu.edu
BAKER, Ingrid 503-821-8976 375 F
ibaker@pnca.edu
BAKER, James 210-999-8076 452 A
jbaker5@trinity.edu
BAKER, James, P 417-836-8501 256 E
jbaker@missouristate.edu
BAKER, Janet 610-740-3765 381 A
jlbaker@cedarcrest.edu
BAKER, Jean 214-860-8885 435 D
jeanbaker@dcccd.edu
BAKER, Jeff 859-371-9393 179 A
jbaker@beckfield.edu
BAKER, Jeff 760-862-1340 39 A
jebaker@collegeofthedesert.edu
BAKER, Jeffrey, A 704-687-8457 342 E
jbaker88@uncc.edu
BAKER, Jennifer 410-516-7490 199 D
jbaker94@jhu.edu
BAKER, Jerry 229-391-4782 113 F
jbaker@abac.edu
BAKER, Jim 817-272-2261 454 J
jimbaker@uta.edu
BAKER, Jimmy 513-562-8762 347 K
jbaker@artacademy.edu
BAKER, Jimmy, H 334-293-4524 1 C
jimmy.baker@accs.edu
BAKER, Jo Nell 909-593-3511 70 D
jbaker@laverne.edu
BAKER, John 802-257-4333 462 E
johnnyb@marlboro.edu
BAKER, John, C 517-355-6509 227 D
bakerjj@cvm.msu.edu
BAKER, Joseph, J 610-499-4151 403 B
jjbaker@widener.edu
BAKER, Josh 719-502-3019 81 F
josh.baker@ppcc.edu
BAKER, Joshua, C 630-515-7277 143 G
jbaker@midwestern.edu
BAKER, Judith, G 585-389-2824 308 B
jbaker51@naz.edu
BAKER, Julie 567-429-3535 360 B
julie_baker5@owens.edu
BAKER, Kathi 715-232-1121 498 A
bakerk@uwstout.edu
BAKER, Kathleen 206-296-6305 484 F
bakerkat@seattleu.edu
BAKER, Kathryn, R 865-354-3000 425 G
bakerkr@roanestate.edu
BAKER, Kevin 662-227-2222 246 C
kbaker@holmescc.edu
BAKER, Larry 540-868-7283 474 J
lbaker@lfcc.edu
BAKER, Leigh 386-822-8900 111 A
labaker@stetson.edu
BAKER, Lesli 801-863-8286 461 A
bakerle@uvu.edu
BAKER, Libba 205-652-3878 9 A
lmmcclendon@uwa.edu
BAKER, Linda 610-799-1584 388 I
lbaker4@lccc.edu
BAKER, Lisa 989-686-9826 223 G
lisabaker@delta.edu
BAKER, Lisa 252-246-1310 339 C
lbaker@wilsoncc.edu
BAKER, Lori 540-857-6348 476 D
sdeanofstudentservices@virginiawestern.edu
BAKER, Luanne 205-247-8147 7 A
lbaker@stillman.edu

BAKER, Margaret, W 415-422-2959 71 K
mwbaker@usfca.edu
BAKER, Marilyn 816-271-4361 257 A
mbaker3@missouriwestern.edu
BAKER, Matt 660-562-1219 257 E
mcbaker@nwmissouri.edu
BAKER, Matt, D 215-951-6803 400 A
bakerm@philau.edu
BAKER, Matthew 610-527-0200 397 I
matthew.baker@rosemont.edu
BAKER, Maureen 402-844-7258 268 J
maureen@northeast.edu
BAKER, Melinda 859-246-6819 180 K
melinda.baker@kctcs.edu
BAKER, Michael 765-641-4237 153 B
mtbaker@anderson.edu
BAKER, Michael 814-886-6368 391 B
mbaker@mtaloy.edu
BAKER, Michael, F 508-856-3040 212 A
michael.baker@umassmed.edu
BAKER, Michael, L 423-478-7702 423 G
mbaker@ptseminary.edu
BAKER, Mickey 334-556-2485 2 C
mbaker@wallace.edu
BAKER, Mike 859-442-4188 181 B
mike.baker@kctcs.edu
BAKER, Nancy 704-636-6882 330 A
nbaker@hoodseminary.edu
BAKER, Natalie 404-880-6879 116 D
nbaker@cau.edu
BAKER, Neal 765-983-1355 154 G
bakerne@earlham.edu
BAKER, Neil 252-823-5166 334 C
bakern@edgecombe.edu
BAKER, Nelson 404-894-8920 118 F
nelson.baker@pe.gatech.edu
BAKER, Nick 989-275-5000 226 B
nick.baker@kirtland.edu
BAKER, Nikki, M 336-334-4225 343 A
nmwilson@uncg.edu
BAKER, Richard 601-643-8404 245 G
richard.baker@colin.edu
BAKER, Richard 601-643-8302 245 G
richard.baker@colin.edu
BAKER, Richard 713-348-4350 442 K
BAKER, Rick 828-689-1215 331 A
rbaker@mhu.edu
BAKER, Robert 617-984-5959 218 B
rbaker@quincycollege.edu
BAKER, Robert, D 972-238-6174 435 F
rbaker1@dcccd.edu
BAKER, Robert, T 336-758-5224 344 D
bakerrt@wfu.edu
BAKER, Robin, E 503-554-2101 373 C
rbaker@georgefox.edu
BAKER, Russell, D 317-921-4313 157 G
rbaker80@ivytech.edu
BAKER, Ruth, E 410-334-2825 204 F
rbaker@worwic.edu
BAKER, Sallie, C 828-361-6267 338 E
sbaker@tricountycc.edu
BAKER, Sandy 951-222-8408 58 I
sandy.baker@rcc.edu
BAKER, Sarah 910-672-1185 341 E
sdbaker@uncfsu.edu
BAKER, Sarah 903-886-5045 447 B
sarah.baker@tamuc.edu
BAKER, Scott 828-339-4249 338 B
scottb@southwesterncc.edu
BAKER, Scott 802-865-5725 462 B
shbaker@champlain.edu
BAKER, Scott, R 740-427-5148 355 E
bakersr@kenyon.edu
BAKER, Seth 312-850-7038 134 H
sbaker71@ccc.edu
BAKER, Shannon 361-593-3290 447 D
shannon.baker@tamuk.edu
BAKER, Sharon 423-478-7707 423 G
sbaker@ptseminary.edu
BAKER, Shawn 314-340-5095 253 I
bakers@hssu.edu
BAKER, Shawn 402-354-7230 268 C
shawn.baker@methodistcollege.edu
BAKER, Sherry 731-286-3242 425 A
baker@dscc.edu
BAKER, Stephen, N 401-874-2109 406 B
snbaker@uri.edu
BAKER, Steven 561-803-2223 104 C
steven_baker@pba.edu
BAKER, Tamara 504-865-3860 189 F
tbaker@loyno.edu
BAKER, Teresa 417-626-1234 257 F
baker.teresa@occ.edu
BAKER, Thomas, N 315-267-2900 319 D
bakertn@potsdam.edu
BAKER, Todd 208-467-8365 131 D
toddbaker@nnu.edu
BAKER, Tracy, W 325-942-2035 451 A
tracy.baker@angelo.edu
BAKER, Uchenna 253-879-3100 485 E
ubaker@pugetsound.edu
BAKER, Valparisa 863-292-3602 105 A
vbaker@polk.edu
BAKER, Wanda 314-838-8858 261 G
assessment@ugst.edu
BAKER, Wayne 432-335-6574 441 D
wbaker@odessa.edu
BAKER, Wendy 727-873-4851 110 C
wbaker@mail.usf.edu
BAKER, William, J 703-580-4810 401 I
wjbaker@valleyforge.edu
BAKER, Winston 936-468-2601 445 F
bakerwa@sfasu.edu
BAKER, Wren 940-565-2789 454 A
wren.baker@unt.edu
BAKER, Yvonne 513-569-1629 350 K
BAKER, Zeb 513-529-3398 356 E
zeb.baker@miamioh.edu
BAKER-BARNES, Kiki 504-816-4752 186 D
kbarnes@dillard.edu
BAKER-DEMARAY,
Twyla 701-627-4738 346 G
tbaker@nhsc.edu
BAKER-FLOWERS,
Kimberly 510-885-2809 31 C
BAKER-ROUSSAT,
Marilee 203-285-2310 85 E
mroussat@gwcc.commnet.edu
BAKER-WATSON, Stevie 765-658-6075 154 F
steviebaker-watson@depauw.edu
BAKEWELL-SACHS,
Susan 503-494-7445 375 B
sondeansoffice@ohsu.edu
BAKHIT, Norman 574-372-5100 155 B
bakhitn@grace.edu
BAKIC, Rachele 920-683-4711 496 E
bakicr@uwgb.edu
BAKK, Kelly 218-749-7765 238 G
k.bakk@mesabirange.edu
BAKKE, Andrea 703-812-4757 468 G
abakke@leland.edu
BAKKE, Lisa 702-651-4211 271 A
lisa.bakke@csn.edu
BAKKEN, Jeffrey 309-677-3997 133 B
jbakken@bradley.edu
BAKKEN, Phillip 402-472-7554 269 H
pbakken@nebraska.edu
BAKKEN, Turina 608-246-6516 499 H
bakken@madisoncollege.edu
BAKKEN, Virgil 218-755-3370 237 E
virgil.bakken@bemidjistate.edu
BAKKER, Theresa 907-474-6218 10 A
uaf-alumni@alaska.edu
BAKO, Pat 206-726-5052 480 C
pbako@cornish.edu
BAKOYEMA, Bryn 334-229-4100 4 B
bbakoyema@alasu.edu
BAKSH, Joanna 817-735-2264 454 C
joanna.baksh@unthsc.edu
BAKSH-JARRETT, Gail 718-482-5116 294 F
gailbj@lagcc.cuny.edu
BAKSI, Christine 717-245-1916 382 F
baksic@dickinson.edu
BAKST, M, S 248-968-3360 233 F
BAKST, Y 248-968-3360 233 F
BAKTHAKUMAR, Davi 954-545-4500 107 E
dbakthakumar@sfbc.edu
BAKULA, Timothy, L 319-273-2722 163 B
tim.bakula@uni.edu
BAL, Sherilyn 352-245-4119 111 E
sherilyn.bal@taylorcollege.edu
BALABAN, Mark 845-431-8044 298 E
mark.balaban@sunydutchess.edu
BALACEK, Patti 608-785-5201 501 A
balacekp@westerntc.edu
BALAKRISHNAN, Raju 313-593-5248 231 F
rajub@umich.edu
BALAKRISHNAN,
Venkataramanan 216-368-3227 349 F
cse-dean@case.edu
BALANA MOLTER,
Sarah 317-955-6319 158 U
sbalanamolter@marian.edu
BALANOFF, Janet 407-708-2963 107 D
balanoffj@seminolestate.edu
BALARIN, Alfredo 518-629-7348 302 E
a.balarin@hvcc.edu
BALASKI, Keith 320-222-5211 240 E
keith.balaski@ridgewater.edu
BALASON, JR., Severo 661-763-7810 66 J
sbalason@taftcollege.edu
BALASUBRAMANIAN,
Ramprasad 508-999-8024 211 F
r.bala@umassd.edu
BALASUBRAMANYA,
Mirley 210-784-2225 448 A
mbalasub@tamusa.edu
BALASZ, Anne 419-530-2087 363 E
anne.balasz@utoledo.edu
BALATBAT, Joseph 212-924-5900 322 B
jbalatbat@swedishinstitute.edu
BALBACH, Donna 812-357-6525 160 D
dbalbach@saintmeinrad.edu
BALBES, Idellisse 787-738-2161 513 D
idelisse.balbes@upr.edu
BALCAZAR, Genaro 708-524-6562 136 C
gbalcazar@dom.edu
BALCAZAR, Hector 323-563-4815 36 D
hectorbalcazar@cdrewu.edu
BALCER, Jesse 215-248-7046 381 D
balcerj@chc.edu
BALCH, Angela 432-685-4508 440 E
abalch@midland.edu
BALCH, Glenna 512-404-4828 431 C
gbalch@austinseminary.edu
BALCH, Marcus 972-617-4128 449 E
marcus.balch@tstc.edu
BALCH, Robert 575-835-5143 286 I
robert.balch@nmt.edu
BALCH-LINDSAY,
Suzanne 575-562-2314 285 M
suzanne.balch@enmu.edu
BALCHAK, Sharon 216-373-5322 358 B
sbalchak@ndc.edu
BALCOM, David, A 410-651-6199 203 A
dabalcom@umes.edu
BALD, Tim 920-403-3030 495 I
tim.bald@snc.edu
BALDA, Wesley 956-665-3599 455 D
wesley.balda@utrgv.edu
BALDAGUEZ, José, A 787-850-9328 513 E
jose.baldaguez1@upr.edu
BALDERAS, Guillermo 702-254-7577 272 A
guillermo.balderas@
northwestcareercollege.edu
BALDERAZ, Brenda Jo 956-872-5057 444 A
brendajb@southtexascollege.edu
BALDIN, Antoinette 419-995-8065 354 H
baldin.a@rhodesstate.edu
BALDINI, Fred 510-879-0784 59 F
fbaldini@samuelmerritt.edu
BALDONADO, Nandy 713-718-5141 437 I
nandy.baldonado@hccs.edu
BALDONEDO, Claudia 718-482-5236 294 F
claudiab@lagcc.cuny.edu
BALDUCCI, Laureen 408-864-8945 43 C
balduccilaureen@deanza.edu
BALDWIN, Al 561-868-3414 104 D
baldwina@palmbeachstate.edu
BALDWIN, Anne, E 585-245-5547 318 E
baldwina@geneseo.edu
BALDWIN, Chad 307-766-2929 502 H
cbaldwin@uwyo.edu
BALDWIN, Charlene 714-532-7747 36 C
baldwin@chapman.edu
BALDWIN, Christine, A 714-850-4800 84 E
baldwin@taftu.edu
BALDWIN, Darin 334-745-6437 3 G
dbaldwin@suscc.edu
BALDWIN, David, N 508-626-4645 212 D
dbaldwin@framingham.edu
BALDWIN, Deborah, J 501-569-3123 22 B
djbaldwin@ualr.edu
BALDWIN, Diane 617-353-4377 207 D
dbaldwin@bu.edu
BALDWIN, Dirk 262-595-2379 497 C
baldwin@uwp.edu
BALDWIN, Eric 509-313-4100 481 D
baldwine@gonzaga.edu
BALDWIN, Erin 515-294-7971 162 I
baldwine@iastate.edu
BALDWIN, James 518-464-8500 299 G
jbaldwin@excelsior.edu
BALDWIN, Latosha 202-274-6604 93 C
latosha.baldwin@udc.edu
BALDWIN, Laura 215-572-2909 379 A
baldwinl@arcadia.edu
BALDWIN, Mark 509-359-2449 480 E
mbaldwin@ewu.edu
BALDWIN, Melanie, C 302-295-1181 90 I
melanie.c.baldwin@wilmu.edu
BALDWIN, Michael 510-780-4500 47 J
mbaldwin@lifewest.edu
BALDWIN, Michelle 217-732-3155 141 I
mbaldwin@lincolncollege.edu
BALDWIN, Naomi 716-673-3451 317 A
naomi.baldwin@fredonia.edu
BALDWIN, R. Chad 636-584-6609 252 J
robert.baldwin@eastcentral.edu
BALDWIN, Ronda 740-474-8896 358 F
rbaldwin@ohiochristian.edu
BALDWIN, Sarah, T 859-858-3511 178 I
sarah.baldwin@asbury.edu
BALDWIN, Sharon 816-531-5223 251 H
BALDWIN, Stan 601-925-3321 247 C
sbaldwin@mc.edu
BALDWIN, Terri, M 740-588-1210 365 E
tbaldwin2@zanestate.edu
BALDWIN, Tony 704-216-6005 330 H
tbaldwin@livingstone.edu
BALDWIN, Tony 704-216-6272 330 H
tbaldwin@livingstone.edu
BALDWIN-DIMEO,
Caren 603-526-3714 272 H
cbaldwin-dimeo@colby-sawyer.edu
BALEE, Mary 901-678-3848 427 D
mbalee@memphis.edu
BALENTINE, Jerry 516-686-3999 309 F
jerry.balentine@nyit.edu
BALENTINE, Kim 417-626-1234 257 F
kbalentine@occ.edu
BALES, Jennifer 913-621-8733 172 K
jennifer@donnelly.edu
BALES, Kay 765-285-5344 153 C
kbales@bsu.edu
BALES, Michael 276-964-7323 475 I
michael.bales@sw.edu
BALES, Stefany 208-885-6567 131 G
sbales@uidaho.edu
BALES, William, J 615-898-5014 422 H
joe.bales@mtsu.edu
BALESTRA, Elisa 914-813-9242 315 F
ebalestra@sarahlawrence.edu
BALESTRERI, Teresa, A 314-516-5002 261 D
tkb@umsl.edu
BALEY, Heather 503-244-0726 371 G
heatherbaley@achs.edu
BALFOUR, Stephen, P 706-357-0049 125 G
stephen.balfour@uga.edu
BALGE, Daniel, N 507-354-8221 236 I
balgedn@mlc-wels.edu
BALINSKI, Joseph 231-439-6347 228 E
jbalinski@ncmich.edu
BALINSKI, Joseph 231-348-6600 228 E
jbalinski@ncmich.edu
BALINT, William, S 724-357-7854 394 G
wsbalint@iup.edu
BALK, Nicholas 518-694-7328 289 D
nicholas.balk@acphs.edu
BALKANSKY, Andrew 618-453-2466 149 E
cola.dean@siu.edu
BALL, Christine 706-771-4150 114 J
cball@augustatech.edu
BALL, Dave 319-296-4204 166 B
david.ball@hawkeyecollege.edu
BALL, Diane 352-588-8417 106 D
diane.ball@saintleo.edu
BALL, Don 330-494-6170 361 F
dball@starkstate.edu
BALL, Doug 620-235-4107 176 F
dbball@pittstate.edu
BALL, Drexel, B 803-535-5263 407 G
dball@claflin.edu
BALL, Gregory, F 301-405-1691 202 C
gball@umd.edu
BALL, James, D 410-386-8188 197 G
jball@carrollcc.edu
BALL, Jamie 618-650-2333 149 F
jball@siue.edu
BALL, Jason 561-297-3440 108 J
jball@fau.edu
BALL, Jennifer 785-670-1648 177 G
jennifer.ball@washburn.edu
BALL, Jennifer 315-268-4208 296 A
jball@clarkson.edu
BALL, John 504-568-4500 189 B
jball@lsuhsc.edu
BALL, Justin 309-677-3850 133 B
jball@bradley.edu
BALL, Karen 559-791-2420 47 A
kball@portervillecollege.edu
BALL, Kathy 304-384-6009 490 A
bonner@concord.edu

BANNER, Josephina ... 215-646-7300 385 D
banner.j@gmercyu.edu
BANNIGAN, Brendan ... 952-885-5413 242 I
bbannigan@nwhealth.edu
BANNIN, Bernard ... 419-289-5291 348 A
bbannin2@ashland.edu
BANNISTER, Darlene ... 830-792-7356 443 G
registrar@schreiner.edu
BANNISTER, Dustin ... 919-299-4817 340 J
dbannister@umo.edu
BANNISTER, Justin ... 575-646-5981 287 B
jbannist@nmsu.edu
BANNISTER, Kathleen ... 770-426-2787 121 C
kstavovy@life.edu
BANNISTER, Mark ... 208-426-1135 129 I
markbannister724@boisestate.edu
BANNISTER, Shelley ... 973-720-2104 284 I
bannisters@wpunj.edu
BANNON, Stephen ... 401-232-6001 404 F
sbannon@bryant.edu
BANO, Matthew ... 757-499-5447 467 J
BANREY, Vincent ... 718-262-2415 295 F
vbanrey@york.cuny.edu
BANSAL, Vibha ... 787-738-2161 513 D
vibha.bansal1@upr.edu
BANSAVICH, John ... 415-422-5529.. 71 K
bansavich@usfca.edu
BANTON, Cris ... 503-554-2167 373 C
cbanton@georgefox.edu
BANUELOS, Francisco .. 559-730-3942.. 39 E
franciscob@cos.edu
BANUELOS, Javier ... 562-860-2451.. 35 M
jbanuelos@cerritos.edu
BANUSH, David ... 504-865-5131 191 B
dbanush@tulane.edu
BANZ, Martha, L ... 405-325-6984 371 B
mlbanz@ou.edu
BAO, Paul ... 478-471-4394 120 F
pbao@helms.edu
BAOUA, Kesha ... 501-450-3824.. 19 F
baoua@hendrix.edu
BAPASOLA, Elizabeth ... 609-771-2455 276 I
bapasola@tcnj.edu
BAPTISTE, Brian ... 215-951-1425 387 C
BAPTISTE, JoRae ... 808-245-8323 129 C
jorae@hawaii.edu
BAPTISTE, Tyler, J ... 804-257-5630 477 C
tjbaptiste@vuu.edu
BAQUERO, Gloria, E ... 787-780-5134 510 F
gbaquero@nuc.edu
BAR, Rosann ... 732-255-0400 280 A
rbar@ocean.edu
BARABE, Becky ... 559-443-8514.. 66 E
becky.barabe@fresnocitycollege.edu
BARABINO, Gilda ... 212-650-5435 293 D
gbarabino@ccny.cuny.edu
BARAGONA, Michelle ... 662-720-7375 248 C
mabaragona@nemcc.edu
BARAJAS, Daniel ... 480-731-8220.. 12 O
daniel.barajas@domail.maricopa.edu
BARAJAS, Ruben ... 310-303-7293.. 51 B
rbarajas@marymountcalifornia.edu
BARAJAS, Silvia ... 805-378-1412.. 72 H
sbarajas@vcccd.edu
BARAKAT, Nabeel, M ... 310-233-4351.. 49 A
barakanm@lahc.edu
BARAKEH, Zeina ... 415-351-3571.. 60 G
zbarakeh@sfai.edu
BARAN, Kelley ... 508-531-2492 212 B
kelley.baran@bridgew.edu
BARAN-CENTENO,
Barbara ... 210-999-7507 452 A
bbarance@trinity.edu
BARANOWSKI, Carl ... 903-877-7704 456 D
carl.baranowski@uthct.edu
BARATO, Ruben ... 914-606-6777 325 C
ruben.barato@sunywcc.edu
BARATTA, Peter ... 609-626-6080 283 D
peter.baratta@stockton.edu
BARBA, Jesse, D ... 413-542-5485 205 B
jbarba@amherst.edu
BARBARICK, Cliff ... 325-674-3767 429 B
cab11c@acu.edu
BARBARICS, Kristen ... 770-426-2836 121 C
kristen.barbarics@life.edu
BARBATIS, Peter ... 561-868-3142 104 D
barbatip@palmbeachstate.edu
BARBEE, Brent ... 910-410-1809 337 B
btbarbee@richmondcc.edu
BARBEE, Chris ... 616-331-3590 224 E
barbeec@gvsu.edu
BARBEE, Daniel ... 419-530-1448 363 E
daniel.barbee@utoledo.edu

BARBEE, Danielle ... 856-225-2965 281 G
danielle.barbee@camden.rutgers.edu
BARBEE, Holly ... 252-493-7206 336 H
hbarbee@email.pittcc.edu
BARBEE, Julianna ... 505-747-2100 287 G
jbarbee@nnmc.edu
BARBEE, Kelsey ... 719-384-6834.. 81 E
kelsey.barbee@ojc.edu
BARBEITO, Patricia ... 401-709-6575 405 D
pbarbeit@risd.edu
BARBER, Afton ... 903-510-2305 452 C
afton.barber@tjc.edu
BARBER,
Bernadette (BJ) ... 626-584-5238.. 43 H
bjbarber@fuller.edu
BARBER, Billy ... 252-789-0303 335 H
billy.barber@martincc.edu
BARBER, Catherine ... 985-448-5916 187 F
catherine.barber@fletcher.edu
BARBER, Cindy ... 870-307-7527.. 20 A
cindy.barber@lyon.edu
BARBER, Eric ... 402-460-5722 267 F
ebarber@marylanning.org
BARBER, Glynis ... 410-951-3078 203 D
gbarber@coppin.edu
BARBER, Isaac ... 816-584-7401 258 A
isaac.barber@park.edu
BARBER, Jacques ... 516-877-4800 289 C
jbarber@adelphi.edu
BARBER, Jeff ... 843-863-7080 407 E
jbarber@csuniv.edu
BARBER, Jennifer ... 916-278-6295.. 32 E
jbarbar@csus.edu
BARBER, Jeremiah ... 816-501-4587 258 H
jeremiah.barber@rockhurst.edu
BARBER, Kimberly ... 850-644-6127 109 C
kabarber@admin.fsu.edu
BARBER, Lindsay ... 231-591-2697 223 J
lindsaybarber@ferris.edu
BARBER, Lori ... 208-535-5419 130 C
lori.barber@cei.edu
BARBER, Luanne ... 870-612-2119.. 22 I
luanne.barber@uaccb.edu
BARBER, Marcia, A ... 315-470-6611 320 A
mabarber@esf.edu
BARBER, Melinda ... 352-435-6351 102 T
barberm@lssc.edu
BARBER, Michelle ... 563-884-5106 168 I
michelle.barber@palmer.edu
BARBER, Richard ... 724-503-1001 402 E
rbarber@washjeff.edu
BARBER, Sarah ... 315-229-5083 314 F
sbarber@stlawu.edu
BARBER, Tracy ... 719-255-7507.. 83 B
tbarber@uccs.edu
BARBER, Trent, J ... 860-512-3283.. 85 G
tbarber@manchestercc.edu
BARBERA, Anthony ... 516-876-3135 319 A
barberaa@oldwestbury.edu
BARBERICH, Kim ... 609-896-5000 281 B
kbarberich@rider.edu
BARBIER GIBSON,
Yolanda ... 540-665-4795 471 E
ygibson@su.edu
BARBIERI, Lina ... 610-282-1100 382 E
lina.barbieri@desales.edu
BARBOSA, Amarildo ... 617-349-8643 210 H
abarbosa@lesley.edu
BARBOSA, Faviola ... 509-793-2305 478 H
faviolab@bigbend.edu
BARBOSA, Francisco ... 787-264-1912 509 F
fbarbosa@intersg.edu
BARBOSA, Mary Kate ... 207-768-9613 196 E
mary.barbosa@maine.edu
BARBOSA, Miguel ... 570-422-3545 394 E
mbarbosa@esu.edu
BARBOUR, A. Sandy ... 814-865-1086 392 B
asb25@psu.edu
BARBOUR, Channell ... 859-985-3251 179 C
barbourc@berea.edu
BARBOUR, Cheryl ... 303-546-3565.. 81 B
cheryl@naropa.edu
BARBOUR, Darrell ... 641-585-8138 170 B
darrell.barbour@waldorf.edu
BARBOUR, Jeffery ... 757-340-2121 465 M
librariancvab@centura.edu
BARBOUR, Monica ... 313-993-1951 231 B
barboumm@udmercy.edu
BARBOUR, Suzanne ... 706-542-6392 125 G
sbarbour@uga.edu
BARBU, Diana ... 305-237-7450 103 D
dbarbu@mdc.edu
BARBU, Diana ... 305-625-6576 106 F
dbarbu@stu.edu

BARCHI, Robert ... 848-932-7454 281 G
president@rutgers.edu
BARCHI, Robert ... 848-932-7454 282 A
president@rutgers.edu
BARCHI, Robert ... 848-932-7454 282 B
president@rutgers.edu
BARCLAY, Beth ... 563-884-5586 168 I
beth.barclay@palmer.edu
BARCLAY, Kent ... 978-232-2282 209 B
kbarclay@endicott.edu
BARCO, Jessica ... 657-278-5256.. 31 E
jbarco@fullerton.edu
BARCUS, Krista ... 660-562-1128 257 E
kbarcus@nwmissouri.edu
BARD, Sharon, K ... 704-463-3428 339 E
sharon.bard@pfeiffer.edu
BARDEGUEZ, Lemuel ... 405-682-7814 367 H
lbardeguez@occc.edu
BARDELL, Kathleen ... 617-449-7430 219 C
kathleen.bardell@urbancollege.edu
BARDEN, John ... 203-432-3262.. 89 D
john.barden@yale.edu
BARDEN, JR ... 512-404-4805 431 C
jrbarden@austinseminary.edu
BARDILL MOSCARITOLO,
Lisa ... 914-773-3860 311 E
lbardillmoscaritolo@pace.edu
BARDINE, Hunt ... 610-526-6012 385 G
hbardine@harcum.edu
BARDNEY, Eileen ... 845-569-3254 307 J
eileen.bardney@msmc.edu
BARE, Benita ... 276-944-6800 467 G
bbare@ehc.edu
BAREFIELD, Kevin ... 662-685-4771 245 D
kbarefield@bmc.edu
BAREFOOT, Jon ... 317-921-4882 157 G
jon.barefoot@ivytech.edu
BAREFOOT, Russell ... 908-526-1200 281 A
russell.barefoot@raritanval.edu
BARELMAN, Jason ... 402-375-7327 268 G
jabarel1@wsc.edu
BARENDS, Frans ... 404-894-5000 118 F
frans.barends@business.gatech.edu
BARENTINE, Julie ... 504-816-8595 190 A
jbarentine@nobts.edu
BARFIELD, Craig ... 919-760-8516 331 B
craigb@meredith.edu
BARFIELD, Julie ... 817-272-2584 454 J
barfield@uta.edu
BARFIELD, Kem ... 860-215-9210.. 86 F
kbarfield@threerivers.edu
BARFIELD, Kem ... 860-215-9210.. 86 F
kbarfield@trcc.commnet.edu
BARFOOT, D. Scott ... 214-887-5151 436 B
sbarfoot@dts.edu
BARFUSS, Blair ... 435-652-7515 460 G
blair.barfuss@dixie.edu
BARGA, Brian ... 619-201-8951.. 65 A
brian.barga@socalsem.edu
BARGAR, Mollie ... 601-928-6345 247 E
mollie.bargar@mgccc.edu
BARGAS, DeLynn ... 575-562-2175 285 M
delynn.bargas@enmu.edu
BARGE, Gayle ... 425-564-2282 478 F
gayle.barge@bellevuecollege.edu
BARGE, Scott ... 540-432-4304 466 G
scott.barge@emu.edu
BARGE-MILES, Linda ... 850-599-3225 108 I
linda.bargemiles@famu.edu
BARGER, Adam, P ... 757-221-1635 466 C
apbarger@wm.edu
BARGER, Debbie, M ... 515-263-6012 165 I
dbarger@grandview.edu
BARGER, Eric, C ... 503-943-7337 377 E
barger@up.edu
BARGER, Judith ... 678-916-2653 114 I
jbarger@johnmarshall.edu
BARGER, Peter, S ... 630-637-5362 144 H
psbarger@noctrl.edu
BARGER, Teresa ... 412-809-5100 396 H
barger.teresa@ptcollege.edu
BARGERON, Jay ... 703-784-2105 503 H
BARGO, Sarah ... 417-447-7813 257 G
bargos@otc.edu
BARHAM, James ... 731-286-3371 425 A
jbarham@dscc.edu
BARHAM, Kelly ... 757-455-3366 477 F
kbarham@vwu.edu
BARHAM, Treva ... 903-233-3470 439 E
trevabarham@letu.edu
BARIA, Jo Ann ... 253-964-6640 483 D
jbaria@pierce.ctc.edu

BARIL, Kathleen, T ... 419-772-2180 358 H
k-baril@onu.edu
BARILAR, Stephen, J ... 570-577-3333 379 F
steve.barilar@bucknell.edu
BARILE, Brandon ... 315-781-3051 302 A
barile@hws.edu
BARILLO, Madeline, K .. 203-857-7039.. 86 D
mbarillo@norwalk.edu
BARILOVITS, Karlyn ... 866-492-5336 244 F
karlyn.barilovits@mail.waldenu.edu
BARIOLA, Kristi ... 662-246-6376 247 D
kbariola@msdelta.edu
BARISH, Robert ... 312-413-0340 151 B
rbarish@uic.edu
BARKALOW, Susan ... 252-823-5166 334 C
barkalows@edgecombe.edu
BARKAN, Chester ... 516-572-7131 308 A
chester.barkan@ncc.edu
BARKE, Brady, L ... 573-651-2227 259 K
bbarke@semo.edu
BARKER, Allyn, S ... 304-896-7404 489 E
allyn.barker@southernwv.edu
BARKER, Anita, S ... 530-898-6470.. 31 A
abarker@csuchico.edu
BARKER, Blake ... 214-648-2168 457 B
blake.barker@utsouthwestern.edu
BARKER, Brett ... 843-377-2149 407 D
bbarker@charlestonlaw.edu
BARKER, Brian ... 970-945-8691.. 77 K
BARKER, Bruce, A ... 715-833-6221 499 D
bbarker@cvtc.edu
BARKER, Curtis ... 336-841-9372 329 G
cbarker@highpoint.edu
BARKER, Eddie ... 606-337-3196 179 G
BARKER, Jeanette ... 919-530-6735 342 A
jbarker@nccu.edu
BARKER, Jeffrey, H ... 864-596-9091 409 B
jeff.barker@converse.edu
BARKER, John, D ... 864-294-2106 410 A
john.barker@furman.edu
BARKER, John, F ... 716-286-8220 310 D
jfb@niagara.edu
BARKER, Lee ... 773-256-3000 143 C
lbarker@meadville.edu
BARKER, Lisa ... 941-359-4340 110 D
lisab@usf.edu
BARKER, Marco ... 402-472-3751 269 J
marco.barker@unl.edu
BARKER, MarQuita ... 336-278-7300 328 K
mbarker4@elon.edu
BARKER, Michael ... 919-843-5684 342 D
michael_barker@unc.edu
BARKER, Neva ... 909-621-8306.. 63 E
neva.barker@scrippscollege.edu
BARKER, Randy ... 910-892-3178 329 F
rbarker@heritagebiblecollege.edu
BARKER, Rhonda ... 850-872-3857 100 N
rbarker@gulfcoast.edu
BARKER, Ryan ... 315-470-5710 291 H
ryanbarker@crouse.org
BARKER, Stephen ... 949-824-8792.. 68 G
barker@uci.edu
BARKER, Tess ... 810-762-3322 231 G
tessba@umich.edu
BARKER, Yvette ... 713-313-7201 449 C
yvette.barker@tsu.edu
BARKHAMER, Kim ... 215-596-8800 401 G
BARKLEY, Alexander ... 914-323-3172 305 J
alexander.barkley@mville.edu
BARKLEY, Beatrice, L ... 215-368-5000 390 F
bbarkley@missio.edu
BARKLEY, Bill ... 866-492-5336 244 F
william.barkley@mail.waldenu.edu
BARKLEY, Brian ... 770-836-6830 127 A
brian.barkley@westgatech.edu
BARKLEY, Jordan ... 254-968-9089 446 E
jbarkley@tarleton.edu
BARKLEY, Susan, E ... 972-238-6943 435 F
sbarkley@dcccd.edu
BARKLEY-GIFFIN,
Adrienne ... 618-985-3741 139 I
adriennebarkley@jalc.edu
BARKO, James, N ... 972-881-5847 433 M
jbarko@collin.edu
BARKO, Valerie ... 808-245-8336 129 C
vabarko@hawaii.edu
BARKOFF, Larry ... 734-677-5413 232 B
lbarkoff@wccnet.edu
BARKOW, Aisha ... 414-297-7035 500 B
barkowa@matc.edu
BARKOWITZ, Daniel, T . 407-582-1458 112 K
dbarkowitz@valenciacollege.edu

BARKSCHAT, Kate .... 828-395-1163 335 D kbarkschat@isothermal.edu
BARKSDALE, Glasetta ... 312-850-7288 134 H gbarksdale@ccc.edu
BARKSDALE, Tina, M ... 302-356-6940.. 90 I tina.m.barksdale@wilmu.edu
BARKWILL, Joseph .... 516-463-6623 302 B joseph.barkwill@hofstra.edu
BARLAND, Karen .... 410-951-3704 203 D kbarland@coppin.edu
BARLETT, Paul .... 913-234-0632 172 E paul.barlett@cleveland.edu
BARLEY, Tracy .... 225-771-2304 190 H tracy_barley@subr.edu
BARLOK, Tracy .... 508-793-3776 208 B tbarlok@holycross.edu
BARLOW, Angela .... 501-450-3124.. 23 H abarlow5@uca.edu
BARLOW, Charlene .... 859-344-3348 184 F barlowc@thomasmore.edu
BARLOW, Christopher .. 405-744-7665 368 B christopher.barlow@okstate.edu
BARLOW, Felicia, R ...... 336-633-0244 337 A frbarlow@randolph.edu
BARLOW, Jean Ann ...... 918-647-1213 365 H jbarlow@carlalbert.edu
BARLOW, Justin .... 678-839-5000 126 E jbarlow@westga.edu
BARLOW, Marlene, T .... 215-968-8000 379 G barlowm@bucks.edu
BARLOW, Michael .... 270-706-8614 181 A mbarlow0002@kctcs.edu
BARLOW, Sarah .... 225-216-8687 186 K barlows@mybrcc.edu
BARLOW, Steve .... 307-855-2029 501 V sbarlow@cwc.edu
BARLOW-KELLEY, Jill ... 207-801-5633 193 F jbk@coa.edu
BARMANN, Terry .... 303-797-5738.. 76 I terrence.barmann@arapahoe.edu
BARNABY, Mike .... 218-855-8039 237 F mbarnaby@clcmn.edu
BARNARD, Cheryl .... 619-388-7313.. 60 E cbarnard@sdccd.edu
BARNARD, Cindy .... 865-573-4517 420 G cbarnard@johnsonu.edu
BARNARD, DeeDee .... 828-395-1292 335 D ddbarnard@isothermal.edu
BARNARD, James .... 513-556-6014 362 D james.barnard@uc.edu
BARNARD, Kathy .... 208-885-7372 131 G kathybarnard@uidaho.edu
BARNARD, Laura .... 440-525-7096 355 H lbarnard@lakelandcc.edu
BARNARD, Mimi .... 615-460-8397 418 F mimi.barnard@belmont.edu
BARNARD, Susan .... 201-447-7938 275 H sbarnard@bergen.edu
BARNDS, W. Kent .... 309-794-7314 132 C wkentbarnds@augustana.edu
BARNELLO, Inga .... 315-445-4321 304 C barnello@lemoyne.edu
BARNER, Becky .... 308-535-3625 267 K barnerb@mpcc.edu
BARNES, Andre .... 844-283-2246.. 93 A
BARNES, Andrew .... 850-973-1604 103 K barnesa@nfcc.edu
BARNES, Andrew .... 718-636-3570 311 J awbarnes@pratt.edu
BARNES, Benjamin .... 860-723-0000.. 84 H
BARNES, Bradley .... 205-934-4073.... 8 A bbarnes1@uab.edu
BARNES, Brian, M .... 907-474-7649.. 10 A bmbarnes@alaska.edu
BARNES, Cory .... 706-233-7681 124 B cbarnes@shorter.edu
BARNES, David .... 907-474-6222.. 10 A dlbarnesl@alaska.edu
BARNES, David .... 251-981-3771.... 5 B david.barnes@columbiasouthern.edu
BARNES, David .... 303-914-6260.. 82 C david.barnes@rrcc.edu
BARNES, Dewayne .... 415-703-9573.. 28 D dbarnes@cca.edu
BARNES, Elizabeth, A ... 248-689-8282 232 A bbarnes@walshcollege.edu
BARNES, Emily .... 800-686-1883 222 E ebarnes@cleary.edu
BARNES, Eric .... 303-964-3628.. 82 E ebarnes002@regis.edu
BARNES, Gary .... 806-742-9000 450 F
BARNES, Huston .... 270-384-8250 183 C barnesh@lindsey.edu
BARNES, III, James, H . 651-638-6230 234 C j-barnes@bethel.edu
BARNES, Jeffrey .... 951-552-8639.. 27 J jbarnes@calbaptist.edu
BARNES, Jimmy .... 575-624-8021 287 A jimmyb@nmmi.edu
BARNES, Joanne .... 765-677-2090 157 D joanne.barnes@indwes.edu
BARNES, Joseph .... 646-717-9704 300 G eadp@gts.edu
BARNES, Julianna .... 619-660-4221.. 44 H julianna.barnes@gcccd.edu
BARNES, Katharine, T ... 401-863-1914 404 E katharine_barnes@brown.edu
BARNES, Kathleen .... 978-232-2292 209 B kbarnes@endicott.edu
BARNES, Kathleen .... 978-542-6000 213 C
BARNES, Kathryn, M .... 336-917-5565 340 D kathym.barnes@salem.edu
BARNES, Kathy .... 423-461-8710 422 J mkbarnes@milligan.edu
BARNES, Keith .... 601-977-4479 249 C kbarnes4@tougaloo.edu
BARNES, Keith .... 719-502-2828.. 81 F keith.barnes@ppcc.edu
BARNES, Kelly .... 706-295-6842 119 A kbarnes@gntc.edu
BARNES, Kerry .... 413-205-3703 205 A kerry.barnes@aic.edu
BARNES, Kevin .... 501-370-5367.. 20 G kbarnes@philander.edu
BARNES, Kim .... 989-386-6622 227 F kbarnes@midmich.edu
BARNES, Lori .... 607-746-4692 320 G
BARNES, Lori .... 941-727-2273 111 B lbarnes@schnursing.edu
BARNES, Lynn .... 979-458-0971 446 G lbarnes@tamu.edu
BARNES, M. Craig .... 609-497-7800 280 D president@ptsem.edu
BARNES, Marc .... 504-816-4359 186 D mbarnes@dillard.edu
BARNES, Mario, L .... 206-543-2586 485 F mbarnes3@uw.edu
BARNES, Mark .... 217-443-8871 135 H mbarnes@dacc.edu
BARNES, Melissa .... 757-823-8131 469 F mbarnes@nsu.edu
BARNES, Mike .... 800-686-1883 222 E mbarnes@my.cleary.edu
BARNES, Nancy .... 909-667-4470.. 37 H nbarnes@claremontlincoln.edu
BARNES, Nicole .... 724-287-8711 380 A nicole.barnes@bc3.edu
BARNES, Nicole .... 281-478-3628 443 C nicole.barnes@sjcd.edu
BARNES, Nina, M .... 651-628-3416 244 D nmbarnes@unwsp.edu
BARNES, Pamela .... 217-424-6244 143 H pjbarnes@millikin.edu
BARNES, Randy .... 619-388-3489.. 60 C rbarnes@sdccd.edu
BARNES, Rebecca .... 315-781-3341 302 A barnes@hws.edu
BARNES, Rita .... 931-372-3797 426 E ritabarnes@tntech.edu
BARNES, Saralyn .... 702-968-1611 272 C sbarnes@roseman.edu
BARNES, Scott .... 541-737-0123 375 D
BARNES, Scott, F .... 724-847-6787 384 G sfbarnes@geneva.edu
BARNES, Shelly .... 252-527-6223 335 G swbarnes16@lenoircc.edu
BARNES, Susan .... 405-491-6365 370 A sbarnes@snu.edu
BARNES, Travis .... 218-755-3988 237 E travis.barnes@bemidjistate.edu
BARNES, Vicki .... 251-981-3771.... 5 B vicki.barnes@columbiasouthern.edu
BARNES-TILLEY, Mary, E .... 972-881-5891 433 M mbarnestilley@collin.edu
BARNES WHYTE, Susan .... 503-883-2517 373 H swhyte@linfield.edu
BARNETT, Alan .... 660-359-3948 257 D abarnett@mail.ncmissouri.edu
BARNETT, Amy .... 765-998-5565 160 F ambarnett@tayloru.edu
BARNETT, Brad .... 540-568-7820 468 F barnetbd@jmu.edu
BARNETT, Brandy .... 352-245-4119 111 E brandy.barnett@taylorcollege.edu
BARNETT, Bryant .... 828-227-7303 344 A barnett@wcu.edu
BARNETT, Darryl .... 580-774-3178 370 C darryl.barnett@swosu.edu
BARNETT, David .... 630-960-7927 136 A dbarnett@devry.edu
BARNETT, David, L .... 770-531-3116 115 D dlbarnett@brenau.edu
BARNETT, Dawn .... 610-902-1071 380 C dawn.barnett@cabrini.edu
BARNETT, Erin .... 906-487-7324 223 K erin.barnett@finlandia.edu
BARNETT, Fatima .... 832-813-6571 439 G fatima.barnett@lonestar.edu
BARNETT, Jahnae, H ...... 800-995-3159 262 G jahnae.barnett@williamwoods.edu
BARNETT, Jeffrey .... 410-617-2608 199 F jbarnett@loyola.edu
BARNETT, Jenifer .... 707-664-3102.. 34 C jenifer.barnett@sonoma.edu
BARNETT, Jonathan ...... 509-682-6835 486 E jbarnett@wvc.edu
BARNETT, Kristine .... 413-565-1000 205 G kbarnett@baypath.edu
BARNETT, Lee .... 251-981-3771.... 5 B lee.barnett@columbiasouthern.edu
BARNETT, Lenice .... 954-486-7728 112 D registrar@uftl.edu
BARNETT, Martha .... 731-881-7052 428 B mbarne37@utm.edu
BARNETT, Mike .... 785-628-4251 173 B mbarnett@fhsu.edu
BARNETT, Monica .... 918-444-2230 367 A barnettm@nsuok.edu
BARNETT, Nora .... 503-760-3131 371 H nora@birthingway.edu
BARNETT, Randy .... 580-774-6051 370 C randy.barnett@swosu.edu
BARNETT, Robert .... 810-766-6878 231 G rbarnett@umich.edu
BARNETT, Ron .... 641-472-1110 167 F rbarnett@mum.edu
BARNETT-PARKER, Janie .... 425-640-1787 480 F jbarnett@edcc.edu
BARNETTE, Andrew .... 724-925-4047 403 A barnettea@westmoreland.edu
BARNETTE, Jeffrey .... 270-686-4359 179 D jeffrey.barnette@brescia.edu
BARNETTE, Kelli .... 740-376-4604 356 A kmb003@marietta.edu
BARNETTE, Todd .... 864-656-4926 408 A tebarne@clemson.edu
BARNETTE, Vivian, D .... 336-334-7727 341 F vdbarnet@ncat.edu
BARNEY, Patti .... 954-201-7520.. 95 H pbarney@broward.edu
BARNEY, Tammy .... 504-286-5343 190 I tbarney@suno.edu
BARNHARDT, Carmen, N .... 714-449-7423.. 51 A cbarnhardt@ketchum.edu
BARNHARDT, David ...... 304-214-8820 489 F dbarnhardt@wvncc.edu
BARNHARDT, Wendy .... 704-216-3700 337 F wendy.barnhardt@rccc.edu
BARNHART, Amy .... 336-744-0900 327 F ccc@outfitters4.com
BARNHART, Amy .... 937-327-7318 364 H barnharta1@wittenberg.edu
BARNHART, Ben .... 970-351-2551.. 83 E ben.barnhart@unco.edu
BARNHART, Bruce .... 724-938-4407 394 B barnhart@calu.edu
BARNHART, Cynthia ..... 617-253-9742 215 G
BARNHART, Daniel .... 410-455-3619 202 E barnhart@umbc.edu
BARNHART, Kristin .... 989-275-5000 226 B kristin.barnhard@kirtland.edu
BARNHART, Michael ..... 740-351-3212 360 K mbarnhart@shawnee.edu
BARNHART, Mitch, S ... 859-257-8015 185 B mbarn@email.uky.edu
BARNHART, Ross .... 719-549-3365.. 81 K ross.barnhart@pueblocc.edu
BARNHART, Ryan .... 724-938-4418 394 B barnhart_r@calu.edu
BARNHILL, Anita .... 606-248-0137 182 E anita.barnhill@kctcs.edu
BARNHILL, Carol .... 870-972-2028.. 17 G cbarnhil@astate.edu
BARNHILL, John .... 850-644-1224 109 C jbarnhill@admin.fsu.edu
BARNHILL, Rob, M .... 262-243-5700 493 B rob.barnhill@cuw.edu
BARNHILL, Tapp .... 802-254-6370 464 B stb08170@ccv.vsc.edu
BARNHOUSE, Richard ... 941-752-5301 108 G barnhr@scf.edu
BARNIKOW, Thomas, E 989-964-4000 230 B
BARNOW, Blyth .... 510-549-4719.. 66 B bbarnow@sksm.edu
BARNUM, Chrisopher, C .... 563-333-6157 169 A barnumchristopherc@sau.edu
BARNUM, David, L .... 402-280-2307 266 I davidbarnum@creighton.edu
BARNUM, Laura, J .... 716-878-4311 318 C barnumlj@buffalostate.edu
BARNUM, Siv Serene ... 503-338-2407 372 E sbarnum@clatsopcc.edu
BARNWELL, Brenda ...... 630-947-8933 132 D bbarnwell@aurora.edu
BARNWELL, Jon, R .... 252-328-6964 341 C barnwellj17@ecu.edu
BARNWELL, Michael ..... 716-286-8637 310 D barnwell@niagara.edu
BARNWELL, Vollie .... 828-251-6700 342 C vbarnwel@unca.edu
BARON, Bruce .... 909-382-4091.. 59 G bbaron@sbccd.cc.ca.us
BARON, David .... 909-469-8835.. 74 I dbaron@westernu.edu
BARON, Kit .... 626-396-2200.. 26 E
BARON, Melissa, M ..... 724-946-7927 402 G baronmm@westminster.edu
BARON, Sara .... 412-396-6130 383 C barons1@duq.edu
BARONAS, James .... 410-328-8792 202 D jbaro001@umaryland.edu
BARONAS, Lynn .... 860-768-4388.. 88 H baronas@hartford.edu
BARONE, OSF, Ann Carmen .... 419-824-3703 355 K acarmen@lourdes.edu
BARONE, Joseph .... 848-445-6814 282 A jbarone@pharmacy.rutgers.edu
BARONET, Mary .... 318-487-5443 187 C marybaronet@cltcc.edu
BARONI, Mitch .... 715-831-7229 499 D mbaroni@cvtc.edu
BARONIO, Lisa .... 816-235-2672 261 C lbbk2y@umkc.edu
BAROODY, Fadi, N .... 843-349-2058 408 C fadi@coastal.edu
BAROUDI, George .... 516-299-3790 304 G george.baroudi@liu.edu
BARQUINERO, James, M .... 203-365-4763.. 88 B barquineroj@sacredheart.edu
BARR, Carol, A .... 413-545-6330 211 D cbarr@provost.umass.edu
BARR, Chris .... 618-252-5400 149 C chris.barr@sic.edu
BARR, Cindy .... 828-262-7244 341 B barrcl@appstate.edu
BARR, Danielle .... 240-895-4202 201 E ddbarr@smcm.edu
BARR, Elizabeth .... 352-588-8824 106 D elizabeth.barr@saintleo.edu
BARR, Jason .... 803-536-8749 412 C jbarr2@scsu.edu
BARR, K. Jill .... 410-455-1337 202 E jbarr@umbc.edu
BARR, Kevin .... 812-237-3600 155 G kevin.barr@indstate.edu
BARR, Krispin, W .... 336-721-2627 340 D krispin.barr@salem.edu
BARR, Lisa .... 661-291-3411.. 28 K lbarr@calarts.edu
BARR, Michael, S .... 734-763-2258 231 E msbarr@umich.edu
BARR, Nakia .... 517-355-6560 227 D nwhite@msu.edu
BARR, Rick .... 903-886-5744 447 B rick.barr@tamuc.edu
BARR, Robin .... 386-506-4473.. 97 D robin.barr@daytonastate.edu
BARR, Rodney .... 660-562-1620 257 E rbarr@nwmissouri.edu
BARR, Sarah .... 402-465-2193 268 H sbarr@nebrwesleyan.edu
BARR, Victor .... 865-974-2196 427 G vbarr@utk.edu
BARR-GILLESPIE, Ann ... 503-352-7200 375 G barr-gillespie@pacificu.edu

BARR-GILLESPIE, Peter . 503-494-8311 375 B
BARR-JEFFREY, Sharon 206-281-2887 484 D
barrs@spu.edu
BARRA, Frank 201-692-2237 277 K
frank_barra@fdu.edu
BARRACATO, Denee 718-262-5115 295 F
dbarracato@york.cuny.edu
BARRACK, Keith, D 973-655-4213 279 C
barrackk@mail.montclair.edu
BARRACLOUGH, Diana . 610-499-4153 403 B
dbarraclough@widener.edu
BARRACLOUGH,
Jessica 785-670-1723 177 G
jessica.barraclough@washburn.edu
BARRAGAN, Joseph 254-526-1427 432 H
joseph.barragan@ctcd.edu
BARRALE, Ralph 636-227-2100 254 G
BARRAR, Elena 610-558-5516 391 D
barrare@neumann.edu
BARRAS, Brittney 504-278-6427 188 A
bbarras@nunez.edu
BARRAZA, Ana Lilia 562-907-4912.. 75 A
abarraza@whittier.edu
BARREDO, Ronald 615-963-5924 426 D
rbarredo@tnstate.edu
BARREE, Zita, M 434-223-6265 468 A
zbarree@hsc.edu
BARRENTINE, Debra, A . 256-228-6001.... 3 B
barrentined@nacc.edu
BARRENTINE, Jim 719-502-2148.. 81 F
jim.barrentine@ppcc.edu
BARRENTINE, Roger 636-481-3106 254 A
rbarrent@jeffco.edu
BARRERA, Adriana, D ... 213-891-2081.. 48 G
barrerad@email.laccd.edu
BARRERA, Leonor 956-295-3436 449 D
leonor.barrera@tsc.edu
BARRERA, Rosa, M 316-284-5241 171 F
rbarrera@bethelks.edu
BARRERAS, Lysette 787-758-2525 513 G
lysette.barreras@upr.edu
BARRESI, JR., Joseph .. 401-598-1000 404 I
jbarresi@jwu.edu
BARRETO, Betsy 240-895-4410 201 E
cbbarreto@gmail.com
BARRETO, Wanda 787-758-2480 513 G
wanda.barreto@upr.edu
BARRETT, Adam 203-582-3250.. 87 G
adam.barrett@quinnipiac.edu
BARRETT, Audra 972-860-8261 435 A
audrabarrett@dcccd.edu
BARRETT, Brian, D 817-515-6960 445 G
brian.barrett@tccd.edu
BARRETT, David 714-816-0366.. 67 I
david.barrett@trident.edu
BARRETT, Dustin 912-650-6250 124 E
dbarrett@southuniversity.edu
BARRETT, Gaylon 903-434-8250 441 B
gbarrett@ntcc.edu
BARRETT, Gretchen 412-362-8500 396 G
librarian@pims.edu
BARRETT, James 920-924-6431 500 C
jbarrett8@morainepark.edu
BARRETT, James, F 330-325-6274 357 G
jbarrett@neomed.edu
BARRETT, Joan 417-447-6914 257 G
barrettj@otc.edu
BARRETT, Kimberly 920-832-7451 493 K
kimberly.a.barrett@lawrence.edu
BARRETT, Laura 845-257-3520 317 B
barrettl@newpaltz.edu
BARRETT, Lawrence 386-752-1822.. 99 A
lawrence.barrett@fgc.edu
BARRETT, Leah 307-675-0121 502 F
lbarrett@sheridan.edu
BARRETT, Linda 401-874-2509 406 B
lindab@uri.edu
BARRETT, Mary, C 607-735-1790 299 D
mbarrett@elmira.edu
BARRETT, Michael 616-432-3412 229 I
michael.barrett@prts.edu
BARRETT, Micheal 845-938-4041 504 H
8sja@usma.edu
BARRETT, Pam, J 770-534-6176 115 D
pbarrett@brenau.edu
BARRETT, Pamela 505-438-8884 288 C
BARRETT, Sarah 518-244-2441 313 D
barres2@sage.edu
BARRETT, Scott 765-998-4917 160 F
scott_barrett@taylor.edu
BARRETT, Steve 507-389-2015 239 C
steve.barrett@mnsu.edu

BARRETT, William 570-740-0305 389 D
wbarrett@luzerne.edu
BARRETT, Zunilka 617-287-7050 211 C
zbarrett@umassp.edu
BARRETTA, Jacqueline .. 503-370-6004 378 B
jbarretta@willamette.edu
BARRETTE, Catherine .... 313-577-1615 232 I
c.barrette@wayne.edu
BARREZUETA, Carlos .... 908-709-7509 284 C
carlos.barrezueta1@ucc.edu
BARRICELLI, Franca 978-665-3627 212 C
fbarrice@fitchburgstate.edu
BARRICK, Jane 218-312-1529 238 C
janebarrick@hibbing.edu
BARRIENTOS, Joe 206-934-6788 484 B
joe.barrientos@seattlecolleges.edu
BARRIER, Jeremy 256-766-6610.... 5 F
jbarrier@hcu.edu
BARRINGER, Al 409-882-3077 450 A
al.barringer@lsco.edu
BARRINGER, Judy 212-659-7215 304 B
jbarringer@tkc.edu
BARRINGER, Susan, J .. 336-217-7221 329 D
susan.barringer@greensboro.edu
BARRINGER, Tony 239-590-7849 108 K
tbarring@fgcu.edu
BARRINGHAUS, Jill 660-248-6977 251 B
jbarring@centralmethodist.edu
BARRINGTON, Beverly .. 850-599-8316 108 I
beverly.barrington@famu.edu
BARRINGTON, Ruth, A . 401-825-2184 404 H
rbarrington@ccri.edu
BARRIO, Brian 860-832-3000.. 84 I
BARRIO-SOTILLO,
Ramona 818-240-1000.. 44 B
rbarrio@glendale.edu
BARRIOS, Kristin 626-568-8850.. 48 F
kristin@lacm.edu
BARRIOS, Sharon, A 530-898-4473.. 31 A
sbarrios@csuchico.edu
BARRIS, Brad 706-236-2272 115 B
bbarris@berry.edu
BARRISH, David, J 804-523-5934 474 H
dbarrish@reynolds.edu
BARRON, Alexandra, L . 512-464-8878 442 M
alexb@stedwards.edu
BARRON, Caulyne 602-648-5750.. 12 D
cbarron@dunlap-stone.edu
BARRON, David 706-731-7951 115 A
david.barron@augusta.edu
BARRON, Deborah 314-539-5220 259 C
deborahbarron@stlcc.edu
BARRON, Dori 828-448-3170 339 A
dbarron@wpcc.edu
BARRON, Eric, J 814-865-7611 392 B
president@psu.edu
BARRON, Jose 575-624-8263 287 A
barron@nmmi.edu
BARRON, Kim 303-605-5281.. 80 N
kbarron3@msudenver.edu
BARRON, Lee 314-275-3510 146 E
lee.barron@principia.edu
BARRON, Matthew 906-217-4054 221 O
barronm@baycollege.edu
BARRON, Nicole 312-341-2114 147 H
nbarron03@roosevelt.edu
BARRON, Robert 515-263-6195 165 I
rbarron@grandview.edu
BARRON, Sebastian 903-434-8260 441 B
sbarron@ntcc.edu
BARROSS, Ben 419-530-7877 363 E
ben.barros@utoledo.edu
BARROTT, James 423-697-3211 424 E
jim.barrott@chattanoogastate.edu
BARROW, Carla 229-225-5077 125 A
cbarrow@southernregional.edu
BARROW, Christine, E .. 301-546-0419 201 C
barowce@pgcc.edu
BARROW, Danny 225-578-1175 188 I
dbarrow1@lsu.edu
BARROW, Deborah, L ... 940-397-4212 440 F
debbie.barrow@msutexas.edu
BARROW, Laurie 717-901-5143 385 K
lbarrow@harrisburgu.edu
BARROWS, India 603-428-2293 273 H
ibarrows@nec.edu
BARROWS, Karen, A 585-475-2396 313 A
karen.barrows@rit.edu
BARROWS, Robert 617-228-2241 214 A
rbarrows@bhcc.mass.edu
BARRY, Carol 225-578-1480 188 I
carolbarry@lsu.edu

BARRY, Catherine 603-578-8900 273 A
cbarry@ccsnh.edu
BARRY, Chris 217-786-2410 142 B
chris.barry@llcc.edu
BARRY, Danyell 478-827-3232 118 A
barnesd@fvsu.edu
BARRY, Ernie 214-768-2004 444 E
ebarry@smu.edu
BARRY, James 215-242-7764 381 D
barryj@chc.edu
BARRY, James (Tim) .... 304-457-6317 487 B
barryjt@ab.edu
BARRY, Jeannette 402-375-7466 268 G
jebarry1@wsc.edu
BARRY, Jessica 937-294-0592 356 H
jessica.barry@themodern.edu
BARRY, John, M 804-289-8778 472 L
jbarry2@richmond.edu
BARRY, Kevin, G 302-295-1170.. 90 I
kevin.g.barry@wilmu.edu
BARRY, Lisa 508-856-6507 212 A
lisa.barry@umassmed.edu
BARRY, Liz 858-566-1200.. 41 E
lbarry@disd.edu
BARRY, Maria 202-885-2121.. 90 J
mariab@american.edu
BARRY, Michael, F 713-646-1819 444 B
mbarry@stcl.edu
BARRY, Richard 610-526-6532 379 E
rbarry@brynmawr.edu
BARRY, Sandra 617-254-2610 218 D
sandy.barry@sjs.edu
BARRY, Seana 541-318-3772 372 B
sbarry@cocc.edu
BARRY, Terry 570-422-3377 394 E
tbarry1@esu.edu
BARRY, Theresa 262-524-7334 492 E
tbarry@carrollu.edu
BARRY-ARQUIT,
Rachel, E 503-943-8223 377 E
rbarry@up.edu
BARSTAD, Joel 412-312-8383 380 B
jbarstad@bcs.edu
BARSTAD, Joel 303-715-3184.. 82 H
joel.barstad@archden.org
BARTA, Gary 319-335-9435 163 A
gary-barta@uiowa.edu
BARTA, Jim 218-755-2965 237 E
jim.barta@bemidjistate.edu
BARTA, Lou 217-641-4215 140 A
lbarta@jwcc.edu
BARTEAU, Mark, A 979-845-8585 446 G
barteau@tamu.edu
BARTEE, Robert 402-559-4203 270 A
bbartee@unmc.edu
BARTEK, Jennifer, J 724-738-2339 395 F
jennifer.bartek@sru.edu
BARTEL, Charles, R 412-396-1090 383 C
bartelc@duq.edu
BARTEL, Mae 918-223-1363 368 D
mbartel@osugiving.com
BARTEL, Steven, J 605-256-5146 416 J
steve.bartel@dsu.edu
BARTEL, Tonia 660-831-4105 256 G
bartelt@moval.edu
BARTELL, LaNeil, R 605-336-6588 416 E
BARTELL, William 605-331-6703 417 E
bill.bartell@usiouxfalls.edu
BARTELS, Dennis 614-416-6200 349 B
dbartels@bradfordschoolcolumbus.edu
BARTELS, Kirsten 318-357-4577 192 C
bartelsk@nsula.edu
BARTELS, Michael 563-387-1352 167 E
bartmi03@luther.edu
BARTELS, Paige 802-440-4300 462 A
pbartels@bennington.edu
BARTELS, Paul, J 828-771-2083 344 E
pbartels@warren-wilson.edu
BARTELS, Suzanne, M .. 336-316-2046 329 E
bartelssm@guilford.edu
BARTELSON,
Gretchen, G 712-324-5061 168 G
gbartelson@nwicc.edu
BARTELSON, Jon 401-456-8200 405 C
jbartelson@ric.edu
BARTELT, Jason 920-923-8090 494 A
jbartelt@marianuniversity.edu
BARTFIELD, Joel 518-262-7302 289 F
bartfij@amc.edu
BARTGES, Ellyn 320-308-5123 240 H
elbartges@stcloudstate.edu
BARTH, Christopher 845-938-3833 504 H
christopher.barth@usma.edu

BARTH, Doug 785-594-4526 170 I
doug.barth@bakeru.edu
BARTH, Michael 406-496-4233 265 A
mbarth@mtech.edu
BARTH, Richard, P 410-706-7794 202 D
rbarth@ssw.umaryland.edu
BARTHA, Jaimee 847-628-2514 140 C
jbartha@judsonu.edu
BARTHEL, Jamie 763-422-6082 237 C
jbarthel@anokatech.edu
BARTHELEMY, Diana 773-577-8100 135 G
dberthelemy@coynecollege.edu
BARTHELL, John 405-974-3371 370 K
jbarthell@uco.edu
BARTHELMAS, Rick 518-244-2200 313 D
barthf@sage.edu
BARTHOLOMEW, Diane 660-831-4146 256 G
bartholomewd@moval.edu
BARTHOLOMEW,
James 630-515-4566 136 A
BARTHOLOMEW,
Jennifer 414-425-8300 495 H
jbartholomew@shsst.edu
BARTHOLOMEW,
Melody 810-762-0453 228 C
melody.bartholomew@mcc.edu
BARTHOLOMEW-FEIS,
Dixee 712-749-1803 163 D
bartholomew@bvu.edu
BARTINDALE, Becky 650-949-6107.. 43 B
bartindalebecky@fhda.edu
BARTINI, Michael, D .... 207-725-3146 193 D
mbartini@bowdoin.edu
BARTKUS, Carolyn 262-422-1686 495 B
cbartkus@nashotah.edu
BARTL, Noelle 575-562-2412 285 M
noelle.bartl@enmu.edu
BARTLE, John, R 402-554-3989 270 B
jbartle@unomaha.edu
BARTLETT, Abby 913-360-7400 171 D
abartlett@benedictine.edu
BARTLETT, Andy 218-755-2746 237 E
andy.bartlett@bemidjistate.edu
BARTLETT, Anne 979-230-3202 432 D
anne.bartlett@brazosport.edu
BARTLETT, Annemarie ... 401-847-6650 406 A
annemarie.bartlett@salve.edu
BARTLETT, Jason, T 718-390-4080 314 B
bartletj@stjohns.edu
BARTLETT, Michael 715-394-8233 498 B
mbartle2@uwsuper.edu
BARTLETT, Raymond 832-842-5544 452 F
rbartlett@uh.edu
BARTLETT, Raymond 713-743-5544 452 E
rbartlett@uh.edu
BARTLETT, Stacey 530-242-7730.. 63 H
sbartlett@shastacollege.edu
BARTLETT, Stacy 706-385-1100 123 C
stacy.bartlett@point.edu
BARTLEY, Mary, E 515-961-1511 169 D
mimi.bartley@simpson.edu
BARTLEY, Patricia, A .... 773-256-0717 142 G
pbartley@lstc.edu
BARTLEY, Phyllis 540-863-2824 474 D
pbartley@dslcc.edu
BARTLEY, Terry 530-251-8834.. 47 F
tbartley@lassencollege.edu
BARTLING, Jonathan 615-248-1258 427 A
jdbartling@trevecca.edu
BARTLING, Kaitlyn 641-648-4611 166 J
kaitlyn.bartling@iavalley.edu
BARTLING, Kelly, H 308-865-8455 269 I
bartlingkh@unk.edu
BARTLOW, Jon, A 620-235-4761 176 F
jbartlow@pittstate.edu
BARTO, Christopher, E . 212-752-1530 304 D
cbarto@limcollege.edu
BARTO, Daniel 727-341-3051 106 E
barto.daniel@spcollege.edu
BARTO, Robert 630-466-7900 152 C
rbarto@waubonsee.edu
BARTOLD, Milissa 312-949-7440 138 E
mbartold@ico.edu
BARTOLI, Andrea 973-313-6174 283 B
andrea.bartoli@shu.edu
BARTOLINI, Brian, J 401-865-1554 405 B
bbartoli@providence.edu
BARTOLOMEI, Chris, J . 716-645-2227 316 F
cbartolo@buffalo.edu
BARTOLOMEO, Jamin ... 240-567-1993 200 C
jamin.bartolomeo@montgomerycollege.edu
BARTOLOTTA, Charles .. 631-451-4790 321 F
bartolc@sunysuffolk.edu

BARTON, Allison 615-220-7826 425 C abarton@mscc.edu
BARTON, Andrea, M 503-943-8715 377 E barton@up.edu
BARTON, April 412-396-6280 383 C ambarton@duq.edu
BARTON, Charles (Lennie) 919-760-8375 331 B bartonl@meredith.edu
BARTON, David 660-284-4800 253 J
BARTON, Gayle 413-748-3532 218 G gbarton@springfield.edu
BARTON, Jennifer, K 520-626-2465 16 G barton@email.arizona.edu
BARTON, Mary 940-565-2085 454 A mary.barton@unt.edu
BARTON, Michelle 760-744-1150 55 I mbarton@palomar.edu
BARTON, Michelle, C 713-834-6268 456 B michelle.barton@uth.tmc.edu
BARTON, Patricia 510-136-1220 45 D barton@hnu.edu
BARTON, Sara 310-506-4275 56 C sara.barton@pepperdine.edu
BARTON, Scott 717-477-1375 395 E swbarton@ship.edu
BARTOW, Patricia 619-216-6694 65 F pbartow@swccd.edu
BARTRUG, Reba 740-374-8716 364 C rbartrug@wscc.edu
BARTS, Bryan 715-232-1469 498 A bartsb@uwstout.edu
BARTSCH, Jonathan 617-236-8873 209 D jbartsch@fisher.edu
BARTSCH, Melissa 859-622-1303 180 B melissa.bartsch@eku.edu
BARTUNEK, Tami 913-288-7166 174 F tbartunek@kckcc.edu
BARTUSIK, LisaMarie 850-484-2007 104 H lbartusik@pensacolastate.edu
BARUA, Susamma 657-278-3362 31 E sbarua@fullerton.edu
BARWICK, Daniel, W 620-331-4100 174 C dbarwick@indycc.edu
BARZACCHINI, Mike 847-925-6510 137 H mbarzacc@harpercollege.edu
BARZILAY, Jessica 908-737-0322 278 E jbarzila@kean.edu
BASALA, Nissim 732-370-1560 275 G
BASCH, Hersch 718-438-1002 306 G
BASCO, Jared 202-884-9504 93 B bascoj@trinitydc.edu
BASCOM, Shawn 208-282-5304 130 H bascshaw@isu.edu
BASCOMB, Cheryl, A 603-646-2258 273 E cheryl.a.bascomb@dartmouth.edu
BASER, Ric 210-486-4908 429 C rbaser@alamo.edu
BASER, Ric, N 210-486-4900 429 E rbaser@alamo.edu
BASFORD, Jerry, L 801-581-3435 460 E jbasford@sa.utah.edu
BASH, Cassaundra 574-936-8898 153 A cassaundra.bash@ancilla.edu
BASHANT, Wendy 619-239-0391 34 F wbashant@cwsl.edu
BASHARA, Teri 318-678-6000 187 A tbashara@bpcc.edu
BASHAW, Ed 620-341-5274 172 L ebashaw@emporia.edu
BASHET, Abuzafar, M 972-860-7158 435 B azbashet@dcccd.edu
BASHIR, Rashid 217-333-2150 151 D rbashir@illinois.edu
BASIC, Mia 909-593-3511 70 D mbasic@laverne.edu
BASICK, Mary 213-738-6813 65 G mbasick@swlaw.edu
BASIL, Meredith 657-278-3341 31 E mbasil@fullerton.edu
BASIL, Natalie 802-440-4390 462 A
BASILE, Carole 480-965-4064 10 I carole.basile@asu.edu
BASILE, Elizabeth 718-368-4539 294 E ebasile@kbcc.cuny.edu
BASILE, Julia 201-200-2016 279 E jbasile@njcu.edu
BASILEO, Paul 631-451-4854 321 G basilep@sunysuffolk.edu
BASILIO, Shelle 315-781-3880 302 A basilio@hws.edu
BASINGER, Cyndie 434-791-5671 464 O cbasinger@averett.edu
BASINGER, David 585-594-6550 312 K basingerd@roberts.edu
BASINGER, Randall, G 717-796-5375 390 E rbasinge@messiah.edu
BASINSKI, Judith, B 716-878-4611 318 C basinsjb@buffalostate.edu
BASIRATMAND, Mehran 561-297-0230 108 J mehran@fau.edu
BASKARAN, Christiana 323-953-4000 48 I baskarc@lacitycollege.edu
BASKEL, Elise 719-598-0200 79 C ebaskel@coloradotech.edu
BASKER, Judy 541-956-7291 376 D jbasker@roguecc.edu
BASKERVILLE, Carly 804-862-6100 470 I cwinfield@rbc.edu
BASKERVILLE, Elizabeth 323-563-5929 36 D ebaskerville@cdrewu.edu
BASKERVILLE, Rebecca 402-472-5393 269 J rlbaskerville@unl.edu
BASKETT, James 770-426-2613 121 C james.baskett@life.edu
BASKETTE, Shawna 562-860-2451 35 M sbaskette@cerritos.edu
BASKI, Alison 909-869-3600 30 D aabaski@cpp.edu
BASKIN, Brent 706-233-7281 124 B bbaskin@shorter.edu
BASKO, Aaron, M 410-543-6161 203 F ambasko@salisbury.edu
BASLER, Danielle 573-518-2307 256 B dbasler@mineralarea.edu
BASLER, Joella 618-634-3274 149 A joellab@shawneecc.edu
BASLER, Julie 303-369-5151 81 J julie.basler@plattcolorado.edu
BASLEY, Carolyn 312-935-4556 147 D cbasley@robertmorris.edu
BASNEY, Janet 541-956-7831 376 D jbasney@roguecc.edu
BASS, Brenda, L 319-273-2221 163 B brenda.bass@uni.edu
BASS, Candace 405-425-5931 367 G candace.bass@oc.edu
BASS, Charles 619-260-4819 71 J charlesb@sandiego.edu
BASS, Donna 334-222-6591 2 I dbass@lbwcc.edu
BASS, Gordon 904-357-8891 100 B gbass@fscj.edu
BASS, Hilarie 305-284-4025 112 E
BASS, Inga 601-484-8823 247 A ibass@meridiancc.edu
BASS, Jake 563-425-5311 170 A bassj323@uiu.edu
BASS, Jimmy 910-962-4292 343 C bassj@uncw.edu
BASS, Kengie, R 919-516-4160 340 C krbass@st-aug.edu
BASS, Leonard, C 407-582-2745 112 K lbass11@valenciacollege.edu
BASS, Mary, T 252-823-5166 334 C bassm@edgecombe.edu
BASS, Randall 202-687-6400 92 A bassr@georgetown.edu
BASS KEER, Wendy 818-712-2619 49 C basskew@piercecollege.edu
BASSALE, Parfait 360-596-5356 485 B pbassale@spscc.edu
BASSETT, Carolyn, S 413-577-1057 211 D cbassett@umass.edu
BASSETT, Claire, M 713-798-4710 431 I bassett@bcm.edu
BASSETT, Heidi, M 972-860-7255 435 B hbassett@dcccd.edu
BASSETT, John 309-649-6303 150 A john.bassett@src.edu
BASSETT, Steven 972-758-3831 433 M sbassett@collin.edu
BASSETT, Susan 607-274-3209 303 B sbassett@ithaca.edu
BASSETTI, Mimi 215-572-2941 379 A bassetti@arcadia.edu
BASSHAM, Mia, W 570-740-0420 389 D mbassham@luzerne.edu
BASSI-COOK, Teresa 724-838-4295 398 H tbassicook@setonhill.edu
BASSIE, Carol 973-408-3838 277 C cbassie@drew.edu
BASSINGER, Donnie 828-726-2214 332 G dbassinger@cccti.edu
BASSO, Sharon 909-621-8485 37 E sharon.basso@cmc.edu
BASSO, Susan, M 614-292-1050 358 I basso.22@osu.edu
BASSUK, Bill 210-233-1102 433 E
BAST, Andy 616-392-8555 233 E andy@westernsem.edu
BAST, EJ 269-488-4755 225 E ebast@kvcc.edu
BASTA, Tania 270-745-7003 185 E tania.basta@wku.edu
BASTECKI-PEREZ, Victoria 215-641-6482 390 H vbasteck@mc3.edu
BASTIAN, Joni 618-537-6555 143 B jjbastian@mckendree.edu
BASTIAN, Kayla 605-773-3455 416 G kayla.bastian@sdbor.edu
BASTIN, Judy 316-322-3235 171 G jbastin@butlercc.edu
BASTINE, Michael 661-362-3111 38 H michael.bastine@canyons.edu
BASTIONY, Peter 305-273-4499 96 L
BASTON, Michael, A 845-574-4214 313 C president@sunyrockland.edu
BASTONE, Linda 914-251-6000 319 E
BASU, Andra 570-422-3494 394 E abasu@esu.edu
BASU, Sukulpa 610-989-1200 402 B sbasu@vfmac.edu
BASUALDO, Maria 607-778-5030 318 A basualdomi@sunybroome.edu
BATCHELDER, Joseph 518-255-5620 319 F batchejb@cobleskill.edu
BATCHELDER, Rick 518-562-4106 296 B rick.batchelder@clinton.edu
BATCHELLER, Tamara 313-993-1246 231 B batchets@udmercy.edu
BATCHELOR, Chelle 503-838-8886 377 H batchelorc@wou.edu
BATCHELOR, Grady 304-724-3700 487 E gbatchelor@apus.edu
BATCHELOR, Jennifer 603-626-9100 274 D j.batchelor@snhu.edu
BATCHELOR, Laura 609-343-5632 275 D lbatchel@atlantic.edu
BATCHELOR, Susan 618-545-3033 140 E sbatchelor@kaskaskia.edu
BATCHER, Shelly 770-426-2653 121 C sbatcher@life.edu
BATE, Jeff, B 801-375-5125 459 L jeff.bate@rm.edu
BATE, Jennifer 201-327-8877 277 H jbate@eastwick.edu
BATE, Joel, C 208-732-6836 130 E jbate@csi.edu
BATEMAN, Bradley, W 434-947-8140 470 E bbateman@randolphcollege.edu
BATEMAN, David 870-230-5150 19 E batemad@hsu.edu
BATEMAN, Douglas, R 318-678-6000 187 A rbateman@bpcc.edu
BATEMAN, Heather 800-686-1883 222 E hbateman@cleary.edu
BATEMAN, Heather 517-796-8628 225 C batemanheathera@jccmi.edu
BATEMAN, Jamie 863-784-7181 107 F jamie.bateman@southflorida.edu
BATEMAN, Joyce 417-447-6966 257 G batemanj@otc.edu
BATEMAN, Mathew 814-866-8148 388 A mbateman@lecom.edu
BATES, Anthony 708-235-7431 137 F abates99@govst.edu
BATES, Aryana 206-934-3612 483 J aryana.bates@seattlecolleges.edu
BATES, Brent 660-596-7252 260 D bbates@sfccmo.edu
BATES, Brian 408-924-6518 34 B brian.bates@sjsu.edu
BATES, Christin 989-275-5000 226 B christin.bates@kirtland.edu
BATES, Damien 928-317-5892 10 J damien.bates@azwestern.edu
BATES, Doug 931-372-3408 426 E dbates@tntech.edu
BATES, Evola 202-274-6016 93 C evola.bates@udc.edu
BATES, Holly 770-533-7007 121 B hbates@laniertech.edu
BATES, Jeffrey 301-736-3631 199 G jbates@msbbcs.edu
BATES, Jennifer 606-218-5253 185 D jenniferbates@upike.edu
BATES, Joan 423-472-7141 424 F jbates@clevelandstatecc.edu
BATES, Julie 501-660-1002 17 E jbates@asusystem.edu
BATES, Kay 662-472-9023 246 C kbates@holmescc.edu
BATES, Larry 865-694-6404 425 F lbates@pstcc.edu
BATES, Lynette 719-846-5559 82 K lynette.bates@trinidadstate.edu
BATES, Lynette 909-558-4561 48 C lbates@llu.edu
BATES, Mary Lou, W 518-580-5588 316 A mbates@skidmore.edu
BATES, Michael 847-925-6304 137 H mbates@harpercollege.edu
BATES, Michele 575-624-8096 287 A bates@nmmi.edu
BATES, Patrick, M 585-292-2820 307 H pbates@monroecc.edu
BATES, Reid 225-578-2457 188 I rbates@lsu.edu
BATES, Starnell 803-822-3235 410 G batess@midlandstech.edu
BATES, Suzanne 314-434-4044 252 B suzanne.bates@covenantseminary.edu
BATES, Tierney, J 804-257-5875 477 C tjbates@vuu.edu
BATES, Trevor 419-251-8968 356 C trevor.bates@mercycollege.edu
BATES, Wendy 707-476-4140 39 D wendy-bates@redwoods.edu
BATES-REESE, Fannie 205-391-2331 3 E freese@sheltonstate.edu
BATESON, Carrie 918-595-7871 370 E carrie.bateson@tulsacc.edu
BATH, Michael, J 906-227-2151 228 F mbath@nmu.edu
BATHANTI, Karen, L 248-341-2037 229 A klbathan@oaklandcc.edu
BATHOLOMEW, Lindsay 864-488-4557 410 E lbartholomew@limestone.edu
BATIATO, Dolores, A 239-513-1122 101 C dbatiato@hodges.edu
BATIC, Marjorie 317-955-6150 158 U mbatic@marian.edu
BATIE, Larry 205-929-1446 6 B lbatie@miles.edu
BATIS, Jeffrey 540-261-8400 471 H jeff.batis@svu.edu
BATISTA, Adrian 440-775-8472 358 C adrian.batista@oberlin.edu
BATISTA, Angela 802-651-5851 462 B abatista@champlain.edu
BATISTA, Freddie 239-992-4624 95 G
BATISTA, Hector 646-664-9100 292 K
BATISTA, Jorge 347-964-8600 291 I jbatista@boricuacollege.edu
BATISTA, Maria, E 787-728-1515 514 D mariae.batista@sagrado.edu
BATISTA-SANTIAGO, Gerardo 787-993-8950 513 B gerardo.batista@upr.edu
BATISTE, Lynda 256-372-8653 1 A lyda.batiste@aamu.edu
BATLAN, Libby 541-346-3873 377 D batlan@uoregon.edu
BATSON, Deborah 918-595-8920 370 E debbie.batson@tulsacc.edu
BATSON, Marie 251-442-2370 8 C mbatson@umobile.edu
BATSON, Rebecca 302-857-7887 89 F rbatson@desu.edu
BATSON, Robert 937-775-2869 364 I robert.batson@wright.edu
BATSON, Trice 269-488-4794 225 E tbatson@kvcc.edu
BATT, Marylou 617-349-8564 210 H mbatt@lesley.edu
BATT, Megan 419-267-1366 358 A mbatt@northweststate.edu
BATTAGLIA, Andrea 417-873-7353 252 F abattaglia@drury.edu
BATTAGLIA, Janet, M 540-464-7213 476 G battagliajm@vmi.edu
BATTAGLIA, John, A 417-268-1000 250 E battagliaj@evangel.edu
BATTAGLINO, JR., John 617-353-3511 207 D jbattag@bu.edu

BATTEE-FREEMAN, Katherine ... 217-206-8503 151 C kathyy@uis.edu
BATTELL, Victoria, L ... 518-438-3111 305 K vbattell@mariacollege.edu
BATTEN, Debbie ... 252-823-5166 334 C battend@edgecombe.edu
BATTEN, Melissa ... 843-349-5228 410 C melissa.batten@hgtc.edu
BATTEN-MICKENS, Melodye ... 301-546-0656 201 C mbatte10373@pgcc.edu
BATTIATA, Russell ... 941-355-9080.. 97 H admissions@ewcollege.org
BATTIATA, Russell ... 941-355-9080.. 97 H rbattiata@ewcollege.org
BATTINKOFF, Robert ... 989-686-9145 223 G robertbattinkoff@delta.edu
BATTISTA, Joe, N ... 407-582-6622 112 K jbattista@valenciacollege.edu
BATTISTA, Marc ... 847-635-1423 145 G mbattista@oakton.edu
BATTISTA, Russ ... 603-862-0700 274 F russell.battista@usnh.edu
BATTISTA, Vince ... 312-567-8625 139 B vbattista@iit.edu
BATTISTE, Leilani ... 415-241-2294.. 37 A lbattist@ccsf.edu
BATTISTELLA, Diane ... 630-829-6415 132 E dbatistella@ben.edu
BATTISTI, Francis ... 607-778-5138 318 A battistifl@sunybroome.edu
BATTLE, Ashley ... 603-428-2230 273 H abattle@nec.edu
BATTLE, Bernadette ... 434-949-1063 475 H bernadette.battle@southside.edu
BATTLE, Donna ... 919-760-8346 331 B battledo@meredith.edu
BATTLE, Kiana ... 708-608-4360 144 C battlek@morainevalley.edu
BATTLE, Lydée ... 301-891-4128 204 C lbattle@wau.edu
BATTLE-BROWN, LaToya ... 973-353-5213 282 B lbbrown@rutgers.edu
BATTLES, Denise, A ... 585-245-5501 318 E battles@geneseo.edu
BATTLES, Linnea ... 251-380-2240.... 6 H lbattles@shc.edu
BATTRAW, Danny ... 928-428-8605.. 12 E danny.battraw@eac.edu
BATTRICK, Sam ... 541-245-7715 376 D sbattrick@roguecc.edu
BATTURS, Beth Anne ... 410-777-7352 197 C babatturs@aacc.edu
BATTY, Philip ... 616-331-8650 224 E battyp@gvsu.edu
BATTY-HERBERT, Kimberly ... 928-226-4362.. 11 O kimberly.batty-herbert@coconino.edu
BATTYE, Anna ... 603-542-7744 273 C abattye@ccsnh.edu
BATWAY, Jody ... 734-432-5744 227 A jbatway@madonna.edu
BATZER, Caren ... 718-990-6366 314 B batzerc@stjohns.edu
BAUBLITZ, Ivan, V ... 419-866-0261 361 H ivbaublitz@stautzenberger.com
BAUCOM, Ian, B ... 434-924-4611 473 A ibb4n@virginia.edu
BAUCUM, Natasha ... 601-928-6281 247 E natasha.baucum@mgccc.edu
BAUDER, Sarah ... 717-720-4000 393 K sbauder@passhe.edu
BAUDRY YOUNG, Rebecca ... 513-529-3438 356 E baudryrm@miamioh.edu
BAUER, Amanda ... 661-763-7853.. 66 J abauer@taftcollege.edu
BAUER, Amie ... 785-227-3380 171 E baueral@bethanylb.edu
BAUER, Angela, C ... 336-841-9501 329 G abauer@highpoint.edu
BAUER, Blanca ... 337-482-6306 192 E blanca.bauer@louisiana.edu
BAUER, C. Jon ... 636-584-6501 252 J jon.bauer@eastcentral.edu
BAUER, Christine ... 208-426-5903 129 I christinebauer@boisestate.edu
BAUER, Cortney, A ... 402-280-3533 266 I cortneybauer@creighton.edu
BAUER, Cynthia, M ... 414-288-7343 494 B cindy.bauer@marquette.edu
BAUER, Daniel, C ... 314-367-8700 259 B daniel.bauer@stlcop.edu
BAUER, Danny ... 724-738-2773 395 F dan.bauer@sru.edu
BAUER, David ... 859-858-3581 178 H
BAUER, Denise ... 845-451-1345 298 A denise.bauer@culinary.edu
BAUER, Dennis ... 479-308-2282.. 17 C dennis.bauer@acheedu.org
BAUER, Glen ... 248-204-3532 226 G gbauer@ltu.edu
BAUER, Jackie ... 320-308-5486 241 A jbauer@sctcc.edu
BAUER, James ... 863-680-4186.. 99 H jbauer@flsouthern.edu
BAUER, Jason, K ... 515-263-2887 165 I jbauer@grandview.edu
BAUER, Jeffrey ... 740-351-3208 360 K jbauer@shawnee.edu
BAUER, Jeffrey, C ... 513-732-5209 362 F jeff.bauer@uc.edu
BAUER, Jeremi ... 203-596-8359.. 87 F jebauer@post.edu
BAUER, Jody ... 215-751-8060 382 A jbauer@ccp.edu
BAUER, Joy ... 918-540-6720 366 I joyb@neo.edu
BAUER, Julie ... 662-562-3274 248 D
BAUER, Kara ... 619-594-0489.. 33 E kbauer@sdsu.edu
BAUER, Karen ... 918-495-7371 368 I kbauer@oru.edu
BAUER, Kelli ... 620-252-7180 172 G bauer.kelli@coffeyville.edu
BAUER, Marc ... 308-865-8332 269 I bauermd@unk.edu
BAUER, Mark, D ... 507-354-8221 236 I bauermd@mlc-wels.edu
BAUER, Mary ... 718-405-3233 296 G mary.bauer@mountsaintvincent.edu
BAUER, Matt ... 919-735-5151 338 H mattb@waynecc.edu
BAUER, Nancy ... 617-627-4230 219 B nancy.bauer@tufts.edu
BAUER, Patrick ... 847-925-6827 137 H pbauer@harpercollege.edu
BAUER, Scott ... 951-222-8920.. 58 I scott.bauer@rcc.edu
BAUER, Scott ... 760-921-5428.. 55 H scott.bauer@paloverde.edu
BAUER, Stacy ... 605-229-8405 416 C stacy.bauer@presentation.edu
BAUER, Susan ... 646-592-4090 326 E susan.bauer@yu.edu
BAUER, Tom ... 650-358-6782.. 61 N bauert@smccd.edu
BAUER, Warren, K ... 515-574-1120 166 E bauer@iowacentral.edu
BAUERLE, Cynthia ... 540-568-3508 468 F bauerlcm@jmu.edu
BAUGH, Anita, G ... 320-308-5936 241 A abaugh@sctcc.edu
BAUGH, Frank ... 601-318-6772 249 H frank.baugh@wmcarey.edu
BAUGH, Josh ... 773-298-3132 148 G baugh@sxu.edu
BAUGH, Robbie ... 940-668-3338 441 A rbaugh@nctc.edu
BAUGH, Shirley, A ... 618-537-6533 143 B sabaugh@mckendree.edu
BAUGH, Stephanie ... 478-757-5209 126 H sbaugh@wesleyancollege.edu
BAUGHMAN, Linda, M . 651-962-6053 244 E lmbaughman@stthomas.edu
BAUGHMAN, Matthew .. 618-453-2341 149 E baughman@siu.edu
BAUGHMAN, Philip ... 515-271-1340 164 I philip.baughman@dmu.edu
BAUGHMAN, Rebecca, L ... 512-471-2303 455 A rbaughman@austin.utexas.edu
BAUGHMAN, Sara ... 828-669-8012 331 J sara.baughman@montreat.edu
BAUGUESS, Seth ... 937-912-0622 364 I seth.bauguess@wright.edu
BAUGUS, John ... 626-815-4622.. 26 H jbaugus@apu.edu
BAUM, Benjamin ... 410-626-2522 201 D benjamin.baum@sjc.edu
BAUM, Christina ... 801-524-8195 459 F christinabaum@ldsbc.edu
BAUM, Courtney ... 724-805-2253 398 E courtney.baum@email.stvincent.edu
BAUM, Courtney ... 724-805-2253 398 F courtney.baum@stvincent.edu
BAUM, Dan, B ... 410-777-2011 197 C dbbaum@aacc.edu
BAUM, Robert ... 724-805-2590 398 E bob.baum@stvincent.edu
BAUMAN, Dallas ... 631-632-6974 317 D dallas.bauman@stonybrook.edu
BAUMAN, Joel ... 386-822-7100 111 A jbauman@stetson.edu
BAUMAN, Mark ... 570-389-4308 394 A mbauman@bloomu.edu
BAUMAN, Michael ... 312-935-4242 139 H mbauman@icsw.edu
BAUMAN, Sandra ... 406-447-6928 264 C sandra.bauman@helenacollege.edu
BAUMANN, Erick ... 708-524-5054 136 C ebauman@dom.edu
BAUMANN, Lawra ... 513-569-1759 350 K lawra.baumann@cincinnatistate.edu
BAUMANN, Melissa, J . 513-745-3837 365 B baumannm@xavier.edu
BAUMANN, Robert ... 913-684-2741 504 D robert.baumann@leavenworth.army.mil
BAUMBACH, Kirk ... 804-752-7263 470 F kirkbaumbach@rmc.edu
BAUMEISTER, Barbara .. 405-736-0208 369 I bbaumeister@rose.edu
BAUMEISTER, Bo ... 503-493-6587 372 I bbaumeister@cu-portland.edu
BAUMER, Brian ... 718-990-3292 314 B baumerb@stjohns.edu
BAUMET, Robert ... 315-279-5328 304 A rbaumet@keuka.edu
BAUMGARDNER, Brice, D ... 573-629-3280 253 H bbaumgardner@hlg.edu
BAUMGARDNER, Deidra ... 317-738-8189 154 J dbaumgardner@franklincollege.edu
BAUMGARDNER, Julie, M ... 606-474-3200 180 G jmbaumgardner@kcu.edu
BAUMGARDNER, William, B ... 606-474-3151 180 G wbbaumgardner@kcu.edu
BAUMGART, Reilly ... 618-262-8641 139 A baumgartr@iecc.edu
BAUMGARTEN, Matthew, J ... 757-822-1780 476 B mbaumgarten@tcc.edu
BAUMGARTNER, Aileen 914-241-3500 306 A abaumgartner@mmm.edu
BAUMGARTNER, Bruce . 814-732-2776 394 F bbaumgartner@edinboro.edu
BAUMGARTNER, Eric ... 414-277-7190 494 G
BAUMGARTNER, Erin ... 503-838-8348 377 H baumgare@wou.edu
BAUMGARTNER, Gretchen ... 530-283-0202.. 42 H gbaumgartner@frc.edu
BAUMGARTNER, Holly, L ... 419-772-2130 358 H h-baumgartner@onu.edu
BAUMGARTNER, Neil ... 262-595-2151 497 C baumgarn@uwp.edu
BAUMGARTNER, Renee . 408-554-5344.. 62 D rbaumgartner@scu.edu
BAUMGARTNER, Timothy, K ... 713-348-4867 442 K timothy.k.baumgartner@rice.edu
BAUMHOVER, Lynne ... 563-589-0300 170 D lbaumhover@wartburgseminary.edu
BAUMUNK, Jeffrey ... 310-660-3593.. 41 L jbaumunk@elcamino.edu
BAUN, Dan ... 507-537-6978 241 D dan.baun@smsu.edu
BAUN, Jeff ... 610-436-2705 396 A jbaun@wcupa.edu
BAUN, Kathy ... 707-668-5663.. 41 D
BAUR, Cathy ... 760-750-4400.. 33 B cbaur@csusm.edu
BAUR, Cheryl ... 570-740-0368 389 D cbaur@luzerne.edu
BAUR, John ... 309-438-2583 139 E jebaur@ilstu.edu
BAURAIN, Thomas ... 816-311-0110 250 K thomas.baurain@calvary.edu
BAUS, Amy ... 563-589-3132 169 I abaus@dbq.edu
BAUSANO, Carrie, J ... 719-333-4293 504 C carrie.bausano@usafa.edu
BAUSERMAN, Judy ... 304-263-0979 488 H
BAUSHKE, Ken ... 270-745-3056 185 E ken.baushke@wku.edu
BAUSINGER, Patricia, E 570-321-4049 389 E baus@lycoming.edu
BAUSLEY, Gwen ... 304-766-4366 491 B gbausley@wvstateu.edu
BAUSS, Celia, N ... 864-592-4754 412 F baussc@sccsc.edu
BAUTE, Brian ... 704-229-2070 339 G bauteb@queens.edu
BAUTISTA, Maria ... 808-734-9519 128 I mariab@hawaii.edu
BAUTISTA MOLLER, Lydia, B ... 954-607-4344 112 B
BAUTTI, Joann ... 757-446-5244 466 I bauttij@evms.edu
BAVA, Brian ... 208-459-5271 130 D bbava@collegeofidaho.edu
BAVADRA, Verenaisi ... 692-625-3394 505 F
BAVER, Chad ... 406-683-7382 264 B chad.baver@umwestern.edu
BAVISI, Lata ... 505-922-2889 286 B lata@eccu.edu
BAVISI, Sanjay ... 505-922-2889 286 B
BAWA, Opinder ... 415-422-2787.. 71 K osbawa@usfca.edu
BAWOROWSKY, John ... 414-288-4976 494 B john.baworowsky@marquette.edu
BAX, John ... 573-681-5860 254 E baxj2@lincolnu.edu
BAXLEY, Amy ... 812-288-8878 159 A abaxley@mid-america.edu
BAXTER, Agnes ... 919-546-8212 340 E abaxter@shawu.edu
BAXTER, Aimee, F ... 318-257-2641 191 F abaxter@latech.edu
BAXTER, Aryn ... 208-885-1150 131 G abaxter@uidaho.edu
BAXTER, Hilary ... 617-327-6777 220 B hilary_baxter@williamjames.edu
BAXTER, Keith ... 580-745-2250 369 K kbaxter@se.edu
BAXTER, Leigh ... 804-706-5214 474 I lbaxter@jtcc.edu
BAXTER, Melissa ... 315-568-3271 308 F mbaxter@nycc.edu
BAXTER, Randy, A ... 662-720-7576 248 C rabaxter@nemcc.edu
BAY, Kelly ... 309-467-6431 137 B kbay@eureka.edu
BAY, Willow, C ... 213-740-6180.. 72 B wbay@usc.edu
BAYARDELLE, Eddy ... 718-289-5185 293 B eddy.bayardelle@bcc.cuny.edu
BAYER, Deborah ... 989-358-7458 221 A bayerd@alpenacc.edu
BAYERL, Sue ... 320-308-2111 240 H sjbayerl@stcloudstate.edu
BAYLES, Kenneth ... 402-559-4945 270 A kbayles@unmc.edu
BAYLESS, Debi ... 573-518-1330 256 B dbayless@mineralarea.edu
BAYLESS, Laura ... 978-665-3215 212 C lbayless@fitchburgstate.edu
BAYLESS, Rita ... 620-227-9313 172 J rbayless@dc3.edu
BAYLISS-CARR, Sandy .. 252-638-4755 333 H bayliss-carrs@cravencc.edu
BAYLOR, Bridget ... 540-453-2358 474 B baylorb@brcc.edu
BAYLOR, Chiquita ... 401-341-2225 406 A chiquita.baylor@salve.edu
BAYLOR, Jeff, S ... 806-651-2020 448 C jbaylor@wtamu.edu
BAYLOR, Kara ... 262-551-5812 492 F kbaylor@carthage.edu
BAYNE, Deann ... 402-872-2226 268 F dbayne@peru.edu
BAYNE, Suzanne ... 423-472-7141 424 F sbayne@clevelandstatecc.edu
BAYNES, Leonard, M ... 713-743-2478 452 F lbaynes@central.uh.edu
BAYOUMI, Magdy, A ... 337-482-6147 192 E mab@louisiana.edu
BAYSINGER, Anne ... 630-829-1123 132 E abaysinger@ben.edu
BAYTO, Tammy ... 478-274-7852 122 H tbayto@oftc.edu
BAZAN, David ... 425-889-5322 482 F david.bazan@northwestu.edu
BAZAN, Yamilet ... 951-785-2100.. 47 C ybazan@lasierra.edu

BAZANT, Robert, S 724-222-5330 392 A rbazant@penncommercial.edu
BAZARSKY, Debbie 717-396-7833 393 E dbazarsky@pcad.edu
BAZEMORE, Alisha 757-823-8462 469 F albazemore@nsu.edu
BAZEMORE, Dennis 910-893-1540 327 E bazemored@campbell.edu
BAZIAN, Hatem 510-356-4760 76 E hbazian@zaytuna.edu
BAZIL, Ted 914-961-8313 315 C ted@svots.edu
BAZILE, Samantha 845-398-4102 315 B sbazile@stac.edu
BAZILE, Stanley 718-960-8241 294 A stanley.bazile@lehman.cuny.edu
BAZLEY, Lisa 210-829-3959 453 D lisa@uiwtx.edu
BAZZEL, Matthew 706-419-1126 117 B matthew.bazzel@covenant.edu
BAZZEL, Mitchell 256-233-8161 4 D mitchell.bazzel@athens.edu
BAZZELL, Darrell 512-471-1422 455 A bazzell@austin.utexas.edu
BEA, David 520-206-4519 15 D dbea@pima.edu
BEACH, Adam, R 765-285-1300 153 C arbeach@bsu.edu
BEACH, Alison 607-844-8222 322 H beacha@tompkinscortland.edu
BEACH, Bradley 330-244-4732 364 B bbeach@walsh.edu
BEACH, Cora 541-962-3368 373 B cbeach@eou.edu
BEACH, Janis 302-857-1293 90 D janis.beach@dtcc.edu
BEACH, Justin 406-377-9410 263 E jbeach@dawson.edu
BEACH, Lisa 253-589-5603 479 G lisa.beach@cptc.edu
BEACH, Michael 913-288-7645 174 F mbeach@kckcc.edu
BEACH, Nancy, S 540-365-4529 467 I nbeach@ferrum.edu
BEACH, Natalie 503-399-5105 372 C natalie.beach@chemeketa.edu
BEACH, Scott, R 412-624-4141 401 B scottb@pitt.edu
BEACH, Steven 432-552-2170 457 A beach_s@utpb.edu
BEACH, Vincent 641-585-8133 170 B vince.beach@waldorf.edu
BEACH, Wendy 906-635-2213 226 E wbeach@lssu.edu
BEACHAM, David, M 864-597-4206 414 H beachamdm@wofford.edu
BEACHAM, Ralph 620-724-0390 173 C ralphb@fortscott.edu
BEACHE, Vidda, P 240-500-2357 198 H vpbeache@hagerstowncc.edu
BEACHLER, Kelly 941-309-4022 105 K kbeachle@ringling.edu
BEACHNAU, Andrew 616-331-2120 224 E beachnaa@gvsu.edu
BEACHY, Jeff 408-554-5360 62 D jdbeachy@scu.edu
BEADLES, Mary 706-245-7226 117 E mbeadles@ec.edu
BEAGHAN, John, W 248-370-2445 229 G beaghan@oakland.edu
BEAGLE, Donald 704-461-6740 327 A donaldbeagle@bac.edu
BEAGLE, Mike 541-552-6127 376 E beaglem@sou.edu
BEAHM, John, A 617-873-0430 207 F john.beahm@cambridgecollege.edu
BEAIL, Linda 619-849-2408 57 E lindabeail@pointloma.edu
BEAKMAN, Andrew, W 315-792-3111 324 B awbeakma@utica.edu
BEAL, Jean 413-572-8574 213 D jbeal@westfield.ma.edu
BEAL, Judy 617-521-2139 218 E judy.beal@simmons.edu
BEAL, Lee 828-835-4233 338 E lbeal@tricountycc.edu
BEAL, Stephen 510-594-3630 28 D sbeal@cca.edu
BEAL, Timothy 216-368-4437 349 F
BEALE, Connie, L 973-761-9401 283 B concetta.beale@shu.edu
BEALE, Rachel 757-569-6791 475 E rbeale@pdc.edu
BEALES, Sharon 610-861-5451 391 F sbeales@northampton.edu
BEALL, David 773-508-2391 142 D dbeall@luc.edu
BEALS, Brandi 602-383-8228 16 F bbeals@uat.edu
BEALS, Michael, J 714-556-3610 72 F officeofthepresident@vanguard.edu
BEAM, Brian 309-438-8404 139 E babeam@ilstu.edu
BEAM, John 510-464-3474 56 G jbeam@peralta.edu
BEAM, Julie 574-807-7020 153 E julie.beam@betheluniversity.edu
BEAM, Sandra 513-244-8628 350 I sandra.beam@ccuniversity.edu
BEAM, Tony 864-977-2009 411 E tony.beam@ngu.edu
BEAMAN, Cynthia, A 812-888-5004 162 C cbeaman@vinu.edu
BEAMON, Jefff 912-650-6206 124 E jbeamon@southuniversity.edu
BEAN, Al 207-780-5588 196 F albean@maine.edu
BEAN, Andrew 312-942-3589 148 A
BEAN, Brent 413-485-7362 213 D bbean@westfield.ma.edu
BEAN, Christopher, A 540-665-4553 471 E cbean@su.edu
BEAN, Gary 315-792-7222 321 E gary.bean@sunypoly.edu
BEAN, James, C 617-373-2170 217 F
BEAN, Joanna 719-255-3180 83 B jbean2@uccs.edu
BEAN, Joanne 207-893-7895 195 F jbean@sjcme.edu
BEAN, Kellie 607-431-4400 301 D bwank@hartwick.edu
BEAN, Leslie 865-573-4517 420 G lbean@johnsonu.edu
BEAN, Linda 479-964-3217 18 C lbean@atu.edu
BEAN, Miho 603-206-8101 272 L msbean@ccsnh.edu
BEAN, Paul 785-242-5200 176 D paul.bean@ottawa.edu
BEAN, Shirley 253-833-9111 481 F sbean@greenriver.edu
BEAN, Stacey 937-778-7844 352 J sbean@edisonohio.edu
BEAN, Steve 218-322-2351 238 E steve.bean@itascacc.edu
BEANE, Michael 508-854-4334 215 D mbeane@qcc.mass.edu
BEANE-BOOSE, Linda 509-533-3567 480 B linda.beane-boose@sfcc.spokane.edu
BEANESS KING, Deborah 708-596-2000 149 B dking@ssc.edu
BEANS, Jessica 937-395-8601 355 F jessica.beans@kc.edu
BEAR, Jill 970-207-4550 80 M jillb@mckinleycollege.edu
BEAR, Marca 813-257-3280 112 J mbear@ut.edu
BEAR, Thomas 812-877-8691 159 J bear@rose-hulman.edu
BEARBOWER, Sarah 608-796-3860 498 N sbearbower@viterbo.edu
BEARCE, John 702-651-7454 271 A john.bearce@csn.edu
BEARD, Alison 828-726-2311 332 G abeard@cccti.edu
BEARD, Ashley 601-477-5454 246 F ashley.beard@jcjc.edu
BEARD, Audrey, W 919-530-5327 342 A awbeard@nccu.edu
BEARD, Brian, C 302-356-6989 90 I bcbeard@wilmu.edu
BEARD, Christopher 808-675-3368 127 E christopher.beard@byuh.edu
BEARD, Gerald 662-562-3319 248 D
BEARD, Jason 206-296-2499 484 F beardj@seattleu.edu
BEARD, Jonathan 419-448-3018 361 J beardjw@tiffin.edu
BEARD, Jordan 229-391-5050 113 F jbeard2@abac.edu
BEARD, Julia 208-426-1459 129 I juliabeard@boisestate.edu
BEARD, Katie 205-652-3528 9 A kbeard@uwa.edu
BEARD, Kenya 516-572-7775 308 A kenya.beard@ncc.edu
BEARD, Kyanna 501-812-2230 23 B kbeard@uaptc.edu
BEARD, Richard, L 717-867-6363 388 H rbeard@lvc.edu
BEARD, Scott 304-876-5176 490 E sbeard@shepherd.edu
BEARD, Susan 508-286-8232 220 A beard_susan@wheatoncollege.edu
BEARD, Tanika, L 803-535-5471 407 G tbeard@claflin.edu
BEARD, Timothy, L 727-816-3400 104 F beardt@phsc.edu
BEARD, Virginia 616-395-7544 225 B beard@hope.edu
BEARDEN, Katherine 318-869-5039 186 B kbearden@centenary.edu
BEARDMORE, Kevin 270-686-4504 182 B kevin.beardmore@kctcs.edu
BEARDMORE, Melissa, A 410-777-2532 197 C mabeardmore@aacc.edu
BEARDSALL, Christopher 210-486-2082 429 G cbeardsall@alamo.edu
BEARDSLEE, Gene 402-872-2270 268 F gbeardslee@peru.edu
BEARDSLEY, Kathleen 215-572-2838 379 A beardsley@arcadia.edu
BEARDSLEY, Scott, C 434-924-7481 473 A scb4v@virginia.edu
BEARE, Iris 903-468-8181 447 B iris.beare@tamuc.edu
BEARMAN, Alan 785-670-1855 177 G alan.bearman@washburn.edu
BEARROWS, Thomas, R 312-996-7762 151 B bearrows@uillinois.edu
BEARROWS, Thomas, R 312-996-7762 151 A bearrows@uillinois.edu
BEARSS, Carrie 810-989-5501 230 C cbearss@sc4.edu
BEASIMER, Linda, M 845-431-8979 298 E beasimer@sunydutchess.edu
BEASLAND, Matthew 708-596-2000 149 B mbeasland@ssc.edu
BEASLEY, Elizabeth 848-932-4748 282 A houghliz@docs.rutgers.edu
BEASLEY, Gerald, R 607-255-2000 297 F
BEASLEY, Joan 386-822-7251 111 A jlbeasle@stetson.edu
BEASLEY, Laura 507-433-0676 240 F laura.beasley@riverland.edu
BEASLEY, Paula 276-326-4269 465 B pbeasley@bluefield.edu
BEASLEY, Sarah 304-384-6035 490 A sbeasley@concord.edu
BEASLEY, Stephanie 901-678-5021 427 D sbeasly1@memphis.edu
BEASLEY, Vanessa 615-322-4948 428 D vanessa.beasley@vanderbilt.edu
BEASON, Stephanie 417-667-8181 252 A sbeason@cottey.edu
BEASSIE, Rhonda 936-294-2424 450 C rbeassie@shsu.edu
BEATA, Tony 402-461-7733 267 D tbeata@hastings.edu
BEATON, Kim 530-283-0202 42 H kbeaton@frc.edu
BEATON-GARCIA, Sunem 954-201-7350 95 H
BEATSON, Bonnie 808-235-7374 129 F beatson@hawaii.edu
BEATTIE, Eric, L 508-831-6231 220 E elbeattie@wpi.edu
BEATTIE, Matthew 734-432-5386 227 A mbeattie@madonna.edu
BEATTIE, Ross 414-326-2330 493 A
BEATTIE, Terry 610-436-3317 396 A tbeattie@wcupa.edu
BEATTY, Alan 903-223-3049 448 B alan.beatty@sscserv.com
BEATTY, Amy 863-667-5523 107 K arbeatty@seu.edu
BEATTY, Anthany 859-257-8200 185 B anthany.beatty@uky.edu
BEATTY, Bernadette 575-624-8001 287 A noriega@nmmi.edu
BEATTY, Brian 415-338-6833 34 A bjbeatty@sfsu.edu
BEATTY, Del 435-652-7514 460 G beatty@dixie.edu
BEATTY, Fran 707-668-5663 41 D fran@dellarte.com
BEATTY, Jane 301-846-2657 198 E jbeatty@frederick.edu
BEATTY, Kimberly 816-604-1011 255 D kimberly.beatty@mcckc.edu
BEATTY, Laura 615-361-7555 419 I lbeatty@daymarcollege.edu
BEATTY, Lisa, L 563-588-8000 165 F lbeatty@emmaus.edu
BEATTY, Luke 217-245-3020 138 D luke.beatty@ic.edu
BEATTY, Michael 415-338-1124 34 A mbeatty@sfsu.edu
BEATTY, Robert 903-566-7346 456 A rbeatty@uttyler.edu
BEATTY, Tracy 269-965-3931 225 F beattyt@kellogg.edu
BEATY, Andrew 309-846-3544 144 B andrew.beaty@moody.edu
BEATY, Deborah 229-317-6735 113 H deborah.beaty@asurams.edu
BEATY, Kimberly, L 716-888-2301 292 D beatyk@canisius.edu
BEATY, Lori 254-968-9430 446 E lbeaty@tarleton.edu
BEAUCHAMP, Cheryl, L 518-629-8177 302 E c.beauchamp@hvcc.edu
BEAUCHAMP, Edwin 941-359-4200 110 D erb1@usf.edu
BEAUCHAMP, Lance 904-588-2104 101 G lbeauch@ju.edu
BEAUCHAMP, Norman 616-234-2785 227 D beauch66@msu.edu
BEAUCHAMP, Robbin 617-989-4112 219 E beauchampr1@wit.edu
BEAUDIN, Giselda 407-646-2466 105 M gbeaudin@rollins.edu
BEAUDIN, Paul, M 631-451-4000 321 F beaudip@sunysuffolk.edu
BEAUDOIN, Shikara 920-693-1139 499 G shikara.beaudoin@gotoltc.edu
BEAUDRY, Matt 313-593-5070 231 F mdbeau@umich.edu
BEAUGENE, Rosa 281-649-3801 437 H rbeaugene@hbu.edu
BEAUJON, Francis 530-257-6181 47 F fbeaujon@lassencollege.edu
BEAULIER, Scott 701-231-8804 345 G scott.beaulier@ndsu.edu
BEAULIEU, Elizabeth 203-932-7257 89 A ebeaulieu@newhaven.edu
BEAULIEU, Ellen 207-602-2334 196 G ebeaulieu@une.edu
BEAULIEU, Gary, R 317-940-9624 153 F gbeaulie@butler.edu
BEAUMONT, Patricia, L 412-578-8772 380 E plbeaumont@carlow.edu
BEAUMONT, Samuel (Lee) 210-690-9000 437 E sbeaumont@hallmarkuniversity.edu
BEAUMONT DOSS, Katherine 210-486-3936 429 F kbeaumont@alamo.edu
BEAUPRE, David, R 610-660-1320 398 C dbeaupre@sju.edu
BEAUPREWHITE, Renee 802-468-1339 464 A renee.beauprewhite@castleton.edu
BEAUREGARD, Amy 419-866-0261 361 H abeauregard@stautzenberger.com
BEAUREGARD, Jill 320-589-6036 244 B beaureja@morris.umn.edu
BEAUREGARD, Kathy, B 269-387-3061 232 K kathy.beauregard@wmich.edu
BEAUREGARD, Stephen 508-565-1375 218 H sbeauregard@stonehill.edu
BEAVEN, Liz 415-575-6105 29 B ebeaven@ciis.edu
BEAVER, David 304-293-2545 491 C david.beaver@mail.wvu.edu
BEAVER, Hillary 619-849-2388 57 E hbeaver@pointloma.edu
BEAVER, Jeff, S 864-388-8208 410 D jbeaver@lander.edu
BEAVER, Nancy 770-533-7001 121 B nbeaver@laniertech.edu
BEAVER, Noele 641-422-4004 168 D noele.beaver@niacc.edu
BEAVER, Randy, L 843-953-6802 408 E beaverr@cofc.edu
BEAVER, Robert 651-779-5744 237 G robert.beaver@century.edu

BEAVERS, Gayonne 940-397-3298 440 F gayonne.beavers@msutexas.edu
BEAVERS, Judy 517-321-0242 224 F jbeavers@glcc.edu
BEAVERS, Kristin 714-289-2020.. 36 C kbeavers@chapman.edu
BEAVERS, Kristy 714-289-2020.. 36 C kbeavers@chapman.edu
BEAVERS, Leslie 937-328-6062 350 L beaversl@clarkstate.edu
BEAVERS, Philip, E 517-321-0242 224 F pbeavers@glcc.edu
BEAVERS, Robin 503-517-1220 377 G rbeavers@warnerpacific.edu
BEAZER, Ken 435-652-7919 460 G ken.beazer@dixie.edu
BEAZLEY, Michael 906-632-6841 226 E
BEBBER, Glenda, H 704-233-8742 344 G gbebber@wingate.edu
BEBER, Melissa 531-622-2236 267 H mlbeber@mccneb.edu
BECCARIA, Michael 518-327-6376 311 G mbeccaria@paulsmiths.edu
BECENTI, Nathalie 505-786-4180 286 G n.becenti@navajotech.edu
BECENTI, Tonilee 505-786-4151 286 G tbecenti@navajotech.edu
BECERRA, Cynthia 209-478-0800.. 45 H cbecerra@humphreys.edu
BECERRA, Gilberto 210-486-3930 429 F gbecerra8@alamo.edu
BECERRA, Irma 703-284-5781 469 C ibecerra@marymount.edu
BECERRA, Irma 703-284-1598 469 C ibecerra@marymount.edu
BECERRA, Kimberly 361-825-2639 447 C kimberly.becerra@tamucc.edu
BECERRA, Mary 657-278-2850.. 31 E mbecerra@fullerton.edu
BECERRIL, Gina 323-259-2548.. 54 E gbecerril@oxy.edu
BECHARD, Deanna 603-646-9100 274 D d.bechard@snhu.edu
BECHARD, Matthew 785-243-1435 172 F mbechard@cloud.edu
BECHDEL, Gwen 570-484-2001 395 B gbechdel@lockhaven.edu
BECHEN, Linda 319-363-1323 168 C lbechen@mtmercy.edu
BECHER, Amy 412-365-1139 381 C abecher@chatham.edu
BECHER, Dave 305-284-4020 112 E davebecher@miami.edu
BECHER, Gregory, J 805-525-4417.. 67 D gbecher@thomasaquinas.edu
BECHERER, Jeffery 212-431-2888 309 G jeff.becherer@nyls.edu
BECHERER, Jennifer 903-463-8648 437 D bechererj@grayson.edu
BECHTEL, Brian 816-604-1059 255 D brian.bechtel@mcckc.edu
BECHTEL, Brian 816-604-3036 255 H brian.bechtel@mcckc.edu
BECICKA, Kim 319-398-5525 167 C kim.becicka@kirkwood.edu
BECK, Anne, D 313-664-7473 222 F abeck@collegeforcreativestudies.edu
BECK, Bruce 617-850-1253 210 D bbeck@hchc.edu
BECK, Carina 406-994-7627 264 D cbeck@montana.edu
BECK, Cathy 402-354-7709 268 C cathy.beck@methodistcollege.edu
BECK, Cherie 517-371-5140 233 A beckc@cooley.edu
BECK, Daniel 405-733-7459 369 I dbeck@rose.edu
BECK, Deborah, C 803-777-3957 413 C dbeck@sc.edu
BECK, Erika, D 805-437-8410.. 30 F erika.beck@csuci.edu
BECK, Gretchen 814-332-2754 378 D gbeck@allegheny.edu
BECK, Jacob 214-887-5067 436 B jbeck@dts.edu
BECK, Jeffery 765-361-6346 162 E beckj@wabash.edu
BECK, Jen 512-245-5500 450 E jb32@txstate.edu
BECK, Jeneane 319-384-0005 163 A jeneane-beck@uiowa.edu
BECK, Jennifer, M 512-448-8516 442 M jbeck@stedwards.edu
BECK, Judy 803-641-3269 413 D judyb@usca.edu
BECK, Leesa 805-893-4165.. 70 A leesa.beck@sa.ucsb.edu
BECK, Maryann, M 334-833-4443.... 5 H mbeck@hawks.huntingdon.edu
BECK, Michael 864-592-4634 412 F beckm@sccsc.edu
BECK, Michael, J 310-825-2411.. 69 A michaelbeck@ucla.edu
BECK, Mike 479-394-7622.. 23 C mbeck@uarichmountain.edu
BECK, Raphe 541-346-6317 377 D apheb@uoregon.edu
BECK, Richard 918-343-7615 369 F rbeck@rsu.edu
BECK, Robert, J 414-229-3713 497 A rjbeck@uwm.edu
BECK, Ronda 517-371-5140 233 A beckr@cooley.edu
BECK, Stacie 480-423-6536.. 13 H stacie.beck@scottsdalecc.edu
BECK, Tamara 336-757-3345 334 E tbeck@forsythtech.edu
BECK-DUDLEY, Caryn 408-554-4523.. 62 D cbeckdudley@scu.edu
BECKA, Roberta 310-973-3134.. 41 L rbecka@elcamino.edu
BECKEL, Constance 724-838-4219 398 H beckel@setonhill.edu
BECKEMEYER, Wendy, C 412-397-5212 397 G beckemeyer@rmu.edu
BECKER, Alex 870-460-1022.. 22 D beckera@uamont.edu
BECKER, Amy 612-874-3799 236 K amy_naughton@mcad.edu
BECKER, Ashley 618-545-3015 140 E abecker@kaskaskia.edu
BECKER, Brian 512-492-3017 430 G bbecker@aoma.edu
BECKER, Carol 212-854-9847 297 C cbecker@columbia.edu
BECKER, Charles, P 304-384-5190 490 A beckerc@concord.edu
BECKER, Dennis, M 303-871-3897.. 83 D dbecker@du.edu
BECKER, Gerrie 505-224-4551 285 J gbecker1@cnm.edu
BECKER, Janine 570-945-8112 386 I janine.becker@keystone.edu
BECKER, Jim 812-855-4884 156 A jambecke@iu.edu
BECKER, Joan 617-287-5862 211 E joan.becker@umb.edu
BECKER, Joe 503-768-7971 373 G jbecker@lclark.edu
BECKER, Jonathan 845-758-7378 290 G jbecker@bard.edu
BECKER, Joseph 516-773-5000 504 G beckerj@usmma.edu
BECKER, Karen 815-802-8405 140 D kbecker@kcc.edu
BECKER, Karl 267-295-2311 397 F kbecker@walnuthillcollege.edu
BECKER, Karl, D 267-295-2307 397 F kbecker@walnuthillcollege.edu
BECKER, Keri 616-331-8800 224 E beckeker@gvsu.edu
BECKER, Kristen 928-428-8308.. 12 E kristen.becker@eac.edu
BECKER, Laurel 970-943-7004.. 84 D lbecker@western.edu
BECKER, Lois 312-341-3615 147 H lbecker05@roosevelt.edu
BECKER, Mark, P 404-413-1300 119 E mbecker@gsu.edu
BECKER, Maureen 718-262-5310 295 F mbecker@york.cuny.edu
BECKER, Milissa, M 651-641-8268 235 F becker@csp.edu
BECKER, Pete, D 708-209-3092 135 F pete.becker@cuchicago.edu
BECKER, Ronald 201-761-6415 282 I rbecker@saintpeters.edu
BECKER, Sara, M 856-225-6409 281 G sara.becker@rutgers.edu
BECKER, Scott 517-884-6546 227 D beckersc@msu.edu
BECKER, Sheila, R 563-556-5110 168 E beckers@nicc.edu
BECKER, Stefan 201-684-7529 280 H sbecker@ramapo.edu
BECKER, Steven 973-278-5400 275 I steven-becker@berkeleycollege.edu
BECKER, Steven 973-278-5400 291 D steven-becker@berkeleycollege.edu
BECKER, Zerryl 760-862-1328.. 39 A zbecker@collegeofthedesert.edu
BECKER-LUTZ, Jill 303-797-5882.. 76 I jill.becker-lutz@arapahoe.edu
BECKER-RICHARDS, Joicy 609-497-7901 280 D joicy.becker@ptsem.edu
BECKERMANN, Corie 320-308-4848 240 H cabeckermann@stcloudstate.edu
BECKETT, Karen, J 305-284-5749 112 E kbeckett@miami.edu
BECKFORD, Dillon 803-535-5301 407 G dbeckford@claflin.edu
BECKHAM, Paul 410-462-7754 197 E pbeckham@bccc.edu
BECKHAM, Terry 913-722-0272 174 E terry.beckham@kansaschristian.edu
BECKHAM, Tim 605-229-8378 416 C tim.beckham@presentation.edu
BECKHORN, Roy 916-568-3190.. 50 E beckhor@losrios.edu
BECKLER, Larry 843-525-8282 412 H lbeckler@tcl.edu
BECKLES, Claude 918-836-6886 370 D claude.beckles@spartan.edu
BECKLEY, Clark 913-234-0609 172 E clark.beckley@cleveland.edu
BECKLEY, David, L 662-252-2491 248 G dlbeckley@rustcollege.edu
BECKMAN, Amy 620-242-0400 175 F beckmana@mcpherson.edu
BECKMAN, John, H 212-998-6848 310 B john.beckman@nyu.edu
BECKMAN, Seth 765-285-5495 153 C
BECKNER, Christine 718-368-5051 294 E cbeckner@kbcc.cuny.edu
BECKNER, Rebecca 319-385-6284 167 A rebecca.beckner@iw.edu
BECKNER, Scott 319-335-5026 163 A scott-beckner@uiowa.edu
BECKRICH, Chris 817-531-4444 451 E
BECKS, Crystal 661-654-3012.. 30 E cbecks@csub.edu
BECKSTROM, Amy, D 303-492-6494.. 83 A amy.beckstrom@colorado.edu
BECKSTROM, Brian 319-352-8217 170 C brian.beckstrom@wartburg.edu
BECKSTROM, Ron 218-755-2743 237 E ronald.beckstrom@bemidjistate.edu
BECKVOLD, John 304-462-6181 490 C john.beckvold@glenville.edu
BECKWITH, LaSharnda 800-477-2254.. 30 A
BECKWITH, Melissa 317-940-9900 153 F mbeckwit@butler.edu
BECKWITH, Rachel 413-559-5765 210 A
BEDA, Cheri 308-398-7437 266 A cheribeda@cccneb.edu
BEDARD, Brooke 413-265-2314 208 C bedardb@elms.edu
BEDDARD, Wesley 919-807-7098 331 L
BEDELL, Honey 563-336-3302 165 B hbedell@eicc.edu
BEDELL, Michael, D 773-442-6100 145 B m-bedell@neiu.edu
BEDELL, Todd 603-271-6484 273 B tbedell@ccsnh.edu
BEDFORD, Allen 218-755-2016 237 E allen.bedford@bemidjistate.edu
BEDFORD, April 718-951-5214 293 C abedford@brooklyn.cuny.edu
BEDFORD, Carter 817-515-1193 445 G carter.bedford@tccd.edu
BEDFORD, Dan 801-626-8091 461 B dbedford@weber.edu
BEDFORD, Grant 209-946-2537.. 70 E gbedford@pacific.edu
BEDFORD, John 405-208-5322 367 I jbedford@okcu.edu
BEDFORD, Michelle 770-412-4005 124 G michelle.bedford@sctech.edu
BEDFORD, Norm 702-774-8000 271 E norm.bedford@unlv.edu
BEDI, Param, S 570-577-1557 379 F param.bedi@bucknell.edu
BEDILLION, Charlene 724-503-1001 402 E cbedillion@washjeff.edu
BEDINGFIELD, Eric 864-250-8700 410 B eric.bedingfield@gvltec.edu
BEDINI, Ken 860-231-5430.. 89 B kbedini@usj.edu
BEDNAR, Gerald, J 440-943-7600 360 J jerrybednar@juno.com
BEDNARZ, Bridgette 254-968-9271 446 E bednarz@tarleton.edu
BEDNARZ, Jeffrey 413-205-3208 205 A jeffrey.bednarz@aic.edu
BEDNEY, Elynda, A 269-471-6040 221 B bedney@andrews.edu
BEDOYA, Eduardo 231-777-0332 228 D eduardo.bedoya@muskegoncc.edu
BEDOYA, Theresa 410-225-2434 199 H tbedoya@mica.edu
BEDRYK, Michael 516-726-5644 504 G bedrykm@usmma.edu
BEDSOLE, C. Blake 479-968-0343.. 18 C bbedsole@atu.edu
BEDTKE, James 507-457-1458 243 B jbedtke@smumn.edu
BEDWELL, Teresa, M 937-775-2313 364 I teresa.bedwell@wright.edu
BEE, Richard 562-944-0351.. 27 C richard.e.bee@biola.edu
BEEBE, Barbara, R 325-574-6501 458 E bbeebe@wtc.edu
BEEBE, Craig 970-943-2314.. 84 D cbeebe@western.edu
BEEBE, Gayle, D 805-565-6024.. 74 K president@westmont.edu
BEEBE, Jennifer 716-338-1404 303 D jenniferbeebe@mail.sunyjcc.edu
BEEBE, Norman 413-775-1333 214 C beebe@gcc.mass.edu
BEEBE, Robert 951-571-6113.. 58 G robert.beebe@mvc.edu
BEEBE-STEVENS, Heather 509-434-5123 480 A heather.beebe-stevens@ccs.spokane.edu
BEEBE-STEVENS, Heather 509-434-5125 480 B heather.beebe-stevens@ccs.spokane.edu
BEEBE STEVENS, Heather 509-434-5123 479 I h.beebe-stevens@ccs.spokan.edu
BEEBY, James, M 812-464-1735 161 E jmbeeby@usi.edu
BEECH, Amanda 661-255-1050.. 28 K abeech@calarts.edu
BEECH, Bettina 601-984-1020 249 E bbeech@umc.edu
BEECHER, Brian 616-234-3869 224 D brianbeecher@grcc.edu
BEECHER, Michael 603-456-2656 274 A mbeecher@northeastcatholic.edu
BEECHER, Shan, L 515-574-1985 166 E beecher@iowacentral.edu
BEEHLER, Jeff 509-865-0446 481 G beehler_j@heritage.edu
BEEHLER, John, M 256-782-5881.... 5 J president@jsu.edu
BEEKE, Joel, R 616-432-3403 229 I joel.beeke@prts.edu
BEEKE, Jonathon 616-432-3408 229 I jonathon.beeke@prts.edu
BEEKMAN, William, R 517-355-1623 227 D beekman@msu.edu
BEELEN, Joan 616-957-6027 221 P jrb44@calvinseminary.edu
BEELER, Jeremy 908-835-2301 284 G jbeeler@warren.edu
BEELER, Sydney 724-925-4050 403 A beelers@westmoreland.edu
BEEMAN, Greg 845-675-4417 310 G greg.beeman@nyack.edu
BEEMAN, Meredith 252-249-1851 336 F mbeeman@pamlicocc.edu
BEEMER, Matthew 904-596-2473 111 F mbeemer@tbc.edu
BEEMER, Pamela 847-491-7505 145 F p-beemer@northwestern.edu
BEEN, Sharon, A 501-882-8836.. 17 F sabeen@asub.edu
BEENEY, Jake 309-694-5520 138 C jacob.beeney@icc.edu
BEERS, David 253-879-3902 485 E dbeers@pugetsound.edu
BEERS, Di 425-235-2426 483 G dbeers@rtc.edu
BEERS, Josh 717-560-8240 388 B jbeers@lbc.edu

BEERS, Kelly 330-941-3582 365 C kbeers@ysu.edu

BEERS, Maggie 415-338-3613 34 A mbeers@sfsu.edu

BEERS, Stephen, T 479-524-7252 19 H sbeers@jbu.edu

BEERT, Brian 563-386-3570 166 A bbeert@hamiltontechcollege.com

BEESE, Cheryl 918-895-9401 369 C cheryl.beese@plattcollege.org

BEESON, Duane, L 712-707-7116 168 H beeson@nwciowa.edu

BEETS, Shannon 775-831-1314 272 D sbeets@sierranevada.edu

BEGANY, James 502-852-5555 185 C jim.begany@louisville.edu

BEGARLY, Brandon, J 718-960-8357 294 A brandon.begarly@lehman.cuny.edu

BEGAY, Janice 785-749-8419 173 G janice.begay@bie.edu

BEGAY, Karen, F 520-626-9809 16 G kfbegay@email.arizona.edu

BEGAYE, Nolan, S 928-724-6857 12 C nsbegaye@dinecollege.edu

BEGG, Melissa, D 212-854-2691 297 C mdb3@columbia.edu

BEGIN, Gene, P 508-286-3223 220 A begin_gene@wheatoncollege.edu

BEGIN, Russell 207-453-5123 194 I rbegin@kvcc.me.edu

BEGLEY, John, B 270-384-8505 183 C begleyj@lindsey.edu

BEGLEY, Mary Ann 386-752-1822 99 A maryanne.begley@fgc.edu

BEGLEY, Shannon 215-670-9072 391 H svbegley@peirce.edu

BEGLY, Mark, L 757-221-1009 466 C mlbegly@wm.edu

BEGOR, Alison 859-233-8520 184 G abegor@transy.edu

BEHAN, Lawrence 413-662-5245 213 A l.behan@mcla.edu

BEHAN KRAUS, Carolyn, A 203-773-8521 84 F cbehan@albertus.edu

BEHAUNEK, Luke 515-961-1562 169 D luke.behaunek@simpson.edu

BEHEN, Joseph 312-499-4272 148 I jbehen@saic.edu

BEHL, Josh, J 218-477-4654 239 D joshua.behl@mnstate.edu

BEHLING, Laura 253-879-3205 485 E provost@pugetsound.edu

BEHM, Bonnie Lee 610-519-6456 402 D bonnie.behm@villanova.edu

BEHM, Sarah 616-988-3639 226 C sbehm@kuyper.edu

BEHMAND, Mojgan 415-485-3276 41 H mojgan.behmand@dominican.edu

BEHMER, Scott 440-610-2240 124 E sbehmer@southuniversity.edu

BEHNEN, Bob 660-626-2395 250 A bbehnen@atsu.edu

BEHNEY, Melissa 860-343-5833 86 A mbehney@mxcc.edu

BEHR, Eileen, W 215-571-3548 383 B eileen.w.behr@drexel.edu

BEHR, Fred, C 507-786-3636 243 C behr@stolaf.edu

BEHR, Julie 706-778-8500 123 B jbehr@piedmont.edu

BEHR, Kate, E 914-337-9300 297 D kate.behr@concordia-ny.edu

BEHR, Kevin 361-354-2338 433 C kevind@coastalbend.edu

BEHR, Michelle 320-589-6035 244 B

BEHR, Richard, A 239-590-7399 108 K rbehr@fgcu.edu

BEHRE, William 724-738-2000 395 F william.behre@sru.edu

BEHRENDT, Todd 315-792-5679 307 D tbehrendt@mvcc.edu

BEHRENS, Christina 407-708-4570 107 D behrensc@seminolestate.edu

BEHRENS, Eric 610-499-1036 403 B ebehrens@widener.edu

BEHRENS, Kim 559-791-2322 47 A kbehrens@portervillecollege.edu

BEHRENS, Michael 217-351-2433 146 C mbehrens@parkland.edu

BEHRENS, Susanne 713-623-2040 430 K sbehrens@aii.edu

BEHRENS, Timothy 414-229-5663 497 A behrens5@uwm.edu

BEHRMANN, Clare 314-256-8807 250 D behrmann@ai.edu

BEHRNS, Kevin 314-977-9801 259 H kevin.behrns@health.slu.edu

BEIDLEMAN, David, C 717-361-1493 383 E beidlemand@etown.edu

BEIER, Nancy, A 410-777-2834 197 C nabeier@aacc.edu

BEIGHLEY, David 304-367-4726 489 D david.beighley@pierpont.edu

BEIGHTS, Chad 765-677-2497 157 D chad.beights@indwes.edu

BEIKIRCH, Dale 432-685-5539 440 E dbeikirch@midland.edu

BEIL, Cheryl 202-994-6712 91 F cbeil@gwu.edu

BEILHARZ, Peter, J 512-448-8521 442 M peterb@stedwards.edu

BEILOCK, Sian, L 212-854-2021 290 J beilock@barnard.edu

BEILSTEIN, Daniel, A 724-847-6115 384 G

BEIMER, Connie 505-277-2498 288 G cbeimer@unm.edu

BEISE, Elizabeth, J 301-405-6836 202 C beise@umd.edu

BEISECKER, Mark 805-893-4071 70 A mark.beisecker@bookstore.ucsb.edu

BEISNER, John 657-278-4937 31 E jbeisner@fulllerton.edu

BEISSNER, Katherine 315-464-6560 317 F beissnek@upstate.edu

BEISWANGER, Chris 719-255-3088 83 B cbeiswan@uccs.edu

BEITEL, Leland, R 443-334-2064 201 H lbeitel@stevenson.edu

BEITLER, Sidney 561-868-3484 104 D beitlers@palmbeachstate.edu

BEITZEL, Vernon, L 540-464-7211 476 G beitzelvl@vmi.edu

BEIZA, Rocio 713-221-8562 453 B beizar@uhd.edu

BEJAR, Elizabeth 305-348-2151 109 A elizabeth.bejar@fiu.edu

BEJARANO, Hope 602-384-2555 11 F hope.bejarano@bryanuniversity.edu

BEJARANO, Ricky 505-747-5050 287 G ricky.bejarano@nnmc.edu

BEJNAROWICZ, Ewa 312-553-3193 134 B ebejnarowicz@ccc.edu

BEJUNE, Matthew 508-929-8511 213 E mbejune@worcester.edu

BEKCHIAN, Arina 510-925-4282 25 Q abekchya@aua.am

BEKISZ, Peter 315-279-5262 304 A pbekisz@keuka.edu

BEKKER, Corne 757-352-4401 470 H clbekker@regent.edu

BELANGER, Annie 616-331-2621 224 E belange1@gvsu.edu

BELANGER, OFM, Brian, C 518-783-5047 315 J bbelanger@siena.edu

BELANGER, David, J 413-585-2530 218 F dbelange@smith.edu

BELANGER, Lisa 207-780-5411 196 F lisa.belanger@maine.edu

BELANGER, Marc 414-930-3119 495 A belangem@mtmary.edu

BELANGER-HAAS, Aimee 937-328-6038 350 L haasa@clarkstate.edu

BELCASTRO, Richard 678-331-4459 121 C richard.belcastro@life.edu

BELCHER, Carol 843-574-6230 413 B carol.belcher@tridenttech.edu

BELCHER, Chris 417-865-2815 253 B belcherc@evangel.edu

BELCHER, Dana 580-559-5564 366 C dbelcher@ecok.edu

BELCHER, Jim 866-323-0233 57 J president@providencecc.edu

BELCHER, Lawrence 317-788-2397 161 B belcherl@uindy.edu

BELD, Jo, M 507-786-3632 243 C beld@stolaf.edu

BELDEN, Donna 401-874-7049 406 B

BELDEN, Doug 651-290-6360 242 G doug.belden@mitchellhamline.edu

BELDEN, Eric 330-490-7337 364 B ebelden@walsh.edu

BELDEN, William 360-992-2103 479 F wbelden@clark.edu

BELETE, Yared 303-797-5092 76 I yared.belete@arapahoe.edu

BELEW, Amy, C 731-881-7901 428 B abelew@utm.edu

BELEW, Katherine 903-434-8264 441 B kbelew@ntcc.edu

BELFIELD, Kevin, D 973-596-3676 279 F kevin.d.belfield@njit.edu

BELFIELD, Sherri 704-378-1032 330 D sbelfield@jcsu.edu

BELFIORE, Michael 914-606-7895 325 C michael.belfiore@sunywcc.edu

BELICS, Patrick 312-621-9650 144 F pbelics@nl.edu

BELIN, Jacki 908-526-1200 281 A jacki.belin@raritanval.edu

BELINER, Janice 413-565-1000 205 G jberliner@baypath.edu

BELISLE, Andria 320-308-3117 240 H aebelisle@stcloudstate.edu

BELISLE, William, R 504-284-5539 190 I wbelisle@suno.edu

BELK, Peter 913-469-8500 174 D pbelk@jccc.edu

BELKNAP, Peggy 928-536-6231 14 J peggy.belknap@npc.edu

BELKO, Dawn 763-424-0715 239 G dbelko@nhcc.edu

BELL, Aimee 330-569-5279 353 J bella1@hiram.edu

BELL, Angela 404-962-3069 126 F angela.bell@usg.edu

BELL, Barbara 216-987-4851 351 G barbara.bell@tri-c.edu

BELL, Bill 765-494-7395 159 E

BELL, Brett 619-388-7815 60 E bbell@sdccd.edu

BELL, Brigitte 815-740-3447 151 J bbell@stfrancis.edu

BELL, Brittany, M 920-832-7030 493 K brittany.m.bell@lawrence.edu

BELL, Brooke 615-687-6906 418 A bbell@abcnash.edu

BELL, Carla 334-727-8014 7 D cbell@tuskegee.edu

BELL, Carmen 575-624-8080 287 A carmen@nmmi.edu

BELL, Christine 909-607-3306 37 D christine.bell@cgu.edu

BELL, Christopher 207-768-9511 196 E chris@maine.edu

BELL, Cindy 406-657-2363 264 E cindy.bell@msubillings.edu

BELL, Corinne 802-387-6863 462 D corinnebell@landmark.edu

BELL, Cynthia, M 330-941-3101 365 C cmbell02@ysu.edu

BELL, Dana 580-745-2132 369 K dbell@se.edu

BELL, Danielle 803-321-5128 411 D danielle.bell@newberry.edu

BELL, Darrell 585-594-6202 310 F bell_darrell@roberts.edu

BELL, Darrell 585-594-6200 312 K bell_darrell@roberts.edu

BELL, David 718-990-1305 314 B belld@stjohns.edu

BELL, David 646-565-6000 322 J david.bell@touro.edu

BELL, Dean, P 312-322-1791 149 I dbell@spertus.edu

BELL, Denise 508-793-2397 208 B dbell@holycross.edu

BELL, Denise 850-973-9481 103 K belld@nfcc.edu

BELL, Don 205-391-2327 3 E dbell@sheltonstate.edu

BELL, Eve 940-565-2759 454 A eve.bell@unt.edu

BELL, Gregory, J 570-321-4395 389 E bell@lycoming.edu

BELL, Harold 404-270-5269 125 B hbell@spelman.edu

BELL, Hershey 814-866-6641 388 A hbell@lecom.edu

BELL, III, J. Edward 843-377-2426 407 D ebell@charlestonlaw.edu

BELL, Jacqueline, B 843-377-1327 407 D jbell@charlestonlaw.edu

BELL, James, L 580-327-8590 367 E jlbell@nwosu.edu

BELL, Jenny 205-665-6565 8 D jbell8@montevallo.edu

BELL, Jessica 602-286-8330 13 B jessica.bell@gatewaycc.edu

BELL, John, D 808-675-3703 127 E john.bell@byuh.edu

BELL, John, W 256-761-6318 7 B jwbell@talladega.edu

BELL, Julie 217-228-5432 146 F bellju@quincy.edu

BELL, Kati 415-482-2483 41 H kathrina.bell@dominican.edu

BELL, Katrina 973-328-5064 277 B kbell@ccm.edu

BELL, Kelli 563-425-5274 170 A bellk59@uiu.edu

BELL, Kelly 864-662-6064 406 G kbell@andersonuniversity.edu

BELL, Kimberly 256-216-5364 4 D kimberly.bell@athens.edu

BELL, Lauren, C 804-752-7268 470 F lbell@rmc.edu

BELL, Lauren, P 615-353-3604 425 D lauren.bell@nscc.edu

BELL, Leslie, T 910-521-6760 343 B leslie.bell@uncp.edu

BELL, Linda 212-854-2708 290 J labell@barnard.edu

BELL, Linda 610-372-4721 397 B lbell@racc.edu

BELL, Lisa, G 859-246-6564 180 K lisag.bell@kctcs.edu

BELL, Marty 217-228-5432 146 F bellma@quincy.edu

BELL, Melanie 919-735-5151 338 H mjbell@waynecc.edu

BELL, Melleta 432-837-8388 450 D mbell@sulross.edu

BELL, Norma, G 205-853-1200 2 G ngbell@jeffersonstate.edu

BELL, Patricia 931-431-9700 423 D pbell@nci.edu

BELL, Paul 864-379-8881 409 H paul.bell@erskine.edu

BELL, Peter 434-592-6515 468 H pabell2@liberty.edu

BELL, Randall, E 479-248-7236 19 C rbell@ecollege.edu

BELL, Rebecca 432-685-4556 440 E rbell@midland.edu

BELL, Rhonda 281-476-1858 443 C rhonda.bell@sjcd.edu

BELL, Richette 310-900-1600 40 A rbell@elcamino.edu

BELL, Robert, H 626-585-7205 55 K rhbell@pasadena.edu

BELL, Robin 229-931-2352 124 D rbell@southgatech.edu

BELL, Sheree 636-481-3119 254 A sbell6@jeffco.edu

BELL, Staci 402-465-2501 268 H sbell@nebrwesleyan.edu

BELL, Stephen 610-558-5549 391 D bells@neumann.edu

BELL, Steven 410-626-2502 201 D skbell@sjc.edu

BELL, Stuart, R 205-348-5100 7 G stuart.bell@ua.edu

BELL, Tamra 360-442-2621 482 B tbell@lowercolumbia.edu

BELL, Tom, J 828-884-8142 327 C bellt@brevard.edu

BELL, Wylie 910-410-1826 337 B wdbell@richmondcc.edu

BELL ADAMS, Sandra 718-262-2363 295 F sadams@york.cuny.edu

BELL-JORDAN, Katrina 773-442-5711 145 B k-bell1@neiu.edu

BELL-OWENS, Nora 585-395-2501 318 B nbell@brockport.edu

BELL-ROBINSON, Vicka 513-529-1809 356 E

BELLA, Andres 510-763-7787 24 C abella@acchs.edu

BELLACERO, Cynthia 252-737-3614 341 C bellacero18@ecu.edu

BELLAFIORE, April 508-678-2811 213 G april.bellafiore@bristolcc.edu

BELLAH, Eric 865-981-8225 421 F eric.bellah@maryvillecollege.edu

BELLALTA, Maria 617-585-0200 206 F maria.bellalta@the-bac.edu

BELLAMKONDA, Ravi 919-660-5389 328 G ravi@duke.edu

BELLAMY, Antoinette, P 910-630-7257 331 C abellamy@methodist.edu
BELLAMY, James 419-267-1267 358 A jbellamy@northweststate.edu
BELLAMY, Johnnie, O 972-860-7619 435 B johnniebellamy@dcccd.edu
BELLAMY, Reagan 509-682-6445 486 E rbellamy@wvc.edu
BELLAMY, Sandra 212-694-1000 291 I sbellamy@boricuacollege.edu
BELLAMY, Scott 304-357-6696 488 G scottbellamy@ucwv.edu
BELLAMY-BENNETT, Sonja, A 803-813-1147 412 C sbennet5@scsu.edu
BELLANCA, Rose, B 734-973-3491 232 B rbellanca@wccnet.edu
BELLANGER, Angela 218-477-2211 239 D angela.bellanger@mnstate.edu
BELLANI, Rajesh 740-587-5034 352 G bellanir@denison.edu
BELLANTONI, Jeffrey 803-323-2323 414 G bellantonij@winthrop.edu
BELLAVIA, Rand 716-829-7616 298 F bellavia@dyc.edu
BELLE ISLE, Denell 651-213-4678 236 B
BELLEFEUILLLE, Barbara, K 574-807-7255 153 E barb.bellefeuille@betheluniversity.edu
BELLEMER, Jess 828-898-8770 330 E bellemerj@lmc.edu
BELLENGER, Lauren 713-221-8197 453 B bellengerl@uhd.edu
BELLEW, Kevin 859-858-3511 178 I kevin.bellew@asbury.edu
BELLI, Keith, L 864-656-3013 408 A kbelli@clemson.edu
BELLINA, Amy 732-571-3586 279 B abellina@monmouth.edu
BELLING, Karen 630-752-5021 152 F karen.belling@wheaton.edu
BELLING, Shawn 608-243-4180 499 H sbelling@madisoncollege.edu
BELLINGER, Andrew 315-792-7141 321 E abellinger@sunypoly.edu
BELLINGER, Eunice 304-205-6613 488 K eunice.bellinger@bridgevalley.edu
BELLINGS, Andy 563-588-6420 163 F andy.bellings@clarke.edu
BELLINI, Michel 217-265-5297 151 D bellini@illinois.edu
BELLINO, Maria 480-517-8220.. 13 G maria.bellino@riosalado.edu
BELLIVEAU, Cynthia, L . 802-656-3890 463 E cynthia.belliveau@uvm.edu
BELLO, Chippi 360-992-2260 479 F cbello@clark.edu
BELLO, Diane 631-632-6179 317 D diane.bello@stonybrook.edu
BELLO-DECASTRO, Leigh 973-877-3483 277 I bellodecastro@essex.edu
BELLOMY, Chasley 256-228-6001.... 3 B bellomyc@nacc.edu
BELLOTTI, Michael, G ... 617-984-1776 218 B mbellotti@quincycollege.edu
BELLOW, Kathleen, D ... 504-520-7691 193 A ibcs@xula.edu
BELLOWS, Alan 801-649-5230 459 G technicalsupport@midwifery.edu
BELLOWS, Charlene 508-793-2514 208 B cbellows@holycross.edu
BELLOWS, Laurie 402-472-3755 269 J lbellows1@unl.edu
BELLUCCI, Anthony, D .. 973-378-2655 283 B anthony.bellucci@shu.edu
BELLUCCI, Debbie 413-755-4334 215 F dbellucci@stcc.edu
BELLUCCI, Keith 617-732-2145 216 B keith.bellucci@mcphs.edu
BELLUM, Kim 605-882-5284 415 F bellumk@lakeareatech.edu
BELMAN, David 925-473-7423.. 40 J dbelman@losmedanos.edu
BELMAR, Ricardo 305-607-6123 103 M belmar@nova.edu
BELMODIS, Cassie 503-399-5159 372 C cassie.belmodis@chemeketa.edu
BELMONT, Amanda 701-349-5416 346 J amandabelmont@trinitybiblecollege.edu
BELMONT, Heather 772-462-7215 101 E hbelmont@irsc.edu
BELOBRAJDIC, Scott 618-650-2298 149 F sbelobr@siue.edu
BELONNI-ROSARIO, Ruth-Aimee 404-687-4516 116 H belonni-rosarior@ctsnet.edu
BELOTE, Eve 757-789-1767 474 F ebelote@es.vccs.edu
BELOTE, Faith, D 757-594-7618 466 B faith.belote@cnu.edu
BELOTE, Michael, R 478-301-2850 121 E belote_mr@mercer.edu
BELOW, Debbie 573-986-6888 259 K dbelow@semo.edu
BELSHER, Judy 602-243-8200.. 14 A judy.belsher@southmountaincc.edu
BELSKY, Marianne 202-651-5031.. 91 E marianne.belsky@gallaudet.edu
BELSTRA, James, E 708-239-4720 150 F jim.belstra@trnty.edu
BELT, Mazel 603-456-2656 274 A mbelt@northeastcatholic.edu
BELTER, Joe 541-888-7634 376 F joseph.belter@socc.edu
BELTON, Ada, A 803-705-4327 407 A ada.belton@benedict.edu
BELTON, Allan 253-535-7101 482 H allan.belton@plu.edu
BELTON, Allan 253-535-7121 482 H allan.belton@plu.edu
BELTON, Ray 225-771-4680 190 H ray_belton@sus.edu
BELTON, Ray, L 225-771-4680 190 G ray_belton@sus.edu
BELTON, Tammie 216-791-5000 351 A tamatha.belton@cim.edu
BELTON, Victor 678-662-7989 297 D victor.belton@concordia-ny.edu
BELTRAN, Dulce 305-348-7347 109 A dulce.beltran@fiu.edu
BELTRAN, Philip 408-554-4161.. 62 D pjbeltran@scu.edu
BELTRAN, Renz 808-954-4934 127 G rbeltran@hmi.edu
BELTZ, Marah 386-481-2928.. 95 F beltzm@cookman.edu
BELUE, Jake, A 804-828-6568 473 F jabelue@vcu.edu
BELVINS, Walter 510-723-6648.. 35 O wbelvins@clpccd.org
BEM, Greg 425-739-8100 482 A greg.bem@lwtech.edu
BEMIS, Scot, R 603-646-3768 273 E scot.r.bemis@dartmouth.edu
BENABESS, Najiba 217-424-6285 143 H nbenabess@millikin.edu
BENABESS, Najibu 217-424-6285 143 H nbenabess@millikin.edu
BENAICHA, Hedi 617-349-8836 210 H hbenaich@lesley.edu
BENALI, Emily 425-640-1516 480 F emily.benali@edcc.edu
BENANDER, Mark 413-565-1000 205 G mbenander@baypath.edu
BENANTI, Jennifer 217-479-7031 142 I jennifer.benanti@mac.edu
BENAVIDES, Elma, F 512-863-1441 445 D benavide@southwestern.edu
BENAVIDES, Julie 323-265-8779.. 48 H benavijr@elac.edu
BENAVIDES, Letty 956-665-2255 455 D letty.benavides@utrgv.edu
BENAVIDES, Lewis 940-898-3555 451 F lbenavides@twu.edu
BENAVIDES-DOMINGUEZ, Patricia 361-698-2474 436 C pbdominguez@delmar.edu
BENBOW, Camilla, P 615-322-8407 428 D camilla.benbow@vanderbilt.edu
BENBOW, Sarah 952-446-4350 235 G benbows@crown.edu
BENBROOK, Tabitha 918-335-6854 368 G tbenbrook@okwu.edu
BENCHOFF, Bryan 225-578-3811 188 I bbenchoff@lsufoundation.org
BENCIVENGO, Alycia 732-247-5241 279 D abencivengo@nbts.edu
BENDAPUDI, Neeli 502-852-5417 185 C neeli@louisville.edu
BENDARSH, Joe 212-960-0110 326 E joe.bednarsh@yu.edu
BENDECK, Yvette 281-283-3022 453 A bendeck@uhcl.edu
BENDEL, Colleen 740-593-1642 359 G bendl@ohio.edu
BENDELE, Jennifer 419-227-3141 363 C jennifer@unoh.edu
BENDER, Christina 267-341-3017 386 A cbender@holyfamily.edu
BENDER, Dave 614-823-1876 360 A dbender@otterbein.edu
BENDER, David, L 989-837-4374 228 H bender@northwood.edu
BENDER, Donna 504-314-2148 191 B dbender@tulane.edu
BENDER, Jennie, M 606-474-3226 180 G jbender@kcu.edu
BENDER, Jim 651-635-2378 234 C j-bender@bethel.edu
BENDER, Judy 585-475-4315 313 A jebpsn@rit.edu
BENDER, Karla 713-718-8247 437 I karla.bender@hccs.edu
BENDER, Kim 307-778-4337 502 D kbender@lccc.wy.edu
BENDER, Linda 307-855-2102 501 V lbender@cwc.edu
BENDER, Loren, J 407-582-3408 112 K lbender2@valenciacollege.edu
BENDER, Marian 814-472-3931 398 B mbender@francis.edu
BENDER, Michael 845-207-0330 290 D
BENDER, Rick 432-685-4529 440 E rbender@midland.edu
BENDER, Starr, S 407-303-5765.. 94 D starr.bender@ahu.edu
BENDER, IV, Thomas, B 504-866-7426 190 B librarian@nds.edu
BENDER, Virginia 201-761-6024 282 I vbender@saintpeters.edu
BENDER, Yaakov 718-868-2300 291 B
BENDERS, Alison 510-549-5040.. 62 D ambenders@scu.edu
BENDES, Caren 313-993-3354 231 B bendescm@udmercy.edu
BENDICKSON, Alisa 414-930-3578 495 A bendicka@mtmary.edu
BENDICKSON, Kimberly 941-487-4668 109 D kbendickson@ncf.edu
BENEDETTI, Brian 253-864-3235 483 D bbenedetti@pierce.ctc.edu
BENEDETTI, Marco, F ... 716-888-2480 292 D benedet2@canisius.edu
BENEDICT, Barbara 719-549-3039.. 81 K barbara.benedict@pueblocc.edu
BENEDICT, David 860-486-2725.. 88 E david.benedict@uconn.edu
BENEDICT, Jody, C 585-385-8322 314 A jbenedict@sjfc.edu
BENEDICT, Kristen 505-224-4000 285 J kbenedict1@cnm.edu
BENEDICT, Mary 931-372-3503 426 E mbenedict@tntech.edu
BENEDICT, Michael 330-569-5134 353 J benedictm@hiram.edu
BENEDIK, Michael 979-845-4016 446 G benedik@tamu.edu
BENEFIEL, Lori 541-383-7572 372 B lbenefiel@cocc.edu
BENEFIEL, Patricia 619-574-6909.. 54 K pbenefiel@pacificcollege.edu
BENEFIEL, Ron 619-849-2613.. 57 E ronbenefiel@pointloma.edu
BENEKE, Thomas, J 515-574-1050 166 E beneke@iowacentral.edu
BENET, Micol, A 415-485-9502.. 39 C mabenet@marin.edu
BENET, Suzeanne 616-331-2400 224 E benets@gvsu.edu
BENEVENTO, Erin 410-386-4821 200 B ebenevento@mcdaniel.edu
BENFANTI, William, J ... 716-878-5557 318 C benfanwj@buffalostate.edu
BENFER, Pamela, A 570-577-1561 379 F pam.benfer@bucknell.edu
BENFORD, Gladys 870-575-8405.. 22 E benfordg@uapb.edu
BENFORD, Jeffrey 925-473-7425.. 40 J jbenford@losmedanos.edu
BENFORD, Michael 713-221-8129 453 B benfordm@uhd.edu
BENGE, Robert 423-236-2855 424 B rcbenge@southern.edu
BENGEL, Kristi 513-244-4624 357 A kristi.bengel@msj.edu
BENGFORT, Joseph 415-353-4273.. 69 E joe.bengfort@ucsf.edu
BENGINIA, Francis, A ... 610-330-5090 387 E benginif@lafayette.edu
BENGTSON, Kathy 612-767-7068 233 H katherine.bengtson@alfredadler.edu
BENHAM, Brad, T 325-674-4877 429 B bjb00c@acu.edu
BENHAM, Maenette 808-689-2770 128 G mbenham@hawaii.edu
BENHAM-DEAL, Tami ... 307-766-4286 502 H benham@uwyo.edu
BENI, Devendra 973-353-3569 282 B dbeni@afc.rutgers.edu
BENIASH, Jessica 860-906-5000.. 85 D jbeniash@capitalcc.edu
BENIGER, Joe 920-565-1000 493 J benigerjw@lakeland.edu
BENINGHOVE, Linda 201-216-5412 283 C linda.beninghove@stevens.edu
BENISH, Amy, L 262-554-2010 494 D albenish@aol.com
BENITEZ, Aristalia 570-484-2344 395 B aab38@lockhaven.edu
BENITEZ, Hubert 816-936-8711 259 I hbenitez@saintlukescollege.edu
BENITEZ, Karen 714-556-3610.. 72 F admissions@vanguard.edu
BENITEZ, Leyda, L 610-519-3976 402 D leyda.benitez@villanova.edu
BENITEZ, Michael 253-879-3929 485 E mbenitez@pugetsound.edu
BENITIZ, Yvette 575-527-7552 287 E ybenitiz@nmsu.edu
BENJAMIN, Daneida 954-486-7728 112 D dbenjamin@uftl.edu
BENJAMIN, Eric, M 240-567-5048 200 C eric.benjamin@montgomerycollege.edu
BENJAMIN, Eric, V 931-598-1241 423 M ebenjami@sewanee.edu
BENJAMIN, Helen 805-730-4011.. 62 C hbenjamin@sbcc.edu
BENJAMIN, Jack 803-641-3327 413 D jackb@usca.edu
BENJAMIN, Jodi 402-941-6102 267 L benjamin@midlandu.edu
BENJAMIN, Robert 269-471-3310 221 B robertb@andrews.edu
BENJAMIN, Robert 617-745-3595 208 G robert.j.benjamin@enc.edu
BENKE, Jack 573-592-5515 262 E jack.benke@westminster-mo.edu
BENKE, Meg 518-587-2100 321 A meg.benke@esc.edu
BENKE, Robin, P 276-328-0151 473 B rpb@virginia.edu
BENKESER, Kristina 724-738-2052 395 F kristina.benkeser@sru.edu
BENKO, Hope 512-472-4133 443 H hope.benko@ssw.edu
BENKO, Richard, A 724-287-8711 380 A richard.benko@bc3.edu
BENLOLO, Henri 352-854-2322.. 96 O benloloh@cf.edu
BENMAMOUN, Abbas ... 919-684-4997 328 G elabbas.benmamoun@duke.edu
BENN, Delores 704-403-3502 327 D delores.benn@carolinashealthcare.org
BENN, Sherri 512-245-2278 450 E sb17@txstate.edu
BENN, Valerie 919-718-7423 333 C vbenn159@cccc.edu
BENNANI, Farah 609-586-4800 278 F bennanif@mccc.edu
BENNE, Jennifer 573-681-5125 254 E bennej@lincolnu.edu
BENNEDUM-KASHAN, Cindy 845-434-5750 322 A ckashan@sunysullivan.edu
BENNEIAN, Teresa 717-290-8748 388 D tbenneian@lancasterseminary.edu
BENNER, Brent, W 813-253-6211 112 J bbenner@ut.edu
BENNER, Matthew 480-947-6644.. 15 A matthew.benner@pennfoster.edu
BENNER, Patrick 707-965-6242.. 55 D pbenner@puc.edu
BENNER, Patrick, B 804-289-8930 472 L pbenner@richmond.edu
BENNER, Tracy 614-823-1580 360 A tbenner@otterbein.edu
BENNETT, Amber 906-487-2538 227 E ambennet@mtu.edu
BENNETT, Amy 317-955-6768 158 U abennett@marian.edu
BENNETT, Anthony, T ... 910-672-1314 341 E abennett@uncfsu.edu

BERBRIER, Mitch ... 256-824-6200 ... 8 B
berbrim@uah.edu
BERCEGEAY, Angelia ... 225-490-1690 186 F
angelia.bercegeay@franu.edu
BERCH, Angela ... 678-664-0506 127 A
angela.berch@westgatech.edu
BERCHENI, Mark ... 307-766-5600 502 H
BERCZY, Josten ... 847-866-3995 137 E
josten.berczy@garrett.edu
BERDANIER, Bruce ... 605-688-4161 417 C
bruce.berdanier@sdstate.edu
BERENBAUM, Asher ... 917-645-0536 307 C
phecht@thejnet.com
BERENBAUM, Devorah .. 718-645-0536 307 C
mirrer@thejnet.com
BERENBAUM, Rachel ... 718-645-0536 307 C
mirrer@thejnet.com
BERENS-FUNK, Tracy ... 317-921-4371 157 H
tfunk@ivytech.edu
BERESFORD, Jack ... 619-388-6914.. 60 B
jberesford@sdccd.edu
BERG, Allison, S ... 404-686-2980 117 F
allison.berg@emory.edu
BERG, Amy ... 607-753-5942 318 D
amy.berg@cortland.edu
BERG, Beth ... 413-585-2106 218 F
bberg@smith.edu
BERG, Brandon ... 724-480-3368 381 K
brandon.berg@ccbc.edu
BERG, Cyndi ... 612-330-1212 233 K
bergc2@augsburg.edu
BERG, Cynthia ... 801-581-8620 460 E
cynthia.berg@psych.utah.edu
BERG, Dale ... 520-326-1600.. 15 M
BERG, Daniel ... 305-284-4215 112 E
dberg@miami.edu
BERG, Denise, D ... 717-871-7551 395 D
denise.berg@millersville.edu
BERG, Emily ... 701-231-8263 345 G
emily.a.berg@ndsu.edu
BERG, James ... 212-220-8323 293 A
jberg@bmcc.cuny.edu
BERG, Jean ... 413-559-6042 210 A
BERG, Jessica, W ... 216-368-3283 349 F
jessica.berg@case.edu
BERG, Jody ... 402-354-7034 268 C
jody.berg@methodistcollege.edu
BERG, Kara ... 970-339-6407.. 76 G
kara.odell@aims.edu
BERG, Kevin ... 509-682-6815 486 E
kberg@wvc.edu
BERG, Kevin, A ... 253-535-7890 482 H
bergka@plu.edu
BERG, Lindsay ... 406-791-5302 265 H
lindsay.berg@uprovidence.edu
BERG, Nancy ... 740-587-5620 352 G
bergn@denison.edu
BERG, Shane, A ... 609-524-1958 280 D
comm-pub@ptsem.edu
BERG, Shelton, G ... 305-284-2241 112 E
sberg@miami.edu
BERG, Tamara ... 507-457-5460 241 F
tberg@winona.edu
BERG, Thomas ... 914-968-6200 314 E
ftb@fatherberg.com
BERGAMASCO, Carla, R 412-578-6174 380 E
crbergamasco@carlow.edu
BERGANT, Amy ... 417-447-2629 257 G
berganta@otc.edu
BERGEN, Lori ... 303-492-5007.. 83 A
lori.bergen@colorado.edu
BERGEN, Randy ... 651-635-8041 234 C
r-bergen@bethel.edu
BERGENGREN, Audrey .. 651-793-1828 238 H
audrey.bergengren@metrostate.edu
BERGER, Amy, C ... 818-677-2932.. 32 D
amy.berger@csun.edu
BERGER, Andy ... 312-935-4100 147 D
aberger@robertmorris.edu
BERGER, Aron ... 845-426-3276 325 E
ydm@thejnet.com
BERGER, David ... 212-960-5253 326 E
dberger@yu.edu
BERGER, Donna, S ... 845-575-3000 305 L
donna.berger@marist.edu
BERGER, Doris ... 212-217-3400 299 H
doris_berger@fitnyc.edu
BERGER, Joseph ... 617-287-7600 211 E
joseph.berger@umb.edu
BERGER, Joseph, B ... 434-971-3301 503 G
joseph.b.berger2.mil@mail.mil
BERGER, Kelly ... 425-388-9202 480 G
kberger@everettcc.edu

BERGER, Leslie ... 405-208-5348 367 I
lberger@okcu.edu
BERGER, Lynn ... 518-255-5465 319 F
bergerla@cobleskill.edu
BERGER, Lynn ... 518-255-5423 319 F
bergerla@cobleskill.edu
BERGER, Mark ... 404-364-8303 122 J
mberger@oglethorpe.edu
BERGER, Michael ... 602-639-7500.. 12 J
BERGER, Scott ... 320-762-4475 237 B
scottb@alextech.edu
BERGER, Sheri ... 818-710-2281.. 49 C
bergersl@piercecollege.edu
BERGER, William ... 814-732-1107 394 F
wberger@edinboro.edu
BERGER, Yaakov ... 845-393-4308 325 H
admin@kessertorah.org
BERGER-SWEENEY,
Joanne ... 860-297-2086.. 88 C
president@trincoll.edu
BERGERON, Bette, S ... 315-267-2108 319 D
bergerbs@potsdam.edu
BERGERON, Ian ... 413-662-5592 213 A
ian.bergeron@mcla.edu
BERGERON, Iva ... 214-860-8735 435 D
ibergeron@dcccd.edu
BERGERON, Katherine .. 860-439-2666.. 86 H
katherine.bergeron@conncoll.edu
BERGERON, Mindy ... 925-969-3300.. 46 H
mbergeron@jfku.edu
BERGESON, Patricia ... 312-369-7478 135 E
pbergeson@colum.edu
BERGESON, Rachel ... 631-632-6740 317 D
rachel.bergeson@stonybrook.edu
BERGESON, Rachel, D .. 218-299-4728 235 E
bergeson@cord.edu
BERGETZ, Carl ... 312-942-6886 148 A
carl_bergetz@rush.edu
BERGGREN, Kent, E ... 208-535-5373 130 C
kent.berggren@cei.edu
BERGGREN, Stacey ... 208-467-8543 131 D
sberggren@nnu.edu
BERGH, David ... 315-655-7126 292 F
dbergh@cazenovia.edu
BERGHOFF, Carolyn ... 312-788-1151 152 B
cberghoff@vandercook.edu
BERGHOLZ, John ... 202-462-2101.. 92 C
jbergholz@iwp.edu
BERGIN, Bonita, M ... 707-545-3647.. 26 J
bonnie@berginu.edu
BERGLER, Michael ... 949-214-3187.. 40 F
michael.bergler@cui.edu
BERGLUND, Lars ... 916-703-9120.. 68 E
lberglund@ucdavis.edu
BERGLUND, Lori ... 712-749-2444 163 D
berglundl@bvu.edu
BERGMAN, Cheryl ... 904-256-7626 101 G
cbergma@ju.edu
BERGMAN, Donald, M .. 410-323-6211 198 C
BERGMAN, Greg ... 218-855-8145 237 F
gbergman@clcmn.edu
BERGMAN, Helen ... 903-813-2468 430 N
hbergman@austincollege.edu
BERGMAN, Joe ... 309-694-5367 138 C
joe.bergman@icc.edu
BERGMAN, Martha ... 336-334-4822 335 A
mabergman@gtcc.edu
BERGMAN, Matthew ... 217-228-5432 146 F
bergmma@quincy.edu
BERGMAN, Michael ... 334-683-5169 ... 6 A
mbergman@judson.edu
BERGMAN, Rebecca, M 507-933-7538 235 I
president@gustavus.edu
BERGMAN, JR.,
William, T ... 215-204-7405 399 F
william.bergman@temple.edu
BERGMANN, Donald, J . 570-941-7400 401 H
donald.bergmann@scranton.edu
BERGMANN, Leah ... 785-738-9062 176 A
lbergmann@ncktc.edu
BERGMANN, Michelle ... 541-440-4620 377 C
michelle.bergmann@umpqua.edu
BERGMANN, Ronald ... 718-960-8421 294 A
ronald.bergmann@lehman.cuny.edu
BERGMANN, Tom ... 847-947-5516 144 F
tbergmann@nl.edu
BERGQUIST, David ... 951-827-2228.. 69 C
david.bergquist@ucr.edu
BERGQUIST, Viola ... 320-308-5177 241 A
vbergquist@sctcc.edu
BERGREN, Rebecca, A .. 717-337-6866 384 H
rbergren@gettysburg.edu

BERGRUD, Erik ... 816-584-6412 258 A
erik.bergrud@park.edu
BERGS, Thomas ... 651-846-1676 241 B
thomas.bergs@saintpaul.edu
BERGSMA, Brad ... 785-890-3641 176 C
brad.bergsma@nwktc.edu
BERGSTROM, Mary, C .. 843-953-0193 408 E
bergstrom@cofc.edu
BERGSTROM, Tracey ... 361-582-2565 457 E
tracey.bergstrom@victoriacollege.edu
BERGTRAUM, Judy ... 646-664-2603 292 K
judy.bergtraum@cuny.edu
BERGUNDE, Gail ... 415-575-6107.. 29 B
gbergunde@ciis.edu
BERHE, Annette ... 901-435-1351 421 A
annette.berhe@loc.edu
BERHORST, Todd ... 323-463-2500.. 67 C
toddb@toa.edu
BERHORST, Todd ... 323-860-1199.. 53 B
toddb@mi.edu
BERICH, Anthony ... 434-947-8537 470 E
aberich@randolphcollege.edu
BERIGAN, Jennifer ... 513-936-1734 362 E
jennifer.berigan@uc.edu
BERK, Steven, L ... 806-743-3000 451 C
steven.berk@ttuhsc.edu
BERKE, Deborah ... 203-432-2279.. 89 D
deborah.berke@yale.edu
BERKENPAS, Barb ... 507-537-6215 241 D
barb.berkenpas@smsu.edu
BERKEY, Jessica ... 864-294-2267 410 A
jessica.berkey@furman.edu
BERKEY, Jonathan ... 704-894-2529 328 F
joberkey@davidson.edu
BERKHEIMER, Eric, J ... 410-677-6553 203 F
ejberkheimer@salisbury.edu
BERKHEIMER, Karen ... 410-334-2915 204 F
kberkheimer@worwic.edu
BERKINSHAW,
Stewart, M ... 405-325-1271 371 B
sberkinshaw@ou.edu
BERKLAS, Jennifer, L ... 909-607-7976.. 63 E
jberklas@scrippscollege.edu
BERKLEY, Shelley ... 702-777-1776.. 67 F
shelley.berkley@tun.touro.edu
BERKNER, Donna ... 817-202-6214 444 I
dberkner@swau.edu
BERKNER, Donna ... 817-202-6279 444 I
berkner@swau.edu
BERKNER, Paul, D ... 207-859-4460 193 E
paul.berkner@colby.edu
BERKOW, Dan ... 209-667-3381.. 33 C
dberkow@csustan.edu
BERKOWITZ, Bobbie ... 212-305-3582 297 C
bb2509@columbia.edu
BERKOWITZ, David ... 256-824-6952 ... 8 B
david.berkowitz@uah.edu
BERKOWITZ, Irving ... 561-868-3218 104 D
berkowii@palmbeachstate.edu
BERKOWITZ, Justin ... 386-267-0565.. 97 C
director@daytonacollege.edu
BERKSHIRE, Jacki ... 864-833-8006 411 I
jberkshire@presby.edu
BERLEY, Susan, A ... 828-448-6125 339 A
sberley@wpcc.edu
BERLIN, Linda ... 231-995-1533 228 G
lberlin@nmc.edu
BERLINER, Donna ... 630-942-2475 135 A
berliner@cod.edu
BERLINER, Herman, A .. 516-463-5402 302 B
herman.a.berliner@hofstra.edu
BERLO, Josh ... 218-726-8168 243 F
jpberlo@d.umn.edu
BERMAN, Ari ... 212-960-5300 326 E
president@yu.edu
BERMAN, Art ... 651-290-7522 242 G
art.berman@mitchellhamline.edu
BERMAN, Bruce ... 714-895-8315.. 38 D
bberman@gwc.cccd.edu
BERMAN, Daniel ... 215-204-2044 399 F
daniel.berman@temple.edu
BERMAN, Harris ... 617-636-2177 219 B
harris.berman@tufts.edu
BERMAN, Ila ... 434-924-7019 473 A
ilb8r@virginia.edu
BERMAN, Joel ... 954-262-2130 103 M
jb@nsu.nova.edu
BERMAN, Larry, S ... 404-413-5570 119 E
larryberman@gsu.edu
BERMAN, Leah ... 907-474-7608.. 10 A
lwberman@alaska.edu
BERMAN, Lou Ann ... 903-566-7052 456 A
lberman@uttyler.edu

BERMAN, Marc ... 619-961-4271.. 67 E
mberman@tjsl.edu
BERMAN, Mark, A ... 518-782-6957 315 J
mberman@siena.edu
BERMAN, Paula ... 617-277-3915 207 C
bermanp@bgsp.edu
BERMEA, Gabriel ... 254-968-9707 446 E
bermea@tarleton.edu
BERMEA, Gilbert, S ... 830-758-4111 444 G
gbermea@swtjc.edu
BERMEL, John ... 507-222-4427 234 F
jbermel@carleton.edu
BERMEL, Patricia ... 619-680-4430.. 28 E
patricia.bermel@cc-sd.edu
BERMEL, Rhea ... 903-463-8628 437 D
bermelr@grayson.edu
BERMOSK, Kendra ... 419-995-8133 354 H
bermosk.k@rhodesstate.edu
BERMUDEZ, Eliezer ... 453-879-4817 460 G
eliezer.bermudez@dixie.edu
BERMUDEZ, Glenda ... 787-766-1717 511 H
glbermudez@suagm.edu
BERMUDEZ, Pedro, A ... 787-786-3030 512 B
pbermudez@ucb.edu.pr
BERMUDEZ, Sixto ... 787-766-1717 511 H
sibermudez@suagm.edu
BERMUDEZ, Sixto ... 787-875-4150 511 H
sibermudez@suagm.edu
BERNA, Francis, J ... 215-951-1346 387 C
berna@lasalle.edu
BERNABE, Arnaldo ... 718-518-6888 294 B
abernabe@hostos.cuny.edu
BERNADELLE, Guary ... 815-967-7300 147 F
gbernadelle@rockfordcareercollege.edu
BERNAHL, Joni ... 217-786-9627 142 B
joni.bernahl@llcc.edu
BERNAIX, Laura ... 618-650-3969 149 F
lbernai@siue.edu
BERNAL, Jesse, M ... 616-331-3296 224 E
bernalje@gvsu.edu
BERNAL, Omar ... 708-237-5050 145 E
obernal@nc.edu
BERNAL-OLSON,
Patricia ... 937-229-4211 362 G
pbernalolson1@udayton.edu
BERNARD, Barbara ... 781-239-2629 214 E
bbernard@massbay.edu
BERNARD, Eugene ... 713-221-8679 453 B
bernarde@uhd.edu
BERNARD, Frances ... 518-461-2528 305 K
franb@mariacollege.edu
BERNARD, Gregory ... 203-392-6501.. 85 A
bernardg2@southerct.edu
BERNARD, Kacey ... 610-341-1459 383 D
kbernard@eastern.edu
BERNARD, Ken ... 803-778-6668 407 C
bernardkd@cctech.edu
BERNARD, Kyle ... 518-580-5820 316 A
kbernar1@skidmore.edu
BERNARD, Michelle ... 706-379-3111 127 C
mmbernard@yhc.edu
BERNARD, Pamela ... 919-684-3955 328 G
pam.bernard@duke.edu
BERNARD, Philip ... 617-989-4162 219 E
bernardp@wit.edu
BERNARD, Renee ... 814-472-2766 398 B
rbernard@francis.edu
BERNARD, Vicki ... 314-340-5089 253 I
bernardv@hssu.edu
BERNARD-AMOS,
Marion ... 484-365-7224 389 C
mba@lincoln.edu
BERNARD-DONALS,
Michael ... 608-262-5246 496 C
mfbernarddon@wisc.edu
BERNARDIS, Tim ... 406-638-3113 263 H
tim@lbhc.edu
BERNARDO, Lisa, M ... 209-667-3094.. 33 C
lbernardo@csustan.edu
BERNARDO, Peter ... 216-397-4217 354 I
pbernardo@jcu.edu
BERNARDO-SOUSA,
Marie ... 401-598-1754 404 I
marie.bernardo-sousa@jwu.edu
BERNATZ, Richard ... 563-387-2000 167 E
bernatzr@luther.edu
BERNAUER, Edmund ... 808-521-2288 128 B
dean@orientalmedicine.edu
BERNAUER, Jeanne ... 808-521-2288 128 B
BERNDT, Michael ... 651-450-3641 238 D
mberndt@inverhills.edu
BERNDT, Michael ... 651-423-8000 237 H
BERNE, Jennifer ... 413-236-2101 213 F
jberne@berkshirecc.edu

BERNECKER, Kim 972-825-4634 445 A kbernecker@sagu.edu
BERNER, JR., Howard, E 314-275-3514 146 E howard.berner@principia.edu
BERNER, Jason 510-215-4131 40 H jberner@contracosta.edu
BERNER, Nancy 931-598-1101 423 M nberner@sewanee.edu
BERNHARD, Anne 860-439-2030 86 H aeber@conncoll.edu
BERNHARD, Robert, J 574-631-3902 161 C bernhard.9@nd.edu
BERNHARD, William 217-333-6677 151 D bernhard@illinois.edu
BERNHARDSON, Bonnie 218-879-0828 238 A bonnie@fdltcc.edu
BERNHARDSON, Mark 218-879-0703 238 A mbernhar@fdltcc.edu
BERNHARDT, Jay, M 512-471-8100 455 A jay.bernhardt@austin.utexas.edu
BERNHARDT, Kevin, J 608-342-1365 497 D bernhark@uwplatt.edu
BERNHARDT, Regina 215-248-7021 381 D bernhardtr@chc.edu
BERNHARDT, Starr 509-793-2065 478 H starrb@bigbend.edu
BERNHARDT, Thomas 804-763-6300 92 G
BERNIER, Carrie 203-857-7270 86 D cbernier@norwalk.edu
BERNIER, Jose 386-822-7045 111 A jbernier@stetson.edu
BERNOI, Verna, A 443-518-4773 199 C vbernoi@howardcc.edu
BERNOT, C. Tina 270-809-3250 183 G cbernot@murraystate.edu
BERNOTAS, Scott, C 412-624-9510 401 B bernotas@pitt.edu
BERNOTSKY, R. Lorraine 610-436-6977 396 A lbernotsky@wcupa.edu
BERNOUSSI, Reda 972-883-2676 455 B rbernou@utdallas.edu
BERNSTEIN, Aimee 718-409-5979 321 C abernstein@sunymaritime.edu
BERNSTEIN, Alan 229-333-5860 126 G abernste@valdosta.edu
BERNSTEIN, David 845-406-4308 325 H
BERNSTEIN, Melissa 801-581-3386 460 E melissa.bernstein@law.utah.edu
BERNSTEIN, Michael 631-632-4360 317 D michael.bernstein@stonybrook.edu
BERNSTEIN, Pamela 603-880-8308 274 E pbernstein@thomasmorecollege.edu
BERNSTEIN, Robin 402-557-7300 265 J robin.bernstein@bellevue.edu
BERNSTEIN, Zeke 802-440-4594 462 A zbernstein@bennington.edu
BERNSTEIN CHARGIN, Jan 408-852-2826 43 J alumni@gavilan.edu
BERNSTEIN-CHARGIN, Jan 408-848-4724 43 J jbchargin@gavilan.edu
BERO, Maggie 603-578-8900 273 A mbero@ccsnh.edu
BEROKOFF, Mark 405-912-9030 369 D mberokoff@ru.edu
BEROWSKI, Alfred 315-866-0300 301 G berowskfj@herkimer.edu
BERQUAM, Lori 480-461-7000 13 D
BERQUE, David 765-658-4735 154 F vpaa@depauw.edu
BERQUIST, Gina 503-255-0332 374 D ginab@multnomah.edu
BERRAHOU, Catherine 248-689-8282 232 A cberraho@walshcollege.edu
BERRIDGE, Bob 773-256-0783 142 G bberridg@lstc.edu
BERRIGAN, Edward 210-341-1366 441 C eberrigan@ost.edu
BERRIOS, Carmen 787-738-2161 513 D carmen.berrios@upr.edu
BERRIOS, Eduardo 787-603-1515 509 A eberrios@bayamon.inter.edu
BERRIOS, Eric 814-864-6666 385 B
BERRIOS, Iris 787-743-7979 511 I ac_irberrios@suagm.edu
BERRIOS, Jonathan 787-738-2161 513 D jonathan.berrios@upr.edu
BERRIOS, Marianne 787-852-1430 508 C mberrios@hccpr.edu
BERRIOS, William 212-592-2043 315 H wberrios@sva.edu
BERRY, Anthony, T 860-297-2177 88 C anthony.berry@trincoll.edu
BERRY, Benny 423-652-4333 420 H blberry@king.edu
BERRY, Brian 870-777-5722 22 A brian.berry@uaht.edu
BERRY, Brian 848-932-2695 282 A brian.berry@ofa.rutgers.edu
BERRY, Brooke, C 804-257-5720 477 C bcberry@vuu.edu
BERRY, Cammie, S 803-536-8961 412 C cberry@scsu.edu
BERRY, Carolynn 336-750-2110 344 B berryc@wssu.edu
BERRY, Clay 870-508-6124 18 A cberry@asumh.edu
BERRY, Donna 559-638-0300 66 F donna.berry@reedleycollege.edu
BERRY, Doug 602-285-7607 13 F doug.berry@phoenixcollege.edu
BERRY, Doug 602-787-7113 13 E doug.berry@paradisevalley.edu
BERRY, Elizabeth, D 607-746-4573 320 G berryee@delhi.edu
BERRY, Emily 513-529-9625 356 E emily.berry@miamioh.edu
BERRY, Evan 772-462-7945 101 E eberry@irsc.edu
BERRY, Gwennette, C 319-273-2820 163 B gwenne.berry@uni.edu
BERRY, Jessica 207-778-7295 196 B jess.berry@maine.edu
BERRY, Joan 254-295-4010 453 E joan.berry@umhb.edu
BERRY, Joan, E 610-566-1776 403 E jberry@williamson.edu
BERRY, Joanne 603-427-7609 272 J jberry@ccsnh.edu
BERRY, John 740-364-9510 349 H berry.19@cotc.edu
BERRY, John 865-981-8145 421 F john.berry@maryvillecollege.edu
BERRY, Joshua 203-582-8695 87 G joshua.berry@quinnipiac.edu
BERRY, Keith 813-253-7714 101 A kberry@hccfl.edu
BERRY, Kimberly, G 518-629-8007 302 E k.berry@hvcc.edu
BERRY, Larry 423-614-8086 420 J lberry@leeuniversity.edu
BERRY, Laura 870-743-3000 20 C lberry@northark.edu
BERRY, Laura Lea 802-586-7711 463 D lberry@sterlingcollege.edu
BERRY, Linda, C 708-209-3209 135 F linda.berry@cuchicago.edu
BERRY, Mario 713-313-7011 449 C
BERRY, Mark 302-736-2567 90 G mark.berry@wesley.edu
BERRY, Mark, E 843-953-7645 408 E berrym@cofc.edu
BERRY, Mary 605-677-5370 416 H mary.berry@usd.edu
BERRY, Molly 217-424-6335 143 H mberry@millikin.edu
BERRY, Nicole 718-270-6413 295 A nberry@mec.cuny.edu
BERRY, Ronald 318-342-1103 192 F rberry@ulm.edu
BERRY, Steve 530-541-4660 47 E sberry@ltcc.edu
BERRY, Steve 530-541-4660 47 E
BERRY, Steve 919-365-7711 340 H
BERRY, Steven 410-386-8145 197 G sberry@carrollcc.edu
BERRY, Tina 520-494-5334 11 K tina.berry@centralaz.edu
BERRY, Trey 870-235-4001 21 D tcberry@saumag.edu
BERRY-GUERIN, Daneen 509-793-2053 478 H daneenb@bigbend.edu
BERRY-HUNG, Rima 313-593-5190 231 F
BERRYHILL, Kelly, M 989-774-2849 222 C berry1km@cmich.edu
BERRYMAN, Cynthia 708-237-5050 145 E cberryman@nc.edu
BERRYMAN, Jennifer 508-856-2900 212 A jennifer.berryman@umassmed.edu
BERRYMAN, Todd 501-450-1322 19 F berryman@hendrix.edu
BERRÍOS, José 787-264-1912 509 F jfberrio@intersg.edu
BERRÍOS, José, E 787-257-7373 511 G jberrios34@suagm.edu
BERRÍOS, Olga, L 787-850-9340 513 E olga.berrios@upr.edu
BERSCHEIDT, Jim 940-369-5158 454 A james.berscheidt@unt.edu
BERSHAD, Carolyn 607-753-4728 318 D carolyn.bershad@cortland.edu
BERSHAD, Robert 215-576-0800 397 C rbershad@rrc.edu
BERSOFF, Edward 703-522-5600 469 C
BERT, Melissa 320-589-6017 244 B mbert@morris.umn.edu
BERTAGNOLE, Jennifer 866-680-2756 459 G fundraising@midwifery.edu
BERTE, Hope 718-982-2400 293 E hope.berte@csi.cuny.edu
BERTEAUX, Susan 508-830-5035 213 B sberteaux@maritime.edu
BERTELSEN, Kevin 707-654-1726 32 B kbertelsen@csum.edu
BERTELSEN, Kevin 510-466-7269 56 H kbertelsen@peralta.edu
BERTHEL, Michael 516-299-2606 304 H michael.berthel@liu.edu
BERTHELOT, Yves 404-385-3383 118 F yves.berthelot@provost.gatech.edu
BERTHELSEN, Michael 612-624-3557 243 E berth004@umn.edu
BERTHIAUME, Joe 209-946-2331 70 E jberthiaume@pacific.edu
BERTHIAUME, Peter, L 603-526-3675 272 H pberthia@colby-sawyer.edu
BERTHIAUME, Scott 972-708-7338 435 H dean-academic@diu.edu
BERTHOUMIEUX, Rachel 516-686-1140 309 F rberthou@nyit.edu
BERTI, David, M 617-422-7209 217 C dberti@nesl.edu
BERTINI, Deanna 212-812-4045 309 D dbertini@nycda.edu
BERTLING, Crystal 954-545-4500 107 E cbertling@sfbc.edu
BERTOLINI, David 701-231-9588 345 G david.bertolini@ndsu.edu
BERTOLINO, Joe 203-392-5250 85 A president@southernct.edu
BERTOLUCCI, Linda 619-644-7799 44 I linda.bertolucci@gcccd.edu
BERTONAZZI, Laura 781-768-7060 218 C laura.bertonazzi@regiscollege.edu
BERTONE, Alicia, L 614-292-9490 358 I bertone.1@osu.edu
BERTONE, David, J 914-694-1122 275 I djb@berkeleycollege.edu
BERTONE, David, J 914-694-1122 291 D djb@berkeleycollege.edu
BERTONI, Alex 802-654-2536 463 B abertoni@smcvt.edu
BERTOT, John 301-405-4252 202 C jbertot@umd.edu
BERTOTTO, Dwayne 952-806-3958 242 K dwayne.bertotto@rasmussen.edu
BERTRAM, Alissa 401-341-2287 406 A alissa.bertram@salve.edu
BERTRAM, Brian 517-264-7676 230 E bbertram@sienaheights.edu
BERTRAN, Colette 515-576-7201 166 E
BERTSCH, Lynda 701-858-3360 345 F lynda.bertsch@minotstateu.edu
BERTSCH, Tauna 254-968-9921 446 E bertsch@tarleton.edu
BERTSCHE, Allen 719-227-8280 77 H abertsche@coloradocollege.edu
BERTSOS, Daniel 937-775-4172 364 I dan.bertsos@wright.edu
BERUBE, Beth 906-217-4036 221 O beth.berube@baycollege.edu
BERUBE, Patricia 413-572-5415 213 D pberube@westfield.ma.edu
BERUMEN, Yvonne 909-621-8129 56 J yvonne_berumen@pitzer.edu
BERWICK, Robert 904-256-7092 101 G rberwic@ju.edu
BERZ, William 732-932-8860 282 A wberz@mgsa.rutgers.edu
BERZINS, Jonathan 602-285-7569 13 F jonathan.berzins@phoenixcollege.edu
BESANA, GianMario 312-362-5554 135 I gbesana@depaul.edu
BESEAU, Steven, P 614-885-5585 360 E sbeseau@pcj.edu
BESEDA, Michael 415-422-4019 71 K mbeseda@usfca.edu
BESEL, Karl 219-980-6554 156 E kbesel@iun.edu
BESENYEI, Alicia 304-384-6313 490 A abesenyei@concord.edu
BESHARA, Alexa 732-255-0400 280 A abeshara@ocean.edu
BESHEARS, Brenda 217-228-5520 133 A bbeshears@brcn.edu
BESIKOF, Rudolph 510-464-3213 56 G rbesikof@peralta.edu
BESKID, Novella 803-777-0958 413 C novella@sc.edu
BESMER, Matthew 559-243-7103 66 C matthew.besmer@scccd.edu
BESNETTE HAUSER, Carrie 970-945-8691 77 K
BESONG, Jeffrey, D 412-392-3819 397 A jbesong@pointpark.edu
BESONG, Marsha 856-225-6107 281 G mw700@camden.rutgers.edu
BESSETTE, Bill 301-934-4753 198 A wrbessette@csmd.edu
BESSETTE, James 912-279-5704 116 G jbessette@ccga.edu
BESSETTE, Mark 518-381-1353 315 G bessetma@sunysccc.edu
BESSETTE, Ray 207-941-7785 194 A bessetter@husson.edu
BESSLER, Joseph, A 918-270-6448 369 A joe.bessler@ptstulsa.edu
BESSLER, Timothy 210-431-4396 443 A tbessler@stmarytx.edu
BEST, JR., A. Reginald 313-317-1700 224 G arbest1@hfcc.edu
BEST, Kathy 919-635-2788 340 J kbest@umo.edu
BEST, Lisa 712-749-2415 163 D bestl@bvu.edu
BEST, Matthew 716-270-5262 299 F bestm@ecc.edu
BEST, Michael 516-299-2501 304 G michael.best@liu.edu
BEST, Mickey 505-287-6624 287 B mbest@nmsu.edu
BEST, Robert 864-455-9812 414 A best@sc.edu
BEST, Roger 660-543-4112 260 K president@ucmo.edu
BEST, Sara 701-349-5793 346 J sarabest@trinitybiblecollege.edu
BEST, Sharon 386-752-1822 99 A sharon.best@fgc.edu
BESTE, Jeff 937-766-3645 349 G bestej@cedarville.edu
BESTER, Christian 718-780-0352 291 J chris.bester@brooklaw.edu
BESWICK, Patrick, T 724-738-4855 395 F patrick.beswick@sru.edu
BETAGERI, Guru 909-469-5682 74 I gbetageri@westernu.edu
BETANCOURT, Angie 801-626-6033 461 B abetancourt@weber.edu
BETANCOURT, Gigi 619-574-5816 43 E jbetancourt@fst.edu
BETANCOURT, Ilder 408-288-3186 61 M ilder.betancourt@sjcc.edu
BETANCOURT, Tammy, L 217-443-8778 135 H tbetancourt@dacc.edu
BETANCOURT SANTIAGO, Victor 703-284-1677 469 C victor.betancourt@marymount.edu
BETANCOURT VELEZ, Ismael, J 563-425-5832 170 A betancourti@uiu.edu
BETCHER, Tom 937-766-7681 349 G tbetcher@cedarville.edu
BETECK, Ellis 937-255-5894 503 A ellis.beteck@afit.edu
BETHAM, Jason 684-699-4834 505 A j.betham@amsamoa.edu
BETHANY, Lea Ann 601-968-8724 245 C lbethany@belhaven.edu
BETHARDS, Troy 417-328-1757 259 L tbethards@sbuniv.edu
BETHE, Rhonda 785-833-4503 175 B rhonda.bethe@kwu.edu
BETHEA, Edward, E 843-661-8000 409 I ed.bethea@fdtc.edu

BETHEL, Genna .... 903-813-3001 430 N
gbethel@austincollege.edu
BETHKE, Jeffrey .... 312-362-6695 135 I
jbethke@depaul.edu
BETHMAN, Brenda .... 816-235-1643 261 C
bethmanb@umkc.edu
BETHUNE, Andrew, J .... 989-964-4071 230 B
ajbethune@svsu.edu
BETSCHART, Joseph, V . 503-845-3335 374 B
joseph.betschart@mtangel.edu
BETSINGER, Alicia, M ... 603-646-1247 273 E
alicia.m.betsinger@dartmouth.edu
BETSKY, Aaron .... 480-627-5379.. 15 P
abetsky@taliesin.edu
BETSWORTH, Sharon .... 405-208-5602 367 I
sbetsworth@okcu.edu
BETTELYOUN, Kim .... 605-455-6093 416 B
kbettelyoun@olc.edu
BETTENDORF, Anthony . 507-933-7529 235 I
abettend@gustavus.edu
BETTERSWORTH,
Michael, A .... 512-647-8790 449 E
michael.bettersworth@tstc.edu
BETTGER, Bianca .... 518-327-6223 311 G
bbettger@paulsmiths.edu
BETTINGER, Lewis .... 608-342-1221 497 D
bettingerl@uwplatt.edu
BETTINGER, Michael ..... 215-461-1105 390 H
mbettinger@mc3.edu
BETTISON, Joshua .... 314-837-6777 258 J
jbettison@stlchristian.edu
BETTS, Albert .... 856-256-4200 281 E
betts@rowan.edu
BETTS, Charles .... 903-875-7540 440 G
charles.betts@navarrocollege.edu
BETTS, Keith .... 203-837-8600.. 85 B
bettsk@wcsu.edu
BETTS, Rob .... 618-634-3270 149 A
robb@shawneecc.edu
BETTS, Steve .... 405-789-6400 370 A
sbetts@snu.edu
BETZ, Bridgette, K .... 573-341-4282 261 E
berry@mst.edu
BETZ, Cheri .... 517-264-7100 230 E
cbetz@sienaheights.edu
BETZ, Jon .... 505-566-3505 288 A
betzj@sanjuancollege.edu
BETZ, Kimberly .... 609-258-3000 280 E
BETZ, Leslie .... 309-556-3161 139 G
registrar@iwu.edu
BETZ, Philip .... 570-372-4197 399 C
betz@susqu.edu
BETZ, Stacey, A .... 610-799-1737 388 I
sbetz1@lccc.edu
BETZIG, David .... 800-567-2344 492 G
dbetzig@menominee.edu
BETZIG, Kaylen, A .... 262-691-5198 500 H
kbetzig@wctc.edu
BEUK, Donna .... 432-552-2579 457 A
beuk_d@utpb.edu
BEUKELMAN, Doug, D . 712-707-7121 168 H
dougb@nwciowa.edu
BEURY, Carey .... 812-465-7175 161 E
clbeury@usi.edu
BEUS, Ben .... 509-542-4811 479 H
bbeus@columbiabasin.edu
BEUS, Yifen .... 808-675-3618 127 E
yifen.beus@byuh.edu
BEUSCHER, Barbara, A . 330-471-8235 355 L
bbeuscher@malone.edu
BEUTEL, Kate .... 419-517-8880 355 K
kbeutel@lourdes.edu
BEUTLER, Randy, L .... 580-774-3766 370 C
randy.beutler@swosu.edu
BEVER, Edward .... 516-876-3998 319 A
bevere@oldwestbury.edu
BEVERAGE, JR.,
Morris, W .... 440-525-7118 355 H
mbeverage@lakelandcc.edu
BEVERIDGE, Kim .... 800-869-7223 123 G
kbeverid@scad.edu
BEVERIDGE, Thomas .... 805-565-6017.. 74 K
tbeverid@westmont.edu
BEVERLY, Beth .... 270-707-3869 181 E
ebeverly0003@kctcs.edu
BEVERLY, Jason .... 601-928-6267 247 E
jason.beverly@mgccc.edu
BEVERLY, Pearlie .... 254-710-4466 431 J
pearl_beverly@baylor.edu
BEVILACQUA, Amy .... 304-724-3700 487 E
abevilacqua@apus.edu
BEVILACQUA, Linda ...... 305-899-3010.. 95 C
lbevilacqua@barry.edu

BEVILL, Yolanda .... 936-261-2111 446 D
ydbevill@pvamu.edu
BEVILLE, Glenn .... 504-526-4745 189 H
glennb@nationsu.edu
BEVILLE, Jill .... 336-334-4013 343 A
jmbevill@uncg.edu
BEVINS, P. Scott .... 276-376-1066 473 B
pb8q@virginia.edu
BEWERSDORF, Marsha . 321-674-8849.. 99 B
mbewersdorf@fit.edu
BEX, Darcee .... 337-521-8941 188 C
darcee.bex@solacc.edu
BEY, Adrienne, M .... 302-295-1140.. 90 I
adrienne.m.bey@wilmu.edu
BEY, Mohammed .... 920-498-6826 500 F
mohammed.bey@nwtc.edu
BEYDA-LORIE, Sandra .. 773-442-5583 145 B
s-beyda@neiu.edu
BEYDLER, Julie .... 970-542-3129.. 81 A
julie.beydler@morgancc.edu
BEYELER, Jodi .... 574-535-7572 155 A
jodihb@goshen.edu
BEYER, Bryan .... 803-754-4100 409 A
BEYER, Christian .... 814-824-2915 390 C
cbeyer@mercyhurst.edu
BEYER, Christopher ...... 309-794-2686 132 C
christopherbeyer@augustana.edu
BEYER, Neil .... 406-657-1705 264 E
neil.beyer@msubillings.edu
BEYER HOUPT, Julia .... 740-587-6636 352 G
houpt@denison.edu
BEYL, Caula .... 865-974-7303 427 G
cbeyl@utk.edu
BEYRANEVAND, Laurie . 802-831-1035 463 G
lbeyranevande@vermontlaw.edu
BEYROUTY, Craig .... 301-405-2012 202 C
beyrouty@umd.edu
BEZEK, Cory, M .... 716-673-3251 317 A
cory.bezek@fredonia.edu
BEZET, Jared .... 561-912-1211.. 98 D
jbezet@evergladesuniversity.edu
BHADA, Farokh .... 401-232-6005 404 F
fbhada@bryant.edu
BHADURY, Joy .... 540-831-5300 470 C
jbhadury@radford.edu
BHAGA, Asha .... 206-592-3868 481 H
abhaga@highline.edu
BHALLA, Raman, S .... 585-475-2555 313 A
rsbetc@rit.edu
BHASIN, Rohit .... 978-681-0800 216 A
rbhasin@mslaw.edu
BHATI, Divya .... 843-953-9443 408 E
bhatid@cofc.edu
BHATI, Kuldhir, S .... 253-535-7206 482 H
bhati@plu.edu
BHATIA, Rupinder .... 510-464-3437.. 56 G
rbhatia@peralta.edu
BHATTACHARYA,
Kaushik .... 626-395-6365.. 29 C
vpr@caltech.edu
BHATTACHARYA,
Somnath .... 217-206-6600 151 C
BHATTACHARYYA,
Abhijit .... 870-972-3565.. 17 G
abhattacharyya@astate.edu
BHAUMIK, Nila .... 646-313-8000 295 E
nila.bhaumik@guttman.cuny.edu
BIAGAS, Lisa .... 215-972-2038 393 D
lbiagas@pafa.edu
BIALEK, Steve .... 262-547-1211 492 E
sbialek@carrollu.edu
BIALK, Kathy, J .... 319-335-3127 163 A
kathy-bialk@uiowa.edu
BIANCHETTO, Melody ... 434-982-2347 473 A
msb2p@virginia.edu
BIANCHI, Amy, M .... 617-333-2236 208 E
abianchi@curry.edu
BIANCHI, Ashley .... 413-597-4181 220 C
abb5@williams.edu
BIANCHI, Carrie, K .... 914-251-6011 319 E
carrie.bianchi@purchase.edu
BIANCHI, Gina, L .... 217-424-6330 143 H
gbianchi@millikin.edu
BIANCHI, Timothy .... 717-299-7793 399 G
BIANCO, Annamarie ...... 202-687-0100.. 92 A
amb504@georgetown.edu
BIANCO, Gena .... 401-254-5602 405 E
gbianco@rwu.edu
BIANSKI, Marty .... 260-459-4590 157 E
mbianski@ibcfortwayne.edu
BIAS, Jeanine .... 936-294-3026 450 C
jrb023@shsu.edu

BIBB, Sandra .... 316-978-3600 178 A
sandra.bibb@wichita.edu
BIBB-SANDERS,
Angelia .... 323-860-0789.. 50 A
BIBBEE, Mistie .... 304-696-3152 490 D
bibbeem@marshall.edu
BIBBENS, Matthew, G ... 909-607-8966.. 37 E
matthew.bibbens@cmc.edu
BIBBO, Chris, J .... 727-816-3261 104 F
bibboc@phsc.edu
BIBLE, Brice .... 716-645-7979 316 F
bible@buffalo.edu
BIBLE, Robert .... 918-549-2800 365 J
rbible@cmn.edu
BIBLER, Nicole .... 913-758-6123 177 F
nicole.bibler@stmary.edu
BIBO, JR., Tim .... 410-704-4685 204 A
tbibo@towson.edu
BIBY, Catherine .... 704-991-0168 338 C
cbiby0719@stanly.edu
BICAK, Charles, J .... 308-865-8209 269 I
bicakc@unk.edu
BICANOVSKY, Andrew .. 352-435-6301 102 T
bicanova@lssc.edu
BICE, Patricia .... 914-251-6360 319 E
patricia.bice@purchase.edu
BICE, Patty .... 914-251-5985 319 E
patricia.bice@purchase.edu
BICHEL, Rebecca .... 817-272-1413 454 J
rbichel@uta.edu
BICHELMEYER, Barbara . 816-235-1107 261 C
bichelmeyer@umkc.edu
BICKEL, Brice .... 864-644-5337 412 E
bdbickel@swu.edu
BICKEL, Kathy .... 541-737-2351 375 D
kathy.bickel@oregonstate.edu
BICKEL, Teri .... 301-846-2612 198 E
tbickel@frederick.edu
BICKERS, Amy .... 205-226-4922.... 5 A
arbicker@bsc.edu
BICKERTON, Molly .... 912-871-1600 122 I
mbickerton@ogeecheetech.edu
BICKERTON, Sally .... 661-255-1050.. 28 K
BICKETT, Larry .... 304-260-4380 488 J
lbickett@blueridgectc.edu
BICKFORD, Deborah, J . 937-229-5360 362 G
dbickford1@udayton.edu
BICKFORD, Ian .... 413-528-7239 205 F
ibickford@simons-rock.edu
BICKFORD, Jeffrey .... 978-556-3745 215 C
jbickford@necc.mass.edu
BICKING, Michael .... 610-341-1720 383 D
michael.bicking@eastern.edu
BICKLEY, Carol .... 803-321-5124 411 D
carol.bickley@newberry.edu
BICKLEY, Craig .... 724-357-4874 394 G
cbickley@iup.edu
BICKNELL, Brian .... 603-206-8009 272 L
bbicknell@ccsnh.edu
BICKNELL, Patricia .... 215-951-1430 387 C
bicknell@lasalle.edu
BICKNELL-HOLMES,
Tracy .... 208-426-1234 129 I
tracybicknell-holmes@boisestate.edu
BICKSLER, Leslie .... 304-647-6279 491 A
lbicksler@osteo.wvsom.edu
BIDDINGER, Mark .... 863-667-5729 107 K
mbiddinger@seu.edu
BIDDINGS-MURO,
Regina .... 805-493-3828.. 29 H
rbiddingsmuro@callutheran.edu
BIDDLE, Chris .... 615-226-3990 421 B
cbiddle@lincolntech.edu
BIDDLE, Elizabeth, A .... 570-326-3761 393 G
ebiddle@pct.edu
BIDDLE, Megan .... 217-854-5512 132 I
megan.biddle@blackburn.edu
BIDLACK, Allison .... 907-796-6289.. 10 B
albidlack@alaska.edu
BIDLE, Kelly .... 609-895-5418 281 B
kbidle@rider.edu
BIDWELL, Lorena, L ...... 269-471-6124 221 B
lorena@andrews.edu
BIEBER, Ann, D .... 610-799-1581 388 I
abieber@lccc.edu
BIEBER, Joshua .... 785-227-3380 171 E
bieberjb@bethanylb.edu
BIEBIGHAUSER,
Victor, K .... 334-395-8800 124 E
vbiebighauser@southuniversity.edu
BIEBUYCK, Bill .... 563-588-6405 163 F
bill.biebuyck@clarke.edu
BIECHLER, Laura .... 508-531-1341 212 B
lbiechler@bridgew.edu

BIEDERMANN, Heather . 507-389-7223 241 C
heather.biedermann@southcentral.edu
BIEDERMANN, Scott ..... 209-946-2166.. 70 E
sbiedermann@pacific.edu
BIEGEL, Peter .... 561-868-3532 104 D
biegelp@palmbeachstate.edu
BIEGENZAHN, Nathan ... 919-497-3250 330 I
nbiegenzahn@louisburg.edu
BIEGER, Mark .... 845-938-3419 504 H
8sgs@usma.edu
BIEHLS, Kelly .... 716-829-8485 298 F
biehls@dyc.edu
BIEK, David .... 478-757-2544 121 F
david.biek@mga.edu
BIEL, Alan .... 520-452-2656.. 11 M
biela@cochise.edu
BIEL, Michael, J .... 219-989-2510 159 G
bielm@pnw.edu
BIELAVITZ, Thomas ...... 503-725-4576 376 A
bielavit@pdx.edu
BIELAWSKI, Bill .... 312-329-8047 144 B
bill.bielawski@moody.edu
BIELBY, Steve .... 864-977-1249 411 E
steve.bielby@ngu.edu
BIELFELDT, Dennis .... 605-692-9337 415 D
president@ilt.edu
BIELICKI, Shawn .... 434-582-3035 468 H
smbielicki@liberty.edu
BIELITZ, Colleen, Q ...... 203-392-5459.. 85 A
bielitzc1@southernct.edu
BIELMAN, Jess .... 503-517-1140 377 G
jbielman@warnerpacific.edu
BIELSTEIN, Jennifer ...... 415-439-2366.. 25 K
jbielstein@act-sf.org
BIEN, Andrea .... 651-290-6322 242 G
andrea.bien@mitchellhamline.edu
BIENFANG, Kim .... 763-433-1483 237 C
kim.bienfang@anokaramsey.edu
BIENVENUE, Joan, M ... 434-243-2233 473 A
jmb7ug@virginia.edu
BIENVENUE, Scott .... 603-578-8900 273 A
sbienvenue@ccsnh.edu
BIENZ, Richard, A .... 260-399-7700 161 D
rbienz@sf.edu
BIER, Debbie .... 412-521-6200 397 H
debbie.bier@rosedaletech.org
BIERBAUER, Charles ..... 803-777-4105 413 C
bierbauer@sc.edu
BIERIG, Samuel .... 816-414-3731 256 A
sbierig@mbts.edu
BIERLY, Robert .... 864-294-2217 410 A
robert.bierly@furman.edu
BIERMAN, Cindy .... 909-621-8265.. 37 D
cindy.bierman@cgu.edu
BIERMAN, Derek .... 402-844-7060 268 J
derek@northeast.edu
BIERMAN, Luke .... 336-279-9201 328 K
lbierman@elon.edu
BIERMAN, Matt .... 309-556-3527 139 G
mbierman@iwu.edu
BIERMAN, Scott .... 402-557-7245 265 J
scott.bierman@bellevue.edu
BIERMAN, Scott .... 608-363-2201 492 C
biermans@beloit.edu
BIERMANN, Mark .... 219-464-5779 162 A
mark.biermann@valpo.edu
BIERMANN, Matt .... 989-275-5000 226 B
matt.biermann@kirtland.edu
BIERNBAUM, John .... 309-298-3320 152 D
j-biernbaum@wiu.edu
BIERRE, Lisa .... 207-509-7262 195 H
lbierre@unity.edu
BIERSCHBACH, Richard 313-577-3933 232 I
rbierschbach@wayne.edu
BIES, Susan .... 605-274-5503 415 B
susan.bies@augie.edu
BIESCHKE, Kathleen ...... 814-863-7494 392 B
kxb11@psu.edu
BIESECKER, James .... 717-337-6700 384 H
jbieseck@gettsyburg.edu
BIESZKE, Jay .... 608-262-1234 496 C
jay.bieszke@wisc.edu
BIETELCHIES, Wade ...... 517-265-5161 220 F
wbietelchies@adrian.edu
BIG CRANE, Michael .... 406-275-4789 265 F
michael_bigcrane@skc.edu
BIG SPRING, Anita .... 406-275-4974 265 F
anita_bigspring@skc.edu
BIGARD, Heather .... 352-365-3525 102 T
bigardh@lssc.edu
BIGBY, Angela, D .... 702-968-2046 272 C
abigby@roseman.edu

BISHOP, Eric .... 909-652-6502.. 36 A
eric.bishop@chaffey.edu
BISHOP, Janet .... 909-621-8014.. 37 C
janet.bishop@claremont.edu
BISHOP, Jason .... 603-271-6484 273 B
jbishop@ccsnh.edu
BISHOP, Jeff .... 770-720-5966 123 E
wjb@reinhardt.edu
BISHOP, Jeffrey .... 314-977-1060 259 H
jeffrey.bishop@slu.edu
BISHOP, Jesse .... 706-368-7776 118 E
jebishop@highlands.edu
BISHOP, Joseph .... 616-554-5687 223 B
joseph.bishop@davenport.edu
BISHOP, Kaylee .... 405-789-7661 370 B
kaylee.bishop@swcu.edu
BISHOP, Kelley .... 301-314-7236 202 C
kbishop1@umd.edu
BISHOP, Kristy .... 724-925-4212 403 A
bishopkr@westmoreland.edu
BISHOP, Laura .... 918-495-7312 368 I
lbishop@oru.edu
BISHOP, Mary Kay .... 585-389-2012 308 B
mbishop2@naz.edu
BISHOP, Melanie .... 314-392-2323 256 C
melanie.bishop@mobap.edu
BISHOP, Mike .... 951-552-8759.. 27 J
mbishop@calbaptist.edu
BISHOP, Nancy .... 803-778-6638 407 C
bishopnw@cctech.edu
BISHOP, Paul .... 805-965-0581.. 62 C
pwbishop@sbcc.edu
BISHOP, Richard .... 860-832-2201.. 84 I
bishopr@ccsu.edu
BISHOP, Richard .... 209-476-7840.. 66 G
rbishop@clc.edu
BISHOP, Robert, H .... 813-974-3864 110 B
robertbishop@usf.edu
BISHOP, Sandy .... 715-365-4564 500 D
sbishop@nicoletcollege.edu
BISHOP, Sasha .... 843-470-8396 412 H
sbishop@tcl.edu
BISHOP, Stephanie .... 765-983-1628 154 G
bishost@earlham.edu
BISHOP, Steve .... 601-276-3701 249 B
bishop@smcc.edu
BISHOP, Wesley, T .... 504-286-5325 190 I
wbishop@suno.edu
BISHOP, William .... 916-278-5770.. 32 E
william.bishop@csus.edu
BISHOP, Wilsie, S .... 423-439-4219 419 J
bishopws@etsu.edu
BISHOP -SAMUELS,
Kellei .... 334-724-4777.... 7 D
ksamuels@tuskegee.edu
BISHOP BENTLEY,
Ember .... 478-471-2700 121 F
BISHOP-CLARK,
Catherine, U .... 513-529-6721 356 E
bishopcu@miamioh.edu
BISIGNANO, Chris .... 914-251-6530 319 E
chris.bisignanoi@purchase.edu
BISKUPIAK, Walter, H .. 406-447-5521 263 C
bbiskupi@carroll.edu
BISPING, Timothy .... 936-468-3101 445 F
bispingto@sfasu.edu
BISSELL, Michelle .... 304-205-6640 488 K
michelle.bissell@bridgevalley.edu
BISSELL, Monika .... 207-795-2846 194 E
bisselmo@mchp.edu
BISSELL, Sally .... 419-783-2366 352 F
sbissell@defiance.edu
BISSEN, Randi .... 712-325-3428 167 B
rbissen@iwcc.edu
BISSET, Matthew, S .... 727-864-8482.. 97 J
bissetms@eckerd.edu
BISSET, William, J .... 718-862-7200 305 H
william.bisset@manhattan.edu
BISSINGER, Mary .... 805-482-2755.. 58 L
mbissinger@stjohnsem.edu
BISSONETTE, David .... 218-855-8178 237 F
dbissonette@clcmn.edu
BISSONNETTE, Ali .... 530-541-4660.. 47 E
BISWAS, Harun .... 678-466-4240 116 E
harunbiswas@clayton.edu
BITIKOFER, Scott .... 407-646-2137 105 M
sbitikofer@rollins.edu
BITNER, Justin .... 314-246-7464 262 C
justinbitner77@webster.edu
BITNER, Scott .... 410-706-3822 202 D
sbitner@umaryland.edu
BITNER, Teddy .... 816-322-0110 250 K
teddy.bitner@calvary.edu

BITTER, Marlo .... 903-675-6327 452 B
marlo.bitter@tvcc.edu
BITTER, Michael .... 808-932-7095 128 E
bitter@hawaii.edu
BITTERBAUM, Erik, J .... 607-753-2201 318 D
erik.bitterbaum@cortland.edu
BITTERMAN, Annette .... 716-839-8459 298 B
abitterm@daemen.edu
BITTINGER, Dale .... 410-455-2278 202 E
bittinger@umbc.edu
BITTINGER, Randall .... 301-387-3091 198 F
randall.bittinger@garrettcollege.edu
BITTINGER, SaraBeth .... 301-687-3130 203 E
sbittinger@frostburg.edu
BITTLE, Tyler .... 501-882-8880.. 17 F
BITTNER, Lauren .... 605-626-2550 417 A
lauren.bittner@northern.edu
BITTON, Yoram .... 513-824-2261 301 E
ybitton@huc.edu
BITTORF, David, C .... 240-500-2266 198 H
dcbittorf@hagerstowncc.edu
BITZER, Michelle .... 715-682-1227 495 C
mbitzer@northland.edu
BITZER, Steve .... 715-682-4591 501 B
steve.bitzer@witc.edu
BIUNDO, Rachel .... 804-594-1479 474 I
rbiundo@jtcc.edu
BIVINS, Christy .... 706-754-7772 122 F
cbivins@northgatech.edu
BIVINS, Dallas .... 480-941-1993.. 43 I
dallasbivins@gs.edu
BIXBY, David, E .... 626-815-5334.. 26 H
dbixby@apu.edu
BIXBY, Gary .... 610-436-3200 396 A
gbixby@wcupa.edu
BIXBY, John, L .... 305-284-2211 112 E
jbixby@miami.edu
BIXEL, Patricia .... 207-941-7104 194 A
bixelp@husson.edu
BIXLER, Kirk, J .... 317-738-8803 154 J
kbixler@franklincollege.edu
BIXLER, Sharon .... 859-858-3511 178 I
sharon.bixler@asbury.edu
BIZOUKAS, Tim .... 630-466-7900 152 C
tbizoukas@waubonsee.edu
BJARNSON, Corey .... 513-241-4338 347 J
corey.bjarnson@antonellicollege.edu
BJELKE, David .... 941-359-4227 110 D
dbjelke@sar.usf.edu
BJELLA, Traci, A .... 407-582-1016 112 K
tthornton12@valenciacollege.edu
BJELLAND, David .... 320-762-4407 237 B
davidb@alextech.edu
BJERKLIE, J. R .... 607-431-4997 301 D
bjerkliej@hartwick.edu
BJOKNE, Daniel, H .... 515-964-0601 165 G
bjokned@faith.edu
BJORDAHL, Julia .... 509-313-6102 481 D
bjordahl@gonzaga.edu
BJORGAN, Heather .... 309-796-5340 132 G
bjorganh@bhc.edu
BJORK, Johanna .... 208-792-2395 131 A
jcbjork@lcsc.edu
BJORK, Ross .... 979-845-5129 446 G
feedback@athletics.tamu.edu
BJORKLUND, Robert, B 651-638-6396 234 C
robert-bjorklund@bethel.edu
BJORKLUND, Tarah .... 651-846-1415 241 B
tarah.bjorklund@saintpaul.edu
BJORKMAN, Karen .... 419-530-2729 363 E
karen.bjorkman@utoledo.edu
BJORN, Thorr, D .... 401-874-5245 406 B
tbjorn@uri.edu
BJORNSTAD, Thomas ... 414-229-3298 497 A
bjornsta@uwm.edu
BJUNE, Stephanie .... 979-458-6000 446 C
sbjune@tamus.edu
BLACHFORD, Charles ... 215-368-5000 390 F
cblachford@missio.edu
BLACK, Adam .... 801-863-6378 461 A
blackad@uvu.edu
BLACK, Adrian .... 410-617-2000 199 F
BLACK, Amber .... 806-651-2345 448 C
ablack@wtamu.edu
BLACK, Andrew .... 808-956-8310 128 F
ablack22@hawaii.edu
BLACK, Ann .... 505-428-1811 288 B
ann.black@sfcc.edu
BLACK, April .... 405-789-7661 370 B
april.black@swcu.edu
BLACK, Bernadette .... 619-644-7100.. 44 I
bernadette.black@gcccd.edu
BLACK, Chantel .... 509-434-5107 479 I

BLACK, Chantel .... 509-533-7067 480 A
chantel.black@scc.spokane.edu
BLACK, Christine .... 570-941-6645 401 H
christine.black@scranton.edu
BLACK, Connie .... 208-562-3252 130 F
connieblack@cwi.edu
BLACK, David .... 920-565-1104 493 J
blackdr@lakeland.edu
BLACK, Diane .... 251-442-2209.... 8 C
dblack@umobile.edu
BLACK, Donald .... 916-339-4371.. 53 A
dblack@mticollege.edu
BLACK, Downey .... 318-345-9297 187 G
harryblack@ladelta.edu
BLACK, Ellen .... 843-349-5211 410 C
ellen.black@hgtc.edu
BLACK, Ellita .... 904-256-7016 101 G
eblack@ju.edu
BLACK, Gary .... 440-826-2900 348 E
gblack@bw.edu
BLACK, Heather .... 412-365-2776 381 C
hblack@chatham.edu
BLACK, James .... 802-635-1298 464 C
james.black@northernvermont.edu
BLACK, Jared .... 602-489-5300.. 10 E
jared.black@arizonachristian.edu
BLACK, Jason .... 205-726-3673.... 6 E
jjblack@samford.edu
BLACK, Jeffrey, S .... 215-702-4347 380 D
jblack@cairn.edu
BLACK, John .... 248-689-8282 232 A
jblack@walshcollege.edu
BLACK, John Paul .... 252-527-6223 335 G
jpblack73@lenoircc.edu
BLACK, Joshua .... 864-941-8542 411 H
black.j@ptc.edu
BLACK, Joshua .... 423-614-8370 420 J
jblack@leeuniversity.edu
BLACK, Karnell .... 801-832-2231 461 G
kblack@westminstercollege.edu
BLACK, Katherine .... 860-768-4103.. 88 H
kablack@hartford.edu
BLACK, Kedric .... 801-863-8536 461 A
kedric.black@uvu.edu
BLACK, Kevin .... 717-531-4803 392 B
kpb4@psu.edu
BLACK, Kim .... 970-351-1102.. 83 E
kim.black@unco.edu
BLACK, Lendley, C .... 218-726-7106 243 F
chan@d.umn.edu
BLACK, Linda .... 970-351-1638.. 83 E
linda.black@unco.edu
BLACK, Linda .... 207-288-5015 193 F
BLACK, Lisa .... 619-239-0391.. 34 F
lblack@cwsl.edu
BLACK, Lynda, K .... 336-838-6148 339 B
lkblack932@wilkescc.edu
BLACK, Mark .... 615-966-5709 421 D
mark.black@lipscomb.edu
BLACK, Matthew .... 606-337-3196 179 G
BLACK, Michael, E .... 210-567-7103 456 C
blackm@uthscsa.edu
BLACK, Michael, M .... 229-245-6517 126 G
mmblack@valdosta.edu
BLACK, Richard .... 915-215-4300 451 D
richard.black@ttuhsc.edu
BLACK, Rochelle, A .... 248-370-3658 229 G
black@oakland.edu
BLACK, Ruth .... 606-337-3196 179 G
BLACK, Sara .... 864-977-2094 411 E
sara.black@ngu.edu
BLACK, Shaun, C .... 315-445-4569 304 C
blacksc@lemoyne.edu
BLACK, Tanja .... 864-424-8080 414 C
trblack@mailbox.sc.edu
BLACK, Thomas .... 650-723-1550.. 65 J
thomas.black@stanford.edu
BLACK, Tom .... 410-516-0602 199 D
tblack5@jhu.edu
BLACK, Tyrone .... 860-913-2063.. 87 A
BLACKABY, Leslie .... 509-574-6806 487 A
lblackaby@yvcc.edu
BLACKABY, Robert .... 423-478-7723 423 G
rblackaby@ptseminary.edu
BLACKARD, Glynis, D .... 770-720-9205 123 E
gdb@reinhardt.edu
BLACKBOURN,
Richard, L .... 662-325-3717 247 F
rlb277@msstate.edu
BLACKBURN, Amanda .. 404-835-6114 423 K
ablackburn@richmont.edu
BLACKBURN, Amber .... 336-838-6419 339 B
alblackburn893@wilkescc.edu

BLACKBURN, Brenda .... 828-694-1773 332 E
bc_blackburn@blueridge.edu
BLACKBURN, Fred .... 619-201-8780.. 60 A
fred.blackburn@sdcc.edu
BLACKBURN, J. Blair .... 903-923-2222 436 D
bblackburn@etbu.edu
BLACKBURN, Jan .... 706-437-6801 114 J
jan.blackburn@augustatech.edu
BLACKBURN, JR .... 301-405-7766 202 C
jrblack@umd.edu
BLACKBURN, Kristi .... 213-763-7000.. 49 E
BLACKBURN, Kristi .... 323-241-5218.. 49 D
blackbkv@lasc.edu
BLACKBURN, Kristi .... 562-860-2451.. 35 M
kblackburn@cerritos.edu
BLACKBURN, Lisa .... 606-218-5296 185 D
lisablackburn@upike.edu
BLACKBURN, Mark .... 605-274-4124 415 B
mark.blackburn@augie.edu
BLACKBURN, Michael ... 713-500-6087 456 B
michael.r.blackburn@uth.tmc.edu
BLACKBURN,
Michael, R .... 713-500-3019 456 B
michael.r.blackburn@uth.tmc.edu
BLACKBURN, Michele ... 401-841-6597 503 L
michele.blackburn@usnwc.edu
BLACKBURN, Sara .... 785-227-3380 171 E
blackburnsk@bethanylb.edu
BLACKBURN, Scottie .... 404-835-6118 423 K
sblackburn@richmont.edu
BLACKBURN, Sean .... 307-766-5123 502 H
sean.blackburn@uwyo.edu
BLACKBURN-SMITH,
Jefferson .... 614-823-1031 360 A
jblackburnsmith@otterbein.edu
BLACKETER, Leslie .... 409-772-1304 456 F
lmblacke@utmb.edu
BLACKFORD, Nancy .... 330-490-7106 364 B
nblackford@walsh.edu
BLACKHURST, Anne .... 218-477-2243 239 D
anne.blackhurst@mnstate.edu
BLACKIE, Crisanne .... 207-581-1359 195 J
cblackie@maine.edu
BLACKLANCE, Charles .. 218-855-8119 237 F
cblacklance@clcmn.edu
BLACKLAW, Stuart .... 412-237-8182 381 G
sblacklaw@ccac.edu
BLACKLOCK, Kathy .... 979-753-4774.. 27 D
kblacklock@brandman.edu
BLACKMAN, Bret .... 402-554-2227 270 B
bblackman@unomaha.edu
BLACKMAN, Bret, R .... 402-554-2227 269 H
bblackman@nebraska.edu
BLACKMAN, Harold .... 208-426-5732 129 I
haroldblackman@boisestate.edu
BLACKMER, Jennifer .... 765-285-2783 153 C
jsblackmer@bsu.edu
BLACKMON, Bruce .... 704-687-7010 342 E
ablackm8@uncc.edu
BLACKMON, Chianti .... 301-846-2531 198 E
cblackmon@frederick.edu
BLACKMON, Jamie .... 256-352-8461.... 4 A
jamie.blackmon@wallacestate.edu
BLACKMON, Luke .... 843-863-8004 407 E
lblackmon@csuniv.edu
BLACKMON, Paul .... 334-420-4461.... 3 H
pblackmon@trenholmstate.edu
BLACKMON, Terry, W .... 731-426-7601 420 I
tblackmon@lanecollege.edu
BLACKMON, Timothy .... 630-752-5087 152 F
chaplains.office@wheaton.edu
BLACKMORE, Lee .... 307-754-6067 502 G
lee.blackmore@nwc.edu
BLACKSHEAR,
Regina, G .... 314-539-5123 259 C
rblackshear@stlcc.edu
BLACKSHER DIABATE,
Dafina .... 484-365-7785 389 C
ddiabate@lincoln.edu
BLACKSTON, Misty .... 912-650-6233 124 E
mblackston@southuniversity.edu
BLACKSTON, Tim .... 912-201-8007 124 E
jblackston@southuniversity.edu
BLACKSTONE, Barbara .. 207-768-9415 196 E
barbara.blackstone@maine.edu
BLACKWELDER,
Mark, A .... 731-989-6624 420 C
mblackwelder@fhu.edu
BLACKWELDER, Megan . 847-467-1730 145 F
megan.blackwelder@northwestern.edu
BLACKWELL, Amy .... 864-294-3496 410 A
amy.blackwell@furman.edu
BLACKWELL, Barbara .... 314-275-3521 146 E
barbara.blackwell@principia.edu

BLACKWELL, Bill 218-755-2032 237 E
william.blackwell@bemidjistate.edu
BLACKWELL, David, W 859-257-1333 185 B
provost@uky.edu
BLACKWELL, Deanna, M 217-786-2868 142 B
deanna.blackwell@llcc.edu
BLACKWELL, Deborah, L 956-326-2628 446 F
dblackwell@tamiu.edu
BLACKWELL, Dick 202-319-5046 91 B
blackwellr@cua.edu
BLACKWELL, Jody 318-675-6161 189 C
jblack3@lsuhsc.edu
BLACKWELL, Jody 405-912-9463 369 D
jblackwell@ru.edu
BLACKWELL, Jody, B 336-599-6622 336 G
jody.blackwell@piedmontcc.edu
BLACKWELL, Joe 405-789-7661 370 B
joe.blackwell@swcu.edu
BLACKWELL, Rachelle 817-257-5920 448 G
r.blackwell@tcu.edu
BLACKWELL, Scott 601-266-4783 249 F
edward.blackwell@usm.edu
BLACKWELL, Tiffiny 864-646-1492 413 A
tblackw7@tctc.edu
BLACKWOOD, Edwin 412-731-6000 397 E
eblackwood@rpts.edu
BLACKWOOD, Houston 256-306-2664 1 F
houston.blackwood@calhoun.edu
BLACKWOOD, James 706-880-8050 121 A
jblackwood@lagrange.edu
BLACKWOOD, Jeremy 414-425-8300 495 H
jblackwood@shsst.edu
BLACKWOOD, Joan 602-557-1347 16 J
joan.blackwood@phoenix.edu
BLACKWOOD, Jothany 210-486-0950 429 H
jblackwood3@alamo.edu
BLADE, Michael 541-880-2203 373 E
blade@klamathcc.edu
BLAETTNER, Wendy 830-792-7226 443 G
hr@schreiner.edu
BLAGUSZEWSKI, Edward, F 413-545-0444 211 D
edblag@admin.umass.edu
BLAHNIK, Brent 920-465-2190 496 E
blahnikb@uwgb.edu
BLAHNIK, Hannah, K 651-628-3332 244 D
hkblahnik@unwsp.edu
BLAHNIK, Jeffrey, J 405-325-2151 371 B
jblahnik@ou.edu
BLAICH, Charles, F 765-361-6311 162 E
blaichc@wabash.edu
BLAIN, Daniel, S 330-325-6261 357 G
dblain@neomed.edu
BLAIN, Judy 931-221-7691 418 D
blainj@apsu.edu
BLAIR, Alan 413-572-5582 213 D
alan@westfield.ma.edu
BLAIR, Anthony, L 717-866-5775 383 H
ablair@evangelical.edu
BLAIR, Audrey, D 563-333-6364 169 A
blairaudreyd@sau.edu
BLAIR, Brian 202-885-2842 90 J
bblair@american.edu
BLAIR, Brian 267-502-2407 379 D
brian.blair@brynathyn.edu
BLAIR, Caroline 616-234-4164 224 D
carolineblair@grcc.edu
BLAIR, Cinnamon 505-277-1806 288 G
cblair@salud.unm.edu
BLAIR, Dan 304-865-6135 488 E
dan.blair@ovu.edu
BLAIR, Daniel 978-556-3820 215 C
dblair@necc.mass.edu
BLAIR, David, A 512-428-1286 442 M
davidab@stedwards.edu
BLAIR, Doug 574-239-8380 155 D
dblair@hcc-nd.edu
BLAIR, Eric 816-415-5217 262 F
blaire@william.jewell.edu
BLAIR, Jeff 614-251-4735 358 G
blairj@ohiodominican.edu
BLAIR, John Paul 270-745-6520 185 E
jp.blair@wku.edu
BLAIR, Julie 713-646-1793 444 B
jblair@stcl.edu
BLAIR, Kathryn 207-453-5000 194 I
kblair@kvcc.me.edu
BLAIR, Kristine 412-396-6388 383 C
blairk2@duq.edu
BLAIR, Larry 415-575-6120 29 B
lblair@ciis.edu
BLAIR, Matthew 305-899-4013 95 C
mblair@barry.edu
BLAIR, Michael, R 563-387-1040 167 E
blairmic@luther.edu
BLAIR, Neil, B 913-253-5090 176 I
neil.blair@spst.edu
BLAIR, Patricia 707-476-4289 39 D
patricia-blair@redwoods.edu
BLAIR, Patti 805-652-5502 72 G
pblair@vcccd.edu
BLAIR, Paul, G 574-372-5100 155 B
blairp@grace.edu
BLAIR, Robbie, M 806-716-2336 443 I
rblair@southplainscollege.edu
BLAIR, Sara, B 734-764-9290 231 E
sbblair@umich.edu
BLAIR, Shelly 714-241-6251 38 C
sblair12@coastline.edu
BLAIR, Thomas, A 770-216-2960 120 H
tab@ict.edu
BLAIR, Wendell 312-553-5662 134 B
wblair@ccc.edu
BLAIR, Zulema 718-270-6127 295 A
zblair@mec.cuny.edu
BLAISDELL, John 845-575-3000 305 L
john.blaisdell@marist.edu
BLAISDELL, Stephanie 845-257-3260 317 B
blaisdes@newpaltz.edu
BLAISE, Butterfly, L 518-564-3002 319 C
bblai001@plattsburgh.edu
BLAKE, Amy 970-675-3228 78 G
amy.blake@cncc.edu
BLAKE, Brian 215-895-2200 383 B
mb3545@drexel.edu
BLAKE, Christopher 478-471-2712 121 F
christopher.blake@mga.edu
BLAKE, Christopher, T 631-451-4283 321 G
blakec@sunysuffolk.edu
BLAKE, Dave 619-239-0391 34 F
dblake@cwsl.edu
BLAKE, David 912-525-5000 123 G
dblake@scad.edu
BLAKE, Donnesha 989-463-7463 220 H
blakeda@alma.edu
BLAKE, Erin 225-216-8711 186 K
blakee@mybrcc.edu
BLAKE, Ira, K 281-283-2004 453 A
president@uhcl.edu
BLAKE, Jessica 910-898-9617 336 D
blakej@montgomery.edu
BLAKE, Joi Lin 760-744-1150 55 I
jblake@palomar.edu
BLAKE, Karen 203-575-8269 86 B
kblake@nv.edu
BLAKE, Keiana 713-718-5059 437 I
keiana.blake@hccs.edu
BLAKE, Lawrence 651-962-6561 244 E
blak0035@stthomas.edu
BLAKE, Lindsey 970-675-3275 78 G
lindsey.blake@cncc.edu
BLAKE, Lisa, M 843-953-6964 407 F
lisa.blake@citadel.edu
BLAKE, Melody, A 478-757-5229 126 H
mblake@wesleyancollege.edu
BLAKE, Paul, A 231-591-3797 223 J
paulblake@ferris.edu
BLAKE, Scott 906-487-7242 223 K
scott.blake@finlandia.edu
BLAKE, Tahkeya 508-213-2020 217 E
tahkeya.blake@nichols.edu
BLAKELY, Craig, H 502-852-3297 185 C
crag.blakely@louisville.edu
BLAKELY, Dedria, A 573-334-6825 259 J
dblakely@sehcollege.edu
BLAKELY, Dee 618-634-3247 149 A
deeb@shawneecc.edu
BLAKELY, Edie 360-992-2239 479 F
eblakely@clark.edu
BLAKEMAN, Donald, L 502-863-8091 180 E
don_blakeman@georgetowncollege.edu
BLAKEMORE, Jerry, D 336-334-3067 343 A
j_blakem@uncg.edu
BLAKEMORE, Molly 707-476-4254 39 D
molly-blakemore@redwoods.edu
BLAKEMORE, Patricia 401-739-5000 405 A
pblakemore@neit.edu
BLAKENEY, Erin 425-352-8534 479 A
eblakeney@cascadia.edu
BLAKENEY, Nicolas 210-486-3780 429 F
nblakeney@alamo.edu
BLAKES, Cara 205-226-4727 5 A
clblakes@bsc.edu
BLAKESLEE, Amber 707-826-5702 33 D
amber.blakeslee@humboldt.edu
BLAKEY, Leah 417-873-4092 252 F
lblakey@drury.edu
BLAKEY, Linda 734-973-3536 232 B
lblakey@wccnet.edu
BLAKLEY, Jackie 864-646-1305 413 A
jblakle1@tctc.edu
BLAKLEY, Linda 312-362-7734 135 I
lblakley@depaul.edu
BLALARK, Frank 919-684-2813 328 G
registrar@duke.edu
BLALOCK, III, W. Ben 307-766-6300 502 H
bblalock@uwyo.edu
BLANC, Doug 607-729-1581 298 C
dblanc@davisny.edu
BLANCERO, Donna Maria 781-891-2357 206 D
dblancero@bentley.edu
BLANCHARD, Catherine 409-880-8355 449 G
catherine.blanchard@lamar.edu
BLANCHARD, Deborah 901-321-3271 419 C
dblanch2@cbu.edu
BLANCHARD, Gina, A 740-392-6868 357 B
gina.blanchard@mvnu.edu
BLANCHARD, Gordon 847-578-3232 147 I
gordon.blanchard@rosalindfranklin.edu
BLANCHARD, Jack 301-405-8438 202 C
jblancha@umd.edu
BLANCHARD, Jeffrey 201-559-6000 278 A
BLANCHARD, Jon, A 207-768-2795 194 J
jblanch@nmcc.edu
BLANCHARD, Joyce 207-621-3403 196 A
joyceb@maine.edu
BLANCHARD, Lloyd 860-486-4240 88 E
lloyd.blanchard@uconn.edu
BLANCHARD, Lloyd 860-486-0930 88 E
lloyd.blanchard@uconn.edu
BLANCHARD, Loren, J 562-951-4710 30 B
lblanchard@calstate.edu
BLANCHARD, Marsha, L 573-888-0513 259 K
mblanchard@semo.edu
BLANCHARD, Nate 801-302-2879 459 H
nate.blanchard@neumont.edu
BLANCHARD, Troy 225-578-8273 188 I
troy@lsu.edu
BLANCHARD, Will 405-425-5115 367 G
will.blanchard@oc.edu
BLANCHET, Robert, C 315-684-6046 321 D
blanchrc@morrisville.edu
BLANCHETT, Russell 972-882-7520 447 B
russell.blanchett@tamuc.edu
BLANCHETT, Wanda 848-932-7496 282 A
wanda.blanchett@gse.rutgers.edu
BLANCHETTE, Jennifer 815-802-8816 140 D
jblanchette@kcc.edu
BLANCHETTE, Nick 715-675-3331 500 E
blanchet@ntc.edu
BLANCHIER, Andree 530-242-7511 63 H
ablanchier@shastacollege.edu
BLANCO, Jill 215-489-2346 382 D
jill.blanco@delval.edu
BLANCO MASIAS, Eva 408-554-5251 62 D
eblanco@scu.edu
BLAND, Bartholomew, F 718-960-8731 294 A
bartholomew.bland@lehman.cuny.edu
BLAND, Carmen 360-676-2772 482 D
cbland@nwic.edu
BLAND, Glenda 256-215-4302 1 G
gbland@cacc.edu
BLAND, James 937-393-3431 361 B
jbland@sscc.edu
BLAND, Janet, L 740-376-4741 356 A
janet.bland@marietta.edu
BLAND, Marissa 816-415-5938 262 F
blandm@william.jewell.edu
BLAND, Morgan, R 252-451-8258 336 E
mrbland492@nashcc.edu
BLAND, Sharon 240-567-3080 200 C
sharon.bland@montgomerycollege.edu
BLAND, Terry 662-862-8282 246 D
tgbland@iccms.edu
BLANDFORD, David, K 989-463-7147 220 H
blandford@alma.edu
BLANDFORD, Jonathan, W 502-272-7404 179 B
jblandford@bellarmine.edu
BLANDFORD, Rob 804-289-6010 472 L
smcinvest@richmond.edu
BLANDON, Darwin 423-648-2678 423 K
dblandon@richmont.edu
BLANK, Dave, L 336-278-6705 328 K
dblank@elon.edu
BLANK, James 330-672-2650 354 J
jblank@kent.edu
BLANK, Michelle 260-665-4179 160 H
blankm@trine.edu
BLANK, Natalia 802-485-2025 463 A
nblank@norwich.edu
BLANK, Rebecca 608-262-9946 496 C
chancellor@news.wisc.edu
BLANKE, Raymond 405-733-7306 369 I
rblanke@rose.edu
BLANKENBAKER, Zarina 817-515-7750 445 G
zarina.blankenbaker@tccd.edu
BLANKENBUEHLER, Carla 304-205-6706 488 K
carla.blankenbuehler@bridgevalley.edu
BLANKENHEIM, Kim 319-368-6464 168 C
kblankenheim@mtmercy.edu
BLANKENHORN, Stacie 503-359-1082 375 G
bookstore@pacificu.edu
BLANKENSHIP, Brendan 559-251-4215 28 B
admissions@calchristiancollege.edu
BLANKENSHIP, Bruce, A 304-457-6340 487 B
blankenshipba@ab.edu
BLANKENSHIP, Bruce, A 304-457-6213 487 B
blankenshipba@ab.edu
BLANKENSHIP, Bryan, P 859-858-2228 178 H
BLANKENSHIP, Karen 281-476-1850 443 C
karen.blankenship@sjcd.edu
BLANKENSHIP, Kevin 615-230-3428 426 B
kevin.blankenship@volstate.edu
BLANKENSHIP, Mark, V 859-280-1250 183 B
mblankenship@lextheo.edu
BLANKENSHIP, Michelle 212-343-1234 306 J
mblankenship@mcny.edu
BLANKENSHIP, Mike 601-605-3315 246 C
mblankenship@holmescc.edu
BLANKENSHIP, Paul, D 407-582-5415 112 K
pblankenship1@valenciacollege.edu
BLANKENSHIP, Randy 419-755-4767 357 E
rblankenship@ncstatecollege.edu
BLANKENSHIP, Rosalie 765-658-4211 154 F
rosalieblankenship@depauw.edu
BLANKENSHIP, Ruth 276-326-4556 465 B
rblankenship@bluefield.edu
BLANKENSHIP, Vince 903-923-2002 436 D
vblankenship@etbu.edu
BLANKMEYER, Bonnie, L 210-567-2691 456 C
blankmeyer@uthscsa.edu
BLANKSON, Joana 404-297-9522 119 B
blanksonj@gptc.edu
BLANSON, Archie 832-813-6648 439 G
archie.blanson@lonestar.edu
BLANTON, Angela 412-268-4925 380 F
ablanton@andrew.cmu.edu
BLANTON, James 205-929-6317 2 H
jblanton@lawsonstate.edu
BLANTON, Jay, D 859-257-6605 185 B
jay.blanton@uky.edu
BLANTON, Julie 620-665-3510 174 B
BLANTON, Michael 213-740-4577 72 B
michael.blanton@usc.edu
BLANTON, Ryan 580-349-1550 368 A
rblanton@opsu.edu
BLANTON, Sharon 609-771-3353 276 I
blantons@tcnj.edu
BLANTON HIBNER, Amelia 314-256-8806 250 D
blantonhibner@ai.edu
BLASCHKE, Jayme, L 512-245-2180 450 E
jb71@txstate.edu
BLASDEL, Amy 618-537-6330 143 B
bookstores@mckendree.edu
BLASE, Frances, R 610-896-1014 385 L
fblase@haverford.edu
BLASE, Kristen 603-428-2226 273 H
kblase@nec.edu
BLASER, Martin, J 848-445-9834 282 A
blaser@cabm.rutgers.edu
BLASHAK, Theodore 305-474-6957 106 F
tblashak@stu.edu
BLASI, Laura, N 407-582-3486 112 K
lblasi@valenciacollege.edu
BLASIG, Jerry, A 402-557-7075 265 J
jerry.blasig@bellevue.edu

BLASS, Tammy .... 323-409-6509.. 49 H
tblass@dhs.lacounty.gov
BLASSINGAME, Susan .. 806-720-7602 439 H
susan.blassingame@lcu.edu
BLASZAK, Julie .... 616-632-2945 221 C
jab008@aquinas.edu
BLASZCZAK, SJ, Gerry .. 203-254-4000.. 86 I
gblaszczak@fairfield.edu
BLATCHFORD, Alicia ..... 305-284-5155 112 E
awb49@miami.edu
BLATT, Keath .... 212-678-8000 303 G
keblatt@jtsa.edu
BLATTNER, Alan .... 919-962-2211 342 D
allan_blattner@unc.edu
BLATTNER, Carolyn .... 919-508-2048 344 F
cmblattner@peace.edu
BLATTNER, Nancy .... 973-618-3217 276 D
nblattner@caldwell.edu
BLAYLOCK, Andrew .... 217-786-4533 142 B
andrew.blaylock@llcc.edu
BLAYLOCK, John, V ...... 402-844-7124 268 J
johnb@northeast.edu
BLAYLOCK, Reginald, S 909-869-3805.. 30 D
rsblaylock@cpp.edu
BLAYLOCK, Stephen ...... 813-988-5131.. 98 Q
blaylocks@floridacollege.edu
BLAYLOCK, Terry .... 936-294-1049 450 C
tab064@shsu.edu
BLAZ, Amy .... 651-638-6125 234 C
a-blaz@bethel.edu
BLAZAK, Joe .... 724-964-8811 391 E
jblazak@ncstrades.edu
BLAZEI, Theresa .... 414-288-5163 494 B
theresa.blazei@marquette.edu
BLAZEK, Brent .... 816-501-4375 258 H
brent.blazek@rockhurst.edu
BLAZEKOVIC, Brenda ...... 509-359-6060 480 E
bblazeko@ewu.edu
BLAZEY, Jerry .... 815-753-1883 145 C
gblazey@niu.edu
BLAZIS, Enoch .... 507-786-3002 243 C
blazis@stolaf.edu
BLEA, Kimberly .... 505-454-3566 286 H
kjvaldez@nmhu.edu
BLECHMAN, Mindy .... 215-635-7300 385 A
mblechman@gratz.edu
BLEDSOE, Chad, A .... 910-898-9601 336 D
bledsoec@montgomery.edu
BLEDSOE, Christopher .. 212-998-2040 310 B
christopher.bledsoe@nyu.edu
BLEDSOE, Gary, L .... 713-313-1071 449 C
gary.bledsoe@tmslaw.tsu.edu
BLEDSOE, Jennifer .... 423-472-7141 424 F
jbledsoe01@clevelandstatecc.edu
BLEDSOE, Lisa .... 971-722-5852 375 J
lbledsoe@pcc.edu
BLEDSOE, Mary .... 817-515-6792 445 G
mary.bledsoe@tccd.edu
BLEDSOE, Ruth .... 213-763-7189.. 49 E
bledsoerj@lattc.edu
BLEDSOE, W. Craig ...... 615-966-1789 421 D
craig.bledsoe@lipscomb.edu
BLEE, Kathleen, M .... 412-624-6094 401 B
kblee@pitt.edu
BLEGEN, Mark .... 262-524-7364 492 E
mglegen@carrollu.edu
BLEIFIELD, Elaina .... 763-576-4113 237 D
ebleifileld@anokatech.edu
BLEIKAMP, Kerry .... 303-963-3350.. 77 G
kbleikamp@ccu.edu
BLEMINGS, Kenneth, P . 304-293-2100 491 C
ken.blemings@mail.wvu.edu
BLEMINGS, Keri .... 304-293-2395 491 C
keri.blemings@mail.wvu.edu
BLENIS, Brian .... 484-664-3631 391 C
brianblenis@muhlenberg.edu
BLENKER, Shawn, A ..... 208-467-8950 131 D
sablenker@nnu.edu
BLESSO, Thomas .... 480-947-6644.. 15 A
thomas.blesso@pennfoster.edu
BLEVINS, Anita, F .... 423-478-7021 423 G
ablevins@ptseminary.edu
BLEVINS, Donna .... 907-563-7575.... 9 C
donna.blevins@alaskacareercollege.edu
BLEVINS, Elisabeth .... 336-838-6145 339 B
ekblevins580@wilkescc.edu
BLEVINS, Elizabeth .... 417-690-2470 251 E
eblevins@cofo.edu
BLEVINS, Elizabeth .... 740-351-3112 360 K
eblevins@shawnee.edu
BLEVINS, Karen .... 606-326-2063 180 I
karen.blevins@kctcs.edu
BLEVINS, Lori .... 336-249-8186 334 A
lori_blevins@davidsonccc.edu
BLEVINS,
Phillip Andrew .... 479-575-4140.. 21 G
BLEVINS, Rick .... 785-442-6110 174 A
rblevins@highlandcc.edu
BLEVINS, Robert .... 601-318-6155 249 H
robert.blevins@wmcarey.edu
BLEVINS, Ryan .... 219-464-5413 162 A
ryan.blevins@valpo.edu
BLEVINS, Scarlett .... 276-944-6229 467 G
scblevins@ehc.edu
BLEW, Chad .... 405-744-6604 368 B
chad.blew@okstate.edu
BLEW, Denise, M .... 610-758-3179 388 J
dmb3@lehigh.edu
BLEWETT, Patrick, A ..... 530-226-4033.. 63 K
pblewett@simpsonu.edu
BLEZA, Michelle .... 760-674-7828.. 39 A
mbleza@collegeofthedesert.edu
BLICKHAN, Lynn .... 217-641-4206 140 A
lblickhan@jwcc.edu
BLIER, Helen .... 412-924-1346 396 I
hblier@pts.edu
BLIESZNER, Rosemary .. 540-231-6779 477 A
rmb@vt.edu
BLIGH, Michelle .... 909-621-8647.. 37 D
michelle.bligh@cgu.edu
BLINKA, Sonja .... 409-933-8474 433 L
sblinka@com.edu
BLISS, Lucinda .... 603-623-0313 273 I
lucindabliss@nhia.edu
BLISS, Patricia, J .... 315-445-4141 304 C
blisspj@lemoyne.edu
BLISS, Shannon .... 831-755-6875.. 44 K
sbliss@hartnell.edu
BLITSTEIN, Peter, A ...... 920-832-6528 493 K
peter.a.blitstein@lawrence.edu
BLITZ, Y .... 248-968-3360 233 F
BLIWISE, Nancy .... 404-727-7452 117 F
nancy.bliwise@emory.edu
BLIZINSKI, Bob .... 626-585-7502.. 55 K
rblizinski@pasadena.edu
BLIZZARD, Mary .... 304-205-6750 488 K
mary.blizzard@bridgevalley.edu
BLOCHER, Larry .... 334-670-3869.... 7 C
lblocher@troy.edu
BLOCK, Debbie .... 507-457-2412 241 F
dblock@winona.edu
BLOCK, Derryl .... 815-753-6155 145 C
dblock@niu.edu
BLOCK, Gene, D .... 310-825-2151.. 69 A
chancellor@conet.ucla.edu
BLOCK, Jayme, E .... 410-543-6156 203 F
jeblock@salisbury.edu
BLOCK, Joel .... 212-686-9244 290 A
BLOCK, Kailey .... 970-339-6433.. 76 G
kailey.block@aims.edu
BLOCK, Kelly, J .... 217-244-0102 151 A
kjb@uillinois.edu
BLOCK, Steven .... 956-665-2175 455 D
steven.block@utrgv.edu
BLOCK, William, A .... 423-439-6317 419 J
block@etsu.edu
BLOCKER, Bill .... 832-252-4624 433 D
bill.blocker@cbshouston.edu
BLOCKER, Robert, L ...... 203-432-4160.. 89 D
robert.blocker@yale.edu
BLOCKSIDGE, Katie .... 740-364-9513 349 H
blocksidge.3@osu.edu
BLODGETT, Bruce, M .... 315-294-8544 292 E
blodgett@cayuga-cc.edu
BLOEBAUM, Christina ... 330-672-2892 354 J
cbloebau@kent.edu
BLOEMENDAAL, Mark ... 712-707-7127 168 H
markb@nwciowa.edu
BLOEMKER,
Geraldine, A .... 610-499-4107 403 B
gabloemker@widener.edu
BLOHM, John .... 337-482-0911 192 E
jib@louisiana.edu
BLOHM, Melvin .... 248-218-2119 229 J
mblohm@rc.edu
BLOM, Alyssa .... 616-988-3624 226 C
ablom@kuyper.edu
BLOMBERG, Brock .... 610-409-3587 402 A
brock@ursinus.edu
BLOMBERG, Thomas ..... 850-644-7380 109 C
tblomber@fsu.edu
BLOME, Christian .... 812-482-3030 162 C
cblome@vinu.edu
BLOME, Shelley .... 701-671-2191 346 E
shelley.blome@ndscs.edu
BLOMGREN, Laura .... 610-892-1536 393 J
lblomgren@pit.edu
BLOMGREN, Rebecca .... 336-272-7102 329 D
blomgrenr@greensboro.edu
BLONDE, Mitchell .... 419-448-3584 361 J
blondemp@tiffin.edu
BLONDEL, Elizabeth ...... 312-662-4003 131 H
eblondel@adler.edu
BLONDIN, Jo, A .... 937-328-6001 350 L
blondinj@clarkstate.edu
BLONDIN, Monica, M .. 508-767-7157 205 D
mm.blondin@assumption.edu
BLONIGEN, Bruce .... 541-346-3902 377 D
bruceb@uoregon.edu
BLOOM, Deborah .... 802-322-1624 462 C
deborah.bloom@goddard.edu
BLOOM, Homer .... 724-589-2040 399 H
hbloom@thiel.edu
BLOOM, Joel, S .... 973-596-3102 279 F
joel.s.bloom@njit.edu
BLOOM, John, S .... 214-887-5591 436 B
jbloom@dts.edu
BLOOM, Ronald .... 914-606-6912 325 C
ronald.bloom@sunywcc.edu
BLOOM, Steven .... 617-243-2440 210 G
sbloom@lasell.edu
BLOOM, Sue .... 814-393-2045 394 D
sbloom@clarion.edu
BLOOM, Tara .... 315-279-5465 304 A
tbloom@keuka.edu
BLOOM, Vicki .... 574-520-4448 157 A
vdbloom@iusb.edu
BLOOM, William .... 760-384-6221.. 46 M
william.bloom@cerrocoso.edu
BLOOM, Yvonne .... 314-539-5150 259 C
ybloom1@stlcc.edu
BLOOMBERG, Laura ...... 612-625-0608 243 E
bloom004@umn.edu
BLOOMBERG, Stephen .. 870-543-5907.. 21 C
sbloomberg@seark.edu
BLOOME, Meghan .... 267-295-2376 397 F
mbloome@walnuthillcollege.edu
BLOOMER, Dennis, L .... 864-488-4561 410 E
dbloomer@limestone.edu
BLOOMER, Richard, J .... 901-678-4316 427 D
rbloomer@memphis.edu
BLOOMFIELD, Ellen ...... 859-846-5755 183 E
ebloomfield@midway.edu
BLOOMFIELD, Stewart .. 212-938-5540 320 B
sbloomfield@sunyopt.edu
BLOOMINGDALE,
Mary, E .... 641-422-4351 168 D
bloommar@niacc.edu
BLOSHINSKI, John .... 570-422-3631 394 E
jbloshinski@esu.edu
BLOSS, Adrienne, G ...... 540-665-4525 471 E
abloss@su.edu
BLOSS, Kim .... 870-235-4057.. 21 D
kkbloss@saumag.edu
BLOSS, Kim, K .... 870-235-4055.. 21 D
kkbloss@saumag.edu
BLOSSER, Joseph, D .... 336-841-9337 329 G
jblosser@highpoint.edu
BLOSSER, Kim .... 540-868-7101 474 J
kblosser@lfcc.edu
BLOSSOM, Marcus .... 508-793-2571 208 B
mblossum@holycross.edu
BLOUCH, Christine .... 309-677-2395 133 B
blouch@fsmail.bradley.edu
BLOUIN, Bob, A .... 919-962-2198 342 D
bob_blouin@unc.edu
BLOUIN, Mike .... 770-962-7580 120 E
mblouin@gwinnetttech.edu
BLOUNT, Brian, K .... 804-278-4200 472 E
bblount@upsem.edu
BLOUNT, Lori .... 610-558-5630 391 D
blountl@neumann.edu
BLOUNT, Nicole .... 513-556-3233 362 D
nicole.blount@uc.edu
BLOUNT, Pamela .... 850-412-5072 108 I
pamela.blount@famu.edu
BLOUNT, Sally, E .... 847-491-2840 145 F
sallyblount@kellogg.northwestern.edu
BLOUNT, Stuart .... 910-378-8212 340 J
sblount@umo.edu
BLOWERS, Kelsy .... 218-683-8543 240 A
kelsy.blowers@northlandcollege.edu
BLOYE, Alex .... 231-995-2914 228 G
abloye@nmc.edu
BLUE, Bob .... 318-869-5127 186 B
vpfa@centenary.edu
BLUE, Jean .... 910-695-3739 337 H
bluej@sandhills.edu
BLUE, Joe .... 270-824-1828 181 G
joe.blue@kctcs.edu
BLUE, Kevin .... 530-752-4557.. 68 E
athleticsdirector@ucdavis.edu
BLUE, Lynn, M .... 616-331-2500 224 E
bluel@gvsu.edu
BLUE, Shella .... 847-578-8807 147 I
shella.blue@rosalindfranklin.edu
BLUEBAUGH, Wade ...... 301-687-3175 203 E
ewadebluebaugh@frostburg.edu
BLUM, Avrim .... 773-834-2500 150 E
ablum@ttic.edu
BLUM, Christopher .... 303-937-4420.. 76 L
christopher.blum@augustineinstitute.
org
BLUM, Dominika .... 605-626-7802 417 A
dominika.blum@northern.edu
BLUM, Harrison .... 617-824-8500 208 H
harrison_blum@emerson.edu
BLUM, Janice .... 317-274-1020 156 F
jblum@iupui.edu
BLUM, Janice, S .... 317-274-5845 156 F
jblum@iupui.edu
BLUM, Jennifer .... 866-492-5336 244 F
jennifer.blum@laureate.edu
BLUM, Jonathan .... 712-274-5408 168 B
blumj@morningside.edu
BLUM, Kim .... 608-785-8616 496 F
kblum@uwlax.edu
BLUM, Robert .... 817-272-2771 454 J
rwblum@uta.edu
BLUM, Stacey, L .... 210-486-4111 429 F
sblum6@alamo.edu
BLUM, Susan .... 631-444-8250 317 D
susan.blum@stonybrook.edu
BLUM, Thomas .... 914-395-2203 315 F
tblum@sarahlawrence.edu
BLUM, Thomas, L .... 914-395-2203 315 F
tblum@sarahlawrence.edu
BLUM MALLEY,
Suzanne .... 312-369-8111 135 E
sbmalley@colum.edu
BLUMBERG, Audrey, S . 516-877-3159 289 C
blumberg@adelphi.edu
BLUMBERG, Bruce, K ... 803-938-3838 414 B
bruceb@uscsumter.edu
BLUMBERG, Elizabeth ... 781-239-2762 214 E
eblumberg@massbay.edu
BLUMBERG, James, J ... 309-556-3066 139 G
jblumber@iwu.edu
BLUME, Travis .... 906-217-4116 221 O
travis.blume@baycollege.edu
BLUMENFELD, Lee .... 858-646-3100.. 62 A
lblumenfeld@sbpdiscovery.org
BLUMENSTEIN, Robert .. 610-282-1100 382 E
robert.blumenstein@desales.edu
BLUMENTHAL, Eric .... 971-722-2913 375 J
eric.blumenthal2@pcc.edu
BLUMENTHAL, Jeff .... 989-358-7317 221 A
blumenthalj@alpenacc.edu
BLUMENTHAL, Pam ...... 971-722-4532 375 J
pamela.blumenthal15@pcc.edu
BLUMENTRITT, Timothy 470-578-2075 120 L
tblument@kennesaw.edu
BLUMER, Lindsay, A ..... 920-748-8316 495 G
blumerl@ripon.edu
BLUML, Joel .... 785-670-2100 177 G
joe.bluml@washburn.edu
BLUNDELL, Keith .... 361-582-2535 457 E
keith.blundell@victoriacollege.edu
BLUNDERS, Lisa .... 802-651-5911 462 B
lblunders@champlain.edu
BLUNK, Shelly, R .... 515-574-1901 166 E
blunk@iowacentral.edu
BLUNT, Lisa .... 406-874-6214 263 I
bluntl@milescc.edu
BLUNT, Shelly, B .... 812-465-1617 161 E
sblunt@usi.edu
BLUST, Robert .... 303-458-1843.. 82 E
rblust@regis.edu
BLUTH, Ellen .... 563-336-3331 165 B
ebluth@eicc.edu
BLUTREICH, Peter .... 912-478-5406 119 C
pblutreich@georgiasouthern.edu
BLY, Scott .... 323-856-7643.. 25 M
sbly@afi.com
BLYTHE, Gretchen, S .... 816-604-2251 255 G
gretchen.blythe@mcckc.edu
BLYTHE, Janett .... 270-534-3079 182 F
janett.blythe@kctcs.edu
BLYTHE, Keith .... 336-734-7212 334 E
kblythe@forsythtech.edu
BLYTHE, Richard, J .... 540-231-6416 477 A
richardblythe@vt.edu

BOHREN, Karen .... 231-591-2607 223 J
karenbohren@ferris.edu
BOHRER, Joseph, S ..... 610-330-3161 387 E
bohrerj@lafayette.edu
BOHRER, Monty .... 605-995-2997 415 C
monty.bohrer@dwu.edu
BOICE, Daniel .... 870-460-1080.. 22 D
boice@uamont.edu
BOICE, Paul .... 708-239-4837 150 F
paul.boice@trnty.edu
BOICE-PARDEE, Heath .. 585-475-2268 313 A
hbpvsa@rit.edu
BOIES, Brandy .... 540-868-7161 474 J
bboies@lfcc.edu
BOIKE, Allan .... 216-707-8004 354 J
aboike1@kent.edu
BOISE, Craig, M .... 315-443-9580 322 C
cmboise@law.syr.edu
BOISEN, Beth .... 715-232-1363 498 A
boisenb@uwstout.edu
BOISSELLE, Juliet .... 315-781-3952 302 A
jhboiselle@hws.edu
BOISSELLE, Vincent ...... 315-781-3549 302 A
boisselle@hws.edu
BOISVERT, Craig .... 304-647-6363 491 A
cboisvert@osteo.wvsom.edu
BOISVERT, David .... 717-262-2002 403 F
david.boisvert@wilson.edu
BOITER, Christine .... 253-964-6500 483 D
cboiter@pierce.ctc.edu
BOIVIN, Janet .... 808-544-1187 127 H
jboivin@hpu.edu
BOJORQUEZ, Cathy ...... 805-289-6354.. 73 B
cbojorquez@vcccd.edu
BOKOSKI, Leslie .... 610-647-4400 386 C
lbokoski@immaculata.edu
BOKSAN, George .... 610-861-1421 391 A
boksang@moravian.edu
BOKTOR, Monir .... 949-794-9090.. 65 I
mboktor@stanbridge.edu
BOLAND, Carolyn .... 513-244-4717 357 A
carolyn.boland@msj.edu
BOLAND, Christopher ... 570-504-9619 384 F
cboland@som.geisinger.edu
BOLAND, Kristine .... 419-783-2469 352 F
kboland@defiance.edu
BOLAND, Mary, G .... 808-956-8522 128 F
mgboland@hawaii.edu
BOLAND, Mary Kate ..... 610-647-4400 386 C
mboland@immaculata.edu
BOLAND, Wendy .... 202-885-1976.. 90 J
boland@american.edu
BOLAND-CHASE, Ann ... 570-961-4728 389 G
chase@marywood.edu
BOLDMAN, Rachael ...... 815-479-7572 143 A
rboldman@mchenry.edu
BOLDON, Diana .... 330-672-2210 354 J
dboldon@kent.edu
BOLDT, Bill .... 503-725-5037 376 A
boldtb@psuf.org
BOLDT, Deborah .... 505-428-1704 288 B
deborah.boldt@sfcc.edu
BOLDUC, Michael, C .... 561-237-7180 102 V
mbolduc@lynn.edu
BOLEK, Catherine .... 410-651-6714 203 A
csbolek@umes.edu
BOLEN, Deb, L .... 717-245-1798 382 F
bolend@dickinson.edu
BOLEN, Tom .... 913-684-5495 504 D
BOLERATZ, David .... 606-693-5000 182 G
dboleratz@kmbc.edu
BOLES, Janie, A .... 334-844-6176.... 4 E
bolesja@auburn.edu
BOLEY, Johanna .... 832-519-2898 439 G
johanna.m.boley@lonestar.edu
BOLEY, Paula .... 419-995-8218 354 H
boley.p@rhodesstate.edu
BOLGER, Eric .... 417-690-2278 251 E
bolger@cofo.edu
BOLIN, Joseph .... 951-343-4714.. 27 J
jbolin@calbaptist.edu
BOLIN, Mark .... 256-352-8102.... 4 A
mark.bolin@wallacestate.edu
BOLIN, Mary, C .... 859-257-8701 185 B
marychandler.bolin@uky.edu
BOLINDER, Megan .... 479-936-5145.. 20 D
mbolinder@nwacc.edu
BOLINE, Krista .... 678-331-4399 121 C
krista.boline@life.edu
BOLING, Carrie .... 859-846-5326 183 E
cboling@midway.edu
BOLING, Cindy .... 405-974-2547 370 K
cboling@uco.edu

BOLLENBACHER, Brian . 773-252-6464 147 B
brian.bollenbacher@resu.edu
BOLLERUD, Julie .... 760-795-6610.. 52 E
jbollerud@miracosta.edu
BOLLHEIMER, Meredith 814-824-3363 390 C
mbollheimer@mercyhurst.edu
BOLLHORST, Robin .... 217-875-7200 147 C
rbollhorst@richland.edu
BOLLIER, John, H .... 203-432-6754.. 89 D
john.bollier@yale.edu
BOLLING, Phyllis .... 973-596-3420 279 F
phyllis.bolling@njit.edu
BOLLINGER, Aaron .... 412-392-8118 397 A
abollinger@pointpark.edu
BOLLINGER, Bruce .... 701-231-6177 345 G
bruce.bollinger@ndsu.edu
BOLLINGER, Larry .... 617-745-3730 208 G
larry.bollinger@enc.edu
BOLLINGER, Lee, C ...... 212-854-9970 297 C
bollinger@columbia.edu
BOLLMAN, Dan .... 517-355-3366 227 D
dbollman@ipf.msu.edu
BOLLMAN-DALANSKY,
Terri, L .... 814-641-3424 386 H
bollmat@juniata.edu
BOLLMANN, Janice, A .. 314-286-4805 258 E
jabollmann@ranken.edu
BOLLOW, Jillian .... 630-617-3564 136 G
jillian.bollow@elmhurst.edu
BOLMAN, Ann .... 605-718-2401 417 F
ann.bolman@wdt.edu
BOLMAN, Dave .... 602-383-8228.. 16 F
dbolman@uat.edu
BOLNET, Carolle .... 718-270-6202 295 A
bolnet@mec.cuny.edu
BOLOGNA, Brynn .... 816-584-6714 258 A
brynn.bologna@park.edu
BOLOGNONE,
John (Buddy) .... 213-624-1200.. 42 I
bbolognone@fidm.edu
BOLSINGER, Tod .... 626-304-3711.. 43 H
bolsinger@fuller.edu
BOLSTER, Damian .... 315-781-3309 302 A
bolster@hws.edu
BOLSTER, Jeff .... 619-849-2480.. 57 E
jeffbolster@pointloma.edu
BOLSTRIDGE, Ronald .... 207-755-5384 194 G
rbolstridge@cmcc.edu
BOLT, Barb .... 814-868-9900 383 F
barbb@erieit.edu
BOLT, Barbara .... 814-864-6666 385 B
barbarab@glit.edu
BOLT, Corrine .... 606-218-5327 185 D
corrinebolt@upike.edu
BOLT, Joy .... 706-864-1514 126 A
joy.bolt@ung.edu
BOLT, Susan .... 614-823-1354 360 A
bolt1@otterbein.edu
BOLT, Tracy, L .... 443-334-2270 201 H
tbolt@stevenson.edu
BOLTON, Adrienne .... 985-448-4091 192 B
adrienne.bolton@nicholls.edu
BOLTON, Brooke .... 513-618-1927 350 J
bbolton@ccms.edu
BOLTON, David .... 417-328-1538 259 L
dbolton@sbuniv.edu
BOLTON, JR., G. Allen . 205-934-5493.... 8 A
abolton@uab.edu
BOLTON, Harry .... 707-654-1192.. 32 B
hbolton@csum.edu
BOLTON, James .... 484-664-3400 391 C
jimbolton@muhlenberg.edu
BOLTON, Jeff .... 313-577-2027 232 I
jbolton@wayne.edu
BOLTON, Kathy, E .... 410-777-2028 197 C
kebolton@aacc.edu
BOLTON, Lance .... 719-502-2200.. 81 F
lance.bolton@ppcc.edu
BOLTON, Lillie, M .... 662-252-8000 248 G
lbolton@rustcollege.edu
BOLTON, Meghann .... 512-313-3000 434 E
meghann.bolton@concordia.edu
BOLTON, Sarah .... 330-263-2311 351 C
sbolton@wooster.edu
BOLTON, Shantay .... 504-865-5000 191 B
BOLTON, Tonya, D .... 870-759-4130.. 23 J
tbolton@williamsbu.edu
BOLYAI, Stephen .... 973-720-2233 284 I
bolyais@wpunj.edu
BOLYARD, Adrienne, M 206-726-5021 480 C
abolyard@cornish.edu
BOMAN, Victoria .... 205-366-8817.... 7 A
vboman@stillman.edu

BOMAR, Charles .... 715-232-4053 498 A
bomarc@uwstout.edu
BOMAR, Jimmy .... 731-352-4034 418 G
bomarj@bethelu.edu
BOMBACK, Larry .... 215-717-3171 382 B
larry.bomback@curtis.edu
BOMBARD, Charles ...... 802-654-0505 464 B
clb10040@ccv.vsc.edu
BOMBERY, Kathleen ..... 912-443-5828 124 A
kbombery@savannahtech.edu
BOMER, Dee .... 615-687-6907 418 A
dbomer@abcnash.edu
BOMER, Randy .... 940-565-2231 454 A
randy.bomer@unt.edu
BOMOTTI, Gerry .... 951-827-7310.. 69 C
gerry.bomotti@ucr.edu
BONA, Dennis .... 218-793-2465 240 A
dennis.bona@northlandcollege.edu
BONACCORSO, Roberto 206-934-5487 484 A
roberto.bonaccorso@seattlecolleges.
edu
BONACIC, Patricia .... 310-900-1600.. 40 A
pbonacic@elcamino.edu
BONACK, Anne, E .... 715-365-4415 500 D
abonack@nicoletcollege.edu
BONADIE, Heidi .... 909-599-5433.. 47 K
hbonadie@lifepacific.edu
BONADUCE DE NIGRIS,
Francesca .... 713-646-1811 444 B
fbonaducedenigris@stcl.edu
BONAGURA, Thom .... 712-749-2271 163 D
bonagura@bvu.edu
BONAHUE, Edward .... 352-381-3822 107 A
ed.bonahue@sfcollege.edu
BONAMICI, Andrew .... 973-408-3322 277 C
abonamici@drew.edu
BONANNO, Joseph, A .. 812-855-4440 156 B
jbonanno@indiana.edu
BONAPARTE, Donna ..... 781-239-6434 205 E
dbonaparte@babson.edu
BONATH, Kyle, K .... 806-742-3931 451 B
kyle.k.bonath@ttu.edu
BONATO, Frederick .... 201-761-6020 282 I
fbonato@saintpeters.edu
BONAVIA, Jan .... 708-709-7844 146 D
jbonavia@prairiestate.edu
BONAVIST, Kathy .... 610-921-7260 378 C
kbonavist@albright.edu
BONCHI, Joseph .... 973-596-3002 279 F
joseph.bonchi@njit.edu
BOND, Alicia .... 570-408-6024 403 D
alicia.bond@wilkes.edu
BOND, Bradley .... 815-753-9403 145 C
bbond@niu.edu
BOND, Dawn .... 413-545-2100 211 D
dbond@umass.edu
BOND, Debra .... 540-674-3607 475 B
dbond@nr.edu
BOND, Emma .... 601-426-6346 249 A
ebond@southeasternbaptist.edu
BOND, Erin .... 212-431-2199 309 G
erin.bond@nyls.edu
BOND, Helen .... 202-806-0870.. 92 B
hbond@howard.edu
BOND, Inge .... 408-855-5204.. 74 D
inge.bond@missioncollege.edu
BOND, Lynette .... 413-662-5106 213 A
lynette.bond@mcla.edu
BOND, Melisa .... 910-898-9634 336 D
bondm@montgomery.edu
BOND, Meredith, R .... 216-687-5580 351 B
m.bond40@csuohio.edu
BOND, Michelle .... 334-386-7275.... 5 D
mbond@faulkner.edu
BOND, Millie .... 610-526-7805 379 E
mbond@brynmawr.edu
BOND, Mollie .... 312-329-4177 144 B
mollie.bond@moody.edu
BOND, Susan, E .... 610-359-1222 382 C
sbond@dccc.edu
BOND, Terrance .... 309-268-8238 137 I
terrance.bond@heartland.edu
BOND-MAUPIN, Lisa .... 707-826-4491.. 33 D
ljb20@humboldt.edu
BONDAD, Theresa .... 435-652-7502 460 G
theresa.bondad@dixie.edu
BONDAVALLI, Bonnie ... 815-836-5691 141 G
bondavbo@lewisu.edu
BONDAVALLI, Bonnie ... 815-836-5242 141 G
bondavbo@lewisu.edu
BONDAVALLI, Bruno ..... 773-878-3439 148 D
bbondavalli@staugustine.edu
BONDEROFF, Mary, H .. 315-684-6038 321 D
bondermh@morrisville.edu

BONDI, Nathanael .... 303-273-3537.. 78 I
nbondi@mines.edu
BONDS, Dorothea .... 214-648-7500 457 B
dorothea.bonds@utsouthwestern.edu
BONDS, Jess .... 209-478-0800.. 45 H
jbonds@humphreys.edu
BONDS, Nechell, T .... 417-836-5517 256 E
nbonds@missouristate.edu
BONDS, Nell .... 870-743-3000.. 20 C
nbonds@northark.edu
BONDS, Robert .... 561-586-0121 100 O
BONDS, Thomas .... 662-862-8130 246 D
tabonds@iccms.edu
BONDS-RAACKE,
Jennifer .... 920-403-3001 495 I
jennifer.bonds-raacke@snc.edu
BONDURANT, Jennifer .. 434-947-4113 470 E
jbondurant@randolphcollege.edu
BONDY, Jeff .... 406-994-2661 264 D
jbondy@montana.edu
BONDY, Kaylyn .... 701-774-4585 346 F
kaylyn.bondy@willistonstate.edu
BONE, Rodney .... 256-228-6001.... 3 B
BONEBRIGHT, Terri ...... 501-450-1273.. 19 F
bonebright@hendrix.edu
BONELLI, Vicky .... 618-544-8657 138 H
bonelliv@iecc.edu
BONERI, Jacqueline ...... 954-776-4476 102 A
jboneri@keiseruniversity.edu
BONES, Whit .... 816-802-3532 254 B
wbones@kcai.edu
BONEWALD, Karen .... 603-526-3748 272 H
kbonewald@colby-sawyer.edu
BONFANTI, Phil .... 601-928-8402 247 E
phil.bonfanti@mgccc.edu
BONGARTZ, Michael ..... 816-235-1515 261 C
bongartzm@umkc.edu
BONGIORNO, Laurel ..... 802-651-5978 462 B
bongiorno@champlain.edu
BONGIOVANNI, Lynne .. 718-405-3753 296 G
lynne.bongiovanni@mountsaintvincent.
edu
BONHARD, Gary .... 520-322-6330.. 12 K
gary@hanuniversity.edu
BONI, Bethyn .... 315-568-3252 308 F
bboni@nycc.edu
BONIADI, Ani .... 818-252-5224.. 75 C
ani.boniadi@woodbury.edu
BONIECKI, Kelli .... 843-525-8307 412 H
kboniecki@tcl.edu
BONIECKI, Kurt, A .... 501-450-3126.. 23 H
kurtb@uca.edu
BONIFAS, Angela .... 309-298-2010 152 D
aj-bonifas@wiu.edu
BONIFER, Duane .... 309-457-2321 144 A
dbonifer@monmouthcollege.edu
BONIFORTI, Chris, G .... 561-237-7163 102 V
cboniforti@lynn.edu
BONILLA, Angelita .... 973-353-1494 282 B
bonillan@newark.rutgers.edu
BONILLA, Anie .... 954-492-5353.. 96 H
abonilla@citycollege.edu
BONILLA, Carlos .... 626-529-8403.. 55 A
cbonilla@pacificoaks.edu
BONILLA, David .... 406-771-4425 264 G
dbonilla@gfcmsu.edu
BONILLA, Kathleen .... 559-489-2221.. 66 E
kathy.bonilla@fresnocitycollege.edu
BONILLA, Mary Kay ...... 406-771-5123 264 G
mbonilla@gfcmsu.edu
BONILLA, Matthew .... 212-463-0400 322 J
matthew.bonilla3@touro.edu
BONILLA, Ray .... 979-458-6128 446 C
rbonilla@tamus.edu
BONILLA, Ruth .... 787-746-1400 508 B
rbonilla@huertas.edu
BONJIONE, Frank .... 407-708-2579 107 D
bonjionef@seminolestate.edu
BONK, Sharon, B .... 617-588-1356 206 C
sbonk@bfit.edu
BONKOWSKI, Janet .... 920-465-2527 496 E
bonkowsj@uwgb.edu
BONLARRON,
Rachael, E .... 561-868-3140 104 D
bonlarr@palmbeachstate.edu
BONN, Brenda .... 719-255-3317.. 83 B
bbonn@uccs.edu
BONN, Cynthia, L .... 401-874-7100 406 B
cynthia_bonn@uri.edu
BONN, Kristina .... 630-637-5601 144 H
klbonn@noctrl.edu
BONNELL, Chris .... 801-274-3280 461 F
chris.bonnell@wgu.edu

BORNHORST, Mary ...... 937-778-7837 352 J
mbornhorst@edisonohio.edu
BORNSTEIN, Eva .... 718-960-8232 294 A
eva.bornstein@lehman.cuny.edu
BORNSTEIN, Leah, L .... 970-339-6210.. 76 G
leah.bornstein@aims.edu
BORNUS, Susan .... 651-523-2929 236 A
sbornus@hamline.edu
BOROFF, Karen, A .... 973-761-9655 283 B
karen.boroff@shu.edu
BORONICO, Jess .... 516-686-7838 309 F
jboronic@nyit.edu
BOROS-KAZAI, Mary .... 608-363-2640 492 C
boroskaz@beloit.edu
BOROUGHS, SJ,
Philip, L .... 508-793-2525 208 B
hcpresident@holycross.edu
BOROWICK, Matthew .... 973-378-9801 283 B
matthew.borowick@shu.edu
BOROWICK, Matthew .... 973-378-9847 283 B
matthew.borowick@shu.edu
BOROWICZ, Laurie .... 815-825-9333 140 F
lborowicz@kish.edu
BOROWICZ, Mark .... 608-757-7723 499 C
mborowicz@blackhawk.edu
BOROZAN, Susan .... 941-309-5455 105 K
sborozan@ringling.edu
BORQUEZ, Leslie .... 510-883-2068.. 41 G
lborquez@dspt.edu
BORR, Mike .... 701-231-9535 345 G
mike.borr@ndsu.edu
BORRACCINI, Martha .... 610-647-4400 386 C
mborraccini@immaculata.edu
BORRAS, Kevin .... 808-237-5147 127 G
kborras@hmi.edu
BORREGARD, Andrea .... 270-686-4521 182 B
andrea.borregard@kctcs.edu
BORREGO, Joaquin .... 503-352-7330 375 G
jborrego@pacificu.edu
BORREGO, Susan, E ...... 810-762-3322 231 G
sborrego@umich.edu
BORRELL, Anthony .... 813-757-2111 101 A
aborrell2@hccfl.edu
BORREN, Tammy .... 931-540-2697 424 G
tborren@columbiastate.edu
BORRERO, Alejandro .... 787-850-9109 513 E
alejandro.borrero@upr.edu
BORRERO, Jennifer, S .. 718-982-2335 293 E
jennifer.borrero@csi.cuny.edu
BORRERO-RICE,
Carlos, J .... 787-998-8997 510 N
BORRETT, Stuart .... 919-962-7430 343 C
borretts@uncw.edu
BORS, Lisa .... 585-340-9647 296 E
lbors@crcds.edu
BORSKI, Brian .... 972-860-4116 434 L
bborski@dcccd.edu
BORSTING, Eric .... 714-449-7473.. 51 A
eborsting@ketchum.edu
BORSZ, Michael .... 315-498-2097 311 B
m.a.borsz@sunyocc.edu
BORTH, Adam .... 620-223-2700 173 C
adamb@fortscott.edu
BORTMAN, Lisa .... 310-506-4393.. 56 C
lisa.bortman@pepperdine.edu
BORTNER, Arlis .... 209-384-6000.. 51 G
BORTON, Jeffrey .... 734-462-4400 230 D
jborton@schoolcraft.edu
BORTONE, Jody .... 203-396-8023.. 88 B
bortonej@sacredheart.edu
BORTUNK, Ayelet .... 305-653-8770 113 E
abortunk@lecfl.com
BORTZ, Carolyn .... 610-861-5434 391 F
cbortz@northampton.edu
BORUCKI, Jennifer, C ... 818-947-2433.. 49 F
fongjc@lavc.edu
BORUFF-JONES, Polly .. 765-455-9343 156 D
pboruffj@iuk.edu
BORUM, John .... 214-333-5973 434 I
johnb@dbu.edu
BORUSZEWSKI,
Richard .... 810-762-0533 228 C
richard.boruszewski@mcc.edu
BORYCZKA, Jocelyn ..... 203-254-4000.. 86 I
jboryczka@fairfield.edu
BOS, James .... 712-722-6030 164 K
jim.bos@dordt.edu
BOSACK-KOSEK,
Carol, A .... 570-408-4063 403 D
carol.bosack@wilkes.edu
BOSCH, Agnes .... 787-767-4300 514 B
agnes.bosch@upr.edu

BOSCHINI, JR.,
Victor, J .... 817-257-7783 448 G
v.boschini@tcu.edu
BOSCO, SJ, Mark .... 202-687-1395.. 92 A
mb2263@georgetown.edu
BOSE, Janet .... 602-286-8327.. 13 B
janet.bose@gatewaycc.edu
BOSE, Mohua .... 518-782-6737 315 J
mbose@siena.edu
BOSE, Shantanu .... 630-829-0281 136 A
sbose@devry.edu
BOSEMAN, Shelby .... 817-272-2142 454 J
sboseman@uta.edu
BOSEN, Patricia .... 518-580-5550 316 A
pbosen@skidmore.edu
BOSHEARS, Shannon .... 501-812-2221.. 23 B
sboshears@uaptc.edu
BOSHKOFF, Katharine ... 617-746-1990 210 E
katharine.boshkoff@hult.edu
BOSKET, David .... 570-585-9218 381 E
dbosket@clarkssummitu.edu
BOSLEY, Amy, N .... 407-582-8255 112 K
abosley@valenciacollege.edu
BOSLEY, Barry .... 717-358-4663 384 D
barry.bosley@fandm.edu
BOSLEY, Gabriele, W .... 502-272-8476 179 B
gbosley@bellarmine.edu
BOSLEY, Mike .... 407-582-7007 112 K
mbosley@valenciacollege.edu
BOSLEY-BOYCE,
Annette .... 203-773-6685.. 84 F
abosleyboyce@albertus.edu
BOSMAN, Linda .... 920-565-1023 493 J
bosmanlr@lakeland.edu
BOSS, Diane .... 479-936-5172.. 20 D
dboss@nwacc.edu
BOSS, Shannon .... 215-780-1318 398 G
sboss@salus.edu
BOSSA, Susan, G .... 617-984-1656 218 B
sbossa@quincycollege.edu
BOSSE, Jeannine .... 207-859-1105 195 G
sfs@thomas.edu
BOSSERMAN,
Sharon, S .... 540-887-7026 469 B
sbosserman@marybaldwin.edu
BOSSERT,
Elizabeth (Becky) .... 909-558-4517.. 48 C
bbossert@llu.edu
BOSSIE, George .... 304-205-6615 488 K
george.bossie@bridgevalley.edu
BOST, Rachel, R .... 662-915-7448 249 D
rbost@olemiss.edu
BOSTANIC, George .... 909-599-5433.. 47 K
gbostanic@lifepacific.edu
BOSTIAN, Susan .... 605-626-2520 417 A
susan.bostian@northern.edu
BOSTIC, Blake .... 704-991-0183 338 C
sbostic2222@stanly.edu
BOSTIC, Heather .... 314-340-3544 253 I
bostich@hssu.edu
BOSTIC, Joy, R .... 216-368-8877 349 F
joy.bostic@case.edu
BOSTIC, Melodie .... 314-505-7626 251 I
bosticm@csl.edu
BOSTIC, Peter .... 310-233-4288.. 49 A
bosticpf@lahc.edu
BOSTIC, Renee .... 410-532-3586 201 B
rbostic@ndm.edu
BOSTICK, William .... 504-520-5243 193 A
wbostick@xula.edu
BOSTOCK, John .... 435-797-9095 460 H
john.bostock@usu.edu
BOSTON, Denise .... 866-492-5336 244 F
denise.boston@mail.waldenu.edu
BOSTON, Ed .... 478-825-6347 118 A
bostone@fvsu.edu
BOSTON, Genyne .... 850-599-3276 108 I
genyne.boston@famu.edu
BOSTON, Kay .... 318-678-6000 187 A
kboston@bpcc.edu
BOSTON, Melissa .... 914-798-2734 305 J
melissa.boston@mville.edu
BOSTON, Pamela, F ...... 757-823-2293 469 F
pfboston@nsu.edu
BOSTON, Troy .... 641-673-1170 170 F
troy.boston@wmpenn.edu
BOSTON, Wallace .... 304-724-3700 487 E
BOSTROM, Steve .... 425-889-5584 482 F
steve.bostrom@northwestu.edu
BOSWELL, Angela .... 870-230-5320.. 19 E
boswela@hsu.edu
BOSWELL, Chris .... 307-766-2238 502 H
chris.boswell@uwyo.edu

BOSWELL, Ellen .... 303-556-5047.. 80 N
boswelle@msudenver.edu
BOSWELL, Erin .... 314-529-9333 254 H
eboswell@maryville.edu
BOSWELL, Katherine ..... 817-598-6216 458 A
kboswell@wc.edu
BOSWELL, Kathryn .... 413-644-4299 205 F
kboswell@simons-rock.edu
BOSWELL, Robert .... 303-735-1332.. 83 A
robert.boswell@colorado.edu
BOSWELL-FORD,
Kirstin .... 617-258-5484 215 G
BOSWORTH, Michelle ... 765-455-9226 156 D
mboswor@iu.edu
BOSWORTH, Sarah .... 401-739-5000 405 A
sbosworth@neit.edu
BOSWORTH, Susan, L .. 757-221-3584 466 C
slbosw@wm.edu
BOSWORTH, Theresa .... 541-278-5957 372 A
tbosworth@bluecc.edu
BOTANA, Joseph .... 276-944-7213 467 G
jbotana@ehc.edu
BOTCHAN, Michael, R .. 510-642-5716.. 68 D
mbotchan@berkeley.edu
BOTENGAN, Tim .... 760-252-2411.. 26 I
rbotengan@barstow.edu
BOTERO, Cecilia .... 662-915-5858 249 D
cbotero@olemiss.edu
BOTEZ, Christian .... 856-256-4850 281 E
botez@rowan.edu
BOTHE, Dan .... 619-849-2290.. 57 E
danbothe@pointloma.edu
BOTHMA, Inge .... 512-492-3005 430 G
ibothma@aoma.edu
BOTHNER, Peter, G ...... 585-389-2196 308 B
pbothne4@naz.edu
BOTHOF, Ken .... 859-572-6639 184 A
bothofk1@nku.edu
BOTMAN, Selma .... 212-960-5217 326 E
selma.botman@yu.edu
BOTONE, Merle .... 701-255-3285 347 B
mbotone@uttc.edu
BOTSTEIN, Leon .... 845-758-7423 290 G
president@bard.edu
BOTSTEIN, Leon .... 914-758-7423 205 F
president@bard.edu
BOTT, Jennifer, P .... 269-387-1000 232 K
BOTT, Rebecca .... 605-688-6361 417 C
rebecca.bott@sdstate.edu
BOTT, Rosa .... 276-328-0312 473 B
grb5u@virginia.edu
BOTTA, Michael .... 412-392-3833 397 A
mfbotta@pointpark.edu
BOTTA, Samuel .... 757-352-4491 470 H
sambott@regent.edu
BOTTARO, Kathy .... 210-805-2591 453 D
bottaro@uiwtx.edu
BOTTELBERGHE, John ... 303-360-4718.. 79 D
john.bottelberghe@ccaurora.edu
BOTTEM, Lisa .... 218-683-8557 240 A
lisa.bottem@northlandcollege.edu
BOTTEMILLER, Sandi .... 503-768-7183 373 G
sjb@lclark.edu
BOTTI, Romayne .... 848-932-1991 282 A
romayne.botti@rutgers.edu
BOTTINELLI, Stasi .... 303-751-8700.. 77 A
bottinelli@bel-rea.com
BOTTO, Karin .... 315-445-4155 304 C
bottoka@lemoyne.edu
BOTTOMS, Rebecca .... 336-725-8344 339 F
bottomsb@piedmontu.edu
BOTTORFF, Allen .... 423-354-5370 425 E
BOTZHEIM, Luke .... 425-640-1946 480 F
luke.botzheim@edcc.edu
BOTZMAN, Thomas, J ... 570-674-6215 390 G
tbotzman@misericordia.edu
BOU, Nydia .... 787-743-7979 511 I
ut_nbou@suagm.edu
BOUABIDI, Debra .... 845-574-4492 313 C
moppenhe@sunyrockland.edu
BOUARÉ, Boubacar .... 509-359-6200 480 E
BOUCHARD, Norma .... 619-594-5456.. 33 E
nbouchard@sdsu.edu
BOUCHARD, Ryan .... 608-363-2350 492 C
bouchardr@beloit.edu
BOUCHER, Gery .... 252-638-7283 333 H
boucherg@cravencc.edu
BOUCHER, J. Cliff .... 903-510-2546 452 C
cliff.boucher@tjc.edu
BOUCHER, Richard .... 657-278-2800.. 31 E
rboucher@fullerton.edu
BOUCHER, Robert .... 207-755-5100 194 G
rboucher@cmcc.edu

BOUCHER-JARVIS,
Allison .... 973-720-2287 284 I
boucherjarvis@wpunj.edu
BOUCHER MORRIS,
Kelly .... 212-228-1888 312 H
BOUCHEREAU, Chantal . 336-750-3471 344 B
housing@wss.edu
BOUDINOT, Ann .... 703-284-3809 469 C
ann.boudinot@marymount.edu
BOUDINOT, F. Douglas 804-828-2233 473 F
fdboudinot@vcu.edu
BOUDO, Lori .... 978-542-6000 213 C
lboudo@salemstate.edu
BOUDOURIS, Jeff .... 937-512-2537 361 A
jeff.boudouris@sinclair.edu
BOUDREAU, Charles ...... 630-466-7900 152 C
cboudreau@waubonsee.edu
BOUDREAU, Mark .... 413-775-1311 214 C
boudreaum@gcc.mass.edu
BOUDREAU, Timothy ...... 516-364-0808 309 A
tboudreau@nycollege.edu
BOUDREAU, Vincent, G 212-650-7285 293 D
vboudreau@ccny.cuny.edu
BOUDREAUX, Gregory .. 330-494-6170 361 F
gboudreaux@starkstate.edu
BOUGHER, Michelle ...... 574-936-8898 153 A
michelle.bougher@ancilla.edu
BOUGHIDA, Karim, B ... 401-874-4602 406 B
boughida@uri.edu
BOUGHMAN, Joann .... 301-445-1992 202 B
jboughman@usmd.edu
BOUIE, Archie .... 850-561-2888 108 I
archie.bouie@famu.edu
BOUIE, Archie .... 850-599-3270 108 I
archie.bouie@famu.edu
BOUIE, II, Archie .... 850-599-8003 108 I
archie.bouie@famu.edu
BOUILLON, Rick .... 801-957-5158 461 D
rick.bouillon@slcc.edu
BOUKHMAN, Anna .... 718-522-9073 290 C
aboukhman@asa.edu
BOULANGER, Brie .... 316-295-5525 173 D
brie_boulanger@friends.edu
BOULANGER, Rebecca .. 920-735-2407 499 E
boulanger@fvtc.edu
BOULDER, James .... 814-732-1047 394 F
jboulder@edinboro.edu
BOULDIN, Randy .... 615-966-5711 421 D
randy.bouldin@lipscomb.edu
BOULDING, William ..... 919-660-7822 328 G
bb1@duke.edu
BOULES, Raouf .... 860-231-5803.. 89 B
rboules@usj.edu
BOULGER, Lynn .... 207-801-5620 193 F
lboulger@coa.edu
BOULTON, April .... 301-696-3811 199 B
boulton@hood.edu
BOULTON, Kenneth .... 605-626-2497 417 A
kenneth.boulton@northern.edu
BOULUKOS, Tracy .... 561-297-2738 108 J
tbouluko@fau.edu
BOUNDS, Hank .... 402-472-8636 269 H
hbounds@nebraska.edu
BOUNDS, Roger, G .... 928-523-6159.. 14 H
roger.bounds@nau.edu
BOUQUOT, Gregory ...... 860-486-3903.. 88 E
gregory.bouquot@uconn.edu
BOURA, Ahmad .... 530-898-5830.. 31 A
aboura@csuchico.edu
BOURANIS, Christin ..... 978-921-4242 216 F
christin.bouranis@montserrat.edu
BOURDON, Marsha ...... 603-524-3207 272 K
mbourdon@ccsnh.edu
BOURG, Chris .... 617-253-5297 215 G
BOURGEAULT, Lucy ...... 802-828-8600 463 F
lucy.bourgeault@vcfa.edu
BOURGEOIS, Angi .... 662-325-2202 247 F
abourgeois@caad.msstate.edu
BOURGEOIS, David, L .. 919-658-7747 340 J
dbourgeois@umo.edu
BOURGEOIS, Donna ..... 504-865-3523 189 F
dhbourg@loyno.edu
BOURGEOIS, Gene .... 512-245-2205 450 E
eb04@txstate.edu
BOURGEOIS, Jack, R .... 864-592-4618 412 F
bourgeois@sccsc.edu
BOURGEOIS, Karen .... 914-337-9300 297 D
karen.bourgeois@concordia-ny.edu
BOURGEOIS, Peggy .... 504-398-2109 191 C
pbourgeois@uhcno.edu
BOURGEOIS, Sheryl ...... 714-997-6523.. 36 C
sbourgeo@chapman.edu

BOXDORFER, Bill .... 573-288-6571 252 E
bboxdorfer@culver.edu
BOXILL, David .... 212-817-7700 293 F
dboxill@gc.cuny.edu
BOXILL, Lavinia .... 848-932-7899 282 A
lavinia.boxill@ruf.rutgers.edu
BOYAN, Barbara, D ...... 804-828-0190 473 F
bboyan@vcu.edu
BOYCE, Eric .... 828-251-6951 342 C
eboyce@unca.edu
BOYCE, Glenn .... 662-915-7111 249 D
chancellor@olemiss.edu
BOYCE, Greg .... 719-846-5530.. 82 K
greg.boyce@trinidadstate.edu
BOYCE, Jessica .... 704-330-6710 333 D
jessica.boyce@cpcc.edu
BOYCE, Justin .... 304-865-6034 488 E
justin.boyce@ovu.edu
BOYCE, Mary, C .... 212-854-1123 297 C
boyce@columbia.edu
BOYCE, Richard, N .... 704-337-2450 472 E
rboyce@upsem.edu
BOYCE, Robert .... 301-687-4043 203 E
rjboyce@frostburg.edu
BOYD, Amanda .... 419-720-6670 360 F
amanda.boyd@proskills.edu
BOYD, Angela .... 757-727-5328 468 B
angela.boyd@hamptonu.edu
BOYD, Betsy, A .... 541-346-0946 377 D
eaboyd@uoregon.edu
BOYD, Bill .... 910-323-5614 327 G
billboyd@ccbs.edu
BOYD, Brandon .... 931-372-6285 426 E
bboyd@tntech.edu
BOYD, Brian .... 407-823-3016 109 E
brian.boyd@ucf.edu
BOYD, Carla .... 520-515-5337.. 11 M
boydc@cochise.edu
BOYD, Carla, L .... 218-726-8795 243 F
clboyd@d.umn.edu
BOYD, Carla, M .... 217-443-8753 135 H
cboyd@dacc.edu
BOYD, Carrie .... 540-887-7220 469 B
cboyd@marybaldwin.edu
BOYD, Catherine .... 310-265-6202.. 59 E
cathi.boyd@usw.salvationarmy.org
BOYD, Chantel .... 334-727-8254.... 7 D
cboyd@tuskegee.edu
BOYD, Clarence .... 918-495-7703 368 I
cboyd@oru.edu
BOYD, Cristine .... 330-972-6476 362 B
BOYD, Cynthia .... 770-426-2756 121 C
cboyd@life.edu
BOYD, Cynthia, E .... 312-942-6915 148 A
cynthia_e_boyd@rush.edu
BOYD, Danielle .... 618-634-3298 149 A
danielleb@shawneecc.edu
BOYD, David, L .... 714-850-4800.. 67 A
boyd@taftu.edu
BOYD, Deborah .... 615-966-5708 421 D
deborah.boyd@lipscomb.edu
BOYD, Elizabeth .... 276-328-0128 473 B
egb4d@virginia.edu
BOYD, JR., Eulas .... 718-780-0395 291 J
eulas.boyd@brooklaw.edu
BOYD, Evan, E .... 215-248-6330 400 I
eboyd@uls.edu
BOYD, Frank .... 336-316-2205 329 E
boydfa@guilford.edu
BOYD, Gary .... 304-357-4704 488 G
garyboyd@ucwv.edu
BOYD, Gerald .... 240-629-7840 198 E
gboyd@frederick.edu
BOYD, Jeffery .... 507-285-7215 240 G
jeffery.boyd@rctc.edu
BOYD, John, C .... 828-766-1270 336 A
jboyd@mayland.edu
BOYD, Keishea .... 816-235-1047 261 C
boydkm@umkc.edu
BOYD, Kevin .... 773-702-5305 150 J
kevin.boyd@chicagobooth.edu
BOYD, Kim .... 918-495-7108 368 I
kboyd@oru.edu
BOYD, Laura .... 417-625-9501 256 D
boyd-l@mssu.edu
BOYD, Lonnie .... 620-229-6136 177 A
lonnie.boyd@sckans.edu
BOYD, Lynn .... 870-972-3079.. 17 G
lyboyd@astate.edu
BOYD, Mary .... 970-945-8691.. 77 K
BOYD, Mary, K .... 706-236-2216 115 B
mboyd@berry.edu
BOYD, Michael .... 706-754-7807 122 F
mboyd@northgatech.edu
BOYD, Michael .... 815-802-8110 140 D
president@kcc.edu
BOYD, Michael, D .... 901-333-4318 426 A
mdboyd@southwest.tn.edu
BOYD, Monica .... 336-917-5579 340 D
monica.boyd@salem.edu
BOYD, Nick .... 530-283-0202.. 42 H
nboyd@frc.edu
BOYD, Randy .... 865-974-2241 427 F
utpresident@tennessee.edu
BOYD, Reginald .... 704-636-6455 330 A
rboyd@hoodseminary.edu
BOYD, Rick .... 803-775-8727 414 B
boydrl@uscsumter.edu
BOYD, Ruth .... 580-774-3177 370 C
ruth.boyd@swosu.edu
BOYD, Shane .... 757-455-3384 477 F
sboyd@vwu.edu
BOYD, Sharon, H .... 910-962-7769 343 C
boyds@uncw.edu
BOYD, Steven .... 916-484-8428.. 50 F
boyds@arc.losrios.edu
BOYD, Susan .... 734-432-5578 227 A
sboyd@madonna.edu
BOYD, Susan .... 586-445-7408 226 H
boyds@macomb.edu
BOYD, Thomas .... 303-273-3221.. 78 I
hboyd@mines.edu
BOYD, Todd .... 580-774-3782 370 C
todd.boyd@swosu.edu
BOYD, Tyler .... 281-649-3209 437 H
tboyd@hbu.edu
BOYD, William .... 805-565-6043.. 74 K
wboyd@westmont.edu
BOYD, Yuko .... 252-638-7229 333 H
boydy@cravencc.edu
BOYD MCELROY, Diana 816-604-2326 255 G
diana.mcelroy@mcckc.edu
BOYD-OWENS,
Margaret .... 501-374-6305.. 21 A
margaret.boyd-owens@shortercollege.edu
BOYD-PUGH,
Jennifer, N .... 305-899-4057.. 95 C
jboydpugh@barry.edu
BOYDL, Loni .... 414-443-8702 498 O
loni.boyd@wlc.edu
BOYDSTON, Glynn .... 806-291-3766 457 J
boydstong@wbu.edu
BOYDSTUN, Morris .... 479-394-7622.. 23 C
mboydstun@uarichmountain.edu
BOYER, Annette .... 724-925-4101 403 A
boyera@westmoreland.edu
BOYER, Brian .... 603-428-2375 273 H
bboyer@nec.edu
BOYER, Bruce .... 508-565-1380 218 H
bboyer@stonehill.edu
BOYER, Bruce, E .... 573-875-7251 251 F
beboyer@ccis.edu
BOYER, Debra, A .... 617-228-2403 214 A
dboyer@bhcc.mass.edu
BOYER, John, W .... 773-702-8576 150 J
jwboyer@uchicago.edu
BOYER, Karen .... 808-734-9569 128 I
kboyer@hawaii.edu
BOYER, Kim, L .... 518-956-8241 316 D
kboyer3@albany.edu
BOYER, Mary .... 215-702-4541 380 D
mboyer@cairn.edu
BOYER, Mary Jo .... 610-450-6524 382 C
mboyer@dccc.edu
BOYER, Sara .... 812-535-5114 160 B
sboyer@smwc.edu
BOYER, Stuart .... 541-776-9942 375 E
stuart.b@pacificbible.edu
BOYER, Suzanne, L .... 410-777-2045 197 C
slboyer1@aacc.edu
BOYER-OWENS, Linda .. 210-485-0230 429 C
lboyer-owens@alamo.edu
BOYERS, Jayson .... 517-586-3012 222 E
jboyers@cleary.edu
BOYERS, Pamela .... 402-559-2442 270 A
pamela.boyers@unmc.edu
BOYES, Jerry, S .... 716-878-6533 318 C
boyesjs@buffalostate.edu
BOYES, Monica .... 530-895-2936.. 27 F
boyesmo@butte.edu
BOYETT, Chad .... 912-287-5808 116 F
cboyett@coastalpines.edu
BOYETT, Chris .... 419-995-8222 354 H
boyett.c@rhodestate.edu
BOYETT, Jennifer .... 870-230-5401.. 19 E
boyettj@hsu.edu
BOYETT, Patricia .... 504-865-7880 189 F
BOYETTE, Alan, J .... 336-334-5494 343 A
jaboyett@uncg.edu
BOYETTE, Rick .... 903-823-3274 446 B
ricky.boyette@texarkanacollege.edu
BOYK, Linda .... 610-902-8131 380 C
linda.boyk@cabrini.edu
BOYKIN, Celyn .... 504-280-6625 189 E
ccboykin@uno.edu
BOYKIN, Coretta .... 251-578-1313.... 3 D
cboykin@rstc.edu
BOYKIN, Gregory .... 252-985-5117 339 D
gboykin@ncwc.edu
BOYKIN, Melinda .... 254-867-3761 449 E
melinda.boykin@tstc.edu
BOYKIN, Regena .... 601-635-2111 245 I
rboykin@eccc.edu
BOYKIN, Sutonia .... 845-574-4306 313 C
sboykin@sunyrockland.edu
BOYKIN, Ted .... 570-585-9327 381 E
tboykin@clarkssummitu.edu
BOYKIN, Tiffany, F .... 410-777-2305 197 C
tfboykin@aacc.edu
BOYLAN, Ellen .... 352-588-8691 106 D
ellen.boylan@saintleo.edu
BOYLAN, Erin .... 607-753-2516 318 D
erin.boylan@cortland.edu
BOYLAN, Stanley, L ...... 646-565-6000 322 J
stanley.boylan@touro.edu
BOYLE, Allison, J .... 410-576-6316 201 E
aboyle@oag.state.md.us
BOYLE, Amy .... 504-865-2445 189 F
aboyle@loyno.edu
BOYLE, Ann .... 480-219-6107 250 A
aboyle@atsu.edu
BOYLE, Antonio .... 302-857-7172.. 89 F
aboyle@desu.edu
BOYLE, Carol, A .... 516-877-3775 289 C
boyle@adelphi.edu
BOYLE, Christine .... 201-761-7390 282 I
cboyle@saintpeters.edu
BOYLE, Jeffery .... 864-592-4823 412 F
boylej@sccsc.edu
BOYLE, Kate .... 360-438-4310 483 H
kboyle@stmartin.edu
BOYLE, Kevin .... 973-618-3372 276 D
kboyle@caldwell.edu
BOYLE, Lori .... 619-239-0391.. 34 F
lboyle@cwsl.edu
BOYLE, Nuala .... 585-389-2670 308 B
nboyle5@naz.edu
BOYLE, Robert, J .... 904-620-4663 110 A
rboyle@unf.edu
BOYLE, Roger .... 202-464-6464 463 C
roger.boyle@worldlearning.org
BOYLE, Sharon, I .... 215-926-2200 399 F
sharon.boyle@temple.edu
BOYLE, Taggart .... 617-984-1771 218 B
tboyle@quincycollege.edu
BOYLE, Thomas, A .... 630-515-6147 143 G
tboyle@midwestern.edu
BOYLES, Bruce .... 704-406-3275 329 A
bboyles@gardner-webb.edu
BOYLES, Elinda .... 740-351-3265 360 K
eboyles@shawnee.edu
BOYLES, Erin, I .... 412-578-8774 380 E
eiboyles@carlow.edu
BOYLES, Joel .... 662-562-3240 248 D
jboyles@northwestms.edu
BOYLES, John Dixon .... 903-823-3192 446 B
johndixon.boyles@texarkanacollege.edu
BOYLES, Patrice .... 773-995-3764 133 K
pboyles@csu.edu
BOYLES, Patricia .... 912-443-4107 124 A
pboyles@savannahtech.edu
BOYLES, Robert .... 253-879-3633 485 E
bboyles@pugetsound.edu
BOYLES, Shery .... 919-760-8581 331 B
boyless@meredith.edu
BOYMAN, Robert .... 626-529-8033.. 55 A
rboyman@pacificoaks.edu
BOYMELGREEN, Shaya . 718-774-3430 292 H
BOYNTON, Andrew, C .. 617-552-4107 207 B
andy.boynton@bc.edu
BOYNTON, Antoine .... 706-583-2552 114 F
aboynton@athenstech.edu
BOYNTON,
Christopher, E .... 207-581-1484 195 J
christopher.boynton@maine.edu
BOYNTON, Eric .... 608-363-2667 492 C
boyntone@beloit.edu
BOYS, Kevin, S .... 937-393-3431 361 B
kboys@sscc.edu
BOYSUN, Virginia .... 406-377-9404 263 E
vboysun@dawson.edu
BOYUM-BREEN, Trenda 952-806-3910 242 K
trenda.boyum-breen@rasmussen.edu
BOZARTH, Diane .... 573-288-6473 252 E
dbozarth@culver.edu
BOZINSKI, Glenn .... 570-674-6434 390 G
gbozinski@misericordia.edu
BOZON, Brandon .... 254-298-8606 446 A
bozonb819@templejc.edu
BOZYLINSKY, Gary .... 860-465-5537.. 84 J
bozylinskyg@easternct.edu
BOZYM, Rebecca .... 412-536-1158 387 B
rebecca.bozym@laroche.edu
BOZZA, Brian .... 239-590-1250 108 K
bbozza@fgcu.edu
BRAATZ, Brady, J .... 913-971-3452 175 G
bbraatz@mnu.edu
BRABHAM, Sherry, F .... 212-217-4020 299 H
sherry_brabham@fitnyc.edu
BRABY, Randy .... 435-283-7058 461 C
randy.braby@snow.edu
BRACCIANO, Susan ...... 816-271-4214 257 A
braccian@missouriwestern.edu
BRACCO, Anthony .... 212-237-8613 294 D
abracco@jjay.cuny.edu
BRACE, Vickie .... 215-635-7300 385 A
vbrace@gratz.edu
BRACERO, Carmen, A ... 787-844-8181 514 A
carmen.bracero@upr.edu
BRACERO-LUGO,
Carmen .... 787-844-8959 512 G
carmen.bracero@upr.edu
BRACEROS, Amy .... 909-537-3224.. 33 A
abracero@csusb.edu
BRACEY, Carol .... 951-343-4456.. 27 J
cbracey@calbaptist.edu
BRACEY,
Christopher, A .... 202-994-6510.. 91 F
cabracey@gwu.edu
BRACEY,
Christopher, A .... 202-994-1000.. 91 F
cabracey@gwu.edu
BRACEY, David .... 714-772-3330.. 26 A
BRACEY, Matthew .... 615-675-5329 428 G
mbracey@welch.edu
BRACHE-MELLO,
Allison, M .... 787-993-8886 513 B
allison.brache@upr.edu
BRACK, Jonathan, M .... 215-572-3878 402 H
jbrack@wts.edu
BRACKE, Paul, J .... 509-313-6533 481 D
bracke@gonzaga.edu
BRACKEN, Carol .... 817-515-5137 445 G
carol.bracken@tccd.edu
BRACKEN, Damien, S ... 617-747-2221 206 E
admissions@berklee.edu
BRACKEN, Diane .... 850-484-1175 104 H
dbracken@pensacolastate.edu
BRACKEN, Gary .... 251-380-3030.... 6 H
gbracken@shc.edu
BRACKEN, Lisa .... 803-778-6652 407 C
brackenlm@cctech.edu
BRACKEN, Steven .... 713-226-5276 453 B
brackens@uhd.edu
BRACKETT, Geoffrey, L . 845-575-3000 305 L
geoffrey.brackett@marist.edu
BRACKETT, Robert .... 708-563-1577 139 B
rbrackett@iit.edu
BRACKETT, Stacey .... 828-328-7309 330 F
stacey.brackett@lr.edu
BRACKETT, Suzanne ...... 252-985-5102 339 D
sbrackett@ncwc.edu
BRACKIN, Anita .... 901-333-4018 426 A
abrackin@southwest.tn.edu
BRACKIN, Chad .... 225-578-4736 188 H
cmb@lsu.edu
BRACKIN, Rebekah .... 325-942-2248 451 A
rebekah.brackin@angelo.edu
BRACKIN, Stewart .... 731-989-6911 420 C
sbrackin@fhu.edu
BRACKMANN, Sarah ...... 512-863-1987 445 D
brackmas@southwestern.edu
BRACKNELL, Ann .... 205-391-2958.... 3 E
ann.bracknell@sheltonstate.edu
BRACY, Judy .... 504-520-7317 193 A
jbracy@xula.edu
BRACY, Marion .... 504-520-7507 193 A
mbracy@xula.edu
BRACY, JR., Randolph .. 386-481-2115.. 95 F
bracyr@cookman.edu
BRACY KNIGHT, Becca . 310-954-5080.. 27 E

BRAND, Jonathan .... 319-895-4324 164 B
jbrand@cornellcollege.edu
BRAND, Kathleen, C ..... 864-646-1774 413 A
kbrand@tctc.edu
BRAND, Richard .... 423-652-4728 420 H
rjbrand@king.edu
BRAND, Todd .... 606-326-2163 180 I
todd.brand@kctcs.edu
BRAND, Tricia .... 971-722-6111 375 J
tricia.brand@pcc.edu
BRANDAU-HYNEK, Ann 608-785-9585 501 A
brandauhyneka@westerntc.edu
BRANDAUER,
Samantha, C .... 717-245-8068 382 F
brandaus@dickinson.edu
BRANDEBURY, Jessica . 260-459-4501 157 E
jbrandebury@ibcfortwayne.edu
BRANDENBURG,
Aurelia .... 859-985-3173 179 C
aurelia_brandenburg@berea.edu
BRANDENBURG,
Mark, C .... 843-953-5252 407 F
mark.brandenburg@citadel.edu
BRANDER, Ann .... 540-545-7335 471 E
abrander12@su.edu
BRANDES, David .... 610-625-7753 391 A
brandesd@moravian.edu
BRANDES, Derek, R ...... 509-527-4274 485 G
derek.brandes@wwcc.edu
BRANDES, Paul .... 620-278-2173 177 B
paul.brandes@sterling.edu
BRANDES, Rand .... 828-328-7077 330 F
rand.brandes@lr.edu
BRANDI, Anne, E .... 516-572-7205 308 A
anne.brandi@ncc.edu
BRANDI, Erica .... 610-398-5300 389 A
ebrandi@lincolntech.edu
BRANDKAMP, Katelyn .. 660-263-4100 257 B
katelynb@macc.edu
BRANDL-REEVES, Sara .. 715-346-2123 497 F
sbrandlr@uwsp.edu
BRANDON, Alonzo, C ... 757-683-5383 469 G
abrandon@odu.edu
BRANDON, Carolyn ...... 828-327-7000 333 B
cbrandon@cvcc.edu
BRANDON, Deborah, L . 909-869-3427.. 30 D
dlbrandon@cpp.edu
BRANDON, Elvis .... 615-230-3375 426 B
elvis.brandon@volstate.edu
BRANDON, Eric .... 828-328-7301 330 F
eric.brandon@lr.edu
BRANDON, Felicia .... 914-674-7718 306 F
fbrandon@mercy.edu
BRANDON, Lisa, K .... 618-537-6865 143 B
lkbrandon@mckendree.edu
BRANDON, Mark, E ...... 205-348-5117.... 7 G
mbrandon@law.ua.edu
BRANDON, Robert .... 276-964-7200 475 I
robert.brandon@sw.edu
BRANDON, Ronald .... 901-321-3256 419 C
ronald.brandon@cbu.edu
BRANDON, Sonia Zoe .. 765-285-2191 153 C
sschaiblebra@bsu.edu
BRANDSEN, Cheryl .... 616-526-6102 222 A
brac@calvin.edu
BRANDSTATER, Nate ..... 937-395-8618 355 F
nate.brandstater@kc.edu
BRANDT, Alexander ...... 910-521-6573 343 B
alexander.brandt@uncp.edu
BRANDT, Amy .... 607-778-5014 318 A
brandtac@sunybroome.edu
BRANDT, Deanna .... 405-974-2753 370 K
dbrandt@uco.edu
BRANDT, John .... 731-425-2624 425 B
jbrandt@jscc.edu
BRANDT, Kimberly .... 208-426-1594 129 I
kimberlybrandt@boisestate.edu
BRANDT, Martin .... 631-420-2333 321 B
martin.brandt@farmingdale.edu
BRANDT, Scott .... 831-459-2425.. 70 B
sbrandt@ucsc.edu
BRANDT, Tony .... 903-886-5761 447 B
charles.brandt@tamuc.edu
BRANDT-PEARCE,
Manté .... 434-924-1470 473 A
mb9q@virginia.edu
BRANDT-RAUF, Paul ..... 215-895-2215 383 B
paul.w.brandt-rauf@drexel.edu
BRANDVOLD, Kelli .... 808-734-9575 128 I
kellib@hawaii.edu
BRANGAITIS, David ...... 845-758-7225 290 G
dbrangaitis@bard.edu
BRANHAM, Carla .... 606-886-3863 180 J
cbranham0022@kctcs.edu
BRANHAM, LaTonya ..... 765-658-4141 154 F
latonyabranham@depauw.edu
BRANHAM, Rich, A ...... 651-631-5285 244 D
rabranham@unwsp.edu
BRANIGAN, David, E .... 814-863-9150 392 B
deb7@psu.edu
BRANKLE, Steve .... 479-524-7209.. 19 H
sbrankle@jbu.edu
BRANNAN, Angie, R ..... 262-524-7335 492 E
abrannan@carrollu.edu
BRANNAN, Colleen, E .. 607-436-2748 317 C
colleen.brannan@oneonta.edu
BRANNAN, Jessica .... 215-951-1355 387 C
brannan@lasalle.edu
BRANNAN, Thomas, I ... 205-934-0177.... 8 A
tbrannan@uab.edu
BRANNEN, Andrew .... 908-737-7023 278 E
abrannen@kean.edu
BRANNEN, Melissia ...... 803-786-3888 408 F
mbrannen@columbiasc.edu
BRANNEN, Tammy .... 912-443-4797 124 A
tbrannen@savannahtech.edu
BRANNER, Wade, H ...... 540-464-7253 476 G
brannerwh@vmi.edu
BRANNIGAN, Michael ... 518-485-3789 296 H
brannigm@strose.edu
BRANNON, Brett .... 618-664-6410 137 G
brett.brannon@greenville.edu
BRANNON, Jennifer .... 478-934-3352 121 F
jennifer.brannon@mga.edu
BRANNON, Mark .... 256-306-2500.... 1 F
mark.brannon@calhoun.edu
BRANNON, Porter .... 704-878-3203 336 C
pbrannon@mitchellcc.edu
BRANON, Rovy .... 206-685-6313 485 F
rbranon@uw.edu
BRANSCOME, Tara .... 256-331-5438.... 3 C
tbranscome@nwscc.edu
BRANSON, Angela .... 312-942-9523 148 A
angela_branson@rush.edu
BRANSON, Carol .... 904-819-6255.. 98 E
cbranson@flagler.edu
BRANSON, Cathy .... 606-487-3550 181 C
cathy.branson@kctcs.edu
BRANSON, Jeff .... 217-234-5253 141 D
jbranson@lakelandcollege.edu
BRANSON, Mark .... 312-662-4121 131 H
mbranson@adler.edu
BRANSON, Salinda Jo .. 309-649-6217 150 A
jo.branson@src.edu
BRANSON, Walter, J .... 937-775-3221 364 I
walt.branson@wright.edu
BRANTLEY, Allison .... 205-652-3665.... 9 A
abrantley@uwa.edu
BRANTLEY, Brenda .... 318-678-6000 187 A
bbrantley@bpcc.edu
BRANTLEY, Kyle .... 601-925-7634 247 C
brantley@mc.edu
BRANTLEY, Linda .... 978-762-4000 215 B
lbrantley@northshore.edu
BRANTLEY, Michael ...... 972-860-7640 435 B
mbrantley@dcccd.edu
BRANTLEY, Will .... 405-585-4455 367 F
will.brantley@okbu.edu
BRANTON-HOUSLEY,
Mary .... 970-204-8121.. 79 J
mary.branton-housley@frontrange.edu
BRANTON SMITH,
Carolyn .... 312-935-6600 147 D
cbsmith@robertmorris.edu
BRANUM, Candise .... 503-253-3443 374 H
cbranum@ocom.edu
BRANUM, Scott .... 409-944-1216 437 B
tbranum@gc.edu
BRAS, Rafael .... 404-385-5700 118 F
provost@gatech.edu
BRASE, Don .... 503-399-6149 372 C
don.brase@chemeketa.edu
BRASE, Heather .... 314-744-5342 256 C
matlock@mobap.edu
BRASE, Terry .... 559-934-2709.. 74 A
terrybrase@whccd.edu
BRASE, Wendell .... 949-824-5107.. 68 G
wcbrase@uci.edu
BRASEL, Steve .... 312-329-4194 144 B
steve.brasel@moody.edu
BRASFIELD, Logan .... 870-633-4480.. 19 B
lbrasfield@eacc.edu
BRASHEAR, Bridgette .... 606-218-5268 185 D
bridgettebrashear@upike.edu
BRASHEAR, Jenna .... 270-852-3291 183 A
jbrashear@kwc.edu
BRASHEAR, Kurth .... 402-643-7408 266 G
kurth.brashear@cune.edu
BRASHEAR, Kurth .... 402-643-7487 266 G
kurth.brashear@cune.edu
BRASHEAR, Pam .... 714-895-8234.. 38 D
pbrashear@gwc.cccd.edu
BRASHEARS, Randolph . 978-934-2384 211 G
randolph_brashears@uml.edu
BRASHEARS,
Thomas, A .... 540-464-7221 476 G
tbrashears@vmiaa.org
BRASHIER, Jason .... 731-989-6571 420 C
jbrashier@fhu.edu
BRASHIER, Samuel .... 864-231-2000 406 G
sbrashier@andersonuniversity.edu
BRASIER, Terry .... 828-398-7146 332 B
terrygbrasier@abtech.edu
BRASKAMP, Corey .... 605-256-5227 416 J
corey.braskamp@dsu.edu
BRASKICH, Brian .... 901-843-2430 423 J
braskichb@rhodes.edu
BRASSARD, Kevin, F ..... 508-213-2213 217 E
kevin.brassard@nichols.edu
BRASSIL, Kristoffer, W .. 617-358-7000 207 D
kbrassil@bu.edu
BRASSORD, James, D .. 413-542-2202 205 B
jdbrassord@amherst.edu
BRASTETER, Christina ... 856-256-5173 281 E
brasteter@rowan.edu
BRASURE, III, Ralph ..... 860-515-3873.. 84 G
BRASWELL, Cara Mia ... 334-244-3498.... 4 F
cbraswe2@aum.edu
BRASWELL, Debbi .... 601-968-5920 245 C
dbraswell@belhaven.edu
BRASWELL, Don .... 318-257-2120 191 F
braswell@latech.edu
BRASWELL, Jody .... 417-690-3376 251 E
braswell@cofo.edu
BRASWELL, Kevin .... 931-372-6092 426 E
kbraswell@tntech.edu
BRASWELL, Macy .... 870-235-4991.. 21 D
macybraswell@saumag.edu
BRASWELL, Macy .... 870-235-4078.. 21 D
macybraswell@saumag.edu
BRASWELL, Mavour ...... 432-264-5092 438 C
mbraswell@howardcollege.edu
BRAT, Dave .... 434-582-2000 468 H
BRATHWAITE, Joy .... 612-874-3700 236 K
joy_brathwaite@mcad.edu
BRATHWAITE, Ormond . 216-987-5008 351 G
ormond.brathwaite@tri-c.edu
BRATHWAITE, Renea, C 612-343-4166 242 H
rcbrathw@northcentral.edu
BRATSCH, John .... 559-730-3830.. 39 E
johnbr@cos.edu
BRATSCH-PRINCE,
Dawn .... 515-294-6410 162 I
deprince@iastate.edu
BRATTEN, Amy .... 863-667-5238 107 K
anbratten@seu.edu
BRATTOLI, Tamara .... 815-280-2470 140 B
tbrattol@jjc.edu
BRATTON, Jason .... 903-923-1643 458 G
jbratton@wileyc.edu
BRATTON, Kevin .... 248-942-3214 229 A
kmbratto@oaklandcc.edu
BRATTON, Marissa .... 808-544-0249 127 H
mbratton@hpu.edu
BRATTON, Phyllis, K .... 701-252-3467 347 C
pbratton@uj.edu
BRATTON, Tara .... 501-337-5000.. 18 J
tbratton@coto.edu
BRATULIN, Paul .... 909-384-8978.. 59 I
pbratulin@sbccd.cc.ca.us
BRATZ, Jennifer .... 406-657-1032 265 E
jen.bratz@rocky.edu
BRAUBURGER, Analea .. 253-566-5124 485 C
abrauburger@tacomacc.edu
BRAUCKMULLER, Lois .. 352-854-2322.. 96 O
brauckml@cf.edu
BRAUD, Terry .... 985-448-4017 192 B
terry.braud@nicholls.edu
BRAUER, Cynthia, A ..... 757-221-1693 466 C
cabra1@wm.edu
BRAUER, William, L ..... 757-594-7040 466 B
wbrauer@cnu.edu
BRAULT, Kelly, N .... 248-370-4921 229 G
brault@oakland.edu
BRAUN, Amanda .... 414-229-6599 497 A
abraun25@uwm.edu
BRAUN, Bernie .... 225-578-1295 188 I
bbraun@lsu.edu
BRAUN, Dale, K .... 715-425-3840 497 E
dale.k.braun@uwrf.edu
BRAUN, Dennis .... 508-767-7541 205 D
dbraun@assumption.edu
BRAUN, Eric .... 740-351-3542 360 K
ebraun@shawnee.edu
BRAUN, Eric .... 740-351-3257 360 K
ebraun@shawnee.edu
BRAUN, Frank .... 440-826-3566 348 E
fbraun@bw.edu
BRAUN, Gregory .... 815-280-2263 140 B
gbraun@jjc.edu
BRAUN, Gretchen .... 864-294-3137 410 A
gretchen.braun@furman.edu
BRAUN, Janice, E .... 510-430-2255.. 52 D
jbraun@mills.edu
BRAUN, Keith, V .... 727-816-3336 104 F
braunk@phsc.edu
BRAUN, Lynn .... 419-783-2548 352 F
lbraun@defiance.edu
BRAUN, Mark, J .... 515-281-6426 162 H
mark.braun@iowaregents.edu
BRAUN, Mary, C .... 319-273-6144 163 B
mary.braun@uni.edu
BRAUN, Neil, S .... 212-346-1962 311 E
nbraun@pace.edu
BRAUN, Raymond .... 419-372-3411 348 H
rwbraun@bgsu.edu
BRAUN, Robert, D .... 303-492-7006.. 83 A
bobby.braun@colorado.edu
BRAUN, Ronald .... 620-947-3121 177 C
ronb@tabor.edu
BRAUNGARD,
Elizabeth (Liz), A .... 717-361-1525 383 E
braungarde@etown.edu
BRAUNGARD, John .... 518-629-4507 302 E
j.braungard@hvcc.edu
BRAUNSCHWEIG, Jim .... 712-274-6400 170 E
jim.braunschweig@witcc.edu
BRAUSCH, Anthony, R .. 513-231-2223 348 C
abrausch@athenaeum.edu
BRAUTIGAN, John .... 216-397-1737 354 I
jbrautigan@jcu.edu
BRAVEMAN, Daan .... 585-389-2004 308 B
dbravem7@naz.edu
BRAVER, Joel .... 845-782-1380 326 H
BRAVERMAN,
Janette, M .... 414-410-4004 492 D
jmbraverman@stritch.edu
BRAVERMAN, Lisa .... 201-692-2671 277 K
lbraverman@fdu.edu
BRAVMAN, John, C ...... 570-577-1511 379 F
john.bravman@bucknell.edu
BRAVO, Bruce .... 210-999-7601 452 A
bbravo@trinity.edu
BRAVO, Deyse .... 423-236-2789 424 B
dbravo@southern.edu
BRAWNER, Dan .... 615-277-7453 428 F
dbrawner@watkins.edu
BRAXTON, Asella .... 404-270-5078 125 B
aybraxton@spelman.edu
BRAXTON, Joanne, E .... 631-451-4160 321 F
braxtoj@sunysuffolk.edu
BRAXTON, Nancy .... 413-369-4044 208 D
braxton@csld.edu
BRAXTON, Pamela .... 610-519-4032 402 D
pamela.braxton@villanova.edu
BRAXTON, Weldon .... 218-322-2380 238 E
weldon.braxton@itascacc.edu
BRAY, Brian .... 207-859-4730 193 E
brain.bray@colby.edu
BRAY, Carrie .... 916-558-2120.. 50 I
brayc@scc.losrios.edu
BRAY, Corey .... 417-873-7290 252 F
cbray003@drury.edu
BRAY, Jane, S .... 757-683-3938 469 G
jsbray@odu.edu
BRAY, John .... 765-677-1771 157 D
john.bray@indwes.edu
BRAY, Laura .... 414-297-6048 500 B
braylm@matc.edu
BRAY, Lee .... 252-493-7264 336 H
lbray@email.pittcc.edu
BRAY, Lisa .... 816-604-2207 255 G
lisa.bray@mcckc.edu
BRAY, Lisa .... 724-357-4820 394 G
lisa.bray@iup.edu
BRAY, Paul .... 515-964-0601 165 G
brayp@faith.edu
BRAY, Rich .... 979-209-7285 432 C
richard.bray@blinn.edu
BRAY, Russell .... 616-526-6481 222 A
rtb2@calvin.edu
BRAY, Sean .... 410-617-2838 199 F
sbray@loyola.edu

BREWER, Jay .... 401-841-7008 503 L jay.brewer@usnwc.edu
BREWER, Jerry, T .... 803-777-5783 413 C jerry-brewer@sc.edu
BREWER, Joan .... 620-341-5367 172 L jbrewer@emporia.edu
BREWER, JR., John, B . 301-447-5043 200 E brewer@msmary.edu
BREWER, Mondy .... 806-720-7803 439 H mondy.brewer@lcu.edu
BREWER, Nancy, A .... 631-451-4064 321 F brewern@sunysuffolk.edu
BREWER, Regina, L ...... 336-628-4554 337 A rlbrewer@randolph.edu
BREWER, Rick .... 318-487-7400 186 I rick.brewer@lacollege.edu
BREWER, Robert, W ...... 336-272-7102 329 D rbrewer@greensboro.edu
BREWER, Tim .... 704-878-3205 336 C tbrewer@mitchellcc.edu
BREWER, Timothy .... 310-825-9570.. 69 A tbrewer@conet.ucla.edu
BREWINGTON, Donald, E .... 512-505-3054 438 E debrewington@htu.edu
BREWINGTON, Donald, E .... 512-505-3044 438 E debrewington@htu.edu
BREWINGTON, Holly .... 910-592-8084 337 G hbrewington@sampsoncc.edu
BREWINGTON, Mark ...... 910-630-7149 331 C sbrewington@methodist.edu
BREWINGTON, Mazie ... 530-741-6723.. 76 A mbrewing@yccd.edu
BREWINGTON, Teare .... 803-536-8775 412 C tbrewing@scsu.edu
BREWS, Peter, J .... 803-777-3176 413 C peter.brews@moore.sc.edu
BREWSTER, Geoffrey ..... 918-610-8303 369 A geoff.brewster@ptstulsa.edu
BREWSTER, Julie .... 812-749-1234 159 C jbrewster@oak.edu
BREWSTER, Mariesa ..... 937-294-0592 356 H mariesa@saa.edu
BREWSTER, Tom .... 276-326-4240 465 B tbrewster@bluefield.edu
BREY, Amanda .... 805-893-2529.. 70 A amanda.brey@ucsb.edu
BREYER, Julia .... 760-773-2507.. 39 A jbreyer@collegeofthedesert.edu
BREZIL, Chris .... 212-229-5300 308 C brezilc@newschool.edu
BREZINSKI, Donald ...... 603-645-3109 274 D d.brezinski@snhu.edu
BRIAN, Robert, M .... 912-583-3107 115 E rbrian@bpc.edu
BRIAND, Simone .... 913-234-0810 172 E simone.briand@cleveland.edu
BRIAR, Jason .... 620-278-4218 177 B jason.briar@sterling.edu
BRIAR, John .... 559-325-3600.. 28 H jbriar@chsu.edu
BRICE, Diane .... 806-371-5028 430 A kdbrice@actx.edu
BRICE, Eloise, D .... 713-743-8165 452 E edstuhr@central.uh.edu
BRICE, Eloise, D .... 713-743-8165 452 F edstuhr@central.uh.edu
BRICELAND, Cynthia ..... 724-503-1001 402 E cbriceland@washjeff.edu
BRICHTA, William .... 215-780-1307 398 G wbrichta@salus.edu
BRICK, George .... 575-624-8023 287 A brick@nmmi.edu
BRICKER, Erin .... 707-527-4679.. 62 F ebricker@santarosa.edu
BRICKER, J. Douglas .... 412-396-6377 383 C bricker@duq.edu
BRICKER, Lauren, W ..... 909-869-2704.. 30 D lwbricker@cpp.edu
BRICKER, Lizette .... 650-574-6590.. 61 P lizette.bricker@smccd.edu
BRICKHOUSE, Nancy, W .... 254-710-3555 431 J
BRICKLE, Colleen .... 952-358-8158 239 F colleen.brickle@normandale.edu
BRIDDES, Bill .... 610-902-8526 380 C 0290mgr@follett.com
BRIDEL, David .... 213-821-4035.. 72 B bridel@usc.edu
BRIDENSTINE, Amy ...... 620-417-1111 176 K amy.bridenstine@sccc.edu
BRIDGE, Holly .... 417-328-1806 259 L hbridge@sbuniv.edu
BRIDGE, Louise .... 801-863-8689 461 A bridgelo@uvu.edu
BRIDGEFORTH, Valerie . 601-318-6188 249 H vbridgeforth@wmcarey.edu
BRIDGEMAN, Curtis ..... 503-370-6402 378 B cbridgem@willamette.edu
BRIDGEMAN, Doris .... 601-977-7836 249 C dbridgeman@tougaloo.edu
BRIDGEMAN, Lindsay ... 800-955-2527 173 F lbridgeman@grantham.edu
BRIDGEMAN, Valerie ..... 740-362-3482 356 D jbridgeman@mtso.edu
BRIDGERS, Brenda .... 662-246-6275 247 D bbridgers@msdelta.edu
BRIDGES, Antoinette ..... 815-753-6727 145 C abridges3@niu.edu
BRIDGES, Clarence, F ... 312-413-5946 151 B cbridges@uic.edu
BRIDGES, Dan .... 707-864-7000.. 64 C daniel.bridges@solano.edu
BRIDGES, Darryl .... 843-661-1295 409 K dbridges@fmarion.edu
BRIDGES, David .... 229-391-5050 113 F dbridges@abac.edu
BRIDGES, Edward .... 304-647-6439 491 A ebridges@osteo.wvsom.edu
BRIDGES, Felicia, L ...... 510-981-2852.. 56 E fbridges@peralta.edu
BRIDGES, George, S ..... 360-867-6100 481 A bridges@evergreen.edu
BRIDGES, Harold, A ...... 310-338-2700.. 50 J drew.bridges@lmu.edu
BRIDGES, J. Thomas .... 704-847-5600 340 I jbridges@ses.edu
BRIDGES, Karl .... 208-282-4131 130 H bridkarl@isu.edu
BRIDGES, Katie .... 202-462-2101.. 92 C kbridges@iwp.edu
BRIDGES, Kermit, S ...... 972-825-4652 445 A president@sagu.edu
BRIDGES, Kristina .... 319-399-8100 164 A kbridges@coe.edu
BRIDGES, LaDonna .... 508-626-4906 212 D lbridges@framingham.edu
BRIDGES, Martin .... 910-410-1818 337 B mwbridges@richmondcc.edu
BRIDGES, Michael, W ..... 412-396-1813 383 C bridgesm@duq.edu
BRIDGES, Robert .... 417-690-3448 251 E rbridges@cofo.edu
BRIDGES, Robert .... 470-578-3622 120 L rbridge7@kennesaw.edu
BRIDGES, Ruth .... 254-298-8309 446 A ruth.bridges@templejc.edu
BRIDGES, Scott .... 618-536-2384 149 E irsdept@siu.edu
BRIDGES, Scott, D .... 618-453-6239 149 E bridges@siu.edu
BRIDGES, Sharekka .... 843-921-6903 411 F sbridges@netc.edu
BRIDGES, Shelton .... 502-451-0815 184 E sbridges@sullivan.edu
BRIDGES, Steven, J .... 812-464-1849 161 E sjbridge@usi.edu
BRIDGES, Vernon, D ..... 818-947-2541.. 49 F bridgevd@lavc.edu
BRIDGES, Vincent .... 405-682-1611 367 H vincent.e.bridges@occc.edu
BRIDGES-CARTER, Shenay .... 773-995-2386 133 K sbridg21@csu.edu
BRIDGESMITH, Lance ... 310-506-4700.. 56 C lance.bridgesmith@pepperdine.edu
BRIDGEWATER, Laura ... 801-422-0684 458 H laura_bridgewater@byu.edu
BRIDGMON, Phillip .... 660-543-4116 260 K bridgmon@ucmo.edu
BRIDWELL, Joy .... 406-395-4875 265 G jbridwell@stonechild.edu
BRIELL, Nicole .... 641-784-5083 165 H nbriell1@graceland.edu
BRIELL, Scott .... 641-784-5110 165 H sbriell1@graceland.edu
BRIEN, Jane .... 845-758-4294 290 G brien@bard.edu
BRIESKE, Sonya .... 480-732-7308.. 12 P sonya.brieske@cgc.edu
BRIGANTTY GONZALEZ, Luis, J .... 787-725-8120 507 N lbrigantty0007@eap.edu
BRIGATI, Arthur, J .... 205-929-1448.... 6 B
BRIGDON, Beth, P .... 706-721-9667 115 A bbrigdon@augusta.edu
BRIGETY, Reuben, E ..... 202-994-6240.. 91 F rbrigety@gwu.edu
BRIGGANCE, Richard .... 615-963-5171 426 D rbriggance@tnstate.edu
BRIGGLE, Jennifer .... 970-207-4550.. 80 M jenniferbr@mckinleycollege.edu
BRIGGMAN, Deitra .... 803-376-5716 406 F dbriggman@allenuniversity.edu
BRIGGS, Catherine, R ... 856-222-9311 281 C cbriggs@rcbc.edu
BRIGGS, Chad .... 847-628-2018 140 C chad.briggs@judsonu.edu
BRIGGS, Darcy .... 303-797-5623.. 76 I darcy.briggs@arapahoe.edu
BRIGGS, Douglas, S ...... 540-636-2900 466 A dougb@christendom.edu
BRIGGS, Jeff .... 785-628-4200 173 B jdbriggs@fhsu.edu
BRIGGS, Jeff .... 864-977-7257 411 E jeff.briggs@ngu.edu
BRIGGS, Jeffrey .... 727-341-3785 106 E briggs.jeffrey@spcollege.edu
BRIGGS, Jeffrey, C .... 513-244-4803 357 A jeffrey.briggs@msj.edu
BRIGGS, Jeneise, S ...... 920-923-8577 494 A jsbriggs26@marianuniversity.edu
BRIGGS, Jennifer .... 812-488-2602 161 A jb610@evansville.edu
BRIGGS, SR., Jerryl ...... 662-254-3425 248 B jerryl.briggs@mvsu.edu
BRIGGS, Julie, A .... 585-245-5616 318 E briggsja@geneseo.edu
BRIGGS, Justine .... 585-395-5118 318 B jbriggs@brockport.edu
BRIGGS, Karen .... 619-260-2762.. 71 J karenbriggs@sandiego.edu
BRIGGS, Kelsey .... 508-791-9241 206 B kelsey.briggs@becker.edu
BRIGGS, Kenneth .... 860-215-9259.. 86 F kbriggs@trcc.commnet.edu
BRIGGS, Kristin .... 336-249-8186 334 A kristin_briggs@davidsonccc.edu
BRIGGS, Larry .... 208-769-3474 131 C ljbriggs@nic.edu
BRIGGS, Lynn .... 509-359-2258 480 E lbriggs@ewu.edu
BRIGGS, Mary, K .... 276-944-6836 467 G mkbriggs@ehc.edu
BRIGGS, Nolan .... 718-270-6069 295 A nbriggs@mec.cuny.edu
BRIGGS, Phillip .... 805-289-6036.. 73 B pbriggs@vcccd.edu
BRIGGS, Stephen, R ..... 706-236-2281 115 B sbriggs@berry.edu
BRIGGS, Tammie .... 334-876-9236.... 2 D tammie.briggs@wccs.edu
BRIGGS, Thyra .... 909-607-4408.. 45 A thyra_briggs@hmc.edu
BRIGGS, William .... 406-477-6215 263 D wbriggs@cdkc.edu
BRIGHAM, Brook .... 508-849-3313 205 C bbrigham@annamaria.edu
BRIGHAM, David, R ...... 215-972-2056 393 D dbrigham@pafa.edu
BRIGHAM, Doug .... 208-459-5268 130 D dbrigham@collegeofidaho.edu
BRIGHAM, Jim .... 256-782-5820.... 5 J jbrigham@jsu.edu
BRIGHT, Brett .... 620-665-3579 174 B brightb@hutchcc.edu
BRIGHT, Cynthia .... 832-813-6568 439 G cynthia.i.bright@lonestar.edu
BRIGHT, David .... 863-667-5310 107 K drbright@seu.edu
BRIGHT, George, L .... 252-335-3396 341 D glbright@ecsu.edu
BRIGHT, Harold .... 480-219-6036 250 A hbright@atsu.edu
BRIGHT, Harry .... 641-472-1178 167 F hbright@mum.edu
BRIGHT, Jessica .... 512-637-5677 442 M seubookstore@texasbook.com
BRIGHT, Sarah .... 636-481-3218 254 A sbright@jeffco.edu
BRIGHT, Steve .... 434-544-8208 472 G bright@lynchburg.edu
BRIGHTON, Robyn, M .. 407-582-2089 112 K rbrighton1@valenciacollege.edu
BRIGHTSMAN, David .... 414-443-8739 498 O david.brightsman@wlc.edu
BRIGNONI, Linda, M .... 818-677-2085.. 32 D linda.brignoni@csun.edu
BRIJBASI, Monique ...... 305-628-6648 106 F mbrijbasi@stu.edu
BRIKER, Olga .... 610-795-6079 385 L obriker@haverford.edu
BRILEY, Jana .... 912-478-1301 119 C janawms@georgiasouthern.edu
BRILEY, Pat .... 540-840-1305.. 19 C pbriley@ecollege.edu
BRILL, Ann, M .... 785-864-4755 177 D abrill@ku.edu
BRILL, Jon .... 610-436-3311 396 A jbrill@wcupa.edu
BRILLEY, Amy .... 217-362-6488 143 H abrilley@millikin.edu
BRILLHART, David .... 740-366-9319 349 H brillhart.5@cotc.edu
BRIMHALL, Carrie .... 218-736-1503 239 B carrie.brimhall@minnesota.edu
BRIMHALL, Joseph .... 503-251-5712 377 F jebrimhall@uws.edu
BRIMHALL-VARGAS, Mark .... 781-736-4411 207 E mbv@brandeis.edu
BRIMLEY, Pamela .... 501-420-1219.. 17 B pamela.brimley@arkansasbaptist.edu
BRIMMER, Suzette .... 713-718-6158 437 I suzette.brimmer@hccs.edu
BRIMMERMAN, Roger .. 620-242-0424 175 F brimmerr@mcpherson.edu
BRINDLE, Denise .... 978-665-3454 212 C dbrindl1@fitchburgstate.edu
BRINDLEY, Roger .... 813-974-1218 110 B brindley@usf.edu
BRINER, Clare .... 708-974-5376 144 C brinerc@morainevalley.edu
BRINER, Sean .... 760-750-4404.. 33 B sbriner@csusm.edu
BRINEY, Colleen, M ...... 479-575-2551.. 21 G cbriney@uark.edu
BRINGAZE, Tammy .... 413-572-5491 213 D tbringaze@westfield.ma.edu
BRINGER, Michael .... 573-288-6528 252 E mbringer@culver.edu
BRINGHAM, Holly .... 509-682-6705 486 E hbringham@wvc.edu
BRINGSJORD, Elizabeth 518-320-1251 316 C elizabeth.bringsjord@suny.edu
BRINING, Patricia .... 215-968-8091 379 G patricia.brining@bucks.edu
BRINK, Benita .... 719-587-7426.. 76 F babrink@adams.edu
BRINK, Laura .... 617-521-2127 218 E laura.brink@simmons.edu
BRINK, Stephanie .... 573-823-8594 251 B sbrink@centralmethodist.edu
BRINK-DRESCHER, Judith .... 516-323-3925 307 F jdrescher@molloy.edu
BRINKER, JR., Thomas, M .... 215-572-4039 379 A brinkert@arcadia.edu
BRINKERHOFF, Robert .. 401-454-6183 405 D rbrinker@risd.edu
BRINKLEY, David .... 270-745-6140 185 E david.brinkley@wku.edu
BRINKLEY, Derek .... 312-369-7493 135 E dbrinkley@colum.edu
BRINKLEY, Frank .... 336-770-3349 343 D brinkleyt@uncsa.edu
BRINKLEY, Martin .... 919-962-4417 342 D martin92@unc.edu
BRINKLEY, Tom .... 336-278-7452 328 K tbrinkley@elon.edu
BRINKLEY-KENNEDY, Rhonda .... 513-861-6400 361 L
BRINKMAN, Kevin .... 513-618-1926 350 J kbrinkman@ccms.edu
BRINKMAN, Matt .... 423-614-8395 420 J mmbrinkman@leeuniversity.edu
BRINKMAN, Sue .... 920-403-3210 495 I sue.brinkman@snc.edu
BRINN, Greg .... 610-989-1330 402 B bgrinn@vfmac.edu
BRINSON, Bruce .... 214-379-5573 441 I bbrinson@pqc.edu
BRINSON, Donna .... 770-533-6921 121 B dbrinson@laniertech.edu
BRINSON, Leigh, T .... 309-341-7130 141 A ltbrinson@knox.edu
BRINSON, Marla .... 732-906-2513 279 A mbrinson@middlesexcc.edu
BRINSON, Reginald .... 404-756-8458 122 E rwbrinson@msm.edu

BRINSON, Willie, L ...... 919-735-5151 338 H wlbrinson@waynecc.edu
BRINSON-BROWN, Angela .... 305-626-3139.. 99 D angela.brinson-brown@fmuniv.edu
BRIONES, Eloisa, M ..... 650-738-4227.. 61 Q briones@smccd.edu
BRISACK, Al .... 608-663-3289 493 C abrisack@edgewood.edu
BRISBON, T. Muriel ...... 610-896-1250 385 L tbrisbon@haverford.edu
BRISCOE, Chad, C .... 574-372-5100 155 B chad.briscoe@grace.edu
BRISCOE, Connie .... 407-646-2194 105 M cbriscoe@rollins.edu
BRISCOE-ALBA, Susana 845-569-3414 307 J susana.alba@msmc.edu
BRISENO, Jason .... 512-223-7550 431 A jbrisen2@austincc.edu
BRISKEY, Marvin .... 614-947-6002 353 C marv.briskey@franklin.edu
BRISLIN, Shawn, P .... 607-746-4670 320 G brislisp@delhi.edu
BRISOLARA, Sharon ...... 530-242-7750.. 63 H sbrisolara@shastacollege.edu
BRISSON, Caitrin .... 617-603-6900 216 H caitrin.brisson@necb.edu
BRISSON, E. Carson ..... 804-355-0671 472 E cbrisson@upsem.edu
BRISSON, Michelle .... 973-408-3454 277 C mbrisson@drew.edu
BRISTLE, Shawn .... 928-758-3926.. 14 F sbristle@mohave.edu
BRISTOL, Amanda .... 423-461-8490 422 J abristol@milligan.edu
BRISTOL, Lori .... 610-225-5010 383 D lbristol@eastern.edu
BRISTOR, Valerie .... 561-297-3357 108 J bristor@fau.edu
BRISTOW, Aimee .... 573-592-5365 262 E aimee.bristow@westminster-mo.edu
BRISTOW, Cliff .... 405-912-9037 369 D cbristow@ru.edu
BRISTOW, Troy .... 630-637-5559 144 H tbbristow@noctrl.edu
BRITE, Chris .... 660-944-2863 251 G cbrite@conception.edu
BRITIGAN, Bradley, E ... 402-599-8878 270 A bradley.britigan@unmc.edu
BRITT, Amber, N .... 601-643-8301 245 G nikki.britt@colin.edu
BRITT, Denise .... 404-752-1500 122 E dbritt@msm.edu
BRITT, Eddie .... 601-643-8628 245 G eddie.britt@colin.edu
BRITT, Frank .... 480-947-6644.. 15 A frank.britt@pennfoster.edu
BRITT, Jeanette .... 814-824-2247 390 C jbritt@mercyhurst.edu
BRITT, Josh .... 843-921-6997 411 F jbritt@netc.edu
BRITT, Julianne .... 781-891-3456 206 D jbritt@bentley.edu
BRITT, Kenith .... 317-955-6209 158 U kbritt@marian.edu
BRITT, Kimbrly, A .... 804-523-5191 474 H kbritt@reynolds.edu
BRITT, Tamara .... 718-862-7858 305 H tamara.britt@manhattan.edu
BRITT, Tammy, T .... 704-233-8111 344 G tbritt@wingate.edu
BRITT-PETTY, Debra ...... 408-848-4711.. 43 J dbrittpetty@gavilan.edu
BRITTAIN, Jordan, S ..... 805-525-4417.. 67 D jbrittain@thomasaquinas.edu
BRITTAIN, Linda, D ...... 717-264-3787 403 F lbrittain@wilson.edu
BRITTAIN, Tiffany .... 817-722-1765 439 B tiffany.brittain@tku.edu
BRITTO, Vanessa, M ..... 401-863-5970 404 E vanessa_britto@brown.edu
BRITTON, Bill .... 805-756-2190.. 30 C bibritto@calpoly.edu
BRITTON, Dana, J .... 800-233-4220 390 E dbritton@messiah.edu
BRITTON, Ida .... 240-567-5264 200 C ida.britton@montgomerycollege.edu
BRITTON, Karen .... 781-239-3101 214 E kbritton@massbay.edu
BRITTON, Keith, E .... 803-938-3882 414 B kbritton@uscsumter.edu
BRITTON, Mark .... 419-289-5057 348 A mbritto3@ashland.edu
BRITTON-SPEARS, Ona . 918-463-2931 366 B ona.britton-spears@connorsstate.edu
BRITZ, Johannes .... 412-229-4501 497 A britz@uwm.edu
BRIX, Timothy .... 636-922-8211 258 I tbrix@stchas.edu
BRIXEY, Shawn .... 804-828-0100 473 F brixey@vcu.edu
BRIZICKY, Amelia .... 940-898-3207 451 F abrizicky@twu.edu
BRIZUELA, Erika .... 310-289-5123.. 73 H erika.brizuela@wcui.edu
BRNCICH, Lisa .... 815-479-7589 143 A lbrncich@mchenry.edu
BROADAWAY, Barbara, D .... 919-516-4234 340 C bdbroadaway@st-aug.edu
BROADDUS, Henry, R ... 757-221-3987 466 C hrbroa@wm.edu
BROADDUS, Matthew ... 865-573-4517 420 G mbroaddus@johnsonu.edu
BROADHURST, Gary ..... 315-792-5573 307 D gbroadhurst@mvcc.edu
BROADIE, II, Paul .... 203-332-5224.. 85 F pbroadie@hcc.commnet.edu
BROADIE, II, Paul .... 203-285-2060.. 85 E
BROADUS, Nariah .... 802-860-2747 462 B nbroadus@champlain.edu
BROADWATER, Bonnie . 301-387-3050 198 F bonnie.broadwater@garrettcollege.edu
BROADWATER, Kimberly .... 662-254-3484 248 B kbroadwater@mvsu.edu
BROADWATER, Larry .... 865-251-1800 424 A lbroadw@south.edu
BROADWATER, Melanie, R .... 724-589-2754 399 H mbroadwater@thiel.edu
BROADWAY, Shane ...... 501-660-1001.. 17 E sbroadway@asusystem.edu
BROADWELL, Phyllis .... 912-279-5816 116 G pbroadwell@ccga.edu
BROBERG, Sarah .... 828-251-6967 342 C sbroberg@unca.edu
BROBERG, Vic .... 610-292-9852 397 D vic.broberg@reseminary.edu
BROCCOLI, Christina .... 914-674-7415 306 F cbroccoli@mercy.edu
BROCK, Ashleigh .... 804-289-8749 472 L ash.brock@richmond.edu
BROCK, Casson .... 501-337-5000.. 18 J cbrock@coto.edu
BROCK, Greg .... 541-684-7252 374 G gbrock@nwcu.edu
BROCK, III, Harry, B .... 205-726-4071.... 6 E bbrock@samford.edu
BROCK, Jennifer .... 602-384-2555.. 11 F jennifer.brock@bryanuniversity.edu
BROCK, Jessica .... 479-356-2188.. 18 C jbrock15@atu.edu
BROCK, Kathy .... 620-792-9233 171 C brockk@bartonccc.edu
BROCK, Marcius .... 507-389-1180 239 C marcius.brock@mnsu.edu
BROCK, Marty, A .... 662-329-7152 248 A mabrock@muw.edu
BROCK, Michael, G .... 610-989-1246 402 B mbrock@vfmac.edu
BROCK, Michele .... 559-737-5441.. 39 E michelebr@cos.edu
BROCK, Michelle .... 704-290-5357 337 I mbrock@spcc.edu
BROCK, Sarah .... 812-488-2151 161 A sb484@evansville.edu
BROCK-SMITH, Cynthia 202-806-2530.. 92 B cynthia.brocksmith@howard.edu
BROCKBANK, Kevin ...... 509-533-7042 480 A kevin.brockbank@scc.spokane.edu
BROCKBANK, Kevin ...... 509-533-7042 479 I kevin.brockbank@scc.spokane.edu
BROCKEL, Amber .... 605-229-8427 416 C amber.brockel@presentation.edu
BROCKEL, Sarah .... 406-377-3396 263 E sbrockel@dawson.edu
BROCKELBANK, Steve ... 740-826-6109 357 C stevenb@muskingum.edu
BROCKETT, Lori .... 760-750-4405.. 33 B brockett@csusm.edu
BROCKGREITENS, Kathy .... 636-922-8229 258 I kbrockgreitens@stchas.edu
BROCKHOFF, Jennifer ... 502-585-9911 184 D jbrockhoff@spalding.edu
BROCKIE, Clarena .... 406-353-2607 262 H cbrockie@ancollege.edu
BROCKIE, Dixie .... 406-353-2607 262 H dbrockie@ancollege.edu
BROCKIE, Kimberly .... 406-353-2607 262 H kbrockie@ancollege.edu
BROCKIE, Michele .... 406-353-2607 262 H mbrockie@ancollege.edu
BROCKMAN, Diane .... 660-596-7205 260 D dbrockman@sfccmo.edu
BROCKMAN, Mark .... 513-745-4842 365 B brockmanm1@xavier.edu
BROCKMAN, Tracy .... 614-985-2324 360 E tbrockman@pcj.edu
BROCKMEIER, Ric .... 913-971-3261 175 G rbrockmeier@mnu.edu
BROCKMYER, Richard, A .... 801-832-2516 461 G rbrockmyer@westminstercollege.edu
BROCKWAY, Celia .... 804-862-6100 470 I cbrockway@rbc.edu
BROD, Catherine .... 914-251-6014 319 E catherine.brod@purchase.edu
BROD, David .... 540-857-7731 476 D dbrod@virginiawestern.edu
BRODA, Joanna .... 212-346-1652 311 E jbroda@pace.edu
BRODA, Mary .... 517-750-1200 230 H mary.broda@arbor.edu
BRODERICK, Christopher .... 503-725-3773 376 A christopher.broderick@pdx.edu
BRODERICK, Debra, J ... 651-962-6780 244 E djbroderick@stthomas.edu
BRODERICK, Jo .... 978-921-4242 216 F jo.broderick@montserrat.edu
BRODERICK, John, R ..... 757-683-3159 469 G jbroderi@odu.edu
BRODERICK, Kimberley 413-755-4490 215 F kebroderick@stcc.edu
BRODERICK, Mac .... 603-513-1327 274 H mac.broderick@granite.edu
BRODERICK, Marybeth . 845-848-7824 298 D marybeth.broderick@dc.edu
BRODERICK, Michael .... 860-515-3885.. 84 G mbroderick@charteroak.edu
BRODERICK, Victor, K .. 217-786-2414 142 B victor.broderick@llcc.edu
BRODERICK BOTTERI, Anne .... 386-226-6013.. 98 A botteria@erau.edu
BRODERSON, Maureen, A .... 817-552-3700 439 B mbroderson@tku.edu
BRODEUR, Lynne .... 508-678-2811 213 G lynne.brodeur@bristolcc.edu
BRODEUR, Thomas .... 860-832-2531.. 84 I brodeur@ccsu.edu
BRODIGAN, Rebecca, H .... 207-859-4692 193 E becky.brodigan@colby.edu
BRODL, Mark .... 309-556-3101 139 G provost@iwu.edu
BRODLEY, Carla, E .... 617-373-2462 217 F
BRODMERKEL, Darcy ..... 570-674-6466 390 G dbrodmerkel@misericordia.edu
BRODRICK, Jeff .... 616-538-2330 224 C jbrodrick@gracechristian.edu
BRODSKIY, Iren .... 201-216-9901 277 D iren.brodskiy@eicollege.edu
BRODSKY, Aryeh .... 732-765-9126 284 L ygocb@yeshivanet.com
BRODSKY, Mikhail .... 510-208-2803.. 48 A president@lincolnuca.edu
BRODSKY, Stephen .... 212-346-1274 311 E sbrodksy@pace.edu
BRODY, Charmain .... 610-398-5300 389 A cbrody@lincolntech.edu
BRODY, Matthew .... 919-962-4651 341 A msbrody@northcarolina.edu
BRODY, Michael .... 503-777-7521 376 C brodym@reed.edu
BRODZINSKI, James .... 219-464-6758 162 A jim.brodzinski@valpo.edu
BROEKER, Camy .... 317-274-4511 156 F cbroeker@iupui.edu
BROETJE, Whitney .... 206-281-2831 484 D broetw@spu.edu
BROFFT, Jeremy .... 757-388-2862 471 D jbrofft@sentara.edu
BROGAN, Jamey .... 304-243-2385 491 I jbrogan@wju.edu
BROGAN, Michael, S ..... 716-839-8227 298 B mbrogan@daemen.edu
BROGAN, William .... 301-985-7000 203 B william.brogan@umuc.edu
BROGDEN, Jeff, D .... 919-658-7171 340 J jbrogden@umo.edu
BROGDON, Christina .... 678-839-6403 126 E cbrogdon@westga.edu
BROGDON, Jarrod .... 229-333-2100 127 B jarrod.brogdon@wiregrass.edu
BROGE, Jason .... 989-275-5000 226 B jason.broge@kirtland.edu
BROGHAMMER, Sean, M .... 970-351-2806.. 83 E sean.broghammer@unco.edu
BROIDO, Chelsea .... 510-859-1300.. 24 D admissions@aimc.edu
BROILES, Janet .... 870-575-8471.. 22 E broilesj@uapb.edu
BROKENBURR, Shenita . 608-262-8299 496 B sbrokenburr@uwsa.edu
BROKKE, Dan .... 952-829-2470 234 A dan.brokke@bethfel.org
BROKKE, Derek .... 952-829-1320 234 A derek.brokke@bethfel.org
BROKKEN, Patricia .... 540-362-6016 468 C brokkenpe@hollins.edu
BROKVIST, Randi .... 904-632-3301 100 B r.brokvis@fscj.edu
BROLINSON, Gunnar .... 540-231-4981 467 F pbrolins@vcom.vt.edu
BROLLEY, Francis, R .... 815-224-0466 139 F fran_brolley@ivcc.edu
BROMAN, Erica .... 413-572-5244 213 D ebroman@westfield.ma.edu
BROMANDER, Lowell .... 651-523-2225 236 A lbromander@hamline.edu
BROMFIELD, Christopher .... 305-626-0207.. 99 D christopher.bromfield@fmuniv.edu
BROMFIELD, Elaine .... 334-727-8508.... 7 D ebromfield@tuskegee.edu
BROMFIELD, Robert, L . 415-422-2786.. 71 K rlbromfield@usfca.edu
BROMLEY, Casey .... 870-612-2034.. 22 I casey.bromley@uaccb.edu
BROMLEY, Dennis .... 801-957-4322 461 D dennis.bromley@slcc.edu
BROMSTRUP, Bryan, T . 812-877-8222 159 J bromstru@rose-hulman.edu
BRONDER, James, S .... 419-998-3143 363 C jsbronde@unoh.edu
BRONET, Frances .... 718-636-3646 311 J fbronet@pratt.edu
BRONFMAN, Jane .... 860-906-5103.. 85 D jbronfman@capitalcc.edu
BRONKEMA, F. David ... 610-225-5068 383 D dbronkem@eastern.edu
BRONNER, Gwethalyn ... 847-543-2685 135 B gbronner@clcillinois.edu
BRONNER, Jennifer, L .. 740-826-8463 357 C jbronner@muskingum.edu
BRONSON, Eric .... 401-254-3369 405 E ebronson@rwu.edu
BRONSON, Ivanie .... 866-492-5336 244 F ivanie.bronson@laureate.net
BRONSTEIN, Daniel ...... 706-821-8249 122 K dbronstein@paine.edu
BRONSTEIN, Fred .... 410-234-4700 199 D fred.bronstein@jhu.edu
BRONSTEIN, Ken .... 360-383-3359 486 G kbronstein@whatcom.edu
BRONSTEIN, Laura .... 607-777-5572 316 E lbronst@binghamton.edu
BRONSTEIN, Susan .... 239-489-9357 100 A sbronstein@fsw.edu
BROOK, Ryan .... 949-582-4722.. 64 G rbrook@saddleback.edu
BROOKBANK, Julie .... 605-995-7104 415 G julie.brookbank@mitchelltech.edu
BROOKER, Mark .... 765-674-6901 157 D
BROOKER, Paulita .... 281-649-3283 437 H pbrooker@hbu.edu
BROOKEY, Lauren .... 405-325-1701 371 B lbrookey@ou.edu
BROOKING, David .... 662-329-7138 248 A dmbrooking@muw.edu
BROOKMAN, Kim .... 413-236-1003 213 F kbrookman@berkshirecc.edu
BROOKMAN, Lori .... 910-630-7128 331 C brookman@methodist.edu
BROOKNER, Laurie .... 415-565-8813.. 68 F brookner@uchastings.edu
BROOKOVER, Joe .... 515-643-6611 168 A jbrookover@mercydesmoines.org

BROOKS, Aaron .... 662-329-7377 248 A
abrooks1@muw.edu
BROOKS, Ann Marie ..... 614-234-5800 356 I
abrooks@mccn.edu
BROOKS, Anne .... 918-302-3603 366 D
abrooks@eosc.edu
BROOKS, Anthony .... 919-719-1983 340 E
anthony.brooks@shawu.edu
BROOKS, Barry .... 270-926-1188 419 I
bbrooks@daymarcollege.edu
BROOKS, Blake .... 317-632-5553 158 S
bbrooks@lincolntech.edu
BROOKS, Browning ...... 850-644-8343 109 C
bbrooks@fsu.edu
BROOKS, Carlton .... 719-502-2003.. 81 F
carlton.brooks@ppcc.edu
BROOKS,
Carrie Allison .... 901-272-5160 422 B
cbrooks@mca.edu
BROOKS, Chad .... 931-221-7414 418 D
brooksc@apsu.edu
BROOKS, Charles, R ..... 973-596-2875 279 F
brooks@njit.edu
BROOKS, Cindy, L .... 610-799-1121 388 I
cbrooks@lccc.edu
BROOKS, Constance ..... 702-889-8426 270 K
constance_brooks@nshe.nevada.edu
BROOKS, Danny, K .... 336-841-9131 329 G
dbrooks@highpoint.edu
BROOKS, Darlene, D .... 901-843-3901 423 J
brooksd@rhodes.edu
BROOKS, Donnie .... 601-974-1190 247 B
brookda@millsaps.edu
BROOKS, Donnie, A ..... 651-696-6366 236 H
dbrooks@macalester.edu
BROOKS, II, Earl, D ..... 260-665-4101 160 H
brookse@trine.edu
BROOKS, Eric .... 520-515-3624.. 11 M
brookse@cochise.edu
BROOKS, Erin .... 603-428-2314 273 H
ebrooks@nec.edu
BROOKS, Gene .... 402-643-7411 266 G
gene.brooks@cune.edu
BROOKS, II,
H. Gordon .... 337-482-6224 192 E
gbrooks@louisiana.edu
BROOKS, Ian .... 510-883-2056.. 41 G
ibrooks@dspt.edu
BROOKS, Jacquelyne .... 706-817-6966 180 C
jacquelyne.brooks@frontier.edu
BROOKS, James .... 614-825-6255 347 F
jbrooks@aiam.edu
BROOKS, James, L .... 323-856-7600.. 25 M
jbrooks@afi.com
BROOKS, Janelle .... 716-878-3051 318 C
BROOKS, Jessie .... 404-270-5323 125 B
jlbrooks@spelman.edu
BROOKS, Jim, J .... 541-346-6121 377 D
brooksja@uoregon.edu
BROOKS, John, I .... 910-672-1060 341 E
jibrooks@uncfsu.edu
BROOKS, Juliette .... 201-692-7050 277 K
juliette_brooks@fdu.edu
BROOKS, Justin, P .... 619-239-0391.. 34 F
jbrooks@cwsl.edu
BROOKS, Karl .... 847-635-1739 145 G
kbrooks@oakton.edu
BROOKS, Katharine, S .. 615-875-8136 428 D
katharine.s.brooks@vanderbilt.edu
BROOKS, Kelly .... 575-527-7551 287 E
kebrooks@nmsu.edu
BROOKS, Kent .... 307-268-2703 501 U
kbrooks@caspercollege.edu
BROOKS, Krista .... 559-453-2289.. 43 G
krista.brooks@fresno.edu
BROOKS, L. Rayburn .... 864-941-8301 411 H
brooks.r@ptc.edu
BROOKS, Larry .... 701-228-5452 346 C
larry.brooks@dakotacollege.edu
BROOKS, Larry .... 701-228-5457 346 C
larry.brooks@dakotacollege.edu
BROOKS, LaShon, F ..... 662-254-3425 248 B
lfbrooks@mvsu.edu
BROOKS, Lauren .... 937-298-3399 355 F
lauren.brooks@kc.edu
BROOKS, Letha .... 317-921-4976 157 H
lbrooks29@ivytech.edu
BROOKS, Lisa .... 818-240-1000.. 44 B
lbrooks@glendale.edu
BROOKS, Lois .... 608-262-5381 496 C
lois.brooks@wisc.edu
BROOKS, Lyvette .... 215-751-8046 382 A
lbrooks@ccp.edu

BROOKS, Marilyn, A ..... 804-257-5846 477 C
mabrooks2@vuu.edu
BROOKS, Mark .... 229-931-2246 124 D
mbrooks@southgatech.edu
BROOKS, Marty .... 804-758-6771 475 G
mbrooks@rappahannock.edu
BROOKS, Michael .... 701-858-3000 345 F
michael.brooks@minotstateu.edu
BROOKS, Monica .... 304-696-6474 490 D
brooks@marshall.edu
BROOKS, NaQuindra ..... 479-880-4358.. 18 C
nbrooks3@atu.edu
BROOKS, Natalie .... 212-353-4100 297 E
nbrooks@cooper.edu
BROOKS, Patricia .... 972-825-4652 445 A
pabrooks@sagu.edu
BROOKS, Paul .... 972-825-4616 445 A
pbrooks@sagu.edu
BROOKS, Randy, M ...... 217-424-6205 143 H
rbrooks@millikin.edu
BROOKS, Ray, O .... 903-657-6543 448 E
BROOKS, Ron .... 901-678-2077 427 D
rbrooks@memphis.edu
BROOKS, Shannon .... 864-644-5072 412 E
sbrooks@swu.edu
BROOKS, Sharon, D ..... 410-651-6621 203 A
sdbrooks@umes.edu
BROOKS, Shawn .... 478-445-5169 118 C
shawn.brooks@gcsu.edu
BROOKS, Terence .... 864-250-8211 410 B
terence.brooks@gvltec.edu
BROOKS, Teresa .... 903-693-2060 441 F
tbrooks@panola.edu
BROOKS, Thom, R .... 828-339-4202 338 B
tbrooks@southwesterncc.edu
BROOKS, Thomas .... 641-472-1205 167 F
tbrooks@mum.edu
BROOKS, Todd .... 404-364-8469 122 J
tbrooks7@oglethorpe.edu
BROOKS, Tom .... 703-416-1441 466 F
tbrooks@divinemercy.edu
BROOKS, Tyia .... 601-403-1211 248 E
tbrooks@prcc.edu
BROOKS, Tyrone .... 509-542-4408 479 H
tbrooks@columbiabasin.edu
BROOKS, Vanessa .... 734-973-3491 232 B
vbrooks@wccnet.edu
BROOKS, Wendy .... 989-358-7299 221 A
brooksw@alpenacc.edu
BROOKS, Wesley .... 309-794-7533 132 C
wesleybrooks@augustana.edu
BROOKS BLAIR,
Sarah, D .... 937-529-2201 362 A
sblair@united.edu
BROOKSHER, Jamie ...... 620-235-4136 176 F
jbrooksher@pittstate.edu
BROOKSHIRE, David ..... 276-244-1211 464 L
dbrookshire@asl.edu
BROOME, Barbara .... 330-672-8799 354 J
bbroome1@kent.edu
BROOME, Marion .... 919-684-9444 328 G
marion.broome@duke.edu
BROOME, Melba .... 202-274-6118.. 93 C
mbroome@udc.edu
BROOME, Tonia .... 704-922-6310 334 F
broome.tonia@gaston.edu
BROOME, William .... 404-880-8016 116 D
william.broome@cwservices.com
BROOMHEAD, Keiko ..... 617-989-4034 219 E
broomheadk@wit.edu
BROPHY, Ann .... 314-246-7422 262 C
annbrophy26@webster.edu
BROPHY, Dale, G .... 801-585-2677 460 E
dale.brophy@dps.utah.edu
BROPHY, Katharine ...... 305-348-2560 109 A
katharine.brophy@fiu.edu
BROPHY, Michael, S .... 716-926-8923 301 H
mbrophy@hilbert.edu
BROPHY, Thomas .... 760-634-1771.. 28 I
BROPHY, Timothy, S .... 352-273-4476 109 F
tbrophy@aa.ufl.edu
BROPHY, JR.,
William, E .... 256-824-6144.... 8 B
william.brophy@uah.edu
BROPHY-BAERMANN,
Bryan .... 401-825-1000 404 H
BROQUARD, Andre .... 479-524-7229.. 19 H
abroquard@jbu.edu
BROSCHEIT, James ...... 406-994-2452 264 D
BROSCHINSKY, Bradley 208-282-7898 130 H
brosbrad@isu.edu
BROSHOUS, Robert, D .. 563-589-3199 169 I
bbroshou@dbq.edu

BROSKE, Kathleen, M ... 920-924-2139 500 C
kbroske@morainepark.edu
BROSKY, Lisa .... 520-206-4850.. 15 D
lbrosky@pima.edu
BROSKY, Tony .... 502-272-8375 179 B
jbrosky@bellarmine.edu
BROSNAN, JoAnna, M . 607-746-4727 320 G
brosnajm@delhi.edu
BROSNAN, Mary .... 516-323-3468 307 F
mbrosnan@molloy.edu
BROSS, Scott .... 309-268-8385 137 I
scott.bross@heartland.edu
BROSTROM, Nathan ...... 209-228-4417.. 69 B
chancellor@ucmerced.edu
BROSTROM, Nathan, E . 510-987-9029.. 68 C
nathan.brostrom@ucop.edu
BROTHERS, Gregory, A . 713-646-1888 444 B
gbrothers@stcl.edu
BROTHERS, James, F ... 937-229-2829 362 G
jbrothers1@udayton.edu
BROTHERS, Kirk .... 256-766-6610.... 5 F
kbrothers@hcu.edu
BROTHERS, Scott .... 304-829-7151 487 G
sbrothers@bethanywv.edu
BROTHERS, William ...... 828-339-4366 338 B
w_brothers@southwesterncc.edu
BROTHERTON,
Thomas, S .... 712-852-5224 166 F
tbrotherton@iowalakes.edu
BROTZMAN, Kelly .... 508-531-2147 212 B
kbrotzman@bridgew.edu
BROUGH, Aimee, B ...... 717-736-4122 385 E
abbrough@hacc.edu
BROUGHMAN, Lisa ...... 434-947-8481 470 E
llee@randolphcollege.edu
BROUGHTON, Nancy .... 218-879-0837 238 A
sam@fdltcc.edu
BROUILLARD-BRUCE,
Torry .... 415-422-6824.. 71 K
tbrouillard@usfca.edu
BROUILLET, Susan .... 603-230-3576 272 I
sbrouillet@ccsnh.edu
BROUILLETTE,
Domenick, R .... 816-604-1370 255 D
domenick.brouillette@mcckc.edu
BROUNK, Thomas, M ... 314-935-5955 262 A
tom_brounk@wustl.edu
BROUSSARD, Camille ... 212-431-2354 309 G
camille.broussard@nyls.edu
BROUSSARD, Carly .... 409-880-7029 449 H
cmwright1@lamar.edu
BROUSSARD, Dawn ...... 603-899-4075 273 F
broussardd@franklinpierce.edu
BROUSSARD, Michael .. 337-550-1292 189 A
mpbrouss@lsue.edu
BROUWER, Tom .... 800-280-0307 152 H
tom.brouwer@ace.edu
BROW, Carl .... 919-735-5151 338 H
brow@waynecc.edu
BROW, Richard, K .... 573-341-7784 261 E
brow@mst.edu
BROWDER, Kathy .... 706-737-1422 115 A
kbrowder@augusta.edu
BROWER, Aaron .... 608-265-8692 496 B
aaron.brower@uwex.edu
BROWER, Beth .... 609-586-4800 278 F
browerb@mccc.edu
BROWER, Bill .... 315-445-5441 304 C
browewih@lemoyne.edu
BROWER, Bob .... 619-849-2216.. 57 E
bobbrower@pointloma.edu
BROWER, Keith .... 718-862-7345 305 H
keith.brower@manhattan.edu
BROWER, Paul, O .... 508-213-2271 217 E
paul.brower@nichols.edu
BROWER, Pearl, K .... 907-852-3333.... 9 F
pearl.brower@ilisagvik.edu
BROWER, Roderick .... 910-695-3994 337 H
browerr@sandhills.edu
BROWN, Aaron .... 951-222-8789.. 58 F
aaron.brown@rccd.edu
BROWN, Adam .... 937-395-7653 355 F
adam.brown@kc.edu
BROWN, Adell .... 203-332-5015.. 85 F
abrown1@hcc.commnet.edu
BROWN, Aimee .... 800-955-2527 173 F
BROWN, Albert .... 360-596-5268 485 B
abrown@spscc.edu
BROWN, Alesia .... 864-941-8611 411 H
brown.a@ptc.edu
BROWN, Alfreda .... 330-672-2442 354 J
abbrown@kent.edu
BROWN, Alison .... 256-761-6310.... 7 B
akbrown@talladega.edu

BROWN, Allen .... 816-268-5400 257 C
b2legal@aol.com
BROWN, Amanda .... 419-207-6301 348 A
abrown18@ashland.edu
BROWN, Amon .... 202-651-5007.. 91 E
amon.brown@gallaudet.edu
BROWN, Amy, L .... 607-746-4584 320 G
brownal@delhi.edu
BROWN, Andrea .... 435-652-7595 460 G
abrown@dixie.edu
BROWN, Andrew .... 651-696-6069 236 H
dabrown@macalester.edu
BROWN, Angela .... 315-312-4100 319 B
angela.brown@oswego.edu
BROWN, Angela .... 817-735-0295 454 C
angela.brown@untsystem.edu
BROWN, Angelyne .... 803-327-7402 408 B
abrown@clintoncollege.edu
BROWN, Ann .... 919-516-5083 340 C
abrown@st-aug.edu
BROWN, Anne .... 704-687-5770 342 E
abrow316@uncc.edu
BROWN, Annette .... 415-749-4595.. 60 G
abrown@sfai.edu
BROWN, Ansel, E .... 919-530-7477 342 A
browna@nccu.edu
BROWN, Anthony .... 718-951-5000 293 C
anthony.brown@brooklyn.cuny.edu
BROWN, Art .... 515-964-6394 164 C
acbrown9@dmacc.edu
BROWN, Barbara .... 229-430-3504 113 I
bbrown@albanytech.edu
BROWN, Barbara .... 601-925-3968 247 C
brown16@mc.edu
BROWN, Barry .... 406-243-6800 264 A
barry.brown@umontana.edu
BROWN, Becki .... 513-875-3344 350 G
becki.brown@chatfield.edu
BROWN, Beverly .... 718-262-2238 295 F
bbrown@york.cuny.edu
BROWN, Beverly, D ...... 239-590-1051 108 K
bdbrown@fgcu.edu
BROWN, Bill .... 919-760-2367 331 B
brownw@meredith.edu
BROWN, Bill .... 757-455-5730 477 F
bbrown@vwu.edu
BROWN, Bob .... 707-476-4239.. 39 D
bob-brown@redwoods.edu
BROWN, Bob .... 940-565-2055 454 A
bob.brown@unt.edu
BROWN, Bobbie .... 806-742-3661 451 B
bobbie.brown@ttu.edu
BROWN, Bonita .... 859-572-5172 184 A
brownb33@nku.edu
BROWN, Bradley .... 435-586-7871 460 F
brown@suu.edu
BROWN, Brent, K .... 801-581-3003 460 E
brent.brown@osp.utah.edu
BROWN, Brian .... 315-364-3207 325 B
bbrown@wells.edu
BROWN, JR., Buck, F .. 864-379-8805 409 H
brown@erskine.edu
BROWN, Calvin .... 404-880-6042 116 D
cbrown@cau.edu
BROWN, Calvin .... 205-348-5966.... 7 G
cbrown@alumni.ua.edu
BROWN, Carl .... 614-947-6080 353 C
carl.brown@franklin.edu
BROWN, Carmen .... 803-812-7318 413 G
cdbrown@mailbox.sc.edu
BROWN, Carolanne ...... 561-803-2050 104 C
carolanne_brown@pba.edu
BROWN, Catherine .... 716-614-5950 310 C
cbrown@niagaracc.suny.edu
BROWN, Chad .... 918-647-1375 365 H
cbrown@carlalbert.edu
BROWN, Chad, M .... 740-588-1201 365 E
cbrown@zanestate.edu
BROWN, Charles .... 502-456-6773 184 E
cbrown@sullivan.edu
BROWN, Chelsea .... 301-934-2251 198 A
crclute@csmd.edu
BROWN, Chelsea, B ..... 717-358-4391 384 D
chelsea.brown@fandm.edu
BROWN, Cheryl-Ann .... 321-674-7581.. 99 B
cbrown@fit.edu
BROWN, Chris .... 205-934-1294.... 8 A
csbrown@uab.edu
BROWN, Chris .... 816-235-1141 261 C
umkc-stuaff@umkc.edu
BROWN, Christi .... 985-545-1500 187 H
BROWN, Christopher .... 785-864-4904 177 D
jcbrown2@ku.edu

BROWN, Christopher .... 949-376-6000.. 47 D cbrown@lcad.edu
BROWN, Cindy .... 417-455-5540 252 D cindybrown@crowder.edu
BROWN, Cinnamon ...... 573-592-5192 262 E cinnamon.brown@westminster-mo.edu
BROWN, Colleen .... 405-789-6400 370 A cbrown@snu.edu
BROWN, Courtney, L .... 540-365-4201 467 I cbrown@ferrum.edu
BROWN, Craig .... 208-562-3412 130 F craigbrown@cwi.edu
BROWN, Craig .... 740-474-8896 358 F jcbrown@ohiochristian.edu
BROWN, Curressia .... 662-254-3600 248 B cbrown@mvsu.edu
BROWN, Cynthia .... 706-754-7714 122 F cbrown@northgatech.edu
BROWN, Danene .... 619-388-2803.. 60 D dmbrown@sdccd.edu
BROWN, Daniel .... 512-245-3579 450 E db70@txstate.edu
BROWN, Daniel .... 806-291-3416 457 J dbrown@wbu.edu
BROWN, Danielle .... 215-951-5038 387 C browndd@lasalle.edu
BROWN, Darrell .... 254-968-9497 446 E dwbrown@tarleton.edu
BROWN, Darryl .... 301-295-3412 504 B darryl.brown@usuhs.edu
BROWN, David .... 314-434-4044 252 B david.brown@covenantseminary.edu
BROWN, David .... 256-233-8187.... 4 D david.brown@athens.edu
BROWN, David .... 352-638-9721.. 95 D dbrown@beaconcollege.edu
BROWN, David .... 949-794-9090.. 65 I dbrown@stanbridge.edu
BROWN, David .... 213-740-5371.. 72 B davidb@usc.edu
BROWN, David .... 262-691-5346 500 H dbrown@wctc.edu
BROWN, David .... 910-668-3331 441 A dbrown@nctc.edu
BROWN, David, A .... 409-772-3001 456 F davibrow@utmb.edu
BROWN, Davin .... 916-558-2142.. 50 I brownd@scc.losrios.edu
BROWN, Davin .... 916-608-6768.. 50 H brownd@flc.losrios.edu
BROWN, Deanie .... 217-206-6222 151 C brown.deanie@uis.edu
BROWN, Deborah .... 202-319-6915.. 91 B browndl@cua.edu
BROWN, Deborah, R .... 757-446-5828 466 I browndr@evms.edu
BROWN, Demetrius ...... 601-974-1225 247 B browndl@millsaps.edu
BROWN, Denelle .... 570-577-2071 379 F denelle.brown@bucknell.edu
BROWN, Dennis .... 281-425-6300 439 D dbrown@lee.edu
BROWN, Derek .... 303-404-5492.. 79 J derek.brown@frontrange.edu
BROWN, Derrick .... 903-593-8311 448 H dbrown@texascollege.edu
BROWN, DeShanna, K .. 904-470-8250.. 97 L dbrown@ewc.edu
BROWN, Diane, M .... 484-365-8055 389 C dbrown@lincoln.edu
BROWN, Dina .... 603-897-8232 274 B dbrown@rivier.edu
BROWN, Dolores, M ..... 262-524-7133 492 E docampo@carrollu.edu
BROWN, Donna, L .... 218-477-2721 239 D donna.brown@mnstate.edu
BROWN, Donna, P .... 479-248-7236.. 19 C registrar@ecollege.edu
BROWN, Donnie .... 806-291-1168 457 J brownd@wbu.edu
BROWN, Douglas .... 508-588-9100 214 F dbrown43@massasoit.mass.edu
BROWN, Douglas, E ..... 515-964-0601 165 G brownd@faith.edu
BROWN, D'Andrea .... 318-274-6100 191 E brownd@gram.edu
BROWN, Ed .... 406-657-1746 264 E edward.brown2@msubillings.edu
BROWN, Elaine .... 803-705-4529 407 A elaine.brown@benedict.edu
BROWN, Eric .... 530-221-4275.. 63 G ebrown@shasta.edu
BROWN, Erik .... 218-726-8891 243 F etbrown@d.umn.edu
BROWN, Erika .... 404-752-1723 122 E ebrown@msm.edu
BROWN, Erin .... 405-789-7661 370 B erin.brown@swcu.edu
BROWN, Erinn .... 308-345-8112 267 K browne@mpcc.edu
BROWN, Evert .... 719-589-7017.. 82 K evert.brown@trinidadstate.edu
BROWN, Fran .... 248-476-1122 227 C fbrown@msp.edu
BROWN, Gary .... 608-785-9167 501 A browng@westerntc.edu
BROWN, Gary, L .... 252-335-3277 341 D glbrown@ecsu.edu
BROWN, Gary, M .... 919-497-3213 330 I gmbrown@louisburg.edu
BROWN, Geeta, A .... 714-712-7900.. 46 C
BROWN, George, H ...... 828-227-7028 344 A ghbrown@wcu.edu
BROWN, Giles .... 903-463-8620 437 D browng@grayson.edu
BROWN, Glenn .... 973-684-5402 280 B gbrown@pccc.edu
BROWN, Gloria, M .... 252-335-3268 341 D gmbrown@ecsu.edu
BROWN, Glory .... 850-599-3531 108 I glory.brown@famu.edu
BROWN, Gregory, N ..... 610-328-8316 399 D gbrown1@swarthmore.edu
BROWN, Guilbert .... 717-871-4087 395 D guilbert.brown@millersville.edu
BROWN, H. David .... 816-271-4327 257 A browndav@missouriwestern.edu
BROWN, Harold .... 415-452-5163.. 37 A hbrown@ccsf.edu
BROWN, Haywood .... 813-974-4373 110 B haywood@usf.edu
BROWN, Heather .... 909-869-2717.. 30 D heatherbrown@cpp.edu
BROWN, Heather .... 916-686-7400.. 29 J
BROWN, Ian .... 361-593-3065 447 D ian.brown@tamuk.edu
BROWN, Ivey .... 336-750-2108 344 B browniv@wssu.edu
BROWN, J. Lee .... 910-672-1592 341 E jbrown84@uncfsu.edu
BROWN, J. Steven .... 202-319-4738.. 91 B brownj@cua.edu
BROWN, J. T .... 650-508-3521.. 54 D jtbrown@ndnu.edu
BROWN, J.J .... 828-262-2060 341 B brownjj@appstate.edu
BROWN, Jackie .... 803-705-4971 407 A jackie.brown@benedict.edu
BROWN, James .... 570-389-4410 394 A jbrown@bloomu.edu
BROWN, James .... 615-230-3787 426 B james.brown@volstate.edu
BROWN, James, M .... 570-340-6044 389 G jmbrown@marywood.edu
BROWN, Janice .... 301-846-2484 198 E jbrown@frederick.edu
BROWN, Jared .... 610-436-3305 396 A jbrown@wcupa.edu
BROWN, Jasmin, K .... 910-630-7034 331 C jabrown@methodist.edu
BROWN, Jazmane .... 504-520-7577 193 A jbrown77@xula.edu
BROWN, Jeff .... 801-832-2900 461 G jbrown@westminstercollege.edu
BROWN, Jeff .... 802-865-6421 462 B jbrown@champlain.edu
BROWN, Jeff .... 509-533-7373 480 A jeff.brown@scc.spokane.edu
BROWN, Jeffery .... 202-885-3165.. 90 J jtbrown@american.edu
BROWN, Jeffrey .... 217-333-2747 151 D brownjr@illinois.edu
BROWN, Jeffrey .... 618-545-3198 140 E jbrown2@kaskaskia.edu
BROWN, Jeffrey .... 804-862-6100 470 I jbrown@rbc.edu
BROWN, Jefrey .... 309-298-1544 152 D j-brown2@wiu.edu
BROWN, Jennifer .... 785-738-9085 176 A jbrown@ncktc.edu
BROWN, Jennifer, G ..... 203-582-3246.. 87 G jennifer.brown@quinnipiac.edu
BROWN, Jeremy .... 951-639-5404.. 52 I jebrown@msjc.edu
BROWN, Jeremy .... 530-741-6700.. 76 C jbrown2@yccd.edu
BROWN, Jeremy .... 970-248-1962.. 77 I jbrown@coloradomesa.edu
BROWN, Jerri .... 928-350-2113.. 15 N jbrown@prescott.edu
BROWN, Jesse .... 765-998-5344 160 F jesse_brown@taylor.edu
BROWN, Jessica .... 610-330-5338 387 E brownjes@lafayette.edu
BROWN, Jessyca .... 254-659-7504 437 G jbrown@hillcollege.edu
BROWN, Jill, A .... 781-891-2407 206 D jbrown@bentley.edu
BROWN, JoAnn .... 318-274-6238 191 E brownj@gram.edu
BROWN, JoAnn .... 318-670-9651 190 J jwarren@susla.edu
BROWN, John .... 404-270-5227 125 B jbrow109@spelman.edu
BROWN, John .... 817-461-8741 430 H jbrown@abu.edu
BROWN, John .... 614-236-6771 349 D jbrown18@capital.edu
BROWN, Jonathan .... 206-592-3257 481 H jbrown@highline.edu
BROWN, Joseph .... 903-923-2270 436 D jbrown@etbu.edu
BROWN, Joseph .... 910-246-4957 337 H brownjo@sandhills.edu
BROWN, Joshua .... 812-749-1456 159 C jobrown@oak.edu
BROWN, Joyce .... 443-885-3015 200 D joyce.brown@morgan.edu
BROWN, Joyce, F .... 212-217-4000 299 H joyce_brown@fitnyc.edu
BROWN, Julia .... 662-472-9011 246 C jubrown@holmescc.edu
BROWN, June, E .... 918-631-2584 371 E june-brown@utulsa.edu
BROWN, Justin, C .... 402-472-3484 269 J justin.brown@unl.edu
BROWN, Kali .... 253-492-2061 338 F brownk@vgcc.edu
BROWN, Karen, A .... 607-436-2524 317 C karen.brown@oneonta.edu
BROWN, Karen, J .... 603-899-4280 273 F brownkj@franklinpierce.edu
BROWN, Kate .... 410-651-6348 203 A kbrown@umes.edu
BROWN, Kathleen .... 641-844-5670 166 K kathleen.brown@iavalley.edu
BROWN, Kathleen, M ... 574-284-4557 160 C kbrown@saintmarys.edu
BROWN, Kathren .... 801-863-8517 461 A kbrown@uvu.edu
BROWN, Kathryn, F ...... 612-625-8515 243 E brown059@umn.edu
BROWN, Katie .... 303-333-4224.. 76 J registrar@aspen.edu
BROWN, Katie .... 843-377-2432 407 D kbrown@charlestonlaw.edu
BROWN, Katrina, M ...... 307-675-0221 502 F kbrown@sheridan.edu
BROWN, Keith .... 440-366-7692 355 J
BROWN, Keith, A .... 205-853-1200.... 2 G kbrown@jeffersonstate.edu
BROWN, Kelli, R .... 828-227-7100 344 A kbrown@wcu.edu
BROWN, Kelly .... 443-482-6575 201 D kelly.brown@sjc.edu
BROWN, Ken .... 620-278-4217 177 B kbrown@sterling.edu
BROWN, Kendra .... 580-774-3785 370 C kendra.brown@swosu.edu
BROWN, Kendrick .... 909-748-8359.. 71 G kendrick_brown@redlands.edu
BROWN, Kenneth .... 318-675-3395 189 C kbrown@lsuhsc.edu
BROWN, Kenneth .... 509-777-4486 486 I kbrown@whitworth.edu
BROWN, Kevin .... 660-263-3900 251 A kevinbrown@cccb.edu
BROWN, Kevin .... 641-784-5149 165 H brown@graceland.edu
BROWN, Kevin .... 843-349-5398 410 C kevin.brown@hgtc.edu
BROWN, Kevin .... 517-750-1200 230 H kbrown@arbor.edu
BROWN, Kevin .... 812-866-7061 155 C brownk@hanover.edu
BROWN, Kevin .... 812-866-7040 155 C brownk@hanover.edu
BROWN, Kevin .... 423-236-2874 424 B kbrown@southern.edu
BROWN, Kevin, A .... 919-866-5475 338 G kabrown@waketech.edu
BROWN, Kevin, H .... 206-239-4500 479 E khbrown@cityu.edu
BROWN, Kevin, J .... 859-858-3511 178 I president@asbury.edu
BROWN, Kim .... 859-985-3912 179 C kimberly_brown@berea.edu
BROWN, Kim, S .... 757-455-3275 477 F kbrown@vwu.edu
BROWN, Kimberley .... 641-673-1182 170 F kimberley.brown@wmpenn.edu
BROWN, Kimberly .... 515-271-1462 164 I kimberly.brown@dmu.edu
BROWN, Kimberly .... 205-726-4582.... 6 E kbrown7@samford.edu
BROWN, Kirby .... 816-584-6308 258 A kirby.brown@park.edu
BROWN, Kristen .... 585-594-6803 310 F brown_kristen@roberts.edu
BROWN, Kristine, A ...... 609-896-5192 281 B kbrown@rider.edu
BROWN, Kyle .... 315-386-7164 320 E brownk@canton.edu
BROWN, Kyle .... 405-945-3252 368 E kyle.j.brown@osuokc.edu
BROWN, Kyris .... 205-366-8817.... 7 A kbrown@stillman.edu
BROWN, Lanette .... 404-413-1515 119 E lanettebrown@gsu.edu
BROWN, Larry .... 804-524-1162 477 B lbrown@vsu.edu
BROWN, Laura .... 847-925-6133 137 H lbrown@harpercollege.edu
BROWN, Laura .... 781-239-3118 214 E lbrown@massbay.edu
BROWN, Laura, C .... 863-667-5041 107 K lcbrown@seu.edu
BROWN, Lawrence .... 714-628-2876.. 36 C
BROWN, LeAnn .... 651-213-4092 236 B ltbrown@hazeldenbettyford.edu
BROWN, Lenice .... 936-261-1068 446 D ldbrown@pvamu.edu
BROWN, JR., Leonard, E .... 240-895-4208 201 E lebrown1@smcm.edu
BROWN, Levy .... 252-492-2061 338 F brownl@vgcc.edu
BROWN, Linda .... 660-359-3948 257 D lbrown@mail.ncmissouri.edu
BROWN, Linda, J .... 218-299-4206 235 E linbrown@cord.edu
BROWN, Lindsey .... 208-885-2020 131 G lindseyb@uidaho.edu
BROWN, Lisa .... 405-682-7896 367 H lbrown@occc.edu
BROWN, Lisa .... 314-918-2537 253 A lbrown@eden.edu
BROWN, Lisa .... 440-366-7559 355 J
BROWN, Lisa, M .... 202-687-6457.. 92 A lbrown@georgetown.edu
BROWN, Lisa, M .... 903-813-2218 430 N lbrown@austincollege.edu
BROWN, Lori, A .... 973-313-6132 283 B lori.brown@shu.edu
BROWN, Lorie .... 973-596-3336 279 F lorie.brown@njit.edu
BROWN, Lucas, A .... 920-993-6027 493 K lucas.a.brown@lawrence.edu
BROWN, Lynne .... 212-998-2350 310 B lynne.brown@nyu.edu
BROWN, II, M. Christopher .... 502-597-6260 182 H president@kysu.edu
BROWN, Madelyn .... 706-649-1883 117 A mnbrown@columbustech.edu
BROWN, Maggie .... 252-527-6223 335 G mlbrown46@lenoircc.edu
BROWN, Mandy .... 641-844-5715 166 K mandy.brown@iavalley.edu
BROWN, Marcia, W ...... 973-353-5541 282 B mwbrown@newark.rutgers.edu
BROWN, Marcus .... 661-654-2713.. 30 E mbrown59@csub.edu
BROWN, Marie .... 470-639-0339 122 D marie.brown@morehouse.edu
BROWN, Mark .... 712-324-5061 168 G mbrown@nwicc.edu
BROWN, Martha .... 806-742-2120 451 B martha.brown@ttu.edu
BROWN, Martha .... 806-742-0012 450 F

BROWN, Mary .... 573-875-7201 251 F
mbrown10@ccis.edu
BROWN, Matthew .... 585-271-3657 313 E
admissions@stbernards.edu
BROWN, Max .... 603-524-3207 272 K
mbrown@ccsnh.edu
BROWN, Melanie, A ..... 904-808-7410 106 C
melaniebrown@sjrstate.edu
BROWN, Melissa .... 412-809-5100 396 H
brown.melissa@ptcollege.edu
BROWN, Melissa, S ..... 909-607-0109.. 37 G
melissa_brown@kgi.edu
BROWN, Merv, R .... 208-496-2010 130 A
brownme@byui.edu
BROWN, Michael .... 406-447-6947 264 C
michael.brown@helenacollege.edu
BROWN, Michael .... 614-891-3200 357 D
BROWN, Michael .... 256-761-6246.... 7 B
mbrown@talladega.edu
BROWN, Michael .... 510-987-9120.. 68 C
michael.brown@ucop.edu
BROWN, Michael .... 937-376-2946 360 D
mbrown@payne.edu
BROWN, Michele .... 847-635-1981 145 G
mbrown@oakton.edu
BROWN, Michelle .... 706-310-6205 126 A
michelle.brown@ung.edu
BROWN, Michelle .... 215-641-6323 390 H
mbrown2@mc3.edu
BROWN, Michelle .... 435-283-7127 461 C
michelle.brown@snow.edu
BROWN, Michelle, L .... 203-837-9400.. 85 B
brownm@wcsu.edu
BROWN, Mike .... 440-375-7060 355 G
mbrown@lec.edu
BROWN, Mike .... 903-463-8772 437 D
mbrown@grayson.edu
BROWN, Mikell .... 804-706-5171 474 I
mbrown@jtcc.edu
BROWN, Monica .... 530-893-7737.. 27 F
brownmo@butte.edu
BROWN, Monica, R ...... 240-567-4341 200 C
monica.brown@montgomerycollege.edu
BROWN, Morgan .... 310-846-2648.. 54 I
mbrown@otis.edu
BROWN, Naima .... 352-395-5648 107 A
naima.brown@sfcollege.edu
BROWN, Nancy .... 801-832-2731 461 G
nbrown@westminstercollege.edu
BROWN, Nancy .... 516-876-3275 319 A
brownn@oldwestbury.edu
BROWN, Narren .... 507-389-7462 241 C
narren.brown@southcentral.edu
BROWN, Natalya .... 541-440-4632 377 C
natalya.brown@umpqua.edu
BROWN, Nicholas .... 303-410-2407.. 82 J
nicholas.brown@spartan.edu
BROWN, Pam .... 843-574-6246 413 B
pam.brown@tridenttech.edu
BROWN, Pamela .... 510-987-9251.. 68 C
pamela.brown@ucop.edu
BROWN, Pamela .... 718-260-5008 295 B
pbrown@citytech.cuny.edu
BROWN, Patrick .... 217-245-3176 138 D
patrick.brown@ic.edu
BROWN, Patrick .... 253-566-6006 485 C
pbrown@tacomacc.edu
BROWN, Patty .... 423-697-2437 424 E
patty.brown@chattanoogastate.edu
BROWN, Paul .... 254-659-7860 437 G
pbrown@hillcollege.edu
BROWN, Peter .... 304-724-5000 487 H
pbrown@cdu.edu
BROWN, Phillip, J .... 410-864-3613 201 F
brownpj@stmarys.edu
BROWN, Phillip, M ...... 618-650-3415 149 F
phbrown@siue.edu
BROWN, R. McKenna ... 804-828-8471 473 F
mbrown@vcu.edu
BROWN, R. Michael ..... 724-357-5924 394 G
rmbrown@iup.edu
BROWN, Rachel .... 901-678-5664 427 D
rbrown33@memphis.edu
BROWN, Rachel, A .... 202-994-6495.. 91 F
rabrown@gwu.edu
BROWN, Ralph .... 303-273-3538.. 78 I
rabrown@mines.edu
BROWN, Randy .... 408-848-4847.. 43 J
rbrown@gavilan.edu
BROWN, Randy .... 517-884-1119 227 D
brownra@uadv.msu.edu

BROWN, Rashayla .... 312-629-6869 148 I
maffai@saic.edu
BROWN, Ray .... 219-464-6896 162 A
ray.brown@valpo.edu
BROWN, Raymond .... 504-520-5439 193 A
rbrown@xula.edu
BROWN, Raymond, A ... 610-527-0200 397 I
bbrown@rosemont.edu
BROWN, Rebecca .... 303-751-8700.. 77 A
brown@bel-rea.com
BROWN, Rebecca .... 850-599-3090 108 I
rebecca.brown@famu.edu
BROWN, Rebecca, L ..... 314-935-4947 262 A
rebeccabrown@wustl.edu
BROWN, Rebekkah, L ... 484-664-3247 391 C
rebekkahbrown@muhlenberg.edu
BROWN, Regena .... 704-687-0030 342 E
rybrown1@uncc.edu
BROWN, Reynolda .... 314-340-3383 253 I
brownre@hssu.edu
BROWN, Richard .... 423-425-4393 428 A
richard-brown@utc.edu
BROWN, Richard, B ...... 801-585-7498 460 E
brown@utah.edu
BROWN, Rick .... 435-586-7700 460 F
BROWN, Ricky .... 252-493-7259 336 H
rbrown@email.pittcc.edu
BROWN, Robert .... 570-321-4250 389 E
brownr@lycoming.edu
BROWN, Robert .... 410-386-8224 197 G
rbrown@carrollcc.edu
BROWN, Robert .... 310-342-5200.. 72 D
BROWN, Robert .... 859-622-1693 180 B
bob.brown@eku.edu
BROWN, Robert, A .... 617-353-2200 207 D
rabrown@bu.edu
BROWN, Robert, L .... 803-981-7375 415 A
rbrown@yorktech.edu
BROWN, Robert, M ...... 251-460-6151.... 8 F
rbrown@southalabama.edu
BROWN, Robin .... 256-395-2211.... 3 G
rbrown@suscc.edu
BROWN, Rod .... 317-921-4384 157 H
rsbrown@ivytech.edu
BROWN, Roger, H .... 617-747-2316 206 E
ootp@berklee.edu
BROWN, Rolanda .... 662-621-4244 245 E
rbrown@coahomacc.edu
BROWN, Ron .... 773-371-5400 133 E
rbrown@ctu.edu
BROWN, Ron .... 254-295-4517 453 E
rbrown@umhb.edu
BROWN, Ronald, H ...... 919-516-4859 340 C
rbrown@st-aug.edu
BROWN, Ronald, T .... 702-895-3693 271 E
ronald.brown@unlv.edu
BROWN, Rosann .... 814-641-3133 386 H
brownr@juniata.edu
BROWN, **III**, Roy .... 206-726-5004 480 C
rbrown@cornish.edu
BROWN, Russ .... 772-462-6004 101 E
rbrown@irsc.edu
BROWN, Ryan .... 415-503-6309.. 60 H
rbrown@sfcm.edu
BROWN, Ryan .... 408-561-6172.. 61 K
ryan.brown@sjeccd.edu
BROWN, Sabrina .... 434-395-2021 469 A
browncs2@longwood.edu
BROWN, Saketta .... 428-274-7643 122 H
sdbrown@oftc.edu
BROWN, Samantha .... 425-352-8514 479 A
sbrown@cascadia.edu
BROWN, Sandra .... 858-534-3526.. 69 D
sandrabrown@ucsd.edu
BROWN, Sandra .... 386-481-2510.. 95 F
browns@cookman.edu
BROWN, Sandra .... 605-668-1555 415 H
sbrown@mtmc.edu
BROWN, Santarvis .... 305-442-9223 103 F
sbrown@mru.edu
BROWN, Sarah .... 918-647-1471 365 H
sbrown@carlalbert.edu
BROWN, Scott, C .... 330-263-2011 351 C
scbrown@wooster.edu
BROWN, Scott, E .... 801-957-2020 461 D
scott.e.brown@slcc.edu
BROWN, Shanita .... 804-342-3812 477 C
BROWN, Shanita, L .... 901-333-5325 426 A
sbrown@southwest.tn.edu
BROWN, Shannon .... 828-726-2288 332 G
sbrown@cccti.edu
BROWN, Shannon .... 267-341-3314 386 A
sbrown10@holyfamily.edu

BROWN, Shannon .... 214-768-4909 444 E
shannonbrown@smu.edu
BROWN, Sharon .... 252-335-0821 333 G
sharon_brown@albemarle.edu
BROWN, Shawn .... 914-606-6434 325 C
shawn.brown@sunywcc.edu
BROWN, Sheila .... 937-376-6349 350 D
sbrown@centralstate.edu
BROWN, Shelly .... 254-968-9083 446 E
sbrown@tarleton.edu
BROWN, Shirl .... 254-710-2000 431 J
shirl_johnson@baylor.edu
BROWN, Shirley .... 615-329-8756 419 K
sbrown@fisk.edu
BROWN, Shondae .... 256-395-2211.... 3 G
sbrown@suscc.edu
BROWN, Simon .... 215-751-8039 382 A
sbrown@ccp.edu
BROWN, Sondra .... 703-891-1787 471 K
dean@standardcollege.edu
BROWN, Stephanie .... 954-262-7456 103 M
browstep@nova.edu
BROWN, Stephanie .... 561-237-7784 102 V
scbrown@lynn.edu
BROWN, Stephen, G ..... 530-221-4275.. 63 G
sbrown@shasta.edu
BROWN, Stephen, R ..... 478-301-2683 121 E
brown_sr@mercer.edu
BROWN, Steve .... 605-677-6703 416 H
steve.brown@usdfoundation.org
BROWN, Steven .... 850-474-3340 110 E
sbrown4@uwf.edu
BROWN, Steven, D .... 906-227-1188 228 F
stebrown@nmu.edu
BROWN, Sue, C .... 309-655-2206 148 E
sue.c.brown@osfhealthcare.org
BROWN, Susan .... 575-646-5858 287 B
susanbro@nmsu.edu
BROWN, Susan .... 956-665-2383 455 D
susan.brown@utrgv.edu
BROWN, Susan, M .... 859-233-8225 184 G
subrown@transy.edu
BROWN, Suzi .... 601-928-8480 247 E
suzana.brown@mgccc.edu
BROWN, Sylvia .... 252-744-6422 341 C
brownsy@ecu.edu
BROWN, T. Rhett .... 704-233-8111 344 G
r.brown@wingate.edu
BROWN, Takeshia .... 912-478-5409 119 C
fbrown@georgiasouthern.edu
BROWN, Tamara .... 940-565-2046 454 A
tamara.brown@unt.edu
BROWN, Tamara, L ...... 936-261-3521 446 D
tlbrown@pvamu.edu
BROWN, Tammy .... 304-384-5358 490 A
tbrown@concord.edu
BROWN, Tanya .... 804-594-1414 474 I
tbrown01@jtcc.edu
BROWN, Tavonda .... 870-743-3000.. 20 C
tbrown@northark.edu
BROWN, Teresa .... 404-225-4700 114 H
tbrown@atlantatech.edu
BROWN, Teresa .... 507-280-2816 240 G
teresa.brown@rctc.edu
BROWN, Terrence .... 901-751-8453 422 E
tbrown@mabts.edu
BROWN, Terry .... 716-673-3335 317 A
terry.brown@fredonia.edu
BROWN, Terry .... 610-683-4120 395 A
tbrown@kutztown.edu
BROWN, Theodore .... 256-726-7070.... 6 C
tbrown@oakwood.edu
BROWN, Thomas, W .... 507-933-7005 235 I
brownie@gustavus.edu
BROWN, Tim .... 843-574-6424 413 B
tim.brown@tridenttech.edu
BROWN, Timothy .... 630-637-5556 144 H
tjbrown@noctrl.edu
BROWN, Timothy, J ..... 704-337-2384 339 G
brownt4@queens.edu
BROWN, Tom .... 352-638-9762.. 95 D
tbrown@beaconcollege.edu
BROWN, Tomeka, K ..... 318-670-9319 190 J
tbrown@susla.edu
BROWN, Tony .... 202-685-2207 503 I
browna@ndu.edu
BROWN, Tracy, H .... 512-471-0000 455 A
tracy.brown@austin.utexas.edu
BROWN, Travis .... 419-372-6067 348 H
brownst@bgsu.edu
BROWN, Travis .... 503-491-7219 374 C
travis.brown@mhcc.edu

BROWN, Trevor, L .... 614-292-4533 358 I
brown.2296@osu.edu
BROWN, Troy .... 310-342-5200.. 72 D
BROWN, Tucker .... 931-221-7725 418 D
brownt@apsu.edu
BROWN, Venessa .... 618-650-5867 149 F
vbrown@siue.edu
BROWN, Veronica .... 334-876-9395.... 2 D
veronica.brown@wccs.edu
BROWN, Victor .... 201-879-7033 275 H
vmbrown@bergen.edu
BROWN, Vintress .... 864-503-5553 414 D
vbrown@uscupstate.edu
BROWN, Wallace .... 912-478-5421 119 C
wbrown@georgiasouthern.edu
BROWN, Wanda .... 336-750-2446 344 B
brownwa@wssu.edu
BROWN, Warren .... 206-934-3601 483 J
warren.brown@seattlecolleges.edu
BROWN, Warren .... 206-934-3601 483 I
warren.brown@seattlecolleges.edu
BROWN, Wilfred, E .... 805-893-4155.. 70 A
willie.brown@auxiliary.ucsb.edu
BROWN, Will .... 478-445-1283 118 C
will.brown@gcsu.edu
BROWN, William .... 301-696-3402 199 B
brownw@hood.edu
BROWN, William .... 775-753-2009 271 B
william.brown@gbcnv.edu
BROWN, William, F ...... 806-834-7548 451 B
william.f.brown@ttu.edu
BROWN, William, T ...... 615-353-3326 425 D
william.brown@nscc.edu
BROWN, Zachariah, D .. 508-565-1058 218 H
zbrown@stonehill.edu
BROWN, Zachary .... 607-431-4547 301 D
brownz@hartwick.edu
BROWN-CORNELIUS,
Denise .... 502-272-8270 179 B
dbrowncornelius@bellarmine.edu
BROWN CORNELIUS,
Lisa .... 216-397-4408 354 I
lmbrown@jcu.edu
BROWN-DOLINSKI,
Trace .... 304-696-3157 490 D
browndolinsk@marshall.edu
BROWN GORDAN,
Loria .... 601-979-2107 246 E
loria.c.brown@jsums.edu
BROWN-JOHNSON,
Leah .... 973-748-9000 276 A
leah_brown@bloomfield.edu
BROWN-LAVEIST,
Cynthia .... 443-885-4720 200 D
cynthia.brownlaveist@morgan.edu
BROWN MARSDEN,
Margaret .... 940-397-4253 440 F
margaret.brownmarsden@msutexas.edu
BROWN-MCCLURE,
Fran 'Cee .... 518-388-6116 323 G
BROWN MCCLURE,
Fran'Cee .... 404-270-5133 125 B
fbrownmc@spelman.edu
BROWN-NAGIN,
Tomiko .... 617-495-8602 210 B
tbrownnagin@radcliffe.harvard.edu
BROWN-WILLIAMS,
Janice, L .... 248-233-2712 229 A
jlbrownw@oaklandcc.edu
BROWN-WRIGHT,
Lynda .... 601-979-2943 246 E
lynda.brownwright@jsums.edu
BROWN WYATT, Donna 660-626-2790 250 A
dbrown@atsu.edu
BROWN YOUNG,
Danita .... 217-300-1300 151 D
dbyoung@illinois.edu
BROWNAWELL,
Carolyn .... 303-556-2400.. 83 C
carolyn.brownawell@ucdenver.edu
BROWNE, Brian .... 718-990-2762 314 B
browneb@stjohns.edu
BROWNE, Doug .... 620-417-1201 176 K
doug.browne@sccc.edu
BROWNE, Jacob .... 727-864-8846.. 97 J
brownejh@eckerd.edu
BROWNE, Janelle .... 214-648-7101 457 B
janelle.browne@utsouthwestern.edu
BROWNE, Joan, M .... 202-806-7513.. 92 B
jmbrowne@howard.edu
BROWNE, Kathleen .... 740-587-8646 352 G
brownek@denison.edu

BRUNO, Dave 615-966-7133 421 D
dave.bruno@lipscomb.edu
BRUNO, Gene 865-524-8079 420 E
gene.bruno@huhs.edu
BRUNO, Joanne, Z 570-422-3539 394 E
provost@esu.edu
BRUNO, Laura 646-664-3620 292 K
laura.bruno@cuny.edu
BRUNO, Michael 808-956-8447 128 F
mbruno2@hawaii.edu
BRUNO, Nick, J 318-342-1010 192 F
bruno@ulm.edu
BRUNO, SC, Teresa 973-957-0188 275 C
academicdean@acs350.org
BRUNOLD, Timothy 213-740-6753 72 B
admdean@usc.edu
BRUNS, Clara 802-322-1603 462 C
clara.bruns@goddard.edu
BRUNS, David 419-995-8177 354 H
bruns.d@rhodesstate.edu
BRUNS, Lisa 631-420-2245 321 B
lisa.bruns@farmingdale.edu
BRUNS, Michelle 605-867-5856 416 B
mbruns@olc.edu
BRUNSON, Rod 973-353-5030 282 B
rod.brunson@rutgers.edu
BRUNSON, Teesa 803-376-5724 406 F
tbrunson@allenuniversity.edu
BRUNSTING, Diane 708-293-4918 150 F
diane.brunsting@trnty.edu
BRUNSWICK, Carl 954-492-5353 96 H
cbrunswick@citycollege.edu
BRUNT, Bonnie 509-533-3339 480 B
bonnie.brunt@sfcc.spokane.edu
BRUNTMYER, Eric, I 325-670-1227 437 F
ebruntmyer@hsutx.edu
BRUSATI, Gerianne 845-341-4020 311 C
gerianne.brusati@sunyorange.edu
BRUSCATO, Brandon 318-342-5314 192 F
bruscato@ulm.edu
BRUSH, Shannon 972-721-5203 452 D
sbrush@udallas.edu
BRUSTEIN, William 304-293-9298 491 C
william.brustein@mail.wvu.edu
BRUSTKERN, Kari 406-447-5422 263 C
kbrustkern@carroll.edu
BRUSUELAS-JAMES,
Rebecca 949-824-7092 68 G
rbrusuel@uci.edu
BRUTON, Muniece 323-241-5338 49 D
brutonmr@lasc.edu
BRUTSMAN, Lauren 732-224-2392 276 B
lbrutsman@brookdalecc.edu
BRUXVOORT, Debra 641-628-7671 163 E
bruxvoortb@central.edu
BRUXVOORT, Diane 940-565-3025 454 A
diane.bruxvoort@unt.edu
BRY, Jay 978-665-3131 212 C
jbry@fitchburgstate.edu
BRYAN, Angela 850-474-2894 110 E
abryan@uwf.edu
BRYAN, Burcu 360-438-4584 483 H
bbryan@stmartin.edu
BRYAN, Christine 978-934-3936 211 G
christine_bryan@uml.edu
BRYAN, Christopher 206-239-4500 479 E
cbryan@cityu.edu
BRYAN, Dave 718-951-5352 293 C
dbryan@brooklyn.cuny.edu
BRYAN, Karla 903-675-6229 452 B
kbryan@tvcc.edu
BRYAN, Mitzi 718-636-3430 311 J
mbryan@pratt.edu
BRYAN, Neva 276-328-0126 473 B
njd8r@virginia.edu
BRYAN, JR.,
Norman, B 864-833-8757 411 I
nbbryan@presby.edu
BRYAN, Paul 215-893-5252 382 B
paul.bryan@curtis.edu
BRYAN, Robert (Bob) 216-987-4684 351 G
bob.bryan@tri-c.edu
BRYAN, Susan 417-865-2815 253 B
bryans@evangel.edu
BRYAN, Terry 832-252-4676 433 D
terry.bryan@cbshouston.edu
BRYAN, Timothy, A 330-471-8539 355 L
tbryan@malone.edu
BRYAN, Warren, J 540-464-7287 476 G
bbryan@vmiaa.org
BRYAN, William, B 804-289-8438 472 L
wbryan@richmond.edu

BRYAN WILLIAMS,
Pamela 314-529-9614 254 H
pbryanwilliams@maryville.edu
BRYANT, Amanda 252-222-6225 333 A
bryanta@carteret.edu
BRYANT, Amie 970-247-7212 79 I
arbryant@fortlewis.edu
BRYANT, Angela, V 229-928-1378 119 D
angela.bryant@gsw.edu
BRYANT, Angie 615-460-6407 418 F
angie.bryant@belmont.edu
BRYANT, Brigette 215-572-2900 379 A
bryantb@arcadia.edu
BRYANT, Bruce 870-236-6901 19 A
bbryant@crc.edu
BRYANT, Bryan 303-914-6346 82 C
bryan.bryant@rrcc.edu
BRYANT, Chip 865-974-9557 427 G
bryant00@utk.edu
BRYANT, Chris 931-393-1663 425 C
cbryant@mscc.edu
BRYANT, Christopher 434-832-7293 474 C
bryantc@centralvirginia.edu
BRYANT, Clint 706-737-1626 115 A
cbryant1@augusta.edu
BRYANT, Cody 931-372-3292 426 E
cdbryant@tntech.edu
BRYANT, Courtney 501-852-0804 23 H
cbryant13@uca.edu
BRYANT, Courtney 509-527-2613 485 H
courtney.bryant@wallawalla.edu
BRYANT, Cynthia, D 225-771-3631 190 H
cynthia_bryant@subr.edu
BRYANT, Don 910-521-6648 343 B
don.bryant@uncp.edu
BRYANT, Elisa 417-625-3039 256 D
bryant-e@mssu.edu
BRYANT, Essie, L 662-254-3440 248 B
elbryant@mvsu.edu
BRYANT, Felicia 856-227-7200 276 E
fbryant@camdencc.edu
BRYANT, Gerard 646-781-5625 294 D
gwbryant@jjay.cuny.edu
BRYANT, Jack 405-422-1260 369 E
jack.bryant@redlandscc.edu
BRYANT, III, James, S 803-535-1330 411 G
bryantj@octech.edu
BRYANT, Jody 864-231-2000 406 G
jbryant@andersonuniversity.edu
BRYANT, John 309-556-3449 139 G
jbryant@iwu.edu
BRYANT, Kelly 704-314-4920 330 A
kbryant@hoodseminary.edu
BRYANT, Kimberly 336-734-7236 334 E
kbryant@forsythtech.edu
BRYANT, III, Lewis 434-832-7615 474 C
bryantl@centralvirginia.edu
BRYANT, Lora, R 304-457-6354 487 B
bryantlr@ab.edu
BRYANT, Luke 214-887-3904 436 B
lbryant@dts.edu
BRYANT, Marcean 510-522-7221 56 F
mbryant@peralta.edu
BRYANT, Matthew 504-816-8077 190 A
internetdeanasst@nobts.edu
BRYANT, Michael 843-863-7518 407 E
mbryant@csuniv.edu
BRYANT, Morgan 601-925-3354 247 C
mbryant@mc.edu
BRYANT, Nate 978-542-6134 213 C
nate.bryant@salemstate.edu
BRYANT, Pam 325-649-8401 438 D
pbryant@hputx.edu
BRYANT, Paul 318-274-2374 191 E
bryantp@gram.edu
BRYANT, Paul 606-248-2001 182 E
pbryant0006@kctcs.edu
BRYANT, Rachel 415-575-6100 29 B
rbryant@ciis.edu
BRYANT, Rick 352-294-0963 109 F
rjbryant@ufl.edu
BRYANT, Robbie 417-328-1550 259 L
rbryant@sbuniv.edu
BRYANT, Robert, G 540-828-5749 465 D
rbryant@bridgewater.edu
BRYANT, Ronnie 910-755-7483 332 F
bryantr@brunswickcc.edu
BRYANT, Rosalynn 314-362-9253 253 E
rosalynn.bryant@bjc.org
BRYANT, Scott 903-923-2069 436 D
sbryant@etbu.edu
BRYANT, Sheila, M 931-221-7178 418 D
bryantsm@apsu.edu

BRYANT, Stephan 712-325-3310 167 B
sbryant@iwcc.edu
BRYANT, Steven, P 734-487-6790 223 H
sbryan16@emich.edu
BRYANT, Susan 334-214-4847 1 H
susan.bryant@cv.edu
BRYANT, Thomas 203-596-5609 87 F
tbryant@post.edu
BRYANT, Ulyssess 912-358-3009 123 H
bryantu@savannahstate.edu
BRYANT, Vickie 817-461-8741 430 H
vbryant@abu.edu
BRYANT, Wayne, H 318-670-9230 190 J
wbryant@ssla.edu
BRYANT, Wilber 251-662-5363 1 E
wbryant@bishop.edu
BRYANT-FRIEDRICH,
Amanda 419-530-4968 363 E
amanda.bryant-friedrich@utoledo.edu
BRYANT HOWE,
Marcio 501-812-2342 23 B
mbryanthowe@uaptc.edu
BRYANT-SHANKS,
Cheryl 336-334-4822 335 A
cmbryantshanks@gtcc.edu
BRYARS, Beth 251-580-2227 1 I
beth.bryars@coastalalabama.edu
BRYCE, Jeanne 928-428-8261 12 E
jeanne.bryce@eac.edu
BRYCH, Jarda 415-581-8902 68 F
brychj@uchastings.edu
BRYDE, Beverly 610-902-8331 380 C
beverly.reilly.bryde@cabrini.edu
BRYDEN, Alexander 518-327-6291 311 G
abryden@paulsmiths.edu
BRYDEN, David, L 336-841-9101 329 G
dbryden@highpoint.edu
BRYDON, Lucinda, C 607-746-4603 320 G
brydonlm@delhi.edu
BRYENTON, John 270-686-4615 182 B
john.bryenton@kctcs.edu
BRYMER, Allison 205-726-2762 6 E
abrymer@samford.edu
BRYNE, Dara 212-484-1347 294 D
dbyrne@jjay.cuny.edu
BRYS-WILSON, Jessica 252-985-5186 339 D
jbrys-wilson@ncwc.edu
BRYSON, Allison 541-880-2202 373 E
bryson@klamathcc.edu
BRYSON, Cynthia 713-771-5336 120 H
zbertrm@ict.edu
BRYSON, Matthew, S 601-923-1600 248 F
mbryant@rts.edu
BRYSON, Terri 931-393-1688 425 C
tbryson@mscc.edu
BRYSON, Todd 618-453-1186 149 E
tsb32@siu.edu
BRYSON, Tony 480-461-7284 13 D
tony.bryson@mesacc.edu
BRYSON, Tonya, K 864-597-4000 414 H
BRZEZINSKI, Karen 715-422-5325 500 A
karen.brzezinski@mstc.edu
BRZORAD, John 828-328-7606 330 F
john.brzorad@lr.edu
BRZOZOWSKI, Eileen 321-433-5493 97 I
brzozowskie@easternflorida.edu
BRZYCKI, Shelly 847-578-8355 147 I
shelly.brzycki@rosalindfranklin.edu
BRZYTWA, MaryClare 415-503-6263 60 H
mcbrzytwa@sfcm.edu
BSULLAK, Nik 207-699-5060 194 D
nbsullak@meca.edu
BUBB, David 772-546-5534 101 B
davidbubb@hsbc.edu
BUBB, Kevin 517-483-9764 226 F
bubbk@lcc.edu
BUBB, Terry 615-230-3398 426 B
terry.bubb@volstate.edu
BUBBLE, Tara 315-228-6581 296 F
tbubble@colgate.edu
BUBNOVA, Elena 775-673-8240 271 D
ebubnova@tmcc.edu
BUBOLTZ, Karen 218-846-3714 239 B
karen.buboltz@minnesota.edu
BUCALOS, Anne 502-272-8405 179 B
abucalos@bellarmine.edu
BUCARO, S. Ted 937-229-4122 362 G
sbucaro1@udayton.edu
BUCCARELLI, Sarah 212-355-1501 292 J
sbuccarelli@christies.edu
BUCCIARELLI, Roseann 732-906-4681 279 A
rbucciarelli@middlesexcc.edu
BUCCILLA, Jerry 419-559-2164 361 I
jbuccil01@terra.edu

BUCCINO, Mike 410-455-2766 202 E
mbuccino@umbc.edu
BUCELLO, Glenn, R 716-878-4128 318 C
bucellgr@buffalostate.edu
BUCHA, Edward 724-738-9000 395 F
edward.bucha@sru.edu
BUCHAN, Kristina 208-535-5477 130 C
kristina.buchan@cei.edu
BUCHANAN, Amanda 828-766-1224 336 A
albuchanan@mayland.edu
BUCHANAN, April 864-455-4145 414 A
abuchanan@ghs.org
BUCHANAN, Barbara 336-322-2106 336 G
barbara.buchanan@piedmontcc.edu
BUCHANAN, Connie 830-703-1555 444 G
cwbuchanan@swtjc.edu
BUCHANAN, David 701-231-7426 345 G
david.s.buchanan@ndsu.edu
BUCHANAN, Eddie 828-766-1227 336 A
ebuchanan@mayland.edu
BUCHANAN, Kelly 619-201-8702 60 A
kelly.buchanan@sdcc.edu
BUCHANAN, Ken 336-917-5472 340 D
ken.buchanan@salem.edu
BUCHANAN, Lauren, A 724-772-5520 380 A
lauren.buchanan@bc3.edu
BUCHANAN, Linda, R 229-732-5926 114 B
lindabuchanan@andrewcollege.edu
BUCHANAN, Pamela 828-227-7640 344 A
pbuchanan@wcu.edu
BUCHANAN, Russell 610-292-9852 397 D
rbuchanan@reseminary.edu
BUCHANAN, Sally 916-608-6643 50 H
howards@flc.losrios.edu
BUCHANAN,
Thomas, R 410-293-1000 504 I
BUCHANAN, Trey 512-313-3000 434 E
trey.buchanan@concordia.edu
BUCHANAN, Wayne 561-803-2000 104 C
wayne_buchanan@pba.edu
BUCHBAUER, Victoria 717-477-1484 395 E
vmbuchbauer@ship.edu
BUCHE, Nathan 620-665-3569 174 B
buchen@hutchcc.edu
BUCHELE, Ann 541-917-4211 374 A
buchela@linnbenton.edu
BUCHELI, Hernan 650-508-3500 54 D
hbucheli@ndnu.edu
BUCHER, Denise 303-404-5481 79 J
denise.bucher@frontrange.edu
BUCHER, Jacob 708-524-6694 136 C
jbucher@dom.edu
BUCHER, Jennifer 570-372-4157 399 C
bucherjennifer@susqu.edu
BUCHER, Karen, H 540-665-4621 471 E
kbucher@su.edu
BUCHER, Mary 864-503-5197 414 D
mbucher@uscupstate.edu
BUCHER, Oskar 541-684-7273 374 G
obucher@nwcu.edu
BUCHHEIT, Rudolph 859-257-1687 185 B
rudolph.buchheit@uky.edu
BUCHHOLZ, Cindy 361-582-2587 457 E
cindy.buchholz@victoriacollege.edu
BUCHHOLZ, Richard 405-422-6204 369 E
richard.buchholz@redlandscc.edu
BUCHHOLZ, Ron 262-472-1498 498 C
buchholr@uww.edu
BUCHKO, Lindsay 202-448-7037 91 E
lindsay.buchko@gallaudet.edu
BUCHMAN, Ashley 870-512-7812 18 B
ashley_buchman@asun.edu
BUCHMAN, Lorne, M 626-396-2301 26 E
president@artcenter.edu
BUCHMANN, Teresa 253-833-9111 481 F
tbuchmann@greenriver.edu
BUCHTERKIRCHEN,
Rebekah 503-517-1975 378 A
rbuchterkirchen@westsernseminary.edu
BUCHWALD, Adam 503-768-7227 373 G
buchwald@lclark.edu
BUCHWALD, Carrie 847-574-5164 141 C
cbuchwald@lfgsm.edu
BUCHWALD, Rosalinda 626-914-8897 36 K
rbuchwald@citruscollege.edu
BUCHWALD, Staci 541-552-6998 376 E
buchwalds@sou.edu
BUCHWALDER,
Mary, P 937-229-3131 362 G
mbuchwalder1@udayton.edu
BUCK, Charles 208-292-1737 131 G
buck@uidaho.edu

BUCK, James, E ... 937-393-3431 361 B jbuck@sscc.edu
BUCK, Jason ... 603-428-2241 273 H jbuck@nec.edu
BUCK, John ... 314-968-6980 262 C
BUCK, Joseph, E ... 610-758-4711 388 J job316@lehigh.edu
BUCK, Karen ... 979-209-7280 432 C karenbuck@blinn.edu
BUCK, Katherine ... 973-290-4203 277 A kbuck@cse.edu
BUCK, Kevan, C ... 918-631-3245 371 E kevan-buck@utulsa.edu
BUCK, Leah ... 207-768-2768 194 J lbuck@nmcc.edu
BUCK, Mark ... 888-556-8226 133 F
BUCK, Sharon ... 360-417-6235 483 B sbuck@pencol.edu
BUCK, Teresa ... 254-295-4640 453 E tbuck@umhb.edu
BUCKALEW, Danielle ... 205-652-3852 ... 9 A bdbuckalew@uwa.edu
BUCKEL, Maria ... 314-889-4533 253 C mbuckel@fontbonne.edu
BUCKELS, Carol ... 386-738-6686 111 A cbuckels@stetson.edu
BUCKENMEYER, Janet ... 812-237-2919 155 G janet.buckenmeyer@indstate.edu
BUCKHAULTS, Tex ... 806-874-3571 433 B tex.buckhaults@clarendoncollege.edu
BUCKHAULTS, Tresea, L ... 318-342-5247 192 F buckhaults@ulm.edu
BUCKHEISTER, Lori ... 678-407-5362 118 D lbuckheister@ggc.edu
BUCKINGHAM, Bob, S . 304-457-6588 487 B buckinghamrs@ab.edu
BUCKINGHAM, David ... 302-736-2529.. 90 G david.buckingham@wesley.edu
BUCKINGHAM, Judith, P ... 936-468-4048 445 F jpbuckingham@sfasu.edu
BUCKINGHAM, Richard 617-573-8605 219 A rbuckingham@suffolk.edu
BUCKINGHAM, Stacy ... 618-985-3741 139 I stacybuckingham@jalc.edu
BUCKIUS, Danielle ... 614-947-6554 353 C danielle.buckius@franklin.edu
BUCKLAND, Steve ... 517-264-3109 220 F sbuckland@adrian.edu
BUCKLER, C. Adam ... 317-896-9324 160 I abuckler@ubca.org
BUCKLES, Beverly, J ... 909-558-4528.. 48 C bbuckles@llu.edu
BUCKLES, Dale ... 270-706-8431 181 A dale.buckles@kctcs.edu
BUCKLES, Jennifer ... 423-425-4677 428 A jennifer-buckles@utc.edu
BUCKLES, Michael ... 337-475-5192 192 A mbuckles@mcneese.edu
BUCKLESS, Frank ... 919-515-5560 342 B buckless@ncsu.edu
BUCKLEW, Andrea, J ... 304-457-6438 487 B bucklewaj@ab.edu
BUCKLEW, Kathy ... 863-297-1016 105 A kbucklew@polk.edu
BUCKLEY, Anne ... 205-934-9518 ... 8 A abuckley@uab.edu
BUCKLEY, Bri ... 801-832-2529 461 G bbuckley@westminstercollege.edu
BUCKLEY, Cynthia, S ... 405-466-3204 366 F cynthia.buckley@langston.edu
BUCKLEY, David ... 530-898-6411.. 31 A dbuckley@csuchico.edu
BUCKLEY, Dawn ... 228-897-3835 247 E dawn.buckley@mgccc.edu
BUCKLEY, Emily ... 913-621-8731 172 K ebuckley@donnelly.edu
BUCKLEY, Erin ... 610-519-8881 402 D erin.buckley@villanova.edu
BUCKLEY, Gerard ... 315-781-3701 302 A buckley@hws.edu
BUCKLEY, Gerard, J ... 585-475-6317 313 A gbuckley@ntid.rit.edu
BUCKLEY, Irene ... 914-674-7308 306 F ibuckley@mercy.edu
BUCKLEY, Jennifer ... 630-844-6155 132 D jbuckley@aurora.edu
BUCKLEY, Jerry, L ... 559-638-0300.. 66 F jerry.buckley@reedleycollege.edu
BUCKLEY, John, M ... 302-857-1200.. 90 D john.buckley@dtcc.edu
BUCKLEY, John, W ... 718-817-4000 300 E jbuckley@fordham.edu
BUCKLEY, Larry ... 805-652-5509.. 72 G
BUCKLEY, Mary ... 314-966-3000 255 A maryb@metrobusinesscollege.edu
BUCKLEY, Merdis ... 615-329-8712 419 K mbuckley@fisk.edu
BUCKLEY, Neil ... 781-239-3193 214 E nbuckley@massbay.edu
BUCKLEY, Noah ... 541-737-4411 375 D osuadmit@oregonstate.edu
BUCKLEY, Patricia ... 518-458-5444 296 H buckleyp@strose.edu
BUCKLEY, Paul ... 719-389-6338.. 77 H paul.buckley@coloradocollege.edu
BUCKLEY, Peter ... 212-353-4274 297 E buckley@cooper.edu
BUCKLEY, Peter, F ... 804-828-9788 473 F peter.buckley@vcuhealth.org
BUCKLEY, Sally ... 508-286-3857 220 A buckley_sally@wheatoncollege.edu
BUCKLEY, Tera ... 701-777-4941 345 C tera.buckley@und.edu
BUCKLEY, Toni ... 413-236-3075 213 F tbuckley@berkshirecc.edu
BUCKLIN, Carolyn ... 515-643-6744 168 A cbucklin@mercydesmoines.org
BUCKMAN, Cathy, M ... 574-520-4451 157 A cmbuckma@iusb.edu
BUCKMAN, Michael, R . 724-458-3355 385 C mrbuckman@gcc.edu
BUCKMAN, Ty ... 540-887-7030 469 B tbuckman@marybaldwin.edu
BUCKMASTER, Emily ... 417-873-7257 252 F ebuckmaster@drury.edu
BUCKNER, Edmond ... 601-877-6137 244 H ebuckner@alcorn.edu
BUCKNER, Forrest ... 509-777-4506 486 I fbuckner@whitworth.edu
BUCKNER, Jeremy ... 865-471-3219 419 A jbuckner@cn.edu
BUCKNER, Melody, J ... 520-626-9484.. 16 G mbuckner@email.arizona.edu
BUCKNER, Nichole ... 828-689-1103 331 A nbuckner@mhu.edu
BUCKNER, R. Ty ... 336-316-2248 329 E rbuckner@guilford.edu
BUCKNER, S. Jamila ... 415-442-7079.. 44 D sjbuckner@ggu.edu
BUCKNER, Terry ... 859-246-6397 180 K terry.buckner@kctcs.edu
BUCKO, Kate ... 901-722-3311 424 C kbucko@sco.edu
BUCKOVICH, John ... 912-525-5000 123 G jbuckovi@scad.edu
BUCKOVICH, Lucas ... 912-525-5000 123 G lbuckovi@scad.edu
BUCKRIDGE, Brett ... 610-902-8781 380 C beb99@cabrini.edu
BUCKSER, Andrew, S ... 518-564-3150 319 C abuck005@plattsburgh.edu
BUCKSON, Ryan ... 803-750-2500.. 92 G
BUCKWALTER, John, B . 785-532-5500 174 G jbb3@ksu.edu
BUCKWALTER, Kristine . 828-669-8012 331 J kristine.buckwalter@montreat.edu
BUCKWALTER, Laura ... 828-669-8012 331 J laura.buckwalter@montreat.edu
BUCY, Brandon, R ... 540-458-8651 478 A bucyb@wlu.edu
BUCZYNSKI, Chris ... 313-845-9615 224 G cbuczynski@hfcc.edu
BUDDE, Bruce ... 309-694-5477 138 C bbudde@icc.edu
BUDDE, Jill ... 641-683-5165 166 C jill.budde@indianhills.edu
BUDDE, Mitzi, J ... 703-370-6600 470 B
BUDDEN, LaNae, R ... 803-786-3856 408 F lrbriggs@columbiasc.edu
BUDDIE, Mike ... 845-938-3701 504 H
BUDDO, Christopher ... 252-328-1283 341 C buddoj@ecu.edu
BUDELL, Andrew ... 615-343-3896 428 D andrew.m.budell@vanderbilt.edu
BUDESKI, Brittany ... 406-791-5207 265 H brittany.budeski@uprovidence.edu
BUDINE, Julie ... 217-228-5432 146 F hendrju@quincy.edu
BUDNIK, Lindsay ... 802-485-2824 463 A lbudnik@norwich.edu
BUDNOVITCH, Keri ... 848-445-1762 282 A kbudnov@oit.rutgers.edu
BUDNY, Jill ... 724-925-4185 403 A budnyj@westmoreland.edu
BUDNY, Steve ... 724-925-4085 403 A budnys@westmoreland.edu
BUDZBAN, Gregory ... 618-650-5047 149 F gbudzba@siue.edu
BUDZIAK, Chase ... 815-825-1708 140 F cbudziak@kish.edu
BUDZILOWICZ, Mary ... 610-902-8352 380 C mary.m.budzilowicz@cabrini.edu
BUDZYNSKI, John ... 312-949-7020 138 E jbudzynski@ico.edu
BUECHELE, Angela, K ... 937-229-2941 362 G abuechele1@udayton.edu
BUECHELE, Thomas ... 312-899-7420 148 I tbuechele@saic.edu
BUECHER, Eileen, C ... 805-756-5726.. 30 C ebuecher@calpoly.edu
BUECHNER, Marybeth ... 916-558-2512.. 50 I buechnm@scc.losrios.edu
BUEHLER, Julie ... 585-245-5601 318 E buehler@geneseo.edu
BUEHLER, Lesley ... 510-742-3126.. 54 F lbuehler@ohlone.edu
BUEHRER, Anna ... 309-672-5513 143 D abuehrer@methodistcol.edu
BUEHRER, Danielle ... 470-578-4426 120 L dbuehrer@kennesaw.edu
BUEL, Kevin, A ... 845-675-4597 310 G kevin.buel@nyack.edu
BUELL, Denise ... 413-597-4351 220 C dbuell@williams.edu
BUELL, Katie ... 630-829-6128 132 E kbuell@ben.edu
BUELL, Lige ... 606-589-3040 182 E e.buell@kctcs.edu
BUENAVENTURA, Lisa .. 716-375-2388 313 F lbuenave@sbu.edu
BUENTELLO, Gracy ... 903-566-7480 456 A gbuentello@uttyler.edu
BUERGER, Paula ... 251-460-6641 ... 8 F pbuerger@southalabama.edu
BUERMANN, Sharon ... 218-935-0417 244 G sharon.buermann@wetcc.edu
BUERSTER, Tara ... 618-393-2982 138 F buerstert@iecc.edu
BUETTNER, John ... 443-352-4494 201 H jbuettner@stevenson.edu
BUETTNER, Rita ... 410-617-2146 199 F rfbuettner@loyola.edu
BUFANO, Suzanne ... 843-953-6799 407 F suzanne.bufano@citadel.edu
BUFF, Sam ... 704-825-6260 334 F buff.sam@gaston.edu
BUFF, Stacy ... 828-652-0663 336 B stacybuff@mcdowelltech.edu
BUFFAMANTI, Sara ... 646-825-4610 309 D sbuffamanti@nycda.edu
BUFFINGTON, Heidi ... 314-977-2500 259 H
BUFFINGTON, James ... 714-437-9697.. 38 A
BUFFONE, Nancy ... 413-577-1101 211 D buffone@admin.umass.edu
BUFFUM, Don ... 662-325-2861 247 F dbuffum@procurement.msstate.edu
BUGADO, Lai Sha ... 808-932-7365 128 E sdelo@hawaii.edu
BUGAIGHIS, Elizabeth .. 610-332-6272 391 F ebugaighis@northampton.edu
BUGAJSKI, Kenneth, A . 260-399-7700 161 D kbugajski@sf.edu
BUGAJSKI, OFS, Trish, J ... 260-399-7700 161 D tbugajski@sf.edu
BUGG, Gary, D ... 859-238-5535 179 F gary.bugg@centre.edu
BUGGLIN, Tracy, F ... 740-826-8142 357 C tbugglin@muskingum.edu
BUGGS, Richard ... 415-575-6116.. 29 B rbuggs@ciis.edu
BUGLIONE, Suzanne ... 508-678-2811 213 G suzanne.buglione@bristolcc.edu
BUGOS, Michelle ... 309-694-5422 138 C michelle.bugos@icc.edu
BUHL, Patrick ... 952-358-8595 239 F patrick.buhl@normandale.edu
BUHL, Patti ... 918-444-2170 367 A buhl@nsuok.edu
BUHLER, Doug ... 517-355-0123 227 D buhler@anr.msu.edu
BUHLIG, Gretchen, E ... 480-965-5769.. 10 I gretchen.buhlig@asu.edu
BUHR, Brian ... 612-625-4772 243 E bbuhr@umn.edu
BUHR, Connie ... 319-296-4281 166 B connie.buhr@hawkeyecollege.edu
BUHR, Heather ... 812-866-7097 155 C buhr@hanover.edu
BUHR, Moira ... 413-528-7297 205 F finaid@simons-rock.edu
BUHRANDT, Jeff ... 608-262-1312 496 B jbuhrandt@uwsa.edu
BUHRMASTER, John ... 305-899-3336.. 95 C jbuhrmaster@barry.edu
BUHROW, William, C ... 503-554-2340 373 C bbuhrow@georgefox.edu
BUI, Derek ... 714-241-6594.. 38 C vbui34@coastline.edu
BUI, Tami ... 657-278-5403.. 31 E tbui@fullerton.edu
BUISMAN, Kevin ... 507-389-6111 239 C kevin.buisman@mnsu.edu
BUITER, Mike ... 864-242-5100 407 B
BUJAK, Jeanette, K ... 704-233-8149 344 G jbujak@wingate.edu
BUKER, Jennifer ... 807-859-1319 195 G pr@thomas.edu
BUKOWSKI, Bruce, J ... 410-293-2934 504 I bukowski@usna.edu
BUKOWSKI, Mark ... 239-489-9067 100 A mbukowski@fsw.edu
BUKOWSKI, Tamzin ... 320-762-4415 237 B tamzinb@alextech.edu
BULCOCK, Jennifer ... 610-902-8297 380 C jennifer.bulcock@cabrini.edu
BULEY, Paula Marie ... 603-897-8202 274 B pbuley@rivier.edu
BULGER, Stepahnie ... 619-388-6965.. 60 B sbulger@sdccd.edu
BULITTA, Sue ... 309-694-5522 138 C sue.bulitta@icc.edu
BULL, Bernard ... 802-322-1600 462 C presidents.office@goddard.edu
BULL, Kam ... 530-895-2376.. 27 F bullka@butte.edu
BULL, Prince ... 704-406-4402 329 A pbull@gardner-webb.edu
BULLARD, Anthony ... 662-685-4771 245 D abullard@bmc.edu
BULLARD, Cora ... 910-521-6219 343 B cora.bullard@uncp.edu
BULLARD, Eric, A ... 323-343-4907.. 32 A ebullard@calstatela.edu
BULLARD, Jayne ... 417-269-3473 252 C jayne.bullard@coxcollege.edu
BULLARD, Roland ... 904-766-6762 100 B roland.bullard@fscj.edu
BULLARD, Roland ... 504-816-4916 186 D rbullard@dillard.edu
BULLARD, Scott, W ... 704-463-3030 339 E scott.bullard@pfeiffer.edu
BULLARD, Steven, H ... 936-468-2707 445 F bullardsh@sfasu.edu
BULLEN, James ... 305-821-3333.. 99 E jbullen@fnu.edu
BULLER, Pierce ... 717-358-5963 384 D pierce.buller@fandm.edu
BULLINGHAM, Bree ... 212-517-0532 306 A bbullingham@mmm.edu
BULLINGTON, Jeffrey ... 719-587-7820.. 76 F jsbullington@adams.edu
BULLINS, Chris ... 419-372-2343 348 H chrishb@bgsu.edu
BULLINS, David ... 704-978-5446 336 C dbullins@mitchellcc.edu
BULLOCK, Ann ... 336-278-5900 328 K abullock9@elon.edu
BULLOCK, Brian ... 610-519-4070 402 D brian.bullock@villanova.edu
BULLOCK, Casey, D ... 801-626-6750 461 B caseybullock@weber.edu
BULLOCK, Damay, J ... 757-569-6704 475 E dbullock@pdc.edu
BULLOCK, Doris ... 919-719-1998 340 E dbullock@shawu.edu
BULLOCK, Doug ... 435-797-1812 460 H doug.bullock@usu.edu
BULLOCK, James ... 704-337-2217 339 G bullockj@queens.edu
BULLOCK, James ... 949-824-7727.. 68 G bullock@uci.edu
BULLOCK, Jeffrey, F ... 563-589-3224 169 I jbullock@dbq.edu
BULLOCK, John ... 802-440-4406 462 A jbullock@bennington.edu
BULLOCK, Josh ... 217-234-5222 141 D jbullock@lakeland.cc.il.us

BULLOCK, Kelly .... 602-386-4104.. 10 E
kelly.bullock@arizonachristian.edu
BULLOCK, Quintin, B .... 412-237-4413 381 G
brichardson@ccac.edu
BULLS, Derald .... 903-785-7661 441 G
dbulls@parisjc.edu
BULLUCK, Bruce .... 256-551-5210.... 2 E
bruce.bulluck@drakestate.edu
BULLUCK, Travis .... 828-227-7733 344 A
tlbulluck@email.wcu.edu
BULLWINKEL,
Michelle, L .... 727-816-3212 104 F
bullwim@phsc.edu
BULMER, Sandra .... 203-392-6993.. 85 A
bulmers1@southernct.edu
BULZONI, Donna, R ..... 570-422-3117 394 E
dbulzoni@esu.edu
BUMANN, Susan .... 218-879-0808 238 A
sbumann@fdltcc.edu
BUMBA, Maureen .... 704-330-6729 333 D
maureen.bumba@cpcc.edu
BUMGARDNER,
Lydia, R .... 212-870-1233 310 A
registrarlb@nyts.edu
BUMGARNER, Brittany .. 704-233-8303 344 G
b.bumgarner@wingate.edu
BUMGARNER, Jennifer . 252-514-6715 333 H
bumgarnerj@cravencc.edu
BUMILLER, Taylor .... 636-327-4645 255 L
taylorbumiller@gmail.com
BUMPERS, Claude .... 251-665-4139.... 1 E
cbumpers@bishop.edu
BUMPOUS, Debbi .... 605-626-2283 417 A
debbi.bumpous@northern.edu
BUMPUS, Danielle .... 508-830-5037 213 B
dbumpus@maritime.edu
BUMPUS, Rexann .... 931-393-1938 425 C
rbumpus@mscc.edu
BUNCE, Heather .... 517-321-0242 224 F
hbunce@glcc.edu
BUNCE, Larry .... 419-289-5032 348 A
lbunce@ashland.edu
BUNCH, Brandon .... 252-940-6426 332 C
brandon.bunch@beaufortccc.edu
BUNCH, Ella .... 252-335-0821 333 G
ella_bunch64@albemarle.edu
BUNCH, Janice .... 573-986-6191 259 K
jlbunch@semo.edu
BUNCH, John .... 903-334-6628 448 B
jbunch@tamut.edu
BUNCH, Kenneth .... 434-832-6691 474 C
bunchk@centralvirginia.edu
BUNCH, Kirsten .... 828-694-1804 332 E
kirstenb@blueridge.edu
BUNCH, Martha, M .... 336-272-7102 329 D
bunchm@greensboro.edu
BUNCH, Tom .... 817-202-6207 444 I
buncht@swau.edu
BUNCH, Wes .... 828-327-7000 333 B
wbunch@cvcc.edu
BUNCH, Wilma .... 417-269-3051 252 C
wilma.bunch@coxcollege.edu
BUNDRA, Judy .... 216-791-5000 351 A
judy.bundra@cim.edu
BUNDY, Bailey .... 859-344-3346 184 F
bundyb@thomasmore.edu
BUNDY, Barbara .... 213-624-1200.. 42 I
bbundy@fidm.edu
BUNDY, James, A .... 203-432-1505.. 89 D
james.bundy@yale.edu
BUNDY, III, O. Richard 814-863-4826 392 B
orb100@psu.edu
BUNGAY, Sophia .... 505-438-8884 288 C
admissions@acupuncturecollege.edu
BUNGE, Sacha .... 415-338-2204.. 34 A
sbunge@sfsu.edu
BUNGER, Ron .... 404-835-6120 423 K
rbunger@richmont.edu
BUNIS, David .... 508-831-4993 220 E
dabunis@wpi.edu
BUNJER, Jeff .... 515-964-0601 165 G
bunjerj@faith.edu
BUNKELMANN, Jeff ...... 480-677-7701.. 11 K
jeffrey.bunkelmann@centralaz.edu
BUNKER, Aaron .... 918-335-6875 368 G
abunker@okwu.edu
BUNKER, Larissa .... 208-467-8588 131 D
lbunker@nnu.edu
BUNKER, Laurel .... 651-638-6372 234 C
l-bunker@bethel.edu
BUNKO, Tracy, A .... 719-333-7731 504 C
tracy.bunko@usafa.edu
BUNN, Doug .... 541-888-1673 376 F
doug.bunn@socc.edu
BUNNELL, Bob .... 856-351-2239 283 A
bbunell@salemcc.edu
BUNNELL, Robin .... 541-888-7339 376 F
rbunnell@socc.edu
BUNNELL, Stephen, P .. 208-496-3000 130 A
bunnells@byui.edu
BUNNELL-RHYNE,
Melinda, A .... 301-369-2800 197 F
melindabunnell@captechu.edu
BUNS, Thomas, J .... 847-578-3405 147 I
thomas.buns@rosalindfranklin.edu
BUNT, Stephanie .... 714-556-3610.. 72 F
stephanie.bunt@vanguard.edu
BUNTEN, Tricia .... 218-726-6995 243 F
tbunten@d.umn.edu
BUNTING, Gene .... 336-841-9583 329 G
gbunting@highpoint.edu
BUNTING, Taryn .... 618-395-7777 138 I
buntingt@iecc.edu
BUNTON, Kristie .... 817-257-6550 448 G
k.bunton@tcu.edu
BUNTON, Nancy .... 734-432-5315 227 A
nbunton@madonna.edu
BUNTON, Thomas .... 501-916-3010.. 22 B
tebunton@ualr.edu
BUNTON, Tim, M .... 217-443-8780 135 H
tbunton@dacc.edu
BUNYARD, Magen .... 325-649-8613 438 D
mbunyard@hputx.edu
BUONICONTI, Bridget ... 781-768-7895 218 C
bridget.buoniconti@regiscollege.edu
BUONO, Jack .... 516-773-5000 504 G
BUONO, Lisa .... 805-493-3663.. 29 H
llbuono@callutheran.edu
BUOSCIO, Amy .... 708-237-5050 145 E
abuoscio@nc.edu
BURAK, Deborah .... 610-861-4137 391 F
dburak@northampton.edu
BURAK, Marshall, J .... 510-254-3749.. 48 A
mburak@lincolnuca.edu
BURBA, Dave .... 530-541-4660.. 47 E
burba@ltcc.edu
BURBA, Randy .... 714-997-6763.. 36 C
burba@chapman.edu
BURBACK, Michael .... 202-884-9812.. 93 B
burbackm@trinitydc.edu
BURBANTE, Gilberto ..... 985-448-4208 192 B
gilberto.burbante@nicholls.edu
BURBEY, Denise .... 716-338-1250 303 D
deniseburbey@mail.sunyjcc.edu
BURCAT, Dina .... 646-592-4486 326 E
burcat@yu.edu
BURCH, Ann Lee .... 480-219-6061 250 A
aburch@atsu.edu
BURCH, Beth .... 503-568-9941 374 H
bburch@ocom.edu
BURCH, Chuck, S .... 704-406-4342 329 A
cburch@gardner-webb.edu
BURCH, David .... 575-769-4744 285 K
david.burch@clovis.edu
BURCH, Doug .... 801-622-1573 459 N
doug.burch@stevenshenager.edu
BURCH, Jim .... 912-443-5874 124 A
jburch@savannahtech.edu
BURCH, John .... 731-881-7070 428 B
jburch5@utm.edu
BURCH, Stacie .... 410-777-1963 197 C
sqburch@aacc.edu
BURCHARD,
Elizabeth, B .... 802-443-5201 462 H
eboudah@middlebury.edu
BURCHARD, Eric .... 740-593-1804 359 G
burchard@ohio.edu
BURCHETT, Amy .... 432-264-5063 438 C
aburchett@howardcollege.edu
BURCHETT, Bonnie, L ... 423-439-4446 419 J
bonnie@etsu.edu
BURCHETT, Kevin .... 734-423-2139 227 B
BURCHETT, Lance .... 470-578-6033 120 L
BURCHETT, Rachelle ..... 606-886-3863 180 J
rachelle.burchett@kctcs.edu
BURCHFIELD, Doug ...... 828-627-4632 335 C
ddburchfield@haywood.edu
BURCK, Renee .... 517-264-3999 220 F
rburck@adrian.edu
BURCKEL, Daryl .... 337-475-5556 192 A
dburckel@mcneese.edu
BURD, Gail, D .... 520-626-4099.. 16 G
gburd@email.arizona.edu
BURD, Randy .... 516-299-2917 304 G
randy.burd@liu.edu
BURDA, Ed .... 304-457-6238 487 B
burdaep@ab.edu
BURDA, Jeffrey .... 860-768-4482.. 88 H
burda@hartford.edu
BURDEN, John .... 502-585-9911 184 D
jburden@spalding.edu
BURDEN, Kathleen, K ... 937-255-6234 503 A
kathleen.burden@afit.edu
BURDEN, Matthew .... 630-637-5433 144 H
mburden@noctrl.edu
BURDEN, Susan .... 660-263-4100 257 B
susanburden@macc.edu
BURDETTE, Vinson .... 803-508-7244 406 E
burdettv@atc.edu
BURDETTE, William .... 304-696-6523 490 D
burdette@marshall.edu
BURDICK, Alexis .... 805-765-9307.. 62 B
alexisburdick@collegesoflaw.edu
BURDICK, David .... 607-962-9000 320 F
dburdic4@corning-cc.edu
BURDICK, Evelyn, P ..... 708-209-3259 135 F
evelyn.burdick@cuchicago.edu
BURDICK, Gary .... 269-471-3501 221 B
gburdick@andrews.edu
BURDICK, Kirsten, N .... 205-934-4319.... 8 A
knburdick@uab.edu
BURDINE, Mike .... 208-459-5663 130 D
mburdine@collegeofidaho.edu
BURDUE, JoEllen .... 414-277-7117 494 G
burdue@msoe.edu
BURDZINSKI, Donna, R 352-797-5001 104 F
burdzid@phsc.edu
BUREAU, Daniel, A .... 901-678-5271 427 D
daniel.bureau@memphis.edu
BURESH, Amy .... 817-735-5149 454 C
amy.buresh@unthsc.edu
BURFITT, William .... 619-849-2540.. 57 E
williamburfitt@pointloma.edu
BURFORD, Kristina .... 501-450-1362.. 19 F
burford@hendrix.edu
BURFORD, Kyla .... 618-252-5400 149 C
kyla.burford@sic.edu
BURG, James .... 260-481-4146 159 F
burgj@pfw.edu
BURGARD, Bambi .... 816-802-3455 254 B
bburgard@kcai.edu
BURGARD, Daniel .... 817-735-2589 454 C
daniel.burgard@unthsc.edu
BURGAU, Tam .... 715-858-1377 499 D
tburgau@cvtc.edu
BURGAY, Stephen, P .... 617-353-1168 207 D
burgay@bu.edu
BURGE, Danielle .... 251-981-3771.... 5 B
danielle.burge@columbiasouthern.edu
BURGE, David .... 703-993-5487 467 L
dburge@gmu.edu
BURGE, Gary .... 616-957-6032 221 P
gb051@calvinseminary.edu
BURGE, Jennifer, G ...... 309-677-4939 133 B
jgruening@bradley.edu
BURGENER, Kelly, T ..... 208-496-1123 130 A
burgenerk@byui.edu
BURGER, Arnold .... 615-329-8516 419 K
aburger@fisk.edu
BURGER, Cindy, L .... 717-796-1800 390 E
cburger@messiah.edu
BURGER, Crystal .... 870-733-6831.. 17 H
ccburger@asumidsouth.edu
BURGER, Dexter, E .... 214-768-4767 444 E
dburger@smu.edu
BURGER, Edward, B ..... 512-863-1454 445 D
burger@southwestern.edu
BURGER, Glenn .... 718-997-5190 295 C
glenn.burger@qc.cuny.edu
BURGER, James .... 724-805-2212 398 F
james.burger@stvincent.edu
BURGER, Lisa .... 701-777-4706 345 C
lisa.burger@und.edu
BURGER, Mark .... 417-667-8181 252 A
mburger@cottey.edu
BURGER, Martha .... 405-208-5032 367 I
maburger@okcu.edu
BURGER, Rosemary ...... 570-348-6280 389 G
burger@marywood.edu
BURGESS, Aaron .... 513-244-8148 350 I
aaron.burgess@ccuniversity.edu
BURGESS, Brandy .... 303-273-3282.. 78 I
burgess@mines.edu
BURGESS, Brenda, K .... 580-774-3000 370 C
brenda.burgess@swosu.edu
BURGESS, Dayle .... 315-229-5011 314 F
dburgess@stlawu.edu
BURGESS, Douglas .... 513-556-9900 362 D
douglas.burgess@uc.edu
BURGESS, Eric .... 573-681-5609 254 E
burgesse@lincolnu.edu
BURGESS, Esther .... 252-985-5134 339 D
eburgess@ncwc.edu
BURGESS, Frederick ...... 607-255-2000 297 F
BURGESS, Jodi .... 540-863-2835 474 D
jburgess@dslcc.edu
BURGESS, John .... 540-568-6131 468 F
burgesjg@jmu.edu
BURGESS, Kimberly ...... 912-279-5770 116 G
kburgess@ccga.edu
BURGESS, Leandra, H ... 803-705-4604 407 A
leandra.burgess@benedict.edu
BURGESS, Linda .... 913-288-7450 174 F
lburgess@kckcc.edu
BURGESS, Marcus .... 803-535-5238 407 G
mburgess@claflin.edu
BURGESS, Norma .... 615-966-5062 421 D
norma.burgess@lipscomb.edu
BURGESS, Robert .... 870-512-8617.. 18 B
robert_burgess@asun.edu
BURGESS, Ronald, L ..... 334-844-4650.... 4 E
rlb0029@auburn.edu
BURGESS, Shane, C ..... 520-621-7621.. 16 G
shaneburgess@email.arizona.edu
BURGESS, Shane, C ..... 520-621-2211.. 16 G
sburgess@cals.arizona.edu
BURGESS, Valerie .... 603-880-8308 274 E
vburgess@thomasmorecollege.edu
BURGGRAFF, Lucy .... 919-573-5350 340 F
lburggraff@shepherds.edu
BURGIN, David .... 419-251-7331 356 C
david.burgin@mercycollege.edu
BURGIN, JR.,
Jeffery, T .... 502-597-5911 182 H
jeffery.burgin@kysu.edu
BURGIN, Jeffrey .... 256-761-6231.... 7 B
jburgin@talladega.edu
BURGMAYER, Sharon .... 610-526-5106 379 E
sburmay@brynmawr.edu
BURGNER, Daniel .... 806-742-0502 451 B
daniel.burgner@ttu.edu
BURGNER, Ryan, C ...... 308-635-6798 270 D
burgnerr@wncc.edu
BURGOS, Blanca .... 305-485-7700 112 C
BURGOS, Gerardo .... 787-279-1912 509 A
gburgos@bayamon.inter.edu
BURGOS, Henry .... 361-593-2258 447 D
henry.burgos@tamuk.edu
BURGOS, Kathy .... 562-860-2451.. 35 M
kburgos@cerritos.edu
BURGOS, Maida .... 305-821-3333.. 99 E
mburgos@fnu.edu
BURGOS CARRION,
Jorge, A .... 787-720-4476 512 D
decanatoestudiantes@mizpa.edu
BURGRAFF, Tom .... 970-943-2237.. 84 D
tburgraff@western.edu
BURHANNA, Kenneth ... 330-672-1660 354 J
kburhann@kent.edu
BURILLO, Madeline ...... 713-718-7748 437 I
madeline.burillo@hccs.edu
BURISH, Thomas, G ..... 574-631-6631 161 C
burish.2@nd.edu
BURK, Ann, M .... 308-432-6311 268 E
aburk@csc.edu
BURK, Thomas .... 973-328-5037 277 B
tburk@ccm.edu
BURKE, Alison .... 610-921-2381 378 C
aburke@albright.edu
BURKE, Andrew .... 575-646-2431 287 B
aburke@nmsu.edu
BURKE, Barbara .... 718-260-5173 295 B
bburke@citytech.cuny.edu
BURKE, Belinda .... 828-771-2000 344 E
bburke@warren-wilson.edu
BURKE, Brenda .... 801-581-7466 460 E
bburke@sa.utah.edu
BURKE, Brian, W .... 413-545-2204 211 D
bwburke@umass.edu
BURKE, Bridgit .... 307-766-2474 502 H
BURKE, Brigid .... 973-443-8520 277 K
brigid_burke@fdu.edu
BURKE, Carson .... 440-934-3101 358 E
cburke@ohiobusinesscollege.edu
BURKE, Cathleen, C ..... 804-828-0179 473 F
ccburke@vcu.edu
BURKE, Christie .... 907-852-1720.... 9 F
christie.burke@ilisagvik.edu
BURKE, Christy .... 740-376-4708 356 A
christy.burke@marietta.edu
BURKE, Clarence .... 919-572-1625 326 L
cburke@apexsot.edu

BURKE, Colleen .... 215-572-2785 379 A
burkec@arcadia.edu
BURKE, Courtney .... 518-262-9590 289 F
burkec4@amc.edu
BURKE, Dennis .... 617-984-1713 218 B
dburke@quincycollege.edu
BURKE, Derek, A .... 252-398-6369 328 D
burked@chowan.edu
BURKE, Donald, S .... 412-624-3001 401 B
donburke@pitt.edu
BURKE, Greg .... 812-749-1288 159 C
gburke@oak.edu
BURKE, Greg .... 318-357-5251 192 C
burkeg@nsula.edu
BURKE, Indy .... 203-432-5109.. 89 D
indy.burke@yale.edu
BURKE, James .... 216-397-4484 354 I
burke@jcu.edu
BURKE, Jeanmarie, R ... 315-568-3869 308 F
jburke@nycc.edu
BURKE, Jim .... 601-974-1036 247 B
BURKE, Joe .... 256-306-2555.... 1 F
joe.burke@calhoun.edu
BURKE, Joe .... 620-421-6700 175 C
joeburke@labette.edu
BURKE, John .... 845-848-4079 298 D
john.burke@dc.edu
BURKE, John .... 361-570-4840 453 C
burkej@uhv.edu
BURKE, John, D .... 617-552-3387 207 B
john.burke.7@bc.edu
BURKE, Jon .... 816-604-5229 255 F
jon.burke@mcckc.edu
BURKE, Jonathan .... 949-376-6000.. 47 D
jburke@lcad.edu
BURKE, Jonathan, L ..... 816-604-6620 255 E
jon.burke@mcckc.edu
BURKE, Joy .... 814-371-2090 400 D
jburke@triangle-tech.edu
BURKE, Judith, M .... 978-656-3116 214 G
BURKE, Kathleen, F ..... 949-582-4840.. 64 E
kburke@socccd.edu
BURKE, Kelly, J .... 336-334-5375 343 A
kjburke@uncg.edu
BURKE, Keri .... 503-883-2269 373 H
kburke@linfield.edu
BURKE, Kevin .... 202-319-6977.. 91 B
burkek@cua.edu
BURKE, Kevin, F .... 303-458-4087.. 82 E
kburke@regis.edu
BURKE, Kimberly, G ..... 601-974-1250 247 B
burkekg@millsaps.edu
BURKE, Letitia .... 201-327-8877 277 H
lburke@eastwick.edu
BURKE, Lisa .... 630-617-5197 136 G
lisab@elmhurst.edu
BURKE, Marcilynn .... 541-346-3836 377 D
maburke@uoregon.edu
BURKE, Matthew .... 978-665-3313 212 C
mburke4@fitchburgstate.edu
BURKE, Melinda, W .... 520-621-3557.. 16 G
mwburke@email.arizona.edu
BURKE, Neva .... 901-435-1601 421 A
neva_burke@loc.edu
BURKE, Pamela, B .... 540-665-4925 471 E
pburke2@su.edu
BURKE, Patty .... 513-487-1287 361 L
patty.burke@myunion.edu
BURKE, Sandra .... 662-252-8000 248 G
sburke@rustcollege.edu
BURKE, Scott, M .... 404-413-2088 119 E
sburke@gsu.edu
BURKE, Sean .... 563-387-2110 167 E
burke.sean@luther.edu
BURKE, Seth .... 540-665-6257 471 E
sburke@su.edu
BURKE, Stephen .... 570-348-6282 389 G
burke@marywood.edu
BURKE, Taylor .... 541-552-6652 376 E
burketa@sou.edu
BURKE, Ted .... 508-541-1774 208 F
tburke@dean.edu
BURKE, Thomas .... 410-864-3602 201 F
tburke@stmarys.edu
BURKE, Thomas, J .... 661-336-5104.. 46 K
tburke@kccd.edu
BURKE, Tracie, L .... 901-321-3357 419 C
tburke@cbu.edu
BURKE, Vic .... 912-443-5500 124 A
vburke@savannahtech.edu
BURKE, William .... 570-702-8907 386 G
wburke@johnson.edu
BURKE, William, R .... 570-941-7887 401 H
william.burke@scranton.edu
BURKE-SULLIVAN,
Eileen, C .... 402-280-3285 266 I
e_burkesullivan@creighton.edu
BURKEE, James .... 914-337-9300 297 D
james.burkee@concordia-ny.edu
BURKERT, Amy, L .... 412-268-5865 380 F
ak11@andrew.cmu.edu
BURKES, Kate .... 479-619-4299.. 20 D
kburkes@nwacc.edu
BURKETT, Bonnie .... 252-862-1239 337 C
bsburkett3197@roanokechowan.edu
BURKETT, Holly, L .... 865-981-5302 425 F
hlburkett@pstcc.edu
BURKETT, Kaia .... 510-587-7890.. 56 H
kburkett@peralta.edu
BURKETT, Nancy .... 610-328-8651 399 D
nburket1@swarthmore.edu
BURKETT, Norvel .... 865-974-3181 427 G
nburkett@utk.edu
BURKETT, Timothy .... 704-847-5600 340 I
itadmin@ses.edu
BURKEY, Robert .... 816-604-4062 255 I
robert.burkey@mcckc.edu
BURKHALTER,
Carmen, L .... 256-765-4288.... 8 E
cburkhalter@una.edu
BURKHALTER, Scott .... 903-693-1112 441 F
sburkhalter@panola.edu
BURKHALTER, Sheila .... 803-323-2251 414 G
burkhalters@winthrop.edu
BURKHARD, Englert ..... 970-351-2877.. 83 E
englert.burkhard@unco.edu
BURKHARDT, Janet .... 303-871-4757.. 83 D
janet.burkhardt@du.edu
BURKHARDT, Paul .... 928-350-4100.. 15 N
pburkhardt@prescott.edu
BURKHARDT, Ronald .... 856-351-2608 283 A
rburkhardt@salemcc.edu
BURKHART, Bethani ..... 330-569-5132 353 J
burkhartbm@hiram.edu
BURKHART, Brad .... 812-749-1442 159 C
bburkhart@oak.edu
BURKHART, Cindy .... 910-938-6145 333 F
burkhartc@coastalcarolina.edu
BURKHART, Jenny .... 859-858-2318 178 H
BURKHOLDER,
Brian, M .... 540-432-4132 466 G
brian.burkholder@emu.edu
BURKHOLDER, Mary, E 419-783-2360 352 F
mburkholder@defiance.edu
BURKHOLDER,
Robert, C .... 215-503-6249 400 A
robert.burkholder@jefferson.edu
BURKINK, Tim, J .... 308-865-1547 269 I
burkinktj@unk.edu
BURKITT, David .... 419-517-8968 355 K
dburkitt@lourdes.edu
BURKLO, Daniel .... 419-267-1273 358 A
dburklo@northweststate.edu
BURKMAN, Roger .... 502-585-9911 184 D
rburkman@spalding.edu
BURKS, A. Welsley .... 919-962-2211 342 D
BURKS, A. Wesley .... 919-962-2211 342 D
BURKS, Brent .... 254-295-4514 453 E
bburks@umhb.edu
BURKS, Bryan .... 501-279-4312.. 19 D
bburks@harding.edu
BURKS, Cherryl .... 770-229-3409 124 G
cherryl.burks@sctech.edu
BURKS, Eric .... 785-738-9057 176 A
eburks@ncktc.edu
BURKS, Gwenevera, E .. 559-453-2010.. 43 G
gwen.burks@fresno.edu
BURKS, Laura .... 334-580-2144.... 1 I
laura.burks@coastalalabama.edu
BURKS, Scott, A .... 502-852-4661 185 C
scott.burks@louisville.edu
BURKWHAT, Louis, E ... 530-226-4979.. 63 K
lburkwhat@simpsonu.edu
BURKY, Heather .... 717-391-6935 399 G
BURLAGE, Robert, S ..... 262-243-5700 493 B
robert.burlage@cuw.edu
BURLEIGH-JONES,
Bronté .... 717-245-1943 382 F
jonesbro@dickinson.edu
BURLESON, Brooke .... 828-766-1269 336 A
bburleson@mayland.edu
BURLESON, Burt .... 254-710-3517 431 J
burt_burleson@baylor.edu
BURLESON, Rachel .... 603-899-4080 273 F
burlesonr@franklinpierce.edu
BURLESON, Rea .... 727-873-4552 110 C
rea@mail.usf.edu
BURLESON, Susan .... 336-249-8186 334 A
sdburl@davidsonccc.edu
BURLEW, Jon .... 606-679-8501 182 C
jon.burlew@kctcs.edu
BURLEW, Lynette .... 318-473-6401 188 J
lburlew@lsua.edu
BURLING, Rachel .... 262-691-5266 500 H
rburling@wctc.edu
BURLINGAME, Kathy .... 502-410-6200 180 D
kburlingame@galencollege.edu
BURMA, William, H .... 515-263-2975 165 I
bburma@grandview.edu
BURMAN, Tom .... 307-766-2292 502 H
tburman@uwyo.edu
BURMASTER, Elizabeth . 301-846-2440 198 E
eburmaster@frederick.edu
BURMEISTER, Justin ..... 718-429-6600 324 D
justin.burmeister@vaughn.edu
BURMENKO, Neil .... 510-464-3520.. 56 G
nburmenko@peralta.edu
BURNAM, Paul .... 740-362-3435 356 D
pburnam@mtso.edu
BURNAMAN, Jerry .... 318-473-6497 188 J
jburnaman@lsua.edu
BURNER, Emily .... 540-665-3489 471 E
eburner@su.edu
BURNETT, Amber .... 909-599-5433.. 47 K
aburnett@lifepacific.edu
BURNETT, Benjamin .... 601-318-6144 249 H
bburnett@wmcarey.edu
BURNETT, Bradley, T .... 405-325-9899 371 B
bburnett@ou.edu
BURNETT, Brian .... 612-626-5845 243 E
burnett@umn.edu
BURNETT, Catherine, G 713-646-1831 444 B
cburnett@stcl.edu
BURNETT, Denita .... 276-223-4769 476 E
dburnett@wcc.vccs.edu
BURNETT, Edward, T .... 508-286-8214 220 A
burnett_edward@wheatoncollege.edu
BURNETT, Farah .... 718-270-2488 317 E
farah.burnett@downstate.edu
BURNETT, Grace .... 208-882-1566 131 B
registrar@nsa.edu
BURNETT, John .... 724-938-4014 394 B
burnett@calu.edu
BURNETT, Kimberly .... 205-226-4906.... 5 A
kmburnet@bsc.edu
BURNETT, Linda, G .... 409-882-3998 450 A
linda.burnett@lsco.edu
BURNETT, Lindsay .... 870-972-2586.. 17 G
lburnett@astate.edu
BURNETT, Lonnie .... 251-442-2201.... 8 C
lburnett@umobile.edu
BURNETT, Marc .... 931-372-3411 426 E
mburnett@tntech.edu
BURNETT, Mary .... 717-477-1279 395 E
meburnett@ship.edu
BURNETT, Myra .... 404-270-5027 125 B
mburnett@spelman.edu
BURNETT, Sharron, T ... 334-727-8692.... 7 D
sburnett@tuskegee.edu
BURNETTE, Brittany .... 832-252-0737 433 D
brittany.burnette@cbshouston.edu
BURNETTE, Daarel, E .... 601-979-3060 246 E
daarel.e.burnette@jsums.edu
BURNETTE, Diane, M .... 803-536-7187 412 C
dburnet1@scsu.edu
BURNETTE, Stephanie ... 321-433-7271.. 97 I
burnettes@easternflorida.edu
BURNETTE, Steve .... 276-223-4705 476 E
sburnette@wcc.vccs.edu
BURNETTE, Teri .... 706-396-8132 122 K
tburnette@paine.edu
BURNEY, Christina, M .. 508-565-1325 218 H
cburney@stonehill.edu
BURNEY, David .... 479-524-7427.. 19 H
dburney@jbu.edu
BURNEY, Linda .... 910-879-5519 332 D
lburney@bladencc.edu
BURNEY, Michelle .... 662-227-2304 246 C
mburney@holmescc.edu
BURNEY, Rolanda, C .... 413-545-2300 211 D
BURNEY, Rolanda, C .... 413-545-2211 211 D
rburney@umass.edu
BURNHAM, Don .... 601-605-3301 246 C
dburnham@holmescc.edu
BURNHAM, Heather ..... 540-373-2200 466 H
hburnham@evcc.edu
BURNHAM, Lorrie .... 909-384-8650.. 59 I
lburnham@sbccd.cc.ca.us
BURNIM, Mickey, L .... 410-951-3838 203 D
BURNIP, David, W .... 330-471-8251 355 L
dburnip@malone.edu
BURNLEY, Chris .... 540-365-4231 467 I
cburnley@ferrum.edu
BURNLEY, Lawrence, A 937-229-4073 362 G
lburnley1@udayton.edu
BURNLEY, Linda .... 646-888-6639 305 E
burnleyl@sloankettering.edu
BURNS, Alana .... 603-629-3467 274 D
a.burns1l@snhu.edu
BURNS, Andrew .... 718-862-7958 305 H
aburns01@manhattan.edu
BURNS, Angelina, L ..... 302-327-4809.. 90 I
angelina.l.burns@wilmu.edu
BURNS, Ann, K .... 716-673-3333 317 A
ann.burns@fredonia.edu
BURNS, Barbara .... 478-471-2502 121 F
barbara.burns@mga.edu
BURNS, Bob .... 617-989-4516 219 E
burnsr5@wit.edu
BURNS, Cathy .... 918-343-7791 369 F
cburns@rsu.edu
BURNS, Cindy .... 910-678-8564 334 D
griffinw@faytechcc.edu
BURNS, Craig, D .... 617-552-3310 207 B
craig.burns@bc.edu
BURNS, Daniel, P .... 985-867-2225 190 F
acdean@sjasc.edu
BURNS, Edward, R .... 718-430-2000 289 G
BURNS, Elizabeth .... 920-735-5795 499 E
burnse@fvtc.edu
BURNS, Ellen .... 386-312-4149 106 C
ellenburns@sjrstate.edu
BURNS, Eric .... 479-308-2235.. 17 C
eric.burns@acheedu.org
BURNS, Erick .... 530-741-6838.. 76 C
eburns@yccd.edu
BURNS, Erin .... 510-849-8222.. 55 B
eburns@psr.edu
BURNS, Felecia .... 432-552-2712 457 A
burns_f@utpb.edu
BURNS, Gary .... 816-501-4854 258 H
gary.burns@rockhurst.edu
BURNS, J. Joseph .... 617-552-3273 207 B
joe.burns@bc.edu
BURNS, Jack .... 734-384-4249 227 G
jburns@monroeccc.edu
BURNS, IVD, James, P 507-457-1503 243 B
jburns@smumn.edu
BURNS, James, T .... 215-670-9235 391 H
jtburns@peirce.edu
BURNS, Jamie .... 252-862-1261 337 C
jburns6896@roanokechowan.edu
BURNS, Jared .... 601-928-6297 247 E
jared.burns@mgccc.edu
BURNS, Jeffrey, S .... 804-752-7367 470 F
jburns@rmc.edu
BURNS, Jennifer, A .... 412-365-1849 381 C
jburns@chatham.edu
BURNS, Kelli .... 314-539-5371 259 C
kburns@stlcc.edu
BURNS, Keri .... 972-883-2943 455 B
keri.burns@utdallas.edu
BURNS, Laura .... 315-364-3289 325 B
lburns@wells.edu
BURNS, Lisa, A .... 434-223-6118 468 A
lburns@hsc.edu
BURNS, Lita .... 208-769-3302 131 C
lita_burns@nic.edu
BURNS, Lori .... 478-289-2036 117 D
lburns@ega.edu
BURNS, Lucy .... 502-272-8234 179 B
lburns@bellarmine.edu
BURNS, Lynda .... 760-366-3791.. 40 K
lburns@cmccd.edu
BURNS, Marie-Elaine .... 510-436-2501.. 56 H
meburns@peralta.edu
BURNS, Matthew .... 585-275-4085 323 J
matthew.burns@rochester.edu
BURNS, Matthew .... 718-780-0305 291 J
matthew.burns@brooklaw.edu
BURNS, Michael .... 254-295-4589 453 E
mburns@umhb.edu
BURNS, Patrick .... 970-491-1833.. 78M
patrick.burns@colostate.edu
BURNS, Patrick .... 928-776-2055.. 16M
patrick.burns@yc.edu
BURNS, Peter .... 914-323-5129 305 J
peter.burns@mville.edu
BURNS, Philip .... 404-835-6112 423 K
pburns@richmont.edu

BURNS, R. Scott .... 716-878-3395 318 C
burnsrs@buffalostate.edu
BURNS, Rachelle .... 850-484-1817 104 H
rburns@pensacolastate.edu
BURNS, Raymond .... 218-335-4268 236 E
BURNS, Rick .... 405-208-5758 176 I
rick.burns@spst.edu
BURNS, Shawn, G .... 806-651-2300 448 C
sburns@wtamu.edu
BURNS, Susan, E .... 313-577-0157 232 I
sburns@wayne.edu
BURNS, Susan, R .... 563-588-6540 163 F
susan.burns@clarke.edu
BURNS, Tenika .... 312-553-3161 134 B
tburns33@ccc.edu
BURNS, Thomas .... 716-286-8580 310 D
tburns@niagara.edu
BURNS, Thomas, D .... 615-460-6400 418 F
thomas.burns@belmont.edu
BURNS, Tiffany .... 304-647-6349 491 A
tburns@osteo.wvsom.edu
BURNS, Todd .... 309-268-8020 137 I
todd.burns@heartland.edu
BURNS, William .... 732-224-2426 276 B
wburns@brookdalecc.edu
BURNS, William .... 701-231-7671 345 G
william.burns@ndsu.edu
BURNSIDE, Michael .... 404-225-4448 114 H
mburnside@atlantatech.edu
BURNWORTH, Karen .... 253-752-2020 481 B
admissions@faithseminary.edu
BURPO, Jessie .... 405-789-7661 370 B
jessie.burpo@swcu.edu
BURR, Alan .... 941-487-4245 109 D
aburr@ncf.edu
BURR, Jason, H .... 864-597-4231 414 H
burrjh@wofford.edu
BURR, Kim .... 828-766-1350 336 A
kburr@mayland.edu
BURR, Robin .... 801-581-6510 460 E
robin.burr@utah.edu
BURR, Stephen .... 313-883-8563 229 K
burr.stephen@shms.edu
BURRAGE, Alexandra .... 216-421-7412 350 M
amburrage@cia.edu
BURRAGE, Gabrielle .... 216-421-7493 350 M
geburrage@cia.edu
BURRAGE, Sean .... 580-745-2500 369 K
sburrage@se.edu
BURRELL, Angie, S .... 662-472-9013 246 C
aburrell@holmescc.edu
BURRELL, Becky .... 410-462-8564 197 E
bburrell@bccc.edu
BURRELL, James .... 937-376-6121 350 D
jburrell@centralstate.edu
BURRELL, LaToya .... 612-343-4180 242 H
ljburrel@northcentral.edu
BURRELL, Scott .... 318-357-4522 192 C
nfburrellc@nsula.edu
BURRELL, Steven, C .... 928-523-9998 .. 14 H
steven.burrell@nau.edu
BURRELL, Todd, C .... 618-650-3705 149 F
tburrel@siue.edu
BURRELL-MCRAE,
Karlene, A .... 207-859-4780 193 E
karlene.burrellmcrae@colby.edu
BURRHUS, Don .... 386-822-4259 111 A
dburrhus@stetson.edu
BURRICHTER, William .. 585-567-9622 302 D
bill.burrichter@houghton.edu
BURRILL, Jennifer, R .... 269-471-6601 221 B
burrillj@andrews.edu
BURRIS, David .... 530-283-0202 .. 42 H
dburris@frc.edu
BURRIS, Deborah, J .... 314-516-5695 261 D
dburris@umsl.edu
BURRIS, Kendra .... 806-743-2786 451 C
kendra.burris@ttuhsc.edu
BURRIS, Thomas .... 314-367-8700 259 B
thomas.burris@stlcop.edu
BURRISS, Matthew .... 740-284-7217 353 B
mburriss@franciscan.edu
BURROUGHS, Carolyn .. 318-678-6000 187 A
cburroughs@bpcc.edu
BURROUGHS, Cynthia .. 501-370-5337 .. 20 G
cburroughs@philander.edu
BURROUGHS, Mary .... 202-546-4734 484 G
mburroughs@shoreline.edu
BURROUGHS DAVIS,
Robin .... 603-526-3752 272 H
rdavis@colby-sawyer.edu
BURROW, Susan .... 256-215-4300 .... 1 G
sburrow@cacc.edu
BURROWES, Nathalia .... 214-329-4447 431 D
nathalia.burrowes@bgu.edu
BURROWS, Bill .... 909-706-8431 .. 74 I
bburrows@westernu.edu
BURROWS, Eguan .... 414-297-6870 500 B
burrowse1@matc.edu
BURROWS-SCHUMACHER,
Molly, A .... 563-588-4981 167 D
molly.burrowsschumacher@loras.edu
BURRUS, Ken .... 509-533-7220 479 I
kburrus@ccs.spokane.edu
BURRUS, Robert .... 910-962-3226 343 C
burrusr@uncw.edu
BURRUSS, Nancy, M .... 920-433-6632 492 B
nancy.burruss@bellincollege.edu
BURRUTO, James .... 315-781-3319 302 A
burruto@hws.edu
BURRY, Leslie .... 816-995-2820 258 F
leslie.burry@researchcollege.edu
BURSI, Megan, M .... 901-572-2853 418 E
megan.bursi@bchs.edu
BURSIK, Nick .... 715-395-4619 498 B
nbursik@uwsuper.edu
BURSON, Patricia .... 310-434-4961 .. 62 E
burson_patricia@smc.edu
BURSON, Todd, E .... 740-427-5181 355 E
bursont@kenyon.edu
BURSTEIN, Mark .... 920-832-6525 493 K
mark.burstein@lawrence.edu
BURSTON, Sam .... 404-880-6316 116 D
sburston@cau.edu
BURSTYN, Yaakov .... 305-534-7050 111 D
rabbibursty@talmudicu.edu
BURT, Andrea .... 517-264-3100 220 F
aburt@adrian.edu
BURT, Ashley .... 727-864-8318 .. 97 J
burtaf@eckerd.edu
BURT, Charles .... 617-745-3725 208 G
charles.burt@enc.edu
BURT, DeAnna .... 507-389-7228 241 C
deanna.burt@southcentral.edu
BURTCHAELL, Treasure . 504-278-6479 188 A
BURTI, Ellen .... 718-940-5852 314 C
eburti@sjcny.edu
BURTLE, Melissa .... 229-217-4210 125 A
mburtle@southernregional.edu
BURTNETT, Jody .... 217-875-7211 147 C
jburtnett@richland.edu
BURTON, Adam .... 951-343-4286 .. 27 J
aburton@calbaptist.edu
BURTON, Adrienne .... 714-892-7711 .. 38 D
aburton@gwc.cccd.edu
BURTON, Alan .... 580-745-2731 369 K
aburton@se.edu
BURTON, Andre, L .... 330-325-6733 357 G
aburton@neomed.edu
BURTON, Becky .... 706-583-2818 114 F
bburton@athenstech.edu
BURTON, Ben .... 317-921-4712 157 G
bburton@ivytech.edu
BURTON, Carol .... 828-227-7495 344 A
burton@wcu.edu
BURTON, Carolyn .... 410-778-2800 204 D
cburton2@washcoll.edu
BURTON, Clen .... 409-933-8261 433 L
clenburton@com.edu
BURTON, David .... 740-284-5276 353 B
dburton@franciscan.edu
BURTON, Deborah .... 800-856-9544 265 H
deborah.burton@uprovidence.edu
BURTON, Derrick .... 641-585-8671 170 B
derrick.burton@waldorf.edu
BURTON, Donald, N .... 602-648-5750 .. 12 D
dburton@dunlap-stone.edu
BURTON, Elisabeth .... 610-399-2710 394 C
eburton@cheyney.edu
BURTON, Gregory, A .... 973-761-9362 283 B
gregory.burton@shu.edu
BURTON, Heather .... 540-868-7201 474 J
hburton@lfcc.edu
BURTON, J.D .... 612-624-7324 243 E
jdburton@umn.edu
BURTON, Khalilah .... 251-981-3771 .... 5 B
khalilah.burton@columbiasouthern.edu
BURTON, Larry .... 336-272-7102 329 D
lwburton@greensboro.edu
BURTON, Mel .... 770-426-2986 121 C
mel.burton@life.edu
BURTON, Melody .... 503-517-1369 377 G
mburton@warnerpacific.edu
BURTON, Nathan .... 304-766-4354 491 B
nburton2@wvstateu.edu
BURTON, Raymond, A .. 804-523-5374 474 H
rburton@reynolds.edu
BURTON, Robert .... 808-984-3245 129 E
reburton@hawaii.edu
BURTON, Sharon .... 270-831-9646 181 D
sharon.burton@kctcs.edu
BURTON, Terrance .... 508-999-8664 211 F
tburton@umassd.edu
BURTON-GOSS, Sadie .... 781-239-6334 205 E
sburtongoss@babson.edu
BURWASH, Laura .... 270-384-8065 183 C
burwashl@lindsey.edu
BURWELL, Elissia .... 903-593-8311 448 H
eburwell@texascollege.edu
BURWELL, Jessica .... 425-640-1654 480 F
jessica.e.burwell@edcc.edu
BURWELL, Sylvia, M .... 202-885-2121 .. 90 J
president@american.edu
BURY, John .... 918-631-2359 371 E
john-bury@utulsa.edu
BURZICHELLI,
Dominick .... 856-415-2292 281 D
dburzichelli@rcgc.edu
BURZINSKI, Jody .... 620-421-6700 175 C
jodyb@labette.edu
BUSAKOWSKI, Bret .... 218-879-0810 238 A
bret.busakowski@fdltcc.edu
BUSALACCHI, Richard ... 414-297-6969 500 B
busalacr@matc.edu
BUSAM KLENOWSKI,
Leah .... 513-745-4879 365 B
busaml@xavier.edu
BUSANO, Josephine .... 808-237-5141 127 G
jbusano@hmi.edu
BUSBEE, Walter .... 803-508-7254 406 E
busbeew@atc.edu
BUSBY, Bruce .... 309-694-5477 138 C
bruce.busby@icc.edu
BUSBY, Dwayne .... 281-283-2019 453 A
busby@uhcl.edu
BUSBY, Joshua .... 405-466-3445 366 F
jabusby@langston.edu
BUSBY, Katie .... 662-915-7387 249 D
kbusby@olemiss.edu
BUSBY, Laura .... 801-863-8456 461 A
lbusby@uvu.edu
BUSBY, Martha .... 404-835-6121 423 K
mbusby@richmont.edu
BUSBY, Matthew .... 864-379-8869 409 H
estep@erskine.edu
BUSBY, Michael .... 662-243-1904 246 A
mbusby@eastms.edu
BUSCH, Austin .... 585-395-5829 318 B
abusch@brockport.edu
BUSCH, Brian .... 252-789-0244 335 H
brian.busch@martincc.edu
BUSCH, Caroline, C .... 804-752-3267 470 F
cbusch@rmc.edu
BUSCH, Tanika .... 314-516-5502 261 D
tanika@umsl.edu
BUSCH-ZURLENT,
Valerie .... 773-907-4350 134 C
vbuschzurlent@ccc.edu
BUSCHER, Frank .... 630-844-5252 132 D
fbuscher@aurora.edu
BUSCHER, Frank, M .... 630-844-5252 132 D
fbuscher@aurora.edu
BUSCHER, Kristin .... 402-872-2298 268 F
kbuscher@peru.edu
BUSCHHAUS,
Rosemary .... 608-246-6904 499 H
rbuschhaus@madisoncollege.edu
BUSCHMAN, John, E .... 973-761-9005 283 B
john.buschman@shu.edu
BUSE, Carol .... 806-371-5994 430 A
acbuse@actx.edu
BUSE, Jon .... 319-398-4977 167 C
jon.buse@kirkwood.edu
BUSE, William .... 212-799-5000 303 H
BUSEL, Yaakov .... 732-985-6533 280 F
BUSEY, Laura .... 304-260-4380 488 J
lbusey@blueridgectc.edu
BUSH, Catherine .... 440-525-7119 355 H
cbush@lakelandcc.edu
BUSH, Cathy .... 440-525-7112 355 H
cbush@lakelandcc.edu
BUSH, Cody .... 931-221-7561 418 D
bushc@apsu.edu
BUSH, Delsa .... 561-868-3968 104 D
bushd@palmbeachstate.edu
BUSH, Edward, C .... 916-691-7321 .. 50 G
bushe@crc.losrios.edu
BUSH, Janis .... 301-387-3049 198 F
janis.bush@garrettcollege.edu
BUSH, Joel .... 479-394-7622 .. 23 C
jbush@uarichmountain.edu
BUSH, John, L .... 314-505-7258 251 I
bushj@csl.edu
BUSH, Joseph .... 202-885-8603 .. 93 E
jbush@wesleyseminary.edu
BUSH, Justin .... 352-588-8361 106 D
justin.bush@saintleo.edu
BUSH, Keith .... 218-751-8670 242 J
it@oakhills.edu
BUSH, Kristen .... 540-231-1796 477 A
khbush@vt.edu
BUSH, Lisa, F .... 828-398-7202 332 B
lbush@abtech.edu
BUSH, Lonica .... 409-933-8413 433 L
lbush@com.edu
BUSH, Maureen .... 410-617-5817 199 F
mwfaux@loyola.edu
BUSH, Michael .... 626-585-7172 .. 55 K
mbush5@pasadena.edu
BUSH, Mickie .... 503-494-7800 375 B
regohsu@ohsu.edu
BUSH, Mike .... 505-526-4745 189 H
mikeb@dmisys.com
BUSH, Polly .... 585-340-9500 296 E
pbush@crcds.edu
BUSHEY, Ann, M .... 804-371-3000 474 H
abushey@reynolds.edu
BUSHEY, Jane, L .... 480-245-7930 .. 12 N
jane.bushey@ibcs.edu
BUSHKIN, Alan .... 954-492-5353 .. 96 H
abushkin@citycollege.edu
BUSHMAN, David, W .... 540-828-5605 465 D
dbushman@bridgewater.edu
BUSHNELL, Elizabeth, J 260-982-5241 158 T
ejbushnell@manchester.edu
BUSHNELL, Ryan .... 517-321-0242 224 F
rbushnell@glcc.edu
BUSHONG, Sara .... 419-372-2856 348 H
sbushon@bgsu.edu
BUSHWAY, Deborah .... 952-888-4777 242 I
dbushway@nwhealth.edu
BUSING, Michael .... 540-568-3254 468 F
busingme@jmu.edu
BUSKIRK, Joseph .... 443-412-2377 199 A
jbuskirk@harford.edu
BUSKIRK, Susan .... 410-706-4937 202 D
sbuskirk@umaryland.edu
BUSS, Brian .... 920-735-5792 499 E
buss@fvtc.edu
BUSS, James .... 859-572-5946 184 A
bussj1@nku.edu
BUSS, Marney .... 508-213-2101 217 E
marney.buss@nichols.edu
BUSSE, Max .... 214-333-5104 434 I
maxwellb@dbu.edu
BUSSELL, Helena .... 817-531-4405 451 E
hbussell@txwes.edu
BUSSELL, Jeff .... 714-619-6615 .. 72 F
jeff.bussell@vanguard.edu
BUSSELL, Paige .... 903-468-3209 447 B
paige.bussell@tamuc.edu
BUSSELL, Rachelle .... 909-558-4544 .. 48 C
rbussell@llu.edu
BUSSEY, Brenda .... 508-929-8455 213 E
bbussey@worcester.edu
BUSSEY, Tosha .... 404-225-4596 114 H
tbussey@atlantatech.edu
BUSSIKI, Marcelo .... 979-209-7460 432 C
mbussiki@blinn.edu
BUSTAMANTE,
Alexander .... 510-987-9090 .. 68 C
alexander.bustamante@ucop.edu
BUSTAMANTE, Camilla . 505-428-1388 288 B
camilla.bustamante@sfcc.edu
BUSTAMANTE, Tom .... 909-218-3253 .. 25 I
tbustamante@americancareercollege.
edu
BUSTARD, James .... 217-351-2211 146 C
jbustard@parkland.edu
BUSTER, Marcella .... 406-657-1043 265 E
marcella.buster@rocky.edu
BUSTER-WILLIAMS,
Kimberley .... 540-654-1618 472 I
kwilli23@umw.edu
BUSTINZA, Reggie .... 815-753-8821 145 C
rbustinza@niu.edu
BUSTOS, Adam .... 505-454-3053 286 H
adambustos@nmhu.edu
BUTCARIS, Michael .... 203-857-7309 .. 86 D
mbutcaris@norwalk.edu
BUTCHER, Claudette .... 918-293-5256 368 D
claudette.butcher@okstate.edu

BUTCHER, Emily .... 716-664-5100 303 C
ebutcher@jbc.edu
BUTCHER, Greg .... 724-589-2031 399 H
gbutcher@thiel.edu
BUTCHER, Marilea .... 304-647-6367 491 A
mbutcher@osteo.wvsom.edu
BUTCHER, Melissa .... 712-749-2049 163 D
butcherm@bvu.edu
BUTCHER, Michael .... 912-279-5815 116 G
mbutcher@ccga.edu
BUTCHER, Michelle .... 859-858-3511 178 I
michelle.butcher@asbury.edu
BUTCHER, Thomas, A ... 616-331-2067 224 E
butchert@gvsu.edu
BUTCHKO, Thomas .... 570-208-5928 387 A
thomasbutchko@kings.edu
BUTDORFF, Carla .... 419-747-5401 357 E
196mgr@fheg.follett.com
BUTERA, Jeffrey .... 508-791-9241 206 B
jeffrey.butera@becker.edu
BUTERA, Peter .... 716-286-8060 310 D
pbutera@niagara.edu
BUTERA, Rae-Anne .... 781-292-2321 209 E
rae-anne.butera@olin.edu
BUTERA, Vince .... 847-578-8374 147 I
vince.butera@rosalindfranklin.edu
BUTKOVICH, Michelle ... 248-204-2111 226 G
mbutkovic@ltu.edu
BUTLER, Aja .... 510-748-2327.. 56 F
abutler@peralta.edu
BUTLER, Alison .... 805-893-2622.. 70 A
alison.butler@ucsb.edu
BUTLER, Allen, P .... 815-455-8999 143 A
abutler@mchenry.edu
BUTLER, Andra .... 606-546-1224 184 H
abutler@unionky.edu
BUTLER, Andrea .... 402-466-4774 267 A
andrea.butler@doane.edu
BUTLER, Andrea .... 803-934-3167 411 C
abutler@morris.edu
BUTLER, Andrew .... 508-831-6634 220 E
abutler@wpi.edu
BUTLER, Andrew, J .... 205-934-5149.... 8 A
andrewbutler@uab.edu
BUTLER, Barry .... 386-226-6000.. 98 A
butlerb@erau.edu
BUTLER, Blake .... 501-760-4176.. 20 B
blake.butler@np.edu
BUTLER, Brady .... 412-536-1300 387 B
brady.butler@laroche.edu
BUTLER, Bruce, D .... 713-500-3369 456 B
bruce.d.butler@uth.tmc.edu
BUTLER, Bryant .... 601-968-5930 245 C
bbutler@belhaven.edu
BUTLER, Carmen .... 704-406-3980 329 A
cbutler@gardner-webb.edu
BUTLER, Connie .... 402-643-7332 266 G
connie.butler@cune.edu
BUTLER, David, L .... 615-898-2182 422 H
david.butler@mtsu.edu
BUTLER, Debra .... 662-252-8000 248 G
dbutler@rustcollege.edu
BUTLER, Duan .... 540-374-4300.. 92 G
BUTLER, Greg .... 601-477-4113 246 F
greg.butler@jcjc.edu
BUTLER, Henry .... 703-993-8644 467 L
hnbutler@gmu.edu
BUTLER, Isaac .... 314-446-8438 259 B
isaac.butler@stlcop.edu
BUTLER, Jacob .... 803-934-3274 411 C
jbutler@morris.edu
BUTLER, Jay .... 215-702-4401 380 D
jbutler@cairn.edu
BUTLER, John, L .... 773-442-4200 145 B
j-butler1@neiu.edu
BUTLER, S.J., John, T .. 617-552-6855 207 B
john.butler@bc.edu
BUTLER, Kevin .... 702-992-2000 271 C
kevin.butler@nsc.edu
BUTLER, Kijaffe .... 410-462-8311 197 E
kbutler@bccc.edu
BUTLER, Kim, I .... 515-263-2841 165 I
maintenance@grandview.edu
BUTLER, Lee .... 817-598-6345 458 A
cbutler@wc.edu
BUTLER, LeRoy .... 815-836-5923 141 G
butlerle@lewisu.edu
BUTLER, Lisa .... 660-543-4001 260 K
ljbutler@ucmo.edu
BUTLER, Margie .... 504-282-4455 190 A
mbutler@nobts.edu
BUTLER, Mark .... 815-479-7677 143 A
mbutler535@mchenry.edu
BUTLER, Mark .... 864-231-2000 406 G
BUTLER, Mary Edith .... 630-466-7900 152 C
mbutler@waubonsee.edu
BUTLER, Meghan .... 617-732-1679 209 A
butlerm2@emmanuel.edu
BUTLER, Michael .... 909-469-5534.. 74 I
mbutler@westernu.edu
BUTLER, Monique .... 510-594-3725.. 28 D
mbutler@cca.edu
BUTLER, Rebecca .... 614-287-2180 351 E
rbutler17@cscc.edu
BUTLER, Rebekah .... 617-364-3510 207 A
rbutler@boston.edu
BUTLER, Renee .... 470-578-5414 120 L
rbutle35@kennesaw.edu
BUTLER, Rhett .... 334-833-4474.... 5 H
chaplain@hawks.huntingdon.edu
BUTLER, Robert .... 617-824-8953 208 H
robert_butler@emerson.edu
BUTLER, Sandy .... 404-364-8325 122 J
sbutler@oglethorpe.edu
BUTLER, Shai .... 518-337-2306 296 H
butlers@strose.edu
BUTLER, Sharon .... 517-884-0101 227 D
sbutler@msu.edu
BUTLER, Sheri .... 318-371-3035 187 I
sheributler@nwltc.edu
BUTLER, Tamaka .... 313-577-6606 232 I
tamaka.butler@wayne.edu
BUTLER, Tammy .... 215-702-4395 380 D
tbutler@cairn.edu
BUTLER, Vicki .... 206-239-4500 479 E
vbutler@cityu.edu
BUTLER, Walter .... 731-352-4000 418 G
butlerw@bethelu.edu
BUTLER-JOHNSON,
Serena .... 202-274-5670.. 93 C
sbutlerjohnson@udc.edu
BUTLER-PURRY, Karen . 979-845-3631 446 G
ogaps@tamu.edu
BUTRON, Jo Anna .... 831-646-4099.. 52 F
jbutron@mpc.edu
BUTT, Darryl, P .... 801-581-8767 460 E
darryl.butt@utah.edu
BUTT, Debi, S .... 336-841-9202 329 G
debib@highpoint.edu
BUTT, Ryan .... 815-836-5267 141 G
rbutt@lewisu.edu
BUTTAFARRO, JR.,
Thomas .... 716-375-2155 313 F
tbuttafa@sbu.edu
BUTTARS, Ryan, J .... 208-496-3405 130 A
buttarsr@byui.edu
BUTTENSCHON,
Marianne .... 315-792-5631 307 D
mbuttenschon@mvcc.edu
BUTTERFIELD, Heather .. 608-796-3930 498 N
hmbutterfield@viterbo.edu
BUTTERFIELD, Kevin ..... 804-289-8456 472 L
kbutterf@richmond.edu
BUTTERFIELD,
Sherri-Ann, P .... 973-353-5541 282 B
sbutter@newark.rutgers.edu
BUTTERFIELD, Valerie ... 616-234-4105 224 D
registrars@grcc.edu
BUTTERMORE, Jim .... 724-964-8811 391 E
jbuttermore@ncstrades.edu
BUTTLEMAN, Kurt .... 206-934-4111 483 I
kurt.buttleman@seattlecolleges.edu
BUTTON, Emiley .... 270-384-7442 183 C
buttone@lindsey.edu
BUTTON, Mark .... 402-472-6262 269 J
mbutton2@unl.edu
BUTTRY, Tonya .... 573-334-6825 259 J
tbuttry@sehcollege.edu
BUTTS, III, Calvin, O .... 516-876-3160 319 A
buttsc@oldwestbury.edu
BUTTS, Dawn .... 803-508-7332 406 E
buttsd@atc.edu
BUTTS, Gary .... 212-241-8276 302 F
gary.butts@mssm.edu
BUTTS, Jeffrey .... 212-237-8486 294 D
jbutts@jjay.cuny.edu
BUTTS, Montez .... 970-351-3403.. 83 E
montez.butts@unco.edu
BUTTS, Nicole, L .... 909-869-4714.. 30 D
nlbutts@cpp.edu
BUTTS, Sue .... 251-981-3771.... 5 B
sue.butts@columbiasouthern.edu
BUTTS, Tracy .... 530-898-5146.. 31 A
tbutts@csuchico.edu
BUTTY, David, C .... 313-496-2526 232 C
dbutty1@wcccd.edu
BUTWELL, Ann .... 859-985-3924 179 C
butwella@berea.edu
BUTWELL, Justin .... 845-575-3000 305 L
justin.butwell@marist.edu
BUTWIN, Bridget, K ...... 812-237-4141 155 G
bridget.butwin@indstate.edu
BUTZ, Carl, R .... 262-243-5700 493 B
carl.butz@cuw.edu
BUTZ, John .... 252-823-5166 334 C
butzj@edgecombe.edu
BUTZER, Hans, W .... 405-325-3505 371 B
butzer@ou.edu
BUVINGER, Nancy .... 562-860-2451.. 35 M
nbuvinger@cerritos.edu
BUWICK, Amy .... 309-298-2453 152 D
aj-buwick@wiu.edu
BUXBAUM, Hannah ...... 812-855-8669 156 B
ovpia@iu.edu
BUXBAUM, Hannah ...... 812-855-4350 156 A
hbuxbaum@iu.edu
BUXTON, Bonnie .... 678-225-7465 396 D
bonnieb@pcom.edu
BUXTON, Jasmine .... 302-857-6300.. 89 F
jbuxton@desu.edu
BUYS, Cindy, G .... 618-453-8743 149 E
cbuys@siu.edu
BUZAK, Anne .... 702-836-9900.. 26 F
abuzak@asher.edu
BUZANSKI, Catherine ... 315-279-5646 304 A
cbuzanski@keuka.edu
BUZARD, Erica .... 814-371-2090 400 D
ebuzard@triangle-tech.edu
BUZBEE, Brandon .... 303-871-2702.. 83 D
brandon.buzbee@du.edu
BUZHARDT, Landee ...... 803-321-5106 411 D
landee.buzhardt@newberry.edu
BUZZANCA, Cristine ...... 239-280-2511.. 94 O
cristine.buzzanca@avemaria.edu
BUZZARD, Curtis .... 845-938-4041 504 H
8uscc@usma.edu
BUZZARD, Janet .... 918-444-2900 367 A
buzzardj@nsuok.edu
BUZZELLI, Andrew .... 423-636-7391 427 B
abuzzelli@tusculum.edu
BUZZETTA, Mary .... 210-784-1336 448 A
mary.buzzetta@tamusa.edu
BYAM, Latrice .... 202-806-2705.. 92 B
latrice.byam@howard.edu
BYAM, Stephan, A .... 410-462-7410 197 E
sbyam@bccc.edu
BYARD, Brenda .... 540-868-7208 474 J
bbyard@lfcc.edu
BYARS, Susan .... 239-590-7980 108 K
sbyars@fgcu.edu
BYBEE, David .... 808-675-4300 127 E
david.bybee@byuh.edu
BYBEE, Paivi .... 816-501-4832 258 H
paivi.bybee@rockhurst.edu
BYBEE, Tamika .... 757-825-2851 476 A
bybeet@tncc.edu
BYCURA, Samantha ...... 412-809-5100 396 H
bycura.samantha@ptcollege.edu
BYCZEK, Sara .... 313-593-5430 231 F
sbyczek@umich.edu
BYELICH, David, S .... 517-355-9271 227 D
byelich@msu.edu
BYEON, Soon, C .... 636-327-4645 255 L
aviation@midwest.edu
BYER, Shanda .... 217-786-2290 142 B
shanda.byer@llcc.edu
BYERLY, Alison, R .... 610-330-5200 387 E
byerlya@lafayette.edu
BYERLY, Thomas, L ...... 540-887-7000 469 B
tbyerly@marybaldwin.edu
BYERS, Fred .... 970-675-3407.. 78 G
fred.byers@cncc.edu
BYERS, Gary .... 909-869-3704.. 30 D
gbyers@cpp.edu
BYERS, Merrie .... 970-675-3204.. 78 G
merrie.byers@cncc.edu
BYERS, Michael .... 304-260-4380 488 J
mbyers@blueridgectc.edu
BYERS, Michelle, C ...... 319-273-2422 163 B
michelle.byers@uni.edu
BYERS, Mike .... 828-227-7321 344 A
mtbyers@wcu.edu
BYERS, Randy .... 214-333-5691 434 I
randy@dbu.edu
BYERS, Rhonda .... 573-341-4241 261 E
byersrf@mst.edu
BYFORD, Tina .... 575-646-2867 287 B
tbyford@nmsu.edu
BYHAM, Joseph .... 215-503-3997 400 A
joseph.byham@jefferson.edu
BYINGTON, Carrie, L .... 979-436-0202 446 G
svp@tamhsc.edu
BYINGTON, Kathleen .... 631-632-6265 317 D
BYINGTON, Scott .... 919-718-7425 333 C
sbyington@cccc.edu
BYLAND, KK .... 800-280-0307 152 H
kk.byland@ace.edu
BYLAND, Tamara, C ..... 513-556-1100 362 D
bylandtc@ucmail.uc.edu
BYLER, Charles .... 262-547-1211 492 E
cbyler@carrollu.edu
BYLSMA, Thomas, W .... 616-395-7781 225 B
bylsma@hope.edu
BYMAN, Gregory, P ...... 260-422-5561 155 H
gpbyman@indianatech.edu
BYNUM, Chris .... 616-949-5300 222 I
chris.bynum@cornerstone.edu
BYNUM, Leroy .... 503-725-3340 376 A
lbynumjr@pdx.edu
BYNUM, Lynn, M .... 502-272-8236 179 B
lbynum@bellarmine.edu
BYNUM, Torrance .... 415-550-4348.. 37 A
tbynum@ccsf.edu
BYNUM, JR., William ... 601-979-2323 246 E
william.b.bynum@jsums.edu
BYRD, Alan .... 314-516-6471 261 D
byrdak@umsl.edu
BYRD, Bonita, E .... 410-651-6088 203 A
bebyrd@umes.edu
BYRD, Cal .... 847-608-5457 136 F
cbyrd@elgin.edu
BYRD, Caroline .... 210-436-3441 443 A
cbyrd@stmarytx.edu
BYRD, Christopher, D ... 803-777-3343 413 C
cbyrd@sc.edu
BYRD, David .... 401-874-5484 406 B
dbyrd@uri.edu
BYRD, David .... 919-546-8237 340 E
david.byrd@shawu.edu
BYRD, Debbie, C .... 423-439-2068 419 J
byrddc1@etsu.edu
BYRD, Devin .... 912-650-5642 124 E
dbyrd@southuniversity.edu
BYRD, Donna .... 404-880-8411 116 D
dbyrd@cau.edu
BYRD, Herb .... 865-974-6621 427 F
hbyrdiii@tennessee.edu
BYRD, James .... 918-293-4940 368 D
james.w.byrd@okstate.edu
BYRD, Jason, D .... 540-365-4295 467 I
jbyrd@ferrum.edu
BYRD, Jennifer, D .... 615-353-3249 425 D
jennifer.byrd@nscc.edu
BYRD, Jimmy .... 979-209-7287 432 C
jimmy.byrd@blinn.edu
BYRD, Katheryn .... 865-694-6523 425 F
kbyrd@pstcc.edu
BYRD, Kim .... 307-268-2210 501 U
kbyrd@caspercollege.edu
BYRD, Laura .... 352-365-3515 102 T
byrdl@lssc.edu
BYRD, Marcia .... 937-529-2201 362 A
mbyrd@united.edu
BYRD, Marcus .... 410-951-6410 203 D
mbyrd@coppin.edu
BYRD, Maria .... 202-274-6878.. 93 C
mbyrd@udc.edu
BYRD, Marlon .... 410-225-2355 199 H
mbyrd01@mica.edu
BYRD, Michelle, E .... 864-250-8423 410 B
michelle.byrd@gvltec.edu
BYRD, Nita .... 315-781-3671 302 A
byrd@hws.edu
BYRD, Paula .... 850-471-4679 104 H
pbyrd@pensacolastate.edu
BYRD, Rodney .... 678-466-4230 116 E
rodneybyrd@clayton.edu
BYRD, Sylvia .... 803-508-7494 406 E
byrds@atc.edu
BYRD, T. Michelle .... 423-439-4210 419 J
byrdt@etsu.edu
BYRD, Theresa .... 619-260-2370.. 71 J
tsbyrd@sandiego.edu
BYRD, Traevena .... 202-885-3285.. 90 J
tbyrd@american.edu
BYRD, Wendy .... 678-359-5011 119 F
wendyb1@gordonstate.edu
BYRD DANSO, Kellie .... 203-857-6887.. 86 D
kbyrd-danso@norwalk.edu
BYRD-HARRIS, Marie .... 559-638-0300.. 66 F
marie.harris@reedleycollege.edu

BYRD-MURPHY, Melinda .... 251-580-2140.... 1 I
melinda.byrd-murphy@coastalalabama.edu
BYRD-POLLER, Lynda ... 757-825-2730 476 A
byrd-pollerl@tncc.edu
BYRNE, Brian .... 405-208-5640 367 I
babyrne@okcu.edu
BYRNE, Faith .... 610-527-0200 397 I
fbyrne@rosemont.edu
BYRNE, Greg .... 205-348-8850.... 7 G
gkbyrne@ua.edu
BYRNE, Jason .... 817-257-7019 448 G
j.byrne@tcu.edu
BYRNE, Ken .... 413-369-4044 208 D
byrne@csld.edu
BYRNE, Matthew .... 845-569-3508 307 J
matthew.byrne@msmc.edu
BYRNE, Molly .... 209-946-2780.. 70 E
mbyrne@pacific.edu
BYRNE, Ryan .... 415-485-9591.. 39 C
rbyrne@marin.edu
BYRNES, Kathleen, J ..... 610-519-4550 402 D
kathleen.byrnes@villanova.edu
BYRNES, Mark, E .... 615-898-2953 422 H
mark.byrnes@mtsu.edu
BYRNES, Steve .... 314-977-7363 259 H
steve.byrnes@health.slu.edu
BYRON, Joseph .... 323-860-0789.. 50 A
BYRON, Shelley .... 607-729-1581 298 C
sbyron@davisny.edu
BYSTRY, Richard, L ...... 217-245-3030 138 D
rlbystry@ic.edu

C

CABALLERO, Cesar .... 909-537-5099.. 33 A
ccaballe@csusb.edu
CABALLERO, Deanna ..... 909-607-8254.. 56 J
deanna_caballero@pitzer.edu
CABALLERO, Maria .... 323-409-2774.. 49 H
mcaballero@dhs.lacounty.gov
CABAN, Jose .... 352-588-8362 106 D
jose.caban@saintleo.edu
CABAN, Jose .... 787-891-0925 508 K
jcaban@aguadilla.inter.edu
CABAN, Mariveliz .... 787-766-1717 511 H
marcaban@suagm.edu
CABANERO, Janett .... 408-498-5145.. 38 F
jcabanero@cogswell.edu
CABASCO, Tony .... 802-440-4887 462 A
tonycabasco@bennington.edu
CABELLO, Connie .... 508-626-4515 212 D
ccabello@framingham.edu
CABELLO, Iris, R .... 787-765-1915 510 B
icabello@opto.inter.edu
CABELLON, Edmund ..... 508-678-2811 213 G
edmund.cabellon@bristolcc.edu
CABIN, Robert, J .... 828-883-8112 327 C
cabinrj@brevard.edu
CABLE, Brett .... 606-759-7141 182 A
brett.cable@kctcs.edu
CABLE, Cyrus, R .... 601-877-6114 244 H
ckruss@alcorn.edu
CABLE, Dwayne .... 901-435-1627 421 A
dwayne_cable@loc.edu
CABLE, Nancy, J .... 828-251-6500 342 C
chanoffi@unca.edu
CABLER, JR., Robert ..... 434-528-5276 477 E
rcabler@vul.edu
CABONI, Timothy, C ..... 270-745-4493 185 E
caboni@wku.edu
CABORN, Peter .... 313-577-2308 232 I
pcaborn@wayne.edu
CABOT, Jeri, O .... 843-953-5522 408 E
cabotj@cofc.edu
CABRAL, Jennifer, G ..... 740-427-5171 355 E
cabral@kenyon.edu
CABRAL, Joyce .... 304-876-5484 490 E
jcabral@shepherd.edu
CABRAL, Kathleen .... 808-455-0524 129 D
kcabral@hawaii.edu
CABRAL, Robert .... 805-678-5824.. 73 A
rcabral@vcccd.edu
CABRALES, Joe .... 909-389-3368.. 59 H
jcabrale@craftonhills.edu
CABRERA, Isabel .... 212-343-1234 306 J
icabrera@mcny.edu
CABRERA, Leonor .... 650-306-3201.. 61 O
cabreral@smccd.edu
CABRERA, Mario .... 212-217-4999 299 H
mario_cabrera@fitnyc.edu
CABRERA, Moises .... 787-841-2000 510 K
mcabrera@pucpr.edu
CABRERA, Rafael .... 787-766-1912 508 J
rcabrera@inter.edu
CABRERA, Rene .... 607-592-3030 216 B
rene.cabrera@mcphs.edu
CABRERA, Zuleika .... 787-852-1430 508 C
zuleika.cabrera@hccpr.edu
CABRERA-RIVERA, Janet .... 787-993-8858 513 B
janet.cabrera@upr.edu
CABUCO, Tracy .... 818-299-5500.. 73 K
tcabuco@westcoastuniversity.edu
CABUNGCAL, Christi, L 614-947-6542 353 C
christi.cabungcal@franklin.edu
CACCAVERI, Peter .... 513-861-6400 361 L
peter.caccaveri@myunion.edu
CACCIOLA, Jaime .... 301-663-3131 199 B
cacciola@hood.edu
CACEDA, Luz .... 410-532-5544 201 B
lcaceda@ndm.edu
CACERES, George .... 201-216-9901 277 D
george.caceres@eicollege.edu
CADA, Beth .... 708-534-5000 137 F
bcada@govst.edu
CADDY, Kurt .... 417-328-1900 259 L
kcaddy@sbuniv.edu
CADDY, Sheryl .... 503-491-6701 374 C
sheryl.caddy@mhcc.edu
CADE, Eulanda .... 402-872-2230 268 F
ecade@peru.edu
CADE, Heather .... 530-541-4660.. 47 E
cade@ltcc.edu
CADE, Jami .... 816-444-0669 258 H
bookstore@rockhurst.edu
CADE, John .... 615-963-5107 426 D
jcade@tnstate.edu
CADE, Tina, Q .... 804-289-8032 472 L
tcade@richmond.edu
CADENA, Rosa .... 978-232-2064 209 B
rcadena@endicott.edu
CADENA-SMITH, Marisela .... 972-758-3896 433 M
mcsmith@collin.edu
CADIENTE-BROWN, Ronalda .... 907-796-6058.. 10 B
rcadientebrown@alaska.edu
CADLE, Anne .... 501-977-2085.. 23 A
cadle@uaccm.edu
CADLE, David .... 314-286-4480 258 E
dacadle@ranken.edu
CADLE, Julie .... 229-732-5927 114 B
juliecadle@andrewcollege.edu
CADLE, Shirley, A .... 719-884-5000.. 81 C
sacadle@nbc.edu
CADOFF, Roy .... 434-924-1074 473 A
rec2qn@virginia.edu
CADRAY, Lynell .... 404-727-2611 117 F
lynell.cadray@emory.edu
CADWALLADER, Dawn .. 770-426-2601 121 C
dawn.callwallader@life.edu
CADWALLADER, Sarah .. 620-431-2820 175 H
scadwallader@neosho.edu
CADWELL, Brian, J .... 906-487-2216 227 E
bjcadwel@mtu.edu
CADY, Alyssa .... 216-421-7957 350 M
arcady@cia.edu
CADY, Cathy .... 321-433-7419.. 97 I
cadyc@easternflorida.edu
CADY MELZER, Deborah, M .... 315-445-4527 304 C
cadymedm@lemoyne.edu
CADZOW, Renee .... 716-829-8287 298 F
cadzowr@dyc.edu
CAFASSO, Frank .... 718-420-4220 324 F
fcafasso@wagner.edu
CAFFELLE, John .... 508-588-9100 214 F
jcaffelle1@massasoit.mass.edu
CAFFERA, Paul .... 662-915-1537 249 D
pcaffera@olemiss.edu
CAFFERTY, Jack .... 208-459-5168 130 D
jcafferty@collegeofidaho.edu
CAFFEY, Kevin .... 903-923-2011 436 D
kcaffey@etbu.edu
CAFFEY, Walter .... 508-286-3782 220 A
caffey_walter@wheatoncollege.edu
CAFFEY, Walter, F .... 203-932-7205.. 89 A
wcaffey@newhaven.edu
CAFFIE, Janique .... 973-328-5149 277 B
jcaffie@ccm.edu
CAFFO, David, C .... 302-356-2474.. 90 I
david.c.caffo@wilmu.edu
CAFFREY, James, L .... 570-941-6267 401 H
james.caffrey@sranton.edu
CAFONCELLI, Kathy, L .. 610-921-7600 378 C
kcafoncelli@albright.edu
CAGE, Beverly .... 361-698-1279 436 C
bacage@delmar.edu
CAGE, John .... 608-342-6188 497 D
cagej@uwplatt.edu
CAGE, Stephanie .... 636-481-3298 254 A
scage@jeffco.edu
CAGIGAS, Marcia .... 323-415-5383.. 48 H
cagigamp@elac.edu
CAGLE, Andrew, R .... 336-334-4225 343 A
racagle@uncg.edu
CAGLE, David .... 815-802-8128 140 D
dcagle@kcc.edu
CAGLE, DeVonne .... 903-510-2417 452 C
dcag@tjc.edu
CAGLE, Kathy .... 703-993-8627 467 L
kcagle@gmu.edu
CAGLE, Pat .... 870-248-4000.. 18 F
pat.cagle@blackrivertech.edu
CAGLE, Sam .... 985-448-4420 192 B
sam.cagle@nicholls.edu
CAGLE, Sheri .... 815-802-8822 140 D
scagle@kcc.edu
CAGNA, Robert .... 252-399-6501 326 M
rcagna@barton.edu
CAGNET, Danny .... 248-218-2190 229 J
dcagnet@rc.edu
CAGWIN, Amber .... 907-474-5655.. 10 A
accagwin@alaska.edu
CAHALAN, Jodi .... 515-271-1369 164 I
jodi.cahalan@dmu.edu
CAHALL, Perry, J .... 614-885-5585 360 E
pcahall@pcj.edu
CAHAN, Susan .... 215-777-9894 399 F
susan.cahan@temple.edu
CAHILL, Diane .... 740-593-4330 359 G
cahilld@ohio.edu
CAHILL, Elena .... 203-576-2389.. 88 D
ecahill@bridgeport.edu
CAHILL, Elizabeth .... 215-965-4037 390 J
ecahill@moore.edu
CAHILL, Gregoria .... 415-920-6001.. 37 A
gcahill@ccsf.edu
CAHILL, Holly .... 701-477-7862 347 A
hcahill@tm.edu
CAHILL, Kevin .... 619-849-2413.. 57 E
kevincahill@pointloma.edu
CAHILL, Margaret, D ..... 651-962-6131 244 E
mdcahill@stthomas.edu
CAHILL, Melissa, L .... 410-888-9048 200 A
mcahill@muih.edu
CAHILL, Michael, T .... 718-780-7901 291 J
michael.cahill@brooklaw.edu
CAHILL, Richard .... 859-985-3451 179 C
richard_cahill@berea.edu
CAHILL, Ryan .... 313-883-8696 229 K
cahill.ryan@shms.edu
CAHILL, Tina .... 617-405-5942 218 B
tcahill@quincycollege.edu
CAHILL-MUSICK, Elizabeth, J .... 304-384-6003 490 A
lcahill@concord.edu
CAHN, Judith .... 212-484-1193 294 D
jcahn@jjay.cuny.edu
CAHOON, Kirsten .... 507-786-3268 243 C
cahoon@stolaf.edu
CAI, Maoyi .... 512-444-8082 449 A
cai@thsu.edu
CAILLOUX, Laura .... 360-679-5333 485 A
laura.cailloux@skagit.edu
CAIN, Bryan .... 978-232-2321 209 B
bcain@endicott.edu
CAIN, Candace .... 334-386-7182.... 5 D
ccain@faulkner.edu
CAIN, Darrell, L .... 253-840-8421 483 D
dcain@pierce.ctc.edu
CAIN, Greg .... 208-885-5541 131 G
gcain@uidaho.edu
CAIN, Holly .... 318-357-5351 192 C
cainh@nsula.edu
CAIN, Joel .... 601-477-2258 246 F
joel.cain@jcjc.edu
CAIN, Katherine .... 314-977-4180 259 H
katherine.cain@slu.edu
CAIN, Michael, E .... 716-829-3955 316 F
mcain@buffalo.edu
CAIN, Michael, E .... 716-829-2100 316 F
vphs@buffalo.edu
CAIN, Pam .... 515-294-6162 162 I
pelliott@iastate.edu
CAIN, Ruth .... 816-235-6084 261 C
cainre@umkc.edu
CAIN, Sandra .... 508-541-1658 208 F
scain@dean.edu
CAIN, Sara Beth .... 619-388-2721.. 60 D
scain@sdccd.edu
CAIN, Stephen, D .... 240-567-1796 200 C
stephen.cain@montgomerycollege.edu
CAIN, Tabi .... 910-775-4201 343 B
tabitha.cain@uncp.edu
CAIN, Wendy .... 270-809-2318 183 G
wcain@murraystate.edu
CAIN, Wingate .... 820-652-0632 336 B
wingatecain@mcdowelltech.edu
CAIRES, Matthew .... 406-994-2826 264 D
mcaires@montana.edu
CAIRNS, Janet .... 918-631-3101 371 E
janet-cairns@utulsa.edu
CAIRNS, Jill .... 207-834-7602 196 C
jillb@maine.edu
CAIRO, Jimmy, R .... 504-568-4246 189 B
jcairo@lsuhsu.edu
CAIRO, Michael .... 859-233-8121 184 G
mcairo@transy.edu
CAIROL, Miguel .... 718-260-5600 295 B
mcairol@citytech.cuny.edu
CAIRY, Timothy, J .... 610-499-1193 403 B
tjcairy@widener.edu
CAISON, Anthony .... 919-866-6101 338 G
amcaison@waketech.edu
CAKMAK, Burak .... 212-229-8966 308 C
cakmakb@newschool.edu
CAL, John .... 305-348-4001 109 A
john.cal@fiu.edu
CAL, Mark .... 575-439-3622 287 C
mcal@nmsu.edu
CALABA, George .... 610-799-1114 388 I
gcalaba@lccc.edu
CALABRESE, Nancy .... 410-626-2553 201 D
nancy.calabrese@sjc.edu
CALABRESE, Walter ...... 252-444-0739 333 H
calabresew@cravencc.edu
CALABRIA, Patrick .... 631-420-2400 321 B
patrick.calabria@farmingdale.edu
CALAHAN, John .... 936-468-1025 445 F
calahanje@sfasu.edu
CALAIS, Debra .... 337-482-6199 192 E
dcalais@louisiana.edu
CALAIS, Erica .... 225-342-6950 191 D
erica.calais@ulsystem.edu
CALAMAIO, Caprice .... 913-234-0733 172 E
caprice.calamaio@cleveland.edu
CALAMARE, Susan, S ... 617-422-7387 217 C
scalamare@nesl.edu
CALAMETTI, Jeffrey, D .. 251-442-2242.... 8 C
jcalametti@umobile.edu
CALAMIA, James .... 732-255-0400 280 A
jcalamia@ocean.edu
CALANDRA, Viviana ...... 407-303-7894.. 94 D
viviana.calandra@ahu.edu
CALARESE, Mary .... 508-831-5423 220 E
mcalarese@wpi.edu
CALARESO, Jack .... 617-217-9046 206 A
CALARESO, Joe .... 305-595-9500.. 94 B
admissions@amcollege.edu
CALDARELLO, Beth .... 660-359-3948 257 D
bcaldarello@mail.ncmissouri.edu
CALDERA, Nancy .... 509-527-2315 485 H
nancy.caldera@wallawalla.edu
CALDERO FIGUEROA, Ana, J .... 407-582-1431 112 K
acalderofigueroa@valenciacollege.edu
CALDERON, Ann Marie . 615-230-3401 426 B
annmarie.calderon@volstate.edu
CALDERON, Christina ... 760-252-2411.. 26 I
ccalderon@barstow.edu
CALDERON, Gerardo ..... 209-954-5052.. 60 J
gcalderon@deltacollege.edu
CALDERON, Hermes ...... 787-780-0070 506 F
hcalderon@caribbean.edu
CALDERON, Janet .... 407-303-6108.. 94 D
janet.calderon@ahu.edu
CALDERON, Nancy, T ... 408-554-4400.. 62 D
ntcalderon@scu.edu
CALDERON, Paula .... 985-549-2217 192 D
paula.calderon@selu.edu
CALDERON, Rosa .... 310-338-8839.. 50 J
rosa.calderon@lmu.edu
CALDERONE, Jackie ...... 508-541-1530 208 F
0558mgr@fheg.follett.com
CALDERONE, Jill .... 574-631-2622 161 C
jcalder2@nd.edu
CALDWELL, Adonna ...... 901-572-2592 418 E
adonna.caldwell@bchs.edu
CALDWELL, Agnes .... 419-783-2402 352 F
acaldwell@defiance.edu

CALDWELL, Benjamin ... 903-233-3200 439 E benjamincaldwell@letu.edu
CALDWELL, Benjamin, D .... 540-831-5431 470 C
CALDWELL, Brinda, W .. 828-398-7134 332 B bcaldwell@abtech.edu
CALDWELL, Bryan .... 305-899-3250.. 95 C bcaldwell@barry.edu
CALDWELL, Cary .... 704-406-3939 329 A ccaldwell@gardner-webb.edu
CALDWELL, Cheryl .... 417-255-7960 256 F cherylcaldwell@missouristate.edu
CALDWELL, Chris .... 502-776-1443 184 B ccaldwell@simmonscollegeky.edu
CALDWELL, Craig .... 801-957-5180 461 D craig.caldwell@slcc.edu
CALDWELL, Dallas .... 405-974-2631 370 K dcaldwell@uco.edu
CALDWELL, Daniel .... 601-318-6115 249 H daniel.caldwell@wmcarey.edu
CALDWELL, Derrick .... 601-977-7720 249 C dcaldwell@tougaloo.edu
CALDWELL, Donna .... 706-864-1410 126 A donna.caldwell@ung.edu
CALDWELL, Gail .... 256-726-7024.... 6 C gcaldwell@oakwood.edu
CALDWELL, Helen .... 704-378-1014 330 D hcaldwell@jcsu.edu
CALDWELL, Jacqueline, H .... 918-631-2691 371 E jacqueline-caldwell@utulsa.edu
CALDWELL, James .... 970-675-3236.. 78 G james.caldwell@cncc.edu
CALDWELL, James .... 215-780-1311 398 G jcaldwell@salus.edu
CALDWELL, James .... 215-780-1306 398 G jcaldwell@salus.edu
CALDWELL, Jeff .... 405-736-0243 369 I jcaldwell@rose.edu
CALDWELL, Jim .... 215-780-1313 398 G jcaldwell@salus.edu
CALDWELL, Jodi, K .... 912-478-5541 119 C jodic@georgiasouthern.edu
CALDWELL, Katrina, M . 662-915-2934 249 D kmcaldw1@olemiss.edu
CALDWELL, Kisha .... 423-697-3250 424 E kisha.caldwell@chattanoogastate.edu
CALDWELL, Larry, W .... 605-336-6588 416 E lcaldwell@sfseminary.edu
CALDWELL, Mike .... 817-257-7523 448 G m.a.caldwell@tcu.edu
CALDWELL, Nina .... 314-529-9485 254 H ncaldwell@maryville.edu
CALDWELL, Patrice .... 575-562-2315 285 M patrice.caldwell@enmu.edu
CALDWELL, Richard .... 402-898-1000 266 H rich_c@creativecenter.edu
CALDWELL, Robert, M .. 802-865-6400 462 B rcaldwell@champlain.edu
CALDWELL, Sheila .... 630-752-7551 152 F sheila.caldwell@wheaton.edu
CALDWELL, Stephanie ... 973-408-3061 277 C scaldwell@drew.edu
CALDWELL, OSB, Teresio .... 503-845-3169 374 B teresio.caldwell@mtangel.edu
CALDWELL, Timothy ..... 509-777-3749 486 I tcaldwell@whitworth.edu
CALDWELL, Trish .... 916-484-8354.. 50 F caldwet@arc.losrios.edu
CALDWELL, Troy .... 740-695-9500 348 F tcaldwell@belmontcollege.edu
CALDWELL, IV, William, B .... 478-387-4775 118 G wcaldwell@gmc.edu
CALE, Benjamin .... 304-877-6428 487 F admissions@abc.edu
CALEB, Peter .... 917-493-4507 305 I library@msmnyc.edu
CALEFFI-PRICHARD, Vivi .... 503-365-4723 372 C vivi.caleffi.prichard@chemeketa.edu
CALERO, Teofilo .... 773-878-2998 148 D tcalero@staugustine.edu
CALFAS, Karen, J .... 858-822-7552.. 69 D kcalfas@ucsd.edu
CALFIN, Matt .... 619-644-7390.. 44 I matt.calfin@gcccd.edu
CALFIN, Matthew .... 805-378-1448.. 72 H mcalfin@vcccd.edu
CALHOUN, Cheryl .... 352-395-5719 107 A cheryl.calhoun@sfcollege.edu
CALHOUN, Dominique .. 713-313-7640 449 C dominique.calhoun@tsu.edu
CALHOUN, Elizabeth ..... 520-626-9921.. 16 G ecalhoun@email.arizona.edu
CALHOUN, Jay .... 401-863-9075 404 E jay_calhoun@brown.edu
CALHOUN, John .... 619-849-2784.. 57 E johncalhoun@pointloma.edu
CALHOUN, Kirk, A .... 903-877-7750 456 D kirk.calhoun@uthct.edu
CALHOUN, Larry .... 912-538-3101 124 F lcalhoun@southeasterntech.edu
CALHOUN, Linda .... 270-686-4473 182 B linda.calhoun@kctcs.edu
CALHOUN, Lozanne ...... 870-543-5952.. 21 C lcalhoun@seark.edu
CALHOUN, M. Grace .... 215-898-7215 400 K athdir@pobox.upenn.edu
CALHOUN, Matthew ...... 601-276-3718 249 B mattc@smcc.edu
CALHOUN, Mitch .... 325-574-7612 458 E mcalhoun@wtc.edu
CALHOUN, Pat .... 409-839-2956 449 G pcalhoun@lit.edu
CALHOUN, Paula, M ..... 330-471-8236 355 L pcalhoun@malone.edu
CALHOUN, Ralph .... 901-435-1276 421 A ralph_calhoun@loc.edu
CALHOUN, Ric .... 678-359-5018 119 F ricc@gordonstate.edu
CALHOUN, Rica .... 850-412-5479 108 I rica.calhoun@famu.edu
CALHOUN, Rochelle ...... 609-258-3056 280 E rochelle.calhoun@princeton.edu
CALHOUN, Roy .... 229-430-1729 113 I rcalhoun@albanytech.edu
CALHOUN, Thomas .... 601-979-1611 246 E thomas.c.calhoun@jsums.edu
CALHOUN, JR., Thomas, J .... 904-470-8000.. 97 L
CALHOUN, Vaughn, A .. 508-373-9736 206 B vaughn.calhoun@becker.edu
CALHOUN-BROWN, Allison .... 404-413-2067 119 E acalhounbrown@gsu.edu
CALHOUN-BROWN, Allison .... 404-413-1500 119 E acalhounbrown@gsu.edu
CALHOUN-FRENCH, Diane .... 502-213-2621 181 F diane.calhoun-french@kctcs.edu
CALHOUN-WARD, Stephanie .... 860-906-5259.. 85 D scalhoun-ward@capitalcc.edu
CALILAN, James (Kimo) .... 707-864-7264.. 64 C
CALISE, Lisa .... 617-287-7050 211 C lcalise@umassp.edu
CALISE, Thomasina, L .. 203-857-7003.. 86 D tcalise@norwalk.edu
CALISSI, Barbara .... 516-323-3035 307 F bcalissi@molloy.edu
CALISTO, George, W ..... 312-553-3149 134 B gcalisto@ccc.edu
CALKINS, Nancy .... 336-334-4822 335 A nfgriffincalkins@gtcc.edu
CALL, Patrick .... 970-339-6657.. 76 G patrick.call@aims.edu
CALLAGHAN, Carolyn ... 717-477-1502 395 E cmcallaghan@ship.edu
CALLAGHAN, James ..... 478-445-4789 118 C james.callaghan@gcsu.edu
CALLAGHAN, Karen, A .. 305-899-3401.. 95 C kcallaghan@barry.edu
CALLAGHAN, MaryEllen 914-633-2512 302 G mcallaghan@iona.edu
CALLAGHAN, Sandra .... 817-257-6483 448 G s.callaghan@tcu.edu
CALLAHAN, Aimee .... 432-335-6701 441 D acallahan@odessa.edu
CALLAHAN, Amy .... 503-352-2838 375 G amy.callahan@pacificu.edu
CALLAHAN, Angela .... 508-910-6454 211 F angela.callahan@umassd.edu
CALLAHAN, Audra .... 508-999-8620 211 F acallahan@umassd.edu
CALLAHAN, Brigid .... 847-947-5409 144 F bcallahan2@nl.edu
CALLAHAN, Caitlin .... 617-449-7038 219 C caitlin.callahan@urbancollege.edu
CALLAHAN, Candice ..... 718-779-1499 311 I cmc2@plazacollege.edu
CALLAHAN, Caroline ..... 718-779-1499 311 I cmc@plazacollege.edu
CALLAHAN, III, Charles, E .... 718-779-1499 311 I cec3@plazacollege.edu
CALLAHAN, IV, Charles, E .... 718-779-1499 311 I cec4@plazacollege.edu
CALLAHAN, Christena ... 321-674-8927.. 99 B ccallahan@fit.edu
CALLAHAN, Christopher .... 602-496-5012.. 10 I christopher.callahan@asu.edu
CALLAHAN, Clara, A ..... 215-955-6983 400 A clara.callahan@jefferson.edu
CALLAHAN, Erica .... 315-568-3213 308 F ecallahan@nycc.edu
CALLAHAN, JR., Jack, F .... 203-432-1185.. 89 D jack.callahan@yale.edu
CALLAHAN, Janet .... 906-487-2005 227 E callahan@mtu.edu
CALLAHAN, Joy, T .... 919-209-2027 335 F jtcallahan@johnstoncc.edu
CALLAHAN, Keith .... 540-887-7201 469 B mkcallahan@marybaldwin.edu
CALLAHAN, Margaret .... 215-517-2654 379 A callahanm@arcadia.edu
CALLAHAN, Margaret, F .... 708-216-9222 142 D mcallahan3@luc.edu
CALLAHAN, Mark .... 402-461-5177 267 F
CALLAHAN, Mary .... 617-258-6432 215 G
CALLAHAN, Michael ...... 805-289-6344.. 73 B mcallahan@vcccd.edu
CALLAHAN, Pat .... 215-489-2208 382 D patrick.callahan@delval.edu
CALLAHAN, Patricia ...... 978-762-4000 215 B tcallaha@northshore.edu
CALLAHAN, Phyllis .... 513-529-6721 356 E callahp@miamioh.edu
CALLAHAN, Robert .... 920-686-6238 496 A robert.callahan@sl.edu
CALLAHAN, Ryan .... 262-472-4661 498 C callahanrm19@uww.edu
CALLAHAN, Sean .... 678-872-8542 118 E scallaha@highlands.edu
CALLAHAN, Tristin .... 256-840-4219.... 3 F tristin.callahan@snead.edu
CALLAN, Pam .... 325-481-8300 438 C pcallan@howardcollege.edu
CALLANAN, Cara .... 978-921-4242 216 F cara.callanan@montserrat.edu
CALLAND, Dana .... 606-759-7141 182 A dana.calland@kctcs.edu
CALLAND, David .... 434-592-7336 468 H dcalland@liberty.edu
CALLAWAY, Cynthia ...... 757-825-2725 476 A callawayc@tncc.edu
CALLAWAY, J. Lea .... 919-497-3325 330 I jleacallaway@louisburg.edu
CALLEJA, Eduardo .... 956-380-8183 442 L psecretary@riogrande.edu
CALLEN, Chad .... 304-296-8282 491 F ctcallen@wvjc.edu
CALLEN, Patricia .... 304-296-8282 491 F pcallen@wvjc.edu
CALLENDER, David, L ... 409-772-1902 456 F dcallender@utmb.edu
CALLICOTT, Robin .... 803-641-3342 413 D robinc@usca.edu
CALLIER, Theodore .... 504-816-4018 186 D tcallier@dillard.edu
CALLIES, Kathryn .... 605-256-5143 416 J kathy.callies@dsu.edu
CALLIES, Mona .... 941-309-4009 105 K mcallies@ringling.edu
CALLIHAM, Marty .... 512-444-8082 449 A mcalliham@thsu.edu
CALLINAN, Dennis .... 845-574-4481 313 C dcallina@sunyrockland.edu
CALLIS, Jennifer .... 785-309-3120 176 J jennifer.callis@salinatech.edu
CALLISTER, Melanie ...... 507-285-7461 240 G melanie.callister@rctc.edu
CALLISTO, Anthony .... 315-443-2225 322 C acallist@syr.edu
CALLOW-WRIGHT, Katie .... 773-795-3361 150 J ccallow@uchicago.edu
CALLOWAY, Brad .... 336-841-9841 329 G scallowa@highpoint.edu
CALLOWAY, Terence ..... 850-599-3256 108 I terence.calloway@famu.edu
CALLWOOD-BRATHWAITE, Denise .... 305-623-1415.. 99 D denise.callwood-brathwaite@fmuniv.edu
CALNAN, Kerry .... 508-213-2207 217 E kerry.calnan@nichols.edu
CALOBRISI, Charlotte, M .... 703-323-3110 475 C ccalobrisi@nvcc.edu
CALOCA, Luis .... 208-562-3396 130 F luiscaloca@cwi.edu
CALOGRIDES, JR., Thomas, G .... 757-822-7330 476 B tcalogrides@tcc.edu
CALOHAN, Jess .... 606-672-2312 180 C
CALORE, Lucille, A .... 401-865-1199 405 B tomasell@providence.edu
CALOVINE, Iris .... 203-932-7297.. 89 A icalovine@newhaven.edu
CALPIN, Fran .... 570-945-8170 386 I fran.calpin@keystone.edu
CALTABIANO, Ronald .... 312-362-7256 135 I rcalt@depaul.edu
CALUS-MCLAIN, Martha 503-352-2764 375 G martha@pacificu.edu
CALUZA, Kimberly .... 206-296-6090 484 F caluzak@seattleu.edu
CALVELLI, Louis .... 718-862-7977 305 H lcalvelli01@manhattan.edu
CALVERT, Carolyn, A .... 325-793-3808 440 B ccalvert@mcm.edu
CALVERT, Chandra .... 605-718-2419 417 F chandra.calvert@wdt.edu
CALVERT, Christopher ... 513-569-1586 350 K christopher.calvert@cincinnatistate.edu
CALVERT, Linda .... 423-323-0222 425 E lwcalvert@northeaststate.edu
CALVERT, Lisa .... 509-335-3564 486 A
CALVERT, Mike .... 620-672-2700 176 G michaelc@prattcc.edu
CALVERT, Phillip .... 334-386-7415.... 5 D pcalvert@faulkenr.edu
CALVERT, Raymond, J .. 727-816-3418 104 F calverr@phsc.edu
CALVEY, Deborah .... 414-955-8225 494 C dcalvey@mcw.edu
CALVIN, Brent .... 559-730-3745.. 39 E brentc@cos.edu
CALVIN, Cathy .... 209-490-4591.. 24 E ccalvin@advancedcollege.edu
CALVIN, Dennis, D .... 814-865-4028 392 B ifa@psu.edu
CALVO, Dean .... 909-621-8211.. 63 E dcalvo@scrippscollege.edu
CALZADA, Maria .... 504-865-2011 189 F calzada@loyno.edu
CALZONETTI, Frank, J ... 419-530-6171 363 E frank.calzonetti@utoledo.edu
CAMACHO, Anita, C ...... 670-237-6824 506 A anita.camacho@marianas.edu
CAMACHO, Carmen, S .. 805-922-6966.. 24 J ccamacho@hancockcollege.edu
CAMACHO, Delia, M ..... 787-798-3001 512 C delia.camacho@uccaribe.edu
CAMACHO, Dennis .... 617-588-1365 206 C dcamacho@bfit.edu
CAMACHO, Francisco, C .... 671-734-0540 505 C mis@guamcc.edu
CAMACHO, Helen, B ..... 670-237-6702 506 A helen.camacho@marianas.edu
CAMACHO, Lawrence, F .... 671-735-2292 505 E lcamacho@triton.uog.edu
CAMACHO, Luis .... 787-725-6500 506 G lcamacho@albizu.edu
CAMACHO, Martin .... 940-397-4274 440 F martin.camacho@msutexas.edu
CAMACHO, Mildred ...... 787-264-1912 509 F milcama@intersg.edu
CAMACHO-MARON, Wanda .... 617-670-4429 209 D wcamacho-maron@fisher.edu
CAMACHO-MELENDEZ, Iris, M .... 787-751-1912 510 A icamacho@juris.inter.edu
CAMAHALAN, Faye, M .. 812-941-2136 157 B fcamahal@ius.edu
CAMANIA, Sarah .... 504-762-3021 187 E scaman@dcc.edu
CAMARA, Lydia .... 508-588-9100 214 F lcamara5@massasoit.mass.edu
CAMARA, Wanda, L ...... 787-894-2828 514 C wanda.camara@upr.edu

CAMARDA-WEBB, Shelata .... 724-938-4444 394 B camardawebb@calu.edu
CAMARENA, Phame, M 989-774-3902 222 C camar1pm@cmich.edu
CAMARGO, Judy, V ...... 210-486-4951 429 E jcamargo@alamo.edu
CAMARILLO, Jane .... 925-631-4235.. 59 B jc11@stmarys-ca.edu
CAMARILLO, Richard .... 805-546-3100.. 41 A richard_camarillo@cuesta.edu
CAMBIA, Barbara .... 561-237-7360 102 V bcambia@lynn.edu
CAMBONE, Joseph .... 978-542-6266 213 C jcambone@salemstate.edu
CAMBRA, Ronald .... 808-956-6231 128 F cambra@hawaii.edu
CAMBRAY, Joseph .... 805-969-3626.. 55 E jcambray@pacifica.edu
CAMBRE, Charles .... 225-743-8500 188 B ccambre@rpcc.edu
CAMBRE, Charles .... 985-549-2244 192 D charles.cambre@selu.edu
CAMBRIA, James .... 212-517-0685 306 A jcambria@mm.edu
CAMBRON, Jerrilyn .... 630-889-6853 144 G jcambron@nuhs.edu
CAMELIO, Jason .... 617-747-2700 206 E jcamelio@berklee.edu
CAMELO, Kathleen, M .. 518-564-2187 319 C camelokm@plattsburgh.edu
CAMERLENGO, Renee ... 412-268-2075 380 F reneec@andrew.cmu.edu
CAMERON, JR., A. Neill .... 864-656-2123 408 A cameron@clemson.edu
CAMERON, Antwone ..... 859-344-4069 184 F cameroa@thomasmore.edu
CAMERON, Aundreia, M .... 323-343-3040.. 32 A acamero6@calstatela.edu
CAMERON, Charley .... 318-678-6000 187 A ccameron@bpcc.edu
CAMERON, Cheryl, A .... 206-221-1405 485 F ccameron@uw.edu
CAMERON, Cori .... 719-549-2456.. 79 A cori.cameron@csupueblo.edu
CAMERON, J. Scott ...... 301-243-2118 503 J
CAMERON, Jennifer ...... 254-526-1264 432 H jennifer.cameron@ctcd.edu
CAMERON, Kenneth ...... 508-373-9452 206 B kenneth.cameron@becker.edu
CAMERON, Kimberly ..... 859-246-6279 180 K kcameron0004@kcts.edu
CAMERON, Maryanne ... 315-279-5179 304 A mcameron@keuka.edu
CAMERON, Matthew, R . 305-899-3875.. 95 C mcameron@barry.edu
CAMERON, Richard, L .. 478-301-5500 121 E cameron_rl@mercer.edu
CAMERON, Ryan, M ..... 402-280-3434 266 I ryancameron@creighton.edu
CAMERON, Samantha ... 906-248-8429 221 N scameron@bmcc.edu
CAMERON, Spencer ...... 303-220-1200.. 77 B spencer.cameron@cffp.edu
CAMERON, Suzette .... 386-506-4506.. 97 D suzette.cameron@daytonastate.edu
CAMERON-KELLY, Diann, E .... 516-877-4426 289 C kelly5@adelphi.edu
CAMEY, John .... 315-792-3055 324 B jpcamey@utica.edu
CAMFIELD, Gregg .... 209-228-4400.. 69 B
CAMILLE, Marc, M .... 203-773-8529.. 84 F mcamille@albertus.edu
CAMILLE, Michael .... 318-342-3011 192 F camille@ulm.edu
CAMILLE, Milton .... 603-752-1113 273 D mcamille@ccsnh.edu
CAMILLERI, Michael ..... 507-284-9328 234 I camilleri.michael@mayo.edu
CAMILLO, Thomas, P .... 814-871-7413 384 E camillo001@gannon.edu
CAMMACK, Cindy .... 402-872-2313 268 F ccammack@peru.edu
CAMMARATA, Jessica ... 814-472-3217 398 B jcammarata@francis.edu
CAMMARATA, Maria ..... 510-430-3322.. 52 D mcammarata@mills.edu
CAMMARATA, Miki .... 973-720-2179 284 I cammaratamj@wpunj.edu
CAMMARATA, Rita .... 212-217-3820 299 H rita_cammarata@fitnyc.edu
CAMOU, Fernando .... 623-845-3677.. 13 C f.camou@gccaz.edu
CAMP, Andy .... 518-580-5745 316 A acamp@skidmore.edu
CAMP, Billy .... 334-386-7255.... 5 D bcamp@faulkner.edu
CAMP, Carol .... 251-442-2213.... 8 C ccamp@umobile.edu
CAMP, Cathryn .... 301-546-0412 201 C
CAMP, Jamie .... 804-862-6100 470 I jcamp@rbc.edu
CAMP, Jon, P .... 863-680-4192.. 99 H jcamp@flsouthern.edu
CAMP, Keith .... 864-424-8091 414 C ckcamp@mailbox.sc.edu
CAMP, Robert, C .... 724-357-7889 394 G bobcamp@iup.edu
CAMP, Skip, L .... 239-513-1122 101 C bcamp@hodges.edu
CAMP, Susan .... 580-581-5952 365 G susanc@cameron.edu
CAMPA, Jeff .... 816-322-0110 250 K jeff.campa@calvary.edu
CAMPAGNA, Gina .... 573-592-5023 262 E gina.campagna@westminster-mo.edu
CAMPANA, Karen .... 630-829-6345 132 E kcampana@ben.edu
CAMPANA, Maryjo .... 570-484-2181 395 B drt831@lockhaven.edu
CAMPANELLI, Kenneth .. 718-482-5502 294 F kcampanelli@lagcc.cuny.edu
CAMPANINI, Albino, P . 321-674-8434.. 99 B bcampanini@fit.edu
CAMPBELL, Aaron .... 661-255-1050.. 28 K
CAMPBELL, Alan .... 563-336-3308 165 B acampbell@eicc.edu
CAMPBELL, Alec .... 425-564-2728 478 F alec.campbell@bellevuecollege.edu
CAMPBELL, Amanda ..... 812-488-2241 161 A ac283@evansville.edu
CAMPBELL, Andrea .... 315-279-5217 304 A acampbell@keuka.edu
CAMPBELL, Andrew, G . 401-863-2532 404 E andrew_campbell@brown.edu
CAMPBELL, Angela .... 802-831-1071 463 G acampbell@vermontlaw.edu
CAMPBELL, Barbara ...... 606-759-7141 182 A barbara.campbell@kctcs.edu
CAMPBELL, Bernice ...... 919-278-2665 340 E bernice.campbell@shawu.edu
CAMPBELL, Bill .... 412-365-1140 381 C bcampbell@chatham.edu
CAMPBELL, Bonnie, L ... 815-224-0408 139 F bonnie_campbell@ivcc.edu
CAMPBELL, Carol .... 936-261-2111 446 D ccampbell@pvamu.edu
CAMPBELL, Carson .... 503-838-8141 377 H campbellcg@wou.edu
CAMPBELL, Catherine, C .... 252-638-7271 333 H campbelc@cravencc.edu
CAMPBELL, Celia, K ..... 617-627-3313 219 B celia.campbell@tufts.edu
CAMPBELL, Charles ...... 334-386-7528.... 5 D ccampbell@faulkner.edu
CAMPBELL, Charlie .... 859-985-3674 179 C campbellc@berea.edu
CAMPBELL, Charria .... 931-372-3381 426 E cycampbell@tntech.edu
CAMPBELL, Christie ...... 512-233-1635 442 M christie@stedwards.edu
CAMPBELL, Connan ...... 509-533-7081 480 A connan.campbell@scc.spokane.edu
CAMPBELL, Conway, C . 508-767-7325 205 D ccampbel@assumption.edu
CAMPBELL, Corey .... 315-786-6561 303 F ccampbell@sunyjefferson.edu
CAMPBELL, Cory .... 724-838-4260 398 H ccampbell@setonhill.edu
CAMPBELL, Curtis .... 503-838-8094 377 H campbellc@wou.edu
CAMPBELL, Dan .... 413-552-2705 214 D dcampbell@hcc.edu
CAMPBELL, Danny .... 432-264-3752 438 C dcampbell@howardcollege.edu
CAMPBELL, David .... 662-562-3231 248 D
CAMPBELL, Deanna ...... 760-872-5301.. 46 M dcampbel@cerrocoso.edu
CAMPBELL, Debra .... 231-843-5819 232 J djcampbell@westshore.edu
CAMPBELL, Diane .... 609-586-4800 278 F campbeld@mccc.edu
CAMPBELL, Donald .... 415-422-5368.. 71 K dmcampbell2@usfca.edu
CAMPBELL, Donald .... 610-896-1100 385 L dcampbel@haverford.edu
CAMPBELL, Douane ...... 212-343-1234 306 J dcampbellr@mcny.edu
CAMPBELL, Elaine .... 912-358-3000 123 H campbele@savannahstate.edu
CAMPBELL, Elreo .... 765-658-4190 154 F elreocampbell@depauw.edu
CAMPBELL, Emily .... 225-922-2373 186 J emilycampbell@lctcs.edu
CAMPBELL, Eric .... 248-218-2080 229 J ecampbell@rc.edu
CAMPBELL, Erika .... 870-368-2013.. 20 F erika.campbell@ozarka.edu
CAMPBELL, Fran .... 937-766-7653 349 G campf@cedarville.edu
CAMPBELL, Gail .... 928-289-6535.. 14 J gail.campbell@npc.edu
CAMPBELL, Gail .... 423-697-5718 424 E gail.campbell@chattanoogastate.edu
CAMPBELL, Heather ...... 757-455-3389 477 F hmcampbell@vwu.edu
CAMPBELL, Ian .... 334-347-2623.... 2 A
CAMPBELL, J. David ..... 256-228-6001.... 3 B campbelld@nacc.edu
CAMPBELL, James, F .... 401-865-2676 405 B james.campbell@providence.edu
CAMPBELL, Jamie, L .... 920-433-6665 492 B jamie.campbell@bellincollege.edu
CAMPBELL, Jane .... 302-622-8000.. 89 E jcampbell@dcad.edu
CAMPBELL, Janell .... 701-224-5431 346 B janell.i.campbell@bismarckstate.edu
CAMPBELL, Jason .... 773-291-6100 134 E
CAMPBELL, Jenni, L ..... 321-682-4981 112 K jcampbell60@valenciacollege.edu
CAMPBELL, Jenny .... 907-474-6265.. 10 A jlcampbell@alaska.edu
CAMPBELL, Jo .... 805-756-7990.. 30 C jcampb33@calpoly.edu
CAMPBELL, Joann, N .... 904-620-2002 110 A jcampbel@unf.edu
CAMPBELL, Joanne .... 479-248-7236.. 19 C jcampbell@ecollege.edu
CAMPBELL, John, B ...... 901-722-3372 424 C jbcampbell@sco.edu
CAMPBELL, Jonathan .... 870-230-5098.. 19 E campbej@hsu.edu
CAMPBELL, Joseph .... 870-680-8725.. 18 B joe_campbell@asun.edu
CAMPBELL, Joseph .... 856-256-4199 281 E campbellj@rowan.edu
CAMPBELL, Kai .... 828-251-6470 342 C kai@unca.edu
CAMPBELL, Karen .... 757-822-1447 476 B kcampbell@tcc.edu
CAMPBELL, Karen .... 610-921-7643 378 C kcampbell@albright.edu
CAMPBELL, Karen, D .... 757-822-1447 476 B kcampbell@tcc.edu
CAMPBELL, Karen, M ... 608-822-2300 500 G kcampbell@swtc.edu
CAMPBELL, Katherine ... 313-664-7428 222 F kcampbell@collegeforcreativestudies.edu
CAMPBELL, Keisha .... 443-885-3300 200 D keisha.campbell@morgan.edu
CAMPBELL, Keith, E ..... 404-413-4465 119 E kcampbell@gsu.edu
CAMPBELL, Kellie, B ..... 802-728-1511 464 E
CAMPBELL, Kelly, D ..... 404-687-4547 116 H campbellk@ctsnet.edu
CAMPBELL, Keni .... 907-796-6509.. 10 B klcampbell4@alaska.edu
CAMPBELL, Kerri .... 901-843-3846 423 J campbellk@rhodes.edu
CAMPBELL, Kevin .... 325-674-6552 429 B kac96b@acu.edu
CAMPBELL, Kim .... 614-234-5144 356 I kcampbell@mccn.edu
CAMPBELL, Kimberly .... 405-491-6335 370 A kcampbel@snu.edu
CAMPBELL, Laurel .... 509-434-5325 479 I laurel.campbell@ccs.spokane.edu
CAMPBELL, Lauren .... 267-341-3331 386 A lcampbell@holyfamily.edu
CAMPBELL, Lea .... 713-221-5548 453 B campbellc@uhd.edu
CAMPBELL, Lenora .... 336-285-3508 341 F lrcampbell@ncat.edu
CAMPBELL, Lindsey ...... 916-608-6572.. 50 H campbel@flc.losrios.edu
CAMPBELL, Lisa .... 775-623-4824 271 B lisa.campbell@gbcnv.edu
CAMPBELL, Lisa, M ...... 724-287-8711 380 A lisa.campbell@bc3.edu
CAMPBELL, Maria .... 985-448-5943 187 F maria.campbell@fletcher.edu
CAMPBELL, Marshall .... 979-230-3474 432 D marshall.campbell@brazosport.edu
CAMPBELL, Mary, B ..... 314-935-3617 262 A marycampbell@wustl.edu
CAMPBELL, Mary, B ..... 864-488-8280 410 E mcampbell@limestone.edu
CAMPBELL, Mason .... 501-812-2211.. 23 B mcampbell@uaptc.edu
CAMPBELL, Matthew ..... 253-840-8419 483 D mcampbell@pierce.ctc.edu
CAMPBELL, Maurice, W 804-257-5606 477 C mwcampbell@vuu.edu
CAMPBELL, Melanie ...... 434-381-6332 472 D mhcampbell@sbc.edu
CAMPBELL, Michael ...... 760-384-6159.. 46 M michael.campbell@cerrocoso.edu
CAMPBELL, Michael ...... 816-279-7000 250 B michael.campbell@abtu.edu
CAMPBELL, Michael ...... 216-881-1700 359 F mcampbell@ohiotech.edu
CAMPBELL, Michael, A . 419-372-2346 348 H campbem@bgsu.edu
CAMPBELL, Michael, A . 423-585-2682 426 C mike.campbell@ws.edu
CAMPBELL, Michelle ..... 732-906-2551 279 A mcampbell@middlesexcc.edu
CAMPBELL, Mitchell ..... 906-217-4012 221 O mitchell.campbell@baycollege.edu
CAMPBELL, Mitchell, L . 916-558-2426.. 50 I campbem@scc.losrios.edu
CAMPBELL, Nicole, J .... 405-325-1978 371 B njudice@ou.edu
CAMPBELL, Patricia ...... 209-946-2424.. 70 E pcampbell@pacific.edu
CAMPBELL, Peter .... 201-684-7363 280 H pcampbel@ramapo.edu
CAMPBELL, Philip .... 434-528-5276 477 E
CAMPBELL, Phyllis .... 731-352-4046 418 G campbellp@bethelu.edu
CAMPBELL, Ralph .... 623-935-8872.. 13 A ralph.campbell@estrellamountain.edu
CAMPBELL, Randy .... 607-778-5196 318 A campbellrj@sunybroome.edu
CAMPBELL, Rebecca ..... 215-368-5000 390 F
CAMPBELL, Rina .... 619-201-8760.. 60 A rina.campbell@sdcc.edu
CAMPBELL, Rina .... 619-201-8753.. 60 A rina.campbell@sdcc.edu
CAMPBELL, Robert .... 410-704-4862 204 A rcampbell@towson.edu
CAMPBELL, Robert, D ... 212-817-7300 293 F rcampbell@gc.cuny.edu
CAMPBELL, Robin .... 336-517-2229 327 B rcampbell@bennett.edu
CAMPBELL, Rosana .... 570-484-2723 395 B rcampbel@lockhaven.edu
CAMPBELL, Samerah ..... 559-243-7122.. 66 C samerah.campbell@scccd.edu
CAMPBELL, Sara .... 423-614-8525 420 J scampbell@leeuniversity.edu
CAMPBELL, Saskia .... 703-993-3738 467 L scampb22@gmu.edu
CAMPBELL, Scott .... 773-834-3390 150 J scottcampbell@uchicago.edu
CAMPBELL, Scott, L ...... 740-392-6868 357 B scott.campbell@mvnu.edu
CAMPBELL, Sean .... 518-580-5663 316 A scampbel@skidmore.edu
CAMPBELL, Sharon .... 919-760-8011 331 B sharonca@meredith.edu
CAMPBELL, Shoshanna, M .... 718-780-7501 291 J shoshanna.campbell@brooklaw.edu
CAMPBELL, Sierra .... 708-802-6181 137 D scampbell@foxcollege.edu
CAMPBELL, Staphea ...... 404-527-7767 120 K sscampbell@itc.edu
CAMPBELL, Stephanie ... 904-470-8114.. 97 L s.campbell@ewc.edu
CAMPBELL, Stephen ...... 409-772-9751 456 F stepcamp@utmb.edu
CAMPBELL, Stephen, M 216-368-5555 349 F stephen.campbell@case.edu
CAMPBELL, Susan .... 623-845-3876.. 13 C susan.j.campbell@gccaz.edu

CAPELO, Jenny .... 509-682-6662 486 E
jcapelo@wvc.edu

CAPERS, Jamie .... 903-593-8311 448 H
jcapers@texascollege.edu

CAPERS, Meggin .... 610-341-5902 383 D
mcapers@eastern.edu

CAPERS, Willette .... 605-274-4313 415 B
willette.capers@augie.edu

CAPETS, OP,
Mary Rachel .... 615-297-7545 418 C
srmrachel@aquinascollege.edu

CAPEZZA, Kristen .... 516-877-3021 289 C
kcapezza@adelphi.edu

CAPILOUTO, Eli, I .... 859-257-1703 185 B
pres@uky.edu

CAPISCIOLTO, Ken .... 616-988-3676 226 C
kcapisciolto@kuyper.edu

CAPLES, Gwen .... 601-979-2282 246 E
gwendolyn.caples@jsums.edu

CAPLES, Philip .... 318-487-7946 186 I
philip.caples@lacollege.edu

CAPLINGER, Chris .... 912-478-3939 119 C
caplinca@georgiasouthern.edu

CAPLOW, Stacy .... 718-780-7944 291 J
stacy.caplow@brooklaw.edu

CAPO, Jeremy .... 712-325-3402 167 B
jcapo@iwcc.edu

CAPO, Laura .... 714-556-3610.. 72 F
laura.capo@vanguard.edu

CAPO, Leslie, L .... 504-568-4806 189 B
lcapo@lsuhsc.edu

CAPOCCIA-WHITE,
Rozanne .... 714-432-5991.. 38 E
rcapoccia@occ.cccd.edu

CAPON, Sandy .... 515-964-0601 165 G
capons@faith.edu

CAPONE, Lisa .... 337-482-0927 192 E
lisa.capone@louisiana.edu

CAPONI, Kimberly .... 630-466-7900 152 C
kcaponi@waubonsee.edu

CAPORALE, Jay .... 978-837-5308 216 D
caporalej@merrimack.edu

CAPORALE, Matthew .... 203-479-4858.. 89 A
mcaporale@newhaven.edu

CAPORUSCIO, Josie .... 718-636-3649 311 J
jcaporus@pratt.edu

CAPOZZI, James .... 718-368-5069 294 E
james.capozzi@kbcc.cuny.edu

CAPOZZOLI, John .... 410-287-1469 197 H
jcapozzoli@cecil.edu

CAPP, Maureen .... 561-868-3333 104 D
cappm@palmbeachstate.edu

CAPPARELLI, Tim .... 312-225-1700 138 E
tcapparelli@ico.edu

CAPPELLANO, Christina 516-323-4835 307 F
ccappellano@molloy.edu

CAPPELLERI,
Mary Anne .... 508-565-1067 218 H
mcappelleri@stonehill.edu

CAPPELLO, Phillip .... 516-572-7300 308 A
phillip.cappello@ncc.edu

CAPPELLO, Rocco .... 309-694-8970 138 C
rocco.cappello@icc.edu

CAPPLEMAN, Amy .... 662-862-8028 246 D
accappleman@iccms.edu

CAPPS, Jennifer .... 303-615-1439.. 80 N
jcapps5@msudenver.edu

CAPPS, John .... 434-832-7601 474 C
cappsj@centralvirginia.edu

CAPPS, Matthew .... 940-397-4138 440 F
matthew.capps@msutexas.edu

CAPPS, Patricia .... 314-371-0236 258 E
pacapps@ranken.edu

CAPPS, Steve .... 936-633-5281 430 F
scapps@angelina.edu

CAPPS, Tammy .... 618-634-3280 149 A
tammyc@shawneecc.edu

CAPPS, Wanda .... 910-592-8081 337 G
wcapps@sampsoncc.edu

CAPRA, Jack .... 850-729-6648 103 L
capraj@nwfsc.edu

CAPRARIO, Janet .... 619-849-2958.. 57 E
janetcaprario@pointloma.edu

CAPRILES, Jose .... 787-758-2525 513 G
jose.capriles@upr.edu

CAPRIO, Anthony, S .... 413-782-1243 219 F
anthony.caprio@wne.edu

CAPRIO, Patty .... 315-228-7442 296 F
pcaprio@colgate.edu

CAPRIOGLIO, Helen .... 719-549-2207.. 79 A
helen.caprioglio@csupueblo.edu

CAPRON, Clara .... 360-650-2422 486 F
capron@wwu.edu

CAPRON, Clara .... 360-650-3470 486 F
clara.capron@wwu.edu

CAPSOURAS, Barbara .... 973-328-5059 277 B
bcapsour@ccm.edu

CAPUANO, Christopher . 201-692-7100 277 K
capuano@fdu.edu

CAPUANO, Rebecca .... 413-565-1000 205 G
rcapuano@baypath.edu

CAPUANO, Sharon, Q .... 401-341-2904 406 A
sharon.capuano@salve.edu

CAPUNAY, Martin .... 718-429-6600 324 D
martin.capunay@vaughn.edu

CAPUNO, Jayson .... 818-575-6800.. 67 G
jayson.capuno@tuw.edu

CAPUTO, Brian .... 630-942-2800 135 A
caputob@cod.edu

CAPUTO, Gail, A .... 856-225-2926 281 G
gcaputo@rutgers.edu

CAPUTO, Michael .... 845-575-3000 305 L
michael.caputo@marist.edu

CAPUTO, Michael, P .... 843-792-6246 410 F
caputom@musc.edu

CAQUIAS, Karen .... 787-284-1912 509 E
kcaquias@ponce.inter.edu

CARA, Robert .... 704-688-4222 248 F
rcara@rts.edu

CARABALLO, Ada .... 787-863-2390 509 B
ada.caraballo@fajardo.inter.edu

CARABALLO, Darryl .... 702-651-2677 271 A
darryl.caraballo@csn.edu

CARABALLO, Frances .... 787-892-2315 509 F
frances_caraballo@intersg.edu

CARABALLO, Luis .... 787-725-6500 506 G

CARABALLO,
Maragnette .... 787-832-6000 508 D

CARABALLO, Omayra .... 787-284-1912 509 E
ocarabal@ponce.inter.edu

CARABALLO, Pablo .... 787-264-1912 509 F
pablo_caraballo_rodriguez@intersg.edu

CARABALLO, Samuel .... 787-761-0640 512 F
escuelagraduada@utcpr.edu

CARABALLO TURRELL,
Gloria, N .... 787-841-2000 510 K
gloria_caraballo@pucpr.edu

CARACCIOLI, Pamela .... 315-312-3699 319 B
pamela.caraccioli@oswego.edu

CARACOGLIA, Erica, S .. 252-940-6203 332 C
erica.caracoglia@beaufortccc.edu

CARAWAY, Tom .... 907-852-1852.... 9 F
tom.caraway@ilisagvik.edu

CARBAJAL, Brent .... 360-650-3480 486 F
brent.carbajal@wwu.edu

CARBALLO, Lauren .... 516-671-8355 324 G
lcarballo@webb.edu

CARBALLO, Manuel .... 440-775-8411 358 C
manuel.carballo@oberlin.edu

CARBERRY, Joseph .... 203-285-2011.. 85 E
jcarberry@gwcc.commnet.edu

CARBO-PORTER, Laurie 518-464-8406 299 G
lporter@excelsior.edu

CARBONARO, Dennis .... 610-785-6525 398 A
dcarbonaro@scs.edu

CARBONARO, Gene .... 562-938-4624.. 48 D
gcarbonaro@lbcc.edu

CARBONE, Cindy, L .... 248-246-2512 229 A
clcarbon@oaklandcc.edu

CARBONELL, Ivette .... 787-720-1022 506 E
icarbonell@atlanticu.edu

CARBONELL, John .... 731-661-5081 427 C
jcarbone@uu.edu

CARBONI, Michelle, L .. 815-224-0417 139 F
michelle_carboni@ivcc.edu

CARCANAGUES, Amy .... 210-829-3912 453 D
amyc@uiwtx.edu

CARCILLO, Antony, J .... 302-356-3475.. 90 I
anthony.j.carcillo@wilmu.edu

CARCOPA, Joshua, R .... 239-513-1122 101 C
jcarcopa@hodges.edu

CARD, Christopher, D ... 920-832-6596 493 K
christopher.card@lawrence.edu

CARD, Michael .... 605-677-6926 416 H
michael.card@usd.edu

CARD, Steven .... 360-650-3109 486 F
steven.card@wwu.edu

CARDELLE, Alberto .... 978-665-3295 212 C
acardelle@fitchburgstate.edu

CARDEN, Gloria .... 864-250-8114 410 B
gloria.carden@gvltec.edu

CARDEN, Monica, W .... 540-674-3600 475 B
mcarden@nr.edu

CARDENA, Sonia .... 860-297-4193.. 88 C
sonia.cardena@trincoll.edu

CARDENAS, Elizabeth .... 773-878-3921 148 D
ecardenas@staugustine.edu

CARDENAS, Eric, D .... 813-253-6232 112 J
ecardenas@ut.edu

CARDENAS, Jenni .... 520-494-5420.. 11 K
jenni.cardenas@centralaz.edu

CARDENAS, Jose, A .... 480-965-6479.. 10 I
jcardenas@asu.edu

CARDENAS, Kerstin .... 507-222-4068 234 F
kcardena@carleton.edu

CARDENAS, Maria .... 970-542-3169.. 81 A
maria.cardenas@morgancc.edu

CARDENAS, Miguel, A .. 619-934-0797.. 60 F

CARDENAS, JR.,
Miguel, A .... 619-934-0797.. 60 F

CARDENAS, Monique .... 248-689-8282 232 A
mcardena@walshcollege.edu

CARDENAS, Raul .... 303-315-2109.. 83 C
raul.cardenas@ucdenver.edu

CARDENAS-ADAME,
Patricia .... 623-935-8812.. 13 A
patricia.cardenas-adame@estrellamountain.edu

CARDENAS-CLAGUE,
Adeline .... 909-593-3511.. 70 D
acardenas-clague@laverne.edu

CARDILLO, Charlie .... 323-259-2937.. 54 E
ccardillo@oxy.edu

CARDILLO, Rosaleen .... 845-437-5843 324 C
roecardillo@vassar.edu

CARDIN, Chad .... 706-295-6552 119 A
ccardin@gntc.edu

CARDIN, Matt .... 254-267-7038 442 E
mcardin@rangercollege.edu

CARDIN, Matthew .... 914-633-2462 302 G
mcardin@iona.edu

CARDINAL, Jason .... 952-358-9462 239 F
jason.cardinal@normandale.edu

CARDINAL, Mark .... 218-733-2032 238 F
mark.cardinal@lsc.edu

CARDINE, Darla, S .... 630-466-7900 152 C
dcardine@waubonsee.edu

CARDONA, Felix .... 718-518-6664 294 B
fcardona@hostos.cuny.edu

CARDONA, Joe .... 856-256-4236 281 E
cardona@rowan.edu

CARDONA, Manuel .... 787-758-2525 513 G
manuel.cardona1@upr.edu

CARDONA, Melissa .... 845-938-6947 504 H
8drm@usma.edu

CARDONA, Nelida .... 787-262-5786 511 D
directora_camuy@unitecpr.net

CARDONA, Niurka .... 787-815-0000 513 A
niurka.cardona@upr.edu

CARDONA, Teresa .... 787-754-8000 512 E
tcardona@pupr.edu

CARDONA-CORTÉS,
Ivelice .... 787-890-2681 512 G
ivelice.cardona@upr.edu

CARDONA-CORTÉS,
Ivelice .... 787-890-2681 512 H
ivelice.cardona@upr.edu

CARDONE, Stephen .... 609-497-7730 280 D
housing@ptsem.edu

CARDONICK, Mariann ... 215-717-6187 400 J
mcardonick@uarts.edu

CARDOZA, Carla .... 915-831-2638 436 E
ccardoza@epcc.edu

CARDOZA, Emy .... 212-854-2096 290 J
ecardoza@barnard.edu

CARDOZA, II, Frederick 574-372-5100 155 B
freddy.cardoza@grace.edu

CARDOZA, Lisa .... 916-278-7043.. 32 E
lisa.cardoza@csus.edu

CARDOZO, Karen .... 540-362-6609 468 C
cdc@hollins.edu

CARDUCCI, Vince .... 313-664-1488 222 F
vcarducci@collegeforcreativestudies.edu

CARDWELL, Becky .... 916-361-1660.. 35 C
bcardwell@carrington.edu

CARDWELL, Catherine ... 727-873-4400 110 C
ccardwell@nelson.usf.edu

CAREAGA, Andrew, P .... 573-341-4183 261 E
acareaga@mst.edu

CARELLA, Terry .... 517-371-5140 233 A
carellat@cooley.edu

CARET, Robert, L .... 301-445-1901 202 B
rcaret@usmd.edu

CAREW, Tara .... 410-777-2204 197 C
tcarew@aacc.edu

CAREY, Alexa .... 616-632-2882 221 C
ajc004@aquinas.edu

CAREY, Amy .... 316-295-5888 173 D
abcarey@friends.edu

CAREY, Catherine .... 812-465-1681 161 E

CAREY, Cathy, T .... 801-524-1958 459 F
cathycarey@ldsbc.edu

CAREY, Cullen .... 251-626-3303.... 7 E
registrar@ussa.edu

CAREY, Elaine .... 219-989-2401 159 G
elaine.carey@pnw.edu

CAREY, Felicia .... 336-917-5558 340 D
felicia.carey@salem.edu

CAREY, Jason .... 718-951-5882 293 C
jcarey@brooklyn.cuny.edu

CAREY, Jessica .... 253-583-8747 479 G
jessica.carey@cptc.edu

CAREY, Joe .... 317-896-9324 160 I
jcarey@ubca.org

CAREY, Karen .... 907-796-6256.. 10 B
ktcarey@alaska.edu

CAREY, Kevin .... 309-556-3850 139 G
kcarey@iwu.edu

CAREY, Marita .... 404-876-1227 115 F
marita.carey@bccr.edu

CAREY, Michael .... 718-862-8000 305 H
michael.carey@manhattan.edu

CAREY, Peter, M .... 716-878-6332 318 C
careypm@buffalostate.edu

CAREY, Russell, C .... 401-863-9650 404 E
russell_carey@brown.edu

CAREY, Seamus .... 914-633-2203 302 G
president@iona.edu

CAREY, Seamus .... 859-233-8111 184 G
president@transy.edu

CAREY, Sherri .... 706-245-7226 117 E
scarey@ec.edu

CAREY, Tim .... 607-274-3225 303 B
tcarey@ithaca.edu

CAREY, Val .... 303-282-3427.. 82 H
val.carey@archden.org

CAREY, William .... 845-451-1300 298 A
william.carey@culinary.edu

CAREY-BUTLER, Sylvia .. 470-578-5129 120 L
scareybu@kennesaw.edu

CAREY-BUTLER, Sylvia .. 920-424-0348 497 B
careybus@uwosh.edu

CARFAGNA, Angelo .... 201-692-7025 277 K
angelo@fdu.edu

CARGILL, Tyler .... 202-644-7210.. 91 A
tcargill@bau.edu

CARIKER, Heath .... 903-983-8657 439 A
hcariker@kilgore.edu

CARILLI, Vincent .... 865-974-7449 427 G
vincent.carilli@tennessee.edu

CARILLO, Ryan .... 401-874-9463 406 B
ryancarrillo@uri.edu

CARIN, Lawrence .... 919-681-6438 328 G
lcarin@duke.edu

CARIO, William, R .... 262-243-5700 493 B
william.cario@cuw.edu

CARISTA, Jessica .... 315-268-3873 296 A
jcarista@clarkson.edu

CARITO, Paige .... 860-932-4098.. 86 E
pcarito@qvcc.edu

CARL, Ashley .... 813-253-7158 101 A
acarl@hccfl.edu

CARL, Cathy .... 845-431-8635 298 E
cathy.carl@sunydutchess.edu

CARL, Diane .... 570-321-4101 389 E
carl@lycoming.edu

CARL, Heidi, A .... 765-494-4600 159 E

CARL, Rebecca .... 812-855-9634 156 A
rebcarl@iu.edu

CARL, Steven, B .... 508-767-7267 205 D
sb.carl@assumption.edu

CARL LINK, Edward .... 713-221-8001 453 B
linke@uhd.edu

CARLAND, J. Paul .... 407-708-2280 107 D
carlandp@seminolestate.edu

CARLAND, Tammy Rae . 510-594-3649.. 28 D
tcarland@cca.edu

CARLBLOM, Shelia .... 765-677-2191 157 D
sheila.carlblom@indwes.edu

CARLESSO, Dennis .... 313-993-3360 231 B
carlesdm@udmercy.edu

CARLETON, Taylor .... 830-372-8026 449 B
tcarleton@tlu.edu

CARLEY, Michael .... 559-791-2275.. 47 A
mcarley@portervillecollege.edu

CARLILE, Kimberly, L .... 806-371-5017 430 A
k0153833@actx.edu

CARLIN, Donna .... 409-944-1387 437 B
dcarlin@gc.edu

CARLIN, Jane 253-879-3118 485 E jcarlin@pugetsound.edu
CARLIN, Laurence 920-424-7364 497 B carlin@uwosh.edu
CARLIN, Melanie 217-357-9117 147 D mcarlin@robertmorris.edu
CARLIN, Michael 704-687-5500 342 E mike.carlin@uncc.edu
CARLINEO, Renee 607-735-1730 299 D rcarlineo@elmira.edu
CARLISLE, Brian, A 706-880-8976 121 A bcarlisl@lagrange.edu
CARLISLE, David, M 323-563-4987 36 D davidcarlisle@cdrewu.edu
CARLISLE, Elizabeth 812-749-1241 159 C lcarlisle@oak.edu
CARLISLE, Nadis 256-372-5555 1 A nadis.carlisle@aamu.edu
CARLISLE, Sandi 320-629-5140 240 C sandi.carlisle@pine.edu
CARLISLE, Susan 931-424-4063 421 E scarlisle@martinmethodist.edu
CARLO, Alex 585-245-5716 318 E carlo@geneso.edu
CARLOCK, Danielle 480-423-6653 13 H d.carlock@scottsdalecc.edu
CARLOCK, Myra 731-352-4090 418 G carlockm@bethelu.edu
CARLOCK, Ruth 402-363-5704 270 E rmcarlock@york.edu
CARLOS, Raymond 909-384-8253 59 I rcarlos@sbccd.cc.ca.us
CARLOW, Regina 505-277-2112 288 G rcarlow@unm.edu
CARLS, Franca 262-595-2211 497 C carls@uwp.edu
CARLSEN, Paul 920-693-1123 499 G paul.carlsen@gotoltc.edu
CARLSON, Beth, L 724-847-6666 384 G bcarlson@geneva.edu
CARLSON, Bob 630-682-6002 139 B carlson@iit.edu
CARLSON, Britt 978-867-4221 209 F britt.carlson@gordon.edu
CARLSON, Bryan 951-827-4592 69 C bryan.carlson@ucr.edu
CARLSON, Cameron 316-942-4291 175 I carlsonc@newmanu.edu
CARLSON, Caroline 949-376-6000 47 D ccarlson@lcad.edu
CARLSON, Casey 530-893-7544 27 F carlsonca@butte.edu
CARLSON, Catherina 781-891-2989 206 D ccarlson@bentley.edu
CARLSON, Catherine 419-448-3436 361 J carlsonc@tiffin.edu
CARLSON, Cathy 507-222-4075 234 F ccarlson@carleton.edu
CARLSON, Christopher 978-867-4073 209 F chris.carlson@gordon.edu
CARLSON, Craig 203-857-3344 86 D ccarlson@norwalk.edu
CARLSON, David 540-362-6675 468 C dcarlson@hollins.edu
CARLSON, David, H 979-845-8160 446 G davidcarlson@tamu.edu
CARLSON, Deb 402-354-7000 268 C deb.carlson@methodistcollege.edu
CARLSON, Deb 402-354-7257 268 C deb.carlson@methodistcollege.edu
CARLSON, Don 925-424-1322 35 P dcarlson@laspositascollege.edu
CARLSON, Donald 661-362-3035 38 H donald.carlson@canyons.edu
CARLSON, Douglas 415-476-4527 69 E doug.carlson@ucsf.edu
CARLSON, Jeffrey 708-524-6813 136 C jcarlson@dom.edu
CARLSON, Jennifer 517-264-3124 220 F jennycarlson@adrian.edu
CARLSON, Jim 985-545-1500 187 H
CARLSON, Julie 402-844-7142 268 J juliec@northeast.edu
CARLSON, Karen 413-565-6850 205 G kcarlson@baypath.edu
CARLSON, Kathleen 574-284-4543 160 C kcarlson@saintmarys.edu
CARLSON, Kathleen 773-298-3305 148 G carlson@sxu.edu
CARLSON, Kenna Lee 402-486-2032 269 F kennalee.carlson@ucollege.edu
CARLSON, Kevin, R 563-333-6070 169 A carlsonkevinr@sau.edu
CARLSON, Kirk 507-933-6362 235 I kcarlson@gustavus.edu
CARLSON, Laina 651-450-3654 238 D lcarlso@inverhills.edu
CARLSON, Laina 651-423-8000 237 H
CARLSON, Laura 574-631-8052 161 C lcarlson@nd.edu
CARLSON, Laura 801-863-5704 461 A lcarlson@uvu.edu
CARLSON, Marta 508-767-7275 205 D mcarlson@assumption.edu
CARLSON, Mary 704-669-6000 333 E
CARLSON, Matt 503-725-9554 376 A carlsonm@pdx.edu
CARLSON, Melinda 214-768-2422 444 E mpcarlson@smu.edu
CARLSON, Neil 616-526-6420 222 A nec4@calvin.edu
CARLSON, Nicki 218-683-8546 240 A nicki.carlson@northlandcollege.edu
CARLSON, Nicole 763-493-0597 239 G ncarlson@nhcc.edu
CARLSON, Paul 815-802-8652 140 D pcarlson@kcc.edu
CARLSON, Ria, M 949-824-7911 68 G ria.carlson@uci.edu
CARLSON, Rich 402-486-2508 269 F rich.carlson@ucollege.edu
CARLSON, Robert 785-227-3380 171 E carlsonr@bethanylb.edu
CARLSON, Ruth 906-217-4032 221 O ruth.carlson@baycollege.edu
CARLSON, Skye 253-272-1126 482 C scarlson@ncad.edu
CARLSON, Steve 937-298-3399 355 F steve.carlson@ketteringhealth.org
CARLSON, Steven 269-782-1305 230 F scarlson01@swmich.edu
CARLSON, Susan 315-787-4005 300 C susan.carlson@flhcon.edu
CARLSON, Susan 510-987-0728 68 C susan.carlson@ucop.edu
CARLSON-ZINK, DeAnna 701-777-2611 345 C deannac@undfoundation.org
CARLSTON, Gary, L 435-283-7010 461 C gary.carlston@snow.edu
CARLTON, Christopher 717-477-1481 395 E cocarlton@ship.edu
CARLTON, Edith 731-286-3300 425 A carlton@dscc.edu
CARLTON, Keitha 903-785-7661 441 G kcarlton@parisjc.edu
CARLTON, William 912-279-5892 116 G wcarlton@ccga.edu
CARMAN, Kevin 775-784-1740 271 F kcarman@unr.edu
CARMAN, Philip 505-224-4000 285 J pcarman@cnm.edu
CARMEL, Julie 508-929-8754 213 E jcarmel@worcester.edu
CARMELO CRUZ-ALVARADO, Marcos 888-488-4968 46 F
CARMEN, Joseph 203-582-7654 87 G joseph.carmen@quinnipiac.edu
CARMEN, Kim 318-675-5207 189 C shvreg@lsuhsc.edu
CARMENATTY, Sylvia 787-834-9595 511 E sylviac@uaa.edu
CARMEY, Emily 989-328-1245 228 A emily.carmey@montcalm.edu
CARMICAL, Beth 910-272-3343 337 D bcarmical@robeson.edu
CARMICHAEL, Ann, C 803-812-7330 413 G anncar@mailbox.sc.edu
CARMICHAEL, Brenda 620-343-4600 173 A bcarmichael@fhtc.edu
CARMICHAEL, Demetrius, L 309-677-3155 133 B dcarmichael@fsmail.bradley.edu
CARMICHAEL, John 360-867-6500 481 A carmichj@evergreen.edu
CARMICHAEL, Lisandra 904-620-2615 110 A l.carmichael@unf.edu
CARMICHAEL, Matthew 541-346-4127 377 D mecarmic@uoregon.edu
CARMICHAEL, Paul 860-343-5787 86 A pcarmichael@mxcc.commnet.edu
CARMICHAEL, Peggy 304-214-8901 489 F pcarmichael@wvncc.edu
CARMICHAEL, Stacey 770-394-8300 114 C stacey.carmichael@cbre.com
CARMINE, Kevin 718-319-7965 294 B kcarmine@hostos.cuny.edu
CARMODY, Mark 508-678-2811 213 G mark.carmody@bristolcc.edu
CARMODY, Patricia 507-537-6206 241 D patricia.carmody@smsu.edu
CARMONA, Josefina 575-527-7639 287 E jocarmon@nmsu.edu
CARNAHAN, Diane 209-468-9155 67 B dcarnahan@sjcoe.net
CARNAROLI, Craig 215-898-6693 400 K carnarol@upenn.edu
CARNATHAN, Janice 575-234-9211 287 D jcarnath@nmsu.edu
CARNAVAS, Ria 718-390-3131 324 F ria.carnavas@wagner.edu
CARNE, Kim 906-217-4027 221 O carnek@baycollege.edu
CARNES, Gregory, A 256-765-4245 8 E gacarnes@una.edu
CARNES, Kathy, M 252-493-7220 336 H kcarnes@email.pittcc.edu
CARNEVALE, David 714-532-6049 36 C carneva@chapman.edu
CARNEY, Chuck 812-855-1892 156 A ccarney@indiana.edu
CARNEY, Ginger 208-885-6195 131 G gingercarney@uidaho.edu
CARNEY, Jennifer 585-785-1388 300 B jennifer.carney@flcc.edu
CARNEY, John 615-460-6000 418 F
CARNEY, Martin 216-421-7424 350 M mcarney@cia.edu
CARNEY, Michael, J 715-836-4353 496 D carneymj@uwec.edu
CARNEY, Michelle 785-864-8975 177 D mmcarney@ku.edu
CARNEY, Paige 304-766-3313 491 B carney3@wvstateu.edu
CARNEY, Paul, B 937-775-4271 364 I pau.carney@wright.edu
CARNEY, RSM, Sheila, A 412-578-6424 380 E sacarney@carlow.edu
CARNEY, Susie 620-278-4228 177 B susie.carney@sterling.edu
CARNEY, Timothy 202-319-5619 91 B carneyt@cua.edu
CARNEY-DEBORD, Nan 740-587-6428 352 G carneydebord@denison.edu
CARNEY-HALL, Karla 309-556-3111 139 G dstudent@iwu.edu
CARNIE, Andrew, H 520-621-3471 16 G carnie@email.arizona.edu
CARNLEY, Lisa 334-222-6591 2 I lcarnley@lbwcc.edu
CARNS, Mary Lee 843-525-5692 412 H mcarns@tcl.edu
CARNZ, Scott 206-239-4500 479 E provost@cityu.edu
CARO, Mary Ellen 215-545-6400 391 H
CAROL, Chris 770-537-6065 127 A chris.carol@westgatech.edu
CAROL, Steve 732-987-2414 278 B scarol@georgian.edu
CAROLAN, Brian, V 203-365-4657 88 B carolanb2@sacredheart.edu
CAROLIN, Robert 760-750-4089 33 B rcarolin@csusm.edu
CAROLINA, Dorinda 305-243-0876 112 E dcarolina@miami.edu
CAROLINA, Kimberly 203-575-8056 86 B kcarolina@nv.edu
CAROLINO, Josiane 404-627-2681 115 C
CAROLLO, Sandy 212-616-7200 301 F scarollo@helenefuld.edu
CARON, Bob 817-552-3700 439 B bcaron@tku.edu
CARON, Elaine 215-641-6300 390 H
CARON, Elizabeth 620-241-0723 172 D elizabeth.caron@centralchristian.edu
CARON, Julie 503-725-4410 376 A jucaron@pdx.edu
CARON, Lenn 410-455-3260 202 E carlen@umbc.edu
CARON, Linda 937-775-2225 364 I linda.caron@wright.edu
CARON, Paul 310-506-4621 56 C paul.caron@pepperdine.edu
CARONNA, Gina 815-921-4043 147 E g.caronna@rockvalleycollege.edu
CAROTHERS, Amy 775-784-6620 271 F acarothers@unr.edu
CAROTHERS, Brad 408-274-7900 61 L brad.carothers@evc.edu
CAROTHERS, Cat 425-640-1112 480 F cat.carothers@edcc.edu
CAROTHERS, John 775-784-1394 271 F jcarothers@adv.unr.edu
CAROW, Ken, A 317-274-2481 156 F kcarow@iupui.edu
CARP, Ralph 267-341-3031 386 A rcarp@holyfamily.edu
CARPENTER, Amanda 805-437-3565 30 F amanda.carpenter@csuci.edu
CARPENTER, Ariel 909-607-0434 37 D ariel.carpenter@cgu.edu
CARPENTER, Barbara 225-771-2613 190 H barbara_carpenter@subr.edu
CARPENTER, Barbara 225-771-2016 190 G barbara_carpenter@subr.edu
CARPENTER, Beth 615-230-3560 426 B beth.carpenter@volstate.edu
CARPENTER, Brenda 405-682-1611 367 H bcarpenter@occc.edu
CARPENTER, Carol 505-984-6102 201 D carol.carpenter@sjc.edu
CARPENTER, Carol 616-977-5520 222 I carol.carpenter@cornerstone.edu
CARPENTER, Catherine 213-738-6875 65 G ccarpenter@swlaw.edu
CARPENTER, David 913-722-0272 174 E david.carpenter@kansaschristian.edu
CARPENTER, Debra 281-283-2150 453 A carpenter@uhcl.edu
CARPENTER, Harold, V 913-722-0272 174 E harold.carpenter@kansaschristian.edu
CARPENTER, Hedy, L 818-677-2138 32 D hcarpenter@csun.edu
CARPENTER, Holly 716-829-7671 298 F carpenth@dyc.edu
CARPENTER, James 417-447-6981 257 G carpentj@otc.edu
CARPENTER, Jan 509-533-3535 480 B jan.carpenter@sfcc.spokane.edu
CARPENTER, Jane 785-670-1526 177 G jane.carpenter@washburn.edu
CARPENTER, Jenna 910-814-4018 327 E carpenter@campbell.edu
CARPENTER, Jennifer 509-527-2683 485 H jennifer.carpenter@wallawalla.edu
CARPENTER, Jessica 607-735-1812 299 D jcarpenter@elmira.edu
CARPENTER, Kae 931-372-3269 426 E kcarpenter@tntech.edu
CARPENTER, Karen 843-383-8000 408 D kcarpenter@coker.edu
CARPENTER, Kathryn, H 312-996-8974 151 B khc@uic.edu
CARPENTER, Kelly 920-693-1172 499 G kelly.carpenter@gotoltc.edu
CARPENTER, Kimberly 323-241-5321 49 D carpenkc@lasc.edu
CARPENTER, Kristy 208-732-6209 130 E kcarpenter@csi.edu
CARPENTER, Larry 423-614-8440 420 J lcarpenter@leeuniversity.edu
CARPENTER, Marla 336-770-3337 343 D carpem@uncsa.edu
CARPENTER, Mary 615-256-1463 418 A mcarpenter@abcnash.edu
CARPENTER, Megan, M 603-513-5100 274 G megan.carpenter@unh.edu
CARPENTER, Michael 315-792-7234 321 E mcarpenter@sunypoly.edu
CARPENTER, Michael 757-823-8104 469 F mcarpenter@nsu.edu
CARPENTER, Mike 402-826-6781 267 A mike.carpenter@doane.edu
CARPENTER, Mike 618-262-8641 139 A carpenterm@iecc.edu
CARPENTER, Monica, S 828-682-7315 336 A mscarpenter@mayland.edu
CARPENTER, Patrick 413-552-2746 214 D pcarpenter@hcc.edu
CARPENTER, Paula 217-234-5217 141 D pcarpent@lakeland.cc.il.us
CARPENTER, Robert 410-455-8942 202 E bobc@umbc.edu
CARPENTER, Robert 423-323-0259 425 E rccarpenter@northeaststate.edu
CARPENTER, Rosalie 724-838-4242 398 H rcarpenter@setonhill.edu
CARPENTER, Scott 541-881-5773 377 B scarpenter@tvcc.cc

CARPENTER, Shelia .... 601-925-3200 247 C
carpenter@mc.edu
CARPENTER, Stacey ...... 765-641-4190 153 B
slcarpenter@anderson.edu
CARPENTER, Suzanne ... 603-899-4246 273 F
caroenters@franklinpierce.edu
CARPENTER, Thomas .... 563-333-6124 169 A
carpenterthomas@sau.edu
CARPENTER, Tiffany ...... 865-974-8184 427 F
tcarpenter@tennessee.edu
CARPENTER, Wayne, D . 413-782-1565 219 F
wayne.carpenter@wne.edu
CARPENTER-DAVIS,
Cheryl .... 913-234-0665 172 E
cheryl.carpenterdavis@cleveland.edu
CARPENTER-HUBIN,
Julie .... 614-292-5915 358 I
carpenter-hubin.16@osu.edu
CARPENTIER, Mark .... 718-631-6325 295 D
mcarpentier@qcc.cuny.edu
CARPENTIER, Mark .... 570-740-0390 389 D
mcarpentier@luzerne.edu
CARPENTIERI, Karen, J . 201-291-1111 291 D
kjc@berkeleycollege.edu
CARPENTIERI, Karen, J . 201-291-1111 275 I
kjc@berkeleycollege.edu
CARPI, Anthony .... 212-237-8944 294 D
acarpi@jjay.cuny.edu
CARPIO, Joseph .... 505-346-2324 288 F
joseph.carpio@bie.edu
CARPIO, Joseph .... 505-346-2361 288 F
joseph.carpio@bie.edu
CARR, Amy .... 303-762-6888.. 79 H
amy.carr@denverseminary.edu
CARR, Bailey .... 816-501-3780 250 F
bailey.carr@avila.edu
CARR, Brenda .... 678-466-4300 116 E
brendacarr@clayton.edu
CARR, Candy .... 937-376-6686 350 D
ccarr@centralstate.edu
CARR, Chuck .... 307-855-2143 501 V
ccarr@cwc.edu
CARR, Connie, L .... 318-345-9262 187 G
ccarr@ladelta.edu
CARR, Daryl, B .... 800-747-2687 144 A
dcarr@monmouthcollege.edu
CARR, Denine .... 585-395-2980 318 B
dcarr@brockport.edu
CARR, Dennis .... 541-463-5583 373 F
carrd@lanecc.edu
CARR, Derrick .... 334-229-4667.... 4 B
dcarr@alasu.edu
CARR, Diane .... 803-822-3599 410 G
carrd@midlandstech.edu
CARR, Ellen .... 617-879-7067 212 E
ecarr@massart.edu
CARR, Frances .... 229-317-6744 113 H
frances.carr@asurams.edu
CARR, Fredrick .... 318-274-3175 191 E
carrf@gram.edu
CARR, Jeffrey .... 619-849-2415.. 57 E
jeffreycarr@pointloma.edu
CARR, Jeffrey .... 321-433-5600.. 97 I
carrj@easternflorida.edu
CARR, Karen .... 212-757-1190 290 B
kcarr@aami.edu
CARR, Kevin .... 207-780-5127 195 J
kevin.carr@maine.edu
CARR, Kevin .... 319-208-5069 169 F
kcarr@scciowa.edu
CARR, Leslie .... 661-362-3100.. 38 H
leslie.carr@canyons.edu
CARR, Matthew, S .... 315-792-3226 324 B
mcarr@utica.edu
CARR, Michael .... 312-261-3468 144 F
mcarr8@nl.edu
CARR, Nancy .... 315-498-2834 311 B
carrn@sunyocc.edu
CARR, Nicole, T .... 251-460-6475.... 8 F
ntcarr@southalabama.edu
CARR, Randall .... 865-251-1800 424 A
rcarr1@south.edu
CARR, Rebecca .... 513-562-8773 347 K
rebecca.carr@artacademy.edu
CARR, Robert .... 870-575-8475.. 22 E
carrro@uapb.edu
CARR, Robin .... 606-546-1206 184 H
rcarr@unionky.edu
CARR, Rodney .... 229-259-2586 126 G
rodneycarr@valdosta.edu
CARR, Scott .... 304-326-1259 488 F
scott.carr@salemu.edu
CARR, Sherrean .... 408-848-4757.. 43 J
scarr@gavilan.edu
CARR, Suzanne, M .... 401-825-1000 404 H
scarr7@ccri.edu
CARR, Timothy .... 402-472-7940 269 J
tcarr2@unl.edu
CARR, Tobin, R .... 706-542-8096 125 G
carr@uga.edu
CARR, Vikki .... 760-355-6244.. 45 I
vikki.carr@imperial.edu
CARR, Yolanda .... 706-864-1800 126 A
yolanda.carr@ung.edu
CARR-CHELLMAN,
Alison .... 208-885-6773 131 G
alicarrchellman@uidaho.edu
CARR ROBINETT, Angie 816-501-4541 258 H
angie.carr@rockhurst.edu
CARRA, Gary .... 860-253-3128.. 85 C
gcarra@asnuntuck.edu
CARRADINE, Sherrye .... 318-342-1012 192 F
carradine@ulm.edu
CARRADINE, Tania .... 504-671-5155 187 E
tcarra@dcc.edu
CARRAFIELLO, Susan .... 937-775-2660 364 I
susan.carrafiello@wright.edu
CARRANCO, Emilio .... 512-245-2161 450 E
ec05@txstate.edu
CARRANO, Julia, L .... 972-721-5000 452 D
jcarran@udallas.edu
CARRANZA, Elsy .... 214-860-8705 435 D
ecarranza@dcccd.edu
CARRANZA, Elsy .... 972-273-3316 435 E
ecarranza@dcccd.edu
CARRANZA, Gabriel ...... 337-482-6819 192 E
gabriel@louisiana.edu
CARRANZA, James .... 650-306-3350.. 61 O
carranza@smccd.edu
CARRANZA, Kylie .... 406-791-5305 265 H
kylie.carranza@uprovidence.edu
CARRANZA, Mike .... 956-872-3420 444 A
mcarranz@southtexascollege.edu
CARRASCO, Alicia .... 210-688-3101 432 L
CARRASCO, Kafi .... 214-329-4447 431 D
kafi.carrasco@bgu.edu
CARRASCO-JACQUEZ,
Diane .... 432-335-6342 441 D
dcarrasco@odessa.edu
CARRASQUILLO,
Felix, A .... 787-743-7979 511 I
ut_fcarrasqu@suagm.edu
CARRASQUILLO, Ralph . 607-753-4724 318 D
ralph.carrasquillo@cortland.edu
CARRAWAY, Jay .... 910-296-2400 335 E
CARRAWAY, Kevin .... 252-328-6434 341 C
carrawayc@ecu.edu
CARRAWAY, Pauline ..... 757-352-4007 470 H
paulcar@regent.edu
CARREIRO, Jane .... 207-602-2898 196 G
jcarreiro@une.edu
CARRENO, Cynthia .... 619-482-6330.. 65 F
ccarreno@swccd.edu
CARRERA, Bonnie .... 405-695-5533 366 E
bcarrera@familyoffaith.edu
CARRERA, Magali .... 508-999-8024 211 F
mcarrera@umassd.edu
CARRERAS, Gisela .... 787-279-1912 509 A
gcarreras@bayamon.inter.edu
CARRERE, Carol, G .... 919-658-7771 340 J
ccarrere@umo.edu
CARRESCIA, John .... 718-420-4264 324 F
jcarresc@wagner.edu
CARRICK, Stacy .... 660-562-1579 257 E
carrick@nwmissouri.edu
CARRICO, Alyona .... 714-533-1495.. 64 D
alyona@southbaylo.edu
CARRICO, Kathryn .... 213-740-2311.. 72 B
CARRICO, Sarah .... 651-846-1424 241 B
sarah.carrico@saintpaul.edu
CARRIER, Bryan .... 731-661-5090 427 C
bcarrier@uu.edu
CARRIER, Heather .... 423-585-2620 426 C
heather.carrier@ws.edu
CARRIER, Jonathan .... 307-778-1157 502 D
jcarrier@lccc.wy.edu
CARRIERE, Patrick .... 225-771-5290 190 G
patrick_carriere@subr.edu
CARRIERE, Patrick .... 225-771-5290 190 H
patrick_carriere@subr.edu
CARRIGAN, Edward .... 415-338-7211.. 34 A
edwardc@sfsu.edu
CARRIGAN, Tena .... 501-812-2217.. 23 B
tcarrigan@uaptc.edu
CARRILLO, Jose .... 760-355-6487.. 45 I
jose.carrillo@imperial.edu
CARRILLO, Jose Raul ... 340-693-1043 514 E
jcarril@uvi.edu
CARRILLO, Lee .... 505-224-3093 285 J
lcarrillo@cnm.edu
CARRILLO, Renae .... 319-226-2515 162 F
renae.carrillo@allencollege.edu
CARRINGTON, Glenn, R 757-823-8005 469 F
grcarrington@nsu.edu
CARRINGTON, Margie ... 650-306-3174.. 61 O
carringtonm@smccd.edu
CARRINO, Amy .... 859-442-1104 181 B
amy.carrino@kctcs.edu
CARRION, Ingrid .... 787-743-4041 507 D
icarrion@columbiacentral.edu
CARRION, Lourdes .... 787-878-5475 508 L
lcarrion@arecibo.inter.edu
CARRION, Yesenia .... 787-258-1501 507 D
ycarrion@columbiacentral.edu
CARRISALEZ, Albert, A . 210-458-5138 455 E
albert.carrisalez@utsa.edu
CARROCCI, Noreen .... 316-942-4291 175 I
carroccin@newmanu.edu
CARROLL, Alicia .... 203-392-5301.. 85 A
carrolla8@southernct.edu
CARROLL, Anne .... 610-683-4575 395 A
acarroll@kutztown.edu
CARROLL, Barbara .... 615-875-9201 428 D
barbara.carroll@vanderbilt.edu
CARROLL, Betsy .... 845-905-4615 298 A
betsy.carroll@culinary.edu
CARROLL, Brett .... 860-768-5708.. 88 H
bcarroll@hartford.edu
CARROLL, Brian .... 909-794-1084.. 39 H
bcarroll@cccollege.edu
CARROLL, Brooke .... 808-687-7051 127 H
CARROLL, Charley .... 575-492-2660 286 J
ccarroll@nmjc.edu
CARROLL, Chris .... 434-592-6463 468 H
cccarroll2@liberty.edu
CARROLL, Christine ...... 540-373-2200 466 H
christine.carroll@evcc.edu
CARROLL,
Christopher, D .... 719-333-6164 504 C
christopher.carroll.1@us.af.mil
CARROLL,
Constance, M .... 619-388-6957.. 60 B
ccarroll@sdccd.edu
CARROLL, Dan .... 802-485-2035 463 A
dcarroll@norwich.edu
CARROLL, Dana .... 617-373-3004 217 F
CARROLL, Dennis, G .... 336-841-9229 329 G
dcarroll@highpoint.edu
CARROLL, Donna, M .... 708-524-6817 136 C
dompres@dom.edu
CARROLL, Erik, P .... 623-572-3326 143 G
ecarro@midwestern.edu
CARROLL, Felicia .... 606-248-0257 182 E
felicia.carroll@kctcs.edu
CARROLL, Gracie .... 325-670-1480 437 F
gcarroll@hsutx.edu
CARROLL, III, James, J 734-487-3200 223 H
jcarroll@emich.edu
CARROLL, Jasmin .... 323-856-7881.. 25 M
jcarroll@afi.com
CARROLL, Jeannie .... 432-264-5603 438 C
jcarroll@howardcollege.edu
CARROLL, Jennifer .... 989-686-3617 223 G
jennifercarroll@delta.edu
CARROLL, Jerry .... 864-503-5168 414 D
jcarroll@uscupstate.edu
CARROLL, Jim .... 530-754-1073.. 68 E
jimcarroll@ucdavis.edu
CARROLL, John .... 718-817-4075 300 E
jcarroll@fordham.edu
CARROLL, John .... 701-224-5491 346 B
john.w.carroll@bismarckstate.edu
CARROLL, Jonathan ...... 203-254-4059.. 86 I
jcarroll@fairfield.edu
CARROLL, Karen .... 410-225-2297 199 H
kcarroll@mica.edu
CARROLL, Kenneth .... 513-487-1265 361 L
kenneth.carroll@myunion.edu
CARROLL, Laura .... 325-674-2459 429 B
lbc01c@acu.edu
CARROLL, Leanne, M ... 334-833-4453.... 5 H
leanne.mallory@hawks.huntingdon.edu
CARROLL, Lisa .... 425-640-1248 480 F
lisa.carroll@edcc.edu
CARROLL, Maria .... 716-270-5735 299 F
carrollm@ecc.edu
CARROLL, Mary Ellen ... 563-588-7575 167 D
maryellen.carroll@loras.edu
CARROLL, Melinda .... 940-668-3315 441 A
mcarroll@nctc.edu
CARROLL, Melissa .... 540-545-7245 471 E
CARROLL, Monique, M . 803-536-7200 412 C
CARROLL, Pamela, S .... 407-823-1463 109 E
pamela.carroll@ucf.edu
CARROLL, Patricia .... 410-386-8184 197 G
pcarroll@carrollcc.edu
CARROLL, Randy .... 931-540-2791 424 G
rcarroll14@columbiastate.edu
CARROLL, Rebecca .... 912-478-5468 119 C
rcarroll@georgiasouthern.edu
CARROLL, Richard .... 409-772-3762 456 F
rcarroll@utmb.edu
CARROLL, Robyn .... 617-873-0172 207 F
robyn.carroll@cambridgecollege.edu
CARROLL, Sandra .... 903-983-8242 439 A
scarroll@kilgore.edu
CARROLL, Sean, M .... 724-658-1938 380 A
sean.carroll@bc3.edu
CARROLL, Shannon .... 806-457-4200 436 G
scarroll@fpctx.edu
CARROLL, Thomas .... 617-236-8829 209 D
tcarroll@fisher.edu
CARROLL, Tim .... 209-946-7710.. 70 E
tcaroll@pacific.edu
CARROLL, Timothy .... 708-534-4503 137 F
tcarroll@govst.edu
CARROLL, Tom .... 612-330-1352 233 K
carrollt@augsburg.edu
CARROLL, William .... 617-217-9240 206 A
wcarroll@baystate.edu
CARRON, Jennifer .... 254-710-3435 431 J
jennifer_carron@baylor.edu
CARROTHERS, Terri, C .. 303-556-2400.. 83 C
CARRUTH, Ann .... 985-549-3772 192 D
acarruth@selu.edu
CARRUTHERS, Brian, A . 864-242-5100 407 B
CARSON, Barrett, H ...... 404-894-1868 118 F
barrett.carson@dev.gatech.edu
CARSON, Bonnie, C ...... 864-503-5349 414 D
bcarson@uscupstate.edu
CARSON, Brenda, B ...... 601-635-2111 245 I
bcarson@eccc.edu
CARSON, Bryan .... 660-831-4123 256 G
carsonb@moval.edu
CARSON, Carol .... 706-754-7703 122 F
ccarson@northgatech.edu
CARSON, Chad, M .... 205-726-2308.... 6 E
cmcarson@samford.edu
CARSON, Connie, L .... 864-294-2202 410 A
connie.carson@furman.edu
CARSON, David, L .... 904-819-6230.. 98 E
dcarson@flagler.edu
CARSON, Denise, K .... 785-227-3380 171 E
carsond@bethanylb.edu
CARSON, Elizabeth, M .. 815-282-7900 148 C
bethcarson@sacn.edu
CARSON,
Jacqueline, M .... 585-292-2523 307 H
jcarson@monroecc.edu
CARSON, Jeffrey .... 732-235-7122 282 A
jeffrey.carson@rutgers.edu
CARSON, Jessica .... 212-237-8717 294 D
jcarson@jjay.cuny.edu
CARSON, Nathan .... 918-495-7127 368 I
ncarson@oru.edu
CARSON, Paula .... 417-625-9394 256 D
carson-p@mssu.edu
CARSON, Rachel .... 314-838-8858 261 G
rcarson@ugst.edu
CARSON, Rebecca .... 310-506-4558.. 56 C
rebecca.carson@pepperdine.edu
CARSON, Scott .... 601-426-6346 249 A
scarson@southeasternbaptist.edu
CARSON, Sylvia .... 678-717-2373 126 A
sylvia.carson@ung.edu
CARSON, Tamika .... 312-850-7070 134 H
tdavenport13@ccc.edu
CARSON, Warren .... 864-503-5634 414 D
wcarson@uscupstate.edu
CARSTARPHEN, Minnie . 334-876-9345.... 2 D
mcarstarphen@wccs.edu
CARSTENS, Joel, B .... 603-862-3671 274 G
joel.carstens@unh.edu
CARSTENS, John .... 336-734-7313 334 E
jcarstens@forsythtech.edu
CARSTENS, Lisa .... 503-352-3065 375 G
carstens@pacificu.edu
CARSTENSEN, Lundie .... 619-201-8705.. 60 A
lundie.carstensen@sdcc.edu
CARSWELL, Justin .... 417-690-3446 251 E
carswell@cofo.edu

CARSWELL, Linda .... 828-448-3110 339 A lcarswell@wpcc.edu
CARSWELL, Pamela .... 386-752-1822.. 99 A pamela.carswell@fgc.edu
CARSWELL, William .... 843-383-8063 408 D wcarswell@coker.edu
CARTAGENA, Milagros .. 787-704-1020 507 K mcartagena@ediccollege.edu
CARTAGENA, Moises .... 787-850-9376 513 E moises.cartagena@upr.edu
CARTAGENA, Moises .... 787-850-9390 513 E moises.cartagena@upr.edu
CARTAGENA-SANTIAGO, Aramilda .... 787-857-3600 508M aramildacartagena@br.inter.edu
CARTE, Mandy .... 216-368-2595 349 F mmc111@case.edu
CARTEE, Dawn, H .... 706-542-3451 125 G cartee@uga.edu
CARTER, Abby .... 229-227-3177 125 A acarter@southernregional.edu
CARTER, Alfonza .... 919-546-8527 340 E alcarter@shawu.edu
CARTER, Allia .... 804-257-5719 477 C alcarter@vuu.edu
CARTER, Allison, A .... 906-487-1888 227 E aagranik@mtu.edu
CARTER, Amber .... 859-442-1712 181 B amber.carter@kctcs.edu
CARTER, Andy .... 701-858-3042 345 F andy.carter@minotstateu.edu
CARTER, Angela, M .... 336-334-4822 335 A amcarter@gtcc.edu
CARTER, Angelique .... 434-528-5276 477 E
CARTER, Anna .... 937-708-5683 364 D acarter2@wilberforce.edu
CARTER, Ashley .... 770-534-6164 115 D acarter@brenau.edu
CARTER, Bates .... 302-622-8000.. 89 E bcarter@dcad.edu
CARTER, Bessie .... 405-945-3211 368 E cartebm@osuokc.edu
CARTER, Beth .... 910-630-7425 331 C bcarter@methodist.edu
CARTER, Bobbi Jo .... 802-635-1381 464 C bobbijo.carter@northernvermont.edu
CARTER, Brenda, C .... 214-491-6271 433M bcarter@collin.edu
CARTER, Brent .... 509-682-6795 486 E bcarter@wvc.edu
CARTER, Brett .... 336-334-5514 343 A bacarter@uncg.edu
CARTER, Brett .... 607-778-5003 318 A carterbd@sunybroome.edu
CARTER, Carolyn .... 313-496-2633 232 C ccarter1@wcccd.edu
CARTER, Christopher .... 425-235-2352 483 G ccarter@rtc.edu
CARTER, Christopher, C .... 610-758-5802 388 J ccc317@lehigh.edu
CARTER, Christy .... 316-295-8701 173 D christy_carter@friends.edu
CARTER, Cindy .... 641-585-8130 170 B carterc@waldorf.edu
CARTER, Cindy .... 906-217-4107 221 O carterc@baycollege.edu
CARTER, Clark .... 843-863-8008 407 E ccarter@csuniv.edu
CARTER, Clay .... 252-940-6357 332 C clay.carter@beaufortccc.edu
CARTER, Cynthia .... 229-931-2057 124 D ccarter@southgatech.edu
CARTER, Danielle .... 414-326-2337 493 A
CARTER, Danita .... 314-918-2625 253 A dcarter@eden.edu
CARTER, Darryl .... 716-878-6522 318 C carterdc@buffalostate.edu
CARTER, David .... 909-607-7692.. 37 G david_carter@kgi.edu
CARTER, David .... 909-667-4493.. 37 H dcarter@claremontlincoln.edu
CARTER, David .... 512-232-6400 455 A david.carter@austin.utexas.edu
CARTER, Dawn .... 910-962-2659 343 C carterdb@uncw.edu
CARTER, Deena .... 909-687-1465.. 43 I deenacarter@gs.edu
CARTER, Derek .... 410-951-3748 203 D dcarter@coppin.edu
CARTER, Derrell .... 708-456-0300 150 I derrellcarter@triton.edu
CARTER, Dione .... 310-434-4858.. 62 E carter_dione@smc.edu
CARTER, Don .... 928-523-1605.. 14 H don.carter@nau.edu
CARTER, Edythe, L .... 806-371-5335 430 A elcarter@actx.edu
CARTER, Emery .... 281-487-1170 448 F ecarter@txchiro.edu
CARTER, Emily .... 609-258-5391 280 E eac@princeton.edu
CARTER, Evonne .... 252-335-0821 333 G evonne_carter@albemarle.edu
CARTER, FeRita .... 951-222-8837.. 58 I ferita.carter@rcc.edu
CARTER, Gary, L .... 731-661-5204 427 C gcarter@uu.edu
CARTER, Glenn .... 423-236-2811 424 B gcarter@southern.edu
CARTER, Glenn .... 302-831-3358.. 90 F gcarter@udel.edu
CARTER, Helene .... 706-821-8233 122 K hcarter@paine.edu
CARTER, Holly .... 812-488-1040 161 A hc110@evansville.edu
CARTER, Hope .... 601-974-1000 247 B
CARTER, Hugh .... 334-222-6591.... 2 I hcarter@lbwcc.edu
CARTER, Jacque .... 402-826-8253 267 A jacque.carter@doane.edu
CARTER, Jasmine .... 940-898-3869 451 F jcarter21@twu.edu
CARTER, Jeffrey .... 252-335-0821 333 G jeffrey_carter@albemarle.edu
CARTER, Jeffrey, J .... 919-866-5148 338 G
CARTER, Jeffrey, W .... 800-287-8822 153 D president@bethanyseminary.edu
CARTER, Jennifer .... 318-257-4730 191 F jcarter@latech.edu
CARTER, Jennings .... 618-545-3169 140 E jcarter@kaskaskia.edu
CARTER, Jessica .... 276-656-0312 475 D jcarter@patrickhenry.edu
CARTER, John .... 334-953-5159 503 B john.carter@us.af.mil
CARTER, John, B .... 413-542-2771 205 B jbcarter@amherst.edu
CARTER, IHM, Joseph Marie .... 610-647-4400 386 C jcarter@immaculata.edu
CARTER, Julien, C .... 617-627-3271 219 B julien.carter@tufts.edu
CARTER, June .... 864-503-5881 414 D jcarter@uscupstate.edu
CARTER, Kara .... 804-594-1578 474 I kcarter@jtcc.edu
CARTER, Kathleen .... 706-778-8500 123 B kcarter@piedmont.edu
CARTER, Kathryn .... 508-999-8421 211 F kcarter1@umassd.edu
CARTER, Keith .... 662-915-7546 249 D jkcarter@olemiss.edu
CARTER, Kendall .... 785-833-4339 175 B kendall.carter@kwu.edu
CARTER, Kim, C .... 859-257-9420 185 B kccarter.1@uky.edu
CARTER, Lana .... 719-296-6108.. 81 K lana.carter@pueblocc.edu
CARTER, Laurie, A .... 717-477-1301 395 E lacarter@ship.edu
CARTER, Lawrence, E .... 470-639-0323 122 D lawrence.carter@morehouse.edu
CARTER, Lawrence, L .... 517-321-0242 224 F lcarter@glcc.edu
CARTER, Linda .... 816-604-3081 255 H linda.carter@mcckc.edu
CARTER, Linnie, S .... 717-780-2321 385 E lscarter@hacc.edu
CARTER, Lisa .... 608-262-1234 496 C lisa.carter@wisc.edu
CARTER, Luther, F .... 843-661-1210 409 K lcarter@fmarion.edu
CARTER, Malika .... 315-464-4924 317 F cartemal@upstate.edu
CARTER, Malika .... 315-470-6866 320 A mcarte06@esf.edu
CARTER, Malinda .... 815-280-2515 140 B mcarter@jjc.edu
CARTER, Matt .... 505-277-3003 288 G mdcarter@unm.edu
CARTER, Melanie .... 202-806-2550.. 92 B melcarter@howard.edu
CARTER, Michael .... 270-789-5001 179 E mvcarter@campbellsville.edu
CARTER, Michael .... 213-738-6800.. 65 G administrativeservices@swlaw.edu
CARTER, Michele .... 254-526-1331 432 H michele.carter@ctcd.edu
CARTER, Michelle, R .... 202-806-7540.. 92 B
CARTER, Mike .... 918-495-7150 368 I mcarter@oru.edu
CARTER, Miranda .... 406-656-9950 265 I mcarter@yellowstonechristian.edu
CARTER, Ninette .... 580-581-2226 365 G ncarter@cameron.edu
CARTER, Pam .... 215-751-8737 382 A pcarter@ccp.edu
CARTER, Paula .... 831-582-3004.. 32 C pcarter@csumb.edu
CARTER, Peggy .... 731-352-4096 418 G carterp@bethelu.edu
CARTER, Prudence .... 510-643-6644.. 68 D pcarter@berkeley.edu
CARTER, Quamina .... 909-621-8965.. 37 D quamina.carter@cgu.edu
CARTER, R. Daphne .... 843-661-1188 409 K rcarter@fmarion.edu
CARTER, Regina, W .... 501-569-3408.. 22 B rswade@ualr.edu
CARTER, Richard .... 251-460-6283.... 8 F rcarter@southalabama.edu
CARTER, Robin .... 916-278-3551.. 32 E carterr@csus.edu
CARTER, Rock .... 562-907-4972.. 75 A rcarter@whittier.edu
CARTER, Ronald, L .... 909-558-7616.. 48 C rcarter@llu.edu
CARTER, Ronald, L .... 909-558-4528.. 48 C rcarter@llu.edu
CARTER, Saundra .... 202-274-5531.. 93 C scarter@udc.edu
CARTER, Scott .... 620-278-4290 177 B scarter@sterling.edu
CARTER, Scott, N .... 423-439-4343 419 J cartersn@etsu.edu
CARTER, Seth, M .... 785-460-5400 172 H seth.carter@colbycc.edu
CARTER, Sharon, L .... 714-879-3901.. 45 F slcarter@hiu.edu
CARTER, Shawna, M .... 608-246-6249 499 H smcarter@madisoncollege.edu
CARTER, Sheila .... 312-369-7187 135 E scarter@colum.edu
CARTER, Sherry .... 626-472-5121.. 41 K scarter@esgvrop.org
CARTER, Shree .... 714-556-3610.. 72 F scarter@vanguard.edu
CARTER, Shree .... 714-556-3610.. 72 F vutrustees@vanguard.edu
CARTER, Shree .... 714-556-3610.. 72 F vaschoolcertifyingofficial@vanguard.edu
CARTER, Steven, J .... 215-887-5511 402 H scarter@wts.edu
CARTER, Sue .... 831-459-3275.. 70 B sacarter@ucsc.edu
CARTER, Sue, V .... 434-223-6220 468 A svcarter@hsc.edu
CARTER, Terrell .... 618-664-7009 137 G terrell.carter@greenville.edu
CARTER, Thomas, E .... 315-470-6691 320 A tecarter@esf.edu
CARTER, Tina, P .... 919-866-5000 338 G tcarter@waketech.edu
CARTER, Todd .... 316-322-3201 171 G tcarter@butlercc.edu
CARTER, Tom .... 256-331-5263.... 3 C tom.carter@nwscc.edu
CARTER, Tracie .... 334-420-4426.... 3 H tcarter@trenholmstate.edu
CARTER, Veronika .... 802-656-0589 463 E vlcarter@uvm.edu
CARTER, JR., Walter, E . 410-293-1000 504 I
CARTER, William, E .... 713-718-8708 437 I william.carter@hccs.edu
CARTER, Yoli .... 509-313-6115 481 D cartery@gonzaga.edu
CARTER, Zina .... 979-532-6417 458 F zinac@wcjc.edu
CARTER-CHAPMAN, Renee .... 907-786-6486.... 9 H rmcarterchapman@alaska.edu
CARTER-ELIZONDO, Stacy .... 409-880-8379 449 H stacy.carter-elizondo@lamar.edu
CARTER-FISHER, Andrea .... 910-879-5512 332 D acarterfisher@bladencc.edu
CARTER-HARBOUR, Courtney .... 972-860-7335 435 B courtneycarter@dcccd.edu
CARTER-HARBOUR, Courtney .... 972-860-7156 435 B courtneycarter@dcccd.edu
CARTER-HORN, Cynthia, A .... 254-519-5498 447 A cynthia.carter@tamuct.edu
CARTER-STEVENS, Marilyn .... 718-862-7958 305 H marilyn.carter@manhattan.edu
CARTER-TELLISON, Katrina .... 561-237-7412 102 V kcartertellison@lynn.edu
CARTIER, Cheryl .... 203-582-8431.. 87 G cheryl.cartier@quinnipiac.edu
CARTIER, Jennifer .... 207-509-7282 195 H jcartier@unity.edu
CARTIER, Jolie, L .... 619-239-0391.. 34 F jcartier@cwsl.edu
CARTIER, Missy, M .... 559-323-2100.. 60 I mcartier@sjcl.edu
CARTLEDGE, Ernest .... 240-567-7991 200 C ernest.cartledge@montgomerycollege.edu
CARTMILL, Christopher . 716-375-7888 313 F
CARTMILL, Mark .... 859-985-3922 179 C cartmillm@berea.edu
CARTNAL, Ryan .... 805-546-3933.. 41 A rcartnal@cuesta.edu
CARTNEY, Michael, D ... 605-882-5284 415 F cartneym@lakeareatech.edu
CARTOLANO, Joseph .... 718-631-6231 295 D jcartolano@qcc.cuny.edu
CARTRIGHT, Jonathan ... 573-882-2011 261 A cartrightj@umsystem.edu
CARTWRIGHT, Alexander, N .... 573-882-3387 261 B chancellor@missouri.edu
CARTWRIGHT, Bill .... 415-422-5417.. 71 K jcartwri@usfca.edu
CARTWRIGHT, Cathy .... 206-592-3339 481 H ccartwright@highline.edu
CARTWRIGHT, Cynthia .. 716-664-5100 303 C cindycartwright@jbc.edu
CARTWRIGHT, David .... 401-598-4826 404 I dcartwright@jwu.edu
CARTWRIGHT, Marla .... 931-540-2618 424 G mcartwright1@columbiastate.edu
CARTWRIGHT, Michael, G .... 317-788-3233 161 B mcartwright@uindy.edu
CARTWRIGHT, Natalie ... 610-683-4153 395 A cartwright@kutztown.edu
CARTY, Cheryl .... 478-471-5235 121 F cheryl.carty@mga.edu
CARTY, Karenann .... 718-933-6700 307 G kcarty@monroecollege.edu
CARTY, Raymond, W .... 573-629-3094 253 H rcarty@hlg.edu
CARULLO, Susan, H .... 843-792-2071 410 F carullos@musc.edu
CARUOLO, Michael .... 401-341-2334 406 A michael.caruolo@salve.edu
CARUSO, Anne-Marie ... 617-989-4174 219 E carusoa@wit.edu
CARUSO, Britni .... 217-814-5440 148 F britni.caruso@sjcs.edu
CARUSO, Janet .... 516-572-7472 308 A janet.caruso@ncc.edu
CARUSO, Kelly .... 318-487-5443 187 C kellycaruso@cltcc.edu
CARUSO, Michele, E .... 985-448-4081 192 B michele.caruso@nicholls.edu
CARUTHERS, Janet .... 573-875-7372 251 F jaocaruthers@ccis.edu
CARUTHERS, Michelle, P .... 540-464-7992 476 G caruthersmp@vmi.edu
CARVAJAL, Lorelei .... 623-845-3729.. 13 C lorelei.carvajal@gccaz.edu
CARVAJAL, Richard .... 229-333-5952 126 G rcarvajal@valdosta.edu
CARVALHO, Corrine, I .. 651-962-5826 244 E clcarvalho@stthomas.edu
CARVALHO, Marco .... 321-674-8020.. 99 B mcarvalho@fit.edu
CARVALHO, Ron .... 972-721-4058 452 D rcarvalo@udallas.edu
CARVALHO, Susan .... 205-348-8280.... 7 G secarvalho@ua.edu
CARVALLOZA, Anthony . 212-327-7161 313 B anthony.carvalloza@rockefeller.edu

CARVELL, Regina .... 508-286-3408 220 A
carvell_regina@wheatoncollege.edu

CARVER, Andrea .... 701-774-4242 346 F
andrea.carver@willistonstate.edu

CARVER, Andrew .... 618-453-5774 149 E
acarver@siu.edu

CARVER, Billy .... 828-898-3542 330 E
carverb@lmc.edu

CARVER, Charles, M ..... 304-462-6131 490 C
marty.carver@glenville.edu

CARVER, JR., Curtis, A . 205-975-0250.... 8 A
carverc@uab.edu

CARVER, David, S .... 402-559-7276 270 A
dcarver@unmc.edu

CARVER, Doris, W .... 336-322-2111 336 G
doris.carver@piedmontcc.edu

CARVER, Eric .... 727-341-3664 106 E
carver.eric@spcollege.edu

CARVER, Jerelene .... 919-546-8525 340 E
jcarver@shawu.edu

CARVER, JR., Keith, S .. 731-881-7500 428 B
kcarver@utm.edu

CARVER, Leslie .... 858-534-4004.. 69 D
tmcprovost@ucsd.edu

CARVER, Maureen .... 215-641-6565 390 H
mcarver@mc3.edu

CARVER, Molly .... 785-227-3380 171 E
carvermm@bethanylb.edu

CARVER, Petra .... 207-326-2241 195 D
petra.carver@mma.edu

CARVER, II, William, S . 252-451-8328 336 E
wscarver671@nashcc.edu

CARWILE, Kathie .... 434-528-5276 477 E

CARY, Alice .... 410-706-7032 202 D
acary@police.umaryland.edu

CARY, Ann .... 239-590-7071 108 K

CARY, Ann .... 816-235-1700 261 C
caryah@umkc.edu

CARY, Charles .... 570-408-4553 403 D
charles.cary@wilkes.edu

CARY, Kim .... 417-447-6933 257 G
caryk@otc.edu

CARY, Stacey .... 309-796-5225 132 G
carys@bhc.edu

CARY, Tom .... 206-239-4500 479 E
tcary@cityu.edu

CASADA, Tracy, L .... 606-679-8501 182 C
tracy.casada@kctcs.edu

CASAINE, Wil .... 609-771-2602 276 I
casainew@tcnj.edu

CASALEGNO, Gina .... 412-268-2075 380 F
ginac@andrew.cmu.edu

CASALES, Isel .... 305-821-3333.. 99 E
icasales@fnu.edu

CASALINO, Francine ..... 860-773-1346.. 86 G
fcasalino@tunxis.edu

CASALINUOVO-ADAMS,
Christine .... 585-292-2215 307 H
ccasalinuovo-adams@monroecc.edu

CASAMENTO, Charlene . 860-832-0033.. 84 I
casamentoc@ccsu.edu

CASAMENTO, Laura ...... 315-792-3222 324 B
lcasamento@utica.edu

CASANOVA, Carmen, L . 302-356-6897.. 90 I
carmen.l.casanova@wilmu.edu

CASARES, Jason, A ...... 410-651-7848 203 A
jacasares@umes.edu

CASARES, Jeanne .... 585-475-4455 313 A
jvccio@rit.edu

CASAS, Alexander .... 305-348-1657 109 A
alexander.casas@fiu.edu

CASAS, Andrew .... 832-325-7317 456 B
andrew.casas@uth.tmc.edu

CASAS, Tanya .... 215-489-4865 382 D
tanya.casas@delval.edu

CASAS HERNANDEZ,
Veronica .... 650-949-7200.. 43 D
casashernandezveronica@fhda.edu

CASAZZA, Jacqualyn ..... 847-491-4302 145 F
jcasazza@northwestern.edu

CASCAMO, John .... 805-546-3973.. 41 A
john_cascamo@cuesta.edu

CASCARDI, Anthony ...... 510-642-5396.. 68 D
ajcascardi@berkeley.edu

CASCELLA, Joseph .... 315-801-8253 313 G
jcascella@mvhealthsystem.org

CASCIANO, Tony .... 413-572-5468 213 D
tcasciano@westfield.ma.edu

CASCIO, Joseph .... 559-791-2260.. 47 A
joseph.cascio@portervillecollege.edu

CASDORPH, Michael ..... 706-721-3364 115 A
mcasdorph@augusta.edu

CASE, Beau .... 419-530-4286 363 E
barbara.floyd@utoledo.edu

CASE, Chad .... 662-862-8232 246 D
cgcase@iccms.edu

CASE, Corrine .... 716-338-1072 303 D
corrinecase@mail.sunyjcc.edu

CASE, Daniel .... 601-643-8385 245 G
daniel.case@colin.edu

CASE, Danuta .... 585-582-8258 299 A
danutacase@elim.edu

CASE, David .... 601-635-2111 245 I
dcase@eccc.edu

CASE, Del .... 218-723-6460 235 D
dcase@css.edu

CASE, Jim .... 432-837-8036 450 D
jcase@sulross.edu

CASE, John .... 404-752-1500 122 E
jcase@msm.edu

CASE, Karyn .... 860-512-3103.. 85 G
kcase@manchestercc.edu

CASE, Keith .... 979-532-6369 458 F
casek@wcjc.edu

CASE, Kim .... 765-998-4557 160 F
kmcase@taylor.edu

CASE, Mark, R .... 203-837-8657.. 85 B
casem@wcsu.edu

CASE, Mary .... 312-996-2716 151 B
marycase@uic.edu

CASE, Michael .... 260-982-5431 158 T
mcase@manchester.edu

CASE, Michael, A .... 607-587-3535 320 C
casema@alfredstate.edu

CASEBEER, Clarice .... 417-967-5466 260 H

CASEL, Michael .... 610-896-1000 385 L
mcasel@haverford.edu

CASERIO, Mark .... 215-596-7432 401 G
m.caseri@usciences.edu

CASEY, Anne, M .... 386-226-6000.. 98 A
caseya3@erau.edu

CASEY, Bonnie-Jeanne .. 617-521-2489 218 E
bonniejeanne.casey@simmons.edu

CASEY, Brian .... 530-754-4105.. 68 E
bscasey@ucdavis.edu

CASEY, Brian, W .... 315-228-7444 296 F
president@colgate.edu

CASEY, Carolyn .... 509-434-5109 480 B
carolyn.casey@ccs.spokane.edu

CASEY, Carolyn .... 509-434-5109 479 I
carolyn.casey@ccs.spokane.edu

CASEY, Carolyn .... 509-434-5108 480 A
carolyn.casey@ccs.spokane.edu

CASEY, Derrick .... 217-732-3155 141 I
dcasey@lincolncollege.edu

CASEY, Greg .... 414-277-4510 494 G

CASEY, Janet, G .... 518-580-5705 316 A
jcasey@skidmore.edu

CASEY, Joanne .... 518-472-5875 289 E
jcase@albanylaw.edu

CASEY, Kaitlin .... 973-408-3039 277 C
kcasey2@drew.edu

CASEY, Karla .... 617-253-0260 215 G

CASEY, Kevin .... 414-382-6225 492 A
kevin.casey@alverno.edu

CASEY, Kevin .... 207-453-5141 194 I
kcasey@kvcc.me.edu

CASEY, Mary .... 414-382-6127 492 A
mary.casey@alverno.edu

CASEY, Mary .... 781-283-2223 219 D
mc4@wellesley.edu

CASEY, Mia .... 254-710-3555 431 J
mia_casey@baylor.edu

CASEY, Michael .... 860-297-2361.. 88 C
michael.casey@trincoll.edu

CASEY, Patrick .... 269-965-3931 225 F
caseyp@kellogg.edu

CASEY, Paul .... 831-755-6860.. 44 K
pcasey@hartnell.edu

CASEY, Peter .... 978-934-2310 211 G
peter_casey@uml.edu

CASEY, Randy .... 414-297-7872 500 B
caseyr@matc.edu

CASEY, Richard .... 610-989-1491 402 B
rcasey@vfmac.edu

CASEY, Roger, N .... 410-857-2222 200 B
presoffice@mcdaniel.edu

CASEY, Terry .... 256-782-5492.... 5 J
tcasey@jsu.edu

CASEY, Tricia .... 401-874-2378 406 B
pcasey@uri.edu

CASEY, Warren .... 501-279-4056.. 19 D
casey@harding.edu

CASEY-LOVELESS,
Tasha .... 405-208-5000 367 I
tasha.loveless@okcu.edu

CASEY POWELL,
Deborah .... 253-833-9111 481 F
dcasey@greenriver.edu

CASH, Arlene .... 301-687-4000 203 E

CASH, Bradley .... 252-398-6259 328 D
bacash0306@chowan.edu

CASH, David .... 617-287-5511 211 E
david.cash@umb.edu

CASH, Erin .... 859-280-1249 183 B
ecash@lextheo.edu

CASH, Jared .... 207-780-4770 196 F
jared.cash@maine.edu

CASH, Jason .... 616-395-7085 225 B
cash@hope.edu

CASH, John .... 904-596-2452 111 F
jcash@tbc.edu

CASH, JR., John .... 904-596-2494 111 F
jcashjr@tbc.org

CASH, Regina .... 323-343-4967.. 32 A
regina.cash@calstatela.edu

CASH, Tammie, L .... 501-569-8474.. 22 B
tlcash@ualr.edu

CASHBURLESS, Marty ... 325-793-4775 440 B
cashburless.marty@mcm.edu

CASHELL, Andrea .... 859-622-4484 180 B
andrea.cashell@eku.edu

CASHEN-THOMPSON,
Kathy .... 641-628-5186 163 E
cashenthompsonk@central.edu

CASHION, Robert .... 212-998-1212 310 B

CASHMAN, Jesse .... 507-222-5992 234 F
jcashman@carleton.edu

CASHWELL, Candace .... 252-985-5232 339 D
ccashwell@ncwc.edu

CASHWELL, Debbie .... 910-410-1803 337 B
dccashwell@richmondcc.edu

CASHWELL, Michael, B . 804-278-4205 472 E
mcashwell@upsem.edu

CASIELLO, Andrew, R ... 757-683-3726 469 G
acasiell@odu.edu

CASILLAS, Caroline .... 773-291-6315 134 E
cgrajeda1@ccc.edu

CASINI, Michelle .... 312-935-4810 147 D
mcasini@robertmorris.edu

CASKEY, Amy .... 580-387-7000 366 H
acaskey@mscok.edu

CASKEY, Brad .... 205-226-4650.... 5 A
bjcaskey@bsc.edu

CASKEY-JAMES,
Jacqueline .... 478-825-6174 118 A
caskeyj@fvsu.edu

CASLEN, Robert .... 864-503-5200 413 C
rcaslen@uscupstate.edu

CASLER, Adam .... 518-782-2919 315 J
acasler@siena.edu

CASLER, Tess, C .... 315-268-7882 296 A
tcasler@clarkson.edu

CASLIN, Miriam .... 770-228-7372 124 G
miriam.caslin@sctech.edu

CASNER, Heather .... 618-634-3228 149 A
heatherca@shawneecc.edu

CASO, Ann .... 508-626-4043 212 D
acaso@framingham.edu

CASON, Craig .... 719-549-2211.. 79 A
craig.cason@csupueblo.edu

CASON, Denise .... 940-668-3307 441 A
dcason@nctc.edu

CASON, Jeff .... 802-443-5404 462 H
cason@middlebury.edu

CASON, Scott .... 785-628-4206 173 B
sacason@fhsu.edu

CASPAR, Timothy .... 517-607-2238 225 A
tcaspar@hillsdale.edu

CASPARIS, Cynthia .... 936-633-5203 430 F
ccasparis@angelina.edu

CASPER, George .... 208-282-3398 130 H
caspgeor@isu.edu

CASPER, Jennifer, A ...... 509-527-5132 486 H
casper@whitman.edu

CASPER, Ruth .... 252-398-6269 328 D
wommar@chowan.edu

CASPER, Scott .... 410-455-2386 202 E
secasper@umbc.edu

CASPER, Steven .... 909-607-0132.. 37 G
steven_casper@kgi.edu

CASPER, Timothy, L ...... 608-246-6033 499 H
tcasper@madisoncollege.edu

CASPERSON, Shanna, E 608-342-1854 497 D
caspersons@uwplatt.edu

CASS, Lori .... 570-662-4873 395 C
lcass@mansfield.edu

CASS, Robin .... 585-475-2683 313 A
robin.cass@rit.edu

CASS, Rose .... 508-830-5080 213 B
rcass@maritime.edu

CASSADY, David .... 502-863-8300 178 K
david.cassady@bsk.edu

CASSADY, Sandra, L ..... 563-333-6409 169 A
cassadysandral@sau.edu

CASSADY, Steve .... 209-384-6000.. 51 G
cassady.s@mccd.edu

CASSAR, Josephine .... 810-989-5539 230 C
jcassar@sc4.edu

CASSARD, Courtney ...... 985-448-4405 192 B
courtney.cassard@nicholls.edu

CASSEL, Kimberly, R ..... 570-326-3761 393 G
kcassel@pct.edu

CASSEL, Stephen .... 215-702-4243 380 D
scassel@cairn.edu

CASSEL, Susie .... 214-333-6806 434 I
susie@dbu.edu

CASSELL, Adam .... 217-479-7105 142 I
adam.cassell@mac.edu

CASSENS, David .... 314-977-3095 259 H
david.cassens@slu.edu

CASSENS, Treisa .... 714-484-7002.. 53 K
tcassens@cypresscollege.edu

CASSIDY, Annamarie .... 610-892-1520 393 J
acassidy@pit.edu

CASSIDY, Carleen .... 406-496-4249 265 A
ccassidy@mtech.edu

CASSIDY, Derrah .... 803-738-7582 410 G
cassidyd@midlandstech.edu

CASSIDY, Jane .... 225-578-5513 188 I
jcassid@lsu.edu

CASSIDY, Jennie, M ...... 843-349-2305 408 C
jcassidy@coastal.edu

CASSIDY, Joseph .... 630-942-2316 135 A
cassidyj1180@cod.edu

CASSIDY, Joseph, L ...... 207-741-5501 195 A
jcassidy@smccme.edu

CASSIDY, Kimberly .... 610-526-5165 379 E
president@brynmawr.edu

CASSIDY, Lisa .... 714-992-7803.. 51 A
lcassidy@ketchum.edu

CASSIDY, Margot .... 602-384-2555.. 11 F
margot.cassidy@bryanuniversity.edu

CASSIDY, Michael .... 312-341-3500 147 H

CASSIDY, Paul .... 650-738-7174.. 61 Q
cassidyp@smccd.edu

CASSIDY, Susan .... 516-323-3601 307 F
scassidy@molloy.edu

CASSIMUS, Randy .... 405-682-1611 367 H
rcassimus@occc.edu

CASSIS, Lisa, A .... 859-257-5294 185 B
lcassis@uky.edu

CASSITY, Kathy .... 503-838-8226 377 H
cassityk@wou.edu

CASTADIO, Paula .... 559-278-6050.. 31 D
pcastadio@csufresno.edu

CASTALDO, Annalisa ...... 610-499-1112 403 B
acastaldo@widener.edu

CASTALDO, John .... 609-771-2082 276 I
castaldo@tcnj.edu

CASTANDEA, Angelica ... 312-935-6015 147 D
acastaneda@robertmorris.edu

CASTANEDA, Alex .... 210-829-6071 453 D
mcasta1@uiwtx.edu

CASTANEDA-CALLEROS,
Russell .... 562-463-7234.. 58 E
rcastanedacalleros@riohondo.edu

CASTANO, Beatriz .... 631-451-4435 321 F
castanb@sunysuffolk.edu

CASTANO, Vincent .... 910-678-8535 334 D
castanov@faytechcc.edu

CASTANON, Miriam .... 619-594-6298.. 33 E
castanon@sdsu.edu

CASTANON, Norma .... 830-792-7283 443 G
reslife@schreiner.edu

CASTAÑEDA, Monica ..... 623-845-3053.. 13 C
monica.castaneda@gccaz.edu

CASTEEL, Matt .... 918-631-2960 371 E
matthew-casteel@utulsa.edu

CASTEELE, Karen .... 540-831-5426 470 C
bov@radford.edu

CASTELBUONO, Audrey 269-471-6667 221 B
audreyc@andrews.edu

CASTELINO, Paul .... 740-593-1616 359 G
castelin@ohio.edu

CASTELLANI, Patrick, E . 570-348-6283 389 G
pcastellani@marywood.edu

CASTELLANO, Ana .... 787-622-8000 512 E
acastellano@pupr.edu

CASTELLANO, Cecilia .... 419-372-7803 348 H
ccast@bgsu.edu
CASTELLANO, Melissa .. 562-903-4883.. 27 C
melissa.c.castellano@biola.edu
CASTELLANOS, Grisel .... 787-878-5475 508 L
gcastellanos@arecibo.inter.edu
CASTELLANOS, Joshua .. 562-938-4343.. 48 D
jcastellanos@lbcc.edu
CASTELLINI, Michael ..... 907-474-7229.. 10 A
macastellini@alaska.edu
CASTELLINO, Lisa .... 707-826-5339.. 33 D
lisa.castellino@humboldt.edu
CASTELLO, Ellen, J .... 575-646-2090 287 B
castello@nmsu.edu
CASTELLOE, Stephen ..... 336-334-4822 335 A
srcastelloe@gtcc.edu
CASTELLUCCI, Paul .... 847-467-6072 145 F
pjcastel@northwestern.edu
CASTENEDA, Debbie ..... 970-542-3140.. 81 A
debbie.casteneda@morgancc.edu
CASTERTON, Deanna ..... 563-387-1038 167 E
castde01@luther.edu
CASTETE, Ralynn, F .... 337-475-5140 192 A
rcastete@mcneese.edu
CASTIGLIA, Patricia, T .. 915-747-7223 455 C
pcastigl@utep.edu
CASTIGLIONE,
Joseph, R .... 405-325-8208 371 B
jcastiglione@ou.edu
CASTIGLIONI, Randy ..... 713-348-5241 442 K
castigr@rice.edu
CASTILAW, Timothy ...... 660-543-4113 260 K
castilaw@ucmo.edu
CASTILE, Robert .... 913-722-0272 174 E
robert.castile@kansaschristian.edu
CASTILLA, Rafael .... 201-327-8877 277 H
rcastilla@eastwick.edu
CASTILLE, Laura .... 575-646-3635 287 B
castille@nmsu.edu
CASTILLO, Arleska .... 973-353-5500 282 B
arleska.castillo@rutgers.edu
CASTILLO, Carlos .... 305-348-2103 109 A
carlos.castillo8@fiu.edu
CASTILLO, Dale .... 785-309-3108 176 J
dale.castillo@salinatech.edu
CASTILLO, David .... 559-934-2166.. 73 M
davidcastillo2@whccd.edu
CASTILLO, Diana .... 254-526-1348 432 H
diana.castillo@ctcd.edu
CASTILLO, Elisa .... 978-542-6410 213 C
elisa.castillo@salemstate.edu
CASTILLO, Evelyn .... 787-891-0925 508 K
ecastillo@aguadilla.inter.edu
CASTILLO, Henry .... 718-862-7249 305 H
bookstore@manhattan.edu
CASTILLO, Jay .... 510-436-1648.. 45 D
jcastillo@hnu.edu
CASTILLO, JR., Juan, J . 956-326-2380 446 F
jjcastillo@tamiu.edu
CASTILLO, Katherine ...... 787-728-1515 514 D
katherine.castillo@sagrado.edu
CASTILLO, Keith .... 951-552-8720.. 27 J
kcastillo@calbaptist.edu
CASTILLO, Maggie .... 623-935-8839.. 13 A
maggie.castillo@estrellamountain.edu
CASTILLO, Mario .... 832-813-6655 439 G
mario.k.castillo@lonestar.edu
CASTILLO, Nicole .... 209-946-2496.. 70 E
ncastillo@pacific.edu
CASTILLO, Pio .... 818-364-7866.. 49 B
castilpg@lamission.edu
CASTILLO, Raul, V .... 818-947-2618.. 49 F
castilrv@lavc.edu
CASTILLO, Ruth .... 276-944-6754 467 G
rcastillo@ehc.edu
CASTILLO, Salvador ...... 541-737-8083 375 D
salvador.castillo@oregonstate.edu
CASTILLO, Santiago ...... 432-837-8885 450 D
santiago.castillo@sulross.edu
CASTILLO, Saundra .... 575-527-7076 287 E
scastillo@nmsu.edu
CASTILLO, Toni .... 405-733-7498 369 I
tcastillo@rose.edu
CASTILLO-ALANIZ,
Jo Elda .... 361-593-2382 447 D
jcastillo-alaniz@tamuk.edu
CASTILLO CLARK,
Evette .... 925-631-4238.. 59 B
ecc4@stmarys-ca.edu
CASTILLO-FRICK, Iliana . 305-237-0294 103 D
ifrick@mdc.edu
CASTILLO-GARRISON,
Estella .... 307-675-0819 502 F
egarrison@sheridan.edu
CASTILLO JOHNSON,
Grace .... 909-537-5241.. 33 A
CASTILLON, Carrie .... 209-478-0800.. 45 H
carrie.castillon@humphreys.edu
CASTILLON, Nicole .... 307-382-1642 502 I
ncastillon@westernwyoming.edu
CASTLE, Ashley .... 757-493-6000.. 92 G
CASTLE, Carey .... 606-679-8501 182 C
carey.castle@kctcs.edu
CASTLE, Clinton .... 218-683-8600 240 A
clinton.castle@northlandcollege.edu
CASTLE, David .... 605-394-4800 416 A
CASTLE, Tom .... 319-363-1323 168 C
tcastle@mtmercy.edu
CASTLEBERRY, Annette . 870-307-7227.. 20 A
annette.castleberry@lyon.edu
CASTLEBERRY, Joseph .. 425-889-4202 482 F
joseph.castleberry@northwestu.edu
CASTLEBERRY, Phillip ... 585-385-5251 314 A
pcastleberry@sfjc.edu
CASTLEBURY, Lisa .... 812-357-6515 160 D
lcastlebury@saintmeinrad.edu
CASTLEMAN, Louanna .. 910-678-0141 334 D
castleml@faytechcc.edu
CASTLES, Steve .... 661-253-3071.. 28 K
scastles@calarts.edu
CASTON, Gay Lynn .... 601-857-3396 246 B
glcaston@hindscc.edu
CASTONGUAY, Sharon .. 860-685-3377.. 89 C
scastonguay@wesleyan.edu
CASTONGUAY, Suzette .. 937-769-1375 347 H
scastonguay@antioch.edu
CASTOR, Tamela .... 661-362-3516.. 38 H
tammy.castor@canyons.edu
CASTORENA, Christina .. 425-640-1668 480 F
christina.castorena@edcc.edu
CASTRO, Adam .... 914-674-7548 306 F
acastro@mercy.edu
CASTRO, Corinne .... 830-372-6334 449 B
ccastro@tlu.edu
CASTRO, Cynthia .... 208-885-6307 131 G
cynthiacastro@uidaho.edu
CASTRO, Daisy .... 787-753-6335 508 D
dcastro@icprjc.edu
CASTRO, Evelyn .... 718-804-8805 295 A
ecastro@mec.cuny.edu
CASTRO, Francia, L .... 212-694-1000 291 I
fcastro@boricuacollege.edu
CASTRO, Ida, L .... 570-504-9647 384 F
icastro@som.geisinger.edu
CASTRO, Jose .... 787-250-1912 509 D
jlcastro@intermetro.edu
CASTRO, Joseph, I .... 559-278-2324.. 31 D
josephcastro@csufresno.edu
CASTRO, Juan, C .... 787-743-3038 511 A
jcastro@sanjuanbautista.edu
CASTRO, Juan, C .... 787-850-9375 513 E
juan.castro@upr.edu
CASTRO, Juan, C .... 787-850-9367 513 E
juan.castro@upr.edu
CASTRO, Judy .... 925-969-3300.. 46 H
jcastro@jfku.edu
CASTRO, Kaye .... 239-687-5343.. 94 N
kcastro@avemarialaw.edu
CASTRO, Lorna .... 787-764-0000 514 B
lorna.castro@upr.edu
CASTRO, Louise, P .... 915-747-8820 455 C
lpcastro@utep.edu
CASTRO, Luis, A .... 787-751-0160 507 F
lcastro@cmpr.pr.gov
CASTRO, Madelyn .... 813-253-6201 112 J
macastro@ut.edu
CASTRO, Mandy .... 817-257-7490 448 G
m.castro@tcu.edu
CASTRO, Manny .... 670-237-6772 506 A
manny.castro@marianas.edu
CASTRO, Melba .... 657-278-5579.. 31 E
melbacastro@fullerton.edu
CASTRO, Rosalinda .... 325-942-2043 451 A
rosalinda.castro@angelo.edu
CASTRO, Roz .... 630-953-3681 133 G
rcastro@chamberlain.edu
CASTRO, Sarah .... 202-624-1426 485 F
smcastro@uw.edu
CASTRO, Toni .... 206-934-3669 483 J
toni.castro@seattlecolleges.edu
CASTRO-DUARTE, Betsy 915-747-5640 455 C
bcastro@utep.edu
CASTRO-QUIRINO,
Sonya .... 806-743-3949 451 C
sonya.castro@ttuhsc.edu
CASTRUITA, Javier .... 408-741-2042.. 74 C
javier.castruita@wvm.edu
CASUCCIO, Anthony ...... 716-896-0700 324 E
acasuccio@villa.edu
CASWELL, Roger .... 620-341-5372 172 L
rcaswekk@emporia.edu
CATALANA, Paul .... 864-455-8201 414 A
pcatalana@ghs.org
CATALANO, Francesca .. 815-802-8758 140 D
fcatalano@kcc.edu
CATALANO, John .... 864-424-8019 414 C
jcat@mailbox.sc.edu
CATALANO, Megan .... 573-288-6570 252 E
mcatalano@culver.edu
CATALANO, Philip .... 315-279-5252 304 A
pcatalano@keuka.edu
CATALANO, Steven .... 718-489-5309 313 H
scatalano@sfc.edu
CATALDI, Amy, E .... 405-208-5446 367 I
acataldi@okcu.edu
CATALDI, Jennifer .... 317-738-8256 154 J
jcataldi@franklincollege.edu
CATALDO, Adrienne ...... 803-938-3906 414 B
cataldo@uscsumter.edu
CATALFAMO, Kevin .... 856-351-2701 283 A
kcatalfamo@salemcc.edu
CATALLOZZI, Lori, A ..... 617-228-2048 214 A
lacatallozzi@bhcc.mass.edu
CATALON, Linda, H ...... 225-771-2520 190 G
linda_catalon@sus.edu
CATANIA, Colette .... 615-230-3204 426 B
colette.catania@volstate.edu
CATANIA, Nancy, M ...... 610-566-1776 403 E
ncatania@williamson.edu
CATANZARO, Sam .... 309-438-7018 139 E
catanzar@ilstu.edu
CATARELLI, Rebecca ..... 802-258-9217 462 E
rcatarelli@marlboro.edu
CATCHING,
Christopher, C .... 609-652-4225 283 D
christopher.catching@stockton.edu
CATCHINGS, Robert ...... 202-806-6700.. 92 B
rcatchings@howard.edu
CATE, Fred, H .... 812-856-2096 156 A
fcate@iu.edu
CATE, Fred, H .... 812-856-2096 156 B
vpr@iu.edu
CATE, Patrick .... 603-524-3207 272 K
CATE, Richard, H .... 802-656-0219 463 E
richard.cate@uvm.edu
CATER, Lisa .... 870-460-1420.. 22 D
caterl@uamont.edu
CATES, Adreanne .... 918-495-7442 368 I
acates@oru.edu
CATES, Brenda .... 940-565-2321 454 A
brenda.cates@unt.edu
CATES, Brenda, B .... 919-658-7853 340 J
bcates@umo.edu
CATES, Carl .... 870-972-3973.. 17 G
ccates@astate.edu
CATES, Cheryl .... 419-755-4800 357 E
ccates@ncstatecollege.edu
CATES, Chris .... 423-585-2618 426 C
chris.cates@ws.edu
CATES, Jared .... 417-255-7233 256 F
jaredcated@missouristate.edu
CATES, Jo .... 312-942-8735 148 A
jo_cates@rush.edu
CATES, Joe .... 503-943-8303 377 E
cates@up.edu
CATES, John .... 256-824-6633.... 8 B
john.cates@uah.edu
CATH, Tom .... 219-464-5005 162 A
tom.cath@valpo.edu
CATHCART, Steve .... 704-216-3777 337 F
steve.cathcart@rccc.edu
CATHELINE, Jim .... 724-964-8811 391 E
jcatheline@ncstrades.edu
CATHELYN, Lisa .... 414-382-6352 492 A
lisa.cathelyn@alverno.edu
CATHERMAN, David ...... 504-398-2279 191 C
dcatherman@uhcno.edu
CATHERWOOD, Ryan ..... 434-395-4804 469 A
catherwoodrp@longwood.edu
CATHEY, Imogene .... 724-552-4499 398 H
icathey@setonhill.edu
CATHEY, Patrice, A .... 716-878-4055 318 C
catheypc@mail.buffalostate.edu
CATHEY, Ron .... 318-257-4336 191 F
rcathey@latech.edu
CATLETT, Deborrah, L ... 859-246-6810 180 K
deborrah.catlett@kctcs.edu
CATLETT, Hilary .... 509-257-2542 485 H
hilary.catlett@wallawalla.edu
CATLETT, Jennifer .... 865-471-3530 419 A
jcatlett@cn.edu
CATLETT, Nick .... 217-443-8864 135 H
ncatlett@dacc.edu
CATLIN, Carter .... 615-963-5319 426 D
ccatlin@tnstate.edu
CATLIN, Michele, E .... 812-221-1714 162 B
michelecatlin@vbc.edu
CATO, Amie .... 903-785-7661 441 G
acato@parisjc.edu
CATO, Jim .... 937-766-7610 349 G
catoj@cedarville.edu
CATON, Brock, E .... 207-778-7033 196 B
brock.caton@maine.edu
CATON, Claire .... 713-646-1799 444 B
ccaton@stcl.edu
CATON, Lisa .... 979-627-0286 432 C
lisa.caton@blinn.edu
CATON, Rebecca, A ...... 630-515-6190 143 G
rcaton@midwestern.edu
CATON, Rhonda .... 479-788-7073.. 21 H
rhonda.caton@uafs.edu
CATON, Sheron .... 325-794-4530 433 A
sheron.caton@cisco.edu
CATOTA, Claudia .... 661-654-2137.. 30 E
ccatota@csub.edu
CATRON, Susan, D .... 530-754-9158.. 68 E
sdcatron@ucdavis.edu
CATRON-WOOD,
Rhonda, K .... 276-223-4772 476 E
rcatronwood@wcc.vccs.edu
CATT, Helen .... 229-430-3506 113 I
hcatt@albanytech.edu
CATTANACH, John, R .... 315-516-4100 261 D
cattanachj@umsl.edu
CATTANI, Jessica .... 213-624-1200.. 42 I
jcattani@fidm.edu
CATTIER, Alan, R .... 603-646-1349 273 E
alan.r.cattier@dartmouth.edu
CATTOLICA, Carolee ...... 707-256-7161.. 53 C
ccattolica@napavalley.edu
CATTON, Heather .... 936-468-5597 445 F
hcatton@sfasu.edu
CATTOOR, Chad, A .... 314-505-7304 251 I
cattoorc@csl.edu
CATULLO, Patrick .... 540-654-2489 472 I
pcatullo@umw.edu
CAUBLE, Christie .... 828-884-8250 327 C
caublecl@brevard.edu
CAUCE, Ana Mari .... 206-543-5010 485 F
pres@uw.edu
CAUDA, Lisa .... 585-475-7721 313 A
lisa.cauda@rit.edu
CAUDILL, Alicia, D .... 843-953-5522 408 E
caudillad@cofc.edu
CAUDILL, Helene .... 209-667-3407.. 33 C
hcaudill@csustan.edu
CAUDILL, Sarah .... 859-985-3193 179 C
sarah_caudill@berea.edu
CAUDILL, Whitney, A .... 260-982-2658 158 T
wjcaudill@manchester.edu
CAUDLE, Mary Anne ..... 252-789-0280 335 H
maryanne.caudle@martincc.edu
CAUDLE, Patricia, M ..... 909-748-8171.. 71 G
pat_caudle@redlands.edu
CAUGHELL, Leslie .... 757-233-8853 477 F
lcaughell@vwu.edu
CAUGHMAN, Gretchen .. 706-721-4014 115 A
gcaughma@augusta.edu
CAULEY, Cleon .... 302-857-7827.. 89 F
ccauley@desu.edu
CAULEY, Phil .... 828-227-2923 344 A
cauley@wcu.edu
CAULFIELD, Jack .... 508-213-2398 217 E
jack.caulfield@nichols.edu
CAULFIELD, Kim .... 267-341-3481 386 A
kcaulfield@holyfamily.edu
CAULFIELD, Richard ..... 907-796-6509.. 10 B
racaulfield@alaska.edu
CAUSBY, Cory .... 828-227-7218 344 A
causby@wcu.edu
CAUSEY, Bruce .... 256-306-2569.... 1 F
bruce.causey@calhoun.edu
CAUSEY, Jana .... 601-554-5506 248 E
jcausey@prcc.edu
CAUSEY, Katherine .... 901-435-1259 421 A
katherine_causey@loc.edu
CAUSLAND, Luann .... 678-407-5231 118 D
lcausland@ggc.edu
CAUTIN, Robin .... 203-396-8020.. 88 B
cautinr@sacredheart.edu
CAUWELS, Beth .... 805-565-6101.. 74 K
bcauwels@westmont.edu

CAVALIER, Deborah ...... 617-747-2146 206 E advisors@online.berklee.edu
CAVALIER, Philip, A ...... 731-881-7010 428 B pcavalie@utm.edu
CAVALIER, Wayne .... 210-341-1366 441 C wcavalier@ost.edu
CAVALIERI, Correne ...... 718-779-1499 311 I ccavalieri@plazacollege.edu
CAVALIERI, Cristina, G . 215-503-9496 400 A cristina.cavalieri@jefferson.edu
CAVALIERI, Thomas ...... 856-566-6995 281 E cavalita@rowan.edu
CAVALIERI-GROVER, Jeanne .... 215-635-7300 385 A jcavalieri@gratz.edu
CAVALLARO, Ronald, A 401-825-1000 404 H rcavallaro@ccri.edu
CAVALLARO, Vito .... 212-938-5500 320 B vito@sunyopt.edu
CAVALLO, Julia .... 724-805-2372 398 E julia.cavallo@stvincent.edu
CAVALLO, Julia .... 724-805-2592 398 F julia.cavallo@stvincent.edu
CAVALLUZZI, Martin ..... 360-475-7100 482 G mcavalluzzi@olympic.edu
CAVALOVITCH, Renee, T .... 412-397-6061 397 G cavalovitch@rmu.edu
CAVANAGH, Debbie ...... 310-338-4493.. 50 J debbie.cavanagh@lmu.edu
CAVANAGH, Jon .... 765-998-4161 160 F jon.cavanagh@taylor.edu
CAVANAGH, Kelly .... 614-508-7277 354 F kcavanagh@hondros.edu
CAVANAGH, Kevin .... 973-748-9000 276 A kevin_cavanagh@bloomfield.edu
CAVANAGH, Paul .... 631-348-3169 309 F pcavanag@nyit.edu
CAVANAGH-DICK, Maura .... 856-351-2754 283 A mdick@salemcc.edu
CAVANAUGH, Amy, E ... 503-943-7201 377 E cavanaug@up.edu
CAVANAUGH, Brian ...... 716-829-7878 298 F cavanaub@dyc.edu
CAVANAUGH, SSJ, Cecelia .... 215-753-3623 381 D ccavanau@chc.edu
CAVANAUGH, Kyle .... 919-684-2826 328 G kyle.cavanaugh@duke.edu
CAVANAUGH, Mary ...... 212-396-7549 294 C mary.cavanaugh@hunter.cuny.edu
CAVANAUGH, Megan .... 717-264-2630 403 F megan.cavanaugh@wilson.edu
CAVANAUGH, Michael .. 585-582-8201 299 A michaelcavanaugh@elim.edu
CAVANESS, Kerrie .... 509-574-4870 487 A kcavaness@yvcc.edu
CAVANUAGH, Rachel .... 910-362-7317 332 H rcavenaugh@cfcc.edu
CAVAZOS, Christopher .. 505-224-4000 285 J ccavazos@cnm.edu
CAVAZOS, Raul .... 361-593-2173 447 D raul.cavazos@tamuk.edu
CAVAZOS, Rebecca .... 956-664-4680 444 A beckyc@southtexascollege.edu
CAVE, Brandi, M .... 903-434-8103 441 B bcave@ntcc.edu
CAVE, Erin, L .... 503-943-7125 377 E cave@up.edu
CAVE, Nancy .... 210-688-3101 432 L
CAVELIER, Amy .... 617-873-0106 207 F amy.cavelier30@go.cambridgecollege.edu
CAVENAUGH, Andy .... 910-296-2480 335 E acavenaugh@jamessprunt.edu
CAVENAUGH, Jennifer .. 407-691-1268 105 M jcavenaugh@rollins.edu
CAVENDER, Wayne .... 214-388-5466 435 G wcavender@dallasinstitute.edu
CAVENER, Douglas, R ... 814-865-9591 392 B drc9@psu.edu
CAVENY, Deanna, M ..... 843-953-5731 408 E cavenyd@cofc.edu
CAVERHILL, Wendy .... 207-768-2708 194 J wcaverhill@nmcc.edu
CAVERLEY, Darla .... 320-629-5118 240 C darla.caverley@pine.edu
CAVI, Sandra .... 309-438-8489 139 E skcavi@ilstu.edu
CAVICCHI, Dan .... 401-454-6134 405 D dcavicch@risd.edu
CAVIEUX, Lydia .... 617-603-6935 216 H lydia.cavieux@necb.edu
CAVINESS, Andrea .... 646-660-6596 292 L andrea.caviness@baruch.cuny.edu
CAVINESS, Debbie, J .... 315-470-6632 320 A dcavines@esf.edu
CAVINESS, Ken .... 423-236-2856 424 B caviness@southern.edu
CAVINS-TULL, Kathryn .. 817-257-7820 448 G k.cavins@tcu.edu
CAVITT, Deborah .... 817-531-4298 451 E dcavitt@txwes.edu
CAVITT, Mary Ellen .... 512-245-2205 450 E mc58@txstate.edu
CAWLEY, James, F .... 215-204-5860 399 F jim.cawley@temple.edu
CAWLEY, Patrick, J .... 843-792-4000 410 F cawleypj@musc.edu
CAWLFIELD, Jeffrey .... 573-341-4557 261 E jdc@mst.edu
CAWOOD, J. Scott .... 215-702-4216 380 D scawood@cairn.edu
CAWTHON, Elisabeth .... 817-272-3291 454 J cawthon2@uta.edu
CAWTHORNE, Jon, G .... 313-577-4020 232 I jon.cawthorne@wayne.edu
CAWYER, Carol, S .... 406-466-6012 366 F cscawyer@langston.edu
CAYCHO, Maura .... 845-434-5750 322 A mcaycho@sunysullivan.edu
CAYEA, Cynthia .... 516-364-0808 309 A library@nycollege.edu
CAYLOR, Deborah, Z ..... 540-458-8730 478 A dcaylor@wlu.edu
CAYWOOD, Carter .... 850-729-6922 103 L caywoodc@nwfsc.edu
CAYWOOD, Steven .... 620-278-4240 177 B scaywood@sterling.edu
CAZARES, Becky .... 559-934-2159.. 73 M beckycazares@whccd.edu
CAZARES, Javier .... 559-934-2176.. 74 A javiercazares@whccd.edu
CAZZETTA, Vinnie .... 845-341-4726 311 C vinnie.cazzetta@sunyorange.edu
CEA, Cara .... 914-694-2200 305 J
CEA, Jorge .... 925-473-7430.. 40 J jcea@losmedanos.edu
CEBINA, Jody .... 704-687-1283 342 E jcebina@uncc.edu
CEBRICK, Daniel, T .... 570-208-5870 387 A dtcebric@kings.edu
CEBULA, Thomas .... 330-490-7051 364 B tcebula@walsh.edu
CECALA, Dianna .... 843-349-5207 410 C dianna.cecala@hgtc.edu
CECCHINI, Bernard .... 315-568-3127 308 F bcecchini@nycc.edu
CECCHINI, Dan .... 541-383-7700 372 B dcecchini@cocc.edu
CECE, Heidi .... 757-352-4809 470 H hcece@regent.edu
CECH, John .... 406-447-4401 263 C jcech@carroll.edu
CECI, David, F .... 248-232-4224 229 A dfceci@oaklandcc.edu
CECIL, Dale .... 270-686-4239 179 D dale.cecil@brescia.edu
CECIL, Matt .... 507-389-1713 239 C matt.cecil@mnsu.edu
CECIL, Patrick, A .... 502-895-3411 183 D pcecil@lpts.edu
CEDERBERG, Alisha ...... 269-488-4231 225 E acederberg@kvcc.edu
CEDERHOLM, Annette ... 256-840-4142.... 3 F annette.cederholm@snead.edu
CEDILLO, Arnulfo .... 510-436-2478.. 56 H acedillo@peralta.edu
CEDRONE, David .... 617-994-6904 211 B dcedrone@bhe.mass.edu
CELA, Suela .... 406-377-9403 263 E scela@dawson.edu
CELAYA, Aintzane .... 305-284-4969 112 E a.celaya@miami.edu
CELELLI, Anthony .... 361-991-9403 445 E
CELENZA, Christopher .. 202-687-4043.. 92 A ccelenza@georgetown.edu
CELENZA, John .... 617-353-2445 207 D celenza@bu.edu
CELHAY, Lilia .... 510-748-2234.. 56 F lcelhay@peralta.edu
CELIAN, Doris, M .... 734-487-0324 223 H dcelian@emich.edu
CELIZ, Jason .... 847-578-8481 147 I jason.celiz@rosalindfranklin.edu
CELL, Paul, M .... 973-655-5123 279 C cellp@mail.montclair.edu
CELLANA, Curt .... 413-662-5245 213 A curt.cellana@mcla.edu
CELLEMME, Patricia ...... 518-292-1710 313 D cellep@sage.edu
CELLI, David, S .... 570-389-4882 394 A dcelli@bloomu.edu
CELLINI, Roger .... 909-748-8020.. 71 G roger_cellini@redlands.edu
CELLINI, Todd .... 918-836-6886 370 D todd.cellini@spartan.edu
CELNIK, Rachel .... 845-352-3431 326 B shaareitorah@optonline.net
CELSO, Jeanne .... 315-470-7256 291 H jeannecelso@crouse.org
CELTEK, Serkan .... 956-872-5577 444 A sbceltek@southtexascollege.edu
CEMAN, Jamie .... 714-997-6582.. 36 C ceman@chapman.edu
CENDANA, Trish .... 304-293-4686 491 C trish.cendana@mail.wvu.edu
CENINA, Angela .... 714-547-9625.. 28 C acenina@calcoast.edu
CENSON, Sora .... 516-255-4748 312 D
CENTENO, Ilsa .... 787-743-3484 511 A icenteno@sanjuanbautista.edu
CENTLIVRE, Becky .... 913-469-8500 174 D bcentliv@jccc.edu
CENTOFANTI-FIELDS, Chantal .... 740-376-4649 356 A cgc002@marietta.edu
CENTOR, Josh .... 412-268-3894 380 F jcentor@andrew.cmu.edu
CEO, Raymond .... 928-445-7300.. 16 M raymond.ceo@yc.edu
CEPEDA, Adrian .... 312-935-6683 147 D acepeda@robertmorris.edu
CEPEDA, Charlotte .... 670-237-6767 506 A charlotte.cepeda@marianas.edu
CEPERO, Ana .... 787-761-0640 512 F desarrollo@utcpr.edu
CEPHAS, Marcia .... 410-951-3812 203 D mcephas@coppin.edu
CERAR-DERBISH, Amanda .... 406-604-4300 263 A
CERCONE, Suzanne .... 570-504-7954 387 D cercones@lackawanna.edu
CERDA, Manuel .... 626-585-7400.. 55 K mcerda4@pasadena.edu
CERES, Joanne .... 910-362-7040 332 H jtceres154@mail.cfcc.edu
CEREZO, Sabrina .... 718-951-5622 293 C scerezo@brooklyn.cuny.edu
CERILLI, Annette .... 401-232-6323 404 F acerilli@bryant.edu
CERINO, Michael, H ...... 864-488-4564 410 E mcerino@limestone.edu
CERIO, Thea .... 508-541-1565 208 F tcerio@dean.edu
CERNY, Glenn .... 734-462-4400 230 D gcerny@schoolcraft.edu
CERRA, Susan .... 845-848-7404 298 D susan.cerra@dc.edu
CERRONI, Keith .... 412-578-8776 380 E kccerroni@carlow.edu
CERRUTO, Joe .... 319-363-1323 168 C jcerruto@mtmercy.edu
CERSLEY, Tracy .... 434-961-5211 475 F tcersley@pvcc.edu
CERVANTES, Cynthia ..... 619-594-6202.. 33 E cynthia.cervantes@sdsu.edu
CERVANTES, Eduardo .... 408-848-4702.. 43 J ecervantes@gavilan.edu
CERVANTES, George ...... 202-495-3828.. 92 E advance@dhs.edu
CERVANTES, Javier .... 541-917-4999 374 A cervanj@linnbenton.edu
CERVANTES, Juana .... 915-779-8031 457 F jcervantes@computercareercenter.com
CERVANTES, Leslie .... 575-646-3616 287 B leslie86@nmsu.edu
CERVANTES, Lynda .... 915-532-3737 458 C lcervantes@westerntech.edu
CERVANTES, Melissa ...... 650-949-7777.. 43 D cervantesmelissa@foothill.edu
CERVANTES, Mike .... 361-592-9335 447 D mike.cervantes@tamuk.edu
CERVANTES, Rafael .... 651-690-6857 242 R rcervantes@stkate.edu
CERVANTES, Richard ..... 979-830-4123 432 C richard.cervantes@blinn.edu
CERVENKA, Katie .... 713-348-6012 442 K cervenka@rice.edu
CERVENKA, Mark .... 713-221-8043 453 B cervenkam@uhd.edu
CERVENY, Terri, A .... 518-388-6180 323 G cervenyt@union.edu
CERVINI, John .... 517-607-2670 225 A jcervini@hillsdale.edu
CERZA, Donna .... 570-674-6460 390 G dcerza@misericordia.edu
CESAREO, Francesco, C 508-767-7321 205 D fcesareo@assumption.edu
CESCA, Michele .... 562-985-5195.. 31 F michele.cesca@csulb.edu
CESELSKI, Teresa .... 660-831-4139 256 G ceselskit@moval.edu
CESMEBASI, Erol .... 201-216-5576 283 C erol.cesmebasi@stevens.edu
CESSNA, Tammy .... 859-858-2306 178 H
CESTERO, Nicolle, M .... 413-205-3800 205 A nicolle.cestero@aic.edu
CESTONE, Amy .... 610-604-7700.. 92 G
CETNARSKI, Eric .... 415-561-6555.. 57 H eric.cetnarski@presidio.edu
CETTIN, Matthew .... 814-732-1304 394 F mcettin@edinboro.edu
CEVALLOS, F. Javier ..... 508-626-4575 212 D jcevallos@framingham.edu
CEZEAUX, Judy .... 479-968-0353.. 18 C jcezeaux@atu.edu
CHÁVEZ-KORELL, Shannon .... 248-416-1122 227 C schavez-korell@msp.edu
CHA, Jason .... 805-565-6132.. 74 K jacha@westmont.edu
CHABNER, Shayna .... 626-395-6762.. 29 C schabner@caltech.edu
CHABOLLA, Edgar .... 213-477-2653.. 52 G echabolla@msmu.edu
CHABON, Shelly .... 503-725-3419 376 A chabonr@pdx.edu
CHABOT, Joseph .... 203-596-6187.. 87 F jchabot@post.edu
CHABOT, Lisabeth .... 607-274-3182 303 B lchabot@ithaca.edu
CHABOT-WIEFERICH, Nicole .... 781-891-2362 206 D nchabotwieferich@bentley.edu
CHABOT-WIEFERICH, Rebecca .... 617-585-0200 206 F rebecca.chabot-wieferich@the-bac.edu
CHABRIES, Carole .... 414-382-6400 492 A carole.chabries@alverno.edu
CHACKO, Jacob .... 678-466-4500 116 E jacobchacko@clayton.edu
CHACKRAVARTHY, Swapna .... 813-974-7555 110 B schackra@health.usf.edu
CHACON, Arnold .... 202-685-3924 503 I arnold.chacon.civ@ndu.edu
CHACON, Fabio .... 301-860-3933 203 C fchacon@bowiestate.edu
CHACON, Jean Pierre ... 305-595-9500.. 94 B
CHACON, Michael .... 208-562-2089 130 F michaelchacon@cwi.edu
CHACONA, Julie, A .... 814-732-1779 394 F jchacona@edinboro.edu
CHACONIS, Alexis .... 718-260-5250 295 B achaconis@citytech.cuny.edu
CHADDOCK, Noelle .... 207-786-6031 193 B nchaddoc@bates.edu
CHADEN, Caryn .... 312-362-8885 135 I cchaden@depaul.edu
CHADHA, Ravneet .... 520-621-3030.. 16 G rschadha@email.arizona.edu
CHADOS, Stacey .... 340-693-1446 514 E schados@uvi.edu
CHADWELL, Faye .... 541-737-3411 375 D faye.chadwell@oregonstate.edu
CHADWELL, Lindsey ..... 907-786-6190.... 9 H lnchadwell@alaska.edu
CHADWICK, Gregory ..... 252-737-7703 341 C chadwickg@ecu.edu
CHADWICK, Stephanie .. 425-388-9392 480 G schadwick@everettcc.edu
CHADWICK, Susan .... 610-526-7922 379 E schadwick@brynmawr.edu
CHAE, Ki Byung .... 910-521-6352 343 B kibyung.chae@uncp.edu
CHAFFEE, Brandy .... 218-281-8434 244 A brandy@umn.edu
CHAFFEE, Cynthia .... 312-567-3084 139 B cchaffee@iit.edu

CHANG, Otto .... 626-656-2101.. 72 C ochang@uwest.edu
CHANG, Peter, M .... 703-333-5904 478 B mchang@wuv.edu
CHANG, Susan, I .... 714-997-6940.. 36 C suschang@chapman.edu
CHANG, Wendy .... 305-237-0244 103 D wchang1@mdc.edu
CHANG, Yae .... 213-487-0110.. 41 I dean@dula.edu
CHANG-RUSSELL, Jessica .... 646-768-5300 301 B
CHANSLOR, Mike .... 918-444-3627 367 A chanslor@nsuok.edu
CHANTUNG, Margaret ... 760-750-4407.. 33 B mchantung@csusm.edu
CHAO, Gloria .... 212-220-8304 293 A gchao@bmcc.cuny.edu
CHAPA, Angela .... 559-453-2170.. 43 G angela.chapa@fresno.edu
CHAPA, Paul .... 210-999-8328 452 A paul.chapa@trinity.edu
CHAPARRO, Eric .... 787-620-2040 506 C echaparro@aupr.edu
CHAPDELAINE, Andrea, E .... 301-696-3855 199 B chapdelaine@hood.edu
CHAPDELAINE, Anne .... 413-565-1000 205 G achapdelaine@baypath.edu
CHAPELLE, Kelby .... 860-701-5043.. 87 D chapelle_k@mitchell.edu
CHAPIN, Timothy .... 850-644-8515 109 C tchapin@fsu.edu
CHAPIN, Wesley .... 715-425-0629 497 E wes.chapin@uwrf.edu
CHAPIN LAVIGNE, Kerry .... 518-564-2090 319 C chapinkg@plattsburgh.edu
CHAPMAN, Adam .... 606-326-2114 180 I
CHAPMAN, Angela .... 203-575-8208.. 86 B achapman@nv.edu
CHAPMAN, April .... 707-836-2904.. 62 F achapman@santarosa.edu
CHAPMAN, Brenda, J .... 404-413-3505 119 E bchapman@gsu.edu
CHAPMAN, Bryce .... 314-744-7631 256 C bryce.chapman@mobap.edu
CHAPMAN, Chris .... 903-233-3561 439 E chrischapman@letu.edu
CHAPMAN, Dale, T .... 618-468-2001 141 F dchapman@lc.edu
CHAPMAN, Daniel, W .... 774-354-0679 206 B daniel.chapman@becker.edu
CHAPMAN, Elaine .... 626-585-7608.. 55 K efchapman@pasadena.edu
CHAPMAN, Eric .... 301-405-7136 202 C echapman@umd.edu
CHAPMAN, Honora .... 559-278-3056.. 31 D
CHAPMAN, J. Quincy ... 715-836-3630 496 D chapmajq@uwec.edu
CHAPMAN, John .... 540-261-8400 471 H john.chapman@svu.edu
CHAPMAN, John, T ...... 919-267-1640 330 B
CHAPMAN, Josh .... 918-781-7225 365 F chapmanj@bacone.edu
CHAPMAN, Kathryn ...... 773-481-8634 134 G kchapman17@ccc.edu
CHAPMAN, Katrina .... 615-248-1268 427 A klchapman@trevecca.edu
CHAPMAN, Kelly .... 603-206-8004 272 L kchapman@ccsnh.edu
CHAPMAN, Linda .... 618-468-4000 141 F lchapman@lc.edu
CHAPMAN, Lindsay ...... 660-543-4730 260 K lchapman@ucmo.edu
CHAPMAN, Lisa, M ...... 919-718-7246 333 C lchapman@cccc.edu
CHAPMAN, Lorna .... 706-754-7789 122 F lchapman@northgatech.edu
CHAPMAN, Matt .... 707-668-5663.. 41 D matt@dellarte.com
CHAPMAN, Merv .... 816-414-3700 256 A mchapman@mbts.edu
CHAPMAN, Michelle ..... 404-756-4000 114 G
CHAPMAN, Nick .... 706-355-5048 114 F nchapman@athenstech.edu
CHAPMAN, Richard, L .. 615-898-2988 422 H richard.chapman@mtsu.edu
CHAPMAN, Sharon, H .. 803-938-3810 414 B hamptons@uscsumter.edu
CHAPMAN, William .... 808-956-3469 128 F wchapman@hawaii.edu
CHAPP, Belena .... 215-568-4010 390 J bchapp@moore.edu
CHAPPA, Kelley .... 706-245-7226 117 E kchappa@ec.edu
CHAPPEL, Jessica .... 802-225-3220 462 I jessica.chappel@neci.edu
CHAPPELL, Cindy .... 619-849-2531.. 57 E cindychappell@pointloma.edu
CHAPPELL, Jean .... 434-961-5446 475 F jchappell@pvcc.edu
CHAPPELL, Joy, G .... 336-342-4261 337 E chappellj@rockinghamcc.edu
CHAPPELL, Paul .... 661-946-2274.. 73 G
CHAPPELL, Susan .... 318-342-5424 192 F chappell@ulm.edu
CHAPPELL-WILLIAMS, Lynette .... 607-255-3976 297 F lc75@cornell.edu
CHAPPIE, Tarana .... 650-574-6196.. 61 P chappiet@smccd.edu
CHAPPUIE, Anita .... 620-331-4100 174 C achappuie@indycc.edu
CHAPPY, Sharon, L ...... 262-243-5700 493 B sharon.chappy@cuw.edu
CHAPUT, Barbara .... 413-662-5596 213 A barbara.chaput@mcla.edu
CHAPUT, JR., Maury, L 410-777-2324 197 C mlchaput@aacc.edu
CHAR, Cheryl .... 808-237-5140 127 G char@hmi.edu
CHARBONNEAU, Leticia 832-813-6246 439 G leticia.t.charbonneau@lonestar.edu
CHARD, David .... 617-353-3213 207 D seddean@bu.edu
CHAREK, Terry .... 978-867-4263 209 F terry.charek@gordon.edu
CHARETTE, Ace .... 701-477-7862 347 A acharette1@tm.edu
CHARETTE, Martin .... 860-932-4157.. 86 E mcharette@qvcc.edu
CHARETTE, Melodie ...... 406-657-1022 265 E melodie.charette@rocky.edu
CHARETTE, Reno .... 406-657-2144 264 E rcharette@msubillings.edu
CHARETTE, Sharon .... 401-739-5000 405 A scharette@neit.edu
CHARI, Kaushal .... 414-229-6256 497 A kchari@uwm.edu
CHARITY, Sherika .... 804-523-5137 474 H scharity@reynolds.edu
CHARLES, Amy .... 608-822-2324 500 G acharles@swtc.edu
CHARLES, Cynthia .... 504-816-4263 186 D ccharles@dillard.edu
CHARLES, Harvey .... 518-591-8183 316 D hcharles@albany.edu
CHARLES, Jeffrey, R ..... 408-554-4607.. 62 D jcharles@scu.edu
CHARLES, Jennifer .... 512-448-8542 442 M jennifercharles@stedwards.edu
CHARLES, John .... 217-545-8080 149 D jcharles@siu.edu
CHARLES, Katy, A .... 717-871-5702 395 D katy.charles@millersville.edu
CHARLES, Kelly .... 910-962-2689 343 C charlesk@uncw.edu
CHARLES, Kerwin .... 203-432-6035.. 89 D kerwin.charles@yale.edu
CHARLES, Kevin, E .... 603-862-1098 274 G kevin.charles@unh.edu
CHARLES, Kristin .... 402-461-7732 267 D kristin.charles@hastings.edu
CHARLES, Kristin .... 415-239-3303.. 37 A kcharles@ccsf.edu
CHARLES, Madonna ...... 718-951-5133 293 C mcharles@brooklyn.cuny.edu
CHARLES, Maurice .... 773-702-1234 150 J
CHARLES, Mitch .... 916-388-2800.. 35 B mpcharles@carrington.edu
CHARLES, Olivier .... 334-347-2623.... 2 A ocharles@escc.edu
CHARLES, Pam .... 504-278-6418 188 A pcharles@nunez.edu
CHARLES, Renee .... 309-677-3260 133 B rcharles@fsmail.bradley.edu
CHARLES, Robert .... 843-921-6900 411 F
CHARLES, Robiaun, R .... 404-471-6000 113 G rcharles@agnesscott.edu
CHARLES, Shawn, M ..... 504-286-5348 190 I scharles@suno.edu
CHARLES, Stacy .... 906-635-2626 226 E scharles1@lssu.edu
CHARLEY, Susan .... 731-286-3226 425 A charley@dscc.edu
CHARLIER, Hara, D .... 218-855-8053 237 F hcharlier@clcmn.edu
CHARLOT, Pascale .... 305-237-2154 103 D pcharlot@mdc.edu
CHARLTON, Patricia, A . 702-651-3598 271 A patty.charlton@csn.edu
CHARNEY, Dennis, S .... 212-241-5674 302 F
CHARNEY, Len .... 617-585-0200 206 F len.charney@the-bac.edu
CHARNOW, Rebecca ..... 917-493-4404 305 I rcharnow@msmnyc.edu
CHAROENSIRI, Kanitta .. 540-231-5313 477 A charkx@vt.edu
CHARPENTIER, Jennifer 262-564-2866 499 F charpentierj@gtc.edu
CHARPENTIER, Paul ...... 207-741-5503 195 A pcharpentier@smccme.edu
CHARRIEZ CORDERO, Mayra .... 787-754-2744 514 B mayra.charriez@upr.edu
CHARRON, Michael ...... 507-457-1606 243 B mcharron@smumn.edu
CHARTRAW, Yuko .... 253-589-6089 479 G yuko.chartraw@cptc.edu
CHASE, A.J .... 865-251-1800 424 A achase@south.edu
CHASE, Christy .... 203-582-8738.. 87 G christy.chase@quinnipiac.edu
CHASE, Del .... 719-336-1514.. 80 K del.chase@lamarcc.edu
CHASE, Dom .... 317-921-4882 157 G dchase@ivytech.edu
CHASE, Gregory .... 304-336-8536 490 F gregory.chase@westliberty.edu
CHASE, Horace .... 615-963-7411 426 D
CHASE, Julie .... 207-741-5874 195 A jchase@smccme.edu
CHASE, Kelley .... 410-837-6149 204 B kchase@ubalt.edu
CHASE, Marilyn, O .... 317-788-2192 161 B chase@uindy.edu
CHASE, Mary, E .... 402-280-2703 266 I marychase@creighton.edu
CHASE, MaryEtta .... 801-957-4799 461 D maryetta.chase@slcc.edu
CHASE, Norris .... 309-677-2648 133 B nchase@fsmail.bradley.edu
CHASE, Susie .... 410-810-5059 204 D schase2@washcoll.edu
CHASE-LANSDALE, Lindsay .... 847-491-8543 145 F lcl@northwestern.edu
CHASNOV, Robert .... 937-766-7683 349 G chasnovr@cedarville.edu
CHASON, Myra .... 310-289-5123.. 73 H myra.chason@wcui.edu
CHASSAPIS, Constantin 201-216-5564 283 C constantin.chassapis@stevens.edu
CHASTAIN, Celina .... 864-225-7653 409 J celinachastain@forrestcollege.edu
CHASTAIN, Donna .... 541-737-0123 375 D donna.chastain@oregonstate.edu
CHASTAIN, Melissa .... 502-585-9911 184 D mchastain@spalding.edu
CHASTAIN, Tricia .... 470-578-4828 120 L pchast11@kennesaw.edu
CHASTANT, Jane .... 713-623-2040 430 K jchastant@aii.edu
CHASTEEN, Denny .... 678-839-5560 126 E dchasteen@westga.edu
CHASTEEN, Jon .... 817-722-1610 439 B jon.chasteen@tku.edu
CHATFIELD, Shoshana .. 401-841-3089 503 L
CHATHAM, David, W ..... 864-833-7028 411 I dchatham@presby.edu
CHATMAN, Anthony ...... 706-233-7315 124 B achatman@shorter.edu
CHATMAN, Cheryl, T .... 651-603-6151 235 F chatman@csp.edu
CHATMAN, Christal .... 215-619-7330 390 H cchatman@mc3.edu
CHATMAN, Jesse .... 901-435-1470 421 A jesse_chatman@loc.edu
CHATMAN, Patricia .... 313-317-6603 224 G pchatman@hfcc.edu
CHATMAN, Rodney .... 937-229-2131 362 G rchatman1@udayton.edu
CHATMON, Angelo, V ... 804-257-5856 477 C achatmon@vuu.edu
CHATMON, Anthony ...... 706-233-7315 124 B achatmon@shorter.edu
CHATRIAND, Craig .... 509-777-4655 486 I cchatriand@whitworth.edu
CHATTERJEE, Somnath .. 850-644-5716 109 C schatterjee@admin.fsu.edu
CHATTERJEE-SUTTON, Eva .... 724-503-1001 402 E echatterjeesutton@washjeff.edu
CHATTERS, Katie .... 402-941-6053 267 L chattersk@midlandu.edu
CHATTERS, Lawrence .... 402-941-6400 267 L chatters@midlandu.edu
CHAU, Lindy .... 805-378-1437.. 72 H lchau@vcccd.edu
CHAUBEY, Indrajeet ...... 860-486-2917.. 88 E indrajeet.chaubey@uconn.edu
CHAUDHRY, Ahmad ...... 864-646-1437 413 A
CHAUDRI, Aamer .... 734-973-3408 232 B achauhdri@wccnet.edu
CHAUFFEE, Gary .... 832-230-5555 440 H gchaffee@na.edu
CHAULK, Amanda .... 802-728-1732 464 E achaulk@vtc.edu
CHAUNG, Amy .... 888-488-4968.. 46 F achaung@itu.edu
CHAURET, Christian ...... 765-455-9371 156 D cchauret@iuk.edu
CHAUVIN, Marc .... 985-545-1500 187 H
CHAVAN, Shiraz .... 415-703-9520.. 28 D schavan@cca.edu
CHAVERS, LaToya .... 901-381-3939 428 E latoya@visible.edu
CHAVES, William .... 701-777-2794 345 C william.chaves@und.edu
CHAVEZ, Antonio, T ..... 512-428-1246 442 M tonyc@stedwards.edu
CHAVEZ, April .... 575-769-4061 285 K april.chavez@clovis.edu
CHAVEZ, Augustine .... 916-691-7418.. 50 G chaveza@crc.losrios.edu
CHAVEZ, Augustine .... 916-608-6733.. 50 H chaveza@flc.losrios.edu
CHAVEZ, Carolyn .... 505-454-2503 286 D cchavez@luna.edu
CHAVEZ, Christine .... 310-568-6691.. 50 J cchavez@lmu.edu
CHAVEZ, Coni .... 209-575-6959.. 75 H chavezc@yosemite.edu
CHAVEZ, Consuelo, E ... 575-461-4413 286 E conniec@mesalands.edu
CHAVEZ, Diana .... 415-703-9575.. 28 D diana@cca.edu
CHAVEZ, Israel .... 563-588-8000 165 F ichavez@emmaus.edu
CHAVEZ, Lilia .... 510-436-2595.. 56 H lchavez@peralta.edu
CHAVEZ, Lisa .... 562-908-3467.. 58 E lchavez@riohondo.edu
CHAVEZ, Lisa, M .... 323-343-3500.. 32 A lisa.chavez@calstatela.edu
CHAVEZ, Mary .... 719-549-3353.. 81 K mary.chavez@pueblocc.edu
CHAVEZ, Matilda .... 619-388-3400.. 60 C mchavez001@sdccd.edu
CHAVEZ, Melanie .... 831-582-5404.. 32 C mchavez@csumb.edu
CHAVEZ, Michael .... 661-654-3181.. 30 E mchavez14@csub.edu
CHAVEZ, Miguel .... 330-490-7341 364 B mchavez@walsh.edu
CHAVEZ, Olga .... 915-831-3322 436 E ochave30@epcc.edu
CHAVEZ, Patricia .... 201-684-7622 280 H pchavez@ramapo.edu
CHAVEZ, Robert .... 215-576-0800 397 C rchavez@rrc.edu
CHAVEZ, Robert .... 615-460-6670 418 F robert.chavez@belmont.edu
CHAVEZ, Robert .... 210-829-6030 453 D rgchavez@uiwtx.edu
CHAVEZ, Steven .... 575-538-6671 289 B steven.chavez@wnmu.edu
CHAVEZ, Susan .... 505-425-7511 286 H srchavez@nmhu.edu
CHAVEZ, Todd .... 813-974-1642 110 B tchavez@usf.edu
CHAVEZ-SILVA, Monica 641-269-3900 165 J chavezsm@grinnell.edu
CHAVIRA, Rejoice .... 909-389-3456.. 59 H rchavira@craftonhills.edu
CHAVIS, Gordon .... 407-823-3004 109 E gordon.chavis@ucf.edu
CHAVIS, Kimberly .... 847-925-6507 137 H kchavis@harpercollege.edu

CHICK, Phil .... 513-745-3445 365 B
chickp@xavier.edu
CHICKERING, Fran .... 603-427-7629 272 J
fchickering@ccsnh.edu
CHICO HURST, Karen ... 518-442-5540 316 D
kchicohurst@albany.edu
CHIDDICK, Troy .... 610-527-0200 397 I
tchiddick@rosemont.edu
CHIDIAC, George .... 626-585-7424.. 55 K
gchidiac@pasadena.edu
CHIELLI, Jack, J .... 301-447-5366 200 E
j.j.chielli@msmary.edu
CHIEN, Amy .... 909-537-3723.. 33 A
ychien2@csusb.edu
CHIEVES, Kevin .... 912-443-5491 124 A
kchieves@savannahtech.edu
CHIGAS, Diana .... 617-627-5870 219 B
diana.chigas@tufts.edu
CHIGAZOLA, Deborah ... 707-527-4525.. 62 F
dchigazola@santarosa.edu
CHIGLINSKY, Brian .... 202-885-2121.. 90 J
brianc@american.edu
CHIGOS, Lisa .... 619-961-4326.. 67 E
lchigos@tjsl.edu
CHILCOAT, Cindy .... 928-523-6120.. 14 H
CHILCOAT, Cynthia, A .. 928-523-6120.. 14 H
cindy.chilcoat@nau.edu
CHILDERS, Amber .... 501-337-5000.. 18 J
amber@coto.edu
CHILDERS, Camille .... 316-978-3620 178 A
camille.childers@wichita.edu
CHILDERS, Mark .... 254-710-2211 431 J
mark_childers@baylor.edu
CHILDERS, JR.,
William, A .... 304-336-5100 490 F
bill.childers@westliberty.edu
CHILDRES, Donna .... 706-368-7742 118 E
dchildre@highlands.edu
CHILDRESS, Amanda ..... 256-840-4210.... 3 F
amanda.childress@snead.edu
CHILDRESS, Kathy .... 864-225-7653 409 J
kathychildress@forrestcollege.edu
CHILDRESS, Marc .... 913-344-1236 170 I
marc.childress@bakeru.edu
CHILDREY, Cynthia, A .. 928-523-6838.. 14 H
cynthia.childrey@nau.edu
CHILDREY, Lauren, T .... 336-272-7102 329 D
lauren.childrey@greensboro.edu
CHILDS, David, E .... 304-877-6428 487 F
david.childs@abc.edu
CHILDS, Gladys .... 817-531-4444 451 E
gchilds@txwes.edu
CHILDS, Jennifer, A ...... 240-500-2259 198 H
jachilds@hagerstowncc.edu
CHILDS, K. Paige .... 864-941-8688 411 H
childs.p@ptc.edu
CHILDS, Kimberly, M ... 936-468-2805 445 F
kchilds@sfasu.edu
CHILDS, Linda, J .... 304-877-6428 487 F
linda.childs@abc.edu
CHILDS, M. Dee .... 979-845-9999 446 G
mdeechilds@tamu.edu
CHILDS, Richard, G ...... 410-864-4274 201 F
rchilds@stmarys.edu
CHILDS, Shannon .... 541-880-2210 373 E
childs@klamathcc.edu
CHILDS, Sidney, R .... 989-964-2932 230 B
schilds@svsu.edu
CHILDS, Tammy .... 423-636-7300 427 B
tchilds@tusculum.edu
CHILES, Rebecca .... 503-838-8481 377 H
chilesr@wou.edu
CHILES, Thomas .... 617-552-0840 207 B
thomas.chiles@bc.edu
CHILICKI, Stacy .... 207-216-4312 195 C
schilicki@yccc.edu
CHILL, Jessica .... 330-941-1526 365 C
jchill@ysu.edu
CHILLO, Joseph, L .... 859-344-3348 184 F
chilloj@thomasmore.edu
CHILSON, Fred .... 208-792-2400 131 A
fmchilson@lcsc.edu
CHILTON, Bette .... 815-825-9308 140 F
bchilton@kish.edu
CHILTON, Elizabeth .... 607-777-2145 316 E
harpdean@binghamton.edu
CHILUKURI, Lakshmi .... 858-246-0428.. 69 D
lchilukuri@ucsd.edu
CHIMBLE, Aaron .... 716-375-2040 313 F
achimble@sbu.edu
CHIMENTI, Vito, R .... 215-670-9297 391 H
vrchimenti@peirce.edu
CHIMIENTI, Sonia .... 508-856-2300 212 A
sonia.chimienti@umassmed.edu
CHIN, Brady .... 310-577-3000.. 75 G
bchin@yosan.edu
CHIN, Christine .... 202-885-6365.. 90 J
cchin@american.edu
CHIN, Penny, J .... 516-876-3137 319 A
chinp@oldwestbury.edu
CHINA, Jennifer .... 813-259-6151 101 A
jchnia@hccfl.edu
CHINERY, Mary .... 732-987-2341 278 B
mchinery@georgian.edu
CHING, Denny .... 617-236-8811 209 D
dching@fisher.edu
CHING, Erik .... 864-294-3347 410 A
erik.ching@furman.edu
CHING, Sheri .... 808-689-2503 128 G
ching@hawaii.edu
CHINN, Clark, A .... 848-932-7496 282 A
clark.chinn@rutgers.edu
CHINN, Derek .... 503-255-0332 374 D
dchinn@multnomah.edu
CHINN, Jeffrey .... 619-961-4235.. 67 E
jchinn@tjsl.edu
CHINNI, Brian .... 201-684-7613 280 H
bchinni@ramapo.edu
CHINNOCK PETROSKI,
Mary, J .... 308-865-8655 269 I
petroskimj@unk.edu
CHIODO, Gary, T .... 206-543-5980 485 F
gchiod@uw.edu
CHIPMAN, Karin .... 412-365-2714 381 C
kchipman@chatham.edu
CHIPMAN, Nelson .... 412-392-4306 397 A
nchipman@pointpark.edu
CHIPMAN, Stephanie .... 217-245-3030 138 D
stephanie.chipman@ic.edu
CHIPMAN, Wayne .... 417-873-7258 252 F
wchipman@drury.edu
CHIQUITO, Yug Fon ..... 626-529-8246.. 55 A
ychiquito@pacificoaks.edu
CHIRICO, Donna .... 718-262-2804 295 F
dchirico@york.cuny.edu
CHISCHILLY, AnnMarie . 928-523-9651.. 14 H
ann-marie.chischilly@nau.edu
CHISEM, Lori .... 205-929-3409.... 2 H
lchisem@lawsonstate.edu
CHISHOLM, Brendan, H 508-856-4031 212 A
brendan.chisholm@umassmed.edu
CHISHOLM,
Douglas, W .... 937-766-7992 349 G
chisd@cedarville.edu
CHISHOLM, Rex .... 312-503-3209 145 F
r-chisholm@northwestern.edu
CHISHOLM, Ryan .... 804-862-6100 470 I
rchisholm@rbc.edu
CHISM, Jenny .... 314-889-1413 253 C
jchism@fontbonne.edu
CHISMAR, William, G ... 808-956-8866 128 F
chismar@hawaii.edu
CHISOLM, Theresa, H ... 813-974-2281 110 B
chisolm@usf.edu
CHISOM, Brian, T .... 540-375-2592 471 B
chisom@roanoke.edu
CHITRE, Manoj .... 909-607-9828.. 37 D
manoj.chitre@cgu.edu
CHITWOOD, Charles ..... 405-491-6455 370 A
cchitwood@snu.edu
CHITWOOD, Vickie .... 336-342-4261 337 E
chitwoodv@rockinghamcc.edu
CHIU, Agnes .... 626-917-9482.. 36 H
agnesc@cesna.edu
CHIU, Edward .... 781-239-5199 205 E
echiu4@babson.edu
CHIU, Monica, E .... 603-862-2880 274 G
monica.chiu@unh.edu
CHIUDIONI, Kathy .... 317-813-2320 157 E
kchiudioni@ibcindianapolis.edu
CHIVUKULA, Anu .... 214-333-6942 434 I
anu@dbu.edu
CHIVUKULA, Sekhar ..... 517-353-5380 227 D
sekhar@msu.edu
CHLEBOWSKI, Angela ... 203-857-7154.. 86 D
achlebowski@norwalk.edu
CHMIEL, Senta .... 304-367-4884 490 B
senta.chmiel@fairmontstate.edu
CHMIELESKI, Guy .... 316-295-5844 173 D
guy_chmieleski@friends.edu
CHMIELESKI, Guy .... 316-295-5488 173 D
guy_chmieleski@friends.edu
CHMIELEWSKI, Jerry ..... 724-738-2170 395 F
jerry.chmielewski@sru.edu
CHMURA, Michael .... 781-239-4549 205 E
mchmura@babson.edu
CHO, Andrew .... 213-252-5100.. 23 K
acho@alu.edu
CHO, Esther .... 714-683-1210.. 27 A
vp.esthercho@buc.edu
CHO, Hyun Sung .... 770-220-7910 118 B
revdrcho@gmail.com
CHO, Hyun Sung .... 770-220-7926 118 B
revdrcho@gmail.com
CHO, Hyun Sung .... 770-220-7910 118 B
revdrcho@gmail.com
CHO, James .... 703-206-0508 466 D
CHO, Karen .... 808-235-7404 129 F
kcho@hawaii.edu
CHO, Peter .... 504-762-3188 187 E
plcho@dcc.edu
CHO,
Seung Je Jeremiah .... 714-517-1945.. 27 A
CHO, Sung .... 323-643-0301.. 25 L
shcho3152@gmail.com
CHOATE, Jim .... 319-398-7612 167 C
jchoate@kirkwood.edu
CHOATE, Michael, J ...... 972-883-2943 455 B
mchoate@utdallas.edu
CHOCK, Kasey "Keala" .. 808-845-9229 129 B
kaseyc@hawaii.edu
CHODOSH, Hiram, E ..... 909-621-8111.. 37 E
hiram.chodosh@cmc.edu
CHODZKO-ZAJKO,
Wojciech .... 217-333-6715 151 D
wojtek@illinois.edu
CHOE, Tina .... 310-338-2833.. 50 J
tina.choe@lmu.edu
CHOI, Andreas .... 213-487-0110.. 41 I
CHOI, Augustine M.K .... 212-746-6005 297 F
dean@med.cornell.edu
CHOI, Eugene .... 312-341-3620 147 H
echoi01@roosevelt.edu
CHOI, Henry .... 714-533-1495.. 64 D
hchoi@southbaylo.edu
CHOI, Jayoung .... 718-262-2297 295 F
jchoi@york.cuny.edu
CHOI, Karen .... 562-926-1023.. 57 G
karenchoi@ptsa.edu
CHOI, Kyunam .... 714-525-0088.. 44 E
ceo@gm.edu
CHOI, Mun, Y .... 573-882-2011 261 A
president@umsystem.edu
CHOI, Paul .... 510-592-9688.. 54 C
paul.choi@npu.edu
CHOI, Sungyi .... 909-623-0302.. 59 A
CHOICE, Jannie .... 864-294-3609 410 A
jannie.choice@furman.edu
CHOJNACKI, David .... 561-868-3465 104 D
chojnacd@palmbeachstate.edu
CHOJNICKI, Linda, M ... 413-782-1315 219 F
linda.chojnicki@wne.edu
CHOKSI, Amit .... 312-949-7505 138 E
achoksi@ico.edu
CHOLETTE, Beth, K .... 585-245-5716 318 E
cholette@geneseo.edu
CHOLOKIS, Kate .... 413-369-4044 208 D
cholokis@csld.edu
CHONCEK,
Christopher, E .... 412-392-3421 397 A
cchoncek@pointpark.edu
CHONG, Bruce .... 386-822-7452 111 A
bchong@stetson.edu
CHONG, Dawn .... 419-372-2723 348 H
dchong@bgsu.edu
CHONG, Frank .... 707-527-4431.. 62 F
fchong@santarosa.edu
CHOO, Brooke .... 949-451-5390.. 64 F
bchoo@ivc.edu
CHOO, Jeff .... 617-327-6777 220 B
jeff_choo@williamjames.edu
CHOONG, Yen Wei .... 510-763-7787.. 24 C
ywchoong@acchs.edu
CHOONOO, John .... 646-312-2196 292 L
john.choonoo@baruch.cuny.edu
CHOPIN, Connie .... 337-521-9027 188 C
connie.chopin@solacc.edu
CHOPIN, Marc .... 208-885-6071 131 G
mchopin@uidaho.edu
CHOPKA, John, A .... 800-233-4220 390 E
jchopka@messiah.edu
CHORAM, Iotaka .... 671-734-1812 505 D
ichoram@piu.edu
CHORNIY, Nataliya .... 770-216-2960 120 H
nchorniy@ict.edu
CHOROSZY, Melisa, N .. 775-784-6181 271 F
choroszy@admin.unr.edu
CHOTTINER, Gregg, M .. 973-596-2937 279 F
gregg.m.chottiner@njit.edu
CHOU, Emily .... 212-812-4040 309 D
echou@nycda.edu
CHOU, Kassi .... 864-379-6516 409 H
chou@erskine.edu
CHOU, Lexer .... 808-455-0248 129 D
achou@hawaii.edu
CHOUDHARY, Mujahid . 708-534-5000 137 F
mchoudhary@govst.edu
CHOUDHRY, Wajid .... 413-545-7090 211 D
wajid.choudhry@umass.edu
CHOUDHURY, Vivek ..... 303-871-6858.. 83 D
vivek.choudhury@du.edu
CHOW, Rebekah .... 718-429-6600 324 D
rebekah.chow@vaughn.edu
CHOW, Soong Min .... 269-387-5879 232 K
soongmin.chow@wmich.edu
CHOW, Timothy .... 812-877-8910 159 J
chow@rose-hulman.edu
CHOWDHURY, Faruque 908-737-5061 278 E
fchowdhu@kean.edu
CHOWN, Deborah .... 413-775-1832 214 C
chown@gcc.mass.edu
CHOWN, Mary .... 610-796-8379 378 F
mary.chown@alvernia.edu
CHOWN, Paul .... 707-476-4164.. 39 D
paul-chown@redwoods.edu
CHOWNING, John .... 270-789-5520 179 E
jechowning@campbellsville.edu
CHOY, Sam .... 312-329-2016 144 B
sam.choy@moody.edu
CHREIST, Ryan .... 303-402-1660.. 83 A
ryan.chreist@colorado.edu
CHRENKO, Sarah, A ..... 517-264-7179 230 E
schrenko@sienaheights.edu
CHRESFIELD, Rae .... 509-527-5195 486 H
chresfr@whitman.edu
CHRESTMAN, Angie ...... 662-325-3344 247 F
achrestman@career.msstate.edu
CHRISLER, Jennifer .... 508-999-8801 211 F
jchrisler@umassd.edu
CHRISLER, Jennifer .... 413-559-5590 210 A
CHRISMAN, Dana .... 319-208-5017 169 F
dchrisman@scciowa.edu
CHRISMAN, Tammy, A . 757-446-8447 466 I
chrismta@evms.edu
CHRISPENS, Pamela ..... 951-785-2002.. 47 C
pchrispe@lasierra.edu
CHRISSOTIMOS, Anna ... 917-493-4463 305 I
achrissotimos@msmnyc.edu
CHRIST, Andrew, P .... 973-596-5774 279 F
andrew.p.christ@njit.edu
CHRIST, Brad .... 509-359-2099 480 E
brad.christ@ewu.edu
CHRIST, Carol .... 510-642-7464.. 68 D
chancellor@berkeley.edu
CHRIST, Suzanne .... 618-545-3069 140 E
schrist@kaskaskia.edu
CHRISTAKIS,
Michael, N .... 518-956-8140 316 D
mchristakis@albany.edu
CHRISTALDI, Antoinette 610-526-1357 378 G
antoinette.christaldi@
theamericancollege.edu
CHRISTEL, Mark .... 641-269-3352 165 J
christelm@grinnell.edu
CHRISTEN, Amy .... 414-382-6040 492 A
amy.christen@alverno.edu
CHRISTEN, Michael, T .. 308-865-8448 269 I
christenmt2@unk.edu
CHRISTENSEN, Angela .. 612-659-6229 238 I
angela.christensen@minneapolis.edu
CHRISTENSEN, Bert .... 510-231-5000.. 46 J
bert.c.christensen@kp.org
CHRISTENSEN, Cody ...... 208-376-7731 129 H
cchristensen@boisebible.edu
CHRISTENSEN, Dan .... 503-316-3382 373 A
dchristensen@corban.edu
CHRISTENSEN, Edward . 732-263-5500 279 B
echriste@monmouth.edu
CHRISTENSEN, Eric .... 505-922-6547 288 F
eric.christensen@bie.edu
CHRISTENSEN, Erik .... 773-256-0696 142 G
erik.christensen@lstc.edu
CHRISTENSEN, Erik .... 863-784-7424 107 F
erik.christensen@southflorida.edu
CHRISTENSEN, Eva .... 727-341-3166 106 E
christensen.eva@spcollege.edu
CHRISTENSEN,
Jeffrey, T .... 217-333-1216 151 D
jchriste@illinois.edu
CHRISTENSEN, Jolene ... 563-588-6436 163 F
jolene.christensen@clarke.edu

CIHLAR, Margaret .... 317-955-6080 158 U
0777mgr@follett.com
CILLAY, David .... 509-335-5454 486 A
dcillay@wsu.edu
CIMA, Dennis .... 650-949-6149.. 43 C
cimadennis@fhda.edu
CIMA, Dennis .... 650-949-6231.. 43 B
cimadennis@fhda.edu
CIMALORE, Ann .... 205-853-1200.... 2 G
acimalore@jeffersonstate.edu
CIMAROSSA, Valerie ..... 602-383-8228.. 16 F
vcimarossa@uat.edu
CIMILLUCA, Maria .... 617-373-2009 217 F
CIMINELLI, Thomas, E .. 716-888-2250 292 D
ciminel1@canisius.edu
CIMINO, Chris .... 865-974-9880 427 G
cimino@utk.edu
CIMITILE, Maria, C .... 616-331-2400 224 E
provost@gvsu.edu
CIMITILE, Matthew .... 727-873-4840 110 C
mcimitile@mail.usf.edu
CIMORELLI, Nick .... 843-863-7581 407 E
ncimorel@csuniv.edu
CIMPL-WIEMER, Jamie . 414-229-5923 497 A
cimplwie@uwm.edu
CINGEL, Pamela .... 305-474-6866 106 F
pcingel@stu.edu
CINGRANELLI, Jeremy .. 315-866-0300 301 G
cingranjs@herkimer.edu
CINSON, Michael .... 330-490-4969 364 B
mcinson@walsh.edu
CINTORINO, Salvatore .. 860-832-1889.. 84 I
cintorino@ccsu.edu
CINTRÓN, Myriam .... 787-850-9302 513 E
myriam.cintron1@upr.edu
CINTRON, Amarilis .... 787-894-2828 514 C
amarilis.cintronlopez@upr.edu
CINTRON, Arnaldo .... 787-864-2222 509 C
arnaldo.cintron@guayama.inter.edu
CINTRON, José, R .... 787-766-1717 511 H
jrcintron@suagm.edu
CINTRON, Rene .... 225-922-2373 186 J
renecintron@lctcs.edu
CINTRON-SERRANO,
Filomena .... 787-857-3600 508 M
fcintron@br.inter.edu
CINTRON-VEGA,
Edgardo .... 787-857-3600 508 M
ecintron@br.inter.edu
CIOCCO, Ronalee .... 724-503-1001 402 E
rciocco@washjeff.edu
CIOCE, Michael, A .... 856-222-9311 281 C
president@rcbc.edu
CIOFFI, Laura .... 212-752-1530 304 D
laura.cioffi@limcollege.edu
CIOLFI, Michael, A .... 203-576-4278.. 88 D
mciolfi@bridgeport.edu
CIONE, Brett .... 212-472-1500 309 I
bcione@nysid.edu
CIORRA, Anthony .... 203-371-7912.. 88 B
ciorraa@sacredheart.edu
CIOTOLI, Carlo .... 212-443-1297 310 B
carlo.ciotoli@nyu.edu
CIPOLLA, Anthony .... 845-848-7814 298 D
anthony.cipolla@dc.edu
CIPOLLA, Michael .... 708-974-5208 144 C
cipollam2@morainevalley.edu
CIPOLLA, Robert, D ...... 401-825-2221 404 H
rcipolla@ccri.edu
CIPRES, Elizabeth .... 949-451-5410.. 64 F
ecipres@ivc.edu
CIPRIANI, Colleen .... 614-234-5828 356 I
ccipriani@mccn.edu
CIPRIANO, Matt, J .... 215-968-8255 379 G
cipriano@bucks.edu
CIPRIANO, Michael .... 978-934-2654 211 G
michael_cipriano@uml.edu
CIPRIANO, JR.,
Thomas .... 215-635-7300 385 A
tcipriano@gratz.edu
CIRCE, Shana .... 845-257-3231 317 B
circes@newpaltz.edu
CIRCELLI, William, A .... 518-564-5022 319 C
circelwa@plattsburgh.edu
CIRCLE, Kelly .... 303-914-6213.. 82 C
kelly.circle@rrcc.edu
CIRELLI, Joyce .... 724-480-3474 381 K
joyce.cirelli@ccbc.edu
CIRELLI, Rachel .... 718-862-7308 305 H
rcirelli01@manhattan.edu
CIRI, Michael .... 907-796-6534.. 10 B
maciri@alaska.edu
CIRI, Michael .... 907-796-6100.. 10 B
CIRI, Michael .... 907-796-6452.. 10 B
maciri@alaska.edu
CIRILLO, Laureen .... 413-565-1006 205 G
lcirillo@baypath.edu
CIRILLO, Robert .... 914-606-6981 325 C
robert.cirillo@sunywcc.edu
CIRIONI, Frank .... 714-895-8700.. 38 D
fcirioni@gwc.cccd.edu
CIRRINCIONE,
AnnaMaria .... 607-753-2336 318 D
annamaria.cirrincione@cortland.edu
CISCO, OSB, Bede .... 812-357-6696 160 D
bcisco@saintmeinrad.edu
CISEWSKI, Greg .... 715-675-3331 500 E
cisewski@ntc.edu
CISLER, Valerie .... 715-346-4920 497 F
vcisler@uwsp.edu
CISNA, Shawn .... 309-796-5000 132 G
cisnas@bhc.edu
CISNEROS, Maria .... 504-671-5603 187 E
mcisne@dcc.edu
CISNEROS, Steven .... 912-443-4155 124 A
scisneros@savannahtech.edu
CISSELL, Jason, A .... 502-272-8329 179 B
jcissell@bellarmine.edu
CITRON, Chaim .... 323-937-3763.. 75 F
ccitron@yoec.edu
CITTI, Lori, A .... 410-516-6760 199 D
lcitti1@jhu.edu
CITZLER, Annette .... 830-372-8002 449 B
acitzler@tlu.edu
CIUFFO, Patricia .... 646-565-6000 322 J
patricia.ciuffo@touro.edu
CIULLO, Carol .... 304-724-5000 487 H
cciullo@cdu.edu
CIVIELLO, Joshua .... 506-206-3210 377 F
jciviello@uws.edu
CLACK, Olivia .... 870-574-4481.. 21 E
oclack@sautech.edu
CLAERBOUT, Libby .... 701-858-4155 345 F
libby.claerbout@minotstateu.edu
CLAERHOUT, Cathryn .... 231-995-1034 228 G
cclaerhout@nmc.edu
CLAEYS, Aimee, K .... 515-281-6456 162 H
aimee.claeys@iowaregents.edu
CLAFFEY, George .... 860-832-3000.. 84 I
george@ccsu.edu
CLAFFEY, Joseph .... 609-586-4800 278 F
claffeyj@mccc.edu
CLAGETT, Craig, A .... 410-386-8163 197 G
cclagett@carrollcc.edu
CLAGHORN, Patricia .... 856-415-5504 281 D
pclaghorn@rcgc.edu
CLAIBORNE, Evelyn ...... 816-604-4824 255 I
evelyn.clairborne@mcckc.edu
CLAIRE, Michael .... 650-574-6222.. 61 P
clairem@smccd.edu
CLAIRE, MIchael .... 650-574-6550.. 61 N
CLANCY, Amanda .... 303-678-3736.. 79 J
amanda.clancy@frontrange.edu
CLANCY, Gerard .... 918-631-3244 371 E
gerard-clancy@utulsa.edu
CLANCY, Patricia .... 718-390-3422 324 F
patricia.clancy@wagner.edu
CLANTON, Andre .... 770-426-2708 121 C
andre.clanton@life.edu
CLANTON, Ann .... 251-405-7055.... 1 E
aclanton@bishop.edu
CLANTON, Daniel .... 828-327-7000 333 B
dclanton@cvcc.edu
CLANTON, Janet .... 573-897-5000 260 E
CLANTON, Karen .... 256-824-6013.... 8 B
karen.clanton@uah.edu
CLAPHAM LAVIN,
Theresa .... 303-352-6625.. 79 E
theresa.clapham@ccd.edu
CLAPP, John .... 213-740-2311.. 72 B
CLAPP, Kenneth, W ...... 704-637-4446 328 A
kclapp@catawba.edu
CLAPP, Marlene .... 508-830-5069 213 B
mclapp@maritime.edu
CLAPP, Shay .... 918-540-6188 366 I
shay.clapp@neo.edu
CLAPPER, Mark, A .... 717-361-1499 383 E
clapperm@etown.edu
CLARDY, Betsy, B .... 409-772-8789 456 F
bbclardy@utmb.edu
CLARDY, JR., Mike .... 334-844-9996.... 4 E
clardch@auburn.edu
CLARENSAU, Michael ... 972-825-4827 445 A
mclarensau@sagu.edu
CLARK, Adon .... 478-374-6407 121 F
adon.clark@mga.edu
CLARK, Adrian, R .... 816-654-7095 254 C
arclark@kcumb.edu
CLARK, Amanda .... 509-777-4482 486 I
amandaclark@whitworth.edu
CLARK, Amy .... 859-572-6145 184 A
clarka17@nku.edu
CLARK, Amy .... 313-845-9615 224 G
CLARK, Amy .... 402-354-7258 268 C
amy.clark@methodistcollege.edu
CLARK, Amy .... 503-838-8187 377 H
clarkaj@wou.edu
CLARK, Ann, B .... 860-727-6761.. 87 A
aclark@goodwin.edu
CLARK, Annette, C .... 206-398-4000 484 F
annclark@seattleu.edu
CLARK, Benita, I .... 919-866-7894 338 G
biclark@waketech.edu
CLARK, III, Beverly .... 402-562-1267 266 A
beverlyclark@cccneb.edu
CLARK, Bill .... 626-584-5588.. 43 H
billclark@fuller.edu
CLARK, Bob .... 310-506-4798.. 56 C
bob.clark@pepperdine.edu
CLARK, Brian, J .... 207-859-4612 193 E
bjclark@colby.edu
CLARK, Brock .... 228-497-7634 247 E
brock.clark@mgccc.edu
CLARK, Bryon .... 580-745-2064 369 K
bclark@se.edu
CLARK, Caitlin .... 330-823-6050 363 B
clarkce@mountunion.edu
CLARK, Carlos .... 501-420-1204.. 17 B
carlos.clark@arkansasbaptist.edu
CLARK, Carol, D .... 931-221-7570 418 D
clarkc@apsu.edu
CLARK, Catherine .... 434-791-5764 464 O
coclark@averett.edu
CLARK, Chad .... 937-529-2201 362 A
cclark@united.edu
CLARK, Charade .... 757-340-2121 465 M
CLARK, Charles .... 919-546-8320 340 E
charles.clark@shawu.edu
CLARK, Cheryl .... 318-487-7601 186 I
cheryl.clark@lacollege.edu
CLARK, Chris .... 618-634-3233 149 A
chrisc@shawneecc.edu
CLARK, Christina .... 703-284-1560 469 C
christina.clark@marymount.edu
CLARK, Christopher ...... 334-833-4498.... 5 H
cclark@hawks.huntingdon.edu
CLARK, Connie .... 912-443-5485 124 A
cclark@savannahtech.edu
CLARK, Curtis .... 860-701-7708.. 87 D
clark_c@mitchell.edu
CLARK, Dallas, B .... 540-464-7321 476 G
clarkdb@vmi.edu
CLARK, Daniel .... 419-448-3349 361 J
clarkds@tiffin.edu
CLARK, Daniel .... 630-752-5593 152 F
daniel.clark@wheaton.edu
CLARK, Daniel .... 616-234-4354 224 D
dbclark@grcc.edu
CLARK, Darrell, L .... 727-816-3427 104 F
clarkda@phsc.edu
CLARK, David .... 559-638-0300.. 66 F
david.clark@reedleycollege.edu
CLARK, Dean .... 620-229-6364 177 A
dean.clark@sckans.edu
CLARK, Debbie .... 502-863-8149 180 E
debbie_clark@georgetowncollege.edu
CLARK, Debra .... 865-694-6602 425 F
dclark@pstcc.edu
CLARK, Denise .... 301-405-4282 202 C
djclark@umd.edu
CLARK, Deron .... 575-392-2741 286 J
dclark@nmjc.edu
CLARK, Dewey .... 252-985-5140 339 D
dclark@ncwc.edu
CLARK, Donna .... 254-442-5001 433 A
donna.clark@cisco.edu
CLARK, Douglas, R .... 951-785-2244.. 47 C
dclark@lasierra.edu
CLARK, Douglas, S .... 510-642-4192.. 68 D
cocdean@berkeley.edu
CLARK, Duwon .... 615-329-8588 419 K
dclark@fisk.edu
CLARK, Edmund, U .... 651-962-6266 244 E
clar7281@stthomas.edu
CLARK, Ehrin .... 570-945-8119 386 I
ehrin.clark@keystone.edu
CLARK, Elaine .... 801-581-7968 460 E
el.clark@utah.edu
CLARK, Elizabeth .... 660-785-7200 260 J
eclark@truman.edu
CLARK, Erica .... 620-343-4600 173 A
CLARK, Ferlin .... 918-781-6284 365 F
clarkf@bacone.edu
CLARK, Frederick .... 508-531-1201 212 B
fred.clark@bridgew.edu
CLARK, Gary, A .... 785-532-5590 174 G
gac@ksu.edu
CLARK, Gary, A .... 310-825-5108.. 69 A
gclark@admission.ucla.edu
CLARK, Gary, C .... 405-744-6384 368 B
gary.clark@okstate.edu
CLARK, Gaye .... 910-410-1804 337 B
agclark@richmondcc.edu
CLARK, Ginger .... 813-253-7755 101 A
gclark@hccfl.edu
CLARK, Holly .... 530-226-4941.. 63 K
hclark@simpsonu.edu
CLARK, Jacqueline .... 256-549-8695.... 2 B
jclark@gadsdenstate.edu
CLARK, Jacqueline .... 718-270-6994 295 A
jaclark@mec.cuny.edu
CLARK, Jaime .... 618-453-5371 149 E
jaimec@siu.edu
CLARK, Jake .... 406-791-5230 265 H
jacob.clark@uprovidence.edu
CLARK, James .... 818-690-8441 250 I
james.clark@calvary.edu
CLARK, James, A .... 334-844-4765.... 4 E
clarkj3@auburn.edu
CLARK, James, E .... 803-536-7013 412 C
jclark@scsu.edu
CLARK, James, J .... 850-644-4752 109 C
jclark5@fsu.edu
CLARK, Janet .... 812-535-5182 160 B
jclark@smwc.edu
CLARK, Jeanian .... 540-868-7122 474 J
jclark@lfcc.edu
CLARK, Jeff, D .... 860-253-3163.. 85 C
kclark@asnuntuck.edu
CLARK, Jennifer .... 724-589-2858 399 H
jclark@thiel.edu
CLARK, Jennifer, M ...... 210-567-6536 456 C
clarkjm@uthscsa.edu
CLARK, Jennifer, R .... 773-508-7450 142 D
jclark7@luc.edu
CLARK, Jesse .... 970-351-1785.. 83 E
jesse.clark@unco.edu
CLARK, Jill .... 712-325-3285 167 B
jclark@iwcc.edu
CLARK, Jimmy .... 479-979-1484.. 23 I
jclark@ozarks.edu
CLARK, Joan .... 304-357-4750 488 G
joanclark@ucwv.edu
CLARK, John, B .... 203-837-8300.. 85 B
clarkj@wcsu.edu
CLARK, John, S .... 865-694-6601 425 F
jclark@pstcc.edu
CLARK, Joy .... 334-244-3539.... 4 F
jclark@aum.edu
CLARK, Joye .... 313-577-2161 232 I
joye.clark@wayne.edu
CLARK, Kacey .... 617-603-6928 216 H
kacey.clark@necb.edu
CLARK, Karen, J .... 937-529-2201 362 A
kclark@united.edu
CLARK, Karen .... 765-973-8242 156 C
krclark@iue.edu
CLARK, Karen .... 254-299-8689 440 A
kclark@mclennan.edu
CLARK, Karen, M .... 708-344-4700 142 A
kclark@lincolntech.edu
CLARK, Karisa, A .... 304-877-6428 487 F
publicrelations@abc.edu
CLARK, Kathleen .... 305-809-3188.. 99 C
kathleen.clark@fkcc.edu
CLARK, Kathy .... 630-844-5443 132 D
kclark@aurora.edu
CLARK, Kelly .... 918-595-7000 370 E
kelly.clark@tulsacc.edu
CLARK, Kevin, G .... 215-204-2452 399 F
keviclar@temple.edu
CLARK, Kimberlee .... 425-352-8204 479 A
kclark@cascadia.edu
CLARK, Kimberley .... 215-248-6301 400 I
kclark@uls.edu
CLARK, Kirstie .... 704-355-8894 327 H
kirstie.clark@carolinascollege.edu
CLARK, Kristin .... 559-925-3217.. 74 B
kristinclark@whccd.edu
CLARK, Kyle .... 850-644-4242 109 C
kyle@fsu.edu

CLARK, Kym ... 432-264-5144 438 C kclark@howardcollege.edu
CLARK, L. Nathan, N ... 775-241-4445 270 G nclark@ccnn4u.com
CLARK, Lanette ... 406-758-6328 263 G lclark@fpcc.edu
CLARK, Larry ... 253-589-5602 479 G larry.clark@cptc.edu
CLARK, Laura ... 870-777-5722.. 22 A laura.clark@uaht.edu
CLARK, Laura, K ... 229-391-4993 113 F laura.clark@abac.edu
CLARK, Laurie ... 979-830-4336 432 C laurie.clark@blinn.edu
CLARK, Lawrence, S ... 318-797-5234 189 D larry.clark@lsus.edu
CLARK, Leanna ... 303-315-7734.. 83 C leanna.clark@ucdenver.edu
CLARK, Lena ... 801-818-8900 459 K lena.clark@provocollege.edu
CLARK, Lesa, C ... 757-683-4406 469 G lclark@odu.edu
CLARK, Letitia ... 949-582-4920.. 64 E
CLARK, Letitia ... 714-438-4606.. 38 B lclark35@cccd.edu
CLARK, Linda ... 662-332-8750 247 D liclark@msdelta.edu
CLARK, Linda, J ... 360-442-2100 482 B lclark@lowercolumbia.edu
CLARK, Lisa ... 910-788-6320 338 A lisa.clark@sccnc.edu
CLARK, Mandi ... 541-885-1087 375 C mandi.clark@oit.edu
CLARK, Marcy, R ... 413-545-3359 211 D mroeclark@umass.edu
CLARK, Margie ... 517-483-1461 226 F clarkm@lcc.edu
CLARK, Maria ... 614-222-6175 351 D mclark@ccad.edu
CLARK, Mark ... 515-964-6213 164 C maclark@dmacc.edu
CLARK, Marla ... 269-927-8762 226 D mclark@lakemichigancollege.edu
CLARK, Marta ... 718-289-5113 293 B marta.clark@bcc.cuny.edu
CLARK, Martha ... 760-872-2000.. 41 C mclark@deepsprings.edu
CLARK, Mary ... 202-885-2155.. 90 J mlclark@american.edu
CLARK, Mary ... 501-977-2011.. 23 A clark@uaccm.edu
CLARK, Mary ... 863-297-1009 105 A mclark@polk.edu
CLARK, Matthew ... 612-626-4734 243 E mclark@umn.edu
CLARK, Matthew ... 417-268-1059 250 E clarkm@evangel.edu
CLARK, OSB, Matthew .. 985-867-2245 190 F mrclark@sjasc.edu
CLARK, Melinda ... 813-226-4858 106 D melinda.clark@saintleo.edu
CLARK, Michael ... 570-321-4249 389 E clark@lycoming.edu
CLARK, Michelle ... 954-262-1384 103 M miclark@nova.edu
CLARK, Michelle ... 817-257-5262 448 G m.clark@tcu.edu
CLARK, Nelson ... 256-782-5884.... 5 J nclark@jsu.edu
CLARK, Nora ... 301-846-2565 198 E nclark@frederick.edu
CLARK, Pam ... 989-686-9225 223 G pamelaclark@delta.edu
CLARK, Patricia ... 910-272-3505 337 D pclark@robeson.edu
CLARK, Patrick, E ... 513-556-2628 362 D patrick.clark@uc.edu
CLARK, Richard ... 702-895-1469 271 E richard.clark@unlv.edu
CLARK, Richard ... 404-894-4154 118 F rick.clark@admission.gatech.edu
CLARK, Richard ... 865-573-4517 420 G rclark@johnsonu.edu
CLARK, Rob ... 585-275-5931 323 J rclark@rochester.edu
CLARK, Robert ... 404-880-6623 116 D rclark@cau.edu
CLARK, Robert, A ... 207-941-7138 194 A clarkr@husson.edu
CLARK, Robert, E ... 757-683-3018 469 G reclark@odu.edu
CLARK, II, Robert, E ... 302-736-2508.. 90 G robert.clark@wesley.edu
CLARK, Rodney ... 508-678-2811 213 G rodney.clark@bristolcc.edu
CLARK, Rodney, E ... 316-978-5520 178 A
CLARK, Ron, M ... 972-238-6277 435 F rclark@dcccd.edu
CLARK, Ryan ... 971-722-7724 375 J ryan.clark13@pcc.edu
CLARK, Sandra ... 410-857-2217 200 B sgclark@mcdaniel.edu
CLARK, Sara ... 419-530-4039 363 E sara.clark2@utoledo.edu
CLARK, Sarah ... 215-951-1732 387 C clarks@lasalle.edu
CLARK, Sarah ... 406-657-1007 265 E sarah.clark@rocky.edu
CLARK, Sarah, E ... 863-667-5463 107 K seclark@seu.edu
CLARK, Scott, D ... 716-888-8357 292 D clarks@canisius.edu
CLARK, Sharon ... 607-844-8222 322 H dovis@tompkinscortland.edu
CLARK, Sharon, L ... 813-988-5131.. 98 Q clarks@floridacollege.edu
CLARK, Sherri ... 606-248-2224 182 E sherril.clark@kctcs.edu
CLARK, Stephanie ... 850-474-2492 110 E sclark2@uwf.edu
CLARK, Steve ... 541-737-4875 375 D steve.clark@oregonstate.edu
CLARK, Steven, C ... 801-863-8082 461 A steven.clark@uvu.edu
CLARK, Susan ... 517-629-0798 220 G sclark@albion.edu
CLARK, Tammie, L ... 252-451-8372 336 E tlckark215@nashcc.edu
CLARK, Tammy, L ... 813-258-7522 112 J tclark@ut.edu
CLARK, Terri ... 601-554-5515 248 E tclark@prcc.edu
CLARK, Terry ... 618-453-7967 149 E tclark@business.siu.edu
CLARK, Tim ... 801-302-2800 459 H tim.clark@neumont.edu
CLARK, Timothy ... 432-335-6848 441 D tclark@odessa.edu
CLARK, Todd ... 870-972-2947.. 17 G tclark@astate.edu
CLARK, Todd ... 909-469-5473.. 74 I tclark@westernu.edu
CLARK, Traci ... 318-345-9185 187 G traciclark@ladelta.edu
CLARK, Tracie ... 704-330-6022 333 D tracie.clark@cpcc.edu
CLARK, Treka ... 870-236-6901.. 19 A
CLARK, Tricia ... 316-394-5227 171 F tclark@bethelks.edu
CLARK, Tyler ... 502-897-4203 184 C tclark@sbts.edu
CLARK, V. Allen, A ... 940-565-2628 454 A allen.clark@unt.edu
CLARK, Victoria ... 425-822-8266 482 F victoria.clark@northwestu.edu
CLARK, Walter ... 715-346-2320 497 F walter.clark@uwsp.edu
CLARK, Wayne, N ... 208-496-2510 130 A clarkw@byui.edu
CLARK, Wesley ... 512-863-1227 445 D clarkw@southwestern.edu
CLARK, William ... 856-351-2602 283 A clark@salemcc.edu
CLARK, William (Bill) ... 740-376-4601 356 A wbc001@marietta.edu
CLARK, Yvette ... 603-645-9623 274 D y.clark@snhu.edu
CLARK, Yvette ... 931-372-3004 426 E yrclark@tntech.edu
CLARK-EICH, Catherine, M ... 740-245-7205 363 D cmclark@rio.edu
CLARK-EVANS, Barbara . 913-288-7504 174 F bclark@kckcc.edu
CLARK-GOFF, Kylah ... 325-649-8148 438 D kclarkgoff@hputx.edu
CLARK-SHAW, Kimberly 410-651-7660 203 A kclarkshaw@umes.edu
CLARK-TALLEY, Christine ... 703-993-8757 467 L cclarkta@gmu.edu
CLARK-WHITE, Patricia . 949-585-2987.. 27 D pwhite@brandman.edu
CLARKBERG, Marin, E .. 607-255-9101 297 F mec30@cornell.edu
CLARKE, Anthony ... 910-788-6270 338 A anthony.clarke@sccnc.edu
CLARKE, Anthony ... 336-334-4822 335 A
CLARKE, Arlene, V ... 404-527-5264 120 K avclarke@itc.edu
CLARKE, Calaundra ... 225-771-2552 191 A cclarke@sulc.edu
CLARKE, Cara ... 606-759-7141 182 A cara.clarke@kctcs.edu
CLARKE, Christopher ... 212-431-2871 309 G christopher.clarke@nyls.edu
CLARKE, Courtney ... 216-987-5504 351 G courtney.clarke@tri-c.edu
CLARKE, Cyril, R ... 540-231-6122 477 A provost@vt.edu
CLARKE, Edmond ... 570-577-3215 379 F ed.clarke@bucknell.edu
CLARKE, Ivan ... 310-233-4436.. 49 A clarkein@lahc.edu
CLARKE, Jaime ... 503-594-3220 372 D jaimec@clackamas.edu
CLARKE, Karen ... 808-853-1040 128 C karenclarke@pacrim.edu
CLARKE, Karen ... 330-672-8533 354 J kclarke8@kent.edu
CLARKE, Kathy ... 916-348-4689.. 42 C kclarke@epic.edu
CLARKE, Kenneth, I ... 607-255-6002 297 F kic2@cornell.edu
CLARKE, Kristen ... 815-226-2840 147 G kclarke@rockford.edu
CLARKE, Lisa ... 202-651-5075.. 91 E lisa.clarke@gallaudet.edu
CLARKE, Malanie ... 212-621-4101 294 D maclarke@jjay.cuny.edu
CLARKE, Mark ... 713-743-9854 452 F mclarke@uh.edu
CLARKE, Megan ... 906-248-8435 221 N mclarke@bmcc.edu
CLARKE, Patrick ... 435-586-5479 460 F clarke@suu.edu
CLARKE, Rachel, M ... 218-299-4816 235 E rclarke@cord.edu
CLARKE, Rachelle ... 480-517-8544.. 13 G rachelle.clark@riosalado.edu
CLARKE, Shari ... 509-359-4705 480 E sclarke5@ewu.edu
CLARKE, Ursala ... 754-312-2898 102 Q uclarke@keycollege.edu
CLARKE-ANDERSON, Shannon ... 718-270-5143 295 A shannon@mec.cuny.edu
CLARKE EBERT, Helen .. 507-222-4183 234 F hebert@carleton.edu
CLARKE-GLOVER, Jazzmine ... 718-390-3280 324 F j.clarke-glover@wagner.edu
CLARKSON, Kris ... 208-282-2794 130 H clarkri3@isu.edu
CLARKSON, Sallie ... 843-349-2448 408 C sallie@coastal.edu
CLARKSTON, Deborah ... 276-739-2440 476 C dclarkston@vhcc.edu
CLARO, Aida ... 305-899-3674.. 95 C aclaro@barry.edu
CLARY, Bruce ... 620-242-0506 175 F claryb@mcpherson.edu
CLARY, Dean ... 309-649-6316 150 A dean.clary@src.edu
CLARY, Gail ... 229-931-2318 124 D gclary@southgatech.edu
CLARY, Henry ... 276-326-4471 465 B hclary@bluefield.edu
CLARY, Joshua, R ... 270-686-4332 179 D josh.clary@brescia.edu
CLARY, Stephanie ... 270-686-9550 179 D stephanie.clary@brescia.edu
CLASEMANN-RYAN, Corey ... 317-917-5707 157 G cclasemann@ivytech.edu
CLAUDIO, Alex ... 787-780-0070 506 F aclaudio@caribbean.edu
CLAUDIO, Leshia ... 415-338-1381.. 34 A leshia@sfsu.edu
CLAUDIO, Nararly ... 787-891-0925 508 K nclaudio@aguadilla.inter.edu
CLAUDIO-VILLAFAÑE, Carlos ... 787-993-8896 513 B carlos.claudio2@upr.edu
CLAUSEN, Beth ... 651-793-1618 238 H beth.clausen@metrostate.edu
CLAUSEN, Dave ... 760-252-2411.. 26 I dclausen@barstow.edu
CLAUSEN, Janice ... 661-654-3360.. 30 E jclausen@csub.edu
CLAUSEN, Terry ... 870-850-8606.. 21 C tclausen@seark.edu
CLAUSON BASH, Kathleen, M ... 641-784-5064 165 H clauson@graceland.edu
CLAUSS, Daniel ... 949-582-4547.. 64 G dclauss@saddleback.edu
CLAUSS, Karl ... 610-328-8317 399 D kclauss1@swarthmore.edu
CLAUSS, Sandy ... 210-366-2701 442 D
CLAUSSEN, Linda, C ... 540-674-3614 475 B lclaussen@nr.edu
CLAUSSEN, Nicole ... 605-256-5744 416 J nicole.claussen@dsu.edu
CLAVELL, Edward ... 602-489-5300.. 10 E edward.clavell@arizonachristian.edu
CLAVELLE, Martha ... 619-644-7000.. 44 I martha.clavelle@gcccd.edu
CLAVERIE, Mark ... 518-587-2100 321 A mark.claverie@esc.edu
CLAVETTE, Jane ... 603-897-8211 274 B jclavette@rivier.edu
CLAVIER, Cheri ... 423-439-7483 419 J clavier@etsu.edu
CLAVIER, Sophie ... 415-338-7160.. 34 A sclavier@sfsu.edu
CLAWSON, Dana ... 318-677-3100 192 C roed@nsula.edu
CLAWSON, Jeff ... 336-725-8344 339 F clawsonj@piedmontu.edu
CLAWSON, Laura ... 540-665-4505 471 E lclawson@su.edu
CLAWSON, Michelle ... 757-727-5474 468 B michelle.clawson@hamptonu.edu
CLAXTON, Brenda ... 432-264-5160 438 C bclaxton@howardcollege.edu
CLAXTON, Marquez ... 803-780-1112 414 E mclaxton@voorhees.edu
CLAXTON, Patricia ... 325-574-7607 458 E pclaxton@wtc.edu
CLAXTON, Stephanie, L 315-267-2154 319 D claxtosc@potsdam.edu
CLAY, Aileen ... 603-206-8175 272 L aclay@ccsnh.edu
CLAY, Antoinette, M ... 732-255-0400 280 A aclay@ocean.edu
CLAY, Brian ... 501-370-5336.. 20 G bclay@philander.edu
CLAY, Claire ... 419-358-3456 348 G clayc@bluffton.edu
CLAY, Daniel ... 319-335-5380 163 A daniel-clay@uiowa.edu
CLAY, Doreen ... 818-710-2510.. 49 C claydj@piercecollege.edu
CLAY, George, W ... 864-656-0723 408 A gclay@clemson.edu
CLAY, John, L ... 256-469-7333.... 5 I president@hbc1.edu
CLAY, Karen ... 662-329-7104 248 A kgclay@muw.edu
CLAY, Karen ... 541-962-3792 373 B karen.clay@eou.edu
CLAY, Lauren ... 601-484-8618 247 A lclay1@meridiancc.edu
CLAY, Martyn ... 813-757-2110 101 A mclay6@hccfl.edu
CLAY, Melanie, N ... 678-839-0627 126 E melaniec@westga.edu
CLAY, Mercedes ... 419-783-2362 352 F mclay@defiance.edu
CLAY, Patricia ... 201-360-4351 278 C pclay@hccc.edu
CLAY, Philip, N ... 508-831-5507 220 E pclay@wpi.edu
CLAY, Rex ... 704-922-6243 334 F clay.rex@gaston.edu
CLAY, Rosetta ... 309-556-3127 139 G rclay@iwu.edu
CLAY, Victor, A ... 626-395-4187.. 29 C vclay@caltech.edu
CLAY-ROOLS, Paul ... 703-425-4143 468 E
CLAYBAUGH, Tracy, L .. 603-535-2550 275 B tlclaybaugh@plymouth.edu
CLAYBON, John ... 405-682-1611 367 H jclaybon@occc.edu
CLAYBORN, Eleanor ... 662-252-8000 248 G eclayborn@rustcollege.edu
CLAYBORNE, Hannah ... 614-234-5021 356 I hclayborne@mccn.edu

CLAYBROOK,
Jennifer, D .... 706-880-8032 121 A
jclaybrook@lagrange.edu
CLAYCOMB, Ann .... 304-293-9919 491 C
ann.claycomb@mail.wvu.edu
CLAYPOLE, Rita .... 304-263-6262 488 C
rclaypole@martinsburgcollege.edu
CLAYPOOL, Joe .... 859-323-5445 185 B
joseph.claypool@uky.edu
CLAYPOOL, Joni .... 503-883-2636 373 H
jclaypool@linfield.edu
CLAYPOOLE, Jack .... 803-777-4113 413 C
jclaypoole@mycarolina.org
CLAYPOOLE, Jennifer .... 765-973-8646 156 C
jenc@iu.edu
CLAYPOOLE, Lou .... 443-412-2655 199 A
lclaypoole@harford.edu
CLAYTER, Seth .... 207-699-5032 194 D
sclayter@meca.edu
CLAYTON, Dana .... 812-488-2500 161 A
dc26@evansville.edu
CLAYTON, Jan, L .... 918-595-7901 370 E
jan.clayton@tulsacc.edu
CLAYTON, Janet, S .... 803-934-3246 411 C
jclayton@morris.edu
CLAYTON, Jay .... 412-809-5100 396 H
clayton.jay@ptcollege.edu
CLAYTON, John .... 913-469-8500 174 D
claytonj@jccc.edu
CLAYTON, Kayci .... 732-255-0400 280 A
kclayton@ocean.edu
CLAYTON, Kirk .... 757-490-1241 464 F
kclayton@auto.edu
CLAYTON, Kori .... 501-337-5000.. 18 J
kclayon@coto.edu
CLAYTON, Patricia, I ..... 336-322-2105 336 G
patti.clayton@piedmontcc.edu
CLAYTON, Ralph .... 205-348-9828.... 7 G
rclayton@fa.ua.edu
CLAYTON, Susan .... 304-367-0205 490 B
susan.clayton@fairmontstate.edu
CLAYTON, Tiffany .... 610-921-6619 378 C
tclayton@albright.edu
CLAYTON, Yvette .... 256-372-5690.... 1 A
yvette.clayton@aamu.edu
CLEARFIELD, Michael ... 707-638-5982.. 67 F
michael.clearfield@tu.edu
CLEARWATER, Bonnie ... 954-262-0225 103M
bclearwater@moafl.org
CLEARY, Anita .... 509-452-5100 483 A
acleary@pnwu.edu
CLEARY, Brian .... 860-512-2612.. 85 G
bcleary@manchestercc.edu
CLEARY, Charles .... 860-773-3403.. 86 G
ccleary@tunxis.edu
CLEARY, Delores .... 509-963-2152 479 B
delores.cleary@cwu.edu
CLEARY, Kathleen .... 937-512-3159 361 A
kathleen.cleary@sinclair.edu
CLEARY, Lynn .... 315-464-5387 317 F
clearyl@upstate.edu
CLEARY, Rose .... 207-780-4640 196 F
rcleary@maine.edu
CLEARY, Sally .... 973-290-4449 277 A
scleary@cse.edu
CLEARY, Thomas .... 210-485-0500 429 C
tcleary1@alamo.edu
CLEARY, Valerie .... 503-725-9744 376 A
vcleary@pdx.edu
CLEAVINGER, Aubrie ..... 719-336-1571.. 80 K
aubrie.cleavinger@lamarcc.edu
CLEBSCH, Bill .... 650-725-0056.. 65 J
clebsch@stanford.edu
CLECKNER, Lisa .... 315-781-4381 302 A
cleckner@hws.edu
CLEEK, Stu .... 805-565-6029.. 74 K
scleek@westmont.edu
CLEGG, Neill .... 336-272-7102 329 D
cleggn@greensboro.edu
CLEM, Monica .... 814-732-1460 394 F
mclem@edinboro.edu
CLEMENCE, Patrick .... 319-398-1274 167 C
patrick.clemence@kirkwood.edu
CLEMENS, Bonnie .... 909-621-8924.. 37 D
bonnieclemens@claremont.edu
CLEMENS, Jacob, E ...... 419-372-9623 348 H
clemenj@bgsu.edu
CLEMENT,
Christopher, D .... 603-862-3081 274 G
christopher.clement@unh.edu
CLEMENT, Dawn .... 901-843-3745 423 J
clementd@rhodes.edu
CLEMENT, Fred .... 512-472-4133 443 H
fred.clement@ssw.edu
CLEMENT, James, A ...... 205-726-2395.... 6 E
jaclemen@samford.edu
CLEMENT, James, F ...... 585-292-3921 307 H
jclement@monroecc.edu
CLEMENT, Jane .... 901-678-2068 427 D
jclement@memphis.edu
CLEMENT, Julia .... 617-327-6777 220 B
julia_clement@williamjames.edu
CLEMENT, Kendra .... 318-345-9187 187 G
kclement@ladelta.edu
CLEMENT, Linda, M ...... 301-314-8430 202 C
lclement@umd.edu
CLEMENT, Lynnette .... 215-991-3682 387 C
clementl@lasalle.edu
CLEMENT, Mercedes ..... 386-506-3440.. 97 D
mercedes.clement@daytonastate.edu
CLEMENT, Nancy .... 985-448-7915 187 F
nancy.clement@fletcher.edu
CLEMENT, Richard .... 505-277-4241 288 G
riclement@unm.edu
CLEMENT, William .... 757-822-7373 476 B
wclement@tcc.edu
CLEMENTS, Blayne .... 931-221-7466 418 D
clementsb@apsu.edu
CLEMENTS, Carole .... 303-546-3584.. 81 B
carole@naropa.edu
CLEMENTS, Gary .... 252-527-6223 335 G
glclements03@lenoircc.edu
CLEMENTS, Geri .... 478-553-2066 122 G
gclements@oftc.edu
CLEMENTS, James, P .... 864-656-3413 408 A
president@clemson.edu
CLEMENTS, Jana .... 307-675-0810 502 F
jclements@sheridan.edu
CLEMENTS, Kieran .... 706-886-6831 125 D
clements@tfc.edu
CLEMENTS, Mari, L .... 626-584-5501.. 43 H
clements@fuller.edu
CLEMENTS, Mari, L .... 626-584-5205.. 43 H
clements@fuller.edu
CLEMENTS, Michelle ..... 206-296-5870 484 F
hr@seattleu.edu
CLEMENTS, Stephen, K . 859-858-3511 178 I
steve.clements@asbury.edu
CLEMENTS, Tommy .... 276-523-7431 475 A
tclements@mecc.edu
CLEMENTS, Vickie .... 814-864-6666 385 B
vickiec@glit.edu
CLEMENTS, William .... 802-485-2370 463 A
bclements@norwich.edu
CLEMES, Karen, M .... 801-863-8898 461 A
kclemes@uvu.edu
CLEMMER, Kristi .... 432-335-6865 441 D
kclemmer@odessa.edu
CLEMMONS, Brian .... 301-860-4363 203 C
bclemmons@bowiestate.edu
CLEMMONS, Raechelle .. 940-898-3980 451 F
rclemmons@twu.edu
CLEMMONS, Sarah .... 850-718-2288.. 96 F
clemmonss@chipola.edu
CLEMMONS, Val .... 910-362-7373 332 H
vclemmons@cfcc.edu
CLEMO, Lorrie .... 716-829-7673 298 F
clemo@dyc.edu
CLEMONS, Benjamin, P 507-354-8221 236 I
clemonbp@mlc-wels.edu
CLEMONS, Brian .... 816-415-7802 262 F
clemonsb@william.jewell.edu
CLEMONS, Cassie .... 912-287-5834 116 F
cclemons@coastalpines.edu
CLEMONS, Cheryl .... 270-686-4250 179 D
cheryl.clemons@brescia.edu
CLEMONS, Chuck .... 352-395-5202 107 A
chuck.clemons@sfcollege.edu
CLEMONS, Neil .... 386-506-3813.. 97 D
neil.clemons@daytonastate.edu
CLEMONS, Rita .... 909-635-0250 207 F
rita.clemons@cambridgecollege.edu
CLEMONS, Teresa, G .... 806-345-5548 430 A
t0155151@actx.edu
CLENCY, Charles .... 718-862-7944 305 H
cclency01@manhattan.edu
CLENDENEN, Holly .... 608-822-2362 500 G
hclendenen@swtc.edu
CLENDENEN, Mike .... 252-493-7608 336 H
mclendenen@email.pittcc.edu
CLERE, Ray, R .... 859-257-1987 185 B
ray.clere@uky.edu
CLERIE, Carole .... 706-568-2005 116 I
clerie_carole@columbusstate.edu
CLERKIN, Elizabeth .... 440-775-8450 358 C
liz.clerkin@oberlin.edu
CLERKIN, Shawn .... 814-871-7493 384 E
clerkin001@gannon.edu
CLESCERI, Michael .... 815-479-7833 143 A
mclesceri@mchenry.edu
CLEVELAND, SR.,
Alvin, A .... 334-872-2533.... 6 F
aclevesr@aol.com
CLEVELAND, Andrew ..... 715-232-2692 498 A
clevelanda@uwstout.edu
CLEVELAND, Angela ...... 269-965-3931 225 F
clevelanda@kellogg.edu
CLEVELAND, III,
Carl, S .... 913-234-0603 172 E
carl.clevelandiii@cleveland.edu
CLEVELAND, Chris .... 515-576-7201 166 E
CLEVELAND, Conne .... 559-934-2383.. 73M
connecleveland@whccd.edu
CLEVELAND, David .... 219-465-7852 162 A
david.cleveland@valpo.edu
CLEVELAND, Jon .... 970-491-5709.. 78M
jon.cleveland@colostate.edu
CLEVELAND, Tracey ...... 716-851-1844 299 F
clevelandt@ecc.edu
CLEVENGER, Brian .... 217-206-6174 151 C
clevenger.brian@uis.edu
CLEVENGER, Ernie .... 504-526-4745 189 H
eclevenger@carehere.com
CLEVENGER, Julie .... 217-786-2365 142 B
julie.clevenger@llcc.edu
CLEVENGER, Leah .... 704-406-4255 329 A
lclevenger@gardner-webb.edu
CLIATT, Cass .... 401-863-2453 404 E
cass_cliatt@brown.edu
CLICK, Sally, E .... 317-940-9854 153 F
sclick@butler.edu
CLIFFORD, Alexamder ... 207-795-2858 194 E
cliffo@mchp.edu
CLIFFORD, Alexander .... 207-795-2858 194 E
cliffoal@mchp.edu
CLIFFORD, Craig .... 254-968-1887 446 E
cliffor@tarleton.edu
CLIFFORD, Dale .... 912-525-5000 123 G
dcliffor@scad.edu
CLIFFORD, Heather .... 802-440-4325 462 A
hclifford@bennington.edu
CLIFFORD, Joan .... 518-244-2410 313 D
cliffj3@sage.edu
CLIFFORD, John .... 216-397-4963 354 I
jclifford@jcu.edu
CLIFFORD, Patrick .... 203-773-6989.. 84 F
pclifford@albertus.edu
CLIFFORD, Paul, J .... 814-865-6516 392 B
pjc37@psu.edu
CLIFT, Carla .... 256-551-3120.... 2 E
carla.clift@drakestate.edu
CLIFT BRELAND,
Byron, D .... 408-274-6700.. 61 K
byron.breland@sjeccd.edu
CLIFTON, Jamie .... 951-571-6293.. 58 G
jamie.clifton@mvc.edu
CLIFTON, Lonzy .... 334-876-9251.... 2 D
lonzy.clifton@wccs.edu
CLIFTON, Mary Beth ..... 407-582-8263 112 K
mclifton4@valenciacollege.edu
CLINARD, Lesley, J ...... 269-337-5767 225 D
lesley.clinard@kzoo.edu
CLINARD, Rhonda .... 931-363-9820 421 E
rclinard@martinmethodist.edu
CLINE, Angela .... 252-493-7679 336 H
acline@email.pittcc.edu
CLINE, Betsy .... 803-508-7457 406 E
clinee@atc.edu
CLINE, Cathie .... 870-633-4480.. 19 B
ccline@eacc.edu
CLINE, Jack .... 240-477-9505 177 D
jackcline@ku.edu
CLINE, James .... 864-231-2000 406 G
bcline@andersonuniversity.edu
CLINE, Jon .... 602-489-5300.. 10 E
jon.cline@arizonachristian.edu
CLINE, Josette .... 479-575-5276.. 21 G
jcline@uark.edu
CLINE, Josh .... 276-326-4208 465 B
jcline@bluefield.edu
CLINE, Kim .... 704-894-2584 328 F
CLINE, Kimberly, R .... 516-299-2501 304 G
kim.cline@liu.edu
CLINE, Kimberly, R .... 516-299-2501 304 H
kim.cline@liu.edu
CLINE, Laurel .... 610-796-8317 378 F
laurel.cline@alvernia.edu
CLINE, Lisa .... 802-635-1279 464 C
lisa.cline@northernvermont.edu
CLINE, Nicky .... 319-398-5629 167 C
nicky.cline@kirkwood.edu
CLINE, Penny .... 785-462-3984 172 H
penny.cline@colbycc.edu
CLINE, Scott .... 415-551-9316.. 28 D
scline2@cca.edu
CLINE, Stacy .... 585-582-8241 299 A
stacycline@elim.edu
CLINE, Tamara .... 530-283-0202.. 42 H
tcline@frc.edu
CLINES, Amy .... 912-279-5775 116 G
aclines@ccga.edu
CLINGER, Andrew .... 775-784-4901 270 K
CLINGINGSMITH, Aaron 406-874-6165 263 I
president@milescc.edu
CLINKSCALES, Sherard .. 812-237-4091 155 G
sherard.clinkscales@indstate.edu
CLINTON, Antwan, D .... 202-806-1361.. 92 B
aclinton@howard.edu
CLINTON, Christine, M . 814-886-6380 391 B
cclinton@mtaloy.edu
CLINTON, Darren .... 803-705-4372 407 A
darren.clinton@benedict.edu
CLINTON, Don .... 903-693-2055 441 F
dclinton@panola.edu
CLINTON, Ericka .... 212-924-5900 322 B
eclinton@swedishinstitute.edu
CLINTON, John .... 212-229-5400 308 C
clintonj@newschool.edu
CLINTON, Joseph .... 845-848-7700 298 D
joseph.clinton@dc.edu
CLINTON, Leslie .... 717-477-1377 395 E
lfclin@sufoundation.org
CLINTON, Ron .... 903-434-8101 441 B
rclinton@ntcc.edu
CLINTON, Tiffany .... 310-342-5200.. 72 D
CLINTON, Veronica .... 732-906-4661 279 A
vclinton@middlesexcc.edu
CLINTON JONES,
Karen, A .... 716-878-6210 318 C
joneska@buffalostate.edu
CLIPPERTON, Alan .... 903-233-3160 439 E
alanclipperton@letu.edu
CLISH, Colleen .... 651-290-6328 242 G
colleen.clish@mitchellhamline.edu
CLODFELTER, Elaine ...... 704-272-5302 337 I
eclodfelter@spcc.edu
CLODFELTER, JR.,
Roger, D .... 336-841-9156 329 G
rclodfel@highpoint.edu
CLOKEY, Diane .... 860-253-3015.. 85 C
dclokey@asnuntuck.edu
CLONINGER, Jason .... 217-854-5654 132 I
jason.cloninger@blackburn.edu
CLONINGER, Mindy, E .. 620-235-4241 176 F
mcloninger@pittstate.edu
CLOONAN, Patricia .... 202-687-7318.. 92 A
cloonanp@georgetown.edu
CLOOS, Kevin, P .... 716-673-3452 317 A
kevin.cloos@fredonia.edu
CLOPTON, John, D .... 319-296-4004 166 B
john.clopton@hawkeyecollege.edu
CLOPTON, Lynn .... 936-294-1780 450 C
clopton@shsu.edu
CLOS, Karen .... 254-519-5744 447 A
karen.clos@tamuct.edu
CLOSE, Cathy .... 715-232-1235 498 A
closec@uwstout.edu
CLOSE, Deidra .... 423-354-2405 425 E
dlclose@northeaststate.edu
CLOSE, Stacey .... 860-465-5791.. 84 J
closes@easternct.edu
CLOSSER, James, B ...... 615-868-6503 422 G
jclosser@mtsa.edu
CLOSTERMAN, Wendy .... 267-502-4849 379 D
wendy.closterman@brynathyn.edu
CLOTHIER, Rebecca ...... 816-331-5700 258 B
rclothier@pcitraining.edu
CLOUD, Andy .... 432-837-8179 450 D
wacloud@sulross.edu
CLOUD, Gary .... 480-219-6013 250 A
gcloud@atsu.edu
CLOUD, Jessica .... 510-549-4711.. 66 B
jcloud@sksm.edu
CLOUD, Melissa .... 918-595-7809 370 E
melissa.cloud@tulsacc.edu
CLOUD, Rodney .... 800-351-4040.... 4 C
CLOUGH, Susan .... 970-542-3127.. 81 A
susan.clough@morgancc.edu
CLOUGHERTY, Helen ...... 832-813-6514 439 G
helen.clougherty@lonestar.edu
CLOUNCH, Teresa .... 785-628-5824 173 B
clounch@fhsu.edu

COGGINS, Patrick .... 940-397-4239 440 F
patrick.coggins@msutexas.edu
COGHLAN, Cathan .... 817-257-7475 448 G
c.coghlan@tcu.edu
COGSWELL, Bob .... 910-893-1217 327 E
cogswell@campbell.edu
COGSWELL, Katherine ... 315-445-6124 304 C
cogswek@lemoyne.edu
COHEA, Melissa .... 707-654-1789.. 32 B
mcohea@csum.edu
COHEN, Alise .... 845-848-4036 298 D
alise.cohen@dc.edu
COHEN, Bernadette .... 404-270-5091 125 B
bcohen@spelman.edu
COHEN, Brad .... 740-593-1220 359 G
cohenb@ohio.edu
COHEN, Brian .... 646-664-2004 292 K
brian.cohen@cuny.edu
COHEN, Chaim .... 410-486-0006 197 D
COHEN, Dan .... 617-373-5001 217 F
COHEN, David .... 631-656-2157 300 D
david.cohen@ftc.edu
COHEN, David .... 800-371-6105.. 14 G
david@nationalparalegal.edu
COHEN, Eliot .... 202-663-5622 199 D
ecohen@jhu.edu
COHEN, Henry .... 707-638-5221 322 J
henry.cohen@touro.edu
COHEN, Ilene .... 732-255-0400 280 A
icohen@ocean.edu
COHEN, Jason .... 413-755-4438 215 F
jlcohen@stcc.edu
COHEN, Jennifer .... 206-543-2212 485 F
huskyad@uw.edu
COHEN, Jerry .... 631-656-2102 300 D
jerry.cohen@ftc.edu
COHEN, John .... 662-325-8082 247 F
jcohen@athletics.msstate.edu
COHEN, Jonah .... 203-285-2289.. 85 E
jcohen@gwcc.commnet.edu
COHEN, Laurie .... 480-423-6511.. 13 H
laurie.cohen@scottsdalecc.edu
COHEN, Lee .... 662-915-7178 249 D
leecohen@olemiss.edu
COHEN, Linda .... 949-824-5189.. 68 G
chair@uci.edu
COHEN, Mark, J .... 202-687-7610.. 92 A
cohenm@georgetown.edu
COHEN, Megan, S .... 617-353-2200 207 D
mseiler@bu.edu
COHEN, Michael .... 828-884-8366 327 C
cohenmw@brevard.edu
COHEN, Michael, E .... 772-466-4822.. 94 P
m.cohen@aviator.edu
COHEN, Michelle, E ...... 215-596-8540 401 G
m.cohen@usciences.edu
COHEN, Neil .... 864-578-8770 412 B
ncohen@sherman.edu
COHEN, Paul, R .... 412-624-5139 401 B
prcohen@pitt.edu
COHEN, Paula .... 215-895-1266 383 B
paula.marantz.cohen@drexel.edu
COHEN, Peter .... 602-557-1555.. 16 J
peter.cohen@phoenix.edu
COHEN, Peter .... 718-368-5563 294 E
pcohen@kbcc.cuny.edu
COHEN, Pinchas .... 213-740-1354.. 72 B
hassy@usc.edu
COHEN, Richard .... 215-985-2500 403 H
rjc@phmc.org
COHEN, Scott .... 731-425-2615 425 B
scohen@jscc.edu
COHEN, Shaya .... 347-619-9074 326 G
COHEN, Todd .... 303-964-6404.. 82 E
tcohen@regis.edu
COHEN, Veronica, M .... 601-979-2282 246 E
veronica.m.cohen@jsums.edu
COHEN, Vicki .... 201-692-2132 277 K
cohen@fdu.edu
COHEN, William, A .... 301-405-9354 202 C
wcohen@umd.edu
COHEN, Yehuda .... 347-619-9074 326 G
COHEN-ROSE, Amy .... 617-277-3915 207 C
cohenrose@bgsp.edu
COHEN-VOGEL, Dan ...... 919-962-4554 341 A
dcohen-vogel@northcarolina.edu
COHENOUR, LeeDel ...... 303-360-4914.. 79 D
leedel.cohenour@ccaurora.edu
COHICK, Lynn, H .... 303-762-6900.. 79 H
provost@denverseminary.edu
COHRS, Daniel, L .... 303-963-3352.. 77 G
dcohrs@ccu.edu

COHUNE, Ellen .... 805-756-2527.. 30 C
ecohune@calpoly.edu
COILE, Julie .... 678-466-4227 116 E
juliecoile@clayton.edu
COINER, Jeff, P .... 417-836-5770 256 E
jeffcoiner@missouristate.edu
COKE, Kim .... 573-875-7420 251 F
kjcoke@ccis.edu
COKER, Amber .... 850-913-3293 100 N
acoker@gulfcoast.edu
COKER, Bryan, F .... 410-337-6150 198 G
bryan.coker@goucher.edu
COKER, Dawn, C .... 706-880-8267 121 A
dcoker@lagrange.edu
COKER, Jacqueline .... 703-812-4757 468 G
jcoker@leland.edu
COKER, Jeffrey .... 540-665-4587 471 E
jcoker2@su.edu
COKER, Jeffrey, S .... 724-946-7123 402 G
cokerjs@westminster.edu
COKER, Keller .... 212-229-5896 308 C
cokerk@newschool.edu
COKER, Kim .... 870-574-4533.. 21 E
kcoker@sautech.edu
COKER, Megan .... 918-836-6886 370 D
megan.coker@spartan.edu
COKER, Melissa, A .... 843-355-4117 414 F
cokerm@wiltech.edu
COKER, Renee .... 646-592-4336 326 E
renee.coker@yu.edu
COKER, Sherry .... 417-447-8907 257 G
cokers@otc.edu
COLÓN, José, C .... 787-815-0000 513 A
jose.colon14@upr.edu
COLÓN, Lizzie .... 787-891-0925 508 K
lcolon@aguadilla.inter.edu
COLÓN, Maria, J .... 787-250-1912 509 D
mjcolon@intermetro.com
COLÓN-ALCARAZ,
Divya, C .... 787-753-9171 512 G
divya.colon@upr.edu
COLAGROSS, Glenda ..... 256-331-5214.... 3 C
colg@nwscc.edu
COLAHAN, Michael .... 610-896-1350 385 L
mcolahan@haverford.edu
COLANER, Kevin, T .... 909-869-3365.. 30 D
ktcolaner@cpp.edu
COLANGELO, Carmon ... 314-935-9300 262 A
colangelo@wustl.edu
COLAPIETRO, Cathy, L .. 913-971-3298 175 G
ccolapietro@mnu.edu
COLASURDO,
Giuseppe, N .... 713-500-3000 456 B
giuseppe.n.colasurdo@uth.tmc.edu
COLATOS, Chris .... 510-637-7326.. 58 K
c.colatos@sae.edu
COLBAN, Tom .... 201-360-4393 278 C
tcolban@follett.com
COLBECK, Ellen .... 217-875-7200 147 C
ecolbeck@richland.edu
COLBERT, Carly, J .... 315-445-4312 304 C
colbercj@lemoyne.edu
COLBERT, Debbie .... 541-737-0123 375 D
COLBERT, Mary, J .... 410-857-2214 200 B
mcolbert@mcdaniel.edu
COLBERT, Monica .... 212-774-4842 306 A
mcolbert@mmm.edu
COLBROOK, William ..... 217-351-2884 146 C
wcolbrook@parkland.edu
COLBS, Sandy .... 309-438-3655 139 E
slcolbs@ilstu.edu
COLBURN, Brent .... 609-258-4611 280 E
brent.colburn@princeton.edu
COLBURN, Jill .... 716-338-1009 303 D
jillcolburn@mail.sunyjcc.edu
COLBY, Adam .... 727-864-7732.. 97 J
colbyac@eckerd.edu
COLBY, Andrew, G .... 603-862-1568 274 G
andy.colby@unh.edu
COLBY, Glenn .... 425-352-8420 479 A
gcolby@cascadia.edu
COLBY BOND,
Courtney .... 208-562-3084 130 F
courtneybond@cwi.edu
COLBY-CLEMENTS,
Paula .... 978-681-0800 216 A
pcolby@mslaw.edu
COLDREN, Brian .... 404-364-8418 122 J
bcoldren@oglethorpe.edu
COLDREN, Mark .... 716-645-8155 316 F
mcoldren@buffalo.edu
COLDREN, Stephanie .... 410-337-6118 198 G
stephanie.coldren@goucher.edu

COLE, Amantha, L .... 304-367-4981 490 B
amantha.cole@fairmontstate.edu
COLE, Amy .... 816-235-1211 261 C
coleamy@umkc.edu
COLE, Andrew .... 859-344-3683 184 F
colea@thomasmore.edu
COLE, Anthony .... 239-687-5332.. 94 N
acole@avemarialaw.edu
COLE, Brad .... 435-797-2631 460 H
brad.cole@usu.edu
COLE, Brian .... 336-770-3200 343 D
coleb@uncsa.edu
COLE, Brian .... 336-631-1226 343 D
coleb@uncsa.edu
COLE, Bruce .... 704-669-6000 333 E
COLE, Cathy .... 406-243-2311 264 A
catherine.cole@umontana.edu
COLE, Christy .... 423-636-7300 427 B
ccole@tusculum.edu
COLE, Crystal .... 563-425-5786 170 A
colec42@uiu.edu
COLE, Dan .... 402-363-5609 270 E
dcole@york.edu
COLE, David .... 817-722-1614 439 B
david.cole@tku.edu
COLE, David, J .... 843-792-2211 410 F
coledj@musc.edu
COLE, Donna .... 480-423-6310.. 13 H
donna.cole@scottsdalecc.edu
COLE, Doug .... 678-450-0550 120 H
rfauer@ict.edu
COLE, Elizabeth, R .... 734-764-0322 231 E
ecole@umich.edu
COLE, Elyne .... 217-244-0784 151 D
egcole@illinois.edu
COLE, Frank .... 505-566-3511 288 A
colef@sancollege.edu
COLE, Graham .... 847-317-8086 150 H
gacole@tiu.edu
COLE, Jack, T .... 717-796-1800 390 E
jcole@messiah.edu
COLE, Jason .... 510-466-5398.. 56 D
jcole@peralta.edu
COLE, Jean .... 260-356-6000 155 F
jcole@huntington.edu
COLE, Jeffrey .... 860-439-2030.. 86 H
jcole1@conncoll.edu
COLE, Jeffrey, S .... 724-847-4696 384 G
jscole@geneva.edu
COLE, Jill .... 716-926-8933 301 H
jillcole@hilbert.edu
COLE, Jim .... 478-301-2737 121 E
cole_jm@mercer.edu
COLE, Jodi .... 616-526-6642 222 A
jlc23@calvin.edu
COLE, John, J .... 304-293-8470 491 C
jay.cole@mail.wvu.edu
COLE, Julie .... 252-328-9520 341 C
coleju17@ecu.edu
COLE, Karin .... 540-857-7236 476 D
kcole@virginiawestern.edu
COLE, Katharine .... 410-455-2859 202 E
kcole@umbc.edu
COLE, Kathryn, B .... 601-857-3502 246 B
kathryn.cole@hindscc.edu
COLE, Keri .... 601-857-3624 246 B
kbcole@hindscc.edu
COLE, Keri .... 601-857-3250 246 B
kbcole@hindscc.edu
COLE, Kevin .... 760-366-5295.. 40 K
kcole@cmccd.edu
COLE, Kimberly, M .... 330-972-2603 362 B
kmorgan@uakron.edu
COLE, Kristie .... 864-231-2067 406 G
kcole@andersonuniversity.edu
COLE, Lauren .... 334-670-3216.... 7 C
lscole@troy.edu
COLE, Lindsay .... 304-865-6077 488 E
lindsay.cole@ovu.edu
COLE, Lisa, L .... 318-257-5222 191 F
lcole@latech.edu
COLE, Marcus, G .... 574-631-6789 161 C
gcole2@nd.edu
COLE, Mark .... 305-237-3798 103 D
mcole@mdc.edu
COLE, Megan .... 402-399-2455 266 F
mcole@csm.edu
COLE, Nadara, L .... 662-720-7277 248 C
ncole@nemcc.edu
COLE, Nathan .... 901-751-8453 422 E
ncole@mabts.edu
COLE, Nathan .... 937-381-1555 352 J
ncole@edisonohio.edu

COLE, Pamela .... 470-578-6023 120 L
pcole@kennesaw.edu
COLE, Phil .... 912-358-3062 123 H
colep@savannahstate.edu
COLE, Richard .... 732-906-4153 279 A
rcole@middlesexcc.edu
COLE, JR., Rick .... 516-463-6750 302 B
rick.cole@hofstra.edu
COLE, Robert .... 413-205-3336 205 A
robert.cole@aic.edu
COLE, Ronald, B .... 814-332-3393 378 D
rcole@allegheny.edu
COLE, Steve .... 870-584-1173.. 22 G
scole@cccua.edu
COLE, Susan, A .... 973-655-4212 279 C
coles@mail.montclair.edu
COLE, Tricia .... 605-331-6635 417 E
tricia.cole@usiouxfalls.edu
COLE, Trudi .... 406-791-5300 265 H
trudi.cole@uprovidence.edu
COLE, III, W. Allen .... 859-572-5225 184 A
colew1@nku.edu
COLE, W. Scott .... 407-823-2482 109 E
scott.cole@ucf.edu
COLE, Wayne .... 563-441-4011 165 E
wcole@eicc.edu
COLE, Xavier, A .... 414-288-7206 494 B
xavier.a.cole@marquette.edu
COLE, Yolanda .... 215-248-7153 381 D
coley@chc.edu
COLE EIMERS, Lisa .... 573-592-1125 262 G
lisa.coleeimers@williamwoods.edu
COLE-JONES, Lisa .... 619-388-6692.. 60 B
lcole@sdccd.edu
COLEAL, Sharlene .... 661-362-3405.. 38 H
sharlene.coleal@canyons.edu
COLELLA, Carlo .... 301-405-1106 202 C
ccolella@umd.edu
COLELLA, Christine .... 215-885-2360 389 F
ccolella@manor.edu
COLELLA, Kurt, J .... 860-444-8275 504 F
kurt.j.colella@uscg.mil
COLELLA, Laurie .... 508-831-4922 220 E
lcolella@wpi.edu
COLELLI, Leonard .... 724-938-4302 394 B
colelli@calu.edu
COLEMAN, Andre .... 916-558-2376.. 50 I
colemaa@scc.losrios.edu
COLEMAN, Angela .... 251-460-7475.... 8 F
macoleman@southalabama.edu
COLEMAN, Angela .... 919-530-6023 342 A
angela.coleman@nccu.edu
COLEMAN, Anne Marie . 401-874-5270 406 B
acoleman@uri.edu
COLEMAN, Antoinette ... 301-445-1917 202 B
acoleman@usmd.edu
COLEMAN, Bob, J .... 904-620-5834 110 A
jcoleman@unf.edu
COLEMAN, Chad .... 574-535-7292 155 A
chadc@goshen.edu
COLEMAN, Daniel .... 205-226-4620.... 5 A
president@bsc.edu
COLEMAN, Danny .... 256-378-2022.... 1 G
dcoleman@cacc.edu
COLEMAN, Darin .... 843-921-6936 411 F
dcoleman@netc.edu
COLEMAN, David .... 859-622-1403 180 B
david.coleman@eku.edu
COLEMAN, Deidra .... 210-436-3135 443 A
dcoleman@stmarytx.edu
COLEMAN, Dennis .... 214-379-5514 441 I
dcoleman@pqc.edu
COLEMAN, Diane .... 206-934-3842 484 A
diane.coleman@seattlecolleges.edu
COLEMAN, Djuan .... 314-454-8515 253 E
djuan.coleman@bjc.org
COLEMAN, Donald .... 423-697-4467 424 E
donald.coleman@chattanoogastate.edu
COLEMAN, Ellen .... 302-736-2508.. 90 G
ellen.coleman@wesley.edu
COLEMAN, Emily .... 606-539-4230 185 A
emily.coleman@ucumberlands.edu
COLEMAN, Frances, N .. 662-325-7661 247 F
fcoleman@library.msstate.edu
COLEMAN, Gerald .... 585-594-6530 312 K
colemang@roberts.edu
COLEMAN, James .... 479-575-5459.. 21 G
jscolema@uark.edu
COLEMAN, John .... 612-624-2535 243 E
coleman@umn.edu
COLEMAN, Jonathan ..... 920-206-2346 493 L
jonathan.coleman@mbu.edu

COLLINS, Melanie ... 985-448-4415 192 B
melanie.collins@nicholls.edu
COLLINS, Michael ... 805-482-2755.. 58 L
mcollins@stjohnsem.edu
COLLINS, Michael ... 951-372-7157.. 58 H
michael.collins@norcocollege.edu
COLLINS, Michael ... 641-673-1393 170 F
collinsm@wmpenn.edu
COLLINS, Michael ... 269-488-4255 225 E
mcollins@kvcc.edu
COLLINS, Michael, F ... 508-856-8100 212 A
michael.collins@umassmed.edu
COLLINS, Miranda ... 740-376-4458 356 A
miranda.collins@marietta.edu
COLLINS, Monique ... 850-484-1552 104 H
mcollins@pensacolastate.edu
COLLINS, Nicole, N ... 423-439-6900 419 J
collinsnn@etsu.edu
COLLINS, Patrick ... 617-627-4173 219 B
patrick.collins@tufts.edu
COLLINS, Rebecca ... 701-224-5476 346 B
rebecca.collins@bismarckstate.edu
COLLINS, Richard ... 407-708-2430 107 D
collinsr@seminolestate.edu
COLLINS, Ron ... 205-934-4423.... 8 A
ronc@uab.edu
COLLINS, Ronnie ... 304-645-6336 491 A
rcollins@osteo.wvsom.edu
COLLINS, SR.,
Ronnie, L ... 410-951-3392 203 D
rcollins@coppin.edu
COLLINS, Roy ... 575-646-2446 287 B
collins0@nmsu.edu
COLLINS, Scott ... 518-736-3622 300 F
scollins@fmcc.suny.edu
COLLINS, Sean ... 401-825-2109 404 H
stcollins@ccri.edu
COLLINS, Shawn ... 304-865-6015 488 E
shawn.collins@ovu.edu
COLLINS, Sheila ... 701-662-1533 346 D
sheila.collins@lrsc.edu
COLLINS,
Sibrina Nichelle ... 248-204-2227 226 G
scollins@ltu.edu
COLLINS, Steve ... 870-612-2026.. 22 I
steve.collins@uaccb.edu
COLLINS, Steven ... 831-242-5291 503 D
COLLINS, Susan, H ... 925-631-4571.. 59 B
susan.collins@stmarys-ca.edu
COLLINS, Tana ... 205-387-0511.... 1 D
tana.collins@bscc.edu
COLLINS, Valerie, H ... 516-572-7664 308 A
valerie.collins@ncc.edu
COLLINS, Wanda ... 404-727-7450 117 F
wanda.collins@emory.edu
COLLINS, II, William ... 716-888-8208 292 D
collinsw@canisius.edu
COLLINS-HALL, Lori ... 937-319-0069 347 G
lcollinshall@antiochcollege.edu
COLLINS JUDD, Cristle 914-395-2201 315 F
president@sarahlawrence.edu
COLLINS PIENTA,
Norah ... 708-524-6822 136 C
ncollins@dom.edu
COLLINS-SMITH,
LaTonia ... 314-340-3512 253 I
collinsl@hssu.edu
COLLINWOOD, Nancy ... 801-626-7538 461 B
ncollinwood@weber.edu
COLLINWOOD, Nancy ... 801-626-6569 461 B
ncollinwood@weber.edu
COLLOGAN, Jessica ... 904-256-7269 101 G
jcollog@ju.edu
COLLOTON, Paul ... 614-251-4563 358 G
collotop@ohiodominican.edu
COLLUM, Lara ... 601-484-8745 247 A
lcollum@meridiancc.edu
COLLUM, Tammy ... 770-975-4125 116 C
tcollum@chattahoocheetech.edu
COLLUMBIEN, Bill, S ... 651-696-6686 236 H
wcollumb@macalester.edu
COLLURA, Jessica ... 718-982-2676 293 E
jessica.collura@csi.cuny.edu
COLMAN, Gabriela ... 254-710-8300 431 J
gabriela_colman@baylor.edu
COLMENERO,
Jacinto (JC) ... 361-354-2559 433 C
jcolmenero@coastalbend.edu
COLMERAUER, Joanne .. 716-270-2826 299 F
colmerauer@ecc.edu
COLOM, Albert ... 715-836-2637 496 D
COLOMBAT, Andre ... 410-617-2910 199 F
acp@loyola.edu
COLOMBO, John ... 785-864-3661 177 D
colombo@ku.edu
COLOMBO, Lisa ... 508-856-4393 212 A
lisa.colombo@umassmed.edu
COLON,
Adabel-Vanessa ... 787-250-1912 509 D
avcolon@metro.inter.edu
COLON, Angie ... 787-863-2390 509 B
angie.colon@fajardo.inter.edu
COLON, Brenda ... 787-765-4210 506 K
bcolon@cempr.edu
COLON, Carmen ... 215-751-8167 382 A
ccolon@ccp.edu
COLON, Denisse ... 787-288-1118 512 A
COLON, Eddie ... 816-279-7000 250 B
eddie.colon@abtu.edu
COLON, Efrain ... 787-738-2161 513 D
efrain.colon@upr.edu
COLON, Hector, W ... 787-284-1912 509 E
hwcolon@ponce.inter.edu
COLON, Ingrid, Y ... 787-884-3838 506 D
icolon@atenascollege.edu
COLON, Iris ... 787-746-1400 508 B
icolon@huertas.edu
COLON, Isaac ... 787-844-8181 514 A
isaaccolondegro@upr.edu
COLON, Jaime ... 787-279-1912 509 A
jcolon@bayamon.inter.edu
COLON, Lesbia ... 787-844-8181 514 A
lesbia.colon@upr.edu
COLON, Luis ... 787-815-0000 513 A
luis.colon19@upr.edu
COLON, Maggie ... 787-763-1912 508 J
mcolon@inter.edu
COLON, Manuel ... 787-758-2525 513 G
manuel.colon8@upr.edu
COLON, Michelle ... 407-888-8689.. 98 R
mcolon@fcim.edu
COLON, Mirta ... 787-754-8000 512 E
mcolon@pupr.edu
COLON, Nidia ... 787-786-3030 512 B
ncolon@ucb.edu.pr
COLON, Olga ... 787-738-2161 513 D
olga.colon1@upr.edu
COLON, Vilma, E ... 787-284-1912 509 E
vcolon@ponce.inter.edu
COLON ALICEA,
Leandro ... 787-841-2000 510 K
leandro_colon@pucpr.edu
COLON-ALONSO, Ana, I 787-857-3600 508 M
aicolon@br.inter.edu
COLON-CANALES,
Wanda ... 301-891-4093 204 C
wcanales@wau.edu
COLON COSME,
Edwin, J ... 787-744-1060 510 C
edwincolon@mechtech.edu
COLON-RIVERA,
Damaris ... 787-857-3600 508 M
dcolon@br.inter.edu
COLON SOTO, Ana ... 787-848-5739 511 C
COLONNA, Corry ... 562-985-4187.. 31 F
corry.colonna@csulb.edu
COLONNO, Daniel ... 413-662-5281 213 A
d.colonno@mcla.edu
COLORADO, Ana ... 787-725-8120 507 N
acolorado0013@eap.edu
COLORITO, Angela ... 724-503-1001 402 E
acolorito@washjeff.edu
COLOSIMO, Beth ... 801-957-5259 461 D
beth.colosimo@slcc.edu
COLSON, Darrel, D ... 319-352-8450 170 C
president@wartburg.edu
COLSON, Jessica ... 413-265-2454 208 C
colsonj@elms.edu
COLSON, John ... 951-639-5201.. 52 I
jcolson@msjc.edu
COLSON, Matthew ... 631-632-4932 317 D
matthew.colson@stonybrook.edu
COLSTON, Karen ... 719-884-5000.. 81 C
kecolston@nbc.edu
COLTER-BRABHAM,
Constance ... 803-780-1189 414 E
cbrabham@voorhees.edu
COLTHARP, Brent ... 314-838-8858 261 G
bcoltharp@ugst.edu
COLTHARP, Duane ... 210-999-8201 452 A
dcolthar@trinity.edu
COLTHARP, Glenn ... 417-455-5534 252 D
glenncoltharp@crowder.edu
COLTMAN, Heather ... 540-568-3429 468 F
coltmahj@jmu.edu
COLTON, Chris ... 518-445-3208 289 E
COLUCCI, III,
Anthony, P ... 330-972-7231 362 B
apc6@uakron.edu
COLUCCI, David ... 718-779-1499 311 I
dcolucci@plazacollege.edu
COLUCCI, Debbie ... 860-685-2000.. 89 C
COLUCCI, Rita ... 978-542-8600 213 C
rita.colucci@salemstate.edu
COLUMBUS, Kristi ... 319-895-4153 164 B
kcolumbus@cornellcollege.edu
COLVER, Mike ... 714-241-6160.. 38 C
mcolver@coastline.edu
COLVEY, Kirsten, S ... 909-389-3327.. 59 H
kcolvey@craftonhills.edu
COLVILLE, John ... 903-988-3747 439 A
jcolville@kilgore.edu
COLVIN, Carol ... 865-251-1800 424 A
ccolvin@south.edu
COLVIN, Gail, B ... 719-333-4510 504 C
gail.colvin@usafa.edu
COLVIN, Jenna ... 706-867-4518 126 A
jenna.colvin@ung.edu
COLVIN, Larry ... 269-749-7668 229 H
lcolvin@olivetcollege.edu
COLVIN, Mike ... 318-345-9107 187 G
mcolvin@ladelta.edu
COLVIN, Ryan ... 601-974-1200 247 B
COLVSON, W. Mark ... 845-257-3719 317 B
colvsonm@newpaltz.edu
COLWELL, Joy ... 219-989-2367 159 G
colwell@pnw.edu
COLWELL, Ken ... 361-570-4230 453 C
colwellk@uhv.edu
COLYAR, Jana ... 801-818-8900 459 K
jana.colyar@provocollege.edu
COLYAR, Mike ... 318-257-2893 191 F
colyar@latech.edu
COLYER, Dominique ... 773-252-5392 147 B
dominique.colyer@resu.edu
COMAGE, Rebecca ... 978-542-2404 213 C
rebecca.comage@salemstate.edu
COMAIR, Claude ... 425-558-0299 480 D
COMANDA, Peter ... 815-280-6606 140 B
pcomanda@jjc.edu
COMBS, Brandon ... 859-858-3511 178 I
brandon.combs@asbury.edu
COMBS, Brandon ... 281-425-6822 439 D
bcombs@lee.edu
COMBS, Carrie ... 540-568-6234 468 F
teicheca@jmu.edu
COMBS, Charles, D ... 757-446-6090 466 I
combscd@evms.edu
COMBS, Delcie ... 606-487-3100 181 C
delcie.combs@kctcs.edu
COMBS, Joseph, L ... 423-585-2675 426 C
joseph.combs@ws.edu
COMBS, Joshua ... 671-734-1812 505 D
jcombs@piu.edu
COMBS, Kevin ... 509-524-5162 485 G
kevin.combs@wwcc.edu
COMBS, Kristina, A ... 415-485-9504.. 39 C
kcombs@marin.edu
COMBS, Lisa, H ... 704-894-2000 328 F
licombs@davidson.edu
COMBS, Patricia ... 256-228-6001.... 3 B
combsp@nacc.edu
COMBS, Travis ... 620-417-1312 176 K
travis.combs@sccc.edu
COMBS, Vickie ... 606-487-3110 181 C
vickie.combs@kctcs.edu
COMEAU, Juanita ... 608-246-6596 499 H
jcomeau@madisoncollege.edu
COMEAUX, David, P ... 337-482-0922 192 E
dcomeaux@louisiana.edu
COMEAUX, Linda ... 303-914-6403.. 82 C
linda.comeaux@rrcc.edu
COMEAUX, Mark ... 714-879-3901.. 45 F
mcomeaux@hiu.edu
COMEDY-HOLMES,
Jennifer ... 210-486-4857 429 E
jcomedy-holmes@alamo.edu
COMEN, Todd ... 978-232-2402 209 B
tcomen@endicott.edu
COMER, Alberta, D ... 801-585-6887 460 E
alberta.comer@utah.edu
COMER, Anthony, C ... 724-847-6711 384 G
accomer@geneva.edu
COMER, Kimberly ... 229-928-1373 119 D
kim.comer@gsw.edu
COMER, Linda, S ... 863-680-3951.. 99 H
lcomer@flsouthern.edu
COMER, Sean ... 513-745-4868 365 B
comers@xavier.edu
COMER-WOODS, Ann ... 941-487-4150 109 D
awoods@ncf.edu
COMERFORD, John, L .. 614-823-1420 360 A
comerford1@otterbein.edu
COMERFORD, Nicholas . 808-956-8234 128 F
nbc6@hawaii.edu
COMERFORD,
Sandra Stefani ... 650-574-6404.. 61 P
comerford@smccd.edu
COMET, Kimberly ... 707-826-3305.. 33 D
kim.comet@humboldt.edu
COMETSEVAH, Cecelia .. 505-922-4093 288 F
cecelia.cometsevah@bie.edu
COMEY, William ... 301-934-7509 198 A
wlcomey@csmd.edu
COMFORT, Randy ... 530-226-4770.. 63 K
rcomfort@simpsonu.edu
COMMANDER, Patricia .. 704-636-6779 330 A
pcommander@hoodseminary.edu
COMMERFORD, Mary ... 212-854-2092 290 J
mcommerf@barnard.edu
COMMETTE, Jeanne ... 978-232-2344 209 B
jcommett@endicott.edu
COMMON, Brandon ... 309-556-3111 139 G
bcommon@iwu.edu
COMMONS, Mary ... 803-508-7413 406 E
commonsm@atc.edu
COMPARY, Kirsten ... 361-593-3606 447 D
kirsten.compary@tamuk.edu
COMPITIELLO, Dan ... 617-745-3714 208 G
dan.compitiello@enc.edu
COMPTON, Betsy ... 205-652-3892.... 9 A
bcompton@uwa.edu
COMPTON, Duane, A ... 603-650-1200 273 E
duane.a.compton@dartmouth.edu
COMPTON, Tonia ... 660-831-4622 256 G
comptont@moval.edu
COMVALIUS-GODDARD,
Sharon ... 617-552-8259 207 B
sharon.comvalius-goddard@bc.edu
CONAHAN, Kathleen ... 800-686-1883 222 E
kconahan@cleary.edu
CONANT, Nicole, A ... 315-267-2128 319 D
conantna@potsdam.edu
CONATY, Donna, M ... 619-594-4464.. 33 E
dconaty@sdsu.edu
CONATY, William ... 401-232-6000 404 F
CONAWAY,
Kathleen, M ... 814-332-4799 378 D
kconaway@allegheny.edu
CONBOY, Bridget ... 704-461-6663 327 A
CONBOY, Sheila (Katie) 617-521-2077 218 E
katie.conboy@simmons.edu
CONCANNON, Chris ... 360-992-2411 479 F
cconcannon@clark.edu
CONCEPCION, Ange ... 718-390-3801 324 F
angelica.concepcion@wagner.edu
CONCEPCION, Beth ... 404-364-8865 122 J
bconcepcion@oglethorpe.edu
CONCEPCION, Lillian ... 787-250-1912 509 D
lconcepcion@metro.inter.edu
CONCHA, Lee ... 847-578-8848 147 I
lee.concha@rosalindfranklin.edu
CONCHA THIA,
Mary Chries ... 650-306-3243.. 61 O
conchathiam@smccd.edu
CONCODORA, Jackie ... 803-323-2206 414 G
concodoraj@winthrop.edu
CONDE, Maria ... 956-882-8201 455 D
maria.conde@utrgv.edu
CONDON, Eileen ... 314-246-7954 262 C
econdon@webster.edu
CONDON, Jennifer ... 813-974-4141 110 B
jcondon@usf.edu
CONDON, Jennifer, M .. 515-574-1190 166 E
condon@iowacentral.edu
CONDON, John (Sean) . 978-837-5599 216 D
sean.condon@merrimack.edu
CONDON, Katherine ... 850-474-2230 110 E
kcondon@uwf.edu
CONDON, Lisa ... 860-768-4007.. 88 H
lcondon@hartford.edu
CONDON, Steve ... 336-725-8344 339 F
condons@piedmontu.edu
CONDRA, Shawn, M ... 785-539-3571 175 E
scondra@mccks.edu
CONDREAY, Jennifer ... 303-722-5724.. 80 L
jcondreay@lincolntech.edu
CONDRON, Lucille ... 814-641-3171 386 H
condrol@juniata.edu
CONDUAH, Dorothy ... 608-243-4746 499 H
dconduah@madisoncollege.edu
CONE, Angela, W ... 334-420-4216.... 3 H
acone@trenholmstate.edu

CONE, Christopher 816-322-0110 250 K
CONE, Diana 912-478-5258 119 C dcone@georgiasouthern.edu
CONE, Janet, R 828-251-6922 342 C jcone@unca.edu
CONEAL, Wanda, B 919-516-4116 340 C wbconeal@st-aug.edu
CONEGLIO, Rebecca 330-490-7190 364 B rconeglio@walsh.edu
CONEJO, Mauricio 787-725-8120 507 N mconejo0014@eap.edu
CONELLI, Maria, A 718-951-3180 293 C mconelli@brooklyn.cuny.edu
CONEWAY, Raydor 478-275-6589 122 H rconeway@oftc.edu
CONEWAY, Raydor 478-553-2065 122 G rconeway@oftc.edu
CONEY, Kareem 305-626-3108 99 D kconey@fmuniv.edu
CONFER, Chris 864-644-5142 412 E cconfer@swu.edu
CONGDON, Bruce 206-281-2508 484 D bcongdon@spu.edu
CONGDON, Marybeth 203-432-5471 89 D marybeth.congdon@yale.edu
CONGDON, Thomas, J 414-410-4002 492 D tjcongdon@stritch.edu
CONGELIO, Paula 304-293-7304 491 C pacongelio@mail.wvu.edu
CONGER, Heather 609-894-9311 281 C hconger@rcbc.edu
CONGER, Kristy, M 865-539-7333 425 F kmconger@pstcc.edu
CONGLETON, Dawn, L 434-223-6203 468 A dcongleton@hsc.edu
CONGLETON, Jonell 973-877-3068 277 I jcongleton@essex.edu
CONGLETON, Randi 412-365-2499 381 C r.congleton@chatham.edu
CONGLETON, Yasemin 859-246-6487 180 K yasemin.congleton@kctcs.edu
CONGRESSI, Karyn 386-752-1822 99 A karyn.congressi@fgc.edu
CONIGLIO, Michael 706-880-8184 121 A mconiglio@lagrange.edu
CONINE, Chris 423-614-8102 420 J cconine@leeuniversity.edu
CONINE, Darren 978-837-5154 216 D conine@merrimack.edu
CONINE, Darren 978-837-5154 216 D conined@merrimack.edu
CONINE, Frances 318-357-5285 192 C coninef@nsula.edu
CONINE, Richard 518-832-7791 320 D coniner@sunyacc.edu
CONKLIN, Barbara 252-399-6445 326 M baconklin@barton.edu
CONKLIN, Christina 716-488-3023 303 C chrissyconklin@jbc.edu
CONKLIN, David 716-488-3026 303 C davidconklin@jbc.edu
CONKLIN, Eileen, G 915-831-4432 436 E econklin@epcc.edu
CONKLIN, Elizabeth 860-486-2943 88 E elizabeth.conklin@uconn.edu
CONKLIN, Kathleen 517-371-5140 233 A conklink@cooley.edu
CONKLIN, Lara, L 217-443-8798 135 H lconklin@dacc.edu
CONKLIN, Margaret 212-355-1501 292 J mconklin@christies.edu
CONKLIN, Peter 603-513-1384 274 H peter.conklin@granite.edu
CONKLIN, Robin 845-574-4484 313 C rconklin@sunyrockland.edu
CONKLIN, Sandra 607-729-1581 298 C sconklin@davisny.edu
CONKLIN, Shane, R 413-545-1581 211 D sconklin@admin.umass.edu
CONKLIN, Shannon 215-204-7981 399 F shannon.conklin@temple.edu
CONLEY, Carlotta 847-543-2345 135 B chd340@clcillinois.edu
CONLEY, Cary 270-831-9610 181 D cary.conley@kctcs.edu
CONLEY, Cherisse 614-837-4088 364 A conleyc@valorcollege.edu
CONLEY, Cindy 501-374-6305 21 A cindy.conley@shortercollege.edu
CONLEY, Dennis 618-395-7777 138 I conleyd@iecc.edu
CONLEY, Jeremy, D 515-574-1086 166 E conley@iowacentral.edu
CONLEY, Jerome 513-529-2800 356 E conleyj@miamioh.edu
CONLEY, Katharine 757-221-2470 466 C kconley@wm.edu
CONLEY, Kelli 256-840-4101 3 F kelli.conley@snead.edu
CONLEY, Laura, H 330-972-5793 362 B lhc1@uakron.edu
CONLEY, Maria 978-934-2383 211 G maria_conley@uml.edu
CONLEY, Mark 206-543-4211 485 F mconley@uw.edu
CONLEY, Marsha, A 717-866-5775 383 H mconley@evangelical.edu
CONLEY, MeShawn 405-974-5944 370 K mconley@uco.edu
CONLEY, Nikki 800-505-4338 347 J
CONLEY, Tony 870-759-4166 23 J tconley@williamsbu.edu
CONLEY, Valerie 719-255-4119 83 B vconley@uccs.edu
CONLEY, William, T 570-577-1618 379 F bill.conley@bucknell.edu
CONLEY-HOLT, Jaime 618-453-2391 149 E jbcholt@siu.edu
CONLIN, Katryn 651-385-6364 239 A kconlin@southeastmn.edu
CONLIN, Pam 419-372-7678 348 H pconlin@bgsu.edu
CONLOGUE, Jon 413-572-5572 213 D jconlogue@westfield.ma.edu
CONLOGUE, Jon 203-576-4226 88 D jconlogu@bridgeport.edu
CONLON, Cindy, H 256-765-4293 8 E chconlon@una.edu
CONLON, Jim 609-896-5188 281 B jconlon@rider.edu
CONLON, Maureen 732-255-0400 280 A mconlon@ocean.edu
CONN, Brian 423-614-8621 420 J bconn@leeuniversity.edu
CONN, C. Paul 423-614-8600 420 J pconn@leeuniversity.edu
CONN, Cameron, A 901-572-2538 418 E cameron.conn@bchs.edu
CONN, Melinda 314-434-4044 252 B melinda.conn@covenantseminary.edu
CONN, Michael 618-395-7777 138 I connm@iecc.edu
CONN, Michael 740-283-6319 353 B mconn@franciscan.edu
CONN, Robert 618-262-8641 139 A connr@iecc.edu
CONN, Steve 903-233-4431 439 E steveconn@letu.edu
CONNAGHAN, Stephen 202-319-5055 91 B connaghan@cua.edu
CONNAUGHTON, David, M 409-747-2606 456 F dmconnau@utmb.edu
CONNEELY, James 706-864-1818 126 A james.conneely@ung.edu
CONNELL, Dan, J 606-783-2612 183 F d.connell@moreheadstate.edu
CONNELL, Gregory 321-674-8095 99 B gconnell@fit.edu
CONNELL, Jack 617-745-3000 208 G
CONNELL, James 440-646-8120 363 G jconnell@ursuline.edu
CONNELL, Jason, R 267-359-5780 383 B jason.r.connell@drexel.edu
CONNELL, Joseph 201-684-7462 280 H jconnell@ramapo.edu
CONNELL, Matthew, J 570-688-2466 391 F mconnell@northampton.edu
CONNELL, Steven 215-972-2027 393 D sconnell@pafa.edu
CONNELLY, Christian 914-888-5226 306 F cconnelly@mercy.edu
CONNELLY, David 801-863-8642 461 A dconnelly@uvu.edu
CONNELLY, Judy 815-280-2265 140 B jconnell@jjc.edu
CONNELLY, Katherine 212-875-4515 290 F kconnelly@bankstreet.edu
CONNELLY, Krysti, H 618-537-6861 143 B khconnelly@mckendree.edu
CONNELLY, Pamela, W 412-624-4685 401 B pwc4@pitt.edu
CONNELLY, Patrick 802-258-9238 462 E pconnelly@marlboro.edu
CONNELLY, Shannon 406-338-5441 263 B shannon@bfcc.edu
CONNELLY-WEIDA, Cecelia, A 610-799-1630 388 I cconnellyweida@lccc.edu
CONNELY, Anne 610-398-5300 389 A aconnely@lincolntech.edu
CONNELY, Kristen 425-564-2388 478 F kristen.connely@bellevuecollege.edu
CONNER, Arabie 785-242-5200 176 D arabie.conner@ottawa.edu
CONNER, Barbara 207-741-5571 195 A bconner@smccme.edu
CONNER, Cassandra 228-702-1829 249 H cconner@wmcarey.edu
CONNER, Courtney, L 276-619-4317 473 B clc5z@virginia.edu
CONNER, Cynthia 713-221-8614 453 B connerc@uhd.edu
CONNER, Deborah 843-349-2300 408 C dconner@coastal.edu
CONNER, Dyonne 601-979-2021 246 E 0364mgr@follett.com
CONNER, III, Frank, M 202-662-5986 473 A frank.conner@virginia.edu
CONNER, Jamelle 727-341-3344 106 E conner.jamelle@spcollege.edu
CONNER, Jean 218-726-6202 243 F jconner@d.umn.edu
CONNER, Kristin 707-864-7000 64 C kristin.conner@solano.edu
CONNER, Lori 276-656-0286 475 D lconner@patrickhenry.edu
CONNER, Marc 540-458-8702 478 A connerm@wlu.edu
CONNER, Sheila 304-384-5385 490 A conners@concord.edu
CONNER, Shelly 559-675-4800 66 F shelly.conner@scccd.edu
CONNER, Steven 850-644-2145 109 C sconner@fsu.edu
CONNER-KERR, Teresa 706-867-4507 126 A teresa.conner-kerr@ung.edu
CONNERAT, Carolyn, K 512-475-9223 455 A cconnerat@austin.utexas.edu
CONNERLEY, Gail 800-287-8822 153 D gailc@bethanyseminary.edu
CONNERY, Elizabeth, A 570-348-6200 389 G connery@marywood.edu
CONNICK, George 212-757-1190 290 B gconnick@aami.edu
CONNIFF, Brian, P 570-941-7560 401 H brian.conniff@scranton.edu
CONNIRY, Charles 503-517-1876 378 A cconniry@westernseminary.edu
CONNOLLY, Adam 843-857-4126 408 D aconnolly@coker.edu
CONNOLLY, Ann Marie 313-883-8500 229 K connolly.annmarie@shms.edu
CONNOLLY, Barbara 845-569-3202 307 J barbara.connolly@msmc.edu
CONNOLLY, Daniel 515-271-2872 165 A daniel.connolly@drake.edu
CONNOLLY, Derry 858-653-6740 46 I dconnolly@jpcatholic.com
CONNOLLY, James 203-332-5090 85 F jconnolly@hcc.commnet.edu
CONNOLLY, Jon, H 973-300-2120 283 E jconnolly@sussex.edu
CONNOLLY, Justin 256-766-6610 5 F jconnolly@hcu.edu
CONNOLLY, Laura 970-351-2707 83 E laura.connolly@unco.edu
CONNOLLY, Lidy 858-653-6740 46 I lconnolly@jpcatholic.com
CONNOLLY, Mary 314-977-7121 259 H mary.connolly@slu.edu
CONNOLLY, Melissa, A 516-463-4160 302 B melissa.a.connolly@hofstra.edu
CONNOLLY, Michael 320-363-3512 243 A mconnolly@csbsju.edu
CONNOLLY, Michael 320-363-2737 243 A mconnolly@csbsju.edu
CONNOLLY, Patricia, A 412-536-1243 387 B patricia.connolly@laroche.edu
CONNOLLY, Robert 404-894-2500 118 F robert.connolly@police.gatech.edu
CONNOLLY, Shawn, M 973-655-5427 279 C connollys@mail.montclair.edu
CONNOLLY, Tara 515-964-6447 164 C tkconnolly@dmacc.edu
CONNOR, Francis, P 260-399-7700 161 D fconnor@sf.edu
CONNOR, James 510-592-9688 54 C jim.connor@npu.edu
CONNOR, Joanne, M 856-256-4102 281 E connorj@rowan.edu
CONNOR, Kate 773-907-4452 134 C kconnor@ccc.edu
CONNOR, Lorri, B 704-403-3207 327 D lorri.connor@carolinashealthcare.org
CONNOR, Pat 812-855-0973 156 B connorp@indiana.edu
CONNOR, Pat 812-855-0973 156 A connorp@indiana.edu
CONNOR, Rianne 707-476-4187 39 D rianne-connor@redwoods.edu
CONNOR, Roger 203-837-9301 85 B connorr@wcsu.edu
CONNOR, Rosie 435-283-7160 461 C rosie.connor@snow.edu
CONNOR, Shane 216-687-2084 351 B s.c.connor@csuohio.edu
CONNOR, Terry, D 859-344-3308 184 F connort@thomasmore.edu
CONNORS, Brian 516-323-3504 307 F bconnors@molloy.edu
CONNORS, Chalese 940-898-2378 451 F cconnors@twu.edu
CONNORS, Cheryl, C 401-739-5000 405 A cconnors@neit.edu
CONNORS, John 215-596-8973 401 G j.connors@usciences.edu
CONNORS, Kerry 901-843-3512 423 J connorsk@rhodes.edu
CONNORS, Nancy 631-420-2142 321 B nancy.connors@farmingdale.edu
CONNORS, Natalie 219-989-2600 159 G natalie.connors@pnw.edu
CONNUCK, Wendy 215-489-2921 382 D wendy.connuck@delval.edu
CONOLEY, Jane, C 562-985-4121 31 F csulb-president@csulb.edu
CONOVER, David 541-346-2090 377 D dconover@uoregon.edu
CONOVER, David 419-267-1462 358 A dconover@northweststate.edu
CONOVER, Dustin 307-382-1644 502 I dconover@westernwyoming.edu
CONOVER, Melanie 801-524-1927 459 F conoverm@ldsbc.edu
CONOVER, Ross 301-696-3566 199 B conover@hood.edu
CONQUE, Chasse, S 501-569-3167 22 B csconque@ualr.edu
CONRAD, Ann 216-987-2464 351 G ann.conrad@tri-c.edu
CONRAD, Deb 775-445-4236 271 G deb.conrad@wnc.edu
CONRAD, Eric, W 405-325-3917 371 B eric.conrad@ou.edu
CONRAD, Jacqueline 617-873-0621 207 F jacqueline.conrad@cambridgecollege.edu
CONRAD, James, A 509-535-4051 144 B jim.conrad@moody.edu
CONRAD, Jeffrey 617-236-8831 209 D jconrad@fisher.edu
CONRAD, Jon, B 610-861-1527 391 A conradj@moravian.edu
CONRAD, Karen 518-861-2529 305 K kconrad@mariacollege.edu
CONRAD, Kari, M 570-577-1217 379 F kari.conrad@bucknell.edu
CONRAD, Kelley 231-777-0321 228 D kelley.conrad@muskegoncc.edu
CONRAD, Kristin 434-582-7602 468 H klconrad@liberty.edu
CONRAD, Lara 614-251-4718 358 G conradl@ohiodominican.edu
CONRAD, Rhonda 641-683-5115 166 C rhonda.conrad@indianhills.edu
CONRAD, Scott 707-524-1553 62 F sconrad@santarosa.edu
CONRAD, Sonya 484-664-3126 391 C sonyaconrad@muhlenberg.edu
CONRAD WEISMAN, Sarah 315-312-3557 319 B sarah.weisman@oswego.edu
CONRADSEN, Susan 706-236-5494 115 B sconradsen@berry.edu
CONREY, Meredith 936-294-3602 450 C meredithconrey@shsu.edu
CONROE, Nicole 716-829-7645 298 F conroen@dyc.edu
CONROY, Kevin 802-224-3016 463 H kevin.conroy@vsc.edu
CONROY, Nina 646-313-8000 295 E nina.conroy@guttman.cuny.edu

CONROY, Shelley, F ..... 214-820-3361 431 J shelley_conroy@baylor.edu
CONROY, Spencer ..... 713-525-6960 454 H conroysc@stthom.edu
CONSELYEA, Mark, E .... 614-293-2562 358 I conselyea.1@osu.edu
CONSIDINE-FONTES, Lisa, M ..... 401-825-2444 404 H lfontes@ccri.edu
CONSOLAZIO, Beth Anne ..... 386-822-7151 111 A bconsolazio@stetson.edu
CONSOLVO, Justin ..... 843-953-5600 407 F consolvoj1@citadel.edu
CONSTABLE, Jean ..... 830-372-8090 449 B jconstable@tlu.edu
CONSTABLE, Peter ..... 217-333-2760 151 D constabl@illinois.edu
CONSTANCE, Eric, F ..... 315-786-2252 303 F econstance@sunyjefferson.edu
CONSTANT, Kristin, P ... 515-294-3337 162 I constant@iastate.edu
CONSTANTINE, Christopher ..... 870-508-6180.. 18 A cconstantine@asumh.edu
CONSTANTINE, OSB, Cyprian, G ..... 724-805-2332 398 F cyprian.constantine@stvincent.edu
CONSTANTINEAU RIES, Tressa ..... 303-273-3005.. 78 I tries@mines.edu
CONSTANTINI, Imad ..... 512-223-1200 431 A imad.constantini@austincc.edu
CONSTANTINO, John ..... 808-245-8245 129 C johncons@hawaii.edu
CONSTANTINO, Patricia 617-745-3724 208 G patricia.constantino@enc.edu
CONSTANTINO, Rocco .. 805-965-0581.. 62 C rfconstantino@sbcc.edu
CONSTANTINOU, Constantia ..... 215-898-7091 400 K cc1@upenn.edu
CONSTON, Marcia ..... 704-330-6647 333 D marcia.conston@cpcc.edu
CONTARDI, Heather ..... 570-558-1818 384 C hcontardi@fortisinstitute.edu
CONTARINO, Sue ..... 847-925-6200 137 H scontari@harpercollege.edu
CONTE, Andrew ..... 412-392-8055 397 A aconte@pointpark.edu
CONTE, John ..... 214-637-3530 457 I jconte@wadecollege.edu
CONTEH, Alpha ..... 212-961-3370 290 F aconteh@bankstreet.edu
CONTINO-CONNER, Cheryl ..... 828-339-4245 338 B cheryl@southwesterncc.edu
CONTOMANOLIS, Laurel ..... 585-275-3166 323 J laurel.contomanolis@rochester.edu
CONTOMANOLIS, Manny ..... 617-373-3440 217 F
CONTRERAS, Eduardo, R ..... 503-943-8266 377 E contrera@up.edu
CONTRERAS, Gilbert ..... 714-992-7074.. 53 L gcontreras@fullcoll.edu
CONTRERAS, Lisa ..... 312-935-6620 147 D lcontreras@robertmorris.edu
CONTRERAS, Lorraine ... 787-753-6000 508 D
CONTRERAS, Maribel .... 787-746-1400 508 B mcontreras@huertas.edu
CONTRERAS, Raquel, J . 864-656-2451 408 A rcontre@clemson.edu
CONTRERAS, Rosalie .... 212-799-5000 303 H
CONTRERAS, JR., Sebastian ..... 847-635-1756 145 G scontrer@oakton.edu
CONTRERAS-TANORI, Maria ..... 650-949-6163.. 43 C contrerastanorimaria@fhda.edu
CONTRERAS-TANORI, Maria ..... 650-949-6166.. 43 B contrerastanorimaria@fhda.edu
CONVERSE, Sharon, K .. 248-341-2154 229 A skconver@oaklandcc.edu
CONVERSINO, Mark, J .. 334-953-5613 503 B
CONWAY, Andrew ..... 909-607-9406.. 37 D andrew.conway@cgu.edu
CONWAY, Francine ..... 848-445-2325 282 A francine.conway@gsapp.rutgers.edu
CONWAY, Heidi ..... 443-997-8113 199 D heidiconway@jhu.edu
CONWAY, John ..... 601-974-1138 247 B john.conway@millsaps.edu
CONWAY, Karen ..... 901-321-3536 419 C kconway@cbu.edu
CONWAY, Katie ..... 212-678-6625 322 G conway@tc.edu
CONWAY, Morri ..... 402-878-2380 267 E mconway@littlepriest.edu
CONWAY, Pete ..... 701-255-3285 347 B pconway@uttc.edu
CONWAY, Sharon ..... 301-891-4005 204 C sconway@wau.edu
CONWAY-TURNER, Katherine, S ..... 716-878-4101 318 C conwayks@buffalostate.edu
CONYERS, Lance ..... 270-831-9632 181 D lance.conyers@kctcs.edu
CONYERS, Rhyan, M ..... 859-233-8500 184 G rconyers@transy.edu
CONZATTI, Maria, P ..... 516-572-7600 308 A maria.conzatti@ncc.edu
CONZELMAN, Karen ..... 623-845-3612.. 13 C karen.ann.conzelman@gccaz.edu
COOK, Aaron ..... 303-546-5284.. 81 B acook@naropa.edu
COOK, Aaron ..... 828-694-1845 332 E
COOK, Alicia ..... 973-748-9000 276 A alicia_cook@bloomfield.edu
COOK, Allen, P ..... 203-576-4206.. 88 D acook@bridgeport.edu
COOK, Amber ..... 814-871-7421 384 E cook069@gannon.edu
COOK, Amy ..... 904-826-8665.. 98 E acook@flagler.edu
COOK, Andrea, P ..... 503-517-1246 377 G acook@warnerpacific.edu
COOK, Angela ..... 336-734-7618 334 E acook@forsythtech.edu
COOK, Barbara Jo ..... 770-467-6038 124 G barbarajo.cook@sctech.edu
COOK, Barry ..... 614-825-6255 347 F bcook@aiam.edu
COOK, Bree ..... 626-529-8204.. 55 A breecook@pacificoaks.edu
COOK, Brett ..... 208-496-2710 130 A cookb@byui.edu
COOK, Bruce ..... 386-506-4417.. 97 D bruce.cook@daytonastate.edu
COOK, Cameron ..... 657-278-1982.. 31 E ccook@fullerton.edu
COOK, Carey, W ..... 208-467-8643 131 D cwcook@nnu.edu
COOK, Charles ..... 512-223-7612 431 A charles.cook@austincc.edu
COOK, Chris ..... 806-742-2136 451 B chris.cook@ttu.edu
COOK, Christopher ..... 208-885-6739 131 G chrisco@uidaho.edu
COOK, Cindy ..... 281-283-2595 453 A cookc@uhcl.edu
COOK, Corey ..... 208-426-1368 129 I coreydcook@boisestate.edu
COOK, Craig, A ..... 518-276-3777 312 I cookc5@rpi.edu
COOK, Daniel ..... 856-225-2816 281 G dtcook@camden.rutgers.edu
COOK, Darrell ..... 202-885-3546.. 90 J dcook@american.edu
COOK, David ..... 309-694-8551 138 C dcook@icc.edu
COOK, David ..... 913-897-8400 177 D davidcook@ku.edu
COOK, David ..... 978-762-4000 215 B dcook@northshore.edu
COOK, David ..... 214-333-5117 434 I davidc@dbu.edu
COOK, Debra ..... 918-335-6264 368 G dcook@okwu.edu
COOK, Don ..... 954-201-7538.. 95 H dcook@broward.edu
COOK, Donelda ..... 410-617-5171 199 F dcook@loyola.edu
COOK, Donna, M ..... 401-341-2435 406 A donna.cook@salve.edu
COOK, Douglas ..... 757-352-4331 470 H dougcoo@regent.edu
COOK, Durwood ..... 580-745-2869 369 K dcook@se.edu
COOK, Ed ..... 870-733-6026.. 17 H jecook@asumidsouth.edu
COOK, Edith, L ..... 412-578-6043 380 E elcook@carlow.edu
COOK, Gary ..... 214-333-5130 434 I chancellor@dbu.edu
COOK, Greg ..... 262-472-1918 498 C cookg@uww.edu
COOK, Holly ..... 970-207-4500.. 84 B hollyc@uscareerinstitute.edu
COOK, Holly ..... 970-207-4550.. 80 M hollyc@mckinleycollege.edu
COOK, James ..... 336-734-7311 334 E jcook@forsythtech.edu
COOK, Jamie ..... 207-509-7200 195 H jcook@unity.edu
COOK, Jason, D ..... 254-710-1412 431 J jason_cook@baylor.edu
COOK, Jeff ..... 562-985-8816.. 31 F jeff.cook@csulb.edu
COOK, John, B ..... 413-755-4906 215 F jbcook@stcc.edu
COOK, Karen ..... 410-777-7370 197 C kcook@aacc.edu
COOK, Karen ..... 650-723-2300.. 65 J kcook@stanford.edu
COOK, Kathy ..... 503-883-2408 373 H kcook@linfield.edu
COOK, Kevin ..... 601-984-4100 249 E kcook@umc.edu
COOK, Larry ..... 909-389-3384.. 59 H lcook@craftonhills.edu
COOK, Les ..... 406-496-4129 265 A les@mtech.edu
COOK, Leslee ..... 435-283-7221 461 C leslee.cook@snow.edu
COOK, Linda, J ..... 785-532-6221 174 G ljcook@ksu.edu
COOK, Lisa, R ..... 510-981-2939.. 56 E lrcook@peralta.edu
COOK, Lori ..... 918-495-7708 368 I lcook@oru.edu
COOK, M. Celeste ..... 330-972-5787 362 B mcook@uakron.edu
COOK, Margaret ..... 630-617-3267 136 G cookm@elmhurst.edu
COOK, Melinda ..... 800-567-2344 492 G melcook@menominee.edu
COOK, Melissa ..... 207-801-5610 193 F mcook@coa.edu
COOK, Michelle, G ..... 706-542-0415 125 G mgcook@uga.edu
COOK, Patrick ..... 978-656-3134 214 G
COOK, Phil ..... 423-614-8500 420 J pcook@leeuniversity.edu
COOK, Robert, G ..... 617-627-2546 219 B robert.cook@tufts.edu
COOK, Ron ..... 314-837-6777 258 J rcook@stlchristian.edu
COOK, Rosalie ..... 650-493-4430.. 64 A rosalie.cook@sofia.edu
COOK, Royrickers ..... 334-844-5700.... 4 E cookroy@auburn.edu
COOK, Sara ..... 608-796-3382 498 N slcook@viterbo.edu
COOK, Sarah ..... 404-727-8878 117 F sccook@emory.edu
COOK, Scott ..... 270-824-2250 181 G scott.cook@kctcs.edu
COOK, Scott, A ..... 304-336-8137 490 F cookscot@westliberty.edu
COOK, Sharon, L ..... 972-860-7629 435 B scook@dcccd.edu
COOK, Stephen ..... 325-670-1487 437 F stephen.cook@hsutx.edu
COOK, Stephen ..... 585-395-5152 318 B scook@brockport.edu
COOK, Steve ..... 502-895-3411 183 D scook@lpts.edu
COOK, Teresa ..... 803-822-3216 410 G cookta@midlandstech.edu
COOK, Terri ..... 231-591-2504 223 J terricook@ferris.edu
COOK, Terry ..... 410-455-2939 202 E tcook@umbc.edu
COOK, Theodosia, S ..... 603-646-3197 273 E theodosia.s.cook@dartmouth.edu
COOK, Tim ..... 909-599-5433.. 47 K tcook@lifepacific.edu
COOK, Tim ..... 503-594-3000 372 D tim.cook@clackamas.edu
COOK, Tom ..... 304-896-7415 489 E tom.cook@southernwv.edu
COOK, Tracey ..... 404-962-3233 126 F tracey.cook@usg.edu
COOK, Tracy, M ..... 601-877-6385 244 H tmcook@alcorn.edu
COOK, Vicki ..... 231-995-1144 228 G vcook@nmc.edu
COOK-BENJAMIN, Lorie ..... 402-466-4774 267 A lorie.cookbenjamin@doane.edu
COOK-NOBLES, Robin ... 784-283-2839 219 D rcooknob@wellesley.edu
COOKE, Connie, F ..... 716-878-4902 318 C cookecf@buffalostate.edu
COOKE, Harry ..... 704-922-6355 334 F cooke.harry@gaston.edu
COOKE, Ilene ..... 845-437-7200 324 C ilcooke@vassar.edu
COOKE, Kristen ..... 501-977-2033.. 23 A cookekristen@uaccm.edu
COOKE, Paul ..... 706-769-1472 114 E pcooke@acmin.org
COOKE, Peggy, S ..... 248-370-2197 229 G cooke@oakland.edu
COOKE, Sandy, P ..... 434-223-6340 468 A scooke@hsc.edu
COOKE, Sean ..... 253-840-8472 483 D scooke@pierce.ctc.edu
COOKE, Shonny ..... 540-857-6325 476 D scooke@virginiawestern.edu
COOKE, Sunita ..... 760-757-2121.. 52 E scooke@miracosta.edu
COOKMAN, John ..... 972-825-4659 445 A jcookman@sagu.edu
COOKS, Kendra ..... 765-361-6485 162 E cooksk@wabash.edu
COOKS, Quentin ..... 706-771-4000 114 J gcooks@augustatech.edu
COOKSEY, Gaye, M ..... 469-365-1808 433 M gcooksey@collin.edu
COOKSEY, Scott ..... 801-863-8568 461 A scott.cooksey@uvu.edu
COOLEY, Francis ..... 203-287-3029.. 87 E paierdean@snet.net
COOLEY, Lisa, K ..... 336-322-2106 336 G lisa.cooley@piedmontcc.edu
COOLEY, Lynn ..... 203-432-2733.. 89 D lynn.cooley@yale.edu
COOLEY, Marianne, B ... 784-283-3344 219 D mcooley@wellesley.edu
COOLEY, Maurice, R ..... 304-696-5430 490 D cooley@marshall.edu
COOLEY, Nanette ..... 410-810-8505 204 D ncooley2@washcoll.edu
COOLEY, Stacey ..... 505-224-4000 285 J scooley3@cnm.edu
COOLEY, Thomas ..... 412-268-4731 380 F tkcooley@andrew.cmu.edu
COOMAR, Parmeshwar . 734-384-4209 227 G pcoomar@monroeccc.edu
COOMBS, Gary, F ..... 619-201-8989.. 65 A
COOMBS, Natalie ..... 718-758-8128 293 C nataliec@brooklyn.cuny.edu
COOMBS, Robert ..... 207-741-5569 195 A rcoombs@smccme.edu
COOMER, Marc ..... 509-574-4855 487 A mcoomer@yvcc.edu
COOMER, Marc ..... 509-882-7049 487 A mcoomer@yvcc.edu
COOMES, Kerrie ..... 620-431-2820 175 H kcoomes@neosho.edu
COON, David, W ..... 415-485-9502.. 39 C dcoon@marin.edu
COON, Karla, J ..... 217-283-4170 135 H kcoon@dacc.edu
COON, Katelynn ..... 906-635-2650 226 E kcoon2@lssu.edu
COON, Lynda ..... 479-575-2089.. 21 G llcoon@uark.edu
COON, Omayra ..... 910-221-2224 329 B
COON, Sharon ..... 216-987-4863 351 G sharon.coon@tri-c.edu
COON, Thomas ..... 405-744-2474 368 B thomas.coon@okstate.edu
COONER, Elizabeth ..... 908-527-7213 284 C elizabeth.cooner@ucc.edu
COONEY, Anita ..... 718-636-3630 311 J acooney@pratt.edu
COONEY, J.P ..... 330-494-6170 361 F jcooney@starkstate.edu
COONEY, Marcia, J ..... 570-577-1631 379 F marcia.cooney@bucknell.edu
COONEY, Terry ..... 410-704-2129 204 A tcooney@towson.edu
COONEY-CONNOR, Erica ..... 315-781-3103 302 A econnor@hws.edu

CORBETT, Lisa .... 607-431-4162 301 D corbettl@hartwick.edu
CORBETT, Marcus .... 803-793-5289 409 C corbettm@denmarktech.edu
CORBETT, Martin .... 315-781-3656 302 A corbett@hws.edu
CORBETT, Mickey .... 432-837-8059 450 D mcorbett@sulross.edu
CORBETT, Patricia .... 603-428-2215 273 H pcorbett@nec.edu
CORBETT, Toya .... 919-530-7466 342 A tcorbet7@nccu.edu
CORBIN, Edith .... 856-222-9311 281 C ecorbin@rcbc.edu
CORBIN, Kirsten .... 916-484-8363.. 50 F corbink@arc.losrios.edu
CORBIN, Michael .... 318-257-3066 191 F mcorbin@latech.edu
CORBIN, Russ .... 315-498-2831 311 B corbinr@sunyocc.edu
CORBIN, Sue .... 216-373-5429 358 B scorbin@ndc.edu
CORBIN, Ty .... 804-523-5726 474 H tcorbin@reynolds.edu
CORBITT, Sandra, K ..... 540-338-1776 470 A slife@phc.edu
CORBITT, Timothy .... 315-229-5392 314 F tcorbitt@stlawu.edu
CORBITT, Zach .... 864-596-9215 409 B zach.corbitt@converse.edu
CORBY, John, T .... 330-972-7345 362 B jcorby@uakron.edu
CORCORAN, D.J .... 978-934-3328 211 G dj_corcoran@uml.edu
CORCORAN, Heather, A 314-935-6525 262 A hcorcoran@wustl.edu
CORCORAN, Janet .... 718-482-5010 294 F jcorcoran@lagcc.cuny.edu
CORCORAN, Jeanne ...... 978-542-7015 213 C eanne.corcoran@salemstate.edu
CORCORAN, Jerry, M ... 815-224-0404 139 F jerry_corcoran@ivcc.edu
CORCORAN, Kevin, J .... 248-370-2140 229 G corcoran@oakland.edu
CORCORAN, Paul .... 507-389-2267 239 C paul.corcoran@mnsu.edu
CORCORAN, Ryan .... 262-547-1211 492 E rcorcora@carrollu.edu
CORCORAN, Thomas .... 315-294-8557 292 E tcorcoran@cayuga-cc.edu
CORCORAN, Tim .... 619-644-7572.. 44 G tim.corcoran@gcccd.edu
CORCORAN, William ..... 201-612-5234 275 H wcorcoran@bergen.edu
CORCORAN, William, M .... 570-208-5846 387 A wmcorcor@kings.edu
CORDANO, Roberta (Bobbi) .... 202-651-5005.. 91 E roberta.cordano@gallaudet.edu
CORDEIRO, Aaron .... 541-485-1780 374 F aaroncordeiro@newhope.edu
CORDEIRO, Uilani .... 541-485-1780 374 F uilanicordeiro@newhope.edu
CORDEIRO, Wayne .... 541-485-1780 374 F waynecordeiro@newhope.edu
CORDEIRO, Wayne .... 808-853-1040 128 C waynecordeiro@pacrim.edu
CORDEIRO, William ...... 916-278-6578.. 32 E william.cordeiro@csus.edu
CORDELL, Janice, K ..... 563-387-1018 167 E cordellj@luther.edu
CORDELL, Michelle .... 479-619-4361.. 20 D mcordell@nwacc.edu
CORDELL, Peggy .... 706-295-6959 119 A pcordell@gntc.edu
CORDELL, Penny .... 706-272-4498 117 C pcordell@daltonstate.edu
CORDELL, Stacey .... 318-342-1982 192 F ulm@campuscornerinc.com
CORDERO, Edwin .... 864-578-8770 412 B ecordero@sherman.edu
CORDERO, Irma, L .... 787-740-1611 512 C irma.cordero@uccaribe.edu
CORDERO, Javier .... 575-646-3553 287 B javierco@nmsu.edu
CORDERO, Zain .... 787-882-2065 511 D mis@unitecpr.net
CORDERO-RIVERA, Marisol .... 787-993-8874 513 B marisol.cordero@upr.edu
CORDERY, Simon .... 706-864-1819 126 A simon.cordery@ung.edu
CORDES, Amanda .... 620-450-2219 176 G amandac@prattcc.edu
CORDES, Mark .... 815-753-0380 145 C mcordes@niu.edu
CORDIA, Judith .... 775-445-3295 271 G judith.cordia@wnc.edu
CORDISCO, Shelli .... 607-778-5222 318 A cordiscosl@sunybroome.edu
CORDLE, David .... 620-341-5171 172 L dcordle@emporia.edu
CORDLE, Emma .... 706-236-2267 115 B ecordle@berry.edu
CORDLE, Robbie, L .... 301-687-4403 203 E rcordle@frostburg.edu
CORDOBA-VELASQUEZ, Natalia .... 619-388-6723.. 60 B ncordoba@sdccd.edu
CORDOVA, Adrian .... 623-245-4600.. 16 E acordova@uti.edu
CORDOVA, Andrea .... 719-255-3056.. 83 B andrea.cordova@uccs.edu
CORDOVA, David .... 773-878-4014 148 D dcordova@staugustine.edu
CORDOVA, Ferando ...... 318-342-1537 192 F fcordova@ulm.edu
CORDOVA, Francie .... 505-277-5251 288 G fcordova3@unm.edu
CORDOVA, John .... 661-362-5586.. 38 H john.cordova@canyons.edu
CORDOVA, Jose, A .... 787-704-1020 507 K jcordova@ediccollege.edu
CORDOVA, Kelly .... 757-455-5709 477 F kcordova@vwu.edu
CORDOVA, Lonita .... 209-381-6410.. 51 G lonita.cordova@mccd.edu
CORDOVA, Lucy .... 714-850-4800.. 67 A cordova@taftu.edu
CORDOVA, Matthew ...... 505-454-2559 286 D mcordova@luna.edu
CORDOVA, Mitch .... 239-590-1522 108 K mcordova@fgcu.edu
CORDOVA, Ryan .... 505-747-2288 287 G rcordova@nnmc.edu
CORDOVA-FIGUEROA, Ubaldo, M .... 787-765-5955 512 G ubaldom.cordova@upr.edu
CORDOVA QUERO, Hugo .... 510-549-4705.. 66 B hquero@sksm.edu
CORDOVES, Jose .... 787-284-1912 509 E jcordoves@ponce.inter.edu
CORDRAY, Mary .... 843-208-8139 413 E marymac@uscb.edu
CORDRAY, Mitch .... 417-455-5712 252 D mitchcordray@crowder.edu
CORDREY, Terri .... 605-882-5284 415 F terri.cordrey@lakeareatech.edu
CORDULACK, Tricia ...... 217-875-7211 147 C tcordulack@richland.edu
COREIL, Paul .... 318-473-6444 188 J chancellor@lsua.edu
CORENO, Kendra .... 440-449-5368 363 G kcoreno@follett.com
COREY, Barry, H .... 562-903-4701.. 27 C president@biola.edu
COREY, Frederick, C ..... 602-496-0624.. 10 I frederick.corey@asu.edu
COREY, George, A .... 413-577-5211 211 D gcorey@uhs.umass.edu
COREY, Jane .... 304-637-1344 487 I coreym@dewv.edu
COREY, Shannon .... 404-413-1800 119 E scorey@gsu.edu
COREY, Steven .... 312-369-7844 135 E scorey@colum.edu
COREY, Steven, M .... 269-749-7642 229 H scorey@olivetcollege.edu
CORIA, Elizabeth .... 415-239-3382.. 37 A ecoria@ccsf.edu
CORIALE, Mary .... 585-785-1442 300 B mary.coriale@flcc.edu
CORINO, Mark, A .... 973-618-3412 276 D mcorino@caldwell.edu
CORK, Mark .... 208-467-8773 131 D mcork@nnu.edu
CORKILL, Jim, R .... 805-893-5882.. 70 A jim.corkill@bfs.ucsb.edu
CORKRAN, Ken .... 508-541-1700 208 F kcorkran@dean.edu
CORKRUM, Dalia, L ...... 509-527-5193 486 H corkrum@whitman.edu
CORKUM, David .... 617-552-4500 207 B david.corkum@bc.edu
CORLE, Trish .... 814-262-3841 393 H tcorle@pennhighlands.edu
CORLEW, Amy .... 931-221-6131 418 D corlewa@apsu.edu
CORLEY, David .... 530-257-6181.. 47 F dcorley@lassencollege.edu
CORLEY, Scott .... 615-460-5547 418 F scott.corley@belmont.edu
CORLEY, Stacey .... 941-359-7674 105 K scorley@ringling.edu
CORLEY, Thomas .... 785-242-5200 176 D thomas.corley@ottawa.edu
CORLISS, Bruce .... 401-874-6222 406 B bcorliss@uri.edu
CORLISS, Carolyn .... 251-442-2276.... 8 C ccorliss@umobile.edu
CORLISS, Cindy .... 603-622-9941 272 L 0970mgr@follett.com
CORLISS, Elizabeth .... 603-271-6484 273 B ecorliss@ccsnh.edu
CORMACK, Jody .... 562-985-4128.. 31 F jody.cormack@csulb.edu
CORMICAN, Beverly ...... 864-242-5100 407 B
CORMIER, Barbara .... 603-358-2355 275 A bhamel@keene.edu
CORMIER, Cathy .... 318-473-6459 188 J ccormier@lsua.edu
CORMIER, Craig, C .... 207-768-3425 196 E craig.cormier@maine.edu
CORMIER, Curtis .... 781-239-2602 214 E ccormier@massbay.edu
CORMIER, Garth .... 207-941-7626 194 A cormierg@husson.edu
CORMIER, Linda .... 213-621-2200.. 38 G
CORMIER, Marissa .... 410-857-2223 200 B mcormier@mcdaniel.edu
CORMIER, Matthew .... 508-362-2131 214 B mcormier@capecod.edu
CORN, Melanie .... 614-222-3220 351 D mcorn@ccad.edu
CORNACCHIA, Eugene, J .... 201-761-6010 282 I ecornacchia@saintpeters.edu
CORNEA, Sheila .... 423-614-8630 420 J scornea@leeuniversity.edu
CORNEJO, Silvia .... 619-216-6755.. 65 F scornejo@swccd.edu
CORNELISON, Steve ...... 731-424-3520 425 B scornelison@jscc.edu
CORNELIUS, Adrian, R .. 301-314-8249 202 C adrianc@umd.edu
CORNELIUS, Barbara ..... 903-813-2536 430 N bcornelius@austincollege.edu
CORNELIUS, Carrie .... 785-832-6659 173 G
CORNELIUS, Katherine .. 615-460-6856 418 F katherine.cornelius@belmont.edu
CORNELIUS, Michael .... 480-423-6573.. 13 H michael.cornelius@scottsdalecc.edu
CORNELIUS, Tim .... 479-619-3117.. 20 D tcornelius@nwacc.edu
CORNELL, Bette .... 757-789-1774 474 F bcornell@es.vccs.edu
CORNELL, Craig .... 740-597-3280 359 G cornellc@ohio.edu
CORNELL, Dona, H .... 832-842-0949 452 E dhcornell@uh.edu
CORNELL, Dona, H .... 713-743-0949 452 F dhcornell@uh.edu
CORNELL, Ken .... 425-889-7800 482 F ken.cornell@northwestu.edu
CORNELL, Thomas .... 314-968-7087 262 C thomascornell28@webster.edu
CORNELL-SCOTT, Andrea .... 540-887-7270 469 B ascott@marybaldwin.edu
CORNELL-SWANSON, LaVonne .... 320-308-4785 240 H lcornellswanson@stcloudstate.edu
CORNELY, Joe .... 513-244-4955 357 A joseph.cornely@msjl.edu
CORNER, Kimberly .... 402-465-7783 268 H kcorner@nebrwesleyan.edu
CORNER, William, T ..... 616-526-6451 222 A wtc2@calvin.edu
CORNERO, Robert .... 732-571-3424 279 B rcornero@monmouth.edu
CORNETT, Doug .... 859-622-7286 180 B doug.cornett@eku.edu
CORNETT, Jeff .... 606-368-6134 178 D jdcornett@alc.edu
CORNETT, Jessalynn ...... 502-863-8302 178 K jessalyn.cornett@bsk.edu
CORNETT, Scott .... 606-368-6120 178 D scottcornett@alc.edu
CORNETT, Vicki .... 785-227-3380 171 E cornettv@bethanylb.edu
CORNIER, Wilfredo .... 787-841-2000 510 K wcornier@pucpr.edu
CORNILLE, Keith .... 309-268-8106 137 I keith.cornille@heartland.edu
CORNISH, Charles .... 903-927-3253 458 G chcornish@wileyc.edu
CORNISH, Garrick .... 302-736-2436.. 90 G garrick.cornish@wesley.edu
CORNISH, La Jerne ...... 410-337-6210 198 G lcornish@goucher.edu
CORNISH, La Jerne, T .. 607-274-3113 303 B lcornish@ithaca.edu
CORNMAN, Thomas ...... 503-375-7015 373 A tcornman@corban.edu
CORNNER, Ryan, M ...... 213-891-2134.. 48 G cornnerm@laccd.edu
CORNOG, Jackie .... 617-588-1364 206 C jcornog@bfit.edu
CORNWELL, Elena .... 402-486-2523 269 F elena.cornwell@ucollege.edu
CORNWELL, Grant, H .... 407-646-2120 105 M president@rollins.edu
CORNWELL, John, M .... 713-348-3227 442 K cornwell@rice.edu
CORNWELL, Julia .... 817-272-2194 454 J cornwell@uta.edu
CORNWELL, Shirley, A .. 937-393-3431 361 B scornwell@sscc.edu
CORONA, Guadalupe .... 619-482-6544.. 65 F gcorona@swccd.edu
CORONA, Jamie, L .... 248-232-4513 229 A jlcorona@oaklandcc.edu
CORONA, Lorena .... 909-652-7459.. 36 A lorena.corona@chaffey.edu
CORONA, Nayeli .... 610-574-6909.. 54 K ncorona@pacificcollege.edu
CORONA, Robert .... 315-464-4238 317 F coronar@upstate.edu
CORONA, Stacie .... 530-898-5103.. 31 A scorona@csuchico.edu
CORONADO, John .... 312-413-1401 151 B jcoronad@uic.edu
CORONADO, Ricardo .... 817-515-5234 445 G ricardo.coronado@tccd.edu
CORONEL, Roberto .... 714-744-7959.. 36 C coronel@chapman.edu
CORP, Cory .... 803-786-3886 408 F bookstore@columbiasc.edu
CORP, Stephanie .... 518-587-2100 321 A stephanie.corp@esc.edu
CORPENING, Brian .... 831-582-3366.. 32 C bcorpening@csumb.edu
CORR, Daniel, P .... 928-344-7500.. 10 J daniel.corr@azwestern.edu
CORR, Jane .... 508-793-2590 208 B jcorr@holycross.edu
CORR, Marianne .... 574-631-6411 161 C mcorr1@nd.edu
CORR, Michael .... 610-861-1365 391 A corrm@moravian.edu
CORRADETTI, Arthur ..... 718-631-6350 295 D acorradetti@qcc.cuny.edu
CORRADO, Colleen .... 610-436-2552 396 A ccorrado@wcupa.edu
CORRAL, Elsa .... 817-272-2101 454 J corral@uta.edu
CORRAL, Nohel .... 562-938-4268.. 48 D ncorral@lbcc.edu
CORREA, Frank .... 714-966-8500.. 73 C fcorrea@ves.edu
CORREA, Omar .... 402-554-2200 270 B ogcorrea@unomaha.edu
CORREA, Sharon .... 787-288-1118 512 A
CORREDERA, Enrique .... 802-656-2005 463 E enrique.corredera@uvm.edu
CORRELL, Christin .... 864-250-8969 410 B christin.correll@gvltec.edu
CORRELL, Jen .... 717-728-2362 381 B jencorrell@centralpenn.edu
CORRELL, Mary .... 610-409-3698 402 A mcorrell@ursinus.edu
CORRELL, Scott .... 701-777-2711 345 C scott.correll@und.edu
CORRELL-HUGHES, Larry .... 386-822-7201 111 A lcorrell-hughes@stetson.edu
CORRIGAN, Boo .... 919-515-2109 342 B ecorrig@ncsu.edu

CORRIGAN, Constance . 215-497-8717 379 G constance.corrigan@bucks.edu
CORRIGAN, Matthew ..... 904-256-7030 101 G mcorrig2@ju.edu
CORRIGAN, Megan .... 417-667-8181 252 A mcorrigan@cottey.edu
CORRIGAN, JR., Robert, F .... 713-798-6392 431 I corrigan@bcm.edu
CORRIGLIANO, Paul ..... 425-235-5555 483 G pcorrigliano@rtc.edu
CORRINGAN, Terrance .. 713-718-7278 437 I terrance.corrigan@hccs.edu
CORRINNE-HARVEY, Janet, K .... 724-925-4091 403 A corrinnej@westmoreland.edu
CORRISS, Mary Jean .... 540-362-6332 468 C corrissmj@hollins.edu
CORRY, David, M .... 434-592-4008 468 H dcorry@liberty.edu
CORRY, Janie .... 864-488-4473 410 E jcorry@limestone.edu
CORRY, Shauna .... 208-885-9301 131 G scorry@uidaho.edu
CORSARO, Louis .... 412-392-6190 397 A lcorsaro@pointpark.edu
CORSELLO, Christine, L 704-403-4336 327 D christine.corsello@carolinashealthcare.org
CORSI, Dan .... 318-345-9250 187 G dcorsi@ladelta.edu
CORSI, Richard .... 503-725-8393 376 A rcorsi@pdx.edu
CORSO, Michael .... 973-720-2202 284 I corsom1@wpunj.edu
CORSO, Phaedra .... 470-578-6354 120 L pcorso@kennesaw.edu
CORSON-RIKERT, Janet, L .... 607-255-3564 297 F jlc18@cornell.edu
CORTÉS, Gloria .... 787-891-0925 508 K gcortes@aguadilla.inter.edu
CORTE, Judith .... 707-638-5824.. 67 F judith.corte@tu.edu
CORTELL, Sabrina .... 619-594-0336.. 33 E scortell@sdsu.edu
CORTES, Chris .... 559-638-0300.. 66 F chris.cortes@reedleycollege.edu
CORTES, Felix .... 787-841-2000 510 K fcortes@pucpr.edu
CORTES, Frances .... 787-878-5475 508 L fcortes@arecibo.inter.edu
CORTES, Gabriel .... 210-924-4338 431 H gabriel.cortes@bua.edu
CORTES, Maria .... 787-738-2161 513 D maria.cortes1@upr.edu
CORTES, Stephanie .... 352-854-2322.. 96 O cortess@cf.edu
CORTES, Tammy .... 831-813-6820 439 G tammy.a.cortes@lonestar.edu
CORTES-HUERTAS, Myrna .... 787-480-2372 507 C mcortes@sanjuanciudadpatria.com
CORTESE, Mike .... 615-460-6328 418 F mike.cortese@belmont.edu
CORTESIO, Cynthia .... 865-354-3000 425 G cortesiocl@roanestate.edu
CORTEZ, Alicia .... 408-864-5338.. 43 C cortezalicia@deanza.edu
CORTEZ, Carrie .... 985-448-7936 187 F carrie.cortez@fletcher.edu
CORTEZ, Christina .... 210-486-2894 429 G ccortez109@alamo.edu
CORTEZ, Dorinna .... 808-934-2510 129 A dorinna@hawaii.edu
CORTEZ, Jack .... 973-748-9000 276 A jack_cortez@bloomfield.edu
CORTEZ, Lori, A .... 815-835-6260 148 H lori.a.cortez@svcc.edu
CORTEZ, Lorissa, M ..... 956-326-2857 446 F lorissam.cortez@tamiu.edu
CORTEZ, Luisa .... 323-953-4000.. 48 I cortezly@lacitycollege.edu
CORTEZ, Ronald .... 949-824-5109.. 68 G rscortez@uci.edu
CORTEZ, Ruben .... 510-849-8931.. 55 B rcortez@psr.edu
CORTEZ, Sandra .... 956-794-4982 439 C sandra.cortez@laredo.edu
CORTI, Tom .... 631-420-2264 321 B tom.corti@farmingdale.edu
CORTINA, Mary .... 516-877-3259 289 C cortina@adelphi.edu
CORTINAS, Debra .... 361-825-5743 447 C debra.cortinas@tamucc.edu
CORTNER, Laquetta .... 614-837-4088 364 A cortnerl@valorcollege.edu
CORUM, Amanda .... 719-549-3163.. 81 K amanda.corum@pueblocc.edu
CORUM, Debbie .... 435-865-8330 460 F debbiecorum@suu.edu
CORVIN, Clay, L .... 504-282-4455 190 A clay@lifesongs.com
CORVIN, Thim .... 540-231-7189 467 F tcorvin@com.vt.edu
CORVINO, John .... 505-224-4639 285 J jcorvino@cnm.edu
CORVINO, John .... 313-577-3030 232 I ae9123@wayne.edu
CORWIN, Courtney Lee 501-450-1352.. 19 F corwin@hendrix.edu
CORWIN, Rhonda .... 620-665-3500 174 B corwinr@hutchcc.edu
COSBY, Felicia .... 804-257-5616 477 C fdcosby@vuu.edu
COSBY, Glen .... 509-533-7015 480 A glen.cosby@scc.spokane.edu
COSBY, Glen .... 509-533-7015 479 I glen.cosby@scc.spokane.edu
COSBY, Kevin, W .... 502-776-1443 184 B srpastor1@aol.com
COSBY, Laura .... 269-488-4440 225 E lcosby@kvcc.edu
COSBY, Sheliah .... 423-869-6353 421 C sheliah.cosby@lmunet.edu
COSBY-GAITHER, Christine .... 502-776-1443 184 B ccosby@simmonscollegeky.edu
COSCIA, Danielle .... 914-395-2365 315 F dcoscia@sarahlawrence.edu
COSCIA, Paul .... 336-917-5577 340 D paul.coscia@salem.edu
COSENTINO, Guy, T ...... 315-294-8627 292 E gcosentin@cayuga-cc.edu
COSENTINO, Lauren ...... 310-506-6202.. 56 C lauren.cosentino@pepperdine.edu
COSENTINO, Richard, E 864-388-8300 410 D cosentino@lander.edu
COSEY, Arnel .... 504-671-5055 187 E acosey@dcc.edu
COSGRIFF, Lawrence .... 202-462-2101.. 92 C lcosgriff@iwp.edu
COSGROVE, John .... 570-662-4586 395 C jcosgrov@mansfield.edu
COSGROVE, Mark .... 517-483-1345 226 F cosgrom1@lcc.edu
COSH, Ian .... 870-245-5321.. 20 E coshi@obu.edu
COSIMO, Julie .... 630-829-6037 132 E jcosimo@ben.edu
COSPER, Emily .... 504-762-3224 187 E ecospe@dcc.edu
COSS, Laura .... 724-852-7629 402 F lcoss@waynesburg.edu
COSSAR, Nigel .... 215-898-9073 400 K ncossar@upenn.edu
COSSE, Ted .... 626-584-5501.. 43 H ted_cosse@fuller.edu
COSSICH, Marc .... 850-474-2022 110 E mcossich@uwf.edu
COSSITT, Brenda .... 307-755-2244 502 K brenda.cossitt@zenith.org
COST, Timothy, P .... 904-256-7016 101 G tcost@ju.edu
COSTA, Daniel .... 831-459-2464.. 70 B costa@ucsc.edu
COSTA, Erik .... 860-701-5182.. 87 D costa_e@mitchell.edu
COSTA, Guilherme .... 607-274-3836 303 B gcosta@ithaca.edu
COSTA, Kris .... 559-925-3218.. 74 B kriscosta@whccd.edu
COSTA, Linda, J .... 848-932-7711 282 A smeds@gradadm.rutgers.edu
COSTA, Maria, D .... 423-439-7737 419 J costa@etsu.edu
COSTALAS, Georgia .... 570-408-7854 403 D georgia.costalas@wilkes.edu
COSTANTINI, Camilla .... 203-332-5222.. 85 F ccostantini@housatonic.edu
COSTANTINIDIS, Teresa 505-277-7520 288 G tcostant@unm.edu
COSTANTINO, Tracie ..... 661-255-1050.. 28 K tcostantino@calarts.edu
COSTANZA, Laina, T .... 334-387-3878.... 4 C lainacostanza@amridgeuniversity.edu
COSTANZO, Brian .... 570-961-7841 387 D costanzob@lackawanna.edu
COSTANZO, Elisabeth ... 607-778-5001 318 A costanzoes@sunybroome.edu
COSTAS, Carolyn .... 787-841-2000 510 K ccostas@pucpr.edu
COSTE, Mike .... 303-914-6636.. 82 C mike.coste@rrcc.edu
COSTELLO, Bernard, J ... 412-648-1938 401 B bjc1@pitt.edu
COSTELLO, Dana .... 410-225-2338 199 H dcostello@mica.edu
COSTELLO, Dave .... 815-921-4516 147 E d.costello@rockvalleycollege.edu
COSTELLO, Dennis .... 586-445-7318 226 H costellod@macomb.edu
COSTELLO, Gregory, W . 507-344-7305 234 B gregory.costello@blc.edu
COSTELLO, Jamie .... 617-879-7703 212 E jcostello@massart.edu
COSTELLO, Kevin .... 617-327-6777 220 B kevin_costello@williamjames.edu
COSTELLO, Leon .... 406-994-4226 264 D lcostello@msubobcats.com
COSTELLO, Richard, J ... 219-989-2539 159 G rick@pnw.edu
COSTELLO, Ron .... 610-647-4400 386 C rcostello@immaculata.edu
COSTIGAN, Harry .... 610-359-5288 382 C hcostigan@dccc.edu
COSTIGAN, Rosemary ... 401-825-2142 404 H rcostigan@ccri.edu
COSTIN, Dondi, E .... 843-863-7502 407 E dcostin@csuniv.edu
COSTLEY, Lucien .... 830-895-7116 443 G avpipfs@schreiner.edu
COSTNER, Carl .... 828-652-0614 336 B carlc@mcdowelltech.edu
COSTNER, Kelly .... 866-492-5336 244 F kelley.costner@mail.waldenu.edu
COSTOLA, Sergio .... 512-863-1373 445 D costolas@southwestern.edu
COSTON, Linda .... 229-430-2751 113 I lcoston@albanytech.edu
COSTON, Robert, H .... 304-647-6574 489 C rcoston@newriver.edu
COSTON, Todd .... 661-395-4601.. 46 L tcoston@bakersfieldcollege.edu
COT, Alea .... 504-280-7484 189 E acot@uno.edu
COTA, Clarissa .... 702-651-4000 271 A clarissa.cota@csn.edu
COTA, Marco .... 909-384-8630.. 59 I mcota@sbccd.cc.ca.us
COTE, Christine .... 509-453-0374 483 C christine.cote@perrytech.edu
COTE, Christy .... 907-745-3201.... 9 B ccote@akbible.edu
COTE, Matthew .... 907-745-3201.... 9 B mcote@akbible.edu
COTE-BONANNO, Joanne, F .... 973-655-6234 279 C bonannoj@mail.montclair.edu
COTHAM, Brian .... 559-278-2111.. 31 D bcotham@csufresno.edu
COTHRAN, Ginger .... 580-387-7112 366 H gcothran@mscok.edu
COTHRAN, Rick .... 864-646-1701 413 A rcothran@tctc.edu
COTHREN, Gary .... 352-395-5567 107 A gary.cothren@sfcollege.edu
COTNER, Dave, R .... 570-326-3761 393 G dcotner@pct.edu
COTO, Jennifer .... 714-628-4967.. 58 A coto_jennifer@sccollege.edu
COTRONE, Allan, L .... 651-962-4561 244 E cotr6990@stthomas.edu
COTRONEO, Keith, J ..... 304-710-3355 489 B cotroneo@mctc.edu
COTSONES, Rena .... 815-753-0834 145 C rcotsones@niu.edu
COTSONIS, Joachim ...... 617-850-1243 210 D jcotsonis@hchc.edu
COTTAM, Michael .... 314-246-5972 262 C michaelcottam@webster.edu
COTTEN, Brian .... 501-686-5684.. 22 C cottenbrian@uams.edu
COTTEN-BROWN, Floya 919-572-1625 326 L fbrown@apexsot.edu
COTTER, Bob .... 513-487-1144 361 L bob.cotter@myunion.edu
COTTER, Carol .... 719-587-7746.. 76 F ccotter@adams.edu
COTTER, Dan, J .... 802-258-9297 462 E dcotter@marlboro.edu
COTTER, George .... 813-974-3340 110 B gcotter@usf.edu
COTTER, Michael .... 914-594-3675 309 H michael_cotter@nymc.edu
COTTER, Regina .... 757-455-3352 477 F rcotter@vwu.edu
COTTET, Sarah .... 914-594-4574 309 H sarah_cottet@nymc.edu
COTTINGHAM, Ryan, T . 517-750-1200 230 H ryanc@arbor.edu
COTTO, Evelyn .... 787-746-1400 508 B ecoto@huertas.edu
COTTO, Marguerite, C ... 231-995-1775 228 G mcotto@nmc.edu
COTTO, Pedro .... 787-850-9551 513 E
COTTO, Sugelenia .... 787-766-1717 511 H sucotto@suagm.edu
COTTON, Anthony, J ..... 334-953-2044 503 B
COTTON, George .... 870-575-8701.. 22 E cottong@uapb.edu
COTTON, Gregory .... 319-895-4454 164 B gcotton@cornellcollege.edu
COTTON, Michael .... 336-517-2286 327 B mcotton@bennett.edu
COTTON, Sabrina .... 256-726-7408.... 6 C cotton@oakwood.edu
COTTON, Todd .... 205-726-4144.... 6 E tcotton@samford.edu
COTTON KELLY, Montique .... 860-486-2240.. 88 E montique.cotton.kelly@uconn.edu
COTTONE, John .... 607-753-2701 318 D john.cottone@cortland.edu
COTTONER, Brittany ...... 812-952-9791 154 A bcottoner@cariscollege.edu
COTTONHAM, Patricia ... 337-482-6266 192 E patcottonham@louisiana.edu
COTTRELL, Bryan .... 254-442-5173 433 A bryan.cottrell@cisco.edu
COTTRELL, Danny .... 501-337-5000.. 18 J dcottrell@coto.edu
COTTRELL, Debbie .... 254-295-5059 453 E dcottrell@umhb.edu
COTTRELL, Debbie .... 830-372-8001 449 B president@tlu.edu
COTTRELL, Liesl .... 773-252-5114 147 B liesl.cottrell@resu.edu
COTTRELL, Terrance, L .. 815-740-5041 151 J tcottrell@stfrancis.edu
COTTRILL, F. Layton ..... 304-696-6295 490 D cottrill@marshall.edu
COTY, Mark .... 941-782-5980 388 A mcoty@lecom.edu
COUCH, A. Kate .... 757-233-8785 477 F
COUCH, Charlie .... 970-351-2231.. 83 E charlie.couch@unco.edu
COUCH, Laurie, L .... 606-783-2434 183 F l.couch@moreheadstate.edu
COUCH, Lisa .... 760-384-6230.. 46 M lcouch@cerrocoso.edu
COUCH, Michael .... 317-921-4990 157 H mcouch28@ivytech.edu
COUCHEY, Evangeline ... 845-675-4733 310 G evangeline.couchey@nyack.edu
COUGHENOUR, Kevin ... 703-539-6890 472 A kcoughenour@stratford.edu
COUGHENOUR, Russ .... 931-372-6153 426 E rcoughenour@tntech.edu
COUGHLIN, Cass .... 620-341-5264 172 L ccoughli@emporia.edu
COUGHLIN, Chris .... 623-845-3205.. 13 C chris.coughlin@gccaz.edu
COUGHLIN, Elizabeth .... 207-509-7189 195 H ecoughlin@unity.edu
COUGHLIN, OFM, F. Edward .... 518-783-2302 315 J ecoughlin@siena.edu
COUGHLIN, III, Jay, J .. 443-518-4032 199 C jcoughlin@howardcc.edu
COUGHLIN, Kathleen .... 210-829-6012 453 D coughlin@uiwtx.edu
COUGHLIN, Kevin .... 305-348-2320 109 A kevin.coughlinjr@fiu.edu
COUGHLIN, Mary Ann .. 413-748-3959 218 G mcoughlin@springfield.edu
COUGHLIN, Meredith .... 772-462-7304 101 E mcoughli@irsc.edu
COUGHLIN, Robert, D .. 860-685-2543.. 89 C rdcoughlin@wesleyan.edu
COUILLARD, Michael .... 719-502-3352.. 81 F mike.couillard@ppcc.edu

COULBY, Susan .... 302-622-8000.. 89 E
scoulby@dcad.edu
COULE, Phillip, L .... 706-721-1083 115 A
pcoule@augusta.edu
COULIER, Laura .... 616-988-1000 222 G
laura.c@compass.edu
COULING, Mike .... 972-660-5701 439 F
mcouling@lincolntech.com
COULLIETTE, Holly .... 904-808-7441 106 C
hollycoulliette@sjrstate.edu
COULOMBE,
Jennifer, B .... 336-734-7723 334 E
jcoulombe@forsythtech.edu
COULON, Richard .... 949-824-6510.. 68 G
rcoulon@uci.edu
COULOUTE, Clifford ...... 718-997-5100 295 C
clifford.couloute@qc.cuny.edu
COULSON, Joseph .... 877-248-6724.. 12 L
jcoulson@hmu.edu
COULSTON, Susan .... 269-782-1396 230 F
scoulston@swmich.edu
COULTER, Ann .... 641-782-1340 169 H
coulter@swcciowa.edu
COULTER, Chris .... 719-389-6568.. 77 H
chris.coulter@coloradocollege.edu
COULTER, Cindy .... 828-327-7000 333 B
ccoulter@cvcc.edu
COULTER, Denise .... 609-343-5007 275 D
dcoulter@atlantic.edu
COULTER, Laurie .... 903-813-2900 430 N
lcoulter@austincollege.edu
COULTER, Lisa .... 610-683-4072 395 A
coulter@kutztown.edu
COULTER, Martha .... 802-468-1314 464 A
martha.coulter@castleton.edu
COULTER, Seana .... 443-885-3110 200 D
seana.coulter@morgan.edu
COUNCIL, Juanette .... 910-672-1208 341 E
jcouncil@uncfsu.edu
COUNCIL, Mark .... 910-362-7009 332 H
mcouncil@cfcc.edu
COUNCIL, Timothy .... 909-607-7811.. 37 D
admissions@cgu.edu
COUNSIL, Brian .... 620-901-6339 170 G
counsil@allencc.edu
COUNTEE, Jerome .... 559-243-7262.. 66 C
jerome.countee@scccd.edu
COUNTIS, Amber .... 903-468-8187 447 B
amber.countis@tamuc.edu
COUNTS, LaNeta .... 404-471-6483 113 G
lcounts@agnesscott.edu
COUPE, Maria .... 845-398-4038 315 B
mcoupe@stac.edu
COURCY, Jane .... 619-239-0391.. 34 F
jcourcy@cwsl.edu
COURET, Esther .... 845-431-8673 298 E
esther.couret@sunydutchess.edu
COUREY, Scott .... 616-394-4287 222 I
scott.courey@cornerstone.edu
COURNOYER, Jeff .... 617-287-7050 211 C
jcournoyer@umassp.edu
COURNOYER, Jennifer .. 603-542-7744 273 C
jcournoyer@ccsnh.edu
COURS, Deborah, A ...... 818-677-2455.. 32 D
dcours@csun.edu
COURSEY, Greg .... 706-437-6808 114 J
gcoursey@augustatech.edu
COURSEY, Laura .... 903-923-2326 436 D
lcoursey@etbu.edu
COURT, Christine .... 330-363-6347 348 D
registrar@aultmancollege.edu
COURT, Cynthia .... 706-236-2261 115 B
ccourt@berry.edu
COURTEMANCHE,
Barbara .... 617-585-0200 206 F
barbara.courtemanche@the-bac.edu
COURTEMANCHE, Brian 978-927-2278 209 B
bcourtem@endicott.edu
COURTEY, Susan .... 818-240-1000.. 44 B
susan@glendale.edu
COURTLEY-TODD,
Laura, J .... 305-628-6677 106 F
lcourtle@stu.edu
COURTMANCHE, John .. 413-559-6180 210 A
jccm@hampshire.edu
COURTNEY, Catherine ... 617-670-4529 209 D
ccourtney@fisher.edu
COURTNEY, Dan .... 765-641-4004 153 B
dacourtney@anderson.edu
COURTNEY, Justin, F .... 419-772-2145 358 H
j-courtney@onu.edu
COURTNEY, Nycole .... 307-766-3296 502 H
nf@uwyo.edu
COURTNEY, Sharon, P .. 504-988-3390 191 B
sharonc@tulane.edu
COURTNEY-BIEDRZYCKI,
Caitlin .... 978-816-7627 209 B
ccourtne@endicott.edu
COURTRIGHT, Amy .... 209-954-5151.. 60 J
acourtright@deltacollege.edu
COURTRIGHT, Caren ..... 509-793-2038 478 H
carenc@bigbend.edu
COUSINO, Thomas .... 262-564-2812 499 F
cousinot@gtc.edu
COUSINS, Amirah .... 718-289-5155 293 B
amirah.cousins@bcc.cuny.edu
COUTS, LeeAnn .... 740-392-6868 357 B
leeann.couts@mvnu.edu
COUTS, Suzann .... 325-793-4608 440 B
couts.suzann@mcm.edu
COUTTS, Christopher .... 540-351-1513 474 J
ccoutts@lfcc.edu
COUTURE, Marie .... 414-847-3334 494 F
mariecouture@miad.edu
COVAL, Scott .... 610-282-1100 382 E
scott.coval@desales.edu
COVAR, Tom .... 864-388-8305 410 D
tcovar@lander.edu
COVARRUBIAS, Henry ... 760-355-6153.. 45 I
henry.covarrubias@imperial.edu
COVARRUBIAS, Leticia .. 626-472-5121.. 41 K
lcovarrubias@esgvrop.org
COVAULT, Pamela .... 785-242-2067 175 H
pcovault@neosho.edu
COVE, Lorraine, D .... 617-573-8160 219 A
lcove@acad.suffolk.edu
COVELLI, Maria .... 305-289-1121.. 97 E
maria.covelli@dolphins.org
COVERDALE, Tonjia ...... 937-376-6028 350 D
tcoverdale@ceentralstate.edu
COVERSON, Stefani ...... 360-992-2986 479 F
scoverson@clark.edu
COVERT, Orrie .... 903-566-7038 456 A
ocovert@uttyler.edu
COVERT, Sarah .... 706-542-9389 125 G
covert@uga.edu
COVERT, Sheree, S .... 319-352-8272 170 C
sheree.covert@wartburg.edu
COVEY, Angie, E .... 540-674-3655 475 B
acovey@nr.edu
COVEY, Bruce .... 404-727-6223 117 F
bcovey@emory.edu
COVEY, Jay .... 623-845-3950.. 13 C
jay.covey@gccaz.edu
COVEY, Lori .... 848-445-4777 282 A
covey@biology.rutgers.edu
COVEY, Mary Ann .... 979-845-4427 446 G
mcovey@tamu.edu
COVEY, Matthew, V .... 212-327-8909 313 B
mcovey@rockefeller.edu
COVILL, Mesa .... 715-232-1259 498 A
covillm@uwstout.edu
COVILLE, Jan .... 603-452-1507 274 H
jan.coville@granite.edu
COVINGTON,
Adrienne, S .... 252-451-8240 336 E
ascovington197@nashcc.edu
COVINGTON, Anthony ... 425-235-2352 483 G
acovington@rtc.edu
COVINGTON, Dave, R ... 208-467-8060 131 D
dcovington@nnu.edu
COVINGTON, David .... 212-650-5263 293 D
dcovington@ccnyalumni.org
COVINGTON, Donna ..... 859-858-2391 178 H
COVINGTON, Janet .... 713-348-6312 442 K
jcov@rice.edu
COVINGTON, Lisa .... 281-649-3704 437 H
lcovington@hbu.edu
COVINGTON, Mary .... 919-966-9176 342 D
mary_covington@unc.edu
COVINGTON, Philip ...... 402-554-3537 270 A
philip.covington@unmc.edu
COVINGTON, R. Dean ... 501-450-5202.. 23 H
dcovington@uca.edu
COVINGTON, Sim .... 585-785-1790 300 B
sim.covington@flcc.edu
COVINGTON, Sirena ...... 312-788-1146 152 B
scovington@vandercook.edu
COVINO, Nicholas .... 617-327-6777 220 B
nicholas_covino@williamjames.edu
COVINO, Paul, F .... 508-767-7057 205 D
pf.covino@assumption.edu
COVINO, William, A ...... 323-343-3030.. 32 A
bill.covino@calstatela.edu
COVIO-CALZADA, Lilia .. 817-515-7602 445 G
lilia.covio-calzada@tccd.edu
COVONE, Michael .... 305-899-3551.. 95 C
mcovone@barry.edu
COWAN, Anthony .... 901-435-1470 421 A
anthony_cowan@loc.edu
COWAN, Carl .... 918-360-9147 365 F
cowanc@bacone.edu
COWAN, Cindy .... 864-977-2058 411 E
cindy.cowan@ngu.edu
COWAN, David .... 507-389-2267 239 C
david.cowan@mnsu.edu
COWAN, Judith .... 803-327-7402 408 B
jcowan@clintoncollege.edu
COWAN, Kenneth, H ..... 402-559-4238 270 A
kcowan@unmc.edu
COWAN, Michelle .... 901-435-1386 421 A
michelle_cowan@loc.edu
COWAN, Patricia .... 501-686-8493.. 22 C
pacowan@uams.edu
COWAN, Sharaya .... 970-248-1958.. 77 I
scowan@coloradomesa.edu
COWAN, Theresa .... 954-201-7554.. 95 H
tcowan@broward.edu
COWAN, Vickie, M .... 718-862-7398 305 H
vickie.cowan@manhattan.edu
COWART, Lisa .... 803-323-2273 414 G
cowartl@winthrop.edu
COWART, Monica, R ..... 717-867-6208 388 H
cowart@lvc.edu
COWDEN, Belle .... 812-465-1061 161 E
bcowden@usi.edu
COWDERY, Aaron .... 740-376-4452 356 A
aaron.cowdery@marietta.edu
COWDIN, Terry .... 503-251-5727 377 F
tcowdin@uws.edu
COWDREY, Scott .... 828-250-2350 342 C
COWELL, Elizabeth .... 831-459-2076.. 70 B
mcowell@ucsc.edu
COWELL, JR.,
James, W .... 626-395-4464.. 29 C
jcowell@caltech.edu
COWELL, John, K .... 706-721-0570 115 A
jcowell@augusta.edu
COWELL, Leslie .... 334-386-7106.... 5 D
lcowell@faulkner.edu
COWELL-OATES, June .... 314-454-8694 253 E
jcowell-oates@bjc.org
COWEN, Emily .... 304-829-7630 487 G
ecowen@bethanywv.edu
COWETT, Allen .... 508-791-9241 206 B
COWGER, John .... 701-594-8192 346 D
john.cowger@lrsc.edu
COWGER, Tiffany .... 618-395-7777 138 F
cowgert@iecc.edu
COWGER, Tiffany .... 618-262-8641 139 A
cowgert@iecc.edu
COWHEY, Peter .... 858-534-3939.. 69 D
pcowhey@ucsd.edu
COWING, Michelle .... 503-493-6392 372 I
mcowing@cu-portland.edu
COWLES, John .... 317-917-5702 157 H
jcowles2@ivytech.edu
COWLEY, Dave .... 435-797-1146 460 H
dave.cowley@usu.edu
COWLEY, Jennifer .... 940-565-3952 454 A
jennifer.cowley@unt.edu
COWLEY, Julie, A .... 512-863-1720 445 D
cowleyj@southwestern.edu
COWLEY, Kate .... 218-235-2121 241 E
COWLIN, Lynn .... 815-455-8688 143 A
lcowlin@mchenry.edu
COWSER, Angela .... 502-895-3411 183 D
acowser@lpts.edu
COWSER, Erin, K .... 985-549-5861 192 D
erin.moore@selu.edu
COWSERT, Stephanie .... 858-513-9240.. 26 G
stephanie.stewart@ashford.edu
COX, Amber .... 407-708-4574 107 D
coxa@seminolestate.edu
COX, Angela .... 518-525-6858 306 E
angela.cox@sphp.com
COX, Ann .... 212-875-4416 290 F
acox@bankstreet.edu
COX, Brandy, A .... 479-575-2801.. 21 G
brandyac@uark.edu
COX, Brant, M .... 757-446-5800 466 I
coxbm@evms.edu
COX, Caitlin .... 256-761-6377.... 7 B
ccox@talladega.edu
COX, Cameron .... 253-964-6598 483 D
cmcox@pierce.ctc.edu
COX, Cathy .... 478-301-2602 121 E
cox_c@law.mercer.edu
COX, Cathy .... 707-476-4264.. 39 D
cathy-cox@redwoods.edu
COX, Cheryl .... 864-592-4613 412 F
coxc@sccsc.edu
COX, Christopher, N ..... 864-656-0229 408 A
cnc2@clemson.edu
COX, Christy .... 252-639-7340 340 J
ccox@umo.edu
COX, Colleen .... 978-656-3284 214 G
COX, Dave .... 217-234-5376 141 D
dcox5612@lakeland.cc.il.us
COX, Dave .... 509-533-7179 480 A
dave.cox@scc.spokane.edu
COX, David .... 575-835-5615 286 I
david.cox@nmt.edu
COX, David, W .... 716-878-5336 318 C
coxdw@buffalostate.edu
COX, Dennis .... 727-376-6911 111 G
dcox@trinitycollege.edu
COX, Donna .... 870-543-5968.. 21 C
dcox@seark.edu
COX, Ed .... 845-431-8071 298 E
ecox@sunydutchess.edu
COX, Elease .... 863-638-7202 113 A
elease.cox@warner.edu
COX, Erika, M .... 210-458-4859 455 E
erika.cox@utsa.edu
COX, G. Paul .... 216-987-0271 351 G
g.cox@tri-c.edu
COX, Hali .... 423-323-0201 425 E
COX, Helen .... 808-245-8210 129 C
helencox@hawaii.edu
COX, J. Ben .... 254-710-2414 431 J
ben_cox@baylor.edu
COX, James .... 518-738-8500 299 G
jcox@excelsior.edu
COX, Jamie, S .... 256-766-6610.... 5 F
jcox@hcu.edu
COX, Jana .... 707-524-1579.. 62 F
jcox@santarosa.edu
COX, Janet .... 513-244-4466 357 A
janet.cox@msj.edu
COX, Jeff, A .... 336-838-6112 339 B
jacox302@wilkescc.edu
COX, Jeffrey, N .... 303-492-5491.. 83 A
avcjeff.cox@colorado.edu
COX, Jeffrey, W .... 585-475-7433 313 A
jwccst@rit.edu
COX, Jennifer .... 580-559-5714 366 C
jcox@ecok.edu
COX, Jesse .... 734-432-5839 227 A
jdcox@madonna.edu
COX, John "Sam" .... 813-253-7495 101 A
jcox53@hccfl.edu
COX, John, L .... 508-362-2131 214 B
jcox@capecod.edu
COX, Josh .... 816-654-7305 254 C
jcox@kcumb.edu
COX, Karen .... 888-556-8226 133 F
COX, Kelli .... 816-235-2760 261 C
kellicox@umkc.edu
COX, Kenneth .... 540-831-7600 470 C
kcox3@radford.edu
COX, Kevin .... 214-887-5233 436 B
kcox@dts.edu
COX, Lady, D .... 334-844-5672.... 4 E
ldc0006@auburn.edu
COX, Lane .... 205-348-8697.... 7 G
lcox@fa.ua.edu
COX, LaShanta' .... 770-962-7580 120 E
lcox@gwinnetttech.edu
COX, Leah .... 410-704-0203 204 A
lcox@towson.edu
COX, Leana .... 970-675-3334.. 78 G
leana.cox@cncc.edu
COX, Linda .... 843-792-9562 410 F
coxl@musc.edu
COX, Lori .... 618-252-5400 149 C
lori.cox@sic.edu
COX, Lynn .... 606-589-3073 182 E
lynn.cox@kctcs.edu
COX, Marianne .... 252-493-7210 336 H
mcox@email.pittcc.edu
COX, Michele, D .... 804-289-8838 472 L
mcox@richmond.edu
COX, Michelle .... 503-251-5726 377 F
mcox@uws.edu
COX, Monte .... 501-279-4808.. 19 D
mcox@harding.edu
COX, Nancy, M .... 859-257-4772 185 B
ncox@email.uky.edu
COX, Nathan .... 864-231-2000 406 G
ncox@andersonuniversity.edu

CRAVEN, Kendra .... 402-354-7848 268 C kendra.craven@methodistcollege.edu
CRAVEN, Nora .... 715-365-4576 500 D ncraven@nicoletcollege.edu
CRAVEN, Randy .... 423-236-2076 424 B rlcraven@southern.edu
CRAVENS, Keith .... 713-920-1120 120 H kcravens@ict.edu
CRAVENS, Michael .... 419-824-3620 355 K mcravens@sistersosf.org
CRAVER, Ken .... 903-510-2591 452 C kcra@tjc.edu
CRAVER, Robert .... 303-369-5151.. 81 J robert.craver@plattcolorado.edu
CRAVER, III, William .... 678-225-7509 396 D williamcr@pcom.edu
CRAWFORD, Abby .... 863-638-7248 113 A abby.crawford@warner.edu
CRAWFORD, Andrew ..... 216-987-2053 351 G andrew.crawford@tri-c.edu
CRAWFORD, Andrew, B 757-594-7663 466 B andrew.crawford@cnu.edu
CRAWFORD, Ann .... 860-509-9560.. 87 B acrawford@hartsem.edu
CRAWFORD, Anna .... 304-260-4380 488 J acrawfor@blueridgectc.edu
CRAWFORD, Arminda ... 614-985-2241 360 E acrawford@pcj.edu
CRAWFORD, Audrey ..... 205-665-6030.... 8 D acrawford@montevallo.edu
CRAWFORD, Brian, L .... 304-336-8004 490 F brian.crawford@westliberty.edu
CRAWFORD, Brittany .... 334-683-2382.... 3 A bcrawford@marionmilitary.edu
CRAWFORD, Bruce .... 205-929-6312.... 2 H bcrawford@lawsonstate.edu
CRAWFORD, Bryan .... 719-562-7002.. 81 K bryan.crawford@pueblocc.edu
CRAWFORD, Cardon, B 843-953-6966 407 F cardon.crawford@citadel.edu
CRAWFORD, Charlie ..... 425-640-1557 480 F charlie.crawford@edcc.edu
CRAWFORD, Chris .... 605-642-6262 416 I chris.crawford@bhsu.edu
CRAWFORD, Chris .... 903-923-2223 436 D chrisc@etbu.edu
CRAWFORD, Chyna, N . 252-335-3113 341 D cncrawford@ecsu.edu
CRAWFORD, Clinton ..... 718-270-5140 295 A crawford@mec.cuny.edu
CRAWFORD, Colin .... 502-852-6373 185 C colin.crawford@louisville.edu
CRAWFORD, David .... 303-797-5762.. 76 I david.crawford@arapahoe.edu
CRAWFORD, David .... 773-947-6301 142 J dcrawford@mccormick.edu
CRAWFORD, David .... 773-947-6250 142 J dcrawford@mccormick.edu
CRAWFORD, David, S ... 202-526-3799.. 92 F dcrawford@johnpaulii.edu
CRAWFORD, Debbie ...... 970-945-8691.. 77 K
CRAWFORD, Deborah ... 703-993-2268 467 L dcrawfo7@gmu.edu
CRAWFORD, Deena .... 601-266-4829 249 F deena.crawford@usm.edu
CRAWFORD, Dickie .... 318-257-2445 191 F crawford@latech.edu
CRAWFORD, Eboni .... 973-803-5000 280 C ecrawford@pillar.edu
CRAWFORD, Galen .... 415-351-3509.. 60 G gcrawford@sfai.edu
CRAWFORD, Gregory .... 513-529-2345 356 E president@miamioh.edu
CRAWFORD, Holly .... 585-275-2800 323 J hcrawford@admin.rochester.edu
CRAWFORD, Isiaah .... 253-879-3201 485 E president@pugetsound.edu
CRAWFORD, James .... 336-517-1818 327 B jcrawford@bennett.edu
CRAWFORD, John, D .... 229-333-5939 126 G jdcrawford@valdosta.edu
CRAWFORD, John, P ..... 716-880-2879 306 C jpc334@medaille.edu
CRAWFORD, Jonas .... 805-678-5870.. 73 A jcrawford@vcccd.edu
CRAWFORD, Karen .... 603-358-2487 275 A kcrawford@keene.edu
CRAWFORD, Kevin .... 803-641-3495 413 D kevincr@usca.edu
CRAWFORD, Kevin, L ... 240-500-2412 198 H klcrawford@hagerstowncc.edu
CRAWFORD, Malinda .... 406-756-3828 263 F mcrawfor@fvcc.edu
CRAWFORD, Martha, J . 203-371-7999.. 88 B
CRAWFORD, Matthew ... 612-659-6701 238 I matthew.crawford@minneapolis.edu
CRAWFORD, Michael .... 617-670-4427 209 D mcrawford@fisher.edu
CRAWFORD, Michael .... 773-995-3973 133 K mcrawf28@csu.edu
CRAWFORD, Michael .... 773-602-5000 134 D
CRAWFORD, Mike .... 863-680-6211.. 99 H mcrawford@flsouthern.edu
CRAWFORD, Peg .... 617-732-2132 216 B peg.crawford@mcphs.edu
CRAWFORD, Ray Scott . 318-678-6000 187 A rcrawford@bpcc.edu
CRAWFORD, Rhia, M .... 828-448-6048 339 A rcrawford@wpcc.edu
CRAWFORD, Scott .... 309-341-7662 141 A rscrawford@knox.edu
CRAWFORD, Steve .... 614-823-3200 360 A crawford2@otterbein.edu
CRAWFORD, Teresa ...... 863-784-7061 107 F teresa.crawford@southflorida.edu
CRAWFORD, Teri .... 281-998-6151 443 B teri.crawford@sjcd.edu
CRAWFORD, Thomas, P .... 412-624-5822 401 B tom.crawford@ia.pitt.edu
CRAWFORD, Tim .... 254-295-4180 453 E tcrawford@umhb.edu
CRAWFORD, Valerie ...... 309-268-8150 137 I val.crawford@heartland.edu
CRAWFORD, Vicinda ...... 404-756-4477 114 G vcrawford@atlm.edu
CRAWFORD, Wendy ...... 870-733-6711.. 17 H wcrawford@asumidsouth.edu
CRAWFORD, William .... 212-280-1396 323 H wcrawford@uts.columbia.edu
CRAWFORD-FOWLER, Sally .... 620-341-5221 172 L scrowfo4@emporia.edu
CRAWFORD-PARKER, Sarah .... 785-864-4225 177 D scrawpar@ku.edu
CRAWFORD-SPINELLI, John, R .... 330-672-2760 354 J jcrawfo1@kent.edu
CRAWFORD-WHITE, Demarus .... 937-376-6574 350 D dcrawford-white@centralstate.edu
CRAWFORT, Denise ...... 212-799-5000 303 H
CRAWLEY, William .... 850-474-2769 110 E wcrawley@uwf.edu
CRAWMER, Martha .... 989-686-9291 223 G marthacrawmer@delta.edu
CRAWSHAW, Taylor ...... 620-331-4100 174 C tcrawshaw@indycc.edu
CRAYS, Linda, L .... 713-500-2080 456 B linda.l.crays@uth.tmc.edu
CRAYTON, DiOnetta ...... 617-253-5010 215 G
CRAZY THUNDER, Susan .... 715-365-4434 500 D scrazythunder@nicoletcollege.edu
CREAGER, Carol .... 540-887-7310 469 B ccreager@marybaldwin.edu
CREAGER, Kristina .... 260-481-6140 159 F creagerk@pfw.edu
CREAGH, CM, Kevin, G 716-652-8900 292 I kcreagh@cks.edu
CREAHAN, Patricia, H ... 716-888-2616 292 D creahan@canisius.edu
CREAMER, Barry .... 214-818-1300 434 F bcreamer@criswell.edu
CREAMER, David .... 513-529-4225 356 E creamerd@miamioh.edu
CREAMER, Elizabeth ...... 804-523-2280 474 I ecreamer@ccwa.vccs.edu
CREAMER, Jenni .... 864-646-1615 413 A jevans12@tctc.edu
CREAMER, Julie .... 507-222-4280 234 F jcreamer@carleton.edu
CREAMER, Kelli .... 205-853-1200.... 2 G kcreamer@jeffersonstate.edu
CREAMER, Scott, F .... 321-682-4971 112 K screamer@valenciacollege.edu
CREAMER, Stephen .... 978-762-4000 215 B screamer@northshore.edu
CREASMAN, Boyd .... 301-447-5218 200 E b.creasman@msmary.edu
CREASON, Paul .... 562-938-4171.. 48 D pcreason@lbcc.edu
CREASON, Rita, A .... 270-789-5233 179 E racreason@campbellsville.edu
CREDE, Brad .... 573-897-5000 260 E
CREE, Robert .... 315-268-6689 296 A rcree@carkson.edu
CREE, Robert, A .... 315-364-3408 325 B rcree@wells.edu
CREECH, Bill .... 918-595-7000 370 E bill.creech@tulsacc.edu
CREECH, Derek .... 423-585-6759 426 C derek.creech@ws.edu
CREECH, Jennifer, M .... 937-229-4141 362 G jcreech1@udayton.edu
CREECH, Karlton .... 303-871-3399.. 83 D karlton.creech@du.edu
CREECH, Michael .... 903-589-7118 438 G mcreech@jacksonville-college.edu
CREECY, Scott .... 870-762-3159.. 17 D screecy@smail.anc.edu
CREED, J. Bradley .... 910-893-1205 327 E creed@campbell.edu
CREED, Mickey .... 812-221-1714 162 B mickeycreed@vbc.edu
CREED-DIKEOGU, Gloria .... 785-242-5200 176 D creeddikeogu@ottawa.edu
CREEHAN, Juliet, A .... 412-578-6123 380 E jacreehan@carlow.edu
CREEHAN, Kenneth .... 314-968-6969 262 C creehan@webster.edu
CREEK, Cassandra .... 202-759-4988.. 91 D
CREEKMORE, Carol .... 201-692-2379 277 K creekmor@fdu.edu
CREEKMORE, Crystal .... 256-233-8174.... 4 D crystal.creekmore@athens.edu
CREEKMORE, Paul, R .... 630-515-7217 143 G pcreek@midwestern.edu
CREEL, Angie .... 928-344-7776.. 10 J angela.creel-erb@azwestern.edu
CREEL, Rickey .... 256-215-4321.... 1 G rcreel@cacc.edu
CREEL, Ronnie .... 334-670-3496.... 7 C rcreel@troy.edu
CREEL, Shane .... 361-593-2237 447 D randolph.creel@tamuk.edu
CREELY, Hilliary, E .... 724-357-2655 394 G hcreely@iup.edu
CREFT, Dawn, H .... 407-303-9706.. 94 D dawn.creft@ahu.edu
CREGER, LeAnn .... 517-607-2305 225 A lcreger@hillsdale.edu
CREGGER, Crystal, Y .... 276-233-4762 476 E ccregger@wcc.vccs.edu
CREIGHTON, Grace .... 914-674-7369 306 F gcreighton@mercy.edu
CREIGHTON, Jill .... 509-335-3564 486 A
CREIGHTON, Joslyn ...... 816-559-5622 258 A joslyn.creighton@park.edu
CREMEENS, Brady .... 217-732-3168 141 H blcremeens@lincolnchristian.edu
CREMERS, Martijn .... 574-631-1691 161 C mcremers@nd.edu
CRENSHAW, Chris .... 601-266-4414 249 F christopher.crenshaw@usm.edu
CRENSHAW, Pamela ..... 714-556-3610.. 72 F pcrenshaw@vanguard.edu
CRESPIE, Nancie .... 301-891-4147 204 C ncrespie@wau.edu
CRESPIN, Andrea .... 505-454-3424 286 H arcrespin@nmhu.edu
CRESPIN, Inca .... 505-454-3437 286 H imcrespin@nmhu.edu
CRESPINO, Curt, J .... 816-235-1105 261 C crespinocj@umkc.edu
CRESPO, Antonio .... 617-349-8541 210 H antonio.crespo@lesley.edu
CRESPO, Evelyza .... 787-257-7373 511 G crespoe2@suagm.edu
CRESPO, Jorge .... 787-751-0178 511 F ac_jcrespo@suagm.edu
CRESPO, Jorge, L .... 787-751-0178 511 F ac_jcrespo@suagm.edu
CRESPO, Lyliana .... 787-863-2390 509 B lyliana.crespo@fajardo.inter.edu
CRESPO, Natalie .... 410-386-8229 197 G ncrespo@carrollcc.edu
CRESPO, Ricardo .... 787-751-1912 510 A rcnevarez@juris.inter.edu
CRESPO-KEBLER, Elizabeth .... 787-993-8864 513 B elizabeth.crespo1@upr.edu
CRESPO-LOPEZ, Sylvia . 212-237-8897 294 D sylopez@jjay.cuny.edu
CRESPO-REYES, José, A .... 787-993-8872 513 B jose.crespo5@upr.edu
CRESPO-RIVERA, Waleska .... 787-798-6904 512 C waleska.crespo@uccaribe.edu
CRESPO VALENTIN, Wilson .... 787-764-0000 514 B wilson.crespo1@upr.edu
CRESS, Pam .... 509-527-2421 485 H pam.cress@wallawalla.edu
CRESS, Trina .... 402-486-2540 269 F trina.cress@ucollege.edu
CREVISTON, Thomas, E 913-684-2738 504 D
CREW, Dwayne .... 706-821-8336 122 K dcrew@paine.edu
CREW, Rudolph, F .... 718-270-5000 295 A rcrew@mec.cuny.edu
CREWE, Sandra .... 202-806-7300.. 92 B screwe@howard.edu
CREWELL, Don .... 626-395-6280.. 29 C dcrewell@caltech.edu
CREWS, Annie .... 301-546-0916 201 C crewsad@pgcc.edu
CREWS, Bradford .... 216-368-4303 349 F bradford.crews@case.edu
CREWS, Chris .... 812-941-2000 157 B cmcrews@ius.edu
CREWS, DeMarcus .... 470-653-7850 122 D demarcus.crews@morehouse.edu
CREWS, Denise .... 217-875-7200 147 C dcrews@richland.edu
CREWS, CSA, Edie, A .... 920-923-7624 494 A eacrews27@marianuniversity.edu
CREWS, Kimberly .... 202-274-5857.. 93 C kcrews@udc.edu
CREWS, LaJada .... 336-744-0900 327 F frontoffice@carolina.edu
CREWS, Patricia, S .... 850-484-1700 104 H pcrews@pensacolastate.edu
CREWS, Roslyn .... 256-372-8889.... 1 A roslyn.crews@aamu.edu
CREWS, Sharon .... 205-929-6307.... 2 H sharon.crews@lawsonstate.edu
CREWS, Tena .... 803-777-6727 413 C tcrews@mailbox.sc.edu
CRIBB, Alastair .... 508-887-4558 219 B alastair.cribb@tufts.edu
CRICK, Summer .... 270-852-3144 183 A summer.crick@kwc.edu
CRICKARD, Valerie .... 704-687-1862 342 E vcrickar@uncc.edu
CRICKENBERGER, Leslie .... 931-372-3034 426 E lcrickenberger@tntech.edu
CRICKETTE, Grace .... 262-472-1918 498 C
CRIDER, Joseph .... 817-923-1921 445 B jcrider@swbts.edu
CRIDER, Kevin, L .... 518-580-5929 316 A kcrider@skidmore.edu
CRIDER, Kyle .... 559-934-2129.. 73 M kylecrider@whccd.edu
CRIDER, Ryan, E .... 816-604-2631 255 G ryan.crider@mcckc.edu
CRIDER, Wayne .... 706-245-7226 117 E wcrider@ec.edu
CRIGLER, Jeremy, T ...... 203-716-8470 191 B jcrigler@tulane.edu
CRILL-HORNSBY, Cherylyn .... 559-243-7511.. 66 C cherylyn.crill-hornsby@scccd.edu
CRILLEY, Bonnie .... 814-866-8144 388 A bcrilley@lecom.edu
CRIMMIN, Nancy, P ...... 508-373-1900 206 B nancy.crimmin@becker.edu
CRIMMINS, Cindy .... 717-815-1216 404 A ccrimmins@ycp.edu
CRIMMINS, Kate .... 410-837-6135 204 B kcrimmins@ubalt.edu
CRINO, Sally, E .... 563-333-6080 169 A crinosallye@sau.edu
CRIPE, Andy .... 989-837-4387 228 H cripe@northwood.edu
CRIPPEN, Carol .... 719-884-5000.. 81 C cacrippen@nbc.edu
CRIPPEN, Julia .... 252-493-7335 336 H jcrippen@email.pittcc.edu
CRIPPIN-HAAKE, Tracy, L .... 515-574-1192 166 E crippin@iowacentral.edu
CRIPPS, Kimberly .... 205-726-4180.... 6 E kcripps@samford.edu
CRISAFULLI, Susan .... 317-738-8240 154 J scrisafulli@franklincollege.edu
CRISCI, David .... 781-768-7843 218 C david.crisci@regiscollege.edu

CROWE, Jeremy .... 610-372-4721 397 B
jcrowe@racc.edu
CROWE, Karen .... 718-960-5746 294 A
karen.crowe@lehman.cuny.edu
CROWE, Kellie .... 276-739-2456 476 C
kcrowe@vhcc.edu
CROWE, Ken .... 706-864-1499 126 A
ken.crowe@ung.edu
CROWE, Lindsey .... 270-852-3118 183 A
lcrowe@kwc.edu
CROWE, Mary, L .... 863-680-4181.. 99 H
mcrowe@flsouthern.edu
CROWE, Peggy .... 270-745-3159 185 E
peggy.crowe@wku.edu
CROWE, Richard .... 818-343-2890.. 39 G
rcrowe@columbiacollege.edu
CROWE, Stephanie .... 406-496-4568 265 A
scrowe@mtech.edu
CROWE, JR., Terry, M .. 865-694-6619 425 F
tmcrowe1@pstcc.edu
CROWE, Thomas .... 847-543-2473 135 B
tcrowe@clcillinois.edu
CROWELL, Anthony .... 212-431-2840 309 G
anthony.crowell@nyls.edu
CROWELL, Heidi .... 603-897-8630 274 B
hcrowell@rivier.edu
CROWELL, Scott .... 507-537-6844 241 D
scott.crowell@smsu.edu
CROWETIPTON, Vaughn 864-294-2138 410 A
vaughn.crowetipton@furman.edu
CROWFOOT, Dara .... 312-996-8586 151 B
CROWL, Ronald .... 330-829-2756 363 B
crowlrl@mountunion.edu
CROWLEY, Cara, J .... 806-345-5518 430 A
cjcrowley@actx.edu
CROWLEY, Janelle .... 262-472-1918 498 C
CROWLEY, Kimberly, A . 806-354-6087 430 A
kacrowley@actx.edu
CROWLEY, Merritt .... 508-286-3464 220 A
crowley_merritt@wheatoncollege.edu
CROWLEY, Michael .... 408-554-4300.. 62 D
mcrowley@scu.edu
CROWLEY, Tanya .... 978-665-4789 212 C
tcrowle7@fitchburgstate.edu
CROWLEY, Timothy, D .. 207-768-2811 194 J
tcrowley@nmcc.edu
CROWN, Deborah, F ..... 407-646-2405 105 M
dcrown@rollins.edu
CROWNOVER,
Konstance .... 405-491-6350 370 A
kcrownover@snu.edu
CROWSON, Allan .... 615-675-5277 428 G
acrowson@welch.edu
CROWSON, Natalie .... 978-626-7111 209 G
ncrowson@gcts.edu
CROWTHER, Cameron ... 540-261-8400 471 H
cameron.crowther@svu.edu
CROWTHER, Cameron ... 540-261-8528 471 H
cameron.crowther@svu.edu
CROWTHER,
Cameron, T .... 540-261-8483 471 H
cameron.crowther@svu.edu
CROWTHER, Lori .... 620-792-9216 171 C
crowtherl@bartonccc.edu
CROWTHER, Steven ...... 910-221-2224 329 B
scrowther@gcd.edu
CROY, Jason .... 706-245-7226 117 E
jcroy@ec.edu
CROY, Kyle .... 541-888-7316 376 F
kcroy@socc.edu
CROYLE, Kristin .... 315-312-2285 319 B
kristin.croyle@oswego.edu
CROZIER, Nate .... 305-284-5766 112 E
nac132@miami.edu
CRUCITTI, Thomas .... 203-837-9090.. 85 B
crucittit@wcsu.edu
CRUICKSHANK,
Cameron .... 734-432-5495 227 A
ccruickshank@madonna.edu
CRUICKSHANK, Laura ... 860-486-2086.. 88 E
laura.cruickshank@uconn.edu
CRUIKSHANK, Alexis .... 206-281-2752 484 D
acruikshank@spu.edu
CRUIKSHANK,
Nancy, L .... 724-738-4831 395 F
nancy.cruikshank@sru.edu
CRULL, Matthew .... 815-825-2086 140 F
mcrull@kish.edu
CRUM, Claude .... 606-368-6061 178 D
claudecrum@alc.edu
CRUM, Lyndsey .... 970-351-2551.. 83 E
lyndsey.crum@unco.edu
CRUM, Wes .... 304-865-6171 488 E
wes.crum@ovu.edu
CRUMBAKER, Chad ...... 304-424-8242 491 D
chad.crumbaker@wvup.edu
CRUME, Gene .... 847-628-2002 140 C
gene.crume@judsonu.edu
CRUMEDY, Ron, C .... 409-944-1237 437 B
rcrumedy@gc.edu
CRUMIT-HANCOCK,
Lisa .... 419-783-2332 352 F
lcrumithancock@defiance.edu
CRUMLEY, Christopher . 281-476-1810 443 C
christopher.crumley@sjcd.edu
CRUMLEY, Kristie .... 410-386-8408 197 G
kcrumley@carrollcc.edu
CRUMP, Amanda .... 315-386-7019 320 E
crumpa@canton.edu
CRUMP, D'adra .... 718-940-5869 314 C
dcrump@sjcny.edu
CRUMP, Lori .... 573-518-2190 256 B
lcrump@mineralarea.edu
CRUMP, Tammy .... 704-991-0267 338 C
tcrump5648@stanly.edu
CRUMPACKER, Jill .... 314-838-8858 261 G
jcrumpacker@ugst.edu
CRUMPTON-YOUNG,
Lesia .... 443-885-3350 200 D
lesia.young@morgan.edu
CRUMRIN, Robin .... 812-237-3700 155 G
robin.crumrin@indstate.edu
CRUMRINE, Stephen ..... 208-562-3371 130 F
stephencrumrine@cwi.edu
CRUSCIEL, Robert .... 814-472-3021 398 B
rcrusciel@francis.edu
CRUSE, David .... 517-265-5161 220 F
dcruse@adrian.edu
CRUSE, Michele .... 971-722-5307 375 J
michele.cruse@pcc.edu
CRUSE, Terry .... 601-484-0220 247 F
tdcruse@meridian.msstate.edu
CRUSER, Kevin .... 940-898-2000 451 F
kcruser@twu.edu
CRUSTO-WAY,
Kathy, M .... 817-515-3065 445 G
kathy.crusto-way@tccd.edu
CRUTCHER, Caicey .... 620-792-9386 171 C
crutcherc@bartonccc.edu
CRUTCHER, Richard ...... 603-983-8144 439 A
rcrutcher@kilgore.edu
CRUTCHER, Ronald, A .. 804-289-8100 472 L
ronald.crutcher@richmond.edu
CRUTCHER, Terri .... 615-230-3343 426 B
terri.crutcher@volstate.edu
CRUTCHFIELD, Anne ..... 276-944-6674 467 G
acrutchfield@ehc.edu
CRUTCHFIELD, Carla ..... 501-337-5000.. 18 J
ccrutchfield@coto.edu
CRUTCHFIELD, Russell .. 678-839-6442 126 E
rcrutchf@westga.edu
CRUZ, Anthony .... 305-237-8714 103 D
acruz11@mdc.edu
CRUZ, Anthony .... 314-539-5000 259 C
acruz@stlcc.edu
CRUZ, Beatriz .... 718-429-6600 324 D
beatriz.cruz@vaughn.edu
CRUZ, Carlos .... 210-486-3338 429 F
ccruz77@alamo.edu
CRUZ, Erin .... 559-791-2332.. 47 A
ecruz@portervillecollege.edu
CRUZ, Esteban .... 217-786-2200 142 B
esteban.cruz@llcc.edu
CRUZ, Evelyn .... 979-230-3119 432 D
evelyn.cruz@brazosport.edu
CRUZ, Evelyn .... 787-850-9203 513 E
evelyn.cruz1@upr.edu
CRUZ, S.M.,
Faustino, M .... 718-817-4802 300 E
fcruz16@fordham.edu
CRUZ, Hilda .... 787-264-1912 509 F
hmcruz@intersg.edu
CRUZ, Irma del Pilar .... 787-828-1319 511 H
um_idelpilar@suagm.edu
CRUZ, Israel .... 787-264-1912 509 F
icruz@intersg.edu
CRUZ, Jackie .... 831-755-6810.. 44 K
jcruz@hartnell.edu
CRUZ, Jaclyn .... 815-802-8842 140 D
jcruz@kcc.edu
CRUZ, Jennifer .... 603-921-1089 273 A
jcruz@ccsnh.edu
CRUZ, Jessica .... 906-227-2000 228 F
jecruz@nmu.edu
CRUZ, Jessica .... 310-233-4112.. 49 A
cruzj@lahc.edu
CRUZ, Johnny .... 951-827-6047.. 69 C
johnny.cruz@ucr.edu
CRUZ, Jose, M .... 787-279-1912 509 A
jcruz@bayamon.inter.edu
CRUZ, Juan .... 787-750-4100 513 C
juan.cruz18@upr.edu
CRUZ, Lambert .... 602-489-5300.. 10 E
lambert.cruz@arizonachristian.edu
CRUZ, Larry .... 787-850-9342 513 E
larry.cruz@upr.edu
CRUZ, Lourdes .... 203-575-8091.. 86 B
lcruz@nv.edu
CRUZ, Madeline .... 787-834-9595 511 E
mcruz@uaa.edu
CRUZ, Marco Antonio ... 909-607-7283.. 56 J
marcoantonio_cruz@pitzer.edu
CRUZ, Mariela .... 787-884-6000 508 D
CRUZ, Mayra .... 787-751-0178 511 F
mcruz@suagm.edu
CRUZ, Milagros .... 787-852-1430 508 C
milagros.cruz@hccpr.edu
CRUZ, Nathaniel .... 718-518-4253 294 B
ncruz@hostos.cuny.edu
CRUZ, Octavio .... 408-270-6423.. 61 L
octavio.cruz@evc.edu
CRUZ, Odalis .... 352-335-2332.. 93 F
odalis.cruz@acupuncturist.edu
CRUZ, Oscar .... 787-250-1912 509 D
ocruz@metro.inter.edu
CRUZ, Raymind .... 857-701-1552 215 E
rcruz@rcc.mass.edu
CRUZ, Rosalia .... 212-694-1000 291 I
rcruz@boricuacollege.edu
CRUZ, Roxanna .... 305-899-7826.. 95 C
rpcruz@barry.edu
CRUZ, Ruben .... 787-841-2000 510 K
ruben_cruz@pucpr.edu
CRUZ, Tessie, H .... 787-844-8181 514 A
tessie.cruz@upr.edu
CRUZ-GONZALEZ,
Carlos, R .... 719-333-8718 504 C
carlos.cruzgonzalez@usafa.edu
CRUZ-JOHNSON, Celia . 408-288-3719.. 61 M
celia.cruz-johnson@sjcc.edu
CRUZ LUGO, Clarisa .... 787-764-0000 514 B
clarisa.cruz@upr.edu
CRUZ-PABÓN, Olga, I ... 787-751-1912 510 A
oicruz@juris.inter.edu
CRUZ-URIBE, Kathryn ... 765-973-8201 156 C
kathcruz@iue.edu
CRUZADO, Waded .... 406-994-2341 264 D
president_cruzado@montana.edu
CRUZADO ROSADO,
Geserie .... 787-720-4476 512 D
recaudacion@mizpa.edu
CRYER, Byron, L .... 214-648-2590 457 B
byron.cryer@utsouthwestern.edu
CRYSTAL, Jonathan .... 718-817-0136 300 E
crystal@fordham.edu
CRYSTAL, Maureen .... 718-270-1976 317 E
maureen.crystal@downstate.edu
CSIKOS, Erik .... 610-799-1877 388 I
ecsikos@lccc.edu
CSOMAN, Kati, R .... 814-641-3184 386 H
csomank@juniata.edu
CUADRAS, Michele .... 386-752-1822.. 99 A
michele.cuadras@fgc.edu
CUBBA, Stephanie .... 213-477-2766.. 52 G
scubba@msmu.edu
CUBBINS, Elaine .... 520-383-8401.. 16 D
ecubbins@tocc.edu
CUBERO, Chris .... 724-738-4267 395 F
chris.cubero@sru.edu
CUBILLOS, Sergio .... 786-331-1000 103 G
scubillos@maufl.edu
CUBRIEL, III, Robert ..... 361-572-6406 457 E
robert.cubriel@victoriacollege.edu
CUCARESE, Lisa .... 304-829-7831 487 G
lcucarese@bethanywv.edu
CUCCIA, Christopher ..... 973-761-7554 283 B
christopher.cuccia@shu.edu
CUCCO, Jeremy, L .... 253-879-2710 485 E
jcucco@pugetsound.edu
CUCCURULLO, Suzanne 781-891-2741 206 D
scuccurullo@bentley.edu
CUCHENS, Pat .... 281-283-3065 453 A
cuchens@uhcl.edu
CUCURELLA-ADORNO,
Ana, E .... 787-780-0070 506 F
president@caribbean.edu
CUCUZZA, Valentina ..... 717-337-6998 384 H
vacucuzza@gettysburg.edu
CUDD, Ann, E .... 412-624-4141 401 B
CUDJOE, Ashton .... 808-237-5143 127 G
ashton@hmi.edu
CUDZILO, Cheryl, B ...... 443-518-3103 199 C
ccudzilo@howardcc.edu
CUELLAR, Leana .... 847-635-1655 145 G
lcuellar@oakton.edu
CUELLAR, Toni .... 254-298-8808 446 A
toni.cuellar@templejc.edu
CUERVO, Merry .... 334-291-4958.... 1 H
merry.cuervo@cv.edu
CUESTA, Zoraya .... 305-237-1191 103 D
zcuesta@mdc.edu
CUEVA, Patricia .... 360-676-2772 482 D
pcueva@nwic.edu
CUEVAS, Carmen .... 312-935-4180 147 D
ccuevas@robertmorris.edu
CUEVAS, Frank .... 865-974-2571 427 G
fcuevas@utk.edu
CUEVAS, Jessica .... 213-477-2570.. 52 G
jcuevas@msmu.edu
CUEVAS, Monica .... 559-442-4600.. 66 E
monica.cuevas@fresnocitycollege.edu
CUEVAS, Patricia .... 312-553-6029 134 B
pcuevas@ccc.edu
CUFF, Michael .... 508-830-5016 213 B
mcuff@maritime.edu
CUFF, Shannon .... 417-873-7755 252 F
scuff@drury.edu
CUKANNA, Paul-James 412-396-6207 383 C
cukanna@duq.edu
CUKROWSKI, Ken, R .... 325-674-3700 429 B
cukrowskik@acu.edu
CULBERSON, Brent .... 615-966-1962 421 D
brent.culberson@lipscomb.edu
CULBERSON, Jeanne ..... 573-681-5477 254 E
CULBERSON, Matt .... 915-747-5594 455 C
mdculberson@utep.edu
CULBERSON, Pam .... 912-344-2527 119 C
pculberson@georgiasouthern.edu
CULBERSON, Roy .... 940-498-6282 441 A
rculberson@nctc.edu
CULBERT, John .... 773-325-7954 135 I
jculbert@depaul.edu
CULBERTSON,
Marianne .... 620-223-2700 173 C
mariannec@fortscott.edu
CULBREATH, Jahan .... 937-376-6373 350 D
jculbreath@centralstate.edu
CULHANE, Corrin, M ..... 412-578-8818 380 E
cmculhane@carlow.edu
CULKIN, Mary, E .... 512-448-8652 442 M
marya@stedwards.edu
CULLARS, Kyle .... 478-445-1976 118 C
kyle.cullars@gcsu.edu
CULLEN, Andrew .... 303-871-3740.. 83 D
andrew.a.cullen@du.edu
CULLEN, Ann .... 843-525-8247 412 H
acullen@tcl.edu
CULLEN, Cathleen, R .... 508-767-7533 205 D
ccullen@assumption.edu
CULLEN, Daryl .... 408-260-0208.. 42 M
sjfinaid@fivebranches.edu
CULLEN, Daryl .... 408-260-0208.. 43 A
sjfinaid@fivebranches.edu
CULLEN, Jim .... 570-961-7864 387 D
cullenj@lakcawanna.edu
CULLEN, Keith .... 251-981-3771.... 5 B
keith.cullen@columbiasouthern.edu
CULLEN, Laura .... 734-462-4400 230 D
lcullen@schoolcraft.edu
CULLEN, Sharon .... 703-993-8700 467 L
scullen1@gmu.edu
CULLENS, Linda .... 831-477-3222.. 27 G
licullen@cabrillo.edu
CULLER, Angela .... 336-758-4010 344 D
culleraa@wfu.edu
CULLER, Kevin, J .... 313-845-9755 224 G
kjculler@hfcc.edu
CULLER, Lori, L .... 260-359-4213 155 F
lculler@huntington.edu
CULLER, Valerie .... 734-384-4139 227 G
vculler@monroeccc.edu
CULLERTON, Laura .... 303-369-5151.. 81 J
laura.cullerton@plattcolorado.edu
CULLEY,
Christopher, M .... 614-292-0611 358 I
culley.8@osu.edu
CULLIGAN, Rob .... 320-363-3388 243 A
rculligan@csbsju.edu
CULLINAN, Carol .... 716-880-2211 306 C
carol.cullinan@medaille.edu
CULLINAN, Mary .... 509-359-6362 480 E
president@ewu.edu
CULLINAN, Shannon, B 574-631-4700 161 C
scullina@nd.edu

CURRIER, Christine .... 785-248-2562 176 D
christine.currier@ottawa.edu
CURRIER, Nicole .... 301-891-4146 204 C
ncurrier@wau.edu
CURRIN, Alicia .... 903-886-5034 447 B
alicia.currin@tamuc.edu
CURRIN, Bruce, A .... 402-472-3105 269 J
bcurrin1@unl.edu
CURRIVAN, Megan, D .. 617-322-3568 210 F
CURRY, Alicia .... 205-247-8001.... 7 A
acurry@stillman.edu
CURRY, Carolyn, S .... 240-895-4282 201 E
cscurry@smcm.edu
CURRY, Christa .... 513-244-4614 357 A
christa.curry@msj.edu
CURRY, Christine, R ..... 330-325-6263 357 G
ccurry@neomed.edu
CURRY, JR., Chuck ...... 336-316-2104 329 E
curryrc@guilford.edu
CURRY, Cynthia .... 305-626-3619.. 99 D
cynthia.curry@fmuniv.edu
CURRY, Cynthia, S .... 304-367-4386 490 B
cindy.curry@fairmontstate.edu
CURRY, Deborah .... 256-549-8321.... 2 B
dcurry@gadsdenstate.edu
CURRY, Dwayne .... 217-786-2261 142 B
dwayne.curry@llcc.edu
CURRY, Evan .... 215-702-4271 380 D
ecurry@cairn.edu
CURRY, Gina .... 916-278-5992.. 32 E
curryg@skymail.csus.edu
CURRY, James .... 402-844-7063 268 J
jamesc@northeast.edu
CURRY, Janel .... 978-867-4063 209 F
janel.curry@gordon.edu
CURRY, Jason .... 615-329-8582 419 K
jcurry@fisk.edu
CURRY, Jason, R .... 615-329-8697 419 K
jcurry@fisk.edu
CURRY, Judson .... 815-825-9532 140 F
jcurry2@kish.edu
CURRY, Kathleen .... 413-265-2412 208 C
curryk@elms.edu
CURRY, Keith .... 310-900-1600.. 40 A
kcurry@elcamino.edu
CURRY, Mike .... 352-395-5204 107 A
michael.curry@sfcollege.edu
CURRY, Milton, S .... 213-740-2723.. 72 B
archdean@usc.edu
CURRY, Ralph .... 906-217-4080 221 O
curryr@baycollege.edu
CURRY, Reva .... 989-686-9298 223 G
revacurry@delta.edu
CURRY, Robert .... 662-252-8000 248 G
rcurry@rustcollege.edu
CURRY, Robert .... 805-922-6966.. 24 J
rcurry@hancockcollege.edu
CURRY, Susan .... 618-514-3110 146 E
susan.curry@principia.edu
CURRY, Susan .... 601-318-6773 249 H
scurry@wmcarey.edu
CURRY, Terri, A .... 712-274-5259 168 B
curryte@morningside.edu
CURRY, II,
Theodore, H .... 517-353-5300 227 D
thcurry@msu.edu
CURRY, Theresa .... 413-577-1418 211 D
tcurry@umass.edu
CURRY, Theresa, M ...... 413-545-5867 211 D
theresa.curry@umass.edu
CURRY, Tim .... 606-546-1682 184 H
tcurry@unionky.edu
CURRY, Valerie .... 510-594-6957.. 58 K
v.curry@sae.edu
CURRY, William .... 601-318-6153 249 H
bcurry@wmcarey.edu
CURRY, William, N .... 601-318-6103 249 H
bill.curry@wmcarey.edu
CURRY, Zadie .... 580-477-2000 371 F
CURRY-ROBERTS,
April, E .... 615-327-6453 422 A
acurry@mmc.edu
CURTIN, Jason, E .... 410-546-6938 203 F
jecurtin@salisbury.edu
CURTIN, Katie, M .... 410-548-4773 203 F
kmcurtin@salisbury.edu
CURTIN, Maria .... 508-565-1311 218 H
mcurtin@stonehill.edu
CURTIN, Shawn, P .... 717-867-6207 388 H
curtin@lvc.edu
CURTIN, Valerie .... 406-447-6913 264 C
valerie.curtin@helenacollege.edu

CURTIS, Amy .... 207-879-8757 194 B
acurtis@idsva.edu
CURTIS, Ardys, E .... 253-535-7149 482 H
acurtis@plu.edu
CURTIS, Chris .... 912-344-2535 119 C
ccurtis@georgiasouthern.edu
CURTIS, Christine .... 256-824-6335.... 8 B
provost@uah.edu
CURTIS, Deborah .... 812-237-4000 155 G
president@indstate.edu
CURTIS, Deborah .... 716-286-8711 310 D
dcurtis@niagara.edu
CURTIS, Elaine .... 931-540-2534 424 G
bcurtis@columbiastate.edu
CURTIS, III, Guy, E ...... 540-868-4079 474 J
gcurtis@lfcc.edu
CURTIS, Jason .... 805-546-3125.. 41 A
jason_curtis@cuesta.edu
CURTIS, Jeanne, F .... 215-898-6300 400 K
curtis@isc.upenn.edu
CURTIS, Jena .... 607-753-2979 318 D
jena.curtis@cortland.edu
CURTIS, Jennifer .... 760-384-6212.. 46 M
jennifer.curtis@cerrocoso.edu
CURTIS, Jennifer .... 928-213-6060.. 11 Q
jennifer.curtis@collegeamerica.edu
CURTIS, Jerri .... 301-295-3638 504 B
jerri.curtis@usuhs.edu
CURTIS, Joanna .... 901-678-3951 427 D
jecurtis@memphis.edu
CURTIS, Joe .... 207-326-2276 195 D
joe.curtis@mma.edu
CURTIS, Kelly, T .... 864-488-4601 410 E
kcurtis@limestone.edu
CURTIS, Linda, H .... 919-516-4297 340 C
lrhubbard@st-aug.edu
CURTIS, Marvin .... 574-520-4170 157 A
mvcurtis@iusb.edu
CURTIS, Matt .... 914-831-0313 297 A
mcurtis@cw.edu
CURTIS, Michael, T .... 304-704-9111 487 I
curtism@dewv.edu
CURTIS, Regina .... 413-775-1426 214 C
curtis@gcc.mass.edu
CURTIS, Rick .... 406-243-2122 264 A
richard.curtis@umontana.edu
CURTIS, Roxie .... 816-802-3437 254 B
rcurtis@kcai.edu
CURTIS, Sandra .... 406-243-2611 264 A
sandra.curtis@umontana.edu
CURTIS, Shannon .... 508-767-7248 205 D
sj.curtis@assumption.edu
CURTIS, Timothy .... 928-428-8915.. 12 E
tim.curtis@eac.edu
CURTIS, Trina .... 828-726-2303 332 G
tcurtis@cccti.edu
CURTIS-CHAVEZ, Mark .. 630-942-2800 135 A
CURTO, Stephen, A .... 732-224-2593 276 B
scurto@brookdalecc.edu
CURTRIGHT,
Jonathan, W .... 573-884-8738 261 B
curtrightj@health.missouri.edu
CURVIN, Nicole .... 802-443-3000 462 H
deanofadmissions@middlebury.edu
CUSACK, Emma .... 949-794-9090.. 65 I
ecusack@stanbridge.edu
CUSACK, Jacqueline, L . 973-596-6445 279 F
jacqueline.l.cusack@njit.edu
CUSACK, Kristen .... 303-360-4701.. 79 D
kristen.cusack@ccaurora.edu
CUSACK, Mary .... 810-762-0474 228 C
CUSATO, Brian .... 859-238-5218 179 F
b.cusato@centre.edu
CUSEO, Vincent .... 323-259-2700.. 54 E
vcuseo@oxy.edu
CUSHENBERRY,
Shalither .... 225-743-8500 188 B
scushenberry@rpcc.edu
CUSHING, Lesleigh .... 315-228-7696 296 F
lcushing@colgate.edu
CUSHING, Ryan .... 815-394-5047 147 G
rcushing@rockford.edu
CUSHMAN, Brooke .... 208-792-2675 131 A
blcushman@lcsc.edu
CUSHMAN, Charles, B .. 202-685-8685 503 I
cushmanc@ndu.edu
CUSHMAN, Jenni .... 515-520-9040 356 A
jmc014@marietta.edu
CUSHMAN, Robert .... 585-395-2032 318 B
rcushman@brockport.edu
CUSHMAN, JR.,
Robert, A .... 707-965-6211.. 55 D
president@puc.edu

CUSICK, Dianna .... 612-659-6319 238 I
dianna.cusick@minneapolis.edu
CUSICK, Sherry .... 563-589-3721 169 I
scusick@dbq.edu
CUSICK, Susan .... 773-896-2400 133 L
scusick@ctschicago.edu
CUSIMANO,
Domonic, A .... 443-518-4448 199 C
dcusimano@howardcc.edu
CUSSEN, Susan .... 845-451-1471 298 A
susan.cussen@culinary.edu
CUSTARDO, Lisa .... 815-394-3600 147 G
lcustardo@rockford.edu
CUSTER, Carole, A .... 515-294-3134 162 I
cacuste@iastate.edu
CUSTER, Laura .... 859-344-3314 184 F
custerl@thomasmore.edu
CUSTODIA-LORA,
Noemi .... 978-738-7401 215 C
ncustodialora@necc.mass.edu
CUTCHENS, Melinda ..... 229-333-5952 126 G
cutchens@valdosta.edu
CUTCHINS, Cathy .... 757-569-6712 475 E
ccutchins@pdc.edu
CUTHRELL, Patrick .... 252-335-0821 333 G
patrick_cuthrell@albemarle.edu
CUTIETTA, Robert, A ..... 213-740-5389.. 72 B
musicdean@thornton.usc.edu
CUTLER, Amy .... 509-777-4733 486 I
acutler@whitworth.edu
CUTLER, Brooke .... 310-506-4246.. 56 C
brooke.cutler@pepperdine.edu
CUTLER, Chris .... 315-268-6745 296 A
ccutler@clarkson.edu
CUTLER, Iris .... 206-517-4541 484 C
admissions@gmail.com
CUTLER, Jerry .... 212-229-5671 308 C
jerry.cutler@newschool.edu
CUTLER, Nancy .... 408-554-4915.. 62 D
ncutler@scu.edu
CUTLER, Peter, J .... 315-267-2434 319 D
cutlerpj@potsdam.edu
CUTLER, Spencer .... 208-732-6600 130 E
scutler@csi.edu
CUTLER, Stephen, J ...... 803-777-8310 413 C
ashley@sccp.sc.edu
CUTONE, Joan .... 412-536-1079 387 B
joan.cutone@laroche.edu
CUTRELL, Lori .... 615-230-4834 426 B
lori.cutrell@volstate.edu
CUTRI, David .... 419-530-6294 363 E
david.cutri@utoledo.edu
CUTRIGHT, Bruce .... 402-461-5177 267 F
CUTRIGHT, Kelsey .... 740-474-8896 358 F
kcutright@ohiochristian.edu
CUTRIGHT, Robyn, E ..... 859-238-5573 179 F
robyn.cutright@centre.edu
CUTSHAW, Kathleen, D . 808-956-9190 128 F
cutshaw@hawaii.edu
CUTSPEC, John .... 828-251-6868 342 C
jcutspec@unca.edu
CUTTING, Judith .... 831-646-4000.. 52 F
jcutting@mpc.edu
CUTTLE-OLIVER, Ellen ... 508-531-2691 212 B
e2oliver@bridgew.edu
CUTTRISS, Christopher . 661-253-7732.. 28 K
ccuttriss@calarts.edu
CUZ, Julio .... 951-571-6380.. 58 G
julio.cuz@mvc.edu
CUZYDLO, Karen .... 810-762-3300 231 G
karenicu@umich.edu
CUZZO, Maria .... 715-394-8449 498 B
mcuzzo@uwsuper.edu
CVETIC, Diane .... 925-969-3300.. 46 H
dcvetic@jfku.edu
CVETIC, Mike .... 412-237-4146 381 G
mcvetic@ccac.edu
CVITKOVIC, Vicki .... 847-543-6504 135 B
vcvitkovic@clcillinois.edu
CWYK, Alysson .... 215-965-4050 390 J
acwyk@moore.edu
CYGAN, Brian, L .... 570-326-3761 393 G
brian.cygan@pct.edu
CYPHERS,
Christopher, J .... 212-592-2550 315 H
ccyphers@sva.edu
CYPHERS, Russell .... 276-523-7473 475 A
rcyphers@mecc.edu
CYPRESS, Sharen .... 731-989-6074 420 C
scypress@fhu.edu
CYR, Cheryl .... 619-298-1829.. 65 E
CYR, Cheryl, A .... 860-253-3050.. 85 C
ccyr@asnuntuck.edu

CYREE, Kendall, B .... 662-915-1103 249 D
kbcyree@olemiss.edu
CYRUS, Cynthia, J .... 615-322-4474 428 D
cynthia.j.cyrus@vanderbilt.edu
CYRUS, Danielle .... 906-487-2510 227 E
dcyrus@mtu.edu
CZAJKA, Darcy .... 518-388-6101 323 G
czajkad@union.edu
CZARAPATA, Paul .... 859-256-3100 180 H
paul.czarapata@kctcs.edu
CZARDA, Lawrence, D .. 336-217-7221 329 D
lczarda@greensboro.edu
CZARNECKI, John .... 607-431-4318 301 D
czarneckij@hartwick.edu
CZEKANSKI, Kathleen ... 215-951-1432 387 C
czekanski@lasalle.edu
CZENSZAK, Richard ...... 407-831-9816.. 96 G
rczenszak@citycollege.edu
CZERNIECKI,
Thomas, J .... 856-222-9311 281 C
tczerniecki@rcbc.edu
CZERWINSKI, Rick .... 540-887-7336 469 B
rczerwin@marybaldwin.edu
CZUCHRY, Michael .... 830-372-6047 449 B
mczuchry@tlu.edu
CZYZ, Vito .... 716-926-8925 301 H
vczyz@hilbert.edu

D

DA CUNHA, Ana .... 617-236-8810 209 D
adacunha@fisher.edu
DA GRACA, John .... 956-447-3361 447 D
john.dagraca@tamuk.edu
DA SILVA, Dawn .... 201-216-5000 283 C
DA SILVA, Jose .... 815-802-8510 140 D
jdasilva@kcc.edu
DAAR, Judith .... 859-572-5717 184 A
daarj1@nku.edu
DAAR, Karen .... 818-947-2378.. 49 F
daarkl@lavc.edu
DAAS, Mahesh .... 785-864-3114 177 D
mahesh@ku.edu
DAAS, Mahesh .... 617-585-0200 206 F
mahesh.daas@the-bac.edu
DABIDAT, Mike Vishol . 212-812-4040 309 D
mdabidat@nycda.edu
DABIRIAN, Amir .... 657-278-5000.. 31 E
adabirian@fullerton.edu
DABNEY, Emily, C .... 662-846-4040 245 H
edabney@deltastate.edu
DABNEY, Natasha .... 619-961-4256.. 67 E
ndabney@tjsl.edu
DABOLL-LAVOIE,
Kathleen .... 585-389-2591 308 B
kdaboll9@naz.edu
DABOVICH, Ann .... 415-749-4577.. 60 G
adabovich@sfai.edu
DACE, Karen, L .... 317-278-3820 156 F
kdace@iupui.edu
DACEY, Joe .... 508-565-1804 218 H
jdacey@stonehill.edu
DACEY, Susan .... 973-748-9000 276 A
susan_dacey@bloomfield.edu
DACHELET, Derek .... 608-822-2417 500 G
ddachelet@swtc.edu
DACHILLE, Nancy .... 215-248-7048 381 D
ndachill@chc.edu
DACOSTA, Romario .... 914-632-5400 307 G
rdacosta@monroecollege.edu
DACOSTA, Tracy, M ...... 401-254-3541 405 E
tdacosta@rwu.edu
DACRUZ, Becky .... 229-333-5800 126 G
DACUNHA,
Rhiannon, L .... 315-684-6020 321 D
dacunhrl@morrisville.edu
DACUS, Kent .... 951-343-4687.. 27 J
kdacus@calbaptist.edu
DADABHOY, Khushnur . 805-378-1408.. 72 H
kdadabhoy@vcccd.edu
DADABHOY, Zavareh .... 661-395-4204.. 46 L
zav.dadabhoy@bakersfieldcollege.edu
DADARRIA, Nikki .... 908-835-9222 284 G
ndadarria@warren.edu
DADEY, Cheryl .... 702-254-7577 272 A
cheryl.dadey@northwestcareercollege.edu
DADIAN PEREZ, Sara ... 603-623-0313 273 I
saradadian@nhia.edu
DAELY, Ben .... 619-929-9748.. 45 C
bdaley@hightechhigh.org
DAFFER, Steve .... 405-733-7424 369 I
sdaffer@rose.edu

DAMRON, Steve .... 254-968-9227 446 E
sdamron@tarleton.edu
DAMROW, Bobbi .... 715-422-5421 500 A
bobbi.damrow@mstc.edu
DAMS, Scott .... 610-861-1601 391 A
damss@moravian.edu
DAMSCHRODER,
Matthew .... 814-641-3151 386 H
damschm@juniata.edu
DAN, Chong .... 704-216-6035 330 H
cdan@livingstone.edu
DANA, Arthur, B .... 706-385-1106 123 C
arthur.dana@point.edu
DANA, Robert, Q .... 207-581-1405 195 J
rdana@maine.edu
DANA, Samantha .... 253-589-4520 479 G
samantha.data@cptc.edu
DANAJOVITS, Joseph ... 860-738-6409.. 86 C
jdanajovits@nwcc.edu
DANALS, Brandt .... 920-686-6135 496 A
brandt.danals@sl.edu
DANCE, Andrea .... 252-335-0821 333 G
andrea_dance@albemarle.edu
DANCER, Erin .... 770-426-2974 121 C
erin.dancer@life.edu
DANCY, Gerlinde .... 963-638-2941 113 B
dancygl@webber.edu
DANCY, Regina, M .... 704-636-6454 330 A
rdancy@hoodseminary.edu
DANDO, Mary .... 303-492-2975.. 83 A
mary.dando@colorado.edu
DANDORPH, Michael .... 312-942-5756 148 A
michael_dandorph@rush.edu
DANE, Jane, H .... 757-683-6702 469 G
jhdane@odu.edu
DANES, Mark .... 515-271-1661 164 I
mark.danes@dmu.edu
DANFORD, Richard, K .. 740-376-4736 356 A
richard.danford@marietta.edu
DANFORTH, Dave .... 218-281-8490 244 A
danfo002@umn.edu
DANFORTH, Elizabeth ... 406-994-3836 264 D
danforth@montana.edu
DANFORTH, Meridith .... 972-860-4823 434 L
mdanforth@dcccd.edu
DANG, Hung, D .... 805-437-8918.. 30 F
hung.dang@csuci.edu
DANG, Tuan .... 425-564-2460 478 F
tuan.dang@bellevuecollege.edu
DANG, Tuan .... 425-739-8818 482 A
tuan.dang@lwtech.edu
DANG-WILLIAMS, Thao 314-246-8757 262 C
thaodangwilliams@webster.edu
DANGELANTONIO,
Sarah .... 603-899-4278 273 F
dangelantonios@franklinpierce.edu
DANGERFIELD, Deneen . 410-777-2830 197 C
drdangerfield@aacc.edu
DANHEISER,
Priscilla, R .... 478-301-2084 121 E
danheiser_p@mercer.edu
DANICA, Kathleen .... 518-244-4552 313 D
bouchk2@sage.edu
DANIEL, Andrea, D .... 706-355-5111 114 F
adaniel@athenstech.edu
DANIEL, Brett .... 903-675-6393 452 B
bdaniel@tvcc.edu
DANIEL, Chett .... 417-455-5750 252 D
chettdaniel@crowder.edu
DANIEL, Chris .... 770-229-3327 124 G
chris.daniel@sctech.edu
DANIEL, Chris .... 813-974-2972 110 B
cldaniel@usf.edu
DANIEL, Eileen .... 585-395-5505 318 B
edaniel@brockport.edu
DANIEL, Ethel .... 617-217-9887 206 A
edaniel@baystate.edu
DANIEL, Gregory, B ...... 540-231-4621 477 A
gdaniel@vt.edu
DANIEL, Juliet .... 828-225-3993 328 E
admissions@daoisttraditions.edu
DANIEL, Karina .... 325-649-8806 438 D
kdaniel@hputx.edu
DANIEL, Kathleen .... 305-809-3248.. 99 C
kathleen.daniel@fkcc.edu
DANIEL, Kevin, S .... 719-587-7741.. 76 F
ksdaniel@adams.edu
DANIEL, Larry .... 432-552-2120 457 A
daniel_l@utpb.edu
DANIEL, Meredith .... 864-941-8442 411 H
meredith.d@ptc.edu
DANIEL, Mick .... 864-977-7160 411 E
mick.daniel@ngu.edu
DANIEL, Nancy .... 828-448-3160 339 A
ndaniel@wpcc.edu
DANIEL, Robin .... 434-949-1018 475 H
robin.daniel@southside.edu
DANIEL, Robin, L .... 336-272-7102 329 D
rdaniel@greensboro.edu
DANIEL, Sharlene .... 423-775-6596 423 F
finance@ogs.edu
DANIEL, Sherman .... 680-488-2471 506 B
shermand1961@yahoo.com
DANIEL, W. John .... 205-934-3474.... 8 A
wdaniel@uab.edu
DANIEL, William .... 214-648-5308 457 B
william.daniel@utsouthwestern.edu
DANIELE, Christina .... 845-575-3000 305 L
christina.daniele@marist.edu
DANIELL, Steven .... 817-531-4405 451 E
sdaniell@txwes.edu
DANIELS, Andrea .... 910-410-1724 337 B
asdaniels@richmondcc.edu
DANIELS, Ashley .... 504-520-5166 193 A
adaniels@xula.edu
DANIELS, Brian .... 865-974-6611 427 F
brian.daniels@tennessee.edu
DANIELS, C. Wess .... 336-316-2445 329 E
danielscw@guilford.edu
DANIELS, Christy .... 252-328-6212 341 C
danielsc@ecu.edu
DANIELS, Clayton .... 706-379-3111 127 C
cpdaniels@yhc.edu
DANIELS, Cordelia .... 503-821-8881 375 F
cdaniels@pnca.edu
DANIELS, Debra .... 661-763-7710.. 66 J
ddaniels@taftcollege.edu
DANIELS, Denise .... 478-289-2145 117 D
dmdaneils@ega.edu
DANIELS, Dennis, E ...... 936-261-3085 446 D
dedaniels@pvamu.edu
DANIELS, Diane .... 617-588-1376 206 C
ddaniels@bfit.edu
DANIELS, Edward .... 541-885-1117 375 C
edward.daniels@oit.edu
DANIELS, George, T ...... 919-572-1625 326 L
gdaniels14@apexsot.edu
DANIELS, Gerri, L .... 906-227-2650 228 F
gdaniels@nmu.edu
DANIELS, Heather, M ... 608-263-1011 496 C
soas@soas.wisc.edu
DANIELS, III, Jack, E ... 608-246-6676 499 H
jdanielsiii@madisoncollege.edu
DANIELS, Joan .... 559-737-6242.. 39 E
joand@cos.edu
DANIELS, Joseph .... 414-288-3368 494 B
joseph.daniels@marquette.edu
DANIELS, Julie .... 601-974-1443 247 B
julie.daniels@millsaps.edu
DANIELS, Kacey .... 405-422-1203 369 E
kacey.daniels@redlandscc.edu
DANIELS, LaMetrius ...... 615-248-1521 427 A
ldaniels@trevecca.edu
DANIELS, Linda .... 601-977-4462 249 C
ldaniels@tougaloo.edu
DANIELS, Lisa .... 518-608-8398 299 G
ldaniels@excelsior.edu
DANIELS, Mark .... 425-235-5839 483 G
mdaniels@rtc.edu
DANIELS, Martin, C .... 518-276-6813 312 I
daniem@rpi.edu
DANIELS, Matt .... 641-844-5708 166 K
matt.daniels@iavalley.edu
DANIELS, Michael .... 617-585-0200 206 F
michael.daniels@the-bac.edu
DANIELS, Michael .... 828-448-3564 339 A
mdaniels@wpcc.edu
DANIELS, JR., Mitchell . 317-208-5311 159 D
DANIELS, JR.,
Mitchell, E .... 765-494-4600 159 E
president@purdue.edu
DANIELS, Patti, J .... 618-537-6936 143 B
pjdaniels@mckendree.edu
DANIELS, Randell, W .... 734-384-4224 227 G
rdaniels@monroeccc.edu
DANIELS, Robin .... 325-793-4601 440 B
daniels.robin@mcm.edu
DANIELS, Ronald, J .... 410-516-4170 199 D
president@jhu.edu
DANIELS, Shedrick .... 847-635-1699 145 G
sdaniels@oakton.edu
DANIELS, Terri, G .... 407-582-6801 112 K
tdaniels31@valenciacollege.edu
DANIELS, Tonya .... 615-230-3214 426 B
tonya.daniels@volstate.edu
DANIELS, Von .... 870-338-6474.. 22 H
DANIELSON, Eric, M .... 301-447-5505 200 E
danielson@msmary.edu
DANIELSON, Lisa, M .... 920-424-3007 497 B
danielsn@uwosh.edu
DANIELSON, Marsha ..... 507-389-7426 241 C
marsha.danielson@southcentral.edu
DANIELSON, Michelle ... 507-285-7180 240 G
michelle.danielson@rctc.edu
DANIELSON, Timothy ... 414-229-4463 497 A
danieltj@uwm.edu
DANIEU, Paul, F .... 716-851-1856 299 F
danieu@ecc.edu
DANIK, Steve .... 410-951-3575 203 D
sdanik@coppin.edu
DANKEL, Richard .... 401-232-6117 404 F
rdankel@bryant.edu
DANKO, James .... 413-755-4812 215 F
jdanko@stcc.edu
DANKO, James, M .... 317-940-9900 153 F
president@butler.edu
DANLEY, Roger .... 316-295-5836 173 D
rogerd@friends.edu
DANLEY, Stacy, L .... 803-533-3743 412 C
sdanley@scsu.edu
DANNA, Debra .... 504-864-7550 189 F
danna@loyno.edu
DANNA, Sasha .... 530-898-6116.. 31 A
sdanna@calstate.edu
DANNA, Stephen .... 518-792-5425 319 C
dann1253@plattsburgh.edu
DANNEMILLER,
Stanley, D .... 330-325-6558 357 G
sdannemiller@neomed.edu
DANNEN, Troy .... 504-865-5500 191 B
tdannen@tulane.edu
DANNENBAUM,
Martha, C .... 979-458-8300 446 G
mdannenbaum@tamu.edu
DANNENBERG, Dave ..... 907-786-4447.... 9 H
ddannenberg@alaska.edu
DANNENHOFFER,
Patrick .... 914-606-8541 325 C
patrick.dannenhoffer@sunywcc.edu
DANNER, Deborah .... 509-359-2383 480 E
ddanner2@ewu.edu
DANNER, John, P .... 210-458-4105 455 E
john.danner@utsa.edu
DANOWITZ, Mary Ann . 919-515-5900 342 B
mdanowi@ncsu.edu
DANSER, Dolores, A ..... 717-245-1589 382 F
danserd@dickinson.edu
DANTLEY, Michael .... 513-529-6317 356 E
dantleme@miamioh.edu
DANUFF, Allan .... 352-854-2322.. 96 O
danuffa@cf.edu
DANVER, Steven .... 866-492-5336 244 F
steven.danver@mail.waldenu.edu
DANZ, Nick .... 715-394-8161 498 B
ndanz@uwsuper.edu
DANZ, Stephanie .... 518-629-7158 302 E
s.danz@hvcc.edu
DANZI, SJ, Rocco .... 201-761-6014 282 I
rdanzi@saintpeters.edu
DANZY, Jamia .... 585-292-3010 307 H
jdanzy1@monroecc.edu
DAO, Chau .... 909-274-4450.. 52 H
cdao@mtsac.edu
DAOAS, Doman .... 691-320-2480 505 B
daoas@comfsm.fm
DAOOD, Christopher .... 262-691-5314 500 H
cdaood@wctc.edu
DAOUST, Carolyn .... 989-358-7211 221 A
daoust@alpenacc.edu
DAPICE-WONG,
Stephanie .... 631-665-1600 322 J
stephanie.wong@touro.edu
DAPP, Kelly .... 661-362-3983.. 38 H
kelly.dapp@canyons.edu
DAPRA, Joe .... 816-322-0110 250 K
joe.dapra@calvary.edu
DAQUILA, August .... 609-343-5116 275 D
adaquila@atlantic.edu
DARABI, Rachelle .... 417-836-8346 256 E
rachelledarabi@missouristate.edu
DARBANDI, Shiva .... 207-699-5090 194 D
sdarbandi@meca.edu
DARBEAU, Ron .... 479-788-7611.. 21 H
ron.darbeau@uafs.edu
DARBONE, Davidson .... 337-421-6940 188 D
david.darbone@sowela.edu
DARBY, Kadia .... 212-616-7263 301 F
kadia.darby@helenefuld.edu
DARBY, Shani .... 212-431-2896 309 G
shani.darby@nyls.edu
DARCY, Kip .... 810-762-7331 225 H
kdarcy@kettering.edu
DARDEN, Alyssa .... 614-947-6685 353 C
alyssa.darden@franklin.edu
DARDEN, Elbert .... 816-501-4275 258 H
elbert.darden@rockhurst.edu
DARDEN, Joanna .... 901-572-2448 418 E
joanna.darden@bchs.edu
DARDEN-BEAUFORD,
Yulonda .... 404-225-4488 114 H
ybeauford@atlantatech.edu
DARE, Akinola .... 478-257-5825.. 92 G
DARGA, Richard .... 773-995-2378 133 K
rdarga@csu.edu
DARGAN, Benardo .... 909-869-3850.. 30 D
bjdargan@cpp.edu
DARIAROW, Esmail ...... 239-939-4766 107 L
edariarow@southerntech.edu
DARIN, Jessica .... 805-756-6000.. 30 C
darin@calpoly.edu
DARK, Shawna .... 562-985-8115.. 31 F
shawna.dark@csulb.edu
DARKEN, Kristin .... 831-646-4001.. 52 F
kdarken@mpc.edu
DARLAND, Suzanne ...... 270-706-8460 181 A
suzanne.darland@kctcs.edu
DARLAND, Zane .... 606-693-5000 182 G
zdarland@kmbc.edu
DARLEY, Maria .... 706-729-2306 115 A
mdarley@augusta.edu
DARLING, Candida .... 801-957-4186 461 D
candida.darling@slcc.edu
DARLING, David .... 608-262-3488 496 C
david.darling@wisc.edu
DARLING, Douglas, D .. 701-662-1506 346 D
doug.darling@lrsc.edu
DARLING, Hilary .... 661-253-7724.. 28 K
hdarling@calarts.edu
DARLING, Kyle .... 206-934-3869 484 A
kyle.darling@seattlecolleges.edu
DARLING, Mary .... 619-594-8299.. 33 E
mdarling@sdsu.edu
DARMON, Robin .... 619-260-4654.. 71 J
rdarmon@sandiego.edu
DARMSTAEDTER,
Nicholous .... 901-272-5177 422 B
ndarmstaedter@mca.edu
DARNELL, Charles .... 435-797-1952 460 H
charles.darnell@usu.edu
DARNELL, Kacey .... 254-867-3009 449 E
kacey.darnell@tstc.edu
DARR, Eric, D .... 717-901-5111 385 K
edarr@harrisburgu.edu
DARR, Kristi .... 515-294-6458 162 I
kdarr@iastate.edu
DARRAGH, Alex .... 847-467-5810 145 F
DARRAH, Joseph .... 610-527-0200 397 I
DARRAH, Thom .... 541-885-1600 375 C
thom.darrah@oit.edu
DARRELL, Christopher .. 973-408-3553 277 C
cdarrell@drew.edu
DARROCH, Jenny .... 909-607-3811.. 37 D
jenny.darroch@cgu.edu
DARROUZET, Hunter ..... 563-588-8192 163 F
hunter.darrouzet@clarke.edu
DARROW, David .... 906-932-4231 224 B
DARROW, Louis .... 330-490-7373 364 B
ldarrow@walsh.edu
DARS, Lori .... 848-932-4481 282 A
lori.dars@rutgers.edu
DARS, Lori .... 848-932-4481 282 B
lori.dars@rutgers.edu
DARSCH, Lisa .... 540-665-4530 471 E
ldarsch@su.edu
DARSEE, Jon .... 319-335-3565 163 A
DARST, Abbie .... 859-985-3019 179 C
darsta@berea.edu
DART, Lucas .... 308-698-5270 269 I
ldart@nufoundation.org
DARWIN, John, W .... 402-280-3994 266 I
johndarwin@creighton.edu
DARWIN, Mike .... 205-726-4241..... 6 E
mdarwin@samford.edu
DAS, A. Andrew .... 630-617-3541 136 G
adas@elmhurst.edu
DAS, Carolyn .... 352-395-5226 107 A
carolyn.das@sfcollege.edu
DAS, Joggeshwar .... 716-829-8006 298 F
dasj@dyc.edu
DAS, Pradeep, K .... 404-627-2681 115 C
pradeep.das@beulah.edu
DASBURG, Deanne .... 828-884-8129 327 C
dasburg@brevard.edu

DAVIS, Britt 910-893-1200 327 E davisb@campbell.edu
DAVIS, Brittany 334-833-4428 5 H finaid@hawks.huntingdon.edu
DAVIS, Bruce 801-626-6789 461 B brucedavis@weber.edu
DAVIS, Bryan 951-343-4721 27 J bdavis@calbaptist.edu
DAVIS, Bryan, P 229-931-5140 119 D bryan.davis@gsw.edu
DAVIS, Bryson 270-745-2051 185 E bryson.davis@wku.edu
DAVIS, Carole 269-965-3931 225 F davisc@kellogg.edu
DAVIS, Catherine, C 609-497-7882 280 D student.relations@ptsem.edu
DAVIS, Chad 701-477-7832 347 A cdavis@tm.edu
DAVIS, Charity 330-325-6726 357 G
DAVIS, III, Charles, E 540-887-7240 469 B cedavis@marybaldwin.edu
DAVIS, Charles, N 706-542-1704 125 G cndavis@uga.edu
DAVIS, Cheryl 270-745-6733 185 E cheryl.davis@wku.edu
DAVIS, Chris 706-385-1041 123 C chris.davis@point.edu
DAVIS, Chris 757-455-3114 477 F ctdavis@vwu.edu
DAVIS, Chrissy 509-533-3514 480 B chrissy.davis@sfcc.spokane.edu
DAVIS, Christine 479-619-3156 20 D cdavis22@nwacc.edu
DAVIS, Christine 239-433-6950 100 A christine.davis@fsw.edu
DAVIS, Christopher, A 410-293-6381 504 I cdavis@usna.edu
DAVIS, Cindy 785-442-6054 174 A cdavis@highlandcc.edu
DAVIS, Claire 818-677-2160 32 D claire.davis@csun.edu
DAVIS, Cliff 708-344-4700 142 A cdavis@lincolntech.edu
DAVIS, Cliff 417-447-2652 257 G davisc@otc.edu
DAVIS, Cody 501-977-2087 23 A davis@uaccm.edu
DAVIS, Colin 309-649-6395 150 A colin.davis@src.edu
DAVIS, Connie 985-549-2094 192 D cdavis@selu.edu
DAVIS, D. Scott 478-301-2110 121 E davis_ds@mercer.edu
DAVIS, Dan 701-228-5451 346 C danny.davis@dakotacollege.edu
DAVIS, Dana 478-445-2301 116 A ddavis@centralgatech.edu
DAVIS, Daniel 212-854-6939 290 J ddavis@barnard.edu
DAVIS, Daniel 817-722-1614 439 B daniel.davis@tku.edu
DAVIS, Danny, R 252-398-6250 328 D drdavis@chowan.edu
DAVIS, Darin 405-789-7661 370 B darin.davis@swcu.edu
DAVIS, Daryl, J 407-582-1255 112 K djdavis@valenciacollege.edu
DAVIS, Deborah 804-828-0100 473 F deborah.davis@vcuhealth.org
DAVIS, Debra, C 251-445-9404 8 F ddavis@southalabama.edu
DAVIS, Deidra 207-326-2138 195 D deidra.davis@mma.edu
DAVIS, Derek 816-268-5400 257 C dldavis@nts.edu
DAVIS, Diana 513-244-4301 357 A diana.davis@msj.edu
DAVIS, Dirk 951-343-3905 27 J ddavis@calbaptist.edu
DAVIS, Don 626-815-3828 26 H ddavis@apu.edu
DAVIS, Donna 760-757-2121 52 E ddavis@miracosta.edu
DAVIS, Donna 636-922-8300 258 I ddavis@stchas.edu
DAVIS, Donna 724-964-8811 391 E ddavis@ncstrades.edu
DAVIS, Donna, J 415-422-6822 71 K davisdj@usfca.edu
DAVIS, Drew, H 704-637-4227 328 A dhdavis18@catawba.edu
DAVIS, Elizabeth 410-871-3376 200 B emdavis@mcdaniel.edu
DAVIS, Elizabeth 317-896-9324 160 I edavis@ubca.org
DAVIS, Elizabeth 864-294-2100 410 A elizabeth.davis@furman.edu
DAVIS, Ellen 254-298-8591 446 A ellen.davis@templejc.edu
DAVIS, Ember 870-460-1274 22 D davisel@uamont.edu
DAVIS, Emily 859-622-1501 180 B emily.davis@eku.edu
DAVIS, Eric 505-424-2351 286 C eric.davis@iaia.edu
DAVIS, Eric 651-201-1827 237 A
DAVIS, Erika 610-558-5613 391 D davise@neumann.edu
DAVIS, Erin 319-895-4296 164 B edavis@cornellcollege.edu
DAVIS, Faye, M 972-548-6866 433 M fdavis@collin.edu
DAVIS, G. Todd 559-638-0300 66 F todd.davis@reedleycollege.edu
DAVIS, G. William 443-518-3209 199 C gdavis@howardcc.edu
DAVIS, Gilda 504-286-5176 190 I gdavis@suno.edu
DAVIS, Glenda 214-379-5526 441 I gdavis@pqc.edu
DAVIS, Glenn 320-308-5272 240 H gmdavis@stcloudstate.edu
DAVIS, Glenn 212-463-0400 322 J glenn.davis2@touro.edu
DAVIS, Grant 610-647-4400 386 C gdavis@immaculata.edu
DAVIS, Greg 360-438-8772 483 H gdavis@stmartin.edu
DAVIS, Gregory 802-865-5435 462 B gdavis@champlain.edu
DAVIS, Guy 423-697-4466 424 E guy.davis@chattanoogastate.edu
DAVIS, Harriet, F 919-530-6151 342 A hfdavis@nccu.edu
DAVIS, Hazel 480-517-8273 13 G hazel.davis@riosalado.edu
DAVIS, Heather 207-602-2629 196 G hdavis@une.edu
DAVIS, Heather 336-750-3350 344 B davish@wssu.edu
DAVIS, Heidi, L 504-865-3086 189 F heidi@loyno.edu
DAVIS, Herbert, R 919-572-1625 326 L hdavis@apexsot.edu
DAVIS, Hope 574-520-4339 157 A hsdavis@iusb.edu
DAVIS, Houston, D 501-450-5286 23 H hdavis@uca.edu
DAVIS, Howard 805-378-4133 72 H hdavis@vcccd.edu
DAVIS, Jackie 712-707-7114 168 H jackie.davis@nwciowa.edu
DAVIS, Jake 270-686-2111 179 D jake.davis@brescia.edu
DAVIS, James 310-206-0011 69 A jdavis@conet.ucla.edu
DAVIS, James 512-471-3434 455 A jim.davis@austin.utexas.edu
DAVIS, James, F 308-865-8517 269 I davisjf@unk.edu
DAVIS, James, J 202-806-6700 92 B jdavis@howard.edu
DAVIS, Jamie 850-412-7994 108 I jamie.davis@famu.edu
DAVIS, Jamie 912-443-4162 124 A jdavis@savannahtech.edu
DAVIS, Jarred 214-860-8680 435 D jarreddavis@dcccd.edu
DAVIS, Jason 218-726-8782 243 F jdavis@d.umn.edu
DAVIS, Jeff 912-871-1640 122 I jdavis@ogeecheetech.edu
DAVIS, Jeff 706-802-5105 118 E jdavis@highlands.edu
DAVIS, Jeff 541-757-8944 374 A jeff.davis@linnbenton.edu
DAVIS, Jeffery 706-507-8909 116 I davis_jeffery6@columbusstate.edu
DAVIS, Jeffrey 662-325-3444 247 F jdavis@alumni.msstate.edu
DAVIS, Jeffry 630-752-5786 152 F jeffry.davis@wheaton.edu
DAVIS, Jenna 719-336-1589 80 K jenna.davis@lamarcc.edu
DAVIS, Jennifer 903-334-6752 448 B jdavis@tamut.edu
DAVIS, Jennifer 216-987-4236 351 G jennifer.davis@tri-c.edu
DAVIS, Jerold 212-592-2829 315 H jdavis8@sva.edu
DAVIS, Jerome 212-854-5017 297 C jd2145@columbia.edu
DAVIS, Jerry, C 417-690-2470 251 E pres@cofo.edu
DAVIS, Joe, D 641-422-4121 168 D davisjoe@niacc.edu
DAVIS, John 937-766-7886 349 G davisjo@cedarville.edu
DAVIS, John 603-641-7770 274 C jdavis@anselm.edu
DAVIS, John 502-863-8044 180 E john_davis@georgetowncollege.edu
DAVIS, John 870-460-1189 22 D davisjc@uamont.edu
DAVIS, John 910-843-5304 331 K johnruedavis@gmail.com
DAVIS, John 920-206-2332 493 L john.davis@mbu.edu
DAVIS, John 920-206-2371 493 L john.davis@mbu.edu
DAVIS, John 307-766-6225 502 H jdavis71@uwyo.edu
DAVIS, John, M 540-423-9043 474 G jdavis@germanna.edu
DAVIS, Jon 360-676-2772 482 D jdavis@nwic.edu
DAVIS, Jon 843-863-7218 407 E jdavis@csuniv.edu
DAVIS, Jonathan 704-669-4124 333 E davisj@clevelandcc.edu
DAVIS, Jonathan, M 802-626-6418 464 C jonathan.davis@northernvermont.edu
DAVIS, Jordan 214-333-6830 434 I jordan@dbu.edu
DAVIS, Joy 970-207-4550 80 M joyd@mckinleycollege.edu
DAVIS, Joyce, E 404-270-5871 125 B jdavis44@spelman.edu
DAVIS, Julia, T 478-301-2644 121 E davis_jt@mercer.edu
DAVIS, Julie 478-934-3518 121 F julie.davis3@mga.edu
DAVIS, Julie 630-752-5079 152 F julie.davis@wheaton.edu
DAVIS, Julie 315-268-6713 296 A davisju@clarkson.edu
DAVIS, Julie, A 207-778-7264 196 B jadavis@maine.edu
DAVIS, June 910-296-2424 335 E jdavis@jamessprunt.edu
DAVIS, Karen 805-493-3164 29 H kdavis@callutheran.edu
DAVIS, Katherine 423-746-5301 426 F kdavis@tnwesleyan.edu
DAVIS, Kathleen 314-977-2500 259 H
DAVIS, Kathy 207-602-2373 196 G kdavis17@une.edu
DAVIS, Katie 478-274-7775 122 H kdavis@oftc.edu
DAVIS, Kelly 479-968-0242 18 C kdavis@atu.edu
DAVIS, Kelly 817-272-2194 454 J kdavis@uta.edu
DAVIS, Kelvin 662-846-4698 245 H kddavis@deltastate.edu
DAVIS, Kelvin 803-376-5700 406 F kdavis@allenuniversity.edu
DAVIS, Ken 803-536-7017 412 C ken.davis@scsu.edu
DAVIS, Kenneth, L 212-659-9003 302 F
DAVIS, JR., Kenneth, M 919-658-2502 340 J kdavis@umo.edu
DAVIS, Kenny 910-272-3500 337 D kdavis@robeson.edu
DAVIS, Kery 202-806-7141 92 B kery.davis@howard.edu
DAVIS, Kevin 205-391-2290 3 E kdavis@sheltonstate.edu
DAVIS, Kevin 704-894-2405 328 F kedavis@davidson.edu
DAVIS, Kevin, L 936-468-1285 445 F daviskl2@sfasu.edu
DAVIS, Kim 843-661-1210 409 K kdavis@fmarion.edu
DAVIS, Koshua 910-362-7187 332 H jldavis393@mail.cfcc.edu
DAVIS, Kristy 479-968-0329 18 C kdavis51@atu.edu
DAVIS, Kyle 270-789-5556 179 E kpdavis@campbellsville.edu
DAVIS, Larry 254-501-5833 447 A lmdavis@tamuct.edu
DAVIS, Larry, J 314-516-5606 261 D ldavis@umsl.edu
DAVIS, LaTricia 870-235-4001 21 D ldavis@saumag.edu
DAVIS, Lautauscha 773-291-6740 134 E ldavis315@ccc.edu
DAVIS, Lee 229-333-5351 126 G escdavis@valdosta.edu
DAVIS, Len, L 516-876-3191 319 A davisl@oldwestbury.edu
DAVIS, Linda 810-989-5765 230 C ldavis@sc4.edu
DAVIS, Lonette 410-287-1034 197 H ldavis@cecil.edu
DAVIS, Loren 253-589-5771 479 G loren.davis@cptc.edu
DAVIS, Lorna 559-934-2203 74 A lornadavis@whccd.edu
DAVIS, Louis 706-855-8233 92 G
DAVIS, Lowell, K 828-227-7495 344 A lkdavis@wcu.edu
DAVIS, LuAnn 402-486-2503 269 F luann.davis@ucollege.edu
DAVIS, Lynne 508-270-4021 214 E ldavis@massbay.edu
DAVIS, MacArthur 336-744-0900 327 F macarthur.davis@carolina.edu
DAVIS, Malcolm 832-842-4719 452 F mdavis@uh.edu
DAVIS, Maria 269-749-7643 229 H mdavis@olivetcollege.edu
DAVIS, Marilyn 404-880-8550 116 D mdavis@cau.edu
DAVIS, Marilyn, S 217-424-6379 143 H mdavis@millikin.edu
DAVIS, Marissa 814-506-8318 393 H mdavis@pennhighlands.edu
DAVIS, Marjorie 509-533-4152 480 B marjorie.davis@sfcc.spokane.edu
DAVIS, Mark 205-652-5456 9 A mdavis@uwa.edu
DAVIS, Mark 205-652-3570 9 A mdavis@uwa.edu
DAVIS, Mark, E 706-880-8257 121 A mdavis@lagrange.edu
DAVIS, Mark, L 515-964-0601 165 G davism@faith.edu
DAVIS, Marsha 706-542-0939 125 G davism@uga.edu
DAVIS, Marsha 845-758-7433 290 G davis@bard.edu
DAVIS, Marty 678-839-6614 126 E gdavis@westga.edu
DAVIS, Mary 540-828-5706 465 D mdavis@bridgewater.edu
DAVIS, Mary, E 212-217-4300 299 H mary_davis@fitnyc.edu
DAVIS, Mary Ann 513-241-4338 347 J
DAVIS, Matt 330-337-6403 347 E proffice@awc.edu
DAVIS, Matthew 402-557-7232 265 J matthew.davis@bellevue.edu
DAVIS, Matthew 920-206-2310 493 L matthew.davis@mbu.edu
DAVIS, Matthew, D 812-877-8421 159 J matthew.davis@rose-hulman.edu
DAVIS, Matthew, H 302-356-2491 90 I matthew.h.davis@wilmu.edu
DAVIS, Meadow 207-725-3037 193 D mdavis1@bowdoin.edu
DAVIS, Meagon 478-757-3803 126 H mdavis@wesleyancollege.edu
DAVIS, Megan, W 603-862-2450 274 G megan.davis@unh.edu
DAVIS, Meghan 970-675-3239 78 G meghan.davis@cncc.edu
DAVIS, Melissa 281-873-0262 434 A library@commonwealth.edu
DAVIS, Melvin, D 843-349-2401 408 C mdavis10@coastal.edu
DAVIS, Meredith 901-843-3529 423 J davism@rhodes.edu
DAVIS, Michael 318-342-5171 192 F mdavis@ulm.edu
DAVIS, Michael 770-381-7200 120 B
DAVIS, Michael 770-457-2021 120 C
DAVIS, Michael 770-859-9779 120 D mdavis@medtech.edu
DAVIS, Michael 617-373-2121 217 F

DAVIS, Michelle .... 701-228-5670 346 C michelle.r.davis@dakotacollege.edu
DAVIS, Michelle .... 912-681-2758 122 I mdavis@ogeecheetech.edu
DAVIS, Michelle .... 617-989-4590 219 E
DAVIS, Michelle .... 610-398-5300 389 A mdavis@lincolntech.edu
DAVIS, Michelle .... 409-984-6341 450 B davisml1@lamarpa.edu
DAVIS, Mike .... 215-489-2931 382 D michael.davis@delval.edu
DAVIS, Mike .... 580-745-2392 369 K mdavis@se.edu
DAVIS, Miles .... 503-883-2408 373 H miles.davis@linfield.edu
DAVIS, Miracle .... 225-216-8311 186 K davism@mybrcc.edu
DAVIS, Mitchel, W .... 603-646-2643 273 E mitchel.w.davis@dartmouth.edu
DAVIS, Monique .... 610-861-1475 391 A davism06@moravian.edu
DAVIS, Myriah .... 740-753-7020 354 A davism@hocking.edu
DAVIS, Natalie .... 601-643-8354 245 G natalie.davis@colin.edu
DAVIS, NaTashua, R ..... 573-884-7267 261 B davisnat@missouri.edu
DAVIS, Nevaler .... 813-253-7068 101 A ndavis5@hccfl.edu
DAVIS, Nicole .... 740-474-8896 358 F ndavis1@ohiochristian.edu
DAVIS, Nyla .... 850-201-6048 111 C davisn@tcc.fl.edu
DAVIS, Pam .... 772-546-5534 101 B admissions@hsbc.edu
DAVIS, Pamela, B .... 216-368-2825 349 F pamela.davis@case.edu
DAVIS, Patrice .... 843-574-6010 413 B patrice.davis@tridenttech.edu
DAVIS, Patricia .... 207-780-5911 196 F patdavis@maine.edu
DAVIS, Patricia .... 970-860-8180 435 A pdavis@dcccd.edu
DAVIS, Patricia, A .... 251-380-3063.... 6 H pdavis@shc.edu
DAVIS, Patrick .... 772-546-5534 101 B patrickdavis@hsbc.edu
DAVIS, Patti .... 410-386-8066 197 G pdavis@carrollcc.edu
DAVIS, Paul, J .... 641-784-5422 165 H pjdavis@graceland.edu
DAVIS, Paul, R .... 530-226-4719.. 63 K pdavis@simpsonu.edu
DAVIS, Paula .... 609-343-5083 275 D pdavis@atlantic.edu
DAVIS, Paula, M .... 269-387-8411 232 K paula.davis@wmich.edu
DAVIS, Peggy .... 804-524-5030 477 B pdavis@vsu.edu
DAVIS, Pete .... 701-477-7862 347 A pdavis@tm.edu
DAVIS, Pete, D .... 608-342-1155 497 D davisp@uwplatt.edu
DAVIS, Phylesia .... 870-543-8611.. 21 C pdavis@seark.edu
DAVIS, Raeanne .... 212-237-8604 294 D radavis@jjay.cuny.edu
DAVIS, Ralph .... 323-241-5261.. 49 D davisrw@lasc.edu
DAVIS, Ralph .... 605-394-2493 417 B ralph.davis@sdsmt.edu
DAVIS, Ralph, U .... 843-661-1110 409 K rdavis@fmarion.edu
DAVIS, Rance .... 315-229-5551 314 F rdavis@stlawu.edu
DAVIS, Randy .... 502-213-2122 181 F randall.davis@kctcs.edu
DAVIS, Rebecca, F .... 512-637-1949 442 M rebeccad@stedwards.edu
DAVIS, Renee .... 334-386-7230.... 5 D rdavis@faulkner.edu
DAVIS, Rhonda .... 817-722-1618 439 B rhonda.davis@tku.edu
DAVIS, Richard, K .... 312-942-6909 148 A richard_k_davis@rush.edu
DAVIS, Rick .... 850-973-9492 103 K davisr@nfcc.edu
DAVIS, Rick .... 617-373-2134 217 F
DAVIS, Rick .... 703-993-8624 467 L rdavi4@gmu.edu
DAVIS, Rick, C .... 402-280-1785 266 I richarddavis@creighton.edu
DAVIS, Robert .... 413-545-1706 211 D robert.davis@umass.edu
DAVIS, JR., Robert, W . 570-941-7500 401 H robert.davis@scranton.edu
DAVIS, Robin .... 804-257-5710 477 C
DAVIS, Rodell .... 773-602-5359 134 D rdavis@ccc.edu
DAVIS, Rodney, L .... 573-999-2145 174 E revrod1983@aol.com
DAVIS, Rodrigo .... 727-712-5720 106 E davis.rod@spcollege.edu
DAVIS, Roger .... 615-966-7161 421 D roger.davis@lipscomb.edu
DAVIS, Roger, W .... 724-480-3400 381 K roger.davis@ccbc.edu
DAVIS, Sandra, S .... 803-535-1218 411 G davisss@octech.edu
DAVIS, Scott .... 575-562-2425 285 M scott.davis@enmu.edu
DAVIS, Shannon .... 901-321-3545 419 C 0478mgr@follett.com
DAVIS, Sharon .... 803-765-6029 406 F sdavis@allenuniversity.edu
DAVIS, Sharon .... 254-526-1346 432 H sharon.davis@ctcd.edu
DAVIS, Sharon .... 214-860-8700 435 D sdavis1@dcccd.edu
DAVIS, Sheila, J .... 706-542-9167 125 G sjames@uga.edu
DAVIS, Shelly .... 207-893-7726 195 F sdavis@sjcme.edu
DAVIS, Sheri .... 401-874-5654 406 B sdavis@uri.edu
DAVIS, Sherri .... 205-929-6357.... 2 H sdavis@lawsonstate.edu
DAVIS, Sherri .... 828-398-7900 332 B sherrijdavis@abtech.edu
DAVIS, Sherry .... 812-221-1714 162 B sherrydavis@vbc.edu
DAVIS, Sherry .... 254-659-7818 437 G sdavis@hillcollege.edu
DAVIS, Staci .... 765-285-5753 153 C sldavis@bsu.edu
DAVIS, Stephanie .... 615-547-1387 419 F sdavis@cumberland.edu
DAVIS, Stephen .... 360-475-7805 482 G sdavis2@olympic.edu
DAVIS, Stephen .... 301-295-3062 504 B stephen.davis@usuhs.edu
DAVIS, Steven .... 707-638-5270.. 67 F steven.davis@tu.edu
DAVIS, Steven .... 252-222-6224 333 A daviss@carteret.edu
DAVIS, Steven, J .... 208-496-3305 130 A daviss@byui.edu
DAVIS, Stewart .... 256-549-8603.... 2 B sdavis@gadsdenstate.edu
DAVIS, Stormy, M .... 417-268-1000 250 E daviss@evangel.edu
DAVIS, Sue .... 225-768-1802 186 F sue.davis@franu.edu
DAVIS, Sue, E .... 330-941-2000 365 C sedavis@ysu.edu
DAVIS, Susan, M .... 434-924-4639 473 A smd5r@virginia.edu
DAVIS, Suzanne .... 618-664-7004 137 G suzanne.davis@greenville.edu
DAVIS, Suzanne, E .... 315-268-6493 296 A sdavis@clarkson.edu
DAVIS, Tamara .... 317-274-8363 156 B tamsdavi@iu.edu
DAVIS, Tamara, S .... 317-274-8362 156 F tamsdavi@iu.edu
DAVIS, Tammy .... 325-574-7695 458 E tdavis@wtc.edu
DAVIS, Teresa .... 336-433-5570 341 F tmdavis4@ncat.edu
DAVIS, Terry .... 619-660-4505.. 44 H terry.davis@gcccd.edu
DAVIS, Theresa, A .... 626-395-4638.. 29 C theresa.davis@caltech.edu
DAVIS, Thom .... 661-654-2287.. 30 E tdavis31@csub.edu
DAVIS, Thomas .... 803-705-4687 407 A thomas.davis@benedict.edu
DAVIS, Tom .... 334-670-3981.... 7 C tomdavis@troy.edu
DAVIS, Tonya .... 661-336-5141.. 46 K tdavis@kccd.edu
DAVIS, Traci .... 309-796-5408 132 G davist@bhc.edu
DAVIS, Tracy .... 951-763-0500.. 54 H
DAVIS, Tracy .... 713-222-5323 453 B davisjam@uhd.edu
DAVIS, Troy .... 413-748-3108 218 G tdavis10@springfield.edu
DAVIS, Ty .... 770-457-2021 120 C
DAVIS, Tyler .... 843-863-7523 407 E tdavis@csuniv.edu
DAVIS, Wain .... 618-393-2982 138 F davisw@iecc.edu
DAVIS, Warren .... 972-860-2944 435 A wldavis@dcccd.edu
DAVIS, Wayne .... 214-333-5163 434 I wayned@dbu.edu
DAVIS, Wendy .... 520-515-3623.. 11 M davisd@cochise.edu
DAVIS, Wendy .... 501-812-2273.. 23 B wdavis@uaptc.edu
DAVIS, Wesley .... 701-477-7862 347 A wdavis1@tm.edu
DAVIS, Whitney .... 478-757-5170 126 H wdavis@wesleyancollege.edu
DAVIS, William .... 708-534-4105 137 F wdavis3@govst.edu
DAVIS, William .... 830-792-7415 443 G deanoffaculty@schreiner.edu
DAVIS, William .... 610-359-6500 382 C wdavis@dccc.edu
DAVIS, Zabe .... 662-562-3308 248 D
DAVIS-AJAMI, Mary Lynn .... 812-855-7089 156 B mdavisaj@iu.edu
DAVIS-BAXTER, Angela . 704-636-6023 330 A adavisbaxter@hoodseminary.edu
DAVIS-BLAKE, Alison .... 781-891-2101 206 D adavisblake@bentley.edu
DAVIS-EYENE, Mishawn 508-854-4576 215 D meyene@qcc.mass.edu
DAVIS-EYENE, Mishawn 857-701-1230 215 E mdeyene@rcc.mass.edu
DAVIS-FREEMAN, Juana .... 803-934-3464 411 C jdavis@morris.edu
DAVIS FREEMAN, Louisa, M .... 413-755-4333 215 F ldavisfreeman@stcc.edu
DAVIS-JOHNSON, Max . 208-426-3033 129 I maxdavisjohnson@boisestate.edu
DAVIS JONES, Chrissy . 509-533-3514 479 I chrissy.davis@sfcc.spokane.edu
DAVIS-LONG, Tasha ..... 217-234-5253 141 D tdavis-long@lakelandcollege.edu
DAVIS-LOWE, Eda .... 321-682-4938 112 K edavislowe@valenciacollege.edu
DAVIS-SAMUELS, Ivanetta .... 615-327-6141 422 A isamuel@mmc.edu
DAVIS-STREET, Jeanean 508-531-6151 212 B jeanean.davisstreet@bridgew.edu
DAVIS-WHITE EYES, Allison .... 541-737-0123 375 D
DAVISON, Brent .... 423-652-4832 420 H bedavison@king.edu
DAVISON, Colette .... 312-893-7173 137 A cdavison@erikson.edu
DAVISON, Frieda, M ..... 864-503-5610 414 D fdavison@uscupstate.edu
DAVISON, Ian, R .... 989-774-1870 222 C davis1ir@cmich.edu
DAVISON, Jane, M .... 989-774-1870 222 C j.davison@cmich.edu
DAVISON, Kimberly, K . 972-985-3781 433 M kdavison@collin.edu
DAVISON, MacKenzie ... 617-731-7083 217 H
DAVITT, Jeffrey .... 904-819-6489.. 98 E jdavitt@flagler.edu
DAVITT, Kristin .... 412-647-6504 401 B davitt@pitt.edu
DAVITZ, Pamela, K .... 314-505-7010 251 I davitzp@csl.edu
DAVOLT, David .... 208-376-7731 129 H ddavolt@boisebible.edu
DAVOUD, Mohammad .. 912-478-7412 119 C mdavoud@georgiasouthern.edu
DAVRAY, Niranjan .... 315-228-7995 296 F ndavray@colgate.edu
DAVROS, Harry .... 214-637-3530 457 I hdavros@wadecollege.edu
DAVSON, Victor .... 848-445-0536 282 B vd240@newark.rutgers.edu
DAVY, Catherine, A ...... 313-593-5030 231 F kdavy@umich.edu
DAW, Michael .... 415-442-6682.. 44 D mdaw@ggu.edu
DAWE, Richard, L .... 870-368-2006.. 20 F rdawe@ozarka.edu
DAWES, Daniel .... 404-752-1833 122 E ddawes@msm.edu
DAWES, Douglas .... 707-826-3351.. 33 D douglas.dawes@humboldt.edu
DAWES, Elliott .... 518-587-2100 321 A
DAWES, Nadraqua .... 770-394-8300 114 C ndawes@aii.edu
DAWES, Trevor, A .... 302-831-2231.. 90 F tadawes@udel.edu
DAWKINS, E. Janyce .... 706-542-7912 125 G edawkins@uga.edu
DAWKINS, Lisa .... 304-357-4374 488 G lisadawkins@ucwv.edu
DAWKINS, Mark .... 904-620-2590 110 A mark.dawkins@unf.edu
DAWKINS, Norman .... 212-431-2142 309 G norman.dawkins@nyls.edu
DAWKINS, Phyllis, W ... 336-517-2225 327 B phyllis.dawkins@bennett.edu
DAWKINS, Sandra, C ... 662-252-8000 248 G sdawkins@rustcollege.edu
DAWKINS, Tom .... 213-763-7361.. 49 E dawkintl@lattc.edu
DAWLEY, Anna Marie ... 315-268-6475 296 A adawley@clarkson.edu
DAWN, Russell .... 708-771-8300 135 F
DAWN DETORO, Emilah .... 505-467-6603 288 E emilahdetoro@swc.edu
DAWOOD, Clark .... 810-237-6571 231 G cdawood@umich.edu
DAWOUD, Sandy .... 973-748-9000 276 A sandy_dawoud@bloomfield.edu
DAWSEY, Brian .... 912-358-4154 123 H dawseyb@savannahstate.edu
DAWSON, Barbara, E .... 304-293-4874 491 C barbara.dawson@mail.wvu.edu
DAWSON, Bridgette ...... 304-336-8215 490 F bdawson@westliberty.edu
DAWSON, Christian ...... 425-889-6934 482 F christian.dawson@northwestu.edu
DAWSON, Cole .... 937-481-2242 364 E cole_dawson@wilmington.edu
DAWSON, Darren .... 256-824-1000.... 8 B
DAWSON, Dave .... 479-575-5451.. 21 G daved@uark.edu
DAWSON, Frank .... 310-434-4585.. 62 E dawson_frank@smc.edu
DAWSON, Greg .... 615-248-1507 427 A gdawson@trevecca.edu
DAWSON, Imara .... 765-285-5422 153 C ivdawson@bsu.edu
DAWSON, J. Lin .... 404-880-8123 116 D jldawson@cau.edu
DAWSON, Katie .... 318-342-3119 192 F dawson@ulm.edu
DAWSON, Keith .... 574-520-4480 157 A khdawson@iusb.edu
DAWSON, Kevin .... 202-806-6100.. 92 B
DAWSON, Marcus .... 517-629-0224 220 G mdawson@albion.edu
DAWSON, Patrick .... 410-455-2356 202 E pdawson@umbc.edu
DAWSON, Rachel .... 660-596-7478 260 D rdawson1@sfccmo.edu
DAWSON, Randall .... 210-486-2534 429 G rdawson@alamo.edu
DAWSON, Renita .... 919-735-5151 338 H rddawson@waynecc.edu
DAWSON, Royal .... 909-607-9501.. 37 G royal_dawson@kgi.edu
DAWSON, Scott .... 805-756-1302.. 30 C scdawson@calpoly.edu
DAWSON, Teresa, U ..... 256-765-4328.... 8 E tdawson2@una.edu
DAWSON, JR., Thomas, E .... 410-951-3792 203 D thdawson@coppin.edu
DAWSON, Wayde .... 864-596-9056 409 B wayde.dawson@converse.edu
DAWTON, Dennis .... 215-965-4073 390 J academic@moore.edu
DAY, Barton .... 953-923-3201 449 E bart.day@tstc.edu
DAY, Cathy .... 406-447-5437 263 C cdday@carroll.edu
DAY, David .... 412-536-1070 387 B david.day@laroche.edu
DAY, Ian, S .... 716-888-2502 292 D dayi@canisius.edu

DAY, John, R ... 404-413-2564 119 E
jday@gsu.edu
DAY, Lawrence ... 315-792-3099 324 B
lday@utica.edu
DAY, Mark ... 949-376-6000.. 47 D
mday@lcad.edu
DAY, Mellani, J ... 303-963-3434.. 77 G
mday@ccu.edu
DAY, Michael ... 812-941-2244 157 B
micaday@ius.edu
DAY, Michelle ... 406-768-6351 263 G
mday@fpcc.edu
DAY, Mitzi ... 231-591-3800 223 J
mitziday@ferris.edu
DAY, Patricia ... 518-828-4181 297 B
day@sunycgcc.edu
DAY, Patrick, K ... 408-924-1000.. 34 B
DAY, Richard ... 216-397-1904 354 I
rday@jcu.edu
DAY, Rondall, H ... 470-578-6074 120 L
rday9@kennesaw.edu
DAY, Thelma ... 323-953-4000.. 48 I
dayt@lacitycollege.edu
DAY, Valerie ... 630-617-6422 136 G
valerie.day@elmhurst.edu
DAY-PERROOTS, Sue ... 304-293-6967 491 C
sue.day-perroots@mail.wvu.edu
DAYHOFF, Brenda ... 301-846-2663 198 E
bdayhoff@frederick.edu
DAYHOFF, Sharon, S ... 717-337-6276 384 H
sdayhoff@gettysburg.edu
DAYNES, Gary ... 252-399-6343 326 M
gdaynes@barton.edu
DAYRIES, Sonje ... 831-459-2686.. 70 B
sdayries@ucsc.edu
DAYRIT, George ... 310-791-9975.. 45 E
DAYTNER, Katrina ... 309-298-1690 152 D
km-daytner@wiu.edu
DAYTON-JOHNSON,
Jeffrey ... 831-647-4647 462 H
jdaytonjohnson@miis.edu
DAYZIE, Meryl ... 928-724-6950.. 12 C
mtdayzie@dinecollege.edu
DE ANGELIS, John ... 212-678-3012 322 G
deangelis@tc.edu
DE BAEZ SNYDER,
Tracey ... 724-830-1125 398 H
snyderdebaez@setonhill.edu
DE BERLY, Geraldine ... 413-755-4434 215 F
DE BOER, David ... 616-451-3511 223 B
ddeboer@davenport.edu
DE BONO, Chad ... 719-336-1517.. 80 K
chad.debono@lamarcc.edu
DE BOTTON, Leonard ... 973-278-5400 291 D
len@berkeleycollege.edu
DE BOTTON, Leonard ... 973-278-5400 275 I
len@berkeleycollege.edu
DE CHANT, Richard ... 216-987-3193 351 G
richard.dechant@tri-c.edu
DE COOKE, Peggy, A ... 315-386-7202 320 E
decookep@canton.edu
DE DIOS, Paul ... 714-484-7335.. 53 K
pdedios@cypresscollege.edu
DE DIOS UNANUE,
Teresa ... 787-720-0596 506 E
DE FATIMA LIMA,
Maria ... 615-327-6505 422 A
mflima@mmc.edu
DE FATIMA LIMA,
Maria ... 615-327-6505 422 A
DE FILIPPIS,
Daisy Cocco ... 203-575-8044.. 86 B
ddefilippis@nv.edu
DE FREITAS, Lisa, H ... 864-597-4203 414 H
defreitaslh@wofford.edu
DE FRIES, Carol ... 215-496-6122 382 A
cdefries@ccp.edu
DE GROAT, II,
Arthur, S ... 785-532-0369 174 G
degroata@ksu.edu
DE HAAS PHILLIPS,
Sylvia ... 413-565-1000 205 G
sdphillips@baypath.edu
DE HARO, Oscar ... 707-256-7365.. 53 C
odeharo@napavalley.edu
DE JESUS, Christian ... 787-780-0070 506 F
cdejesus@caribbean.edu
DE JESUS, Keyshla ... 787-725-8120 507 N
programaextension@eap.edu
DE JESUS, Norma ... 312-369-7465 135 E
ndejesus@colum.edu
DE JESUS, Ruth ... 715-682-1350 495 C
rdejesus@northland.edu
DE JESUS, Victoria ... 787-751-0178 511 F
ac_vdejesus@suagm.edu
DE JESUS-ALICEA,
Angela ... 787-864-2222 509 C
angela.dejesus@guayama.inter.edu
DE JESÚS, Dámaso ... 787-844-8181 514 A
damaso.dejesus@upr.edu
DE JESÚS, Eigna ... 787-728-1515 514 D
eigna.dejesus@sagrado.edu
DE JESÚS, Marcos ... 787-993-8953 513 B
marcos.dejesus@upr.edu
DE JESÚS, Marien ... 787-765-3560 507 L
mjesus@edpuniversity.edu
DE JESÚS, Sandra ... 787-815-0000 513 A
sandra.dejesus@upr.edu
DE JESÚS, Victoria ... 787-257-7373 511 G
ac_vdejesus@suagm.edu
DE JONG, Carol ... 616-395-7760 225 B
cdejong@hope.edu
DE JONG, Shawn ... 508-793-3570 208 B
sdejong@holycross.edu
DE LA CERDA, Paul ... 323-265-8198.. 48 H
delacep@elac.edu
DE LA FUENTE, Ariel ... 956-295-3498 449 D
ariel.delafuente@tsc.edu
DE LA FUENTE,
Marta, A ... 915-831-4029 436 E
mdelafu7@epcc.edu
DE LA GARZA, Katy ... 802-257-7751 463 C
katy.delagarza@worldlearning.org
DE LA GARZA,
Marco, J ... 559-325-5214.. 66 D
marco.delagarza@cloviscollege.edu
DE LA GARZA, Ricardo 956-872-3714 444 A
rickdlg@southtexascollege.edu
DE LA GUARDIA,
Teresa, S ... 305-284-2928 112 E
tdelaguardia@miami.edu
DE LA PAZ, Gloria ... 914-606-6744 325 C
gloria.delapaz@sunywcc.edu
DE LA PENA, Nataly ... 310-303-7222.. 51 B
ndelapena@marymountcalifornia.edu
DE LA ROSA, Casar ... 301-369-2800 197 F
DE LA ROSA, Jennifer .. 714-564-6212.. 57 L
de_la_rosa_jennifer@sac.edu
DE LA ROSA,
Jose Manuel ... 915-215-4300 451 D
jmanuel.delarosa@ttuhsc.edu
DE LA ROSA, Shirley ... 684-699-9155 505 A
s.delarosa@amsamoa.edu
DE LA TORRE, Adela ... 619-594-5201.. 33 E
presidents.office@sdsu.edu
DE LA TORRE, Etelvina 310-287-4378.. 49 G
delatoe@wlac.edu
DE LA TORRE, Jorge ... 425-640-1233 480 F
jorge.delatorre@edcc.edu
DE LA TORRE,
Marisela ... 213-356-5376.. 64 H
marisela_delatorre@sciarc.edu
DE LA TORRE, Susana . 510-436-2598.. 56 H
sdelatorre@peralta.edu
DE LA VEGA, Gabriela .. 415-442-7297.. 44 D
gdelavega@ggu.edu
DE LA VEGA, Kristina ... 818-677-2118.. 32 D
kristina.delavega@csun.edu
DE LACEY, Lora ... 630-844-5510 132 D
ldelacey@aurora.edu
DE LEON, Beatriz ... 787-743-3038 511 A
bdeleon@sanjuanbautista.edu
DE LEON, Darcy, L ... 269-471-3327 221 B
darcy@andrews.edu
DE LEON, Yvonne ... 210-458-4101 455 E
yvonne.deleon@utsa.edu
DE LEON MULLERT,
Maureen ... 787-720-4476 512 D
decanatofinanzas@mizpa.edu
DE LEONARDIS,
David, J ... 614-885-5585 360 E
ddeleon@pcj.edu
DE LONG, Linda ... 909-593-3511.. 70 D
ldelong@laverne.edu
DE LONG, Renee ... 714-432-5764.. 38 E
rdelong2@occ.cccd.edu
DE LOS REYES, Jose ... 415-749-4519.. 60 G
jdelosreyes@sfai.edu
DE LOS REYES, Maria .. 210-486-0918 429 H
mdelosreyes10@alamo.edu
DE LUCA, James, P ... 843-953-6861 407 F
jdeluca@citadel.edu
DE MELLO, Duilia ... 202-319-5244.. 91 B
demello@cua.edu
DE MUCHA FLORES,
Martin ... 510-981-5083.. 56 E
mdemuchaflores@peralta.edu
DE NOBLE, Timothy ... 785-532-5950 174 G
tdenoble@ksu.edu
DE OLIVEIRA,
Glenisson ... 940-565-3971 454 A
glenisson.deoliveira@unt.edu
DE PABLO, Juan ... 773-702-1383 150 J
depablo@uchicago.edu
DE PAULA, Anna ... 201-761-7450 282 I
adepaula@saintpeters.edu
DE PILLIS, Emmeline ... 808-932-7272 128 E
depillis@hawaii.edu
DE PRATER, Victoria, L 209-468-9155.. 67 B
vdeprater@sjcoe.net
DE ROSE, John ... 203-287-3034.. 87 E
paier.fad@snet.net
DE ROSSI, Scott, S ... 919-537-3236 342 D
scott_derossi@unc.edu
DE RUBERTIS, Andrew . 414-410-4221 492 D
aderubertis@stritch.edu
DE VELASCO, Joanna ... 305-284-3441 112 E
jdevelasco@miami.edu
DE VEYGA, Guillermo ... 201-200-2440 279 E
gdeveyga@njcu.edu
DE YAMPERT, Fredi ... 906-487-7301 223 K
fredi.deyampert@finlandia.edu
DE YOUNG, Gene ... 541-684-7219 374 G
gdeyoung@nwcu.edu
DEACY, Deborah, S ... 909-593-3511.. 70 D
ddeacy@laverne.edu
DEAHL, Anne, D ... 414-288-6786 494 B
anne.deahl@marquette.edu
DEAL, Charles, T ... 731-881-7015 428 B
cdeal@utm.edu
DEAL, David ... 276-656-0258 475 D
ddeal@patrickhenry.edu
DEAL, Kelley, P ... 252-451-8235 336 E
kpdeal870@nashcc.edu
DEAL, Lisa ... 352-392-1331 109 F
lsd@ufl.edu
DEAL, Michael ... 307-268-2211 501 U
mdeal@caspercollege.edu
DEAL, Scott ... 803-754-4100 409 A
DEAL, Shannon ... 731-881-7750 428 B
sdeal@utm.edu
DEAN, Adam, S ... 417-667-8181 252 A
adean@cottey.edu
DEAN, Amy ... 508-791-9241 206 B
amy.dean@becker.edu
DEAN, Amy ... 740-593-1711 359 G
deana@ohio.edu
DEAN, Barbara ... 502-942-8503 184 E
bsdean@sullivan.edu
DEAN, Brian ... 626-914-8597.. 36 K
bdean@citruscollege.edu
DEAN, Cindy ... 704-991-0329 338 C
cdean5600@stanly.edu
DEAN, Don ... 914-323-5219 305 J
donald.dean@mville.edu
DEAN, Gayle ... 505-566-3204 288 A
deang@sanjuancollege.edu
DEAN, Henry ... 504-671-5468 187 E
hwdean@dcc.edu
DEAN, James, H ... 941-359-7524 105 K
jdean@ringling.edu
DEAN, JR., James, W .. 603-862-2450 274 G
presidents.office@unh.edu
DEAN, Jeffrey ... 502-272-8014 179 B
jdean@bellarmine.edu
DEAN, Jeffrey, L ... 856-225-2747 281 G
jldean@camden.rutgers.edu
DEAN, Jennifer ... 313-993-1090 231 B
deanjl@udmercy.edu
DEAN, Jonathan, E ... 828-339-4614 338 B
j_dean@southwesterncc.edu
DEAN, Justin ... 740-389-4636 356 B
deanj@mtc.edu
DEAN, Karol ... 914-674-7517 306 F
kdean@mercy.edu
DEAN, Kathy, L ... 251-442-2215.... 8 C
kdean@umobile.edu
DEAN, Kayla ... 501-882-8867.. 17 F
kidean@asub.edu
DEAN, Kevin ... 608-785-9539 501 A
deank@westerntc.edu
DEAN, Kevin ... 610-436-2996 396 A
kdean@wcupa.edu
DEAN, Kristina ... 410-888-9048 200 A
kdean@muih.edu
DEAN, LeAnn ... 320-589-6173 244 B
deanl@morris.umn.edu
DEAN, Lynne ... 210-486-4135 429 E
ldean12@alamo.edu
DEAN, Mark ... 620-792-9235 171 C
deanm@bartonccc.edu
DEAN, Matt ... 901-843-3946 423 J
deanm@rhodes.edu
DEAN, Matt ... 864-681-1457 414 C
mcdean@mailbox.sc.edu
DEAN, Miles ... 410-287-1147 197 H
mdean@cecil.edu
DEAN, Paul, M ... 603-862-1427 274 G
paul.dean@unh.edu
DEAN, Rachel ... 406-265-3720 264 F
rachel.dean1@msun.edu
DEAN, Samuel, J ... 614-985-2226 360 E
sdean@pcj.edu
DEAN, Shawna ... 209-575-6518.. 75 H
deans@yosemite.edu
DEAN, Takeem ... 704-378-1132 330 D
tdean@jcsu.edu
DEAN, Thomas, K ... 319-335-1995 163 A
thomas-k-dean@uiowa.edu
DEAN, Tonya ... 972-524-3341 445 C
tdean@swcc.edu
DEAN, Troy ... 541-684-7293 374 G
tdean@nwcu.edu
DEAN, Willow ... 316-322-3124 171 G
wdean@butlercc.edu
DEAN-BAAR, Susan ... 314-516-6066 261 D
deanbaar@umsl.edu
DEAN-OUSLEY, Tyra, L . 773-995-4517 133 K
tdean21@csu.edu
DEANE, Julie ... 816-654-7000 254 C
jdeane@kcumb.edu
DEANE, Lynne, P ... 804-289-8064 472 L
ldeane@richmond.edu
DEANGELIS, Beth ... 518-782-6109 315 J
bdeangelis@siena.edu
DEANGELIS, Dave ... 617-573-8320 219 A
ddeangelis@suffolk.edu
DEANGELIS, Gennaro ... 860-253-3048.. 86 G
gdeangelis@acc.commnet.edu
DEANGELIS, Gennaro ... 860-253-3048.. 85 C
gdeangelis@asnuntuck.edu
DEANGELIS, JR.,
Peter, L ... 215-955-4773 400 A
peter.deangelis@jefferson.edu
DEANGELO, Jane ... 530-221-4275.. 63 G
jdeangelo@shasta.edu
DEANGELO, OFM CONV,
Jude ... 202-319-5575.. 91 B
deangelo@cua.edu
DEANNA, Linda ... 312-996-4857 151 B
ldeanna@uic.edu
DEANS, Beverly ... 919-735-5151 338 H
bdeans@waynecc.edu
DEANS, Greg ... 252-451-8275 336 E
gddeans098@nashcc.edu
DEAR, Carley ... 601-857-3357 246 B
carley.dear@hindscc.edu
DEAR, Michael ... 760-757-2121.. 52 E
mdear@miracosta.edu
DEARBORN, Heidi ... 360-596-5358 485 B
hdearborn@spscc.edu
DEARBORN, Philip, E ... 717-560-8233 388 B
pdearborn@lbc.edu
DEARCORN, Casey ... 307-754-6084 502 G
casey.dearcorn@nwc.edu
DEARDORFF, Lori ... 918-343-7573 369 F
ldeardorff@rsu.edu
DEARDURFF, Mindy, J . 651-696-6143 236 H
mdeardur@macalester.edu
DEARMAN, Heather ... 601-928-6225 247 E
heather.dearman@mgccc.edu
DEARSTYNE, Kenneth ... 610-607-6265 397 B
kdearstyne@racc.edu
DEARTH, Chris ... 276-328-0322 473 B
gk6ne@virginia.edu
DEAS, Deborah ... 951-827-4564.. 69 C
deborah.deas@ucr.edu
DEASE, Dennis, J ... 651-962-8520 244 E
djdease@stthomas.edu
DEASE, Mary Ann ... 203-837-8248.. 85 B
deasem@wcsu.edu
DEASIS, Mark ... 951-372-7014.. 58 H
mark.deasis@norcocollege.edu
DEASON, Michael ... 972-860-4670 434 L
mdeason@dcccd.edu
DEATER, Kate ... 814-472-3222 398 B
kdeater@francis.edu
DEATHERAGE, Eric ... 417-455-5610 252 D
ericdeatherage@crowder.edu
DEATLEY, Carry ... 361-354-2275 433 C
cdeatley@coastalbend.edu
DEATON, Andrea, D ... 405-325-1646 371 B
adeaton@ou.edu

DEGIULIO, Jules .... 541-440-7648 377 C jules.degiulio@umpqua.edu
DEGN, Jason .... 479-619-4337.. 20 D jdegn@nwacc.edu
DEGNER, Katie .... 352-424-1719 106 D katie.degner@saintleo.edu
DEGRAFFENREID, Pamela .... 828-227-7346 344 A degraffen@wcu.edu
DEGRANGE, Karen, A ... 812-877-8285 159 J degrange@rose-hulman.edu
DEGRAW, Heather .... 425-739-8200 482 A heather.degraw@lwtech.edu
DEGRAW, Julie .... 219-464-5411 162 A julie.degraw@valpo.edu
DEGROAT, Kevin .... 718-405-3400 296 G kevin.degroat@mountsaintvincent.edu
DEGROFT, Michael .... 717-391-3506 399 G degroft@stevenscollege.edu
DEGROOT, Laurie .... 641-422-4322 168 D laurie.degroot@niacc.edu
DEHAAN, Brandon .... 616-331-3255 224 E dehaanb@gvsu.edu
DEHAAN, Laura .... 616-526-7114 222 A ldehaan@calvin.edu
DEHAEMERS, Jennifer, E .... 618-453-1440 149 E jennifer.dehaemers@siu.edu
DEHART, Carrick .... 805-375-8919.. 30 F carrick.dehart@csuci.edu
DEHART, Jennifer .... 207-509-7100 195 H jdehart@unity.edu
DEHART, Joe .... 515-791-1721 164 C jcdehart@dmacc.edu
DEHART, Katy .... 301-369-2800 197 F kdehart@captechu.edu
DEHAVEN, Barbara .... 201-216-8762 283 C barbara.dehaven@stevens.edu
DEHAY, Galen .... 864-646-1773 413 A gdehay@tctc.edu
DEHAYES, Donald, H .... 401-874-4410 406 B donald_dehayes@uri.edu
DEHAZE, Danny .... 541-506-6097 372 G ddehaze@cgcc.edu
DEHGHANI, Mohammad .... 573-341-4114 261 E chancellor@mst.edu
DEHN, Paula .... 270-852-3117 183 A pdehn@kwc.edu
DEHNE, Nate .... 320-363-3036 235 C ndehne001@csbsju.edu
DEHNE, Nathan .... 320-363-3036 243 A ndehne001@csbsju.edu
DEHOOGH-KLIEWER, Michelle .... 605-331-6619 417 E michelle.dehoogh-kliewer@usiouxfalls.edu
DEHORN, Thomas .... 574-239-8383 155 D tdehorn@hcc-nd.edu
DEHOYOS, Diane, N ..... 915-747-5601 455 C dndehoyos@utep.edu
DEI, Michael .... 281-649-3406 437 H mdei@hbu.edu
DEIANA, Maureen .... 508-831-5099 220 E mdeiana@wpi.edu
DEIBEL, Michael .... 765-983-1459 154 G deibemi@earlham.edu
DEIBERT, Glenn .... 912-287-5827 116 F gdeibert@coastalpines.edu
DEIBERT, Renee .... 706-439-6314 122 F rdeibert@northgatech.edu
DEIBLER, Lauren, C ...... 717-361-1162 383 E deiblerl@etown.edu
DEICHEN, Michael, G ... 407-823-2094 109 E michael.deichen@ucf.edu
DEIGHTON, Joseph .... 314-889-1410 253 C jdeighton@fontbonne.edu
DEIGNAN, Kathleen ...... 609-258-5431 280 E kdeignan@princeton.edu
DEIKE, Terri .... 903-233-3769 439 E terrideike@letu.edu
DEINNOCENTIIS, Maria . 212-517-0482 306 A mdeinnocentiis@mmm.edu
DEITCH, Elaine, C .... 610-861-1364 391 A deitche@moravian.edu
DEITCH, Marissa .... 215-572-2972 379 A deitchm@arcadia.edu
DEITCHMAN, Jay .... 518-629-7567 302 E j.deitchman@hvcc.edu
DEITEMEYER, Kandi, W 704-330-6566 333 D kandi.deitemeyer@cpcc.edu
DEITRICK, Becky .... 570-372-4015 399 C deitrick@susqu.edu
DEITZ, Jennifer .... 907-563-7575.... 9 C jennifer.deitz@alaskacareercollege.edu
DEIULIO, Gina .... 863-583-9050 109 B
DEJAGER, Brad .... 218-751-8670 242 J braddejager@oakhills.edu
DEJESUS, Sadi .... 787-780-5134 510 F sdejesus@nuc.edu
DEJESUS-AVILES, Desire .... 212-924-5900 322 B ddejesusaviles@swedishinstitute.edu
DEJI, Deborah .... 312-939-0111 136 D deborah@eastwest.edu
DEJOICE, Mary Jo .... 304-637-1359 487 I dejoicem@dewv.edu
DEJONG, David, N .... 412-624-4228 401 B dejong@pitt.edu
DEJONG, Debbie .... 516-299-3438 304 H debbie.dejong@liu.edu
DEJOY, Jennifer .... 207-326-2256 195 D jennifer.dejoy@mma.edu
DEJTHAI, Eddie .... 239-280-2507.. 94 O eddie.dejthai@avemaria.edu
DEKAN, Doug, D .... 715-833-6238 499 D ddekan@cvtc.edu
DEKAY, Amy .... 716-880-2177 306 C adekay@medaille.edu
DEKAY, Amy, M .... 716-880-2224 306 C amy.marie.dekay@medaille.edu
DEKAY, Todd .... 575-624-7059 286 A todd.dekay@roswell.enmu.edu
DEKAY, Todd .... 717-358-6021 384 D todd.dekay@fandm.edu
DEKETELAERE, Vicki ..... 419-995-8357 354 H deketelaere.v@rhodesstate.edu
DEKKER NETTLEMAN, Mary .... 605-357-1309 416 H med@usd.edu
DEKLOTZ, Steve .... 503-493-6286 372 I sdeklotz@cu-portland.edu
DEKOVEN, Aram .... 860-701-6930 504 F aram.dekoven@uscg.mil
DEL BALZO, Mary Beth 914-831-0343 297 A mbdelbalzo@cw.edu
DEL BELLO, Wendy ...... 281-756-3600 429 I wdelbello@alvincollege.edu
DEL BELLO, Wendy ...... 281-756-3600 429 I wdebello@alvincollege.edu
DEL BELLO, Wendy ...... 281-756-3600 429 I wdelbello@alvincollege.edu
DEL CASINO, Vincent ... 408-924-2400.. 34 B provost@sjsu.edu
DEL CONTE, Christopher .... 512-471-5757 455 A ad@athletics.utexas.edu
DEL GIUDICE, Michale . 303-724-0731.. 83 C michael.delguidice@ucdenver.edu
DEL GIUDICE, Tristan, S .... 814-641-3390 386 H delgiut@juniata.edu
DEL PILAR BONNIN OROZCO, Maria .... 787-848-5739 511 C
DEL REAL, Remberto .... 630-960-8016 136 A
DEL RIO, Esteban .... 619-260-7455.. 71 J edelrio@sandiego.edu
DEL RIO, Roxanne .... 940-668-7731 441 A
DEL ROSARIO, Heather 661-763-7809.. 66 J hdelrosario@taftcollege.edu
DEL TONDO, Bruce ...... 719-587-7227.. 76 F bdeltond@adams.edu
DEL VALLE, Maritza ...... 787-780-0070 506 F mvalle@caribbean.edu
DEL VALLE, Nilkaliz ...... 787-852-1430 508 C n.delvalle.f@hccpr.edu
DEL VALLE, Wilfredo .... 787-863-2390 509 B wilfredo.delvalle@fajardo.inter.edu
DEL VECCHIO, Teri .... 954-776-4476 102 A tdelvecchio@keiseruniversity.edu
DELA CRUIZ, Jose .... 972-860-8312 435 B josedelacruz@dcccd.edu
DELA CRUZ, Lisa .... 512-863-1957 445 D delacrul@southwestern.edu
DELA CRUZ, Maria .... 714-564-6093.. 57 L dela_cruz_maria@sac.edu
DELA ROSA, Chris .... 510-659-6038.. 54 F cdelarosa@ohlone.edu
DELA ROSA, Chris .... 510-659-6514.. 54 F cdelarosa@ohlone.edu
DELA ROSA, John .... 671-735-5638 505 C pio@guamcc.edu
DELABY, Lisa .... 530-895-2937.. 27 F delabyli@butte.edu
DELACH, Ruth .... 412-809-5100 396 H delach.ruth@ptcollege.edu
DELACRUZ, Marisa .... 646-312-1000 292 L marisa.delacruz@baruch.cuny.edu
DELAET, Lee .... 314-889-4539 253 C ldelaet@fontbonne.edu
DELAGUERRA, Christy .. 201-327-8877 277 H cdelaguerra@eastwick.edu
DELAHOYDE, Theresa ... 402-481-8843 265 K theresa.delahoyde@bryanhealthcollege.edu
DELAHUNT, Tom, F ...... 512-863-1200 445 D delahunt@southwestern.edu
DELALUE, Shontay .... 401-863-2216 404 E shontay_delalue@brown.edu
DELAND, Michael .... 606-337-1015 179 G michael.deland@ccbbc.edu
DELAND, Robert .... 312-788-1142 152 B rdeland@vandercook.edu
DELANDSHEER, Alyson . 906-487-7339 223 K alyson.delandsheer@finlandia.edu
DELANEY, Christopher .. 717-337-6235 384 H cdelaney@gettysburg.edu
DELANEY, Collette .... 610-647-4400 386 C cdelaney@immaculata.edu
DELANEY, Connie, J ..... 612-624-1410 243 E delaney@umn.edu
DELANEY, Jeff .... 470-578-6755 120 L jdelaney@kennesaw.edu
DELANEY, John, T .... 202-885-1985.. 90 J jdelaney@american.edu
DELANEY, Kevin, J .... 215-204-3745 399 F kevin.delaney@temple.edu
DELANEY, Marymichele 617-243-2176 210 G mdelaney@lasell.edu
DELANEY, Matthew .... 610-683-4778 395 A mdelaney@kutztown.edu
DELANEY, Michara .... 229-903-3605 113 H michara.delaney@asurams.edu
DELANEY, Peggy .... 831-459-4317.. 70 B pdelaney@ucsc.edu
DELANEY, Sean .... 410-532-5371 201 B sdelaney@ndm.edu
DELANEY, Timothy, J ... 740-284-5211 353 B tdelaney@franciscan.edu
DELANEY, Ute .... 212-563-6647 323 F registrar@uts.edu
DELANOY, Debra .... 845-687-5088 323 E delanoyd@sunyulster.edu
DELANY, Karen .... 406-275-4820 265 F karen_delany@skc.edu
DELANY, Michelle .... 860-465-5244.. 84 J delanym@easternct.edu
DELAP, Joe .... 256-233-8203.... 4 D joe.delap@athens.edu
DELAPP, Jan .... 916-484-8633.. 50 F delappj@arc.losrios.edu
DELARGE, Kimberly, F .. 585-685-6191 307 H kdelarge@monroecc.edu
DELARGY, Deborah .... 714-966-8500.. 73 C ddelargy@ves.edu
DELAROSSA, Arnie .... 860-215-9236.. 86 F adelarossa@trcc.commnet.edu
DELASHMIT, Margaret .. 662-252-8000 248 G mdelashmit@rustcollege.edu
DELASHMUTT, Michael . 646-717-9781 300 G delashmutt@gts.edu
DELATE, John, J .... 585-292-2128 307 H jdelate@monroecc.edu
DELAUDER, Saundra ..... 302-857-6117.. 89 F sfdelauder@desu.edu
DELAVAN, Katharine ..... 440-375-7389 355 G kdelavan@lec.edu
DELAWALLA, Noorali .... 562-860-2451.. 35M ndelawalla@cerritos.edu
DELAY, Mary, G .... 210-567-2010 456 C delay@uthscsa.edu
DELBAGNO, Julia .... 973-748-9000 276 A
DELBELSO, Debra .... 518-783-2339 315 J ddelbelso@siena.edu
DELBRUGGE, Laura .... 814-393-2225 394 D ldelbrugge@clarion.edu
DELCOURE, Natalya ...... 361-593-5989 447 D natalya.delcoure@tamuk.edu
DELCOURT, Carrie .... 309-796-5318 132 G delcourtc@bhc.edu
DELEON, Christian .... 775-831-1314 272 D cdeleon@sierranevada.edu
DELEON, Cynthia, I .... 670-237-6706 506 A cynthia.dlguerrero@marianas.edu
DELEON, Hilda .... 713-798-4612 431 I hildad@bcm.edu
DELEON, Jozi .... 805-756-2262.. 30 C jozi@calpoly.edu
DELEON, Rocio .... 310-954-4025.. 52 G rdeleon@msmu.edu
DELEON, Rolando .... 262-691-5175 500 H rdeleon5@wctc.edu
DELEON, Zelma .... 940-565-3901 454 A zelma.deleon@unt.edu
DELESKEY, Sharon .... 617-873-0154 207 F sharon.deleskey@cambridgecollege.edu
DELFFS, Erin .... 614-236-6814 349 D edelffs@capital.edu
DELFORTE, Joseph, L ... 585-785-1227 300 B joseph.delforte@flcc.edu
DELGADILLO, Carlos .... 509-527-4282 485 G carlos.delgadillo@wwcc.edu
DELGADO, AnneMarie .. 252-335-3222 341 D adelgado@ecsu.edu
DELGADO, Antonio .... 610-436-3086 396 A adelgado@wcupa.edu
DELGADO, Christina ..... 949-451-5693.. 64 F cdelgado@ivc.edu
DELGADO, Edwin .... 843-921-6929 411 F edelgado@netc.edu
DELGADO, Fernando ..... 218-726-7104 243 F vcaa@d.umn.edu
DELGADO, Gabriel .... 760-872-2000.. 41 C gabriely.delgado@deepsprings.edu
DELGADO, Irene, R .... 718-289-5869 293 B irene.delgado@bcc.cuny.edu
DELGADO, Junior .... 413-572-5546 213 D jdelgado@westfield.ma.edu
DELGADO, Maria .... 787-852-1430 508 C mariadelosangeles@hccpr.edu
DELGADO, Nelson .... 210-434-6711 441 E ndelgado@ollusa.edu
DELGADO, Ricardo .... 636-949-4735 254 F rdelgado@lindenwood.edu
DELGADO, Rosite .... 423-425-5760 428 A rosite-delgado@utc.edu
DELGADO, Yanit .... 787-780-0070 506 F yadelgado@caribbean.edu
DELGIORNO, Christopher, M .... 845-575-3000 305 L christopher.delgiorno@marist.edu
DELGRECO, Michael ..... 978-837-5292 216 D delgrecom@merrimack.edu
DELHOUSAYE, Darryl, L .... 602-429-4932.. 15 C ddelhousaye@ps.edu
DELIA, Al .... 301-687-3017 203 E aadelia@frostburg.edu
DELISA, Kenneth, J .... 860-465-5269.. 84 J delisak@easternct.edu
DELISA, Monica .... 478-445-5768 118 C monica.delisa@gcsu.edu
DELISIO, Therese .... 773-380-6787 132 F tdelisio@bexleyseabury.edu
DELISLE, David, W .... 315-268-6666 296 A ddelisle@clarkson.edu
DELISLE, Joseph .... 781-239-2571 214 E jdelisle@massbay.edu
DELITTO, Anthony .... 412-383-6560 401 B delitto@pitt.edu
DELIZIO, Carissa .... 401-456-8126 405 C cdelizio@ric.edu
DELL, Kyle .... 336-316-2196 329 E kdell@guilford.edu
DELL, Troy .... 301-687-4471 203 E tadell@frostburg.edu
DELLA COLETTA, Cristina .... 858-534-6270.. 69 D cdellacoletta@ucsd.edu
DELLA POSTA, Joseph, B .... 315-445-4564 304 C dellapjb@lemoyne.edu
DELLA ROCCA, Jodi ...... 518-262-4303 289 F dellarj@amc.edu
DELLA TORRE, Thomas 845-574-4465 313 C tdellato@sunyrockland.edu
DELLACONTRADA, John .... 716-645-4601 316 F dellacon@buffalo.edu
DELLAPIETRA, Lynn ...... 215-968-8272 379 G lynn.dellapietra@bucks.edu
DELLAPORTA, Pamela ... 718-933-6700 307 G pdellaporta@monroecollege.edu
DELLAR, Dan .... 231-843-5985 232 J ddellar@westshore.edu
DELLAROCAS, Chris ...... 617-358-0831 207 D dell@bu.edu
DELLASALA, Kristen ...... 845-569-3439 307 J kristen.dellasala@msmc.edu
DELLATORRE, Bonnie ... 714-449-7495.. 51 A bdellatorre@ketchum.edu

DENNIS, Matt ... 229-430-3602 113 I mdennis@albanytech.edu

DENNIS, Pam ... 704-406-4298 329 A pdennis@gardner-webb.edu

DENNIS, Paul ... 909-384-8286 .. 59 I pdennis@sbccd.cc.ca.us

DENNIS, Peggy ... 419-372-8495 348 H fayed@bgsu.edu

DENNIS, Roger, J ... 215-571-4755 383 B rjd45@drexel.edu

DENNIS, Terry ... 863-680-4148 .. 99 H vdennis@flsouthern.edu

DENNIS, Vicki ... 318-678-6000 187 A vdennis@bpcc.edu

DENNIS, Yolanda ... 508-588-9100 214 F ydennis@massasoit.mass.edu

DENNISON, Anne ... 207-699-5054 194 D adennison@meca.edu

DENNISON, Corley ... 304-558-0261 489 O corley.dennison@wvhepc.edu

DENNISON, Lori, R ... 315-859-4412 301 C ldenniso@hamilton.edu

DENNISON, Sondra, R .. 724-357-2696 394 G sondra.dennison@iup.edu

DENNISON, Wayne ... 812-877-8858 159 J dennison@rose-hulman.edu

DENNISTON, Marsha .... 605-331-6633 417 E marsha.denniston@usiouxfalls.edu

DENNISTON, Terry ... 423-425-4203 428 A terry-denniston@utc.edu

DENNY, Bryan ... 918-465-1818 366 D bdenny@eosc.edu

DENON, Gregory ... 978-934-2418 211 G gregory_denon@uml.edu

DENSE, Angela ... 417-865-2815 253 B densea@evangel.edu

DENSLOW, Kathy ... 325-793-4903 440 B kdenslow@mcm.edu

DENSMORE, Timothy .... 607-844-8222 322 H tad@tompkinscortland.edu

DENSON, Jeff ... 510-845-5373 .. 29 G jeff@cjc.edu

DENSON, John ... 205-665-6235 .... 8 D jdenson1@montevallo.edu

DENSON, Michael ... 415-476-1414 .. 69 E mike.denson@ucsf.edu

DENSON, Rob ... 515-964-6638 164 C rjdenson@dmacc.edu

DENT, Christopher ... 310-609-2704 .. 76 D

DENT, Deborah ... 601-979-4299 246 E deborah.f.dent@jsums.edu

DENT, Sara ... 304-829-7744 487 G sdent@bethanywv.edu

DENT, Valeda, F ... 718-990-6559 314 B dentv@stjohns.edu

DENTINO, Daniel, A ... 716-888-2130 292 D dentinod@canisius.edu

DENTLER, James ... 330-337-6403 347 E registrar@awc.edu

DENTLER, Kellie ... 336-316-2165 329 E dentlerkf@guilford.edu

DENTON, Amy ... 800-686-1883 222 E adenton@cleary.edu

DENTON, Andrew, C ... 612-343-4745 242 H acdenton@northcentral.edu

DENTON, Carol ... 704-922-6484 334 F denton.carol@gaston.edu

DENTON, Christine ... 808-739-8597 127 F christine.denton@chaminade.edu

DENTON, Melissa ... 913-234-0750 172 E melissa.denton@cleveland.edu

DENTON, SaVana ... 580-477-7712 371 F

DENVER, Genae ... 785-539-3571 175 E gdenver@mccks.edu

DENYER, Susan ... 321-674-7259 .. 99 B sdenyer@fit.edu

DENYS, Mark ... 215-204-7500 399 F mark.denys@temple.edu

DEOLALIKAR, Anil ... 951-827-2310 .. 69 C anil.deolalikar@ucr.edu

DEOLIVEIRA, Shushawna ... 718-270-4744 317 E shushawna.deoliveira@downstate.edu

DEORSEY, Ellen, M ... 802-654-2212 463 B edeorsey@smcvt.edu

DEPACE, Paul ... 401-874-2725 406 B pauldepace@uri.edu

DEPAOLA, John ... 518-262-6008 289 F depaolj@amc.edu

DEPAOLA, Natacha ... 312-567-3009 139 B depaola@iit.edu

DEPAOLIS, Cheryl ... 412-924-1384 396 I cdepaolis@pts.edu

DEPAS, Jacob ... 920-465-2000 496 E depasj@uwgb.edu

DEPASQUALE, Dana ... 412-365-1517 381 C ddepasquale@chatham.edu

DEPAULL, Mark ... 607-753-2111 318 D mark.depaull@cortland.edu

DEPAUW, Karen, P ... 540-231-7581 477 A kpdepauw@vt.edu

DEPEDER, Suzanne ... 312-362-8648 135 I sdepeder@depaul.edu

DEPERRO, Dennis, R .... 716-375-2222 313 F drdeperro@sbu.edu

DEPEW, Chris ... 845-434-5750 322 A cdepew@sunysullivan.edu

DEPEW, Dennis, R ... 423-439-4289 419 J depewd@etsu.edu

DEPEW, Sally ... 231-591-3823 223 J sallydepew@ferris.edu

DEPINET, Andrea ... 419-372-8844 348 H adepine@bgsu.edu

DEPINTO, Michael ... 908-526-1200 281 A michael.depinto@raritanval.edu

DEPOO, Tilokie ... 212-343-1234 306 J tdepoo@mcny.edu

DEPOUTOT, Al ... 727-376-6911 111 G adepoutot@trinitycollege.edu

DEPOY, Bryan ... 440-375-7028 355 G bdepoy@lec.edu

DEPPONG, Greg ... 517-355-5020 227 D deppong@msu.edu

DEPRANO, Corinne ... 937-229-1025 362 G cdaprano1@udayton.edu

DEPREY, Brynn ... 201-216-9901 277 D brynn.deprey@eicollege.edu

DEPRON, Dianna ... 225-771-5050 190 H dianna_gilbert@subr.edu

DEPTA, Linda ... 269-488-4821 225 E ldepta@kvcc.edu

DEPUTY, Meghan ... 386-312-4169 106 C meghandeputy@sjrstate.edu

DEPUY, Rebecca ... 817-598-6388 458 A rdepuy@wc.edu

DER, Brenda ... 410-837-4813 204 B bder@ubalt.edu

DERAMUS, Danny ... 501-279-4339 .. 19 D dderamus@harding.edu

DERAVI, Fariba, S ... 334-244-3249 .... 4 F fderav1@aum.edu

DERBY, Andre ... 954-532-9614 101 D

DERBY, Dustin, C ... 563-884-5682 168 I dustin.derby@palmer.edu

DERBYSHIRE, Lynne ... 401-874-4732 406 B derbyshire@uri.edu

DERCOLA, Corinne ... 585-271-3657 313 E corinne.dercola@stbernards.edu

DERDA, Bob ... 412-392-6157 397 A rderda@pointpark.edu

DERDEN, Wade ... 501-760-4203 .. 20 B wade.derden@np.edu

DERDERIAN, Todd ... 508-767-7392 205 D tderderi@assumption.edu

DERDIK, Ari ... 347-619-9074 326 G

DEREMER, Dennis ... 970-204-8255 .. 79 J dennis.deremer@frontrange.edu

DERIA, Jamilla ... 413-545-3517 211 D jderia@umass.edu

DERICO, Amanda ... 513-244-8149 350 I amanda.derico@ccuniversity.edu

DERIEUX, Anne ... 206-726-5171 480 C aderieux@cornish.edu

DERIGGI, Nancy ... 914-923-2699 311 E

DERING, Allison ... 337-421-6955 188 D allison.dering@sowela.edu

DERK, Malcolm ... 570-372-4571 399 C derk@susqu.edu

DERMER, Shannon ... 708-534-8396 137 F sdermer@govst.edu

DERMISHYAN, Sima ... 916-877-7977 .. 58 J sima@sui.edu

DERMODY, Sean, B ... 518-564-2539 319 C dermodsb@plattsburgh.edu

DEROCHE, Jessica ... 972-899-8402 441 A jderoche@nctc.edu

DEROCHER, Cynthia ... 989-356-9021 221 A derocherc@alpenacc.edu

DEROCHI, Jack ... 803-323-2204 414 G derochij@winthrop.edu

DEROEUN, Sheila, D ... 225-771-5808 190 G sheila_duplechain@subr.edu

DEROSA, John ... 203-837-9806 .. 85 B derosaj@wcsu.edu

DEROSA, Michael ... 510-869-8821 .. 59 F mderosa@samuelmerritt.edu

DEROSE, Angela ... 203-287-3032 .. 87 E paier.admin@snet.net

DEROSE, Angela ... 203-287-3033 .. 87 E paier.admin@snet.net

DEROSE, Michelle ... 616-632-2826 221 C derosmic@aquinas.edu

DEROSE, Paul ... 602-285-7517 .. 13 F paul.derose@phoenixcollege.edu

DEROSIER, Stephen ... 603-752-1113 273 D sderosier@ccsnh.edu

DEROUIN, Erika ... 719-587-7901 .. 76 F ederouin@adams.edu

DEROUIN, Karen ... 413-552-2248 214 D kderouin@hcc.edu

DERR, Colleen ... 765-677-3467 157 D colleen.derr@indwes.edu

DERR, Ed ... 417-873-7418 252 F ederr@drury.edu

DERR, Gary, L ... 802-656-2212 463 E gary.derr@uvm.edu

DERR, Matthew, A ... 802-586-7711 463 D mderr@sterlingcollege.edu

DERRICK, Ann ... 512-451-5743 430 M

DERRICK, Damon ... 936-468-4305 445 F derrickdc@sfasu.edu

DERRICK, Diahann ... 541-881-5827 377 B dderrick@tvcc.cc

DERRICK, Gwen ... 918-270-6424 369 A gwen.derrick@ptstulsa.edu

DERRICK, Joey ... 803-777-3205 413 C jcderric@mailbox.sc.edu

DERRICO, Cindy ... 805-437-3340 .. 30 F cindy.derrico@csuci.edu

DERRINGER, Daniel ... 540-362-7433 468 C dderringer@hollins.edu

DERRITT, Shawn ... 913-288-7437 174 F sderritt@kckcc.edu

DERRY, John, L ... 714-879-3901 .. 45 F jderry@hiu.edu

DERSTINE, Andria ... 440-775-8665 358 C andria.derstine@oberlin.edu

DERUBBO, Jeff ... 724-938-4415 394 B derubbo@calu.edu

DERUE, Scott ... 734-764-1361 231 E dsderue@umich.edu

DERUITER, Mark ... 269-749-7133 229 H

DERVIN, Alice ... 618-374-5106 146 E alice.dervin@principia.edu

DESAI, Amanda ... 508-213-2092 217 E amanda.desai@nichols.edu

DESAI, Anand ... 316-978-3200 178 A anand.desai@wichita.edu

DESAI, Rebekah ... 512-637-1924 442 M rebekahn@stedwards.edu

DESALVO, Dianne, S ... 989-774-4308 222 C desal1ds@cmich.edu

DESANCTIS, Greg ... 908-526-1200 281 A greg.desanctis@raritanval.edu

DESANCTIS, Marielena .. 954-201-6511 .. 95 H mdesanct@broward.edu

DESANTIS, Charles, E ... 202-687-1787 .. 92 A ced33@georgetown.edu

DESANTIS, Linda ... 609-343-5093 275 D desantis@atlantic.edu

DESANTIS, Matthew ... 512-448-8726 442 M mdesant1@stedwards.edu

DESANTIS, Melanie, A .. 717-358-4278 384 D melanie.desantis@fandm.edu

DESANTIS, Melissa ... 303-724-1748 .. 83 C melissa.desantis@ucdenver.edu

DESANTIS, Susan ... 239-489-9234 100 A susan.desantis@fsw.edu

DESANTIS, Victor, S ... 717-871-7001 395 D victor.desantis@millersville.edu

DESAUTELS-POLIQUIN, Lisa ... 207-859-1243 195 G desautelsl@thomas.edu

DESBROW, Susan ... 850-484-1605 104 H sdesbrow@pensacolastate.edu

DESCAK, Carol ... 410-837-6859 204 B cdescak@ubalt.edu

DESCH, Andrew, P ... 920-748-8849 495 G descha@ripon.edu

DESCHAMPS, Eric, N .... 928-523-8334 .. 14 H eric.deschamps@nau.edu

DESHIELDS, Richard ... 406-874-6226 263 I deshieldsr@milescc.edu

DESHLER, Kirsten ... 805-893-4588 .. 70 A kirsten.deshler@ia.ucsb.edu

DESHONG, Jelanie ... 718-270-1490 317 E jelanie.deshong@downstate.edu

DESHOTEL, Al ... 713-522-7911 454 H deshotak@stthom.edu

DESHPANDE, Satish ... 269-387-5067 232 K satish.deshpande@wmich.edu

DESIMONE, Albert, J .... 269-337-7292 225 D al.desimone@kzoo.edu

DESIMONE, Barbara ... 716-614-6220 310 C murphy@niagaracc.suny.edu

DESIR, JR., Serge ... 727-873-4974 110 C swdesir@mail.usf.edu

DESJARDINS, Karla ... 860-932-4000 .. 86 E kdesjardins@qvcc.edu

DESJARDINS, Linda ... 413-775-1105 214 C desjardins@gcc.mass.edu

DESJEANS, Karen ... 413-552-2221 214 D kdesjeans@hcc.edu

DESLATTE, Daniel ... 903-877-7561 456 D daniel.deslatte@uthct.edu

DESMARAIS, Rachel, M 252-492-2061 338 F desmarais@vgcc.edu

DESMARTEAU, Doug ... 620-901-6245 170 G desmarteau@allencc.edu

DESMOND, Bill ... 309-796-5437 132 G desmondw@bhc.edu

DESMOND, Jill ... 414-382-6067 492 A jill.desmond@alverno.edu

DESMOND, Nell ... 540-887-7225 469 B hdesmond@marybaldwin.edu

DESORMEAUX, Amy ... 337-482-1325 192 E amyd@louisiana.edu

DESOUZA, Priscila ... 650-543-3786 .. 51 F priscila.desouza@menlo.edu

DESPAIN, Trenton ... 540-261-8453 471 H trenton.despain@svu.edu

DESPATHY, Carol ... 603-206-8136 272 L cdespathy@ccsnh.edu

DESPLAS, Edward ... 505-566-3253 288 A desplase@sanjuancollge.edu

DESRAVINES, Melissa ... 212-280-1531 323 H finaid@utsnyc.edu

DESROCHES, Reginald .. 713-348-4009 442 K rdr@rice.edu

DESROSIERS, Candace .. 281-649-3049 437 H cdesrosiers@hbu.edu

DESSER, Kari ... 360-417-6291 483 B kdesser@pencol.edu

DESSOYE, Jane, F ... 570-408-3839 403 D jane.dessoye@wilkes.edu

DESTEFANO, Joanne, M ... 607-255-4242 297 F jmd11@cornell.edu

DESTEIGUER, John ... 405-425-5100 367 G john.desteiguer@oc.edu

DESTEPHANO, Andrew .. 212-986-4343 291 D afd@berkeleycollege.edu

DESTEPHANO, Andrew .. 212-986-4343 275 I afd@berkeleycollege.edu

DESTER, Lisa ... 518-743-2232 320 D desterl@sunyacc.edu

DESVIGNE, LaVora ... 718-482-5114 294 F ldesvigne@lagcc.cuny.edu

DESWERT, David ... 413-585-2200 218 F ddeswert@smith.edu

DETAMPEL, SuAnn ... 920-465-2302 496 E detampes@uwgb.edu

DETAR, Dave ... 412-521-6200 397 H dave.detar@rosedaletech.org

DETAR, Eric ... 315-279-5378 304 A edetar@keuka.edu

DETEMPLE, Jon Jay ... 610-526-6119 385 G jdetemple@harcum.edu

DETER, Daniel ... 434-592-4172 468 H ddeter@liberty.edu

DETERMAN, Scott ... 651-423-8000 237 H

DETGEN, Jim ... 580-327-8645 367 E ejdetgen@nwosu.edu

DETIEGE, Jacques ... 504-398-2242 191 C jdetiege@uhcno.edu

DETLAFF, Alan ... 713-743-7819 452 F ajdettlaff@uh.edu

DETLEV, Angela ... 703-993-8969 467 L adetlev@gmu.edu

DETREUX, Keneth ... 610-989-1276 402 B kdetreux@vfmac.edu

DETRICK, Jeffrey ... 979-230-3383 432 D jeffrey.detrick@brazosport.edu

DETRIE, Pam ... 901-843-3835 423 J detriep@rhodes.edu

DETROW, David, A ... 540-432-4110 466 G detrowd@emu.edu

DETTELBACH, Michael .. 781-736-4052 207 E dettelbach@brandeis.edu

DETTINGER, Jacob ... 435-283-7255 461 C jacob.dettinger@snow.edu

DETTLOFF, Kathy ... 410-455-1720 202 E

DIAZ, Ande ... 603-641-7150 274 C
adiaz@anselm.edu
DIAZ, Angelica ... 480-994-9244.. 16 B
angelicav@swiha.edu
DIAZ, Arelis ... 787-753-6335 508 D
adiaz@icprjc.edu
DIAZ, Armando ... 210-567-0372 456 C
diaza@uthscsa.edu
DIAZ, Daniel ... 336-316-2351 329 E
diazdf@guilford.edu
DIAZ, Edgar, I ... 787-766-1717 511 H
eddiaz@suagm.edu
DIAZ, Emma ... 909-384-8611.. 59 I
ediaz@sbccd.cc.ca.us
DIAZ, Ester ... 219-473-4388 153 G
ediaz@ccsj.edu
DIAZ, Francisco ... 973-720-3244 284 I
diazf@wpunj.edu
DIAZ, Franco, L ... 787-284-1912 509 E
fldiaz@ponce.inter.edu
DIAZ, Gladys, M ... 787-841-2000 510 K
gdiaz@pucpr.edu
DIAZ, Glenda ... 787-863-2390 509 B
glenda.diaz@fajardo.inter.edu
DIAZ, Ivan ... 970-542-3157.. 81 A
ivan.diaz@morgancc.edu
DIAZ, Jillian ... 203-591-5619.. 87 F
jdiaz@post.edu
DIAZ, Joel ... 805-678-5810.. 73 A
jdiaz@vcccd.edu
DIAZ, Jorge, L ... 787-786-3030 512 B
jdiaz@ucb.edu.pr
DIAZ, Karen ... 304-293-5277 491 C
karen.diaz@mail.wvu.edu
DIAZ, Kris ... 440-826-2900 348 E
kdiaz@bw.edu
DIAZ, Leticia, M ... 321-206-5602.. 95 C
ldiaz@barry.edu
DIAZ, Luis, R ... 787-751-0160 507 F
lrdiaz@cmpr.pr.gov
DIAZ, Mario ... 312-850-7492 134 H
mdiaz103@ccc.edu
DIAZ, Marisol ... 787-894-6918 514 C
marisol.diaz2@upr.edu
DIAZ, Mark ... 202-994-9610.. 91 F
markdiaz@gwu.edu
DIAZ, Mary ... 210-458-4101 455 E
mary.diaz@utsa.edu
DIAZ, Mauro ... 818-252-5297.. 75 C
mauro.diaz@woodbury.edu
DIAZ, Minerva ... 787-738-2161 513 D
minerva.diaz@upr.edu
DIAZ, Mischelle, R ... 512-448-8404 442 M
mischeld@stedwards.edu
DIAZ, Olga ... 760-744-1150.. 55 I
odiaz@palomar.edu
DIAZ, Ramonita ... 787-878-5475 508 L
rdiaz@arecibo.inter.edu
DIAZ, Roberto ... 215-717-3107 382 B
roberto.diaz@curtis.edu
DIAZ, Russell ... 845-848-4048 298 D
russell.diaz@dc.edu
DIAZ, Sam ... 570-504-9069 384 F
sdiaz@som.geisinger.edu
DIAZ, Santos ... 830-591-7342 444 G
sdiaz2@swtjc.edu
DIAZ, Sylvia ... 631-451-4486 321 F
diazs@sunysuffolk.edu
DIAZ, Veronica ... 310-434-4224.. 62 E
diaz_veronica@smc.edu
DIAZ, Walter ... 860-465-5247.. 84 J
diazw@easternct.edu
DIAZ, Walter ... 956-665-3553 455 D
walter.diaz@utrgv.edu
DIAZ, Zaida ... 787-257-0199 513 C
zaida.diaz@upr.edu
DIAZ ALONSO, Herman 213-613-2200.. 64 H
directors_office@sciarc.edu
DIAZ ESPARZA,
Ruben Dario ... 202-646-1337.. 92 D
DIAZ PIÑEIRO, Odalys . 718-997-5646 295 C
odalys.diazpineiro@qc.cuny.edu
DIAZ-RODRIGUEZ,
Nereida ... 787-798-6732 512 C
nereida.diaz@uccaribe.edu
DIAZ-TORRES, Marie ... 973-353-5089 282 B
mdtorres@rutgers.edu
DIBARTOLO, Gerard, R . 410-548-3503 203 F
grdibartolo@salisbury.edu
DIBARTOLO, Patricia ... 413-585-3913 218 F
pdibarto@smith.edu
DIBB, Andrew M, T ... 267-502-2582 379 D
andrew.dibb@brynathyn.edu
DIBBERT, Douglas, S ... 919-962-7050 342 D
doug_dibbert@unc.edu
DIBBLE, Deborah, A ... 716-673-3131 317 A
deborah.dibble@fredonia.edu
DIBBLE, Jessica ... 620-229-6155 177 A
jessica.dibble@sckans.edu
DIBBLE, Rita ... 651-793-1805 238 H
rita.dibble@metrostate.edu
DIBELLA, Jeannette ... 603-206-8006 272 L
jdibella@ccsnh.edu
DIBELLA, Sue ... 702-895-4317 271 E
sue.dibella@unlv.edu
DIBENEDETTO,
Jonathan, J ... 724-450-4045 385 C
dibenedettojj@gcc.edu
DIBERT, Cregg ... 814-262-3837 393 H
cdibert@pennhighlands.edu
DIBIASIO, Daniel, A ... 419-772-2030 358 H
d-dibiasio@onu.edu
DIBLEY, Paula ... 704-216-3467 337 F
paula.dibley@rccc.edu
DIBONA, Brian ... 815-479-7510 143 A
bdibona@mchenry.edu
DIBRITO, Kyle, J ... 717-736-4117 385 E
kjdibrit@hacc.edu
DICAPRIO, Deborah, A . 845-575-3000 305 L
deborah.dicaprio@marist.edu
DICARLO, Joseph ... 508-929-8090 213 E
jdicarlo1@worcester.edu
DICARO, David ... 585-385-8025 314 A
ddicaro@sjfc.edu
DICARO, Kim ... 313-496-2625 232 C
kdicaro1@wcccd.edu
DICCE, Lisa ... 718-951-5065 293 C
lisa.dicce@brooklyn.cuny.edu
DICE, Douglas ... 989-463-7162 220 H
dice@alma.edu
DICENZO, Robert ... 540-665-1280 471 E
dicenzo@su.edu
DICESARE, Deborah, A . 818-778-5522.. 49 F
dicesad@lavc.edu
DICHELE, Anne, M ... 203-582-3463.. 87 G
anne.dichele@quinnipiac.edu
DICHRISTINA, Joseph ... 860-297-2156.. 88 C
joseph.dichristina@trincoll.edu
DICHTEL, Julie ... 248-370-3915 229 G
dichtel@oakland.edu
DICK, Andrew ... 814-864-6666 385 B
DICK, Dave ... 276-223-4868 476 E
ddick@wcc.vccs.edu
DICK, Denise ... 516-299-2522 304 G
denise.dick@liu.edu
DICK, Melissa, L ... 724-357-2550 394 G
m.l.dick@iup.edu
DICK, Nancy ... 206-546-4741 484 G
ndick@shoreline.edu
DICKEN, Jill ... 217-732-3168 141 H
jmdicken@lincolnchristian.edu
DICKENS, Anne ... 281-459-7634 443 D
anne.dickens@sjcd.edu
DICKENS, Lauren ... 636-922-8533 258 I
ldickens@stchas.edu
DICKENS, Linda, N ... 512-232-2646 455 A
linda.dickens@austin.utexas.edu
DICKENS, Reginald ... 704-216-6025 330 H
rdickens@livingstone.edu
DICKENS, Robert, L ... 210-458-4065 455 E
robert.dickens@utsa.edu
DICKENS, Sarah, B ... 512-464-8818 442 M
sarahbd@stedwards.edu
DICKENSON, Deb ... 703-993-3767 467 L
ddicken2@gmu.edu
DICKER, James ... 302-831-0530.. 90 F
jwdicker@udel.edu
DICKERMAN, Robert ... 413-755-4606 215 F
dickerman@stcc.edu
DICKERSON, Charles ... 864-622-6001 406 G
cdickerson@andersonuniversity.edu
DICKERSON, Chris ... 910-323-5614 327 G
cdickerson@ccbs.edu
DICKERSON, Dee Ann .. 918-647-1307 365 H
ddickerson@carlalbert.edu
DICKERSON, Diane ... 828-395-1495 335 D
ddickerson@isothermal.edu
DICKERSON, Hannah ... 704-233-8291 344 G
h.dickerson@wingate.edu
DICKERSON, Jeremy ... 910-962-3030 343 C
DICKERSON, John ... 662-325-2663 247 F
jdickerson@registrar.msstate.edu
DICKERSON, John, R ... 662-325-2663 247 F
jdickerson@registrar.msstate.edu
DICKERSON, Kenny ... 252-985-5438 339 D
kdickerson@ncwc.edu
DICKERSON, Kent ... 252-940-6205 332 C
kent.dickerson@beaufortccc.edu
DICKERSON, Kyle ... 615-966-7600 421 D
kyle.dickerson@lipscomb.edu
DICKERSON, Leslie ... 406-496-4879 265 A
ldickerson@mtech.edu
DICKERSON,
Maniphone ... 408-270-6434.. 61 L
maniphone.dickerson@evc.edu
DICKERSON, Mark ... 626-387-5763.. 26 H
mdickerson@apu.edu
DICKERSON, Mary Ann 913-469-8500 174 D
mdkerson@jccc.edu
DICKERSON, Michelle ... 219-980-6618 156 E
mtdicker@iun.edu
DICKERSON, Shirley ... 936-468-4109 445 F
sdickerson@sfasu.edu
DICKERT, Gerry ... 409-984-6342 450 B
dickertgl@lamarpa.edu
DICKESS, Clarice ... 907-564-8880.... 9 D
cdickess@alaskapacific.edu
DICKEY, Daryl ... 678-839-6534 126 E
ddickey@westga.edu
DICKEY, JP ... 417-455-5466 252 D
jamesdickey@crowder.edu
DICKEY, Kelly ... 580-559-5219 366 C
kelmdic@ecok.edu
DICKEY, M. Thaxter ... 813-988-5131.. 98 Q
dickeyt@floridacollege.edu
DICKEY, Wanda ... 813-988-5131.. 98 Q
library@floridacollege.edu
DICKEY, Wyman ... 904-269-7086 100 I
wdickey@fortiscollege.edu
DICKEY-KOTZ, Michele . 641-784-5202 165 H
dickey@graceland.edu
DICKIE, George ... 406-874-6196 263 I
dickieg@milescc.edu
DICKINSON, Adam ... 989-686-9029 223 G
adamdickinson@delta.edu
DICKINSON, J. Barry ... 267-341-3440 386 A
jdickinson@holyfamily.edu
DICKINSON, Jennifer ... 802-656-2232 463 E
jennifer.dickinson@uvm.edu
DICKINSON, Kyle ... 503-554-2119 373 C
kdickinson@georgefox.edu
DICKINSON, Lindsey ... 231-995-1037 228 G
ldicksinson@nmc.edu
DICKINSON, Maureen ... 309-796-5052 132 G
dickinsonm@bhc.edu
DICKINSON, Michael ... 617-873-0547 207 F
michael.dickinson@cambridgecollege.edu
DICKINSON, Robyn ... 570-945-8506 386 I
robyn.dickinson@keystone.edu
DICKINSON, Rosie, A ... 956-326-2202 446 F
rosie@tamiu.edu
DICKINSON, Steve ... 864-242-5100 407 B
DICKMAN, Brent ... 212-280-1402 323 H
bdickman@uts.columbia.edu
DICKMEYER, Lou ... 507-389-1268 239 C
louise.dickmeyer@mnsu.edu
DICKS, Karin ... 512-448-8405 442 M
karind@stedwards.edu
DICKS, Nikasha ... 803-508-7477 406 E
dicksn@atc.edu
DICKSON, Brook, E ... 540-362-6287 468 C
bdickson@hollins.edu
DICKSON, Chris, M ... 260-422-5561 155 H
cmdickson@indianatech.edu
DICKSON, Kari ... 806-743-2946 451 C
kari.dickson@ttuhsc.edu
DICKSON, Laura, M ... 515-281-3939 162 H
laura.dickson@iowaregents.edu
DICKSON, Laurie ... 928-523-6771.. 14 H
laurie.dickson@nau.edu
DICKSON, Michael ... 972-758-3832 433 M
mdickson@collin.edu
DICKSON, Phillip ... 870-248-4000.. 18 F
phillipd@blackrivertech.edu
DICKSON, Risa ... 650-433-3830.. 55 G
rdickson@paloaltou.edu
DICKSTEIN, Gary ... 937-775-2808 364 I
gary.dickstein@wright.edu
DICOLLA, Maura ... 919-497-3228 330 I
mdicolla@louisburg.edu
DICORLETO, Paul, E ... 330-672-1733 354 J
dicorlp@kent.edu
DICOSTANZO, Elina ... 910-755-8517 332 F
dicostanzoe@brunswickcc.edu
DICRESCIO, Michael ... 516-877-3745 289 C
dicresci@adelphi.edu
DIDDAMS, Margaret ... 630-752-5004 152 F
margaret.diddams@wheaton.edu
DIDIER, Kim ... 515-965-7064 164 C
kmdidier@dmacc.edu
DIDIER, Meredith ... 919-962-1591 341 A
mbdidier@northcarolina.edu
DIDION, Judy, A ... 248-364-8787 229 G
jdidion@oakland.edu
DIDLAKE, Ralph, H ... 601-984-5009 249 E
rdidlake@umc.edu
DIEBOLD, Ann ... 610-519-4560 402 D
ann.diebold@villanova.edu
DIECKMAN, Stacy ... 402-844-7288 268 J
stacyd@northeast.edu
DIECKMEYER, Diane ... 760-757-2121.. 52 E
ddieckmeyer@miracosta.edu
DIEDRICH, Todd ... 701-349-3621 346 J
tdied@charter.net
DIEGEL, James ... 202-865-6660.. 92 B
DIEHL, Amy ... 717-477-1476 395 E
DIEHL, Beatrice ... 518-454-2142 296 H
diehlb@strose.edu
DIEHL, Bert ... 440-525-7140 355 H
rdiehl@lakelandcc.edu
DIEHL, David ... 615-248-1291 427 A
ddiehl@trevecca.edu
DIEHL, David, W ... 630-844-4933 132 D
ddiehl@aurora.edu
DIEHL, Elizabeth ... 717-337-6501 384 H
ediehl@gettysburg.edu
DIEHL, Hope, L ... 610-359-5333 382 C
hdiehl@dccc.edu
DIEHL, Joan ... 570-348-6248 389 G
1226mgr@fheg.follett.com
DIEHL, Melissa, M ... 570-577-3776 379 F
melissa.diehl@bucknell.edu
DIEHL, Michele ... 215-646-7300 385 D
diehl.m@gmercyu.edu
DIEHL, Nathan ... 610-896-1298 385 L
ndiehl@haverford.edu
DIEHL, Randy, L ... 512-471-4141 455 A
diehl@austin.utexas.edu
DIEHL, Timothy ... 207-725-3716 193 D
tdiehl@bowdoin.edu
DIEHM, Perry ... 405-789-6400 370 A
pdiehm@snu.edu
DIEKER, R. Joseph ... 319-895-4210 164 B
jdieker@cornellcollege.edu
DIEKMAN, Larry ... 269-467-9945 224 A
ldiekman@glenoaks.edu
DIEKMANN, Beth ... 507-285-7259 240 G
beth.diekmann@rctc.edu
DIEL-HUNT, Sarah ... 309-268-8593 137 I
sarah.dielhunt@heartland.edu
DIEMER, Robert ... 352-588-8974 106 D
robert.diemer@saintleo.edu
DIENGER, Rebecca, J ... 715-836-4423 496 D
diengerj@uwec.edu
DIENNO, Linda ... 703-370-6600 470 B
DIERENFIELD, Bruce, J . 716-888-2683 292 D
derenfb@canisius.edu
DIERINGER, Deanna, L . 907-474-6629.. 10 A
dldieringer@alaska.edu
DIERKS, David, R ... 319-335-3305 163 A
david-dierks@uiowa.edu
DIERMEIER, Daniel ... 773-702-8810 150 J
provost@uchicago.edu
DIETER, Mary ... 765-658-4286 154 F
marydieter@depauw.edu
DIETERICH, Scott ... 718-409-7204 321 C
sdieterich@sunymaritime.edu
DIETRICH, Kim, E ... 260-399-7700 161 D
kdietrich@sf.edu
DIETRICH, Robb ... 570-321-4401 389 E
dietrich@lycoming.edu
DIETRICH, Robert ... 617-373-4827 217 F
DIETRICH, Robin ... 540-887-7025 469 B
rdietrich@marybaldwin.edu
DIETRICH, Sandra, L ... 919-866-5674 338 G
sldietrich@waketech.edu
DIETZ, Carol ... 216-397-4310 354 I
cdietz@jcu.edu
DIETZ, Fred ... 940-397-4533 440 F
fred.dietz@msutexas.edu
DIETZ, Jonathan ... 620-792-9281 171 C
dietzj@bartonccc.edu
DIETZ, Kelley ... 919-508-2220 344 F
kelley.dietz@peace.edu
DIETZ, Kenneth ... 502-852-6176 185 C
kenneth.dietz@louisville.edu
DIETZ, Larry ... 309-438-5451 139 E
ldietz@ilstu.edu
DIETZ, Maya ... 618-374-5162 146 E
maya.dietz@principia.edu

DIRKS, Kurt, T .... 314-935-4074 262 A
dirks@wustl.edu
DIRKS, Randy .... 952-829-1388 234 A
randy.dirks@bethfel.org
DIRKSCHNEIDER, Carla 402-552-6295 266 E
dirkschneider@clarksoncollege.edu
DIRKSEN, Andrew .... 507-452-4430 243 B
adirksen@smumn.edu
DIRKSEN, Dawn .... 866-323-0233.. 57 J
admin@providencecc.edu
DIRKSEN, Debra .... 575-538-6427 289 B
debra.dirksen@wnmu.edu
DIRMYER, Richard .... 585-395-5816 318 B
rdirmyer@brockport.edu
DISABATINO, Gail .... 617-287-5800 211 E
gail.d@umb.edu
DISALVIO, Philip .... 617-287-7926 211 E
philip.disalvio@umb.edu
DISALVO, Anthony .... 909-652-6257.. 36 A
anthony.disalvo@chaffey.edu
DISALVO, Stephen .... 314-529-9521 254 H
sdisalvo@maryville.edu
DISALVO, Steven .... 978-232-2000 209 B
sdisalvo@endicott.edu
DISALVO, Tony .... 760-366-5277.. 40 K
tdisalvo@cmccd.edu
DISANO, Maria .... 401-874-7078 406 B
mdisano@uri.edu
DISANTI, Francis, J ...... 610-660-1506 398 C
disanti@sju.edu
DISBROW, Lynn .... 470-578-3550 120 L
ldisbrow@kennesaw.edu
DISCALA, Anthony .... 480-517-8411.. 13 G
anthony.discala@riosalado.edu
DISCENZA, Tobias .... 239-489-9329 100 A
tjdiscenza@fsw.edu
DISCHINGER, Rainier .... 928-344-7726.. 10 J
rainier.dischinger@azwestern.edu
DISCHINO, Maureen ..... 617-989-4009 219 E
dischinom@wit.edu
DISHMAM, Julie .... 765-983-1523 154 G
dishmju@earlham.edu
DISHMAN, Marcie .... 919-718-7491 333 C
mdishman@cccc.edu
DISHMAN, Melissa .... 307-778-1372 502 D
mdishman@lccc.wy.edu
DISHMAN, Mike .... 470-578-7588 120 L
mdishma2@kennesaw.edu
DISION, Maria .... 691-320-2480 505 B
mdison@comfsm.fm
DISKIN, Becca, L .... 417-659-5422 256 D
diskin-b@mssu.edu
DISMUKES, David .... 225-578-4400 188 I
dismukes@lsu.edu
DISMUKES,
Mary Claire .... 615-460-6490 418 F
maryclaire.dismukes@belmont.edu
DISNEW, Carolyn .... 212-752-1530 304 D
carolyn.disnew@limcollege.edu
DISPIGNO, OFM,
Francis, J .... 716-375-2142 313 F
fdispigno@sbu.edu
DISQUE, Carol .... 336-506-4138 332 A
carol.disque@alamancecc.edu
DISS, Brian .... 574-631-5646 161 C
bdiss@nd.edu
DISTASI, Vincent, F ...... 724-458-2116 385 C
vfdistasi@gcc.edu
DISTEFANO, Ann, L ...... 570-577-3200 379 F
ann.distefano@bucknell.edu
DISTEFANO, Augustine . 215-596-8800 401 G
DISTEFANO, Phillip, P .. 303-492-8908.. 83 A
phil.distefano@colorado.edu
DISTEFANO, Tammy ..... 716-829-7639 298 F
distefan@dyc.edu
DITCHFIELD, Dora .... 205-726-2980.... 6 E
dditchfi@samford.edu
DITLEFSEN, Ed .... 208-732-6847 130 E
editlefsen@csi.edu
DITMAN, Mark .... 713-348-5441 442 K
mditman@rice.edu
DITOMMASO OWEN,
Kathy .... 541-684-7206 374 G
kowen@nwcu.edu
DITOMMSO, Anthony .... 412-237-4413 381 G
adtommaso@ccac.edu
DITORO, Tim .... 936-633-5204 430 F
tditoro@angelina.edu
DITTEMORE, Nancy .... 951-785-2300.. 47 C
ndittemo@lasierra.edu
DITTMAN, Jeff, L .... 605-256-5229 416 J
jeff.dittman@dsu.edu
DITTMAN, Judy .... 605-256-5270 416 J
judy.dittman@dsu.edu
DITTMAN, Scott .... 540-458-8455 478 A
sdittman@wlu.edu
DITTMAR, Amy .... 734-763-1282 231 E
adittmar@umich.edu
DITTMER, Michael .... 513-244-4619 357 A
michael.dittmer@msj.edu
DITTO, John .... 979-230-3157 432 D
john.ditto@brazosport.edu
DITTO, Liz .... 419-434-4510 363 A
dittoe@findlay.edu
DITTRICH, Linda .... 315-786-2323 303 F
lditrich@sunyjefferson.edu
DITULLIO, Daniel, F ..... 508-767-7321 205 D
df.ditullio@assumption.edu
DITZLER, Mauri, A .... 517-629-0210 220 G
mditzler@albion.edu
DIVALERIO, Thomas, J . 856-225-6050 281 G
tdivaler@camden.rutgers.edu
DIVELY, Mary Jo .... 412-268-9519 380 F
mjdively@andrew.cmu.edu
DIVEN-BROWN, Laura .. 662-915-5788 249 D
ldivenbr@olemiss.edu
DIVINCENZO, Mark .... 617-452-2082 215 G
DIVINE, Christine, E ..... 916-278-7702.. 32 E
christine.miller@csus.edu
DIVINE, Darren, D .... 307-268-2548 501 U
darrendivine@caspercollege.edu
DIVINITY, Darrell .... 312-935-6800 147 D
ddivinity@robertmorris.edu
DIVINO, Claudio, F ...... 252-334-2049 331 D
claudio.divino@macuniversity.edu
DIVIRGILIO, Mark .... 425-640-1582 480 F
mark.divirgilio@edcc.edu
DIVJAK, Robert .... 203-575-8235.. 86 B
rdivjak@nv.edu
DIWARA, Patrica .... 719-502-2037.. 81 F
patricia.diawar@ppcc.edu
DIX, Julie .... 508-849-3401 205 C
jdix@annamaria.edu
DIXEY, Mary .... 413-552-2261 214 D
mdixey@hcc.edu
DIXIE, Wendy, D .... 502-597-7000 182 H
wendy.dixie@kysu.edu
DIXON, Andrew .... 800-462-7845.. 78 N
andrew.dixon@csuglobal.edu
DIXON, Brad .... 660-248-6267 251 B
bdixon@centralmethodist.edu
DIXON, Brian .... 509-335-9711 486 A
DIXON, Cassie .... 704-403-1798 327 D
cassie.dixon@carolinashealthcare.org
DIXON, Catherine .... 410-626-2548 201 D
cathy.dixon@sjc.edu
DIXON, Clay-Edward .... 510-649-2540.. 44 F
cedixon@gtu.edu
DIXON, Colin .... 812-749-1454 159 C
cdixon@oak.edu
DIXON, David .... 216-649-8700 354 J
ddixon@kent.edu
DIXON, Dawn, S .... 919-464-2373 335 F
dsdixon@johnstoncc.edu
DIXON, Deanna .... 413-585-2523 218 F
ddixon@smith.edu
DIXON, Doreen, O .... 804-257-5630 477 C
dodixon@vuu.edu
DIXON, Jacqueline .... 727-553-3369 110 B
jdixon@usf.edu
DIXON, Jennifer .... 206-934-4101 483 I
jennifer.dixon@seattlecolleges.edu
DIXON, Jenny .... 928-681-5656.. 14 F
jdixon@mohave.edu
DIXON, Jesse .... 618-482-8326 149 F
jessdix@siue.edu
DIXON, John .... 843-661-1335 409 K
jdixon@fmarion.edu
DIXON, Joyce, A .... 662-254-3308 248 B
jadixon@mvsu.edu
DIXON, Karrie, G .... 252-335-3228 341 D
chancellor@ecsu.edu
DIXON, Kathy .... 541-888-7408 376 F
kathy.dixon@socc.edu
DIXON, Kristin .... 503-375-7080 373 A
kdixon@corban.edu
DIXON, Leon .... 301-447-6122 200 E
l.s.dixon@msmary.edu
DIXON, Lisa .... 615-329-8775 419 K
ldixon@fisk.edu
DIXON, Lynn .... 512-223-1222 431 A
cdixon@austincc.edu
DIXON, Margaret .... 662-621-4670 245 E
mdixon@coahomacc.edu
DIXON, Melanie .... 916-568-3130.. 50 E
dixonm@losrios.edu
DIXON, Michael .... 432-685-4616 440 E
mdixon@midland.edu
DIXON, Michael, D .... 812-465-7015 161 E
mdixon@usi.edu
DIXON, Michael, G .... 260-982-5276 158 T
mgdixon@manchester.edu
DIXON, Michelle .... 336-757-3710 334 E
mdixon@forsythtech.edu
DIXON, Patrick .... 336-315-7800.. 92 G
DIXON, Patrick .... 919-466-4400.. 92 G
DIXON, Paul .... 785-628-4536 173 B
pgdixon@fhsu.edu
DIXON, Ramona .... 610-399-2220 394 C
rdixon@cheyney.edu
DIXON, Robert .... 312-413-1878 151 B
robd@uic.edu
DIXON, Robert .... 405-744-6512 368 B
robert.dixon@okstate.edu
DIXON, Roger .... 478-471-2720 121 F
roger.dixon@mga.edu
DIXON, Samuel .... 678-466-4200 116 E
samdixon@clayton.edu
DIXON, Sean .... 602-212-0501.. 11 B
sean.dixon@brightoncollege.edu
DIXON, Sean .... 602-212-0501.. 14 Q
sdixon@brightoncollege.edu
DIXON, Sonja .... 806-796-8800 439 H
DIXON, Steve .... 918-540-6275 366 I
steve.dixon10@neo.edu
DIXON, Terrance .... 404-954-6520 122 D
terrance.dixon@morehouse.edu
DIXON, Todd .... 386-312-4190 106 C
todddixon@sjrstate.edu
DIXON, William .... 270-831-9650 181 D
bill.dixon@kctcs.edu
DIXON, William .... 585-292-3031 307 H
wdixon5@monroecc.edu
DIXON-PETERS, Earic ... 818-710-2911.. 49 C
peterseb@piercecollege.edu
DIXON-SAXON, Savitri . 866-492-5336 244 F
savitri.dixon-saxon@mail.waldenu.edu
DIZAZZO, Laura .... 206-934-5492 484 A
laura.dizazzo@seattlecolleges.edu
DIZON, Mike, M .... 773-442-4226 145 B
m-dizon@neiu.edu
DIZON, Richard .... 650-289-3332.. 59 C
richard.dizon@stpsu.edu
DJALALI, Chaden .... 740-593-2600 359 G
djalali@ohio.edu
DJEUKENG, Benji .... 804-627-5300 465 C
benjamin_djeukeng@bshsi.org
DJUKIC, Stevan .... 918-876-2529 368 G
sdjukic@okwu.edu
DJUNAIDI, Harry .... 931-540-2523 424 G
hdjunaidi@columbiastate.edu
DJURIC, Teresa, A .... 540-887-7243 469 B
tdjuric@marybaldwin.edu
DLUGOS, James, S .... 207-893-7711 195 F
jdlugos@sjcme.edu
DLUGOS, Joseph 252-399-6366 326M
jadlugos@barton.edu
DLUGOS, OSA,
Raymond .... 978-837-5130 216 D
dlugosr@merrimack.edu
DLUGOSZ, Joy .... 610-225-5660 383 D
jdlugosz@eastern.edu
DMARJIAN, Steve .... 312-850-7140 134 H
sdamarjian@ccc.edu
DO, Dao .... 714-484-7316.. 53 K
ddo@cypresscollege.edu
DOAK, Bryan, E .... 928-344-7617.. 10 J
bryan.doak@azwestern.edu
DOAK, Joshua, M .... 417-659-4460 256 D
doak-j@mssu.edu
DOAN, Hannah .... 478-757-5272 126 H
hdoan@wesleyancollege.edu
DOAN, Kathleen .... 207-741-5805 195 A
kdoan@smccme.edu
DOAN, Linh .... 714-903-2762.. 67 L
DOAN, Viet .... 701-231-5143 345 G
viet.doan@ndsu.edu
DOANE, Dudley, J .... 434-924-3371 473 A
djd4j@virginia.edu
DOANE, Dudley, J .... 434-982-3013 473 A
djd4j@virginia.edu
DOBBELMANN, Duncan 802-440-4400 462 A
duncand@bennington.edu
DOBBERSTEIN, Trina ..... 440-826-2111 348 E
tdobbers@bw.edu
DOBBINS, Kenneth .... 336-506-4126 332 A
kenneth.dobbins@alamancecc.edu
DOBBS, Brian .... 208-732-6266 130 E
bdobbs@csi.edu
DOBBS, Chris .... 406-994-6543 264 D
chris.dobbs@montana.edu
DOBBS, Gwen .... 479-636-9222.. 20 D
gdobbs@nwacc.edu
DOBBS, Lynn .... 662-329-7231 248 A
rldobbs@muw.edu
DOBBS, Ricky .... 903-468-8707 447 B
ricky.dobbs@tamuc.edu
DOBBS, Trent .... 405-425-5913 367 G
trent.dobbs@oc.edu
DOBBS, Trish .... 315-268-4443 296 A
tdobbs@clarkson.edu
DOBBS, Wendell .... 304-696-2964 490 D
dobbs@marshall.edu
DOBELL, Dan .... 318-628-4342 292 E
dan.dobell@cayuga-cc.edu
DOBELL, Daniel .... 845-574-4156 313 C
ddobell@sunyrockland.edu
DOBI, Hanko, H .... 203-932-7191.. 89 A
hdobi@newhaven.edu
DOBIAS, Dale .... 651-255-6144 243 D
ddobias@unitedseminary.edu
DOBIE, Elizabeth, A ...... 607-871-2137 289 H
dobie@alfred.edu
DOBIS, David .... 805-756-1104.. 30 C
ddobis@calpoly.edu
DOBISH, Rodney, W ..... 412-396-4781 383 C
dobish@duq.edu
DOBIYANSKI, Victoria ... 850-644-2428 109 C
vdobiyanski@admin.fsu.edu
DOBKIN, Bethami .... 801-832-2550 461 G
bdobkin@westminstercollege.edu
DOBRANSKY, Mary .... 402-557-7160 265 J
mary.dobransky@bellevue.edu
DOBRIN, Ben .... 757-455-3412 477 F
bdobrin@vwu.edu
DOBRINSKY,
Herbert, C .... 212-960-0850 326 E
dobrinsk@yu.edu
DOBROTA, Joseph .... 757-221-2420 466 C
jdobrota@wm.edu
DOBROVOLNY,
Shannon .... 215-965-4097 390 J
sdobrovolny@moore.edu
DOBROWSKI, Pauline ... 508-565-1363 218 H
pdobrowski@stonehill.edu
DOBSON, Alyssa .... 724-738-2220 395 F
alyssa.dobson@sru.edu
DOBSON, Catherine ...... 417-208-0636 254 C
cdobson@kcumb.edu
DOBSON, Cheryl .... 417-625-9389 256 D
dobson-c@mssu.edu
DOBSON, Lark, T .... 301-546-0616 201 C
dobsonlt@pgcc.edu
DOBSON, Laura .... 828-328-7028 330 F
laura.dobson@lr.edu
DOBSON, Melissa .... 318-257-2377 191 F
mkdobson@latech.edu
DOBSON, Van .... 757-221-2255 466 C
vdobson@wm.edu
DOBSON-HOPKINS,
Nina .... 443-885-3130 200 D
nina.hopkins@morgan.edu
DOCKENDORF, Amy, L . 605-256-5130 416 J
amy.dockendorf@dsu.edu
DOCKENS, Samuel .... 409-880-8195 449 G
sjdockens@lit.edu
DOCKERY, Jonathan ..... 847-317-7083 150 H
jsdockery@tiu.edu
DOCKERY, Kirbie .... 910-630-7167 331 C
kdockery@methodist.edu
DOCKERY, Rachael, M .. 417-836-8507 256 E
rmdockery@missouristate.edu
DOCKERY, Sheila .... 910-788-6250 338 A
sheila.dockery@sccnc.edu
DOCKING, Jeffrey, R ..... 517-265-5161 220 F
jdocking@adrian.edu
DOCKINS, Waynna .... 870-612-2009.. 22 I
waynna.dockins@uaccb.edu
DOCTOR, John .... 650-738-4166.. 61 Q
doctorj@smccd.edu
DOCTOR, OFM, John .... 217-228-5432 146 F
docotjo@quincy.edu
DOCTOR, OFM, John .... 218-228-5432 146 F
doctojo@quincy.edu
DODANI, Sunita .... 757-446-7944 466 I
dodanis@evms.edu
DODD, Daran .... 828-694-1832 332 E
d_dodd@blueridge.edu
DODD, David .... 502-456-6504 184 E
dhdodd@sullivan.edu
DODD, David .... 201-216-5491 283 C
david.dodd@stevens.edu

DONCITS, Diane .... 651-641-3472 236 F ddoncits@luthersem.edu
DONCSECZ, Joseph, J .. 814-865-1355 392 B jjd7@psu.edu
DONDERO, Susan .... 414-326-1797 493 A
DONE, Karen .... 662-621-4153 245 E kwdone@coahomacc.edu
DONE, Kenneth .... 662-254-3624 248 B kenneth.done@mvsu.edu
DONEGAN, Helen .... 407-235-3935 109 E helen.donegan@ucf.edu
DONEGAN, Jean .... 985-448-4595 192 B jean.donegan@nicholls.edu
DONEGAN, John, P ...... 734-487-3591 223 H jdonega1@emich.edu
DONELAN, Pam .... 605-229-8401 416 C pam.donelan@presentation.edu
DONELL, Katherine .... 978-837-5125 216 D donellk@merrimack.edu
DONELSON, Rollin .... 336-334-3004 343 A rollin_donelson@uncg.edu
DONES, Abraham .... 919-536-7200 334 B donesa@durhamtech.edu
DONES, Carmen .... 310-287-4522.. 49 G donescm@wlac.edu
DONEZ, Norma, C .... 787-751-0178 511 I nodonez@suagm.edu
DONG, Jianyu (Jane) .... 323-343-4510.. 32 A jdong2@calstatela.edu
DONG, Suhua .... 717-337-6487 384 H sdong@gettysburg.edu
DONG, XinQi .... 848-932-3818 282 A xdong@ifh.rutgers.edu
DONGHIA, Mike .... 717-866-5775 383 H mike.donghia@evangelical.edu
DONHAM, Brent .... 903-886-5390 447 B brent.donham@tamuc.edu
DONHAM, Marilyn .... 734-973-3630 232 B mdonham@wccnet.edu
DONINI, Joseph .... 845-398-4040 315 B jdonini@stac.edu
DONIUS, Mary Alice ..... 203-365-4508.. 88 B doniusm@sacredheart.edu
DONKERSLOOT, Norman .... 616-392-8555 233 E norman@westernsem.edu
DONLAY, Joe .... 970-491-6321.. 78 M joe.donlay@colostate.edu
DONLEY, Laurre .... 330-339-3391 354 J ldonley@kent.edu
DONLEY, Michael .... 903-566-7284 456 A mdonley@uttyler.edu
DONLEY, Victoria .... 440-934-3101 358 E vdonley@ohiobusinesscollege.edu
DONNAY, Brent .... 320-308-3039 240 H btdonnay@stcloudstate.edu
DONNELL, Jameson ...... 704-403-3000 327 H jameson.donnell@carolinascollege.edu
DONNELL, Richard .... 731-426-7523 420 I rdonnell@lanecollege.edu
DONNELLEY, Jason ...... 864-294-2000 410 A
DONNELLI, Amber .... 775-753-2135 271 B amber.donnelli@gbcnv.edu
DONNELLY, Eileen, G ... 302-356-6812.. 90 I eileen.g.donnelly@wilmu.edu
DONNELLY, Jeffrey .... 732-987-2427 278 B jdonnelly@georgian.edu
DONNELLY, Jilian .... 610-361-5261 391 D donnellj@neumann.edu
DONNELLY, John .... 434-961-5205 475 F jdonnelly@pvcc.edu
DONNELLY, JR., Joseph .... 617-373-2520 217 F
DONNELLY, Lucinda, J . 516-877-3268 289 C cdonnelly@adelphi.edu
DONNELLY, Sarah .... 908-526-1200 281 A sarah.donnelly@raritanval.edu
DONNELLY, Sharon .... 215-489-2317 382 D sharon.donnelly@delval.edu
DONNELLY, Sherri .... 518-445-2396 289 E sdonn@albanylaw.edu
DONNHAUSER, Marc .... 951-639-5670.. 52 I mdonnhauser@msjc.edu
DONOFF, R. Bruce .... 617-432-1401 210 B bruce_donoff@hsdm.harvard.edu
DONOFF, Susan .... 503-808-7993 377 F sdonoff@uws.edu
DONOFRIO, Joseph ...... 864-578-8770 412 B jdonofrio@sherman.edu
DONOGHUE, Karen, A .. 203-254-4000.. 86 I kdonoghue@fairfield.edu
DONOHOE, Cheryl .... 313-593-5639 231 F cdonohoe@umich.edu
DONOHOE, Janet .... 678-839-6636 126 E jdonohoe@westga.edu
DONOHOE, Kerry .... 978-934-2542 211 G kerry_donohoe@uml.edu
DONOHOE, Nancy .... 312-935-4804 147 D ndonohoe@robertmorris.edu
DONOHOO, Daniel .... 650-325-5621.. 59 C daniel.donohoo@stpatricksseminary.org
DONOHUE, Beth .... 315-568-3115 308 F bdonohue@nycc.edu
DONOHUE, John .... 609-771-2393 276 I jdonohue@tcnj.edu
DONOHUE, Mary .... 518-736-3622 300 F mdonohue@fmcc.suny.edu
DONOHUE, Michael, T . 212-752-1530 304 D mdonohue@limcollege.edu
DONOHUE, Michelle ...... 831-479-6525.. 27 G midonohu@cabrillo.edu
DONOHUE, Patrick, R ... 570-941-4072 401 H patrick.donohue@scranton.edu
DONOHUE, OSA, Peter, M .... 610-519-8881 402 D peter.donohue@villanova.edu
DONOTO, Chris .... 847-317-8113 150 H cdonoto@tiu.edu
DONOVAN, Amy .... 978-232-2048 209 B adonovan@endicott.edu
DONOVAN, SND, Anne . 617-735-9822 209 A donovan@emmanuel.edu
DONOVAN, Anthony ...... 615-460-5802 418 F anthony.donovan@belmont.edu
DONOVAN, Celeste .... 620-417-1016 176 K celeste.donovan@sccc.edu
DONOVAN, Donald .... 920-206-2314 493 L donald.donovan@mbu.edu
DONOVAN, Elizabeth ..... 978-556-3940 215 C edonovan@necc.mass.edu
DONOVAN, James .... 657-278-2777.. 31 E jdonovan@fullerton.edu
DONOVAN, Janine, E .... 860-444-8322 504 F janine.e.donovan@uscg.mil
DONOVAN, Jennifer ...... 412-809-5100 396 H donovan.jennifer@ptcollege.edu
DONOVAN, Jody .... 970-491-5312.. 78 M jody.donovan@colostate.edu
DONOVAN, Maura .... 414-288-5006 494 B maura.donovan@marquette.edu
DONOVAN, Michael .... 617-353-8630 207 D donovanm@bu.edu
DONOVAN, Scott .... 201-761-6109 282 I sdonovan@saintpeters.edu
DONOVAN, Steve .... 860-297-2281.. 88 C steve.donovan@trincoll.edu
DONOVAN, Susan, M .... 502-272-8234 179 B sdonovan@bellarmine.edu
DONOVAN, Suzette .... 865-981-8102 421 F suzette.donovan@maryvillecollege.edu
DONOVAN, Terry .... 209-667-3566.. 33 C tdonovan1@csustan.edu
DONOWAY, Troy .... 301-687-7003 203 E dtdonoway@frostburg.edu
DONSBACH, Dave .... 217-351-2393 146 C ddonsbach@parkland.edu
DONSBACH, James .... 585-343-0055 301 A jadonsbach@genesee.edu
DONTES, Arnim .... 214-648-3572 457 B arnim.dontes@utsouthwestern.edu
DOODY, Josh .... 650-508-3685.. 54 D jdoody@ndnu.edu
DOOLEN, Toni .... 541-737-6400 375 D toni.doolen@oregonstate.edu
DOOLEN, Toni .... 541-737-0123 375 D toni.doolen@oregonstate.edu
DOOLEY, Andrea .... 619-594-2314.. 33 E adooley@sdsu.edu
DOOLEY, Chris .... 912-583-3221 115 E cdooley@bpc.edu
DOOLEY, David, M .... 401-874-2444 406 B davedooley@uri.edu
DOOLEY, Elizabeth .... 407-823-2373 109 E elizabeth.dooley@ucf.edu
DOOLEY, Frank, J .... 765-494-1874 159 E dooleyf@purdue.edu
DOOLEY, John, E .... 540-231-2265 477 A jdooley@vt.edu
DOOLEY, Jon .... 336-278-7220 328 K jdooley4@elon.edu
DOOLEY, Joseph, M ..... 203-392-5375.. 85 A dooleyj1@southernct.edu
DOOLEY, Kathleen A, M .... 630-515-6078 143 G kdoole@midwestern.edu
DOOLEY, Lisa .... 701-858-3447 345 F lisa.dooley@minotstateu.edu
DOOLEY, Marella .... 754-312-2898 102 Q mdooley@keycollege.edu
DOOLEY, Margaret .... 520-494-5215.. 11 K margaret.dooley1@centralaz.edu
DOOLEY, Marietta .... 215-780-1260 398 G mdooley@salus.edu
DOOLEY, Robert .... 423-425-4313 428 A robert-dooley@utc.edu
DOOLEY, Ron .... 754-312-2898 102 Q admissions@keycollege.edu
DOOLEY, Ronald, H ...... 754-312-2898 102 Q rdooley@keycollege.edu
DOOLEY, Sue .... 831-656-3023 503 K sgdooley@nps.edu
DOOLITTLE, Eric .... 630-637-5104 144 H edoolittle@noctrl.edu
DOORE, Brian, E .... 207-974-4664 194 H bdoore@emcc.edu
DOORN, Dawn .... 760-480-8474.. 74 J ddoorn@wscal.edu
DOPP, Kristi .... 206-592-3504 481 H kdopp@highline.edu
DOPSON, Brian .... 386-752-1822.. 99 A brian.dopson@fgc.edu
DOPSON, Lea, R .... 909-869-3464.. 30 D lrdopson@cpp.edu
DOPSON, Nicole .... 505-277-2611 288 G nicole14@unm.edu
DORADO, Luis .... 310-233-4031.. 49 A doradol@lahc.edu
DORAN, Dru, A .... 810-762-3322 231 G drudoran@umich.edu
DORAN, Marcia .... 203-285-2389.. 85 E mdoran@gwcc.commnet.edu
DORAN, Pam .... 803-777-2752 413 C pdoran@mailbox.sc.edu
DORAN, Sandra, J .... 336-721-2605 340 D sandra.doran@salem.edu
DORAN, Stacy .... 920-735-5698 499 E doran@fvtc.edu
DORANTES, Andrew, R . 909-621-8126.. 45 A andrew_dorantes@hmc.edu
DORCEY, Penny, R .... 734-384-4311 227 G pdorcey@monroeccc.edu
DORCEY MCINTOSH, Alicia .... 402-375-7321 268 G aldorce1@wsc.edu
DORCHEUS, Greg .... 503-338-2489 372 E gdorcheus@clatsopcc.edu
DORE, David .... 520-206-7100.. 15 D ddore@pima.edu
DOREN, Douglas .... 302-831-2054.. 90 F doren@udel.edu
DORER, Thomas .... 617-725-4117 219 A tdorer@suffolk.edu
DORF, Laurie .... 718-997-3920 295 C laurie.dorf@qc.cuny.edu
DORFF, Robin, H .... 603-535-3500 275 B rhdorff@plymouth.edu
DORGAN, Mark, W .... 802-656-0518 463 E mark.dorgan@uvm.edu
DORGAN, Sheila .... 508-910-6527 211 F sdorgan@umassd.edu
DORHOUT, Peter, K ...... 785-532-5110 174 G dorhout@ksu.edu
DORIA, Joseph .... 201-761-6195 282 I jdoria@saintpeters.edu
DORIANI, Daniel, M ..... 314-434-4044 252 B dan.doriani@covenantseminary.edu
DORITY, Nancy .... 657-278-2350.. 31 E ndority@fullerton.edu
DORMAN, Jay, A .... 334-833-4406.... 5 H jdorman@hawks.huntingdon.edu
DORMAN, Jeremy .... 903-693-2009 441 F jdorman@panola.edu
DORMAN, Jesse .... 402-872-2246 268 F jdorman@peru.edu
DORMAN, Laura .... 217-206-6005 151 C dorman.laura@uis.edu
DORMAN, Steve, M ...... 478-445-4444 118 C steve.dorman@gcsu.edu
DORMINY, Bill .... 706-385-1466 123 C bill.dorminy@point.edu
DORMITORIO, Edgar, J 949-824-4476.. 68 G ejdormit@uci.edu
DORN, Charles .... 207-725-3290 193 D cdorn@bowdoin.edu
DORN, Sara .... 314-421-0949 260 G sdorn@siba.edu
DORNBUSH, Mathew .... 920-465-2454 496 E dornbusm@uwgb.edu
DORNE, Clifford .... 989-964-7072 230 B cdorne@svsu.edu
DORNER, Michael, H .... 651-641-8811 235 F dorner@csp.edu
DORNES, Delfina .... 618-468-5200 141 F ddornes@lc.edu
DORNES, Stephanie ...... 909-607-7894.. 37 C stephanie.dornes@claremont.edu
DORNEVIL, James .... 954-532-9614 101 D
DORPH, Martin .... 212-992-8282 310 B martin.dorph@nyu.edu
DORR, Jodi, L .... 810-762-7996 225 H jdorr@kettering.edu
DORR, Mary, I .... 913-288-7145 174 F mdorr@kckcc.edu
DORRELL, Martha .... 803-321-5373 411 D martha.dorrell@newberry.edu
DORRELL, Natalie .... 760-384-6260.. 46 M ndorrell@cerrocoso.edu
DORRIAN, John .... 843-953-6779 407 F jdorrian@citadel.edu
DORSETT, Al .... 302-857-6252.. 89 F adorsett@desu.edu
DORSETT, James .... 517-353-1720 227 D jdorsett@msu.edu
DORSEY, Alan, T .... 706-542-1561 125 G atdorsey@uga.edu
DORSEY, Andrew, R ..... 303-404-5481.. 79 J andy.dorsey@frontrange.edu
DORSEY, Brynnmarie .... 484-664-3199 391 C brynnmariedorsey@muhlenberg.edu
DORSEY, Christopher ... 860-465-4398.. 84 J dorseyc@easternct.edu
DORSEY, David, F .... 440-775-5191 358 C david.dorsey@oberlin.edu
DORSEY, Denice .... 225-768-1734 186 F denice.dorsey@franu.edu
DORSEY, J. Kevin .... 618-536-3471 149 D kdorsey@siumed.edu
DORSEY, Judith .... 718-270-1867 317 E judith.dorsey@downstate.edu
DORSEY, Melanie .... 917-493-4588 305 I mdorsey@msmnyc.edu
DORSEY, Michael, W .... 508-831-5609 220 E mwdorsey@wpi.edu
DORSEY, Peter, A .... 301-447-7435 200 E dorsey@msmary.edu
DORSEY, Tim .... 216-987-5602 351 G tim.dorsey@tri-c.edu
DORSEY, Victor .... 757-455-3351 477 F vdorsey@vwu.edu
DORTCH, Derrick .... 202-462-2101.. 92 C ddortch@iwp.edu
DORTH, Kari .... 415-561-6555.. 57 H kari.dorth@presidio.edu
DORTON, Alicia .... 678-359-5585 119 F aliciad@gordonstate.edu
DORTON, Kim .... 276-523-2400 475 A kdorton@mecc.edu
DORTON, Lauren .... 843-661-8002 409 I lauren.dorton@fdtc.edu
DORY, Ondrea .... 641-784-5447 165 H dory@graceland.edu
DOS SANTOS, Linda ..... 212-960-5300 326 E linda.dossantos@yu.edu
DOSAL, Paul, J .... 813-974-5649 110 B pdosal@usf.edu
DOSANJOS, Joelisio ..... 201-684-6818 280 H jdosanjos@ramapo.edu
DOSCH, Myron .... 907-450-8079.... 9 G myron.dosch@alaska.edu
DOSKAL, Darese .... 607-844-8222 322 H doskald@tompkinscortland.edu
DOSREIS, Catrina, S ..... 919-530-6198 342 A cdosreis@nccu.edu
DOSS, Brad .... 507-433-0523 240 F brad.doss@riverland.edu
DOSS, Julie .... 806-743-2786 451 C julie.doss@ttuhsc.edu
DOSS, Khalilah .... 602-242-0501 175 F dossk@mcpherson.edu
DOSS, Lauren .... 205-726-2915.... 6 E ledoss@samford.edu
DOSS, Peggy .... 870-460-1033.. 22 D dossp@uamont.edu
DOSTER, Aurora .... 765-641-4171 153 B acdoster@anderson.edu
DOSTER, Betty .... 704-687-5769 342 E betty.doster@uncc.edu
DOSTER, Robert .... 201-684-7870 280 H rdoster@ramapo.edu
DOSTER, Ronda .... 937-258-8251 354 G ronda.doster@icb.edu

DOWNING, Jay .... 432-837-8368 450 D jdowning@sulross.edu
DOWNING, John .... 910-362-7846 332 H jfdowning296@mail.cfcc.edu
DOWNING, Kimberly .... 513-556-5028 362 D kimberly.downing@uc.edu
DOWNING, Michael ...... 508-336-8700 404 I mdowning@jwu.edu
DOWNING, Scott .... 620-278-2173 177 B scott.downing@sterling.edu
DOWNING, Stacy, L ..... 302-857-6300.. 89 F sdowning@desu.edu
DOWNING, Steve .... 317-955-6351 158 U sdowning@marian.edu
DOWNING, Valerie .... 610-606-4609 381 A vdowning@cedarcrest.edu
DOWNS, Amy .... 717-815-1781 404 A adowns@ycp.edu
DOWNS, Jeffrey .... 775-445-3271 271 G jeffrey.downs@wnc.edu
DOWNS, Jesse, G .... 225-578-7180 188 I jdowns@lsu.edu
DOWNS, Nate .... 580-774-3700 370 C nate.downs@swosu.edu
DOWNS, Timothy .... 605-626-2521 417 A president@northern.edu
DOWNS, William .... 252-328-6249 341 C downsw14@ecu.edu
DOWNS, William, M ..... 704-406-4236 329 A presidentdowns@gardner-webb.edu
DOWNS-BURNS, Kim .... 802-443-5158 462 H kdowns@middlebury.edu
DOWTY, Dean .... 310-233-4216.. 49 A dowtydl@lahc.edu
DOXEY, Tia, M .... 919-530-7269 342 A tdoxey@nccu.edu
DOYLE, Amanda .... 337-482-6730 192 E amandad@louisiana.edu
DOYLE, Anne .... 617-663-7054 210 G adoyle@lasell.edu
DOYLE, Barbara .... 805-765-9300.. 62 B
DOYLE, Bill .... 804-758-6706 475 G bdoyle@rappahannock.edu
DOYLE, Catherine .... 585-389-2123 308 B cdoyle0@naz.edu
DOYLE, Cathleen, H ...... 410-777-2902 197 C chdoyle@aacc.edu
DOYLE, Christy .... 208-769-3481 131 C cadoyle@nic.edu
DOYLE, Clare .... 215-248-7071 381 D doylecm@chc.edu
DOYLE, Creig .... 904-819-6200.. 98 E cdoyle@flagler.edu
DOYLE, Damian .... 410-455-3872 202 E damian.doyle@umbc.edu
DOYLE, Denise .... 210-829-3900 453 D ddoyle@uiwtx.edu
DOYLE, Diana, M .... 303-797-5701.. 76 I diana.doyle@arapahoe.edu
DOYLE, Dorothy (Darcy) .... 610-647-4400 386 C ddoyle1@immaculata.edu
DOYLE, Eileen .... 914-633-2483 302 G edoyle@iona.edu
DOYLE, Fiona, M .... 510-642-5472.. 68 D graddean@berkeley.edu
DOYLE, Francis, J .... 617-495-5829 210 B dean@seas.harvard.edu
DOYLE, Jamie .... 877-559-3621.. 29 A info@ciat.edu
DOYLE, Jeanette .... 508-373-5733 216 B jeanette.doyle@mcphs.edu
DOYLE, Jeff .... 254-710-3100 431 J jeff_doyle@baylor.edu
DOYLE, Jillian .... 323-469-3300.. 25 E jdoyle@amda.edu
DOYLE, John .... 734-432-5737 227 A jdoyle@madonna.edu
DOYLE, Johnna .... 719-549-2130.. 79 A johnna.doyle@colostate.edu
DOYLE, Kara .... 812-888-7777 162 C kdoyle@vinu.edu
DOYLE, Leslie .... 641-472-1241 167 F ldoyle@mum.edu
DOYLE, Leslie .... 816-501-3590 258 H leslie.doyle@rockhurst.edu
DOYLE, Lori, N .... 215-895-2613 383 B lori.n.doyle@drexel.edu
DOYLE, Michael .... 973-294-4449 282 A midoyle@rutgers.edu
DOYLE, Michael, H .... 563-588-7823 167 D mike.doyle@loras.edu
DOYLE, Oliver, J .... 406-791-5300 265 H

DOYLE, Pam .... 316-677-9400 178 B pdoyle@watc.edu
DOYLE, Rock, D .... 716-878-6711 318 C doylerd@buffalostate.edu
DOYLE, Sheila .... 607-777-3844 316 E sdoyle@binghamton.edu
DOYLE, Susan .... 205-726-2375.... 6 E sdoyle@samford.edu
DOYLE, Teresa .... 530-895-2568.. 27 F doylete@butte.edu
DOYLE, Timothy .... 901-321-3548 419 C tdoyle1@cbu.edu
DOYLEN, Michael .... 414-229-4781 497 A doylenm@uwm.edu
DOZIER, John .... 803-777-9943 413 C jdozier@mailbox.sc.edu
DOZIER, Ken .... 252-399-6596 326 M kdozier@barton.edu
DOZIER, Luann, D .... 504-865-5794 191 B ldozier@tulane.edu
DOZIER, Monique .... 470-639-0545 122 D monique.dozier@morehouse.edu
DOZIER, Rodney .... 620-276-9603 173 E rodney.dozier@gcccks.edu
DRABIK, Joshua .... 954-545-4500 107 E webmaster@sfbc.edu
DRABIK, Mary, A .... 954-545-4500 107 E mdrabik@sfbc.edu
DRABIK, Thomas .... 954-637-2268 107 E financialaid@sfbc.edu
DRACHMAN, Annette, R .... 843-792-4063 410 F drachmar@musc.edu
DRACOS, Bill .... 703-993-8742 467 L wdracos@gmu.edu
DRAEGER, James .... 262-691-5323 500 H jdraeger5@wctc.edu
DRAGAN, Kimberly .... 860-738-6418.. 86 C kdragan@nwcc.edu
DRAGNA, Janine .... 916-686-7382.. 29 J
DRAGON, Emily .... 207-602-2451 196 G edragon@une.edu
DRAGOUN, Mary Beth .. 805-581-1233.. 42 D mdragoun@eternitybiblecollege.com
DRAGUSHANSKAYA, Ludmilla .... 718-522-9073 290 C mdragush@asa.edu
DRAIN, Cecil, B .... 804-828-7247 473 F cbdrain@vcu.edu
DRAIN, Deborah .... 315-279-5210 304 A ddrain@keuka.edu
DRAIN, Jerome .... 713-718-5261 437 I jerome.drain@hccs.edu
DRAIN, Timothy, S .... 903-510-2458 452 C tdra@tjc.edu
DRAKE, Bo .... 423-697-2514 424 E bo.drake@chattanoogastate.edu
DRAKE, Brent .... 702-895-1073 271 E brent.drake@unlv.edu
DRAKE, Brent .... 702-895-3011 271 E brent.drake@unlv.edu
DRAKE, Brian .... 713-221-8045 453 B drakeb@uhd.edu
DRAKE, Brittney .... 714-816-0366.. 67 I brittney.drake@trident.edu
DRAKE, David .... 706-865-2134 125 E ddrake@truett.edu
DRAKE, Edna .... 601-977-7876 249 C edrake@tougaloo.edu
DRAKE, JR., George, P 717-871-7333 395 D george.drake@millersville.edu
DRAKE, Howard .... 863-669-2321 105 A hdrake@polk.edu
DRAKE, James .... 214-648-2088 457 B james.drake@utsouthwestern.edu
DRAKE, Jeff .... 704-991-0274 338 C jdrake5284@stanly.edu
DRAKE, Jennifer .... 704-847-5600 340 I jdrake@ses.edu
DRAKE, Jennifer .... 360-867-6400 481 A provost@evergreen.edu
DRAKE, Jill .... 678-839-6445 126 E jdrake@westga.edu
DRAKE, Julie .... 608-267-9066 499 B julie.drake@wtcsystem.edu
DRAKE, Kay, L .... 859-238-5467 179 F kay.drake@centre.edu
DRAKE, Kourtney .... 816-279-7000 250 B registrar@abtu.edu
DRAKE, Lynette .... 217-581-3221 136 E ldrake@eiu.edu
DRAKE, Matthew .... 585-582-8200 299 A matthewdrake@elim.edu

DRAKE, Michael, V .... 614-292-2424 358 I drake.379@osu.edu
DRAKE, Paul .... 671-734-1812 505 D pdrake@piu.edu
DRAKE, Peter .... 212-842-5970 308 D pdrake@nyaa.edu
DRAKE, Roger, D .... 660-248-6221 251 B rdrake@centralmethodist.edu
DRAKE, Susan, K .... 217-245-3041 138 D sdrake@ic.edu
DRAKE, Tyler .... 480-212-1704.. 15 Q tyler@sessions.edu
DRAKE, Web .... 864-977-7000 411 E web.drake@ngu.edu
DRAKE-DEESE, Kent ...... 603-358-2346 275 A kdrakedeese@keene.edu
DRALE, Christina, S ...... 501-569-3204.. 22 B csdrale@ualr.edu
DRAMMEH, Lamin .... 205-366-8817.... 7 A ldrammeh@stillman.edu
DRANKA, Scott .... 413-748-3110 218 G sdranka@springfield.edu
DRAPEAU, Guy .... 860-297-4210.. 88 C guy.drapeau@trincoll.edu
DRAPER, Diana, M .... 203-254-4125.. 86 I ddraper@fairfield.edu
DRAPER, Erin .... 315-268-3995 296 A edraper@clarkson.edu
DRAPER, Frances .... 303-492-7531.. 83 A frances.draper@colorado.edu
DRAPER, Jason .... 724-830-1014 398 H jdraper@setonhill.edu
DRAPER, Mark .... 717-866-5775 383 H mdraper@evangelical.edu
DRAPER, Marla .... 303-273-3297.. 78 I mdraper@mines.edu
DRAPER, Matthew .... 315-268-6763 296 A mdraper@clarkson.edu
DRAPER, Nancy, J .... 405-912-9024 369 D ndraper@ru.edu
DRAPER, Sherry .... 785-670-2312 177 G sherry.draper@washburn.edu
DRASGOW, Fritz .... 217-333-1480 151 D fdrasgow@illinois.edu
DRASIN, Joseph .... 301-314-1019 202 C jdrasin@umd.edu
DRATCH, Joseph .... 845-848-7600 298 D joseph.dratch@dc.edu
DRAUD, Matthew .... 517-264-7667 230 E mdraud@sienaheights.edu
DRAUDE, Barbara, J ..... 615-904-8383 422 H barbara.draude@mtsu.edu
DRAUGHON, Katherine, A .... 812-465-1630 161 E kdraughon@usi.edu
DRAVES, Patricia, H ...... 641-784-5111 165 H pat.draves@graceland.edu
DRAWDY, Lester, W ..... 770-720-5927 123 E lwd@reinhardt.edu
DRAYER, Judy .... 602-274-1885.. 15 B jdrayer@pihma.edu
DRAYFAHL, Perry, M .... 610-499-1291 403 B pmdrayfahl@widener.edu
DRAYTON, Rebecca ...... 610-398-5300 389 A rdrayton@lincolntech.edu
DRAZKOWSKI, Amy ...... 507-453-1479 239 A amy.drazkowski@southeastmn.edu
DREBIN, Diane .... 541-278-5796 372 A ddrebin@bluecc.edu
DREES, Betty .... 816-926-4400 253 G
DREES, Bill .... 210-297-9630 431 E wfdrees@baptisthealthsystem.com
DREES, John .... 502-852-6739 185 C john.drees@exchange.louisville.edu
DREESE, Dawn .... 610-989-1307 402 B ddreese@vfmac.edu
DREGER, Barb .... 920-735-4776 499 E dreger@fvtc.edu
DREGIER, Denise, M .... 443-412-2428 199 A ddregier@harford.edu
DREHER, Heyward, M ... 718-270-5011 295 A mdreher@mec.cuny.edu
DREHER, Karolina .... 610-796-8218 378 F karolina.dreher@alvernia.edu
DREIER, Alexander .... 203-432-4949.. 89 D alexander.dreier@yale.edu
DREIZLER, Robin .... 310-660-5487.. 41 L rdreizle@elcamino.edu
DRELL, Persis .... 650-724-4074.. 65 J provost@stanford.edu
DRENKOW, Daniel, D ... 605-274-5251 415 B dan.drenkow@augie.edu

DRENNEN, Michelle ...... 509-777-4974 486 I mdrennen@whitworth.edu
DRENNEN, Rebecca, J .. 212-986-4343 291 D rjd@berkeleycollege.edu
DRENNEN, Rebecca, J .. 973-278-5400 275 I rjd@berkeleycollege.edu
DRENNING, Caleb .... 814-472-3035 398 B cdrenning@francis.edu
DRESCHER, Debra .... 518-631-9847 296 A ddresche@clarkson.edu
DRESCHER, Greg .... 916-416-6476 298 A greg.drescher@culinary.edu
DRESCHER, Marc .... 310-434-4547.. 62 E drescher_mark@smc.edu
DRESDNER, Lisa .... 203-575-8004.. 86 B ldresdner@nv.edu
DRESSEN, Barbara, J .... 507-344-7317 234 B barb.dressen@blc.edu
DRESSEN, Dan .... 507-786-3420 243 C dressen@stolaf.edu
DRESSER, Kathy .... 914-337-9300 297 D kathy.dresser@concordia-ny.edu
DRESSER-RECKTENWALD, Wendy .... 607-587-4025 320 C dressews@alfredstate.edu
DREW, Daniel, J .... 716-888-2569 292 D drewd@canisius.edu
DREW, Nichole .... 503-554-2182 373 C ndrew@georgefox.edu
DREW, Phil .... 405-425-1842 367 G philip.drew@oc.edu
DREWELOW, Lonna ...... 319-363-1323 168 C ldrewelow@mtmercy.edu
DREWENSKI, Shirley ..... 708-596-2000 149 B sdrewenski@ssc.edu
DREWES, James .... 419-267-1439 358 A jdrewes@northweststate.edu
DREXEL, Penny, M .... 814-332-4311 378 D pdrexel@allegheny.edu
DREXLER, Brad .... 610-861-5475 391 F bdrexler@northampton.edu
DREXLER, Jim .... 706-419-1407 117 B jim.drexler@covenant.edu
DREXLER, Julie .... 229-333-2100 127 B julie.drexler@wiregrass.edu
DREYER, Allen, R .... 570-585-9317 381 E adreyer@clarkssummitu.edu
DREYER, Thomas .... 978-934-4801 211 G thomas_dreyer@uml.edu
DREYFUS, Kristen .... 252-328-9492 341 C springerk@ecu.edu
DREYFUS, Mark, B .... 757-671-7171 467 A president@ecpi.edu
DREYFUSS, Shannon .... 303-963-3411.. 77 G sdreyfuss@ccu.edu
DRIBBEN, Anthony .... 772-462-7520 101 E adribben@irsc.edu
DRIEBE, Caroline .... 404-727-1552 117 F caroline.driebe@emory.edu
DRIEDGER, Derek .... 605-995-2635 415 C derek.driedger@dwu.edu
DRIES, Kelly .... 414-297-6263 500 B driesk@matc.edu
DRIES, Kelly, J .... 414-410-4390 492 D kjdries@stritch.edu
DRIESSEN, Daniel .... 701-662-1508 346 D daniel.driessen@lrsc.edu
DRIESSNER, Johnnie .... 503-493-6549 372 I jddriessner@cu-portland.edu
DRIESSNER, Johnnie .... 503-493-6549 372 I jdriessner@cu-portland.edu
DRIGGINS, Steffani .... 803-376-5734 406 F sdriggins@allenuniversity.edu
DRIGGS, Bethany .... 207-509-7169 195 H bdriggs@unity.edu
DRIGGS, Jeff .... 801-832-2737 461 G jdriggs@westminstercollege.edu
DRIMMER, Alan .... 301-985-7000 203 B alan.drimmer@umuc.edu
DRINAN, Helen, G .... 617-521-2070 218 E helen.drinan@simmons.edu
DRINDAK, Desiree .... 518-587-2100 321 A desiree.drindak@esc.edu
DRINKWATER, Norman . 608-262-7992 496 C norman.drinkwater@wisc.edu
DRISCOLL, Daniel .... 630-889-6609 144 G ddriscoll@nuhs.edu
DRISCOLL, Debbie .... 434-544-8125 472 G driscoll@lynchburg.edu
DRISCOLL, Diane, H ..... 603-526-3673 272 H ddriscoll@colby-sawyer.edu
DRISCOLL, Frederick ..... 617-989-4135 219 E driscollf@wit.edu

DUFFY, Elizabeth 240-629-7886 198 E
eduffy@frederick.edu
DUFFY, James, P 717-337-6240 384 H
jpduffy@gettysburg.edu
DUFFY, Julia, A 203-254-4000.. 86 I
jduffy@fairfield.edu
DUFFY, Kelly 315-470-5922 291 H
kellyduffy@crouse.org
DUFFY, Kelly 937-481-2243 364 E
DUFFY, Kevin 609-586-4800 278 F
duffyk@mccc.edu
DUFFY, Kristine 518-743-2237 320 D
duffyk@sunyacc.edu
DUFFY, Matthew 218-726-8829 243 F
duffy@d.umn.edu
DUFFY, Michael 517-265-5161 220 F
mduffy@adrian.edu
DUFFY, Pamela, A 619-239-0391.. 34 F
pduffy@cwsl.edu
DUFFY, Peter 508-999-9216 211 F
pduffy@umassd.edu
DUFFY, Rachelle, M 517-265-5161 220 F
rduffy@adrian.edu
DUFFY, Sophia 610-526-1255 378 G
sophia.duffy@theamericancollege.edu
DUFFY, Stephen, M 956-326-2543 446 F
sduffy@tamiu.edu
DUFFY, Susan 781-239-6425 205 E
sduffy@babson.edu
DUFFY, Thomas 845-431-8305 298 E
thomas.duffy1@sunydutchess.edu
DUFFY, II, William, R .. 563-425-5221 170 A
duffyw@uiu.edu
DUFNER, Sally 320-308-5538 241 A
sally.dufner@sctcc.edu
DUFORT, Linda 630-617-3059 136 G
dufortl@elmhurst.edu
DUFOUR, Graciela 815-836-5270 141 G
dufourgr@lewisu.edu
DUFOUR, Jeff 518-694-7395 289 D
jeff.dufour@acphs.edu
DUFRENE, Uric 812-941-2208 157 B
udufrene@ius.edu
DUFRESNE, Edwidge 478-825-6200 118 A
edwidge.dufresne@fvsu.edu
DUFRESNE, Sarah 989-686-9386 223 G
sarahdufresne@delta.edu
DUGAN, James 816-654-7219 254 C
jdugan@kcumb.edu
DUGAN, Jennifer 606-218-5219 185 D
jenniferdugan@upike.edu
DUGAN, Lyndsey 304-367-4135 490 B
lyndsey.dugan@fairmontstate.edu
DUGAN, Mary 775-784-3941 271 F
mdugan@unr.edu
DUGAN-WOOD, Joyce .. 205-929-1458.... 6 B
jduganwood@miles.edu
DUGAR, Curtis 570-422-3460 394 E
cdugar@esu.edu
DUGAT, Nathan 713-525-2152 454 H
registrar@stthom.edu
DUGGAN, Chris 636-949-4913 254 F
cduggan@lindenwood.edu
DUGGAN, Gary 413-572-5243 213 D
gduggan@westfield.ma.edu
DUGGAN, Michael 617-824-8268 208 H
michael_duggan@emerson.edu
DUGGAN, Sean 806-742-2661 451 B
s.duggan@ttu.edu
DUGGER, Neil 214-333-5202 434 I
neil@dbu.edu
DUGGIN, Josh 731-286-3338 425 A
duggin@dscc.edu
DUGUID, Brent 601-643-8261 245 G
brent.duguid@colin.edu
DUGUID, Iain 215-887-5511 402 H
iduguid@wts.edu
DUGUID, James 864-231-2000 406 G
jduguid@andersonuniversity.edu
DUGUID, Stephanie 601-643-5341 245 G
stephanie.duguid@colin.edu
DUHAI, Karen 800-287-8822 153 D
duhaika@bethanyseminary.edu
DUHAME-SCHMIDT,
Donna, L 248-522-3505 229 A
dlduhame@oaklandcc.edu
DUHE, Christen 601-928-6205 247 E
christen.duhe@mgccc.edu
DUHON, Gail 616-222-1431 222 I
gail.duhon@cornerstone.edu
DUHON, Stacey, D 318-274-6174 191 E
duhons@gram.edu

DUIN, Diane 605-229-8379 416 C
diane.duin@presentation.edu
DUININK, Leslie 641-628-7643 163 E
duininkl@central.edu
DUITCH, Suri 504-865-5555 191 B
sduitch@tulane.edu
DUKE, Buddy 601-426-6346 249 A
bduke@southeasternbaptist.edu
DUKE, Christopher 615-329-8505 419 K
cduke@fisk.edu
DUKE, Del, G 870-235-4171.. 21 D
dgduke@saumag.edu
DUKE, Jaime 406-265-3582 264 F
jaime.duke@msun.edu
DUKE, Labin, L 262-646-6517 495 B
lduke@nashotah.edu
DUKE, Lynda 309-556-3255 139 G
lduke@iwu.edu
DUKE, Robert 626-815-5441.. 26 H
rrduke@apu.edu
DUKE, Russell 980-495-3978 329 C
DUKE, Stacey 479-524-7371.. 19 H
sduke@jbu.edu
DUKE, Steven, T 402-472-8845 269 H
sduke@nebraska.edu
DUKE, Todd 765-973-8611 156 C
mtduke@iu.edu
DUKERICH, Janet, M 512-232-3310 455 A
janet.dukerich@austin.utexas.edu
DUKES, Bonita 386-822-8808 111 A
bdukes@stetson.edu
DUKES, Charlene, M 301-546-0400 201 C
dukescm@pgcc.edu
DUKES, Gary 503-838-8221 377 H
dukesg@wou.edu
DUKES, Keith, M 301-736-3631 199 G
keith.dukes@msbbcs.edu
DULABAUM, Mary 847-628-2089 140 C
mdulabaum@judsonu.edu
DULANEY, Kimberly 540-831-5000 470 C
DULANEY, Wes 931-540-2617 424 G
wdulaney@columbiastate.edu
DULANY, Ann 740-284-5254 353 B
adulany@franciscan.edu
DULAY, Sarah 708-237-5050 145 E
sdulay@nc.edu
DULEK, Krissy 630-829-6522 132 E
kdulek@ben.edu
DULEPSKI, Deborah, L . 203-576-2388.. 88 D
ddulepsk@bridgeport.edu
DULEY, Melody 775-445-4235 271 G
melody.duley@wnc.edu
DULGAR, Laura 623-935-8808.. 13 A
laura.dulgar@estrellamountain.edu
DULL, Katiina 951-493-6753.. 75 K
DULLEA, Robert 206-296-2590 484 F
dullea@seattleu.edu
DULSKI-BUCHOLZ,
Andi, L 701-788-4833 345 E
andrea.dulskibucholz@mayvillestate.
edu
DULUDE, Ryan 802-654-0505 464 B
rxd04120@ccv.vsc.edu
DUMANCELA, Fanny 718-518-4434 294 B
fdumancela@hostos.cuny.edu
DUMAS, Brandon 903-927-3233 458 G
bkdumas@wileyc.edu
DUMAS, Brandon, K 903-927-3233 458 G
bkdumas@wileyc.edu
DUMAS, Carolyn 618-634-3260 149 A
carolynd@shawneecc.edu
DUMAS, Jacky 254-295-4567 453 E
jdumas@umhb.edu
DUMAS, Maureen 401-598-2350 404 I
mdumas@jwu.edu
DUMAS-DYER, Heather . 408-554-4900.. 62 D
hdumasdyer@scu.edu
DUMAS SERFES,
Pamela 860-439-5226.. 86 H
pdserfes@conncoll.edu
DUMAUAL, Roberto 718-522-9073 290 C
rdumaual@asa.edu
DUMAY, Harry, E 413-265-2293 208 C
hdumay@elms.edu
DUMBLETON, Eric 415-565-4616.. 68 F
dumbletoneric@uchastings.edu
DUMDEI, Mike 903-823-3107 446 B
michael.dumdei@texarkanacollege.edu
DUMIRE, William 724-852-3382 402 F
wdumire@waynesburg.edu
DUMITRU, Dariu 661-362-2607.. 51 C
ddumitru@masters.edu

DUMM, Pamela 502-213-2109 181 F
pamela.dumm@kctcs.edu
DUMONT, Betsy 209-228-2969.. 69 B
edumont@ucmerced.edu
DUMONT, Gregory, L ... 412-578-6088 380 E
gldumont@carlow.edu
DUMONT, Sara, E 202-885-1321.. 90 J
dumont@american.edu
DUMONTELLE, Janine .... 714-997-6553.. 36 C
jpdumont@chapman.edu
DUMONTIER, Raelyn 406-275-4800 265 F
raelyn_dumontier@skc.edu
DUMOUCHEL, Jerrett 904-632-3307 100 B
jerrett.dumouchel@fscj.edu
DUMPSON,
Kimberly, C 401-456-8460 405 C
kdumpson@ric.edu
DUNAGAN, Pam 706-368-6397 115 B
pdunagan@berry.edu
DUNAVIN, Callie 870-733-6840.. 17 H
cdunavin@asumidsouth.edu
DUNAWAY, Donna, H ... 615-230-3551 426 B
donna.dunaway@volstate.edu
DUNAWAY, Greg, A 804-594-1430 474 I
gdunaway@jtcc.edu
DUNAWAY, Gregory 304-293-4611 491 C
gregory.dunaway@mail.wvu.edu
DUNBAR, Deirdre, M 262-554-2010 494 D
midwestcollege@aol.com
DUNBAR, Dorlena 516-572-7759 308 A
dorlena.dunbar@ncc.edu
DUNBAR, Joan 313-577-1912 232 I
aj0824@wayne.edu
DUNBAR, John 770-533-7028 121 B
jdunbar@laniertech.edu
DUNBAR, Kelly 215-619-7314 390 H
kdunbar@mc3.edu
DUNBAR, Melanie 814-866-8160 388 A
mdunbar@lecom.edu
DUNBAR, Nelia 575-835-7625 286 I
nelia.dunbar@nmt.edu
DUNBAR, Sandra 407-303-7894.. 94 D
sandra.dunbar@ahu.edu
DUNBAR, William, J 262-554-2010 494 D
dunbarphd@yahoo.com
DUNBAR-JACOB,
Jacqueline 412-624-2400 401 B
dunbar@pitt.edu
DUNCAN, Alfonzo 803-327-7402 408 B
aduncan@clintoncollege.edu
DUNCAN, C. Michael ... 413-782-1240 219 F
cmichael.duncan@wne.edu
DUNCAN, Charles 919-508-2395 344 F
cduncan@peace.edu
DUNCAN, Christopher .. 314-977-2244 259 H
chris.duncan@slu.edu
DUNCAN, Christopher .. 973-353-5255 282 B
chris.duncan@rutgers.edu
DUNCAN, Darrell 615-966-6166 421 D
darrell.duncan@lipscomb.edu
DUNCAN, Dennis, L 574-372-5100 155 B
duncandl@grace.edu
DUNCAN, Heather 904-620-1000 110 A
heather.duncan@unf.edu
DUNCAN, Holly 864-596-9704 409 B
holly.duncan@converse.edu
DUNCAN, Issac 270-686-4324 179 D
issac.duncan@brescia.edu
DUNCAN, J. Ligon 601-923-1600 248 F
lduncan@rts.edu
DUNCAN, Jay, R 770-720-5543 123 E
jrd@reinhardt.edu
DUNCAN, Jenny 918-293-5488 368 D
jenny.duncan@okstate.edu
DUNCAN, Jenny 918-293-4987 368 D
jenny.duncan@okstate.edu
DUNCAN, Jerelyn, L 501-420-1242.. 17 B
jerelyn.duncan@arkansasbaptist.edu
DUNCAN, Jim 901-843-3850 423 J
duncanjb@rhodes.edu
DUNCAN, John 313-883-8599 229 K
duncan.john@shms.edu
DUNCAN, John 864-231-2000 406 G
jduncan@andersonuniversity.edu
DUNCAN, John 864-977-7156 411 E
john.duncan@ngu.edu
DUNCAN, K. Michael 843-953-6356 408 E
duncanm@cofc.edu
DUNCAN, Kimberly 818-785-2726.. 35 J
kimberly.duncan@casalomacollege.edu
DUNCAN, Kimberly 240-629-7961 198 E
kduncan@frederick.edu
DUNCAN, Krystal 650-574-6440.. 61 P
duncank@smccd.edu

DUNCAN, Lewis, M 401-841-7004 503 L
lewis.duncan@usnwc.edu
DUNCAN, Linda 773-244-5697 145 A
lduncan@northpark.edu
DUNCAN, Lynette 479-524-7225.. 19 H
lduncan@jbu.edu
DUNCAN, Martina 207-725-3358 193 D
mduncan@bowdoin.edu
DUNCAN, Matthew 408-554-4583.. 62 D
mduncan@scu.edu
DUNCAN, Michael, W ... 724-847-6528 384 G
mwduncan@geneva.edu
DUNCAN, Randall, S 262-243-5700 493 B
DUNCAN, Randy 704-687-7323 342 E
rduncan@uncc.edu
DUNCAN, Robert 419-267-1202 358 A
rduncan@northweststate.edu
DUNCAN, Robin 951-552-8948.. 27 J
rduncan@calbaptist.edu
DUNCAN, Susan 662-915-6900 249 D
sduncan@olemiss.edu
DUNCAN, Suzanne 757-388-3693 471 D
sxduncan@sentara.com
DUNCAN, Tammy, W 336-322-2101 336 G
tammy.duncan@piedmontcc.edu
DUNCAN, Teresa, S 865-882-4648 425 G
duncants@roanestate.edu
DUNCAN, Tim 504-280-6459 189 E
tduncan@uno.edu
DUNCAN, Todd 513-556-4200 362 D
todd.duncan@uc.edu
DUNCAN, Wendy 559-325-3600.. 28 H
wduncan@chsu.edu
DUNCAN, William, H 916-660-7000.. 63 I
president@sierracollege.edu
DUNCAN, William, R 423-439-6000 419 J
duncanw@etsu.edu
DUNCAN-HERRING,
Chevene 270-534-3209 182 F
chevene.duncan-herring@kctcs.edu
DUNCAN-POITIER,
Johanna 518-320-1303 316 C
johanna.duncan-poitier@suny.edu
DUNCAN RAINES, Lisa . 757-594-7846 466 B
duncanl@cnu.edu
DUNCAN SMITH, Shá 610-690-5744 399 D
sdsmith1@swarthmore.edu
DUNCKLEE, Mary 508-565-3360 218 H
stonehillbkstr@fheg.follett.com
DUNCOMBE,
Kemmoree 269-927-8183 226 D
kduncombe@lakemichigancollege.edu
DUNEGAN, Kent 432-837-8100 450 D
kdunegan@sulross.edu
DUNEK, Susan 319-208-5193 169 F
sdunek@scciowa.edu
DUNFORD, Brandon 276-326-4282 465 B
bdunford@bluefield.edu
DUNGAN, Bonnie, J 607-871-2612 289 H
dunganbj@alfred.edu
DUNGEY, Deborah, J 936-361-1000 446 D
djdungey@pvamu.edu
DUNHAM, Andrew 517-629-0216 220 G
ddunham@albion.edu
DUNHAM, Andrew, M .. 517-629-0477 220 G
ddunham@albion.edu
DUNHAM, David 209-228-4264.. 69 B
ddunham@ucmerced.edu
DUNHAM, Dennis 405-974-2374 370 K
ddunham1@uco.edu
DUNHAM, Douglas, N .. 816-501-4617 258 H
douglas.dunham@rockhurst.edu
DUNHAM, Mark, E 660-263-3900 251 A
markdunham@cccb.edu
DUNHAM, Nikki 313-577-2116 232 I
gz1101@wayne.edu
DUNHAM, Rhonda, J 660-263-3900 251 A
rhondadunham@cccb.edu
DUNHAM, Robert 812-888-5555 162 C
rdunham@vinu.edu
DUNHAM, Stephen, S .. 814-867-4088 392 B
ssd13@psu.edu
DUNHAM, Thomas 773-907-4477 134 C
tdunham@ccc.edu
DUNHAM HOWIE,
Jules 937-376-2946 360 D
juleshouse@payne.edu
DUNHAM STRAND,
Amy 616-632-8900 221 C
stranamy@aquinas.edu
DUNIFUN, Rachel 607-255-2138 297 F
red26@cornell.edu
DUNIVAN, Daniel 812-749-1239 159 C
ddunivan@oak.edu

DURBIN, Bryce 706-236-2282 115 B bdurbin@berry.edu
DURBIN, Daniel 502-852-5555 185 C daniel.durbin.1@louisville.edu
DURBIN, Kelly 505-428-1814 288 B kelly.durbin@sfcc.edu
DURBIN, Rachel 503-494-7800 375 B finaid@ohsu.edu
DURDELLA, Caroline 562-908-3412 58 E cdurdella@riohondo.edu
DURDEN, Lori, S 912-871-1638 122 I ldurden@ogeecheetech.edu
DURDEN, Robert 434-924-0311 473 A
DURDEN, Tracey 734-432-5673 227 A tdurden@madonna.edu
DUREN, Brad 580-349-1498 368 A duren@opsu.edu
DUREN, Marion 608-249-6611 493 E careers@msn.herzing.edu
DURFEE, Carissa 617-989-4086 219 E durfeec@wit.edu
DURFEE, Jeffrey, A 904-620-2820 110 A jdurfee@unf.edu
DURGLO, Dan 406-275-4972 265 F dan_durglo@skc.edu
DURHAM, Bettye 901-321-3254 419 C bettye.durham@cbu.edu
DURHAM, Danielle 660-831-4172 256 G durhamd@moval.edu
DURHAM, David, L 304-293-8220 491 C david.durham@mail.wvu.edu
DURHAM, Dawn, W 864-833-8477 411 I dwdurham@presby.edu
DURHAM, Ed 410-287-1010 197 H edurham@cecil.edu
DURHAM, Gesele 703-993-5883 467 L gedurham@gmu.edu
DURHAM, John, R 610-519-7164 402 D john.durham@villanova.edu
DURHAM, Kathy, F 828-448-3102 339 A kdurham@wpcc.edu
DURHAM, Kimberly 954-262-8730 103 M durham@nova.edu
DURHAM, Leslie 208-426-1414 129 I ldurham@boisestate.edu
DURHAM, Lynn 404-894-8261 118 F lynn.durham@carnegie.gatech.edu
DURHAM, Monica 419-755-4896 357 E mdurham@ncstatecollege.edu
DURHAM, Rhonda 501-882-4442 17 F rsdurham@asub.edu
DURHAM, Tammara 785-864-4060 177 D tdurham@ku.edu
DURHAM, Teresa 269-965-3931 225 F durhamt@kellogg.edu
DURHAM, Terry 615-220-7885 425 C tdurham@mscc.edu
DURHAM, William, H 704-233-8811 344 G durham@wingate.edu
DURHAM DECESARO, Genevieve 806-742-3601 451 B genevieve.durham@ttu.edu
DURIAN-GAMBELL, Angella 641-673-1076 170 F gambella@wmpenn.edu
DURIAN-GAMBELL, Angella, M 641-673-1076 170 F gambella@wmpenn.edu
DURICK, Brian 949-480-4018 64 B bdurick@soka.edu
DURKEE, Gene 603-428-2358 273 H edurkee@nec.edu
DURKIN, Karen 856-415-2284 281 D kdurkin@rcgc.edu
DURKIN, Lisa 330-569-5109 353 J durkinls@hiram.edu
DURKIN, Mary 718-429-6600 324 D mary.durkin@vaughn.edu
DURKIN, Rebecca 847-578-8351 147 I rebecca.durkin@rosalindfranklin.edu
DURKLE, Robert, F 937-229-4411 362 G rdurkle1@udayton.edu
DURMOWICZ, Meredith 443-334-2414 201 H mdurmowicz@stevenson.edu
DURNIN, Ellen 203-392-5356 85 A durnine1@southernct.edu
DURNIN, Mike, J 563-589-3270 169 I mdurnin@dbq.edu
DUROCHER, Becky, L 985-448-4510 192 B becky.durocher@nicholls.edu
DUROCHER, Robert 315-229-5850 314 F bdur@stlawu.edu
DUROCHER, Sean 419-448-5136 361 J durochersm@tiffin.edu
DUROJAIYE, Ande 859-572-5379 184 A durojaiye1@nku.edu
DURON, Kety 626-256-4673 37 B kduron@coh.org
DUROSS, Frank 315-792-5526 307 D fduross@mvcc.edu
DUROUSSEAU, Erica 504-816-4696 186 D edurousseau@dillard.edu
DURR, David, W 270-809-6912 183 G ddurr@murraystate.edu
DURR, Elaine 336-278-5229 328 K edurr@elon.edu
DURR, Kimberly, H 618-650-2475 149 F kdurr@siue.edu
DURRETT, Duane 817-598-6222 458 A ddurrett@wc.edu
DURSO, Mary 215-568-9215 403 H mdurso@phmc.org
DURSO, Tom 215-489-6371 382 D thomas.durso@delval.edu
DURST, Devoiry 732-414-2834 285 D yeshivatoraschaim@gmail.com
DURST, Ellen 415-575-6153 29 B edurst@ciis.edu
DURST, Steve 231-591-2254 223 J stephendurst@ferris.edu
DUS-ZASTROW, Joanne 848-445-1928 282 A joanne.dz@rutgers.edu
DUSEK, Craig 620-417-1204 176 K craig.dusek@sccc.edu
DUSEK, Summer 850-201-6209 111 C washinsu@tcc.fl.edu
DUSENBURY, Renata 919-546-8252 340 E rdusenbury@shawu.edu
DUSING, Roger 816-584-6386 258 A roger.dusing@park.edu
DUSSEAU, Daniel 703-425-5369 475 C ddusseau@nvcc.edu
DUSSERT, Alain 805-969-3626 55 E adussert@pacifica.edu
DUSTIN, Kevin, M 801-957-4083 461 D kevin.dustin@slcc.edu
DUSTMAN, Teresa 904-596-2400 111 F tdustman@tbc.edu
DUTCH, Jennifer 402-363-5719 270 E jdutch@york.edu
DUTCHER, Debra 518-327-6082 311 G ddutcher@paulsmiths.edu
DUTCHER, Donald 315-866-0300 301 G dutcherdm@herkimer.edu
DUTIL, Stacey 718-429-6600 324 D stacey.dutil@vaughn.edu
DUTKIEWICZ, Mary 617-746-1990 210 E mary.dutkiewicz@hult.edu
DUTKO, Teresa 513-618-1928 350 J tdutko@ccms.edu
DUTLER, Sue 312-935-2210 147 D sdutler@robertmorris.edu
DUTMER, Brendan, C 815-599-3493 138 B brendan.dutmer@highland.edu
DUTREMBLE, Kathy 850-484-2076 104 H kdutremble@pensacolastate.edu
DUTRISAC, Gordon 425-352-8288 479 A gdutrisac@cascadia.edu
DUTSON, Tanya 716-926-8835 301 H tdutson@hilbert.edu
DUTTON, Ashley 860-231-5245 89 B adutton@usj.edu
DUTTON, Ashley 860-297-2048 88 C ashley.dutton@trincoll.edu
DUTTON, Colleen 972-883-2130 455 B colleen.dutton@utdallas.edu
DUTTON, Dennis 620-278-4364 177 B ddutton@sterling.edu
DUTTON, Katelyn 212-854-2021 290 J kdutton@barnard.edu
DUTTON, Lisa 651-690-8126 242 R lldutton@stkate.edu
DUTTON, Timothy 937-752-2189 355 F timothy.dutton@ketteringhealth.org
DUTTON COX, Deborah 603-862-1627 274 G debbie.dutton@unh.edu
DUVAL, Amanda 989-463-7255 220 H duvalal@alma.edu
DUVALL, Elizabeth 309-298-1971 152 D el-duvall@wiu.edu
DUVALL, Kathleen 509-793-2050 478 H kathleend@bigbend.edu
DUVALL, Steve 740-389-4636 356 B duvalls@mtc.edu
DUVALL, William 864-231-2144 406 G wduvall@andersonuniversity.edu
DUXBURY-EDWARDS, Chris 303-329-6355 78 K recruiting@cstcm.edu
DUZGOREN-AYDIN, Nurdan, S 201-200-3003 279 E naydin@njcu.edu
DVERGSDAL, Stacy, M 303-556-5740 80 N
DVORACSEK, Joe 727-341-6108 106 E dvoracsek.joe@spcollege.edu
DVORAK, Jerome 570-389-4995 394 A jdvorak@bloomufdn.org
DVORAK, Jessica 402-844-7045 268 J jessicad@northeast.edu
DVORAK, Leah, M 262-243-5700 493 B leah.dvorak@cuw.edu
DVORAK, Michele 574-936-8898 153 A michele.dvorak@ancilla.edu
DVORAK, Robert 909-687-1560 43 I robertdvorak@gs.edu
DVORAK, Sarah 574-284-4587 160 C sdvorak@saintmarys.edu
DVORAK, Susan 414-464-9777 499 A dvorak.susan@wspp.edu
DVORKIN, Ariel 212-431-7959 309 G ariel.dvorkin@nyls.edu
DWIGHT, Beverly, J 413-796-2210 219 F beverly.dwight@wne.edu
DWIRE, Steven, W 518-337-4915 296 H dwires@strose.edu
DWORKIN, Natasha 206-726-5169 480 C dworkin@cornish.edu
DWORKIS, Paul, S 301-405-2584 202 C pdworkis@umd.edu
DWYER, James, P 989-964-4209 230 B jdwyer@svsu.edu
DWYER, Jeff 517-355-2308 227 D dwyerje@msu.edu
DWYER, Johanna 360-596-5234 485 B jdwyer@spscc.edu
DWYER, John 510-204-0717 36 J jdwyer@cdsp.edu
DWYER, Katelyn 617-322-3535 210 F katelyn_dwyer@laboure.edu
DWYER, Ken 508-854-4579 215 D krd@qcc.mass.edu
DWYER, Susan, J 301-405-1102 202 C dwyer@umd.edu
DWYER, Thomas, P 804-752-7244 470 F tdwyer@rmc.edu
DYBA, Chris 252-328-9565 341 C dyba@ecu.edu
DYBA, Christopher 252-328-9565 341 C dybac@ecu.edu
DYBERG, Patrik 304-724-3700 487 E pdyberg@apus.edu
DYBWAD, Peter 510-841-9230 75 E pdybwad@wi.edu
DYCK-LAUMANN, Rebecca 901-678-2814 427 D rlaumann@memphis.edu
DYCZKO, Moira 574-520-4383 157 A mdyczko@iusb.edu
DYE, Christine 910-755-7304 332 F dyec@brunswickcc.edu
DYE, James 276-964-7278 475 I james.dye@sw.edu
DYE, John 330-337-6403 347 E college@awc.edu
DYE, Larry 580-628-6217 367 D larry.dye@noc.edu
DYE, Lisa 618-252-5400 149 C lisa.dye@sic.edu
DYE, Ronald 256-761-0949 7 B rdye@talladega.edu
DYE, Sheila 806-720-7233 439 H sheila.dye@lcu.edu
DYE, Steve, M 304-457-6324 487 B dyesm@ab.edu
DYER, Chris 408-741-2119 74 E chris.dyer@westvalley.edu
DYER, Cynthia, M 515-961-1519 169 D cyd.dyer@simpson.edu
DYER, Esther, L 865-971-5216 425 F eldyer@pstcc.edu
DYER, Jennifer 213-821-5002 72 B jennifer.dyer@stevens.usc.edu
DYER, John 214-887-5101 436 B jdyer@dts.edu
DYER, Karen 812-535-5101 160 B kdyer@smwc.edu
DYER, Kent 484-664-3140 391 C kentdyer@muhlenberg.edu
DYER, Kristyn, M 508-793-2418 208 B kdyer@holycross.edu
DYER, Nazly 713-226-5594 453 B dyern@uhd.edu
DYER, Nicolas 518-828-4181 297 B nicolas.dyer@sunycgcc.edu
DYER, Robin 704-669-4128 333 E dyer@clevelandcc.edu
DYER, Tricia 207-621-3390 196 A triciad@maine.edu
DYER, Una 340-693-1002 514 E udyer@uvi.edu
DYER, Wayne, R 973-803-5000 280 C wdyer@pillar.edu
DYERLY, Kevin, M 909-748-8026 71 G kevin_dyerly@redlands.edu
DYESS, Hubert 601-426-6346 249 A hdyess@southeasternbaptist.edu
DYKEMA, Ann, C 616-432-3404 229 I ann.dykema@prts.edu
DYKES, Alllison, K 404-727-9895 117 F allison.dykes@emory.edu
DYKES, Donald, E 860-444-8213 504 F donald.e.dykes@uscga.edu
DYKES, Stephanie 206-934-3656 483 J stephanie.dykes@seattlecolleges.edu
DYKES, Wes 601-318-6053 249 H wdykes@wmcarey.edu
DYKES-ANDERSON, Michele 606-589-3049 182 E michelle.dykes-anderson@kctcs.edu
DYKI, Judy 248-645-3300 223 A
DYKMANN, Melony 816-322-0110 250 K melony.dykmann@calvary.edu
DYKSHOORN, Sharon 712-274-6400 170 E sharon.dykshoorn@witcc.edu
DYKSTRA, Frank 520-515-5311 11 M poncho@cochise.edu
DYKSTRA, Gail 972-708-7547 435 H gail_dykstra@diu.edu
DYKSTRA, Joel 575-624-8203 287 A dykstra@nmmi.edu
DYKSTRA, Kurt, D 708-239-4791 150 F kurt.dykstra@trnty.edu
DYKSTRA, Philip 714-484-7311 53 K pdykstra@cypresscollege.edu
DYLAK, Sandy 914-251-6953 319 E sandy.dylak@purchase.edu
DYMOWSKI, Tom 210-829-3131 453 D dymowski@uiwtx.edu
DYMSKI, M, L 617-349-8208 210 H mld@lesley.edu
DYNAN, Sheila 201-360-4230 278 C sdynan@hccc.edu
DYNAN-DOBBERTIEN, Lisa 904-620-2900 110 A n00914995@unf.edu
DYRUD, Lars 218-683-8616 240 A lars.dyrud@northlandcollege.edu
DYSARD, Nancy, J 443-412-2408 199 A ndysard@harford.edu
DYSART, Charles 334-876-9248 2 D charles.dysart@wccs.edu
DYSON, Carolyn 941-359-4200 110 D cdyson@sar.usf.edu
DYSON, Greg 765-998-5284 160 F greg_dyson@taylor.edu
DYSON, Melissa, J 217-245-3080 138 D mdyson@ic.edu
DYTON-WHITE, Rayna 860-231-5487 89 B rdytonwhite@usj.edu
DZAPO, Kyle 309-677-2596 133 B kdzapo@bradley.edu
DZIDZIENYO, Vishnu 202-722-8100 92 G
DZIEDZIAK, Michael 610-341-1376 383 D mdziedzi@eastern.edu
DZIEKAN, Rebecca 585-343-0055 301 A rldziekan@genesee.edu
DZIELSKI, Mark 716-851-1073 299 F dzielski@ecc.edu
DZIESINSKI, Lori 989-356-9021 221 A dziesinl@alpenacc.edu
DZIEWATKOSKI, Julius, J 740-264-5591 352 H jdziewatkoski@egcc.edu
DZINANKA, John, S 631-420-2017 321 B john.dzinanka@farmingdale.edu
DZIURA, William 413-265-2213 208 C dziuraw@elms.edu
DZWONKOWSKI, David, R 315-470-6626 320 A drdzwonk@esf.edu
DÍAZ, Ángel 787-764-0000 514 B angel.diaz10@upr.edu
DÍAZ-PÉREZ, Carlos, R 787-474-0402 512 G carlos.diaz14@upr.edu

EBBERTS, Judy ..... 814-262-6442 393 H
jebberts@pennhighlands.edu

EBBESMEYER, Karen ..... 660-248-6246 251 B
kebbesme@centralmethodist.edu

EBBING, Jeff ..... 319-208-5060 169 F
jebbing@scciowa.edu

EBBS, George, H ..... 757-594-7184 466 B
george.ebbs@cnu.edu

EBEL, Malia ..... 603-526-3375 272 H
malia.ebel@colby-sawyer.edu

EBENHACK, Kori ..... 541-956-7196 376 D
kebenhack@roguecc.edu

EBERHARDT, David ..... 205-226-4731 5 A
deberhar@bsc.edu

EBERHARDT, Russell ..... 605-698-3966 416 F
reberhardt@swc.tc

EBERHART, Becky, J ..... 847-866-3938 137 E
becky.eberhart@garrett.edu

EBERHART, John ..... 269-782-1207 230 F
jeberhart@swmich.edu

EBERLE, Jeanette ..... 863-638-2978 113 B
eberleja@webber.edu

EBERLE, John ..... 615-248-1234 427 A
jeberle@trevecca.edu

EBERLE, Josh ..... 814-871-5592 384 E
eberle003@gannon.edu

EBERLE, Matt ..... 480-245-7969 12 N
matt.eberle@tricityministries.org

EBERLE, Sarah, D ..... 701-355-8126 347 D
sdeberle@umary.edu

EBERLY, Jamie ..... 402-872-2436 268 F
jeberly@peru.edu

EBERSOLE, Susan ..... 718-960-8000 294 A
susan.ebersole@lehman.cuny.edu

EBERT, Chris ..... 559-791-2370 47 A
chris.ebert@portervillecollege.edu

EBERT, Derry ..... 863-638-3818 113 A
derry.ebert@warner.edu

EBERT, Kathleen ..... 607-587-4122 320 C
ebertkb@alfredstate.edu

EBERT, Loretta ..... 518-783-2550 315 J
lebert@siena.edu

EBERT, Stacy ..... 281-756-5601 429 I
sebert@alvincollege.edu

EBERT, Tina, L ..... 417-268-6006 250 G
tebert@gobbc.edu

EBERT-HOLBERG, Olga . 865-539-7283 425 F
odeberthiberg@pstcc.edu

EBERTS, Keirsten ..... 260-665-4675 160 H
ebertsk@trine.edu

EBERTZ, Susan J, S ..... 563-589-0265 170 D
library@wartburgseminary.edu

EBLEN-ZAYAS, Melissa . 507-222-4191 234 F
meblenza@carleton.edu

EBNER, Timothy, J ..... 801-581-5808 460 E
tebner@sa.utah.edu

EBONG, Imeh ..... 661-654-2231 30 E
iebong@csub.edu

EBORALL, Martha ..... 304-327-4152 489 P
meborall@bluefieldstate.edu

EBRAHIMPOUR, Maling 401-874-4244 406 B
mebrahimpour@uri.edu

EBSTEIN, Gemma, F ..... 860-685-2535 89 C
gebstein@wesleyan.edu

EBY, Larry ..... 302-225-6289 90 E
ebylw@gbc.edu

EBY, Tim, J ..... 314-516-6765 261 D
ebyt@umsl.edu

ECABERT, Gayle ..... 859-371-9393 179 A
gecabert@beckfield.edu

ECCLES, Jennifer ..... 507-453-1428 239 A
jennifer.eccles@southeastmn.edu

ECCLES, Tom ..... 845-758-7598 290 G
ccs@bard.edu

ECHAMBADI, Raj ..... 617-373-3232 217 F

ECHEVARRI, Richard ..... 215-780-1410 398 G
rech@salus.edu

ECHOLS, Darren ..... 423-614-8519 420 J
dechols@leeuniversity.edu

ECHOLS, Marti ..... 305-760-7500 102 U

ECHOLS, Steven, F ..... 912-583-2241 115 E
sechols@bpc.edu

ECHOLS TOBE, Dorothy 201-684-7008 280 H
dechols@ramapo.edu

ECK, Jim ..... 770-531-3129 115 D
jeck@brenau.edu

ECK, Kristi ..... 315-312-2212 319 B
kristi.eck@oswego.edu

ECK, Stephen ..... 405-425-5106 367 G
stephen.eck@oc.edu

ECK, Stephen, M ..... 973-596-3306 279 F
steven.eck@njit.edu

ECK, Tammy ..... 405-744-4188 368 B
tammy.eck@okstate.edu

ECK, Tim ..... 801-626-6352 461 B
teck@weber.edu

ECKARDT, Chip, P ..... 715-836-2381 496 D
eckardpp@uwec.edu

ECKARDT, Jill ..... 940-898-3676 451 F
jeckardt@twu.edu

ECKART, Natasha ..... 814-332-2701 378 D
neckart@allegheny.edu

ECKEL, Todd ..... 909-593-3511 70 D
teckel@laverne.edu

ECKENRODE, Jeanine ..... 315-498-2237 311 B
j.a.eckenrode@sunyocc.edu

ECKER, Brian ..... 717-262-2017 403 F
brian.ecker@wilson.edu

ECKERT, Amber ..... 858-635-4535 24 L
aeckert@alliant.edu

ECKERT, Amber ..... 415-955-2100 24 K
amber.eckert@alliant.edu

ECKERT, Barry ..... 215-780-1420 398 G
beckert@salus.edu

ECKERT, Jason, C ..... 937-229-2045 362 G
jeckert1@udayton.edu

ECKERT, Les ..... 231-995-1197 228 G
leckert@nmc.edu

ECKERT, Lisa ..... 906-227-1828 228 F
leckert@nmu.edu

ECKERT, Robin ..... 610-372-4721 397 B
reckert@racc.edu

ECKERT, Steve ..... 928-314-9475 10 J
steve.eckert@azwestern.edu

ECKERT, Wendy ..... 423-439-6052 419 J
research@etsu.edu

ECKHARDT, Libby ..... 504-865-5000 191 B

ECKLES, Blaine ..... 208-885-6757 131 G
beckles@uidaho.edu

ECKLEY, Catherine ..... 304-357-4925 488 G
catherineeckley@ucwv.edu

ECKLUND, Joe ..... 402-280-5531 266 I
josephecklund@creighton.edu

ECKLUND, Todd ..... 719-549-3175 81 K
todd.ecklund@pueblocc.edu

ECKMAN, Angela ..... 715-738-3852 499 D
aeckman@cvtc.edu

ECKMAN, Charles ..... 305-284-1959 112 E
ceckman@miami.edu

ECKMAN, Mark ..... 414-229-4846 497 A
eckmanm@uwm.edu

ECKMAN, Steven, W ..... 402-363-5621 270 E
seckman@york.edu

ECKRICH, Steve, E ..... 541-737-4323 375 D
stevee@osubookstore.com

ECKSTEIN, Mark ..... 716-829-8349 298 F
eckstein@dyc.edu

ECKSTEIN, Melanie ..... 704-461-6877 327 A
melanieeckstein@bac.edu

ECKSTEIN, Rebecca ..... 914-633-2702 302 G
reckstein@iona.edu

ECKSTROM, Jessica ..... 508-849-3271 205 C
jeckstrom@annamaria.edu

ECTOR, Goldie ..... 303-765-3114 80 F
gector@iliff.edu

EDAMALA, Charles ..... 309-438-3618 139 E
cmedama@ilstu.edu

EDBURG, Lisa ..... 573-518-2294 256 B
lisae@mineralarea.edu

EDDINGER, Pam, Y ..... 617-228-2400 214 A
peddinger@bhcc.mass.edu

EDDINGS, Kevin ..... 405-682-1611 367 H
kevin.eddings@occc.edu

EDDINGS, Melissa ..... 971-343-2702 374 B
melissa.eddings@mtangel.edu

EDDINGTON, Natalie, D 410-706-2176 202 D
neddingt@rx.umaryland.edu

EDDLEMAN, Donna ..... 909-748-8917 71 G
donna_eddleman@redlands.edu

EDDS-ELLIS, Stacy ..... 270-686-4573 182 B
stacy.edds@kctcs.edu

EDDY, Brant ..... 360-867-6358 481 A
eddyb@evergreen.edu

EDDY, Corbin ..... 906-487-7239 223 K
corbin.eddy@finlandia.edu

EDDY, Doug ..... 301-369-2454 197 F
dbeddy@captechu.edu

EDDY, Eired ..... 727-614-7292 106 E
eddy.eired@spcollege.edu

EDDY, James, M ..... 336-315-7044 343 A
jmeddy@uncg.edu

EDDY, Rick ..... 309-341-5234 133 C
reddy@sandburg.edu

EDDY, Shayna ..... 508-626-4506 212 D
seddy@framingham.edu

EDEL, Logan ..... 515-961-1579 169 D
logan.edel@simpson.edu

EDELMAN, Adam ..... 406-994-5091 264 D
aedelman@montana.edu

EDELMAN, Daniel ..... 406-657-2300 264 E
dedelman@msubillings.edu

EDELMAN, Debbie ..... 618-468-2010 141 F
dedelman@lc.edu

EDELMAN, Vladimir ..... 989-328-1206 228 A
vladimir.edelman@montcalm.edu

EDELMAN-BLANK,
Deborah ..... 978-934-6800 211 G
deborah_edelmanblank@uml.edu

EDELSON, Jeffrey ..... 510-642-5039 68 D
swdean@berkeley.edu

EDELSON, Maurice, F ... 212-799-5000 303 H

EDELSTEIN, Ronald, A .. 323-563-4980 36 D
ronaldedelstein@cdrewu.edu

EDEN, Gene, F ..... 610-799-1146 388 I
geden@lccc.edu

EDEN, James, R ..... 920-924-3317 500 C
jeden@morainepark.edu

EDEN, Peter, A ..... 802-387-6730 462 D
petereden@landmark.edu

EDEN, SM, Tim ..... 210-436-3786 443 A
teden@stmarytx.edu

EDENS, Ashley ..... 423-636-7376 427 B
aedens@tusculum.edu

EDENS, Barb ..... 423-236-2587 424 B
barbedens@southern.edu

EDENS, Byron ..... 423-308-9652 339 F
edensb@piedmontu.edu

EDENS, Gary ..... 915-747-7471 455 C
gedens@utep.edu

EDENS, Mike ..... 903-693-2021 441 F
medens@panola.edu

EDGAR, Kimberly, S ..... 615-898-5825 422 H
kimberly.edgar@mtsu.edu

EDGAR, Richard, J ..... 240-895-3206 201 E
rjedgar@smcm.edu

EDGAR-SMITH, Susan ... 610-341-5865 383 D
sedgarsm@eastern.edu

EDGE, LaJill ..... 920-565-1000 493 J
edgely@lakeland.edu

EDGENS, Jeff ..... 307-268-2713 502 H
jedgens@uwyo.edu

EDGEWORTH, Lori ..... 419-251-1614 356 C
lori.edgeworth@mercycollege.edu

EDGHILL-WALDEN,
Vernese ..... 815-753-2638 145 C
vedghillwalden@niu.edu

EDGINGTON, Kyle ..... 972-883-6527 455 B
kyle.edgington@utdallas.edu

EDGINGTON, Rick ..... 580-628-6220 367 D
rick.edgington@noc.edu

EDGINGTON, Steve ..... 714-879-3901 45 F
sedgington@hiu.edu

EDGINGTON,
Thomas, J ..... 574-372-5100 155 B
edgingtj@grace.edu

EDGMON, Angie ..... 615-675-5278 428 G
finaid@welch.edu

EDGREN, JR., Gerald .... 618-842-3711 138 G
edgreng@iecc.edu

EDIB, Melek ..... 202-644-7210 91 A

EDICK, Nancy ..... 402-554-2719 270 B
nedick@unomaha.edu

EDIE, Shawn ..... 315-498-2762 311 B
s.l.edie@sunyocc.edu

EDINGTON, Julie ..... 870-248-4000 18 F
julie.edington@blackrivertech.edu

EDINGTON, Maurice ..... 850-599-3276 108 I
maurice.edington@famu.edu

EDINGTON, Pamela, R .. 845-431-8980 298 E
pamela.edington@sunydutchess.edu

EDIRISINGHE, Chanaka 518-276-6590 312 I
edirin@rpi.edu

EDIZEL, Gerar ..... 607-871-2412 289 H
fedizel@alfred.edu

EDKINS, Charles ..... 570-674-6294 390 G
cedkins@misericordia.edu

EDLUND, Erin ..... 651-423-8233 237 H
erin.edlund@dctc.edu

EDLUND, Erin, M ..... 712-274-5411 168 B
edlunde@morningside.edu

EDLUND, Matt ..... 828-771-2000 344 E
medlund@warren-wilson.edu

EDMAN, Patricia ..... 612-381-3308 235 H
pedman@dunwoody.edu

EDMAN, Sally ..... 712-707-7321 168 H
sedman@nwciowa.edu

EDMINSTER, David ..... 303-546-3514 81 B
davee@naropa.edu

EDMISTON, Carie ..... 360-417-6205 483 B
cedmiston@pencol.edu

EDMOND, Cara ..... 512-454-7001 430 G
cedmond@aoma.edu

EDMOND, Steven ..... 512-505-6472 438 E
ssedmond@htu.edu

EDMOND, Yolanda ..... 713-313-7011 449 C
yolanda.edmond@tsu.edu

EDMONDS, Charles, W . 570-321-4347 389 E
edmonds@lycoming.edu

EDMONDS, Heather ..... 617-587-5579 217 A
edmondsh@neco.edu

EDMONDS, Jane ..... 781-239-4998 205 E
jedmonds@babson.edu

EDMONDS, Jennifer ..... 732-987-2662 278 B
jedmonds@georgian.edu

EDMONDS, III, Jerry ..... 252-536-7376 335 B
jedmonds@halifaxcc.edu

EDMONDS, John ..... 812-221-1714 162 B
johnedmonds@vbc.edu

EDMONDS, Joshua ..... 931-372-3556 426 E
jedmonds@tntech.edu

EDMONDS, Kerry ..... 540-362-6630 468 C
kedmonds@hollins.edu

EDMONDS, Lawson ..... 205-652-3545 9 A
ledmonds@uwa.edu

EDMONDS, Lawson, C . 205-652-3545 9 A
ledmonds@uwa.edu

EDMONDS, Lorna Jean . 740-593-1889 359 G
edmonds@ohio.edu

EDMONDS, Mabel ..... 253-589-5510 479 G
mabel.edmonds@cptc.edu

EDMONDS, Michelle, K 434-949-1006 475 H
michelle.edmonds@southside.edu

EDMONDS, Mike ..... 719-389-6684 77 H
medmonds@coloradocollege.edu

EDMONDS, Silvia, R ..... 518-276-2564 312 I
edmons@rpi.edu

EDMONDS, William ..... 814-732-2761 394 F
eup_admissions@edinboro.edu

EDMONDSON, Jackie .... 256-549-8224 2 B
jedmondson@gadsdenstate.edu

EDMONDSON,
Melanie, M ..... 443-334-2272 201 H
medmondson@stevenson.edu

EDMONDSON, Michael . 201-200-2085 279 E
medmondson@njcu.edu

EDMONDSON, William . 814-871-7298 384 E
edmondso002@gannon.edu

EDMONSON, Stacey ..... 936-294-1101 450 C
edu_sle01@shsu.edu

EDMUND, Devon ..... 866-492-5336 244 F
devon.edmund@mail.waldenu.edu

EDMUNDS, Heidi ..... 307-532-8261 502 A
heidi.edmunds@ewc.wy.edu

EDMUNDSON, John ..... 928-314-9500 10 J
john.edmundson@azwestern.edu

EDONICK, Jessica ..... 717-396-7833 393 E
jedonick@pcad.edu

EDOUARD, Randall ..... 607-777-4787 316 E
redouard@binghamton.edu

EDRICH, Terri ..... 972-860-4825 434 L
tedrich@dcccd.edu

EDSALL, Denese ..... 954-201-7502 95 H
dedsall@broward.edu

EDSON, Brenda ..... 434-947-4287 470 E
bedson@randolphcollege.edu

EDUARDO, Marcelo ..... 601-925-3214 247 C
eduardo@mc.edu

EDWARD, David ..... 973-353-2506 282 B
dedward@oit.rutgers.edu

EDWARD, Marcus ..... 781-239-2523 214 E
medward@massbay.edu

EDWARDS, Amanda ..... 828-398-7176 332 B
amandaedwards@abtech.edu

EDWARDS, Amy ..... 217-333-3551 151 D
aledward@illinois.edu

EDWARDS, Ana ..... 470-578-6025 120 L
aedwar50@kennesaw.edu

EDWARDS, Ariel ..... 215-248-7020 381 D
edwardsa@chc.edu

EDWARDS, Bahola ..... 432-685-4520 440 E
bahola@midland.edu

EDWARDS, Betty ..... 334-420-4321 3 H
bedwards@trenholmstate.edu

EDWARDS, Brad ..... 479-524-7212 19 H
bedwards@jbu.edu

EDWARDS, Brad ..... 703-993-3212 467 L
bedwards@gmu.edu

EDWARDS, Bretta ..... 320-308-1595 241 A
bedwards@sctcc.edu

EDWARDS, Brian ..... 504-865-5000 191 B

EDWARDS, Brian 252-335-0821 333 G
brian_edwards@albemarle.edu
EDWARDS, Brian, J 412-397-5295 397 G
edwardsb@rmu.edu
EDWARDS, Byron 615-514-2787 423 E
dredwards@nossi.edu
EDWARDS, Candace 410-386-8505 197 G
cedwards@carrollcc.edu
EDWARDS, Carmen 432-685-4589 440 E
cedwards@midland.edu
EDWARDS, Cathy 214-860-8715 435 D
cedwards@dcccd.edu
EDWARDS, Chris 601-481-1316 247 A
cedwards@meridiancc.edu
EDWARDS, Cody 703-993-4564 467 L
cedward7@gmu.edu
EDWARDS, Connie 724-738-2226 395 F
constance.edwards@sru.edu
EDWARDS, Dan 417-865-2815 253 B
edwardsd@evangel.edu
EDWARDS, Dave 657-278-7740 31 E
daveedwards@fullerton.edu
EDWARDS, David 856-227-7200 276 E
dredwards@camdencc.edu
EDWARDS, David 330-941-3394 365 C
dwedwards@ysu.edu
EDWARDS, Delyssa 740-245-7431 363 D
dedwards@rio.edu
EDWARDS, Donald 828-689-1246 331 A
dedwards@mhu.edu
EDWARDS, Doreen 585-475-2146 313 A
ddeen@rit.edu
EDWARDS, Earl, W 858-534-8750 69 D
ewedwards@ucsd.edu
EDWARDS, Edra 832-230-5188 440 H
registrar@na.edu
EDWARDS, Elizabeth 662-862-8265 246 D
etedwards@iccms.edu
EDWARDS, Emory 201-761-6108 282 I
eedwards@saintpeters.edu
EDWARDS, Eugene 503-375-7010 373 A
eedwards@corban.edu
EDWARDS, Francine 302-857-6628 89 F
fedwards@desu.edu
EDWARDS, Frank 404-880-8672 116 D
fedwards@cau.edu
EDWARDS, Gail 404-225-4126 114 H
gedwards@atlantatech.edu
EDWARDS, Gay 252-940-6264 332 C
gay.edwards@beaufortcc.edu
EDWARDS, Geoffrey, M 812-488-1102 161 A
ge21@evansville.edu
EDWARDS, Hazel 202-806-6100 92 B
EDWARDS, Hollly 325-670-1026 437 F
holly.edwards@hsutx.edu
EDWARDS, Ian, C 412-396-6204 383 C
edwards181@duq.edu
EDWARDS, Ishmell, H 662-252-8000 248 G
iedwards@rustcollege.edu
EDWARDS, Jakki 952-885-5465 242 I
jedwards@nwhealth.edu
EDWARDS, James 757-822-5201 476 B
jeedwards@tcc.edu
EDWARDS, Jan 719-884-5000 81 C
jmedwards@nbc.edu
EDWARDS, Jan 719-227-8294 77 H
jan.edwards@coloradocollege.edu
EDWARDS, Jane 203-432-8680 89 D
jane.edwards@yale.edu
EDWARDS, Jeff 513-745-2987 365 B
edwardsj11@xavier.edu
EDWARDS, John 212-343-1234 306 J
jedwards@mcny.edu
EDWARDS, John 214-333-5525 434 I
johne@dbu.edu
EDWARDS, John, P 610-519-3507 402 D
john.p.edwards@villanova.edu
EDWARDS, Jon 781-239-2732 214 E
jedwards@massbay.edu
EDWARDS, Jonathan, P 843-661-1181 409 K
jedwards@fmarion.edu
EDWARDS, Judson 334-670-3989 7 C
jcedwards@troy.edu
EDWARDS, Karen 251-460-7092 8 F
cedwards@southalabama.edu
EDWARDS, Karen 281-756-3639 429 I
kedwards@alvincollege.edu
EDWARDS, Karen, K 641-269-3703 165 J
edwardsk@grinnell.edu
EDWARDS, Karin 971-722-5302 375 J
karin.edwards@pcc.edu
EDWARDS, Katherine 415-422-5209 71 K
kedwards3@usfca.edu
EDWARDS, Kendra 816-604-5249 255 D
kendra.edwards@mcckc.edu
EDWARDS, Keston 708-344-4700 142 A
kedwards@lincolntech.edu
EDWARDS, Lauralea 801-957-4888 461 D
lauralea.edwards@slcc.edu
EDWARDS, Lola 229-430-1702 113 I
ledwards@albanytech.edu
EDWARDS, Mark, H 315-655-7334 292 F
medwards@cazenovia.edu
EDWARDS, Mary, A 304-336-8000 490 F
edwardsm@westliberty.edu
EDWARDS, Mary Ann 304-336-8000 490 F
edwardsm@westliberty.edu
EDWARDS, Michael 641-673-2120 170 F
edwardsml@wmpenn.edu
EDWARDS, Mike 615-675-5333 428 G
mike.edwards@welch.edu
EDWARDS, Natasha 718-489-2035 313 H
nedwards2@sfc.edu
EDWARDS, Nigel 850-599-3183 108 I
nigel.edwards@famu.edu
EDWARDS, Paul 978-867-4900 209 F
paul.edwards@gordon.edu
EDWARDS, Paul 804-861-6100 470 I
pedwards@rbc.edu
EDWARDS, JR.,
Quinton, T 662-915-3785 249 D
qtedward@olemiss.edu
EDWARDS, Randy 828-262-2090 341 B
edwardsk@appstate.edu
EDWARDS, Richard 518-629-7356 302 E
r.edwards@hvcc.edu
EDWARDS, Rosie 334-514-5063 2 F
rosie.edwards@istc.edu
EDWARDS, Sarah 270-706-8447 181 A
sarah.edwards@kctcs.edu
EDWARDS, Shawn 843-953-6989 407 F
shawn.edwards@citadel.edu
EDWARDS, Sheryl 870-235-5090 21 D
saedwards@saumag.edu
EDWARDS, Stephen 719-884-5000 81 C
sfedwards@nbc.edu
EDWARDS, Steve 912-583-3218 115 E
sedwards@bpc.edu
EDWARDS, Susan 937-775-3035 364 I
susan.edwards@wright.edu
EDWARDS, Tania 816-322-0110 250 K
tania.edwards@calvary.edu
EDWARDS, Tawni 918-610-0027 366 A
tedwards@communitycarecollege.edu
EDWARDS, Terry 334-386-7940 5 D
tedwards@faulkner.edu
EDWARDS, Thomas 207-859-1362 195 G
edwardst@thomas.edu
EDWARDS, Tim 205-652-3457 9 A
tedwards@uwa.edu
EDWARDS, Timothy 907-786-1381 9 G
tmedwards202@alaska.edu
EDWARDS, Timothy 208-882-1566 131 B
timedwards@nsa.edu
EDWARDS, Tina, L 260-982-5001 158 T
tledwards@manchester.edu
EDWARDS, Tony 740-392-6868 357 B
tony.edwards@mvnu.edu
EDWARDS, Tracy 405-945-3376 368 E
tracyle@osuokc.edu
EDWARDS, Ulrica, S 318-274-7297 191 E
edwardsu@gram.edu
EDWARDS, Wanda 910-296-1812 335 E
wedwards@jamessprunt.edu
EDWARDS, Wayne 516-876-3207 319 A
edwardsw@oldwestbury.edu
EDWARDS LANGE,
Sheila 206-934-4454 484 A
sheila.edwardslange@seattlecolleges.edu
EDWARDS LANGE,
Sheila 206-934-4144 483 I
sheila.edwardslange@seattlecolleges.edu
EDYTHE, Abdullah, E 904-620-5408 110 A
e.abdullah@unf.edu
EE, Marvin 254-295-8620 453 E
mee@umhb.edu
EELLS, Gregory 215-898-7021 400 K
geells@upenn.edu
EELLS, Rachel 708-209-3255 135 F
rachel.eells@cuchicago.edu
EFFLANDT, Scott 913-684-3443 504 D
EFFORD, Lelia 305-626-3180 99 D
lefford@fmuniv.edu
EFTHIMIOU, Chris 718-289-5169 293 B
chris.efthimiou@bcc.cuny.edu
EFTHYMIOU,
Lampeto (Betty) 718-631-6611 295 D
lefthymiou@qcc.cuny.edu
EFURD, Melissa 479-308-2284 17 C
melissa.efurd@arcomedu.org
EGAN, Beth-Anne 860-253-3030 85 C
began@asnuntuck.edu
EGAN, Brian 973-684-5999 280 B
began@pccc.edu
EGAN, Carolyn 850-644-4440 109 C
cegan@fsu.edu
EGAN, Eric 760-921-5520 55 H
eegan@paloverde.edu
EGAN, Jonathon 562-947-8755 65 C
jonathonegan@scuhs.edu
EGAN, Kristen 847-628-2017 140 C
kristen.egan@judsonu.edu
EGAN, Margaret 646-664-3254 292 K
margaret.egan@cuny.edu
EGAN, Maryan 239-590-1234 108 K
megan@fgcu.edu
EGAN, Michael 309-794-8965 132 C
mikeegan@augustana.edu
EGAN, Michelle 574-284-4601 160 C
mlegan@saintmarys.edu
EGAN, Russi 530-541-4660 47 E
egan@ltcc.edu
EGAN, Thomas 215-572-2900 379 A
egant@arcadia.edu
EGBE, Daniel 501-370-5268 20 G
degbe@philander.edu
EGBE, Emmanuel 718-270-5170 295 A
egbe@mec.cuny.edu
EGBERT, Edwin, C 605-342-0317 415 E
eegbert@jwc.edu
EGBERT, Jeb 949-783-4800 73 K
jegbert@westcoastuniversity.edu
EGBERT, Jessica, D 801-375-5125 459 L
jessica.egbert@rm.edu
EGELER, William, G 207-768-2792 194 J
wegeler@nmcc.edu
EGENESS, Cynthia 651-690-6864 242 R
cnegeness@stkate.edu
EGERSON, Veronica, V 414-464-9777 499 A
egerson.veronica@wspp.edu
EGGEBRECHT, Erin 815-967-7302 147 F
eeggebrecht@rockfordcareercollege.edu
EGGENSPERGER,
Martin 870-248-4000 18 F
martin.eggensperger@blackrivertech.edu
EGGERS, Daniel, W 512-245-1555 450 E
dwe16@txstate.edu
EGGERS, Jeremy 425-564-2193 478 F
jeremy.eggers@bellevuecollege.edu
EGGERS, John, M 320-308-0121 240 H
jmeggers@stcloudstate.edu
EGGERS, Marilyn 909-558-7658 48 C
meggers@llu.edu
EGGERS, Ron 252-399-6417 326 M
reggers@barton.edu
EGGERS, Troy 212-854-5939 297 C
te99@columbia.edu
EGGERSTEDT, Jane 318-675-6124 189 C
jegger@lsuhsc.edu
EGGIMANN, Becky 630-752-5646 152 F
becky.eggimann@wheaton.edu
EGGLESTON, Chad 254-299-8672 440 A
ceggleston@mclennan.edu
EGGLESTON, Joseph 562-947-8755 65 C
josepheggleston@scuhs.edu
EGGLESTON,
Kathryn, K 972-238-6364 435 F
keggleston@dcccd.edu
EGGLESTON, Meghan 276-656-0285 475 D
meggleston@patrickhenry.edu
EGGLESTON, Tami 618-537-6926 143 B
teggleston@mckendree.edu
EGGLESTON WILLIAMS,
Latrice, E 773-995-2548 133 K
legglest@csu.edu
EGIEBOR, Nosa 315-470-6510 320 A
noegiebo@esf.edu
EGLE, Don 903-233-3290 439 E
donegle@letu.edu
EGLI, Ryan 215-368-5000 390 F
regli@missio.edu
EGLSAER, Richard 936-294-1001 450 C
eglsaer@shsu.edu
EGUARAS, Agnes 818-240-1000 44 B
aeguaras@glendale.edu
EHASZ, Maribeth 407-823-4372 109 E
maribeth.ehasz@ucf.edu
EHLER, Gina, M 262-524-7247 492 E
gehler@carrollu.edu
EHLERS, Chris 918-781-7233 365 F
ehlersc@bacone.edu
EHLERS, Kathleen 617-670-4501 209 D
kehlers@fisher.edu
EHLERS, Nancy, M 716-652-8900 292 I
nehlers@cks.edu
EHLERS, Pam 405-744-2122 368 B
pam.ehlers@okstate.edu
EHLERT, Alycia 386-506-3769 97 D
alycia.ehlert@daytonastate.edu
EHLERT, Kim 262-691-5594 500 H
kehlert@wctc.edu
EHLING, Andrew 620-242-0582 175 F
ehlinga@mcpherson.edu
EHLING, William 252-328-6387 341 C
ehlingw16@ecu.edu
EHLINGER-SAJ,
Jennifer 716-827-2412 323 D
ehlinger-sajj@trocaire.edu
EHMAN, Amanda 740-245-7443 363 D
amandae@rio.edu
EHMANN, William 607-431-4405 301 D
ehmannw@hartwick.edu
EHMEN, Stacy, L 217-443-8746 135 H
stacy@dacc.edu
EHMIG, Ashley 503-244-0726 371 G
EHNOT, Jillian 406-791-5307 265 H
jillian.ehnot@uprovidence.edu
EHRESMAN, Terry 620-278-4264 177 B
tehresman@sterling.edu
EHRHARDT, Emily 319-399-8663 164 A
eehrhardt@coe.edu
EHRLICH, Anne, R 309-341-7221 141 A
arehrlich@knox.edu
EHRLICH, Brian 321-674-8832 99 B
behrlich@fit.edu
EHRLICH, Robert 660-626-2297 250 A
rehrlich@atsu.edu
EHRLICH, Sam 830-372-8155 449 B
sehrlich@tlu.edu
EHRMAN, James, E 717-866-5775 383 H
james.ehrman@evangelical.edu
EHRMAN, Sheryl 408-924-3800 34 B
sheryl.ehrman@sjsu.edu
EHRMANTRAUT,
Dominic 901-321-3286 419 C
dehrmant@cbu.edu
EHST, Suzanne 574-535-7839 155 A
sehst@goshen.edu
EIB, Rod 765-998-5157 160 F
rdeib@taylor.edu
EICHELBERGER, Lisa 678-466-4900 116 E
lisaeichelberger@clayton.edu
EICHELBERGER, Travis 301-696-3563 199 B
eichelberger@hood.edu
EICHELROTH, Kathleen 508-929-8098 213 E
keichelroth@worcester.edu
EICHENBERGER, Julie 620-223-2700 173 C
juliee@fortscott.edu
EICHENSTEIN, Joseph 732-985-6533 280 F
EICHER, Michael 614-292-9858 358 I
eicher@osu.edu
EICHER, Paul 918-343-7707 369 F
peicher@rsu.edu
EICHFIELD, Tara 912-287-5809 116 F
teichfield@coastalpines.edu
EICHHORN, Kristen, C 315-312-3152 319 B
kristen.eichhorn@oswego.edu
EICHHORST, Amy 301-405-2102 202 C
aeich@umd.edu
EICHHORST, Carly 507-786-3357 243 C
eichho1@stolaf.edu
EICHLER, Richard 212-854-2878 297 C
re1@columbia.edu
EICHNER, John 716-614-5931 310 C
jeichner@niagaracc.suny.edu
EICHNER, Kevin 785-242-5200 176 D
kevin.eichner@ottawa.edu
EICHOLTZ, Kristin 610-282-1100 382 E
kristin.eicholtz@desales.edu
EICHORST, Christopher 509-777-4780 486 I
ceichorst@whitworth.edu
EICKEN, Hajo 907-474-7331 10 A
heicken@alaska.edu
EICKHOFF, Chad, A 928-523-7141 14 H
chad.eickhoff@nau.edu
EICKHOFF, Jeffrey 402-643-4052 269 A
sggs@sggs.edu
EICKHOLT, Marcia 419-227-3141 363 C
marcia@unoh.edu

EICKHORST, Lindsay ..... 309-268-8031 137 I
lindsay.eickhorst@heartland.edu
EID, Haitham .... 504-286-5010 190 I
heid@suno.edu
EIDELMAN, Lipa .... 732-370-1560 275 G
EIDSON, Kristi .... 270-686-4216 179 D
kristi.eidson@brescia.edu
EIDSON, Paul .... 406-799-1515 263 A
dreidson@apollos.edu
EIDSON, Rebecca, W .... 864-646-1507 413 A
reidson@tctc.edu
EIDSON, Scott .... 406-604-4320 263 A
drscott@apollos.edu
EIDSON, Steve .... 229-430-6619 113 I
seidson@albanytech.edu
EIFERT, Robert .... 217-824-4004 141 D
reifert@lakeland.cc.il.us
EIGHMY, Sunny .... 641-628-5272 163 E
eighmys@central.edu
EIGHMY, Taylor .... 210-458-4101 455 E
taylor.eighmy@utsa.edu
EIKE, Claire .... 312-629-9379 148 I
ceike@saic.edu
EIKENBERRY, Michael .. 317-940-8940 153 F
meikenbe@butler.edu
EIKENS, Anita .... 414-382-6343 492 A
anita.eikens@alverno.edu
EILER, Claire, M .... 610-917-1487 401 I
cmeiler@valleyforge.edu
EIMER, Greg, A .... 217-732-3155 141 I
geimer@lincolncollege.edu
EIMERS, Mardy, T .... 573-882-3412 261 B
eimersm@missouri.edu
EIMERS, Megan .... 563-425-4180 170 A
eimersm00@uiu.edu
EINESMAN, Floralynn ... 619-239-0391.. 34 F
fle@cwsl.edu
EINFELD, Aaron .... 616-957-7035 221 P
aaron@calvinseminary.edu
EINHELLIG, Frank, E ..... 417-836-5119 256 E
frankeinhellig@missouristate.edu
EINOLF, Karl, W .... 260-399-2800 155 H
kweinolf@indianatech.edu
EINSPAHR, Kent .... 402-643-7315 266 G
kent.einspahr@cune.edu
EINSTEIN, Heath, A .... 817-257-7490 448 G
h.einstein@tcu.edu
EIOLA, William, T .... 419-772-2261 358 H
w-eiola@onu.edu
EIS, Linda .... 417-625-3797 256 D
eis-l@mssu.edu
EISELE, Chad, E .... 434-223-6151 468 A
ceisele@hsc.edu
EISEMAN, Margaret .... 412-396-6061 383 C
eiseman@duq.edu
EISEN, Arnold, M .... 212-678-8072 303 G
areisen@jtsa.edu
EISEN, Jeffrey, M .... 919-658-7759 340 J
jeisen@umo.edu
EISEN, Karen .... 718-780-0343 291 J
karen.eisen@brooklaw.edu
EISENBACH, Regina ...... 760-750-4253.. 33 B
regina@csusm.edu
EISENBACH, Theresa ..... 203-285-2534.. 85 E
teisenbach@hcc.commnet.edu
EISENBACH, Theresa ..... 203-332-5013.. 85 F
teisenbach@hcc.commnet.edu
EISENBEISER, Colleen ... 410-777-1249 197 C
ckeisenbeiser@aacc.edu
EISENBERG, Eric .... 813-974-2804 110 B
eisenberg@usf.edu
EISENBERG, Judith .... 718-289-5132 293 B
judith.eisenberg@bcc.cuny.edu
EISENBERG, Larry, A .... 314-516-6469 261 D
eisenbergl@umsl.edu
EISENBERGER, Israel .... 845-362-3053 291 A
EISENHART, Pamela ...... 717-337-6010 384 H
peisenha@gettysburg.edu
EISENHAUER, James ..... 218-879-0743 238 A
james.eisenhauer@fdltcc.edu
EISENHAUER, Jay .... 304-829-7465 487 G
jeisenhauer@bethanywv.edu
EISENHAUER, Joseph .... 313-993-1204 231 B
eisenhjg@udmercy.edu
EISENHAUER, Thomas .. 816-415-5990 262 F
eisenhauer@william.jewell.edu
EISENHAUER, Walt .... 570-484-2168 395 B
weisenha@lockhaven.edu
EISENHOUR, Lyn .... 425-352-8548 479 A
leisenhour@cascadia.edu
EISENMAN, Ann .... 563-244-7040 165 C
aeisenman@eicc.edu
EISENMAN, Elaine .... 781-239-4355 205 E
eeisenman@babson.edu
EISENMENGER,
Paul, W .... 309-341-7212 141 A
pweisenmenger@knox.edu
EISENSTEIN, Laya .... 718-268-4700 312 G
EISENSTEIN, Paul .... 614-823-1609 360 A
peisenstein@otterbein.edu
EISENTRAGER, Pete ...... 816-235-2665 261 C
eisentragerp@umkc.edu
EISFELDER, Aaron .... 217-479-7124 142 I
aaron.eisfelder@mac.edu
EISGRUBER,
Cristopher, L .... 609-258-3026 280 E
eisgrube@princeton.edu
EISLER, David, L .... 231-591-2500 223 J
davideisler@ferris.edu
EISNAUGLE, Eva .... 704-978-1344 336 C
eeisnaugle@mitchellcc.edu
EISNER, SND, Janet ...... 617-735-9825 209 A
president@emmanuel.edu
EISSES, Effie .... 360-650-7610 486 F
eissese@wwu.edu
EITEL, Norine .... 660-626-2391 250 A
neitel@atsu.edu
EIZENGA, Shannon .... 510-549-4718.. 66 B
seizenga@sksm.edu
EJIGIRI, Damien .... 225-771-3103 190 H
dejigiri@yahoo.com
EJIMA, Tricia, R .... 808-956-4304 128 F
ejimat@hawaii.edu
EKANGER, Holger .... 716-338-1332 303 D
holgerekanger@mail.sunyjcc.edu
EKARIUS, John .... 215-503-5017 400 A
john.ekarius@jefferson.edu
EKE, Kenoye .... 903-730-4890 438 H
keke@jarvis.edu
EKKER, David, A .... 757-822-7198 476 B
dekker@tcc.edu
EKMAN, Tom .... 615-230-3357 426 B
thomas.ekman@volstate.edu
EKNESS, Ray .... 406-243-4088 264 A
ray.ekness@umontana.edu
EKOUE-TOTOU, Patrick . 415-883-2211.. 39 C
pekouetotou@marin.edu
EKPO, NseAbasi .... 937-376-6411 350 D
nekpo@centralstate.edu
EKSTROM, Rodney .... 603-535-2217 275 B
raekstrom@plymouth.edu
EL-AMIN, Aisha .... 312-413-3450 151 B
aelami2@uic.edu
EL-DWEIK, Majed .... 573-681-5134 254 E
dweikm@lincolnu.edu
EL FATTAL, David .... 805-652-5536.. 72 G
delfattal@vcccd.edu
EL-HAGGAN, Ahmed ..... 410-951-3850 203 D
elhaggan@coppin.edu
EL-HAGGAN,
Ahmed, M .... 410-951-3896 203 D
EL-HASHEMY, Shehab .. 503-552-1848 374 E
selhashemy@nunm.edu
EL-KHOURY, Nadim ...... 413-748-3925 218 G
nel-khoury@springfield.edu
EL-KHOURY, Rodolphe . 305-284-9092 112 E
rxe66@miami.edu
EL-OSERY, Aly .... 575-835-5481 286 I
aly.elosery@nmt.edu
EL-REWINI, Hesham ..... 703-284-1550 469 C
hesham.el-rewini@marymount.edu
ELAM, Harry, J .... 650-723-2300.. 65 J
helam@stanford.edu
ELAM, Michael, A .... 252-536-7217 335 B
melam@halifaxcc.edu
ELAM, Terry, D .... 706-771-4005 114 J
telam@augustatech.edu
ELAND, Tom .... 612-659-6286 238 I
thomas.eland@minneapolis.edu
ELARDE, Chris .... 914-923-2804 311 E
ELAZIER, Molly .... 209-382-4508.. 69 B
melazier@ucmerced.edu
ELBASSIOUNY, Samir ... 908-835-2334 284 G
selbassiouny@warren.edu
ELBE, Michael .... 217-641-4101 140 A
melbe@jwcc.edu
ELBERT, Erickia .... 336-285-3772 341 F
edelbert@ncat.edu
ELDAYRIE, Elias, G .... 352-273-1788 109 F
eldayrie@ufl.edu
ELDEMIRE, Flavia .... 803-255-4742 406 F
feldemire@allenuniversity.edu
ELDER, Britni .... 501-812-2724.. 23 B
belder@uaptc.edu
ELDER, Britni .... 501-205-8923.. 18 H
belder@cbc.edu
ELDER, Darla .... 814-732-2743 394 F
delder@edinboro.edu
ELDER, Jackie .... 903-223-3110 448 B
jackie.elder@tamut.edu
ELDER, Jill .... 605-718-2411 417 F
jill.elder@wdt.edu
ELDER, Keith .... 205-726-4655.... 6 E
kelder@samford.edu
ELDER, Kelly .... 412-268-8977 380 F
kelder@andrew.cmu.edu
ELDER, Matthew .... 502-585-9911 184 D
melder@spalding.edu
ELDER, Paul .... 269-471-3284 221 B
elderp@andrews.edu
ELDER, Shelia .... 404-962-3002 126 F
shelia.elder@usg.edu
ELDER, Steve .... 501-205-8893.. 18 H
selder@cbc.edu
ELDER, Thomas .... 903-510-3038 452 C
teld@tjc.edu
ELDER, Vivian .... 417-447-8114 257 G
elderv@otc.edu
ELDERS, Candice .... 269-927-8198 226 D
cedlers@lakemichigancollege.edu
ELDRED, Jessica .... 315-801-4459 313 G
jeldred@secon.edu
ELDRIDGE, Audrey .... 208-562-3509 130 F
audreyeldridge@cwi.edu
ELDRIDGE, Connie .... 847-574-5264 141 C
celdridge@lfgsm.edu
ELDRIDGE, Daryl .... 866-931-4300 258 G
daryl.eldridge@rockbridge.edu
ELDRIDGE, Jacqueline .. 501-420-1252.. 17 B
jacqueline.eldridge@arkansasbaptist.edu
ELDRIDGE, Jonathan ..... 415-485-9619.. 39 C
jeldridge@marin.edu
ELDRIDGE, Karen .... 865-981-8207 421 F
karen.eldridge@maryvillecollege.edu
ELDRIDGE, Mark .... 402-486-2507 269 F
mark.eldridge@ucollege.edu
ELDRIDGE, Paul, J .... 951-343-4492.. 27 J
peldridge@calbaptist.edu
ELDRIDGE, Randy .... 610-527-0200 397 I
reldridge@rosemont.edu
ELDRIDGE, Ray .... 615-966-5946 421 D
ray.eldridge@lipscomb.edu
ELEBARIO, Jessica .... 575-461-4413 286 E
jessicae@mesalands.edu
ELEFF, Zev .... 847-982-2500 138 A
eleff@htc.edu
ELENICH, Richard .... 906-487-2763 227 E
rjelenic@mtu.edu
ELENWO, Elizabeth .... 619-549-3974.. 65 A
elizabeth.elenwo@socalsem.edu
ELFRING, Lisa, K .... 520-621-1671.. 16 G
ELFRINK, John .... 309-298-2442 152 D
ja-elfrink@wiu.edu
ELFRINK, Stephanie ...... 314-529-9370 254 H
selfrink@maryville.edu
ELGARICO, Michael .... 805-493-3049.. 29 H
elgarico@callutheran.edu
ELGENDY, Rick .... 202-885-8670.. 93 E
relgendy@wesleyseminary.edu
ELHINDI, Mohamed .... 608-785-8309 496 F
melhindi@uwlax.edu
ELI, Lisa, G .... 407-582-6649 112 K
leli@valenciacollege.edu
ELIAS, Benjamin .... 888-775-1514.. 68 A
belias@unitekcollege.edu
ELIAS, Charles .... 718-482-5052 294 F
celias@lagcc.cuny.edu
ELIAS, Jack .... 401-863-3330 404 E
jack_elias@brown.edu
ELIAS, Michael .... 610-896-1228 385 L
melias@haverford.edu
ELIAS, Stephanny, J ..... 617-333-2010 208 E
selias0104@curry.edu
ELIAS, Steven, M .... 970-247-7010.. 79 I
selias@fortlewis.edu
ELIAS BLOOMER,
Michelle .... 617-228-2025 214 A
meliacbl@bhcc.mass.edu
ELIASON, Eric, J .... 218-299-3001 235 E
vpaa@cord.edu
ELIASSON-CREEK, Fia .... 253-833-9111 481 F
feliasson-creek@greenriver.edu
ELIAV, Eli .... 585-275-5688 323 J
eli_eliav@urmc.rochester.edu
ELICKER, Beth .... 207-699-5045 194 D
belicker@meca.edu
ELICKER, Elizabeth .... 207-699-5043 194 D
belicker@meca.edu
ELIMIMIAN, Jonathan ... 256-761-6277.... 7 B
jelimimian@talladega.edu
ELIPTICO, Frankie, M .... 670-237-6700 506 A
frankie.eliptico@marianas.edu
ELISH-PIPER, Laurie ..... 815-753-9055 145 C
laurieep@niu.edu
ELIZA, Lourdes .... 787-852-1430 508 C
leliza@hccpr.edu
ELIZONDO, Laura, M .... 956-326-2213 446 F
laura@tamiu.edu
ELIZONDO, Maria, G .... 956-872-3559 444 A
marye@southtexascollege.edu
ELIZONDO, Priscilla ..... 512-444-8082 449 A
registrar@thsu.edu
ELKESHK, Abed .... 718-405-3300 296 G
abed.elkeshk@mountsaintvincent.edu
ELKINS, Germaine .... 910-695-3706 337 H
elkinsg@sandhills.edu
ELKINS, Julie, B .... 617-228-2436 214 A
jelkins@bhcc.mass.edu
ELKINS, Leah, C .... 513-241-4338 347 J
leah.elkins@antonellicollege.edu
ELKINS, Lindsay .... 901-722-3378 424 C
lelkins@sco.edu
ELKINS, Mark .... 904-596-2445 111 F
melkins@tbc.edu
ELKINS, Mary Jane .... 434-949-1051 475 H
mary.elkins@southside.edu
ELKINS, Paula, S .... 706-886-6831 125 D
pelkins@tfc.edu
ELKINS, Penny, L .... 478-301-2120 121 E
elkins_pl@mercer.edu
ELKINS, Susan .... 803-777-7695 413 C
selkins@mailbox.sc.edu
ELKS, Martha .... 404-752-1881 122 E
melks@msm.edu
ELLARD, Katherine .... 662-472-9134 246 C
kellard@holmescc.edu
ELLARD, Mark, D .... 662-329-7145 248 A
mdellard@muw.edu
ELLARD, Owen, H .... 210-567-2413 456 C
ellard@uthscsa.edu
ELLENBERG, George, B . 850-474-2035 110 E
gellenberg@uwf.edu
ELLENBERG, Kristi .... 304-205-6622 488 K
kristi.ellenberg@bridgevalley.edu
ELLENBURG, Aaron .... 434-200-7033 465 H
aaron.ellenburg@centrahealth.com
ELLENBURG, Phil .... 615-966-5841 421 D
phil.ellenburg@lipscomb.edu
ELLENS, Timothy, L .... 616-526-6475 222 A
tje6@calvin.edu
ELLERBE, Laverne .... 757-822-1994 476 B
lellerbe@tcc.edu
ELLERKER, Charla .... 863-784-7176 107 F
charla.ellerker@southflorida.edu
ELLERMAN, Brittany ...... 217-228-5432 146 F
ellerbr@quincy.edu
ELLERMAN, Paige, L ..... 513-244-4393 357 A
paige.ellerman@msj.edu
ELLERTSON, Shari .... 208-426-1614 129 I
shariellertson@boisestate.edu
ELLIBEE, Margaret .... 501-812-2216.. 23 B
mellibee@uaptc.edu
ELLIFF POUND, Lee ...... 417-625-9355 256 D
pound-l@mssu.edu
ELLIG, Tracy .... 406-994-5607 264 D
tellig@montana.edu
ELLINGER, John, M ...... 419-372-2006 348 H
johne@bgsu.edu
ELLINGER, Paul .... 217-333-5503 151 D
pellinge@illinois.edu
ELLINGHUYSEN, Scott .. 507-457-5696 241 F
sellinghuysen@winona.edu
ELLINGSON, Mike .... 701-231-7307 345 G
michael.ellingson@ndsu.edu
ELLINGTON, Keri, A ...... 317-738-8333 154 J
kellington@franklincollege.edu
ELLINGTON, Michael, A 304-293-2702 491 C
michael.ellington@mail.wvu.edu
ELLINWOOD, Dawn, M . 802-654-2566 463 B
dellinwood@smcvt.edu
ELLINWOOD, Suzanne .. 970-248-1337.. 77 I
sellinwo@coloradomesa.edu
ELLIOT, Jillian .... 415-575-6135.. 29 B
jelliot@ciis.edu
ELLIOT, Robert .... 646-717-9764 300 G
elliot@gts.edu
ELLIOT BROWN,
Karin, A .... 323-343-3820.. 32 A
kbrown5@calstatela.edu

EMERSON, Brian .... 716-896-0700 324 E
bemerson@villa.edu
EMERSON, Colleen .... 401-341-2908 406 A
emersonc@salve.edu
EMERSON, Dana .... 714-241-6184.. 38 C
demerson3@coastline.edu
EMERSON, Jim .... 434-200-3070 465 H
jim.emerson@centrahealth.com
EMERSON, Kimberly ..... 307-382-1661 502 I
kemerson@westernwyoming.edu
EMERSON, Michael .... 630-617-3178 136 G
michael.emerson@elmhurst.edu
EMERSON, Michael, O .. 773-244-5570 145 A
moemerson@northpark.edu
EMERSON, Mitchell, R .. 623-572-3501 143 G
memers@midwestern.edu
EMERSON, Peter .... 985-549-3894 192 D
peter.emerson@selu.edu
EMERSON, Sally .... 608-789-6083 501 A
emersons@westerntc.edu
EMERSON, Steve .... 208-467-8528 131 D
sdemerson@nnu.edu
EMERSON, Steve .... 951-343-4415.. 27 J
semerson@calbaptist.edu
EMERSON, Wendy, R .... 336-734-7540 334 E
wemerson@forsythtech.edu
EMERSON, Yolanda ...... 562-692-0921.. 58 E
yemerson@riohondo.edu
EMERT, John .... 765-285-1024 153 C
jemert@bsu.edu
EMERY, Lea .... 914-337-9300 297 D
EMERY, P. Michael .... 713-221-5806 453 B
emeryp@uhd.edu
EMILIO, Linda .... 909-469-8421.. 74 I
lemilio@westernu.edu
EMIRU, Tadael .... 916-691-7284.. 50 G
emirut@crc.losrios.edu
EMISON, Barry .... 662-407-1409 246 D
blemison@iccms.edu
EMM, William, T .... 585-345-6811 301 A
wtemm@genesee.edu
EMMA, Janine .... 732-255-0400 280 A
jemma@ocean.edu
EMMER, Karen .... 520-515-5417.. 11 M
emmerk@cochise.edu
EMMERICH, Linda, E .... 443-518-3825 199 C
lemmerich@howardcc.edu
EMMERSON, Janet .... 515-964-6476 164 C
jeemmerson@dmacc.edu
EMMICK, Joe .... 847-866-3923 137 E
joe.emmick@garrett.edu
EMMIL, Bruce .... 701-224-5758 346 B
bruce.emmil@bismarckstate.edu
EMMONS, Carol-Ann .... 312-567-3827 139 B
emmons@iit.edu
EMMONS, David .... 360-475-7120 482 G
demmons@olympic.edu
EMMONS, Gillian .... 617-358-5293 207 D
gcemmons@bu.edu
EMMONS, Larry, K .... 989-964-2558 230 B
lkemmons@svsu.edu
EMMONS, Lee .... 270-534-3084 182 F
lee.emmons@kctcs.edu
EMMONS, Scott .... 414-229-4762 497 A
semm@uwm.edu
EMODOGO, Yolanda ..... 901-435-1585 421 A
yolanda_emodogo@loc.edu
EMOND, Gean Ann .... 850-484-1728 104 H
gemond@pensacolastate.edu
EMORY, Cynthia, M ...... 717-264-2192 403 F
cynthia.emory@wilson.edu
EMORY, Douglas, J ...... 425-739-8311 482 A
doug.emory@lwtech.edu
EMORY, Julie, W .... 252-398-6252 328 D
emoryj@chowan.edu
EMORY, LaTonya .... 615-361-7555 419 I
lemory@daymarinstitute.edu
EMPET, Audriana, L ...... 570-326-3761 393 G
alm56@pct.edu
EMPET, David .... 607-962-9540 320 F
dempet@corning-cc.edu
EMRICH, Whitney .... 601-974-1105 247 B
whitney.emrich@millsaps.edu
EMSELLEM, Dawn .... 401-341-2336 406 A
dawn.emsellem@salve.edu
EMSWELLER, David, W . 419-434-4578 363 A
emsweller@findlay.edu
ENAMAIT, John .... 704-991-0220 338 C
jenamait1211@stanly.edu
ENCARNACION, Zaneta . 619-216-6613.. 65 F
zencarnacion@swccd.edu
ENCINA, Rosalinda .... 210-486-4609 429 E
rencina@alamo.edu
ENDARA, Miguel, A ...... 714-966-8500.. 73 C
mendara@ves.edu
ENDERS, Jessica .... 760-636-7972.. 39 A
jenders@collegeofthedesert.edu
ENDERS, Naulayne, R ... 606-474-3276 180 G
nenders@kcu.edu
ENDERS, Tom .... 323-343-6510.. 32 A
thomas.enders@calstatela.edu
ENDICOTT, Alicia .... 660-359-3948 257 D
aendicott@mail.ncmissouri.edu
ENDICOTT, Daniel, D .... 904-620-2019 110 A
dendicot@unf.edu
ENDICOTT, Jon .... 559-453-3484.. 43 G
jon.endicott@fresno.edu
ENDICOTT, Patricia .... 812-749-1435 159 C
pendicott@oak.edu
ENDRASKE, Mark, C ..... 530-226-4108.. 63 K
mendraske@simpsonu.edu
ENDRES, David .... 513-231-2223 348 C
dendres@athenaeum.edu
ENDRES, Judy .... 507-389-7351 241 C
judy.endres@southcentral.edu
ENDRESS, Wendy .... 360-867-6296 481 A
endressw@evergreen.edu
ENDRIJONAS, Erika, A .. 626-585-7201.. 55 K
eendrijonas@pasadena.edu
ENDSLEY, Douglas .... 210-829-6004 453 D
douge@uiwtx.edu
ENDSLEY, Kara .... 919-530-5597 342 A
kendsley@nccu.edu
ENDY, Michael .... 817-598-6211 458 A
mendy@wc.edu
ENDY, Stephanie .... 216-368-2000 349 F
stephanie.endy@case.edu
ENFIELD, Jeff .... 708-239-4803 150 F
jeff.enfield@trnty.edu
ENGBROCK, M. Jeff ...... 409-944-1215 437 B
mengbrock@gc.edu
ENGEBRETSON, Pam .... 651-779-3994 237 G
pam.engebretson@century.edu
ENGEL, Amy .... 631-687-5149 314 C
aengel@sjcny.edu
ENGEL, Angela .... 309-438-3305 139 E
akengel@ilstu.edu
ENGEL, Deidre .... 712-279-5448 163 C
deidre.engel@briarcliff.edu
ENGEL, Karen .... 650-306-3145.. 61 O
engelk@smccd.edu
ENGEL, Michelle .... 414-382-6037 492 A
michelle.engel@alverno.edu
ENGEL, Renata, S .... 814-863-6726 392 B
rse1@psu.edu
ENGEL, Richard, R .... 530-752-9960.. 68 E
rrengel@ucdavis.edu
ENGEL, Steven .... 912-478-0357 119 C
sengel@georgiasouthern.edu
ENGELBACH, Karl, M .... 530-754-7237.. 68 E
kmengelbach@ucdavis.edu
ENGELBOURG, Karen .... 617-638-4560 207 D
engelbou@bu.edu
ENGELBRIDE, Ed .... 518-956-8140 316 D
eengelbride@albany.edu
ENGELDINGER, Lyle ...... 760-252-2511.. 26 I
lengeldinger@barstow.edu
ENGELHARDT, Kelli .... 406-791-5237 265 H
kelli.engelhardt@uprovidence.edu
ENGELHARDT, Nichole .. 573-897-5000 260 E
ENGELHART, Brian, W .. 260-422-5561 155 H
bwengelhart@indianatech.edu
ENGELHART, Rene .... 919-646-2774.. 59 F
rengelhart@samuelmerritt.edu
ENGELHART, Rene .... 916-646-2774.. 59 F
rengelhart@samuelmerritt.edu
ENGELKEMIER, John ..... 312-329-2145 144 B
john.engelkemier@moody.edu
ENGELKING, Heather .... 407-708-2103 107 D
engelkingh@seminolestate.edu
ENGELLANT, Roxanne ... 406-683-7305 264 B
roxanne.engellant@umwestern.edu
ENGELMAN, Kevin .... 843-349-5393 410 C
kevin.engelman@hgtc.edu
ENGELMAN, Laura .... 507-285-7206 240 G
laura.engelman@rctc.edu
ENGELSCHALL,
Emily, D .... 951-827-3986.. 69 C
emily.engelschall@ucr.edu
ENGELSEN, Karen .... 760-245-4271.. 73 D
karen.engelsen@vvc.edu
ENGELSMA, Chris .... 616-432-3406 229 I
chris.engelsma@prts.edu
ENGEMANN, Andy .... 973-408-3378 277 C
aengemann@drew.edu
ENGEN, Stuart .... 701-671-2446 346 E
stuart.engen@ndscs.edu
ENGER, Lee .... 217-228-5432 146 F
engerle@quincy.edu
ENGERMAN, Kimarie .... 340-692-4110 514 E
kengerman@uvi.edu
ENGFER, Tom .... 323-856-7747.. 25 M
tengfer@afi.com
ENGLAND, A, W .... 313-593-5290 231 F
england@umich.edu
ENGLAND, Amy .... 918-631-3288 371 E
amy-england@utulsa.edu
ENGLAND, Christy .... 850-245-0466 108 H
christy.england@flbog.edu
ENGLAND, David .... 615-966-6210 421 D
david.england@lipscomb.edu
ENGLAND, Jerry .... 615-547-1240 419 F
jengland@cumberland.edu
ENGLAND, Kenneth, W . 404-471-6278 113 G
kengland@agnesscott.edu
ENGLAND, Rebecca ...... 276-244-1231 464 L
bengland@asl.edu
ENGLAND, Richard .... 217-581-2017 136 E
rengland@eiu.edu
ENGLAR, Samantha .... 618-537-6548 143 B
smenglar@mckendree.edu
ENGLE, Cathy .... 360-417-6347 483 B
cengle@pencol.edu
ENGLE, Chris .... 810-762-0242 228 C
chris.engle@mcc.edu
ENGLE, Diane .... 620-792-9271 171 C
engled@bartonccc.edu
ENGLE, Jason .... 509-544-4935 479 H
jengle@columbiabasin.edu
ENGLE, Patricia, A .... 248-370-4223 229 G
pengle@oakland.edu
ENGLE, Sara .... 406-377-9441 263 E
sengle@dawson.edu
ENGLEHARDT,
Richard, E .... 606-693-5000 182 G
registrar@kmbc.edu
ENGLEHARDT, Thomas . 617-236-5467 209 D
tenglehardt@fisher.edu
ENGLEHART, Kathy .... 207-453-5117 194 I
kenglehart@kvcc.me.edu
ENGLERT, Jeannine .... 212-960-5274 326 E
englert@yu.edu
ENGLERT, Mark, G .... 307-681-6201 502 F
menglert@sheridan.edu
ENGLERT, Patrick .... 502-272-8323 179 B
penglert@bellarmine.edu
ENGLERT, Richard, M ... 215-204-7405 399 F
president@temple.edu
ENGLESTATTER,
Pauline, A .... 301-447-5086 200 E
englesta@msmary.edu
ENGLIN, Peter, D .... 515-294-5636 162 I
penglin@iastate.edu
ENGLISH, Ana .... 928-317-6092.. 10 J
ana.english@azwestern.edu
ENGLISH, Andrew .... 870-307-7225.. 20 A
andrew.english@lyon.edu
ENGLISH, Andy .... 515-961-1547 169 D
andy.english@simpson.edu
ENGLISH, Ashley .... 334-808-6539.... 7 C
englisha@troy.edu
ENGLISH, Cara .... 480-285-1761.. 12 A
ENGLISH, Chris .... 828-694-1728 332 E
chrise@blueridge.edu
ENGLISH, Claude .... 816-584-6492 258 A
claude.english@park.edu
ENGLISH, Cyndy .... 504-865-5738 191 B
cenglish@tulane.edu
ENGLISH, David, A .... 740-587-6262 352 G
englishda@denison.edu
ENGLISH, Eva .... 406-353-2607 262 H
eenglish@ancollege.edu
ENGLISH, Garrett .... 951-552-8865.. 27 J
genglish@calbaptist.edu
ENGLISH, Jill .... 616-392-8555 233 E
jill@westernsem.edu
ENGLISH, John .... 479-575-3054.. 21 G
jre@uark.edu
ENGLISH, John .... 610-989-1200 402 B
jenglish@vfmac.edu
ENGLISH, Josh .... 661-362-2245.. 51 C
jenglish@masters.edu
ENGLISH, Kristen .... 309-457-2210 144 A
kenglish@monmouthcollege.edu
ENGLISH, Lindsay .... 216-987-3610 351 G
lindsay.english@tri-c.edu
ENGLISH, Sarah, H .... 845-575-3000 305 L
sarah.english@marist.edu
ENGLISH, Susan .... 848-932-7821 282 A
chancellornb@rutgers.edu
ENGLISH, Susan .... 616-632-8900 221 C
ENGLISH, Susan .... 757-825-3527 476 A
englishs@tncc.edu
ENGLISH, Susan .... 757-825-2952 476 A
englishs@tncc.edu
ENGLOT, Peter .... 973-353-5541 282 B
peter.englot@rutgers.edu
ENGLUND, Elizabeth ..... 425-352-8432 479 A
eenglund@cascadia.edu
ENGLUND, Tim .... 509-963-1866 479 B
tim.englund@cwu.edu
ENGSTROM, Dan, M ..... 724-938-1523 394 B
engstrom@calu.edu
ENGSTROM, Larry .... 775-682-8803 271 F
engstrom@unr.edu
ENGSTROM, Rick .... 425-889-6397 482 F
rick.engstrom@northwestu.edu
ENKE, Kathryn .... 320-363-5070 235 C
kenke@csbsju.edu
ENLOE, Donald .... 303-871-2463.. 83 D
denloe@du.edu
ENLOE, Jeremy .... 303-871-3142.. 83 D
jeremy.enloe@du.edu
ENNELLO-BUTLER,
Deanna .... 518-694-7305 289 D
deanna.ennello-butler@acphs.edu
ENNIS, Daniel, G .... 410-516-2373 199 D
danielgennis@jhu.edu
ENNIS, Daniel, J .... 843-349-2089 408 C
dennis@coastal.edu
ENNIS, Jackie .... 252-399-6571 326 M
jennis@barton.edu
ENNIS, Kim .... 205-387-0511.... 1 D
kim.ennis@bscc.edu
ENNIS, Matt .... 941-752-5574 108 G
ennism@scf.edu
ENNIS, Theresa .... 931-372-6124 426 E
tennis@tntech.edu
ENNIST, Phyllis .... 937-529-2201 362 A
pjennist@united.edu
ENNS-REMPEL, Kevin .... 559-453-2300.. 43 G
kevin.enns.rempel@fresno.edu
ENO, Alisha .... 303-765-3102.. 80 F
aeno@iliff.edu
ENOKAWA, Jerilyn .... 808-734-9899 128 I
jilorenz@hawaii.edu
ENOMA, Benjamin .... 212-463-0400 322 J
benjamin.enoma@touro.edu
ENOS, Chris .... 785-670-1153 177 G
chris.enos@washburn.edu
ENRIGHT, Jan Brue .... 605-256-5205 416 J
jan.enright@dsu.edu
ENRIGHT, John .... 213-613-2200.. 64 H
john_enright@sciarc.edu
ENRIGHT, Nancy .... 973-275-2545 283 B
nancy.enright@shu.edu
ENRIGHT, Patrick .... 973-328-5700 277 B
penright@ccm.edu
ENRIGHT, Sara .... 401-825-1084 404 H
senright@ccri.edu
ENRIQUEZ, Anita, B ...... 671-735-2994 505 E
abe@triton.uog.edu
ENRIQUEZ, Igrí .... 787-765-3560 507 L
enriquez@edpuniversity.edu
ENRIQUEZ-FERNANDEZ,
Gustavo .... 805-922-6966.. 24 J
gustavo.enriquez@hancockcollege.edu
ENRIQUEZ FIELD,
Diana .... 650-508-3761.. 54 D
denriquezfield@ndnu.edu
ENROTH, Kevin .... 662-325-7404 247 F
enroth@osp.msstate.edu
ENS, Allison .... 559-453-2204.. 43 G
allison.ens@fresno.edu
ENS, Terry .... 620-947-3121 177 C
terryens@tabor.edu
ENSER, Jason .... 802-728-1434 464 E
jenser@vtc.edu
ENSER, Pamela .... 518-580-4709 321 A
pamela.enser@esc.edu
ENSIGN, Margee, M ...... 717-245-1322 382 F
ensignm@dickinson.edu
ENSING, Kim .... 805-922-6966.. 24 J
kensing@hancockcollege.edu
ENSLEY, Cynthia .... 252-638-7201 333 H
ensleyc@cravencc.edu
ENSLEY, Dana .... 706-379-3111 127 C
ddensley@yhc.edu
ENSLEY, Kevin .... 817-923-1921 445 B
kensley@swbts.edu
ENSLIN, Jon .... 920-403-3016 495 I
jon.enslin@snc.edu

ESCALANTE, Maria .... 800-567-2344 492 G
mescalante@menominee.edu
ESCALERA, Liya .... 617-228-2173 214 A
lescalera@bhcc.mass.edu
ESCALERA MUÑOZ,
Jorge .... 787-620-2040 506 C
jescalera@aupr.edu
ESCALLIER, Lori, A .... 718-270-7632 317 E
lori.escallier@downstate.edu
ESCAMILLA, Cindy .... 210-829-3136 453 D
cyescami@uiwtx.edu
ESCAMILLA, Mark .... 361-698-1203 436 C
mescamilla@delmar.edu
ESCARRAMAN, Iris .... 202-884-9400.. 93 B
escarramani@trinitydc.edu
ESCH, Marj .... 989-275-5000 226 B
marj.esch@kirtland.edu
ESCH, Rod .... 970-351-3192.. 83 E
rodney.esch@unco.edu
ESCHBACH, Jeanne .... 607-962-9335 320 F
eschbach@corning-cc.edu
ESCHENBAUM, Matt ...... 303-871-4256.. 83 D
matt.eschenbaum@du.edu
ESCHENBERG, Ardis ...... 808-235-7402 129 F
ardise@hawaii.edu
ESCHENBRENNER,
Nancy .... 860-773-1304.. 86 G
neschenbrenner@tunxis.edu
ESCHER, Nancy .... 401-341-2157 406 A
nancy.escher@salve.edu
ESCHHOLZ, Ingrid .... 303-315-2600.. 83 C
ingrid.eschholz@ucdenver.edu
ESCLAVON, Annette .... 972-241-3371 434 J
ESCOBAR, Estrella .... 915-747-5555 455 C
estrella@utep.edu
ESCOBAR, Fabio .... 716-270-6688 299 F
escobar@ecc.edu
ESCOBAR, Jorge, L .... 408-274-6700.. 61 K
jorge.escobar@sjeccd.edu
ESCOBAR, Luis .... 650-738-4124.. 61 Q
escobarluis@smccd.edu
ESCOBAR, Maria .... 408-855-5147.. 74 D
maria.escobar@missioncollege.edu
ESCOBEDO, Beatriz .... 619-934-0797.. 60 F
ESCOBEDO, Maria .... 805-591-6220.. 41 A
maria_escobedo@cuesta.edu
ESCOE, Gigi .... 513-556-9193 362 D
gisela.escoe@uc.edu
ESCOE, Gisela .... 513-556-9193 362 D
gisela.escoe@uc.edu
ESCOLAS, Roger .... 614-222-3264 351 D
rescolas@ccad.edu
ESHLEMAN, Kristen ...... 704-894-2583 328 F
kreshleman@davidson.edu
ESHLEMAN, Robert .... 406-656-9950 265 I
reshleman@yellowstonechristian.edu
ESHWAR, Naina .... 206-934-5411 484 A
naina.eshwar@seattlecolleges.edu
ESKAM, Shannon .... 307-268-2596 501 U
seskam@caspercollege.edu
ESKANDARI, Sepehr ..... 909-869-4182.. 30 D
seskandari@cpp.edu
ESKANDARIAN, Ali .... 202-994-8192.. 91 F
ea1102@gwu.edu
ESKER, Brian .... 312-899-5177 148 I
besker@saic.edu
ESKES, Todd .... 909-599-5433.. 47 K
teskes@lifepacific.edu
ESKEW, Sherry .... 918-631-2550 371 E
sherry-eskew@utulsa.edu
ESKINS, Katrina .... 304-696-7096 490 D
eskinsk@marshall.edu
ESKRIDGE, Steve .... 206-546-4553 484 G
eskridge@shoreline.edu
ESLAND, Melanie .... 248-689-8282 232 A
mesland@walshcollege.edu
ESLINGER, Elise .... 507-222-5597 234 F
eeslinger@carleton.edu
ESLINGER, Robert .... 906-227-2212 228 F
reslinge@nmu.edu
ESMAEILI, Ali .... 956-872-7270 444 A
esmaeili@southtexascollege.edu
ESNES-JOHNSON, Terry 631-420-2104 321 B
terry.esnes-johnson@farmingdale.edu
ESPARZA, Jazmine .... 863-680-3004.. 99 H
jesparza@flsouthern.edu
ESPARZA, Lou .... 214-333-5289 434 I
lou@dbu.edu
ESPERANZA, JR.,
Emmanuel .... 708-974-5344 144 C
esperanzajre2@morainevalley.edu
ESPERIAS, Kelly .... 909-607-9651.. 37 G
kelly_esperias@kgi.edu
ESPESET, Rick .... 260-982-5390 158 T
rbespeset@manchester.edu
ESPICH, Whitney, T ...... 617-253-8231 215 G
ESPINA, John .... 516-686-7791 309 F
jespina@nyit.edu
ESPINA, Maritza .... 563-333-6266 169 A
espinamaritza@sau.edu
ESPINAL, Jeanette .... 727-736-3812 107 C
jeanette.espinal@schiller.edu
ESPING, David .... 417-447-7552 257 G
espingd@otc.edu
ESPINOSA, Dora .... 847-578-8524 147 I
dora.espinosa@rosalindfranklin.edu
ESPINOSA, Juan Carlos 305-348-4100 109 A
juancarlos.espinosa@fiu.edu
ESPINOSA, Martin .... 615-687-6960 418 A
mespinosa@abcnash.edu
ESPINOSA, Philip .... 810-762-0566 228 C
philip.espinosa@mcc.edu
ESPINOSA, Rene .... 210-341-1366 441 C
respinosa@ost.edu
ESPINOSA, Zoila .... 305-642-4104 105 D
ESPINOSA-PIEB,
Christina, G .... 408-864-8705.. 43 C
espinosapiebchristina@deanza.edu
ESPINOZA, Anthony ...... 936-468-5822 445 F
espinozaea1@sfasu.edu
ESPINOZA, Ernesto .... 787-743-7979 511 I
eespinoza@suagm.edu
ESPINOZA, Juan, P ...... 540-231-6267 477 A
juespino@vt.edu
ESPINOZA, Judy .... 316-978-3540 178 A
judy.espinoza@wichita.edu
ESPINOZA, Julissa .... 909-593-3511.. 70 D
jespinoza@laverne.edu
ESPINOZA, Roberta .... 310-338-4405.. 50 J
roberta.espinoza@lmu.edu
ESPINOZA, Suzanne ..... 510-885-7636.. 31 C
suzanne.espinoza@csueastbay.edu
ESPINOZA-MOLINA,
Humberto .... 210-434-6711 441 E
hespinoza-mol@ollusa.edu
ESPINOZA-PARRA,
Oscar .... 760-674-7792.. 39 A
oespinoza-parra@collegeofthedesert.edu
ESPIRITU, David .... 619-216-6759.. 65 F
despiritu@swccd.edu
ESPIRITU, Kira, A .... 619-260-4598.. 71 J
kespiritu@sandiego.edu
ESPIZONA, Yolanda ...... 623-845-3305.. 13 C
yolanda.espinoza@gccaz.edu
ESPLIN, Daniel .... 928-774-3890.. 12 M
desplin@indianbible.org
ESPOSITO, Augustine .... 610-785-6252 398 A
aesposito@scs.edu
ESPOSITO, James .... 212-678-8095 303 G
jaesposito@jtsa.edu
ESPOSITO, Joseph, P ... 213-738-5743.. 65 G
jesposito@swlaw.edu
ESPOSITO, Juliana .... 508-854-4276 215 D
jesposito@qcc.mass.edu
ESPOSITO, Mark .... 309-796-5427 132 G
espositom@bhc.edu
ESPOSITO, Richard .... 843-863-8044 407 E
resposito@csuniv.edu
ESPOSITO, Richard, C .. 412-396-6607 383 C
esposito@duq.edu
ESPOSITO, Samantha .... 304-296-8282 491 F
sesposito@wvjc.edu
ESPOSITO, Scott .... 203-254-4000.. 86 I
sesposito@fairfield.edu
ESPOSITO-NOY, Celia ... 707-864-7112.. 64 C
celia.esposito-noy@solano.edu
ESPY, Tracy, Y .... 704-463-3440 339 E
tracy.espy@pfeiffer.edu
ESQUEDA, Angie .... 805-730-4011.. 62 C
esqueda@sbcc.edu
ESQUEDA, Melissa, G .. 512-448-8400 442 M
mellissaesqueda@stedwards.edu
ESQUITH, Stephen, L .... 517-355-0212 227 D
esquith@msu.edu
ESQUIVEL, Carlos .... 212-875-4615 290 F
cesquivel@bankstreet.edu
ESQUIVEL, Daniel .... 806-379-2702 430 A
dmesquivel@actx.edu
ESQUIVEL, Ruben, E ..... 214-648-0448 457 B
ruben.esquivel@utsouthwestern.edu
ESSAK KOPP, Erin .... 740-593-4303 359 G
erinek@ohio.edu
ESSENBURG, Curt .... 616-988-3654 226 C
cessenburg@kuyper.edu
ESSER, Kurt .... 407-708-2148 107 D
esserk@seminolestate.edu
ESSES, Levi .... 301-447-6122 200 E
l.k.esses@msmary.edu
ESSEX, Don .... 301-891-4222 204 C
dessex@wau.edu
ESSEX, T.A .... 972-773-8300.. 92 G
ESSIG, Linda .... 323-343-4001.. 32 A
linda.essig@calstatela.edu
ESSIG, Mary .... 304-647-6213 491 A
messig@osteo.wvsom.edu
ESSL, Michael (Mike) ... 212-353-4203 297 E
essl@cooper.edu
ESTABROOK,
Madeleine, A .... 617-373-2772 217 F
ESTAPHAN, Charles ...... 508-793-3014 208 B
cestapha@holycross.edu
ESTEBAN, A. Gabriel ..... 312-362-8890 135 I
president@depaul.edu
ESTELLA, Marlon .... 909-599-5433.. 47 K
mestella@lifepacific.edu
ESTEN, Phil, J .... 651-962-5901 244 E
este0003@stthomas.edu
ESTENSON, Chad .... 701-662-1521 346 D
chad.estenson@lrsc.edu
ESTEP, Alison .... 206-378-5056 484 D
estep@spu.edu
ESTEP, Jim .... 660-263-3900 251 A
ESTEPP, Stella .... 304-896-7382 489 E
stella.estepp@southernwv.edu
ESTER, Joyce, C .... 952-358-8150 239 F
joyce.ester@normandale.edu
ESTERBERG, Kristin, G .. 315-267-2100 319 D
president@potsdam.edu
ESTERHUIZEN, Amy ...... 814-393-2337 394 D
aesterhuizen@clarion.edu
ESTERLINE, David, V .... 412-924-1366 396 I
desterline@pts.edu
ESTERS, Llatetra .... 410-837-5429 204 B
lesters@ubalt.edu
ESTERS, Randy .... 870-743-3000.. 20 C
randy.esters@northark.edu
ESTES, Amy .... 404-835-6124 423 K
aestes@richmont.edu
ESTES, IV, Edward, R .... 757-479-3706 473 C
eestes@vbts.edu
ESTES, Eric, S .... 401-863-1800 404 E
eric_estes@brown.edu
ESTES, James .... 202-885-8696.. 93 E
jestes@wesleyseminary.edu
ESTES, Kelly .... 865-573-4517 420 G
kestes@johnsonu.edu
ESTES, Lane .... 205-226-4640.... 5 A
lestes@bsc.edu
ESTES, Wendy .... 678-717-3845 126 A
wendy.estes@ung.edu
ESTES, William .... 423-614-8175 420 J
bestes@leeuniversity.edu
ESTEY, Alicia .... 208-426-1417 129 I
aliciaestey@boisestate.edu
ESTEY, Amanda .... 641-648-4611 166 J
amanda.estey@iavalley.edu
ESTILL, Donna .... 256-306-2756.... 1 F
donna.estill@calhoun.edu
ESTILL, Gabe .... 773-481-8816 134 G
jestill@ccc.edu
ESTILL, Sandi, L .... 606-759-7141 182 A
sandi.estill@kctcs.edu
ESTLACK, Scarlet .... 806-874-3571 433 B
scarlet.estlack@clarendoncollege.edu
ESTOCK, Steven .... 575-562-2632 285 M
steven.estock@enmu.edu
ESTRADA, Adriana .... 310-660-3593.. 41 L
aestrada@elcamino.edu
ESTRADA, Donna .... 985-448-7954 187 F
donna.estrada@fletcher.edu
ESTRADA, Ella Mae ...... 212-431-2827 309 G
ellamae.estrada@nyls.edu
ESTRADA, George .... 203-576-4330.. 88 D
gestrada@bridgeport.edu
ESTRADA, George .... 530-242-7929.. 63 H
gestrada@shastacollege.edu
ESTRADA, Hadda .... 509-533-3844 480 B
hadda.estrada@ccs.spokane.edu
ESTRADA, Jeri .... 970-521-6730.. 81 D
jeri.estrada@njc.edu
ESTRADA, Lorraine .... 915-779-8031 457 F
lestrada@computercareercenter.com
ESTRADA, Maria .... 787-780-5134 510 F
mestrada@nuc.edu
ESTRADA, Nicolas .... 406-791-5261 265 H
nicolas.estrada@uprovidence.edu
ESTRADA, Rebecca .... 505-428-1604 288 B
rebecca.estrada@sfcc.edu
ESTRADA, Robert .... 925-473-7540.. 40 J
restrada@losmedanos.edu
ESTRADA-HAMBY, Lisa . 940-397-4076 440 F
lisa.hamby@msutexas.edu
ESTRIN, David .... 718-522-9073 290 C
david@asa.edu
ETCHISON, Matt .... 317-921-5739 157 G
metchison@ivytech.edu
ETE, Sonia .... 310-360-8888.. 27 B
ETE, Thierry .... 310-360-8888.. 27 B
ETHEREDGE, Susan .... 413-585-4900 218 F
sethered@smith.edu
ETHERIDGE, Joey .... 479-213-0022.. 23 I
jetheridge@ozarks.edu
ETHERIDGE, Lori .... 270-852-3284 183 A
letheridge@kwc.edu
ETHERTON, Scott .... 503-370-6707 378 B
swetherton@willamette.edu
ETHIER, Maria .... 575-527-7540 287 E
ethierm@nmsu.edu
ETHIER, Richard .... 802-224-3023 463 H
richard.ethier@vsc.edu
ETHINGTON, Robert .... 707-527-4573.. 62 F
rethington@santarosa.edu
ETHRIDGE, Jennifer .... 815-740-2286 151 J
jethridge@stfrancis.edu
ETIENNE, Guy .... 754-312-2898 102 Q
registrar@keycollege.edu
ETIENNE, John .... 904-276-6859 106 C
johnetienne@sjrstate.edu
ETIENNE, Sabrina .... 301-891-4177 204 C
setienne@wau.edu
ETINGE, Elias, E .... 706-396-7609 122 K
eetinge@paine.edu
ETSCHMAIER, Gale .... 850-644-5211 109 C
getschmaier@fsu.edu
ETTARO, Barbara .... 814-863-1030 392 B
bxm7@psu.edu
ETTENSOHN, Clare .... 973-290-4240 277 A
cettensohn@cse.edu
ETTINGER, Sherri .... 617-521-2451 218 E
sherri.ettinger@simmons.edu
ETTLE, Violeta .... 202-885-2720.. 90 J
vi@american.edu
ETTLICH, Sherry .... 541-552-6576 376 E
ettlich@sou.edu
ETTLING, John .... 518-564-2010 319 C
president_office@plattsburgh.edu
ETTORE, JD .... 567-661-7974 360 B
johndavid_ettore@owens.edu
ETTRICH, Rudi .... 305-760-7500 102 U
ETZEL, Brent .... 479-968-0417.. 18 C
betzel@atu.edu
EUBANK, Charlotte .... 573-840-9105 260 I
ceubank@trcc.edu
EUBANK, Chelsea .... 352-638-9747.. 95 D
ceubank@beaconcollege.edu
EUBANK, Janet .... 316-295-5452 173 D
eubankj@friends.edu
EUBANKS, David .... 864-294-2024 410 A
david.eubanks@furman.edu
EUBANKS, Gail .... 912-443-5443 124 A
geubanks@savannahtech.edu
EUBANKS, Karen .... 904-516-8749.. 98 P
keubanks@fcsl.edu
EUBANKS, Karla .... 912-427-5899 116 F
keubanks@coastalpines.edu
EUBANKS, Kathleen, L .. 508-999-8086 211 F
keubanks@umassd.edu
EUBANKS, Matthew .... 479-979-1414.. 23 I
meubanks@ozarks.edu
EUBANKS, Michelle .... 256-765-4225.... 8 E
meubanks@una.edu
EUBANKS, Nekita .... 704-216-3778 337 F
nekita.eubanks@rccc.edu
EUEN, Mandy, L .... 513-529-8776 356 E
euenal@miamioh.edu
EUGENE, Nicholas .... 410-951-3462 203 D
neugene@coppin.edu
EULE, Anne .... 603-578-8900 273 A
aeule@ccsnh.edu
EUNICE, E, E .... 850-201-7000 111 C
eunicee@tcc.fl.edu
EURE, Darius, D .... 252-335-8530 341 D
ddeure@ecsu.edu
EURICH, David .... 610-526-1171 378 G
dave.eurich@theamericancollege.edu
EURY, Brian .... 610-902-8734 380 C
brian.eury@cabrini.edu
EUSTROM, Jim .... 503-399-5144 372 C
jim.eustrom@chemeketa.edu
EVAN, Joseph .... 570-208-5895 387 A
josephevan@kings.edu

EWING, James .... 954-262-8082 103 M
jewing@nova.edu
EWING, Jennifer .... 619-201-8967 .. 65 A
EWING, Mike, J .... 320-363-5605 235 C
mjewing@csbsju.edu
EWING, Nadia .... 574-284-4560 160 C
newing@saintmarys.edu
EWING, II, Rick, M .... 419-289-5893 348 A
pewing@ashland.edu
EWING, Rob .... 510-845-5373 .. 29 G
rob@cjc.edu
EWING, Sarah .... 814-871-7618 384 E
ewing003@gannon.edu
EWING, Sim, E .... 276-328-0133 473 B
see4r@virginia.edu
EWING, Sunnie .... 901-722-3231 424 C
sewing@sco.edu
EWING, Susan .... 248-645-3300 223 A
EWING-MORGAN,
Dawn .... 718-960-8111 294 A
dawn.ewing-morgan@lehman.cuny.edu
EXELER, Brandy .... 859-371-9393 179 A
bexeler@beckfield.edu
EXLER, Michael, J .... 215-895-6488 383 B
mexler@drexel.edu
EXLEY, Robert .... 256-840-4100 .... 3 F
robert.exley@snead.edu
EXLINE, Teresa, D .... 812-237-7783 155 G
teresa.exline@indstate.edu
EXNER, Allen .... 301-369-2470 197 F
ahexner@captechu.edu
EXSTEEN, Shaun .... 561-237-7839 102 V
exsteen@lynn.edu
EXSTROM, Bruce .... 402-323-3389 269 C
bexstrom@southeast.edu
EYE, John .... 601-266-4241 249 F
john.eye@usm.edu
EYE, Kurt .... 518-244-4536 313 D
eyek@sage.edu
EYERLY, Mark .... 610-330-5120 387 E
eyerlym@lafayette.edu
EYERLY, Rita .... 531-622-2203 267 H
reyerly@mccneb.edu
EYERMAN, Sandra .... 518-629-7737 302 E
s.eyerman@hvcc.edu
EYLER, Robert .... 707-664-2396 .. 34 C
robert.eyler@sonoma.edu
EYLERS, Hinrich .... 602-557-7428 .. 16 J
hinrich.eylers@phoenix.edu
EYNON, Bret .... 718-482-5478 294 F
beynon@lagcc.cuny.edu
EYNON, Craig, S .... 330-325-6663 357 G
ceynon@neomed.edu
EYNON, Matthew .... 717-358-4144 384 D
matthew.eynon@fandm.edu
EYNOUF, Erica .... 413-755-4816 215 F
eweynouf@stcc.edu
EYRING, Henry, J .... 208-496-1111 130 A
eyringh@byui.edu
EYSTER, Kevin .... 734-432-5307 227 A
keyster@madonna.edu
EZELL, Cyn, D .... 813-257-3028 112 J
cezell@ut.edu
EZELL, Monica .... 251-460-6111 .... 8 F
monicae@southalabama.edu
EZEOKE, Benedict .... 507-457-5331 241 F
bezeoke@winona.edu
EZEONU, Rolita .... 253-833-9111 481 F
rezeonu@greenriver.edu
EZZEDDINE, Ahmad .... 313-577-4450 232 I
oip@wayne.edu
EZZELL, Russell .... 325-649-8040 438 D
rezzell@hputx.edu

F

FAAS, Charles .... 408-924-1500 .. 34 B
charlie.faas@sjsu.edu
FAASUA, Linda .... 805-678-5170 .. 73 A
lrobison@vcccd.edu
FABBI, Jennifer .... 760-750-4330 .. 33 B
jfabbi@csusm.edu
FABE, Barbara, A .... 718-862-7392 305 H
barbara.fabe@manhattan.edu
FABER, Andrea .... 419-448-3375 361 J
faberad@tiffin.edu
FABER, Charles .... 208-376-7731 129 H
cfaber@boisebible.edu
FABER, David .... 620-947-3121 177 C
davidf@tabor.edu
FABER, Paul, W .... 785-628-4234 173 B
pfaber@fhsu.edu
FABIANI, Steve .... 516-463-4426 302 B
steve.fabiani@hofstra.edu
FABIN, Justin .... 724-805-2669 398 F
justin.fabin@stvincent.edu
FABOS, Kristin .... 831-479-6158 .. 27 G
krfabos@cabrillo.edu
FABOZZI, Kirsten .... 651-779-3298 237 G
kirsten.fabozzi@century.edu
FABREGAS, Belkis .... 787-764-0000 514 B
belkis.fabregas@upr.edu
FABRIZI, Cheryl .... 814-865-5423 392 B
cxt295@psu.edu
FABRIZIO, Eve .... 740-389-4636 356 B
fabrizioe@mtc.edu
FABRIZIO, Linda .... 212-614-6113 311 H
linda.fabrizio@mountsinai.org
FACCINI-VITO, Lorena .... 832-813-6537 439 G
lorena.faccini.vito@lonestar.edu
FACKRELL, Brady, R .... 307-675-0550 502 F
bfackrell@sheridan.edu
FADDOUL, Jill .... 716-731-8850 310 C
jmfaddoul@niagaracc.suny.edu
FADEL-BAZZI, Nadia .... 248-204-2316 226 G
nfadelbaz@ltu.edu
FADIA, Vijay .... 310-791-9975 .. 45 E
FADICH, Matt .... 541-463-3573 373 F
fadichm@lanecc.edu
FADLER, Lisa .... 517-371-5140 233 A
fadlerl@cooley.edu
FAEH, John .... 920-922-8611 500 C
jfaeh@morainepark.edu
FAEHNER, David, A .... 269-471-3122 221 B
dfaehner@andrews.edu
FAEHNER, Frances, M .. 269-471-6686 221 B
frances@andrews.edu
FAERMAN, Larry .... 561-297-3542 108 J
lfaerman@fau.edu
FAERMAN, Susie .... 713-683-3817 443 F
FAFFLER, Ken .... 972-241-3371 434 J
FAGAN, Sean .... 850-484-1538 104 H
sfagan@pensacolastate.edu
FAGAN-MURDOCK,
Calette .... 914-632-5400 307 G
cfaganmurdock@monroecollege.edu
FAGBEYIRO, Betty, C .... 318-670-9679 190 J
bfagbeyiro@susla.edu
FAGBEYIRO, Gabriel .... 225-771-5091 190 G
gabriel_fagbeyiro@sus.edu
FAGBEYIRO, Gabriel .... 225-771-5091 190 H
gabriel_fagbeyiro@sus.edu
FAGEN, Jeffrey, W .... 718-990-6068 314 B
fagenj@stjohns.edu
FAGER, Jennifer .... 989-386-6607 227 F
jfager@midmich.edu
FAGG, Meghan .... 865-981-8191 421 F
meghan.fagg@maryvillecollege.edu
FAGIOLI, Loris .... 949-451-5513 .. 64 F
lfagioli@ivc.edu
FAGLER, Mitchell .... 478-289-2272 124 F
mfagler@southeasterntech.edu
FAGNONI, Nick .... 813-253-6230 112 J
FAGO, Stephanie .... 724-805-2534 398 E
stephanie.fago@stvincent.edu
FAGO, Stephanie .... 724-805-2923 398 F
stephanie.fago@stvincent.edu
FAGRE, Dale .... 763-424-0909 239 G
dfagre@nhcc.edu
FAGUY, David, M .... 928-523-6117 .. 14 H
david.faguy@nau.edu
FAHEY, Katie .... 847-866-3929 137 E
katherine.fahey@garrett.edu
FAHEY, Stephen .... 909-537-3165 .. 33 A
stephen.fahey@csusb.edu
FAHEY, William, E .... 603-880-8308 274 E
wfahey@thomasmorecollege.edu
FAHEY-SMITH, Ellen .... 718-817-3040 300 E
faheysmith@fordham.edu
FAHIMI, Traci .... 949-451-5204 .. 64 F
tfahimi@ivc.edu
FAHNER, Dawn .... 513-529-5716 356 E
fahnerdm@miamioh.edu
FAHNESTOCK, Bethene . 918-540-6202 366 I
bfahnestock@neo.edu
FAHRENWALD, Nancy ... 979-436-0111 446 G
nfahrenwald@tamu.edu
FAHY, Greg .... 207-621-3255 196 A
gregory.fahy@maine.edu
FAIGMAN, David, L .... 415-565-4700 .. 68 F
chancellorfaigman@uchastings.edu
FAILEY, Rhonda .... 318-797-5139 189 D
rhonda.failey@lsus.edu
FAILING, Kate .... 662-246-6361 247 D
kfailing@msdelta.edu
FAIMON, Peg .... 812-855-2561 156 B
pfaimon@indiana.edu
FAIN, Juanita .... 702-895-4387 271 E
juanita.fain@unlv.edu
FAIN, Starr .... 334-387-3877 .... 4 C
starrfain@amridgeuniversity.edu
FAIOLA, Norman .... 603-899-4073 273 F
faiolan@franklinpierce.edu
FAIR, George, W .... 972-883-4566 455 B
gwfair@utdallas.edu
FAIR, George, W .... 972-883-2350 455 B
gwfair@utdallas.edu
FAIR, Terry .... 404-894-9396 118 F
terry.fair@business.gatech.edu
FAIR, Vickie .... 202-994-9633 .. 91 F
vvfair14@gwu.edu
FAIRBAIRN, Donald .... 704-527-9909 209 G
dfairbairn@gcts.edu
FAIRBAIRN, Katie .... 707-468-3164 .. 51 E
kfairbairn@mendocino.edu
FAIRBANKS, Daniel .... 801-863-6440 461 A
daniel.fairbanks@uvu.edu
FAIRBANKS, Diana .... 231-995-1019 228 G
dfairbanks@nmc.edu
FAIRBANKS, Ken .... 276-739-2462 476 C
kfairbanks@vhcc.edu
FAIRCHILD, Joseph, J .. 757-822-7208 476 B
jfairchild@tcc.edu
FAIRCLOTH, Brad .... 828-669-8012 331 J
bfaircloth@montreat.edu
FAIRCLOTH, Jimmy .... 478-218-3385 116 A
jfaircloth@centralgatech.edu
FAIRLEY, Danny .... 913-360-7256 171 D
dfairley@benedictine.edu
FAIRMAN, Jerilyn .... 315-786-6542 303 F
jfairman@sunyjefferson.edu
FAIRWEATHER, Alisa .... 503-847-2550 377 F
afairweather@uws.edu
FAISAL, Ali .... 321-674-6211 .. 99 B
afaisal@fit.edu
FAISON, JR.,
A. Zachary .... 904-470-8012 .. 97 L
azfaison@ewc.edu
FAISON, Frederick .... 484-365-7527 389 C
ffaison@lincoln.edu
FAISON, Frederick .... 484-365-8075 389 C
ffaison@lincoln.edu
FAIT, Jacob .... 423-636-7300 427 B
jfait@tusculum.edu
FAITH, Helen .... 541-463-5266 373 F
faithh@lanecc.edu
FAJACK, Matt .... 205-348-4530 .... 7 G
mfajack@fa.ua.edu
FAKHARI, Reza .... 718-489-2036 313 H
rfakhari@sfc.edu
FAKHIR, Bazra .... 304-205-6630 488 K
bazra.fakhir@bridgevalley.edu
FALA, Gregory .... 215-951-1907 387 C
fala@lasalle.edu
FALABELLA, Deneb .... 410-888-9048 200 A
dfalabella@muih.edu
FALACCI, Andrew .... 508-856-4653 212 A
andrew.falacci@umassmed.edu
FALASTER, Marilyn .... 618-985-3741 139 I
marilynfalaster@jalc.edu
FALCHER, Rosanna .... 315-792-3015 324 B
refalche@utica.edu
FALCI, David .... 315-470-5767 291 H
davidfalci@crouse.org
FALCIANI-WHITE,
Nancy, K .... 804-752-7256 470 F
nancyfalcianiwhite@rmc.edu
FALCK, Brian, G .... 717-245-1686 382 F
falckb@dickinson.edu
FALCK, Larry, B .... 843-661-1251 409 K
lfalck@fmarion.edu
FALCK-YI, Suzanne .... 641-585-8225 170 B
falckyis@waldorf.edu
FALCO, James .... 608-524-7825 499 H
jsfalco@madisoncollege.edu
FALCO, Kathleen, P .... 207-778-7280 196 B
kathleen.falco@maine.edu
FALCON, Luis .... 978-934-3843 211 G
luis_falcon@uml.edu
FALCON-CHANDLER,
Carole .... 406-353-2607 262 H
cfalconchan@hotmail.com
FALCONE, Alice, A .... 978-867-4208 209 F
alice.falcone@gordon.edu
FALCONE, Andrea .... 859-572-5483 184 A
falconeal@nku.edu
FALCONER, John .... 308-865-8702 269 I
falconerj@unk.edu
FALCONETTI, Angela .... 863-297-1098 105 A
agarciafalconetti@polk.edu
FALDER, Mike .... 765-998-5538 160 F
mcfalder@taylor.edu
FALDUTO, Ellen .... 330-263-2230 351 C
efalduto@wooster.edu
FALDUTO, Matt .... 319-398-1274 167 C
matt.falduto@kirkwood.edu
FALE, Tauvela .... 684-699-7834 505 A
t.fale@amsamoa.edu
FALES, Julia .... 269-749-7595 229 H
jfales@olivetcollege.edu
FALES, Michael, F .... 269-749-7624 229 H
mfales@olivetcollege.edu
FALESE, Joseph .... 815-836-5275 141 G
falesejo@lewisu.edu
FALEY, Heather .... 802-440-4423 462 A
hfaley@bennington.edu
FALK, Ann .... 206-546-4701 484 G
afalk@shoreline.edu
FALK, Barry, L .... 804-828-1803 473 F
blfalk@vcu.edu
FALK, Dan .... 620-229-6267 177 A
dan.falk@sckans.edu
FALK, Stephanie, A .... 717-867-6696 388 H
falk@lvc.edu
FALK, William .... 920-403-3943 495 I
william.falk@snc.edu
FALKENBERG, Janice .... 414-297-8718 500 B
falkenjm@matc.edu
FALKENSTEIN, Marc .... 209-946-2738 .. 70 E
mfalkenstein@pacific.edu
FALKNER, Amy .... 315-443-3627 322 C
apfalkne@syr.edu
FALKNER, Jay .... 918-647-1210 365 H
jfalkner@carlalbert.edu
FALKNER, Tina .... 612-626-0302 243 E
rovic001@umn.edu
FALKOWITZ, Getzel .... 718-302-7500 326 F
FALKS, Delisa, F .... 979-458-5311 446 G
delisa@tamu.edu
FALL, Matt .... 517-483-1953 226 F
fallm@lcc.edu
FALLAVOLLITA, John .... 603-623-0313 273 I
johnfallavollita@nhia.edu
FALLDINE, Cory .... 620-341-5297 172 L
cfalldin@emporia.edu
FALLERT, Danelle .... 323-265-8797 .. 48 H
fallerd@elac.edu
FALLERT, Lynn .... 314-367-8700 259 B
lynn.fallert@stlcop.edu
FALLETA, David, A .... 304-457-6213 487 B
falletada@ab.edu
FALLETTA, Eva, R .... 480-732-7231 .. 12 P
eva.falletta@cgc.edu
FALLETTA, Margaret, F .. 304-637-1363 487 I
fallettam@dewv.edu
FALLING, Cary .... 405-425-5290 367 G
cary.falling@oc.edu
FALLING, Sali, K .... 765-285-5162 153 C
sfalling@bsu.edu
FALLIS, Drew .... 210-292-6280 504 B
drew.fallis@us.af.mil
FALLON, Ann Marie .... 585-385-8477 314 A
afallon@sjfc.edu
FALLON, Anne Marie .... 508-830-6485 213 B
afallon@maritime.edu
FALLON, Greg .... 973-684-5895 280 B
gfallon@pccc.edu
FALLON, Kevin, C .... 410-543-6075 203 F
kcfallon@salisbury.edu
FALLON-KORB,
Melissa, A .... 607-436-3368 317 C
melissa.fallon@oneonta.edu
FALLONE, Deborah, A ... 914-323-5224 305 J
deborah.fallone@mville.edu
FALLOWS, Noel .... 706-542-2202 125 G
nfallows@uga.edu
FALLS, Meda .... 731-925-5722 425 B
mfalls@jscc.edu
FALLS, Sarah .... 336-770-3266 343 D
fallss@uncsa.edu
FALLS, William, A .... 802-656-3166 463 E
william.falls@uvm.edu
FALOTICO, Michael .... 312-467-2328 .. 36 F
mfalotico@thechicagoschool.edu
FALSETTI, Ryan .... 951-552-8516 .. 27 J
rfalsetti@calbaptist.edu
FALSO, Katie .... 518-244-4527 313 D
gardnk2@sage.edu
FALTER, Corey .... 641-628-7604 163 E
falterc@central.edu
FALTER, James .... 330-494-6170 361 F
jfalter@starkstate.edu

FATCHERIC, Michelle .... 774-354-0462 206 B michelle.fatcheric@becker.edu
FATH, Stephen, J .... 713-500-5202 456 B stephen.j.fath@uth.tmc.edu
FATHALLAH, Fadi .... 530-754-9707.. 68 E fathallah@ucdavis.edu
FATHERLY, Sarah .... 704-337-2568 339 G fatherlys@queens.edu
FATIMA, Nasrin .... 607-777-2365 316 E nfatima@binghamton.edu
FATOOH, Coleen .... 415-239-3151.. 37 A cfatooh@ccsf.edu
FATOOL, Kirk .... 765-448-1986 154 H
FATTA, Libby .... 805-289-6474.. 73 B lfatta@vcccd.edu
FATTIG, Teri, L .... 208-732-6501 130 E tfattig@csi.edu
FATTOUH, Said .... 713-221-8059 453 B fattouhs@uhd.edu
FAUBERT, Bob .... 928-757-0840.. 14 F bfaubert@mohave.edu
FAUCHET, Philippe, M .. 615-322-0720 428 D philippe.m.fauchet@vanderbilt.edu
FAUCI, Darcy .... 607-777-2131 316 E dfauci@binghamton.edu
FAUDREE, Donna .... 574-807-7752 153 E donna.faudree@betheluniversity.edu
FAUGHANAN, Timothy . 607-777-2275 316 E tfaughn@binghamton.edu
FAUGHT, Jerry .... 580-481-5243 457 J jerry.faught@wbu.edu
FAUGHT, Norma .... 575-392-5018 286 J nfaught@nmjc.edu
FAUGHT, Shelbie .... 575-492-2121 289 A sfaught@usw.edu
FAULCON, Gaddius .... 919-516-4200 340 C
FAULCONER, Christian . 801-422-4690 458 H christian_faulconer@byu.edu
FAULK, Daniel .... 724-503-1001 402 E dfaulk@washjeff.edu
FAULK, Jason, C .... 434-395-2908 469 A faulkjc@longwood.edu
FAULK, Randy .... 361-570-4397 453 C faulkr@uhv.edu
FAULK, Sancy .... 501-205-8799.. 18 H sfaulk@cbc.edu
FAULKENBERRY, Scott .. 865-471-4369 419 A sfaulkenberry@cn.edu
FAULKNER, Brenda .... 254-968-9044 446 E faulkne@tarleton.edu
FAULKNER, Jacqueline, A .... 901-333-5722 426 A jfaulkner@southwest.tn.edu
FAULKNER, Jerry .... 615-230-3500 426 B jerry.faulkner@volstate.edu
FAULKNER, Jessica ...... 501-205-8800.. 18 H jfaulkner@cbc.edu
FAULKNER, Karen, R .... 812-888-5640 162 C kfaulkner@vinu.edu
FAULKNER, Keith .... 434-592-5305 468 H bkfaulkner@liberty.edu
FAULKNER, Michael ..... 336-386-3436 338 D faulknerm@surry.edu
FAULKNER, Ted .... 540-231-5618 477 A thfaulkn@vt.edu
FAULKNER, William ...... 718-631-6244 295 D wfaulkner@qcc.cuny.edu
FAULSTICK, Donald, R .. 413-542-8266 205 B drfaulstick@amherst.edu
FAULSTICK, Lindsay ...... 812-866-7079 155 C faulstick@hanover.edu
FAUOLO-MANILA, Okenaisa .... 684-699-9155 505 A o.fauolo@amsamoa.edu
FAUROT, Sara .... 609-652-4469 283 D sara.faurot@stockton.edu
FAUST, Brian .... 715-346-3511 497 F brian.faust@uwsp.edu
FAUST, Brian, A .... 502-852-2898 185 C brian.faust@louisville.edu
FAUST, Joanne .... 860-343-5890.. 86 A jfaust@mxcc.edu
FAUST, Kimberly, A ...... 803-323-2225 414 G faustk@winthrop.edu
FAUST, Lucas .... 414-443-8720 498 O lucas.faust@wlc.edu
FAUST, Mary Catherine 770-426-2771 121 C cfaust@life.edu
FAUST, Scott .... 831-755-6858.. 44 K sfaust@hartnell.edu
FAUST, Teresa .... 352-854-2322.. 96 O faustt@cf.edu
FAUST, William Bryant . 504-568-4829 189 B wfaust@lsuhsc.edu
FAUSTIN, Ketsia .... 617-585-0200 206 F ketsia.faustin@the-bac.edu
FAUSTINO, James .... 808-675-3739 127 E james.faustino@byuh.edu
FAUSZ, Kevin .... 210-434-6711 441 E kpfausz@ollusa.edu
FAUTAS, Jason .... 330-490-7437 364 B jfautas@walsh.edu
FAUVER, James .... 304-734-6614 488 K james.fauver@bridgevalley.edu
FAVARA, JR., Leonard .. 620-241-0723 172 D lenny.favara@centralchristian.edu
FAVATA, Joanne .... 201-684-7115 280 H jfavata@ramapo.edu
FAVAZZA, Erin .... 301-985-7077 203 B erin.favazza@umuc.edu
FAVAZZA, Joseph, A .... 603-641-7010 274 C jfavazza@anselm.edu
FAVEDE, Ginny .... 304-243-2233 491 I president@wju.edu
FAVERTY, Patrick .... 916-520-7472.. 70 E pfaverty@pacific.edu
FAVOR, Jessica .... 803-536-8743 412 C jfavor@scsu.edu
FAVORIT, Mike, D .... 407-582-1336 112 K mfavorit@valenciacollege.edu
FAVORS, Gretchen .... 601-877-4063 244 H gretchen.favors@sodexo.com
FAVORS, Regina .... 501-420-1202.. 17 B president@arkansasbaptist.edu
FAVORS, Toney .... 903-223-3061 448 B toney.favors@tamut.edu
FAVRE, Martha .... 978-665-3216 212 C mfavre@fitchburgstate.edu
FAW, Justin, D .... 260-359-4035 155 F jfaw@huntington.edu
FAW, Kim, E .... 336-838-6293 339 B kefaw728@wilkescc.edu
FAWBUSH, Greg .... 615-675-5255 428 G gfawbush@welch.edu
FAWCETT, Andrew .... 631-451-4879 321 F fawceta@sunysuffolk.edu
FAWCETT, Carol .... 708-709-2947 146 D cfawcett@prairiestate.edu
FAWCETT, Jeffrey, K ...... 574-372-5100 155 B fawcettj@grace.edu
FAWCETT, Sean .... 207-985-7976 194 C seanfawcett@landingschool.edu
FAWCETT, Tonya, L .... 574-372-5100 155 B fawcettl@grace.edu
FAWKS, Melinda, D ...... 717-477-1121 395 E mdfawk@ship.edu
FAWTHROP, Lynn .... 401-739-5000 405 A lmfawthrop@neit.edu
FAY, Dana .... 630-515-7166 143 G dfayxx@midwestern.edu
FAY, Derek, R .... 208-496-7310 130 A fayd@byui.edu
FAY, Jake .... 360-623-8400 479 C jake.fay@centralia.edu
FAY, Laurie .... 518-783-2307 315 J fay@siena.edu
FAY, Patrick .... 414-229-2222 497 A fayp@uwm.edu
FAY, Sue .... 847-543-2218 135 B sfay@clcillinois.edu
FAY-REILLY, Tara .... 718-862-7939 305 H tfayreilly01@manhattan.edu
FAYAD, Barbara, H .... 864-938-3722 411 I bfayad@presby.edu
FAYEK, Moaty .... 408-864-8896.. 43 C fayekmoaty@deanza.edu
FAYLOR, David, L .... 256-469-7333.... 5 I deaninst@hbc1.edu
FAYMONVILLE, Carmen 920-424-0890 497 B faymonvc@uwosh.edu
FAZ, Isaac .... 214-378-1793 434 K isaac.faz@dcccd.edu
FAZAL, Shafeek .... 631-632-1067 317 D shafeek.fazal@stonybrook.edu
FAZEKAS, Evelyn .... 315-792-3002 324 B efazekas@utica.ucsu.edu
FAZEKAS, Jennifer .... 203-932-7274.. 89 A jfazekas@newhaven.edu
FAZIO, James, I .... 619-201-8978.. 65 A
FAZIO, Jamie .... 585-389-2308 308 B jfazio1@naz.edu
FAZIO, Jennifer .... 732-255-0400 280 A jfazio@ocean.edu
FAZIO, Josephine .... 708-456-0300 150 I josephinefazio@triton.edu
FAZIO, Kari .... 610-526-5160 379 E kfazio@brynmawr.edu
FAZIO, Patricia .... 860-486-5634.. 88 E patricia.fazio@uconn.edu
FAZZANO FICANO, Adriana .... 954-201-7518.. 95 H afazzano@broward.edu
FAZZI, Diane .... 323-343-4303.. 32 A dfazzi@calstatela.edu
FEAGANS, Frank .... 972-883-6900 455 B frank.feagans@utdallas.edu
FEAKES, Debra .... 317-791-6129 161 B feakesd@uindy.edu
FEAN, Judith .... 574-284-4886 160 C jfean@saintmarys.edu
FEAR, Kevin, G .... 724-653-2222 383 A kfear@dec.edu
FEARN, Odell .... 865-882-4679 425 G fearnao@roanestate.edu
FEARN, Odell .... 865-354-3000 425 G fearnao@roanestate.edu
FEASEL, Brenda .... 740-389-4636 356 B feaselb@mtc.edu
FEASEL, Edward, M ...... 949-480-4133.. 64 B efeasel@soka.edu
FEASTER, Blanton .... 903-589-7144 438 G bfeaster@jacksonville-college.edu
FEASTER, Glenn .... 865-573-4517 420 G gfeaster@johnsonu.edu
FEATHERLING, Adam .... 740-366-9301 349 H
FEATHERSTON, Guy ...... 972-775-7250 440 G guy.featherston@navarrocollege.edu
FEATHERSTONE, Andrea .... 577-577-2405 379 F a.featherstone@bucknell.edu
FEATHERSTONE, Richard .... 541-917-4594 374 A feather@linnbenton.edu
FEAVER, John, H .... 405-224-3140 371 D jfeaver@usao.edu
FEBBO, Jenny .... 216-987-4854 351 G jenny.febbo@tri-c.edu
FEBO-GOMEZ, Yamillet . 732-906-2602 279 A yfebo-gomez@middlesexcc.edu
FECHNER, Mary .... 575-439-3696 287 C mfechner@nmsu.edu
FECHO, Susan .... 252-399-6480 326 M sfecho@barton.edu
FECHTER, Sharon .... 240-567-7563 200 C sharon.fechter@montgomerycollege.edu
FEDDER, Carolyn .... 631-420-2239 321 B fedderc@farmingdale.edu
FEDELE, Genine .... 610-359-5148 382 C gfedele@dccc.edu
FEDER, Mary, M .... 631-451-4256 321 F federm@sunysuffolk.edu
FEDERER, Gina .... 972-273-3006 435 E gfederer@dcccd.edu
FEDERMAN, Robin .... 213-884-4133.. 24 A rfederman@ajrca.edu
FEDEROWICZ, Jane .... 610-527-0200 397 I jfederowicz@rosemont.edu
FEDIN, Audrey .... 408-498-5151.. 38 F afedin@cogswell.edu
FEDORCHAK, David ...... 410-704-3974 204 A dfedorchak@towson.edu
FEDORCHAK, Lynn .... 607-778-5319 318 A fedorchaklm@sunybroome.edu
FEDORKO, Kathleen, C . 215-968-8220 379 G fedorkok@bucks.edu
FEDRICK, Marion .... 229-500-2000 113 H marion.fedrick@asurams.edu
FEDRIZZI-WILLIAMS, Linda .... 717-728-2219 381 B lindafedrizzi@centralpenn.edu
FEE, Andy .... 562-985-7976.. 31 F andy.fee@csulb.edu
FEE, Richard .... 714-484-7152.. 53 K rfee@cypresscollege.edu
FEE, T. Joshua .... 859-858-3511 178 I josh.fee@asbury.edu
FEEHAN, Patrick .... 240-567-3087 200 C patrick.feehan@montgomerycollege.edu
FEELER, William .... 432-685-4626 440 E bfeeler@midland.edu
FEELEY, Brian .... 336-278-7446 328 K bfeeley@elon.edu
FEELEY, Maria .... 860-768-4275.. 88 H feeley@hartford.edu
FEELY, SND, Katherine . 216-397-1966 354 I kfeely@jcu.edu
FEENEY, Gregory .... 859-246-6329 180 K greg.feeney@kctcs.edu
FEERER, Pam .... 620-252-7355 172 G feerer.pam@coffeyville.edu
FEES, Megan .... 910-775-4403 343 B megan.fees@uncp.edu
FEEST, Amy .... 860-773-1631.. 86 G afeest@tunxis.edu
FEEZELL, Travis .... 402-461-7326 267 D tfeezell@hastings.edu
FEGAN, Kevin, G .... 972-293-5449 228 H fegan@northwood.edu
FEGAN, Kevin, G .... 903-875-7306 440 G kevin.fegan@navarrocollege.edu
FEGAN, Maryanne .... 908-852-1400 276 G maryanne.fegan@centenaryuniversity.edu
FEGETT, Greg .... 217-443-8888 135 H gfegett@dacc.edu
FEHER, Katie .... 567-661-7532 360 B katie_feher2@owens.edu
FEHLING, Patricia .... 518-580-5742 316 A pfehling@skidmore.edu
FEHN, Heather .... 609-771-2101 276 I hfehn@tcnj.edu
FEHNRICH, Jennifer ...... 567-661-7101 360 B jennifer_fehnrich@owens.edu
FEHOKO, Lakiesha .... 801-957-4278 461 D lakiesha.fehoko@slcc.edu
FEHR, Chad .... 310-377-5501.. 51 B cfehr@marymountcalifornia.edu
FEHRENBACHER, Rick ... 206-220-8269 484 F fehrenbacher@seattleu.edu
FEICHTER, Kathryn .... 330-966-5452 361 F kfeichter@starkstate.edu
FEICK, Andrew .... 610-328-8276 399 D afeick1@swarthmore.edu
FEICK, Lawrence, F .... 814-362-5140 401 B feick@pitt.edu
FEIERMAN, Michael ...... 212-678-3438 322 G mf192@tc.columbia.edu
FEIERTAG, Jason .... 484-664-3140 391 C jasonfeiertag@muhlenberg.edu
FEIFER, Amy .... 610-896-1181 385 L afeifer@haverford.edu
FEIGELSTOCK, Yitzchok . 516-255-4700 312 D rcli@mlb.edu
FEIGENBAUM, Peter ...... 718-817-2243 300 E pfeigenbaum@fordham.edu
FEIGERT, James, M ...... 949-582-4342.. 64 G jfeigert@saddleback.edu
FEIGERT, Kendra, M ..... 717-867-6126 388 H feigert@lvc.edu
FEIL, Hallie .... 308-635-6032 270 D feilh@wncc.edu
FEIN, Adam .... 940-565-2624 454 A adam.fein@unt.edu
FEIN, Gene .... 718-817-3900 300 E fein@fordham.edu
FEIN, Jason .... 207-786-6341 193 B jfein@bates.edu
FEIN, Michael, R .... 401-598-1736 404 I mfein@jwu.edu
FEIN, Michael, T .... 434-832-7751 474 C feinm@centralvirginia.edu
FEINBERG, Diane .... 405-974-2658 370 K dfeinberg@uco.edu
FEINBERG, Elisha .... 718-268-4700 312 G
FEINGOLD, Ruth, P ...... 503-370-6285 378 B feingold@willamette.edu
FEINMAN, Shannon, V . 434-949-1005 475 H shannon.feinman@southside.edu
FEINSTEIN, Andrew .... 970-351-2121.. 83 E andy.feinstein@unco.edu
FEINSTEIN, David .... 212-964-2830 306 H
FEINSTEIN, Lee .... 812-856-7900 156 B lafeinst@indiana.edu
FEIST, Donna, L .... 610-758-3156 388 J dlf210@lehigh.edu
FEIST, K. Cameron .... 315-859-4413 301 C cfeist@hamilton.edu
FEIST, Wes .... 406-447-5465 263 C wfeist@carroll.edu
FEIST-PRICE, Sonja, M . 859-257-9293 185 B sonja.feist-price@uky.edu
FEISTHAMEL, Kevin, P .. 330-569-5952 353 J
FEISTRITZER, Emily .... 844-283-2246.. 93 A
FEISTRITZER, Richard ... 844-283-2246.. 93 A
FEIT, Christopher, R ..... 563-588-7109 167 D christopher.feit@loras.edu
FEITZ, David, A .... 801-321-7211 460 D dfeitz@ushe.edu

FERNANDER, Kevin, A .. 561-868-3143 104 D
fernandk@palmbeachstate.edu
FERNANDES, Brian .... 845-848-7807 298 D
brian.fernandes@dc.edu
FERNANDES, Jamie ...... 404-894-7162 118 F
jamie.fernandes@business.gatech.edu
FERNANDES, Jane, K .... 336-316-2146 329 E
fernandesjk@guilford.edu
FERNANDES, Jill .... 304-829-7601 487 G
jfernandes@bethanywv.edu
FERNANDES, Kim .... 816-604-1418 255 D
kim.fernandes@mcckc.edu
FERNANDES, Sidney ..... 813-974-7927 110 B
sfernand@health.usf.edu
FERNANDEZ, Edith .... 702-992-2358 271 C
edith.fernandez@nsc.edu
FERNANDEZ, Ernie .... 305-284-8281 112 E
erniefernandez@miami.edu
FERNANDEZ, Eva .... 718-997-2867 295 C
eva.fernandez@qc.cuny.edu
FERNANDEZ, Frank .... 614-236-6504 349 D
ffernand@capital.edu
FERNANDEZ, Henry, B .. 954-486-7728 112 D
uftlchancellor@uftl.edu
FERNANDEZ, Jazmine ... 954-776-4476 102 A
jazminef@keiseruniversity.edu
FERNANDEZ, Jeffrey ..... 508-289-2325 220 D
jfernandez@whoi.edu
FERNANDEZ, Jose .... 973-684-6107 280 B
jfernandez@pccc.edu
FERNANDEZ, Jose, A .... 407-582-1701 112 K
jfernandez145@valenciacollege.edu
FERNANDEZ, Julie .... 281-649-3000 437 H
jfernandez@hbu.edu
FERNANDEZ, Marco, A . 915-831-6498 436 E
mferna56@epcc.edu
FERNANDEZ, Marla .... 660-785-4130 260 J
mfernandez@truman.edu
FERNANDEZ, Mayra ...... 509-453-0374 483 C
mayra.fernandez@perrytech.edu
FERNANDEZ, Miguel ..... 802-443-5792 462 H
fernande@middlebury.edu
FERNANDEZ, Mike .... 615-966-5186 421 D
mike.fernandez@lipscomb.edu
FERNANDEZ,
Rodolfo, J .... 305-284-4085 112 E
rudyfernandez@miami.edu
FERNANDEZ, Sam .... 602-212-0501.. 14 Q
sfernandez@brightoncollege.edu
FERNANDEZ,
Stephanie, M .... 603-641-7465 274 C
sfernandez@anselm.edu
FERNANDEZ, Thomas ... 516-572-7775 308 A
thomas.fernandez@ncc.edu
FERNANDEZ, Yaniris ..... 413-559-5781 210 A
ymfpr@hampshire.edu
FERNANDEZ MORAL,
Leticia .... 787-751-0500 514 B
leticia.fernandez@upr.edu
FERNANDEZ-TORRES,
Luis, C .... 305-474-6014 106 F
fernandez@stu.edu
FERNANDO, Gihan .... 202-885-1829.. 90 J
gihan@american.edu
FERNANDO, Shane .... 910-362-7890 332 H
sfernando@cfcc.edu
FERNENDEZ, Sam .... 602-212-0501.. 11 B
sam.fernendez@brightoncollege.edu
FERNETTE, Eric .... 713-500-3110 456 B
eric.fernette@uth.tmc.edu
FERNHALL, Bo .... 312-996-6695 151 B
fernhall@uic.edu
FERNIANY, Will .... 205-975-5362.... 8 A
ferniany@uab.edu
FERNOS, Manuel, J ...... 787-766-1912 509 C
mfernos@inter.edu
FERNOS, Manuel, J ...... 787-766-1912 510 A
mfernos@inter.edu
FERNOS, Manuel, J ...... 787-763-4203 508 J
mfernos@inter.edu
FERNS, Nathalie .... 603-206-8132 272 L
nferns@ccsnh.edu
FERO, Laura .... 651-690-6358 242 R
ljfero284@stkate.edu
FEROE, Louise, H .... 914-323-5262 305 J
louise.feroe@mville.edu
FERRAN, Peggy .... 315-781-3311 302 A
ferran@hws.edu
FERRANTE, John .... 516-918-2787 324 G
jferrante@webb.edu
FERRANTE, Regina .... 860-512-3632.. 85 G
rferrante@manchestercc.edu
FERRAO-DELGADO,
Luis, A .... 787-763-7099 512 G
luis.ferrao@upr.edu
FERRAO DELGADO,
Luis, A .... 787-763-3930 514 B
rectoria.rrp@upr.edu
FERRARA, Brandi .... 315-781-3517 302 A
bferrara@hws.edu
FERRARA, Catherine ..... 718-982-2250 293 E
catherine.ferrara@csi.cuny.edu
FERRARA, Hania .... 201-692-2381 277 K
ferrara@fdu.edu
FERRARA, Maria .... 201-447-7236 275 H
mferrara@bergen.edu
FERRARA, Michael .... 603-862-1178 274 G
mike.ferrara@unh.edu
FERRARA, Victoria .... 914-674-3094 306 F
vferrara@mercy.edu
FERRARE, Dino .... 805-898-4018.. 42 L
dferrare@fielding.edu
FERRARI, Cynthia .... 724-830-4639 398 H
ferrari@setonhill.edu
FERRARI, John .... 305-821-3333.. 99 E
jferrari@fnu.edu
FERRARI, Loretta .... 212-229-5860 308 C
ferraril@newschool.edu
FERRARI, Susan .... 641-269-4983 165 J
ferraris@grinnell.edu
FERRARO, Johnathan .... 419-434-4749 363 A
ferraro@findlay.edu
FERRARO, Michael .... 212-217-4018 299 H
michael_ferraro@fitnyc.edu
FERRATO, Christy .... 505-566-3299 288 A
ferratoc@sanjuancollege.edu
FERRAUILO-DAVIS,
Mary-Jo .... 518-736-3622 300 F
mferraui@fmcc.suny.edu
FERRAUILO-DAVIS,
Mary-Jo .... 518-736-3622 300 F
mary-jo.ferrauilo-davis@fmcc.suny.edu
FERRE, Loren .... 785-670-1794 177 G
loren.ferre@washburn.edu
FERREIRA, David .... 860-738-6319.. 86 C
dferreira@nwcc.edu
FERREIRA, Debora, D ... 413-545-3464 211 D
ferreira@admin.umass.edu
FERREIRA, Kenneth ...... 603-899-4186 273 F
ferreirak@franklinpierce.edu
FERREIRA, Lara .... 561-929-3405 107 E
admissions@sfbc.edu
FERREIRA, Lisa .... 619-961-4202.. 67 E
lisaf@tjsl.edu
FERREIRA, Milagros ..... 954-763-9840.. 94 L
registrar@atom.edu
FERREIRA, Paul .... 207-326-2419 195 D
paul.ferreira@mma.edu
FERREIRA, Robert .... 401-865-2407 405 B
rferreir@providence.edu
FERREL, Kathleen .... 715-365-4416 500 D
kferrel@nicoletcollege.edu
FERRELL, Amber .... 910-296-2400 335 E
aferrell@jamessprunt.edu
FERRELL, Danny .... 513-556-6001 362 D
danny.ferrell@uc.edu
FERRELL, David .... 620-241-0723 172 D
david.ferrell@centralchristian.edu
FERRELL, Justin, L .... 801-863-7575 461 A
justin.ferrell@uvu.edu
FERRELL, Martin .... 336-631-1561 343 D
ferrellm@uncsa.edu
FERRENCE, Steve .... 315-792-7100 321 E
sferrence@sunypoly.edu
FERRENTINO,
Robert, C .... 989-328-1221 228 A
bobf@montcalm.edu
FERRER, Alba .... 787-765-3560 507 L
aferrer@edpuniversity.edu
FERRER, Brunilda .... 787-264-1912 509 F
bferrer@intersg.edu
FERRER, Laura .... 787-864-2222 509 C
laura.ferrer@guayama.inter.edu
FERRER, Yolanda .... 787-834-9595 511 E
yferrer@uaa.edu
FERRER-MUNIZ, Karen . 518-629-7234 302 E
k.ferrermuniz@hvcc.edu
FERRERO, JR., Ray .... 954-262-7575 103 M
ferrero@nova.edu
FERRES, Steven .... 845-574-4770 313 C
sferres@sunyrockland.edu
FERRETTI, Anthony, J ... 941-756-0690 388 A
aferretti@lecom.edu
FERRETTI, Bruce, S .... 610-330-5375 387 E
ferrettb@lafayette.edu
FERRETTI, John, M .... 814-866-6641 388 A
hmckenzie@lecom.edu
FERRETTI, Kenneth, M .. 215-965-4007 390 J
kferretti@moore.edu
FERRETTI, Richard .... 814-666-6641 388 A
rferretti@lecom.edu
FERRETTI, Silvia, M ...... 814-866-6641 388 A
jzboyovski@lecom.edu
FERRETTI, Stephanie ..... 215-871-6486 396 D
stephanief@pcom.edu
FERRI, Bonnie .... 404-894-3145 118 F
bonnie.ferri@gatech.edu
FERRI, Donna Marie ..... 617-587-5678 217 A
ferrid@neco.edu
FERRICK, Courtney .... 914-633-2336 302 G
cferrick@iona.edu
FERRIER, Douglas, M ... 956-326-2400 446 F
douglas.ferrier@tamiu.edu
FERRIER, Michelle .... 850-599-3379 108 I
michelle.ferrierr@famu.edu
FERRIERA, Lara .... 954-637-2268 107 E
admissions@sfbc.edu
FERRIGAN, MaryAnn .... 989-275-5000 226 B
maryann.ferrigan@kirtland.edu
FERRIN, Kenton .... 714-556-3610.. 72 F
campussafety@vanguard.edu
FERRINI, Cynthia .... 909-469-8205.. 74 I
cferrini@westernu.edu
FERRINI-MUNDY, Joan . 207-581-1865 195 J
FERRIS, Adriaan .... 510-780-4500.. 47 J
aferris@lifewest.edu
FERRIS, Bill .... 206-543-9004 485 F
bferris@uw.edu
FERRIS, Diane, L .... 727-864-7761.. 97 J
ferrisdl@eckerd.edu
FERRIS, Jo .... 760-757-2121.. 52 E
jferris@miracosta.edu
FERRIS, John .... 619-594-4967.. 33 E
jferris@sdsu.edu
FERRIS, Mary .... 805-893-2251.. 70 A
mary.ferris@sa.ucsb.edu
FERRIS, Steve .... 765-285-5100 153 C
spferris@bsu.edu
FERRITTO, Joe .... 216-421-7314 350 M
jbferritto@cia.edu
FERRO, David .... 801-626-6303 461 B
dferro@weber.edu
FERRO, Deanna .... 315-731-5797 307 D
dferro@mvcc.edu
FERRO, Jennifer .... 310-450-4613.. 62 E
ferro_jennifer@smc.edu
FERRO, Lynn, P .... 717-815-1558 404 A
lferro@ycp.edu
FERRO, Robert .... 617-989-4557 219 E
ferrob@wit.edu
FERRO, Rosanna .... 607-274-3376 303 B
rferro@ithaca.edu
FERRUCCI, Rosemary .... 516-686-1081 309 F
rferrucc@nyit.edu
FERRUOLO, Stephen, C 619-260-4527.. 71 J
lawdean@sandiego.edu
FERRY, Patrick, T .... 262-243-5700 493 B
patrick.ferry@cuw.edu
FERRY, Richard, E .... 610-921-7825 378 C
rferry@albright.edu
FERRY, Tamara, R .... 262-243-5700 493 B
tamara.ferry@cuw.edu
FERSHEE, Joshua, P ..... 402-280-2874 266 I
joshuafershee@creighton.edu
FERULLO, Tony .... 978-232-2384 209 B
aferullo@endicott.edu
FERUS, Kenneth, S .... 401-456-8033 405 C
kferus@ric.edu
FESCOE, Michael .... 973-290-4498 277 A
mfescoe@cse.edu
FESER, Ed .... 541-737-2111 375 D
osu.provost@oregonstate.edu
FESKO, John .... 760-480-8474.. 74 J
jvfesko@wscal.edu
FESSENDEN, June, S .... 623-845-3406.. 13 C
june.fessenden@gccaz.edu
FESSLER, Bob .... 573-592-5372 262 E
bob.fessler@westminster-mo.edu
FESSLER, Brent .... 210-690-9000 437 E
bfessler@hallmarkuniversity.edu
FESSLER, Karen, P .... 570-326-3761 393 G
kfessler@pct.edu
FESSLER, Matthew .... 201-360-4131 278 C
mfessler@hccc.edu
FESTER, Rachel .... 646-660-6519 292 L
rachel.fester@baruch.cuny.edu
FETICK, Fay .... 314-529-9673 254 H
ffetick@maryville.edu
FETROW, Aaron, L .... 540-375-2592 471 B
fetrow@roanoke.edu
FETROW, Jacquelyn, S . 610-921-7600 378 C
jfetrow@albright.edu
FETSCH, Cindy .... 701-777-4156 345 C
cynthia.fetsch@und.edu
FETTER, Steve .... 301-405-5793 202 C
sfetter@umd.edu
FETTERMAN, Les .... 814-871-5678 384 E
FETTEROLF,
Bernadette, M .... 785-354-5853 170 I
bfetterolf@stormontvail.org
FETTERS, Luke .... 260-359-4008 155 F
lfetters@huntington.edu
FEUCHT-HAVIAR,
Joyce, A .... 818-677-4711.. 32 D
joyce.feucht-haviar@csun.edu
FEUDO, John .... 978-934-4814 211 G
john_feudo@uml.edu
FEUER, Avraham .... 732-367-1060 275 J
afeuer@bmg.edu
FEUER, Michael, J .... 202-994-6160.. 91 F
mjfeuer@gwu.edu
FEUERBORN, Matthew .. 320-234-8509 240 E
FEULING, Michael .... 503-838-8449 377 H
feulingm@wou.edu
FEUNE, David .... 650-574-6550.. 61 N
FEUSTEL, Paul .... 518-262-5339 289 F
feustep@amc.edu
FEUSTLE, Judith .... 443-352-4292 201 H
jfeustle@stevenson.edu
FEVIG, David .... 219-464-5304 162 A
david.fevig@valpo.edu
FEVOLA,
Christopher, N .... 516-299-3149 304 G
christopher.fevola@liu.edu
FEVOLA, Michael .... 516-299-2222 304 H
michael.fevola@liu.edu
FEW, Tamaria .... 417-836-6616 256 E
tammyfew@missouristate.edu
FEWOX, Keli .... 706-227-5375 114 F
kfewox@athenstech.edu
FEY, Jo .... 660-263-4100 257 B
jof@macc.edu
FEY-YENSAN, Nancy ..... 603-358-2112 275 A
nancy.fey-yensan@keene.edu
FEYEN, Deanna .... 979-532-6304 458 F
deannaf@wcjc.edu
FEYEN, Mike .... 979-532-6358 458 F
mikef@wcjc.edu
FEYERHERM, Dianne, E 254-299-8843 440 A
dfeyerherm@mclennan.edu
FEYERHERM, Katrina ..... 860-701-5045.. 87 D
feyerherm_k@mitchell.edu
FEYERHERM, Sarah .... 410-778-7752 204 D
sfeyerherm2@washcoll.edu
FEYTEN, Carine .... 940-898-3201 451 F
cfeyten@twu.edu
FIALA, Bill .... 626-815-2109.. 26 H
bfiala@apu.edu
FIALA, Kelly, A .... 410-548-2022 203 F
kafiala@salisbury.edu
FIALA, Lisa .... 904-819-6351.. 98 E
lfiala@flagler.edu
FICK, Steve .... 512-313-3000 434 E
steve.fick@concordia.edu
FICK, Verlyn .... 520-515-5414.. 11 M
fickv@cochise.edu
FICKEN, Bob .... 707-638-5200.. 67 F
bob.ficken@tu.edu
FICKEN-DAVIS, Amanda 619-388-6957.. 60 B
aficken@sdccd.edu
FICKENSCHER, II,
Carl, C .... 260-452-2131 154 E
carl.fickenscher@ctsfw.edu
FICO, Marie .... 585-385-8042 314 A
mfico@sjfc.edu
FIDATI, Brian .... 484-664-3110 391 C
brianfidati@muhlenberg.edu
FIDDELKE, Deb .... 402-472-0088 269 J
deb.fiddelke@unl.edu
FIDELI, Baycan .... 631-451-4212 321 F
fidelib@sunysuffok.edu
FIDLER-SHEPPARD,
Rebecca .... 856-227-7200 276 E
rsheppard@camdencc.edu
FIEBIG, Andrea .... 847-925-6371 137 H
afiebig@harpercollege.edu
FIEDLER, Scott .... 417-447-6903 257 G
fiedlers@otc.edu
FIEDLER, Thomas .... 617-353-3488 207 D
tfiedler@bu.edu
FIEDLER, Tristan .... 321-674-7723.. 99 B
fiedler@fit.edu

FINN, Kevin 248-204-4100 226 G
kfinn@ltu.edu

FINN, Laurie Ann 757-352-4036 470 H
lfinn@regent.edu

FINN, Mary Beth 801-883-8335 459 I
mfinn@new.edu

FINN, Nancy 617-585-0200 206 F
nancy.finn@the-bac.edu

FINN, Nathan 864-977-7011 411 E
nathan.finn@ngu.edu

FINN, Robert 207-454-1011 195 B
rfinn@wccc.me.edu

FINN, William 708-974-5727 144 C
finn@morainevalley.edu

FINNEGAN, Andrea 773-256-0784 142 G
andrea.finnegan@lstc.edu

FINNEGAN, John 612-625-1179 243 E
finne001@umn.edu

FINNEGAN, Paul, J 617-495-1000 210 B

FINNEGAN, Robert 802-828-2800 464 B
rjf12090@ccv.vsc.edu

FINNEGAN-HOSEY, David 252-399-6368 326 M
dfinneganhosey@barton.edu

FINNEL, Kristen 360-442-2651 482 B
kfinnel@lowercolumbia.edu

FINNEL, Kristin, M 920-924-3319 500 C
kfinnel@morainepark.edu

FINNELL, JoRene 831-646-4272.. 52 F
jfinnell@mpc.edu

FINNELLY, Ryan 210-999-8490 452 A
rfinnell@trinity.edu

FINNEMORE, Cathi 207-236-8581 195 E

FINNEN, Mary 646-660-6549 292 L
mary.finnen@baruch.cuny.edu

FINNERAN, Christina, M 207-725-3897 193 D
cfinnera@bowdoin.edu

FINNERTY, James, M 716-878-4324 318 C
finnerjm@buffalostate.edu

FINNERTY, Mary Beth 518-782-6818 315 J
mfinnerty@siena.edu

FINNERTY, Robert 585-475-4733 313 A
bob.finnerty@rit.edu

FINNEY, Andy 208-769-3266 131 C
andy_finney@nic.edu

FINNEY, George 214-768-3950 444 E
gfinney@smu.edu

FINNEY, Jack 540-231-2350 477 A
jfinney@vt.edu

FINNEY, Lesley, M 717-361-1445 383 E
finneylm@etown.edu

FINNEY, Maureen 716-829-7713 298 F
finneym@dyc.edu

FINNEY, Rebecca 707-668-5663.. 41 D
becca@dellarte.com

FINNEY, Sarah 206-296-6390 484 F
sfinney@seattleu.edu

FINNEY, Terry 870-972-2398.. 17 G
tfinney@astate.edu

FINNIE, David, A 937-775-2056 364 I
david.finnie@wright.edu

FINNIN, Meredith 212-752-1530 304 D
meredith.finnin@limcollege.edu

FINNING, Shannon 508-999-8640 211 F
sfinning@umassd.edu

FINNKENNEY, Rebecca 610-796-8221 378 F
rebecca.finnkenney@alvernia.edu

FINO, Mike 760-757-2121.. 52 E
mfino@miracosta.edu

FINOCH, Todd 314-446-8402 259 B
todd.finoch@stlcop.edu

FINSTUEN, Andrew 208-426-1205 129 I
andrewfinstuen@boisestate.edu

FINTON, Tabby 612-343-4743 242 H
tjfinton@northcentral.edu

FINUF, Danny, D 304-326-1522 488 F
dan.finuff@salemu.edu

FIOCHETTA, Joseph 570-484-2083 395 B
jfiochetta@lockhaven.edu

FIORAVANTI, Emil 508-999-8106 211 F
efioravanti@umassd.edu

FIORE, Douglas, J 515-643-6601 168 A
dfiore@mercydesmoines.org

FIORE, Maria 703-993-4739 467 L
mfiore1@gmu.edu

FIORE CONTE, Johann 607-777-2221 316 E
jmfconte@binghamton.edu

FIORELLA, Cynthia 270-686-4445 182 B
cindy.fiorella@kctcs.edu

FIORELLO, Christopher 703-284-1615 469 C
chris.fiorello@marymount.edu

FIORENTINO, Chris 610-436-6973 396 A
cfiorentino@wcupa.edu

FIORENZA, Anthony 305-237-2867 103 D
afiorenz@mdc.edu

FIORENZA, Jennifer 863-297-1000 105 A
jfiorenza@polk.edu

FIORI, Christopher 781-280-3292 214 G
fioric@middlesex.mass.edu

FIREMAN, Gary 617-305-6368 219 A
gfireman@suffolk.edu

FIRESTONE, Douglas 717-901-5100 385 K
dfirestone@harrisburgu.edu

FIRESTONE, Elizabeth, E 865-694-6457 425 F
eefirestone@pstcc.edu

FIRESTONE, Lauren, A 717-544-9051 384 D
lauren.firestone@fandm.edu

FIRMIN, RET., Lisa, C 210-458-6097 455 E
lisa.firmin@utsa.edu

FIRMIN, Sally 254-710-8696 431 J
sally_firmin@baylor.edu

FIRTH, Ann, M 574-631-9164 161 C
firth.2@nd.edu

FISCHER, Alex 718-817-3085 300 E
afischer9@fordham.edu

FISCHER, Andrew 734-384-4202 227 G
afischer@monroeccc.edu

FISCHER, Barry 212-217-3560 299 H
barry_fischer@fitnyc.edu

FISCHER, Beth 336-334-3876 343 A
beth.fischer@uncg.edu

FISCHER, Bruce 618-545-3173 140 E
bfischer@kaskaskia.edu

FISCHER, Dwight 315-498-2183 311 B
d.w.fischer@sunyocc.edu

FISCHER, Emily 626-395-1462.. 29 C
efischer@caltech.edu

FISCHER, OSU, Helena 270-686-4248 179 D
helena.fischer@brescia.edu

FISCHER, Howard 602-749-5120 176 D
howard.fischer@ottawa.edu

FISCHER, Jacqueline 660-263-4100 257 B
jackiefischer@macc.edu

FISCHER, Katie, J 651-641-8735 235 F
laviolette@csp.edu

FISCHER, Luke 319-895-4133 164 B
lfischer@cornellcollege.edu

FISCHER, Mark, T 585-275-3340 323 J
mfische8@ur.rochester.edu

FISCHER, Marsha 573-884-3222 261 A
fischermb@umsystem.edu

FISCHER, Megan 605-367-4624 417 D
megan.fischer@southeasttech.edu

FISCHER, Melissa 614-825-6255 347 F
mfischer@aiam.edu

FISCHER, Paige 580-327-8533 367 E
plfischer@nwosu.edu

FISCHER, Patty 573-875-7260 251 F
pafischer@ccis.edu

FISCHER, Rachel 920-686-6278 496 A
rachel.fischer@sl.edu

FISCHER, JR., Robert, U 615-898-2613 422 H
bud.fischer@mtsu.edu

FISCHER, Samuel 718-302-7500 326 F

FISCHER, Stacy 973-408-3047 277 C
sfischer@drew.edu

FISCHER, Timothy 602-386-4105.. 10 E
tim.fischer@arizonachristian.edu

FISCHER, Tracy 414-410-4266 492 D
tfischer@stritch.edu

FISCHER, Tracy, A 414-410-4266 492 D
tafischer@stritch.edu

FISCHER, William, M 937-229-3682 362 G
wfischer1@udayton.edu

FISCHER-FREE, Todd 815-226-3385 147 G
tfree@rockford.edu

FISCHER-FREE, Todd 815-226-3385 147 G
tfischer-free@rockford.edu

FISCUS, Tricia 541-880-2351 373 E
fiscus@klamathcc.edu

FISCUS, Wendy 607-735-1750 299 D
wfiscus@elmira.edu

FISH, H. Woodrow 704-406-4254 329 A
hwfish@gardner-webb.edu

FISH, Jacqueline 843-863-7504 407 E
jfish@csuniv.edu

FISH, Jennifer, N 757-683-4903 469 G
jfish@odu.edu

FISH, Robb 715-422-5327 500 A
robb.fish@mstc.edu

FISHBACK, Bill 325-649-8012 438 D
bfishback@hputx.edu

FISHBACK, Lauren 559-730-3921.. 39 E
laurenfi@cos.edu

FISHBONE, Alexis 978-556-3615 215 C
afishbone@necc.mass.edu

FISHEL, Teresa 651-696-6343 236 H
fishel@macalester.edu

FISHER, Amy 479-524-7128.. 19 H
afisher@jbu.edu

FISHER, Andrew 507-222-4300 234 F
afisher@carleton.edu

FISHER, Andrew 940-668-4234 441 A
afisher@nctc.edu

FISHER, Anne, E 941-487-4254 109 D
fisher@ncf.edu

FISHER, Anthony 912-525-5000 123 G
afisher@scad.edu

FISHER, Barrett 651-638-6083 234 C
fisbar@bethel.edu

FISHER, Barry 620-450-2179 176 G
barryf@prattcc.edu

FISHER, Beth 901-722-3285 424 C
bfisher@sco.edu

FISHER, Brian 239-590-1786 108 K
bfisher@fgcu.edu

FISHER, Brock 815-455-8561 143 A
bfisher@mchenry.edu

FISHER, Brock 201-447-7100 275 H

FISHER, Bryan 479-968-0400.. 18 C
pfisher1@atu.edu

FISHER, Bryan 479-968-0674.. 18 C
pfisher1@atu.edu

FISHER, Courtney 870-762-3105.. 17 D
cfisher@smail.anc.edu

FISHER, Craig 325-674-4985 429 B
cdf11a@acu.edu

FISHER, Dalene 918-335-6217 368 G
dfisher@okwu.edu

FISHER, David 918-540-6233 366 I
dfisher@neo.edu

FISHER, David, A 864-242-5100 407 B

FISHER, Dawn 940-397-4787 440 F
dawn.fisher@msutexas.edu

FISHER, Dianna, L 657-278-2586.. 31 E
difisher@fullerton.edu

FISHER, D'Andre 206-934-3655 483 J
dandre.fisher@seattlecolleges.edu

FISHER, Ed 202-885-2167.. 90 J
edfisher@american.edu

FISHER, Edward 714-872-5692.. 51 A
efisher@ketchum.edu

FISHER, Elisa 704-461-6895 327 A
elisafisher@bac.edu

FISHER, Ellen 212-472-1500 309 I
efisher@nysid.edu

FISHER, Emily 501-812-2366.. 23 B
efisher@uaptc.edu

FISHER, Glenn, R 570-577-1921 379 F
glenn.fisher@bucknell.edu

FISHER, Gloria 817-515-5777 445 G
gloria.fisher@tccd.edu

FISHER, Hilry 212-817-7523 293 F
hfisher@gc.cuny.edu

FISHER, Howard 903-927-0183 458 G
hlfisher@wileyc.edu

FISHER, Jane 516-877-3220 289 C
fisher2@adelphi.edu

FISHER, Jay 931-598-1142 423 M
jafisher@sewanee.edu

FISHER, Jeff 616-988-3678 226 C
jfisher@kuyper.edu

FISHER, Jennifer, L 304-293-8531 491 C
jennifer.fisher@mail.wvu.edu

FISHER, Jeremy, M 402-280-3819 266 I
jfisher@creighton.edu

FISHER, Joseph, B 210-690-9000 437 E
jfisher@hallmarkuniversity.edu

FISHER, Joy 310-233-4033.. 49 A
fisherjp@lahc.edu

FISHER, Joy 208-885-4000 131 G
joyfish@uidaho.edu

FISHER, Judith 269-471-3470 221 B
jfisher@andrews.edu

FISHER, Julie 773-896-2400 133 L
julie.fisher@ctschicago.edu

FISHER, Karla 480-731-8164.. 12 O
karla.fisher@domail.maricopa.edu

FISHER, Katie 828-328-7247 330 F
katie.fisher@lr.edu

FISHER, Kelly 978-232-2328 209 B
kfisher@endicott.edu

FISHER, Kevin 859-233-8889 184 G
kfisher@transy.edu

FISHER, Kristie 641-752-7106 166 K

FISHER, Kristie 641-844-5720 166 I
kristie.fisher@iavalley.edu

FISHER, L. Dean 607-962-9264 320 F
lfisher6@corning-cc.edu

FISHER, Lee 216-687-2300 351 B
l.fisher@law.csuohio.edu

FISHER, Linda 916-660-7605.. 63 I
lfisher@sierracollege.edu

FISHER, Marc 510-642-3507.. 68 D

FISHER, Maurissa 503-330-5012 374 B
maurissa.fisher@mtangel.edu

FISHER, Michael 440-525-7788 355 H
mfisher@lakelandcc.edu

FISHER, Michael 858-785-1458 300 B
michael.fisher@flcc.edu

FISHER, Michael 541-383-7238 372 B
mfisher@cocc.edu

FISHER, Nevan 585-389-2370 308 B
nfisher2@naz.edu

FISHER, Ocie 903-593-8311 448 H
ofisher@texascollege.edu

FISHER, P. Brian 843-953-7532 408 E
fisherb@cofc.edu

FISHER, Patti, J 574-807-7625 153 E
patti.fisher@bethelunivesity.edu

FISHER, Rebecca 877-248-6724.. 12 L
rfisher@hmu.edu

FISHER, Robert 317-931-2318 154 C
rfisher@cts.edu

FISHER, Robert 507-457-6658 243 B
rfisher@smumn.edu

FISHER, Robert, C 615-460-6793 418 F
bob.fisher@belmont.edu

FISHER, Susan 814-262-3833 393 H
sfisher@pennhighlands.edu

FISHER, Tabor 315-445-4256 304 C
fisherct@lemoyne.edu

FISHER, Thomas 574-520-4207 157 A
fishert@iu.edu

FISHER, Tiffany 574-936-8898 153 A
tiffany.fisher@ancilla.edu

FISHER, Timothy 860-570-5127.. 88 E
timothy.fisher@uconn.edu

FISHER, Tom 505-323-9282 457 J
twfisher@wbu.edu

FISHER, William 978-468-7111 209 G
wfisher@gcts.edu

FISHER, Witney 864-592-4051 412 F
fisherw@sccsc.edu

FISHER-BAMMER, Doreen 717-221-1309 385 E
dmfisher@hacc.edu

FISHMAN, David 845-406-4308 325 H

FISHMAN, Joan, R 212-431-2850 309 G
joan.fishman@nyls.edu

FISHMAN, Yisroel 718-645-0536 307 C

FISHNER, Carrie, J 607-746-4635 320 G
fishnecj@delhi.edu

FISHSTEIN, Janet 781-239-5840 205 E
jfishstein@babson.edu

FISK, Cheryl 952-446-4172 235 G
fiskc@crown.edu

FISK, Deanna 815-280-2701 140 B
dfisk@jjc.edu

FISK, Francine, J 918-631-2495 371 E
francine-fisk@utulsa.edu

FISK, Gerald 716-673-3101 317 A
gerald.fisk@fredonia.edu

FISK, Janessa 724-266-3838 400 H
janessa.fisk@tsm.edu

FISKAA, Evelyn 845-848-4032 298 D
evelyn.fiskaa@dc.edu

FISKE, Joshua, A 315-268-6718 296 A
jfiske@clarkson.edu

FISSINGER, Matthew, X 310-338-2750.. 50 J
mfissing@lmu.edu

FISTER, Cherie 314-529-9563 254 H
cfister@maryville.edu

FISTER, K. Renee 270-809-2491 183 G
kfister@murraystate.edu

FISTER-TUCKER, Mary 859-257-2956 185 B
mary.fister@uky.edu

FITCH, CD 620-862-5252 171 B
cd.fitch@barclaycollege.edu

FITCH, Gene 972-883-6236 455 B
gene.fitch@utdallas.edu

FITCH, James 814-332-2381 378 D
jfitch@allegheny.edu

FITCH, James 940-668-4271 441 A
jfitch@nctc.edu

FITCH, Jerome, H 803-535-5549 407 G
jfitch@claflin.edu

FITCH, Marilyn .... 919-573-5350 340 F mfitch@shepherds.edu
FITCH, Megan .... 610-896-2958 385 L mfitch@haverford.edu
FITCH, Michelle .... 712-279-3503 169 B michelle.fitch@stlukescollege.edu
FITCH, Poppy .... 858-513-9240.. 26 G poppy.fitch@ashford.edu
FITE-MORGAN, Amber .. 256-765-4487.... 8 E afitemorgan@una.edu
FITHIAN, David, B .... 773-702-2305 150 J fithian@uchicago.edu
FITSIMMONS, Gary, N .. 423-775-7196 418 H gary.fitsimmons@bryan.edu
FITTA, Kevin, J .... 401-456-9885 405 C kfitta@ric.edu
FITTERLING, Lori .... 816-654-7262 254 C lfitterling@kcumb.edu
FITTS, Alex .... 907-474-7980.. 10 A affitts@alaska.edu
FITTS, Bev .... 503-517-1031 377 G bfitts@warnerpacific.edu
FITTS, Michael, A .... 504-865-5201 191 B maf@tulane.edu
FITZ, Franzetta .... 850-599-3460 108 I franzetta.fitz@famu.edu
FITZ, SM, James, F ...... 937-229-2899 362 G jfitz1@udayton.edu
FITZGERALD, Annette .... 802-322-1671 462 C annette.fitzgerald@goddard.edu
FITZGERALD, Barrie, D . 229-333-7836 126 G bdfitzgerald@valdosta.edu
FITZGERALD, Brian .... 603-456-2656 274 A bfitzgerald@northeastcatholic.edu
FITZGERALD, Ed .... 618-252-5400 149 C eddie.fitzgerald@sic.edu
FITZGERALD, Ed .... 765-973-8422 156 C efitzger@iue.edu
FITZGERALD, Erin .... 860-723-0013.. 84 H fitzgeralde@ct.edu
FITZGERALD, Erin .... 401-341-3108 406 A erin.fitzgerald@salve.edu
FITZGERALD, Faith, M .. 757-823-8407 469 F fmfitzgerald@nsu.edu
FITZGERALD, Frank .... 540-231-1216 477 A fitzgera@vt.edu
FITZGERALD, Glynis ..... 610-796-8340 378 F glynis.fitzgerald@alvernia.edu
FITZGERALD, Gregory ... 410-532-5109 201 B gfitzgerald@ndm.edu
FITZGERALD, Hiram, E . 517-353-8977 227 D fitzger9@msu.edu
FITZGERALD, Ione .... 312-461-0600 132 A ifitzgerald@aaart.edu
FITZGERALD, Jamie .... 253-833-9111 481 F jfitzgerald@greenriver.edu
FITZGERALD, Joanne .... 585-389-2070 308 B jfitzge0@naz.edu
FITZGERALD, Margaret . 701-231-8211 345 G margaret.fitzgerald@ndsu.edu
FITZGERALD, Marty ...... 773-371-5400 133 E mfitzgerald@ctu.edu
FITZGERALD, Nathan .... 509-559-2445 480 E nfitzgerald1@ewu.edu
FITZGERALD, Paul .... 814-868-9900 383 F paulf@erieit.edu
FITZGERALD, SJ, Paul, J .... 415-422-6762.. 71 K pjfitzgerald@usfca.edu
FITZGERALD, Paula .... 440-646-8327 363 G paula.fitzgerald@ursuline.edu
FITZGERALD, Robert, F . 401-863-2500 404 E robert_fitzgerald@brown.edu
FITZGERALD, Ryan .... 806-716-2341 443 I rfitzgerald@southplainscollege.edu
FITZGERALD, Scott .... 614-823-0113 360 A sfitzgerald@otterbein.edu
FITZGERALD, Susan ...... 860-768-4011.. 88 H fitzgeral@hartford.edu
FITZGERALD, Teresa ..... 786-331-1000 103 G tfitzgerald@maufl.edu
FITZGERALD, Thomas ... 617-850-1212 210 D tfitzgerald@hchc.edu
FITZGERALD, JR., Walter, L .... 208-282-2175 130 H fitzwalt@isu.edu
FITZGERALD-BOCARSLY, Patricia .... 973-972-5233 282 A bocarsly@njms.rutgers.edu
FITZGIBBON, Cecelia .... 215-965-4000 390 J cfitzgibbon@moore.edu
FITZGIBBON, James ..... 510-231-5000.. 46 J james.x.fitzgibbon@kp.org
FITZGIBBONS, Courtney .... 212-431-2859 309 G courtney.fitzgibbons@nyls.edu
FITZGIBBONS, SJ, John, P .... 303-458-4190.. 82 E president@regis.edu
FITZHUGH, Keena .... 215-785-0111 393 C
FITZMAURICE, Patricia .. 212-752-1530 304 D patricia.fitzmaurice@limcollege.edu
FITZPATRICK, Colleen ... 802-443-3177 462 H cfitzpatrick@middlebury.edu
FITZPATRICK, Daniel ..... 304-384-5276 490 A dfitzpatrick@concord.edu
FITZPATRICK, Holly ...... 413-775-1813 214 C fitzpatrickh@gcc.mass.edu
FITZPATRICK, James, D 203-254-4000.. 86 I jfitzpatrick@fairfield.edu
FITZPATRICK, Jane .... 606-783-2053 183 F j.fitzpatrick@moreheadstate.edu
FITZPATRICK, Kenneth .. 209-476-7840.. 66 G kfitzpatrick@clc.edu
FITZPATRICK, Laura ...... 432-264-5009 438 C lfitzpatrick@howardcollege.edu
FITZPATRICK, SC, Margaret, M .... 845-398-4013 315 B mfitzpat@stac.edu
FITZPATRICK, Mark .... 212-229-5300 308 C fitzpame@newschool.edu
FITZPATRICK, Mary Anne .... 803-777-4621 413 C fitzpatm@mailbox.sc.edu
FITZPATRICK, Michael .. 620-450-2175 176 G michaelf@prattcc.edu
FITZPATRICK, Paula, A . 508-767-7550 205 D pfitzpat@assumption.edu
FITZPATRICK, Ralph ...... 502-852-6026 185 C ralph.fitzpatrick@louisville.edu
FITZPATRICK, Sharon ... 405-945-3292 368 E shfitzp@osuokc.edu
FITZPATRICK, Susan ..... 906-635-2831 226 E sfitzpatrick@lssu.edu
FITZPATRICK, Tamara ... 209-476-7840.. 66 G tfitzpatrick@clc.edu
FITZPATRICK, Thomas .. 916-577-2200.. 75 B tfitzpatrick@jessup.edu
FITZPATRICK, Timothy, J .... 352-273-1325 109 F timf@ufl.edu
FITZPATRICK, Tracy ...... 914-251-6105 319 E tracy.fitzpatrick@purchase.edu
FITZSIMMONS, Joanne . 518-445-2324 289 E jfitz@albanylaw.edu
FITZSIMMONS, Katie ..... 701-328-4109 345 B katie.fitzsimmons@ndus.edu
FITZSIMMONS, Linda .... 207-454-1033 195 B lfitzsimmons@wccc.me.edu
FITZSIMMONS, Stephanie .... 732-224-2369 276 B sfitzsimmons@brookdalecc.edu
FITZSIMMONS, Tracy .... 540-665-4505 471 E tfitzsim@su.edu
FIVECOAT, Frederick ..... 610-892-1519 393 J ffivecoat@pit.edu
FIXEN, Randall .... 701-662-1518 346 D randy.fixen@lrsc.edu
FLAA, Carol .... 701-224-5519 346 B carol.flaa@bismarckstate.edu
FLACK, Anna .... 631-451-4008 321 F flacka@sunysuffolk.edu
FLACK, Felecia, J .... 906-227-1272 228 F fflack@nmu.edu
FLACK, Lisa .... 217-228-5432 146 F flackli@quincy.edu
FLACK, Tamala .... 315-228-7014 296 F tflack@colgate.edu
FLACK, Toney .... 316-978-3919 178 A toney.flack@wichita.edu
FLADELAND, Diane .... 701-355-8140 347 D dflade@umary.edu
FLADRY, Robert .... 303-753-6046.. 82 F rfladry@rmcad.edu
FLAGEL, Jennifer .... 781-891-2740 206 D jflagel@bentley.edu
FLAGG, Chuck, S .... 248-232-4811 229 A csflagg@oaklandcc.edu
FLAGGERT, James .... 703-539-6890 472 A jflaggert@stratford.edu
FLAGSTAD, Lois .... 605-642-6599 416 I lois.flagstad@bhsu.edu
FLAGSTAD, Paul .... 952-446-4152 235 G flagstadp@crown.edu
FLAHERTY, Amy .... 808-245-8230 129 C
FLAHERTY, John .... 212-817-7769 293 F jflaherty@gc.cuny.edu
FLAHERTY, Kathryn .... 843-857-4227 408 D kflaherty@coker.edu
FLAHERTY, Mary .... 585-594-6533 312 K flahertym@roberts.edu
FLAHERTY, Michael .... 315-312-2106 319 B michael.flaherty@oswego.edu
FLAHERTY, Pamela, B ... 781-280-3631 214 G flahertyp@middlesex.mass.edu
FLAMER, Keith .... 707-476-4170.. 39 D keith-flamer@redwoods.edu
FLAMER, Latonya .... 336-517-2115 327 B lflamer@bennett.edu
FLAMER, Thelma .... 301-243-2178 503 J thelma.flamer@dodiis.mil
FLAMINIO, Becca .... 630-844-5475 132 D bflaminio@aurora.edu
FLAMM, Adele .... 302-736-2566.. 90 G adele.flamm@wesley.edu
FLAMM, Andrew, R .... 574-372-5100 155 B drew.flamm@grace.edu
FLAMMER, Rachel .... 716-827-4348 323 D flammerr@trocaire.edu
FLANAGAN, Erin .... 619-388-3453.. 60 C eflanaga@sdccd.edu
FLANAGAN, Hilary .... 206-220-6088 484 F hflanagan@seattleu.edu
FLANAGAN, J. Kelly ..... 801-422-3142 458 H kelly_flanagan@byu.edu
FLANAGAN, James .... 212-247-3434 305 G jflanagan@mandl.edu
FLANAGAN, James, L ... 770-484-1204 121 D vanessa@lutherrice.edu
FLANAGAN, James, P ... 603-641-6025 274 C jflanagan@anselm.edu
FLANAGAN, John .... 510-642-3414.. 68 D jgflanagan@berkeley.edu
FLANAGAN, Jon .... 414-443-8826 498 O jon.flanagan@wlc.edu
FLANAGAN, Joseph ...... 716-375-2375 313 F jflan@sbu.edu
FLANAGAN, Lori .... 314-516-5661 261 D flanagamlo@umsl.edu
FLANAGAN, Mary Jane . 989-774-3131 222 C flana1mj@cmich.edu
FLANAGAN, Maureen .... 215-574-9600 386 B maureen.flanagan@hussiancollege.edu
FLANAGAN, Melissa ..... 770-962-7580 120 E mflanagan@gwinnetttech.edu
FLANAGAN, Paige, S .... 570-321-4082 389 E flanagan@lycoming.edu
FLANAGAN, Scott .... 608-663-2262 493 C sflanagan@edgewood.edu
FLANAGAN, Wendy .... 417-873-7276 252 F wflanagan@drury.edu
FLANDERS, Lorene .... 251-460-7021.... 8 F lflanders@southalabama.edu
FLANIGAN, Alyce .... 256-352-8295.... 4 A alyce.malcolm@wallacestate.edu
FLANIGAN, Karen .... 480-988-8884.. 12 P karen.flanigan@cgc.edu
FLANIGAN, JR., Robert, D .... 404-270-5072 125 B rflaniga@spelman.edu
FLANIGAN, Rod .... 520-515-4516.. 11 M flaniganr@cochise.edu
FLANIGAN, Virginia ...... 973-877-3056 277 I vflaniga@essex.edu
FLANIK, Greg, G .... 440-826-2700 348 E gflanik@bw.edu
FLANNERY, Brenda .... 507-389-9423 239 C brenda.flannery@mnsu.edu
FLANNERY, Chad .... 618-252-5400 149 C chad.flannery@sic.edu
FLANNERY, Christopher 419-289-5413 348 A cflanner@ashland.edu
FLANNERY, John .... 608-246-6052 499 H jflannery1@madisoncollege.edu
FLANNERY, Kathleen ..... 620-235-4769 176 F kflannery@pittstate.edu
FLANNERY, Kim .... 262-595-2301 497 C bookstore@uwp.edu
FLANNERY, Patrick .... 517-607-2239 225 A pflannery@hillsdale.edu
FLANNERY, Patrick .... 570-577-3775 379 F patrick.flannery@bucknell.edu
FLASCHNER, Maura ...... 706-667-4946 115 A mflaschner@augusta.edu
FLASH, Kevin .... 916-558-2254.. 50 I flashk@scc.losrios.edu
FLATEBY, Teresa .... 912-478-2482 119 C tflateby@georgiasouthern.edu
FLATEN, Mike .... 218-262-6749 238 C mikeflaten@hibbing.edu
FLATLEY, Kate .... 314-889-1447 253 C kflatley@fontbonne.edu
FLATZ, Connor .... 914-968-6200 314 E
FLAUGHER, Amanda ..... 989-317-4760 230 A aflaugher@sagchip.edu
FLAVIN, Stephen, P ...... 508-831-5095 220 E sflavin@wpi.edu
FLAX-HYMAN, Cheryl, L .... 850-747-3215 100 N cflax-hyman@gulfcoast.edu
FLAYTON, Brad .... 605-331-6575 417 E brad.flayton@usiouxfalls.edu
FLEAGLE, Steven, R ...... 319-384-0595 163 A steve-fleagle@uiowa.edu
FLECK, Lauren .... 410-287-1087 197 H lfleck@cecil.edu
FLECK, Theresa .... 636-227-2100 254 G
FLEEGER, Christina, M . 724-287-8711 380 A tina.fleeger@bc3.edu
FLEEGER, Christina, M . 724-287-8711 380 A christine.fleeger@bc3.edu
FLEENER, Katie .... 559-453-7121.. 43 G katie.fleener@fresno.edu
FLEENOR, James .... 478-757-5140 126 H jfleenor@wesleyancollege.edu
FLEENOR, Rick .... 606-539-4154 185 A rick.fleenor@ucumberlands.edu
FLEETWOOD, Nick .... 619-596-2766.. 24 F nfleetwood@advancedtraining.edu
FLEISCHER, Amy .... 805-756-2132.. 30 C afleisch@calpoly.edu
FLEISCHER, Sheila .... 516-239-9002 315 I sfleischer@shoryoshuv.org
FLEISCHER ROWLAND, Theresa .... 925-485-5244.. 35 N
FLEISCHMAN, Linda ...... 704-337-2543 339 G fleischmanl@queens.edu
FLEISCHMAN, Robert .... 507-389-5567 239 C robert.fleischman@mnsu.edu
FLEISCHMANN, Anne .... 916-660-8000.. 63 I afleischmann@sierracollege.edu
FLEISCHMANN, Kenneth .... 314-367-8700 259 B kenneth.fleischmann@stlcop.edu
FLEISHER, Greg, E .... 443-518-4644 199 C gfleisher@howardcc.edu
FLEITAS, Dionisio .... 214-333-5481 434 I dionisio@dbu.edu
FLEMING, Alicia .... 773-235-5572 147 B alicia.fleming@resu.edu
FLEMING, Allyson .... 615-327-6235 422 A afleming@mmc.edu
FLEMING, Amanda .... 910-962-3122 343 C flemingac@uncw.edu
FLEMING, Andrea .... 419-251-2182 356 C andrea.fleming@mercycollege.edu
FLEMING, Angela .... 607-962-9458 320 F aflemin2@corning-cc.edu
FLEMING, Arkeem .... 229-430-4660 113 H al.fleming@asurams.edu
FLEMING, Candace, C .. 973-655-4040 279 C flemingc@mail.montclair.edu
FLEMING, Damon .... 901-678-3633 427 D dmflmng1@memphis.edu
FLEMING, David .... 269-782-1201 230 F dfleming@swmich.edu
FLEMING, David .... 540-654-1058 472 I dflemin3@umw.edu
FLEMING, Elizabeth ...... 413-565-1000 205 G lfleming@baypath.edu
FLEMING, Erika .... 305-428-5700 103 E efleming@aii.edu
FLEMING, Estefania, S .. 863-667-5253 107 K esfleming@seu.edu
FLEMING, J. Christopher .... 757-683-3685 469 G jcflemin@odu.edu
FLEMING, Jennifer .... 479-498-6020.. 18 C jfleming@atu.edu
FLEMING, John .... 512-245-2308 450 E jf18@txstate.edu
FLEMING, OP, John Mary .... 615-256-5486 418 C education@op-tn.org
FLEMING, Joshua .... 518-736-3622 300 F joshua.fleming@fmcc.suny.edu
FLEMING, Julie, C .... 770-720-5527 123 E jcf@reinhardt.edu
FLEMING, Justin .... 507-786-3615 243 C flemingj@stolaf.edu
FLEMING, Katherine ...... 212-998-3660 310 B katherine.fleming@nyu.edu
FLEMING, Kay .... 618-985-3741 139 I kayfleming@jalc.edu

FLEMING, Kevin .... 951-739-7880.. 58 H
kevin.fleming@norcocollege.edu
FLEMING, Kirsty .... 562-985-4128.. 31 F
kirsty.fleming@csulb.edu
FLEMING, Mark .... 973-655-5225 279 C
flemingm@mail.montclair.edu
FLEMING, Philip .... 714-484-7390.. 53 K
pfleming@cypresscollege.edu
FLEMING, Robert .... 617-824-8670 208 H
robert_fleming@emerson.edu
FLEMING, Saundra, K ... 773-878-4699 148 D
sfleming@staugustine.edu
FLEMING, Tawny .... 707-826-4273.. 33 D
tb36@humboldt.edu
FLEMING, Thomas, O ... 310-338-2738.. 50 J
tfleming@lmu.edu
FLEMING, Tracey .... 773-777-7900 134 G
tfleming22@ccc.edu
FLEMING, Tricia .... 610-526-6001 385 G
tfleming@harcum.edu
FLEMING, Wanda .... 601-877-6188 244 H
wcfleming@alcorn.edu
FLEMING, William, M ... 561-803-2001 104 C
william_fleming@pba.edu
FLEMING-RANDLE,
Marche .... 316-978-5932 178 A
marche.fleming-randle@wichita.edu
FLENIKEN, Tracey .... 940-668-4207 441 A
tfleniken@nctc.edu
FLENNER, Ronald, W .... 757-446-5829 466 I
flennerw@evms.edu
FLESCHNER, Julius .... 706-368-7732 118 E
jfleschn@highlands.edu
FLESHLER, David .... 216-368-2399 349 F
david.fleshler@case.edu
FLESNER, Brian .... 402-826-8228 267 A
brian.flesner@doane.edu
FLETCHER, Bill .... 502-852-4740 185 C
bill.fletcher@louisville.edu
FLETCHER, Carol .... 575-562-2611 285 M
carol.fletcher@enmu.edu
FLETCHER, Daryl .... 912-583-3230 115 E
dfletcher@bpc.edu
FLETCHER, David .... 334-291-4938.... 1 H
david.fletcher@cv.edu
FLETCHER, James .... 920-424-3030 497 B
fletcher@uwosh.edu
FLETCHER, Jennifer .... 304-473-8017 491 H
fletcher.j@wvwc.edu
FLETCHER, Jereial .... 276-964-7224 475 I
jereial.fletcher@sw.edu
FLETCHER, Jerrod .... 352-371-2833.. 97 G
clinicdirector@dragonrises.edu
FLETCHER, John .... 252-328-5817 341 C
fletcherjo@ecu.edu
FLETCHER, Kiely .... 312-996-5563 151 B
kfletch@uic.edu
FLETCHER, Lauronda ..... 610-399-2224 394 C
lfletcher@cheyney.edu
FLETCHER, Leah .... 816-584-6407 258 A
leah.fletcher@park.edu
FLETCHER, Linda .... 252-492-2061 338 F
fletcherl@vgcc.edu
FLETCHER, Martha .... 615-675-5264 428 G
mfletcher@welch.edu
FLETCHER, Pam .... 352-365-3351 102 T
fletchep@lssc.edu
FLETCHER, Randy .... 815-280-2246 140 B
rfletcher@jjc.edu
FLETCHER, Richard, L ... 440-826-2323 348 E
rfletche@bw.edu
FLETCHER, Rob .... 773-291-6143 134 E
FLETCHER, Scott .... 503-768-6001 373 G
graddean@lclark.edu
FLETCHER, Scott, H ...... 512-233-1436 442 M
scottf@stedwards.edu
FLETCHER, Thomas .... 570-389-5161 394 A
tfletche@bloomu.edu
FLETCHER, Tracee .... 713-942-9505 438 A
tfletcher@hgst.edu
FLETCHER, Wanda .... 252-335-0821 333 G
wanda_fletcher@albemarle.edu
FLEURISMOND, Jude ..... 845-574-4224 313 C
jfleuri2@sunyrockland.edu
FLEURY, Karl .... 715-425-3133 497 E
karl.fleury@uwrf.edu
FLICK, Chuch .... 540-568-3825 468 F
flickco@jmu.edu
FLICK, Kay .... 508-849-3228 205 C
kflick@annamaria.edu
FLICK, Matt .... 937-294-0592 356 H
matt.flick@themodern.edu
FLICK, Zeke .... 641-683-5282 166 C

FLICKEMA, Aubree .... 847-628-1572 140 C
aubree.flickema@judsonu.edu
FLICKER, John .... 928-350-4100.. 15 N
john.flicker@prescott.edu
FLICKER, Thomas .... 315-279-5217 304 A
help@keuka.edu
FLICKINGER, Catherine . 516-686-7792 309 F
catherine.flickinger@nyit.edu
FLIDER, Robert .... 217-300-5348 151 D
rfflider@illinois.edu
FLIGER, Jerry .... 409-933-8229 433 L
jfliger@com.edu
FLINDERS, Tracy .... 801-422-6101 458 H
tracyf@byu.edu
FLING, Corey .... 619-849-2583.. 57 E
coreyfling@pointloma.edu
FLINK, Sara .... 413-265-2447 208 C
flinks@elms.edu
FLINN, Cara .... 479-979-1467.. 23 I
cflinn@ozarks.edu
FLINN, Eileen .... 724-805-2897 398 F
eileen.flinn@stvincent.edu
FLINN, Steve .... 309-694-5512 138 C
steve.flinn@icc.edu
FLINT, Brenda .... 802-728-1000 464 E
bflint@vtc.edu
FLINT, Juanita .... 972-860-4694 434 L
juanitazf@dcccd.edu
FLINT, Mary Ann .... 601-643-8414 245 G
maryann.flint@colin.edu
FLINT, Michelle .... 508-793-4378 208 A
mflint@clarku.edu
FLINT, Tora .... 310-577-3000.. 75 G
registrar@yosan.edu
FLINT, Wendy .... 503-554-2332 373 C
wflint@georgefox.edu
FLINT-HAMILTON,
Kimberly .... 315-229-5011 314 F
kflint@stlawu.edu
FLINTJER, Nathan .... 845-451-1405 298 A
nathan.flintjer@culinary.edu
FLINTOFT, Rebecca .... 303-273-3050.. 78 I
rflintof@mines.edu
FLIPPO, Angela .... 870-759-4120.. 23 J
aflippo@williamsbu.edu
FLIPSE, Vanessa .... 785-628-4494 173 B
vmflipse@fhsu.edu
FLISS, Susan .... 413-585-2902 218 F
sfliss@smith.edu
FLOCK, Gretchen .... 724-805-2209 398 E
gretchen.flock@email.stvincent.edu
FLOCKEN, Lise .... 760-757-2121.. 52 E
lflocken@miracosta.edu
FLODEN, Robert .... 517-355-1734 227 D
floden@msu.edu
FLOOD, Malia .... 619-482-6369.. 65 F
mflood@swccd.edu
FLOOD, Malinali .... 559-934-2306.. 74 A
malinaliflood@whccd.edu
FLOOD, Thomas .... 718-489-5443 313 H
thomasflood@sfc.edu
FLOOD, Tim .... 760-757-2121.. 52 E
FLOOD, Tim .... 619-482-6310.. 65 F
tflood@swccd.edu
FLOOD, Tom .... 336-278-6549 328 K
tflood@elon.edu
FLOOD-WEINER,
Christie .... 614-253-3502 358 G
weinerc@ohiodominican.edu
FLOOR, Gregory .... 617-850-1285 210 D
gfloor@hchc.edu
FLORA, Bethany .... 423-279-7633 425 E
bhflora@northeaststate.edu
FLORA, David .... 606-783-9404 183 F
d.flora@moreheadstate.edu
FLORA, Kristen .... 317-738-8784 154 J
kflora@franklincollege.edu
FLORAK, Mike .... 740-284-5860 353 B
mflorak@franciscan.edu
FLOREA, Carleen .... 716-896-0700 324 E
cflorea@villa.edu
FLORENCE, Brad .... 563-876-3353 164 J
bflorence@dwci.edu
FLORENDO, Heather ..... 808-844-2310 129 B
heather.florendo@hawaii.edu
FLORENTINE, Dennis .... 908-835-2326 284 G
dflorentine@warren.edu
FLORES, Abraham .... 713-221-8685 453 B
floresa@uhd.edu
FLORES, Anna .... 480-517-8171.. 13 G
anna.flores@riosalado.edu
FLORES, Aubrey .... 775-784-4805 271 F
aubreyf@unr.edu

FLORES, Beatriz .... 787-753-6000 508 D
FLORES, Brian .... 713-221-8978 453 B
floresbr@uhd.edu
FLORES, Carmen .... 787-744-8519 507 K
cflores@ediccollege.edu
FLORES, Chio .... 509-682-6805 486 E
cflores@wvc.edu
FLORES, Dan .... 530-674-9199.. 34 H
FLORES, Daniel .... 321-674-7281.. 99 B
dflores@fit.edu
FLORES, Daniel .... 616-392-8555 233 E
dan.flores@westernsem.edu
FLORES, Deanna, L .... 407-303-1851.. 94 D
deanna.flores@ahu.edu
FLORES, Eddie .... 575-538-6321 289 B
flores4@wnmu.edu
FLORES, Elizabeth .... 616-632-2868 221 C
floreeli@aquinas.edu
FLORES, Esmarelda .... 210-434-6711 441 E
emflores@lake.ollusa.edu
FLORES, Fernando .... 915-831-6391 436 E
fflore63@epcc.edu
FLORES, Gustavo .... 707-664-4388.. 34 C
gustavo.flores@sonoma.edu
FLORES, Hector .... 409-880-8305 449 H
hector.flores@lamar.edu
FLORES, Javier .... 325-942-2047 451 A
javier.flores@angelo.edu
FLORES, Jorge .... 210-486-2505 429 G
flores375@alamo.edu
FLORES, Juan, S .... 915-831-7866 436 E
jflor242@epcc.edu
FLORES, Laureano .... 661-722-6300.. 26 D
lflores@avc.edu
FLORES, Lucinda .... 210-297-9638 431 E
lgflores@baptisthealthsystem.com
FLORES, Maria, E .... 787-743-7979 511 I
ut_mflores@suagm.edu
FLORES, Marilyn .... 714-628-4880.. 58 A
flores_marilyn@sccollege.edu
FLORES, Mary .... 208-792-2325 131 A
mflores@lcsc.edu
FLORES, Maureen, E ..... 781-891-2818 206 D
mflores@bentley.edu
FLORES, Mike .... 210-485-0020 429 C
rflores@alamo.edu
FLORES, Minerva .... 707-468-3011.. 51 E
mflores@mendocino.edu
FLORES, Nanette .... 413-755-4418 215 F
nflores@stcc.edu
FLORES, Ramon .... 540-444-4175 464 G
rflores@an.edu
FLORES, Ricardo .... 301-891-4000 204 C
FLORES, Ricardo .... 787-665-7910 507 K
riflores@ediccollege.edu
FLORES, Robert, E .... 863-453-6661 107 F
robert.flores@southflorida.edu
FLORES, Rolando .... 575-646-3748 287 B
rolflo@nmsu.edu
FLORES, Ruben .... 201-692-2250 277 K
ruben771_flores@fdu.edu
FLORES CHARTER,
Patricia .... 619-421-6700.. 65 F
pflores@swccd.edu
FLORES-CHURCH,
Adriana .... 562-860-2451.. 35 M
achurch@cerritos.edu
FLORES-LOPEZ, Brenda 423-236-2277 424 B
bfloreslopez@southern.edu
FLORES-MEDINA,
Donna .... 505-454-5328 286 D
dflores@luna.edu
FLORES-MILLS, Maria ... 704-337-2227 339 G
FLORES-SOTO, Yaly ...... 305-595-9500.. 94 B
dean@amcollege.edu
FLORESCA, Ann .... 270-745-2466 185 E
ann.floresca@wku.edu
FLOREY, Nancy .... 717-947-6098 393 F
neflorey@pacollege.edu
FLOREZ-NEVAREZ, Tina 254-519-8015 447 A
t.flores@tamuct.edu
FLORIAN, Greg, E .... 217-875-7200 147 C
gflorian@richland.edu
FLORIAN, James, S ...... 520-621-3680.. 16 G
florianj@email.arizona.edu
FLORIAN, Kelley .... 804-627-5300 465 C
kelley_florian@bshsi.org
FLOROS, John .... 575-646-2035 287 B
president.floros@nmsu.edu
FLORY, Julie, A .... 314-935-5408 262 A
julie.flory@wustl.edu
FLORY, Nathan .... 903-923-2137 436 D
nflory@etbu.edu

FLOT, Rob .... 323-259-2500.. 54 E
rflot@oxy.edu
FLOTKOETTER, Pauline . 406-874-6188 263 I
flotkoetterp@milescc.edu
FLOTRON, Rich .... 573-518-2341 256 B
rflotron@mineralarea.edu
FLOTTE, Terence, R .... 508-856-8000 212 A
terry.flotte@umassmed.edu
FLOUHOUSE, Steve .... 606-326-2055 180 I
steve.flouhouse@kctcs.edu
FLOURNOY, Carrie .... 318-257-3785 191 F
flournoy@latech.edu
FLOURNOY, Eric .... 706-385-1459 123 C
FLOURNOY, Jacob .... 361-593-2410 447 D
jacob.flournoy@tamuk.edu
FLOURNOY, Jacob, W .. 501-686-2901.. 21 F
jwflournoy@uasys.edu
FLOWER, Hannah .... 912-525-5000 123 G
hcrocket@scad.edu
FLOWER KIM, Laura ..... 626-395-6330.. 29 C
laura.flowerkim@caltech.edu
FLOWERS, Alisa .... 657-278-2998.. 31 E
aflowers@fullerton.edu
FLOWERS, Carol, A .... 404-727-0833 117 F
caflowe@emory.edu
FLOWERS, Gayle .... 318-678-6000 187 A
gflowers@bpcc.edu
FLOWERS, George .... 334-844-4700.... 4 E
flowegt@auburn.edu
FLOWERS, Kathleen ...... 315-781-3825 302 A
kflowers@hws.edu
FLOWERS, Ken .... 269-927-4103 226 D
flowers@lakemichigancollege.edu
FLOWERS, Laura .... 615-550-3168 429 A
laura@williamsoncc.edu
FLOWERS, Lisa .... 406-791-5295 265 H
lisa.flower@uprovidence.edu
FLOWERS, Madison ...... 617-745-3675 208 G
madison.flowers@enc.edu
FLOWERS, Marshall ...... 276-326-4355 465 B
mflowers@bluefield.edu
FLOWERS, Nicole .... 213-283-4218.. 36 F
nflowers@thechicagoschool.edu
FLOWERS, Patricia, J .... 850-644-0415 109 C
pjflowers@fsu.edu
FLOWERS, Robert .... 315-781-3827 302 A
flowers@hws.edu
FLOYD, Andrew .... 229-317-6725 113 H
andrew.floyd@asurams.edu
FLOYD, David .... 225-765-2437 188 I
dfloyd@lsu.edu
FLOYD, Dawn .... 828-328-7040 330 F
dawn.floyd@lr.edu
FLOYD, Gina .... 706-233-7205 124 B
gfloyd@shorter.edu
FLOYD, James, J .... 909-621-8351.. 37 E
james.floyd@cmc.edu
FLOYD, Krystal .... 334-727-8540.... 7 D
kfloyd@tuskegee.edu
FLOYD, Morris .... 316-942-4291 175 I
floydm@newmanu.edu
FLOYD, Polly, K .... 850-263-3261.. 95 B
pkfloyd@baptistcollege.edu
FLOYD, Shawnda .... 972-273-3590 435 E
shawndafloyd@dcccd.edu
FLOYD, Steven .... 405-585-5132 367 F
steven.floyd@okbu.edu
FLOYD, Stuart .... 864-977-7669 411 E
stuart.floyd@ngu.edu
FLOYD, Tony .... 828-689-1141 331 A
tony_floyd@mhu.edu
FLOYD, Wesley .... 662-720-7594 248 C
wcfloyd@nemcc.edu
FLOYD-SMITH, Tamara . 334-727-8953.... 7 D
tfloyd@tuskegee.edu
FLUCKEY, Kari .... 402-461-7300 267 D
kfluckey@hastings.edu
FLUECKIGER,
Joseph, T .... 413-542-2220 205 B
mflueckiger@amherst.edu
FLUET, Gregoire, J .... 845-569-3154 307 J
gregoire.fluet@msmc.edu
FLUGSTAD, Bjorn .... 928-523-4240.. 14 H
bjorn.flugstad@nau.edu
FLUGUM, Deborah .... 818-677-2301.. 32 D
deborah.flugum@csun.edu
FLUHARTY, Steven, J ... 215-898-7320 400 K
sasdean@sas.upenn.edu
FLUKE, Donald, W .... 574-372-5100 155 B
dwfluke@grace.edu
FLUKE, Lauri, A .... 405-585-5130 367 F
lauri.fluke@okbu.edu

FORD, Jermaine 337-521-9049 188 C jermaine.ford@solacc.edu
FORD, Jesse 617-670-4536 209 D jford02@fisher.edu
FORD, Kelsey 314-837-6777 258 J kford@stlchristian.edu
FORD, Kimberly 843-863-7050 407 E kcford@csuniv.edu
FORD, Kimberly 330-337-6403 347 E college@awc.edu
FORD, Kristie, A 518-580-5425 316 A kford@skidmore.edu
FORD, Lacy 803-777-7798 413 C ford@mailbox.sc.edu
FORD, Laura, C 309-794-7452 132 C lauraford@augustana.edu
FORD, Lisa 323-241-5200 49 D fordld@lasc.edu
FORD, Lynne, E 843-953-6531 408 E fordl@cofc.edu
FORD, Madeline 718-518-4211 294 B mford@hostos.cuny.edu
FORD, Mark, C 913-971-3614 175 G mford@mnu.edu
FORD, Mary Beth 412-396-2061 383 C fordmb@duq.edu
FORD, Michael 312-341-2322 147 H mford@roosevelt.edu
FORD, Nadine 919-536-7200 334 B fordn@durhamtech.edu
FORD, Nancy 620-365-5116 170 G ford@allencc.edu
FORD, Patrick 704-461-6545 327 A patrickford@bac.edu
FORD, Ricky, G 662-720-7730 248 C rgford@nemcc.edu
FORD, Robert 909-607-1554 37 D robert.ford@cgu.edu
FORD, Rochelle 336-278-5724 328 K rford9@elon.edu
FORD, Sharhonda 305-626-3102 99 D sharhonda.ford@fmuniv.edu
FORD, Shelly 601-928-6222 247 E shelly.ford@mgccc.edu
FORD, Sheree 407-265-8383 96 A
FORD, Sherry 970-943-7052 84 D sford@western.edu
FORD, Tracey 336-770-3283 343 D fordt@uncsa.edu
FORD, Tracey 615-963-5644 426 D tford@tnstate.edu
FORD, Tracey, D 419-783-2354 352 F tford@defiance.edu
FORD, Tracy 601-968-8840 245 C tford@belhaven.edu
FORD FISHER, Margaret 713-718-8011 437 I margaret.fordfisher@hccs.edu
FORD-KEE, Dianthia 662-254-3550 248 B dfkee@mvsu.edu
FORD MULLINS, Maquisha 256-726-8205 6 C mfordmullins@oakwood.edu
FORDE, Althea 718-960-8066 294 A althea.forde@lehman.cuny.edu
FORDE, Christopher 617-544-8657 138 H fordec@iecc.edu
FORDE, Dermot, M 419-372-9475 348 H dforde@bgsu.edu
FORDE, Nokoia 484-365-7275 389 C nforde@lincoln.edu
FORDE, Timothy 859-622-6587 180 B tim.forde@eku.edu
FORDHAM, Traci 971-722-4667 375 J traci.fordham@pcc.edu
FORDHAM, Tracy 941-377-4880 103 C tfordham@meridian.edu
FORDIS, JR., C. Michael 713-798-8256 431 I fordis@bcm.edu
FORE, Marilyn, J 843-349-5201 410 C marilyn.fore@hgtc.edu
FORE, Robert 415-439-2305 25 K rfore@act-sf.org
FOREE, Amy 870-612-2144 22 I amy.foree@uaccb.edu
FOREHAND, Cynthia, J 802-656-8060 463 E cynthia.forehand@uvm.edu
FOREMAN, Adam 601-484-8615 247 A tforeman@meridiancc.edu
FOREMAN, Artie 601-635-2111 245 I aforeman@eccc.edu
FOREMAN, Hank, T 828-262-2040 341 B foremanht@appstate.edu
FOREMAN, Kyle 509-793-2299 478 H kylef@bigbend.edu
FOREMAN, Margo 515-294-0143 162 I mrforma@iastate.edu
FOREMAN, Marquis, D 312-942-7117 148 A marquis_d_foreman@rush.edu
FOREMAN, Michelle 717-477-1475 395 E mtforeman@ship.edu
FOREMAN, Pamela, B 804-257-5821 477 C pforeman@vuu.edu
FOREMAN, Todd 518-956-8120 316 D todd.foreman@albany.edu
FOREST, Colleen 805-437-8537 30 F colleen.forest@csuci.edu
FOREST, John 918-270-6421 369 A john.forest@ptstulsa.edu
FOREST, Mark 609-771-2247 276 I forestm@tcnj.edu
FOREST, Rebecca 978-630-9597 215 A r_forest@mwcc.mass.edu
FOREST, Robert 610-647-4400 386 C rforest@immaculata.edu
FORESTER, Anne 206-934-4554 483 J anne.forester@seattlecolleges.edu
FORESTER, David 252-536-7213 335 B dforester@halifaxcc.edu
FORESTER, Robin 334-244-3676 4 F rforeste@aum.edu
FORESTER, Sherri, L 270-901-1115 182 D sherri.forester@kctcs.edu
FORGER, James 517-355-4583 227 D forger@msu.edu
FORGETTE, Adrienne 505-566-3217 288 A forgettea@sanjuancollege.edu
FORGEY, Glendon 620-227-9213 172 J gforgey@dc3.edu
FORGUES, David 657-278-8351 31 E dforgues@fullerton.edu
FORINA, Olga 718-517-7722 315 A oforina@edaff.com
FORISTER, J. Glenn 817-735-2762 454 C glenn.forister@unthsc.edu
FORKNER, Peter 781-891-2274 206 D pforkner@bentley.edu
FORLINES, Jon 615-675-5299 428 G jforlines@welch.edu
FORLINES, Susan 615-675-5259 428 G susan@welch.edu
FORMAN, Kristi 901-321-4208 419 C kforman@cbu.edu
FORMAN, Robert, J 718-990-7552 314 B formanj@stjohns.edu
FORMAN, Robin 504-865-5261 191 B rforman@tulane.edu
FORMAN, Scheherazade, W 301-546-0886 201 C formansw@pgcc.edu
FORMICA, Melinda 203-582-3735 87 G melinda.formica@quinnipiac.edu
FORMICA, Nick 216-373-5316 358 B nformica@ndc.edu
FORNERIS, Glenda 815-802-8835 140 D gforneris@kcc.edu
FORNERO, Sarah 312-662-4234 131 H sfornero@adler.edu
FORNEY, Heather 605-394-2373 417 B heather.forney@sdsmt.edu
FORNEY, Heather 605-394-2371 417 B heather.forney@sdsmt.edu
FORNEY, Heather 605-773-3455 416 G
FORNIERI, Diane, K 516-323-3204 307 F dfornieri@molloy.edu
FOROUDASTAN, Hooshang 434-381-6130 472 D hforoudastan@sbc.edu
FOROUDASTAN, Hooshang 434-381-6387 472 D hforoudastan@sbc.edu
FORREST, Anderson 610-372-4721 397 B aforrest@racc.edu
FORREST, Barbara 205-665-6055 8 D forrestb@montevallo.edu
FORREST, Christian 248-204-2204 226 G cforrest@ltu.edu
FORREST, Christy 336-249-8186 334 A clforrest@davidsonccc.edu
FORREST, Danae 585-567-9493 302 D danae.forrest@houghton.edu
FORREST, Jeffrey 661-362-3144 38 H jeffrey.forrest@canyons.edu
FORREST, Lisa 704-894-2599 328 F liforrest@davidson.edu
FORREST, Seth 410-951-6183 203 D sforrest@coppin.edu
FORRESTER, Cynthia 913-758-6114 177 F cynthia.forrester@stmary.edu
FORRESTER, Djuna 903-463-8759 437 D forresterd@grayson.edu
FORRESTER, Don 812-221-1714 162 B donforrester@vbc.edu
FORRESTER, Jill, M 717-245-1669 382 F forrestj@dickinson.edu
FORRESTER, Leslie, Y 719-333-7819 504 C leslie.forrester@usafa.edu
FORRESTER, Liane 406-683-7530 264 B liane.forrester@umwestern.edu
FORRESTER, Maureen 781-891-2000 206 D mforrester@bentley.edu
FORRESTER, Michael, P 864-592-4805 412 F forresterm@sccsc.edu
FORRESTER, Risa 405-425-5106 367 G risa.forrester@oc.edu
FORRIDER, Timothy 330-337-6403 347 E college@awc.edu
FORRY, Jennifer 617-735-9746 209 A forryj@emmanuel.edu
FORSBERG, LeAnn 817-257-7516 448 G leann.forsberg@tcu.edu
FORSETH, Eric, A 712-722-6004 164 K eric.forseth@dordt.edu
FORSHEE, Jennifer 208-282-2566 130 H jennforshee@isu.edu
FORSSTROM, Janice, M 978-762-4000 215 B jforsstr@northshore.edu
FORSTEIN, David 646-981-4500 322 J david.forstein@touro.edu
FORSTER, Dan 413-572-5365 213 D dforster@westfield.ma.edu
FORSTER, Jerry 304-929-1478 488 G jerryforster@ucwv.edu
FORSTER, Kathy 716-673-3341 317 A kathy.forster@fredonia.edu
FORSTMAN, Valerie 817-257-7513 432 E v.forstman@tcu.edu
FORSYTH, Anne, S 805-525-4417 67 D aforsyth@thomasaquinas.edu
FORSYTH, Nate 641-648-4611 166 J nate.forsyth@iavalley.edu
FORSYTHE, Micah 406-586-3585 263 J micah.forsythe@montanabiblecollege.edu
FORSYTHE, Robert, E 313-577-4501 232 I robert.forsythe@wayne.edu
FORSYTHE, Ryan 508-929-8498 213 E rforsythe@worcester.edu
FORT, Lindsay 763-424-0736 239 G lfort@nhcc.edu
FORT, Rebecca, L 330-471-8313 355 L rfort@malone.edu
FORTE, Allana 303-871-2036 83 D allana.forte@du.edu
FORTE, Marcel 831-582-4796 32 C mforte@csumb.edu
FORTE, Paul, D 828-262-2030 341 B fortepd@appstate.edu
FORTE, Teresa (Terrie) 413-747-0204 207 F teresa.forte@cambridgecollege.edu
FORTGANG, William 631-656-3189 300 D william.fortgang@ftc.edu
FORTHMAN, Emily 618-634-3223 149 A emilyf@shawneecc.edu
FORTHMAN, Jennifer 870-245-5299 20 E forthmanj@obu.edu
FORTHOFER, Scott 406-496-4500 265 A sforthofer@mtech.edu
FORTIER, Breean 617-373-2416 217 F
FORTIER, Shareka 253-589-5500 479 G shareka.fortier@cptc.edu
FORTIN, Barbara 530-898-4113 31 A bfortin@csuchico.edu
FORTIN, Elizabeth 207-453-5858 194 I efortin@kvcc.me.edu
FORTINI, Mary-Ellen 408-554-4806 62 D mfortini@scu.edu
FORTINI, Nick 619-201-8676 60 A nfortini@sdcc.edu
FORTINO, Matthew 212-924-5900 322 B mfortino@swedishinstitute.edu
FORTMAN, Brian, J 864-833-8287 411 I bjfortman@presby.edu
FORTMAN, Susan 516-323-4311 307 F sfortman@molloy.edu
FORTNER, Everette 434-243-7755 473 A ewf5db@virginia.edu
FORTNER, James 404-894-4615 118 F james.fortner@business.gatech.edu
FORTNER, Martin 318-670-9322 190 J mfortner@susla.edu
FORTNER, Melissa 706-865-2134 125 E mfortner@truett.edu
FORTNER, Thomas, H 601-984-1100 249 E tfortner@umc.edu
FORTRESS, Marty 517-750-1200 230 H marty.fortress@arbor.edu
FORTSCH, Peggy 319-226-2031 162 F peggy.fortsch@allencollege.edu
FORTSON, Carolyn 803-793-5213 409 C fortsonc@denmarktech.edu
FORTSON, Daniel 415-442-7000 44 D dfortson@ggu.edu
FORTSON, Jill 325-674-2653 429 B jill.fortson@acu.edu
FORTUNATO, Frank 904-264-2172 105 L frank.fortunato@om.org
FORTUNE, Diana 518-891-2915 310 E dfortune@nccc.edu
FOSCHIA, Christine 724-805-2524 398 E chris.foschia@stvincent.edu
FOSCHIA, Christine, L 724-805-2524 398 F christine.foschia@stvincent.edu
FOSDYCK, Rick 641-683-5117 166 C rick.fosdyck@indianhills.edu
FOSGARD, Steven 989-275-5000 226 B steven.fosgard@kirtland.edu
FOSHANG, Trevor 952-885-5462 242 I tfoshang@nwhealth.edu
FOSHEE, Brian, E 901-843-3870 423 J foshee@rhodes.edu
FOSHEE, Kenneth, H 205-348-2857 7 G ken.foshee@ua.edu
FOSS, Ben 941-487-4777 109 D bfoss@ncf.edu
FOSS, Deborah 413-662-5242 213 A deborah.foss@mcla.edu
FOSS, Erica 620-278-4213 177 B efoss@sterling.edu
FOSS, Jennifer, J 757-683-3132 469 G jfoss@odu.edu
FOSS, Lisa, H 320-308-4028 240 H lhfoss@stcloudstate.edu
FOSSETT, Christine 360-623-8451 479 C christine.fossett@centralia.edu
FOSSUM, Dallas 218-299-4533 235 E dfossum@cord.edu
FOSSUM, Dallas 701-671-2314 346 E dallas.fossum@ndscs.edu
FOSSUM, Michael, E 409-740-4408 446 G fossum@tamug.edu
FOSSUM, Scott 605-995-7178 415 G scott.fossum@mitchelltech.edu
FOSSUM, Theresa, W 630-515-7663 143 G tfossum@midwestern.edu
FOSTER, Alicia 315-792-7347 321 E alicia.foster@sunypoly.edu
FOSTER, Andrew 203-773-8542 84 F afoster@albertus.edu
FOSTER, Angelique 303-860-5600 82 N angelique.foster@cu.edu
FOSTER, Ben 972-524-3341 445 C bfost@swcc.edu
FOSTER, Cherie, A 248-341-2117 229 A cafoster@oaklandcc.edu
FOSTER, Claybourne 901-435-1307 421 A clay_foster@loc.edu
FOSTER, Colleen 575-835-5525 286 I colleen.foster@nmt.edu
FOSTER, Diane 610-359-5100 382 C dfoster@dccc.edu
FOSTER, Donna 864-941-8430 411 H foster.d@ptc.edu
FOSTER, Doug 803-777-0707 413 C drdofster@mailbox.sc.edu
FOSTER, Dyrell 951-571-6384 58 G dyrell.foster@mvc.edu
FOSTER, Elaine 303-991-1575 76 H elaine.foster@americansentinel.edu
FOSTER, Gretchen, K 308-635-6183 270 D fosterg2@wncc.edu
FOSTER, Isaac 646-378-6125 310 G isaac.foster@nyack.edu
FOSTER, Jackie 910-362-7019 332 H jfoster@cfcc.edu
FOSTER, James, D 503-554-2144 373 C jfoster@georgefox.edu
FOSTER, Janet 562-985-5459 31 F janet.foster@csulb.edu
FOSTER, Jasmine 661-362-3101 38 H jasmine.foster@canyons.edu

FOY, Morna, K .... 608-267-9066 499 B
president@wtcsystem.edu
FOY, Richard .... 715-425-3505 497 E
richard.foy@uwrf.edu
FOY-BURROUGHS,
Wanda .... 704-378-1023 330 D
wfburroughs@jcsu.edu
FOYE, Shanen .... 949-675-4451.. 46 D
shanen@idi.edu
FOYLE, Kevin, J .... 713-500-4472 456 B
kevin.j.foyle@uth.tmc.edu
FOZARD, John, D .... 405-692-3176 366 G
alecia.shannon@macu.edu
FRAASE, Justin .... 605-626-2552 417 A
justin.fraase@northern.edu
FRABONI, Dave .... 678-839-6447 126 E
dfraboni@westga.edu
FRADEN, Rena .... 209-946-2023.. 70 E
rfraden@pacific.edu
FRADEN, Sarah .... 904-538-1000.. 92 G
FRAGALE, Stephen .... 518-381-1339 315 G
fragalsa@sunysccc.edu
FRAGOSO, Marcos .... 210-805-3014 453 D
fragoso@uiwtx.edu
FRAHM, Karyn .... 661-726-1911.. 68 B
karyn.frahm@uav.edu
FRAIMAN, Keren .... 312-322-1728 149 I
FRAINIER, Janine, L .... 317-940-9228 153 F
jfrainie@butler.edu
FRAIRE, John .... 773-442-4046 145 B
j-fraire@neiu.edu
FRAIZER, Bob .... 660-626-2380 250 A
rfraizer@atsu.edu
FRAKES, Robert .... 661-654-6728.. 30 E
rfrakes@csub.edu
FRALEY, Bill .... 304-384-6334 490 A
bfraley@concord.edu
FRALEY, Meghann .... 740-245-7267 363 D
mfraley@rio.edu
FRALEY, Priscilla .... 606-368-6045 178 D
priscillafraley@alc.edu
FRALEY, Taryn .... 806-457-4200 436 G
tfraley@fpctx.edu
FRALIC, Bradley .... 713-348-4927 442 K
bradley.w.fralic@rice.edu
FRALIX, Brandon .... 973-748-9000 276 A
brandon_fralix@bloomfield.edu
FRAME, Brenda .... 507-280-2814 240 G
brenda.frame@rctc.edu
FRAME, J. Davidson .... 703-516-0035 472 H
davidson.frame@umtweb.edu
FRAME, Michael .... 315-792-7400 321 E
mframe@sunypoly.edu
FRAMPTON, Danica, D .... 512-448-8418 442 M
danicad@stedwards.edu
FRAMPTON, Travis .... 830-792-7371 443 G
provost@schreiner.edu
FRANCA, Whitney, R .... 405-325-1693 371 B
wfranca@ou.edu
FRANCAVILLA,
Theodore .... 914-337-9300 297 D
theodore.francavilla@concordia-ny.edu
FRANCE, Lucy .... 406-243-4742 264 A
lucy.france@umontana.edu
FRANCE, Melissa, H .... 918-631-2516 371 E
melissa-france@utulsa.edu
FRANCE, Trisha .... 651-255-6162 243 D
tfrance@unitedseminary.edu
FRANCESCHINI,
Geralynn .... 202-885-2121.. 90 J
geralynn@american.edu
FRANCHAK, Jen .... 513-529-3831 356 E
jen.franchak@miamioh.edu
FRANCIES, Karen .... 281-649-3450 437 H
kfrancies@hbu.edu
FRANCIOSI, Adrienne .... 617-243-2214 210 G
afranciosi@lasell.edu
FRANCIS, Aisha .... 617-588-1342 206 C
afrancis@bfit.edu
FRANCIS, Amy .... 419-783-2376 352 F
afrancis@defiance.edu
FRANCIS, Charlie .... 402-472-3886 269 J
cfrancis3@unl.edu
FRANCIS, JR.,
D. Morgan .... 336-838-6102 339 B
dmfrancis058@wilkescc.edu
FRANCIS, Diana .... 219-473-4211 153 G
dfrancis@ccsj.edu
FRANCIS, Heather .... 972-825-4627 445 A
hfrancis@sagu.edu
FRANCIS, Jeff .... 972-825-4731 445 A
jfrancis@sagu.edu
FRANCIS, Jeffrey .... 918-631-2084 371 E
jeffrey-francis@utulsa.edu
FRANCIS, Jennifer .... 919-613-6814 328 G
jfrancis@duke.edu
FRANCIS, Kathy .... 240-629-7804 198 E
kfrancis@frederick.edu
FRANCIS, Krista .... 360-417-6212 483 B
kfrancis@pencol.edu
FRANCIS, Laurie, S .... 208-496-9510 130 A
francisl@byui.edu
FRANCIS, Leon .... 610-558-5584 391 D
francisl@neumann.edu
FRANCIS, CSV, Mark, R .... 773-371-5420 133 E
president@ctu.edu
FRANCIS, Melanie .... 916-306-1628.. 66 I
mfrancis@sum.edu
FRANCIS, Melissa, A .... 252-940-6236 332 C
melissa.francis@beaufortccc.edu
FRANCIS, Morgan .... 336-838-6102 339 B
dmfrancis058@wilkescc.edu
FRANCIS, Rebecca .... 270-852-3222 183 A
rfrancis@kwc.edu
FRANCIS, Sean .... 410-617-5922 199 F
sefrancis@loyola.edu
FRANCIS-CONNOLLY,
Elizabeth .... 860-231-5471.. 89 B
efrancisconnolly@usj.edu
FRANCISCHETTI,
Jessica .... 406-657-1041 265 E
francisj@rocky.edu
FRANCISCO, Michael .... 218-733-5976 238 F
m.francisco@lsc.edu
FRANCKE, Daniel .... 989-686-9027 223 G
danielfrancke@delta.edu
FRANCO, Barry .... 843-574-6796 413 B
barry.franco@tridenttech.edu
FRANCO, Darlery .... 201-360-4191 278 C
dfranco@hccc.edu
FRANCO, Dennis .... 510-215-3900.. 40 H
dfranco@contracosta.edu
FRANCO, Maria .... 386-226-6225.. 98 A
francom@erau.edu
FRANCO, Rita .... 209-478-0800.. 45 H
rfranco@humphreys.edu
FRANCO, Robert .... 808-734-9514 128 I
bfranco@hawaii.edu
FRANCO, Vilma .... 708-237-5050 145 E
vfranco@nc.edu
FRANCOIS, Jason .... 206-546-4514 484 G
jfrancois@shoreline.edu
FRANCOIS, Kelvin, M .... 225-771-2790 190 H
kelvin_francois@subr.edu
FRANCOIS-SEENY,
Denise .... 610-861-5066 391 F
dfrancois@northampton.edu
FRANCZYK, Wendi .... 800-785-0585.. 39 G
wendi.franczyk@columbiacollege.edu
FRANDER, Tyler, P .... 719-333-2250 504 C
tyler.frander@usafa.edu
FRANDSEN, Michael .... 937-327-7916 364 H
frandsenm@wittenberg.edu
FRANDSEN, Todd .... 657-278-8569.. 31 E
tfrandsen@fullerton.edu
FRANEY, Laura .... 601-974-1304 247 B
franele@millsaps.edu
FRANGAKIS, Evelyn .... 609-497-3631 280 D
evelyn.frangakis@ptsem.edu
FRANK, Allison .... 505-467-6839 288 E
allisonfrank@swc.edu
FRANK, April .... 713-221-8422 453 B
franka@uhd.edu
FRANK, Brian .... 727-341-4143 106 E
frank.brian@spcollege.edu
FRANK, Dawn .... 605-455-6035 416 B
dfrank@olc.edu
FRANK, Deborah .... 315-655-7122 292 F
dfrank@cazenovia.edu
FRANK, Donna .... 419-448-3508 361 J
frankd@tiffin.edu
FRANK, Gregory, P .... 757-822-7261 476 B
gfrank@tcc.edu
FRANK, Jay .... 509-574-6870 487 A
jfrank@yvcc.edu
FRANK, Josh .... 919-508-2418 344 F
josh.frank@peace.edu
FRANK, Katherine .... 509-963-1400 479 B
katherine.frank@cwu.edu
FRANK, Linda .... 415-485-9528.. 39 C
lfrank@marin.edu
FRANK, Marie .... 337-482-2148 192 E
mcf3023@louisiana.edu
FRANK, Peter .... 704-233-8147 344 G
pfrank@wingate.edu
FRANK, Sandy, K .... 812-464-1761 161 E
sfrank@usi.edu
FRANK, Thomas .... 607-753-2511 318 D
thomas.frank@cortland.edu
FRANK, Tony .... 303-534-6290.. 78 L
chancellor@colostate.edu
FRANK, Vincent, P .... 717-901-5115 385 K
vfrank@harrisburgu.edu
FRANK, Wendy .... 765-641-4115 153 B
wsfrank@anderson.edu
FRANK-ALSTON,
Melissa .... 706-771-4171 114 J
mfalston@augustatech.edu
FRANK MAYS, Karen .... 978-665-3712 212 C
kfrankmays@fitchburgstate.edu
FRANKBERRY,
Constance .... 701-627-4738 346 G
cfrank@nhsc.edu
FRANKE, James .... 660-263-3900 251 A
jamiefranke@cccb.edu
FRANKEN, AJ .... 605-658-3668 416 H
aj.franken@usd.edu
FRANKEN, Kathy .... 563-425-5200 170 A
frankenk@uiu.edu
FRANKER, Karen .... 608-663-3408 493 C
kfranker@edgewood.edu
FRANKEWICZ, Walter .... 303-751-8700.. 77 A
frankewicz@bel-rea.com
FRANKHAUSER,
Frederick .... 617-732-2800 216 B
fred.frankhauser@mcphs.edu
FRANKLAND, Dinelle .... 904-264-2172 105 L
dfrankland@iws.edu
FRANKLAND, Phil .... 603-578-8900 273 A
pfrankland@ccsnh.edu
FRANKLIN, Alison .... 315-792-3111 324 B
ahfrannkl@utica.edu
FRANKLIN, Andrew .... 270-789-5005 179 E
anfranklin@campbellsville.edu
FRANKLIN, Audrey .... 336-517-2247 327 B
afranklin@bennett.edu
FRANKLIN, Bernard .... 301-447-6122 200 E
b.franklin@msmary.edu
FRANKLIN, Beverly .... 202-274-6258.. 93 C
bfranklin@udc.edu
FRANKLIN, Celeste .... 215-972-7600 393 D
cfranklin@pafa.edu
FRANKLIN, David .... 202-274-6912.. 93 C
david.franklin@udc.edu
FRANKLIN, Geralyn .... 337-482-6491 192 E
c00466754@louisiana.edu
FRANKLIN, Janice .... 334-229-4106.... 4 B
franklin@alasu.edu
FRANKLIN, Joseph .... 575-835-5964 286 I
joe.franklin@nmt.edu
FRANKLIN, Julie .... 801-422-2387 458 H
julie_franklin@byu.edu
FRANKLIN, Karen .... 575-624-7138 286 A
karen.franklin@roswell.enmu.edu
FRANKLIN, Kathy, C .... 434-528-5276 477 E
kfranklin@vul.edu
FRANKLIN, Katrina, V .... 434-528-5276 477 E
tfranklin@vul.edu
FRANKLIN, Laura, A .... 608-342-1817 497 D
franklinl@uwplatt.edu
FRANKLIN, Laurie .... 425-388-9035 480 G
lfranklin@everettcc.edu
FRANKLIN, Lecia .... 870-230-5350.. 19 E
frankll@hsu.edu
FRANKLIN, Milton, S .... 540-828-5761 465 D
mfranklin@bridgewater.edu
FRANKLIN, Mona .... 785-749-8448 173 G
mona.franklin@bie.edu
FRANKLIN, Randall .... 434-832-7617 474 C
franklinr@centralvirginia.edu
FRANKLIN, Rebekah .... 706-754-7704 122 F
rfranklin@northgatech.edu
FRANKLIN, Renee .... 712-324-5061 168 G
rfranklin@nwicc.edu
FRANKLIN, JR.,
Robert, M .... 404-727-4176 117 F
rmfrank@emory.edu
FRANKLIN, Roschoune .... 323-856-7621.. 25 M
rfranklin@afi.com
FRANKLIN, Shannon .... 541-278-5951 372 A
sfranklin@bluecc.edu
FRANKLIN, Sherry .... 601-885-7002 246 B
sdfranklin@hindscc.edu
FRANKLIN, Somer .... 936-294-1009 450 C
somer@shsu.edu
FRANKLIN, Susan .... 402-461-7410 267 D
sfranklin@hastings.edu
FRANKLIN, Timothy, V .... 973-596-5515 279 F
timothy.v.franklin@njit.edu
FRANKLIN, Truitt .... 706-865-2134 125 E
tfranklin@truett.edu
FRANKLIN, Whitney .... 931-598-1981 423 M
wpfrankl@sewanee.edu
FRANKLIN, William .... 310-243-3784.. 31 B
wfranklin@csudh.edu
FRANKLIN-OWENS,
Alyce .... 908-737-3153 278 E
franklia@kean.edu
FRANKO, Debra .... 617-373-5454 217 F
FRANKOVICH, Lauren .... 917-493-4543 305 I
lfrankovich@msmnyc.edu
FRANKOWSKI, Brian .... 215-991-3736 387 C
frankowski@lasalle.edu
FRANKOWSKI, Brian .... 215-991-3736 387 C
frankowskib1@lasalle.edu
FRANKS, Billie .... 606-589-3029 182 E
billie.franks@kctcs.edu
FRANKS, Brian .... 817-531-4452 451 E
bfranks@txwes.edu
FRANKS, Debra, J .... 864-388-8749 410 D
jfranks@lander.edu
FRANKS, Dennis .... 336-278-5555 328 K
dfranks3@elon.edu
FRANKS, Mark .... 920-498-6269 500 F
mark.franks@nwtc.edu
FRANKS, Tammy .... 228-497-7700 247 E
tammy.franks@mgccc.edu
FRANKS, Tiffany, M .... 434-791-5670 464 O
tfranks@averett.edu
FRANKS, Traci .... 580-387-7221 366 H
tfranks@mscok.edu
FRANKY, Jason .... 914-606-6745 325 C
jason.franky@sunywcc.edu
FRANQUI, Alicia .... 718-262-2137 295 F
afranqui@york.cuny.edu
FRANTZ, Alan .... 208-282-2285 130 H
franalan@isu.edu
FRANTZ, Amy .... 319-385-6246 167 A
amy.frantz@iw.edu
FRANTZ, Jane .... 859-442-1175 181 B
jane.frantz@kctcs.edu
FRANTZ, Meg .... 609-633-9658 284 B
mfrantz@tesu.edu
FRANZ, Brad .... 580-327-8632 367 E
bmfranz@nwosu.edu
FRANZ, Chris .... 303-963-3415.. 77 G
cfranz@ccu.edu
FRANZ, Jennifer .... 920-748-8192 495 G
franzj@ripon.edu
FRANZ, Mark .... 563-387-1007 167 E
FRANZ, Matt .... 937-328-6045 350 L
franzm@clarkstate.edu
FRANZ, Michelle .... 407-708-2396 107 D
franzm@seminolstate.edu
FRANZ, Scott .... 620-947-3121 177 C
scottf@tabor.edu
FRANZA, Richard, M .... 706-737-1418 115 A
rfranza@augusta.edu
FRANZEN, Kristine .... 563-387-1330 167 E
frankr03@luther.edu
FRANZEN, Matthew .... 402-826-8583 267 A
matt.franzen@doane.edu
FRANZEN, Rhonda .... 307-268-2025 501 U
rhonda.franzen@caspercollege.edu
FRANZEN, Sarah .... 260-665-4849 160 H
franzens@trine.edu
FRASCA, Melissa Sue .... 617-873-0474 207 F
melissasue.frasca@cambridgecollege.edu
FRASCATORE, Mark .... 716-286-8050 310 D
frascatore@niagara.edu
FRASCIELLO, Michael .... 315-443-3281 322 C
mfrascie@syr.edu
FRASCO, Mark .... 970-542-3174.. 81 A
mark.frasco@morgancc.edu
FRASER, Cathryn .... 507-284-9024 234 J
fraser.cathryn@mayo.edu
FRASER, Cathy .... 507-266-7095 234 I
cathy.fraser@mayo.edu
FRASER, Dori .... 919-735-5151 338 H
dori@waynecc.edu
FRASER, Greg .... 313-664-7660 222 F
gfraser@collegeforcreativestudies.edu
FRASER, Jeanmarie .... 508-362-2131 214 B
jfraser@capecod.edu
FRASER, Lynne .... 401-865-1534 405 B
lfraser1@providence.edu
FRASER, Oswald .... 718-482-5080 294 F
ofraser@lagcc.cuny.edu
FRASER, Robin .... 845-368-7241 315 D
robin.fraser@use.salvationarmy.org
FRASER, Sheri .... 207-621-3136 196 A
fraser@maine.edu

FREIRE, Ken .... 952-996-1316 234 A
kenneth.freire@bethfel.org
FREITAG, Nancy .... 312-413-2411 151 B
nfreitag@uic.edu
FREITAG, Rodd, D .... 715-836-2542 496 D
freitard@uwec.edu
FREIWALD, Susan .... 415-422-6304.. 71 K
freiwald@usfca.edu
FREKING, Lise .... 651-423-8000 237 H
FRELICH, Daryl .... 202-250-2282.. 91 E
daryl.frelich@gallaudet.edu
FRELING, Matthew .... 410-951-3000 203 D
FRENCH, Alexandra .... 808-956-5495 128 F
afrench@hawaii.edu
FRENCH, Angie .... 870-248-4000.. 18 F
angie.french@blackrivertech.edu
FRENCH, Brian .... 406-243-2565 264 A
brian.french@umontana.edu
FRENCH, Brian .... 215-572-2900 379 A
frenchb@arcadia.edu
FRENCH, Christopher .... 860-297-5204.. 88 C
christopher.french@trincoll.edu
FRENCH, Cortney .... 603-513-1345 274 H
cortney.french@granite.edu
FRENCH, Dan .... 409-880-8603 449 H
dfrench2@lamar.edu
FRENCH, Dan .... 419-251-1967 356 C
dan.french@mercycollege.edu
FRENCH, Daniel, J .... 315-443-9732 322 C
djfrench@syr.edu
FRENCH, Daphne .... 912-260-4232 124 C
daphne.french@sgsc.edu
FRENCH, Heather .... 314-367-8700 259 B
heather.french@stlcop.edu
FRENCH, Joy .... 303-724-2516.. 83 C
joy.french@ucdenver.edu
FRENCH, Kelly .... 859-344-3619 184 F
frenchk@thomasmore.edu
FRENCH, Mark .... 614-287-2810 351 E
mfrench1@cscc.edu
FRENCH, Mary Ann ...... 617-353-5168 207 D
mafrench@bu.edu
FRENCH, Paige .... 540-515-3749 465 D
pfrench@bridgewater.edu
FRENCH, CSSP,
Raymond .... 412-396-5286 383 C
french@duq.edu
FRENCH, Staley .... 918-495-6890 368 I
FRENCH, Steve .... 404-894-3380 118 F
steve.french@coa.gatech.edu
FRENCH, Vickie .... 870-248-4000.. 18 F
vickief@blackrivertech.edu
FRENCH-HART, Holly .... 318-678-6000 187 A
ltaylordupre@bpcc.edu
FRENDO, Cristina .... 313-593-5156 231 F
vatalaro@umich.edu
FRENK, Julio .... 305-284-5155 112 E
jfrenk@miami.edu
FRENTZOS, Karla, W ..... 734-462-4400 230 D
kfrentzo@schoolcraft.edu
FRENZA, Linda .... 909-469-5356.. 74 I
lfrenza@westernu.edu
FRENZEL, Michelle .... 218-755-2075 237 E
michelle.frenzel@bemidjistate.edu
FRERE, Leslie .... 540-828-5380 465 D
lfrere@bridgewater.edu
FRERICHS, Chris .... 515-961-1711 169 D
chris.frerichs@simpson.edu
FRESA, Kerin .... 215-871-6864 396 D
kerinf@pcom.edu
FRESCAS, Christina, C .. 915-831-6735 436 E
ccasta16@epcc.edu
FRESCH, Cathy .... 814-871-5842 384 E
fresch001@gannon.edu
FRESE, Philip .... 814-393-2600 394 D
pfrese@clarion.edu
FRESE, Sandra .... 518-454-5244 296 H
freses@strose.edu
FRESHOUR, Brett .... 724-552-4372 398 H
bfreshour@setonhill.edu
FRESHWATER,
Laurie, A .... 252-222-6281 333 A
freshwaterl@carteret.edu
FRESQUEZ, Julie .... 951-343-4302.. 27 J
jfresquez@calbaptist.edu
FRESSE, Daliana .... 787-815-0000 513 A
daliana.fresse@upr.edu
FREUND, Debra .... 860-512-3107.. 85 G
dfreund@manchestercc.edu
FREUND, Rachel .... 312-341-3500 147 H
FREUND, Scott .... 401-739-5000 405 A
sfreund@neit.edu

FREW, Jeremy .... 517-796-8409 225 C
frewjeremy@jccmi.edu
FREY, Carolyn, A .... 859-238-5275 179 F
carrie.frey@centre.edu
FREY, Eva, R .... 253-535-7159 482 H
eva.frey@plu.edu
FREY, Fernanda, C .... 606-546-1232 184 H
ffrey@unionky.edu
FREY, Isabel, D .... 516-463-4779 302 B
isabel.d.frey@hofstra.edu
FREY, James .... 229-931-2039 124 D
jfrey@southgatech.edu
FREY, Jason .... 773-896-2400 133 L
jason.frey@ctschicago.edu
FREY, Len, T .... 870-972-3303.. 17 G
lfrey@astate.edu
FREY, Lori .... 717-262-2012 403 F
lfrey@wilson.edu
FREY, Margot .... 415-503-6265.. 60 H
mfrey@sfcm.edu
FREY, Melissa .... 304-724-3700 487 E
mfrey@apus.edu
FREY, Melissa .... 503-589-7652 372 C
melissa.frey@chemeketa.edu
FREY, Michelle .... 660-263-4100 257 B
michellefrey@macc.edu
FREY, Steven .... 936-294-2739 450 C
saf001@shsu.edu
FREY, Tim .... 402-826-8648 267 A
timothy.frey@doane.edu
FREYBERG, Ian .... 606-539-4219 185 A
FREYERMUTH, John ...... 409-984-6520 450 B
freyermuthje@lamarpa.edu
FREYTAG, Peter .... 303-373-2008.. 82 G
pfreytag@rvu.edu
FREYTES, Liza .... 787-279-1912 509 A
lfreytes@bayamon.inter.edu
FREZZA, Daniel, H .... 757-221-1156 466 C
dhfrezza@wm.edu
FRIANT, Jakim .... 910-362-7212 332 H
jfriant@cfcc.edu
FRIAR, Shirley .... 334-724-4667.... 7 D
sfriar@tuskegee.edu
FRIAR, Tobyn, L .... 773-508-8636 142 D
tfriar@luc.edu
FRIAS, Frank .... 626-529-8064.. 55 A
ffrias@pacificoaks.edu
FRICK, Jeffrey .... 724-503-1001 402 E
jfrick@washjeff,.edu
FRICK, Lillian, K .... 989-386-6605 227 F
lfrick@midmich.edu
FRICK, Richard, A .... 201-692-2001 277 K
rfrick@fdu.edu
FRICK, Wanda .... 910-898-9637 336 D
frickw@montgomery.edu
FRICK CARDELLE,
Rachel .... 978-630-9161 215 A
rfrickcardelle@mwcc.mass.edu
FRICK-RUPPERT,
Jennifer, E .... 828-884-8144 327 C
jefrick@brevard.edu
FRICKE, David .... 732-906-2519 279 A
dfricke@middlesexcc.edu
FRICKE, Erik .... 805-965-0581.. 62 C
fricke@sbcc.edu
FRIDAY, Alicia .... 832-813-6738 439 G
alicia.r.friday@lonestar.edu
FRIDAY, Brenda .... 570-422-3455 394 E
bfriday@esu.edu
FRIDAY, Nkenge .... 740-376-3267 356 A
nrf001@marietta.edu
FRIDAY, Nkenge .... 740-376-4737 356 A
nrf001@marietta.edu
FRIDAY, Yolanda .... 909-652-7405.. 36 A
yolanda.fridayl@chaffey.edu
FRIDAY-STROUD,
Shawnta .... 850-599-3491 108 I
shawnta.friday@famu.edu
FRIDAY-STROUD,
Shawnta .... 850-599-3565 108 I
shawnta.fridaystroud@famu.edu
FRIDIE, Stan .... 903-730-4890 438 H
sfridie@jarvis.edu
FRIDLEY, Kenneth .... 205-348-5506.... 7 G
kfridley@ua.edu
FRIED, Barry, J .... 608-796-3811 498 N
bjfried@viterbo.edu
FRIED, David .... 814-866-8116 388 A
dfried@lecom.edu
FRIED, Linda, P .... 212-305-9300 297 C
lpfried@columbia.edu
FRIED, Marc .... 785-670-1712 177 G
marc.fried@washburn.edu

FRIED, Michael .... 973-408-4250 277 C
mfried@drew.edu
FRIED, Ray .... 325-235-7320 449 E
ray.fried@tstc.edu
FRIEDEL, Kristin, M ...... 315-859-4637 301 C
kfriedel@hamilton.edu
FRIEDER, Steven, W ..... 414-288-7752 494 B
steven.frieder@marquette.edu
FRIEDHOFF, Scott .... 330-263-2118 351 C
sfriedhoff@wooster.edu
FRIEDLANDER,
Helaine, R .... 617-559-8775 210 C
hfriedlander@hebrewcollege.edu
FRIEDLANDER,
Michael, J .... 540-231-2013 477 A
friedlan@vt.edu
FRIEDLEN, Karen .... 414-930-3349 495 A
friedlek@mtmary.edu
FRIEDLEY, Margret .... 360-623-8410 479 C
margret.friedley@centralia.edu
FRIEDLINE, Patrick .... 312-329-4414 144 B
patrick.friedline@moody.edu
FRIEDMAN, Al .... 425-388-9399 480 G
afriedman@everettcc.edu
FRIEDMAN, Avraham .... 847-982-2500 138 A
friedman@htc.edu
FRIEDMAN, Bruce .... 610-647-4400 386 C
bfriedman@immaculata.edu
FRIEDMAN, Carol .... 516-572-9786 308 A
carol.friedman@ncc.edu
FRIEDMAN, Carol Ann .. 408-855-5579.. 74 D
carol.friedman@missioncollege.edu
FRIEDMAN, David .... 410-484-7200 201 A
dfreidman@nirc.edu
FRIEDMAN, Deanna ...... 603-427-7600 272 J
FRIEDMAN, Elea .... 213-884-4133.. 24 A
registrar@ajrca.edu
FRIEDMAN, Elizabeth .... 718-518-4314 294 B
efriedman@hostos.cuny.edu
FRIEDMAN, Eric .... 201-360-4012 278 C
efriedman@hccc.edu
FRIEDMAN, Erica .... 212-650-7624 293 D
ericafriedman@med.cuny.edu
FRIEDMAN, Erik .... 312-369-7790 135 E
efriedman@colum.edu
FRIEDMAN, Frank .... 434-977-1620 475 F
ffriedman@pvcc.edu
FRIEDMAN, Jay, R .... 530-898-4890.. 31 A
jfriedman1@csuchico.edu
FRIEDMAN, Jill, D .... 314-935-5261 262 A
jill.friedman@wustl.edu
FRIEDMAN, Joshua .... 305-284-4111 112 E
jmfriedman@miami.edu
FRIEDMAN, Lauren, H .. 860-231-5323.. 89 B
lfriedman@usj.edu
FRIEDMAN, Lori .... 617-989-4233 219 E
friedmanl@wit.edu
FRIEDMAN, Melissa .... 212-280-6001 303 G
mefriedman@jtsa.edu
FRIEDMAN, Natalie .... 212-854-2024 290 J
nfriedma@barnard.edu
FRIEDMAN, Robert .... 212-960-5269 326 E
rfriedm2@yu.edu
FRIEDMAN, Sandra, V .. 516-572-7326 308 A
sandra.friedman@ncc.edu
FRIEDMAN, Scott .... 310-825-8607.. 69 A
friedman@idre.ucla.edu
FRIEDMAN, Scott .... 708-974-5359 144 C
friedmans5@morainevalley.edu
FRIEDMAN, Yaakov .... 847-982-2500 138 A
yfriedman@htc.edu
FRIEDMANN, Jonathan . 213-884-4133.. 24 A
jfriedmann@ajrca.edu
FRIEDRICH, Brian, L ..... 402-643-7364 266 G
brian.friedrich@cune.edu
FRIEDRICH, II, Charles 850-644-2825 109 C
friedrich@fsu.edu
FRIEDRICH, Dan .... 605-256-5555 416 J
dan.friedrich@dsu.edu
FRIEDRICHSEN,
Steven, W .... 909-706-3911.. 74 I
sfriedrichsen@westernu.edu
FRIEHS, Curt .... 718-429-6600 324 D
curt.friehs@vaughn.edu
FRIEL, Lydia .... 215-780-1251 398 G
lfriel@salus.edu
FRIEL, Wm. Jake .... 724-287-8711 380 A
jake.friel@bc3.edu
FRIEND, Damian .... 303-273-3154.. 78 I
dfriend@mines.edu
FRIEND, Dane .... 713-798-1544 431 I
dfriend@bcm.edu
FRIEND, Jennifer .... 816-501-4076 258 H
jennifer.friend@rockhurst.edu

FRIEND, Michael, P ...... 563-588-7810 167 D
michael.friend@loras.edu
FRIEND, Micheal .... 860-701-6728 504 F
micheal.friend@uscg.mil
FRIEND, Ricky .... 205-348-1370.... 7 G
rdfriend@bama.ua.edu
FRIERSON, Henry, T ..... 352-392-6622 109 F
hfrierson@ufl.edu
FRIES, Jane .... 970-542-3106.. 81 A
jane.fries@morgancc.edu
FRIES, Ruth, A .... 651-628-3241 244 D
rafries@unwsp.edu
FRIESEMA, Nathan .... 607-735-1821 299 D
nfriesema@elmira.edu
FRIESEN, Brandon .... 805-893-8125.. 70 A
brandon.friesen@ucsb.edu
FRIESEN, Joshua .... 864-250-8994 410 B
joshua.friesen@gvltec.edu
FRIESSEN, Lisa .... 580-774-3149 370 C
lisa.friessen@swosu.edu
FRIEZ-LEWINTER, Cara . 412-392-4304 397 A
cfriez@pointpark.edu
FRIGGE, Maria .... 334-670-3736.... 7 C
lfrigge@troy.edu
FRIMOTH, Margaret, R . 503-338-2440 372 E
mfrimoth@clatsopcc.edu
FRINK, Brian .... 920-565-1000 493 J
brinkbt@lakeland.edu
FRINK, Dorothy .... 219-980-6994 156 E
defrink@iun.edu
FRINK, Kandy .... 307-382-1602 502 I
kfrink@westernwyoming.edu
FRISBEE, Bob .... 620-235-4365 176 F
rfrisbee@pittstate.edu
FRISBEE, Sean .... 304-293-4731 491 C
sean.frisbee@mail.wvu.edu
FRISBEE, Stephen .... 315-792-5399 307 D
sfrisbee@mvcc.edu
FRISBIE, Kathy .... 970-542-3240.. 81 A
kathy.frisbie@morgancc.edu
FRISBY, Anthony .... 215-503-8848 400 A
anthony.frisby@jefferson.edu
FRISBY, Anthony .... 215-503-4990 400 A
anthony.frisby@jefferson.edu
FRISCH, Connie .... 320-629-5166 240 C
connie.frisch@pine.edu
FRISCH, Kevin .... 315-279-5889 304 A
kfrisch@keuka.edu
FRISCH, Kim .... 303-458-4909.. 82 E
kfrisch@regis.edu
FRISCH, Randy, C .... 206-239-4500 479 E
president@cityu.edu
FRISCH, Rick .... 208-426-3276 129 I
rickfrisch@boisestate.edu
FRISHMAN, Niki .... 760-872-2000.. 41 C
nikif@deepsprings.edu
FRISINA, Warren .... 516-463-4783 302 B
warren.frisina@hofstra.edu
FRISKICS, Scott .... 406-353-2607 262 H
friskics@hotmail.com
FRISKNEY, Paul .... 513-244-8128 350 I
paul.friskney@ccuniversity.edu
FRISONE, Al .... 510-409-7939.. 59 F
afrisone@samuelmerritt.edu
FRISQUE, Megan .... 512-863-1584 445 D
frisquem@southwestern.edu
FRIST, Matthew, J .... 412-396-6063 383 C
frist@duq.edu
FRITCH, John, E .... 319-273-2725 163 B
john.fritch@uni.edu
FRITCH, Margie .... 760-744-1150.. 55 I
mfritch@palomar.edu
FRITSCH, Denise .... 859-442-4162 181 B
denise.fritsch@kctcs.edu
FRITSCHE, Teresa .... 570-422-3422 394 E
tfritsche@esu.edu
FRITSCHI, Ramona .... 717-697-6027 390 E
rfritschi@messiah.edu
FRITSKY, Wren .... 570-389-4070 394 A
wfritsky@bloomu.edu
FRITTS, Jack .... 630-829-6060 132 E
jfritts@ben.edu
FRITZ, Brandon, J .... 515-964-0601 165 G
fritzb@faith.edu
FRITZ, John .... 410-455-6596 202 E
fritz@umbc.edu
FRITZ, Kelli .... 605-626-2550 417 A
kelli.fritz@northern.edu
FRITZ, Sarah .... 608-246-6559 499 H
fritz@madisoncollege.edu
FRITZ, Simon .... 315-228-7144 296 F
sfritz@colgate.edu

FULLER, Mickey .... 405-945-8645 368 E
mickedf@osuokc.edu
FULLER, Norine .... 202-822-9633.. 42 I
nfuller@fidm.edu
FULLER, Peggy .... 318-678-6000 187 A
pfuller@bpcc.edu
FULLER, Rex .... 503-838-8888 377 H
rfuller@wou.edu
FULLER, Roger, D .... 817-257-7199 448 G
r.fuller@tcu.edu
FULLER, Sunny .... 417-328-1512 259 L
sfuller@sbuniv.edu
FULLER, Theresa .... 330-569-5214 353 J
fullertd@hiram.edu
FULLERTON, Adam .... 712-274-5247 168 B
fullertona@morningside.edu
FULLERTON, Darren, S . 417-625-3135 256 D
fullerton-d@mssu.edu
FULLERTON, Fred, C .... 208-467-8530 131 D
ffullerton@nnu.edu
FULLINGTON, Joseph ... 262-564-2638 499 F
fullingtonj@gtc.edu
FULMER, David .... 478-387-4890 118 G
dfulmer@gmc.edu
FULMER, Gregory, L ..... 610-921-7749 378 C
gfulmer@albright.edu
FULMER, Hal .... 334-670-3112.... 7 C
hfulmer@troy.edu
FULMER, Judy .... 334-670-3102.... 7 C
jfulmer@troy.edu
FULMER, Phillip .... 865-974-4886 427 G
fulmersr@utk.edu
FULMORE, Robbin, S ... 757-683-4756 469 G
rfulmore@odu.edu
FULOP, Ann .... 309-467-6301 137 B
afulop@eureka.edu
FULOP, Ann .... 309-467-6440 137 B
afulop@eureka.edu
FULOP, Timothy .... 434-791-5630 464 O
tfulop@averett.edu
FULTINEER, Scheri .... 401-454-6100 405 D
sfultine@risd.edu
FULTON, Cara, E .... 724-847-6636 384 G
cefulton@geneva.edu
FULTON, Dean .... 360-752-8378 478 G
dfulton@btc.edu
FULTON, Deborah, M ... 540-231-0735 477 A
dfulton@vt.edu
FULTON, DoVeanna ...... 713-221-8009 453 B
fultond@uhd.edu
FULTON, Erica .... 870-575-8491.. 22 E
fultone@uapb.edu
FULTON, Jodie .... 541-956-7200 376 D
jfulton@roguecc.edu
FULTON, Lori .... 509-452-5100 483 A
lfulton@pnwu.edu
FULTON, Neil .... 605-658-3508 416 H
neil.fulton@usd.edu
FULTON, Richard .... 970-247-7150.. 79 I
fulton_r@fortlewis.edu
FULTON, Sandra .... 713-718-7444 437 I
sandra.fulton@hccs.edu
FULTON, Tara Lynn ...... 603-862-1506 274 G
taralynn.fulton@unh.edu
FULTON, Tom .... 412-924-1434 396 I
tfulton@pts.edu
FULTZ, Angela .... 606-759-7141 182 A
angela.fultz@kctcs.edu
FULTZ, Bob .... 502-863-8029 180 E
bob_fultz@georgetowncollege.edu
FULTZ, Dan .... 843-863-7026 407 E
dfultz@csuniv.edu
FULTZ, Larenda .... 731-286-3234 425 A
fultz@dscc.edu
FULTZ, Rob .... 423-614-8420 420 J
rfultz@leeuniversity.edu
FUNARO, Janette .... 630-466-7900 152 C
jfunaro@waubonsee.edu
FUNDERBURG,
Stephanie .... 617-873-0238 207 F
stephanie.funderburg@
cambridgecollege.edu
FUNDERBURK, Annette . 334-290-3265.... 2 F
annette.funderburk@istc.edu
FUNICELLO, Lori .... 973-618-3226 276 D
lfunicello@caldwell.edu
FUNK, Andrea .... 805-765-9300.. 62 B
FUNK, Carla .... 321-674-8921.. 99 B
cfunk@fit.edu
FUNK, Chad .... 916-691-7333.. 50 G
funkc@crc.losrios.edu
FUNK, Chad .... 916-484-8452.. 50 F
funkc@arc.losrios.edu
FUNK, David .... 503-255-0332 374 D
davefunk@multnomah.edu
FUNK, David .... 903-510-2026 452 C
dfun@tjc.edu
FUNK, Ed .... 916-348-4689.. 42 C
efunk@epic.edu
FUNK, Tiger .... 435-586-7888 460 F
funk@suu.edu
FUNK-BAXTER, Kathryn 210-458-4201 455 E
kathryn.funk-baxter@utsa.edu
FUNKE, Rebecca .... 515-964-6328 164 C
rsfunke@dmacc.edu
FUNSTON, Terry Lyn .... 815-825-9338 140 F
tfunston@kish.edu
FUQUA, Amy .... 605-642-6221 416 I
amy.fuqua@bhsu.edu
FUQUA, Julie .... 850-718-2478.. 96 F
fuquaj@chipola.edu
FURBECK, Lee, F .... 989-774-3872 222 C
furbe1l@cmich.edu
FURDA, Eric, J .... 215-898-2886 400 K
furda@admissions.upenn.edu
FURDA, Mark .... 740-284-5326 353 B
mfurda@franciscan.edu
FURE-SLOCUM, Carolyn 507-222-4003 234 F
cfureslo@carleton.edu
FURER, Cheryl .... 866-680-2756 459 G
studentservices@midwifery.edu
FURGE, Laura, L .... 269-337-7162 225 D
laura.furge@kzoo.edu
FURLAN, Rogerio .... 787-850-9006 513 E
rogerio.furlan@upr.edu
FURLER, Arthur .... 540-261-4094 471 H
arthur.furler@svu.edu
FURLONE, Jeffrey, C ..... 603-535-2206 275 B
jfurlone@plymouth.edu
FURLONG, Deborah ...... 315-312-2345 319 B
deborah.furlong@oswego.edu
FURLONG, Matthew ...... 409-772-5113 456 F
mfurlong@utmb.edu
FURLONG, Scott, R .... 315-312-2290 319 B
scott.furlong@oswego.edu
FURLONG, Vicki .... 315-312-3636 319 B
victoria.furlong@oswego.edu
FURLONG, Vicki .... 315-312-2250 319 B
victoria.furlong@oswego.edu
FURMAN, Ellen .... 413-205-3503 205 A
ellen.furman@aic.edu
FURMAN, John, A .... 360-650-3496 486 F
john.furman@wwu.edu
FURNESS-FALLIN,
Robyn .... 404-364-8333 122 J
rfurness@oglethorpe.edu
FURNISS, Rochel .... 740-392-6868 357 B
rochel.furniss@mvnu.edu
FURNO, Mike .... 303-871-2361.. 83 D
mike.furno@du.edu
FURQUIM, Fernando ..... 612-659-6000 238 I
fernando.furquim@minneapolis.edu
FURR, Alyssa .... 214-333-5408 434 I
alyssa@dbu.edu
FURR, Angela .... 601-643-8332 245 G
angela.furr@colin.edu
FURR, Brandi .... 903-463-8650 437 D
furrb@grayson.edu
FURR, James, H .... 713-942-9505 438 A
jfurr@hgst.edu
FURR, Jennifer .... 402-643-7341 266 G
alumni@cune.edu
FURR, Laci .... 620-417-1151 176 K
laci.furr@sccc.edu
FURR, Myra .... 704-991-0202 338 C
mfurr7711@stanly.edu
FURR, Timothy, L .... 320-222-5735 240 E
tim.furr@ridgewater.edu
FURROW, Louise, S ..... 206-281-2998 484 D
lfurrow@spu.edu
FURST, Jesse .... 417-626-1234 257 F
furst.jesse@occ.edu
FURST, Mary .... 828-898-8743 330 E
furstm@lmc.edu
FURST-BOWE, Julie ...... 715-858-1857 499 D
jfurstbowe@cvtc.edu
FURTON, Kenneth .... 305-348-2866 109 A
furtonk@fiu.edu
FURUI, Sadaoki .... 773-834-2493 150 E
furui@ttic.edu
FURUKAWA, Karen .... 707-527-4302.. 62 F
kfurukawa-schlereth@santarosa.edu
FURULI, Andrea .... 808-932-7692 128 E
andrea.furuli@uhfoundation.org
FURUSHIMA, Randall ... 808-853-1040 128 C
randallfurushima@pacrim.edu
FURUTA, Lisa .... 808-739-4746 127 F
lisa.furuta@chaminade.edu
FURUTANI, Laurie .... 808-956-8177 128 F
lhf@hawaii.edu
FURUTO, Brian .... 808-734-9572 128 I
bfuruto@hawaii.edu
FURUTO, Sandra, K ...... 808-956-7487 128 D
yano@hawaii.edu
FUSCO, Joseph .... 610-902-8245 380 C
jf693@cabrini.edu
FUSCO, Valerie .... 315-792-7111 321 E
valerie.fusco@sunypoly.edu
FUSELIER, Johnathan .... 254-519-5477 447 A
j.fuselier@tamuct.edu
FUSSEL, Latesha .... 508-565-1411 218 H
lfussell@stonehill.edu
FUSTER, Bradley .... 315-279-5202 304 A
bfuster@keuka.edu
FUSTER, Luis .... 787-765-3560 507 L
lfuster@edpuniversity.edu
FUTHEY, Carol .... 970-248-1657.. 77 I
cfuthey@coloradomesa.edu
FUTHEY, Tracy .... 919-684-8111 328 G
futhey@duke.edu
FUTRELL, Michelle, G ... 843-953-5674 408 E
futrellm@cofc.edu
FUTRELL, Tamara .... 540-458-8766 478 A
tfutrell@wlu.edu
FUTTERER, Julie .... 815-740-3826 151 J
jfutterer@stfrancis.edu
FYDENKEVEZ,
Mary Ellen .... 413-775-1469 214 C
fydenkevezm@gcc.mass.edu
FYE, Marty .... 402-826-8261 267 A
marty.fye@doane.edu
FYFE, Billy .... 414-277-2339 494 G
FYNES, Daniel .... 330-569-6107 353 J
fynesda@hiram.edu
FYRE, Gerald .... 662-846-3000 245 H

G

GAAL, John .... 215-276-6070 398 G
jgaal@salus.edu
GAALSWYK, Terry .... 507-372-3491 239 E
terry.gaalswyk@mnwest.edu
GABA, Barbara .... 609-343-4901 275 D
GABBARD, Clinton, E ... 815-455-8725 143 A
cgabbard@mchenry.edu
GABBARD, Kurt, A .... 609-497-7705 280 D
kurt.gabbard@ptsem.edu
GABBARD, Veronica ..... 281-649-3747 437 H
vgabbard@hbu.edu
GABBERT, Jeri Pat .... 219-981-4242 156 E
jgabbert@iun.edu
GABEHART, Luci .... 432-264-5074 438 C
lgabehart@howardcollege.edu
GABEL, Ann-Marie .... 949-582-4664.. 64 E
agabel@socccd.edu
GABEL, Barb .... 419-448-2183 353 H
bgabel@heidelberg.edu
GABEL, Joan, T .... 612-626-1616 243 E
upres@umn.edu
GABER, Sharon, L .... 419-530-2211 363 E
sharon.gaber@utoledo.edu
GABERT, Susan, S .... 603-641-7231 274 C
sgabert@anselm.edu
GABLE, Carol .... 315-859-4313 301 C
cgable@hamilton.edu
GABLE, Jill .... 312-942-5681 148 A
jill_gable@rush.edu
GABLE, Justin .... 559-453-2215.. 43 G
justin.gable@fresno.edu
GABLE, Nicole .... 412-536-1022 387 B
nicole.gable@laroche.edu
GABOURY, John, D .... 517-355-5767 227 D
gaboury@msu.edu
GABOURY, Mario .... 203-932-7253.. 89 A
mgaboury@newhaven.edu
GABRIEL, Kirsten .... 608-796-3840 498 N
kkgabriel@viterbo.edu
GABRIEL, Lisa .... 281-283-3032 453 A
gabriel@uhcl.edu
GABRIEL, Mary .... 970-339-6248.. 76 G
mary.gabriel@aims.edu
GABRIEL, Peter .... 913-288-7484 174 F
pgabriel@kckcc.edu
GABRIEL, Robert .... 510-742-3102.. 54 F
rgabriel@ohlone.edu
GABRIEL, Sherine, E ..... 312-942-7100 148 A
GABRIELE, Erin .... 610-902-8304 380 C
eg574@cabrini.edu
GABRIELSON, Kerry ...... 719-846-5643.. 82 K
kerry.gabrielson@trinidadstate.edu
GABY FISHER, Robin ..... 973-353-3739 282 B
rofisher@newark.rutgers.edu
GACHETTE, Yves, M ...... 716-878-4521 318 C
gachetym@buffalostate.edu
GACHIGO, David .... 718-390-4345 314 B
gachigod@stjohns.edu
GACKENHEIMER,
Lois, M .... 561-683-1400.. 94 A
admin@anho.edu
GADBERRY, Brad .... 678-341-6615 121 B
bgadberry@laniertech.edu
GADD, Holly .... 423-236-2961 424 B
hgadd@southern.edu
GADE, Chris, W .... 507-284-2073 234 J
cgade@mayo.edu
GADE-JONES, Tish .... 402-465-2114 268 H
tgadejon@nebrwesleyan.edu
GADIKIAN,
Randolph Lee .... 716-673-3181 317 A
randolph.gadikian@fredonia.edu
GADSBY, Peter .... 845-758-7457 290 G
gadsby@bard.edu
GADSON, Mark, P .... 610-409-3164 402 A
mgadson@ursinus.edu
GADZINSKI, James, G .. 906-227-2971 228 F
jgadzins@nmu.edu
GAEB, Amanda .... 603-342-3006 273 D
agaeb@ccsnh.edu
GAECKE, Lauren .... 920-403-3981 495 I
lauren.gaecke@snc.edu
GAERTE, Phyllis .... 585-567-9620 302 D
phyllis.gaerte@houghton.edu
GAERTNER, Michelle .... 615-248-1463 427 A
mgaertner@trevecca.edu
GAETA, Alexa .... 404-471-6054 113 G
agaeta@agnesscott.edu
GAETA, Maria .... 408-288-3725.. 61 M
maria.gaeta@sjcc.edu
GAETA, Maria .... 805-482-2755.. 58 L
mgaeta@stjohnsem.edu
GAETJE, Lisa .... 714-484-7188.. 53 K
lgaetje@cypresscollege.edu
GAETZ, Ivan .... 307-766-3279 502 H
igaetz@uwyo.edu
GAETZ, Patricia .... 502-863-8058 180 E
patricia_gaetz@georgetowncollege.edu
GAFFEY, Pat .... 480-947-6644.. 15 A
pat.gaffey@pennfoster.edu
GAFFIN, Douglas, D ..... 405-325-5291 371 B
ddgaffin@ou.edu
GAFFIN, John .... 859-572-6611 184 A
gaffinj@nku.edu
GAFFNER, Lori .... 618-664-7120 137 G
lori.gaffner@greenville.edu
GAFFNEY, Eva .... 508-531-1337 212 B
egaffney@bridgew.edu
GAFFNEY, Kathryn .... 860-215-9266.. 86 F
kgaffney@trcc.commnet.edu
GAFFNEY, Kevin .... 775-445-4223 271 G
kevin.gaffney@wnc.edu
GAFFNEY, Michelle .... 330-823-2496 363 B
gaffnemi@mountunion.edu
GAFFNEY, Peggy .... 361-825-2621 447 C
peggy.gaffney@tamucc.edu
GAFFNEY, Phillip .... 706-204-2201 118 E
pgaffney@highlands.edu
GAFFNEY, Tiffany, D ..... 401-865-2191 405 B
tgaffne1@providence.edu
GAFFORD, Brian .... 931-393-1576 425 C
bgafford@mscc.edu
GAGAN, Adam .... 212-799-5000 303 H
GAGAN, Kelly .... 585-389-2411 308 B
kgagan8@naz.edu
GAGE, Adrian .... 508-929-8563 213 E
agage@worcester.edu
GAGE, Brent .... 319-335-3839 163 A
brent-gage@uiowa.edu
GAGE, Christopher .... 812-866-7000 155 C
cgage@hanover.edu
GAGE, David .... 315-781-3734 302 A
gage@hws.edu
GAGE, J. Scott .... 978-837-5468 216 D
j.scott.gage@merrimack.edu
GAGE, Jeannie .... 361-825-2332 447 C
jeannie.gage@tamucc.edu
GAGE, Julia .... 401-841-6535 503 L
julia.gage@usnwc.edu
GAGER, Sarah .... 203-575-8034.. 86 B
sgager@nv.edu
GAGLIANO, Patricia ...... 772-462-7565 101 E
pgaglian@irsc.edu
GAGLIARDI, Jonathan ... 718-960-8111 294 A
jonathan.gagliardi@lehman.cuny.edu

GALLO-MURPHY, Meredith .... 773-907-4650 134 C
mgallo-murphy@ccc.edu
GALLONIO, Anthony ..... 401-454-6636 405 D
agalloni@risd.edu
GALLOT, JR., Richard ... 318-274-3811 191 E
prez@gram.edu
GALLOWAY, Carolina .... 806-651-5309 448 C
cgalloway@wtamu.edu
GALLOWAY, David .... 315-781-3304 302 A
galloway@hws.edu
GALLOWAY, David .... 651-603-6263 235 F
galloway@csp.edu
GALLOWAY, Heather ..... 512-245-2266 450 E
hg02@txstate.edu
GALLOWAY, Jeanne ...... 425-602-3007 478 D
jgalloway@bastyr.edu
GALLOWAY, Jeannie ..... 606-368-6113 178 D
jeanniegalloway@alc.edu
GALLOWAY, Merrill .... 606-589-3079 182 E
merrill.galloway@kctcs.edu
GALLOWAY, Pamela ..... 919-760-8360 331 B
davisp@meredith.edu
GALLOWAY, Peter .... 610-436-1015 396 A
pgalloway@wcupa.edu
GALLOWAY, Robin .... 319-296-4292 166 B
robin.galloway@hawkeyecollege.edu
GALLOWAY, Sean .... 717-358-4210 384 D
sean.galloway@fandm.edu
GALLOWAY, Sheila .... 910-755-7312 332 F
galloways@brunswickcc.edu
GALLOWAY, Tami .... 740-389-4636 356 B
gallowayt@mtc.edu
GALLOWAY, Tammy .... 903-875-7573 440 G
tammy.galloway@navarrocollege.edu
GALLOWAY-PERRY, Rulisa .... 212-237-8701 294 D
rgalloway@jjay.cuny.edu
GALLOWGLAS, Robin ..... 916-484-8401.. 50 F
gallowr@arc.losrios.edu
GALM, Ruth .... 509-359-6567 480 E
rgalm@ewu.edu
GALOPE, Richard .... 909-382-4034.. 59 G
rgalope@sbccd.cc.ca.us
GALOVIC, John .... 216-373-5238 358 B
jgalovic@ndc.edu
GALOYAN, Nazy .... 408-864-8292.. 43 C
galoyannazy@deanza.edu
GALT, Cindy .... 561-433-2330 107 J
GALTNEY, Alfred .... 601-877-3965 244 H
agaltney@alcorn.edu
GALUKYAN, Armine .... 626-585-7201.. 55 K
agalukyan@yahoo.com
GALVAN, Betty .... 210-434-6711 441 E
bagalvan@ollusa.edu
GALVAN, Dennis, C ...... 541-346-5851 377 D
dgalvan@uoregon.edu
GALVAN, Efren .... 714-432-5774.. 38 E
egalvan@occ.cccd.edu
GALVAN, Margarita, M . 361-593-3209 447 D
margarita.galvan@tamuk.edu
GALVAN, Michael .... 903-223-3013 448 B
mgalvan@tamut.edu
GALVAN, Racheal .... 785-309-3147 176 J
racheal.galvan@salinatech.edu
GALVANONI, Mark .... 630-889-6661 144 G
mgalvanoni@nuhs.edu
GALVIN, Carroll .... 410-532-5314 201 B
cgalvin@ndm.edu
GALVIN, Garrett .... 619-574-5802.. 43 E
ggalvin@fst.edu
GALVIN, OFM, Garrett .. 619-574-5802.. 43 E
ggalvin@fst.edu
GALVIN, Jeanne .... 718-631-6220 295 D
jgalvin@qcc.cuny.edu
GALVIN, Mary, E .... 574-631-6456 161 C
mgalvin2@nd.edu
GALVIN, Michael .... 973-655-7761 279 C
galvinm@mail.montclair.edu
GALVINHILL, Paul .... 508-793-3363 208 B
pgalvin@holycross.edu
GALYEAN, Michael .... 806-742-2184 451 B
michael.galyean@ttu.edu
GALYEAN, Paul .... 903-589-7135 438 G
pgalyean@jacksonville-college.edu
GAMBILL, Jon .... 816-501-2436 250 F
jon.gambill@avila.edu
GAMBILL, Todd .... 765-455-9360 156 D
tgambill@iuk.edu
GAMBINI, Lindsay .... 661-362-5305.. 38 H
lindsay.gambini@canyons.edu
GAMBINO, Ellen, M ...... 845-431-8954 298 E
gambino@sunydutchess.edu
GAMBLE, Brad .... 417-328-1823 259 L
bgamble@sbuniv.edu
GAMBLE, Brandon .... 256-726-8259.... 6 C
bgamble@oakwood.edu
GAMBLE, Desiree .... 360-442-2202 482 B
dgamble@lowercolumbia.edu
GAMBLE, Geraldine .... 505-786-4118 286 G
ggamble@navajotech.edu
GAMBLE, Gregory .... 856-225-6388 281 G
gambleg@camden.rutgers.edu
GAMBLE, Jim .... 616-538-2330 224 C
jgamble@gracechristian.edu
GAMBLE, John, E .... 361-825-6045 447 C
john.gamble@tamucc.edu
GAMBLE, Mort .... 757-455-3217 477 F
mgamble@vwu.edu
GAMBLE, Suzanne .... 865-251-1800 424 A
sgamble@southtn.edu
GAMBLE, Thomas, J ..... 518-438-3111 305 K
tgamble@mariacollege.edu
GAMBOA, Anthony .... 773-481-8752 134 G
agamboa@ccc.edu
GAMBOA, Benjamin ...... 619-388-7392.. 60 E
bgamboa@sdccd.edu
GAMBOA, Jorge .... 714-992-7048.. 53 L
jgamboa@fullcoll.edu
GAMBOA, Noel .... 718-262-2372 295 F
ngamboa@york.cuny.edu
GAMBRO, John, S .... 815-740-3829 151 J
jgambro@stfrancis.edu
GAMER, Josh .... 608-785-9088 501 A
gamerj@westerntc.edu
GAMEZ, Francisco .... 510-981-2881.. 56 E
fgamez@peralta.edu
GAMLIN, Kim .... 252-246-1290 339 C
kgamlin@wilsoncc.edu
GAMMA, Kristal .... 909-607-7821.. 37 D
kristal.gamma@cgu.edu
GAMMEL-SMITH, Hollie 936-468-7249 445 F
hsmith@sfasu.edu
GAMMELL, William .... 860-723-0054.. 84 H
gammellw@ct.edu
GAMMILL, Brandon ...... 417-873-7219 252 F
bgammill@drury.edu
GAMMON, Jennifer .... 803-325-2874 415 A
jgammon@yorktech.edu
GAMMON, Marcia, L ..... 480-245-7918.. 12 N
marcia.gammon@ibcs.edu
GAMMON, Steven .... 406-496-4207 265 A
sgammon@mtech.edu
GANAC, Lynn .... 657-278-8474.. 31 E
lganac@fullerton.edu
GANAHL, Gina .... 636-949-4501 254 F
gganahl@lindenwood.edu
GANCERES, Lupe .... 361-354-2712 433 C
lupegg@coastalbend.edu
GANCHUK, Thomas .... 512-505-3021 438 E
tganchuk@htu.edu
GANCIO, Charles .... 606-783-2081 183 F
c.gancio@moreheadstate.edu
GANDHI, Jay .... 810-762-3476 231 G
jgandhi@umich.edu
GANDHI, Ketan .... 973-300-2115 283 E
kgandhi@sussex.edu
GANDHI, Pratima, N ..... 309-677-3123 133 B
pratima@fsmail.bradley.edu
GANDIA, Antonio .... 239-992-4624.. 95 G
GANDRE, James .... 917-493-4438 305 I
jgandre@msmnyc.edu
GANDU, Bobby .... 316-978-5675 178 A
bobby.gandu@wichita.edu
GANDY, Fredrick .... 815-836-5125 141 G
gandyfr@lewisu.edu
GANDY, Rex .... 931-221-7676 418 D
gandyr@apsu.edu
GANESAN, Nlck .... 910-672-1477 341 E
nganesan@uncfsu.edu
GANESH, Jaishankar ..... 856-225-6217 281 G
jganesh@camden.rutgers.edu
GANESON, Visakan .... 425-388-9378 480 G
vganeson@everettcc.edu
GANG, Martin .... 207-629-4014 194 F
mgang@mccs.me.edu
GANGER, Trisha .... 224-293-5858 132 B
tganger@aiuniv.edu
GANGI, Maria .... 914-831-0350 297 A
mgangi@cw.edu
GANGL, Brad .... 701-228-2277 346 C
brad.gangl@dakotacollege.edu
GANGSTEAD, Sandra .... 478-445-6848 118 C
sandra.gangstead@gcsu.edu
GANIC, Emir .... 718-758-8125 293 C
eganic@brooklyn.cuny.edu
GANIO, Mary .... 619-482-6301.. 65 F
mganio@swccd.edu
GANLEY, DeLacy .... 909-621-8075.. 37 D
delacy.ganley@cgu.edu
GANN, Alexander .... 516-367-6890 296 D
ganna@cshl.edu
GANN, Brian .... 731-425-8820 425 B
bgann1@jscc.edu
GANN, Heather .... 731-286-3331 425 A
gann@dscc.edu
GANNAWAY, Anne, A ... 563-333-6283 169 A
gannawayannem@sau.edu
GANNON, Debbie, K ..... 515-263-6020 165 I
dgannon@grandview.edu
GANNON, Kim .... 512-245-2371 450 E
kg33@txstate.edu
GANNON, Marcy .... 301-934-7560 198 A
mdgannon@csmd.edu
GANNON, Monica .... 712-279-1614 163 C
monica.gannon@briarcliff.edu
GANNON, Susan .... 908-737-3461 278 E
sgannon@kean.edu
GANNT, Aubra, J .... 817-515-8003 445 G
aubra.gantt@tccd.edu
GANO-PHILLIPS, Susan 810-762-3234 231 G
sganop@umich.edu
GANSCHOW, Darby .... 605-677-6623 416 H
darby.ganschow@usd.edu
GANSERT, Heidi .... 775-784-4778 271 F
hgansert@unr.edu
GANSZ, David .... 202-685-3470 503 I
david.gansz.civ@ndu.edu
GANT, Corey .... 540-458-8251 478 A
cgant@wlu.edu
GANT, Jeffrey, D .... 973-655-6911 279 C
gantj@mail.montclair.edu
GANT, Jon, P .... 919-530-7438 342 A
jpgant@nccu.edu
GANT, Kim .... 423-354-2471 425 E
kbgant@northeaststate.edu
GANTNER, Christine, M 920-424-3414 497 B
gantner@uwosh.edu
GANTT, Bernard .... 718-289-5515 293 B
bernard.gantt@bcc.cuny.edu
GANTT, Calvin .... 607-777-2791 316 E
cgantt@binghamton.edu
GANTT, Calvin, J .... 585-292-2122 307 H
cgant@monroecc.edu
GANTT, Dave .... 406-791-5926 265 H
david.gantt@uprovidence.edu
GANTT, Kevin .... 913-758-6230 177 F
ganttk@stmary.edu
GANTZ, Jennifer .... 316-942-4291 175 I
gantzj@newmanu.edu
GANTZ, Katherine, L ..... 240-895-4922 201 E
klgantz@smcm.edu
GANUES, Jeff .... 567-661-7334 360 B
jeffrey_ganues@owens.edu
GANYARD, Clifton .... 920-465-2033 496 E
ganyardc@uwgb.edu
GANYARD, Paula .... 920-465-2000 496 E
ganyardp@uwgb.edu
GANZEL, Toni .... 502-852-5192 185 C
toni.ganzel@louisville.edu
GAO, Jing .... 215-646-7300 385 D
gao.j@gmercyu.edu
GAO, Lan .... 617-521-2721 218 E
lan.gao@simmons.edu
GAO, Songsong .... 408-206-0208.. 42 M
song@fivebranches.edu
GAO, Su .... 940-369-8289 454 A
su.gao@unt.edu
GARAFALO, Mary .... 518-828-4181 297 B
garafalo@sunycgcc.edu
GARAFOLO, Rich .... 252-527-6223 335 G
rmgarafolo48@lenoircc.edu
GARAS, Alana .... 410-293-1521 504 I
pao@usna.edu
GARAWITZ, Amy .... 212-217-4100 299 H
amy_garawitz@fitnyc.edu
GARBART, Hadley .... 410-225-2231 199 H
hgarbart@mica.edu
GARBE, John .... 585-389-2038 308 B
jgarbe6@naz.edu
GARBE, Theresa .... 423-461-8718 422 J
tmgarbe@milligan.edu
GARBER, Alan .... 617-496-5100 210 B
alan_garber@harvard.edu
GARBER, Jason .... 217-732-3155 141 I
jgarber@lincolncollege.edu
GARBER, Linda .... 408-551-1913.. 62 D
lgarber@scu.edu
GARBER, Lindsay .... 717-728-2214 381 B
lindsaygarber@centralpenn.edu
GARBER, Philip .... 847-214-7285 136 F
pgarber@elgin.edu
GARBER BAX, Sharlene 660-543-4114 260 K
bax@ucmo.edu
GARBO-SHAWHAN, Jennifer .... 414-443-8800 498 O
jennifer.garbo-shawhan@wlc.edu
GARBUTT, Keith .... 405-744-6799 368 B
keith.garbutt@okstate.edu
GARBUTT, Naomi .... 503-338-2450 372 E
ngarbutt@clatsopcc.edu
GARCES, Brenda .... 703-891-1787 471 K
financialaid@standardcollege.edu
GARCIA, Adam .... 702-895-3668 271 E
adam.garcia@unlv.edu
GARCIA, Adlar .... 305-237-3240 103 D
agarci30@mdc.edu
GARCIA, Albert .... 916-558-2226.. 50 I
garciaaj@scc.losrios.edu
GARCIA, Alberto .... 787-844-8181 514 A
alberto.garcia3@upr.edu
GARCIA, Ana, T .... 787-888-1135 510 D
agarcia@monteclaro.edu
GARCIA, Andrea .... 707-638-5272.. 67 F
andrea.garcia@tu.edu
GARCIA, Andrew .... 303-352-3079.. 79 E
andrew.garcia@ccd.edu
GARCIA, Angela .... 520-515-4508.. 11 M
garciaangela@cochise.edu
GARCIA, Angelica .... 650-738-4333.. 61 Q
garciaa@smccd.edu
GARCIA, Anna .... 361-354-2207 433 C
agarcia@coastalbend.edu
GARCIA, Aurelio .... 787-777-0677 514 B
aurelio.garcia@upr.edu
GARCIA, Ava, M .... 671-735-6013 505 C
ava.garcia@guamcc.edu
GARCIA, Bert .... 412-578-8712 380 E
GARCIA, Bo .... 517-483-9639 226 F
garciab@lcc.edu
GARCIA, Brenda, W ...... 575-439-3697 287 C
brgarcia@nmsu.edu
GARCIA, Brett .... 540-261-8401 471 H
brett.garcia@svu.edu
GARCIA, Carlos .... 719-255-3776.. 83 B
cgarci12@uccs.edu
GARCIA, Carlos .... 845-437-7248 324 C
GARCIA, Carlos .... 210-829-2717 453 D
cagarci9@uiwtx.edu
GARCIA, Carol .... 718-779-1430 311 I
cgarcia@plazacollege.edu
GARCIA, Carola .... 787-779-2500 507 B
ccat@coqui.edu
GARCIA, Caroline, M .... 520-626-0631.. 16 G
cmgarcia@email.arizona.edu
GARCIA, Catherine .... 704-216-7290 337 F
catherine.garcia@rccc.edu
GARCIA, Cecilia .... 760-921-5478.. 55 H
cecy.garcia@paloverde.edu
GARCIA, Christian .... 305-284-5451 112 E
christian@miami.edu
GARCIA, Christina, M ... 626-914-8825.. 36 K
cmgarcia@citruscollege.edu
GARCIA, Claire .... 719-389-6510.. 77 H
cgarcia@coloradocollege.edu
GARCIA, Clint .... 719-502-2040.. 81 F
clint.garcia@ppcc.edu
GARCIA, Daisy .... 940-668-3330 441 A
dgarcia@nctc.edu
GARCIA, Dan .... 505-277-8392 288 G
GARCIA, Daniel .... 810-762-9752 225 H
dgarcia@kettering.edu
GARCIA, Danielle .... 657-278-4626.. 31 E
daniellegarcia@fullerton.edu
GARCIA, Dominick .... 610-917-1406 401 I
dagarcia@valleyforge.edu
GARCIA, Donna .... 575-461-4413 286 E
donnag@mesalands.edu
GARCIA, Eda .... 404-270-5244 125 B
egarcia1@spelman.edu
GARCIA, Elena .... 787-780-0070 506 F
egarcia@caribbean.edu
GARCIA, Eliezer .... 787-786-3030 512 B
egarcia@ucb.edu.pr
GARCIA, Emma .... 432-264-5030 438 C
egarcia@howardcollege.edu
GARCIA, Erin .... 561-237-7258 102 V
edgarcia@lynn.edu
GARCIA, Fernando .... 706-272-4600 117 C
fgarcia@daltonstate.edu

GARNER, Bianca .... 601-977-7737 249 C
bgarner@tougaloo.edu
GARNER, Cindy .... 901-722-3223 424 C
cgarner@sco.edu
GARNER, David, B .... 215-572-3811 402 H
dgarner@wts.edu
GARNER, Graham .... 315-684-6041 321 D
garnerg@morrisville.edu
GARNER, Latonya .... 662-254-3421 248 B
lcgarner@mvsu.edu
GARNER, Lyn .... 281-998-6150 443 D
lyn.garner@sjcd.edu
GARNER, Mary Ann ...... 229-468-2018 127 B
maryann.garner@wiregrass.edu
GARNER, MaryAnne ...... 202-462-2101.. 92 C
garner@iwp.edu
GARNER, Porter .... 979-845-7514 446 G
porter-garner@tamu.edu
GARNER, Ray .... 256-824-4688.... 8 B
ray.garner@uah.edu
GARNER, Regina .... 214-860-8561 435 D
garnerre@dcccd.edu
GARNER, Sam .... 402-363-5620 270 E
sgarner@york.edu
GARNER, Sarah .... 302-622-8000.. 89 E
sgarner@dcad.edu
GARNER, Tim .... 256-782-8220.... 5 J
tgarner@jsu.edu
GARNETT, Heather .... 434-544-8431 472 G
garnett.h@lynchburg.edu
GARNETT, Sherman, W . 517-353-6753 227 D
garnetts@msu.edu
GARNICK, Renee .... 302-622-8000.. 89 E
rgarnick@dcad.edu
GARNIER, Todd .... 607-962-9334 320 F
tgarnier@corning-cc.edu
GARNO, Art .... 315-386-7197 320 E
garnoa@canton.edu
GARNSEY HARTER,
Ann .... 206-546-5879 484 G
agarnsey@shorline.edu
GAROFALO, Giovanni ... 412-365-1292 381 C
g.garofalo@chatham.edu
GAROFALO, Teresa .... 605-229-8434 416 C
teresa.garofalo@presentation.edu
GARON, Jon .... 954-262-6101 103 M
garon@nova.edu
GARR, Bethany .... 864-596-9595 409 B
healthservices@converse.edu
GARRANT, Ines .... 617-358-0513 207 D
igarrant@bu.edu
GARRELL, Robin, L .... 310-825-4383.. 69 A
rgarrell@gdnet.ucla.edu
GARREN, Cynthia .... 863-784-7177 107 F
cynthia.garren@southflorida.edu
GARREN, Kenneth, R .... 434-544-8200 472 G
president@lynchburg.edu
GARREN, Mary Ann ...... 870-762-3168.. 17 D
mgarren@smail.anc.edu
GARRETSON, Angela, R 973-596-3101 279 F
angela.r.garretson@njit.edu
GARRETSON, Charlie .... 601-477-4249 246 F
charlie.garretson@jcjc.edu
GARRETT, Allen .... 619-201-8700.. 60 A
algarrett@sdcc.edu
GARRETT, Allison .... 620-341-5551 172 L
agarrett@emporia.edu
GARRETT, Bonnie, J ..... 410-777-2503 197 C
bjgarrett@aacc.edu
GARRETT, Craig .... 504-282-4455 190 A
cgarrett@nobts.edu
GARRETT, Don .... 325-674-2213 429 B
dlg09a@acu.edu
GARRETT, Geoffrey .... 215-898-4715 400 K
ggarrett@wharton.upenn.edu
GARRETT, Gina .... 870-307-7557.. 20 A
gina.garrett@lyon.edu
GARRETT, Glenda .... 214-860-8666 435 D
ghall@dcccd.edu
GARRETT, Helen .... 206-685-2553 485 F
helenbg@uw.edu
GARRETT, JR.,
James, H .... 412-268-2000 380 F
garrett@andrew.cmu.edu
GARRETT, Jason .... 731-661-5365 427 C
jgarrett@uu.edu
GARRETT, Jonathan ...... 513-244-1728 350 I
jonathan.garrett@ccuniversity.edu
GARRETT, Katrina .... 601-484-8724 247 A
kgarret2@meridiancc.edu
GARRETT, Kelly .... 713-623-2040 430 K
kgarrett@aii.edu
GARRETT, Kevin .... 304-384-5340 490 A
garrettad@concord.edu
GARRETT, Krystal .... 217-351-2533 146 C
kgarrett@parkland.edu
GARRETT, LaCharlotte ... 504-284-5435 190 I
lgarrett@suno.edu
GARRETT, Leonard .... 214-860-3697 435 D
lgarrett@dcccd.edu
GARRETT, Lynn .... 407-404-6060 107 D
garrettl@seminolestate.edu
GARRETT, Mark .... 270-901-1065 182 D
mark.garrett@kctcs.edu
GARRETT, Natasha .... 412-536-1296 387 B
natasha.garrett@laroche.edu
GARRETT, Nicole, L ...... 919-658-7896 340 J
ngarrett@umo.edu
GARRETT, Paul .... 864-977-7035 411 E
paul.garrett@ngu.edu
GARRETT, Rachele .... 936-468-2403 445 F
nixonhr@sfasu.edu
GARRETT, Rick .... 765-641-4156 153 B
ragarrett@anderson.edu
GARRETT, Rob, J .... 208-496-1124 130 A
garrettr@byui.edu
GARRETT, Robin .... 254-526-1733 432 H
robin.garrett@ctcd.edu
GARRETT, Schnell, R .... 443-518-4766 199 C
sgarrett@howardcc.edu
GARRETT, Scott .... 216-687-5119 351 B
s.garrett1@csuohio.edu
GARRETT, Shana .... 866-492-5336 244 F
shana.garrett@mail.waldenu.edu
GARRETT, Shelli .... 254-442-5121 433 A
shelli.garrett@cisco.edu
GARRETT, Stephanie ..... 864-225-7653 409 J
stephaniegarrett@forrestcollege.edu
GARRETT, Teresa .... 434-381-6205 472 D
tgarrett@sbc.edu
GARRETT, Todd, L .... 913-971-3278 175 G
tgarrett@mnu.edu
GARRETT FINSTER,
Susan .... 619-239-0391.. 34 F
sgf@cwsl.edu
GARRETT-KOJU, Stacey 615-238-6350 419 K
skoju@bonelaw.com
GARRICK, Connie .... 281-290-2923 439 G
connie.s.garrick@lonestar.edu
GARRICK DUHANEY,
Laurel .... 845-257-3561 317 B
duhaneyl@newpaltz.edu
GARRIDO, Lillian .... 407-303-7747.. 94 D
lillian.garrido@ahu.edu
GARRIGA, Maria .... 859-344-3578 184 F
garrigm@thomasmore.edu
GARRIOCH, Shay .... 845-451-4365 298 A
shay.garrioch@culinary.edu
GARRIS, Daffie, H .... 336-633-0290 337 A
dhgarris@randolph.edu
GARRIS, Eric .... 843-661-1134 409 K
egarris@fmarion.edu
GARRIS, Kim .... 717-477-1523 395 E
kdgarr@ship.edu
GARRIS, Rick .... 303-963-3290.. 77 G
rgarris@ccu.edu
GARRISON, Amy .... 828-689-1295 331 A
agarrison@mhu.edu
GARRISON, Cindy .... 931-526-3660 420 A
cynthia.stephenson@fortisinstitute.edu
GARRISON, Deborah ..... 309-672-5513 143 D
dgarrison@methodistcol.edu
GARRISON, Greg .... 844-283-2246.. 93 A
GARRISON, Helene .... 949-376-6000.. 47 D
hgarrison@lcad.edu
GARRISON, James .... 913-971-3626 175 G
jgarriso@mnu.edu
GARRISON, James, R ... 913-971-3296 175 G
jgarriso@mnu.edu
GARRISON, Joseph, L .. 989-774-5251 222 C
garri2jl@cmich.edu
GARRISON, Julie, A ...... 269-387-5202 232 K
julie.garrison@wmich.edu
GARRISON, Kristen .... 940-397-6305 440 F
kristen.garrison@msutexas.edu
GARRISON, Lissy .... 303-871-2708.. 83 D
lissy.garrison@du.edu
GARRISON, Lorie .... 580-581-2612 365 G
loriebg@cameron.edu
GARRISON, Mark .... 443-885-3185 200 D
mark.garrison@morgan.edu
GARRISON, Melissa ...... 610-330-5005 387 E
garrisom@lafayette.edu
GARRISON, Phil .... 315-568-3268 308 F
pgarrison@nycc.edu
GARRISON, Rebecca ..... 314-539-5154 259 C
rgarrison@stlcc.edu
GARRISON, Ryan .... 828-652-6021 336 B
GARRISON, Samuel ...... 940-898-2911 451 F
sgarrison1@twu.edu
GARRISON, Shane .... 270-789-5541 179 E
msgarrison@campbellsville.edu
GARRISON, Tom .... 208-792-2247 131 A
tgarrison@lcsc.edu
GARRITY, Christopher .. 413-737-7000 205 A
christopher.garrity@aic.edu
GARRITY, Collette .... 212-343-1234 306 J
cgarrity@mcny.edu
GARRITY, Geraldine ...... 928-724-6814.. 12 C
ggarrity@dinecollege.edu
GARRITY, Kathleen, E ... 608-822-2471 500 G
kgarrity@swtc.edu
GARRITY, Mary .... 617-873-0168 207 F
mary.garrity@go.cambridgecollege.edu
GARRITY, Michael .... 708-456-0300 150 I
michaelgarrity@triton.edu
GARRITY, Mitch .... 505-277-0111 288 G
mgarrity@unm.edu
GARRY, Kirby .... 831-582-3015.. 32 C
kgarry@csumb.edu
GARSTECKI, Marcus ...... 605-229-8492 416 C
marcus.garstecki@presentation.edu
GARTENMAYER,
Charles .... 913-360-7583 171 D
cgartenmayer@benedictine.edu
GARTHOFF, Jerry .... 207-621-3067 196 A
garthoff@maine.edu
GARTLAND, Myles .... 816-501-4563 258 H
myles.gartland@rockhurst.edu
GARTMAN, Mark .... 903-510-2252 452 C
mgar3@tjc.edu
GARTNER, Lia .... 212-229-5192 308 C
gartnerl@newschool.edu
GARTON, Jilda .... 404-894-4819 118 F
jilda.garton@gtrc.gatech.edu
GARVER, Beth .... 617-585-0200 206 F
blg@the-bac.edu
GARVER, John, M .... 719-333-4153 504 C
john.garver@usafa.edu
GARVER, Robert, A .... 419-866-0261 361 H
ragarver@stautzenberger.com
GARVEY, Ann, L .... 612-330-1168 233 K
garvey@augsburg.edu
GARVEY, Carol .... 712-274-5178 168 B
garvey@morningside.edu
GARVEY, Elizabeth .... 518-320-1344 316 C
elizabeth.garvey@suny.edu
GARVEY, James .... 618-453-4551 149 E
jgarvey@siu.edu
GARVEY, James .... 267-341-5008 386 A
jgarvey@holyfamily.edu
GARVEY, John, H .... 202-319-5100.. 91 B
cua-president@cua.edu
GARVEY, Judy .... 714-241-6230.. 38 C
jgarvey@coastline.edu
GARVEY, Kathleen, M ... 508-373-9455 206 B
kathleen.garvey@becker.edu
GARVEY, Kevin .... 973-720-2861 284 I
garveyk@wpunj.edu
GARVIN, Lynda .... 318-487-5443 187 C
lyndagarvin@cltcc.edu
GARVIN, Maureen .... 912-525-5000 123 G
mgarvin@scad.edu
GARVIN, Natara .... 615-329-8635 419 K
ngarvin@fisk.edu
GARVIN, William .... 417-873-7482 252 F
wgarvin@drury.edu
GARVIN AQUILINO,
Rose .... 240-567-4249 200 C
rose.garvinaquilino@
montgomerycollege.edu
GARVIN-LEIGHTON,
Timothy .... 706-778-8500 123 B
tleighton@piedmont.edu
GARY, Carole .... 865-539-7025 425 F
cgary2@pstcc.edu
GARY, Cynthia .... 405-682-1611 367 H
cynthia.d.gary@occc.edu
GARY, Cynthia .... 405-682-1611 367 H
cgary@occc.edu
GARY, Jay .... 662-246-6302 247 D
jgary@msdelta.edu
GARY, Linda .... 903-510-3515 452 C
lgar@tjc.edu
GARY, Marc .... 212-678-8080 303 G
magary@jtsa.edu
GARY, William .... 216-987-3110 351 G
william.gary@tri-c.edu
GARZA, Adriana .... 361-593-4979 447 D
adriana.garza@tamuk.edu
GARZA, Ana Lisa .... 512-245-2780 450 E
ag02@txstate.edu
GARZA, Dan .... 210-784-2030 448 A
dan.garza@tamusa.edu
GARZA, Daniel .... 408-288-3163.. 61 M
daniel.garza@sjcc.edu
GARZA, Edwardo .... 773-838-7500 134 F
egarza@ccc.edu
GARZA, Felipe .... 361-593-2611 447 D
felipe.garza@tamuk.edu
GARZA, Fernando .... 830-372-6056 449 B
fgarza@tlu.edu
GARZA, Javier .... 254-968-9104 446 E
garza@tarleton.edu
GARZA, Kim .... 509-793-2010 478 H
kimg@bigbend.edu
GARZA, Nora, R .... 956-721-5868 439 C
nrgarza@laredo.edu
GARZA, Rebecca, J .... 214-860-2618 435 C
rgarza@dcccd.edu
GARZA, Richie .... 806-371-5022 430 A
rrgarza@actx.edu
GARZA, Robert .... 210-486-3963 429 C
GARZA, Robert .... 210-486-3000 429 F
GARZA, Roberto, A .... 956-326-2325 446 F
roberto.garza1@tamiu.edu
GARZA, Rolando .... 361-593-5501 447 D
rolando.garza@tamuk.edu
GARZA, JR., Victor .... 408-270-6434.. 61 L
victor.garza@evc.edu
GARZA-RODERICK,
Jessie .... 209-833-7900.. 60 J
jgarza-roderick@deltacollege.edu
GARZANELLI, Michael .. 660-785-4150 260 J
michaelg@truman.edu
GARZARELLI, Todd .... 724-357-4295 394 G
tgarzare@iup.edu
GASAWAY, Debbie .... 870-460-1622.. 22 D
gasaway@uamont.edu
GASCHE, Currie .... 847-574-5158 141 C
cgasche@lfgsm.edu
GASEVIC, Sarah .... 701-788-4647 345 E
sarah.gasevic@mayvillestate.edu
GASH, Bill .... 678-717-2357 126 A
william.gash@ung.edu
GASH, James, A .... 310-506-4451.. 56 C
jim.gash@pepperdine.edu
GASH, Justin .... 317-738-8213 154 J
jgash@franklincollege.edu
GASHI, Agron .... 845-848-4058 298 D
agron.gashi@dc.edu
GASKELL, Carolyn .... 509-527-2107 485 H
carolyn.gaskell@wallawalla.edu
GASKELL, Millicent .... 610-519-6371 402 D
millicent.gaskell@villanova.edu
GASKIN, Cathy, M .... 503-370-6492 378 B
cmccann@willamette.edu
GASKIN, Elizabeth .... 772-462-5604 101 E
egaskin@irsc.edu
GASKINS, Leebrian, E ... 956-326-2310 446 F
lgaskins@tamiu.edu
GASOSKE, Betsy .... 314-434-4044 252 B
registrar@covenantseminary.edu
GASPAR, Leigh .... 617-824-3877 208 H
leigh_gaspar@emerson.edu
GASPAR, Mario .... 714-564-6319.. 57 L
gaspar_mario@sac.edu
GASPAR, Nicholas .... 810-762-3200 231 G
ngaspar@umich.edu
GASPARD, Harold .... 504-671-6247 187 E
hgaspa@dcc.edu
GASPARD, Rusty .... 318-473-6443 188 J
rgaspard@lsua.edu
GASPARIAN, Albert .... 714-895-8707.. 38 D
agasparian@gwc.cccd.edu
GASPARICH, Gail .... 978-542-6265 213 C
ggasparich@salemstate.edu
GASPARRO, Paul .... 740-699-3037 348 F
pgasparro@belmontcollege.edu
GASPER, Kim .... 916-649-9600.. 26 F
kgasper@asher.edu
GASQUE, Tarlough .... 240-567-7588 200 C
tarlough.gasque@montgomerycollege.
edu
GASS, Beth .... 423-305-7783 419 B
beth.gass@chattanoogacollege.edu
GASS, Melanie .... 704-403-1613 327 D
melanie.gass@carolinashealthcare.org
GASS, Michael .... 828-232-5118 342 C
mgass@unca.edu
GASSELING, Garet .... 509-453-0374 483 C
garet.gasseling@perrytech.edu

GEE, Terry ... 619-594-2853.. 33 E
tgee@sdsu.edu
GEEHAN, Margaret ... 518-629-7151 302 E
m.geehan@hvcc.edu
GEEL, Donna ... 207-454-1013 195 B
dgeel@wccc.me.edu
GEER, Brad ... 814-371-2090 400 D
bgeer@triangle-tech.edu
GEER, Jill ... 800-280-0307 152 H
jill.geer@ace.edu
GEER, John, G ... 615-936-6366 428 D
john.geer@vanderbilt.edu
GEER, Kimberly ... 425-739-8119 482 A
kimberly.geer@lwtech.edu
GEER, Nathan ... 503-375-7010 373 A
ngeer@corban.edu
GEETER, Andy ... 229-732-5934 114 B
andygeeter@andrewcollege.edu
GEETER, Candy ... 248-341-2138 229 A
crgeeter@oaklandcc.edu
GEETTER, Erika ... 617-353-2326 207 D
egeetter@bu.edu
GEFELL, Michele, D ... 315-786-2271 303 F
mgefell@sunyjefferson.edu
GEFFERT, Bryn ... 802-656-2020 463 E
bryn.geffert@uvm.edu
GEGENHEIMER BALDASSARO,
Sarah ... 202-994-5152.. 91 F
sarahgb@gwu.edu
GEGGIE, Steven ... 847-317-8178 150 H
sgeggie@tiu.edu
GEHBAUER, Daryl ... 636-481-3120 254 A
dgehbaue@jeffco.edu
GEHLERT, Sarah ... 803-777-5292 413 C
sgehlert@mailbox.sc.edu
GEHLHAUSEN, Keith ... 812-488-2943 161 A
kg77@evansville.edu
GEHRICH, Michael, D ... 317-381-6000 162 C
mgehrich@vinu.edu
GEHRING, Patrick, D ... 253-535-7119 482 H
gehrinpd@plu.edu
GEHRINGER, Steve ... 610-409-3000 402 A
GEHRIS, Deborah, L ... 417-268-1010 250 E
gehrisd@evangel.edu
GEHRKE, Deb ... 651-793-1278 238 H
deb.gehrke@metrostate.edu
GEHRKE, Sean ... 206-543-9956 485 F
sjgehrke@uw.edu
GEHRMAN-ROTTIER,
Laura ... 715-346-3811 497 F
lgehrman@uwsp.edu
GEIDEL, Jeremy ... 402-643-7330 266 G
jeremy.geidel@cune.edu
GEIER, Doug ... 415-369-5275.. 44 D
dgeier@ggu.edu
GEIER, Marisa ... 360-442-2391 482 B
mgeier@lowercolumbia.edu
GEIGER, Darlene ... 503-594-3271 372 D
darleneg@clackamas.edu
GEIGER, James ... 814-393-2572 394 D
jgeiger@clarion.edu
GEIGER, Kimberly ... 423-775-6596 423 F
GEIGER, Martha ... 513-936-1691 362 E
martha.geiger@uc.edu
GEIGER, Tad ... 847-970-4902 152 A
tgeiger@usml.edu
GEIGER, William ... 903-565-5515 456 A
wgeiger@uttyler.edu
GEIL, Carol ... 641-844-5747 166 K
carol.geil@iavalley.edu
GEIL, Toi ... 307-766-2187 502 H
GEIS, Scott ... 901-321-3349 419 C
sgeis@cbu.edu
GEISER, Laura ... 314-977-2543 259 H
laura.geiser@slu.edu
GEISER-GETZ, Glenn ... 585-245-5531 318 E
geisergetz@geneseo.edu
GEISLER, Allison ... 218-322-2323 238 E
allison.geisler@itascacc.edu
GEISLER, Michael, E ... 914-323-5230 305 J
michael.geisler@mville.edu
GEISLER, Norman, L ... 714-966-8500.. 73 C
info@ves.edu
GEISMAN, Cami ... 225-342-6950 191 D
cami.geisman@ulsystem.edu
GEISSLER, Mary ... 909-607-8451.. 37 G
mary_geissler@kgi.edu
GEISSLER, Nancy ... 217-228-5432 146 F
geissna@quincy.edu
GEIST, Alan ... 937-766-7768 349 G
geista@cedarville.edu
GEIST, Amanda ... 630-466-7900 152 C
ageist@waubonsee.edu
GELB, Ed ... 919-573-5350 340 F
assessment@shepherds.edu
GELBACK-DIAZ, Christy 317-921-4746 157 G
cgelback@ivytech.edu
GELCH, Deborah ... 617-333-2158 208 E
deborah.gelch@curry.edu
GELDENHUYS, Tammie . 620-331-4100 174 C
tgeldenhuys@indycc.edu
GELDER, Tom ... 661-395-4840.. 46 L
tom.gelder@bakersfieldcollge.edu
GELDWORTH, Lipa ... 718-853-8500 322 I
GELDZAHLER, Daniel ... 718-633-4715 312 F
collegeoy@gmail.com
GELERNTER, Mark ... 303-315-1020.. 83 C
mark.gelernter@ucdenver.edu
GELINAS, Cynthia, B ... 803-641-3609 413 D
cindyg@usca.edu
GELINAS, David ... 704-894-2698 328 F
dagelinas@davidson.edu
GELL, Barry ... 518-255-5440 319 F
gellbf@cobleskill.edu
GELLE, Mark ... 507-786-3294 243 C
gelle@stolaf.edu
GELLER, Jack, M ... 813-253-6262 112 J
jgeller@ut.edu
GELLER, Laurie ... 701-858-3310 345 F
laurie.geller@minotstateu.edu
GELLER, Mary, A ... 320-363-5601 235 C
mgeller@csbsju.edu
GELLER, Steve ... 952-358-8954 239 F
steve.geller@normandale.edu
GELLES, Karen ... 631-420-2040 321 B
gelleska@farmingdale.edu
GELLMAN, Sarah, M ... 724-946-7340 402 G
gellmasm@westminster.edu
GELO, Daniel, J ... 210-458-4359 455 E
daniel.gelo@utsa.edu
GELORMINI, John ... 617-745-3719 208 G
john.gelormini@enc.edu
GELOW, Zac ... 954-526-1275 100 O
GELPI-RODRIGUEZ,
Phaedra ... 787-480-2370 507 C
pgelpi@sanjuanciudadpatria.com
GELSINGER, Kim ... 704-922-6515 334 F
gelsinger.kim@gaston.edu
GELSTON, Nicole ... 860-486-5796.. 88 E
nicole.gelston@uconn.edu
GELWICKS, Carla ... 360-383-3222 486 G
cgelwick@whatcom.edu
GELY, Gilda ... 616-554-5183 223 B
gilda.gely@davenport.edu
GEMEDA, Mekbib, L ... 757-446-7151 466 I
gemedam@evms.edu
GEMME, Terese ... 203-392-5499.. 85 A
gemmet1@southernct.edu
GEMMELL, Ann ... 651-290-6476 242 G
ann.gemmell@mitchellhamline.edu
GEMMER, Pete ... 513-936-1632 362 E
peter.gemmer@uc.edu
GEMPERLEIN,
Monica, P ... 919-334-1520 338 G
mpgemperlein@waketech.edu
GEMPERLINE, Paul ... 252-328-6073 341 C
gemperlinep@ecu.edu
GEMPESAW,
Conrado, M ... 718-990-6755 314 B
pres@stjohns.edu
GENANDT, Jim, J ... 785-320-4500 175 D
jimgenandt@manhattantech.edu
GENARD, Daniel, J ... 757-683-3090 469 G
dgenard@odu.edu
GENARD, Giovanna, M . 757-683-3580 469 G
ggenard@odu.edu
GENARDO, Patricia ... 630-889-6597 144 G
pgenardo@nuhs.edu
GEND, Peter ... 800-785-0585.. 39 G
pgend@columbiacollege.edu
GENDRON, Dennis ... 206-296-5556 484 F
gendron@seattleu.edu
GENDRON, Dennis ... 423-425-4000 428 A
dennis-gendron@utc.edu
GENECIN, Paul ... 203-432-0076.. 89 D
paul.genecin@yale.edu
GENELIUS, Sandy ... 413-542-5785 205 B
sgenelius@amherst.edu
GENERALS, Donald ... 215-751-8000 382 A
ggenerals@ccp.edu
GENES, Marna ... 408-924-1550.. 34 B
marna.genes@sjsu.edu
GENESE, Carol ... 914-632-5400 307 G
cgenese@monroecollege.edu
GENETTI, Carol ... 805-893-2013.. 70 A
cgenetti@graddiv.ucsb.edu
GENFI, Henrieta ... 973-618-3589 276 D
hgenfi@caldwell.edu
GENG, Zhong, M ... 570-348-6211 389 G
geng@marywood.edu
GENGLER, Charles, E ... 713-221-8017 453 B
GENIG, Dennis ... 734-462-4400 230 D
dgenig@schoolcraft.edu
GENNA, Angela ... 602-285-7357.. 13 F
angela.genna@phoenixcollege.edu
GENNARO, Gwen ... 719-255-3153.. 83 B
ggennaro@uccs.edu
GENNARO, Susan ... 617-552-1710 207 B
susan.gennaro@bc.edu
GENNETTE, Heather ... 785-243-1435 172 F
hgennette@cloud.edu
GENO, Amanda ... 413-565-1150 205 G
ageno@baypath.edu
GENO, Rita, B ... 802-468-1203 464 A
rita.geno@castleton.edu
GENONI, Mia, R ... 804-289-8468 472 L
mgenoni@richmond.edu
GENOVESE, Lou ... 216-397-1999 354 I
lgenovese@jcu.edu
GENT, Barbara ... 606-589-3020 182 E
barbara.gent@kctcs.edu
GENT, Pamela ... 814-393-2223 394 D
pgent@clarion.edu
GENTHON, Paulette ... 402-556-4456 269 G
paulettegenthon@ucha.edu
GENTILE, Kim ... 330-972-6345 362 B
gentile@uakron.edu
GENTILE, Linda ... 412-268-5231 380 F
lgentile@cmu.edu
GENTILE, Maria ... 415-257-1307.. 41 H
maria.gentile@dominican.edu
GENTILE, Marla ... 828-898-3841 330 E
gentilem@lmc.edu
GENTILE, Patricia, A ... 978-762-4000 215 B
pgentile@northshore.edu
GENTLEWARRIOR,
Sabrina ... 508-531-1429 212 B
sabrina.gentlewarrior@bridgew.edu
GENTNER, John ... 614-236-6544 349 D
jgentner@capital.edu
GENTRY, Ashley ... 757-965-8500 466 I
gentryac@evms.edu
GENTRY, Bradley, D ... 217-786-2278 142 B
brad.gentry@llcc.edu
GENTRY, Elmer, J ... 773-821-2589 133 K
egentry@csu.edu
GENTRY, Eric, C ... 859-572-5129 184 A
egentry@nku.edu
GENTRY, Jeff ... 575-562-2733 285 M
jeff.gentry@enmu.edu
GENTRY, Jodi, D ... 352-392-1075 109 F
jodi-gentry@ufl.edu
GENTRY, Kalonn ... 423-652-4715 420 H
kkgentry@king.edu
GENTRY, Keil ... 703-784-2105 503 H
keil.gentry@usmc.mil
GENTRY, Marichal ... 931-598-1229 423 M
wmgentr@sewanee.edu
GENTRY, Rusty ... 615-868-6503 422 G
rusty.gentry@mtsa.edu
GENTRY, Susan ... 252-335-0821 333 G
susan_gentry@albemarle.edu
GENTRY, William, A ... 336-841-9470 329 G
wgentry@highpoint.edu
GENTRY-WRIGHT,
Susan, C ... 864-833-8100 411 I
sgentry-w@presby.edu
GENTSCH, James ... 205-652-3361.... 9 A
jgentsch@uwa.edu
GENTZLER, Randall ... 410-617-2345 199 F
rdgentzler@loyola.edu
GEOFFRION-SCANNELL,
Kathryn ... 978-837-5211 216 D
geoffrionsck@merrimack.edu
GEOGHEGAN, Michael .. 740-264-5591 352 H
mgeoghegan@egcc.edu
GEORG, Vanessa ... 312-341-3801 147 H
GEORGE, Amanda ... 501-686-5670.. 22 C
adgeorge@uams.edu
GEORGE, Andrew, L ... 616-526-6057 222 A
alg35@calvin.edu
GEORGE, Beena ... 713-525-5903 454 H
georgeb@stthom.edu
GEORGE, Bill ... 816-322-0110 250 K
bill.george@calvary.edu
GEORGE, Chris ... 507-786-3775 243 C
georgec@stolaf.edu
GEORGE, Christi ... 205-652-3840.... 9 A
cjw@uwa.edu
GEORGE, Claudia ... 770-538-4749 115 D
cgeorge@brenau.edu
GEORGE, Deborah ... 770-962-7580 120 E
dgeorge@gwinnetttech.edu
GEORGE, Demetria ... 225-771-2552 191 A
dgeorge@sulc.edu
GEORGE, Dionne ... 478-757-4023 126 H
dgeorge@wesleyancollege.edu
GEORGE, Emily ... 605-995-2601 415 C
emily.george@dwu.edu
GEORGE, Janice, S ... 620-421-6700 175 C
janicec@labette.edu
GEORGE, Jennifer ... 719-255-3820.. 83 B
jennifer.george@uccs.edu
GEORGE, Julie ... 859-622-1778 180 B
julie.george@eku.edu
GEORGE, Karen ... 719-365-1038.. 82 M
karen.george@uchealth.org
GEORGE, Karen ... 636-922-8643 258 I
kgeorge@stchas.edu
GEORGE, Kris ... 954-532-9614 101 D
GEORGE, Lee ... 612-330-1629 233 K
lgeorge@augsburg.edu
GEORGE, Lisa ... 620-327-8217 173 H
lisa.george@hesston.edu
GEORGE, Lynn, E ... 412-578-6115 380 E
legeorge@carlow.edu
GEORGE, Marianne ... 863-297-1000 105 A
mgeorge@polk.edu
GEORGE, Mertha, V ... 601-877-6154 244 H
mgeorge@alcorn.edu
GEORGE, Michel ... 503-768-7850 373 G
mgeorge@lclark.edu
GEORGE, Rani ... 229-430-4832 113 H
rani.george@asurams.edu
GEORGE, Regina ... 251-460-6050.... 8 F
reginageorge@southalabama.edu
GEORGE, Rick ... 303-492-6591.. 83 A
rick.george@colorado.edu
GEORGE, Sarah, B ... 801-581-6927 460 E
sgeorge@nhmu.utah.edu
GEORGE, Sheila ... 202-885-8657.. 93 E
sgeorge@wesleyseminary.edu
GEORGE, Simone, M ... 302-356-6898.. 90 I
simone.m.george@wilmu.edu
GEORGE, Susan ... 304-473-8080 491 H
george@wvwc.edu
GEORGE, T. Chris ... 270-745-3978 185 E
chris.george@wku.edu
GEORGE, Tami, B ... 910-272-3541 337 D
tgeorge@robeson.edu
GEORGE, Teresa ... 989-837-4227 228 H
georget@northwood.edu
GEORGE, Thomas ... 704-991-0387 338 C
tgeorge5857@stanly.edu
GEORGE, Tracey ... 615-322-6310 428 D
tracey.george@vanderbilt.edu
GEORGE, Tree ... 318-257-3036 191 F
tgeorge@latech.edu
GEORGE, William, D ... 570-577-1228 379 F
wdgeorge@bucknell.edu
GEORGE-MERRILL,
Pamela ... 216-397-1908 354 I
pgeorgemerrill@jcu.edu
GEORGE-TAYLOR,
Mosunmola ... 423-697-5731 424 E
mosunmola.georgetaylor@chattanoogastate.edu
GEORGE-WEINSTEIN,
Mindy ... 215-871-6654 396 D
mindygw@pcom.edu
GEORGES, Anthony, C .. 314-516-5508 261 D
tony_georges@umsl.edu
GEORGES, Jane ... 619-260-4550.. 71 J
jgeorges@sandiego.edu
GEORGIEV, Nancy ... 864-294-3274 410 A
nancy.georgiev@furman.edu
GEORGIOPOULOS,
Michael ... 407-823-5338 109 E
michaelg@ucf.edu
GEORGIOU, Thales ... 972-238-6231 435 F
tgeorgiou@dcccd.edu
GEORGIOU, Tina ... 212-343-1234 306 J
tgeorgiou@mcny.edu
GEPHART, Elizabeth ... 217-424-6348 143 H
egephart@millikin.edu
GEPPERTH, James ... 216-201-9025 355 I
GERACE, Christopher ... 716-250-7500 291 K
cpgerace@bryantstratton.edu
GERAMBIA, Becky ... 800-280-0307 152 H
becky.gerambia@ace.edu
GERAMI, Keyvan ... 314-286-3670 258 E
kgerami@ranken.edu

GERAMI, Michelle .... 409-933-8271 433 L
mgerami@com.edu
GERARD, Debra .... 714-480-7450.. 57 K
gerard_debra@rsccd.edu
GERARD, Matthew, C ... 402-280-1773 266 I
matthewgerard@creighton.edu
GERARD, Pam .... 319-895-5267 164 B
pgerard@cornellcollege.edu
GERARD, Phil .... 864-242-5100 407 B
GERARD, Stacey .... 252-940-6241 332 C
stacey.gerard@beaufortccc.edu
GERASSIMIDES, Gus ..... 859-985-3158 179 C
gus_gerassimides@berea.edu
GERATY, Brent, G .... 909-748-8076.. 71 G
brent_geraty@redlands.edu
GERATY, Larry .... 951-785-2160.. 47 C
lgeraty@lasierra.edu
GERBASI, Iris .... 714-997-6676.. 36 C
gerbasi@chapman.edu
GERBER, Cheryl .... 724-946-6173 402 G
gerberca@westminster.edu
GERBER, Elizabeth, L .... 815-599-3421 138 B
liz.gerber@highland.edu
GERBER, Gary .... 870-245-5129.. 20 E
gerberg@obu.edu
GERBER, Molly .... 215-955-1061 400 A
molly.gerber@jefferson.edu
GERBER, Natalie .... 716-673-3529 317 A
natalie.gerber@fredonia.edu
GERBER, Nathan .... 801-863-7973 461 A
nathan.gerber@uvu.edu
GERBER, Stephen, D .... 574-372-5100 155 B
gerbersd@grace.edu
GERBER, Sue .... 201-200-3042 279 E
sgerber@njcu.edu
GERBERICH, Brian .... 214-887-5174 436 B
bgerberich@dts.edu
GERBOTH, Karen .... 937-327-6141 364 H
kgerboth@wittenberg.edu
GERBRACHT, Tonya ...... 319-273-6520 163 B
tonya.gerbracht@uni.edu
GERDA, Joseph .... 661-362-3410.. 38 H
joe.gerda@canyons.edu
GERDES, Christine, M .. 734-936-2254 231 E
cmgerdes@umich.edu
GERDRUM, Kacie .... 541-684-7288 374 G
kgerdrum@nwcu.edu
GERDTS, Adam .... 212-960-0863 326 E
adam.gerdts@yu.edu
GERDTS, Daniel .... 507-344-7777 234 B
dgerdts@blc.edu
GERE, Nicholas .... 207-602-2011 196 G
ngere@une.edu
GEREAUX, Teresa, T ..... 540-375-2282 471 B
gereaux@roanoke.edu
GEREMIA, Kenneth .... 413-528-7291 205 F
kgeremia@simons-rock.edu
GERETY, Emilie .... 559-325-5205.. 66 D
emilie.gerety@cloviscollege.edu
GERG, Julie .... 607-844-8211 322 H
gergj@tompkinscortland.edu
GERGER, Daniel .... 212-217-3315 299 H
daniel_gerger@fitnyc.edu
GERGER, Rick .... 314-246-8708 262 C
rickgerger06@webster.edu
GERHARD, Gesine .... 515-271-3939 165 A
gesine.gerhard@drake.edu
GERHARD, Ronald .... 925-485-5203.. 35 N
rgerhard@clpccd.org
GERHARDSON, Ashley .. 479-308-2311.. 17 C
ashley.gerhardson@arcomedu.org
GERHARDT, Cassie .... 701-777-4200 345 C
cassie.gerhardt@und.edu
GERHARDT, Lyndsay .... 585-345-6800 301 A
lagerhardt@genesee.edu
GERHARDT, Marie, O ... 518-255-5630 319 F
gerharmo@cobleskill.edu
GERHARDT, Winifred .... 440-826-8002 348 E
wgerhard@bw.edu
GERHART, Barry .... 608-262-3895 496 C
bgerhart@bus.wisc.edu
GERHART, Robert .... 229-391-4850 113 F
rgerhart@abac.edu
GERIA, Kellyann, R .... 215-699-5700 388 E
kgeria@lsb.edu
GERICS, Aron .... 810-762-0200 228 C
aron.gerics@mcc.edu
GERIEN, Matt .... 901-843-3874 423 J
gerienm@rhodes.edu
GERIG, Jill .... 912-478-5367 119 C
jgerig@georgiasouthern.edu
GERIGUIS, David .... 951-785-2002.. 47 C
dgerigui@lasierra.edu

GERIK, Debbie .... 254-659-7704 437 G
debgerik@hillcollege.edu
GERING, Carol .... 541-346-3428 377 D
cgering2@uoregon.edu
GERING, Jonathan, C ... 316-284-5241 171 F
jgering@bethelks.edu
GERINGER, Sandra .... 251-626-3303.... 7 E
sgeringer@ussa.edu
GERISCH, Carl .... 541-888-7707 376 F
carl.gerisch@socc.edu
GERKEN, Heather .... 203-432-1660.. 89 D
heather.gerken@yale.edu
GERKEN, Kevin .... 419-267-1226 358 A
kgerken@northweststate.edu
GERKEN, Stacey .... 715-346-3553 497 F
sgerken@uwsp.edu
GERKIN, Jeffrey, G .... 865-974-3131 427 G
jgerkin@utk.edu
GERKIN GUERRANT,
Emily .... 517-355-3853 227 D
emilyg@msu.edu
GERL, Beth .... 217-234-5250 141 D
bgerl@lakeland.cc.il.us
GERLACH, Alysa .... 617-373-5144 217 F
GERLACH, David, M ..... 217-732-3155 141 I
dgerlach@lincolncollege.edu
GERLACH, Karen .... 202-884-9203.. 93 B
gerlachk@trinitydc.edu
GERLACH, Matthew .... 313-883-8541 229 K
gerlach.matthew@shms.edu
GERLICH, Bella .... 806-742-2261 451 B
bella.gerlich@ttu.edu
GERMAIN, Lauren .... 315-464-5193 317 F
germainl@upstate.edu
GERMAN, Deborah .... 407-266-1000 109 E
deborah.german@ucf.edu
GERMAN, James .... 916-278-5344.. 32 E
james.german@csus.edu
GERMAN, Lisa .... 256-352-8306 .... 4 A
lisa.german@wallacestate.edu
GERMAN, Lisa, A .... 713-743-0291 452 F
lagerman@uh.edu
GERMANO, Dorothy .... 707-986-4153.. 45 B
GERMANO, William .... 516-796-4800 308 F
wgermano@nycc.edu
GERMANY, Carole, H ... 601-635-6201 245 I
cgermany@eccc.edu
GERMANY, Debbie .... 803-754-4100 409 A
GERMERAAD,
Stephanie .... 310-954-5080.. 27 E
GERMIC, Stephen, A ..... 406-657-1020 265 E
stephen.germic@rocky.edu
GERNANDER, Scott, R .. 281-478-2771 443 C
scottr.gernander@sjcd.edu
GERNER, Steven, W ...... 262-243-5700 493 B
steven.gerner@cuw.edu
GERNES, Todd, S .... 508-565-1946 218 H
tgernes@stonehill.edu
GERODIMOS, Ashley ..... 219-989-2414 159 G
afclark@pnw.edu
GEROUX, Joni .... 715-833-6397 499 D
jgeroux3@cvtc.edu
GEROW, Gary .... 207-941-7907 194 A
gerowg@husson.edu
GERRAIN, Dawn .... 518-608-8271 299 G
dgerrainl@excelsior.edu
GERRETSEN, Amy, L ..... 920-748-8353 495 G
gerretsena@ripon.edu
GERRIETS, Carla .... 402-399-2391 266 F
cgerriets@csm.edu
GERRIG, Richard, J ...... 631-632-7035 317 D
richard.gerrig@stonybrook.edu
GERRISH, James .... 973-290-4479 277 A
jgerrish@cse.edu
GERRY, Bobbi, J .... 208-885-6111 131 G
bgerry@uidaho.edu
GERSBACHER, Holly ...... 937-327-6374 364 H
gersbacherh@wittenberg.edu
GERSH, Sheila .... 914-674-7339 306 F
sgersh@mercy.edu
GERSHEN, Jay, A .... 330-325-6263 357 G
president@neomed.edu
GERSHMAN, Richard ..... 615-277-7434 428 F
rgershman@watkins.edu
GERSICH, Frank .... 309-457-2119 144 A
fgersich@monmouthcollege.edu
GERSTEN, Karen .... 760-591-3012.. 71 H
kgersten@usa.edu
GERSTENBERGER, Julie 806-716-2019 443 I
jgerstenberger@southplainscollege.edu
GERSTENBERGER,
Shawn .... 702-895-1565 271 E
shawn.gerstenberger@unlv.edu

GERSTL-PEPIN, Cynthia 413-545-2705 211 D
cgerstlp@umass.edu
GERSTMAN, Josh .... 206-878-3710 481 H
GERSTMAYR, Andrew .... 973-748-9000 276 A
andrew_gerstmayr@bloomfield.edu
GERTLER, Sara .... 909-667-4413.. 37 H
sgertler@claremontlincoln.edu
GERTNER, Kimberly, A . 843-953-5758 408 E
gertnerka@cofc.edu
GERTSON, Katherine ..... 212-799-5000 303 H
GERTZ, Genie .... 202-651-5653.. 91 E
genie.gertz@gallaudet.edu
GERVASI, Robert .... 614-251-4690 358 G
robert.gervasi@ohiodominican.edu
GERWITZ, Jim .... 573-518-2134 256 B
jgerwitz@mineralarea.edu
GERZINA, Gretchen .... 413-577-3902 211 D
dean@honors.umass.edu
GERZINA, Holly, A .... 330-325-6740 357 G
hgerzina@neomed.edu
GESELE, Scott .... 757-594-7863 466 B
scott.gesele@cnu.edu
GESO, Cristina .... 215-955-8164 400 A
cristina.geso@jefferson.edu
GESSELE, Symonne .... 701-483-2314 345 D
dsu.symonne.gessele@dickinsonstate.
edu
GESSLER, Benjamin ...... 740-283-6466 353 B
bgessler@franciscan.edu
GESSNER, Bob, F .... 407-582-1321 112 K
rgessner@valenciacollege.edu
GESTOSO, Lloyd .... 215-702-4275 380 D
lgestoso@cairn.edu
GESTRING, Sheila, K .... 605-677-5641 416 H
sheila.gestring@usd.edu
GETCHELL, JR.,
Charles, M .... 603-641-7320 274 C
cgetchell@anselm.edu
GETMAN, Meghan .... 315-792-7264 321 E
meghan.getman@sunypoly.edu
GETSINGER, Joseph ...... 856-415-6209 281 D
jgetsinger@rcgc.edu
GETTY, Marc, D .... 304-326-1258 488 F
mgetty@salemu.edu
GETTYS, Rob .... 269-471-3215 221 B
rgettys@andrews.edu
GETZ, Beth .... 765-285-5131 153 C
bgoetz@bsu.edu
GETZ, Karen .... 724-266-3838 400 H
kgetz@tsm.edu
GETZ, Kathleen .... 410-617-2301 199 F
kgetz@loyola.edu
GETZ, Rob .... 610-902-8147 380 C
rag44@cabrini.edu
GETZ, Roger .... 207-768-9595 196 E
roger.getz@maine.edu
GEVAIS, Alissa .... 207-974-4796 194 H
agervais@emcc.edu
GEVITZ, Norman .... 660-626-2371 250 A
ngevitz@atsu.edu
GEWEKE, Christina .... 319-273-7505 163 B
christina.geweke@uni.edu
GEWOLB, Matthew .... 212-431-2352 309 G
matthew.gewolb@nyls.edu
GEYE, Trina .... 254-968-9400 446 E
geye@tarleton.edu
GEYER, Eileen .... 978-232-2129 209 B
egeyer@endicott.edu
GEYER, Enid .... 518-262-6008 289 F
geyere@amc.edu
GEYER, Jon .... 614-236-6955 349 D
jgeyer@capital.edu
GEYER, Mariann, K .... 412-392-3805 397 A
mgeyer@pointpark.edu
GFELLER, Josh .... 785-320-4530 175 D
joshgfeller@manhattantech.edu
GHAFFAR, Abdul .... 910-521-6577 343 B
abdul.ghaffar@uncp.edu
GHAHRAMANI, Saeed ... 413-782-1218 219 F
sghahram@wne.edu
GHALI, Ghali, E .... 318-675-5240 189 C
gghali@lsuhsc.edu
GHAN, Mark .... 775-445-4468 271 G
mark.ghan@wnc.edu
GHANA, Julani .... 610-399-2048 394 C
jghana@cheyney.edu
GHANEM, Salma .... 312-362-8875 135 I
sghanem@depaul.edu
GHANNADIAN,
F. Frank .... 813-253-6221 112 J
fghannadian@ut.edu
GHARAKANIAN, Anahid 213-738-6786.. 65 G
agharakanian@swlaw.edu

GHAZARIAN, Esther, A . 781-768-7280 218 C
esther.ghazarian@regiscollege.edu
GHAZARYAN, Ashot ...... 510-925-4282.. 25 Q
ashot.ghazaryan@aua.am
GHERBI, Naima .... 860-439-2411.. 86 H
nghe@conncoll.edu
GHIDIU, Katherine, E ... 585-292-2320 307 H
kghidiu@monroecc.edu
GHIDOTTI, Lisa .... 540-831-5000 470 C
lghidotti@radford.edu
GHILONI, Adam .... 864-646-1583 413 A
aghiloni@tctc.edu
GHINASSI, Frank .... 848-932-3818 282 A
ghinassi@ubhc.rutgers.edu
GHOLSON, Robert, D .... 601-266-4466 249 F
robert.gholson@usm.edu
GHOLSON, Shari .... 270-534-3372 182 F
shari.gholson@kctcs.edu
GHORAYEB, Samir .... 409-984-6484 450 B
samir.ghorayeb@lamarpa.edu
GHORI, Zaid .... 650-738-7088.. 61 Q
ghoriz@smccd.edu
GHORMOZ, Jacquelyn .. 570-504-9073 384 F
jghormoz@som.geisinger.edu
GHORPADE, Anuja .... 518-694-7337 289 D
anuja.ghorpade@acphs.edu
GHOSAL, Bobby .... 601-928-6207 247 E
bobby.ghosal@mgccc.edu
GHOSH, Avijit .... 217-265-0263 151 A
ghosha@uillinois.edu
GHOSH, Debarati .... 813-253-7995 101 A
dghosh@hccfl.edu
GHOSH, Guru .... 540-231-3205 477 A
gghosh@vt.edu
GHOSH, Jayati .... 610-499-4300 403 B
jghosh@widener.edu
GHOSH, Melanie Mala . 617-627-2000 219 B
mala.ghosh@tufts.edu
GHOSH, Monica .... 808-956-7205 128 F
monicag@hawaii.edu
GHOSH, Sibdas .... 412-578-6072 380 E
sghosh@carlow.edu
GHOUS, Mostafa .... 831-386-7100.. 44 K
mghous@hartnell.edu
GHRAYEB, Omar .... 815-753-0494 145 C
oghrayeb@niu.edu
GIACOBBE, Jeff .... 973-655-5373 279 C
giacobbej@mail.montclair.edu
GIACOMINI, Mike .... 661-395-4203.. 46 L
mike.giacomini@bakersfieldcollege.edu
GIACOMINI, Mike .... 626-300-5444.. 57 A
GIAGO, Don .... 605-455-6000 416 B
dgiago@olc.edu
GIAMBRA, Leonard, M . 860-701-6679 504 F
leonard.m.giambra@uscg.mil
GIAMPIETRO, Michael .. 413-565-1000 205 G
mgiampietro@baypath.edu
GIANCATARINO, Kate ... 610-519-6285 402 D
kate.giancatarino@villanova.edu
GIANCOLI, Adriana .... 607-735-1770 299 D
agiancoli@elmira.edu
GIANFORTE, Danna .... 951-827-4888.. 69 C
danna.gianforte@ucr.edu
GIANFRANCESCO,
Laura .... 423-636-7300 427 B
lgianfrancesco@tusculum.edu
GIANNELLIS,
Emmanuel, P .... 607-255-7200 297 F
epg2@cornell.edu
GIANNESCHI, Matt .... 970-945-8691.. 77 K
mgianneschi@coloradomtn.edu
GIANNET, Stanley, M ... 727-816-3490 104 F
giannes@phsc.edu
GIANNINI, Gaetan .... 215-641-6303 390 H
ggiannini@mc3.edu
GIANNINI, John .... 856-256-5414 281 E
giannini@rowan.edu
GIANNOTTI, Louis, J .... 410-293-1400 504 I
giannott@usna.edu
GIANOTTI, Margaret ...... 541-278-5775 372 A
mgianotti@bluecc.edu
GIARDULLO, Kelly .... 781-891-2014 206 D
kgiardullo@bentley.edu
GIARRUSSO, John .... 518-956-8090 316 D
jgiarrusso@albany.edu
GIATAS, Domna .... 207-621-3495 196 A
domna.giatas@maine.edu
GIAUQUE, Margie, T .... 218-755-2038 237 E
margie.giauque@bemidjistate.edu
GIBB, Deborah .... 212-229-5667 308 C
gibbd@newschool.edu
GIBB, Katharine .... 864-503-5444 414 D
kgibb@uscupstate.edu

GIBB, Randy .... 602-639-7500.. 12 J
GIBBEL, Mark .... 212-229-5662 308 C
gibbelm@newschool.edu
GIBBISON, Godfrey .... 843-953-3596 408 E
gibbisonga@lowcountrygraduatecenter.org
GIBBISON, Godfrey .... 843-953-3596 408 E
gibbisonga@cofc.edu
GIBBON, Lori .... 316-942-4291 175 I
gibbonl@newmanu.edu
GIBBONS, Arthur .... 845-758-7442 290 G
gibbons@bard.edu
GIBBONS, Dennis .... 315-792-5361 307 D
dgibbons@mvcc.edu
GIBBONS, Earl, F .... 360-650-3308 486 F
earl.gibbons@wwu.edu
GIBBONS, Kristie .... 540-261-4100 471 H
kristie.gibbons@svu.edu
GIBBONS, Michael .... 478-471-2430 121 F
michael.gibbons@mga.edu
GIBBONS, Peter .... 304-724-3700 487 E
pgibbons@apus.edu
GIBBONS, Susan .... 203-432-1810.. 89 D
susan.gibbons@yale.edu
GIBBONS, Thomas, F ... 312-503-3011 145 F
tgibbons@northwestern.edu
GIBBS, Beth, B .... 207-859-1130 195 G
gibbs@thomas.edu
GIBBS, Brian .... 503-494-5657 375 B
cedma@ohsu.edu
GIBBS, Charles .... 205-929-1156.... 6 B
GIBBS, Danny .... 615-366-3921 424 D
danny.gibbs@tbr.edu
GIBBS, Donna .... 360-650-3482 486 F
donna.gibbs@wwu.edu
GIBBS, Hilary, H .... 229-259-5503 126 G
hhgibbs@valdosta.edu
GIBBS, J. D .... 252-527-6223 335 G
jdgibbs27@lenoircc.edu
GIBBS, Jamie .... 252-249-1851 336 F
jgibbs@pamlicocc.edu
GIBBS, Jeffery .... 407-971-5172 107 D
gibbsj@seminolestate.edu
GIBBS, Jeremiah .... 317-788-2058 161 B
gibbsj@uindy.edu
GIBBS, Jim .... 806-651-3287 448 C
jgibbs@wtamu.edu
GIBBS, Kelly .... 510-549-4702.. 66 B
kgibbs@sksm.edu
GIBBS, Lincoln .... 231-591-2273 223 J
lincolngibbs@ferris.edu
GIBBS, Mark, G .... 864-587-4221 412 G
gibbsm@smcsc.edu
GIBBS, Melissa .... 707-967-2911.. 53 C
lissa.gibbs@napavalley.edu
GIBBS, Nicole .... 919-530-6096 342 A
ngibbs2@nccu.edu
GIBBS, Renisha, L .... 850-644-8082 109 C
rgibbs@admin.fsu.edu
GIBBS, Ryan .... 806-716-2207 443 I
rgibbs@southplainscollege.edu
GIBBS, Sarah .... 919-209-2086 335 F
sfgibbs@johnstoncc.edu
GIBBS, Stacy .... 641-784-5221 165 H
institutionalresearch@graceland.edu
GIBBS, Susan .... 620-227-9327 172 J
sgibbs@dc3.edu
GIBBS, Tanya, R .... 203-285-2061.. 85 E
tgibbs@gatewayct.edu
GIBBS, Tricia .... 603-623-0313 273 I
patriciagibbs@nhia.edu
GIBBS DRAYTON,
Marilyn .... 803-535-5309 407 G
mgibbs@claflin.edu
GIBELLINO, Pamela .... 937-778-7856 352 J
pgibellino@edisonohio.edu
GIBERT, Lisa .... 360-992-2677 479 F
lgibert@clark.edu
GIBERTI, Bruno .... 805-756-2246.. 30 C
bgiberti@calpoly.edu
GIBLER, Linda .... 210-341-1366 441 C
lgibler@ost.edu
GIBLER, Rhonda, K .... 573-882-2094 261 B
giblerr@missouri.edu
GIBLIN, Frank .... 248-370-2395 229 G
giblin@oakland.edu
GIBLIN, Patrick .... 314-246-7174 262 C
patrickgiblin61@webster.edu
GIBLIN, Tara .... 714-432-5093.. 38 E
tgiblin@occ.cccd.edu
GIBNEY, Glenn .... 912-344-3248 119 C
ggibney@georgiasouthern.edu
GIBOUT, Holly .... 847-970-4929 152 A
hgibout@usml.edu
GIBRALTER, Jonathan ... 315-364-3265 325 B
president@wells.edu
GIBSON, Amy, B .... 630-515-7198 143 G
agibso@midwestern.edu
GIBSON, Andrea .... 386-506-3337.. 97 D
andrea.gibson@daytonastate.edu
GIBSON, Ashley, M .... 918-270-6405 369 A
ashley.gibson@ptstulsa.edu
GIBSON, Brenda .... 503-255-0332 374 D
bgibson@multnomah.edu
GIBSON, Camille .... 936-261-5205 446 D
cbgibson@pvamu.edu
GIBSON, Cedrick .... 904-779-4045 100 B
cegibson@fscj.edu
GIBSON, Christopher .... 650-738-4343.. 61 Q
gibsonc@smccd.edu
GIBSON, Clayton .... 256-372-5221.... 1 A
clayton.gibson@aamu.edu
GIBSON, Corinne, J ...... 724-738-2700 395 F
corinne.gibson@sru.edu
GIBSON, Cristopher, A . 651-641-8277 235 F
cgibson@csp.edu
GIBSON, Dan .... 214-333-5931 434 I
danielg@dbu.edu
GIBSON, David, J .... 802-443-5834 462 H
djgibson@middlebury.edu
GIBSON, David, W .... 432-837-8702 450 D
dgibson@sulross.edu
GIBSON, Dennis .... 301-387-3051 198 F
dennis.gibson@garrettcollege.edu
GIBSON, Donald .... 207-768-9560 196 E
donald.gibson@maine.edu
GIBSON, Donald .... 718-862-7440 305 H
dgibson01@manhattan.edu
GIBSON, Donna, S .... 212-639-2109 305 E
gibsond@mskcc.org
GIBSON, Edie, B .... 731-881-7508 428 B
edgibson@utm.edu
GIBSON, Emma, C .... 909-869-4351.. 30 D
ecgibson@cpp.edu
GIBSON, Erin .... 419-517-8884 355 K
egibson@lourdes.edu
GIBSON, Ginger .... 352-395-5211 107 A
ginger.gibson@sfcollege.edu
GIBSON, Gloria, J .... 773-442-5400 145 B
gjgibson@neiu.edu
GIBSON, Gregory .... 850-201-6100 111 C
policechief@tcc.fl.edu
GIBSON, J. Murray .... 850-410-6161 108 I
jm.gibson@eng.famu.fsu.edu
GIBSON, Jacqueline ..... 662-254-3636 248 B
jacqueline.gibson@mvsu.edu
GIBSON, James .... 334-683-5157.... 6 A
jgibson@judson.edu
GIBSON, Jane .... 901-375-4400 422 F
janegibson@midsouthchristian.edu
GIBSON, Janell .... 251-981-3771..... 5 B
janell.gibson@columbiasouthern.edu
GIBSON, Janell, E .... 972-438-6932 441 H
jgibson@parker.edu
GIBSON, Jeff .... 319-895-4357 164 B
jgibson@cornellcollege.edu
GIBSON, Jeff .... 417-625-9727 256 D
gibson-j@mssu.edu
GIBSON, Jeffrey .... 302-736-2420.. 90 G
jeffrey.gibson@wesley.edu
GIBSON, Jencie .... 276-656-0202 475 D
jgibson@patrickhenry.edu
GIBSON, Jeremy .... 978-837-5306 216 D
gibsonj@merrimack.edu
GIBSON, Jonathan .... 503-517-1806 378 A
jgibson@westernseminary.edu
GIBSON, Joseph .... 843-574-6311 413 B
joe.gibson@tridenttech.edu
GIBSON, Keith, E .... 540-464-7334 476 G
gibsonke@vmi.edu
GIBSON, Kelly .... 913-971-3392 175 G
krgibson@mnu.edu
GIBSON, Kody .... 502-897-4000 184 C
kgibson@sbts.edu
GIBSON, Lloyd .... 914-674-7159 306 F
lgibson@mercy.edu
GIBSON, Lynn .... 662-685-4771 245 D
lgibson@bmc.edu
GIBSON, Mandi .... 713-646-1702 444 B
mgibson@stcl.edu
GIBSON, Marc .... 318-675-4928 189 C
mgibso@lsuhsc.edu
GIBSON, Michael .... 256-840-4124.... 3 F
michael.gibson@snead.edu
GIBSON, Michele .... 518-388-6104 323 G
gibsonm@union.edu
GIBSON, Murray .... 850-410-6161 109 C
jmgibson@fsu.edu
GIBSON, Nathan .... 719-255-3075.. 83 B
ngibson@uccs.edu
GIBSON, Nola, R .... 601-974-1132 247 B
gibsonk@millsaps.edu
GIBSON, Pamela .... 910-486-3930 334 D
gibsonp@faytechcc.edu
GIBSON, Peggy .... 276-523-2400 475 A
pgibson@mecc.edu
GIBSON, Pippa .... 408-864-8705.. 43 C
gibsonpippa@deanza.edu
GIBSON, Rick .... 310-506-4125.. 56 C
rick.gibson@pepperdine.edu
GIBSON, Rob .... 620-341-6694 172 L
rgibson1@emporia.edu
GIBSON, Ryan .... 606-368-6130 178 D
ryangibson@alc.edu
GIBSON, Sally .... 816-271-4369 257 A
sgibson14@missouriwestern.edu
GIBSON, Sandra, S .... 803-934-3419 411 C
sangibson@morris.edu
GIBSON, Shanan .... 903-886-5178 447 B
shanan.gibson@tamuc.edu
GIBSON, Stacey .... 208-282-3964 130 H
gibsstа2@isu.edu
GIBSON, Susan .... 404-880-8757 116 D
sgibson@cau.edu
GIBSON, Tammy .... 706-379-3111 127 C
tgibson@yhc.edu
GIBSON, Tera .... 325-670-1259 437 F
GIBSON, Terry .... 972-923-6406 440 G
terry.gibson@navarrocollege.edu
GIBSON, Tim .... 212-659-7207 304 B
tgibson@tkc.edu
GIBSON, Tim .... 618-985-3741 139 I
timgibson@jalc.edu
GIBSON, Tim .... 405-692-3287 366 G
GIBSON, Todd, D .... 724-458-2147 385 C
tdgibson@gcc.edu
GIBSON, Tom .... 419-372-2299 348 H
tjgibso@bgsu.edu
GIBSON, Tonia, R .... 270-824-1739 181 G
tonia.gibson@kctcs.edu
GIBSON, Wanda .... 909-621-8144.. 57 F
wanda.gibson@pomona.edu
GIBSON-GAYLE, Gale .... 718-489-5240 313 H
ggibson-gayle@sfc.edu
GIBSON SHEFFIELD,
Gail .... 802-387-6797 462 D
gailsheffield@landmark.edu
GIBSON-SHREVE, Lada . 330-494-6170 361 F
lshreve@starkstate.edu
GIDDENS, Jean .... 804-828-5174 473 F
jgiddens@vcu.edu
GIDDINGS, Matthew ..... 701-224-5789 346 B
matthew.giddings@bismarckstate.edu
GIDEON, Amy, C .... 615-868-6503 422 G
amy@mtsa.edu
GIDEON, Ryan .... 320-363-5225 235 C
rgideon001@csbsju.edu
GIDJUNIS, Rebecca ...... 610-341-1576 383 D
rgidjuni@eastern.edu
GIE, Lori .... 504-520-5730 193 A
lgie@xula.edu
GIELOW, Bob .... 617-559-8610 210 C
bgielow@hebrewcollege.edu
GIENGER, Crystal .... 985-448-7909 187 F
crystal.gienger@fletcher.edu
GIER, David .... 734-764-0584 231 E
dgier@umich.edu
GIERBOLINI, Ángel, M . 787-850-9335 513 E
angel.gierbolini@upr.edu
GIERBOLINI-SANTIAGO,
Rafael, L .... 787-993-8855 513 B
rafael.gierbolini@upr.edu
GIERI, Joe .... 505-454-3168 286 H
jgieri@nmhu.edu
GIEROK, Ed .... 503-554-2090 373 C
egierok@georgefox.edu
GIES, Jason .... 814-254-0564 381 F
jgies@pa.gov
GIESCHEN, Charles, A .. 260-452-2104 154 E
charles.gieschen@ctsfw.edu
GIESE, Martin .... 218-751-8670 242 J
martingiese@oakhills.edu
GIESE, Melissa .... 816-604-1492 255 D
melissa.giese@mcckc.edu
GIESE, Michael .... 202-885-2200.. 90 J
mgiese@american.edu
GIESE, Ralph .... 719-255-4327.. 83 B
rgiese@uccs.edu
GIESECKE, Marian, K .... 806-651-2055 448 C
mgiesecke@wtamu.edu
GIESEKE, Amy .... 515-961-1615 169 D
amy.gieseke@simpson.edu
GIESELMAN, Tammy ..... 812-488-2260 161 A
tg85@evansville.edu
GIETZEN, Garett .... 209-228-2589.. 69 B
ggietzen@ucmerced.edu
GIFFEN, Scott .... 618-664-6768 137 G
scott.giffen@greenville.edu
GIFFORD, Darcy .... 734-487-5375 223 H
dgiffor2@emich.edu
GIFFORD, Rachel .... 870-838-2902.. 17 D
rgifford@smail.anc.edu
GIFFORD, Rhonda .... 724-938-4413 394 B
gifford@calu.edu
GIFFROW, Tammy .... 281-756-3598 429 I
tgiffrow@alvincollege.edu
GIGER, Lisa .... 662-846-4035 245 H
lgiger@deltastate.edu
GIGLIO, Elizabeth .... 845-758-7177 290 G
giglio@bard.edu
GIGLIOTTI, Chandra, M 410-827-5812 197 I
cgigliotti@chesapeake.edu
GIGLIOTTI, Kate .... 413-662-5074 213 A
kate.gigliotti@mcla.edu
GIGLIOTTI, Lori .... 402-354-7044 268 C
lori.gigliotti@methodistcollege.edu
GIGOT, Jeremy .... 620-276-9570 173 E
jeremy.gigot@gcccks.edu
GIGUETTE, Marguerite .. 504-520-7525 193 A
mgiguett@xula.edu
GIL, Andres .... 305-348-2494 109 A
andres.gil@fiu.edu
GIL, Sean .... 951-827-6063.. 69 C
sean.gil@ucr.edu
GILBERT, Aerin .... 410-923-4585.. 92 G
GILBERT, Alan .... 718-951-5116 293 C
agilbert@brooklyn.cuny.edu
GILBERT, Bryan .... 512-313-3000 434 E
bryan.gilbert@concordia.edu
GILBERT, Charlene .... 419-530-2413 363 E
charlene.gilbert@utoledo.edu
GILBERT, Cherry .... 206-281-2009 484 D
cyueh@spu.edu
GILBERT, Corynn .... 541-684-7222 374 G
cgilbert@nwcu.edu
GILBERT, David, H .... 414-906-4670 497 A
dhg@uwm.edu
GILBERT, Demetrius ...... 501-374-6305.. 21 A
demetrius.gilbert@shortercollege.edu
GILBERT, Dianna .... 225-771-7827 190 G
dianna_gilbert@subr.edu
GILBERT, Elizabeth .... 402-399-2458 266 F
egilbert@csm.edu
GILBERT, Emily, R .... 806-371-5403 430 A
e0400185@actx.edu
GILBERT, Faye .... 207-581-1951 195 J
faye.gilbert@maine.edu
GILBERT, Fred .... 928-757-0854.. 14 F
fgilbert@mohave.edu
GILBERT, Glenn .... 574-535-7351 155 A
ggilbert@goshen.edu
GILBERT, Jan .... 308-367-5252 270 C
jgilbert3@unl.edu
GILBERT, Jarett .... 503-594-0699 372 D
jarett.gilbert@clackamas.edu
GILBERT, Jerome, A ..... 304-696-3977 490 D
gilbert@marshall.edu
GILBERT, Jon .... 252-737-4502 341 C
gilbertjo18@ecu.edu
GILBERT, Karen .... 404-471-6435 113 G
kgilbert@agnesscott.edu
GILBERT, Kelsey .... 207-509-7218 195 H
kgilbert@unity.edu
GILBERT, Larry .... 940-498-6282 441 A
lgilbert@nctc.edu
GILBERT, Marita .... 814-641-3173 386 H
gilberm@juniata.edu
GILBERT, Michael .... 860-486-6137.. 88 E
michael.gilbert@uconn.edu
GILBERT, Michael .... 213-624-1200.. 42 I
mgilbert@fidm.edu
GILBERT, Mindy .... 615-514-2787 423 E
mgilbert@nossi.edu
GILBERT, Nancy .... 419-448-3413 361 J
ngilbert@tiffin.edu
GILBERT, Peter, J .... 920-832-7353 493 K
peter.j.gilbert@lawrence.edu
GILBERT, Regina .... 615-277-7421 428 F
rgilbert@watkins.edu

GILBERT, Rhonda .... 319-226-2011 162 F
rhonda.gilbert@allencollege.edu
GILBERT, Robert .... 352-392-1784 109 F
ragilber@ufl.edu
GILBERT, Stacy .... 318-257-4730 191 F
stacyc@latech.edu
GILBERT, Tammy .... 423-869-6306 421 C
sm8218@bncollege.com
GILBERT, Teresa .... 423-478-7702 423 G
tgilbert@ptseminary.edu
GILBERT, Trent .... 205-226-4694.... 5 A
trgilber@bsc.edu
GILBERTSON, Jake .... 619-849-2253.. 57 E
jakegilbertson@pointloma.edu
GILBERTSON, Sandi ...... 701-671-2904 346 E
sandi.gilbertson@ndscs.edu
GILBES SANTAELLA,
Fernando .... 787-265-3828 513 F
decano.arci@uprm.edu
GILCHRIST, Debra .... 253-964-6584 483 D
dgilchrist@pierce.ctc.edu
GILCREASE, Kathy .... 936-294-1012 450 C
gilcrease@shsu.edu
GILCREAST, Emily .... 401-598-1900 404 I
egilcreast@jwu.edu
GILDEA-BRODERICK,
Kate .... 801-957-4914 461 D
kate.gildea@slcc.edu
GILDERSLEEVE,
Elizabeth .... 781-283-2376 219 D
egilders@wellesley.edu
GILDNER, Justin .... 828-771-3029 344 E
jgildner@warren-wilson.edu
GILE, Jason .... 630-620-2105 145 D
jgile@faculty.seminary.edu
GILE, Joseph .... 316-942-4291 175 I
gilej@newmanu.edu
GILES, Daniel .... 330-337-6403 347 E
bookstore@awc.edu
GILES, Gordon .... 513-875-3344 350 G
gordon.giles@chatfield.edu
GILES, JR., Henry, C .... 864-592-4616 412 F
gilesh@sccsc.edu
GILES, Melissa .... 818-677-6111.. 32 D
melissa.giles@csun.edu
GILES, Pam .... 276-523-2400 475 A
pgiles@mecc.edu
GILES, Roger, W .... 870-235-4008.. 21 D
rwgiles@saumag.edu
GILES, Roni .... 724-480-3401 381 K
roni.giles@ccbc.edu
GILES, Ronita .... 412-397-6403 397 G
gilesr@rmu.edu
GILES, Wayne .... 312-996-5939 151 B
wgiles@uic.edu
GILFERT, Christy .... 941-637-5678 100 A
cgilfert@fsw.edu
GILFILLAN, Margaret .... 412-392-3994 397 A
mgilfillan@pointpark.edu
GILFOIL, David .... 610-282-1100 382 E
david.gilfoil@desales.edu
GILGALLON, James ...... 570-208-8103 387 A
jamesgilgallon@kings.edu
GILGER, Jeffrey .... 209-228-4343.. 69 B
jgilger@ucmerced.edu
GILGOUR, Joe .... 573-518-2146 256 B
jgilgour@mineralarea.edu
GILKERSON,
Tammeil, Y .... 510-464-3236.. 56 G
tgilkerson@peralta.edu
GILKEY, Shannon .... 859-256-3100 180 H
shannon.gilkey@kctcs.edu
GILL, Allison .... 978-837-5175 216 D
gilla@merrimack.edu
GILL, Alyson, A .... 479-979-1430.. 23 I
agill@ozarks.edu
GILL, Barbara, A .... 301-314-8350 202 C
bgill@umd.edu
GILL, Barbara, J .... 850-201-6570 111 C
gillb@tcc.fl.edu
GILL, Beth .... 903-813-2226 430 N
bgill@austincollege.edu
GILL, Casey .... 937-327-7801 364 H
gillc@wittenberg.edu
GILL, Chris .... 515-271-3918 165 A
chris.gill@drake.edu
GILL, Coner .... 210-202-3700.. 92 G
GILL, Coner .... 512-568-3300.. 92 G
GILL, D. Christopher .... 573-288-6322 252 E
cgill@culver.edu
GILL, Dana .... 616-395-7775 225 B
gill@hope.edu
GILL, Davie .... 727-341-4314 106 E
gill.davie@spcollege.edu
GILL, Dennis .... 541-881-5915 377 B
dgill@tvcc.cc
GILL, Janet .... 712-274-6400 170 E
janet.gill@witcc.edu
GILL, Jason .... 847-866-3987 137 E
jason.gill@garrett.edu
GILL, Lanae .... 313-993-1230 231 B
gillla@udmercy.edu
GILL, Lee, A .... 864-656-4238 408 A
lagill@clemson.edu
GILL, Mark .... 970-491-6211.. 78 M
mark.gill@colostate.edu
GILL, Mark, A .... 859-846-5364 183 E
mgill@midway.edu
GILL, Michele .... 402-844-7748 268 J
micheleg@northeast.edu
GILL, Nancy .... 805-437-8456.. 30 F
nancy.gill@csuci.edu
GILL, Nicholas .... 207-216-4467 195 C
ngill@yccc.edu
GILL, Paula .... 615-460-8637 418 F
paula.gill@belmont.edu
GILL, Ruth, F .... 410-334-2928 204 F
rgill@worwic.edu
GILL, Steven .... 609-258-3466 280 E
sgill@princeton.edu
GILL, Yug .... 765-658-4500 154 F
yuggill@depauw.edu
GILL-POWELL,
Jacqueline .... 434-797-8400 474 E
jackie.gillpowell@danville.edu
GILLAHAN, Sheila .... 731-286-3316 425 A
gillahan@dscc.edu
GILLAN, Darlene .... 617-879-7050 212 E
sgillan@massart.edu
GILLAN, Maria .... 973-684-5904 280 B
mgillan@pccc.edu
GILLAND, Laura .... 704-637-4410 328 A
lgwimpey@catawba.edu
GILLARD, Natalie .... 575-461-4413 286 E
natalieg@mesalands.edu
GILLARD, Natalie .... 443-352-4489 201 H
ngillard@stevenson.edu
GILLASPIE, Ray .... 270-824-8592 181 G
ray.gillaspie@kctcs.edu
GILLE, Chaudron .... 706-864-1602 126 A
chaudron.gille@ung.edu
GILLECE, Nancy, E .... 301-696-3710 199 B
gillece@hood.edu
GILLEECCE, Eileen .... 215-572-2187 379 A
gilleeccee@arcadia.edu
GILLEN, Dan .... 319-296-4268 166 B
daniel.gillen@hawkeyecollege.edu
GILLESPIE, Adrienne, G 801-626-7243 461 B
adrienneandrews@weber.edu
GILLESPIE, Andrew, R .... 334-844-5009.... 4 E
arg0014@auburn.edu
GILLESPIE, Anne .... 319-363-1323 168 C
agillespie@mtmercy.edu
GILLESPIE, Ashley .... 662-329-7462 248 A
GILLESPIE, Bart .... 678-839-6582 126 E
bgillesp@westga.edu
GILLESPIE, Christine ..... 201-612-7488 275 H
cgillespie@bergen.edu
GILLESPIE, Dave .... 402-941-6545 267 L
gillespie@midlandu.edu
GILLESPIE, Deena .... 928-524-7365.. 14 J
deena.gillespie@npc.edu
GILLESPIE, Denise .... 225-768-1755 186 F
denise.gillespie@franu.edu
GILLESPIE, Denise .... 662-620-5368 246 D
dlgillespie@iccms.edu
GILLESPIE, Greg .... 805-652-5502.. 72 G
ggillespie@vcccd.edu
GILLESPIE, John .... 718-270-2262 317 E
john.gillespie@downstate.edu
GILLESPIE, Jon .... 210-829-3971 453 D
jong@uiwtx.edu
GILLESPIE, Kendra .... 703-284-1554 469 C
kendra.gillespie@marymount.edu
GILLESPIE, Mary Ellen .. 860-768-4989.. 88 H
ad@hartford.edu
GILLESPIE, Melanie .... 864-644-5504 412 E
mlgillespie@swu.edu
GILLESPIE, Michele, K .. 336-758-5000 344 D
gillesmk@wfu.edu
GILLESPIE, Teresa .... 425-889-5290 482 F
teresa.gillespie@northwestu.edu
GILLETE, Kathryn .... 303-937-4420.. 76 L
admissions@augustineinstitute.org
GILLETT, Charisse, L .... 859-280-1230 183 B
cgillett@lextheo.edu
GILLETTE, John .... 509-533-8378 479 I
john.gillette@ccs.spokane.edu
GILLETTE, John .... 509-533-8378 480 B
john.gillette@ccs.spokane.edu
GILLETTE, Kimberly .... 218-282-8442 244 A
gillette@umn.edu
GILLETTE, Lynn .... 906-635-2211 226 E
lgillette@lssu.edu
GILLETTE, Maureen .... 973-761-9024 283 B
maureen.gillette@shu.edu
GILLETTE, Susan .... 410-706-5353 202 D
sgillett@umaryland.edu
GILLEY, Janice .... 850-474-2200 110 E
jgilley@uwf.edu
GILLEY, Michael .... 276-523-2400 475 A
mgilley@mecc.edu
GILLEY, Pam .... 318-255-7950 191 F
pam@latechalumni.org
GILLEY, Ryan .... 513-529-2107 356 E
gilleyrl@miamioh.edu
GILLIAM, Brock .... 803-641-3550 413 D
brockg@usca.edu
GILLIAM, Dara .... 405-273-5331 366 E
dgilliam@familyoffaith.edu
GILLIAM, Dara .... 405-695-5533 366 E
dgilliam@familyoffaith.edu
GILLIAM, Franklin, D .... 336-334-5266 343 A
chancellor@uncg.edu
GILLIAM, Glenna .... 479-308-2209.. 17 C
glenna.gilliam@arcomedu.org
GILLIAM, Keshia .... 864-596-9029 409 B
nikeshiajackson.gilliam@converse.edu
GILLIAM, Kevin .... 616-988-3695 226 C
kgilliam@kuyper.edu
GILLIAM, Melissa .... 773-795-5432 150 J
mgilliam@bsd.uchicago.edu
GILLIAM, Rebecca .... 318-670-9353 190 J
rgilliam@susla.edu
GILLIAM, Thomas, J ..... 850-484-1500 104 H
tgilliam@pensacolastate.edu
GILLIAM, Tom .... 850-484-1500 104 H
tgilliam@pensacolastate.edu
GILLIAM, Trina .... 864-699-4632 412 G
gilliamt@smcsc.edu
GILLIAM-HOLMES,
Sheraine .... 931-221-7179 418 D
gilliams@apsu.edu
GILLIAM JOHNSON,
Patrice .... 302-857-6000.. 89 F
pgjohnson@desu.edu
GILLIAM PHILLIPS,
Ruth .... 919-530-7908 342 A
ruth.gilliam.phillips@nccu.edu
GILLIE, Esther .... 757-352-4182 470 H
egillie@regent.edu
GILLIE, Lynn, L .... 607-735-1804 299 D
lgillie@elmira.edu
GILLIES, Cheryl .... 626-396-2278.. 26 E
cheryl.gillies@artcenter.edu
GILLIES, Pamela .... 646-768-5300 301 B
GILLIGAN, Thomas .... 650-723-1198.. 65 J
GILLIGAN, William .... 617-824-8190 208 H
william_gilligan@emerson.edu
GILLILAND, Brandon ..... 305-284-2258 112 E
bgilliland@miami.edu
GILLILAND,
Brandon, M .... 716-673-3253 317 A
brandon.gilliland@fredonia.edu
GILLILAND, Christie ...... 253-833-9111 481 F
cgilliland@greenriver.edu
GILLILAND, Drew .... 541-552-6319 376 E
gilliland@sou.edu
GILLILAND, Jane, A ...... 607-871-2913 289 H
gilliland@alfred.edu
GILLILAND, Mary, K ...... 520-494-5210.. 11 K
maryk.gilliland@centralaz.edu
GILLIN, Douglas, P ...... 828-262-7781 341 B
gillindp@appstate.edu
GILLING RAYNOR,
Beatrice .... 718-951-6545 293 C
braynor@brooklyn.cuny.edu
GILLINS, Dawn .... 914-606-6844 325 C
dawn.gillins@sunywcc.edu
GILLIS, Arthur .... 225-743-8500 188 B
agillis@rpcc.edu
GILLIS, Chester .... 314-977-2193 259 H
GILLIS, Ed .... 202-994-9259.. 91 F
edgillis@gwu.edu
GILLIS, Graham .... 501-450-3181.. 23 H
ggillis@uca.edu
GILLIS, Lynette .... 512-313-3000 434 E
lynette.gillis@concordia.edu
GILLIS-OLION, Marion .. 910-672-1265 341 E
molion@uncfsu.edu
GILLISPIE, Billy .... 254-267-7059 442 E
bgillispie@rangercollege.edu
GILLISPIE, James .... 540-868-7042 474 J
jgillispie@lfcc.edu
GILLISS, Buster .... 701-224-5512 346 B
buster.gilliss@bismarckstate.edu
GILLISS, Catherine .... 415-476-1805.. 69 E
catherine.gilliss@ucsf.edu
GILLITZER, Nadia .... 319-363-1323 168 C
ngillitzer@mtmercy.edu
GILLLILAN, Kevin, L ..... 256-765-4357.... 8 E
kgillilan@una.edu
GILLMAN, Howard, A ... 949-824-5111.. 68 G
chancellor@uci.edu
GILLMAN, Rick .... 219-464-6718 162 A
rick.gillman@valpo.edu
GILLMAN, Sally .... 605-688-4151 417 C
sally.gillman@sdstate.edu
GILLMING, Kenneth, D . 617-364-3510 207 A
kgillming@boston.edu
GILLOOLY, Jeffrey .... 508-793-7512 208 A
jgillooly@clarku.edu
GILLS, Kristofer .... 907-564-8259.... 9 D
kgills@alaskapacific.edu
GILLS, Twyla .... 214-379-5460 441 I
tgills@pqc.edu
GILLUM, Deborah .... 574-807-7015 153 E
deborah.gillum@betheluniversity.edu
GILLUS, Raynaldo .... 662-254-3636 248 B
raynaldo.gillus@mvsu.edu
GILMAN, Isaac .... 503-352-1401 375 G
gilmani@pacificu.edu
GILMAN, James, T .... 203-932-7015.. 89 A
jgilman@newhaven.edu
GILMAN, Regis, M .... 252-328-9317 341 C
gilmanr16@ecu.edu
GILMAN, Wendy .... 518-255-5520 319 F
gilmanwc@cobleskill.edu
GILMARTIN, Anne .... 914-674-7337 306 F
agilmartin@mercy.edu
GILMARTIN, Kevin, M .. 626-395-6351.. 29 C
kmg@hss.caltech.edu
GILMER, Christopher .... 304-424-8200 491 D
president@wvup.edu
GILMER, Elizabeth .... 478-289-2037 117 D
egilmer@ega.edu
GILMER, Garrett .... 419-372-2081 348 H
ggilmer@bgsu.edu
GILMER, Ray .... 240-567-7970 200 C
ray.gilmer@montgomerycollege.edu
GILMORE, Blaine .... 859-572-6449 184 A
gilmoreb@nku.edu
GILMORE, Calvin, L ...... 336-272-7102 329 D
gilmorec@greensboro.edu
GILMORE, Darwin .... 850-718-2270.. 96 F
gilmored@chipola.edu
GILMORE, David .... 617-989-4328 219 E
gilmored@wit.edu
GILMORE, Derrick, C .... 502-597-5787 182 H
derrick.gilmore@kysu.edu
GILMORE, Don .... 661-362-2811.. 51 C
dgilmore@masters.edu
GILMORE, Eric, J .... 402-280-2100 266 I
ericgilmore@creighton.edu
GILMORE, Grover, C ..... 216-368-2270 349 F
gcg@case.edu
GILMORE, Jessica .... 801-863-7353 461 A
jessica.gilmore@uvu.edu
GILMORE, John, W .... 609-497-7700 280 D
john.gilmore@ptsem.edu
GILMORE, Marcos .... 618-664-6616 137 G
marcos.gilmore@greenville.edu
GILMORE, Paul .... 848-932-0990 282 A
paul.gilmore@rutgers.edu
GILMORE, Robert .... 616-632-8900 221 C
GILMORE, Robert .... 914-323-5357 305 J
robert.gilmore@mville.edu
GILMORE, Wayne .... 617-353-8289 207 D
waygil@bu.edu
GILMORE ENGLISH,
Jessica .... 425-235-2463 483 G
jgilmoreenglishl@rtc.edu
GILMOUR, Davie, J ...... 570-320-8010 392 B
djg120@psu.edu
GILMOUR, Davie Jane .. 570-326-3761 393 G
dgilmour@pct.edu
GILOI, Eva .... 973-353-3885 282 B
evagiloi@rutgers.edu
GILORMINI, Dominique 787-766-1912 510 A
dgilormini@inter.edu
GILORMINI-DE GRACIA,
Dominique .... 787-763-4203 508 J
dgilormini@inter.edu

GILPERT, Jessica .... 610-647-4400 386 C
jgilpert@immaculata.edu
GILPIN, JoAnn .... 208-792-5272 131 A
GILPIN, Sandy .... 505-566-3022 288 A
gilpins@sanjuancollege.edu
GILREATH, Scott .... 765-677-6515 157 D
scott.gilreath@indwes.edu
GILREATH, Scott, A ...... 812-488-2429 161 A
sg157@evansville.edu
GILROY, Janice .... 914-606-6610 325 C
janice.gilroy@sunywcc.edu
GILROY, Maryellen .... 518-783-2328 315 J
mgilroy@siena.edu
GILSON, David .... 216-791-5000 351 A
david.gilson@cim.edu
GILSON, Jannie .... 508-588-9100 214 F
jgilson1@massasoit.mass.edu
GILSON, Ken .... 562-903-4870.. 27 C
ken.gilson@biola.edu
GILSTAD, John .... 301-295-9213 504 B
lester.huff@usuhs.edu
GILSTRAP, Donald .... 205-348-7561.... 7 G
dlgilstrap@ua.edu
GILSTRAP, Linda .... 619-216-6614.. 65 F
lgilstrap@swccd.edu
GILTNER, Greg .... 405-425-5501 367 G
greg.giltner@oc.edu
GILTNER, Scott .... 573-288-6382 252 E
sgiltner@culver.edu
GIMA, Wesley, T .... 671-735-3025 505 C
wesley.gima@guamcc.edu
GIMNESS, Erik .... 253-964-6529 483 D
egimness@pierce.ctc.edu
GIN, Kevin .... 510-436-1204.. 45 D
kgin@hnu.edu
GINDER, Greg .... 317-955-6018 158 U
gginder@marian.edu
GINES, D. Scott .... 302-857-6030.. 89 F
dgines@desu.edu
GINES, Joan .... 801-585-9144 460 E
joan.gines@utah.edu
GINEVAN, Douglas, W .. 207-786-6093 193 B
dginevan@bates.edu
GINEX, Linda .... 800-477-2254.. 30 A
GINGERELLA, David ...... 508-999-8051 211 F
dgingerella@umassd.edu
GINGERICH, Jeff .... 570-941-7520 401 H
jeffrey.gingerich@scranton.edu
GINGERICH, Tamara ..... 219-464-6196 162 A
tamara.gingerich@valpo.edu
GINGERICH, Willard, P . 973-655-4382 279 C
gingerichw@mail.montclair.edu
GINGRAS, Gregory .... 510-879-9267.. 59 F
ggingras@samuelmerritt.edu
GINKEL, Nadine .... 303-762-6955.. 79 H
nadine.ginkel@denverseminary.edu
GINN, Bryan .... 678-225-7500 396 D
bginn@pcom.edu
GINN, Julie .... 781-239-2734 214 E
jginn@massbay.edu
GINN, Mark .... 828-262-2070 341 B
ginnmc@appstate.edu
GINNETTI, Jennifer .... 215-646-7300 385 D
ginnetti.j@gmercyu.edu
GINNEY, Monica .... 937-481-2336 364 E
monica_ginney@wilmington.edu
GINSBERG, Amy .... 973-720-2138 284 I
ginsberga3@wpunj.edu
GINSBERG, Mark, R ...... 703-993-2004 467 L
mginsber@gmu.edu
GINSBERG, Richard ...... 718-289-5770 293 B
richard.ginsberg@bcc.cuny.edu
GINSBERG, Rick .... 785-864-4297 177 D
ginsberg@ku.edu
GINSBURG, Charles, M 214-648-8597 457 B
charles.ginsburg@utsouthwestern.edu
GINTER, Judy .... 859-985-3767 179 C
ginterj@berea.edu
GINTER, Matthew .... 419-434-5624 363 A
ginterm@findlay.edu
GINTHER, Gary .... 760-773-2560.. 39 A
gginther@collegeofthedesert.edu
GINTY, Kevin .... 773-508-2204 142 D
kginty@luc.edu
GIOGLIO, Tom .... 570-484-2102 395 B
tmg252@lockhaven.edu
GIOIOSO, Domenic .... 603-526-3698 272 H
domenic.gioioso@colby-sawyer.edu
GIONFRIDDO, Elizabeth 508-213-2113 217 E
elizabeth.gionfriddo@nichols.edu
GIORDANI, Robert .... 410-704-3508 204 A
rgiordani@towson.edu
GIORDANO, Amy .... 567-661-7883 360 B
amy_giordano@owens.edu
GIORDANO,
Christopher .... 810-762-3434 231 G
giordanc@umich.edu
GIORDANO, Matthew .... 716-896-0700 324 E
giordano@villa.edu
GIORDANO,
Nicholas, J .... 334-844-5737.... 4 E
njg0003@auburn.edu
GIOVAGNOLI, Michelle . 570-208-5847 387 A
michellegiovagnoli@kings.edu
GIOVANNELLI, Tony ..... 724-964-8811 391 E
tgiovannelli@ncstrades.edu
GIOVANNETTI, Dianne .. 847-970-4801 152 A
dgiovannetti@usml.edu
GIOVANNINI,
Eugene, V .... 817-515-5201 445 G
chancellors.office@tccd.edu
GIPKO, Jesse .... 740-699-9500 348 F
jgipko@belmontcollege.edu
GIPSON, Amy .... 386-822-7220 111 A
agipson@stetson.edu
GIPSON, Andre .... 770-216-2960 120 H
agipson@ict.edu
GIPSON, Batanya, M .... 757-822-7701 476 B
bgipson@tcc.edu
GIPSON, Keith .... 719-846-5577.. 82 K
keith.gipson@trinidadstate.edu
GIPSON, Maurice .... 870-972-3081.. 17 G
mgipson@astate.edu
GIPSON, Patrick .... 773-602-5524 134 D
pgipson2@ccc.edu
GIPSON, Richard .... 817-257-2787 448 G
r.gipson@tcu.edu
GIPSON, Tim .... 760-872-2000.. 41 C
tgipson@deepsprings.edu
GIPSON, William .... 215-898-0809 400 K
wgipson@exchange.upenn.edu
GIRALDO, Luis .... 805-965-0581.. 62 C
lggiraldo@sbcc.edu
GIRANDOLA, Joe .... 513-562-8743 347 K
president@artacademy.edu
GIRARD, Angela .... 562-985-5146.. 31 F
angela.girard@csulb.edu
GIRARD, Angie .... 509-452-5100 483 A
agirard@pnwu.edu
GIRARD, Christine .... 503-552-1702 374 E
president@nunm.edu
GIRARD, David .... 719-384-6818.. 81 E
david.girard@ojc.edu
GIRARD, Don .... 310-434-4287.. 62 E
girard_donald@smc.edu
GIRARD, Jerry .... 406-683-7181 264 B
jerry.girard@umwestern.edu
GIRARD, Joseph, C ...... 401-841-2245 503 L
joseph.girard@usnwc.edu
GIRARD, Preble .... 337-475-5243 192 A
preble@mcneese.edu
GIRARD-MALLEY,
Jenny .... 510-436-1081.. 45 D
girard-malley@hnu.edu
GIRARDEAU, Cathy .... 912-650-5672 124 E
cgirardeau@southuniversity.edu
GIRARDOT, Steven .... 404-385-7344 118 F
steven.girardot@gatech.edu
GIRAUD, Gerald .... 307-754-6235 502 G
gerald.giraud@nwc.edu
GIRDWOOD, Anna .... 636-949-4654 254 F
agirdwood@lindenwood.edu
GIRELLI, Carl, A .... 434-947-8126 470 E
cgirelli@randolphcollege.edu
GIRNUS, Josh, C .... 253-535-7476 482 H
girnusjc@plu.edu
GIROD, Carlos .... 214-648-8960 457 B
carlos.girod@utsouthwestern.edu
GIROD, Douglas, A ...... 785-864-3131 177 D
dgirod@ku.edu
GIROD, Mark .... 503-838-8471 377 H
girodm@wou.edu
GIROIR, Elizabeth .... 337-482-5930 192 E
elizabeth.giroir@louisiana.edu
GIRON, Jenny .... 915-831-6571 436 E
jgiron6@epcc.edu
GIROUX, Jenifer .... 401-456-8990 405 C
jgiroux@ric.edu
GISH, Jennifer .... 518-337-5694 296 H
gishj@strose.edu
GISH, Joanne .... 805-565-6066.. 74 K
jgish@westmont.edu
GISS, Gary .... 315-279-2969 304 A
ggiss@keuka.edu
GISSELER, Adam .... 815-825-2086 140 F
agisseler@kish.edu
GISSENDANNER,
Cindy, H .... 410-704-5456 204 A
cgissendanner@towson.edu
GISSY, Cynthia .... 304-424-8259 491 D
cindy.gissy@wvup.edu
GIST, Vicki .... 406-265-3706 264 F
gist@msun.edu
GITAU, Peter .... 435-879-4713 460 G
gitau@dixie.edu
GITTELL, Ross .... 603-230-3501 272 I
rgittell@ccsnh.edu
GITTENS, Brian, E .... 501-603-1159.. 22 C
bgittens@uams.edu
GITTENS, Carol Ann ...... 925-631-4012.. 59 B
cgittens@stmarys-ca.edu
GITTINGS, Carl, W .... 304-457-6243 487 B
gittingscw@ab.edu
GITTLEMAN, John, L .... 706-542-2968 125 G
ecohead@uga.edu
GITTO, Marisa .... 518-438-3111 305 K
mgitto@mariacollege.edu
GIUFFI, Krista .... 312-942-2569 148 A
krista_m_giuffi@rush.edu
GIUFFRE, Joseph .... 973-278-5400 275 I
joseph-giuffre@berkeleycollege.edu
GIUFFRE, Joseph .... 212-986-4343 291 D
joseph-giuffre@berkeleycollege.edu
GIUFFRIDA, Andrea ...... 210-567-4219 456 C
giuffrida@uthscsa.edu
GIUGNI, Terry .... 626-585-7734.. 55 K
tdgiugni@pasadena.edu
GIUNTA, Bridget .... 570-408-4134 403 D
bridget.giunta@wilkes.edu
GIUSTI, Linda .... 916-577-2305.. 75 B
lgiusti@jessup.edu
GIUSTI, Rebecca .... 909-706-3519.. 74 I
rgiusti@westernu.edu
GIUSTI, Stacey, J .... 509-527-5980 486 H
giustisj@whitman.edu
GIVAN, Natalie .... 212-757-1190 290 B
ngivan@aami.edu
GIVENS, Earl .... 704-637-4212 328 A
ebgivens15@catawba.edu
GIVENS, Hali .... 251-442-2212..... 8 C
hgivens@umobile.edu
GIVENS, Natisha .... 704-290-5828 337 I
ngivens@spcc.edu
GIVENS, Patrick .... 732-987-2736 278 B
pgivens@georgian.edu
GIVENS, Rita .... 870-574-4495.. 21 E
rgivens@sautech.edu
GIVHAN, Walter .... 334-670-5991.... 7 C
wgivhan@troy.edu
GIVNER, Christine, E .... 716-673-3311 317 A
christine.givner@fredonia.edu
GIVOGLU, Wendy, L ..... 407-582-2218 112 K
wgivoglu@valenciacollege.edu
GJERDE, Michelle, B .... 719-549-2512.. 79 A
michelle.gjerde@csupueblo.edu
GJERDE, Ryan .... 563-387-1288 167 E
gjerdery@luther.edu
GJERTSON, Sarah .... 303-871-4938.. 83 D
sgjertso@du.edu
GLACKIN, Barbara .... 573-986-6011 259 K
bglackin@semo.edu
GLADCHUK, Chet .... 410-293-2429 504 I
gladchuk@usna.edu
GLADD, Aaron .... 518-587-2100 321 A
aaron.gladd@esc.edu
GLADDEN, James, M .... 317-278-3635 156 F
jamglad@iupui.edu
GLADDEN, Josh .... 662-915-2780 249 D
jgladden@olemiss.edu
GLADEN, Dennis .... 701-671-2217 346 E
dennis.gladen@ndscs.edu
GLADES, Matt .... 620-223-2700 173 C
mattg@fortscott.edu
GLADNEY, Sandra, K .... 541-346-0696 377 D
skgladney@uoregon.edu
GLADNEY, Sherry .... 318-675-5561 189 C
sgladn1@lsuhsc.edu
GLADSTONE, Hannah .... 207-859-1243 195 G
gladstoneh@thomas.edu
GLADU, Frank .... 931-598-3397 423 M
fxgladu@sewanee.edu
GLADUE, Angel .... 701-477-7862 347 A
agladue@tm.edu
GLADWIN, Sonja .... 410-777-2927 197 C
srgladwin@aacc.edu
GLADYS, Niki .... 775-445-3239 271 G
niki.gladys@wnc.edu
GLANCY, Nick .... 206-281-2711 484 D
nglancy@spu.edu
GLANCY, Susan, K .... 212-854-9977 297 C
skg56@columbia.edu
GLANDER, Mindy .... 706-754-7790 122 F
mglander@northgatech.edu
GLANDON, Bert .... 208-562-3200 130 F
bertglandon@cwi.edu
GLANDON,
Constance, J .... 641-422-4332 168 D
glandcon@niacc.edu
GLANZ, IHM, Elaine ..... 610-647-4400 386 C
eglanz@immaculata.edu
GLANZ, Melissa, A .... 330-494-6170 361 F
mglanz@starkstate.edu
GLANZER, Chris .... 620-947-3121 177 C
chrisg@tabor.edu
GLANZER, Jules .... 620-947-3121 177 C
julesg@tabor.edu
GLANZER, Katrina .... 610-896-1293 385 L
kglanzer@haverford.edu
GLAPA-GROSSKLAG,
James .... 661-362-3632.. 38 H
james.glapa-grossklag@canyons.edu
GLASCO, Gerald .... 810-762-3480 231 G
gglasco@umich.edu
GLASCO, Sarah .... 336-278-5813 328 K
sglasco@elon.edu
GLASCOCK, Donna .... 870-307-7253.. 20 A
donna.glascock@lyon.edu
GLASENER, Jacquelyn .... 559-278-2586.. 31 D
jacquig@csufresno.edu
GLASER, Brian .... 309-796-5238 132 G
glaserb@bhc.edu
GLASER, James .... 617-627-4230 219 B
james.glaser@tufts.edu
GLASER, Jodi .... 651-290-6355 242 G
jodi.glaser@mitchellhamline.edu
GLASER, Stacey .... 907-442-3400.. 10 A
slglaser@alaska.edu
GLASER, Stephanie .... 704-894-2114 328 F
stglaser@davidson.edu
GLASER, Thomas, J ...... 443-518-4442 199 C
tglaser@howardcc.edu
GLASFORD,
Theodore, E .... 340-693-1535 514 E
tglasfo@uvi.edu
GLASGAL, Rana .... 617-373-8565 217 F
GLASGOW,
Mary Ellen, S .... 412-396-6554 383 C
glasgowm@duq.edu
GLASGOW, Michael ...... 860-486-3619.. 88 E
michael.glasgow@uconn.edu
GLASGOW, Sara .... 231-348-6604 228 E
sglasgow@ncmich.edu
GLASGOW, Terri .... 269-749-7623 229 H
tglasgow@olivetcollege.edu
GLASGOW, Wayne, C ... 912-721-8201 121 E
glasgow_wc@mercer.edu
GLASHEEN, Jim .... 508-856-5610 212 A
jim.glasheen@umassmed.edu
GLASIER, Jennifer .... 360-475-7128 482 G
GLASMAN, Yvonne .... 270-707-3722 181 E
yvonne.glasman@kctcs.edu
GLASPER, Janice .... 702-651-5698 271 A
janice.glasper@csn.edu
GLASPIE, Henry .... 352-854-2322.. 96 O
glaspieh@cf.edu
GLASS, Amber .... 580-349-1376 368 A
amber.glass@opsu.edu
GLASS, AmyBeth .... 609-652-4298 283 D
amybeth.glass@stockton.edu
GLASS, Andrew .... 360-532-9020 481 E
GLASS, Art .... 845-569-3210 307 J
arthur.glass@msmc.edu
GLASS, Brent .... 651-201-1673 237 A
brent.glass@minnstate.edu
GLASS, Carrie .... 305-284-2211 112 E
cxg949@miami.edu
GLASS, Carrie .... 504-865-3231 189 F
ceglass@loyno.edu
GLASS, Cheryl, A .... 651-631-5344 244 D
caglass@unwsp.edu
GLASS, Chris .... 202-462-2101.. 92 C
cglass@iwp.edu
GLASS, Cynthia .... 502-597-5923 182 H
cindy.glass@kysu.edu
GLASS, Cynthia, M .... 212-217-3650 299 H
cynthia_glass@fitnyc.edu
GLASS, Fred .... 812-855-1966 156 A
athldir@indiana.edu
GLASS, Fred .... 812-855-1966 156 B
iuad@indiana.edu
GLASS, Grace .... 304-724-3700 487 E
gglass@apus.edu

GOELLNER, Marilyn ...... 814-732-1778 394 F
mgoellner@edinboro.edu
GOELZHAUSER,
Michael, J .... 812-465-1649 161 E
mjgoelzh@usi.edu
GOEMAN, Peter .... 919-573-5350 340 F
pgoeman@shepherds.edu
GOEN, Brandon .... 806-720-7313 439 H
brandon.goen@lcu.edu
GOEN, Jennifer .... 239-590-1020 108 K
jgoen@fgcu.edu
GOEPPINGER,
Kathleen, H .... 630-515-7300 143 G
drgoeppinger@midwestern.edu
GOERING, Wynn, M ..... 505-277-7601 288 G
wgoering@unm.edu
GOERS, Jama .... 303-369-5151.. 81 J
jama.goers@plattcolorado.edu
GOERTZEN, Leroy .... 503-375-7103 373 A
lgoertzen@corban.edu
GOERZEN, Les .... 316-284-5261 171 F
lgoerzen@bethelks.edu
GOES, Paulo .... 520-621-2125.. 16 G
pgoes@eller.arizona.edu
GOETCHIUS,
Stephen, H .... 860-215-9002.. 86 F
sgoetchius@trcc.commnet.edu
GOETSCH, John .... 661-946-2274.. 73 G
GOETSCH, Lori, A .... 785-532-7402 174 G
lgoetsch@ksu.edu
GOETSCH, Mark .... 850-478-8496 104 G
mgoetsch@pcci.edu
GOETTING, Matthew ..... 207-699-5011 194 D
mgoetting@meca.edu
GOETTSCH, Gay .... 575-769-4045 285 K
gay.goettsch@clovis.edu
GOETZ, Julie, K .... 260-359-4127 155 F
jgoetz@huntington.edu
GOETZ, Michael, A .... 414-847-3305 494 F
mikegoetz@miad.edu
GOETZ, Michele .... 619-594-1862.. 33 E
mgoetz@sdsu.edu
GOETZ, Stephen .... 907-474-6215.. 10 A
sfgoetz@alaska.edu
GOEWERT, Ed .... 618-374-5109 146 E
ed.goewert@principia.edu
GOFF, Cecelia .... 304-865-6132 488 E
cecelia.goff@ovu.edu
GOFF, David .... 303-724-7304.. 83 C
david.goff@ucdenver.edu
GOFF, David, W .... 870-236-6901.. 19 A
dgoff@crc.edu
GOFF, Erica .... 906-227-1000 228 F
efranich@nmu.edu
GOFF, Karen .... 404-471-6391 113 G
kgoff@agnesscott.edu
GOFF, Katherine .... 302-736-2455.. 90 G
katherin.goff@wesley.edu
GOFF, Kim .... 916-558-2054.. 50 I
goffk@scc.losrios.edu
GOFF, Matthew .... 920-686-6262 496 A
matthew.goff@sl.edu
GOFF, Michelle .... 478-289-2095 117 D
mgoff@ega.edu
GOFF, Patricia, A .... 401-865-1031 405 B
pgoff@providence.edu
GOFF, Sue .... 503-594-3110 372 D
sue.goff@clackamas.edu
GOFF-CREWS, Kimberly 203-432-6602.. 89 D
kimberly.goff-crews@yale.edu
GOFFE, Lorraine .... 814-863-6188 392 B
lag5792@psu.edu
GOFORTH, Cheri, D ...... 501-686-5850.. 22 C
goforthcherid@uams.edu
GOFORTH, Glen .... 936-633-5240 430 F
ggoforth@angelina.edu
GOGA, Nedzad .... 718-636-3599 311 J
ngoga@pratt.edu
GOGA, Robert, D .... 412-624-6609 401 B
rgoga@cfo.pitt.edu
GOGAL, Mark .... 910-521-4615 343 B
mark.gogal@uncp.edu
GOGERTY, Andrew .... 515-964-0601 165 G
gogertya@fatih.edu
GOGGIN, Nan .... 317-278-9470 156 F
ngoggin@iu.edu
GOGOLA, Eva .... 313-593-5495 231 F
egronows@umich.edu
GOGU, Longin .... 281-290-3772 439 G
longin.gogu@lonestar.edu
GOGUE, Jay .... 334-844-4650.... 4 E
president@auburn.edu
GOH, Michael .... 612-624-2590 243 E
mgoh@umn.edu
GOHDE, Amanda .... 715-468-2815 501 B
amanda.gohde@witc.edu
GOHEEN, Peter .... 207-551-5765 194 J
pgoheen@nmcc.edu
GOHL, Pam .... 605-331-5000 417 E
GOHLKE, Brian, B .... 608-757-7773 499 C
bgohlke@blackhawk.edu
GOHMANN, Jennifer ..... 502-585-9911 184 D
jgohmann@spalding.edu
GOHSMAN, John .... 574-631-9700 161 C
jgohsman@nd.edu
GOIN, JR., Randy .... 717-720-4010 393 K
rgoin@passhe.edu
GOINES, Janice .... 979-230-3395 432 D
janice.goines@brazosport.edu
GOINES, Pamela .... 513-792-8625 362 E
pamela.goines@uc.edu
GOINGS, Eric .... 918-335-6257 368 G
egoings@okwu.edu
GOINGS, Tyson .... 419-358-3306 348 G
goingst@bluffton.edu
GOINS, Anita .... 305-443-9170 106 A
agoins@sabercollege.edu
GOINS, Jennifer .... 804-627-5300 465 C
jennifer_goins@bshsi.org
GOINS, Jessica, D .... 864-488-4590 410 E
jgoins@limestone.edu
GOINS, Jody .... 423-869-6725 421 C
jody.goins@lmunet.edu
GOINS, LaKeya .... 205-366-8150.... 7 A
lgoins@stillman.edu
GOINS, Melissa .... 936-633-5215 430 F
mgoins@angelina.edu
GOINS, Rick .... 479-788-7026.. 21 H
rick.goins@uafs.edu
GOINS, Scott, E .... 337-475-5456 192 A
sgoins@mcneese.edu
GOINS, Suzanne .... 251-460-6111.... 8 F
sgoins@southalabama.edu
GOKE-PARIOLA,
Abiodun .... 630-637-5356 144 H
agokepariola@noctrl.edu
GOLABEK, Sue .... 843-208-8144 413 E
sgolabek@uscb.edu
GOLAN, Jay .... 212-817-7130 293 F
jgolan@gc.cuny.edu
GOLAND, Lois .... 518-782-6673 315 J
lgoland@siena.edu
GOLATO, Andrea .... 512-245-2581 450 E
a_g554@txstate.edu
GOLAY, David, R .... 757-446-5890 466 I
golaydr@evms.edu
GOLBA, Gina .... 816-802-3397 254 B
ggolba@kcai.edu
GOLD, Chris .... 310-660-3735.. 41 L
cgold@elcamino.edu
GOLD, E .... 212-964-2830 306 H
egold@mtj.edu
GOLD, Ellen .... 734-487-1107 223 H
ellen.gold@emich.edu
GOLD, Harriet, B .... 270-384-8018 183 C
goldh@lindsey.edu
GOLD, Janice .... 512-505-3002 438 E
jgold@htu.edu
GOLD, Jeffery, P .... 402-559-4201 270 A
jeffrey.gold@unmc.edu
GOLD, Jeffrey, P .... 402-554-2419 270 B
jeffrey.gold@unomaha.edu
GOLD, Jered .... 626-396-2251.. 26 E
jered.gold@artcenter.edu
GOLD, Julie .... 518-783-4239 315 J
jgold@siena.edu
GOLD, Kenneth .... 718-982-3720 293 E
education@csi.cuny.edu
GOLD, Kimberly .... 910-272-3230 337 D
kgold@robeson.edu
GOLD, Mark .... 718-951-5861 293 C
mark@brooklyn.cuny.edu
GOLDBART, Paul .... 512-471-3821 455 A
cnsdean@austin.utexas.edu
GOLDBERG, Bob .... 855-786-6546 146 I
GOLDBERG, Elaine .... 646-565-6000 322 J
elaine.goldberg@touro.edu
GOLDBERG, Jane, F ...... 360-538-4005 481 E
jgoldber@ghc.edu
GOLDBERG, Jeffrey, B .. 520-621-2211.. 16 G
jgoldberg@arizona.edu
GOLDBERG, Maureen ... 805-965-0581.. 62 C
mmgoldberg@pipeline.sbcc.edu
GOLDBERG, Nisse .... 904-256-7326 101 G
ngoldbe@ju.edu
GOLDBERG, Robert .... 212-854-2003 290 J
rgoldber@barnard.edu
GOLDBERG,
Suzanne, B .... 212-854-0411 297 C
sgoldb1@law.columbia.edu
GOLDBERG, Yisroel ...... 973-267-9404 280 G
financialaid@rca.edu
GOLDBERGBELLE,
Jonathan .... 217-206-8319 151 C
goldbergbelle.jonathan@uis.edu
GOLDBERGER, David .... 845-783-9901 324 A
GOLDBERGER, Jo .... 212-229-5192 308 C
jogo@newschool.edu
GOLDBLATT, Noah .... 802-865-6464 462 B
ngoldblatt@champlain.edu
GOLDBLUM, Tom .... 610-989-1329 402 B
tgoldblum@vfmac.edu
GOLDEN, Andrew, K ..... 609-258-4136 280 E
agolden@princeton.edu
GOLDEN, Beverley .... 903-566-7303 456 A
bgolden@uttyler.edu
GOLDEN, Carolyn .... 334-244-3837.... 4 F
cgolden2@aum.edu
GOLDEN, Cheryl .... 316-942-4291 175 I
goldenc@newmanu.edu
GOLDEN, Chris .... 423-614-8020 420 J
cgolden@leeuniversity.edu
GOLDEN, Cynthia .... 412-624-3335 401 B
goldenc@pitt.edu
GOLDEN, Denise .... 814-871-7663 384 E
golden007@gannon.edu
GOLDEN, Heather 216-421-8073 350M
hagolden@cia.edu
GOLDEN, Jay .... 252-328-9479 341 C
goldenj17@ecu.edu
GOLDEN, Kendra, J ...... 509-527-4952 486 H
golden@whitman.edu
GOLDEN, Leslie, B .... 407-582-3466 112 K
lgolden@valenciacollege.edu
GOLDEN, Marthe .... 713-348-4428 442 K
marthe.golden@rice.edu
GOLDEN, Paul .... 570-586-2400 381 E
pgolden@clarkssummitu.edu
GOLDEN, Robert, N ...... 608-263-4910 496 C
rngolden@wisc.edu
GOLDEN-BATTLE, Julia . 617-732-2058 216 B
julia.golden-battle@mcphs.edu
GOLDENBERG,
David, H .... 860-768-4055.. 88 H
goldenber@hartford.edu
GOLDENBERG, Isabel ... 202-741-2656.. 91 F
iag@gwu.edu
GOLDENBERG, Jay .... 646-216-2862 309 D
jgoldenberg@nycda.edu
GOLDENBERG, Mary ..... 847-491-2005 145 F
m-goldenberg@northwestern.edu
GOLDEY, Ellen, S .... 859-238-5226 179 F
ellen.goldey@centre.edu
GOLDFEIZ, Emanuel ..... 410-653-0433 201 A
GOLDGEIER, Eileen ...... 401-863-9900 404 E
eileen_goldgeier@brown.edu
GOLDHABER,
Yochanan .... 718-232-7800 325 J
GOLDIN, Steve .... 703-993-8294 467 L
sgoldin2@gmu.edu
GOLDING, Tena .... 985-549-2316 192 D
provost@selu.edu
GOLDMAN, Gregg .... 310-825-3444.. 69 A
ggoldman@conet.ucla.edu
GOLDMAN, Lee .... 212-305-2752 297 C
lg2379@columbia.edu
GOLDMAN, Lynn, R ...... 202-994-1000.. 91 F
GOLDMAN, Marc .... 717-337-6616 384 H
mgoldman@gettysburg.edu
GOLDMAN, Patricia ...... 914-813-9201 315 F
pgoldman@sarahlawrence.edu
GOLDMAN, Zvi .... 203-591-5651.. 87 F
zgoldman@post.edu
GOLDMON, Moses .... 870-460-1053.. 22 D
goldmon@uamont.edu
GOLDMON, Moses .... 731-426-1722 420 I
mgoldmon@lanecollege.edu
GOLDNER, Lauren .... 213-884-4133.. 24 A
lgoldner@ajrca.edu
GOLDNER, Lauren .... 213-884-4133.. 24 A
lgoldner@arjca.edu
GOLDSBERRY,
Kimberlie .... 262-551-5721 492 F
kgoldsberry@carthage.edu
GOLDSBY, Michael .... 765-285-9002 153 C
mgoldsby@bsu.edu
GOLDSCHMIDT, Erik ...... 251-380-3499.... 6 H
egoldschmidt@shc.edu
GOLDSCHMIDT, Robert . 646-565-6000 322 J
robert.goldschmidt@touro.edu
GOLDSMITH, Carole ..... 559-489-2212.. 66 E
carole.goldsmith@fresnocitycollege.edu
GOLDSMITH, Carolee .... 970-204-5363.. 79 J
carolee.goldsmith@frontrange.edu
GOLDSMITH, Diane .... 401-874-4218 406 B
dgoldsmith@uri.edu
GOLDSMITH, Glenn, A .. 574-269-5344 155 B
goldsmga@grace.edu
GOLDSMITH, Gordon .... 303-404-5799.. 79 J
gordon.goldsmith@frontrange.edu
GOLDSMITH, Kristie ...... 901-678-1782 427 D
kgldsmth@memphis.edu
GOLDSMITH, Rae .... 618-453-7174 149 E
rae.goldsmith@siu.edu
GOLDSMITH, Rae .... 618-453-2518 149 E
rae.goldsmith@siu.edu
GOLDSMITH, Steve .... 903-813-2342 430 N
sgoldsmith@austincollege.edu
GOLDSTEIN, Aaron .... 314-434-4044 252 B
aaron.goldstein@covenantseminary.edu
GOLDSTEIN, Adam .... 336-758-5226 344 D
GOLDSTEIN, Barry .... 251-981-3771.... 5 B
barry.goldstein@columbiasouthern.edu
GOLDSTEIN, Benjamin .. 213-763-3683.. 49 E
goldstbd@lattc.edu
GOLDSTEIN, Benjamin .. 707-527-4880.. 62 F
bgoldstein@santarosa.edu
GOLDSTEIN, Bill .... 641-472-1183 167 F
bgoldstein@mum.edu
GOLDSTEIN, Brian, A .... 215-951-1015 387 C
goldstein@lasalle.edu
GOLDSTEIN, Cheryl ...... 212-517-0683 306 A
cgoldstein@mmm.edu
GOLDSTEIN, Chip, B ..... 415-575-6100.. 29 B
cgoldstein@ciis.edu
GOLDSTEIN, Jeffrey, E .. 610-330-5001 387 E
goldstej@lafayette.edu
GOLDSTEIN, Jody .... 978-934-4574 211 G
jody_goldstein@uml.edu
GOLDSTEIN, Joel .... 304-760-1700.. 92 G
GOLDSTEIN, Leonard .... 480-219-6017 250 A
lgoldstein@atsu.edu
GOLDSTEIN, Matthias ... 410-704-4011 204 A
mmgoldstein@towson.edu
GOLDSTEIN, Robert, S .. 502-852-6169 185 C
rsgold03@louisville.edu
GOLDSTEIN, Serge, J ... 609-258-6059 280 E
serge@princeton.edu
GOLDSTEIN, Sharon ..... 973-684-6919 280 B
sgoldstein@pccc.edu
GOLDSTEIN, Sheri, E .... 561-862-4310 104 D
goldstse@palmbeachstate.edu
GOLDSTEIN, Steve .... 949-824-5011.. 68 G
GOLDSTEIN, Stuart .... 973-720-2978 284 I
goldsteins@wpunj.edu
GOLDSTON, David .... 202-789-1828 215 G
GOLDWATER,
Joanne, A .... 240-895-4270 201 E
jagoldwater@smcm.edu
GOLDYS, Michelle .... 386-506-3331.. 97 D
michelle.goldys@daytonastate.edu
GOLEMBESKI,
Richard, M .... 804-752-3288 470 F
richardgolembesi@rmc.edu
GOLEN, Harriet, S .... 215-670-9328 391 H
hsgolen@peirce.edu
GOLETZ, JR.,
Gregory, J .... 610-799-1172 388 I
ggoletz@lccc.edu
GOLEY, Julie .... 706-737-1604 115 A
jgoley@augusta.edu
GOLICH, Vicki, L .... 303-658-0666.. 80 N
vgolich@gmail.com
GOLIN, Dana .... 212-616-7264 301 F
dana.golin@helenefuld.edu
GOLIS, Kim .... 623-845-3562.. 13 C
kimberly.golis@gccaz.edu
GOLKA, John .... 402-554-2897 270 B
jgolka@unomaha.edu
GOLL, Susan .... 713-718-5041 437 I
susan.goll@hccs.edu
GOLLAHALLI, Anil, V .... 405-325-4124 371 B
agollahalli@ou.edu
GOLLBERG, Linda .... 208-885-4074 131 G
lstrong@uidaho.edu
GOLLEHER, Ashley .... 479-968-0228.. 18 C
agolleher1@atu.edu
GOLLENBERG, Gary .... 914-337-9300 297 D
gary.gollenberg@concordia-ny.edu
GOLLING, Werner, M ... 316-978-3030 178 A
werner.golling@wichita.edu
GOLLNICK, Donna, A .... 844-283-2246.. 93 A

GONZALEZ, Sandra .... 787-882-2065 511 D
administracion_empresas@unitecpr.net
GONZALEZ, Sergio .... 401-863-5402 404 E
sergio_gonzalez@brown.edu
GONZALEZ, Sophia .... 210-486-2247 429 G
fklein@alamo.edu
GONZALEZ, Stacy .... 518-244-4557 313 D
gonzas@sage.edu
GONZALEZ, Steven .... 602-286-8008.. 13 B
steven.gonzalez@gatewaycc.edu
GONZALEZ, Susana ...... 281-998-6129 443 B
susana.gonzalez@sjcd.edu
GONZALEZ, Taima .... 786-391-1167.. 94 I
GONZALEZ, Ted .... 254-526-1668 432 H
ted.gonzalez@ctcd.edu
GONZALEZ, Tina .... 212-799-5000 303 H
GONZALEZ, Tomas .... 585-785-1469 300 B
tomas.gonzalez@flcc.edu
GONZALEZ, Victor .... 956-872-2336 444 A
vgonzalez99@southtexascollege.edu
GONZALEZ, Widalys ..... 787-884-3838 506 D
wgonzalez@atenascollege.edu
GONZALEZ, Yadira .... 541-278-5753 372 A
ygonzalez@bluecc.edu
GONZALEZ, Yaitzaenid .. 787-765-3560 507 L
ygonzalez@edpuniversity.edu
GONZALEZ MEDINA, CMF,
Ruben, A .... 787-848-5265 510 K
ruben_gonzalez@pucpr.edu
GONZALEZ-MELENDEZ,
Saraliz 787-857-3600 508M
sgonzalez@br.inter.edu
GONZALEZ-SALAMANCA,
Julian .... 316-284-5390 171 F
juliangs@bethelks.edu
GOOCH, Darlene .... 919-962-4388 342 D
darlene_gooch@unc.edu
GOOCH, Jackie .... 256-233-8211.... 4 D
jackie.gooch@athens.edu
GOOCH, Janet .... 660-785-4105 260 J
jquinzer@truman.edu
GOOCH, Josh .... 620-665-3594 174 B
goochj@hutchcc.edu
GOOCH, Zanetta .... 615-963-7401 426 D
zgooch@tnstate.edu
GOOCH-GRAYSON,
Cynthia .... 531-622-2649 267 H
cgooch@mccneb.edu
GOOD, Andrew .... 818-364-7800.. 49 B
gooda@lamission.edu
GOOD, Darrin, S .... 402-465-2217 268 H
president@nebrwesleyan.edu
GOOD, Gayle, A .... 402-363-5621 270 E
gagood@york.edu
GOOD, Glenn .... 352-392-3261 109 F
ggood@coe.ufl.edu
GOOD, Jennifer .... 251-380-2278.... 6 H
jgood@shc.edu
GOOD, Lisa .... 717-396-7833 393 E
lgood@pcad.edu
GOOD, Megan, R .... 334-844-6844.... 4 E
mrg0030@auburn.edu
GOOD, Michael, L .... 801-581-7480 460 E
michael.good@hsc.utah.edu
GOOD, Rhonda .... 717-337-6015 384 H
rgood@gettysburg.edu
GOOD, RT .... 561-237-7458 102 V
rgood@lynn.edu
GOOD LUCK, Aldean .... 406-638-3118 263 H
goodluckav@lbhc.edu
GOODALE, Brian .... 518-587-2100 321 A
brian.goodale@esc.edu
GOODALE, Nathan .... 315-859-4615 301 C
ngoodale@hamilton.edu
GOODALE, Timothy, A .. 252-335-3767 341 D
tagoodale@ecsu.edu
GOODARZI, Shirin, M .. 410-777-2148 197 C
smgoodarzi@aacc.edu
GOODBURN, Amy .... 402-472-3751 269 J
agoodburn1@unl.edu
GOODE, Greg, J .... 812-237-7778 155 G
greg.goode@indstate.edu
GOODE, Jess .... 312-567-3970 139 B
jgoode1@iit.edu
GOODE, Jodi .... 325-646-2502 438 D
jgoode@hputx.edu
GOODE, Kevin .... 814-866-8406 388 A
kgoode@lecom.edu
GOODE, Mike .... 704-894-2143 328 F
migoode@davidson.edu
GOODE, Roger .... 781-768-7401 218 C
roger.goode@regiscollege.edu
GOODE, Tyler .... 828-339-4394 338 B
t_goode@southwesterncc.edu

GOODE-CROSS, David .. 410-225-5266 199 H
dgoodecross@mica.edu
GOODELL, Adam .... 201-879-3673 275 H
agoodell@bergen.edu
GOODEN, Benny, L ...... 479-308-2294.. 17 C
benny.gooden@acheedu.org
GOODENOW, Andrew ... 816-235-1107 261 C
goodenowa@umkc.edu
GOODFELLOW,
Geoffrey .... 312-949-7016 138 E
ggoodfel@ico.edu
GOODFELLOW, Sandy .. 615-675-5280 428 G
alex@welch.edu
GOODFELLOW, Tim ...... 503-554-2585 373 C
tgoodfellow@georgefox.edu
GOODFRIEND,
Kimberly .... 972-883-2201 455 B
kimberly.goodfriend@utdallas.edu
GOODGAME, Henry ...... 470-639-0400 122 D
henry.goodgame@morehouse.edu
GOODGE, Marshall, M . 570-561-1818 398 D
mgoodge@stots.edu
GOODGE, Samuel .... 304-829-7905 487 G
sgoodge@bethanywv.edu
GOODHEART, Marc .... 617-496-9480 210 B
marc_goodheart@harvard.edu
GOODHUE LYNCH,
Mary .... 508-588-9100 214 F
mgoodhuel@massasoit.mass.edu
GOODIN, Allison .... 610-606-4666 381 A
agoodin@cedarcrest.edu
GOODIN, Nicole .... 502-413-8882 184 E
ngoodin@sullivan.edu
GOODING, Betsy .... 903-434-8137 441 B
bgooding@ntcc.edu
GOODING, Michelle ..... 941-487-4649 109 D
mgooding@ncf.edu
GOODING, Samuel .... 281-949-1800.. 92 G
GOODING, Samuel .... 281-201-3800.. 92 G
GOODING, Timothy ...... 770-426-2741 121 C
tgooding@life.edu
GOODJOHN, Bunny ...... 434-947-8126 470 E
bgoodjohn@randolphcollege.edu
GOODKIND, Hilary .... 650-574-6196.. 61 P
goodkindh@smccd.edu
GOODLING, Barry, G .... 717-796-5064 390 E
bgoodlin@messiah.edu
GOODMAN, Adam .... 205-853-1200.... 2 G
akgoodman@jeffersonstate.edu
GOODMAN, Ann .... 575-646-1722 287 B
anng@nmsu.edu
GOODMAN, Brent .... 619-849-2371.. 57 E
brentgoodman@pointloma.edu
GOODMAN, Carl .... 850-599-3276 108 I
carl.goodman@famu.edu
GOODMAN, Catie .... 850-201-8281 111 C
goodmanc@tcc.fl.edu
GOODMAN, David, M ... 617-552-3900 207 B
david.goodman@bc.edu
GOODMAN, Dennis, S .. 573-341-4284 261 E
dgoodman@mst.edu
GOODMAN, Elodie .... 509-533-3694 480 B
elodie.goodman@sfcc.spokane.edu
GOODMAN, Grayson .... 407-303-1631.. 94 D
grayson.goodman@ahu.edu
GOODMAN, Guy .... 602-243-8000.. 14 A
guy.goodman@southmountaincc.edu
GOODMAN, Gwen .... 518-327-6242 311 G
ggoodman@paulsmiths.edu
GOODMAN, Hunter, P .. 937-229-4915 362 G
hgoodman1@udayton.edu
GOODMAN, J. Andy ...... 314-516-7133 261 D
goodmanjam@umsl.edu
GOODMAN, Jacque ...... 641-844-5640 166 I
jacque.goodman@iavalley.edu
GOODMAN, James .... 808-455-0668 129 D
goodmanj@hawaii.edu
GOODMAN, Jeremy ...... 781-292-2373 209 E
jeremy.goodman@olin.edu
GOODMAN, Kameron ... 314-838-8858 261 G
ithelpdesk@ugst.edu
GOODMAN, Larry, J ..... 312-942-7073 148 A
larry_j_goodman@rush.edu
GOODMAN, Lena, C ..... 920-433-6638 492 B
lena.goodman@bellincollege.edu
GOODMAN, Marc, P ..... 310-506-4607.. 56 C
marc.goodman@pepperdine.edu
GOODMAN, Mark .... 646-565-6000 322 J
mark.goodman@touro.edu
GOODMAN, Matthew .... 207-741-5500 195 A
mgoodman@smccme.edu
GOODMAN, Michael ..... 504-865-5725 191 B
mgoodman@tulane.edu

GOODMAN, Richard, H 503-494-5078 375 B
goodmanr@ohsu.edu
GOODMAN, Robert, M . 848-932-3600 282 A
execdean@aesop.rutgers.edu
GOODMAN,
Shannon, M .... 940-565-4510 454 A
shannon.goodman@unt.edu
GOODMAN, Sharon ...... 910-410-1734 337 B
sbgoodman@richmondcc.edu
GOODMAN, Willie, F .... 404-527-5735 120 K
wgoodman@itc.edu
GOODNER, Jason .... 501-882-8830.. 17 F
GOODNESS, Gail, C ...... 603-646-3011 273 E
gail.c.goodness@dartmouth.edu
GOODNIGHT, Lisa .... 219-989-2323 159 G
ljgoodni@pnw.edu
GOODNOUGH, Doug .... 517-264-7141 230 E
dgoodnou@sienaheights.edu
GOODNOW, Jean .... 989-686-9200 223 G
jeangoodnow@delta.edu
GOODRICH, James .... 503-352-2814 375 G
jgoodrich@pacificu.edu
GOODRICH, Joy, P .... 804-354-5210 477 C
jgoodrich@vuu.edu
GOODRICH, Mark .... 707-654-1563.. 32 B
mgoodrich@csum.edu
GOODRICH, Rachel .... 717-290-8701 388 D
rgoodrich@lancasterseminary.edu
GOODRICH, Shannon ... 208-769-3303 131 C
sgoodrich@nic.edu
GOODRICH PELLETIER,
Monica .... 508-213-2108 217 E
monica.goodrich-pelletier@nichols.edu
GOODRIDGE, Ellengold 256-726-7093.... 6 C
egoodridge@oakwood.edu
GOODSON, Alyn .... 252-335-2972 341 D
agoodson@ecsu.edu
GOODSON, Drew .... 919-718-7287 333 C
dgoodson@cccc.edu
GOODSON, Leigh .... 918-595-7868 370 E
leigh.goodson@tulsacc.edu
GOODSON, Linda .... 334-699-2266.... 1 B
lgoodson@acom.edu
GOODSON, Michael ...... 507-786-3294 243 C
goodson@stolaf.edu
GOODSPEED, Seth .... 612-874-3745 236 K
agoodspeed@mcad.edu
GOODSTEIN, Eban .... 845-758-7067 290 G
ebangood@bard.edu
GOODSTONE, Michael .. 631-420-2337 321 B
michael.goodstone@farmingdale.edu
GOODWIIN, Christina ... 802-586-7711 463 D
cgoodwin@sterlingcollege.edu
GOODWIN, Amy .... 719-587-7912.. 76 F
1559mgr@follett.com
GOODWIN, Ann, E .... 859-238-5760 179 F
ann.goodwin@centre.edu
GOODWIN, Bryan .... 417-625-3191 256 D
goodwin-b@mssu.edu
GOODWIN, Cheryl .... 978-556-3854 215 C
cgoodwin@necc.mass.edu
GOODWIN, Cheryl .... 206-876-6100 484 E
cgoodwin@theseattleschool.edu
GOODWIN,
Christine, M .... 718-990-1993 314 B
goodwinc@stjohns.edu
GOODWIN, Christy .... 251-578-1313.... 3 D
cbulger@rstc.edu
GOODWIN, Cindi, J ..... 336-633-4475 337 A
cjgoodwin@randolph.edu
GOODWIN, Darrell .... 206-296-6060 484 F
goodwind@seattleu.edu
GOODWIN, Erica, A ...... 937-481-2223 364 E
erica_goodwin@wilmington.edu
GOODWIN, Jerome .... 919-530-6739 342 A
jgoodwin@nccu.edu
GOODWIN, Julie .... 443-885-3220 200 D
julie.goodwin@morgan.edu
GOODWIN, Kristine, C . 401-865-2144 405 B
kgoodwi2@providence.edu
GOODWIN, Laura .... 303-315-2105.. 83 C
laura.goodwin@ucdenver.edu
GOODWIN, Lisa .... 503-883-2492 373 H
lgoodwin@linfield.edu
GOODWIN, Marnie .... 517-355-6560 227 D
goodwin9@msu.edu
GOODWIN, Mary Ann .. 509-533-3820 480 B
maryann.goodwin@ccs.spokane.edu
GOODWIN, Matthew .... 207-893-6601 195 F
mgoodwin@sjcme.edu
GOODWIN, Michelle ..... 301-934-7635 198 A
mlgoodwin@csmd.edu
GOODWIN, Mike .... 541-737-3288 375 D
mike.goodwin@oregonstate.edu

GOODWIN, Peter .... 410-228-9250 202 F
GOODWIN, Steven, D ... 413-545-2211 211 D
sgoodwin@cns.umass.edu
GOODWIN, Valerie .... 803-536-7026 412 C
vgoodwi4@scsu.edu
GOODWIN, Virginia ...... 317-543-4796 158 V
vgoodwin@martin.edu
GOODWIN, Whittington 281-649-3238 437 H
wgoodwin@hbu.edu
GOODYEAR, Anne .... 207-798-4352 193 D
agoodyea@bowdoin.edu
GOODYEAR, Frank .... 207-725-3673 193 D
fgoodyea@bowdoin.edu
GOODYEAR, Jack .... 214-333-5595 434 I
jackg@dbu.edu
GOOKIN, Karen .... 207-454-1054 195 B
kgookin@wccc.me.edu
GOOLSBY, Edwin, G ..... 352-518-1301 104 F
goolsbe@phsc.edu
GOON, Dean .... 419-207-5195 348 A
dgoon@ashland.edu
GOONEWARDENE,
Julie .... 512-499-4355 454 I
jgoonewardene@utsystem.edu
GOORIS, Daniel .... 773-244-5222 145 A
dgooris@northpark.edu
GOOS, Karen .... 660-543-4811 260 K
goos@ucmo.edu
GOOSBY, Gloria .... 912-478-0644 119 C
gtmorgan@georgiasouthern.edu
GOOSEN, Richard .... 231-591-2635 223 J
richardgoosen@ferris.edu
GOOYABADI, Ali .... 858-653-3000.. 29 I
GOPALAN, Sandeep ...... 336-725-8344 339 F
gopalans@piedmontu.edu
GOPLEN, Joanna .... 315-312-3234 319 B
joanna.goplen@oswego.edu
GOPLIN, Scott .... 260-665-4365 160 H
goplins@trine.edu
GOPP, Jeff .... 408-848-4705.. 43 J
jgopp@gavilan.edu
GORBANDT, Melissa .... 859-572-5744 184 A
gorbandt@nku.edu
GORBY, Kristine .... 724-222-5330 392 A
kgorby@penncommercial.edu
GORDEN, JR., Monroe . 310-825-1514.. 69 A
mgorden@saonet.ucla.edu
GORDEN, Noel .... 641-856-5181 166 C
noel.gorden@indianhills.edu
GORDER, Corey .... 701-228-5673 346 C
corey.gorder@dakotacollege.edu
GORDIEN CASE,
Lori, K .... 909-593-3511.. 70 D
lgordien@laverne.edu
GORDLEY, Matthew, E .. 412-578-6262 380 E
megordley@carlow.edu
GORDON, Allen .... 765-285-2983 153 C
agordon@bsu.edu
GORDON, Andrew .... 904-470-8244.. 97 L
andrew.gordon@ewc.edu
GORDON, Andrew .... 315-443-5459 322 C
agordon@syr.edu
GORDON, Bruce .... 402-559-6045 270 A
bgordon@unmc.edu
GORDON, Carin, M ...... 407-582-2556 112 K
cgordon15@valenciacollege.edu
GORDON, Casey .... 320-363-5620 235 C
cgordon@csbsju.edu
GORDON, Casey .... 320-363-5620 243 A
cgordon@csbsju.edu
GORDON, Cristina .... 605-886-6777 415 H
cristina.gordon@mtmc.edu
GORDON, Daniel, L ...... 404-727-3746 117 F
dangordon@emory.edu
GORDON, Dawn .... 507-372-3443 239 E
dawn.gordon@mnwest.edu
GORDON, Delton .... 479-968-0376.. 18 C
dgordon5@atu.edu
GORDON, Donny .... 707-654-1175.. 32 B
dgordon@csum.edu
GORDON, Eric .... 207-992-4925 194 A
gordoner@husson.edu
GORDON, Evelyn .... 765-973-8232 156 C
evgordon@iue.edu
GORDON, James, D ..... 606-783-2122 183 F
j.gordon@moreheadstate.edu
GORDON, Jeffrey .... 518-262-5486 289 F
gordonj@amc.edu
GORDON, Jessie .... 989-317-4626 227 F
jmgordon@midmich.edu
GORDON, John .... 202-274-5998.. 93 C
john.gordon@udc.edu

GORDON, Joyce .... 270-809-2146 183 G
jgordon@murraystate.edu
GORDON, Julie .... 608-262-1803 496 B
jgordon@uwsa.edu
GORDON, Kelly .... 512-313-3000 434 E
kelly.gordon@concordia.edu
GORDON, Leslie .... 907-747-9474.. 10 B
llgordon@alaska.edu
GORDON, Mark, B .... 248-370-3000 229 G
mbgordon@oakland.edu
GORDON, Matthew .... 415-703-9500.. 28 D
mgordon@cca.edu
GORDON, Matthew .... 707-468-3165.. 51 E
mgordon@mendocino.edu
GORDON, Monica .... 692-625-3291 505 F
mgordon@cmi.edu
GORDON, Patti .... 662-560-1103 248 D
GORDON, Paul .... 816-501-3600 250 F
paul.gordon@avila.edu
GORDON, Paul .... 660-831-4176 256 G
gordonp@moval.edu
GORDON, Rebecca, J .... 205-975-6149.... 8 A
rjgordon@uab.edu
GORDON, River .... 612-874-3727 236 K
rgordon182@mcad.edu
GORDON, Ronald .... 937-328-6095 350 L
gordonr@clarkstate.edu
GORDON, Sally .... 814-886-6395 391 B
sgordon@mtaloy.edu
GORDON, Sandra .... 718-473-8701 295 B
sgordon@citytech.cuny.edu
GORDON, Scott .... 509-359-7900 480 E
sgordon@ewu.edu
GORDON, Sharon .... 860-679-2808.. 88 E
sgordon@uchc.edu
GORDON, Sherie .... 229-430-4754 113 H
sherie.gordon@asurams.edu
GORDON, Solomon .... 718-854-8700 322 E
GORDON, Stephanie ..... 304-829-7115 487 G
sgordon@bethanywv.edu
GORDON, Sue, B .... 443-394-9257 201 H
sbgordon@stevenson.edu
GORDON, T. Scott .... 724-458-3352 385 C
tsgordon@gcc.edu
GORDON, Timothy, W .. 716-878-4705 318 C
gordontw@buffalostate.edu
GORDON, Tom .... 914-632-5400 307 G
tgordon@monroecollege.edu
GORDON, Tonia, J .... 814-886-6390 391 B
tgordon@mtaloy.edu
GORDON, Wade .... 218-733-7656 238 F
w.gordon@lsc.edu
GORDON, Wes .... 662-325-9129 247 F
wgordon@foundation.msstate.edu
GORDON-ALLEN, Gail ... 773-907-4384 134 C
ggorden-allen@ccc.edu
GORDON-CANLAS, Liz .. 614-222-3294 351 D
lgordon-canlas@ccad.edu
GORDON-JACKSON,
Yolanda .... 334-872-2533.... 6 F
yolandagordon176@yahoo.com
GORDY, Mary .... 303-300-8740.. 77 D
mary.gordy@collegeamerica.com
GORDY, Reggie .... 334-291-4947.... 1 H
reggie.gordy@cv.edu
GORE, Chris .... 903-988-7446 439 A
cgore@kilgore.edu
GORE, Darvin .... 405-945-6789 368 E
dargore@osuokc.edu
GORE, Fred .... 972-825-4630 445 A
fgore@sagu.edu
GORE, Jacqui .... 432-335-6815 441 D
jgore@odessa.edu
GORE, Paul .... 256-264-5060.... 3 F
paul.gore@snead.edu
GORE, Paul .... 502-272-8184 179 B
pgore@bellarmine.edu
GORE, Scott .... 410-386-8467 197 G
sgore@carrollcc.edu
GORE, Shana .... 850-474-2400 110 E
sgore1@uwf.edu
GORE, Sonya .... 405-682-1611 367 H
sonya.d.gore@occc.edu
GORE, Vennie .... 517-355-7457 227 D
vgore@msu.edu
GORE, Vikki .... 509-452-5100 483 A
vgore@pnwu.edu
GOREHAM, Amber .... 660-543-8225 260 K
agoreham@ucmo.edu
GORES, Greg .... 507-538-5027 234 I
gores.gregory@mayo.edu
GORES, Julie, C .... 608-246-6633 499 H
jgores@madisoncollege.edu
GORETSKY, Andrew ...... 215-572-2934 379 A
goretskya@arcadia.edu
GORETZKY, Andrew ...... 215-572-2934 379 A
goretskya@arcadia.edu
GORGA, Joe .... 925-969-4229.. 40 I
jgorga@dvc.edu
GORHAM, Chad .... 256-228-6001.... 3 B
gorhamchad@nacc.edu
GORHAM, Elizabeth ...... 617-879-5986 216 B
elizabeth.gorham@mcphs.edu
GORHAM, Faust .... 661-654-3425.. 30 E
fgorham@csub.edu
GORHAM, Jonathan ...... 617-243-2315 210 G
jgorham@lasell.edu
GORIN, Beth .... 646-565-6000 322 J
beth.gorin@touro.edu
GORINI, Cathy .... 641-472-1107 167 F
cgorini@mum.edu
GORINSHTEYN, Dasha .. 718-368-4975 294 E
dasha.gorinshteyn@kbcc.cuny.edu
GORKA, Gary .... 415-257-1301.. 41 H
gary.gorka@dominican.edu
GORMAN, Bonnie, B .... 906-487-2212 227 E
bbgorman@mtu.edu
GORMAN, Bridget .... 713-348-4996 442 K
bkgorman@rice.edu
GORMAN, Deb .... 920-996-2813 499 E
gorman@fvtc.edu
GORMAN, June .... 610-647-4400 386 C
jgorman@immaculata.edu
GORMAN, Kimberly ...... 828-227-7469 344 A
ksgorman@wcu.edu
GORMAN, Luke .... 603-526-3797 272 H
luke.gorman@colby-sawyer.edu
GORMAN, Mary .... 646-312-3315 292 L
mary.gorman@baruch.cuny.edu
GORMAN, Michael .... 856-351-2601 283 A
mgorman@salemcc.edu
GORMAN, Patrick .... 504-568-4820 189 B
pgorma@lsuhsc.edu
GORMAN, Robin, A ...... 724-357-2410 394 G
rgorman@iup.edu
GORMAN, Steven .... 603-271-6484 273 B
sgorman@ccsnh.edu
GORMAN, Sue .... 774-243-3488 216 B
sue.gorman@mcphs.edu
GORMAN, Susan, L ...... 617-558-1788 217 D
sgorman@nesa.edu
GORMAN, Susan, T ...... 443-334-2331 201 H
sgorman@stevenson.edu
GORMAN, Wendy .... 715-682-1322 495 C
wgorman@northland.edu
GORMAN, Wil .... 573-651-2297 259 K
wgorman@semo.edu
GORMAN, William, P .... 617-989-4147 219 E
gormanb@wit.edu
GORMAN, William, W .. 740-283-6456 353 B
wgorman@franciscan.edu
GORMAN, Zach .... 309-677-3100 133 B
zgorman@bradley.edu
GORMAN-SMITH,
Deborah .... 773-834-1781 150 J
debgs@uchicago.edu
GORMLEY, Christina, L 717-337-6611 384 H
cgormley@gettysburg.edu
GORMLEY, Kenneth, G . 412-396-6060 383 C
president@duq.edu
GORMLEY, Melissa, E .. 608-342-1151 497 D
gormleym@uwplatt.edu
GORNEAULT, Gregg ...... 860-906-5127.. 85 D
ggorneault@capitalcc.edu
GORR, Nathan .... 612-330-1390 233 K
gorr@augsburg.edu
GORRELL, Cathy .... 303-458-4117.. 82 E
cgorrell@regis.edu
GORRELL, Renee .... 314-454-8171 253 E
reneegorrell@bjc.org
GORSKI, Gary .... 313-593-9953 231 F
gmgorski@umich.edu
GORSKI, Holly .... 253-964-6519 483 D
hgorski@pierce.ctc.edu
GORSKI, Kathleen .... 630-466-7900 152 C
kgorski@waubonsee.edu
GORT, Amy .... 651-793-1920 238 H
amy.gort@metrostate.edu
GORTER, Tracy .... 712-324-5061 168 G
tgorter@nwicc.edu
GORTI, Anantha .... 703-284-1488 469 C
anantha.gorti@marymount.edu
GORTON, Holly, J .... 231-995-1012 228 G
hgorton@nmc.edu
GOSAI, Mayur .... 301-243-2336 503 J
mayur.gosai@dodiis.mil
GOSCH, Judy .... 865-539-7233 425 F
jagosch@pstcc.edu
GOSE, Becca .... 541-737-2474 375 D
GOSE, Carrie .... 307-766-1121 502 H
GOSHORN, Mark .... 859-344-3513 184 F
goshorm@thomasmore.edu
GOSIER, Michelle .... 585-385-8064 314 A
mgosier@sjfc.edu
GOSLIN, Elle .... 860-932-4000.. 86 E
egoslin@qvcc.edu
GOSNELL, Victor .... 434-947-8138 470 E
vgosnell@randolphcollege.edu
GOSNEY, Sue .... 213-356-5330.. 64 H
sue_gosney@sciarc.edu
GOSS, Barbara .... 205-853-1200.... 2 G
bgoss@jeffersonstate.edu
GOSS, Jeanne .... 443-412-2306 199 A
jgoss@harford.edu
GOSS, Jonathan, D .... 315-268-2320 296 A
jgoss@clarkson.edu
GOSS, Leah .... 303-352-3121.. 79 E
leah.goss@ccd.edu
GOSS, Nathan, R .... 770-534-6162 115 D
ngoss@brenau.edu
GOSS, Peter .... 971-722-4490 375 J
peter.goss@pcc.edu
GOSS, Rebecca .... 509-533-8449 480 A
rebecca.goss@scc.spokane.edu
GOSS, Ronald .... 541-956-7494 376 D
rgoss@roguecc.edu
GOSSARD, Sheryl, R ..... 615-353-3305 425 D
sheryl.gossard@nscc.edu
GOSSELIN, Grant, M ..... 617-552-3100 207 B
grant.gosselin@bc.edu
GOSSEN, Timothy .... 507-457-1597 243 B
tgossen@smumn.edu
GOSSETT, Betty .... 716-673-3321 317 A
betty.gossett@fredonia.edu
GOSSETT, John .... 828-652-0630 336 B
johngossett@mcdowelltech.edu
GOSSFELD-BENZING,
Sara .... 715-675-3331 500 E
gossfeld-benzing@ntc.edu
GOSWAMI, Jaya, S .... 361-593-2170 447 D
jaya.goswami@tamuk.edu
GOSWAMI, Utpal .... 816-604-2414 255 D
utpal.goswami@mcckc.edu
GOSWAMI, Utpal, K ...... 816-604-2044 255 G
utpal.goswami@mcckc.edu
GOSZ, Mike .... 312-567-3198 139 B
gosz@iit.edu
GOTANDA, John .... 808-544-0203 127 H
GOTAY, Susanne .... 787-725-8120 507 N
consejerasusanne@eap.edu
GOTCHER, Mike .... 931-372-3366 426 E
mgotcher@tntech.edu
GOTELLI, Luis .... 787-728-1515 514 D
luis.gotelli@sagrado.edu
GOTHAM, Kerry .... 585-395-2068 318 B
kgotham@brockport.edu
GOTHARD, Mathew, J .. 303-963-3223.. 77 G
mgothard@ccu.edu
GOTJEN, Lynne .... 207-795-7166 194 E
gotjenly@mchp.edu
GOTSCH, Kenneth .... 847-543-2631 135 B
kgotsch@clcillinois.edu
GOTSCH, Sarah, A .... 574-631-3903 161 C
sgotsch@nd.edu
GOTSCHALL, Matthew ... 308-398-7300 266 A
mgotschall@cccneb.edu
GOTSMAN, Craig .... 973-596-5488 279 F
craig.gotsman@njit.edu
GOTT, Jared .... 731-989-6649 420 C
jgott@fhu.edu
GOTTARDY, John .... 716-645-2450 316 F
johngott@buffalo.edu
GOTTDIENER, Yitzchok . 718-941-8000 306 I
GOTTLIEB, Jane .... 212-799-5000 303 H
GOTTLIEB, Mel .... 213-884-4133.. 24 A
mgottlieb@ajrca.edu
GOTTLIEB, Neal .... 732-431-1600 284 A
taofnj@gmail.com
GOTTSCHALK,
Katherine .... 765-983-1267 154 G
gottska@earlham.edu
GOTTSCHALK, Mark ...... 806-720-7327 439 H
GOTTSCHALK, Mark ...... 806-894-9611 443 I
mgottschalk@southplainscollege.edu
GOTTSCHALK, Sandy .... 785-623-6150 176 A
sgottschalk@ncktc.edu
GOTTSHALL, Lori .... 954-771-0376 102 R
lgottshall@knoxseminary.edu
GOTTULA, Todd .... 308-865-8454 269 I
gottulatm@unk.edu
GOTZMAN, Ron .... 763-417-8250 234 H
rgotzman@centralseminary.edu
GOTZON, Mary, A .... 610-282-1100 382 E
mary.gotzon@desales.edu
GOUCH, Shawn .... 724-805-2895 398 E
shawn.gouch@stvincent.edu
GOUCH, Shawn .... 724-805-2894 398 F
shawn.guch@stvincent.edu
GOUDEAU, Arthur .... 281-487-1170 448 F
agoudeau@txchiro.edu
GOUDEAU, LaTasha ...... 713-221-8162 453 B
goudeaul@uhd.edu
GOUGER, Tammy .... 585-395-2442 318 B
tgouger@brockport.edu
GOUGH, Allison .... 808-544-1109 127 H
agough@hpu.edu
GOUGH, Annette .... 732-571-3402 279 B
gough@monmouth.edu
GOUGH, Christopher .... 203-332-5022.. 85 F
cgough@hcc.commnet.edu
GOUGH, Daniel .... 315-228-7335 296 F
dgough@colgate.edu
GOUGH, Darby .... 816-501-3660 250 F
darby.gough@avila.edu
GOUGH, Richard, J .... 843-525-8247 412 H
rgough@tcl.edu
GOUKER, Toby .... 301-654-7267 201 G
GOULD, Alicia .... 303-458-4167.. 82 E
agould@regis.edu
GOULD, Amanda .... 413-565-1000 205 G
agould@baypath.edu
GOULD, Dean, J .... 702-889-8426 270 K
dgould@nshe.nevada.edu
GOULD, Deborah, M ..... 413-545-2554 211 D
dmgould@admin.umass.edu
GOULD, Kenneth .... 718-951-3136 293 C
kgould@brooklyn.cuny.edu
GOULD, Kyle .... 765-998-4635 160 F
kygould@taylor.edu
GOULD, Mark .... 978-837-5072 216 D
gouldm@merrimack.edu
GOULD, Shari .... 814-732-1294 394 F
sgould@edinboro.edu
GOULD, Terri .... 989-686-9081 223 G
tlgould@delta.edu
GOULD, Thomas .... 252-493-7406 336 H
tgould@email.pittcc.edu
GOULD, Trent .... 601-266-5253 249 F
trent.gould@usm.edu
GOULD, Trent .... 601-266-4568 249 F
trent.gould@usm.edu
GOULET, Bonnie .... 203-576-8752.. 86 B
bgoulet@nv.edu
GOULET, Caroline .... 210-283-6924 453 D
goulet@uiwtx.edu
GOULET, Stephen, P ..... 508-793-7598 208 A
sgoulet@clarku.edu
GOURDINE, Raji .... 334-876-9292.... 2 D
rgourdine@wccs.edu
GOURJI, Konstantin ...... 650-685-6616.. 44 J
kgourji@gurnick.edu
GOURLEY, Bridget, L .... 765-658-4359 154 F
bgourley@depauw.edu
GOURLEY, Hannah .... 641-628-5381 163 E
gourleyh@central.edu
GOURLEY, Kristin .... 865-981-8215 421 F
kristin.gourley@maryvillecollege.edu
GOURNEAU, Haven .... 406-768-6300 263 G
hgourneau@fpcc.edu
GOURNEAU, Kim .... 218-755-3948 237 E
kim.gourneau@bemidjistate.edu
GOUSE, Richard, I .... 401-739-5000 405 A
rgouse@neit.edu
GOUSY, Norman .... 413-545-3364 211 D
ngousy@admin.umass.edu
GOUVEIA, Jan .... 808-956-6405 128 F
jgouveia@hawaii.edu
GOUVEIA, Jan, N .... 808-956-6405 128 D
jgouveia@hawaii.edu
GOUVEIA, JR.,
Leonard, R .... 808-956-8259 128 F
lgouveia@hawaii.edu
GOVAN, JR., Tom .... 708-596-2000 149 B
tgovan@ssc.edu
GOVEA, Rene .... 815-479-7619 143 A
rgovea@mchenry.edu
GOVEA, Sam .... 972-860-4216 434 L
sgovea@dcccd.edu
GOVENDER, Yogani ...... 787-250-1912 509 D
ygovender@intermetro.onmicrosoft.
com

GOVER, Bruce .... 606-679-8501 182 C
bruce.gover@kctcs.edu
GOVER, Kristie .... 904-256-7070 101 G
kgover1@ju.edu
GOVINDARAJU, Venu ... 716-645-3321 316 F
vpr@buffalo.edu
GOVITZ, Leanne .... 989-686-9490 223 G
leannegovitz@delta.edu
GOVITZ, Scott .... 989-386-6624 227 F
sgovitz@midmich.edu
GOW, Joe .... 608-785-8004 496 F
jgow@uwlax.edu
GOWAN, Mary, A .... 706-864-1800 126 A
GOWANS, Faye .... 803-822-3251 410 G
gowansf@midlandstech.edu
GOWDY, Stephen .... 616-538-2330 224 C
sgowdy@gracechristian.edu
GOWEN, Karla .... 312-553-2500 134 A
kgowen@ccc.edu
GOWER, Ana Maria ...... 510-628-8034.. 48 A
agower@lincolnuca.edu
GOWER, Donna .... 405-224-3140 371 D
dgower@usao.edu
GOWER, Paula .... 405-585-5410 367 F
paula.gower@okbu.edu
GOWER, Ryan .... 618-544-8657 138 H
gowerry@iecc.edu
GOWING, Wendi .... 303-762-6887.. 79 H
wendi.gowing@denverseminary.edu
GOYAL, Arun .... 951-222-8250.. 58 I
arun.goyal@rcc.edu
GOYETTE, John .... 805-525-4417.. 67 D
jgoyette@thomasaquinas.edu
GOYETTE, Sylvain .... 815-836-5974 141 G
goyettsy@lewisu.edu
GOYUNYAN, Gevorg ..... 510-925-4282.. 25 Q
gevorg@aua.am
GOZA, Franklin .... 262-472-1712 498 C
gozaf@uww.edu
GOZIA, Richard .... 660-831-4183 256 G
goziar@moval.edu
GOZIK, Nick .... 617-552-3827 207 B
nick.gozik@bc.edu
GOZUM, Allan .... 937-769-1304 347 H
agozum@antioch.edu
GRABAREK, Christina ... 219-464-5271 162 A
christina.grabarek@valpo.edu
GRABAU, Lauren .... 308-535-3636 267 K
grabaul@mpcc.edu
GRABER, Brent .... 574-296-6221 152 I
it@ambs.edu
GRABER, David .... 402-375-7257 268 G
dagrabe1@wsc.edu
GRABER, Linda .... 866-931-4300 258 G
linda.graber@rockbridge.edu
GRABOWSKI, Janice, T 724-925-4123 403 A
grabowskij@westmoreland.edu
GRABOWSKI, Jeremiah . 716-829-8392 298 F
grabowsj@dyc.edu
GRABOWSKI, John, F ... 410-777-2231 197 C
jfgrabowski@aacc.edu
GRABOWSKI, Mark .... 417-328-1556 259 L
mgrabowski@sbuniv.edu
GRABOWSKI,
Rodney, M .... 716-645-2925 316 F
rodneyg@buffalo.edu
GRABOYS, James .... 334-229-6500.... 4 B
jgraboys@alasu.edu
GRACA, Michael .... 508-286-8235 220 A
graca_michael@wheatoncollege.edu
GRACE, Anna .... 503-253-3443 374 H
anna.grace@ocom.edu
GRACE, Dennis .... 239-304-7093.. 94 O
dennis.grace@avemaria.edu
GRACE, Janet .... 620-441-5564 172 I
janet.grace@cowley.edu
GRACE, Lynn .... 734-973-3507 232 B
lgmartin@wccnet.edu
GRACE, Melissa, H .... 850-474-3423 110 E
mgrace@uwf.edu
GRACE, Michelle, M ..... 847-543-2274 135 B
mgrace@clcillinois.edu
GRACE, Nabil, F .... 248-204-2500 226 G
ngrace@ltu.edu
GRACE, Selena .... 208-373-1874 130 H
gracsele@isu.edu
GRACE, Sherie .... 256-228-6001.... 3 B
graces@nacc.edu
GRACE, Ted, W .... 618-453-4408 149 E
tgrace@siu.edu
GRACHAN, Bart .... 718-482-5900 294 F
bgrachan@lagcc.cuny.edu

GRACIA, Hector .... 787-780-0070 506 F
graciah@caribbean.edu
GRACIA, Jessica, L .... 508-565-1301 218 H
jlgracia@stonehill.edu
GRACIAS, Vicente, H .... 732-235-6300 282 A
graciavh@rbhs.rutgers.edu
GRACYALNY, David .... 410-225-2220 199 H
dgracyal@mica.edu
GRADDY, Elizabeth .... 213-740-6715.. 72 B
graddy@usc.edu
GRADDY, Kathryn .... 781-736-8616 207 E
kgraddy@brandeis.edu
GRADOWSKI, Charles ... 484-365-7404 389 C
cgradowski@lincoln.edu
GRADY, Amber, N .... 870-759-4188.. 23 J
agrady@williamsbu.edu
GRADY, David, L .... 205-348-6670.... 7 G
david.grady@ua.edu
GRADY, Helene .... 443-997-3359 199 D
hgrady1@jhu.edu
GRADY, Joy .... 910-879-5596 332 D
jgrady@bladencc.edu
GRADY, Lynne .... 706-379-3111 127 C
lbgrady@yhc.edu
GRADY, Meghan .... 610-606-4612 381 A
megrady@cedarcrest.edu
GRADY, Sara .... 508-929-8130 213 E
sara.grady@worcester.edu
GRADY, Sarah .... 718-409-7262 321 C
sgrady@sunymaritime.edu
GRAEBERT, James, K .... 414-288-3048 494 B
james.graebert@marquette.edu
GRAEF, Jon .... 206-726-5028 480 C
jgraef@cornish.edu
GRAEM, David .... 903-675-6364 452 B
dgraem@tvcc.edu
GRAESER, Kristin .... 717-736-4103 385 E
kgraeser@hacc.edu
GRAETHER, Anna .... 816-654-7122 254 C
agraether@kcumb.edu
GRAF, Amanda .... 540-636-2900 466 A
agraf@christendom.edu
GRAF, Bob .... 651-696-6280 236 H
rgraf@macalester.edu
GRAF, Katie, M .... 716-839-8364 298 B
kgraf@daemen.edu
GRAF, Mel .... 401-598-4949 404 I
mgraf@jwu.edu
GRAFER, Maggie .... 516-877-3844 289 C
yoon@adelphi.edu
GRAFF, Brenda .... 217-641-4530 140 A
GRAFF, Eric, S .... 614-885-5585 360 E
egraff@pcj.edu
GRAFF, Jennifer .... 920-424-0775 497 B
graff@uwosh.edu
GRAFF, Jonathan, K ...... 575-624-8400 287 A
graff@nmmi.edu
GRAFF, Leslie .... 901-321-4036 419 C
leslie.graff@cbu.edu
GRAFF, Michael .... 440-525-7060 355 H
mgraff@laeklandcc.edu
GRAFF, Nadja .... 212-463-0400 322 J
nadja.graff@touro.edu
GRAFF, Robin .... 914-606-7756 325 C
robin.graff@sunywcc.edu
GRAFFAGNINO, Jason .. 706-865-2134 125 E
jgraffagnino@truett.edu
GRAFFIUS, Jeff .... 740-753-6336 354 A
graffiusj@hocking.edu
GRAFIUS, Brandon .... 313-831-5200 223 I
bgrafius@etseminary.edu
GRAFTON, Anthony .... 870-307-7315.. 20 A
anthony.grafton@lyon.edu
GRAFTON, David .... 860-509-9536.. 87 B
dgrafton@hartsem.edu
GRAFTON, Donald .... 541-485-1780 374 F
donaldgrafton@newhope.edu
GRAFTON, Floria .... 541-485-1780 374 F
floriagrafton@newhope.edu
GRAFTON, Ken .... 701-231-7131 345 G
k.grafton@ndsu.edu
GRAFTON, Ken .... 701-231-7655 345 G
k.grafton@ndsu.edu
GRAFTON, Phillip .... 937-766-7834 349 G
graftonp@cedarville.edu
GRAFTON, Robert .... 318-257-2111 191 F
rgrafton@latec.edu
GRAFTON, Steve, C .... 734-763-9730 231 E
sgrafton@umich.edu
GRAGG, Derrick .... 918-631-2181 371 E
derrick-gragg@utulsa.edu
GRAGG, Matt .... 909-748-8108.. 71 G
matt_gragg@redlands.edu

GRAGG, Philip, T .... 619-239-0391.. 34 F
pgragg@cwsl.edu
GRAHAM, Amy .... 405-422-1263 369 E
amy.graham@redlandscc.edu
GRAHAM, Amy .... 315-470-7858 291 H
amygraham@crouse.org
GRAHAM, Angela .... 540-863-2806 474 D
agraham@dslcc.edu
GRAHAM, Annette .... 845-451-1610 298 A
annette.graham@culinary.edu
GRAHAM, Anthony .... 276-944-6491 467 G
agraham@ehc.edu
GRAHAM, Anthony .... 336-750-2200 344 B
grahama@wssu.edu
GRAHAM, April .... 661-362-3248.. 38 H
april.graham@canyons.edu
GRAHAM, Cara .... 479-979-1304.. 23 I
cgraham@ozarks.edu
GRAHAM, Carleen .... 212-614-6195 311 H
carleen.graham@mountsinai.org
GRAHAM, Carlos .... 573-681-5912 254 E
grahamc@lincolnu.edu
GRAHAM, Carole .... 540-857-6696 476 D
cgraham@virginiawestern.edu
GRAHAM, Christopher .. 214-818-1390 434 F
cgraham@criswell.edu
GRAHAM, Christy .... 423-869-6314 421 C
christy.graham@lmunet.edu
GRAHAM, Chuck .... 412-237-3184 381 G
cgraham@ccac.edu
GRAHAM, Dean .... 207-581-1714 195 J
dean.graham@maine.edu
GRAHAM, Dennis .... 616-949-5300 222 I
dennis.graham@cornerstone.edu
GRAHAM, Doug .... 612-343-4798 242 H
dmgraham@northcentral.edu
GRAHAM, Earl .... 203-332-5290.. 85 F
egraham@housatonic.edu
GRAHAM, Eva .... 661-255-1050.. 28 K
egraham@calarts.edu
GRAHAM, Evelyn .... 757-728-5357 468 B
evelyn.graham@hamptonu.edu
GRAHAM, Greg .... 321-674-7707.. 99 B
ggraham@fit.edu
GRAHAM, Gwen .... 219-464-5115 162 A
gwen.graham@valpo.edu
GRAHAM, James, F .... 660-543-4279 260 K
graham@ucmo.edu
GRAHAM, Jean .... 251-580-2293.... 1 I
jean.graham@fcoastalalabama.edu
GRAHAM, Jeanne .... 906-932-4231 224 B
jeanneg@gogebic.edu
GRAHAM, Jeffrey .... 301-687-4311 203 E
jlgraham@frostburg.edu
GRAHAM, Jeffrey .... 956-665-2683 455 D
jeff.graham@utrgv.edu
GRAHAM, Jennifer .... 254-298-8592 446 A
jennifer.graham@templejc.edu
GRAHAM, Jennifer .... 814-393-2352 394 D
jgraham@clarion.edu
GRAHAM, Joan, E .... 585-475-6079 313 A
jegirp@rit.edu
GRAHAM, Jocelyn .... 910-775-4471 343 B
jocelyn.hunt@uncp.edu
GRAHAM, John, D .... 812-855-1432 156 B
grahamjd@indiana.edu
GRAHAM, John-Bauer .. 256-782-5255.... 5 J
jgraham@jsu.edu
GRAHAM, Jonathan ...... 765-983-1295 154 G
grahajo@earlham.edu
GRAHAM, Jonathan ...... 615-220-7839 425 C
jgraham@mscc.edu
GRAHAM, Kathleen .... 570-577-3607 379 F
kathy.graham@bucknell.edu
GRAHAM, Keith .... 901-375-4400 422 F
keithgraham@midsouthchristian.edu
GRAHAM, Keith .... 570-740-0302 389 D
kgraham@luzerne.edu
GRAHAM, Kerwin .... 336-750-2078 344 B
grahamkw@wssu.edu
GRAHAM, Larry .... 479-979-1425.. 23 I
lgraham@ozarks.edu
GRAHAM, LeRoy .... 802-443-5669 462 H
leroyg@middlebury.edu
GRAHAM, JR.,
Lewis, P .... 803-934-3404 411 C
lgraham@morris.edu
GRAHAM, Lindsey .... 978-556-3621 215 C
lgraham@necc.mass.edu
GRAHAM, Mark, R .... 276-944-6104 467 G
mgraham@ehc.edu
GRAHAM, Mary, S .... 601-928-6280 247 E
mary.graham@mgccc.edu

GRAHAM, Michael .... 847-947-5333 144 F
michael.graham@nl.edu
GRAHAM, SJ,
Michael, J .... 513-745-3502 365 B
GRAHAM, Paula .... 914-964-4282 296 C
pgraham@riversidehealth.org
GRAHAM, Rachael .... 413-559-5724 210 A
GRAHAM, Randy .... 713-525-3813 454 H
grahamra@stthom.edu
GRAHAM, Robbie .... 907-786-1190.... 9 G
rlgraham3@alaska.edu
GRAHAM, Robert .... 773-602-5265 134 D
rgraham24@ccc.edu
GRAHAM, Robin .... 914-282-6087 323 F
r.graham@uts.edu
GRAHAM, Rosmari .... 814-732-1246 394 F
rgraham@edinboro.edu
GRAHAM, Serina .... 360-442-2134 482 B
sgraham@lowercolumbia.edu
GRAHAM, Sharon, D ..... 913-897-8767 177 D
sgraham@ku.edu
GRAHAM, Shelci .... 212-217-3600 299 H
shelci_graham@fitnyc.edu
GRAHAM, Stephanie ..... 909-607-6722.. 45 A
stephanie_graham@hmc.edu
GRAHAM, Stephen .... 650-723-2750.. 65 J
GRAHAM, Stephen, A ... 973-761-9011 283 B
stephen.graham@shu.edu
GRAHAM, Steve .... 252-492-2061 338 F
grahams@vgcc.edu
GRAHAM, Steven, W ..... 573-884-3360 261 A
grahams@umsystem.edu
GRAHAM, Thomas .... 740-264-5591 352 H
tegraham@egcc.edu
GRAHAM, Toby .... 706-542-0621 125 G
tgraham@uga.edu
GRAHAM, Van .... 903-233-3900 439 E
vangraham@letu.edu
GRAHAM, Whitney .... 580-477-7784 371 F
whitney.graham@newmoodle.wosc.edu
GRAHN, Lance .... 330-675-8820 354 J
lgrahn@kent.edu
GRAIOUID, Said .... 802-257-7751 463 C
said.graiouid@worldlearning.org
GRAJEWSKI, Tracy, L ... 814-641-3194 386 H
grajewt@juniata.edu
GRALNEK, Gaelle .... 657-278-2200.. 31 E
ggralnek@fullerton.edu
GRAMELSPACHER,
Dave .... 812-357-8429 160 D
dgramelspacher@saintmeinrad.edu
GRAMELSPACHER,
Mike .... 812-357-8293 160 D
mgramelspacher@saintmeinrad.edu
GRAMENZ, Gary .... 559-453-2291.. 43 G
gary.gramenz@fresno.edu
GRAMLICH, Annalisa ..... 816-501-4122 258 H
annalisa.gramlich@rockhurst.edu
GRAMLING, P.J .... 325-649-8406 438 D
pgramling@hputx.edu
GRAMMER, Jody .... 918-293-4890 368 D
jody.grammer@okstate.edu
GRAMOPADHYE,
Anand .... 864-656-5540 408 A
agramop@clemson.edu
GRAMS, Justin .... 701-671-2189 346 E
justin.grams@ndscs.edu
GRAMZA, Elise .... 231-591-2805 223 J
elisegramza@ferris.edu
GRAN, Tracey .... 651-690-6566 242 R
tlgran@stkate.edu
GRANA, Joe .... 714-879-3901.. 45 F
jgrana@hiu.edu
GRANADE, Ray .... 870-245-5121.. 20 E
granade@obu.edu
GRANADOS, Alex .... 336-725-8344 339 F
granadosa@piedmontu.edu
GRANADOS, Hernan ..... 707-965-6311.. 55 D
hgranados@puc.edu
GRANADOS, Pattie .... 760-252-2411.. 26 I
pgranados@barstow.edu
GRANART, Heather, L ... 630-844-5448 132 D
hgranart@aurora.edu
GRANAT, Bonnie .... 718-613-8534 317 E
bonnie.granat@downstate.edu
GRANATA, Brian .... 215-572-2194 379 A
granatab@arcadia.edu
GRANATOWSKI, Doris ... 480-212-1704.. 15 Q
doris@sessions.edu
GRANBERRY, Jackie ..... 601-857-3630 246 B
jgranberry@hindscc.edu
GRANBERRY-RUSSELL,
Paulette .... 517-353-3924 227 D
prussell@msu.edu

GRAND PRÉ, Paul .... 508-588-9100 214 F
pgrandpre@massasoit.mass.edu
GRAND PRE, Donna ..... 617-573-8460 219 A
dgrandpre@suffolk.edu
GRANDALL, Jerolyn, R . 608-785-9576 501 A
grandallj@westerntc.edu
GRANDCHAMP,
Michael, N .... 401-341-2142 406 A
grandchm@salve.edu
GRANDILLO, Michael ... 734-432-5315 227 A
magrandillo@madonna.edu
GRANDINETTI, Margie .. 610-282-1100 382 E
margie.grandinetti@desales.edu
GRANDJEAN, Peter, W . 662-915-7900 249 D
pwg@olemiss.edu
GRANDO, Victoria .... 816-936-8715 259 I
vgrando@saintlukescollege.edu
GRANDSTAFF, Kelly ...... 850-478-8496 104 G
kgrandstaff@pcci.edu
GRANDSTAFF, Lyla, D .. 304-376-4503 489 D
lyla.grandstaff@pierpont.edu
GRANDY, Jody .... 252-335-3275 341 D
jograndy@ecsu.edu
GRANDY, Mike .... 231-591-2163 223 J
mikegrandy@ferris.edu
GRANEY, Carol .... 215-717-6393 400 J
cgraney@uarts.edu
GRANEY, Daniel .... 401-874-2098 406 B
dgraney@uri.edu
GRANFIELD, Cathy .... 414-955-8566 494 C
mcw@matthewsstores.com
GRANFIELD, Robert ...... 716-645-3594 316 F
rgranfie@buffalo.edu
GRANGER, III, Earl, T .. 757-221-1188 466 C
earl.granger@wm.edu
GRANGER, Gary .... 503-777-7379 376 C
grangerg@reed.edu
GRANGER, Heidi .... 915-747-7390 455 C
hgranger@utep.edu
GRANGER, Jennifer .... 617-243-2475 210 G
jgranger@lasell.edu
GRANGER, Jill .... 828-227-7383 344 A
jngranger@wcu.edu
GRANGER, Joey .... 601-984-1199 249 E
jgranger@umc.edu
GRANGER, Kevin .... 713-313-4378 449 C
kevin.granger@tsu.edu
GRANGER, Robert .... 334-244-3678.... 4 F
rgrange2@aum.edu
GRANGER, Ron .... 970-675-2261.. 78 G
ron.granger@cncc.edu
GRANGER, Sarah .... 323-409-2739.. 49 H
sgranger@dhs.lacounty.gov
GRANGER, Sarah, C ...... 323-409-2739.. 49 H
sgranger@dhs.lacounty.gov
GRANGER, Vern .... 860-486-1478.. 88 E
vern.granger@uconn.edu
GRANHOLD, Kevin, B ... 713-500-3624 456 B
kevin.b.granhold@uth.tmc.edu
GRANICK, Jamal .... 505-467-6823 288 E
jamalgranick@swc.edu
GRANILLO, Lillian .... 718-522-9073 290 C
lgranillo@asa.edu
GRANNAS, Amanda .... 610-519-5858 402 D
amanda.grannas@villanova.edu
GRANOT, Elad .... 419-289-5932 348 A
egranot@ashland.edu
GRANT, Alan .... 540-231-4152 477 A
algrant@vt.edu
GRANT, Allen, C .... 315-267-2515 319 D
grant@potsdam.edu
GRANT, Amy .... 310-660-3350.. 41 L
agrant@elcamino.edu
GRANT, Andi .... 308-632-6933 269 E
GRANT, Andrea, E .... 225-578-4339 188 I
agrant10@lsu.edu
GRANT, Angela .... 617-824-8204 208 H
angela_grant@emerson.edu
GRANT, Armada .... 443-885-3195 200 D
armada.grant@morgan.edu
GRANT, Barry .... 860-512-3403.. 85 G
bgrant@manchestercc.edu
GRANT, Beth, A .... 813-988-5131.. 98 Q
registrar@floridacollege.edu
GRANT, Bob .... 937-775-2771 364 I
bob.grant@wright.edu
GRANT, Brad .... 912-525-5000 123 G
bgrant@scad.edu
GRANT, Brian, T .... 315-268-6463 296 A
bgrant@clarkson.edu
GRANT, Bud .... 563-333-6419 169 A
grantrobert@sau.edu
GRANT, Caleb .... 518-255-5525 319 F
grantcr@cobleskill.edu
GRANT, Carl .... 405-325-2611 371 B
carl.grant@ou.edu
GRANT, Christa, J .... 518-783-2330 315 J
cgrant@siena.edu
GRANT, Christine .... 860-768-4220.. 88 H
cgrant@hartford.edu
GRANT, Christopher ..... 540-665-5597 471 E
cgrant2@su.edu
GRANT, Christy .... 402-354-7077 268 C
christy.grant@methodistcollege.edu
GRANT, Christy .... 615-248-1447 427 A
cgrant@trevecca.edu
GRANT, Dana .... 434-200-3070 465 H
dana.grant@centralhealth.com
GRANT, Donald .... 626-529-8201.. 55 A
dgrant@pacificoaks.edu
GRANT, Ellen .... 252-536-7299 335 B
GRANT, G. Anthony ...... 303-615-0539.. 80 N
ggrant5@msudenver.edu
GRANT, Gary .... 321-674-6160.. 99 B
ggrant@fit.edu
GRANT, George .... 616-331-6850 224 E
grantg@gvsu.edu
GRANT, Gina .... 605-882-5284 415 F
gina.grant@lakeareatech.edu
GRANT, Jamie .... 864-596-9010 409 B
jamie.grant@converse.edu
GRANT, Ja'Wanda .... 504-520-5747 193 A
jgrant4@xula.edu
GRANT, Jeff .... 229-245-3852 126 G
jgrant@valdosta.edu
GRANT, Johnny .... 478-445-5852 118 C
johnny.grant@gcsu.edu
GRANT, Jordan, L .... 206-281-2469 484 D
grantj@spu.edu
GRANT, Karen .... 508-854-4275 215 D
kgrant@qcc.mass.edu
GRANT, Kenna .... 860-768-5433.. 88 H
mckenna@hartford.edu
GRANT, Kizuwanda .... 214-379-5500 441 I
kgrant@pqc.edu
GRANT, Laura .... 636-922-8391 258 I
lgrant@stchas.edu
GRANT, Madeline .... 714-564-6750.. 57 L
grant_madeline@sac.edu
GRANT, Meagan .... 978-921-4242 216 F
meagan.grant@montserrat.edu
GRANT, Michael .... 772-462-7159 101 E
mgrant2@irsc.edu
GRANT, Nancy .... 907-852-1708.... 9 F
nancy.grant@ilisagvik.edu
GRANT, Nathan .... 207-778-7864 196 B
nathan.grant@maine.edu
GRANT, Nina .... 308-635-6104 270 D
grantel@wncc.edu
GRANT, Nina .... 843-863-8020 407 E
ngrant@csuniv.edu
GRANT, Pamela .... 216-987-5020 351 G
pamela.grant@tri-c.edu
GRANT, Ralph .... 973-803-5000 280 C
rgrant@pillar.edu
GRANT, Sabrina .... 973-720-2754 284 I
grants@wpunj.edu
GRANT, Sharone, V ...... 410-651-6597 203 A
svgrant@umes.edu
GRANT, Shauna .... 907-786-1517.... 9 H
GRANT, Shaunette .... 305-899-4888.. 95 C
sgrant@barry.edu
GRANT, Stacey .... 478-289-2105 117 D
skgrant@ega.edu
GRANT, Terry .... 304-724-3700 487 E
tgrant@apus.edu
GRANT, Timothy .... 609-771-2167 276 I
tgrant@tcnj.edu
GRANT, Traci .... 425-889-7823 482 F
traci.grant@northwestu.edu
GRANT, Tyler .... 574-807-7124 153 E
tyler.grant@bethelunivesity.edu
GRANT, Tyler, C .... 574-807-7124 153 E
tyler.grant@betheluniversity.edu
GRANT, Velvet, L .... 757-683-3159 469 G
vlgrant2@odu.edu
GRANTHAM, Bill .... 334-670-3637.... 7 C
bgranth@troy.edu
GRANZOW, Daniel .... 636-922-8508 258 I
dgranzow@stchas.edu
GRASSEL, OSB, Martin . 503-845-3326 374 B
martin.grassel@mtangel.edu
GRASSETTI, J. Vincent .. 413-755-4061 215 F
vgrassetti@stcc.edu
GRASSI, Janel .... 417-447-2601 257 G
grassij@otc.edu
GRASSO, Dominico .... 313-593-5500 231 F
grasso@umich.edu
GRASSO, Eliot .... 541-683-5141 373 D
GRASSO, Richard .... 718-489-3450 313 H
richardgrasso@sfc.edu
GRASWICK, Sharon ...... 412-359-1000 400 G
sgraswick@triangle-tech.edu
GRATE, Cammy .... 803-516-4510 412 C
cgrate2@scsu.edu
GRATSON, Emily .... 616-949-5300 222 I
emily.gratson@cornerstone.edu
GRATTON, John .... 575-234-9200 287 B
jgratton@nmsu.edu
GRATTON, John .... 575-234-9210 287 D
jgratton@nmsu.edu
GRAU, Beverly .... 479-619-3103.. 20 D
bgrau@nwacc.edu
GRAU, Frances .... 787-720-1022 506 E
fgrau@atlanticu.edu
GRAU, Isidro .... 713-221-8494 453 B
graui@uhd.edu
GRAU, Kurt .... 405-208-5240 367 I
kmgrau@okcu.edu
GRAU, Leeann .... 740-389-4636 356 B
graul@mtc.edu
GRAU, Melissa .... 845-848-7602 298 D
melissa.grau@dc.edu
GRAU, Melissa .... 269-927-6172 226 D
grau@lakemichigancollege.edu
GRAU, Monica, C .... 607-436-2255 317 C
monica.grau@oneonta.edu
GRAUBERGER, Renee ... 602-383-8228.. 16 F
rgrauberger@uat.edu
GRAUMAN, Greg .... 808-543-8061 127 H
ggrauman@hpu.edu
GRAUMLICH, Lisa .... 206-221-0908 485 F
graumlic@uw.edu
GRAUSE, Candice .... 850-201-6219 111 C
grausec@tcc.fl.edu
GRAVATT, Tomi .... 217-234-5253 141 D
tgravatt@lakelandcollege.edu
GRAVDAHL, Jeanette .... 605-698-3966 416 F
jgravdahl@swc.tc
GRAVEEN, Melody .... 951-571-6291.. 58 G
melody.graveen@mvc.edu
GRAVEL, Joan .... 413-755-4817 215 F
jegravel@stcc.edu
GRAVEL, Matthew .... 413-755-4623 215 F
mgravel@stcc.edu
GRAVEL, Tammy .... 508-373-5682 216 B
tammy.gravel@mcphs.edu
GRAVELLE, Andrea .... 410-386-8419 197 G
agravelle@carrollcc.edu
GRAVERATTE,
Jacqueline .... 989-317-4760 230 A
jgraveratte@sagchip.edu
GRAVES, Becky .... 256-352-8159.... 4 A
becky.graves@wallacestate.edu
GRAVES, Carla .... 985-867-2232 190 F
cgraves@sjasc.edu
GRAVES, Carla .... 904-470-8237.. 97 L
carla.graves@ewc.edu
GRAVES, Cheryl .... 719-884-5000.. 81 C
cagraves@nbc.edu
GRAVES, Devin .... 620-441-5595 172 I
devin.graves@cowley.edu
GRAVES, Elizabeth, E .... 859-238-5200 179 F
elizabeth.graves@centre.edu
GRAVES, Frank .... 254-299-8126 440 A
fgraves@mclennan.edu
GRAVES, Harold, B .... 719-884-5000.. 81 C
hbgraves@nbc.edu
GRAVES, Howard, E ...... 516-463-6429 302 B
howard.e.graves@hofstra.edu
GRAVES, Kathleen .... 563-884-5102 168 I
kathleen.graves@palmer.edu
GRAVES, Lauren .... 502-597-6229 182 H
lauren.graves@kysu.edu
GRAVES, Lisa .... 269-337-4400 233 D
GRAVES, Loreatha, D .... 336-334-7551 341 F
loretha@ncat.edu
GRAVES, Mallis .... 859-442-1608 181 B
mallis.graves@kctcs.edu
GRAVES, Randy .... 918-647-1370 365 H
rggraves@carlalbert.edu
GRAVES, Randy, K .... 269-471-3854 221 B
gravesr@andrews.edu
GRAVES, Robbie .... 731-661-5008 427 C
rgraves@uu.edu
GRAVES, Sara .... 256-824-6868.... 8 B
sara.graves@uah.edu
GRAVES, Sara, J .... 256-824-6064.... 8 B
sara.graves@uah.edu
GRAVES, Scott .... 907-564-8342.... 9 D
sgraves@alaskapacific.edu
GRAVES, Susan .... 270-534-3155 182 F
susan.graves@kctcs.edu
GRAVES, Theresa, D ..... 405-466-3201 366 F
theresa.graves@langston.edu
GRAVES, Veronica .... 303-273-3056.. 78 I
vgraves@mines.edu
GRAVES, William, R ...... 515-294-2682 162 I
graves@iastate.edu
GRAVES, William, T ...... 318-342-1961 192 F
graves@ulm.edu
GRAVETT, Sharon, L ..... 229-333-5950 126 G
sgravett@valdosta.edu
GRAVIETTE,
Kimberly, K .... 402-461-7387 267 D
kgraviette@hastings.edu
GRAVINA, Kevin .... 303-273-3351.. 78 I
kgravina@mines.edu
GRAVLEY, John, W .... 913-667-5740 172 C
jgravley@cbts.edu
GRAVLEY-STACK, Kara .. 218-477-4000 239 D
kara.gravleystack@mnstate.edu
GRAY, Amanda .... 816-995-2806 258 F
amanda.gray@researchcollege.edu
GRAY, Amy .... 630-844-5467 132 D
agray@aurora.edu
GRAY, Anita .... 260-359-4063 155 F
agray@huntington.edu
GRAY, Bo .... 828-835-4222 338 E
bgray@tricountycc.edu
GRAY, Brandy .... 903-730-4890 438 H
bgray@jarvis.edu
GRAY, Charlotte .... 417-967-5466 260 H
GRAY, Chris .... 815-455-8673 143 A
cgray1@mchenry.edu
GRAY, Chris .... 913-469-8500 174 D
chrisgray@jccc.edu
GRAY, Christine .... 303-722-5724.. 80 L
cgray@lincolntech.edu
GRAY, Corey .... 402-643-3651 266 G
corey.gray@cune.edu
GRAY, Craig .... 205-665-6116.... 8 D
cgray2@montevallo.edu
GRAY, David .... 701-355-8180 347 D
dpgray@umary.edu
GRAY, David, J .... 814-865-6574 392 B
djg36@psu.edu
GRAY, David, R .... 540-868-7154 474 J
dgray@lfcc.edu
GRAY, Gary .... 570-422-3689 394 E
GRAY, Glenn, P .... 319-273-2333 163 B
glenn.gray@uni.edu
GRAY, Gregory, S .... 334-727-8011.... 7 D
gsgray@tuskegee.edu
GRAY, Hannah .... 972-279-6511 430 B
hgray@amberton.edu
GRAY, Holly .... 662-620-5092 246 D
ehgray@iccms.edu
GRAY, Howard .... 631-656-2157 300 D
howard.gray@ftc.edu
GRAY, Isabel .... 856-227-7200 276 E
igray@camdencc.edu
GRAY, Jeff .... 478-387-4781 118 G
jgray@gmc.edu
GRAY, Jeffrey .... 515-271-1506 164 I
jeffrey.gray@dmu.edu
GRAY, Jeffrey, L .... 718-817-4750 300 E
gray@fordham.edu
GRAY, Joe .... 615-547-1255 419 F
jgray@cumberland.edu
GRAY, John .... 910-755-7434 332 F
grayj@brunswickcc.edu
GRAY, John, C .... 302-295-1139.. 90 I
john.c.gray@wilmu.edu
GRAY, Julianna, R .... 607-871-2256 289 H
gray@alfred.edu
GRAY, Karol .... 804-828-6116 473 F
kgray8@vcu.edu
GRAY, Kathleen .... 718-489-5340 313 H
kgray4@sfc.edu
GRAY, Kelly .... 575-769-4179 285 K
kelly.gray@clovis.edu
GRAY, Kelly .... 419-755-4823 357 E
kgray@ncstatecollege.edu
GRAY, Kilen .... 502-895-3411 183 D
kgray@lpts.edu
GRAY, Kristen .... 616-395-7945 225 B
gray@hope.edu
GRAY, Kristina .... 309-341-5456 133 C
kgray@sandburg.edu

GRAY, Leslie .... 510-594-3705.. 28 D lgray@cca.edu
GRAY, Lisa .... 410-455-8478 202 E lisamgray@umbc.edu
GRAY, Lisa, G .... 410-546-6390 203 F lggray@salisbury.edu
GRAY, Lloyd .... 601-974-1000 247 B lloyd.gray@millsaps.edu
GRAY, Lydia, E .... 718-862-7231 305 H lydia.gray@manhattan.edu
GRAY, Marisa .... 913-288-7284 174 F mcgray@kckcc.edu
GRAY, Michaelle .... 580-387-7131 366 H mgray@mscok.edu
GRAY, Michaelle .... 580-387-7000 366 H mgray@mscok.edu
GRAY, Michelle .... 541-245-7754 376 D mgray@roguecc.edu
GRAY, Mike .... 606-546-4151 184 H mgray@unionky.edu
GRAY, Monita, M .... 920-832-6697 493 K monita.m.gray@lawrence.edu
GRAY, Nancy .... 970-339-6392.. 76 G nancy.gray@aims.edu
GRAY, Nancy, O .... 540-362-6321 468 C presoffc@hollins.edu
GRAY, Neil .... 903-566-7368 456 A ngray@uttyler.edu
GRAY, Rebecca .... 254-968-9473 446 E rgray@tarleton.edu
GRAY, Sarah .... 309-649-6265 150 A sarah.gray@src.edu
GRAY, Sean .... 319-385-6271 167 A sean.gray@iw.edu
GRAY, Seneca .... 503-768-6781 373 G seneca@lclark.edu
GRAY, Shashuna .... 540-891-3046 474 G dgray@germanna.edu
GRAY, Shaun .... 207-741-5580 195 A sgray@smccme.edu
GRAY, Shawn .... 409-880-8466 449 H shawn.gray@lamar.edu
GRAY, Sheryl .... 865-471-3240 419 A sgray@cn.edu
GRAY, Shonda .... 443-885-3430 200 D shonda.gray@morgan.edu
GRAY, Simon .... 716-285-1212 310 D sgray@niagara.edu
GRAY, Sissy .... 870-248-4000.. 18 F sissy.gray@blackrivertech.edu
GRAY, Tiffany .... 206-296-6070 484 F grayt@seattleu.edu
GRAY, Tim .... 303-937-4420.. 76 L tim.gray@augustineinstitute.org
GRAY, Tita .... 410-888-9048 200 A tgray@muih.edu
GRAY, Toni, B .... 806-371-2912 430 A tbgray@actx.edu
GRAY, Tracy .... 858-695-8587 155 E tgray@horizonuniversity.edu
GRAY, Tuesday, A .... 225-216-8403 186 K grayt@mybrcc.edu
GRAY, Vance .... 404-756-4033 114 G vgray@atlm.edu
GRAY, Velma .... 901-435-1676 421 A velma_gray@loc.edu
GRAY-DEVINE, Sherry ... 580-387-7212 366 H sgray@mscok.edu
GRAY HAYES, Tracy ..... 610-929-6504 378 C tghayes@albright.edu
GRAY PAYTON, Pamela 619-260-4681.. 71 J grayp@sandiego.edu
GRAY-VICKREY, Peg ..... 254-519-5447 447 A gray-vickrey@tamuct.edu
GRAY WILSON, Stephanie .... 614-236-6894 349 D honors@capital.edu
GRAYBEAL, David .... 252-399-6599 326 M jdgraybeal@barton.edu
GRAYBEAL, Susan .... 423-354-2549 425 E segraybeal@northeaststate.edu
GRAYBILL, Jody, D .... 570-577-3351 379 F jody.graybill@bucknell.edu
GRAYLEE, Laleh .... 657-278-2304.. 31 E lgraylee@fullerton.edu
GRAYS, Rodney, F .... 301-447-7411 200 E grays@msmary.edu
GRAYS, Shantay .... 713-718-5115 437 I shantay.grays@hccs.edu
GRAYSON, Denise, R .... 605-256-5152 416 J denise.grayson@dsu.edu
GRAYSON, Micki .... 951-571-6382.. 58 G micki.clowney@mvc.edu
GRAZIANO, Lisa .... 716-851-1499 299 F grazianol@ecc.edu
GRAZIOSO, Amanda ..... 603-535-2260 275 B ajgrazioso@plymouth.edu
GRAZZINI-OLSON, Nancy .... 952-851-0066 233 G
GREANEY, Bryan .... 917-493-4125 305 I bgreaney@msmnyc.edu
GREANEY, KC .... 707-778-4188.. 62 F kgreaney@santarosa.edu
GREASON, Jessica .... 816-584-6329 258 A jessica.greason@park.edu
GREATHOUSE, Jo .... 979-230-3234 432 D jo.greathouse@brazosport.edu
GREAVES, Matthew, C .. 202-687-3488.. 92 A mcg3@georgetown.edu
GREAVES, Valerie .... 734-973-3345 232 B vgreaves@wccnet.edu
GREBEL, David, A .... 817-257-7130 448 G d.grebel@tcu.edu
GREBENC, Christi .... 303-458-4347.. 82 E cgrebenc@regis.edu
GREBIN, Kevin .... 605-331-6772 417 E kevin.grebin@usiouxfalls.edu
GREBINOSKI, Jeff .... 920-498-7193 500 F jeffrey.grebinoski@nwtc.edu
GRECO, Adrianna .... 845-431-3700 298 E adrianna.greco@sunydutchess.edu
GRECO, Anne .... 215-751-8217 382 A agreco@ccp.edu
GRECO, Frank, M .... 412-365-1680 381 C greco@chatham.edu
GRECO, Gary .... 310-660-3593.. 41 L ggreco@elcamino.edu
GRECO, Gil .... 541-683-5141 373 D ggreco@gutenberg.edu
GRECO, Jared .... 530-226-4101.. 63 K jgreco@simpsonu.edu
GRECO, Juneann .... 570-340-6004 389 G greco@marywood.edu
GRECO, Michelle .... 504-671-5091 187 E mgreco@dcc.edu
GRECO, Michelle .... 504-671-6006 187 E mgreco@dcc.edu
GRECO, Peter .... 801-832-2005 461 G pgreco@westminstercollege.edu
GRECOL, Joseph .... 216-373-5407 358 B
GREDEN, Leigh .... 734-487-8676 223 H lgreden@emich.edu
GREEAR, Amy .... 276-523-7480 475 A agreear@mecc.edu
GREEN, Adam, S .... 423-439-4211 419 J
GREEN, Ann, F .... 828-694-1709 332 E anng@blueridge.edu
GREEN, Ashley .... 817-722-1612 439 B ashley.green@tku.edu
GREEN, Becky .... 806-874-3571 433 B becky.green@clarendoncollege.edu
GREEN, Bevley, W .... 251-460-6188.... 8 F bwgreen@southalabama.edu
GREEN, Bichevia .... 803-535-1249 411 G greenb@octech.edu
GREEN, Brenda .... 479-725-4669.. 20 D bgreen@nwacc.edu
GREEN, Brittany, D .... 662-254-3577 248 B brittany.d.green@mvsu.edu
GREEN, C. Scott .... 208-885-6365 131 G president@uidaho.edu
GREEN, Cara .... 570-348-6211 389 G cgreen@marywood.edu
GREEN, Carol, C .... 517-750-1200 230 H ca368436@arbor.edu
GREEN, Charlotte .... 601-318-6495 249 H cgreen@wmcarey.edu
GREEN, Cheryl .... 262-472-1918 498 C
GREEN, Chris .... 805-546-3902.. 41 A cgreen@cuesta.edu
GREEN, Chris .... 859-985-3727 179 C greenchr@berea.edu
GREEN, Cindy .... 334-222-6591.... 2 I cgreen@lbwcc.edu
GREEN, Cindy .... 314-539-5227 259 C cgreen2@stlcc.edu
GREEN, Clarence .... 660-562-1254 257 E cgreen@nwmissouri.edu
GREEN, Danielle, M .... 217-581-5313 136 E dmgreen@eiu.edu
GREEN, Danny .... 717-815-1924 404 A greend@ycp.edu
GREEN, JR., David, B ... 518-244-4720 313 D greend8@sage.edu
GREEN, David, M .... 818-947-2679.. 49 F greendm@lavc.edu
GREEN, Denise .... 334-670-3712.... 7 C mbgreen@troy.edu
GREEN, Donald .... 217-732-3168 141 H pres@lincolnchristian.edu
GREEN, Donald, J .... 706-295-6328 118 E dgreen@highlands.edu
GREEN, Donna .... 562-985-5468.. 31 F donna.green@csulb.edu
GREEN, Dwayne .... 256-372-8672.... 1 A dwayne.green@aamu.edu
GREEN, Dwayne .... 320-629-4543 240 C dwayne.green@pine.edu
GREEN, Elaine .... 215-248-7063 381 D greene@chc.edu
GREEN, Eleanor, M .... 979-845-5051 446 G emgreen@tamu.edu
GREEN, Elna, C .... 706-737-1738 115 A elngreen@augusta.edu
GREEN, Evan .... 248-218-2114 229 J egreen@rc.edu
GREEN, Finley .... 423-652-4865 420 H flgreen@king.edu
GREEN, Gedalya, A .... 732-367-1060 275 J ggreen@bmg.edu
GREEN, Geoff .... 805-965-0581.. 62 C green@sbccfoundation.org
GREEN, Haley .... 425-352-8258 479 A hgreen@cascadia.edu
GREEN, James "Dub" ... 843-574-6774 413 B james.green@tridenttech.edu
GREEN, James .... 314-340-3502 253 I greenj@hssu.edu
GREEN, Janet .... 903-677-8822 452 B janet.green@tvcc.edu
GREEN, Jasmine .... 773-907-4445 134 C jgreen14@ccc.edu
GREEN, Jeffrey .... 312-662-4401 131 H jgreen@adler.edu
GREEN, Jeffrey .... 281-649-3197 437 H jgreen@hbu.edu
GREEN, Jennifer .... 212-854-3953 290 J jengreen@barnard.edu
GREEN, Jennifer .... 909-621-8000.. 45 A jgreen@hmc.edu
GREEN, Jennifer .... 860-932-4140.. 86 E jgreen@qvcc.edu
GREEN, Jennifer .... 865-524-8079 420 E jennifer.green@huhs.edu
GREEN, Jennifer, K .... 434-395-2944 469 A greenjk@longwood.edu
GREEN, Jeremy .... 410-386-8335 197 G jgreen@carrollcc.edu
GREEN, Jerry .... 718-817-4170 300 E jgreen@fordham.edu
GREEN, John .... 661-362-3684.. 38 H john.green@canyons.edu
GREEN, John .... 252-222-6273 333 A greenj@carteret.edu
GREEN, John, C .... 330-972-7869 362 B green@uakron.edu
GREEN, Jonathan .... 570-372-4130 399 C supres@susqu.edu
GREEN, Judith .... 201-684-7523 280 H jgreen2@ramapo.edu
GREEN, Julie .... 207-941-7129 194 A greenj@husson.edu
GREEN, Kamala .... 510-430-2333.. 52 D kagreen@mills.edu
GREEN, Katherine .... 239-590-1067 108 K
GREEN, Katherine .... 940-898-3250 451 F kgreen33@twu.edu
GREEN, Kelli, L .... 512-448-8768 442 M kellig@stedwards.edu
GREEN, Kelly .... 360-596-5214 485 B kgreen@spscc.edu
GREEN, Kevin .... 336-217-7221 329 D
GREEN, Lillie, F .... 757-727-5057 468 B lillie.green@hamptonu.edu
GREEN, Lisa .... 315-792-3736 324 B lcgreen@utica.edu
GREEN, Lorry .... 864-977-7124 411 E lorry.green@ngu.edu
GREEN, Lynette .... 920-403-3235 495 I lynette.green@snc.edu
GREEN, Mark .... 812-237-2304 155 G mark.green@indstate.edu
GREEN, Mary .... 269-965-3931 225 F greenm@kellogg.edu
GREEN, Matthew .... 845-688-1568 323 E greenm@sunyulster.edu
GREEN, Matthew .... 805-546-3924.. 41 A mgreen@cuesta.edu
GREEN, Maureen .... 252-789-0297 335 H maureen.green@martincc.edu
GREEN, Melanie, H .... 804-627-5300 465 C melanie_green@bshsi.org
GREEN, Melissa .... 530-938-5374.. 39 F mgreen8@siskiyous.edu
GREEN, Meredith .... 864-294-2163 410 A meredith.green@furman.edu
GREEN, Michael .... 508-856-5330 212 A micheal.green@umassmed.edu
GREEN, Mike .... 615-966-6000 421 D mike.green@lipscomb.edu
GREEN, Mike .... 541-737-9275 375 D
GREEN, Mike .... 541-737-2447 375 D
GREEN, Moishe .... 845-352-5852 325 E
GREEN, Monica .... 951-372-7016.. 58 H monica.green@norcocollege.edu
GREEN, Monica .... 951-222-8000.. 58 I
GREEN, Myrtes, D .... 205-929-6305.... 2 H mdgreen@lawsonstate.edu
GREEN, Nancy .... 704-403-3599 327 D nancy.green@carolinashealthcare.org
GREEN, Nathan .... 615-343-7626 428 D nathan.green@vanderbilt.edu
GREEN, Nicole .... 310-825-0768.. 69 A ngreen@caps.ucla.edu
GREEN, O. Jerome .... 501-374-6305.. 21 A jerome.green@shortercollege.edu
GREEN, Patrick .... 918-595-7440 370 E patrick.green@tulsacc.edu
GREEN, Paul .... 785-833-4387 175 B green@kwu.edu
GREEN, Rachel .... 570-662-4815 395 C rgreen@mansfield.edu
GREEN, Ragan .... 478-275-7865 122 H rgreen@oftc.edu
GREEN, Ramona .... 903-223-3058 448 B ramona.green@tamut.edu
GREEN, Ray .... 903-468-3005 447 B raymond.green@tamuc.edu
GREEN, Rebecca .... 760-355-6499.. 45 I becky.green@imperial.edu
GREEN, Richard .... 717-338-3001 400 I rgreen@uls.edu
GREEN, Robert .... 312-369-7002 135 E rgreen@colum.edu
GREEN, Ronnie, D .... 402-472-2116 269 J rgreen@unl.edu
GREEN, Ruvain .... 845-352-5852 325 E
GREEN, Ryan, C .... 773-995-5257 133 K rgreen28@csu.edu
GREEN, Samantha .... 973-720-2107 284 I greens19@wpunj.edu
GREEN, Sandra .... 225-342-6950 191 D sandra.green@ulsystem.edu
GREEN, Sandy, B .... 864-488-8348 410 E sgreen@limestone.edu
GREEN, Saytra .... 518-580-8418 316 A sgreen3@skidmore.edu
GREEN, Sherri .... 503-253-3443 374 H sherri.green@ocom.edu
GREEN, Staci .... 701-483-2562 345 D staci.green@dickinsonstate.edu
GREEN, Stacy .... 207-974-4679 194 H sgreen@emcc.edu
GREEN, Susan .... 802-635-1308 464 C susan.green@northernvermont.edu
GREEN, Susan .... 281-290-3242 439 G susan.green@lonestar.edu
GREEN, Teresa .... 806-716-2205 443 I tgreen@southplainscollege.edu
GREEN, Tica, D .... 336-272-7102 329 D tica.green@greensboro.edu
GREEN, Tiffany .... 256-539-8161.... 2 E
GREEN, Tim .... 256-549-8601.... 2 B tgreen@gadsdenstate.edu
GREEN, Timothy, M .... 615-248-1378 427 A tgreen@trevecca.edu
GREEN, Tom .... 216-421-7491 350 M tgreen@cia.edu
GREEN, Tracie .... 714-480-7489.. 57 K green_tracie@rsccd.edu
GREEN, Tracy, A .... 440-366-4073 355 J
GREEN, Wayne, A .... 301-447-5535 200 E w.a.green@msmary.edu
GREEN, William .... 423-614-8240 420 J wgreen@leeuniversity.edu.edu
GREEN, William .... 336-734-7520 334 E bgreen@forsythtech.edu
GREEN, William, S .... 305-284-2006 112 E wgreen@miami.edu

GREGORY, Melissa .... 240-567-5036 200 C melissa.gregory@montgomerycollege.edu
GREGORY, Miraglia ...... 707-654-4528.. 53 C mgregory@napavalley.edu
GREGORY, Patrick .... 334-386-7259.... 5 D pgregory@faulkner.edu
GREGORY, Rhonda .... 615-230-3668 426 B rhonda.gregory@volstate.edu
GREGORY, Rich .... 818-909-5517.. 51 C rgregory@tms.edu
GREGORY, Seamus .... 715-682-1395 495 C sgregory@northland.edu
GREGORY, Tom, F .... 570-326-3761 393 G tgregory@pct.edu
GREGORY, Tony .... 864-424-8000 414 C gregorga@mailbox.sc.edu
GREGORY, Travis .... 760-750-4954.. 33 B tgregory@csusm.edu
GREGORY, Trisha .... 301-687-4201 203 E tgregory@frostburg.edu
GREGORY WYATT, Denise .... 425-388-9232 480 G dgregorywyatt@everettcc.edu
GREGORYK, Kerry .... 701-845-7480 346 A kerry.gregoryk@vcsu.edu
GREGORYK, Michael, D 909-274-4230.. 52 H mgregoryk@mtsac.edu
GREGSON, Joanna .... 253-535-7126 482 H gregson@plu.edu
GREIDER, Lauren .... 812-941-2280 157 B lgreider@ius.edu
GREIFE, Alice, L .... 660-543-4450 260 K greife@ucmo.edu
GREIFFENDORF, OP, Mary Agnes .... 615-297-7545 418 C srmagnes@aquinascollege.edu
GREIG, Carl .... 903-223-3062 448 B carl.greig@tamut.edu
GREIG, Judith, M .... 650-508-3503.. 54 D jgreig@ndnu.edu
GREIL, Stan .... 405-733-7488 369 I sgreil@rose.edu
GREIMAN, Ann .... 402-891-6600 267 A ann.greiman@doane.edu
GREIMAN, Judith .... 631-632-6302 317 D judith.greiman@stonybrook.edu
GREIMAN, Judith .... 631-632-6538 317 D judith.greiman@stonybrook.edu
GREINER, Gary .... 219-980-4291 156 E gagreine@iun.edu
GREINER, Mary .... 641-269-4818 165 J greinerm@grinnell.edu
GREINER, Stephanie .... 515-271-1386 164 I stephanie.greiner@dmu.edu
GREINER, Stephen, G ... 304-336-8000 490 F stephen.greiner@westliberty.edu
GREINER, Susan, L .... 336-322-2245 336 G sue.greiner@piedmontcc.edu
GRELINGER, Adam .... 316-942-4291 175 I grelingera@newmanu.edu
GREMILLION, Henry ..... 504-619-8500 189 B hgremi@lsuhsc.edu
GREMMELS, Gillian .... 515-271-4776 165 A gillian.gremmels@drake.edu
GRENDER, Teresa .... 606-368-6044 178 D teresagrender@alc.edu
GRENNAN, Jon .... 845-451-1323 298 A jon.grennan@culinary.edu
GRENUS, Steven .... 785-670-1574 177 G steven.grenus@washburn.edu
GRENZ, Jonathan .... 561-803-2543 104 C jon_grenz@pba.edu
GRENZOW, Kelly .... 715-425-3531 497 E kelly.grenzow@uwrf.edu
GRESCH, Mary .... 206-685-3710 485 F mgresch@uw.edu
GRESHAM, Joanne .... 209-476-7840.. 66 G jgresham@clc.edu
GRESHAM, John .... 313-883-7032 229 K gresham.john@shms.edu
GRESHAM, Jonathan ..... 423-636-7300 427 B jgresham@tusculum.edu
GRESHAM, Kathryn .... 828-884-8328 327 C greshakb@brevard.edu
GRESHAM, Ralph .... 209-476-7840.. 66 G rgresham@clc.edu
GRESHAM, Susan .... 812-535-5121 160 B sgresham@smwc.edu
GRESHAN, Mary .... 207-581-2441 195 J
GRESS, Andrew .... 515-643-6637 168 A agress@mercydesmoines.org
GRESS, Michael .... 812-888-4176 162 C mgress@vinu.edu
GRESS, Vicky .... 217-333-4493 151 D gress@illinois.edu
GRETCH, Jim .... 406-791-5320 265 H jim.gretch@uprovidence.edu
GRETEN-HARRISON, Derek .... 703-370-6600 470 B
GRETINA, Lauren .... 718-518-4284 294 B lgretina@hostos.cuny.edu
GREUBEL, Deb .... 540-887-4318 469 B sgreubel@marybaldwin.edu
GREUFE, Sandra .... 641-648-4611 166 J sandra.greufe@iavalley.edu
GREVE, Jennifer .... 402-844-7062 268 J jenniferg@northeast.edu
GREVE, Scott .... 740-284-5891 353 B sgreve@franciscan.edu
GREVI, Laura .... 914-337-9300 297 D laura.grevi@concordia-ny.edu
GREVING, John .... 402-465-2486 268 H jgreving@nebrwesleyan.edu
GREW-GILLEN, Cheryl .. 701-777-4200 345 C cheryl.grewgillen@und.edu
GREWAL, Daman .... 650-574-6550.. 61 N
GREWAL, Parwinder ...... 956-665-3883 455 D parwinder.grewal@utrgv.edu
GREY, Cynthia .... 727-302-6724 106 E grey.cynthia@spcollege.edu
GREY, Gregory, D .... 410-334-2933 204 F ggrey@worwic.edu
GREY, Kimberly .... 314-392-2241 256 C grey@mobap.edu
GREY, Marge .... 209-946-2311.. 70 E mgrey@pacific.edu
GREY, Mary .... 413-796-2267 219 F mary.grey@wne.edu
GREY, Pam .... 408-864-8209.. 43 C greypam@deanza.edu
GREY, Shenequa .... 225-771-2552 191 A
GREY GILBERT, Jeanette .... 406-994-4284 264 D jeanette.greygilbert@montana.edu
GREYBAR MILLIKEN, Shannon .... 216-687-2048 351 B s.greybarmilliken@csuohio.edu
GREYDANUS, John .... 541-737-9099 375 D john.greydanus@oregonstate.edu
GREYWATER, Brigitte .... 701-662-1546 346 D brigitte.greywater@lrsc.edu
GRGICAK, Catherine ..... 856-225-6142 281 G cmg369@camden.rutgers.edu
GRIBB, Molly, M .... 608-342-1561 497 D gribbm@uwplatt.edu
GRIBBEN, Les .... 212-817-7470 293 F lgribben@gc.cuny.edu
GRIBBIN, David .... 478-289-2047 117 D dgribbin@ega.edu
GRIBBLE, Kari .... 608-663-2305 493 C kgribble@edgewood.edu
GRIBBLE, Scott .... 308-632-6933 269 E
GRIBBLE, Shannon, L ... 301-687-7588 203 E slgribble@frostburg.edu
GRIBBONS, Barry .... 661-362-5500.. 38 H barry.gribbons@canyons.edu
GRIBBONS, Barry, C ..... 818-947-2321.. 49 F gribbobc@lavc.edu
GRIBLIN, Diana .... 316-942-4291 175 I griblind@newmanu.edu
GRICAR, Jeff .... 713-718-7431 437 I jeff.gricar@hccs.edu
GRICE, Ronnie, D .... 785-532-1131 174 G raker@ksu.edu
GRICE, Sharon .... 319-895-4162 164 B sgrice@cornellcollege.edu
GRIEGER, Mary .... 414-425-8300 495 H mgrieger@shsst.edu
GRIEGO, Orlando .... 815-740-3452 151 J ogriego@stfrancis.edu
GRIER, Derek .... 703-445-9056 473 D
GRIER, Ed .... 804-828-1062 473 F egrier@vcu.edu
GRIER, Judith .... 757-789-1753 474 F jgrier@es.vccs.edu
GRIER, Lauri .... 909-748-8390.. 71 G lauri_grier@redlands.edu
GRIES, Kathie .... 269-782-1425 230 F kgries@swmich.edu
GRIESHEIMER, Tina ...... 303-797-5901.. 76 I tina.griesheimer@arapahoe.edu
GRIESSE, Sarah .... 612-330-1489 233 K griesse@augsburg.edu
GRIEVE, Kimberly .... 605-677-5331 416 H kimberly.grieve@usd.edu
GRIEVE, Robyn .... 408-260-0208.. 42 M daom@fivebranches.edu
GRIEWISCH, Carl .... 828-898-8862 330 E griewischc@lmc.edu
GRIFFEL, Michael, M .... 541-346-2667 377 D mgriffel@uoregon.edu
GRIFFEN, Emily .... 413-542-2265 205 B egriffen@amherst.edu
GRIFFENBERG, William 210-784-4357 448 A william.griffenberg@tamusa.edu
GRIFFIN, Amy .... 317-917-5956 157 H agriffin76@ivytech.edu
GRIFFIN, Bruce .... 925-485-5213.. 35 N bgriffin@clpccd.org
GRIFFIN, Bryan, L .... 989-774-7112 222 C griff3bl@cmich.edu
GRIFFIN, Cathy .... 908-526-1200 281 A cathy.griffin@raritanval.edu
GRIFFIN, Clifton, P ...... 410-548-3894 203 F cpgriffin@salisbury.edu
GRIFFIN, Colton .... 304-333-3688 490 B colton.griffin@fairmontstate.edu
GRIFFIN, Dan .... 731-661-5120 427 C dgriffin@uu.edu
GRIFFIN, David .... 617-824-8500 208 H david_griffin@emerson.edu
GRIFFIN, David .... 903-923-2340 436 D dgriffin@etbu.edu
GRIFFIN, Donitha .... 334-876-9302.... 2 D donitha.griffin@wccs.edu
GRIFFIN, Drew .... 660-543-4170 260 K dgriffin@ucmo.edu
GRIFFIN, Eddie .... 405-974-2502 370 K egriffin2@uco.edu
GRIFFIN, Elaine .... 615-966-5818 421 D elaine.griffin@lipscomb.edu
GRIFFIN, Erica .... 618-252-5400 149 C erica.griffin@sic.edu
GRIFFIN, Heather .... 502-895-3411 183 D hgriffin@lpts.edu
GRIFFIN, James .... 281-542-2089 443 C james.griffin@sjcd.edu
GRIFFIN, Jason .... 567-661-2692 360 B jason_griffin@owens.edu
GRIFFIN, Jeff .... 765-455-9339 156 D griffon0@purdue.edu
GRIFFIN, Jeff, D .... 504-816-8018 190 A jgriffin@nobts.edu
GRIFFIN, Joe .... 765-973-8633 156 C joegrif@iue.edu
GRIFFIN, Joel .... 864-941-8324 411 H griffin.j@ptc.edu
GRIFFIN, Kara .... 775-682-9013 271 F karag@unr.edu
GRIFFIN, Karen .... 636-584-6575 252 J karen.griffin@eastcentral.edu
GRIFFIN, Karen .... 813-253-7002 101 A kgriffin@hccfl.edu
GRIFFIN, Larry .... 901-375-4400 422 F larrygriffin@midsouthchristian.edu
GRIFFIN, Leslie .... 662-846-4400 245 H lgriffin@deltastate.edu
GRIFFIN, Lisa .... 229-217-4144 125 A lgriffin@southernregional.edu
GRIFFIN, Lonnie .... 912-443-4174 124 A lgriffin@savannahtech.edu
GRIFFIN, Lori .... 253-912-3633 483 D lgriffin@pierce.ctc.edu
GRIFFIN, Lynn .... 843-383-8071 408 D lgriffin@coker.edu
GRIFFIN, Mark .... 785-628-4026 173 B magriffin2@fhsu.edu
GRIFFIN, Mark .... 973-353-1458 282 B markg@newark.rutgers.edu
GRIFFIN, Meghan .... 863-667-5537 107 K mlgriffin@seu.edu
GRIFFIN, Micah .... 256-372-5601.... 1 A micha.griffin@aamu.edu
GRIFFIN, Michael .... 574-239-8307 155 D mgriffin@hcc-nd.edu
GRIFFIN, Michael .... 212-636-6520 300 E mgriffin19@fordham.edu
GRIFFIN, Nancy, D .... 207-780-4021 196 F nancy.d.griffin@maine.edu
GRIFFIN, Neil .... 626-966-4576.. 25 N neil@jamagency.com
GRIFFIN, Neil .... 864-592-4897 412 F griffinn@sccsc.edu
GRIFFIN, Patricia, L ...... 785-628-5377 173 B pgriffin@fhsu.edu
GRIFFIN, CM, Patrick, J .... 718-990-6311 314 B griffinp@stjohns.edu
GRIFFIN, Ragan, K .... 724-357-2218 394 G rgriffin@iup.edu
GRIFFIN, Richard .... 207-755-5224 194 G rgriffin@cmcc.edu
GRIFFIN, Robert .... 901-375-4400 422 F robertgriffin@midsouthchristian.edu
GRIFFIN, Sallie .... 601-877-6377 244 H sgriffin@alcorn.edu
GRIFFIN, Sharon, R .... 919-516-4132 340 C srgriffin@st-aug.edu
GRIFFIN, Stephen, L ..... 651-962-6855 244 E stephen.griffin@stthomas.edu
GRIFFIN, Tamara .... 870-612-2022.. 22 I tamara.griffin@uaccb.edu
GRIFFIN, Tim .... 602-639-7500.. 12 J
GRIFFIN, Tim .... 303-914-6516.. 82 C tim.griffin@rrcc.edu
GRIFFIN, Timothy .... 202-379-7808.. 92 G
GRIFFIN, Timothy .... 201-216-5107 283 C timothy.griffin@stevens.edu
GRIFFIN-DESTA, Jerlena .... 707-664-2880.. 34 C
GRIFFIN-SMITH, Elizabeth .... 972-721-5000 452 D egriffin@udallas.edu
GRIFFIN-SOBEL, Joyce, P .... 212-616-7284 301 F jgriffinsobel@helenefuld.edu
GRIFFING, Joan .... 316-295-5849 173 D joan_griffing@friends.edu
GRIFFIS, Emma .... 303-273-3067.. 78 I egriffis@mines.edu
GRIFFIS, Sarah .... 617-305-1721 219 A sgriffis@suffolk.edu
GRIFFITH, Abby .... 607-871-2082 289 H griffitha@alfred.edu
GRIFFITH, Belinda .... 404-270-6618 125 B bgriff14@spelman.edu
GRIFFITH, Bernard .... 504-284-5523 190 I bgriffith@suno.edu
GRIFFITH, Bradley .... 618-985-3741 139 I bradleygriffith@jalc.edu
GRIFFITH, Claire .... 434-381-6479 472 D cgriffith@sbc.edu
GRIFFITH, Cynthia .... 281-756-3601 429 I cgriffith@alvincollege.edu
GRIFFITH, Darcell .... 302-831-6741.. 90 F darcellg@udel.edu
GRIFFITH, Debra .... 408-741-4616.. 74 E debra.griffith@westvalley.edu
GRIFFITH, Dede .... 318-371-3035 187 I dedegriffith@nwltc.edu
GRIFFITH, Donald .... 559-453-3485.. 43 G donald.griffith@fresno.edu
GRIFFITH, Jackie .... 302-857-6707.. 89 F jgriffith@desu.edu
GRIFFITH, Jolene .... 641-782-1456 169 H griffith@swcciowa.edu
GRIFFITH, Kayin .... 503-554-2322 373 C kgriffith@georgefox.edu
GRIFFITH, Kelly .... 360-417-6201 483 B kgriffith@pencol.edu
GRIFFITH, Kevin .... 574-520-4879 157 A kevgriff@iusb.edu
GRIFFITH, Launey, P .... 337-550-1390 189 A lgriffit@lsue.edu
GRIFFITH, Lauren .... 904-256-7535 101 G lgriffi9@ju.edu
GRIFFITH, Luther, T ...... 434-381-6325 472 D lgriffith@sbc.edu
GRIFFITH, Margo .... 907-474-6600.. 10 A margo.griffith@alaska.edu
GRIFFITH, Mary .... 615-547-1200 419 F mgriffith@cumberland.edu
GRIFFITH, Rebecca (Becki) .... 817-515-1581 445 G rebecca.griffith@tccd.edu
GRIFFITH, Roger, D ...... 304-647-6563 489 C rgriffith@newriver.edu
GRIFFITH, Ryan .... 209-946-2090.. 70 E rgriffith@pacific.edu
GRIFFITH, Sarah .... 360-442-2520 482 B sgriffith@lowercolumbia.edu
GRIFFITH, Tashika .... 727-341-4738 106 E griffith.tashika@spcollege.edu
GRIFFITH-KLINE, Cheryl .... 704-687-7077 342 E cgriffit@uncc.edu
GRIFFITHS, James .... 602-489-5300.. 10 E james.griffiths@arizonachristian.edu
GRIFFITHS, José -Marie .... 605-256-5112 416 J presidentsoffice@dsu.edu

GROVE, Russell .... 208-376-7731 129 H
rgove@boisebible.edu
GROVE, Shannon, D ..... 814-886-6391 391 B
sgrove@mtaloy.edu
GROVENSTEIN,
Elizabeth .... 919-807-7070 331 L
GROVER, Carol .... 315-781-3339 302 A
groverc@hws.edu
GROVER, Dustin .... 918-540-6296 366 I
dugrover@neo.edu
GROVER-BISKER, Edna . 573-341-4292 261 E
egroverb@mst.edu
GROVER-ROOSA,
Janice .... 307-382-1701 502 I
jgrover@westernwyoming.edu
GROVES, Allen, W .... 434-924-7429 473 A
awg8vd@virginia.edu
GROVES, Bob .... 517-884-1003 227 D
grovesr@msu.edu
GROVES, Devany .... 904-620-2506 110 A
dgroves@unf.edu
GROVES, Jason .... 325-674-4977 429 B
jag97a@acu.edu
GROVES, John .... 215-572-2940 379 A
grovesj@arcadia.edu
GROVES, Kathy .... 573-592-1106 262 G
kathy.groves@williamwoods.edu
GROVES, Loren .... 307-681-6460 502 F
lgroves@sheridan.edu
GROVES, Robert, M ...... 202-687-6400.. 92 A
provost@georgetown.edu
GROVES, Suzanne .... 817-515-1541 445 G
suzanne.groves@tccd.edu
GROVES, William .... 937-769-1345 347 H
bgroves@antioch.edu
GROVES-SCOTT,
Victoria .... 501-450-3175.. 23 H
vickigs@uca.edu
GROW, David .... 801-274-3280 461 F
dgrow@wgu.edu
GROYSMAN, Natasga .... 954-492-5353.. 96 H
ngroysman@citycollege.edu
GROZA, Adam .... 909-687-1450.. 43 I
adamgroza@gs.edu
GRUBB, Allyson, D .... 724-847-6532 384 G
adgrubb@geneva.edu
GRUBB, Autumn .... 863-680-5118.. 99 H
agrubb@flsouthern.edu
GRUBB, Dan .... 910-592-8081 337 G
dgrubb@sampsoncc.edu
GRUBB, Derek .... 970-542-3158.. 81 A
derek.grubb@morgancc.edu
GRUBB, John .... 423-354-5144 425 E
jmgrubb@northeaststate.edu
GRUBB, Kevin .... 610-519-4060 402 D
kevin.c.grubb@villanova.edu
GRUBB, Lillie .... 620-223-2700 173 C
lillieg@fortscott.edu
GRUBBS, Laurie .... 850-644-3296 109 C
lgrubbs@fsu.edu
GRUBBS, Norris, C .... 504-282-4455 190 A
provostadmin@nobts.edu
GRUBE, M. Marshall .... 423-439-4150 419 J
grube@etsu.edu
GRUBER,
Christopher, J .... 704-894-2710 328 F
chgruber@davidson.edu
GRUBER, Elizabeth .... 570-484-2858 395 B
egruber@lockhaven.edu
GRUBER, Jay .... 202-687-7014.. 92 A
jg1502@georgetown.edu
GRUEGER, Andrea .... 217-228-5432 146 F
gruegan@quincy.edu
GRUEN, Kris .... 802-322-1721 462 C
kris.gruen@goddard.edu
GRUENIG, Gwendolyn .. 907-450-8190.... 9 G
gdgruenig@alaska.edu
GRUENWALD, John ...... 610-399-2051 394 C
jgruenwald@cheyney.edu
GRUESER, Suzanna .... 213-624-1200.. 42 I
sgrueser@fidm.edu
GRUHLER, Sarah .... 360-992-2406 479 F
sgruhler@clark.edu
GRUICHICH, Dawn .... 480-732-7050.. 12 P
dawn.gruichich@cgc.edu
GRUITS, Christopher, A 215-898-5828 400 K
gruits@ac.upenn.edu
GRULKE, Kimmi .... 928-226-4343.. 11 O
kimmi.grulke@coconino.edu
GRUNBLATT, Akiva .... 718-268-4700 312 G
GRUNDEN, Chelsea ...... 281-487-1170 448 F
cgrunden@txchiro.edu
GRUNDEN, Cynthia .... 312-369-7125 135 E
cgrunden@colum.edu
GRUNDEN, Ken .... 614-837-4088 364 A
grundenk@harvestprep.org
GRUNDER, Mark .... 989-358-7317 221 A
grunderm@alpenacc.edu
GRUNDER, Ty, J .... 563-333-5736 169 A
grundertyj@sau.edu
GRUNDIG, John .... 863-680-6212.. 99 H
jgrundig@flsouthern.edu
GRUNDMAN, Stephen .. 703-416-1441 466 F
sgrundman@divinemercy.edu
GRUNDY, Margaret, S .. 434-982-6409 473 A
mg8r@virginia.edu
GRUNKLEE, David .... 319-296-4042 166 B
david.grunklee@hawkeyecollege.edu
GRUNLOH, Jean Anne .. 217-234-5329 141 D
jgrunloh@lakeland.cc.il.us
GRUNOW, Tamie, L ...... 513-556-1015 362 D
grunowtl@ucmail.uc.edu
GRUNWALD, Gerald ...... 215-503-8982 400 A
gerald.grunwald@jefferson.edu
GRUS, Shannon .... 573-897-5000 260 E
GRUSKA, Julie .... 320-363-3395 243 A
jgruska@csbsju.edu
GRUSKA, Julie, E .... 320-363-3395 235 C
jgruska@csbsju.edu
GRUSKOS, Cynthia .... 732-224-2204 276 B
cgruskos@brookdalecc.edu
GRUSZKA, Bill .... 678-466-4351 116 E
billgruska@clayton.edu
GRUTZIK, Cynthia .... 415-338-2686.. 34 A
cgrutzik@sfsu.edu
GRUVER, Nolan .... 509-533-8481 479 I
nolan.gruver@ccs.spokane.edu
GRUVER, Nolan .... 509-434-8481 480 B
nolan.gruver@ccs.spokane.edu
GRUYS, Melissa .... 260-481-6461 159 F
gruysm@pfw.edu
GRYCENKOV, Tina .... 848-932-7305 282 A
grycenko@irap.rutgers.edu
GRZENDA, Jana, T .... 641-422-4269 168 D
jana.grzenda@niacc.edu
GRZESIAK, Michael, P .. 724-503-1001 402 E
mgrzesiak@washjeff.edu
GRZYBOWSKI, Mark, J . 815-224-0393 139 F
mark_grzybowski@ivcc.edu
GRZYWACZ,
Norberto, M .... 202-687-5603.. 92 A
norberto@georgetown.edu
GSTALDER, Steven .... 203-773-0129.. 84 F
sgstalder@albertus.edu
GUADAGNINO, Frank ... 814-867-4088 392 B
ftg2@psu.edu
GUADALUPE, Sarah ...... 248-370-3266 229 G
saguadal@oakland.edu
GUADALUPE, Sarahi ..... 787-276-0130 513 C
sarahi.guadalupe@upr.edu
GUADALUPE, Yvonne .... 787-766-1717 511 H
yguadalupe@suagm.edu
GUADALUPE-DE JESÚS,
Raúl .... 787-993-8867 513 B
raul.guadalupe@upr.edu
GUADALUPEZ, Elaine .... 787-743-7979 511 I
eguadalupe@suagm.edu
GUADARRAMA, Janet ... 210-436-3725 443 A
jguadarrama2@stmarytx.edu
GUAH, Matthew .... 803-536-8152 412 C
mguah@scsu.edu
GUAJARDO, Francisco .. 956-882-7829 455 D
francisco.guajardo@utrgv.edu
GUAJARDO, George ...... 210-486-3736 429 F
gguajardo41@alamo.edu
GUAJARDO, Nicole, R .. 757-594-8069 466 B
nguajard@cnu.edu
GUALTIERI, Kelly .... 207-326-2215 195 D
kelly.gualtieri@mma.edu
GUAMAN, Luis .... 203-857-7025.. 86 D
lguaman@norwalk.edu
GUAN, Sharon .... 773-325-7726 135 I
xguan@depaul.edu
GUANZON, Kimberly .... 530-898-4177.. 31 A
kguanzon@csuchico.edu
GUARD, Louis .... 315-781-3309 302 A
guard@hws.edu
GUARIGLIA, Daniel, M . 716-286-8431 310 D
dmg@niagara.edu
GUARIN-KLEIN, Natalia 718-951-5696 293 C
nataliag@brooklyn.cuny.edu
GUARINO, Mindy .... 708-344-4700 142 A
mguarino@lincolntech.edu
GUASCONI, Joseph .... 973-378-9850 283 B
joseph.guasconi@shu.edu
GUAY, Sheila .... 401-323-6324 404 F
sguay@bryant.edu
GUAY, Tanya .... 603-428-2440 273 H
tguay@nec.edu
GUBAN, Philip .... 440-943-7676 360 J
pguban@dioceseofcleveland.org
GUBAN, Philip .... 440-943-7600 360 J
pguban@dioceseofcleveland.org
GUBBINS, Jean, E .... 216-368-5557 349 F
jeg2@case.edu
GUBLER, Seth .... 435-652-7571 460 G
sgubler@dixie.edu
GUBSER, Kristin .... 602-286-8000.. 13 B
GUCKER, Jacob .... 903-586-2501 431 G
GUCKERT, Donald, J ..... 319-335-1248 163 A
don-guckert@uiowa.edu
GUDELUNAS, David ...... 813-253-6100 112 J
GUDMUNDSSON,
Markus .... 831-656-3690 503 K
markus.gudmundsson@nps.edu
GUDUR, Jaganmohan ... 303-458-4050.. 82 E
jgudur@regis.edu
GUDVANGEN, John, E .. 303-871-4857.. 83 D
john.gudvangen@du.edu
GUECO, Allan .... 818-766-8151.. 40 C
agueco@concorde.edu
GUEGOLD, Tina .... 614-236-6242 349 D
tguegold@capital.edu
GUEL, Carolyn .... 408-924-6083.. 34 B
carolyn.guel@sjsu.edu
GUELDA, Debbie .... 218-755-2786 237 E
debbie.guelda@bemidjistate.edu
GUELL, Dawn, M .... 920-923-8103 494 A
dmguell22@marianuniversity.edu
GUELLEC, Katell .... 978-837-5000 216 D
guelleck@merrimack.edu
GUENARD, Erik, M .... 906-932-4231 224 B
erikg@gogebic.edu
GUENGERICH, Alison .... 773-481-8186 134 G
aguengerich1@ccc.edu
GUENTER-SCHLESINGER,
Sue .... 360-650-3307 486 F
sue.guenter-schlesinger@wwu.edu
GUENTHER, Jeffrey .... 256-233-8116.... 4 D
jeffrey.guenther@athens.edu
GUENTHER, Thomas ..... 847-543-2264 135 B
tguenther@clcillinois.edu
GUENZLER-STEVENS,
Marsha, A .... 301-314-8505 202 C
mguenzle@umd.edu
GUERIN, Donna .... 215-635-7300 385 A
dguerin@gratz.edu
GUERIN, Melanie .... 413-528-7239 205 F
provostadmin@simons-rock.edu
GUERIN, Thomas, B ..... 513-556-2389 362 D
tom.guerin@uc.edu
GUERRA, Blanca .... 210-567-2621 456 C
guerrabe@uthscsa.edu
GUERRA, Elizabeth .... 909-469-5418.. 74 I
guerra@westernu.edu
GUERRA, Elizabeth .... 214-860-2236 435 C
eguerra@dcccd.edu
GUERRA, JR., Juan, M . 214-648-2400 457 B
juan.guerra@utsouthwestern.edu
GUERRA, Laura .... 563-588-8000 165 F
lguerra@emmaus.edu
GUERRA, Luis .... 510-436-1516.. 45 D
guerra@hnu.edu
GUERRA, Manuel .... 503-399-5076 372 C
manuel.guerra@chemeketa.edu
GUERRA, Manuel .... 503-821-8897 375 F
mguerra@pnca.edu
GUERRA, Michael .... 510-628-8031.. 48 A
mguerra@lincolnuca.edu
GUERRA, Nancy .... 949-824-6094.. 68 G
nguerra1@uci.edu
GUERRA, Sabra .... 254-968-9770 446 E
sguerra@tarleton.edu
GUERRA, Theresa .... 972-438-6932 441 H
tguerra@parker.edu
GUERRA, Yvonne .... 210-486-4339 429 E
yguerra6@alamo.edu
GUERRA-LOPEZ, Ingrid . 313-577-5139 232 I
ay2276@wayne.edu
GUERRERO, Bertha, M . 671-735-5638 505 C
boardoftrustees@guamcc.edu
GUERRERO, Daniel, G .. 310-206-6382.. 69 A
dguerrero@athletics.ucla.edu
GUERRERO, Dolores ..... 361-593-2717 447 D
dolores.guerrero@tamuk.edu
GUERRERO, Jennifer ..... 609-984-1588 284 B
jguerrero@tesu.edu
GUERRERO, Larry .... 405-382-9210 369 J
l.guerrero@sscok.edu
GUERRERO, Rico .... 559-243-7503.. 66 C
rico.guerrero@scccd.edu
GUERRERO, Tammy ...... 219-989-2675 159 G
tsguerre@pnw.edu
GUERRERO, Tim .... 303-410-2429.. 82 J
tim.guerrero@spartan.edu
GUERRERO, William ..... 607-274-3118 303 B
wguerrero@ithaca.edu
GUERRETTE, Leslie .... 207-741-5715 195 A
lguerrette@smccme.edu
GUERRIDO, Samuel .... 787-863-2390 509 B
samuel.guerrido@fajardo.inter.edu
GUERRIERO, William .... 480-732-7004.. 12 P
william.guerriero@cgc.edu
GUESS, Melissa .... 310-660-3492.. 41 L
mguess@elcamino.edu
GUEST, Charles .... 251-460-6261.... 8 F
cguest@southalabama.edu
GUEST, Stephany .... 816-415-5929 262 F
sguest@william.jewell.edu
GUETTI, Joan .... 973-275-2480 283 B
joan.guetti@shu.edu
GUEVERRA, Jonathan ... 305-809-3204.. 99 C
jonathan.gueverra@fkcc.edu
GUEVIN, Todd, G .... 610-917-1493 401 I
tgguevin@valleyforge.edu
GUEZMIR, Jean .... 651-690-6533 242 R
jmguezmir254@stkate.edu
GUFFEY, Patti .... 828-669-8012 331 J
pguffey@montreat.edu
GUGENHEIMER,
Yirmiya .... 718-853-8500 322 I
GUGLIELMO, B. Joseph 415-476-8010.. 69 E
bjoseph.guglielmo@ucsf.edu
GUGLIELMO, JR.,
Michael .... 401-863-7844 404 E
michael_guglielmo_jr@brown.edu
GUGLIELMONI, Mark, J 203-254-4000.. 86 I
mguglielmoni@fairfield.edu
GUICE, Leslie, K .... 318-257-3785 191 F
guice@latech.edu
GUIDO, Deana, L .... 252-451-8244 336 E
dguido744@nashcc.edu
GUIDO, Diane .... 626-812-3034.. 26 H
dguido@apu.edu
GUIDOTTI, Mike .... 312-369-8889 135 E
mguidotti@colum.edu
GUIDRY, Marc .... 936-468-2707 445 F
mguidry@sfasu.edu
GUIDRY, Neichelle .... 404-270-5728 125 B
nguidry@spelman.edu
GUIDUGLI, Kaye .... 410-864-4000 201 F
GUILARTE, Tomas .... 305-348-2000 109 A
tomas.guilarte@fiu.edu
GUILBEAU, Cara .... 256-761-6100.... 7 B
cguilbeau@talladega.edu
GUILBEAULT, Nancy, G 612-330-1169 233 K
guilbeau@augsburg.edu
GUILER, Douglas .... 352-365-3526 102 T
guilerd@lssc.edu
GUILFOILE, Patrick .... 715-232-2421 498 A
guilfoilep@uwstout.edu
GUILFORD, Renate, H ... 703-993-2299 467 L
rguilfor@gmu.edu
GUILFOYLE, Michael, K 508-767-7331 205 D
mk.guilfoyle@assumption.edu
GUILLEN, Christian .... 707-826-3739.. 33 D
cg36@humboldt.edu
GUILLEN, George .... 281-283-3950 453 A
guillen@uhcl.edu
GUILLEN, Oscar .... 510-659-6105.. 54 F
oguillen@ohlone.edu
GUILLEN, Patrick, J ...... 808-932-7170 128 E
pguillen@hawaii.edu
GUILLETTE, Natalie, L ... 802-656-4183 463 E
natalie.guillette@uvm.edu
GUILLIANI, Melissa ...... 787-766-1717 511 H
mguilliani@suagm.edu
GUILLIOM, Allison .... 313-577-2230 232 I
dy9063@wayne.edu
GUILLORY, Angela .... 225-578-2171 188 I
angelagu@lsu.edu
GUILLORY, Ann, V .... 201-559-6154 278 A
guillorya@felician.edu
GUILLORY, Eli .... 225-771-2786 190 G
eli_guillory@subr.edu
GUILLORY, III, Eli, G ... 225-771-2786 190 H
eli_guillory@subr.edu
GUILLORY, Justin .... 360-676-2772 482 D
jguillory@nwic.edu
GUILLORY, Monique ..... 973-290-4418 277 A
mguillory@cse.edu

GUTTENTAG, Christoph, O .... 919-684-2898 328 G
christoph.guttentag@duke.edu
GUTTMAN, Minerva ...... 201-692-2890 277 K
minerva_guttman@fdu.edu
GUTTMAN, Stephen, J .. 610-758-4204 388 J
sjg2@lehigh.edu
GUY, Elmer .... 505-786-4112 286 G
eguy@navajotech.edu
GUY, Georgina .... 949-582-4738.. 64 G
gguy@saddleback.edu
GUY, Kathleen .... 404-261-1441 122 J
kguy1@oglethorpe.edu
GUY, Kip .... 859-257-5290 185 B
kip.guy@uky.edu
GUY, Stephanie .... 206-934-7935 484 B
stephanie.guy@seattlecolleges.edu
GUY, Sunethra .... 901-381-3939 428 E
sunethra@visible.edu
GUY, Todd .... 562-903-6000.. 27 C
GUY-ANDERSON, Adrian .... 504-816-4325 186 D
aguy@dillard.edu
GUY-SHEFTAL, Beverly . 404-270-5624 125 B
bsheftal@spelman.edu
GUYER, Jennifer, L .... 814-863-0205 392 B
jlg337@psu.edu
GUYER, Kim .... 402-898-1000 266 H
kim_g@creativecenter.edu
GUYER, Kimberly .... 607-871-2132 289 H
guyer@alfred.edu
GUYETTE, Daniel .... 269-387-5810 232 K
daniel.guyette@wmich.edu
GUYETTE, Joyce .... 864-379-8858 409 H
jguyette@erskine.edu
GUYETTE, Randy .... 828-835-4253 338 E
rguyette@tricountycc.edu
GUYMON, Christopher . 773-702-1730 150 J
cguymon@uchicago.edu
GUYNES, Del .... 972-923-5437 445 A
dguynes@sagu.edu
GUYTON, Deirdre .... 304-327-4569 489 P
dguyton@bluefieldstate.edu
GUYTON, Don .... 713-743-8000 452 E
dguyton@uh.edu
GUYTON, Sondra .... 910-879-5634 332 D
sguyton@bladencc.edu
GUZELIMIAN, Ara .... 212-799-5000 303 H
GUZMAN, Alejandro ..... 818-523-9026.. 49 B
guzmana4@lamission.edu
GUZMAN, Amanda .... 575-492-2176 289 A
aguzman@usw.edu
GUZMAN, Andre .... 509-793-2077 478 H
andreg@bigbend.edu
GUZMAN, Andrew .... 213-740-7331.. 72 B
andrewgu@usc.edu
GUZMAN, Angelica .... 209-575-6471.. 75 J
guzmana@mjc.edu
GUZMAN, Ariel .... 787-751-0160 507 F
aguzman@cmpr.pr.gov
GUZMAN, Claudia .... 920-465-2464 496 E
guzmanc@uwgb.edu
GUZMAN, Debora .... 210-434-6711 441 E
daguzman@lake.ollusa.edu
GUZMAN, Jill .... 973-720-2257 284 I
guzmanj21@wpunj.edu
GUZMAN, John .... 718-963-4112 291 I
jguzman@boricuacollege.edu
GUZMAN, Juan .... 308-865-8127 269 I
guzmanj@unk.edu
GUZMAN, Juan (Johnny), C .... 830-591-7264 444 G
jcguzman@swtjc.edu
GUZMAN, Katheleen ..... 405-325-4652 371 B
kguzman@ou.edu
GUZMAN, Laura .... 949-214-3099.. 40 F
laura.guzman@cui.edu
GUZMAN, Leslie Ann ... 787-746-1400 508 B
lguzman@huertas.edu
GUZMAN, Ruben .... 949-451-5220.. 64 F
rguzman@ivc.edu
GUZMAN, Tobias .... 970-351-1944.. 83 E
tobias.guzman@unco.edu
GUZMAN-AGUILAR, Mariella .... 530-661-7759.. 76 B
mguzman@yccd.edu
GUZMAN-LOPEZ, Evelyn .... 787-480-2410 507 C
eguzman@sanjuanciudadpatria.com
GUZMAN QUILES, Jaydee, A .... 787-720-4476 512 D
secretariapresidente@mizpa.edu
GUZZARDO, Joseph ..... 215-670-9060 391 H
jguzzardo@peirce.edu
GUZZI, Martin .... 607-778-5245 318 A
guzzimj@sunybroome.edu
GUZZI, Michael, A .... 530-898-4336.. 31 A
maguzzi@csuchico.edu
GUZZO, Linda .... 860-906-5132.. 85 D
lguzzo@capitalcc.edu
GWALTNEY, Darrell .... 615-460-5552 418 F
darrell.gwaltney@belmont.edu
GWALTNEY, Tammy ...... 618-985-3741 139 I
tammygwaltney@jalc.edu
GWARTNEY, Kurt .... 918-270-6470 369 A
kurt.gwartney@ptstulsa.edu
GWATNEY, Bradley .... 432-837-8190 450 D
bradley.gwatney@sulross.edu
GWIN, Matthew .... 201-216-3346 283 C
matthew.gwin@stevens.edu
GWINN, Janice .... 304-357-4383 488 G
janicegwinn@ucwv.edu
GWINNER, Kevin, P ...... 785-532-7227 174 G
kgwinner@ksu.edu
GWYN, Lori .... 580-774-7010 370 C
lori.gwyn@swosu.edu
GWYNN, Diana .... 307-754-6058 502 G
diana.gwynn@nwc.edu
GWYNN, Douglas .... 443-885-3647 200 D
douglas.gwynn@morgan.edu
GWYNN, Tim .... 503-251-5773 377 F
tgwynn@uws.edu
GWYTHER, Chelsea .... 617-243-2152 210 G
cgwyther@lasell.edu
GYERTSON, David .... 859-858-2335 178 H
GYI, Khin Khin .... 260-481-6105 159 F
khinkhin.gyi@pfw.edu
GYLLIN, John .... 407-708-4577 107 D
gyllinj@seminolestate.edu
GYMZIAK, Paul .... 603-623-0313 273 I
paulgymziak@nhia.edu
GYORKE, Allan .... 305-284-6101 112 E
a.gyorke@miami.edu

H

HA, Kevin .... 760-328-5554.. 51 D
HA, Viet, X .... 864-833-8193 411 I
vxha@presby.edu
HA, Won .... 415-476-6296.. 69 E
won.ha@ucsf.edu
HAAB, Brian .... 616-234-5268 231 H
HAAB, Melissa .... 662-862-8251 246 D
mjhaab@iccms.edu
HAACK, Julie, A .... 563-333-6314 169 A
haackjuliea@sau.edu
HAACK, Kristen .... 617-521-2917 218 E
kristen.haack@simmons.edu
HAAG, Adam .... 316-284-5273 171 F
ahaag@bethelks.edu
HAAG, Kelly .... 414-229-4508 497 A
kajohnso@uwm.edu
HAAKE, Anne .... 585-475-4786 313 A
arhics@rit.edu
HAAN, Emily .... 415-565-8981.. 68 F
haanemily@uchastings.edu
HAAN, Mary Beth .... 915-831-6723 436 E
mhaan@epcc.edu
HAAN, Nicole .... 972-860-8054 435 A
nicolehaan@dcccd.edu
HAAR, Annemarie .... 510-594-3657.. 28 D
ahaar@cca.edu
HAAR, Jean .... 507-389-5445 239 C
jean.haar@mnsu.edu
HAAR, Scott .... 417-862-5700 250 J
shaar@bryancolleges.edu
HAARBUSCH, Rainer ..... 651-846-1490 241 B
rainer.haarbusch@saintpaul.edu
HAARSMA, Jill .... 712-707-7100 168 H
jhaarsma@nwciowa.edu
HAAS, Bob .... 740-389-4636 356 B
haasr@mtc.edu
HAAS, Evelyn .... 612-767-7044 233 H
ev@alfredadler.edu
HAAS, Jackie .... 978-542-2149 213 C
jhaas@salemstate.edu
HAAS, Jennifer .... 651-696-6700 236 H
jhaas@macalester.edu
HAAS, Jesse .... 575-528-7548 287 E
jhaas@nmsu.edu
HAAS, Kurt .... 970-248-1881.. 77 I
khaas@coloradomesa.edu
HAAS, Laura, M .... 413-545-2572 211 D
dean@cics.umass.edu
HAAS, Mark, P .... 517-355-5014 227 D
haasmark@msu.edu
HAAS, Mary Ann .... 207-992-4900 194 A
haasm@husson.edu
HAAS, McKenna .... 847-628-5037 140 C
mckenna.haas@judsonu.edu
HAAS, Nate .... 970-351-1763.. 83 E
nate.haas@unco.edu
HAAS, Nicole .... 718-951-5671 293 C
nicole@brooklyn.cuny.edu
HAAS, Ocki .... 417-447-2631 257 G
haaso@otc.edu
HAAS, Sarah .... 563-588-6307 163 F
sarah.haas@clarke.edu
HAAS, Stephen .... 800-371-6105.. 14 G
shaas@nationalparalegal.edu
HAAS, Sue .... 434-961-5229 475 F
shaas@pvcc.edu
HAASE, LuAnn, M .... 712-274-5183 168 B
haasel@morningside.edu
HAASE, Ryan .... 620-862-5252 171 B
rhaase@barclaycollege.edu
HAATVEDT, Chad .... 218-322-2444 238 E
chad.haatvedt@itascacc.edu
HABA, Jerry .... 972-721-5018 452 D
dhaba@udallas.edu
HABAYEB, Omar .... 800-686-1883 222 E
ohabayeb@cleary.edu
HABEGER, Christian ...... 864-379-8812 409 H
habeger@erskine.edu
HABEGGER, Toni .... 509-359-6373 480 E
thabegger@ewu.edu
HABEL, Leah .... 406-771-4327 264 G
lhabel@gfcmsu.edu
HABEN, Kristen .... 858-653-3000.. 29 I
HABER, Jessica .... 914-674-7457 306 F
jhaber@mercy.edu
HABER, Melanie .... 508-588-9100 214 F
mhaber@massasoit.mass.edu
HABERBERGER, Patty, A .... 573-882-4256 261 B
haberbergerp@missouri.edu
HABEREK, Gregory .... 508-588-9100 214 F
ghaberek@massasoit.mass.edu
HABERER, Ronald, J ..... 716-888-8527 292 D
haberern@canisius.edu
HABERLE, Charles, J .... 401-865-1154 405 B
chaberle@providence.edu
HABERMANN, Barbara .. 253-535-7674 482 H
nurs@plu.edu
HABERSHAM, Sherida .. 912-583-3156 115 E
shabersham@bpc.edu
HABERSTICH, Laura ...... 559-297-4500.. 46 A
lhaberstich@iot.edu
HABETZ, Pauline, M ..... 713-500-8425 456 B
pauline.m.habetz@uth.tmc.edu
HABIB, Bob .... 757-352-4840 470 H
robehab@regent.edu
HABIB, Claudia .... 559-791-2316.. 47 A
claudia.habib@portervillecollege.edu
HABIB, Claudia .... 559-675-4800.. 66 F
claudia.habib@scccd.edu
HABICH, Casey .... 704-463-3055 339 E
casey.habich@pfeiffer.edu
HABICH, Maegan .... 704-463-3409 339 E
maegan.habich@pfeiffer.edu
HABROCK, Marty .... 402-554-3408 270 B
mhabrock@unomaha.edu
HABSCHMIDT, Cathy .... 765-983-1772 154 G
habscca@earlham.edu
HABUCHMAI, Joseph .... 691-320-2480 505 B
jhabuchmai@comfsm.fm
HABUKI, Daniel, Y .... 949-480-4005.. 64 B
habuki@soka.edu
HACHE, Jason .... 952-829-2405 234 A
jason.hache@bethfel.org
HACK, Mary, C .... 609-984-1661 284 B
mhack@tesu.edu
HACK-SULLIVAN, Heather .... 503-760-3131 371 H
heather@birthingway.edu
HACKBARTH, Greg .... 270-745-5623 185 E
greg.hackbarth@wku.edu
HACKBARTH, Wade ...... 608-785-9123 501 A
hackbarthw@westerntc.edu
HACKBARTH-ONSON, Annette .... 620-417-1106 176 K
annette.hackbarthons@sccc.edu
HACKE, Keith .... 314-539-5000 259 C
khacke@stlcc.edu
HACKEMER, Kurt .... 605-677-6497 416 H
kurt.hackemer@usd.edu
HACKER, David .... 304-243-2639 491 I
dhacker@wju.edu
HACKER, Eugene .... 540-365-4268 467 I
ehacker@ferrum.edu
HACKET, JR., William, C .... 863-667-5004 107 K
wchacket@seu.edu
HACKETT, Alaysia .... 828-689-1508 331 A
ahackett@mhu.edu
HACKETT, Amy, E .... 253-879-3140 485 E
ahackett@pugetsound.edu
HACKETT, Gail .... 804-828-1345 473 F
ghackett@vcu.edu
HACKETT, Keith .... 319-895-4230 164 B
khackett@cornellcollege.edu
HACKETT, Lorinda .... 417-625-9300 256 D
HACKETT, Royce .... 229-931-2074 119 D
royce.hackett@gsw.edu
HACKETT, Timothy .... 510-436-2464.. 56 H
thackett@peralta.edu
HACKLER, Donald .... 405-682-1611 367 H
donald.r.hackler@occc.edu
HACKLER, Gwen .... 405-789-6400 370 A
ghackler@snu.edu
HACKLER, Yolanda .... 316-322-3104 171 G
yhackler@butlercc.edu
HACKMAN, Erika .... 845-341-4768 311 C
erika.hackman@sunyorange.edu
HACKNEY, James .... 617-373-5149 217 F
HACKNEY, Michele .... 254-295-4148 453 E
mhackney@umhb.edu
HACKWITH, Maggie ...... 402-481-8705 265 K
maggie.hackwith@bryanhealthcollege.edu
HADAWAY, Maura .... 775-674-7600 271 D
mhadaway@tmcc.edu
HADAWAY, Maura .... 307-778-1204 502 D
mhadaway@lccc.wy.edu
HADAWAY-MELLIS, Tina .... 805-756-1211.. 30 C
thadaway@calpoly.edu
HADDAD, Abdallah .... 843-349-2938 408 C
abdallah@coastal.edu
HADDAD, Emily, A .... 207-581-1954 195 J
emily.haddad@maine.edu
HADDAD, Kamel .... 760-750-4050.. 33 B
khaddad@csusm.edu
HADDAD, Linda .... 910-962-7410 343 C
haddadl@uncw.edu
HADDAD, Nicole .... 413-265-2275 208 C
haddadn@elms.edu
HADDAWAY, Deborah .. 504-280-1292 189 E
dleitz@uno.edu
HADDELAND, Patricia ... 503-883-2259 373 H
phaddel@linfield.edu
HADDOCK, Gregory ...... 660-562-1145 257 E
haddock@nwmissouri.edu
HADDOCK, Jennifer ...... 870-743-3000.. 20 C
jhaddock@northark.edu
HADDOCK-ACEVEDO, Jorge .... 787-751-9521 512 G
jorge.haddock@upr.edu
HADDOCK ACEVEDO, Jorge .... 787-759-6061 514 B
presidente.upr@upr.edu
HADDON, Phoebe, A ..... 856-225-6095 281 G
chancellor@camden.rutgers.edu
HADENFELDT, Sharon ... 402-481-8606 265 K
sharon.hadenfeldt@bryanhealthcollege.edu
HADERTHAUER, Janine . 787-264-1912 509 F
janine@intersg.edu
HADIDI, Rassule .... 612-659-7293 238 H
rassule.hadidi@metrostate.edu
HADJU, Amanda .... 816-802-3379 254 B
ahadju@kcai.edu
HADLEY, Craig .... 207-992-1953 194 A
hadleyc@husson.edu
HADLEY, Kim .... 479-524-7117.. 19 H
khadley@jbu.edu
HADLEY, Kristin .... 801-626-6273 461 B
kristinhadley@weber.edu
HADLEY, Linda .... 706-568-2044 116 I
hadley_linda@columbusstate.edu
HADLEY, Pamela .... 610-399-2260 394 C
phadley@cheyney.edu
HADLEY, Robyn, S .... 314-935-7192 262 A
robyn.hadley@wustl.edu
HADLOCK, Heather .... 903-923-2319 436 D
hhadlock@etbu.edu
HADSELL, Krissta .... 740-397-9000 357 B
krissta.hadsell@mvnu.edu
HADVINA, Shellie .... 818-677-5541.. 32 D
shellie.hadvina@csun.edu
HADWIN, Julie .... 803-812-7304 413 G
jhadwin@mailbox.sc.edu
HAEBERLE, Kathleen ..... 559-325-3600.. 28 H
khaeberle@chsu.edu

HAECKER, Nathan .... 402-280-2735 266 I nathanhhaecker@creighton.edu

HAEFNER, Brenda .... 319-363-1323 168 C bhaefner@mtmercy.edu

HAEFNER, Jeremy .... 303-315-7682.. 83 C chancellor@ucdenver.edu

HAEFNER, Jeremy .... 303-871-2111.. 83 D chancellor@du.edu

HAEGER, Loredana, C .. 901-572-2772 418 E loredana.haeger@bchs.edu

HAELEN, Robert .... 518-320-1502 316 C bob.haelen@suny.edu

HAEN, Richard .... 920-565-1000 493 J haenrn@lakeland.edu

HAENNICKE, Sheila ...... 312-893-7161 137 A shaennicke@erikson.edu

HAENSEL, Angela .... 513-569-4845 350 K angela.haensel@cincinnatistate.edu

HAERENS, Joy .... 909-652-6840.. 36 A joy.haerens@chaffey.edu

HAERING, Harold, J ..... 630-515-3976 143 G hhaeri@midwestern.edu

HAESLOOP, Mary .... 650-508-3651.. 54 D mhaesloop@ndnu.edu

HAFEN, Steven, J .... 801-422-2533 458 H stevehafen@byu.edu

HAFFAR, Warren .... 215-572-4094 379 A haffarw@arcadia.edu

HAFFEY, Jim .... 662-472-9013 246 C jhaffey@holmescc.edu

HAFFNER, Peter .... 860-773-1382.. 86 G phaffner@tunxis.edu

HAFFORD, Patrick .... 617-989-4870 219 E haffordp@wit.edu

HAFT, Susan .... 740-245-7276 363 D shaft@rio.edu

HAFT, Tami .... 208-769-7729 131 C tami_haft@nic.edu

HAGA-DUFFY, Laura ...... 541-956-7158 376 D lduffy@roguecc.edu

HAGADON, Shawn .... 269-749-7607 229 H sholt@olivetcollege.edu

HAGAMAN, Bernice ...... 423-323-0208 425 E bdhagaman@northeaststate.edu

HAGAN, Alise .... 337-482-9029 192 E alise@louisiana.edu

HAGAN, Bruce .... 949-451-5254.. 64 F bhagan@ivc.edu

HAGAN, Diane .... 440-934-3101 358 E dhagan@ohiobusinesscollege.edu

HAGAN, Eric .... 610-282-1100 382 E eric.hagan@desales.edu

HAGAN, Joanna .... 480-858-9100.. 16 A j.hagan@scnm.edu

HAGAN, Kacy .... 570-321-4309 389 E hagan@lycoming.edu

HAGAN, Khalli, s .... 985-549-2068 192 D khalli.hagan@selu.edu

HAGAN, Maura .... 435-797-2478 460 H maura.hagan@usu.edu

HAGAN, Scott, A .... 612-343-4741 242 H sahagan@northcentral.edu

HAGAN, Tara .... 229-226-1621 125 C thagan@thomasu.edu

HAGAN, Winifred, M .... 617-994-6912 211 B whagan@bhe.mass.edu

HAGANDER, Sonja .... 612-330-1435 233 K hagander@augsburg.edu

HAGANS, Lori, R .... 405-585-5262 367 F lori.hagans@okbu.edu

HAGARTY, Michael .... 507-457-6695 243 B mhagarty@smumn.edu

HAGE, Nikki .... 928-344-7580.. 10 J nikki.hage@azwestern.edu

HAGELIN, John .... 641-472-8194 167 F president@mum.edu

HAGELMAN, Mark .... 504-816-8002 190 A mhagelman@nobts.edu

HAGELOH, Michael .... 903-983-8187 439 A mhageloh@kilgore.edu

HAGEMAN, Kristin .... 651-773-1780 237 G kristin.hageman@century.edu

HAGEMANN, Melinda ... 719-255-5103.. 83 B melinda.hagemann@uccs.edu

HAGEMANN, Ryan .... 503-838-8809 377 H hagemannr@wou.edu

HAGEN, Cheryl, M .... 734-462-4400 230 D chagen@schoolcraft.edu

HAGEN, Dara .... 952-358-8283 239 F dara.hagen@normandale.edu

HAGEN, Debra .... 608-342-1358 497 D hagende@uwplatt.edu

HAGEN, Joshua .... 605-626-2601 417 A joshua.hagen@northern.edu

HAGEN, Peter .... 609-652-4504 283 D hagenp@stockton.edu

HAGEN, William .... 978-867-4898 209 F william.hagen@gordon.edu

HAGENBAUGH, Stacie .. 413-585-2582 218 F shagenba@smith.edu

HAGENDORF, Ana .... 210-805-3036 453 D wandless@uiwtx.edu

HAGENESS, Sandy .... 701-228-5480 346 C sandy.hageness@dakotacollege.edu

HAGENS, Kathy .... 952-885-5439 242 I khagens@nwhealth.edu

HAGER, Amy .... 660-263-4100 257 B amyh@macc.edu

HAGER, Annie .... 304-724-5000 487 H ahager@cdu.edu

HAGER, Eric .... 402-554-2336 270 B ehager@unomaha.edu

HAGER, Judy .... 701-252-3467 347 C jhager@uj.edu

HAGER, Michael, A .... 319-273-2382 163 B michael.hager@uni.edu

HAGER, Timi .... 941-359-4200 110 D thager@usf.edu

HAGER, Timothy, A ...... 417-268-1010 250 E hagert@evangel.edu

HAGER, Tricia .... 816-415-5946 262 F hagerm@william.jewell.edu

HAGERMAN, Grayson, P .... 270-824-8562 181 G grayson.hagerman@kctcs.edu

HAGERMANN, P. Donald .... 302-356-6844.. 90 I p.donald.hagermann@wilmu.edu

HAGEROTT, Jacqueline . 740-753-7006 354 A hagerottj@hocking.edu

HAGEROTT, Mark .... 701-328-2963 345 B mark.hagerott@ndus.edu

HAGERTY, George, J ..... 352-638-9770.. 95 D ghagerty@beaconcollege.edu

HAGG, Scott .... 760-750-4826.. 33 B shagg@csusm.edu

HAGGARD, Bill .... 828-251-6474 342 C bhaggard@unca.edu

HAGGARD, David, L ..... 423-775-7207 418 H david.haggard@bryan.edu

HAGGARD, Dennis .... 479-248-7236.. 19 C dennishaggard75@yahoo.com

HAGGARD, Luanne .... 816-279-7000 250 B luanne.haggard@abtu.edu

HAGGARD, Michael .... 518-355-4000 422 E mhaggard@mabtsne.edu

HAGGERTY, Blake .... 973-596-2912 279 F blake.haggerty@njit.edu

HAGGERTY, Christina ... 815-455-8694 143 A chaggerty@mchenry.edu

HAGGERTY, Janet, A ..... 918-631-2304 371 E janet-haggerty@utulsa.edu

HAGGERTY, Roy .... 541-737-4811 375 D roy.haggerty@oregonstate.edu

HAGGETT, Rosemary, R 214-752-5535 454 A rosemary.haggett@untsystem.edu

HAGGINS, Debra, L ...... 757-727-5340 468 B debra.haggins@hamptonu.edu

HAGGINS, Isaac .... 216-201-9025 355 I

HAGGINS, Tanya .... 216-201-9025 355 I

HAGGLUND, Kristofer ... 573-884-6705 261 B hagglundk@missouri.edu

HAGGRAY, Annette .... 703-845-6222 475 C ahaggray@nvcc.edu

HAGGY, Marisa .... 218-879-0879 238 A mhaggy@fdltcc.edu

HAGIN, Linwood .... 864-663-0069 411 E linwood.hagin@ngu.edu

HAGOOD, Matthew .... 305-348-2820 109 A matthew.hagood@fiu.edu

HAGOOD, Thomas .... 706-542-7575 125 G tchagood@uga.edu

HAGREEN, Sarah .... 585-292-2352 307 H shagreen@monroecc.edu

HAGUE, Beverly .... 828-898-2417 330 E hagueb@lmc.edu

HAGUE, Martin .... 314-505-7313 251 I haguem@csl.edu

HAGUE, Michael, J .... 810-762-3324 231 G mjhague@umich.edu

HAGY, Joseph .... 540-863-2925 474 D jhagy@dslcc.edu

HAHKA, Curt .... 906-487-7380 223 K curt.hahka@finlandia.edu

HAHN, Ben .... 907-564-8289.... 9 D bhahn@alaskapacific.edu

HAHN, David .... 520-621-6595.. 16 G dwhahn@email.arizona.edu

HAHN, Greg .... 208-426-5391 129 I greghahn@boisestate.edu

HAHN, Karen .... 352-588-8522 106 D karen.hahn@saintleo.edu

HAHN, Katharine .... 216-687-2277 351 B k.hahn@csuohio.edu

HAHN, Kathryn .... 612-330-1013 233 K hahn@augsburg.edu

HAHN, Kelli .... 269-927-6701 226 D khahn@lakemichigancollege.edu

HAHN, Laura .... 707-826-5086.. 33 D lkh9@humboldt.edu

HAHN, Lenell .... 573-986-6012 259 K lhahn@semo.edu

HAHN, Lisa .... 516-572-7169 308 A lisa.hahn@ncc.edu

HAHN, Marc, B .... 816-654-7102 254 C mhahn@kcumb.edu

HAHN, Marcela .... 212-875-4400 290 F mhahn@bankstreet.edu

HAHN, Mary Joan .... 509-313-6095 481 D hahn@gonzaga.edu

HAHN, Rob .... 414-443-8944 498 O rob.hahn@wlc.edu

HAHN, Sarah .... 530-752-8990.. 68 E shahn@shcs.ucdavis.edu

HAHN, Stephen .... 713-792-2121 456 E

HAHN, Steven .... 608-262-2433 496 C steve.hahn@wisc.edu

HAHN, Troy .... 718-997-3009 295 C troy.hahn@qc.cuny.edu

HAHN SCHNIPPER, Jenny .... 636-922-8244 258 I jschnipper@stchas.edu

HAIDLE, Shirley .... 541-881-5842 377 B shaidle@tvcc.cc

HAIDLE, Sue, E .... 740-368-3104 359 N sehaidle@owu.edu

HAIGLER, Steven .... 310-900-1600.. 40 A shaigler@elcamino.edu

HAIK, Kristi .... 231-591-3667 223 J kristihaik@ferris.edu

HAIKKA, Tommi .... 406-447-6935 264 C tommi.haikka@helenacollege.edu

HAILE, Amy .... 207-221-4228 196 G ahaile@une.edu

HAILE, Bob, A .... 309-649-6331 150 A bob.haile@src.edu

HAILE, Dawit .... 804-524-1141 477 B dhaile@vsu.edu

HAILE, Gregory Adam ... 954-201-7401.. 95 H

HAILE, Haley .... 870-307-7425.. 20 A

HAILEY, Christine .... 512-245-2119 450 E ceh138@txstate.edu

HAILEY, Maryann .... 903-875-7305 440 G maryann.hailey@navarrocollege.edu

HAILEY, Mechele .... 620-227-9240 172 J mhailey@dc3.edu

HAILEY, Robert, C .... 504-862-8064 191 B rhailey@tulane.edu

HAILEY PENN, Carla ..... 973-353-5541 282 B carla.hpenn@rutgers.edu

HAILU, Elias .... 713-313-7879 449 C hailu_ex@tsu.edu

HAIN, Cheryl .... 575-538-6174 289 B cheryl.hain@wnmu.edu

HAIN, Peggy, S .... 402-465-2137 268 H phain@nebrwesleyan.edu

HAINES, Amanda .... 360-623-8428 479 C amanda.haines@centralia.edu

HAINES, Asher .... 704-687-8693 342 E ahaines3@uncc.edu

HAINES, Brian .... 816-415-7871 262 F hainesb@william.jewell.edu

HAINES, Chris, M .... 480-423-6310.. 13 H chris.haines@scottsdalecc.edu

HAINES, Chuck .... 805-893-8541.. 70 A chuck.haines@ucsb.edu

HAINES, Gary .... 719-884-5000.. 81 C gwhaines@nbc.edu

HAINES, Lynne .... 912-650-5673 124 E lhaines@southuniversity.edu

HAINES, Melissa .... 610-558-5625 391 D hainesm@neumann.edu

HAINES, Paul Lowell .... 765-998-5201 160 F president@taylor.edu

HAINES, Rachael, M ..... 252-335-3787 341 D rmhaines@ecsu.edu

HAINES, Rhonda .... 315-792-7100 321 E rhaines@sunypoly.edu

HAINES, Terry .... 913-266-8601 176 D terry.haines@ottawa.edu

HAINEY, Dale, E .... 817-202-6519 444 I haineyd@swau.edu

HAINGRAY, Donald ...... 585-567-9287 302 D donald.haingray@houghton.edu

HAINLINE, Benjamin ..... 580-628-6250 367 D ben.hainline@noc.edu

HAIR, Neil, F .... 585-475-6322 313 A nfhbbu@rit.edu

HAIR, Shannon .... 434-797-8495 474 E shannon.hair@danville.edu

HAIRE, Cassandra .... 919-209-2007 335 F cwhaire@johnstoncc.edu

HAIRE, Helen, M .... 319-273-2712 163 B helen.haire@uni.edu

HAIRR, Blair .... 910-592-8081 337 G ahairr@sampsoncc.edu

HAIRSTON, Creasie .... 312-996-3219 151 B cfh@uic.edu

HAISCH, Craig .... 503-883-2675 373 H chaisch@linfield.edu

HAISEN, Michael .... 808-735-4711 127 F

HAISMA, Dale .... 616-632-3037 221 C haismdal@aquinas.edu

HAJ-HARIRI, Hossein ... 803-777-7356 413 C hhh@mailbox.sc.edu

HAJDER, Michelle .... 866-492-5336 244 F michelle.hajder@mail.waldenu.edu

HAJELA, Prabhat .... 518-276-6487 312 I hajelap@rpi.edu

HAJIR, Farshid .... 413-545-6330 211 D hajir@provost.umass.edu

HAJIYEV, Emin .... 518-454-5111 296 H hajiyeve@strose.edu

HAJIZEDAH, Neda .... 212-774-0727 306 A nhajizedah@mmm.edu

HAKA, Clifford, H .... 517-355-2341 227 D hakac@mail.lib.msu.edu

HAKALA, Curtis .... 304-434-8000 489 A curtis.hakala@easternwv.edu

HAKANSON, David .... 314-977-5353 259 H david.hakanson@health.slu.edu

HAKER, Catherine, A .... 518-454-5282 296 H hakerc@strose.edu

HAKES, Joseph .... 312-567-7124 139 B jhakes@iit.edu

HAKIM, George .... 810-762-3223 231 G geohak@umich.edu

HAKIM, Iman, A .... 520-626-7083.. 16 G ihakim@email.arizona.edu

HAKKAKIAN, Eliyahu .... 410-484-7200 201 A

HALABE, Anjali .... 304-293-8768 491 C anjali.halabe@mail.wvu.edu

HALACO, Karen .... 518-464-8500 299 G khalaco@excelsior.edu

HALARIS, Dimitris .... 914-633-2649 302 G dhalaris@iona.edu

HALAS, Wally .... 203-254-4000.. 86 I whalas@fairfield.edu

HALAYCHIK, Corey .... 718-409-7200 321 C

HALBERSTADT, Joseph . 718-438-1002 306 G yhalberstadt@yeshivanet.com

HALBERSTAM, Lisa .... 646-565-6000 322 J lisa.halberstam@touro.edu

HALBERT, Jay .... 325-942-2355 451 A jay.halbert@angelo.edu

HALBERT, Martin .... 336-334-3418 343 A martin.halbert@uncg.edu

HALBESLEBEN, Jonathon .... 205-348-2702.... 7 G jrhalbesleben@ua.edu

HALBROOK, Anna .... 501-208-5310.. 23 A halbrook@uaccm.edu

HALCOMB, Jonda .... 361-698-1218 436 C jhalcomb@delmar.edu

HALCUMB, Cambrea ..... 573-840-9658 260 I chalcumb@trcc.edu

HALDEMAN, Bill .... 612-626-1616 243 E

HALE, Barry .... 903-923-2020 436 D bhale@etbu.edu

HALE, Charles .... 352-588-7531 106 D charles.hale@saintleo.edu

HALE, Charles, R .... 805-893-8354.. 70 A ssdean@ltsc.ucsb.edu

HALE, Cynthia, R .... 301-405-6816 202 C chale@umd.edu

HALE, David, B .... 804-289-8150 472 L dhale2@richmond.edu

HALE, Don .... 404-413-3025 119 E dhale@gsu.edu

HALE, Georgia ... 479-788-7030 .. 21 H
georgia.hale@uafs.edu
HALE, Jerold ... 423-425-4633 428 A
jerold-hale@utc.edu
HALE, Jimmie ... 864-488-4519 410 E
jhale@limestone.edu
HALE, Jonathan ... 620-431-2820 175 H
jhale@neosho.edu
HALE, Jordan ... 479-788-7008 .. 21 H
jordan.hale@uafs.edu
HALE, Kandi ... 207-941-7138 194 A
halek@husson.edu
HALE, Kathy ... 913-234-0649 172 E
kathy.hale@cleveland.edu
HALE, Kayla ... 918-631-2565 371 E
kayla-hale@utulsa.edu
HALE, Kimberly ... 217-228-5432 146 F
haleki@quincy.edu
HALE, LaToya ... 443-394-3377 .. 92 G
HALE, Lloyd ... 816-604-2221 255 G
lloyd.hale@mcckc.edu
HALE, Mallie ... 256-824-6549 .... 8 B
mallie.hale@uah.edu
HALE, Mark ... 214-333-5503 434 I
markh@dbu.edu
HALE, Melina ... 773-702-2102 150 J
mhale@uchicago.edu
HALE, Nori ... 785-242-5200 176 D
nori.hale@ottawa.edu
HALE, Ryan ... 941-408-1405 108 G
haler@scf.edu
HALE, Sheri ... 540-545-7240 471 E
shale2@su.edu
HALE, Ted ... 860-906-5053 .. 85 D
thale@capitalcc.edu
HALE, Tricia, A ... 229-333-5940 126 G
tahale@valdosta.edu
HALEAMAU-KAM,
Raynette Kalei ... 808-969-8804 129 A
haleamau@hawaii.edu
HALES, Cassie ... 319-352-8553 170 C
cassie.hales@wartburg.edu
HALES, Christie, C ... 434-949-1068 475 H
christie.hales@southside.edu
HALES, Jessica ... 410-334-2808 204 F
jhales@worwic.edu
HALES, Mike ... 859-572-5207 184 A
halesm1@nku.edu
HALEY, Christopher ... 207-326-2232 195 D
christopher.haley@mma.edu
HALEY, Donna ... 678-839-6438 126 E
dhaley@westga.edu
HALEY, John ... 315-445-4520 304 C
haleyjr@lemoyne.edu
HALEY, John, R ... 315-445-4689 304 C
haleyjr@lemoyne.edu
HALEY, Kent ... 740-245-7237 363 D
khaley@rio.edu
HALEY, Melissa ... 847-578-8756 147 I
melissa.haley@rosalindfranklin.edu
HALEY, Ted ... 508-767-7215 205 D
thaley@assumption.edu
HALEY, Terence ... 256-824-6674 .... 8 B
terence.haley@uah.edu
HALEY-THOMSON, Lisa 518-454-5239 296 H
thomsonl@strose.edu
HALFMANN, Tina ... 612-351-0631 236 D
thalfmann@ipr.edu
HALGREN, Cara ... 701-777-2724 345 C
cara.halgren@und.edu
HALIBURTON, Tori ... 731-265-1709 420 I
thaliburton@lanecollege.edu
HALICKI, Shannon, D ... 304-336-8075 490 F
shalicki@westliberty.edu
HALIEMUN, Cynthia ... 217-228-5432 146 F
haliecy@quincy.edu
HALING, Linda ... 920-424-1234 497 B
HALKIAS, Carlesha ... 717-477-1161 395 E
cghalkias@ship.edu
HALKITIS, Perry, N ... 732-235-9700 282 A
perry.halkitis@rutgers.edu
HALKITIS, Perry, N ... 732-235-9700 282 B
perry.halkitis@rutgers.edu
HALL, Allyson ... 860-465-5283 .. 84 J
hallall@easternct.edu
HALL, Amber, L ... 501-450-3663 .. 23 H
amberh@uca.edu
HALL, Amy ... 225-214-6979 186 F
amy.hall@franu.edu
HALL, Anders, W ... 615-322-2451 428 D
anders.hall@vanderbilt.edu
HALL, Andy ... 423-585-6801 426 C
andy.hall@ws.edu
HALL, Andy ... 423-585-6801 426 C
robert.hall@ws.edu
HALL, Andy ... 425-889-5212 482 F
andy.hall@northwestu.edu
HALL, Ann ... 989-463-7411 220 H
hall@alma.edu
HALL, Benjamin ... 740-362-3448 356 D
bhall@mtso.edu
HALL, Bobby, L ... 806-291-3401 457 J
hallb@wbu.edu
HALL, Brad, R ... 406-338-5441 263 B
brad@bfcc.edu
HALL, Brian ... 207-768-2707 194 J
nbhall@nmcc.edu
HALL, Brian ... 312-850-7899 134 H
bhall44@ccc.edu
HALL, Bryan ... 303-964-6835 .. 82 E
bhall002@regis.edu
HALL, Bubba ... 307-685-0821 502 F
rhall@sheridan.edu
HALL, Carol ... 860-515-3889 .. 84 G
chall@charteroak.edu
HALL, Carol ... 860-515-3880 .. 84 G
chall@charteroak.edu
HALL, Carrie, M ... 510-430-2050 .. 52 D
cmilliga@mills.edu
HALL, Cassie ... 406-447-4572 263 C
chall@carroll.edu
HALL, Cheryl ... 985-549-5312 192 D
chall@selu.edu
HALL, Chris ... 618-537-6833 143 B
chall@mckendree.edu
HALL, Christopher ... 803-793-5101 409 C
hallch@denmarktech.edu
HALL, Cynthia ... 530-283-0202 .. 42 H
chall@frc.edu
HALL, Daniel, B ... 323-241-5467 .. 49 D
halldb@lasc.edu
HALL, Danielle ... 517-371-5140 233 A
halld@cooley.edu
HALL, David ... 340-693-1000 514 E
dhall@uvi.edu
HALL, David, A ... 417-836-8444 256 E
dhall@missouristate.edu
HALL, Deborah, P ... 706-880-8232 121 A
dhall4@lagrange.edu
HALL, Dennis ... 817-531-4870 451 E
HALL, Dennis ... 817-531-6504 451 E
dhall@txwes.edu
HALL, Derek ... 906-227-2716 228 F
halld@nmu.edu
HALL, Devon ... 910-410-1912 337 B
dghall@richmondcc.edu
HALL, Donald ... 585-273-5000 323 J
donald.hall@rochester.edu
HALL, Elizabeth ... 856-415-2228 281 D
ehall@rcgc.edu
HALL, Frank ... 603-428-2320 273 H
fhall@nec.edu
HALL, Gene ... 503-517-1119 377 G
ghall@warnerpacific.edu
HALL, Gregory ... 860-444-8624 504 F
gregory.hall@uscga.edu
HALL, Gwen ... 304-724-3700 487 E
ghall@apus.edu
HALL, Gwenn ... 318-345-9126 187 G
ghall@ladelta.edu
HALL, Haley ... 803-535-1255 411 G
hallht@octech.edu
HALL, Hollie, M ... 607-587-4200 320 C
hallhm@alfredstate.edu
HALL, Jack, C ... 386-312-4293 106 C
jackhall@sjrstate.edu
HALL, Jackie ... 606-487-3180 181 C
jackie.hall@kctcs.edu
HALL, James ... 520-515-5329 .. 11 M
bohall@cochise.edu
HALL, James ... 262-650-4844 492 E
jkhall@carrollu.edu
HALL, James, R ... 864-597-4351 414 H
halljr@wofford.edu
HALL, Jami ... 706-272-4428 117 C
jhall@daltonstate.edu
HALL, Jason ... 910-893-1291 327 E
hallj@campbell.edu
HALL, Jeffrey ... 229-317-6731 113 H
jeffrey.hall@asurams.edu
HALL, Jeffrey, B ... 706-419-1121 117 B
hall@covenant.edu
HALL, Jennifer ... 334-222-6591 .... 2 I
jmh@lbwcc.edu
HALL, Jennifer ... 330-829-6644 363 B
halljene@mountunion.edu
HALL, Jessica ... 478-934-3458 121 F
jessica.hall@mga.edu
HALL, Jessica ... 614-251-4372 358 G
hallj@ohiodominican.edu
HALL, Jill ... 863-297-1072 105 A
jhall@polk.edu
HALL, Jim ... 479-619-4182 .. 20 D
jhall@nwacc.edu
HALL, Jim ... 631-420-2457 321 B
jim.hall@farmingdale.edu
HALL, JoAnn ... 920-922-8611 500 C
jhall@morainepark.edu
HALL, John, A ... 214-768-3518 444 E
jhall@smu.edu
HALL, John, D ... 817-272-2102 454 J
jhall@uta.edu
HALL, Jon Mark ... 812-464-1846 161 E
jmhall@usi.edu
HALL, Joseph, C ... 757-823-8675 469 F
jchall@nsu.edu
HALL, Joy Lin ... 918-343-7541 369 F
jhall@rsu.edu
HALL, Juanita ... 805-493-3951 .. 29 H
jahall@callutheran.edu
HALL, Karla ... 502-213-2507 181 F
karla.hall@kctcs.edu
HALL, Karyn ... 936-468-3806 445 F
khall@sfasu.edu
HALL, Katherine ... 425-564-2810 478 F
katherine.hall@bellevuecollege.edu
HALL, Katie ... 614-292-8914 358 I
hall.738@osu.edu
HALL, Kellie, M ... 701-477-7862 347 A
kmhall@tm.edu
HALL, Kelly ... 760-776-7344 .. 39 A
khall@collegeofthedesert.edu
HALL, Kenneth ... 570-484-2598 395 B
khall@lockhaven.edu
HALL, Kevin ... 706-886-6831 125 D
khall@tfc.edu
HALL, Kevin ... 651-603-6165 235 F
khall@csp.edu
HALL, Kim ... 360-416-7601 485 A
kim.hall@skagit.edu
HALL, Kim, B ... 865-251-1800 424 A
khall@south.edu
HALL, Kristin, E ... 845-758-7531 290 G
hall@bard.edu
HALL, Kristy ... 276-523-2400 475 A
khall@mecc.edu
HALL, Lareese, M ... 207-859-5100 193 E
lareese.hall@colby.edu
HALL, Lasella ... 508-999-9220 211 F
lhall1@umassd.edu
HALL, Lataria ... 559-442-8267 .. 66 E
lataria.hall@fresnocitycollege.edu
HALL, Lawrence ... 860-832-2298 .. 84 I
halllaw@ccsu.edu
HALL, Lemond ... 850-201-6652 111 C
halla@tcc.fl.edu
HALL, Les ... 803-545-5048 413 C
les.hall@uscmed.sc.edu
HALL, Linda ... 434-544-8126 472 G
hall.l@lynchburg.edu
HALL, Linda, M ... 585-292-2103 307 H
lhall38@monroecc.edu
HALL, Lisa ... 423-236-2900 424 B
lisahall@southern.edu
HALL, Lori ... 207-741-5501 195 A
lhall@smccme.edu
HALL, Lori ... 503-594-3162 372 D
lori.hall@clackamas.edu
HALL, Lydia ... 803-327-8000 415 A
lhall@yorktech.edu
HALL, Lydia ... 936-294-3608 450 C
lth003@shsu.edu
HALL, Lyndon ... 252-257-1900 338 F
halll@vgcc.edu
HALL, Lynn ... 812-866-7385 155 C
hall@hanover.edu
HALL, Marilee ... 801-290-3240 459 E
marilee.hall@indepence.edu
HALL, Mark ... 919-545-8043 333 C
mhall@cccc.edu
HALL, Mark ... 918-495-7742 368 I
mhall@oru.edu
HALL, Marlon, R ... 530-251-8820 .. 47 F
mhall@lassencollege.edu
HALL, Mary ... 828-232-5109 342 C
mhall7@unca.edu
HALL, Matthew ... 805-893-8989 .. 70 A
matthall@ucsb.edu
HALL, Matthew ... 502-897-4897 184 C
mhall@sbts.edu
HALL, Matthew ... 502-897-4043 184 C
mhall@sbts.edu
HALL, Maurice ... 609-771-1855 276 I
hallmau@tcnj.edu
HALL, Michael ... 302-736-2483 .. 90 G
j.michael.hall@wesley.edu
HALL, Michael, R ... 336-841-9235 329 G
mhall@highpoint.edu
HALL, Michael, W ... 540-654-1635 472 I
mhall2@umw.edu
HALL, Micheal ... 770-426-2829 121 C
micheal.hall@life.edu
HALL, Michelle ... 404-364-8336 122 J
mhall@oglethorpe.edu
HALL, Michelle ... 620-278-4211 177 B
mhall@sterling.edu
HALL, Michelle ... 985-549-2077 192 D
mhall@selu.edu
HALL, Myrna ... 303-458-4160 .. 82 E
mhall004@regis.edu
HALL, Nicole ... 312-629-6100 148 I
nhall1@saic.edu
HALL, Nicole ... 336-334-4174 343 A
nrhall@uncg.edu
HALL, Norma ... 317-788-3206 161 B
hallne@uindy.edu
HALL, Norman, D ... 530-226-4130 .. 63 K
nhall@simpsonu.edu
HALL, Otis ... 718-517-7730 315 A
ohall@edaff.com
HALL, Pamela ... 313-845-6410 224 G
phall@hfcc.edu
HALL, Patricia ... 479-394-7622 .. 23 C
phall@uarichmountain.edu
HALL, Paulakay ... 423-775-7308 418 H
phall7036@bryan.edu
HALL, Persephone ... 860-439-2646 .. 86 H
phall3@conncoll.edu
HALL, Philip, D ... 843-792-8979 410 F
hallpd@musc.edu
HALL, Rachel ... 501-882-8912 .. 17 F
HALL, Rachelle ... 623-845-3235 .. 13 C
rachelle.hall@gccaz.edu
HALL, Randolph, W ... 213-740-6709 .. 72 B
rwhall@usc.edu
HALL, Raymond, D ... 810-762-3335 231 G
raydhall@umich.edu
HALL, Rebecca, S ... 269-337-7090 225 D
rebecca.hall@kzoo.edu
HALL, Renardo, A ... 717-871-5840 395 D
renardo.hall@millersville.edu
HALL, Renee ... 662-621-4858 245 E
rsanford@coahomacc.edu
HALL, Ricardo ... 610-758-3890 388 J
rih217@lehigh.edu
HALL, Rickey ... 206-685-0518 485 F
vpomad@uw.edu
HALL, Robert ... 716-829-7657 298 F
hallrm@dyc.edu
HALL, Robert ... 512-223-1053 431 A
robert.hall@austincc.edu
HALL, Rodney ... 804-524-2954 477 B
rhall@vsu.edu
HALL, Ron ... 865-251-1800 424 A
rhall@south.edu
HALL, Ryan ... 701-788-4706 345 E
ryan.o.hall@mayvillestate.edu
HALL, Sandy ... 325-674-2273 429 B
halls@acu.edu
HALL, Seth ... 318-345-9359 187 G
sethhall2@ladelta.edu
HALL, Steven ... 309-341-7823 141 A
shall@knox.edu
HALL, Steven, A ... 617-358-0476 207 D
sahall@bu.edu
HALL, Susan ... 856-415-2185 281 D
shall@rcgc.edu
HALL, Susan, L ... 585-292-2179 307 H
shall60@monroecc.edu
HALL, Tami ... 870-307-7203 .. 20 A
tami.hall@lyon.edu
HALL, Tammy ... 501-279-8756 .. 19 D
thall@harding.edu
HALL, Tammy ... 575-461-4413 286 E
tammyh@mesalands.edu
HALL, Taylor ... 509-865-8613 481 G
hall_t@heritage.edu
HALL, Teri ... 316-978-3021 178 A
teri.hall@wichita.edu
HALL, Terry ... 225-771-2552 191 A
thall@sulc.edu

HAMILTON, Marty .... 423-236-2806 424 B
mlhamil@southern.edu
HAMILTON, Maryanne .. 563-386-3570 166 A
mhamilton@hamiltontechcollege.com
HAMILTON, Matthew .... 276-326-4602 465 B
mhamilton@bluefield.edu
HAMILTON, Michael ..... 757-240-2206 471 A
michael.hamilton@rivhs.com
HAMILTON, Michelle .... 618-985-3741 139 I
michellehamilton@jalc.edu
HAMILTON, Nardos ...... 516-572-7759 308 A
nardos.hamilton@ncc.edu
HAMILTON, Richard ...... 360-442-2263 482 B
rhamilton@lowercolumbia.edu
HAMILTON, Rick .... 601-477-4189 246 F
rick.hamilton@jcjc.edu
HAMILTON, Ronald .... 304-434-8000 489 A
ron.hamilton@easternwv.edu
HAMILTON, Roy .... 219-989-2779 159 G
rhamilt@pnw.edu
HAMILTON, Salina .... 386-481-2628.. 95 F
hamiltonsd@cookman.edu
HAMILTON, Shadel .... 813-221-6302 106 D
shadel.hamilton@saintleo.edu
HAMILTON, Sharalyn .... 909-447-2535.. 37 F
shamilton@cst.edu
HAMILTON, Shelley ...... 760-921-5483.. 55 H
shamilton@paloverde.edu
HAMILTON, Tina .... 201-216-9901 277 D
tina.hamilton@eicollege.edu
HAMILTON, Tina .... 512-313-3000 434 E
tina.hamilton@concordia.edu
HAMILTON-GOLDEN,
Barbara .... 201-447-7113 275 H
bagolden@bergen.edu
HAMILTON-HONEY,
Emily .... 315-386-7071 320 E
hamiltone@canton.edu
HAMILTON SLANE,
Sandra .... 530-242-7799.. 63 H
sslane@shastacollege.edu
HAMLETT, Rebecca .... 816-415-7620 262 F
hamlettr@william.jewell.edu
HAMLETT, Tiffany .... 816-995-2844 258 F
tiffany.hamlett@researchcollege.edu
HAMLETT, Willie .... 626-815-3890.. 26 H
whamlett@apu.edu
HAMLIN, John .... 337-550-1233 189 A
jhamlin@lsue.edu
HAMLIN, Kelly .... 828-652-0629 336 B
khamlin@mcdowelltech.edu
HAMLIN, Lindsey .... 605-688-4154 417 C
lindsey.hamlin@sdstate.edu
HAMLIN, Toby .... 518-608-8218 299 G
thamlin@excelsior.edu
HAMM, Bernard, C .... 804-828-1233 473 F
bchamm2@vcu.edu
HAMM, Darryl .... 562-951-4500.. 31 D
dhamm@calstate.edu
HAMM, Doug .... 920-693-1648 499 G
douglas.hamm@gotoltc.edu
HAMM, Jennifer .... 828-327-7000 333 B
jhamm@cvcc.edu
HAMM, Jolene .... 434-961-5301 475 F
jhamm@pvcc.edu
HAMM, K. Joy .... 941-487-5000 109 D
jhamm@ncf.edu
HAMM, Kimberly .... 215-885-2360 389 F
khamm@manor.edu
HAMM, Lee, L .... 504-988-5462 191 B
lhamm@tulane.edu
HAMM, Leonard .... 410-951-3906 203 D
lhamm@coppin.edu
HAMM, Michelle .... 404-471-5443 113 G
mhamm@agnesscott.edu
HAMM, Rod .... 620-947-3121 177 C
rodneyhamm@tabor.edu
HAMMACK, Brian .... 641-683-4270 166 C
HAMMACK, Mike .... 325-670-1278 437 F
mhammack@hsutx.edu
HAMMAN, John .... 240-567-7794 200 C
john.hamman@montgomerycollege.edu
HAMMAR, Matt .... 503-554-2162 373 C
mhammar@georgefox.edu
HAMMAT, Jennifer, R ... 812-464-1862 161 E
jhammat@usi.edu
HAMMEKE, Curtis .... 785-628-4050 173 B
chammeke@fhsu.edu
HAMMEL, Nicole .... 484-664-3163 391 C
nicolehammel@muhlenberg.edu
HAMMEL, Rachel .... 330-490-7452 364 B
rhammel@walsh.edu
HAMMELL, Rebecca, J .. 717-245-1858 382 F
hammellr@dickinson.edu

HAMMER, Adam .... 320-308-3151 240 H
aehammer@stcloudstate.edu
HAMMER, Amanda .... 575-461-4413 286 E
amandah@mesalands.edu
HAMMER, Bradley, C .... 419-434-6922 363 A
hammer@findlay.edu
HAMMER, Brian .... 802-257-7751 463 C
brian.hammer@sit.edu
HAMMER, Debbie .... 610-989-1200 402 B
dhammer@vfmac.edu
HAMMER, Elizabeth ...... 504-520-5141 193 A
eyhammer@xula.edu
HAMMER, Jaime, S ...... 334-844-5176.... 4 E
jsh0073@auburn.edu
HAMMER, Joyce .... 360-623-8486 479 C
HAMMER, Kimberley, A 412-578-6294 380 E
kahammer@carlow.edu
HAMMER, Larry .... 828-227-7232 344 A
hammer@wcu.edu
HAMMER, Melanie .... 516-572-7775 308 A
melanie.hammer@ncc.edu
HAMMERMAN,
Adam, D .... 914-594-4570 309 H
adam_hammerman@nymc.edu
HAMMERSEN, Frederick 301-243-2183 503 J
frederick.hammersen@dodiis.mil
HAMMERSLEY, Lisa ...... 916-278-4655.. 32 E
hammersley@csus.edu
HAMMES, Meg .... 563-387-1375 167 E
hammma01@luther.edu
HAMMETT, Amy, S .... 216-368-4318 349 F
registrar@case.edu
HAMMETT, Becky .... 870-460-1050.. 22 D
hammettb@uamont.edu
HAMMETT, Fred .... 919-530-7775 342 A
fhammett@nccu.edu
HAMMETT, Maria, A ..... 478-301-2226 121 E
hammett_ma@mercer.edu
HAMMETT, Steve .... 216-421-7000 350 M
shammett@cia.edu
HAMMILL, Graham, L ... 716-645-3786 316 F
ghammill@buffalo.edu
HAMMILL, Viv .... 406-449-9166 263 K
vhammill@montana.edu
HAMMING, Jeanne .... 318-869-5240 186 B
jhamming@centenary.edu
HAMMITT, Stephanie .... 218-879-0804 238 A
shammitt@fdltcc.edu
HAMMOCK, Susan .... 478-240-5162 122 G
shammock@oftc.edu
HAMMON, Kyle .... 360-442-2551 482 B
khammon@lowercolumbia.edu
HAMMOND, Brad .... 541-881-5599 377 B
bhammond@tvcc.cc
HAMMOND, Brady .... 307-772-4245 502 D
bhammond@lccc.wy.edu
HAMMOND, Caroline .... 870-864-7102.. 21 B
chammond@southark.edu
HAMMOND, Charles ...... 646-378-6131 310 G
charles.hammond@nyack.edu
HAMMOND, Charles, A 302-225-6352.. 90 E
hammond@gbc.edu
HAMMOND, Christine ... 816-995-2856 258 F
christine.hammond@researchcollege.edu
HAMMOND,
Christine, M .... 989-386-6602 227 F
chammond@midmich.edu
HAMMOND, Dale .... 509-777-3730 486 I
dhammond@whitworth.edu
HAMMOND, Debbie .... 843-953-7408 408 E
hammonddd@cofc.edu
HAMMOND, Denise ...... 870-584-1118.. 22 G
dhammond@cccua.edu
HAMMOND, Erin .... 314-256-8808 250 D
hammond@ai.edu
HAMMOND, Jaime .... 203-575-8022.. 86 B
jhammond@nv.edu
HAMMOND, Jeff .... 601-266-5001 249 F
jeff.hammond@usm.edu
HAMMOND, Jeremy ...... 909-748-8273.. 71 G
jeremy_hammond@redlands.edu
HAMMOND, Jerome ...... 423-614-8310 420 J
jhammond@leeunivieristy.edu
HAMMOND, Karen, S ... 240-500-2241 198 H
kshammond@hagerstowncc.edu
HAMMOND, Ken .... 573-876-7299 260 F
khammond@stephens.edu
HAMMOND, Mark .... 910-893-1211 327 E
hammond@campbell.edu
HAMMOND, Meg .... 802-322-1685 462 C
meg.hammond@goddard.edu
HAMMOND, Michael ...... 765-998-5203 160 F
mchammond@taylor.edu

HAMMOND, Michelle ... 620-341-5208 172 L
mhammon2@emporia.edu
HAMMOND, Mike .... 803-535-1267 411 G
hammondm@octech.edu
HAMMOND, Troy, D ...... 630-637-5454 144 H
tdhammond@noctrl.edu
HAMMOND, Vanessa .... 423-614-8511 420 J
vhammond@leeuniversity.edu
HAMMOND NASS,
Holly .... 207-602-2306 196 G
hnass@une.edu
HAMMONDS, David ...... 936-294-2709 450 C
david.hammonds@shsu.edu
HAMMONDS, Diane, M 610-526-1409 378 G
diane.hammonds@theamericancollege.edu
HAMMONDS, Jennifer .. 270-745-5030 185 E
jennifer.hammonds@wku.edu
HAMMONDS, Luke .... 601-477-4058 246 F
luke.hammonds@jcjc.edu
HAMMONS, Stacy .... 765-677-3061 157 D
stacy.hammons@indwes.edu
HAMMONTREE, Tonya .. 501-205-8809.. 18 H
thammontree@cbc.edu
HAMMS, Gavin .... 318-274-6328 191 E
hammsg@gram.edu
HAMNER, Elise .... 541-888-7211 376 F
elise.hamner@socc.edu
HAMNER, Mark, S .... 940-898-3013 451 F
mhamner@twu.edu
HAMPEL-KOZAR, Vesna 612-624-9545 243 E
hampe004@umn.edu
HAMPSHIRE, Audrey, N 260-982-5036 158 T
anhampshire@manchester.edu
HAMPSON, Bill .... 816-995-2818 258 F
bill.hampson@researchcollege.edu
HAMPTON, Aletha .... 334-229-4250.... 4 B
dhampton@alasu.edu
HAMPTON, Brian .... 580-559-5225 366 C
bridham@ecok.edu
HAMPTON, Carl .... 608-890-3273 496 B
champton@uwsa.edu
HAMPTON, Diane .... 870-733-6880.. 17 H
dhampton@asumidsouth.edu
HAMPTON, Franki .... 540-453-2285 474 B
hamptonf@brcc.edu
HAMPTON, Iyisha .... 334-244-3674.... 4 F
ihampton@aum.edu
HAMPTON, Jarvis, D .... 806-651-3451 448 C
jhampton@wtamu.edu
HAMPTON, Joyce .... 413-265-2423 208 C
hamptonj@elms.edu
HAMPTON, Julie .... 309-649-6201 150 A
julie.hampton@src.edu
HAMPTON, Lacy .... 210-486-2178 429 G
lhampton14@alamo.edu
HAMPTON, Lee .... 517-787-0800 225 C
hamptonleem@jccmi.edu
HAMPTON, Logan, C .... 731-426-7595 420 I
lhampton@lanecollege.edu
HAMPTON, Marie .... 925-485-5233.. 35 O
mhampton@clpccd.org
HAMPTON, Mark .... 516-686-7925 309 F
mark.hampton@nyit.edu
HAMPTON, Michael ...... 503-883-2442 373 H
mhampton@linfield.edu
HAMPTON, Nancy .... 806-651-2116 448 C
nhampton@wtamu.edu
HAMPTON, Renee .... 417-667-8181 252 A
rhampton@cottey.edu
HAMPTON, Tabatha ...... 870-762-3121.. 17 D
thampton@smail.anc.edu
HAMPTON, Terri .... 951-222-8589.. 58 F
terri.hampton@rccd.edu
HAMPTON, Todd .... 626-585-7162.. 55 K
tjhampton@pasadena.edu
HAMPTON, Victoria .... 860-768-4296.. 88 H
vhampton@hartford.edu
HAMPTON, William .... 903-730-4890 438 H
whampton@jarvis.edu
HAMRICK, David, S ...... 512-232-7604 455 A
dhamrick@utpress.utexas.edu
HAMRICK, Elizabeth ...... 704-290-5251 337 I
ehamrick@spcc.edu
HAMRICK, Jeff .... 415-422-6136.. 71 K
jhamrick@usfca.edu
HAMRICK, Mike .... 304-696-5408 490 D
hamrickm@marshall.edu
HAMRICK, Robin, G ..... 704-406-3996 329 A
rhamrick@gardner-webb.edu
HAMSTRA, Brent .... 423-236-2203 424 B
bhamstra@southern.edu
HAMZE, Cathrine .... 510-356-4760.. 76 E

HAN, Anna .... 408-554-4362.. 62 D
ahan@scu.edu
HAN, David, S .... 423-478-7524 423 G
dhan@ptseminary.edu
HAN, Jenjen .... 407-888-8689.. 98 R
jhan@fcim.edu
HAN, Ki Won .... 714-527-0691.. 42 E
HAN, Luoheng .... 205-348-4890.... 7 G
luoheng.han@ua.edu
HAN, Peter .... 303-273-3131.. 78 I
phan@mines.edu
HAN, Woo Jin .... 714-533-1495.. 64 D
whan@southbaylo.edu
HAN, Yuan-Yuan .... 407-888-8689.. 98 R
y2han@fcim.edu
HANADA, Karen .... 808-984-3527 129 E
tkhanada@hawaii.edu
HANADA,
Tamone Karen .... 808-984-3527 129 E
tkhanada@hawaii.edu
HANAK, Lesley .... 912-525-5000 123 G
lhanak@scad.edu
HANAVAN, Laura .... 816-415-7804 262 F
hanavanl@william.jewell.edu
HANBURY, II,
George, L .... 954-262-7575 103 M
hanbury@nsu.nova.edu
HANBURY, John .... 276-656-0205 475 D
jhanbury@patrickhenry.edu
HANCE, JR., James, H . 401-598-1000 404 I
HANCHETT, James .... 757-594-7699 466 B
jim.hanchett@cnu.edu
HANCKS, Jeffrey .... 309-298-1929 152 D
jl-hancks@wiu.edu
HANCOCK, Barry .... 618-985-3741 139 I
barryhancock@jalc.edu
HANCOCK, Blair .... 336-838-6128 339 B
bmhancock168@wilkescc.edu
HANCOCK, Darryl .... 478-827-3857 118 A
darryl.hancock@fvsu.edu
HANCOCK, Daryl, R .... 618-537-6870 143 B
drhancock@mckendree.edu
HANCOCK, Heather .... 918-595-7842 370 E
heather.hancock@tulsacc.edu
HANCOCK, John .... 713-500-7356 456 B
john.f.hancock@uth.tmc.edu
HANCOCK, John .... 503-768-7160 373 G
hancock@lclark.edu
HANCOCK, Lua .... 386-822-7343 111 A
lhancock@stetson.edu
HANCOCK, Mara .... 510-594-5080.. 28 D
mhancock@cca.edu
HANCOCK, Marcia .... 410-864-4000 201 F
HANCOCK, Merodie, A . 609-984-1105 284 B
president@tesu.edu
HANCOCK, Shannon ...... 913-253-5084 176 I
shannon.hancock@spst.edu
HANCOCK, Wanda .... 229-225-5089 125 A
whancock@southernregional.edu
HANCOX, Robert, E ...... 610-892-1578 393 J
rhancox@pit.edu
HAND, Christie .... 304-358-2000 488 A
christie@future.edu
HAND, David .... 601-968-8703 245 C
dhand@belhaven.edu
HAND, Jason .... 215-751-8806 382 A
jhand@ccp.edu
HAND, Jeffrey .... 856-256-5186 281 E
handj@rowan.edu
HAND, Kelli .... 704-637-4416 328 A
kmhand@catawba.edu
HAND, Mary .... 518-743-2248 320 D
handm@sunyacc.edu
HAND, Mike .... 503-370-6868 378 B
mhand@willamette.edu
HAND, Natalie .... 484-664-3804 391 C
nataliehand@muhlenberg.edu
HAND, Theresa .... 518-244-2301 313 D
handt@sage.edu
HANDCOX, Jenelle .... 910-521-6255 343 B
jenelle.handcox@uncp.edu
HANDEL, Albert .... 509-527-2343 485 H
albert.handel@wallawalla.edu
HANDEL, Greg .... 318-357-5361 192 C
handelg@nsula.edu
HANDELSMAN, Sharon . 410-532-5105 201 B
shandelsman@ndm.edu
HANDFIELD, Sandy .... 321-433-5502.. 97 I
handfields@easternflorida.edu
HANDFORD, Ann .... 262-524-7211 492 E
ahandfor@carrollu.edu
HANDLER, Brittany .... 303-751-8700.. 77 A
handler@bel-rea.com

HANDLER, Lisa, M 414-410-4207 492 D lmhandler@stritch.edu
HANDLEY, Kristen 907-796-6100 10 B
HANDOJO, Jeanne 626-584-5366 43 H jeanne@fuller.edu
HANDS, Ashanti 619-388-2678 60 D ahands@sdccd.edu
HANDS, Colette 847-635-7675 145 G chands@oakton.edu
HANDWERK, Phil 336-758-5244 344 D handwepg@wfu.edu
HANDWORK, David 870-972-2066 17 G dhandwork@astate.edu
HANDY, Cromwell 334-229-4309 4 B chandy@alasu.edu
HANDY, Cynthia, H 404-752-1654 122 E cynthia@msm.edu
HANDY, Linda, B 317-788-3349 161 B handy@uindy.edu
HANDY, Maisha 404-527-7705 120 K mhandy@itc.edu
HANDY, Ty, J 502-213-2121 181 F ty.handy@kctcs.edu
HANDYSIDE, David 920-206-2345 493 L david.handyside@mbu.edu
HANDYSIDES, Robert 909-558-4683 48 C rhandysides@llu.edu
HANDZLIK, Diane, M 716-896-0700 324 E dianeh@villa.edu
HANDZLIK, Summer, L 716-888-3145 292 D handzlis@canisius.edu
HANEFIELD, Robert 580-581-2417 365 G rhanefield@cameron.edu
HANELLY, William 570-484-2002 395 B whanelly@lockhaven.edu
HANES, Barbara 484-840-4604 391 D hanesb@neumann.edu
HANES, Billie 919-530-5086 342 A bhanes@nccu.edu
HANES, Carol 903-875-7594 440 G carol.hanes@navarrocollege.edu
HANES, Jonathan 414-229-3305 497 A jmhanes@uwm.edu
HANES, Julie 336-721-2600 340 D
HANES, Mackenzie 859-846-5385 183 E mhanes@midway.edu
HANES, Madlyn, L 814-863-0327 392 B mqh3@psu.edu
HANES, Rick 937-778-8600 352 J rhanes@edisonohio.edu
HANES-GOODLANDER, Lisa 651-846-1383 241 B lisa.hanes@saintpaul.edu
HANES-RAMOS, Melanie 843-208-8023 413 E hanesml@uscb.edu
HANEWICZ, Cheryl, A 801-863-6539 461 A hanewich@uvu.edu
HANEY, Ashley 281-649-3650 437 H ahaney@hbu.edu
HANEY, Asia 512-505-3023 438 E aehaney@htu.edu
HANEY, Cindy, M 610-799-1122 388 I chaney1@lccc.edu
HANEY, David 931-526-3660 420 A david.haney@fortisinstitute.edu
HANEY, Frank 913-234-0788 172 E frank.haney@cleveland.edu
HANEY, Genelle 770-426-2725 121 C genelle.haney@life.edu
HANEY, Lee Anna 828-694-1885 332 E leeannah@blueridge.edu
HANEY, Michele 303-914-6215 82 C michele.haney@rrcc.edu
HANEY, Mychail 209-476-7840 66 G mhaney@clc.edu
HANEY, Pamela 708-974-5204 144 C haney@morainevalley.edu
HANEY, Regina 806-457-4200 436 G rhaney@fpctx.edu
HANEY, Rich 480-461-7300 13 D richard.haney@mesacc.edu
HANF, Stuart, J 302-327-4894 90 I stuart.j.hanf@wilmu.edu
HANFORD, Thomas 607-753-4702 318 D thomas.hanford@cortland.edu
HANG, Ducha 401-456-8845 405 C dhang@ric.edu
HANG, Foua 920-693-1387 499 G foua.hang@gotoltc.edu
HANG, Phillip 734-432-5662 227 A phang@madonna.edu
HANG, Phillip 248-645-3300 223 A
HANGEN, Susan 201-684-7407 280 H shangen@ramapo.edu
HANIFIN, Martin 785-227-3380 171 E hanifinmj@bethanylb.edu
HANIFIN, Sheila 413-782-1628 219 F shanifin@wne.edu
HANINCIK, Amanda 610-921-7529 378 C ahanincik@albright.edu
HANKEN, Tamera 504-520-5083 193 A thanken@xula.edu
HANKERSON, Brian 954-486-7728 112 D bhankersoncfo@uftl.edu
HANKERSON, Kimberly 850-599-3491 108 I kimberly.hankerson@famu.edu
HANKERSON, Reggie 662-621-4231 245 E rhankerson@coahomacc.edu
HANKES, Doug 334-844-5123 4 E hankedm@auburn.edu
HANKINS, Jeff 501-660-1004 17 E jhankins@asusystem.edu
HANKINS, Kim 815-455-8778 143 A khankins@mchenry.edu
HANKINS, Orlando, E 919-516-4860 340 C oehankins@st-aug.edu
HANKINS, Paul 479-788-7431 21 H paul.hankins@uafs.edu
HANKS, SR., Keith 402-878-2380 267 E keith.hanks@littlepriest.edu
HANKS, Mary 205-652-3668 9 A mhanks@uwa.edu
HANKS, Sharon 928-757-0879 14 F shanks@mohave.edu
HANLEY, Christian 843-863-7517 407 E chanley@csuniv.edu
HANLEY, Darla, S 617-747-2664 206 E dhanley@berklee.edu
HANLEY, James 215-204-5578 399 F sm693@bncollege.com
HANLEY, Madalyn 718-489-5468 313 H mhanley@sfc.edu
HANLEY, Peggy 318-274-6546 191 E peggy@gram.edu
HANLEY, Rodney, S 906-635-2202 226 E rhanley@lssu.edu
HANLEY, Theodore 713-718-8566 437 I theodore.hanley@hccs.edu
HANLEY-MAXWELL, Cheryl 217-333-6677 151 D cherylhm@illinois.edu
HANLON, Chris 610-921-7264 378 C chanlon@albright.edu
HANLON, Erin 617-322-3531 210 F erin_hanlon@laboure.edu
HANLON, Philip, J 603-646-2223 273 E philip.j.hanlon@dartmouth.edu
HANLON, Susan 330-972-7442 362 B hanlon@uakron.edu
HANNA, Aaron 210-431-3335 443 A ahanna1@stmarytx.edu
HANNA, Bashar, W 570-389-4526 394 A bhanna@bloomu.edu
HANNA, Bryce 970-943-2126 84 D bhanna@western.edu
HANNA, Chris 616-432-3407 229 I chris.hanna@prts.edu
HANNA, Dorothy 785-833-4468 175 B dahanna@kwu.edu
HANNA, Jandy 304-647-6366 491 A jhanna@osteo.wvsom.edu
HANNA, Jenette 620-441-5214 172 I jenette.hanna@cowley.edu
HANNA, Kim 931-372-3203 426 E khanna@tntech.edu
HANNA, Kimberly 575-461-4413 286 E kimberlyh@mesalands.edu
HANNA, Mae 513-732-5332 362 F mae.hanna@uc.edu
HANNA, Mark 708-239-4705 150 F mark.hanna@trnty.edu
HANNA, Patricia 610-861-7874 391 A hannap@moravian.edu
HANNA, Randy 850-770-2102 109 C rhanna@fsu.edu
HANNA, Tara 419-517-8908 355 K thanna@lourdes.edu
HANNAFIN, Robert 203-254-4250 86 I rhannafin@fairfield.edu
HANNAFORD, Bo, S 580-327-8406 367 E bshannaford@nwosu.edu
HANNAFORD, Erin, E 717-867-6071 388 H hannafor@lvc.edu
HANNAFORD, Tara 580-327-8540 367 E tlhannaford@nwosu.edu
HANNAH, Felisa 559-791-2316 47 A felisa.hannah@portervillecollege.edu
HANNAH, Katie 269-783-2185 230 F khannah@swmich.edu
HANNAH, Kimberly 413-265-2293 208 C hannahk@elms.edu
HANNAH, Marcus 334-876-9360 2 D marcus.hannah@wccs.edu
HANNAH, Russ 870-972-3303 17 G rhannah@astate.edu
HANNAH-JEFFERSON, Floressa 601-979-2127 246 E floressa.j.hannah-jefferson@jsums.edu
HANNAN, Christopher 319-291-2705 166 B christopher.hannan@hawkeyecollege.edu
HANNAN, James 315-445-4310 304 C hannanjp@lemoyne.edu
HANNAN, Michael 814-732-2729 394 F hannan@edinboro.edu
HANNAN, Steven, M 419-289-5007 348 A shannan@ashland.edu
HANNAR, Christine 636-949-4625 254 F channar@lindenwood.edu
HANNE, Benjamin, C 620-229-6371 177 A ben.hanne@sckans.edu
HANNEMAN, Richard 531-622-2739 267 H rhanneman@mccneb.edu
HANNES, Sarah 307-778-1178 502 D shannes@lccc.wy.edu
HANNIGAN, Robyn 315-268-6544 296 A rhanniga@clarkson.edu
HANNIGAN, Scott 501-279-4407 19 D shannigan@harding.edu
HANNING, Chris 610-430-4178 396 A channing@wcupa.edu
HANNMANN, Richard 518-608-8198 299 G mhannmann@excelsior.edu
HANNO, Dennis 508-286-8244 220 A hanno_dennis@wheatoncollege.edu
HANNON, Daniel 914-323-5253 305 J dan.hannon@mville.edu
HANNON, Dominic 716-878-4631 318 C
HANNON, James 330-672-0566 354 J jhannon5@kent.edu
HANNON, Jed 617-745-3581 208 G jed.hannon@enc.edu
HANNON, Jim, M 563-333-6359 169 A hannonjamesm@ambrose.sau.edu
HANNON, Lauretta 404-756-4666 114 G lhannon@atlm.edu
HANNON, Ron 408-848-4895 43 J rhannon@gavilan.edu
HANNUM, Joshua 520-795-0787 10 H president@asaom.edu
HANNUM, Natalie 925-473-7403 40 J nhannum@losmedanos.edu
HANOFEE, Rose 845-434-5750 322 A rhanofee@sunysullivan.edu
HANOLD, John, W 814-863-0768 392 B jhh6@psu.edu
HANRAHAN, Chelsea 603-428-2291 273 H chanrahan@nec.edu
HANRAHAN, Neil, S 212-998-4581 310 B nsh2@nyu.edu
HANRAHAN, Susan, N 870-972-3112 17 G hanrahan@astate.edu
HANRAHAN, Thomas 718-399-4308 311 J hanrahan@pratt.edu
HANRAHAN, Thomas, M 717-867-6030 388 H hanrahan@lvc.edu
HANS, Peter 919-807-6951 331 L hansp@nccommunitycolleges.edu
HANSARD, Jamie 806-742-1480 451 B jamie.hansard@ttu.edu
HANSBARGER, Tom 845-938-2715 504 H tom.hansbarger@usma.edu
HANSBURG, David 303-273-3300 78 I hansburg@mines.edu
HANSCOM, Marcus 401-254-3345 405 E mhanscom@rwu.edu
HANSEL, Marie, C 708-709-3542 146 D mhansel@prairiestate.edu
HANSEL, Travis 303-722-5724 80 L thansel@lincolntech.edu
HANSELMAN, Jennifer 413-572-8702 213 D jhanselman@westfield.ma.edu
HANSEN, Alan 801-290-3240 459 E alan.hansen@independence.edu
HANSEN, Anne, W 518-564-2090 319 C hansenaw@plattsburgh.edu
HANSEN, Blaine, J 828-898-8838 330 E hansenb@lmc.edu
HANSEN, Brandi 712-324-5061 168 G bhensen@nwicc.edu
HANSEN, Carl, F 707-826-3731 33 D ch1@humboldt.edu
HANSEN, Cheryl 402-494-2311 268 B chansen@thenicc.edu
HANSEN, Chris 423-236-2802 424 B chansen@southern.edu
HANSEN, Christian 207-453-5128 194 I chansen@kvcc.me.edu
HANSEN, Christine 419-372-6389 348 H hachris@bgsu.edu
HANSEN, Corinne 605-642-6215 416 I corinne.hansen@bhsu.edu
HANSEN, Craig 651-793-1727 238 H craig.hansen@metrostate.edu
HANSEN, David 605-367-7568 416 G dave.hansen@sdbor.edu
HANSEN, David 843-574-6021 413 B david.hansen@tridenttech.edu
HANSEN, Dean 662-915-1945 249 D dlhansen@olemiss.edu
HANSEN, Eric 432-264-5046 438 C ehansen@howardcollege.edu
HANSEN, Gregg 978-468-7111 209 G ghansen@gcts.edu
HANSEN, Jill 815-825-9517 140 F jhansen1@kish.edu
HANSEN, John 515-576-7201 166 E hansen_j@iowacentral.edu
HANSEN, John 307-532-8304 502 A john.hansen@ewc.wy.edu
HANSEN, Jon 308-432-6231 268 E jhansen@csc.edu
HANSEN, Jory 605-995-2151 415 C jory.hansen@dwu.edu
HANSEN, Karen 612-626-0051 243 E provost@umn.edu
HANSEN, Kathy 320-363-5307 235 C kghansen@csbsju.edu
HANSEN, Kenneth 402-559-5301 270 A hansenkl@unmc.edu
HANSEN, Kent, A 909-558-2644 48 C khansen@claysonlaw.com
HANSEN, Kevin 319-398-5625 167 C kevin.hansen@kirkwood.edu
HANSEN, Kristine 651-793-1300 238 H kristine.hansen@metrostate.edu
HANSEN, Lynn 407-823-2362 109 E lynn.hansen@ucf.edu
HANSEN, Mandy 719-255-7528 83 B mhansen2@uccs.edu
HANSEN, Marie 207-973-1081 194 A hansenm@my.husson.edu
HANSEN, Matt 563-333-6261 169 A hansenmattb@sau.edu
HANSEN, Micah 605-367-5550 417 D micah.hansen@southeasttech.edu
HANSEN, Michele, J 317-278-2618 156 F mjhansen@iupui.edu
HANSEN, Noah 619-594-4808 33 E nhansen@sdsu.edu
HANSEN, Patricia 417-865-2815 253 B hansenp@evangel.edu
HANSEN, Peter 210-436-3324 443 A phansen@stmarytx.edu
HANSEN, Richard 913-971-3381 175 G rdhanson@mnu.edu
HANSEN, Richard, A 334-844-8348 4 E rah0019@auburn.edu
HANSEN, Robin 414-382-6120 492 A robin.hansen@alverno.edu
HANSEN, Sharon 610-409-3175 402 A shansen@ursinus.edu
HANSEN, Shelley 530-541-4660 47 E hansen@ltcc.edu
HANSEN, Sherri 435-283-7251 461 C sherri.hansen@snow.edu
HANSEN, Steven 405-974-3773 370 K shansen8@uco.edu
HANSEN, Susan 860-727-6782 87 A shansen@goodwin.edu
HANSEN, Terry 432-264-5600 438 C thansen@howardcollege.edu
HANSEN, Zeynep 208-426-4010 129 I zeynephansen@boisestate.edu
HANSEN-KIEFFER, Kristin, M 717-796-5234 390 E khansen@messiah.edu
HANSENS-PASSERI, Catherine 410-651-9314 203 A chpasseri@umes.edu
HANSON, Andrew 208-792-2218 131 A ahanson@lcsc.edu

HANSON, Andrew .... 702-895-2267 271 E
andrew.hanson@unlv.edu
HANSON, Anita .... 218-879-0805 238 A
anita.hanson@fdltcc.edu
HANSON, Brenda .... 406-756-3812 263 F
bhanson@fvcc.edu
HANSON, Charlene .... 401-841-6541 503 L
charlene.hanson@usnwc.edu
HANSON, Cheryl .... 208-282-2533 130 H
hanscher@isu.edu
HANSON, Christina, R .. 717-796-1800 390 E
chanson@messiah.edu
HANSON, Courtney .... 414-288-3577 494 B
courtney.hanson@marquette.edu
HANSON, Daniel .... 402-872-2239 268 F
dhanson@peru.edu
HANSON, Denise .... 319-226-2012 162 F
denise.hanson@allencollege.edu
HANSON, Doug .... 928-774-3890.. 12 M
dhanson@indianbible.org
HANSON, Eric .... 540-261-8400 471 H
eric.hanson@svu.edu
HANSON, Gary, A .... 310-506-4405.. 56 C
gary.hanson@pepperdine.edu
HANSON, Janet, K .... 507-786-3018 243 C
jhanson@stolaf.edu
HANSON, Janna .... 605-688-6304 417 C
jana.hanson@sdstate.edu
HANSON, Julie .... 970-945-8691.. 77 K
HANSON, Katrina .... 510-666-8248.. 24 D
HANSON, Kent .... 763-576-4700 237 D
kent.hanson@anokatech.edu
HANSON, Kent .... 763-433-1179 237 C
kent.hanson@anokaramsey.edu
HANSON, Kristina .... 281-487-1170 448 F
khanson@txchiro.edu
HANSON, Lisa .... 309-341-5212 133 C
lhanson@sandburg.edu
HANSON, Mark .... 920-206-2373 493 L
mark.hanson@mbu.edu
HANSON, Megan .... 810-762-9781 225 H
mhanson@kettering.edu
HANSON, Michelle .... 605-331-6714 417 E
michelle.hanson@usiouxfalls.edu
HANSON, Patti .... 641-422-1521 168 D
patti.hanson@iwd.iowa.gov
HANSON, Paula .... 903-886-5890 447 B
paula.hanson@tamuc.edu
HANSON, Peter .... 513-875-3344 350 G
peter.hanson@chatfield.edu
HANSON, Rhoda .... 503-842-8222 377 A
rhodahanson@tillamookbaycc.edu
HANSON, Richard .... 888-378-9988 416 J
richard.hanson@dsu.edu
HANSON, Sara .... 860-343-5883.. 86 A
shanson@mxcc.edu
HANSON, Sara .... 402-399-2350 266 F
shanson@csm.edu
HANSON, Sara .... 608-663-2329 493 C
sarahanson@edgewood.edu
HANSON, Shirley, M .... 701-788-4767 345 E
shirley.m.hanson@mayvillestate.edu
HANSON, Stephen, E .... 757-221-3590 466 C
sehanson@wm.edu
HANSON, Steven, D ..... 517-355-2352 227 D
ispdean@msu.edu
HANSON, Susan .... 909-469-5329.. 74 I
shanson@westernu.edu
HANSON, Tonya .... 952-358-8213 239 F
tonya.hanson@normandale.edu
HANSON, Virginia .... 773-577-8100 135 G
vhanson@coynecollege.edu
HANSS, Patrick, G .... 315-386-7222 320 E
hanssp@canton.edu
HANSTAD, Kari .... 701-483-2326 345 D
kari.hanstad@dickinsonstate.edu
HANTEN, Joan .... 360-475-7305 482 G
jhanten@olympic.edu
HANTL, Bill .... 216-881-1700 359 F
bhantl@ohiotech.edu
HANTON, Tracy .... 215-496-6175 382 A
thanton@ccp.edu
HANTZSCHEL, Linda, J . 516-463-6903 302 B
linda.j.hantzschel@hofstra.edu
HANUSCIN, R. Douglas 419-755-4871 357 E
dhanusci@ncstatecollege.edu
HANYCZ, Colleen, M .... 215-951-1010 387 C
president@lasalle.edu
HANZLIK, Gilbert .... 804-524-3698 477 B
ghanzik@vsu.edu
HAO, Lan .... 626-914-8521.. 36 K
lhao@citruscollege.edu

HAPGOOD-WHITE,
Jennifer .... 617-253-2811 215 G
HAPPE, Doyle .... 713-529-2778 432 G
happe@paralegal.edu
HAPPEL, Harriet .... 661-362-3653.. 38 H
harriet.happel@canyons.edu
HAPSMITH, Linda, M ... 907-474-1849.. 10 A
lhapsmith@alaska.edu
HARA, Lou .... 785-749-8440 173 G
lhara@haskell.edu
HARA, Michael .... 651-690-6845 242 R
mehara140@stkate.edu
HARARI-RAFUL, Joseph 347-394-1036 291 E
rjraful@ateret.net
HARAWAY, Malcolm ..... 512-505-3009 438 E
mxharaway@htu.edu
HARB, Sam .... 337-521-9041 188 C
sam.harb@solacc.edu
HARBACH, Heather .... 608-663-2212 493 C
hharbach@edgewood.edu
HARBAUGH, Ian .... 251-461-1390.... 8 F
iharbaugh@southalabama.edu
HARBAUGH, Martha ..... 314-529-9360 254 H
mharbaugh@maryville.edu
HARBAUGH, Melinda ... 360-442-2662 482 B
mharbaugh@lowercolumbia.edu
HARBER, Bruce .... 901-678-3888 427 D
bharber@memphis.edu
HARBER, Zachery .... 870-612-2081.. 22 I
zach.harber@uaccb.edu
HARBIN, Averl .... 716-286-8406 310 D
aharbin@niagara.edu
HARBIN, Suzanne .... 256-352-8144.... 4 A
suzanne.harbin@wallacestate.edu
HARBISON, Amanda ..... 205-391-5878.... 3 E
aharbison@sheltonstate.edu
HARBOR, Jon .... 406-243-4689 264 A
jon.harbor@umontana.edu
HARBOUR, Petra .... 952-829-2470 234 A
petra.harbour@bethfel.org
HARBOURT, Ellen, K .... 740-427-5121 355 E
harbourte@kenyon.edu
HARCOURT, Tracy, J .... 315-267-2667 319 D
harcoutj@potsdam.edu
HARDASH, Peter .... 714-480-7340.. 57 K
hardash_peter@rsccd.edu
HARDASH, Peter .... 714-564-6000.. 57 L
hardash_peter@rsccd.edu
HARDAWAY,
Johnathon .... 718-270-5002 295 A
jhardaway@mec.cuny.edu
HARDAWAY, Rex .... 404-727-4332 117 F
purrdh@emory.edu
HARDAWAY, Thelria ..... 615-963-5137 426 D
thardaway@tnstate.edu
HARDCASTLE, Beth .... 734-487-1047 223 H
bhardcas@emich.edu
HARDCASTLE, Bob .... 610-359-5182 382 C
bhardcastle@dccc.edu
HARDCASTLE, Louis, B . 770-484-1204 121 D
louis.hardcastle@lutherrice.edu
HARDEE, Sheri .... 706-864-1800 126 A
HARDEE, Tara .... 310-243-3696.. 31 B
thardee@csudh.edu
HARDEMAN, Jonathan .. 770-720-5551 123 E
jonathan.hardeman@reinhardt.edu
HARDEMON, Rhonda .... 312-850-7894 134 H
rhardemon@ccc.edu
HARDEN, Daniel .... 916-348-4689.. 42 C
dharden@epic.edu
HARDEN, Daphne .... 229-732-5923 114 B
HARDEN, Debra .... 757-727-5477 468 B
debra.harden@hamptonu.edu
HARDEN, Derrick .... 847-543-2113 135 B
dharden@clcillinois.edu
HARDEN, Derrick .... 847-543-2225 135 B
dharden@clcillinois.edu
HARDEN, Erica .... 478-553-2068 122 G
eharden@oftc.edu
HARDEN, Jim .... 906-487-7307 223 K
jim.harden@finlandia.edu
HARDEN, Kelly .... 731-661-5946 427 C
kharden@uu.edu
HARDEN, Kennith .... 360-596-5353 485 B
HARDEN, Mark .... 973-803-5000 280 C
mharden@pillar.edu
HARDEN, Michelle .... 614-508-7219 354 F
mharden@hondros.edu
HARDEN, Ronald, W ..... 916-348-4689.. 42 C
rharden@epic.edu
HARDEN, Siegfried .... 334-670-3660.... 7 C
sbharden@troy.edu

HARDEN, Yoshiko .... 206-934-3851 484 A
yoshiko.harden@seattlecolleges.edu
HARDEN-MOORE, Tai ... 503-554-2115 373 C
thardenmoore@georgefox.edu
HARDENBROOK, Joe .... 262-650-4887 492 E
jhardenb@carrollu.edu
HARDER, Kenette .... 816-414-3730 256 A
kharder@mbts.edu
HARDER, Maria .... 402-465-2117 268 H
mharder@nebrwesleyan.edu
HARDER, Matthew .... 304-336-8006 490 F
mharder@westliberty.edu
HARDER, Natalie .... 337-521-8959 188 C
natalie.harder@solacc.edu
HARDER, Robert .... 503-554-2788 373 C
bharder@georgefox.edu
HARDESKI, Grace, L .... 215-955-6618 400 A
grace.hardeski@jefferson.edu
HARDESTY, Amy .... 806-720-7178 439 H
amy.hardesty@lcu.edu
HARDESTY, Jon, H .... 972-548-6803 433 M
jhardesty@collin.edu
HARDESTY, Karla .... 719-587-8124.. 76 F
karla_hardesty@adams.edu
HARDESTY, Larry, E ...... 724-458-2700 385 C
lehardesty@gcc.edu
HARDGRAVE, Bill, C ..... 334-844-5771.... 4 E
provost@auburn.edu
HARDGROVE, Mark .... 404-627-2681 115 C
mark.hardgrove@beulah.edu
HARDIE, Susan .... 909-652-6531.. 36 A
susan.hardie@chaffey.edu
HARDIN, Brian .... 515-271-2889 165 A
brian.hardin@drake.edu
HARDIN, Carol .... 434-544-8321 472 G
hardin@lynchburg.edu
HARDIN, Dan .... 575-492-2771 286 J
dhardin@nmjc.edu
HARDIN, Elizabeth, A ... 704-687-5750 342 E
eahardin@uncc.edu
HARDIN, Marie .... 814-863-1484 392 B
mch208@psu.edu
HARDIN, Michael .... 205-726-2718.... 6 E
mhardin@samford.edu
HARDIN, Mike, W .... 704-406-4280 329 A
mhardin@gardner-webb.edu
HARDIN, Monica .... 870-245-4281.. 20 E
hardinm@obu.edu
HARDIN, Nathan .... 919-536-7200 334 B
hardinn@durhamtech.edu
HARDIN, Pam .... 828-627-4544 335 C
pahardin@haywood.edu
HARDING, Benjamin ..... 215-702-4321 380 D
bharding@cairn.edu
HARDING, Cathy .... 413-644-4776 205 F
charding@simons-rock.edu
HARDING, Jeanne .... 660-785-7777 260 J
jharding@truman.edu
HARDING, Kelly .... 660-263-3900 251 A
bookstore@cccb.edu
HARDING, Kristin .... 309-438-7304 139 E
klhardi@ilstu.edu
HARDING, Marc, L .... 412-624-7175 401 B
mharding@pitt.edu
HARDING, Millicent ...... 606-759-7141 182 A
millicent.harding@kctcs.edu
HARDING, Sally .... 212-431-2319 309 G
sally.harding@nyls.edu
HARDING, Sam .... 217-854-5617 132 I
sam.harding@blackburn.edu
HARDING, Sarah .... 863-680-4970.. 99 H
sharding@flsouthern.edu
HARDING, Sarah .... 612-874-3737 236 K
sharding@mcad.edu
HARDING, Shannan ...... 218-235-2175 241 E
shannan.harding@vcc.edu
HARDING, Shawn .... 785-864-4535 177 D
shawnharding@ku.edu
HARDING, Sonya .... 502-852-5825 185 C
sonya.harding@louisville.edu
HARDING, Tayloe .... 803-777-4336 413 C
tharding@mozart.sc.edu
HARDING, Tayloe .... 803-777-2808 413 C
tharding@mozart.sc.edu
HARDING, Teresa .... 701-766-1309 345 A
teresa.harding@littlehoop.edu
HARDING, Timothy .... 813-258-7281 112 J
tharding@ut.edu
HARDISON, Al .... 910-893-1441 327 E
hardison@campbell.edu
HARDISON, John .... 910-296-2433 335 E
jhardison@jamessprunt.edu

HARDISON, Sheri .... 210-458-6774 455 E
sheri.hardison@utsa.edu
HARDLEY, Michelle, M . 805-565-7263.. 74 K
mhardley@westmont.edu
HARDMAN,
Alton (Tony) .... 580-349-1542 368 A
ahardman@opsu.edu
HARDMAN, John .... 870-245-5189.. 20 E
hardmanj@obu.edu
HARDMAN, II,
Robert, O .... 304-637-1331 487 I
hardmanr@dewv.edu
HARDMON,
Tamecka, C .... 401-456-8213 405 C
thardmon@ric.edu
HARDRICK, Jaffus .... 305-626-3600.. 99 D
jaffus.hardrick@fmuniv.edu
HARDT, Jim .... 412-392-6186 397 A
jhardt@pointpark.edu
HARDT, John .... 708-327-9200 142 D
jhardt@lumc.edu
HARDT, John .... 804-289-8694 472 L
jhardt@richmond.edu
HARDTKE, Kristy .... 307-855-2161 501 V
khardtke@cwc.edu
HARDWARE, LaKendra . 574-535-7000 155 A
lphardware@goshen.edu
HARDWICK, James .... 813-253-6209 112 J
jhardwick@ut.edu
HARDWICK, Monica ..... 719-549-3024.. 81 K
monica.hardwick@pueblocc.edu
HARDWOOD-ROM,
Melissa .... 479-575-5004.. 21 G
mhardwood@uark.edu
HARDY, Angelic .... 570-484-2628 395 B
anh1227@lockhaven.edu
HARDY, Anthony .... 770-533-7051 121 B
ahardy@laniertech.edu
HARDY, Ashley .... 317-738-8758 154 J
ahardy@franklincollege.edu
HARDY, Beatriz, B .... 410-543-6133 203 F
bbhardy@salisbury.edu
HARDY, Catherine .... 203-575-8080.. 86 B
chardy@nv.edu
HARDY, Charles .... 910-962-3460 343 C
hardyc@uncw.edu
HARDY, SR., Daniel, R . 330-337-6403 347 E
president@awc.edu
HARDY, Deborah, L ...... 440-525-7446 355 H
dhardy@lakelandcc.edu
HARDY, Deborah, L ...... 440-525-7828 355 H
dhardy@lakelandcc.edu
HARDY, D'andre .... 336-272-7102 329 D
dandre.hardy@greensboro.edu
HARDY, Kacee .... 731-286-3238 425 A
hardy@dscc.edu
HARDY, Kevin .... 207-947-4591 193 C
khardy@bealcollege.edu
HARDY, Kia .... 757-822-1421 476 B
khardy@tcc.edu
HARDY, Marriel .... 662-621-4067 245 E
mhardy@coahomacc.edu
HARDY, Mia .... 847-214-7951 136 F
mhardy@elgin.edu
HARDY, Patricia .... 973-341-1600 280 B
phardy@pccc.edu
HARDY, Randall .... 757-727-5640 468 B
randall.hardy@hamptonu.edu
HARDY, Richard, J .... 309-298-2228 152 D
rj-hardy@wiu.edu
HARDY, Robert, M .... 203-396-8390.. 88 B
hardyr@sacredheart.edu
HARDY, Stacia .... 225-216-8247 186 K
hardys@mybrcc.edu
HARDY, Stacy .... 706-233-7358 124 B
shardy@shorter.edu
HARDY, Stephanie, K ... 540-261-4088 471 H
stephanie.hardy@svu.edu
HARDY, Steven .... 973-684-6036 280 B
shardy@pccc.edu
HARDY, Thomas .... 502-852-6636 185 C
thomas.hardy.1@louisville.edu
HARDY, Thomas, P ...... 312-996-3772 151 A
hardyt@uillinois.edu
HARDY, Tyrrell .... 505-786-4183 286 G
thardy@navajotech.edu
HARDY, Virginia .... 252-328-6541 341 C
hardyv@ecu.edu
HARDY-LUCAS, Faye ..... 757-727-5233 468 B
faye.hardy-lucas@hamptonu.edu
HARE, Angela .... 717-796-5360 390 E
ahare@messiah.edu
HARE, Emily .... 919-718-7230 333 C
ehare@cccc.edu

HARE, Michelle 803-323-2189 414 G harem@winthrop.edu
HARE, Sara 605-256-7321 416 J sara.hare@dsu.edu
HARE, Terri 309-298-2446 152 D ta-hare@wiu.edu
HAREL, Elazar 619-260-4258 71 J eharel@sandiego.edu
HAREWOOD, Anita 410-837-4533 204 B aharewood@ubalt.edu
HAREWOOD, Gwendolyn 201-447-7124 275 H
HAREZA, Dennis 216-397-1964 354 I dhareza@jcu.edu
HARF, James 314-529-6851 254 H jharf@maryville.edu
HARGETT, Jack 901-321-3231 419 C jhargett@cbu.edu
HARGIS, Dustin 419-289-5723 348 A dhargis@ashland.edu
HARGIS, Joe 507-222-4327 234 F jhargis@carleton.edu
HARGIS, Kenton 812-488-2142 161 A kh88@evansville.edu
HARGIS, Michael 501-450-3106 23 H mhargis@uca.edu
HARGIS, Randall 318-487-7129 186 I randall.hargis@lacollege.edu
HARGIS, V. Burns 405-744-6384 368 B osupres@okstate.edu
HARGRAVE, Alan 765-285-8011 153 C ahargrave@bsu.edu
HARGRAVE, Chad 936-294-1538 450 C cwhargrave@shsu.edu
HARGRAVE, Stephanie 336-316-2499 329 E hargravesj@gulford.edu
HARGRAVES, Christopher 949-582-4213 64 G chargraves@saddleback.edu
HARGRAVES, Darla 517-338-3323 222 E dhargraves@cleary.edu
HARGRAVES, J. Stanley 804-278-4379 472 E shargraves@upsem.edu
HARGRAVES, Ryan 802-656-4647 463 E ryan.hargraves@uvm.edu
HARGREAVES, Ken 626-395-6256 29 C ken.hargreaves@caltech.edu
HARGROVE, Debra 717-245-1901 382 F hargrove@dickinson.edu
HARGROVE, Demond, T 908-709-7142 284 C demond.hargrove@ucc.edu
HARGROVE, Kristi 615-277-7419 428 F khargrove@watkins.edu
HARGROVE, Kristy 615-277-7419 428 F khargrove@watkins.edu
HARGROVE, S. Keith 615-963-5451 426 D skhargrove@tnstate.edu
HARGROVE, Tony 870-584-1165 22 G thargrove@cccua.edu
HARICHANDRAN, Ronald 203-932-7167 89 A rharichandran@newhaven.edu
HARICOMBE, Lorraine, J 512-495-4350 455 A ljharic@austin.utexas.edu
HARING, Gayle 239-513-1122 101 C gharing@hodges.edu
HARING, Peter 402-399-2332 266 F pharing@csm.edu
HARJO, Kaila 918-781-7322 365 F harjok@bacone.edu
HARJU, Mary Lou 724-266-3838 400 H mharju@tsm.edu
HARKAVY, Ira 215-898-5351 400 K harkavy@upenn.edu
HARKENRIDER, Tom 949-480-4091 64 B harkenrider@soka.edu
HARKER, Heather 202-651-5005 91 E heather.harker@gallaudet.edu
HARKER, Perry, L 252-222-6205 333 A harkerp@carteret.edu
HARKEY, Betsy 940-552-6291 457 C bharkey@vernoncollege.edu
HARKEY, Penny 806-743-3080 451 C penny.harkey@ttuhsc.edu
HARKINS, Anita 402-826-8586 267 A anita.harkins@doane.edu
HARKINS, Brenda 405-422-1410 369 E harkinsb@redlandscc.edu
HARKINS, Keith 434-949-1000 475 H keith.harkins@southside.edu
HARKINS, Mackenzie 706-379-3111 127 C mharkins@yhc.edu
HARKINS, Vincent 202-885-3704 90 J vharkins@american.edu
HARKNESS, Charles 440-826-2426 348 E charkness@bw.edu
HARKNESS, Kyle 209-946-2424 70 E kharkness@pacific.edu
HARKNESS, Suzan 410-532-5316 201 B sharkness@ndm.edu
HARL, Luke 618-393-2982 138 F harll@iecc.edu
HARLACHER, Paul 850-644-0170 109 C pharlacher@fsu.edu
HARLAN, Brian 661-255-1050 28 K bharlan@calarts.edu
HARLAN, Cathy 954-262-5366 103 M charlan@nova.edu
HARLAN, Christine 972-708-7464 435 H christine_harlan@diu.edu
HARLAN, Mark, M 801-581-5605 460 E athleticsdirector@utah.edu
HARLAND, Teresa, L 218-299-3733 235 E harland@cord.edu
HARLESS, Cleta, M 304-357-4736 488 G cletaharless@ucwv.edu
HARLESS, Debra 651-638-6371 234 C d-harless@bethel.edu
HARLESS, Roberta 336-838-6146 339 B rjharless610@wilkescc.edu
HARLEY, Jay 214-333-6812 434 I jay@dbu.edu
HARLEY, Travis 215-951-1861 400 A travis.harley@jefferson.edu
HARLIN, Tim 409-772-6116 456 F tjharlin@utmb.edu
HARLOW, Brian 973-353-3724 282 B bph40@newark.rutgers.edu
HARLOW, Debra, B 336-322-2157 336 G debra.harlow@piedmontcc.edu
HARLOW, Jamie 860-768-4155 88 H harlow@hartford.edu
HARLOW, Laura 574-520-5536 157 A lewhitne@iusb.edu
HARLOW, Renee 603-358-2493 275 A rharlow@keene.edu
HARMAN, Elizabeth 619-260-4682 71 J harman@sandiego.edu
HARMAN, Holli 276-498-5231 464 K hharman@acp.edu
HARMAN, Jacob 212-960-5241 326 E jharman@yu.edu
HARMAN, Joany 916-608-6622 50 H harmanj@flc.losrios.edu
HARMAN, John 504-568-5135 189 B jharman@lsuhsc.edu
HARMAN, Michelle 570-372-4451 399 C harman@susqu.edu
HARMAN, William 801-878-1403 272 C wharman@roseman.edu
HARMELINK, Harlan 712-722-6082 164 K harlan.harmelink@dordt.edu
HARMENING, Todd 651-201-1856 237 A todd.harmening@minnstate.edu
HARMON, Alison 406-994-6338 264 D harmon@montana.edu
HARMON, Benjamin 931-221-6777 418 D harmonb@apsu.edu
HARMON, Cindy, S 573-882-2388 261 A harmonc@umsystem.edu
HARMON, Jason, M 920-923-8599 494 A jmharmon@marianuniversity.edu
HARMON, Jeff 208-732-6210 130 E jharmon@csi.edu
HARMON, Kara 801-689-2160 459 J kharmon@nightingale.edu
HARMON, Kate 503-244-0726 371 G kateharmon@achs.edu
HARMON, Kathryn 704-334-6882 328 C kharmon@charlottechristian.edu
HARMON, Kevin 701-858-3299 345 F kevin.harmon@minotstateu.edu
HARMON, Ladelle 828-652-0626 336 B ladelleh@mcdoweltech.edu
HARMON, LaVerne, T 302-356-6818 90 I laverne.t.harmon@wilmu.edu
HARMON, Martino 515-294-4420 162 I mharmon@iastate.edu
HARMON, Meghan 716-829-8160 298 F harmonm@dyc.edu
HARMON, Melanie, B 260-982-5211 158 T mbharmon@manchester.edu
HARMON, Nathaniel, S 417-268-6007 250 G nharmon@gobbc.edu
HARMON, Patricia 304-929-5460 489 C pharmon@newriver.edu
HARMON, Steve, K 956-326-2180 446 F harmon@tamiu.edu
HARMON, Suzanne 937-328-6085 350 L harmons@clarkstate.edu
HARMON, Terrence 336-770-3374 343 D harmont@uncsa.edu
HARMON, Travis 256-766-6610 5 F tharmon@hcu.edu
HARMON-FRANCIS, Barbara 201-684-7543 280 H bharmonf@ramapo.edu
HARMS, Brenda 715-394-8155 498 B bharms1@uwsuper.edu
HARMS, Cory, L 515-294-2591 162 I clharms@iastate.edu
HARMS, Dennis 708-239-4819 150 F dennis.harms@trnty.edu
HARMS, Matthew 562-860-2451 35 M mharms@cerritos.edu
HARMSEN, Mark 254-526-1365 432 H mark.harmsen@ctcd.edu
HARN, William 409-880-8229 449 H william.harn@lamar.edu
HARNACKE, Jacob 217-732-3155 141 I jharnacke@lincolncollege.edu
HARNE, George, A 603-456-2656 274 A administration@northeastcatholic.edu
HARNER, Holly 215-951-1865 387 C harner@lasalle.edu
HARNER, Kristy 423-614-8110 420 J kharner@leeuniversity.edu
HARNER, Mike 517-607-2303 225 A mharner@hillsdale.edu
HARNEY, Jacob, P 770-720-9102 123 E jph@reinhardt.edu
HARNEY, Jake, P 770-720-9102 123 E jph@reinhardt.edu
HARNEY, Malea 217-773-4441 141 D mharney@lakeland.cc.il.us
HARNISCH, Joe 402-941-6143 267 L harnischj@midlandu.edu
HARNISH, Eric 661-362-3429 38 H eric.harnish@canyons.edu
HARNOIS, Deborah 508-856-2660 212 A deborahl.harnois@umassmed.edu
HARNSBERGER, James 413-748-4826 218 G jharnsberger@springfield.edu
HARNUM, Donald, P 609-896-5054 281 B harnum@rider.edu
HAROLD, Martin 858-653-6740 46 I mharold@jpcatholic.com
HARP, Dennis 406-377-9425 263 E dharp@dawson.edu
HARP, Elizabeth, R 815-282-7900 148 C bethharp@sacn.edu
HARP, Jeff 405-974-2800 370 K jharp@uco.edu
HARP, John, W 319-895-4234 164 B jharp@cornellcollege.edu
HARP, Randy 903-886-5351 447 B randy.harp@tamuc.edu
HARP, Samuel 508-548-1400 220 D
HARP-STEPHENS, Becky 859-246-6498 180 K becky.harp@kctcs.edu
HARPE, Mary 262-564-3018 499 F harpem@gtc.edu
HARPER, Amy 828-395-1292 335 D aharper@isothermal.edu
HARPER, April 704-991-0114 338 C aharper6224@stanly.edu
HARPER, Christine 859-257-3458 185 B christine.harper@email.uky.edu
HARPER, Daniel 512-463-6449 449 F daniel.harper@tsus.edu
HARPER, David 410-827-5806 197 I dharper@chesapeake.edu
HARPER, David 412-396-5589 383 C harperd1@duq.edu
HARPER, Donna, L 540-568-3705 468 F harperdl@jmu.edu
HARPER, Doreen, C 205-934-5360 8 A dcharper@uab.edu
HARPER, E. Royster 734-764-5132 231 E harperer@umich.edu
HARPER, Elizabeth 703-323-3459 475 C eharper@nvcc.edu
HARPER, Heather 615-230-3519 426 B heather.harper@volstate.edu
HARPER, J. Kyle 405-325-3221 371 B kyleharper@ou.edu
HARPER, Jimmy 912-260-4314 124 C jimmy.harper@sgsc.edu
HARPER, Joann 706-245-7226 117 E jharper@ec.edu
HARPER, Josh 503-255-0332 374 D jharper@multnomah.edu
HARPER, Karla 937-376-6444 350 D kharper@centralstate.edu
HARPER, Kimberly, P 540-828-5393 465 D kharper@bridgewater.edu
HARPER, Kristin 205-226-4720 5 A kharper@bsc.edu
HARPER, Lauren 409-933-8232 433 L lharper1@come.edu
HARPER, III, Laurie 256-761-6119 7 B lharper@talladega.edu
HARPER, Lisa 405-974-2553 370 K lharper@uco.edu
HARPER, Lisa, D 859-858-3511 178 I lisa.harper@asbury.edu
HARPER, Marjoree 318-678-6000 187 A mharper@bpcc.edu
HARPER, Mary, J 812-465-1026 161 E mjharper@usi.edu
HARPER, Matt 918-465-2361 366 D mharper@eosc.edu
HARPER, Pam 270-706-8434 181 A pamela.harper@kctcs.edu
HARPER, Patricia 816-654-7162 254 C pharper@kcumb.edu
HARPER, Randy 870-574-4590 21 E rharper@sautech.edu
HARPER, Rosie 601-977-7818 249 C rharper@tougaloo.edu
HARPER, Ross 620-421-6700 175 C rossh@labette.edu
HARPER, Sandra 325-793-3800 440 B harper.sandra@mcm.edu
HARPER, Stephany 304-462-6171 490 C stephany.harper@glenville.edu
HARPER, Teresa, B 502-213-2121 181 F teresa.harper@kctcs.edu
HARPER, Vernon 661-654-2154 30 E vharper@csub.edu
HARPER, Vernon 661-654-3420 30 E vharper@csub.edu
HARPER HAGAN, Mary 305-284-4476 112 E mharperh@miami.edu
HARPER-MARINICK, Maria 480-731-8100 12 O maria.harper@domail.maricopa.edu
HARPHAM, Edward 972-883-6729 455 B harpham@utdallas.edu
HARPHAM, Jennifer, E 330-972-5860 362 B jharpham@uakron.edu
HARPIN, Kimberlee 815-802-8472 140 D kharpin@kcc.edu
HARPINE, Annette 910-938-6789 333 F harpinea@coastalcarolina.edu
HARPOLE, Jessica 662-329-7352 248 A jjharpole@muw.edu
HARPOLE, Pam 217-479-7040 142 I pam.harpole@mac.edu
HARPOLE, Theresa 662-476-5274 246 A tharpole@eastms.edu
HARPOOL, David 866-776-0331 54 A president@ncu.edu
HARPOOL, David 866-776-0331 54 A dharpool@ncu.edu
HARPS, Juanita 706-821-8339 122 K jharps@paine.edu
HARPS, Trynette Lottie 231-777-0559 228 D trynette.lottie-harps@muskegoncc.edu
HARPST, Steve 845-341-4230 311 C steve.harpst@sunyorange.edu
HARR, Brian 661-362-2364 51 C bharr@masters.edu
HARR, Jon 423-652-4773 420 H jharr@king.edu
HARR, Lois 718-862-7142 305 H lois.harr@manhattan.edu
HARR, Shannon, L 606-783-2529 183 F s.harr@moreheadstate.edu
HARRA, Alice 503-517-7421 376 C harraa@reed.edu
HARRAL, Judy 361-825-2495 447 C judy.harral@tamucc.edu
HARRAL, Kevin 650-949-7223 43 D harralkevin@foothill.edu
HARRAL, Nicole, D 928-344-7600 10 J nicole.harral@azwestern.edu
HARRELD, Bruce 319-335-3549 163 A

HARRELL, Alfred, E 225-771-3911 190 H alfred_harrell@sus.edu

HARRELL, III, Alfred, E 225-771-3911 190 G alfred_harrell@sus.edu

HARRELL, Brenda 904-470-8081 97 L b.harrell@ewc.edu

HARRELL, Brian 478-934-3027 121 F brian.harrell@mga.edu

HARRELL, Bryant, L 860-727-6756 87 A bharrell@goodwin.edu

HARRELL, David 972-708-7340 435 H david_harrell@diu.edu

HARRELL, David, L 865-539-7378 425 F dlharrell@pstcc.edu

HARRELL, Evelyn 504-286-5234 190 I eharrell@suno.edu

HARRELL, II, Ivan, L 253-566-5100 485 C iharrell@tacomacc.edu

HARRELL, Jessica 336-506-4113 332 A jessica.harrell@alamancecc.edu

HARRELL, Jonathan 757-352-4453 470 H jonahar@regent.edu

HARRELL, Joseph, H 513-558-4635 362 D joseph.harrell@uc.edu

HARRELL, Katie 605-668-1541 415 H katie.harrell@mtmc.edu

HARRELL, Kimberly 916-691-7390 50 G harrelk@crc.losrios.edu

HARRELL, Lee 941-359-7532 105 K lharrell@ringling.edu

HARRELL, Lisa 229-430-3396 113 I lharrell@albanytech.edu

HARRELL, Pamela, J 919-209-2048 335 F pjharrell@johnstoncc.edu

HARRELL, Shereada 850-599-3700 108 I shereada.harrell@famu.edu

HARRELL, Tracy 870-543-8416 21 C tharrell@seark.edu

HARRELSON, Chris 505-566-3284 288 A harrelsonc@sanjuancollege.edu

HARRI, Ed 360-383-3230 486 G eharri@whatcom.edu

HARRI, Robert 563-387-2103 167 E harrro01@luther.edu

HARRIEL, Mary 770-689-4965 114 C mharriel@aii.edu

HARRIER, Briana, K 515-964-0601 165 G harrierb@faith.edu

HARRIES, Peter, J 919-515-1989 342 B pjharrie@ncsu.edu

HARRIG, Tina, L 920-832-6541 493 K tina.l.harrig@lawrence.edu

HARRIGAN, Maureen 207-288-5015 193 F

HARRIGAN, Tammy 401-598-1012 404 I tharrigan@jwu.edu

HARRIGER, Christine 434-947-8344 470 E charriger@randolphcollege.edu

HARRILL, Thad 828-395-1624 335 D tharrill@isothermal.edu

HARRING, Christopher 410-225-2255 199 H charring@mica.edu

HARRING, Kathleen 484-664-3134 391 C provost's_office@muhlenberg.edu

HARRINGTON, Angela 973-278-5400 291 D angela-harringt@berkeleycollege.edu

HARRINGTON, Angela 973-278-5400 275 I angela-harringt@berkeleycollege.edu

HARRINGTON, Billie 864-578-8770 412 B bharrington@sherman.edu

HARRINGTON, Bonnie 215-751-8253 382 A bharrington@ccp.edu

HARRINGTON, Chris 510-587-6050 68 C chris.harrington@ucop.edu

HARRINGTON, Constance 301-369-2494 197 F cpharrington@captechu.edu

HARRINGTON, Donna 505-467-6831 288 E donnaharrington@swc.edu

HARRINGTON, Jamee 541-956-7017 376 D jharrington@roguecc.edu

HARRINGTON, Kahlil 323-953-4000 48 I harrinkg@lacitycollege.edu

HARRINGTON, Kim 404-894-2499 118 F kim.harrington@ohr.gatech.edu

HARRINGTON, Kimberly 704-216-6151 330 H kharrington@livingstone.edu

HARRINGTON, Krista 843-574-6077 413 B krista.harrington@tridenttech.edu

HARRINGTON, L. Katharine 213-740-7849 72 B vpap@usc.edu

HARRINGTON, Lynn 708-974-5704 144 C harrington@morainevalley.edu

HARRINGTON, Mark, R 716-888-3749 292 D harring4@canisius.edu

HARRINGTON, Melinda 620-276-9514 173 E melinda.harrington@gcccks.edu

HARRINGTON, Michael 631-420-2053 321 B michael.harrington@farmingdale.edu

HARRINGTON, Michael, J 415-422-2790 71 K harrington@usfca.edu

HARRINGTON, Sean, P 540-464-7132 476 G harringtonsp@vmi.edu

HARRINGTON, Shawn, M 860-231-5314 89 B sharrington@usj.edu

HARRINGTON, Sherre Lee 706-236-2285 115 B sharrington@berry.edu

HARRINGTON, Stacey 314-977-7124 259 H stacey.harrington@slu.edu

HARRINGTON, Thomas 504-280-1154 189 E trharrin@uno.edu

HARRINGTON-HOPE, Sharon 617-243-2145 210 G sharrington-hope@lasell.edu

HARRINGTON-MARTIN, Angela 317-543-3250 158 V aharrington@martin.edu

HARRIOTT, Danielle 815-965-8616 147 F dharriott@rockfordcareercollege.edu

HARRIS, Aaron 952-829-2411 234 A aaron.harris@bethfel.org

HARRIS, Alex 208-769-7156 131 C afharris@nic.edu

HARRIS, Alexis 251-981-3771 5 B alexis.harris@columbiasouthern.edu

HARRIS, Alice 304-424-8224 491 D alice.harris@wvup.edu

HARRIS, Allatia 281-459-7140 443 B allatia.harris@sjcd.edu

HARRIS, Allison 432-837-8432 450 D allison.harris@sulross.edu

HARRIS, Alvin 501-370-5284 20 G aharris@philander.edu

HARRIS, Amalia 802-586-7711 463 D

HARRIS, Amelia, J 276-376-4557 473 B ajh7a@virginia.edu

HARRIS, Andrew 312-341-3500 147 H

HARRIS, Andrew 415-338-1471 34 A a1harris@sfsu.edu

HARRIS, Angie 510-430-2039 52 D anharris@mills.edu

HARRIS, Angie 717-245-1556 382 F harrisa@dickinson.edu

HARRIS, Angie 865-981-8201 421 F angie.harris@maryvillecollege.edu

HARRIS, Anjour 804-828-2021 473 F abharris@vcu.edu

HARRIS, Anna-Lize 201-216-5208 283 C anna-lize.harris@stevens.edu

HARRIS, Anne 641-269-3100 165 J harrisanne@grinnell.edu

HARRIS, Anthony 802-828-2800 464 B ajh03150@ccv.vsc.edu

HARRIS, April 714-556-3610 72 F april.harris@vanguard.edu

HARRIS, Becky 214-638-0484 438 I b.harris@kdstudio.com

HARRIS, Bennie, L 404-752-1955 122 E bharris@msm.edu

HARRIS, Beryl 410-951-6280 203 D bharris@coppin.edu

HARRIS, Beth 203-287-3023 87 E paierartlibrary@snet.net

HARRIS, Bethany, W 434-949-1007 475 H bethany.harris@southside.edu

HARRIS, Betsy, A 207-768-2791 194 J bharris@nmcc.edu

HARRIS, Beverly 620-331-4100 174 C bharris@indycc.edu

HARRIS, Beverly 757-823-2409 469 F bbharris@nsu.edu

HARRIS, Bill 972-708-7340 435 H bill_harris@diu.edu

HARRIS, Bruce 435-879-4638 460 G bruce.harris@dixie.edu

HARRIS, Carol, B 605-342-0317 415 E charris@jwc.edu

HARRIS, Caroline 252-536-2551 335 B

HARRIS, Charles, S 434-791-5701 464 O csharris@averett.edu

HARRIS, Chelsy 719-502-3034 81 F chelsy.harris@ppcc.edu

HARRIS, Chonnea 661-726-1911 68 B chonnea.harris@uav.edu

HARRIS, Chris 949-214-3169 40 F chris.harris@cui.edu

HARRIS, Chris 803-947-2110 411 D chris.harris@newberry.edu

HARRIS, Christina 530-422-7923 73 F charris@weimar.edu

HARRIS, Clarissa 828-771-3816 344 E charris@warren-wilson.edu

HARRIS, Clark 307-778-1103 502 D charris@lccc.wy.edu

HARRIS, Clayton 216-987-4425 351 G clayton.harris@tri-c.edu

HARRIS, Cliff 313-664-7403 222 F charris@collegeforcreativestudies.edu

HARRIS, Craig 540-857-7797 476 D charris@virginiawestern.edu

HARRIS, Crystal 816-271-5827 257 A crharris@missouriwestern.edu

HARRIS, Danielle 828-627-4507 335 C ldharris@haywood.edu

HARRIS, Darrell, A 904-264-2172 105 L dharris@iws.edu

HARRIS, David 320-308-4866 240 H djharris@stcloudstate.edu

HARRIS, David 718-268-4700 312 G

HARRIS, David 843-574-6615 413 B david.harris@tridenttech.edu

HARRIS, David, P 909-558-7600 48 C dpharris@llu.edu

HARRIS, David, R 518-388-6101 323 G harrisd@union.edu

HARRIS, David, W 319-273-2470 163 B david.harris@uni.edu

HARRIS, Dawn 225-771-2680 190 H dawn_harris@subr.edu

HARRIS, Debbie 804-751-9191 465 O dharris@ccc-va.com

HARRIS, Delana 601-403-1197 248 E dharris@prcc.edu

HARRIS, Delphia 901-435-1380 421 A delphia_harris@loc.edu

HARRIS, Denise 716-829-7874 298 F harrisd@dyc.edu

HARRIS, Derrell 912-287-5855 116 F dharris@coastalpines.edu

HARRIS, Dina 574-520-4131 157 A dlharris@iusb.edu

HARRIS, Donald 303-871-2267 83 D don.harris@du.edu

HARRIS, Erica 606-539-4167 185 A erica.harris@ucumberlands.edu

HARRIS, Eugenia 903-813-2371 430 N eharris@austincollege.edu

HARRIS, Felicia 937-376-6611 350 D fharris@centralstate.edu

HARRIS, SR., Forrest, E 615-256-1463 418 A officeofthepresident@abcnash.edu

HARRIS, G. Duncan 860-906-5101 85 D gharris@capitalcc.edu

HARRIS, Gail 423-746-5208 426 F gharris@tnwesleyan.edu

HARRIS, Gary, L 202-806-2550 92 B gharris@howard.edu

HARRIS, Gheretta 231-591-3947 223 J gherettaharris@ferris.edu

HARRIS, Greg 602-275-7133 15 O greg.harris@rsiaz.edu

HARRIS, Hayley 607-274-3011 303 B hharris@ithaca.edu

HARRIS, Hubert, D 804-524-1085 477 B hharris@vsu.edu

HARRIS, James 903-593-8311 448 H jharris@texascollege.edu

HARRIS, James 918-647-1310 365 H jharris@carlablert.edu

HARRIS, James, T 619-260-4520 71 J president@sandiego.edu

HARRIS, Janette 530-938-5500 39 F jharris6@siskiyous.edu

HARRIS, Jason 919-301-6500 92 G

HARRIS, Jean 941-487-4570 109 D jharris@ncf.edu

HARRIS, Jeff 205-226-4700 5 A jharris@bsc.edu

HARRIS, Jeff 575-674-2391 285 H jharris@bcomnm.org

HARRIS, Jesse 208-459-5222 130 D jharris@collegeofidaho.edu

HARRIS, Jesse 864-225-7653 409 J jesseharris@forrestcollege.edu

HARRIS, Jessica 618-650-5609 149 F jesharr@siue.edu

HARRIS, Jewell 601-979-1773 246 E jewell.e.harris@jsums.edu

HARRIS, Jim, C 770-216-2960 120 H jharris@ict.edu

HARRIS, John 515-961-1626 169 D john.harris@simpson.edu

HARRIS, John 515-271-1472 164 I john.harris@dmu.edu

HARRIS, John 601-635-2111 245 I jharris@eccc.edu

HARRIS, John 518-244-4582 313 D harrisj8@sage.edu

HARRIS, John 903-923-2181 436 D jharris@etbu.edu

HARRIS, II, John (Jack), P 330-471-8247 355 L jharris@malone.edu

HARRIS, Joshua 252-246-1257 339 C jharris@wilsoncc.edu

HARRIS, Judy 760-744-1150 55 I jharris@palomar.edu

HARRIS, Kelly 773-995-4412 133 K kharri44@csu.edu

HARRIS, Kendall 713-313-1133 449 C kendall.harris@tsu.edu

HARRIS, Kenneth, E 313-831-5200 223 I kharris@etseminary.edu

HARRIS, Kim 662-720-7193 248 C kkharris@nemcc.edu

HARRIS, Kim 865-882-4695 425 G harriskb@roanestate.edu

HARRIS, Kimberly 802-831-1225 463 G kharris@vermontlaw.edu

HARRIS, Krista 785-227-3380 171 E harriskm@bethanylb.edu

HARRIS, Kristi 660-357-6203 257 D kharris@mail.ncmissouri.edu

HARRIS, Kristin 940-855-2203 457 C kharris@vernoncollege.edu

HARRIS, Lakeisha, L 410-651-6507 203 A llharris@umes.edu

HARRIS, Lamel 408-288-3736 61 M lamel.harris@sjcc.edu

HARRIS, Liesl, W 205-853-1200 2 G lwharris@jeffersonstate.edu

HARRIS, Lisa 763-433-1292 237 C lisa.harris@anokaramsey.edu

HARRIS, Lori 757-233-8786 477 F lharris@vwu.edu

HARRIS, Marc 717-867-6208 388 H harris@lvc.edu

HARRIS, Marie 253-964-6500 483 D mharris@pierce.ctc.edu

HARRIS, Marilyn 417-873-7854 252 F mharris016@drury.edu

HARRIS, Mark 609-586-4800 278 F harrisma@mccc.edu

HARRIS, Mark 336-454-1126 335 A meharris@gtcc.edu

HARRIS, Mark, T 414-229-8417 497 A mtharris@uwm.edu

HARRIS, Marty 626-968-1328 47 G

HARRIS, Mary 317-931-4440 154 C mharris@cts.edu

HARRIS, Mary, E 512-223-7705 431 A mharris3@austincc.edu

HARRIS, Matthew 417-447-8290 257 G harrism@otc.edu

HARRIS, Maurice, A 315-443-4734 322 C maharr17@syr.edu

HARRIS, Mel 703-812-4757 468 G mharris@leland.edu

HARRIS, Melvin 256-726-7374 6 C mharris@oakwood.edu

HARRIS, Michael 715-425-3774 497 E michael.harris@uwrf.edu

HARRIS, Michael 580-349-1362 368 A michael.harris12@opsu.edu

HARRIS, Mitzi 903-877-7750 456 D mitzi.harris@uthct.edu

HARRIS, Molly 903-463-8700 437 D harrism@grayson.edu

HARRIS, Nick, L 504-816-4704 186 D nharris@dillard.edu

HARRIS, Patricia 662-252-8000 248 G pharris@rustcollege.edu

HARRIS, Patricia 616-988-3624 226 C pharris@kuyper.edu

HARRIS, Patrick 406-447-4380 263 C pharris@carroll.edu

HARRIS, Paul 585-475-4992 313 A pahdar@rit.edu

HARTHORN, Karen, M .. 651-962-6353 244 E
kmharthorn@stthomas.edu
HARTIGAN, Ellen .... 212-237-8100 294 D
ehartigan@jjay.cuny.edu
HARTIGAN, Gretchen .... 617-358-6361 207 D
hartigan@bu.edu
HARTIGAN, Sheenah ..... 732-255-0400 280 A
shartigan@ocean.edu
HARTING, Troy, R .... 719-333-4130 504 C
troy.harting@usafa.edu
HARTKE, Emily .... 217-234-5430 141 D
ehartke@lakeland.cc.il.us
HARTL, Derek .... 563-387-1433 167 E
hartde01@luther.edu
HARTL, Renae .... 563-387-1244 167 E
hartre01@luther.edu
HARTLAUB, Mark .... 361-825-2659 447 C
mark.hartlaub@tamucc.edu
HARTLESS, Megan .... 540-453-2209 474 B
hartlessm@brcc.edu
HARTLEY, Brian .... 618-664-6821 137 G
brian.hartley@greenville.edu
HARTLEY, Greg, L .... 916-348-4689.. 42 C
ghartley@epic.edu
HARTLEY, James .... 870-762-1020.. 17 D
jehartley@smail.anc.edu
HARTLEY, Laura .... 316-942-4291 175 I
hartleyl@newmanu.edu
HARTLEY, Laura .... 503-554-2143 373 C
lhartley@georgefox.edu
HARTLEY, Leslie .... 205-387-0511.... 1 D
leslie.hartley@bscc.edu
HARTLEY, Roger .... 410-837-5359 204 B
rhartley@ubalt.edu
HARTLEY, Vaughn .... 304-473-8367 491 H
hartley.v@wvwc.edu
HARTLEY-HUTTON,
Kelley .... 260-481-6643 159 F
hartleyk@pfw.edu
HARTLINE, Beverly .... 406-496-4456 265 A
bhartline@mtech.edu
HARTLINE, Michael .... 850-644-4405 109 C
mhartline@cob.fsu.edu
HARTMAN,
Alexander, M .... 508-373-9435 206 B
alexander.hartman@becker.edu
HARTMAN, Brandi, P .... 864-488-4617 410 E
bhartman@limestone.edu
HARTMAN, Brian .... 509-525-2694 485 H
brian.hartman@wallawalla.edu
HARTMAN, Bryan, G ..... 518-564-2280 319 C
hartmabg@plattsburgh.edu
HARTMAN, C. Max .... 650-306-3132.. 61 O
hartmanmax@smccd.edu
HARTMAN, Carolyn, S .. 910-962-4103 343 C
hartmanc@uncw.edu
HARTMAN, Chris, T ...... 215-885-2360 389 F
chartman@manor.edu
HARTMAN, Christine .... 717-796-1800 390 E
chartman@messiah.edu
HARTMAN, Cynthia .... 740-389-4636 356 B
hartmanc@mtc.edu
HARTMAN, Dean, A ...... 706-880-8246 121 A
dhartman@lagrange.edu
HARTMAN, Eric .... 931-598-1443 423 M
ehartman@sewanee.edu
HARTMAN, Fritz .... 574-535-7423 155 A
fritzdh@goshen.edu
HARTMAN, James .... 609-896-5016 281 B
jhartman@rider.edu
HARTMAN, Joel, L .... 407-823-6778 109 E
joel.hartman@ucf.edu
HARTMAN, Joseph .... 978-934-2168 211 G
joseph_hartman@uml.edu
HARTMAN, Joseph .... 972-825-4774 445 A
jhartman@sagu.edu
HARTMAN, Joshua .... 617-627-3248 219 B
joshua.hartman@tufts.edu
HARTMAN, Kerry .... 701-627-4738 346 G
khartm@nhsc.edu
HARTMAN, Kimberly ..... 727-712-5876 106 E
hartman.kimberly@spcollege.edu
HARTMAN, Laurie .... 315-792-7400 321 E
laurie.hartman@sunypoly.edu
HARTMAN, Phil .... 817-257-7727 448 G
p.hartman@tcu.edu
HARTMAN, Rob .... 803-754-4100 409 A
HARTMAN, Robin .... 714-879-3901.. 45 F
rhartman@hiu.edu
HARTMAN, Sherry .... 410-287-1025 197 H
shartman@cecil.edu
HARTMAN, Stephanie ... 304-358-2000 488 A
stephanie@future.edu

HARTMAN, Thomas ...... 336-506-4201 332 A
thomas.hartman@alamancecc.edu
HARTMANN, Angela ..... 361-570-4374 453 C
hartmanna@uhv.edu
HARTMANN,
Gretchen, L .... 605-336-6588 416 E
ghartmann@sfseminary.edu
HARTMANN, Lori, L ..... 859-238-5371 179 F
lori.hartmann@centre.edu
HARTMANN, Richard .... 714-992-7044.. 53 L
rhartmann@fullcoll.edu
HARTMANN, Wendy ..... 636-584-6712 252 J
wendy.hartmann@eastcentral.edu
HARTNESS, Darrin, L .... 336-249-8186 334 A
HARTNET, Amelia .... 309-298-1971 152 D
af-hartnett@wiu.edu
HARTNETT, Christa .... 409-944-1314 437 B
chartnett@gc.edu
HARTNETT, David .... 231-348-6603 228 E
dhartnett@ncmich.edu
HARTNETT, Ryan .... 716-896-0700 324 E
hartnettr@villa.edu
HARTO, Diana, L .... 304-336-8139 490 F
diana.harto@westliberty.edu
HARTOG, John .... 712-324-5066 168 G
jhartog@nwicc.edu
HARTOG, Paul, A .... 515-964-0601 165 G
hartogp@faith.edu
HARTON, Mary Kay .... 847-925-6221 137 H
mharton@harpercollege.edu
HARTS, Melissa, L .... 727-816-3466 104 F
hartsm@phsc.edu
HARTSELL, Angela .... 239-489-9427 100 A
ahartsell1@fsw.edu
HARTSELL, Skip .... 501-450-1348.. 19 F
hartsell@hendrix.edu
HARTSHORN, Tricia ...... 620-242-0441 175 F
hartshot@mcpherson.edu
HARTSOCK, Michael ..... 217-424-6265 143 H
mhartsock@millikin.edu
HARTSOE, Janice .... 864-644-5538 412 E
jhartsoe@swu.edu
HARTSON, Michelle ...... 931-431-9700 423 D
financialaid@nci.edu
HARTSON, Michelle ...... 931-431-9700 423 D
mhartson@nci.edu
HARTUNIAN, Sharon .... 413-528-7350 205 F
shartunian@simons-rock.edu
HARTWELL, Edward ...... 914-674-7562 306 F
ehartwell@mercy.edu
HARTWELL, John .... 435-797-2060 460 H
john.hartwell@usu.edu
HARTWELL, Richard ...... 443-412-2344 199 A
rhartwell@harford.edu
HARTWELL, Stephanie .. 313-577-2519 232 I
gr2312@wayne.edu
HARTWIG, Ryan .... 303-963-3426.. 77 G
rhartwig@ccu.edu
HARTY, Kristin .... 412-365-2769 381 C
kharty@chatham.edu
HARTZ, James .... 270-686-4630 182 B
jim.hartz@kctcs.edu
HARTZ, Ronald, G .... 671-735-5555 505 C
ronald.hartz@guamcc.edu
HARTZELL, Jay, C .... 512-471-5058 455 A
dean.hartzell@mccombs.utexas.edu
HARTZELL, Rick .... 563-425-5293 170 A
hartzellr53@uiu.edu
HARTZLER, Murray, G .. 843-661-1237 409 K
mhartzler@fmarion.edu
HARTZLER, Tracy .... 505-224-4413 285 J
thartzler@cnm.edu
HARVEY, Andrew .... 301-387-3025 198 F
andrew.harvey@garrettcollege.edu
HARVEY, Barron, H .... 202-806-1500.. 92 B
bharvey@howard.edu
HARVEY, Binti .... 909-621-8152.. 63 E
bharvey@scrippscollege.edu
HARVEY, Brian .... 864-250-8417 410 B
brian.harvey@gvltec.edu
HARVEY, Cameron .... 901-381-3939 428 E
cameron@visible.edu
HARVEY, Chad .... 605-995-2830 415 C
chad.harvey@dwu.edu
HARVEY, David .... 941-487-4380 109 D
dharvey@ncf.edu
HARVEY, Diana .... 510-642-6448.. 68 D
diana.harvey@berkeley.edu
HARVEY, George .... 919-761-2203 340 G
harvey@sebts.edu
HARVEY, Janice .... 870-248-4000.. 18 F
janice.harvey@blackrivertech.edu

HARVEY, Jay .... 800-227-2013 248 F
jharvey@rts.edu
HARVEY, Jim .... 805-922-6966.. 24 J
jharvey@hancockcollege.edu
HARVEY, John .... 803-754-4100 409 A
HARVEY, Katie .... 304-345-2820 491 E
kharvey@wvjc.edu
HARVEY, Kem .... 864-592-4795 412 F
harveyk@sccsc.edu
HARVEY, Kimberly .... 636-481-3200 254 A
kharvey@jeffco.edu
HARVEY, Kimberly .... 585-245-5571 318 E
harvey@geneseo.edu
HARVEY, Laurie .... 516-686-7711 309 F
lharve05@nyit.edu
HARVEY, Linda .... 718-780-0382 291 J
linda.harvey@brooklaw.edu
HARVEY, Marcus .... 816-604-4121 255 I
marcus.harvey@mcckc.edu
HARVEY, Marilyn .... 951-639-5436.. 52 I
mharvey@msjc.edu
HARVEY, Melissa .... 715-682-1674 495 C
mharvey@northland.edu
HARVEY, Michael .... 864-592-4991 412 F
harveym@sccsc.edu
HARVEY, Peter, W .... 509-527-5145 486 H
harvey@whitman.edu
HARVEY, Richard, C ...... 304-367-4101 490 B
richard.harvey@fairmontstate.edu
HARVEY, Roberta .... 856-256-5140 281 E
harvey@rowan.edu
HARVEY, Ryan, D .... 740-826-8051 357 C
harvey@muskingum.edu
HARVEY, Sally .... 480-858-9100.. 16 A
s.harvey@scnm.edu
HARVEY, Sarah, J .... 260-359-4010 155 F
sharvey@huntington.edu
HARVEY, Scott .... 864-646-1556 413 A
sharvey@tctc.edu
HARVEY, Shannon, S ... 717-339-3503 385 E
ssharvey@hacc.edu
HARVEY, Sonja, K .... 217-786-4913 142 B
sonja.harvey@llcc.edu
HARVEY, Stephanie .... 503-517-1026 377 G
sdharvey@warnerpacific.edu
HARVEY, Stephen .... 212-731-3419 302 F
stephen.harvey@mssm.edu
HARVEY, Stewart, A .... 207-581-2668 195 J
stewarth@maine.edu
HARVEY, Trevor, A .... 865-539-7368 425 F
taharvey@pstcc.edu
HARVEY, William, R ...... 757-727-5231 468 B
presidentsoffice@hamptonu.edu
HARVEY-LIVINGSTON,
Kim .... 903-566-7197 456 A
klivingston@uttyler.edu
HARVEY-SAHAK,
Judy, B .... 909-621-8973.. 63 E
judy.sahak@scrippscollege.edu
HARVEY-SMITH, Alicia .. 412-809-5100 396 H
harveysmith.alicia@ptcollege.edu
HARVILLE, Beth .... 417-873-4085 252 F
bharville@drury.edu
HARVIN, Lillian .... 510-869-8785.. 59 F
lharvin@samuelmerritt.edu
HARVIN, Peter .... 864-231-2000 406 G
pharvin@andersonuniversity.edu
HARVISON,
Mary Catherine .... 318-795-2400 189 D
mary.harvison@lsus.edu
HARWARD, Brian .... 814-332-3027 378 D
bharward@allegheny.edu
HARWELL, Becky .... 501-603-1315.. 22 C
bwharwell@uams.edu
HARWELL, Neal .... 870-248-4000.. 18 F
neal.harwell@blackrivertech.edu
HARWOOD, Gina .... 718-960-8245 294 A
gina.harwood@lehman.cuny.edu
HARWOOD, Jessica ...... 864-587-4000 412 G
harwoodj@smcsc.edu
HARWOOD, Melissa ..... 802-831-1339 463 G
mharwood@vermontlaw.edu
HARWOOD, Mike .... 541-346-8267 377 D
maharwoo@uoregon.edu
HARWOOD, Scott .... 518-891-2915 310 E
sharwood@nccc.edu
HASAN, Abul .... 918-293-4809 368 D
abul.hasan@okstate.edu
HASAN, Nash .... 704-461-6257 327 A
nashhasan@bac.edu
HASAN, Zia .... 803-535-5219 407 G
hasan@claflin.edu
HASART, Lisa .... 360-992-2488 479 F
lnelson@clark.edu

HASCALL, Corey .... 207-780-4883 196 F
corey.hascall@maine.edu
HASE, Heath .... 816-415-7641 262 F
haseh@william.jewell.edu
HASEGAWA, Betsy .... 206-934-5300 484 B
betsy.hasegawa@seattlecolleges.edu
HASELEY, Amanda .... 716-614-6271 310 C
ahaseley@niagaracc.suny.edu
HASELHORST, Christina 620-227-9541 172 J
chaselhorst@dc3.edu
HASELOFF, Gregory, K . 859-858-3511 178 I
greg.haseloff@asbury.edu
HASENKAMP,
Mindy-Kate .... 503-255-0332 374 D
mhasenkamp@multnomah.edu
HASH, Jennifer .... 303-722-5724.. 80 L
jhash@lincolntech.edu
HASH, Joseph .... 707-476-4242.. 39 D
joe-hash@redwoods.edu
HASHIM, Sharief .... 315-267-2310 319 D
hashimms@potsdam.edu
HASHIM, Susanne .... 937-319-0163 347 G
shashim@antiochcollege.edu
HASHIMOTO, Fumie ..... 360-438-4333 483 H
fhashimoto@stmartin.edu
HASHIZUME, John .... 415-485-3227.. 41 H
john.hashizume@dominican.edu
HASIK, Michelle .... 815-802-8552 140 D
mhasik@kcc.edu
HASKAMP, Misty .... 573-875-7582 251 F
mrhaskamp@ccis.edu
HASKELL, Candis .... 502-863-8376 180 E
candis_haskell@georgetowncollege.edu
HASKEY, Glennita .... 928-724-6736.. 12 C
ghaskey@dinecollege.edu
HASKINS, Brenda .... 985-448-4518 192 B
brenda.haskins@nicholls.edu
HASKINS, Eileen, T .... 401-598-1035 404 I
ehaskins@jwu.edu
HASKINS, Michael .... 251-460-6211.... 8 F
mhaskins@southalabama.edu
HASKINS, Thomas, D .... 903-927-3216 458 G
tdhaskins@wileyc.edu
HASL, Rudy .... 714-444-4141.. 75 A
rhasl@law.whittier.edu
HASLAG, Dan .... 573-642-3361 262 E
dan.haslag@westminster-mo.edu
HASLAM, Kent .... 406-243-5348 264 A
kent.haslam@umontana.edu
HASLAM, Kevin, R .... 256-765-5018.... 8 E
khaslam@una.edu
HASLAM, Lacey .... 513-562-8743 347 K
lacey.haslam@artacademy.edu
HASLER, Dan .... 765-494-4600 159 E
HASLER, Dan .... 765-494-4600 159 E
djhasler@purdue.edu
HASLER, Paul .... 715-346-3059 497 F
phasler@uwsp.edu
HASLER, Susan .... 410-617-1619 199 F
sahasler@loyola.edu
HASS, Amy, M .... 352-392-1358 109 F
amhass@ufl.edu
HASS, Chris, J .... 352-392-4792 109 F
cjhass@ufl.edu
HASS, Marjorie .... 901-843-3730 423 J
hassm@rhodes.edu
HASS, Martha .... 518-694-7238 289 D
martha.hass@acphs.edu
HASS, Moshe .... 845-425-1370 311 A
HASSABELNABY,
Hassan .... 859-572-6642 184 A
hassabelnh1@nku.edu
HASSAN, Ali .... 408-554-5739.. 62 D
ahassan@scu.edu
HASSANPOUR, Zinat ..... 704-403-1698 327 D
zinat.hassanpour@carolinashealthcare.org
HASSEL, George, E .... 610-499-4182 403 B
gehassel.sr@widener.edu
HASSELL, Rusty .... 706-385-1503 123 C
rusty.hassell@point.edu
HASSEN, Marjorie .... 207-725-3281 193 D
mhassen@bowdoin.edu
HASSENBEIN, Ashley .... 570-702-8953 386 G
ahassenbein@johnson.edu
HASSENZAHL,
David, M .... 530-898-3865.. 31 A
dhassenzahl@csuchico.edu
HASSENZAHL,
David, M .... 530-898-6121.. 31 A
dhassenzahl@csuchico.edu
HASSENZAHL, Roger .... 765-285-1532 153 C
rahassenzahl@bsu.edu

HAWKINS, Josh .... 502-852-7002 185 C
josh.hawkins@louisville.edu
HAWKINS, Julie .... 601-318-6298 249 H
jhawkins@wmcarey.edu
HAWKINS,
Katherine, W .... 757-683-4423 469 G
kwhawkin@odu.edu
HAWKINS, Kennosha .... 229-430-3510 113 I
khawkins@albanytech.edu
HAWKINS, Lauren .... 218-869-5748 186 B
lcarleton@centenary.edu
HAWKINS, Marcia .... 606-546-1700 184 H
mhawkins@unionky.edu
HAWKINS, Marcy, T .... 260-359-4097 155 F
mhawkins@huntington.edu
HAWKINS, Margaret, E . 941-752-5307 108 G
hawkinm@scf.edu
HAWKINS, Martin, E ..... 972-224-5481 444 D
HAWKINS, Mary, B .... 402-557-7005 265 J
mary.hawkins@bellevue.edu
HAWKINS, MaryAnn ..... 765-641-4535 153 B
mahawkins@anderson.edu
HAWKINS, Matt .... 317-921-4882 157 G
matthawkins@ivytech.edu
HAWKINS, Melissa .... 617-274-3355 216 B
melissa.hawkins@mcphs.edu
HAWKINS, Michele .... 561-297-3069 108 J
mhawkins@fau.edu
HAWKINS, Mike .... 816-414-3700 256 A
registrar@mbts.edu
HAWKINS, Ray .... 662-915-7234 249 D
rahawkin@olemiss.edu
HAWKINS, Reynani .... 559-325-5295.. 66 D
reynani.hawkins@cloviscollege.edu
HAWKINS, Robin .... 773-995-3755 133 K
rhawkins@csu.edu
HAWKINS, Ronald, E .... 434-592-4030 468 H
rehawkins@liberty.edu
HAWKINS, Ryan .... 618-393-2982 138 F
hawkinsr@iecc.edu
HAWKINS, Tim .... 620-862-5252 171 B
tim.hawkins@barclaycollege.edu
HAWKINS, Tony .... 301-846-2491 198 E
thawkins@frederick.edu
HAWKINS, Vernon, L .... 922-860-4221 434 L
vhawkins@dcccd.edu
HAWKINS, Wesley, E .... 561-297-4168 108 J
whawkins@fau.edu
HAWKINS, William, B ... 203-773-8516.. 84 F
wbhawkins@albertus.edu
HAWKINS-HILKE,
Annika .... 802-860-2711 462 B
ahawkinshilke@champlain.edu
HAWKINSON, Carrie ...... 309-341-5360 133 C
chawkinson@sandburg.edu
HAWKINSON,
Kenneth, S .... 610-683-4102 395 A
hawkinson@kutztown.edu
HAWKINSON, Paul .... 828-669-8012 331 J
paul.hawkinson@montreat.edu
HAWKS, Brenda .... 617-735-9920 209 A
hawksb@emmanuel.edu
HAWKS, Matt .... 407-646-2104 105 M
mhawks@rollins.edu
HAWLEY, Bill .... 660-543-4710 260 K
hawley@ucmo.edu
HAWLEY, Dawn .... 360-752-8574 478 G
dhawley@btc.edu
HAWLEY, Doug .... 660-562-1588 257 E
dhawley@nwmissouri.edu
HAWLEY, Elizabeth .... 516-572-7472 308 A
elizabeth.hawley@ncc.edu
HAWLEY, Eric .... 435-797-8146 460 H
eric.hawley@usu.edu
HAWLEY, Harold .... 843-349-5279 410 C
harold.hawley@hgtc.edu
HAWLEY, Jana .... 940-565-2925 454 A
jana.hawley@unt.edu
HAWLEY, Michelle .... 207-755-5370 194 G
mhawley@cmcc.edu
HAWLEY, Michelle .... 323-343-3830.. 32 A
mhawley@calstatela.edu
HAWLEY, Pamela .... 410-455-2832 202 E
mcinnis@umbc.edu
HAWLEY, Thomas, A .... 231-843-5803 232 J
tahawley@westshore.edu
HAWORTH, John .... 423-697-2692 424 E
john.haworth@chattanoogastate.edu
HAWORTH, Karen .... 847-947-5246 144 F
khaworth@nl.edu
HAWORTH, Timothy ..... 310-338-7760.. 50 J
thaworth@lmu.edu
HAWS, Joann .... 610-282-1100 382 E
joann.haws@desales.edu
HAWSEY, David .... 815-394-5003 147 G
dhawsey@rockford.edu
HAWTHORNE, Laura ..... 434-982-2791 473 A
lfh4c@virginia.edu
HAWTIN, Mary .... 810-989-5546 230 C
mhawtin@sc4.edu
HAWTON, Noelle .... 651-201-1801 237 A
noelle.hawton@minnstate.edu
HAXTON, Lori .... 660-626-2236 250 A
lhaxton@atsu.edu
HAY, April .... 812-237-2020 155 G
april.hay@indstate.edu
HAY, David .... 859-858-3511 178 I
david.hay@asbury.edu
HAY, Kuniko .... 510-981-2933.. 56 E
khay@peralta.edu
HAY, Laura .... 912-583-3202 115 E
lhay@bpc.edu
HAY, Mary .... 828-771-2046 344 E
mhay@warren-wilson.edu
HAY, Sharon, L .... 401-865-2750 405 B
sharhay@providence.edu
HAYASHI, Lori Lei .... 808-455-0657 129 D
lhayashi@hawaii.edu
HAYASHI-PETERSEN,
Elaine .... 360-867-5195 481 A
peach@evergreen.edu
HAYASHIDA, Peter, A ... 951-827-5203.. 69 C
peter.hayashida@ucr.edu
HAYDARI, Shahram ...... 978-934-6546 211 G
shahram_haydari@uml.edu
HAYDEL, Sheryl, K .... 504-816-4024 186 D
shaydel@dillard.edu
HAYDEN, Angie, N .... 410-572-8712 204 F
ahayden@worwic.edu
HAYDEN, Arthur .... 502-597-6893 182 H
arthur.hayden@kysu.edu
HAYDEN, Cathy, C .... 601-857-3322 246 B
cchayden@hindscc.edu
HAYDEN, Chris .... 617-585-1181 217 B
chris.hayden@necmusic.edu
HAYDEN, Jacob .... 913-758-6146 177 F
jacob.hayden@stmary.edu
HAYDEN, Jeffrey .... 413-538-7000 214 D
jhayden@hcc.edu
HAYDEN, John .... 610-526-6005 385 G
jhayden@harcum.edu
HAYDEN, Kevin .... 315-470-6500 320 A
kmhayden@esf.edu
HAYDEN, Ruby .... 425-739-8208 482 A
ruby.hayden@lwtech.edu
HAYDEN-ROY, Patrick ... 402-465-2440 268 H
phr@nebrwesleyan.edu
HAYDON, Darrell .... 209-667-3077.. 33 C
dhaydon@csustan.edu
HAYE, Erin .... 207-216-4311 195 C
ehaye@yccc.edu
HAYE, Jack .... 540-338-1776 470 A
president@phc.edu
HAYE, Melissa .... 304-327-4145 489 P
mhaye@bluefieldstate.edu
HAYEK, John .... 512-463-7281 449 F
joh.hayek@tsus.edu
HAYEN, Christopher, M 518-388-6358 323 G
hayenc@union.edu
HAYEN, Janet .... 605-995-2648 415 C
janet.hayen@dwu.edu
HAYEN, Joseph .... 361-592-1615 433 C
jchayen@coastalbend.edu
HAYES, Alastair .... 802-828-8600 463 F
alastair.hayes@vcfa.edu
HAYES, Amy .... 706-865-2134 125 E
ahayes@truett.edu
HAYES,
Andrea (Andy), S .... 573-882-2824 261 B
hayesas@missouri.edu
HAYES, Ann, C .... 717-867-6416 388 H
hayes@lvc.edu
HAYES, Ann, K .... 573-651-2552 259 K
ahayes@semo.edu
HAYES, Anne, C .... 336-517-2243 327 B
anne.hayes@bennett.edu
HAYES, B. Grant .... 252-328-1000 341 C
hayesb15@ecu.edu
HAYES, Blair .... 301-985-7940 203 B
blair.hayes@umuc.edu
HAYES, Caroline .... 617-746-1990 210 E
caroline.hayes@hult.edu
HAYES, Charles .... 231-348-6619 228 E
chayes3@ncmich.edu
HAYES, Chris .... 806-720-7156 439 H
chris.hayes@lcu.edu
HAYES, Clint .... 606-451-6601 182 C
clint.hayes@kctcs.edu
HAYES, Dale .... 772-462-7809 101 E
lhayes@irsc.edu
HAYES, Dan .... 434-791-7252 464 O
dhayes@averett.edu
HAYES, Daniel, J .... 315-267-2147 319 D
hayesdj@potsdam.edu
HAYES, David .... 337-421-6960 188 D
david.hayes@sowela.edu
HAYES, David .... 319-399-8555 164 A
dhayes@coe.edu
HAYES, Debra .... 816-265-1954 250 B
debra.hayes@abtu.edu
HAYES, Eden-Renee ...... 413-528-7226 205 F
erhayes@simons-rock.edu
HAYES, Eileen, M .... 262-472-1221 498 C
hayese@uww.edu
HAYES, Eric .... 773-602-5062 134 D
ehayes@ccc.edu
HAYES, Erik, Z .... 812-877-8230 159 J
hayesez@rose-hulman.edu
HAYES, Gail .... 563-589-3000 169 I
ghayes@dbq.edu
HAYES, Gaye .... 229-928-1273 119 D
gaye.hayes@gsw.edu
HAYES, George .... 212-431-2837 309 G
george.hayes@nyls.edu
HAYES, Ingrid .... 404-270-5186 125 B
ihayes1@spelman.edu
HAYES, Jack .... 401-863-2972 404 E
jack_hayes@brown.edu
HAYES, Janet .... 229-430-3525 113 I
jhayes@albanytech.edu
HAYES, Jerry .... 216-373-5211 358 B
jhayes@ndc.edu
HAYES, John .... 970-491-6675.. 78 M
john.hayes@colostate.edu
HAYES, John, J .... 508-856-3507 212 A
john.hayes@umassmed.edu
HAYES, Josh .... 317-788-3219 161 B
hayesje@uindy.edu
HAYES, Joshua .... 270-745-5121 185 E
joshua.hayes@wku.edu
HAYES, Julie, C .... 413-545-4169 211 D
jhayes@hfa.umass.edu
HAYES, Kellee .... 815-802-8828 140 D
khayes@kcc.edu
HAYES, Kristi .... 678-359-5022 119 F
kristih@gordonstate.edu
HAYES, LaTonya .... 501-370-5341.. 20 G
lhayes@philander.edu
HAYES, Lee, W .... 717-736-4121 385 E
lhhayes@hacc.edu
HAYES, Libby .... 937-481-2282 364 E
libby_hayes@wilmington.edu
HAYES, Maggie .... 406-994-2343 264 D
maggie.hammett@montana.edu
HAYES, Margaret .... 928-314-9515.. 10 J
peggy.hayes@azwestern.edu
HAYES, Marion .... 888-488-4968.. 46 F
mhayes@itu.edu
HAYES, Mary Jo .... 208-562-3329 130 F
maryjohayes@cwi.edu
HAYES, Matthew, D ...... 304-696-2523 490 D
hayes2@marshall.edu
HAYES, Megan .... 828-262-7525 341 B
hayesme@appstate.edu
HAYES, JR., Michael, F 716-888-2420 292 D
hayes28@canisius.edu
HAYES, Michelle .... 312-935-4106 147 D
mhayes@robertmorri.edu
HAYES, Mike .... 423-614-8406 420 J
mhayes@leeuniversity.edu
HAYES, Rebecca, L .... 330-325-6498 357 G
rlhayes@neomed.edu
HAYES, Rhonda .... 252-335-3103 341 D
rmhayes@ecsu.edu
HAYES, Richard .... 773-291-6180 134 E
rhayes13@ccc.edu
HAYES, Scott .... 434-582-2777 468 H
smhayes@liberty.edu
HAYES, Susan .... 781-891-2275 206 D
shayes@bentley.edu
HAYES, Susan .... 973-618-3553 276 D
shayes@caldwell.edu
HAYES, Terri, L .... 928-523-6608.. 14 H
terri.hayes@nau.edu
HAYES, Thomas .... 513-745-3528 365 B
hayes@xavier.edu
HAYES, Tony .... 608-342-1421 497 D
hayesto@uwplatt.edu
HAYES, Trent .... 513-862-1678 353 G
trent.hayes@email.gscollege.edu
HAYES, Tyler .... 541-383-7700 372 B
thayes1@cocc.edu
HAYES, Valerie .... 609-652-4693 283 D
valerie.hayes@stockton.edu
HAYES, Wendy .... 937-376-6332 350 D
whayes@centralstate.edu
HAYES, Ziette, H .... 757-727-5361 468 B
ziette.hayes@hamptonu.edu
HAYES-CARTER, Arnella 501-374-6305.. 21 A
arnella.carter@shortercollege.edu
HAYES-MARTIN,
Melville .... 510-204-0705.. 36 J
mhayes-martin@cdsp.edu
HAYGOOD, Courtney ..... 870-574-4458.. 21 E
chaygood@sautech.edu
HAYGOOD, Jennifer ...... 919-807-7021 331 L
haygoodj@nccommunitycolleges.edu
HAYLER, David, E .... 828-262-6276 341 B
haylerd@appstate.edu
HAYLES, JR., Rupert, A 973-803-5000 280 C
rhayles@pillar.edu
HAYMAN, Jared .... 765-455-9291 156 D
jahayman@iu.edu
HAYMAN, Jerry .... 207-974-4685 194 H
jhayman@emcc.edu
HAYMOND, Jeffrey .... 937-766-4442 349 G
jhaymond@cedarville.edu
HAYMORE, Teresa .... 706-865-2134 125 E
thaymore@truett.edu
HAYNER, Kate .... 510-869-6511.. 59 F
khayner@samuelmerritt.edu
HAYNER, Leon .... 407-646-2649 105 M
lhayner@rollins.edu
HAYNES, Allison .... 770-533-7003 121 B
ahaynes@laniertech.edu
HAYNES, Anthony .... 615-741-8220 427 F
anthony.haynes@tennessee.edu
HAYNES, Brian .... 951-827-4641.. 69 C
brian.haynes@ucr.edu
HAYNES, Carolyn, A ..... 513-529-6722 356 E
haynesca@miamioh.edu
HAYNES, Dawna .... 719-502-3198.. 81 F
dawna.haynes@ppcc.edu
HAYNES, Douglas, M ... 949-824-1540.. 68 G
dhaynes@uci.edu
HAYNES, Jamil .... 918-343-7728 369 F
jhaynes@rsu.edu
HAYNES, Jerry .... 301-846-2459 198 E
jhaynes@frederick.edu
HAYNES, John, G .... 806-743-7387 451 C
john.g.haynes@ttuhsc.edu
HAYNES, Karen, S .... 760-750-4040.. 33 B
pres@csusm.edu
HAYNES, Leticia .... 413-597-4376 220 C
lseh1@williams.edu
HAYNES, Lisa .... 616-331-7204 224 E
haynesl@gvsu.edu
HAYNES, Mike .... 254-968-9354 446 E
rhaynes@tarleton.edu
HAYNES, Pamela, J ...... 336-888-9055 329 G
phaynes@highpoint.edu
HAYNES, Penny, A .... 518-381-1374 315 G
haynespa@sunysccc.edu
HAYNES, Samuel, C ..... 316-284-5324 171 F
shaynes@bethelks.edu
HAYNES, Sandra .... 509-335-3564 486 A
HAYNES, Scot .... 912-201-8000 124 E
HAYNES, Stephanie, C . 304-637-1335 487 I
hayness@dewv.edu
HAYNES, Tiffany .... 559-791-2447.. 47 A
tduke@portervillecollege.edu
HAYNES, Warren .... 816-604-5353 255 F
warren.haynes@mcckc.edu
HAYNES, Warren, E ...... 816-604-6430 255 E
warren.haynes@mcckc.edu
HAYNES, Wendy .... 254-968-9128 446 E
haynes@tarleton.edu
HAYNES STEPHENS,
Kimberly .... 803-705-4747 407 A
kimberly.haynes@benedict.edu
HAYNIE, Glenda, D .... 804-333-6719 475 G
ghaynie@rappahannock.edu
HAYNIE, Janice .... 910-672-1211 341 E
jhaynie@uncfsu.edu
HAYNIE, Michael .... 315-443-8016 322 C
jmhaynie@syr.edu
HAYNIE, Stacia .... 225-578-2534 188 I
pohayn@lsu.edu
HAYNIE, Stacia, J .... 225-578-2534 188 H
pohayn@lsu.edu
HAYNIE, Todd .... 928-428-8231.. 12 E
todd.haynie@eac.edu

HEDAYAT, Nasser .... 407-582-3326 112 K
nhedayat@valenciacollege.edu
HEDBERG, Rick .... 701-858-3000 345 F
rick.hedberg@minotstateu.edu
HEDBERG, William, B ... 518-956-8030 316 D
whedberg@albany.edu
HEDDERICK,
Malgorzata .... 617-324-7239 215 G
HEDDLESTON, George .. 423-425-4363 428 A
george-heddleston@utc.edu
HEDDLESTON,
Patrick, D .... 330-823-6599 363 B
heddlepd@mountunion.edu
HEDEEN, Deborah .... 406-683-7115 264 B
deborah.hedeen@umwestern.edu
HEDEGARD, Heidi .... 603-862-0967 274 F
heidi.hedegard@usnh.edu
HEDGE, Allison .... 205-226-4910.... 5 A
akhedge@bsc.edu
HEDGE, Dennis .... 605-688-4173 417 C
dennis.hedge@sdstate.edu
HEDGEPATH, Donna ..... 270-789-5231 179 E
drhedgepath@campbellsville.edu
HEDGES, Denise, C ...... 417-667-8181 252 A
dhedges@cottey.edu
HEDGES, Don .... 847-317-7001 150 H
dhedges@tiu.edu
HEDGES, Jerris, R .... 808-692-0899 128 F
jerris@hawaii.edu
HEDGES, Tammy .... 901-678-2843 427 D
thedges@memphis.edu
HEDIN, Norma .... 214-333-5599 434 I
norma@dbu.edu
HEDLAND HANSEN,
Katherine .... 425-235-2356 483 G
khedlandhansen@rtc.edu
HEDLUN, Randy, J .... 417-862-9533 253 D
rhedlun@globaluniversity.edu
HEDLUND, Traci .... 816-960-2008 251 D
billing@cityvision.edu
HEDMAN, Shawn .... 507-537-6292 241 D
shawn.hedman@smsu.edu
HEDRICK, Van .... 940-668-7347 441 A
vhedrick@nctc.edu
HEDSTROM, Lori .... 843-953-7777 407 F
lhedstro@citadel.edu
HEE LEE, Seong .... 714-636-1722.. 28 G
HEEMSTRA, John .... 605-995-7204 415 G
john.heemstra@mitchelltech.edu
HEERDINK, Joe .... 270-831-9615 181 D
joe.heerdink@kctcs.edu
HEERDINK, Joe .... 270-831-9615 181 G
joe.heerdink@kctcs.edu
HEEREN, Diana .... 210-999-7163 452 A
dheeren@trinity.edu
HEEREN, Matthew .... 660-626-2064 250 A
mheeren@atsu.edu
HEERMAN, Heather, L .. 508-565-1301 218 H
hheerman@stonehill.edu
HEERMANN, Keith .... 417-862-9533 253 D
kheermann@globaluniversity.edu
HEERSINK, Heather .... 719-587-7759.. 76 F
heather_heersink@adams.edu
HEERSINK, Jordan .... 303-963-3388.. 77 G
joheersink@ccu.edu
HEESACKER-SMITH,
Angela .... 402-354-7256 268 C
angela.heesackersmith@
methodistcollege.edu
HEETLAND, David, L ..... 847-866-3970 137 E
david.heetland@garrett.edu
HEFFER, David .... 410-337-6112 198 G
david.heffer@goucher.edu
HEFFERIN, Cathy, D ..... 336-633-0208 337 A
cdhefferin@randolph.edu
HEFFERNAN,
Thomas, J .... 561-237-7270 102 V
theffernan@lynn.edu
HEFFERNAN, Tom .... 262-524-7343 492 E
HEFFNER, Brian .... 231-995-1283 228 G
bheffner@nmc.edu
HEFFRON, Timothy .... 740-284-5177 353 B
theffron@franciscan.edu
HEFLEY, Jacqueline, D . 512-404-4826 431 C
jhefley@austinseminary.edu
HEFLIN, David .... 903-589-7121 438 G
dheflin@jacksonville-college.edu
HEFLIN, David .... 270-534-3388 182 F
david.heflin@kctcs.edu
HEFLIN, David .... 605-394-4800 416 A
HEFLIN, Sherry .... 717-815-1257 404 A
sheflin@ycp.edu
HEFNER, Alana .... 254-968-9078 446 E
hefner@tarleton.edu

HEFNER, Beth .... 770-533-6607 121 B
bhefner@laniertech.edu
HEFTON, Ryan .... 214-333-5424 434 I
ryanh@dbu.edu
HEGAB, Hisham .... 318-257-4647 191 F
hhegab@latech.edu
HEGARTY, James .... 618-374-5157 146 E
james.hegarty@principia.edu
HEGARTY, Kevin, P .... 734-764-7272 231 E
hegartyk@umich.edu
HEGEDUS, Mary Ellen .. 574-239-8391 155 D
mhegedus@hcc-nd.edu
HEGEDUS, Stephen .... 203-392-5900.. 85 A
schoolofeducation@southernct.edu
HEGEL, Johanna .... 303-751-8700.. 77 A
hegel@bel-rea.com
HEGEMAN, Jay .... 301-687-4738 203 E
jhegeman@frostburg.edu
HEGENBARTH, Chris ..... 218-235-2164 241 E
chris.hegenbarth@vcc.edu
HEGER, Laura .... 570-389-4179 394 A
lheger@bloomu.edu
HEGGEMEYER, Terri ...... 402-844-7263 268 J
terrih@northeast.edu
HEGGOY, Liv .... 540-868-4091 474 J
lheggoy@lfcc.edu
HEGRANES, Colleen ...... 414-382-6126 492 A
colleen.hegranes@alverno.edu
HEGWER, Kim .... 757-352-4005 470 H
khegwer@regent.edu
HEGWOOD, Johnetta .... 310-342-5200.. 72 D
HEHL, Jim .... 239-590-1313 108 K
jhehl@fgcu.edu
HEIDA, Debbie .... 706-236-2227 115 B
dheida@berry.edu
HEIDBREDER, Kay, K .... 540-231-6293 477 A
heidbred@vt.edu
HEIDEMAN, Carl, E ...... 616-395-7670 225 B
heideman@hope.edu
HEIDEMAN, Gail .... 618-664-6609 137 G
gail.heideman@greenville.edu
HEIDEMANN, Molly .... 513-529-8600 356 E
mheidemann@miamioh.edu
HEIDENDAL, Egon .... 660-562-1965 257 E
egon@nwmissouri.edu
HEIDENFELDER, Jason . 630-829-1389 132 E
jheidenfelder@ben.edu
HEIDENREICH, Kari .... 262-472-1921 498 C
heidenreka12@uww.edu
HEIDENREICH, Lisa ...... 651-290-7678 242 G
lisa.heidenreich@mitchellhamline.edu
HEIDER, Don .... 408-554-7898.. 62 D
dheider@scu.edu
HEIDERICH, Gail .... 504-526-4745 189 H
gailh@nationsu.edu
HEIDERSBACH, Annie ... 440-826-3530 348 E
aheiders@bw.edu
HEIDICK, Venesa, A ...... 979-845-1059 446 G
vheidick@tamu.edu
HEIDINGSFIELD,
Michael, J .... 512-499-4688 454 I
mheidingsfield@utsystem.edu
HEIDKE, Stephen .... 314-392-2372 256 C
heidkesj@mobap.edu
HEIDLE, Wayne .... 714-463-7589.. 51 A
wheidle@ketchum.edu
HEIDORF, Marc .... 414-930-3219 495 A
heidorfm@mtmary.edu
HEIDRICH, Mark .... 208-459-5199 130 D
mheidrich@collegeofidaho.edu
HEIDRICK, Judy .... 785-738-9058 176 A
jheidrick@ncktc.edu
HEIDT, Mason .... 276-244-1226 464 L
mheidt@asl.edu
HEIDT, Matthew .... 716-926-8792 301 H
mheidt@hilbert.edu
HEIDTKE, Staci, L .... 715-836-5358 496 D
heidtksl@uwec.edu
HEIFNER, Bryan .... 432-335-6512 441 D
bheifner@odessa.edu
HEIGHES, Robert .... 734-487-1222 223 H
rheighes@emich.edu
HEIGHT, Linda, L .... 248-204-2159 226 G
lheight@ltu.edu
HEIGLE, Chris .... 870-633-4480.. 19 B
cheigle@eacc.edu
HEIKKILA, Christina ...... 910-362-7313 332 H
cheikkila@cfcc.edu
HEIKKINEN, Melinda .... 651-523-2100 236 A
mheikkinen@hamline.edu
HEIL, Elissa .... 717-262-2018 403 F
elissa.heil@wilson.edu

HEIL, Mark .... 208-426-1200 129 I
markheil@boisestate.edu
HEIL, Marti .... 517-355-1855 227 D
HEIL, Scott .... 951-827-3296.. 69 C
scott.heil@ucr.edu
HEILAND, Donna .... 718-636-3744 311 J
dheiland@pratt.edu
HEILBRON, Shawn, R ... 631-632-7205 317 D
shawn.heilbron@stonybrook.edu
HEILEMAN, Greg .... 859-257-1701 185 B
greg.heileman@uky.edu
HEILGEIST, Pete .... 360-650-3127 486 F
pete.heilgeist@wwu.edu
HEILMAN, Carl, R .... 620-792-9301 171 C
heilmanc@bartonccc.edu
HEILMAN, Todd .... 212-774-0704 306 A
theilman@mmm.edu
HEILSTEDT, Sally .... 425-739-8233 482 A
sally.heilstedt@lwtech.edu
HEIM, Edward .... 610-796-2838 378 F
edward.heim@alvernia.edu
HEIM, Peggy, M .... 610-799-1532 388 I
pheim@lccc.edu
HEIMANN, Anne .... 402-552-3100 266 E
HEIMBAUGH, Sharon ... 773-442-5805 145 B
s-heimbaugh@neiu.edu
HEIMBURGER, David, F 314-977-3139 259 H
david.heimburger@slu.edu
HEIMMERMANN, Dan ... 432-552-2110 457 A
heimmermann_d@utpb.edu
HEIMOVITZ, Issac .... 718-438-1002 306 G
HEIMS, Daniel .... 716-878-5336 318 C
HEIN, Anna .... 386-481-2894.. 95 F
heina@cookman.edu
HEIN, Beth .... 651-779-3438 237 G
beth.hein@century.edu
HEIN, Bruxanne .... 912-478-0580 119 C
bhein@georgiasouthern.edu
HEIN, Steven, M .... 912-478-0831 119 C
shein@georgiasouthern.edu
HEINBUCH, Danielle ..... 714-895-8970.. 38 D
dheinbuch@gwc.cccd.edu
HEINDEL, Patricia .... 973-290-4102 277 A
pheindel@cse.edu
HEINDL, Michael, J .... 662-562-3227 248 D
mheindl@northwestms.edu
HEINE, Gillian .... 541-684-7211 374 G
gheine@nwcu.edu
HEINE, Kelly .... 620-341-5473 172 L
kheinri1@emporia.edu
HEINEMAN, Linda .... 978-656-3228 214 G
heinemanl@middlesex.mass.edu
HEINEMAN, Pete .... 402-557-7146 265 J
pete.heineman@bellevue.edu
HEINEMAN, Ronald, E .. 513-244-8492 350 I
ron.heineman@ccuniversity.edu
HEINEMAN, William ..... 978-556-3327 215 C
wheineman@necc.mass.edu
HEINEN, Jack .... 828-669-8012 331 J
jheinen@montreat.edu
HEINEN, James .... 847-970-4809 152 A
jheinen@usml.edu
HEINERICHS, Scott .... 610-436-2733 396 A
sheinerichs@wcupa.edu
HEINLE, Nicole .... 701-252-3467 347 C
nicole.heinle@uj.edu
HEINLE, Sharon .... 703-726-1087.. 91 F
sheinle@gwu.edu
HEINRICH, Peggy .... 847-214-7635 136 F
pheinrich@elgin.edu
HEINRICH, Robert .... 609-652-6039 283 D
robert.heinrich@stockton.edu
HEINS, Marshall .... 713-718-7564 437 I
marshall.heins@hccs.edu
HEINSELMAN, Gregg .... 509-963-1515 479 B
gregory.heinselman@cwu.edu
HEINTZ, Jill .... 315-792-5584 307 D
jheintz@mvcc.edu
HEINTZ, Tim .... 303-292-0015.. 79 G
theintz@denvercollegeofnursing.edu
HEINZ, Cheryl .... 630-829-6581 132 E
cheinz@ben.edu
HEINZ, Jessica, J .... 417-836-6105 256 E
jessicaheinz@missouristate.edu
HEINZ, Kartha .... 206-876-6100 484 E
kheinz@theseattleschool.edu
HEINZEKEHR, Justin ..... 574-535-7000 155 A
justinbh@goshen.edu
HEINZEKEHR, Justin ..... 574-535-7110 155 A
justinbh@goshen.edu
HEINZELMAN, Wendi .... 585-275-4151 323 J
wendi.heinzelman@rochester.edu

HEINZERLING, Kelly ..... 734-384-4275 227 G
kheinzerling@monroeccc.edu
HEINZMAN, Mary, B .... 563-333-6241 169 A
heinzmanmaryb@sau.edu
HEISER, Andy .... 360-416-7745 485 A
andy.heiser@skagit.edu
HEISER, Donna .... 239-687-5402.. 94 N
dheiser@avemarialaw.edu
HEISER, Eric .... 801-957-5009 461 D
eric.heiser@slcc.edu
HEISER, Gregory, M ..... 405-325-8679 371 B
gheiser@ou.edu
HEISEY, Jennifer .... 513-556-4344 362 D
heiseyj@ucmail.uc.edu
HEISS, Beth, L .... 517-265-5161 220 F
bheiss@adrian.edu
HEISSERER, Nick .... 218-855-8038 237 F
nheisserer@clcmn.edu
HEIST, Daniel, P .... 814-865-1359 392 B
dph3@psu.edu
HEIST, Richard, H .... 203-254-4000.. 86 I
rheist@fairfield.edu
HEISTAD, Deirdre, A ..... 319-273-2633 163 B
d.heistad@uni.edu
HEITHAUS, Michael ...... 305-348-2866 109 A
michael.heithaus@fiu.edu
HEITING, Jordan .... 308-432-6415 268 E
jheiting@csc.edu
HEITKAMP, Andrew ...... 701-858-4002 345 F
andy.heitkamp@minotstateu.edu
HEITKAMP, Gordon .... 507-372-3465 239 E
gordy.heitkamp@mnwest.edu
HEITKEMPER, Mary .... 509-313-4231 481 D
heitkemper@gonzaga.edu
HEITMAN, Dave .... 916-577-2200.. 75 B
dheitman@jessup.edu
HEITZ, Nadine .... 609-896-5157 281 B
nheitz@rider.edu
HEITZENRATER, Kim, D 931-598-1121 423M
kheitzen@sewanee.edu
HEITZINGER, Karen ...... 716-375-2328 313 F
kheitzin@sbu.edu
HEIZ, Andrew .... 845-341-4251 311 C
andrew.heiz@sunyorange.edu
HEIZER NEWQUIST,
Leslie .... 425-564-2191 478 F
leslie.newquist@bellevuecollege.edu
HEJL, Cindy .... 303-964-5758.. 82 E
chejl@regis.edu
HELBIG, Suzanne, C ..... 949-824-7366.. 68 G
shelbig@uci.edu
HELBIG, Tuesdi .... 270-745-3250 185 E
tuesdi.helbig@wku.edu
HELBLE, Joseph, J .... 603-646-2404 273 E
joseph.j.helble@dartmouth.edu
HELBLING, Brenda .... 208-885-9191 131 G
brendah@uidaho.edu
HELD, II, John .... 573-341-6533 261 E
heldjohn@mst.edu
HELD, Joshua .... 847-317-4188 150 H
jrheld@tiu.edu
HELDEROP, Sue .... 248-364-6135 229 G
helderop@oakland.edu
HELDMAN, Lou .... 316-978-7114 178 A
lou.heldman@wichita.edu
HELEAN, Cathy .... 251-380-3868.... 6 H
chelean@shc.edu
HELEEN, Pamela, A ...... 315-294-8508 292 E
pamela.heleen@cayuga-cc.edu
HELENS, Joyce .... 775-753-2265 271 B
joyce.helens@gbcnv.edu
HELGESEN, Pete .... 913-360-7476 171 D
phelgesen@benedictine.edu
HELGESON, Grant .... 808-455-0645 129 D
helgeson@hawaii.edu
HELGESON, Stu .... 610-989-1276 402 B
shelgeson@vfmac.edu
HELIEISAR, Jennifer ...... 691-320-2480 505 B
jenniferh@comfsm.fm
HELITZER, Deborah ...... 602-496-0789.. 10 I
deborah.helitzer@asu.edu
HELLA, Lori, L .... 989-774-7194 222 C
hella1ll@cmich.edu
HELLAMS, J, T .... 864-379-8873 409 H
hellams@erskine.edu
HELLAR, Mark .... 415-351-3536.. 60 G
mhellar@sfai.edu
HELLDOBLER, Richard .. 973-720-2222 284 I
helldoblerr@wpunj.edu
HELLEMAN, Kathryn ...... 419-434-4256 364 G
khelleman@winebrenner.edu
HELLEN, Sharla .... 870-743-3000.. 20 C
sharla.hellen@northark.edu

HELLER, Adam 623-245-4600 16 E aheller@uti.edu
HELLER, Dana 734-487-4344 223 H dheller@emich.edu
HELLER, Dennis 605-882-5284 415 F dennis.heller@lakeareatech.edu
HELLER, Donald 415-422-6136 71 K deheller@usfca.edu
HELLER, Jacob 516-628-5076 319 A hellerj@oldwestbury.edu
HELLER, James 262-595-2455 497 C james.heller@uwp.edu
HELLER, Jennifer 816-584-6755 258 A jennifer.heller@park.edu
HELLER, Joshua, W 585-785-1335 300 B joshua.heller@flcc.edu
HELLER, Lauren 706-290-2688 115 B lheller@berry.edu
HELLER, Laurent 608-263-2467 496 C lheller@wisc.edu
HELLER, Mary 406-265-4198 264 F mary.heller@msun.edu
HELLER, Mary 610-989-1345 402 B mheller@vfmac.edu
HELLER, Matthew, D 607-587-3992 320 C hellermd@alfredstate.edu
HELLER, Tracy 858-635-4772 24 L theller@alliant.edu
HELLER, Tracy 858-635-4535 24 K theller@alliant.edu
HELLER DE MESSER, Kirk 414-930-3221 495 A hellerk@mtmary.edu
HELLER-ROSS, Holly, B 518-564-5180 319 C hellerhb@plattsburgh.edu
HELLER ROSS, Holly, B 518-564-5192 319 C hellerhb@plattsburgh.edu
HELLERMANN, David 651-290-6457 242 G david.hellermann@mitchellhamline.edu
HELLERSTEIN, Laurel 978-232-2153 209 B lhellers@endicott.edu
HELLERUD, Nancy 314-246-7440 262 C nancyhellerud@webster.edu
HELLING, Mary Kay 605-688-4173 417 C mary.helling@sdstate.edu
HELLING, Nathan, M 605-336-6588 416 E nhelling@sfseminary.edu
HELLMAN, Frances 510-642-5872 68 D fhellman@berkeley.edu
HELLMAN, Joel 202-687-0100 92 A jhellman@georgetown.edu
HELLMAN, Shari 419-434-4570 363 A shellman@findlay.edu
HELLMICH, David, M 815-835-6303 148 H david.m.hellmich@svcc.edu
HELLRUNG, Scott, A 414-410-4697 492 D shellrung@stritch.edu
HELLUMS, Paula 337-421-6965 188 D paula.hellums@sowela.edu
HELLWIG, Brant, J 540-458-5352 478 A hellwig@wlu.edu
HELLYER, Brenda 281-998-6100 443 B brenda.hellyer@sjcd.edu
HELM, Jonathan, C 254-710-1181 431 J jonathan_helm@baylor.edu
HELM, Lloyd 503-594-6793 372 D lloyd.helm@clackamas.edu
HELM, Scott 641-782-1481 169 H helm@swcciowa.edu
HELM, Steven 540-831-5471 470 C shelm@radford.edu
HELMBOLT, Shawn 605-688-4008 417 C shawn.helmbolt@sdstate.edu
HELMBRECHT, Alex 308-432-6212 268 E ahlembrecht@csc.edu
HELMER, Robert, C 440-826-2424 348 E rhelmer@bw.edu
HELMER, Shannon 610-799-1857 388 I shelmer@lccc.edu
HELMICK, Mary 540-231-6221 477 A mhelmick@vt.edu
HELMICK, Michael, S 828-448-3102 339 A mhelmick@wpcc.edu
HELMICK, Tom 724-852-3210 402 F thelmick@waynesburg.edu
HELMINCK, Aloysius 808-956-6451 128 F helminck@hawaii.edu
HELMLINGER, Barb 419-473-2700 352 E bhelmlinger@daviscollege.edu
HELMS, Barbara 440-375-7015 355 G bhelms@lec.edu
HELMS, Bryan 334-293-4522 1 C bryan.helms@accs.edu
HELMS, Carol 509-453-0374 483 C carol.helms@perrytech.edu
HELMS, Chris 828-766-1291 336 A chelms@mayland.edu
HELMS, Clint 706-233-7265 124 B chelms@shorter.edu
HELMS, Joel 715-232-3485 498 A helmsj@uwstout.edu
HELMS, Lance 912-538-3207 124 F lhelms@southeasterntech.edu
HELMS, LuAnn 435-797-1012 460 H luann.helms@usu.edu
HELMS, Marilyn 706-272-2600 117 C mhelms@daltonstate.edu
HELMS, Mark 704-330-6127 333 D mark.helms@cpcc.edu
HELMS, Michael 334-347-2623 2 A mhelms@escc.edu
HELMS, Paula 334-347-2623 2 A phelms@escc.edu
HELMS, Sherrie 478-289-2360 117 D shelms@ega.edu
HELMS, Steve 334-222-6591 2 I shelms@lbwcc.edu
HELMS, Wanda 505-224-4000 285 J whelms@cnm.edu
HELMSING, Debra, F 260-665-4240 160 H helmsingd@trine.edu
HELMSTETTER, Ashley 419-448-2231 353 H ahelmste@heidelberg.edu
HELMUS, Aimee 910-362-7012 332 H ahelmus@cfcc.edu
HELMUS, Mark 765-285-5555 153 C dmhelmus@bsu.edu
HELOU, Ibrahim (Abe) 909-593-3511 70 D ihelou@laverne.edu
HELSPER, Nancy 320-589-6012 244 B helsper@morris.umn.edu
HELTON, Ed 706-507-8720 116 I helton_ed@columbusstate.edu
HELTON, Karen 903-927-3369 458 G khelton@wileyc.edu
HELTON, Kasey 404-894-1822 118 F kasey.helton@gatech.edu
HELTON, Patricia 727-873-4882 110 C phelton@mail.usf.edu
HELVERING, Christal 765-641-4205 153 B crhelvering@anderson.edu
HELWIG, Anna 708-596-2000 149 B ahelwig@ssc.edu
HELWIG, Susan, M 570-674-6368 390 G shelwig@misericordia.edu
HELYER, Kella 503-838-8684 377 H helyerk@wou.edu
HEMANN, Patty 507-433-0816 240 F patty.hemann@riverland.edu
HEMANS, Peter 828-694-1723 332 E peterh@blueridge.edu
HEMBRECHT, Louise 920-686-6200 496 A louise.hembrecht@sl.edu
HEMBREE, Jennifer 707-654-1780 32 B jhembree@csum.edu
HEMENWAY, Jessica 920-693-1118 499 G jessica.hemenway@gotoltc.edu
HEMENWAY, Michael 303-765-3173 80 F mhemenway@iliff.edu
HEMENWAY, Robin 612-238-4542 243 B rhemenwa@smumn.edu
HEMINGWAY, Liana 727-864-8316 97 J hemingl@eckerd.edu
HEMKER, Judy 618-545-3105 140 E jhemker@kaskaskia.edu
HEMKIN, Sheryl 740-427-5093 355 E themkins@kenyon.edu
HEMLICK, Lisa, M 610-341-5830 383 D lhemlick@eastern.edu
HEMMELER, Curtis 614-891-3200 357 D
HEMMENBACH, Jimmi 808-543-8083 127 H jhemmenbach@hpu.edu
HEMMER, David 906-487-2156 227 E djhemmer@mtu.edu
HEMMER, Katie 212-842-5962 308 D khemmer@nyaa.edu
HEMMER, Laura 314-505-7203 251 I hemmerl@csl.edu
HEMMER, Michelle 919-508-2260 344 F michelle.hemmer@peace.edu
HEMMESCH, Michael 320-363-2595 243 A mhemmesch@csbsju.edu
HEMMIG, Bill 215-504-8611 379 G bill.hemmig@bucks.edu
HEMMILA, Deanna 906-227-2637 228 F dhemmila@nmu.edu
HEMMINGSEN, Jens 614-236-6105 349 D jhemming@capital.edu
HEMPEN, Laurie 319-208-5063 169 F lhempen@scciowa.edu
HEMPHILL, Brian, O 540-831-5401 470 C president@radford.edu
HEMPHILL, Bryon 208-467-8673 131 D bdhemphill@nnu.edu
HEMPHILL, F. Bruce 337-475-5563 192 A bhemphill@mcneese.edu
HEMPHILL, Valory 281-931-7717 120 H gweaver@ict.edu
HEMPSEY, John Paul 928-524-7418 14 J paul.hempsey@npc.edu
HEMPTON, David, N 617-495-4513 210 B dhempton@hds.harvard.edu
HEMRIC, Cheryl 910-296-2070 335 E chemric@jamessprunt.edu
HEMRICK, Robert, D 731-425-2636 425 B dhemrick@jscc.edu
HEMSTOCK, Kaleigh 336-272-7102 329 D kaleigh.hemstock@greensboro.edu
HEMWAY, Joseph 718-399-4293 311 J jhemway@pratt.edu
HENAHAN, David 518-587-2100 321 A david.henahan@esc.edu
HENAN, Carmen 505-424-2336 286 C chenan@iaia.edu
HENARD, Kevin 254-298-8425 446 A kevin.henard@templejc.edu
HENARD, Kevin 254-267-7012 442 E khenard@rangercollege.edu
HENCHEY, Russell 740-245-7358 363 D rhenchey@rio.edu
HENCHY, Dolores 201-355-1133 278 A henchyd@felician.edu
HENCK, Anita 626-815-5348 26 H ahenck@apu.edu
HENDERSHOT, Debra 256-306-2581 1 F debi.hendershot@calhoun.edu
HENDERSHOT, Jason 814-393-2111 394 D jhendershot@clarion.edu
HENDERSHOT, Stephanie, N 412-262-6251 397 G hendershot@rmu.edu
HENDERSON, Aaron 559-453-2207 43 G aaron.henderson@fresno.edu
HENDERSON, Allan 816-322-0110 250 K allen.henderson@calvary.edu
HENDERSON, Allen 817-531-4405 451 E ahenderson@txwes.edu
HENDERSON, Amy 410-287-1910 197 H ahenderson@cecil.edu
HENDERSON, Andre 412-237-2224 381 G ahenderson@ccac.edu
HENDERSON, Andrea 309-298-1977 152 D ad-henderson@wiu.edu
HENDERSON, Brad 806-291-3616 457 J brad.henderson@wbu.edu
HENDERSON, Brad 660-596-7250 260 D rhenderson9@sfccmo.edu
HENDERSON, Brian 276-656-0313 475 D bhenderson@patrickhenry.edu
HENDERSON, Brittany 206-726-5174 480 C bhenderson@cornish.edu
HENDERSON, Carol 315-364-3356 325 B chenderson@wells.edu
HENDERSON, Carol 302-831-3919 90 F ceh@udel.edu
HENDERSON, Carolyn 256-551-3226 2 E carolyn.henderson@drakestate.edu
HENDERSON, Chiquita, A 727-816-3205 104 F henderc@phsc.edu
HENDERSON, Christina 515-271-1501 164 I christina.henderson@dmu.edu
HENDERSON, Christine 773-371-5450 133 E chenderson@ctu.edu
HENDERSON, Cori 859-572-6534 184 A hendersonc5@nku.edu
HENDERSON, Cynthia 903-223-3053 448 B cynthia.henderson@tamut.edu
HENDERSON, Darren 219-473-4346 153 G dhenderson@ccsj.edu
HENDERSON, Darwin, C 505-786-4300 286 G chenderson@navajotech.edu
HENDERSON, Dave 541-917-4331 374 A henderd@linnbenton.edu
HENDERSON, Donna 503-768-7860 373 G dhenderson@lclark.edu
HENDERSON, Eddie, W 806-651-2600 448 C ehenderson@wtamu.edu
HENDERSON, George 704-330-4806 333 D george.henderson@cpcc.edu
HENDERSON, Howard 580-349-1380 368 A howardh@opsu.edu
HENDERSON, Idell 404-527-6360 120 K ihenderson@itc.edu
HENDERSON, James 856-256-4175 281 E henderson@rowan.edu
HENDERSON, James, B 225-342-6950 191 D jim.henderson@ulsystem.edu
HENDERSON, Janice 850-729-5392 103 L hendersonj@nwfsc.edu
HENDERSON, Joe, T 731-881-3506 428 B jhende33@utm.edu
HENDERSON, June 317-738-8028 154 J jhenderson@franklincollege.edu
HENDERSON, Keith 404-756-8919 122 E khenderson@msm.edu
HENDERSON, Keli 724-938-5985 394 B henderson_k@calu.edu
HENDERSON, Ken 617-373-4798 217 F
HENDERSON, Kyle, W 740-427-5729 355 E hendersonk@kenyon.edu
HENDERSON, Lacey 903-886-5108 447 B lacey.henderson@tamuc.edu
HENDERSON, Lisa 440-826-2767 348 E lhenders@bw.edu
HENDERSON, Mantra 662-254-3495 248 B mlhenderson@mvsu.edu
HENDERSON, Michelle 760-252-2411 26 I mhenderson@barstow.edu
HENDERSON, Mitchell 718-482-5534 294 F mhenderson@lagcc.cuny.edu
HENDERSON, Molly, L 304-457-6256 487 B cummingsml@ab.edu
HENDERSON, Nancy 319-296-4448 166 B nancy.henderson@hawkeyecollege.edu
HENDERSON, Nicole 215-641-6545 390 H nhenders@mc3.edu
HENDERSON, Paul 207-602-2302 196 G phenderson@une.edu
HENDERSON, Paula, M 601-984-1010 249 E pmhenderson@umc.edu
HENDERSON, Perry 254-968-9644 446 E phenderson@tarleton.edu
HENDERSON, Peter 410-455-3263 202 E phenders@umbc.edu
HENDERSON, Sean 559-442-8295 66 E sean.henderson@fresnocitycollege.edu
HENDERSON, Stacie 334-727-8643 7 D shenderson@tuskegee.edu
HENDERSON, Sue 201-200-3111 279 E shenderson@njcu.edu
HENDERSON, Susan 843-383-8264 408 D shenderson@coker.edu
HENDERSON, Tammy 850-484-1766 104 H thenderson@pensacolastate.edu
HENDERSON, Toni 910-296-2438 335 E thenderson@jamessprunt.edu
HENDERSON, Triss 217-353-2101 146 C thenderson@parkland.edu
HENDERSON, Vaneshette 903-927-3329 458 G vhenderson@wileyc.edu
HENDERSON, William, J 262-243-5700 493 B william.henderson@cuw.edu
HENDERSON-BROWN, Tessa 415-239-3530 37 A thenders@ccsf.edu
HENDERSON-GASSER, Ellen 217-357-3129 133 C ehenderson@sandburg.edu
HENDLER, Gail 708-216-5303 142 D ghendler@luc.edu
HENDREY, Elizabeth 718-997-5900 295 C elizabeth.hendrey@qc.cuny.edu
HENDRICK, Ronald 517-355-0232 227 D hendric6@msu.edu
HENDRICK, Sarah 661-654-3370 30 E shendrick@csub.edu
HENDRICK, Sarah 860-932-4096 86 E shendrick@qvcc.edu
HENDRICKS, Bill 214-887-5252 436 B bhendricks@dts.edu
HENDRICKS, Constance 334-727-8282 7 D chendricks@tuskegee.edu
HENDRICKS, Cynthia, L 651-696-6145 236 H chendric@macalester.edu
HENDRICKS, Dawn 570-321-4022 389 E henddawn@lycoming.edu
HENDRICKS, George 704-922-6305 334 F hendricks.george@gaston.edu

HENDRICKS, Jeff .... 336-278-5587 328 K
jhendrick4@elon.edu
HENDRICKS, Jeff .... 270-852-8977 182 B
jhendricks0008@kctcs.edu
HENDRICKS, Joan, C .... 215-898-8841 400 K
vetdean@vet.upenn.edu
HENDRICKS, Julie .... 805-893-4581.. 70 A
julie.hendricks@dcs.ucsb.edu
HENDRICKS,
Lynn Nicole .... 203-582-8753.. 87 G
lynn.hendricks@quinnipic.edu
HENDRICKS, Mark .... 916-278-1999.. 32 E
mark.hendricks@csus.edu
HENDRICKS, Michael .... 864-294-3231 410 A
michael.hendricks@furman.edu
HENDRICKS,
Michelle, M .... 570-577-2404 379 F
michelle.jones@bucknell.edu
HENDRICKS, Richard, J 708-974-5203 144 C
hendricksr4@morainevalley.edu
HENDRICKS, Susan ...... 765-455-9288 156 D
shendric@iu.edu
HENDRICKS, Tom, M ... 248-232-4312 229 A
tmhendri@oaklandcc.edu
HENDRICKSEN,
Melanie .... 503-552-1966 374 E
mhendricksen@nunm.edu
HENDRICKSON,
Anthony, R .... 402-280-2852 266 I
anthonyhendrickson@creighton.edu
HENDRICKSON,
Brittney .... 417-447-8656 259 L
bhendrickson@sbuniv.edu
HENDRICKSON, SJ,
Daniel, S .... 402-280-2770 266 I
president@creighton.edu
HENDRICKSON, Ken ..... 936-294-1031 450 C
his_keh@shsu.edu
HENDRICKSON, Kristen 715-346-2641 497 F
khendric@uwsp.edu
HENDRICKSON,
Kristine .... 401-341-2148 406 A
hendrick@salve.edu
HENDRICKSON, Loretta 607-962-9291 320 F
hendrickson@corning-cc.edu
HENDRICKSON, Philip .. 402-643-7358 266 G
philip.hendrickson@cune.edu
HENDRICKSON,
Ryan, C .... 217-581-2220 136 E
rchendrickson@eiu.edu
HENDRICKSON, Sandy . 425-889-5232 482 F
sandy.hendrickson@northwestu.edu
HENDRICKSON, Tracy ... 218-335-4200 236 E
tracy.hendrickson@lltc.edu
HENDRICKSON,
Vicki, A .... 918-631-2526 371 E
vicki-hendrickson@utulsa.edu
HENDRIKSMA, Jane, E . 616-526-6117 222 A
jhendrik@calvin.edu
HENDRIX, Andrew .... 803-641-3490 413 D
andrewh@usca.edu
HENDRIX, Dean, D .... 210-458-4889 455 E
dean.hendrix@utsa.edu
HENDRIX, Grace .... 208-882-1566 131 B
ghendrix@nsa.edu
HENDRIX, Joan .... 228-267-8643 247 E
joan.hendrix@mgccc.edu
HENDRIX, Kristie, F ...... 336-734-7051 334 E
khendrix@forsythtech.edu
HENDRIX, Mary .... 304-876-5107 490 E
mhendrix@shepherd.edu
HENDRIX, Mary Helen .. 803-822-3077 410 G
hendrixca@midlandstech.edu
HENDRIX, Pat .... 931-393-1629 425 C
phendrix@mscc.edu
HENDRIX, Sherri .... 517-750-1200 230 H
shendrix@arbor.edu
HENDRY, David .... 727-873-4475 110 C
davidhendry@mail.usf.edu
HENDRYX, Julie, A .... 260-422-5561 155 H
jahendryx@indianatech.edu
HENEGAR, Kellie .... 618-545-3025 140 E
khenegar@kaskaskia.edu
HENG-MOSS, Tiffany ..... 402-472-2797 269 J
thengmoss2@unl.edu
HENICK, Steven, T .... 410-777-2429 197 C
sthenick@aacc.edu
HENIK, John .... 319-398-5518 167 C
jhenik@kirkwood.edu
HENK, William, A .... 414-288-7376 494 B
william.henk@marquette.edu
HENKE, Corrine .... 208-426-4045 129 I
chenke@boisestate.edu
HENKE, Wanda .... 402-494-2311 268 B
whenke@thenicc.edu
HENKEL, Mandy .... 608-822-2475 500 G
mhenkel@swtc.edu
HENKELMAN, Amy .... 415-257-1304.. 41 H
amy.henkelman@dominican.edu
HENKEN, Celeste .... 262-564-2644 499 F
henkenc@gtc.edu
HENKING, Susan .... 336-721-2617 340 D
susan.henking@salem.edu
HENLEY, Amy .... 701-777-2135 345 C
amy.henley@und.edu
HENLEY, Antonio .... 704-330-1320 330 D
ahenley@jcsu.edu
HENLEY, Blair .... 423-636-7300 427 B
bhenley@tusculum.edu
HENLEY, Brian .... 916-278-7766.. 32 E
brian.henley@csus.edu
HENLEY, Charles .... 936-294-4719 450 C
ceh071@shsu.edu
HENLEY, Jerry, D .... 801-863-6246 461 A
jerry.henley@uvu.edu
HENLEY, Keldon .... 870-245-5405.. 20 E
henleyk@obu.edu
HENLEY, Kyle .... 541-346-2329 377 D
henley@uoregon.edu
HENLEY, Marilynn, D ... 602-614-2337.. 10 D
HENLEY, Marsia .... 215-751-8902 382 A
mhenley@ccp.edu
HENLEY, Wade .... 301-860-3744 203 C
whenley@bowiestate.edu
HENNEKE,
Danette Johnson .... 865-539-7350 425 F
dljohnson11@pstcc.edu
HENNEN, Thomas, J ..... 563-333-6151 169 A
hennenthomasj@sau.edu
HENNESS, Rose .... 816-322-0110 250 K
rose.henness@calvary.edu
HENNESSEY, Brendan ... 575-562-2424 285 M
brendan.hennessey@enmu.edu
HENNESSEY, Catherine . 978-542-6134 213 C
ctr_chennessey@salemstate.edu
HENNESSEY, David .... 617-243-2478 210 G
dhennessey@lasell.edu
HENNESSEY, Patrick ..... 914-606-6638 325 C
patrick.hennessey@sunywcc.edu
HENNESSY, Bill .... 701-349-5779 346 J
bhennessy@trinitybiblecollege.edu
HENNESSY, Catherine ... 516-463-6820 302 B
catherine.hennessy@hofstra.edu
HENNESSY, John, L ...... 650-723-2300.. 65 J
HENNESSY, Kelly .... 609-771-3455 276 I
hennessk@tcnj.edu
HENNESSY, Lynne, M ... 203-773-8529.. 84 F
lhennessy@albertus.edu
HENNIGAN, Ed .... 570-740-0399 389 D
ehennigan@luzerne.edu
HENNIGAN, Paul .... 412-392-3990 397 A
phennigan@pointpark.edu
HENNIGES, Amy .... 920-465-2380 496 E
hennigea@uwgb.edu
HENNIGH, Aimee .... 620-947-3121 177 C
aimeehennigh@tabor.edu
HENNING, Amy .... 215-572-2900 379 A
henninga@arcadia.edu
HENNING, Arnold .... 773-583-4050 145 B
HENNING, John .... 732-571-4484 279 B
jhenning@monmouth.edu
HENNING, Kana .... 773-508-3489 142 D
kwibben@luc.edu
HENNING, Kent, L .... 515-263-2802 165 I
khenning@grandview.edu
HENNING, Patricia .... 505-277-6128 288 G
henning@unm.edu
HENNING, Stefanie .... 617-747-2246 206 E
careercenter@berklee.edu
HENNING, Stephanie ..... 407-646-2258 105 M
shenning@rollins.edu
HENNING, Volker .... 509-527-2615 485 H
volker.henning@wallawalla.edu
HENNINGER, Ed .... 541-962-3672 373 B
ehenninger@eou.edu
HENNINGSEN,
James, D .... 352-873-5835.. 96 O
jim.henningsen@cf.edu
HENRICH, IHM, Mary ... 610-647-4400 386 C
mhenrich@immaculata.edu
HENRICH, William, L .... 210-567-2050 456 C
henrich@uthscsa.edu
HENRICHSEN, Courtney 636-584-6583 252 J
courtney.henrichsen@eastcentral.edu
HENRICKSON, Jay, A .... 701-788-4899 345 E
jay.henrickson@mayvillestate.edu
HENRIE, Stephen, E ...... 313-577-5929 232 I
fj9065@wayne.edu
HENRIKSEN, Deb .... 605-642-6581 416 I
deb.henriksen@bhsu.edu
HENRIKSEN, J.L .... 509-533-7295 480 A
jl.henriksen@scc.spokane.edu
HENRIKSEN, Smokey .... 406-338-5441 263 B
smokeyh@bfcc.edu
HENRIQUES, Richard .... 402-486-2511 269 F
richard.henriqes@ucollege.edu
HENRIQUES, Shilo .... 508-588-9100 214 F
shenrique@massasoit.mass.edu
HENRIS, Dan .... 989-463-7144 220 H
henris@alma.edu
HENRIS, Shawn .... 716-827-2522 323 D
henriss@trocaire.edu
HENRY, Alison .... 609-652-4831 283 D
alison.henry@stockton.edu
HENRY, Amy .... 404-894-7475 118 F
amy.henry@oie.gatech.edu
HENRY, Barb .... 404-364-8443 122 J
bhenry@oglethorpe.edu
HENRY, Barbara, L .... 419-372-4825 348 H
bhenry@bgsu.edu
HENRY, Carolyn, J .... 573-882-3768 261 B
henryc@missouri.edu
HENRY, Charles, E .... 713-313-4343 449 C
henryce@tsu.edu
HENRY, Christy, S .... 478-757-5219 126 H
chenry@wesleyancollege.edu
HENRY, Cynthia .... 850-599-3225 108 I
cynthia.henry@famu.edu
HENRY, Dale .... 731-352-4239 418 G
henryd@bethelu.edu
HENRY, Deena, H .... 919-209-2017 335 F
dhhenry@johnstoncc.edu
HENRY, Donna, P .... 276-328-0122 473 A
dph3p@virginia.edu
HENRY, Donna, P .... 276-328-0122 473 B
dph3p@virginia.edu
HENRY, Earl .... 256-726-8308.... 6 C
ehenry@oakwood.edu
HENRY, II, Edwell .... 215-248-6393 400 I
ehenry@uls.edu
HENRY, Elizabeth .... 602-383-8228.. 16 F
ehenry@uat.edu
HENRY, Etta, A .... 757-683-5889 469 G
ehenry@odu.edu
HENRY, Frank, M .... 405-325-6151 371 B
fhenry@ou.edu
HENRY, Geneva .... 202-994-6455.. 91 F
genevahenry@gwu.edu
HENRY, Glenn .... 706-355-5033 114 F
ghenry@athenstech.edu
HENRY, Jamie .... 618-544-8657 138 H
henryj@iecc.edu
HENRY, Jennifer .... 314-529-9552 254 H
jhenry@maryville.edu
HENRY, Jerlynn .... 505-786-4104 286 G
jhenryi@navajotech.edu
HENRY, Jerry, W .... 361-698-2178 436 C
jhenry12@delmar.edu
HENRY, Jonathan .... 207-621-3304 196 A
jonathan.henry@maine.edu
HENRY, Kevin, C .... 717-866-5775 383 H
khenry@evangelical.edu
HENRY, Kimberly .... 712-325-3207 167 B
khenry@iwcc.edu
HENRY, Kyonna .... 920-748-8190 495 G
henryk@ripon.edu
HENRY, Laurie, A .... 410-543-6335 203 F
lahenry@salisbury.edu
HENRY, Linda .... 913-360-7500 171 D
lhenry@benedictine.edu
HENRY, Marci .... 970-521-6617.. 81 D
marci.henry@njc.edu
HENRY, Melody .... 903-434-8148 441 B
mhenry@ntcc.edu
HENRY, Nick .... 706-272-4435 117 C
nhenry@daltonstate.edu
HENRY, Ronald .... 850-599-3560 108 I
ronald.henry@famu.edu
HENRY, Ryan .... 806-743-9855 451 C
ryan.henry@ttuhsc.edu
HENRY, Sandra .... 334-983-6556.... 7 C
shenry@troy.edu
HENRY, Sandy .... 541-962-3185 373 B
shenry@eou.edu
HENRY, Scott .... 570-662-4900 395 C
shenry@mansfield.edu
HENRY, Shannon, B ..... 336-750-2020 344 B
henrysb@wssu.edu
HENRY, Stuart .... 619-594-5037.. 33 E
shenry2@sdsu.edu
HENRY, Tim .... 817-272-7215 454 J
dr.henry@uta.edu
HENRY, Winfield .... 336-506-4136 332 A
winfield.henry@alamancecc.edu
HENRY POWELL, Jonita 704-379-6800.. 92 G
HENRY ROBINSON,
Shanelle .... 914-773-3775 311 E
shenryrobinson@pace.edu
HENSEL, Chad .... 740-389-4636 356 B
henselc@mtc.edu
HENSEL, Wendy, F .... 404-413-2574 119 E
whensel@gsu.edu
HENSGEN, Brian, C ...... 217-442-3044 135 H
bhensgen@dacc.edu
HENSGEN, Laura, M ..... 217-554-1668 135 H
lhensgen@dacc.edu
HENSHAW, Debbie .... 706-649-1888 117 A
dhenshaw@columbustech.edu
HENSLER, Brandon .... 954-262-5385 103 M
bh623@nova.edu
HENSLEY, Alec .... 812-749-1421 159 C
ahensley@oak.edu
HENSLEY, Chiara .... 734-487-0074 223 H
emu_ombuds@emich.edu
HENSLEY, Kenneth .... 479-308-2361.. 17 C
kenneth.hensley@arcomedu.org
HENSLEY, Linda .... 619-388-2797.. 60 D
lhensley@sdccd.edu
HENSLEY, Mary .... 979-830-4112 432 C
chancellor@blinn.edu
HENSLEY, Michele, R ... 540-432-4139 466 G
michele.hensley@emu.edu
HENSLEY, Ron .... 417-255-7268 256 F
ronhensley@missouristate.edu
HENSON, Alexander, L . 804-828-0138 473 F
alhenson@vcu.edu
HENSON, Amy .... 573-518-2122 256 B
amy@mineralarea.edu
HENSON, Chris .... 931-540-2705 424 G
chenson12@columbiastate.edu
HENSON, Don .... 901-722-4719 424 C
dhenson@sco.edu
HENSON, Gregory, J .... 605-336-6588 416 E
ghenson@sfseminary.edu
HENSON, John, H .... 717-245-1434 382 F
henson@dickinson.edu
HENSON, Joseph .... 415-422-4086.. 71 K
jhenson2@usfca.edu
HENSON, Kevin .... 714-432-5796.. 38 E
khenson@occ.cccd.edu
HENSON, Michael, C .... 606-783-9080 183 F
m.henson@moreheadstate.edu
HENSON, Nicholas .... 937-395-8112 355 F
nicholas.henson@kc.edu
HENSON, Pamella, A .... 314-935-5850 262 A
hensonp@wustl.edu
HENSON, Perry, V .... 864-597-4000 414 H
hensonpv@wofford.edu
HENSON, JR.,
Thomas, M .... 864-597-4213 414 H
HENSON, Travis .... 618-545-3177 140 E
thenson@kaskaskia.edu
HENSRUD, Faith .... 218-333-6600 240 B
fhensrud@bemidjistate.edu
HENSRUD, Faith, C .... 218-755-2011 237 E
faith.hensrud@bemidjistate.edu
HENTHORN, Becky .... 580-387-7000 366 H
bhenthorn@mscok.edu
HENTIES, Brian, B .... 407-582-3337 112 K
mhenties@valenciacollege.edu
HENTSCHEL, Alain, R .... 386-312-4302 106 C
alainhentschel@sjrstate.edu
HENTZ, Paula .... 386-822-7012 111 A
phentz@stetson.edu
HENZE, George .... 920-693-1733 499 G
george.henze@gotoltc.edu
HENZEL, JR., John, R .. 706-245-7226 117 E
jhenzel@ec.edu
HEO, Samuel, S .... 201-981-0009 118 B
sheo1004@gmail.com
HEOS, Pamela .... 517-371-5140 233 A
heosp@cooley.edu
HEPBURN, Deborah ...... 814-453-6016 400 E
dhepburn@triangle-tech.edu
HEPBURN, Deborah, G . 814-371-2090 400 F
dhepburn@triangle-tech.edu
HEPBURN, Deborah, G . 814-371-2090 400 G
dhepburn@triangle-tech.edu
HEPERI, Vernon, L .... 801-422-0556 458 H
vern_heperi@byu.edu

HERNANDEZ-RODRIGUEZ, Raul 787-746-1400 508 B rahernandez@huertas.edu
HERNANDEZ-SIEGEL, Alex 719-389-6639 77 H ahernandezsiegel@coloradocollege.edu
HERNANDEZ-STEVENSON, Britney 270-824-8671 181 G britney.hernandezstevenson@kctcs.edu
HERNDON, Craig 804-819-4782 474 A cherndon@vccs.edu
HERNDON, Doug 916-484-8101 50 F herndod@arc.losrios.edu
HERNDON, Kimmetha, D 205-726-2198 6 E kherndon@samford.edu
HERNDON, OSB, Linda 913-360-7553 171 D lherndon@benedictine.edu
HERNDON, Linda, M 229-226-1621 125 C lherndon@thomasu.edu
HERNDON, Micaela 972-923-6440 440 G micaela.herndon@navarrocollege.edu
HERNDON, Michael (Mike) 817-515-1502 445 G michael.herndon@tccd.edu
HERNDON, Nicole 501-760-4300 20 B nicole.herndon@np.edu
HERNDON, Renee 205-929-3419 2 H rherndon@lawsonstate.edu
HERNDON, Steven, T 937-229-3317 362 G sherndon1@udayton.edu
HERNDON, Tamia 601-877-3540 244 H therndon@alcorn.edu
HERNDON, Tamia 601-629-3568 244 H therndon@alcorn.edu
HERNE, Jaclyn 716-839-8245 298 B jherne@daemen.edu
HERNESS, Scott 973-655-4368 279 C hernesss@mail.montclair.edu
HEROD, Kevin 256-761-8757 7 B krherod@talladega.edu
HEROLD, Brent 504-568-2412 189 B bherol@lsuhsc.edu
HEROLD, Dale 352-638-9778 95 D dherold@beaconcollege.edu
HEROLD, Irene 330-263-2483 351 C iherold@wooster.edu
HERON, Keith 212-217-4210 299 H keith_heron@fitnyc.edu
HERONIMUS, Katie 507-372-3455 239 E katie.heronimus@mnwest.edu
HEROY, Darci 541-346-8136 377 D titleixcoordinator@uoregon.edu
HERR, Audrey 717-871-7612 395 D aherr@ssi.millersville.edu
HERR, Beth, J 402-280-5769 266 I bherr@creighton.edu
HERR, Don 850-201-6168 111 C herrd@tcc.fl.edu
HERR, Duane 410-777-2346 197 C dpherr@aacc.edu
HERR, Elijah 541-463-3000 373 F
HERR, Matthew, F 570-348-6211 389 G mfherr@marywood.edu
HERR, Robert 973-408-3250 277 C rherr@drew.edu
HERRAN, Edward 914-251-6070 319 E edward.herran@purchase.edu
HERRELKO, Edward 214-887-5141 436 B eherrelko@dts.edu
HERREN, Melissa 405-945-3297 368 E herrenm@osuokc.edu
HERRERA, Andrea 719-255-4001 83 B aherrera@uccs.edu
HERRERA, Antoinette 408-274-7900 61 L antoinette.herrera@evc.edu
HERRERA, Cynthia 805-678-5944 73 A cherrera@vcccd.edu
HERRERA, Francisco 510-436-1000 45 D herrera@hnu.edu
HERRERA, Gilberto 787-890-2681 512 H gilberto.herrera@upr.edu
HERRERA, Jesse 605-394-1828 417 B jesse.herrera@sdsmt.edu
HERRERA, Jorge, D 512-404-4829 431 C jherrera@austinseminary.edu
HERRERA, Jose 914-674-7500 306 F jherrera@mercy.edu
HERRERA, Rick 956-364-5002 449 E rick.herrera@tstc.edu
HERRERA, Xochil 303-360-4788 79 D xochil.herrera@ccaurora.edu
HERRERA LINDSTROM, Cynthia, E 312-996-3719 151 B cynthiar@uic.edu
HERRERA-SOBEK, Maria 805-893-5114 70 A maria.sobek@ucsb.edu
HERRICK, Alice 207-326-2445 195 D alice.herrick@mma.edu
HERRICK, Bryan 636-481-3168 254 A bherrick@jeffco.edu
HERRICK, George 304-367-4293 490 B george.herrick@fairmontstate.edu
HERRICK, James, S 619-594-0213 33 E herrick1@sdsu.edu
HERRICK, Jessica 989-328-1228 228 A jessicah@montcalm.edu
HERRICK-PHELPS, Johnna 802-865-5488 462 B jherrickphelps@champlain.edu
HERRIDGE, Curt 214-768-4197 444 E herridge@smu.edu
HERRIFORD, Steven, R 317-781-5767 161 B sherriford@uindy.edu
HERRIG, Becky 563-588-6321 163 F becky.herrig@clarke.edu
HERRIN, Andraea 803-376-5758 406 F aherrin@allenuniversity.edu
HERRIN, Brice 229-732-5980 114 B briceherrin@andrewcollege.edu
HERRIN, Bridget 619-388-2509 60 D bherrin@sdccd.edu
HERRIN, Carl 508-929-8263 213 E cherrin@worcester.edu
HERRIN, Madison 912-583-3211 115 E mherrin@bpc.edu
HERRIN, Timothy, D 704-233-8150 344 G herrin@wingate.edu
HERRIN, William 209-946-2650 70 E wherrin@pacific.edu
HERRING, Angela 252-246-1363 339 C aherring@wilsoncc.edu
HERRING, April 410-386-8444 197 G aherring@carrollcc.edu
HERRING, Charles 410-704-5913 204 A cherring@towson.edu
HERRING, George 972-860-4634 434 L gtherring@dcccd.edu
HERRING, Jack 360-650-3779 486 F jack.herring@wwu.edu
HERRING, Jamie 270-809-3011 183 G jherring5@murraystate.edu
HERRING, Jeff, C 801-585-0928 460 E jeff.herring@utah.edu
HERRING, Mark, Y 803-323-2232 414 G herringm@winthrop.edu
HERRING, Natalie 217-206-8660 151 C nherr4@uis.edu
HERRING, Nathan 765-677-2257 157 D nathan.herring@indwes.edu
HERRING, Paula 229-333-2109 127 B paula.herring@wiregrass.edu
HERRING, Robin 717-262-2017 403 F rherring@wilson.edu
HERRING, Susan 215-968-8364 379 G susan.herring@bucks.edu
HERRINGER, Gretchen, B 413-585-2550 218 F gherringer@smith.edu
HERRINGTON, Ashley 928-344-7501 10 J ashley.herrington@azwestern.edu
HERRINGTON, James 816-654-7910 254 C jherrington@kcumb.edu
HERRINGTON, Jere 662-562-3214 248 D recruiting@northwestms.edu
HERRINGTON, Theophilus 713-313-7827 449 C theo.herrington@tsu.edu
HERRINTON, Thomas, R 619-260-4553 71 J herrinton@sandiego.edu
HERRITAGE, John 518-262-3777 289 F herritj@amc.edu
HERRMAN, Kathy 785-628-4251 173 B kaherrman@fhsu.edu
HERRMANN, Anthony 914-323-5406 305 J anthony.herrmann@mville.edu
HERRMANN, Bryan 320-589-6100 244 B herrmanb@morris.umn.edu
HERRMANN, John, L 740-284-5215 353 B jherrmann@franciscan.edu
HERRMANN, Mark 907-474-7116 10 A mlherrmann@alaska.edu
HERRMANN, Matthew 910-938-6236 333 F herrmannm@coastalcarolina.edu
HERRMANN, Tracy 513-745-5689 362 E tracy.herrmann@ec.edu
HERRNDON, Jessica 704-406-2297 329 A jherndon@gardner-webb.edu
HERROD, Lindsay 724-925-4059 403 A herrodl@westmoreland.edu
HERROLD-MENZIES, Melinda 909-607-7960 56 J melinda_herrold-menzies@pitzer.edu
HERRON, Alex 512-313-3000 434 E alex.herron@concordia.edu
HERRON, Anne, J 315-294-9070 292 E anne.herron@cayuga-cc.edu
HERRON, Chetiqua, M 713-221-2715 453 B matthewsherronc@uhd.edu
HERRON, Crystal 314-286-0236 258 E cherron@ranken.edu
HERRON, David 719-884-5000 81 C dsherron@nbc.edu
HERRON, Jeffrey 732-906-2515 279 A jherron@middlesexcc.edu
HERRON, Kyle 843-953-9888 407 F jherron@citadel.edu
HERRON, Margaret 785-242-5200 176 D margaret.herron@ottawa.edu
HERRON, Martin, T 515-964-0601 165 G herronm@faith.edu
HERRON-WILLIAMS, Sharon 318-670-6337 190 J shwilliams@susla.edu
HERSCH, Lisa 301-687-7085 203 E ldhersh@frostburg.edu
HERSCHEDE, Kathryn, J 610-499-4101 403 B kjherschede@widener.edu
HERSCHER, Silviu 212-229-5192 308 C silviu@newschool.edu
HERSETH SANDLIN, Stephanie 605-274-4111 415 B stephanie.hersethsandlin@augie.edu
HERSH, Amy 212-678-8007 303 G financialaid@jtsa.edu
HERSH, Amy 212-678-8007 303 G registrar@jtsa.edu
HERSH-TUDOR, Andrew 509-682-6715 486 E ehersh-tudor@wvc.edu
HERSHBERGER, Bernie 207-725-3069 193 D bhershbe@bowdoin.edu
HERSHENSON, Jay 718-997-5648 295 C jay.hershenson@qc.cuny.edu
HERSHEY, J. David 717-396-7833 393 E dhershey@pcad.edu
HERSHEY, Jean 717-947-6150 393 F jlhershey@pacollege.edu
HERSHKOWITZ, Meyer 845-207-0330 290 D
HERSHOCK, Martin 313-593-5490 231 F mhershoc@umich.edu
HERSKOWITZ, Issac 212-463-0400 322 J issac.herskowitz@touro.edu
HERSKOWITZ, Mordechai 732-367-1060 275 J
HERSON, Mendy 973-267-9404 280 G ymmherson@rca.edu
HERSON, Moshe 973-267-9404 280 G rabbiherson@rca.edu
HERST, Jared 212-237-8704 294 D jherst@jjay.cuny.edu
HERT, Darlene 406-657-2320 264 E dhert@msubillings.edu
HERTEL, James, W 314-516-5000 261 D hertelj@umsl.edu
HERTEL, Jeffrey 616-395-7770 225 B hertelj@hope.edu
HERTEL, Lori 920-693-1207 499 G lori.hertel@gotoltc.edu
HERTEL, Tina, L 484-664-3550 391 C tinahertel@muhlenberg.edu
HERTIG, Vicky 206-934-6962 484 A vicky.hertig@seattlecolleges.edu
HERTS, George 501-374-6305 21 A gherts@shortercollege.edu
HERTS, Rolando 662-846-4311 245 H rherts@deltastate.edu
HERTZ, Adam 610-328-8325 399 D ahertz1@swarthmore.edu
HERTZ, Amy 828-884-8124 327 C hertzae@brevard.edu
HERTZ, Elisa 646-313-8000 295 E elisa.hertz@guttman.cuny.edu
HERTZ, Kara 509-313-5981 481 D hertzk@gonzaga.edu
HERTZOG, Janet 607-778-5203 318 A hertzogjm@sunybroome.edu
HERTZOG, Janet, M 607-778-5203 318 A hertzogjm@sunybroome.edu
HERTZOG, Laura 973-720-2950 284 I hertzogl@wpunj.edu
HERTZOG, Matthew 773-235-5549 147 B matthew.hertzog@resu.edu
HERVEY, Brian, T 949-824-8941 68 G bhervey@uci.edu
HERZ, Ursula 410-778-7752 204 D uherz2@washcoll.edu
HERZBERG, Tina 864-503-5572 414 D therzberg@uscupstate.edu
HERZIG, Brenda, H 218-726-8794 243 F bherzig@d.umn.edu
HERZING, Renee 608-249-6611 493 E rherzing@herzing.edu
HERZOG, Jennifer 925-631-4108 59 B jgh3@stmarys-ca.edu
HERZOG, Melanie 608-663-2881 493 C mherzog@edgewood.edu
HERZOG, Robert 608-249-6611 493 E rherzog@herzing.edu
HERZOG, Serge 775-784-4546 271 F serge@unr.edu
HESCH, Kim 701-845-7403 346 A kim.hesch@vcsu.edu
HESCHT, Sonya 304-865-6113 488 E sonya.hescht@ovu.edu
HESELIUS, Helen, S 757-446-6065 466 I heselihs@evms.edu
HESHEL, Alan 213-427-2200 35 K
HESKEL, Mitch 310-434-3414 62 E heskel_mitch@smc.edu
HESS, Allison, B 801-626-7948 461 B ahess@weber.edu
HESS, Ann 928-532-6157 14 J ann.hess@npc.edu
HESS, Brandi, S 812-464-1999 161 E bhess@usi.edu
HESS, Cynthia 254-968-9125 446 E hess@tarleton.edu
HESS, Cynthia 918-595-7980 370 E cindy.hess@tulsacc.edu
HESS, Danielle 509-335-2636 486 A danielleh@wsu.edu
HESS, David 706-721-2231 115 A dhess@augusta.edu
HESS, Diana 608-262-1763 496 C dhess@wisc.edu
HESS, E. Clayton 423-869-6391 421 C eugene.hess@lmunet.edu
HESS, Gregory, D 765-361-6221 162 E hessg@wabash.edu
HESS, Heather 269-783-2110 230 F hhess@swmich.edu
HESS, Jay 317-278-0318 156 A jayhess@iu.edu
HESS, Jay, L 317-278-0318 156 B jayhess@iu.edu
HESS, Jay, L 317-274-8157 156 F jayhess@iu.edu
HESS, Kimberly, L 802-656-1467 463 E kimberly.hess@uvm.edu
HESS, Maren 910-893-1907 327 E hess@campbell.edu
HESS, Mitchell, R 314-516-6608 261 D hessmr@umsl.edu
HESS, Pam 440-375-8005 355 G phess@lec.edu
HESS, Patrice 815-224-0462 139 F patrice_hess@ivcc.edu
HESS, Resa 760-384-6259 46 M rhess@cerrocoso.edu
HESS, Richard 858-566-1200 41 E rhess@disd.edu
HESS, Shivon 559-638-0300 66 F shivon.hess@reedleycollege.edu
HESS, Stephen, H 801-581-3100 460 E stephen.hess@utah.edu
HESS, Tim 765-285-1736 153 C trhess@bsu.edu
HESS, William 510-628-8013 48 A whess@lincolnuca.edu
HESS MOLL, Sandra 815-455-8987 143 A smoll@mchenry.edu
HESS SALISBURY, Kelly 508-531-1816 212 B kelly.hess@bridgew.edu
HESSBERG, Lee 518-262-3828 289 F hessbel@amc.edu
HESSE, Carla 510-642-5195 68 D chesse@berkeley.edu
HESSE, Cindy 303-360-4752 79 D cindy.hesse@ccaurora.edu

HIEBERT, Sandra .... 620-327-8231 173 H sandra.hiebert@hesston.edu

HIEDEMAN, Ann .... 218-477-2066 239 D ann.hiedeman@mnstate.edu

HIEL, Edwin .... 619-388-3400.. 60 C ehiel@sdccd.edu

HIEMENZ, Karen, A ...... 320-308-5017 241 A khiemenz@sctcc.edu

HIETAPELTO, Amy .... 218-726-7281 243 F lsbe@d.umn.edu

HIETSCH, Stephen .... 315-229-5896 314 F shietsch@stlawu.edu

HIGA, Pat .... 949-582-4585.. 64 G phiga@saddleback.edu

HIGA-KING, Jennifer ..... 808-845-9110 129 B higaking@hawaii.edu

HIGASHI, Lori .... 541-485-1780 374 F lorihigashi@enewhope.edu

HIGBEE, Isabelle .... 601-974-1220 247 B higbeie@millsaps.edu

HIGDEM, Julie .... 763-488-2453 238 B julie.higdem@hennepintech.edu

HIGDON, Hal, L .... 417-447-2602 257 G higdonh@otc.edu

HIGDON, Jude .... 802-440-4485 462 A judehigdon@bennington.edu

HIGGINBOTHAM, Amanda .... 610-921-7636 378 C ahigginbotham@albright.edu

HIGGINBOTHAM, Debra .... 940-397-4120 440 F debra.higginbotham@msutexas.edu

HIGGINBOTHAM, Karen 212-472-1500 309 I khigginbotham@nysid.edu

HIGGINBOTHAM, Ray ... 931-393-1737 425 C rhigginbotham@mscc.edu

HIGGINBOTHAM, Rocky .... 662-476-5014 246 A rhigginbotham@eastms.edu

HIGGINBOTHOM, Julie . 618-544-8657 138 H higginbothomj@iecc.edu

HIGGINS, Brandon .... 903-823-3024 446 B brandon.higgins@texarkanacollege.edu

HIGGINS, Brenda .... 660-785-4562 260 J bhiggins@truman.edu

HIGGINS, Carla .... 419-783-2571 352 F chiggins@defiance.edu

HIGGINS, Carolyn .... 212-752-1530 304 D carolyn.higgins@limcollege.edu

HIGGINS, Colette .... 808-235-7339 129 F chiggins@hawaii.edu

HIGGINS, Dalton .... 918-335-6865 368 G dhiggins@okwu.edu

HIGGINS, Dawn .... 603-271-6484 273 B dhiggins@ccsnh.edu

HIGGINS, Elizabeth .... 207-780-4632 196 F bhiggins@maine.edu

HIGGINS, Holly .... 207-699-5047 194 D hhiggins@meca.edu

HIGGINS, Kacey .... 325-670-1368 437 F kacey.higgins@hsutx.edu

HIGGINS, Kerena .... 360-650-2040 486 F kerena.higgins@wwu.edu

HIGGINS, Linda, A .... 803-641-3444 413 D lindahi@usca.edu

HIGGINS, Mark .... 314-977-3833 259 H mark.higgins@slu.edu

HIGGINS, Mark .... 802-387-1678 462 D mhiggins@landmark.edu

HIGGINS, Matthew .... 563-425-5200 170 A higginsm69@uiu.edu

HIGGINS, Michael .... 314-434-4044 252 B mike.higgins@covenantseminary.edu

HIGGINS, TOR, Michael, J .... 619-574-5801.. 43 E mjhiggins@fst.edu

HIGGINS, Peter, J .... 678-359-5156 119 F phiggins@gordonstate.edu

HIGGINS, Ronnell, A .... 203-432-9455.. 89 D ronnell.higgins@yale.edu

HIGGINS, Sandra .... 718-260-5700 295 B shiggins@citytech.cuny.edu

HIGGINS, Sarah .... 970-943-2288.. 84 D shiggins@western.edu

HIGGINS, Shana .... 909-748-8097.. 71 G shana_higgins@redlands.edu

HIGGINS, Sharon .... 410-617-5025 199 F sbhiggins@loyola.edu

HIGGINS, Tammy .... 620-235-4240 176 F thiggins@pittstate.edu

HIGGINS, Terri .... 641-782-1431 169 H thiggins@swcciowa.edu

HIGGINS, Thomas, J .... 518-564-3013 319 C higgintj@plattsburgh.edu

HIGGINS, Wendy .... 707-654-1194.. 32 B whiggins@csum.edu

HIGGS, Fred .... 713-348-5923 442 K higgs@rice.edu

HIGGS, Jessica .... 309-677-2700 133 B jhiggs@bradley.edu

HIGGS, John .... 724-480-3558 381 K john.higgs@ccbc.edu

HIGGS, Ronnie .... 831-582-4363.. 32 C rhiggs@csumb.edu

HIGGS, Toni .... 904-256-7184 101 G thiggs@ju.edu

HIGH, Andrew .... 310-289-5123.. 73 H andrew.high@wcui.edu

HIGH, Jennifer .... 252-399-6397 326 M jmhigh@barton.edu

HIGH, Katherine, N .... 731-881-7225 428 B khigh@tennessee.edu

HIGH, Reginald .... 919-572-1625 326 L rhigh@apexsot.edu

HIGHAM, Pamela, S ..... 814-332-3576 378 D phigham@allegheny.edu

HIGHERS, Cami .... 918-444-4200 367 A highersc@nsuok.edu

HIGHFIELD, Richard ...... 914-633-2256 302 G rhighfield@iona.edu

HIGHLEY, Melinda, C ... 606-783-2033 183 F m.highley@moreheadstate.edu

HIGHSMITH, Stephen ... 610-902-1070 380 C smh395@cabrini.edu

HIGHTOWER, Christopher .... 817-257-7156 448 G c.hightower@tcu.edu

HIGHTOWER, Darlene ... 405-744-3555 368 B darlene.hightower@okstate.edu

HIGHTOWER, Jodie ...... 870-612-2016.. 22 I jodie.hightower@uaccb.edu

HIGHTOWER, Tabitha ... 773-947-6309 142 J thightower@mccormick.edu

HIGHTOWER, Zachary ... 706-886-6831 125 D zhightower@tfc.edu

HIGINBOTHAM, Lynn, E .... 212-998-4444 310 B lynn.higinbotham@nyu.edu

HIGLE, Robin .... 978-468-7111 209 G rhigle@gcts.edu

HIGLEY, William, J .... 570-586-2400 381 E whigley@clarkssummitu.edu

HIJEK, Barbara .... 754-312-2898 102 Q

HIJLEH, Mark .... 212-659-7200 304 B mhijleh@tkc.edu

HILBERT, Diane .... 972-238-6250 435 F dhilbert@dcccd.edu

HILBERT, Stephen .... 216-987-3501 351 G stephen.hilbert@tri-c.edu

HILBORN, David .... 216-373-5240 358 B dhilborn@ndc.edu

HILBURN, Nancy .... 843-574-6564 413 B nancy.hilburn@tridenttech.edu

HILDEBRAND, Carol ...... 415-485-9306.. 39 C childebrand@marin.edu

HILDEN, Scott .... 734-677-5306 232 B sjhilden@wccnet.edu

HILDERBRAND, Barbara .... 407-708-2114 107 D hilderbrandb@seminolestate.edu

HILDERBRAND, Carey .. 801-274-3280 461 F carey.hilderbrand@wgu.edu

HILDRETH, James E.K .. 615-327-6904 422 A jhildreth@mmc.edu

HILEMAN, Dylan .... 610-989-1450 402 B dhileman@vfmac.edu

HILES, Jason .... 602-639-7500.. 12 J

HILES, Tom, S .... 573-882-7703 261 B hilest@missouri.edu

HILGEDICK, Brianne ..... 660-248-6210 251 B bhilgedi@centralmethodist.edu

HILGERSOM, Karin .... 775-673-7025 271 D khilgersom@tmcc.edu

HILKE, David .... 805-493-3960.. 29 H dhilke@callutheran.edu

HILL, Abbas, S .... 401-254-3161 405 E ashill@rwu.edu

HILL, Alan, P .... 765-658-4199 154 F alanhill@depauw.edu

HILL, Amber .... 928-524-7311.. 14 J amber.hill@npc.edu

HILL, Angela .... 707-476-4177.. 39 D angela-hill@redwoods.edu

HILL, Araceli .... 214-954-3610 447 B araceli.hill@tamuc.edu

HILL, Ben .... 319-384-3400 163 A benjamin-hill-1@uiowa.edu

HILL, Benjamin .... 540-831-2311 470 C bhill59@radford.edu

HILL, Benjamin .... 920-929-2136 500 C bhill@morainepark.edu

HILL, Beth .... 520-515-3613.. 11 M hillb@cochise.edu

HILL, Beverly .... 479-619-2679.. 20 D bhill3@nwacc.edu

HILL, Brandi .... 931-372-3317 426 E bhill@tntech.edu

HILL, Brandon .... 765-677-2200 157 D brandon.hill@indwes.edu

HILL, Brian .... 412-268-1939 380 F brianhill@cmu.edu

HILL, Brian, W .... 540-231-5107 467 F bhill@vcom.vt.edu

HILL, Calvin, R .... 413-748-3552 218 G chill@springfield.edu

HILL, Carol .... 580-349-1566 368 A carol.hill@opsu.edu

HILL, Charles .... 920-424-1255 497 B hill@uwosh.edu

HILL, Chris .... 760-757-2121.. 52 E chill@miracosta.edu

HILL, Christine .... 614-222-6178 351 D chill@ccad.edu

HILL, Christopher, D .... 404-413-2574 119 E chill@gsu.edu

HILL, Christopher, J .... 412-392-4707 397 A chill@pointpark.edu

HILL, Craig, C .... 214-768-2534 444 E craighill@smu.edu

HILL, Craig, R .... 352-392-1336 109 F craighill@ufl.edu

HILL, Curtis .... 435-865-8621 460 F hillc@suu.edu

HILL, David .... 518-564-5402 319 C hillds@plattsburgh.edu

HILL, Deana .... 570-484-2014 395 B dhill@lockhaven.edu

HILL, Deborah .... 601-318-6197 249 H dhill@wmcarey.edu

HILL, Deborah .... 972-279-6511 430 B acaddean@amberton.edu

HILL, Deborah .... 972-279-6511 430 B dhill@amberton.edu

HILL, Deidra .... 610-796-8376 378 F deidra.hill@alvernia.edu

HILL, Diane .... 973-353-1630 282 B dianeh@newark.rutgers.edu

HILL, Dometrius .... 903-510-2353 452 C dhil2@tjc.edu

HILL, Don .... 620-341-5551 172 L dhill11@emporia.edu

HILL, Doree .... 252-222-6282 333 A hilld@carteret.edu

HILL, Doris .... 763-488-0129 239 G dhill@nhcc.edu

HILL, Edith .... 815-965-8616 147 F ehill@rockfordcareercollege.edu

HILL, Edward .... 254-501-5837 447 A edward.hill@tamuct.edu

HILL, Edward .... 937-708-5814 364 D ehill@wilberforce.edu

HILL, Eileen .... 831-479-6458.. 27 G eihill@cabrillo.edu

HILL, Emilee .... 863-667-5280 107 K echill@seu.edu

HILL, Flo .... 229-430-4735 113 H flo.hill@asurams.edu

HILL, G. Richard .... 801-626-7313 461 B grhill@weber.edu

HILL, Gary .... 573-681-5496 254 E hillg@lincolnu.edu

HILL, Gladys .... 205-391-2457.... 3 E ghill@sheltonstate.edu

HILL, Hamner .... 573-651-2178 259 K hhill@semo.edu

HILL, Heather .... 704-991-0306 338 C hhill7464@stanly.edu

HILL, Holly, L .... 904-826-8636.. 98 E hhill@flagler.edu

HILL, Jacquelinet .... 225-771-2169 190 H jacqueline_hill@subr.edu

HILL, Jamie .... 309-796-5284 132 G hillj@bhc.edu

HILL, Janeen, M .... 714-744-7650.. 36 C jhill@chapman.edu

HILL, Janice .... 973-290-4468 277 A jhill01@cse.edu

HILL, Jennifer .... 256-352-8032.... 4 A jennifer.hill@wallacestate.edu

HILL, Jessica .... 413-755-4320 215 F jehill@stcc.edu

HILL, Jody .... 662-658-4771 245 D jhill@bmc.edu

HILL, John, T .... 562-907-4241.. 75 A jthill@whittier.edu

HILL, Johnny .... 919-546-8612 340 E jhill@shawu.edu

HILL, Jonathan, H .... 212-346-1810 311 E

HILL, Joseph .... 215-503-0033 400 A joseph.hill@jefferson.edu

HILL, Joslyn .... 405-425-5476 367 G joslyn.hill@oc.edu

HILL, Joyce .... 575-439-3879 287 C joyhill@nmsu.edu

HILL, Juddson .... 717-767-4300 404 D juddson.hill@yti.edu

HILL, Kameshia .... 601-979-1325 246 E kameshia.m.hill@jsums.edu

HILL, Karen .... 310-665-6910.. 54 I khill@otis.edu

HILL, Katrina .... 937-298-3399 355 F katrina.hill@kc.edu

HILL, Kelli .... 309-268-8100 137 I kelli.hill@heartland.edu

HILL, Kelly .... 352-588-7560 106 D kelly.hill02@saintleo.edu

HILL, Ken .... 207-801-5630 193 F khill@coa.edu

HILL, Kimberly .... 252-527-6223 335 G krhill01@lenoircc.edu

HILL, Kyle .... 812-749-1459 159 C khill@oak.edu

HILL, Leia .... 601-484-8786 247 A lhill@meridiancc.edu

HILL, Lena .... 540-458-8746 478 A lmhill@wlu.edu

HILL, Lisa .... 252-940-6223 332 C lisa.hill@beaufortccc.edu

HILL, Malcolm .... 207-786-6066 193 B mhill@bates.edu

HILL, Manda .... 907-564-8299.... 9 D mhill@alaskapacific.edu

HILL, Mark .... 651-641-8223 235 F hill@csp.edu

HILL, Mark, J .... 315-470-6670 320 A mjhill@esf.edu

HILL, Mary .... 202-806-6100.. 92 B

HILL, Mary, M .... 989-774-3331 222 C hill1mm@cmich.edu

HILL, Mary Alice .... 515-271-3133 165 A maryalice.hill@drake.edu

HILL, Melissa .... 509-865-0411 481 G hill_m@heritage.edu

HILL, Melissa, D .... 812-941-2359 157 B mhill02@ius.edu

HILL, Michael .... 313-664-7650 222 F mhill@collegeforcreativestudies.edu

HILL, Michael .... 610-328-8067 399 D mhill1@swarthmore.edu

HILL, Michelle, D .... 757-823-8135 469 F mdhill@nsu.edu

HILL, Mike .... 704-687-1054 342 E athleticdirector@uncc.edu

HILL, Miriam .... 651-638-6415 234 C m-hill@bethel.edu

HILL, Nicholas .... 803-535-5689 407 G

HILL, Nicole, R .... 717-477-1373 395 E nrhill@ship.edu

HILL, Penny .... 518-629-7294 302 E p.hill@hvcc.edu

HILL, Reggie .... 479-979-1203.. 23 I rhill@ozarks.edu

HILL, Reinhold, R .... 812-348-7226 156 F reihill@iupuc.edu

HILL, Renee .... 514-287-5146 351 E rhill39@cscc.edu

HILL, Rick .... 252-222-6153 333 A hillr@carteret.edu

HILL, Robert .... 818-240-1000.. 44 B rhill@glendale.edu

HILL, Robert, A .... 617-353-3560 207 D rahill@bu.edu

HILL, Rory .... 216-397-3015 354 I rhill@jcu.edu

HILL, Samantha .... 850-484-4680 104 H smhill@pensacolastate.edu

HILL, Sandra, B .... 973-720-2565 284 I hills21@wpunj.edu

HILL, Sean .... 618-468-6000 141 F shill@lc.edu

HILL, Seddrick .... 256-761-6201.... 7 B shill@talladega.edu

HIONIDES, David 214-887-5201 436 B dhionides@dts.edu
HIOTT, Connie 912-279-5965 116 G chiott@ccga.edu
HIOTT, Henry 843-321-1502 410 E hhiott@limestone.edu
HIPES, Barrett 212-799-5000 303 H
HIPOLITO, Veronica 480-732-7309 12 P veronica.hipolito@cgc.edu
HIPP, Joye, G 803-786-3178 408 F joyehipp@columbiasc.edu
HIPP, Julie 630-844-6503 132 D jhipp@aurora.edu
HIPPEN, Kristi 309-457-2327 144 A khippen@monmouthcollege.edu
HIPPISLEY, Andrew 316-978-6659 178 A andrew.hippisley@wichita.edu
HIPPLER, Stanley 337-562-4290 192 A stan@mcneese.edu
HIPPOLITE WRIGHT, Debbie 808-675-3799 127 E debbie.hippolite.wright@byuh.edu
HIPPOLITE WRIGHT, Debbie 808-675-3999 127 E debbie.hippolite.wright@byuh.edu
HIPPS, Suzanne 602-243-8153 14 A suzanne.hipps@smcmail.maricopa.edu
HIRALDO, Rafael 787-863-2390 509 B rafael.hiraldo@fajardo.inter.edu
HIRASE-STACEY, Joanne 208-282-3924 130 H hirajoan@isu.edu
HIRATA, Heather 808-932-7369 128 E hiratah@hawaii.edu
HIRD, John, A 413-545-4173 211 D jhird@sbs.umass.edu
HIRONAKA-JUTEAU, Jody 559-278-4004 31 D jhironak@csufresno.edu
HIRSCH, Alex 907-474-7931 10 A ahirsch@alaska.edu
HIRSCH, Andy 610-328-8000 399 D ahirsch1@swarthmore.edu
HIRSCH, Michael 512-505-3125 438 E mlhirsch@htu.edu
HIRSCH, Samuel 215-751-8160 382 A shirsch@ccp.edu
HIRSCHBECK, Denise, R 314-935-5320 262 A dhirschbeck@wustl.edu
HIRSCHFELD, Adam 614-251-4234 358 G hirschfa@ohiodominican.edu
HIRSCHFELD, Chloe 970-542-3126 81 A chloe.hirschfeld@morgancc.edu
HIRSCHI, Jill 406-657-1009 265 E jill.hirschi@rocky.edu
HIRSCHY, Margaret 419-434-4260 364 G hirschym@findlay.edu
HIRSHLER, Dave 740-474-8896 358 F dhirshler@ohiochristian.edu
HIRSHMAN, Elliot 443-334-2203 201 H
HIRSHON, Arnold 216-368-5292 349 F arnold.hirshon@case.edu
HIRST, Liz 850-644-1085 109 C lehirst@fsu.edu
HIRST, Martha, K 718-817-3120 300 E mhirst1@fordham.edu
HIRST, Steve 903-886-5523 447 B steve.hirst@tamuc.edu
HIRT, Samuel 540-261-8400 471 H samuel.hirt@svu.edu
HIRT, Sonia, A 706-542-8113 125 G sonia.hirt@uga.edu
HIRTLE, Christopher 413-572-5455 213 D chris@westfield.ma.edu
HISCANO, Lisa 908-965-2358 284 C hiscano@ucc.edu
HISE, Jeremy 580-628-6345 367 D jeremy.hise@noc.edu
HISE, Paul 806-720-7279 439 H paul.hise@lcu.edu
HISER, Larry, R 740-376-4665 356 A larry.hiser@marietta.edu
HISEY, Richard, M 617-747-2018 206 E rhisey@berklee.edu
HISLE, W. Lee 860-439-2650 86 H wlhis@conncoll.edu
HISLOP, Charlotte 619-298-1829 65 E
HISRICH, Matt 765-983-1687 154 G hisrima@earlham.edu
HISSONG, Wesley 315-786-6517 303 F whissong@sunyjefferson.edu
HITCH, Elizabeth, J 801-321-7122 460 D ehitch@ushe.edu
HITCHCOCK, Claude, E 443-885-3938 200 D claude.hitchcock@morgan.edu
HITCHCOCK, Cory 575-492-2158 289 A chitchcock@usw.edu
HITCHCOCK, Patrick 508-831-5577 220 E phitchcock@wpi.edu
HITCHCOCK, Richard 907-796-6493 10 B rhitchc1@alaska.edu
HITCHELL, Dan 860-297-4224 88 C dan.hitchell@trincoll.edu
HITE, Griffin 256-765-4400 8 E una@bkstr.com
HITE, Lisa 618-252-5400 149 C lisa.hite@sic.edu
HITE, Stu 620-235-4624 176 F skhite@pittstate.edu
HITE, Trudy, E 302-356-6965 90 I trudy.e.hite@wilmu.edu
HITE, Vito 850-474-2636 110 E vhite@gmail.com
HITES, Michael, H 214-768-3805 444 E hites@smu.edu
HITT, Anne 248-370-2190 229 G hitt@oakland.edu
HITT, Jennifer 508-793-7318 208 A jhitt@clarku.edu
HITT, Jennifer 901-321-3465 419 C jhitt@cbu.edu
HITT, Richard, J 863-784-7036 107 F richard.hitt@southflorida.edu
HITTLE, Ann 509-452-5100 483 A ahittle@pnwu.edu
HITZEMAN, Adam 312-922-1884 142 H ahitzeman@maccormac.edu
HIVELY, Karla, R 304-457-6317 487 B hivelykr@ab.edu
HIX, Ann 303-273-3052 78 I ahix@mines.edu
HIX, Patty 803-754-4100 409 A
HIXON, Carla 701-224-5580 346 B carla.hixson@bismarckstate.edu
HIXON, Sharon 706-272-4594 117 C shixon@daltonstate.edu
HIXSON, Kim 301-687-4000 203 E
HIXSON, Tom 909-687-1500 43 I tomhixson@gs.edu
HIXSON-WALLACE, Julie 501-279-5205 19 D jahixson@harding.edu
HIYANE-BROWN, Kathi 360-383-3330 486 G presoffice@whatcom.edu
HIZER, Ginny 513-761-2020 350 J ghizer@ccms.edu
HJALTALIN, Lisa 509-434-5210 480 A lisa.hjaltalin@ccs.spokane.edu
HJALTALIN, Lisa 509-434-5275 479 I lisa.hjaltalin@ccs.spokane.edu
HJALTALIN, Lisa 509-434-5210 480 B lisa.hjaltalin@ccs.spokane.edu
HJELLUM, Wilma 531-622-2723 267 H whjellum@mccneb.edu
HJERPE, Karen 724-938-4351 394 B hjerpe@calu.edu
HJERPE, Kelsey 602-386-4115 10 E kelseyhjerpe@arizonachristian.edu
HLADEK, Thomas 718-482-5510 294 F tomhl@lagcc.cuny.edu
HLADIS, Jirka 303-245-4702 81 B jirka@naropa.edu
HLASNY, Robert, G 603-535-2461 275 B rhlasny@plymouth.edu
HLAVENKA, Lawrence 201-689-7057 275 H lhlavenka@bergen.edu
HLAVIN, Karen 847-543-2384 135 B adr016@clcillinois.edu
HLEBOWITSH, Peter 205-348-6052 7 G phlebowitsh@bama.ua.edu
HLINAK, Matthew, J 773-612-5797 136 C mhlinak@dom.edu
HLINKA, Karen 270-534-3236 182 F karen.hlinka@kctcs.edu
HLUBB, Emma 931-424-7366 421 E ehlubb@martinmethodist.edu
HLUBB, James, R 931-424-7379 421 E jhlubb@martinmethodist.edu
HLUCH, Dale, A 330-325-6191 357 G dhluch@neomed.edu
HMIELEWSKI, Christopher 507-537-7984 241 D christopher.hmielewski@smsu.edu
HO, C. Christina 301-405-2583 202 C cchrisho@umd.edu
HO, Co 714-992-7021 53 L cho@fullcoll.edu
HO, Katy, W 971-722-4005 375 J kho@pcc.edu
HO, Nan 925-424-1182 35 P nho@laspositascollege.edu
HO, Sam 408-223-6798 61 K sam.ho@sjeccd.edu
HO, Sandra 603-427-7614 272 J sho@ccsnh.edu
HO, Victor 415-565-4624 68 F hov@uchastings.edu
HO, Wendall, K 808-956-2144 128 F wendall@hawaii.edu
HOAG, David, A 863-638-7209 113 A david.hoag@warner.edu
HOAG, Jamie, D 508-793-2011 208 B jhoag@holycross.edu
HOAG, William 857-701-1380 215 E whoag@rcc.mass.edu
HOAGLAND, Andrea 517-483-1077 226 F hoaglana@lcc.edu
HOAGLAND, Christopher 610-341-5934 383 D 0713mgr@follett.com
HOANG, Ann, D 973-596-5798 279 F ann.d.hoang@njit.edu
HOANG, Christina 714-816-0366 67 I christina.hoang@trident.edu
HOANG, Minh-Ha 619-260-4506 71 J hoangm@sandiego.edu
HOANG, SVD, Thang 563-876-3353 164 J hthang@dwci.edu
HOANG POE, Linh 808-734-9570 128 I lhoang@hawaii.edu
HOARD, Phil 317-896-9324 160 I phoard@ubca.org
HOBAN, Elizabeth 973-328-5160 277 B ehoban@ccm.edu
HOBAN, Patricia, K 503-375-5477 378 B phoban@willamette.edu
HOBART, Will 361-825-2616 447 C will.hobart@tamucc.edu
HOBBS, Bill 301-696-3622 199 B hobbs@hood.edu
HOBBS, Brenna 541-440-4617 377 C brenna.hobbs@umpqua.edu
HOBBS, Clinton, G 478-757-5161 126 H chobbs@wesleyancollege.edu
HOBBS, Jeanie 817-598-6267 458 A hobbs@wc.edu
HOBBS, Jennifer, E 404-727-7202 117 F jennifer.e.hobbs@emory.edu
HOBBS, Jessica, W 910-630-7005 331 C jhobbs@methodist.edu
HOBBS, Lynn 410-626-2504 201 D lynn.hobbs@sjc.edu
HOBBS, Morgan 215-972-2199 393 D mhobbs@pafa.edu
HOBBS, Patrick, E 732-445-8610 282 A patrick.hobbs@rutgers.edu
HOBBS, Phillip, M 205-853-1200 2 G mhobbs@jeffersonstate.edu
HOBBS, Ryan 435-879-4653 460 G ryan.hobbs@dixie.edu
HOBBS, Tommy 205-929-3521 2 H thobbs@lawsonstate.edu
HOBBS, III, William 305-430-1166 99 D william.hobbs@fmuniv.edu
HOBBY, Angela 229-333-2100 127 B angela.hobby@wiregrass.edu
HOBBY, Brett 713-221-5075 453 B hobbyb@uhd.edu
HOBBY-MEARS, Michelle 949-480-4134 64 B mhobby@soka.edu
HOBELMAN, Greg 317-896-9324 160 I ghobelman@ubca.org
HOBERMAN, Chaim 516-255-4700 312 D
HOBERMAN, Evan 646-565-6000 322 J evan.hoberman@touro.edu
HOBGOOD, Kathy, B 864-656-1151 408 A kbhob@clemson.edu
HOBIN, Caron, T 413-565-1333 205 G chobin@baypath.edu
HOBLER, Dean 419-998-3103 363 C dahobler@unoh.edu
HOBLET, Kent, H 662-325-1418 247 F hoblet@cvm.msstate.edu
HOBSON, Elizabeth 847-214-6945 136 F ehobson@elgin.edu
HOBSON, Katie 507-389-7344 241 C katie.hobson@southcentral.edu
HOBSON, Lynn, M 620-341-5267 172 L lhobson@emporia.edu
HOBSON, Paula, L 603-535-2901 275 B phobson@plymouth.edu
HOBSON, Sheila 301-860-3451 203 C shobson@bowiestate.edu
HOBSON-PAPE, Karri 706-542-8083 125 G karri@uga.edu
HOBYAK, Michael, S 215-785-0111 393 C
HOCH, Cathy 515-961-1398 169 D cathy.hoch@simpson.edu
HOCHMAN, Alex 415-422-2437 71 K ahochman@usfca.edu
HOCHNER, Rose 713-500-3824 456 B rose.hochner@uth.tmc.edu
HOCHSTEIN, Dale 212-517-0571 306 A phochstein@mmm.edu
HOCHSTEIN, Jessica 402-399-2664 266 F jhochstein@csm.edu
HOCHSTETLER, Stephanie 574-807-7354 153 E stephanie.hochstetler@betheluniversity.edu
HOCK, Joan 215-489-2975 382 D joan.hock@delval.edu
HOCK, Nathan 802-828-2800 464 B nxh08030@ccv.vsc.edu
HOCKENBERRY, Frederick 301-846-2544 198 E fhockenberry@frederick.edu
HOCKENHULL, Ben 440-775-6727 358 C ben.hockenhull@oberlin.edu
HOCKER, Elizabeth 405-491-6609 370 A ehocker@snu.edu
HOCKMAN, Joan 814-371-2090 400 D jhockman@triangle-tech.edu
HOCKSTALL, April 202-274-2303 93 D marketing@potomac.edu
HOCOY, Dan 716-842-2770 299 F
HOCUTT, Kirby 806-742-3355 451 B kirby.hocutt@ttu.edu
HODA-KEARSE, Rebecca 315-498-2119 311 B r.a.hoda-kearse@sunyocc.edu
HODEL, Laura 607-778-5028 318 A hodellj@sunybroome.edu
HODGE, Andrea 213-740-4225 72 B ahodge@usc.edu
HODGE, Angela 512-223-1102 431 A angela.hodge@austincc.edu
HODGE, Brad, K 215-670-9206 391 H bhodge@peirce.edu
HODGE, Christina 860-701-5024 87 D hodge_c@mitchell.edu
HODGE, David 334-291-4928 1 H david.hodge@cv.edu
HODGE, Duane 937-328-6054 350 L hodged@clarkstate.edu
HODGE, Evelyn 334-229-4139 4 B ehodge@alasu.edu
HODGE, Frank 206-543-9132 485 F fhodge@uw.edu
HODGE, Jeremy 334-229-4156 4 B jhodge@alasu.edu
HODGE, Johnesa 313-496-2796 232 C jdimick1@wcccd.edu
HODGE, Margaret 706-385-1069 123 C margaret.hodge@point.edu
HODGE, Marilyn, R 757-822-7245 476 B mhodge@tcc.edu
HODGE, Michael 470-639-0801 122 D michael.hodge@morehouse.edu
HODGE, Michel 718-260-4999 295 B mhodge@citytech.cuny.edu
HODGE, Paula 661-362-5108 38 H paula.hodge@canyons.edu
HODGE, Rick 323-242-5388 49 D hodgerl@lasc.edu
HODGE, Tiffani 404-523-8520 125 B thodge3@spelman.edu
HODGEN, Danielle 509-527-4301 485 G danielle.hodgen@wwcc.edu
HODGES, Bridget 716-827-2425 323 D hodgesb@trocaire.edu
HODGES, Caryl 650-508-3621 54 D chodges@ndnu.edu
HODGES, Christopher 215-717-3117 382 B christopher.hodges@curtis.edu
HODGES, Courtney 434-395-2823 469 A hodgesmc@longwood.edu
HODGES, Greg 276-656-0315 475 D ghodges@patrickhenry.edu
HODGES, Hannah 859-256-3132 180 H hannah.hodges@kctcs.edu

HOIDA, Will .... 775-881-1314 272 D
whoida@sierranevada.edu
HOIE, Stephanie .... 619-260-7414.. 71 J
shoie@sandiego.edu
HOILAND, Eric .... 530-893-7528.. 27 F
hoilander@butte.edu
HOILAND, Erin .... 360-412-6149 483 H
ehoiland@stmartin.edu
HOILE, Linda .... 209-575-6498.. 75 J
hoilel@yosemite.edu
HOILMAN, Sandra, K .... 828-448-6025 339 A
shoilman@wpcc.edu
HOIT, Marc, I .... 919-515-0141 342 B
mark_hoit@ncsu.edu
HOJAN, Elizabeth, M .... 262-554-2010 494 D
mwcfinancialaid@aol.com
HOJAN-CLARK, Jane ..... 212-853-0469 297 C
jh3574@columbia.edu
HOJSACK, Dana .... 619-849-2678.. 57 E
danahojsack@pointloma.edu
HOKANSON, SND,
Karen .... 617-735-9976 209 A
hokanson@emmanuel.edu
HOKANSON, Kimberly .. 781-768-7222 218 C
kimberly.hokanson@regiscollege.edu
HOKE, Chris .... 701-252-3467 347 C
choke@uj.edu
HOKE, Cynthia .... 912-358-4000 123 H
hokec@savannahstate.edu
HOKE, Franklin .... 212-327-8998 313 B
fhoke@rockefeller.edu
HOKE, Rick .... 818-243-1131.. 44 A
HOKOANA, Lui .... 808-984-3636 129 E
lhokoana@hawaii.edu
HOLADAY, Stephanie .... 304-326-1311 488 F
stephanie.holaday@salemu.edu
HOLAHAN, Barbara .... 516-686-7755 309 F
bholahan@nyit.edu
HOLAHAN, Cindy .... 262-524-7361 492 E
cholahan@carrollu.edu
HOLAK, Susan, L .... 718-982-2920 293 E
schoolofbusiness@csi.cuny.edu
HOLAN, Craig .... 618-650-2560 149 F
cholan@siue.edu
HOLANDA, Shelly .... 800-686-1883 222 E
sholanda@cleary.edu
HOLBERG, Connie .... 315-786-2402 303 F
cholberg@sunyjefferson.edu
HOLBERG, John .... 706-419-1565 117 B
john.holberg@covenant.edu
HOLBROOK, Carl .... 334-347-2623.... 2 A
cholbrook@escc.edu
HOLBROOK, Catherine . 413-662-5231 213 A
catherine.holbrook@mcla.edu
HOLBROOK, Christine .. 413-552-2319 214 D
cholbrook@hcc.edu
HOLBROOK, Jamirae .... 606-539-4120 185 A
HOLBROOK, Jennifer .... 870-230-5275.. 19 E
holbroj@hsu.edu
HOLBROOK, Karen .... 941-359-4340 110 B
kholbrook@usf.edu
HOLBROOK, Karen .... 941-359-4200 110 D
kholbrook@usf.edu
HOLBROOK, Peter .... 419-448-5864 361 J
holbrookpj@tiffin.edu
HOLBROOK, Tim .... 404-712-0353 117 F
tholbrook@emory.edu
HOLCOMB, David .... 254-295-4184 453 E
dholcomb@umhb.edu
HOLCOMB, Debra .... 903-510-2261 452 C
dhol2@tjc.edu
HOLCOMB, Donna .... 757-352-4662 470 H
dholcomb@regent.edu
HOLCOMB, Gay .... 859-858-3511 178 I
gay.holcomb@asbury.edu
HOLCOMB, Glen .... 405-491-6309 370 A
gholcomb@snu.edu
HOLCOMB, Mark .... 815-939-5236 146 A
mholcomb@olivet.edu
HOLCOMB, Robert .... 707-527-4615.. 62 F
rholcomb@santarosa.edu
HOLCOMB, Todd .... 319-296-4201 166 B
todd.holcomb@hawkeyecollege.edu
HOLCOMB, Todd, R ...... 308-635-6101 270 D
holcombt@wncc.edu
HOLCOMB-MCCOY,
Cheryl .... 202-885-3720.. 90 J
cholcomb@american.edu
HOLCOMBE, Kara .... 503-554-2189 373 C
kholcombe@georgefox.edu
HOLCOMBE, Randall ..... 808-586-3013 128 F
rfh6979@hawaii.edu

HOLCOMBE, Robert ...... 864-424-8024 414 C
reholcom@mailbox.sc.edu
HOLDEMAN, Lisa, K ..... 713-743-8408 452 E
lkholdeman@uh.edu
HOLDEMAN, Lisa, K ..... 713-743-0945 452 F
lkholdeman@uh.edu
HOLDEN, Brad .... 541-278-5783 372 A
bholden@bluecc.edu
HOLDEN, Cheryl .... 509-542-4761 479 H
cholden@columbiabasin.edu
HOLDEN, Christy .... 719-846-5550.. 82 K
christy.holden@trinidadstate.edu
HOLDEN, Dave .... 618-664-6750 137 G
dave.holden@greenville.edu
HOLDEN, Elaine, P .... 704-645-4402 328 A
epholden@catawba.edu
HOLDEN, Ginger .... 209-954-5040.. 60 J
gholden@deltacollege.edu
HOLDEN, Joan .... 773-508-2530 142 D
jholde1@luc.edu
HOLDEN, Joseph, M .... 714-966-8500.. 73 C
info@ves.edu
HOLDEN, Kathleen .... 727-873-4986 110 C
kholden1@mail.usf.edu
HOLDEN, Kimberly .... 706-771-4019 114 J
kholden@augustatech.edu
HOLDEN, Larry .... 615-327-6339 422 A
lholden@mmc.edu
HOLDEN, Leslie .... 540-365-4460 467 I
lholden@ferrum.edu
HOLDEN, Randy .... 540-231-3171 477 A
rholden@vt.edu
HOLDEN, Ronald .... 330-823-2138 363 B
holdenrf@mountunion.edu
HOLDEN, Scott, A .... 212-799-5000 303 H
HOLDEN, Teresa .... 618-664-6844 137 G
teresa.holden@greenville.edu
HOLDEN, Wesley .... 772-546-5534 101 B
wesleyholden@hsbc.edu
HOLDEN-DUFFY,
Cheryl .... 410-651-6460 203 A
clduffy@umes.edu
HOLDER, Amy .... 931-393-1643 425 C
aholder@mscc.edu
HOLDER, Beth .... 910-521-6221 343 B
beth.holder@uncp.edu
HOLDER, Candace .... 336-386-3382 338 D
holderc@surry.edu
HOLDER, Cheryl .... 618-842-3711 138 G
holderc@iecc.edu
HOLDER, Connie .... 573-518-2119 256 B
cholder@mineralarea.edu
HOLDER, Debra .... 817-274-4284 432 A
dholder@bhcarroll.edu
HOLDER, Jayne .... 423-425-4785 428 A
jayne-holder@utc.edu
HOLDER, Kenneth .... 251-405-7172.... 1 E
kholder@bishop.edu
HOLDER, Mike .... 405-744-7231 368 B
mike.holder@okstate.edu
HOLDER, Mitchell .... 660-359-3948 257 D
mholder@mail.ncmissouri.edu
HOLDERBY, Kindle .... 620-341-5421 172 L
kholderb@emporia.edu
HOLDING, Frederick ..... 910-962-1123 343 C
holdingf@uncw.edu
HOLDNAK, John, R .... 850-872-3800 100 N
jholdnak@gulfcoast.edu
HOLDREN, Chris .... 503-375-7173 373 A
choldren@corban.edu
HOLEHOUSE, Fonda .... 304-357-4766 488 G
fondaholehouse@ucwv.edu
HOLEMAN, Jeff .... 603-358-2181 275 A
jeff.holeman@keene.edu
HOLFORD, Kenneth ...... 219-989-2469 159 G
cholford@pnw.edu
HOLGUIN, Emilsen .... 518-608-8356 299 G
eholguin@excelsior.edu
HOLIDA, Pamela .... 256-726-8328.... 6 C
pholiday@oakwood.edu
HOLIDAY, Jana .... 978-468-7111 209 G
jholiday@gordonconwell.edu
HOLIFIELD, Brenda .... 870-780-1227.. 17 D
bholifield@smail.anc.edu
HOLIGROCKI, Rick .... 805-493-3528.. 29 H
rholigrocki@callutheran.edu
HOLL, Karolina .... 315-792-3179 324 B
kmholl@utica.edu
HOLLAAR, Jean .... 218-477-2070 239 D
jean.hollaar@mnstate.edu
HOLLADAY, Allison .... 570-321-4220 389 E
holladay@lycoming.edu

HOLLADAY, Clare, M .... 563-333-6346 169 A
holladayclarem@sau.edu
HOLLAND, Alex .... 520-322-6330.. 12 K
info@hanuniversity.edu
HOLLAND, Alex .... 520-322-6330.. 12 K
alex@hanuniversity.edu
HOLLAND, Alice .... 610-328-8058 399 D
ahollan3@swarthmore.edu
HOLLAND, Ann, T .... 270-707-3724 181 E
ann.holland@kctcs.edu
HOLLAND, Beth .... 828-726-2200 332 G
HOLLAND, Colleen .... 417-455-5588 252 D
colleenholland@crowder.edu
HOLLAND, Don .... 574-936-8898 153 A
don.holland@ancilla.edu
HOLLAND, Jeff .... 304-424-8229 491 D
jeff.holland@wvup.edu
HOLLAND, Kevin .... 940-552-6291 457 C
kholland@vernoncollege.edu
HOLLAND, Kimberly ..... 334-727-8881.... 7 D
kholland@tuskegee.edu
HOLLAND, Kristine .... 567-661-7172 360 B
kristine_holland@owens.edu
HOLLAND, LaTonya ...... 301-546-0007 201 C
hollanlt@pgcc.edu
HOLLAND, Leslie .... 901-722-3238 424 C
lholland@sco.edu
HOLLAND, Linda .... 501-354-7565.. 23 A
holland@uaccm.edu
HOLLAND, Lynne .... 270-745-2683 185 E
lynne.holland@wku.edu
HOLLAND, Mario .... 405-466-3370 366 F
mario.holland@langston.edu
HOLLAND, Melinda .... 919-658-7702 340 J
mholland@umo.edu
HOLLAND, Michelle ...... 904-819-6223.. 98 E
mholland@flagler.edu
HOLLAND, Rolanda, J .. 919-572-1625 326 L
rholland@apexsot.edu
HOLLAND, Sam .... 214-768-2880 444 E
sholland@smu.edu
HOLLAND, Scott .... 800-287-8822 153 D
hollasc@bethanyseminary.edu
HOLLAND, Sharon .... 301-295-3578 504 B
sharon.holland@usuhs.edu
HOLLAND, Steven, C .... 520-621-1556.. 16 G
sholland@email.arizona.edu
HOLLAND, Tina .... 225-768-1710 186 F
tina.holland@franu.edu
HOLLAND, Tony .... 334-293-4668.... 1 C
tony.holland@accs.edu
HOLLAND, Tracey .... 845-437-7360 324 C
trholland@vassar.edu
HOLLANDER, Lisa .... 219-464-6882 162 A
lisa.hollander@valpo.edu
HOLLANDSWORTH,
Heather .... 540-365-4282 467 I
hhollandsworth@ferrum.edu
HOLLAWAY, Jamie .... 319-352-8521 170 C
jamie.hollaway@wartburg.edu
HOLLDORF, Barry .... 206-878-3710 481 H
bholldorf@highline.edu
HOLLEMAN, Clate .... 662-472-9087 246 C
cholleman@holmescc.edu
HOLLEMON, John .... 434-223-7154 468 A
jhollemon@hsc.edu
HOLLENBAUGH, David . 724-805-2590 398 F
david.hollenbaugh@stvincent.edu
HOLLENBECK, Dean ...... 620-343-4600 173 A
dhollenbeck@fhtc.edu
HOLLENBECK, Nicole .... 480-627-5384.. 15 P
nhollenbeck@taliesin.edu
HOLLENBECK, Peter ...... 765-494-9709 159 E
phollenb@purdue.edu
HOLLENBERGER, Leah .. 802-635-1657 464 C
leah.hollenberger@northernvermont.edu
HOLLENHORST, Steven . 360-650-3521 486 F
steve.hollenhorst@wwu.edu
HOLLER, Juanita .... 805-756-2100.. 30 C
jmholler@calpoly.edu
HOLLER, Stacy .... 301-387-3045 198 F
stacy.holler@garrettcollege.edu
HOLLERAN, Meghan ..... 660-263-4100 257 B
meghanh@macc.edu
HOLLERICH, Mary .... 612-330-1603 233 K
holleric@augsburg.edu
HOLLEY, Debra .... 434-797-8410 474 E
debra.holley@danville.edu
HOLLEY, Earle .... 843-208-8143 413 E
eholley@uscb.edu
HOLLEY, Joey .... 334-347-2623.... 2 A
jholley@escc.edu

HOLLEY, John .... 256-306-2865.... 1 F
john.holley@calhoun.edu
HOLLEY, Steven .... 909-607-9192.. 37 C
steven.holley@claremont.edu
HOLLEY, Suzy .... 813-253-7000 101 A
sholley7@hccfl.edu
HOLLEY, Tracy, S .... 540-365-4216 467 I
tholley@ferrum.edu
HOLLEY-WALKER,
Danielle, R .... 202-806-8000.. 92 B
danielle.holley-walker@howard.edu
HOLLIDAY, Chrissy .... 719-549-2997.. 79 A
chrissy.holliday@csupueblo.edu
HOLLIDAY, Deann .... 425-352-8324 479 A
dholliday@cascadia.edu
HOLLIDAY, Greg .... 256-233-8106.... 4 D
greg.holliday@athens.edu
HOLLIDAY, Lisa, C .... 503-370-6574 378 B
lcjones@willamette.edu
HOLLIDAY, Odell, P ...... 252-451-8221 336 E
moholliday690@nashcc.edu
HOLLIDAY, Paul .... 213-356-5348.. 64 H
paul_holliday@sciarc.edu
HOLLIDAY, Roxann .... 402-461-2463 266 A
roxannholliday@cccneb.edu
HOLLIDAY, Shawn, P ... 580-327-8410 367 E
spholliday@nwosu.edu
HOLLIDAY, Theresa ...... 913-288-7110 174 F
tholliday@kckcc.edu
HOLLIDAY, Wendy .... 801-626-6403 461 B
wendyholliday@weber.edu
HOLLIER, Larry, H .... 504-568-4800 189 B
lhholl@lsuhsc.edu
HOLLIFIELD, Jim .... 901-722-3264 424 C
jhollifield@sco.edu
HOLLIMAN-DOUGLAS,
Chassity .... 360-867-5133 481 A
hollimac@evergreen.edu
HOLLIMAN-GINKENS,
Stephanie .... 641-683-5751 166 C
HOLLINGER-SMITH,
Linda .... 888-556-8226 133 F
HOLLINGSHEAD, Brad .. 863-680-4124.. 99 H
bhollingshead@flsouthern.edu
HOLLINGSHEAD,
Jennifer .... 848-445-1910 282 A
jh1509@echo.rutgers.edu
HOLLINGSWORTH,
Clifford .... 914-632-5400 307 G
chollingsworth@monroecollege.edu
HOLLINGSWORTH,
Guy, M .... 801-524-1928 459 F
ghollingsworth@ldsbc.edu
HOLLINGSWORTH,
Jeffrey, K .... 301-405-7700 202 C
hollings@umd.edu
HOLLINGSWORTH,
Kimberly .... 773-291-6313 134 E
khollingsworth@ccc.edu
HOLLINGSWORTH,
Rusty .... 270-789-5009 179 E
rhollingsworth@campbellsville.edu
HOLLINGSWORTH,
Stacey .... 601-635-6406 245 I
sholling@eccc.edu
HOLLINS, Cary .... 225-771-5662 190 H
cary_hollins@subr.edu
HOLLINS, Cassandra .... 205-929-2091.... 2 H
creneehollins@lawsonstate.edu
HOLLINS, Emily .... 540-665-4914 471 E
ehollins2@su.edu
HOLLINS, Kayla .... 413-662-5585 213 A
kayla.hollins@mcla.edu
HOLLIS, Debra .... 704-378-1128 330 D
dhollis@jcsu.edu
HOLLIS, Denson .... 662-915-5092 249 D
dhollis@olemiss.edu
HOLLIS, Erika, M .... 303-964-5387.. 82 E
ehollis@regis.edu
HOLLIS, John .... 870-777-5722.. 22 A
john.hollis@uaht.edu
HOLLIS, Keith .... 978-837-5356 216 D
hollisk@merrimack.edu
HOLLIS, Mark .... 440-943-7600 360 J
mhollis@dioceseofcleveland.org
HOLLIS, Quintress .... 478-757-5175 126 H
qhollis@wesleyancollege.edu
HOLLIS, Stephanie .... 423-697-4477 424 E
stephanie.hollis@chattanoogastate.edu
HOLLISTER, Laurie .... 516-686-7499 309 F
lhollist@nyit.edu
HOLLISTER, Ryan .... 503-552-1665 374 E
rhollister@nunm.edu

HOLLISTER, Ryan .... 215-780-1235 398 G
rhollister@salus.edu
HOLLISTER, Thomas ..... 617-496-2650 210 B
thomas_hollister@harvard.edu
HOLLMAN, Suzanne, N . 703-416-1441 466 F
shollman.ips@divinemercy.edu
HOLLOMAN, Anthony ... 478-827-3677 118 A
hollomana@fvsu.edu
HOLLOMAN,
Brittany, A .... 256-372-5230.... 1 A
brittany.holloman@aamu.edu
HOLLOMAN, Darryl .... 404-270-5138 125 B
dholloman@spelman.edu
HOLLOMAN, Eric .... 910-755-7343 332 F
hollomane@brunswickcc.edu
HOLLOMAN, Marc .... 919-365-7711 340 H
HOLLOMAN, Mike .... 919-497-3249 330 I
mholloman@louisburg.edu
HOLLOMAN, Scotty ...... 575-492-2791 286 J
sholloman@nmjc.edu
HOLLOW, Jeffrey .... 414-297-6663 500 B
hollowj4@matc.edu
HOLLOWAY, Amy .... 478-757-3510 116 A
aholloway@centralgatech.edu
HOLLOWAY, Antonio .... 512-444-8082 449 A
faid@thsu.edu
HOLLOWAY, Betsy, B ... 205-726-4109.... 6 E
bbhollow@samford.edu
HOLLOWAY, C. Allen .... 501-977-2031.. 23 A
holloway@uaccm.edu
HOLLOWAY, Charles .... 502-597-6388 182 H
charles.holloway@kysu.edu
HOLLOWAY, David, J ... 304-877-6428 487 F
dave.holloway@abc.edu
HOLLOWAY, Denise, W 478-757-5211 126 H
dholloway@wesleyancollege.edu
HOLLOWAY, Gregg .... 765-998-5295 160 F
grholloway@taylor.edu
HOLLOWAY, James ...... 505-277-2611 288 G
provost@unm.edu
HOLLOWAY, Jerry, R .... 918-631-2539 371 E
jerry-holloway@utulsa.edu
HOLLOWAY, Jessica ..... 312-850-7152 134 H
jholloway@ccc.edu
HOLLOWAY, Jessica ..... 479-968-0269.. 18 C
jholloway@atu.edu
HOLLOWAY, John .... 276-944-6122 467 G
jholloway@ehc.edu
HOLLOWAY,
Jonathan, S .... 847-491-5117 145 F
nu-provost@northwestern.edu
HOLLOWAY, Kelly, L .... 478-301-2650 121 E
holloway_kl@mercer.edu
HOLLOWAY, Linda, C ... 217-581-2979 136 E
lcholloway@eiu.edu
HOLLOWAY, Lorretta ..... 508-626-4926 212 D
lholloway@framingham.edu
HOLLOWAY, Mary .... 803-738-7699 410 G
hollowaym@midlandstech.edu
HOLLOWAY, Melissa .... 336-285-2431 341 F
mjholloway@ncat.edu
HOLLOWAY, Michelle ... 386-752-1822.. 99 A
michelle.holloway@fgc.edu
HOLLOWAY, Rachel, L .. 540-231-4167 477 A
rholloway@vt.edu
HOLLOWAY, Saletta ...... 615-327-6869 422 A
sholloway@mmc.edu
HOLLOWAY, Stacy .... 618-985-3741 139 I
stacyholloway@jalc.edu
HOLLOWAY, Thadeus ... 912-423-0498 115 E
thadeusholloway@rts.hush.com
HOLLOWELL, Lorna ...... 218-281-8580 244 A
lholl0we@umn.edu
HOLLOWELL,
Meghan, E .... 513-585-4841 350 H
meghan.hollowell@thechristcollege.edu
HOLLY, Julie .... 205-226-4761.... 5 A
jbholly@bsc.edu
HOLLY, Shelly .... 918-631-2550 371 E
shelly-holly@utulsa.edu
HOLM, Cyndi .... 507-537-7854 241 D
cyndi.holm@smsu.edu
HOLM, Janet .... 253-589-5545 479 G
janet.holm@cptc.edu
HOLM, Jeffrey .... 701-777-5964 345 C
jeffrey.holm@und.edu
HOLM, Kim .... 330-569-5288 353 J
holmka@hiram.edu
HOLM, Rachel .... 703-370-6600 470 B
HOLMAN, Cale .... 202-379-7808.. 92 G
HOLMAN, Dena .... 828-726-2737 332 G
dnholman@cccti.edu
HOLMAN, Fred, B .... 775-784-4853 271 F
fholman@unr.edu
HOLMAN, George .... 308-865-8519 269 I
holmangp@unk.edu
HOLMAN, James .... 414-443-8566 498 O
james.holman@wlc.edu
HOLMAN, Jill .... 763-576-4073 237 D
jholman@anokatech.edu
HOLMAN, Jill .... 706-867-2532 126 A
jill.holman@ung.edu
HOLMAN, John .... 606-218-5194 185 D
johnholman@upike.edu
HOLMAN, Keisha .... 254-526-1106 432 H
keisha.holman@ctcd.edu
HOLMAN, Lucy .... 910-962-7703 343 C
holmanl@uncw.edu
HOLMAN, Mark .... 701-854-8024 346 I
mark.holman@sittingbull.edu
HOLMAN, Neil .... 847-574-5230 141 C
nholman@lfgsm.edu
HOLMAN, Pat .... 505-984-6144 287 J
pat.holman@sjc.edu
HOLMAN-BROOKS,
Leslie .... 803-793-5287 409 C
holmanbrooksl@denmarktech.edu
HOLMANS, Jim .... 325-674-4974 429 B
holmansj@acu.edu
HOLMBOE, Janelle .... 410-857-2273 200 B
jholmboe@mcdaniel.edu
HOLME, Susan, H .... 509-527-5790 486 H
holmesl@whitman.edu
HOLMES, JR.,
Archie, L .... 434-982-2016 473 A
ah7sj@virginia.edu
HOLMES, Barbara, J ..... 202-274-6156.. 93 C
bholmes@udc.edu
HOLMES, Betsy .... 603-623-0313 273 I
betsyholmes@nhia.edu
HOLMES, Beverly .... 309-341-7755 141 A
bholmes@knox.edu
HOLMES, Brian .... 301-243-2112 503 J
brian.holmes@dodiis.mil
HOLMES, Carlos .... 302-857-6062.. 89 F
cholmes@desu.edu
HOLMES, Cassandra ..... 941-752-5389 108 G
holmesc@scf.edu
HOLMES, Cayce .... 910-410-1721 337 B
ccholmes@richmondcc.edu
HOLMES, Charley .... 903-586-2501 431 G
charley.holmes@bmats.edu
HOLMES, Christine, L ... 508-849-3418 205 C
cholmes@annamaria.edu
HOLMES,
Christopher, W .... 254-710-3821 431 J
christopher_holmes@baylor.edu
HOLMES, Claire .... 510-987-9195.. 68 C
claire.holmes@ucop.edu
HOLMES, Clayton .... 479-308-6020.. 17 C
clayton.holmes@acheedu.org
HOLMES, Debra .... 912-279-5787 116 G
dholmes@ccga.edu
HOLMES, Emily .... 336-272-7102 329 D
emily.holmes@greensboro.edu
HOLMES, Emily .... 570-702-8956 386 G
eholmes@johnson.edu
HOLMES, Erin .... 907-786-1544.... 9 H
ejholmes@alaska.edu
HOLMES, Frank .... 936-294-3625 450 C
holmes@shsu.edu
HOLMES, Greg .... 541-463-5516 373 F
holmesg@lanecc.edu
HOLMES, Heather, W .... 410-677-4865 203 F
hwholmes@salisbury.edu
HOLMES, Ilona, M .... 954-486-7728 112 D
uftlpresident@uftl.edu
HOLMES, Jennifer .... 972-883-6852 455 B
jholmes@utdallas.edu
HOLMES, Jimmy .... 256-395-2211.... 3 G
jholmes@suscc.edu
HOLMES, John .... 281-649-3402 437 H
jholmes@hbu.edu
HOLMES, Joseph .... 386-752-1822.. 99 A
joseph.holmes@fgc.edu
HOLMES, Kathryn .... 801-832-2565 461 G
kholmes@westminstercollege.edu
HOLMES, Kelly .... 845-575-3000 305 L
kelly.holmes@marist.edu
HOLMES, Kenneth, M ... 202-806-2100.. 92 B
kenneth.holmes@howard.edu
HOLMES, Kimberly .... 229-430-2799 113 H
kimberly.holmes@asurams.edu
HOLMES, Kristen .... 256-352-8118.... 4 A
kristen.holmes@wallacestate.edu
HOLMES, Leasa, O .... 919-735-5151 338 H
loh@waynecc.edu
HOLMES, Leslie .... 864-379-6571 409 H
lholmes@erskine.edu
HOLMES, Lisa .... 760-252-2411.. 26 I
lholmes@barstow.edu
HOLMES, Lloyd, A .... 585-292-2120 307 H
lholmes20@monroecc.edu
HOLMES, Lucina .... 508-362-2131 214 B
lholmes@capecod.edu
HOLMES, Malcolm .... 540-654-1617 472 I
mholmes3@umw.edu
HOLMES, Merlyn .... 903-988-7521 439 A
mholmes@kilgore.edu
HOLMES, Michael, S ..... 563-333-6229 169 A
holmesmichaels@sau.edu
HOLMES, Nathaniel .... 504-520-6753 193 A
nholmes@xula.edu
HOLMES, O'Neal, C .... 334-683-2350.... 3 A
oholmes@marionmilitary.edu
HOLMES, Paige .... 207-992-1939 194 A
holmesp@husson.edu
HOLMES, Phillip .... 302-857-6326.. 89 F
pholmes@desu.edu
HOLMES, Phillip .... 601-923-1600 248 F
pholmes@rts.edu
HOLMES, Phillip, M ...... 478-387-4905 118 G
mholmes@gmc.edu
HOLMES, Radonna .... 972-825-4762 445 A
rholmes@sagu.edu
HOLMES, IV, Richard ... 805-493-3586.. 29 H
holmes@callutheran.edu
HOLMES, Rodney .... 480-461-7325.. 13 D
rodney.holmes@mesacc.edu
HOLMES, Ryan, C .... 305-284-5353 112 E
rch88@miami.edu
HOLMES, Shade' .... 803-786-3476 408 F
sholmes@columbiasc.edu
HOLMES, Shandria .... 773-602-5517 134 D
sholmes65@ccc.edu
HOLMES, Stephanie ...... 309-694-8420 138 C
stephanie.holmes@icc.edu
HOLMES, Terrell .... 302-857-6375.. 89 F
tholmes@desu.edu
HOLMES, Tiffany .... 312-759-1671 148 I
tholmes@saic.edu
HOLMES, Wendy .... 845-341-4662 311 C
wendy.holmes@sunyorange.edu
HOLMES-BUTLER,
Layna .... 610-399-2544 394 C
laynaholmes@cheyney.edu
HOLMES CAMPBELL,
Kathlene, L .... 651-962-4455 244 E
camp1012@stthomas.edu
HOLMES-LEOPOLD, R.J 507-222-4295 234 F
rholmes@carleton.edu
HOLMES-LEOPOLD, RJ . 319-895-4445 164 B
rholmes-leopold@cornellcollege.edu
HOLMES-SULLIVAN,
Robin .... 503-768-7220 373 G
rholmes-sullivan@lclark.edu
HOLMGREN,
Richard, A .... 814-332-2898 378 D
rholmgre@allegheny.edu
HOLMOE, Tom .... 801-422-7649 458 H
tom_holmoe@byu.edu
HOLMQUEST, Kate .... 312-645-8300 501 T
kate@wrightgrad.edu
HOLMQUIST, Jake .... 718-862-7449 305 H
jake.holmquist@manhattan.edu
HOLMQUIST, Loren .... 619-644-7653.. 44 I
loren.holmquist@gcccd.edu
HOLOHAN-MOYER,
Irene .... 716-839-7213 298 B
imoyer@daemen.edu
HOLOMAN,
Christopher .... 318-869-5101 186 B
president@centenary.edu
HOLS, Eric .... 703-284-1601 469 C
eric.hols@marymount.edu
HOLSCHER, Jennifer, L . 812-888-4959 162 C
jholscher@vinu.edu
HOLSCLAW, Brent .... 270-706-8427 181 A
bholsclaw0004@kctcs.edu
HOLSER, Derek, P .... 757-481-5005 478 C
HOLSINGER, Kent .... 860-486-2182.. 88 E
kent.holsinger@uconn.edu
HOLSINGER-FUCHS,
Pamela .... 360-688-2101 483 H
pholsingerfuchs@stmartin.edu
HOLSOPPLE, Lee .... 202-885-3409.. 90 J
lee.holsopple@american.edu
HOLST, Barry .... 651-635-8500 234 C
barry-holst@bethel.edu
HOLSTAD, Deb .... 320-308-3277 241 A
dholstad@sctcc.edu
HOLSTAD, Deb, A .... 320-308-3227 241 A
dholstad@sctcc.edu
HOLSTEGE, Christopher 434-924-5185 473 A
ch2fx@virginia.edu
HOLSTEN, Robert .... 252-246-1254 339 C
rholsten@wilsoncc.edu
HOLSTER, Melissa .... 617-228-2271 214 A
mholster@bhcc.mass.edu
HOLSTON, J.B .... 303-871-3787.. 83 D
jb.holston@du.edu
HOLSTON, Jo-Ann, M .. 334-833-4410.... 5 H
jholston@hawks.huntingdon.edu
HOLSTON, Tavarez .... 404-297-9522 119 B
HOLSTON, William .... 336-841-9221 329 G
bookstor@highpoint.edu
HOLT, Anthony .... 313-577-2056 232 I
aa6479@wayne.edu
HOLT, Bruce .... 865-981-8035 421 F
bruce.holt@maryvillecollege.edu
HOLT, Christine .... 573-882-2011 261 A
holtcj@umsystem.edu
HOLT, Daniel .... 816-415-5977 262 F
holtd@william.jewell.edu
HOLT, Fred .... 318-487-7439 186 I
fred.holt@lacollege.edu
HOLT, Gail, W .... 413-542-2296 205 B
financialaid@amherst.edu
HOLT, Herman .... 828-250-3880 342 C
hholt@unca.edu
HOLT, Kenneth .... 281-649-3014 437 H
kholt@hbu.edu
HOLT, Mary Margaret ... 405-325-7370 371 B
marymholt@ou.edu
HOLT, Melissa .... 573-288-6417 252 E
mholt@culver.edu
HOLT, Michelle, M .... 208-535-5381 130 C
michelle.holt@cei.edu
HOLT, Raymond .... 229-931-2001 124 D
rholt@southgatech.edu
HOLT, Rosalind .... 770-216-2960 120 H
rholt@ict.edu
HOLT, Rosalyn, J .... 318-670-9436 190 J
rholt@susla.edu
HOLT, Russ .... 925-473-7375.. 40 J
rholt@losmedanos.edu
HOLT, Ruth Ann .... 931-540-2750 424 G
rholt@columbiastate.edu
HOLT, Ryan, C .... 828-884-8217 327 C
holtrc@brevard.edu
HOLT, Sam .... 580-387-7311 366 H
sholt@mscok.edu
HOLT, Shari .... 870-743-3000.. 20 C
sholt@northark.edu
HOLT, Tina .... 706-419-1275 117 B
tina.holt@covenant.edu
HOLT-MANCUSO, Tracy 928-532-6170.. 14 J
tracy.mancuso@npc.edu
HOLTE, Lane .... 920-924-6378 500 C
lholte@morainepark.edu
HOLTE, Lane .... 920-924-3163 500 C
lholte@morainepark.edu
HOLTEN, Kathryn .... 828-884-8373 327 C
holtenki@brevard.edu
HOLTGRAVE, David .... 518-402-0281 316 D
dholtgrave@albany.edu
HOLTGREIVE, Shaun ..... 989-774-3111 222 C
holtg1s@cmich.edu
HOLTGREN, Shawn, M . 574-807-7215 153 E
holtgrs@betheluniversity.edu
HOLTHAUS, Barbara ..... 217-641-4104 140 A
bholthaus@jwcc.edu
HOLTHAUS, Cynthia ..... 785-670-1560 177 G
cynthia.holthaus@washburn.edu
HOLTHOUSER,
David, M .... 704-894-2220 328 F
daholthouser@davidson.edu
HOLTMAN, Kaity .... 660-944-2823 251 G
communications@conception.edu
HOLTMANN, Miranda ... 503-251-5712 377 F
mholtmann@uws.edu
HOLTMYER-JONES,
Larissa .... 515-294-6511 162 I
larissah@foundation.iastate.edu
HOLTON, Anne .... 703-993-8700 467 L
president@gmu.edu
HOLTON, Benjamin .... 404-894-1420 118 F
benjamin.holton@health.gatech.edu
HOLTON, Carol .... 910-898-9605 336 D
holtonc@montgomery.edu
HOLTON, Kristina .... 541-917-4416 374 A
holtonk@linnbenton.edu

HOLTROP, Steve 712-722-6214 164 K steve.holtrop@dordt.edu
HOLTSCHNEIDER, CM, Dennis, H 312-362-8712 135 I dholtsch@depaul.edu
HOLTSCLAW, Ben 828-898-8830 330 E holtsclawb@lmc.edu
HOLTZ, Daniel, F 320-222-5205 240 E daniel.holtz@ridgewater.edu
HOLTZ, Edwin 712-325-3227 167 B eholtz@iwcc.edu
HOLTZ, Ryan 410-706-7481 202 D rholtz@umaryland.edu
HOLTZCLAW, Rhonda 239-590-1037 108 K rholtzcl@wgcu.edu
HOLTZHAUSEN, Derina 409-880-8137 449 H derina.holtzhausen@lamar.edu
HOLUBIK, Donna 734-487-0455 223 H dholubik@emich.edu
HOLVEY BOWLES, Joanna 315-228-7216 296 F jholveybowles@colgate.edu
HOLWERDA, Jane 620-227-9359 172 J jholwerda@dc3.edu
HOLWICK, Jana, W 770-426-2697 121 C jana.holwick@life.edu
HOLYFIELD, Patrick 704-991-0235 338 C pholyfield8286@stanly.edu
HOLZ, Doris 212-220-8021 293 A dholz@bmcc.cuny.edu
HOLZ, Marina 914-594-4110 309 H mholz@nymc.edu
HOLZ, Richard 303-273-3003 78 I rholz@mines.edu
HOLZ-CLAUSE, Mary 218-281-8343 244 A mhclause@umn.edu
HOLZBERLEIN, Anne 405-974-2770 370 K aholzberlein@uco.edu
HOLZCLAW, Mike 925-551-1822 40 I mholzclaw@dvc.edu
HOLZEMER, William, L 973-353-5149 282 A holzemer@sn.rutgers.edu
HOLZEMER, William, L 973-353-5149 282 B holzemer@sn.rutgers.edu
HOLZHEUSER, Christina 361-825-5975 447 C christina.holzheuser@tamucc.edu
HOLZMAN, Terri, L 920-748-8850 495 G holzmant@ripon.edu
HOLZMER, OSF, M. Anita 260-399-7700 161 D aholzmer@sf.edu
HOMAN, Elizabeth, S 443-518-4073 199 C ehoman@howardcc.edu
HOMAN, Judi 901-375-4400 422 F judihoman@midsouthchristian.edu
HOMAN, Pamela 605-274-5016 415 B pamela.homan@augie.edu
HOMAN, Richard, V 757-446-5800 466 I homanrv@evms.edu
HOMANY, Garry 216-397-1982 354 I ghomany@jcu.edu
HOMARD, Jennifer 352-395-5493 107 A jen.homard@sfcollege.edu
HOMER, Cory 973-300-2116 283 E chomer@sussex.edu
HOMER, Rollin 626-396-2263 26 E rollin.homer@artcenter.edu
HOMFELDT, Mike 541-880-2244 373 E homfeldt@klamathcc.edu
HOMIAK, JR., Albert, J 302-831-7285 90 F homiak@udel.edu
HOMICH, John 617-627-6333 219 B john.homich@tufts.edu
HOMOLKA, Karen, K 217-245-3094 138 D khomolk@ic.edu
HOMSHER, Betsy, E 810-762-9540 225 H bhomsher@kettering.edu
HON, Ken 808-932-7332 128 E kenhon@hawaii.edu
HONADEL, Tim 661-362-3699 38 H tim.honadel@canyons.edu
HONAKER, Lisa 609-652-4505 283 D lisa.honaker@stockton.edu
HONAN, Lisa 203-932-7264 89 A lhonan@newhaven.edu
HONDA, Herminia 323-409-6301 49 H hhonda@dhs.lacounty.gov
HONDA, Hirosuke 207-621-3216 196 A hirosuke.honda@maine.edu
HONDA, Jacqueline 408-274-7900 61 L jacqueline.honda@evc.edu
HONEBRINK, Emily 952-446-4112 235 G honebrinke@crown.edu
HONEYCUTT, Andrew, E 714-772-3330 26 A
HONEYCUTT, Del Ray 607-871-2300 289 H honeycutt@alfred.edu
HONEYCUTT, Del Rey 607-871-2134 289 H honeycutt@alfred.edu
HONG, Luoluo 415-338-2032 34 A luoluo@sfsu.edu
HONG, Marcus 502-895-3411 183 D mhong@lpts.edu
HONG, Michael 323-860-1122 53 B hongm@mi.edu
HONG, Michael 323-463-2500 67 C michaelh@toa.edu
HONG, Peter 909-621-8099 37 E
HONG, Rebecca 310-338-7371 50 J rebecca.hong@lmu.edu
HONG, Sung Wook 512-444-8082 449 A whong@thsu.edu
HONG, Tran 951-343-3907 27 J thong@calbaptist.edu
HONG, Ye (Solar) 218-755-3773 237 E ye.hong@bemidjistate.edu
HONG, Z. George 718-817-0029 300 E zhong4@fordham.edu
HONNELL, Cherie 503-494-7878 375 B acad@ohsu.edu
HONNY, Jean 619-216-6670 65 F jhonny@swccd.edu
HONTZ, Rachel 816-322-0110 250 K rachel.hontz@calvary.edu
HOO, Karlene 406-994-4145 264 D karlene.hoo@montana.edu
HOO, Karlene 509-313-6117 481 D hook@gonzaga.edu
HOOD, Amanda 601-643-8619 245 G amanda.hood@colin.edu
HOOD, Carra 609-652-4514 283 D carra.hood@stockton.edu
HOOD, Chester 850-599-3796 108 I chester.hood@famu.edu
HOOD, David 973-655-4280 279 C hoodd@montclair.edu
HOOD, Donna 828-395-1404 335 D dhood@isothermal.edu
HOOD, Gwendolyn, D 205-348-5855 7 G ghood@aalan.ua.edu
HOOD, Jean 817-272-5554 454 J jmhood@uta.edu
HOOD, Joshua, D 423-775-7574 418 H jhood3724@bryan.edu
HOOD, Mattie 850-599-3203 108 I mattie.hood@famu.edu
HOOD, Michael 210-829-3957 453 D hood@uiwtx.edu
HOOD, Mike 903-233-4115 439 E mikehood@letu.edu
HOOD, Robin 931-363-9800 421 E rhood@martinmethodist.edu
HOOD, Scott, W 207-725-3256 193 D shood@bowdoin.edu
HOOD, Steven 435-283-7301 461 C steve.hood@snow.edu
HOOD, Tim 815-599-3513 138 B tim.hood@highland.edu
HOOD, W.C. (Chip) 864-656-3414 408 A chip@clemson.edu
HOOGEWERF, Arlene 616-526-8668 222 A ahoogewe@calvin.edu
HOOK, Amy 617-353-2399 207 D amyhook@bu.edu
HOOK, Beth 314-362-6590 253 E beth.hook@bjc.org
HOOKER, Kendricks 608-243-4088 499 H khooker@madisoncollege.edu
HOOKER, Mike 970-217-3134 78 L mike.hooker@colostate.edu
HOOKER, Steven, P 619-594-6516 33 E shooker@sdsu.edu
HOOKS, Alicia 913-288-7388 174 F ahokks@kckcc.edu
HOOKS, Ariana 580-349-1396 368 A ariana.hooks@opsu.edu
HOOKS, Deborah 850-484-2116 104 H dhooks@pensacolastate.edu
HOOKS, Jeffery 269-783-2159 230 F jhooks@swmich.edu
HOOKS, Jodi 563-588-6553 163 F jodi.hooks@clarke.edu
HOOKS, Karin 440-366-7102 355 J
HOOKS, Rebecca 704-216-3488 337 F rebecca.hooks@rccc.edu
HOOLE, Thomas 978-934-3509 211 G thomas_hoole@uml.edu
HOON, William 309-298-1552 152 D wg-hoon@wiu.edu
HOOPER, Brooke 757-446-7439 466 I hooperab@evms.edu
HOOPER, Celia 336-750-2567 344 B hoopercr@wssu.edu
HOOPER, Christy 615-966-1000 421 D christy.hooper@lipscomb.edu
HOOPER, Elizabeth, A 253-535-7337 482 H hooperea@plu.edu
HOOPER, Heath 706-292-3906 124 B hhooper@shorter.edu
HOOPER, Julie 510-642-7374 68 D jhooper@berkeley.edu
HOOPER, Ricardo 310-287-4513 49 G hopperra@wlac.edu
HOOPER, Robert, D 740-427-5109 355 E hooperr@kenyon.edu
HOOPER-PORTER, Tracey 740-588-1377 365 E tporter2@zanestate.edu
HOOPES, Robbin 513-569-1511 350 K robbin.hoopes@cincinnatistate.edu
HOOPES, Tom 913-360-7529 171 D thoopes@benedictine.edu
HOOPS, James 419-267-1368 358 A jhoops@northweststate.edu
HOOPS, Lisa 937-778-7955 352 J lhoops@edisonohio.edu
HOOPS, Tony 316-284-5279 171 F thoops@bethelks.edu
HOORMAN, Rachel 504-865-2011 189 F rchoorma@loyno.edu
HOORNBEEK, Corbin 626-815-5328 26 H choornbeek@apu.edu
HOOT, Dustin 414-847-3233 494 F dustinhoot@miad.edu
HOOTEN, Jon 805-922-6966 24 J jon.hooten@hancockcollege.edu
HOOTEN, Michael 806-414-9683 451 C michael.hooten@ttuhsc.edu
HOOTS, Cathy 336-750-2265 344 B hoots@wssu.edu
HOOVER, Amy, K 712-778-2466 266 I amyhoover@creighton.edu
HOOVER, Angela 336-725-8344 339 F hoovera@piedmontu.edu
HOOVER, Chris 620-341-5337 172 L choover@emporia.edu
HOOVER, Diane 541-956-7011 376 D dhoover@roguecc.edu
HOOVER, Douglas 724-938-4096 394 B hoover@calu.edu
HOOVER, James, W 214-887-5347 436 B jhoover@dts.edu
HOOVER, Jean, B 717-262-2007 403 F jhoover@wilson.edu
HOOVER, Josie 202-664-5682 93 E jhoover@wesleyseminary.edu
HOOVER, Karelyn 909-274-4570 52 H khoover@mtsac.edu
HOOVER, Kathleen 610-558-5560 391 D hooverk@neumann.edu
HOOVER, Kathy 360-596-5409 485 B khoover@spscc.edu
HOOVER, Kelly 410-704-2516 204 A khoover@towson.edu
HOOVER, Kevin 559-325-3600 28 H khoover@chsu.edu
HOOVER, Linda 806-742-3031 451 B linda.hoover@ttu.edu
HOOVER, Lisa 214-637-3530 457 I lhoover@wadecollege.edu
HOOVER, Myrna 850-644-6089 109 C mhoover@fsu.edu
HOOVER, Robert 563-588-6338 163 F robert.hoover@clarke.edu
HOOVER, Susan 405-425-5961 367 G susan.hoover@oc.edu
HOOVER, Thomas 318-342-1050 192 F hoover@ulm.edu
HOOYMAN, Jamie 660-562-1122 257 E jhooyman@nwmissouri.edu
HOPE, Alana 510-780-4500 47 J ahope@lifewest.edu
HOPE, Deryle 864-503-5769 414 D dhope@uscupstate.edu
HOPE, Henry 404-471-6355 113 G hhope@agnesscott.edu
HOPE, John 251-981-3771 5 B john.hope@columbiasouthern.edu
HOPE, John 617-603-6903 216 H john.hope@necb.edu
HOPE, Joseph, S 315-228-7422 296 F jshope@colgate.edu
HOPE, Kelly 203-332-5973 85 F khope@hcc.commnet.edu
HOPE, Laura 909-652-6131 36 A laura.hope@chaffey.edu
HOPE, Nancy 276-739-2412 476 C nhope@vhcc.edu
HOPE, Oral 212-431-2300 309 G oral.hope@nyls.edu
HOPEWELL, Mitchell 661-362-2683 51 C mhopewell@masters.edu
HOPEWELL, JR., Woodson, H 757-727-5303 468 B woodson.hopewell@hamptonu.edu
HOPEY, Christopher, E 978-837-5110 216 D christopher.hopey@merrimack.edu
HOPF, Jim 252-328-6105 341 C hopfj16@ecu.edu
HOPKIN, Fran 435-797-8380 460 H fran.hopkin@usu.edu
HOPKINS, Alexander, M 713-798-4262 431 I ahopkins@bcm.edu
HOPKINS, Barry 773-256-0734 142 G bhopkins@jkmlibrary.org
HOPKINS, Boone 864-596-9227 409 B boone.hopkins@converse.edu
HOPKINS, Bruce 229-430-2837 113 I bhopkins@albanytech.edu
HOPKINS, Christi 620-242-0414 175 F hopkinsc@mcpherson.edu
HOPKINS, David 903-675-6214 452 B david.hopkins@tvcc.edu
HOPKINS, Drew, W 609-984-3430 284 B dhopkins@tesu.edu
HOPKINS, Elijah 406-768-6371 263 G ehopkins@fpcc.edu
HOPKINS, Gena 260-459-4512 157 E ghopkins@ibcfortwayne.edu
HOPKINS, Jamal 803-376-5834 406 F jhopkins@allenuniversity.edu
HOPKINS, Jessica 618-537-6817 143 B jlhopkins@mckendree.edu
HOPKINS, John, L 203-596-4652 87 F jhopkins@post.edu
HOPKINS, Joseph 205-726-2778 6 E jhopkins@samford.edu
HOPKINS, Kent 480-965-2408 10 I kent.hopkins@asu.edu
HOPKINS, Kevin 785-594-8553 170 I kevin.hopkins@bakeru.edu
HOPKINS, Mark 706-236-2231 115 B mhopkins@berry.edu
HOPKINS, Melissa 573-518-2177 256 B mhopkins@mineralarea.edu
HOPKINS, Michael 773-702-6490 150 J mhopkins@uchicago.edu
HOPKINS, Paulette 619-388-7350 60 E phopkins@sdccd.edu
HOPKINS, Randy 816-501-4659 258 H randy.hopkins@rockhurst.edu
HOPKINS, Rebecca 507-457-6620 243 B rhopkins@smumn.edu
HOPKINS, Ronnie 803-780-1179 414 E rhopkins@voorhees.edu
HOPKINS, Sara 615-248-1653 427 A shopkins@trevecca.edu
HOPKINS, Sarah 707-527-4831 62 F shopkins@santarosa.edu
HOPKINS, Stacy 724-357-2230 394 G stacy.hopkins@iup.edu
HOPKINS, T. Hampton 704-355-5316 327 H hampton.hopkins@carolinascollege.edu
HOPKINS, Threasa 605-692-9337 415 D thopkins@ilt.edu
HOPKINS, Timothy 630-829-6449 132 E thopkins@ben.edu
HOPKINS-GROSS, Anne 518-255-5214 319 F hopkinam@cobleskill.edu
HOPKINS-JENKINS, Amber 212-938-5607 320 B aehopkinsjenkins@sunyopt.edu
HOPKINS-POSELLE, Denise 914-637-2757 302 G dhopkins@iona.edu
HOPP, Lisa 219-989-2823 159 G ljhopp@pnw.edu
HOPP, Melissa 443-840-3176 198 B mhopp@ccbcmd.edu
HOPP, Susan 503-883-2278 373 H shopp@linfield.edu

HOTTINGER, Sara .... 843-349-2473 408 C
shottinge@coastal.edu
HOTZFIELD, Brian .... 773-298-3096 148 G
hotzfield@sxu.edu
HOTZLER, Russell, K ..... 718-260-5400 295 B
rhotzler@citytech.cuny.edu
HOUBECK, JR.,
Robert, L .... 810-762-3410 231 G
rhoubeck@umich.edu
HOUCH, Chad .... 760-384-6201.. 46 M
chad.houch@cerrocoso.edu
HOUCHEN-CLAGETT,
Denise, A .... 910-755-7472 332 F
houchen-clagettd@brunswickcc.edu
HOUCHENS, Brianna ..... 513-875-3344 350 G
brianna.houchens@chatfield.edu
HOUCHIN, Janeane .... 785-833-4462 175 B
janeane.houchin@kwu.edu
HOUCK, Beth .... 864-977-7200 411 E
beth.houck@ngu.edu
HOUCK, Clarence, M .... 803-934-3235 411 C
chouck@morris.edu
HOUCK, Jancy .... 803-777-8315 413 C
jancyh@mailbox.sc.edu
HOUCK, Laurie .... 407-646-2124 105 M
lhouck@rollins.edu
HOUDE, Dorothy .... 671-734-1812 505 D
HOUDE, Joe .... 858-653-6740.. 46 I
jhoude@jpcatholic.edu
HOUDYSCHELL,
Jendonnae .... 304-696-6704 490 D
houdyschell2@marshall.edu
HOUFER, Michael .... 651-747-4085 237 G
michael.houfer@century.edu
HOUFF, Bekah .... 260-982-5243 158 T
rlhouff@manchester.edu
HOUGE, Melanie .... 406-791-5210 265 H
melanie.houge@uprovidence.edu
HOUGH, Andy .... 314-744-7623 256 C
andy.hough@mobap.edu
HOUGH, Barbara, J ...... 518-276-6426 312 I
houghb2@rpi.edu
HOUGH, Brad .... 636-227-2100 254 G
HOUGH, David .... 417-836-5254 256 E
davidhough@missouristate.edu
HOUGH, Kristy, M .... 770-720-5542 123 E
kristy.hough@reinhardt.edu
HOUGH, Melanie, J ...... 419-772-2024 358 H
m-hough@onu.edu
HOUGH, Tony .... 803-738-7695 410 G
hought@midlandstech.edu
HOUGHTON, Brian .... 808-675-3209 127 E
brian.houghton@byuh.edu
HOUGHTON, David, C .. 405-585-4400 367 F
david.houghton@okbu.edu
HOUGLAND, Dawn .... 312-341-3531 147 H
dhougland@roosevelt.edu
HOUK, Christopher .... 270-686-4241 179 D
chris.houk@brescia.edu
HOUK, Suzanne, N .... 724-458-2208 385 C
snhouk@gcc.edu
HOULIHAN, Janet, M ... 714-895-8307.. 38 D
jhoulihan@gwc.cccd.edu
HOULIHAN, Jill .... 501-760-4206.. 20 B
jill.houlihan@np.edu
HOULT, Kevin, J .... 334-844-3466.... 4 E
kjh0029@auburn.edu
HOUPIS, James .... 209-575-6498.. 75 J
houpisj@mjc.edu
HOUPT, Andrew, M .... 724-589-2175 399 H
ahoupt@thiel.edu
HOURANY, Lance .... 925-631-4767.. 59 B
lph5@stmarys-ca.edu
HOURIGAN,
Christopher, P .... 401-456-8998 405 C
chourigan@ric.edu
HOURIGAN, Gerard ...... 216-987-4706 351 G
gerard.hourigan@tri-c.edu
HOUSE, DeAndre .... 601-857-3701 246 B
deandre.house@hindscc.edu
HOUSE, H. Wayne .... 888-777-7675 481 B
hwhouse@faithseminary.edu
HOUSE, J. Daniel .... 815-753-6002 145 C
jhouse@niu.edu
HOUSE, Kamesia .... 910-672-1325 341 E
kmhouse@uncfsu.edu
HOUSE, Karen .... 978-542-6120 213 C
khouse@salemstate.edu
HOUSE, Kevin .... 509-244-6851 480 A
kevin.house@scc.spokane.edu
HOUSE, Ron .... 618-985-2637 139 I
ronhouse@jalc.edu
HOUSE, Stephanie .... 208-769-3368 131 C
stephanie.house@nic.edu
HOUSE, Steven, D .... 336-278-6647 328 K
shouse@elon.edu
HOUSE, Vicki .... 325-670-1276 437 F
vhouse@hsutx.edu
HOUSEKNECHT, Karen .. 207-602-2872 196 G
khouseknecht@une.edu
HOUSEKNECHT, Rick .... 215-368-5000 390 F
rhouseknecht@missio.edu
HOUSEMAN, Jennifer .... 215-951-1070 387 C
houseman@lasalle.edu
HOUSENICK, Joseph ..... 570-408-4630 403 D
joseph.housenick@wilkes.edu
HOUSER, Janet .... 303-458-1843.. 82 E
jhouser@regis.edu
HOUSER, John .... 575-562-2123 285 M
john.houser@enmu.edu
HOUSER, Katie .... 843-953-5606 408 E
houserkk@cofc.edu
HOUSER, Kay .... 910-788-6219 338 A
kay.houser@sccnc.edu
HOUSER, Nate .... 785-594-8316 170 I
HOUSER, Robert .... 970-351-1759.. 83 E
robert.houser@ucno.edu
HOUSER, Sue .... 302-736-2438.. 90 G
susan.houser@wesley.edu
HOUSEWORTH, Julie .... 573-592-4260 262 G
julie.houseworth@williamwoods.edu
HOUSHMAND, Ali .... 856-256-4100 281 E
presidenthoushmand@rowan.edu
HOUSHOWER, Hans ..... 419-358-3234 348 G
houshowerh@bluffton.edu
HOUSKA, Nila .... 712-749-2233 163 D
houskan@bvu.edu
HOUSLEY, Brooks .... 334-387-3877.... 4 C
brookshousley@amridgeuniversity.edu
HOUSLEY, Harold .... 903-875-7307 440 G
harold.housley@navarrocollege.edu
HOUSLEY, Heather, L ... 404-413-2070 119 E
heatherh@gsu.edu
HOUSLEY, La Royce ..... 310-954-4191.. 52 G
ldodd@msmu.edu
HOUSMAN, Naomi .... 215-635-7300 385 A
nhousman@gratz.edu
HOUSMAN, Yosef .... 732-367-1060 275 J
yhousman@bmg.edu
HOUSTON, Adam .... 760-921-5463.. 55 H
ahouston@paloverde.edu
HOUSTON, Angela .... 620-331-4100 174 C
ahouston@indycc.edu
HOUSTON, Angela .... 601-318-6231 249 H
lhouston@wmcarey.edu
HOUSTON, Annazette .... 865-539-7401 425 F
ahouston1@pstcc.edu
HOUSTON, Anne .... 610-330-5150 387 E
houstona@lafayette.edu
HOUSTON, Chrystal ...... 402-363-5607 270 E
chrystal.houston@york.edu
HOUSTON, Don .... 408-855-5428.. 74 D
don.houston@wvm.edu
HOUSTON, Doug .... 636-584-6732 252 J
doug.houston@eastcentral.edu
HOUSTON, Douglas, B . 530-741-6971.. 76 A
dhouston@yccd.edu
HOUSTON, Hope .... 781-891-2450 206 D
hhouston@bentley.edu
HOUSTON, Jason .... 509-328-4220 481 D
houston@gonzaga.edu
HOUSTON, Jean .... 707-765-1836.. 51 H
HOUSTON, Kathryn .... 816-235-6211 261 C
houstonk@umkc.edu
HOUSTON, Kristen .... 206-876-6100 484 E
khouston@theseattleschool.edu
HOUSTON, Michael ...... 662-621-4853 245 E
mhouston@coahomacc.edu
HOUSTON, Michael ...... 662-621-4205 245 E
mhouston@coahomacc.edu
HOUSTON, Michelle ..... 631-499-7100 304 F
mhouston@libi.edu
HOUSTON, Nainsi .... 740-826-8260 357 C
nhouston@muskingum.edu
HOUSTON, Rachel .... 704-403-1228 327 D
rachel.houston@carolinashealthcare.org
HOUSTON, Raymond .... 914-606-6789 325 C
raymond.houston@sunywcc.edu
HOUSTON, Renee .... 253-879-3207 485 E
rhouston@pugetsound.edu
HOUSTON, Richard .... 662-846-4690 245 H
rhouston@deltastate.edu
HOUSTON, Rick .... 978-867-4130 209 F
ric.houston@gordon.edu
HOUSTON, Sue .... 419-372-2211 348 H
shousto@bgsu.edu
HOUSTON, Vinson .... 256-782-5993.... 5 J
vhouston@jsu.edu
HOUSTON-BROWN,
Clive .... 909-469-7037.. 74 I
choustonbrown@westernu.edu
HOUT-REILLY, Daniel .... 216-791-5000 351 A
daniel.hout-reilly@cim.edu
HOUTMAN, Anne .... 765-983-1211 154 G
earlhampresident@earlham.edu
HOUTZ, Tracy .... 816-523-9140 262 D
tracy.houtz@wellspring.edu
HOUZE, Shea, K .... 865-974-3179 427 G
shouze@utk.edu
HOVATTER, Angela, L ... 301-687-4301 203 E
ahovatter@frostburg.edu
HOVEKAMP, Tina .... 541-383-7563 372 B
thovekamp@cocc.edu
HOVEN, Kierstin .... 218-755-4135 237 E
kierstin.hoven@bemidjistate.edu
HOVENGA, Danielle ...... 918-631-3303 371 E
danielle-hovenga@utulsa.edu
HOVERSTEN, Mark .... 919-515-8347 342 B
mark_hoversten@ncsu.edu
HOVESTOL, Dan .... 406-586-3585 263 J
dan.hovestol@montanabiblecollege.edu
HOVET, Jami .... 701-788-4761 345 E
jami.hovet@mayvillestate.edu
HOVEY, Jeff .... 314-977-8375 259 H
jeff.hovey@slu.edu
HOVEY, Mark .... 860-685-2337.. 89 C
mhovey@wesleyan.edu
HOVEY, Rebecca .... 413-585-2697 218 F
rhovey@smith.edu
HOVEY, Roger, S .... 308-635-6012 270 D
rhovey@wncc.edu
HOW, Christine .... 402-557-7002 265 J
chow@bellevue.edu
HOWAR, Julie .... 309-690-6909 138 C
julie.howar@icc.edu
HOWARD, Aimee .... 225-490-1652 186 F
aimee.howard@franu.edu
HOWARD, Alistair .... 215-204-0720 399 F
alistair.howard@temple.edu
HOWARD, Andrew .... 806-743-2870 451 C
andrew.howard@ttuhsc.edu
HOWARD, Ann .... 202-884-9608.. 93 B
howarda@trinitydc.edu
HOWARD, April .... 540-986-1800 464 G
ahoward@an.edu
HOWARD, Armando .... 718-270-6484 295 A
ahoward@mec.cuny.edu
HOWARD, Barry .... 615-514-2787 423 E
bhoward@nossi.edu
HOWARD, Bobby .... 870-743-3000.. 20 C
robert.howard@northark.edu
HOWARD, Brandy .... 510-215-3836.. 40 H
bhoward@contracosta.edu
HOWARD, Bree .... 661-255-1050.. 28 K
bhoward@calarts.edu
HOWARD, Catherine ..... 903-823-3285 446 B
catherine.howard@texarkanacollege.edu
HOWARD,
Catherine, W .... 804-828-8790 473 F
choward@vcu.edu
HOWARD, Cedric, B ..... 716-673-3271 317 A
cedric.howard@fredonia.edu
HOWARD, Chad, E .... 479-248-7236.. 19 C
choward@ecollege.edu
HOWARD, Charles, L ... 215-898-8456 400 K
choward@upenn.edu
HOWARD, Christopher . 412-397-6400 397 G
president@rmu.edu
HOWARD, Cindy .... 816-268-5424 257 C
choward@nts.edu
HOWARD, Courtney, A . 843-953-7629 408 E
howardca1@cofc.edu
HOWARD, Dale, S .... 330-490-7303 364 B
dhoward@walsh.edu
HOWARD, Dana, K .... 318-274-3133 191 E
howardd@gram.edu
HOWARD, Daniel .... 601-925-3350 247 C
drhoward@mc.edu
HOWARD, Donna .... 443-885-3535 200 D
donna.howard@morgan.edu
HOWARD, Doris .... 415-503-6214.. 60 H
finaid@sfcm.edu
HOWARD, Doug .... 615-460-6306 418 F
doug.howard@belmont.edu
HOWARD, Douglas .... 603-888-1311 274 B
dhoward@rivier.edu
HOWARD, Drew .... 863-680-4266.. 99 H
ahoward@flsouthern.edu
HOWARD, JR., Eddie .... 330-941-2018 365 C
ejhoward01@ysu.edu
HOWARD, Elizabeth ...... 817-531-6582 451 E
ehoward@txwes.edu
HOWARD, Elizabeth ...... 215-646-7300 385 D
howard.e@gmercyu.edu
HOWARD, Ezra .... 662-621-4083 245 E
ehoward@coahomacc.edu
HOWARD, Gary, E .... 859-858-3511 178 I
gary.howard@asbury.edu
HOWARD, Gene .... 205-726-2366.... 6 E
wehoward@samford.edu
HOWARD, Genevieve .... 360-992-2936 479 F
ghoward@clark.edu
HOWARD, Gerard, L ..... 601-979-1073 246 E
gerard.l.howard@jsums.edu
HOWARD, Gregory .... 804-257-5717 477 C
gmhoward@vuu.edu
HOWARD, Hugh .... 330-263-2145 351 C
hhoward@wooster.edu
HOWARD, Jane .... 620-792-9208 171 C
howardj@bartonccc.edu
HOWARD, Jay, R .... 317-940-9874 153 F
jrhoward@butler.edu
HOWARD, Jeffery, S ..... 423-439-4210 419 J
howardjs@etsu.edu
HOWARD, Jeffrey .... 605-626-2415 417 A
jeffrey.howard@northern.edu
HOWARD, Jessica .... 503-399-6591 372 C
jessica.howard@chemeketa.edu
HOWARD, Joe .... 814-824-2829 390 C
jhoward@mercyhurst.edu
HOWARD, John .... 303-273-3646.. 78 I
jkhoward@mines.edu
HOWARD, Jordan .... 620-768-2909 173 C
jordanh@fortscott.edu
HOWARD, Karleen .... 410-857-2234 200 B
kphoward@mcdaniel.edu
HOWARD, Kevin .... 706-821-8232 122 K
khoward@paine.edu
HOWARD, Kimberly, A . 802-656-4296 463 E
kimberly.howard@uvm.edu
HOWARD, Lelia .... 267-502-2680 379 D
lelia.howard@brynathyn.edu
HOWARD, Leon .... 662-252-8000 248 G
lhoward@rustcollege.edu
HOWARD, Lonnie .... 409-880-8185 449 G
llhoward@lit.edu
HOWARD, Luke .... 662-621-4168 245 E
lhoward@coahomacc.edu
HOWARD, Manny .... 610-292-9852 397 D
manny.howard@reseminary.edu
HOWARD, Martin, J ...... 617-353-2290 207 D
mjhoward@bu.edu
HOWARD, Mary Ann .... 478-757-5137 126 H
mhoward@wesleyancollege.edu
HOWARD, Michael .... 617-627-3331 219 B
michael.howard@tufts.edu
HOWARD, Michael, P ... 518-564-3140 319 C
mhowa001@plattsburgh.edu
HOWARD, Penelope ..... 716-851-1701 299 F
howardp@ecc.edu
HOWARD, Predita .... 478-934-3092 121 F
predita.howard@mga.edu
HOWARD, Randy, B ..... 386-226-6000.. 98 A
randy.howard@erau.edu
HOWARD, Ron .... 601-925-3870 247 C
howard@mc.edu
HOWARD, Rosetta .... 662-252-8000 248 G
rhoward@rustcollege.edu
HOWARD, II, Ruben ..... 847-635-1807 145 G
rhoward@oakton.edu
HOWARD, Sherry .... 870-864-7193.. 21 B
showard@southark.edu
HOWARD, Stefanie .... 310-393-0411.. 55 J
stefanie_howard@rand.org
HOWARD, Steven .... 619-596-2766.. 24 F
showard@advancedtraining.edu
HOWARD, Tammy, L .... 217-443-8552 135 H
thoward@dacc.edu
HOWARD, Tiffany .... 318-876-2401 187 B
HOWARD, Vikki .... 218-335-4255 236 E
vikki.howard@lltc.edu
HOWARD, Will .... 253-566-5344 485 C
whoward@tacomacc.edu
HOWARD, Yaffa .... 215-635-7300 385 A
yhoward@gratz.edu
HOWARD, Yelitza, M .... 956-326-4483 446 F
yelitza.howard@tamiu.edu
HOWARD-WEISSMAN,
Linda .... 646-565-6125 322 J
lindah@tourolaw.edu

HUBBARD, Susan, G .... 334-844-4790.... 4 E hubbasg@auburn.edu
HUBBARD, Tatum .... 432-552-3102 457 A hubbard_t@utpb.edu
HUBBELL, Melody .... 417-255-7234 256 F melodyhubbell@missouristate.edu
HUBBELL, Sarah .... 269-488-4207 225 E shubbell@kvcc.edu
HUBBERT, Daron .... 951-343-4229.. 27 J dhubbert@calbaptist.edu
HUBBS, Jocelyn .... 541-684-7291 374 G jhubbs@nwcu.edu
HUBER, Amy .... 973-803-5000 280 C ahuber@pillar.edu
HUBER, E. Kim .... 303-315-2252.. 83 C
HUBER, Heidi .... 410-857-2769 200 B hhuber@mcdaniel.edu
HUBER, Karrie, K .... 701-355-8226 347 D kkhuber@umary.edu
HUBER, Lane .... 701-224-5714 346 B lane.huber@bismarckstate.edu
HUBER, Laurie, G .... 248-232-4543 229 A lghuber@oaklandcc.edu
HUBER, Lindsey .... 309-341-5213 133 C lhuber@sandburg.edu
HUBER, Lydia .... 361-572-6461 457 E lydia.huber@victoriacollege.edu
HUBER, Lynn .... 336-278-5709 328 K lhuber@elon.edu
HUBER, Margaret .... 605-229-8405 416 C margaret.huber@presentation.edu
HUBER, Morgan .... 605-995-7250 415 G morgan.huber@mitchelltech.edu
HUBER, Patricia, B .... 540-674-3601 475 B phuber@nr.edu
HUBERMAN, Jeffrey, H . 309-677-2360 133 B huberman@bradley.edu
HUBERMAN, Steven ...... 212-463-0400 322 J steven.huberman@touro.edu
HUBERS, Todd, K .... 616-526-8754 222 A thubers@calvin.edu
HUBERT, David .... 801-957-4280 461 D david.hubert@slcc.edu
HUBERT, Jennifer .... 404-385-7604 118 F jennifer.hubert@business.gatech.edu
HUBERT, Jennifer .... 404-894-7894 118 F jennifer.hubert@business.gatech.edu
HUBERT, Lydia .... 229-468-2000 127 B lydia.hubert@wiregrass.edu
HUBIN, Kert .... 303-245-4797.. 81 B khubin@naropa.edu
HUBRIC, Kimberly, A .... 610-921-7629 378 C khubric@albright.edu
HUCH, Robert, E .... 540-261-4098 471 H bob.huch@svu.edu
HUCK, Jack .... 402-323-3411 269 C jhuck@southeast.edu
HUCKABA, Sam .... 850-644-4404 109 C shuckaba@fsu.edu
HUCKABAY, Sonia .... 559-791-2403.. 47 A shuckaba@portervillecollege.edu
HUCKABY, Deborah ...... 706-769-1472 114 E dhuckaby@acmin.org
HUCKS, Tracey, E .... 315-228-7222 296 F thucks@colgate.edu
HUCKSTEAD, Seth .... 616-432-3411 229 I seth.huckstead@prts.edu
HUDACK, John, J .... 716-827-2512 323 D hudackj@trocaire.edu
HUDAK, David .... 614-247-8670 358 I dhudak@osu.edu
HUDAK, Jane, E .... 484-664-3300 391 C janehudak@muhlenberg.edu
HUDAK, Sharon .... 570-674-6295 390 G shudak@misericordia.edu
HUDANICK, Richard ..... 636-584-6500 252 J richard.hudanick@eastcentral.edu
HUDDLESON, Colleen ... 260-399-7700 161 D chuddleson@sf.edu
HUDDLESTON, Sean, L . 317-543-3235 158 V
HUDGENS, Kevin .... 719-502-2000.. 81 F kevin.hudgens@ppcc.edu
HUDGIN, Denise .... 419-251-1324 356 C denise.hudgin@mercycollege.edu
HUDGINS, Debra .... 757-825-3513 476 A hudgins@tncc.edu
HUDGINS, Jamie .... 770-720-5634 123 E jth@reinhardt.edu
HUDGINS, Karen .... 904-819-6252.. 98 E khudgins@flagler.edu
HUDGINS, Molly .... 636-949-4192 254 F mhudgins@lindenwood.edu
HUDGINS, V. Lavoyed .. 859-985-3240 179 C hudginsv@berea.edu
HUDMAN, Steve .... 936-633-5292 430 F shudman@angelina.edu
HUDNELL, Jason .... 501-760-4374.. 20 B jason.hudnell@np.edu
HUDSICK, Walter .... 360-752-8323 478 G whudsick@btc.edu
HUDSON, Adair .... 864-488-4370 410 E ahudson@limestone.edu
HUDSON, Angela .... 501-686-2504.. 21 F ahudson@uasys.edu
HUDSON, April .... 407-618-5900.. 92 G
HUDSON, April .... 407-926-2000.. 92 G
HUDSON, April .... 407-264-9400.. 92 G
HUDSON, Bo .... 918-293-4912 368 D steven.w.hudson@okstate.edu
HUDSON, Bobby .... 615-230-3445 426 B bobby.hudson@volstate.edu
HUDSON, Crystal .... 903-730-4890 438 H chudson@jarvis.edu
HUDSON, David, D .... 714-895-8104.. 38 D dhudson@gwc.cccd.edu
HUDSON, Dean, P .... 843-349-2739 408 C dhudson@coastal.edu
HUDSON, DeVaria .... 318-342-1295 192 F dhudson@ulm.edu
HUDSON, Donald, M .... 609-652-4883 283 D donald.hudson@stockton.edu
HUDSON, Edith .... 414-288-7700 494 B edith.hudson@marquette.edu
HUDSON, El Pagnier .... 305-348-2190 109 A elpagnier.hudson@fiu.edu
HUDSON, Elizabeth .... 617-373-2170 217 F
HUDSON, Garien .... 614-236-6232 349 D ghudson@capital.edu
HUDSON, Holly .... 251-460-7053.... 8 F hhudson@southalabama.edu
HUDSON, Holly .... 979-845-0544 446 G studyabroad@tamu.edu
HUDSON, Jennifer, M .. 713-646-1819 444 B jhudson@stcl.edu
HUDSON, Jennifer, M .. 713-646-1899 444 B jhudson@stcl.edu
HUDSON, John .... 713-221-8664 453 B hudsonj@uhd.edu
HUDSON, Karen .... 615-550-3165 429 A karen.hudson@williamsoncc.edu
HUDSON, Lea Ann .... 404-471-6402 113 G lhudson@agnesscott.edu
HUDSON, Lyla .... 843-792-8721 410 F hudsonly@musc.edu
HUDSON, Malinda, S .... 270-831-9626 181 D malinda.hudson@kctcs.edu
HUDSON, Mark, A .... 217-581-3923 136 E mahudson@eiu.edu
HUDSON, Matthew .... 417-447-8102 257 G hudsonm@otc.edu
HUDSON, Mattie .... 256-352-8170.... 4 A mattie.hudson@wallacestate.edu
HUDSON, Maureen .... 781-280-3506 214 G hudsonm@middlesex.mass.edu
HUDSON, Michael, J .... 630-637-5661 144 H mjhudson@noctrl.edu
HUDSON, Patrick .... 816-414-3700 256 A phudson@mbts.edu
HUDSON, Richard .... 502-585-9911 184 D rhudson@spalding.edu
HUDSON, Rob .... 719-502-3193.. 81 F rob.hudson@ppcc.edu
HUDSON, Rob .... 563-425-5270 170 A hudsonr68@uiu.edu
HUDSON, Robert .... 314-889-1488 253 C rhudson@fontbonne.edu
HUDSON, Robert .... 864-644-5001 412 E rhudson@swu.edu
HUDSON, Sean .... 716-827-2567 323 D hudsons@trocaire.edu
HUDSON, Sean .... 773-907-4428 134 C shudson52@ccc.edu
HUDSON, Sid .... 405-224-3140 371 D shudson@usao.edu
HUDSON, Stephanie ..... 601-857-3280 246 B stephanie.hudson@hindscc.edu
HUDSON, Stephanie ..... 864-379-8718 409 H hudson@erskine.edu
HUDSON, Thomas .... 601-979-2323 246 E thomas.k.hudson@jsums.edu
HUDSON, Tijuana, R .... 803-535-5197 407 G thudson@claflin.edu
HUDSON, Tim .... 931-221-7779 418 D hudsont@apsu.edu
HUDSON, Violina .... 684-699-9155 505 A v.hudson@amsamoa.edu
HUDSON, JR., William . 850-599-3183 108 I william.hudsonjr@famu.edu
HUDSON HOSEK, Hilary .... 312-567-3012 139 B hhudsonhosek@iit.edu
HUDSON-WARD, Alexia 440-775-5024 358 C ahudsonw@oberlin.edu
HUDSPETH, Donald ...... 585-475-7077 313 A don.hudspeth@croatia.rit.edu
HUDSPETH, Josie .... 541-885-1392 375 C josie.hudspeth@oit.edu
HUDSPETH, Philip .... 541-463-5898 373 F hudspethp@lanecc.edu
HUDSPETH, Phillip .... 503-399-2532 372 C phillip.hudspeth@chemeketa.edu
HUDSPETH, William ...... 770-426-2833 121 C william.hudspeth2@life.edu
HUEBER, Charlie .... 830-792-7278 443 G deanofstudents@schreiner.edu
HUEBLER, Deborah .... 808-956-2980 128 F dhuebler@hawaii.edu
HUEBNER, Casey .... 425-576-5807 482 A casey.huebner@lwtech.edu
HUEBNER, Janet .... 319-352-8227 170 C janet.huebner@wartburg.edu
HUEBNER, MJ .... 432-552-2645 457 A huebner_m@utpb.edu
HUEBNER, JR., Thomas .... 601-484-8618 247 A thuebner@meridiancc.edu
HUEBOTTER, Chris .... 573-288-6542 252 E chuebotter@culver.edu
HUEG, Kurt .... 650-949-7394.. 43 D huegkurt@foothill.edu
HUELSBECK, Tom, A ..... 253-535-7200 482 H tom.huelsbeck@plu.edu
HUELSKAMP, Benjamin 610-527-0200 397 I benjamin.huelskamp@rosemont.edu
HUELSMAN, Shelly .... 620-227-9285 172 J shuelsman@dc3.edu
HUENEMANN, Kurt .... 419-448-2351 353 H keh@heidelberg.edu
HUERTA, David .... 559-278-8400.. 31 D dhuerta@csufresno.edu
HUERTA, Flor .... 714-484-7335.. 53 K fhuerta@cypresscollege.edu
HUERTA, Homer, J .... 512-428-1385 442M homerh@stedwards.edu
HUERTA, Patricia .... 312-362-8601 135 I phuerta@depaul.edu
HUERTA, Paul .... 312-935-4559 147 D phuerta@robertmorris.edu
HUERTA, Yvette, V .... 915-831-2654 436 E yhuerta@epcc.edu
HUERTAS, Carmelo, V .. 973-353-5581 282 B carmelo.huertas@rutgers.edu
HUERTAS, Felix, R .... 787-743-7979 511 I fhuertas@suagm.edu
HUERTAS, Linda .... 773-481-8453 134 G lhuertas@ccc.edu
HUERTAS SOLÁ, Mildred .... 787-257-7373 511 G ue_mhuertas@suagm.edu
HUESER, Kyle .... 712-274-6400 170 E kyle.hueser@witcc.edu
HUESTON, William, J ... 414-955-8220 494 C whueston@mcw.edu
HUET, Yvette .... 704-687-8696 342 E ymhuet@uncc.edu
HUEWITT, Kenneth .... 713-313-1301 449 C kenneth.huewitt@tsu.edu
HUEY, Keith .... 248-218-2124 229 J khuey@rc.edu
HUFF, Eugene, C .... 925-229-6851.. 40 G ehuff@4cd.edu
HUFF, Kim .... 803-535-1204 411 G huffk@octech.edu
HUFF, Mary .... 502-272-8359 179 B mhuff@bellarmine.edu
HUFF, Michael .... 216-987-4294 351 G michael.huff@tri-c.edu
HUFF, Peter .... 630-829-6664 132 E phuff@ben.edu
HUFF, Rick .... 772-546-5534 101 B rickhuff@hsbc.edu
HUFF, Tim, T .... 405-744-5459 368 B tim.huff@okstate.edu
HUFFAKER, Joshua .... 470-322-1200 424 A jhuffaker@south.edu
HUFFARD, Lorri .... 276-223-4794 476 E lhuffard@wcc.vccs.edu
HUFFMAN, Donald .... 440-366-7397 355 J
HUFFMAN, Jessica .... 419-559-2326 361 I jhuffman02@terra.edu
HUFFMAN, Keith .... 740-362-3380 356 D khuffman@mtso.edu
HUFFMAN, Kenny .... 903-877-5043 456 D kenny.huffman@uthct.edu
HUFFMAN, Lisa .... 940-898-2204 451 F lhuffman1@twu.edu
HUFFMAN, Lori .... 574-936-8898 153 A lori.huffman@ancilla.edu
HUFFMAN, Mari .... 815-965-7314 147 F mhuffman@rockfordcareercollege.edu
HUFFMAN, Mari, L .... 419-866-0261 361 H mlhuffman@stautzenberger.com
HUFFMAN, Monica, R .. 660-543-4106 260 K mhuffman@ucmo.edu
HUFFMAN, Rebecca ...... 276-328-0139 473 B reg5a@virginia.edu
HUFFMAN, Robin .... 260-399-7700 161 D rhuffman@sf.edu
HUFFMAN, Tammy, S .. 740-588-1212 365 E thuffman@zanestate.edu
HUFFMAN, Virginia, A .. 212-327-8300 313 B huffman@rockefeller.edu
HUFFMAN, Xander .... 510-549-4749.. 66 B xhuffman@sksm.edu
HUFFORD, Adela .... 574-535-7706 155 A ahufford@goshen.edu
HUFFSTUTLER, Steven .. 618-650-5234 149 F shuffst@siue.edu
HUFFT, Anita .... 940-898-2401 451 F ahufft@twu.edu
HUFNAGEL, Michele ..... 724-503-1001 402 E mhufnagel@washjeff.edu
HUFSTETLER, Catrice .... 770-975-4031 116 C chufsteller@chattahoocheetech.edu
HUFTALIN, Deneece ...... 801-957-4226 461 D deneece.huftalin@slcc.edu
HUFTON, Maren .... 805-756-6770.. 30 C mhufton@calpoly.edu
HUG-ENGLISH, Cheryl .. 775-784-6122 271 F cherylh@med.unr.edu
HUGANIR, Gail .... 717-815-1425 404 A ghuganir@ycp.edu
HUGE, Samantha .... 757-221-3332 466 C skhuge@wm.edu
HUGGETT, Monica .... 212-799-5000 303 H
HUGGINS, Brian .... 314-340-3335 253 I hugginsb@hssu.edu
HUGGINS, Derrick, E .... 803-777-3150 413 C dhuggins@mailbox.sc.edu
HUGGINS, Elise .... 503-491-7589 374 C elise.huggins@mhcc.edu
HUGGINS, Jennifer .... 815-802-8702 140 D jhuggins@kcc.edu
HUGGINS, Jonathan ..... 706-236-2217 115 B jhuggins@berry.edu
HUGGINS, Lance .... 816-654-7702 254 C lhuggins@kcumb.edu
HUGGINS, Regina, M ... 919-866-5408 338 G rmhuggins@waketech.edu
HUGGINS, Tim .... 864-977-7505 411 E tim.huggins@ngu.edu
HUGHES, Adam .... 765-658-4293 154 F adamhughes@depauw.edu
HUGHES, Ally .... 912-525-5000 123 G ahughes@scad.edu
HUGHES, Andrew .... 775-673-7240 271 D ahughes@tmcc.edu
HUGHES, Bernice .... 229-391-5130 113 F bhughes@abac.edu
HUGHES, Blanche, M ... 970-491-1101.. 78M blanche.hughes@colostate.edu
HUGHES, Bonnie .... 506-865-8588 481 G hughes_b@heritage.edu
HUGHES, JR., Byron, A 540-231-3787 477 A tbrown@vt.edu
HUGHES, Carol .... 312-362-8592 135 I chughe23@depaul.edu
HUGHES, Cathie .... 423-775-6596 423 F chughes.omegagradschool@gmail.com
HUGHES, Chris .... 870-236-6901.. 19 A chughes@crc.edu
HUGHES, Christine .... 617-824-8908 208 H christine_hughes@emerson.edu
HUGHES, Christy .... 812-866-7012 155 C hughes@hanover.edu
HUGHES, Cory .... 410-290-7100 199 E
HUGHES, David .... 435-586-7735 460 F hughes@suu.edu
HUGHES, Deborah .... 786-279-2643 290 C dhughes@asa.edu

HUMPHRIES, Brian, L ... 651-286-7620 244 D
blhumphries@unwsp.edu
HUMPHRIES,
Gregory, G .... 704-406-4647 329 A
ghumphries@gardner-webb.edu
HUMPHRIES, Karl .... 903-875-7600 440 G
karl.humphries@navarrocollege.edu
HUMPHRIES, OP,
Mary Edith .... 615-297-7545 418 C
srmedith@aquinascollege.edu
HUMPHRIES, Tara .... 919-735-5151 338 H
tarah@waynecc.edu
HUMPHRIES, Trish .... 304-558-2104 489 O
patricia.humphries@wvhepc.edu
HUNDLEY, Christina ..... 602-787-6622.. 13 E
christina.hundley@paradisevalley.edu
HUNDLEY, Stephen, P .. 317-274-4111 156 F
shundley@iupui.edu
HUNEYCUTT, Richy .... 252-527-6223 335 G
rshuneycutt78@lenoircc.edu
HUNG, Alex .... 626-571-5110.. 48 B
alexhung@les.edu
HUNGER, Suzanne .... 406-265-3568 264 F
suzanne.hunger@msun.edu
HUNGERFORD,
H. Daniel .... 716-375-2017 313 F
dhungerf@sbu.edu
HUNHOFF, Christian ..... 605-668-5126 415 H
christian.hunhoff@mtmc.edu
HUNKERSTORM,
Louisa .... 307-855-2235 501 V
lhunker@cwc.edu
HUNN, Jonathan .... 636-949-4528 254 F
jhunn@lindenwood.edu
HUNN, Martha, S .... 843-349-2962 408 C
mhunn@coastal.edu
HUNN, II, Marvin, T .... 214-887-5281 436 B
mhunn@dts.edu
HUNNEWELL, Lila .... 617-358-4915 207 D
lilawell@bu.edu
HUNNICUTT, Marianne . 630-942-4306 135 A
hunnicutt@cod.edu
HUNSADER, Tricia .... 423-636-7300 427 B
thunsader@tusculum.edu
HUNSAKER, Deanna ..... 660-626-2356 250 A
dhunsaker@atsu.edu
HUNSAKER, Wayne .... 801-622-1573 459 N
wayne.hunsaker@stevenhenager.edu
HUNSBERGER, Jill .... 734-481-2324 223 H
jhunsberg1@emich.edu
HUNSICKER, Donald ..... 617-585-0200 206 F
don.hunsicker@the-bac.edu
HUNSICKER-WALBURN,
Melissa .... 785-628-5865 173 B
mjhunsickerwalburn@fhsu.edu
HUNSINGER, Elizabeth . 540-654-1000 472 I
ehunsing@umw.edu
HUNSINGER PATTEN,
Rachael .... 610-359-5131 382 C
rpatten@dccc.edu
HUNSTAD, Carla, J .... 719-333-0056 504 C
carla.hunstad@usafa.edu
HUNSUCKER, Scott, E .. 704-233-8221 344 G
scotth@wingate.edu
HUNT, Ana .... 501-812-2206.. 23 B
ahunt@uaptc.edu
HUNT, Bill (William) ..... 918-495-7750 368 I
whunt@oru.edu
HUNT, Blanchie .... 870-762-1020.. 17 D
bhunt@smail.anc.edu
HUNT, Chris .... 610-330-5320 387 E
huntgc@lafayette.edu
HUNT, Corey .... 304-367-4729 490 B
corey.hunt@fairmontstate.edu
HUNT, Daphne .... 254-968-1852 446 E
djhunt@tarleton.edu
HUNT, Darnell .... 310-267-4304.. 69 A
dhunt@soc.ucla.edu
HUNT, Dave .... 816-501-4890 258 H
dave.hunt@rockhurst.edu
HUNT, Denise .... 256-782-5151.... 5 J
dhunt@jsu.edu
HUNT, Denise .... 760-921-5510.. 55 H
dhunt@paloverde.edu
HUNT, Edward, L .... 212-870-1227 310 A
ehunt@nyts.edu
HUNT, Emily .... 806-651-5330 448 C
ehunt@wtamu.edu
HUNT, Gerri .... 336-342-4261 337 E
huntg0780@rockinghamcc.edu
HUNT, Gerry .... 405-208-5582 367 I
ghunt@okcu.edu
HUNT, Hallie .... 657-278-4168.. 31 E
hhunt@fullerton.edu
HUNT, Jamer .... 212-229-8950 308 C
huntj@newschool.edu
HUNT, James .... 850-644-4041 109 C
jhunt@fsu.edu
HUNT, James .... 325-793-3806 440 B
hunt.james@mcm.edu
HUNT, Jamie .... 336-750-3148 344 B
huntj@wssu.edu
HUNT, Jamie .... 843-661-1318 409 K
jhunt@fmarion.edu
HUNT, Janet .... 501-337-5000.. 18 J
jhunt@coto.edu
HUNT, Janette .... 727-341-3229 106 E
hunt.janette@spcollege.edu
HUNT, Jeff .... 303-963-3254.. 77 G
jhunt@ccu.edu
HUNT, Jeff .... 864-592-4727 412 F
huntj@sccsc.edu
HUNT, Jeffrey .... 559-486-1166.. 24 G
HUNT, Jeffrey .... 808-235-7442 129 F
jwhunt@hawaii.edu
HUNT, Jennifer .... 765-641-4063 153 B
jehunt@anderson.edu
HUNT, Judith, L .... 973-655-4301 279 C
huntjl@mail.montclair.edu
HUNT, Karen .... 304-829-7591 487 G
khunt@bethanywv.edu
HUNT, Lisa .... 910-521-6357 343 B
lisa.hunt@uncp.edu
HUNT, Lori .... 509-533-7378 480 A
lori.hunt@scc.spokane.edu
HUNT, Louis, D .... 919-515-1428 342 B
ldhunt@ncsu.edu
HUNT, Mark .... 334-386-7140.... 5 D
mhunt@faulkner.edu
HUNT, Michelle .... 760-750-8362.. 33 B
mihunt@csusm.edu
HUNT, Patrick, G .... 240-895-4307 201 E
pghunt@smcm.edu
HUNT, Paul, M .... 517-432-4499 227 D
pmhunt@msu.edu
HUNT, Philip .... 605-394-2497 417 B
philip.hunt@sdsmt.edu
HUNT, Rusty .... 252-527-6223 335 G
rthunt78@lenoircc.edu
HUNT, Shari .... 315-866-0300 301 G
huntsl@herkimer.edu
HUNT, Skyler .... 304-357-4741 488 G
skylerhunt@ucwv.edu
HUNT, Steve .... 828-327-7000 333 B
shunt@cvcc.edu
HUNT, T. Jill .... 270-809-3763 183 G
thunt@murraystate.edu
HUNT, Terry, L .... 520-621-3015.. 16 G
tlhunt@email.arizona.edu
HUNT, Tolif, R .... 319-273-3217 163 B
tolif.hunt@uni.edu
HUNT, Valerie .... 206-934-4085 484 A
valerie.hunt@seattlecolleges.edu
HUNT, Wendy .... 402-465-2135 268 H
whunt@nebrwesleyan.edu
HUNT-BULL, Nicholas ... 518-327-6247 311 G
nhuntbull@paulsmiths.edu
HUNTER, Barbara .... 904-361-6352 100 B
barbara.hunter@fscj.edu
HUNTER, Ben .... 208-885-6534 131 G
bhunter@uidaho.edu
HUNTER, Benjamin .... 812-855-4296 156 A
bdhunter@iu.edu
HUNTER, Bill .... 850-973-9448 103 K
hunterb@nfcc.edu
HUNTER, Carolyn .... 513-585-2068 350 H
carolyn.hunter@thechristcollege.edu
HUNTER, Chip .... 509-335-3596 486 A
chip.hunter@wsu.edu
HUNTER, Derek .... 919-735-5151 338 H
mdhunter@waynecc.edu
HUNTER, Elizabeth .... 910-775-6400 343 B
elizabeth.hunter@uncp.edu
HUNTER, Gayle .... 386-752-1822.. 99 A
gayle.hunter@fgc.edu
HUNTER, Gerald, E .... 757-823-8011 469 F
gehunter@nsu.edu
HUNTER, Grant .... 402-984-8825 267 D
ghunter@hastings.edu
HUNTER, James .... 270-707-3713 181 E
james.hunter@kctcs.edu
HUNTER, Jane .... 520-621-4248.. 16 G
jhunter@arizona.edu
HUNTER, Janet .... 563-387-2229 167 E
hunterja@luther.edu
HUNTER, Jasmine .... 225-771-2552 191 A
jhunter@sulc.edu
HUNTER, Jeff, C .... 304-462-6201 490 C
jeff.hunter@glenville.edu
HUNTER, Kim .... 513-244-4248 357 A
kim.hunter@msj.edu
HUNTER, Kymm .... 803-705-4519 407 A
kymm.hunter@benedict.edu
HUNTER, Lai-Monte ...... 870-307-7313.. 20 A
laimonte.hunter@lyon.edu
HUNTER, Larry, T .... 614-236-6641 349 D
lhunter2@capital.edu
HUNTER, LeAnn .... 509-452-5100 483 A
lhunter@pnwu.edu
HUNTER, Lorna .... 410-778-7114 204 D
lhunter2@washcoll.edu
HUNTER, Lynn .... 781-239-3111 214 E
lhunter@massbay.edu
HUNTER, Maggie .... 510-430-3220.. 52 D
mhunter@mills.edu
HUNTER, Marc .... 405-382-9950 369 J
m.hunter@sscok.edu
HUNTER, Noah .... 212-659-3604 304 B
nhunter@tkc.edu
HUNTER, Noah .... 212-659-3615 304 B
nhunter@tkc.edu
HUNTER, Noelle .... 304-865-6085 488 E
noelle.hunter@ovu.edu
HUNTER, Pam .... 760-773-2508.. 39 A
phunter@collegeofthedesert.edu
HUNTER, Patti .... 805-565-7262.. 74 K
phunter@westmont.edu
HUNTER, Rebecca .... 212-229-5620 308 C
hunterr@newschool.edu
HUNTER, Richie, C .... 518-276-2800 312 I
hunter3@rpi.edu
HUNTER, Rosey .... 509-313-3564 481 D
hunterr2@gonzaga.edu
HUNTER, Sean .... 614-947-6103 353 C
sean.hunter@franklin.edu
HUNTER, Susan, S .... 804-523-5375 474 H
shunter@reynolds.edu
HUNTER, Teressa .... 405-466-3274 366 F
teressa.hunter@langston.edu
HUNTER, Tiffany .... 937-328-6025 350 L
huntert@clarkstate.edu
HUNTER, Timothy .... 704-216-3694 337 F
timothy.hunter@rccc.edu
HUNTER, Tracie .... 415-338-2611.. 34 A
tnhunter@sfsu.edu
HUNTER, Valerie .... 201-684-7502 280 H
vhunter@ramapo.edu
HUNTER, W. Bingham .. 602-429-4431.. 15 C
bhunter@ps.edu
HUNTER, William .... 670-237-6719 506 A
william.hunter@marianas.edu
HUNTER-MCKINNEY,
Shaunna, E .... 434-223-6193 468 A
shunter@hsc.edu
HUNTER-RAINEY,
Sharon .... 919-278-2673 340 E
sharon.hunter-rainey@shawu.edu
HUNTINGTON, Lucas .... 225-768-1732 186 F
lucas.huntington@franu.edu
HUNTINGTON, Robert ... 419-448-2202 353 H
president@heidelberg.edu
HUNTLEY, Deborah, R .. 989-964-4296 230 B
huntley@svsu.edu
HUNTLEY, Julie .... 918-495-7040 368 I
jhuntley@oru.edu
HUNTLEY, Kristy .... 203-479-4559.. 89 A
khuntley@newhaven.edu
HUNTLEY, Richard .... 972-721-4142 452 D
rhuntley@udallas.edu
HUNTLEY, Steve, E .... 904-264-2172 105 L
steve.huntley@iws.edu
HUNTON, Ladonna, L .... 270-745-6867 185 E
ladonna.hunton@wku.edu
HUNTOON,
Jacqueline, E .... 906-487-2440 227 E
jeh@mtu.edu
HUNTSINGER, Trish ...... 828-395-1297 335 D
thuntsing@isothermal.edu
HUNZER, Kathleen .... 715-425-3843 497 E
kathleen.hunzer@uwrf.edu
HUNZIGER, Lucas .... 913-367-6204 174 A
lhunziger@highlandcc.edu
HUO,
Xiaoming (Sharon) ..... 931-372-3463 426 E
xhuo@tntech.edu
HUOPPI, Jennifer .... 860-465-4357.. 84 J
huoppij@easternct.edu
HUPFER, Mary, A .... 812-464-1627 161 E
mhupfer@usi.edu
HUPKE, Jennifer .... 219-989-2953 159 G
jhupke@pnw.edu
HUPP, Stephen .... 304-424-8273 491 D
stephen.hupp@wvup.edu
HUPPE, Alicia, L .... 972-377-1749 433 M
ahuppe@collin.edu
HUPPE, Maureen .... 913-360-7384 171 D
mhuppe@benedictine.edu
HUPPERT, Susan .... 515-271-1384 164 I
susan.huppert@dmu.edu
HUPPON, Dana .... 561-433-2330 107 J
HURBANIS, Julie, T ...... 651-696-6475 236 H
jhurbani@macalester.edu
HURD, Anne, J .... 336-272-7102 329 D
anne.hurd@greensboro.edu
HURD, Brian .... 216-397-1974 354 I
bhurd@jcu.edu
HURD, James, R .... 850-474-2214 110 E
jhurd@uwf.edu
HURD, Roy .... 707-546-4000.. 42 B
rhurd@empcol.edu
HURD, Sherie .... 707-546-4000.. 42 B
shurd@empcol.edu
HURD-CRANK, Cathy .... 606-886-3863 180 J
cathy.hurdcrank@kctcs.edu
HURDLE-WINSLOW,
Lynn .... 252-335-0821 333 G
lynnhw@albermarle.edu
HURDT, Emily .... 704-669-4321 333 E
hurdte@clevelandcc.edu
HURLBURT, Rob .... 716-375-2622 313 F
rhurl@sbu.edu
HURLBUT, Bradford, D . 201-692-2170 277 K
hurlbut@fdu.edu
HURLBUT, Jeffrey .... 949-451-5546.. 64 F
jhurlbut@ivc.edu
HURLBUT, Trent .... 509-453-0374 483 C
trent.hurlburt@perrytech.edu
HURLEY, Charles, T ...... 574-631-7495 161 C
hurley.32@nd.edu
HURLEY, Deanne .... 440-646-8320 363 G
dhurley@ursuline.edu
HURLEY, James .... 423-636-7301 427 B
jhurley@tusculum.edu
HURLEY, Jeff .... 513-244-4465 357 A
jeff.hurley@msj.edu
HURLEY, John, J .... 716-888-2100 292 D
hurleyj@canisius.edu
HURLEY, Kristin, M ...... 301-447-5372 200 E
k.hurley@msmary.edu
HURLEY, Leah, A .... 214-648-7986 457 B
leah.hurley@utsouthwestern.edu
HURLEY, Rachel .... 937-529-2201 362 A
rehurley@united.edu
HURLEY, Ronald .... 201-200-3127 279 E
rhurley@njcu.edu
HURLEY, Sam .... 903-928-3288 452 B
shurley@tvcc.edu
HURLEY, Wanda .... 601-635-2111 245 I
whurley@eccc.edu
HURN, Jeffrey .... 785-442-6077 174 A
jhurn@highlandcc.edu
HURN, Patricia, D .... 734-764-7185 231 E
phurn@umich.edu
HURNS, Kimberly .... 734-973-3488 232 B
khurns@wccnet.edu
HURRELL, Rockie .... 719-502-2007.. 81 F
rockie.hurrell@ppcc.edu
HURSE, Jeremy .... 828-669-8012 331 J
jeremy.hurse@montreat.edu
HURSSEY, Elizabeth ...... 662-254-3531 248 B
ejhurssey@mvsu.edu
HURSSEY, Terrence .... 662-254-3584 248 B
terrence.hurssey@mvsu.edu
HURST, Andrew .... 719-590-6797.. 79 C
ahurst@coloradotech.edu
HURST, Angela .... 334-420-4483.... 3 H
alhurst@trenholmstate.edu
HURST, Ashley .... 940-397-4461 440 F
ashley.hurst@msutexas.edu
HURST, Jamie .... 303-615-2044.. 80 N
jhurst7@msudenver.edu
HURST, Jason .... 704-669-6000 333 E
HURST, Jeffrey, J .... 801-626-7256 461 B
jhurst@weber.edu
HURST, Kevin .... 972-860-4838 434 L
khurst@dcccd.edu
HURST, Mark .... 423-585-6876 426 C
mark.hurst@ws.edu
HURST, Susan .... 870-245-5567.. 20 E
hursts@obu.edu
HURT, Aaron .... 620-235-4680 176 F
ahurt@pittstate.edu
HURT, Aaron .... 317-940-9697 153 F
ahurt@butler.edu

I

IACULLO, Gerald .... 973-642-3888 291 D gji@berkeleycollege.edu
IADEVAIA, Norma .... 310-506-4149.. 56 C norma.iadevaia@pepperdine.edu
IAMSIRITHAWORN, Chalaiporn .... 702-463-2122 272 G chalai@wongu.org
IAMUNNO, Janine .... 910-962-2445 343 C iamunnoj@uncw.edu
IANNACE, John-Paul .... 914-606-8501 325 C john-paul.iannace@sunywcc.edu
IANNAZZI, Michael, L .. 203-371-7899.. 88 B iannazzim@sacredheart.edu
IANNELLA, Lori .... 610-902-8255 380 C lni723@cabrini.edu
IANNELLI, Clare .... 281-998-6150 443 C clare.iannelli@sjcd.edu
IANNELLI, Clare .... 281-998-1357 443 B clare.iannelli@sjcd.edu
IANNELLI, Clare .... 281-998-6150 443 D clare.iannelli@sjcd.edu
IANNELLI, Clare .... 281-998-6150 443 E clare.iannelli@sjcd.edu
IANNELLO, Lisa .... 607-431-4061 301 D iannellol@hartwick.edu
IANNESSA, Katherine .... 512-499-4204 454 I kiannessa@utsystem.edu
IANNINI, Joseph .... 212-217-3359 299 H joseph_iannini@fitnyc.edu
IANNO, Daniel .... 315-792-5356 307 D dianno@mvcc.edu
IANNONE, Frank .... 321-674-8113.. 99 B fiannone@fit.edu
IANNUZZI, Maria Lise .. 909-447-2552.. 37 F miannuzzi@cst.edu
IAPALUCCI, Philip .... 574-520-4218 157 A piapaluc@iusb.edu
IARATE-CERVANTES, Rebeca .... 888-491-8686.. 74 F rebecacervantes@westcliff.edu
IATRIDIS, Ioanna .... 530-661-5795.. 76 B iiatridi@yccd.edu
IATRIDIS, Ioanna .... 530-339-3610.. 63 H iiatridis@shastacollege.edu
IAVARONE, William .... 309-794-7357 132 C williamiavarone@augustana.edu
IBARRA, Clotilde .... 212-343-1234 306 J cibarra@mcny.edu
IBARRA, Ruben .... 909-448-4959.. 70 D ssmith3@laverne.edu
IBARRONDO, Daniel ..... 617-984-1619 218 B dibarrondo@quincycollege.edu
IBE, Basil .... 310-233-4160.. 49 A ibebo@lahc.edu
IBEANUSI, Victor .... 850-599-3550 108 I victor.ibeanusi@famu.edu
IBRAHIM, Atallah .... 313-845-9615 224 G
IBRAHIM, Olla .... 425-640-1957 480 F olla.ibrahim@edcc.edu
IBSEN, Brian .... 907-786-1263.... 9 H bpibsen@alaska.edu
ICE, James, W .... 412-578-6557 380 E jwice@carlow.edu
ICE, Jerry .... 617-873-0224 207 F jerry.ice@cambridgecollege.edu
ICE, Richard .... 320-363-5503 243 A rice@csbsju.edu
ICE, Richard .... 320-363-5503 235 C rice@csbsju.edu
ICHIGAYA, Frank .... 925-473-7391.. 40 J fichigaya@losmedanos.edu
ICHON, Eric .... 310-287-4305.. 49 G ichone@wlac.edu
ICHSAN, Tony .... 971-722-4338 375 J tony.ichsan@pcc.edu
ICKES, Jessica .... 321-674-7569.. 99 B jickes@fit.edu
IDE, Susan .... 248-218-2059 229 J side@rc.edu
IDELL, Steven .... 903-877-7556 456 D steven.idell@uthct.edu
IDETA, Lori .... 808-956-3290 128 F ideta@hawaii.edu
IDNURM, Tom .... 302-736-2461.. 90 G tom.idnurm@wesley.edu
IERIEN, Kim .... 503-281-4181 372 H
IFRAH, Joseph .... 443-548-6037 201 A jifrah@nirc.edu
IGHODARO, Osaro .... 602-243-8036.. 14 A osaro.ighodaro@southmountaincc.edu
IGO, Leah .... 207-699-5010 194 D ligo@meca.edu
IGO, Mary .... 304-883-2424 489 C migo@newriver.edu
IGONOR, Andy .... 614-947-6226 353 C andy.igonor@franklin.edu
IGWEBUIKE, John .... 601-877-6142 244 H jigwe@alcorn.edu
IGWIKE, Richard .... 504-816-4830 186 D rigwike@dillard.edu
IGYARTO, Mia .... 630-942-3410 135 A igyartom@cod.edu
IHEKWEAZU, Stanley, N .... 803-536-8392 412 C sihekwea@scsu.edu
IHMELS, Michelle .... 208-426-2701 129 I michelleihmels@boisestate.edu
IHRER, Kenneth .... 212-650-7400 293 D kihrer@ccny.cuny.edu
IHRKE, Barbara .... 765-677-1578 157 D barbara.ihrke@indwes.edu
IJIRI, Lisa .... 617-349-8706 210 H lijiri@lesley.edu
IKACH, Yugo .... 724-938-4187 394 B ikach@calu.edu
IKEGAMI, Robin .... 916-558-2337.. 50 I ikegamr@scc.losrios.edu
IKEM, Fidelis, M .... 937-376-6441 350 D fikem@centralstate.edu
IKHARO, Sadiq .... 510-466-7336.. 56 H sikharo@peralta.edu
ILARDI, Kristin .... 949-794-9090.. 65 I
ILES, Linda .... 530-221-4275.. 63 G finaid@shasta.edu
ILIAKIS-DOHERTY, Sophia .... 360-417-6219 483 B sdoherty@pencol.edu
ILICETO, Thomas .... 212-229-5101 308 C ilicetot@newschool.edu
ILIEVA, Vessela, K .... 801-863-5183 461 A vessela.ilieva@uvu.edu
ILINCA, Ingrid .... 573-592-5323 262 E ingrid.ilinca@westminster-mo.edu
ILLICH, Paul .... 402-323-3415 269 C pillich@southeast.edu
ILLIES, Diane .... 320-308-5572 241 A diane.illies@sctcc.edu
ILLINGWORTH, Theresa, M .... 414-425-8300 495 H tillingworth@shsst.edu
IM, Dou Ho .... 562-926-1023.. 57 G
IM, Manyul .... 203-576-4234.. 88 D manyulim@bridgeport.edu
IM, Sam .... 215-887-5511 402 H sim@wts.edu
IMAI, Geri .... 808-235-7430 129 F gerii@hawaii.edu
IMALA, Mabel .... 703-416-1441 466 F mimala@divinemercy.edu
IMASUEN, Edwin .... 252-536-7239 335 B
IMBER, Margaret, A ...... 207-786-6280 193 B mimber@bates.edu
IMBRAGULIO, Lisa .... 205-726-4172.... 6 E lcimbrag@samford.edu
IMBRESCIA, Janelle ...... 724-653-2192 383 A janelle@dec.edu
IMBRESCIA, Jeffrey, D .. 724-653-2200 383 A jimbrescia@dec.edu
IMBRESCIA, Julian .... 724-653-2213 383 A julian@dec.edu
IMBRIALE, William .... 718-409-7348 321 C wimbriale@sunymaritime.edu
IMBRIGLIO, Sarah .... 908-526-1200 281 A sarah.imbriglio@raritanval.edu
IMEL, Philip .... 304-327-4012 489 P pimel@bluefieldstate.edu
IMEL, Travis .... 202-651-5064.. 91 E travis.imel@gallaudet.edu
IMES, Amber .... 480-994-9244.. 16 B amberi@swiha.edu
IMES, Melissa, J .... 717-262-2000 403 F melissa.imes@wilson.edu
IMHOFF, Dan .... 608-822-2401 500 G dimhoff@swtc.edu
IMHOFF, Donna .... 216-987-5125 351 G donna.imhoff@tri-c.edu
IMHOFF, Maren, E .... 212-327-8682 313 B imhoff@rockefeller.edu
IMLER, Mary Elizabeth .. 815-740-2274 151 J mimler@stfrancis.edu
IMMLER, Eric .... 410-386-4639 200 B eimmler@mcdaniel.edu
IMPERATO, Pascal .... 718-270-1056 317 E pascal.imperato@downstate.edu
IMPERIALE, Michael, J . 734-763-3472 231 E imperial@umich.edu
IMWALLE, Todd, W ...... 937-229-3299 362 G timwalle1@udayton.edu
INABINET, Chad, E .... 231-843-5965 232 J ceinabinet@westshore.edu
INAFUKU, Derek .... 808-845-9123 129 B dinafuku@hawaii.edu
INBASEKARAM, Pamela 212-228-1888 312 H
INBODY, Brian, L .... 620-431-2820 175 H binbody@neosho.edu
INCANDELA, Joe .... 805-893-8270.. 70 A incandela@research.ucsb.edu
INCANDELA, Joseph ..... 630-829-6247 132 E jincandela@ben.edu
INCANDELA, Marybeth .. 631-420-2107 321 B marybeth.incandela@farmingdale.edu
INCERA, Vivian .... 718-982-2430 293 E vivian.incera@csi.cuny.edu
INCH, Edward .... 510-885-3711.. 31 C edward.inch@csueastbay.edu
INCH, Megan .... 336-841-9166 329 G minch@highpoint.edu
INCITTI, Merri, S .... 304-367-4832 490 B merri.incitti@fairmontstate.edu
INCORVAIN, James .... 310-204-1666.. 58 D
INDA, Darlene .... 805-678-5813.. 73 A dinda@vcccd.edu
INES, Caryn, L .... 603-535-2981 275 B clines1@plymouth.edu
INFANTI, Steven, M ...... 717-901-5146 385 K sinfanti@harrisburgu.edu
INFUSINO, Melissa .... 562-938-3217.. 48 D minfusino@lbcc.edu
INGALLS, Keith .... 413-748-3946 218 G kingalls@springfield.edu
INGARGIOLA, Janet, M 217-443-8760 135 H jingarg@dacc.edu
INGBER, Marc .... 303-556-2870.. 83 C marc.ingber@ucdenver.edu
INGE, Brittany .... 502-213-5155 181 F brittany.inge@kctcs.edu
INGERMAN, Bret .... 850-201-6082 111 C ingermab@tcc.fl.edu
INGERSOLL, Christopher .... 419-530-5453 363 E christopher.ingersoll@utoledo.edu
INGERSOLL, Julia .... 610-526-6132 385 G jingersoll@harcum.edu
INGERSOLL, Melinda .... 215-951-1374 387 C ingersoll@lasalle.edu
INGERSOLL, Ryan .... 503-554-2411 373 C ringersoll@georgefox.edu
INGHAM, Joanne .... 212-431-2876 309 G joanne.ingham@nyls.edu
INGIOSI, Regina .... 610-527-0200 397 I
INGLAND, Susan .... 620-417-1400 176 K susan.ingland@sccc.edu
INGLE, Jeffery, S .... 865-981-8199 421 F jeff.ingle@maryvillecollege.edu
INGLE, Karen .... 616-331-3688 224 E inglek@gvsu.edu
INGLE, III, Kenneth, G . 704-216-3577 337 F ken.ingle@rccc.edu
INGLE, Kent .... 863-667-5002 107 K kingle@seu.edu
INGLEHART, Hope .... 770-593-2257 120 A higlehart@gupton-jones.edu
INGLES, Roger .... 614-236-6528 349 D ringles@capital.edu
INGLES, Susan, L .... 414-410-4236 492 D slingles@stritch.edu
INGLESIAS, Kaylynn, C . 315-684-6046 321 D inglesike@morrisville.edu
INGLIS, Mark .... 216-421-7403 350 M minglis@cia.edu
INGLISH, Darla .... 940-397-4321 440 F darla.inglish@msutexas.edu
INGMIRE, Eric .... 785-442-6020 174 A eingmire@highlandcc.edu
INGMIRE, MacKenzie .... 309-467-6748 137 B mingmire@eureka.edu
INGRAHAM, Barry .... 207-768-2706 194 J bingraham@nmcc.edu
INGRAHAM, Timothy .... 978-468-7111 209 G tingraham@gcts.edu
INGRAM, Archinya .... 803-327-7402 408 B aingram@clintoncollege.edu
INGRAM, Beth .... 815-753-0493 145 C bingram@niu.edu
INGRAM, Beverly .... 318-487-7694 186 I beverly.ingram@lacollege.edu
INGRAM, Brian, C .... 731-881-7069 428 B cingram@utm.edu
INGRAM, Casey .... 318-257-4917 191 F casey@latech.edu
INGRAM, Cathy .... 413-528-7266 205 F cingram@simons-rock.edu
INGRAM, David .... 817-461-8741 430 H dingram@abu.edu
INGRAM, Donnie .... 803-327-7402 408 B dingram@clintoncollege.edu
INGRAM, Donnie, L ...... 563-333-5826 169 A ingramdonniel@sau.edu
INGRAM, Earl .... 334-670-3104.... 7 C ingram@troy.edu
INGRAM, Geoff .... 951-785-2000.. 47 C gingram@lasierra.edu
INGRAM, Iris .... 310-660-3593.. 41 L iingram@elcamino.edu
INGRAM, J. Kevin .... 785-539-3571 175 E kingram@mccks.edu
INGRAM, Jim .... 662-862-8047 246 D jingram@iccms.edu
INGRAM, Joyce .... 850-599-3211 108 I joyce.ingram@famu.edu
INGRAM, Joyce .... 850-412-5146 108 I joyce.ingram@famu.edu
INGRAM, Kaycee .... 919-735-5151 338 H klingram@waynecc.edu
INGRAM, Kendra .... 303-871-6544.. 83 D kendra.ingram@du.edu
INGRAM, Kimberly .... 360-623-8444 479 C kimberly.ingram@centralia.edu
INGRAM, Lashawanda, T .... 315-386-7128 320 E ingraml@canton.edu
INGRAM, Maleka .... 866-492-5336 244 F maleka.ingram@mail.waldenu.edu
INGRAM, Mark, T .... 205-934-0766.... 8 A mingram@uab.edu
INGRAM, Mike .... 423-746-5316 426 F mingram@tnwesleyan.edu
INGRAM, SR., Roderick, L .... 330-325-6673 357 G ringram@neomed.edu
INGRAM, Trent .... 870-248-4000.. 18 F trent.ingram@blackrivertech.edu
INGRAM, Wanda Rhea . 334-244-3476.... 4 F wingram4@aum.edu
INGRAM, William .... 615-460-6568 418 F william.ingram@belmont.edu
INGRAM, William, G .... 919-536-7200 334 B ingramb@durhamtech.edu
INGRAM PILE, Judy ..... 501-202-7433.. 18 E
INGRAM-WALLACE, Brenda, J .... 610-921-7585 378 C bingramwallace@albright.edu
INGS, Margaret Ann ..... 617-824-8299 208 H margaret_ann_ings@emerson.edu
INIGUEZ, Edmond .... 719-549-3206.. 81 K edmond.iniguez@pueblocc.edu
INIGUEZ, Elizabeth .... 323-463-2500.. 67 C lizm@toa.edu
INIGUEZ, Maria .... 509-682-6400 486 E miniguez@wvc.edu
INKSTER, Kathy .... 606-546-4151 184 H kyinkster@unionky.edu
INLOW, Laura .... 618-468-3255 141 F linlow@lc.edu
INMAN, Barbara, L .... 757-727-5264 468 B barbara.inman@hamptonu.edu
INMAN, Dean .... 870-864-7142.. 21 B dinman@southark.edu
INMAN, James, P .... 540-464-7104 476 G inmanjp@vmi.edu
INMAN, John, G .... 724-458-2176 385 C jginman@gcc.edu
INMAN, Leigh .... 619-961-4278.. 67 E glinman@tjsl.edu
INMAN, Lisa, D .... 919-536-7200 334 B inmanl@durhamtech.edu
INMAN, Stan, D .... 801-585-5028 460 E sinman@sa.utah.edu
INMAN, Steve, G .... 814-868-8258 388 A sinman@mch1.org
INNIGER, Alyssa, K ...... 507-344-7874 234 B alyssa.inniger@blc.edu
INNISS, Tasha .... 404-270-5897 125 B tinniss@spelman.edu
INOCENCIO, Leticia ...... 210-486-3117 429 F linocencio@alamo.edu
INOUYE, Carolyn .... 805-678-5803.. 73 A cinouye@vcccd.edu
INOUYE, Richard .... 435-797-3981 460 H richard.inouye@usu.edu

IVIE, Wendy 541-885-1539 375 C wendy.ivie@oit.edu
IVIS, Dan 515-965-7029 164 C drivis@dmacc.edu
IVORY, Audrey 919-516-4201 340 C laivory@st-aug.edu
IVORY, Janice 501-374-6305 21 A
IVORY, Joanne 847-925-6341 137 H jivory@harpercollege.edu
IVY, Mike 706-867-2712 126 A mike.ivy@ung.edu
IWAGOSHI, Thawi 510-592-9688 54 C thawi.iwagoshi@npu.edu
IWAMA, Kenichi 718-982-2394 293 E kenichi.iwama@csi.cuny.edu
IWAMIYA, Shigeo 617-305-2500 219 A siwamiya@suffolk.edu
IWAMURA, Jane 626-571-8811 72 C janei@uwest.edu
IWANAGA-BECKER, Kelly 847-635-1973 145 G kbecker@oakton.edu
IWANE, David 213-615-7268 36 F diwane@thechicagoschool.edu
IWANENKO, JR., Walter 814-871-7401 384 E iwanenko001@gannon.edu
IWANOWICZ, Susan 518-694-7217 289 D susan.iwanowicz@acphs.edu
IWASA, Mark 916-278-6851 32 E miwasa@csus.edu
IWATA, Chris 916-558-2552 50 I iwatac@scc.losrios.edu
IYENGAR, Sundararaj 305-348-3549 109 A undararaj.iyengar@fiu.edu
IYER, Anand 757-727-5071 468 B anand.iyer@hamptonu.edu
IYER, Aruna 860-701-5161 87 D iyer_a@mitchell.edu
IYER, Nalini 206-296-6161 484 F niyer@seattleu.edu
IYER, Sandhya, L 603-646-0101 273 E sandhya.l.iyer@dartmouth.edu
IZADIAN, Ali 657-278-2122 31 E izadian@fullerton.edu
IZAGUIRRE, Minelia 281-998-6150 443 D mini.izaguirre@sjcd.edu
IZBRAND, Joe 210-458-8754 455 E joe.izbrand@utsa.edu
IZIENICKI, Kylie 303-369-5151 81 J kylie.izienicki@plattcolorado.edu
IZQUIERDO, Julio 973-877-3259 277 I izquierdo@essex.edu
IZZI, Louis 203-576-4558 88 D louizzi@bridgeport.edu

J

JABAR, Abdul 212-346-1521 311 E ajabar@pace.edu
JABAUT, Gregory 617-573-8034 219 A gjabaut@suffolk.edu
JABBOUR, Alice 804-862-6100 470 I ajabbour@rbc.edu
JABLONSKI, Allison 434-544-8266 472 G jablonski@lynchburg.edu
JABLONSKI, Anna 661-255-1050 28 K ajablonski@calarts.edu
JABLONSKI, Jack 608-262-4046 496 B jjablonski@uwsa.edu
JABLONSKI, John 518-743-2236 320 D jablonski@sunyacc.edu
JABLONSKY, Carol 516-686-1014 309 F cjablons@nyit.edu
JABOUR, Albert 214-768-3054 444 E ajabour@smu.edu
JABRASSIAN, Vic 213-613-2200 64 H vic@sciarc.edu
JABS, Carol, A 708-209-3145 135 F carol.jabs@cuchicago.edu
JACCARINO, David 305-626-3766 99 D david.jaccarino@fmuniv.edu
JACCUZZO, Craig, M 985-448-7131 192 B craig.jaccuzzo@nicholls.edu
JACELON, Cynthia 413-545-5093 211 D dean@nursing.umass.edu
JACHIM-MOORE, Darrell, K 585-292-2185 307 H djachim-moore@monroecc.edu
JACHNA, Timothy, J 513-556-9808 362 D timothy.jachna@uc.edu
JACIEN, Julia 570-702-8929 386 G jjacein@johnson.edu
JACK, Eric 205-934-8800 8 A ejack@uab.edu
JACK, Grilly 691-320-3795 505 B gjack@comfsm.fm
JACK, Jill 319-399-8023 164 A jjack@coe.edu
JACK, Laura 315-228-7407 296 F ljack@colgate.edu
JACKANICZ, Jeffrey 510-430-2380 52 D jjackanicz@mills.edu
JACKEY, Ben 502-213-2400 181 F ben.jackey@kctcs.edu
JACKIEWICZ, Thomas, E 323-442-9775 72 B thomas.jackiewicz@med.usc.edu
JACKLITCH, Bert 626-584-5506 43 H bert@fuller.edu
JACKLITSCH, Anthony 845-341-4710 311 C
JACKLOSKY, Robert 718-405-3301 296 G robert.jacklosky@mountsaintvincent.edu
JACKMAN, Guy 305-595-9500 94 B finaid@amcollege.edu
JACKO, Mariusz 787-250-1912 509 D mjacko@intermetro.com
JACKS, Almeda 864-656-2161 408 A arogers@clemson.edu
JACKSON, Addie 530-226-4788 63 K ajackson@simpsonu.edu
JACKSON, Adrian 210-486-2712 429 G ajackson202@alamo.edu
JACKSON, Alfred 215-335-0800 389 B
JACKSON, Alfred, B 601-979-2300 246 E alfred.b.jackson@jsums.edu
JACKSON, Alicia 229-430-4014 113 H alicia.jackson@asurams.edu
JACKSON, Amy 620-450-2135 176 G amyj@prattcc.edu
JACKSON, Andrew 412-731-6000 397 E ajackson@rpts.edu
JACKSON, Angela 434-949-1004 475 H angela.jackson@southside.edu
JACKSON, Anthony 225-771-5781 190 H anthony_jackson@subr.edu
JACKSON, Antonio 910-678-0058 334 D jacksona@faytechcc.edu
JACKSON, Arrick 231-591-2702 223 J arrickjackson@ferris.edu
JACKSON, Arrick, L 218-477-4377 239 D arrick.jackson@mnstate.edu
JACKSON, Bradley, A 513-585-0116 350 H bradley.jackson@thechristcollege.edu
JACKSON, Brenda 910-695-3731 337 H jacksonbr@sandhills.edu
JACKSON, Brenda 251-578-1313 3 D bjackson@rstc.edu
JACKSON, Brenda, W 504-586-5274 190 I bjackson@suno.edu
JACKSON, Brian, A 859-257-7132 185 B brian.jackson@uky.edu
JACKSON, Brian, K 609-652-4900 283 D brian.jackson@stockton.edu
JACKSON, Bridgett 334-291-4972 1 H bridgett.jackson@cv.edu
JACKSON, Brittany 501-975-8557 20 G bjackson@philander.edu
JACKSON, Brittany 330-569-5380 353 J jacksonb1@hiram.edu
JACKSON, Buddy 334-386-7293 5 D bjackson@faulkner.edu
JACKSON, Cameron 704-233-8739 344 G c.jackson@wingate.edu
JACKSON, Carol 212-517-0756 306 A cjackson@mmm.edu
JACKSON, Chris 636-922-8271 258 I chubbard@stchas.edu
JACKSON, Chris 213-615-7284 36 F cjackson4@thechicagoschool.edu
JACKSON, Clint 901-435-1233 421 A clint_jackson@loc.edu
JACKSON, Corey 415-476-1000 69 E corey.jackson@ucsf.edu
JACKSON, Corey, A 610-566-1776 403 E cjackson@williamson.edu
JACKSON, Courtney 508-270-4005 214 E cjackson@massbay.edu
JACKSON, Craig 478-757-3508 116 A cjackson@centralgatech.edu
JACKSON, Craig 541-440-7729 377 C craig.jackson@umpqua.edu
JACKSON, Craig, R 909-558-4545 48 C cjackson@llu.edu
JACKSON, Dalen, C 502-863-8300 178 K dalen.jackson@bsk.edu
JACKSON, Danielle 406-353-2607 262 H djackson@ancollege.edu
JACKSON, Darlene 916-660-7800 63 I djackson@sierracollege.edu
JACKSON, Darryl 256-372-4854 1 A darryl.jackson1@aamu.edu
JACKSON, JR., David 850-599-3505 108 I david.jackson@famu.edu
JACKSON, David, H 941-309-0166 105 K djackson@ringling.edu
JACKSON, Deanne 573-341-4362 261 E registrar@mst.edu
JACKSON, Deborah, C 617-873-0112 207 F deborah.jackson@cambridgecollege.edu
JACKSON, Debra 309-677-3085 133 B dsjackson@bradley.edu
JACKSON, Deirdre 910-630-7150 331 C dejackson@methodist.edu
JACKSON, Derek, A 785-532-6453 174 G derekaj@ksu.edu
JACKSON, Dexter 334-214-4815 1 H dexter.jackson@cv.edu
JACKSON, Diana, K 510-231-5000 46 J diana.k.jackson@kp.org
JACKSON, Emily, S 302-225-6271 90 E emily@gbc.edu
JACKSON, Equilla 936-261-1890 446 D eqjackson@pvamu.edu
JACKSON, Eric 208-467-8061 131 D ericjackson@nnu.edu
JACKSON, Eric, W 601-977-7814 249 C ewjackson@tougaloo.edu
JACKSON, Ericka 313-577-1981 232 I emjackson@wayne.edu
JACKSON, Eugene 973-877-3276 277 I ejackson@essex.edu
JACKSON, Flossie 772-462-7467 101 E fjackson@irsc.edu
JACKSON, Gary 662-325-3036 247 F gary@ext.msstate.edu
JACKSON, Gary 254-298-8456 446 A gary.jackson@templejc.edu
JACKSON, Gayla 251-626-3303 7 E gjackson@ussa.edu
JACKSON, Grace 713-623-2040 430 K gjackson@aii.edu
JACKSON, Gregory 256-372-8653 1 A gregory.jackson@aamu.edu
JACKSON, Gregory 508-626-4698 212 D gjackson@framingham.edu
JACKSON, Heidi 308-635-6395 270 D jacksonh@wncc.edu
JACKSON, J. Brooks 319-335-8064 163 A brooks-jackson@uiowa.edu
JACKSON, Jacob 425-235-7863 483 G jjackson@rtc.edu
JACKSON, Jacqueline 443-412-2233 199 A jajackson@harford.edu
JACKSON, Jacqueline 803-535-5047 407 G jajackson@claflin.edu
JACKSON, Jane 615-963-7427 426 D jjackson@tnstate.edu
JACKSON, Jannett 650-738-4110 61 Q jacksonjannett@smccd.edu
JACKSON, Jay 864-592-4723 412 F jacksonj@sccsc.edu
JACKSON, Jean 919-760-8556 331 B jacksonj@meredith.edu
JACKSON, Jerry 606-539-4250 185 A jerry.jackson@ucumberlands.edu
JACKSON, Jim, C 580-581-2460 365 G jjackson@cameron.edu
JACKSON, John 916-577-2210 75 B jjackson@jessup.edu
JACKSON, John 540-231-8508 477 A johnj1@vt.edu
JACKSON, JR., John, L 215-898-4407 400 K dean@asc.upenn.edu
JACKSON, Julie 662-846-4151 245 H jjackson@deltastate.edu
JACKSON, Justin 973-408-3957 277 C jjackson@drew.edu
JACKSON, Karen 323-563-5930 36 D karenjackson@cdrewu.edu
JACKSON, Kashanta 601-857-3395 246 B kashanta.jackson@hindscc.edu
JACKSON, Kathryn 773-508-7716 142 D kjackson9@luc.edu
JACKSON, Kathy 512-492-3118 442 M kathyj@stedwards.edu
JACKSON, Keith 334-876-9238 2 D keith.jackson@wccs.edu
JACKSON, Keith 304-293-4532 491 C keith.jackson@mail.wvu.edu
JACKSON, Keith 414-326-2335 493 A kjackso4@ccon.edu
JACKSON, Kelly 970-339-6583 76 G kelly.jackson@aims.edu
JACKSON, Kelly 910-592-8081 337 G kjackson@sampsoncc.edu
JACKSON, Ken, L 208-496-1610 130 A jacksonken@byui.edu
JACKSON, Kenneth 219-989-2366 159 G kjackson@pnw.edu
JACKSON, Kevin, P 254-710-1314 431 J kevin_jackson@baylor.edu
JACKSON, Kim 509-793-2067 478 H kimj@bigbend.edu
JACKSON, Kimberly 252-940-6252 332 C kimberly.jackson@beaufortccc.edu
JACKSON, Kremiere 509-963-1425 479 B kremiere.jackson@cwu.edu
JACKSON, Lachanna 513-569-1230 350 K lachanna.jackson@cincinnatistate.edu
JACKSON, LaTisha 501-370-5229 20 G ljackson@philander.edu
JACKSON, LaToya 916-660-7102 63 I ljackson7@sierracollege.edu
JACKSON, LaToya 646-313-8000 295 E latoya.jackson@guttman.cuny.edu
JACKSON, Laura 903-565-5936 456 A laurajackson@uttyler.edu
JACKSON, Lauren 318-357-5961 192 C potterl@nsula.edu
JACKSON, Leah 318-357-4553 192 C jacksonl@nsula.edu
JACKSON, Leah 440-375-7223 355 G ljackson@lec.edu
JACKSON, Lenora 404-270-5209 125 B lenoraj@spelman.edu
JACKSON, Linda 804-257-5807 477 C lrjackson@vuu.edu
JACKSON, Linda, Y 512-505-3006 438 E lyjackson@htu.edu
JACKSON, Lisa 301-985-7077 203 B lisa.jackson@umuc.edu
JACKSON, Loreto 617-228-2088 214 A lmjackson@bhcc.mass.edu
JACKSON, Lydia 618-650-2712 149 F ljackso@siue.edu
JACKSON, Madonna 810-762-0500 228 C madonna.jackson@mcc.edu
JACKSON, Margaret, W 931-363-9836 421 E mjackson@martinmethodist.edu
JACKSON, Marian, D 903-510-2759 452 C mjac@tjc.edu
JACKSON, Mark 610-519-4110 402 D m.w.jackson@villanova.edu
JACKSON, Marquise 619-216-6718 65 F mjackson@swccd.edu
JACKSON, Mary 504-286-5388 190 I mjackson@suno.edu
JACKSON, Mary 901-375-4400 422 F maryjackson@midsouthchristian.edu
JACKSON, Mary Anne 816-235-1808 261 C jacksonmar@umkc.edu
JACKSON, Mckenzie 910-630-7108 331 C mjackson@methodist.edu
JACKSON, Melodie, R 717-361-1404 383 E jacksonmr@etown.edu
JACKSON, Micah 773-380-6780 132 F mjackson@bexleyseabury.edu
JACKSON, Michael 858-646-3100 62 A mjackson@sbpdiscovery.org
JACKSON, Michael 256-766-6610 5 F mjackson@hcu.edu
JACKSON, Michele, H 517-353-6480 227 D mhj@msu.edu
JACKSON, Michelle 678-916-2600 114 I
JACKSON, Michelle 858-635-4772 24 L
JACKSON, Mike 717-871-4292 395 D michael.jackson@millersville.edu
JACKSON, Mike 918-463-2931 366 B mike.jackson@connorsstate.edu
JACKSON, Miles 360-992-2934 479 F mjackson@clark.edu
JACKSON, Myesha 619-216-6631 65 F mjackson@swccd.edu
JACKSON, Nan 850-484-1721 104 H njackson@pensacolastate.edu
JACKSON, Nancy 334-833-4482 5 H hcbookstore@hawks.huntingdon.edu

JACKSON, Nick ... 903-434-8147 441 B njackson@ntcc.edu
JACKSON, Pam ... 970-491-2359.. 78 M pam.jackson@colostate.edu
JACKSON, Pamela ... 540-423-9039 474 G pjackson@germanna.edu
JACKSON, Pamela ... 910-672-1460 341 E pjackson@uncfsu.edu
JACKSON, Pat ... 618-985-3741 139 I patjackson@jalc.edu
JACKSON, Patricia ... 401-863-9383 404 E patricia_jackson@brown.edu
JACKSON, Patrick ... 815-599-3485 138 B pat.jackson@highland.edu
JACKSON, Patrick, T ... 202-885-6194.. 90 J ptjack@american.edu
JACKSON, Paul ... 603-880-8308 274 E pjackson@thomasmorecollege.edu
JACKSON, Paul ... 603-880-8308 274 E tmc@thomasmorecollege.edu
JACKSON, Paul ... 585-245-6128 318 E jackson@geneseo.edu
JACKSON, Peggy ... 870-612-2030.. 22 I peggy.jackson@uaccb.edu
JACKSON, Philip ... 870-972-3362.. 17 E pjackson@asusystem.edu
JACKSON, Rasheedah ... 662-252-8000 248 G rjackson@rustcollege.edu
JACKSON, Raymond, L . 817-272-3186 454 J jackson@uta.edu
JACKSON, Richard ... 615-687-6892 418 A rjackson@abcnash.edu
JACKSON, Rickey ... 928-532-6141.. 14 J rickey.jackson@npc.edu
JACKSON, Robert ... 270-809-6912 183 G rjackson@murraystate.edu
JACKSON, Robert ... 901-678-8324 427 D rjax@memphis.edu
JACKSON, Robert, D ... 847-578-3248 147 I robert.jackson@rosalindfranklin.edu
JACKSON, Ron ... 864-592-4817 412 F jacksonr@sccsc.edu
JACKSON, Ronald ... 718-951-5352 293 C rcjackson@brooklyn.cuny.edu
JACKSON, Rose Mary ... 501-882-4407.. 17 F rmjackson@asub.edu
JACKSON, Ruth ... 207-859-4350 193 E ruth.jackson@colby.edu
JACKSON, Ruth ... 405-466-3424 366 F ruth.jackson@langston.edu
JACKSON, Ruth, R ... 405-466-3265 366 F ruth.jackson@langston.edu
JACKSON, Sally ... 509-533-3123 480 B sally.jackson@sfcc.spokane.edu
JACKSON, Shanna, L ... 615-353-3236 425 D shanna.jackson@nscc.edu
JACKSON, Sharon, S ... 804-752-3747 470 F sjackson@rmc.edu
JACKSON, Shawn, L ... 773-907-4450 134 C sljackson@ccc.edu
JACKSON, Shelbra ... 919-735-5151 338 H sbjackson@waynecc.edu
JACKSON, Shirley, J ... 202-806-7565.. 92 B sjackson@howard.edu
JACKSON, Shirley Ann . 518-276-6211 312 I president@rpi.edu
JACKSON, Smith ... 336-278-5837 328 K jacksons@elon.edu
JACKSON, Stacy, N ... 313-447-3905 232 I stacy.jackson@wayne.edu
JACKSON, Stanley ... 410-455-1336 202 E jackson@umbc.edu
JACKSON, Stephanie ... 912-525-5000 123 G sjackson@scad.edu
JACKSON, Susan ... 406-586-3585 263 J susan.jackson@montanabiblecollege.edu
JACKSON, Tekesha ... 229-732-5962 114 B tekeshajackson@andrewcollege.edu
JACKSON, Teresa ... 314-652-0300 259 A tjackson@slchc.edu
JACKSON, Terrence ... 334-872-2533.... 6 F tejack3@gmail.com
JACKSON, Terry ... 215-489-2324 382 D terry.jackson@delval.edu
JACKSON, Theron ... 318-670-6000 190 J tjackson@susla.edu
JACKSON, Tom ... 336-256-0543 341 F htjackson@ncat.edu
JACKSON, JR., Tom ... 707-826-3311.. 33 D tom.jackson@humboldt.edu
JACKSON, Tondaleya ... 803-705-4726 407 A tondaleya.jackson@benedict.edu
JACKSON, Tony ... 803-712-7430 413 G tonyjack@mailbox.sc.edu
JACKSON, Tonya ... 919-516-4127 340 C tjackson@st-aug.edu
JACKSON, Torie ... 304-424-8000 491 D
JACKSON, Tracey ... 504-520-7364 193 A tjacks33@xula.edu
JACKSON, Tracey ... 317-543-3235 158 V
JACKSON, Trevor, S ... 240-500-2330 198 H tsjackson@hagerstowncc.edu
JACKSON, Twana ... 304-929-6716 489 C tjackson@newriver.edu
JACKSON, Tyrone ... 323-343-2800.. 32 A tjackso4@calstatela.edu
JACKSON, Tyrone ... 662-246-6301 247 D tjackson@msdelta.edu
JACKSON, Vince, E ... 912-287-5818 116 F vjackson@costalpines.edu
JACKSON, Vincent ... 213-763-7035.. 49 E vjackson@lattc.edu
JACKSON, Wanda ... 205-932-3221.... 1 D wanda.jackson@bscc.edu
JACKSON, Wayne ... 407-823-2716 109 E wayne.jackson@ucf.edu
JACKSON, Wendy ... 704-216-6158 330 H wjackso@livingstone.edu
JACKSON, William ... 301-891-4475 204 C wjackson@wau.edu
JACKSON, William ... 217-234-5296 141 D wjackson60312@lakeland.cc.il.us
JACKSON, Wilma ... 402-826-8620 267 A wilma.jackson@doane.edu
JACKSON, Zena ... 817-515-3010 445 G zena.jackson@tccd.edu
JACKSON-DAVIS, Dorothy, G ... 601-877-6460 244 H djdavis@alcorn.edu
JACKSON-ELMOORE, Cynthia ... 517-355-2326 227 D jacks174@msu.edu
JACKSON-HAMMOND, Cynthia ... 937-376-6332 350 D chammond@centralstate.edu
JACKSON-LEE, Sophia .. 318-670-9355 190 J slee@susla.edu
JACKSON-NEWSOM, Julia ... 336-334-3218 343 A j_jackso@uncg.edu
JACKSON-STENLUND, Laura ... 785-227-3380 171 E stenlundl@bethanylb.edu
JACKSON-WILLIAMS, Loretta ... 601-984-5006 249 E ljackson@umc.edu
JACO, Jason ... 870-338-6474.. 22 H
JACOB, Jeffrey ... 212-678-8000 303 G jejacob@jtsa.edu
JACOB, Karen ... 978-478-3400 217 G kjacob@northpoint.edu
JACOB, Robert, W ... 570-577-1791 379 F rjw003@bucknell.edu
JACOB, Sinu ... 718-368-4645 294 E sinu.jacob@kbcc.cuny.edu
JACOB, Sybil ... 810-762-9514 225 H sjacob@kettering.edu
JACOBI, Keli ... 870-307-7242.. 20 A keli.jacobi@lyon.edu
JACOBOWITZ, Chanie ... 732-367-1060 275 J cjacobowitz@bmg.edu
JACOBS, Andrew ... 334-386-7657.... 5 D ajacobs@faulkner.edu
JACOBS, Bernadette ... 505-428-1778 288 B bernadette.jacobs@sfcc.edu
JACOBS, Bonita ... 706-864-1993 126 A president@ung.edu
JACOBS, Brandi, D ... 304-696-3328 490 D jacobs2@marshall.edu
JACOBS, Bret ... 504-865-3979 189 F bljacobs@loyno.edu
JACOBS, Carmela ... 785-320-4530 175 D carmelajacobs@manhattantech.edu
JACOBS, Cathleen ... 412-536-1033 387 B cathleen.jacobs@laroche.edu
JACOBS, Cecilia ... 254-968-1620 446 E cjacobs@tarleton.edu
JACOBS, Cindi ... 413-644-4700 205 F cjacobs@simons-rock.edu
JACOBS, Cody ... 214-887-5088 436 B cjacobs@dts.edu
JACOBS, Craig, M ... 610-892-1509 393 J cjacobs@pit.edu
JACOBS, Danny, O ... 503-494-8252 375 B president@ohsu.edu
JACOBS, Dennis, C ... 718-817-3040 300 E dcjacobs@fordham.edu
JACOBS, Derya, A ... 412-397-6363 397 G jacobs@rmu.edu
JACOBS, Diane ... 412-237-3064 381 G djacobs@ccac.edu
JACOBS, Holly, A ... 330-941-2340 365 C hajacobs@ysu.edu
JACOBS, Jeanne ... 305-237-5006 103 D jfjacobs@mdc.edu
JACOBS, Jeff ... 701-231-7537 345 G jeffrey.jacobs@ndsu.edu
JACOBS, Jenny ... 573-897-5000 260 E
JACOBS, Jo-Ann ... 718-270-6024 295 A jo-ann@mec.cuny.edu
JACOBS, Joshua ... 660-248-6214 251 B jejacobs@centralmethodist.edu
JACOBS, Joshua ... 312-942-5450 148 A
JACOBS, Judy ... 620-792-9349 171 C jacobsj@bartonccc.edu
JACOBS, Ken ... 830-792-7450 443 G security2@schreiner.edu
JACOBS, Kevin ... 708-239-4735 150 F kevin.jacobs@trnty.edu
JACOBS, Kristen ... 401-254-3428 405 E kjacobs@rwu.edu
JACOBS, Lacie ... 910-879-5505 332 D ljacobs@bladencc.edu
JACOBS, Laura ... 479-575-7910.. 21 G laura@uark.edu
JACOBS, Mark ... 480-965-2354.. 10 I mark.jacobs@asu.edu
JACOBS, Mary, R ... 513-875-3344 350 G mary.jacobs@chatfield.edu
JACOBS, Michael ... 419-267-1330 358 A mjacobs@northweststate.edu
JACOBS, Michael ... 585-292-3369 307 H mjacobs20@monroecc.edu
JACOBS, Mike ... 251-442-2228.... 8 C mjacobs@umobile.edu
JACOBS, Mike ... 404-364-8535 122 J mjacobs@oglethorpe.edu
JACOBS, Morenika ... 253-680-7014 478 E mjacobs@batestech.edu
JACOBS, Nicole ... 410-617-2271 199 F nmjacobs@loyola.edu
JACOBS, Sheila ... 479-508-3317.. 18 C sjacobs3@atu.edu
JACOBS, Tina ... 405-422-1454 369 E tina.jacobs@redlandscc.edu
JACOBS, OFS, Vicki, L . 260-399-7700 161 D vjacobs@sf.edu
JACOBS, Walt ... 408-924-5300.. 34 B walt.jacobs@sjsu.edu
JACOBS ANDERSON, Laura ... 503-370-6206 378 B ljacobsa@willamette.edu
JACOBS ELSON, Claire . 609-258-4131 280 E celson@princeton.edu
JACOBSEN, Brandy ... 318-670-9371 190 J bjacobsen@susla.edu
JACOBSEN, Christie ... 610-625-7797 391 A jacobsen@moravian.edu
JACOBSEN, Gabe ... 206-281-2043 484 D jacobseng@spu.edu
JACOBSEN, James ... 888-378-9988 416 J
JACOBSEN, Joyce ... 860-685-2357.. 89 C jjacobsen@wesleyan.edu
JACOBSEN, Joyce, P ... 315-781-3309 302 A jacobsen@hws.edu
JACOBSEN, Ruth ... 206-281-2114 484 D rjacobsen@spu.edu
JACOBSEN, Stan ... 828-884-8381 327 C jacobssf@brevard.edu
JACOBSEN, Steven ... 707-638-5270.. 67 F steven.jacobsen@tu.edu
JACOBSMA, Kelly, G ... 616-395-7790 225 B jacobsma@hope.edu
JACOBSON, Annie ... 231-845-3329 232 J ajacobson@westshore.edu
JACOBSON, Bob ... 510-642-6000.. 68 D bjacobson@berkeley.edu
JACOBSON, Cynthia ... 620-901-6213 170 G jacobson@allencc.edu
JACOBSON, Dan ... 808-488-8570 457 J dan.jacobson@wbu.edu
JACOBSON, Jennifer ... 218-846-3769 239 B jennifer.jacobson@minnesota.edu
JACOBSON, Karin ... 620-431-2800 175 H kjacobson@neosho.edu
JACOBSON, Kristie ... 765-998-4886 160 F kristie_jacobson@taylor.edu
JACOBSON, Leigh Ann . 570-408-4608 403 D leighann.jacobson@wilkes.edu
JACOBSON, Mark ... 414-416-9503 497 A markj@uwm.edu
JACOBSON, Mark ... 804-862-6100 470 I mjacobson@rbc.edu
JACOBSON, Mary ... 763-433-1315 237 C mary.jacobson@anokaramsey.edu
JACOBSON, Mary ... 763-433-1315 237 D mary.jacobson@anokaramsey.edu
JACOBSON, Renee, R ... 231-995-1256 228 G jacobsr@nmc.edu
JACOBSON, Ron ... 718-817-1000 300 E rjacobson@fordham.edu
JACOBSON, Ronald ... 509-777-4574 486 I rjacobson@whitworth.edu
JACOBSON, Shane ... 802-656-6626 463 E shane.jacobson@uvm.edu
JACOBSON, Terra ... 708-974-5467 144 C jacobsont6@morainevalley.edu
JACOBSON, Tim ... 952-995-1471 238 B tim.jacobson@hennepintech.edu
JACOBSON-SCHULTE, Marah ... 612-330-1034 233 K jacobsm@augsburg.edu
JACOBSON-SCHULTE, Patrick ... 651-423-8000 237 H
JACOBSON-SCHULTE, Patrick ... 651-450-3522 238 D pjacobs@inverhills.edu
JACOBSON-SCHULTE, Patrick ... 651-450-3000 238 D pjacobs@inverhills.edu
JACOBY, JoAnn ... 719-389-6070.. 77 H jjacoby@coloradocollege.edu
JACOBY, Robin, M ... 214-648-2288 457 B robin.jacoby@utsouthwestern.edu
JACOBY, Susan ... 202-651-5005.. 91 E susan.jacoby@gallaudet.edu
JACOT, Jaclyn ... 509-279-6234 480 A jaclyn.jacot@scc.spokane.edu
JACQUE, Mark ... 410-837-6875 204 B mjacque@ubalt.edu
JACQUES, Kevin ... 256-765-5760.... 8 E kljacques@una.edu
JACQUES, Theresa ... 901-321-2474 419 C tjacque2@cbu.edu
JACQUES, Theresa, K ... 906-487-2936 227 E tjacques@mtu.edu
JACSO, Jeff ... 812-237-3525 155 G jeff.jacso@indstate.edu
JACZYNSKI, Linda ... 610-519-4080 402 D linda.jaczynski@villanova.edu
JADALLAH, Edward ... 843-349-2773 408 C ejadalla@coastal.edu
JADHAV, Esther ... 859-858-3511 178 I esther.jadhav@asbury.edu
JADLOS, Melissa ... 585-385-8164 314 A mjadlos@sjfc.edu
JADUSHLEVER, Renee ... 510-430-2033.. 52 D reneejad@mills.edu
JAECKEL, Andrea ... 928-350-4006.. 15 N andrea.jaeckel@prescott.edu
JAEGER, David ... 239-590-2315 108 K djaeger@fgcu.edu
JAEGER, Meridith ... 920-498-6995 500 F meridith.jaeger@nwtc.edu
JAEGER, Naftalie ... 515-239-9002 315 I mgross@shoryoshuv.org
JAEGER, Timothy, J ... 949-214-3179.. 40 F tim.jaeger@cui.edu
JAEN, Ulysses ... 239-687-5501.. 94 N ujaen@avemarialaw.edu
JAFERIAN, Warren ... 978-232-2272 209 B wjaferia@endicott.edu
JAFFE, Daniel ... 512-471-2877 455 A vp-research-sr@austin.utexas.edu
JAFFE, David, L ... 561-237-7099 102 V djaffe@lynn.edu
JAFFE, Denise ... 802-387-1682 462 D denisejaffe@landmark.edu
JAFFE, Judith, A ... 781-736-2104 207 E jjaffe@brandeis.edu
JAFFE, Robert ... 718-482-5037 294 F rjaffe@lagcc.cuny.edu
JAFFE, Susan ... 336-770-3207 343 D jaffes@uncsa.edu
JAFFE, Victoria ... 602-206-8115 272 L vjaffe@ccsnh.edu
JAFFE, Yaakov ... 347-619-9074 326 G
JAFFEE, Victoria ... 949-214-3042.. 40 F victori.jaffe@cui.edu
JAFFER, Nori ... 212-687-3730 275 I naj@berkeleycollege.edu

JAFFER, Nori .... 212-687-3730 291 D
naj@berkeleycollege.edu
JAFFRAY, Shelly .... 714-564-6500.. 57 L
jaffray_shelly@sac.edu
JAGENDORF, Susan ...... 518-255-5558 319 F
jagends@cobleskill.edu
JAGER, Tim .... 712-274-5313 168 B
jager@morningside.edu
JAGERSON, Todd .... 651-450-3373 238 D
tjagerson@inverhills.edu
JAGERSON, Todd .... 651-423-8000 237 H
JAGGARS, Damon, E .... 614-292-4241 358 I
jaggars.1@osu.edu
JAGGERS, Dametraus .... 610-436-3260 396 A
djaggers@wcupa.edu
JAGGERS, Misty .... 405-789-6400 370 A
mjaggers@snu.edu
JAGNE-SHAW,
Marcel, E .... 410-651-7859 203 A
mjagneshaw@umes.edu
JAGODZINSKE, Scott .... 785-833-4529 175 B
campus.ministry@kwu.edu
JAGODZINSKI, Paul, W 928-523-2408.. 14 H
paul.jagodzinski@nau.edu
JAGORD, Mary-Jo .... 716-878-6001 318 C
jagordmj@buffalostate.edu
JAH, Cassaundra .... 575-758-8914 286 F
cassaundraj@midwiferycollege.edu
JAHANIAN, Farnam .... 412-268-2201 380 F
president@andrew.cmu.edu
JAHNKE, Tamera, S ...... 417-836-5249 256 E
tamerajahnke@missouristate.edu
JAHR, Helen .... 507-433-0527 240 F
helen.jahr@riverland.edu
JAIME, Andres .... 210-434-6711 441 E
aijaime@ollusa.edu
JAIN, Anil .... 323-953-4000.. 48 I
jainak@lacitycollege.edu
JAIN, Madhu .... 312-939-0111 136 D
madhu@eastwest.edu
JAKO, Robert .... 925-969-3300.. 46 H
rjako@jfku.edu
JAKUBOWSKI, Jason .... 716-286-8405 310 D
jjakubowski@niagara.edu
JAKUBOWSKI, Laura ..... 802-468-6072 464 A
laura.jakubowski@castleton.edu
JAKUBS, Deborah .... 919-660-5800 328 G
deborah.jakubs@duke.edu
JAKWAY, Julie .... 941-752-5326 108 G
jakwayj@scf.edu
JALBERT, Kenneth .... 401-739-5000 405 A
kjalbert@neit.edu
JALOMO, Romero .... 831-755-6822.. 44 K
rjalomo@hartnell.edu
JALOWIEC, Tammi .... 218-935-0417 244 G
tammi.jalowiec@wetcc.edu
JALSEVAC, Paul .... 540-636-2900 466 A
pjalsevac@christendom.edu
JAMEISON, Linda .... 864-646-1562 413 A
ljameiso@tctc.edu
JAMERISON, Alex .... 501-279-5126.. 19 D
ajamerison@harding.edu
JAMERSON, JR.,
Londell .... 816-604-1453 255 D
londell.jamerson@mcckc.edu
JAMERSON, Sun Kyong 440-366-7569 355 J
JAMES, JR.,
Advergus, D .... 334-727-8088.... 7 D
ajames@tuskegee.edu
JAMES, Anisa .... 606-546-1704 184 H
ajames@unionky.edu
JAMES, Arthur .... 972-860-4417 435 E
ajames@dcccd.edu
JAMES, Beverly .... 803-786-3107 408 F
bjames@columbiasc.edu
JAMES, Blake .... 305-284-6381 112 E
bjames@miami.edu
JAMES, Bruce .... 501-370-5234.. 20 G
bjames@philander.edu
JAMES, Catherine .... 269-965-3931 225 F
jamesc@kellogg.edu
JAMES, Cheryl .... 850-973-9416 103 K
jamesc@nfcc.edu
JAMES, Christene, A ..... 206-726-5020 480 C
cjames@cornish.edu
JAMES, Deborah .... 804-862-6100 470 I
djames@rbc.edu
JAMES, Denise .... 708-209-3337 135 F
denise.james@cuchicago.edu
JAMES, Derrick .... 504-286-5295 190 I
djames@suno.edu
JAMES, Erika .... 404-727-6377 117 F
erika.james@emory.edu
JAMES, Errin .... 870-633-4480.. 19 B
ejames@eacc.edu
JAMES, III, Frank .... 215-368-5000 390 F
fjames@missio.edu
JAMES, Glenn .... 210-829-3940 453 D
gjames@uiwtx.edu
JAMES, Gwendolyn .... 509-533-8883 480 A
gwendolyn.james@scc.spokane.edu
JAMES, Holly .... 502-863-7094 180 E
holly_james@georgetowncollege.edu
JAMES, II, Hubert, L .... 386-481-2524.. 95 F
jamesh@cookman.edu
JAMES, Jacqueline .... 404-270-5111 125 B
jjames@spelman.edu
JAMES, Jamie .... 603-314-1474 274 D
j.james@snhu.edu
JAMES, Janet, C .... 972-238-6974 435 F
jjames@dcccd.edu
JAMES, Jennifer, N .... 718-270-5083 295 A
jenjames@mec.cuny.edu
JAMES, Jeremy .... 334-556-2361.... 2 C
jjames@wallace.edu
JAMES, Jill .... 856-351-2910 283 A
jjames@salemcc.edu
JAMES, Jim .... 404-962-3155 126 F
jim.james@usg.edu
JAMES, Justin .... 504-286-5117 190 I
jjames@suno.edu
JAMES, Karen .... 336-517-1565 327 B
kjames@bennett.edu
JAMES, Kathy .... 325-649-8409 438 D
kjames@hputx.edu
JAMES, Kelly .... 785-890-3641 176 C
kelly.james@nwktc.edu
JAMES, Kelly .... 815-394-5045 147 G
kjames@rockford.edu
JAMES, Kesha .... 205-929-6450.... 2 H
kjames@lawsonstate.edu
JAMES, Kevin, L .... 336-334-7632 341 F
kljames@ncat.edu
JAMES, Lance .... 360-538-4120 481 E
ljames@ghc.edu
JAMES, Lisa .... 256-726-7270.... 6 C
ljames@oakwood.edu
JAMES, Lisa .... 719-502-2056.. 81 F
lisa.james@ppcc.edu
JAMES, Makila .... 202-685-4242 503 I
makila.james.civ@ndu.edu
JAMES, Mark .... 806-874-3571 433 B
mark.james@clarendoncollege.edu
JAMES, Mary .... 509-865-8654 481 G
james_m@heritage.edu
JAMES, Mary, B .... 503-777-7250 376 C
mjames@reed.edu
JAMES, Matricia .... 716-375-2000 313 F
mjames@sbu.edu
JAMES, Michael .... 620-947-3121 177 C
michaeljames@tabor.edu
JAMES, Michelle .... 412-536-1139 387 B
michelle.james@laroche.edu
JAMES, Mike .... 501-279-4529.. 19 D
james@harding.edu
JAMES, Mike .... 956-665-2451 455 D
mike.james@utrgv.edu
JAMES, Misha .... 719-502-2012.. 81 F
misha.james@ppcc.edu
JAMES, Naja .... 310-377-5501.. 51 B
njames@marymountcalifornia.edu
JAMES, Nancy .... 916-660-7900.. 63 I
njames3@sierracollege.edu
JAMES, Novia .... 520-383-8401.. 16 D
njames@tocc.edu
JAMES, Patrick .... 256-824-6942.... 8 B
patrick.james@uah.edu
JAMES, Patrick .... 312-629-6600 148 I
pjames@saic.edu
JAMES, Peggy .... 262-595-2101 497 C
james@uwp.edu
JAMES, Penny .... 402-354-7225 268 C
penny.james@methodistcollege.edu
JAMES, Regina .... 225-771-2552 191 A
rjames@sulc.edu
JAMES, Rhonda .... 904-770-3584.. 71 H
rjames@usa.edu
JAMES, Ruben .... 310-900-1600.. 40 A
rjames@elcamino.edu
JAMES, Ruby, F .... 217-420-6029 143 H
rubyjames@millikin.edu
JAMES, Scott .... 978-542-6243 213 C
sjames@salemstate.edu
JAMES, Shashanta .... 269-387-6000 232 K
shanta.james@wmich.edu
JAMES, Shauna .... 256-765-4279.... 8 E
sljames@una.edu
JAMES, Skip .... 850-973-9477 103 K
jamess@nfcc.edu
JAMES, Stephen .... 865-251-1800 424 A
sjames1@south.edu
JAMES, Steven .... 802-322-1676 462 C
steven.james@goddard.edu
JAMES, Susan, M .... 757-822-1084 476 B
sjames@tcc.edu
JAMES, Sylvia .... 253-964-6710 483 D
JAMES, Tessa .... 800-567-2344 492 G
tjames@menominee.edu
JAMES, Timmy .... 256-331-6281.... 3 C
timmy.james@nwscc.edu
JAMES, Tracy .... 636-481-3187 254 A
tjames@jeffco.edu
JAMES, W. Brian .... 706-245-7226 117 E
bjames@ec.edu
JAMES, Wayne .... 219-980-7222 156 E
wljames@iun.edu
JAMES-BATTELLE, Brice 870-733-6790.. 17 H
bjames-battelle@asumidsouth.edu
JAMES BLACKWELL,
Leanna .... 413-565-1000 205 G
ljamesblackwell@baypath.edu
JAMES-MOORE,
Annette .... 901-272-5153 422 B
amoore@mca.edu
JAMES WALKER,
Cherena .... 323-259-2623.. 54 E
cwalker2@oxy.edu
JAMESON, Dennis .... 916-577-2200.. 75 B
djameson@jessup.edu
JAMESON, Gretchen, M 262-243-5700 493 B
gretchen.jameson@cuw.edu
JAMESON, J, L .... 215-898-6796 400 K
ljameson@mail.med.upenn.edu
JAMESON, Kim .... 405-682-1611 367 H
kjameson@occc.edu
JAMESON, Kim .... 405-682-7534 367 H
kjameson@occc.edu
JAMESON, Maisha .... 510-464-3236.. 56 G
mjameson@peralta.edu
JAMESON, Sean .... 914-395-2494 315 F
sjameson@sarahlawrence.edu
JAMESON, Susan .... 507-389-7211 241 C
susan.jameson@southcentral.edu
JAMIESON, Kristine ...... 330-263-2000 351 C
kjamieson@wooster.edu
JAMIESON, Michelle, E 724-287-8711 380 A
michelle.jamieson@bc3.edu
JAMIESON, Richard, J .. 216-368-3720 349 F
rjj@case.edu
JAMIESON-DRAKE,
David .... 919-684-0736 328 G
david.jamieson.drake@duke.edu
JAMIESOON,
Michelle, E .... 724-287-8711 380 A
michelle.jamieson@bc3.edu
JAMISON, Calvin, D ..... 972-883-2213 455 B
cjamison@utdallas.edu
JAMISON, Charles .... 610-409-3607 402 A
cjamison@ursinus.edu
JAMISON, Joey .... 601-857-3584 246 B
joey.jamison@hindscc.edu
JAMISON, Larry, W ...... 814-393-1926 394 D
ljamison@cuf-inc.org
JAMISON, Leslie .... 609-343-5004 275 D
ljamison@atlantic.edu
JAMISON, Lucretzia ...... 773-451-3798 134 D
ljamison@ccc.edu
JAMISON, Matt .... 303-678-3845.. 79 J
matt.jamison@frontrange.edu
JAMISON, Todd .... 507-222-4292 234 F
tjamison@carleton.edu
JAMISON, Wayne .... 803-786-3343 408 F
wjamison@columbiasc.edu
JAMOUS, Danielly .... 401-739-5000 405 A
djamous@neit.edu
JAMROS, Brian .... 503-280-8554 372 I
bjamros@cu-portland.edu
JANARO, Walter, A .... 540-636-2900 466 A
walter@christendom.edu
JANCHENKO, Michael ... 312-329-4495 144 B
michael.janchenko@moody.edu
JANCHESON, Linda .... 321-674-7277.. 99 B
ljancheson@fit.edu
JANELLE, Sherri .... 304-876-5043 490 E
sjanelle@shepherd.edu
JANELLE, William, P ..... 603-862-1903 274 G
william.janelle@unh.edu
JANES, Jennifer .... 315-364-3483 325 B
jjanes@wells.edu
JANES, Kristin .... 828-669-8012 331 J
kjanes@montreat.edu
JANESCH, Cynthia, D ... 570-577-3763 379 F
cindy.janesch@bucknell.edu
JANG, Michelle .... 714-533-1495.. 64 D
michelle@southbaylo.edu
JANGER, Edward .... 718-780-0314 291 J
edward.janger@brooklaw.edu
JANICKI, Thomas .... 715-394-8596 498 B
tjanicki@uwsuper.edu
JANIESCH, Mark .... 636-481-3130 254 A
mjaniesc@jeffco.edu
JANIS, Robert, J .... 312-362-8762 135 I
bjanis@depaul.edu
JANIS, Sofia, A .... 412-359-1000 400 G
sjanis@triangle-tech.edu
JANISIN, Matthew .... 262-564-3942 499 F
janisinm@gtc.edu
JANITZ, Suzanne .... 607-431-4244 301 D
janitzs@hartwick.edu
JANKE, Louise, L .... 608-785-8604 496 F
ljanke@uwlax.edu
JANKOWSKI, Mark .... 518-587-2100 321 A
mark.jankowski@esc.edu
JANKOWSKI NIEMCZURA,
Leslie .... 614-222-3225 351 D
ljankowski@ccad.edu
JANMOHAMMAD,
Shenaaz .... 510-430-2292.. 52 D
shjanmohammad@mills.edu
JANNEY, Cindy .... 507-389-1011 239 C
cynthia.janney@mnsu.edu
JANNEY, Dell Ann .... 573-288-6388 252 E
djanney@culver.edu
JANNEY, Justin .... 912-478-5224 119 C
jjjaney@georigasouthern.edu
JANNIFER, Seth .... 917-493-4420 305 I
sjannifer@msmnyc.edu
JANOSKY, Amanda .... 716-896-0700 324 E
ajanosky@villa.edu
JANOSKY, Janine, E ..... 773-838-7511 134 F
jjanosky@ccc.edu
JANOW, Merit, E .... 212-854-4604 297 C
mj60@columbia.edu
JANOWSKI, Lori .... 212-650-3133 294 C
lori.janowski@hunter.cuny.edu
JANOYAN, Kerop .... 315-268-6506 296 A
kjanoyan@clarkson.edu
JANS, Briget .... 832-842-3701 452 F
bajans@uh.edu
JANS, Roger .... 201-684-7231 280 H
rjans@ramapo.edu
JANSE, Korey .... 661-255-1050.. 28 K
JANSEN, James, S .... 402-280-1804 266 I
jimjansen@creighton.edu
JANSEN, Jennifer .... 510-594-3763.. 28 D
jjansen@cca.edu
JANSEN, Mark .... 815-599-3455 138 B
mark.jansen@highland.edu
JANSEN, Shelley .... 970-943-2101.. 84 D
sjansen@western.edu
JANSMA, Dana .... 269-337-7210 225 D
dana.jansma@kzoo.edu
JANSMA, Pamela .... 303-556-2557.. 83 C
pamela.jansma@ucdenver.edu
JANSSEN, Emma .... 360-417-6503 483 B
ejanssen@pencol.edu
JANSSEN, Jessica .... 402-941-6523 267 L
janssen@midlandu.edu
JANSSEN, Jill, M .... 815-599-3412 138 B
jill.janssen@highland.edu
JANSSEN, John .... 913-722-0272 174 E
john.janssen@kansaschristian.edu
JANSSEN, Michelle, L .... 765-361-6365 162 E
janssenm@wabash.edu
JANSSEN-ROBINSON,
Aimee .... 812-535-5219 160 B
a.janssen-robinson@smwc.edu
JANSSON, Jimilea .... 580-628-6771 367 D
jimilea.jansson@noc.edu
JANUARY, Shennell ...... 703-445-9056 473 D
JANUS, Janet .... 530-339-3655.. 63 H
jjanus@shastacollege.edu
JANUSCH, Barry .... 360-475-7458 482 G
bjanusch@olympic.edu
JANUTIS, Rachel .... 614-236-6383 349 D
rjanutis@law.capital.edu
JANVIER, Lydie .... 305-821-3333.. 99 E
ljanvier@fnu.edu
JANZ, Curtis .... 479-788-7591.. 21 H
curtis.janz@uafs.edu
JANZ, Jeff .... 414-288-7206 494 B
jeff.janz@marquette.edu

JENKINS, Anthony, L 304-766-3112 491 B anthony.jenkins@wvstateu.edu
JENKINS, Brandon 919-739-6841 338 H bmjenkins@waynecc.edu
JENKINS, Brent 317-632-5553 158 S bjenkins@lincolntech.edu
JENKINS, Bryan 919-807-7147 331 L jenkinsb@nccommunitycolleges.edu
JENKINS, Cara 610-436-3513 396 A cjenkins@wcupa.edu
JENKINS, Caren 304-462-6182 490 C caren.jenkins@glenville.edu
JENKINS, Carri, P 801-422-1166 458 H carri_jenkins@byu.edu
JENKINS, Cheryl, S 919-760-8338 331 B jenkinsc@meredith.edu
JENKINS, David, A 502-852-7997 185 C d.jenkins@louisville.edu
JENKINS, Dora 912-921-2900.. 92 G
JENKINS, Doug 417-865-2815 253 B jenkinsd@evangel.edu
JENKINS, Ernest 919-530-7639 342 A ernest.jenkins@nccu.edu
JENKINS, Freddie 229-732-5919 114 B freddiejenkins@andrewcollege.edu
JENKINS, Garry 612-625-4841 243 E gjenkins@umn.edu
JENKINS, Geraldine, M 440-646-8322 363 G gerri.jenkins@ursuline.edu
JENKINS, Gloria 574-284-4723 160 C gjenkins@saintmarys.edu
JENKINS, H. E 713-942-5079 454 H jenkinhe@stthom.edu
JENKINS, J. Marshall 706-236-2259 115 B mjenkins@berry.edu
JENKINS, Jacqueline 212-217-4000 299 H jacqueline_jenkins1@fitnyc.edu
JENKINS, Jan 479-968-0456.. 18 C ejenkins@atu.edu
JENKINS, Jason 701-777-6345 345 C jjenkins@nd.gov
JENKINS, Jeffrey, L 812-877-8209 159 J jenkins@rose-hulman.edu
JENKINS, SR., Jimmy, R 704-216-6098 330 H jjenkins@livingstone.edu
JENKINS, Jo Ann 708-608-4199 144 C jenkinsj52@morainevalley.edu
JENKINS, Joanna 215-965-4059 390 J jjenkins@moore.edu
JENKINS, CSC, John, I 574-631-3903 161 C jenkins.1@nd.edu
JENKINS, Juanita, M 570-422-3961 394 E jjenkins20@esu.edu
JENKINS, Katrina 407-646-2115 105 M kejenkins@rollins.edu
JENKINS, Keith 585-475-7404 313 A kbjgpt@rit.edu
JENKINS, Keith 936-294-1759 450 C rca_kej@shsu.edu
JENKINS, Kevin 870-307-7220.. 20 A kevin.jenkins@lyon.edu
JENKINS, Lidia 415-239-3267.. 37 A ljenkins@ccsf.edu
JENKINS, Louis 301-736-3631 199 G
JENKINS, Lucy 603-578-8900 273 A ljenkins@ccsnh.edu
JENKINS, Malia 619-201-8728.. 60 A malia.jenkins@sdcc.edu
JENKINS, Margo 315-268-6478 296 A mjohnsto@clarkson.edu
JENKINS, Melanie 804-484-1581 472 L mjenkin3@richmond.edu
JENKINS, Mike 903-983-8189 439 A mjenkins@kilgore.edu
JENKINS, Nicole 540-373-2200 466 H njenkins@evcc.edu
JENKINS, Patricia 865-354-3000 425 G jenkinsp@roanestate.edu
JENKINS, Patsy 318-473-6474 188 J pjenkins@lsua.edu
JENKINS, Paul 603-899-4142 273 F jenkinsp@franklinpierce.edu
JENKINS, Quincy 706-272-4573 117 C qjenkins@daltonstate.edu
JENKINS, Rebecca 419-434-5692 363 A jenkinsr1@findlay.edu
JENKINS, Robert 909-384-8662.. 59 I rjenkins@sbccd.cc.ca.us
JENKINS, Robert 713-500-3334 456 B robert.jenkins@uth.tmc.edu
JENKINS, Robert 903-877-7777 456 D robert.jenkins@uth.tmc.edu
JENKINS, Rod 972-708-7369 435 H rod_jenkins@diu.edu
JENKINS, Rodney 928-776-2280.. 16 M rodney.jenkins@yc.edu
JENKINS, Ronny 202-319-5492.. 91 B jenkinsr@cua.edu
JENKINS, Safia 504-286-5101 190 I sjenkins@suno.edu
JENKINS, Sam 770-537-6012 127 A sam.jenkins@westgatech.edu
JENKINS, Scott 402-643-7482 266 G finaid@cune.edu
JENKINS, Sharon 575-439-3806 287 C djenkins@nmsu.edu
JENKINS, Sonja 478-218-3308 116 A sjenkins@centralgatech.edu
JENKINS, Stancia, J 402-472-5270 269 H sjenkins@nebraska.edu
JENKINS, Stephen 678-466-4115 116 E stephenjenkins@clayton.edu
JENKINS, Steve 619-201-8716.. 60 A steve.jenkins@sdcc.edu
JENKINS, Steven 740-392-6868 357 B steven.jenkins@mvnu.edu
JENKINS, Sylvia 708-974-5201 144 C president@morainevalley.edu
JENKINS, Timothy, S 219-464-5411 162 A tim.jenkins@valpo.edu
JENKINS, Toni, P 972-758-3804 433 M tjenkins@collin.edu
JENKINS, Vanessa, C 757-823-8173 469 F vcjenkins@nsu.edu
JENKINS-EVANS, Janie 802-387-6814 462 D janiejenkinsevans@landmark.edu
JENKINS-UNTERBERG, Michelle 314-529-9625 254 H munterberg@maryville.edu
JENKS, Ann, M 269-337-7297 225 D ann.jenks@kzoo.edu
JENKS, Catherine 678-839-6449 126 E cjenks@westga.edu
JENKS, David 678-839-6445 126 E djenks@westga.edu
JENKS, Dean 503-517-1093 377 G djenks@warnerpacific.edu
JENKS, Laura 617-358-5207 207 D ljenks@bu.edu
JENKS, Salli 402-486-2600 269 F salli.jenks@ucollege.edu
JENKS, Wayne 919-761-2277 340 G wjenks@sebts.edu
JENNEMAN, Eugene, A 231-995-1572 228 G ejenneman@nmc.edu
JENNER, Mark 618-664-6551 137 G mark.jenner@greenville.edu
JENNESS, Jennier 701-845-7276 346 A jennifer.jenness@vcsu.edu
JENNETTE, Judy 252-789-0310 335 H judy.jennette@martincc.edu
JENNETTEN, Tory 309-677-2259 133 B tory@fsmail.bradley.edu
JENNINGS, Amani 732-987-2601 278 B ajennings@georgian.edu
JENNINGS, Arbolina, L 713-313-7661 449 C jennings_al@tsu.edu
JENNINGS, Barbara 641-844-5522 166 I barb.jennings@iavalley.edu
JENNINGS, Bill 541-880-2247 373 E jenningsb@klamathcc.edu
JENNINGS, Carlette 404-876-1227 115 F carlette.jennings@bccr.edu
JENNINGS, Charla 870-743-3000.. 20 C charlam@northark.edu
JENNINGS, Chris 626-387-5763.. 26 H cjennings@apu.edu
JENNINGS, Chris 213-624-1200.. 42 I cjennings@fidm.edu
JENNINGS, Cyndean 262-564-2672 499 F jenningsc@gtc.edu
JENNINGS, David, C 845-675-4616 310 G david.jennings@nyack.edu
JENNINGS, Eli 808-853-1040 128 C elijennings@pacrim.edu
JENNINGS, Eva 510-748-2318.. 56 F ejennings@peralta.edu
JENNINGS, Hope 937-775-4818 364 I hope.jennings@wright.edu
JENNINGS, Jamie 541-880-2228 373 E jennings@klamathcc.edu
JENNINGS, Jarvis 423-585-6845 426 C jarvis.jennings@ws.edu
JENNINGS, Jody 864-977-7058 411 E jody.jennings@ngu.edu
JENNINGS, John 415-955-2100.. 24 K jjennings@alliant.edu
JENNINGS, Logan 423-652-4895 420 H ljennings@king.edu
JENNINGS, Lynn 252-335-0821 333 G lynn_jennings@albemarle.edu
JENNINGS, Michael, E 864-294-2149 410 A michael.jennings3@furman.edu
JENNINGS, Patricia 203-596-4693.. 87 F pjennings@post.edu
JENNINGS, Robert 402-559-5899 270 A robert.jennings@unmc.edu
JENNINGS, Sarah, E 870-235-4040.. 21 D sejennings@saumag.edu
JENNINGS, Shawna 312-935-4234 139 H sjennings@icsw.edu
JENNINGS, Susan 423-697-2576 424 E susan.jennings@chattanoogastate.edu
JENNINGS, Thomas, W 850-645-9655 109 C tjennings@fsu.edu
JENNINGS, Todd 909-537-5655.. 33 A tjennin@csusb.edu
JENNISON, Barry 423-697-2614 424 E barry.jennison@chattanoogastate.edu
JENNUM, Joe 909-274-4630.. 52 H jjennum@mtsac.edu
JENNY, Paul 415-476-4148.. 69 E paul.jenny@ucsf.edu
JENOURE, Rita 202-651-5005.. 91 E rita.jenoure@gallaudet.edu
JENRETTE, John 310-423-8294.. 35 L
JENSCHKE, Danielle 830-792-7217 443 G admissions@schreiner.edu
JENSEN, Al 360-752-8571 478 G ajensen@btc.edu
JENSEN, Anna 812-856-2548 156 B anjensen@iu.edu
JENSEN, Anna, K 812-856-2548 156 A anjensen@indiana.edu
JENSEN, Brenda 808-236-3533 127 H bjensen@hpu.edu
JENSEN, Christopher 270-745-5065 185 E christopher.jensen@wku.edu
JENSEN, Chuck 970-339-6509.. 76 G chuck.jensen@aims.edu
JENSEN, Dan 712-279-3734 169 B dan.jensen@stlukescollege.edu
JENSEN, Dan 817-735-2500 454 C danny.jensen@unthsc.edu
JENSEN, David, H 512-404-4821 431 C djensen@austinseminary.edu
JENSEN, Doug 909-274-5517.. 52 H djenson@mtsac.edu
JENSEN, Doug 661-722-6300.. 26 D djensen@avc.edu
JENSEN, Douglas, J 815-921-4001 147 E d.jensen@rockvalleycollege.edu
JENSEN, Dustin 701-252-3467 347 C dustin.jensen@uj.edu
JENSEN, Gail 951-487-3040.. 52 I gjensen@msjc.edu
JENSEN, Gail, M 402-280-3727 266 I gailjensen@creighton.edu
JENSEN, Genevieve 718-517-7711 315 A gjensen@edaff.com
JENSEN, Jed 307-681-6100 502 F jjensen@sheridan.edu
JENSEN, Jennifer, M 610-758-3705 388 J jmj313@lehigh.edu
JENSEN, John, A 540-458-8604 478 A jensenj@wlu.edu
JENSEN, Joshua 509-527-5768 486 H jensenj@whitman.edu
JENSEN, Kae 208-562-3336 130 F kaejensen@cwi.edu
JENSEN, Karen 907-474-7224.. 10 A kjensen@alaska.edu
JENSEN, Katie 425-388-9581 480 G kjensen@everettcc.edu
JENSEN, Kevin 607-436-2158 317 C kevin.jensen@oneonta.edu
JENSEN, Kimberly 303-494-7988.. 76 K
JENSEN, Kirsten 218-477-2175 239 D kirsten.jensen@mnstate.edu
JENSEN, Laura 970-491-5939.. 78 M l.jensen@colostate.edu
JENSEN, Lauren 616-526-7269 222 A lauren.jensen@calvin.edu
JENSEN, Lauren, J 616-526-6106 222 A lauren.jensen@calvin.edu
JENSEN, Laurie 575-624-7157 286 A laurie.jensen@roswell.enmu.edu
JENSEN, Lori 507-529-2720 240 G lori.jensen@rctc.edu
JENSEN, Megan 509-574-4635 487 A mjensen@yvcc.edu
JENSEN, Melissa 319-398-5491 167 C melissa.jensen@kirkwood.edu
JENSEN, Michael, A 801-422-4327 458 H jensen@byu.edu
JENSEN, Michelle 785-833-4316 175 B kmichelj@kwu.edu
JENSEN, Mitch 574-936-8898 153 A mitch.jensen@ancilla.edu
JENSEN, Nathan 714-432-5909.. 38 E njensen@occ.cccd.edu
JENSEN, Paul 708-456-0300 150 I pauljensen@triton.edu
JENSEN, Paul, E 215-895-2122 383 B paul.eric.jensen@drexel.edu
JENSEN, Peter, E 605-677-5341 416 H pete.jensen@usd.edu
JENSEN, Riki 989-328-1220 228 A riki.jensen@montcalm.edu
JENSEN, Robert 559-453-2058.. 43 G robert.jensen@fresno.edu
JENSEN, Sandra 319-234-5748 166 B sandra.jensen@hawkeyecollege.edu
JENSEN, Scott 316-978-3693 178 A scott.jensen@wichita.edu
JENSEN, Scott 435-879-4603 460 G scott.jensen@dixie.edu
JENSEN, Sol 815-753-2253 145 C sjensen1@niu.edu
JENSEN, Steve 713-942-3464 454 H jensensj@stthom.edu
JENSEN, Steve, M 563-588-8000 165 F smjensen@emmaus.edu
JENSEN, Steven, M 330-471-8521 355 L sjensen@malone.edu
JENSEN, Trisha 801-832-2598 461 G tjensen@westminstercollege.edu
JENSEN, Tyler 307-675-0777 502 F tjensen@sheridan.edu
JENSEN, Valerie 408-855-5464.. 74 D valerie.jensen@missioncollege.edu
JENSON, Hal, B 269-337-4400 233 D
JENSON, Jody 406-477-6215 263 D jjenson@cdkc.edu
JENSON, John 671-735-2694 505 E jjenson@triton.uog.edu
JENT, Laura 931-393-1544 425 C ljent@mscc.edu
JENUWIN, Daniel 248-341-2138 229 A djenuwin@oaklandcc.edu
JENUWINE, Dan, J 248-341-2035 229 A djjenuwi@oaklandcc.edu
JEON, Isaac 323-643-0301.. 25 L
JEON, John 213-487-0150.. 41 I
JEONG, Hayoung 213-385-2322.. 75 D hayoungjeong@wmu.edu
JEONG, Peter, K 973-748-9000 276 A peter_jeong@bloomfield.edu
JEONG, Seongeun 909-623-0302.. 59 A
JEONG, Wooseob 620-341-5203 172 L wjeong1@emporia.edu
JEPPESEN, Vicki 715-675-3331 500 E jeppesen@ntc.edu
JEPSON, Darla 815-802-8832 140 D djepson@kcc.edu
JERABEK, Megan 610-436-2205 396 A mjerabek@wcupa.edu
JERAK, Susan 630-942-3324 135 A jeraks@cod.edu
JERALDS, Jeri Ann 314-837-6777 258 J jjeralds@stlchristian.edu
JERDAN, David 215-968-8184 379 G david.jerdan@bucks.edu
JERDINE, Kimberly 248-204-3943 226 G kosantows@ltu.edu
JEREBKO, Peter, J 716-851-1221 299 F jerebko@ecc.edu
JEREMIAH, David 619-201-8995.. 65 A david.jeremiah@socalsem.edu
JEREMIAH, Jacob 847-638-1640 145 G jjeremia@oakton.edu
JERGOVIC, Diana 626-395-6214.. 29 C jergovic@caltech.edu
JERMAN, Willa, H 919-866-5701 338 G whjerman@waketech.edu
JERMIER, James 563-387-1506 167 E jermja01@luther.edu
JERMIER, Jim 319-273-2487 163 B jim.jermier@uni.edu

JOHNSON, Anna .... 740-753-6553 354 A johnsona@hocking.edu
JOHNSON, Anne .... 651-423-8000 237 H
JOHNSON, Antoinette ... 757-925-6340 475 E ajohnson@pdc.edu
JOHNSON, April .... 301-860-4406 203 C ajohnson@bowiestate.edu
JOHNSON, April .... 334-670-3402.... 7 C acjohnson@troy.edu
JOHNSON, Arvid, C ...... 815-740-3369 151 J ajohnson@stfrancis.edu
JOHNSON, Ashlee .... 314-392-2305 256 C ashlee.johnson@mobap.edu
JOHNSON, Ashlee .... 314-392-2305 256 C johnsona@mobap.edu
JOHNSON, Autumn .... 310-954-4347.. 52 G ajohnson@msmu.edu
JOHNSON, Barbara .... 601-968-5974 245 C bjohnson@belhaven.edu
JOHNSON, Barbara .... 609-777-4351 284 B bjohnson@tesu.edu
JOHNSON, Barbara, J ... 479-968-0319.. 18 C bjohnson@atu.edu
JOHNSON, Barry .... 408-864-5678.. 43 C johnsonbarry@deanza.edu
JOHNSON, Barry .... 704-406-4440 329 A bjohnson@gardner-webb.edu
JOHNSON, Bart .... 218-322-2388 238 E bart.johnson@itascacc.edu
JOHNSON, Becky .... 903-983-8223 439 A rjohnson@kilgore.edu
JOHNSON, Ben .... 812-488-2862 161 A bj23@evansville.edu
JOHNSON, Betsy .... 419-372-2651 348 H betsyj@bgsu.edu
JOHNSON, Bill .... 952-446-4352 235 G
JOHNSON, Billy .... 404-627-2681 115 C billy.johnson@beulah.edu
JOHNSON, Bonnie .... 641-673-1036 170 F johnsonb@wmpenn.edu
JOHNSON, Brad .... 859-858-3511 178 I bjohnson@asbury.edu
JOHNSON, Brad .... 417-328-1805 259 L bjohnson@sbuniv.edu
JOHNSON, Brad .... 360-650-6400 486 F brad.johnson@wwu.edu
JOHNSON, Brandi .... 978-232-3096 209 B bjohnson@endicott.edu
JOHNSON, Brandon ...... 931-372-3636 426 E bjjohnson@tntech.edu
JOHNSON, Brenda .... 510-780-4500.. 47 J bjohnson@lifewest.edu
JOHNSON, Brenda .... 510-981-2830.. 56 E bjohnson@peralta.edu
JOHNSON, Brian .... 504-314-2486 191 B johnson@tulane.edu
JOHNSON, Brian, D ...... 208-885-6246 131 G johnsonb@uidaho.edu
JOHNSON, Brian, T ...... 219-464-6732 162 A brian.johnson1@valpo.edu
JOHNSON, Brooke .... 608-757-7654 499 C bjohnson97@blackhawk.edu
JOHNSON, Bruce .... 520-621-1081.. 16 G brucej@email.arizona.edu
JOHNSON, Bryan .... 610-526-1582 378 G bryan.johnson@theamericancollege.edu
JOHNSON, Bryan, M .... 205-726-4036.... 6 E bmjohnso@samford.edu
JOHNSON, Calvin, M ... 334-844-4546.... 4 E johncal@auburn.edu
JOHNSON, Carl .... 847-317-7005 150 H cjohnson@tiu.edu
JOHNSON, Carl .... 817-461-8741 430 H cjohnson@abu.edu
JOHNSON, Carla .... 831-759-6006.. 44 K cjohnson@hartnell.edu
JOHNSON, Carley .... 215-717-6380 400 J cajohnson@uarts.edu
JOHNSON, Carlos .... 843-349-2876 408 C
JOHNSON, Carol .... 906-227-2947 228 F carjohns@nmu.edu
JOHNSON, Carol .... 704-878-3225 336 C cjohnson@mitchellcc.edu
JOHNSON, Casie .... 507-453-2663 239 A cjohnson@southeastmn.edu
JOHNSON, Cassandra, M .... 903-927-3201 458 G cmjohnson@wileyc.edu
JOHNSON, Cassandra, M .... 903-927-3336 458 G cmjohnson@wileyc.edu
JOHNSON, Catherine .... 585-785-1212 300 B catherine.johnson@flcc.edu
JOHNSON, Catherine .... 207-780-4141 196 F catherine.johnson@maine.edu
JOHNSON, Cathy .... 478-218-3309 116 A cajohnson@centralgatech.edu
JOHNSON, Chad .... 952-888-4777 242 I cgjohnson@nwhealth.edu
JOHNSON, Charlene ..... 803-780-1039 414 E cjohnson@voorhees.edu
JOHNSON, Charles, R .. 812-888-4208 162 C president@vinu.edu
JOHNSON, Charles, S .. 334-724-4715.... 7 D cjohnson@tuskegee.edu
JOHNSON, Charlie .... 405-974-2315 370 K chjohnson@uco.edu
JOHNSON, Charlotte ..... 909-621-8277.. 63 E deanofstudentsoffice@scrippscollege.edu
JOHNSON, Charlotte ..... 870-584-1115.. 22 G cjohnson@cccua.edu
JOHNSON, Cheryl .... 707-826-4503.. 33 D cheryl.johnson@humboldt.edu
JOHNSON, Cheryl, L .... 412-624-8030 401 B clj@pitt.edu
JOHNSON, Chris .... 251-580-2222.... 1 I chris.johnson@coastalalabama.edu
JOHNSON, Chris .... 303-762-6924.. 79 H chris.johnson@denverseminary.edu
JOHNSON, Chris .... 315-443-1899 322 C cejohns@syr.edu
JOHNSON, Christine ..... 509-434-5006 480 A christine.johnson@ccs.spokane.edu
JOHNSON, Christine ..... 509-434-5006 479 I cjohnson@ccs.spokane.edu
JOHNSON, Christine, L 859-858-2176 178 H
JOHNSON, Christol ...... 214-860-2627 435 C christoljohnson@dcccd.edu
JOHNSON, Christopher 805-965-0581.. 62 C ckjohnson2@sbcc.edu
JOHNSON, Christopher 940-898-3206 451 F cjohnson44@twu.edu
JOHNSON, Cindi Beth .. 651-255-6137 243 D cbjohnson@unitedseminary.edu
JOHNSON, Cindy .... 620-235-4185 176 F cynthia.johnson@pittstate.edu
JOHNSON, Cindy, K ..... 816-604-1011 255 D cindy.johnson@mcckc.edu
JOHNSON, Clint .... 816-604-6538 255 E clint.johnson@mcckc.edu
JOHNSON, JR., Clyde .. 443-552-1659 199 H cjohnson01@mica.edu
JOHNSON, Connie .... 719-598-0200.. 79 C cjohnson@coloradotech.edu
JOHNSON, Cornelia ...... 302-857-1126.. 90 D cornelia@dtcc.edu
JOHNSON, Cornelius .... 214-860-2496 435 C cjohnson@dcccd.edu
JOHNSON, Courtney ..... 610-341-5840 383 D courtney.johnson@eastern.edu
JOHNSON, Craig .... 870-972-2852.. 17 G crjohnso@astate.edu
JOHNSON, Craig .... 847-491-3741 145 F
JOHNSON, Craig .... 320-222-5202 240 E craig.johnson@ridgewater.edu
JOHNSON, Croslena ..... 864-646-1568 413 A cjohnso5@tctc.edu
JOHNSON, Cuthrell ...... 336-750-2230 344 B johnsonc@wssu.edu
JOHNSON, Cynda Ann . 540-231-6000 477 A cajohnson@vt.edu
JOHNSON, Cynthia .... 360-486-8131 483 H cjohnson@stmartin.edu
JOHNSON, D. Nichole .. 614-236-6945 349 D njohnson@capital.edu
JOHNSON, Dacia .... 218-736-1512 239 B dacia.johnson@minnesota.edu
JOHNSON, Damon .... 512-505-3060 438 E damonjohnson@htu.edu
JOHNSON, Dan .... 763-417-8250 234 H djohnson@centralseminary.edu
JOHNSON, Danette ...... 804-524-5070 477 B dljohnson@vsu.edu
JOHNSON, Daniel .... 803-812-7353 413 G johns943@mailbox.sc.edu
JOHNSON, Daniel .... 701-662-1515 346 D dan.johnson@lrsc.edu
JOHNSON, Daniel .... 206-934-6709 484 B daniel.johnson@seattlecolleges.edu
JOHNSON, Daniel .... 918-444-4211 367 A johnso89@nsuok.edu
JOHNSON, Daniel, C .... 909-869-3047.. 30 D danielj@cpp.edu
JOHNSON, Daniel, W ... 414-443-8952 498 O daniel.johnson@wlc.edu
JOHNSON, Danny .... 714-895-8334.. 38 D djohnson@gwc.cccd.edu
JOHNSON, Danny .... 406-586-3585 263 J djohnson@montanabiblecollege.edu
JOHNSON, Dara .... 765-455-9533 156 D darnjohn@iu.edu
JOHNSON, Darryl .... 336-517-2358 327 B djohnson@bennett.edu
JOHNSON, Daryl .... 651-793-1227 238 H daryl.johnson@metrostate.edu
JOHNSON, David .... 314-838-8858 261 G djohnson@ugst.edu
JOHNSON, David .... 716-338-1002 303 D davejohnson@mail.sunyjcc.edu
JOHNSON, David .... 606-368-6031 178 D davidjohnson@alc.edu
JOHNSON, David .... 510-531-4911.. 56 H dmjohnson@peralta.edu
JOHNSON, David .... 812-855-8908 156 B vpem@indiana.edu
JOHNSON, David .... 256-824-6288.... 8 B david.johnson@uah.edu
JOHNSON, David, B ..... 812-855-8908 156 A dj44@indiana.edu
JOHNSON, David, J ...... 513-745-3202 365 B johnsond8@xavier.edu
JOHNSON, David, N ..... 919-209-2050 335 F dnjohnson@johnstoncc.edu
JOHNSON, Dañáe .... 229-226-1621 125 C djohnson@thomasu.edu
JOHNSON, Deadre .... 202-885-2721.. 90 J deadrej@american.edu
JOHNSON, Dean, L ...... 906-487-2668 227 E dean@mtu.edu
JOHNSON, Debbie .... 218-733-6904 238 F debra.johnson@lsc.edu
JOHNSON, Deborah ...... 419-251-1821 356 C deborah.johnson@mercycollege.edu
JOHNSON, Deborah ...... 618-634-3374 149 A deborahj@shawneecc.edu
JOHNSON, Deborah ...... 806-457-4200 436 G djohnson@fpctx.edu
JOHNSON, Deborah ...... 484-365-7429 389 C dejohnson@lincoln.edu
JOHNSON, Deidre .... 410-951-2654 203 D deijohnson@coppin.edu
JOHNSON, Deirdra, G .. 410-334-2902 204 F djohnson@worwic.edu
JOHNSON, Demetrius ... 703-284-5960 469 C demetrius.johnson@marymount.edu
JOHNSON, Denise .... 425-889-7829 482 F denise.johnson@northwestu.edu
JOHNSON, Dennis .... 719-549-3035.. 81 K dennis.johnson@pueblocc.edu
JOHNSON, Deshawn ..... 248-204-2117 226 G djohnson@ltu.edu
JOHNSON, Diana .... 479-725-4681.. 20 D djohnson@nwacc.edu
JOHNSON, Diane .... 518-828-4181 297 B diane.johnson@sunycgcc.edu
JOHNSON, Diane .... 801-883-8336 459 I djohnson@new.edu
JOHNSON, Dianna .... 508-373-9468 206 B diana.johnson@becker.edu
JOHNSON, Donielle, R . 972-860-7372 435 B doniellejohnson@dcccd.edu
JOHNSON, Donna .... 318-383-5758 191 F donnaj@latech.edu
JOHNSON, Donnie .... 309-672-5513 143 D djohnson@methodistcol.edu
JOHNSON, Doris .... 972-524-3341 445 C
JOHNSON, Doug .... 317-274-1383 156 F johnsodo@indiana.edu
JOHNSON, Doug .... 785-460-5411 172 H doug.johnson@colbycc.edu
JOHNSON, Doug .... 315-228-6624 296 F djohnson@colgate.edu
JOHNSON, Douglas, P . 207-581-1392 195 J douglasj@maine.edu
JOHNSON, Dreand .... 816-604-1206 255 D dreand.johnson@mcckc.edu
JOHNSON, Dustin .... 715-394-8122 498 B djohns75@uwsuper.edu
JOHNSON, Dustin .... 803-793-5170 409 C johnsond@denmarktech.edu
JOHNSON, Earl .... 918-631-3142 371 E earl-johnson@utulsa.edu
JOHNSON, Eartha .... 504-816-4723 186 D ejohnson@dillard.edu
JOHNSON, Edward .... 716-827-2456 323 D johnsone@trocaire.edu
JOHNSON, Edward .... 732-224-2899 276 B edjohnson@brookdalecc.edu
JOHNSON, Elise .... 586-498-4119 226 H johnsonem@macomb.edu
JOHNSON, Elizabeth ..... 203-596-4638.. 87 F ejohnson@post.edu
JOHNSON, Eric .... 815-224-0440 139 F eric_johnson@ivcc.edu
JOHNSON, Eric .... 219-464-5085 162 A eric.johnson@valpo.edu
JOHNSON, Eric .... 813-253-7560 101 A ejohnson71@hccfl.edu
JOHNSON, Eric .... 906-227-2313 228 F ericjohn@nmu.edu
JOHNSON, Eric .... 402-844-7236 268 J eric@northeast.edu
JOHNSON, Eric, C .... 617-627-5484 219 B eric.johnson@tufts.edu
JOHNSON, Eric, P .... 218-299-3447 235 E johnson@cord.edu
JOHNSON, Eric, S .... 207-859-4460 193 E eric.johnson@colby.edu
JOHNSON, Eric, W .... 985-549-3860 192 D ejohnson@selu.edu
JOHNSON, Erica .... 801-832-2206 461 G eljohnson@westminstercollege.edu
JOHNSON, Erik .... 541-885-1151 375 C erik.johnson@oit.edu
JOHNSON, Erin .... 865-981-8011 421 F erin.johnson@maryvillecollege.edu
JOHNSON, Faith .... 320-222-7645 240 E
JOHNSON, Felicia .... 804-342-1264 477 C fmjohnson@vuu.edu
JOHNSON, Fengling, M .... 651-628-3372 244 D fmjohnson@unwsp.edu
JOHNSON, Frank .... 620-947-3121 177 C frankj@tabor.edu
JOHNSON, G. David ..... 251-460-6261.... 8 F djohnson@southalabama.edu
JOHNSON, G. Michael . 816-654-7641 254 C mjohnson@kcumb.edu
JOHNSON, Gary .... 828-328-7112 330 F gary.johnson@lr.edu
JOHNSON, George .... 210-486-2174 429 G gjohnson@alamo.edu
JOHNSON, George, W .. 803-535-5077 407 G geojohnson@claflin.edu
JOHNSON, Glen .... 276-739-2467 476 C gjohnson@vhcc.edu
JOHNSON, Glenn .... 304-929-1495 488 G glennjohnson@ucwv.edu
JOHNSON, Gloria, C .... 615-963-7518 426 D gjohnson@tnstate.edu
JOHNSON, Greg .... 804-862-6100 470 I gjohnson@rbc.edu
JOHNSON, Greg, L .... 612-343-3545 242 H gljohnso@northcentral.edu
JOHNSON, Gregg .... 412-392-3898 397 A gjohnson@pointpark.edu
JOHNSON, Hannah .... 662-685-4771 245 D hjohnson@bmc.edu
JOHNSON, Harper .... 719-255-3594.. 83 B hjohnson@uccs.edu
JOHNSON, Heather .... 847-628-2597 140 C hjohnson@judsonu.edu
JOHNSON, Heather .... 810-237-6648 231 G hejo@umich.edu
JOHNSON, Heidi .... 217-333-1676 151 D johnso19@illinois.edu
JOHNSON, Holly .... 319-296-4283 166 B holly.johnson@hawkeyecollege.edu
JOHNSON, J. Lee .... 517-264-7108 230 E ljohnson@sienaheights.edu
JOHNSON, Jacqueline .. 731-881-3612 428 B jjohn253@utm.edu
JOHNSON, Jacy, R .... 515-294-5672 162 I jacyjohn@iastate.edu
JOHNSON, James, F .... 215-898-2173 400 K johnsonj@isc.upenn.edu
JOHNSON, Janet, L ...... 812-464-1924 161 E jljohnson@usi.edu
JOHNSON, Janett .... 575-769-4753 285 K janett.johnson@clovis.edu
JOHNSON, Jared, W ..... 202-994-1135.. 91 F jaredw@gwu.edu
JOHNSON, Jason .... 303-534-6270.. 78 L jason.johnson@colostate.edu
JOHNSON, Jason .... 423-869-6028 421 C jason.johnson02@lmunet.edu
JOHNSON, Jason .... 580-628-6240 367 D jason.johnson@noc.edu
JOHNSON, Jason .... 405-466-2957 366 F jason.k.johnson@langston.edu

JOHNSON, Jason .... 580-774-7152 370 C
jason.johnson@swosu.edu
JOHNSON, Jay .... 660-562-1277 257 E
jayj@nwmissouri.edu
JOHNSON, Jayde .... 217-245-3298 138 D
jayde.johnson@ic.edu
JOHNSON, Jeff .... 303-292-0015.. 79 G
jjohnson@denvercollegeofnursing.edu
JOHNSON, Jeff .... 318-628-4342 187 D
JOHNSON, Jeff .... 214-333-5759 434 I
jeff@dbu.edu
JOHNSON, Jeffrey .... 850-718-2237.. 96 F
johnsonj@chipola.edu
JOHNSON, Jeffrey, A .... 757-446-6100 466 I
johnsonja@evms.edu
JOHNSON, Jeffrey, C .... 561-237-7333 102 V
jjohnson@lynn.edu
JOHNSON, Jeffrey, W ... 515-294-6561 162 I
jjohnsn@iastate.edu
JOHNSON, Jennie .... 785-539-3571 175 E
jennie.johnson@mccks.edu
JOHNSON, Jennifer ...... 503-768-6626 373 G
jjj@lclark.edu
JOHNSON, Jenny .... 731-989-6378 420 C
jjohnson@fhu.edu
JOHNSON, Jerry .... 713-221-2720 453 B
johnsonj@uhd.edu
JOHNSON, Jesse .... 317-931-2387 154 C
jwjohnson@cts.edu
JOHNSON, Jessica .... 918-335-6854 368 G
jjohnson@okwu.edu
JOHNSON, Jessica, R ... 800-747-2687 144 A
jjohnson@monmouthcollege.edu
JOHNSON, Jill, K .... 904-632-5016 100 B
jill.johnson@fscj.edu
JOHNSON, Jill, R .... 864-587-4232 412 G
johnsoj@smcsc.edu
JOHNSON, Jim .... 620-235-4389 176 F
jjohnson@pittstate.edu
JOHNSON, Jodi .... 706-272-4475 117 C
jjohnson@daltonstate.edu
JOHNSON, Joel .... 863-667-5400 107 K
jkjohnson@seu.edu
JOHNSON, John, J .... 361-698-1269 436 C
jjohnson@delmar.edu
JOHNSON, JR.,
John, R .... 704-406-4303 329 A
jrjohnson@gardner-webb.edu
JOHNSON, Johnny .... 903-742-4910 458 G
jfjohnson@wileyc.edu
JOHNSON, Joselyn .... 410-837-5714 204 B
jjohnson@ubalt.edu
JOHNSON, Joyce .... 951-639-5439.. 52 I
jajohnso@msjc.edu
JOHNSON, Joyce, Y ..... 478-825-6253 118 A
johnsonj@fvsu.edu
JOHNSON, Joycelyn ..... 225-771-2770 190 G
joycelyn_johnson@subr.edu
JOHNSON, Joycelyn ..... 225-771-2770 190 H
joycelyn_johnson@subr.edu
JOHNSON, Juanita .... 850-599-3491 108 I
juanita.johnson@famu.edu
JOHNSON, Judith .... 212-961-3399 290 F
jjohnson@bankstreet.edu
JOHNSON, Julie .... 870-612-2165.. 22 I
julie.johnson@uaccb.edu
JOHNSON, Julie .... 309-556-3134 139 G
jjohns11@iwu.edu
JOHNSON, Julie .... 209-667-3351.. 33 C
jjohnson34@csustan.edu
JOHNSON, Julie .... 605-455-6011 416 B
jjohnson@olc.edu
JOHNSON, Julie, A .... 352-273-6309 109 F
johnson@cop.ufl.edu
JOHNSON, Kara .... 706-385-1477 123 C
kara.johnson@point.edu
JOHNSON, Karen .... 507-457-5300 241 F
kjohnson@winona.edu
JOHNSON, Karen .... 713-798-4951 431 I
karenj@bcm.edu
JOHNSON, Karen .... 903-813-2444 430 N
kjohnson@austincollege.edu
JOHNSON, Karen .... 610-526-6008 385 G
kgreen@harcum.edu
JOHNSON, Karen, A ...... 574-284-4571 160 C
kjohnson@saintmarys.edu
JOHNSON, Karen, D ..... 630-515-7268 143 G
kjohns@midwestern.edu
JOHNSON, Karen, L ..... 607-735-1827 299 D
kajohnson@elmira.edu
JOHNSON, Kathaerine .. 602-787-7106.. 13 E
kathaerine.johnson@paradisevalley.edu
JOHNSON, Kathryn .... 916-649-9600.. 26 F
kjohnson@asher.edu
JOHNSON, Kathy .... 269-488-4223 225 E
kjohnson@kvcc.edu
JOHNSON, Kathy .... 269-488-4223 225 E
mkjohnson@kvcc.edu
JOHNSON, Kathy, E ...... 317-274-4500 156 F
kjohnso@iupui.edu
JOHNSON, Kathy, J ...... 605-642-6512 416 I
kathy.johnson@bhsu.edu
JOHNSON, Kay .... 936-468-2206 445 F
JOHNSON, Keesha .... 501-337-5000.. 18 J
kjohnson@coto.edu
JOHNSON, Keith .... 831-477-3548.. 27 G
kejohnso@cabrillo.edu
JOHNSON, Keith .... 205-453-6300.. 92 G
JOHNSON, Keith .... 701-671-2218 346 E
keith.johnson@ndscs.edu
JOHNSON, Keith, V ...... 423-439-4445 419 J
johnsonk@etsu.edu
JOHNSON, Kellye .... 405-789-7661 370 B
kellye.johnson@swcu.edu
JOHNSON, Ken .... 903-233-3510 439 E
kenjohnson@letu.edu
JOHNSON, Kendall .... 512-568-3300.. 92 G
JOHNSON, Kendall .... 210-202-3700.. 92 G
JOHNSON, Kenneth ...... 850-644-9396 109 C
ken.johnson@fsu.edu
JOHNSON, Kenneth ...... 740-593-2247 359 G
johnsok9@ohio.edu
JOHNSON, Kent, M ...... 319-273-2122 163 B
kent.johnson@uni.edu
JOHNSON, Kenyatta ...... 229-430-2799 113 H
kenyatta.johnson@asurams.edu
JOHNSON, Kerry .... 562-985-4128.. 31 F
kerry.johnson@csulb.edu
JOHNSON, Kevin .... 620-341-5667 172 L
kjohnson@emporia.edu
JOHNSON, Kevin .... 651-450-3894 238 D
jjohnson@inverhills.edu
JOHNSON, Kevin, R ..... 530-752-7225.. 68 E
krjohnson@ucdavis.edu
JOHNSON, Kim .... 714-556-3610.. 72 F
officevpem@vanguard.edu
JOHNSON, Kim .... 507-389-7270 241 C
kim.johnson@southcentral.edu
JOHNSON, Kim, M .... 773-896-2400 133 L
kjohnson@ctschicago.edu
JOHNSON, Kimberly ..... 765-361-6209 162 E
johnsonk@wabash.edu
JOHNSON, Kimberly, T 301-447-5916 200 E
kjohnson@msmary.edu
JOHNSON, Kinte .... 707-476-4293.. 39 D
kinte-johnson@redwoods.edu
JOHNSON, Kristen .... 719-502-3363.. 81 F
kristen.johnson@ppcc.edu
JOHNSON, Kristina .... 518-320-1355 316 C
chancellor@suny.edu
JOHNSON, Kyle .... 808-739-8552 127 F
kyle.johnson@chaminade.edu
JOHNSON, LaJoyya .... 214-860-2111 435 C
lajoyya.johnson@dcccd.edu
JOHNSON, LaKenya ...... 229-931-2057 124 D
ljohnson@southgatech.edu
JOHNSON, Lamont .... 919-546-8434 340 E
lamont.johnson@shawu.edu
JOHNSON, Larry .... 870-236-6901.. 19 A
ljohnson@crc.edu
JOHNSON, Larry .... 202-685-2128 503 I
johnsonl@ndu.edu
JOHNSON, JR., Larry ... 602-285-7433.. 13 F
larry.johnson@phoenixcollege.edu
JOHNSON, Latesha .... 757-822-1054 476 B
ldjohnson@tcc.edu
JOHNSON, Laura .... 704-216-6029 330 H
ljohnson@livingstone.edu
JOHNSON, Laura .... 870-574-4513.. 21 E
ljohnson@sautech.edu
JOHNSON, Laura .... 410-778-7204 204 D
ljohnson3@washcoll.edu
JOHNSON, Laura .... 906-217-4022 221 O
lauralee.johnson@baycollege.edu
JOHNSON, Laura, T ...... 520-621-3175.. 16 G
ltj@email.arizona.edu
JOHNSON, Laurie .... 605-995-2901 415 C
laurie.johnson@dwu.edu
JOHNSON, Lawrence, J 513-556-2322 362 D
lawrence.johnson@uc.edu
JOHNSON, Le Keisha ... 210-567-2651 456 C
johnsonld@uthscsa.edu
JOHNSON, Leda .... 623-935-8868.. 13 A
leda.johnson@estrellamountain.edu
JOHNSON, Lee Ann ...... 229-333-5666 126 G
1493mgr@follett.com
JOHNSON, Lennor .... 760-355-6472.. 45 I
lennor.johnson@imperial.edu
JOHNSON, Les .... 218-281-8345 244 A
ljohnson@umn.edu
JOHNSON, Leslie .... 706-872-8072 118 E
ljohnson@highlands.edu
JOHNSON, Leslie .... 626-396-2200.. 26 E
leslie.johnson@artcenter.edu
JOHNSON, Leslie, R ..... 217-786-2848 142 B
leslie.johnson@llcc.edu
JOHNSON, Levester ...... 309-438-5451 139 E
ljohn13@ilstu.edu
JOHNSON, Lewis .... 850-599-3276 108 I
lewis.johnson@famu.edu
JOHNSON, Lillian .... 410-337-6040 198 G
lillian.johnson@goucher.edu
JOHNSON, Lillian, T ...... 323-953-4000.. 48 I
johnsolj@lacitycollege.edu
JOHNSON, Lindsay .... 618-833-3399 149 A
lindsayj@shawneecc.edu
JOHNSON, Linsay .... 402-280-2703 266 I
lindsayjohnson@creighton.edu
JOHNSON, Lisa .... 701-328-4143 345 B
lisa.a.johnson@ndus.edu
JOHNSON, Lisa .... 407-646-2391 105 M
adjohnson@rollins.edu
JOHNSON, Lisa .... 631-632-6265 317 D
lisa.johnson@stonybrook.edu
JOHNSON, Lisa .... 701-328-4143 345 B
lisa.a.johnson@ndus.edu
JOHNSON, Lisa .... 423-636-7305 427 B
ljohnson@tusculum.edu
JOHNSON, Lisa .... 804-862-6100 470 I
lsjohnson@rbc.edu
JOHNSON, Lisa, K .... 262-243-5700 493 B
lisa.johnson@cuw.edu
JOHNSON, Liz .... 512-448-8621 442 M
ekjohnson@stedwards.edu
JOHNSON, Lizzie .... 479-575-4140.. 21 G
ejohns@uark.edu
JOHNSON, Lori .... 208-282-3899 130 H
johnlori@isu.edu
JOHNSON, Louise, N ... 563-589-0200 170 D
ljohnson@wartburgseminary.edu
JOHNSON, Lydia .... 907-564-8269.... 9 D
ljohnson@alaskapacific.edu
JOHNSON, Lynn .... 970-491-1550.. 78 M
lynn.johnson@colostate.edu
JOHNSON, Lynn .... 631-632-6151 317 D
lynn.johnson@stonybrook.edu
JOHNSON, Lynn .... 218-755-2068 237 E
lynn.johnson@bemidjistate.edu
JOHNSON, Lynn .... 541-440-7690 377 C
lynn.johnson@umpqua.edu
JOHNSON, Lynne .... 907-796-6416.. 10 B
lejohnson@alaska.edu
JOHNSON, M. Eric .... 615-322-2534 428 D
eric.johnson@vanderbilt.edu
JOHNSON, Maggie .... 972-708-7573 435 H
maggie_johnson@diu.edu
JOHNSON, Malonda ...... 740-351-3484 360 K
mjohnson@shawnee.edu
JOHNSON, Marc .... 775-784-4805 271 F
marc.johnson@unr.edu
JOHNSON, Marco .... 661-726-1911.. 68 B
marco.johnson@uav.edu
JOHNSON, Marcus .... 702-651-4148 271 A
marcus.johnson@csn.edu
JOHNSON, Maren, A ..... 701-788-4743 345 E
allison.johnson.3@mayvillestate.edu
JOHNSON, Marguerite .. 617-274-3377 216 B
peg.johnson@mcphs.edu
JOHNSON, Maria .... 909-748-8333.. 71 G
maria_johnson@redlands.edu
JOHNSON,
Marianne, H .... 215-699-5700 388 E
mjohnson@lsb.edu
JOHNSON, Marie .... 657-278-2638.. 31 E
mariejohnson@fullerton.edu
JOHNSON, Marie, D ...... 802-656-5700 463 E
marie.johnson@uvm.edu
JOHNSON, Mark .... 507-389-2555 239 C
mark.johnson@mnsu.edu
JOHNSON, Mark .... 704-894-2681 328 F
majohnson@davidson.edu
JOHNSON, Mark .... 651-690-6824 242 R
majohnson6@stkate.edu
JOHNSON, Mark .... 919-735-5151 338 H
mrjohnson@waynecc.edu
JOHNSON, Martin .... 225-578-9294 188 I
martinj@lsu.edu
JOHNSON, Marviette ..... 513-487-3215 301 E
mjohnson@huc.edu
JOHNSON, Mary .... 334-291-4973.... 1 H
mary.johnson@cv.edu
JOHNSON, Mary .... 919-760-8535 331 B
mbjohnson@meredith.edu
JOHNSON, Mary Jean .. 419-358-3272 348 G
johnsonmj@bluffton.edu
JOHNSON, Matt .... 906-217-4134 221 O
matt.c.johnson@baycollege.edu
JOHNSON, Matthew ...... 413-205-3532 205 A
matthew.johnson@aic.edu
JOHNSON, Megan .... 302-622-8000.. 89 E
mjohnson@dcad.edu
JOHNSON, Melanie .... 817-272-2099 454 J
melanie.johnson@uta.edu
JOHNSON, Melissa .... 701-671-2520 346 E
melissa.j.johnson@ndscs.edu
JOHNSON, Melvina .... 866-492-5336 244 F
melvina.johnson@laureate.net
JOHNSON, Meredith, G 404-814-8813 125 G
mgurley@uga.edu
JOHNSON, Micah .... 209-476-7840.. 66 G
mjohnson@clc.edu
JOHNSON, Michael .... 216-397-4281 354 I
president@jcu.edu
JOHNSON, Michael .... 903-468-8175 447 B
michael.johnson@tamuc.edu
JOHNSON, Michael .... 713-743-8859 452 E
cmj@uh.edu
JOHNSON, Michael .... 615-248-7735 427 A
mjohnson@trevecca.edu
JOHNSON, Michael, A .. 205-929-1851.... 6 B
JOHNSON, Michael, C . 404-627-2681 115 C
michael.johnson@beulah.edu
JOHNSON, Michael, C . 214-860-2167 435 C
mcjohnson@dcccd.edu
JOHNSON, Michael, D . 407-823-1911 109 E
michael.johnson@ucf.edu
JOHNSON, Michael, L .. 270-824-8567 181 G
michael.johnson@kctcs.edu
JOHNSON, Michele .... 253-864-3100 483 D
mjohnson@pierce.ctc.edu
JOHNSON, Michelle ...... 631-420-2369 321 B
michelle.johnson@farmingdale.edu
JOHNSON, Michelle ...... 626-815-4550.. 26 H
mmjohnson@apu.edu
JOHNSON, Michelle ...... 309-341-5258 133 C
mljohnson@sandburg.edu
JOHNSON, Michelle ...... 605-688-4128 417 C
michelle.johnson@sdstate.edu
JOHNSON, Michelle ...... 414-229-6444 497 A
john3453@uwm.edu
JOHNSON, Mike .... 479-575-6601.. 21 G
mrj03@uark.edu
JOHNSON, Mike .... 713-743-8859 452 F
cmj@uh.edu
JOHNSON, Mike .... 405-585-5130 367 F
mike.johnson@okbu.edu
JOHNSON, Mike .... 541-506-6068 372 G
mjohnson@cgcc.edu
JOHNSON, Mikki .... 559-442-4600.. 66 E
mikki.johnson@fresnocitycollege.edu
JOHNSON, Mimi .... 334-420-4243.... 3 H
mjohnson@trenholmstate.edu
JOHNSON, Mitchell .... 336-334-4822 335 A
mjohnson@gtcc.edu
JOHNSON, Monika, L ... 901-333-5065 426 A
mljohnson@southwest.tn.edu
JOHNSON, Morgan .... 858-513-9240.. 26 G
morgan.johnson@ashford.edu
JOHNSON, Morgan .... 605-882-5284 415 F
morgan.johnson@lakeareatech.edu
JOHNSON, Nakikke .... 662-846-4646 245 H
njohnson@deltastate.edu
JOHNSON, Nancy .... 952-885-5428 242 I
njohnson@nwhealth.edu
JOHNSON, Nathan .... 616-538-2330 224 C
njohnson@gracechristian.edu
JOHNSON, Neil, A .... 303-867-1155.. 84 E
johnson@taft.edu
JOHNSON, Nellie .... 402-354-7014 268 C
nellie.johnson@methodistcollege.edu
JOHNSON, Nina .... 218-755-3760 237 E
nina.johnson@bemidjistate.edu
JOHNSON, Pam .... 256-835-5456.... 2 B
pjohnson@gadsdenstate.edu
JOHNSON, Pamela, D ... 937-766-7765 349 G
johnsonp@cedarville.edu
JOHNSON, Patricia .... 202-274-5946.. 93 C
patricia.johnson3@udc.edu
JOHNSON, Patricia, A .. 610-758-3178 388 J
paj214@lehigh.edu

JOHNSON, Patrick .... 240-567-5288 200 C
patrick.johnson@montgomerycollege.edu
JOHNSON, Patrick, H ... 615-327-6061 422 A
pjohnson@mmc.edu
JOHNSON, Paul .... 404-727-7707 117 F
rpaul.johnson@emory.edu
JOHNSON, Paul, C .... 303-273-3280.. 78 I
presoffice@mines.edu
JOHNSON, Paula, A ..... 781-283-2237 219 D
pjohnson@wellesley.edu
JOHNSON, CRM,
Paula, J .... 858-534-2552.. 69 D
pjjohnson@ucsd.edu
JOHNSON, Paulette, M . 269-471-3275 221 B
JOHNSON, Peggy, A .... 814-865-2631 392 B
paj6@psu.edu
JOHNSON, Peter, B ...... 701-777-2731 345 C
peter.johnson@und.edu
JOHNSON, Phil .... 706-385-1000 123 C
pjohnson@teamnational.com
JOHNSON, Philip .... 906-487-7201 223 K
philip.johnson@finlandia.edu
JOHNSON, Philip, M .... 503-255-0332 374 D
pjohnson@multnomah.edu
JOHNSON, Phill .... 334-244-3202.... 4 F
pjohns23@aum.edu
JOHNSON, Phillip .... 205-391-2665.... 3 E
pjohnson@sheltonstate.edu
JOHNSON, Quentin, R .. 434-949-1000 475 H
quentin.johnson@southside.edu
JOHNSON, R .... 504-283-8822 186 D
JOHNSON, Rachel .... 916-660-8103.. 63 I
rjohnson45@sierracollege.edu
JOHNSON, Rachelle ...... 502-597-5824 182 H
rachelle.johnson@kysu.edu
JOHNSON, Ralph .... 301-891-4028 204 C
rejohnson@wau.edu
JOHNSON, Ralph, F ..... 706-542-7369 125 G
rfj@uga.edu
JOHNSON, Rana .... 207-509-7140 195 H
rjohnson@unity.edu
JOHNSON, Randi .... 406-377-9401 263 E
rjohnson@dawson.edu
JOHNSON, Randolph .... 864-644-5220 412 E
rjohnson@swu.edu
JOHNSON, Randy .... 217-228-5432 146 F
johnsra@quincy.edu
JOHNSON, Raniyah ...... 408-223-6768.. 61 L
raniyah.johnson@evc.edu
JOHNSON, Rebecca ...... 541-322-3100 375 D
rebecca.johnson@osucascades.edu
JOHNSON, Rebecca, D . 203-932-7176.. 89 A
rjohnson@newhaven.edu
JOHNSON, Rebecca, J .. 703-784-2105 503 H
JOHNSON, Rhea .... 925-969-3300.. 46 H
rjohnson1@jfku.edu
JOHNSON, Richard .... 870-236-6901.. 19 A
rjohnson@crc.edu
JOHNSON, Richard, A .. 864-597-4090 414 H
johnsonra@wofford.edu
JOHNSON, Rick .... 239-590-7072 108 K
rjohnson@wgcu.edu
JOHNSON, Robert .... 928-524-7695.. 14 J
robert.johnson@npc.edu
JOHNSON, Robert .... 973-972-4538 282 A
rjohnson@njms.rutgers.edu
JOHNSON, Robert, E .... 508-999-8004 211 F
chancellor@umassd.edu
JOHNSON, Robert, E .... 913-667-5715 172 C
rjohnson@cbts.edu
JOHNSON, Robert, E .... 704-687-8242 342 E
robejohn@uncc.edu
JOHNSON, Roberta, L .. 515-294-0109 162 I
rljohns@iastate.edu
JOHNSON, Rodney .... 937-766-4114 349 G
johnsonr@cedarville.edu
JOHNSON, Roger .... 540-261-8400 471 H
roger.johnson@svu.edu
JOHNSON, Romaneir .... 510-466-7282.. 56 D
rjohnson@peralta.edu
JOHNSON, Ronald .... 714-432-5605.. 38 E
rgjohnson@occ.cccd.edu
JOHNSON, Ronald, W ... 310-206-0401.. 69 A
rojohnso@saonet.ucla.edu
JOHNSON, Ronnie, J .... 903-586-2501 431 G
ronnie.johnson@bmats.edu
JOHNSON, Rory .... 707-465-2300.. 39 D
rory-johnson@redwoods.edu
JOHNSON, Ruben .... 972-860-8161 435 A
rjohnson@dcccd.edu
JOHNSON, JR.,
Rushton .... 865-694-6552 425 F
rwjohnson2@pstcc.edu
JOHNSON, Russell, R ... 207-859-4776 193 E
margaret.mcfadden@colby.edu
JOHNSON, Ryan .... 501-205-8815.. 18 H
rjohnson@cbc.edu
JOHNSON, Sabrina, C .. 540-654-1213 472 I
sjohnson@umw.edu
JOHNSON, Sabrina, J ... 920-923-8082 494 A
sjjohnson41@marianuniversity.edu
JOHNSON, Sandra .... 661-726-1911.. 68 B
sandra.johnson@uav.edu
JOHNSON, Sandra, S ... 585-475-2267 313 A
ssjvsa@rit.edu
JOHNSON, Sarah .... 419-448-3039 361 J
depughst@tiffin.edu
JOHNSON, Scott .... 831-479-5663.. 27 G
scjohnso@cabrillo.edu
JOHNSON, Scott .... 810-762-3160 231 G
scotjohn@umich.edu
JOHNSON, Scott .... 419-448-2280 353 H
sjohnson@heidelberg.edu
JOHNSON, Scott .... 714-449-7439.. 51 A
scottjohnson@ketchum.edu
JOHNSON, Scott .... 715-682-1369 495 C
skjohnson@northland.edu
JOHNSON, Scott .... 336-838-6141 339 B
sajohnson366@wilkescc.edu
JOHNSON, Sean .... 707-664-4032.. 34 C
spjohnson@sonoma.edu
JOHNSON, Sean .... 701-252-3467 347 C
sean.johnson@uj.edu
JOHNSON, Seth .... 716-375-2382 313 F
sjohnson@sbu.edu
JOHNSON, Sharon .... 314-516-6817 261 D
sharon_johnson@umsl.edu
JOHNSON, Sharon .... 262-564-3164 499 F
johnsonsh@gtc.edu
JOHNSON, Shatealy ...... 912-443-5347 124 A
sjohnson@savannahtech.edu
JOHNSON, Sheila, G .... 405-744-6321 368 B
sheila.johnson@okstate.edu
JOHNSON, Sheila, M ... 727-376-6911 111 G
registrar@trinitycollege.edu
JOHNSON, Shelia .... 304-327-4040 489 P
sjohnson@bluefieldstate.edu
JOHNSON, Sherrick, L . 706-771-4008 114 J
sjohnson@augustatech.edu
JOHNSON, Shirley .... 763-424-0776 239 G
sjohnson@nhcc.edu
JOHNSON, Sonia .... 870-236-6901.. 19 A
sjohnson@crc.edu
JOHNSON, Sonya .... 803-705-4815 407 A
sonya.johnson@benedict.edu
JOHNSON, Stacey .... 718-368-1193 304 F
sjohnson@libi.edu
JOHNSON, Stacey, R .... 407-582-2216 112 K
srjohnson@valenciacollege.edu
JOHNSON, Stacy .... 248-689-8282 232 A
sjohnso6@walshcollege.edu
JOHNSON, Stephanie ... 573-875-7357 251 F
sgjohnson@ccis.edu
JOHNSON, Stephanie ... 704-886-6500.. 92 G
JOHNSON, Stephen ...... 626-812-3020.. 26 H
sjohnson@apu.edu
JOHNSON, Stephen ...... 214-305-9500 429 B
scj98d@acu.edu
JOHNSON, Steve .... 504-280-6303 189 E
sgjohnso@uno.edu
JOHNSON, Steve .... 913-360-7415 171 D
stevej@benedictine.edu
JOHNSON, Steven .... 816-604-5396 255 F
steven.johnson@mcckc.edu
JOHNSON, Steven .... 816-604-6748 255 E
steven.johnson@mcckc.edu
JOHNSON, Steven .... 906-635-2160 226 E
sjohnson18@lssu.edu
JOHNSON, Steven, L .... 937-512-2525 361 A
president@sinclair.edu
JOHNSON, Susan .... 775-831-1314 272 D
sjohnson@sierranevada.edu
JOHNSON, Susan, E ..... 651-631-5333 244 D
snjohnson@unwsp.edu
JOHNSON, Suzanne ...... 253-833-9111 481 F
sjohnson@greenriver.edu
JOHNSON, Tamara .... 312-662-4043 131 H
tajohnson@adler.edu
JOHNSON, Tammy .... 304-696-3161 490 D
johnson73@marshall.edu
JOHNSON, Tara .... 863-680-4110.. 99 H
tjohnson@flsouthern.edu
JOHNSON, Tara .... 229-903-3622 113 H
tara.johnson@asurams.edu
JOHNSON, Tardis .... 212-217-3082 299 H
tardis_johnson@fitnyc.edu
JOHNSON, TaRita .... 616-526-6484 222 A
tdj4@calvin.edu
JOHNSON, Tasha .... 252-527-6223 335 G
tvjohnson90@lenoircc.edu
JOHNSON, Ted .... 858-822-5949.. 69 D
edjohnson@ucsd.edu
JOHNSON, Teisha .... 312-949-7407 138 E
tjohnson@ico.edu
JOHNSON, Tera .... 216-373-5181 358 B
tjohnson@ndc.edu
JOHNSON, Teresa .... 573-840-9660 260 I
tjohnson@trcc.edu
JOHNSON, Terrence ..... 231-843-5874 232 J
tjohnson@westshore.edu
JOHNSON, Terri .... 512-863-1342 445 D
tjohnson@southwestern.edu
JOHNSON, Terry, L .... 937-481-2222 364 E
terry_johnson@wilmington.edu
JOHNSON, Theodore ..... 630-889-6512 144 G
tjohnson@nuhs.edu
JOHNSON, Thomas ...... 323-343-3488.. 32 A
tjohnson@cslanet.calstatela.edu
JOHNSON, Thomas ...... 641-628-5276 163 E
johnsont@central.edu
JOHNSON, Thomas, A .. 409-882-3314 450 A
thomas.johnson@lsco.edu
JOHNSON, Thomasine .. 202-319-6065.. 91 B
johnsotn@cua.edu
JOHNSON, Tianna .... 507-457-1635 243 B
tpjohnso@smumn.edu
JOHNSON, Tiffany .... 870-972-3025.. 17 G
tijohnson@astate.edu
JOHNSON, Timothy ...... 336-334-5636 343 A
tjjohns3@uncg.edu
JOHNSON, Timothy ...... 843-953-5770 408 E
johnsonts@cofc.edu
JOHNSON, Todd, K ...... 757-683-3415 469 G
tjohnso@odu.edu
JOHNSON, Tom .... 910-221-2224 329 B
tjohnson@gcd.edu
JOHNSON, Tonjanita .... 865-974-8886 427 F
tonjanita.johnson@tennessee.edu
JOHNSON, Tony .... 903-983-8102 439 A
tjohnson@kilgore.edu
JOHNSON, Tony .... 206-592-4320 481 H
tjohnson@highline.edu
JOHNSON, Toya .... 312-850-7267 134 H
tjohnson616@ccc.edu
JOHNSON, Tracci .... 818-252-5114.. 75 C
tracci.johnson@woodbury.edu
JOHNSON, Tracey .... 618-634-3271 149 A
traceyj@shawneecc.edu
JOHNSON, Tracie .... 615-277-7424 428 F
tjohnson@watkins.edu
JOHNSON, Tracy .... 214-860-2033 435 C
tracy.johnson@dcccd.edu
JOHNSON, Trent .... 270-534-3302 182 F
trent.johnson@kctcs.edu
JOHNSON, Tricia .... 303-360-4735.. 79 D
tricia.johnson@ccaurora.edu
JOHNSON, Troy .... 334-244-3110.... 4 F
ljohns90@aum.edu
JOHNSON, Troy .... 817-272-5401 454 J
troy.johnson@uta.edu
JOHNSON, Trygve, D ... 616-395-7145 225 B
johnsont@hope.edu
JOHNSON, Ursa .... 540-365-4323 467 I
ujohnson@ferrum.edu
JOHNSON, Valen, E ..... 979-845-7361 446 G
vejohnson@tamu.edu
JOHNSON, Velena .... 225-771-5050 190 G
velena_johnson@subr.edu
JOHNSON, Veronica ..... 773-947-6319 142 J
vjohnson@mccormick.edu
JOHNSON, Vicki .... 731-989-6095 420 C
vjohnson@fhu.edu
JOHNSON, Victoria, D .. 504-865-5591 191 B
victoria@tulane.edu
JOHNSON, Vincent .... 210-436-3684 443 A
vjohnson@stmarytx.edu
JOHNSON, Vivian .... 937-529-2201 362 A
vjohnson@united.edu
JOHNSON, Wallace .... 909-384-8502.. 59 I
wjohnson@sbccd.cc.ca.us
JOHNSON, Walter .... 864-977-7068 411 E
walter.johnson@ngu.edu
JOHNSON, Warren .... 601-979-1541 246 E
warren.b.johnson@jsums.edu
JOHNSON, Wayne, E .... 704-406-4269 329 A
wjohnson@gardner-webb.edu
JOHNSON, Wendy .... 225-743-8500 188 B
wjohnson@rpcc.edu
JOHNSON, Wesley .... 910-892-3178 329 F
JOHNSON, William .... 510-885-4602.. 31 C
william.johnson@csueastbay.edu
JOHNSON, William .... 734-973-3490 232 B
billjohnson@wccnet.edu
JOHNSON, William, H .. 203-254-4000.. 86 I
wjohnson@fairfield.edu
JOHNSON, William, P .. 314-977-2788 259 H
william.johnson@slu.edu
JOHNSON, Willie .... 715-232-1151 498 A
johnsonw@uwstout.edu
JOHNSON, Zak .... 218-755-2226 237 E
zachary.johnson@bemidjistate.edu
JOHNSON-BAILEY,
Juanita .... 706-542-2846 125 G
jjb@uga.edu
JOHNSON-CASSULO,
Nancy .... 208-459-5680 130 D
njohnsoncassulo@collegeofidaho.edu
JOHNSON-CHANDLER,
Sabrina .... 718-262-2719 295 F
sjohnson25@york.cuny.edu
JOHNSON-CRAMER,
Michael .... 781-891-2921 206 D
mjohnsoncramer@bentley.edu
JOHNSON-DEAN, Carol 901-435-1676 421 A
JOHNSON-HAWKINS,
Alma .... 909-447-2534.. 37 F
ajohnson-hawkins@cst.edu
JOHNSON HOLSINGER,
Valerie .... 214-777-6433 442 A
JOHNSON-HOUSTON,
Debbie, L .... 337-475-5716 192 A
djohnsonhouston@mcneese.edu
JOHNSON JONES,
Sylvia, M .... 847-543-2404 135 B
cps086@clcillinois.edu
JOHNSON-MILLS,
Jessica .... 818-401-1151.. 39 G
jjohnsonmills@columbiacollege.edu
JOHNSON RENVALL,
Poppy .... 505-224-4435 285 J
pjohnsonrenvall@cnm.edu
JOHNSON-RUSCANSKY,
Abigail .... 207-985-7976 194 C
abigail@landingschool.edu
JOHNSON SHAHEED,
Karen .... 301-860-3555 203 C
kshaheed@bowiestate.edu
JOHNSON-SHAW,
Joanne .... 252-862-1308 337 C
jjohnson-shaw@roanokechowan.edu
JOHNSON SUSKI,
Katharine .... 515-294-0815 162 I
ksuski@iastate.edu
JOHNSON-TAYLOR,
Sabrina .... 607-962-9385 320 F
sjohns49@corning-cc.edu
JOHNSON-WALKER,
Heather .... 334-556-2397.... 2 C
hwalker@wallace.edu
JOHNSON-WEEKS,
Demetria .... 713-313-7940 449 C
weeks_dj@tsu.edu
JOHNSRUD, Jason .... 202-462-2101.. 92 C
johnsrud@iwp.edu
JOHNSSON,
Magnus, H .... 804-827-1363 473 F
johnssonm@vcu.edu
JOHNSTON, Alysia .... 620-223-2700 173 C
alysiaj@fortscott.edu
JOHNSTON, Angela ...... 330-263-2313 351 C
ajohnston@wooster.edu
JOHNSTON, Ann .... 970-943-2493.. 84 D
afjohnston@western.edu
JOHNSTON, Barbara, A 972-985-3732 433 M
bjohnston@collin.edu
JOHNSTON, Brian .... 319-385-6241 167 A
brian.johnston@iw.edu
JOHNSTON, Brian .... 216-373-5252 358 B
bjohnston@ndc.edu
JOHNSTON, Brian, A .... 202-319-6425.. 91 B
johnston@cua.edu
JOHNSTON, Carol .... 213-477-2617.. 52 G
cjohnston@msmu.edu
JOHNSTON, Caroline .... 321-674-7400.. 99 B
cjohnston@fit.edu
JOHNSTON, Chad .... 318-678-6000 187 A
cjohnston@bpcc.edu

JONES, Donald ... 860-768-4751 88 H
djones@hartford.edu
JONES, Donald, A ... 502-371-8330 178 J
djones@ata.edu
JONES, Donald, E ... 803-754-4100 409 A
JONES, Doug ... 423-636-7322 427 B
djones@tusculum.edu
JONES, Douglas, W ... 805-565-6048 74 K
vpfinance@westmont.edu
JONES, Eddie, V ... 989-964-4228 230 B
evjones@svsu.edu
JONES, Edward ... 312-329-4354 144 B
edward.jones@moody.edu
JONES, JR., Edward ... 202-274-7441 93 C
ejones@udc.edu
JONES, Eli ... 979-845-4712 446 G
elijones@tamu.edu
JONES, Elizabeth, R ... 404-413-3003 119 E
bethjones@gsu.edu
JONES, Elliot ... 318-274-3811 191 E
jonese@gram.edu
JONES, Elliot ... 248-218-2036 229 J
ejones@rc.edu
JONES, Elwin ... 251-981-3771 5 B
elwin.jones@columbiasouthern.edu
JONES, Emily, M ... 413-542-2267 205 B
ejones@amherst.edu
JONES, Eric ... 641-628-5420 163 E
jonese@central.edu
JONES, Ericka ... 512-505-3035 438 E
edjones@htu.edu
JONES, Erin ... 619-260-4523 71 J
ekjones@sandiego.edu
JONES, Esther ... 508-793-7141 208 A
esjones@clarku.edu
JONES, II, Eugene, G ... 407-582-1635 112 K
ejones102@valenciacollege.edu
JONES, Faye, M ... 615-353-3556 425 D
faye.jones@nscc.edu
JONES, Garry ... 407-679-0100 100 K
gjones@fullsail.com
JONES, Garry ... 662-243-2643 246 A
gjones@eastms.edu
JONES, Garth ... 909-593-3511 70 D
gjones@laverne.edu
JONES, Gary ... 405-425-5904 367 G
gary.jones@oc.edu
JONES, Gena, W ... 575-646-1694 287 B
genaj@nmsu.edu
JONES, Gerald ... 850-201-6140 111 C
jonesge@tcc.fl.edu
JONES, Gerald ... 334-386-7600 5 D
gjones@faulkner.edu
JONES, Geraldine ... 724-938-4400 394 B
jones_gm@calu.edu
JONES, Gina ... 612-330-1051 233 K
jonesg@augsburg.edu
JONES, Gina, G ... 803-323-2194 414 G
jonesgg@winthrop.edu
JONES, Gloria ... 803-323-3900 414 G
jonesg@winthrop.edu
JONES, Gordon ... 208-426-2975 129 I
gojones@boisestate.edu
JONES, Harold ... 903-675-6256 452 B
hjones@tvcc.edu
JONES, Hollie ... 718-270-5010 295 A
hjones@mec.cuny.edu
JONES, J. Pernell ... 610-341-5948 383 D
pjones1@eastern.edu
JONES, James, C ... 334-699-2266 1 B
JONES, Jamie ... 319-363-1323 168 C
jjones@mtmercy.edu
JONES, Janice ... 270-707-3707 181 E
jjones0004@kctcs.edu
JONES, Jarian, R ... 770-220-7926 118 B
libray@gcuniv.edu
JONES, Jason ... 850-245-0466 108 H
jason.jones@flbog.edu
JONES, Jeannette ... 830-372-6061 449 B
jjones@tlu.edu
JONES, Jeff ... 407-823-1582 109 E
jeffrey.jones@ucf.edu
JONES, Jeff ... 928-226-4297 11 O
jeff.jones@coconino.edu
JONES, Jeff ... 909-687-1750 43 I
jeffjones@gs.edu
JONES, Jeffrey ... 610-399-2042 394 C
jjones@cheyney.edu
JONES, Jen ... 254-295-8645 453 E
jen.jones@umhb.edu
JONES, Jennifer ... 815-455-8770 143 A
jjones@mchenry.edu
JONES, Jennifer ... 201-200-3005 279 E
jjones@njcu.edu
JONES, Jennifer ... 304-367-4233 490 B
jennifer.jones@fairmontstate.edu
JONES, Jennifer ... 920-465-2111 496 E
jonesj@uwgb.edu
JONES, Jennifer ... 252-536-7254 335 B
JONES, Jenny ... 859-246-6653 180 K
jenny.jones@kctcs.edu
JONES, Jenny, B ... 662-472-9035 246 C
jbailey@holmescc.edu
JONES, Jenny, L ... 404-880-8549 116 D
jjones@cau.edu
JONES, Jeremy ... 541-962-3553 373 B
jdjones1@eou.edu
JONES, Jerry ... 254-519-5446 447 A
jerry.jones@tamuct.edu
JONES, Jessica ... 252-246-1221 339 C
jjones@wilsoncc.edu
JONES, Jill ... 309-438-3135 139 E
jajones2@ilstu.edu
JONES, Jim ... 517-787-0800 225 C
jonesjamesl@jccmi.edu
JONES, Jim ... 325-670-1207 437 F
jjones@hsutx.edu
JONES, Jim ... 972-860-8058 435 A
s.jimjones@dcccd.edu
JONES, John ... 316-978-7751 178 A
john.jones@wichita.edu
JONES, John ... 904-596-2304 111 F
jjones@tbc.edu
JONES, John ... 765-677-2387 157 D
john.jones@indwes.edu
JONES, John ... 479-788-7456 21 H
john.jones@uafs.edu
JONES, John, P ... 520-621-1112 16 G
jpjones@email.arizona.edu
JONES, III, John, R ... 205-996-0132 8 A
jrjones3@uab.edu
JONES, John, S ... 772-546-5534 101 B
johnjones@hsbc.edu
JONES, Jon ... 417-268-6049 250 G
jjones@gobbc.edu
JONES, Joree ... 334-291-4913 1 H
joree.jones@cv.edu
JONES, Joseph ... 678-359-5468 119 F
jjones1@gordonstate.edu
JONES, Joseph ... 559-453-2010 43 G
fpupres@fresno.edu
JONES, Josh ... 785-864-6414 177 D
joshjones@ku.edu
JONES, Joshua ... 309-677-1000 133 B
jejones@bradley.edu
JONES, Joshua ... 864-503-5093 414 D
jjones3@uscupstate.edu
JONES, Joy ... 386-481-2959 95 F
jonesjo@cookman.edu
JONES, Joy ... 304-865-6102 488 E
joy.jones@ovu.edu
JONES, Joyce ... 404-962-3105 126 F
joyce.jones@usg.edu
JONES, Joye ... 205-391-2283 3 E
jjones1@sheltonstate.edu
JONES, Judy ... 979-532-6561 458 F
judyj@wcjc.edu
JONES, Julia, A ... 801-581-7569 460 E
julia.jones@utah.edu
JONES, Justin, D ... 801-863-7578 461 A
justin.jones@uvu.edu
JONES, Kaiser ... 614-882-2551 353 A
JONES, Karen ... 803-323-3708 414 G
jonesk@winthrop.edu
JONES, Karen, S ... 478-289-2012 117 D
kjones@ega.edu
JONES, Kathy ... 713-348-5460 442 K
kjones@rice.edu
JONES, Katie ... 704-330-6758 333 D
katie.jones@cpcc.edu
JONES, Kayla ... 361-354-2532 433 C
kdjones@coastalbend.edu
JONES, Keisha ... 336-249-8186 334 A
keisha_jones@davidsonccc.edu
JONES, Kelli ... 317-738-8019 154 J
kjones2@franklincollege.edu
JONES, Kelly ... 802-586-7711 463 D
kjones@sterlingcollege.edu
JONES, Kelsey ... 678-664-0515 127 A
kelsey.jones@westgatech.edu
JONES, Ken ... 919-735-5151 338 H
kwjones@waynecc.edu
JONES, Kenneth, E ... 615-329-8738 419 K
kjones@fisk.edu
JONES, Kent ... 256-228-6001 3 B
jonesk@nacc.edu
JONES, Kevin ... 740-474-8896 358 F
kjones7@ohiochristian.edu
JONES, Kevin ... 518-736-3622 300 F
kevin.jones@fmcc.suny.edu
JONES, Kim ... 270-831-9617 181 D
kim.jones@kctcs.edu
JONES, Kim ... 270-824-8649 181 G
kim.jones@kctcs.edu
JONES, Kim ... 530-895-2298 27 F
joneski@butte.edu
JONES, Kim ... 903-823-3004 446 B
kimberly.jones@texarkanacollege.edu
JONES, Kimberly ... 904-256-7642 101 G
kmarian@ju.edu
JONES, Kimberly, B ... 334-670-3113 7 C
kbrink@troy.edu
JONES, Kirsten ... 425-564-2206 478 F
kirsten.jones@bellevuecollege.edu
JONES, Kona ... 217-875-7211 147 C
kona@richland.edu
JONES, Kristen ... 425-564-2260 478 F
kristen.jones@bellevuecollege.edu
JONES, Kristine ... 919-497-3217 330 I
kjones@louisburg.edu
JONES, L. Gregory ... 919-660-3434 328 G
gjones@div.duke.edu
JONES, Lance ... 386-752-1822 99 A
christopher.jones@fgc.edu
JONES, Lance ... 303-458-3673 82 E
ljones007@regis.edu
JONES, Landon ... 816-415-6335 262 F
jonesl@william.jewell.edu
JONES, Larry ... 443-885-3022 200 D
larry.jones@morgan.edu
JONES, Laura, A ... 928-523-9084 14 H
laura.jones@nau.edu
JONES, Laura, B ... 734-764-7423 231 E
laurabj@umich.edu
JONES, Laurene ... 609-586-4800 278 F
jonesl@mccc.edu
JONES, Laurie ... 229-430-4623 113 H
laurie.jones@asurams.edu
JONES, Lenroy ... 419-289-5067 348 A
ljones31@ashland.edu
JONES, Leonard ... 360-650-2953 486 F
leonard.jones@wwu.edu
JONES, II, LeRoy ... 773-995-2438 133 K
ljones27@csu.edu
JONES, Levi ... 816-268-5414 257 C
ljones@nts.edu
JONES, Liesl ... 908-709-7465 284 C
liesl.jones@ucc.edu
JONES, Linda ... 205-387-0511 1 D
linda.jones@bscc.edu
JONES, Linda, E ... 413-782-1247 219 F
linda.jones@wne.edu
JONES, Linda, T ... 240-895-3246 201 E
ltjones1@smcm.edu
JONES, Lindsey ... 337-421-6917 188 D
lindsey.jones@sowela.edu
JONES, Lisa ... 845-257-3216 317 B
jonesl@newpaltz.edu
JONES, Logan ... 816-271-4476 257 A
jones@missouriwestern.edu
JONES, Loree ... 856-225-6542 281 G
ldjones@camden.rutgers.edu
JONES, Louisa ... 203-857-7301 86 D
ljones@norwalk.edu
JONES, Luke ... 208-447-1005 129 I
lukejones@boisestate.edu
JONES, Marcia ... 678-466-4250 116 E
marciajones@clayton.edu
JONES, Marcus ... 318-357-5701 192 C
marcusj@nsula.edu
JONES, Marcy ... 217-479-7028 142 I
marcy.jones@mac.edu
JONES, Margaret ... 914-422-4043 311 E
mjones@pace.edu
JONES, Marian ... 704-378-1074 330 D
myjones@jcsu.edu
JONES, Marie ... 828-884-8248 327 C
jonesmf@brevard.edu
JONES, Marie ... 334-876-9284 2 D
marie.jones@wccs.edu
JONES, Marlynn ... 904-620-2513 110 A
marlynn.jones@unf.edu
JONES, Mary ... 805-289-6346 73 B
mjones@vcccd.edu
JONES, OP, Mary ... 517-264-7109 230 E
mjones@sienaheights.edu
JONES, Mary, O ... 845-575-3000 305 L
mary.jones@marist.edu
JONES, Matteel ... 864-250-8177 410 B
matteel.jones@gvltec.edu
JONES, Matthew ... 630-829-6135 132 E
mjones@ben.edu
JONES, Mautra ... 405-466-2937 366 F
mautra.jones@langston.edu
JONES, Megan ... 732-571-3465 279 B
mjones@monmouth.edu
JONES, Megan ... 423-323-0226 425 E
majones@northeaststate.edu
JONES, Melanie, E ... 803-327-8012 415 A
mjones@yorktech.edu
JONES, Melinda, L ... 901-678-2690 427 D
mljones6@memphis.edu
JONES, Melissa ... 864-622-6011 406 G
melissajones@andersonuniversity.edu
JONES, Melissa ... 217-854-5514 132 I
melissa.k.jones@blackburn.edu
JONES, Melissa, A ... 910-678-8474 334 D
jonesma@faytechcc.edu
JONES, Meredith ... 580-559-5668 366 C
mjones@ecok.edu
JONES, Michael ... 909-607-8585 37 G
michael_jones@kgi.edu
JONES, Michael ... 518-292-8615 313 D
jonesm4@sage.edu
JONES, Michael ... 412-578-6378 380 E
mbjones@carlow.edu
JONES, Mike ... 601-925-3819 247 C
jones01@mc.edu
JONES, Mike ... 434-544-8538 472 G
jones.mj@lynchburg.edu
JONES, Molly ... 513-618-1933 350 J
mjones@ccms.edu
JONES, Monica ... 859-985-3795 179 C
jonesmo@berea.edu
JONES, Monterrio ... 803-780-1209 414 E
mjones@voorhees.edu
JONES, Nancy ... 714-241-6209 38 C
njones@coastline.edu
JONES, Natalie ... 207-780-5113 196 F
natalie.jones@maine.edu
JONES, Nathaniel ... 951-571-6341 58 G
nathaniel.jones@mvc.edu
JONES, Ned, J ... 518-783-2423 315 J
jones@siena.edu
JONES, Nicholas ... 678-916-2600 114 I
JONES, Nicholas, P ... 814-865-2505 392 B
provost@psu.edu
JONES, Nicole ... 619-660-4302 44 H
nicole.jones@gcccd.edu
JONES, Nina ... 662-915-7690 249 D
nina@olemiss.edu
JONES, Nolan ... 972-825-7970 445 A
nojones@sagu.edu
JONES, Norm ... 316-942-4291 175 I
jonesn@newmanu.edu
JONES, Norm ... 413-542-5822 205 B
njones@amherst.edu
JONES, Olivia ... 919-530-7713 342 A
ojones@nccu.edu
JONES, Orion ... 419-434-4544 363 A
orion.jones@findlay.edu
JONES, Pam ... 501-882-8956 17 F
pljones@asub.edu
JONES, Para, M ... 330-494-6170 361 F
pjones@starkstate.edu
JONES, Parago ... 303-329-6355 78 K
dean@cstcm.edu
JONES, Patrice ... 703-892-5100 92 G
JONES, Patrice ... 301-548-5500 92 G
JONES, Patricia ... 301-736-3631 199 G
patricia.jones@msbbcs.edu
JONES, Patrick ... 904-256-7502 101 G
pjones15@ju.edu
JONES, Paul ... 478-825-6315 118 A
jonesp@fvsu.edu
JONES, Peter ... 415-575-6100 29 B
pjones@ciis.edu
JONES, Phil ... 772-546-5534 101 B
philjones@hsbc.edu
JONES, Philip ... 717-245-1509 382 F
jonesph@dickinson.edu
JONES, Randy ... 805-565-7048 74 K
rjones@westmont.edu
JONES, Randy, P ... 214-768-2146 444 E
rpjones@smu.edu
JONES, Rebecca ... 352-254-4119 111 E
rebecca.jones@taylorcollege.edu
JONES, Rebecca ... 503-255-0332 374 D
beccajones@multnomah.edu

JOSEPH, Cynthia .... 562-907-4830.. 75 A
cjoseph@whittier.edu
JOSEPH, Daniel, P .... 410-951-3549 203 D
djoseph@coppin.edu
JOSEPH, Darnell .... 713-313-1826 449 C
djoseph@tsu.edu
JOSEPH, James, E .... 315-445-4279 304 C
josepjae@lemoyne.edu
JOSEPH, Jann, L .... 678-407-5000 118 D
JOSEPH, Jerry .... 217-206-6003 151 C
gjose1@uis.edu
JOSEPH, Joanne .... 315-792-7326 321 E
joanne.joseph@sunypoly.edu
JOSEPH, Josh .... 212-960-0083 326 E
josh.joseph@yu.edu
JOSEPH, Laly .... 212-614-6153 311 H
laly.joseph@mountsinai.org
JOSEPH, Laura .... 631-420-2003 321 B
laura.joseph@farmingdale.edu
JOSEPH, Laurel .... 281-756-3513 429 I
ljoseph@alvincollege.edu
JOSEPH, Mark .... 740-284-5870 353 B
mjoseph@franciscan.edu
JOSEPH, Michael .... 312-369-7114 135 E
mijoseph@colum.edu
JOSEPH, Michiko .... 808-689-2710 128 G
msjoseph@hawaii.edu
JOSEPH, Nicole .... 208-282-2123 130 H
rosenico@isu.edu
JOSEPH, Noson .... 718-601-3523 326 D
njoseph@ytariverdale.org
JOSEPH, Patricia .... 484-365-7659 389 C
joseph@lincoln.edu
JOSEPH, Rabi .... 707-654-1782.. 32 B
JOSEPH, Sonya, F .... 407-582-7734 112 K
sjoseph@valenciacollege.edu
JOSEPH, Stephen, M .... 724-287-8711 380 A
steve.joseph@bc3.edu
JOSEPH, Susan .... 423-697-3136 424 E
susan.joseph@chattanoogastate.edu
JOSEPHSON, David .... 973-655-6956 279 C
josephsond@mail.montclair.edu
JOSEPHSON, Jyl .... 973-353-5125 282 B
jylj@newark.rutgers.edu
JOSEY, Peige .... 334-222-6591.... 2 I
pjosey@lbwcc.edu
JOSHEE, Jeet .... 562-985-4106.. 31 F
jeet.joshee@csulb.edu
JOSHEE, Jeet .... 562-985-8330.. 31 F
jeet.joshee@csulb.edu
JOSHI, Maulin .... 973-618-3519 276 D
mjoshi@caldwell.edu
JOSHUA, Donald .... 212-280-1462 323 H
djoshua@uts.columbia.edu
JOSHUA, Kazi .... 509-527-5158 486 H
joshuake@whitman.edu
JOSLIN, Michael .... 661-362-3260.. 38 H
michael.joslin@canyons.edu
JOSLIN, Randall .... 530-251-8836.. 47 F
rjoslin@lassencollege.edu
JOSS, Jamie .... 304-637-1342 487 I
jossj@dewv.edu
JOSSELL, Steven .... 662-621-4304 245 E
sjossell@coahomacc.edu
JOSSERAND,
Tamara, M .... 909-748-8840.. 71 G
tamara_josserand@redlands.edu
JOST, Muktha, B .... 336-285-2496 341 F
mjost@ncat.edu
JOST, Steve, A .... 301-860-4212 203 C
sjost@bowiestate.edu
JOUGHIN, Sarah .... 207-581-3437 195 J
joughin@maine.edu
JOUNG, Christina .... 636-327-4645 255 L
mio@midwest.edu
JOURDAN, Lee Ann ...... 317-738-8755 154 J
ljourdan@franklincollege.edu
JOUVENAS, Anthony ..... 334-556-2474.... 2 C
ajouvenas@wallace.edu
JOVEN, Robert .... 203-582-3468.. 87 G
robert.joven@quinnipiac.edu
JOWERS, Angel .... 205-652-3547.... 9 A
ajowers@uwa.edu
JOY, Alonzo, F .... 202-806-6100.. 92 B
JOY, Steaven .... 731-426-7523 420 I
sjoy@lanecollege.edu
JOYCE, Christine .... 317-632-5553 158 S
cjoyce@lincolntech.edu
JOYCE, Christopher, J .. 781-891-2003 206 D
cjoyce@bentley.edu
JOYCE, Colman .... 503-206-3205 377 F
cjoyce@uws.edu
JOYCE, SJ, Dan .... 610-660-3291 398 C
djoyce@sju.edu
JOYCE, Daniel .... 215-951-1881 387 C
joyced@lasalle.edu
JOYCE, David, C .... 828-884-8264 327 C
president@brevard.edu
JOYCE, Elizabeth .... 201-692-7071 277 K
ejoyce@fdu.edu
JOYCE, Gerard .... 610-282-1100 382 E
gerard.joyce@desales.edu
JOYCE, Jeff .... 828-884-8202 327 C
joycejj@brevard.edu
JOYCE, Kelly .... 812-866-7160 155 C
joyce@hanover.edu
JOYCE, Kevin .... 914-674-7775 306 F
kjoyce@mercy.edu
JOYCE, Kimberly .... 410-287-1022 197 H
kjoyce@cecil.edu
JOYCE, Maureen .... 617-588-1363 206 C
mjoyce@bfit.edu
JOYCE, Michelle .... 574-631-2786 161 C
mjoyce@nd.edu
JOYCE-BRADY, Jean, M 617-573-8260 219 A
jmjoyce-brady@suffolk.edu
JOYE, Teresa .... 510-649-2410.. 44 F
tjoye@gtu.edu
JOYNER, Barry .... 912-478-5322 119 C
joyner@georgiasouthern.edu
JOYNER, Chartarra .... 336-334-7631 341 F
cmjoyne2@ncat.edu
JOYNER, Joseph, G ...... 904-819-6288.. 98 E
jjoyner@flagler.edu
JOYNER, Laurie, M ...... 773-298-3000 148 G
joyner@sxu.edu
JOYNER, Marie .... 973-408-3097 277 C
mjoyner@drew.edu
JOYNER, Scott .... 803-321-5617 411 D
scott.joyner@newberry.edu
JOYNER, SR., Stephen . 704-330-1406 330 D
sjoyner@jcsu.edu
JOYNER-GRAHAM,
JoAnn .... 718-270-4832 295 A
jjoyner@mec.cuny.edu
JOYNES, Stephanie, N .. 434-223-6325 468 A
sjoynes@hsc.edu
JOYNES-STURGIS,
Jicola, R .... 410-651-7018 203 A
jrsturgis@umes.edu
JOZAITIS, Judy .... 217-786-2200 142 B
judy.jozaitis@llcc.edu
JUARBE, Lorraine .... 787-763-6425 508 J
ljuarbe@inter.edu
JUARBE REY, Myriam ... 787-720-4476 512 D
asistenciaeconomica@mizpa.edu
JUAREZ, Anabel .... 972-273-3000 435 E
JUAREZ, Elisa .... 520-494-5426.. 11 K
elisa.juarez@centralaz.edu
JUAREZ, Raelene .... 209-588-5087.. 75 I
juarezr@yosemite.edu
JUAREZ, Reina .... 858-534-3755.. 69 D
rjuarez@ucsd.edu
JUAREZ, Sylvia .... 206-934-4710 483 J
sylvia.juarez@seattlecolleges.edu
JUDAH, Courtney .... 541-506-6151 372 G
cjudah@cgcc.edu
JUDD, Daniel .... 801-422-2736 458 H
daniel_judd@byu.edu
JUDD, Matthew .... 909-274-4425.. 52 H
mjudd@mtsac.edu
JUDD, Summer .... 731-989-6662 420 C
sjudd@fhu.edu
JUDD, Tim .... 270-789-5027 179 E
tmjudd@campbellsville.edu
JUDE, Willie, L .... 615-329-8595 419 K
wjude@fisk.edu
JUDGE, Jeffrey .... 952-358-8585 239 F
jeff.judge@normandale.edu
JUDGE, John .... 202-319-5160.. 91 B
judge@cua.edu
JUDGE, Joseph .... 610-282-1100 382 E
jjudge@follett.com
JUDGE, Kristin, O .... 215-572-2928 379 A
judgek@arcadia.edu
JUDGE, Linda .... 925-631-4686.. 59 B
ljudge@stmarys-ca.edu
JUDGE, Rebecca .... 507-786-3358 243 C
judge@stolaf.edu
JUDGE, Sheila .... 504-816-4370 186 D
sjudge@dillard.edu
JUDGE CRIPE,
Stephanie .... 317-940-9351 153 F
sjudge@butler.edu
JUDKINS, Jason .... 760-245-4271.. 73 D
jason.judkins@vvc.edu
JUDSON, Frank .... 570-585-9444 381 E
fjudson@clarkssummitu.edu
JUDY, Allison .... 308-635-6081 270 D
judya2@wncc.edu
JUDY, Dan .... 304-637-1268 487 I
judyd@dewv.edu
JUDY, Joyce, M .... 802-828-2800 464 B
jmj10300@ccv.vsc.edu
JUEHNE, Elizabeth .... 618-537-6529 143 B
bjuehne@mckendree.edu
JUELE, Lilia .... 845-574-4480 313 C
ljuele@sunyrockland.edu
JUELG, Earl .... 832-246-0055 439 G
butch@lonestar.edu
JUERGENS, Kristin, A ... 414-464-9777 499 A
juergens.kristin@wspp.edu
JUERGENS, Valorie .... 269-467-9945 224 A
vjuergens@glenoaks.edu
JUGOVICH, Shelly .... 218-748-2416 240 D
shelly.jugovich@mesabirange.edu
JUHLIN, Eric .... 801-281-7603.. 28 E
eric.juhlin@collegeamerica.edu
JUKKALA, Clint, A .... 215-972-7623 393 D
cjukkala@pafa.edu
JUKOSKI, Mary Ellen ..... 860-215-9001.. 86 F
mjukoski@trcc.commnet.edu
JULIA, Jake .... 847-491-2912 145 F
jjulia@northwestern.edu
JULIAN, Betsy .... 541-383-7530 372 B
bjulian@cocc.edu
JULIAN, Charity .... 812-749-1235 159 C
cjulian@oak.edu
JULIAN, Elizabeth, A ..... 706-771-4049 114 J
ejulian@augustatech.edu
JULIAN, James .... 617-287-7050 211 C
evp@umassp.edu
JULIAN, Janelle .... 314-719-8057 253 C
jjulian@fontbonne.edu
JULIAN, Karen, M .... 651-962-6176 244 E
kmjulian@stthomas.edu
JULIAN, Leisa .... 765-973-8348 156 C
lejulian@iu.edu
JULIAN, Tijuana, S .... 417-873-7215 252 F
tjulian@drury.edu
JULIAN BOWDEN,
Kimberly .... 404-727-8782 117 F
kjulian@emory.edu
JULIEN, Earlye, A .... 563-884-5476 168 I
earlye.julien@palmer.edu
JULIG, Suzanne .... 212-355-1501 292 J
sjulig@christies.edu
JULIN, Paul .... 202-651-5410.. 91 E
paul.julin@gallaudet.edu
JULIO, Liz .... 906-524-8111 226 A
ljulio@kbocc.edu
JULIUS, Greg .... 805-482-2755.. 58 L
greg@stjohnsem.edu
JULIUS, James .... 760-757-2121.. 52 E
jjulius@miracosta.edu
JUMA, Stephan .... 901-333-5000 426 A
JUMONVILLE, Jennifer .. 504-314-2602 191 B
jjumonvi@tulane.edu
JUMP, Jonathon, D ...... 765-361-6206 162 E
jumpj@wabash.edu
JUMPER, Cynthia .... 806-743-3107 451 C
cynthia.jumper@ttuhsc.edu
JUMPER, G. Robin .... 850-263-3261.. 95 B
grjumper@baptistcollege.edu
JUMPER, Jonathan .... 217-479-7079 142 I
jonathan.jumper@mac.edu
JUMPER, Kevin .... 870-633-4480.. 19 B
kjumper@eacc.edu
JUNCO, Maite .... 646-664-9100 292 K
JUNE, Vincent .... 337-521-9032 188 C
vincent.june@solacc.edu
JUNEAU-BUTLER,
Allyson .... 801-649-5230 459 G
admissions@midwifery.edu
JUNEK, Shauna .... 605-642-6203 416 I
shauna.junek@bhsu.edu
JUNG, Alan .... 205-726-2716.... 6 E
apjung@samford.edu
JUNG, Alan .... 415-338-1111.. 34 A
JUNG, Anne .... 518-438-3111 305 K
ajung@mariacollege.edu
JUNG, Barnabas .... 951-763-0500.. 54 H
JUNG, Daniel .... 213-252-5100.. 23 K
djung@alu.edu
JUNG, Jackie .... 310-756-0001.. 72 A
JUNG, Jimmy .... 713-221-8100 453 B
jungj@uhd.edu
JUNG, Wonho .... 703-333-5904 478 B
whjung@wuv.edu
JUNG-MATHEWS,
Anne, M .... 603-535-2458 275 B
amjung@plymouth.edu
JUNGBLUT, Bernadette . 509-963-1404 479 B
bernadette.jungblut@cwu.edu
JUNGBLUT, Heather, L . 563-588-7103 167 D
heather.jungblut@loras.edu
JUNGERS, Christin .... 740-284-7220 353 B
cjungers@franciscan.edu
JUNGKUNTZ, David ...... 360-752-8355 478 G
djungkun@btc.edu
JUNKER, OP, Gianna .... 615-297-7545 418 C
srgianna@aquinascollege.edu
JUNKER, Tercio .... 847-866-3969 137 E
tercio.junker@garrett.edu
JUNKERMAN,
Charles, L .... 650-723-6866.. 65 J
clj@stanford.edu
JUNN, Ellen .... 209-667-3201.. 33 C
president@csustan.edu
JUNOR, Bill .... 914-251-6460 319 E
bill.junor@purchase.edu
JUNOR, Laura, J .... 202-685-4379 503 I
laura.j.junor.civ@ndu.edu
JUNQUERA, Belinda ...... 787-766-1717 511 H
junquerab1@suagm.edu
JUNTUNEN, Cindy .... 701-777-2674 345 C
cindy.juntunen@und.edu
JURAN, Victor .... 651-690-6826 242 R
vbjuran@stkate.edu
JURAS, Jennifer .... 415-703-9522.. 28 D
jjuras@cca.edu
JURENOVICH,
David, M .... 210-829-6007 453 D
davidj@uiwtx.edu
JURGENS, Amy .... 402-643-3651 266 G
amy.jurgens@cune.edu
JURGENS, Ronald .... 920-686-6131 496 A
ronald.jurgens@sl.edu
JURGENS, William, K ... 321-674-8032.. 99 B
bjurgens@fit.edu
JURNAK, Sheila .... 505-277-6331 288 G
sjurnak@unm.edu
JURY, Michael .... 323-463-2500.. 67 C
michaelj@toa.edu
JURY, Veronica .... 559-638-0300.. 66 F
veronica.jury@reedleycollege.edu
JUSINO, Lidis, L .... 787-284-1912 509 E
ljusino@ponce.inter.edu
JUSKEVICE, Leigh .... 207-509-7208 195 H
ljuskevice@unity.edu
JUSKIEWICZ, Scott .... 406-496-4523 265 A
sjuskiewicz@mtech.edu
JUSSEAUME, Richard .... 330-490-7102 364 B
rjusseaume@walsh.edu
JUSSEL, Adam .... 414-229-4632 497 A
jussel@uwm.edu
JUST, Eric .... 785-670-1860 177 G
eric.just@washburn.edu
JUSTESON, Rebecca ...... 530-898-6421.. 31 A
rjusteson@csuchico.edu
JUSTICE, Brooke .... 270-901-1001 182 D
brooke.justice@kctcs.edu
JUSTICE, Greg .... 260-481-6785 159 F
justiceg@pfw.edu
JUSTICE, Jessica .... 606-546-1214 184 H
jjustice@unionky.edu
JUSTICE, Josh .... 276-376-4517 473 B
jvj6e@virginia.edu
JUSTICE, Lillian .... 310-660-6960.. 41 L
ljustice@elcamino.edu
JUSTICE, Madeline .... 903-886-5181 447 B
madeline.justice@tamuc.edu
JUSTICE, Richard .... 317-299-0333 160 G
richard@tcmi.org
JUSTICE, Shannon .... 843-921-6913 411 F
sjustice@netc.edu
JUSTINGER, Doreen ...... 716-250-7500 291 K
dajustinger@bryantstratton.edu
JUSTINIANO, Jonna ...... 510-501-5075.. 58 B
jjustiniano@reachinst.org
JUSTISON, Brian, K ...... 217-424-6300 143 H
bjustison@millikin.edu
JUVERA, Susie .... 210-999-7298 452 A
sjuvera@trinity.edu

K

KAAI, Elmer .... 808-956-3816 128 F
elmerk@hawaii.edu
KAAKOUSH, Walid .... 847-756-4317 132 B
wkaakoush@aiuniv.edu
KAANE, Sophia .... 432-552-2373 457 A
kaane_s@utpb.edu

KAANOI, Aulani ... 808-739-8394 127 F
akaanoi@chaminade.edu
KAATZ, Forrest ... 575-461-4413 286 E
forrestk@mesalands.edu
KABALA, Heather ... 724-805-2960 398 F
heather.kabala@stvincent.edu
KABALA, Heather ... 724-805-2960 398 E
heather.kabala@stvincent.edu
KABASELE, Mutombo ... 803-641-3671 413 D
andyk@usca.edu
KABBAZ, Michael, S ... 513-529-2075 356 E
mkabbaz@miamioh.edu
KABETZKE, Donald ... 214-333-5477 434 I
donaldk@dbu.edu
KABOUREK, Chris ... 402-472-7102 269 H
ckabourek@nebraska.edu
KABRICH, Renee ... 509-453-0374 483 C
renee.kabrich@perrytech.edu
KACELI, Sali ... 215-702-4555 380 D
skaceli@cairn.edu
KACELI, Stephanie ... 215-702-4376 380 D
stephaniekaceli@cairn.edu
KACENGA, George, F ... 219-989-1104 159 G
gkacenga@pnw.edu
KACHANI, Soulaymane . 212-854-1804 297 C
kachani@columbia.edu
KACHUR, John ... 412-434-6626 383 C
kachurj@duq.edu
KACIR, Chris ... 740-351-3491 360 K
ckacir@shawnee.edu
KACSKOS, Janet, E ... 717-871-7870 395 D
janet.kacskos@millersville.edu
KACZMAR, Debra ... 831-770-6145.. 44 K
dkaczmar@hartnell.edu
KACZMARCZYK, Joseph 215-871-6652 396 D
josephk@pcom.edu
KACZMAREK, Melissa ... 845-257-3454 317 B
kaczmarm@newpaltz.edu
KACZMAREK, Shannon . 325-674-2036 429 B
srb04a@acu.edu
KACZUK, Edward ... 440-943-7600 360 J
ekaczuk@gmail.com
KACZVINSKY, Don ... 318-257-4805 191 F
dkaczv@latech.edu
KACZYNSKI, John, L ... 989-964-7481 230 B
jlkaczyn@svsu.edu
KADAD, Solange ... 707-256-7186.. 53 C
skada@napavalley.edu
KADDEN, Jerome, H ... 443-548-6064 201 A
jhk@nirc.edu
KADING, Linda ... 515-271-1465 164 I
linda.kading@dmu.edu
KADISH, Alan ... 212-463-0400.. 67 F
alan.kadish@touro.edu
KADISH, Alan ... 646-565-6000 322 J
alan.kadish@touro.edu
KADISH, Alan, H ... 914-594-4600 309 H
alan_kadish@nymc.edu
KADOWAKI, Ted ... 562-985-8831.. 31 F
ted.kadowaki@csulb.edu
KADUC, Maria ... 701-671-2616 346 E
maria.kaduc@ndscs.edu
KAECHELE, Dana ... 847-574-5268 141 C
dkaechele@lfgsm.edu
KAEHNE, Bruce ... 218-751-8670 242 J
brucekaehne@oakhills.edu
KAELI, Dianne ... 617-277-3915 207 C
kaelid@bgsp.edu
KAELKE, Christopher ... 217-641-4556 140 A
ckaelke@jwcc.edu
KAEMPFER, Seth ... 320-308-5166 240 H
skaempfer@stcloudstate.edu
KAEMPFER, William, H . 303-492-8861.. 83 A
vcaa@colorado.edu
KAENZIG, Lisa ... 315-781-3467 302 A
kaenzig@hws.edu
KAESERMANN, Kathryn . 414-297-6520 500 B
kaesermk@matc.edu
KAESS, Almabeth ... 719-384-6857.. 81 E
almabeth.kaess@ojc.edu
KAEUPER, Edith ... 415-452-5448.. 37 A
ekaeuper@ccsf.edu
KAFF, Pinches ... 718-854-2290 291 F
KAFFEN, Annie, M ... 503-943-8004 377 E
kaffen@up.edu
KAFSKY, Jennifer, L ... 828-884-8216 327 C
kafskyjl@brevard.edu
KAHAN, Miriam ... 818-299-5500.. 73 K
mkahan@westcoastuniversity.edu
KAHANOV, Leamor ... 607-436-2517 317 C
leamor.kahanov@oneonta.edu
KAHL, Anne ... 414-930-3248 495 A
kahla@mtmary.edu
KAHL, Jay ... 605-274-4190 415 B
jay.kahl@augie.edu
KAHL, Jenna ... 480-732-7000.. 12 P
jenna.kahl@cgc.edu
KAHL, Michael, D ... 585-389-2890 308 B
mkahl6@naz.edu
KAHLDEN, Dawn ... 817-598-6350 458 A
dkahlden@wc.edu
KAHLE, Jacinda ... 620-343-4600 173 A
jkahle@fhtc.edu
KAHLE, Lisa ... 607-753-5793 318 D
lisa.kahle@cortland.edu
KAHLEH, Saleim ... 281-649-3485 437 H
skahleh@hbu.edu
KAHLER, Dean ... 208-885-5690 131 G
dkahler@uidaho.edu
KAHLER, Jay, L ... 402-465-2169 268 H
jlk@nebrwesleyan.edu
KAHLER, Jeff ... 715-394-8473 498 B
jkahler@uwsuper.edu
KAHLER, Kari, L ... 231-995-1228 228 G
kkahler@nmc.edu
KAHLER, Lewis, J ... 315-792-5301 307 D
lkahler@mvcc.edu
KAHLER, Mark ... 847-317-8103 150 H
mdkahler@tiu.edu
KAHLER, Michael ... 213-382-1136.. 53 I
drmkahler@yahoo.com
KAHLER, William ... 619-239-0391.. 34 F
wkahler@cwsl.edu
KAHLIG, Charla ... 254-295-5436 453 E
ckahlig@umhb.edu
KAHN, Avi ... 718-382-8702 325 I
KAHN, Douglas ... 631-451-4578 321 F
kahnd@sunysuffolk.edu
KAHN, Eleanor ... 309-341-7303 141 A
efkahn@knox.edu
KAHN, Erin ... 952-888-4777 242 I
ekahn@nwhealth.edu
KAHN, Hilary, E ... 317-278-1265 156 F
hkahn@iu.edu
KAHN, Jack ... 760-744-1150.. 55 I
jkahn1@palomar.edu
KAHN, Jeannine ... 225-342-6950 191 D
jeannine.kahn@ulsystem.edu
KAHN, Patricia ... 718-982-2209 293 E
patricia.kahn@csi.cuny.edu
KAHN, Rachel ... 207-509-7221 195 H
rkahn@unity.edu
KAHN-FOSS, Aimee, S .. 404-471-6423 113 G
akahnfoss@agnesscott.edu
KAHOL, Pawan ... 620-235-4223 176 F
pkahol@pittstate.edu
KAHR, Audra, J ... 610-606-4630 381 A
ajhoffma@cedarcrest.edu
KAHWAJY-ANDERSON,
Joan ... 434-791-5624 464 O
jkahwajy@averett.edu
KAIL, Pam ... 870-933-7903.. 17 E
pkail@asusystem.edu
KAILI, Tevita ... 808-675-3907 127 E
tevita.kaili@byuh.edu
KAIN, Brian ... 610-526-1434 378 G
brian.kain@theamericancollege.edu
KAIN, Daniel ... 928-523-7122.. 14 H
daniel.kain@nau.edu
KAIN, Douglas ... 209-384-6344.. 51 G
kain.d@mccd.edu
KAIN, Gregory ... 708-709-3579 146 D
gkain@prairiestate.edu
KAIN, William ... 865-882-4512 425 G
kainwn@roanestate.edu
KAINE, Kryztofr ... 805-765-9300.. 62 B
KAINTH, Pritpal ... 516-876-3207 319 A
kainthp@oldwestbury.edu
KAINTZ, Paula ... 314-256-8850 250 D
kaintz@ai.edu
KAIRISS, Edward ... 401-232-6000 404 F
ekairiss@bryant.edu
KAIRO, Moses, T ... 410-651-6072 203 A
mkairo@umes.edu
KAISER, Carla ... 803-738-7610 410 G
kaiserc@midlandstech.edu
KAISER, Kenneth, H ... 215-204-6545 399 F
ken.kaiser@temple.edu
KAISER, Kim ... 720-279-8990.. 80 C
kkaiser@holmesinstitute.edu
KAISER, Larry ... 215-707-8773 399 F
larry.kaiser@temple.edu
KAISER, Larry, R ... 215-707-8773 399 F
larry.kaiser@temple.edu
KAISER, Lyn ... 757-352-4773 470 H
lkaiser@regent.edu
KAISER, Michelle ... 620-792-9232 171 C
kaiserm@bartonccc.edu
KAISER, Nancy ... 618-468-3315 141 F
nkaiser@lc.edu
KAISER, Sandra ... 360-867-5612 481 A
kaisers@evergreen.edu
KAIVOLA, Karen ... 612-330-1024 233 K
kaivola@augsburg.edu
KAJIWARA, Robert ... 808-245-8236 129 C
kajiwara@hawaii.edu
KAKISH, William ... 770-729-8400 114 D
KAKLIS, Nicole ... 276-326-4370 465 B
nicole.kaklis@bluefield.edu
KAKOULIDIS, Sofia ... 516-463-6810 302 B
sofia.kakoulidis@hofstra.edu
KAKUGAWA-LEONG,
Alyson ... 808-932-7669 128 E
alyson@hawaii.edu
KAKUGAWA-LEONG,
Alyson, Y ... 808-932-7669 128 E
alyson@hawaii.edu
KALASKY, Tom ... 540-458-8242 478 A
tkalasky@wlu.edu
KALATOZI, Nino ... 308-635-6033 270 D
kalatozn@wncc.edu
KALAVIK, James ... 267-502-2436 379 D
james.kalavik@brynathyn.edu
KALB, Melanie, T ... 740-368-3377 359 N
mtkalb@owu.edu
KALBFLEISCH, Gary ... 206-546-5813 484 G
garyk@shoreline.edu
KALDOR, Teresa ... 323-259-2966.. 54 E
tkaldor@oxy.edu
KALE, Kathy ... 408-554-5021.. 62 D
kkale@scu.edu
KALE, Sheetal ... 718-862-7512 305 H
skale01@manhattan.edu
KALEEL, Joe, D ... 503-943-7523 377 E
kaleel@up.edu
KALEIWAHEA,
Kenneth, K ... 808-934-2508 129 A
kjakalei@hawaii.edu
KALER, Robin ... 217-333-5010 151 D
rkaler@illinois.edu
KALEVELA, Sylvester ... 719-549-2696.. 79 A
sylvester.kalevela@csupueblo.edu
KALEVITCH, Maria, V ... 412-397-4020 397 G
kalevitch@rmu.edu
KALFAYAN, Stephanie .. 650-725-2788.. 65 J
kalfayan@stanford.edu
KALFSBEEK-GOETZ,
Jennifer ... 805-289-6406.. 73 B
jkgoetz@vcccd.edu
KALICH, Karrie ... 603-358-2885 275 A
kkalich@keene.edu
KALIKOW, Theo ... 970-351-2305.. 83 E
theo.kalikow@unco.edu
KALIL, Aida ... 787-850-9107 513 E
aida.kalil@upr.edu
KALINA, Susan ... 907-786-1988.... 9 H
smkalina@alaska.edu
KALINOWSKI, Patricia .. 508-373-1901 206 B
patricia.kalinowski@becker.edu
KALINOWSKI, Teresa ... 716-270-5112 299 F
kalinowski@ecc.edu
KALINSKY, Yosef ... 646-592-4068 326 E
kalinsky@yu.edu
KALIS, Kevin, J ... 301-447-5654 200 E
kalis@msmary.edu
KALIS, Michelle ... 860-231-5229.. 89 B
mkalis@usj.edu
KALISA, Marie-Chantal . 402-472-3747 269 J
mkalisa2@unl.edu
KALITA, Tish ... 260-982-5083 158 T
lnkalita@manchester.edu
KALK, Bruce ... 203-392-5468.. 85 A
kalkb1@southernct.edu
KALKA, Alicia ... 304-367-4917 490 B
alicia.kalka@fairmontstate.edu
KALKBRENNER,
Suzanne, K ... 518-629-4530 302 E
s.kalkbrenner@hvcc.edu
KALKSTEIN,
Yasmine, L ... 845-569-3631 307 J
yasmine.kalkstein@msmc.edu
KALLEND, Jennifer ... 213-621-2200.. 38 G
KALLERGIS, Sophia, D . 440-826-2180 348 E
skallerg@bw.edu
KALLIERIS, Nick, C ... 847-543-2476 135 B
nkallieris@clcillinois.edu
KALMANOFSKY, Amy ... 212-678-8826 303 G
amkalmanofsky@jtsa.edu
KALMANOWITZ, Osher . 718-645-0536 307 C
phecht@thejnet.com
KALMANSON, Dan, P ... 973-378-9856 283 B
daniel.kalmanson@shu.edu
KALMEY, Jon ... 814-866-8147 388 A
jkalmey@lecom.edu
KALOGIANNIS, Natalie .. 707-664-2874.. 34 C
natalie.kalogiannis@sonoma.edu
KALOOSTIAN, Damita ... 602-243-8021.. 14 A
damita.kaloostian@smcmail.maricopa.edu
KALSCHEUR, S.J.,
Gregory ... 617-552-2393 207 B
gregory.kalscheur@bc.edu
KALSTROM, Sally ... 503-552-1616 374 E
skalstrom@nunm.edu
KALTCHEV, Matey ... 414-277-7544 494 G
kaltchev@msoe.edu
KALTENMARK, Michael . 317-940-9672 153 F
mkaltenm@butler.edu
KALTMAN, Steven ... 954-262-7332 103 M
skaltman@nova.edu
KALUARACHCHI,
Jagath ... 435-797-2776 460 H
jagath.kaluarachchi@usu.edu
KALYAYEVA, Julia ... 510-845-0752.. 75 E
jkalyayeva@wi.edu
KALYN, Andrea ... 617-585-1200 217 B
andrea.kalyn@necmusic.edu
KALYNOVSKYI, Serhii ... 707-965-6218.. 55 D
skalynovskyi@puc.edu
KALYON, Dilhan ... 201-216-8225 283 C
dilhan.kalyon@stevens.edu
KAM, Moshe ... 973-596-6506 279 F
moshe.kam@njit.edu
KAMAGU, Wanjiku ... 318-274-3811 191 E
kamaguw@gram.edu
KAMAHELE, Ron ... 907-786-1419.... 9 H
rckamahele@alaska.edu
KAMARA, Sheku ... 414-277-7416 494 G
kamara@msoe.edu
KAMARADOS,
Georgenne ... 740-264-5591 352 H
gkamarados@egcc.edu
KAMAT, Deborah ... 440-484-7027 363 G
deborah.kamat@ursuline.edu
KAMATANI, Kathy ... 732-224-2453 276 B
kkamatani@brookdalecc.edu
KAMATH, Karishma ... 808-932-7472 128 E
karishma@hawaii.edu
KAMENETSKY, Shmuel . 215-473-1212 399 E
talmudicalyeshiva@yahoo.com
KAMENETSKY, Sholom . 215-477-1000 399 E
talmudicalyeshvia@yahoo.com
KAMEOKA, Velma ... 808-956-0813 128 F
velmak@hawaii.edu
KAMERER, Caitlin ... 610-921-6608 378 C
ckamerer@albright.edu
KAMERON, Keith ... 815-836-5130 141 G
kameroke@lewisu.edu
KAMHI, Victoria ... 309-655-7100 148 E
victoria.kamhi@osfhealthcare.org
KAMIAB, Jane ... 336-770-3297 343 D
kamiabj@uncsa.edu
KAMICKER, Andrea ... 724-847-6610 384 G
amkamick@geneva.edu
KAMIMURA-JIMENEZ,
Mark ... 817-257-5557 448 G
m.kamimura@tcu.edu
KAMINSKI, Janice, M ... 724-480-3423 381 K
jan.kaminski@ccbc.edu
KAMINSKI, Linda ... 509-574-4635 487 A
lkaminski@yvcc.edu
KAMINSKI, Michael ... 213-624-1200.. 42 I
mkaminski@fidm.edu
KAMINSKY, Margaret, I 585-292-3398 307 H
mkaminsky@monroecc.edu
KAMINSKY, Paul, A ... 615-353-3615 425 D
paul.kaminsky@nscc.edu
KAMITSUKA, David ... 440-775-8410 358 C
david.kamitsuka@oberlin.edu
KAMMER, Dan ... 573-876-7273 260 F
dkammer@stephens.edu
KAMMER, Roy ... 651-213-4863 236 B
rkammer@hazeldenbettyford.edu
KAMMERMAN, Amy ... 615-277-7440 428 F
akammerman@watkins.edu
KAMMERZELL, Joan ... 360-752-8436 478 G
jkammerzell@btc.edu
KAMOCHE, Njambi ... 847-925-6764 137 H
nkamoche@harpercollege.edu
KAMP, Cyndi ... 317-955-6103 158 U
ckamp@marian.edu
KAMPE, Brent, S ... 626-584-5423.. 43 H
brentkampe@fuller.edu

KAMPF, Stephen .... 419-372-7485 348 H
skampf@bgsu.edu
KAMPFSCHULTE, Darcy . 616-632-2894 221 C
kampfdar@aquinas.edu
KAMPHAUS, Lisa .... 412-536-1526 387 B
lisa.kamphaus@laroche.edu
KAMPHAUS, Randy, W . 541-346-1601 377 D
randyk@uoregon.edu
KAMPS, Anne .... 920-498-6367 500 F
anne.kamps@nwtc.edu
KAMPS, Larissa .... 866-323-0233.. 57 J
admissions@providencecc.edu
KAMWITHI, Gina .... 419-755-4554 357 E
gkamwithi@ncstatecollege.edu
KANAK, Daniel .... 610-359-5135 382 C
dkanak@dccc.edu
KANAKALA, Raghunath . 972-238-6211 435 F
rkanakala@dcccd.edu
KANAKIS, Chris .... 312-942-2831 148 A
chris_kanakis@rush.edu
KANALIS, Mike .... 724-938-4409 394 B
kanalis@calu.edu
KANARAS, Elizabeth ...... 610-902-8283 380 C
KANAREK, Berel .... 914-736-1500 310 I
KANAREK, E .... 914-736-1500 310 I
KANAVLE, Judith .... 707-468-3280.. 51 E
jkanavle@mendocino.edu
KANAWADA, Christine .. 518-694-7357 289 D
christine.kanawada@acphs.edu
KANBAR, Hiam .... 831-242-5618 503 D
hiam.n.kanbar@dliflc.edu
KANDER, Ron .... 215-951-0252 400 A
kanderr@philau.edu
KANDLER, Mike .... 850-769-1551 100 N
mkandler@gulfcoast.edu
KANDOLA, Amandeep ... 530-741-6700.. 76 C
akandola@yccd.edu
KANDUS-FISHER,
Christopher .... 617-747-2231 206 E
studentaffairs@berklee.edu
KANE, Andrew .... 609-258-3469 280 E
kane@princeton.edu
KANE, Barry, S .... 212-854-1458 297 C
barry@columbia.edu
KANE, Brian .... 610-785-6265 398 A
bkane@scs.edu
KANE, Christopher .... 215-951-1585 387 C
kanec@lasalle.edu
KANE, Colleen .... 715-422-5510 500 A
colleen.kane@mstc.edu
KANE, Daniel, C .... 207-768-9475 196 E
daniel.c.kane@maine.edu
KANE, Gina .... 315-781-3064 302 A
kane@hws.edu
KANE, Hillary .... 213-738-6825.. 65 G
co-mark@swlaw.edu
KANE, Jane .... 908-709-7169 284 C
jane.kane@ucc.edu
KANE, Jesse .... 478-825-6291 118 A
kanej@fvsu.edu
KANE, Karen .... 760-252-2411.. 26 I
kkane@barstow.edu
KANE, Katherine, J .... 864-938-3913 411 I
kjkane@presby.edu
KANE, Kathleen .... 856-227-7200 276 E
kkane@camdencc.edu
KANE, Kerri .... 413-755-4115 215 F
kpkane@stcc.edu
KANE, Kim .... 707-638-5280.. 67 F
kim.kane@tu.edu
KANE, Laura .... 580-581-5502 365 G
laurak@cameron.edu
KANE, Luanne .... 763-433-1297 237 C
luanne.kane@anokaramsey.edu
KANE, Marie .... 210-485-0020 429 C
KANE, Michael .... 650-738-4248.. 61 Q
KANE, Michael .... 859-858-3511 178 I
mike.kane@asbury.edu
KANE, Robert, C .... 202-685-3927 503 I
robert.kane@ndu.edu
KANE, Ryan, D .... 407-582-3421 112 K
rkane8@valenciacollege.edu
KANE, Sara, F .... 863-638-7602 113 A
sara.kane@warner.edu
KANE, Sylvia .... 714-556-3610.. 72 F
KANE, Thomas .... 781-891-2340 206 D
tkane@bentley.edu
KANE, Thomas, F .... 570-674-6223 390 G
tkane@misericordia.edu
KANE, Vicki .... 814-944-5643 404 D
vicki.kane@yti.edu
KANELOS, Gwen, E .... 708-209-3101 135 F
gwen.kanelos@cuchicago.edu
KANELOS, Peter .... 410-626-2510 201 D
pkanelos@sjc.edu
KANEPS, Katherine, D ... 610-330-5200 387 E
kanepsk@lafayette.edu
KANEVSKAYA, Svetlana 212-752-1530 304 D
svetlana.kanevskaya@limcollege.edu
KANG, David .... 303-492-4212.. 83 A
david.kang@colorado.edu
KANG, Hyo Jeong .... 714-533-1495.. 64 D
hjkang@southbaylo.edu
KANG, Jerry .... 310-825-3935.. 69 A
jkang@equity.ucla.edu
KANG, Mia .... 770-220-7906 118 B
academic@gcuniv.edu
KANG, Richard .... 310-756-0001.. 72 A
KANG, Soonhae .... 714-527-0691.. 42 E
KANG, Yunn .... 215-702-4461 380 D
ykang@cairn.edu
KANGAS, Richard .... 218-322-2319 238 E
richard.kangas@itascacc.edu
KANIA, Dan .... 314-371-0236 258 E
dkania@ranken.edu
KANIA, Ed .... 407-646-2117 105 M
ekania@rollins.edu
KANICH, Amy .... 814-886-6483 391 B
akanich@mtaloy.edu
KANIKKEBERG,
Dee Dee .... 208-885-6571 131 G
deedeek@uidaho.edu
KANIPES, Margaret .... 336-285-2030 341 F
mikanipe@ncat.edu
KANIS, David .... 773-995-2497 133 K
dkanis@csu.edu
KANISS, John .... 253-589-5529 479 G
john.kaniss@cptc.edu
KANLIOGLU, Osman ..... 832-230-5555 440 H
osman@na.edu
KANMORE, John .... 575-562-2511 285 M
john.kanmore@enmu.edu
KANN, Andrea .... 212-824-2208 301 E
akann@huc.edu
KANN, Sam .... 773-583-4050 145 B
s-kann@neiu.edu
KANNAN, Govind .... 478-825-6802 118 A
govindak@fvsu.edu
KANNARKAT, Mily .... 757-446-8910 466 I
kannarmj@evms.edu
KANNE, Lynn .... 206-934-4072 484 A
lynn.kanne@seattlecolleges.edu
KANNENWISCHER,
Susan, E .... 614-236-6511 349 D
skannenwischer@capital.edu
KANONIK, Robert .... 815-836-5813 141 G
kanoniro@lewisu.edu
KANOY, David .... 910-362-7695 332 H
dkanoy@cfcc.edu
KANT, Sudarsan .... 314-340-5787 253 I
kants@hssu.edu
KANTARDJIEFF,
Katherine .... 760-750-7204.. 33 B
kkantard@csusm.edu
KANTENWEIN, Heidi, L . 574-372-5100 155 B
biehlehl@grace.edu
KANTER, Connie .... 206-296-6148 484 F
kanterc@seattleu.edu
KANTERMAN, Kathy ...... 401-254-3531 405 E
kkanterman@rwu.edu
KANTNER, Joanne .... 815-825-9450 140 F
mkantner@kish.edu
KANTNER, John .... 904-620-2455 110 A
j.kantner@unf.edu
KANTNER, John .... 904-620-1360 110 A
j.kantner@unf.edu
KANTNER, Michael .... 856-256-4566 281 E
kantner@rowan.edu
KANTO, Kind .... 691-330-2620 505 B
kank@comfsm.fm
KANTOR, Ali .... 617-521-1038 218 E
ali.kantor@simmons.edu
KANTOR, Rebecca .... 303-315-6343.. 83 C
rebecca.kantor@ucdenver.edu
KANU, Andrew .... 804-524-5930 477 B
akanu@vsu.edu
KANWISCHER, Charlie .. 419-372-9395 348 H
ckanwis@bgsu.edu
KANZ, Maryellen .... 507-453-2673 239 A
mkanz@southeastmn.edu
KAO, Chi-Chang .... 650-723-2300.. 65 J
KAO, Patrick .... 415-422-5380.. 71 K
pk@usfca.edu
KAO, Teresa .... 626-571-5110.. 48 B
teresakao@les.edu
KAOPUA, Heipua .... 808-235-7370 129 F
heipua@hawaii.edu
KAOPUIKI, Ryon .... 765-641-4337 153 B
rkaopuiki@anderson.edu
KAOUDIS, Kathryn .... 303-352-3356.. 79 E
kathy.kaoudis@ccd.edu
KAPASI, Zoher, F .... 843-792-3328 410 F
kapasi@musc.edu
KAPCSOS, Kathy .... 610-861-5499 391 F
kkapcsos@northampton.edu
KAPFHAMMER, Sean ..... 410-777-2836 197 C
srkapfhammer@aacc.edu
KAPILESHWAR, Sameer 850-599-8033 108 I
sameer.kapileshwar@famu.edu
KAPINUS, Carolyn .... 940-898-3301 451 F
ckapinus@twu.edu
KAPLA, Dale, P .... 906-227-2920 228 F
dkapla@nmu.edu
KAPLAN, Alan .... 608-263-8025 496 C
akaplan@uwhealth.org
KAPLAN, Anita, S .... 561-868-4102 104 D
kaplana1@palmbeachstate.edu
KAPLAN, Anne, C .... 815-753-9503 145 C
akaplan@niu.edu
KAPLAN, John .... 208-426-1304 129 I
johnkaplan@boisestate.edu
KAPLAN, Judith .... 216-987-4613 351 G
judith.kaplan@tri-c.edu
KAPLAN, Leonard, I ...... 973-596-3638 279 F
leonard.i.kaplan@njit.edu
KAPLAN, Mark .... 352-392-4574 109 F
mark.kaplan@ufl.edu
KAPLAN, Richard .... 617-732-2808 216 B
richard.kaplan@mcphs.edu
KAPLAN, Ronald, S .... 847-578-8538 147 I
ronald.kaplan@rosalindfranklin.edu
KAPLAN, Steven, H .... 203-932-7276.. 89 A
skaplan@newhaven.edu
KAPLAN, Thomas, E ...... 260-422-5561 155 H
tekaplan@indianatech.edu
KAPLINSKY, Yoheved ... 212-799-5000 303 H
KAPOCIUS, Andrew .... 219-980-6841 156 E
ajkapoci@iun.edu
KAPOUN, Jim .... 717-815-1353 404 A
jkapoun@ycp.edu
KAPP, Alisha .... 217-854-5511 132 I
alisha.kapp@blackburn.edu
KAPPANADZE,
Margaret .... 607-735-1867 299 D
mkappanadze@elmira.edu
KAPPEL, Rachel .... 518-828-4181 297 B
rachel.kappel@sunycgcc.edu
KAPPEL, Stephanie .... 304-214-8801 489 F
skappel@wvncc.edu
KAPPELER, Victor .... 859-622-3565 180 B
victor.kappeler@eku.edu
KAPPENMAN, Angi .... 605-256-5134 416 J
angi.kappenman@dsu.edu
KAPPES, Christiaan .... 412-321-8383 380 B
dean@bcs.edu
KAPRIVE, Mark .... 561-803-2542 104 C
mark_kaprive@pba.edu
KAPSAL, Sean .... 859-344-3600 184 F
kapsals@thomasmore.edu
KAPTAIN, Laurence .... 303-352-3559.. 83 C
laurence.kaptain@ucdenver.edu
KAPTIK, Michael .... 425-564-2752 478 F
michael.kaptik@bellevuecollege.edu
KAPUR, Anup .... 609-771-2859 276 I
kapura@tcnj.edu
KAPURCH, Jason .... 508-929-8045 213 E
jkapurch@worcester.edu
KARABETSOS,
Michael, L .... 517-264-7109 230 E
mkarabet@sienaheights.edu
KARACAL, Cem .... 618-650-2861 149 F
skaraca@siue.edu
KARAFA, Andy .... 716-673-3173 317 A
andy.karafa@fredonia.edu
KARAFIN, Diana, L .... 212-998-4426 310 B
diana.karafin@nyu.edu
KARAGEZIAN, Vardan ... 818-240-6900.. 25 P
KARAGIANNIS, Aliki, E . 508-565-1537 218 H
akaragiannis@stonehill.edu
KARAGOSIAN, Nico ...... 740-593-4764 359 G
nico@ohio.edu
KARAHADIAN, Milton ... 619-849-2649.. 57 E
miltonkarahadian@pointloma.edu
KARAM, Robert .... 318-342-5014 192 F
karam@ulm.edu
KARAM, Vanessa .... 626-571-8811.. 72 C
vanessak@uwest.edu
KARAMAN, Ana .... 503-838-8459 377 H
vpfa@wou.edu
KARAMOL, Mark .... 567-661-7988 360 B
mark_karamol@owens.edu
KARANFIL, Tanju .... 864-656-7701 408 A
tkaranf@clemson.edu
KARANJA, Benson, M .. 404-627-2681 115 C
benson.karanja@beulah.edu
KARANJA, Peter .... 404-627-2681 115 C
peter.karanja@beulah.edu
KARANTINOS,
Patroklos .... 802-224-3000 463 H
patroklos.karantinos@vsc.edu
KARAS, Jane, A .... 406-756-3801 263 F
jkaras@fvcc.edu
KARAS, Jennifer .... 303-871-6793.. 83 D
jkaras@du.edu
KARAS, Tara .... 941-487-5001 109 D
tkaras@ncf.edu
KARAS, Tim .... 510-748-2273.. 56 F
tkaras@peralta.edu
KARASEK, III,
Raymond, N .... 401-825-2298 404 H
mkarasek@ccri.edu
KARASINSKI, Tracy .... 401-825-2305 404 H
tkarasinski@ccri.edu
KARASS, Alan .... 617-585-1247 217 B
alan.karass@necmusic.edu
KARATAN, Ece .... 828-262-7459 341 B
karatane@appstate.edu
KARAVOKIRIS, Marina .. 760-471-1316.. 71 I
mkaravokiris@usk.edu
KARAVOLAS, Susan ...... 518-694-7278 289 D
susan.karavolas@acphs.edu
KARAZIM, Jan .... 269-965-3931 225 F
karazimj@kellogg.edu
KARAZSIA, Bryan .... 330-263-2632 351 C
bkarazsia@wooster.edu
KARBHARI, Vistasp, M . 817-272-2101 454 J
vkarbhari@uta.edu
KARCH, Lisa .... 218-477-2699 239 D
lisa.karch@mnstate.edu
KARCHER, Larry .... 602-384-2555.. 11 F
larry.karcher@bryanuniversity.edu
KARDAN, Sel .... 213-621-2200.. 38 G
KARDOS, Shane .... 330-569-5205 353 J
kardossd@hiram.edu
KARDOW, Vivian, D ..... 409-772-2636 456 F
vdkardow@utmb.edu
KARELS, Tara .... 218-894-5172 237 F
tkarels@clcmn.edu
KARGES, Teri .... 843-863-7050 407 E
tkarges@csuniv.edu
KARIM, Anwar .... 240-567-3212 200 C
anwar.karim@montgomerycollege.edu
KARIM, Mohammad .... 508-999-8024 211 F
provost@umassd.edu
KARIMBUX, Nadeem .... 617-636-6636 219 B
nadeem.karimbux@tufts.edu
KARIMIGEVARI, Reza .... 503-352-7276 375 G
karimir@pacificu.edu
KARIUKI, Benson .... 903-730-4890 438 H
bkaruiku@jarvis.edu
KARL, Stacy .... 715-425-4481 497 E
stacy.karl@uwrf.edu
KARLBERG,
Anne Marie .... 360-383-3302 486 G
amkarlberg@whatcom.edu
KARLE, Christie .... 949-794-9090.. 65 I
ckarle@stanbridge.edu
KARLGAARD, Joseph .... 713-348-4077 442 K
joe.karlgaard@rice.edu
KARLIN, Angela .... 785-864-4700 177 D
akarlin@ku.edu
KARLIN, Barbara, H ...... 415-442-7882.. 44 D
bkarlin@ggu.edu
KARLIN, Craig .... 785-628-4222 173 B
ckarlin@fhsu.edu
KARLOFF, Glee .... 352-245-4119 111 E
glee.karloff@taylorcollege.edu
KARLOFF, Michael .... 402-461-7473 267 D
mkarloff@hastings.edu
KARLSSON, Anette .... 216-687-2558 351 B
a.karlsson@csuohio.edu
KARMANOVA, Tatiana ... 909-537-3986.. 33 A
tkarma@csusb.edu
KARMIS, Beth .... 312-949-7415 138 E
bkarmis@ico.edu
KARMON, Rachel .... 937-433-3410 352 M
rkarmon@fortiscollege.edu
KARNBACH, Lee .... 321-674-7442.. 99 B
lkarnbach@fit.edu
KARNES, Michael, S ...... 585-753-3700 307 H
mkarnes@monroecc.edu

KAWALL, Scott 815-825-9837 140 F
skawall@kish.edu
KAWAMOTO, Judy 610-436-3282 396 A
jkawamoto@wcupa.edu
KAWANNA, JR., Ronald 708-596-2000 149 B
rkawanna@ssc.edu
KAWAR, Ferris 310-434-3911 62 E
kawar_ferris@smc.edu
KAWAUCHI, John 906-635-2674 226 E
jkawauchi@lssu.edu
KAY, Carol 915-831-6725 436 E
ckay@epcc.edu
KAY, Catherine 313-577-3049 232 I
catherine.kay@wayne.edu
KAY, Colin 973-761-9478 283 B
colin.kay@shu.edu
KAY, Gwen 518-320-1376 316 C
gwen.kay@suny.edu
KAY, Julie 209-954-5093 60 J
jkay@deltacollege.edu
KAY, Peggy 209-946-7358 70 E
pkay@pacific.edu
KAY, Sabrina 562-809-5100 43 F
sabrina.kay@fremont.edu
KAY-WONG, Chelsea 808-932-7442 128 E
ckwong@hawaii.edu
KAYALAR, Dee 718-940-5566 314 C
dkayalar@sjcny.edu
KAYE, Anders 619-961-4259 67 E
anderskaye@tjsl.edu
KAYE, Johanna 503-554-2235 373 C
kayej@georgefox.edu
KAYE, Joyce 212-592-2011 315 H
jkaye3@sva.edu
KAYE, Matthew 641-628-5376 163 E
kayem@central.edu
KAYLOR, Debbie 208-426-4351 129 I
debbiekaylor@boisestate.edu
KAYLOR, Sean, P 845-575-3000 305 L
sean.kaylor@marist.edu
KAYNAMA, Shohreh, A 410-704-6309 204 A
skaynama@towson.edu
KAYNARD, Meryl, R 212-220-1237 293 A
mkaynard@bmcc.cuny.edu
KAYS, Brenda, S 903-983-8100 439 A
bkays@kilgore.edu
KAYSEN-LUZBETAK, Angie 815-280-6679 140 B
akaysen@jjc.edu
KAZAMA, Susan 808-845-9158 129 B
smurata@hawaii.edu
KAZANECKI-KEMPTER, Diane 631-420-2065 321 B
diane.kazanecki-kempter@farmingdale.edu
KAZARIAN, Julie 508-929-8077 213 E
jkazarian@worcester.edu
KAZDA, Kathleen 262-691-5464 500 H
kkazda@wctc.edu
KAZEN, James, D 210-567-0390 456 C
kazen@uthscsa.edu
KAZEN, Tom 708-239-4866 150 F
thomas.kazen@trnty.edu
KAZER, Meredith, W 203-254-4150 86 I
mkazer@fairfield.edu
KAZEROUNIAN, Kazem 860-486-2221 88 E
kazem.kazerounian@uconn.edu
KAZI, Javeria 518-276-6177 312 I
kazij@rpi.edu
KAZIC, Ivana 606-546-1281 184 H
ivana.kazic@unionky.edu
KAZMAN, Nelly 909-593-3511 70 D
nkazman@laverne.edu
KAZMIR, Darin 361-582-2417 457 E
darin.kazmir@victoriacollege.edu
KAZUMA, Clement 680-488-2471 506 B
clementk@palau.edu
KAZYAKA, Carrie 619-961-4324 67 E
ckazyaka@tjsl.edu
KEADY, Thomas, J 617-552-6795 207 B
thomas.keady@bc.edu
KEAL, Aaron, J 620-421-6700 175 C
aaronk@labette.edu
KEALA, David 808-675-3572 127 E
david.keala@byuh.edu
KEAN, Christopher, S 719-333-9338 504 C
christopher.kean@usafa.edu
KEAN, Joy 970-943-2114 84 D
jkean@western.edu
KEAN, Linda 781-239-4284 205 E
kean@babson.edu
KEANE, Christopher 509-335-3574 486 A
chris.keane@wsu.edu

KEANE, James 610-896-1023 385 L
jkeane@haverford.edu
KEANE, John 212-752-1530 304 D
john.keane@limcollege.edu
KEARN, Tim 559-297-4500 46 A
tkearn@iot.edu
KEARNEY, Anne, E 315-445-4195 304 C
kearneae@lemoyne.edu
KEARNEY, Janice 870-575-8283 22 E
kearneyj@uapb.edu
KEARNEY, Joseph, D 414-288-1955 494 B
joseph.kearney@marquette.edu
KEARNEY, Kimberly 540-261-8542 471 H
kim.kearney@svu.edu
KEARNEY, Matt 573-651-2039 259 K
mkearney@semo.edu
KEARNEY, Tyler 225-578-8200 188 I
tkearney@lsu.edu
KEARNS, Chris 406-994-2828 264 D
chris.kearns@montana.edu
KEARNS, Gayle 405-470-2636 370 B
gayle.kearns@swcu.edu
KEARNS, Jane 802-728-1231 464 E
jkearns@vtc.edu
KEARNS, Jennifer 619-388-2759 60 D
jnkearns@sdccd.edu
KEARNS, Joanne 973-328-5044 277 B
jkearns@ccm.edu
KEARNS, Kevin 716-673-3758 317 A
kevin.kearns@fredonia.edu
KEARNS, Lorna, R 412-624-6786 401 B
lrkearns@pitt.edu
KEARNS, Michelle 801-863-8976 461 A
michelle.kearns@uvu.edu
KEARNS, Richard 918-631-2150 371 E
richard-kearns@utulsa.edu
KEARNS, Tom 765-361-6188 162 E
kearnst@wabash.edu
KEARNS-BARRETT, Marybeth 508-793-2448 208 B
mkearns@holycross.edu
KEARY, Chris 785-864-5900 177 D
ckeary@ku.edu
KEAS, Lenora 361-698-1207 436 C
lkeas@delmar.edu
KEASLER, Robert, L 540-665-4533 471 E
rkeasler@su.edu
KEASLING, Diane 423-461-8968 422 J
dlkeasling@milligan.edu
KEAST, Cindy 620-665-3565 174 B
keastc@hutchcc.edu
KEATHLEY, Gwynne 410-225-5242 199 H
gkeathley@mica.edu
KEATING, Frederick 856-415-2100 281 D
fkeating@rcgc.edu
KEATING, Jeffery 909-469-5205 74 I
keating@westernu.edu
KEATING, Joseph 740-588-1242 365 E
jkeating@zanestate.edu
KEATING, Kathy 616-234-4953 224 D
kkeating@grcc.edu
KEATING, Lisa 518-454-2833 296 H
keatingl@strose.edu
KEATON, Alicia 407-823-2827 109 E
alicia.keaton@ucf.edu
KEATY, Anthony 781-899-5500 218 A
akeaty@psjs.edu
KEBER, Hope 630-829-1801 132 E
hkeber@ben.edu
KEBREAB, Ermias 530-754-9707 68 E
ekebreab@ucdavis.edu
KECHICHIAN, Avedis (Avo) 909-593-3511 70 D
akechichian2@laverne.edu
KECK, Julie 740-695-9500 348 F
jkeck@belmontcollege.edu
KECK, Kay 269-965-3931 225 F
keckk@kellogg.edu
KECK, III, Ray, M 903-886-5011 447 B
ray.keck@tamuc.edu
KECKLEY, Kim 540-665-4841 471 E
kkeckley@su.edu
KEDROSKI, Cristie 850-729-5357 103 L
kedroskc@nwfsc.edu
KEDROWSKI, Karen 218-748-2418 238 C
kkedrowski@nhed.edu
KEDROWSKI, Karen 218-312-1511 238 E
kkedrowski@nhed.edu
KEDROWSKI, Karen 218-748-2418 238 G
kkedrowski@nhed.edu
KEDROWSKI, Karen 218-312-1511 238 E
kkedrowski@nhed.edu
KEDSKI, Cathy 508-830-5042 213 B
ckedski@maritime.edu

KEE, Josh 870-235-4321 21 D
jrkee@saumag.edu
KEE, Mindi 918-781-7260 365 F
keem@bacone.edu
KEE, Shomari 859-572-5198 184 A
kees1@nku.edu
KEEBLER, Patrick 440-826-3745 348 E
pkeebler@bw.edu
KEECH, Brian, T 215-895-2244 383 B
brian.keech@drexel.edu
KEECH, Renee 860-465-4596 84 J
keechr@easternct.edu
KEEDY, Thomas, E 765-361-6227 162 E
keedyt@wabash.edu
KEEFE, Maureen 617-879-7705 212 E
mkeefe@massart.edu
KEEFE, Terri, K 610-799-1580 388 I
tkeefe@lccc.edu
KEEFER, Cassandra 907-786-1480 9 H
ckeefer@alaska.edu
KEEFER, Charles 620-450-2120 176 G
charlesk@prattcc.edu
KEEFER, Elizabeth, J 216-368-4286 349 F
elizabeth.keefer@case.edu
KEEFER, Elizabeth, J 216-368-5555 349 F
elizabeth.keefer@case.edu
KEEFER, Jessica 303-384-2601 78 I
jkeefer@mines.edu
KEEFER, Matthew, W 618-453-7313 149 E
keefer@siu.edu
KEEFER, Maureen, H 412-397-6484 397 G
keefer@rmu.edu
KEEFER, Michael, R 814-393-1610 394 D
mkeefer@cuf-inc.org
KEEGAN, Bridget, M 402-280-4015 266 I
bmkeegan@creighton.edu
KEEGAN, Joe 518-355-5282 310 E
jkeegan@nccc.edu
KEEGAN, Kim 603-206-8005 272 L
kkeegan@ccsnh.edu
KEEGAN, Thomas 360-416-7997 485 A
thomas.keegan@skagit.edu
KEEHN, Aybuke 928-344-7699 10 J
aybuke.keehn@azwestern.edu
KEEHN, Jay 305-653-7141 361 L
jay.keehn@myunion.edu
KEEL, Brooks, A 706-721-2301 115 A
president@augusta.edu
KEEL, Darla 901-678-5755 427 D
darkeel@memphis.edu
KEEL, Dave 804-758-6731 475 G
dkeel@rappahannock.edu
KEELE, Layne 334-386-7547 5 D
lkeele@faulkner.edu
KEELER, Anne, B 540-828-5470 465 D
akeeler@bridgewater.edu
KEELER, Bruce 714-241-6257 38 C
bkeeler@coastline.edu
KEELER, Chuck 609-586-4800 278 F
keelerc@mccc.edu
KEELER, John, T 412-624-7605 401 B
keeler@pitt.edu
KEELER, Karen 603-206-8002 272 L
kkeeler@ccsnh.edu
KEELER-STROM, Michela 402-844-7122 268 J
michela@northeast.edu
KEELEY, Brian 360-383-3375 486 G
bkeeley@whatcom.edu
KEELEY, Dan 845-574-4452 313 C
dkeeley@sunyrockand.edu
KEELEY, Edward, J 608-663-2223 493 C
ekeeley@edgewood.edu
KEELEY, Eileen, M 704-894-2422 328 F
eikeeley@davidson.edu
KEELEY, Gloria 312-996-2860 151 B
gkeeley@uic.edu
KEELING, Amy 865-354-3000 425 G
keelinga@roanestate.edu
KEELS, Carl 301-736-3631 199 G
genekeels@aol.com
KEEN, Cathy 352-395-5829 107 A
cathy.keen@sfcollege.edu
KEEN, Larry 910-678-8321 334 D
keenl@faytechcc.edu
KEEN, Mike 423-775-7111 418 H
mkeen8126@bryan.edu
KEEN, Ralph 312-413-2267 151 B
rkeen01@uic.edu
KEEN, Russell 706-721-2301 115 A
rukeen@augusta.edu
KEEN, Suzanne 315-859-4607 301 C
skeen@hamilton.edu

KEEN, Suzette 574-936-8898 153 A
suzette.keen@ancilla.edu
KEENAHAN, Patty 585-340-9638 296 E
pkeenahan@crcds.edu
KEENAN, Claudine 609-652-3593 283 D
claudine.keenan@stockton.edu
KEENAN, SJ, James, F 617-552-3880 207 B
james.keenan.2@bc.edu
KEENAN, John 978-542-6400 213 C
jkeenan@salemstate.edu
KEENAN, Laurie 518-464-8575 299 G
laurie@excelsior.edu
KEENAN, Mary 218-726-7009 243 F
mkeenan@d.umn.edu
KEENAN, Maura 215-780-1266 398 G
mkeenan@salus.edu
KEENAN, Ruth 281-998-6368 443 B
ruth.keenan@sjcd.edu
KEENAN, Stuart 800-686-1883 222 E
skeenan@cleary.edu
KEENAN, Timothy 920-924-3420 500 C
tkeenan@morainepark.edu
KEENE, David 502-456-6504 184 E
dkeene@sullivan.edu
KEENE, Frances 540-231-6205 477 A
fbabb@vt.edu
KEENE, Jennifer 714-997-6947 36 C
keene@chapman.edu
KEENE, Jennifer 702-895-3401 271 E
jennifer.keene@unlv.edu
KEENE, Joanne 928-523-7478 14 H
joanne.keene@nau.edu
KEENE, John 973-353-3899 282 B
john.keene@rutgers.edu
KEENE, Vickie 276-498-5230 464 K
vkeene@acp.edu
KEENE, Vincent 276-326-4209 465 B
vkeene@bluefield.edu
KEENER, Barb 419-755-4539 357 E
bkeener@ncstatecollege.edu
KEENER, Donna 813-974-5711 110 B
dlkeener@usf.edu
KEENER, Dorie 609-343-4920 275 D
dkeener@atlantic.edu
KEENER, Gary, S 540-863-2900 474 D
gkeener@dslcc.edu
KEENER, John, F 434-947-8367 470 E
jkeener@randolphcollege.edu
KEENEY, Hunter 409-882-3312 450 A
hunter.keeney@lsco.edu
KEENEY, Jeffrey 918-335-6883 368 G
jkeeney@okwu.edu
KEENEY, Madonna 815-599-3449 138 B
madonna.keeney@highland.edu
KEENEY, Michael, S 843-953-5843 407 F
mkeeney@citadel.edu
KEENUM, Mark, E 662-325-3221 247 F
president@msstate.edu
KEENUM, Nancy 256-306-2850 1 F
nancy.keenum@calhoun.edu
KEEP, William 609-771-1855 276 I
keep@tcnj.edu
KEERY, Nina 781-239-2463 214 E
nkeery@massbay.edu
KEESE, Russelle 502-597-5759 182 H
russelle.keese@kysu.edu
KEESE, Wallace 478-825-6931 118 A
keesew@fvsu.edu
KEESEY, Aiza 661-255-1050 28 K
KEETER, Brian, C 334-844-4650 4 E
bck0001@auburn.edu
KEETER, Howell, W 417-690-2370 251 E
dock@cofo.edu
KEETER, Tara 252-536-7223 335 B
tkeeter618@halifaxcc.edu
KEETON, Kristi 913-971-3544 175 G
kkeeton@mnu.edu
KEETON, Tim 913-971-3607 175 G
tkeeton@mnu.edu
KEFAUVER, Lucy 304-336-8432 490 F
KEFERL, Joseph, E 937-775-2821 364 I
joseph.keferl@wright.edu
KEGEL, Gregory, D 406-265-3720 264 F
kegel@msun.edu
KEGELMAN, Nancy 732-224-2221 276 B
nkegelman@brookdalecc.edu
KEGLEY, Jacquelyn 661-654-2249 30 E
jkegley@csub.edu
KEHL, Maria 760-921-5415 55 H
maria.kehl@paloverde.edu
KEHL, Susan 501-279-4941 19 D
skehl@harding.edu

KELLY, Carrie .... 928-692-3085.. 14 F
ckelly@mohave.edu
KELLY, Chassie .... 662-720-7239 248 C
cmkelly@nemcc.edu
KELLY, Chris .... 479-788-7510.. 21 H
chris.kelly@uafs.edu
KELLY, Christine .... 909-621-8177.. 37 D
christine.kelly@cgu.edu
KELLY, Daniel .... 775-831-1314 272 D
dkelly@sierranevada.edu
KELLY, Daniel .... 734-487-2031 223 H
dkelly20@emich.edu
KELLY, Darin .... 215-717-3108 382 B
darin.kelly@curtis.edu
KELLY, OSB, David .... 724-805-2644 398 E
david.kelly@email.stvincent.edu
KELLY, OSB, David .... 724-805-2644 398 F
david.kelly@stvincent.edu
KELLY, David, E .... 845-368-7210 315 D
KELLY, Dean .... 253-589-6066 479 G
dean.kelly@cptc.edu
KELLY, Debra .... 609-771-2161 276 I
dkelly@tcnj.edu
KELLY, Debra, D .... 716-880-2524 306 C
debra.d.kelly@medaille.edu
KELLY, Dennis .... 937-481-2555 364 E
dennis_kelly@wilmington.edu
KELLY, Drew .... 610-526-6669 385 G
dkelly@harcum.edu
KELLY, Francis, E .... 845-575-3000 305 L
francis.kelly@marist.edu
KELLY, George, N .... 615-327-6800 422 A
gkelly@mmc.edu
KELLY, Georgetta .... 480-731-8103.. 12 O
georgetta.kelly@domail.maricopa.edu
KELLY, Grayson .... 864-646-1548 413 A
gkelly1@tctc.edu
KELLY, Hank .... 740-474-8896 358 F
hkelly@ohiochristian.edu
KELLY, Heather, A .... 302-831-2021.. 90 F
hkelly@udel.edu
KELLY, Hilton .... 704-894-2270 328 F
hikelly@davidson.edu
KELLY, Inesha, B .... 773-291-6275 134 E
ikelly1@ccc.edu
KELLY, James .... 256-726-7356.... 6 C
jbkelly@oakwood.edu
KELLY, Janet .... 478-218-3319 116 A
jkelly@centralgatech.edu
KELLY, Jeffrey, M .... 443-352-4012 201 H
jkelly@stevenson.edu
KELLY, Jeneen .... 914-323-5337 305 J
jeneen.kelly@mville.edu
KELLY, Jess, P .... 972-860-7141 435 B
jesskelly@dcccd.edu
KELLY, John .... 617-735-9710 209 A
kellyjo@emmanuel.edu
KELLY, John .... 561-297-3450 108 J
president@fau.edu
KELLY, Julie, A .... 860-444-8508 504 F
julie.a.kelly@uscg.mil
KELLY, Kathleen .... 518-244-2030 313 D
kellyk5@sage.edu
KELLY, Kathleen .... 617-585-1154 217 B
kathleen.kelly@necmusic.edu
KELLY, Kathy .... 513-244-4418 357 A
kathy.kelly@msj.edu
KELLY, Kelly .... 608-822-2305 500 G
kkelly@swtc.edu
KELLY, Kevin .... 860-215-9325.. 86 F
kkelly@trcc.commnet.edu
KELLY, Kevin, P .... 410-269-5087 202 D
kkelly@umaryland.edu
KELLY, Kevin, R .... 937-229-3557 362 G
kellyker@udayton.edu
KELLY, Kieran .... 617-254-2610 218 D
kieran.kelly@sjs.edu
KELLY, Kirk .... 503-725-6246 376 A
kkelly@pdx.edu
KELLY, Laura .... 315-312-3151 319 B
laura.kelly@oswego.edu
KELLY, Lauren, E .... 407-582-8125 112 K
lkelly22@valenciacollege.edu
KELLY, Lee .... 718-997-4455 295 C
lee.kelly@qc.cuny.edu
KELLY, Leslie, E .... 207-834-7522 196 C
lesliek@maine.edu
KELLY, Lyn .... 585-475-2946 313 A
lyn.kelly@rit.edu
KELLY, Lynn .... 912-260-4324 124 C
lynn.kelly@sgsc.edu
KELLY, Margaret, S .... 267-341-3651 386 A
mkelly@holyfamily.edu
KELLY, Marie, C .... 508-565-1169 218 H
mkelly1@stonehill.edu
KELLY, Marisa .... 617-573-8120 219 A
mjkelly@suffolk.edu
KELLY, Mark .... 269-927-8100 226 D
kelly@lakemichigancollege.edu
KELLY, Maureen .... 708-235-7556 137 F
mkelly7@govst.edu
KELLY, Michael .... 813-974-1442 110 B
michaelskelly@usf.edu
KELLY, Michele .... 734-462-4400 230 D
KELLY, Paige .... 276-739-2461 476 C
pkelly@vhcc.edu
KELLY, Patricia .... 662-246-6417 247 D
pkelly@msdelta.edu
KELLY, Peter .... 540-654-1464 472 I
pkelly3@umw.edu
KELLY, Peter, T .... 570-389-4674 394 A
pkelly@bloomu.edu
KELLY, Rob .... 410-617-2842 199 F
rkelly1@loyola.edu
KELLY, Robert .... 620-665-3417 174 B
kellyr@hutchcc.edu
KELLY, Rosemary .... 910-678-8325 334 D
kellyr@faytechcc.edu
KELLY, Roxanne .... 218-285-2202 240 D
roxanne.kelly@rainyriver.edu
KELLY, Ryan, J .... 517-750-1200 230 H
jo776328@arbor.edu
KELLY, Sandra .... 601-968-8909 245 C
skelly@belhaven.edu
KELLY, Sandra .... 803-777-2808 413 C
sjkelly@mailbox.sc.edu
KELLY, Sara .... 585-395-2369 318 B
skelly@brockport.edu
KELLY, Sarah .... 504-865-2011 189 F
KELLY, Sarah, J .... 330-972-6134 362 B
sarah30@uakron.edu
KELLY, Sean .... 210-458-6463 455 E
sean.kelly@utsa.edu
KELLY, Sean Ann .... 570-702-8963 386 G
skelly@johnson.edu
KELLY, Stephanie .... 773-995-2462 133 K
skelly24@csu.edu
KELLY, Stephanie .... 317-788-6099 161 B
spkelly@uindy.edu
KELLY, Steve .... 757-481-5005 478 C
KELLY, Susan .... 617-287-7050 211 C
skelly@umassp.edu
KELLY, T. Liisa .... 910-843-5304 331 K
lkelly@nabc.edu
KELLY, Tami .... 281-459-7653 443 D
tami.kelly@sjcd.edu
KELLY, Tiffany .... 719-389-6772.. 77 H
tkelly@coloradocollege.edu
KELLY, Todd .... 719-549-2380.. 79 A
todd.kelly@csupueblo.edu
KELLY, Tracy .... 716-338-1042 303 D
tracykelly@mail.sunyjcc.edu
KELLY, Troy .... 703-284-1614 469 C
bstore@marymount.edu
KELLY, Valerie, I .... 330-672-0020 354 J
vkelly@kent.edu
KELLY, William .... 605-642-6371 416 I
william.kelly@bhsu.edu
KELLY, William, G .... 860-444-8285 504 F
william.g.kelly@uscg.mil
KELLY BATES, Martha ... 847-578-8582 147 I
martha.bates@rosalindfranklin.edu
KELLY-BOWRY, Tanya ... 303-831-6192.. 82 N
tanya.kellybowry@cu.edu
KELLY KLEESE,
Christine .... 919-536-7200 334 B
kleesec@durhamtech.edu
KELLY-VERGONA,
Barbara .... 973-957-0188 275 C
registrar@acs350.org
KELSCH, Anne .... 701-777-3325 345 C
anne.kelsch@und.edu
KELSCH, Tyler .... 303-546-3569.. 81 B
tkelsch@naropa.edu
KELSER, Sandra, B .... 334-833-4409.... 5 H
skelser@hawks.huntingdon.edu
KELSEY, Anita .... 765-285-8101 153 C
akelsey@bsu.edu
KELSEY, Barb .... 608-789-6199 501 A
kelseyb@westerntc.edu
KELSEY, Kathleen, A ..... 570-326-3761 393 G
kathy.kelsey@pct.edu
KELSEY, Katie, M .... 402-280-1715 266 I
katiekelsey@creighton.edu
KELSEY, Madelaine .... 203-596-4624.. 87 F
mkelsey@post.edu
KELSEY, Ross .... 281-998-6150 443 E
ross.kelsey@sjcd.edu
KELSO, Amanda .... 919-684-2174 328 G
amanda.kelso@duke.edu
KELSO, Anne-Marie ...... 541-881-5838 377 B
akelso@tvcc.cc
KELSO, Geni .... 903-813-2445 430 N
gkelso@austincollege.edu
KELSO, William .... 912-478-6028 119 C
wkelso@georgiasouthern.edu
KELTON, Emily .... 303-273-3148.. 78 I
ekelton@mines.edu
KELVEY, Bill .... 410-386-8214 197 G
bkelvey@carrollcc.edu
KEM, John .... 717-245-4400 504 E
KEMENY, Paul, C .... 724-458-2025 385 C
pckemeny@gcc.edu
KEMKER, Brett .... 941-359-4200 110 D
kemker@sar.usf.edu
KEMNITZ, Marcie .... 308-398-7400 266 A
mkemnitz@cccneb.edu
KEMP, Arnold .... 312-899-1294 148 I
akemp@saic.edu
KEMP, Camilla .... 810-762-9937 225 H
ckemp@kettering.edu
KEMP, Claudia .... 501-623-2272.. 18 I
KEMP, Connie .... 713-743-5703 452 F
ckemp2@uh.edu
KEMP, Connie .... 713-743-5703 452 E
ckemp2@uh.edu
KEMP, Danny .... 540-831-7167 470 C
dmkemp@radford.edu
KEMP, Dawn .... 317-632-5553 158 S
dkemp@lincolntech.edu
KEMP, Gloria .... 501-686-6128.. 22 C
kempgloriad@uams.edu
KEMP, Jerylle .... 212-237-8964 294 D
jkemp@jjay.cuny.edu
KEMP, John .... 864-294-3717 410 A
john.kemp@furman.edu
KEMP, Katie .... 847-317-8177 150 H
katiek@tiu.edu
KEMP, Lisa .... 301-985-7000 203 B
lisa.kemp@umuc.edu
KEMP, Rick .... 480-517-8508.. 13 G
rick.kemp@riosalado.edu
KEMP, Shirley .... 304-829-7485 487 G
skemp@bethanywv.edu
KEMP, Stephen .... 515-292-9694 162 G
stephen.kemp@antiochschool.edu
KEMP, Steve .... 760-366-5283.. 40 K
skemp@cmccd.edu
KEMPA, Richard .... 307-382-1731 502 I
rkempa@westernwyoming.edu
KEMPE, Amy, P .... 401-825-2028 404 H
apkempe@ccri.edu
KEMPE, Michael, A .... 330-325-6481 357 G
mkempe@neomed.edu
KEMPEL, Leo .... 517-355-5114 227 D
kempel@egr.msu.edu
KEMPER, James .... 740-588-1209 365 E
jkemper@zanestate.edu
KEMPER, Kenneth, B .... 616-538-2330 224 C
preskemper@gracechristian.edu
KEMPER-PELLE, Cathy .. 541-956-7000 376 D
ckemperpelle@roguecc.edu
KEMPF, Cory .... 715-394-8366 498 B
ckempf1@uwsuper.edu
KEMPF, Kimberly .... 802-387-6723 462 D
kimberlykempf@landmark.edu
KEMPF-LEONARD,
Kimberly .... 502-852-2234 185 C
asdean@louisville.edu
KEMPSTER, James .... 718-636-3471 311 J
jkempster@pratt.edu
KEMPTON, Daniel .... 740-283-6228 353 B
dkempton@franciscan.edu
KENAUSIS, Veronica ...... 203-837-9109.. 85 B
kenausisv@wcsu.edu
KENCH, Brian .... 203-932-7115.. 89 A
bkench@newhaven.edu
KENDALL, Curtis, L .... 540-828-5476 465 D
ckendall@bridgewater.edu
KENDALL, David .... 574-535-7030 155 A
davidk15@goshen.edu
KENDALL, Donna .... 781-891-3441 206 D
dkendall@bentley.edu
KENDALL, Elizabeth .... 845-574-4269 313 C
ekendall@sunyrockland.edu
KENDALL, Joel .... 580-774-3252 370 C
joel.kendall@swosu.edu
KENDALL, Justin .... 620-862-5252 171 B
justin.kendall@barclaycollege.edu
KENDALL, Kenny .... 315-470-7749 291 H
kennethkendall@crouse.org
KENDALL, Mallory .... 662-846-4640 245 H
KENDALL, Mark .... 909-607-9660.. 57 F
mark.kendall@pomona.edu
KENDALL, Peter .... 828-328-7100 330 F
peter.kendall@lr.edu
KENDALL, Rex .... 812-237-6100 155 G
rkendall@indstatefoundation.org
KENDALL, Stephanie ..... 978-837-5321 216 D
kendalls@merrimack.edu
KENDALL-LEKKA,
Meitaka .... 692-625-3394 505 F
mkendall@cmi.edu
KENDER, Joseph, P ...... 610-660-2309 398 C
jkender@sju.edu
KENDERDINE, Linda ..... 410-706-5036 202 D
lcassard@umaryland.edu
KENDIG, P. Tysen .... 860-486-6713.. 88 E
tysen.kendig@uconn.edu
KENDJORIA, Barrett ...... 864-656-2354 408 A
bkendjo@clemson.edu
KENDREX, Bradley, S ... 480-732-7379.. 12 P
bradley.kendrex@cgc.edu
KENDRICK, Bethany ...... 620-421-6700 175 C
bethanyk@labette.edu
KENDRICK, Curtis .... 607-777-4550 316 E
kendrick@binghamton.edu
KENDRICK, Emory .... 478-757-2038 126 H
ekendrick@wesleyancollege.edu
KENDRICK, Haley .... 704-406-3957 329 A
hkendrick@gardner-webb.edu
KENDRICK, Marsha .... 405-692-3241 366 G
marsha.kendrick@macu.edu
KENDRICK, R. Ryan ...... 716-286-8708 310 D
rkendrick@niagara.edu
KENDZIERSKI,
Christian .... 410-532-3191 201 B
ckendzierski@ndm.edu
KENERSON, Laura .... 401-874-5271 406 B
lkenerson@uri.edu
KENERSON, Murle .... 615-963-5203 426 D
mkenerson@tnstate.edu
KENESSON, Summer, S 253-535-8145 482 H
kenessss@plu.edu
KENFIELD, Mikal, C ...... 218-299-3872 235 E
kenfield@cord.edu
KENIMER, Ann .... 979-845-3210 446 G
a-kenimer@tamu.edu
KENISTON, Joseph, C .. 315-229-1858 314 F
jkeniston@stlawu.edu
KENISTON, Leonda .... 434-961-5380 475 F
lkeniston@pvcc.edu
KENKEL, Kevin .... 605-995-2617 415 C
kevin.kenkel@dwu.edu
KENMILLE, Cleo .... 406-275-4864 265 F
cleo_kenmille@skc.edu
KENN, Jim .... 617-559-8688 210 C
jkenn@hebrewcollege.edu
KENNA-SCHENK, Becca 360-951-3733 486 F
becca.kenna-schenk@wwu.edu
KENNAMER, Mike .... 256-228-6001.... 3 B
kennamerm@nacc.edu
KENNARD, Douglas ...... 304-876-5330 490 E
dkennard@shepherd.edu
KENNARD, Janet .... 713-942-9505 438 A
jkennard@hgst.edu
KENNEDY, Aaron .... 575-461-4413 286 E
aaronk@mesalands.edu
KENNEDY, Anne .... 312-553-2641 134 D
akennedy10@ccc.edu
KENNEDY, Barbara .... 724-222-5330 392 A
bkennedy@penncommercial.edu
KENNEDY, Bill .... 406-657-2244 264 E
foundation@msubillings.edu
KENNEDY, Brenda, J .... 251-580-2185.... 1 I
brenda.kennedy@coastalalabama.edu
KENNEDY, Brianne .... 619-388-3513.. 60 C
bkennedy@sdccd.edu
KENNEDY, Carol, M ..... 570-577-1511 379 F
carol.kennedy@bucknell.edu
KENNEDY, Catherine, B 401-739-5000 405 A
ckennedy@neit.edu
KENNEDY,
Catherine, C .... 727-394-6202 106 E
kennedy.catherine@spcollege.edu
KENNEDY, Christopher . 843-661-1557 409 K
ckennedy@fmarion.edu
KENNEDY, Colleen .... 773-371-5417 133 E
ckennedy@ctu.edu
KENNEDY, Damon .... 432-685-4524 440 E
dkennedy@midland.edu
KENNEDY, Dana .... 330-263-2317 351 C
dakennedy@wooster.edu

KERRIGAN, John, E ...... 408-554-4968.. 62 D
jekerrigan@scu.edu
KERRIGAN, Noreen .... 718-430-2000 289 G
KERRUISH, Diane .... 847-214-7374 136 F
dkerruish@elgin.edu
KERRY, Susan .... 218-723-6083 235 D
skerry@css.edu
KERRY, Susan, E .... 906-487-1060 227 E
skerry@mtu.edu
KERSAINT, Gladis .... 860-486-3815.. 88 E
kersaint@uconn.edu
KERSCHNER, Joseph, E 414-955-8213 494 C
jkerschner@mcw.edu
KERSEY, Pam .... 619-660-4453.. 44 H
pam.kersey@gcccd.edu
KERSEY, Robert, N .... 843-953-5542 408 E
kerseyr@cofc.edu
KERSH, Rogan .... 336-758-3128 344 D
kersh@wfu.edu
KERSHNER, Megan, N .. 316-284-5305 171 F
mkershner@bethelks.edu
KERSHNER, Scott, M .... 570-372-4220 399 C
kershner@susqu.edu
KERSTEN, Andrew .... 314-516-5404 261 D
kerstenan@umsl.edu
KERSTEN, Belen .... 559-730-3794.. 39 E
belenk@cos.edu
KERSTEN, David, W ...... 773-244-6235 145 A
dwkersten@northpark.edu
KERSTEN, James, B ...... 515-574-1132 166 E
kersten@iowacentral.edu
KERSTENS, Margaret ..... 832-813-6272 439 G
margaret.kerstens@lonestar.edu
KERTULIS-TARTAR,
Gina .... 706-272-4516 117 C
gkertulistartar@daltonstate.edu
KERTZ, Nancy, K .... 515-643-6615 168 A
nkertz@mercydesmoines.org
KERWICK, Sean .... 201-360-4023 278 C
skerwick@hccc.edu
KERWIN, Linda .... 716-827-2454 323 D
kerwinl@trocaire.edu
KERWITZ, Ann .... 815-921-4001 147 E
a.kerwitz@rockvalleycollege.edu
KERYLOW, Tiffany .... 802-387-6725 462 D
tiffanykerylow@landmark.edu
KESERAUSKIS, Beth ...... 314-446-8207 259 B
beth.keserauskis@stlcop.edu
KESHNER, Larry .... 708-344-4700 142 A
lkeshner@lincolntech.edu
KESHVALA, Seelpa .... 281-290-3940 439 G
seelpa.h.keshvala@lonestar.edu
KESICKI, Michael .... 814-871-5873 384 E
kesicki001@gannon.edu
KESKULA, Douglas, R ... 828-227-7271 344 A
drkeskula@wcu.edu
KESLER, David .... 740-264-5591 352 H
dkesler@egcc.edu
KESNER, Idalene, F .... 812-855-8489 156 B
ikesner@indiana.edu
KESNER, Idalene, F .... 812-855-8489 156 A
ikesner@indiana.edu
KESSELMAN, Harvey ..... 609-652-4521 283 D
harvey.kesselman@stockton.edu
KESSELRING-QUAKENBUSH,
Heather .... 616-632-2151 221 C
hkq001@aquinas.edu
KESSIE, Michael .... 941-487-4212 109 D
mkessie@ncf.edu
KESSINGER, David .... 618-664-7109 137 G
david.kessinger@greenville.edu
KESSINGER, Whitney .... 513-244-4389 357 A
whitney.kessinger@msj.edu
KESSLER, Brian .... 423-869-7077 421 C
brian.kessler@lmunet.edu
KESSLER, H. Charles .... 216-881-1700 359 F
ckessler@ohiotech.edu
KESSLER, Jeffrey, A ...... 516-877-3660 289 C
kessler@adelphi.edu
KESSLER, Joyce .... 216-421-7411 350 M
jkessler@cia.edu
KESSLER, Kathleen .... 802-839-8317 462 I
kathleen.kessler@neci.edu
KESSLER, Lisa .... 909-869-2203.. 30 D
lakessler@cpp.edu
KESSLER, Lisa .... 512-313-3000 434 E
lisa.kessler@concordia.edu
KESSLER, Mary .... 812-488-2569 161 A
mk43@evansville.edu
KESSLER, Michael .... 701-231-7494 345 G
michael.r.kessler@ndsu.edu
KESSLER, Richard .... 212-580-0210 308 C
kesslerr@newschool.edu
KESSLER, Samantha ...... 510-723-6824.. 35 O
skessler@chabotcollege.edu
KESSLER, Sheryl .... 215-972-7600 393 D
skessler@pafa.org
KESSLER, Susan, B .... 386-312-4021 106 C
susankessler@sjrstate.edu
KESSLER-CLEARY,
Timothy .... 973-618-3484 276 D
tcleary@caldwell.edu
KESTEN, Philip, R .... 408-554-4311.. 62 D
pkesten@scu.edu
KESTENBAUM, Yoel ...... 845-782-1380 326 H
KESTER, John .... 910-410-1778 337 B
jikester@richmondcc.edu
KESTER, Kelly .... 360-383-3245 486 G
kkester@whatcom.edu
KESTER, Lori .... 303-273-3639.. 78 I
lkester@mines.edu
KESTERSON, Donald ..... 863-784-7132 107 F
donald.kesterson@southflorida.edu
KESTERSON, Ronald, L . 865-694-6608 425 F
rkesterson@pstcc.edu
KESTNER-RICKETTS,
Laura .... 309-794-7338 132 C
laurakestnerricketts@augustana.edu
KETCHEN, John .... 865-573-4517 420 G
jketchen@johnsonu.edu
KETCHER, Sam .... 417-690-2211 251 E
ketcher@cofo.edu
KETCHESON, Kathi, A ... 503-725-3425 376 A
ketchesonk@pdx.edu
KETCHUM, Kendra .... 210-458-4011 455 E
KETELS, Margo .... 563-589-3765 169 I
mketels@dbq.edu
KETJEN, William .... 330-823-2293 363 B
ketjenwl@mountunion.edu
KETNER, Annette .... 619-260-2925.. 71 J
aketner@sandiego.edu
KETO, Stephen, W .... 218-726-7101 243 F
vcfo@d.umn.edu
KETTEMAN, P. Greg ...... 615-675-5312 428 G
gketteman@welch.edu
KETTENBEIL, Kenneth ... 313-593-5140 231 F
kketten@umich.edu
KETTERING, Rocky .... 706-507-8954 116 I
kettering_rocky@columbusstate.edu
KETTERING-LANE,
Denise .... 800-287-8822 153 D
kettede@bethanyseminary.edu
KETTERLING, Jayme ...... 208-732-6552 130 E
jketterling@csi.edu
KETTERLING, Kate .... 612-343-4442 242 H
kaketter@northcentral.edu
KETTERMAN, Beth .... 252-744-2212 341 C
kettermane@ecu.edu
KETTING-WELLER,
Ginger .... 951-785-2266.. 47 C
gketting@lasierra.edu
KETTINGER, Kevin .... 585-567-9350 302 D
kevin.kettinger@houghton.edu
KETTINGER, Kirk .... 585-594-6415 312 K
kettinger_kirk@roberts.edu
KETTLER, Karen .... 304-336-8070 490 F
kkettler@westliberty.edu
KETTLEWELL, Kelly .... 570-577-1604 379 F
kelly.kettlewell@bucknell.edu
KETTNER, Valrey, V ...... 701-231-9608 345 G
val.kettner@ndsu.edu
KEUFFEL, Elizabeth ...... 603-641-7203 274 C
ekeuffel@anselm.edu
KEUSS, Theresa .... 314-516-4602 261 D
keusst@umsl.edu
KEVARI, Jacob .... 760-366-5279.. 40 K
jkevari@cmccd.edu
KEVIL, Chris .... 318-675-4102 189 C
ckevil@lsuhsc.edu
KEVIL, Tim .... 903-875-7443 440 G
tim.kevil@navarrocollege.edu
KEVORKIAN, Meline ...... 954-262-8523 103 M
melinek@nova.edu
KEVORKIAN,
Theresa, R .... 305-684-6020 321 D
kevorktr@morrisville.edu
KEW-FICKUS, Olivia ...... 615-343-2746 428 D
olivia.m.kew-fickus@vanderbilt.edu
KEY, Charles .... 865-471-3447 419 A
ckey@cn.edu
KEY, Dan .... 641-844-5741 166 K
dan.key@iavalley.edu
KEY, Dillon .... 864-977-7122 411 E
dillon.key@ngu.edu
KEY, Randal .... 281-655-3701 439 G
rand.key@lonestar.edu
KEY, Shelly .... 361-593-5991 447 D
shelly.key@tamuk.edu
KEYES, Pat .... 401-841-6594 503 L
patrick.keyes@usnwc.edu
KEYNTON, Robert, S ..... 502-852-6356 185 C
robert.keynton@louisville.edu
KEYS, James, A .... 910-843-5304 331 K
jamesakeys@gmail.com
KEYS, Margo, A .... 715-858-1825 499 D
mkeys@cvtc.edu
KEYS, Marina .... 503-845-3550 374 B
marina.keys@mtangel.edu
KEYS, Mattie .... 918-463-2931 366 B
mattie.keys@connorsstate.edu
KEYS, Staci .... 417-667-8181 252 A
skeys@cottey.edu
KEYS, Terrance .... 585-292-3432 307 H
tkeys@monroecc.edu
KEYTON, Victoria .... 503-352-2705 375 G
victoria.keyton@pacificu.edu
KHACHATRYAN, Davit ... 949-451-5326.. 64 F
dkhachatryan@ivc.edu
KHADANGA, Dave .... 334-386-7113.... 5 D
dkhadanga@faulkner.edu
KHADEM, Farnaz .... 650-723-2300.. 65 J
KHADKA, Chandni .... 256-782-8304.... 5 J
ckhadka@jsu.edu
KHAGRAM, Sanjeev ...... 602-978-7203.. 10 I
sanjeev.khagram@asu.edu
KHALDEN, Jeff .... 817-598-6485 458 A
jkhalden@wc.edu
KHALEDI, Morteza .... 817-272-3491 454 J
morteza.khaledi@uta.edu
KHALILI, Kambiz .... 734-763-1291 231 E
kkhalili@umich.edu
KHALSA, Barbara .... 480-517-8778.. 13 G
barbara.khalsa@riosalado.edu
KHAMIS, Hanan .... 508-999-8845 211 F
hkhamis@umassd.edu
KHAMOUNA, Mo .... 308-367-5213 270 C
mkhamouna1@unl.edu
KHAN, Adil .... 636-227-2100 254 G
KHAN, Ali .... 402-559-4950 270 A
ali.khan@unmc.edu
KHAN, Feroze .... 703-539-6890 472 A
fkhan@stratford.edu
KHAN, Kafi .... 312-939-0111 136 D
kafikhan@eastwest.edu
KHAN, M. Rehan .... 502-852-7997 185 C
rehan.khan@louisville.edu
KHAN, M. Wasiullah ..... 312-939-0111 136 D
chancellor@eastwest.edu
KHAN, Raza .... 410-386-8222 197 G
rkhan@carrollcc.edu
KHAN, Robert .... 201-360-4033 278 C
rkhan@hccc.edu
KHAN, Rumaana, R .... 209-290-0333.. 24 E
rkhan@advancedcollege.edu
KHAN, Sadya .... 708-974-5283 144 C
khans46@morainevalley.edu
KHAN, Sobia .... 210-486-0947 429 H
skhan32@alamo.edu
KHAN-MARCUS,
Zaveeni .... 805-893-8411.. 70 A
zaveeni.khan-marcus@sa.ucsb.edu
KHANEJA, Gurvinder ..... 201-684-7766 280 H
gkhaneja@ramapo.edu
KHANI, Anthony .... 646-717-9743 300 G
khani@gts.edu
KHANNA, Pradeep .... 217-333-9525 151 D
pkhanna@illinois.edu
KHANOYAN, Gayane ...... 818-988-2300.. 53 D
KHARGONEKAR,
Pramod .... 949-824-5796.. 68 G
pkhargon@uci.edu
KHARKOVYY, Andriy ..... 269-471-3591 221 B
alumni@andrews.edu
KHARTABIL, Basim .... 312-935-3036 147 D
bkhartabil@robertmorris.edu
KHASIDOVA, Albina ...... 212-776-7299 293 A
akhasidova@bmcc.cuny.edu
KHATOR, Renu .... 713-743-8820 452 F
rkhator@uh.edu
KHATOR, Renu .... 713-743-8820 452 E
rkhator@uh.edu
KHATRI, Achal .... 617-873-0235 207 F
achal.khatri@cambridgecollege.edu
KHATTAB, Ahmed .... 337-482-6166 192 E
khattab@louisiana.edu
KHAVARI, Jenn .... 207-974-4673 194 H
jkhavari@emcc.edu
KHAWAR, Mariam .... 607-735-1932 299 D
mkhawar@elmira.edu
KHAYUM, Mohammed .. 812-465-1617 161 E
mkhayum@usi.edu
KHIDEKEL, Nelly .... 626-395-6454.. 29 C
nkhidekel@caltech.edu
KHOJA, Faiza .... 713-221-8218 453 B
khojafai@uhd.edu
KHOL, Justin .... 740-366-9171 349 H
khol.4@osu.edu
KHOO-ROBINSON,
Cynthia .... 716-645-3313 316 F
ckr5@buffalo.edu
KHOR, Henry .... 909-895-7138.. 45 G
KHOSLA, Pradeep, K ..... 858-534-3135.. 69 D
chancellor@ucsd.edu
KHOSRAVANI, Mariam . 714-241-6159.. 38 C
mkhosravani@coastline.edu
KHOSROWPANAH,
Shahram .... 671-735-2694 505 E
khosrow@triton.uog.edu
KHOURY, Melik Peter ... 207-509-7221 195 H
mkhoury@unity.edu
KHOURY, Philip, S .... 617-253-0887 215 G
KHOZA, Lombuso, S ..... 410-651-8385 203 A
lskhoza@umes.edu
KHURANA, Rakesh .... 617-495-1555 210 B
deankhurana@fas.harvard.edu
KHURANA-BAUGH,
Nikki .... 845-569-3216 307 J
nikki.khurana-baugh@msmc.edu
KIA, Norman .... 575-769-4074 285 K
norman.kia@clovis.edu
KIAKU, Junior .... 404-627-2681 115 C
junior.kiaku@beulah.edu
KIAN, David .... 561-297-3007 108 J
dkian@fau.edu
KIBBE REED, Trudie ..... 386-481-2000.. 95 F
KIBLER, Bill .... 432-837-8000 450 D
president@sulross.edu
KIBLER, Matthew .... 410-778-7862 204 D
mkibler2@washcoll.edu
KIBLER, Michele .... 614-222-4009 351 D
mkibler@ccad.edu
KICKER, Darrell .... 808-983-4100 128 A
KICKLIGHTER, Barry ..... 678-359-5680 119 F
bkicklighter@gordonstate.edu
KIDD, Anessa .... 334-876-9303.... 2 D
anessa.kidd@wccs.edu
KIDD, Ayesha .... 702-651-7456 271 A
ayesha.kidd@csn.edu
KIDD, Beth Ann .... 903-675-6223 452 B
bkidd@tvcc.edu
KIDD, Jimmy .... 502-213-2446 181 F
jimmy.kidd@kctcs.edu
KIDD, Kevin .... 617-989-9095 219 E
kiddk@wit.edu
KIDD, Lisa, L .... 920-923-8115 494 A
llkidd60@marianuniversity.edu
KIDD, Quentin .... 757-594-0723 466 B
qkidd@cnu.edu
KIDD, Twyla .... 704-463-3067 339 E
twyla.kidd@pfeiffer.edu
KIDD, Windy .... 859-280-1237 183 B
wkidd@lextheo.edu
KIDDER, Micki .... 574-631-6526 161 C
mkidder@nd.edu
KIDDIE, Thomas .... 304-766-4116 491 B
tkiddie@wvstateu.edu
KIDDOO, Sandra .... 606-487-3091 181 C
sandra.kiddoo@kctcs.edu
KIDDOO, Sandy .... 715-422-5476 500 A
sandy.kiddoo@mstc.edu
KIDESS LUCEY, Tamie .. 413-748-3161 218 G
tkidessl@springfield.edu
KIDNEIGH, Gina .... 307-675-0331 502 F
gkidneigh@sheridan.edu
KIDO, Kengo .... 323-860-1173.. 53 B
kengok@mi.edu
KIDSTON, Nicole .... 212-353-4136 297 E
nkidston@cooper.edu
KIDWELL, Eric, A .... 334-833-4420..... 5 H
ekidwell@hawks.huntingdon.edu
KIDWELL, John .... 870-460-1083.. 22 D
kidwell@uamont.edu
KIDWELL, Kim .... 217-333-0460 151 D
kkidwell@illinois.edu
KIDWELL, Martin .... 503-253-3443 374 H
mkidwell@ocom.edu
KIEBA-TOLKSDORF,
Helen, C .... 248-689-8282 232 A
hkieba@walshcollege.edu
KIEC, Michael .... 216-373-5227 358 B
mkiec@ndc.edu

KIMBLE, Robert ... 304-473-8438 491 H kimble.r@wvwc.edu
KIMBLE, Thomas, D ... 757-446-5615 466 I kimbletd@evms.edu
KIMBLE, Treina ... 318-342-1004 192 F landrum@ulm.edu
KIMBLE-TUSZYNSKI, Kate ... 707-654-1406.. 32 B kkimble@csum.edu
KIMBRIEL, William ... 870-508-6107.. 18 A wkimbriel@asumh.edu
KIMBROUGH, B. J ... 205-652-3531.... 9 A bkimbrough@uwa.edu
KIMBROUGH, B.J ... 205-652-3421.... 9 A bkimbrough@uwa.edu
KIMBROUGH, II, Richard (Rick) ... 210-436-3138 443 A rkimbrough@stmarytx.edu
KIMBROUGH, Scott ... 904-256-7118 101 G skimbro@ju.edu
KIMBROUGH, Walter, M ... 504-816-4640 186 D wkimbrough@dillard.edu
KIMBROW, Terry ... 501-205-8904.. 18 H tkimbrow@cbc.edu
KIME, Kevin ... 814-886-6481 391 B kkime@mtaloy.edu
KIMERY, Millard ... 325-649-8181 438 D mkimery@hputx.edu
KIMES, Diane, K ... 810-762-7491 225 H dkimes@kettering.edu
KIMLER, Robert ... 732-224-2355 276 B rkimler@brookdalecc.edu
KIMMEL, Kate ... 631-656-2145 300 D kate.kimmel@ftc.edu
KIMMEL, Peter ... 802-468-1344 464 A peter.kimmel@castleton.edu
KIMMEL, Rhonda ... 262-595-2237 497 C rhonda.kimmel@uwp.edu
KIMMELMAN, Barbara .. 215-951-2612 400 A barbara.kimmelman@jefferson.edu
KIMMELMAN, Scott ... 772-462-7760 101 E skimmelm@irsc.edu
KIMMINS, William, P ... 516-876-3179 319 A kimminsw@oldwestbury.edu
KIMPAN, John ... 412-359-1000 400 G jkimpan@triangle-tech.edu
KIMREY, Phil ... 205-726-2736.... 6 E ppkimrey@samford.edu
KIMSEY, Phillip ... 706-204-2283 118 E pkimsey@highlands.edu
KIN, Amanda, E ... 205-853-1200.... 2 G akin@jeffersonstate.edu
KINANE, Michael, G ... 516-876-3162 319 A kinanem@oldwestbury.edu
KINARD, Mary ... 205-387-0511.... 1 D mary.kinard@bscc.edu
KINARD, Trent ... 803-812-7468 413 G tkinard@mailbox.sc.edu
KINARD, Zeolean, F ... 864-941-8688 411 H kinard.z@ptc.edu
KINCAID, Brenda, L ... 615-297-7545 418 C kincaid@aquinascollege.edu
KINCAID, Heather ... 740-374-8716 364 C hkincaid@wscc.edu
KINCANNON, Mary ... 817-257-7237 448 G m.kincannon@tcu.edu
KINCART, Joel ... 605-394-2436 417 B joel.kincart@sdsmt.edu
KINCHEN, Thomas, A ... 850-263-3261.. 95 B takinchen@baptistcollege.edu
KINCHENS, Eulish ... 229-931-2249 124 D ekinchens@southgatech.edu
KIND, Gene ... 970-542-3248.. 81 A gene.kind@morgancc.edu
KIND, Jule ... 765-677-2980 157 D jule.kind@indwes.edu
KIND-KEPPEL, Heather . 262-595-2239 497 C kindkepp@uwp.edu
KINDER, Angelic, M ... 304-260-4380 488 J akinder@blueridgectc.edu
KINDER, Chad, L ... 580-774-3790 370 C chad.kinder@swosu.edu
KINDER, Terri ... 419-866-0291 361 H tkinder@stautzenberger.com
KINDERS, Mark ... 405-974-5560 370 K mkinders@uco.edu
KINDHART, Randi ... 217-228-5432 146 F kindhra@quincy.edu
KINDL, Christine ... 724-938-5492 394 B kindl@calu.edu
KINDLE, Derek ... 608-262-3060 496 C derek.kindle@wisc.edu
KINDLE, Joan ... 563-336-3488 165 B jkindle@eicc.edu
KINDLER, Andreas ... 309-677-3107 133 B akindler@bradley.edu
KINDLER, Lisa ... 704-406-3923 329 A lkindler@gardner-webb.edu
KINDON, Victoria ... 434-395-2001 469 A kindonv@longwood.edu
KINEAVY, Jacqueline ... 973-684-6300 280 B jkineavy@pccc.edu
KINEAVY, John ... 617-573-8406 219 A jkineavy@suffolk.edu
KINEL, Janine, S ... 860-297-2255.. 88 C janine.kinel@trincoll.edu
KINERNEY, Donna ... 240-567-8827 200 C donna.kinerney@montgomerycollege.edu
KINERSON, Sara ... 802-635-1257 464 C sara.kinerson@northernvermont.edu
KINES, James ... 864-231-2177 406 G jkines@andersonuniversity.edu
KINES, Teresa ... 336-249-8186 334 A tkines@davidsonccc.edu
KING, Adrienne ... 419-530-2002 363 E adrienne.king@utoledo.edu
KING, Albert ... 419-289-5959 348 A aking@ashland.edu
KING, Alissa ... 601-318-6474 249 H aking@wmcarey.edu
KING, Allyson ... 229-732-5956 114 B allysonking@andrewcollege.edu
KING, Andrew ... 207-780-5670 196 F andrew.king@maine.edu
KING, Andrew, B ... 904-620-2602 110 A a.king@unf.edu
KING, Angella ... 859-246-6696 180 K angie.king@kctcs.edu
KING, Ann ... 847-214-7228 136 F aking@elgin.edu
KING, Anne ... 805-289-6503.. 73 B aking@vcccd.edu
KING, Anthony ... 937-255-6565 503 A anthony.king@afit.edu
KING, Art ... 646-312-4570 292 L art.king@baruch.cuny.edu
KING, B, J ... 423-439-5884 419 J kingbj@etsu.edu
KING, Barabara ... 903-533-5468 452 C bkin2@tjc.edu
KING, Bayard ... 212-217-4020 299 H bayard_king@fitnyc.edu
KING, Beth ... 304-637-1243 487 I kinge@dewv.edu
KING, Bill, L ... 972-985-3796 433 M blking@collin.edu
KING, Blythe ... 228-896-2503 247 E blythe.king@mgccc.edu
KING, Bob ... 210-999-7011 452 A bob.king@trinity.edu
KING, Brenda, M ... 304-336-8076 490 F kingbren@westliberty.edu
KING, Brian ... 916-568-3021.. 50 E kingb@losrios.edu
KING, Brian ... 814-866-6641 388 A bking@lecom.edu
KING, Bruce ... 510-215-4853.. 40 H bking@contracosta.edu
KING, Bruce ... 507-786-3334 243 C kingb@stolaf.edu
KING, Carolee ... 409-772-1904 456 F caaking@utmb.edu
KING, Charles ... 501-370-5392.. 20 G cking@philander.edu
KING, Charles ... 409-933-8404 433 L cking@com.edu
KING, Charles, W ... 540-568-6434 468 F kingcw@jmu.edu
KING, Chris ... 276-244-1303 464 L cking@asl.edu
KING, Chris ... 412-397-4913 397 G kingc@rmu.edu
KING, Clifton ... 662-246-6462 247 D cking@msdelta.edu
KING, Corey ... 561-297-3988 108 J cking14@fau.edu
KING, Corinna ... 515-263-2802 165 I cking@grandview.edu
KING, Craig ... 212-870-1238 310 A cking@nyts.edu
KING, Curt ... 978-542-6446 213 C cking@salemstate.edu
KING, Cynthia, L ... 610-861-5510 391 F cking@northampton.edu
KING, D. Wayne ... 859-238-5550 179 F wayne.king@centre.edu
KING, Dan ... 218-679-2860 242 P
KING, Dana ... 706-622-5006 124 B dking@shorter.edu
KING, Daniel, P ... 334-844-4810.... 4 E dpk0002@auburn.edu
KING, Danielle ... 606-487-3524 181 C danielle.king@kctcs.edu
KING, Darin ... 701-777-4237 345 B darin.r.king@ndus.edu
KING, David ... 815-772-7218 144 D dking@morrisontech.edu
KING, David, A ... 540-432-4440 466 G david.king@emu.edu
KING, David, A ... 330-471-8121 355 L dking@malone.edu
KING, David, A ... 541-737-2676 375 D ecampus@oregonstate.edu
KING, David, S ... 252-334-2084 331 D david.king@macuniversity.edu
KING, David, W ... 805-565-6036.. 74 K dking@westmont.edu
KING, Deborah ... 870-338-6474.. 22 H
KING, Del ... 404-727-7567 117 F dking2@emory.edu
KING, Denise ... 423-472-7141 424 F dking05@clevelandstatecc.edu
KING, Dennis ... 785-628-4276 173 B dking@fhsu.edu
KING, Dennis ... 828-398-7112 332 B dennisfking@abtech.edu
KING, Donald ... 508-999-8575 211 F dking@umassd.edu
KING, Dottie ... 812-535-5296 160 B president@smwc.edu
KING, Ebony ... 712-749-2379 163 D kinge@bvu.edu
KING, Elizabeth, H ... 316-978-3510 178 A elizabeth.king@wichita.edu
KING, Fleurette ... 970-351-3012.. 83 E fleurette.king@unco.edu
KING, Fred, L ... 304-293-3449 491 C fred.king@mail.wvu.edu
KING, Garrett ... 580-774-3267 370 C garrett.king@swosu.edu
KING, Gillian, M ... 315-859-4101 301 C gking@hamilton.edu
KING, Greg ... 309-556-3031 139 G gking@iwu.edu
KING, Greg ... 423-236-2975 424 B gking@southern.edu
KING, Gregory ... 330-823-2282 363 B kinggl@mountunion.edu
KING, Henry, D ... 260-422-5561 155 H hdking@indianatech.edu
KING, Herbert, L ... 828-898-8785 330 E kingl@lmc.edu
KING, Jackie, E ... 585-275-9900 323 J jking@admin.rochester.edu
KING, James ... 615-336-4460 424 D james.king@tbr.edu
KING, James ... 615-366-4400 424 D james.king@tbr.edu
KING, James ... 304-876-5236 490 E jking@shepherd.edu
KING, Jason ... 850-484-1337 104 H jking@pensacolastate.edu
KING, Jeff ... 615-230-3461 426 B jeff.king@volstate.edu
KING, Jennifer ... 406-377-9458 263 E jking@dawson.edu
KING, Jeremy, R ... 864-656-4275 408 A jking2@clemson.edu
KING, Jerry ... 903-675-6211 452 B jking@tvcc.edu
KING, Jim, M ... 318-257-2445 191 F king@latech.edu
KING, Joel ... 308-398-7315 266 A joelking@cccneb.edu
KING, John ... 541-552-6261 376 E kingjo@sou.edu
KING, John ... 806-720-7211 439 H john.king@lcu.edu
KING, John ... 304-877-6428 487 F
KING, John, J ... 401-254-3042 405 E jjking@rwu.edu
KING, Jonathan ... 530-541-4660.. 47 E jking@ltcc.edu
KING, Jonathan ... 619-482-6379.. 65 F jking@swccd.edu
KING, Jovanna, J ... 864-656-0663 408 A jovanna@clemson.edu
KING, Julie ... 803-786-3650 408 F juking@columbiasc.edu
KING, Karen, D ... 423-439-5654 419 J kingk@etsu.edu
KING, Katherine ... 949-480-4161.. 64 B kking@soka.edu
KING, Keith ... 850-474-2503 110 E kcking@uwf.edu
KING, Kenneth ... 801-878-1419 272 C kking@roseman.edu
KING, Khristian, J ... 716-673-3398 317 A khristian.king@fredonia.edu
KING, Kim ... 937-376-2946 360 D kking@payne.edu
KING, Kimberly ... 239-280-2484.. 94 O kimberly.king@avemaria.edu
KING, Kwanna ... 307-766-5272 502 H regirtrar@uwyo.edu
KING, Laura ... 651-846-1316 241 B laura.king@saintpaul.edu
KING, Leslie ... 718-518-4377 294 B lking@hostos.cuny.edu
KING, Leslie ... 770-426-2713 121 C lesliek@life.edu
KING, Linda ... 864-231-2000 406 G dking@andersonuniversity.edu
KING, Linda ... 903-886-5013 447 B linda.king@tamuc.edu
KING, Lynn ... 910-879-5520 332 D lking@bladencc.edu
KING, Marsha, M ... 260-399-7700 161 D mking@sf.edu
KING, Mary ... 940-552-6291 457 C mking@vernoncollege.edu
KING, Mary Jo ... 270-706-8530 181 A maryjo.king@kctcs.edu
KING, Meade, B ... 540-464-7328 476 G mking@vmiaa.org
KING, Melinda ... 205-348-4904.... 7 G mjking@ua.edu
KING, Meredith ... 508-793-7739 208 A meking@clarku.edu
KING, Michael ... 913-360-7633 171 D mking@benedictine.edu
KING, Michael ... 706-754-7711 122 F mking@northgatech.edu
KING, Michelle ... 310-434-3323.. 62 E king_michelle@smc.edu
KING, Mike ... 617-747-2363 206 E enrollment@berklee.edu
KING, Mike ... 812-535-5273 160 B mking2@smwc.edu
KING, Mikki ... 567-268-6022 361 J kingmr@tiffin.edu
KING, Mindy ... 715-346-2321 497 F mking@uwsp.edu
KING, Natalie ... 831-582-3609.. 32 C nmking@csumb.edu
KING, Natasha ... 912-287-5827 116 F nking@coastalpines.edu
KING, Nathan ... 828-669-8012 331 J nathan.king@montreat.edu
KING, Nathaniel ... 702-992-2806 271 C nathaniel.king@nsc.edu
KING, Paula Kay ... 765-973-8331 156 C pkayking@iue.edu
KING, Peter, D ... 843-661-1281 409 K pking@fmarion.edu
KING, Phillip ... 206-546-4651 484 G pking@shoreline.edu
KING, Phyllis ... 414-229-6175 497 A pking@wm.edu
KING, Queen ... 661-654-2251.. 30 E qking@csub.edu
KING, Robert ... 707-654-1245.. 32 B rking@csum.edu
KING, Roch ... 251-626-3303.... 7 E rking@ussa.edu
KING, Rodmon ... 315-312-4478 319 B rodmon.king@oswego.edu
KING, Ronan ... 276-944-6125 467 G rking@ehc.edu
KING, Ryan ... 207-326-0136 195 D ryan.king@mma.edu
KING, S. Bruce ... 336-758-5774 344 D kingsb@wfu.edu
KING, Samuel ... 901-435-1509 421 A samuel_king@loc.edu
KING, Sasha ... 310-434-3404.. 62 E king_sasha@smc.edu
KING, Shawn ... 509-359-6878 480 E sking@ewu.edu

KING, Sheila, D .... 310-506-4151.. 56 C
sheila.king@pepperdine.edu
KING, Shelly .... 816-415-5963 262 F
kings@william.jewell.edu
KING, Stephanie .... 413-565-1000 205 G
sking@baypath.edu
KING, Steven .... 413-662-5410 213 A
steven.king@mcla.edu
KING, Susan, L .... 207-780-4681 196 F
susank@maine.edu
KING, Susan, R .... 919-962-1204 342 D
susanking@unc.edu
KING, JR.,
Talmadge, E .... 415-476-2342.. 69 E
talmadge.king@ucsf.edu
KING, Tamara .... 215-898-6081 400 K
tamking@upenn.edu
KING, Tammy, A .... 330-941-3321 365 C
taking@ysu.edu
KING, Terry .... 419-267-1251 358 A
tking@northweststate.edu
KING, Theresa .... 201-684-7800 280 H
0396mgr@fheg.follett.com
KING, Thomas .... 610-896-1111 385 L
tking@haverford.edu
KING, Tim .... 256-782-5020.... 5 J
tbking@jsu.edu
KING, Tom .... 610-896-1111 379 E
tking01@brynmawr.edu
KING, Tommy .... 601-318-6495 249 H
pres@wmcarey.edu
KING, Victor, I .... 323-343-3054.. 32 A
vking@cslanet.calstatela.edu
KING, W. Cody .... 229-931-2066 119 D
cody.king@gsw.edu
KING, W. Joseph .... 870-307-7201.. 20 A
president@lyon.edu
KING, William .... 734-764-0277 231 E
wwking@umich.edu
KING, William .... 540-231-5992 467 F
wiking1@vcom.vt.edu
KING, Yolanda .... 440-684-6085 363 G
yolanda.king@ursuline.edu
KING, Zachery .... 701-477-7978 347 A
zachery.king@tm.edu
KING-CROCKETT, Carla . 305-626-3666.. 99 D
ccrockett@fmuniv.edu
KING-LEROY,
Cynthia, B .... 518-783-2420 315 J
kingleroy@siena.edu
KING LIU, Tsu-Jae .... 510-642-5771.. 68 D
tking@eecs.berkeley.edu
KINGAN, Michael .... 203-392-6191.. 85 A
kinganm1@southernct.edu
KINGERY, Bobbi .... 217-581-7462 136 E
rkingery@eiu.edu
KINGHAM, Margret, T .. 610-566-1776 403 E
mkingham@williamson.edu
KINGKADE, H.K .... 502-863-8209 180 E
hk_kingkade@georgetowncollege.edu
KINGREY, Deb .... 337-475-5556 192 A
dkingrey@mcneese.edu
KINGREY, Tiffany .... 719-549-2708.. 79 A
tiffany.kingrey@csupueblo.edu
KINGSBURY, Judy .... 507-285-7216 240 G
judy.kingsbury@rctc.edu
KINGSLEY, Lindsay .... 623-245-4600.. 16 E
likingsley@uti.edu
KINGSLEY, Margery ...... 580-581-6900 365 G
margeryk@cameron.edu
KINGSLEY, Patty .... 402-463-2402 267 D
pkingsley@hastings.edu
KINGSTON, Linda .... 507-457-5138 241 F
lkingston@winona.edu
KINGSTONE, Peter .... 973-655-4228 279 C
KINGTON, Raynard, S .. 641-269-3000 165 J
kington@grinnell.edu
KINIKINI, Lea Lani .... 801-957-4228 461 D
lealani.kinikini@slcc.edu
KINIMAKA, Malia .... 562-985-4296.. 31 F
malia.kinimaka@csulb.edu
KINKADE, Mike .... 870-584-1320.. 22 G
mkinkade@cccua.edu
KINLAW, Mark, O .... 336-342-4261 337 E
kinlawm@rockinghamcc.edu
KINLEY, Billie .... 360-676-2772 482 D
bjkinley@nwic.edu
KINLEY, Naomi .... 718-489-5260 313 H
nkinley@sfc.edu
KINLOCH, Valerie .... 412-648-1773 401 B
vkinlock@pitt.edu
KINNAIRD, Jennifer ...... 440-375-7115 355 G
jkinnaird@lec.edu

KINNAMAN, Mindy .... 303-404-5254.. 79 J
mindy.kinnaman@frontrange.edu
KINNAMON, Jeffrey ...... 617-747-2240 206 E
registrar@berklee.edu
KINNAMON, Joel, L ..... 760-773-2500.. 39 A
jkinnamon@collegeofthedesert.edu
KINNARD, Rob .... 510-436-1035.. 45 D
kinnard@hnu.edu
KINNARD-PAYTON,
Tiffany .... 330-490-7538 364 B
tkpayton@walsh.edu
KINNESTON, Susan ...... 920-693-1224 499 G
susan.kinneston@gotoltc.edu
KINNEY, Amy, J .... 419-434-4241 364 G
kinney@winebrenner.edu
KINNEY, Dan .... 712-325-3201 167 B
dkinney@iwcc.edu
KINNEY, Daniel, P .... 515-574-1150 166 E
kinney@iowacentral.edu
KINNEY, Doug .... 315-294-8411 292 E
doug.kinney@cayuga-cc.edu
KINNEY, Frank .... 321-674-8745.. 99 B
fkinney@fit.edu
KINNEY, Katie .... 256-765-4252.... 8 E
kckinney@una.edu
KINNEY, Kevin .... 408-795-5600.. 34 B
kevin.kinney@sjsu.edu
KINNEY, Lee, M .... 575-439-3605 287 C
kinney@nmsu.edu
KINNEY, Mark .... 231-845-6211 232 J
mkinney@westshore.edu
KINNEY, Michael .... 607-778-5031 318 A
kinneym@sunybroome.edu
KINNEY, Michael, J ...... 203-371-7872.. 88 B
mike.kinney@sacredheart.edu
KINNEY, Paula .... 319-385-6315 167 A
pkinney@iw.edu
KINNEY, Susan .... 205-226-4646.... 5 A
skinney@bsc.edu
KINNEY, Wendi .... 585-245-5501 318 E
kinney@geneseo.edu
KINNISON, Mike .... 662-846-4300 245 H
mkinnisn@deltastate.edu
KINSELLA, Denise .... 310-434-3466.. 62 E
kinsella_denise@smc.edu
KINSELLA, Jill, H .... 478-301-2717 121 E
kinsella_jh@mercer.edu
KINSELLA, Susan .... 352-588-8272 106 D
susan.kinsella@saintleo.edu
KINSER, Beth .... 276-326-4260 465 B
bkinser@bluefield.edu
KINSERVIK, Matt .... 302-831-2101.. 90 F
matthewk@udel.edu
KINSEY, Barry, C .... 734-384-4124 227 G
bkinsey@monroeccc.edu
KINSEY, Bill .... 608-262-1696 496 C
wjkinsey@uhs.wisc.edu
KINSEY, Chris, S .... 229-391-5001 113 F
ckinsey@abac.edu
KINSEY, Marisa .... 610-647-4400 386 C
mkinsey@immaculata.edu
KINSEY, Ronda .... 308-635-6361 270 D
kinseyr2@wncc.edu
KINSEY, Sheila, C .... 910-630-7668 331 C
skinsey@methodist.edu
KINSHUK, ... 940-565-2731 454 A
kinshuk@unt.edu
KINSINGER,
Mitchell, G .... 605-274-4724 415 B
mitch.kinsinger@augie.edu
KINSLEY, Chris .... 850-245-0466 108 H
chris.kinsley@flbog.edu
KINSLEY-DAME, Gail .... 925-969-3300.. 46 H
gkinsley@jfku.edu
KINSLOW, Tony .... 585-275-2815 323 J
akinslow@ur.rochester.edu
KINTZI, Audrey .... 507-457-1486 243 B
akintzi@smumn.edu
KINUCAN, Robert, J ..... 432-837-8201 450 D
kinucan@sulross.edu
KINYATTI, Njoki .... 718-262-2021 295 F
nkinyatti@york.cuny.edu
KINZEL, Erin, C .... 574-807-7382 153 E
erin.kinzel@bethelуniversity.edu
KINZEL, Lisa .... 303-384-2470.. 78 I
lkinzel@mines.edu
KINZER, Esther .... 951-785-2175.. 47 C
ekinzer@lasierra.edu
KINZER, Jay .... 903-675-6220 452 B
jkinzer@tvcc.edu
KINZER, Jay .... 903-675-6213 452 B
jkinzer@tvcc.edu
KINZER, Marlin, L .... 605-394-2375 417 B
marlin.kinzer@sdsmt.edu

KINZLER, Robert, J .... 215-951-1048 387 C
kinzler@lasalle.edu
KINZY, Terri, G .... 269-387-8294 232 K
terri.kinzy@wmich.edu
KIP, Margaret .... 215-898-6636 400 K
mkip@upenn.edu
KIPER, Melissa .... 318-342-5420 192 F
kiper@ulm.edu
KIPFER, Julie .... 406-994-5737 264 D
jkipfer@montana.edu
KIPNES, Ethan .... 540-458-8427 478 A
ekipnes@wlu.edu
KIPP, Deborah, J .... 484-664-3223 391 C
debkipp@muhlenberg.edu
KIPP, Tom, E .... 414-410-4157 492 D
tekipp@stritch.edu
KIPPENHAN, Heidi .... 701-483-2566 345 D
heidi.kippenhan@dickinsonstate.edu
KIPPES, John .... 605-995-2160 415 C
john.kippes@dwu.edu
KIRALLA, John .... 310-338-2366.. 50 J
john.kiralla@lmu.edu
KIRALLA, Laura .... 310-665-6961.. 54 I
lkiralla@otis.edu
KIRBY, Claire, J .... 704-687-7292 342 E
ckirby@uncc.edu
KIRBY, SJ, Donald .... 315-445-4110 304 C
kirby@lemoyne.edu
KIRBY, Elizabeth, A ...... 989-774-6995 222 C
kirby2ea@cmich.edu
KIRBY, John .... 401-874-2957 406 B
jdkirby@uri.edu
KIRBY, Jonathan .... 913-758-6173 177 F
jonathan.kirby@stmary.edu
KIRBY, Joseph .... 410-455-3020 202 E
kirby@umbc.edu
KIRBY, Kevin .... 859-572-6544 184 A
kirby@nku.edu
KIRBY, Kevin .... 713-348-6040 442 K
kevin.kirby@rice.edu
KIRBY, Kim .... 870-673-4201.. 22 H
KIRBY, Marie .... 979-209-7337 432 C
marie.kirby@blinn.edu
KIRBY, Renee .... 262-595-2610 497 C
kirby@uwp.edu
KIRBY, Vickie, S .... 903-813-2414 430 N
vkirby@austincollege.edu
KIRBY, Yvonne .... 860-832-1784.. 84 I
ykirby@ccsu.edu
KIRCH, Michael .... 952-358-8164 239 F
michael.kirch@normandale.edu
KIRCHER, Jason .... 630-752-5011 152 F
jason.kircher@wheaton.edu
KIRCHGRABER, Paul ..... 928-445-7300.. 16 M
paul.kirchgraber@yc.edu
KIRCHMAIER, Michael .. 617-850-1239 210 D
mkirchmaier@hchc.edu
KIRCHMAN, Paul .... 941-359-4200 110 D
pkirchman@sar.usf.edu
KIRCHNER, Tom, A .... 440-525-7138 355 H
tkirchner@lakelandcc.edu
KIRGIS, Julianne .... 510-594-3656.. 28 D
jkirgis@cca.edu
KIRGIS, Paul .... 406-243-2549 264 A
paul.kirgis@umontana.edu
KIRIAKOS, Christopher . 541-485-1780 374 F
christopherkiriakos@newhop.edu
KIRK, Artemis, G .... 202-687-7425.. 92 A
agk3@georgetown.edu
KIRK, Barrie .... 803-691-3875 410 G
kirkb@midlandstech.edu
KIRK, Bruce .... 434-582-7220 468 H
bmkirk@liberty.edu
KIRK, Daniel .... 507-457-2570 241 F
daniel.kirk@winona.edu
KIRK, Donna, R .... 904-620-2819 110 A
d.kirk@unf.edu
KIRK, Donnie .... 940-696-8752 457 C
dkirk@vernoncollege.edu
KIRK, Ella .... 330-569-5150 353 J
kirkew@hiram.edu
KIRK, Gary, R .... 717-254-8917 382 F
kirkg@dickinson.edu
KIRK, Jimmy .... 415-452-5534.. 37 A
jkirk@ccsf.edu
KIRK, Kenneth .... 336-249-8186 334 A
kenneth_kirk@davidsonccc.edu
KIRK, Kevin .... 334-683-5105.... 6 A
kkirk@judson.edu
KIRK, Kristi .... 512-313-3000 434 E
kristi.kirk@concordia.edu
KIRK, Lisa .... 212-842-5977 308 D
lkirk@nyaa.edu

KIRK, Michael .... 860-486-0715.. 88 E
michael.kirk@uconn.edu
KIRK, Tanya, K .... 662-252-8400 248 G
tkirk@rustcollege.edu
KIRK, Tim .... 870-864-7154.. 21 B
wtkirk@southark.edu
KIRK-HOLLAND,
Marcie .... 530-752-0752.. 68 E
makirk@ucdavis.edu
KIRKBRIDE, Robert .... 212-229-8955 308 C
kirkbride@newschool.edu
KIRKEMO, William .... 816-268-5400 257 C
bkirkemo@nts.edu
KIRKEN, Robert .... 915-747-5000 455 C
rakirken@utep.edu
KIRKENDALL-BAKER,
Heyke .... 503-768-6235 373 G
hkirkendall-baker@lclark.edu
KIRKENDALL-BAKER,
Heyke .... 503-493-8625 372 I
hkirkendallbaker@cu-portland.edu
KIRKER, Elizabeth .... 302-225-6256.. 90 E
kirkere@gbc.edu
KIRKHART, Chandler .... 620-417-1135 176 K
chandler.kirkhart@sccc.edu
KIRKLAND, Cecil, E ...... 304-326-1519 488 F
ekirkland@salemu.edu
KIRKLAND, Jennifer ...... 540-458-8929 478 A
jkirkland@wlu.edu
KIRKLAND, Joe .... 828-669-8012 331 J
jkirkland@montreat.edu
KIRKLAND, Keith .... 973-877-3070 277 I
kirkland@essex.edu
KIRKLAND, LeeAnn ...... 478-471-2717 121 F
leeann.kirkland@mga.edu
KIRKLAND, Michael ...... 229-243-3160 113 F
mkirkland@abac.edu
KIRKLAND, Nick .... 601-581-3526 247 A
nkirkla1@meridiancc.edu
KIRKLAND, Sandra .... 804-594-1556 474 I
skirkland@jtcc.edu
KIRKLAND, Susan, M ... 336-278-5428 328 K
skirkland3@elon.edu
KIRKLAND, William, B . 803-777-0066 413 C
kirkland@sc.edu
KIRKLAND, Willie .... 504-816-4428 186 D
wkirkland@dillard.edu
KIRKLAND-GORDON,
Sharon, E .... 301-314-7651 202 C
skirklan@umd.edu
KIRKPATRICK,
Bonnie, L .... 302-356-6804.. 90 I
bonnie.l.kirkpatrick@wilmu.edu
KIRKPATRICK, Brian, J . 973-596-3427 279 F
brian.j.kirkpatrick@njit.edu
KIRKPATRICK,
Christopher .... 906-227-2355 228 F
ckirkpat@nmu.edu
KIRKPATRICK,
Deleanor, A .... 405-466-3228 366 F
dekirkp@langston.edu
KIRKPATRICK,
Elizabeth, L .... 240-500-2265 198 H
elkirkpatrick@hagerstowncc.edu
KIRKPATRICK, Heather .. 650-362-3997.. 24 H
KIRKPATRICK, Holly, R . 215-572-4475 379 A
kirkpath@arcadia.edu
KIRKPATRICK, John, T . 603-862-2053 274 G
ted.kirkpatrick@unh.edu
KIRKPATRICK, Laura ..... 931-363-9864 421 E
lkirkpatrick@martinmethodist.edu
KIRKPATRICK, Lisa, L ... 512-448-8408 442 M
lisak@stedwards.edu
KIRKPATRICK, Mac .... 864-338-8090 410 D
mkirkpatrick@lander.edu
KIRKSEY, Jason .... 405-744-9154 368 B
jason.kirksey@okstate.edu
KIRKSEY, Jeffrey .... 617-745-3718 208 G
jeffrey.kirksey@enc.edu
KIRKSEY, Jennifer .... 740-593-1804 359 G
kirkseyj@ohio.edu
KIRKWOOD, Jeffrey, D . 301-243-2119 503 J
jeffrey.kirkwood@dodiis.mil
KIRKWOOD,
William, G .... 423-439-5049 419 J
kirkwood@etsu.edu
KIRLEIS, Kathleen .... 617-287-5100 211 E
kathleen.kirleis@umb.edu
KIRMER, Lisa .... 620-343-4600 173 A
lkirmer@fhtc.edu
KIRMSE, David .... 415-422-2057.. 71 K
dkirmse@usfca.edu
KIRON, Gopu .... 570-504-7929 387 D
kirong@lackawanna.edu

KIRSCH, Breanne .... 712-279-1771 163 C
breanne.kirsch@briarcliff.edu
KIRSCH, Emily .... 707-826-3781.. 33 D
emily@humboldt.edu
KIRSCH, Laurie, J .... 412-624-5749 401 B
lkirsch@pitt.edu
KIRSCH, OSB, Myron ... 724-805-2111 398 E
myron.kirsch@email.stvincent.edu
KIRSCH, OSB, Myron ... 724-805-2111 398 F
myron.kirsch@stvincent.edu
KIRSCHBAUM, Steven ... 563-588-6326 163 F
steven.kirschbaum@clarke.edu
KIRSCHE, Stephen .... 860-685-4124.. 89 C
skirsche@wesleyan.edu
KIRSCHEN, Alyse .... 714-449-7835.. 51 A
akirschen@ketchum.edu
KIRSCHLING, Jane, M .. 410-706-6741 202 D
kirschling@son.umaryland.edu
KIRSCHNER, Kelly .... 727-864-8880.. 97 J
kirschkm@eckerd.edu
KIRSHLING, Jeff .... 715-394-8218 498 B
jkirschl@uwsuper.edu
KIRSININKAS, Becky ..... 858-695-8587 155 E
bkirsininkas@horizonuniversity.edu
KIRSTAETTER, Dawn ..... 410-462-7432 197 E
dkirstaetter@bccc.edu
KIRSTEN, Jan .... 732-255-0400 280 A
jkirsten@ocean.edu
KIRTLEY, Adam, M .... 509-522-4449 486 H
kirtleam@whitman.edu
KIRTMAN, Janet .... 212-346-1700 311 E
jkirtman@pace.edu
KIRTMAN, Lisa .... 657-278-4021.. 31 E
lkirtman@fullerton.edu
KIRVES, Carol .... 270-707-3751 181 E
carol.kirves@kctcs.edu
KIRWIN, Luanne .... 617-373-2520 217 F
KISER, Dan .... 828-328-7154 330 F
dan.kiser@lr.edu
KISER, Joseph, B .... 276-328-0143 473 B
jbk5b@virginia.edu
KISER, Lee .... 828-448-6707 339 A
lkiser@wpcc.edu
KISER, Liz .... 252-399-6453 326 M
epkiser@barton.edu
KISER, Lyda .... 540-869-0623 474 J
lkiser@lfcc.edu
KISH, Anne .... 406-683-7492 264 B
anne.kish@umwestern.edu
KISH, Deborah .... 850-729-5363 103 L
kishd@nwfsc.edu
KISH, Deborah .... 970-339-6459.. 76 G
deb.kish@aims.edu
KISH, Joy .... 828-689-1140 331 A
jkish@mhu.edu
KISH, Kelly .... 440-375-7480 355 G
kkish@lec.edu
KISH-GOODLING,
Donna, M .... 484-664-3479 391 C
donnakish-goodling@muhlenberg.edu
KISHBAUGH, Amanda ... 570-389-4297 394 A
akishba2@bloomu.edu
KISHPAUGH, Melva .... 540-654-1084 472 I
mkishpau@umw.edu
KISLER, Adam .... 816-604-3007 255 H
adam.kisler@mcckc.edu
KISLER, Jeffrey .... 215-717-6415 400 J
jkisler@uarts.edu
KISLING, Reid .... 503-517-1820 378 A
rkisling@westernseminary.edu
KISLYUK, Paulina .... 413-369-4044 208 D
KISONGO, Ibuchwa .... 763-424-0806 239 G
ikisongo@nhcc.edu
KISPERT, Craig, G .... 206-281-2536 484 D
ckispert@spu.edu
KISPERT, John, J .... 843-661-1110 409 K
jkispert@fmarion.edu
KISS, John, Z .... 336-334-5241 343 A
jzkiss@uncg.edu
KISS DOUGHERTY,
Alison .... 610-499-4182 403 B
akdougherty@widener.edu
KISSACK, Heather .... 719-389-6202.. 77 H
hkissack@coloradocollege.edu
KISSAL, Carol, D .... 703-993-8750 467 L
ckissal@gmu.edu
KISSEBERTH, Sara .... 419-358-3484 348 G
kisseberths@bluffton.edu
KISSEL, Chuck .... 657-278-4101.. 31 E
ckissel@fullerton.edu
KISSELL, Joseph .... 570-389-4263 394 A
jkissell@bloomu.edu

KISSINGER, Kurt, A ...... 814-865-6574 392 B
kak47@psu.edu
KISSINGER, Sue .... 715-346-3361 497 F
skissing@uwsp.edu
KISSLER, Lance .... 509-359-4257 480 E
lkissler@ewu.edu
KIST-KLINE, Gail, E ...... 513-585-1414 350 H
gail.kistkline@thechristcollege.edu
KISTLER, Eric .... 843-863-7933 407 E
ekistler@csuniv.edu
KISTNER, Angie .... 618-437-5321 147 A
kistner@rlc.edu
KISTNER, Frances .... 508-373-5749 216 B
frances.kistner@mcphs.edu
KISTNER, Janet .... 850-644-7836 109 C
jkistner@fsu.edu
KISTNER, Warren .... 309-556-3071 139 G
wkistner@iwu.edu
KISTULENTZ, Steven ..... 352-588-7218 106 D
steven.kistulentz@saintleo.edu
KITCH, Rhonda .... 701-231-7987 345 G
rhonda.k.kitch@ndsu.edu
KITCHELL, Jeni .... 530-898-5910.. 31 A
jkitchell@csuchico.edu
KITCHEN, Augusta .... 803-780-1159 414 E
akitchen@voorhees.edu
KITCHEN, Herbert .... 510-466-7374.. 56 H
hkitchen@peralta.edu
KITCHEN, Mark .... 307-754-6405 502 G
mark.kitchen@nwc.edu
KITCHEN, Todd .... 479-619-4232.. 20 D
tkitchen@nwacc.edu
KITCHENS, Elizabeth ..... 605-999-7136 415 G
elizabeth.kitchens@mitchelltech.edu
KITCHENS, Joann .... 701-662-1502 346 D
joann.kitchens@lrsc.edu
KITCHENS, Penny .... 478-553-2060 122 G
pkitchens@oftc.edu
KITCHIN, Dolores .... 785-594-7884 170 I
KITCHIN, Steven, H .... 401-739-5000 405 A
skitchin@neit.edu
KITCHINGS, Dorcas ...... 803-822-3584 410 G
kitchings@midlandstech.edu
KITCHINGS, Dorcas ...... 803-822-3584 410 G
kitchingsd@midlandstech.edu
KITCHINGS, Maribeth ... 601-974-1002 247 B
kitchme@millsaps.edu
KITE, Michelle .... 269-782-1302 230 F
mkite@swmich.edu
KITE, Terry .... 636-481-3273 254 A
tkite@jeffco.edu
KITHCART, Jane .... 845-687-5111 323 E
kithcarj@sunyulster.edu
KITLEY, Barry, S .... 336-841-9363 329 G
bkitley@highpoint.edu
KITTEL, Jane .... 262-691-5214 500 H
jkittel@wctc.edu
KITTELSON, Laura .... 651-846-1703 241 B
KITTINGER, Fred .... 407-823-1208 109 E
fred.kittinger@ucf.edu
KITTLE, Daniel .... 319-352-8745 170 C
daniel.kittle@wartburg.edu
KITTNER, Missy .... 254-299-8514 440 A
mkittner@mclennan.edu
KITTO, Kathy .... 360-650-2884 486 F
kitto@wwu.edu
KITTREDGE,
Cynthia Briggs .... 512-472-4133 443 H
cynthia.kittredge@ssw.edu
KITTRELL-MIKELL,
Deborah .... 706-729-2211 117 D
dkittrell@ega.edu
KITTS, Justin .... 828-898-8797 330 E
kittsj@lmc.edu
KITTS, Kenneth .... 256-765-4211.... 8 E
kkitts@una.edu
KITZINGER, Denis .... 603-880-8308 274 E
dkitzinger@thomasmorecollege.edu
KITZINGER, Sara .... 603-566-5017 274 E
skitzinger@thomasmorecollege.edu
KIWUS, Christopher ...... 540-231-6291 477 A
chkiwus@vt.edu
KIYOSAKI, Donna .... 808-956-7616 128 F
donnafay@hawaii.edu
KIYOSAKI, Donna, F ..... 808-956-7616 128 D
donnafay@hawaii.edu
KJAR, Daniel .... 607-735-1826 299 D
dkjar@elmira.edu
KJELLEREN, Donald, J .. 413-597-2312 220 C
donald.f.kjelleren@williams.edu
KLAAS, Brian .... 816-235-1333 261 C
klaasb@umkc.edu

KLAAS, Carlene .... 312-362-8146 135 I
cklaas@depaul.edu
KLAASSEN, Sara .... 816-322-0110 250 K
sara.klaassen@calvary.edu
KLABE, Kimberly, S ...... 301-447-5377 200 E
klabe@msmary.edu
KLAEHN, Scott .... 651-450-3462 238 D
sklaehn@inverhills.edu
KLAFFKE, David .... 360-383-3016 486 G
dklaffke@whatcom.edu
KLAIBER, Beverly, G ..... 530-226-4179.. 63 K
bklaiber@simpsonu.edu
KLAIBER, James, S .... 440-775-5603 358 C
jim.klaiber@oberlin.edu
KLAPATAUSKAS,
Kyle, J .... 563-588-7829 167 D
kyle.klapatauskas@loras.edu
KLAPPER, Robert .... 770-729-8400 114 D
KLASEK, Angie .... 402-466-4774 267 A
angie.klasek@doane.edu
KLASEN, James .... 617-588-1344 206 C
jklasen@bfit.edu
KLASKO, Stephen, K ..... 215-955-6617 400 A
stephen.klasko@jefferson.edu
KLASKOW, Sam .... 810-762-7870 225 H
sklaskow@kettering.edu
KLASS, Stephen, P .... 413-597-3118 220 C
stephen.p.klass@williams.edu
KLASSY, Garrett .... 312-996-2695 151 B
gklassy@uic.edu
KLATT, Sara .... 712-274-6400 170 E
sara.klatt@witcc.edu
KLAUBER, SR.,
James, S .... 240-500-2233 198 H
jklauber@hagerstowncc.edu
KLAUS, Amanda .... 732-571-3653 279 B
aklaus@monmouth.edu
KLAUS, Chad, L .... 609-258-5498 280 E
klaus@princeton.edu
KLAUS, Courtney .... 785-242-5200 176 D
courtney.klaus@ottawa.edu
KLAUS, Sky .... 575-234-9414 287 D
sklaus@nmsu.edu
KLAUSMEYER, Robert ... 573-875-7304 251 F
rklausmeyer@ccis.edu
KLAVER, Lenny .... 660-359-3948 257 D
lklaver@mail.ncmissouri.edu
KLAWE, Maria, M .... 909-921-8120.. 45 A
klawe@hmc.edu
KLAWUNN, Margaret .... 805-893-3651.. 70 A
margaret.klawunn@sa.ucsb.edu
KLEBE, Kelli .... 719-255-3779.. 83 B
kklebe@uccs.edu
KLECKNER, Joan .... 610-902-8201 380 C
joan.d.kleckner@cabrini.edu
KLEDZIK, Eric .... 321-674-8107.. 99 B
ekledzik@fit.edu
KLEE-TIESMAN,
Kerry, J .... 517-750-1200 230 H
ke497810@arbor.edu
KLEEMAN, Amy, E .... 407-582-1238 112 K
akleeman@valenciacollege.edu
KLEEMAN, Kathryn .... 217-206-4847 151 C
kklee1@uis.edu
KLEICH, Tammie .... 308-635-6072 270 D
kleicht@wncc.edu
KLEIMAN, Adriana .... 213-615-7295.. 36 F
akleiman@thechicagoschool.edu
KLEIN, Andrew, O .... 508-849-3313 205 C
aklein@annamaria.edu
KLEIN, Andrew, R .... 317-274-2581 156 F
anrklein@iupui.edu
KLEIN, Barb .... 641-648-4611 166 J
barb.klein@iavalley.edu
KLEIN, Bart .... 816-501-4780 258 H
bart.klein@rockhurst.edu
KLEIN, Cynthia .... 412-809-5100 396 H
klein.cynthia@ptcollege.edu
KLEIN, Daniel .... 617-559-8637 210 C
dklein@hebrewcollege.edu
KLEIN, Erick, P .... 651-631-5141 244 D
epklein@unwsp.edu
KLEIN, Erin .... 701-252-3467 347 C
eklein@uj.edu
KLEIN, Gary .... 608-663-6713 493 C
garyklein@edgewood.edu
KLEIN, Jacob .... 248-689-8282 232 A
jklein@walshcollege.edu
KLEIN, Jacqueline .... 518-454-2851 296 H
jklein@strose.edu
KLEIN, Jeff .... 909-652-6317.. 36 A
jeff.klein@chaffey.edu
KLEIN, Jennifer .... 949-582-4565.. 64 G
jklein26@saddleback.edu

KLEIN, Jill .... 202-885-5990.. 90 J
jklein@american.edu
KLEIN, Jim .... 502-456-6508 184 E
jklein@sullivan.edu
KLEIN, June .... 650-433-3849.. 55 G
jklein@paloaltou.edu
KLEIN, Kara .... 843-953-3721 407 F
kklein1@citadel.edu
KLEIN, Karen .... 580-774-3268 370 C
karen.klein@swosu.edu
KLEIN, Leslie, G .... 410-358-3144 204 E
KLEIN, Lori .... 907-796-6540.. 10 B
laklein@alaska.edu
KLEIN, Lori .... 907-796-6057.. 10 B
laklein@alaska.edu
KLEIN, Marjorie, S .... 814-332-5910 378 D
mklein@allegheny.edu
KLEIN, Mendel .... 718-384-5460 325 M
KLEIN, Michael .... 718-368-5087 294 E
mklein@kbcc.cuny.edu
KLEIN, Michael .... 215-204-1927 399 F
mike.klein@temple.edu
KLEIN, Michelle, W .... 504-866-7426 190 B
finance@nds.edu
KLEIN, Nate .... 319-363-1323 168 C
nklein@mtmercy.edu
KLEIN, Patti .... 651-523-2421 236 A
pklein01@hamline.edu
KLEIN, Peg .... 401-841-3665 503 L
margaret.klein@usnwc.edu
KLEIN, Phil .... 704-272-5300 337 I
KLEIN, Ray .... 812-941-2457 157 B
rayklein@ius.edu
KLEIN, Sara .... 201-216-3543 283 C
sara.klein@stevens.edu
KLEIN, Steve .... 503-352-2822 375 G
kleinsk@pacificu.edu
KLEIN, Stuart .... 212-431-2170 309 G
stuart.klein@nyls.edu
KLEIN, Terry .... 715-468-2815 501 B
terry.klein@witc.edu
KLEIN-WILLIAMS,
Marcella .... 805-678-5262.. 73 A
mkleinwilliams@vcccd.edu
KLEINBERG, David .... 630-829-6304 132 E
dkleinberg@ben.edu
KLEINE, Patricia, A .... 715-836-2320 496 D
kleinepa@uwec.edu
KLEINER, Zev .... 347-394-1036 291 E
zkleiner@ateret.net
KLEINHANS, Randy .... 574-372-5100 155 B
kleinhrp@grace.edu
KLEINKAUFMAN, Dovid 718-327-7600 325 F
info@yofr.org
KLEINLEIN, Tom .... 912-478-5047 119 C
tkleinlein@georgiasouthern.edu
KLEINMAN, Daniel, L .... 617-353-2230 207 D
dlklein@bu.edu
KLEINMAN, Kent .... 607-255-9110 297 F
aapdean@cornell.edu
KLEINMAN, Kent .... 401-454-6406 405 D
kkleinman@risd.edu
KLEINMAN, Kim .... 314-246-7768 262 C
kleinman@webster.edu
KLEINMAN, Yisroel .... 718-853-8500 322 I
KLEINSCHMIDT, Robert . 609-586-4800 278 F
kleinscr@mccc.edu
KLEINWORTH, Tom ...... 713-798-6498 431 I
tklein@bcm.edu
KLEISER, Richele .... 559-325-3600.. 28 H
rkleiser@chsu.edu
KLEMANN, M. Adam ..... 330-471-8308 355 L
aklemann@malone.edu
KLEMENS, Kristina .... 262-595-2004 497 C
klemens@uwp.edu
KLEMENT, Emily .... 940-872-4002 441 A
eklement@nctc.edu
KLEMIUK, Christy .... 817-515-7778 445 G
christy.klemiuk@tccd.edu
KLEMM, Jotisa .... 817-515-3083 445 G
jotisa.klemm@tccd.edu
KLEMM, Mary .... 269-927-1000 226 D
KLEMME, Kari .... 906-932-4231 224 B
KLEMPNER, Mark, D ..... 617-474-3250 212 A
mark.klempner@umassmed.edu
KLEN, Joseph, R .... 765-361-6052 162 E
klenj@wabash.edu
KLENK, Jesse .... 251-544-1510.... 6 D
KLENKE, James, W .... 618-650-2020 149 F
jklenke@siue.edu
KLEPACKI, Rebecca .... 863-638-2918 113 B
klepackirm@webber.edu

KNIGHT, David .... 256-726-7389.... 6 C
dknight@oakwood.edu
KNIGHT, David .... 765-983-1298 154 G
knighda@earlham.edu
KNIGHT, Debra, L .... 217-443-8865 135 H
dknight@dacc.edu
KNIGHT, Derric .... 906-635-6244 226 E
dknight@lssu.edu
KNIGHT, Gabe .... 563-244-7021 165 C
gknight@eicc.edu
KNIGHT, Gary, E .... 803-705-4559 407 A
gary.knight@benedict.edu
KNIGHT, Gina, R .... 252-335-4822 341 D
grknight@ecsu.edu
KNIGHT, J. Aaron .... 713-718-2445 437 I
aaron.knight@hccs.edu
KNIGHT, Jack .... 540-568-5242 468 F
knigh2jf@jmu.edu
KNIGHT, Jacob, E .... 317-738-8080 154 J
jknight@franklincollege.edu
KNIGHT, Jaime .... 508-531-2337 212 B
j2knight@bridgew.edu
KNIGHT, John, C .... 423-585-6882 426 C
john.knight@ws.edu
KNIGHT, Joseph .... 601-484-8779 247 A
jknight5@meridiancc.edu
KNIGHT, Lance .... 404-364-8542 122 J
lknight@oglethorpe.edu
KNIGHT, Leonard .... 760-245-4271.. 73 D
leonard.knight@vvc.edu
KNIGHT, Robert .... 360-992-2101 479 F
rknight@clark.edu
KNIGHT, Roger, A .... 601-403-1206 248 E
rknight@prcc.edu
KNIGHT, Stephanie, L .. 214-768-4242 444 E
slknight@smu.edu
KNIGHT, Tamara .... 804-751-9191 465 O
tknight@ccc-va.com
KNIGHT, Tim .... 870-245-5528.. 20 E
knightt@obu.edu
KNIGHT, Tracey .... 870-245-5401.. 20 E
knightte@obu.edu
KNIGHT, Wendy, S .... 563-556-5110 168 E
knightw@nicc.edu
KNIGHT, William, E ...... 513-529-1660 356 E
knightw3@miamioh.edu
KNIGHT, Xavier .... 218-723-5966 235 D
xknight@css.edu
KNIGHTON, Denise .... 662-915-7792 249 D
denisek@olemiss.edu
KNIGHTON, Diana .... 205-929-1442.... 6 B
dknighton@miles.edu
KNIGHTON, Jeffery .... 678-359-5018 119 F
jknighton@gordonstate.edu
KNIGHTON, JR.,
Lewis, J .... 864-656-3184 408 A
knightl@clemson.edu
KNIGHTS, John, E .... 407-582-5197 112 K
jknights@valenciacollege.edu
KNILEY, Mary Lynne .... 585-582-8317 299 A
marykniley@elim.edu
KNILL, Michael .... 717-728-2272 381 B
michaelknill@centralpenn.edu
KNILLE, Noel .... 415-703-9560.. 28 D
nknille@cca.edu
KNIOUM, Jay .... 361-698-1247 436 C
jknioum@delmar.edu
KNIPFEL, Shirley, J ...... 515-294-1781 162 I
sknipfel@iastate.edu
KNIPPEL, Dianne .... 661-722-6300.. 26 D
dknippel@avc.edu
KNISELY, Emilia .... 513-875-3344 350 G
emilia.knisely@chatfield.edu
KNISLEY, Joel .... 828-232-5121 342 C
jknisley@unca.edu
KNISLEY, Patrick .... 212-217-4320 299 H
patrick_knisley@fitnyc.edu
KNISLEY, Sharon .... 513-244-8443 350 I
sharon.knisley@ccuniversity.edu
KNISPEL, Todd .... 620-431-2820 175 H
tknispel@neosho.edu
KNISS, Fred, L .... 540-432-4105 466 G
fred.kniss@emu.edu
KNISS, Rob .... 517-629-0440 220 G
rkniss@albion.edu
KNITIG, Sherri .... 785-890-3641 176 C
sherri.knitig@nwktc.edu
KNOBBE, Amy .... 402-481-8847 265 K
amy.knobbe@bryanhealthcollege.edu
KNOBLICH, Julie .... 620-792-9275 171 C
knoblichj@bartonccc.edu
KNODEL, Becky .... 701-252-3467 347 C
bknodel@uj.edu
KNODLE-BRAGIEL, Lisa 503-883-2214 373 H
lbragiel@linfield.edu
KNOEBEL, Thomas .... 414-425-8300 495 H
tknoebel@shsst.edu
KNOEPPEL, Robert, C ... 813-974-3400 110 B
rkc3@usf.edu
KNOETTGEN, Amber ..... 785-243-1435 172 F
aknoettgen@cloud.edu
KNOETTGEN, Suzi .... 785-243-1435 172 F
sknoettgen@cloud.edu
KNOLL, Eric .... 314-446-8375 259 B
eric.knoll@stlcop.edu
KNOLL, Joseph .... 617-824-8112 208 H
joseph_knoll@emerson.edu
KNOLL, Molly, H .... 641-422-4404 168 D
knollmol@niacc.edu
KNOLL-FINN, MJ .... 212-998-4553 310 B
mjknollfinn@nyu.edu
KNOLLE, Jon .... 831-646-3030.. 52 F
jknolle@mpc.edu
KNOLLMAN, Paul, L ..... 734-384-4282 227 G
pknollman@monroeccc.edu
KNOLTON, Cristina, C .. 213-738-5774.. 65 G
cknolton@swlaw.edu
KNOOR, Robert .... 616-957-6039 221 P
rknoor@calvinseminary.edu
KNOP, Joachim, W .... 202-994-6506.. 91 F
knop@gwu.edu
KNOPP, David .... 423-472-7141 424 F
dknopp@clevelandstatecc.edu
KNORR, Dan .... 570-389-4655 394 A
dknorr@bloomu.edu
KNOTHE, Thomas, E ..... 608-796-3376 498 N
teknothe@viterbo.edu
KNOTT, Allan .... 214-860-8531 435 D
aknott@dcccd.edu
KNOTT, Blythe .... 503-768-7296 373 G
blythe@lclark.edu
KNOTT, Catherine .... 812-866-7087 155 C
knott@hanover.edu
KNOTT, Dana .... 937-769-1881 347 H
dknott@antioch.edu
KNOTT, Dorothea .... 434-949-1012 475 H
dorothea.knott@southside.edu
KNOTT, Gail .... 308-535-3605 267 K
knottg@mpcc.edu
KNOTT, Greg .... 860-486-6135.. 88 E
gknott@foundation.uconn.edu
KNOTT, Jack, H .... 213-740-0350.. 72 B
jhknott@usc.edu
KNOTT, Kevin .... 217-351-2239 146 C
kknott@parkland.edu
KNOTT, Krista .... 970-247-7177.. 79 I
klknott@fortlewis.edu
KNOTTS, Brad .... 812-749-1215 159 C
bknotts@oak.edu
KNOTTS, Cecil .... 318-357-5965 192 C
knottsc@nsula.edu
KNOTTS, Debby .... 505-277-5765 288 G
debby@unm.edu
KNOTTS, Gibbs .... 843-953-6792 408 E
knottshg@cofc.edu
KNOUSE, Christine .... 717-262-2016 403 F
cknouse@wilson.edu
KNOUSE, Elizabeth .... 717-477-1123 395 E
eaknouse@ship.edu
KNOWLES, Ann .... 864-522-2000 410 A
ann.knowles@prismahealth.org
KNOWLES, Bill .... 405-382-9272 369 J
b.knowles@sscok.edu
KNOWLES, Harley .... 423-746-5201 426 F
hknowles@tnwesleyan.edu
KNOWLES, James, M ..... 409-984-6432 450 B
knowlejm@lamarpa.edu
KNOWLES, Melody, D .. 703-370-6600 470 B
KNOWLES, Monica .... 360-992-2904 479 F
mknowles@clark.edu
KNOWLES, Susan .... 315-268-6633 296 A
sknowles@clarkson.edu
KNOWLES, Tamece .... 305-348-7882 109 A
knowles@fiu.edu
KNOWLTON, Eloise .... 508-767-7487 205 D
eknowlton@assumption.edu
KNOWLTON, James ...... 510-642-5316.. 68 D
athletic.director@berkeley.edu
KNOX, Amy .... 414-930-3563 495 A
knoxa@mtmary.edu
KNOX, Chrisanne .... 925-969-2048.. 40 I
cknox@dvc.edu
KNOX, Craig .... 850-201-8660 111 C
KNOX, Darby .... 503-226-4391 375 F
KNOX, George .... 336-750-2146 344 B
knoxge@wssu.edu
KNOX, Gordon .... 415-749-4549.. 60 G
gknox@sfai.edu
KNOX, Linda, B .... 219-989-3169 159 G
lbknox@pnw.edu
KNOX, Lindsay .... 503-554-2242 373 C
lknox@georgefox.edu
KNOX, Michael, J .... 806-651-2050 448 C
mknox@wtamu.edu
KNOX, Ramon .... 562-938-4362.. 48 D
rknox@lbcc.edu
KNOX, Ryan .... 309-248-8189 137 I
ryan.knox@heartland.edu
KNOX, Tracey .... 970-521-6643.. 81 D
tracey.knox@njc.edu
KNOX, Wayne .... 512-505-3003 438 E
wknox@htu.edu
KNUCKLES, Jill .... 970-248-1426.. 77 I
jknuckle@coloradomesa.edu
KNUCKLES, Leator .... 410-238-9000.. 92 G
KNUDSEN, J. Todd .... 315-568-3146 308 F
dodiorne@nycc.edu
KNUDSEN, Jeffrey .... 802-831-1285 463 G
jknudsen@vermontlaw.edu
KNUDSEN, Ross .... 208-376-7731 129 H
rknudsen@boisebible.edu
KNUDSON, Chris .... 319-352-8580 170 C
chris.knudson@wartburg.edu
KNUDSON, Dan .... 218-299-6521 239 B
dan.knudson@minnesota.edu
KNUDSON, Edward, T .. 661-722-6300.. 26 D
eknudson@avc.edu
KNUDSON, Kari .... 701-224-5604 346 B
kari.l.knudson@bismarckstate.edu
KNUDSON, Paula, M .... 319-273-2332 163 B
paula.knudson@uni.edu
KNUDSON, Timothy ...... 540-261-8400 471 H
tim.knudson@svu.edu
KNUDSON-CARL, Tara .. 402-399-2449 266 F
tknudsoncarl@csm.edu
KNUPPEL, Lisa .... 714-432-5575.. 38 E
lknuppel@occ.cccd.edu
KNUST, Alyse .... 217-424-3769 143 H
aknust@millikin.edu
KNUTEL, Phillip .... 781-239-4225 205 E
pknutel@babson.edu
KNUTH, Barbara, A .... 607-255-5864 297 F
bak3@cornell.edu
KNUTH, Doug .... 775-784-6900 271 F
dknuth@unr.edu
KNUTSEN, Mark .... 423-697-4785 424 E
mark.knutsen@chattanoogastate.edu
KNUTSON, Jennifer .... 605-331-6611 417 E
jennifer.knutson@usiouxfalls.edu
KNUTSON, Kailani .... 559-791-2294.. 47 A
kknutson@portervillecollege.edu
KNUTSON, Karen .... 320-363-5922 235 C
kknutson@csbsju.edu
KNUTSON, Ryan .... 605-688-4988 417 C
ryan.knutson@sdstate.edu
KNUTSON, Todd .... 605-331-6813 417 E
todd.knutson@usiouxfalls.edu
KO, Jeanne .... 212-472-1500 309 I
jko@nysid.edu
KO, Kristina .... 202-554-0578 231 E
kdko@umich.edu
KO, Lester, D .... 717-245-1102 382 F
kole@dickinson.edu
KO, Shinsaeng .... 404-727-0825 117 F
shinsaeng.ko@emory.edu
KO, Yoo, K .... 571-730-4750 255 L
wdc@midwest.edu
KO, Yoo, K .... 636-327-4645 255 L
ykko9191@yahoo.com
KOAN, Mark .... 480-731-8895.. 12 O
mark.koan@domail.maricopa.edu
KOBALLA, Thomas .... 912-478-5648 119 C
tkoballa@georgiasouthern.edu
KOBALLA, JR.,
Thomas, R .... 478-301-5397 121 E
rothenhoffer_w@mercer.edu
KOBAYASHI, Frank .... 916-484-8202.. 50 F
kobayaf@arc.losrios.edu
KOBER, Kevin .... 262-547-1211 492 E
kkober@carrollu.edu
KOBERNUSZ, Bob .... 605-995-7128 415 G
bob.kobernusz@mitchelltech.edu
KOBES, Patricia .... 845-574-4280 313 C
pkobes@sunyrockland.edu
KOBLER, Soheila .... 973-618-3724 276 D
skobler@caldwell.edu
KOBLER, Wendy .... 607-274-3115 303 B
wkobler@ithaca.edu
KOBMAN, Lisa .... 513-244-4979 357 A
lisa.kobman@msj.edu
KOBOLAKIS, Evan .... 516-876-3379 319 A
kobolakise@oldwestbury.edu
KOBRINSKY, Natasha ... 310-665-6837.. 54 I
nkobrinsky@otis.edu
KOBUS, James .... 641-673-1046 170 F
james.kobus@wmpenn.edu
KOBYELSKI, Kammie .... 928-445-7300.. 16 M
kammie.kobyelski@yc.edu
KOBYLSKI, Gerald .... 845-938-5608 504 H
gerald.kobylski@usma.edu
KOBYLSKI, Janet .... 570-408-4501 403 D
janet.kobylski@wilkes.edu
KOCAK, Taskin .... 504-280-4384 189 E
tkocak@uno.edu
KOCAR, Deb .... 617-349-8800 210 H
ugadm@lesley.edu
KOCER, Ken .... 605-668-1589 415 H
kkocer@mtmc.edu
KOCH, Amy .... 317-955-6021 158 U
akoch@marian.edu
KOCH, Bill .... 252-328-6166 341 C
kochb@ecu.edu
KOCH, Bradley .... 610-902-8571 380 C
bradley.r.koch@cabrini.edu
KOCH, Chris .... 901-321-3259 419 C
chris.koch@cbu.edu
KOCH, Don .... 618-634-3289 149 A
donk@shawneecc.edu
KOCH, Doug .... 660-543-8059 260 K
koch@ucmo.edu
KOCH, Erec .... 212-650-8166 293 D
ekoch1@ccny.cuny.edu
KOCH, Eric .... 785-242-5200 176 D
eric.koch@ottawa.edu
KOCH, Greg .... 770-960-1298 120 H
gkoch@ict.edu
KOCH, Jo Ann .... 770-216-2960 120 H
jkoch@ict.edu
KOCH, John .... 607-777-6757 316 E
jkoch@binghamton.edu
KOCH, Kathie .... 312-369-7436 135 E
kkoch@colum.edu
KOCH, Kevin .... 781-762-1211 209 C
kkoch@fmc.edu
KOCH, Matthew .... 919-890-7500.. 92 G
KOCH, Paul .... 563-333-6212 169 A
kochpaulc@sau.edu
KOCH, Paul .... 831-459-2931.. 70 B
plkoch@ucsc.edu
KOCH, Sheena .... 270-707-3921 181 E
bkshopkinsville@bncollege.com
KOCH, Susan .... 217-206-6634 151 C
koch@uis.edu
KOCH, Susan .... 217-206-6634 151 A
koch@uis.edu
KOCH, Thomas, L .... 520-621-2448.. 16 G
tlkoch@email.arizona.edu
KOCHAN, Julie .... 518-454-5145 296 H
kochanj@strose.edu
KOCHAN, Roman .... 562-985-4047.. 31 F
roman.kochan@csulb.edu
KOCHANEK, Lea .... 210-341-1366 441 C
lkochanek@ost.edu
KOCHARYAN, Armine ... 916-877-7977.. 58 J
armine@sui.edu
KOCHER, Andy, M .... 317-788-3493 161 B
akocher@uindy.edu
KOCHER, Craig, T .... 804-289-8500 472 L
ckocher@richmond.edu
KOCHER, Rebecca .... 937-327-7430 364 H
KOCHERA, Melissah ..... 203-596-4652.. 87 F
mkochera@post.edu
KOCHEVAR, Brenda ...... 218-749-0314 238 G
b.kochevar@mesabirange.edu
KOCHIS, Stephen, J ...... 845-575-3000 305 L
stephen.kochis@marist.edu
KOCHON, Barbara .... 413-565-1000 205 G
bkochon@baypath.edu
KOCHUBA, Sara .... 724-503-1001 402 E
skochuba@washjeff.edu
KOCIAN, Bryce .... 979-532-6315 458 F
brycek@wcjc.edu
KOCIAN, Justin .... 402-494-2311 268 B
jkocian@thenicc.edu
KOCIK, Piotr .... 718-518-6610 294 B
pkocik@hostos.cuny.edu
KOCIOLEK, Patrick .... 303-492-8464.. 83 A
patrick.kociolek@colorado.edu
KOCOUR, Bruce .... 865-471-3240 419 A
bkocour@cn.edu

KOCSIS, Katie, L .... 716-286-8669 310 D kkocsis@niagara.edu
KODAT, Catherine .... 920-832-6528 493 K catherine.g.kodat@lawrence.edu
KOEBEL, Dave .... 531-622-2391 267 H dkoebel@mccneb.edu
KOEBEL, Derek .... 786-534-0517.. 98 K koebeld@floridacareercollege.edu
KOEGL, Evan, S .... 516-463-8000 302 B evan.koegl@hofstra.edu
KOEGLER, Jason, W ..... 304-336-8302 490 F jkoegler@westliberty.edu
KOEHLER, Al .... 636-922-8452 258 I alkoehler@stchas.edu
KOEHLER, David .... 308-635-6021 270 D koehlerd@wncc.edu
KOEHLER, Laurie .... 607-274-1555 303 B lkoehler@ithaca.edu
KOEHLER, Martha Kaye 813-253-7007 101 A mkoehler@hccfl.edu
KOEHLER, R. Brien .... 262-646-6545 495 B rkoehler@nashotah.edu
KOEHLER, II, Randy ..... 513-244-8449 350 I randy.koehler@ccuniversity.edu
KOEHN, Michelle .... 316-226-2002 162 F michelle.koehn@allencollege.edu
KOEHNEKE, Mary, A ...... 716-888-2300 292 D mkoehneke@canisius.edu
KOEHNKE, Paul .... 704-330-6121 333 D paul.koehnke@cpcc.edu
KOELKER, June .... 817-257-7106 448 G j.koelker@tcu.edu
KOELLER, Martin, E ...... 973-761-9782 283 B martin.koeller@shu.edu
KOELSCH, Chris .... 305-284-1356 112 E chriskoelsch@miami.edu
KOELTZOW, Dawn .... 309-677-2510 133 B dkoeltzow@fsmail.bradley.edu
KOENECKE, David .... 660-626-2410 250 A dkoenecke@atsu.edu
KOENEN, Gary .... 414-930-3534 495 A koeneng@mtmary.edu
KOENIG, Deanna .... 612-659-6509 238 I deanna.koenig@minneapolis.edu.edu
KOENIG, Jason, T .... 864-833-8490 411 I jtkoenig@presby.edu
KOENIG, Linda .... 740-351-3655 360 K lkoenig@shawnee.edu
KOEPKE, Janelle .... 507-433-0695 240 F janelle.koepke@riverland.edu
KOEPKE, Sarah .... 651-793-1304 238 H sarah.koepke@metrostate.edu
KOEPPEL, Edmund .... 516-572-7126 308 A edmund.koeppel@ncc.edu
KOEPPEN, Bruce .... 203-582-5301.. 87 G bruce.koeppen@quinnipiac.edu
KOEPSELL, Kelli .... 888-378-9988 416 J
KOERBER, Brent .... 614-236-7167 349 D bkoerber@capital.edu
KOERMER, Kelly .... 443-412-2382 199 A kkoermer@harford.edu
KOERNERT, Andrew, H . 757-594-8480 466 B andrew.koernert@cnu.edu
KOERSELMAN, Corky .... 712-707-7000 168 H corky.koerselman@nwciowa.edu
KOERT, Carol Ann .... 973-290-4208 277 A ckoert@cse.edu
KOERWER, Venard, S ... 570-504-7000 384 F vkoerwer@som.geisinger.edu
KOESER, Bryan .... 920-693-1731 499 G bryan.koeser@gotoltc.edu
KOETTING, Sandy .... 573-681-5073 254 E koetting@lincolnu.edu
KOEVEN, Gary, J .... 435-652-7770 460 G koeven@dixie.edu
KOFF, Gordon, D .... 603-646-2451 273 E gordon.d.koff@dartmouth.edu
KOFFLER, Jeromy, A ..... 503-943-7470 377 E koffler@up.edu
KOGAN, Alexander .... 212-327-8001 313 B kogana@rockefeller.edu
KOGUT, Matthew .... 207-602-2077 196 G mkogut@une.edu
KOH, Alex .... 978-468-7111 209 G akoh@gordonconwell.edu
KOH, Jonathan .... 205-391-2471.... 3 E jkoh@sheltonstate.edu
KOHL, Bunny .... 856-227-7200 276 E bkohl@camdencc.edu
KOHL, Erin .... 608-243-4052 499 H ekohl@madisoncollege.edu
KOHL, James .... 978-934-2108 211 G james_kohl@uml.edu
KOHL, Laura .... 401-232-6000 404 F lkohl@bryant.edu
KOHL, Raymond .... 312-922-1884 142 H
KOHL, Troy .... 920-735-5766 499 E kohlt@fvtc.edu
KOHLER, Dave .... 360-867-6451 481 A kohlerd@evergreen.edu
KOHLER, Donald .... 712-325-3262 167 B dkohler@iwcc.edu
KOHLER, Kurt .... 402-844-7722 268 J kurtk@northeast.edu
KOHLES, Paula, S .... 402-280-2731 266 I paulakohles@creighton.edu
KOHLI, Vandana .... 805-437-8400.. 30 F vandana.kohli@csuci.edu
KOHLMAN, Bradley, A .. 316-284-5349 171 F bkohlman@bethelks.edu
KOHLMAN, Mark .... 740-427-5000 355 E kohlmanm@kenyon.edu
KOHLMEYER, Bill .... 503-399-6505 372 C bill.kohlmeyer@chemeketa.edu
KOHN, David .... 845-341-4388 311 C david.kohn@sunyorange.edu
KOHN, Edward .... 802-485-2410 463 A ekohn@norwich.edu
KOHN, Gary .... 630-829-6095 132 E gkohn@ben.edu
KOHN, Paul .... 404-385-3708 118 F paul.kohn@ssc.gatech.edu
KOHN, Rebecca .... 215-572-2018 379 A kohnr@arcadia.edu
KOHN, Selina .... 706-821-8467 122 K skohn@paine.edu
KOHN, Shayeh .... 718-327-7600 325 F skohn@yofr.org
KOHN-WOOD, Laura ..... 305-284-1316 112 E l.kohnwood@miami.edu
KOHNKE, Maria .... 805-493-3105.. 29 H kohnke@callutheran.edu
KOHR, Lesa .... 585-594-6220 310 F kohrl@roberts.edu
KOHR, Lesa, J .... 585-594-6966 312 K kohrl@roberts.edu
KOHRMAN, Elaine .... 606-451-6918 182 C elaine.kohrman@kctcs.edu
KOHRMAN, Robert .... 605-688-4920 417 C robert.kohrman@sdstate.edu
KOHRN, Lynn, M .... 203-254-4288.. 86 I lkohrn@fairfield.edu
KOHUT, Byron .... 724-925-6713 403 A kohutb@westmoreland.edu
KOIRALA-AZAD, Shabnam .... 415-422-6525.. 71 K skoirala@usfca.edu
KOKAJKO, Hillary, C .... 336-841-9118 329 G hkokajko@highpoint.edu
KOKER, John .... 920-424-2220 497 B koker@uwosh.edu
KOKILEPERSAUD, Premdat .... 443-885-3177 200 D prem.kokilepersaud@morgan.edu
KOKINOVA, Margarita, D .... 330-325-6333 357 G mkokinov@neomed.edu
KOKKALA, Irene .... 706-864-1862 126 A irene.kokkala@ung.edu
KOKOLUS, Cait .... 610-785-6280 398 A ckokolus@scs.edu
KOKONAS, Georgios ..... 914-961-8313 315 C gkokonas@svots.edu
KOKOS, Jon .... 828-898-8809 330 E kokosj@lmc.edu
KOKX-TEMPLET, Ann .... 281-998-6103 443 B ann.kokx-templet@sjcd.edu
KOLACINSKI, John .... 602-384-2555.. 11 F john.kolacinski@bryanuniversity.edu
KOLANDER, John, D .... 414-443-8816 498 O john.kolander@wlc.edu
KOLAR, Steve .... 210-297-9630 431 E sxkolar@baptisthealthsystem.com
KOLAREVIC, Branko, R . 973-596-6370 279 F branko.r.kolarevic@njit.edu
KOLB, Christine .... 630-620-2101 145 D ckolb@seminary.edu
KOLB, Daniel .... 812-357-6566 160 D dkolb@saintmeinrad.edu
KOLB, Donna .... 352-294-3220 109 F dkolb@ufl.edu
KOLB, George, R .... 610-519-4580 402 D george.kolb@villanova.edu
KOLB, John, E .... 518-276-2122 312 I kolbj@rpi.edu
KOLB, Susan .... 301-696-3494 199 B kolb@hood.edu
KOLBABA, Tia, M .... 848-932-9638 282 A kolbaba@rci.rutgers.edu
KOLBE, Ken .... 616-331-6775 224 E kolbek@gvsu.edu
KOLBE, Rick .... 574-520-4346 157 A rkolbe@iusb.edu
KOLDER, Stacey .... 815-921-4158 147 E s.kolder@rockvalleycollege.edu
KOLDIN, Hillary .... 518-608-8382 299 G hkoldin@excelsior.edu
KOLENBRANDER, Kirk .. 603-665-7344 274 D k.kolenbrander@snhu.edu
KOLENOVIC, Zeke .... 212-472-1500 309 I zkolenovic@nysid.edu
KOLIMAGA, Karen .... 978-630-9365 215 A k_kolimaga@mwcc.mass.edu
KOLISON, Stephen .... 317-788-3212 161 B kolisons@uindy.edu
KOLISZ, Karin .... 219-757-6132 160 A karin.kolisz@franciscanalliance.org
KOLK-CONNER, Theresa .... 740-588-1221 365 E tkolk@zanestate.edu
KOLLAR, Lisa, S .... 386-226-7068.. 98 A lisa.kollar@erau.edu
KOLLASCH, Jair .... 314-529-9564 254 H jkollasch@maryville.edu
KOLLATH, Carissa .... 402-844-7159 268 J carissa@northeast.edu
KOLLBAUM, Kristin, E .. 712-324-5061 168 G kkollbaum@nwicc.edu
KOLLER, Craig, A .... 610-799-1073 388 I ckoller@lccc.edu
KOLLER, Tim .... 303-762-6944.. 79 H tim.koller@denverseminary.edu
KOLLIEN, Mike .... 989-358-7339 221 A kollienm@alpenacc.edu
KOLLIGIAN, John .... 609-258-3285 280 E jkjr@princeton.edu
KOLLMAN, Willy .... 330-972-2575 362 B wrk1@uakron.edu
KOLLMANN, Linda .... 513-562-6288 347 K linda.kollman@artacademy.edu
KOLLMEYER, Will .... 662-720-7443 248 C wakollmeyer@nemcc.edu
KOLLMORGEN, Terry .... 918-495-6175 368 I tmk@oru.edu
KOLLROSS, Crystal .... 626-585-7759.. 55 K cakollross@pasadena.edu
KOLLURU, Ramesh .... 337-482-6541 192 E rxk6962@louisiana.edu
KOLODZIEJSKI, Gwynne .... 610-796-8325 378 F gwynne.kolodziejski@alvernia.edu
KOLOJACO, Leslie .... 979-532-4560 458 F lesliek@wcjc.edu
KOLOMITZ, Kara .... 781-768-7055 218 C kara.kolomitz@regiscollege.edu
KOLSTAD, Michael .... 417-865-2815 253 B kolstadm@evangel.edu
KOLVOORD, Robert ...... 540-568-2752 468 F kolvoora@jmu.edu
KOLWINSKA, Jeremy, W .... 651-631-5100 244 D jwkolwinska@unwsp.edu
KOM, Sheila .... 208-792-2288 131 A sheilak@lcsc.edu
KOMANECKI, William ... 309-655-2180 148 E william.g.komanecki@osfhealthcare.org
KOMARRAJU, Meera ..... 618-453-5744 149 E provost@siu.edu
KOMMER, Richard .... 575-439-3611 287 C rick1574@nmsu.edu
KOMORA, Melissa .... 570-372-4103 399 C komora@susqu.edu
KOMOTO, Cary .... 952-358-9007 239 F cary.komoto@normandale.edu
KOMP, Chuck .... 715-365-4537 500 D ckomp@nicoletcollege.edu
KOMPELIEN, Ken .... 701-671-2297 346 E ken.kompelien@ndscs.edu
KONA, Mijana .... 215-335-0800 389 B mkona@lincolntech.edu
KONAN, Denise, E .... 808-956-6570 128 F konan@hawaii.edu
KONAN, LaCretia .... 815-825-2086 140 F lkonan1@kish.edu
KONCZAL, Timothy, J ... 330-672-9192 354 J tkonczal@kent.edu
KONDA, Kevin, J .... 316-978-7022 178 A kevin.konda@wichita.edu
KONDRACKI, Lacey ...... 912-279-4540 116 G lkondracki@ccga.edu
KONDRAK, Mark .... 907-450-8389.... 9 G
KONDZIELAWA, Eric ..... 804-862-6100 470 I ekondzielawa@rbc.edu
KONE, Drissa .... 212-563-6647 323 F d.kone@uts.edu
KONEN, Judee, L .... 402-461-7434 267 D jkonen@hastings.edu
KONG, Amy .... 406-447-6364 264 C amy.kong@helenacollege.edu
KONG, Xiangping .... 609-626-6025 283 D xiangping.kong@stockton.edu
KONGATS, Tracey .... 716-880-2362 306 C tracey.l.kongats@medaille.edu
KONIECZKA, Matthew ... 603-899-1130 273 F konieczkam@franklinpierce.edu
KONING, Shawnn .... 951-343-4224.. 27 J skoning@calbaptist.edu
KONISIEWICZ, Richard . 440-646-8355 363 G richard.konisiewicz@ursuline.edu
KONKOL, Brian .... 315-443-2902 322 C bkonkol@syr.edu
KONKOLESKI, II, Raymond, J .... 740-695-9500 348 F rkonkoleski@belmontcollege.edu
KONKOTH, Shanthi .... 718-522-9073 290 C skonkoth@asa.edu
KONKRIGHT, Ryan .... 210-436-3126 443 A rkonkright@stmarytx.edu
KONO, Brian, S .... 517-750-1200 230 H bkono@arbor.edu
KONOPA AIGOTTI, Claire .... 317-940-9900 153 F caigotti@butler.edu
KONOPKA, Joseph .... 732-255-0400 280 A jkonopka@ocean.edu
KONOPSKI, Michael, J . 570-321-4126 389 E konopski@lycoming.edu
KONRAD, Jim .... 847-491-8121 145 F j-konrad@northwestern.edu
KONSCHAK, Norma ...... 952-358-8243 239 F norma.konschak@normandale.edu
KONSTALID, Daniel, T .. 717-337-6200 384 H dkonstal@gettysburg.edu
KONSTANTINOVA, Iana . 540-261-8400 471 H iana.konstantinova@svu.edu
KONWERSKI, Peter .... 518-276-6201 312 I konwep@rpi.edu
KONYA, Jeffrey .... 617-373-2000 217 F
KONYAOLE, Cederic ..... 504-816-4872 186 D ckonyaole@dillard.edu
KOO, Jahyuk .... 714-525-0088.. 44 E administration@gm.edu
KOO, Jason .... 571-633-9651 472 J jason.koo@uona.edu
KOO, Kyung Mo .... 562-926-1023.. 57 G kmkoo@ptsa.edu
KOO, Laura .... 650-543-3732.. 51 F laura.koo@menlo.edu
KOOB, Colleen .... 207-947-4591 193 C ckoob@bealcollege.edu
KOOB, Sondra .... 215-785-0111 393 C
KOOCHER, Gerald, P .... 617-984-1640 218 B gkoocher@quincycollege.edu
KOODALI, Ranjit .... 605-658-6129 416 H ranjit.koodali@usd.edu
KOOHANG, Alex .... 478-471-2801 121 F alex.koohang@mga.edu
KOOI, Jana .... 904-997-2649 100 B jana.kooi@fscj.edu
KOOI, Janeen, W .... 260-982-5202 158 T jwkooi@manchester.edu
KOOK, Kathleen .... 510-649-2464.. 44 F kkook@gtu.edu
KOOMER, Ajoy .... 714-872-5695.. 51 A akoomer@ketchum.edu
KOON, Chi .... 718-270-6107 295 A chi@mec.cuny.edu
KOON, Mike .... 304-214-8800 489 F mkoon@wvncc.edu
KOONCE, JR., George, E .... 923-923-7154 494 A gkoonce@marianuniversity.edu
KOONG, Kia .... 334-727-8705.... 7 D kkoong@tuskegee.edu
KOONTS, Christina .... 703-591-7042 476 F
KOONTZ, David .... 562-903-4760.. 27 C dave.koontz@biola.edu
KOONTZ, Megan .... 866-680-2756 459 G graduatedean@midwifery.edu
KOONTZ, Nikki .... 435-586-5400 460 F nikkikootz@suu.edu
KOONTZ, Stephanie ...... 330-244-4943 364 B skoontz@walsh.edu

KOOPMAN, Daniel .... 541-888-2525 376 F
daniel.koopman@socc.edu
KOOPMANS, Ken .... 517-607-2609 225 A
kkoopmans@hillsdale.edu
KOOREN, Lisa .... 209-478-0800.. 45 H
lkooren@humphreys.edu
KOOS, Agnes .... 530-283-0202.. 42 H
akoos@frc.edu
KOOTI, John .... 717-477-1435 395 E
jgkooti@ship.edu
KOOTTUNGAL, Yvette ... 305-899-3600.. 95 C
ybrown@barry.edu
KOPACH,
Christopher, M .... 520-241-6482.. 16 G
ckopach@email.arizona.edu
KOPAS, Michael .... 914-251-6916 319 E
michael.kopas@purchase.edu
KOPAS, William .... 954-262-4412 103 M
wk128@nsu.nova.edu
KOPECKY, Lisa .... 508-362-2131 214 B
lkopecky@capecod.edu
KOPER, Francis .... 248-683-0310 231 A
fkoper@sscms.edu
KOPERA, Ken .... 864-646-1770 413 A
kkopera@tctc.edu
KOPERSKI, Kate .... 716-286-8288 310 D
kjk@niagara.edu
KOPERSKI, Mike .... 415-442-7082.. 44 D
mkoperski@ggu.edu
KOPISCHKE, Connie ..... 612-455-3420 234 D
connie.kopischke@bcsmn.edu
KOPKOWSKI, Renee ...... 404-894-0870 118 F
renee.kopkowski@gatech.edu
KOPP, Courtney, A .... 515-574-1020 166 E
kopp@iowacentral.edu
KOPP, Jason .... 952-995-1626 238 B
jason.kopp@hennepintech.edu
KOPP, Nikki .... 715-675-3331 500 E
kopp@ntc.edu
KOPP, Sacha, E .... 402-554-2907 270 B
sacha.kopp@unomaha.edu
KOPP, Sonya .... 251-981-3771.... 5 B
sonya.kopp@columbiasouthern.edu
KOPP, Will, E .... 740-368-3108 359 N
wekopp@owu.edu
KOPP-MILLER, Barbara . 419-530-4488 363 E
barbara.kopp-miller@utoledo.edu
KOPPEL, Michael .... 202-885-8610.. 93 E
mkoppel@wesleyseminary.edu
KOPPELL, Jonathan ...... 602-496-0402.. 10 I
koppell@asu.edu
KOPPEN, Jason .... 928-774-3890.. 12 M
jkoppen@indianbible.org
KOPPI, Stefan .... 508-831-5260 220 E
skoppi@wpi.edu
KOPPI, Susan, W .... 518-580-5700 316 A
skoppi@skidmore.edu
KOPPY, Katie .... 320-625-5114 240 C
katie.koppy@pine.edu
KOPS, Christopher .... 414-955-8703 494 C
ckops@mcw.edu
KOPSTAIN, Eric .... 615-875-8617 428 D
eric.kopstain@vanderbilt.edu
KORALESKY, Barron ...... 413-597-3072 220 C
barron.koralesky@williams.edu
KORB-NICE, Jobe, S ..... 206-281-2564 484 D
jobe@spu.edu
KORBEL, Linda .... 847-635-1952 145 G
lkorbel@oakton.edu
KORD, JoLanna .... 620-341-6829 172 L
jkord@emporia.edu
KORDENBROCK,
William, R .... 906-487-2200 227 E
billk@mtu.edu
KORENEK, Rebecca .... 409-747-2210 456 F
bbkorene@utmb.edu
KORETOFF, Lisa, A .... 336-334-4822 335 A
lakoretoff@gtcc.edu
KORETSKY, Carla, M .... 269-387-4360 232 K
carla.koretsky@wmich.edu
KORETZKY, Gary .... 212-746-1363 297 F
gak2008@med.cornell.edu
KORF, Abraham .... 305-673-5664 113 E
rabbikorf@hotmail.com
KORF, Benzion .... 305-653-8770 113 E
bkorf@lecfl.com
KORFF, Zamira .... 781-736-4002 207 E
zkorff@brandeis.edu
KORGAN, Christos .... 760-471-1316.. 71 I
ckorgan@usk.edu
KORGAN, Kate, H .... 702-895-0446 271 E
kate.korgan@unlv.edu
KORINKE, Kim .... 805-378-1463.. 72 H
kkorinke@vcccd.edu

KORITARI, Andi .... 312-261-3317 144 F
andi.koritari@nl.edu
KORKLAN, Michael .... 816-604-1000 255 I
michael.korklan@mcckc.edu
KORKMAZ, Ali .... 816-235-1045 261 C
korkmaza@umkc.edu
KORKUS, Tisha .... 512-863-1538 445 D
templet@southwestern.edu
KORMAN, Caryn .... 312-996-7125 151 B
caryn1@uic.edu
KORMAN, Thomas, P ... 517-750-1200 230 H
tkorman@arbor.edu
KORMANAK, Steve .... 608-757-7766 499 C
skormanak@blackhawk.edu
KORN, Judy .... 320-589-6011 244 B
kornjr@morris.umn.edu
KORN, Timothy .... 716-829-7640 298 F
kornt@dyc.edu
KORNACKI, Kelly .... 414-425-8300 495 H
kkornacki@shsst.edu
KORNAHRENS, Chris .... 650-508-3640.. 54 D
ckornahrens@ndnu.edu
KORNBERG, Judith .... 212-986-4343 291 D
jdk@berkeleycollege.edu
KORNBERG, Judith .... 212-986-4343 275 I
jdk@berkeleycollege.edu
KORNBERG, Mindy .... 206-685-4730 485 F
mindyk@uw.edu
KORNBLUH, Mark, L .... 859-257-1375 185 B
kornbluh@uky.edu
KORNBLUTH, Jerry .... 516-572-7775 308 A
jerry.kornbluth@ncc.edu
KORNBLUTH, Sally .... 919-684-2631 328 G
sally.kornbluth@duke.edu
KORNEGAY, Jeffrey .... 910-879-5574 332 D
jkornegay@bladencc.edu
KORNEGAY, Joy .... 919-735-5151 338 H
jmkornegay@waynecc.edu
KORNER, Barbara, O .... 814-865-2591 392 B
bok2@psu.edu
KORNER, Christoph ...... 818-394-3325.. 75 C
christoph.korner@woodbury.edu
KORNFUEHRER, Dana ... 512-313-3000 434 E
dana.kornfuehrer@concordia.edu
KORNGIEBEL, Aaron ..... 206-934-4532 483 J
aaron.korngiebel@seattlecolleges.edu
KORNKVEN, Kelly, J ..... 701-788-4816 345 E
kelly.kornkven@mayvillestate.edu
KORNS, Linda .... 409-839-2022 449 G
ldkorns@lit.edu
KORNWEIBEL, Karen, R 423-439-7881 419 J
kornweib@etsu.edu
KOROIVULAONO,
Theresa, B .... 692-625-3394 505 F
tkoroivulaono@cmi.edu
KOROMA, Joseph .... 510-464-3414.. 56 G
jkoroma@peralta.edu
KORONKIEWICZ, Talia .. 815-455-8584 143 A
tkoronkiewica@mchenry.edu
KOROS, Shadrack .... 678-422-4100.. 92 G
KOROSEC, Ronnie .... 407-823-0676 109 E
ronnie@ucf.edu
KORPELA, Doreen .... 906-487-7201 223 K
doreen.korpela@finlandia.edu
KORPI, Jeff .... 906-227-2620 228 F
jkorpi@nmu.edu
KORSAKOV, Stephan .... 212-966-0300 308 D
skorsakov@nyaa.edu
KORSCHINOWSKI,
Claire .... 253-589-5516 479 G
claire.korschinowski@cptc.edu
KORSTAD, Donna .... 509-542-4401 479 H
dkorstad@columbiabasin.edu
KORSTAD, John .... 918-495-6942 368 I
jkorstad@oru.edu
KORT, J. Thomas .... 609-497-7782 280 D
j.thomas.kort@ptsem.edu
KORTA, Allison .... 716-614-6231 310 C
akorta@niagaracc.suny.edu
KORTE, Andrea .... 910-695-3767 337 H
kortea@sandhills.edu
KORTENDICK, Kyle .... 715-634-4790 493 I
kkortendick@lco.edu
KORUS, Daniel .... 361-698-1065 436 C
dkorus@delmar.edu
KORVAS, Ronald .... 617-824-8544 208 H
ronald_korvas@emerson.edu
KORVER, Bill .... 910-323-5614 327 G
president@ccbs.edu
KORZENDORFER, Kate .. 781-768-7340 218 C
kate.korzendorfer@regiscollege.edu
KORZENIEWSKI,
Noelle, J .... 920-748-8116 495 G
korzeniewskin@ripon.edu

KORZINEK, Sue .... 616-331-2035 224 E
korzines@gvsu.edu
KOSAKA, Timothy .... 817-202-6628 444 I
tim@swau.edu
KOSAKOWSKI, Sheryl ... 413-565-1000 205 G
skosakowski@baypath.edu
KOSARUE, Lori .... 517-264-7132 230 E
lshearer@sienaheights.edu
KOSBOTH, Michele .... 440-775-6392 358 C
mkosboth@oberlin.edu
KOSCHMEDER,
Douglas, D .... 319-352-8761 170 C
doug.koschmeder@wartburg.edu
KOSCHWANEZ, Jeanne . 760-795-6840.. 52 E
jkoschwanez@miracosta.edu
KOSCIW, Dennis .... 850-718-2244.. 96 F
kosciwd@chipola.edu
KOSER, Ashley .... 570-484-2128 395 B
ashley.koser@lhufoundation.org
KOSHI, Deanne .... 808-245-8226 129 C
deannesy@hawaii.edu
KOSHLAND, Cathy .... 510-643-7384.. 68 D
ckoshland@berkeley.edu
KOSHMIDER, III,
John, W .... 330-471-8326 355 L
jkoshmider@malone.edu
KOSHORK, Lori .... 206-726-5027 480 C
lkoshork@cornish.edu
KOSHUT, Thomas, M ... 256-824-6100.... 8 B
tom.koshut@uah.edu
KOSIEK, Timothy, J ...... 708-709-3702 146 D
tkosiek@prairiestate.edu
KOSIK, Jamie, F .... 304-293-7202 491 C
jamie.kosik@mail.wvu.edu
KOSINE, Brandon .... 307-268-2550 501 U
bkosine@caspercollege.edu
KOSINSKI, Mark .... 203-285-2077.. 85 E
mkosinski@gwcc.commnet.edu
KOSINSKI, Ross, J .... 630-515-6470 143 G
rkosin@midwestern.edu
KOSINSKY, James, A ..... 708-209-3519 135 F
jim.kosinsky@cuchicago.edu
KOSKI, Janet .... 906-227-2420 228 F
jakoski@nmu.edu
KOSKI, Mary .... 309-794-7208 132 C
marykoski@augustana.edu
KOSKINEN, Michael ...... 201-200-3449 279 E
mkoskinen@njcu.edu
KOSKY, Kristy .... 740-695-9500 348 F
kkosky@belmontcollege.edu
KOSLOSKY, Jill .... 307-637-1154 502 D
jkoslosk@lccc.wy.edu
KOSLOW MARTIN, Jodi 708-456-0300 150 I
jodikoslowmartin@triton.edu
KOSMOSKI, Kathleen .... 912-486-7409 122 I
kkosmoski@ogeecheetech.edu
KOSOBUCKI, Dave .... 858-695-8587 155 E
dkosobucki@horizonuniversity.edu
KOSS, Kim .... 706-721-0140 115 A
kkoss@augusta.edu
KOSS, Michelle .... 586-286-2172 226 H
kossm26@macomb.edu
KOSSE, Glenn, F .... 502-272-8328 179 B
gkosse@bellarmine.edu
KOSSO, Cynthia .... 610-861-1348 391 A
kossoc@moravian.edu
KOSSUTH, Joanne .... 860-701-5155.. 87 D
kossuth_j@mitchell.edu
KOST, Patricia, L .... 216-368-2165 349 F
patricia.kost@case.edu
KOSTECKI, David .... 808-356-5256 127 H
KOSTELIS, Kimberly ...... 860-832-3000.. 84 I
KOSTELL, Stacey, R ...... 802-656-1394 463 E
stacey.kostell@uvm.edu
KOSTEN, Linda .... 303-871-7922.. 83 D
linda.kosten@du.edu
KOSTER, Ed .... 402-761-8224 269 C
ekoster@southeast.edu
KOSTIC, Jennifer .... 937-512-4191 361 A
jennifer.kostic@sinclair.edu
KOSTIHOVA, Marcela .... 651-523-2252 236 A
mkostihova01@hamline.edu
KOSTJUK, Todd .... 661-362-2734.. 51 C
tkostjuk@masters.edu
KOSTOFF, Marcia, R ..... 419-772-2192 358 H
m-kostoff@onu.edu
KOSTRZEWA,
Waldemar .... 203-575-8297.. 86 B
wkostrzewa@nv.edu
KOSTRZEWSKI, Diana ... 701-777-4354 345 C
diana.kostrzewski@und.edu
KOSTYUKOV, Victoria ... 718-522-9073 290 C
victoria_kostyukov@asa.edu

KOTAKIS, Paul .... 978-921-4242 216 F
paul.kotakis@montserrat.edu
KOTCAMP, Butch .... 740-351-3429 360 K
bkotcamp@shawnee.edu
KOTECKI, Kathy .... 406-657-1660 264 E
kkotecki@msubillings.edu
KOTH, Jason .... 212-592-2259 315 H
jkoth@sva.edu
KOTH, Kent .... 206-296-2329 484 F
kothk@seattleu.edu
KOTHANDARAMAN,
Prabakar .... 315-312-3168 319 B
pk@oswego.edu
KOTLAS, Maureen .... 301-405-3960 202 C
mkotlas@umd.edu
KOTLER, A. Malkiel ...... 732-367-1060 275 J
KOTLER, Aaron .... 732-367-1060 275 J
akotler@bmg.edu
KOTLER, Yitzchok, S ..... 732-367-1060 275 J
KOTLIKOFF, Michael, I . 607-255-2364 297 F
provost@cornell.edu
KOTLINSKI, Michael, J . 717-337-6363 384 H
mkotlinski@gettysburg.edu
KOTOISUVA, Agnes .... 692-625-3394 505 F
KOTORI, Chiaki .... 570-321-4029 389 E
kotori@lycoming.edu
KOTOWICZ, Keith, A .... 414-847-3301 494 F
keithkotowicz@miad.edu
KOTOWSKI, Jenni .... 352-365-3571 102 T
kotoskj@lssc.edu
KOTOWSKI, Kelli .... 740-597-1819 359 G
kotowskk@ohio.edu
KOTSCHEVAR, Joel .... 218-736-1560 239 B
joel.kotschevar@minnesota.edu
KOTT, Micheal .... 708-656-8000 144 E
micheal.kott@morton.edu
KOTTAS, Kathy .... 620-792-9355 171 C
kottask@bartonccc.edu
KOTTAYIL, Joseph .... 305-223-4561 106 B
josephpothen@hotmail.com
KOTTENSTETTE, Kathy ... 970-675-3237.. 78 G
kathy.kottenstette@cncc.edu
KOTTER, David .... 303-963-3336.. 77 G
dkotter@ccu.edu
KOTTICH, Sarah .... 402-399-2427 266 F
skottich@csm.edu
KOTTON, Stevenson ...... 692-625-3394 505 F
skotton@cmi.edu
KOTTRE, Chris .... 805-581-1233.. 42 D
ckottre@eternitybiblecollege.edu
KOTWICKI, Lee .... 941-363-7218 108 G
kotwicl@scf.edu
KOUA, Deb .... 515-965-7025 164 C
dkkoua@dmacc.edu
KOUANCHAO, Ketmani .. 626-585-7560.. 55 K
kkouanchao@pasadena.edu
KOUBEK, Richard, J ..... 906-487-2200 227 E
koubek@mtu.edu
KOUCOUMARIS,
John, S .... 740-695-9500 348 F
jkoucoumaris@belmontcollege.edu
KOUDELIK-JONES,
Rachelle .... 540-857-6187 476 D
rkoudelikjones@virginiawestern.edu
KOUDOU, Nick .... 816-559-6182 258 A
nicolas.koudou@park.edu
KOUGH, Katherine .... 717-262-2006 403 F
kkough@wilson.edu
KOUKARI, Ray .... 262-619-6712 499 F
koukarir@gtc.edu
KOUKOL, June .... 617-333-2091 208 E
jkoukol@curry.edu
KOULIK, Chet .... 845-451-1347 298 A
chet.koulik@culinary.edu
KOULOS, Elleni, R .... 909-593-3511.. 70 D
ekoulos@laverne.edu
KOUMAS, Sokratis .... 508-999-8859 211 F
skoumas@umassd.edu
KOURY, Kevin, A .... 724-938-4125 394 B
koury@calu.edu
KOURY, Regina .... 856-225-2828 281 G
regina.koury@rutgers.edu
KOUTSIDIS, Anastasia .. 646-313-8000 295 E
anastasia.koutsidis@guttman.cuny.edu
KOVAC, Jason .... 503-594-3390 372 D
jason.kovac@clackamas.edu
KOVAC, Matt .... 724-287-8711 380 A
matt.kovac@bc3.edu
KOVACH, Jacalyn, E ..... 330-325-6369 357 G
jkovach1@neomed.edu
KOVACH, Ronald .... 703-591-7042 476 F
KOVACICH, Christine, L 330-325-6551 357 G
ckovacich@neomed.edu

KREHBIEL, Lee .... 479-788-7304.. 21 H
lee.krehbiel@uafs.edu
KREIDER, Paul .... 304-293-7119 491 C
paul.kreider@mail.wvu.edu
KREIDLER, Kathleen ...... 713-500-3968 456 B
kathleen.kreidler@uth.tmc.edu
KREILICK, Amy .... 419-559-2121 361 I
akreilick01@terra.edu
KREINER, Thane .... 408-551-6043.. 62 D
tkreiner@scu.edu
KREISER, Valerie .... 610-740-3785 381 A
valerie@cedarcrest.edu
KREISS, Andrew .... 309-556-3031 139 G
akreiss@iwu.edu
KREITZER, Ilene .... 516-773-5000 504 G
kreitzeri@usmma.edu
KREJCI, Teresa .... 815-836-5200 141 G
KREMENEK, Amy .... 315-498-7252 311 B
kremenea@sunyocc.edu
KREMENS, Zdzislaw ...... 860-832-1801.. 84 I
kremensz@ccsu.edu
KREMER, Anne .... 515-271-3181 165 A
anne.kremer@drake.edu
KREMER, Cheryl, E .... 717-245-1098 382 F
kremerc@dickinson.edu
KREMER, Ed .... 913-288-7111 174 F
ekremer@kckcc.edu
KREMER, Jacalyn .... 978-665-3833 212 C
jkremer@fitchburgstate.edu
KREMER, Kathy, S .... 815-834-6450 141 G
kremerka@lewisu.edu
KREMER, Peter, W .... 502-272-8334 179 B
pkremer@bellarmine.edu
KREMER, Rachel .... 501-420-1208.. 17 B
rachel.kremer@arkansasbaptist.edu
KREMS, Ruth .... 860-906-5141.. 85 D
rkrems@capitalcc.edu
KRENGEL, Jennifer .... 415-458-3785.. 41 H
jennifer.krengel@dominican.edu
KRENTZ, Shelby .... 859-815-7648 181 B
shelby.krentz@kctcs.edu
KRENTZMAN, Lily, A ..... 508-565-1105 218 H
lkrentzman@stonehill.edu
KRESCH, Dow .... 845-426-3110 325 O
KRESKEN, Jonathan ...... 843-953-1411 407 F
jkresken@citadel.edu
KRESS, Anne, M .... 585-292-2100 307 H
akress@monroecc.edu
KRESS, Cathann .... 614-292-6164 358 I
kress.98@osu.edu
KRESS, Dillon .... 540-373-2200 466 H
dkress@evcc.edu
KRESS, Lisa, P .... 785-864-3911 177 D
lpkress@ku.edu
KRESS, Ruth .... 812-357-6561 160 D
rkress@saintmeinrad.edu
KRETSCHMAR, Lani .... 413-205-3202 205 A
lani.kretschmar@aic.edu
KRETSCHMER, Mark ...... 805-525-4417.. 67 D
mkretschmer@thomasaquinas.edu
KREUSER, Ryan .... 715-394-8538 498 B
rkreuser@uwsuper.edu
KREUTTER, Tayler .... 585-594-6391 312 K
kreutter_tayler@roberts.edu
KREUTZER, Steven .... 973-748-9000 276 A
steven_kreutzer@bloomfield.edu
KREUZER, Charlene ...... 507-457-5090 241 F
ckreuzer@winona.edu
KREVH, Janet .... 216-397-4349 354 I
jkrevh@jcu.edu
KREYE, Judy .... 330-244-4757 364 B
jkreye@walsh.edu
KREYNIS, Ilona .... 408-498-5104.. 38 F
ikreynis@cogswell.edu
KREYS, Tiffany-Jade ..... 916-686-7400.. 29 J
KRHIN, Daniel, J .... 920-748-8394 495 G
krhind@ripon.edu
KRIARAS, Dimitrios ...... 708-237-5050 145 E
dkriaras@nc.edu
KRIBBE, Bridget .... 574-631-4061 161 C
bkibbe@nd.edu
KRIBS, Rick, A .... 812-888-4176 162 C
rkribs@vinu.edu
KRICHMAR, Lee .... 707-664-2880.. 34 C
KRICKX, Guido .... 415-338-1111.. 34 A
KRIEB, Dennis .... 618-468-4300 141 F
dkrieb@lc.edu
KRIEG, Eric, J .... 716-878-5550 318 C
kriegej@buffalostate.edu
KRIEG, John .... 360-650-7405 486 F
john.krieg@wwu.edu
KRIEG, Lisa, M .... 412-268-5399 380 F
krieg@andrew.cmu.edu

KRIEGE, Bill .... 816-501-4855 258 H
bill.kriege@rockhurst.edu
KRIEGER, Andrea .... 850-484-1477 104 H
akrieger@pensacolastate.edu
KRIEGER, Jill .... 412-397-5279 397 G
krieger@rmu.edu
KRIEGER, Marcos .... 570-372-4292 399 C
kriegerm@susqu.edu
KRIEGERMEIER, Pat ...... 815-455-8726 143 A
pkriegermeier@mchenry.edu
KRIEGH, David .... 650-321-5655.. 59 C
david.kriegh@stpsu.edu
KRIEPS, Kevin .... 219-473-4330 153 G
kkrieps@ccsj.edu
KRIER, Jacob, C .... 507-344-7519 234 B
jake.krier@blc.edu
KRIESE, Theresa .... 605-995-2621 415 C
theresa.kriese@dwu.edu
KRIETE, Jennie .... 321-433-7055.. 97 I
krietej@easternflorida.edu
KRIGEL, Belinda .... 256-233-8100.... 4 D
belinda.krigel@athens.edu
KRIKAU, Paul .... 920-923-7666 494 A
pwkrikau25@marianuniversity.edu
KRIKORIAN,
Gregory, H .... 717-867-6238 388 H
krikoria@lvc.edu
KRILEY, Taylor .... 785-628-5826 173 B
tkriley@fhsu.edu
KRIMMEL, Jon .... 626-815-4570.. 26 H
KRIMMEL, Thomas .... 262-595-2591 497 C
krimmel@uwp.edu
KRIMPELBEIN, Kristi ..... 715-232-2149 498 A
krimpelbeink@uwstout.edu
KRINGEL, Dawny .... 575-492-2114 289 A
dkringel@usw.edu
KRISAK, Wendy .... 610-282-1100 382 E
wendy.krisak@desales.edu
KRISE, Thomas, W .... 671-735-2990 505 E
tkrise@triton.uog.edu
KRISHNAIAH, Raghu ..... 816-943-9600.. 16 J
raghu.krishnaiah@phoenix.edu
KRISHNAMOORTI,
Ramanan .... 713-743-4307 452 F
rkrishna@central.uh.edu
KRISHNAMURTHY,
Sushma .... 318-342-1041 192 F
krishnamurthy@ulm.edu
KRISHNAN, G, V .... 713-221-8478 453 B
krishnang@uhd.edu
KRISHNAN, Kris .... 661-654-2124.. 30 E
skrishnan@csub.edu
KRISHNAN, Ramayya .... 412-268-2159 380 F
rk2x@andrew.cmu.edu
KRISHNAN, Ranga .... 312-563-2033 148 A
ranga_krishnan@rush.edu
KRISHNASWAMY,
Vidya .... 972-377-1575 433 M
vkrishnaswamy@collin.edu
KRISHNASWAMY,
Vidya .... 972-860-8152 435 A
vkrishnaswamy@dcccd.edu
KRISLOV, Marvin .... 212-346-1097 311 E
president@pace.edu
KRISNAN, Kris .... 661-654-2124.. 30 E
skrishnan@csub.edu
KRISPIN, Joy .... 847-628-1546 140 C
joy.krispin@judsonu.edu
KRISS, George .... 618-537-6425 143 B
gnkriss@mckendree.edu
KRISS, OSF, M. Elise ... 260-399-7700 161 D
ekriss@sf.edu
KRISSOFF BOEHM,
Lisa .... 508-531-2809 212 B
lkrissoffboehm@bridgew.edu
KRIST, Paula, S .... 619-260-7878.. 71 J
pkrist@sandiego.edu
KRISTENSEN,
Douglas, A .... 308-865-8208 269 I
kristensend@unk.edu
KRITSCHER, Matthew .... 510-723-6743.. 35 O
mkritscher@chabotcollege.edu
KRITSKY, Gene .... 513-244-4401 357 A
gene.kritsky@msj.edu
KRIVONIAK,
Christopher .... 740-283-6860 353 B
ckrivoniak@franciscan.edu
KRIZ, Christine .... 540-868-7094 474 J
ckriz@lfcc.edu
KROB, Jay, C .... 785-833-4440 175 B
jayk@kwu.edu
KROBOTH, Patricia, D .. 412-624-3270 401 B
pkroboth@pitt.edu

KROEGER, Brian .... 573-288-6450 252 E
bkroeger@culver.edu
KROEKER, Dean .... 620-241-0723 172 D
dean.kroeker@centralchristian.edu
KROENING, Mike .... 507-453-2752 239 A
mkroening@southeastmn.edu
KROENKE, Paul .... 309-677-2325 133 B
pkroenke@bradley.edu
KROGDAHL, Renate ...... 650-493-4430.. 64 A
renate.krogdahl@sofia.edu
KROGH, Mary Anne ...... 605-688-5178 417 C
maryanne.krogh@sdstate.edu
KROH, Lynne .... 417-862-9533 253 D
enroll@globaluniversity.edu
KROHN, Lisa .... 712-274-5100 168 B
krohn@morningside.edu
KROL, Naz .... 814-866-8152 388 A
nkrol@lecom.edu
KROLAK, Steven .... 812-941-2470 157 B
skrolak@ius.edu
KROLICK, Sandy .... 505-747-2191 287 G
sandyk@nnmc.edu
KROLL, Ann .... 510-723-7637.. 35 P
akroll@clpccd.edu
KROLL, Dana .... 262-551-5858 492 F
KROLL, Jason .... 201-200-3344 279 E
jkroll@njcu.edu
KROLOFF, Reed .... 312-567-3000 139 B
KROMPF, Steven .... 703-425-4143 468 E
KRONE, Rhiannon .... 714-533-1495.. 64 D
rhiannon@southbaylo.edu
KRONEMAN, Ann .... 517-483-1604 226 F
kronemaa@lcc.edu
KRONENBERGER, Judy . 513-862-5010 353 G
judy.kronenberger@email.gscollege.edu
KRONENBITTER,
Jennifer .... 607-753-2221 318 D
jennifer.kronenbitter@cortland.edu
KRONFELD, Michelle .... 608-796-3025 498 N
mlkronfeld@viterbo.edu
KRONISER, Maria .... 412-365-1862 381 C
mkroniser@chatham.edu
KROOT, Irwin .... 212-229-5671 308 C
krooti@newschool.edu
KROPF, Kevin .... 417-873-7524 252 F
kkropf@drury.edu
KROPF, Nancy, P .... 678-891-2700 119 E
nkropf@gsu.edu
KROPFF, Robert .... 330-972-7048 362 B
bobk@uakron.edu
KROPIEWNICKI, Mary ... 912-358-4100 123 H
sote@savannahstate.edu
KROPP-ANDERSON,
Pamela .... 207-941-7107 194 A
kroppandersonp@husson.edu
KROTINGER, Nicole ...... 802-485-2126 463 A
nkroting@norwich.edu
KROTZER, Mary, J .... 205-247-8164.... 7 A
mkrotzer@stillman.edu
KROUSE, Alisa .... 713-963-8979 124 E
akrouse@southuniversity.edu
KROUSE, Anne, M .... 610-499-4214 403 B
amkrouse@widener.edu
KROUSE, John .... 956-296-1445 455 D
john.krouse@utrgv.edu
KRSTIC, Miroslav .... 858-534-5556.. 69 D
mkrstic@ucsd.edu
KRTINIC, Marina .... 708-709-7921 146 D
mkrtinic@prairiestate.edu
KRUCKEBERG, Tara .... 626-395-8661.. 29 C
tkruckeb@caltech.edu
KRUEGER, Amy .... 619-688-0800.. 40 E
KRUEGER, Beth Ann ..... 913-288-7100 174 F
bkrueger@kckcc.edu
KRUEGER, Bryon, D ...... 651-631-5392 244 D
bdkrueger@unwsp.edu
KRUEGER, Carr .... 801-422-3760 458 H
carr@byu.edu
KRUEGER, Christopher . 410-626-2558 201 D
chris.krueger@sjc.edu
KRUEGER, Cindy .... 419-267-1233 358 A
ckrueger@northweststate.edu
KRUEGER, Conrad .... 210-486-0915 429 H
ckrueger@alamo.edu
KRUEGER, Dave .... 406-265-4157 264 F
david.krueger@msun.edu
KRUEGER, Joni .... 605-274-4015 415 B
joni.krueger@augie.edu
KRUEGER, Kurt, J .... 949-214-3194.. 40 F
kurt.krueger@cui.edu
KRUEGER, Laura .... 480-423-6133.. 13 H
laura.krueger@scottsdalecc.edu

KRUEGER, Mablene ...... 312-935-6645 147 D
mkrueger@robertmorris.edu
KRUEGER, Matthew ...... 218-855-8115 237 F
mkrueger@clcmn.edu
KRUEGER, Michelle ...... 941-359-4200 110 D
mkrueger@sar.usf.edu
KRUEGER, Todd .... 252-335-0821 333 G
todd_krueger@albemarle.edu
KRUEKEBERG, Adam ..... 617-552-3300 207 B
adam.krueckeberg@bc.edu
KRUEMMLING, Brooke . 215-780-1364 398 G
KRUG, Anita, K .... 312-567-3000 139 B
KRUG, Cherie .... 301-387-3100 198 F
cherie.krug@garrettcollege.edu
KRUG, Stefan .... 617-521-3929 218 E
stefan.krug@simmons.edu
KRUGER, Darrell, P ...... 828-262-2070 341 B
krugerdp@appstate.edu
KRUGER, Jenny .... 712-325-3326 167 B
jkruger@iwcc.edu
KRUGER, Michael .... 605-677-5221 416 H
michael.kruger@usd.edu
KRUGER, Michael, J ..... 704-688-4233 248 F
mkruger@rts.edu
KRUGER, Severa .... 920-923-7600 494 A
KRUGLER, DeeAnn, M .. 218-299-3000 235 E
krugler@cord.edu
KRUHLY, Leslie, L .... 215-898-7005 400 K
kruhly@upenn.edu
KRUIZENGA, Alicia .... 714-564-6971.. 57 L
kruizenga_alicia@sac.edu
KRUKONES, James .... 216-397-4762 354 I
jkrukones@jcu.edu
KRUKOVITZ, Robyn, M . 570-348-6231 389 G
rmkrukovitz@marywood.edu
KRULL, Kimberly .... 316-322-3100 171 G
kim.krull@butlercc.edu
KRULL, Lucille .... 509-527-2145 485 H
lucy.krull@wallawalla.edu
KRUMBACH, Carol .... 562-467-5053.. 35 M
ckrumbach@cerritos.edu
KRUMBACH, Carol .... 310-578-1080 347 H
ckrumbach@antioch.edu
KRUMER, Walter .... 718-522-9073 290 C
vkrumer@asa.edu
KRUMHANSL, Ezra .... 502-585-9911 184 D
ekrumhansl@spalding.edu
KRUML, Susan .... 402-941-6200 267 L
kruml@midlandu.edu
KRUMM, Beth .... 314-516-4151 261 D
krumme@umsl.edu
KRUMM, Brenda, L .... 620-431-2820 175 H
bkrumm@neosho.edu
KRUMM, Javier .... 951-785-2295.. 47 C
jkrumm@lasierra.edu
KRUMMEN SCHRAVEN,
Ginger, B .... 920-433-6631 492 B
ginger.krummen@bellincollege.edu
KRUMMENACHER, Alan 512-404-4803 431 C
akrummenacher@austinseminary.edu
KRUMPELMAN, Jacqui . 330-363-6347 348 D
jacqui.krumpelman@aultman.com
KRUPA, Heather .... 419-289-5048 348 A
hkrupa@ashland.edu
KRUPICKA, Ted .... 503-352-1515 375 G
tedk@pacificu.edu
KRUPIN, Maria .... 845-451-1385 298 A
maria.krupin@culinary.edu
KRUPITSKIY, Anna .... 201-714-7100 278 C
KRUPKA, Ben .... 413-528-7413 205 F
benkrupk@simons-rock.edu
KRUPKA, Moshe, D ...... 646-565-6000 322 J
moshe.krupka@touro.edu
KRUPNICK-WALSH,
Kayla .... 415-442-7228.. 44 D
kkrupnick@ggu.edu
KRUPP, David .... 808-235-7416 129 F
krupp@hawaii.edu
KRUPP, Jason .... 727-341-3339 106 E
krupp.jason@spcollege.edu
KRUPPS, Gina .... 309-341-5264 133 C
gkrupps@sandburg.edu
KRUPPSTADT, Tom .... 877-476-8674 437 C
KRUPSKI, Eric, A .... 617-422-7298 217 C
ekrupski@nesl.edu
KRUPSKI, Katrina .... 950-565-1000 493 J
krupskika@lakeland.edu
KRUS, Haley .... 309-677-2242 133 B
hkrus@fsmail.bradley.edu
KRUSCHINSKA, Kurt ..... 313-577-6748 232 I
registrar@wayne.edu
KRUSE, Amy .... 320-629-5129 240 C
amy.kruse@pine.edu

KUNSELMAN, Scott, G .. 248-370-4287 229 G
skunselman@oakland.edu
KUNSMAN, Kip .... 410-777-2961 197 C
kakunsman@aacc.edu
KUNST, Malia .... 619-388-7834.. 60 E
mkunst@sdccd.edu
KUNTZ, Daniel .... 805-493-3855.. 29 H
kuntz@callutheran.edu
KUNTZ, David .... 216-987-4790 351 G
david.kuntz@tri-c.edu
KUNTZ, F. Douglas ...... 570-321-4116 389 E
kuntz@lycoming.edu
KUNTZ, Jason .... 717-391-7322 399 G
kuntz@stevenscollege.edu
KUNTZ, Jim .... 215-335-0800 389 B
KUNTZ, John .... 973-300-2252 283 E
jkuntz@sussex.edu
KUNTZ, Kristi .... 217-333-6677 151 D
kakuntz@illinois.edu
KUNTZ, Nicole .... 570-321-4081 389 E
kuntzn@lycoming.edu
KUNTZ, Twyla .... 701-349-5438 346 J
twyla@trinitybiblecollege.edu
KUNTZ, Wayne .... 228-897-4361 247 E
wayne.kuntz@mgccc.edu
KUNYCZKA,
Cristiana, A .... 973-596-3602 279 F
crisitana.kunyczka@njit.edu
KUNZ, Kent .... 208-334-4781 130 H
kunzkent@isu.edu
KUNZ, Leonard .... 908-852-1400 276 G
kunzl01@centenaryuniversity.edu
KUNZE, Joel .... 563-425-5259 170 A
kunzej@uiu.edu
KUNZELMAN, Ryan .... 248-689-8282 232 A
rkunzelm@walshcollege.edu
KUNZLER, Rachael .... 641-472-1104 167 F
stuact@mum.edu
KUO, David .... 215-871-6690 396 D
davidku@pcom.edu
KUO, David .... 215-871-7128 396 D
davidku@pcom.edu
KUO, Kent .... 541-737-3525 375 D
kent.kuo@oregonstate.edu
KUO, Ling Ling .... 626-571-8811.. 72 C
linglingk@uwest.edu
KUO, Wai Lan .... 512-444-8082 449 A
wkuo@thsu.edu
KUPERMAN, Eli .... 732-367-1060 275 J
ekuperman@bmg.edu
KUPERSMITH, Peter, A . 215-489-2254 382 D
peter.kupersmith@delval.edu
KUPPER, Jodi .... 402-471-2505 268 D
jkupper@nscs.edu
KUPPINGER, Karen .... 585-389-2100 308 B
kkuppin9@naz.edu
KURACINA, William ...... 903-886-5166 447 B
william.kuracina@tamuc.edu
KURAI, Mark .... 925-969-3300.. 46 H
mkurai@jfku.edu
KURAPATI, Raaj .... 901-678-2121 427 D
kurapati@memphis.edu
KURDA, Linda .... 907-543-4502.. 10 A
lrcurda@alaska.edu
KURDOWSKA, Anna ...... 903-877-7967 456 D
anna.kurdowska@uthct.edu
KURIMAY, Mary Beth ... 610-436-6931 396 A
mkurimay@wcupa.edu
KURISKY, Brian .... 757-455-3216 477 F
bkurisky@vwu.edu
KURKER-STEWART,
Nicole .... 860-768-5101.. 88 H
kurkerste@hartford.edu
KUROKAWA, Linda .... 760-757-2121.. 52 E
lkorokawa@miracosta.edu
KUROPAS, Michael .... 217-420-6765 143 H
mkuropas@millikin.edu
KURPIUS, David, D ...... 573-882-6686 261 B
kurpius@missouri.edu
KURR, Brigitte .... 918-610-0027 366 A
bkurr@communitycarecollege.edu
KURTH, Ann .... 203-785-2393.. 89 D
ann.kurth@yale.edu
KURTH, Christine .... 614-251-4513 358 G
kurthc@ohiodominican.edu
KURTINITIS, Sandra, L . 443-840-1015 198 B
skurtinitis@ccbcmd.edu
KURTZ, Andrew .... 419-372-0623 348 H
kurtz@bgsu.edu
KURTZ, Diane, L .... 517-750-1200 230 H
dkurtz@arbor.edu
KURTZ, Josef .... 617-735-9979 209 A
kurtzj@emmanuel.edu
KURTZ, Rick .... 507-389-7369 241 C
rick.kurtz@southcentral.edu
KURTZ, Terri .... 361-572-6463 457 E
terri.kurtz@victoriacollege.edu
KURTZ HOFFMAN,
Linda, A .... 330-471-8145 355 L
lhoffman@malone.edu
KURTZ-SHAW, Brad ...... 208-467-8539 131 D
bradshaw@nnu.edu
KURZDORFER, Max .... 585-340-9588 296 E
mkurzdorfer@crcds.edu
KURZY, Tracy .... 626-256-4673.. 37 B
tkurzy@coh.org
KUSCH, Bruce, C .... 801-524-8113 459 F
bkusch@ldsbc.edu
KUSCH, Joshua .... 740-392-6868 357 B
josh.kusch@mvnu.edu
KUSER, Janet .... 617-236-5458 209 D
jkuser@fisher.edu
KUSHMIDER, Kristin ..... 303-724-8488.. 83 C
kristin.kushmider@ucdenver.edu
KUSHNER, Cynthia .... 440-366-7610 355 J
KUSHNER, Larry .... 410-706-3911 202 D
lkushner@umaryland.edu
KUSHNER, Melissa .... 610-647-4400 386 C
mkushner@immaculata.edu
KUSHNER, Mikhel, A .... 410-706-1852 202 D
mikhel.kushner@umaryland.edu
KUSHNER, Tiffany .... 908-852-1400 276 G
kushnert@centenaryuniversity.edu
KUSKOWSKI, David ...... 864-656-5463 408 A
dkuskow@clemson.edu
KUSPA, Adam .... 713-798-1060 431 I
akuspa@bcm.edu
KUSPA, Adam .... 713-798-4032 431 I
akuspa@bcm.edu
KUSSE, Debra .... 585-475-3947 313 A
dskpur@rit.edu
KUSTER, Brian .... 270-745-2791 185 E
brian.kuster@wku.edu
KUSTER-DALE, Kim .... 308-635-6103 270 D
kusterdk@wncc.edu
KUTATELADZE, Andrei .. 303-871-2995.. 83 D
akutatel@du.edu
KUTCH, Jason .... 219-464-5917 162 A
jason.kutch@valpo.edu
KUTCHER, Gene .... 609-895-5152 281 B
ekutcher@rider.edu
KUTCHER, Kevin .... 856-351-2612 283 A
kkutcher@salemcc.edu
KUTHY, Anna .... 270-686-4277 179 D
anna.kuthy@brescia.edu
KUTI, Morakinyo .... 937-376-6547 350 D
mkuti@centralstate.edu
KUTLENIOS, Rose, M .... 304-336-8108 490 F
rose.kutlenios@westliberty.edu
KUTNER, Sender .... 847-982-2500 138 A
kutner@htc.edu
KUTNEY, Joshua .... 920-565-1000 493 J
kutneyjp@lakeland.edu
KUTSHIED, Mandy .... 828-771-2048 344 E
mkutshied@warren-wilson.edu
KUTSKO, Jim .... 505-438-8884 288 C
KUTTEN, Shmuel .... 718-941-8000 306 I
KUTTENKULER, Scott .... 870-850-4826.. 21 C
skuttenkuler@seark.edu
KUTZKE, Mike .... 320-222-5218 240 E
mike.kutzke@ridgewater.edu
KUTZKE, Mike .... 320-222-5218 240 E
KUVAAS, Laura .... 320-222-6090 240 E
KUWASAKI,
L. Michelle .... 206-592-3693 481 H
mkuwasaki@highline.edu
KUYKENDALL, Brad ...... 915-532-3737 458 C
KUYKENDALL, John ...... 870-575-8000.. 22 E
kuykendallj@upab.edu
KUYKENDALL, John ...... 870-575-8498.. 22 E
kuykendallj@uapb.edu
KUYKENDALL, John ...... 317-788-3778 161 B
kuykendallj@uindy.edu
KUYKENDALL, Michelle 208-467-8521 131 D
mlkuykendall@nnu.edu
KUYKENDALL, Robin .... 575-769-4916 285 K
robin.kuykendall@clovis.edu
KUYKENDALL, Robin .... 575-769-4001 285 K
robin.kuykendall@clovis.edu
KUZMA, Marta .... 203-432-2606.. 89 D
marta.kuzma@yale.edu
KVAAL, Kimberly .... 512-448-8413 442 M
kimkvaal@stedwards.edu
KVIGNE, Eric .... 530-752-1247.. 68 E
epkvigne@ucdavis.edu
KWAK, Kyueil .... 770-220-7908 118 B
kkwak@gcuniv.edu
KWAN, Billy .... 212-472-1500 309 I
bkwan@nysid.edu
KWANBUNBUMPEN,
Ada .... 204-286-5244 190 I
akwanbunbumpen@suno.edu
KWANDRANS, Karen ..... 716-614-6472 310 C
kkwandrans@niagaracc.suny.edu
KWANG CHUNG, Sae ... 714-222-1110.. 27 I
KWAPONG, Sam .... 619-849-2524.. 57 E
samkwapong@pointloma.edu
KWASIGROH, Catherine 731-661-5281 427 C
ckwasigroh@uu.edu
KWASIKPUI, Tremaine .. 713-221-8563 453 B
kwasikpuit@uhd.edu
KWASITSU, Lishi .... 503-517-1023 377 G
lkwasitsu@warnerpacific.edu
KWENDA, Maxwell .... 509-313-6948 481 D
kwenda@gonzaga.edu
KWESKIN, Amy, B .... 314-935-9842 262 A
amy.b.kweskin@wustl.edu
KWIATKOWSKI, Amy .... 415-955-2100.. 24 K
akwiatkowski@alliant.edu
KWIATKOWSKI,
Anthony .... 773-907-4784 134 C
akwiatkowski@ccc.edu
KWIATKOWSKI, Christa 304-367-4796 490 B
christa.kwiatkowski@fairmontstate.edu
KWIECIEN, Garth .... 415-452-7768.. 37 A
gkwiecien@ccsf.edu
KWILINSKI, Kathie .... 206-934-7965 484 B
kathie.kwilinski@seattlecolleges.edu
KWIST, Sabrina, T .... 925-473-7314.. 40 J
skwist@losmedanos.edu
KWOLEK, Katherine ...... 617-585-0200 206 F
katherine.kwolek@the-bac.edu
KWON, P .... 323-641-7009.. 63 J
KYLE, James, R .... 619-596-2766.. 24 F
jkyle@advancedtraining.edu
KYLE, Jean .... 507-433-0568 240 F
jean.kyle@riverland.edu
KYLE, Michael .... 507-786-3025 243 C
kylem@stolaf.edu
KYLE, Paul .... 913-469-8500 174 D
pkyle@jccc.edu
KYLE, Roberta .... 508-929-8811 213 E
rkyle@worcester.edu
KYNARD, Olivia, L .... 413-538-7000 214 D
okynard@hcc.edu
KYNOR, James .... 303-352-3221.. 79 E
james.kynor@ccd.edu
KYPRIOS, Linda, A .... 972-881-5726 433 M
lkyprios@collin.edu
KYPUROS, Javier .... 903-566-7267 456 A
jkypuros@uttyler.edu
KYRIAKIDES, Michelle .. 516-463-6060 302 B
michelle.kyriakides@hofstra.edu
KYRKANIDES,
Stephanos .... 859-323-1884 185 B
stephanos@uky.edu
KYTE, Richard, L .... 608-796-3704 498 N
rlkyte@viterbo.edu

L

LA BARBERA,
Christopher .... 781-239-3114 214 E
clabarbera@massbay.edu
LA BELLE, Brian .... 312-488-6062.. 36 F
blabelle@thechicagoschool.edu
LA BRANCHE, Mark, D . 931-363-9802 421 E
mlabranche@martinmethodist.edu
LA CHAPELLE,
Jacqueline .... 337-550-1282 189 A
jlachape@lsue.edu
LA HARA, Maura .... 212-752-1530 304 D
maura.walters@limcollege.edu
LA MAZZA, Bernadette . 480-732-7019.. 12 P
bernadette.la.mazza@cgc.edu
LA PIERRE, Mary .... 518-562-4125 296 B
mary.lapierre@clinton.edu
LA POINT, Kris .... 262-554-2010 494 D
krisbob1@cs.com
LA POINT, Kristine, L ... 773-975-1295 494 D
krisbob1@cs.com
LA ROCCA, Chris .... 252-492-2061 338 F
laroccac@vgcc.edu
LA SALA, Lisa .... 815-599-3724 138 B
lisa.lasala@highland.edu
LA TORRA, Grace .... 206-876-6100 484 E
glatorra@theseattleschool.edu
LA VENTURE, Kelly .... 218-755-4404 237 E
kelly.laventure@bemidjistate.edu
LA VIGNE, Steven .... 562-860-2451.. 35 M
slavigne@cerritos.edu
LA VOY, Sharon, A .... 301-405-5590 202 C
slavoy@umd.edu
LABACH, Elaine .... 406-657-2296 264 E
elaine.labach@msubillings.edu
LABAN, Danielle .... 312-261-3162 144 F
dlaban@nl.edu
LABARBERA, Mark .... 219-464-6894 162 A
mark.labarbera@valpo.edu
LABARBERA, Paul .... 845-758-7819 290 G
labarbera@bard.edu
LABAT, Nichole .... 985-545-1500 187 H
LABAT, Tony .... 415-351-3574.. 60 G
tlabat@sfai.edu
LABAUGH, Amy, R .... 208-496-1155 130 A
labaugha@byui.edu
LABAY, Theodore .... 251-405-7240.... 1 E
tlabay@bishop.edu
LABBERTON, Mark, A ... 626-584-5201.. 43 H
LABE, Geoffey .... 610-896-1806 385 L
glabe@haverford.edu
LABEFF, Toni .... 903-434-8105 441 B
tlabeff@ntcc.edu
LABELL, Yitzi .... 301-649-7077 204 G
ylabell@yeshiva.edu
LABELLE, Heather .... 312-553-5914 134 B
hlabelle@ccc.edu
LABENSKI, Paula .... 570-740-0388 389 D
plabenski@luzerne.edu
LABIG, John .... 865-524-8079 420 E
john.labig@huhs.edu
LABKOWSKI, Zalman .... 718-774-3430 292 H
LABOE, Mark .... 773-325-4004 135 I
mlaboe@depaul.edu
LABOE, Timothy .... 313-883-8556 229 K
laboe.timothy@shms.edu
LABONTE, Angela .... 603-342-3041 273 D
alabonte@ccsnh.edu
LABONTE, Gene, R .... 978-542-6542 213 C
glabonte@salemstate.edu
LABONTE, Jason .... 631-656-2113 300 D
jason.labonte@ftc.edu
LABONTE, Kim .... 618-650-2789 149 D
klabont@siue.edu
LABONTE, Melissa .... 718-817-4400 300 E
labonte@fordham.edu
LABONTE, Robert .... 978-630-9272 215 A
r_labonte@mwcc.mass.edu
LABOR, Jennifer .... 918-465-1828 366 D
jlabor@eosc.edu
LABORDE, Tais .... 787-704-1020 507 K
tlaborde@edicollege.edu
LABOUNTY, Jennifer ..... 714-992-7085.. 53 L
jlabounty@fullcoll.edu
LABOY, Gloryber .... 787-751-0160 507 F
glaboy@cmpr.pr.gov
LABOY FUSTER, Rafael . 787-720-4476 512 D
relacionespublicas@mizpa.edu
LABRADOR, Victoria ...... 510-666-8248.. 24 D
faofficer@aimc.edu
LABRANCHE, Matthew .. 413-782-1503 219 F
matthew.labranche@wne.edu
LABRANCHE, Michael ... 504-398-2241 191 C
mlabranche@uhcno.edu
LABRIE, Lori, A .... 713-313-7040 449 C
labrie_la@tsu.edu
LABRIOLA, Elisabeth, S 860-439-2064.. 86 H
elisabeth.labriola@conncoll.edu
LABRIOLA, Toni Ann .... 954-753-6869.. 98 C
LABRON, Wendy .... 617-735-9778 209 A
labronw@emmanuel.edu
LABROSSE, Tonya, B .... 603-535-2846 275 B
tblabrosse@plymouth.edu
LABRY, Daniel .... 877-476-8674 437 C
LABS, Jeff .... 715-365-4406 500 D
jlabs@nicoletcollege.edu
LACASCIO, Joe .... 508-286-3405 220 A
lacascio_joe@wheatoncollege.edu
LACEY, Kasi .... 573-592-5269 262 E
kasi.lacey@westminster-mo.edu
LACEY, Kristin .... 864-455-7981 414 A
klacey@ghs.org
LACEY, Mark .... 904-632-3319 100 B
mark.lacey@fscj.edu
LACEY, Pete .... 810-989-5561 230 C
placey@sc4.edu
LACEY, Roshae .... 601-877-6333 244 H
rlacey@alcorn.edu
LACEY, Sherry Leigh ..... 334-833-4562.... 5 H
internships@hawks.huntingdon.edu
LACH, Carolyn .... 773-244-5506 145 A
clach@northpark.edu

LAMANQUE, Andrew ..... 510-659-6220.. 54 F
alamanque@ohlone.edu
LAMAR, Melissa .... 860-773-1407.. 86 G
mlamar@tunxis.edu
LAMAR, Sharmaine .... 610-690-5675 399 D
slamar1@swarthmore.edu
LAMARAND, Donita, M 757-446-6009 466 I
lamaradm@evms.edu
LAMARCH, Jessica .... 906-217-4086 221 O
jessica.lamarch@baycollege.edu
LAMARCHE, Gilles .... 770-426-2674 121 C
gilles.lamarche@life.edu
LAMARCHE, Paul .... 609-258-4999 280 E
lamarche@princeton.edu
LAMAS, Frank .... 559-278-2541.. 31 D
flamas@csufresno.edu
LAMASCUS, Scott .... 405-425-5469 367 G
scott.lamascus@oc.edu
LAMB, Audrey .... 785-864-8040 177 D
lamb@ku.edu
LAMB, Barry, P .... 217-786-2334 142 B
barry.lamb@llcc.edu
LAMB, Bill .... 319-398-5509 167 C
blamb@kirkwood.edu
LAMB, Colin .... 620-276-9683 173 E
colin.lamb@gcccks.edu
LAMB, Craig .... 585-345-6969 301 A
crlamb@genesee.edu
LAMB, Craig .... 704-216-3500 337 F
craig.lamb@rccc.edu
LAMB, David .... 716-829-7652 298 F
kavinokytheater@dyc.edu
LAMB, David .... 215-368-5000 390 F
dlamb@missio.edu
LAMB, Duane .... 205-348-8092.... 7 G
dlamb@fa.ua.edu
LAMB, Earnest .... 218-477-2764 239 D
earnest.lamb@mnstate.edu
LAMB, Jason .... 540-261-8509 471 H
jason.lamb@svu.edu
LAMB, Jeffrey, N .... 714-564-6080.. 57 L
lamb_jeffrey@sac.edu
LAMB, Jennifer .... 276-326-4397 465 B
jlamb@bluefield.edu
LAMB, Jon .... 734-462-4400 230 D
jlamb@schoolcraft.edu
LAMB, Keith .... 940-397-4291 440 F
keith.lamb@msutexas.edu
LAMB, Ken .... 513-861-6400 361 L
ken.lamb@myunion.edu
LAMB, Kevin, D .... 859-238-5367 179 F
kevin.lamb@centre.edu
LAMB, Kyle .... 731-989-6020 420 C
klamb@fhu.edu
LAMB, Linda .... 315-866-0300 301 G
lamblc@herkimer.edu
LAMB, Margaret .... 619-388-6957.. 60 B
mlamb@sdccd.edu
LAMB, Mary .... 707-468-3071.. 51 E
mlamb@mendocino.edu
LAMB, Marybeth .... 508-531-1353 212 B
marybeth.lamb@bridgew.edu
LAMB, Melissa .... 912-427-5840 116 F
mlamb@coastalpines.edu
LAMB, Michael .... 316-978-3804 178 A
mike.lamb@wichita.edu
LAMB, Noah, B .... 239-513-1122 101 C
nlamb@hodges.edu
LAMB, Rosemary .... 662-246-6256 247 D
rlamb@msdelta.edu
LAMB, Susan .... 925-969-2001.. 40 I
slamb@dvc.edu
LAMBA, Sandy .... 707-864-7000.. 64 C
sandy.lamba@solano.edu
LAMBDIN, Brandon ...... 423-746-5337 426 F
bslambdin@tnwewsleyan.edu
LAMBE, Joan .... 212-772-5462 294 C
joan.lambe@hunter.cuny.edu
LAMBERSON, Jeffrey ..... 843-953-7962 407 F
jlamber6@citadel.edu
LAMBERSON, Shannon . 817-531-4444 451 E
slamberson@txwes.edu
LAMBERT, Ame .... 401-254-3079 405 E
aolambert@rwu.edu
LAMBERT, Angela .... 304-327-4480 489 P
alambert@bluefieldstate.edu
LAMBERT, Anne .... 713-525-2160 454 H
lambera@stthom.edu
LAMBERT, Barry .... 254-968-9104 446 E
blambert@tarleton.edu
LAMBERT, Bill .... 909-274-4215.. 52 H
wlambert@mtsac.edu
LAMBERT, Brooke .... 402-557-7087 265 J
blambert@bellevue.edu
LAMBERT, Chip .... 276-326-4603 465 B
clambert@bluefield.edu
LAMBERT, Chris .... 304-829-7281 487 G
clambert@bethanywv.edu
LAMBERT, Christopher .. 414-425-8300 495 H
clambert@shsst.edu
LAMBERT, David .... 740-377-2520 361 K
david.lambert@tsbc.edu
LAMBERT, Dewayne ...... 985-732-6640 187 H
LAMBERT, Elizabeth ...... 607-735-1806 299 D
llambert@elmira.edu
LAMBERT,
Huntington, D .... 617-495-2930 210 B
dean@extension.harvard.edu
LAMBERT, Ian .... 313-664-1474 222 F
ilambert@collegeforcreativestudies.edu
LAMBERT, James .... 540-261-8400 471 H
james.lambert@svu.edu
LAMBERT, James .... 419-372-9970 348 H
jlamber@bgsu.edu
LAMBERT, Jay .... 361-570-4290 453 C
lambertj1@uhv.edu
LAMBERT, Kathy .... 919-508-2028 344 F
kplambert@peace.edu
LAMBERT, Kim, D .... 315-792-3341 324 B
klambert@utica.edu
LAMBERT, III, Lake .... 812-866-7056 155 C
lambert@hanover.edu
LAMBERT, Lee, D .... 520-206-4747.. 15 D
llambert@pima.edu
LAMBERT, Lori, A .... 513-745-3203 365 B
lambert@xavier.edu
LAMBERT, Matthew, T .. 757-221-1001 466 C
mtlambert@wm.edu
LAMBERT, Patrick .... 845-398-4396 315 B
plambert@stac.edu
LAMBERT, Sarah .... 423-775-6596 423 F
slambert@ogs.edu
LAMBERT, Stacey .... 617-327-6777 220 B
stacey_lambert@williamjames.edu
LAMBERT, Tamatha .... 478-471-2700 121 F
LAMBERT, Toni .... 434-949-1017 475 H
toni.lambert@southside.edu
LAMBERTON, Jill .... 765-361-6154 162 E
lambertj@wabash.edu
LAMBERTON, Ryan .... 925-631-4015.. 59 B
rml4@stmarys-ca.edu
LAMBETH, Gregory .... 208-885-6716 131 G
lambeth@uidaho.edu
LAMBIE-SIMPSON,
Yasmin .... 415-749-4524.. 60 G
ylambie-simpson@sfai.edu
LAMBLEY, Jennifer .... 605-367-5990 417 D
jennifer.lambley@southeasttech.edu
LAMBORN, Kim .... 503-251-5798 377 F
klamborn@uws.edu
LAMBOY, Camille .... 787-743-7979 511 I
calamboy@suagm.edu
LAMBOY, Maritza .... 787-834-9595 511 E
mlamboy@uaa.edu
LAMBRAKIS, Christine .. 602-286-8227.. 13 B
christine.lambrakis@gwmail.maricopa.edu
LAMBRECHT, Anne, K ... 989-463-7225 220 H
lambrechtak@alma.edu
LAMBRECHT, Jessica .... 920-565-1043 493 J
lambrechtjn@lakeland.edu
LAMBRECHT, John .... 708-456-0300 150 I
johnlambrecht@triton.edu
LAMBRECHTSEN, Karen 916-577-2200.. 75 B
klambrechtsen@jessup.edu
LAMBRUNO, Joyce .... 270-707-3844 181 E
joyce.lambruno@kctcs.edu
LAMELZA, George .... 417-447-2664 257 G
lamelzag@otc.edu
LAMENDOLA, Nicholas . 585-389-2072 308 B
nlamend7@naz.edu
LAMERE, Thomas .... 914-674-7442 306 F
tlamere@mercy.edu
LAMERS, Chet .... 920-498-5723 500 F
chet.lamers@nwtc.edu
LAMICA, Lauren .... 413-545-3016 211 D
llamica@finaid.umass.edu
LAMICA, Thomas .... 805-922-6966.. 24 J
thomas.lamica@hancockcollege.edu
LAMIMAN, Lynne .... 972-708-7536 435 H
LAMIQUIZ, Jason .... 509-453-0374 483 C
jason.lamiquiz@perrytech.edu
LAMKIN, Fletcher .... 573-592-5315 262 E
president@westminster-mo.edu
LAMM, Edward .... 920-403-3007 495 I
edward.lamm@snc.edu
LAMM, Gary .... 254-295-4545 453 E
glamm@umhb.edu
LAMMATHA, Kranthi ..... 888-488-4968.. 46 F
klammatha@itu.edu
LAMMERS, Amanda ...... 770-534-6108 115 D
alammers@brenau.edu
LAMMERS, Jenna .... 618-545-3044 140 E
jlammers@kaskaskia.edu
LAMMERS, Kimberly ..... 419-289-5306 348 A
klammers@ashland.edu
LAMMONS, Anthony ...... 951-343-4309.. 27 J
alammons@calbaptist.edu
LAMONS, Jerisia .... 270-706-8841 181 A
jlamons0001@kctcs.edu
LAMONTAGNE, Ramona 815-836-5291 141 G
lamontra@lewisu.edu
LAMONTAGNE, Susan ... 413-572-5425 213 D
slamontagne@westfield.ma.edu
LAMOTT, Eric, E .... 651-641-8729 235 F
lamott@csp.edu
LAMOUREUX, Joshua ... 603-542-7744 273 C
jlamoureux@ccsnh.edu
LAMOUREUX, AA,
Richard, E .... 508-767-7033 205 D
re.lamoureux@assumption.edu
LAMOUREUX, Wayne .... 617-243-2291 210 G
wlamoureux@lasell.edu
LAMPE, Lawrence, P ..... 513-556-2201 362 D
lampelp@ucmail.uc.edu
LAMPE, Paul .... 636-584-6581 252 J
paul.lampe@eastcentral.edu
LAMPING, Patrick .... 859-442-4175 181 B
patrick.lamping@kctcs.edu
LAMPKIN, Patricia, M ... 434-924-7984 473 A
pml@virginia.edu
LAMPKIN-WILLIAMS,
Ann .... 313-593-5090 231 F
lampkin@umich.edu
LAMPKIN-WILLIAMS,
Ann .... 313-593-5321 231 F
lampkin@umich.edu
LAMPLEY, Dearl .... 615-790-4419 424 G
dlampley@columbiastate.edu
LAMPLEY, Katherine ...... 781-891-2243 206 D
klampley@bentley.edu
LAMPLEY, Paul, C .... 662-252-8000 248 G
plampley@rustcollege.edu
LAMPO, Jane .... 816-654-7109 254 C
jlampo@kcumb.edu
LAMPO, Jane .... 816-654-7282 254 C
jlampo@kcumb.edu
LAMPSON, Dawayne ..... 715-682-1399 495 C
dlampson@northland.edu
LAMSMA, Matt .... 509-313-4100 481 D
lamsma@gonzaga.edu
LAMURAGLIA, Rose ...... 619-388-3488.. 60 C
rlamurag@sdccd.edu
LAMY, Patrick, J .... 973-748-9000 276 A
patrick_lamy@bloomfield.edu
LAN, Stan .... 206-378-5094 484 D
lans@spu.edu
LANA, Peter .... 585-389-2344 308 B
plana0@naz.edu
LANAGAN, Keni .... 865-981-8308 421 F
keni.lanagan@maryvillecollege.edu
LANAGAN, Pete .... 702-651-5664 271 A
peter.lanagan@csn.edu
LANAHAN, Richard .... 570-208-6069 387 A
richardlanahan@kings.edu
LANCASTER, Adrianna ... 580-559-5368 366 C
alancaster@ecok.edu
LANCASTER, Amy, E ..... 864-597-4430 414 H
lancasterae@wofford.edu
LANCASTER, Brad .... 717-337-6377 384 H
blancast@gettysburg.edu
LANCASTER, David .... 304-424-8346 491 D
david.lancaster@wvup.edu
LANCASTER, Dennis ...... 417-255-7272 256 F
dennislancaster@missouristate.edu
LANCASTER, James .... 630-844-5144 132 D
jlancast@aurora.edu
LANCASTER, James .... 323-953-4000.. 48 I
lancasj@lacitycollege.edu
LANCASTER, Jennifer .... 718-489-5323 313 H
jlancaster@sfc.edu
LANCASTER, Karen .... 443-997-9909 199 D
klancaster@jhu.edu
LANCASTER, Kelly .... 406-604-4300 263 A
LANCASTER, Rich .... 484-365-7440 389 C
rlancaster@lincoln.edu
LANCASTER, Robin .... 501-882-4547.. 17 F
rglancaster@asub.edu
LANCE, Amanda .... 870-777-5722.. 22 A
amanda.lance@uaht.edu
LANCE, Ann, H .... 507-284-2915 234 J
lance.ann@mayo.edu
LAND, Christopher .... 508-289-2900 220 D
cland@whoi.edu
LAND, Elizabeth .... 504-280-6723 189 E
eland@uno.edu
LAND, Mark, D .... 864-656-4233 408 A
mdland@clemson.edu
LAND, Matt .... 260-665-4143 160 H
landm@trine.edu
LAND, Richard, D .... 704-847-5600 340 I
cwoodside@ses.edu
LAND, Roderic .... 801-957-4024 461 D
roderic.land@slcc.edu
LAND, Sabrina .... 773-821-4976 133 K
sland20@csu.edu
LANDA, Carrie .... 617-353-3569 207 D
clanda@bu.edu
LANDA, Keith .... 914-251-6435 319 E
keith.landa@purchase.edu
LANDAU, Joshua .... 717-815-6632 404 A
jlandau@ycp.edu
LANDEN, Jenny .... 505-428-1837 288 B
jenny.landen@sfcc.edu
LANDEN, Marcia .... 601-266-4119 249 F
marcia.landen@usm.edu
LANDEN, Robyn .... 307-268-2362 501 U
rlanden@caspercollege.edu
LANDENBERGER, Lacey 316-295-5407 173 D
lacey_landenberger@friends.edu
LANDENBERGER,
Rebecca .... 906-217-4266 221 O
becky.landenberger@baycollege.edu
LANDENBURGER,
Marguerite .... 540-665-4618 471 E
mlandenb@su.edu
LANDER, Janice .... 303-273-3266.. 78 I
jslander@mines.edu
LANDER, Laura .... 903-730-4890 438 H
llander@jarvis.edu
LANDER, Maria .... 704-290-5267 337 I
mlander@spcc.edu
LANDERS, Joanne .... 973-290-4720 277 A
jlanders@cse.edu
LANDERS, Mary, G .... 336-256-2014 343 A
mglander@uncg.edu
LANDERS, Michael .... 903-875-7488 440 G
michael.landers@navarrocollege.edu
LANDERS, Ty .... 615-244-5848 423 L
LANDGAARD, Jodi .... 507-372-3403 239 E
jodi.landgaard@mnwest.edu
LANDGRAF, Kurt, M ..... 410-778-7201 204 D
klandgraf2@washcoll.edu
LANDGRAF, Tanya .... 712-749-2212 163 D
landgraft@bvu.edu
LANDGREBE, Jessica .... 217-424-3965 143 H
jlandgrebe@millikin.edu
LANDGREN, Peter .... 513-556-6703 362 D
peter.landgren@uc.edu
LANDHERR, Ashlyn .... 517-607-2625 225 A
alandherr@hillsdale.edu
LANDING, Haydee .... 787-725-8120 507 N
hlandiing0030@eap.edu
LANDINI, Marlene .... 405-682-7879 367 H
marlene.t.landini@occc.edu
LANDIS, Amy .... 303-273-3871.. 78 I
amylandis@mines.edu
LANDIS, Bethany, L .... 517-750-1200 230 H
blandis@arbor.edu
LANDIS, David .... 620-278-4235 177 B
dlandis@sterling.edu
LANDIS, Jean, W .... 215-951-1020 387 C
landis@lasalle.edu
LANDIS, Jennifer .... 717-299-7754 399 G
LANDIS, Kristi .... 712-324-5061 168 G
klandis@nwicc.edu
LANDIS, SCC,
Marie Cecelia .... 973-957-0188 275 C
criss@acs350.org
LANDIS, Michelle .... 928-344-7526.. 10 J
michelle.landis@azwestern.edu
LANDIS, Sarah .... 540-828-5334 465 D
slandis@bridgewater.edu
LANDIS, Susan .... 540-665-4513 471 E
slandis@su.edu
LANDISS, Leslie .... 615-966-6194 421 D
leslie.landiss@lipscomb.edu
LANDOWSKI, Anthony .. 608-757-7726 499 C
alandowski@blackhawk.edu
LANDPHAIR, Juliette ..... 540-654-1656 472 I
jlandpha@umw.edu

LANDRAU-ESPINOSA, Barbara .... 787-993-8856 513 B barbara.landrau@upr.edu
LANDREMAN, Lisa .... 401-254-3032 405 E llandreman@rwu.edu
LANDRIEU, Madeleine .. 504-861-5550 189 F landrieu@loyno.edu
LANDRITH, James .... 864-231-2000 406 G wlandrith@andersonuniversity.edu
LANDRUM, Beverly, J ... 843-349-2399 408 C blandrum@coastal.edu
LANDRUM, Kay .... 817-598-6499 458 A klandrum@wc.edu
LANDRUM, Rodney, J .. 205-391-2211.... 3 E rlandrum@sheltonstate.edu
LANDRUM, Zalika .... 773-602-5116 134 D zlandrum@ccc.edu
LANDRY, Abbie .... 318-357-4403 192 C landry@nsula.edu
LANDRY, Brett .... 972-721-5276 452 D cobdean@udallas.edu
LANDRY, David, M .... 504-398-2109 191 C dlandry@uhcno.edu
LANDRY, Debborah .... 918-444-2060 367 A landryd@nsuok.edu
LANDRY, Fred .... 318-869-5136 186 B flandry@centenary.edu
LANDRY, Lisa, C .... 337-482-5430 192 E ldlandry@louisiana.edu
LANDRY, Patrick .... 337-482-6402 192 E pml@louisiana.edu
LANDRY, Sandra .... 704-878-3325 336 C slandry@mitchellcc.edu
LANDRY, Shawntel, D ... 800-280-0307 152 H shawntel.landry@ace.edu
LANDRY, Stephen .... 973-761-7386 283 B stephen.landry@shu.edu
LANDRY-THOMAS, Kerii .... 225-771-2552 191 A klandry-thomas@sulc.edu
LANDSAW, Christy .... 918-444-2192 367 A landsaw@nsuok.edu
LANDSTROM, Corey ...... 563-387-1020 167 E clandstrom@luther.edu
LANDWER, Allan, J .... 325-670-2222 437 F alandwer@hsutx.edu
LANDWERMEYER, Elizabeth .... 817-515-3049 445 G elizabeth.landwermeyer@tccd.edu
LANDY, Kathleen .... 718-281-5161 295 D klandy@qcc.cuny.edu
LANDY, Margo .... 209-946-3267.. 70 E mlandy@pacific.edu
LANE, Anne .... 717-337-6579 384 H alane@gettysburg.edu
LANE, Austin, A .... 713-313-1179 449 C austin.lane@tsu.edu
LANE, Barbara .... 573-329-5160 254 E laneb@lincolnu.edu
LANE, Bradley .... 206-934-5481 484 A bradley.lane@seattlecolleges.edu
LANE, Charles, E .... 352-392-9122 109 F charlielane@ufl.edu
LANE, Dean .... 202-462-2101.. 92 C dlane@iwp.edu
LANE, Deborah .... 405-744-6384 368 B debbie.lane@okstate.edu
LANE, Deborah .... 865-573-4517 420 G dlane@johnsonu.edu
LANE, Derek .... 859-257-9538 185 B derek.lane@uky.edu
LANE, Diane, L .... 217-362-6416 143 H dlane@millikin.edu
LANE, Edwin, H .... 816-415-7587 262 F lanee@william.jewell.edu
LANE, Gower .... 845-451-1309 298 A gower.lane@culinary.edu
LANE, Jason, E .... 518-442-5080 316 D jlane@albany.edu
LANE, Jennifer .... 808-675-4971 127 E jennifer.lane@byuh.edu
LANE, Jill, L .... 678-466-4100 116 E jilllane@clayton.edu
LANE, John .... 713-221-8292 453 B lanej@uhd.edu
LANE, Jolene, A .... 330-972-6237 362 B jolenealane@uakron.edu
LANE, Jolene, A .... 330-972-7522 362 B jolenealane@uakron.edu
LANE, Jon .... 940-397-4241 440 F jon.lane@msutexas.edu
LANE, Joseph .... 304-829-7311 487 G jlane@bethanywv.edu
LANE, Kelsi-Leandra ..... 315-445-4194 304 C lanekl@lemoyne.edu
LANE, Kimberly, A .... 864-833-8379 411 I kalane@presby.edu
LANE, Kristi .... 218-683-8631 240 A kristi.lane@northlandcollege.edu
LANE, Laura .... 248-476-1122 227 C llane@msp.edu
LANE, Marguerite .... 516-323-4014 307 F mlane@molloy.edu
LANE, Mark .... 808-455-0213 129 D marklane@hawaii.edu
LANE, Mary Ellen .... 508-856-4018 212 A maryellen.lane@umassmed.edu
LANE, Michael .... 516-686-7723 309 F mlane@nyit.edu
LANE, Natalie .... 307-382-1673 502 I nlane@westernwyoming.edu
LANE, Nathan .... 561-803-2754 104 C nathan_lane@pba.edu
LANE, Phillip .... 618-985-2828 139 I philliplane@jalc.edu
LANE, Robert, J .... 515-961-1417 169 D bob.lane@simpson.edu
LANE, Sadonia .... 620-947-3121 177 C sadonialane@tabor.edu
LANE, Scott .... 603-428-2411 273 H slane@nec.edu
LANE, Shannon .... 870-759-4143.. 23 J slane@williamsbu.edu
LANE, Stephanie .... 707-826-3132.. 33 D sml19@humboldt.edu
LANE, Thomas, A .... 785-532-6237 174 G talane@ksu.edu
LANE, Tracey, R .... 817-722-1621 439 B tracey.lane@tku.edu
LANE, Tracy .... 252-246-1202 339 C tlane@wilsoncc.edu
LANE RASMUS, Fran .... 253-535-7141 482 H lanerafr@plu.edu
LANEAR, John .... 866-776-0331.. 54 A provost@ncu.edu
LANEEL TANNER, Beth . 732-247-5241 279 D btanner@nbts.edu
LANESSKOG, Stig .... 909-621-8026.. 37 C stig.lanesskog@claremont.edu
LANEVE, Melissa .... 508-849-3280 205 C mlaneve@annamaria.edu
LANEY, Brenda .... 816-501-4122 258 H brenda.laney@rockhurst.edu
LANEY, Candy .... 406-874-6165 263 I laneyc@milescc.edu
LANEY, Jennifer .... 201-621-3422 196 A jennifer.laney@maine.edu
LANFEAR, Jeffery .... 773-325-8308 135 I jlanfear@depaul.edu
LANFORD, Coty .... 540-863-2861 474 D clanford@dslcc.edu
LANG, Bob .... 970-248-1754.. 77 I bllang@coloradomesa.edu
LANG, Christopher .... 304-865-6107 488 E christopher.lang@ovu.edu
LANG, Dirk .... 651-641-3476 236 F dlang001@luthersem.edu
LANG, Heather .... 971-722-4008 375 J heather.lang@pcc.edu
LANG, Jennifer, R .... 718-780-0679 291 J jennifer.lang@brooklaw.edu
LANG, John .... 605-995-2937 415 C john.lang@dwu.edu
LANG, Katherine .... 580-559-5424 366 C klang@ecok.edu
LANG, Lisa, K .... 502-597-5945 182 H lisa.lang@kysu.edu
LANG, Mandy .... 715-422-5446 500 A mandy.lang@mstc.edu
LANG, Marjorie .... 313-993-1802 231 B langma@udmercy.edu
LANG, Mark .... 608-262-2321 496 B mark.lange@uwex.edu
LANG, Michelle .... 503-517-1190 377 G mlang@warnerpacific.edu
LANG, Mindy .... 212-353-4212 297 E lang@cooper.edu
LANG, Natasha .... 925-424-1634.. 35 P nlang@laspositascollege.edu
LANG, Samuel .... 909-593-3511.. 70 D slang@laverne.edu
LANG, Stephen, W .... 432-837-8061 450 D slang@sulross.edu
LANGAN, Frances .... 570-945-8000 386 I fran.langan@keystone.edu
LANGAN, Nicole .... 570-945-8274 386 I nicole.langan@keystone.edu
LANGAN, Rikki .... 217-479-7030 142 I rikki.langan@mac.edu
LANGDON, Dawn .... 585-785-1277 300 B dawn.langdon@flcc.edu
LANGDON, Deb .... 740-389-4636 356 B langdond@mtc.edu
LANGDON, Heather, H .. 828-262-2093 341 B langdonhh@appstate.edu
LANGDON, Steven, D ... 573-334-6825 259 J slangdon@sehcollege.edu
LANGE, Barbara .... 352-365-3521 102 T langeb@lssc.edu
LANGE, Douglas .... 843-661-8300 409 I douglas.lange@fdtc.edu
LANGE, Janet .... 309-677-2523 133 B lange@bradley.edu
LANGE, Janet .... 309-677-2374 133 B lange@fsmail.bradley.edu
LANGE, Karen, M .... 651-962-6120 244 E kmlange@stthomas.edu
LANGE, Richard .... 915-215-4300 451 D richard.lange@ttuhsc.edu
LANGE, Robert, J .... 757-594-7015 466 B robert.lange@cnu.edu
LANGE, Shane .... 815-224-0219 139 F shane_lange@ivcc.edu
LANGE, Steven .... 320-629-5155 240 C steve.lange@pine.edu
LANGE, Tom, J .... 715-831-7285 499 D tlange8@cvtc.edu
LANGE, Tyana .... 660-785-4114 260 J tyana@truman.edu
LANGE, Tyana .... 570-484-2087 395 B tsl400@lockhaven.edu
LANGE, Tyler .... 206-616-5631 485 F langet2@uw.edu
LANGEMAK, Elizabeth ... 215-951-1145 387 C langemak@lasalle.edu
LANGEMEIER, Ryan ...... 507-379-3335 240 F ryan.langemeier@riverland.edu
LANGEN, Jill .... 989-729-3350 221 D jill.langen@baker.edu
LANGENBERG, Todd ..... 410-704-4679 204 A tlangenberg@towson.edu
LANGENEGGER, Joyce .. 979-830-4000 432 C joyce.langenegger@blinn.edu
LANGER, Dan .... 608-262-4766 496 C dan.langer@wisc.edu
LANGER, Jenna .... 323-860-0789.. 50 A
LANGER, Katherine .... 803-323-4746 414 G langerk@winthrop.edu
LANGER, Manfred .... 740-377-2520 361 K manfred.langer@tsbc.edu
LANGER, Patricia, M .... 651-696-6562 236 H planger@macalester.edu
LANGERBEIN, Helmut ... 870-235-4200.. 21 D hblangerbein@saumag.edu
LANGEVIN, Duetta .... 909-274-4230.. 52 H dlangevin@mtsac.edu
LANGEVIN, Patrice .... 909-607-2226.. 56 J patrice_langevin@pitzer.edu
LANGFORD, Allison .... 417-328-2093 259 L alangford@sbuniv.edu
LANGFORD, Chris .... 503-253-3443 374 H clangford@ocom.edu
LANGFORD, Curt .... 806-742-3641 451 B curt.langford@ttu.edu
LANGFORD, Debra .... 304-876-5216 490 E dlangfor@shepherd.edu
LANGFORD, Joel, C ...... 770-720-5585 123 E jcl@reinhardt.edu
LANGFORD, Pamela ...... 909-537-7454.. 33 A plangfor@csusb.edu
LANGFORD, Russ .... 417-862-9533 253 D rlangford@globaluniversity.edu
LANGHAM, Gay .... 601-643-8307 245 G gay.langham@colin.edu
LANGHAM, Julie .... 706-595-0166 114 J jlangham@augustatech.edu
LANGHAM, Lynda .... 936-468-2503 445 F llangham@sfasu.edu
LANGHAM, Pamela .... 850-474-3420 110 E plangham@uwf.edu
LANGHAMMER, Paul .... 401-874-5526 406 B langhammer@uri.edu
LANGHART, Alex .... 662-915-1101 249 D langhart@olemiss.edu
LANGHART, Maura .... 662-915-2760 249 D mmwakefi@olemiss.edu
LANGLAND, Meg .... 573-592-5381 262 E meg.langland@westminster-mo.edu
LANGLEN, Terrell .... 541-917-4999 374 A langlet@linnbenton.edu
LANGLEY, Anne .... 860-486-4035.. 88 E anne.langley@uconn.edu
LANGLEY, Dorothy .... 903-730-4890 438 H dlangley@jarvise.edu
LANGLEY, Goldie .... 614-947-6509 353 C goldie.langley@franklin.edu
LANGLEY, Jesse .... 252-985-5177 339 D jlangley@ncwc.edu
LANGLEY, Maia .... 502-418-5638 181 F maia.langley@kctcs.edu
LANGLEY, Seth .... 718-270-7763 317 E seth.langley@downstate.edu
LANGLEY-TURNBAUGH, Samantha .... 859-572-7528 184 A langleys1@nku.edu
LANGLOIS, OP, John .... 202-495-3831.. 92 E president@dhs.edu
LANGLOIS, Jon .... 406-377-9465 263 E jlanglois@dawson.edu
LANGLOIS, Mary Ann ... 716-888-2103 292 D langloim@canisius.edu
LANGOLF, Judi .... 810-762-9585 225 H jlangolf@kettering.edu
LANGONI, Kerri .... 505-566-3515 288 A langonik@sanjuancollege.edu
LANGREHR, Andrew ...... 314-539-5364 259 C andrewlangrehr@stlcc.edu
LANGRIDGE, Nick .... 540-568-3197 468 F langrinl@jmu.edu
LANGROCK, Adela .... 802-443-3440 462 H alangroc@middlebury.edu
LANGSETH, Kay .... 319-895-4242 164 B klangseth@cornellcollege.edu
LANGSTON, Carol .... 409-944-1302 437 B clangston@gc.edu
LANGSTON, Emily .... 410-972-3303 201 D emily.langston@sjc.edu
LANGSTON, Ginna, V ... 918-631-2641 371 E ruth-langston@utulsa.edu
LANGSTON, James .... 209-476-7840.. 66 G jlangston@clc.edu
LANGSTON, Louanne .... 601-857-3749 246 B louanne.langston@hindscc.edu
LANGSTON, Randall ...... 940-898-3010 451 F rlangston1@twu.edu
LANGSTRAAT, Jim .... 503-352-1621 375 G jim.langstraat@pacificu.edu
LANGSTRAAT, Nate .... 360-383-3350 486 G nlangstraat@whatcom.edu
LANGUTH, Christine ..... 860-215-9260.. 86 F clanguth@trcc.commnet.edu
LANGVARDT, Guy .... 310-756-0001.. 72 A
LANGWELL, Teri .... 806-457-4200 436 G tlangwell@fpctx.edu
LANHAM, Chuck .... 360-650-3917 486 F chuck.lanham@wwu.edu
LANHAM, Heather .... 937-778-7803 352 J hlanham@edisonohio.edu
LANHAM, Jeff .... 740-245-7485 363 D jlanham@rio.edu
LANHAM, Terri .... 270-686-4548 182 B terri.lanham@kctcs.edu
LANHAM, Tracey, M ..... 239-513-1122 101 C tlanham@hodges.edu
LANIER, Anna .... 316-978-3001 178 A anna.weyers@wichita.edu
LANIER, Annette .... 503-768-7685 373 G annette@lclark.edu
LANIER, John .... 706-385-1065 123 C john.lanier@point.edu
LANIER, Lisa .... 912-871-1606 122 I llanier@ogeecheetech.edu
LANIER, Mandy .... 334-556-2235.... 2 C mlanier@wallace.edu
LANIER, Mark .... 910-962-3030 343 C lanierm@uncw.edu
LANIER, Percy .... 205-929-1663.... 6 B finaid@miles.edu
LANIER, Stephen, M ..... 313-577-5600 232 I stephen.lanier@wayne.edu
LANIER, Walter .... 414-297-7710 500 B lanierw@matc.edu
LANK, Kristy .... 207-985-7976 194 C kristy@landingschool.edu
LANKES, Susan .... 716-652-8900 292 I slankes@buffalodiocese.org
LANKFORD, Lisa .... 828-398-7540 332 B lisahlankford@abtech.edu
LANN, Jennifer .... 802-387-6764 462 D jlann@landmark.edu

LANNEN, Dan .... 610-282-1100 382 E daniel.lannen@desales.edu
LANNERT, Mary .... 406-447-6944 264 C mary.lannert@helenacollege.edu
LANNING, Brek .... 828-565-4027 335 C bwlanning@haywood.edu
LANNING, Crystal .... 715-425-3246 497 E crystal.lanning@uwrf.edu
LANOUE, David .... 870-235-4004.. 21 D davidlanoue@saumag.edu
LANOUE, Kevin .... 540-568-4777 468 F lanoueka@jmu.edu
LANPHER, Jim .... 803-754-4100 409 A
LANSING, Corey .... 231-439-6349 228 E clansing@ncmich.edu
LANSING, Sean, T .... 414-410-4583 492 D stlansing@stritch.edu
LANSING, Travis .... 801-957-4009 461 D travis.lansing@slcc.edu
LANSIQUOT, Beverley, A .... 340-692-4117 514 E beverley.lansiquot@uvi.edu
LANTER, Jennifer .... 920-735-2520 499 E lanter@fvtc.edu
LANTER, Rebecca .... 859-572-5493 184 A lanterr1@nku.edu
LANTHIER, Eric .... 617-243-2433 210 G elanthier@lasell.edu
LANTHIER-BANDY, Julie .... 760-744-1150.. 55 I jlanthierbandy@palomar.edu
LANTIS, Glenda .... 541-318-3753 372 B glantis@cocc.edu
LANTZ, David .... 301-387-3011 198 F david.lantz@garrettcollege.edu
LANTZ, Dona .... 614-222-6171 351 D dlantz@ccad.edu
LANTZ, Mary Jan .... 409-944-1281 437 B mlantz@gc.edu
LANTZ, Susan .... 570-372-4415 399 C lantzs@susqu.edu
LANTZKY-EATON, Kristina .... 716-926-8854 301 H klantzky@hilbert.edu
LANUEZ, Jeffrey .... 520-206-4637.. 15 D jlanuez@pima.edu
LANYON, Scott .... 612-625-2809 243 E slanyon@umn.edu
LANZA, Donald .... 865-354-3000 425 G lanzad@roanestate.edu
LANZA, Michael .... 718-951-5000 293 C mlanza@brooklyn.cuny.edu
LANZEROTTI, Robert .... 309-794-7374 132 C robertlanzerotti@augustana.edu
LANZI, Lesley .... 518-736-3622 300 F lesley.lanzi@fmcc.suny.edu
LANZO, Caryn .... 216-802-3143 351 B c.lanzo@csuohio.edu
LAOUTARIS, Kathy .... 914-337-9300 297 D kathy.laoutaris@concordia-ny.edu
LAOYZA, Matt .... 507-389-5308 239 C matthew.laoyza@mnsu.edu
LAP, James .... 718-260-5565 295 B jlap@citytech.cuny.edu
LAPALOMBARA, Catherine .... 301-546-0414 201 C lapalocx@pgcc.edu
LAPANNE, Susan .... 603-358-2014 275 A susan.lapanne@keene.edu
LAPAYOVER, Alan .... 215-576-0800 397 C alapayover@rrc.edu
LAPERLE, Kimberly .... 508-856-8992 212 A kimberlymuri.laperle@umassmed.edu
LAPETINO, Kelly .... 708-709-3795 146 D klapetino@prairiestate.edu
LAPHAM, Steve .... 301-891-4161 204 C slapham@wau.edu
LAPIANA, William, P .... 212-431-2840 309 G william.lapiana@nyls.edu
LAPIDUS, Chaim, D .... 443-548-6063 201 A cdl@nirc.edu
LAPIDUS, Richard, S .... 978-665-3101 212 C rlapidus@fitchburgstate.edu
LAPIER, Terrance .... 407-265-8383.. 96 A
LAPIER, Terrence .... 561-381-4990.. 95 I
LAPIERRE DREGER, Miah .... 860-906-5010.. 85 D mlapierre-dreger@capitalcc.edu
LAPIKAS, Ken .... 814-724-0700 388 F klapikas@laurel.edu
LAPIKAS, Sonya, L .... 724-589-2172 399 H slapikas@thiel.edu
LAPINSKI, Scott .... 903-566-7181 456 A slapinski@uttyler.edu
LAPLANT, James, T .... 229-333-5800 126 G jtlaplant@valdosta.edu
LAPLANTE, Brian .... 518-445-2381 289 E blapl@albanylaw.edu
LAPLANTE, Jane .... 701-858-3855 345 F jane.laplante@minotstateu.edu
LAPLANTE, Kim .... 920-498-5487 500 F kim.laplante@nwtc.edu
LAPLANTE, Melissa .... 603-342-3086 273 D mlaplante@ccsnh.edu
LAPLANTE, Mike .... 970-943-7038.. 84 D mlaplante@western.edu
LAPOINTE, Laurence .... 860-465-5113.. 84 J lapointel@easternct.edu
LAPOINTE, Matthew .... 202-884-9135.. 93 B lapointem@trinitydc.edu
LAPOINTE, Michael .... 219-980-7106 156 E mslapoin@iun.edu
LAPOINTE, Robert .... 312-567-7135 139 B lapointe@iit.edu
LAPORTE, Christopher .. 860-773-1362.. 86 G claporte@tunxis.edu
LAPORTE, Laura .... 518-736-3622 300 F llaporte@fmcc.suny.edu
LAPORTE, Sandra .... 312-567-5199 139 B laporte@iit.edu
LAPOS, Christopher .... 570-389-4740 394 A clapos@bloomu.edu
LAPP, Beverly, K .... 574-296-6267 152 I bklapp@ambs.edu
LAPP, Ian .... 781-239-5700 205 E ilapp@babson.edu
LAPP, Katherine, N .... 617-495-1524 210 B katie_lapp@harvard.edu
LAPPIN, Julie, M .... 909-537-5002.. 33 A jlappin@csusb.edu
LAPPLE, James, H .... 212-327-8371 313 B james.lapple@rockefeller.edu
LAPRADE, Kimberly .... 602-639-7500.. 12 J
LAPRAY, Kim .... 208-732-6299 130 E klapray@csi.edu
LAPREY, Amy .... 508-286-3522 220 A laprey_amy@wheatoncollege.edu
LAPREZIOSA, Mark .... 215-572-2900 379 A laprezim@arcadia.edu
LAPRISE, John .... 423-585-6829 426 C john.laprise@ws.edu
LAPSLEY, Jacqueline, E 609-497-3622 280 D academic.dean@ptsem.edu
LAQUEY, Karen .... 325-649-8014 438 D klaquey@hputx.edu
LARA, Jessika .... 214-379-5494 441 I jlara@pqc.edu
LARA, Larry .... 714-992-7025.. 53 L llara@fullcoll.edu
LARA, María de Lourdes .... 787-850-9204 513 E maria.lara1@upr.edu
LARA, Rosa .... 717-720-4010 393 K rlara@passhe.edu
LARANGE, Shannon .... 413-775-1410 214 C larange@gcc.mass.edu
LARCOM, Geoffrey .... 734-487-4401 223 H glarcom@emich.edu
LARDIZABAL, Alana .... 541-552-8110 376 E lardizaba@sou.edu
LARDNER, Emily .... 206-878-3711 481 H elardner@highline.edu
LARDNER, Patrick .... 803-777-2036 413 C lardnerp@mailbox.sc.edu
LAREAU, Martin .... 708-596-2000 149 B mlareau@ssc.edu
LAREY, Franklin .... 309-556-3061 139 G flarey@iwu.edu
LAREY, Keith, L .... 903-813-2431 430 N klarey@austincollege.edu
LAREZ, Joseph .... 509-961-4674 481 G larez_j@heritag.edu
LARGE, Ron .... 509-313-6767 481 D large@gonzaga.edu
LARGEN, Kristin .... 717-337-6280 384 H klargen@gettysburg.edu
LARGENT, Trudy .... 510-466-7252.. 56 H tlargent@peralta.edu
LARICK, Duane, K .... 919-515-2196 342 B duane_larick@ncsu.edu
LARIMORE, Jennifer .... 715-425-4603 497 E jennifer.larimore@uwrf.edu
LARIOS, Jose .... 828-669-8012 331 J jose.larios@montreat.edu
LARIOS, Liza .... 718-631-6356 295 D llarios@qcc.cuny.edu
LARIVE, Cynthia .... 831-459-2058.. 70 B chancellor@ucsc.edu
LARIVEE, Lisa .... 802-322-1644 462 C lisa.larivee@goddard.edu
LARK, Catherine .... 603-646-2442 273 E catherine.lark@dartmouth.edu
LARKAN, Kara .... 210-999-7479 452 A klarkans@trinity.edu
LARKIN, Anne .... 508-856-4250 212 A anne.larkin@umassmed.edu
LARKIN, Conal .... 203-575-8173.. 86 B clarkin@nv.edu
LARKIN, SSJ, Mary Josephine .... 215-248-7055 381 D mjlarkin@chc.edu
LARKIN, Michael .... 210-283-5096 453 D mlarkin@uiwtx.edu
LARKIN, Patti .... 619-482-6325.. 65 F plarkin@swccd.edu
LARKIN, Susan .... 757-233-8809 477 F slarkin@vwu.edu
LARKIN-BEENE, Bridgett .... 815-280-2476 140 B blarkin@jjc.edu
LARKINS, Mike .... 870-574-4516.. 21 E mlarkins@sautech.edu
LARKINS, Tammy .... 870-574-4564.. 21 E tlarkins@sautech.edu
LARMON, Natalie .... 661-255-1050.. 28 K
LARNER, Eve .... 914-606-6562 325 C eve.larner@sunywcc.edu
LAROBINA, Michael, D . 203-371-7859.. 88 B larobinam@sacredheart.edu
LAROCCA, Sandy .... 402-898-1000 266 H sandy_l@creativecenter.edu
LAROCCO, Susan .... 845-569-3429 307 J susan.larocco@msmc.edu
LAROCHELLE, Josee .... 518-564-2130 319 C jlaro007@plattsburgh.edu
LAROCQUE, Alyssa .... 580-349-1356 368 A alyssa.fox@opsu.edu
LAROCQUE, Edward, A . 260-399-7700 161 D elarocque@sf.edu
LAROCQUE, Monique, M .... 207-581-3143 195 J mlarocque@maine.edu
LAROCQUE, Sandra .... 701-477-7862 347 A salrocqu@tm.edu
LAROI, Heather .... 608-265-3195 496 B hlaroi@uwsa.edu
LAROSEE, Howie .... 617-879-7938 212 E hlarosee@massart.edu
LARRABEE, Ashley .... 361-825-3020 447 C ashley.larrabee@tamucc.edu
LARRAT, Paul .... 401-874-5003 406 B larrat@uri.edu
LARRIVEE, Linda .... 508-929-8333 213 E llarrivee@worcester.edu
LARRY, Latasha .... 773-291-6210 134 E llarry4@ccc.edu
LARSEN, Carl .... 423-636-7313 427 B clarsen@tusculum.edu
LARSEN, Curt .... 801-957-4186 461 D curt.larsen@slcc.edu
LARSEN, Cynde .... 608-822-2642 500 G clarsen@swtc.edu
LARSEN, Daniel .... 630-466-7900 152 C dlarsen@waubonsee.edu
LARSEN, David .... 253-833-9111 481 F dlarsen@greenriver.edu
LARSEN, Erik .... 909-748-8035.. 71 G erik_larsen@redlands.edu
LARSEN, Geri .... 610-647-4400 386 C hr@immaculata.edu
LARSEN, Jennifer .... 402-559-4837 270 A jlarsen@unmc.edu
LARSEN, Jon-Erik .... 503-352-7221 375 G larsenj@pacificu.edu
LARSEN, Kerstin .... 609-258-9289 280 E klarsen@princeton.edu
LARSEN, Kevin, W .... 252-334-2044 331 D kevin.larsen@macuniversity.edu
LARSEN, Kevin, W .... 252-334-2009 331 D kevin.larsen@macuniversity.edu
LARSEN, Kody .... 801-281-1069 459 E kody.larsen@collegeamerica.edu
LARSEN, Marci .... 435-283-7013 461 C marci.larsen@snow.edu
LARSEN, Matt .... 701-231-5614 345 G matt.larsen@ndsu.edu
LARSEN, Ron .... 406-994-4371 264 D ronl@montana.edu
LARSEN, Sarah .... 713-743-7948 452 F sclarsen@central.uh.edu
LARSEN, Susan .... 575-562-2211 285 M susan.larsen@enmu.edu
LARSEN, Whitney, M .... 540-261-8530 471 H whitney.larsen@svu.edu
LARSON, Barb .... 308-398-7359 266 A blarson@cccneb.edu
LARSON, Barbara .... 913-469-8500 174 D
LARSON, Cate .... 651-631-0204 233 I clarson@aaaom.edu
LARSON, Chelsea .... 701-777-4409 345 C chelsea.larson@und.edu
LARSON, Craig .... 763-424-0733 239 G clarson@nhcc.edu
LARSON, Dale, C .... 214-887-5021 436 B dlarson@dts.edu
LARSON, Dan .... 541-737-8748 375 D deanofstudents@oregonstate.edu
LARSON, Dan .... 541-737-3626 375 D dan.larson@oregonstate.edu
LARSON, Dan .... 541-737-4771 375 D dan.larson@oregonstate.edu
LARSON, David .... 864-231-2000 406 G dlarson@andersonuniversity.edu
LARSON, Debra .... 618-537-6816 143 B dlarson@mckendree.edu
LARSON, Debra, S .... 530-898-6101.. 31 A dslarson@csuchico.edu
LARSON, Doreen .... 937-778-7801 352 J dlarson@edisonohio.edu
LARSON, Elena .... 916-278-6845.. 32 E larsone@csus.edu
LARSON, Gary, N .... 630-752-5990 152 F gary.larson@wheaton.edu
LARSON, Gayle .... 651-423-8307 237 H gayle.larson@dctc.edu
LARSON, Heidi .... 701-252-3467 347 C hlarson@uj.edu
LARSON, Jamie .... 409-880-7126 449 H jamie.larson@lamar.edu
LARSON, Jan .... 605-995-2614 415 C jan.larson@dwu.edu
LARSON, Jennifer .... 701-845-7401 346 A jennifer.larson@vcsu.edu
LARSON, Jens .... 509-359-6584 480 E jlarson@ewu.edu
LARSON, Jon, H .... 732-255-0330 280 A jlarson@ocean.edu
LARSON, Julianna .... 574-936-8898 153 A julianna.larson@ancilla.edu
LARSON, Kelly .... 815-740-3610 151 J klarson@stfrancis.edu
LARSON, Ken .... 630-752-5085 152 F kenneth.larson@wheaton.edu
LARSON, Kristin .... 906-635-2453 226 E klarsen1@lssu.edu
LARSON, Lawrence, E ... 401-863-1422 404 E lawrence_larson@brown.edu
LARSON, Lesley .... 570-321-4456 389 E larsonl@lycoming.edu
LARSON, Lisa .... 207-974-4691 194 H llarson@emcc.edu
LARSON, Lois .... 651-793-1411 238 H lois.larson@metrostate.edu
LARSON, Matthew .... 860-486-2616.. 88 E matthew.larson@uconn.edu
LARSON, Paul, V .... 805-565-6286.. 74 K plarson@westmont.edu
LARSON, Rebecca .... 630-752-5566 152 F rebecca.a.larson@wheaton.edu
LARSON, Rick .... 952-446-4190 235 G larsonr@crown.edu
LARSON, Robert .... 503-255-0332 374 D rlarson@multnomah.edu
LARSON, Ruth .... 315-470-4716 320 A rlarson@esf.edu
LARSON, Samantha .... 712-325-3341 167 B slarson@iwcc.edu
LARSON, Sandra .... 847-578-3400 147 I sandra.larson@rosalindfranklin.edu
LARSON, Sandy .... 229-931-2450 124 D slarson@southgatech.edu
LARSON, Shane .... 970-945-8691.. 77 K
LARSON, Shane .... 620-441-5246 172 I shane.larson@cowley.edu
LARSON, Steve .... 406-756-3821 263 F slarson@fvcc.edu
LARSON, Susan, J .... 218-299-3001 235 E larson@cord.edu
LARSON, Thomas .... 309-694-5225 138 C thomas.larson@icc.edu
LARSON, Thomas, R .... 423-652-4765 420 H trlarson@king.edu

LAVES, Beth .... 270-745-5308 185 E
beth.laves@wku.edu
LAVIAL, Pierre .... 772-466-4822.. 94 P
pierre.lavial@aviator.edu
LAVIGNE, Brent .... 405-491-6311 370 A
blavigne@snu.edu
LAVIGNE, Robert, W ..... 508-213-2217 217 E
robert.lavigne@nichols.edu
LAVIN, Gabrielle .... 215-965-4027 390 J
glavin@moore.edu
LAVIN, Lindsie .... 413-565-1000 205 G
llavin@baypath.edu
LAVIN, Terri .... 419-267-1364 358 A
tlavin@northweststate.edu
LAVINDER,
Katherine, W .... 610-758-4159 388 J
kwl211@lehigh.edu
LAVINE, Danielle .... 860-509-9511.. 87 B
dlavine@hartsem.edu
LAVOIE, Chuck .... 802-468-1250 464 A
chuck.lavoie@castleton.edu
LAVOIE, Lisa .... 860-773-1543.. 86 G
llavoie@tunxis.edu
LAW, Amir .... 925-424-1275.. 35 P
alaw@laspositascollege.edu
LAW, Courtney .... 509-313-5658 481 D
lawc@gonzaga.edu
LAW, Donna .... 435-865-8182 460 F
law@suu.edu
LAW, John .... 413-236-3001 213 F
jlaw@berkshirecc.edu
LAW, Mike .... 503-253-3443 374 H
mlaw@ocom.edu
LAW, Nancy .... 903-983-8101 439 A
nlaw@kilgore.edu
LAW, Scott .... 515-271-3860 165 A
scott.law@drake.edu
LAW, Shirley .... 646-313-8000 295 E
shirley.law@guttman.cuny.edu
LAW, Theresa .... 505-454-3198 286 H
tlaw@nmhu.edu
LAW, William .... 630-829-6532 132 E
wlaw@ben.edu
LAWDERMILT, Sherry .... 701-777-6373 345 C
sherry.lawdermilt@und.edu
LAWERANCE, Adrea ...... 406-243-4911 264 A
adrea.lawerance@umontana.edu
LAWERENCE, Gail .... 325-235-7333 449 E
gail.lawerence@tstc.edu
LAWHORN, Janice .... 928-428-8509.. 12 E
janice.lawhorn@eac.edu
LAWHORN, Paul .... 423-775-6596 423 F
registrar@ogs.edu
LAWHORN, Paul .... 423-775-6596 423 F
vp-admin@ogs.edu
LAWHORNE, Angela ...... 757-569-6064 475 E
alawhorne@pdc.edu
LAWHORNE, Jeffrey, L .. 540-464-7215 476 G
lawhornejl@vmi.edu
LAWKIS, Nicholas .... 251-460-7277.... 8 F
nlawkis@southalabama.edu
LAWLER, Ann .... 563-441-4201 165 E
alawler@eicc.edu
LAWLER, Hannah .... 310-434-3472.. 62 E
lawler_hannah@smc.edu
LAWLER, Michael, J ..... 509-452-5100 483 A
president@pnwu.edu
LAWLER, Shirley, A ...... 417-255-7900 256 E
slawler@missouristate.edu
LAWLER-SAGARIN,
Kimberly .... 630-617-3202 136 G
ksagarin@elmhurst.edu
LAWLESS, Daniel, M ..... 843-349-2021 408 C
dan@coastal.edu
LAWLESS, J. Alan .... 918-343-7715 369 F
alawless@rsu.edu
LAWLESS, Jacob .... 248-218-2080 229 J
jlawless@rc.edu
LAWLESS, John .... 315-460-3161 321 A
john.lawless@esc.edu
LAWLESS, Kimberly .... 814-865-2526 392 B
klr5825@psu.edu
LAWLESS, Richard .... 516-572-7222 308 A
richard.lawless@ncc.edu
LAWLOR, Andrew .... 410-857-2762 200 B
alawlor@mcdaniel.edu
LAWLOR, John .... 518-276-6266 312 I
lawlej4@rpi.edu
LAWLOR, Kevin, P .... 203-254-4000.. 86 I
klawlor@fairfield.edu
LAWLOR, Sarah .... 406-447-4515 263 C
slawlor@carroll.edu
LAWLOR, William .... 402-559-5838 270 A
wlawlor@unmc.edu

LAWRENCE, Alicia .... 212-854-5561 290 J
alawrenc@barnard.edu
LAWRENCE, Alvin .... 352-392-1575 109 F
alaw@ufl.edu
LAWRENCE, Barbara ...... 336-316-2196 329 E
blawrenc@guilford.edu
LAWRENCE, Charles ...... 206-296-6384 484 F
lawrence@seattleu.edu
LAWRENCE, Craig, D .... 205-929-3427.... 2 H
clawrence@lawsonstate.edu
LAWRENCE, Dan .... 303-360-4740.. 79 D
dan.lawrence@ccaurora.edu
LAWRENCE, David .... 616-233-2595 223 B
david.lawrence@davenport.edu
LAWRENCE, David, A .... 740-245-7032 363 D
lawrence@rio.edu
LAWRENCE, Deborah .... 518-244-2466 313 D
lawred@sage.edu
LAWRENCE, Deborah .... 518-292-1704 313 D
lawresd@sage.edu
LAWRENCE, Deborah .... 317-955-6208 158 U
dlawrence@marian.edu
LAWRENCE, Derrick .... 605-698-3966 416 F
dlawrence@swc.tc
LAWRENCE, DeShawn ... 701-766-1342 345 A
deshawn.lawrence@littlehoop.edu
LAWRENCE, Diana .... 502-456-6506 184 E
dlawrence@sullivan.edu
LAWRENCE, Gary .... 805-893-3781.. 70 A
gary@ucen.ucsb.edu
LAWRENCE, Jason .... 860-231-5700.. 89 B
jmlawrence@usj.edu
LAWRENCE, Jason .... 870-368-2058.. 20 F
jason.lawrence@ozarka.edu
LAWRENCE, Jennifer ..... 318-678-6000 187 A
jelawrence@bpcc.edu
LAWRENCE, John, D ..... 515-294-5390 162 I
jdlaw@iastate.edu
LAWRENCE, Kalista .... 812-535-5102 160 B
kalista.lawrence@smwc.edu
LAWRENCE, Kevin .... 757-388-2862 471 D
klawrence@sentara.edu
LAWRENCE, Lara .... 660-263-3900 251 A
laralawrence@cccb.edu
LAWRENCE, Larry, D ..... 501-450-3196.. 23 H
larryl@pplant.uca.edu
LAWRENCE, Laura .... 870-368-2010.. 20 F
llawrence@ozarka.edu
LAWRENCE, Lesa .... 218-755-4142 237 E
lesa.lawrence@bemidjistate.edu
LAWRENCE, Leslie .... 518-276-6287 312 I
lawrel@rpi.edu
LAWRENCE, Mark .... 757-352-4295 470 H
marklaw@regent.edu
LAWRENCE, Melody, L . 828-339-4224 338 B
mlawrence@southwesterncc.edu
LAWRENCE, Paul .... 212-241-7892 302 F
paul.lawrence@mssm.edu
LAWRENCE, Paul .... 412-624-6620 401 B
plawrence@bc.pitt.edu
LAWRENCE, Randall, K . 817-554-5950 440 C
rlawrence@messengercollege.edu
LAWRENCE, Robin, P .... 864-388-8234 410 D
rlawrence@lander.edu
LAWRENCE, Ross .... 406-874-6172 263 I
lawrencer@milescc.edu
LAWRENCE, Sharee .... 478-825-6282 118 A
lawrencs@fvsu.edu
LAWRENCE, Stephanie .. 229-317-6936 113 H
stephanie.lawrence@asurams.edu
LAWRENCE,
Stewart "Scott" .... 615-547-1281 419 F
slawrence@cumberland.edu
LAWRENCE, Tena .... 701-252-3467 347 C
tlawrenc@uj.edu
LAWRENCE, Tom .... 864-646-1429 413 A
tlawrenc@tctc.edu
LAWRENCE, Tonya .... 662-605-3413 246 C
tlawrence@holmescc.edu
LAWRENCE, Torrey .... 208-885-7941 131 G
tlawrence@uidaho.edu
LAWRENCE KEANE,
Loretta .... 212-217-4700 299 H
loretta_keane@fitnyc.edu
LAWRENCE-PHILLIPS,
Teresa .... 615-963-1545 426 D
tphillips@tnstate.edu
LAWRENCE-RAMAEKER,
Janice .... 715-232-2114 498 A
ramaekerj@uwstout.edu
LAWRENSON, Lisa .... 916-484-8411.. 50 F
lawrenl@arc.losrios.edu
LAWRIE, Joshua .... 419-372-2011 348 H
jlawrie@bgsu.edu

LAWS, David .... 423-869-6418 421 C
david.laws@lmunet.edu
LAWS, Frank .... 601-968-8978 245 C
flaws@belhaven.edu
LAWS, Michaele, D .... 423-439-8245 419 J
lawsm@etsu.edu
LAWS, Mishelle .... 562-985-8356.. 31 F
mishelle.laws@csulb.edu
LAWS, Page .... 757-823-8208 469 F
prlaws@nsu.edu
LAWS, Paige .... 870-633-4480.. 19 B
plaws@eacc.edu
LAWSON, Abby .... 803-934-3298 411 C
alawson@morris.edu
LAWSON, Andrea .... 608-265-5600 496 C
ajlawson@uhs.wisc.edu
LAWSON, Angela .... 615-230-3576 426 B
angela.lawson@volstate.edu
LAWSON, Carey .... 337-457-6135 189 A
clawson@lsue.edu
LAWSON, Cassandra .... 415-452-7689.. 37 A
clawson@ccsf.edu
LAWSON, Dan .... 419-289-5244 348 A
dlawson@ashland.edu
LAWSON, Daniel, L ...... 415-422-4222.. 71 K
lawson@usfca.edu
LAWSON, Danny, L ...... 423-323-0234 425 E
dllawson@northeaststate.edu
LAWSON, Darren, P ...... 864-242-5100 407 B
LAWSON, Deneen .... 864-242-5100 407 B
LAWSON, Diana .... 616-331-7100 224 E
lawsond1@gvsu.edu
LAWSON, Donald .... 864-424-8040 414 C
lawsondr@mailbox.sc.edu
LAWSON, Earl .... 831-582-3062.. 32 C
elawson@csumb.edu
LAWSON, Jacob .... 918-463-2931 366 B
jacob.lawson@connorsstate.edu
LAWSON, Jason .... 270-789-5031 179 E
jklawson@campbellsville.edu
LAWSON, Kelvin .... 904-281-9800 108 I
kelvin.lawson@famu.edu
LAWSON, Kenneth .... 360-416-7732 485 A
kenneth.lawson@skagit.edu
LAWSON, Melanie .... 713-313-7762 449 C
lawson_mw@tsu.edu
LAWSON, Melanie, E .... 260-982-5052 158 T
melawson@manchester.edu
LAWSON, Patricia .... 312-893-7120 137 A
plawson@erikson.edu
LAWSON, Peter .... 541-880-2363 373 E
lawson@klamathcc.edu
LAWSON, Raymond .... 847-635-1979 145 G
rlawson@oakton.edu
LAWSON, Rebecca, L ... 843-661-1841 409 K
rlawson@fmarion.edu
LAWSON, Regina, G ..... 336-758-6066 344 D
lawsonrg@wfu.edu
LAWSON, Scott .... 276-328-0211 473 B
msl6r@virginia.edu
LAWSON, Steve .... 859-985-3050 179 C
steve_lawson@berea.edu
LAWSON, Thomas .... 661-255-1050.. 28 K
tlawson@calarts.edu
LAWSON, Tonia .... 850-872-3843 100 N
tlawson@gulfcoast.edu
LAWSON, Valerie, S ..... 276-376-4523 473 B
vas7k@virginia.edu
LAWSON, Victoria .... 206-221-6075 485 F
lawson@uw.edu
LAWSON, Von .... 951-487-3440.. 52 I
vlawson@msjc.edu
LAWSON-BORDERS,
Gracie .... 202-806-7694.. 92 B
gracie.lawsonborders@howard.edu
LAWTER, JR., Vernon ... 352-746-6721.. 96 O
lawterv@cf.edu
LAWTON, Elizabeth .... 603-366-5257 272 K
elawton@ccsnh.edu
LAWTON, Kenneth, B .... 570-662-4913 395 C
klawton@mansfield.edu
LAWTON, Margaret, M . 843-377-2423 407 D
mlawton@charlestonlaw.edu
LAWTON-RAUH,
Amy, L .... 864-656-9867 408 A
apfa@clemson.edu
LAWVER, Miranda .... 906-932-4231 224 B
mirandal@gogebic.edu
LAWYER, Becky .... 952-888-4777 242 I
blawyer@nwhealth.edu
LAWYER, Mary, K .... 518-783-4288 315 J
mlawyer@siena.edu

LAWYER, Scott .... 901-321-3104 419 C
mlawyer@cbu.edu
LAXAMANA, Grace .... 650-289-3336.. 59 C
grace.laxamana@stpsu.edu
LAXMI, Priti .... 210-297-9634 431 E
pxlaxmi@baptisthealthsystem.com
LAY, Bethany .... 931-540-2837 424 G
blay@columbiastate.edu
LAY, Brian, K .... 734-384-4188 227 G
blay@monroeccc.edu
LAY, Mary .... 660-248-6221 251 B
mlay@centralmethodist.edu
LAY, Robin .... 423-636-7300 427 B
rlay@tusculum.edu
LAYCOCK, Sharon .... 318-487-5443 187 C
sharonlaycock@cltcc.edu
LAYE, Don .... 229-430-3577 113 I
dlaye@albanytech.edu
LAYER, Paul .... 907-450-8019.... 9 G
LAYISH, Michael, D ...... 781-239-4022 205 E
mlayish@babson.edu
LAYMAN, Amy, T .... 717-358-4263 384 D
amy.layman@fandm.edu
LAYMAN, Leslie .... 773-907-4059 134 C
llayman1@ccc.edu
LAYMAN, Susan .... 918-631-3244 371 E
susan-layman@utulsa.edu
LAYNE, Barbara .... 978-542-8036 213 C
LAYNE, Candace .... 304-357-4862 488 G
candacelayne@ucwv.edu
LAYNE, Donnell .... 951-571-6118.. 58 G
donnell.layne@mvc.edu
LAYNE, Preston .... 276-523-7491 475 A
playne@mecc.edu
LAYNE, Ron .... 910-246-4109 337 H
layner@sandhills.edu
LAYNE, Rosemary .... 321-674-8137.. 99 B
rlayne@fit.edu
LAYTHAM, D. Brent ...... 410-864-4202 201 F
blaytham@stmarys.edu
LAYTON, Bruce .... 847-491-5680 145 F
b-layton@northwestern.edu
LAYTON, Christopher .... 281-873-0262 434 A
c.layton@commonwealth.edu
LAYTON, David, B .... 724-847-6508 384 G
dblayton@geneva.edu
LAYTON, Rebecca .... 601-928-6230 247 E
rebecca.layton@mgccc.edu
LAYTON, Susan .... 303-458-1638.. 82 E
slayton@regis.edu
LAYTON, Wayne .... 928-428-8225.. 12 E
wayne.layton@eac.edu
LAYTON, III,
William, C .... 207-859-4342 193 E
bill.layton@colby.edu
LAYZELL, Daniel .... 225-578-4342 188 I
dlayzell@lsu.edu
LAYZELL, Daniel .... 225-578-2111 188 H
dlayzell@lsu.edu
LAZENBY, Paul .... 805-525-4417.. 67 D
plazenby@thomasaquinas.edu
LAZROE, Tony .... 732-571-4491 279 B
alazroe@monmouth.edu
LAZU, Carlos .... 787-850-9804 513 E
carlos.lazu@upr.edu
LAZZARI, John (JW) ..... 775-445-3259 271 G
john.lazzari@wnc.edu
LE, Hao .... 713-313-7950 449 C
hao.le@tsu.edu
LE, Hung, V .... 310-506-4307.. 56 C
hung.le@pepperdine.edu
LE CLAIR, Denise, Y ..... 402-280-2166 266 I
leclair@creighton.edu
LE MASTERS, Philip ..... 325-793-3898 440 B
plemasters@mcm.edu
LE ROY, Michael, K ...... 616-526-6100 222 A
president@calvin.edu
LE SAUX, Catherine ...... 812-866-7399 155 C
lesaux@hanover.edu
LEA, Brette, E .... 512-223-7611 431 A
blea@austincc.edu
LEA, Jernice .... 215-590-8231 389 C
jlea@lincoln.edu
LEA, Kizzy .... 704-216-7235 337 F
kizzy.lea@rccc.edu
LEACH, Adria .... 978-542-7524 213 C
adria.leach@salemstate.edu
LEACH, Barbara .... 815-825-2086 140 F
bleach1@kish.edu
LEACH, David .... 267-502-6083 379 D
david.leach@brynathyn.edu
LEACH, Evan .... 610-436-2930 396 A
eleach@wcupa.edu

LEE, Craig .... 949-480-4235.. 64 B
clee@soka.edu
LEE, Crystal .... 281-649-3244 437 H
clee@hbu.edu
LEE, Curtis .... 253-964-6595 483 D
clee@pierce.ctc.edu
LEE, Cynthia .... 713-313-7523 449 C
lee_cl@tsu.edu
LEE, Daniel, J .... 253-535-7177 482 H
daniel.lee@plu.edu
LEE, Darriona .... 985-732-6640 187 H
LEE, David .... 303-273-3155.. 78 I
dlee@mines.edu
LEE, David .... 510-464-3215.. 56 G
delee@peralta.edu
LEE, David .... 626-289-7719.. 24 I
dlee@amu.edu
LEE, David, C .... 706-542-5969 125 G
dclee@uga.edu
LEE, David, Y .... 703-333-5904 478 B
dylee@wuv.edu
LEE, Deanna .... 312-935-4860 147 D
dlee@robertmorris.edu
LEE, Deborah .... 949-214-3433.. 40 F
deborah.lee@cui.edu
LEE, Debra, A .... 330-471-8406 355 L
dlee@malone.edu
LEE, Delores .... 310-243-3189.. 31 B
dslee@csudh.edu
LEE, Dennis .... 229-227-2414 125 A
dlee@southernregional.edu
LEE, Dewain .... 812-866-7078 155 C
lee@hanover.edu
LEE, Don .... 662-246-6441 247 D
dlee@msdelta.edu
LEE, Dongjin .... 510-639-7879.. 54 G
LEE, Donna .... 651-696-6220 236 H
donnalee@macalester.edu
LEE, Donny .... 501-279-4187.. 19 D
dlee@harding.edu
LEE, Doug .... 724-852-3212 402 F
dlee@waynesburg.edu
LEE, Douglas .... 319-335-0444 163 A
douglas-lee@uiowa.edu
LEE, D'Andrea, J .... 225-771-2552 191 A
djlee@sulc.edu
LEE, Ed .... 715-346-3612 497 F
ed.lee@uwsp.edu
LEE, Eliot .... 562-926-1023.. 57 G
eliotlee@ptsa.edu
LEE, Elizabeth .... 503-943-7485 377 E
leeel@up.edu
LEE, Elwyn, C .... 832-842-5090 452 F
eclee@uh.edu
LEE, Eun Moo .... 770-220-7929 118 B
emlee@gcuniv.edu
LEE, Eunjo .... 770-220-7911 118 B
eunjol@gmail.com
LEE, Gloria .... 203-392-5200.. 85 A
leeg1@southernct.edu
LEE, Grace .... 415-442-7859.. 44 D
glee@ggu.edu
LEE, Hannah .... 213-381-0081.. 46 E
library@irus.edu
LEE, Harkmore .... 323-343-4907.. 32 A
hlee55@calstatela.edu
LEE, Harlan .... 425-564-4042 478 F
harlan.lee@bellevuecollege.edu
LEE, Hee, C .... 636-327-4645 255 L
hcleeshep@gmail.com
LEE, Hee, C .... 636-327-4645 255 L
hclee@midwest.edu
LEE, Hee Cheol .... 636-327-4645 255 L
hcleeshep@gmail.com
LEE, Heeseung .... 215-717-6046 400 J
helee@uarts.edu
LEE, Helen Elaine .... 617-253-2642 215 G
LEE, Herbert .... 831-459-1349.. 70 B
vpaa@ucsc.edu
LEE, Holly .... 580-628-6274 367 D
holly.lee@noc.edu
LEE, Hubert .... 610-361-2499 391 D
leeh@neumann.edu
LEE, Hyang .... 213-381-0081.. 46 E
office@irus.edu
LEE, Hyejoo .... 703-629-1281 473 E
LEE, HyeKyung .... 303-360-4737.. 79 D
hyekyung.lee@ccaurora.edu
LEE, Ilses-Mari .... 406-994-4689 264 D
ilselee@montana.edu
LEE, Jadie .... 951-827-1431.. 69 C
jadie.lee@ucr.edu
LEE, Jaewon .... 909-623-0302.. 59 A
LEE, James .... 760-252-2411.. 26 I
jlee@barstow.edu
LEE, James .... 617-873-0236 207 F
james.lee@cambridgecollege.edu
LEE, James, A .... 713-467-4501 444 F
LEE, James, D .... 808-675-3289 127 E
james.lee@byuh.edu
LEE, James, S .... 626-448-0023.. 46 G
president@itsla.edu
LEE, Jason .... 216-397-4795 354 I
jlee@jcu.edu
LEE, Jason .... 937-766-7674 349 G
jasonlee@cedarville.edu
LEE, Jay .... 970-521-6607.. 81 D
jay.lee@njc.edu
LEE, Jay .... 507-537-7285 241 D
jay.lee@smsu.edu
LEE, Jeffrey .... 973-877-4447 277 I
lee@essex.edu
LEE, Jeffrey, C .... 904-808-7492 106 C
jeffreylee@sjrstate.edu
LEE, Joanne .... 406-496-4769 265 A
jlee@mtech.edu
LEE, Joanne, C .... 714-995-9988.. 47 B
LEE, John .... 651-255-6156 243 D
jlee@unitedseminary.edu
LEE, John .... 703-812-4757 468 G
jlee@leland.edu
LEE, Jonathan .... 508-626-4697 212 D
jlee8@framingham.edu
LEE, Jonathan .... 310-233-4471.. 49 A
leej@lahc.edu
LEE, JongOh .... 909-447-6305.. 37 F
jolee@cst.edu
LEE, Joni, C .... 501-569-3186.. 22 B
jclee@ualr.edu
LEE, Joseph .... 251-380-3865.... 6 H
jlee@shc.edu
LEE, Judy .... 718-818-6470 315 A
jlee@edaff.com
LEE, Julian, C .... 626-455-0312.. 58 C
LEE, Ka Yee .... 773-702-3109 150 J
kayeelee@uchicago.edu
LEE, Karen .... 619-849-2535.. 57 E
karenlee@pointloma.edu
LEE, Karen .... 808-845-9225 129 B
karenlee@hawaii.edu
LEE, Karen .... 406-791-5280 265 H
karen.lee@uprovidence.edu
LEE, Karen .... 864-644-5032 412 E
klee@swu.edu
LEE, Kathleen, F .... 317-917-5935 157 H
klee@ivytech.edu
LEE, Katrina, K .... 919-658-2502 340 J
klee@umo.edu
LEE, Kenneth .... 603-645-9691 274 D
k.lee7@snhu.edu
LEE, Kenya, N .... 646-312-3322 292 L
kenya.lee@baruch.cuny.edu
LEE, Kesha, T .... 919-530-6976 342 A
klee@nccu.edu
LEE, Kimberly .... 229-420-1284 113 I
klee@albanytech.edu
LEE, Kwang Hoon .... 213-381-0081.. 46 E
khlee@irus.edu
LEE, Kyu, H .... 253-752-2020 481 B
klee@faithseminary.edu
LEE, Kyuboem .... 215-368-5000 390 F
klee@missio.edu
LEE, LeBlanc .... 210-486-0560 429 H
lleblanc7@alamo.edu
LEE, Lenetta .... 484-365-7222 389 C
llee@lincoln.edu
LEE, Lily .... 240-567-5272 200 C
lily.lee@montgomerycollege.edu
LEE, Linda, S .... 657-725-7789.. 65 J
lslee@stanford.edu
LEE, Lisa .... 212-410-8007 309 B
llee@nycpm.edu
LEE, Malisa .... 559-278-4639.. 31 D
malisal@csufresno.edu
LEE, Marilyn .... 701-483-2330 345 D
marilyn.lee@dickinsonstate.edu
LEE, Marsha .... 662-246-6314 247 D
mlee@msdelta.edu
LEE, Mary W, L .... 630-515-7311 143 G
mleexx@midwestern.edu
LEE, Matt .... 225-578-7155 188 I
mlee@lsu.edu
LEE, Matthew .... 913-722-0272 174 E
matt.lee@kansaschristian.edu
LEE, Melissa .... 863-784-7123 107 F
melissa.lee@southflorida.edu
LEE, Miae .... 888-777-7675 481 B
mlee@faithseminary.edu
LEE, Michael, D .... 229-226-1621 125 C
mlee@thomasu.edu
LEE, Michael, J .... 216-368-4306 349 F
michael.j.lee6@case.edu
LEE, Michele .... 864-424-8038 414 C
michele@mailbox.sc.edu
LEE, Michelle .... 910-362-7555 332 H
mlee@cfcc.edu
LEE, Michelle .... 910-362-7555 332 H
mslee36@mail.cfcc.edu
LEE, Mike .... 916-686-7300.. 29 J
LEE, Mike, C .... 818-947-2336.. 49 F
leemc@lavc.edu
LEE, Min .... 714-525-0088.. 44 E
gmu@gm.edu
LEE, Norman .... 315-294-8412 292 E
norman.lee@cayuga-cc.edu
LEE, Ok-Hee .... 218-477-2095 239 D
okheelee@mnstate.edu
LEE, Otto .... 310-233-4010.. 49 A
leeow@lahc.edu
LEE, Patricia, A .... 843-355-4127 414 F
leepa@wiltech.edu
LEE, Patrick .... 210-486-3282 429 F
plee18@alamo.edu
LEE, Paul .... 310-756-0001.. 72 A
LEE, Paula .... 225-216-8732 186 K
leep@mybrcc.edu
LEE, Peter .... 301-624-2738 198 E
plee@frederick.edu
LEE, Phyllis .... 815-967-7306 147 F
plee@rockfordcareercollege.edu
LEE, Raeann .... 614-416-6239 349 B
rlee@bradfordschoolcolumbus.edu
LEE, Randall .... 601-635-6375 245 I
rlee@eccc.edu
LEE, Randolph .... 860-297-2413.. 88 C
randolph.lee@trincoll.edu
LEE, Rebecca .... 270-901-1019 182 D
rebecca.lee@kctcs.edu
LEE, Robert .... 660-543-4272 260 K
relee@ucmo.edu
LEE, Robert, W .... 260-399-7700 161 D
rlee@sf.edu
LEE, Samuel .... 951-372-7199.. 58 H
samuel.lee@norcocollege.edu
LEE, Sang Meyng .... 562-926-1023.. 57 G
sangmeynglee@msn.com
LEE, Sanghhoon .... 323-643-0301.. 25 L
president@aeu.edu
LEE, Sanghoon .... 323-643-0301.. 25 L
dean@aeu.edu
LEE, Sasha .... 302-736-2425.. 90 G
sasha.lee@wesley.edu
LEE, Seung Deok .... 213-487-0110.. 41 I
president@dula.edu
LEE, Shad .... 760-921-5431.. 55 H
shad.lee@paloverde.edu
LEE, Shane .... 605-394-2347 417 B
shane.lee@sdsmt.edu
LEE, Shannon .... 203-773-8550.. 84 F
slee1@albertus.edu
LEE, Sharon .... 919-572-1625 326 L
slee14@apexsot.edu
LEE, Sheng Chien, R .... 956-326-2323 446 F
sheng.lee@tamiu.edu
LEE, Sooyeon .... 248-232-4175 229 A
sxkim@oaklandcc.edu
LEE, Staci .... 760-921-5512.. 55 H
staci.lee@paloverde.edu
LEE, Stephen .... 435-652-7651 460 G
stephen.lee@dixie.edu
LEE, Stephen .... 304-293-0141 491 C
stephen.lee@mail.wvu.edu
LEE, Steven .... 757-446-5221 466 I
leect@evms.edu
LEE, Sun Kyu .... 562-926-1023.. 57 G
LEE, Susan .... 808-956-5852 128 H
susanlee@hawaii.edu
LEE, Susan .... 406-791-5318 265 H
susan.lee@uprovidence.edu
LEE, Teresa .... 785-670-1538 177 G
teresa.lee@washburn.edu
LEE, Terri, S .... 919-209-2125 335 F
tslee@johnstoncc.edu
LEE, Theresa .... 865-974-4337 427 G
artscidean@utk.edu
LEE, Tiffany .... 562-944-0351.. 27 C
tiffany.lee@biola.edu
LEE, Tiffany .... 484-365-7842 389 C
tlee@lincoln.edu
LEE, Timothy .... 773-995-2002 133 K
tlee27@csu.edu
LEE, Timothy .... 315-445-4300 304 C
leetm@lemoyne.edu
LEE, Tony .... 310-825-1633.. 69 A
tlee@ucpd.ucla.edu
LEE, Traci .... 480-314-2102.. 15 R
LEE, Treva, A .... 504-520-7566 193 A
tlee@xula.edu
LEE, Trisha .... 907-796-6294.. 10 B
tclee@alaska.edu
LEE, Trudy .... 573-651-2332 259 K
tglee@semo.edu
LEE, Tyjaun .... 816-604-4205 255 D
tyjaun.lee@mcckc.edu
LEE, Tyjaun .... 816-604-4203 255 I
tyjaun.lee@mcckc.edu
LEE, Tyjuan, A .... 816-604-3044 255 H
tyjuan.lee@mcckc.edu
LEE, Unjoo .... 323-267-3774.. 48 H
leeuh@elac.edu
LEE, Vina .... 845-672-0550 300 A
LEE, W. P. Andrew .... 214-648-8712 457 B
wpandrew.lee@utsouthwestern.edu
LEE, Wendy .... 415-257-1354.. 41 H
wendy.lee@dominican.edu
LEE, Willie .... 201-761-7125 282 I
wlee@saintpeters.edu
LEE, Y. Ben .... 260-422-5561 155 H
yblee@indianatech.edu
LEE, Yuet .... 203-576-4644.. 88 D
yuetlee@bridgeport.edu
LEE, Yung Jae .... 925-631-4610.. 59 B
ylee@stmarys-ca.edu
LEE, Zelda .... 803-535-5348 407 G
zlee@claflin.edu
LEE-BARBER, Jill .... 404-413-1640 119 E
jleebarber@gsu.edu
LEE-LEWIS, Sherri .... 310-434-4419.. 62 E
lee-lewis_sherri@smcv.edu
LEE MURPHY, Karen .... 954-201-7350.. 95 H
LEE-OPERARIO, Tam .... 510-436-1348.. 45 D
lee-operario@hnu.edu
LEE SANG, Brian .... 202-885-6108.. 90 J
leesang@american.edu
LEE-THOMAS, Victoria .... 860-723-0011.. 84 H
thomasv@ct.edu
LEE-YUAN, Mona .... 516-739-1545 309 C
clinicdirector@nyctcm.edu
LEEBRON, David, W .... 713-348-5050 442 K
president@rice.edu
LEEBRON TUTELMAN,
Elizabeth .... 215-204-8660 399 F
elizabeth.leebron@temple.edu
LEECH, Jackie .... 870-733-6741.. 17 H
jleech@asumidsouth.edu
LEECK, Henry .... 618-437-5321 147 A
leeckh@rlc.edu
LEECY, Melissa .... 804-752-3205 470 F
melissaleecy@rmc.edu
LEEDER, Mike .... 229-931-2222 119 D
mike.leeder@gsw.edu
LEEDS, Charles .... 920-206-2339 493 L
charles.leeds@mbu.edu
LEEDS, Mark .... 817-923-1921 445 B
mleeds@swbts.edu
LEEDS CARSON, Ben .... 831-459-4512.. 70 B
blc@ucsc.edu
LEEDY, David .... 212-659-0741 304 B
dleedy@tkc.edu
LEEDY, Debbie .... 623-845-4770.. 13 C
debbie.leedy@gccaz.edu
LEEK, Linda .... 859-985-3205 179 C
leekl@berea.edu
LEEK, Marilyn, J .... 515-961-1675 169 D
marilyn.leek@simpson.edu
LEEMAN, Julia .... 847-585-2267 132 B
jleeman@careered.com
LEEMAN BARTZIS,
Opal .... 517-353-8920 227 D
bartziso@msu.edu
LEEMON, Donna .... 334-683-2362.... 3 A
dleemon@marionmilitary.edu
LEENEY-PANAGROSSI,
Anne .... 203-773-8595.. 84 F
panagrossi@albertus.edu
LEEPER, Greg .... 612-343-4457 242 H
gjleeper@northcentral.edu
LEEPER, Karla .... 706-721-7406 115 A
kleeper@augusta.edu
LEES, David .... 215-991-2015 387 C
leesp@lasalle.edu

LEMONS, Daniel .... 718-960-8111 294 A
president.lemons@lehman.cuny.edu
LEMONS, Daniel .... 718-960-8222 294 A
daniel.lemons@lehman.cuny.edu
LEMONS, James .... 434-832-7680 474 C
lemonsj@centralvirginia.edu
LEMPERLE, Monica .... 973-300-2100 283 E
mlemperle@sussex.edu
LEMUEL, Robert, L .... 989-964-4393 230 B
lemuel@svsu.edu
LEMURA, Linda, M .... 315-445-4120 304 C
president14@lemoyne.edu
LEMUS,
Maria De Jesus .... 773-371-5453 133 E
mlemus@ctu.edu
LENA, III, Hugh, F .... 401-865-2155 405 B
hlena@providence.edu
LENAGHAN, Andrew ..... 815-836-5015 141 G
lenaghan@lewisu.edu
LENAGHAN, Janet, A .... 516-463-5676 302 B
janet.lenaghan@hofstra.edu
LENAHAN, Robert .... 631-632-6350 317 D
robert.lenahan@stonybrook.edu
LENCZOWSKI, John ...... 202-462-2101.. 92 C
lenczowski@iwp.edu
LENEZ, Nicole .... 540-365-4456 467 I
nlenez@ferrum.edu
LENFEST, Richard .... 413-572-5405 213 D
rlenfest@westfield.ma.edu
LENGA, Kirk .... 818-333-3558.. 53 G
kirk.lenga@nyfa.edu
LENGNICK, Todd .... 305-919-5305 109 A
todd.lengnick@fiu.edu
LENGREN, Les .... 909-447-2545.. 37 F
llengren@cst.edu
LENGSFELD, Corinne .... 303-871-2966.. 83 D
clengsfe@du.edu
LENGSFELD, Corinne .... 303-871-4843.. 83 D
clengsfe@du.edu
LENHARDT, Andrew, R . 812-465-7115 161 E
alenhardt@usi.edu
LENHART, Jeff .... 704-847-5600 340 I
jlenhart@ses.edu
LENIG, Joni, L .... 931-540-2752 424 G
jlenig@columbiastate.edu
LENIHAN, David .... 787-840-2575 510 J
dlenihan@psm.edu
LENIO, Jim .... 866-492-5336 244 F
jim.lenio@mail.waldenu.edu
LENK, Robert .... 405-789-7661 370 B
robert.lenk@swcu.edu
LENKER, Caitlin .... 717-867-6231 388 H
lenker@lvc.edu
LENN, Michael .... 608-262-1234 496 C
mlenn@wisc.edu
LENNA, Nila .... 413-205-3310 205 A
nila.lenna@aic.edu
LENNEMAN, Marc .... 406-447-4869 263 C
mlenneman@carroll.edu
LENNERTON, Mark .... 718-289-5655 293 B
mark.lennerton@bcc.cuny.edu
LENNERTZ, Reid .... 239-590-7960 108 K
rlennert@fgcu.edu
LENNEY, Raina .... 202-885-5936.. 90 J
lenney@american.edu
LENNO, Chip .... 831-582-4700.. 32 C
clenno@csumb.edu
LENNO, Matthew .... 410-704-2332 204 A
mlenno@towson.edu
LENNON, Craig .... 203-576-4273.. 88 D
clennon@bridgeport.edu
LENNON, John .... 845-848-4061 298 D
john.lennon@dc.edu
LENO, Melissa .... 218-733-5903 238 F
m.leno@lsc.edu
LENO, Tom .... 701-224-5497 346 B
thomas.leno@bismarckstate.edu
LENOIR, Nina .... 714-997-6622.. 36 C
lenoir@chapman.edu
LENORE, Leila .... 405-682-1611 367 H
leila.c.lenore@occc.edu
LENORE, Shani .... 314-529-9359 254 H
slenore@maryville.edu
LENOSKY, Charles .... 402-280-2540 266 I
charleslenosky@creighton.edu
LENOX, Jill .... 816-936-8729 259 I
jlenox@saintlukescollege.edu
LENOX, Richard .... 806-742-3671 451 B
richard.lenox@ttu.edu
LENROW, Jon .... 215-670-9359 391 H
jlenrow@peirce.edu
LENSER, Leslie, A .... 615-460-6456 418 F
LENSING, Peggy .... 563-387-1015 167 E
lensinpe@luther.edu
LENSING TATE, Amy ..... 414-229-3844 497 A
lensing@uwm.edu
LENSMIRE, Emily .... 920-686-6205 496 A
emily.lensmire@sl.edu
LENSON, Jacob, G .... 219-989-3120 159 G
lenson@pnw.edu
LENT, Tina .... 209-954-5151.. 60 J
tlent@deltacollege.edu
LENTINI, James, P .... 248-370-2193 229 G
jlentini@oakland.edu
LENTINO, Nicholas .... 860-727-6765.. 87 A
nlentino@goodwin.edu
LENTSCH, Matt .... 574-807-7120 153 E
matt.lentsch@betheluniversity.edu
LENTZ, Brannon .... 334-514-8607.... 2 F
brannon.lentz@istc.edu
LENTZ, Heather .... 605-995-7227 415 G
heather.lentz@mitchelltech.edu
LENTZ, Kristi, L .... 701-788-4772 345 E
kristi.lentz@mayvillestate.edu
LENTZ, Tracy .... 212-757-1190 290 B
tlentz@aami.edu
LENTZ, Victoria, A .... 410-543-6262 203 F
valentz@salisbury.edu
LENWAY, Stefanie, A .... 651-962-4201 244 E
lenw0002@stthomas.edu
LENZ, Mary .... 320-762-4648 237 B
maryl@alextech.edu
LENZ, Patrick, J .... 510-987-9101.. 68 C
patrick.lenz@ucop.edu
LENZER, Julie .... 301-405-2960 202 C
jlenzer@umd.edu
LENZMEIER, Brian .... 712-749-2243 163 D
lenzmeier@bvu.edu
LENZO, Diana, D .... 607-778-5100 318 A
lenzodd@sunybroome.edu
LEO, Donald .... 706-542-1653 125 G
donleo@engr.uga.edu
LEO, Jonathan .... 423-869-7094 421 C
jonathan.leo@lmunet.edu
LEO, Laurie .... 585-594-6861 312 K
leo_laurie@roberts.edu
LEO, Laurie .... 585-594-6861 310 F
leo_laurie@roberts.edu
LEOMITI, Sonny, J .... 684-699-9155 505 A
s.leomiti@amsamoa.edu
LEON, Christine .... 714-564-6230.. 57 L
leon_christine@sac.edu
LEON, Dante .... 386-506-4153.. 97 D
dante.leon@daytonastate.edu
LEON, Gabriela .... 281-756-3524 429 I
gleon@alvincollege.edu
LEON, Linda, J .... 330-471-8442 355 L
lleon2@malone.edu
LEON, Martha .... 661-654-3965.. 30 E
mleon7@csub.edu
LEON, Nelson .... 212-752-1530 304 D
nelson.leon@limcollege.edu
LEON, Orlando .... 559-278-3923.. 31 D
oleon@csufresno.edu
LEON, Tony .... 559-297-4500.. 46 A
tleon@iot.edu
LEON, Victor .... 505-224-4000 285 J
vleon@cnm.edu
LEON GUERRERO,
Ann S, A .... 671-735-2941 505 E
annsalg@triton.uog.edu
LEON-GUERRERO,
Anna, Y .... 253-535-7196 482 H
ayl@plu.edu
LEON GUERRERO,
Deborah, D .... 671-735-2585 505 E
deborah@triton.uog.edu
LEON GUERRERO,
Latisha Ann, N .... 671-735-5518 505 C
csi@guamcc.edu
LEON GUERRERO,
Rachael, T .... 671-735-2170 505 E
rachaeltlg@triton.uog.edu
LEON-JORDAN,
Jordania .... 262-595-2010 497 C
leonjord@uwp.edu
LEONARD, Alice .... 866-294-3974 154 D
alice.leonard@ccr.edu
LEONARD, Andy .... 704-461-6200 327 A
andyleonard@bac.edu
LEONARD, Bethany .... 262-695-6520 500 H
bleonard3@wctc.edu
LEONARD, Bob .... 765-658-4161 154 F
bobleonard@depauw.edu
LEONARD, Bryan .... 217-245-3048 138 D
bryan.leonard@ic.edu
LEONARD, Courtney ..... 563-588-6585 163 F
courtney.leonard@clarke.edu
LEONARD, Daniel .... 303-282-3427.. 82 H
father.leonard@archden.org
LEONARD, David, M ..... 540-458-8752 478 A
dleonard@wlu.edu
LEONARD, J. Rich .... 919-865-5878 327 E
leonardjr@campbell.edu
LEONARD, Jesse, W ..... 814-641-3162 386 H
leonarj@juniata.edu
LEONARD, John .... 804-758-6842 475 G
jleonard@rappahannock.edu
LEONARD, Katie .... 570-702-8925 386 G
kleonard@johnson.edu
LEONARD, Lindsey .... 319-352-8526 170 C
lindsey.leonard@wartburg.edu
LEONARD, Marjolie .... 631-632-6280 317 D
marjolie.leonard@stonybrook.edu
LEONARD,
Mary Kathleen .... 814-871-7430 384 E
leonard010@gannon.edu
LEONARD, Patricia, L ... 910-962-3117 343 C
leonard@uncw.edu
LEONARD, Raychelle .... 928-724-6683.. 12 C
rleonard@dinecollege.edu
LEONARD, Robert .... 256-824-2233.... 8 B
robert.leonard@uah.edu
LEONARD, Roberta .... 724-589-2024 399 H
rleonard@thiel.edu
LEONARD, Steve .... 317-738-8316 154 J
sleonard@franklincollege.edu
LEONARD, Tammy .... 214-388-5466 435 G
tleonard@dallasinstitute.edu
LEONARD, Timothy .... 410-704-3936 204 A
tleonard@towson.edu
LEONARD, Vee .... 239-590-1101 108 K
vleonard@fgcu.edu
LEONARD, William .... 610-361-5217 391 D
leonardw@neumann.edu
LEONE, Charles .... 215-204-7900 399 F
charles.leone@temple.edu
LEONE, Deanna .... 657-278-2097.. 31 E
dleone@fullerton.edu
LEONE, Gerard .... 617-287-7050 211 C
gleone@umassp.edu
LEONE, John .... 518-828-4181 297 B
john.leone@sunycgcc.edu
LEONE, Lucian .... 269-782-1238 230 F
lleone@swmich.edu
LEONETTI, Marc .... 401-254-3843 405 E
mleonetti@rwu.edu
LEONI, Amy .... 740-284-7214 353 B
aleoni@franciscan.edu
LEONOR, JR.,
Samuel, E .... 951-785-2090.. 47 C
sleonor@lasierra.edu
LEOPARD, Tim .... 205-348-8157.... 7 G
tleopard@fa.ua.edu
LEOPOLD, Emily .... 617-588-1347 206 C
eleopold@bfit.edu
LEOPOLD, Joseph .... 727-341-3719 106 E
leopold.joseph@spcollege.edu
LEOPOLD, Lillian .... 619-482-6564.. 65 F
lleopold@swccd.edu
LEOS, Jonathan, S .... 323-856-7742.. 25 M
jleos@afi.com
LEOUSIS, Kim .... 251-442-2290.... 8 C
kleousis@umobile.edu
LEPAGE, Sharon .... 808-440-4263 127 F
slepage@chaminade.edu
LEPAGE, Shaun .... 816-322-0110 250 K
shaun.lepage@calvary.edu
LEPERA, John .... 410-323-6211 198 C
admissions@fts.edu
LEPHART, Scott, M .... 859-323-1100 185 B
scott.lephart@uky.edu
LEPLEY, Pamela, D .... 804-828-6057 473 F
pdlepley@vcu.edu
LEPPER, Charles .... 801-957-4285 461 D
charles.lepper@slcc.edu
LEPPER, David .... 989-275-5000 226 B
david.lepper@kirtland.edu
LEPPING, Lou .... 802-586-7711 463 D
llepping@sterlingcollege.edu
LEPRE, Dave .... 575-835-5091 286 I
dave.lepre@nmt.edu
LEPRE, Lyn, R .... 845-575-3000 305 L
lyn.lepre@marist.edu
LERCH, Derek .... 530-283-0202.. 42 H
dlerch@frc.edu
LERER, Nava .... 516-877-3236 289 C
lerer@adelphi.edu
LERMAN, Linda .... 203-857-7211.. 86 D
llerman@norwalk.edu
LERMAN, Steven, R ...... 831-656-2371 503 K
slerman@nps.edu
LEROY, Antonio .... 229-430-3635 113 H
antonio.leroy@asurams.edu
LEROY, Fabrice .... 337-482-0195 192 E
fleroy@louisiana.edu
LEROY, Francois .... 859-572-7976 184 A
leroy@nku.edu
LEROY, Lindsay .... 910-962-2684 343 C
leroyl@uncw.edu
LEROY, Terri .... 620-421-6700 175 C
terril@labette.edu
LEROY, Thomas .... 315-470-6667 320 A
tjleroy@esf.edu
LESA, Elsie .... 684-699-9155 505 A
e.lesa@amsamoa.edu
LESAGE, Jasper .... 316-295-5881 173 D
jasper_lesage@friends.edu
LESAN, Thomas, L .... 641-782-1443 169 H
lesan@swcciowa.edu
LESANE, II, Cornell ...... 814-332-2102 378 D
clesane@allegheny.edu
LESANE, Steven .... 919-546-8534 340 E
slesane@shawu.edu
LESCARBEAU, Lisa .... 413-662-5205 213 A
lisa.lescarbeau@mcla.edu
LESCAULT, JR.,
Maurice, A .... 434-971-3291 503 G
maurice.a.lescault.civ@mail.mil
LESCHES, Elchonon .... 718-363-2034 322 F
bmotzal@gmail.com
LESCINSKI, CSJ, Joan ... 563-333-6213 169 A
officeofthepresident@sau.edu
LESCZINSKI, Michael .... 518-608-8450 299 G
mlesczinski@excelsior.edu
LESEANE, Reginald .... 912-358-3389 123 H
leseaner@savannahstate.edu
LESEN, Beth .... 916-278-6060.. 32 E
beth.lesen@csus.edu
LESESNE, David, L .... 804-752-7305 470 F
davidlesesne@rmc.edu
LESH, Aja .... 626-815-6000.. 26 H
alesh@apu.edu
LESHAN, Tim, E .... 617-373-8528 217 F
LESHIN, Laurie .... 508-831-5200 220 E
president@wpi.edu
LESHINSKIE, Eric .... 602-787-7668.. 13 E
eric.leshinskie@paradisevalley.edu
LESHKEVICH, Peter .... 734-973-3729 232 B
pleshkev@wccnet.edu
LESHOK, Paul .... 414-930-3305 495 A
leshokp@mtmary.edu
LESIAK, Erin .... 308-398-7406 266 A
erinlesiak@cccneb.edu
LESKIW, Christopher ..... 606-539-4214 185 A
christopher.leskiw@ucumberlands.edu
LESKO, Kathleen .... 518-454-5154 296 H
leskok@strose.edu
LESLEY, Kimberly .... 215-965-8582 390 J
klesley@moore.edu
LESLIE, Benjamin, C ..... 704-406-4239 329 A
bleslie@gardner-webb.edu
LESLIE, Bethany .... 330-823-8440 363 B
lesliebe@mountunion.edu
LESLIE, Colleen, M .... 617-253-7086 215 G
LESLIE, Donald .... 434-528-5276 477 E
drlcpa75@hotmail.com
LESLIE, Frances, M .... 949-824-6351.. 68 G
fmleslie@uci.edu
LESLIE, Howard .... 973-278-5400 291 D
hdl@berkeleycollege.edu
LESLIE, Howard .... 973-278-5400 275 I
hdl@berkeleycollege.edu
LESLIE, Jerry .... 325-649-8097 438 D
jleslie@hputx.edu
LESLIE, Julie .... 419-251-1598 356 C
julie.leslie@mercycollege.edu
LESLIE, Ken .... 802-635-1315 464 C
ken.leslie@northernvermont.edu
LESLIE, Meinya .... 404-225-4712 114 H
LESLIE, Paul, L .... 336-272-7102 329 D
lesliep@greensboro.edu
LESLIE, Robert .... 704-978-5410 336 C
rleslie@mitchellcc.edu
LESLIE, Robin .... 704-463-3442 339 E
robin.leslie@pfeiffer.edu
LESLIE, Sarah-Jane .... 609-258-3035 280 E
sjleslie@princeton.edu
LESLIE, Steve .... 512-322-3789 454 I
sleslie@utsystem.edu
LESMEISTER, Heather .... 417-625-9365 256 D
lesmeister-h@mssu.edu

LEWIS, Don .... 763-433-1116 237 C
donald.lewis@anokaramsey.edu
LEWIS, Donald .... 763-433-1116 237 D
donald.lewis@anokaramsey.edu
LEWIS, Donna .... 601-925-3967 247 C
dlewis@mc.edu
LEWIS, Dorothy .... 607-431-4320 301 D
lewisd@hartwick.edu
LEWIS, E. Charles .... 817-202-6720 444 I
lewis@swau.edu
LEWIS, Edward .... 336-770-3329 343 D
lewise@uncsa.edu
LEWIS, Elizabeth (Beth) 919-866-5768 338 G
ealewis@waketech.edu
LEWIS, Erica, D .... 336-841-9039 329 G
elewis@highpoint.edu
LEWIS, Erin .... 972-238-6132 435 F
erinlewis@dcccd.edu
LEWIS, Erin .... 206-934-3881 484 A
erin.lewis2@seattlecolleges.edu
LEWIS, Eva .... 205-934-2384.... 8 A
aqi-iea@uab.edu
LEWIS, Eva .... 423-425-2127 428 A
eva-lewis@utc.edu
LEWIS, Gabe .... 254-267-7021 442 E
glewis@rangercollege.edu
LEWIS, JR., Gary, D ..... 502-852-6111 185 C
gary.lewis.1@louisville.edu
LEWIS, Gerald .... 210-458-4249 455 E
gerald.lewis@utsa.edu
LEWIS, Gregory .... 804-257-5750 477 C
gelewis@vuu.edu
LEWIS, Jackie .... 252-985-5170 339 D
jlewis@ncwc.edu
LEWIS, Jacqueline, A .... 301-405-4680 202 C
jalewis@umd.edu
LEWIS, James .... 610-399-2092 394 C
james.lewis@cheyney.edu
LEWIS, James, E .... 206-934-5157 484 B
james.lewis@seattlecolleges.edu
LEWIS, Jamie .... 813-988-5131.. 98 Q
lewisj@floridacollege.edu
LEWIS, Jan .... 252-328-2267 341 C
lewisja@ecu.edu
LEWIS, Jan, P .... 253-535-7283 482 H
lewisjp@plu.edu
LEWIS, Janet, L .... 740-368-3002 359 N
jllewis@owu.edu
LEWIS, Jarelle .... 701-483-2370 345 D
jarelle.lewis@dickinsonstate.edu
LEWIS, Jeff .... 561-803-2702 104 C
jeff_lewis@pba.edu
LEWIS, Jennifer .... 619-482-6375.. 65 F
jlewis@swccd.edu
LEWIS, Jerry .... 260-481-6710 159 F
jerry.lewis@pfw.edu
LEWIS, Jim .... 806-743-2530 451 C
jim.lewis@ttuhsc.edu
LEWIS, Jim .... 817-531-4404 451 E
jimlewis@txwes.edu
LEWIS, Jim, D .... 704-637-4720 328 A
jdlewis@catawba.edu
LEWIS, John .... 860-932-4172.. 86 E
jlewis@qvcc.edu
LEWIS, John .... 501-812-2233.. 23 B
jlewis@uaptc.edu
LEWIS, John .... 304-327-4191 489 P
jlewis@bluefieldstate.edu
LEWIS, Judith .... 936-294-3160 450 C
judith.lewis@shsu.edu
LEWIS, Judith .... 513-745-3134 365 B
LEWIS, K. Lynn .... 281-646-1109 432 B
LEWIS, Karen .... 704-355-5585 327 H
karen.lewis@carolinascollege.edu
LEWIS, Karla .... 618-252-5400 149 C
karla.lewis@sic.edu
LEWIS, Kay .... 206-543-6107 485 F
sklewis@uw.edu
LEWIS, Keisha .... 205-929-1604.... 6 B
catcenter@miles.edu
LEWIS, Kelley .... 800-785-0585.. 39 G
klewis@columbiacollege.edu
LEWIS, Kendrick, D ...... 803-536-8227 412 C
klewis19@scsu.edu
LEWIS, JR., Kenneth, A 252-492-2061 338 F
lewisj@vgcc.edu
LEWIS, Keri .... 617-745-3774 208 G
keri.lewis@enc.edu
LEWIS, Kristin .... 219-464-5093 162 A
kristin.lewis@valpo.edu
LEWIS, Larry .... 620-862-5252 171 B
larry.lewis@barclaycollege.edu

LEWIS, Leigh .... 402-643-7240 266 G
leigh.lewis@cune.edu
LEWIS, JR., Leon .... 501-882-8887.. 17 F
LEWIS, Leontye .... 410-951-3010 203 D
llewis@coppin.edu
LEWIS, Lisa .... 623-845-3784.. 13 C
lisa.lewis@gccaz.edu
LEWIS, Lisa .... 612-624-6142 243 E
lrlewis@umn.edu
LEWIS, Lori .... 828-227-7124 344 A
lalewis@wcu.edu
LEWIS, Lori .... 828-771-2082 344 E
llewis@warren-wilson.edu
LEWIS, Luca .... 360-383-3076 486 G
llewis@whatcom.edu
LEWIS, Marcus .... 252-536-2551 335 B
LEWIS, Marianne, W ..... 513-556-7001 362 D
marianne.lewis@uc.edu
LEWIS, Mark .... 952-358-8405 239 F
mark.lewis@normandale.edu
LEWIS, Mark .... 607-871-2649 289 H
lewism@alfred.edu
LEWIS, Mark .... 813-253-7017 101 A
mlewis73@hccfl.edu
LEWIS, Mark .... 325-674-2772 429 B
lewism@acu.edu
LEWIS, Marsha, L .... 716-829-2533 316 F
ubnursingdean@buffalo.edu
LEWIS, Mary .... 772-462-7444 101 E
mlewis@irsc.edu
LEWIS, Maryjo .... 937-376-2946 360 D
mlewis@payne.edu
LEWIS, Melissa .... 931-526-3660 420 A
melissa.lewis@fortisinstitute.edu
LEWIS, Michelle .... 314-977-3065 259 H
michelle.lewis@slu.edu
LEWIS, Mike .... 918-463-2931 366 B
mike.lewis@connorsstate.edu
LEWIS, Mildred .... 510-464-3413.. 56 G
mildredlewis@peralta.edu
LEWIS, Mitchell, R .... 607-735-1709 299 D
mlewis@elmira.edu
LEWIS, Monique .... 281-487-1170 448 F
mlewis@txchiro.edu
LEWIS, Myra .... 704-978-1309 336 C
mlewis@mitchellcc.edu
LEWIS, Nadia .... 419-448-3433 361 J
lewisna@tiffin.edu
LEWIS, Nora, E .... 215-746-1172 400 K
nlewis@sas.upenn.edu
LEWIS, Orlando .... 704-216-6185 330 H
olewis@livingstone.edu
LEWIS, Pamela .... 661-362-3875.. 38 H
pamela.lewis@canyons.edu
LEWIS, Pat .... 704-355-2029 327 H
pat.lewis@carolinascollege.edu
LEWIS, Patricia .... 936-294-4265 450 C
pal007@shsu.edu
LEWIS, Paul, W .... 417-268-1014 250 E
lewisp@evangel.edu
LEWIS, Paula .... 740-376-4701 356 A
lewisp@marietta.edu
LEWIS, Peggy .... 202-884-9621.. 93 B
lewisp@trinitydc.edu
LEWIS, Pericles .... 203-432-2517.. 89 D
pericles.lewis@yale.edu
LEWIS, Rachel .... 801-957-4563 461 D
rachel.lewis@slcc.edu
LEWIS, Raynold .... 508-929-8883 213 E
rlewis1@worcester.edu
LEWIS, Rebecca .... 817-272-3365 454 J
rebeccal@uta.edu
LEWIS, Rebecca, B .... 423-439-6155 419 J
bakerr@etsu.edu
LEWIS, Rhiannon .... 415-503-6291.. 60 H
rlewis@sfcm.edu
LEWIS, Rob .... 214-333-5821 434 I
robertl@dbu.edu
LEWIS, Robin .... 606-326-2423 180 I
robin.lewis@kctcs.edu
LEWIS, Rob'n .... 253-680-7123 478 E
rlewis@batestech.edu
LEWIS, Ronald, J .... 605-342-0317 415 E
president@jwc.edu
LEWIS, Rossana .... 954-486-7728 112 D
roslewis@uftl.edu
LEWIS, Sally .... 254-968-1694 446 E
slewis@tarleton.edu
LEWIS, Shannon .... 626-584-5458.. 43 H
slewis@fuller.edu
LEWIS, Sheila .... 818-575-6800.. 67 G
sheila.lewis@tuw.edu

LEWIS, Shirley .... 707-864-7000.. 64 C
shirley.lewis@solano.edu
LEWIS, Stacy .... 415-422-5540.. 71 K
lewiss@usfca.edu
LEWIS, Stephanie .... 909-384-8534.. 59 I
slewis@sbccd.cc.ca.us
LEWIS, Susan .... 325-674-2024 429 B
lewiss@acu.edu
LEWIS, Susan .... 541-506-6047 372 G
slewis@cgcc.edu
LEWIS, Tammy .... 718-951-5024 293 C
tlewis@brooklyn.cuny.edu
LEWIS, Ted .... 304-327-4161 489 P
tlewis@bluefieldstate.edu
LEWIS, Thomas .... 443-287-9900 199 D
tomlewis@jhu.edu
LEWIS, Tiffany .... 765-677-2102 157 D
tiffany.lewis@indwes.edu
LEWIS, Tracie, O .... 888-498-6752 341 F
tolewis@ncat.edu
LEWIS, Trevor .... 305-626-3750.. 99 D
trevor.lewis@fmuniv.edu
LEWIS, Trevor, C .... 215-898-1135 400 K
lewistc@upenn.edu
LEWIS, Vivian .... 585-273-2760 323 J
vivian.lewis@rochester.edu
LEWIS, Walter .... 518-587-2100 321 A
walter.lewis@esc.edu
LEWIS, Whitney .... 404-364-8470 122 J
wlewis@oglethorpe.edu
LEWIS-GUMP, Kelly ...... 248-645-3300 223 A
LEWIS-JASPER, Vera ..... 409-944-1496 437 B
vlewis@gc.edu
LEWIS-SEVILLA, Nadine 305-474-6871 106 F
nlewis-sevilla@stu.edu
LEWLESS, Scott .... 989-686-9042 223 G
scottlewless@delta.edu
LEWTER, John, A .... 731-881-7710 428 B
jlewter@utm.edu
LEY, David .... 907-745-3201.... 9 B
dley@akbible.edu
LEY-SOTO, Javier .... 305-237-3694 103 D
jleysoto@mdc.edu
LEYBA, John .... 706-864-1958 126 A
john.leyba@ung.edu
LEYBA-FRANK, Marylou 415-239-3291.. 37 A
mleyba@ccsf.edu
LEYBA RUIZ, Teresa ..... 623-845-3010.. 13 C
president@gccaz.edu
LEYKAM, Scott, R .... 503-943-8420 377 E
leykam@up.edu
LEYVA-PUEBLA,
Ricardo .... 206-934-3890 484 A
ricardo.leyvapuebla@seattlecolleges.edu
LEZAK JANOW,
Roseann .... 860-509-9501.. 87 B
rlezak@hartsem.edu
LE'I, Emilia .... 684-699-9155 505 A
e.lei@amsamoa.edu
LI, Brian .... 612-343-4745 242 H
bdli@northcentral.edu
LI, Dai .... 602-235-4179 176 F
dli@pittstate.edu
LI, Haipeng .... 209-228-2579.. 69 B
hli58@ucmerced.edu
LI, Holly .... 815-479-7573 143 A
hli82@mchenry.edu
LI, Joanne .... 305-348-2751 109 A
joli@fiu.edu
LI, Kevin .... 708-456-0300 150 I
kevinli@triton.edu
LI, King .... 217-300-2424 151 D
kingli@illinois.edu
LI, Kuiyuan .... 850-473-7716 110 E
kli@uwf.edu
LI, Ming .... 269-387-2966 232 K
ming.li@wmich.edu
LI, Peter .... 361-593-4340 447 D
peter.li@tamuk.edu
LI, Rui .... 610-430-4959 396 A
rli@wcupa.edu
LI, Sharon, F .... 415-422-2790.. 71 K
lis@usfca.edu
LI, Suling .... 815-836-5878 141 G
lisu@lewisu.edu
LI, Xiaofan .... 312-567-3135 139 B
lix@iit.edu
LI, Xiaohong .... 661-763-7978.. 66 J
xli@taftcollege.edu
LI, Xun .... 954-776-4476 102 A
xli@keiseruniversity.edu
LI, Yi .... 212-237-8801 294 D
yili@jjay.cuny.edu

LI, Yongmei .... 864-596-9752 409 B
yongmei.li@converse.edu
LI, Zhan .... 203-254-4070.. 86 I
zli2@fairfield.edu
LI-BUGG, Cherry .... 714-808-4787.. 53 J
clibugg@nocccd.edu
LI-ROSI, AnaMaria .... 239-280-7398.. 94 O
anamaria.lirosi@avemaria.edu
LIANG, Heng .... 707-621-7000.. 41 F
LIANG, John Paul .... 713-780-9777 430 C
jpliang@acaom.edu
LIANG, Mark .... 714-564-6040.. 57 L
liang_mark@sac.edu
LIANG, Sherry .... 510-628-8027.. 48 A
sliang@lincolnuca.edu
LIAO, Min-Ken .... 864-294-2248 410 A
minken.liao@furman.edu
LIAUTAUD, Danielle ...... 973-720-2121 284 I
liautaudd@wpunj.edu
LIBBY, Betsy .... 207-755-5250 194 G
blibby@cmcc.edu
LIBBY, John .... 240-567-7951 200 C
john.libby@montgomerycollege.edu
LIBBY, Wendy, B .... 386-822-7250 111 A
wlibby@stetson.edu
LIBENGOOD, Desiree .... 612-343-4796 242 H
dslibeng@northcentral.edu
LIBERATI, Dennis .... 267-295-2314 397 F
dliberati@walnuthillcollege.edu
LIBERATORI, Ellen, A ... 607-746-4612 320 G
liberaem@delhi.edu
LIBERATOSCIOLI,
Daniel .... 267-295-2316 397 F
president@walnuthillcollege.edu
LIBERATOSCIOLI,
Peggy .... 267-295-2325 397 F
pl@walnuthillcollege.edu
LIBERATOSCIOLI,
Peggy .... 267-295-2315 397 F
pl@walnuthillcollege.edu
LIBERMAN, Ira .... 718-438-1002 306 G
yliberman@yeshivanet.com
LIBERONA, Ann .... 215-242-7989 381 D
liberonaa@chc.edu
LIBERTO, Salvadore, A . 617-873-0167 207 F
salvadore.liberto@cambridgecollege.edu
LIBERTO, Terri .... 412-536-1813 387 B
terri.liberto@laroche.edu
LIBERTY, Bob .... 254-526-1310 432 H
bob.liberty@ctcd.edu
LIBERTY, Cynthia .... 336-770-3333 343 D
libertyc@uncsa.edu
LIBERTY, Paul .... 703-993-8860 467 L
pliberty@gmu.edu
LIBET, Alice, Q .... 843-792-4930 410 F
libeta@musc.edu
LIBHART, Bonnie .... 423-775-6596 423 F
drbonnie@me.com
LIBOLT, Kay .... 707-826-3311.. 33 D
kay.libolt@humboldt.edu
LIBUNAO, Arte .... 949-783-4800.. 73 K
alibunao@westcoastuniversity.edu
LIBUTTI, Dean .... 401-874-4405 406 B
deanlibutti@uri.edu
LIBUTTI, Ken .... 561-868-3239 104 D
libuttik@palmbeachstate.edu
LIBUTTI, Steven, K .... 732-235-8064 282 A
steven.libutti@cinj.rutgers.edu
LICARI, Frank .... 702-990-4433 272 C
flicari@roseman.edu
LICARI, Michael, J .... 812-237-2309 155 G
mike.licari@indstate.edu
LICATA, Betty Jo .... 330-941-3064 365 C
bjlicata@ysu.edu
LICATA, Christine, M .... 585-475-2953 313 A
cmlnbt@rit.edu
LICATA, Christine, M .... 585-475-6399 313 A
cmlnbt@rit.edu
LICHT, Daniel .... 914-395-2301 315 F
dlicht@sarahlawrence.edu
LICHT, Jodi, N .... 212-752-1530 304 D
jodi.licht@limcollege.edu
LICHT, William .... 920-206-2320 493 L
william.licht@mbu.edu
LICHTBLAU, Jobey .... 710-231-7672 345 G
jobey.lichtblau@ndsu.edu
LICHTENBERG, Anne, V 859-257-5068 185 B
anne.lichtenberg@uky.edu
LICHTENSTEIN, Mark .... 315-470-4748 320 A
malichte@esf.edu
LICHTI, Benjamin .... 316-284-5349 171 F
blichti@bethelks.edu

LINDGREN, Dianne 828-339-4269 338 B diannel@southwesterncc.edu
LINDGREN, Rita 701-224-5427 346 B rita.lindgren@bismarckstate.edu
LINDGREN, Robert, R 804-752-7211 470 F rlindgren@rmc.edu
LINDGREN, Teresa, C 606-783-2449 183 F t.lindgren@moreheadstate.edu
LINDLEY, Carolyn, V 847-491-8557 145 F c-lindley@northwestern.edu
LINDLEY, Holly 650-433-3881.. 55 G hlindley@paloaltou.edu
LINDLEY, Kelli 208-467-8825 131 D klindley@nnu.edu
LINDLEY, Kendall 208-732-6204 130 E klindley@csi.edu
LINDLEY, Korey 714-484-7464.. 53 K klindley@cypresscollege.edu
LINDLEY, Lori 814-871-7522 384 E lindley001@gannon.edu
LINDMARK, Elaine 949-872-2224.. 29 D
LINDNER, Angela 352-273-1102 109 F alindner@aa.ufl.edu
LINDNER, Bill 850-644-7572 109 C blindner@fsu.edu
LINDNER, Janet 203-432-2188.. 89 D janet.lindner@yale.edu
LINDO, Patricia 860-512-3613.. 85 G plindo@manchestercc.edu
LINDOERFER, Brian 303-735-0716.. 83 A brian.lindoerfer@colorado.edu
LINDON, Jennifer 606-487-3100 181 C jennifer.lindon@kctcs.edu
LINDOW, Claudio 718-262-5337 295 F clindow@york.cuny.edu
LINDOW, Tracy 901-722-3230 424 C tlindow@sco.edu
LINDQUIST, Brent 806-742-2566 451 B brent.lindquist@ttu.edu
LINDQUIST, Cynthia, A 701-766-4055 345 A president@littlehoop.edu
LINDQUIST, Joyce 970-207-4500.. 84 B joycel@uscareerinstitute.edu
LINDQUIST, Joyce 970-207-4550.. 80 M joycel@mckinleycollege.edu
LINDQUIST, Kelsey 510-436-1245.. 45 D lindquist@hnu.edu
LINDQUIST, Kimberly 734-384-4101 227 G klindquist@monroeccc.edu
LINDQUIST, Robert 256-824-2882.... 8 B robert.lindquist@uah.edu
LINDQUIST, Robert 256-824-6100.... 8 B robert.lindquist@uah.edu
LINDQUIST, Vern, L 217-786-2885 142 B vern.lindquist@llcc.edu
LINDSAY, Caryn 270-745-2571 185 E caryn.lyndsey@wku.edu
LINDSAY, Charles, W 607-735-1790 299 D clindsay@elmira.edu
LINDSAY, D. Michael 978-867-4800 209 F president@gordon.edu
LINDSAY, Dawn, S 410-777-1177 197 C dslindsay@aacc.edu
LINDSAY, Dennis 541-684-7253 374 G dlindsay@nwcu.edu
LINDSAY, Haley 620-450-2169 176 G haleyl@prattcc.edu
LINDSAY, Jonathan 603-623-0313 273 I jonathanlindsay@nhia.edu
LINDSAY, Kristen 419-559-2350 361 I klindsay01@terra.edu
LINDSAY, Nathan 406-243-4689 264 A nathan.lindsay@umontana.edu
LINDSAY, Shawn 417-626-1234 257 F lindsay.shawn@occ.edu
LINDSAY, Terry 518-327-6490 311 G tlindsay@paulsmiths.edu
LINDSAY, Thomas 312-553-5600 134 B
LINDSAY, Timika 410-293-1881 504 I
LINDSETH, Lori 602-787-7102.. 13 E lori.lindseth@paradisevalley.edu
LINDSETH, Paul 701-777-2791 345 C lindseth@aero.und.edu
LINDSEY, Beverly 662-846-4021 245 H blindsey@deltastate.edu
LINDSEY, Chuck 239-590-7168 108 K clindsey@fgcu.edu
LINDSEY, Connie 773-947-6300 142 J clindsey@mccormick.edu
LINDSEY, Dana 352-395-4409 107 A dana.lindsey@sfcollege.edu
LINDSEY, Heidie 337-482-6272 192 E hlindsey@louisiana.edu
LINDSEY, Jill 540-545-7324 471 E jlindsey@su.edu
LINDSEY, Jonathan 602-274-1885.. 15 B jlindsey@pihma.edu
LINDSEY, Jordan 503-375-7156 373 A jlindsey@corban.edu
LINDSEY, Melissa 320-308-5377 241 A mlindsey@sctcc.edu
LINDSEY, Pam 217-420-6774 143 H plindsey@millikin.edu
LINDSEY, Patrick, O 313-577-4228 232 I patrick.lindsey@wayne.edu
LINDSEY, Shannon 785-628-4462 173 B sdlindsey@fhsu.edu
LINDSEY, Steve 602-557-7537.. 16 J steve.lindsey@phoenix.edu
LINDSEY, Terryl 918-293-4730 368 D terryl.lindsey@okstate.edu
LINDSEY, Valarie 773-252-5318 147 B valarie.lindsey@resu.edu
LINDSEY, Victor 434-381-6346 472 D vlindsey@sbc.edu
LINDSKOOG, Marie 765-455-9468 156 D mlindsk@iuk.edu
LINDSTAEDT, William 415-502-2422.. 69 E bill.lindstaedt@ucsf.edu
LINDSTEDT, John 508-856-2198 212 A john.lindstedt@umassmed.edu
LINDSTEDT, Monique 815-394-4376 147 G mlindstedt@rockford.edu
LINDSTROM, Chris 207-581-1640 195 J chris.lindstrom@maine.edu
LINDSTROM, David 509-527-2664 485 H david.lindstrom@wallawalla.edu
LINDSTROM, Derrick 612-659-6030 238 I derrick.lindstrom@minneapolis.edu
LINDSTROM, Lauren 530-752-4663.. 68 E lelindstrom@ucdavis.edu
LINDSTROM, Lynne 563-884-5313 168 I lynne.lindstrom@palmer.edu
LINDSTROM, Peter 303-352-6785.. 79 E peter.lindstrom@ccd.edu
LINDSTROM, Richard, W 323-563-5832.. 36 D richardlindstrom@cdrewu.edu
LINDSTROM, Ryan 801-863-8303 461 A lindstry@uvu.edu
LINDSTROM, Yvonne 313-578-0328 231 B lindstym@udmercy.edu
LINDZEY, Jonathan 570-484-2204 395 B jlindzey@lockhaven.edu
LINE, Josh 740-389-4636 356 B linej@mtc.edu
LINEBACH, Jared 706-233-7294 124 B jlinebach@shorter.edu
LINEBACK, Carla 802-258-3266 463 C carla.lineback@worldlearning.org
LINEBAUGH, Donald 301-405-6309 202 C dwline@umd.edu
LINEBERGER, Susanne, B 386-312-4050 106 C susannelineberger@sjrstate.edu
LINEBERRY, Gene, T 859-323-6630 185 B gt.lineberry@uky.edu
LINEBURG, Robert 540-831-5228 470 C rlineburg@radford.edu
LINEGAR, Malinda 308-432-6399 268 E mlinegar@csc.edu
LINEHAN, Rob 765-998-4905 160 F rblinehan@taylor.edu
LINEHAN, Sarah, J 518-743-2263 320 D linehans@sunyacc.edu
LINEHAN, Stephen 781-899-5500 218 A rev.linehan@psjs.edu
LINENBERG, Harry 305-237-7469 103 D hlinenbe@mdc.edu
LINENBURG, Savannah, C 812-888-4354 162 C slinenburg@vinu.edu
LINFANTE, Patrick 973-761-9328 283 B patrick.linfante@shu.edu
LINFOOT, Rose 585-245-5596 318 E andersonr@geneseo.edu
LINFORD, Jon, F 208-496-1123 130 A linfordj@byui.edu
LINGEN, Scott 701-224-5441 346 B scott.lingen@bismarckstate.edu
LINGER, Frederick, S 740-427-5250 355 E lingerf@kenyon.edu
LINGER, Roberta 304-336-8990 490 F roberta.linger@westliberty.edu
LINGLE, Earl, W 336-841-9552 329 G elingle@highpoint.edu
LINGLE, Richard 816-279-7000 250 B richard.lingle@abtu.edu
LINGNER, Jackie 321-674-8053.. 99 B jlingner@fit.edu
LINGO, Amy 502-852-6411 185 C amy.lingo@louisville.edu
LINGRELL, Scot 912-478-1863 119 C slingrell@georgiasouthern.edu
LINGROSSO, Samuel 805-378-1443.. 72 H slingrosso@vcccd.edu
LINGUA, Jane 310-954-4132.. 52 G jlingua@msmu.edu
LINHART, Steve 719-255-3838.. 83 B slinhart@uccs.edu
LINK, Christine, A 626-914-8821.. 36 K clink@citruscollege.edu
LINK, Harvey 701-671-2112 346 E harvey.link@ndscs.edu
LINK, Heather 216-687-7359 351 B heather.link@csuohio.edu
LINK, Hilary, L 814-332-5380 378 D hlink@allegheny.edu
LINK, John 314-968-6982 262 C johnlink24@webster.edu
LINK, Laura 612-874-3700 236 K llink@mcad.edu
LINK, Lisa 616-222-1426 222 I lisa.link@cornerstone.edu
LINK, Robert 419-434-4528 363 A link@findlay.edu
LINK, Stephen 202-687-1747.. 92 A spl8@georgetown.edu
LINK, Terri 419-289-4142 348 A tlink@ashland.edu
LINKER, Kari 970-542-3113.. 81 A kari.linker@morgancc.edu
LINKER, Maureen 313-593-5445 231 F mlinker@umich.edu
LINKHAUER, SC, Vivien 724-830-1052 398 H linkhauer@setonhill.edu
LINKS, Jonathan 410-516-6880 199 D jlinks1@jhu.edu
LINMAN, Eric 503-255-0332 374 D elinman@multnomah.edu
LINN, Joseph, G 785-628-4277 173 B jlinn@fhsu.edu
LINN, Richard, T 716-827-3451 323 D linnr@trocaire.edu
LINN-ADDISON, Margaret 303-964-3657.. 82 E mlinnaddison@regis.edu
LINNANE, SJ, Brian, F 410-617-2201 199 F president@loyola.edu
LINNELL, Michael 701-858-3065 345 F michael.linnell@minotstateu.edu
LINNEMAN, Scott 360-650-7207 486 F scott.linneman@wwu.edu
LINNEVERS, David 510-592-9688.. 54 C david.linnevers@npu.edu
LINNEWEBER, Travis, W 765-658-4175 154 F travislinneweber@depauw.edu
LINNEY, Vincent 828-726-2471 332 G vlinney@cccti.edu
LINO, Paulette 510-723-2665.. 35 O plino@chabotcollege.edu
LINSENMEYER, Machelle 304-793-6871 491 A alinsenmeyer@osteo.wvsom.edu
LINSEY, Carolyn, R 203-576-2374.. 88 D clinsey@bridgeport.edu
LINSEY, Troy 678-513-5202 121 B tlinsey@laniertech.edu
LINSON, Marci 417-690-2636 251 E linson@cofo.edu
LINSON, Robert 202-885-6013.. 90 J rlinson@american.edu
LINSTER, Michelle 336-517-2155 327 B mlinster@bennett.edu
LINSTRA, Ralph 434-582-2330 468 H rlinstra@liberty.edu
LINTHICUM, Glen 615-248-1243 427 A glinthicum@trevecca.edu
LINTNER, Tim 803-641-3564 413 D tlintner@usca.edu
LINTON, Greg 865-573-4517 420 G glinton@johnsonu.edu
LINTON, Jill 814-732-1346 394 F jlinton@edinboro.edu
LINTON, Peggy 334-493-3573.... 2 I plinton@lbwcc.edu
LINTON, Richard, H 919-515-2668 342 B richard_linton@ncsu.edu
LINVILLE, Joe 304-896-7366 489 E joe.linville@southernwv.edu
LINZEY, Scott 912-525-5000 123 G slinzey@scad.edu
LINZMEYER, Kathryn 510-723-6751.. 35 O klinzmeyer@chabotcollege.edu
LION, Ben, C 407-582-1388 112 K blion@valenciacollege.edu
LION, Benjamin 314-392-2211 256 C benjamin.lion@mobap.edu
LIOSATOS, Alexandra 920-565-1527 493 J liosatosa@lakeland.edu
LIOTTA, Robert 301-295-9172 504 B robert.liotta@usuhs.edu
LIOTTA, Sheila, A 401-865-2600 405 B sadamus@providence.edu
LIPAN, Petruta 314-977-3571 259 H petruta.lipan@slu.edu
LIPE, Kaiwipuni 808-956-2697 128 F kaiwipun@hawaii.edu
LIPFORD, Michael 662-846-4667 245 H mlipford@deltastate.edu
LIPHART, Jodi 904-826-0084.. 71 H jliphart@usa.edu
LIPHART, Kristin 920-693-1854 499 G kristin.liphart@gotoltc.edu
LIPINSKI, Tomas 414-229-4709 497 A tlipinski@uwm.edu
LIPITZ, Jon 410-225-2516 199 H jlipitz@mica.edu
LIPIZ GONZALEZ, Elaine 714-992-7088.. 53 L elipizgonzalez@fullcoll.edu
LIPMAN, Elizabeth, D 610-799-1165 388 I elipman@lccc.edu
LIPMAN, Howard 305-348-6298 109 A howard.lipman@fiu.edu
LIPNITZKY, April, M 815-282-7900 148 C aprillipnitzky@sacn.edu
LIPP, Evan, E 978-232-2005 209 B elipp@endicott.edu
LIPP, Jacob 713-226-5585 453 B lippp@uhd.edu
LIPPARD, Jed 212-875-4422 290 F jlippard@bankstreet.edu
LIPPARD, Rodney 803-641-3460 413 D rodneyl@usca.edu
LIPPE, Diane 954-262-4932 103 M lipped@nova.edu
LIPPENS, Susan 419-720-6670 360 F susan.lippens@proskills.edu
LIPPERT, Patricia, A 812-488-2152 161 A pl23@evansville.edu
LIPPERT, Rebecca 215-702-4353 380 D blippert@cairn.edu
LIPPERT, Robert 559-453-2189.. 43 G robert.lippert@fresno.edu
LIPPIELLO, Steve 724-925-4071 403 A lippiellos@westmoreland.edu
LIPPMAN, Fred 954-262-1508 103 M flippman@nsu.nova.edu
LIPPMAN, Stuart 646-565-6000 322 J stuart.lippman@touro.edu
LIPPMANN, Ryan 714-484-7194.. 53 K rlippmann@cypresscollege.edu
LIPSCOMB, Benjamin 585-567-9374 302 D benjamin.lipscomb@houghton.edu
LIPSCOMB, Kevin 434-791-7273 464 O klipscomb@averett.edu
LIPSCOMB, Natasha 704-216-3622 337 F natasha.lipscomb@rccc.edu
LIPSCOMB, Sharyon 225-578-8833 188 H slipsc1@lsu.edu
LIPSCOMB, Tom 336-517-2304 327 B tlipscomb@bennett.edu
LIPSETT, Teresa 787-743-7979 511 I ut_tlipsett@suagm.edu
LIPSHITZ, Rita 773-973-0241 138 A lipshitz@htc.edu
LIPSKIER, Hershel 973-267-9404 280 G info@rca.edu
LIPSTREU, Tiffany 614-823-1414 360 A tlipstreu@otterbein.edu
LIPTAK, Kathy 304-384-6303 490 A liptakka@concord.edu
LIQUET, Antoinette 212-752-1530 304 D antoinette.liquet@limcollege.edu
LIRA, Ken 949-451-5435.. 64 F klira@ivc.edu
LIRLEY, Sean 719-336-1543.. 80 K sean.lirley@lamarcc.edu
LISCHIN, Renee 973-408-3955 277 C rlischin@drew.edu

LISCHKE, Douglas, E .... 434-982-3485 473 A
del8s@virginia.edu

LISCHWE, Sheila, T ...... 864-656-1661 408 A
slischw@clemson.edu

LISCIO, Gina .... 315-792-7288 321 E
gina.liscio@sunypoly.edu

LISEA, Scott .... 805-565-6210.. 74 K
slisea@westmont.edu

LISK, Patti .... 540-423-9824 474 G
plisk@germanna.edu

LISLE, Kristy .... 650-949-7209.. 43 D
lislekristy@foothill.edu

LISLE, Tara .... 432-264-5646 438 C
tlisle@howardcollege.edu

LISNER, Lydia .... 804-627-5300 465 C
lydia_lisner@bshsi.org

LISS, Donna .... 660-785-4163 260 J
dliss@truman.edu

LISS, Joshua .... 267-341-3100 386 A
jliss@holyfamily.edu

LISS, Katrina .... 618-664-7014 137 G
katrina.liss@greenville.edu

LISS, Ron .... 928-717-7778.. 16 M
ron.liss@yc.edu

LISS, Tony .... 212-650-8261 293 D
tliss@ccny.cuny.edu

LIST, Allison .... 631-687-5198 314 C
alist@sjcny.edu

LIST, Edith .... 618-374-5147 146 E
edith.list@principia.edu

LISTAU, Lynsey .... 850-484-2128 104 H
llistau@pensacolastate.edu

LISTER, Basil .... 816-604-4206 255 I
basil.lister@mcckc.edu

LISTER, Tommy .... 626-584-5338.. 43 H
tommylister@fuller.edu

LISTI, Garnette .... 504-762-3032 187 E
glisti@dcc.edu

LISTON, Brenda .... 614-947-6532 353 C
brenda.liston@franklin.edu

LISTON, Jed .... 406-243-5211 264 A
jed.liston@umontana.edu

LISTWAK, Jeffrey, A ...... 412-397-5263 397 G
listwak@rmu.edu

LISZKA, Justin .... 336-272-7102 329 D
justin.liszka@greensboro.edu

LITANT, Josiah .... 507-453-1420 239 A
josiah.litant@southeastmn.edu

LITCHFIELD, Brad .... 609-896-5001 281 B
blitchfield@rider.edu

LITCHFIELD, Charles ..... 719-255-3678.. 83 B
clitchfi@uccs.edu

LITCHMAN, Jennifer, B . 410-706-3477 202 D
jlitchman@umaryland.edu

LITHERLAND, Steve, E .. 757-822-1944 476 B
slitherland@tcc.edu

LITKE, Russ .... 419-995-8342 354 H
litke.r@rhodeesstate.edu

LITMAN, Kay .... 610-372-4721 397 B
klitman@racc.edu

LITOLFF, Edwin .... 225-342-6950 191 D
edwin.litolff@ulsystem.edu

LITSITSA, Anna .... 650-433-3807.. 55 G
alitsitsa@paloaltou.edu

LITT, Eleni .... 212-229-8947 308 C
litte@newschool.edu

LITT, Jacquelyn, S .... 848-932-3047 282 A
jlitt@echo.rutgers.edu

LITTEN, Joyce .... 419-824-3708 355 K
jlitten@lourdes.edu

LITTERAL, Dan .... 602-557-1616.. 16 J
dan.litteral@phoenix.edu

LITTERAL, David .... 606-783-2000 183 F
d.litteral@moreheadstate.edu

LITTERAL, David, J .... 606-783-2000 183 F
d.litteral@moreheadstate.edu

LITTERAL, Samuel, M ... 304-896-7426 489 E
samuel.litteral@southernwv.edu

LITTKY, Dennis .... 401-752-2640 404 G
LITTLE, Albert .... 904-632-5167 100 B
al.little@fscj.edu

LITTLE, Andrew, P .... 410-777-2227 197 C
aplittle1@aacc.edu

LITTLE, Chris .... 530-895-4047.. 27 F
littlech@butte.edu

LITTLE, Christopher ...... 765-983-1400 154 G
littlech@earlham.edu

LITTLE, Crystal .... 619-594-5901.. 33 E
little@sdsu.edu

LITTLE, Glenn, W .... 863-784-7218 107 F
glenn.little@southflorida.edu

LITTLE, Janie, D .... 330-672-4050 354 J
sdlittle@kent.edu

LITTLE, Jennifer .... 864-592-4808 412 F
littlej@sccsc.edu

LITTLE, Kevin, K .... 831-656-2508 503 K
kllittle@nps.edu

LITTLE, Lara .... 704-463-3353 339 E
lara.little@pfeiffer.edu

LITTLE, Laura .... 570-702-8946 386 G
llittle@johnson.edu

LITTLE, Leeann .... 918-335-6234 368 G
llittle@okwu.edu

LITTLE, Michael .... 678-466-4477 116 E
michaellittle@clayton.edu

LITTLE, Pamela .... 256-551-1711.... 2 E
pamela.little@drakestate.edu

LITTLE, Rebecca, K .... 812-888-4220 162 C
rlittle@vinu.edu

LITTLE, Scott .... 601-968-5956 245 C
slittle@belhaven.edu

LITTLE, Sylvester .... 863-292-3762 105 A
slittle@polk.edu

LITTLE, Tony .... 310-243-3301.. 31 B
adlittle@csudh.edu

LITTLE-STOETZEL,
Sharon .... 816-833-0524 165 H
stoetzel@graceland.edu

LITTLE WHITEMAN,
Iona .... 701-627-4738 346 G
ilittl@nhsc.edu

LITTLEBEAR, Richard ..... 406-477-6215 263 D
rlbear@cdkc.edu

LITTLEFIELD,
Elizabeth, S .... 804-523-5181 474 H
blittlefield@reynolds.edu

LITTLEFOX, Allie .... 510-430-2232.. 52 D
afox@mills.edu

LITTLEJOHN, Dee .... 214-887-5006 436 B
dlittlejohn@dts.edu

LITTLEJOHN, Quincina .. 973-748-9000 276 A
quincina_littlejohn@bloomfield.edu

LITTLEJOHN, Sylvia ...... 803-738-7764 410 G
littlejohns@midlandstech.edu

LITTLES, Kathy .... 925-631-4000.. 59 B
LITTLETON, Robert, A ... 423-652-6022 420 H
ralittle@king.edu

LITTLETON STEIB,
Larissa .... 504-762-3000 187 E
llsteib@dcc.edu

LITTMAN, Cheryl .... 718-997-2805 295 C
cheryl.littman@qc.cuny.edu

LITTMAN, Jared, E .... 718-990-2920 314 B
littmanj@stjohns.edu

LITTON, Fred .... 361-570-4261 453 C
littonf@uhv.edu

LITTRELL, Beth .... 402-461-7372 267 D
blittrell@hastings.edu

LITTRELL, Johnny .... 931-540-2840 424 G
jlittrell@columbiastate.edu

LITTRELL, Meghann ...... 513-244-4524 357 A
meghann.littrell@msj.edu

LITVACK, Steven, B .... 201-489-5836 278 D
LITWACK, Kim .... 414-229-4189 497 A
litwack@uwm.edu

LITWILLER, Hannah ...... 620-241-0723 172 D
hannah.litwiller@centralchristian.edu

LITWIN, Daveen, H .... 603-646-3780 273 E
daveen.h.litwin@dartmouth.edu

LITZ, Kerri .... 410-225-2277 199 H
klitz@mica.edu

LITZIN, Louise .... 928-724-6633.. 12 C
louise@dinecollege.edu

LIU, Bei .... 408-733-1878.. 70 C
bei.liu@uewm.edu

LIU, Chris .... 657-278-8205.. 31 E
cyliu@fullerton.edu

LIU, Fengshan .... 302-857-6646.. 89 F
fliu@desu.edu

LIU, Frank .... 626-917-9482.. 36 H
frankliu@cesna.edu

LIU, John .... 315-443-2492 322 C
johnliu@syr.edu

LIU, Jun .... 631-632-7653 317 D
jun.liu@stonybrook.edu

LIU, Keming .... 718-270-4951 295 A
kliu@mec.cuny.edu

LIU, Monika .... 415-452-5730.. 37 A
mliu@ccsf.edu

LIU, Patrick .... 218-755-4096 237 E
patrick.liu@bemidjistate.edu

LIU, Samuel .... 626-571-5110.. 48 B
samuelliu@les.edu

LIU, Shuang .... 410-337-6062 198 G
shuang.liu@goucher.edu

LIU, Susan .... 626-448-0023.. 46 G

LIU, Yuxiang .... 212-960-5400 326 E
yuxiang.liu@yu.edu

LIU, Yuxing .... 512-454-1188 430 G
info@aoma.edu

LIVELY, Alisa .... 304-473-8441 491 H
lively_a@wvwc.edu

LIVELY, Amanda .... 478-538-3160 124 F
alively@southeasterntech.edu

LIVELY, David .... 847-491-2094 145 F
david.lively@northwestern.edu

LIVELY, Jason .... 636-949-4696 254 F
jlively@lindenwood.edu

LIVELY, Kathryn, J .... 603-646-3113 273 E
kathryn.j.lively@dartmouth.edu

LIVELY, Shane .... 203-596-8507.. 87 F
slively@post.edu

LIVENGOOD, Naomi ..... 269-965-3931 225 F
livengoodn@kellogg.edu

LIVERMAN, Deborah, L . 617-715-5329 215 G
LIVERPOOL, Patrick, R .. 919-530-6230 342 A
pliverpool@nccu.edu

LIVERS, Regina .... 513-569-5735 350 K
regina.livers@cincinnatistate.edu

LIVESAY, Dennis .... 316-978-6513 178 A
dennis.livesay@wichita.edu

LIVESAY, Stephen, D .... 423-775-7201 418 H
livesast@bryan.edu

LIVINGOOD,
Susannah, B .... 405-325-5065 371 B
slivingood@ou.edu

LIVINGSTON, Carolyn ... 507-222-4248 234 F
clivingston@carleton.edu

LIVINGSTON, David, J .. 815-836-5230 141 G
dlivingston@lewisu.edu

LIVINGSTON, Esther ...... 859-985-3065 179 C
livginstone@berea.edu

LIVINGSTON, Jane .... 850-644-2525 109 C
jane.livingston@fsu.edu

LIVINGSTON, Lynette .... 715-858-1849 499 D
livingston3@cvtc.edu

LIVINGSTON, Mike .... 281-283-2976 453 A
livingston@uhcl.edu

LIVINGSTON, Omar .... 432-552-2629 457 A
livingston_o@utpb.edu

LIVINGSTON, Omar .... 203-332-5049.. 85 F
olivingston@housatonic.edu

LIVINGSTON, Randy ...... 650-724-0213.. 65 J
livingston@stanford.edu

LIVINGSTON, Shannon . 715-675-3331 500 E
livingst@ntc.edu

LIVINGSTON, Stan .... 601-477-4006 246 F
stan.livingston@jcjc.edu

LIVINGSTON, Tina .... 903-886-5667 447 B
tina.livingston@tamuc.edu

LIVINGSTONE, Linda, A 254-710-3555 431 J
linda_livingstone@baylor.edu

LIVIO, Michael, D .... 609-497-7805 280 D
michael.livio@ptsem.edu

LIVORNO, Charles .... 317-632-5553 158 S
clivorno@lincolntech.edu

LIZAN, Rey .... 757-490-1241 464 F
rlizan@auto.edu

LIZER, Shannon, K .... 815-282-7900 148 C
shannonlizer@sacn.edu

LJUBENKO, Bojan .... 920-924-3229 500 C
bljubenko@morainepark.edu

LJUTIC, Peter .... 718-270-8650 317 E
peter.ljutic@downstate.edu

LLAMAS, Jennifer, C ..... 209-476-7840.. 66 G
jllamas@clc.edu

LLANOS, Angela .... 239-304-7096.. 94 O
angela.llanos@avemaria.edu

LLANOS, Keren .... 787-620-2040 506 C
kllanos@aupr.edu

LLERANDI, Joanne, A ... 718-990-1487 314 B
llerandj@stjohns.edu

LLERANDI, Mariel .... 787-878-5475 508 L
mllerandi@arecibo.inter.edu

LLERENA, Luis .... 305-273-4499.. 96 L
luis@cbt.edu

LLERENA, Monica .... 305-273-4499.. 96 L
monica@cbt.edu

LLEWELLYN, Nada`, M . 718-990-6334 314 B
llewelln@stjohns.edu

LLOPIZ, Maria .... 773-481-8323 134 G
mllopiz@ccc.edu

LLORENS, Ashley, J ...... 410-955-5107 199 D
ashley.llorens@jhuapl.edu

LLORENS, James .... 239-590-7000 108 K
jllorens@fgcu.edu

LLORENS, Jared .... 225-578-0936 188 I
jared1@lsu.edu

LLOSA, Talia .... 845-341-4090 311 C
talia.llosa@sunyorange.edu

LLOSA, Tulio .... 217-206-7755 151 C
tllos1@uis.edu

LLOVIO, Kay .... 916-577-2200.. 75 B
kllovio@jessup.edu

LLOYD, Alicia .... 616-632-2455 221 C
aal006@aquinas.edu

LLOYD, Betsy .... 910-592-8081 337 G
blloyd@sampsoncc.edu

LLOYD, Brent .... 608-263-3045 496 C
brent.lloyd@wisc.edu

LLOYD, Celia, P .... 212-650-7859 293 D
clloyd@ccny.cuny.edu

LLOYD, Charles .... 603-752-1113 273 D
clloyd@ccsnh.edu

LLOYD, Charmaine, R ... 203-392-5250.. 85 A
lloydc1@southernct.edu

LLOYD, Chris .... 215-702-4339 380 D
clloyd@cairn.edu

LLOYD, Curtis .... 518-320-1192 316 C
curtis.lloyd@suny.edu

LLOYD, David .... 765-998-4634 160 F
dvlloyd@taylor.edu

LLOYD, Giovina .... 607-871-2966 289 H
lloydgm@alfred.edu

LLOYD, Gweneth .... 845-257-2920 317 B
lloydg@newpaltz.edu

LLOYD, James .... 513-244-8435 350 I
james.lloyd@ccuniversity.edu

LLOYD, Jan .... 407-708-2144 107 D
lloydj@seminolestate.edu

LLOYD, Jayson .... 208-732-6547 130 E
jlloyd@csi.edu

LLOYD, Leslie, M .... 252-638-7367 333 H
lloydl@cravencc.edu

LLOYD, Lisa .... 512-245-2121 450 E
ll12@txstate.edu

LLOYD, Mary, J .... 815-599-3418 138 B
mary.lloyd@highland.edu

LLOYD, Michael .... 501-450-3117.. 23 H
mlloyd3@uca.edu

LLOYD, Patrick, M .... 614-292-9755 358 I
lloyd.256@osu.edu

LLOYD, Rachel .... 918-540-6971 366 I
rlloyd@neo.edu

LLOYD, Richard .... 402-481-8781 265 K
rich.lloyd@bryanhealthcollege.edu

LLOYD, Robert .... 561-803-2252 104 C
robert_lloyd@pba.edu

LLOYD, Rodie, F .... 207-725-3963 193 D
rlloyd@bowdoin.edu

LLOYD, Scott .... 513-244-4351 357 A
scott.lloyd@msj.edu

LLOYD, Steve .... 706-864-1445 126 A
steve.lloyd@ung.edu

LLOYD-DENNIS, Diann . 617-217-9216 206 A
dlloyddennis@baystate.edu

LLYWELYN, SJ, Dorian . 408-551-1951.. 62 D
dllywelyn@scu.edu

LO, Angie .... 888-488-4968.. 46 F
alo@itu.edu

LO, Christina, T .... 617-253-1747 215 G
LO LEE, Mai .... 920-465-2021 496 E
lom@uwgb.edu

LO MONACO, Bethany .. 978-837-5616 216 D
lomonacob@merrimack.edu

LO RE, Mary .... 212-742-8770 322 J
mary.lo-re@touro.edu

LOAFMAN, Lucas .... 254-519-5724 447 A
loafman@tamuct.edu

LOAIZA, Rodrigo .... 305-821-3333.. 99 E
rloaiza@fnu.edu

LOBASSO, Lisa, M .... 570-941-7459 401 H
lisa.lobasso@scranton.edu

LOBASSO, Thomas .... 386-506-3200.. 97 D
thomas.lobasso@daytonastate.edu

LOBATO, Richard, L ...... 915-831-7810 436 E
rlobato@epcc.edu

LOBB, Monty .... 740-474-8896 358 F
mlobb@ohiochristian.edu

LOBB, William, K .... 414-288-7485 494 B
william.lobb@marquette.edu

LOBBAN-VIRAVONG,
Heather .... 610-409-3000 402 A
hlobbanviravong@ursinus.edu

LOBDELL, Keri .... 509-542-4422 479 H
klobdell@columbiabasin.edu

LOBDELL, Stephanie ..... 740-392-6868 357 B
stephanie.lobdell@mvnu.edu

LOBERG, Lisa .... 310-338-1973.. 50 J
lisa.loberg@lmu.edu

LOBERTINI, Jo .... 423-636-7300 427 B
jlobertini@tusculum.edu
LOBO, Andre .... 301-243-2332 503 J
andre.lobo@dodiis.mil
LOBO, Teri, A .... 610-409-3000 402 A
tlobo@ursinus.edu
LOBO-TORRES, Sally ..... 219-473-4219 153 G
slobotorres@ccs.edu
LOBOA, Elizabeth, G ..... 573-882-0948 261 B
egloboa@missouri.edu
LOBOSCO, Victoria .... 775-831-1314 272 D
vlobosco@sierranevada.edu
LOBOVITS, Adriana .... 415-703-9500.. 28 D
a.lopez-lobovits@cca.edu
LOBUONO, Joseph .... 978-665-4614 212 C
jlobuono@fitchburgstate.edu
LOCASCIO, Laurie .... 301-405-6499 202 C
lel@umd.edu
LOCASCIO, Nicola .... 304-696-3963 490 D
locascio@marshall.edu
LOCASCIO, Patti, P .... 352-395-5169 107 A
patti.locascio@sfcollege.edu
LOCH, Bob .... 319-226-2040 162 F
bob.loch@allencollege.edu
LOCH, OSB, Killian .... 724-805-2350 398 E
killian.loch@email.stvincent.edu
LOCH, Robert .... 319-226-2040 169 B
robert.loch@stlukescollege.edu
LOCHER, Karen .... 361-570-4170 453 C
locherk@uhv.edu
LOCHHEAD, Michael, J 617-552-3255 207 B
michael.lochhead@bc.edu
LOCHMANN, Steve .... 870-575-8165.. 22 E
assessment@uapb.edu
LOCHMUELLER,
Stephen .... 859-622-2120 180 B
stephen.lochmueller@eku.edu
LOCHNER, Elizabeth ...... 610-341-5930 383 D
elizabeth.lochner@eastern.edu
LOCHSTAMPFOR, Mike . 770-534-6230 115 D
mlochstampfor@brenau.edu
LOCHTE, Lynne .... 410-337-6572 198 G
lynne.lochte@goucher.edu
LOCK, Cory .... 512-448-8720 442 M
julial@stedwards.edu
LOCK, Robin .... 806-742-1988 451 B
robin.lock@ttu.edu
LOCK, Vickie .... 920-498-5447 500 F
victoria.lock@nwtc.edu
LOCKABY, Dorothy, C ... 540-464-7573 476 G
lockabydc@vmi.edu
LOCKBEAM, Kaila .... 509-453-0374 483 C
kaila.lockbeam@perrytech.edu
LOCKE, Barbara .... 718-429-6600 324 D
barbara,locke@vaughn.edu
LOCKE, Benjamin, D ..... 814-863-0395 392 B
bdl10@psu.edu
LOCKE, Dot, M .... 662-685-4771 245 D
dlocke@bmc.edu
LOCKE, Gillian .... 903-813-2192 430 N
glocke@austincollege.edu
LOCKE, Jason .... 607-255-2000 297 F
jcl31@cornell.edu
LOCKE, Lisa .... 517-629-0206 220 G
llocke@albion.edu
LOCKE, Richard, M .... 401-863-2706 404 E
richard_locke@brown.edu
LOCKE, Steven, S .... 781-736-3017 207 E
slocke@brandeis.edu
LOCKE, Teb .... 717-358-4339 384 D
teb.locke@fandm.edu
LOCKER, Rick .... 615-366-4417 424 D
rick.locker@tbr.edu
LOCKERBIE, Andrew ..... 858-695-8587 155 E
alockerbie@horizonuniversity.edu
LOCKETT, JR.,
Eugene, D .... 301-985-7330 203 B
eugene.lockett@umuc.edu
LOCKETT, Rose .... 662-621-4287 245 E
rlockett@coahomacc.edu
LOCKHART,
Calandra, D .... 215-885-2360 389 F
clockhart@manor.edu
LOCKHART, Felicia .... 818-299-5517.. 73 K
flockhart@westcoastuniversity.edu
LOCKHART, Janet .... 310-506-4301.. 56 C
janet.lockhart@pepperdine.edu
LOCKHART, Michael ...... 917-493-4460 305 I
mlockhart@msmnyc.edu
LOCKLEAR, Alexis .... 910-521-6333 343 B
alexis.locklear@uncp.edu
LOCKLEAR, Amy .... 386-506-3079.. 97 D
amy.locklear@daytonastate.edu

LOCKLEAR, Patricia .... 910-272-3356 337 D
plocklear@robeson.edu
LOCKLEAR, Ronnie .... 910-272-3347 337 D
rlocklear@robeson.edu
LOCKLEAR, William, L .. 910-272-3304 337 D
wlocklea@robeson.edu
LOCKLEAR, Zoe .... 910-775-4009 343 B
zoe.locklear@uncp.edu
LOCKREM, Michael .... 605-688-6161 417 C
michael.lockrem@sdstate.edu
LOCKRIDGE, Ann .... 504-280-6501 189 E
alockridg@uno.edu
LOCKWARD, Ana, C ...... 516-323-4209 307 F
alockward@molloy.edu
LOCKWOOD, Charles .... 813-974-0553 110 B
cjlockwood@health.usf.edu
LOCKWOOD,
Lawrence, J .... 319-335-0217 163 A
larry-lockwood@uiowa.edu
LOCKWOOD,
Matthew, T .... 313-577-9098 232 I
mlockwood@wayne.edu
LOCKWOOD, Monica .... 203-576-2400.. 88 D
monical@bridgeport.edu
LOCURTO, Chuck .... 401-232-6196 404 F
clocurto@bryant.edu
LOCUST, Jonathan .... 507-457-5597 241 F
jlocust@winona.edu
LOCY, Caitlin .... 608-796-3017 498 N
calocy@viterbo.edu
LODATO, Michelle .... 864-388-8340 410 D
mlodato@lander.edu
LODGE, Jennifer, K .... 314-747-0515 262 A
lodgejk@wustl.edu
LODHOLZ, Amy .... 503-847-2574 377 F
alodholz@uws.edu
LODMELL, Joseph .... 912-279-5896 116 G
jlodmell@ccga.edu
LODOVICO, John .... 860-773-1321.. 86 G
jlodovico@tunxis.edu
LODWICK, David .... 216-687-6956 351 B
d.lodwick@csuohio.edu
LOEFFEL, Linda, L .... 414-443-8842 498 O
linda.loeffel@wlc.edu
LOEFFELHOLZ, Mary ..... 617-373-2400 217 F
LOEFFLER, Lauren .... 610-861-5580 391 F
lloeffler@northampton.edu
LOEHFELM, Courtney .... 303-797-5914.. 76 I
courtney.loehfelm@arapahoe.edu
LOEPER, Catherine .... 918-836-6886 370 D
catherine.loeper@spartan.edu
LOERA, Audrey .... 908-526-1200 281 A
audrey.loera@raritanval.edu
LOERA, Daniel, L .... 909-593-3511.. 70 D
dloera@laverne.edu
LOESCH, Richard .... 224-570-7946 147 I
rick.loesch@rosalindfranklin.edu
LOETTERLE, Jon .... 402-461-7424 267 D
jloetterle@hastings.edu
LOEW, Cody .... 513-569-1898 350 K
cody.loew@cincinnatistate.edu
LOEW, Timothy .... 508-373-9460 206 B
timothy.loew@becker.edu
LOEWEN, Kerry .... 707-524-1519.. 62 F
kloewen@santarosa.edu
LOEWEN, Sherrie .... 909-652-6696.. 36 A
sherrie.loewen@chaffey.edu
LOEWEN, Steve .... 620-343-4600 173 A
sloewen@fhtc.edu
LOEWRIGKEIT, Kirsten .. 201-684-7621 280 H
kloewrig@ramapo.edu
LOEWY-WELLISCH,
Peggy .... 310-233-4321.. 49 A
loewywp@lahc.edu
LOFFLER, Alicia .... 847-491-4647 145 F
a-loffler@kellogg.northwestern.edu
LOFFREDO, Joe .... 585-475-2829 313 A
jjlrgr@rit.edu
LOFLIN, Gene .... 828-398-7240 332 B
williamgloflin@abtech.edu
LOFLIN, Reine .... 620-901-6252 170 G
loflin@allencc.edu
LOFMAN, Brian .... 831-755-6809.. 44 K
blofman@hartnell.edu
LOFQUIST, Les .... 919-573-5350 340 F
llofquist@shepherds.edu
LOFRUMENTO, Kristin .. 740-362-3126 356 D
klofrumento@mtso.edu
LOFTEN, Larry .... 970-351-4899.. 83 E
larry.loften@unco.edu
LOFTESNES, Teresa .... 701-858-3062 345 F
teresa.loftesnes@minotstateu.edu
LOFTHOUSE, David, R .. 951-785-2938.. 47 C
dlofthou@lasierra.edu

LOFTIN, Loren .... 903-223-3002 448 B
lloftin@tamut.edu
LOFTIN, Virginia, G ...... 205-226-4938.... 5 A
vgloftin@bsc.edu
LOFTON, Antwan .... 202-238-5960.. 92 B
antwan.lofton@howard.edu
LOFTON, Robynne .... 510-430-3295.. 52 D
rlofton@mills.edu
LOFTSGAARDEN,
Michael .... 773-508-2106 142 D
mloftsgaarden@luc.edu
LOFTUS, Craig .... 207-221-4750 196 G
cloftus1@une.edu
LOFTUS, James, K .... 412-624-4216 401 B
ja1216@pitt.edu
LOFTUS, James, P .... 563-333-6480 169 A
loftusjamesp@sau.edu
LOFTUS, Kate .... 262-472-1392 498 C
loftusk@uww.edu
LOFTUS-BERLIN, Eileen 973-278-5400 275 I
eml@berkeleycollege.edu
LOFTUS-BERLIN, Eileen 973-278-5400 291 D
eml@berkeleycollege.edu
LOFTUS WHEELER,
Rosemary .... 336-721-2605 340 D
rosemary.wheeler@salem.edu
LOGAN, Caleb .... 334-683-2304.... 3 A
registrar@marionmilitary.edu
LOGAN, Cynthia .... 931-393-1588 425 C
clogan@mscc.edu
LOGAN, Doug .... 509-527-2074 485 H
doug.logan@wallawalla.edu
LOGAN, Drew .... 773-697-2143 136 B
dlogan@devry.edu
LOGAN, Ethan .... 806-742-1482 451 B
ethan.logan@ttu.edu
LOGAN, Frank .... 843-953-5256 407 F
frank.logan@citadel.edu
LOGAN, Gary .... 210-999-7306 452 A
glogan@trinity.edu
LOGAN, Jake .... 765-285-8314 153 C
jakelogan@bsu.edu
LOGAN, James .... 765-983-1528 154 G
jlogan@earlham.edu
LOGAN, Julie .... 619-594-6578.. 33 E
logan1@sdsu.edu
LOGAN, Katherine .... 706-272-4524 117 C
klogan@daltonstate.edu
LOGAN, Mark .... 562-860-2451.. 35 M
mlogan@cerritos.edu
LOGAN, Martin .... 425-352-8262 479 A
mlogan@cascadia.edu
LOGAN, Matt .... 601-403-1111 248 E
mlogan@prcc.edu
LOGAN, Michael, F .... 336-334-4104 343 A
mflogan@uncg.edu
LOGAN, Mike .... 712-274-6400 170 E
mike.logan@witcc.edu
LOGAN, Ruth .... 585-594-6408 310 F
loganr@roberts.edu
LOGAN, Ruth .... 585-594-6408 312 K
loganr@roberts.edu
LOGAN, Steve .... 901-678-4666 427 D
selogan@memphis.edu
LOGAN, Timothy, M ..... 254-710-2115 431 J
tim_logan@baylor.edu
LOGAN, Traci .... 617-587-5711 217 A
logant@neco.edu
LOGAN-BENNETT, Lorie 410-704-2386 204 A
lloganbennett@towson.edu
LOGGINS, Jeffery .... 662-254-3325 248 B
jloggins@mvsu.edu
LOGHIN, Sarah .... 512-313-3000 434 E
sarah.loghin@concordia.edu
LOGLISCI, Marlene .... 856-415-2113 281 D
mloglisc@rcgc.edu
LOGSDON, Michael .... 301-387-3333 198 F
michael.logsdon@garrettcollege.edu
LOGSDON, Paul .... 417-865-2815 253 B
logsdonp@evangel.edu
LOGUE, Heather .... 847-317-8192 150 H
hlogue@tiu.edu
LOH, Wallace, D .... 301-405-5803 202 C
wdloh@umd.edu
LOHAN-BREMER,
Maureen .... 845-257-3256 317 B
lbremerm@newpaltz.edu
LOHDEN, Bethany, L .... 636-584-6503 252 J
bethany.lohden@eastcentral.edu
LOHMANN, Janet .... 207-725-3490 193 D
jlohmann@bowdoin.edu
LOHOCZKY, Maria .... 863-297-1000 105 A
mlehoczky@polk.edu

LOHR, Joel .... 860-509-9502.. 87 B
jlohr@hartsem.edu
LOHRENZ, Steven .... 508-910-6550 211 F
slohrenz@umassd.edu
LOHREY, Adam .... 937-481-2266 364 E
adam_lohrey@wilmington.edu
LOHRSTORFER, Chris ... 601-366-8880 249 G
clohrstorfer@wbs.edu
LOHRUM, Kitty .... 314-889-4701 253 C
clohrum@fontbonne.edu
LOHSE, MaryPat .... 617-349-8669 210 H
mlohse@lesley.edu
LOHSTROH, Tracy .... 618-634-3203 149 A
tracyl@shawneecc.edu
LOILAND, Sharon .... 701-777-3178 345 C
sharon.loiland@und.edu
LOIODICE, Melissa .... 413-236-1022 213 F
mloiodice@berkshirecc.edu
LOISEAU, Marvin .... 617-588-1337 206 C
mloiseau@bfit.edu
LOIZEAUX, Elizabeth ..... 617-353-2230 207 D
ebloiz@bu.edu
LOJOWSKY, MacAdam . 707-468-3081.. 51 E
mlojowsky@mendocino.edu
LOKAR, William .... 434-544-8631 472 G
lokar@lynchburg.edu
LOKENI, Lokeni .... 684-699-9155 505 A
l.lokeni@amsamoa.edu
LOKEY, Scott .... 717-947-6161 393 F
selokey@pacollege.edu
LOKIE, Kirky .... 970-943-3069.. 84 D
klokie@western.edu
LOKKEN, Pamela, S .... 314-935-5752 262 A
lokken@wustl.edu
LOKMAN, Lawrence, H . 814-863-1028 392 B
lhl11@psu.edu
LOKUTA, Sharon .... 260-422-5561 155 H
slokuta@indianatech.edu
LOLLAND, Sonja .... 831-770-7091.. 44 K
slolland@hartnell.edu
LOLLATHIN, Eric .... 740-245-7438 363 D
ericl@rio.edu
LOMASTRO, Joseph, A . 508-373-9546 206 B
oseph.lomastro@becker.edu
LOMBARD, Anne, E ...... 315-470-6658 320 A
aelombard@esf.edu
LOMBARDI, Annie .... 845-398-4016 315 B
alombard@stac.edu
LOMBARDI, Mark .... 314-529-9330 254 H
president@maryville.edu
LOMBARDI, Phillip .... 401-232-6374 404 F
plombard@bryant.edu
LOMBARDI, Ryan, T ..... 607-255-7595 297 F
ryan.lombardi@cornell.edu
LOMBARDO, Joann .... 860-486-5519.. 88 E
joann.lombardo@uconn.edu
LOMBARDO, John .... 631-851-6225 321 F
lombarj@sunysuffolk.edu
LOMBARDO, Kristina .... 904-826-8583.. 98 E
klombardo@flagler.edu
LOMBARDO, Michael .... 503-777-7542 376 C
lombardm@reed.edu
LOMBARDO, Roberto .... 386-506-3159.. 97 D
roberto.lombardo@daytonastate.edu
LOMBARDO, Tony .... 225-578-0552 188 I
lauramorrow@lsu.edu
LOMBELLA, James, P ... 860-773-1419.. 86 G
jlombella@acc.commnet.edu
LOMBELLA, James, P ... 860-253-3001.. 85 C
jlombella@asnuntuck.edu
LOMELI, Nestor .... 559-925-3135.. 74 B
nestorlomeli@whccd.edu
LOMELI, Susan .... 909-593-3511.. 70 D
slomeli@laverne.edu
LOMIDZE, Kote .... 202-464-6973 463 C
kote.lomidze@worldlearning.org
LOMMEL, John, M .... 574-372-5110 155 B
lommeljm@grace.edu
LONDOIRO, Carol .... 631-632-6267 317 D
carol.londoiro@stonybrook.edu
LONDON, Allen, S .... 478-301-2715 121 E
london_a@mercer.edu
LONDON, Lauren .... 734-487-8079 223 H
llondon2@emich.edu
LONDON, Manuel .... 631-632-8304 317 D
manuel.london@stonybrook.edu
LONDON, Michael, E .... 415-422-4400.. 71 K
melondon@usfca.edu
LONDON, Priscilla, A ... 410-651-6349 203 A
palondon@umes.edu
LONDON, Samuel .... 256-726-7223.... 6 C
slondon@oakwood.edu

LOPEZ, Gloria .... 413-572-5272 213 D glopez@westfield.ma.edu
LOPEZ, Heather .... 509-335-2001 486 A hlopez@wsu.edu
LOPEZ, Ignacio .... 312-553-5901 134 B ilopez@ccc.edu
LOPEZ, Ines .... 915-831-2659 436 E ivelazco@epcc.edu
LOPEZ, Irene .... 530-226-4112.. 63 K ilopez@simpsonu.edu
LOPEZ, Iris .... 787-738-2161 513 D iris.lopez7@upr.edu
LOPEZ, Iris .... 787-744-8519 507 K ilopez@ediccollege.edu
LOPEZ, Isabel .... 910-843-5304 331 K sisterisabel.lopez@gmail.com
LOPEZ, Isiah .... 215-871-6609 396 D isiahlo@pcom.edu
LOPEZ, Israel .... 787-852-1430 508 C ilopez@hccpr.edu
LOPEZ, Jaime .... 787-834-9595 511 E jlopez@uaa.edu
LOPEZ, Jane, A .... 757-221-3965 466 C jalope@wm.edu
LOPEZ, Jerry .... 415-476-4181.. 69 E jerry.lopez@ucsf.edu
LOPEZ, Jerry .... 415-439-2411.. 25 K jlopez@act-sf.org
LOPEZ, Jesse .... 619-388-7392.. 60 E jlopez006@sdccd.edu
LOPEZ, Jilian .... 702-254-7577 272 A jilian.lopez@northwestcareercollege.edu
LOPEZ, John .... 732-255-0400 280 A john_lopez@ocean.edu
LOPEZ, Jose Israel .... 347-964-8600 291 I jilopez@boricuacollege.edu
LOPEZ, Keila .... 787-882-2065 511 D utcpresident@yahoo.com
LOPEZ, Kim .... 650-574-6118.. 61 P lopezk@smccd.edu
LOPEZ, Kimberly .... 912-525-5000 123 G klopez@scad.edu
LOPEZ, Lauren .... 404-880-6294 116 D llopez@cau.edu
LOPEZ, Lidby .... 213-252-5100.. 23 K
LOPEZ, Lillian .... 817-202-6290 444 I lillian.lopez@swau.edu
LOPEZ, Lillian, L .... 712-274-5030 168 B lopez@morningside.edu
LOPEZ, Lisa .... 503-251-5703 377 F llopez@uws.edu
LOPEZ, Lorena .... 818-719-6449.. 49 C lopezl6@piercecollege.edu
LOPEZ, Luis .... 787-738-2161 513 D luis.lopez16@upr.edu
LOPEZ, Luis .... 787-743-4041 507 D llopez@columbiacentral.edu
LOPEZ, Luis .... 210-486-2355 429 G llopez@alamo.edu
LOPEZ, Magdalis .... 787-786-3030 512 B mlopez@ucb.edu.pr
LOPEZ, Maggie .... 312-949-7701 138 E mho@ico.edu
LOPEZ, Marcos, A .... 845-697-7241 315 D
LOPEZ, Maria .... 510-780-4500.. 47 J mlopez@lifewest.edu
LOPEZ, Maria .... 915-831-2676 436 E mlopez35@epcc.edu
LOPEZ, Maria del Mar .. 787-746-1400 508 B
LOPEZ, Maribel .... 203-285-2029.. 85 E mlopez@gwcc.commnet.edu
LOPEZ, Mark .... 972-860-4152 434 L mlopez@dcccd.edu
LOPEZ, Mary .... 909-706-3860.. 74 I mlopez@westernu.edu
LOPEZ, Mayra, I .... 787-754-8000 512 E mlopez@pupr.edu
LOPEZ, Michael .... 586-286-2189 226 H lopezm263@macomb.edu
LOPEZ, Miguel .... 541-881-5583 377 B mlopez@tvcc.cc
LOPEZ, Monique .... 413-572-8066 213 D mlopez@westfield.ma.edu
LOPEZ, Myriam .... 956-664-4600 444 A myriaml@southtexascollege.edu
LOPEZ, Myriam, D .... 787-841-2000 510 K mdlopez@pucpr.edu
LOPEZ, Nataly .... 210-841-7365 453 D nagutie1@uiwtx.edu
LOPEZ, Nicolas .... 972-721-5080 452 D nicklopez@udallas.edu
LOPEZ, Oscar .... 972-860-4837 434 L olopez@dcccd.edu
LOPEZ, Paulette .... 509-574-4901 487 A plopez@yvcc.edu
LOPEZ, Priscilla .... 310-233-4605.. 49 A lopezpa@lahc.edu
LOPEZ, Priscilla .... 310-233-4450.. 49 A lopezpa@lahc.edu
LOPEZ, Rebecca .... 254-526-1302 432 H ctc.international@ctcd.edu
LOPEZ, Regina .... 209-476-7840.. 66 G rlopez@clc.edu
LOPEZ, Robert .... 323-343-3050.. 32 A robert.lopez@calstatela.edu
LOPEZ, Robert .... 305-821-3333.. 99 E rlopez@fnu.edu
LOPEZ, Ruben .... 787-746-1400 508 B rublopez@huertas.edu
LOPEZ, Sam, M .... 213-740-1219.. 72 B sam.lopez@usc.edu
LOPEZ, Santa, E .... 209-478-0800.. 45 H selopez@humphreys.edu
LOPEZ, Silvia .... 305-629-2929 106 H slopez@sanignaciouniversity.edu
LOPEZ, Sonia .... 323-267-3794.. 48 H lopezms@elac.edu
LOPEZ, Stacey, J .... 215-573-5836 400 K staceylo@upenn.edu
LOPEZ, Stephen .... 646-768-5300 301 B
LOPEZ, Tammy, L .... 719-587-7122.. 76 F tllopez@adams.edu
LOPEZ, Theresa .... 562-860-2451.. 35 M tmlopez@cerritos.edu
LOPEZ, Tom .... 818-947-2988.. 49 F lopezt@lavc.edu
LOPEZ, Vanessa .... 718-779-1499 311 I vlopez@plazacollege.edu
LOPEZ, Vidal .... 973-443-8935 277 K vidal903_lopez@fdu.edu
LOPEZ, Vince .... 323-343-3844.. 32 A vlopez@cslanet.calstatela.edu
LOPEZ, Yiselle .... 787-844-8181 514 A yiselle.lopez@upr.edu
LOPEZ-CEPERO RAMOS, Maria, C .... 787-720-1022 506 E orientador@atlanticu.edu
LOPEZ-GARRETT, Bernadette .... 702-651-5620 271 A bernadette.lopez@csn.edu
LOPEZ GONZALEZ, Myrna .... 787-783-4125 514 B myrna.lopez2@upr.edu
LOPEZ-HURTADO, Ivan . 505-747-2225 287 G ilopez@nnmc.edu
LOPEZ-JANOVE, Lorraine .... 845-235-2764 311 C
LOPEZ-JIMINEZ, Jessica .... 626-852-6413.. 36 K slopezjiminez@citrsucollege.edu
LOPEZ-MATTHEWS, Amy, L .... 937-229-3333 362 G amatthews1@udayton.edu
LOPEZ-MEDERO, Lilliana, M .... 787-765-4210 506 K llopez@cempr.edu
LOPEZ-NUNCI, Adrián ... 787-250-0000 512 G adria.lopeznunci@upr.edu
LOPEZ-PHILLIPS, Matthew .... 209-667-3177.. 33 C mlopezphillips@csustan.edu
LOPEZ-ROSADO, Jorge . 239-590-1210 108 K jlopez@fgcu.edu
LOPEZ SIERRA, Beda .... 773-878-2473 148 D blopezsierra@staugustine.edu
LOPEZ-STRONG, Maria . 806-894-9611 443 I mstrong@southplainscollege.edu
LOPEZ-VALLES, Ilsa .... 787-863-2390 509 B ilsa.lopez@fajardo.inter.edu
LOPEZ-WAGNER, Muriel .... 909-537-5000.. 33 A
LOPIANSKY, Aaron .... 301-649-7077 204 G alopiansky@yeshiva.edu
LOPICCOLO, Joseph ...... 831-656-2994 503 K jlopiccolo@nps.edu
LOPP, Phillip .... 704-216-3602 337 F phillip.lopp@rccc.edu
LOPRESTI, James, M .... 724-458-3795 385 C jmlopresti@gcc.edu
LOPRESTI-GOODMAN, Stacy .... 703-284-1546 469 C stacy.lopresti-goodman@marymount.edu
LOR, Kia .... 262-243-5700 493 B kia.lor@cuw.edu
LORAINE, Donna .... 916-388-2800.. 35 B dloraine@carrington.edu
LORANG, Amy .... 406-496-4429 265 A alorang@mtech.edu
LORANGER, Cathy .... 540-665-4510 471 E clorange@su.edu
LORBER, Jeffrey, D .... 217-206-7822 151 C jlorber@uis.edu
LORCH, Chris .... 870-368-2004.. 20 F clorch@ozarka.edu
LORD, Annette .... 702-651-5600 271 A annette.lord@csn.edu
LORD, David .... 304-294-2010 489 E david.lord@southernwv.edu
LORD, Evelyn .... 510-464-3496.. 56 G elord@peralta.edu
LORD, Jeanne, F .... 202-687-4056.. 92 A lordj@georgetown.edu
LORD, Jess .... 610-896-1350 385 L jlord@haverford.edu
LORD, Jonathan .... 208-732-6484 130 E jlord@csi.edu
LORD, Kenneth .... 734-487-4140 223 H cob_dean@emich.edu
LORD, Lisa .... 337-482-6863 192 E lisa@louisiana.edu
LORD, Mara .... 414-955-8298 494 C mlord@mcw.edu
LORDEN, Joan, F .... 704-687-5962 342 E jflorden@uncc.edu
LORDS, Kristie .... 208-496-9200 130 A lordsk@byui.edu
LORE, Peggy .... 303-352-3526.. 83 C peggy.lore@ucdenver.edu
LORENCE, Mark, S .... 252-823-5166 334 C lorencem@edgecombe.edu
LORENTZEN, Marcia, H 203-576-4139.. 88 D marcia@bridgeport.edu
LORENZ, Aaron, S .... 201-684-7624 280 H alorenz@ramapo.edu
LORENZ, Britt .... 605-626-2371 417 A britt.lorenz@northern.edu
LORENZ, Dan, P .... 701-788-4676 345 E daniel.lorenz@mayvillestate.edu
LORENZ, Georgia .... 407-708-2009 107 D lorenzg@seminolestate.edu
LORENZ, Heather .... 603-626-9100 274 D h.lorenz@snhu.edu
LORENZ, Kristen .... 304-876-5212 490 E klorenz@shepherd.edu
LORENZ, Michael .... 402-280-2775 266 I michaellorenz@creighton.edu
LORENZA WHEELER, Edward .... 404-527-7702 120 K ewheeler@itc.edu
LORENZEN, Chris .... 307-268-3088 501 U chris.lorenzen@caspercollege.edu
LORENZEN, Michael ..... 309-298-2762 152 D mg-lorenzen@wiu.edu
LORENZO, Janice .... 787-891-0925 508 K jalorenzo@aguadilla.inter.edu
LORENZO, Susan .... 650-738-4253.. 61 Q lorenzo@smccd.edu
LORENZO, Vivian .... 607-274-3177 303 B vlorenzo@ithaca.edu
LORETO, David, P .... 716-878-5519 318 C loretodp@buffalostate.edu
LORGAN, Jason .... 530-752-9075.. 68 E jplorgan@ucdavis.edu
LORGE-GROVER, Christina .... 715-422-5526 500 A christina.lorgegrover@mstc.edu
LORIA, Anne .... 616-250-7500 291 K alloria@bryantstratton.edu
LORIA, Tonia .... 504-278-6278 188 A tloria@nunez.edu
LORICK, Piper .... 803-750-2510.. 92 G
LORIMER, David, W ...... 606-693-5000 182 G dlorimer@kmbc.edu
LORIMER, Steve, A .... 606-693-5000 182 G slorimer@kmbc.edu
LORIMER, Thomas .... 606-693-5000 182 G tlorimer@kmbc.edu
LORINCZOVA, Klaudia .. 315-279-5699 304 A klorincz@keuka.edu
LORING, Trish .... 603-271-6484 273 B tloring@ccsnh.edu
LORING, Trish .... 603-271-6984 273 B tloring@ccsnh.edu
LORIUS, Billie Jo .... 701-328-4107 345 B billiejo.lorius@ndus.edu
LORKOVICH, Malinda ... 312-996-4366 151 B mlork@uic.edu
LORTA, Danielle .... 510-780-4500.. 47 J dlorta@lifewest.edu
LORTON-ROWLAND, Julie .... 317-921-4715 157 G jlorton@ivytech.edu
LORTZ, Peter .... 206-934-3701 483 J peter.lortz@seattlecolleges.edu
LOSASSO, Joseph .... 609-652-4235 283 D joe.losasso@stockton.edu
LOSCHIAVO, Linda .... 718-817-3570 300 E loschiavo@fordham.edu
LOSCHIAVO, Melissa .... 770-426-2741 121 C melissa.loschiavo@life.edu
LOSHIN, David .... 954-262-1167 103 M loshin@nsu.nova.edu
LOSS, Amy .... 618-842-3711 138 G lossa@iecc.edu
LOTANO, Vincent .... 908-709-7046 284 C vincent.lotano@ucc.edu
LOTH, Karen, M .... 616-331-6000 224 E lothk@gvsu.edu
LOTHRINGER, Bobby .... 940-898-3031 451 F rlothringer@twu.edu
LOTHRINGER, Rebecca . 940-565-3903 454 A rebecca.lothringer@unt.edu
LOTKOWICTZ, Bob .... 315-464-4448 317 F lotkowir@upstate.edu
LOTRIONTE, John, D .... 901-321-3550 419 C jlotrion@cbu.edu
LOTT, Ileo .... 847-635-1660 145 G ilott@oakton.edu
LOTT, Jesse .... 315-655-7161 292 F jlott@cazenovia.edu
LOTT, Shevallanie .... 757-727-5251 468 B shevallanie.lott@hamptonu.edu
LOTT, Theresa .... 904-633-8173 100 B theresa.lott@fscj.edu
LOTTO, Benjamin .... 845-437-7437 324 C lotto@vassar.edu
LOTURCO, Jennifer .... 212-217-4000 299 H jennifer_loturco@fitnyc.edu
LOTYCZEWSKI, Halina ... 315-792-3087 324 B halotycz@utica.edu
LOTZ, Cindy .... 309-556-3536 139 G clotz@iwu.edu
LOTZ, Erin .... 928-350-2307.. 15 N elotz@prescott.edu
LOTZE, Conrad .... 304-724-3700 487 E clotze@apus.edu
LOTZGESELL, John .... 956-380-8179 442 L jlotzgesell@riogrande.edu
LOU, Kris .... 503-370-5328 378 B klou@willamette.edu
LOUALLEN, Cheryl .... 937-481-2337 364 E cheryl_louallen@wilmington.edu
LOUCKS, Susan .... 718-940-5564 314 C sloucks@sjcny.edu
LOUCY, Brian, M .... 315-445-4174 304 C loucyb@lemoyne.edu
LOUDEN, Jennifer .... 410-617-2000 199 F
LOUDEN, Sandy .... 731-352-4095 418 G loudens@bethelu.edu
LOUDER, Corey .... 660-626-2203 250 A clouder@atsu.edu
LOUDERMILK, Jessica .. 210-784-1612 448 A jloudermilk@tamusa.edu
LOUDIN, Katie .... 304-473-8165 491 H loudin_k@wvwc.edu
LOUDIN, Rose Ellen ...... 304-473-8600 491 H loudin_r@wvwc.edu
LOUFEK, Michelle .... 321-433-7765.. 97 I loufekm@easternflorida.edu
LOUGEE, Barbara .... 619-260-4886.. 71 J blougee@sandiego.edu
LOUGEE, Wendy, P .... 612-624-1807 243 E wlougee@umn.edu
LOUGH, Pam .... 808-544-0292 127 H
LOUGHERY, James, F ... 215-968-8041 379 G loughery@bucks.edu
LOUGHMAN, Ann .... 518-262-5435 289 F loughma@amc.edu
LOUGHRAN, Kristine ..... 513-732-5218 362 F kris.loughran@uc.edu
LOUGHRAN, Sean .... 203-837-9330.. 85 B loughrans@wcsu.edu
LOUGHREN, Joseph ..... 718-997-5910 295 C joseph.loughren@qc.cuny.edu
LOUIMA, Gariot .... 937-767-1286 347 G
LOUIS, Debra .... 800-375-9878.. 67 I debra.louis@trident.edu
LOUIS, Germaine .... 703-993-1918 467 L chhsdean@gmu.edu
LOUIS, Louisana .... 727-341-3640 106 E louis.louisana@spcollege.edu

LOUIS, Michael 314-505-7301 251 I
louism@csl.edu

LOUIS, Naomi 937-328-6031 350 L
louisn@clarkstate.edu

LOUIS, Naomi 937-778-7814 352 J
nlouis@edisonohio.edu

LOUIS, Zachary 478-508-4139 126 G
zlouis@valdosta.edu

LOUIS CRUZ, Jose 646-664-9100 292 K

LOULA, Karianne 651-423-8298 237 H
karianne.loula@dctc.edu

LOUNDER, Lee 406-265-3711 264 F
lee.lounder@msun.edu

LOUNEY, Mark 617-747-2682 206 E
publicsafety@berklee.edu

LOUNSBERY, Monica 562-985-4691 31 F
monica.lounsbery@csulb.edu

LOUREIRO, Rita, D 561-237-7035 102 V
rloureiro@lynn.edu

LOURO, Jeffrey 508-999-8171 211 F
jlouro@umassd.edu

LOUTHAN, Katherine 314-529-9671 254 H
mlouthan@maryville.edu

LOUTHERBACK, George 254-295-4698 453 E
gloutherback@umhb.edu

LOUTTIT, Julianne, E 724-287-8711 380 A
juli.louttit@bc3.edu

LOVAS, Judy 973-300-2100 283 E
jlovas@sussex.edu

LOVATO, Heather 575-769-4039 285 K
heather.lovato@clovis.edu

LOVATO, Jeremy 505-428-1767 288 B
jeremy.lovato@sfcc.edu

LOVATO, Stella 210-486-0903 429 H
slovato@alamo.edu

LOVATO, Todd 505-428-1217 288 B
todd.lovato@sfcc.edu

LOVATO, Vanessa 301-846-2607 198 E
vlovato@frederick.edu

LOVE, Andrea 225-771-2552 191 A
alove@sulc.edu

LOVE, Brandolyn 843-355-4131 414 F
loveb@wiltech.edu

LOVE, Ceshia 713-221-8454 453 B
lovec@uhd.edu

LOVE, Charles 864-503-5733 414 D
clove@uscupstate.edu

LOVE, Cindy 919-516-5082 340 C
clove@st-aug.edu

LOVE, David 413-597-4237 220 C
dlove@williams.edu

LOVE, Edna 972-860-4806 434 L
elove@dcccd.edu

LOVE, Eric 574-631-2859 161 C
elove1@nd.edu

LOVE, James, S 512-464-8817 442 M
jlove2@stedwards.edu

LOVE, Jan 404-727-6324 117 F
jlove3@emory.edu

LOVE, Janice 714-564-6000 57 L
love_janice@sac.edu

LOVE, Julie, N 970-247-7503 79 I
love_j@fortlewis.edu

LOVE, Kathy, S 912-443-3024 124 A
klove@savannahtech.edu

LOVE, Kelly 360-992-2921 479 F
klove@clark.edu

LOVE, Kensey 740-753-7007 354 A
lovek@hocking.edu

LOVE, Latonya, J 713-500-6054 456 B
latanya.d.jones@uth.tmc.edu

LOVE, Mark 616-538-2330 224 C
mlove@gracechristian.edu

LOVE, Patrick 413-748-3100 218 G
plove@springfield.edu

LOVE, Paula 903-730-4890 438 H
plove@jarvis.edu

LOVE, Vanessa 412-391-4100 397 A
vlove@pointpark.edu

LOVE-SMITH, Ashley 310-206-6361 69 A
alovesmith@volunteer.ucla.edu

LOVE-VAUGHN, Devonia 318-257-2532 191 F
dlvaughn@latech.edu

LOVECCHIO, Francis 570-941-7500 401 H
francis.lovecchio@scranton.edu

LOVEDAY, Joyce 253-589-5500 479 G
joyce.loveday@cptc.edu

LOVEDAY, Travis, C 865-694-6415 425 F
tcloveday@pstcc.edu

LOVEJOY, Jon 210-832-5668 453 D
lovejoy@uiwtx.edu

LOVEJOY, Mike 469-348-2500 434 D

LOVELACE, Rhonda 501-370-5297 20 G
rlovelace@philander.edu

LOVELACE, Vanessa 717-290-8723 388 D

LOVELACE PETR, Carrie 402-826-8111 267 A
carrie.petr@doane.edu

LOVELADY, III, Artis 832-252-4617 433 D
artis@cbshouston.edu

LOVELAND, David, A 607-746-4013 320 G
lovelada@delhi.edu

LOVELESS, Alyssa 405-736-0373 369 I
aloveless@rose.edu

LOVELESS, Cecelia 360-438-4366 483 H
cloveless@stmartin.edu

LOVELESS, Debra 937-327-6131 364 H
registrar@wittenberg.edu

LOVELESS, Jill 304-214-8856 489 F
jloveless@wvncc.edu

LOVELESS-MORRIS, Judy 253-566-5000 485 C

LOVELL, Cheryl, D 719-587-7341 76 F
president@adams.edu

LOVELL, Donna 650-723-2300 65 J
dlovell@stanford.edu

LOVELL, JR., Ernest, L 601-403-1183 248 E
elovell@prcc.edu

LOVELL, Janet 706-754-7833 122 F
jlovell@northgatech.edu

LOVELL, Kenya 386-481-2275 95 F
lovellk@cookman.edu

LOVELL, Matthew 814-886-6388 391 B
mlovell@mtaloy.edu

LOVELL, Matthew, D 812-877-8318 159 J
lovellmd@rose-hulman.edu

LOVELL, Michael, R 414-288-7223 494 B
michael.lovell@marquette.edu

LOVELL, Sharon 540-568-2705 468 F
lovellse@jmu.edu

LOVELY, Christine 530-752-1011 68 E

LOVETT, Christopher, M 814-886-6400 391 B
clovett@mtaloy.edu

LOVETT, Greg 806-743-2952 451 C
greg.lovett@ttuhsc.edu

LOVETT, Myra 318-342-1266 192 F
mlovett@ulm.edu

LOVETT, Patricia 270-686-4336 179 D
patricia.lovett@brescia.edu

LOVICK, Reed 252-527-6223 335 G
wrlovick87@lenoircc.edu

LOVIK, Eric 540-831-5099 470 C
elovik@radford.edu

LOVIN, Eddie 615-547-1231 419 F
elovin@cumberland.edu

LOVITT, Timm 253-833-9111 481 F
tlovitt@greenriver.edu

LOVORN, Beth 228-497-7685 247 E
beth.lovorn@mgccc.edu

LOVSETH, Stephanie 618-374-5215 146 E
stephanie.lovseth@principia.edu

LOVSTUEN, Brenda, C 319-895-4292 164 B
blovstuen@cornellcollege.edu

LOVVORN, Judi 229-217-4198 125 A
jlovvorn@southernregional.edu

LOW, Avrum Yehuda 718-600-8897 325 K

LOW, Catherine Yu-Ling 808-371-5443 128 B
cfo@orientalmedicine.edu

LOW, Douglas 812-749-1280 159 C
dlow@oak.edu

LOW, George 510-885-3291 31 C
george.low@csueastbay.edu

LOW, Greg 949-794-9090 65 I
glow@stanbridge.edu

LOW, Hershel 718-600-8897 325 K
hershellow@yktiferetheliezer.com

LOW, Rochel 718-600-8897 325 K

LOW, Ryan 207-581-1554 195 I
ryan.low@maine.edu

LOW, Ryan 207-581-1554 195 J
ryan.low@maine.edu

LOW, Wai Hoa 808-521-2288 128 B
whlow@orientalmedicine.edu

LOWDEN, Paul 616-732-1194 223 B
plowden@davenport.edu

LOWDER, Diane, M 804-752-7218 470 F
dianelowder@rmc.edu

LOWDER, Michael 405-789-7661 370 B
michael.lowder@swcu.edu

LOWDER, Theresa 859-985-3313 179 C
lowdert@berea.edu

LOWDERMILK, Robert, S 336-342-4261 337 E
lowdermilkb@rockinghamcc.edu

LOWE, Allyson 716-827-2480 323 D
lowea@trocaire.edu

LOWE, Amy 573-592-5315 262 E
amy.lowe@westminster-mo.edu

LOWE, Brenda 806-720-7307 439 H
brenda.lowe@lcu.edu

LOWE, Calvin 757-727-5239 468 B

LOWE, Carmen 617-627-4239 219 B
carmen.lowe@tufts.edu

LOWE, Carrie Beth 865-573-4517 420 G
cblowe@johnsonu.edu

LOWE, Charles 973-720-2200 284 I
lowec1@wpunj.edu

LOWE, Charm 864-592-4624 412 F
lowec@sccsc.edu

LOWE, Dawn, Y 443-518-4256 199 C
dlowe@howardcc.edu

LOWE, JR., Eugene, Y 847-491-8409 145 F
eyljr@northwestern.edu

LOWE, Grant 706-419-1360 117 B
grant.lowe@covenant.edu

LOWE, James 765-285-2805 153 C
jlowe@bsu.edu

LOWE, James, R 860-486-0566 88 E
jim.lowe@uconn.edu

LOWE, Jeanette 706-771-4000 114 J
jlowe@augustatech.edu

LOWE, Jody 662-915-7911 249 D
jplowe@olemiss.edu

LOWE, John-Martin 402-552-3001 270 A
jjlowe@unmc.edu

LOWE, Judy 423-697-2686 424 E
judy.lowe@chattanoogastate.edu

LOWE, Kathy 606-886-3863 180 J
kathy.lowe@kctcs.edu

LOWE, Larry 803-705-4573 407 A
larry.lowe@benedict.edu

LOWE, Laura 253-833-9111 481 F
llowe@greenriver.edu

LOWE, Lisa 404-876-1227 115 F
lisa.lowe@bccr.edu

LOWE, Megan 318-342-3041 192 F
lowe@ulm.edu

LOWE, Melinda 662-241-6088 248 A
mslowe@muw.edu

LOWE, Melissa 303-492-0025 83 A
melissa.lowe@colorado.edu

LOWE, Nathan 541-962-3098 373 B
nlowe@eou.edu

LOWE, Pamela 847-578-8786 147 I
pamela.lowe@rosalindfranklin.edu

LOWE, Patricia 617-552-3334 207 B
patricia.lowe@bc.edu

LOWE, Rick, D 910-630-7027 331 C
rlowe@methodist.edu

LOWE, Rosemary 870-762-3182 17 D
rlowe@smail.anc.edu

LOWE, Sharon 419-289-5035 348 A
slowe3@ashland.edu

LOWE, Stephen 815-939-5231 146 A
slowe@olivet.edu

LOWE, Susan, L 276-964-7304 475 I
susan.lowe@sw.edu

LOWE, Thomas 716-286-8360 310 D
tlowe@niagara.edu

LOWE, Tiffany, P 254-710-6978 431 J
tiffany_lowe@baylor.edu

LOWE, William, J 219-980-6701 156 E
wjlowe@iun.edu

LOWE-JENKINS, Alesia 864-587-4229 412 G
lowejenkinsa@smcsc.edu

LOWE-SCHNEIDER, Katy 812-866-7081 155 C
lowe@hanover.edu

LOWELL, Hillary 406-683-7151 264 B
hillary.lowell@umwestern.edu

LOWELL, Randy 864-424-8046 414 C
lowell@mailbox.sc.edu

LOWENBERG, Ron 714-895-8373 38 D
rlowenberg@gwc.cccd.edu

LOWENSTEIN, Daniel, H 415-476-4451 69 E
lowenstein@ucsf.edu

LOWENSTEIN, Noah 425-278-9318 63 A
nlowenstein@saybrook.edu

LOWENTHAL, Barbara 212-472-1500 309 I
blowenthal@nysid.edu

LOWENTHAL, Tina 626-395-2758 29 C
tina.lowenthal@caltech.edu

LOWENTHALL, Benjamin 410-704-2151 204 A
blowenthal@towson.edu

LOWERY, Andrew 229-209-5239 114 B
andrewlowery@andrewcollege.edu

LOWERY, Carla 662-329-7197 248 A
cmlowery@muw.edu

LOWERY, Chris 317-921-4882 157 G
crlowery@ivytech.edu

LOWERY, Christina 207-780-5240 196 F
christina.smith1@maine.edu

LOWERY, Kathryn 601-266-6775 249 F
kathryn.lowery@usm.edu

LOWERY, Misa, D 910-843-5304 331 K
mlowery@nabc.edu

LOWERY, Randall 912-358-4350 123 H
loweryr@savannahstate.edu

LOWERY, Wendy 540-831-5407 470 C
wlowery@radford.edu

LOWERY-HART, Russell, D 806-371-5123 430 A
rdloweryhart@actx.edu

LOWMAN, Anthony 856-256-5300 281 E
lowman@rowan.edu

LOWMAN, Sara 713-348-2457 442 K
lowman@rice.edu

LOWN, Maris 908-709-7006 284 C
maris.lown@ucc.edu

LOWNDS, Kristen 269-782-1462 230 F
klownds@swmich.edu

LOWNES-JACKSON, Millicent 615-963-7127 426 D
mlownes@tnstate.edu

LOWRANCE, Jeffrey 704-330-6666 333 D
jeff.lowrance@cpcc.edu

LOWREY, Andrew 352-854-2322 96 O
lowreya@cf.edu

LOWREY, James, S 336-841-9283 329 G
jlowrey@highpoint.edu

LOWREY, Jason, H 507-344-7378 234 B
jason.lowrey@blc.edu

LOWREY, Pamela 262-564-2670 499 F
lowreyp@gtc.edu

LOWREY, Tammy 325-649-8043 438 D
tlowrey@hputx.edu

LOWREY, Will 662-685-4771 245 D
wlowrey@bmc.edu

LOWRY, Alexander 978-867-4276 209 F
alexander.lowry@gordon.edu

LOWRY, Christian 217-732-3168 141 H
cjlowry@lincolnchristian.edu

LOWRY, Genny 218-335-4253 236 E
genny.lowry@lltc.edu

LOWRY, John 615-966-3000 421 D
john.lowry@lipscomb.edu

LOWRY, III, L. Randolph 615-966-1787 421 D
randy.lowry@lipscomb.edu

LOWRY, Laura 303-273-3064 78 I
dleclair@mines.edu

LOWRY, Lee 813-253-7671 101 A
llowry2@hccfl.edu

LOWRY, Rebekah, R 910-272-3235 337 D
relowry@robeson.edu

LOWY, Vivien 213-624-1200 42 I
vlowy@fidm.edu

LOX, Curt 904-620-2810 110 A
c.lox@unf.edu

LOY, Marty 715-346-3169 497 F
mloy@uwsp.edu

LOYA, Karla 956-665-8756 455 D
karla.loya@utrgv.edu

LOYA, Leanne 307-268-2111 501 U
leanne.loya@caspercollege.edu

LOYA, Leanne 307-268-2662 501 U
leanne.loya@caspercollege.edu

LOYACK, John, R 610-796-8203 378 F
john.loyack@alvernia.edu

LOYD, Ashley 512-492-3011 430 G
registrar@aoma.edu

LOYD, James 706-649-1449 117 A
jloyd@columbustech.edu

LOYD, James 256-306-2784 1 F
james.loyd@calhoun.edu

LOYD, Jeff 731-989-6009 420 C
jloyd@fhu.edu

LOYD, Jo Lynn 972-279-6511 430 B
jloyd@amberton.edu

LOYD, Kristen, J 812-877-8484 159 J
loyd1@rose-hulman.edu

LOYD, Nic 256-824-3025 8 B
nicholas.loyd@uah.edu

LOYD, Nicole, L 610-861-1502 391 A
loydn@moravian.edu

LOYD, Sage 870-460-1422 22 D
coons@uamont.edu

LOYD-PAIGE, Michelle 616-526-8703 222 A
lopa@calvin.edu

LOZADA, Fuji, P .... 704-894-2035 328 F
erlozada@davidson.edu
LOZADA-CRUZ, Isabel .. 787-480-2380 507 C
ilozada@sanjuanciudadpatria.com
LOZANO, Franz .... 707-654-1032.. 32 B
flozano@csum.edu
LOZANO, Marlene .... 323-259-2558.. 54 E
lozanom@oxy.edu
LOZANO, Ruth, V .... 214-768-4708 444 E
rlozano@smu.edu
LOZIER, Chris .... 812-535-5186 160 B
chris.lozier@smwc.edu
LOZINA, Mary .... 914-674-7651 306 F
mlozina@mercy.edu
LOZOYA, Karna .... 202-319-5100.. 91 B
lozoya@cua.edu
LU, Arthur .... 315-792-7116 321 E
xinjian.lu@sunypoly.edu
LU, Elissa .... 508-793-7513 208 A
ellu@clarku.edu
LU, Flora .... 831-459-5852.. 70 B
floralu@ucsc.edu
LU, Jeffrey .... 408-433-2280.. 36 I
LU, Kuang Kai .... 323-731-2383.. 55 C
rex@psuca.edu
LU, Kuang Kai .... 323-731-2383.. 55 C
registrar@psuca.edu
LU, Michael, C .... 510-664-4219.. 68 D
mclu@berkeley.edu
LU, Zhaoxue .... 503-253-3443 374 H
zlu@ocom.edu
LUAN, Jing .... 650-358-6880.. 61 N
luan@smccd.edu
LUBA, Kristen .... 845-675-4400 310 G
kristen.luba@nyack.edu
LUBARSKY, David, A .... 916-734-0751.. 68 E
dalubarsky@ucdavis.edu
LUBAS, Rebecca .... 509-963-1981 479 B
rebecca.lubas@cwu.edu
LUBBEN, Richard .... 559-730-3735.. 39 E
richardl@cos.edu
LUBBERS, Tony .... 660-543-8266 260 K
lubbers@ucmo.edu
LUBBERTS, Rhonda .... 616-331-2525 224 E
lubbertr@gvsu.edu
LUBELL, Courtney .... 707-765-1836.. 51 H
LUBELL, David .... 607-431-4031 301 D
lubelld@hartwick.edu
LUBELL, Ellen .... 212-410-8479 309 B
elubell@nycpm.edu
LUBIENECKI, Teresa ...... 716-652-8900 292 I
tlubienecki@cks.edu
LUBIG, Joe .... 906-227-1880 228 F
jlubig@nmu.edu
LUBIN, James .... 212-686-9244 290 A
LUBINGER, Bill .... 216-368-4443 349 F
william.lubinger@case.edu
LUBINSKY, Hindy .... 718-787-1602 322 J
hindy.lubinsky@touro.edu
LUBNOW, Jeff .... 973-328-5155 277 B
jlubnow@ccm.edu
LUCAS, Bryan .... 817-257-7682 448 G
b.lucas@tcu.edu
LUCAS, Carol, A .... 516-877-3154 289 C
lucas@adelphi.edu
LUCAS, Catherine .... 303-605-5229.. 80 N
lucascat@msudenver.edu
LUCAS, Cathy .... 910-221-2224 329 B
clucas@gcd.edu
LUCAS, Cecilia .... 808-455-0325 129 D
cblucas@hawaii.edu
LUCAS, Daniel .... 850-474-3380 110 E
dlucas@uwf.edu
LUCAS, Dawn .... 704-463-1360 339 E
dawn.lucas@pfeiffer.edu
LUCAS, Dawn .... 704-463-3207 339 E
dawn.lucas@pfeiffer.edu
LUCAS, Dwayne .... 315-781-3304 302 A
lucas@hws.edu
LUCAS, Evonna .... 662-254-3579 248 B
evonna.lucas@mvsu.edu
LUCAS, Hakim, J .... 804-257-5835 477 C
hjlucas@vuu.edu
LUCAS, Jane, K .... 205-934-4636.... 8 A
jklucas@uab.edu
LUCAS, Janet .... 209-946-2392.. 70 E
jlucas@pacific.edu
LUCAS, Jennifer, R .... 717-337-6211 384 H
jlucas@gettysburg.edu
LUCAS, Jenny .... 610-647-4400 386 C
jlucas@immaculata.edu
LUCAS, Joan .... 662-325-8131 247 F
jlucas@legal.msstate.edu
LUCAS, John .... 608-262-8287 496 C
jplucas@wisc.edu
LUCAS, Julie .... 617-253-3952 215 G
LUCAS, Kendall .... 619-849-2680.. 57 E
kendalllucas@pointloma.edu
LUCAS, Lynn .... 330-972-7920 362 B
plynn@uakron.edu
LUCAS, Mark .... 785-227-3380 171 E
lucas@bethanylb.edu
LUCAS, Matt .... 765-677-2408 157 D
matt.lucas@indwes.edu
LUCAS, Michelle .... 717-796-1800 390 E
mlucas@messiah.edu
LUCAS, Miguel .... 623-845-3528.. 13 C
miguel.lucas@gccaz.edu
LUCAS, Pam, A .... 214-860-2097 435 C
plucas@dcccd.edu
LUCAS, Paul, M .... 724-287-8711 380 A
paul.lucas@bc3.edu
LUCAS, Sandra .... 520-383-8401.. 16 D
slucas7578@aol.com
LUCAS, Scott .... 316-677-9536 178 B
slucas@watc.edu
LUCAS, Sharron .... 913-758-6102 177 F
sharron.lucas@stmary.edu
LUCAS, Sheri .... 614-222-3220 351 D
slucas@ccad.edu
LUCAS, Tamara, F .... 973-655-5167 279 C
lucast@mail.montclair.edu
LUCAS, Tara .... 919-718-7245 333 C
tlucas@cccc.edu
LUCAS-ROSS, Jennifer .. 239-687-5351.. 94 N
jlross@avemarialaw.edu
LUCAS-YOUMANS,
Tasha .... 386-481-2181.. 95 F
youmanst@cookman.edu
LUCASCHI-DECKER,
Silvia .... 803-754-4100 409 A
LUCCHESI, Michael .... 718-270-3776 317 E
michael.lucchesi@downstate.edu
LUCCHI, Addison .... 913-971-3567.. 81 C
amlucchi@mnu.edu
LUCCI, Elaine .... 724-266-3838 400 H
elucci@tsm.edu
LUCENA, Lisa .... 812-221-1714 162 B
lisalucena@vbc.edu
LUCERO, Cori .... 209-228-4440.. 69 B
clucero2@ucmerced.edu
LUCERO, Edwin .... 206-546-4503 484 G
elucero@shoreline.edu
LUCERO, Gabe .... 307-755-2613 502 K
gabe.lucer@zenith.org
LUCERO, Kathy .... 909-652-6620.. 36 A
kathy.lucero@chaffey.edu
LUCERO, Louis .... 661-722-6300.. 26 D
llucero@avc.edu
LUCERO-MILLER,
Denise .... 940-898-3801 451 F
dluceromiller@twu.edu
LUCETTE, Kisha .... 706-821-8495 122 K
klucette@paine.edu
LUCHAU, Michael .... 575-527-7604 287 E
mluchau@nmsu.edu
LUCIA, Joseph, P .... 215-204-8231 399 F
joseph.lucia@temple.edu
LUCIA, Megan .... 203-591-7425.. 87 F
mlucia@post.edu
LUCIANI, Michael .... 802-387-6713 462 D
mluciani@landmark.edu
LUCIANO, Carol .... 787-878-6000 508 D
LUCIANO, Jack .... 910-755-7336 332 F
lucianoj@brunswickcc.edu
LUCIANO, Jennifer, K ... 201-200-2220 279 E
jluciano@njcu.edu
LUCIDO, Michael .... 314-977-8173 259 H
michael.lucido@slu.edu
LUCK, Deborah, S .... 336-633-0272 337 A
dsluck@randolph.edu
LUCK, Garrett .... 847-317-8118 150 H
gmluck@tiu.edu
LUCK, Janice, J .... 610-921-7824 378 C
jluck@albright.edu
LUCK, Jessica, E .... 540-828-5720 465 D
jluck@bridgewater.edu
LUCK, Renita .... 229-317-6732 113 H
renita.luck@asurams.edu
LUCK, Tonya .... 910-898-9631 336 D
luckt@montgomery.edu
LUCKER, Lucy .... 860-231-5405.. 89 B
llucker@usj.edu
LUCKES, Kim .... 757-727-5773 468 B
kim.luckes@hamptonu.edu
LUCKETT, Jenni .... 503-352-3006 375 G
jluckett@pacificu.edu
LUCKETT, Jerry .... 605-995-2647 415 C
jerry.luckett@dwu.edu
LUCKETT, Matt .... 270-824-1757 181 G
matt.luckett@kctcs.edu
LUCKEY, JR.,
William, T .... 270-384-8001 183 C
luckeyw@lindsey.edu
LUCKING, Rachel .... 508-626-4615 212 D
rlucking@framingham.edu
LUCKY, Jana .... 318-357-4616 192 C
luckyj@nsula.edu
LUCUS-FLANNERY,
Mary .... 510-780-4500.. 47 J
mary@lifewest.edu
LUCY, John .... 904-596-2507 111 F
jlucy@tbc.edu
LUCZYK, Sarah .... 419-448-2061 353 H
sluczuk@heidelberg.edu
LUDEMAN, Randall .... 218-755-3750 237 E
randall.ludeman@bemidjistate.edu
LUDEMANN, Martin ...... 406-243-2277 264 A
marty.ludemann@umontana.edu
LUDESCHER,
Sandra, M .... 563-589-3223 169 I
sludescher@dbq.edu
LUDLAM, David .... 970-248-1868.. 77 I
dludlam@coloradomesa.edu
LUDLOW, Allison, J ...... 610-799-1216 388 I
aludlow1@lccc.edu
LUDLUM, Beth .... 202-885-8616.. 93 E
bludlum@wesleyseminary.edu
LUDLUM, Kevin .... 806-291-3428 457 J
ludlumk@wbu.edu
LUDWICK, Richard .... 713-525-2160 454 H
president@stthom.edu
LUDWIG, Allison .... 718-430-2000 289 G
LUDWIG, Amy .... 479-394-7622.. 23 C
aludwig@uarichmountain.edu
LUDWIG, Amy .... 479-397-7622.. 23 C
aludwig@uarichmountain.edu
LUDWIG, Deborah .... 785-628-4539 173 B
dmludwig@fhsu.edu
LUDWIG, Mary .... 515-574-1145 166 E
ludwig@iowacentral.edu
LUDWIG, Scott .... 408-741-2031.. 74 E
scott.ludwig@westvalley.edu
LUDWIG, Stephen .... 660-562-1749 257 E
sludwig@nwmissouri.edu
LUEBBERING, Kevin ...... 417-447-8188 257 G
luebberk@otc.edu
LUEBBERT, Paula, J ...... 217-782-1086 142 B
paula.luebbert@llcc.edu
LUEBKE, Miriam .... 651-651-8825 235 F
luebke@csp.edu
LUEBKE, Patricia .... 414-382-6368 492 A
patricia.luebke@alverno.edu
LUECKE, Chris .... 435-797-2452 460 H
chris.luecke@usu.edu
LUEDTKE-JONES, Sarah 651-641-3434 236 F
sluedtkejones001@luthersem.edu
LUEKEN, Joel .... 605-394-2352 417 B
joel.lueken@sdsmt.edu
LUEKEN, Paul, A .... 724-738-2021 395 F
paul.lueken@sru.edu
LUEKENGA, Chris .... 765-641-4219 153 B
cdluekenga@anderson.edu
LUEKENGA, Chris .... 970-943-2616.. 84 D
cluekenga@western.edu
LUEKENGA, Julie .... 303-718-5307.. 76 G
julie.luekenga@aims.edu
LUELLEN, Jannie .... 662-252-8000 248 G
jluellen@rustcollege.edu
LUER, Mark, S .... 618-650-5153 149 F
mluer@siue.edu
LUERA, Kayla .... 785-890-3641 176 C
kayla.luera@nwktc.edu
LUESSE, Amy .... 952-446-4122 235 G
luessea@crown.edu
LUETH, Brian .... 269-488-4777 225 E
blueth@kvcc.edu
LUETKEHANS, Lara, M .. 724-357-2482 394 G
lara.luetkehans@iup.edu
LUEVANOS, Aida .... 432-837-8000 450 D
aluevanos@sulross.edu
LUFF, Libby .... 615-514-2787 423 E
lfunke@nossi.edu
LUFF, Paula .... 312-362-8520 135 I
pluff@depaul.edu
LUFKIN, Daniel, W .... 757-569-6712 475 E
dlufkin@pdc.edu
LUFKIN, MB .... 937-769-1323 347 H
mlufkin@antioch.edu
LUFKINS, Lorraine .... 218-935-0417 244 G
lorraine.lufkins@wetcc.edu
LUFT, John, P .... 717-796-1800 390 E
jluft@messiah.edu
LUGAR, Emma .... 434-791-7116 464 O
elugar@averett.edu
LUGDON, Shannon .... 207-834-7800 196 C
shannon.lugdon@maine.edu
LUGG, Carol, A .... 570-326-3761 393 G
cal7@pct.edu
LUGO, Daniel, G .... 704-337-2216 339 G
LUGO, Efrain .... 787-620-2040 506 C
elugo@aupr.edu
LUGO, Eric .... 312-553-2500 134 A
eblugo@ccc.edu
LUGO, Eric .... 646-660-6095 292 L
eric.lugo@baruch.cuny.edu
LUGO, Francisco .... 787-841-2000 510 K
flugo@pucpr.edu
LUGO, Irma .... 787-263-3770 513 D
irma.lugonazario@upr.edu
LUGO, Javier .... 787-894-2828 514 C
javier.lugo3@upr.edu
LUGO, Nilsa .... 787-850-9337 513 E
nilsa.lugo@upr.edu
LUGO, Udeth .... 407-646-2573 105 M
ulugo@rollins.edu
LUGO-VÉLEZ, Samuel ... 787-993-8878 513 B
samuel.lugo1@upr.edu
LUHTA, Brad .... 440-375-7585 355 G
bluhta@lec.edu
LUI, Joyce .... 408-288-3177.. 61 M
joyce.lui@sjcc.edu
LUIKART, Nancy .... 563-288-6073 165 D
nluikart@eicc.edu
LUINENBURG, Amber ... 507-372-3499 239 E
amber.luinenburg@mnwest.edu
LUING, Kevin, L .... 973-278-5400 291 D
kevin@berkeleycollege.edu
LUING, Kevin, L .... 973-278-5400 275 I
kevin@berkeleycollege.edu
LUING, Randy .... 201-291-1111 275 I
rl@berkeley.org
LUING, Randy .... 201-291-1111 291 D
rl@berkeley.org
LUING, Tim .... 212-986-4343 291 D
tim@berkeleycollege.edu
LUING, Tim .... 973-278-5400 275 I
tim@berkeleycollege.edu
LUIS, Silvio .... 202-646-1337.. 92 D
LUJAN, Linda .... 719-336-1511.. 80 K
linda.lujan@lamarcc.edu
LUJIC, Branislav .... 239-513-1122 101 C
blujic@hodges.edu
LUKAC, Dan .... 513-244-4617 357 A
dan.lukac@msj.edu
LUKACH, Matt .... 701-777-1234 345 C
matthew.lukach@und.edu
LUKACSKO, Debbie .... 201-684-7535 280 H
dlukacsk@ramapo.edu
LUKAS, Veronica .... 718-281-5196 295 D
vlukas@qcc.cuny.edu
LUKASIEWICZ, Mark ..... 516-463-5213 302 B
mark.lukasiewicz@hofstra.edu
LUKE, Amy .... 807-956-9704 128 F
aluke@hawaii.edu
LUKE, Amy, M .... 808-956-8207 128 D
aluke@hawaii.edu
LUKE, Don, J .... 570-326-3761 393 G
dluke@pct.edu
LUKE, Kristie .... 580-745-2176 369 K
kluke@se.edu
LUKE, Learie, B .... 803-536-7180 412 C
lluke@scsu.edu
LUKE, Sarah .... 207-801-5670 193 F
sluke@coa.edu
LUKE, Victoria .... 308-367-5200 270 C
vluke1@unl.edu
LUKEHART, Debra .... 641-269-3400 165 J
lukehart@grinnell.edu
LUKENS, Michael .... 661-654-2241.. 30 E
mlukens@csub.edu
LUKES, Don .... 812-855-4206 156 B
dlukes@iu.edu
LUKES, Donald .... 812-855-4206 156 A
dlukes@iu.edu
LUKESH, Michelle .... 575-528-7245 287 E
mlukesh@nmsu.edu
LUKKES, Nathan .... 605-773-3455 416 G
nathan.lukkes@sdbor.edu
LUKKES, Nathan .... 605-773-3455 416 G
LUKSA, Jennifer .... 570-674-6224 390 G
jluksa@misericordia.edu

LULGJURAJ, Diana .... 718-817-4914 300 E
dlulgjuraj2@fordham.edu
LULING, Jennifer .... 267-341-3479 386 A
jluling@holyfamily.edu
LULJAK, Thomas, L ...... 414-229-4035 497 A
tluljak@uwm.edu
LULLO, Ronald .... 708-656-8000 144 E
LUM, Grande, H .... 650-543-3757.. 51 F
grande.lum@menlo.edu
LUMAN, Karl .... 601-366-8880 249 G
kluman@wbs.edu
LUMM, Werner .... 920-390-2820 493 L
werner.lumm@mbu.edu
LUMM, Werner .... 920-206-2322 493 L
werner.lumm@mbu.edu
LUMPE, Mike .... 614-885-5585 360 E
mlumpe@pcj.edu
LUMPKIN, James .... 940-898-3005 451 F
jlumpkin@twu.edu
LUMPKIN, Maria .... 229-434-8446 113 H
maria.lumpkin@asurams.edu
LUMSDEN, Mark .... 712-749-2386 163 D
mark@bvu.edu
LUNA, Andrew .... 931-221-6184 418 D
lunaa@apsu.edu
LUNA, Carmen, M .... 787-766-1717 511 H
cmluna@suagm.edu
LUNA, Christine .... 210-829-3900 453 D
chluna1@uiwtx.edu
LUNA, David .... 520-515-5485.. 11 M
lunad@cochise.edu
LUNA, Elaina .... 505-454-5301 286 D
eluna@luna.edu
LUNA, Kaitlin .... 202-651-5410.. 91 E
kaitlin.luna@gallaudet.edu
LUNA, Leslie .... 520-383-8401.. 16 D
lluna@tocc.edu
LUNA, Mickey .... 314-977-3948 259 H
mickey.luna@slu.edu
LUNA, Olga .... 787-758-6260 508 J
oluna@inter.edu
LUNA, Raul .... 509-453-0374 483 C
raul.luna@perrytech.edu
LUNA, Shirley, A .... 936-468-2605 445 F
sluna@sfasu.edu
LUNA-DE LOS SANTOS,
Heriberto .... 787-766-1399 512 G
heriberto.luna@upr.edu
LUNBECK, Jo .... 501-660-1030.. 17 E
jlunbeck@asusystem.edu
LUNCEFORD, Casey ...... 772-462-2505 101 E
cluncefo@irsc.edu
LUND, Brenda .... 360-438-4307 483 H
blund@stmartin.edu
LUND, James .... 760-480-8474.. 74 J
jlund@wscal.edu
LUND, Jon .... 563-387-1428 167 E
lundjon@luther.edu
LUND, Lisa .... 989-328-1284 228 A
lisal@montcalm.edu
LUND, Robin .... 210-486-4134 429 E
rlund4@alamo.edu
LUNDAHL, Deb .... 402-375-7209 268 G
delunda1@wsc.edu
LUNDAY, Bobbi, J .... 701-662-1501 346 D
bobbi.lunday@lrsc.edu
LUNDAY, Tammy .... 605-688-6415 417 C
tammy.lunday@sdstate.edu
LUNDBERG, Alessandra 860-932-4170.. 86 E
alundberg@qvcc.edu
LUNDBERG, Erik .... 734-615-4445 231 E
lerikl@umich.edu
LUNDBERG, Phil .... 503-253-3443 374 H
phil.lundberg@ocom.edu
LUNDBERG, Stacey .... 218-335-4222 236 E
stacey.lundberg@lltc.edu
LUNDBLAD, Jeffrey, K .. 773-244-5542 145 A
jlundblad@northpark.edu
LUNDBLAD, Larry .... 507-453-2721 239 A
LUNDBLAD, Tracey .... 302-736-2372.. 90 G
tracey.lundblad@wesley.edu
LUNDBURG, P. Wesley 631-451-4259 321 G
lundbuw@sunysuffolk.edu
LUNDE, Allen, K .... 530-898-4412.. 31 A
aklunde@csuchico.edu
LUNDE, Beth .... 757-822-1711 476 B
blunde@tcc.edu
LUNDE, Beth .... 757-789-1789 474 F
blunde@tcc.edu
LUNDE-STOCKERO,
Beth .... 906-487-3310 227 E
blunde@mtu.edu
LUNDEEN, Kate .... 414-382-6103 492 A
kate.lundeen@alverno.edu
LUNDELL, Candy .... 714-895-8736.. 38 D
clundell@gwc.ccc.edu
LUNDERMAN, Dedria .... 850-729-6031 103 L
lundermand@nwfsc.edu
LUNDGREN, Jennifer .... 816-235-1301 261 C
lundgrenj@umkc.edu
LUNDGREN, LaRae .... 951-827-2587.. 69 C
larae.lundgren@ucr.edu
LUNDGREN, LouAnne ... 505-224-4000 285 J
llundgren1@cnm.edu
LUNDI, Barbara .... 407-265-8383.. 96 A
LUNDQUIST, Lisa, M .... 678-547-6308 121 E
lundquist_lm@mercer.edu
LUNDQUIST, Lynn .... 651-641-8232 235 F
lundquist@csp.edu
LUNDSTREM, Karen ...... 718-260-5140 295 B
klundstrem@citytech.cuny.edu
LUNDSTROM, Alicia ...... 601-318-6709 249 H
alundstrom@wmcarey.edu
LUNDSTROM, Joel .... 712-792-8308 164 C
jtlundstrom@dmacc.edu
LUNDY, Jennifer .... 724-838-4236 398 H
jlundy@setonhill.edu
LUNDY, Tony .... 703-233-7469 124 B
tlundy@shorter.edu
LUNGER, Steve .... 616-632-2916 221 C
LUNN, Ardelia, M .... 334-727-8147.... 7 D
alunn@tuskegee.edu
LUNN, D. Paul .... 919-513-6210 342 B
paul_lunn@ncsu.edu
LUNN, Sheri, V .... 651-628-3321 244 D
svlunn@unwsp.edu
LUNNERMON, II,
James, G .... 410-651-7606 203 A
jglunnermonii@umes.edu
LUNNIE, Leisha .... 701-228-5669 346 C
leisha.lunnie@dakotacollege.edu
LUNSFORD, Dale, A ...... 903-233-3100 439 E
dalelunsford@letu.edu
LUNSFORD, Donald ...... 502-863-7035 180 E
donald_lunsford@georgetowncollege.edu
LUNSFORD, Justin, P ... 260-982-5280 158 T
jplunsford@manchester.edu
LUNT, Andrew .... 575-538-6181 289 B
andrew.lunt@wnmu.edu
LUNT, Dennis .... 218-755-2737 237 E
dennis.lunt@bemidjistate.edu
LUNTSFORD, Becky ...... 850-474-2449 110 E
rluntsford@uwf.edu
LUO, Pengju George .... 864-578-8770 412 B
lpengju@sherman.edu
LUONG, Carmen .... 718-482-5511 294 F
carmenl@lagcc.cuny.edu
LUONG, Huan .... 972-860-8102 435 A
hluong@dcccd.edu
LUONGO, Ann Marie .... 516-323-3200 307 F
presidents-office@molloy.edu
LUPE, Mark .... 239-433-6948 100 A
mlupe@fsw.edu
LUPIANI, Blanca .... 979-845-4274 446 G
blupiani@tamu.edu
LUPIEN, Todd .... 575-624-8110 287 A
todd@nmmi.edu
LUPTAK, Marcia .... 847-214-6917 136 F
mluptak@elgin.edu
LUPTON, Brendan .... 847-970-4891 152 A
blupton@usml.edu
LUPTON, Deborah .... 410-337-6135 198 G
dlupton@goucher.edu
LUPU, Peter .... 623-845-3747.. 13 C
peter.lupu@gccaz.edu
LUQUETTE, Heidi .... 503-842-8222 377 A
heidiluquette@tillamookbaycc.edu
LUQUIRE, Heath .... 704-991-0122 338 C
rluquire5455@stanly.edu
LURSEN, Cara .... 704-403-1614 327 D
cara.lursen@carolinashealthcare.org
LURZ, Carol .... 910-938-6343 333 F
lurzc@coastalcarolina.edu
LUSBY, Catie .... 620-252-7135 172 G
LUSHBAUGH, Jeffery .... 609-777-3083 284 B
jlushbaugh@tesu.edu
LUSHNIAK, Boris, D ..... 301-405-2437 202 C
lushniak@umd.edu
LUSK, Carol .... 615-966-5256 421 D
carol.lusk@lipscomb.edu
LUSK, D. Claude .... 806-291-3436 457 J
luskc@wbu.edu
LUSK, Kent .... 312-553-5628 134 B
klusk1@ccc.edu
LUSK, Laurel .... 330-244-4762 364 B
llusk@walsh.edu
LUSK, Susie .... 304-384-5323 490 A
lusks@concord.edu
LUSSIER, Michel .... 207-741-5519 195 A
mlussier@smccme.edu
LUSSON, Keith .... 312-369-7283 135 E
klusson@colum.edu
LUST, Kevin .... 217-789-1017 142 B
kevin.lust@llcc.edu
LUSTER, Pamela, T .... 619-388-2721.. 60 D
pluster@sdccd.edu
LUSTER, Stacey .... 508-929-8022 213 E
sluster@worcester.edu
LUSTIG, Derek .... 315-781-3123 302 A
lustig@hws.edu
LUTCHEN, Kenneth, R ... 617-353-2800 207 D
klutch@bu.edu
LUTER, Gary, S .... 813-253-3333 112 J
gluter@ut.edu
LUTES, David .... 703-284-5993 469 C
david.lutes@marymount.edu
LUTES, Morris .... 404-835-6122 423 K
mlutes@richmont.edu
LUTGEN, Roxanne .... 715-675-3331 500 E
lutgen@ntc.edu
LUTGRING, Ray .... 812-488-2589 161 A
rl5@evansville.edu
LUTHER, Kathy .... 314-256-8851 250 D
luther@ai.edu
LUTHI, John, R .... 570-577-3332 379 F
john.luthi@bucknell.edu
LUTNER, Rachel .... 216-687-2223 351 B
r.lutner@csuohio.edu
LUTON, Sally .... 315-498-2466 311 B
lutons@sunyocc.edu
LUTRICK, Donny .... 972-825-4824 445 A
dlutrick@sagu.edu
LUTTJEBOER, Jared .... 219-864-2400 159 B
jluttjeboer@midamerica.edu
LUTTON, Margaret, K .... 817-515-5140 445 G
margaret.lutton@tccd.edu
LUTTRELL, Cori .... 254-968-1683 446 E
luttrell@tarleton.edu
LUTTRELL, Curt .... 760-776-7441.. 39 A
cluttrell@collegeofthedesert.edu
LUTUS, Peter, E .... 302-356-6920.. 90 I
peter.e.lutus@wilmu.edu
LUTY, Paul, J .... 503-943-8874 377 E
luty@up.edu
LUTZ, Andrew, J .... 563-333-5842 169 A
lutzandrewj@sau.edu
LUTZ, JR., Ben .... 865-573-4517 420 G
blutz@johnsonu.edu
LUTZ, Bob .... 561-803-2661 104 C
bob_lutz@pba.edu
LUTZ, Bob .... 561-803-2000 104 C
LUTZ, Brock .... 517-607-2561 225 A
blutz@hillsdale.edu
LUTZ, Bryan .... 740-753-6489 354 A
lutzb@hocking.edu
LUTZ, Cathleen, A .... 570-321-4069 389 E
lutz@lycoming.edu
LUTZ, Cheryl .... 717-391-3595 399 G
lutz@stevenscollege.edu
LUTZ, Dan .... 765-285-8984 153 C
dlutz@bsu.edu
LUTZ, John, M .... 615-875-8895 428 D
john.lutz@vanderbilt.edu
LUTZ, Kimberley .... 843-661-8005 409 I
kimberley.lutz@fdtc.edu
LUTZ, Nate, K .... 612-874-3780 236 K
nate_lutz@mcad.edu
LUTZ, Paula .... 307-766-4106 502 H
plutz@uwyo.edu
LUTZ, Susan .... 303-871-2118.. 83 D
susan.lutz@du.edu
LUTZ, Todd .... 254-519-5708 447 A
todd.lutz@tamuct.edu
LUX, Jace, T .... 270-745-2551 185 E
jace.lux@wku.edu
LUXNER, Catherine .... 570-961-4703 389 G
luxner@marywood.edu
LUXTON, Andrea, T ...... 269-471-3100 221 B
aluxton@andrews.edu
LUY, Peg .... 607-431-4026 301 D
luyp@hartwick.edu
LUYCKX, April .... 214-637-3530 457 I
aluyckx@wadecollege.edu
LUZURIAGA, Katherine . 508-856-6282 212 A
katherine.luzuriaga@umassmed.edu
LUZURIAGA, Suzana, H 513-556-0364 362 D
susana.luzuriaga@uc.edu
LUZZI, David .... 617-373-4160 217 F
LWANGA, Elizabeth .... 847-866-3902 137 E
liz.lwanga@garrett.edu
LY, Geisce .... 415-267-6521.. 37 A
jly@ccsf.edu
LY, Geisce .... 415-267-6521.. 37 A
gly@ccsf.edu
LY, Lisa .... 650-949-6204.. 43 D
lylisa@foothill.edu
LY, Pearl .... 760-744-1150.. 55 I
ply@palomar.edu
LY, Tey .... 949-872-2224.. 29 D
LYALL, Rachel .... 610-861-1304 391 A
lyallr@moravian.edu
LYBYER, Debra .... 208-792-2313 131 A
dlybyer@lcsc.edu
LYDEN MURPHY,
Diane .... 315-443-5582 322 C
dlmurphy@syr.edu
LYDON, Carol Ann .... 828-694-1882 332 E
ca_lydon@blueridge.edu
LYDON, Christopher, P 202-319-5305.. 91 B
lydon@cua.edu
LYDON, JR.,
Theodore, M .... 415-422-6396.. 71 K
lydon@usfca.edu
LYERLY, Claudia .... 678-839-2981 126 E
clyerly@westga.edu
LYKE, Alan, D .... 719-884-5000.. 81 C
adlyke@nbc.edu
LYKE, Heather, R .... 412-648-8230 401 B
lykeh@pitt.edu
LYKINS, Karen .... 931-372-3084 426 E
klykins@tntech.edu
LYKOUDIS, Michael, N . 574-631-7473 161 C
lykoudis.1@nd.edu
LYLE, William .... 215-489-4987 382 D
william.lyle@delval.edu
LYM, Brian .... 212-772-4144 294 C
blym@hunter.cuny.edu
LYMANSTALL, Judy .... 419-783-2300 352 F
jlymanstall@defiance.edu
LYN, Rodney .... 404-413-1130 119 E
ryn1@gsu.edu
LYNCH, Alice, D .... 804-752-3039 470 F
alicelynch@rmc.edu
LYNCH, Alicia .... 515-271-1457 164 I
alicia.lynch@dmu.edu
LYNCH, Andrea .... 626-256-4673.. 37 B
alynch@coh.org
LYNCH, Andrea .... 609-586-4800 278 F
lyncha@mccc.edu
LYNCH, April .... 313-993-1524 231 B
lynchap@udmercy.edu
LYNCH, Carly .... 212-517-0584 306 A
clynch@mmm.edu
LYNCH, Chad .... 531-622-2929 267 H
celynch@mccneb.edu
LYNCH, Christoher .... 951-827-6374.. 69 C
christopher.lynch@ucr.edu
LYNCH, Christopher ...... 251-460-6494.... 8 F
clynch@southalabama.edu
LYNCH, Christopher ...... 251-460-7725.... 8 F
clynch@southalabama.edu
LYNCH, Cynthia .... 414-847-3340 494 F
cynthialynch@miad.edu
LYNCH, Cynthia, D .... 414-847-3340 494 F
cynthialynch@miad.edu
LYNCH, Darlene .... 219-980-6614 156 E
darlynch@iun.edu
LYNCH, Deborah .... 407-708-2144 107 D
lynchd@seminolestate.edu
LYNCH, Diane .... 973-761-9175 283 B
diane.lynch@shu.edu
LYNCH, Diane .... 908-852-1400 276 G
diane.lynch@centenaryuniversity.edu
LYNCH, Dianne .... 573-876-7210 260 F
president@stephens.edu
LYNCH, Eileen .... 773-838-7984 134 F
elynch4@ccc.edu
LYNCH, Jacqueline .... 708-456-0300 150 I
jacquelinelynch@triton.edu
LYNCH, Jacqueline .... 315-792-3111 324 B
jlynch@utica.edu
LYNCH, James .... 315-792-5316 307 D
jlynch@mvcc.edu
LYNCH, James .... 508-588-9100 214 F
jlynch@massasoit.mass.edu
LYNCH, James .... 912-279-5713 116 G
jlynch@ccga.edu
LYNCH, Joanna .... 502-213-2410 181 F
joanna.lynch@kctcs.edu

LYNCH, Joe .... 717-337-6518 384 H
jlynch@gettysburg.edu
LYNCH, Julia .... 512-499-4309 454 I
jlynch@utsystem.edu
LYNCH, Kelly .... 781-239-4220 205 E
klynch@babson.edu
LYNCH, Laura .... 912-279-4548 116 G
llynch@ccga.edu
LYNCH, Lisa, M .... 781-736-2503 207 E
lisalynch@brandeis.edu
LYNCH, Lynn .... 727-873-4143 110 C
lynnlynch@usf.edu
LYNCH, Marilyn, K .... 972-860-4181 434 L
mklynch@dcccd.edu
LYNCH, Marlon .... 212-998-1409 310 B
m.lynch@nyu.edu
LYNCH, Michael .... 781-239-4528 205 E
mlynch4@babson.edu
LYNCH, Michael .... 678-916-2661 114 I
mlynch@johnmarshall.edu
LYNCH, Molly .... 703-257-6664 475 C
mlynch@nvcc.edu
LYNCH, Patricia .... 336-334-9725 343 A
pmlynch2@uncg.edu
LYNCH, Paul, F .... 315-445-4551 304 C
lynchpf@lemoyne.edu
LYNCH, Richard .... 972-708-7340 435 H
dick_lynch@diu.edu
LYNCH, Robert .... 240-567-7306 200 C
bob.lynch@montgomerycollege.edu
LYNCH, Scott .... 970-207-4550.. 80 M
scottl@mckinleycollege.edu
LYNCH, Stephanie, J .... 202-687-4560.. 92 A
sjl28@georgetown.edu
LYNCH, Stephen, J .... 401-865-2233 405 B
sjlynch@providence.edu
LYNCH, Susan .... 218-322-2451 238 E
susan.lynch@itascacc.edu
LYNCH, Sylvia .... 562-938-4280.. 48 D
slynch@lbcc.edu
LYNCH, Sylvia .... 423-869-6372 421 C
sylvia.lynch@lmunet.edu
LYNCH, III, Thomas ..... 617-973-1175 219 A
tlynch@suffolk.edu
LYNCH, Tim .... 909-869-4379.. 30 D
tlynch@cpp.edu
LYNCH, Timothy .... 718-631-6222 295 D
tlynch@qcc.cuny.edu
LYNCH, Timothy, G ...... 734-764-0304 231 E
timlynch@umich.edu
LYNCH, Valerie .... 217-234-5270 141 D
vlynch@lakeland.cc.il.us
LYNCH, Viron .... 941-359-7518 105 K
vlynch@ringling.edu
LYNCH, Wayne .... 716-614-5980 310 C
wlynch@niagaracc.suny.edu
LYNCH GADALETA,
Margaret, A .... 401-456-8387 405 C
mlynchgadaleta@ric.edu
LYNCH-SOSA, Jill .... 402-472-7488 269 J
jlynch-sosa@nebraskamed.com
LYNDON, Laura .... 510-436-1658.. 45 D
lyndon@hnu.edu
LYNES, Julie .... 559-265-5763.. 66 E
julie.lynes@fresnocitycollege.edu
LYNETT, Christopher ..... 617-243-2211 210 G
clynett@lasell.edu
LYNETT, Sharon .... 570-955-1456 387 D
lynetts@lackwanna.edu
LYNG-GLIDDI, Diana, L 518-327-6314 311 G
dlyngglidi@paulsmiths.edu
LYNHAM, Sandra .... 207-741-5923 195 A
slynham@smccme.edu
LYNN, Angela .... 309-298-1891 152 D
an-lynn@wiu.edu
LYNN, David .... 405-425-5645 367 G
david.lynn@oc.edu
LYNN, Erin .... 212-752-1530 304 D
erin.lynn@limcollege.edu
LYNN, Jeff .... 334-293-4709.... 1 C
jeff.lynn@accs.edu
LYNN, Laura .... 866-492-5336 244 F
laura.lynn@mail.waldenu.edu
LYNN, Mac .... 504-526-4745 189 H
macl@nationsu.edu
LYNN, Martha .... 206-546-4634 484 G
mlynn@shoreline.edu
LYNN, Marty .... 504-526-4745 189 H
martyl@nationsu.edu
LYNN, Marvin .... 503-725-4697 376 A
marvinlynn@pdx.edu
LYNN, Michael .... 219-785-5380 159 G
mlynn@pnw.edu
LYNN, Richard .... 251-809-1556.... 1 I
richard.lynn@coastalalabama.edu
LYNN, Steve .... 803-777-2128 413 C
lynns@mailbox.sc.edu
LYNN, Vicki .... 501-450-1494.. 19 F
lynn@hendrix.edu
LYNN, Vivian .... 732-255-0400 280 A
vlynn@ocean.edu
LYNNE, Chris .... 602-557-5760.. 16 J
chris.lynne@phoenix.edu
LYNOTT, Patricia .... 603-645-9794 274 D
p.lynott@snhu.edu
LYON, Alexandra .... 478-757-5216 126 H
alyon@wesleyancollege.edu
LYON, Brett .... 712-274-5234 168 B
lyon@morningside.edu
LYON, Brooke .... 256-782-5449.... 5 J
bbell@jsu.edu
LYON, Charles .... 661-362-3545.. 38 H
chuck.lyon@canyons.edu
LYON, James .... 706-721-8106 115 A
jlyon@augusta.edu
LYON, Jonathan .... 978-837-5280 216 D
lyonj@merrimack.edu
LYON, L. Andrew .... 714-997-6930.. 36 C
lyon@chapman.edu
LYON, Larry .... 504-282-4455 190 A
llyon@nobts.edu
LYON, Larry .... 254-710-3588 431 J
larry_lyon@baylor.edu
LYON, Larry .... 919-761-2372 340 G
llyon@sebts.edu
LYON, Leah .... 580-559-5259 366 C
llyon@ecok.edu
LYON, Mary Eilleen ...... 616-331-2221 224 E
lyonme@gvsu.edu
LYON, Melissa .... 714-895-8284.. 38 D
mlyon@gwc.cccd.edu
LYON, Misty .... 309-341-5422 133 C
mlyon@sandburg.edu
LYON, Mollie .... 515-271-1400 164 I
mollie.lyon@dmu.edu
LYON, Rachele .... 541-888-7259 376 F
rachele.lyon@socc.edu
LYON, Sue .... 413-644-4282 205 F
slyon@simons-rock.edu
LYON, Tammy .... 910-938-6247 333 F
lyont@coastalcarolina.edu
LYON, Wade .... 620-417-1064 176 K
wade.lyon@sccc.edu
LYONS, Angelica .... 323-473-5673.. 73 K
alyons@westcoastuniversity.edu
LYONS, Becky .... 406-657-2168 264 E
blyons@msubillings.edu
LYONS, Bridget .... 540-665-4646 471 E
blyons@su.edu
LYONS, Bruce .... 646-313-8000 295 E
bruce.lyons@guttman.cuny.edu
LYONS, Cheryl, C .... 501-450-3140.. 23 H
clyons@uca.edu
LYONS, Cindy .... 434-947-8722 470 E
clyons@randolphcollege.edu
LYONS, Ellen .... 617-236-8812 209 D
elyons@fisher.edu
LYONS, Florence .... 229-430-4847 113 H
florence.lyons@asurams.edu
LYONS, Heather .... 910-695-3701 337 H
lyonsh@sandhills.edu
LYONS, James .... 408-551-1691.. 62 D
jlyons@scu.edu
LYONS, James, E .... 919-516-4373 340 C
jelyons@st-aug.edu
LYONS, Jason, C .... 757-594-8175 466 B
jason.lyons@cnu.edu
LYONS, Joseph .... 804-524-6453 477 B
jlyons@vsu.edu
LYONS, Larry .... 309-438-5626 139 E
lelyons@ilstu.edu
LYONS, Laura .... 808-956-5971 128 F
lelyons@hawaii.edu
LYONS, Marybeth .... 315-792-7505 321 E
smbl@sunypoly.edu
LYONS, Matt .... 202-664-5703.. 93 E
mlyons@wesleyseminary.edu
LYONS, Melanie, N .... 616-526-7745 222 A
mnl2@calvin.edu
LYONS, Michael .... 781-239-2443 214 E
mlyons@massbay.edu
LYONS, Nicholas, A ...... 315-312-2222 319 B
nicholas.lyons@oswego.edu
LYONS, Patrick, G .... 973-761-9011 283 B
LYONS, Paul .... 909-580-9661.. 34 E
LYONS, Phil .... 715-232-1683 498 A
lyonsp@uwstout.edu
LYONS, Phillip .... 936-294-1700 450 C
icc_pml@shsu.edu
LYONS, Richard, K .... 510-643-2027.. 68 D
lyons@haas.berkeley.edu
LYONS, Shane .... 304-293-5621 491 C
shlyons@mail.wvu.edu
LYONS, Shawn .... 859-238-5500 179 F
shawn.lyons@centre.edu
LYONS, Sheena .... 410-704-5074 204 A
slyons@towson.edu
LYONS, Steve .... 218-723-6167 235 D
slyons@css.edu
LYONS, Steven, J .... 937-775-5745 364 I
steven.lyons@wright.edu
LYONS, Suzette, M .... 951-827-3989.. 69 C
suzette.lyons@ucr.edu
LYONS, Theresa .... 907-786-1240.... 9 H
tlyons@alaska.edu
LYSACK, Catherine .... 313-577-1574 232 I
c.lysack@wayne.edu
LYSIONEK, Christine ..... 610-902-8416 380 C
christine.lysionek@cabrini.edu
LYSLE, Jane, H .... 302-225-6274.. 90 E
lyslej@gbc.edu
LYSNE, Josh, D .... 218-299-3645 235 E
jlysne@cord.edu
LYSNE, Marit .... 507-222-4080 234 F
mlysne@carleton.edu
LYTCH, Carol, E .... 717-290-8701 388 D
president@lancasterseminary.edu
LYTHGOE, Maren .... 801-524-8103 459 F
mlythgoe@ldsbc.edu
LYTLE, Anne .... 212-772-4242 294 C
alytle@hunter.cuny.edu
LYTLE, Daniel .... 715-233-5358 499 D
dlytle@cvtc.edu
LYTLE, James, R .... 570-586-2400 381 E
jlytle@clarkssummitu.edu
LYTLE, Jesse .... 610-896-1000 385 L
jlytle@haverford.edu
LYTLE, Roy .... 505-566-3990 288 A
lytler@sanjuancollege.edu
LYTTLE, Darylnet .... 804-524-5674 477 B
dlyttle@vsu.edu
LYTTON, Billy .... 704-922-6480 334 F
lytton.billy@gaston.edu
LYZUN, Nancy .... 317-940-8029 153 F
nlyzun@butler.edu
L'ALLIER, Kristi .... 763-424-0725 239 G
k.l'allier@nhcc.edu
L'AMOREAUX, Neal ...... 330-972-7535 362 B
neal@uakron.edu
L'ESPERANCE, Mark ...... 540-568-6572 468 F
lesperme@jmu.edu
L'ETOILE, Michelle .... 617-422-7210 217 C
mletoile@nesl.edu
L'HEUREUX, Andrea ..... 970-542-3166.. 81 A
andrea.lheureux@morgancc.edu

M

MA, Carolyn .... 808-932-8116 128 E
csjma@hawaii.edu
MA, Duc, D .... 520-626-1188.. 16 G
mad2@email.arizona.edu
MA, Elise .... 516-739-1545 309 C
financial_aid@nyctcm.edu
MA, Jennifer .... 925-473-7521.. 40 J
jma@losmedanos.edu
MA, Patricia .... 215-965-4069 390 J
pma@moore.edu
MA, Qing .... 626-289-7719.. 24 I
qma@amu.edu
MA, Wei .... 928-524-7350.. 14 J
wei.ma@npc.edu
MA, Wonsuk .... 918-495-6868 368 I
wma@oru.edu
MA, Yanli .... 630-617-3653 136 G
yanlima@elmhurst.edu
MA, Yue .... 773-298-5516 148 G
ma@sxu.edu
MAALOUF, Kathy .... 305-237-7356 103 D
kmaalouf@mdc.edu
MAAS, Brendan .... 562-902-3305.. 65 C
MAAS, John .... 912-201-8000 124 E
jmaas@southuniversity.edu
MAAS, Lisa .... 920-498-6829 500 F
lisa.maas@nwtc.edu
MAAS, Lisa .... 931-372-3384 426 E
lmaas@tntech.edu
MAAS, Lyndsay .... 805-965-0581.. 62 C
lmmaas@sbcc.edu
MAAS, Paula .... 212-229-8947 308 C
maasp@newschool.edu
MAAS, Tammy .... 307-778-1258 502 D
tmaas@lccc.wy.edu
MAAS-STEED, Deaun ..... 405-692-3263 366 G
MAASJO, Bryan .... 212-772-4582 294 C
bm514@hunter.cuny.edu
MAASS, Kern .... 504-865-3039 189 F
kdmaass@loyno.edu
MABE, Scotty .... 910-410-1684 337 B
samabe@richmondcc.edu
MABERY, Dan .... 918-444-2120 367 A
mabery@nsuok.edu
MABERY, Dan .... 918-444-2017 367 A
mabery@nsuok.edu
MABERY, Mary, V .... 504-526-4745 189 H
registrar@nationsu.edu
MABEUS, Amy .... 319-385-6478 167 A
amy.mabeus@iw.edu
MABOKELA, Reitumetse 217-333-1828 151 D
mabokela@illinois.edu
MABRY, Doug .... 503-517-1935 378 A
dmabry@westernseminary.edu
MABRY, James, C .... 978-656-3101 214 G
mabry@middlesex.mass.edu
MABRY, Lisa .... 804-862-6100 470 I
lmabry@rbc.edu
MABRY, Tom, R .... 719-333-2229 504 C
tom.mabry@usafa.edu
MABUS, John .... 402-463-2402 267 D
john.mabus@hastings.edu
MAC PHERSON, Garry .. 805-893-3132.. 70 A
gmacpherson@ucsb.edu
MACALESTER, Tom .... 704-461-6721 327 A
tommacalester@bac.edu
MACALUSO, Danielle .... 513-562-8752 347 K
danielle.macaluso@artacademy.edu
MACAN, Drew .... 386-822-7472 111 A
dmacan@stetson.edu
MACAPINLAC, Jonas, D 671-735-2944 505 E
jmac@triton.uog.edu
MACARTHUR, John .... 989-463-7241 220 H
macarthurjr@alma.edu
MACAULAY, Alaina .... 413-265-2343 208 C
macaulaya@elms.edu
MACAULAY, Barbara ..... 508-373-5897 216 B
barbara.macaulay@mcphs.edu
MACAULAY,
Jennifer, M .... 508-565-1238 218 H
jmacaulay@stonehill.edu
MACAULEY, Robert .... 201-200-3171 279 E
rmacauley@njcu.edu
MACCARONE, Ellen, M . 509-313-6136 481 D
maccarone@gonzaga.edu
MACCARTHY,
Stephen, J .... 215-898-8724 400 K
smaccar@upenn.edu
MACCARTNEY, Teresa ... 404-962-3016 126 F
teresa.maccartney@usg.edu
MACCHI, Thomas, J ..... 215-572-2942 379 A
macchit@arcadia.edu
MACCHIARELLA, Sue, A 386-226-7740.. 98 A
macchis1@erau.edu
MACCLAREN, Jon .... 802-387-6721 462 D
jmacclaren@landmark.edu
MACCLAREN, Jon, A ..... 802-387-6721 462 D
jonmacclaren@landmark.edu
MACCORMACK,
Jennifer .... 206-616-7933 485 F
jmaccorm@uw.edu
MACCUISH, Spencer ..... 805-581-1233.. 42 D
smaccuish@eternitybiblecollege.com
MACCULLOCH, Heather . 646-312-5045 292 L
heather.macculloch@baruch.cuny.edu
MACDONALD, Amy .... 919-866-5076 338 G
ajmacdonald@waketech.edu
MACDONALD, Ashley ... 207-454-1020 195 B
amacdonald@wccc.me.edu
MACDONALD, Beth .... 701-228-2277 346 C
beth.macdonald@dakotacollege.edu
MACDONALD, Brian ...... 610-282-1100 382 E
brian.macdonald@desales.edu
MACDONALD, Bruce ..... 619-239-0391.. 34 F
bmacdonald@cwsl.edu
MACDONALD, David, E 419-772-2200 358 H
d-macdonald@onu.edu
MACDONALD, Elizabeth 636-949-4396 254 F
emacdonald@lindenwood.edu
MACDONALD, Gail .... 802-225-3261 462 I
gail.macdonald@neci.edu
MACDONALD, Gregory . 610-330-5069 387 E
macdonag@lafayette.edu
MACDONALD, Ian .... 518-337-4853 296 H
macdonai@strose.edu

MADDOX, Timothy .... 252-527-6223 335 G
tdmaddox07@lenoircc.edu
MADDOX, Yvonne .... 301-295-3303 504 B
yvonne.maddox@usuhs.edu
MADDUX, Gary .... 256-824-2679.... 8 B
gary.maddux@us.army.mil
MADDUX, Pat .... 563-588-6366 163 F
pat.maddux@clarke.edu
MADDUX, Susan .... 864-294-2140 410 A
susan.maddux@furman.edu
MADDY, Angela .... 620-792-9322 171 C
maddya@bartonccc.edu
MADELONE LINCOLN,
Laura .... 607-436-2526 317 C
laura.madelone@oneonta.edu
MADER, Mary .... 603-641-7174 274 C
mmader@anselm.edu
MADER, Pamela .... 909-621-8856.. 56 J
pamela_mader@pitzer.edu
MADERE, Whit .... 804-819-4951 474 A
wmadere@vccs.edu
MADIA, Sherrie .... 201-200-2472 279 E
smadia@njcu.edu
MADIA, William, J .... 650-723-2300.. 65 J
MADIGAN, Dennis, J .... 617-603-6900 216 H
dennis.madigan@necb.edu
MADIGAN, Karen .... 802-225-3230 462 I
karen.madigan@neci.edu
MADIGAN, Kay .... 330-652-9919 352 K
kaymadigan@eticollege.edu
MADIGAN, Kaye .... 320-762-4684 237 B
kayem@alextech.edu
MADIGAN, Marc .... 906-932-4231 224 B
MADISON, Stephen, S .. 817-515-1002 445 G
stephen.madison@tccd.edu
MADISON-CANNON,
Sabrina .... 541-346-1000 377 D
smadison@uoregon.edu
MADLOCK, Calvin .... 510-466-5398.. 56 H
cmadlock@peralta.edu
MADLOCK, Krystal .... 319-352-8434 170 C
krystal.madlock@wartburg.edu
MADONNA, Richard ...... 860-439-2044.. 86 H
rich.madonna@conncoll.edu
MADOR, Jonathan .... 212-517-0540 306 A
jmador@mmm.edu
MADORE, Keith .... 860-253-3041.. 85 C
kmadore@asnuntuck.edu
MADORE, Ketih .... 860-253-3041.. 86 G
kmadore@acc.commnet.edu
MADORIN, Jeanne .... 336-334-5167 343 A
j_madori@uncg.edu
MADRAY, Van .... 704-216-3900 337 F
van.madray@rccc.edu
MADRIAN, Brigitte .... 801-422-4122 458 H
brigitte_madrian@byu.edu
MADRIGAL, Richard ...... 949-359-0045.. 29 E
MADSEN, Jan, E .... 402-280-2131 266 I
janmadsen@creighton.edu
MADSEN, Lois .... 620-241-0723 172 D
lois.madsen@centralchristian.edu
MADSEN, Monte .... 210-688-3101 432 L
MADSEN, Patrick .... 704-687-0784 342 E
pmadsen@uncc.edu
MADSEN, Reva .... 210-688-3101 432 L
MADSEN, Ruthanne ...... 617-824-8600 208 H
ruthanne_madsen@emerson.edu
MADSEN, Thor .... 816-414-3700 256 A
academicdean@mbts.edu
MADSON, Gregory .... 406-791-5359 265 H
gregory.madson@uprovidence.edu
MADUKO, O. John .... 940-668-7731 441 A
jmaduko@nctc.edu
MADULI, Ed .... 408-741-2082.. 74 C
ed.maduli@wvm.edu
MADURA, Angela .... 303-245-4751.. 81 B
amadura@naropa.edu
MADUTA, John .... 360-992-2505 479 F
jmaduta@clark.edu
MAEA, Cheri .... 540-834-1980 474 G
cmaea@germanna.edu
MAEDA, Donna, K .... 651-696-6581 236 H
maeda@macalester.edu
MAEDER, Deb .... 402-481-8065 265 K
deb.maeder@bryanhealth.org
MAENE, Sara .... 304-876-5112 490 E
smaene@shepherd.edu
MAESTAS, Belen .... 719-587-7321.. 76 F
bmaestas@adams.edu
MAESTAS, Henrietta ...... 505-454-2596 286 D
hmaestas@luna.edu
MAESTAS, Michael .... 785-864-2277 177 D
mvm1@ku.edu
MAESTAS, Stacy .... 307-778-1240 502 D
smaestas@lccc.wy.edu
MAFFEI, Melody .... 209-667-3623.. 33 C
mmaffei@csustan.edu
MAFFEO, Angie .... 815-740-3711 151 J
amaffeo@stfrancis.edu
MAFFIA, Robert .... 201-216-3542 283 C
robert.maffia@stevens.edu
MAGALDI, Thomas, G .. 646-888-6639 305 E
magaldit@mskcc.org
MAGALLON, Eric .... 626-914-8624.. 36 K
emagallon@citruscollege.edu
MAGALONG, Mariles .... 510-215-3847.. 40 H
mmagalong@contracosta.edu
MAGANA, Elbi .... 818-677-2121.. 32 D
elbi.magana@csun.edu
MAGANA, Keri .... 828-898-8896 330 E
maganak@lmc.edu
MAGARY, Diane .... 812-866-7364 155 C
magary@hanover.edu
MAGAZU, Daniel .... 508-626-4539 212 D
dmagazu@framingham.edu
MAGAZU, Jessica .... 678-331-4276 121 C
jessica.magzu@life.edu
MAGBIE-CARR, Shawna 704-886-6500.. 92 G
MAGEE, Colin .... 270-824-8674 181 G
colin.magee@kctcs.edu
MAGEE, Edward .... 304-558-0281 489 O
edward.magee@wvhepc.edu
MAGEE, Frances .... 508-793-7423 208 A
fmagee@clarku.edu
MAGEE, Gwen .... 601-477-4028 246 F
gwen.magee@jcjc.edu
MAGEE, Jeanette .... 323-241-5274.. 49 D
mageejm@lasc.edu
MAGEE, Jennifer .... 214-637-3530 457 I
jmagee@wadecollege.edu
MAGEE, John .... 734-432-5656 227 A
jmagee@madonna.edu
MAGEE, Patrick .... 415-351-3542.. 60 G
pmagee@sfai.edu
MAGEEHON, Ali .... 541-888-7417 376 F
ali.mageehon@socc.edu
MAGET, Douglas .... 212-854-5204 290 J
dmaget@barnard.edu
MAGGARD, Bryan .... 337-482-5393 192 E
athleticdirector@louisiana.edu
MAGGARD, Ginger .... 620-862-5252 171 B
MAGGARD, Shawn .... 615-277-7415 428 F
smaggard@watkins.edu
MAGGARD, Trent .... 620-862-5252 171 B
trent.maggard@barclaycollege.edu
MAGGELAKIS, Sophia ... 585-475-2483 313 A
sxmsma@rit.edu
MAGGIO, Chris .... 318-357-6441 192 C
maggioc@nsula.edu
MAGGIO, Marielena ...... 216-368-2519 349 F
mxm346@case.edu
MAGGIO, Michelle .... 413-572-5591 213 D
mmaggio@westfield.ma.edu
MAGGIONI, Susan .... 781-239-2461 214 E
smaggioni@massbay.edu
MAGGIORE, Ray .... 516-876-2031 319 A
maggiorer@oldwestbury.edu
MAGGITTI, Patrick, G .... 610-519-4521 402 D
patrick.maggitti@villanova.edu
MAGGITTI, Sara .... 610-902-8561 380 C
sara.t.maggitti@cabrini.edu
MAGGS, Mark .... 814-234-7755 399 B
mmaggs@southhills.edu
MAGHSOUD,
Amanda, F .... 803-323-4891 414 G
maghsouda@winthrop.edu
MAGIDA, David .... 802-485-2145 463 A
davem@norwich.edu
MAGIE, CM, Sandra, C . 713-686-4345 454 H
smagie@stthom.edu
MAGIERA, Steve, L .... 239-590-1119 108 K
smagiera@fgcu.edu
MAGILL, M. Elizabeth ... 434-924-3728 473 A
mem2a@virginia.edu
MAGINNIS, JR.,
Edward .... 301-405-4939 202 C
maginnis@umd.edu
MAGLES, Christy .... 310-791-9975.. 45 E
MAGLOIRE, Yves, M ..... 516-628-5007 319 A
magloirey@oldwestbury.edu
MAGNAN, Carolyn .... 860-832-3715.. 84 I
magnanc@ccsu.edu
MAGNANI, Holly .... 914-337-9300 297 D
holly.magnani@concordia-ny.edu
MAGNER, Brent .... 402-363-5636 270 E
brent.magner@york.edu
MAGNER, Johnette .... 318-257-0211 191 F
jmagner@latech.edu
MAGNER, Lois, B .... 620-417-1011 176 K
lois.magner@sccc.edu
MAGNER, Michael .... 978-837-5019 216 D
magnerm@merrimack.edu
MAGNONI, Dee .... 848-932-7129 282 A
dee.magnoni@rutgers.edu
MAGNUS, Keith, B .... 317-940-9385 153 F
kmagnus@butler.edu
MAGNUSON, Amy .... 850-644-8868 109 C
amagnuson@admin.fsu.edu
MAGNUSON, Gretchen . 802-258-3117 463 C
gretchen.magnuson@worldlearning.org
MAGNUSON, Kelly, J ... 320-222-6094 240 E
kelly.magnuson@ridgewater.edu
MAGNUSON, Kendyl ..... 760-744-1150.. 55 I
kmagnuson@palomar.edu
MAGNUSON, Matthew .. 559-934-2403.. 74 A
matthewmagnuson@whccd.edu
MAGNUSON, Terry .... 919-962-1319 342 D
tmagnuson@unc.edu
MAGNUSSON, Selena ... 706-295-6866 119 A
smagnusson@gntc.edu
MAGORIAN, Cortney ..... 916-660-7391.. 63 I
cmagorian@sierracollege.edu
MAGORIAN, Kathy .... 605-668-1206 415 H
kathy.magorian@mtmc.edu
MAGRETTA, Dawn .... 734-462-4400 230 D
dmagrett@schoolcraft.edu
MAGRO, Edward .... 401-232-6000 404 F
MAGUET, Kathryn, L ..... 570-577-3700 379 F
kathryn.maguet@bucknell.edu
MAGUIRE, Karen .... 212-355-1501 292 J
kmaguire@christies.edu
MAGUIRE, Kevin, C ...... 617-627-3502 219 B
kevin.maguire@tufts.edu
MAGUIRE, Kim .... 267-341-3494 386 A
kmaguire315@holyfamily.edu
MAGUIRE, Robert .... 973-278-5400 291 D
robert-maguire@berkeleycollege.edu
MAGUIRE, Robert .... 973-278-5400 275 I
robert-maguire@berkeleycollege.edu
MAGUSIAK, Henry .... 724-738-4898 395 F
henry.magusiak@sru.edu
MAHADY, Sarah .... 812-535-5143 160 B
sarah.mahady@smwc.edu
MAHAFFEY, Danny .... 225-578-3962 188 H
dmahaf1@lsu.edu
MAHAFFEY, Sharon ...... 334-420-4252.... 3 H
smahaffey@trenholmstate.edu
MAHAFFY, Kevin .... 312-329-4134 144 B
kevin.mahaffy@moody.edu
MAHALINGAM,
Shankar .... 256-824-6474.... 8 B
shankar.mahalingam@uah.edu
MAHAN, Christine, P .... 610-341-1706 383 D
cmahan@eastern.edu
MAHAN, Forest, E .... 803-508-7247 406 E
MAHAN, Karl .... 806-720-7122 439 H
karl.mahan@lcu.edu
MAHAN, Kim, B .... 806-371-5050 430 A
kbmahan@actx.edu
MAHAN, Melissa .... 210-784-1350 448 A
melissa.mahan@tamusa.edu
MAHAN, Mickie .... 417-455-5536 252 D
mickiemahan@crowder.edu
MAHANY, Patrick .... 310-665-6995.. 54 I
pmahany@otis.edu
MAHAR, Alissa .... 503-594-3009 372 D
alissa.mahar@clackamas.edu
MAHAR, Eddie .... 903-785-7661 441 G
emahar@parisjc.edu
MAHAR, Kate .... 530-242-7769.. 63 H
kmahar@shastacollege.edu
MAHARAJ, Peter .... 714-484-7109.. 53 K
pmaharaj@cypresscollege.edu
MAHARAJ,
Sandhya (Sandy), G ... 304-766-3236 491 B
smaharaj@wvstateu.edu
MAHARAS, Marian .... 303-404-5285.. 79 J
marian.maharas@frontrange.edu
MAHDY, Ahmed .... 361-825-2577 447 C
ahmed.mahdy@tamucc.edu
MAHER, Brian .... 973-278-5400 275 I
bdm@berkeleycollege.edu
MAHER, Brian .... 212-986-4343 291 D
bdm@berkeleycollege.edu
MAHER, CM, James .... 716-286-8350 310 D
president@niagara.edu
MAHER, Jason .... 641-269-3450 165 J
maherjas@grinnell.edu
MAHER, Jeffrey .... 207-725-3178 193 D
jmaher@bowdoin.edu
MAHER, Jerelyn .... 309-676-7611 133 B
jmaher2@fsmail.bradley.edu
MAHER, John .... 304-696-4748 490 D
maherj@marshall.edu
MAHER, Judith .... 724-805-2900 398 E
judith.maher@email.stvincent.edu
MAHER, Judith .... 724-805-2581 398 F
judith.maher@stvincent.edu
MAHER, Tracy .... 701-854-8039 346 I
tracy.maher@sittingbull.edu
MAHER, Walter .... 210-829-3939 453 D
maher@uiwtx.edu
MAHER, William, J .... 716-888-2986 292 D
maherw@canisius.edu
MAHFOOD, Sebastian ... 860-632-3010.. 87 C
smahfood@holyapostles.edu
MAHINDRA, Ankush ...... 310-665-6916.. 54 I
amahindra@otis.edu
MAHITAB, Frank .... 478-825-6754 118 A
mahitabf@fvsu.edu
MAHLBERG, Raye .... 918-610-0027 366 A
rmahlberg@communitycarecollege.edu
MAHLER, Craig .... 615-675-5292 428 G
cmahler@welch.edu
MAHLER, Stephen, J ..... 337-482-6418 192 E
mahler@louisiana.edu
MAHLER, Steve .... 337-482-6780 192 E
mahler@louisiana.edu
MAHLMANN, Jaclyn ..... 361-825-2321 447 C
jaclyn.mahlmann@tamucc.edu
MAHLMEISTER,
Kenneth, J .... 718-990-5883 314 B
mahlmeik@stjohns.edu
MAHMOOD, Ghazanfar . 209-490-4591.. 24 E
gmahmood@advancedcollege.edu
MAHMOUD, Ghina .... 856-256-5747 281 E
najjar@rowan.edu
MAHNKE, Corrynn .... 715-836-2327 496 D
mahnkecm@uwec.edu
MAHON, Cathryn, A ..... 843-953-5432 408 E
mahonc@cofc.edu
MAHON,
Gwendolyn, M .... 973-972-4892 282 A
mahongm@shp.rutgers.edu
MAHON, James .... 718-960-8675 294 A
james.maho@lehman.cuny.edu
MAHON, Patricia, G ...... 605-394-2416 417 B
patricia.mahon@sdsmt.edu
MAHON, Richard .... 805-922-6966.. 24 J
richard.mahon@hancockcollege.edu
MAHON, Richard .... 909-274-5414.. 52 H
rmahon@mtsac.edu
MAHONE, Reshunda ...... 804-524-5045 477 B
rmahone@vsu.edu
MAHONE-LEIWS,
Gerald .... 254-526-1166 432 H
gerald.mahone-lewis@ctcd.edu
MAHONEY, Angela .... 336-770-3317 343 D
mahoneya@uncsa.edu
MAHONEY, Erin, A .... 765-658-4278 154 F
emahoney@depauw.edu
MAHONEY, Jack, D ...... 518-437-4928 316 D
jmahoney@albany.edu
MAHONEY, Janet .... 732-263-5271 279 B
jmahoney@monmouth.edu
MAHONEY, John .... 530-898-3276.. 31 A
jmahoney@csuchico.edu
MAHONEY, JR., John ... 617-552-3100 207 B
john.mahoney.2@bc.edu
MAHONEY, Kathryn ...... 303-352-6165.. 79 E
kathryn.mahoney@ccd.edu
MAHONEY, Kelly .... 401-874-5569 406 B
kellymahoney@uri.edu
MAHONEY, Kevin, B ..... 215-662-2203 400 K
kevin.mahoney@uphs.upenn.edu
MAHONEY, Kim .... 907-786-1110.... 9 H
MAHONEY, Leo .... 440-366-7738 355 J
MAHONEY, Lynn .... 415-338-1381.. 34 A
president@sfsu.edu
MAHONEY, Mary Ellen . 508-373-9510 206 B
maryellen.mahoney@becker.edu
MAHONEY, Melissa ...... 804-862-6100 470 I
mmahoney@rbc.edu
MAHONEY, Peter .... 724-805-2241 398 F
peter.mahoney@stvincent.edu
MAHONEY, Peter, E ...... 724-805-2241 398 E
peter.mahoney@email.stvincent.edu
MAHONEY, Sandra .... 337-550-1308 189 A
smahoney@lsue.edu
MAHONEY, Sharon, A .. 508-767-7322 205 D
shmahone@assumption.edu

MAHONEY, Thomas ...... 609-771-2734 276 I
tmahoney@tcnj.edu
MAHONEY, Trina .... 208-885-4387 131 G
tmahoney@uidaho.edu
MAHONEY, Yemi .... 765-983-1606 154 G
mahonye@earlham.edu
MAHONY, Daniel, F ...... 803-323-2225 414 G
mahonyd@winthrop.edu
MAHONY, James .... 517-264-3525 220 F
jmahony@adrian.edu
MAHOWALD, Rose .... 310-660-3111.. 41 L
rmahowald@elcamino.edu
MAI, Bill .... 307-766-4941 502 H
william.mai@uwyo.edu
MAI, Brent .... 503-493-6560 372 I
bmai@cu-portland.edu
MAI, Christy .... 785-227-3380 171 E
maicl@bethanylb.edu
MAI, Laura .... 309-268-8103 137 I
laura.mai@heartland.edu
MAI, Uyen .... 909-274-4121.. 52 H
umai@mtsac.edu
MAIBEN, Dina .... 215-635-7300 385 A
dmaiben@gratz.edu
MAIDEN, Michael .... 732-263-5285 279 B
mmaiden@monmouth.edu
MAIDOU, Nikoleta .... 617-850-1231 210 D
nmaidou@hchc.edu
MAIENSHEIN,
Richard, W .... 215-887-5511 402 H
rmaienshein@wts.edu
MAIER, Kim .... 608-822-2463 500 G
kmaier@swtc.edu
MAIER, Mark .... 517-607-2445 225 A
mmaier@hillsdale.edu
MAIER-O'SHEA,
Kathryn .... 773-244-5582 145 A
kmaier@northpark.edu
MAIERHOFER, Jean ...... 763-488-2633 238 B
jean.maierhofer@hennepintech.edu
MAIETTA, Heather .... 978-837-5038 216 D
maiettah@merrimack.edu
MAIGA, Harouna .... 218-281-8107 244 A
hmaiga@umn.edu
MAILE, Kristin .... 914-395-2560 315 F
kmaile@sarahlawrence.edu
MAILEY, Sharon .... 304-876-5344 490 E
smailey@shepherd.edu
MAILHOT, John .... 413-748-3145 218 G
jmailhot@springfield.edu
MAILLET, Becky .... 504-278-6477 188 A
bmaillet@nunez.edu
MAILLEY, Kimberly .... 718-940-5902 314 C
kmailley@sjcny.edu
MAIMON, Elaine, P ...... 708-534-4130 137 F
emaimon@govst.edu
MAIMONE, Charles, A .. 336-334-5200 343 A
camaimon@uncg.edu
MAIN, James, E .... 972-780-3600 454 B
MAIN, Jean .... 860-773-1494.. 86 G
jmain@tunxis.edu
MAIN, Jeremy .... 314-434-4044 252 B
jeremy.main@covenantseminary.edu
MAIN, Mary, E .... 540-458-8920 478 A
mmain@wlu.edu
MAIN, Nathan .... 269-927-8169 226 D
nmain@lakemichigancollege.edu
MAINE, Kate .... 706-864-1950 126 A
kate.maine@ung.edu
MAIO, James .... 315-792-5401 307 D
jmaio@mvcc.edu
MAIORANO, Andrew ..... 661-654-2782.. 30 E
MAIRS, Julie .... 520-325-0123.. 16 C
MAIRS, Rob .... 520-325-0123.. 16 C
rmairs@suva.edu
MAISENBACHER,
Melissa .... 863-667-5010 107 K
mamaisen@seu.edu
MAISON, Amy .... 229-225-3977 125 A
amaison@southernregional.edu
MAISTER, Eric .... 215-568-9215 403 H
emaister@phmc.org
MAISTO, Jeremy, A .... 717-867-6215 388 H
maisto@lvc.edu
MAITINO, Jennifer .... 617-333-3165 208 E
jmaitino0615@curry.edu
MAITLAND, Jason, R ..... 585-785-1437 300 B
jason.maitland@flcc.edu
MAITLEN, Caitlyn .... 641-782-1453 169 H
maitlen@swcciowa.edu
MAIYER, Mark .... 678-331-4356 121 C
mmaiyer@life.edu
MAIZE, David .... 210-883-1000 453 D
maize@uiwtx.edu
MAJAK, Julieta .... 845-257-3295 317 B
majakj@newpaltz.edu
MAJEBE, Mary Cissy .... 828-225-3993 328 E
president@daoisttraditions.edu
MAJEED, Hameedah ...... 281-756-3584 429 I
hmajeed@alvincollege.edu
MAJEROVIC, Chaim ...... 516-239-9002 315 I
rcm@shoryoshuv.org
MAJESKY, Mark .... 541-917-4245 374 A
majeskm@linnbenton.edu
MAJETTE, Yolanda .... 252-398-6249 328 D
majety@chowan.edu
MAJEWSKI, Deborah ..... 508-999-8060 211 F
dmajewski@umassd.edu
MAJEWSKI, John .... 805-893-4327.. 70 A
majewski@ltsc.ucsb.edu
MAJEWSKI, Marc .... 415-338-2596.. 34 A
majewski@sfsu.edu
MAJID, Anouar .... 206-221-4447 196 G
amajid@une.edu
MAJKA, David, R .... 412-397-5443 397 G
majka@rmu.edu
MAJOCHA, Kristen .... 724-938-4240 394 B
majocha@calu.edu
MAJOR, Carla .... 504-762-3003 187 E
cmajor@dcc.edu
MAJOR, Carrie .... 865-251-1800 424 A
cmajor@south.edu
MAJOR, Phillip .... 561-803-2034 104 C
phillip_major@pba.edu
MAJOR, Tonya .... 817-722-1700 439 B
tonya.major@tku.edu
MAJORS, Cristina .... 615-550-3170 429 A
cris@williamsoncc.edu
MAJUMDAR, Sutanu ..... 513-487-3259 301 E
smajumdar@huc.edu
MAJZNER, Kathy .... 561-803-2080 104 C
MAKARCZUK, Meghan .. 914-323-5484 305 J
meghan.makarczuk@mville.edu
MAKARECHI, Pejman .... 215-503-7841 400 A
pejman.makarechi@jefferson.edu
MAKAROFF, JR.,
Christopher, A .... 513-529-4432 356 E
makaroca@miamioh.edu
MAKEE, Susan .... 603-271-6484 273 B
smakee@ccsnh.edu
MAKEVICH, John .... 661-362-3384.. 38 H
john.makevich@canyons.edu
MAKHIJA, Anil, K .... 614-292-7899 358 I
makhija.1@osu.edu
MAKI, David, W .... 906-227-1262 228 F
dmaki@nmu.edu
MAKI, Kristen .... 508-856-1870 212 A
kristen.maki@umassmed.edu
MAKI, Laura .... 209-575-6173.. 75 J
makil@mjc.edu
MAKI, William .... 651-201-1732 237 A
MAKI, William, D .... 218-312-1510 238 E
wmaki@nhed.edu
MAKIN, Linda .... 801-863-8457 461 A
linda.makin@uvu.edu
MAKINEN, Bryan .... 859-622-2421 180 B
bryan.makinen@eku.edu
MAKOFSKE, Rose .... 215-619-7383 390 H
rmakofske@mc3.edu
MAKREZ ALLEN,
Heather .... 978-934-4809 211 G
heather_makrezallen@uml.edu
MAL, Mirlen .... 617-333-2193 208 E
mirlen.mal@curry.edu
MALAFA, Jeanette .... 217-652-6467 152 D
j-malafa@wiu.edu
MALAGIERE, Kenneth .... 732-255-0400 280 A
kmalagiere@ocean.edu
MALAGON, Blanca .... 305-284-2605 112 E
bmalagon@miami.edu
MALAGRINO, Tony .... 562-985-4131.. 31 F
tony.malagrino@csulb.edu
MALANCA, Donna .... 630-617-3550 136 G
donnas@elmhurst.edu
MALANDRA, Theresa .... 215-951-1619 387 C
malandrat1@lasalle.edu
MALANI, Upendra .... 703-284-1491 469 C
upendra.malani@marymount.edu
MALAS, JR., William .... 617-745-3828 208 G
william.malas@enc.edu
MALASKI, Donna .... 269-965-3931 225 F
malaskid@kellogg.edu
MALASPINA, Margaret .. 860-906-5096.. 85 D
mmalaspina@capitalcc.edu
MALASRI, Pong .... 901-321-3419 419 C
pong@cbu.edu
MALAT, Heide .... 651-690-6805 242 R
hlmalat@stkate.edu
MALATESTA, Addy .... 570-408-4020 403 D
adelene.malatesta@wilkes.edu
MALATESTA,
Matthew, J .... 518-388-6026 323 G
malatesm@union.edu
MALATRAS, Jim .... 518-587-2100 321 A
jim.malatras@esc.edu
MALAVE, Cesar .... 979-845-2217 446 G
dean@qatar.tamu.edu
MALAVE, Sarah .... 787-738-2161 513 D
sarah.malave@upr.edu
MALAVE-LASSO, Mara .. 787-480-2418 507 C
mamalave@sanjuanciudadpatria.com
MALAVET, Carmen .... 787-840-2575 510 J
cmalavet@psm.edu
MALAVOLTI, TOR,
Nathan .... 740-283-6407 353 B
nmalavolti@franciscan.edu
MALBAURN, Scott .... 541-552-8484 376 E
malbaurns@sou.edu
MALBROUGH, Russell .. 631-451-4630 321 F
malbror@sunysuffolk.edu
MALBY, Jeff .... 406-238-7376 265 E
jeff.malby@rocky.edu
MALCOLM, III,
Everett, J .... 904-620-2600 110 A
emalcolm@unf.edu
MALCOLM,
Jacquelyn, L .... 716-878-3694 318 C
malcoljl@buffalostate.edu
MALCOLM, John .... 216-791-5000 351 A
john.malcolm@cim.edu
MALCOLM, Joshua .... 910-775-4336 343 B
joshua.malcolm@uncp.edu
MALCOLM, Kathy .... 309-796-5038 132 G
malcolmk@bhc.edu
MALCOLM, Kim .... 309-694-8815 138 C
kmalcolm@icc.edu
MALCOLM, Molly Beth . 512-223-7683 431 A
mollybeth.malcolm@austincc.edu
MALCOM-PIQUEUX,
Lindsey, E .... 626-395-1567.. 29 C
malcom@caltech.edu
MALDAR, Mustafa .... 832-230-5555 440 H
maldar@na.edu
MALDONA VLAAR,
Carmen .... 787-764-0000 514 B
carmen.maldonado7@upr.edu
MALDONADO, Amelia ... 787-850-9327 513 E
amelia.maldonado1@upr.edu
MALDONADO,
Bernadette .... 301-405-1995 202 C
blm@umd.edu
MALDONADO, Candice . 325-481-8300 438 C
cdraper@howardcollege.edu
MALDONADO, Carlos ... 760-773-2566.. 39 A
cmaldonado@collegeofthedesert.edu
MALDONADO, Cesar .... 713-718-5059 437 I
cesar.maldonado@hccs.edu
MALDONADO, Gilda ..... 619-388-2817.. 60 D
gmaldona@sdccd.edu
MALDONADO, Ileana .... 787-725-8120 507 N
imaldonado@eap.edu
MALDONADO, Israel ..... 718-270-3161 317 E
israel.maldonado@downstate.edu
MALDONADO, Kenneth . 787-751-0178 511 F
kenmaldona@suagm.edu
MALDONADO, Lourdes . 787-766-1717 511 H
lmaldonado@suagm.edu
MALDONADO,
Maria del Carmen ...... 787-751-0160 507 F
mcmaldon@cmpr.gov.pr
MALDONADO, Nichole . 787-753-6000 508 D
MALDONADO, Orlando . 787-751-0160 507 F
omaldonado@cmpr.pr.gov
MALDONADO, Theresa . 915-747-6921 455 C
tamaldonado@utep.edu
MALDONADO, Victor .... 787-878-5475 508 L
vmaldonado@arecibo.inter.edu
MALDONADO, Víctor .... 787-815-0000 513 A
victor.maldonado1@upr.edu
MALDONADO, Wanda ... 787-758-2525 513 G
wanda.maldonado1@upr.edu
MALDONADO,
Wendy, E .... 787-888-1135 510 D
wmaldonado@monteclaro.edu
MALDONADO, Yesenia . 630-889-6546 144 G
ymaldonado@nuhs.edu
MALDONADO-RIVERA,
Irving .... 787-743-3038 511 A
imaldonado@sanjuanbautista.edu
MALDONADO-ROJAS,
Jose, E .... 787-288-1118 512 A
MALDOON, Gladys .... 718-960-8111 294 A
gladys.maldoon@lehman.cuny.edu
MALE, Taylor .... 989-328-1275 228 A
taylor.male@montcalm.edu
MALECHA, Marvin .... 619-684-8777.. 53 H
mmalecha@newschoolarch.edu
MALECHA, Ryan .... 731-989-6022 420 C
rmalecha@fhu.edu
MALEKI, Soroush .... 206-934-6070 483 J
soroush.maleki@seattlecolleges.edu
MALEKPOUR, Susan ..... 719-598-0200.. 79 C
MALEKZADEH, Ali .... 312-341-3800 147 H
amalekzadeh@roosevelt.edu
MALEPEAI-RHODES,
Alexis .... 208-562-3505 130 F
alexisrhodes@cwi.edu
MALESH, Rashmi .... 718-262-2916 295 F
rmalesh@york.cuny.edu
MALESPINI, Al .... 719-846-5707.. 82 K
al.malespini@trinidadstate.edu
MALESZEWSKI, Joseph . 850-412-5480 108 I
joseph.maleszewski@famu.edu
MALEY, Brian .... 513-745-3315 365 B
maley@xavier.edu
MALEY, David, C .... 607-274-3480 303 B
maley@ithaca.edu
MALEY, Joelle .... 605-773-3455 416 G
MALFITANO,
Gregory, J .... 561-237-7277 102 V
gmalfitano@lynn.edu
MALHOTRA, Devinder ... 651-201-1638 237 A
devinder.malhotra@minnstate.edu
MALHOTRA, Manoj .... 216-368-1156 349 F
manoj.malhotra@case.edu
MALHOTRA, Rajiv, R .... 401-825-1176 404 H
rrmalhotra@ccri.edu
MALHOTRA, Rishab ...... 312-567-3909 139 B
rmalhot1@iit.edu
MALIA, Marcia .... 352-588-8242 106 D
marcia.malia@saintleo.edu
MALICK, Cassie .... 859-622-2101 180 B
cassie.malick@eku.edu
MALIEKAL, Jose .... 585-395-2394 318 B
jmalieka@brockport.edu
MALIG, Jannet .... 562-860-2451.. 35M
jmalig@cerritos.edu
MALIGO, Pedro .... 402-826-8221 267 A
pedro.maligo@doane.edu
MALIK, Elyas .... 352-638-9723.. 95 D
emalik@beaconcollege.edu
MALIK, Nish .... 415-405-4105.. 34 A
nish@sfsu.edu
MALIK, Rick .... 312-788-1188 152 B
rmalik@vandercook.edu
MALIK, Zafar, A .... 312-939-0111 136 D
zafar@eastwest.edu
MALIN, Adam .... 608-796-3913 498 N
ammalin@viterbo.edu
MALIN, Burke .... 650-685-6616.. 44 J
bmalin@gurnick.edu
MALIN, Jay .... 712-274-5116 168 B
malin@morningside.edu
MALIN, Jennifer, L .... 620-417-2102 176 K
jennifer.malin@sccc.edu
MALIN, John .... 217-854-5572 132 I
john.malin@blackburn.edu
MALINA, Joel, M .... 607-255-9029 297 F
vp-university@cornell.edu
MALINAK, Steven .... 724-503-1001 402 E
smalinak@washjeff.edu
MALINOWSKI, Gayle ..... 802-468-1389 464 A
gayle.malinowski@castleton.edu
MALINOWSKI-FERRARY,
Sarah .... 201-761-6239 282 I
smalinowski@saintpeters.edu
MALISCH, Susan, M ..... 773-508-7750 142 D
smalisc@luc.edu
MALIWESKY, Martin ..... 614-287-3674 351 E
mmaliwes@cscc.edu
MALKIC, Amela .... 941-359-4314 110 D
amela@usf.edu
MALKOWSKI, Keith, J ... 989-774-7226 222 C
malko1kj@cmich.edu
MALLABO, Jose .... 470-639-0543 122 D
jose.mallabo@morehouse.edu
MALLARD, Cindy .... 731-352-4000 418 G
mallardc@bethel.edu
MALLARD, Jessica .... 806-651-2777 448 C
jmallard@wtamu.edu

MALLARD, Kina, S 770-720-5502 123 E ksm@reinhardt.edu

MALLARI, Kelly 336-517-2179 327 B kmallari@bennett.edu

MALLE, Connie, D 620-235-4793 176 F cmalle@pittstate.edu

MALLER, Jennifer 847-543-2375 135 B jmaller@clcillinois.edu

MALLERY, Mary 718-951-5611 293 C mary.mallery@brooklyn.cuny.edu

MALLERY, Michael 541-506-6050 372 G mmallery@cgcc.edu

MALLERY, Taniecea 337-482-6464 192 E taniecea.mallery@louisiana.edu

MALLET, Colleen 845-437-5276 324 C comallet@vassar.edu

MALLETT, Chris 617-373-6440 217 F

MALLETT, Veronica, T 615-327-6204 422 A vmallett@mmc.edu

MALLETTE, Constance 336-750-2703 344 B mallettec@wssu.edu

MALLETTE, Kirk 402-363-5696 270 E kmallette@york.edu

MALLEY, Rebecca 601-266-4466 249 F rebecca.malley@usm.edu

MALLIE, Andre 619-260-5951 71 J amallie@sandiego.edu

MALLOL, Ramon 787-765-3560 507 L ramon@edpuniversity.edu

MALLORY, Brian 843-521-4137 413 E malloryb@uscb.edu

MALLORY, Caroline 812-237-3683 155 G caroline.mallory@indstate.edu

MALLORY, Jeff 412-396-1117 383 C malloryj@duq.edu

MALLORY, Kristen 909-621-8267 37 E kristen.mallory@cmc.edu

MALLORY, Kristin, L 410-334-2813 204 F kmallory@worwic.edu

MALLORY, Lisa 404-756-4013 114 G lmallory@atlm.edu

MALLORY, Rob 270-852-3330 183 A rmallory@kwc.edu

MALLORY, Timothy, L 757-822-1783 476 B tmallory@tcc.edu

MALLOY, Dannel, P 207-973-3220 195 I dannel.malloy@maine.edu

MALLOY, Gary 843-953-5118 407 F malloyg1@citadel.edu

MALLOY, Sarah, L 479-575-4140 21 G

MALLOY, Stephanie 419-227-3141 363 C sadavis@unoh.edu

MALLOY, Thomas, K 610-499-4174 403 B tkmalloy@widener.edu

MALM, Loren 765-285-1034 153 C lmalm@bsu.edu

MALMGREN, Jodi 507-786-3375 243 C malmgren@stolaf.edu

MALO, Trudi 704-461-6717 327 A trundimalo@bac.edu

MALONE, Allison 501-337-5000 18 J amalone@coto.edu

MALONE, Anne, B 412-924-1379 396 I amalone@pts.edu

MALONE, Barbara 903-463-8730 437 D maloneb@grayson.edu

MALONE, Brian 505-277-8900 288 G bmalone@unm.edu

MALONE, David 616-526-6072 222 A dbm9@calvin.edu

MALONE, Dean, P 630-515-7145 143 G dmalon@midwestern.edu

MALONE, Deborah 610-282-1100 382 E debbie.malone@desales.edu

MALONE, Dennis, C 404-713-1069 123 D dennis.malone@runiv.edu

MALONE, Elbert, R 803-536-8213 412 C malone@scsu.edu

MALONE, Emmanuel 480-245-7903 12 N

MALONE, Gregory 216-987-2340 351 G gregory.malone@tri-c.edu

MALONE, Judith 781-891-2016 206 D jmalone@bentley.edu

MALONE, Kate 216-397-4909 354 I kmalone@jcu.edu

MALONE, Kathy 219-980-6701 156 E kalmalon@iun.edu

MALONE, Laurie 513-936-1537 362 E laurie.malone@uc.edu

MALONE, Marc 620-276-9595 173 E marc.malone@gcccks.edu

MALONE, Matt 620-241-0723 172 D matthew.malone@centralchristian.edu

MALONE, Maureen 610-989-1453 402 B mmalone@vfmac.edu

MALONE, Michael 860-768-7793 88 H malone@hartford.edu

MALONE, Michael 740-826-8086 357 C

MALONE, Michael, F 413-545-5270 211 D mmalone@umass.edu

MALONE, Pamela 528-587-2100 321 A pamela.malone@esc.edu

MALONE, Shannon 970-247-7358 79 I smmalone@fortlewis.edu

MALONE, Susan, C 478-301-2233 121 E malone_sc@mercer.edu

MALONE, Tamra 562-777-4085 27 C tamra.j.malone@biola.edu

MALONE, Travis 757-455-3256 477 F tmalone@vwu.edu

MALONE, Walter 502-597-6693 182 H walter.malone@kysu.edu

MALONE-COLON, Linda 757-727-5400 468 B linda.malone-colon@hamptonu.edu

MALONE-HADDOX, Kimberly 615-871-2260 92 G

MALONEY, Anne, O 570-961-4581 389 G maloney@marywood.edu

MALONEY, Barry, M 508-929-8020 213 E bmaloney@worcester.edu

MALONEY, Caroline 760-674-7640 39 A cmaloney@collegeofthedesert.edu

MALONEY, Catherine 617-984-1787 218 B cmaloney@quincycollege.edu

MALONEY, Cory 740-283-6944 353 B cmaloney@franciscan.edu

MALONEY, Dena, P 310-660-3111 41 L dmaloney@elcamino.edu

MALONEY, Edward, J 202-687-9858 92 A ejm@georgetown.edu

MALONEY, Heather 513-745-5710 362 E heather.maloney@uc.edu

MALONEY, Kimberly 732-255-0400 280 A kmalony@ocean.edu

MALONEY, Marcy 805-756-1281 30 C mmaloney@calpoly.edu

MALONEY, Mary 508-791-9241 206 B

MALONEY, Michael 212-280-1534 323 H mmaloney@uts.columbia.edu

MALONEY, Rebecca, S 504-866-7426 190 B rmaloney@nds.edu

MALONEY, Shari 320-762-4466 237 B sharim@alextech.edu

MALONEY, Vinnie 803-786-3608 408 F vmaloney@columbiasc.edu

MALOOF, Eric 210-999-7273 452 A emaloof@trinity.edu

MALOTKY, Daniel 336-272-7102 329 D dmalotky@greensboro.edu

MALOTT, Michelle 765-973-8320 156 C mimalott@iue.edu

MALOTT, Pat 719-384-6823 81 E pat.malott@ojc.edu

MALOTT, Richard 763-433-1204 237 D richard.malott@anokaramsey.edu

MALOY, Frances, J 518-388-6739 323 G maloyf@union.edu

MALPASS, Scott, C 574-631-8877 161 C malpass.1@nd.edu

MALTA, Anthony 318-342-3547 192 F malta@ulm.edu

MALTBY, Marc 270-686-4544 182 B marc.maltby@kctcs.edu

MALTER, Dave 215-635-7300 385 A dmalter@gratz.edu

MALTZMAN, Forrest 202-994-6510 91 F forrest@gwu.edu

MALUTICH, Stephen, M 602-275-7133 15 O stephen.malutich@rsiaz.edu

MALVEAUX, Gregory 240-567-8077 200 C greg.malveaux@montgomerycollege.edu

MALY, Lonn 651-641-8203 235 F maly@csp.edu

MALY, Mike 312-341-3769 147 H mmaly@roosevelt.edu

MALYN, Justin 816-235-5294 261 C malynj@umkc.edu

MAMA, Robin 732-571-3607 279 B rmama@monmouth.edu

MAMAY, Fred 973-300-2119 283 E fmamay@sussex.edu

MAMMEN, Tanya 641-673-2123 170 F tanyamammen@wmpenn.edu

MAMMENGA, Brenda 605-626-2433 417 A brenda.mammenga@northern.edu

MANAHAN, Jamie 219-989-3252 159 G jmanahan@pnw.edu

MANAKAS, Sharon 805-378-1413 72 H smanakas@vcccd.edu

MANAKAS, Vance 805-378-1457 72 H vmanakas@vcccd.edu

MANALLA, Christine 504-568-4800 189 B cmanal@lsuhsc.edu

MANAOIS, Rogelio, A 415-338-6488 34 A jmanaois@sfsu.edu

MANASSAH, Michele 850-474-2420 110 E mmanassah@uwf.edu

MANAUTOU, Teresa 787-864-2222 509 C teresa.manautou@guayama.inter.edu

MANAZIR, Theodore 802-728-1275 464 E tmanazir@vtc.edu

MANCE, Nick, J 618-235-2700 149 H nick.mance@swic.edu

MANCEOR, Thomas 313-993-1508 231 B tmanceor@udmercy.edu

MANCHESTER-MOLAK, Ann 401-865-2406 405 B ammolak@providence.edu

MANCINI, Michael 609-984-1105 284 B mmancini@tesu.edu

MANCINI, Mike 574-520-4415 157 A mmancini@iusb.edu

MANCINI, Sarah 216-881-1700 359 F smancini@ohiotech.edu

MANCINI, Tracy 252-222-6144 333 A mancinit@carteret.edu

MANCINI-BROWN, Darlene 860-512-3660 85 G dmancini-brown@manchestercc.edu

MANCINO, Mary, S 610-861-5415 391 F msinibaldi@northhampton.edu

MANCOSH, Bridget 412-392-3992 397 A bmancosh@pointpark.edu

MANCUSO, Matthew 712-325-3434 167 B mmancuso@iwcc.edu

MANCUSO, Sandra, L 305-899-3072 95 C smancuso@barry.edu

MAND, Claire 608-663-3228 493 C cmand@edgewood.edu

MANDALA, Jim 973-408-3395 277 C jmandala@drew.edu

MANDEL, Carol, A 212-998-2444 310 B carol.mandel@nyu.edu

MANDEL, Christine 315-655-7250 292 F cmandel@cazenovia.edu

MANDEL, Christine 315-655-7174 292 F cmandel@cazenovia.edu

MANDEL, Gregory, M 215-204-8993 399 F gregory.mandel@temple.edu

MANDEL, Jeffrey 570-389-4311 394 A jmandel@bloomu.edu

MANDEL, Jennifer 207-602-2980 196 G jmandel2@une.edu

MANDEL, Larry 562-951-4430 30 B lmandel@calstate.edu

MANDEL, Maud, S 413-597-4233 220 C msm8@williams.edu

MANDELKERN, Michael 714-432-5786 38 E mmandelkern@occ.cccd.edu

MANDEREN, Michael, C 440-775-8413 358 C michael.manderen@oberlin.edu

MANDERSHEID, David 865-974-2445 427 G dmanders@utk.edu

MANDEVILLE, Steve 314-529-6849 254 H shmandeville@maryville.edu

MANDEVILLE-GAMBLE, Steve 951-827-3221 69 C steve.mandeville-gamble@ucr.edu

MANDRELL, Jon, D 815-835-6344 148 H jon.d.mandrell@svcc.edu

MANDRELL, Kara 319-385-6453 167 A kara.mandrell@iw.edu

MANDUJANO, Hazel 310-665-6976 54 I hmandujano@otis.edu

MANDY, Lisa 408-864-8403 43 C mandylisa@deanza.edu

MANDYAM, Raja 512-454-1188 430 G info@aoma.edu

MANERI, Wendy, L 315-568-3262 308 F wmaneri@nycc.edu

MANESS, Terry, S 254-710-3411 431 J terry_maness@baylor.edu

MANESS, Thomas 541-737-4279 375 D thomas.maness@oregonstate.edu

MANESS, Virginia 813-988-5131 98 Q admissions@floridacollege.edu

MANETTA, Edward 914-323-7270 305 J edward.manetta@mville.edu

MANEY, Beth 515-244-3146 313 D maneye@sage.edu

MANFERDINI, Elena 213-613-2200 64 H elena_manferdini@sciarc.edu

MANFRA, Matthew 732-987-2478 278 B mmanfra@georgian.edu

MANFREDA, Teresa 732-224-2638 276 B tmanfreda@brookdalecc.edu

MANGAN, Kim 217-420-6658 143 H kmangan@millikin.edu

MANGANARO, Marc 251-380-2262 6 H mmanganaro@shc.edu

MANGAROVA, Nelly 510-592-9688 54 C nelly.mangarova@npu.edu

MANGELS, Andrew, P 413-545-1581 211 D amangels@admin.umass.edu

MANGELS, Kathy, M 573-651-2570 259 K kmangels@semo.edu

MANGHAM, Kirk 757-490-1241 464 F kmangham@auto.edu

MANGIACAPRA, Vincent, P 203-932-7058 89 A vmangiacapra@newhaven.edu

MANGINE, John, J 814-332-4356 378 D jmangine@allegheny.edu

MANGINO, Christine 718-518-6611 294 B cmangino@hostos.cuny.edu

MANGIONE, Amy 518-445-2361 289 E amang@albanylaw.edu

MANGIONE, Lisa 864-250-8461 410 B lisa.mangione@gvltec.edu

MANGIONE, Terri 310-338-3756 50 J terri.mangione@lmu.edu

MANGLONA, Gregorio, T 671-777-5591 505 C safety@guamcc.edu

MANGLONA-PROPST, Daisy 670-237-6792 506 A daisy.propst@marianas.edu

MANGOLD, Thomas 401-841-2074 503 L thomas.mangold@usnwc.edu

MANGUAL, Marlene 787-766-1912 508 J mmanguals@inter.edu

MANGUM, Genita, D 717-736-4144 385 E gdmangum@hacc.edu

MANGUM, Linda 336-334-7862 341 F lmangum@ncat.edu

MANGUM, Sarah 530-752-2427 68 E semangum@ucdavis.edu

MANGUM, Steve 865-974-5061 427 G smangum@utk.edu

MANGUM, Vincent 404-756-4006 114 G vmangum@atlm.edu

MANGUS, Christy 269-782-1473 230 F cmangus@swmich.edu

MANGUS, Jennifer 814-332-2312 378 D jmangus@allegheny.edu

MANHARDT, Joseph 207-741-5598 195 A jmanhardt@smccme.edu

MANIACI, Vincent, M 413-205-3202 205 A vincent.maniaci@aic.edu

MANIAOL, Albert 909-384-8904 59 I amaniaol@sbccd.cc.ca.us

MANIATIS, Marc 203-932-7218 89 A mmaniatis@newhaven.edu

MANICKAM, Joseph 620-327-8233 173 H joseph.manickam@hesston.edu

MANIER, Tracy, L 512-448-8602 442 M tracym@stedwards.edu

MANIGAULT, Kimberly 412-237-3001 381 G kmanigault@ccac.edu

MANIGO, Jocelyn 610-436-3238 396 A jmanigo@wcupa.edu

MANIGO, Venis 803-777-4115 413 C venis.manigo@sc.edu

MANILAY, Jol 209-946-2236 70 E jmanilay@pacific.edu

MANION, Amy 262-695-3459 500 H amanion@wctc.edu

MANION, Andrew, P 920-923-7617 494 A amanion@marianuniversity.edu

MANION, Sheila, M 314-977-2306 259 H sheila.manion@slu.edu

MANIS, Christopher 619-388-6546 60 B cmanis@sdccd.edu

MANISCALCO, Steven 607-436-2735 317 C steven.maniscalco@oneonta.edu

MANISCALCO, Steven, J 607-436-2735 317 C steven.maniscalco@oneonta.edu

MANJONE, Joe 251-981-3771 5 B joe.manjone@columbiasouthern.edu

MANKEY, Richanne, C 419-783-2300 352 F rmankey@defiance.edu

MANKO, Tammy, P ...... 724-357-2235 394 G
tammy.manko@iup.edu
MANKOWICH, James .... 205-929-3498.... 2 H
jmankowich@lawsonstate.edu
MANLEY, Colleen .... 315-229-5988 314 F
cmanley@stlawu.edu
MANLEY, Denise .... 864-388-8350 410 D
dmanley@lander.edu
MANLEY, James .... 845-451-1760 298 A
james.manley@culinary.edu
MANLEY, Jennifer .... 360-596-5305 485 B
jmanley@spscc.edu
MANLEY, John .... 252-335-3266 341 D
jhmanley@ecsu.edu
MANLEY, Lisa .... 860-727-6788.. 87 A
lmanley@goodwin.edu
MANLEY, Thomas .... 937-319-6164 347 G
MANLEY-ROOK,
Stephanie .... 252-493-7383 336 H
sgmrook@email.pittcc.edu
MANN, Brian .... 813-253-7022 101 A
bmann@hccfl.edu
MANN, Charles, G .... 301-696-3611 199 B
mann@hood.edu
MANN, Christy .... 870-512-7867.. 18 B
christy_mann@asun.edu
MANN, Daniel .... 217-333-9299 151 D
danmann@illinois.edu
MANN, Deanna .... 620-901-6338 170 G
mann@allencc.edu
MANN, Doug .... 423-775-7208 418 H
dmann7365@bryan.edu
MANN, Douglas .... 410-225-2352 199 H
dmann@mica.edu
MANN, Eric .... 251-626-3303.... 7 E
emann@ussa.edu
MANN, Gary .... 734-432-5325 227 A
gmann@madonna.edu
MANN, Gwendolyn .... 334-229-4436.... 4 B
gmann@alasu.edu
MANN, Henry, J .... 614-292-5711 358 I
mann.414@osu.edu
MANN, Janet .... 202-687-1307.. 92 A
mannj2@georgetown.edu
MANN, Karen .... 502-585-9911 184 D
kmann@spalding.edu
MANN, Karen .... 315-279-5289 304 A
kmann@keuka.edu
MANN, Kevin, J .... 410-543-6202 203 F
kjmann@salisbury.edu
MANN, Lara, G .... 317-781-5760 161 B
mannlg@uindy.edu
MANN, Laura .... 507-457-5069 241 F
lmann@winona.edu
MANN, Lucretia .... 914-674-7492 306 F
lmann@mercy.edu
MANN, Lynde .... 256-228-6001.... 3 B
mannl@nacc.edu
MANN, Randy .... 254-295-4618 453 E
rmann@umhb.edu
MANN, Steve .... 732-247-5241 279 D
smann@nbts.edu
MANNARA, Kevin .... 585-385-8196 314 A
kmannara@sjfc.edu
MANNELLA, Stephen ..... 610-436-2242 396 A
smannella@wcupa.edu
MANNELLI, Rita, J .... 585-389-2147 308 B
rmannel5@naz.edu
MANNER, Kimberly .... 310-287-4395.. 49 G
mannerke@wlac.edu
MANNERING,
Susan, M .... 302-225-6232.. 90 E
manners@gbc.edu
MANNINEN, Kevin .... 906-487-7371 223 K
kevin.manninen@finlandia.edu
MANNING, Amanda ...... 207-326-2280 195 D
amanda.manning@mma.edu
MANNING, Amelia .... 603-314-1416 274 D
a.manning@snhu.edu
MANNING, Beth .... 810-762-3150 231 G
bmanning@umich.edu
MANNING, Carmen, K .. 715-836-3671 496 D
manninck@uwec.edu
MANNING, Christopher 773-508-3081 142 D
cmannin@luc.edu
MANNING, Colleen .... 713-646-1729 444 B
cmanning@stcl.edu
MANNING, Danielle ...... 909-869-3019.. 30 D
dmanning@cpp.edu
MANNING, Dawn .... 252-493-7633 336 H
dmanning@email.pittcc.edu
MANNING, Dianne .... 413-662-5249 213 A
dianne.manning@mcla.edu
MANNING, Gaye .... 870-574-4509.. 21 E
gmanning@sautech.edu
MANNING, Jennifer ...... 815-753-9676 145 C
manning@niu.edu
MANNING, Jessica .... 325-942-2021 451 A
jessica.manning@angelo.edu
MANNING, Jessica .... 214-305-9454 429 B
jxm15c@acu.edu
MANNING, John, F .... 617-495-4601 210 B
jmanning@law.harvard.edu
MANNING, Karen .... 910-695-3995 337 H
manningk@sandhills.edu
MANNING, Kirk .... 845-398-4066 315 B
kmanning@stac.edu
MANNING, Linda .... 206-934-6415 484 B
linda.manning@seattlecolleges.edu
MANNING,
Lynn Etta, G .... 214-887-5366 436 B
lmanning@dts.edu
MANNING, Marcus .... 318-869-5087 186 B
mmanning@centenary.edu
MANNING, Mark .... 315-498-2622 311 B
m.r.manning@sunyocc.edu
MANNING, Mark .... 315-498-2268 311 B
m.r.manning@sunyocc.edu
MANNING, Michelle ..... 262-551-5931 492 F
mmanning@carthage.edu
MANNING, Mike .... 765-674-6901 157 D
mike.manning@indwes.edu
MANNING, Noel, T .... 704-406-4631 329 A
ntmanning@gardner-webb.edu
MANNING, Patricia .... 850-201-8994 111 C
manningp@tcc.fl.edu
MANNING, R. Douglas . 714-564-6900.. 57 L
manning_r-douglas@sac.edu
MANNING, Sandra, J .... 919-572-1625 326 L
smanning@apexsot.edu
MANNING, Scott .... 570-372-4256 399 C
manning@susqu.edu
MANNING, Tina .... 912-427-5814 116 F
tmanning@coastalpines.edu
MANNING, Veronica ..... 870-512-7890.. 18 B
veronica_manning@asun.edu
MANNING, Vivian .... 360-992-2104 479 F
vmanning@clark.edu
MANNING-MILLER,
Donald .... 662-252-8000 248 G
manningmiller@rustcollege.edu
MANNINO, Jessica, L .... 315-445-4130 304 C
hammonjl@lemoyne.edu
MANNINO, Sam .... 502-459-3535 184 E
smannino@sullivan.edu
MANNION, Tom, N .... 626-395-6174.. 29 C
mannion@caltech.edu
MANNISTO, Richard ...... 414-443-8788 498 O
rich.mannisto@wlc.edu
MANNIX, William .... 413-236-3036 213 F
wmannix@berkshirecc.edu
MANNO, Kim .... 740-366-9135 349 H
manno.18@osu.edu
MANNO, Mariann, M ..... 508-856-2323 212 A
admissions@umassmed.edu
MANNS, Jennifer .... 970-207-4550.. 80 M
jenniferm@mckinleycollege.edu
MANNS, Jill, R .... 260-982-5050 158 T
jrmanns@manchester.edu
MANOGIN, Toni, L .... 225-771-2273 190 H
toni_manogin@sus.edu
MANOHAR, Aruna, S ..... 410-323-6211 198 C
a.manohar@fts.edu
MANOHAR, John .... 410-323-6211 198 C
j.manohar@fts.edu
MANOHAR, Norman, J . 410-323-6211 198 C
n.manohar@fts.edu
MANOLIS, Lilly .... 617-327-6777 220 B
lilly_manolis@williamjames.edu
MANOR, Scott .... 954-771-0376 102 R
smanor@knoxseminary.edu
MANORD, Wayne .... 256-352-8116.... 4 A
wayne.manord@wallacestate.edu
MANORE, David .... 315-792-7280 321 E
david.manore@sunypoly.edu
MANOS, Dennis, M .... 757-871-9581 466 C
dmanos@wm.edu
MANOUSOS, Carol .... 713-221-8425 453 B
manousosc@uhd.edu
MANRIQUE, Santos .... 620-231-3690 173 C
santosm@fortscott.edu
MANRIQUEZ, Chris .... 310-243-3655.. 31 B
cmanriquez@csudh.edu
MANROSE, Mark .... 310-665-6851.. 54 I
mmanrose@otis.edu
MANRY, J. Mark .... 248-218-2120 229 J
mmanry@rc.edu
MANRY, Mark .... 248-218-2120 229 J
mmanry@rc.edu
MANRY, Robert .... 785-628-4513 173 B
rjmanry@fhsu.edu
MANSAPIT, Felix .... 671-482-8671 505 E
fmansapit@triton.uog.edu
MANSDORF, Geri .... 646-592-4440 326 E
gmansdor@yu.edu
MANSER,
Jacqueline, M .... 330-490-7117 364 B
jmanser@walsh.edu
MANSFIELD, Amy .... 616-234-4226 224 D
amymansfield@grcc.edu
MANSFIELD, Jim .... 217-351-2435 146 C
jmansfield@parkland.edu
MANSFIELD, Jim .... 217-351-2290 146 C
jmansfield@parkland.edu
MANSFIELD, Robin .... 908-737-4880 278 E
rmansfie@kean.edu
MANSFIELD, Tim .... 315-228-7433 296 F
tmansfield@colgate.edu
MANSO, Jose, R .... 212-694-1000 291 I
jmanso@boricuacollege.edu
MANSON, Rachel .... 484-365-7807 389 C
rmanson@lincoln.edu
MANSON, Robert .... 714-564-6247.. 57 L
manson_robert@sac.edu
MANSON, Stephen .... 803-793-5263 409 C
mansons@denmarktech.edu
MANSOUR, Deena .... 406-243-2988 264 A
deena.mansour@umontana.edu
MANSOUR, Nick .... 602-222-9300.. 10 F
nmansour@arizonacollege.edu
MANSOUR, Ruchana ..... 347-394-1036 291 E
rmansour@ateret.net
MANSPERGER, Thomas 419-755-4650 357 E
tmansperger@ncstatecollege.edu
MANSUETO, Anthony .... 214-860-2693 435 C
anthony.mansueto@dcccd.edu
MANSUR, Jay .... 859-858-2305 178 H
MANTELLA,
Philomena, V .... 616-331-2100 224 E
president@gvsu.edu
MANTER, Debbie .... 972-708-7340 435 H
alumni@diu.edu
MANTERNACH, Dean .... 402-354-7058 268 C
dean.manternach@methodistcollege.edu
MANTHE, Theodore, E .. 507-344-7745 234 B
ted.manthe@blc.edu
MANTHEY, Tom .... 406-657-2085 264 E
tom.manthey@msubillings.edu
MANTILLA, Tonya, M .... 414-410-4210 492 D
tmmantilla@stritch.edu
MANTLO, Ryan .... 910-362-7042 332 H
rmantlo@cfcc.edu
MANTONI, Thomas .... 610-282-1100 382 E
thomas.mantoni@desales.edu
MANTOOTH, Brooks, E . 620-665-3497 174 B
mantoothb@hutchcc.edu
MANTOOTH, James, D . 731-881-7053 428 B
jdmantooth@utm.edu
MANTOVANI, Theresa ... 407-265-8383.. 96 A
MANTRANA, Manuel ..... 214-860-3633 435 D
manuelmantrana@dcccd.edu
MANTZ, Tim .... 610-902-8765 380 C
MANUEL, Ann, S .... 410-651-6400 203 A
asmanuel@umes.edu
MANUEL, Barbara .... 276-739-2432 476 C
bmanuel@vhcc.edu
MANUEL, Beulah .... 301-891-4184 204 C
bmanuel@wau.edu
MANUEL, Elizabeth .... 304-558-0655 489 O
elizabeth.manuel@wvhepc.edu
MANUEL, Jeff .... 205-652-3682.... 9 A
jmanuel@uwa.edu
MANUEL, Keith .... 334-291-4950.... 1 H
keith.manuel@cv.edu
MANUEL, Marilyn, G .... 504-286-5020 190 I
mmanuel@suno.edu
MANUEL, Mark .... 859-246-6673 180 K
mark.manuel@kctcs.edu
MANUEL, Mary .... 661-362-3184.. 38 H
mary.manuel@canyons.edu
MANUEL, Robert, L ...... 317-788-3211 161 B
rmanuel@uindy.edu
MANUEL, Thomas, E .... 859-238-5361 179 F
thomas.manuel@centre.edu
MANUEL, Warde .... 734-764-9416 231 E
wardemanuelad@umich.edu
MANUKYAN, Diana .... 510-925-4282.. 25 Q
diana@aua.am
MANULI, Nunziatina, A . 718-990-2401 314 B
manulin@stjohns.edu
MANZANARES, Lucy ..... 828-328-7142 330 F
lucy.manzanares@lr.edu
MANZANAREZ,
Magdaleno .... 575-538-6229 289 B
magdaleno.manzanarez@wnmu.edu
MANZANO, Anna .... 310-665-6951.. 54 I
amanzano@otis.edu
MANZANO, Florentino .. 818-947-2691.. 49 F
manzanf@lavc.edu
MANZANO, Yvonne ...... 575-835-5533 286 I
yvonne.manzano@nmt.edu
MANZKE, Robert .... 715-346-3738 497 F
rmanzke@uwsp.edu
MANZO, Dana .... 352-638-9751.. 95 D
dmanzo@beaconcollege.edu
MANZO, Pablo .... 916-856-3400.. 50 E
manzop@losrios.edu
MANZO, Serena .... 206-281-2598 484 D
serenamanzo@spu.edu
MAO, Ruixuan .... 847-214-7440 136 F
rmao@elgin.edu
MAPES, Chris .... 270-789-5013 179 E
ctmapes@campbellsville.edu
MAPES, Kim .... 570-961-7810 387 D
mapesk@lackawanna.edu
MAPES, Sharon .... 707-965-6232.. 55 D
smapes@puc.edu
MAPHUMULO, Peter ..... 760-245-4271.. 73 D
peter.maphumulo@vvc.edu
MAPIRA, Happiness ...... 614-251-7641 358 G
mapirah@ohiodominican.edu
MAPLE, Makala .... 402-844-7268 268 J
makala@northeast.edu
MAPLE, Vicki .... 740-364-9565 349 H
maple.2571@cotc.edu
MAPLES, Christopher .... 503-821-8881 375 F
presidentsoffice@pnca.edu
MAPLES, John .... 806-720-7478 439 H
john.maples@lcu.edu
MAPLES, Stephen .... 775-784-4700 271 F
smaples@unr.edu
MAPLES, Tracey .... 903-510-3346 452 C
tracey.maples@tjc.edu
MAPPS, Lorianna .... 443-518-4133 199 C
lmapps@howardcc.edu
MAPSTON, Austin .... 406-657-1024 265 E
mapstona@rocky.edu
MARA, Mary .... 206-239-4500 479 E
mmara@cityu.edu
MARA, Stacy, J .... 920-832-6557 493 K
stacy.j.mara@lawrence.edu
MARABETI, Hilary, B .... 615-230-3355 426 B
hilary.marabeti@volstate.edu
MARABLE, Shelia .... 205-929-6437.... 2 H
smarable@lawsonstate.edu
MARAGAKIS,
Emmanuel .... 775-784-6925 271 F
maragaki@ce.unr.edu
MARAH, Andrew, E .... 717-736-4160 385 E
aemarah@hacc.edu
MARAK, Andrae .... 708-534-4101 137 F
amarak@govst.edu
MARAK, Janeil .... 919-735-5151 338 H
janeilm@waynecc.edu
MARAK, Randy .... 713-646-2912 444 B
rmarak@stcl.edu
MARANDI, Susan .... 212-410-8039 309 B
smarandi@nycpm.edu
MARANVILLE, Amy .... 978-478-3400 217 G
amaranville@northpoint.edu
MARASCO, Canio .... 716-829-7846 298 F
marascoc@dyc.edu
MARASINGHE, Madhavi 701-777-5756 345 C
madhavi.marasinghe@und.edu
MARASKA, Monica .... 973-328-5340 277 B
mmaraska@ccm.edu
MARATHE, Tara .... 858-646-3100.. 62 A
tmarathe@sbpdiscovery.org
MARAVETZ, Sarah .... 410-225-2219 199 H
smaravetz@mica.edu
MARAVIGLIA, James, L 805-756-2311.. 30 C
jmaravig@calpoly.edu
MARAZITA, John .... 614-251-4687 358 G
marazitj@ohiodominican.edu
MARBACH, Joseph, R .... 732-987-2252 278 B
president@georgian.edu
MARBLE, Alan .... 417-625-9501 256 D
marble-a@mssu.edu
MARBLE, Amanda, F ..... 208-467-8402 131 D
afmarble@nnu.edu
MARBLE, Jan .... 507-389-5120 239 C
janice.marble@mnsu.edu

MARBLE, Janet .... 607-871-2144 289 H
marblej@alfred.edu
MARBRAY, Antionette ... 619-594-5211.. 33 E
amarbray@sdsu.edu
MARBURY, Diane .... 516-562-0449 299 B
dmarbury@northwell.edu
MARBURY, Kevin .... 541-346-1137 377 D
kmarbury@uoregon.edu
MARBURY, Sonni .... 928-692-3032.. 14 F
smarbury@mohave.edu
MARCANGELI, Karissa .. 918-610-0027 366 A
kmarcangeli@communitycarecollege.edu
MARCANO, Walbert .... 787-257-0000 513 C
walbert.marcano@upr.edu
MARCEAUX, Christi .... 985-545-1500 187 H
MARCEC, Paula .... 920-465-2207 496 E
marcecp@uwgb.edu
MARCEL, Gina .... 985-448-7929 187 F
gina.marcel@fletcher.edu
MARCELLA, Patricia ...... 508-588-9100 214 F
pmarcella@massasoit.mass.edu
MARCELLINO, Sara .... 510-215-3805.. 40 H
smarcellino@contracosta.edu
MARCELO, Cheryl .... 903-813-2025 430 N
cmarcelo@austincollege.edu
MARCH, Debra .... 706-379-3111 127 C
dbmarch@yhc.edu
MARCH, Mandy .... 573-592-5226 262 E
mandy.march@westminster-mo.edu
MARCH, Peter .... 848-932-7896 282 A
peter.march@rutgers.edu
MARCHAL, Anne .... 845-434-5750 322 A
amarchal@sunysullivan.edu
MARCHAND, Nicole ...... 612-861-7554 233 H
nicole.marchand@alfredadler.edu
MARCHAND, William ..... 516-686-7904 309 F
wmarchan@nyit.edu
MARCHANT, Karen .... 605-626-7781 417 A
karen.marchant@northern.edu
MARCHBANKS, Pete ...... 979-845-9999 446 G
pete-marchbanks@tamu.edu
MARCHELLO, Sara, L .... 757-221-2801 466 C
slmarc@wm.edu
MARCHESE, Wendy .... 315-866-0300 301 G
marcheswt@herkimer.edu
MARCHIONE, Susan, M 716-839-8447 298 B
smarchio@daemen.edu
MARCHIONE-TRAINA,
Joyce .... 201-488-9400 277 F
MARCHIONINI, Gary ..... 919-962-8363 342 D
gary@ils.unc.edu
MARCHIORI,
Dennis, M .... 563-884-5500 168 I
dennis.marchiori@palmer.edu
MARCHITELLO, Howard 856-225-6149 281 G
marchitello@camden.rutgers.edu
MARCHWICK,
Colleen, C .... 715-836-4874 496 D
marchwcc@uwec.edu
MARCIAL, Myriam .... 787-891-0925 508 K
mmarcial@aguadilla.inter.edu
MARCIANO, Jackie .... 610-902-8212 380 C
jmm745@cabrini.edu
MARCIL, Michelle .... 518-564-2082 319 C
marcilmm@plattsburgh.edu
MARCIN, Heidi, C .... 585-785-1609 300 B
heidi.marcin@flcc.edu
MARCONE, Luigi .... 203-837-9314.. 85 B
marconel@wcsu.edu
MARCOTTE, Brian .... 310-377-5501.. 51 B
bmarcotte@marymountcalifornia.edu
MARCOTTE, Theresa ...... 618-395-7777 138 I
marcottet@iecc.edu
MARCOU, William, L .... 414-410-4463 492 D
wlmarcou@stritch.edu
MARCOUX, Jamie, P .... 508-767-7416 205 D
jp.marcoux@assumption.edu
MARCOUX, Mollie, D ... 609-258-3535 280 E
mmarcoux@princeton.edu
MARCOZZI, Rudi .... 312-341-3500 147 H
MARCUCCILLI,
Christine, M .... 260-481-6106 159 F
marcuccc@pfw.edu
MARCUS, Bess .... 401-863-9858 404 E
bess_marcus@brown.edu
MARCUS, Lynn .... 978-762-4000 215 B
lmarcus@northshore.edu
MARCUS, Robert, J ...... 317-940-9910 153 F
rmarcus@butler.edu
MARCUS, Susan .... 773-907-4418 134 C
smarcus2@ccc.edu
MARCUS, Terry .... 691-320-2480 505 B
tmarcus@comfsm.fm
MARCUS-NEWHALL,
Amy .... 909-607-3541.. 63 E
amy.marcus-newhall@scrippscollege.edu
MARCUSE, Elizabeth, S . 212-752-1530 304 D
emarcuse@limcollege.edu
MARCUSSEN, Thomas ... 414-229-4537 497 A
marcusse@uwm.edu
MARCY, Mary, B .... 415-485-3200.. 41 H
president@dominican.edu
MARCZYNSKI, Jerry ...... 775-784-4898 271 F
marczyns@unr.edu
MARDEN, Jennifer .... 661-395-4211.. 46 L
jmarden@bakersfieldcollege.edu
MARDEN, Rose .... 210-341-1366 441 C
rmarden@ost.edu
MARDER, Dave .... 404-471-5465 113 G
dmarder@agnesscott.edu
MARDIS, Michael .... 502-852-5787 185 C
m.mardis@louisville.edu
MARDIS, Patrick .... 334-727-8757.... 7 D
pmardis@tuskegee.edu
MAREK, Amy .... 573-592-5195 262 E
amy.marek@westminster-mo.edu
MAREK, Kate .... 708-524-6648 136 C
kmarek@dom.edu
MAREK, Robin .... 731-425-2654 425 B
rmarek@jscc.edu
MAREK-MARTINEZ, Ora 928-523-8532.. 14 H
ora.marek-martinez@nau.edu
MARENTES, Henry .... 619-596-2766.. 24 F
hmarentes@advancedtraining.edu
MARES, Maria .... 787-864-2222 509 C
maria.mares@guayama.inter.edu
MARES, Michaela .... 626-585-7553.. 55 K
mmares5@pasadena.edu
MARESCA, Laura .... 303-871-7436.. 83 D
laura.maresca@du.edu
MARFISE, Larry, J .... 813-253-6240 112 J
lmarfise@ut.edu
MARFOE, Tina .... 708-237-5050 145 E
tmarfoe@nc.edu
MARGERUM-LEYS, Jon . 248-370-3045 229 G
jmargerumleys@oakland.edu
MARGETTS, James .... 308-432-6246 268 E
jmargetts@csc.edu
MARGHEIM, Jeffrey ...... 386-822-7020 111 A
jmarghei@stetson.edu
MARGO, Carlos .... 956-872-6109 444 A
clmargo@southtexascollege.edu
MARGOLIN, Lori .... 201-360-4244 278 C
lmargolin@hccc.edu
MARGOLIS, Leslie .... 267-620-4894 379 A
margolisl@arcadia.edu
MARGRAVE, Alex .... 563-884-5257 168 I
alex.margrave@palmer.edu
MARGRAVE, Carrie .... 207-326-0265 195 D
carrie.margrave@mma.edu
MARGULES, Gary, S ..... 954-262-7507 103 M
margules@nova.edu
MARGULIES, Anne .... 617-495-9092 210 B
anne_margulies@harvard.edu
MARGULIES, L .... 718-853-8500 322 I
MARGULIES,
Mordechai .... 718-854-2290 291 F
MARHENKE, Catherine .. 315-228-7037 296 F
cmarhenke@colgate.edu
MARI, Mike .... 530-242-7595.. 63 H
mmari@shastacollege.edu
MARIANI, Elsa .... 787-257-7373 511 G
emariani@suagm.edu
MARIANO, Anthony, A . 802-485-2230 463 A
tmariano@norwich.edu
MARIANO, Milbert .... 707-965-6234.. 55 D
mmariano@puc.edu
MARIANO, Rosette .... 323-254-2203.. 41 J
MARIC, Radenka .... 860-486-3619.. 88 E
radenka.maric@uconn.edu
MARICHAL-LUGO,
Carlos .... 787-993-8866 513 B
carlos.marichal@upr.edu
MARIELLA-WALROND,
Helena .... 386-481-2349.. 95 F
walrondh@cookman.edu
MARIETTA, Melissa .... 607-436-2534 317 C
melissa.marietta@oneonta.edu
MARIL, Virginia .... 805-493-3577.. 29 H
gmaril@callutheran.edu
MARIN, Anthony, S ...... 575-646-7207 287 B
amarin@nmsu.edu
MARIN, Elsa .... 787-764-0000 514 B
elsa.marin1@upr.edu
MARIN, Joseph, F .... 225-922-1635 186 J
jmarin@lctcs.edu
MARIN, Nicole .... 707-468-3065.. 51 E
nmarin@mendocino.edu
MARIN, Rafael, E .... 787-863-2390 509 B
rafael.marin@fajardo.inter.edu
MARIN ANDRADE,
Claudia, L .... 516-876-3067 319 A
marinandradec@oldwestbury.edu
MARIN-HILL, Angelica .. 214-648-3684 457 B
angelica.marin-hill@utsouthwestern.edu
MARINA, Joseph, G ..... 315-445-4124 304 C
marinaj@lemoyne.edu
MARINACCIO, Jessica ... 212-854-1222 297 C
jm996@columbia.edu
MARINACE, Betsy .... 973-684-6868 280 B
bmarinace@pccc.edu
MARINAK, Barbara, A ... 301-447-5170 200 E
marinak@msmary.edu
MARINAN, Jerilyn .... 516-876-3158 319 A
marinanj@oldwestbury.edu
MARINCH, Maria .... 702-651-7546 271 A
maria.marinch@csn.edu
MARINE, Jason .... 407-264-9400.. 92 G
MARINE, Sharon .... 773-702-0686 150 J
smarine@uchicago.edu
MARINELLI, Bryan, D ... 401-865-1822 405 B
bmarinel@providence.edu
MARINELLI, Roberta ..... 541-737-0123 375 D
MARING, Bayta .... 206-546-6949 484 G
bmaring@shoreline.edu
MARINI, Mario .... 724-589-2022 399 H
mmarini@thiel.edu
MARINI, Stephen, T ..... 508-854-4272 215 D
smarini@qcc.mass.edu
MARINO, Chris .... 864-646-1836 413 A
cmarino@tctc.edu
MARINO, David .... 215-204-7663 399 F
david.marino0001@temple.edu
MARINO, Dennis .... 319-208-5022 169 F
dmarino@scciowa.edu
MARINO, Lucille .... 785-864-7439 177 D
lmarino@ku.edu
MARINO, Marie .... 215-503-7794 400 A
marie.ann.marino@jefferson.edu
MARINO, Michael .... 419-720-6670 360 F
mike.marino@edevolve.org
MARINUCCI, Dorothy .... 718-817-3000 300 E
marinucci@fordham.edu
MARION, D. Keith .... 803-754-4100 409 A
MARION, Jeanne, V ...... 607-871-2094 289 H
marion@alfred.edu
MARION, Joseph .... 504-286-5389 190 I
jmarion@suno.edu
MARION, Lucy, N .... 706-721-3771 115 A
lumarion@augusta.edu
MARION, Michael .... 908-526-1200 281 A
michael.marion@raritanval.edu
MARION, Ron .... 802-322-1717 462 C
ron.marion@goddard.edu
MARIONEAUX, Stachia . 225-490-1628 186 F
stachia.marioneaux@franu.edu
MARISAM, Tina .... 612-626-9357 243 E
marisam@umn.edu
MARISOL, Cortes .... 646-313-8000 295 E
marisol.cortes@guttman.cuny.edu
MARIUCCI, Robert .... 805-546-3210.. 41 A
rmariucc@cuesta.edu
MARIX, Amy .... 225-578-3486 188 I
amarix@lsu.edu
MARK, Allan .... 704-461-6736 327 A
allanmark@bac.edu
MARK, Kevin .... 208-732-6295 130 E
kmark@csi.edu
MARK, Marty, L .... 319-273-6258 163 B
marty.mark@uni.edu
MARKANTONAKIS,
Angelo .... 704-216-3710 337 F
angelo.markantonakis@rccc.edu
MARKEL, Karen .... 907-786-4126.... 9 H
MARKEL, Mark, D .... 608-263-6716 496 C
mark.markel@wisc.edu
MARKELL, Dawn .... 810-762-3085 231 G
dmarkell@umich.edu
MARKER, Brian .... 434-381-6144 472 D
bmarker@sbc.edu
MARKER, James .... 814-254-0404 381 F
jamarker@pa.gov
MARKER, Trish .... 304-214-8960 489 F
pmarker@wvncc.edu
MARKEY, Heidi .... 863-784-7108 107 F
heidi.markey@southflorida.edu
MARKEY, John .... 210-341-1366 441 C
jmarkey@ost.edu
MARKEY-GRABILL,
Mindy .... 937-393-3431 361 B
mmarkey@sscc.edu
MARKGRAF, Jill, S .... 715-836-4827 496 D
markgrjs@uwec.edu
MARKGRAF, Karl .... 218-726-7053 243 F
kmarkgra@d.umn.edu
MARKHAM, Adrianne ..... 860-773-1371.. 86 G
amarkham@tunxis.edu
MARKHAM, Cindy .... 985-867-2263 190 F
rectorsec@sjasc.edu
MARKHAM, Desiree .... 575-769-4131 285 K
desiree.markham@clovis.edu
MARKHAM, Ian, S .... 703-370-6600 470 B
MARKHAM, Mark .... 770-426-2980 121 C
john.markham@life.edu
MARKIDES, Karin .... 510-925-4282.. 25 Q
MARKIN, Karen .... 401-874-5971 406 B
markevicius@uri.edu
MARKIN, Rodney .... 402-559-7687 270 A
rmarkin@unmc.edu
MARKIN, Terrence, C ... 301-243-2260 503 J
terrence.markin@dodiis.mil
MARKLAND, Allie .... 616-632-2948 221 C
acm003@aquinas.edu
MARKLAND, Scott .... 937-512-5502 361 A
scott.markland@sinclair.edu
MARKLE, Suzanne, L .... 412-346-2100 396 F
smarkle@pia.edu
MARKLEY, Ashley .... 856-351-2831 283 A
amarkley@salemcc.edu
MARKLEY, Bradley, A ... 717-796-1800 390 E
bmarkley@messiah.edu
MARKLEY, Neil .... 707-664-4068.. 34 C
neil.markley@sonoma.edu
MARKOFF, Eliane .... 781-891-3102 206 D
emarkoff@bentley.edu
MARKOVICH, Monica ..... 574-239-8405 155 D
mmarkovich@hcc-nd.edu
MARKOVITCH, Matthew 707-524-1849.. 62 F
mmarkovitch@santarosa.edu
MARKOW, David .... 802-828-8535 463 F
david.markow@vcfa.edu
MARKOWITZ, Carol .... 504-865-2011 189 F
carol@loyno.edu
MARKOWITZ, Gary .... 478-471-4394 120 F
MARKOWITZ, Marianne 315-448-5040 314 D
marianne.markowitz@sjhsyr.org
MARKOWITZ, Michael .. 267-341-3286 386 A
mmarkowitz@holyfamily.edu
MARKOWITZ, Sheila ..... 620-341-5211 172 L
smarkowi@emporia.edu
MARKOWSKI, Vincent ... 201-684-7432 280 H
vmarkows@ramapo.edu
MARKS, Alana .... 256-766-6610.... 5 F
amarks@hcu.edu
MARKS, Andrea, M .... 210-567-7020 456 C
marksa@uthscsa.edu
MARKS, Andy .... 219-473-4295 153 G
amarks@ccsj.edu
MARKS, Carl .... 610-796-8392 378 F
carl.marks@alvernia.edu
MARKS, David .... 201-879-7999 275 H
dmarks1@bergen.edu
MARKS, Dennis .... 503-883-2602 373 H
dmarks@linfield.edu
MARKS, Erica .... 845-257-3240 317 B
markse@newpaltz.edu
MARKS, Farah .... 434-947-8056 470 E
fmarks@randolphcollege.edu
MARKS, Howard .... 432-685-4726 440 E
hmarks@midland.edu
MARKS, Janice, L .... 443-518-4617 199 C
jmarks@howardcc.edu
MARKS, Jeffrey .... 760-750-4062.. 33 B
jmarks@csusm.edu
MARKS, John .... 414-382-6360 492 A
john.marks@alverno.edu
MARKS, Katie .... 360-417-6276 483 B
kmarks@pencol.edu
MARKS, Lilly .... 303-724-5369.. 83 C
lilly.marks@ucdenver.edu
MARKS, Mary Beth .... 504-280-7014 189 E
mmarks1@uno.edu
MARKS, Michelle .... 703-993-8705 467 L
mmarks@gmu.edu
MARKS, Nick .... 603-822-5434 274 H
nicholas.marks@granite.edu
MARKS, Patrice .... 908-526-1200 281 A
patrice.marks@raritanval.edu
MARKS, Sandra .... 562-860-2451.. 35 M
smarks@cerritos.edu

MARKS, Steven 718-780-7507 291 J
steven.marks@brooklaw.edu

MARKSON, Alison, W 617-333-2120 208 E
amarkson1109@curry.edu

MARKULY, Mark 206-296-5330 484 F
markulym@seattleu.edu

MARKUM, Michael 254-298-8291 446 A
mmarkum@templejc.edu

MARKWOOD, Chris 706-507-8950 116 I
markwood_chris@columbusstate.edu

MARKWORTH, Ruth 414-425-8300 495 H
rmarkworth@shsst.edu

MARLAIRE, Colin 866-776-0331 54 A
cmarlaire@ncu.edu

MARLAIRE, Natalyn, M 715-852-1399 499 D
nmarlaire@cvtc.edu

MARLATT, Julie 217-351-2531 146 C
jmarlatt@parkland.edu

MARLER, Eric 808-675-3708 127 E
eric.marler@byuh.edu

MARLETT, Jeffrey 518-454-2861 296 H
marlettj@strose.edu

MARLETTE, Marnie, S 336-841-4683 329 G
mmarlett@highpoint.edu

MARLEY, Chad 307-778-1346 502 D
cmarley@lccc.wy.edu

MARLIN, John 201-360-4287 278 C
jmarlin@hccc.edu

MARLIN, John 973-328-5090 277 B
jmarlin@ccm.edu

MARLO, Francis (Frank) 202-462-2101 92 C
fmarlo@iwp.edu

MARLOW, Amber 715-634-4790 493 I
marlowa@lco.edu

MARLOW, Dan 816-279-7000 250 B
dan@abtu.edu

MARLOW, J.J 712-274-5424 168 B
marlow@morningside.edu

MARLOW, Jean 859-622-1986 180 B
jean.marlow@eku.edu

MARLOW, Mike 928-523-5353 14 H
mike.marlow@nau.edu

MARLOW, Peter 619-260-7460 71 J
petermarlow@sandiego.edu

MARLOW, Thomas, J 718-390-4352 314 B
marlowt@stjohns.edu

MARLOWE, Channing, H 205-391-2256 3 E
cmarlowe@sheltonstate.edu

MARLOWE, June 314-991-6245 133 F
jmarlowe@chamberlain.edu

MARLOWE, Michelle 304-357-4944 488 G
michellemarlowe@ucwv.edu

MARLOWE, Wendy, C 252-451-8243 336 E
wcmarlowe937@nashcc.edu

MARMARELLI, Beth 313-593-5542 231 F
bethmar@umich.edu

MARMO, Andrew 303-466-1714 82 J

MARMOLEJO, William 818-710-2955 49 C
marmolwa@piercecollege.edu

MARMORSTEIN, Naomi 856-225-6434 281 G
marmorst@camden.rutgers.edu

MARNEY, Dylan 573-288-6351 252 E
dmarney@culver.edu

MARNEY, Katherine 573-288-6478 252 E
kmarney@culver.edu

MARNICH, Darlene 412-392-3474 397 A
dmarnich@pointpark.edu

MAROHL, Matthew 507-786-3092 243 C
marohl@stolaf.edu

MAROLDO, Brian 516-686-7449 309 F
bmaroldo@nyit.edu

MARONEY, Christopher, S 315-684-6465 321 D
maronecs@morrisville.edu

MARONEY, Dustin 520-494-5237 11 K
dustin.maroney@centralaz.edu

MARONEY, Dustin 480-517-8418 13 G
dustin.maroney@riosalado.edu

MAROUN, Sarah 518-891-2915 310 E
smaroun@nccc.edu

MAROZICK, Jeff 415-485-9467 39 C
jmarozick@marin.edu

MARPLE, Bradley 214-648-2646 457 B
bradley.marple@utsouthwestern.edu

MARQUARDT, Brian 231-591-3755 223 J
brianmarquardt@ferris.edu

MARQUARDT, Christopher 315-229-5250 314 F
cmarquardt@stlawu.edu

MARQUARDT, Robert 405-585-5504 367 F
robert.marquardt@okbu.edu

MARQUARDT, Shelly 714-547-9625 28 C
smarquardt@calcoast.edu

MARQUART, James, W 409-880-8398 449 H
james.marquart@lamar.edu

MARQUES, Javier 305-348-2111 109 A
javier.marques@fiu.edu

MARQUES, Jeffrey 413-775-1700 214 C
marquesj@gcc.mass.edu

MARQUES, Joan 818-394-3391 75 C
joan.marques@woodbury.edu

MARQUEZ, Abigail 407-251-0007 104 B
amarquez@omi.edu

MARQUEZ, Andrew 520-792-1506 457 J
andrew.marquez@wbu.edu

MARQUEZ, Dianne 575-492-2841 286 J
dmarquez@nmjc.edu

MARQUEZ, JR., Felix, J 407-251-0007 104 B
fmarquez@omi.edu

MARQUEZ, Kenneth, L 719-587-7227 76 F
klmarque@adams.edu

MARQUEZ, Korey 360-992-2472 479 F
kmarquez@clark.edu

MARQUEZ, Krishna 787-746-1400 508 B
kmarquez@huertas.edu

MARQUEZ, Loren, L 757-455-3338 477 F
lmarquez@vwu.edu

MARQUEZ, Moses 505-454-5312 286 D
mmarquez@luna.edu

MARQUEZ, Nelson 863-734-1509 113 B
marqueznj@webber.edu

MARQUEZ, Nora 650-433-3865 55 G
nmarquez@paloaltou.edu

MARQUEZ, Patricia 619-260-7795 71 J
pmarquez@sandiego.edu

MARQUEZ, Raymond 805-482-2755 58 L
rmarquez@stjohnsem.edu

MARQUEZ-HUDSON, Christine 303-615-0065 80 N
cmarqu37@msudenver.edu

MARQUEZ-SCALLY, Marline 505-984-6075 287 J
registrar@sjc.edu

MARQUIS, Susan 310-393-0411 55 J
smarquis@rand.org

MARR, Jay, D 502-456-6506 184 E
jmarr@sullivan.edu

MARR, Jena 405-422-1265 369 E
jena.marr@redlandscc.edu

MARR, Ronda 209-946-2206 70 E
rmarr@pacific.edu

MARR, Shannon 406-771-4408 264 G
shannon.marr1@gfcmsu.edu

MARRA, Joseph 845-574-4156 313 C
jmarra2@sunyrockland.edu

MARRA, Michele, L 740-376-4718 356 A
mm011@marietta.edu

MARRANT, Dale 913-234-0612 172 E
dale.marrant@cleveland.edu

MARRAPESE, Patricia 607-777-2510 316 E
pmarra@binghamton.edu

MARRAPODI, Michael, E 617-873-0652 207 F
michael.marrapodi@cambridgecollege.edu

MARRERO, Argelio 860-906-5125 85 D
amarrero@capitalcc.edu

MARRERO, Carmen-Amalia 787-250-1912 509 D
camarrero@metro.inter.edu

MARRERO, Kyle 912-478-5211 119 C
kmarrero@georgiasouthern.edu

MARRERO, Luis, A 787-766-1717 511 H
lumarrero@suagm.edu

MARRERO, Rene 787-841-2000 510 K
rene_marrero@pucpr.edu

MARRERO, Wilma 787-765-1915 510 B
wmarrero@opto.inter.edu

MARRERO-HERNÁNDEZ, Angel 787-993-8852 513 B
angel.marrero@upr.edu

MARRERO PEREZ, Rafael 787-780-0070 506 F
rmarrero@caribbean.edu

MARRETT, Clifford 860-465-0306 84 J
marrettc@easternct.edu

MARRINER, Nigel, R 716-878-4811 318 C
marrinnr@buffalostate.edu

MARRIOTT, Carol 585-343-0055 301 A
cmarriott@genesee.edu

MARRIOTT, Danny 760-480-8474 74 J
dmarriott@wscal.edu

MARRIOTT, Douglas 818-947-2929 49 F
marriodc@lavc.edu

MARRIOTT, Duncan 219-989-3199 159 G
dmarriot@pnw.edu

MARRIOTT, Jean 410-386-8121 197 G
jmarriott@carrollcc.edu

MARRIOTT, Karin 951-487-3060 52 I
kmarriott@msjc.edu

MARRIOTT, Martin 920-206-2310 493 L
marty.marriott@mbu.edu

MARRIOTT, Russell 214-818-1318 434 F
rmarriott@criswell.edu

MARROCCO, Susan 941-752-5201 108 G
marrocs@scf.edu

MARROCHELLO, Drew 617-353-4631 207 D
marroand@bu.edu

MARRON, Timothy 206-296-5990 484 F
marront@seattleu.edu

MARRON, Victoria 281-425-6501 439 D
vmarron@lee.edu

MARRONE-CREECH, Tiana 541-463-5538 373 F
marrone-creecht@lanecc.edu

MARROTT, Ann 845-687-5070 323 E
marrotta@sunyulster.edu

MARROW, Cary 806-894-9611 443 I
cmarrow@southplainscollege.edu

MARROW, Sydne, M 508-531-1754 212 B
smarrow@bridgew.edu

MARROW, Victor 252-536-7283 335 B
vmarrow@halifaxcc.edu

MARRS, Chris 979-691-2069 432 C
chris.marrs@blinn.edu

MARRS, Rick 310-506-4261 56 C
rick.marrs@pepperdine.edu

MARRS, Sherrie 606-218-5261 185 D
sherriemarrs@upike.edu

MARS, Kandace 785-670-2270 177 G
kandace.mars@washburn.edu

MARSAGLIA, JR., Joseph, A 412-362-8500 396 G
jmarsaglia@pims.edu

MARSALEK, Lisa 419-783-2587 352 F
lmarsalek@defiance.edu

MARSALIS, Joyce 865-354-3000 425 G
marsalisje@roanestate.edu

MARSALIS, Wynton 212-799-5000 303 H

MARSCH, Charlotte 417-328-1803 259 L
cmarsch@sbuniv.edu

MARSCHKE, Robyn 719-255-3640 83 B
rmarschk@uccs.edu

MARSDEN, Janet 740-427-5158 355 E
marsden1@kenyon.edu

MARSDEN, John, P 859-846-5310 183 E
jmarsden@midway.edu

MARSELIAN, Zareh 805-493-3119 29 H
marselia@callutheran.edu

MARSH, Anne 540-828-8024 465 D
atmarsh@bridgewater.edu

MARSH, Barry 843-349-7557 410 C
barry.marsh@hgtc.edu

MARSH, Bonnie 724-439-4900 388 F
bmarsh@laurel.edu

MARSH, Brent 662-915-7705 249 D

MARSH, Brent 918-343-7569 369 F
bmarsh@rsu.edu

MARSH, Cecilia 660-359-3948 257 D
cmarsh@mail.ncmissouri.edu

MARSH, Clay, B 304-293-1024 491 C
cbmarsh@hsc.wvu.edu

MARSH, David, F 989-837-4389 228 H
dmarsh@northwood.edu

MARSH, Douglas, K 574-631-4200 161 C
marsh.14@nd.edu

MARSH, Dyremple 302-857-6400 89 F
dmarsh@desu.edu

MARSH, Eric 585-785-1293 300 B
eric.marsh@flcc.edu

MARSH, III, F. Chapin 954-453-9228 34 G

MARSH, Geoff 562-903-4742 27 C
geoff.marsh@biola.edu

MARSH, Gregory 409-880-2100 449 H
gregory.marsh@lamar.edu

MARSH, Heather, A 214-860-3611 435 D
hmarsh@dcccd.edu

MARSH, James, G 254-710-2467 431 J
jim_marsh@baylor.edu

MARSH, Janet 517-607-2341 225 A
jmarsh@hillsdale.edu

MARSH, Jed 609-258-7860 280 E
jmarsh@princeton.edu

MARSH, Jerry 570-702-8927 386 G
jmarsh@johnson.edu

MARSH, Jolee 910-678-8217 334 D
marshj@faytechcc.edu

MARSH, Kent 719-255-3505 83 B
kmarsh@uccs.edu

MARSH, Marilyn 215-324-0746 383 D
mmarsh@eastern.edu

MARSH, MaToya 773-821-2601 133 K
mmarsh@csu.edu

MARSH, Maureen 410-516-8132 199 D
mmarsh9@jhu.edu

MARSH, Nancy, J 770-720-5657 123 E
njm@reinhardt.edu

MARSH, Nicole, Y 510-379-4053 48 A
librarian@lincolnuca.edu

MARSH, Robert 231-439-6353 228 E
rmarsh@ncmich.edu

MARSHAK, Helen Hopp 909-558-4578 48 C
hhoppmarshak@llu.edu

MARSHALECK, Allison 610-341-4375 383 D
amarshal@eastern.edu

MARSHALL, Alycia 410-777-2776 197 C
aamarshall@aacc.edu

MARSHALL, Amy 706-886-6831 125 D
amarshall@tfc.edu

MARSHALL, Amy 510-986-6984 56 G
amarshall@peralta.edu

MARSHALL, Ave 404-270-5288 125 B
amarshall@spelman.edu

MARSHALL, Ben 813-253-7125 101 A
rmarshall10@hccfl.edu

MARSHALL, Bleuzette 513-556-6262 362 D
bleuzette.marshall@uc.edu

MARSHALL, Bryon 609-586-4800 278 F
marshalb@mccc.edu

MARSHALL, Cameron 434-223-6148 468 A
cmarshall@hsc.edu

MARSHALL, Charles, B 504-865-7421 189 F
cbmarsh@loyno.edu

MARSHALL, Chebon 661-255-1050 28 K
cmarshall@calarts.edu

MARSHALL, Cheryl, A 714-808-4797 53 J
cmarshall@nocccd.edu

MARSHALL, Christina 714-997-6517 36 C
cmarsh@chapman.edu

MARSHALL, Christopher 813-529-2640 503 J
christopher.marshall@centcom.mil

MARSHALL, Connie 423-323-0238 425 E
cmarshall@northeaststate.edu

MARSHALL, Connie 423-279-7632 425 E

MARSHALL, Courtney 316-978-3830 178 A
courtney.marshall@wichita.edu

MARSHALL, Darren 801-957-4782 461 D
darren.marshall@slcc.edu

MARSHALL, Darwina 405-692-3196 366 G

MARSHALL, Dave 218-235-2125 241 E
david.marshall@vcc.edu

MARSHALL, David 909-537-5032 33 A
dmarshall@csusb.edu

MARSHALL, David 979-230-3213 432 D
david.marshall@brazosport.edu

MARSHALL, David, B 805-893-2785 70 A
david.marshall@ucsb.edu

MARSHALL, Debbie 858-695-8587 155 E
dmarshall@horizonuniversity.edu

MARSHALL, Donna 252-638-7249 333 H
marshalldo@cravencc.edu

MARSHALL, Elaine 864-503-5331 414 D
emarshall@uscupstate.edu

MARSHALL, Ella 843-383-8060 408 D
emarshall@coker.edu

MARSHALL, Erica 260-359-4290 155 F
emarshall@huntington.edu

MARSHALL, Ericka 801-290-3240 459 E
ericka.marshall@independence.edu

MARSHALL, J, A 413-205-3263 205 A
ja.marshall@aic.edu

MARSHALL, James 559-278-2448 31 D
jamesm@csufresno.edu

MARSHALL, JaNice 216-987-3260 351 G
janice.marshall@tri-c.edu

MARSHALL, Joan 732-247-5241 279 D
jmarshall@nbts.edu

MARSHALL, John 970-248-1366 77 I
marshall@coloradomesa.edu

MARSHALL, Jon 620-901-6212 170 G
marshall@allencc.edu

MARSHALL, Judith 618-536-2626 149 E
jmarshal@siu.edu

MARSHALL, Justin, W 989-837-4279 228 H
marshall@northwood.edu

MARSHALL, Katherine 716-270-2661 299 F
marshallk@ecc.edu

MARSHALL, Kent 708-974-5390 144 C
marshallk34@morainevalley.edu

MARSHALL, Kevin .... 909-460-2000.. 70 D gholmes@laverne.edu
MARSHALL, Kim .... 870-762-1020.. 17 D kmarshall@smail.anc.edu
MARSHALL, Kimberley .. 470-639-0982 122 D kimberley.marshall@morehouse.edu
MARSHALL, Larry .... 724-852-3230 402 F lmarshal@waynesburg.edu
MARSHALL, Lori .... 856-256-4197 281 E marshall@rowan.edu
MARSHALL, Lynette, L .. 319-335-3305 163 A lynette-marshall@foriowa.org
MARSHALL, Margaret, J .... 334-844-7474.... 4 E mjm0030@auburn.edu
MARSHALL, Marianne ... 262-551-8500 492 F mmarshall@carthage.edu
MARSHALL, Maura .... 603-641-7028 274 C mmarshall@anselm.edu
MARSHALL, Michelle .... 904-596-2443 111 F mmarshall@tbc.edu
MARSHALL, Mike .... 502-272-8180 179 B mmarshall2@bellarmine.edu
MARSHALL, Molly, T .... 913-667-5721 172 C mtmarshall@cbts.edu
MARSHALL, Phyllis .... 609-633-6460 284 B pmarshall@tesu.edu
MARSHALL, Richard, A . 309-457-2124 144 A rmarshall@monmouthcollege.edu
MARSHALL, II, Sherman .... 605-856-5880 416 D
MARSHALL, Sheryll .... 843-921-6939 411 F smarshall@netc.edu
MARSHALL, Steven .... 951-372-7040.. 58 H steven.marshall@norcocollege.edu
MARSHALL, Steven .... 610-282-1100 382 E steven.marshall@desales.edu
MARSHALL, Susan .... 401-598-4988 404 I smarshall@jwu.edu
MARSHALL, Susan, D ... 423-652-6006 420 H sdmarsha@king.edu
MARSHALL, Tamara .... 713-269-3876.... 7 A tmarshall@stillman.edu
MARSHALL, Tammy ...... 615-547-1359 419 F tmarshall@cumberland.edu
MARSHALL, Thomas, H 423-775-2041 418 H tmarshall5222@bryan.edu
MARSHALL, Tim .... 212-229-8947 308 C provost@newschool.edu
MARSHALL, Tim .... 214-378-1856 434 K tmarshall@dcccd.edu
MARSHALL, Toni .... 803-508-7242 406 E marshalt@atc.edu
MARSHALL, William ...... 218-322-2340 238 E william.marshall@itascacc.edu
MARSHALL-BIGGINS, Cynthia .... 903-593-8311 448 H cmarshall-biggins@texascollege.edu
MARSHALL BIGGINS, Cynthia .... 903-593-8311 448 H cmarshall-biggins@texascollege.edu
MARSHBURN, Susan .... 951-827-3340.. 69 C susan.marshburn@ucr.edu
MARSILI, Amanda .... 401-254-3774 405 E amarsili@rwu.edu
MARSON, Harry .... 845-938-2022 504 H 8gc@usma.edu
MARSON, Jason .... 419-448-3300 361 J marsonjm@tiffin.edu
MARSON, Wendy .... 651-450-3392 238 D wmarson@inverhills.edu
MARSTELLER, Diane ...... 330-652-9919 352 K dianemarsteller@eticollege.edu
MARSTELLER, Jill, A ..... 610-409-3582 402 A jmarsteller@ursinus.edu
MARSTELLER-KOWALEWSKI, Brenda .... 801-626-7737 461 B bkowalewski@weber.edu
MARSWILLO, Joseph, S .... 973-642-4568 279 F joseph.s.marswillo@njit.edu
MARTE, Maria .... 973-684-5993 280 B mmarte@pccc.edu
MARTEL, Annette .... 701-224-5771 345 D annette.martel@dickinsonstate.edu
MARTEL, David, W .... 434-924-7821 473 A dwm5x@virginia.edu
MARTEL, Holly .... 707-826-4143.. 33 D holly.martel@humboldt.edu
MARTEL, Kristie, A .... 724-847-5751 384 G kamartel@geneva.edu
MARTEL, Mary .... 212-343-1234 306 J mmartel@mcny.edu
MARTEL, Ronald .... 401-598-2848 404 I rmartel@jwu.edu
MARTELL, Corey .... 860-343-5701.. 86 A cmartell@mxcc.edu
MARTELL, Loida .... 859-280-1256 183 B lmartell@lextheo.edu
MARTELLARO, John ...... 816-235-1592 261 C martellaroj@umkc.edu
MARTELLARO, Joseph .. 717-867-6323 388 H martella@lvc.edu
MARTELLO, Michael ...... 716-338-1023 303 D michaelmartello@mail.sunyjcc.edu
MARTEN, Timothy .... 217-544-6464 148 F timothy.marten@sjcs.edu
MARTENS, Anne .... 301-405-4280 202 C amartens@umd.edu
MARTENS, Daniel, R ..... 812-464-1799 161 E dmartens@usi.edu
MARTENS, Kathy .... 503-375-7000 373 A kmartens@corban.edu
MARTENSEN, Brian .... 507-389-5998 239 C brian.martensen@mnsu.edu
MARTENSON, Brian ...... 507-389-1333 239 C brian.martenson@mnsu.edu
MARTERER, Aaron, C .... 803-777-5555 413 C marterer@sc.edu
MARTH, Brian .... 312-369-7933 135 E bmarth@colum.edu
MARTHERS, Paul, P ...... 404-727-3533 117 F paul.p.marthers@emory.edu
MARTI, Tammy, S .... 563-588-7142 167 D tammy.marti@loras.edu
MARTI, Vionex .... 787-738-2161 513 D vionex.marti@upr.edu
MARTICH, Luisa .... 718-289-5732 293 B luisa.martich@bcc.cuny.edu
MARTICKE, Nathan .... 816-584-6844 258 A nathan.marticke@park.edu
MARTIGNETTI, Rick .... 239-280-2424.. 94 O fr.rick.martignetti@avemaria.edu
MARTIN, Aaron .... 570-372-4120 399 C martinaaron@susqu.edu
MARTIN, Aaron .... 740-826-8024 357 C apmartin@muskingum.edu
MARTIN, Abigail .... 850-245-0466 108 H abigail.martin@flbog.edu
MARTIN, Alan, B .... 304-293-7398 491 C alan.martin@mail.wvu.edu
MARTIN, Allison .... 318-678-6000 187 A amartin@bpcc.edu
MARTIN, Alvin .... 213-884-4133.. 24 A amartin@ajrca.edu
MARTIN, Alyssa .... 701-355-8020 347 D amartin@umary.edu
MARTIN, Andrew, D ...... 314-935-5100 262 A admartin@wustl.edu
MARTIN, Angela, A .... 515-574-1064 166 E martin_a@iowacentral.edu
MARTIN, Angela, S .... 859-257-9830 185 B angie.martin@uky.edu
MARTIN, Angelo .... 570-372-4136 399 C martinma@susqu.edu
MARTIN, Angie .... 608-785-9454 501 A martina@westerntc.edu
MARTIN, Anita .... 501-337-5000.. 18 J amartin@coto.edu
MARTIN, SR., Anthony . 708-709-7834 146 D manthony@prairiestate.edu
MARTIN, Barbara .... 601-877-6230 244 H bmartin@alcorn.edu
MARTIN, Bethany, A ..... 315-386-7555 320 E martinb@canton.edu
MARTIN, Billy .... 859-622-7739 180 B billy.martin@eku.edu
MARTIN, Bobby .... 405-491-6339 370 A bgmartin@snu.edu
MARTIN, Bonnie .... 518-255-5402 319 F martinbg@cobleskill.edu
MARTIN, Brad .... 704-894-2612 328 F bcmartin@davidson.edu
MARTIN, Bradford .... 401-232-6000 404 F
MARTIN, Brandon .... 816-235-1020 261 C martinbran@umkc.edu
MARTIN, Bridgit .... 920-403-3963 495 I bridgit.martin@snc.edu
MARTIN, Brint .... 757-727-5425 468 B alumni@hamptonu.edu
MARTIN, Bronwyn .... 601-605-3314 246 C bmartin@holmescc.edu
MARTIN, Byron .... 219-464-6760 162 A byron.martin@vlapo.edu
MARTIN, Cameron, K ... 801-863-8514 461 A cameron.martin@uvu.edu
MARTIN, Carla, M .... 870-575-8873.. 22 E martinm@uapb.edu
MARTIN, Carol .... 503-845-3555 374 B carol.martin@mtangel.edu
MARTIN, Carolyn (Biddy), A ..... 413-542-2234 205 B president@amherst.edu
MARTIN, Cathy .... 615-329-1907 419 K camartin@fisk.edu
MARTIN, Cecelia .... 251-460-6591.... 8 F cgmartin@southalabama.edu
MARTIN, Cecelia .... 503-847-2581 377 F cmartin@uws.edu
MARTIN, Chad .... 580-774-3024 370 C chad.martin@swosu.edu
MARTIN, Charles .... 340-693-1511 514 E cmartin@uvi.edu
MARTIN, Charlie .... 727-376-6911 111 G cmartin@trinitycollege.edu
MARTIN, Cheryl .... 857-701-1200 215 E cmartin@rcc.mass.edu
MARTIN, Chicora .... 510-430-3189.. 52 D chimartin@mills.edu
MARTIN, Chris .... 904-997-2924 100 B chris.martin@fscj.edu
MARTIN, Chris .... 318-257-4526 191 F cmartin@latech.edu
MARTIN, Chris .... 573-651-2322 259 K cmartin@semo.edu
MARTIN, Christa, S ...... 931-540-2644 424 G cmartin@columbiastate.edu
MARTIN, Christopher .... 208-769-3340 131 C camartin@nic.edu
MARTIN, Christy .... 503-255-0332 374 D cmartin@multnomah.edu
MARTIN, Clara .... 843-574-6326 413 B clara.martin@tridenttech.edu
MARTIN, Cole .... 214-333-8877 434 I bookstoremanager@dbu.edu
MARTIN, Corie .... 270-745-2990 185 E corie.martin@wku.edu
MARTIN, Crystle .... 310-660-3593.. 41 L cmartin@elcamino.edu
MARTIN, Curt .... 970-248-1396.. 77 I cumartin@coloradomesa.edu
MARTIN, D. Michael ..... 909-687-1600.. 43 I michaelmartin@gs.edu
MARTIN, Dale .... 318-357-4496 192 C dale@nsula.edu
MARTIN, Dan .... 319-398-4984 167 C dan.martin@kirkwood.edu
MARTIN, Dan, J .... 412-268-2349 380 F djmartin@cmu.edu
MARTIN, Daniel, J .... 206-281-2114 484 D dmartin@spu.edu
MARTIN, David .... 831-646-4060.. 52 F dmartin@mpc.edu
MARTIN, David .... 718-420-4341 324 F dmartin@wagner.edu
MARTIN, David .... 423-636-7319 427 B dmartin@tusculum.edu
MARTIN, David .... 323-469-3300.. 25 E dmartin@amda.edu
MARTIN, David .... 203-837-9600.. 85 B martind@wcsu.edu
MARTIN, David .... 414-847-3213 494 F davidmartin@miad.edu
MARTIN, David .... 409-880-8471 449 H dmartin28@lamar.edu
MARTIN, David, J .... 979-845-0532 446 G david-j-martin@tamu.edu
MARTIN, David, L .... 570-941-7400 401 H david.martin2@scranton.edu
MARTIN, David, W .... 605-394-1269 417 B david.martin@sdsmt.edu
MARTIN, Debbie .... 910-296-1429 335 E dmartin@jamessprunt.edu
MARTIN, Deborah .... 661-336-5124.. 46 K debmarti@kccd.edu
MARTIN, Deborah .... 312-629-6800 148 I dmartin@saic.edu
MARTIN, Deborah .... 662-246-6263 247 D dmartin@msdelta.edu
MARTIN, Debra .... 310-954-4030.. 52 G dmartin@msmu.edu
MARTIN, Deidre .... 229-391-4907 113 F dmartin@abac.edu
MARTIN, Dewey .... 314-246-7560 262 C deweymartin21@webster.edu
MARTIN, Diann .... 708-237-5050 145 E dmartin7008@nc.edu
MARTIN, Dillon .... 719-384-6890.. 81 E dillon.martin@ojc.edu
MARTIN, Donald, L .... 706-233-7203 124 B dmartin@shorter.edu
MARTIN, Donna .... 337-475-5493 192 A dmartin@mcneese.edu
MARTIN, Donna .... 904-548-4414 100 B donna.martin@fscj.edu
MARTIN, Dorothy .... 207-768-2806 194 J ndmartin@nmcc.edu
MARTIN, Doug .... 757-446-5035 466 I martinsd@evms.edu
MARTIN, Dustin .... 765-641-4150 153 B dlmartin@anderson.edu
MARTIN, Earl, F .... 515-271-2191 165 A earl.martin@drake.edu
MARTIN, III, Earl Joe ... 225-752-4230 186 H jmartin@iticollege.edu
MARTIN, Elwyn .... 870-230-5135.. 19 E emartin@hsu.edu
MARTIN, Emily .... 864-231-2000 406 G amartin@andersonuniversity.edu
MARTIN, Eric .... 212-752-1530 304 D eric.martin@limcollege.edu
MARTIN, Etienne .... 614-287-2491 351 E emarti10@cscc.edu
MARTIN, Frank, C .... 803-536-8388 412 C fmartin@scsu.edu
MARTIN, Gale .... 610-526-6143 385 G gmartin@harcum.edu
MARTIN, Galen .... 770-962-7580 120 E gmartin@gwinnetttech.edu
MARTIN, Gary .... 561-237-7157 102 V gmartin@lynn.edu
MARTIN, Gary, D .... 651-696-6735 236 H gmartin6@macalester.edu
MARTIN, George .... 603-526-3604 272 H gmartin@colby-sawyer.edu
MARTIN, George, E ...... 512-448-8411 442M georgem@stedwards.edu
MARTIN, Gerald .... 610-436-1074 396 A gmartin2@wcupa.edu
MARTIN, Greg .... 515-964-6368 164 C gcmartin@dmacc.edu
MARTIN, SR., Harold, L .... 336-334-7940 341 F hmartin@ncat.edu
MARTIN, Heath .... 636-584-6565 252 J heath.martin@eastcentral.edu
MARTIN, Heidi .... 248-476-1122 227 C hmartin@msp.edu
MARTIN, Holly .... 618-393-2982 138 F martinh@iecc.edu
MARTIN, Irene .... 860-343-5740.. 86 A imartin@mxcc.commnet.edu
MARTIN, Isis, C .... 530-226-2177.. 63 K imartin@simpsonu.edu
MARTIN, Jackei .... 601-643-8323 245 G jackie.martin@colin.edu
MARTIN, James .... 913-684-3280 504 D
MARTIN, James, J .... 501-882-8851.. 17 F jjmartin@asub.edu
MARTIN, James, R .... 208-282-2341 130 H martjame@isu.edu
MARTIN, II, James, R .. 412-624-9811 401 B jrmartin@pitt.edu
MARTIN, Jana .... 918-293-5339 368 D jana.s.martin@okstate.edu
MARTIN, Janette .... 203-696-4266 130 G
MARTIN, Jason .... 615-898-8378 422 H jason.martin@mtsu.edu
MARTIN, Jeania .... 704-991-0370 338 C jmartin8295@stanly.edu
MARTIN, Jeanne .... 210-366-2701 442 D
MARTIN, Jeffrey, L .... 401-456-8840 405 C jmartin1@ric.edu
MARTIN, Jenni .... 509-533-7075 479 I jenni.martin@ccs.spokane.edu
MARTIN, Jenni .... 509-533-7075 480 A jenni.martin@scc.spokane.edu
MARTIN, Jenni .... 509-533-7075 479 I jenni.martin@scc.spokane.edu
MARTIN, Jennifer .... 940-898-3406 451 F jmartin@twu.edu
MARTIN, Jeremy, A ...... 513-556-1826 362 D jeremy.martin@uc.edu
MARTIN, Jeremy, P ...... 757-221-1258 466 C jpmartin@wm.edu
MARTIN, Jill .... 571-633-9651 472 J jill.martin@uona.edu
MARTIN, Jim .... 785-670-1634 177 G jim.martin@washburn.edu
MARTIN, Jo Leda .... 303-963-3206.. 77 G jomartin@ccu.edu

MARTIN, Joel, W 718-390-3131 324 F
joel.martin@wagner.edu
MARTIN, John, O 413-545-0361 211 D
jomartin@admin.umass.edu
MARTIN, John, U 941-487-4444 109 D
jmartin@ncf.edu
MARTIN, Joshua 972-825-4821 445 A
jmartin@sagu.edu
MARTIN, Joshua 508-854-7513 215 D
jmartin@qcc.mass.edu
MARTIN, Joshua 740-264-5591 352 H
jmartin@egcc.edu
MARTIN, Juanita, K 330-972-7082 362 B
juanita@uakron.edu
MARTIN, Karla 740-264-5591 352 H
kmartin@egcc.edu
MARTIN, Kathleen 413-748-3408 218 G
MARTIN, Kathy 540-375-2262 471 B
kmartin@roanoke.edu
MARTIN, Keith 918-343-7706 369 F
kmartin@rsu.edu
MARTIN, Keith 713-743-1449 452 F
kmartin@uh.edu
MARTIN, Kelsey, C 310-794-9507.. 69 A
kcmartin@mednet.ucla.edu
MARTIN, Kenneth, M 717-815-1211 404 A
kmartin@ycp.edu
MARTIN, Kevin 618-650-2345 149 F
kemarti@siue.edu
MARTIN, Kevin 215-407-0584 393 D
kmartin@pafa.edu
MARTIN, Kimberly 731-352-7646 418 G
martink@bethelu.edu
MARTIN, Kristina 617-585-1725 217 B
kristina.martin@necmusic.edu
MARTIN, Kyle, R 208-496-1450 130 A
martink@byui.edu
MARTIN, Lara 561-237-7459 102 V
lmartin@lynn.edu
MARTIN, Larry 657-278-2570.. 31 E
larrymartin@fullerton.edu
MARTIN, Laura 304-877-6428 487 F
financialaid@abc.edu
MARTIN, Laurel 859-246-6584 180 K
laurel.martin@kctcs.edu
MARTIN, Leandra 408-855-5182.. 74 D
leandra.martin@wvm.edu
MARTIN, Les, D 831-656-1027 503 K
ldmartin2@nps.edu
MARTIN, Levi 503-255-0332 374 D
lmartin@multnomah.edu
MARTIN, Linda 505-224-4000 285 J
lmartin@cnm.edu
MARTIN, Linda, C 865-974-3843 427 F
lcmartin@tennessee.edu
MARTIN, Lisa 918-343-7621 369 F
lmartin@rsu.edu
MARTIN, Lisa 254-710-2611 431 J
lisa_m_martin@baylor.edu
MARTIN, Llanet 818-778-5764.. 49 F
martinl7@lavc.edu
MARTIN, Lori 225-578-2031 188 I
lkemp1@lsu.edu
MARTIN, Lynne 256-765-5215.... 8 E
flmartin1@una.edu
MARTIN, Machelle 916-278-6078.. 32 E
MARTIN, Maggie 229-391-5135 113 F
mmartin@abac.edu
MARTIN, Marc 510-780-4500.. 47 J
mmartin@lifewest.edu
MARTIN, Marcus, L 434-243-4311 473 A
mlm8n@virginia.edu
MARTIN, Margo 702-651-7545 271 A
margo.martin@csn.edu
MARTIN, Marian 256-378-2001.... 1 G
mmartin8@cacc.edu
MARTIN, Marie 651-604-4131 236 J
mmartin@minneapolisbusinesscollege.edu
MARTIN, Mariel 518-580-8212 316 A
mariel@skidmore.edu
MARTIN, Mark 757-352-4040 470 H
marybun@regent.edu
MARTIN, Mark, A 989-837-4497 228 H
martinm@northwood.edu
MARTIN, Marty 571-633-9651 472 J
marty.martin@uona.edu
MARTIN, Maureen 734-764-1817 231 E
mmartin@umich.edu
MARTIN, Micah 704-406-2135 329 A
mmartin8@gardner-webb.edu
MARTIN, Michael 918-647-1388 365 H
mmartin@carlalbert.edu
MARTIN, Michael, V 239-590-1055 108 K
president@fgcu.edu
MARTIN, Michelle 972-580-7600 432 A
mmartin@bhcarroll.edu
MARTIN, Michelle, D 410-651-6230 203 A
mdmartin1@umes.edu
MARTIN, Mike 704-991-0300 338 C
tmartin7444@stanly.edu
MARTIN, Mirta, M 304-367-4151 490 B
mirta.martin@fairmontstate.edu
MARTIN, Natasha 206-398-4039 484 F
nmartin@seattleu.edu
MARTIN, Nicola 323-563-9318.. 36 D
nicolamartin@cdrewu.edu
MARTIN, Pat 610-328-8451 399 D
pmartin1@swarthmore.edu
MARTIN, Paul, W 518-276-8711 312 I
martip@rpi.edu
MARTIN, Paula 618-537-6952 143 B
phmartin@mckendree.edu
MARTIN, II, Ralph, C 617-373-2101 217 F
MARTIN, Randy 870-972-2093.. 17 G
rmartin@astate.edu
MARTIN, Randy, L 724-357-2244 394 G
rmartin@iup.edu
MARTIN, Renee 318-626-6730 189 D
sm8267@bncollege.com
MARTIN, Renee 303-963-3384.. 77 G
rmartin@ccu.edu
MARTIN, Robert 505-424-2301 286 C
MARTIN, Robert, E 303-233-4697.. 78 J
rm@schooloftrades.edu
MARTIN, Robyn 520-515-3688.. 11 M
martinrc@cochise.edu
MARTIN, Ronald 773-843-7553 134 F
rmartin@ccc.edu
MARTIN, Roneida 847-543-2641 135 B
rmartin@clcillinois.edu
MARTIN, Rosa, L 706-821-8365 122 K
rmartin@paine.edu
MARTIN, Rosalynn 504-568-3916 189 B
rmar11@lsuhsc.edu
MARTIN, Russell 864-941-8669 411 H
martin.r@ptc.edu
MARTIN, Ruth 619-201-8685.. 60 A
ruth.martin@sdcc.edu
MARTIN, Sandra 630-942-2865 135 A
martins14@cod.edu
MARTIN, Sandra, E 870-235-4041.. 21 D
sandrasmith@saumag.edu
MARTIN, Sean 860-439-2058.. 86 H
sean.martin@conncoll.edu
MARTIN, Shane 206-296-2595 484 F
martins@seattleu.edu
MARTIN, Sharon, L 304-293-9091 491 C
sharon.martin@mail.wvu.edu
MARTIN, Stacey 325-670-1253 437 F
smartin@hsutx.edu
MARTIN, Staci 903-983-8200 439 A
smartin@kilgore.edu
MARTIN, Stephanie 219-464-5212 162 A
stephanie.martin1@valpo.edu
MARTIN, Steve 850-478-8496 104 G
smartin@pcci.edu
MARTIN, Steven, J 419-772-2277 358 H
s-martin.11@onu.edu
MARTIN, Susan 352-588-8117 106 D
susan.martin04@saintleo.edu
MARTIN, Susie 310-377-5501.. 51 B
smartin@marymountcalifornia.edu
MARTIN, Terry 225-768-1700 186 F
terry.martin@franu.edu
MARTIN, Thomas, K 972-758-3817 433 M
tmartin@collin.edu
MARTIN, Timothy 856-225-6671 281 G
timartin@camden.rutgers.edu
MARTIN, Timothy, J 515-574-1097 166 E
martin@iowacentral.edu
MARTIN, Timothy, R 508-767-7373 205 D
timartin@assumption.edu
MARTIN, Tod 501-279-4403.. 19 D
registrar@harding.edu
MARTIN, Todd 660-263-4100 257 B
toddmartin@macc.edu
MARTIN, Tom 859-622-2383 180 B
tom.martin@eku.edu
MARTIN, Tom 361-593-2139 447 D
katdm00@tamuk.edu
MARTIN, Tony, L 336-386-3222 338 D
martint@surry.edu
MARTIN, Tracey 281-949-1800.. 92 G
MARTIN, Tracey 281-201-3800.. 92 G
MARTIN, Traci 410-337-6191 198 G
tmartin@goucher.edu
MARTIN, Traycee, F 229-333-5710 126 G
tmartin@valdosta.edu
MARTIN, Troy 617-745-3865 208 G
troy.martin@enc.edu
MARTIN, Troy 607-962-9428 320 F
tmarti13@corning-cc.edu
MARTIN, Valerie, G 570-372-4288 399 C
vmartin@susqu.edu
MARTIN, Vicki, J 414-297-6320 500 B
martinv@matc.edu
MARTIN, Victor 661-654-2161.. 30 E
vmartin4@csub.edu
MARTIN, Wayne 973-754-7192 280 B
wmartin@pccc.edu
MARTIN, Wendy 207-859-1111 195 G
martinw@thomas.edu
MARTIN, Willadean 972-860-4817 434 L
wmartin@dcccd.edu
MARTIN, William, J 614-292-8350 358 I
martin.3047@osu.edu
MARTIN-BROWN,
Karen 352-371-2833.. 97 G
assistantdirector@dragonrises.edu
MARTIN-FEDICH,
Laura, E 253-879-3211 485 E
lmartinfedich@pugetsound.edu
MARTIN-HALL,
Margaret 870-575-8064.. 22 E
hallm@uapb.edu
MARTIN-HATCHER,
Dorothy 212-752-1530 304 D
dorothy.martinhatcher@limcollege.edu
MARTIN LONG, Kim 504-280-1278 189 E
kmlong@uno.edu
MARTIN LOPIT,
Maribeth 206-281-2448 484 D
martinm3@spu.edu
MARTIN-OSORIO,
Carol, J 615-353-3268 425 D
carol.martin-osorio@nscc.edu
MARTIN-PARISIEN,
Terri 701-477-7862 347 A
tmartinparisien@tm.edu
MARTIN-REND, Jill 814-653-8265 380 A
jill.martin-rend@bc3.edu
MARTIN-SCOTT, Mable 517-371-5140 233 A
martinm@cooley.edu
MARTIN-THORNTON,
Renee 951-222-8048.. 58 I
renee.martin-thornton@rcc.edu
MARTIN TSE, Jennifer 315-464-4604 317 F
registrar@upstate.edu
MARTIN-VEGA,
Louis, A 919-515-2311 342 B
louis_martin-vega@ncsu.edu
MARTINCHEK, Mark, E 315-267-3106 319 D
martinme@potsdam.edu
MARTINE, Jason 407-618-5900.. 92 G
MARTINE, Jason 407-926-2000.. 92 G
MARTINEAU, Jim 503-594-3271 372 D
jmartineau@clackamas.edu
MARTINEAU, Kevin 816-584-6225 258 A
kevin.martineau@park.edu
MARTINEAU,
Michael, D 801-581-7481 460 E
mike.martineau@utah.edu
MARTINEC, Jeff 724-925-4237 403 A
martinecj@westmoreland.edu
MARTINELLE, Lorraine 508-213-2219 217 E
lorraine.martinelle@nichols.edu
MARTINELLI, Diana 304-293-5746 491 C
diana.martinelli@mail.wvu.edu
MARTINELLI-FERNANDEZ,
Susan 309-298-1828 152 D
martinelli-fernandez@wiu.edu
MARTINELLO, Peter 330-923-9959 352 N
MARTINELLO, Peter 614-882-2551 353 A
MARTINEZ, Abelardo 787-758-2525 513 G
abelardo.martinez@upr.edu
MARTINEZ, Ana 718-518-4407 294 B
anmartinez@hostos.cuny.edu
MARTINEZ, Angela 407-303-5727.. 94 D
angela.martinez@ahu.edu
MARTINEZ, Art 512-499-4296 454 I
amartinez@utsystem.edu
MARTINEZ, Arti Patel 650-493-4430.. 64 A
artipatel.martinez@sofia.edu
MARTINEZ, Auris 787-878-5475 508 L
amartinez@arecibo.inter.edu
MARTINEZ, Brenda 510-466-7203.. 56 H
bmartinez@peralta.edu
MARTINEZ, Carla 714-895-8705.. 38 D
cmartinez@gwc.cccd.edu
MARTINEZ, Carlos 361-593-2249 447 D
carlos.martinez@tamuk.edu
MARTINEZ, Carlos 817-531-4959 451 E
cmartinez@txwes.edu
MARTINEZ, Carlos, E 512-471-6519 455 A
carlos.martinez@austin.utexas.edu
MARTINEZ, Carolina 505-454-3269 286 H
carolina@nmhu.edu
MARTINEZ, Charles 512-471-7255 455 A
dean.education@austin.utexas.edu
MARTINEZ, Christina 806-742-0012 451 B
christina.martinez@ttu.edu
MARTINEZ, Cristina 787-257-0000 513 C
cristina.martinezlebron@upr.edu
MARTINEZ, Cristina 830-895-7110 443 G
careerdevelopment@schreiner.edu
MARTINEZ, Cynthia 909-607-0121.. 37 G
cynthia_martinez@kgi.edu
MARTINEZ, Daniel 760-776-7212.. 39 A
damartinez@collegeofthedesert.edu
MARTINEZ, Danny 310-338-2893.. 50 J
danny.martinez@lmu.edu
MARTINEZ, Denise 254-968-9924 446 E
dmartinez@tarleton.edu
MARTINEZ, Diana 630-942-3007 135 A
martinezd59@cod.edu
MARTINEZ, Diana 602-285-7821.. 13 F
dr.martinez@phoenixcollege.edu
MARTINEZ, Diana, S 210-458-8000 455 E
diana.martinez1@utsa.edu
MARTINEZ, Didit 806-743-2900 451 C
didit.martinez@ttuhsc.edu
MARTINEZ, Edward 505-454-3366 286 H
eamartinez@nmhu.edu
MARTINEZ, Edward 631-451-4176 321 G
martineze@sunysuffolk.edu
MARTINEZ, Elena, M 956-326-2433 446 F
emartinez@tamiu.edu
MARTINEZ, Elizabeth 310-900-1600.. 40 A
emartinez@elcamino.edu
MARTINEZ, Elizabeth 787-841-2000 510 K
elizabeth_martinez@pucpr.edu
MARTINEZ, Ernie 559-265-5711.. 66 E
ernie.martinez@fresnocitycollege.edu
MARTINEZ, Geraldine 575-528-7244 287 E
gerri66@nmsu.edu
MARTINEZ, German 609-497-7779 280 D
facilities-security@ptsem.edu
MARTINEZ, Gilbert 815-836-5442 141 G
gmartinez9@lewisu.edu
MARTINEZ, Guillermo 512-223-7053 431 A
gmartin1@austincc.edu
MARTINEZ, Hector 787-284-1912 509 E
hmartin@ponce.inter.edu
MARTINEZ, Hector 787-284-1912 509 E
hemart@ponce.inter.edu
MARTINEZ, Henry 972-860-8142 435 A
hmartinez@dcccd.edu
MARTINEZ, J. Leonard 575-646-2035 287 B
jmarti@nmsu.edu
MARTINEZ, Jacqueline 212-938-5500 320 B
jmartinez@sunyopt.edu
MARTINEZ, Janice, A 787-765-1915 510 B
jamartinez@opto.inter.edu
MARTINEZ, Jeffrey 909-748-8400.. 71 G
jeff_martinez@redlands.edu
MARTINEZ, Jenny, S 650-723-2300.. 65 J
MARTINEZ, Jesse 208-885-7716 131 G
jessem@uidaho.edu
MARTINEZ, Jesus 787-738-2161 513 D
jesus.martinez5@upr.edu
MARTINEZ, Joaquin 305-237-7175 103 D
jmarti16@mdc.edu
MARTINEZ, Johanna 787-753-6000 508 D
MARTINEZ, Jose, D 787-288-1118 512 A
MARTINEZ, Juan 787-894-2828 514 C
juan.martinez8@upr.edu
MARTINEZ, Juan 716-851-1257 299 F
martinez@ecc.edu
MARTINEZ, Juan 419-289-5160 348 A
jmarti63@ashland.edu
MARTINEZ, Juan, F 787-763-5845 508 J
jfmartinez@inter.edu
MARTINEZ, Kara 806-716-4600 443 I
kmartinez@southplainscollege.edu
MARTINEZ, Kimberly 303-861-1151.. 79 F
kmartinez@concorde.edu
MARTINEZ, Kristen 617-236-5400 209 D
kmartinez@fisher.edu
MARTINEZ, Kymm 651-962-6486 244 E
mart2073@stthomas.edu

MARTINEZ, Leticia .... 928-344-7644.. 10 J
leticia.martinez@azwestern.edu
MARTINEZ, Loretta .... 505-277-0111 288 G
MARTINEZ, Luis, E .... 786-331-1000 103 G
lmartinez@maufl.edu
MARTINEZ, Luz, E .... 787-894-2828 514 C
luz.martinez6@upr.edu
MARTINEZ, Manuel .... 614-251-4730 358 G
martinem1@ohiodominican.edu
MARTINEZ, Maria .... 415-338-7264.. 34 A
mlmartinez@sfsu.edu
MARTINEZ, Maria .... 787-751-0178 511 F
ac_mmartinez@suagm.edu
MARTINEZ, Maria .... 361-593-2129 447 D
maria.martinez2@tamuk.edu
MARTINEZ, Maria .... 661-362-3418.. 38 H
maria.martinez@canyons.edu
MARTINEZ, Maria .... 918-465-1711 366 D
mmartinez@eosc.edu
MARTINEZ, Maria, D .... 860-486-4040.. 88 E
maria.d.martinez@uconn.edu
MARTINEZ, Marilyn ...... 787-863-2390 509 B
marilyn.martinez@fajardo.inter.edu
MARTINEZ, Marla .... 512-232-7903 455 A
marla.martinez@austin.utexas.edu
MARTINEZ, Marvin .... 714-480-7450.. 57 K
martinez_marvin@rsccd.edu
MARTINEZ, Marvin .... 505-224-4000 285 J
mmartinez188@cnm.edu
MARTINEZ, Melba .... 787-780-0070 506 F
melmartinez@caribbean.edu
MARTINEZ, Melinda ...... 949-214-3050.. 40 F
melinda.martinez@cui.edu
MARTINEZ, Mike .... 575-624-7116 286 A
mike.martinez@roswell.enmu.edu
MARTINEZ, Mildred ...... 214-379-5438 441 I
MARTINEZ, Miriam .... 787-284-1912 509 E
mmartine@ponce.inter.edu
MARTINEZ, Monica .... 760-245-4271.. 73 D
monica.martinez@vvc.edu
MARTINEZ, Nina .... 562-947-8755.. 65 C
ninamartinez@scuhs.edu
MARTINEZ, Nina .... 502-456-6505 184 E
nmartinez@sullivan.edu
MARTINEZ, Pedro .... 707-826-4402.. 33 D
pedro.martinez@humboldt.edu
MARTINEZ, Pedro, L ...... 937-376-6636 350 D
pmartinez@centralstate.edu
MARTINEZ, Raul, J .... 972-985-3725 433 M
rjmartinez@collin.edu
MARTINEZ, Richard ...... 626-812-3002.. 26 H
rsmartinez@apu.edu
MARTINEZ, Roman .... 305-237-0012 103 D
rmartin9@mdc.edu
MARTINEZ, Rosa, J ...... 787-864-2222 509 C
rosa.martinez@guayama.inter.edu
MARTINEZ, Ruben, O .... 407-303-9372.. 94 D
ruben.martinez@ahu.edu
MARTINEZ, Sandra .... 951-571-6267.. 58 G
sandra.martinez@mvc.edu
MARTINEZ, Siria .... 530-668-2536.. 76 B
smartinez@yccd.edu
MARTINEZ, Steve .... 830-591-7280 444 G
srmartinez@swtjc.edu
MARTINEZ, Tara .... 612-659-6761 238 I
tara.martinez@minneapolis.edu
MARTINEZ, Terry .... 315-859-4020 301 C
tmartine@hamilton.edu
MARTINEZ, Veronica ..... 408-848-4725.. 43 J
vmartinez@gavilan.edu
MARTINEZ, Vesta, M ..... 817-515-7795 445 G
vesta.martinez@tccd.edu
MARTINEZ, Windy .... 661-763-7815.. 66 J
wmartinez@taftcollege.edu
MARTINEZ, Xochitl, E ... 909-593-3511.. 70 D
xmartinez@laverne.edu
MARTINEZ, Yuli .... 619-201-8953.. 65 A
yuli.martinez@socalsem.edu
MARTINEZ DE DIOS,
Heri .... 787-720-0596 506 E
hmartinez@atlanticu.edu
MARTINEZ-DOANE,
Karol .... 410-225-2284 199 H
kmartinez@mica.edu
MARTINEZ-GONZALEZ,
Liduvina .... 212-938-4030 320 B
lgonzalez@sunyopt.edu
MARTINEZ-LOPEZ,
Carmen Leonor .... 914-606-6795 325 C
carmen.martinez-lopez@sunywcc.edu
MARTINEZ-ORTIZ,
Javier .... 787-863-2390 509 B
javier.martinez@fajardo.inter.edu
MARTINEZ-QUILES,
Suzette .... 215-635-7300 385 A
smartinez@gratz.edu
MARTINEZ-SAENZ,
Miguel .... 718-489-5486 313 H
president@sfc.edu
MARTINEZ STLUKA,
Rena .... 714-992-7077.. 53 L
rmartinezstluka@fullcoll.edu
MARTINEZ-WOODRUFF,
Regina .... 254-526-1397 432 H
regina.martinez-woodruff@ctcd.edu
MARTINEZ-YADEN,
Camille .... 520-383-8401.. 16 D
cmartinez@tocc.edu
MARTINI, Louis .... 609-777-5696 284 B
lmartini@tesu.edu
MARTINI-HAUSNER,
Mary .... 315-279-5368 304 A
mmartini@keuka.edu
MARTINI-JOHNSON,
Lisa, A .... 610-799-1754 388 I
lmartinijohnson@lccc.edu
MARTINIS, Susan .... 217-244-2405 151 D
martinis@illinois.edu
MARTINO, Andrew, P .... 410-546-6902 203 F
apmartino@salisbury.edu
MARTINO, Bill .... 212-592-2212 315 H
wmartino@sva.edu
MARTINO, Gregory .... 215-972-2079 393 D
gmartino@pafa.edu
MARTINS, Sandra .... 630-942-2174 135 A
martinss14@cod.edu
MARTINSEN, Daniel ...... 254-299-8333 440 A
dmartinsen@mclennan.edu
MARTINSEN, Michael ..... 440-775-5782 358 C
mike.martinsen@oberlin.edu
MARTINSON, Ben .... 651-846-1473 241 B
benjamin.martinson@saintpaul.edu
MARTINSON, Brady ...... 773-244-6203 145 A
bmartinson@northpark.edu
MARTLAND, Paul .... 860-932-4124.. 86 E
pmartland@qvcc.edu
MARTLEY, Karen .... 916-469-8500 174 D
kmartley@jccc.edu
MARTNER, James, E ..... 630-942-2543 135 A
martner@cod.edu
MARTOCCI, DeAnne ...... 518-629-7154 302 E
d.martocci@hvcc.edu
MARTOCHE, Katie .... 716-926-8819 301 H
kmortoche@hilbert.edu
MARTON, Nathan .... 716-829-7583 298 F
martonn@dyc.edu
MARTONE, Eric .... 914-674-7618 306 F
emartone@mercy.edu
MARTORANA,
Anne Marie .... 617-368-1418 217 C
amartorana@nesl.edu
MARTOZA, Roberta .... 209-932-2933.. 70 E
rmartoza@pacific.edu
MARTS, Chad .... 757-490-1241 464 F
cmarts@auto.edu
MARTY, Angela, L .... 630-515-6120 143 G
amarty@midwestern.edu
MARTY, Patrick .... 570-326-3761 393 G
pmarty@pct.edu
MARTZ, Ben .... 304-876-5007 490 E
bmartz@shepherd.edu
MARTZ, Diane .... 585-385-7309 314 A
dmartz@sjfc.edu
MARTÍNEZ, Leticia .... 787-264-1912 509 F
letmarti@sangerman.inter.edu
MARTÍNEZ, María, T ..... 787-728-1515 514 D
mariat.martinez@sagrado.edu
MARTÍNEZ, Sirimarie .... 787-765-1915 510 B
smartinez@opto.inter.edu
MARTÍNEZ, Vilma .... 787-264-0409 509 F
vilma_martinez_toro@intersg.edu
MARTÍNEZ, Waleska ...... 787-751-0160 507 F
wmartinez@cmpr.pr.gov
MARUCHA, Phillip, T .... 503-494-8801 375 B
marucha@ohsu.edu
MARUGGI, Vincent .... 410-822-5400 197 I
vmaruggi@chesapeake.edu
MARUYAMA, Kenichi .... 480-461-7758.. 13 D
kenichi.maruyama@mesacc.edu
MARVI, Hassan .... 202-885-2799.. 90 J
hassan@american.edu
MARVIN, Corey .... 760-384-6201.. 46 M
cmarvin@cerrocoso.edu
MARX, Ben .... 503-253-3443 374 H
bmarx@ocom.edu
MARX, Christopher .... 616-451-3511 223 B
cmarx@davenport.edu
MARX, Christopher .... 845-688-7167 323 E
marxc@sunyulster.edu
MARX, Christopher .... 845-802-7167 323 E
marxc@sunyulster.edu
MARX, Lisa, M .... 410-778-7261 204 D
lmarx2@washcoll.edu
MARXUACH-TORROS,
Gilberto .... 787-727-7033 514 D
gilberto.marxuach@sagrado.edu
MARYATT, Victoria .... 916-608-6925.. 50 H
maryatv@flc.losrios.edu
MARYE, Erica .... 859-442-1163 181 B
erica.marye@kctcs.edu
MARYMONT, John .... 251-460-7189.... 8 F
jmarymont@southalabama.edu
MARYOTT, Megan .... 402-354-7111 268 C
megan.maryott@methodistcollege.edu
MARZAN, Marissa .... 559-297-4500.. 46 A
mmarzan@iot.edu
MARZANO, Maria .... 212-517-0428 306 A
mmarzano@mmm.edu
MARZCAK, Kelly .... 906-932-4231 224 B
kellym@gogebic.edu
MARZILLI, T. Scott .... 713-221-8007 453 B
marzillis@uhd.edu
MARZITELLI, Ron .... 518-381-1449 315 G
marzitrd@sunysccc.edu
MARZO, Sam, J .... 708-216-9183 142 D
smarzo@luc.edu
MARZULLO, Frank .... 708-656-8000 144 E
frank.marzullo@morton.edu
MARZULLO, Keith .... 301-405-2861 202 C
marzullo@umd.edu
MASAU, Traci .... 406-377-9418 263 E
tmasau@dawson.edu
MASCARENAS, Malinda 303-404-5630.. 79 J
malinda.mascarenas@frontrange.edu
MASCARI, OP, Michael 314-256-8881 250 D
mascari@ai.edu
MASCARO, Elizabeth ..... 951-487-3210.. 52 I
emascaro@msjc.edu
MASCARO, Jennifer .... 207-262-7836 196 A
jennifer.mascaro@maine.edu
MASCARO, Juan, C .... 828-884-8219 327 C
mascarjc@brevard.edu
MASCARO, Maria, S ..... 787-841-2000 510 K
exaluminos@pucpr.edu
MASCETTI, Kris .... 205-665-6392.... 8 D
kmascett@montevallo.edu
MASCH, Michael .... 202-806-2400.. 92 B
michael.masch@howard.edu
MASCHMAN, Greg, D ... 402-465-2116 268 H
gdm@nebrwesleyan.edu
MASCIANTONIO, John .. 215-596-8531 401 G
j.mascia@usciences.edu
MASEK, Jessie .... 805-893-3938.. 70 A
jessie.masek@ucsb.edu
MASEK, Phyllis .... 573-592-5213 262 E
phyllis.masek@westminster-mo.edu
MASELLA, Joanne .... 561-803-2827 104 C
joanne_masella@pba.edu
MASELLI, Gennaro .... 914-606-6856 325 C
gennaro.maselli@sunywcc.edu
MASENTHIN,
Kimberly, R .... 262-243-5700 493 B
kimberly.masenthin@cuw.edu
MASHARIKI, Opio .... 912-358-3449 123 H
ssuathletics@savannahstate.edu
MASHBURN, Scott .... 423-746-5203 426 F
smashburn@tnwesleyan.edu
MASHBURN, Ted .... 251-442-2391.... 8 C
tmashburn@umobile.edu
MASHEK, Randy, D .... 563-556-5110 168 E
mashekr@nicc.edu
MASHUDA, Patrick, M .. 252-398-6484 328 D
mashup@chowan.edu
MASI, Jessica .... 207-216-4401 195 C
jmasi@yccc.edu
MASINGILA, Joanna, O 315-443-4751 322 C
jomasing@syr.edu
MASINI, Blase, E .... 773-442-4890 145 B
b-masini@neiu.edu
MASINI, Marco .... 630-829-6006 132 E
mmasini@ben.edu
MASK, Renae .... 901-375-4400 422 F
renaemask@midsouthchristian.edu
MASKEY, Cynthia, L ..... 217-786-2436 142 B
cynthia.maskey@llcc.edu
MASLENNIKOVA, Lena .. 864-663-0258 411 E
lena.maslennikova@ngu.edu
MASLEY, Kelly .... 989-463-7146 220 H
masley@alma.edu
MASLOW, Tamara .... 718-327-7600 325 F
tmaslow@yofr.org
MASMAN, T. Todd .... 419-824-3873 355 K
tmasman@lourdes.edu
MASO, Marta, E .... 773-442-5200 145 B
m-maso@neiu.edu
MASON, Amy .... 340-457-6274 487 B
masonar@ab.edu
MASON, Angel .... 706-236-2260 115 B
amason@berry.edu
MASON, April .... 678-359-5733 119 F
aprilm@gordonstate.edu
MASON, Aprile .... 423-869-7145 421 C
aprile.mason@lmunet.edu
MASON, Ashley .... 903-988-7520 439 A
amason@kilgore.edu
MASON, Bobby, J .... 405-325-3546 371 B
bjm@ou.edu
MASON, Chip .... 601-968-8945 245 C
cmason@belhaven.edu
MASON, Chuck .... 802-443-5717 462 H
cmason@middlebury.edu
MASON, Clif .... 402-557-7512 265 J
clif.mason@bellevue.edu
MASON, Dan, J .... 641-422-4281 168 D
masondan@niacc.edu
MASON, Geri .... 402-557-7020 265 J
geri.mason@bellevue.edu
MASON, Gregory .... 618-634-3325 149 A
gregm@shawneecc.edu
MASON, JR., Herman ... 803-780-1229 414 E
hmason@voorhees.edu
MASON, Holly .... 740-366-9219 349 H
mason.536@cotc.edu
MASON, James .... 314-792-6152 254 D
mason@kenrick.edu
MASON, Jeff .... 678-359-5573 119 F
jeffreym@gordonstate.edu
MASON, Jesse .... 763-424-0712 239 G
jmason@nhcc.edu
MASON, Karol, V .... 212-237-8000 294 D
MASON, Kathryn .... 609-652-4282 283 D
kathryn.mason@stockton.edu
MASON, Krystan .... 615-361-7555 419 I
kmason@daymarinstitute.edu
MASON, Linda .... 423-585-6809 426 C
linda.mason@ws.edu
MASON, Martha .... 907-450-8383.. 10 A
mjmason@alaska.edu
MASON, Mary Ellen ...... 410-777-2707 197 C
memason@aacc.edu
MASON, Melanie .... 443-352-4371 201 H
mmason5@stevenson.edu
MASON, Merle .... 650-508-3739.. 54 D
mmason@ndnu.edu
MASON, Michelle .... 203-932-7067.. 89 A
mmason@newhaven.edu
MASON, Patience .... 678-225-7534 396 D
patiencema@pcom.edu
MASON, Paul .... 325-793-3850 440 B
mason.paul@mcm.edu
MASON, Rachel .... 562-860-2451.. 35 M
rmason@cerritos.edu
MASON, Reni .... 318-487-7503 186 I
reni.mason@lacollege.edu
MASON, Richard .... 757-727-5617 468 B
richard.mason@hamptonu.edu
MASON, Rick .... 606-589-2145 182 E
rick.mason@kctcs.edu
MASON, Rochelle .... 719-389-6800.. 77 H
rmason@coloradocollege.edu
MASON, Ron .... 203-837-8736.. 85 B
masonr@wcsu.edu
MASON, JR., Ronald .... 202-274-6016.. 93 C
ronald.mason@udc.edu
MASON, Shawna .... 479-308-2210.. 17 C
shawna.mason@arcomedu.org
MASON, Stacey, W .... 864-488-4540 410 E
smason@limestone.edu
MASON, Starla .... 307-778-1118 502 D
smason@lccc.wy.edu
MASON, Stephen .... 803-793-5155 409 C
masons@denmarktech.edu
MASON, Steven, D .... 903-233-3200 439 E
stevenmason@letu.edu
MASON, Terrell .... 757-881-5100.. 92 G
MASON, Tiera .... 502-863-8373 180 E
tiera_mason@georgetowncollege.edu
MASON, Tisa .... 785-628-4231 173 B
tisa.mason@fhsu.edu
MASON, Tonya .... 240-567-5052 200 C
tonya.mason@montgomerycollege.edu
MASON, Traci .... 352-873-5808.. 96 O
masont@cf.edu

MATHWEG, Cathy, M ... 920-923-8138 494 A
cmathweg@marianuniversity.edu
MATIC, Katharina .... 717-245-1010 382 F
matick@dickinson.edu
MATIIA, Mike, M .... 717-337-6530 384 H
mmattia@gettysburg.edu
MATIKA, Susan .... 908-709-7548 284 C
matika@ucc.edu
MATIS, Michelle, D .... 407-582-3130 112 K
mmatis@valenciacollege.edu
MATISON, Kim .... 253-566-5194 485 C
kmatison@tacomacc.edu
MATISTA, Theresa .... 916-568-3058.. 50 E
matistt@losrios.edu
MATITIA, Abraham .... 440-943-5300 360 G
MATKIN, Gary, W .... 949-824-5525.. 68 G
gmatkin@uci.edu
MATKIN, H. Neil .... 972-758-3800 433 M
nmatkin@collin.edu
MATLIN, David .... 808-956-7301 128 F
athdir@hawaii.edu
MATLOCK, Debra .... 312-996-7084 151 B
mdebra@uic.edu
MATNEY, Ross .... 540-674-3613 475 B
rmatney@nr.edu
MATONAK, Jessica, M . 724-287-8711 380 A
jessica.matonak@bc3.edu
MATOS, Awilda .... 787-834-9595 511 E
amatos@uaa.edu
MATOS, Bethany .... 559-934-2324.. 74 A
bethanymatos@whccd.edu
MATOS, Carol .... 917-493-4450 305 I
cmatos@msmnyc.edu
MATOS, Dania .... 209-228-4400.. 69 B
MATOS, Daniel .... 212-484-1303 294 D
dmatos@jjay.cuny.edu
MATOS, Elsa .... 787-890-2681 512 H
elsa.matos@upr.edu
MATOS, Emily .... 787-844-8181 514 A
emily.matos@upr.edu
MATOS, Jose .... 787-751-0160 507 F
jamatos@cmpr.pr.gov
MATOS, Jose .... 787-758-2525 513 G
jose.matos5@upr.edu
MATOS, Juan Carlos .... 718-817-0664 300 E
jmatos6@fordham.edu
MATOS, Lillian .... 787-780-0070 506 F
lmatos@caribbean.edu
MATOS AUFFANT, Jose 210-436-3538 443 A
jmatosauffant@stmarytx.edu
MATOS RODRIGUEZ,
Felix, V .... 646-664-9100 292 K
MATOSO, Michael .... 925-631-4399.. 59 B
mjm37@stmarys-ca.edu
MATOTT, Benjamin .... 315-386-7448 320 E
matot104@canton.edu
MATSEN, Maureen .... 757-594-7585 466 B
maureen.matsen@cnu.edu
MATSON, Christine, B .. 671-735-0231 505 C
christine.matson@guamcc.edu
MATSON, Steven, W ..... 919-962-3251 342 D
smatson@bio.unc.edu
MATSUBARA, Melissa ... 808-544-0288 127 H
mmatsubara@hpu.edu
MATSUDA, Matthew, K . 848-932-0990 282 A
mmatsuda@echo.rutgers.edu
MATSUDA, Seiichi .... 713-348-4002 442 K
matsuda@rice.edu
MATSUKADO, Kevin, G . 808-544-1407 127 H
MATSUMORI, Dylan ...... 435-652-7755 460 G
dylan.matsumori@dixie.edu
MATSUMORI, Jessica ... 408-554-4397.. 62 D
jmatsumori@scu.edu
MATSUMOTO, David ..... 510-809-1444.. 45 K
MATSUMOTO, Mark ...... 209-228-4021.. 69 B
mmatsumoto@ucmerced.edu
MATSUMOTO, Rae .... 707-638-5926.. 67 F
rae.matsumoto@tu.edu
MATSUNO, Kenichi .... 781-239-4363 205 E
matsuno@babson.edu
MATSUO, Monica .... 626-396-2268.. 26 E
monica.matsuo@artcenter.edu
MATSUWAKI, Charis ..... 808-369-8593 127 G
charis@hmi.edu
MATT, Kathleen .... 302-831-8370.. 90 F
ksmatt@udel.edu
MATTACOLA, Carl, G .... 336-334-5744 343 A
cgmattac@uncg.edu
MATTEI, Vivien .... 787-284-1912 509 E
vmattei@ponce.inter.edu
MATTEK, Barb .... 414-443-8662 498 O
barbara.mattek@wlc.edu

MATTEO, Jim .... 609-258-1447 280 E
jsmatteo@princeton.edu
MATTER, Shawn .... 765-677-2869 157 D
shawn.matter@indwes.edu
MATTERAZZO, Susan .... 860-832-3002.. 84 I
matterazzo@ccsu.edu
MATTES, Bilita, S .... 717-901-5134 385 K
bmattes@harrisburgu.edu
MATTES, Marty .... 360-596-5227 485 B
mmattes@spscc.edu
MATTESON, Christi, G .. 904-264-2172 105 L
christi.matteson@iws.edu
MATTESON, Kimberly .... 563-333-6339 169 A
mettesonkimberly@sau.edu
MATTESON, Ryan .... 805-756-7676.. 30 C
rmatteso@calpoly.edu
MATTESON, Susan, A ... 574-807-7824 153 E
sue.matteson@betheluniversity.edu
MATTEY, Melissa, L ...... 443-518-4208 199 C
mmattey@howardcc.edu
MATTHEIS, Lacey .... 417-690-3223 251 E
lmattheis@cofo.edu
MATTHES, Kevin .... 575-538-6715 289 B
kevin.matthes@wnmu.edu
MATTHES, Peter .... 319-335-3714 163 A
peter-matthes@uiowa.edu
MATTHEW, Kathryn .... 281-283-3020 453 A
matthew@uhcl.edu
MATTHEWS, Adrienne ... 256-726-7398.... 6 C
amatthews@oakwood.edu
MATTHEWS, Allison ...... 617-449-7041 219 C
allison.matthews@urbancollege.edu
MATTHEWS, Ann .... 573-840-9669 260 I
amatthews@trcc.edu
MATTHEWS, Anne .... 541-888-7612 376 F
amatthews@socc.edu
MATTHEWS, Carolyn, E 510-841-1905.. 25 G
cmatthews@absw.edu
MATTHEWS, Charlotte ... 816-802-3461 254 B
ckmatthews@kcai.edu
MATTHEWS, Cissy .... 409-944-1203 437 B
cmatthews@gc.edu
MATTHEWS, Dan .... 813-419-5100 233 A
matthewd@cooley.edu
MATTHEWS, Daniel .... 405-273-5331 366 E
dmatthews@familyoffaith.edu
MATTHEWS, Daniel, J ... 405-273-5331 366 E
dmatthews@familyoffaith.edu
MATTHEWS, Daniell, C . 412-397-6237 397 G
matthews@rmu.edu
MATTHEWS, Debra .... 478-471-2730 121 F
debra.matthews@mga.edu
MATTHEWS, Dennis, T .. 252-399-6345 326 M
dtmatthews@barton.edu
MATTHEWS, Dennis, W 215-968-8301 379 G
matthews@bucks.edu
MATTHEWS,
Douglas, K .... 859-858-2206 178 H
MATTHEWS, Dustin .... 641-472-1163 167 F
dmatthews@mum.edu
MATTHEWS, Elizabeth ... 760-750-4195.. 33 B
ematthew@csusm.edu
MATTHEWS, Ellen .... 903-510-2380 452 C
emat@tjc.edu
MATTHEWS, Ellery .... 718-636-3603 311 J
matthews@pratt.edu
MATTHEWS, Elyse .... 212-961-3390 290 F
ematthews@bankstreet.edu
MATTHEWS, Emily .... 215-335-0800 389 B
MATTHEWS, Gary, C ..... 858-534-6820.. 69 D
gcmatthews@ucsd.edu
MATTHEWS, Grant .... 541-463-5618 373 F
matthewsg@lanecc.edu
MATTHEWS, Greg .... 802-485-2013 463 A
gmatthe2@norwich.edu
MATTHEWS, Harold, P .. 812-488-2051 161 A
hm3@evansville.edu
MATTHEWS, Janet .... 828-328-7254 330 F
janet.matthews@lr.edu
MATTHEWS, Jeanne ...... 703-284-1580 469 C
jeanne.matthews@marymount.edu
MATTHEWS, Jennifer .... 202-274-5449.. 93 C
jennifer.matthews@udc.edu
MATTHEWS, John, D ..... 864-242-5100 407 B
MATTHEWS, Johnny ...... 618-545-3099 140 E
jmatthews@kaskaskia.edu
MATTHEWS, Jon .... 910-814-8801 333 C
jmatthews@cccc.edu
MATTHEWS, Jonelle ...... 717-396-7833 393 E
jmatthews@pcad.edu
MATTHEWS, Joseph ...... 706-864-1786 126 A
joseph.matthews@ung.edu

MATTHEWS, Julia .... 610-921-2381 378 C
jmatthews@albright.edu
MATTHEWS, Kismet ...... 252-789-0223 335 H
kismet.matthews@martincc.edu
MATTHEWS, Lawrence .. 419-358-3409 348 G
matthewsl@bluffton.edu
MATTHEWS, Leon .... 704-330-6524 333 D
leon.matthews@cpcc.edu
MATTHEWS, Matt .... 352-854-2322.. 96 O
matthewm@cf.edu
MATTHEWS, Matt .... 423-425-4719 428 A
matt-matthews@utc.edu
MATTHEWS, Pamela, R . 979-845-5141 446 G
p-matthews@tamu.edu
MATTHEWS, Paul .... 614-236-6211 349 D
pmatthews@capital.edu
MATTHEWS, Robert .... 810-232-2511 228 C
robert.matthews@mcc.edu
MATTHEWS, Robin .... 252-672-7506 333 H
matthewsr@cravencc.edu
MATTHEWS, Ronald, A . 610-341-5890 383 D
ron.matthews@eastern.edu
MATTHEWS, Ronald, E .. 216-373-6492 358 B
rmatthews@ndc.edu
MATTHEWS, Samuel, W 405-273-5331 366 E
smatthews@familyoffaith.edu
MATTHEWS, Sasha .... 757-481-5005 478 C
MATTHEWS, Stephen, P 518-564-3824 319 C
matthesp@plattsburgh.edu
MATTHEWS, Thomas ..... 216-368-2188 349 F
thomas.matthews@case.edu
MATTHEWS,
Valencia, E .... 850-599-3430 108 I
valencia.matthews@famu.edu
MATTHEWS, Victor .... 417-836-5529 256 E
victormatthews@missouristate.edu
MATTHEWS, Wesley .... 208-885-3478 131 G
wmatthews@uidaho.edu
MATTHEWS-JUAREZ,
Patricia .... 615-327-6526 422 A
pmatthews-juarez@mmc.edu
MATTHEWSON,
Mansfield .... 616-234-3851 224 D
mmatthew@grcc.edu
MATTHIAS, Ryan .... 402-643-7374 266 G
ryan.matthias@cune.edu
MATTHIES, Brad .... 307-268-2036 501 U
bmatthies@caspercollege.edu
MATTIACCI, John, A ..... 215-625-5400 399 F
john.mattiacci@temple.edu
MATTILA, Lisa .... 413-236-1609 213 F
lmattila@berkshirecc.edu
MATTINGLY, Amy .... 304-637-1273 487 I
mattinglya@dewv.edu
MATTINGLY, Bruce .... 607-753-4312 318 D
bruce.mattingly@cortland.edu
MATTINGLY, Carole ...... 270-831-9786 181 D
carole.mattingly@kctcs.edu
MATTINGLY, Chris .... 931-363-9809 421 E
cmattingly@martinmethodist.edu
MATTINGLY, Keith, E .... 269-471-3411 221 B
matt@andrews.edu
MATTINGLY, Linda .... 843-953-6859 407 F
linda.mattingly@citadel.edu
MATTIOLI, Kathy, L ...... 740-283-6267 353 B
kmattioli@franciscan.edu
MATTIS, JR., George, E 276-223-4744 476 E
gmattis@wcc.vccs.edu
MATTIS-PINARD,
Rebecca .... 212-517-0562 306 A
rpinard@mmm.edu
MATTISON, Debra .... 651-213-4282 236 B
dmattison@hazeldenbettyford.edu
MATTISON, Sue .... 515-271-3751 165 A
sue.mattison@drake.edu
MATTIX, Brigit .... 469-941-8300 436 A
rmattix@dni.edu
MATTOX, Bennie .... 229-732-5908 114 B
benniemattox@andrewcollege.edu
MATTOX, Bob, J .... 470-578-6600 120 L
bmattox@kennesaw.edu
MATTOX, Jason .... 662-720-7299 248 C
jlmattox@nemcc.edu
MATTSON, Bob .... 217-443-8856 135 H
rmattson@dacc.edu
MATTSON, Craig .... 708-239-4881 150 F
craig.mattson@trnty.edu
MATTSON, Jean .... 308-865-8202 269 I
mattsonj@unk.edu
MATTSON, Joanne .... 314-889-4514 253 C
jmattson@fontbonne.edu
MATTSON, Michelle .... 937-327-7915 364 H
mattsonm@wittenberg.edu

MATUGA, Julia .... 419-372-5572 348 H
jmatuga@bgsu.edu
MATULIA, Michael, K ... 352-323-3643 102 T
matuliam@lssc.edu
MATURAN, Ashley .... 605-331-6801 417 E
ashley.maturan@usiouxfalls.edu
MATUS, Nelson .... 956-380-8175 442 L
nmatus@riogrande.edu
MATUS, Paul .... 631-451-4518 321 G
matusp@sunysuffolk.edu
MATUSIK, Sharon .... 303-735-5113.. 83 A
sharon.matusik@colorado.edu
MATUSOW-AYRES,
Helen .... 718-636-3639 311 J
hmayres@pratt.edu
MATVEY, Jessica .... 218-262-7384 238 C
jessicamatvey@hibbing.edu
MATVIUK, Sergio .... 918-495-6523 368 I
smatviuk@oru.edu
MATWEYCHUK, Karen ... 610-647-4980 386 C
kmatweychuk@immaculata.edu
MATYE EDWARDS, Lisa 303-797-5601.. 76 I
lisa.matyeedwards@arapahoe.edu
MATYNKA, Paul, J .... 248-232-4662 229 A
pjmatynk@oaklandcc.edu
MATZ, David .... 612-330-1155 233 K
matz@augsburg.edu
MATZ, Kurt, M .... 574-520-5522 157 A
kumatz@iusb.edu
MATZ, Tina .... 517-787-0800 225 C
matztinam@jccmi.edu
MATZKE, Brian .... 616-632-2073 221 C
matzkbri@aquinas.edu
MATZKE, William .... 989-358-7259 221 A
matzkew@alpenacc.edu
MATZKIN, Michael .... 641-472-7000 167 F
webmaster@mum.edu
MATZNER, Alan .... 507-537-6010 241 D
alan.matzner@smsu.edu
MAU, Jeremy .... 563-588-8000 165 F
jmau@emmaus.edu
MAUCH, Elizabeth, K .... 785-227-3380 171 E
mauchek@bethanylb.edu
MAUCH, Tom .... 909-274-4380.. 52 H
tmauch@mtsac.edu
MAUCK, Megan, J .... 330-588-2586 355 L
mmauck@malone.edu
MAUE, Deb .... 630-844-7572 132 D
dmaue@aurora.edu
MAUER, Emily .... 850-201-8258 111 C
maurere@tcc.fl.edu
MAUER, JR.,
Gerard, M .... 202-685-4260 503 I
gerard.m.mauer.civ@ndu.edu
MAUGE, Lucille .... 404-880-6876 116 D
lmauge@cau.edu
MAUI, Lorraine, C .... 670-237-6708 506 A
lorraine.maui@marianas.edu
MAUK, Andy .... 910-962-7638 343 C
mauka@uncw.edu
MAUK, Jean .... 305-809-3266.. 99 C
wjean.mauk@fkcc.edu
MAUK, Teresa .... 401-598-1000 404 I
tmauk@jwu.edu
MAUK, Vera .... 508-373-9768 206 B
vera.mauk@becker.edu
MAULDIN, Brad .... 575-562-2393 285 M
bradley.mauldin@enmu.edu
MAULDIN, Teena, P ...... 704-463-3031 339 E
teena.mauldin@pfeiffer.edu
MAULTSBY, Bill .... 910-788-6310 338 A
bill.maultsby@sccnc.edu
MAUN, Duane, F .... 717-901-5120 385 K
dmaun@harrisburgu.edu
MAUNEY, Bill .... 910-272-3300 337 D
bmauney@robeson.edu
MAUNEY, Richard .... 773-371-5442 133 E
rmauney@ctu.edu
MAUNSELL, Jody .... 802-828-8724 463 F
jody.maunsell@vcfa.edu
MAURANA, Cheryl, A .... 414-955-8075 494 C
cmaurana@mcw.edu
MAURANO, Steven, J .... 401-865-2775 405 B
smaurano@providence.edu
MAURER, Amanda, C .... 813-974-4126 110 B
amaurer@usf.edu
MAURER, Amybeth .... 847-214-7423 136 F
amaurer@elgin.edu
MAURER, Bobby Jo ...... 309-341-7315 141 A
bmaurer@knox.edu
MAURER, Carmen, K ..... 402-472-3906 269 H
cmaurer@nebraska.edu
MAURER, Caroline .... 717-796-5068 390 E
cmaurer@messiah.edu

MAURER, Charles .... 212-757-1190 290 B cmaurer@aami.edu
MAURER, Erin .... 864-622-6074 406 G emaurer@andersonuniversity.edu
MAURER, Gaylyn .... 541-885-1800 375 C gaylyn.maurer@oit.edu
MAURER, Lynn .... 409-880-8508 449 H lmaurer@lamar.edu
MAURER, Paul, J .... 828-669-8012 331 J president@montreat.edu
MAURER, Ryan .... 937-327-6114 364 H rmaurer@wittenberg.edu
MAURER, Stace .... 503-760-3131 371 H stace@birthingway.edu
MAURER, William, M ... 949-824-6802.. 68 G wmmaurer@uci.edu
MAURICE, JR., John, W .... 252-334-2004 331 D president@macuniversity.edu
MAURIELLO, Thomas .... 718-862-7241 305 H thomas.mauriello@manhattan.edu
MAURIN, Kay .... 985-549-2507 192 D kay.maurin@selu.edu
MAURO, Anthony, F ..... 724-938-1653 394 B mauro@calu.edu
MAURO, Brian .... 973-443-8343 277 K brian_mauro@fdu.edu
MAURO, Laurie .... 304-263-6262 488 C lmauro@martinsburgcollege.edu
MAURO, Steven, A .... 814-871-7605 384 E mauro003@gannon.edu
MAUST, Donielle, R ..... 304-293-4245 491 C donielle.maust@mail.wvu.edu
MAUST, Scott .... 309-341-7892 141 A smaust@knox.edu
MAUSZYCKI, Christine .. 605-995-2737 415 C christine.mauszycki@dwu.edu
MAUZERALL, Cynthia ... 208-459-5561 130 D cmauzerall@collegeofidaho.edu
MAUZY, Stephanie .... 314-367-8700 259 B stephanie.hoffmann@stlcop.edu
MAVRINAC, Mary Ann .. 585-275-4461 323 J maryann.mavrinac@rochester.edu
MAVROS, Jeff .... 309-438-2181 139 E jmavros@ilstu.edu
MAX, Claire .... 831-459-2991.. 70 B cemax@ucsc.edu
MAX, Rosemary .... 248-370-3358 229 G rmax@oakland.edu
MAX, Sheryl .... 816-995-2842 258 F sheryl.max@researchcollege.edu
MAXEINER, Amy .... 309-796-5043 132 G maxeinera@bhc.edu
MAXEY, JoAnn .... 501-686-2515.. 21 F jmaxey@uasys.edu
MAXEY, Larry .... 619-388-5940.. 60 D lmaxey@sdccd.edu
MAXEY, Michael, C ...... 540-375-2200 471 B maxey@roanoke.edu
MAXFIELD, John .... 303-963-3228.. 77 G jmaxfield@ccu.edu
MAXFIELD, Sylvia .... 401-865-1224 405 B maxfield@providence.edu
MAXIE, Leslie .... 502-272-3101 179 B lmaxie@bellarmine.edu
MAXIN, Leslie .... 724-503-1001 402 E lmaxin@washjeff.edu
MAXISON, Tony, M ...... 309-467-6408 137 B tmaxison@eureka.edu
MAXON, John .... 256-824-6108.... 8 B john.maxon@uah.edu
MAXSON, Kathi .... 605-718-2401 417 F katherine.maxson@wdt.edu
MAXSON, Krista .... 405-224-3140 371 D kmaxson@usao.edu
MAXWELL, Alice .... 850-201-6049 111 C maxwella@tcc.fl.edu
MAXWELL, Barbara, A .. 509-527-5208 486 H maxwelba@whitman.edu
MAXWELL, Ben .... 864-587-4251 412 G maxwellb@smcsc.edu
MAXWELL, Brandon ...... 404-687-4522 116 H maxwellb@ctsnet.edu
MAXWELL, Cathy .... 303-292-0015.. 79 G cmaxwell@denvercollegeofnursing.edu
MAXWELL, Chris .... 706-245-7226 117 E cmaxwell@ec.edu
MAXWELL, Christopher . 312-939-0111 136 D cmaxwell@eastwest.edu
MAXWELL, Daniel .... 713-743-5390 452 F dmmaxwell@central.uh.edu
MAXWELL, Danita .... 323-259-2613.. 54 E dmaxwell@oxy.edu
MAXWELL, Drew .... 414-847-3317 494 F drewmaxwell@miad.edu
MAXWELL, James .... 423-869-6298 421 C james.maxwell@lmunet.edu
MAXWELL, James .... 972-524-3341 445 C
MAXWELL, Jewerl .... 978-867-4118 209 F jewerl.maxwell@gordon.edu
MAXWELL, Kate .... 410-827-5802 197 I kmaxwell@chesapeake.edu
MAXWELL, Kim .... 970-542-3192.. 81 A kim.maxwell@morgancc.edu
MAXWELL, Lafayette ..... 919-572-1625 326 L lmaxwell@nc.rr.com
MAXWELL, Laura .... 678-407-5726 118 D lmaxwell@ggc.edu
MAXWELL, Mardell .... 832-842-9058 452 F mrmaxwell@central.uh.edu
MAXWELL, Mischka ...... 321-674-8482.. 99 B mmaxwell@fit.edu
MAXWELL, Monique ..... 703-445-9056 473 D
MAXWELL, Noel .... 907-745-3201.... 9 B nmaxwell@akbible.edu
MAXWELL, Rick .... 972-860-4730 434 L rmaxwell@dcccd.edu
MAXWELL, Sharon .... 630-844-5630 132 D smaxwell@aurora.edu
MAXWELL, Tanisha .... 925-473-7421.. 40 J tmaxwell@losmedanos.edu
MAXWELL, Valarie .... 940-397-4346 440 F valarie.maxwell@msutexas.edu
MAXWELL-DOHERTY, Melissa .... 805-493-3330.. 29 H revmmmd@callutheran.edu
MAXWELL-DOHERTY, Scott .... 805-493-3230.. 29 H revsjmd@callutheran.edu
MAXWELL-FRIEDEN, Lisa .... 260-665-4310 160 H friedenl@trine.edu
MAY, Barbara .... 320-363-5401 235 C bmay@csbsju.edu
MAY, Barbara .... 320-363-3147 243 A bmay@csbsju.edu
MAY, Bobbie Jo, C .... 919-496-1567 338 F may@vgcc.edu
MAY, Brian, J .... 325-942-2073 451 A brian.may@angelo.edu
MAY, Bryan .... 803-778-7841 407 C maybw@cctech.edu
MAY, Cathryn .... 601-635-6238 245 I cmay@eccc.edu
MAY, Charles, A .... 573-882-7744 261 B mayc@missouri.edu
MAY, Christopher, V .... 314-977-3167 259 H christopher.may@slu.edu
MAY, Daniel .... 203-932-7262.. 89 A dmay@newhaven.edu
MAY, David .... 509-359-6345 480 E dmay@ewu.edu
MAY, David, J .... 603-862-2727 274 G david.may@unh.edu
MAY, Gary, S .... 530-752-2065.. 68 E chancellor@ucdavis.edu
MAY, Ginny .... 248-218-2018 229 J
MAY, Janet .... 712-279-5227 163 C janet.may@briarcliff.edu
MAY, Janet .... 713-718-8570 437 I janet.may2@hccs.edu
MAY, Joe, D .... 214-378-1601 434 K jmay@dcccd.edu
MAY, Libby .... 603-645-9698 274 D l.may@snhu.edu
MAY, Lindsay .... 800-280-0307 152 H lindsay.may@ace.edu
MAY, Michael .... 724-738-4573 395 F michael.may@sru.edu
MAY, Michelle .... 605-455-6064 416 B mmay@olc.edu
MAY, Mindy .... 937-766-7855 349 G mkmay@cedarville.edu
MAY, Nina .... 609-586-4800 278 F mayn@mccc.edu
MAY, Nita .... 903-434-8113 441 B nmay@ntcc.edu
MAY, Robert, E .... 276-739-2436 476 C rmay@vhcc.edu
MAY, Ronald .... 253-964-6736 483 D rmay@pierce.ctc.edu
MAY, Sarah, E .... 478-301-2413 121 E may_se@mercer.edu
MAY, Susan .... 618-985-2828 139 I susanmay@jalc.edu
MAY, Susan, A .... 920-735-5731 499 E may@fvtc.edu
MAY, Tammie .... 816-604-4018 255 D tammie.may@mcckc.edu
MAY, Walter, P .... 770-720-5540 123 E wpm@reinhardt.edu
MAY-RICCIUTI, Heather . 304-829-7335 487 G hricciuti@bethanywv.edu
MAYABB, Patricia .... 214-887-5022 436 B pmayabb@dts.edu
MAYAN, Kathy .... 410-386-8110 197 G kmayan@carrollcc.edu
MAYBANK, Denise, B ... 517-355-7535 227 D maybank@msu.edu
MAYBERRY, Marla .... 918-877-8116 366 F marla.mayberry@langston.edu
MAYDEN, Sharrie .... 702-895-0970 271 E sharrie.mayden@unlv.edu
MAYEA, Bethany .... 810-989-5537 230 C blmayea@sc4.edu
MAYEAUX, Darryl .... 716-375-2490 313 F dmayeaux@sbu.edu
MAYER, Bob .... 704-527-9909 209 G bmayer@gordonconwell.edu
MAYER, Cathy .... 708-239-4797 150 F cathy.mayer@trnty.edu
MAYER, Charles .... 336-249-8186 334 A cmayer@davidsonccc.edu
MAYER, Connie .... 518-445-2393 289 E cmaye@albanylaw.edu
MAYER, Fritz .... 303-871-6338.. 83 D frederick.mayer@du.edu
MAYER, Kasey .... 913-288-7240 174 F kmayer@kckcc.edu
MAYER, Kathy .... 608-262-4808 496 B kmayer@uwsa.edu
MAYER, Louis .... 201-216-8761 283 C louis.mayer@stevens.edu
MAYER, Lynn .... 202-319-5220.. 91 B mayer@cua.edu
MAYER, Patrick .... 606-679-8501 182 C pmayer0003@kctcs.edu
MAYER, Russell .... 978-837-3499 216 D mayerr@merrimack.edu
MAYER, Russell, K .... 920-923-7604 494 A rkmayer@marianuniversity.edu
MAYER, Susan .... 623-845-3849.. 13 C susan.mayer@gccaz.edu
MAYER, Theresa .... 540-231-7630 477 A tsmayer@vt.edu
MAYER, Thomas .... 803-793-5197 409 C mayert@denmarktech.edu
MAYES, David, M .... 501-882-4420.. 17 F dmmayes@asub.edu
MAYES, John, A .... 203-432-8049.. 89 D john.mayes@yale.edu
MAYES, Larry, D .... 336-334-9876 343 A ldmayes@uncg.edu
MAYES, LaVerne .... 215-871-6560 396 D lavernema@pcom.edu
MAYES, Lisa .... 757-683-6746 469 G lmayes@odu.edu
MAYES, Richard, A .... 336-272-7102 329 D mayesr@greensboro.edu
MAYEUX, Liza .... 225-490-1664 186 F liza.mayeux@franu.edu
MAYEUX, Teresa .... 225-752-4233 186 H registrar@iticollege.edu
MAYFIELD, Amanda, B . 860-439-2088.. 86 H amanda.mayfield@conncoll.edu
MAYFIELD, Donny .... 423-746-5253 426 F dmayfield@tnwesleyan.edu
MAYFIELD, Janet .... 314-392-2355 256 C mayfij@mobap.edu
MAYFIELD, Kimberly ..... 510-436-1396.. 45 D mayfield@hnu.edu
MAYFIELD, Pamela .... 254-867-3118 449 E pamela.mayfield@tstc.edu
MAYHER, Michael, E .... 440-525-7255 355 H mmayher@lakelandcc.edu
MAYHEW, Megan .... 620-450-2113 176 G meganh@prattcc.edu
MAYHEW, Sam .... 423-439-4286 419 J mayhew@etsu.edu
MAYHEW, Steven .... 620-231-7000 176 F smayhew@pittstate.edu
MAYHEW, Susan, L .... 276-498-5201 464 K slmayhew@acp.edu
MAYLE, Chad, A .... 304-457-6410 487 B mayleca@ab.edu
MAYLEY, Errol .... 859-344-3321 184 F mayleye@thomasmore.edu
MAYLOTT, Robbyn .... 423-461-8712 422 J rmaylott@milligan.edu
MAYNARD, Charmel ..... 305-284-9587 112 E cmaynard@miami.edu
MAYNARD, Chris .... 936-294-1006 450 C maynard@shsu.edu
MAYNARD, Craig .... 309-467-6305 137 B cmaynard@eureka.edu
MAYNARD, Francyenne 972-273-3109 435 E fmaynard@dcccd.edu
MAYNARD, Jack, C ...... 812-237-2000 155 G jack.maynard@indstate.edu
MAYNARD, Kimberly, L 304-896-7345 489 E kimberly.maynard@southernwv.edu
MAYNARD, Nelly .... 773-821-2453 133 K nmaynard@csu.edu
MAYNARD, Rebecca, A . 207-768-2715 194 J bmaynard@nmcc.edu
MAYNARD, Thurmond .. 301-696-3546 199 B maynard@hood.edu
MAYNARD-ERRAMI, Nickcole .... 434-381-6478 472 D nmaynarderrami@sbc.edu
MAYNARD NELSON, Jeanette .... 612-767-7043 233 H jeanette@alfredadler.edu
MAYNARD-REID, Pedrito .... 509-527-2028 485 H pedrito.maynard-reid@wallawalla.edu
MAYNE, Kevin .... 802-387-6716 462 D kevinmayne@landmark.edu
MAYNE, Tania .... 310-756-0001.. 72 A
MAYO, Christy .... 616-234-5722 231 H christy.mayo@vai.edu
MAYO, Cindy .... 870-743-3000.. 20 C cmayo@northark.edu
MAYO, Dan .... 252-493-7304 336 H dmayo@email.pittcc.edu
MAYO, Jennifer .... 919-739-6721 338 H jbmayo@waynecc.edu
MAYO, Julia .... 503-517-1856 378 A jmayo@westernseminary.edu
MAYO, Karen .... 859-246-6525 180 K karen.mayo@kctcs.edu
MAYO, Kathy .... 252-249-1851 336 F kmayo@pamlicocc.edu
MAYO, Michele .... 252-940-6233 332 C michele.mayo@beaufortccc.edu
MAYO, Michelle, L .... 919-530-7149 342 A mlmayo@nccu.edu
MAYO, Michelle, P .... 585-292-2370 307 H mmayo@monroecc.edu
MAYO, Rachel .... 831-786-4710.. 27 G ramayo@cabrillo.edu
MAYO, Sandra .... 530-741-6793.. 76 A smayo@yccd.edu
MAYO, Sandra .... 206-281-2515 484 D mayos@spu.edu
MAYO, Stephen, L .... 626-395-4951.. 29 C steve@mayo.caltech.edu
MAYO, Tom .... 239-590-1520 108 K tmayo@fgcu.edu
MAYOR-GLENN, Jennifer, A .... 801-972-3596 460 E j.mayer-glenn@partners.utah.edu
MAYORGA, Erica .... 310-233-4396.. 49 A mayorge@lahc.edu
MAYRAND, Leslie .... 325-486-6247 451 A leslie.mayrand@angelo.edu
MAYRL, Matt .... 608-262-1165 496 C matthew.maryl@wisc.edu
MAYROSE, James .... 716-878-5550 318 C mayrosj@buffalostate.edu
MAYS, Allen .... 660-562-1307 257 E ajmays@nwmissouri.edu
MAYS, Beth, A .... 410-777-2480 197 C bamays@aacc.edu
MAYS, Cathy .... 434-381-6448 472 D cdmays@sbc.edu
MAYS, Florence .... 803-822-3419 410 G maysf@midlandstech.edu
MAYS, Justin .... 678-466-5544 116 E justinmays@clayton.edu
MAYS, Lisa .... 937-433-3410 352 M lmays@fortiscollege.edu
MAYS, Nathaniel .... 617-349-8539 210 H nmays@lesley.edu
MAYS, Susan .... 615-550-3161 429 A susan@williamsoncc.edu
MAYS, Theresa .... 205-853-1200.... 2 G tmays@jeffersonstate.edu
MAYS, Vida .... 662-252-8000 248 G vmays@rustcollege.edu

MAYS-JACKSON, Debra 601-979-2323 246 E
debra.mays-jackson@jsums.edu
MAYSE, Laura .... 302-736-2317.. 90 G
laura.mayse@wesley.edu
MAYSE, Tiffany .... 859-572-5806 184 A
masyset@nku.edu
MAYSENT, Patty .... 858-249-5534.. 69 D
pmaysent@ucsd.edu
MAZA, Antonio .... 703-416-1441 466 F
amaza@divinemercy.edu
MAZA-DUERTO,
Aristides .... 786-331-1000 103 G
amaza@maufl.edu
MAZA-DUERTO, Jenice . 786-331-1000 103 G
jmaza@maufl.edu
MAZACHEK, JuliAnn ..... 785-670-2544 177 G
juliann.mazachek@washburn.edu
MAZANOWSKI, Natalie . 415-442-4877.. 44 D
nmazanowski@ggu.edu
MAZARES, Joe .... 888-488-4968.. 46 F
jmazares@itu.edu
MAZARIEGOS, John ...... 847-947-5086 144 F
jmazariegos@nl.edu
MAZDRA, Brad .... 575-527-7519 287 E
bmazdra@nmsu.edu
MAZE, Joan .... 952-888-4777 242 I
jmaze@nwhealth.edu
MAZE, Mary, C .... 248-341-2051 229 A
mcmaze@oaklandcc.edu
MAZE, Tom .... 252-399-6533 326 M
tmaze@barton.edu
MAZEIKA, Michael .... 413-572-8541 213 D
mmazeika@westfield.ma.edu
MAZELIN, Mark .... 937-766-4155 349 G
mazelinm@cedarville.edu
MAZER, Vickie .... 301-687-4595 203 E
vmmazer@frostburg.edu
MAZGULSKI, Judy .... 860-343-5868.. 86 A
jmazgulski@mxcc.commnet.edu
MAZIAR, Christine, M .. 574-631-2749 161 C
maziar.1@nd.edu
MAZIAR, Lucia .... 860-444-8517 504 F
lucia.maziar@uscga.edu
MAZICH, OSB,
Edward, M .... 724-805-2592 398 F
edward.mazich@stvincent.edu
MAZIERE, Kevin .... 858-653-6740.. 46 I
kmeziere@jpcatholic.com
MAZONE, Dennis .... 718-636-3542 311 J
dmazone@pratt.edu
MAZUK, Mary, E .... 513-244-4828 357 A
mary.mazuk@msj.edu
MAZUR, III, Francis, J . 352-873-5823.. 96 O
mazurf@cf.edu
MAZURE, Sharon .... 304-367-4122 490 B
sharon.mazure@fairmontstate.edu
MAZUROWSKI, James .. 610-282-1100 382 E
james.mazurowski@desales.edu
MAZZA, Diane .... 203-392-5405.. 85 A
mazzad3@southernct.edu
MAZZA, James, A .... 607-255-1989 297 F
jam16@cornell.edu
MAZZA, Jennifer .... 845-398-4034 315 B
jmazza@stac.edu
MAZZA, Joseph .... 760-757-2121.. 52 E
jmazza@miracosta.edu
MAZZA, Lori .... 203-837-9013.. 85 B
mazzal@wcsu.edu
MAZZA, Maralyn .... 814-234-7755 399 B
MAZZA, III, S. Paul ..... 814-234-7755 399 B
pmazza@southhills.edu
MAZZA, Stephen, W ..... 785-864-4550 177 D
smazza@ku.edu
MAZZARINI, Molly .... 202-379-7808.. 92 G
MAZZELLA, Christina .... 215-871-6500 396 D
christinamaz@pcom.edu
MAZZEO, Michael, A .... 248-370-2957 229 G
mazzeo@oakland.edu
MAZZIE, Misty .... 931-668-7010 425 C
mmazzie@mscc.edu
MAZZIOTTA, John .... 310-825-5687.. 69 A
jmazziotta@mednet.ucla.edu
MAZZOCCO, Lisa .... 213-740-6426.. 72 B
lisa.mazzocco@usc.edu
MAZZOLA, Frank .... 603-358-2243 275 A
fmazzola@keene.edu
MAZZOLA, Gregg .... 603-526-3725 272 H
gregg.mazzola@colby-sawyer.edu
MAZZOLLA, Jeanne ...... 201-692-7100 277 K
mazzolla@fdu.edu
MBOMEH, Gabriel, A .... 240-895-4305 201 E
gambomeh@smcm.edu

MBUGUA, Martin, A ..... 528-580-5733 316 A
mmbugua@skidmore.edu
MBUWAYESANGO,
Dora, R .... 704-636-6077 330 A
dmbuwayesango@hoodseminary.edu
MBYIRUKIRA, James .... 256-726-7157.... 6 C
mbyirukira@oakwood.edu
MC CAIG, Robert .... 732-571-3413 279 B
rmccaig@monmouth.edu
MCABEE, Sarah .... 256-233-8102.... 4 D
sarah.mcabee@athens.edu
MCADAM DONEGAN,
Lisa .... 401-598-1000 404 I
lisa.mcadamdonegan@jwu.edu
MCADAMS, Angie .... 434-791-5629 464 O
amcadams@averett.edu
MCADAMS, Beverly .... 864-231-2000 406 G
bmcadams@andersonuniversity.edu
MCADAMS, Charles ...... 662-846-4010 245 H
cmcadams@deltastate.edu
MCADOO, Anthony .... 270-745-5405 185 E
anthony.mcadoo@wku.edu
MCAFFEE, Matthew, J ... 615-675-5330 428 G
mjmcaffee@welch.edu
MCALARY, Christopher . 626-395-3727.. 29 C
cmcalaryr@caltech.edu
MCALEER, Brenda .... 207-621-3425 196 A
mcaleer@maine.edu
MCALEER, Jessica .... 631-687-2667 314 C
jmcaleer@sjcny.edu
MCALEXANDER, Dan ..... 706-880-8230 121 A
dmcalexander@lagrange.edu
MCALHANEY, Kelly .... 864-379-8769 409 H
mcalhaney@erskine.edu
MCALISTER, George ...... 208-769-3393 131 C
glmcalister@nic.edu
MCALISTER, Jean .... 609-343-4901 275 D
mcaliste@atlantic.edu
MCALISTER, Kimberly ... 318-357-6288 192 C
mcalisterk@nsula.edu
MCALLISTER, Alex, M ... 859-238-5205 179 F
alex.mcallister@centre.edu
MCALLISTER,
Annemarie .... 914-964-4282 296 C
amcallister@riversidehealth.org
MCALLISTER, Carol .... 760-750-4802.. 33 B
cmcallis@csusm.edu
MCALLISTER, Craig .... 305-284-3163 112 E
crm1530@miami.edu
MCALLISTER, Dave .... 503-552-2014 374 E
dmcallister@nunm.edu
MCALLISTER, Erin .... 813-988-5131.. 98 Q
mcallistere@floridacollege.edu
MCALLISTER, Eugene .... 320-363-2882 243 A
sjpresident@csbsju.edu
MCALLISTER, Gary .... 501-205-8827.. 18 H
gmcallister@cbc.edu
MCALLISTER,
Latrelle, P .... 704-378-1230 330 D
lmcallister@jcsu.edu
MCALLISTER, Mary, C ... 607-871-2101 289 H
mcallister@alfred.edu
MCALLISTER, Peter .... 941-359-7537 105 K
pmcallis@ringling.edu
MCALLISTER, Steven, G 540-458-8740 478 A
smcallister@wlu.edu
MCALLISTER-WILSON,
David .... 202-885-8601.. 93 E
president@wesleyseminary.edu
MCALPIN, Michael .... 925-631-4222.. 59 B
mdm5@stmarys-ca.edu
MCALPINE, Lynn .... 402-554-3514 270 B
lmcalpine@unomaha.edu
MCANALLY, Kent .... 785-670-1938 177 G
kent.mcanally@washburn.edu
MCANDREW, Jennifer ... 781-239-2557 214 E
jmcandrew@massbay.edu
MCANDREW, John .... 570-208-5958 387 A
johnmcandrew@kings.edu
MCANDREW, Kathleen .. 217-353-2024 146 C
kmcandrew@parkland.edu
MCANDREW, Laura .... 202-885-6294.. 90 J
mcandrew@american.edu
MCANELLEY, Becky, J ... 409-882-3318 450 A
becky.mcanelley@lsco.edu
MCANUFF, Courtney ..... 848-445-6601 282 A
courtney.mcanuff@rutgers.edu
MCARDELL, James .... 218-855-8136 237 F
jmcardell@clcmn.edu
MCARDLE, Eliza .... 413-559-5458 210 A
MCARDLE, Jennifer .... 718-862-7975 305 H
jennifer.mcardle@manhattan.edu
MCARDLE, Karen .... 248-204-2010 226 G
kmcardle@ltu.edu

MCARTHUR, Andrew, L 615-353-3572 425 D
andrew.mcarthur@nscc.edu
MCARTHUR, Bridgette ... 863-616-6411.. 99 H
bmcarthur@flsouthern.edu
MCARTHUR, Douglas .... 517-607-2462 225 A
dmcarthur@hillsdale.edu
MCARTHUR, Jennifer .... 307-675-0571 502 F
jmcarthur@sheridan.edu
MCARTHUR, John, M ... 580-581-2201 365 G
jmcarthur@cameron.edu
MCARTHUR, Marcus ..... 760-480-8474.. 74 J
mmcarthur@wscal.edu
MCARTHUR, Thomas .... 330-263-2263 351 C
tmcarthur@wooster.edu
MCATEE, Christopher .... 847-970-4940 152 A
cmcatee@usml.edu
MCATEE, Christopher .... 414-425-8300 495 H
cmcatee@shsst.edu
MCATEE, Jim .... 765-285-2420 153 C
jfmcatee@bsu.edu
MCATHIE, Regan, M ..... 651-603-6257 235 F
MCAULIFF, Kimberly, B 315-445-4553 304 C
mcaulikb@lemoyne.edu
MCAULIFFE, Lynne .... 307-855-2206 501 V
lynne@cwc.edu
MCAVOY, Eugene .... 425-388-9031 480 G
emcavoy@everettcc.edu
MCAVOY, John .... 304-876-5374 490 E
jmcavoy@shepherd.edu
MCAVOY, Paul .... 518-861-2596 305 K
pmcavoy@mariacollege.edu
MCAVOY, William, J ..... 508-831-5337 220 E
wjmcavoy@wpi.edu
MCBEATH, Trish .... 918-465-1804 366 D
tmcbeath@eosc.edu
MCBEE, Cheryl .... 919-735-5151 338 H
wcc-bookstore@waynecc.edu
MCBEE, Lori, A .... 479-979-1413.. 23 I
lamcbee@ozarks.edu
MCBEE, Russ .... 620-227-9355 172 J
rmcbee@dc3.edu
MCBEE, Whitney .... 903-693-1192 441 F
wmcbee@panola.edu
MCBETH, Valerie .... 360-676-2772 482 D
vmcbeth@nwic.edu
MCBIRTH, Matthew .... 417-626-1234 257 F
mcbirth.matthew@occ.edu
MCBRADY, Allison .... 216-373-6376 358 B
amcbrady@ndc.edu
MCBRAYER, Mike .... 903-463-8753 437 D
mmcbrayer@grayson.edu
MCBRAYER,
Stephanie, H .... 501-450-5932.. 23 H
smcbrayer@uca.edu
MCBRIDE, Amanda .... 303-871-2203.. 83 D
amanda.mcbride@du.edu
MCBRIDE, Ameerah ...... 512-245-2539 450 E
a_m1658@txstate.edu
MCBRIDE, Andrew, S .... 804-289-8964 472 L
amcbride@richmond.edu
MCBRIDE, Becky .... 979-830-4306 432 C
becky.mcbride@blinn.edu
MCBRIDE, Chris .... 805-756-5724.. 30 C
chmcbrid@calpoly.edu
MCBRIDE, Christy .... 618-985-3741 139 I
christymcbride@jalc.edu
MCBRIDE, Connie .... 209-228-4692.. 69 B
cmcbride3@ucmerced.edu
MCBRIDE, Dan .... 859-622-1968 180 B
dan.mcbride@eku.edu
MCBRIDE, David .... 301-314-8117 202 C
dmcbrid2@umd.edu
MCBRIDE, Derrick .... 860-231-5396.. 89 B
dmcbride@usj.edu
MCBRIDE, Dwight, A .... 404-727-6055 117 F
dwight.a.mcbride@emory.edu
MCBRIDE, Faith .... 218-322-2360 238 E
faith.mcbride@itascacc.edu
MCBRIDE, Jeanette .... 910-898-9630 336 D
mcbridej@montgomery.edu
MCBRIDE, Jennifer, N ... 812-941-2020 157 B
mcbridjn@iu.edu
MCBRIDE, John, E .... 512-245-2557 450 E
jm05@txstate.edu
MCBRIDE, Kris .... 928-428-8320.. 12 E
kris.mcbride@eac.edu
MCBRIDE, Maria .... 504-865-2696 189 F
mmcbride@loyno.edu
MCBRIDE, Megan .... 216-397-4212 354 I
mmcbride@jcu.edu
MCBRIDE, Meghan .... 404-297-9522 119 B
MCBRIDE, Michael .... 276-739-2402 476 C
mmcbride@vhcc.edu

MCBRIDE, Phil .... 928-428-8404.. 12 E
phil.mcbride@eac.edu
MCBRIDE, Robert, J ...... 610-660-1351 398 C
rmcbride@sju.edu
MCBRIDE, Ron .... 910-221-2224 329 B
rmcbride@gcd.edu
MCBRIDE, Tara, E .... 215-545-6400 391 H
temcbride@peirce.edu
MCBRINE, Paul .... 617-236-8882 209 D
pmcbrine@fisher.edu
MCBROOM, Michael ..... 806-651-4400 448 C
mmcbroom@wtamu.edu
MCBRYDE, Tennie, S .... 334-420-4306.... 3 H
tmcbryde@trenholmstate.edu
MCCABE, Bryan .... 214-329-4447 431 D
bryan.mccabe@bgu.edu
MCCABE, Colleen .... 608-266-9399 499 B
colleen.mccabe@wtcsystem.edu
MCCABE, Cynthia .... 814-262-6477 393 H
cmccabe@pennhighlands.edu
MCCABE, Daniel .... 516-877-4231 289 C
dmccabe@adelphi.edu
MCCABE, Eileen .... 718-405-3240 296 G
eileen.mccabe@mountsaintvincent.edu
MCCABE, Karen .... 850-471-4639 104 H
kmccabe@pensacolastate.edu
MCCABE, Kenneth, F ..... 401-825-2111 404 H
kfmccabe@ccri.edu
MCCABE, Kevin .... 505-277-2241 288 G
kmccab02@unm.edu
MCCABE, Kevin .... 610-647-4400 386 C
kmccabe1@immaculata.edu
MCCABE, Luke .... 202-759-4988.. 91 D
MCCABE, Margaret .... 479-575-4504.. 21 G
MCCABE, Michael .... 217-228-5432 146 F
mccabmi@quincy.edu
MCCABE, Philip, J .... 203-371-7934.. 88 B
mccabep@sacredheart.edu
MCCABE, Ryan .... 585-785-1683 300 B
ryan.mccabe@flcc.edu
MCCABE, Tonya .... 360-752-8331 478 G
tmccabe@btc.edu
MCCADDEN, Brian, M ... 401-865-2503 405 B
bmccadde@providence.edu
MCCAFFERTY, Bridgit .... 254-519-5484 447 A
bmccaffe@tamuct.edu
MCCAFFERTY, Pamela ... 978-665-3435 212 C
pmccafferty@fitchburgstate.edu
MCCAFFERTY, Patricia ... 978-934-3238 211 G
patricia_mccafferty@uml.edu
MCCAFFREY, Dena .... 636-481-3400 254 A
dmccaffr@jeffco.edu
MCCAFFREY, Kate, E ..... 508-286-8218 220 A
mccaffrey_kate@wheatoncollege.edu
MCCAFFREY, Kayla .... 212-517-0469 306 A
kmccaffrey@mmm.edu
MCCAFFREY,
Michael, H .... 260-399-7700 161 D
mmccaffrey@sf.edu
MCCAGHREN, Chris ...... 251-442-2218.... 8 C
cmccaghren@umobile.edu
MCCAGHREN, Lauren .... 251-442-2220.... 8 C
lmccaghren@umobile.edu
MCCAIN, ALecia .... 830-372-8050 449 B
almccain@tlu.edu
MCCAIN, Gail, C .... 212-772-4000 294 C
gmccain@hunter.cuny.edu
MCCAIN, Lindy .... 662-472-9067 246 C
lmccain@holmescc.edu
MCCAIN, Mark .... 602-872-7748.. 14 A
mark.mccain@southmountaincc.edu
MCCALEB, Colin .... 269-965-3931 225 F
mccalebc@kellogg.edu
MCCALEB, Gary, D .... 325-674-2156 429 B
mccalebg@acu.edu
MCCALEB, George .... 956-872-8396 444 A
gmccaleb@southtexascollege.edu
MCCALEB, Karen .... 361-825-2449 447 C
joann.canales@tamucc.edu
MCCALIP, Rick .... 281-646-1109 432 B
MCCALL, Al .... 706-213-2102 114 F
amccall@athenstech.edu
MCCALL, Anne .... 504-520-7470 193 A
amccall@xula.edu
MCCALL, Becky .... 530-242-7719.. 63 H
bmccall@shastacollege.edu
MCCALL, Brian .... 512-463-1808 449 F
chancellor@tsus.edu
MCCALL, Danielle .... 314-529-9396 254 H
dmccall@maryville.edu
MCCALL, Gloria .... 859-256-3100 180 H
gloria.mccall@kctcs.edu

MCCLELLAND, Theresa 251-580-2120 1 I theresa.mcclelland@coastalalabama.edu

MCCLELLAND, II, Thomas, H 318-257-3247 191 F tmcclelland@latech.edu

MCCLELLON, Leslie, R 313-670-9300 190 J lmcclellon@susla.edu

MCCLENAGAN, Cindy, M 806-291-3410 457 J cindym@wbu.edu

MCCLENDON, Bev 479-788-7082 21 H bev.mcclendon@uafs.edu

MCCLENDON, Dawn 541-278-5937 372 A ddifuria@bluecc.edu

MCCLENDON, Karen 916-686-8602 29 J

MCCLENDON, Mark 940-397-4567 440 F mark.mcclendon@msutexas.edu

MCCLENDON, Michael 918-631-2200 371 E michael-mcclendon@utulsa.edu

MCCLENDON, Rodney, P 412-268-2056 380 F rodneypm@andrew.cmu.edu

MCCLENDON, Vivienne 425-564-3056 478 F vivienne.mcclendon@bellevuecollege.edu

MCCLENNEY, Elizabeth 540-375-2293 471 B mcclenney@roanoke.edu

MCCLIDE, LeMarques 256-761-6337 7 B tchousing@talladega.edu

MCCLIN, Raul 787-761-0640 512 F online@utcpr.edu

MCCLINTOCK, Elizabeth, A 412-578-6333 380 E eamcclintock@carlow.edu

MCCLINTOCK, Grace 831-459-4300 70 B grace@ucsc.edu

MCCLINTOCK, Kate 707-527-4797 62 F kmcclintock@santarosa.edu

MCCLINTOCK, Marta 724-938-4251 394 B mcclintock@calu.edu

MCCLINTOCK, Melvin, A 240-895-4309 201 E mamcclintock@smcm.edu

MCCLINTOCK, Patty 812-237-2305 155 G patty.mcclintock@indstate.edu

MCCLINTON, Flandus 225-771-5550 190 G flandus_mcclinton@sus.edu

MCCLINTON, Flandus 225-771-5550 190 H flandus_mcclinton@sus.edu

MCCLINTON, Leon 405-744-9164 368 B leon.mcclinton@okstate.edu

MCCLINTON, Martin 239-489-9229 100 A martin.mcclinton@fsw.edu

MCCLOSKEY, Anthony 303-329-6355 78 K anthony.mccloskey@cstcm.edu

MCCLOSKEY, Brian 609-586-4800 278 F mccloskb@mccc.edu

MCCLOSKEY, Dan, E 646-664-8910 292 K daniel.mccloskey@cuny.edu

MCCLOSKEY, James, M 302-356-6880 90 I james.m.mccloskey@wilmu.edu

MCCLOSKEY, JR., John, R 610-796-3005 378 F john.mccloskey@alvernia.edu

MCCLOUD, Alyssa 973-761-9107 283 B alyssa.mccloud@shu.edu

MCCLOUD, Amber 806-291-3430 457 J amber.mccloud@wbu.edu

MCCLOUD, Barbara, L 630-515-7687 143 G bmcclo@midwestern.edu

MCCLOUD, Clarence 386-506-6301 97 D clarence.mccloud@daytonastate.edu

MCCLOUD, Jennifer 317-822-3489 158 V jmccloud@martin.edu

MCCLOUD, Mickey 913-469-8500 174 D mmcloud@jccc.edu

MCCLOY, Eric 610-341-1372 383 D eric.mccloy@eastern.edu

MCCLUER, Carol 520-795-0787 10 H cmccluer@asaom.edu

MCCLUNG, Alan 423-614-8410 420 J amcclung@leeuniversity.edu

MCCLUNG, Alex 973-408-3799 277 C amcclung@drew.edu

MCCLUNG, Bruce, D 336-334-5789 343 A bdmcclun@uncg.edu

MCCLUNG, Shemeka 601-979-7030 246 E shemeka.s.mcclung@jsums.edu

MCCLURE, Amber 575-461-4413 286 E amberm@mesalands.edu

MCCLURE, Amy 740-368-3562 359 N aamcclur@owu.edu

MCCLURE, Erin 361-593-2760 447 D erin.mcclure@tamuk.edu

MCCLURE, Gina 731-881-7888 428 B gmcclure@utm.edu

MCCLURE, Jennifer 847-214-7319 136 F jmcclure@elgin.edu

MCCLURE, Judy 828-766-1272 336 A jmmclure@mayland.edu

MCCLURE, Kelly 580-581-2255 365 G kmcclure@cameron.edu

MCCLURE, Krista 801-426-8234 460 C kmcclure@ucdh.edu

MCCLURE, Mike 541-956-7237 376 D mmclure@roguecc.edu

MCCLURE, Shannon 417-865-2815 253 B mcclures@evangel.edu

MCCLURE, Stephanie 801-626-6090 461 B womenscenter@weber.edu

MCCLURE, Tonya 478-757-3467 116 A tmcclure@centralgatech.edu

MCCLURE, William 718-997-5790 295 C wmclure@qc.cuny.edu

MCCLURG, Greg 970-247-7433 79 I mcclurg_g@fortlewis.edu

MCCLURKEN, Jeff 540-654-1475 472 I jmcclurk@umw.edu

MCCLURKEN, Jeffrey 540-654-1475 472 I jmcclurk@umw.edu

MCCLUSKEY, Cindy 815-825-9324 140 F cmccluskey@kish.edu

MCCLUSKEY, Jennifer 314-529-9561 254 H jmccluskey@maryville.edu

MCCLUSKEY, Peter 860-773-1442 86 G pmccluskey@tunxis.edu

MCCLUSKEY, Steph 507-786-3885 243 C mcclus1@stolaf.edu

MCCLUSKY, John 217-854-3231 132 I john.mcclusky@blackburn.edu

MCCLYMONT, Jay, W 717-796-1800 390 E jmcclymont@messiah.edu

MCCOART, Teresa 606-886-7371 180 J teresa.mccoart@kctcs.edu

MCCOEY, Margaret 215-951-1130 387 C mccoey@lasalle.edu

MCCOLGIN, Cathleen, C 315-866-0300 301 G mccolgicc@herkimer.edu

MCCOLLETT, Sherry 207-509-7201 195 H smccollett@unity.edu

MCCOLLOCH, Bruce 304-243-2241 491 I brucemcc@wju.edu

MCCOLLOUGH, LaDonna 913-971-3472 175 G lmccullough@mnu.edu

MCCOLLOUGH, Laura, L 907-474-6625 10 A lcmccollough@alaska.edu

MCCOLLOUGH, William, A 352-392-1202 109 F amccollough@aa.ufl.edu

MCCOLLUM, Jennifer 405-682-1611 367 H jennifer.e.mccollum@occc.edu

MCCOLLUM, Jennifer 503-554-2100 373 C jmccollum@georgefox.edu

MCCOLLUM, Ricky 718-429-6600 324 D ricky.mccollum@vaughn.edu

MCCOLLUM, Scott 937-512-3068 361 A scott.mccullum@sinclair.edu

MCCOLLUM, Shannon, M 530-895-2484 27 F mccollumsh@butte.edu

MCCOLLUM, Shawn 513-861-6400 361 L shawn.mccollum@myunion.edu

MCCOLLUM, Walter 866-492-5336 244 F walter.mccollum@mail.waldenu.edu

MCCOMAS, Katherine 607-255-9970 297 F kam19@cornell.edu

MCCOMBE, John, P 937-229-4615 362 G jmccombe1@udayton.edu

MCCOMBE WALLER, Sandy 301-624-2826 198 E smccombewaller@frederick.edu

MCCOMBS, Jonathan 614-947-6169 353 C jonathan.mccombs@franklin.edu

MCCOMMON, John 731-425-2652 425 B jmccommon@jscc.edu

MCCONAHA, Kristen 425-267-0154 480 G kmcconaha@everettcc.edu

MCCONAHAY, Mark 812-855-2654 156 A mcconaha@indiana.edu

MCCONAHAY, Mark 812-855-2654 156 B mcconaha@indiana.edu

MCCONATHY, Terry, M 318-257-4262 191 F tmm@latech.edu

MCCONICO, Courtney 785-242-5200 176 D courtney.mcconico@ottawa.edu

MCCONICO, Shannon 229-333-2110 127 B shannon.mcconico@wiregrass.edu

MCCONKEY, Susan 415-503-6285 60 H smcconkey@sfcm.edu

MCCONNELL, Blake 618-658-8331 141 D james.mcconnell@doc.illinois.gov

MCCONNELL, Cary 617-573-8575 219 A cmcconnell@suffolk.edu

MCCONNELL, Cheryl, A 610-660-1000 398 C

MCCONNELL, Chris 907-786-6764 9 H ccmcconnell@alaska.edu

MCCONNELL, Dave 405-208-5498 367 I dmcconnell@okcu.edu

MCCONNELL, Frank, J 706-864-1606 126 A mac.mcconnell@ung.edu

MCCONNELL, George 218-755-2027 237 E george.mcconnell@bemidjistate.edu

MCCONNELL, James 512-313-3000 434 E james.mcconnell@concordia.edu

MCCONNELL, Jason 423-869-6333 421 C jason.mcconnell@lmunet.edu

MCCONNELL, Joyce, E 970-491-6211 78 M presofc@colostate.edu

MCCONNELL, Karen, E 253-535-7656 482 H mcconnke@plu.edu

MCCONNELL, Karl 856-227-7200 276 E kmcconnell@camdencc.edu

MCCONNELL, Penny, J 217-443-8747 135 H pmcconn@dacc.edu

MCCONNELL, Sheppard 580-559-5625 366 C smcconnell@ecok.edu

MCCONNELL-BLACK, Karnell 801-832-2231 461 G kblack@westminstercollege.edu

MCCONNELLOGUE, Ken 303-860-5600 82 N ken.mcconnellogue@cu.edu

MCCONNICO, Kelly 336-758-5000 344 D mcconnkm@wfu.edu

MCCONOUGHEY, Gina 815-455-8996 143 A gmcconoughey@mchenry.edu

MCCONVILLE, Haley 978-921-4242 216 F haley.mcconville@montserrat.edu

MCCONVILLE, Jennifer, A 308-367-5259 270 C jmcconville2@unl.edu

MCCOOK, Sonya 336-506-4278 332 A sonya.mccook@alamancecc.edu

MCCOOL, Jeff 575-492-4711 286 J jmccool@nmjc.edu

MCCORCLE, Michael 417-865-2815 253 B mccorclem@evangel.edu

MCCORD-FITHIAN, Regina, L 812-888-5848 162 C rmccord-fithian@vinu.edu

MCCORKLE, Candy 269-387-1000 232 K

MCCORKLE, Kimberly 850-474-2035 110 E kmccorkle@uwf.edu

MCCORMAC, Greg 916-608-6615 50 H mccormg@flc.losrios.edu

MCCORMACK, Amy 219-473-4333 153 G amccormack@ccsj.edu

MCCORMACK, Beth 802-831-1327 463 G bmccormack@vermontlaw.edu

MCCORMACK, Brian 956-295-3585 449 D brian.mccormack@tsc.edu

MCCORMACK, Elizabeth 207-725-3578 193 D emccorma@bowdoin.edu

MCCORMACK, James 570-389-4166 394 A jmccorma@bloomu.edu

MCCORMACK, Jeff 405-425-1933 367 G jeff.mccormack@oc.edu

MCCORMACK, John 708-596-2000 149 B jmccormack@ssc.edu

MCCORMICK, Adrienne 803-323-2220 414 G mccormicka@winthrop.edu

MCCORMICK, Brad 618-985-8340 139 I bradmccormick@jalc.edu

MCCORMICK, Brad 423-697-3264 424 E brad.mccormick@chattanoogastate.edu

MCCORMICK, Brian 319-296-4050 166 B brian.mccormick@hawkeyecollege.edu

MCCORMICK, Cathleen 717-720-4070 394 C cmccormick@passhe.edu

MCCORMICK, Cecilia, M 717-361-1000 383 E mccormickcecilia@etown.edu

MCCORMICK, Charlie 830-792-7345 443 G president@schreiner.edu

MCCORMICK, David 312-567-4972 139 B dmccormick@iitri.org

MCCORMICK, Deanna 517-629-0315 220 G dmccormick@albion.edu

MCCORMICK, Gordon 831-656-2484 503 K gmccormick@navy.edu

MCCORMICK, Heath 610-921-2381 378 C hmccormick@albright.edu

MCCORMICK, Jill 402-872-2257 268 F jmccormick@peru.edu

MCCORMICK, Jim, S 303-963-3363 77 G jimmccormick@ccu.edu

MCCORMICK, Joseph 301-846-2548 198 E jmccormick@frederick.edu

MCCORMICK, Karla, S 334-844-4183 4 E ksm0010@auburn.edu

MCCORMICK, Kevin, M 630-515-6053 143 G kmccor@midwestern.edu

MCCORMICK, Kirsten, M 714-879-3901 45 F kmmccormick@hiu.edu

MCCORMICK, Lisa 830-792-7312 443 G library@schreiner.edu

MCCORMICK, Lucas 785-227-3380 171 E mccormicklf@bethanylb.edu

MCCORMICK, Mark 205-366-8831 7 A mmccormick@stillman.edu

MCCORMICK, Mark 239-304-7827 94 O mark.mccormick@avemaria.edu

MCCORMICK, Mark 732-906-2517 279 A mmccormic@middlesexcc.edu

MCCORMICK, OSU, Mary 440-943-7600 360 J mmccormick@dioceseofcleveland.org

MCCORMICK, Michael 206-221-4344 485 F mccorm50@uw.edu

MCCORMICK, Michael, R 315-386-7222 320 E mccormic@canton.edu

MCCORMICK, Patrick, T 509-313-6715 481 D mccormick@gonzaga.edu

MCCORMICK, CSC, Peter, M 574-631-7800 161 C mccormick.23@nd.edu

MCCORMICK, Reenie 410-334-2939 204 F rmccormick@worwic.edu

MCCORMICK, Robert 312-362-6627 135 I bmccormi@depaul.edu

MCCORMICK, Silas 217-732-3168 141 H smccormick@lincolnchristian.edu

MCCORN, Lester, A 803-327-7402 408 B

MCCORRY, Laurie, K 617-228-2465 214 A lkmccorry@bhcc.mass.edu

MCCORRY, Margaret 908-737-0580 278 E mmccorry@kean.edu

MCCORRY, Wendy 845-688-1980 323 E mccorryw@sunyulster.edu

MCCORRY-ANDALIS, Catherine, M 915-747-5648 455 C cmandalis@utep.edu

MCCORY, Denise 216-987-2296 351 G denise.mccory@tri-c.edu

MCCOTTER, Suzanne 609-771-1855 276 I mccottes@tcnj.edu

MCCOULLUM, Valarie, S 215-898-5337 400 K cade@upenn.edu

MCCOURRY, Maurine 517-607-2402 225 A mmccourry@hillsdale.edu

MCCOURT, MaryFrances 215-898-1005 400 K mfmccourt@upenn.edu

MCCOURT, Richard 440-449-4471 363 G richard.mccourt@ursuline.edu

MCCOURT, Susan 508-678-2811 213 G susan.mccourt@bristolcc.edu

MCCOWAN, Carla 217-333-3701 151 D cmccowan@illinois.edu

MCCOWN, Amber 239-489-9226 100 A amccown@fsw.edu

MCCOWN, Paul 307-332-2930 502 J pmccown@wyomingcatholic.edu

MCCOY, Avis, M 954-201-7401 95 H amccoy@broward.edu

MCCOY, Chris 479-575-3301 21 G cam@uark.edu

MCCOY, Daven 501-374-6305 21 A daven.mccoy@shortercollege.edu

MCCOY, David, M 804-289-8718 472 L dmccoy2@richmond.edu

MCCOY, Holly, M 724-738-2650 395 F holly.mccoy@sru.edu

MCCOY, Isaac 205-247-8149 7 A imccoy@stillman.edu

MCCOY, James 229-732-5950 114 B jamesmccoy@andrewcollege.edu

MCCOY, JR., James, F 813-393-3675 124 E

MCCOY, Jim 540-887-7285 469 B jmccoy@marybaldwin.edu
MCCOY, Julie 803-938-3821 414 B jmccoy@uscsumter.edu
MCCOY, J'Neal 417-447-4817 257 G mccoyj@otc.edu
MCCOY, Kathleen 941-487-4900 109 D kmccoy@ncf.edu
MCCOY, Kevin 785-227-3380 171 E mccoyk@bethanylb.edu
MCCOY, Marilyn 847-491-4335 145 F mmccoy@northwestern.edu
MCCOY, Mark 765-658-4220 154 F president@depauw.edu
MCCOY, Mary 409-882-3080 450 A mary.mccoy@lsco.edu
MCCOY, Matthew, J 541-383-7210 372 B mmccoy@cocc.edu
MCCOY, Mike 620-229-6104 177 A mike.mccoy@sckans.edu
MCCOY, Mike 256-216-3300 4 D mike.mccoy@athens.edu
MCCOY, Nate 217-732-3155 141 I nmccoy@lincolncollege.edu
MCCOY, Patricia 602-212-0501 11 B patricia.mccoy@brightoncollege.edu
MCCOY, Peggy, S 406-496-4404 265 A pmccoy@mtech.edu
MCCOY, Robert 907-474-7500 10 A rpmccoy@alaska.edu
MCCOY, Ryan 303-404-5238 79 J ryan.mccoy@frontrange.edu
MCCOY, Sue 916-484-8211 50 F mccoys@arc.losrios.edu
MCCOY, Tammie, M 662-329-7299 248 A tmmccoy@muw.edu
MCCOY, Ted 641-673-1090 170 F mccoyt@wmpenn.edu
MCCOY, William, K 570-577-1609 379 F bill.mccoy@bucknell.edu
MCCOY, Zaire 407-646-2385 105 M zmccoy@rollins.edu
MCCOY-WILSON, Sonya 404-225-4672 114 H smccoy-wilson@atlantatech.edu
MCCRACKEN, Carolyn 423-354-2509 425 E cgmccracken@northeaststate.edu
MCCRACKEN, Fawn 952-446-4325 235 G mccrackenf@crown.edu
MCCRACKEN, Hailey 302-622-8000 89 E hmccracken@dcad.edu
MCCRACKEN, Jeff, B 919-966-5730 342 D jeff_mccracken@unc.edu
MCCRACKEN, Jennifer, L 570-326-3761 393 G jlm16@pct.edu
MCCRACKIN, Tara 616-254-9303 223 J taramccrackin@ferris.edu
MCCRAE, Byron, P 704-894-2225 328 F bymccrae@davidson.edu
MCCRARY, Chandra 404-270-5394 125 B cmccrary@spelman.edu
MCCRARY, Cheryl 785-594-8327 170 I cheryl.mccrary@bakeru.edu
MCCRARY, Lauren 270-686-4236 179 D lauren.mccrary@brescia.edu
MCCRARY, Victor 202-274-7443 93 C victor.mccrary@udc.edu
MCCRAW, Bethany, J 254-710-1715 431 J bethany_mccraw@baylor.edu
MCCRAW, Liz 580-745-2080 369 K lmccraw@se.edu
MCCRAW, Patti, H 864-488-4571 410 E pmccraw@limestone.edu
MCCRAY, Corey, L 757-822-1184 476 B cmccray@tcc.edu
MCCRAY, Corey, L 757-822-1061 476 B cmccray@tcc.edu
MCCRAY, Suzanne 479-575-4883 21 G smccray@uark.edu
MCCRAY, Sylvia 215-574-9600 386 B sylvia.mccray@hussiancollege.edu
MCCRAY, Tammy 218-751-8670 242 J registrar@oakhills.edu
MCCREA, Larry 816-604-6541 255 E larry.mccrea@mcckc.edu
MCCREADY, John 858-653-3000 29 I
MCCREADY, Randall 412-624-7180 401 B mccready@pitt.edu
MCCREARY, Beverly 808-956-9429 128 F bmccrear@hawaii.edu
MCCREARY, Lynn 940-565-2378 454 A mccreary@unt.edu
MCCREARY, Micah, L 732-247-5241 279 D mmccreary@nbts.edu
MCCREARY, William 419-530-3990 363 E william.mccreary@utoledo.edu
MCCREE, Bernard, L 610-683-4032 395 A mccree@kutztown.edu
MCCREIGHT, Robert 785-738-9031 176 A rmccreight@ncktc.edu
MCCRILLIS, Neal, R 312-413-1468 151 B nealrm@uic.edu
MCCROHAN, Betty, A 979-532-6304 458 F bettym@wcjc.edu
MCCRORY, Cynthia 704-922-6406 334 F mccrory.cynthia@gaston.edu
MCCRORY, Davis 540-654-1042 472 I dmccrory@umw.edu
MCCRORY, Heidi, H 864-294-2475 410 A heidi.mccrory@furman.edu
MCCROSKEY, Lorie, L 336-633-1118 337 A llmccroskey@randolph.edu
MCCROSKEY, Shannen 918-647-1200 365 H
MCCROW, Rich 661-720-2002 46 L rmccrow@bakersfieldcollege.edu
MCCROW, Rich 661-395-4694 46 L rmccrow@bakersfieldcollege.edu
MCCUBBIN, Jeff 970-491-5841 78 M jeff.mccubbin@colostate.edu
MCCUBBIN, Todd, A 573-882-6017 261 B mccubbint@missouri.edu
MCCUDDEN, Suzanne 253-833-9111 481 F smccudden@greenriver.edu
MCCUE, Cindy 631-420-2319 321 B cynthia.mccue@farmingdale.edu
MCCUE, Jennie 949-582-4500 64 G
MCCUEN, Jan 714-997-6862 36 C mccuen@chapman.edu
MCCUIEN-SMITH, Cassandra 501-450-3173 23 H cmccuien@uca.edu
MCCUISTION, Kimberly 254-968-9100 446 E mccuistion@tarleton.edu
MCCULLA, Justin 937-328-7819 350 L mccullaj@clarkstate.edu
MCCULLAH, Anne 773-244-4589 145 A amccullah@northpark.edu
MCCULLAR, Bryan, L 785-833-4398 175 B bryan.mccullar@kwu.edu
MCCULLEN, Ann, S 904-620-2100 110 A amccullen@unf.edu
MCCULLEY, Becky 214-645-5482 457 B becky.mcculley@utsouthwestern.edu
MCCULLOCH, Greg 618-252-5400 149 C greg.mcculloch@sic.edu
MCCULLOCH, Sonja 912-260-4402 124 C sonja.mcculloch@sgsc.edu
MCCULLOH, Edna 330-490-7191 364 B emcculloh@walsh.edu
MCCULLOH, Julie, A 509-313-6591 481 D mccullohj@gonzaga.edu
MCCULLOH, Thayne, M 509-313-6102 481 D president@gonzaga.edu
MCCULLOUGH, Bryan 336-249-4688 334 A bryan_mccullough@davidsonccc.edu
MCCULLOUGH, Catherine 802-728-1247 464 E cmccullough@vtc.edu
MCCULLOUGH, Cheryl, J 803-327-7402 408 B cmccullough@clintoncollege.edu
MCCULLOUGH, Desiree, A 731-881-7014 428 B dmccull1@utm.edu
MCCULLOUGH, James 918-293-5068 368 D james.mccullough@okstate.edu
MCCULLOUGH, Jonathan, W 903-434-8115 441 B jmccullough@ntcc.edu
MCCULLOUGH, Karen 785-628-4260 173 B kamccullough@fhsu.edu
MCCULLOUGH, Laura 912-478-5234 119 C lmccullough@georgiasouthern.edu
MCCULLOUGH, Laura 304-205-6611 488 K laura.mccullough@bridgevalley.edu
MCCULLOUGH, Laurie 304-243-2281 491 I lmccullough@wju.edu
MCCULLOUGH, Mary 310-338-7312 50 J mmccullough@lmu.edu
MCCULLOUGH, Phenicia 657-278-4637 31 E pmccullough@fullerton.edu
MCCULLOUGH, Robert, R 216-368-5445 349 F robert.mccullough@case.edu
MCCULLOUGH, Scott 507-529-2789 240 G scott.mccullough@rctc.edu
MCCULLOUGH, Tami 262-472-6704 498 C mccullot@uww.edu
MCCULLY, Clare 617-724-6399 216 E cmccully@mghihp.edu
MCCUNE, Jennifer 661-654-3405 30 E jmccune@csub.edu
MCCUNE, Kate 562-947-8755 65 C katemccune@scuhs.edu
MCCUNE, L.B 810-762-9629 225 H lbmccune@kettering.edu
MCCUNE, Ryan 620-252-7046 172 G mccune.ryan@coffeyville.edu
MCCURDY, Clantha 617-391-6098 211 B cmccurdy@osfa.mass.edu
MCCURDY, Debra, L 410-462-7799 197 E dlmccurdy@bccc.edu
MCCURDY, Eugene, M 608-796-3921 498 N emmccurdy@viterbo.edu
MCCURDY, Megan 870-235-4094 21 D meganmccurdy@saumag.edu
MCCURDY, Solynn 206-296-6116 484 F mccurdys@seattleu.edu
MCCURLEY, Lisa 603-427-7878 272 J
MCCURREN, Cynthia 616-331-3558 224 E mccurrec@gvsu.edu
MCCURRY, David 864-503-5509 414 D dmccurry@uscupstate.edu
MCCURRY, Elizabeth 985-448-4521 192 B liz.mccurry@nicholls.edu
MCCURRY, Faith 803-535-1230 411 G mccurryf@octech.edu
MCCURRY, Michael 202-885-8600 93 E mmccurry@wesleyseminary.edu
MCCURRY, Roslyn 770-229-3404 124 G roslyn.mccurry@sctech.edu
MCCURTY, Kenyetta 334-387-3877 4 C kenyettamccurty@amridgeuniversity.edu
MCCUTCHEN, Michael 731-989-6901 420 C mmccutchen@fhu.edu
MCCUTCHEON, Andy 661-362-3387 38 H andy.mccutcheon@canyons.edu
MCCUTCHEON, John 805-893-8320 70 A jmccutch@athletics.ucsb.edu
MCDADE, Ben 770-534-6167 115 D bmcdade@brenau.edu
MCDADE, Kate 216-987-4710 351 G kate.mcdade@tri-c.edu
MCDADE, Lucinda 909-625-8767 37 D lucinda.mcdade@cgu.edu
MCDAID, James 617-879-7960 212 E jmcdaid@massart.edu
MCDANIEL, Amy 636-481-3465 254 A amcdanie@jeffco.edu
MCDANIEL, Anna, M 352-273-6324 109 F annammcdaniel@ufl.edu
MCDANIEL, Beth 601-477-4037 246 F beth.mcdaniel@jcjc.edu
MCDANIEL, Cleve 575-835-5606 286 I cleve.mcdaniel@nmt.edu
MCDANIEL, Cliff 817-461-8741 430 H cmcdaniel@abu.edu
MCDANIEL, Diane 765-677-2436 157 D diane.mcdaniel@indwes.edu
MCDANIEL, Donna 903-823-3220 446 B donna.mcdaniel@texarkanacollege.edu
MCDANIEL, Dustin 706-583-2525 114 F dmcdaniel@athenstech.edu
MCDANIEL, Gary, R 949-214-3055 40 F gary.mcdaniel@cui.edu
MCDANIEL, Joy 580-387-7000 366 H jmcdaniel@mscok.edu
MCDANIEL, Juley 620-223-2700 173 C juleym@fortscott.edu
MCDANIEL, Kimberly 916-691-7487 50 G mcdanik@crc.losrios.edu
MCDANIEL, Kristina, D 573-840-9695 260 I kristinamcdaniel@trcc.edu
MCDANIEL, Laura 701-231-8330 345 G laura.mcdaniel@ndsu.edu
MCDANIEL, Mary 620-341-5223 172 L mmcdanie@emporia.edu
MCDANIEL, Mary, W 864-388-8242 410 D mmcdaniel@lander.edu
MCDANIEL, Michael 517-371-5140 233 A mcdanielm@cooley.edu
MCDANIEL, Mick, R 607-844-8222 322 H mcdanim@tompkinscortland.edu
MCDANIEL, Rose 336-249-8186 334 A rose_mcdaniel@davidsonccc.edu
MCDANIEL, Sonya 770-962-7580 120 E smcdaniel@gwinnetttech.edu
MCDANIEL, Wendy 479-394-7622 23 C wmcdaniel@uarichmountain.edu
MCDANIEL-SMITH, Nicole, L 302-356-6928 90 I nicole.l.mcdaniel-smith@wilmu.edu
MCDANIELS, Lisa 814-641-3458 386 H mcdanil@juniata.edu
MCDANIELS, Preselfannie 601-979-2455 246 E preselfannie.w.mcdaniels@jsums.edu
MCDANIELS, Rob, M 573-882-9370 261 B mcdanielsr@missouri.edu
MCDANIELS WILSON, Cathy 614-236-6114 349 D cmcdanielswilson@capital.edu
MCDAVID, Cristina, C 304-696-2248 490 D mcdavidc@marshall.edu
MCDERMOTT, Anastacia, M 563-588-7056 167 D anastacia.mcdermott@loras.edu
MCDERMOTT, Ann, B 508-793-2443 208 B amcdermo@holycross.edu
MCDERMOTT, Anne 401-341-2140 406 A anne.mcdermott@salve.edu
MCDERMOTT, Brian 907-564-8248 9 D bmcdermott@alaskapacific.edu
MCDERMOTT, Brian 308-398-7387 266 A bmcdermott@cccneb.edu
MCDERMOTT, Christine 315-568-3105 308 F cmcdermott@nycc.edu
MCDERMOTT, Christine 302-736-2505 90 G christine.mcdermott@wesley.edu
MCDERMOTT, Colleen 920-424-1217 497 B mcdermot@uwosh.edu
MCDERMOTT, David 617-287-7050 211 C dmcdermott@umassp.edu
MCDERMOTT, Emily 617-287-5600 211 E emily.mcdermott@umb.edu
MCDERMOTT, Joan 415-422-6623 71 K jmcdermott2@usfca.edu
MCDERMOTT, John, R 563-588-7132 167 D john.mcdermott@loras.edu
MCDERMOTT, Marty 231-777-0462 228 D marty.mcdermott@muskegoncc.edu
MCDERMOTT, Patrice 410-455-3150 202 E mcdermot@umbc.edu
MCDERMOTT, Patricia, L 757-594-7222 466 B mcdermot@cnu.edu
MCDERMOTT, Patrick 941-377-4880 103 C pmcdermott@meridian.edu
MCDERMOTT, Randi 208-426-1493 129 I randimcdermott@boisestate.edu
MCDERMOTT, Richard, L 713-500-4963 456 B richard.l.mcdermott@uth.tmc.edu
MCDERMOTT, Suzan 315-386-7611 320 E mcdermotts@canton.edu
MCDERMOTT, Teresa 360-475-7480 482 G tmcdermott@olympic.edu
MCDERMOTT, Virginia, M 336-841-9384 329 G vmcdermo@highpoint.edu
MCDERMOTT, Walter, M 434-223-6112 468 A wmcdermott@hsc.edu
MCDEVITT, Michelle 419-517-8953 355 K mmcdevitt@lourdes.edu
MCDEVITT, Richard, K 704-406-2361 329 A rmcdevitt@gardner-webb.edu
MCDONAGH, David, L 646-888-6639 305 E mcdonagd@sloankettering.edu
MCDONALD, Amee 651-255-6109 243 D amcdonald@unitedseminary.edu
MCDONALD, Ann 508-626-4993 212 D amcdonald3@framingham.edu
MCDONALD, Brian 319-363-1323 168 C bmcdonald@mtmercy.edu
MCDONALD, Bridgette 678-466-4000 116 E bridgettemcdonald@clayton.edu
MCDONALD, Carleigh 415-703-9500 28 D c.mcdonald@cca.edu
MCDONALD, Christopher 949-451-5679 64 F cmcdonald@ivc.edu
MCDONALD, Christy 865-981-8402 421 F christy.mcdonald@maryvillecollege.edu
MCDONALD, Clay 636-227-2100 254 G
MCDONALD, Dana 301-846-2458 198 E dmcdonald@frederick.edu
MCDONALD, Danielle 813-974-6677 110 B dmcdonald@usf.edu

MCDONALD, Dave .... 503-838-8919 377 H mcdonald@wou.edu
MCDONALD, David .... 505-984-6082 287 J gi@sjc.edu
MCDONALD, Debbie ..... 626-966-4576.. 25 N info@agu.edu
MCDONALD, Deborah ... 845-938-5706 504 H admissions@usma.edu
MCDONALD, Dennis ..... 518-454-5126 296 H mcdonald@strose.edu
MCDONALD, Dennis ..... 417-865-2815 253 B mcdonaldd@evangel.edu
MCDONALD, Donna ...... 703-445-9056 473 D
MCDONALD, Dotty .... 337-550-1357 189 A dmcdonal@lsue.edu
MCDONALD, Eric .... 864-587-4200 412 G mcdonalde@smcsc.edu
MCDONALD, Francis, X 508-830-5001 213 B fmcdonald@maritime.edu
MCDONALD, Frank .... 212-346-1800 311 E fmcdonald@pace.edu
MCDONALD, Hannah .... 254-519-5454 447 A h.mcdonald@tamuct.edu
MCDONALD, James ...... 508-830-5096 213 B jmcdonald@maritime.edu
MCDONALD, James, R . 321-682-4401 112 K jmcdonald4@valenciacollege.edu
MCDONALD, Jan .... 864-977-7151 411 E jan.mcdonald@ngu.edu
MCDONALD, Jason, S .. 503-943-7147 377 E mcdonaja@up.edu
MCDONALD, Jennifer .... 714-241-6163.. 38 C jmcdonald@coastline.edu
MCDONALD, John .... 208-426-1258 129 I johnnymcdonald@boisestate.edu
MCDONALD, Joseph ..... 239-590-1102 108 K jmcdonald@fgcu.edu
MCDONALD, Joseph, M .... 518-461-2534 305 K jmcdonald01@mariacollege.edu
MCDONALD, Joy .... 973-353-5953 282 B joymcd@newark.rutgers.edu
MCDONALD, Julia .... 270-745-4346 185 E julia.mcdonald@wku.edu
MCDONALD, Ken .... 314-434-4044 252 B ken.mcdonald@covenantseminary.edu
MCDONALD, Kevin, G .. 573-882-2011 261 A mcdonaldkg@umsystem.edu
MCDONALD, Leander .... 701-255-3285 347 B president@uttc.edu
MCDONALD, Loretta ..... 314-340-3300 253 I mcdonall@hssu.edu
MCDONALD, Lori .... 949-214-3074.. 40 F lori.mcdonald@cui.edu
MCDONALD, Lori .... 801-581-7066 460 E lmcdonald@sa.utah.edu
MCDONALD, Lori, K ..... 801-581-7066 460 E lmcdonald@sa.utah.edu
MCDONALD, Martha, A 626-914-8534.. 36 K mmcdonald@citruscollege.edu
MCDONALD, Mary .... 251-380-2290.... 6 H mmcdonald@shc.edu
MCDONALD, Mary Rae . 575-538-6238 289 B maryrae.mcdonald@wnmu.edu
MCDONALD, MarySheila, A .... 215-951-1059 387 C mcdonaldms@lasalle.edu
MCDONALD, Michelle ... 609-626-3529 283 D michelle.mcdonald@stockton.edu
MCDONALD, Molly .... 408-554-6993.. 62 D mmcdonald@scu.edu
MCDONALD, Nicholas .. 978-837-3597 216 D mcdonaldn@merrimack.edu
MCDONALD, Paul, R .... 626-966-4576.. 25 N paulmcdonald@agu.edu
MCDONALD, Robert, H . 303-492-7511.. 83 A robert.mcdonald-2@colorado.edu
MCDONALD, Scott .... 318-342-5361 192 F mcdonald@ulm.edu
MCDONALD, Sharon ..... 309-268-8143 137 I sharon.mcdonald@heartland.edu
MCDONALD, Steven ...... 401-277-4955 405 D smcdonal@risd.edu
MCDONALD, Tammy ..... 361-698-1133 436 C tmcdonal1@delmar.edu
MCDONALD, Tim .... 770-533-6991 121 B tmcdonal@laniertech.edu
MCDONALD, Timothy ... 207-453-5116 194 I tmcdonal@kvcc.me.edu
MCDONALD, Tracie .... 406-275-4978 265 F tracie_mcdonald@skc.edu
MCDONALD, William .... 315-866-0300 301 G mcdonalwh@herkimer.edu
MCDONALD, William .... 617-322-3516 210 F william_mcdonald@laboure.edu
MCDONALD, William, A .... 973-748-9000 276 A bill_mcdonald@bloomfield.edu
MCDONALD, William, M .... 706-542-7774 125 G bmcdonal@uga.edu
MCDONALD HUTCHINS, Renee .... 202-274-6443.. 93 C renee.hutchins@udc.edu
MCDONELL, Clint .... 313-883-3112 229 K mcdonell.clint@shms.edu
MCDONNELL, Brian, A .. 401-341-2185 406 A mcdonneb@salve.edu
MCDONNELL, Fiona ...... 603-271-6484 273 B fmcdonnell@ccsnh.edu
MCDONNELL, John .... 773-481-8253 134 G jmcdonnell@ccc.edu
MCDONNELL, Karen ...... 470-578-6030 120 L kmcdonn1@kennesaw.edu
MCDONNELL, Pete .... 218-755-2967 237 E pete.mcdonnell@bemidjistate.edu
MCDONNELL, Ryan .... 314-529-9362 254 H rmcdonnell@maryville.edu
MCDONNELL, Tom .... 531-622-2716 267 H tjmcdonnell3@mccneb.edu
MCDONNELL, William, J .... 716-645-3129 316 F mcdonnell@buffalo.edu
MCDONOUGH, Amy, G . 651-962-6030 244 E mcdo0126@stthomas.edu
MCDONOUGH, Ann ...... 702-774-4619 271 E ann.mcdonough@unlv.edu
MCDONOUGH, Eileen ... 305-899-3085.. 95 C emcdonough@barry.edu
MCDONOUGH, Ellin ...... 803-323-2141 414 G mcdonoughe@winthrop.edu
MCDONOUGH, Erin ...... 503-838-9120 377 H mcdonough@wou.edu
MCDONOUGH, Michael 908-526-1200 281 A michael.mcdonough@raritanval.edu
MCDONOUGH, Thomas 401-254-3797 405 E tmcdonough@rwu.edu
MCDONOUGH, Timothy, J .... 410-576-5749 202 B tmcdonough@usmd.edu
MCDORMAN, Heather ... 636-922-8277 258 I hmcdorman@stchas.edu
MCDOUGAL, Bradley, N .... 540-464-7637 476 G mcdougalbn@vmi.edu
MCDOUGALD, Bryan, L 803-981-7063 415 A bcmdougald@yorktech.edu
MCDOUGALD, Sherlock 252-823-5166 334 C mcdougalds@edgecombe.edu
MCDOUGALL, Gordon ... 707-664-2880.. 34 C
MCDOUGALL, Jen .... 218-935-0417 244 G jen.mcdougall@wetcc.edu
MCDOUGLE, James .... 304-205-6710 488 K james.mcdougle@bridgevalley.edu
MCDOW, Robert, S .... 716-880-2288 306 C rsm334@medaille.edu
MCDOWALL, Douglass . 785-460-5484 172 H doug.mcdowall@colbycc.edu
MCDOWALL, Melissa .... 701-355-8181 347 D mpmcdowall@umary.edu
MCDOWALL LONG, Kimberly .... 316-942-4291 175 I longk@newmanu.edu
MCDOWELL, Amy .... 802-763-7170 463 G amcdowell@vermontlaw.edu
MCDOWELL, Denise ...... 507-457-5300 241 F dmcdowell@winona.edu
MCDOWELL, Jackie .... 706-236-2202 115 B jmcdowell@berry.edu
MCDOWELL, Jacqueline 919-530-7827 342 A mcdowelljw@nccu.edu
MCDOWELL, James .... 860-512-3603.. 85 G jmcdowell@manchestercc.edu
MCDOWELL, Jennifer .... 972-883-6301 455 B jpazik@utdallas.edu
MCDOWELL, Jill .... 203-285-2007.. 85 E jmcdowell@gwcc.commnet.edu
MCDOWELL, Mark .... 214-295-8592 248 F mmcdowell@rts.edu
MCDOWELL, N. Renee .. 724-653-2212 383 A rmcdowell@dec.edu
MCDOWELL, Pamela ..... 507-786-3011 243 C mcdowell@stolaf.edu
MCDOWELL, Travis, W . 864-488-4615 410 E tmcdowell@limestone.edu
MCDOWELL, Whitney .... 601-977-7821 249 C wmcdowell@tougaloo.edu
MCDUFFIE, April .... 229-468-2103 127 B april.mcduffie@wiregrass.edu
MCEACHERN, Daniel (JJ) .... 704-330-6395 333 D jj.mceachern@cpcc.edu
MCEACHERN, Patrick .... 509-533-8240 479 I patrick.mceachern@ccs.spokane.edu
MCEACHERN, Patrick .... 509-533-8240 480 B patrick.mceachern@ccs.spokane.edu
MCELANEY-JOHNSON, Ann .... 310-954-4011.. 52 G amcelaney@msmu.edu
MCELDERRY, Stuart ...... 925-424-1383.. 35 P smcelderry@laspositascollege.edu
MCELHANEY, Amy, M ... 402-280-4169 266 I amymcelhaney@creighton.edu
MCELHANEY, Patrick ..... 706-233-7225 124 B pmcelhaney@shorter.edu
MCELHANY, Ryan .... 972-825-4701 445 A rmcelhany@sagu.edu
MCELHENY, Candi .... 225-768-1725 186 F candi.mcelheny@franu.edu
MCELHOE, Dennis .... 704-922-6476 334 F mcelhoe.dennis@gaston.edu
MCELLIGOTT, Abbey ..... 888-556-8226 133 F
MCELMURRY, Chauvette .... 314-340-3601 253 I mcelmurc@hssu.edu
MCELMURRY, James ..... 808-853-1040 128 C jamesmcelmurry@pacrim.edu
MCELMURRY, Mark .... 314-434-4044 252 B mark.mcelmurry@covenantseminary.edu
MCELRATH, William ...... 732-571-3488 279 B wmcelrat@monmouth.edu
MCELROY, Blair .... 662-915-1508 249 D blair@olemiss.edu
MCELROY, Clint .... 704-330-6339 333 D clint.mcelroy@cpcc.edu
MCELROY, Coleetta .... 408-924-6086.. 34 B
MCELROY, Edith .... 704-330-4386 333 D edith.mcelroy@cpcc.edu
MCELROY, Emily, J .... 402-559-7078 270 A emily.mcelroy@unmc.edu
MCELROY, Jeff .... 641-784-5179 165 H jwmcelro@graceland.edu
MCELROY, Joe .... 714-966-8500.. 73 C info@ves.edu
MCELROY, Kathleen ...... 914-633-2201 302 G kmcelroy@iona.edu
MCELROY, Lee .... 518-276-6685 312 I mcelrl@rpi.edu
MCELROY HOOPER, Kellie .... 507-389-7493 241 C kellie.mcelroyhooper@southcentral.edu
MCELVEEN, Dawn .... 352-588-8499 106 D dawn.mcelveen@saintleo.edu
MCELWAIN, Brandon .... 573-897-5000 260 E
MCELWAIN, Karen .... 708-344-4700 142 A kmcelwain@lincolntech.edu
MCELWAIN, Sherman ... 607-729-1581 298 C smcelwain@davisny.edu
MCELYEA, Berna .... 713-223-7927 453 B mcelyeab@uhd.edu
MCENEANY, Barbara ..... 845-848-4031 298 D barbara.mceneany@dc.edu
MCENTEE, Mary .... 413-775-1203 214 C mcenteem@gcc.mass.edu
MCENTIRE, David .... 801-863-7810 461 A david.mcentire@uvu.edu
MCENTIRE, Tina, M ...... 704-687-7019 342 E tmmcenti@uncc.edu
MCEVOY, Ed, M .... 610-526-1290 378 G ed.mcevoy@theamericancollege.edu
MCEWAN, Anna .... 334-833-4236.... 5 H provost@hawks.huntingdon.edu
MCEWEN, Beryl .... 336-334-7965 341 F mcewenb@ncat.edu
MCEWEN, Jill .... 920-996-2847 499 E mcewen@fvtc.edu
MCFADDEN, David, F ... 260-982-5050 158 T dfmcfadden@manchester.edu
MCFADDEN, John .... 305-899-3208.. 95 C jmcfadden@barry.edu
MCFADDEN, Judy .... 970-521-6660.. 81 D judy.mcfadden@njc.edu
MCFADDEN, Margaret, T .... 207-859-4772 193 E margaret.mcfadden@colby.edu
MCFADDEN, Mary .... 845-848-7809 298 D mary.mcfadden@dc.edu
MCFADDEN, Mary Kay .. 208-885-6155 131 G marykaymcfadden@uidaho.edu
MCFADDEN, Melinda, A .... 309-298-1414 152 D ma-mcfadden@wiu.edu
MCFADDEN, Michael .... 202-806-1280.. 92 B michael.mcfadden@howard.edu
MCFADDEN, Paul .... 870-236-6901.. 19 A pmcfadden@crc.edu
MCFADDEN, Scott .... 509-527-2205 485 H scott.mcfadden@wallawalla.edu
MCFADDEN, Shamona .. 305-237-8965 103 D smcfadde@mdc.edu
MCFADDEN, Susan .... 215-955-2867 400 A susan.mcfadden@jefferson.edu
MCFADDEN, Thomas ..... 540-636-2900 466 A tmcfadden@christendom.edu
MCFADDEN, Toney, C .. 423-624-0077 419 B toney.mcfadden@chattanoogacollege.edu
MCFADDIN, David .... 859-622-6220 180 B david.mcfaddin@eku.edu
MCFADIN, Bard .... 575-624-7180 286 A brad.mcfadin@roswell.enmu.edu
MCFADZEN, Molly .... 262-646-6507 495 B mmcfadzen@nashotah.edu
MCFALL-NGAI, Margaret .... 808-956-8838 128 F mcfallng@hawaii.edu
MCFARLAND, Brenda .... 828-398-7669 332 B brendahmcfarland@abtech.edu
MCFARLAND, James ..... 412-731-1177 397 E rptrustees@aol.com
MCFARLAND, Keith .... 903-886-5226 447 B keith.mcfarland@tamuc.edu
MCFARLAND, Michael, S .... 570-389-4050 394 A mcfarland@bloomu.edu
MCFARLAND, Mike .... 919-962-2011 342 D mike_mcfarland@unc.edu
MCFARLAND, Reoungeneria .... 901-435-1213 421 A reo_mcfarland@loc.edu
MCFARLAND, Stacy ...... 304-876-5526 490 E smcfarla@shepherd.edu
MCFARLAND, Tracy ...... 315-279-5215 304 A tmcfarl@keuka.edu
MCFARLANE, Alison ...... 801-957-4103 461 D alison.mcfarlane@lscc.edu
MCFARLANE, Michele ... 208-732-6304 130 E mmcfarlane@csi.edu
MCFARLANE, Zachary ... 970-339-6202.. 76 G zachary.mcfarlane@aims.edu
MCFARLIN, Dean, B ..... 412-396-2554 383 C mcfarlind@duq.edu
MCFARLIN, Diane, H .... 352-392-0466 109 F dmcfarlin@ufl.edu
MCFARLIN, Leslie .... 706-754-8128 122 F lmcfarlin@northgatech.edu
MCFATRIDGE, Michael .. 310-954-4084.. 52 G mmcfatridge@msmu.edu
MCFAYDEN, Andy .... 316-677-9400 178 B amcfayden@watc.edu
MCFAYDEN, Brandon ..... 410-778-7810 204 D bmcfayden2@washcoll.edu
MCFAYDEN, Kenneth, J 804-355-0671 472 E kmcfayden@upsem.edu
MCFEE, Brenda .... 828-766-1330 336 A bmcfee@mayland.edu
MCFEELY, Gareth .... 617-353-9888 207 D garethmc@bu.edu
MCFETRIDGE, Travis ..... 541-881-5825 377 B tmcfetri@tvcc.cc
MCFRAZIER, Michael, L 936-261-2111 446 D mlmcfrazier@pvamu.edu
MCFRY, Kevin .... 256-549-8242.... 2 B kmcfry@gadsdenstate.edu
MCGADNEY, C. Andrew 207-859-4114 193 E andy.mcgadney@colby.edu
MCGAHA, SR., Gary, A . 404-756-4440 114 G gmcgaha@atlm.edu
MCGAHAN, Chris .... 919-515-7277 342 B chris_mcgahan@ncsu.edu
MCGAHEE, Thayer .... 803-641-2823 413 D thayerm@usca.edu
MCGAHERAN, Amy .... 315-268-3788 296 A amcgaher@clarkson.edu
MCGALLIARD, Anna ...... 207-509-7250 195 H amcgalliard@unity.edu
MCGALLIARD, Donna .... 336-758-5000 344 D
MCGALLIARD, Mike ...... 501-279-4640.. 19 D mmcgalliard@harding.edu
MCGANN, Joesph .... 860-465-4514.. 84 J mcgannj@easternct.edu
MCGANN, Matthew .... 413-542-2328 205 B admissions@amherst.edu

MCGRAW, Packy .... 518-694-7257 289 D
packy.mcgraw@acphs.edu
MCGRAW-ROWE, Victoria .... 614-236-6908 349 D
tmcgrawrowe@capital.edu
MCGREAL, Kristy .... 708-974-5335 144 C
mcgrealc2@morainevalley.edu
MCGREEVEY, Michael ... 614-890-3000 360 A
mmcgreevey@otterbein.edu
MCGREEVEY, Sean .... 502-272-8426 179 B
smcgreevey@bellarmine.edu
MCGREEVY, Bill .... 619-644-7141.. 44 I
bill.mcgreevy@gcccd.edu
MCGREEVY, Jeanette ..... 605-256-5663 416 J
jeanette.mcgreevy@dsu.edu
MCGREGOR, Cynthia .... 619-482-6371.. 65 F
cmcgregor@swccd.edu
MCGREGOR, Kyle, W .... 254-968-9890 446 E
mcgregor@tarleton.edu
MCGREGOR, Tiffany ...... 610-361-2487 391 D
mcgregot@neumann.edu
MCGREW, Martha .... 505-272-2165 288 G
mmcgrew@salud.unm.edu
MCGREW, Shea .... 740-826-8473 357 C
MCGRIFF, Elizabeth .... 415-565-4600.. 68 F
mcgriffelizabeth@uchastings.edu
MCGRIFF, Ilona .... 415-239-3677.. 37 A
imcgriff@ccsf.edu
MCGRIFF, Marsha .... 765-285-5316 153 C
mcmcgriff@bsu.edu
MCGRUDER, Janell, J ... 309-341-7492 141 A
jmcgruder@knox.edu
MCGRUDER, Lerla .... 512-313-3000 434 E
lerla.mcgruder@concordia.edu
MCGRUE, Geno .... 256-761-6324.... 7 B
gmcgrue@talladega.edu
MCGUCKIN, Tammy ...... 262-595-2571 497 C
mcgukin@uwp.edu
MCGUFFEE, James .... 901-321-3448 419 C
jmcguffee@cbu.edu
MCGUFFEY, Amy .... 937-327-6342 364 H
amcguffey@wittenberg.edu
MCGUFFEY, Michael, J . 304-696-3648 490 D
mcguffey@marshall.edu
MCGUFFIN, Kurt .... 731-881-7661 428 B
MCGUINNESS, Maureen 940-565-2648 454 A
moe@unt.edu
MCGUINNESS, Scott ..... 724-503-1001 402 E
smcguinness@washjeff.edu
MCGUINNESS, Tom ...... 207-786-8210 193 B
tmcguinn@bates.edu
MCGUIRE, Ann .... 440-646-6033 363 G
ann.mcguire@ursuline.edu
MCGUIRE, Bill .... 713-920-1120 438 F
MCGUIRE, Bud .... 903-233-3000 439 E
MCGUIRE, Carla .... 940-369-8757 454 A
carla.mcguire@unt.edu
MCGUIRE, Catherine ..... 559-737-5410.. 39 E
catherinemc@cos.edu
MCGUIRE, Christine, W 617-353-9814 207 D
chmcguir@bu.edu
MCGUIRE, David, D ...... 561-697-9200 124 E
dmcguire@southuniversity.edu
MCGUIRE, David, T ...... 435-586-7755 460 F
mcguire@suu.edu
MCGUIRE, Dennis .... 312-369-7434 135 E
dmcguire@colum.edu
MCGUIRE, Jack .... 315-267-2131 319 D
mcguirjp@potsdam.edu
MCGUIRE, Jamie .... 902-403-3166 495 I
jamie.mcguire@snc.edu
MCGUIRE, Jamie .... 336-838-6482 339 B
jdmcguire271@wilkescc.edu
MCGUIRE, Kathleen ...... 508-541-1615 208 F
kmcguire@dean.edu
MCGUIRE, Larry .... 309-677-2919 133 B
lmcguire@bradley.edu
MCGUIRE, Mark, T .... 740-284-5249 353 B
mmcguire@franciscan.edu
MCGUIRE, Maureen .... 509-313-6137 481 D
mcguirem@gonzaga.edu
MCGUIRE, Michael .... 303-871-3518.. 83 D
mmcguire@du.edu
MCGUIRE, Michael, J ... 785-670-1763 177 G
michael.mcguire@washburn.edu
MCGUIRE, Nona, S .... 614-236-6908 349 D
nmcguire@capital.edu
MCGUIRE, Patricia, A ... 202-884-9050.. 93 B
mcguirep@trinitydc.edu
MCGUIRE, Rachel, L ..... 641-422-4104 168 D
mcguirac@niacc.edu
MCGUIRE, Ruth, A .... 651-631-5343 244 D
ramcguire@unwsp.edu

MCGUIRE, Shirley .... 415-422-6136.. 71 K
mcguire@usfca.edu
MCGUIRE, Sue .... 828-898-2561 330 E
mcguirer@lmc.edu
MCGUIRE, Tara, S .... 402-280-3973 266 I
taramcguire@creighton.edu
MCGUIRE, Venus .... 903-463-8698 437 D
mcguirev@grayson.edu
MCGUIRE, Venus .... 214-698-0461 435 C
ecc5100@dcccd.edu
MCGUIRE, William, K ... 859-282-8989 120 H
wmcguire@ict.edu
MCGUIRK, Ryan .... 303-273-3062.. 78 I
mcguirk@mines.edu
MCGURGAN, Susan ...... 513-231-2223 348 C
smcgurgan@athenaeum.edu
MCGURIMAN, Timothy . 610-660-1357 398 C
tmcgurim@sju.edu
MCGURK, Mark .... 915-747-5113 455 C
mmcgurk@utep.edu
MCGURN, Joseph, P .... 740-283-6278 353 B
jmcgurn@franciscan.edu
MCGURTY, Thomas, S .. 617-627-3264 219 B
thomas.mcgurty@tufts.edu
MCGUTHRY, John, W ... 909-869-6442.. 30 D
jwmcguthry@cpp.edu
MCHALE, Barbara .... 215-641-5521 385 D
mchale.b@gmercyu.edu
MCHALE, Brendan .... 217-351-2409 146 C
jmchale@parkland.edu
MCHALE, Tammy, J ...... 570-348-6222 389 G
tmchale@marywood.edu
MCHALE, JR., William .. 717-358-3870 384 D
william.mchale@fandm.edu
MCHANEY, Eric .... 251-981-3771.... 5 B
eric.mchaney@columbiasouthern.edu
MCHARGUE, Jackie .... 828-250-2370 342 C
jmchargu@unca.edu
MCHARRIS, Michael ..... 315-792-5489 307 D
mmcharris@mvcc.edu
MCHATTON, Patricia ..... 956-665-2111 455 D
patricia.mchatton@utrgv.edu
MCHENRY, Beau .... 850-484-1146 104 H
bmchenry@pensacolastate.edu
MCHENRY, Erin .... 949-582-4481.. 64 G
emchenry@saddleback.edu
MCHENRY, John .... 760-384-6148.. 46 M
john.mchenry@cerrocoso.edu
MCHENRY, Lepaine .... 405-585-4450 367 F
lepaine.mchenry@okbu.edu
MCHENRY, Thomas ...... 802-831-1237 463 G
tmchenry@vermontlaw.edu
MCHORNEY, Mark .... 630-829-6150 132 E
mmchorney@ben.edu
MCHUGH, Chris .... 563-588-8000 165 F
cmchugh@emmaus.edu
MCHUGH, Elizabeth ...... 360-867-6808 481 A
mchughe@evergreen.edu
MCHUGH, James .... 619-201-8727.. 60 A
james.mchugh@sdcc.edu
MCHUGH, John .... 434-924-4214 473 A
jm7v@virginia.edu
MCHUGH, John .... 704-748-5213 334 F
mchugh.john@gaston.edu
MCHUGH, Kevin .... 609-652-1776 283 D
kevin.mchugh@stockton.edu
MCHUGH, Lindsay .... 508-541-1656 208 F
lmchugh@dean.edu
MCHUGH, Mary .... 845-848-7407 298 D
mary.mchugh@dc.edu
MCHUGH, Patti .... 610-341-5812 383 D
pmchugh@eastern.edu
MCHUGH, Shelley .... 402-465-2123 268 H
smchugh@nebrwesleyan.edu
MCHUGH, Tracy .... 630-889-6605 144 G
tmchugh@nuhs.edu
MCHUGH, Tracy .... 630-889-6607 144 G
tmchugh@nuhs.edu
MCILDUFF, Stacy .... 518-381-1322 315 G
mcildusm@sunysccc.edu
MCILHAGGA, Doug .... 618-650-3605 149 F
dmcilha@siue.edu
MCILLECE, Emily .... 402-354-7249 268 C
emily.mcillece@methodistcollege.edu
MCILROY, Julia .... 208-885-6123 131 G
juliam@uidaho.edu
MCILVANE, Amy .... 770-426-2648 121 C
mcilvane@life.edu
MCILWAINE, Tammi ...... 704-991-0311 338 C
tmcilwaine7455@stanly.edu
MCINALLY, David, W .... 319-399-8686 164 A
dmcinally@coe.edu

MCINERNEY, Todd .... 203-932-7031.. 89 A
tmcinerney@newhaven.edu
MCINNIS, James, P ...... 601-643-8488 245 G
jp.mcinnis@colin.edu
MCINNIS, Kyle .... 978-837-3590 216 D
mcinnisk@merrimack.edu
MCINNIS, Maurie .... 512-232-3300 455 A
provost@utexas.edu
MCINNIS, Robert, L ...... 704-216-6400 330 H
rmcinnis@livingstone.edu
MCINNIS, W. Dale .... 910-410-1806 337 B
wdmcinnis@richmondcc.edu
MCINTEE, Justin .... 714-556-3610.. 72 F
justin.mcintee@vanguard.edu
MCINTIRE, Heidi .... 330-337-6403 347 E
college@awc.edu
MCINTIRE, Kelsey .... 706-754-7768 122 F
kmcintire@northgatech.edu
MCINTIRE, Molly .... 407-582-5588 112 K
mmcintire1@valenciacollege.edu
MCINTOSH, Amy .... 646-664-9109 292 K
amy.mcintosh@cuny.edu
MCINTOSH, Angela .... 937-766-3200 349 G
mcintosh@cedarville.edu
MCINTOSH, Charles ...... 352-854-2322.. 96 O
mcintosc@cf.edu
MCINTOSH, Daniel .... 303-871-4449.. 83 D
daniel.mcintosh@du.edu
MCINTOSH, Gary .... 425-889-7790 482 F
gary.mcintosh@northwestu.edu
MCINTOSH, Gayle .... 253-879-3905 485 E
gmcintosh@pugetsound.edu
MCINTOSH, Glenn .... 248-370-4200 229 G
mcintosh@oakland.edu
MCINTOSH, Joe .... 817-515-5377 445 G
clifford.mcintosh@tccd.edu
MCINTOSH, John .... 256-331-5323.... 3 C
jmcintosh@nwscc.edu
MCINTOSH, Joshua .... 207-786-6219 193 B
jmcintos@bates.edu
MCINTOSH, Julie .... 419-434-4062 363 A
mcintosh@findlay.edu
MCINTOSH, Katy .... 714-556-3610.. 72 F
katy.mcintosh@vanguard.edu
MCINTOSH, Keith, J ...... 804-289-8771 472 L
kmcintosh@richmond.edu
MCINTOSH, Laurel .... 479-308-2212.. 17 C
laurel.mcintosh@arcome3du.org
MCINTOSH, Linda .... 936-294-3974 450 C
lam096@shsu.edu
MCINTOSH, Mark .... 573-882-2011 261 A
mcintoshm@umsystem.edu
MCINTOSH, Mark, A ..... 573-882-3360 261 B
mcintoshm@health.missouri.edu
MCINTOSH-DOTY, Mikail .... 512-313-3000 434 E
mikail.doty@concordia.edu
MCINTURF, Rob .... 940-369-7053 454 A
robert.mcinturf@unt.edu
MCINTYRE, Ellen, C ...... 704-687-8722 342 E
ellen.mcintyre@uncc.edu
MCINTYRE, Faye, S .... 678-839-6467 126 E
fmcintyr@westga.edu
MCINTYRE, Helen, M .... 205-934-8132.... 8 A
hmcintyre@uab.edu
MCINTYRE, Jacqueline .. 516-364-0808 309 A
jmcintyre@nycollege.edu
MCINTYRE, John .... 910-221-2224 329 B
jmcintyre@gcd.edu
MCINTYRE, Kevin .... 806-743-7425 451 C
kevin.mcintyre@ttuhsc.edu
MCINTYRE, Kevin, M .... 712-749-2655 163 D
mcintyrek@bvu.edu
MCINTYRE, Willie .... 910-672-1157 341 E
wmcintyre@uncfsu.edu
MCIVOR, Keith .... 208-885-6469 131 G
keithm@uidaho.edu
MCKAIN, Betty, J .... 269-387-4728 232 K
betty.mckain@wmich.edu
MCKAIN, Joshua .... 617-236-8854 209 D
jmckain@fisher.edu
MCKAIN, Mishele .... 218-751-8670 242 J
mishelemckain@oakhills.edu
MCKANNA, Nate .... 214-887-5041 436 B
nmckanna@dts.edu
MCKAY, Ashley, M .... 812-941-2075 157 B
atronc01@ius.edu
MCKAY, Bill .... 509-542-5531 479 H
bmckay@columbiabasin.edu
MCKAY, Cheryl, A .... 573-341-7060 261 E
cherylan@mst.edu
MCKAY, Janet .... 203-837-8460.. 85 B
mckayj@wcsu.edu

MCKAY, Jeffrey .... 207-778-7009 196 B
jeffrey.d.mckay@maine.edu
MCKAY, Kerri .... 313-664-7441 222 F
kmckay@collegeforcreativestudies.edu
MCKAY, Kevin .... 425-640-1547 480 F
kevin.mckay@edcc.edu
MCKAY, Kimberly .... 432-335-6683 441 D
kmckay@odessa.edu
MCKAY, Mary, M .... 314-935-6693 262 A
mary.mckay@wustl.edu
MCKAY, Monique .... 239-590-1022 108 K
mmckay@fgcu.edu
MCKAY, Rebecca .... 256-761-6306.... 7 B
rmckay@talladega.edu
MCKAY, Richard .... 281-998-6150 443 E
richard.mckay@sjcd.edu
MCKAY, Sally .... 803-777-7161 413 C
mckayst@mailbox.sc.edu
MCKAY, Scott .... 432-552-2220 457 A
mckay_s@utpb.edu
MCKAY JOHNSON, Rebecca .... 903-566-7351 456 A
rjohnson@uttyler.edu
MCKAYLE, Camille, A ... 340-693-1200 514 E
cmckayl@uvi.edu
MCKEAN, Molly .... 603-641-7020 274 C
mmckean@anselm.edu
MCKEAN, Scott .... 425-352-8192 479 A
smckean@cascadia.edu
MCKEARN, Tim .... 608-757-7704 499 C
tmckearn@blackhawk.edu
MCKECHNIE, Janna .... 701-858-3373 345 F
janna.mckechnie@minotstateu.edu
MCKECHNIE, Sally .... 225-578-2307 188 I
smckechnie@lsu.edu
MCKEE, Andy .... 260-399-7700 161 D
amckee@sf.edu
MCKEE, Anne .... 865-981-8298 421 F
anne.mckee@maryvillecollege.edu
MCKEE, Brandi .... 301-369-2800 197 F
bkmckee@captechu.edu
MCKEE, Diann, E .... 812-237-2372 155 G
diann.mckee@indstate.edu
MCKEE, Erin .... 712-325-3204 167 B
emckee@iwcc.edu
MCKEE, John, C .... 409-747-9080 456 F
jcmckee@utmb.edu
MCKEE, Jonathon .... 808-984-3213 129 E
jvmckee@hawaii.edu
MCKEE, Joseph .... 662-621-4156 245 E
jmckee@coahomacc.edu
MCKEE, Judith .... 574-284-4719 160 C
smcbookstore@bkstr.com
MCKEE, Kelli, J .... 724-847-6526 384 G
kelli.mckee@geneva.edu
MCKEE, Larry .... 856-351-2605 283 A
lmckee@salemcc.edu
MCKEE, Lori .... 575-646-8306 287 B
lomckee@nmsu.edu
MCKEE, Lori, L .... 419-755-4828 357 E
lmckee@ncstatecollege.edu
MCKEE, Marites .... 808-687-7014 127 H
mmckee@hpu.edu
MCKEE, Mark .... 419-448-2194 353 H
mmckee@heidelberg.com
MCKEE, Michael .... 352-392-2402 109 F
mckee@ufl.edu
MCKEE, Mike .... 386-752-1822.. 99 A
mike.mckee@fgc.edu
MCKEE, Nancy, C .... 850-245-0466 108 H
nancy.mckee@flbog.edu
MCKEE, Richard .... 432-685-4734 440 E
rmckee@midland.edu
MCKEE, Suzanne .... 334-683-2347.... 3 A
smckee@marionmilitary.edu
MCKEE, William .... 615-547-1311 419 F
bmckee@cumberland.edu
MCKEEGAN, John .... 503-883-2217 373 H
jmckeega@linfield.edu
MCKEEN, Jerry .... 805-493-3139.. 29 H
jmckeen@callutheran.edu
MCKEEVER, Diane, M ... 312-942-6950 148 A
diane_m_mckeever@rush.edu
MCKEEVER, William, P . 716-829-7807 298 F
mckeever@dyc.edu
MCKEIGUE, Elizabeth .... 978-542-6762 213 C
emckeigue@salemstate.edu
MCKEITHEN, Susan, P .. 719-884-5000.. 81 C
spmckeithen@nbc.edu
MCKELLIP, Mark .... 419-251-8989 356 C
mark.mckellip@mercycollege.edu
MCKELLIPS, Steve .... 828-250-3829 342 C
smckelli@unca.edu

MCKELVEY, Brandon ..... 407-582-3046 112 K
jmckelvey@valenciacollege.edu
MCKELVEY, Kathryn ...... 419-267-1327 358 A
kmckelvey@northweststate.edu
MCKENDREE, Lynda ...... 713-525-2151 454 H
mckendla@stthom.edu
MCKENDRICKS, John .... 775-849-4983 374 D
jmckendricks@multnomah.edu
MCKENNA, Andrea .... 805-898-2913.. 42 L
amckenna@fielding.edu
MCKENNA, Crichton ..... 207-453-5155 194 I
cmckenna@kvcc.me.edu
MCKENNA, Doug .... 703-993-2434 467 L
cmckenn@gmu.edu
MCKENNA, Heidi .... 510-883-7160.. 41 G
hmckenna@dspt.edu
MCKENNA, Judith .... 734-432-5465 227 A
jmckenna@madonna.edu
MCKENNA, Kevin .... 914-395-2510 315 F
kmckenna@sarahlawrence.edu
MCKENNA, Kristen, P ... 617-228-2416 214 A
kpmckenn@bhcc.edu
MCKENNA, Lynn, C ...... 413-545-6272 211 D
lmckenna@admin.umass.edu
MCKENNA, Matthew ...... 330-569-5416 353 J
mckennamk@hiram.edu
MCKENNA, Megan .... 814-824-3355 390 C
mmckenna@mercyhurst.edu
MCKENNA, Timothy, J .. 319-273-3241 163 B
tim.mckenna@uni.edu
MCKENNA, Tori .... 860-439-2314.. 86 H
tori.mckenna@conncoll.edu
MCKENNA-JONES, Amy 573-518-2146 256 B
mjones@mineralarea.edu
MCKENNEY, William ..... 574-239-8390 155 D
wmckenney@hcc-nd.edu
MCKENZIE, Andre, A ..... 718-990-1892 314 B
mckenzia@stjohns.edu
MCKENZIE, Bruce .... 937-778-7855 352 J
bmckenzie@edisonohio.edu
MCKENZIE, Connie, L ... 757-965-8500 466 I
mckenzcl@evms.edu
MCKENZIE, Deborah ..... 803-705-4589 407 A
deborah.mckenzie@benedict.edu
MCKENZIE, Helen, R ..... 814-866-8130 388 A
hmckenzie@lecom.edu
MCKENZIE, JoAnn .... 404-727-6052 117 F
jmckenz@emory.edu
MCKENZIE, Justin .... 484-365-8134 389 C
cio@lincoln.edu
MCKENZIE, Laura .... 208-282-2979 130 H
mckelaur@isu.edu
MCKENZIE, Lester .... 903-886-5091 447 B
lester.mckenzie@tamuc.edu
MCKENZIE, Lisa .... 518-454-5114 296 H
mckenzil@strose.edu
MCKENZIE, Michael ...... 828-262-2130 341 B
mckenziemj@appstate.edu
MCKENZIE, Rene .... 541-956-7129 376 D
rmckenzie@roguecc.edu
MCKENZIE, Sarah .... 334-808-6128.... 7 C
smckenzie93530@troy.edu
MCKENZIE, Steve .... 707-476-4385.. 39 D
MCKENZIE, Vandeen ..... 575-646-6014 287 B
vmckenzi@nmsu.edu
MCKEON, Margaret .... 215-871-6826 396 D
margaremc@pcom.edu
MCKEOWN, Joshua, S .. 315-312-2118 319 B
joshua.mckeown@oswego.edu
MCKEOWN, Robert .... 716-614-6201 310 C
mckeown@niagaracc.suny.edu
MCKERALL, Deborah ..... 936-294-3548 450 C
dam004@shsu.edu
MCKERNAN, Sarah .... 620-341-5551 172 L
smckerna@emporia.edu
MCKERNAN, Steve .... 505-272-2071 288 G
smckernan@salud.unm.edu
MCKETHAN, Lisa, H .... 254-710-3817 431 J
lisa_mckethan@baylor.edu
MCKETHER, Willie .... 419-530-5529 363 E
willie.mckether@utoledo.edu
MCKIBBIN, Barbara .... 704-669-4116 333 E
mckibbin@clevelandcc.edu
MCKIE, Angi .... 319-335-3531 163 A
angi-mckie@uiowa.edu
MCKIERNAN, Jack .... 908-737-0600 278 E
jmckiern@kean.edu
MCKIM, Heather .... 970-248-1950.. 77 I
hmckim@coloradomesa.edu
MCKINION, Randall ...... 937-766-7986 349 G
rmkinion@cedarville.edu
MCKINLEY, Bob .... 817-598-6256 458 A
bmckinley@wc.edu
MCKINLEY, Colleen ...... 562-860-2451.. 35 M
cmckinley@cerritos.edu
MCKINLEY, Elizabeth .... 816-501-3767 250 F
elizabeth.mckinley@avila.edu
MCKINLEY, Erika .... 662-915-7014 249 D
mckinley@olemiss.edu
MCKINLEY, Kathy .... 919-536-7244 334 B
mckinleyk@durhamtech.edu
MCKINLEY, Kristin, L .... 920-832-6532 493 K
kristin.l.mckinley@lawrence.edu
MCKINLEY, Michael ...... 716-884-9120 291 L
MCKINLEY, Mike .... 859-253-0621 178 E
mmckinley@national-college.edu
MCKINLEY, Patricia .... 713-525-3575 454 H
mckinley@stthom.edu
MCKINLEY, Robert .... 210-485-0020 429 C
MCKINNEY, Anya .... 865-251-1800 424 A
library@south.edu
MCKINNEY, Bryan .... 870-245-5250.. 20 E
mckinneyb@obu.edu
MCKINNEY, Bryan .... 870-245-5513.. 20 E
mckinneyb@obu.edu
MCKINNEY, David, C ..... 888-491-8686.. 74 F
davidmckinney@westcliff.edu
MCKINNEY, Frances, H 410-651-6668 203 A
fhmckinney@umes.edu
MCKINNEY, Gail .... 303-797-5647.. 76 I
gail.mckinney@arapahoe.edu
MCKINNEY, Jason .... 315-279-5434 304 A
jmckinney@keuka.edu
MCKINNEY, Jermaine ... 386-481-2358.. 95 F
mckinneyj@cookman.edu
MCKINNEY, Jill .... 317-940-8312 153 F
jsmckinn@butler.edu
MCKINNEY, Joan, C ..... 270-789-5214 179 E
jmckinney@campbellsville.edu
MCKINNEY, Marion ...... 610-436-3307 396 A
mmckinney@wcupa.edu
MCKINNEY, Marion, R .. 804-524-5961 477 B
mmckinney@vsu.edu
MCKINNEY, Mica .... 435-797-1156 460 H
mica.mckinney@usu.edu
MCKINNEY, Michael ...... 724-589-2600 399 H
mmckinney@thiel.edu
MCKINNEY, Michele ..... 303-860-5600.. 82 N
michele.mckinney@cu.edu
MCKINNEY, Monica ...... 919-760-8056 331 B
mckinneym@meredith.edu
MCKINNEY, Nancy .... 803-732-5355 410 G
mckinneyn@midlandstech.edu
MCKINNEY, Paul .... 662-325-7428 247 F
kpm137@msstate.edu
MCKINNEY, Rebekah ..... 314-392-2319 256 C
rebekah.mckinney@mobap.edu
MCKINNY, Robert .... 337-482-5308 192 E
mckinney@louisiana.edu
MCKINNEY, Roger .... 866-492-5336 244 F
roger.mckinney@laureate.net
MCKINNEY, Ronnie .... 334-244-3668.... 4 F
ronnie@aum.edu
MCKINNEY, Scott .... 304-473-8041 491 H
mckinney.s@wvwc.edu
MCKINNEY, Shortie ...... 978-934-4460 211 G
shortie_mckinney@uml.edu
MCKINNEY, Teresa .... 940-369-8979 454 A
teresa.mckinney@unt.edu
MCKINNON, Brad .... 256-766-6610.... 5 F
bmckinnon@hcu.edu
MCKINNON, Carol, E .... 301-546-0014 201 C
mckinnce@pgcc.edu
MCKINNON, Charles ..... 770-962-7580 120 E
cmckinnon@gwinnetttech.edu
MCKINNON, Georgia .... 980-495-3978 329 C
MCKINNON, Haley .... 334-670-3178.... 7 C
hmckinnon@troy.edu
MCKINNON, Laura .... 972-238-6107 435 F
lauramckinnon@dcccd.edu
MCKINNON, Maureen .... 816-501-4831 258 H
maureen.mckinnon@rockhurst.edu
MCKINNON, Theresa ..... 615-327-6185 422 A
tmckinnon@mmc.edu
MCKINNON, Will .... 801-863-8922 461 A
will.mckinnon@uvu.edu
MCKINNON-HOWE,
Leah .... 617-585-1284 217 B
leah.mckinnon-howe@necmusic.edu
MCKINNY, Charles .... 361-698-1794 436 C
cmckinn@delmar.edu
MCKINSEY-MABRY,
Kimberly .... 585-262-1616 307 H
kmckinseymabry@monroecc.edu
MCKIRDY, Pam .... 434-791-5618 464 O
pmckirdy@averett.edu
MCKISSICK, Issac .... 864-466-1065 412 F
mckissicki@sccsc.edu
MCKISSON, Kevin .... 281-669-4711 443 B
kevin.mckisson@sjcd.edu
MCKISSON, Kevin .... 281-669-4711 443 C
kevin.mckisson@sjcd.edu
MCKISSON, Kevin .... 281-484-1900 443 E
kevin.mckisson@sjcd.edu
MCKISSON, Kevin .... 281-998-6150 443 D
kevin.mckisson@sjcd.edu
MCKISSON, Kevin .... 281-998-6150 443 E
kevin.mckisson@sjcd.edu
MCKITTRICK, Jerry .... 314-744-5345 256 C
mckittrickj@mobap.edu
MCKNIGHT, Carrie .... 650-508-3717.. 54 D
cmknight@ndnu.edu
MCKNIGHT, Colleen ..... 301-846-2446 198 E
cmcknight@frederick.edu
MCKNIGHT, Cynthia ...... 440-684-6102 363 G
cmcknigh@ursuline.edu
MCKNIGHT, Frank .... 330-490-7226 364 B
fmcknight@walsh.edu
MCKNIGHT, Jeannine ... 570-465-2344 387 D
mcknightj@lackawanna.edu
MCKNIGHT, John .... 860-439-2035.. 86 H
jmcknight@conncoll.edu
MCKNIGHT, Natalie .... 617-353-2852 207 D
njmck@bu.edu
MCKNIGHT, Oscar .... 419-289-5065 348 A
omcknigh@ashland.edu
MCKNIGHT, Sandra ...... 216-987-4832 351 G
sandra.mcknight@tri-c.edu
MCKNIGHT, Steven, H .. 571-858-3000 477 A
shm@vt.edu
MCKNIGHT-TUTEIN,
Gillian .... 303-404-5497.. 79 J
gillian.mcknight-tutein@frontrange.edu
MCKONE, Kevin .... 601-643-8369 245 G
kevin.mckone@colin.edu
MCKOWN, Johnette ...... 254-299-8601 440 A
jmckown@mclennan.edu
MCKOY, Cynthia .... 910-879-5566 332 D
cmckoy@bladencc.edu
MCKUSICK, Jim .... 816-235-2182 261 C
honors@umkc.edu
MCLACKEN, Susan .... 401-232-6881 404 F
smcdonal@bryant.edu
MCLAIN, Chippy .... 423-585-6956 426 C
chippy.mclain@ws.edu
MCLAIN, Chris .... 425-739-8265 482 A
chris.mclain@lwtech.edu
MCLAIN, Mandy .... 336-725-8344 339 F
mclainm@piedmontu.edu
MCLAMB, Alvin .... 803-327-7402 408 B
amclamb@clintoncollege.edu
MCLANE, Margaret .... 518-454-5161 296 H
mclanem@strose.edu
MCLANEY, Carl .... 323-563-4854.. 36 D
carlmclaney@cdrewu.edu
MCLANEY, Jeremy .... 419-559-2465 361 I
jmclaney01@terra.edu
MCLARAN, Diane .... 503-316-3229 372 C
diane.mclaran@chemeketa.edu
MCLAREN, Donna .... 585-594-6114 312 K
mclaren_donna@roberts.edu
MCLAREN, Kate .... 508-531-6502 212 B
kate.mclaren@bridgew.edu
MCLAREN, Robert .... 808-956-8531 128 F
rmclaren@hawaii.edu
MCLARIO, Lisa .... 770-381-7200 120 B
MCLARTY, Bruce, D ...... 501-279-4274.. 19 D
president@harding.edu
MCLAUGHLIN, Annette . 718-817-4350 300 E
lmclaughlin9@fordham.edu
MCLAUGHLIN, Anthony 860-632-3010.. 87 C
amclaughlin@holyapostles.edu
MCLAUGHLIN,
Bryan, S .... 402-280-2386 266 I
bmclaughlin@creighton.edu
MCLAUGHLIN, Chris ..... 541-962-3516 373 B
cjmclaughlin@eou.edu
MCLAUGHLIN, Colin ..... 618-664-7100 137 G
MCLAUGHLIN,
David, B .... 419-207-5555 348 A
dmclaugh@ashland.edu
MCLAUGHLIN,
Edward, K .... 804-828-6692 473 F
athleticsdir@vcu.edu
MCLAUGHLIN, Eric .... 626-350-1500.. 28 J
MCLAUGHLIN,
Francis, X .... 718-817-4300 300 E
mclaughlin@fordham.edu
MCLAUGHLIN, Gerald ... 215-641-5550 385 D
mclaughlin.g@gmercyu.edu
MCLAUGHLIN, Henry, J 646-660-6000 292 L
henry.mclaughlin@baruch.cuny.edu
MCLAUGHLIN, Jack ...... 443-840-1021 198 B
jmclaughlin@ccbcmd.edu
MCLAUGHLIN, James ... 518-388-6284 323 G
mclaughj@union.edu
MCLAUGHLIN, Jane ...... 714-432-5531.. 38 E
jmclaughlin@occ.cccd.edu
MCLAUGHLIN, Jennifer . 215-335-0800 389 B
jmcloughlin@lincolntech.edu
MCLAUGHLIN, John ..... 508-678-2811 213 G
john.mclaughlin2@bristolcc.edu
MCLAUGHLIN, Joyce .... 978-934-4237 211 G
joyce_mclaughlin@uml.edu
MCLAUGHLIN, Keith ..... 708-656-8000 144 E
keith.mclaughlin@morton.edu
MCLAUGHLIN, Kerry ..... 718-933-6700 307 G
kmclaughlin@monroecollege.edu
MCLAUGHLIN, Kevin .... 216-791-5000 351 A
kevin.mclaughlin@cim.edu
MCLAUGHLIN, Kevin .... 401-863-9525 404 E
kevin_mclaughlin@brown.edu
MCLAUGHLIN, Laura, L 217-581-7264 136 E
lmclaughlin@eiu.edu
MCLAUGHLIN,
Laurie, L .... 612-626-1499 243 E
mclau001@umn.edu
MCLAUGHLIN, LaVerne 229-430-4798 113 H
laverne.mclaughlin@asurams.edu
MCLAUGHLIN, Mark ..... 610-785-6216 398 A
mmclaughlin@scs.edu
MCLAUGHLIN, Mark ..... 513-745-3409 365 B
mclaughlin@xavier.edu
MCLAUGHLIN, Mary ..... 603-526-3755 272 H
mmclaughlin@colby-sawyer.edu
MCLAUGHLIN, Mary, R 518-454-5170 296 H
mclaughr@strose.edu
MCLAUGHLIN,
Mary Jane .... 860-701-5162.. 87 D
mclaughlin_mj@mitchell.edu
MCLAUGHLIN,
Maureen .... 215-248-7137 381 D
mclaughlinm1@chc.edu
MCLAUGHLIN, Mike ..... 319-398-4947 167 C
mclaug@kirkwood.edu
MCLAUGHLIN, Nora ...... 503-777-7774 376 C
nora.mclaughlin@reed.edu
MCLAUGHLIN, Paula .... 843-676-8590 409 I
paula.mclaughlin@fdtc.edu
MCLAUGHLIN, Robert ... 713-798-4613 431 I
rmclaughlin@bcm.edu
MCLAUGHLIN, Sean, M 614-823-1576 360 A
smclaughlin@otterbein.edu
MCLAUGHLIN, Steve ..... 612-874-3759 236 K
smclaughlin@mcad.edu
MCLAUGHLIN, Steven ... 404-894-6825 118 F
swm@coe.gatech.edu
MCLAUGHLIN, Tim .... 850-478-8496 104 G
tmclaughlin@pcci.edu
MCLAUGHLIN, ToniAnn 732-987-2264 278 B
tmclaughlin@georgian.edu
MCLAUGHLIN, Tracy ..... 617-873-0150 207 F
tracy.mclaughlin@cambridgecollege.
edu
MCLAUGHLIN, William . 585-785-1561 300 B
william.mclaughlin@flcc.edu
MCLAURINE, Tradara .... 812-237-2584 155 G
tradara.mclaurine@indstate.edu
MCLAWHORN, Toni, D . 540-375-2303 471 B
mclawhorn@roanoke.edu
MCLEAN, Alexis .... 718-270-6049 295 A
amclean@mec.cuny.edu
MCLEAN, Amber .... 906-635-2382 226 E
amclean@lssu.edu
MCLEAN, Angela .... 406-449-9131 263 K
amclean@montana.edu
MCLEAN, Anita .... 609-258-3285 280 E
amclean@princeton.edu
MCLEAN, Beverly .... 925-631-4600.. 59 B
bam12@stmarys-ca.edu
MCLEAN, Brandon .... 402-844-7102 268 J
brandon@northeast.edu
MCLEAN, Connie .... 309-796-5369 132 G
mcleanc@bhc.edu
MCLEAN, David .... 970-491-3366.. 78 M
david.mclean@colostate.edu
MCLEAN, Janna .... 574-807-7191 153 E
janna.mclean@betheluniversity.edu
MCLEAN, Jennifer .... 570-326-3761 393 G
jmclean@pct.edu
MCLEAN, Laura .... 704-378-1295 330 D
lmclean@jcsu.edu
MCLEAN, Michael, F ..... 805-525-4417.. 67 D
mmclean@thomasaquinas.edu

MCLEAN, Monique .... 202-884-9097.. 93 B mcleanmo@trinitydc.edu
MCLEAN, Natalie .... 336-273-4431 327 B nmclean@bennett.edu
MCLEAN, Pat .... 417-690-3441 251 E mclean@cofo.edu
MCLEAN, Robert .... 443-997-8767 199 D bobmclean@jhu.edu
MCLEAN, Sandra .... 972-438-6932 441 H slmclean@parker.edu
MCLEAN, Selvin .... 321-674-7715.. 99 B smclean@fit.edu
MCLEAN, William, H ..... 847-491-7050 145 F wmclean@northwestern.edu
MCLEANE, David .... 870-574-4504.. 21 E dmcleane@sautech.edu
MCLEER, Karen .... 608-342-1615 497 D mcleerk@uwplatt.edu
MCLELLAN, Amy .... 415-442-5285.. 44 D amclellan@ggu.edu
MCLELLAN, Don .... 310-204-1666.. 58 D
MCLELLAN, Mark .... 503-725-9944 376 A mark.mclellan@pdx.edu
MCLELLAND, Brandy ..... 210-784-1204 448 A brandy.mclelland@tamusa.edu
MCLEMORE, Kareem ..... 302-857-6348.. 89 F kmclemore@desu.edu
MCLEMORE, Larry .... 619-660-4064.. 44 H larry.mclemore@gcccd.edu
MCLENDON, Catrenia ... 850-201-8708 111 C mclendc@tcc.fl.edu
MCLENDON, Sandra ..... 864-644-5354 412 E smclendon@swu.edu
MCLENNAN, Dale .... 978-232-2101 209 B dmclenna@endicott.edu
MCLENNON-WIER, Sharon .... 914-694-1122 275 I sharon-mclennon@berkeleycollege.edu
MCLENNON-WIER, Sharon, M .... 914-694-1122 291 D sharon-mclennon@berkeleycollege.edu
MCLEOD, Dale, A .... 571-553-8356.. 91 F damcleod@gwu.edu
MCLEOD, Dwight .... 660-626-2842 250 A dmcleod@atsu.edu
MCLEOD, Gregory .... 252-823-5166 334 C mcleodg@edgecombe.edu
MCLEOD, Michael .... 209-228-4055.. 69 B mmcleod@ucmerced.edu
MCLEOD, Michael, J ..... 516-877-3177 289 C mcleod@adelphi.edu
MCLEOD, Steve .... 706-864-1915 126 A steve.mcleod@ung.edu
MCLERNON-SYKES, Bridget .... 843-953-6378 408 E mclernonsykesb@cofc.edu
MCLESKEY, Stephanie ... 828-689-1128 331 A smcleskey@mhu.edu
MCLODA, Todd .... 309-438-7616 139 E tamclod@ilstu.edu
MCLOGAN, Matthew, E . 616-331-2190 224 E mcloganm@gvsu.edu
MCLOUD, Debbie .... 479-575-2159.. 21 G dmcloud@uark.edu
MCLOUGHLIN, Eileen ... 518-320-1193 316 C eileen.mcloughlin@suny.edu
MCLOUGHLIN, John ..... 914-337-9300 297 D john.mcloughlin@concordia-ny.edu
MCLOUGHLIN, II, Paul, J .... 315-228-7425 296 F pmcloughlin@colgate.edu
MCLOUGHLIN, Suzanne 516-876-3109 319 A mcloughlins@oldwestbury.edu
MCMACKIN, Carolyn ..... 336-734-7382 334 E cmcmackin@forsythtech.edu
MCMAHAN, Carla .... 864-977-7090 411 E carla.mcmahan@ngu.edu
MCMAHAN, Chantel ...... 360-752-8320 478 G cmcmahan@btc.edu
MCMAHAN, Craig, T ..... 478-301-2992 121 E mcmahan_ct@mercer.edu
MCMAHAN, Kerrin .... 323-415-4135.. 48 H mcmahakm@elac.edu
MCMAHAN, Maureen, E .... 260-399-7700 161 D mmcmahan@sf.edu
MCMAHAN, Mendi .... 214-333-5119 434 I mendi@dbu.edu
MCMAHAN, Oliver, L .... 423-478-7037 423 G omcmahan@ptseminary.edu
MCMAHAN, Richard ...... 304-647-6410 491 A rmcmahan@osteo.wvsom.edu
MCMAHAN, Robert, K ... 810-762-9864 225 H mcmahan@kettering.edu
MCMAHAN, Shari .... 909-537-5024.. 33 A smcmahan@csusb.edu
MCMAHILL, Janet, M .... 515-271-3726 165 A janet.mcmahill@drake.edu
MCMAHON, Anne .... 267-341-3615 386 A amcmahon2@holyfamily.edu
MCMAHON, Beth .... 641-628-5345 163 E mcmahone@central.edu
MCMAHON, Cara .... 215-248-7993 381 D mcmahonc@chc.edu
MCMAHON, RSM, Catherine .... 215-646-7300 385 D mcmahon.c@gmercyu.edu
MCMAHON, David .... 413-748-3210 218 G dmcmahon@springfield.edu
MCMAHON, Doug .... 727-864-8587.. 97 J mcmahodh@eckerd.edu
MCMAHON, Jessica ...... 252-527-6223 335 G jlmcmahon67@lenoircc.edu
MCMAHON, Kathleen .... 805-756-0327.. 30 C kmcmah02@calpoly.edu
MCMAHON, Kevin .... 213-356-5323.. 64 H kevin_mcmahon@sciarc.edu
MCMAHON, Lori .... 704-687-5962 342 E lorimcmahon@uncc.edu
MCMAHON, Lori, L .... 205-934-8227.... 8 A mcmahon@uab.edu
MCMAHON, Mary Pat ... 919-684-3737 328 G studentaffairs@duke.edu
MCMAHON, Maura .... 703-658-4304 466 A maura.mcmahon@christendom.edu
MCMAHON, Melissa ..... 580-477-7725 371 F melissa.mcmahon@wosc.edu
MCMAHON, Michael ..... 406-447-5528 263 C msmcmahon@carroll.edu
MCMAHON, Patrice .... 402-472-3235 269 J pmcmahon2@unl.edu
MCMAHON, Renee, M .. 406-447-5501 263 C rmcmahon@carroll.edu
MCMAHON, Roberta ..... 708-524-6790 136 C rmcmahon@dom.edu
MCMAHON, Shelly, A ... 740-368-3201 359 N samcmaho@owu.edu
MCMAHON, Tim .... 414-288-7434 494 B timothy.mcmahon@marquette.edu
MCMAHON, Timothy, J 412-359-1000 400 G tmcmahon@triangle-tech.edu
MCMAHON, Timothy, J 412-359-1000 400 F tmcmahon@triangle-tech.edu
MCMAKIN, Sandy .... 210-805-3005 453 D mcmakin@uiwtx.edu
MCMANN, Daniel .... 716-286-8755 310 D dmcmann@niagara.edu
MCMANNESS, Matthew, S .... 718-862-7357 305 H matthew.mcmanness@manhattan.edu
MCMANON, Karen .... 412-924-1420 396 I kmcmahon@pts.edu
MCMANUS, Ellie, F .... 419-772-2073 358 H e-mcmanus.1@onu.edu
MCMANUS, Joe-Joe ...... 760-750-4039.. 33 B jmcmanus@csusm.edu
MCMANUS, Kim .... 434-961-5207 475 F kmcmanus@pvcc.edu
MCMANUS, Shirley .... 559-442-8215.. 66 E shirley.mcmanus@fresnocitycollege.edu
MCMANUS, Terry .... 704-991-0392 338 C tmcmanus3385@stanly.edu
MCMANUS, Tiffany .... 785-670-1470 177 G tiffany.mcmanus@washburn.edu
MCMANUS, Wendy .... 630-617-3142 136 G wendy.mcmanus@elmhurst.edu
MCMARTIN, David .... 760-750-4171.. 33 B dhmcmart@csusm.edu
MCMASTER, Dennis ...... 304-829-7217 487 G dmcmaster@bethanywv.edu
MCMASTER, Pam .... 402-481-8718 265 K pam.mcmaster@bryanhealthcollege.edu
MCMASTER, Robert ...... 612-626-9425 243 E mcmaster@umn.edu
MCMASTERS, Daniel ..... 856-227-7200 276 E dmcmasters@camdencc.edu
MCMASTERS, Daniel ..... 931-363-9800 421 E dmcmasters@martinmethodist.edu
MCMATH-TURNER, Lavita .... 646-313-8000 295 E lavita.mcmath@guttman.cuny.edu
MCMEANS, Orlando, F .. 304-766-4300 491 B mcmeanso@wvstateu.edu
MCMEEL, Padraic .... 870-460-1058.. 22 D mcmeel@uamont.edu
MCMELLON, Marcus ..... 512-451-5743 430 M
MCMENAMIN, Margaret, M .... 908-709-7100 284 C mcmenamin@ucc.edu
MCMICHAEL, Andrew .... 334-244-3929.... 4 F amcmich1@aum.edu
MCMICHAEL, Brett .... 202-319-5232.. 91 B mcmichaelb@cua.edu
MCMICHAEL, Cody .... 501-362-1125.. 17 F
MCMICHAEL, Dan .... 805-378-4660.. 72 H dmcmichael@vcccd.edu
MCMICHAEL, Darlene, A .... 814-871-7609 384 E theisen001@gannon.edu
MCMILLAN, Byron .... 610-341-5906 383 D bmcmilla@eastern.edu
MCMILLAN, Felicia, L ... 803-516-4914 412 C fmcmilla@scsu.edu
MCMILLAN, Jessica ...... 415-551-9284.. 28 D jmcmillan@cca.edu
MCMILLAN, Karen .... 918-270-6402 369 A karen.mcmillan@ptstulsa.edu
MCMILLAN, Karon .... 601-925-3212 247 C kmcmilla@mc.edu
MCMILLAN, Katie .... 307-268-2488 501 U kmcmillan@caspercollege.edu
MCMILLAN, Michelle .... 918-495-6013 368 I mmcmillan@oru.edu
MCMILLAN, Sean .... 706-542-6128 125 G smcmilla@uga.edu
MCMILLAN, Sheri .... 972-708-7343 435 H discoverdallasinternational@diu.edu
MCMILLEN, Doug .... 574-520-4222 157 A dmcmille@iusb.edu
MCMILLEN, Jeremy, P .. 903-463-8600 437 D mcmillenj@grayson.edu
MCMILLIAN, Carey .... 816-271-4582 257 A mcmilli@missouriwestern.edu
MCMILLIAN, David .... 918-683-4581 365 F mcmilliand@bacone.edu
MCMILLIAN, Josh .... 479-968-0222.. 18 C jmcmillian1@atu.edu
MCMILLIAN, Roger .... 573-518-2157 256 B rmcmilli@mineralarea.edu
MCMILLIAN, Shalliah .... 904-470-8166.. 97 L s.mcmillian@ewc.edu
MCMILLIN, Barbara, C .. 662-685-4771 245 D bmcmillin@bmc.edu
MCMILLIN, David .... 417-626-1234 257 F dmcmillin@occ.edu
MCMILLIN, Donna .... 870-972-3700.. 17 G mcmillin@astate.edu
MCMILLIN, Jennifer ...... 417-626-1234 257 F jmcmillin@occ.edu
MCMILLIN, Nicole .... 203-696-4266 130 G
MCMILLIN, Nicole .... 605-367-4821 417 D nicole.mcmillin@southeasttech.edu
MCMILLION, David .... 706-776-0114 123 B dmcmillion@piedmont.edu
MCMILLION, Eric, C ..... 859-858-3511 178 I eric.mcmillion@asbury.edu
MCMILLION, Neil .... 850-474-2463 110 E nmcmillion@uwf.edu
MCMILLON, Darrell .... 302-857-7499.. 89 F dmcmillon@desu.edu
MCMILLON, Jeff .... 405-425-5919 367 G jeff.mcmillon@oc.edu
MCMILLON, Kimberly ... 813-253-7006 101 A kmcmillon@hccfl.edu
MCMINN, Jamie, G .... 724-946-7121 402 G mcminnjg@westminster.edu
MCMINN, Martha .... 864-231-2061 406 G
MCMONAGLE, Nicole .... 405-224-3140 371 D nmcmonagle@usao.edu
MCMORRAN, Carolyn, R .... 407-582-6700 112 K cmcmorran@valenciacollege.edu
MCMORRIS, Makayla .... 402-554-2762 270 B mmcmorris@unomaha.edu
MCMOY, Johnny .... 256-352-8117.... 4 A johnny.mcmoy@wallacestate.edu
MCMULLEN, Joshua ..... 757-352-4500 470 H jmcmullen@regent.edu
MCMULLEN, Mark .... 918-595-7895 370 E mark.mcmullen@tulsacc.edu
MCMULLEN, Michael .... 315-498-2566 311 B mcmullem@sunyocc.edu
MCMULLEN, Patricia ..... 202-319-5403.. 91 B mcmullep@cua.edu
MCMULLEN, Rebecca .... 478-825-6856 118 A mcmullenr@fvsu.edu
MCMULLEN, Timothy .... 336-750-2889 344 B mcmullent@wssu.edu
MCMULLEN, William ...... 817-515-1268 445 G william.mcmullen@tccd.edu
MCMULLIN, Angeline .... 423-614-8357 420 J amcmullin@leeuniversity.edu
MCMULLIN, Kyle, S ..... 757-594-7420 466 B kyle.mcmullin@cnu.edu
MCMURDOCK, Linda .... 703-284-1615 469 C linda.mcmurdock@marymount.edu
MCMURPHY, Elizabeth .. 580-349-1564 368 A liz@opsu.edu
MCMURRAY, Brock .... 661-763-7811.. 66 J bmcmurray@taftcollege.edu
MCMURRAY, Tim .... 903-886-5568 447 B timm@tamuc.edu
MCMURROUGH, Leili ... 847-808-8444 152 G lmcmurrough@worsham.edu
MCMURRY, Alice, R ...... 717-871-7520 395 D alice.mcmurry@millersville.edu
MCMURRY, Alice, R ...... 717-871-7500 395 D alice.mcmurry@millersville.edu
MCMURTRIE, John .... 865-981-8112 421 F john.mcmurtrie@maryvillecollege.edu
MCMURTRY, Brian .... 270-831-9790 181 D brian.mcmurtry@kctcs.edu
MCMURTRY, Craig .... 254-298-8524 446 A craig.mcmurtry@templejc.edu
MCMURTY, Jerry .... 208-885-6244 131 G mcmurtry@uidaho.edu
MCNAB, Richard .... 305-628-6554 106 F rmcnab@stu.edu
MCNABB, Ann, M .... 773-442-5110 145 B a-mcnabb@neiu.edu
MCNABB, Douglas .... 716-614-6226 310 C dmcnabb@niagaracc.suny.edu
MCNABB, Kathleen, J ... 218-477-4321 239 D mcnabb@mnstate.edu
MCNABB, Mark .... 509-865-8643 481 G mcnabb_m@heritage.edu
MCNABOE, Dennis .... 304-326-1482 488 F dmcnaboe@salemu.edu
MCNAIR, Christopher, L .... 325-670-1211 437 F cmcnair@hsutx.edu
MCNAIR, Lily, D .... 334-727-8011.... 7 D president@tuskegee.edu
MCNAIR, Rebekah .... 706-419-1113 117 B rebekah.mcnair@covenant.edu
MCNAIR, Ronna .... 216-987-4855 351 G ronna.mcnair@tri-c.edu
MCNAIR, Sheila .... 804-524-6948 477 B smcnair@vsu.edu
MCNALL, Mike .... 309-457-2122 144 A mike@monmouthcollege.edu
MCNALLY, Kate .... 610-282-1100 382 E kate.mcnally@desales.edu
MCNALLY, Matthew .... 202-319-5373.. 91 B mcnally@cua.edu
MCNALLY, Michael .... 480-423-6616.. 13 H michael.mcnally@scottsdalecc.edu
MCNALLY, Minta, A ...... 336-758-4237 344 D mcnallma@wfu.edu
MCNALLY, Neal, P .... 330-941-2719 365 C npmcnally@ysu.edu
MCNALLY, Patrick, J ..... 313-496-2524 232 C pmcnall1@wcccd.edu
MCNALLY, Robin .... 508-793-7467 208 A rmcnally@clarku.edu
MCNALLY, Tom .... 803-777-6212 413 C tom@mailbox.sc.edu
MCNAMARA, Ann .... 619-876-4250.. 67 M
MCNAMARA, Cathy .... 315-268-4394 296 A cmcnamar@clarkson.edu
MCNAMARA, Connie ..... 717-245-1813 382 F mcnamarc@dickinson.edu
MCNAMARA, Craig .... 315-786-2256 303 F cmcnamara@sunyjefferson.edu
MCNAMARA, Jeff .... 262-524-7360 492 E jmcnamar@carrollu.edu
MCNAMARA, John .... 862-906-5102.. 85 D jmcnamara@capitalcc.edu
MCNAMARA, Karen .... 215-951-1882 387 C mcnamara@lasalle.edu
MCNAMARA, Kristine, E .... 401-598-1565 404 I kmcnamara@jwu.edu
MCNAMARA, Paul .... 408-741-2623.. 74 E paul.mcnamara@westvalley.edu
MCNAMARA, Paul .... 904-779-4141 100 B paul.mcnamara@fscj.edu
MCNAMARA, Ryan .... 570-662-4848 395 C rmcnamar@mansfield.edu
MCNAMARA, Ryan .... 434-947-8035 470 E rmcnamara@randolphcollege.edu

MEADOWS, Melissa ...... 760-252-2411.. 26 I
mmeadows@barstow.edu
MEADOWS, Michelle .... 434-395-2429 469 A
meadowsme@longwood.edu
MEADOWS, Ricky .... 252-638-4550 333 H
millardj@cravencc.edu
MEADOWS, Shapiro ...... 504-286-5205 190 I
smeadows@suno.edu
MEADOWS, Steve .... 304-384-5180 490 A
meadows@concord.edu
MEADOWS, Terry .... 479-788-7891.. 21 H
terry.meadows@uafs.edu
MEAGER, Kevin .... 419-227-3141 363 C
klmeager@unoh.edu
MEAGHER, Jo-Ann .... 978-630-9101 215 A
j_meagher@mwcc.mass.edu
MEAGHER, Kathy .... 301-387-3095 198 F
kathy.meagher@garrettcollege.edu
MEAGHER, Paula, G ..... 915-831-4530 436 E
pmeagher@epcc.edu
MEAGHER, Sharon .... 212-517-0521 306 A
smeagher@mmm.edu
MEALER, Donna .... 731-286-3312 425 A
mealer@dscc.edu
MEALIE, Monica .... 225-771-3282 190 H
monica_mealie@subr.edu
MEALY, Stephanie .... 414-277-7224 494 G
MEANA, Marta .... 702-895-3201 271 E
marta.meana@unlv.edu
MEANEY, Dorothy .... 617-627-2979 219 B
dorothy.meaney@tufts.edu
MEANEY, Heather, L ..... 518-381-1250 315 G
meaneyhl@sunysccc.edu
MEANEY, Sarah .... 630-617-3191 136 G
sarah.meaney@elmhurst.edu
MEANOR, Nicole .... 470-578-7629 120 L
nmeanor@kennesaw.edu
MEANS, Amanda .... 740-351-3229 360 K
ameans@shawnee.edu
MEANS, Ben .... 217-228-5432 146 F
meansbe@quincy.edu
MEANS, Danyelle .... 505-424-2309 286 C
danyelle.means@iaia.edu
MEANS, Jameelah .... 304-204-4341 491 B
jmeans9@wvstateu.edu
MEANS, John .... 661-336-5036.. 46 K
jmeans@kccd.edu
MEANS, Laurie .... 937-328-6145 350 L
lmeans@clarkstate.edu
MEANS COLEMAN,
Robin, R .... 979-458-2905 446 G
rrmc@tamu.edu
MEANY, Birgit .... 907-852-1818.... 9 F
birgit.meany@ilisagvik.edu
MEANY, David .... 509-359-6335 480 E
dmeany@ewu.edu
MEARA, Mark .... 856-222-9311 281 C
mmeara@rcbc.edu
MEARIG, Sayaka .... 541-485-1780 374 F
sayakamearig@newhope.edu
MEARNS, Geoffrey, S .... 765-285-5555 153 C
gsmearns@bsu.edu
MEARS, Kathy .... 850-645-1328 109 C
kmears@fsu.edu
MEARS, Laura .... 301-846-2429 198 E
lmears@frederick.edu
MEASAMER, Ronnie ...... 919-718-7409 333 C
rmeasamer@cccc.edu
MEASE, Ervin, J .... 610-799-1112 388 I
emease@lccc.edu
MEATTE, Tony .... 208-562-2752 130 F
tonymeatte@cwi.edu
MECCIA, Barbara .... 609-497-7720 280 D
human.resources@ptsem.edu
MECHAM, Melissa, E ..... 206-239-4500 479 E
mmecham@cityu.edu
MECHE, Eddie, P .... 337-475-5501 192 A
emeche@mcneese.edu
MECHE, Lance .... 972-825-4747 445 A
lmeche@sagu.edu
MECHLER, Heather, S .... 505-918-7302 288 G
hsmechler@unm.edu
MECK, Bill .... 641-683-5106 166 C
bill.meck@indianhills.edu
MECKEL, David .... 415-703-9561.. 28 D
dmeckel@cca.edu
MEDA, Pat .... 626-529-8261.. 55 A
pmeda@pacificoaks.edu
MEDASTIN,
Jean-Jacques .... 937-376-6302 350 D
jmedastin@centralstate.edu
MEDBURY, Doug .... 425-235-2352 483 G
dmedbury@rtc.edu
MEDCALF, Elizabeth ...... 301-687-4751 203 E
emedcalf@frostburg.edu
MEDDERS, Elizabeth ...... 817-735-2483 454 C
elizabeth.medders@unthsc.edu
MEDDERS, Mike, W .... 903-566-7393 456 A
mmedders@uttyler.edu
MEDEARIS, Cheryl .... 605-856-5880 416 D
cheryl.medearis@sintegleska.edu
MEDEIROS, Brad .... 508-626-4911 212 D
bmedeiros@framingham.edu
MEDEIROS, Madeline .... 805-546-3123.. 41 A
mmedeiro@cuesta.edu
MEDEL, Michael .... 805-965-0581.. 62 C
medel@sbcc.edu
MEDEMA, Pamela, S .... 815-835-6378 148 H
pamela.s.medema@svcc.edu
MEDENBLIK, Julius, T .. 616-957-6024 221 P
jmedenblik@calvinseminary.edu
MEDFORD, Edna .... 202-806-6700.. 92 B
MEDFORD, Kim .... 254-968-0515 446 E
medford@tarleton.edu
MEDFORD, Lienne .... 864-596-9082 409 B
MEDFORD, Mike .... 404-687-4576 116 H
medfordm@ctsnet.edu
MEDINA, Elizabeth .... 512-313-3000 434 E
elizabeth.medina@concordia.edu
MEDINA, Erica .... 325-793-4801 440 B
medina.erica@mcm.edu
MEDINA, Herbert, A ...... 503-943-7452 377 E
medinah@up.edu
MEDINA, Kimberly .... 303-273-3225.. 78 I
kmedina@mines.edu
MEDINA, Lisa .... 760-750-4813.. 33 B
lmmedina@csusm.edu
MEDINA, Lourdes, E ..... 787-766-1717 511 H
lmedina@suagm.edu
MEDINA, María, C .... 787-884-3838 506 D
mmedinav@atenascollege.edu
MEDINA, Nancy .... 773-442-5240 145 B
n-medina4@neiu.edu
MEDINA, Raúl .... 787-264-0406 509 F
rimedina@intersg.edu
MEDINA, Ricco .... 262-646-6528 495 B
rmedina@nashotah.edu
MEDINA, Robert .... 818-778-5787.. 49 F
medinara@lavc.edu
MEDINA, Tinnah .... 559-278-2373.. 31 D
tinnahcm@mail.fresnostate.edu
MEDINA, Widylia .... 787-890-2681 512 H
widylia.medina@upr.edu
MEDINA-MARTIN,
Flavio .... 661-259-7800.. 38 H
flavio.medina-martin@canyons.edu
MEDINA-ORTIZ,
Roberto .... 787-622-8000 512 E
rmedina@pupr.edu
MEDING, Griselda .... 432-552-2700 457 A
meding_g@utpb.edu
MEDIONTE-PHILIPS,
Krista .... 607-777-4010 316 E
kmediont@binghamton.edu
MEDLEY, Dawn .... 313-577-1090 232 I
dawn.medley@wayne.edu
MEDLEY, Mike .... 435-896-9714 461 C
michael.medley@snow.edu
MEDLEY, Ticily .... 817-515-4742 445 G
ticily.medley@tccd.edu
MEDLEY-WEEKS,
Clarice .... 214-379-5565 441 I
cweeks@pqc.edu
MEDLIN, Melissa, T ...... 256-765-4276.... 8 E
mtmedlin@una.edu
MEDLIN, Rian .... 661-362-3426.. 38 H
rian.medlin@canyons.edu
MEDRANO, Jennifer ...... 801-832-2126 461 G
jmedrano@westminstercollege.edu
MEDRO, Alfred .... 619-265-0107.. 57 D
amedro@platt.edu
MEDVETZ, Betsy .... 603-428-2477 273 H
bmedvetz@nec.edu
MEDWICK, Peter .... 215-972-2017 393 D
pmedwick@pafa.edu
MEE, Christine, L .... 843-349-2091 408 C
christin@coastal.edu
MEE, David .... 615-460-6785 418 F
david.mee@belmont.edu
MEECE, Jill .... 606-451-6625 182 C
jill.meece@kctcs.edu
MEECE, Jill, N .... 606-679-8501 182 C
jill.meece@kctcs.edu
MEEHAN, Barry .... 603-578-8900 273 A
bmeehan@ccsnh.edu
MEEHAN, Gabriel .... 916-558-2097.. 50 I
meehang@scc.losrios.edu
MEEHAN, Lisa .... 425-739-8155 482 A
lisa.meehan@lwtech.edu
MEEHAN, Martin, T ...... 617-287-7050 211 C
umasspresident@umassp.edu
MEEHAN, Sara .... 703-284-6815 469 C
smeehan@marymount.edu
MEEK, Barbara, A .... 419-772-1943 358 H
b-meek@onu.edu
MEEK, Charles Ronald .. 340-693-1421 514 E
charles.meek@uvi.edu
MEEK, Christopher .... 701-483-2565 345 D
christopher.meek@dickinsonstate.edu
MEEK, Marshall .... 785-670-1830 177 G
mmeek@wualumni.org
MEEK, Michelle .... 606-886-3863 180 J
michelle.meek@kctcs.edu
MEEK, Scott .... 602-787-7902.. 13 E
scott.meek@paradisevalley.edu
MEEK, Tracey .... 518-587-2100 321 A
tracey.meek@esc.edu
MEEK, William, D .... 401-863-3422 404 E
will_meek@brown.edu
MEEKER, April, M .... 605-642-6092 416 I
april.meeker@bhsu.edu
MEEKER, Kimberly .... 660-359-3948 257 D
kmeeker@mail.ncmissouri.edu
MEEKER, Melissa .... 618-537-6834 143 B
mlmeeker@mckendree.edu
MEEKER, Steve, L .... 605-642-6385 416 I
steve.meeker@bhsu.edu
MEEKMA, Glenn .... 269-471-3484 221 B
meekma@andrews.edu
MEEKS, Andy .... 859-572-5575 184 A
meeksa@nku.edu
MEEKS, Chris .... 575-624-7155 286 A
chris.meeks@roswell.enmu.edu
MEEKS, Harry, L .... 812-888-4511 162 C
hmeeks@vinu.edu
MEEKS, J. Duane .... 561-803-2610 104 C
duane_meeks@pba.edu
MEEKS, Mark .... 478-445-5851 118 C
mark.meeks@gcsu.edu
MEEKS, Ronald .... 662-685-4771 245 D
rmeeks@bmc.edu
MEEKS, Susan .... 478-387-4801 118 G
smeeks@gmc.edu
MEEKS, Tom .... 216-373-5206 358 B
tmeeks@ndc.edu
MEENTS-DECAIGNY,
Ellen .... 312-362-7298 135 I
emeentsd@depaul.edu
MEER, Jonathan .... 732-571-3411 279 B
jmeer@monmouth.edu
MEEROFF, Diego .... 561-868-3128 104 D
meeroffd@palmbeachstate.edu
MEESKE, Susan .... 402-461-7398 267 D
smeeske@hastings.edu
MEETZE-HOLCOMBE,
Tracy .... 843-661-1558 409 K
tmeetzeholcombe@fmarion.edu
MEFFORD, Angel .... 660-596-7218 260 D
amefford@sfccmo.edu
MEGAHED, Nivine .... 312-261-3232 144 F
nivine.megahed@nl.edu
MEGAN, Piccus .... 413-565-1000 205 G
mpiccus@baypath.edu
MEGAW, Shelly .... 507-389-7289 241 C
shelly.megaw@southcentral.edu
MEGGETT, Paul .... 828-262-2751 341 B
meggettpa@appstate.edu
MEGGIE, Derrick .... 803-777-0112 413 C
meggie@mailbox.sc.edu
MEGGS, Christi .... 843-921-6908 411 F
cmeggs@netc.edu
MEGHREBLIAN, Caren .. 510-925-4282.. 25 Q
cmeghreblian@aua.am
MEGNA, Robert, L .... 518-320-1100 316 C
robert.megna@suny.edu
MEHA, Arapata .... 808-675-3010 127 E
ara.meha@byuh.edu
MEHDIZADEH, Mojdeh . 925-229-6858.. 40 G
modjeh@4cd.edu
MEHDIZADEH,
Mojdheh .... 925-229-6825.. 40 H
mmehdizadeh@4cd.edu
MEHLHOFF, Monte .... 605-626-7781 417 A
monte.mehlhoff@northern.edu
MEHLIG, Lisa .... 815-921-4070 147 E
l.mehlig@rockvalleycollege.edu
MEHRER, Susanne .... 603-646-2236 273 E
susanne.mehrer@dartmouth.edu
MEHRHOFF, Jay .... 636-584-6585 252 J
jay.mehrhoff@eastcentral.edu
MEHRING, Michelle ...... 212-678-8072 303 G
mimehring@jtsa.edu
MEHRING, Tes .... 785-594-8312 170 I
tes.mehring@bakeru.edu
MEHRINGER, Marty .... 317-805-1791 488 F
marty.mehringer@salemu.edu
MEHROTRA, Anuj .... 202-994-1152.. 91 F
anuj_m@gwu.edu
MEHTA, Raj .... 513-556-6252 362 D
raj.mehta@uc.edu
MEHUS, Joseph .... 701-788-4802 345 E
joseph.mehus@mayvillestate.edu
MEI, Jeffrey .... 617-731-7170 217 H
jmei@pmc.edu
MEIDL, Barb .... 704-216-3605 337 F
barb.meidl@rccc.edu
MEIDL, Tynesha .... 920-403-3272 495 I
tynesha.meidl@snc.edu
MEIDLINGER, Peter, K .. 417-873-7469 252 F
pmeidlin@drury.edu
MEIER, Andreea .... 843-863-7095 407 E
ameier@csuniv.edu
MEIER, Beth, A .... 919-760-8427 331 B
meierb@meredith.edu
MEIER, Heather .... 215-641-6603 390 H
hmeier@mc3.edu
MEIER, Jared .... 970-248-1945.. 77 I
jmeier@coloradomesa.edu
MEIER, Jason .... 251-380-3020..... 6 H
bookstore@shc.edu
MEIER, Jay .... 701-224-5666 346 B
jay.meier@bismarckstate.edu
MEIER, John .... 610-330-5927 387 E
meierj@lafayette.edu
MEIER, Karen, F .... 757-683-5026 469 G
kmeier@odu.edu
MEIER, Lori .... 712-279-3518 169 B
lori.meier@stlukescollege.edu
MEIER, Veronica .... 402-872-2218 268 F
vmcasey@peru.edu
MEIER PFEIFER, Donna 620-672-2700 176 G
donnamp@prattcc.edu
MEIFERT, Janeen .... 920-686-6121 496 A
janeen.meifert@sl.edu
MEIKLEJOHN, Scott ...... 207-725-3460 193 D
smeiklej@bowdoin.edu
MEIKSINS, Peter .... 216-687-5520 351 B
p.meiksins@csuohio.edu
MEILMAN, Philip, W ...... 202-687-6985.. 92 A
pwm9@georgetown.edu
MEIN, Dina .... 810-762-7812 225 H
dmein@kettering.edu
MEINDERS, Darin .... 417-268-6065 250 G
dmeinders@gobbc.edu
MEINDL, Lidia .... 212-463-0400 322 J
lidia.meindl@touro.edu
MEINECKE, Dale .... 325-649-8804 438 D
dmeinecke@hputx.edu
MEINEKE, John .... 309-796-5053 132 G
meinekej@bhc.edu
MEINERT, Anita .... 641-673-1063 170 F
meinerta@wmpenn.edu
MEINERT, David .... 641-673-1702 170 F
meinertd@wmpenn.edu
MEINERT, David, B .... 417-836-4408 256 E
davidmeinert@missouristate.edu
MEINHARD, Veronica ... 301-405-3677 202 C
meinhard@umd.edu
MEINZEN, David, L .... 260-399-7700 161 D
dmeinzen@sf.edu
MEIRICK, Craig, R .... 563-562-3263 168 E
meirickc@nicc.edu
MEIS, Aaron .... 513-745-2941 365 B
meisa@xavier.edu
MEIS, Gail, N .... 404-471-6306 113 G
gmeis@agnesscott.edu
MEIS, John .... 229-226-1621 125 C
jmeis@thomasu.edu
MEISCH, Karen .... 931-221-7971 418 D
meischk@apsu.edu
MEISEL, Joseph .... 401-863-9499 404 E
joseph_meisel@brown.edu
MEISEL, Seth .... 262-472-1013 498 C
meisels@uww.edu
MEISELS, Yesoscher ..... 718-600-8897 325 K
ymeisels@yktiferetheliezer.com
MEISENZAHL, Dan .... 808-956-8856 128 F
dmeisenz@hawaii.edu
MEISENZAHL, Dan, T ... 808-956-5941 128 D
dmeisenz@hawaii.edu
MEISNER, Jolene .... 570-662-4696 395 C
jmeisner@mansfield.edu

MEISSNER, Ken .... 712-749-2111 163 D
meissnerk@bvu.edu
MEISTER, Bobbi .... 712-274-5606 168 B
meisterb@morningside.edu
MEISTER, Tony .... 660-944-2899 251 G
tmeister@conception.edu
MEITZNER, June .... 507-285-7213 240 G
june.meitzner@rctc.edu
MEIXSEL-CORDERO,
Terri .... 623-245-4600.. 16 E
tmeixsell@uti.edu
MEJABI, Patricia .... 610-372-4721 397 B
pmejabi@racc.edu
MEJIA, Gary, L .... 626-584-5440.. 43 H
garymejia@fuller.edu
MEJIA, Juan, E .... 903-510-2261 452 C
jmej@tjc.edu
MEJIA, Laurie .... 626-966-4576.. 25 N
lauriemejia@agu.edu
MEJIA KRUG,
Miroslava .... 630-829-6418 132 E
mmkrug@ben.edu
MEJIA MARTINEZ,
Marcela .... 714-997-6711.. 36 C
mamartin@chapman.edu
MEJIAS, Gladys .... 787-264-1912 509 F
gmejias@intersg.edu
MEJIAS, Ida, A .... 787-250-1912 509 D
iamejias@metro.inter.edu
MEJIAS, Jackeline .... 787-765-1915 510 B
jmejias@opto.inter.edu
MEJIAS, Nelson .... 787-753-6335 508 D
nmejias@icprjc.edu
MEJIAS-ORTIZ, Juan, R 787-763-6700 508 A
jrmejias@se-pr.edu
MELÉNDEZ-MATEO,
Katherine .... 787-522-4383 512 G
katherine.melendez@upr.edu
MELANCON, Girard .... 225-216-8055 186 K
melancong@mybrcc.edu
MELANCON, Kimberly ... 225-768-1710 186 F
kimberly.melancon@franu.edu
MELANSON, Christine ... 207-509-7141 195 H
cmelanson@unity.edu
MELANSON,
Leigh Anne .... 603-862-3292 274 G
leigh-anne.melanson@unh.edu
MELARAGNI, Robert ..... 617-670-4401 209 D
rmelaragni@fisher.edu
MELARAGNO, Steven .... 401-254-3667 405 E
smelaragno@rwu.edu
MELBOURNE, Barbara ... 563-884-5290 168 I
barbara.melbourne@palmer.edu
MELBY, Darlene .... 530-938-5220.. 39 F
dmelby@siskiyous.edu
MELBY, Diane .... 210-434-6711 441 E
dmelby@ollusa.edu
MELCHER, Chris .... 706-721-4018 115 A
cmelcher@augusta.edu
MELCHER, Mike .... 806-291-3431 457 J
melcherp@wbu.edu
MELCHER, Rick, W .... 610-921-7748 378 C
rmelcher@albright.edu
MELCHERT, Russell, B .. 816-235-1607 261 C
melchertr@umkc.edu
MELCHIOR, Vonda .... 813-253-7107 101 A
vmelchior@hccfl.edu
MELDE, Vicki .... 903-223-3025 448 B
vmelde@tamut.edu
MELDER, Renee .... 318-487-7340 186 I
renee.melder@lacollege.edu
MELE MAI, Debbie .... 360-676-2772 482 D
dmelemai@nwic.edu
MELEG, Mike .... 309-796-5002 132 G
melegm@bhc.edu
MELEN, Pia .... 714-533-1495.. 64 D
pmelen@southbaylo.edu
MELENDEZ, Andres .... 315-792-7100 321 E
jmelendez@sunypoly.edu
MELENDEZ, Astrid, Y .... 787-884-3838 506 D
amelendez@atenascollege.edu
MELENDEZ, Edwin .... 787-738-2161 513 D
edwin.melendez@upr.edu
MELENDEZ, Georgianna 617-287-4877 211 E
georgianna.melendez@umb.edu
MELENDEZ, Jennifer ..... 914-395-2689 315 F
jmelendez@sarahlawrence.edu
MELENDEZ, Jennifer ..... 212-472-1500 309 I
jmelendez@nysid.edu
MELENDEZ, Luis .... 914-632-5400 307 G
lmelendez@monroecollege.edu
MELENDEZ, Marlene ..... 575-674-2223 285 H
mmelendez@bcomnm.org
MELENDEZ, Rafael .... 787-725-6500 506 G
rmelendez@albizu.edu
MELENDEZ, Ruben .... 908-709-7085 284 C
ruben.melendez@ucc.edu
MELENDEZ LEON,
Leonardo .... 787-720-4476 512 D
registraduria@mizpa.edu
MELENDEZ-ORTEGA,
Maria, M 787-857-3600 508M
mmmelendez@br.inter.edu
MELENDRES, Andrew .... 651-690-6285 242 R
anmelendres676@stkate.edu
MELENDY, Lisa, M .... 413-597-2477 220 C
lisa.m.melendy@williams.edu
MELETIES, Panayiotis .... 718-262-2780 295 F
pmeleties@york.cuny.edu
MELGAREJO, Ricardo .... 787-780-0070 506 F
rmelgarejo@caribbean.edu
MELIKECHI,
Noureddine .... 978-934-3840 211 G
noureddine_melikechi@uml.edu
MELISI, Mary Ann .... 610-558-5611 391 D
melisim@neumann.edu
MELISSARATOS, Aris ..... 443-352-4140 201 H
amelissaratos@stevenson.edu
MELKONIAN,
Madeleine .... 718-405-3236 296 G
madeleine.melkonian@
mountsaintvincent.edu
MELL, Doug .... 715-232-1198 498 A
melld@uwstout.edu
MELLENKAMP,
Kathleen .... 606-759-7141 182 A
kathleen.mellenkamp@kctcs.edu
MELLICHAMP,
James, F .... 706-776-0100 123 B
president@piedmont.edu
MELLING, Alice .... 206-934-3693 483 J
alice.melling@seattlecolleges.edu
MELLINGER, Keith .... 540-654-1052 472 I
kmelling@umw.edu
MELLO, Catherine .... 402-559-4385 270 A
catherine.mello@unmc.edu
MELLO, Heath, M .... 402-472-7156 269 H
hmello@nebraska.edu
MELLO, James .... 740-284-5369 353 B
jmello@franciscan.edu
MELLO, Jeffrey .... 401-456-8036 405 C
jmello1@ric.edu
MELLO, Lynne .... 401-254-3436 405 E
lmello@rwu.edu
MELLO-GOLDNER,
Diane .... 617-731-7106 217 H
dmellogoldner@pmc.edu
MELLON, Brenda .... 215-702-4843 380 D
bmellon@cairn.edu
MELLON, James, P .... 808-932-7467 128 E
mellon@hawaii.edu
MELLON, Suzanne, K .... 412-578-6123 380 E
skmellon@carlow.edu
MELLONI, Suzanne .... 508-999-9299 211 F
smelloni@umassd.edu
MELLOR, Kariena .... 253-589-5588 479 G
kariena.mellor@cptc.edu
MELLOR, Tracey .... 617-747-6600 206 E
studyabroad@berklee.edu
MELLOTT, David, M ...... 317-931-2303 154 C
dmellott@cts.edu
MELLOTT, Ramona, N ... 928-523-7145.. 14 H
ramona.mellott@nau.edu
MELMED, Shlomo .... 310-423-8294.. 35 L
MELNICK, Julie .... 402-844-7123 268 J
juliem@northeast.edu
MELNICK, Patrick .... 216-221-8584 357 F
pmelnick@vmcad.edu
MELNYK, Bernadette ..... 614-292-4844 358 I
melnyk.15@osu.edu
MELOAN, Andrea .... 816-415-7831 262 F
meloana@william.jewell.edu
MELOCHE, Catherine ..... 774-354-0464 206 B
catherine.meloche@becker.edu
MELOCHE, Kyle .... 410-857-2275 200 B
kmeloche@mcdaniel.edu
MELOHUSKY, Lisa .... 716-673-3649 317 A
lisa.melohusky@fredonia.edu
MELONSON, Christie .... 210-829-3129 453 D
melonson@uiwtx.edu
MELOY, Faye, A .... 610-359-5353 382 C
fmeloy@dccc.edu
MELOY, Michelle .... 856-225-2724 281 G
mlmeloy@rutgers.edu
MELROE LEHRMAN,
Bethany .... 605-995-2706 415 C
bethany.melroe@dwu.edu
MELSON, Ben .... 713-792-2121 456 E
MELSON, Rick .... 937-766-7810 349 G
rickmelson@cedarville.edu
MELSON, Vollie, D .... 410-777-1494 197 C
vmelson@aacc.edu
MELTON, Angela .... 402-471-2505 268 D
amelton@nscs.edu
MELTON, Chad, W .... 517-750-1200 230 H
cmelton@arbor.edu
MELTON, Chandy, D ..... 270-824-8635 181 G
chandy.melton@kctcs.edu
MELTON, Chris .... 206-546-4613 484 G
cmelton@shoreline.edu
MELTON, Cindy .... 601-925-3250 247 C
cmelton@mc.edu
MELTON, David, V .... 617-364-3510 207 A
dmelton@boston.edu
MELTON, Eric, E .... 405-325-3701 371 B
emelton@ou.edu
MELTON, Judi .... 214-329-4447 431 D
judi.melton@bgu.edu
MELTON, Judy .... 828-652-0645 336 B
judym@mcdowelltech.edu
MELTON, Julie .... 217-875-7211 147 C
jmelton@richland.edu
MELTON, Leslie, J .... 740-368-3152 359 N
ljdelerm@owu.edu
MELTON, Mark, A .... 919-516-4029 340 C
mamelton@st-aug.edu
MELTON, Matthew .... 423-614-8115 420 J
mmelton@leeuniversity.edu
MELTON, Melissa .... 251-380-2271.... 6 H
mmelton@shc.edu
MELTON, Randy, G .... 517-750-1200 230 H
ra766788@arbor.edu
MELTON, Ryan .... 541-684-7470 374 G
rmelton@nwcu.edu
MELTON, JR., Samuel .. 662-254-3434 248 B
smelton@mvsu.edu
MELTON, Steve .... 828-297-3811 332 G
smelton@cccti.edu
MELTON, Susan, B .... 252-862-1228 337 C
sbmelton1310@roanokechowan.edu
MELTON, Toni .... 901-381-3939 428 E
toni@visible.edu
MELTON, Valerie .... 512-505-3070 438 E
vmelton@htu.edu
MELTON, Valerie .... 512-505-3074 438 E
vmelton@htu.edu
MELTON PAGES, Joyce 817-598-6245 458 A
jpages@wc.edu
MELUSKY, Marie, B ...... 814-472-3126 398 B
mmelusky@francis.edu
MELVILLE, John .... 252-638-7260 333 H
melvillej@cravencc.edu
MELVIN, Dana .... 724-653-2216 383 A
dmelvin@dec.edu
MELVIN, Julie 216-421-7455 350M
jrmelvin@cia.edu
MELVIN, Kari .... 301-846-2442 198 E
kmelvin@frederick.edu
MELVIN, Lee, H .... 716-645-5970 316 F
leemelvi@buffalo.edu
MELVIN, Marilee, A ...... 630-752-5517 152 F
marilee.melvin@wheaton.edu
MELVIN, Matt .... 785-864-4381 177 D
mattmelvin@ku.edu
MELVIN, Sharyl .... 618-985-2828 139 I
sharylmelvin@jalc.edu
MELVIN, Stephanie .... 202-884-9707.. 93 B
melvins@trinitydc.edu
MEMBRINO, Charles ..... 617-585-1239 217 B
itshelp@necmusic.edu
MEN, Su-hua .... 941-752-5250 108 G
mens@scf.edu
MENA, Clara .... 203-285-2123.. 85 E
cmena@gwcc.commnet.edu
MENA, Robert .... 213-738-6716.. 65 G
studentaffairs@swlaw.edu
MENA, Salvador .... 848-932-8576 282 A
salvador.mena@rutgers.edu
MENADIER, Judy .... 352-854-2322.. 96 O
menadiej@cf.edu
MENARD, Connie .... 940-898-3813 451 F
cmenard@twu.edu
MENARD, Jennifer .... 508-678-2811 213 G
jennifer.menard@bristolcc.edu
MENARD, Richard, O .... 509-313-3583 481 D
menardr@gonzaga.edu
MENARD, Richard, R .... 401-841-3589 503 L
richard.menard@usnwc.edu
MENARD, Tim .... 218-281-8585 244 A
menar021@umn.edu
MENARD, William .... 401-739-5000 405 A
bmenard@neit.edu
MENCARELLI, Brent, T .. 574-372-5100 155 B
mencarb@grace.edu
MENCARINI, Steven ...... 336-316-2465 329 E
mencarinism@guilford.edu
MENCHEN, Ann .... 813-253-7018 101 A
amenchen3@hccfl.edu
MENCHION, Byron .... 850-644-1803 109 C
bmenchion@fsu.edu
MENDELSOHN, Kathy ... 831-755-6700.. 44 K
kmendelsohn@hartnell.edu
MENDELSON, Eleonor ... 831-476-9424.. 43 A
admissions@fivebranches.edu
MENDENHALL, James ... 918-463-2931 366 B
james.mendenhall@connorsstate.edu
MENDES, Godfrey .... 614-947-6027 353 C
godfrey.mendes@frankli.edu
MENDES, Steve .... 203-857-7011.. 86 D
smendes@norwalk.edu
MENDES, Susy .... 212-237-8449 294 D
smendes@jjay.cuny.edu
MENDEZ, Angel .... 787-878-5475 508 L
amendez@arecibo.inter.edu
MENDEZ, Celia .... 787-257-0000 513 C
celia.mendez@upr.edu
MENDEZ, David .... 787-743-7979 511 I
edmendez@suagm.edu
MENDEZ, Diana .... 760-921-5536.. 55 H
diana.mendez@paloverde.edu
MENDEZ, Elisaida 216-421-7463 350M
emendez@cia.edu
MENDEZ, Jannette .... 787-856-0945 507 D
jmendez@columbiacentral.edu
MENDEZ, Jesse, P .... 317-274-6862 156 F
jpmendez@iupui.edu
MENDEZ, José, F .... 787-751-0178 511 G
jmendez@suagm.edu
MENDEZ, José, F .... 787-766-1717 511 H
jmendez@suagm.edu
MENDEZ, Jose, F .... 787-751-2262 511 F
jmendez@suagm.edu
MENDEZ, Magaly .... 787-815-0000 513 A
magaly.mendez@upr.edu
MENDEZ, Mike .... 320-308-5353 241 A
mike.mendez@sctcc.edu
MENDEZ, Pedro .... 209-575-6332.. 75 J
mendezp@mjc.edu
MENDEZ, Sheri .... 775-784-4252 271 F
smendez@unr.edu
MENDEZ-GRANT,
Monica .... 940-898-3700 451 F
mmendez@twu.edu
MENDEZ-HERNANDEZ,
Santiago .... 787-296-1101 207 F
santiago.mendez-hernandez@
cambridgecollege.edu
MENDEZ MAQUEO,
Veronica .... 830-279-3023 450 D
veronica.maqueo@sulross.edu
MENDIETA, Juan .... 305-237-7611 103 D
jmendiet@mdc.edu
MENDINI, Shauna .... 435-865-8185 460 F
mendini_s@suu.edu
MENDIOLA, Francisco .. 691-320-2480 505 B
mendiolaf@comfsm.fm
MENDIOLA, Mark .... 671-735-2260 505 E
mendiolam@triton.uog.edu
MENDIOLA, Melanie ..... 671-735-2957 505 E
melanie@uogendowment.org
MENDIS, Chanaka .... 608-342-1262 497 D
mendisc@uwplatt.edu
MENDOLA, Richard, A .. 404-727-6861 117 F
rich.mendola@emory.edu
MENDOLARO,
Angela, J .... 407-582-3011 112 K
amendolaro@valenciacollege.edu
MENDONCA, James ...... 401-456-8888 405 C
jmendonca@ric.edu
MENDONEZ RUSSELL,
Bernadette .... 561-862-4400 104 D
russellb@palmbeachstate.edu
MENDOZA, Daniell .... 909-469-5541.. 74 I
dwitsoe@westernu.edu
MENDOZA, Gaylyn .... 254-267-7040 442 E
gmendoza@rangercollege.edu
MENDOZA, Graciano ..... 650-306-3274.. 61 O
mendozag@smccd.edu
MENDOZA, Kendelynn .. 559-638-0299.. 66 F
kendelynn.mendoza@reedleycollege.
edu
MENDOZA, Mynor .... 760-252-2411.. 26 I
mmendoza@barstow.edu

MENDOZA, Pablo .... 678-696-2462 126 A
pablo.mendoza@ung.edu
MENDOZA, Patricia ...... 714-432-5562.. 38 E
pmendoza31@occ.cccd.edu
MENDOZA, Raúl .... 787-891-0925 508 K
rmendoza@aguadilla.inter.edu
MENDOZA, Rick .... 310-879-0554.. 65 H
rmendoza@spartan.edu
MENDOZA, Rosalyn ...... 541-956-7000 376 D
rmendoza@roguecc.edu
MENDOZA, Stephanie ... 415-503-6280.. 60 H
security@sfcm.edu
MENDOZA, Sylvia, F .... 201-360-4201 278 C
smendoza@hccc.edu
MENDOZA, Tracey .... 210-829-3837 453 D
temendo2@uiwtx.edu
MENDOZA-MILLER,
Marylou .... 559-278-2032.. 31 D
maryloum@csufresno.edu
MENDOZA-WELCH,
Maxine .... 903-886-5851 447 B
maxine.mmendo@tamu.edu
MENEAR, Anne .... 660-263-3900 251 A
annemenear@cccb.edu
MENEAR, Anne, P .... 660-263-3900 251 A
annemenear@cccb.edu
MENEAR, Shelley .... 301-387-3037 198 F
shelley.menear@garrettcollege.edu
MENEELY, J. Andy .... 252-334-2087 331 D
andy.meneely@macuniversity.edu
MENELEY, Theresa .... 713-221-8612 453 B
meneleyt@uhd.edu
MENENDEZ,
Jacqueline, R .... 305-284-5505 112 E
jmenendez@miami.edu
MENENDEZ, Mirizza ...... 305-442-9223 103 F
mmenendez@mru.edu
MENENDEZ, Rasel .... 310-287-4379.. 49 G
menendrm2@wlac.edu
MENGEL, David .... 513-745-3101 365 B
mengel@xavier.edu
MENGELLE, Ervens .... 614-885-5585 360 E
emengelle@pcj.edu
MENGELSDORF,
Sarah, C .... 585-275-8356 323 J
sarah.mengelsdorf@rochester.edu
MENGHINI, Jared .... 570-208-5868 387 A
jaredmenghini@kings.edu
MENGLER, Thomas, M . 210-436-3722 443 A
tmengler@stmarytx.edu
MENIFIELD, Charles ...... 973-353-5253 282 B
charles.menifield@rutgers.edu
MENJARES, Pete .... 714-556-3610.. 72 F
officeoftheprovost@vanguard.edu
MENJIVAR, Claudia, I ... 650-574-6146.. 61 P
menjivarc@smccd.edu
MENJIVAR, Juan .... 562-938-4258.. 48 D
jmenjivar@lbcc.edu
MENK, David, A .... 507-933-6539 235 I
dmenk@gustavus.edu
MENKE, David .... 206-592-3443 481 H
dmenke@highline.edu
MENKE, Scott .... 262-595-2076 497 C
menke@uwp.edu
MENN, Esther .... 773-256-0721 142 G
emenn@lstc.edu
MENNE, Renee, A .... 563-588-7130 167 D
renee.menne@loras.edu
MENNECHEY, Pamela ... 407-708-2380 107 D
mennecheyp@seminolestate.edu
MENNEKE, Beth, R .... 314-505-7761 251 I
mennekeb@csl.edu
MENNELL, Betsy .... 801-626-6002 461 B
betsymennell@weber.edu
MENNELL, Jennifer .... 828-251-6501 342 C
jmennell@unca.edu
MENNELLA, Hillary .... 562-860-2451.. 35 M
hmennella@cerritos.edu
MENNICKE, Sue .... 717-358-7187 384 D
sue.mennicke@fandm.edu
MENNINGER, Jay, E ..... 802-656-3290 463 E
jay.menninger@uvm.edu
MENOGAN, Kelle .... 601-977-7828 249 C
kmenogan@tougaloo.edu
MENON, Sanjay, T .... 318-797-5234 189 D
sanjay.menon@lsus.edu
MENON, Sathyapal .... 415-442-7080.. 44 D
smenon@ggu.edu
MENON, Shaily, A .... 610-660-1282 398 C
casdean@sju.edu
MENSAH, Elfrida .... 336-334-7708 341 F
elfridam@ncat.edu
MENSAH, Ernesta .... 323-860-0789.. 50 A
MENSCH, Deserie .... 254-519-5722 447 A
d.mensch@tamuct.edu
MENSCHING, Ron .... 630-889-6606 144 G
rmensching@nuhs.edu
MENSE, Tobias .... 334-244-3838.... 4 F
tmense@aum.edu
MENTA, Vijay .... 802-443-2929 462 H
vmenta@middlebury.edu
MENTZER, Cathy .... 717-262-2604 403 F
cmentzer@wilson.edu
MENTZER, Stacy, L .... 515-574-1148 166 E
mentzer_s@iowacentral.edu
MENZ, Harald .... 304-829-7915 487 G
hmenz@bethanywv.edu
MENZEL, Carol, A .... 410-334-2946 204 F
cmenzel@worwic.edu
MENZEMER, Craig .... 330-972-7911 362 B
ccmenze@uakron.edu
MENZER, Paul .... 540-887-7058 469 B
pmenzer@marybaldwin.edu
MENZIES, Victoria .... 510-531-4911.. 56 H
vmenzies@peralta.edu
MEOLA, Christine .... 248-204-4000 226 G
MEONSKE, Kali, A .... 330-325-6492 357 G
kmeonske@neomed.edu
MERANDA, Seth .... 402-643-7220 266 G
seth.meranda@cune.edu
MERAR, Roland .... 670-234-5498 506 A
roland.merrar@marianas.edu
MERCADEL, Patrice .... 504-520-7558 193 A
pbellmer@xula.edu
MERCADEL, Robert .... 504-520-7396 193 A
rmercade@xula.edu
MERCADO, Claudia .... 847-925-6622 137 H
cmercado@harpercollege.edu
MERCADO, Harry .... 787-740-3555 512 C
harry.mercado@uccaribe.edu
MERCADO, Jose .... 660-543-8650 260 K
mercado@ucmo.edu
MERCADO, Juan .... 562-860-2451.. 35 M
jmercado@cerritos.edu
MERCADO, Juan Carlos 212-925-6625 293 D
jmercado@ccny.cuny.edu
MERCADO, Lemuel .... 770-228-7383 124 G
lemuel.mercado@sctech.edu
MERCADO, Lillian .... 787-780-0070 506 F
lmercado@caribbean.edu
MERCADO, Maritza .... 718-522-9073 290 C
mmercado@asa.edu
MERCADO, Waddy .... 787-841-2000 510 K
waddy_mercado@pucpr.edu
MERCADO-COTA,
Teresa .... 714-564-6105.. 57 L
mercado-cota_teresa@sac.edu
MERCADO-LÓPEZ,
Damaris .... 787-763-6700 508 A
dmercado@se-pr.edu
MERCANTINI, Jonathan 908-737-0437 278 E
jmercant@kean.edu
MERCANTINI, Rachel ... 828-395-4201 335 D
rmercantini@isothermal.edu
MERCED, Melissa .... 718-368-4911 294 E
melissa.merced@kbcc.cuny.edu
MERCER, Brian .... 217-351-2273 146 C
bmercer@parkland.edu
MERCER, Debbie, K ...... 785-532-5525 174 G
dmercer@ksu.edu
MERCER, Frank .... 386-506-4461.. 97 D
frank.mercer@daytonastate.edu
MERCER, John .... 513-745-4890 365 B
mercerjl@xavier.edu
MERCER, John, D .... 850-872-3807 100 N
jmercer@gulfcoast.edu
MERCER, Leneil .... 318-487-7420 186 I
leneil.mercer@lacollege.edu
MERCER, Louie .... 386-506-4433.. 97 D
louie.mercer@daytonastate.edu
MERCER, Molly .... 724-738-2179 395 F
molly.mercer@sru.edu
MERCER, Peter, P .... 201-684-7607 280 H
pmercer@ramapo.edu
MERCER,
Roberta (Bobby) .... 740-377-2520 361 K
bobby.mercer@tsbc.edu
MERCER, Sally .... 724-480-3379 381 K
sally.mercer@ccbc.edu
MERCER, Shannon .... 850-718-2362.. 96 F
mercershan@chipola.edu
MERCER-BURGESS,
Brenda, D .... 919-739-6736 338 H
bdmercer@waynecc.edu
MERCHANT, Debra, S ... 513-556-4119 362 D
debra.merchant@uc.edu
MERCHANT, Deneene .... 740-753-7080 354 A
merchantm@hocking.edu
MERCHANT, Jason .... 773-702-8523 150 J
merchant@uchicago.edu
MERCHANT, Joshua, D . 904-620-2100 110 A
joshua.merchant@unf.edu
MERCHANT, Joshua, D . 712-749-2103 163 D
merchantj@bvu.edu
MERCHANT, Maeesha ... 661-253-7835.. 28 K
cfo@calarts.edu
MERCHANT, Susan .... 518-608-8420 299 G
smerchant@excelsior.edu
MERCHBAKER, Doug .... 814-332-3357 378 D
wmerchbaker@allegheny.edu
MERCHLEWITZ, Ann, E . 507-457-1587 243 B
amerchle@smumn.edu
MERCIER, Deanna .... 757-340-2121 465 M
registrarcvab@centura.edu
MERCIER, Deborah .... 949-214-3346.. 40 F
deb.mercier@cui.edu
MERCIER, Diane .... 617-585-0200 206 F
diane.mercier@the-bac.edu
MERCIER, Nichole, R .... 314-747-1903 262 A
nmercier@wustl.edu
MERCIER, Stace, L .... 601-266-8525 249 F
stace.mercier@usm.edu
MERCIER, Taylor .... 210-690-9000 437 E
tmercier@hallmarkuniversity.edu
MERCINCAVAGE,
Janet, E .... 570-208-5878 387 A
jemercin@kings.edu
MERCK, Dana .... 252-222-6021 333 A
merckd@carteret.edu
MERCKX, Frank .... 973-408-3391 277 C
fcmerckx@drew.edu
MERCURIO, Sherry .... 614-947-6581 353 C
sherry.mercurio@franklin.edu
MEREDITH, Craig .... 614-797-4700 353 C
craig.meredith@urbana.edu
MEREDITH, Derek .... 252-335-0821 333 G
derek_meredith@albemarle.edu
MEREDITH, Joanne .... 410-455-1000 202 E
jmeredith@umbc.edu
MEREDITH, Joyce .... 740-587-6515 352 G
meredithj@denison.edu
MEREDITH, Nic .... 415-503-6289.. 60 H
nmeredith@sfcm.edu
MEREDITH, Stephanie ... 304-336-8117 490 F
smeredith@westliberty.edu
MEREDITH, Steve .... 435-586-7700 460 F
stevenmeredith@suu.edu
MEREN ACIERTO, Ei ..... 626-448-0023.. 46 G
MERESSI, Tesfay .... 508-999-8542 211 F
tmeressi@umassd.edu
MERFALEN, Vincent ...... 670-237-6764 506 A
vincent.merfalen@marianas.edu
MERGEN, Amy .... 419-251-1842 356 C
amy.mergen@mercycollege.edu
MERGEN, Dennis .... 320-308-3296 240 H
djmergen@stcloudstate.edu
MERGET, Kathleen .... 845-451-1776 298 A
kathy.merget@culinary.edu
MERGUIE, John .... 501-450-3111.. 23 H
jmerguie@uca.edu
MERHAR, Sarah .... 218-262-6713 238 C
sarahmerhar@hibbing.edu
MERIAN, Dan .... 313-593-5151 231 F
dmerian@umich.edu
MERIANO, John .... 203-582-8763.. 87 G
john.meriano@quinnipiac.edu
MERIANS, Linda .... 646-313-8000 295 E
linda.merians@guttman.cuny.edu
MERICA, Michael .... 928-226-4212.. 11 O
michael.merica@coconino.edu
MERICLE, Margaret, E ... 559-442-8210.. 66 E
margaret.mericle@fresnocitycollege.edu
MERIDA, Cindy .... 657-278-4697.. 31 E
cmerida@fullerton.edu
MERIDITH, Pamela .... 870-759-4139.. 23 J
pmeridith@williamsbu.edu
MERILLAT, Jason, C ..... 610-566-1776 403 E
jmerillat@williamson.edu
MERIMEE, Nancy, S ...... 913-971-3427 175 G
nsmerimee@mnu.edu
MERINAR, Whitney, A .. 570-321-4144 389 E
merinar@lycoming.edu
MERINO, Robert .... 281-998-6342 443 C
robert.merino@sjcd.edu
MERINO, Robert .... 281-998-6150 443 B
robert.merino@sjcd.edu
MERINO, Robert .... 281-998-6342 443 E
robert.merino@sjcd.edu
MERINO, Robert .... 281-998-6342 443 D
robert.merino@sjcd.edu
MERIWETHER, Mimi ...... 803-786-3856 408 F
mmeriwether@columbiasc.edu
MERJIL, Mark .... 909-384-8900.. 59 I
mmerjil@sbccd.cc.ca.us
MERKEL, Diane, K .... 518-564-2195 319 C
dmerk001@plattsburgh.edu
MERKEL, Luz .... 509-777-4225 486 I
lmerkel@whitworth.edu
MERKEL, SJ, Tom .... 402-280-1771 266 I
tommerkel2@creighton.edu
MERKIN, Yitzchok .... 301-962-5111 204 G
ymerkin@yeshiva.edu
MERKLE, Ben .... 208-882-1566 131 B
bmerkle@nsa.edu
MERKLE, Jean .... 563-425-5765 170 A
merklej@uiu.edu
MERKLE, Joseph, F ...... 717-815-1460 404 A
jmerkle@ycp.edu
MERKLE, Patricia .... 315-568-3277 308 F
pmerkle@nycc.edu
MERKLIN, Lynn .... 269-471-6066 221 B
merklin@andrews.edu
MERKOW, Russ .... 425-739-8436 482 A
russ.merkow@lwtech.edu
MERKT, Dan .... 518-608-8371 299 G
dmerkt@excelsior.edu
MERLE, Robin .... 212-484-1156 294 D
rmerle@jjay.cuny.edu
MERLIC, Jennifer .... 310-434-4000.. 62 E
MERLINO, Keith .... 412-809-5100 396 H
merlino.keith@ptcollege.edu
MERLINO, Tina .... 209-954-5039.. 60 J
kmerlino@deltacollege.edu
MERLO, Barbara .... 254-526-1223 432 H
barbara.merlo@ctcd.edu
MERLO, Scott, R .... 269-387-5555 232 K
scott.merlo@wmich.edu
MERMANN-JOZWIAK,
Elisabeth .... 570-577-1561 379 F
emmj001@bucknell.edu
MERMELSTEIN, Joanne . 978-837-5117 216 D
mermelsteinj@merrimack.edu
MERO, Neal, P .... 386-822-7406 111 A
nmero@stetson.edu
MERO, Sandi .... 909-607-8592.. 37 G
sandi_mero@kgi.edu
MEROPOL, Ian .... 617-243-2150 210 G
imeropol@lasell.edu
MEROS, Camilla .... 703-591-7042 476 F
MERRELL, Howard .... 671-734-1812 505 D
hmerrell@piu.edu
MERRELL, Kathy .... 671-734-1812 505 D
MERRELL, Tom .... 415-422-2613.. 71 K
merrellt@usfca.edu
MERRICK, Robyn, M ..... 225-771-2000 190 H
robyn_merrick@sus.edu
MERRICK, Robyn, M ..... 225-771-5497 190 G
robyn_merrick@sus.edu
MERRIFIELD, Ann .... 573-875-7210 251 F
amerrifield@ccis.edu
MERRILL, Chad .... 828-694-1704 332 E
chadm@blueridge.edu
MERRILL, Dale .... 657-278-3256.. 31 E
dmerrill@fullerton.edu
MERRILL, H. Donald ..... 704-233-8284 344 G
dmerrill@wingate.edu
MERRILL, Joanne .... 603-897-8257 274 B
jmerrill@rivier.edu
MERRILL, Peter .... 802-586-7711 463 D
pmerrill@sterlingcollege.edu
MERRILL, Scott, M .... 508-793-2438 208 B
smerrill@holycross.edu
MERRILL, Timothy .... 804-523-5131 474 H
tmerrill@reynolds.edu
MERRILL, Traci .... 619-260-7967.. 71 J
tmerrill@sandiego.edu
MERRILL-SANDS,
Deborah, M .... 603-862-1983 274 G
deborah.merrill-sands@unh.edu
MERRIMAN, Gary .... 909-599-5433.. 47 K
gmerriman@lifepacific.edu
MERRIMAN, JR., W, R . 330-823-6050 363 B
merrimdr@mountunion.edu
MERRITT, Bert .... 850-484-1143 104 H
bmerritt@pensacolastate.edu
MERRITT, Brian .... 919-718-7426 333 C
bmerritt@cccc.edu
MERRITT, Cheryl .... 909-607-7853.. 37 G
cheryl_merrit@kgi.edu
MERRITT, Debra .... 860-486-2337.. 88 E
debra.merritt@uconn.edu

MERRITT, Jeffrey .... 919-866-7206 338 G
jlmerritt@waketech.edu
MERRITT, Kevin .... 304-485-5487 488 D
kmerritt@msc.edu
MERRITT, Mark .... 213-740-7922.. 72 B
MERRITT, Nancy .... 412-268-1209 380 F
nmkm@andrew.cmu.edu
MERRITT, Nathan .... 626-584-5364.. 43 H
nathanmerritt@fuller.edu
MERRITT, Pearl, E .... 325-696-0503 451 C
pearl.merritt@ttuhsc.edu
MERRITT, Ronald .... 256-233-6527.... 4 D
ronald.merritt@athens.edu
MERRITT, Scott .... 318-869-5708 186 B
smerritt@centenary.edu
MERRITT, Terence .... 503-845-3564 374 B
terence.merritt@mtangel.edu
MERRY, Nicholas .... 410-293-1010 504 I
nicholas.merry@navy.mil
MERRYMAN, Ed .... 408-554-5076.. 62 D
emerryman@scu.edu
MERRYMAN, Jon .... 870-245-5506.. 20 E
merrymanj@obu.edu
MERSMANN, Tina .... 513-244-4232 357 A
tina.mersmann@msj.edu
MERTENS, Daniel .... 701-662-1654 346 D
danial.mertens@lrsc.edu
MERTENS, Peter .... 718-518-6731 294 B
pmertens@hostos.cuny.edu
MERTES, Michael .... 802-387-7179 462 D
michaelmertes@landmark.edu
MERTES, Scott .... 989-386-6622 227 F
smertes@midmich.edu
MERTH, Paula, B .... 651-290-6376 242 G
paula.merth@mitchellhamline.edu
MERTZ, Jennifer, L .... 610-758-3181 388 J
jlm207@lehigh.edu
MERTZ, Laila .... 714-241-6153.. 38 C
lmertz@coastline.edu
MERTZ-WEIGEL,
Dorothee .... 912-478-0332 119 C
dmertzweigel@georgiasouthern.edu
MERVIUS, Sandra .... 516-463-4335 302 B
sandra.mervius@hofstra.edu
MERWIN, Elizabeth .... 817-272-2776 454 J
elizabeth.merwin@uta.edu
MERY, Pam .... 415-239-3227.. 37 A
pmery@ccsf.edu
MERZ, Marcie, L .... 215-898-6171 400 K
mmerz@dev.upenn.edu
MERZ, Nan .... 408-554-4007.. 62 D
nmerz@scu.edu
MERZIAK, Traci .... 406-447-6914 264 C
traci.merzlak@helenacollege.edu
MESA, Norma .... 805-969-3626.. 55 E
nmesa@pacifica.edu
MESA, Tina .... 210-486-3901 429 F
tmesa@alamo.edu
MESARIS, Nikilos 'Nik' . 951-487-3073.. 52 I
nmesaris@msjc.edu
MESEHA, Manal .... 973-300-2754 283 E
mmeseha@sussex.edu
MESEROLE, Scott .... 618-842-3711 138 G
meseroles@iecc.edu
MESERVE, Linda .... 970-491-5105.. 78 M
linda.meserve@colostate.edu
MESERVE, Mary .... 207-786-6097 193 B
mmeserve@bates.edu
MESHKATY, Shahra .... 619-260-2298.. 71 J
meshkaty@sandiego.edu
MESICS, Linda, L .... 610-799-1585 388 I
lmesics@lccc.edu
MESKER, Bobby, S .... 432-837-8231 450 D
bmesker@sulross.edu
MESLENER, Jennifer .... 301-387-3022 198 F
jennifer.meslener@garrettcollege.edu
MESONAS, Lenny .... 908-526-1200 281 A
lenny.mesonas@raritanval.edu
MESQUITA, Cezar .... 360-650-4350 486 F
cezar.mesquita@wwu.edu
MESSA, Emily .... 832-842-8184 452 E
eamessa@uh.edu
MESSA, Emily .... 832-842-8184 452 F
eamessa@uh.edu
MESSAC, Achille .... 202-806-6565.. 92 B
messac@howard.edu
MESSAROS, Jean .... 570-674-6320 390 G
srjean@misericordia.edu
MESSATZZIA, Amanda .. 410-334-2993 204 F
amessatzzia@worwic.edu
MESSER, Emily, W .... 256-782-5363.... 5 J
emesser@jsu.edu
MESSER, James .... 412-237-3108 381 G
jmesser@ccac.edu
MESSER, Thomas, C .... 904-596-2411 111 F
tmesser@tbc.org
MESSERLI, Jodi .... 605-882-5284 415 F
jodi.messerli@lakeareatech.edu
MESSERVY, Steven .... 256-824-6343.... 8 B
steven.messervy@uah.edu
MESSICK, Gary, A .... 260-422-5561 155 H
gamessick@indianatech.edu
MESSIER, John, D .... 207-778-7457 196 B
john.messier@maine.edu
MESSINA, John, A .... 330-972-6594 362 B
jam125@uakron.edu
MESSINA, Kimberlee .... 509-533-3535 480 B
kimberlee.messina@sfcc.spokane.edu
MESSINA, Kimberlee .... 509-434-5107 479 I
MESSINA, Melissa .... 816-501-3360 258 H
melissa.messina@rockhurst.edu
MESSINA, Rosalia .... 503-847-2555 377 F
rmessina@uws.edu
MESSINGER, Jacquelyn 620-276-9631 173 E
jacquelyn.messinger@gcccks.edu
MESSINGSCHALGER,
Mark .... 859-344-3531 184 F
messinm@thomasmore.edu
MESSITTE, Zachariah, P 920-748-8118 495 G
messittez@ripon.edu
MESSMAN-MANDICOTT,
Lea .... 301-687-4890 203 E
lmessman@frostburg.edu
MESSNER, Leonard, V .. 312-949-7108 138 E
lmessner@ico.edu
MESSNER, Melody .... 816-936-8717 259 I
mmessner@saintlukescollege.edu
MESSNER, Robert, H .... 717-780-2333 385 E
rhmessne@hacc.edu
MESSNER, Stephanie .... 312-949-7013 138 E
smessner@ico.edu
MESSNER, Tom .... 904-646-2175 100 B
tom.messner@fscj.edu
MESSPLAY, Paul .... 540-654-1410 472 I
pmesspla@umw.edu
MESTAN, Michael, A .... 315-568-3100 308 F
mmestan@nycc.edu
MESTAS, Richard .... 301-243-2165 503 J
richard.mestas@dodiis.mil
MESTETH, Leslie .... 605-455-6033 416 B
lmesteth@olc.edu
MESTLER, Nathan, M .... 480-245-7903.. 12 N
MESTRES, Ibrahim .... 787-780-0070 506 F
imestres@caribbean.edu
MESYEF, Masha .... 801-649-5230 459 G
marketing@midwifrey.edu
MESYEF, Whitney .... 866-680-2756 459 G
financialaid@midwifery.edu
METAJ, Dee .... 317-278-5644 156 F
metaj@iupui.edu
METCALF, Amanda .... 304-367-4241 490 B
amanda.metcalf@fairmontstate.edu
METCALF, Christine .... 603-271-6484 273 B
cmetcalf@ccsnh.edu
METCALF, Courtney .... 620-223-2700 173 C
courtneym@fortscott.edu
METCALF, Dustin .... 208-467-8665 131 D
dmetcalf@nnu.edu
METCALF, Gary .... 559-453-2063.. 43 G
gary.metcalf@fresno.edu
METCALF, Jeff, K .... 606-474-3258 180 G
jmetcalf@kcu.edu
METCALF, Jonathan, G . 240-500-2216 198 H
jgmetcalf@hagerstowncc.edu
METCALF, Kim, K .... 702-895-3375 271 E
kim.metcalf@unlv.edu
METCALF, Linda .... 817-531-7530 451 E
lmetcalf@txwes.edu
METCALFE, Sharon .... 740-392-6868 357 B
sharon.metcalfe@mvnu.edu
METE, T.J .... 772-466-4822.. 94 P
tj.mete@aviator.edu
METESH, John, J .... 406-496-4159 265 A
jmetesh@mtech.edu
METEVIER, Robert .... 602-787-7872.. 13 E
robert.metevier@paradisevalley.edu
METH, Clifford .... 646-565-6000 322 J
yehudah.meth2@touro.edu
METHE, Deborah .... 413-265-2485 208 C
methed@elms.edu
METHODIOS,
Metropolitan .... 617-850-1280 210 D
pres_office@hchc.edu
METHVIN, Jennifer .... 501-882-8956.. 17 F
METIANU, Mihaela .... 561-297-3049 108 J
mmetianu@fau.edu
METILLY, Paul .... 617-254-2610 218 D
paul.metilly@sjs.edu
METIVIER SCOTT,
Shelly .... 508-910-6402 211 F
shelly.scott@umassd.edu
METOYER, Regan .... 281-756-3527 429 I
rmetoyer@alvincollege.edu
METRESS, Heather, B .... 706-721-5052 115 A
hmetress@augusta.edu
METS, Lisa, A .... 727-864-8221.. 97 J
metsla@eckerd.edu
METTEN, Michelle .... 618-252-5400 149 C
michelle.metten@sic.edu
METTILLE, Teege .... 262-524-7221 492 E
tmetill@carrollu.edu
METTS, Amanda .... 252-399-6315 326 M
ahmetts@barton.edu
METTS, Deanna .... 931-372-3045 426 E
dmetts@tntech.edu
METZ, Bernice .... 712-279-5400 163 C
bernice.metz@briarcliff.edu
METZ, Catherine, A .... 765-361-6418 162 E
metzc@wabash.edu
METZ, Christine .... 516-562-3403 299 B
cmetz@northwell.edu
METZ, George .... 843-863-7765 407 E
gmetz@csuniv.edu
METZ, Gregory .... 513-745-5720 362 E
gregory.metz@uc.edu
METZ, Matthew .... 716-829-7502 298 F
metzm@dyc.edu
METZ, Robert, C .... 517-264-7117 230 E
rmetz@sienaheights.edu
METZ, Roxanne .... 949-582-4824.. 64 G
rmetz@saddleback.edu
METZ, Starla .... 727-341-4368 106 E
metz.starla@spcollege.edu
METZ, Susan .... 201-216-5245 283 C
susan.metz@stevens.edu
METZ, Terry .... 651-523-2160 236 A
tmetz01@hamline.edu
METZ, Tim .... 323-860-1129.. 53 B
tmetz@mi.edu
METZ, Tim .... 828-227-7239 344 A
tdmetz@wcu.edu
METZCAR, Aaron .... 601-968-8971 245 C
ametzcar@belhaven.edu
METZELAARS, Gretchen 614-688-8011 358 I
metzelaars.1@osu.edu
METZER, Stacy .... 515-574-1148 166 E
mentzer_s@iowacentral.edu
METZGAR, Kim .... 724-805-2601 398 F
kim.metzgar@stvincent.edu
METZGAR, Michael .... 315-498-6061 311 B
m.c.metzgar@sunyocc.edu
METZGER, Amanda .... 585-385-8411 314 A
ametzger@sjfc.edu
METZGER, Carl .... 407-823-5242 109 E
carl.metzger@ucf.edu
METZGER, David, D .... 757-683-4865 469 G
dmetzger@odu.edu
METZGER, Elizabeth .... 505-277-3389 288 G
emetzger@unm.edu
METZGER, Matthew, R .. 574-372-5100 155 B
metzgemr@grace.edu
METZGER, Michael, D .. 716-673-3109 317 A
michael.metzger@fredonia.edu
METZGER, Nan .... 414-930-3338 495 A
metzgern@mtmary.edu
METZGER, Peggy .... 707-826-4321.. 33 D
mam7001@humboldt.edu
METZGER, Stacy .... 413-775-1364 214 C
metzgers@gcc.mass.edu
METZGER, Thomas .... 702-968-2013 272 C
tmetzger@roseman.edu
METZGER, Tina .... 804-627-5300 465 C
METZINGER, Harry .... 856-222-9311 281 C
hmetzinger@rcbc.edu
METZINGER, Michelle ... 913-758-6115 177 F
michelle.metzinger@stmary.edu
METZLER, Christopher .. 717-299-7794 399 G
metzler@stevenscollege.edu
METZLER, Madeleine .... 401-865-2499 405 B
METZO, Vincent .... 212-924-5900 322 B
vmetzo@swedishinstitute.edu
MEULEMANS, Nicole .... 651-423-8403 237 H
nicole.meulemans@dctc.edu
MEULEMANS, Nicole .... 651-450-3311 238 D
nmeulem@inverhills.edu
MEUSCHKE, Daylene .... 661-362-5329.. 38 H
daylene.meuschke@canyons.edu
MEUWISSEN, Daniel, J . 651-962-5100 244 E
djmeuwissen@stthomas.edu
MEWERS, Montgomery . 318-869-5110 186 B
mmewers@centenary.edu
MEWS, Joseph .... 803-938-3731 414 B
mewsj@uscsumter.edu
MEY, Craig, A .... 715-836-3263 496 D
meyca@uwec.edu
MEYDAM, Mark, R .... 715-425-4095 497 E
mark.r.meydam@uwrf.edu
MEYER, Adam .... 212-799-5000 303 H
MEYER, AJ .... 937-327-6471 364 H
meyera@wittenberg.edu
MEYER, Alexis .... 414-955-8246 494 C
alemeyer@mcw.edu
MEYER, Angela .... 573-651-2292 259 K
admeyer@semo.edu
MEYER, Ann .... 312-329-4417 144 B
ann.meyer@moody.edu
MEYER, Brenda .... 479-619-4248.. 20 D
bmeyer@nwacc.edu
MEYER, Bruce, A .... 419-372-3232 348 H
bameyer@bgsu.edu
MEYER, Bruce, A .... 419-372-6821 348 H
bameyer@bgsu.edu
MEYER, Carrie .... 765-998-4554 160 F
crmeyer@taylor.edu
MEYER, Chris .... 405-733-7913 369 I
cmeyer@rose.edu
MEYER, Christopher, G . 559-278-3936.. 31 D
cmeyer@csufresno.edu
MEYER, Dale, A .... 314-505-7010 251 I
meyerd@csl.edu
MEYER, David .... 816-414-3700 256 A
dmeyer@mbts.edu
MEYER, David, D .... 504-865-5930 191 B
meyer@tulane.edu
MEYER, Donald, J .... 319-352-8517 170 C
donald.meyer@wartburg.edu
MEYER, Doug .... 503-493-6471 372 I
dmeyer@cu-portland.edu
MEYER, Dulcie .... 315-781-3082 302 A
dmeyer@hws.edu
MEYER, Eddie .... 860-727-6906.. 87 A
emeyer@goodwin.edu
MEYER, Eric .... 512-471-3821 455 A
dean@ischool.utexas.edu
MEYER, Frederick, B .... 507-538-0554 234 I
frederick.meyer@mayo.edu
MEYER, Fredric, B .... 507-284-3268 234 J
meyer.fredric@mayo.edu
MEYER, Gary .... 917-493-4456 305 I
gmeyer@msmnyc.edu
MEYER, Gary .... 414-288-6350 494 B
gary.meyer@marquette.edu
MEYER, Gregg, A .... 508-531-1237 212 B
gmeyer@bridgew.edu
MEYER, Gregor .... 312-788-1132 152 B
gmeyer@vandercook.edu
MEYER, Heidi .... 612-625-2008 243 E
meyer119@umn.edu
MEYER, Jay .... 847-543-2717 135 B
jmeyer@clcillinois.edu
MEYER, Jean, C .... 610-526-1466 378 G
jean.meyer@theamericancollege.edu
MEYER, Jennifer .... 818-785-2726.. 35 J
MEYER, Jill .... 414-277-7365 494 G
MEYER, John .... 414-443-8910 498 O
john.meyer@wlc.edu
MEYER, John .... 949-451-5200.. 64 F
jmeyer@ivc.edu
MEYER, John, D .... 239-513-1122 101 C
jmeyer@hodges.edu
MEYER, John, E .... 507-354-8221 236 I
meyerjd@mlc-wels.edu
MEYER, Joseph, M .... 512-245-2386 450 E
jm01@txstate.edu
MEYER, Josh .... 540-857-6311 476 D
jmeyer@virginiawestern.edu
MEYER, Kathy .... 701-483-2535 345 D
kathleen.meyer@dickinsonstate.edu
MEYER, Katie .... 270-706-8443 181 A
cmeyer0015@kctcs.edu
MEYER, Kelli, A .... 203-576-4487.. 88 D
kmeyer@bridgeport.edu
MEYER, Kelly .... 518-458-5402 296 H
meyerk@strose.edu
MEYER, Kimberly, J .... 574-807-7021 153 E
kimberly.meyer@betheluniversity.edu
MEYER, Kingsley .... 740-245-7365 363 D
kmeyer@rio.edu
MEYER, Kyle, P .... 402-559-7428 270 A
kpmeyer@unmc.edu

MEYER, Lara .... 509-527-4928 486 H
meyerla@whitman.edu
MEYER, Larry .... 859-572-6117 184 A
meyerl3@nku.edu
MEYER, Lisa .... 503-768-7056 373 G
lmeyer@lclark.edu
MEYER, Liz .... 970-248-1410.. 77 I
lmeyer@coloradomesa.edu
MEYER, Marilyn, S .... 801-863-6076 461 A
marilyn.meyer@uvu.edu
MEYER, Mathys .... 606-218-5467 185 D
mathysmeyer@upike.edu
MEYER, Matthew .... 213-477-2899.. 52 G
mmeyer@msmu.edu
MEYER, Matthew .... 919-807-7155 331 L
meyerm@nccommunitycolleges.edu
MEYER, Merry .... 845-758-7005 290 G
sm568@bncollege.com
MEYER, Michael .... 808-844-2308 129 B
mmeyer@hawaii.edu
MEYER, Michele .... 407-691-1754 105 M
mmeyer@rollins.edu
MEYER, Mike .... 909-599-5433.. 47 K
mmeyer@lifepacific.edu
MEYER, Patricia .... 240-629-7905 198 E
pmeyer@frederick.edu
MEYER, Patricia .... 513-745-1996 365 B
meyerp@xavier.edu
MEYER, Paul, W .... 215-247-5777 400 K
pmeyer@upenn.edu
MEYER, Richard .... 314-246-7429 262 C
richardmeyer33@webster.edu
MEYER, Rick .... 909-599-5433.. 47 K
rmeyer@lifepacific.edu
MEYER, Robert .... 715-232-2441 498 A
meyeb@uwstout.edu
MEYER, Shana .... 816-271-4432 257 A
slmeyer@missouriwestern.edu
MEYER, Shane .... 503-255-0332 374 D
smeyer@multnomah.edu
MEYER, Sheree .... 916-278-6502.. 32 E
meyers@csus.edu
MEYER, Stan .... 602-639-7500.. 12 J
MEYER, Steven .... 202-759-4988.. 91 D
MEYER, Susan .... 320-308-5512 241 A
smeyer@sctcc.edu
MEYER, Terry .... 623-935-8191.. 13 A
terry.meyer@estrellamountain.edu
MEYER, Terry .... 701-328-2963 345 B
terry.meyer@ndus.edu
MEYER, Thomas .... 816-604-5250 255 D
thomas.meyer@mcckc.edu
MEYER, Thomas .... 816-604-5250 255 F
thomas.meyer@mcckc.edu
MEYER, Thomas, W .... 816-604-6544 255 E
thomas.meyer@mcckc.edu
MEYER, Yvonne .... 630-844-3830 132 D
ymeyer@aurora.edu
MEYER REIMER,
Kathryn .... 574-535-7443 155 A
kathymr@goshen.edu
MEYERS, Jeff .... 432-552-2809 457 A
MEYERS, Matthew .... 610-892-1543 393 J
mmeyers@pit.edu
MEYERS, Ruth .... 510-204-0720.. 36 J
rmeyers@cdsp.edu
MEYERS, Shelly .... 864-488-8207 410 E
smeyers@limestone.edu
MEYERS, Tom, J .... 574-535-7346 155 A
tomjm@goshen.edu
MEYERS, Vanessa .... 202-687-5627.. 92 A
vmm8@georgetown.edu
MEZA, Ilda .... 509-865-0710 481 G
meza_i@heritage.edu
MEZA, Jane .... 402-559-6825 270 A
jmeza@unmc.edu
MEZA, Jane, L .... 402-559-6825 270 B
jmeza@unomaha.edu
MEZA, José, I .... 787-769-9965 513 C
jose.meza1@upr.edu
MEZA, Jose .... 787-257-0000 513 C
jose.meza1@upr.edu
MEZA, Kathy .... 610-341-1955 383 D
kathy.meza@eastern.edu
MEZEY, Nancy .... 732-263-5631 279 B
nmezey@monmouth.edu
MEZIERE, Kevin .... 858-653-6740.. 46 I
kmeziere@jpcatholic.com
MEZWA, Duane .... 248-370-2452 229 G
mezwa@oakland.edu
MEZYNSKI, David .... 914-961-8313 315 C
dmezynski@svots.edu

MHLANGA, Fortune ...... 615-966-5073 421 D
fortune.mhlanga@lipscomb.edu
MIAN, Mahreen, N .... 904-620-2371 110 A
mahreen.mian@unf.edu
MIAOULIS, Ioannis .... 401-254-3030 405 E
imiaoulis@rwu.edu
MIARKA-GRZELAK,
Anna .... 518-562-4171 296 B
anna.miarka-grzelak@clinton.edu
MICAL, Kelly .... 910-296-2509 335 E
kmical@jamessprunt.edu
MICARELLI, Stephen ..... 617-349-8705 210 H
smicarel@lesley.edu
MICCO, Melissa, A .... 412-397-5264 397 G
micco@rmu.edu
MICELI, Anthony .... 313-664-7814 222 F
amiceli@collegeforcreativestudies.edu
MICELI, Christy .... 312-629-6706 148 I
cmiceli@saic.edu
MICELI, Paul, E .... 781-899-5500 218 A
rev.miceli@psjs.edu
MICELI, Tara .... 916-361-1660.. 35 C
tara.miceli@carrington.edu
MICHAEL, Cheryl .... 410-334-2884 204 F
cmichael@worwic.edu
MICHAEL, Cynthia .... 937-376-6304 350 D
cmichael@centralstate.edu
MICHAEL, Gage .... 719-549-3011.. 81 K
michael.gage@pueblocc.edu
MICHAEL, Jody .... 810-762-0048 228 C
jody.michael@mcc.edu
MICHAEL, Josh .... 937-766-7846 349 G
jmichael@cedarville.edu
MICHAEL, Magali .... 727-873-4258 110 C
mcmichael2@mail.usf.edu
MICHAEL, Rebecca .... 831-646-5506.. 52 F
rmichael@mpc.edu
MICHAEL, Steve, O .... 323-563-5854.. 36 D
stevemichael@cdrewu.edu
MICHAEL, Thomas, R ... 217-581-2319 136 E
trmichael@eiu.edu
MICHAEL, Timothy .... 313-577-2313 232 I
tmichael@wayne.edu
MICHAEL-PICKETT,
Stephanie .... 704-922-6215 334 F
michael.stephanie@gaston.edu
MICHAELIAN, Katherine 240-567-7695 200 C
katherine.michaelian@
montgomerycollege.edu
MICHAELIDES, Anthony 661-362-3253.. 38 H
anthony.michaelides@canyons.edu
MICHAELIDES, Barbara . 318-342-5550 192 F
michaelides@ulm.edu
MICHAELIS, Joel .... 606-248-0178 182 E
jmichaelis0001@kctcs.edu
MICHAELIS, Michael ...... 785-628-4291 173 B
mwmichaelis@fhsu.edu
MICHAELIS, Randy .... 509-777-4402 486 I
rmichaelis@whitworth.edu
MICHAELS, Alan, C .... 614-292-2631 358 I
michaels.23@osu.edu
MICHAELS, Craig .... 718-997-5220 295 C
craig.michaels@qc.cuny.edu
MICHAELS, Dennis .... 716-614-6744 310 C
dmichaels@niagaracc.suny.edu
MICHAELS, George, H .. 805-893-2378.. 70 A
george.michaels@id.ucsb.edu
MICHAELS, Jeff, A .... 717-477-1171 395 E
jamich@ship.edu
MICHAELS, Lynda .... 570-389-4061 394 A
lmichael@bloomu.edu
MICHAELS, Sheri .... 229-732-5928 114 B
sherimichaels@andrewcollege.edu
MICHAELSEN, Kevin ...... 919-760-8565 331 B
michaelsen@meredith.edu
MICHAELSON, Frank ..... 805-969-3626.. 55 E
fmichaelson@pacifica.edu
MICHALAK, Mary Jane . 317-921-4882 157 G
mmichalak@ivytech.edu
MICHALAK, Russell ...... 302-225-6227.. 90 E
michalr@gbc.edu
MICHALAK, Sarah .... 919-962-1301 342 D
smichala@email.unc.edu
MICHALENKO, John, A . 412-397-6483 397 G
michalenko@rmu.edu
MICHALKO, Nancy .... 801-957-4247 461 D
nancy.michalko@slcc.edu
MICHALOWSKI, Sam ..... 201-692-2060 277 K
ir_sam@fdu.edu
MICHALSKI, Gregory ..... 904-632-3017 100 B
g.michalski@fscj.edu
MICHALSKI, Joshua ...... 817-202-6224 444 I
jmichalski@swau.edu

MICHALSKI, Monica ..... 718-489-5272 313 H
mmichalski@sfc.edu
MICHALSKI, Tim .... 361-570-4820 453 C
michalskit@uhv.edu
MICHAUD, Lisa .... 207-834-7607 196 C
lisa.michaud@maine.edu
MICHAUD, Paul .... 908-526-1200 281 A
paul.michaud@raritanval.edu
MICHAUX, Kimberly, S . 434-223-6102 468 A
kmixhaux@hsc.edu
MICHEALS, Erica .... 770-426-2810 121 C
erica.michaels@life.edu
MICHEL, Bill .... 773-702-2673 150 J
wmichel@uchicago.edu
MICHEL, Brian .... 716-614-5928 310 C
bmichel@niagaracc.suny.edu
MICHEL, Mike .... 410-293-1901 504 I
michel@usna.edu
MICHEL, Pamela .... 315-312-2102 319 B
pamela.michel@oswego.edu
MICHEL, R. Keith .... 516-671-2277 324 G
kmichel@webb.edu
MICHEL, Tabatha .... 404-413-5057 119 E
tmichele@gsu.edu
MICHELBACH,
Andrea, N .... 253-535-7447 482 H
michelan@plu.edu
MICHELLE, Marable, D . 757-823-8600 469 F
MICHELS, Kallie, B .... 734-764-3526 231 E
kallie@umich.edu
MICHELSON, Peggy ...... 314-529-6543 254 H
pmichelson@maryville.edu
MICHIE, Cheryl .... 641-472-7000 167 F
cmichie@mum.edu
MICHIELSSEN, Eric .... 734-647-1793 231 E
emichiel@umich.edu
MICHTAVY, Lesley .... 209-588-5100.. 75 I
MICIAK, Alan .... 216-397-1745 354 I
amiciak@jcu.edu
MICIOTTO, Joseph .... 318-675-8053 189 C
jmicio@lsuhsc.edu
MICKELSEN, Scott, R .... 406-377-9406 263 E
smickelsen@dawson.edu
MICKELSON, Kristine .... 608-663-2374 493 C
kmickelson@edgewood.edu
MICKELSON, Sally .... 702-968-2004 272 C
smickelson@roseman.edu
MICKENS, Charles .... 517-371-5140 233 A
mickensc@cooley.edu
MICKENS, George .... 623-245-4600.. 16 E
gmickens@uti.edu
MICKENS, Kendrick .... 610-359-5340 382 C
kmickens@dccc.edu
MICKENS, Telishia .... 409-944-1285 437 B
tmickens@gc.edu
MICKETTI, Phyllis .... 848-445-6622 282 A
p.micketti@admissions.rutgers.edu
MICKEY, Marty .... 847-947-5580 144 F
mmickey@nl.edu
MICKEY, Travis .... 336-272-7102 329 D
travis.mickey@greensboro.edu
MICKEY-BOGGS, Shari .. 937-775-2120 364 I
shari.mickey-boggs@wright.edu
MICKLE, Angelia .... 937-766-7720 349 G
amickle@cedarville.edu
MICKLER, Michael .... 845-752-3000 323 F
mm@uts.edu
MICKLES, Muriel .... 434-832-7656 474 C
micklesm@centralvirginia.edu
MICKLES, Muriel .... 434-832-7837 474 C
micklesm@centralvirginia.edu
MICKLES, Ryan .... 434-528-5276 477 E
MICKOOL, Richard .... 937-525-3811 364 H
rmickool@wittenberg.edu
MICKOOL, Rick .... 401-709-8479 405 D
rmickool@risd.edu
MIDCAP, Richard .... 301-387-3056 198 F
richard.midcap@garrettcollege.edu
MIDDEKER, Vicki .... 303-466-1714.. 82 J
MIDDEN, Karen .... 618-453-2469 149 E
kmidden@siu.edu
MIDDENDORF, Terry ...... 651-523-2302 236 A
tmiddendorf@hamline.edu
MIDDENDORF, Tom .... 615-248-7712 427 A
tmiddendorf@trevecca.educca.edu
MIDDIS, Amanda .... 419-289-5457 348 A
amiddis@ashland.edu
MIDDLEBROOKS,
Betty, A .... 334-683-5127.... 6 A
bmiddlebrooks@judson.edu
MIDDLEKAUFF, Paul ...... 212-659-0736 304 B
pmiddlekauff@tkc.edu

MIDDLESWARTH,
Jean, E .... 336-757-3288 334 E
jmiddleswarth@forsythtech.edu
MIDDLETON, David .... 412-924-1790 396 I
dmiddleton@pts.edu
MIDDLETON, Dewayne .. 601-849-0112 245 G
dewayne.middleton@colin.edu
MIDDLETON,
Jacqueline .... 330-263-2580 351 C
jkmiddleton@wooster.edu
MIDDLETON, Kenna ...... 859-622-3436 180 B
kenna.middleton@eku.edu
MIDDLETON, Lauren ..... 860-439-2666.. 86 H
lmiddlet@conncoll.edu
MIDDLETON, Lyle .... 501-205-8830.. 18 H
lmiddleton@cbc.edu
MIDDLETON,
Melinda, L .... 812-877-8259 159 J
middleto@rose-hulman.edu
MIDDLETON, Michael ... 212-772-4065 294 C
mm5378@hunter.cuny.edu
MIDDLETON, Natavia .... 727-398-8288 106 E
middleton.natavia@spcollege.edu
MIDDLETON, Renee, A . 740-593-4400 359 G
middletr@ohio.edu
MIDDLETON,
Rodney, C .... 989-328-1202 228 A
rodm@montcalm.edu
MIDDLETON, Tracy .... 803-705-4594 407 A
tracy.middleton@benedict.edu
MIDDLETON,
Whittaker, V .... 803-535-5347 407 G
wmiddleton@claflin.edu
MIDEI, Ron .... 954-262-5224 103 M
ronmidei@nsu.nova.edu
MIDGETT, Pam .... 940-397-4182 440 F
pam.midgett@msutexas.edu
MIDGLEY, Brianna .... 801-832-2257 461 G
bmidgley@westminstercollege.edu
MIDGLEY, Michael, T ... 512-223-7579 431 A
midgley@austincc.edu
MIDHA, Chand .... 330-972-7664 362 B
cmidha@uakron.edu
MIDKIFF, Kittridge .... 270-686-4508 182 B
kitt.midkiff@kctcs.edu
MIDKIFF, Lindsay .... 870-633-4480.. 19 B
lindsay.midkiff@eacc.edu
MIDKIFF, Lori, A .... 304-929-5472 489 C
lmidkiff@newriver.edu
MIDKIFF, Michael .... 831-646-3073.. 52 F
mmidkiff@mpc.edu
MIDKIFF, Robert .... 570-577-1561 379 F
robert.midkiff@bucknell.edu
MIDKIFF, Scott, F .... 540-231-4227 477 A
midkiff@vt.edu
MIDURA, Matthew .... 310-506-4181.. 56 C
matthew.midura@pepperdine.edu
MIDYETTE, Marilyn, W . 757-221-1166 466 C
mwmidyette01@wm.edu
MIEDEMA, Linda, L .... 321-433-7380.. 97 I
miedemal@easternflorida.edu
MIEDZIONOSKI, Paul ... 978-556-3921 215 C
pmiedzionoski@necc.mass.edu
MIELE, Tony .... 480-423-6003.. 13 H
anthony.miele@scottsdalecc.edu
MIELKE, Cindi .... 815-599-3491 138 B
cindi.mielke@highland.edu
MIELKE, John .... 262-595-3226 497 C
mielke@uwp.edu
MIELKE, Larenda .... 214-768-1107 444 E
lmielke@smu.edu
MIELL, Shelley .... 253-864-3390 483 D
smiell@pierce.ctc.edu
MIENE, Peter .... 507-457-5017 241 F
pmiene@winona.edu
MIENIE, Edward .... 678-717-3410 126 A
edward.mienie@ung.edu
MIERA, Joseph .... 702-895-5116 271 E
joe.miera@unlv.edu
MIERS, Brianne .... 781-239-2637 214 E
bmiers@massbay.edu
MIERS, Michael .... 508-849-3416 205 C
mmiers@annamaria.edu
MIERS, Michael .... 508-849-3326 205 C
mmiers@annamaria.edu
MIERTSCHIN, Charla ..... 507-457-5299 241 F
cmiertschin@winona.edu
MIESO, Rob .... 408-864-8330.. 43 C
miesorob@deanza.edu
MIGEL, April .... 224-293-5876 132 B
amigel@aiuniv.edu
MIGHTY, Hugh, E .... 202-806-5677.. 92 B
hugh.mighty@howard.edu

MIGLER, Jerry .... 701-228-5431 345 F
jerome.migler@dakotacollege.edu
MIGLER, Jerry .... 701-228-5403 346 C
jerry.migler@dakotacollege.edu
MIGLIO, Joseph .... 617-873-0490 207 F
joseph.miglio@cambridgecollege.edu
MIGLIO, Sarah .... 630-752-5153 152 F
sarah.miglio@wheaton.edu
MIGLIORINO, Nicholas . 845-398-4084 315 B
nmiglior@stac.edu
MIGNARDOT, Henry ...... 505-428-1225 288 B
henry.mignardot@sfcc.edu
MIGUEL, Francine .... 225-743-8500 188 B
mmiguel@rpcc.edu
MIGUEL, George .... 520-383-8401.. 16 D
gmiguel@tocc.edu
MIGUEL, Joann .... 520-383-8401.. 16 D
jmiguel@tocc.edu
MIGUEL, Rafael .... 770-220-7930 118 B
rmiguel@gcuniv.edu
MIGYANKO,
Stephanie, M .... 724-439-4900 388 F
smigyanko@laurel.edu
MIHAL, Deborah, F .... 843-953-1431 408 E
mihaldf@cofc.edu
MIHAL, Matt .... 570-674-6336 390 G
mmihal@misericordia.edu
MIHAL, Roxanne .... 617-984-1695 218 B
rmihal@quincycollege.edu
MIHAL, Ruthie .... 704-609-1542 327 H
ruthie.mihal@carolinascollege.edu
MIHALIC, Angela .... 214-648-2168 457 B
angela.mihalic@utsouthwestern.edu
MIHALKO, Taras .... 570-674-6246 390 G
tmihalko@misericordia.edu
MIHALY, Christine .... 734-973-3477 232 B
cmihaly@wccnet.edu
MIHALYOV, David .... 585-395-2577 318 B
dmihalyo@brockport.edu
MIHELICH, John .... 701-777-7589 345 C
john.mihelich@und.edu
MIHEVC, Jake .... 315-792-5653 307 D
jmihevc@mvcc.edu
MIHLON, Mildred, A ..... 201-761-6023 282 I
mmihlon@saintpeters.edu
MIHM-HEROLD,
Wendy, A .... 563-562-3263 168 E
mihm-heroldw@nicc.edu
MIHOPULOS, Sheryl, L . 516-877-3365 289 C
mihopulos@adelphi.edu
MIKE, James .... 717-477-1151 395 E
jhmike@ship.edu
MIKE, Nena .... 691-370-3191 505 B
nenam@comfsm.fm
MIKELL, Chaundra, J .... 803-536-8597 412 C
cmikell1@scsu.edu
MIKEMAN, Cindy .... 405-736-0315 369 I
cmikeman@rose.edu
MIKESELL, Brian .... 413-528-7274 205 F
bmikesell@simons-rock.edu
MIKHAIL, Michael, B .... 312-996-2671 151 B
mmikhail@uic.edu
MIKHAIL, Mona .... 626-812-3013.. 26 H
mmikhail@apu.edu
MIKHAIL, Peter .... 408-727-1060.. 45 J
MIKHALEVSKY, Nina ..... 540-654-1655 472 I
nmik@umw.edu
MIKLUSAK, Courtney .... 619-239-0391.. 34 F
cmiklusak@cwsl.edu
MIKNAVICH, Marie .... 315-792-5467 307 D
mmiknavich@mvcc.edu
MIKOS, Shari .... 312-329-6651.. 36 F
smikos@tcsedsystem.edu
MIKOTA, Michael .... 803-778-6640 407 C
mikotagm@cctech.edu
MIKSA, Anthony, R .... 423-585-6770 426 C
tony.miksa@ws.edu
MIKSCH, Joseph, T .... 412-624-4356 401 B
jmiksch@pitt.edu
MIKTARIAN, Christine .. 559-243-7182.. 66 C
christine.miktarian@scccd.edu
MIKUS, Robert, L .... 717-867-6234 388 H
mikus@lvc.edu
MILAM, B. Hofler .... 336-758-3121 344 D
bhm@wfu.edu
MILAM, Dale .... 509-527-2608 485 H
dale.milam@wallawalla.edu
MILAM, Elizabeth .... 864-656-3431 408 A
milamm@clemson.edu
MILAM, Jennifer .... 410-386-8417 197 G
jmilam@carrollcc.edu
MILAM, John .... 540-868-7249 474 J
jmilam@lfcc.edu
MILAM, Kristin .... 859-233-8111 184 G
kmilam@transy.edu
MILAM, Linda .... 918-781-7275 365 F
milam@bacone.edu
MILAM, Rebecca .... 865-694-6560 425 F
bmilam@pstcc.edu
MILAN, Jordan .... 715-394-8213 498 B
jmilan@uwsuper.edu
MILANI, Andrea .... 513-569-1555 350 K
andrea.milani@cincinnatistate.edu
MILANI, Rachel .... 218-262-7258 238 C
rachelmilani@hibbing.edu
MILANICH, Timothy, R . 216-368-4306 349 F
timothy.milanich@case.edu
MILANO, Angela .... 916-484-8050.. 50 F
milanoa@arc.losrios.edu
MILASINOVIC, Milan ..... 216-221-8584 357 F
mmilasinovic@vmcad.edu
MILASINOVIC, Milan .... 802-225-3200 462 I
MILASZEWSKI, Bruncha 775-824-3819 271 D
bmilaszewski@tmcc.edu
MILAVETZ, Barry .... 701-777-4278 345 C
barry.milavetz@und.edu
MILAZZO, Theresa .... 404-727-7404 117 F
theresa.milazzo@emory.edu
MILBERG, Craig .... 503-370-6561 378 B
cmilberg@willamette.edu
MILBERG, William .... 212-229-5901 308 C
milbergw@newschool.edu
MILBOURNE, John, M .. 321-674-7160.. 99 B
jmilbour@fit.edu
MILBOURNE, Lauren ..... 805-922-6966.. 24 J
lauren.milbourne@hancockcollege.edu
MILBRETT, Juanita .... 507-389-5860 239 C
juanita.milbrett@mnsu.edu
MILBURN, John .... 661-362-3245.. 38 H
john.milburn@canyons.edu
MILBURN, Trudy .... 914-251-6507 319 E
trudy.milburn@purchase.edu
MILBURN DOAN,
Natalie .... 740-368-2000 359 N
MILBY, John .... 864-294-2111 410 A
john.milby@furman.edu
MILBY, Kevin, S .... 859-238-5534 179 F
kevin.milby@centre.edu
MILBY, Megan, H .... 859-238-5516 179 F
megan.milby@centre.edu
MILDENHALL, Joseph ... 602-639-7500.. 12 J
MILDER, Kevin, J .... 719-549-3195.. 81 K
kevin.milder@pueblocc.edu
MILEHAM, Trisha .... 219-464-5099 162 A
trisha.mileham@valpo.edu
MILEK, Joseph .... 814-863-2521 392 B
jmm9228@psu.edu
MILEM, Jeffrey .... 805-893-3917.. 70 A
jmilem@education.ucsb.edu
MILEM, Jill .... 936-468-2401 445 F
jmilem@sfasu.edu
MILENDER, Stephanie ... 603-271-6484 273 B
smilender@ccsnh.edu
MILES, Arletha .... 914-773-3856 311 E
lmiles@pace.edu
MILES, Belinda, S .... 914-606-6707 325 C
belinda.miles@sunywcc.edu
MILES, Brad .... 806-291-3750 457 J
milesb@wbu.edu
MILES, Brian .... 727-341-3246 106 E
miles.brian@spcollege.edu
MILES, Byron .... 208-535-5387 130 C
byron.miles@cei.edu
MILES, Catherine .... 225-771-6231 190 H
catherine_miles@sus.edu
MILES, Cindy .... 619-644-7569.. 44 G
cindy.miles@gcccd.edu
MILES, Daniel .... 740-283-6777 353 B
dmiles@franciscan.edu
MILES, David .... 802-225-3240 462 I
david.miles@neci.edu
MILES, David, A .... 201-692-2227 277 K
dmiles@fdu.edu
MILES, Deborah .... 912-279-5750 116 G
dmiles@ccga.edu
MILES, Deidra .... 978-934-4807 211 G
deidra_miles@uml.edu
MILES, Donald .... 814-472-3029 398 B
dmiles@francis.edu
MILES, Elizabeth .... 503-253-3443 374 H
elizabeth.miles@ocom.edu
MILES, Jenifer .... 512-505-3040 438 E
jpmiles@htu.edu
MILES, Jennifer .... 662-329-7129 248 A
jmmiles@muw.edu
MILES, Jessica .... 217-443-8769 135 H
jmiles@dacc.edu
MILES, John, D .... 864-597-4363 414 H
milesjd@wofford.edu
MILES, Jonathan .... 256-215-4251.... 1 G
jmiles@cacc.edu
MILES, Kim .... 941-377-4880 103 C
kmiles@meridian.edu
MILES, Leon .... 319-471-6260 415 D
lmiles@ilt.edu
MILES, Lloyd .... 301-985-7237 203 B
lloyd.miles@umuc.edu
MILES, Martin .... 757-727-5635 468 B
martin.miles@hamptonu.edu
MILES, Mary, E .... 502-852-6688 185 C
maryelizabeth.miles@louisville.edu
MILES, Mary, E .... 248-942-3331 229 A
memiles@oaklandcc.edu
MILES, Michelle .... 304-345-2820 491 E
MILES, Richard .... 513-721-7944 353 F
rmiles@gbs.edu
MILES, Sandra .... 904-818-6238.. 98 E
smiles@flagler.edu
MILES, Sarah, L .... 508-831-4180 220 E
smiles@wpi.edu
MILES, Stephannie .... 704-461-6873 327 A
stephanniemiles@bac.edu
MILES, Thomas .... 773-702-9495 150 J
tmiles@law.uchicago.edu
MILES, Tom .... 478-445-1473 118 C
tom.miles@gcsu.edu
MILES, Tonya .... 202-885-8601.. 93 E
tmiles@wesleyseminary.edu
MILES, Vickie .... 334-670-3732.... 7 C
vmiles@troy.edu
MILESKI, James .... 413-545-9625 211 D
jmileski@oit.umass.edu
MILEWICZ, Mark .... 910-521-6630 343 B
mark.milewicz@uncp.edu
MILEY, Melinda .... 843-953-5426 408 E
mileym@cofc.edu
MILEY, Tamara .... 812-749-1271 159 C
tmiley@oak.edu
MILFORD, Dorie .... 540-373-2200 466 H
dmilford@evcc.edu
MILI, Fatma .... 704-687-8622 342 E
fmili@uncc.edu
MILICI, JR., Roger, A ... 212-636-6545 300 E
milici@fordham.edu
MILIONI, Barbara .... 417-268-6008 250 G
bmilioni@gobbc.edu
MILIONI, Emily .... 417-268-6068 250 G
emilioni@gobbc.edu
MILIONI, Mark, L .... 417-268-6008 250 G
mmilioni@gobbc.edu
MILIONIS, Daren .... 503-375-7012 373 A
dmilionis@corban.edu
MILIOTIS, David .... 507-457-1421 243 B
dmilioti@smumn.edu
MILJEVICH, Greg .... 715-365-4486 500 D
gmiljevich@nicoletcollege.edu
MILKOVICH, Anne .... 920-424-4480 497 B
milkovich@uwosh.edu
MILKOVICH, Patrice ...... 619-575-6176.. 65 F
pmilkovich@swccd.edu
MILKOWSKI, Rose .... 312-629-6182 148 I
rmilkowski@saic.edu
MILKOWSKI, Tracy .... 920-686-6176 496 A
tracy.milkowski@sl.edu
MILLAGE, Mark .... 605-256-7327 416 J
MILLAN, Iris .... 773-481-8765 134 G
imillan3@ccc.edu
MILLAR, Janet .... 661-654-3366.. 30 E
jmillar@csub.edu
MILLAR, Jeremy .... 937-255-6565 503 A
jeremy.millar@afit.edu
MILLARD, Bryan .... 805-546-3205.. 41 A
bryan_millard@cuesta.edu
MILLARD, Christina ...... 801-626-6566 461 B
cmillard@weber.edu
MILLARD, Cristi .... 801-957-4145 461 D
cristi.millard@slcc.edu
MILLARD, Jill .... 704-290-5887 337 I
jmillard@spcc.edu
MILLARD, Jim .... 252-638-7266 333 H
millardj@cravencc.edu
MILLARD, Kent .... 937-529-2201 362 A
kmillard@united.edu
MILLARD, Rachel .... 316-295-5719 173 D
millard@friends.edu
MILLARD, Robert, B ..... 617-253-6700 215 G
MILLARD, Sandy .... 919-209-2011 335 F
sbmillard@johnstoncc.edu
MILLARD, Stacey .... 313-228-7367 296 F
smillard@colgate.edu
MILLAS, Nikoletta .... 610-896-1032 385 L
nmillas@haverford.edu
MILLEN, Jonathan .... 207-283-0171 196 G
MILLEN, Michelle, L ..... 972-548-6677 433 M
mmillen@collin.edu
MILLENBINE, Donnie .... 618-437-5321 147 A
millenbined@rlc.edu
MILLENDER, Angelia ..... 651-779-3368 237 G
angelia.millender@century.edu
MILLER, A.T .... 989-774-3700 222 C
mille4at@cmich.edu
MILLER, Adam .... 509-527-5411 486 H
MILLER, Al .... 251-442-2357.... 8 C
amiller@umobile.edu
MILLER, Alexandria .... 573-876-7106 260 F
almiller@stephens.edu
MILLER, Allen .... 803-777-2930 413 C
pamiller@sc.edu
MILLER, Allyson .... 214-333-2212 434 I
allysonm@dbu.edu
MILLER, Alyce .... 818-710-4332.. 49 C
millerae@piercecollege.edu
MILLER, Amber, D .... 213-740-2531.. 72 B
dean@dornsife.usc.edu
MILLER, Amy .... 616-732-1157 223 B
amy.miller@davenport.edu
MILLER, Amy .... 931-372-3634 426 E
almiller@tntech.edu
MILLER, Andrea .... 940-565-2095 454 A
andrea.miller@unt.edu
MILLER, Andrew, M ...... 269-337-7542 225 D
andrew.miller@kzoo.edu
MILLER, Angela .... 402-878-2380 267 E
angela.miller@littlepriest.edu
MILLER, Angela .... 502-456-6771 184 E
anmiller@sullivan.edu
MILLER, Angela .... 601-718-5900.. 92 G
MILLER, Angela, M .... 608-342-1555 497 D
millerang@uwplatt.edu
MILLER, Angie .... 970-675-3235.. 78 G
angela.miller@cncc.edu
MILLER, Ann .... 440-826-3308 348 E
amiller@bw.edu
MILLER, Anna .... 812-888-6965 162 C
amiller@vinu.edu
MILLER, Anthony .... 763-424-0822 239 G
amiller@nhcc.edu
MILLER, Anthony .... 540-545-7257 471 E
amiller@su.edu
MILLER, Ashley .... 253-272-1126 482 C
amiller@ncad.edu
MILLER, Ashley, C .... 478-757-5212 126 H
amiller@wesleyancollege.edu
MILLER, Ave .... 770-962-7580 120 E
amiller@gwinnetttech.edu
MILLER, B.J .... 202-685-2906 503 I
bj.miller.civ@ndu.edu
MILLER, Baruch .... 718-269-4080 292 G
MILLER, Becky .... 913-360-7410 171 D
beckymiller@benedictine.edu
MILLER, Bert .... 580-559-5760 366 C
bmiller@ecok.edu
MILLER, Bethany .... 562-903-4886.. 27 C
bethany.miller@biola.edu
MILLER, Betsy .... 575-538-6118 289 B
millerb@wnmu.edu
MILLER, Bill .... 830-372-8120 449 B
bmiller@tlu.edu
MILLER, Bo .... 601-968-8777 245 C
bmiller@belhaven.edu
MILLER, Bob .... 610-526-7878 379 E
rmiller03@brynmawr.edu
MILLER, Boise .... 570-484-2255 395 B
bmiller1@lockhaven.edu
MILLER, Brett .... 304-473-8461 491 H
miller_bt@wvwc.edu
MILLER, Brian .... 501-420-1329.. 17 B
brian.miller@arkansasbaptist.edu
MILLER, Brian .... 616-732-1195 223 B
bmiller@davenport.edu
MILLER, Brian .... 414-277-6947 494 G
MILLER, Brian .... 408-855-5247.. 74 D
brian.miller@missioncollege.edu
MILLER, Brian .... 315-781-3574 302 A
bmiller@hws.edu
MILLER, Brian .... 252-493-7421 336 H
bmiller@email.pittcc.edu
MILLER, Brian, E .... 219-989-2994 159 G
mill1817@pnw.edu
MILLER, Bridget .... 718-862-7597 305 H
bmiller02@manhattan.edu

MILLER, Caitlin .... 450-620-2122 176 G caitlinm@prattcc.edu
MILLER, Carey .... 307-754-6114 502 G carey.miller@nwc.edu
MILLER, Carey .... 412-365-1552 381 C cmiller8@chatham.edu
MILLER, Carolann .... 631-656-2134 300 D carolann.miller@ftc.edu
MILLER, Caroline, B ..... 513-556-3379 362 D caroline.miller@uc.edu
MILLER, Cary Beth ...... 615-277-7413 428 F cmiller@watkins.edu
MILLER, Cary Beth .... 615-277-7408 428 F cmiller@watkins.edu
MILLER, Catherine .... 203-857-3342.. 86 D cmiller@norwalk.edu
MILLER, Chad .... 812-488-2775 161 A cm121@evansville.edu
MILLER, Chad, N .... 651-286-7474 244 D cnmiller@unwsp.edu
MILLER, Chana .... 908-354-6057 285 F
MILLER, Chandra .... 580-559-5262 366 C chalmil@ecok.edu
MILLER, Chanti .... 612-359-6491 233 K millerch@augsburg.edu
MILLER, Charles .... 337-521-8990 188 C charles.miller@solacc.edu
MILLER, Cheryl .... 503-552-1510 374 E cmiller@nunm.edu
MILLER, Cheryl, L .... 860-439-2085.. 86 H cheryl.miller@conncoll.edu
MILLER, Chris .... 623-845-3841.. 13 C c.miller@gccaz.edu
MILLER, Chris .... 606-783-2855 183 F c.miller@moreheadstate.edu
MILLER, Chris .... 847-317-7036 150 H cmiller@tiu.edu
MILLER, Chris .... 760-744-1150.. 55 I cmiller@palomar.edu
MILLER, Chris, E .... 570-326-3761 393 G cmiller@pct.edu
MILLER, Christie .... 931-540-2521 424 G cmiller26@columbiastate.edu
MILLER, Christina .... 719-587-7506.. 76 F crmiller@adams.edu
MILLER, Christine, M ... 916-278-6331.. 32 E millercm@csus.edu
MILLER, Cindy .... 314-838-8858 261 G cmiller@ugst.edu
MILLER, Clarence (Hank) .... 845-687-5065 323 E millerh@sunyulster.edu
MILLER, Clinton .... 901-251-7100.. 92 G
MILLER, Cora .... 508-270-4103 214 E cmiller@massbay.edu
MILLER, Craig .... 304-260-4380 488 J rmiller@blueridgectc.edu
MILLER, Curt .... 336-838-6142 339 B cbmiller932@wilkescc.edu
MILLER, Dale .... 518-381-1280 315 G millerdj@sunysccc.edu
MILLER, Daniel, P .... 570-321-4139 389 E millerda@lycoming.edu
MILLER, Darlene .... 973-877-3101 277 I dmiller@essex.edu
MILLER, David .... 205-226-4723.... 5 A wdmiller@bsc.edu
MILLER, David .... 623-845-3707.. 13 C david.miller@gccaz.edu
MILLER, David .... 316-978-5821 178 A david.miller@wichita.edu
MILLER, David .... 606-546-1291 184 H dkmiller@unionky.edu
MILLER, David .... 312-362-8720 135 I miller@cdm.depaul.edu
MILLER, David .... 605-256-5016 416 J david.miller@dsu.edu
MILLER, David, J .... 715-836-3871 496 D milleda@uwec.edu
MILLER, David, L .... 865-974-9080 427 F davidmiller@tennessee.edu
MILLER, Dawn .... 612-330-1216 233 K millerd1@augsburg.edu
MILLER, Deb .... 904-620-1416 110 A deb.miller@unf.edu
MILLER, Debbie .... 262-564-3220 499 F millerd@gtc.edu
MILLER, Deborah, L ...... 419-772-2464 358 H d-miller@onu.edu
MILLER, Debra .... 815-753-1375 145 C dmiller20@niu.edu
MILLER, Debra .... 845-687-5075 323 E millerde@sunyulster.edu
MILLER, Diane .... 419-530-2211 363 E diane.miller@utoledo.edu
MILLER, Diane .... 419-530-5529 363 E diane.miller@utoledo.edu
MILLER, Dianna .... 956-721-5232 439 C dmiller@laredo.edu
MILLER, Dion .... 718-482-5741 294 F dmiller@lagcc.cuny.edu
MILLER, Don .... 314-514-3103 146 E don.miller@principia.edu
MILLER, Don .... 510-748-2301.. 56 F ddmiller@peralta.edu
MILLER, Don, M .... 336-322-2154 336 G don.miller@piedmontcc.edu
MILLER, Donna .... 502-213-4258 181 F donnar.miller@kctcs.edu
MILLER, Doug .... 417-626-1234 257 F miller.doug@occ.edu
MILLER, Doug .... 713-348-6770 442 K doug.miller@rice.edu
MILLER, Drew .... 936-294-1720 450 C adm007@shsu.edu
MILLER, E. John .... 701-231-7933 345 G ej.miller@ndsu.edu
MILLER, Elizabeth .... 562-860-2451.. 35 M emiller@cerritos.edu
MILLER, Elizabeth .... 920-403-3117 495 I elizabeth.miller@snc.edu
MILLER, Elizabeth, K ..... 651-638-6215 234 C e-miller@bethel.edu
MILLER, Ellen .... 317-791-5932 161 B emiller@uindy.edu
MILLER, Emily, A .... 606-474-3212 180 G emilyamiller@kcu.edu
MILLER, Eric .... 724-847-6634 384 G emiller@geneva.edu
MILLER, Fayneese, S .... 651-523-2202 236 A president@hamline.edu
MILLER, Frank .... 314-286-3390 258 E fdmiller@ranken.edu
MILLER, Fredrick, M ...... 864-597-4000 414 H
MILLER, Gary, L .... 920-465-2207 496 E millerg@uwgb.edu
MILLER, Gary Alan .... 919-962-6507 342 D garyalanmiller@unc.edu
MILLER, III, George, E . 757-823-8015 469 F gemiller@nsu.edu
MILLER, Gina .... 412-536-1085 387 B gina.miller@laroche.edu
MILLER, Glen .... 503-399-6520 372 C glen.miller@chemeketa.edu
MILLER, Glenn .... 816-268-5400 257 C gamiller@mmsmidwest.com
MILLER, Glynis .... 512-223-7850 431 A glynis.miller@austincc.edu
MILLER, Grace .... 765-998-4734 160 F grace_miller2@taylor.edu
MILLER, Grant, T .... 208-467-8059 131 D gtmiller@nnu.edu
MILLER, Gregory, J .... 330-471-8119 355 L gmiller@malone.edu
MILLER, Gregory, R ...... 206-543-0350 485 F gmiller@uw.edu
MILLER, Gretchen .... 260-665-4312 160 H millerg@trine.edu
MILLER, Gretchen .... 414-229-3067 497 A gemiller@uwm.edu
MILLER, JR., H. Samuel .... 828-227-7147 344 A sammiller@wcu.edu
MILLER, Heather .... 662-846-4311 245 H hmiller@deltastate.edu
MILLER, Heather, C ...... 704-233-8632 344 G h.miller@wingate.edu
MILLER, Holly .... 321-674-8871.. 99 B hmiller@fit.edu
MILLER, J. Scott .... 801-422-2779 458 H scott_miller@byu.edu
MILLER, Jack .... 619-574-6909.. 54 K jmiller@pacificcollege.edu
MILLER, Jackson .... 503-883-2308 373 H
MILLER, Jaime, M .... 708-709-3513 146 D jmmiller@prairiestate.edu
MILLER, James .... 630-637-5500 144 H jlmiller@noctrl.edu
MILLER, James .... 435-652-7625 460 G miller_j@dixie.edu
MILLER, James, A .... 256-824-2846.... 8 B james.miller@uah.edu
MILLER, James, D .... 740-264-5591 352 H jdmiller@egcc.edu
MILLER, Jan .... 205-652-3421.... 9 A jmiller@uwa.edu
MILLER, Jan .... 205-652-3675.... 9 A jmiller@uwa.edu
MILLER, Jane-Ellen .... 240-567-9195 200 C janeellen.miller@montgomerycollege.edu
MILLER, Jean M, K .... 309-438-8322 139 E jmmill5@ilstu.edu
MILLER, Jeanette .... 206-934-3727 483 J jeanette.miller@seattlecolleges.edu
MILLER, Jeff .... 314-529-9353 254 H jeffmiller@maryville.edu
MILLER, Jeff .... 320-222-5204 240 E
MILLER, Jeffrey, A .... 412-396-5081 383 C millerjeff@duq.edu
MILLER, Jennifer .... 323-343-3103.. 32 A jennifer.miller@calstatela.edu
MILLER, Jeremy .... 802-485-2480 463 A jmille16@norwich.edu
MILLER, Jeremy .... 740-857-1311 360 I jmiller@rosedale.edu
MILLER, Jerry .... 707-524-1506.. 62 F jmiller@santarosa.edu
MILLER, Jess .... 541-440-4698 377 C jess.miller@umpqua.edu
MILLER, Jessca, T .... 412-362-8500 396 G
MILLER, Jim .... 724-503-1001 402 E jbmiller@washjeff.edu
MILLER, Jo Ann .... 770-426-2819 121 C joann.miller@life.edu
MILLER, Joannie .... 541-888-7298 376 F joannie.miller@socc.edu
MILLER, John .... 701-774-4231 346 F john.s.miller@willistonstate.edu
MILLER, John .... 256-840-4195.... 3 F john.miller@snead.edu
MILLER, John .... 503-352-2215 375 G jmiller@pacificu.edu
MILLER, John .... 585-582-8212 299 A johnmiller@elim.edu
MILLER, John .... 802-831-1334 463 G jmiller@vermontlaw.edu
MILLER, John .... 803-705-4788 407 A john.miller@benedict.edu
MILLER, Joise .... 303-797-5813.. 76 I josie.mills@arapahoe.edu
MILLER, Jon .... 630-829-6515 132 E jmiller@ben.edu
MILLER, Jonathan .... 413-597-2502 220 C jm30@williams.edu
MILLER, Jonathan .... 989-686-9472 223 G jonathanmiller3@delta.edu
MILLER, Joseph .... 361-825-5967 447 C joseph.miller@tamucc.edu
MILLER, Joseph, C .... 706-880-8253 121 A jcmiller@lagrange.edu
MILLER, Joseph, R .... 619-201-8955.. 65 A joe.miller@socalsem.edu
MILLER, Joshua .... 205-665-6245.... 8 D millerjd@montevallo.edu
MILLER, Julie, H .... 313-577-2034 232 I julie.h.miller@wayne.edu
MILLER, Julie, L .... 317-940-9714 153 F jlmille5@butler.edu
MILLER, June, B .... 301-447-5188 200 E jmiller@msmary.edu
MILLER, K, C .... 480-994-9244.. 16 B kc@swiha.edu
MILLER, Karen .... 802-443-5275 462 H karenm@middlebury.edu
MILLER, Karen .... 507-223-7252 239 E karen.miller@mnwest.edu
MILLER, Karen .... 270-824-8680 181 G karen.miller@kctcs.edu
MILLER, Karen .... 216-987-3471 351 G karen.miller@tri-c.edu
MILLER, Karen .... 757-822-1504 476 B kmiller@tcc.edu
MILLER, Karen, A .... 770-216-2960 120 H kam@ict.edu
MILLER, Karissa .... 941-359-7970 105 K karissa@ringling.edu
MILLER, Karla .... 256-372-4871.... 1 A karla.miller@aamu.edu
MILLER, Kate .... 307-766-4286 502 H kate.miller@uwyo.edu
MILLER, Kathleen .... 239-590-7600 108 K kmiller@fgcu.edu
MILLER, SSJ, Kathryn ... 215-248-7167 381 D kmiller@chc.edu
MILLER, Katie .... 252-335-0821 333 G kathryn_miller@albemarle.edu
MILLER, Kausha .... 859-246-6417 180 K kausha.miller@kctcs.edu
MILLER, Keila .... 606-487-3287 181 C keila.miller@kctcs.edu
MILLER, Keiona .... 601-979-2914 246 E keiona.miller@jsums.edu
MILLER, Keith .... 864-250-8175 410 B keith.miller@gvltec.edu
MILLER, Kelly .... 217-581-2223 136 E kpmiller@eiu.edu
MILLER, Kelly, M .... 317-788-3437 161 B kmiller@uindy.edu
MILLER, Kelsey .... 410-778-7745 204 D kmiller8@washcoll.edu
MILLER, Ken .... 407-646-2999 105 M kmiller@rollins.edu
MILLER, Kenneth .... 740-857-1311 360 I kmiller@rosedale.edu
MILLER, Kevin .... 847-866-3920 137 E kevin.miller@garrett.edu
MILLER, Kevin, D .... 973-408-3109 277 C theoadm@drew.edu
MILLER, Kevin, J .... 716-878-5601 318 C millerkj@buffalostate.edu
MILLER, Kevyn .... 480-517-8076.. 13 G kevyn.miller@riosalado.edu
MILLER, Kimela .... 575-835-5888 286 I kimela.miller@nmt.edu
MILLER, Kris .... 615-966-5722 421 D kris.miller@lipscomb.edu
MILLER, Kristen .... 603-342-3002 273 D kmiller@ccsnh.edu
MILLER, Kristine .... 435-797-3646 460 H kristine.miller@usu.edu
MILLER, Kyren .... 701-224-2450 346 B kyren.miller@bismarckstate.edu
MILLER, LaKeith .... 251-405-7295.... 1 E kmiller@bishop.edu
MILLER, Larry .... 410-706-7776 202 D larry.miller@umaryland.edu
MILLER, Larry .... 864-250-8058 410 B larry.miller@gvltec.edu
MILLER, Laura, M .... 717-796-1800 390 E lmiller@messiah.edu
MILLER, Lauren .... 312-935-6026 147 D lmiller@robertmorris.edu
MILLER, Leilani, M .... 408-554-4427.. 62 D lmiller@scu.edu
MILLER, Linda, J .... 262-691-5526 500 H lmiller@wctc.edu
MILLER, Lindsay .... 937-775-3207 364 I lindsay.miller@wright.edu
MILLER, Lisa .... 563-244-7002 165 C lmiller@eicc.edu
MILLER, Lisa .... 708-210-5767 149 B lmiller@ssc.edu
MILLER, Lisa .... 561-237-7000 102 V lmiller@lynn.edu
MILLER, Lisa .... 620-450-2185 176 G lisam@prattcc.edu
MILLER, Lisa .... 516-323-3046 307 F lmiller@molloy.edu
MILLER, Lor, M .... 563-562-3263 168 E millerd1533@nicc.edu
MILLER, Lori .... 215-702-4335 380 D lmiller@cairn.edu
MILLER, Mandrake .... 904-470-8216.. 97 L m.miller@ewc.edu
MILLER, Marc .... 870-230-5377.. 19 E millermd@hsu.edu
MILLER, Marc, L .... 520-621-1498.. 16 G marc.miller@law.arizona.edu
MILLER, Marcia, K .... 316-284-5315 171 F mmiller@bethelks.edu
MILLER, Margaret, M .... 609-258-5813 280 E mmmiller@princeton.edu
MILLER, Mark .... 417-447-2655 257 G millerm@otc.edu
MILLER, Mark .... 620-862-5252 171 B registrar@barclaycollege.edu
MILLER, Mark .... 318-869-5117 186 B mmiller@centenary.edu
MILLER, Mark .... 740-376-4811 356 A mark.miller@marietta.edu
MILLER, Martin, J .... 724-287-8711 380 A martin.miller@bc3.edu
MILLER, Matt .... 989-386-6600 227 F mmiller@midmich.edu
MILLER, Matthew .... 903-875-7422 440 G matt.miller@navarrocollege.edu
MILLER, Megan .... 603-526-3409 272 H megan.miller@colby-sawyer.edu
MILLER, Megan, M .... 678-542-7537 213 C mmiller@salemstate.edu

MILLS, Joe .... 304-336-5189 490 F
jmills@westliberty.edu
MILLS, John .... 606-368-6121 178 D
johnmills@alc.edu
MILLS, John .... 814-886-6411 391 B
jmills@mtaloy.edu
MILLS, Juline .... 413-572-8691 213 D
jmills@westfield.ma.edu
MILLS, Kelley .... 817-515-5043 445 G
kelley.mills@tccd.edu
MILLS, Kelly .... 863-638-7254 113 A
kelly.mills@warner.edu
MILLS, Kevin .... 209-932-3014.. 70 E
kmills@pacific.edu
MILLS, Kevin .... 828-398-7200 332 B
kevinsmills@abtech.edu
MILLS, Laura .... 912-344-3073 119 C
lmills@georgiasouthern.edu
MILLS, Leslie .... 406-791-5296 265 H
leslie.mills@uprovidence.edu
MILLS, Linda, G .... 212-992-9712 310 B
linda.mills@nyu.edu
MILLS, Mark .... 215-898-1453 400 K
millsme@upenn.edu
MILLS, Martin .... 512-245-2501 450 E
mm79@txstate.edu
MILLS, Marvin, J .... 240-567-5371 200 C
marvin.mills@montgomerycollege.edu
MILLS, Matthew .... 913-253-5060 176 I
matthew.mills@spst.edu
MILLS, Matthew .... 352-588-8200 106 D
matthew.mills@saintleo.edu
MILLS, Melissa .... 763-433-1332 237 C
melissa.mills@anokaramsey.edu
MILLS, Michael .... 940-397-4590 440 F
michael.mills@msutexas.edu
MILLS, Michael .... 240-567-6001 200 C
michael.mills@montgomerycollege.edu
MILLS, Michael .... 918-631-2510 371 E
michael-mills@utulsa.edu
MILLS, Michelle .... 661-654-2263.. 30 E
mmills@csub.edu
MILLS, Pamela .... 718-960-8764 294 A
pamela.mills@lehman.cuny.edu
MILLS, Priscilla, L .... 928-523-3312.. 14 H
priscilla.mills@nau.edu
MILLS, Rebecca .... 802-651-5965 462 B
rmills@champlain.edu
MILLS, Richard, G .... 603-646-0459 273 E
richard.g.mills@dartmouth.edu
MILLS, Shala .... 845-257-3550 317 B
millss@newpaltz.edu
MILLS, Shirley, D .... 803-777-2001 413 C
smills@mailbox.sc.edu
MILLS, Susan .... 951-222-8381.. 58 F
susan.mills@rccd.edu
MILLS, Thomas .... 817-515-1011 445 G
thomas.mills@tccd.edu
MILLS, William, R .... 617-552-8661 207 B
william.mills@bc.edu
MILLS CAMPBELL,
Dawn .... 803-705-4383 407 A
dawn.campbell@benedict.edu
MILLS-DICK, Melissa ...... 413-559-5316 210 A
MILLS-LEMIRE, Denise .. 218-733-7600 238 F
d.mills-lemire@lsc.edu
MILLSAP, Pamela .... 409-984-6211 450 B
millsappa@lamarpa.edu
MILLSAPPS, Michael ..... 970-339-6376.. 76 G
michael.millsapps@aims.edu
MILLSAPS, Brooke .... 828-771-3015 344 E
bmillsaps@warren-wilson.edu
MILLUSH, Mary Ann ..... 630-942-2269 135 A
millush@cod.edu
MILLWOOD, Kent .... 864-231-2049 406 G
kmillwood@andersonuniversity.edu
MILNARICH, Sarah .... 361-354-2741 433 C
shmilnarich@coastalbend.edu
MILNE, Arryn .... 410-864-4075 201 F
amilne@stmarys.edu
MILNE, Erin .... 413-662-5049 213 A
erin.milne@mcla.edu
MILNE, Sheila .... 252-399-6326 326 M
smilne@barton.edu
MILNER, Andrea .... 517-265-5161 220 F
amilner@adrian.edu
MILNER, Devika, M ...... 305-284-6858 112 E
dmilner@miami.edu
MILNER, Eric .... 401-341-2218 406 A
eric.milner@salve.edu
MILNER, Jocelyn, L ...... 608-263-5658 496 C
jocelyn.milner@wisc.edu
MILNER, Laura .... 608-785-8095 496 F
lmilner@uwlax.edu
MILNER, Wesley .... 812-488-2686 161 A
wm23@evansville.edu
MILO, Elaine .... 978-542-8031 213 C
elaine.milo@salemstate.edu
MILO, Jennifer .... 760-750-7108.. 33 B
jmilo@csusm.edu
MILON, Ronald, A .... 212-217-3070 299 H
ronald_milon@fitnyc.edu
MILONE-NUZZO, Paula 617-726-8002 216 E
pmilone-nuzzo@mghihp.edu
MILOWSKI, Nicholas, B 718-817-4975 300 E
nmilowski@fordham.edu
MILSO, Lisa .... 978-762-4000 215 B
lmilso@northshore.edu
MILSOM, Penny .... 443-840-5426 198 B
mmilsom@ccbcmd.edu
MILSTEIN, Marc .... 214-648-0757 457 B
marc.milstein@utsouthwestern.edu
MILTENBERGER, Chad .. 509-758-1711 485 G
chad.miltenberger@wwcc.edu
MILTER, Rebecca .... 678-916-2621 114 I
rmilter@johnmarshall.edu
MILTON, Alice .... 205-929-6306.... 2 H
amilton@lawsonstate.edu
MILTON, James .... 704-636-6580 330 A
jmilton@hoodseminary.edu
MILTON, John .... 661-362-2287.. 51 C
jmilton@masters.edu
MILTON, Shawntee .... 760-245-4271.. 73 D
shawntee.milton@vvc.edu
MILTON, Shirlette .... 713-313-7551 449 C
milton_sg@tsu.edu
MILTON, Vikki .... 850-718-2371.. 96 F
miltonv@chipola.edu
MILZ, George .... 713-646-1864 444 B
gmilz@stcl.edu
MIMA, Rebecca .... 330-490-7090 364 B
rmima@walsh.edu
MIMMS, Lee, S .... 817-552-3700 439 B
lmimms@tku.edu
MIMS, Christina .... 254-562-3848 440 G
christina.mims@navarrocollege.edu
MIMS, Dana, M .... 570-577-3171 379 F
dana.mims@bucknell.edu
MIMS, Grace .... 308-865-8265 269 I
mimsga@unk.edu
MIMS, Jane .... 210-784-1000 448 A
jane.mims@tamusa.edu
MIMS, Janet .... 843-863-8004 407 E
jmims@csuniv.edu
MIMS, Lloyd .... 561-803-2400 104 C
lloyd_mims@pba.edu
MIMS, Yolanda, L .... 504-286-5335 190 I
ymims@suno.edu
MIMS-DEVEZIN, Lisa .... 504-286-5064 190 I
lmims@suno.edu
MIN, John .... 949-480-4171.. 64 B
min@soka.edu
MIN, Ki Wook .... 510-639-7879.. 54 G
MIN, Sangki .... 785-628-4540 173 B
s_min2@fhsu.edu
MIN, Sarah .... 323-731-2383.. 55 C
sarahmin@psuca.edu
MINA, Jean .... 847-578-3238 147 I
jean.mina@rosalindfranklin.edu
MINAR, Thomas, J .... 317-738-8010 154 J
president@franklincollege.edu
MINARD, Jeff .... 972-708-7340 435 H
vp-operations@diu.edu
MINARD, Tiffany .... 859-815-7683 181 B
tiffany.minard@kctcs.edu
MINATOYA, Lydia .... 206-934-3712 483 J
lydia.minatoya@seattlecolleges.edu
MINCE, Rosalie .... 410-386-8195 197 G
rmince@carrollcc.edu
MINCER, Amy .... 402-872-2239 268 F
amincer@peru.edu
MINCER, Gretta .... 303-615-0872.. 80 N
mincer@msudenver.edu
MINCH, Kevin .... 660-785-4105 260 J
kminch@truman.edu
MINCHEFF, Daniel .... 920-498-5444 500 F
daniel.mincheff@nwtc.edu
MINCHELLO, Carla .... 508-626-4534 212 D
cminchello@framingham.edu
MINCHIN, John .... 562-988-2278.. 25 R
jminchin@auhs.edu
MINCKS, Kathy .... 907-564-8272.... 9 D
kmincks.akpacprop@gci.net
MINDEN, Courtney .... 781-239-5589 205 E
cminden@babson.edu
MINE, Jodi .... 808-934-2742 129 A
mine@hawaii.edu
MINEHART, Heather ...... 760-252-2411.. 26 I
hminehart@barstow.edu
MINEHART, James .... 419-448-2160 353 H
jminehar@heidelberg.edu
MINELLA, Rosenda .... 505-224-4000 285 J
maranjo9@cnm.edu
MINEO, Steve .... 912-525-5000 123 G
smineo@scad.edu
MINER, Anna, D .... 603-526-3655 272 H
anna.miner@colby-sawyer.edu
MINER, Brenda .... 479-394-7622.. 23 C
bminer@uarichmountain.edu
MINER, Jack .... 614-292-9330 358 I
miner.10@osu.edu
MINER, Jerome .... 309-341-7150 141 A
jminer@knox.edu
MINER, Judy, C .... 650-949-6100.. 43 B
minerjudy@fhda.edu
MINER, Madonne .... 801-626-6006 461 B
madonneminer@weber.edu
MINER, Seth .... 575-646-1879 287 B
miners@nmsu.edu
MINERICK, Adrienne ..... 906-487-2259 227 E
minerick@mtu.edu
MINFORD, Joell .... 412-392-3422 397 A
jminford@pointpark.edu
MING, Amanda .... 248-476-1122 227 C
aming@msp.edu
MING, Sally .... 563-387-1527 167 E
mingsa01@luther.edu
MINGEE, Sheila .... 217-709-0923 141 E
smingee@lakeviewcol.edu
MINGO, Doreen .... 319-226-2049 162 F
doreen.mingo@allencollege.edu
MINGO, Rhonda .... 864-596-9140 409 B
rhonda.mingo@converse.edu
MINGO, Susan .... 207-454-1001 195 B
smingo@wccc.me.edu
MINGO, Tracey .... 912-478-5413 119 C
tmingo@georgiasouthern.edu
MINHAS, Omer, I .... 419-772-2529 358 H
o-minhas@onu.edu
MINI, Susan .... 815-753-0495 145 C
smini@niu.edu
MINICK, Amy .... 773-702-5033 150 E
aminick@ttic.edu
MINICK, Thomas .... 610-790-2862 378 F
thomas.minick@alvernia.edu
MINICOLA, Steven .... 215-573-0251 400 K
minicola@upenn.edu
MINIER, Matt .... 502-897-4205 184 C
mrminier@sbts.edu
MINIER-DELGADO,
Jesenia .... 203-837-8277.. 85 B
minierdelgadoj@wcsu.edu
MININGER, Marcus .... 219-864-2400 159 B
mmininger@midamerica.edu
MINIX, Jeannette .... 865-524-8079 420 E
accounting@huhs.edu
MINK, Randy, L .... 412-397-4901 397 G
mink@rmu.edu
MINK, Rose .... 901-751-8453 422 E
rmink@mabts.edu
MINK, Suzy .... 540-362-6363 468 C
minks@hollins.edu
MINKLER, James .... 360-538-4000 481 E
jim.minkler@ghc.edu
MINKLER, Steven .... 860-343-5706.. 86 A
sminkler@mxcc.edu
MINNEMA, Linnea .... 205-726-2735.... 6 E
lminnema@samford.edu
MINNER, Mandy .... 302-831-1234.. 90 F
aminner@udel.edu
MINNER, Sam .... 505-454-3269 286 H
president_office@nmhu.edu
MINNICH, Chad, A .... 401-456-8395 405 C
cminnich@ric.edu
MINNICH, Peggy .... 513-244-4531 357 A
peggy.minnich@msj.edu
MINNICH, Sharon .... 717-720-4100 393 K
sminnich@passhe.edu
MINNICH, William .... 650-738-4484.. 61 Q
minnichw@smccd.edu
MINNICH SPUHLER,
Donna .... 973-720-3258 284 I
minnichspuhlerd@wpunj.edu
MINNICK, Ann, M .... 651-696-6036 236 H
aminnick@macalester.edu
MINNICK, Charlie .... 858-513-9240.. 26 G
charlie.minnick@ashford.edu
MINNICK, Marc .... 215-885-2360 389 F
mminnick@manor.edu
MINNICK, William, C .... 712-707-7226 168 H
bminnick@nwciowa.edu
MINNIEFIELD,
Angela, L .... 323-563-4897.. 36 D
angelaminniefield@cdrewu.edu
MINNIS, Stephen, D ..... 913-360-7400 171 D
sminnis@benedictine.edu
MINNIS, Tia, A .... 804-524-3283 477 B
tminnis@vsu.edu
MINNIS, William .... 217-581-3526 136 E
wcminnis@eiu.edu
MINNITE, Lorraine .... 856-225-2526 281 G
minnite@camden.rutgers.edu
MINNITI, Lea .... 513-745-3711 365 B
minnitil@xavier.edu
MINOR, Frankie .... 401-874-2899 406 B
frankie@uri.edu
MINOR, James .... 704-290-5429 337 I
jminor@spcc.edu
MINOR, Jessica .... 864-242-5100 407 B
MINOR, Karen .... 770-533-7030 121 B
kminor@laniertech.edu
MINOR, Leslie .... 661-763-7871.. 66 J
lminor@taftcollege.edu
MINOR, Lloyd .... 650-723-2300.. 65 J
lminor@stanford.edu
MINOR, Marlene .... 630-620-2177 145 D
mminor@seminary.edu
MINOR, Scott .... 916-631-8363.. 29 J
MINOR, Tamra .... 518-956-8110 316 D
tminor@albany.edu
MINOR, Tracey .... 601-977-7879 249 C
tminor@tougaloo.edu
MINSON, Patrick .... 516-686-7718 309 F
patrick.minson@nyit.edu
MINTEN, Sam, L .... 615-868-6503 422 G
sam@mtsa.edu
MINTER, Doug, O .... 507-933-7527 235 I
dminter@gustavus.edu
MINTER, Douglas .... 309-268-8100 137 I
doug.minter@heartland.edu
MINTER, Michelle .... 609-258-6110 280 E
mminter@princeton.edu
MINTLE, Theresa .... 312-996-8153 151 B
mintlet@uic.edu
MINTO, James .... 718-270-3128 317 E
james.minto@downstate.edu
MINTO, Robert .... 614-508-7246 354 F
rminto@hondros.edu
MINTON, J. Ernest .... 785-532-6147 174 G
eminton@ksu.edu
MINTON, Jessie .... 541-346-1799 377 D
minton@uoregon.edu
MINTZ, Katrina, H .... 205-726-2896.... 6 E
kmintz@samford.edu
MINTZ, Zev .... 732-370-1560 275 G
MINTZER, Jen .... 610-358-4547 391 D
mintzerj@neumann.edu
MINUS, Molly, E .... 512-448-8581 442 M
mollym@stedwards.edu
MINUS, Monica .... 252-633-1764 333 H
minusm@cravencc.edu
MIOTA, Katie .... 414-229-4445 497 A
miota@uwm.edu
MIRABAL, Gloria .... 787-743-4041 507 D
gmirabal@columbiacentral.edu
MIRABAL, Larry .... 505-424-2316 286 C
lmirabal@iaia.edu
MIRABEL, Jonathan ...... 908-852-1400 276 G
jonathan.mirabel@centenaryuniversity.edu
MIRABI, Shayan .... 832-201-3636 132 B
smirabi@aiuniv.edu
MIRABILE, Kathleen ...... 602-212-0501.. 14 Q
kmirabile@theparalegalinstitute.edu
MIRABILE, Robert .... 508-767-7285 205 D
r.mirabile@assumption.edu
MIRABITO, Michael ...... 570-348-6209 389 G
mirabito@marywood.edu
MIRACLE, Ashley .... 912-201-8000 124 E
amiracle@southuniversity.edu
MIRAFTABI, Ellie .... 323-254-2203.. 41 J
emiraftabi@eaglerockcollege.edu
MIRAMONTEZ, Daniel ... 619-388-7333.. 60 E
dmiramon@sdccd.edu
MIRANDA, Aida, W .... 787-864-2222 509 C
walesca.miranda@guayama.inter.edu
MIRANDA, Alex .... 714-895-8180.. 38 D
amiranda42@gwc.cccd.edu
MIRANDA, Candida ...... 312-567-3134 139 B
miranda@iit.edu

MIRANDA, Edmund (Rick) .... 562-860-2451.. 35 M
ermiranda@cerritos.edu
MIRANDA, Eduardo ...... 860-906-5050.. 85 D
emiranda@capitalcc.edu
MIRANDA, Jakelin .... 786-331-1000 103 G
jmiranda@maufl.edu
MIRANDA, Katherine, M .... 330-325-6483 357 G
kmiranda@neomed.edu
MIRANDA, Kenneth, M . 607-254-1150 297 F
kmm446@cornell.edu
MIRANDA, Mark .... 732-571-3593 279 B
mmiranda@monmouth.edu
MIRANDA, Rick .... 970-491-6614.. 78 M
rick.miranda@colostate.edu
MIRANDA, Rick .... 970-491-6614.. 78 L
rick.miranda@colostate.edu
MIRANDA, Yolanda .... 787-743-3038 511 A
ymiranda@sanjuanbautista.edu
MIRANDO, Nicole .... 212-280-1342 323 H
registrar@utsnyc.edu
MIRECKI, Julie .... 920-693-1193 499 G
julie.mirecki@gotoltc.edu
MIRELES, Rod .... 936-261-1905 446 D
rmireles@pvamu.edu
MIRELES, Selina .... 956-665-7899 455 D
selina.mireles@utrgv.edu
MIRENBERG, Mark .... 718-522-9073 290 C
mmirenberg@asa.edu
MIRIJANIAN, Nara .... 586-498-4124 226 H
mirijanian225@macomb.edu
MIRMIRAN, Amir .... 903-566-7104 456 A
amirmiran@uttyler.edu
MIRMIRANI, Maj .... 386-226-6889.. 98 A
mirmiram@erau.edu
MIRNICS, Karoly .... 402-559-5720 270 A
karoly.mirnics@unmc.edu
MIRR, James .... 925-969-3300.. 46 H
jmirr@jfku.edu
MIRRO, Roberta .... 631-249-3048 321 B
sm711/bncollege@bncollege.com
MIRSHAB, Bahman .... 248-204-3050 226 G
bmirshab@ltu.edu
MIRTSCHINK, Steven .... 770-426-2851 121 C
smirtsch@life.edu
MIRUS, Kevin .... 608-246-6478 499 H
kmirus@madisoncollege.edu
MIRUS, Tarrah, N .... 404-413-2273 119 E
tmirus@gsu.edu
MISAK, David .... 580-774-3275 370 C
david.misak@swosu.edu
MISCHE, Terri .... 320-308-6675 240 H
tamische@stcloudstate.edu
MISCHKE, Carly .... 310-506-6738.. 56 C
carly.mischke@pepperdine.edu
MISCHLER, Jeremy .... 309-467-6394 137 B
jmischler@eureka.edu
MISERENDINO, Peter .... 203-287-3026.. 87 E
paier.admin@snet.net
MISEY, Monica .... 414-425-8300 495 H
mmisey@shsst.edu
MISGEN, Sherry .... 312-899-5216 148 I
smisgen@saic.edu
MISHEK, Mark .... 651-213-4006 236 B
mmishek@hazeldenbettyford.org
MISHLER, Jeremy .... 231-591-2345 223 J
jeremymishler@ferris.edu
MISHLER, Richard .... 814-886-6339 391 B
rmishler@mtaloy.edu
MISHOE, Wilma .... 302-857-6001.. 89 F
MISHOU, Stephanie ...... 207-947-4591 193 C
smishou@bealcollege.edu
MISHRA, Ashu .... 916-375-5505.. 50 I
mishraa@scc.losrios.edu
MISHRA, Sharda, D ...... 615-327-6156 422 A
smishra@mmc.edu
MISHRA, Tara .... 479-788-7002.. 21 H
tara.mishra@uafs.edu
MISIANO, Chris .... 434-592-3144 468 H
cjmisiano@liberty.edu
MISKELL, Anita .... 812-749-1240 159 C
amiskell@oak.edu
MISKO, Ashley .... 716-286-8350 310 D
amisko@niagara.edu
MISKUS, Lynn .... 219-473-4310 153 G
lmiskus@ccsj.edu
MISKY, Allison .... 860-727-2117.. 87 A
amisky@goodwin.edu
MISLEVY, Michele .... 610-921-2381 378 C
mmislevy@albright.edu
MISRA, Christopher, P . 413-545-9339 211 D
chris.misra@umass.edu
MISRA, Kalpana .... 918-631-2547 371 E
kalpana-misra@utulsa.edu
MISRA, Ravi, P .... 414-955-4403 494 C
rmisra@mcw.edu
MISRA, Sukant .... 806-742-3667 451 B
sukant.misra@ttu.edu
MISS, Stephen .... 704-461-6802 327 A
stephenmiss@bac.edu
MISSEL, Thomas .... 716-375-2303 313 F
MISSILDINE, Mark .... 903-223-3153 448 B
mmissildine@tamut.edu
MISSINNE, Amy .... 715-394-8449 498 B
amissin1@uwsuper.edu
MISSURELLI, David, S .. 630-637-5680 144 H
dsmissurelli@noctrl.edu
MISTICK, Barbara, K ..... 717-262-2000 403 F
barbara.mistick@wilson.edu
MISTLER, Brian .... 707-826-3146.. 33 D
bjm728@humboldt.edu
MISTRIC, Amy .... 731-881-7040 428 B
amistric@utm.edu
MISTUR, Mark .... 330-672-2917 354 J
mmistur1@kent.edu
MITCHELL, Alan .... 256-331-5362.... 3 C
mitchell@nwscc.edu
MITCHELL, Andrew, J ... 757-446-5199 466 I
mitcheaj@evms.edu
MITCHELL, Angela .... 540-831-6297 470 C
amitchell90@radford.edu
MITCHELL, Anne, L .... 317-278-9230 156 F
amitch29@iupui.edu
MITCHELL, Anne, M ...... 401-254-3207 405 E
amitchell@rwu.edu
MITCHELL, Annette .... 937-229-4122 362 G
amitchell2@udayton.edu
MITCHELL, Annie, S ...... 864-597-4199 414 H
mitchellas1@wofford.edu
MITCHELL, Arden .... 863-680-4131.. 99 H
amitchell@flsouthern.edu
MITCHELL, Ashley .... 503-517-1819 378 A
amitchell@westernseminary.edu
MITCHELL, Bede .... 912-478-5116 119 C
wbmitch@georgiasouthern.edu
MITCHELL, Betsy .... 626-395-6148.. 29 C
betsy.mitchell@caltech.edu
MITCHELL, Bonnie .... 508-626-4651 212 D
bmitchell@framingham.edu
MITCHELL, Bradley, J ... 937-481-2231 364 E
brad_mitchell@wilmington.edu
MITCHELL, Brenda .... 334-244-3464.... 4 F
bmitche8@aum.edu
MITCHELL, Brenda, S .... 301-546-0858 201 C
bmitchell@pgcc.edu
MITCHELL, Brian .... 323-860-0789.. 50 A
MITCHELL, Bryan .... 404-756-4025 114 G
bmitchell@atlm.edu
MITCHELL, Carl .... 910-678-8373 334 D
mitchelc@faytechcc.edu
MITCHELL, Carlton .... 903-233-3482 439 E
carltonmitchell@letu.edu
MITCHELL, Carrie .... 505-277-1758 288 G
carriem@unm.edu
MITCHELL, Cassandra ... 919-719-8880 340 E
c.mitchell@shawu.edu
MITCHELL, Cathy .... 575-392-4510 286 J
cmitchell@nmjc.edu
MITCHELL, Charles .... 409-882-3367 450 A
charles.mitchell@lsco.edu
MITCHELL, Chase .... 435-283-7340 461 C
chase.mitchell@snow.edu
MITCHELL, Chris .... 501-205-8919.. 18 H
cmitchell@cbc.edu
MITCHELL, Chrisie .... 845-431-8976 298 E
chrisie.mitchell@sunydutchess.edu
MITCHELL, Christopher . 419-251-1596 356 C
christopher.mitchell@mercycollege.edu
MITCHELL, Cindy, J .... 207-859-4000 193 E
cindy.mitchell@colby.edu
MITCHELL, Clayton .... 215-503-7268 400 A
clayton.mitchell@jefferson.edu
MITCHELL, Clifton .... 229-226-1621 125 C
cmitchell@thomasu.edu
MITCHELL, Connie .... 803-754-4100 409 A
MITCHELL, Cordelia ...... 501-374-6305.. 21 A
cordelia.mitchell@shortercollege.edu
MITCHELL, Corinne .... 732-987-2766 278 B
cmitchell@georgian.edu
MITCHELL, Craig .... 206-517-4541 484 C
cmitchell@sieam.edu
MITCHELL, David .... 415-503-6218.. 60 H
dlmitchell@sfcm.edu
MITCHELL, David, B ...... 301-405-5726 202 C
dmitche5@umd.edu
MITCHELL, Dawn .... 318-357-5960 192 C
dawnmitchell@nsula.edu
MITCHELL, Dawn, P ...... 336-734-7207 334 E
dmitchell@forsythtech.edu
MITCHELL, Debbie .... 734-432-5613 227 A
doffman@madonna.edu
MITCHELL, Delmer .... 217-222-8020 146 F
MITCHELL, Dennis .... 480-461-7213.. 13 D
dennis.mitchell@mesacc.edu
MITCHELL, Dennis .... 212-854-7161 297 C
dmitchell@columbia.edu
MITCHELL, Dian .... 478-471-6684 121 F
dian.mitchell@mga.edu
MITCHELL, Donald .... 217-206-6690 151 C
mitchell.donald@uis.edu
MITCHELL, Donna .... 740-245-7303 363 D
mitchell@rio.edu
MITCHELL, III, Earnest, L .... 731-426-7604 420 I
emitchell@lanecollege.edu
MITCHELL, Eleanor .... 717-245-1864 382 F
mitchele@dickinson.edu
MITCHELL, Erica .... 573-288-6469 252 E
emitchell@culver.edu
MITCHELL, Erik, T .... 858-534-2230.. 69 D
MITCHELL, Gary .... 575-763-0535 457 J
mitchellg@wbu.edu
MITCHELL, George .... 843-383-8140 408 D
gmitchell@coker.edu
MITCHELL, Glendon, G . 801-587-3784 460 E
gmitchell@purchasing.utah.edu
MITCHELL, Gloria .... 903-927-3304 458 G
gemitchell@wileyc.edu
MITCHELL, Greg .... 727-376-6911 111 G
greg.mitchell@trinitycollege.edu
MITCHELL, Gregory .... 843-477-2032 410 C
greg.mitchell@hgtc.edu
MITCHELL, Gwendolyn, F .... 803-536-8212 412 C
gmitche3@scsu.edu
MITCHELL, Heather .... 850-201-8580 111 C
mitchelh@tcc.fl.edu
MITCHELL, James, M .... 334-876-9231.... 2 D
jmitchell@wccs.edu
MITCHELL, Jennifer .... 229-732-5946 114 B
jennifermitchell@andrewcollege.edu
MITCHELL, Joan .... 801-274-3280 461 F
jmitchell@wgu.edu
MITCHELL, Joann .... 215-898-6630 400 K
joannm@upenn.edu
MITCHELL, Joanne .... 310-665-6963.. 54 I
jmitchell@otis.edu
MITCHELL, Johnnie .... 501-337-5000.. 18 J
jmitchell@coto.edu
MITCHELL, Juanita .... 870-574-4423.. 21 E
jmitchel@sautech.edu
MITCHELL, Jud .... 870-574-4726.. 21 E
jmitchel@sautech.edu
MITCHELL, Judy .... 815-280-2207 140 B
jmitchel@jjc.edu
MITCHELL, Justin, A ..... 770-720-9130 123 E
jam@reinhardt.edu
MITCHELL, Karen .... 615-230-3505 426 B
karen.mitchell@volstate.edu
MITCHELL, Katharyne .... 831-459-2919.. 70 B
kmitch@ucsc.edu
MITCHELL, Kathy .... 407-823-2889 109 E
kathryn.mitchell@ucf.edu
MITCHELL, Katie .... 765-641-4197 153 B
kmmitchell@anderson.edu
MITCHELL, Keith .... 580-581-2211 365 G
kmitchel@cameron.edu
MITCHELL, Ken, H .... 919-209-2112 335 F
khmitchell@johnstoncc.edu
MITCHELL, Kerrie .... 575-492-2560 286 J
kmitchell@nmjc.edu
MITCHELL, Kerry .... 623-845-3693.. 13 C
kerry.mitchell@gccaz.edu
MITCHELL, Kim .... 502-456-6508 184 E
kmitchell@sullivan.edu
MITCHELL, Kimberly, A . 309-655-2230 148 E
kim.mitchell@osfhealthcare.org
MITCHELL, Lori .... 540-674-3790 475 B
lmitchell@nr.edu
MITCHELL, Marcia .... 413-552-2431 214 D
mmitchell@hcc.edu
MITCHELL, Maria .... 610-372-4721 397 B
mmitchell@racc.edu
MITCHELL, Marionette ... 713-525-3120 454 H
marion@stthom.edu
MITCHELL, Mark .... 540-338-1776 470 A
MITCHELL, Matt .... 573-592-5301 262 E
matt.mitchell@westminster-mo.edu
MITCHELL, Melissa .... 308-432-6221 268 E
mmitchell@csc.edu
MITCHELL, Michael .... 251-460-6172.... 8 F
mmitchell@southalabama.edu
MITCHELL, Michelle ...... 731-352-4239 418 G
mitchellm@bethelu.edu
MITCHELL, Mitch .... 812-288-8878 159 A
mmitchell@mid-america.edu
MITCHELL, Nancy .... 636-584-6617 252 J
nancy.mitchell@eastcentral.edu
MITCHELL, Nancy, L ..... 509-527-5168 486 H
mitchenl@whitman.edu
MITCHELL, Pamela .... 860-512-2605.. 85 G
pmitchell1@manchestercc.edu
MITCHELL, Paula .... 915-831-6375 436 E
pmitche8@epcc.edu
MITCHELL, Peg, P .... 302-356-6810.. 90 I
peg.p.mitchell@wilmu.edu
MITCHELL, Randolph .... 904-470-8150.. 97 L
randolph.mitchell@ewc.edu
MITCHELL, Rashida .... 203-576-4665.. 88 D
ramitche@bridgeport.edu
MITCHELL, Reavis .... 615-329-8610 419 K
rmitchel@fisk.edu
MITCHELL, Remegia, A . 585-685-6237 307 H
rmitchell@monroecc.edu
MITCHELL, JR., Robert . 504-816-4864 186 D
rvmitchell@dillard.edu
MITCHELL, Robin .... 563-288-6103 165 D
rmitchell@eicc.edu
MITCHELL, Roland .... 225-578-2156 188 I
rwmitch@lsu.edu
MITCHELL, Rose .... 973-748-9000 276 A
rose_mitchell@bloomfield.edu
MITCHELL, Scott .... 510-809-1444.. 45 K
MITCHELL, Seandra .... 414-277-6762 494 G
MITCHELL, Sharon, L .... 716-645-2720 316 F
smitch@buffalo.edu
MITCHELL, Sheila .... 731-661-5953 427 C
smitchell@uu.edu
MITCHELL, Steve .... 903-823-3269 446 B
steven.mitchell@texarkanacollege.edu
MITCHELL, Tedd, L .... 806-743-2900 451 C
tedd.mitchell@ttuhsc.edu
MITCHELL, Tedd, L .... 806-742-0012 450 F
MITCHELL, Tedd, L .... 806-742-0012 451 B
tedd.mitchell@ttuhsc.edu
MITCHELL, Tee .... 229-333-5791 126 G
rtmitchell@valdosta.edu
MITCHELL, Thomas .... 814-732-2743 394 F
tmitchell@edinboro.edu
MITCHELL, Thomas, J ... 352-392-5407 109 F
tmitchell@uff.ufl.edu
MITCHELL, Thomas, R .. 956-326-2240 446 F
tmitchell@tamiu.edu
MITCHELL, Todd .... 270-534-3256 182 F
todd.mitchell@kctcs.edu
MITCHELL, Trapper .... 608-342-1183 497 D
mitchellt@uwplatt.edu
MITCHELL, Tucker .... 843-661-1332 409 K
cmitchell@fmarion.edu
MITCHELL, Venita .... 573-592-4235 262 G
venita.mitchell@williamwoods.edu
MITCHELL, Vicki .... 740-588-1386 365 E
vmitchell@zanestate.edu
MITCHELL, Victor .... 860-314-4709.. 86 G
vmitchell@tunxis.edu
MITCHELL, William .... 508-588-9100 214 F
wamitchell@massasoit.mass.edu
MITCHELL, JR., Zane, W .... 812-465-7137 161 E
zwmitchell@usi.edu
MITCHELL-FERRIS, Peggy .... 479-964-0532.. 18 C
pmitchellferris@atu.edu
MITCHELSON, Ron .... 252-328-5419 341 C
mitchelsonr@ecu.edu
MITCHEM, Brandi .... 478-445-2313 116 A
bmitchem@centralgatech.edu
MITCHLER, Allan, M ...... 414-410-4059 492 D
admitchler@stritch.edu
MITCHLEY, Jill .... 570-484-2526 395 B
jmitchle@lockhaven.edu
MITCHUM, M.G .... 843-574-6995 413 B
mg.mitchum@tridenttech.edu
MITEZA, Ilir .... 313-593-5030 231 F
imiteza@umich.edu
MITJANS, Dolores .... 787-882-2065 511 D
compras@unitecpr.net
MITNICK, Eric .... 508-985-1169 211 F
emitnick@umassd.edu
MITSUI, Mark .... 971-722-4365 375 J
mark.mitsui@pcc.edu

MITTELSTAEDT, John ..... 937-229-3349 362 G jmittelstaedt1@udayton.edu
MITTEN, Richard .... 646-312-2076 292 L richard.mitten@baruch.cuny.edu
MITTERNDORFER, Sylvia, M .... 757-221-3595 466 C smmitt@wm.edu
MITTLEIDER, Jan .... 208-732-6201 130 E csitrustees@csi.edu
MITTLEMAN, Michael, H .... 215-780-1280 398 G president@salus.edu
MITTLER, Tiina .... 626-852-8047.. 36 K tmittler@citruscollege.edu
MITTMAN, Paul, A .... 480-858-9100.. 16 A p.mittman@scnm.edu
MITTON, Gregory, S ..... 484-664-3175 391 C gregmitton@muhlenberg.edu
MITTON, Lynda .... 816-960-2008 251 D dean@cityvision.edu
MITTUCH, Maggie, A ..... 253-879-3673 485 E mmittuch@pugetsound.edu
MITZEL, Bobbi .... 307-675-0703 502 F rmitzel@sheridan.edu
MITZEL, Thomas .... 701-483-2326 345 D thomas.mitzel@dickinsonstate.edu
MIX, Catherine .... 937-229-4311 362 G cmix01@udayton.edu
MIX, Christina .... 714-484-7309.. 53 K cmix@cypresscollege.edu
MIX, Julie, L .... 253-535-7101 482 H mixjl@plu.edu
MIX, Kerry .... 409-839-2048 449 G kmix@lit.edu
MIX, Shelley .... 484-365-7499 389 C smix@lincoln.edu
MIXON, Connie .... 630-617-3569 136 G mixonc@elmhurst.edu
MIXON, Daardi .... 507-389-5953 239 C daardi.mixon@mnsu.edu
MIXON, Lonnie .... 407-303-8192.. 94 D lonnie.mixon@ahu.edu
MIXON, Melissa .... 206-934-7791 483 J melissa.mixon@seattlecolleges.edu
MIXSON, Anamarie .... 850-474-2200 110 E amixson@uwf.edu
MIXSON, Frank .... 562-860-2451.. 35 M fmixson@cerritos.edu
MIYAKE, Richard .... 310-342-5200.. 72 D
MIYARES, Javier .... 301-985-7077 203 B president-office@umuc.edu
MIYASHIRO, James .... 619-260-7690.. 71 J publicsafety@sandiego.edu
MIYASHIRO, Jane .... 310-660-3401.. 41 L jmiyashiro@elcamino.edu
MIYASHIRO, Ross .... 310-660-3472.. 41 L rmiyashiro@elcamino.edu
MIYAUCHI, Alison .... 615-277-7458 428 F amiyauchi@watkins.edu
MIZAK, Pat .... 941-893-2858 105 K pmizak@ringling.edu
MIZE, Kyle, C .... 325-649-8049 438 D kmize@hputx.edu
MIZE, Lewis .... 620-227-9354 172 J lmize@dc3.edu
MIZELL, Claire .... 903-510-2939 452 C cmiz@tjc.edu
MIZNER, Kevin .... 559-730-3868.. 39 E kevinm@cos.edu
MLODZIK, Leigh, D ...... 920-748-8704 495 G mlodzikl@ripon.edu
MLYNARCZYK, Chuck ... 866-582-8448 107 B
MLYNSKI, Melissa .... 217-206-7148 151 C mmlyn2@uis.edu
MMEJE, Kenechukwu (K.C.) ..... 214-768-2821 444 E kmmeje@smu.edu
MNOOKIN, Jennifer, L .. 310-825-8202.. 69 A mnookin@law.ucla.edu
MO, Huanbiao .... 404-413-1082 119 E hmo@gsu.edu
MOAK, Marvin .... 601-629-6805 246 B memoak@hindscc.edu
MOANANU, Letupu .... 684-699-9155 505 A l.moananu@amsamoa.edu
MOATS, Kyle .... 417-836-5244 256 E kylemoats@missouristate.edu
MOATS, Scott .... 952-446-4210 235 G moatss@crown.edu
MOAVENI, Saeed .... 801-863-8237 461 A saeed.moaveni@uvu.edu
MOAYERI, Al .... 323-254-2203.. 41 J amoayeri@eaglerockcollege.edu
MOBERG, Bret .... 847-578-8308 147 I bret.moberg@rosalindfranklin.edu
MOBERLY, Jonathon ..... 402-643-7430 266 G jonathon.moberly@cune.edu
MOBERLY, Richard .... 402-472-3751 269 J moberly@unl.edu
MOBLEY, Cathryn, B ..... 434-395-2759 469 A mobleycb@longwood.edu
MOBLEY, Cedric .... 478-825-6518 118 A mobleyc@fvsu.edu
MOBLEY, Jill .... 870-307-7226.. 20 A jill.mobley@lyon.edu
MOBLEY, Karen .... 912-871-1638 122 I kmobley@ogeecheetech.edu
MOBLEY, Katie .... 802-654-0505 464 B kjf06010@ccv.vsc.edu
MOBLEY, Wade .... 763-544-9501 233 J
MOCABEE, Todd .... 210-784-2009 448 A todd.mocabee@tamusa.edu
MOCARSKI, Richard, A . 308-865-8496 269 I mocarskira@unk.edu
MOCCIA, Mario .... 575-646-7630 287 B moccia@nmsu.edu
MOCEK, Christian .... 812-357-6479 160 D cmocek@saintmeinrad.edu
MOCK, Kenrick .... 907-786-1956.... 9 H kjmock@alaska.edu
MOCK, Lisa .... 701-228-5432 346 C lisa.mock@minotstateu.edu
MOCK, Robert, C .... 410-651-6101 203 A rcmock@umes.edu
MOCNIK, Joe .... 701-231-6128 345 G joe.mocnik@ndsu.edu
MODDELMOG, Debra ..... 775-784-6805 271 F dmoddelmog@unr.edu
MODDER, Gail .... 916-660-7340.. 63 I gmodder@sierracollege.edu
MODELANE, Dan .... 508-541-1614 208 F dmodelane@dean.edu
MODENA, Shawn .... 478-825-6100 118 A modenas@fvsu.edu
MODENSTEIN, Susan .... 212-592-2208 315 H smodenstein@sva.edu
MODERO, Thomas .... 646-565-6000 322 J thomas.modero@touro.edu
MODESTOU, Jennifer, A .... 319-335-0705 163 A jennifer-modestou@uiowa.edu
MODIC, Jeannette, L ..... 240-895-2260 201 E jlmodic@smcm.edu
MODICA, Joseph .... 909-748-8692.. 71 G joseph_modica@redlands.edu
MODICA, Joseph, B ...... 610-341-5826 383 D jmodica@eastern.edu
MODIG, James, E .... 785-864-3493 177 D jmodig@ku.edu
MODLIN, Andrew, S ..... 336-841-9605 329 G amodlin@highpoint.edu
MODLIN, Eli, J .... 410-548-3316 203 F ejmodlin@salisbury.edu
MODRCIN, Mary Anne .. 423-869-6319 421 C mary.modrcin@lmunet.edu
MODROVSKY, Amanda . 570-408-5534 403 D amanda.modrovsky@wilkes.edu
MODRY-CARON, Irah .... 260-481-6375 159 F modryi@pfw.edu
MOE, Karine, F .... 651-696-6160 236 H moe@macalester.edu
MOE, Keri, L .... 915-831-6526 436 E kmoe@epcc.edu
MOE, Marie .... 701-483-2560 345 D marie.moe@dickinsonstate.edu
MOEDER, Lawrence, E .. 785-532-6250 174 G larrym@ksu.edu
MOEDER, Lawrence, E .. 785-532-6420 174 G larrym@ksu.edu
MOEGGENBERG, Rich .... 517-607-2348 225 A rmoeggenberg@hillsdale.edu
MOEHRING, Richard ..... 913-469-8500 174 D rmoehrin@jccc.edu
MOELLER, Darin .... 712-274-6400 170 E darin.moeller@witcc.edu
MOELLER, Lon, D .... 386-226-6000.. 98 A moellerl@erau.edu
MOELLER, Marcus .... 405-692-3102 366 G
MOELLER, Molly .... 515-271-7497 164 I molly.moeller@dmu.edu
MOEN, Jeremiah, T ...... 701-788-4623 345 E jeremiah.moen@mayvillestate.edu
MOEN, Stuart .... 281-873-0262 434 A s.moen@commonwealth.edu
MOENCH, Gerald .... 816-501-4862 258 H gerald.moench@rockhurst.edu
MOENKHAUS, Kevin, P 515-271-3902 165 A kevin.moenkhaus@drake.edu
MOENTMANN, Elise ...... 503-943-7341 377 E moentman@up.edu
MOERLAND, Timothy, S .... 724-357-2219 394 G tim.moerland@iup.edu
MOERMAN, LeeAnn ...... 712-722-6002 164 K leeann.moerman@dordt.edu
MOERSCHBAECHER, Joseph, M .... 504-568-4804 189 B jmoers@lsuhsc.edu
MOESSNER, Phil .... 320-308-3190 240 H pmmoessner@stcloudstate.edu
MOEZ, Chrystal .... 262-619-6830 499 F moezc@gtc.edu
MOFFAT, Barbara, A ..... 413-782-1630 219 F barbara.moffat@wne.edu
MOFFAT, Heather .... 812-888-4120 162 C hmoffat@vinu.edu
MOFFATT, Tammy, L .... 603-646-2811 273 E tammy.l.moffatt@dartmouth.edu
MOFFATT-LIMOGES, Pamela .... 401-739-5000 405 A pmoffatt-limoges@neit.edu
MOFFETT, David .... 317-738-8221 154 J dmoffett@franklincollege.edu
MOFFETT, Janelle .... 301-689-4493 203 E jamoffett@frostburg.edu
MOFFETT, Jared, E .... 202-274-6858.. 93 C jared.moffett@udc.edu
MOFFETT, Mark .... 614-823-1534 360 A mmoffett@otterbein.edu
MOFFETT LANE, Amanda .... 575-538-6675 289 B amanda.moffett@wnmu.edu
MOFFITT, Jamie, H .... 541-346-3003 377 D jmoffitt@uoregon.edu
MOFFITT, Lisa .... 615-327-3927 420 F moffitt@guptoncollege.edu
MOFFITT, Michael .... 765-674-6901 157 D michael.moffitt@indwes.edu
MOFFITT, Thomas, J ..... 610-566-1776 403 E tmoffitt@williamson.edu
MOGFORD, Jon .... 979-458-0243 446 C jmogford@tamus.edu
MOGHE, Prabhas, V ..... 848-445-6591 282 A moghe@soe.rutgers.edu
MOGULESCU, John .... 646-664-8004 292 K john.mogulescu@cuny.edu
MOHAJIR, Terry .... 870-972-3880.. 17 G tmohajir@astate.edu
MOHAMADIAN, Habib, P .... 225-771-4266 190 H habib_mohamadian@subr.edu
MOHAMED, Rafik .... 909-537-5500.. 33 A rafik.mohamed@csusb.edu
MOHAMMAD, Esam .... 316-323-6426 171 G emohammad@butlercc.edu
MOHAMMAD, Yatty ...... 402-878-2380 267 E ymohammad@littlepriest.edu
MOHAMMADI, Amir ..... 724-738-2002 395 F amir.mohammadi@sru.edu
MOHAMMADI, Jamshid 312-567-7516 139 B mohammadi@iit.edu
MOHAMMADI, Rameen 315-312-2232 319 B rameen.mohammadi@oswego.edu
MOHAPATRA, Prasant ... 530-754-7764.. 68 E pmohapatra@ucdavis.edu
MOHEBBI, Vargha .... 480-425-6903.. 13 H vargha.mohebbi@scottsdalecc.edu
MOHLER, Benjamin .... 859-256-3100 180 H ben.mohler@kctcs.edu
MOHLER, JR., R. Albert .... 502-897-4121 184 C mohler@sbts.edu
MOHNEY, David .... 908-737-4770 278 E dmohney@kean.edu
MOHR, James, R .... 724-946-7116 402 G mohrjr@westminster.edu
MOHR, Jannine, R .... 970-491-6270.. 78 M jannine.mohr@colostate.edu
MOHR, Karl .... 530-752-2063.. 68 E kfmohr@ucdavis.edu
MOHR, Sandra .... 617-587-5587 217 A mohrs@neco.edu
MOHR, Sharon .... 218-855-8054 237 F smohr@clcmn.edu
MOHR, Wayne, C .... 570-389-4303 394 A wmohr@bloomu.edu
MOHRBACHER, Robert .. 360-623-8552 479 C bob.mohrbacher@centralia.edu
MOHRE, Trudy .... 517-264-7185 230 E tmohre@sienaheights.edu
MOHRMANN, Esther ..... 575-769-4122 285 K esther.mohrmann@clovis.edu
MOHSEN, Bashir .... 201-216-9901 277 D bashir.mohsen@eicollege.edu
MOINEAU, Suzanne ...... 760-750-8505.. 33 B smoineau@csusm.edu
MOIOLA, Tena .... 858-566-1200.. 41 E tmoiola@disd.edu
MOIR, Chris .... 216-987-3492 351 G chris.moir@tri-c.edu
MOIR, Joe .... 207-768-9649 196 E joseph.moir@maine.edu
MOISE, Connie .... 760-744-1150.. 55 I cmoise@palomar.edu
MOISEY, Neil .... 406-265-3726 264 F neil.moisey@msun.edu
MOIST, Kirk, L .... 715-833-6224 499 D kmoist@cvtc.edu
MOJ, Cynthia .... 323-469-3300.. 25 E cmoj@amda.edu
MOJE, Elizabeth, B .... 734-647-0621 231 E moje@umich.edu
MOJICA, Agnes .... 787-892-5634 509 F amojica@intersg.edu
MOJICA, Ben .... 413-205-3265 205 A ben.mojica@aic.edu
MOJICA, Francis, J .... 787-723-4481 507 A fmojica@ceaprc.edu
MOJICA, Jorge, E .... 787-852-1430 508 C jmojica@hccpr.edu
MOK, Jacqueline, L ...... 210-567-2004 456 C mok@uthscsa.edu
MOKAMBA, Lilly .... 952-885-5407 242 I lmokamba@nwhealth.edu
MOKHTARI, Kouider ..... 903-566-7177 456 A kmokhtari@uttyler.edu
MOKREN, Jennifer .... 845-257-3860 317 B mokrenj@newpaltz.edu
MOKU, Sam .... 808-544-1406 127 H smoku@hpu.edu
MOKU, Sam .... 808-544-0209 127 H smoku@hpu.edu
MOKUAU, Noreen, K .... 808-956-6300 128 F noreen@hawaii.edu
MOKWA, Robert .... 406-994-4371 264 D mokwa@montana.edu
MOLALENGE, Teshome, H .... 540-828-5750 465 D tmolalen@bridgewater.edu
MOLAPO, Tsooane .... 309-794-7328 132 C tsooanemolapo@augustana.edu
MOLCHANY, Jim .... 610-282-1100 382 E jim.molchany@desales.edu
MOLD, Joseph .... 906-217-4246 221 O moldj@baycollege.edu
MOLDENHAUER, Troy ... 262-595-2495 497 C moldenht@uwp.edu
MOLDER, Kandi .... 918-335-6237 368 G kmolder@okwu.edu
MOLDOVAN, Regina ..... 214-768-7660 444 E rmoldovan@smu.edu
MOLDSTAD, Donald, L . 507-344-7312 234 B don.moldstad@blc.edu
MOLELLA, Holly .... 845-431-8953 298 E molella@sunydutchess.edu
MOLEN, Brent .... 801-426-8234 460 C president@ucdh.edu
MOLEN, Kenneth .... 801-426-8234 460 C director@ucdh.edu
MOLER, Kathryn, A .... 650-723-2300.. 65 J
MOLEY, Linda .... 620-252-7115 172 G moley.linda@coffeyville.edu
MOLIFE, Brenda .... 508-531-2454 212 B bmolife@bridge.edu
MOLIKEN, Laura .... 610-409-3606 402 A lmoliken@ursinus.edu
MOLIN-DUNN, Casey ... 917-493-4486 305 I cmdunn@msmnyc.edu
MOLINA, Alejandra .... 315-781-3319 302 A molina@hws.edu
MOLINA, Carlos .... 202-495-3876.. 92 E cmolina@dhs.edu
MOLINA, David .... 314-838-8858 261 G dmolina@ugst.edu
MOLINA, Graciela .... 209-575-6509.. 75 H molinag@yosemite.edu
MOLINA, Ivan .... 787-878-5475 508 L
MOLINA, Joe .... 843-953-6841 407 F jmolina@citadel.edu
MOLINA, Marc .... 630-617-3042 136 G marc.molina@elmhurst.edu
MOLINA, Michael, S .... 214-768-1265 444 E msmolina@smu.edu

MONTENEGRO, Luis ..... 718-289-5139 293 B
luis.montenegro@bcc.cuny.edu
MONTENEGRO, Luis ..... 718-289-5939 293 B
luis.montenegro@bcc.cuny.edu
MONTERO, Alfred .... 507-222-4985 234 F
amontero@carleton.edu
MONTERO, Diana .... 301-860-3501 203 C
dmontero@bowiestate.edu
MONTERO, Grecia .... 609-771-3132 276 I
montero@tcnj.edu
MONTERO, Joel .... 787-720-1022 506 E
admisiones@atlanticu.edu
MONTEROSO,
Catherine .... 304-336-8231 490 F
cmonteroso@westliberty.edu
MONTES, Angel .... 213-356-5321.. 64 H
angel_montes@sciarc.edu
MONTES, Bruce, A .... 773-508-7601 142 D
bmontes@luc.edu
MONTES, Darlene .... 818-364-7758.. 49 B
montesd@lamission.edu
MONTES, Luis .... 914-594-3723 309 H
luis_montes@nymc.edu
MONTES, Rebecca .... 707-468-3009.. 51 E
rmontes@mendocino.edu
MONTES, Sofia .... 956-665-3650 455 D
sofia.montes@utrgv.edu
MONTES, Susan, R .... 305-284-6021 112 E
smontes@miami.edu
MONTES-HELU, Mario .. 520-383-8401.. 16 D
mmonteshelu@tocc.edu
MONTES-HELU, Mario .. 520-383-8401.. 16 D
mmontes@tocc.edu
MONTESINO,
María del C .... 787-720-1022 506 E
recaudaciones@atlanticu.edu
MONTEVIRGEN, Alexis .. 818-719-6408.. 49 C
MONTEZ, Daniel .... 956-447-6635 444 A
dmontez@southtexascollege.edu
MONTEZ, Nicholas .... 619-482-6306.. 65 F
nmontez@swccd.edu
MONTGOMERY,
Adrienne .... 978-837-5485 216 D
montgomerya@merrimack.edu
MONTGOMERY, Alan .... 772-462-7860 101 E
jmontgom@irsc.edu
MONTGOMERY,
Alisa, L .... 336-322-2213 336 G
alisa.montgomery@piedmontcc.edu
MONTGOMERY,
Barbara .... 478-757-5233 126 H
bmontgomery@wesleyancollege.edu
MONTGOMERY, Cassie . 806-345-5600 430 A
c0353116@actx.edu
MONTGOMERY, Cathy .. 912-427-6265 116 F
cmontgomery@coastalpines.edu
MONTGOMERY, Christy 985-545-1500 187 H
MONTGOMERY, Cindy .. 229-226-1621 125 C
cmontgomery@thomasu.edu
MONTGOMERY, Dale ... 479-619-4234.. 20 D
dmontgom@nwacc.edu
MONTGOMERY, Daron .. 603-641-7107 274 C
dmontgomery@anselm.edu
MONTGOMERY,
Edward, B .... 269-387-2351 232 K
edward.montgomery@wmich.edu
MONTGOMERY, Eric ..... 620-331-4100 174 C
emontgomery@indycc.edu
MONTGOMERY, Isalene 386-506-3961.. 97 D
isalene.montgomery@daytonastate.edu
MONTGOMERY, Jeff ...... 937-393-3431 361 B
jlmontgo@sscc.edu
MONTGOMERY, John .... 951-343-4963.. 27 J
jmontgomery@calbaptist.edu
MONTGOMERY, John ... 734-432-5574 227 A
jmontgomery@madonna.edu
MONTGOMERY, John ... 575-562-2343 285 M
john.montgomery@enmu.edu
MONTGOMERY, John ... 575-562-4002 285 M
john.montgomery@enmu.edu
MONTGOMERY, John ... 575-562-2147 285 M
john.montgomery@enmu.edu
MONTGOMERY,
Joseph, D .... 330-823-2295 363 B
montgojd@mountunion.edu
MONTGOMERY,
Kara, H .... 724-946-7363 402 G
montgokh@westminster.edu
MONTGOMERY, Keisha . 803-705-4601 407 A
keisha.montgomery@benedict.edu
MONTGOMERY,
Laura, M .... 630-752-5227 152 F
laura.montgomery@wheaton.edu
MONTGOMERY, Lisa ..... 312-567-3777 139 B
montgomeryl@iit.edu
MONTGOMERY, Lisa, P 843-792-5050 410 F
montgoml@musc.edu
MONTGOMERY, Mark ... 315-792-5463 307 D
mmontgomery@mvcc.edu
MONTGOMERY, Martha 254-442-5114 433 A
martha.montgomery@cisco.edu
MONTGOMERY, Nancy . 949-451-5273.. 64 F
nmontgomery@ivc.edu
MONTGOMERY, Rob ..... 870-612-2057.. 22 I
rob.montgomery@uacc.edu
MONTGOMERY, Robert . 248-232-4808 229 A
rjmontgo@oaklandcc.edu
MONTGOMERY,
Tamara, F .... 225-771-2200 190 G
tamara_montgomery@subr.edu
MONTGOMERY,
Tamara, F .... 225-771-2200 190 H
tamara_montgomery@subr.edu
MONTGOMERY, Tammy 916-568-3207.. 50 E
montgot@losrios.edu
MONTGOMERY, Terri .... 314-362-6255 253 E
terri.montgomery@bjc.org
MONTGOMERY,
Toni-Marie .... 847-491-7552 145 F
t-montgomery@northwestern.edu
MONTGOMERY, Tony ... 662-476-5062 246 A
tmontgomery@eastms.edu
MONTGOMERY,
Walter, C .... 336-322-2258 336 G
walter.montgomery@piedmontcc.edu
MONTGOMERY, Wendy 301-405-6279 202 C
wmont@umd.edu
MONTGOMERY RICE,
Valerie .... 404-752-1740 122 E
vmrice@msm.edu
MONTI, Joseph .... 407-644-1408 105 M
jmonti@rollins.edu
MONTICCIOLO, Cheryl .. 516-686-1080 309 F
cheryl.monticciolo@nyit.edu
MONTIEL, Arthuro .... 956-488-5808 444 A
amontiel@southtexascollege.edu
MONTILEAUX, Kateri ..... 605-455-6142 416 B
kmontileaux@olc.edu
MONTILLA, Hector .... 787-834-9595 511 E
h.montilla@uaa.edu
MONTORIO, Lois .... 914-337-9300 297 D
lois.montorio@concordia-ny.edu
MONTOYA, Carlos .... 925-473-7341.. 40 J
MONTOYA, Dan .... 619-594-8236.. 33 E
dmontoya@sdsu.edu
MONTOYA, III, David ... 707-826-5084.. 33 D
david.montoyaiii@humboldt.edu
MONTOYA, Denise .... 505-426-2240 286 H
montoyad@nmhu.edu
MONTOYA, Jimi .... 505-747-2139 287 G
jimi.montoya@nnmc.edu
MONTOYA, Michael .... 505-454-2534 286 D
mimontoya@luna.edu
MONTOYA, Mitzi .... 541-737-6024 375 D
MONTOYA, Valerie .... 505-346-2351 288 F
valerie.montoya@bie.edu
MONTOYA, Vanessa ..... 757-340-2121 465 M
finaid2cvab@centura.edu
MONTOYO, Mitzi .... 509-335-5581 486 A
mitzi.montoyo@wsu.edu
MONTPLAISIR, Daniel ... 909-869-4789.. 30 D
dmontplaisir@cpp.edu
MONTREAL, Steven, R .. 262-243-5700 493 B
steven.montreal@cuw.edu
MONTROSE, Lee .... 910-410-1813 337 B
ljmontrose@richmondcc.edu
MONTROSS, Julia, H .... 989-774-3332 222 C
montr1jh@cmich.edu
MONYPENY, Derek .... 760-366-3791.. 40 K
dmonypeny@cmccd.edu
MOO-YOUNG, Keith ...... 518-276-2244 312 I
mooyoh2@rpi.edu
MOODY, Anissa .... 718-940-5853 314 C
amoody@sjcny.edu
MOODY, Barbara .... 207-941-7000 194 A
moodyb@husson.edu
MOODY, Debra .... 334-222-6591.... 2 I
djmoody@lbwcc.edu
MOODY, Jeff, T .... 866-294-3974 154 D
jmoody@ccr.edu
MOODY, Kari .... 920-465-2226 496 E
moodyk@uwgb.edu
MOODY, Kay .... 866-294-3974 154 D
kay.moody@ccr.edu
MOODY, Krystal .... 903-927-3312 458 G
kmoody@wileyc.edu
MOODY, Kyle .... 620-241-0723 172 D
kyle.moody@centralchristian.edu
MOODY, Lisa .... 941-893-2863 105 K
lmoody@ringling.edu
MOODY, Marla .... 417-447-4842 257 G
moodym@otc.edu
MOODY, Mary .... 615-366-4438 424 D
mary.moody@tbr.edu
MOODY, Michelle, L .... 757-594-8819 466 B
mlmoody@cnu.edu
MOON, Alan .... 903-693-1113 441 F
amoon@panola.edu
MOON, Beverly .... 662-846-4873 245 H
bmoon@deltastate.edu
MOON, Bryonie .... 651-690-6525 242 R
bamoon@stkate.edu
MOON, Daniel, C .... 904-620-5955 110 A
dmoon@unf.edu
MOON, Don .... 434-592-3235 468 H
donmoon@liberty.edu
MOON, Freddie, P .... 256-766-6610.... 5 F
pmoon@hcu.edu
MOON, Greg .... 503-517-1880 378 A
gmoon@westernseminary.edu
MOON, Greta .... 760-245-4271.. 73 D
greta.moon@vvc.edu
MOON, Hope .... 440-366-7183 355 J
MOON, Hyon, J .... 949-480-4139.. 64 B
hmoon@soka.edu
MOON, Joshua .... 605-626-3336 417 A
joshua.moon@northern.edu
MOON, Lee, L .... 904-620-2833 110 A
l.moon@unf.edu
MOON, Lisa .... 866-492-5336 244 F
lisa.moon@mail.waldenu.edu
MOON, Lisa, T .... 804-257-5605 477 C
ltmoon@vuu.edu
MOON, Michael, J .... 503-370-6017 378 B
mmoon@willamette.edu
MOON, Randy .... 251-460-6121.... 8 F
rmoon@southalabama.edu
MOON, Sandra .... 502-895-3411 183 D
smoon@lpts.edu
MOON, Sarah .... 585-785-1373 300 B
sarah.moon@flcc.edu
MOON, Shin .... 973-618-3000 276 D
smoon@caldwell.edu
MOON, Sunny .... 323-343-2739.. 32 A
sunny.moon@calstatela.edu
MOON, Susan .... 573-288-6441 252 E
smoon@culver.edu
MOON, Won, W .... 224-425-2854 123 D
wonwmoon@runiv.edu
MOON JOHNSON,
Joshua .... 916-484-8925.. 50 F
johnso2j@arc.losrios.edu
MOONEY, Debra .... 513-745-3204 365 B
mooney@xavier.edu
MOONEY, Denise .... 617-353-9814 207 D
dmooney@bu.edu
MOONEY, Dewanna ...... 706-886-6831 125 D
dmooney@tfc.edu
MOONEY, Ken .... 704-669-4030 333 E
mooneyk@clevelandcc.edu
MOONEY, Kim .... 603-899-4128 273 F
president@franklinpierce.edu
MOONEY, Laura .... 413-662-5411 213 A
laura.mooney@mcla.edu
MOONEY, Lisa .... 434-395-2074 469 A
mooneylj@longwood.edu
MOONEY, Michael, C ... 585-245-5343 318 E
mooney@geneseo.edu
MOONEY, Sandra .... 281-649-3256 437 H
smooney@hbu.edu
MOONEY, Thelma .... 936-294-4047 450 C
tgm001@shsu.edu
MOONEY BURNS,
Mary .... 816-501-4199 258 H
mary.burns@rockhurst.edu
MOONEYHAN, Allen ..... 870-512-7864.. 18 B
allen_mooneyhan@asun.edu
MOONFLOWER, Nandi .. 206-239-4500 479 E
nandim@cityu.edu
MOONO, Steady .... 518-381-1304 315 G
moonosh@sunysccc.edu
MOONSWE, Isaac .... 301-548-5500.. 92 G
MOONZWE, Isaac .... 703-892-5100.. 92 G
MOORADIAN, Jody .... 401-341-2268 406 A
jody.mooradian@salve.edu
MOORADIAN, Todd .... 502-852-4812 185 C
tamoor10@louisville.edu
MOORE, Al .... 205-387-0511.... 1 D
al.moore@bscc.edu
MOORE, Albert .... 408-741-2060.. 74 C
albert.moore@wvm.edu
MOORE, Albert .... 408-741-2060.. 74 E
albert.moore@wvm.edu
MOORE, Alfred .... 336-316-2151 329 E
mooread2@guilford.edu
MOORE, Alicia .... 541-383-7262 372 B
amoore@cocc.edu
MOORE, Alissa .... 815-479-7563 143 A
amoore189@mchenry.edu
MOORE, Angela .... 719-549-2967.. 79 A
angela.moore@csupueblo.edu
MOORE, Angela .... 417-667-8181 252 A
amore@cottey.edu
MOORE, Angelica .... 925-631-4533.. 59 B
anmoore@stmarys-ca.edu
MOORE, Anita, W .... 662-252-8000 248 G
amoore@rustcollege.edu
MOORE, Anne .... 413-236-1641 213 F
amoore@berkshirecc.edu
MOORE, Anne, C .... 704-687-0145 342 E
amoor168@uncc.edu
MOORE, Annette .... 636-584-6704 252 J
annette.moore@eastcentral.edu
MOORE, Barbara .... 914-251-6018 319 E
barbara.moore@purchase.edu
MOORE, Barbara .... 714-879-3901.. 45 F
bmoore@hiu.edu
MOORE, Barbara .... 724-357-4077 394 G
bmoore@iup.edu
MOORE, Barbara, N ...... 662-252-8000 248 G
bmoore@rustcollege.edu
MOORE, Beata .... 913-758-3033 504 D
MOORE, Becca .... 706-419-1262 117 B
becca.moore@covenant.edu
MOORE, III, Berrien ..... 405-325-3095 371 B
berrien@ou.edu
MOORE, Beth .... 513-862-3188 353 G
beth.moore@email.gscollege.edu
MOORE, Billy .... 662-846-4200 245 H
bmoore@deltastate.edu
MOORE, Bonnie .... 217-238-8260 141 D
bmoore71258@lakeland.cc.il.us
MOORE, Brad .... 505-224-4423 285 J
bmoore28@cnm.edu
MOORE, Brad, D .... 336-278-5492 328 K
bmoore6@elon.edu
MOORE, Brandon .... 951-639-5426.. 52 I
bmoore@msjc.edu
MOORE, Brian .... 845-569-3275 307 J
brian.moore@msmc.edu
MOORE, Brooks .... 812-237-3890 155 G
brooks.moore@indstate.edu
MOORE, Brooks .... 979-458-6144 446 G
rbm@tamus.edu
MOORE, Bryan .... 309-467-6377 137 B
bmoore@eureka.edu
MOORE, Caitlan .... 970-675-3205.. 78 G
caitlan.moore@cncc.edu
MOORE, Caitlin .... 352-323-3677 102 T
moorec@lssc.edu
MOORE, Candice .... 252-399-6393 326 M
cbmoore@barton.edu
MOORE, Carla .... 336-342-4261 337 E
moorec@rockinghamcc.edu
MOORE, Carol, A .... 803-786-3178 408 F
camoore@columbiasc.edu
MOORE, Cassandra ...... 757-240-2404 471 A
cassandra.moore@rivhs.com
MOORE, Cassandra, S .. 410-777-2151 197 C
csmoore@aacc.edu
MOORE, Cathy, D .... 678-407-5000 118 D
cmoore@ggc.edu
MOORE, Charles .... 904-256-7062 101 G
cmoore@ju.edu
MOORE, Charlette .... 501-812-2299.. 23 B
cmoore@uaptc.edu
MOORE, Chase .... 678-466-4464 116 E
chasemoore@clayton.edu
MOORE, Chris .... 760-744-1150.. 55 I
cmoore@palomar.edu
MOORE, Christine .... 602-285-7454.. 13 F
christine.moore@phoenixcollege.edu
MOORE, Christopher, A 617-353-2704 207 D
mooreca@bu.edu
MOORE, Christy .... 318-678-6000 187 A
cmoore@bpcc.edu
MOORE, Cyndee .... 706-310-6219 126 A
cyndee.moore@ung.edu
MOORE, Cynthia .... 310-434-4305.. 62 E
moore_cynthia@smc.edu
MOORE, Cynthia, C ...... 412-624-6623 401 B
ccm20@pitt.edu

MOOSE, Megan .... 415-869-2900 210 E
megan.moose@hult.edu
MOOT, Bradley .... 212-678-8035 303 G
brmoot@jtsa.edu
MOOTHART, Kathy .... 319-385-6209 167 A
kathy.moothart@iw.edu
MOOTISPAW, Angel ...... 937-393-3431 361 B
amootispaw@sscc.edu
MOOTZ, Allison, C .... 215-885-2360 389 F
amootz@manor.edu
MOQTADERI, Emily .... 718-951-5074 293 C
emily.moqtaderi@brooklyn.cuny.edu
MOQUAY, Alexandra ..... 480-800-5449.. 15 P
amoquay@taliesin.edu
MORA, Cecilio .... 559-934-2430.. 73 M
ceciliomora@whccd.edu
MORA, Flora .... 808-984-3517 129 E
fmora@hawaii.edu
MORA, Joshua .... 806-291-1100 457 J
moraj@wbu.edu
MORA, Michelle .... 818-240-1000.. 44 B
mmora@glendale.edu
MORA, Priscilla .... 805-965-0581.. 62 C
mora@sbcc.edu
MORA-ALVAREZ,
Gabriela .... 626-968-1328.. 47 G
MORA RIVERA, Aida ..... 787-765-4210 506 K
MORADILLOS, Alicia ..... 787-834-9595 511 E
amoradillos@uaa.edu
MORALE, Mary .... 937-376-2911 364 D
mmorale@wilberforce.edu
MORALES, Adelina, C ... 325-942-2073 451 A
adelina.morales@angelo.edu
MORALES, Alba, G .... 787-884-3838 506 D
amorales@atenascollege.edu
MORALES, Angelica, C . 212-870-1251 310 A
amorales@nyts.edu
MORALES, Aurea .... 718-963-4112 291 I
amorales@boricuacollege.edu
MORALES, Awilda .... 787-761-0640 512 F
oficialderegistroacademico@utcpr.edu
MORALES, Betsy .... 787-265-3807 513 F
decasac@uprm.edu
MORALES, Brenda, L .... 787-852-1430 508 C
bmorales@hccpr.edu
MORALES, Carlos .... 817-515-5024 445 G
carlos.morales@tccd.edu
MORALES, David .... 409-984-6304 450 B
moralesdp@lamarpa.edu
MORALES, David .... 801-274-3280 461 F
david.morales@wgu.edu
MORALES, Erica .... 713-221-8443 453 B
moralese@uhd.edu
MORALES, Hector .... 787-746-1400 508 B
hmorales@huertas.edu
MORALES, Ileana .... 787-878-5475 508 L
imorales@arecibo.inter.edu
MORALES, Ingrid .... 845-569-3262 307 J
ingrid.morales@msmc.edu
MORALES, James .... 435-797-1712 460 H
james.morales@usu.edu
MORALES, Jessica .... 575-538-6139 289 B
jessica.morales@wnmu.edu
MORALES, Julie .... 575-538-6238 289 B
moralesj@wnmu.edu
MORALES, Karen, G ...... 787-841-2000 510 K
karen_morales@pucpr.edu
MORALES, Kathy .... 954-453-9228.. 34 G
MORALES, Luis, R .... 201-200-2070 279 E
lmorales@njcu.edu
MORALES, Margarita ..... 620-227-9594 172 J
mmorales@dc3.edu
MORALES, Nancy .... 787-882-2065 511 D
controller@unitecpr.net
MORALES, Nora .... 361-354-2239 433 C
moralesn@coastlbend.edu
MORALES, Ofelia, A ...... 303-492-8223.. 83 A
ofelia.morales@colorado.edu
MORALES, Patricia .... 949-824-6701.. 68 G
patricia.morales@uci.edu
MORALES, Rachel .... 207-780-5758 196 F
rachel.morales@maine.edu
MORALES, Ray .... 212-678-8000 303 G
ramorales@jtsa.edu
MORALES, Ray .... 917-493-4445 305 I
rmorales@msmnyc.edu
MORALES, Robert .... 805-965-0581.. 62 C
moralesr@sbcc.edu
MORALES, Rosalia .... 787-864-2222 509 C
rosalia.morales@guayama.inter.edu
MORALES, Rosalie .... 787-780-0070 506 F
rmorales@caribbean.edu

MORALES, Sulmarie ...... 787-264-1912 509 F
smorales@intersg.edu
MORALES, Tamara .... 787-765-3560 507 L
tmorales@edpuniversity.edu
MORALES, Tomas .... 909-537-5002.. 33 A
president_morales@csusb.edu
MORALES-DIAZ,
Enrique .... 413-572-8580 213 D
emoralesdiaz@westfield.ma.edu
MORALES-ORTIZ,
Javier .... 440-826-2452 348 E
jmorales@bw.edu
MORALES-RODRIGUEZ,
Sandra, M .... 787-857-3600 508 M
smmorales@br.inter.edu
MORALES TORRES,
Jessica, A .... 787-764-0000 514 B
jessica.morales1@upr.edu
MORALES TORRES,
Nilsa .... 787-890-2681 512 H
nilsa.morales@upr.edu
MORAMARCO, Jacques 310-453-8300.. 42 A
jacques@emperors.edu
MORAN, Al .... 850-201-6079 111 C
morana@tcc.fl.edu
MORAN, Awilda .... 787-720-1022 506 E
recursos@atlanticu.edu
MORAN, Bradley .... 907-474-7210.. 10 A
sbmoran@alaska.edu
MORAN, Carmella .... 630-844-5132 132 D
cmoran@aurora.edu
MORAN, Christyn .... 610-527-0200 397 I
christyn@rosemont.edu
MORAN, David .... 413-236-3015 213 F
dmoran@berkshirecc.edu
MORAN, Demetria .... 401-456-8031 405 C
dmoran@ric.edu
MORAN, Eileen, P .... 940-565-3687 454 A
eileen.moran@unt.edu
MORAN, Ellen, L .... 412-624-7355 401 B
emoran@pitt.edu
MORAN, James .... 314-977-3490 259 H
james.moran@slu.edu
MORAN, Jason, E .... 814-641-3419 386 H
moranj@juniata.edu
MORAN, Jay .... 203-392-6025.. 85 A
moranj1@southernct.edu
MORAN, Jim .... 605-256-5136 416 J
jim.moran@dsu.edu
MORAN, Karen .... 718-420-4164 324 F
karen.moran@wagner.edu
MORAN, Kathy .... 518-464-8784 299 G
kmoran@excelsior.edu
MORAN, Kelly .... 724-938-4400 394 B
moran@calu.edu
MORAN, Lady .... 931-221-1013 418 D
moranl@apsu.edu
MORAN, Laura, P .... 615-353-3217 425 D
laura.moran@nscc.edu
MORAN, Mark .... 425-869-6843 421 C
mark.moran@lmunet.edu
MORAN, Meghan .... 973-618-3000 276 D
mmoran@caldwell.edu
MORAN, Patrick .... 307-766-4175 502 H
pmoran5@uwyo.edu
MORAN, Paul, J .... 570-208-5948 387 A
pjmoran@kings.edu
MORAN, Raymond .... 775-784-1641 271 F
rmoran@unr.edu
MORAN, Timothy .... 973-761-9172 283 B
timothy.moran@shu.edu
MORAN, Virginia .... 760-245-4271.. 73 D
virginia.moran@vvc.edu
MORANO, Joe .... 845-451-1314 298 A
joe.morano@culinary.edu
MORANO, Lori .... 518-464-8648 299 G
lmorano@excelsior.edu
MORANO, Nancy .... 914-633-2494 302 G
nmorano@iona.edu
MORASKI, Ron .... 518-276-8439 312 I
morasr@rpi.edu
MORAVEC, Todd, A ...... 518-564-2072 319 C
moraveta@plattsburgh.edu
MORAVITZ, Judy .... 909-667-4411.. 37 H
jmoravitz@claremontlincoln.edu
MORAWIEC, SCJ,
Zbigniew .... 414-425-8300 495 H
zmorawiec@shsst.edu
MORAY, Yvonne .... 212-472-1500 309 I
ymoray@nysid.edu
MORBER, Timothy, T .... 330-471-8279 355 L
tmorber@malone.edu
MORCOMB, Mike .... 952-829-2459 234 A
mike.morcomb@bethfel.org

MORDACH, John .... 312-942-5600 148 A
john_mordach@rush.edu
MORDAN-MCCOMBS,
Sarah .... 317-738-8301 154 J
smordan-mccombs@franklincollege.edu
MORDEN, Erik .... 909-384-8671.. 59 I
emorden@sbccd.cc.ca.us
MOREA, John .... 757-822-1932 476 B
jmorea@tcc.edu
MOREAU, Donald .... 603-641-7350 274 C
dmoreau@anselm.edu
MOREAU, Elizabeth .... 617-745-3101 208 G
elizabeth.moreau@enc.edu
MOREAU, Joe .... 650-949-6120.. 43 C
moreaujoe@fhda.edu
MOREAU, Joseph .... 650-949-6119.. 43 B
moreaujoe@fhda.edu
MOREAU, Sandra, E ..... 619-239-0391.. 34 F
sem@cwsl.edu
MOREAU, Scott .... 630-752-5933 152 F
scott.moreau@wheaton.edu
MORECI, Rick .... 773-325-4283 135 I
rmoreci@depaul.edu
MOREFIELD, Bill, R ...... 423-318-2735 426 C
bill.morefield@ws.edu
MOREHEAD, Jere, W .... 706-542-1214 125 G
president@uga.edu
MOREHEAD, Krystal ...... 704-379-6800.. 92 G
MOREHOUSE, Karissa ... 530-257-6181.. 47 F
kmorehouse@lassencollege.edu
MOREIRA, Antonio, R ... 410-455-6576 202 E
moreira@umbc.edu
MOREIRA, Catarina .... 610-527-0200 397 I
MOREIRA, Rubén .... 787-850-9354 513 E
ruben.moreira@upr.edu
MOREL, Nina .... 615-966-2501 421 D
nina.morel@lipscomb.edu
MORELAND, Doran .... 317-921-4467 157 G
doran.moreland@ivytech.edu
MORELAND, Jeremy, L . 305-628-6720 106 F
jlmoreland@stu.edu
MORELAND, Kristen ...... 317-921-4858 157 G
kmoreland@ivytech.edu
MORELAND, Milton .... 901-843-3795 423 J
morelandm@rhodes.edu
MORELL, Christina .... 434-924-3417 473 A
cm5c@virginia.edu
MORELLO, Chanell .... 828-327-7000 333 B
cmorello@cvcc.edu
MORELLO, John, T .... 540-654-1269 472 I
jmorello@umw.edu
MORELLO, JR., Joseph 650-738-4271.. 61 Q
morelloj@smccd.edu
MORELLO, Kay, F .... 508-213-2114 217 E
kay.morello@nichols.edu
MORELLO, Terry .... 661-253-7707.. 28 K
tmorello@calarts.edu
MORELOCK, Luann .... 309-655-7353 148 E
luann.morelock@osfhealthcare.org
MORELOCK, Tommy ..... 352-854-2322.. 96 O
moreloct@cf.edu
MORELON, Carla .... 770-962-7580 120 E
cmorelon@gwinnetttech.edu
MORENA, Pat .... 212-650-7997 293 D
pmorena@ccny.cuny.edu
MORENCY, Douglass .... 207-786-6254 193 B
dmorency@bates.edu
MORENCY, Maurice ...... 212-752-1530 304 D
maurice.morency@limcollege.edu
MORENO, Ben .... 650-723-9406.. 65 J
MORENO, Cynthia .... 773-838-7606 134 F
cmoreno38@ccc.edu
MORENO, Francisco ..... 787-738-2161 513 D
francisco.moreno@upr.edu
MORENO, Gettie .... 210-485-0374 429 C
gmoreno107@alamo.edu
MORENO, Jose .... 410-857-2791 200 B
jmoreno@mcdaniel.edu
MORENO, Judith .... 207-755-5265 194 G
jmoreno@cmcc.edu
MORENO, Laura .... 785-227-3380 171 E
morenoc@bethanylb.edu
MORENO, Linda .... 773-298-3379 148 G
moreno@sxu.edu
MORENO, Marcio .... 910-962-2029 343 C
morenom@uncw.edu
MORENO, Melissa .... 805-683-8292.. 62 C
melissa.moreno@sbcc.edu
MORENO, Nancy .... 713-798-8200 431 I
nmoreno@bcm.edu
MORENO, Patricia .... 281-873-0262 434 A
p.moreno@commonwealth.edu

MORENO, Valerie .... 360-992-2888 479 F
vmoreno@clark.edu
MORENO ORAMA,
Fernando .... 787-841-2000 510 K
fernando_moreno@pucpr.edu
MORENO-RIANO,
Gerson .... 757-352-4320 470 H
agast@regent.edu
MORENO-WEINERT,
Inez .... 602-243-8134.. 14 A
inez.moreno-weinert@smcmail.maricopa.edu
MORENZ, Angie .... 217-854-5536 132 I
angie.morenz@blackburn.edu
MORENZ, Ronald .... 440-525-7321 355 H
rmorenz@lakelandcc.edu
MORENZ, Tim .... 217-854-5759 132 I
tim.morenz@blackburn.edu
MOREO, Patrick .... 941-359-4200 110 D
pmoreo@sar.usf.edu
MORERA, Joachim .... 310-287-4307.. 49 G
morerajj@wlac.edu
MORERA-GONZÁLEZ,
Angel .... 787-993-8871 513 B
angel.morera1@upr.edu
MORESCHI, Robert, W .. 540-464-7212 476 G
moreschirw@vmi.edu
MORESCHI, Tracy, L ..... 503-255-0332 374 D
tmoreschi@multnomah.edu
MOREST, Vanessa .... 914-606-6712 325 C
vanessa.morest@sunywcc.edu
MORETON, April, L .... 651-286-7773 244 D
almoreton@unwsp.edu
MORETTI, Linda .... 716-829-7811 298 F
moretti@dyc.edu
MORETZ, Drew .... 919-962-7096 341 A
jkappler@northcarolina.edu
MORETZ, Patsy .... 334-387-3877.... 4 C
patsymoretz@amridgeuniversity.edu
MOREY, Ann, N .... 818-677-2878.. 32 D
ann.morey@csun.edu
MOREY, Debby .... 404-727-4583 117 F
dmorey@emory.edu
MOREY, Joshua .... 951-343-4235.. 27 J
jmorey@calbaptist.edu
MOREY, Megan .... 413-597-4217 220 C
megan.e.morey@williams.edu
MOREY, Robin .... 404-727-8561 117 F
robin.morey@emory.edu
MORGAN, Amanda .... 864-388-8971 410 D
amorgan@lander.edu
MORGAN, Andrea .... 303-273-3021.. 78 I
asalazar@mines.edu
MORGAN, Andy .... 812-237-8111 155 G
andy.morgan@indstate.edu
MORGAN, Anna Beth .... 507-284-9595 234 I
annabeth.morgan@mayo.edu
MORGAN, Anna Beth .... 507-293-7480 234 J
morgan.annabeth@mayo.edu
MORGAN, Annie .... 866-492-5336 244 F
ann.morgan@mail.waldenu.edu
MORGAN, Betsy .... 608-785-8042 496 F
bmorgan@uwlax.edu
MORGAN, Bruce, A .... 423-775-7233 418 H
bruce.morgan@bryan.edu
MORGAN, Camella .... 253-833-9111 481 F
cmorgan@greenriver.edu
MORGAN, Carlene, J .... 919-516-4084 340 C
cjmorgan@st-aug.edu
MORGAN, Cassie .... 256-549-8263.... 2 B
cmorgan@gadsdenstate.edu
MORGAN, Catherine, A 423-439-4300 419 J
morganca1@etsu.edu
MORGAN, Catherine L .. 802-860-2729 462 B
cmorgan@champlain.edu
MORGAN, Chris .... 951-343-4369.. 27 J
cmorgan@calbaptist.edu
MORGAN, Chris .... 717-361-1407 383 E
morganc@etown.edu
MORGAN, David .... 765-361-6382 162 E
morgand@wabash.edu
MORGAN, David, A .... 423-775-7597 418 H
morganda@bryan.edu
MORGAN, Deborah .... 918-540-6312 366 I
demorgan@neo.edu
MORGAN, Derek .... 303-273-3288.. 78 I
dmorgan@mines.edu
MORGAN, Elizabeth ...... 909-621-8101.. 37 E
elizabeth.morgan@cmc.edu
MORGAN, Erin, K .... 530-752-3619.. 68 E
ekmmorgan@ucdavis.edu
MORGAN, Gilbert .... 443-885-3125 200 D
gilbert.morgan@morgan.edu

MORGAN, Ginny .... 510-841-9230.. 75 E
vmorgan@wi.edu
MORGAN, Heath .... 660-831-4087 256 G
morganh@moval.edu
MORGAN, Helen .... 912-525-5000 123 G
hmorgan@scad.edu
MORGAN, J. Reid .... 336-758-5122 344 D
jrm@wfu.edu
MORGAN, Janie, M ...... 608-785-8495 496 F
jspencer@uwlax.edu
MORGAN, Jason .... 256-306-2545.... 1 F
jason.morgan@calhoun.edu
MORGAN, Jason .... 919-278-2676 340 E
jmorgan@shawu.edu
MORGAN, Jeff .... 501-279-4305.. 19 D
jrmorgan@harding.edu
MORGAN, Jeff .... 713-743-3455 452 F
jjmorgan@central.uh.edu
MORGAN, Jeffrey .... 480-219-6111 250 A
jmorgan@atsu.edu
MORGAN, Jim .... 575-461-4413 286 E
jimm@mesalands.edu
MORGAN, Joanne, L .... 919-658-8558 340 J
jmorgan@umo.edu
MORGAN, John .... 928-717-7721.. 16 M
john.morgan@yc.edu
MORGAN, John .... 203-582-5359.. 87 G
john.morgan@quinnipiac.edu
MORGAN, Joseph, A .... 606-783-2022 183 F
j.morgan@moreheadstate.edu
MORGAN, Joshua .... 575-492-2769 286 J
jmorgan@nmjc.edu
MORGAN, Kara, A .... 814-871-7610 384 E
morgan013@gannon.edu
MORGAN, Karen .... 201-200-2150 279 E
kmorgan@njcu.edu
MORGAN, Karrie .... 605-331-6672 417 E
karrie.morgan@usiouxfalls.edu
MORGAN, Kelly .... 863-638-7244 113 A
kelly.morgan@warner.edu
MORGAN, Kristi .... 865-251-1800 424 A
kmorgan@southtn.edu
MORGAN, Kristy .... 903-233-4410 439 E
kristymorgan@letu.edu
MORGAN, JR., Leroy .... 706-821-8235 122 K
lmorgan@paine.edu
MORGAN, Lissa .... 901-572-2441 418 E
lissa.morgan@bchs.edu
MORGAN, Louis .... 423-614-8567 420 J
lmorgan@leeuniversity.edu
MORGAN, Lucas .... 318-798-4107 189 D
lucas.morgan@lsus.edu
MORGAN, Mark .... 407-708-2224 107 D
morganm@seminolestate.edu
MORGAN, Mark, D .... 910-962-3719 343 C
morganm@uncw.edu
MORGAN, Mary .... 724-357-7942 394 G
morgan@iup.edu
MORGAN, Matt .... 215-893-5252 382 B
matt.morgan@curtis.edu
MORGAN, Maunka .... 402-878-2380 267 E
maunka.morgan@littlepriest.edu
MORGAN, Melissa .... 717-901-5173 385 K
mmorgan@harrisburgu.edu
MORGAN, Michael .... 901-843-3810 423 J
morganm@rhodes.edu
MORGAN, Michael, D .... 205-726-2727.... 6 E
mmorgan@samford.edu
MORGAN, Michelle .... 216-397-1525 354 I
MORGAN, Natasha .... 432-685-4534 440 E
nmorgan@midland.edu
MORGAN, Patricia .... 707-256-7305.. 53 C
pmorgan@napavalley.edu
MORGAN, Patricia .... 315-470-8851 291 H
patriciamorgan@crouse.org
MORGAN, Rachel, A ..... 651-631-5249 244 D
ramorgan@unwsp.edu
MORGAN, Rebecca .... 714-432-5670.. 38 E
rmorgan@occ.cccd.edu
MORGAN, Robin, W ..... 302-831-2101.. 90 F
morgan@udel.edu
MORGAN, Romena .... 434-528-5276 477 E
rmorgan@vul.edu
MORGAN, Russell .... 309-298-1066 152 D
re-morgan@wiu.edu
MORGAN, Samuel .... 559-638-0300.. 66 F
samuel.morgan@reedleycollege.edu
MORGAN, Scott .... 360-867-6913 481 A
sustainabilitydirector@evergreen.edu
MORGAN, Sharon, E .... 973-596-5560 279 F
sharon.e.morgan@njit.edu
MORGAN, Silas .... 651-255-6107 243 D
smorgan@unitedseminary.edu
MORGAN, Sonja .... 253-566-5322 485 C
smorgan@tacomacc.edu
MORGAN, Steve .... 504-398-2228 191 C
smorgan@uhcno.edu
MORGAN, Terry .... 334-683-5119.... 6 A
tmorgan1@judson.edu
MORGAN, Timothy .... 217-443-8803 135 H
tmorgan@dacc.edu
MORGAN, Tracy .... 603-641-7402 274 C
tmorgan@anselm.edu
MORGAN, Wendy .... 304-637-1341 487 I
morganw@dewv.edu
MORGAN, Whitney .... 417-626-1234 257 F
morgan.whitney@occ.edu
MORGAN, William, E .... 972-438-6932 441 H
wmorgan@parker.edu
MORGAN, Zachary .... 661-222-2733.. 28 K
zmorgan@calarts.edu
MORGAN AGARD,
Nicole .... 201-684-7503 280 H
nmagard@ramapo.edu
MORGAN DAVIS,
Pamela .... 940-397-4785 440 F
pamela.morgan@msutexas.edu
MORGAN-RUSSELL,
Simon .... 419-372-2340 348 H
smorgan@bgsu.edu
MORGAN-ZAYACHEK,
Eileen .... 607-436-2855 317 C
eileen.morgan@oneonta.edu
MORGANSTEIN, Penny . 212-472-1500 309 I
pmorganstein@mysid.edu
MORGANTE, Nicole .... 315-464-8812 317 F
morgantm@upstate.edu
MORGENSTERN,
Patricia .... 269-467-9945 224 A
pmorgenstern@glenoaks.edu
MORGENTHALER,
Diane, S .... 203-392-6300.. 85 A
morgenthald1@southernct.edu
MORI, Darryl .... 626-396-4288.. 26 E
darryl.mori@artcenter.edu
MORIARITY, Marlene .... 830-372-8009 449 B
mmoriarity@tlu.edu
MORIARTY, Deb .... 410-704-2055 204 A
dmoriarty@towson.edu
MORIARTY, Joan .... 973-618-3394 276 D
jmoriarty@caldwell.edu
MORIARTY, John .... 305-899-3957.. 95 C
jmoriarty@barry.edu
MORIARTY, Laura .... 732-571-3405 279 B
lmoriart@monmouth.edu
MORIARTY, Martha .... 843-521-3137 413 E
mamoriar@uscb.edu
MORIARTY, Maureen .... 802-831-1265 463 G
mmoriarty@vermontlaw.edu
MORIARTY, Michael, J . 860-515-3760.. 84 G
mjmoriarty@charteroak.edu
MORIARTY, Sean .... 315-312-5500 319 B
sean.moriarty@oswego.edu
MORIARTY, Sean .... 718-780-7505 291 J
sean.moriarty@brooklaw.edu
MORIATY, Erin, T .... 773-508-3079 142 D
emoriar@luc.edu
MORICLE, Jeanne .... 304-327-4000 489 P
jmoricle@bluefieldstate.edu
MORICONI, Jill .... 814-254-0400 381 F
jmoriconi@pa.gov
MORICONI,
Kimberly, A .... 816-604-6544 255 E
kim.moriconi@mcckc.edu
MORIKANG, Marilyn ..... 408-288-3187.. 61 M
marilyn.morikang@sjcc.edu
MORIKANG, Marilyn ..... 408-288-3119.. 61 M
marilyn.morikang@sjcc.edu
MORILLO, Janell .... 559-278-0276.. 31 D
janellt@csufresno.edu
MORIMOTO, Mandy ...... 808-954-4937 127 G
mmorimoto@hmi.edu
MORIMOTO, Yash .... 505-428-1765 288 B
yash.morimoto@sfcc.edu
MORIN, Anna .... 508-373-5649 216 B
anna.morin@mcphs.edu
MORIN, Erin .... 336-770-3296 343 D
morine@uncsa.edu
MORIN, Jeff .... 414-847-3210 494 F
jeffreymorin@miad.edu
MORIN, Jodie .... 712-749-2097 163 D
morinj@bvu.edu
MORIN, Karen, M .... 570-577-3293 379 F
karen.morin@bucknell.edu
MORIN, Kevin .... 414-277-7129 494 G
morin@msoe.edu
MORIN, Roland .... 765-361-6096 162 E
morinr@wabash.edu
MORIN, Sheila .... 701-477-7862 347 A
smorin1@tm.edu
MORIN, Shirley .... 701-477-7862 347 A
smorin@tm.edu
MORIN, Stephen, J .... 203-932-7268.. 89 A
smorin@newhaven.edu
MORINEC, Maire .... 707-864-7000.. 64 C
maire.morinec@solano.edu
MORIOKA, Brennon ...... 808-956-7727 128 F
bmorioka@hawaii.edu
MORISHITA, Leroy, M .. 510-885-3877.. 31 C
leroy.morishita@csueastbay.edu
MORISSEAU, Natalia ..... 973-353-5872 282 B
natalia.morisseau@rutgers.edu
MORITA, Denise .... 510-649-2469.. 44 F
dmorita@gtu.edu
MORLEY, Deborah, G ... 610-499-4087 403 B
dgmorley@widener.edu
MORLEY, John .... 312-850-7230 134 H
jmorley@ccc.edu
MORLEY, Kathleen .... 254-710-2061 431 J
kathleen_morley@baylor.edu
MORLEY, Maureen .... 212-938-5945 320 B
mmorley@sunyopt.edu
MORLEY, Sandy .... 517-264-7193 230 E
smorley@sienaheights.edu
MORLEY, Yvonne, Y ..... 859-238-5220 179 F
yvonne.morley@centre.edu
MORLEY-MOWER,
Cynthia .... 213-763-7074.. 49 E
morleycn@lattc.edu
MORMANDO, Karin, W . 215-204-8556 399 F
karin.mormando@temple.edu
MORNINGSTAR, Kevin .. 760-750-4775.. 33 B
kmorningstar@csusm.edu
MORO, Nicole .... 617-228-1913 214 A
nmoro@bhcc.mass.edu
MORO, Simonetta .... 347-966-1096 194 B
smoro@idsva.edu
MORODOMI, Joyce, K .. 559-323-2100.. 60 I
jmorodomi@sjcl.edu
MORONEY, Donney ...... 414-410-4329 492 D
dmoroney@stritch.edu
MORONEY, James .... 617-254-2610 218 D
rector@sjs.edu
MORONEY, Maryclaire .. 216-397-6674 354 I
mmoroney@jcu.edu
MORONG, Andrew .... 207-755-5273 194 G
amorong@cmcc.edu
MORONSKI-CHAPMAN,
Karen .... 716-566-7879 298 B
kmoronsk@daemen.edu
MOROSKO, Linda .... 330-494-6170 361 F
lmorosko@starkstate.edu
MOROSOFF, Wendy ...... 914-251-6370 319 E
wendy.morosoff@purchase.edu
MOROTE, Elsa-Sofia ..... 631-420-2723 321 B
morotee@farmingdale.edu
MOROWSKI, James, R .. 701-788-4619 345 E
james.morowski@mayvillestate.edu
MOROZOWICH, Mark ... 202-319-5683.. 91 B
morozowich@cua.edu
MORPHEW,
Christopher .... 410-516-7820 199 D
christopher.morphew@jhu.edu
MORPHEW, Vonnie .... 254-659-7502 437 G
ymorphew@hillcollege.edu
MORR, Alex .... 617-873-0475 207 F
alex.morr@cambridgecollege.edu
MORRA, Elizabeth .... 202-216-4365 341 A
emorra@northcarolina.edu
MORREALE, Robert .... 716-286-8344 310 D
rmorreale@niagara.edu
MORREALE, Thirza .... 315-228-6776 296 F
tmorreale@colgate.edu
MORRELL, Christopher . 217-424-6360 143 H
cmorrell@millikin.edu
MORRELL, Erin .... 203-773-8541.. 84 F
emorrell@albertus.edu
MORRELL, Matthew, D . 763-417-8250 234 H
mmorrell@centralseminary.edu
MORREN, Glen .... 313-664-1162 222 F
gmorren@collegeforcreativestudies.edu
MORRICE, Pelema .... 603-427-7601 272 J
MORRILL, Allen .... 724-589-2124 399 H
amorrill@thiel.edu
MORRILL, Deborah, H .. 210-567-6395 456 C
morrill@uthscsa.edu
MORRILL, Donald, D .... 813-258-7409 112 J
dmorrill@ut.edu
MORRILL, Lucas .... 479-979-1448.. 23 I
lmorrill@ozarks.edu
MORRIN, Jeffrey, R ...... 208-496-1155 130 A
morrinj@byui.edu
MORRIN, Matthew .... 207-834-7562 196 C
matthew.morrin@maine.edu
MORRIN, Matthew .... 207-768-9432 196 E
matthew.morrin@maine.edu
MORRIS, Adam .... 562-903-4714.. 27 C
adam.morris@biola.edu
MORRIS, Adam .... 417-455-5740 252 D
adammorris@crowder.edu
MORRIS, Adam .... 360-475-7100 482 G
amorris@olympic.edu
MORRIS, Amanda .... 912-287-6584 116 F
amorris@coastalpines.edu
MORRIS, Amy .... 785-242-2067 175 H
amorris@neosho.edu
MORRIS, Andrew .... 585-389-2113 308 B
amorris8@naz.edu
MORRIS, Ann .... 419-824-3694 355 K
amorris@lourdes.edu
MORRIS, Annie, K .... 757-683-3152 469 G
akmorris@odu.edu
MORRIS, Ashley .... 912-443-5783 124 A
amorris@savannahtech.edu
MORRIS, Barbara .... 607-436-2500 317 C
barbara.morris@oneonta.edu
MORRIS, Ben .... 252-940-6374 332 C
ben.morris@beaufortccc.edu
MORRIS, Brenda .... 870-584-1107.. 22 G
bmorris@cccua.edu
MORRIS, Brenda .... 903-468-3020 447 B
brenda.morris@tamuc.edu
MORRIS, Brett, E .... 706-867-2991 126 A
brett.morris@ung.edu
MORRIS, Carlene .... 785-830-2702 173 G
cmorris@haskell.edu
MORRIS, Carlton, E ...... 334-724-8784.... 7 D
cmorris@tuskegee.edu
MORRIS, Carmeline ...... 910-695-3952 337 H
morrisc@sandhills.edu
MORRIS, Caroline .... 512-492-3157 442 M
carolim@stedwards.edu
MORRIS, Chad .... 661-654-3271.. 30 E
cmorris@csub.edu
MORRIS, Chad, T .... 540-375-4926 471 B
morris@roanoke.edu
MORRIS, Charles .... 304-865-6025 488 E
charles.morris@ovu.edu
MORRIS, Clark .... 816-415-5997 262 F
morrisc@william.jewell.edu
MORRIS, Clark, W .... 816-415-5997 262 F
morrisc@william.jewell.edu
MORRIS, Claudia .... 352-365-3523 102 T
morrisc@lssc.edu
MORRIS, Connie .... 843-661-8315 409 I
connie.morris@fdtc.edu
MORRIS, Corinne .... 402-844-7361 268 J
corinne@northeast.edu
MORRIS, Craig .... 651-793-1272 238 H
craig.morris@metrostate.edu
MORRIS, Daryl .... 334-244-3295.... 4 F
dmorris@aum.edu
MORRIS, David .... 205-853-1200.... 2 G
dmorris@jeffersonstate.edu
MORRIS, Deborah .... 304-357-4849 488 G
deborahmorris@ucwv.edu
MORRIS, Delesa .... 561-803-2022 104 C
delesa_morris@pba.edu
MORRIS, Diana .... 800-567-2344 492 G
dmorris@menominee.edu
MORRIS, Don .... 314-968-7444 262 C
morrisdo@webster.edu
MORRIS, Donna .... 325-574-7914 458 E
dmorris@wtc.edu
MORRIS, Dottie .... 603-358-2206 275 A
dmorris@keene.edu
MORRIS, Earl .... 435-797-1939 460 H
earl.morris@usu.edu
MORRIS, Elizabeth .... 951-343-4507.. 27 J
emorris@calbaptist.edu
MORRIS, Gary .... 315-312-2255 319 B
gary.morris@oswego.edu
MORRIS, Gary .... 512-448-8731 442 M
gmorris1@stedwards.edu
MORRIS, Gary, Z .... 304-462-6113 490 C
gary.morris@glenville.edu
MORRIS, Gerard .... 253-879-3700 485 E
gmorris@pugetsound.edu
MORRIS, Geri .... 419-998-3106 363 C
geri@unoh.edu
MORRIS, Greg .... 214-860-2677 435 C
cmorris@dcccd.edu

MORRIS, Greg .... 972-860-5094 435 C
cmorris@dcccd.edu
MORRIS, Heather .... 716-338-1056 303 D
heathermorris@mail.sunyjcc.edu
MORRIS, Heather .... 614-251-4690 358 G
morrish@ohiodominican.edu
MORRIS, Henry .... 507-389-1150 239 C
henry.morris@mnsu.edu
MORRIS, Jacqueline ..... 262-564-2200 499 F
morrisj@gtc.edu
MORRIS, Jaime .... 620-341-5457 172 L
jmorri12@emporia.edu
MORRIS, James, H .... 512-448-1271 442 M
jmorris9@stedwards.edu
MORRIS, Jason .... 325-674-2830 429 B
morrisj@acu.edu
MORRIS, Jeff .... 620-252-7177 172 G
morris.jeff@coffeyville.edu
MORRIS, Jeffery, B .... 785-532-6415 174 G
jbmorris@ksu.edu
MORRIS, Jennifer .... 800-567-2344 492 G
jmorris@menominee.edu
MORRIS, Jennifer .... 801-689-2160 459 J
jmorris@nightingale.edu
MORRIS, Jessica .... 610-921-2381 378 C
jmorris@albright.edu
MORRIS, John .... 808-739-8555 127 F
jmorris@chaminade.edu
MORRIS, John .... 617-627-3232 219 B
john.morris@tufts.edu
MORRIS, John, P .... 843-953-1325 408 E
morrisjp2@cofc.edu
MORRIS, Joseph .... 303-797-5801.. 76 I
joseph.morris@arapahoe.edu
MORRIS, Julia, M .... 304-457-6205 487 B
auviljm@ab.edu
MORRIS, Julie .... 404-876-1227 115 F
julie.morris@bccr.edu
MORRIS, Justin .... 620-278-4324 177 B
jmorris@sterling.edu
MORRIS, Kathleen .... 315-786-2236 303 F
kmorris@sunyjefferson.edu
MORRIS, Kathryn .... 317-940-9903 153 F
kmorris@butler.edu
MORRIS, Kelli .... 256-326-2602.... 1 F
kelli.morris@calhoun.edu
MORRIS, Ken .... 510-666-8248.. 24 D
clinicdirector@aimc.edu
MORRIS, Kevin .... 281-922-3479 443 E
kevin.morris@sjcd.edu
MORRIS, Kevin .... 936-294-1794 450 C
kmorris@shsu.edu
MORRIS, Kimberly .... 478-825-6605 118 A
morrisk01@fvsu.edu
MORRIS, Kizzy .... 610-399-2279 394 C
kmorris@cheyney.edu
MORRIS, Kyle .... 307-755-2129 502 K
kyle.morris@zenith.org
MORRIS, Laura, M .... 302-295-1179.. 90 I
laura.m.morris@wilmu.edu
MORRIS, Lawrence, J ... 202-319-5100.. 91 B
morrisl@cua.edu
MORRIS, Loren, L .... 620-665-3523 174 B
morrisl@hutchcc.edu
MORRIS, Malcolm, L .... 678-916-2603 114 I
mmorris@johnmarshall.edu
MORRIS, Marie .... 765-641-4020 153 B
msmorris@anderson.edu
MORRIS, Mary Ann .... 918-270-6464 369 A
maryann.morris@ptstulsa.edu
MORRIS, Matthew .... 417-836-5233 256 E
mattmorris@missuristate.edu
MORRIS, Melissa, M .... 334-844-7771.... 4 E
morrimm@auburn.edu
MORRIS, Mellasenah .... 765-658-4394 154 F
mellasenahmorris@depauw.edu
MORRIS, Michael .... 805-437-8881.. 30 F
michael.morris@csuci.edu
MORRIS, Mike .... 208-376-7731 129 H
mmorris@boisebible.edu
MORRIS, Nathan .... 859-846-5417 183 E
nmorris.ca@midway.edu
MORRIS, Nora .... 763-433-1632 237 C
nora.morris@anokaramsey.edu
MORRIS, Nora .... 763-433-1632 237 D
nora.morris@anokaramsey.edu
MORRIS, Paul .... 435-652-7504 460 G
pmorris@dixie.edu
MORRIS, Raymond .... 706-769-1472 114 E
rmorris@acmin.org
MORRIS, Regina .... 573-840-9606 260 I
rmorris@trcc.edu
MORRIS, Renea .... 303-871-2711.. 83 D
renea.morris@du.edu
MORRIS, Rick .... 864-977-7777 411 E
publicsafety@ngu.edu
MORRIS, Robert .... 815-280-2884 140 B
romorris@jjc.edu
MORRIS, Sara, R .... 716-888-2120 292 D
morriss@canisius.edu
MORRIS, Scott .... 713-683-3817 443 F
MORRIS, Sheila .... 405-382-9501 369 J
s.morris@sscok.edu
MORRIS, Stephanie .... 716-286-8539 310 D
smorris@niagara.edu
MORRIS, Steve .... 217-854-5513 132 I
steve.morris@blackburn.edu
MORRIS, Steve .... 270-789-5017 179 E
srmorris@campbellsville.edu
MORRIS, Tama .... 704-337-2363 339 G
morrist@queens.edu
MORRIS, Tommy .... 256-824-6576.... 8 B
tommy.morris@uah.edu
MORRIS, Traci .... 405-912-9111 369 D
MORRIS, Tracy, L .... 304-293-1788 491 C
tracy.morris@mail.wvu.edu
MORRIS, Trevor .... 806-291-3636 457 J
morrist@wbu.edu
MORRIS, Valerie, B .... 843-953-8222 408 E
morrisv@cofc.edu
MORRIS, Vicky .... 252-399-6330 326 M
vamorris@barton.edu
MORRIS, Wanda .... 310-900-1600.. 40 A
wmorris@elcamino.edu
MORRIS, Wanda .... 310-660-3281.. 41 L
wmorris@elcamino.edu
MORRIS, Wendi .... 478-296-6179 122 H
wmorris@oftc.edu
MORRIS, William .... 336-517-2236 327 B
rwmorris@bennett.edu
MORRIS-CAFIERO,
Haley .... 901-272-5107 422 B
MORRIS-DUEER, Vicky . 972-265-5744 452 D
vmorrisdueer@udallas.edu
MORRISETT, Gregory, J 607-255-9188 297 F
greg.morrisett@cornell.edu
MORRISETTE, Joanna .... 919-735-5151 338 H
jmmorrisette@waynecc.edu
MORRISON, Alison .... 202-379-7808.. 92 G
MORRISON, Amy .... 425-739-8200 482 A
amy.morrison@lwtech.edu
MORRISON, Andrew ..... 740-588-1388 365 E
amorrison@zanestate.edu
MORRISON, Angel .... 785-460-5418 172 H
angel.morrison@colbycc.edu
MORRISON, Barry, F ..... 401-232-6017 404 F
bmorriso@bryant.edu
MORRISON, Brenda, M 443-412-2409 199 A
bmorrison@harford.edu
MORRISON, Cammie .... 856-225-2949 281 G
cammor@camden.rutgers.edu
MORRISON, Dan .... 848-932-4371 282 A
dm1218@echo.rutgers.edu
MORRISON, Darrell ...... 816-271-4226 257 A
morrison@missouriwestern.edu
MORRISON, Edwina ...... 406-449-9150 263 K
emorrison@montana.edu
MORRISON,
Elizabeth, N .... 630-515-7600 143 G
emorri@midwestern.edu
MORRISON,
Hassel Andre .... 507-786-3503 243 C
morrison@stolaf.edu
MORRISON, Jason .... 870-574-4501.. 21 E
jmorriso@sautech.edu
MORRISON, Jean .... 617-353-2230 207 D
morrison@bu.edu
MORRISON, Jennifer .... 503-244-0726 371 G
jennifermorrison@achs.edu
MORRISON, Jennifer, K 508-767-7007 205 D
jemorrison@assumption.edu
MORRISON, Jessica ...... 559-730-3755.. 39 E
jessicamo@cos.edu
MORRISON, John .... 856-351-2628 283 A
jmorrison@salemcc.edu
MORRISON, Julia .... 707-476-4172.. 39 D
julia-morrison@redwoods.edu
MORRISON, Julie .... 623-845-4761.. 13 C
julie.morrison@gccaz.edu
MORRISON, Julie .... 734-973-5010 232 B
jmorriso@wccnet.edu
MORRISON, Karen .... 407-823-6479 109 E
karen.morrison@ucf.edu
MORRISON, Kim .... 510-723-6762.. 35 O
kmorrison@chabotcollege.edu
MORRISON, Larry .... 402-481-8752 265 K
larry.morrison@bryanhealthcollege.edu
MORRISON, Laura .... 252-335-0821 333 G
laura_morrison@albemarle.edu
MORRISON, Lexi .... 215-717-6362 400 J
lmorrison@uarts.edu
MORRISON, Lisa .... 712-325-3287 167 B
lmorrison@iwcc.edu
MORRISON, Lolita .... 404-297-9522 119 B
morrisonl@gptc.org
MORRISON, Marty, G ... 540-654-2287 472 I
mmorris3@umw.edu
MORRISON, Melanie .... 650-433-3895.. 55 G
mmorrison@paloaltou.edu
MORRISON, Michael .... 980-495-3978 329 C
MORRISON, Michael, L 812-888-5736 162 C
mmorrison@vinu.edu
MORRISON, Nancy, J ... 212-998-4924 310 B
nancy.morrison@nyu.edu
MORRISON, Pamela ..... 916-558-2088.. 50 I
morrisp@scc.losrios.edu
MORRISON, Philip .... 413-528-7204 205 F
pmorrison@simons-rock.edu
MORRISON,
Rebecca, L .... 414-955-4949 494 C
rmorriso@mcw.edu
MORRISON, Regina ...... 650-738-4350.. 61 Q
morrison@smccd.edu
MORRISON, Robert .... 312-261-3372 144 F
rob.morrison@nl.edu
MORRISON, Rodney ..... 631-632-6857 317 D
rodney.morrison@stonybrook.edu
MORRISON, Rodney ..... 419-448-2391 353 H
rmorriso@heidelberg.edu
MORRISON, Roxanne .... 619-260-7579.. 71 J
roxannemorrison@sandiego.edu
MORRISON, Sarah .... 740-366-9209 349 H
morrison.415@cotc.edu
MORRISON, Sarah, B ... 276-656-0322 475 D
sbmorrison@patrickhenry.edu
MORRISON, Scott .... 775-445-4401 271 G
scott.morrison@wnc.edu
MORRISON, Scott, D .... 540-828-5376 465 D
smorriso@bridgewater.edu
MORRISON, Thomas .... 812-855-6992 156 A
morrisot@iu.edu
MORRISON, Thomas, A 812-855-6992 156 B
morrisot@iu.edu
MORRISON, William ..... 508-588-9100 214 F
wmorrison@massasoit.mass.edu
MORRISON-FRONCKOWIAK,
Lisa, T .... 716-878-4500 318 C
morrislt@buffalostate.edu
MORRISON-MONGER,
Heather .... 865-524-8079 420 E
heather.monger@huhs.edu
MORRISON-WILLAIMS,
Suzanne .... 954-492-5353.. 96 H
smw@citycollege.edu
MORRISS, Andrew, P .... 216-272-9187 446 G
amorriss@tamu.edu
MORRISS-OLSON,
Melissa .... 413-565-1000 205 G
mmolson@baypath.edu
MORRISSEY, Ann, M .... 401-874-4402 406 B
morrissey@uri.edu
MORRISSEY, Kelly, A .... 401-333-7173 404 H
kamorrissey@ccri.edu
MORRISSEY, Sharon ..... 804-819-4972 474 A
smorrissey@vccs.edu
MORRISSEY, Shawn ...... 508-856-2265 212 A
shawn.morrissey@umassmed.edu
MORRO, Robert .... 610-519-4589 402 D
robert.morro@villanova.edu
MORRONE, Anastasia ... 317-274-3479 156 F
amorrone@iu.edu
MORRONE, Anthony ..... 702-992-2150 271 C
finaid@nsc.edu
MORROW, Andrea .... 567-661-7104 360 B
andrea_morrow@owens.edu
MORROW, Annette, L ... 218-477-2477 239 D
morrowan@mnstate.edu
MORROW, Barbara, A ... 314-340-5763 253 I
morrowb@hssu.edu
MORROW, Bill, J .... 302-857-1245.. 90 D
bmorrow@dtcc.edu
MORROW, David .... 267-295-2357 397 F
dmorrow@walnuthillcollege.edu
MORROW, David, M ..... 518-736-3622 300 F
dmorrow@fmcc.suny.edu
MORROW, Donnie .... 828-835-4309 338 E
dmorrow@tricountycc.edu
MORROW, Dorothy .... 402-557-7296 265 J
dorothy.morrow@bellevue.edu
MORROW, Elizabeth ..... 573-681-6107 254 E
morrowe@lincolnu.edu
MORROW, Eric .... 254-968-9141 446 E
morrow@tarleton.edu
MORROW, Erik .... 512-472-4133 443 H
emorrow@ssw.edu
MORROW, Frances .... 330-490-7312 364 B
fmorrow@walsh.edu
MORROW, Jeff .... 509-574-4691 487 A
jmorrow@yvcc.edu
MORROW, Joyce, S ...... 319-273-2244 163 B
joyce.morrow@uni.edu
MORROW, Marjann ...... 325-574-7608 458 E
mmorrow@wtc.edu
MORROW, Michael .... 651-523-1660 236 F
mmorrow001@luthersem.edu
MORROW, Rebecca ...... 304-793-6591 491 A
rmorrow@osteo.wvsom.edu
MORROW, Wanda .... 713-646-1825 444 B
wmorrow@stcl.edu
MORSBERGER,
Michael, J .... 407-882-1250 109 E
mike.mors@ucf.edu
MORSCHES, Michael .... 708-974-5310 144 C
morschesm@morainevalley.edu
MORSE, Alicia .... 410-777-2587 197 C
ammorse@aacc.edu
MORSE, Andrew .... 319-273-2570 163 B
andrew.morse@uni.edu
MORSE, Austin .... 616-988-1000 222 G
austin.m@compass.edu
MORSE, Charles, C .... 508-831-5540 220 E
cmorse@wpi.edu
MORSE, Kimberly .... 201-219-9901 277 D
kimberly.morse@eicollege.edu
MORSE, Micael .... 903-589-7114 438 G
mmorse@jacksonville-college.edu
MORSE, Paris .... 231-995-2822 228 G
pmorse@nmc.edu
MORSE, Saul .... 518-608-8472 299 G
smorse@excelsior.edu
MORSE, Stephen .... 478-471-2724 121 F
stephen.morse@mga.edu
MORSE, Stephen, C ...... 770-720-5591 123 E
scm@reinhardt.edu
MORSE, Susan .... 740-427-5926 355 E
morses@kenyon.edu
MORSE, Terry .... 410-706-2456 202 D
tmorse@umaryland.edu
MORSE, William .... 909-607-9506.. 57 F
william.morse@pomona.edu
MORSMAN, Elaine .... 607-587-4061 320 C
morsmaem@alfredstate.edu
MORSOVILLO, Michael . 708-524-6793 136 C
morsomike@dom.edu
MORSS, Susan .... 520-515-3662.. 11 M
morsss@cochise.edu
MORT, Jane .... 605-688-6197 417 C
jane.mort@sdstate.edu
MORT, Kristin .... 970-248-1908.. 77 I
kmort@coloradomesa.edu
MORTALI, Jill, M .... 603-646-3007 273 E
jill.m.mortali@dartmouth.edu
MORTAZAVI, Mansour .. 870-575-7140.. 22 E
mortazavim@uapb.edu
MORTELA, Cecilia .... 805-267-1690.. 47 H
cecilia.mortela@lauruscollege.edu
MORTENSEN, Alan .... 217-234-5253 141 D
amortens@lakelandcollege.edu
MORTENSEN, Brad, L ... 801-626-6001 461 B
bmortensen@weber.edu
MORTENSEN, Erin .... 262-551-5911 492 F
emortensen@carthage.edu
MORTENSEN, John .... 435-797-1110 460 H
john.mortensen@usu.edu
MORTENSEN, Larry .... 719-587-7402.. 76 F
lsmorten@adams.edu
MORTENSEN, Norm ...... 304-734-6680 488 K
norm.mortensen@bridgevalley.edu
MORTENSEN, Stacey ..... 701-627-4738 346 G
smorte@nhsc.edu
MORTENSON, Gary .... 254-710-1161 431 J
gary_mortenson@baylor.edu
MORTENSON, Pam .... 402-280-4341 266 I
pammortenson@creighton.edu
MORTHLAND, Betsey .... 309-796-5049 132 G
morthlandb@bhc.edu
MORTIMER, Gayle .... 620-862-5252 171 B
gayle.mortimer@barclaycollege.edu
MORTIMER, Ian .... 585-475-6637 313 A
ijmoem@rit.edu
MORTIMER, Nathan, J .. 330-972-6501 362 B
njm9@uakron.edu

MORTLAND, Stephen .... 765-998-5206 160 F
stmortlan@taylor.edu
MORTLEY, Preston .... 323-241-5059.. 49 D
mortlepc@lasc.edu
MORTON, Amy .... 508-831-6556 220 E
ammorton@wpi.edu
MORTON, Ben .... 907-786-1214.... 9 H
MORTON, Bradley .... 732-906-2601 279 A
bmorton@middlesexcc.edu
MORTON, Cassandra .... 909-748-8391.. 71 G
cassandra_morton@redlands.edu
MORTON, Christina ...... 412-392-4207 397 A
cmorton@pointpark.edu
MORTON, Clarresa .... 717-736-4139 385 E
cmmorton@hacc.edu
MORTON, Doug .... 919-515-8851 342 B
dgmorton@ncsu.edu
MORTON, Jack .... 512-936-8202 454 A
jack.morton@untsystem.edu
MORTON, James, P ...... 910-362-7555 332 H
jpmorton634@mail.cfcc.edu
MORTON, Jordan .... 661-362-2234.. 51 C
jmorton@masters.edu
MORTON, Josh .... 605-274-4316 415 B
josh.morton@augie.edu
MORTON, Kimberly .... 907-786-1215.... 9 H
kmorton11@alaska.edu
MORTON, Lynn, M .... 828-771-2070 344 E
president@warren-wilson.edu
MORTON, Mary, B .... 607-746-4430 320 G
mortonmb@delhi.edu
MORTON, Matt .... 949-376-6000.. 47 D
mmorton@lcad.edu
MORTON, Pierre .... 603-899-4045 273 F
mortonp@franklinpierce.edu
MORTON, Robert .... 678-466-4663 116 E
robertmorton@clayton.edu
MORTON, Sally, C .... 540-231-6394 477 A
scmorton@vt.edu
MORTON, Tonya, L .... 910-938-6211 333 F
mortont@coastalcarolina.edu
MORTON, Tracy, L .... 757-446-5800 466 I
mortontl@evms.edu
MORTON, Wendy .... 918-495-6817 368 I
wmorton@oru.edu
MORVANT, Mark .... 254-968-9103 446 E
morvant@tarleton.edu
MORVICE, Michael .... 714-432-5741.. 38 E
mmorvice@occ.cccd.edu
MORY, Scott .... 412-268-2135 380 F
mory@cmu.edu
MORY, Scott .... 412-268-2135 380 F
mory@andrew.cmu.edu
MORYAN, James .... 215-489-4889 382 D
james.moryan@delval.edu
MOSBURG, Calleb, N .... 580-327-8415 367 E
cnmosburg@nwosu.edu
MOSBY, David, C .... 301-546-0655 201 C
mosbydc@pgcc.edu
MOSBY, Gary .... 913-288-7305 174 F
gmosby@kckcc.edu
MOSBY, John .... 206-878-3710 481 H
jmosby@highline.edu
MOSBY-WILSON,
Shatiqua, A .... 504-286-5030 190 I
swilson@suno.edu
MOSCA, David .... 443-367-0035 202 B
dmosca@usmd.edu
MOSCATO, Robin, A ..... 609-258-3330 280 E
moscato@princeton.edu
MOSCHELLA, Jayne .... 972-438-6932 441 H
jmoschella@parker.edu
MOSCHENROSS, Sarah . 641-269-3702 165 J
moschenr@grinnell.edu
MOSCHINA, Justin .... 949-214-3613.. 40 F
justin.mochina@cui.edu
MOSCOVITZ, Yechezkel . 718-269-4080 292 G
MOSELEY, Bruce .... 315-228-7451 296 F
bmoseley@colgate.edu
MOSELEY, John .... 573-681-5333 254 E
moseleyj@lincolnu.edu
MOSELY-HAWKINS,
Elizabeth .... 803-376-5717 406 F
ehawkins@allenuniversity.edu
MOSER, Brett .... 701-252-3467 347 C
brett.moser@uj.edu
MOSER, Derek .... 417-626-1234 257 F
library@occ.edu
MOSER, Drew .... 765-998-5384 160 F
drmoser@taylor.edu
MOSER, Gary .... 661-336-5143.. 46 K
gmoser@kccd.edu
MOSER, Gary .... 707-654-1224.. 32 B
gmoser@csum.edu
MOSER, Jeremy .... 714-556-3610.. 72 F
jeremy.moser@vanguard.edu
MOSER, Kristin, M .... 319-273-3103 163 B
kristin.moser@uni.edu
MOSER, Patrick .... 503-838-8063 377 H
moserp@wou.edu
MOSER, Rachael .... 757-352-4858 470 H
rachwri@regent.edu
MOSER, Stephanie .... 605-668-1293 415 H
stephanie.moser@mtmc.edu
MOSER, Steven .... 601-266-5002 249 F
steven.moser@usm.edu
MOSER, Tina, L .... 724-738-2000 395 F
tina.moser@sru.edu
MOSER, Tracy, S .... 662-685-4771 245 D
tmoser@bmc.edu
MOSES, Bernard .... 912-358-4169 123 H
mosesb@savannahstate.edu
MOSES, Bruce .... 520-206-4514.. 15 D
bmoses3@pima.edu
MOSES, Carl .... 515-263-2835 165 I
cmoses@grandview.edu
MOSES, Charles .... 415-422-2508.. 71 K
cmoses1@usfca.edu
MOSES, Darren .... 215-489-6370 382 D
darren.moses@delval.edu
MOSES, David .... 316-978-6791 178 A
david.moses@wichita.edu
MOSES, Henry .... 615-327-6266 422 A
hmoses@mmc.edu
MOSES, James .... 202-644-7210.. 91 A
jmoses@bau.edu
MOSES, Orrin Douglas . 831-656-3218 503 K
dmoses@nps.edu
MOSES, Rhonda, M ...... 512-505-3030 438 E
rmmoses@htu.edu
MOSES, Seidel .... 303-914-6303.. 82 C
seidel.moses@rrcc.edu
MOSES, Shirley .... 504-520-5229 193 A
sbmoses@xula.edu
MOSES, Tara .... 509-359-7911 480 E
tmoses@ewu.edu
MOSES-HOLMES,
Jeanette .... 803-934-3989 411 C
jholmes@morris.edu
MOSESON, Mottie .... 732-367-1060 275 J
mmoseson@bmg.edu
MOSESSO, Lynn .... 479-575-6247.. 21 G
mosesso@uark.edu
MOSHAVI, Dan .... 408-924-3400.. 34 B
dan.moshavi@sjsu.edu
MOSHER, George .... 312-329-4268 144 B
george.mosher@moody.edu
MOSHER, Mike .... 641-844-5551 166 I
mike.mosher@iavalley.edu
MOSHER, Sharon .... 512-471-6048 455 A
smosher@jsg.utexas.edu
MOSHER, Tricia .... 614-891-3200 357 D
MOSIER, Greg .... 913-288-7123 174 F
gmosier@kckcc.edu
MOSIER, Gregory .... 775-784-4912 271 F
greg.mosier@unr.edu
MOSIER, Julianna .... 559-243-7132.. 66 C
julianna.mosier@scccd.edu
MOSIER, Roger .... 212-854-6031 290 J
rmosier@barnard.edu
MOSKALA, Jiri .... 269-471-3648 221 B
moskala@andrews.edu
MOSKE, Amanda .... 701-777-4358 345 C
amanda.moske@und.edu
MOSKOVITZ, Joy .... 908-737-7030 278 E
jmoskovi@kean.edu
MOSKOWITZ,
Yechezkel .... 347-619-9074 326 G
MOSLEY, Alisa .... 615-963-2923 426 D
MOSLEY, Crystal .... 410-951-3579 203 D
cmosley@coppin.edu
MOSLEY, David .... 409-880-2207 449 G
dpmosley@lit.edu
MOSLEY, Dawn .... 302-857-6272.. 89 F
dmosely@desu.edu
MOSLEY, Debra .... 417-255-7900 256 F
debbiemosley@missouristate.edu
MOSLEY, Eartha, J .... 803-536-7048 412 C
emosely1@scsu.edu
MOSLEY, Juliana .... 215-242-7751 381 D
mosleyj@chc.edu
MOSLEY, Julie .... 479-788-7404.. 21 H
julie.mosley@uafs.edu
MOSLEY, Lisa .... 203-785-4689.. 89 D
lisa.mosley@yale.edu
MOSLEY, Melissa .... 662-476-5074 246 A
mmosley@eastms.edu
MOSQUEDA, Leticia ...... 212-659-7200 304 B
lmosqueda@tkc.edu
MOSQUEDA, Margarita . 989-686-9512 223 G
momosque@delta.edu
MOSQUEDA, Rolando ... 702-651-4245 271 A
rolando.mosqueda@csn.edu
MOSS, Alan .... 918-465-1802 366 D
amoss@eosc.edu
MOSS, Brendan .... 660-944-2928 251 G
brendan@conception.edu
MOSS, Carol, L .... 216-368-8769 349 F
carol.moss@case.edu
MOSS, Dana .... 802-485-2176 463 A
dmoss1@norwich.edu
MOSS, Edwin .... 718-390-3165 324 F
edwin.moss@wagner.edu
MOSS, Elizabeth .... 410-455-2540 202 E
emoss@umbc.edu
MOSS, Glen .... 402-463-2402 267 D
gmoss@commmonwealthelectric.com
MOSS, Joshua .... 951-343-5045.. 27 J
jmoss@calbaptist.edu
MOSS, Orianna, M .... 786-331-1000 103 G
omaza@maufl.edu
MOSS, Pamela .... 901-722-3318 424 C
pmoss@sco.edu
MOSS, Paula .... 816-501-4418 258 H
paula.moss@rockhurst.edu
MOSS, Sara .... 870-512-7874.. 18 B
sara_moss@asun.edu
MOSS, Sarah .... 712-722-6078 164 K
sarah.moss@dordt.edu
MOSS, Zahra .... 701-228-5678 346 C
zahra.moss@dakotacollege.edu
MOSS-LINNEAR, Kim .... 817-515-5379 445 G
kim.moss-linnear@tccd.edu
MOSSER, John .... 760-862-1324.. 39 A
jmosser@collegeofthedesert.edu
MOSSETTE, Mary Beth .. 559-442-8286.. 66 E
marybeth.mossette@fresnocitycollege.edu
MOSSEY, Christopher ... 215-893-5252 382 B
MOSSMAN, Mark .... 309-298-1066 152 D
ma-mossman@wiu.edu
MOSTAFAVI, Mohsen .... 617-495-4364 210 B
mohsen_mostafavi@harvard.edu
MOSTELLER, Kate .... 480-947-6644.. 15 A
kate.mosteller@pennfoster.edu
MOSTILLER, Donna .... 716-286-8689 310 D
dmostiller@niagara.edu
MOTE, Jerry .... 724-266-3838 400 H
jmote@tsm.edu
MOTE, Tanya .... 360-596-5229 485 B
tmote@spscc.edu
MOTHERSBAUGH, Erik .. 312-949-7405 138 E
emothersbaugh@ico.edu
MOTHERSHEAD, Peggy . 641-784-5224 165 H
peggym@graceland.edu
MOTHERSHED, Lorraine 607-735-1728 299 D
lmothershed@elmira.edu
MOTHERWELL, Mary ..... 734-487-2229 223 H
mmotherwe@emich.edu
MOTL, Lori .... 870-245-5110.. 20 E
motll@obu.edu
MOTLEY, Clay .... 239-590-7368 108 K
cmotley@fgcu.edu
MOTLEY, Darlene .... 412-365-2970 381 C
dmotley@chatham.edu
MOTSCHENBACHER,
Jill .... 701-231-6404 345 G
jill.motschenbacher@ndsu.edu
MOTSCHENBACHER,
Russell .... 406-771-4362 264 G
r.motschenbacher1@gfcmsu.edu
MOTT, Asena .... 863-784-7041 107 F
asena.mott@southflorida.edu
MOTT, Jennifer .... 832-813-6512 439 G
jennifer.mott@lonestar.edu
MOTT, Judy .... 859-985-3521 179 C
judy_mott@berea.edu
MOTT, Molly .... 315-386-7425 320 E
mottma@canton.edu
MOTT, Molly, A .... 315-386-7425 320 E
mottma@canton.edu
MOTT, Penne .... 205-387-0511.... 1 D
penne.mott@bscc.edu
MOTTEN, Luisa .... 206-934-6782 484 B
luisa.motten@seattlecolleges.edu
MOTTER, Kristi .... 256-824-4158.... 8 B
kristi.motter@uah.edu
MOTTET, Timothy .... 719-549-2951.. 79 A
president.office@csupueblo.edu
MOTTLER, Christopher .. 301-295-3654 504 B
christopher.mottler@usuhs.edu
MOTTLEY, Juanita, D .... 530-898-5241.. 31 A
jmottley@csuchico.edu
MOTYKA, Konrad .... 914-888-5315 306 F
kmotyka@mercy.edu
MOTYL, Lynne, M .... 724-738-2070 395 F
lynne.motyl@sru.edu
MOTZER, Bill .... 402-465-2551 268 H
wmotzer@nebrwesleyan.edu
MOUCH, Sarah .... 740-362-3335 356 D
smouch@mtso.edu
MOUCK, Eric .... 707-256-7542.. 53 C
eric.mouck@napavalley.edu
MOUDGIL, Virinder, K .. 248-204-2000 226 G
president@ltu.edu
MOUDIAB, Jamilah .... 973-748-9000 276 A
jamilah_moudiab@bloomfield.edu
MOUDY, Quentin, J ...... 260-982-5267 158 T
qjmoudy@manchester.edu
MOULDS, Perry .... 615-460-6434 418 F
perry.moulds@belmont.edu
MOULTON, Jeff .... 225-578-6916 188 I
jmoulton@lsu.edu
MOULTON, Katie .... 508-213-2402 217 E
katie.moulton@nichols.edu
MOULTON, Patricia, L .. 802-728-1251 464 E
pmoulton@vtc.edu
MOULTON, Paul .... 208-459-5217 130 D
pmoulton@collegeofidaho.edu
MOULTRIE, C. Maxille .. 504-286-5033 190 I
cmoultrie@suno.edu
MOULTRIE, Cynthia ...... 610-399-2131 394 C
cmoultrie@cheyney.edu
MOULTRIE, Gloria, B .... 504-286-5341 190 I
gmoultrie@suno.edu
MOULTRIE, Nicolette ..... 925-473-7410.. 40 J
nmoultrie@losmedanos.edu
MOULTRIE, William, R .. 919-530-6693 342 A
wmoultri@nccu.edu
MOUNDS, Paul .... 860-512-3634.. 85 G
pmounds@manchestercc.edu
MOUNGA, DJ .... 605-229-8366 416 C
djmounga@presentation.edu
MOUNT, Charles .... 480-732-7281.. 12 P
charles.mount@cgc.edu
MOUNT, Jeanine .... 617-732-2192 216 B
jeanine.mount@mcphs.edu
MOUNT, Judy .... 316-677-1619 178 B
jmount@watc.edu
MOUNT, Marianne, E .... 304-724-5000 487 H
mmount@cdu.edu
MOUNTAIN, Carel .... 916-558-2275.. 50 I
mountac@scc.losrios.edu
MOUNTAIN, Mark .... 815-928-5794 146 A
mcmountain@olivet.edu
MOUNTJOY, Jeff .... 520-452-2601.. 11 M
mountjoyj@cochise.edu
MOUNTJOY, Shane .... 402-363-5614 270 E
mountjoy@york.edu
MOUNTS, Melody .... 309-467-6312 137 B
mmounts@eureka.edu
MOUNTS, William .... 912-279-5851 116 G
wmounts@ccga.edu
MOURACADE, John ...... 907-786-1086.... 9 H
jmmouracade@alaska.edu
MOURAD, Roger .... 734-677-5328 232 B
mou@wccnet.edu
MOURITSEN, Matthew .. 801-626-6063 461 B
mmouritsen@weber.edu
MOURNIGHAN, Jim ...... 401-341-2200 406 A
jim.mournighan@salve.edu
MOURTZANOS,
Emmanuel .... 661-395-4406.. 46 L
emmanuel.mourtzanos@bakersfieldcollege.edu
MOUSER, Lisa .... 636-922-8319 258 I
lmouser@stchas.edu
MOUTON, Charles, P .... 409-772-3619 456 F
cpmouton@utmb.edu
MOUTOS, Don .... 503-654-8000 375 H
dmoutos@pioneerpacific.edu
MOUTRAY, Tonya .... 518-244-2406 313 D
moutrt@sage.edu
MOUTSATSON, Kelly ..... 541-552-6411 376 E
moutsatsk@sou.edu
MOUTTET, Nate .... 206-281-2652 484 D
natem@spu.edu
MOW, Lauren .... 269-782-1316 230 F
lmow@swmich.edu
MOWDY, Cheryl .... 205-348-4530.... 7 G
cmowdy@fa.ua.edu
MOWEN, Brenda .... 804-828-3361 473 F
bmowen@vcu.edu

MOWEN, David ... 540-375-2283 471 B
mowen@roanoke.edu

MOWERY, Chris ... 423-472-7141 424 F
cmowery@clevelandstatecc.edu

MOWERY, Richard ... 570-784-3123 394 A
frmowery@bloomu.edu

MOWITZ, Marlane, A ... 910-521-6270 343 B
marlane.mowitz@uncp.edu

MOWRER, Julie ... 808-932-7826 128 E
jmowrer@hawaii.edu

MOWRY, Cynthia ... 253-589-5570 479 G
cynthia.mowry@cptc.edu

MOWRY, Harold ... 308-432-6227 268 E
hmowry@csc.edu

MOX, Andrea ... 530-895-4007.. 27 F
moxan@butte.edu

MOXLEY, Gary, D ... 585-475-4515 313 A
gdmcps@rit.edu

MOY, James, S ... 813-974-7380 110 B
moy@usf.edu

MOYA, Will ... 212-986-4343 275 I
will@berkeleycollege.edu

MOYA, Will ... 212-986-4343 291 D
will@berkeleycollege.edu

MOYANO, Angelica ... 954-607-4344 112 B

MOYE, Holly ... 310-506-6285.. 56 C
holly.moye@pepperdine.edu

MOYE, Robert, L ... 478-757-2083 126 H
rmoye@wesleyancollege.edu

MOYER, Andrew ... 215-489-4665 382 D
andrew.moyer@delval.edu

MOYER, Anna ... 618-235-2700 149 H
anna.moyer@swic.edu

MOYER, Caleigh ... 870-235-4360.. 21 D
csmoyer@saumag.edu

MOYER, Cheryl ... 215-489-4898 382 D
cheryl.moyer@delval.edu

MOYER, Cheryl ... 215-345-1500 382 D

MOYER, Christina, L ... 610-799-1136 388 I
cmoyer@lccc.edu

MOYER, Cole ... 510-430-3131.. 52 D
cmoyer@mills.edu

MOYER, James ... 863-638-7613 113 A
james.moyer@warner.edu

MOYER, James, G ... 863-638-7613 113 A
james.moyer@warner.edu

MOYER, Jane ... 617-373-2230 217 F

MOYER, Lorraine ... 912-279-5757 116 G
lmoyer@ccga.edu

MOYER, Monica ... 352-588-8646 106 D
monica.moyer@saintleo.edu

MOYER, Paul ... 410-386-4660 200 B
pmoyer@mcdaniel.edu

MOYICH, Kelly ... 636-255-2275 254 F
kmoyich@lindenwood.edu

MOYLAN, Deana, K ... 713-500-3279 456 B
deana.k.moylan@uth.tmc.edu

MOYLAN, Shannon ... 607-735-1782 299 D
smoylan@elmira.edu

MOYNIHAN, Daniel ... 781-280-3625 214 G

MOZAFFARIAN,
Dariush ... 617-636-3702 219 B
dariush.mozaffarian@tufts.edu

MOZEE, JR., Sam ... 601-979-1400 246 E
sam.mozee@jsums.edu

MOZELESKI, Dee Dee ... 212-650-7396 293 D
dmozeleski@ccny.cuny.edu

MOZIE, Jeanine ... 708-597-3000 150 F

MOZIE-ROSS, Yvette ... 410-455-3799 202 E
mozie@umbc.edu

MOZLEY, Peter ... 575-835-5172 286 I
peter.mozley@nmt.edu

MOZOLIK, Erik ... 414-464-9777 499 A
mozolik.erik@wspp.edu

MOZQUEDA, Andrea ... 909-607-0896.. 37 G
andrea_mozqueda@kgi.edu

MOZRALL, Jacqueline ... 585-475-7181 313 A
jrmeie@rit.edu

MRASEK, Jean ... 817-257-5566 448 G
j.mrasek@tcu.edu

MROCZKOWSKI, Mark .. 863-583-9050 109 B

MROZEK, John ... 281-487-1170 448 F
jmrozek@txchiro.edu

MROZIK, Jacek ... 701-858-3110 345 F
jacek.mrozik@minotstateu.edu

MROZINSKI, Mark ... 847-925-6540 137 H
mmrozins@harpercollege.edu

MRSNY, Jason ... 402-375-7195 268 G
jamrsny1@wsc.edu

MRUK, Kristen ... 585-345-6832 301 A
kemruk@genesee.edu

MRVOS, Dessa ... 412-396-1653 383 C
mrvosds@duq.edu

MUASAU, Jarad ... 719-365-8218.. 82 M
jarad.muasau@uchealth.org

MUCCINO, SJ, Keith ... 708-216-8763 142 D
kmuccino@luc.edu

MUCH, Kari ... 507-389-1455 239 C
karen.much@mnsu.edu

MUCHANE, Mary, W ... 704-894-2644 328 F
mamuchane@davidson.edu

MUCHANE, Muchane ... 336-758-4016 344 D
mmuchane@wfu.edu

MUCHER, Walter ... 787-738-2161 513 D
walter.mucher@upr.edu

MUCHIRI, Rosalind ... 301-860-4335 203 C
rmuchiri@bowiestate.edu

MUDD, Bryan ... 941-359-4200 110 D
bmudd@sar.usf.edu

MUDD, Kira ... 361-570-4869 453 C
muddk@uhv.edu

MUDD, Michael, A ... 508-929-8746 213 E
mmudd@worcester.edu

MUDD, Sarah, G ... 859-846-5390 183 E
smudd@midway.edu

MUDLOFF, Scott ... 316-942-9491 175 I
mudloffs@newmanu.edu

MUECK, Robert ... 410-626-6931 201 D
robert.mueck@sjc.edu

MUECKE, Mary ... 718-409-7444 321 C
mmuecke@sunymaritime.edu

MUEGGE, Dave ... 417-836-4040 256 E
davemuegge@missouristate.edu

MUEHSAM, Mitchell ... 936-294-1254 450 C
mmuehsam@shsu.edu

MUELLER, II, Alfred, G . 610-558-5508 391 D
muellera@neumann.edu

MUELLER, Beverley, D .. 757-594-7002 466 B
bmueller@cnu.edu

MUELLER, Brian ... 602-639-7500.. 12 J

MUELLER, Edward, A ... 603-862-3272 274 G
edward.mueller@unh.edu

MUELLER, Erin, R ... 773-298-3319 148 G
emueller@sxu.edu

MUELLER, Glen, C ... 607-255-5070 297 F
gcm37@cornell.edu

MUELLER, Janis ... 810-762-9500 225 H
jmueller1@kettering.edu

MUELLER, Jennifer ... 320-308-3023 240 H
jjmueller@stcloudstate.edu

MUELLER, Joanna ... 605-668-1514 415 H
joanna.mueller@mtmc.edu

MUELLER, Joe, B ... 307-675-0501 502 F
jbmueller@sheridan.edu

MUELLER, Kate ... 714-241-6160.. 38 C
kmueller@coastline.edu

MUELLER, Kimberloy ... 866-680-2756 459 G
studentfinances@midwifery.edu

MUELLER, Lloyd ... 503-338-2412 372 E
lmueller@clatsopcc.edu

MUELLER, Maggie ... 913-253-5036 176 I
maggim@spst.edu

MUELLER, Michelle ... 734-477-8976 232 B
mimueller@wccnet.edu

MUELLER, OSU, Pam ... 270-686-4319 179 D
pam.mueller@brescia.edu

MUELLER, Shelia ... 412-536-1180 387 B
sheila.mueller@laroche.edu

MUELLER, Steven, P ... 949-214-3386.. 40 F
steve.mueller@cui.edu

MUELLER, Teri ... 405-425-5104 367 G
teri.mueller@oc.edu

MUELLER, Tom ... 319-296-4418 166 B
thomas.mueller@hawkeyecollege.edu

MUELLER, Tony ... 909-748-8288.. 71 G
tony_mueller@redlands.edu

MUELLER, Valerie ... 252-335-0821 333 G
valerie_mueller50@albemarle.edu

MUENCH, Kim ... 414-382-6091 492 A
kim.muench@alverno.edu

MUERTZ, Julie, A ... 618-235-2700 149 H
julie.muertz@swic.edu

MUGG, Heather ... 404-727-9326 117 F
hmugg@emory.edu

MUGGEO, Louis ... 845-398-4174 315 B
lmuggeo@stac.edu

MUGGLI, Darrin ... 913-360-7961 171 D
dmuggli@benedictine.edu

MUGRAUER, Darrah ... 215-489-2236 382 D
darrah.mugrauer@delval.edu

MUGRIDGE, Rebecca ... 518-442-3568 316 D
rmugridge@albany.edu

MUHA, Beth ... 202-885-2451.. 90 J
bmuha@american.edu

MUHA, David ... 609-771-2132 276 I
muhad@tcnj.edu

MUHA, Priscilla ... 707-654-1275.. 32 B
pmuha@csum.edu

MUHAMMAD,
Darrick, D ... 313-496-2650 232 C
dmuhamm1@wcccd.edu

MUHAMMAD, Devissi ... 903-927-3374 458 G
dmuhammad@wileyc.edu

MUHAMMAD, Kareem .. 803-376-8091 406 F
kmuhammad@allenuniversity.edu

MUHAMMED, Robert ... 336-750-3299 344 B
muhammedr@wssu.edu

MUHL, Erica ... 213-740-6267.. 72 B
artdean@usc.edu

MUHLEMAN, Aimee ... 309-796-5505 132 G
muhlemana@bhc.edu

MUHLFELDER, Leslie, F 610-330-5060 387 E
muhlfell@lafayette.edu

MUHSIN, Karen ... 504-671-6138 187 E
kmuhsi@dcc.edu

MUHSIN, Karen ... 504-671-6100 187 E
kmuhsi@dcc.edu

MUHVIC, Marie ... 203-576-4896.. 88 D
mmuhvic@bridgeport.edu

MUI, Eva Marie, L ... 671-735-8889 505 C
evamarie.mui@guamcc.edu

MUIR, Bernard ... 650-723-2300.. 65 J

MUIR, Eleanor ... 717-796-1800 390 E
emuir@messiah.edu

MUIR, Janette ... 703-993-8891 467 L
jmuir@gmu.edu

MUIR, Pete ... 616-949-5300 222 I
pete.muir@cornerstone.edu

MUIR, Scott ... 856-256-4981 281 E
muir@rowan.edu

MUIR, Thorton ... 770-426-2624 121 C
tmuir@life.edu

MUIRHEAD, Tracy, H ... 914-323-5304 305 J
tracy.muirhead@mville.edu

MUJICA, Andrea ... 641-422-4438 168 D
andrea.mujica@niacc.edu

MUKHARJI, Indrani ... 312-503-2903 145 F
indrani@northwestern.edu

MUKHERJEE,
Avinandan ... 304-696-2659 490 D
mukherjeea@marshall.edu

MUKHERJEE, Chaitali ... 415-476-1683.. 69 E
chaitali.mukherjee@ucsf.edu

MUKHERJEE, Sue ... 717-477-7447 395 E
smukherjee@ship.edu

MUKOOZA,
Margaret, N ... 803-934-3439 411 C
mmukooza@morris.edu

MULADORE, James, G .. 989-964-4190 230 B
jgm@svsu.edu

MULBAY, Emily ... 717-262-2003 403 F
conferences@wilson.edu

MULCAHY, Grace ... 913-360-7621 171 D
gmulcahy@benedictine.edu

MULCAHY, Meghan ... 580-349-1342 368 A
meghan.mulcahy@opsu.edu

MULCAHY, Sean ... 913-360-7500 171 D
smulcahy@benedictine.edu

MULCAIRE, Carrie ... 831-479-3566.. 27 G
camulcai@cabrillo.edu

MULCAIRE, Heather ... 928-445-7300.. 16 M
heather.mulcaire@yc.edu

MULDER, Joey ... 806-874-3571 433 B
joey.mulder@clarendoncollege.edu

MULDER, Lori ... 616-395-7811 225 B
mulderl@hope.edu

MULDOON, Kevin ... 215-572-4076 379 A
muldoonk@arcadia.edu

MULERO, Daritza ... 787-258-1501 507 D
dmulero@columbiacentral.edu

MULES, Mary ... 602-384-2555.. 11 F
mary.mules@bryanuniversity.edu

MULFORD, Joe ... 320-629-5140 240 C
joe.mulford@pine.edu

MULFORD, Shannon, L 417-268-6037 250 G
smulford@gobbc.edu

MULHALL, Lawrence, P 864-833-8300 411 I
lmulhall@presby.edu

MULHERIN, April, C ... 207-778-7081 196 B
april.mulherin@maine.edu

MULHERN, John ... 480-461-7627.. 13 D
john.mulhern@mesacc.edu

MULHERN, Maureen ... 845-398-4067 315 B
mmulhern@stac.edu

MULHERN,
Michelle, M ... 330-325-6259 357 G
mmulhern@neomed.edu

MULHOLLAND,
Angela, B ... 843-953-5502 408 E
mulhollandab@cofc.edu

MULICK, Patrick ... 870-307-7247.. 20 A
patrick.mulick@lyon.edu

MULIK, James ... 425-640-1610 480 F
james.mulik@edcc.edu

MULINEX, Stacey ... 614-287-5128 351 E
smulinex@cscc.edu

MULKA, Christine ... 616-988-3626 226 C
cmulka@kuyper.edu

MULKIN, Alan ... 315-386-7777 320 E
mulkina@canton.edu

MULL, Diane ... 803-754-4100 409 A

MULL, Stephen, D ... 434-924-8612 473 A
sdm9rg@virginia.edu

MULLAHY, Michael ... 617-725-4140 219 A
mmullahy@suffolk.edu

MULLANE, Patrick ... 216-397-4495 354 I
pmullane@jcu.edu

MULLANE, William, S ... 512-223-1024 431 A
wmullane@austincc.edu

MULLANEY, William, P . 607-962-9232 320 F
mullaney@corning-cc.edu

MULLEN, Bill ... 706-233-7336 124 B
bmullen@shorter.edu

MULLEN, Bonnie ... 302-736-2300.. 90 G
pastor@wesley.edu

MULLEN, Daniel ... 916-306-1628.. 66 I
dmullen@sum.edu

MULLEN, Eric ... 616-234-3673 224 D
emullen@grcc.edu

MULLEN, Frank ... 508-541-1574 208 F
fmullen@dean.edu

MULLEN, Greg ... 864-656-2222 408 A
gmullen@clemson.edu

MULLEN, John ... 785-227-3380 171 E
mullenj@bethanylb.edu

MULLEN, Kate ... 518-327-6480 311 G
kmullen@paulsmiths.edu

MULLEN, Ken ... 209-946-2345.. 70 E
kmullen@pacific.edu

MULLEN, Laurie ... 410-704-2048 204 A
lmullen@towson.edu

MULLEN, Megan ... 585-224-3222 321 A
megan.mullen@esc.edu

MULLEN, Michael ... 610-361-5222 391 D
mullenm@neumann.edu

MULLEN, Michael, D ... 919-515-2446 342 B
mike.mullen@ncsu.edu

MULLEN, Robert ... 434-582-3326 468 H
ramullen2@liberty.edu

MULLEN, Sally ... 618-650-3839 149 F
smullen@siue.edu

MULLEN, Shane ... 978-630-9384 215 A
smullen@mwcc.mass.edu

MULLEN, Shirley, A ... 585-567-9310 302 D
shirley.mullen@houghton.edu

MULLEN, Steve, L ... 716-851-1294 299 F
mullens@ecc.edu

MULLEN, William ... 925-631-4060.. 59 B

MULLENIX,
Elizabeth, R ... 513-529-6010 356 E
mullener@miamioh.edu

MULLENS, Deborah, K .. 304-473-8181 491 H
mullens_d@wvwc.edu

MULLENS, Michelle ... 405-789-6400 370 A
mmullens@snu.edu

MULLENS, Rob, A ... 541-346-5455 377 D
athleticdirector@uoregon.edu

MULLER, Andrew ... 843-355-4150 414 F
mullera@wiltech.edu

MULLER, Brook ... 704-687-0090 342 E
brookmuller@uncc.edu

MULLER, Dalia, A ... 716-645-3020 316 F
daliamul@buffalo.edu

MULLER, David ... 212-241-8716 302 F

MULLER, Jacquelyn, P . 724-458-3302 385 C
jpmuller@gcc.edu

MULLER, Joseph ... 860-253-3055.. 85 C
jmuller@asnuntuck.edu

MULLER, Kathy, A ... 712-362-0433 166 F
kmuller@iowalakes.edu

MULLER, Kimberly ... 906-635-2170 226 E
kmuller@lssu.edu

MULLER, Paul ... 218-755-2040 237 E
paul.muller@bemidjistate.edu

MULLER, Robert ... 847-947-5065 144 F
rmuller@nl.edu

MULLER, Stephen ... 352-638-9706.. 95 D
smuller@beaconcollege.edu

MULLER, Tammy ... 828-327-7000 333 B
tmuller@cvcc.edu

MULLER, Wade ... 541-278-5971 372 A
wmuller@bluecc.edu

MURPHREE, Rick .... 202-274-2303.. 93 D
president@potomac.edu
MURPHREY,
Hiram Todd .... 252-638-7263 333 H
murphret@cravencc.edu
MURPHY, Alexandra ..... 312-362-7964 135 I
amurphy1@depaul.edu
MURPHY, Allison .... 801-622-1573 459 N
allison.murphy@stevenhenager.edu
MURPHY, Allison .... 518-828-4181 297 B
MURPHY, Allison .... 503-517-1807 378 A
amurphy@westserseminary.edu
MURPHY, Amanda .... 561-364-3064.. 95 E
amandakm@baptisthealth.net
MURPHY, Amy .... 508-793-3880 208 B
amurphy@holycross.edu
MURPHY, Amy .... 815-280-1418 140 B
amurphy@jjc.edu
MURPHY, Amy .... 618-252-5400 149 C
amy.murphy@sic.edu
MURPHY, Angela .... 910-362-7014 332 H
amurphy@cfcc.edu
MURPHY, Ann, B .... 303-615-1113.. 80 N
murphann@msudenver.edu
MURPHY, Antoinette ..... 417-269-3083 252 C
antoinette.murphy@coxcollege.edu
MURPHY, Becca .... 269-337-7192 225 D
becca.murphy@kzoo.edu
MURPHY, Beverly, J ...... 336-322-2128 336 G
beverly.murphy@piedmontcc.edu
MURPHY, Brent, D .... 574-232-2408 159 I
bmurphy@rtuvt.com
MURPHY, Bret .... 775-753-2217 271 B
bret.murphy@gbcnv.edu
MURPHY, Brian .... 802-440-4335 462 A
brianmurphy@bennington.edu
MURPHY, Brian .... 530-895-2987.. 27 F
murphybr@butte.edu
MURPHY, Brian .... 914-606-6846 325 C
brian.murphy@sunywcc.edu
MURPHY, Brian .... 936-468-2803 445 F
murphybm1@sfasu.edu
MURPHY, Brian .... 360-416-7690 485 A
brian.murphy@skagit.edu
MURPHY, Britt Anne ...... 501-450-1303.. 19 F
johnsen@hendrix.edu
MURPHY, Carolyn .... 402-471-2505 268 D
cmurphy@nscs.edu
MURPHY, Catherine ...... 615-460-6418 418 F
catherine.murphy@belmont.edu
MURPHY, Chad .... 309-649-6266 150 A
chad.murphy@src.edu
MURPHY, Charles, J .... 509-313-6139 481 D
murphyc@gonzaga.edu
MURPHY, Chetara .... 718-270-6067 295 A
cmurphy@mec.cuny.edu
MURPHY, Chris .... 662-720-7280 248 C
cdmurphy@nemcc.edu
MURPHY, Chris .... 805-756-5692.. 30 C
cmurph18@calpoly.edu
MURPHY, Christine .... 617-217-9733 206 A
cmurphy@baystate.edu
MURPHY, Christine .... 718-940-5800 314 C
cmurphy@sjcny.edu
MURPHY, Colleen .... 919-508-2206 344 F
cfmurphy@peace.edu
MURPHY, Colleen, K .... 781-891-2630 206 D
cmurphy@bentley.edu
MURPHY, Corinne .... 270-745-4664 185 E
corinne.murphy@wku.edu
MURPHY, David .... 414-288-4810 494 B
david.murphy@marquette.edu
MURPHY, David .... 608-262-1234 496 C
dlmurphy3@wisc.edu
MURPHY, Davis .... 530-251-8890.. 47 F
dmurphy@lassencollege.edu
MURPHY, Denise .... 301-687-4457 203 E
dmurphy@frostburg.edu
MURPHY, Doris .... 716-839-8272 298 B
dmurphy@daemen.edu
MURPHY, Eileen .... 845-398-4316 315 B
emurphy@stac.edu
MURPHY, Elizabeth .... 773-878-3752 148 D
emurphy@staugustine.edu
MURPHY, Erin .... 812-288-8878 159 A
emurphy@mid-america.edu
MURPHY, Erin .... 509-452-5100 483 A
emurphy@pnwu.edu
MURPHY, Gail .... 239-732-3953 100 A
gail.murphy@fsw.edu
MURPHY, Gene .... 601-857-3330 246 B
temurphy@hindscc.edu
MURPHY, Ginger .... 423-746-5289 426 F
gmurphy@tnwesleyan.edu
MURPHY, Gregory .... 818-677-2201.. 32 D
MURPHY, OSB, Isaac ... 603-641-7150 274 C
imurphy@anselm.edu
MURPHY, Jack .... 773-481-8124 134 G
jmurphy@ccc.edu
MURPHY, James, H ...... 573-341-4292 261 E
murphyj@mst.edu
MURPHY, Jamie .... 814-866-8117 388 A
jmurphy@lecom.edu
MURPHY, Jan .... 309-438-7018 139 E
jshane@ilstu.edu
MURPHY, Jenni .... 916-278-4433.. 32 E
jmurphy@csus.edu
MURPHY, Jessica, C .... 972-883-3536 455 B
ugdean@utdallas.edu
MURPHY, Jim .... 916-388-2812.. 35 B
jmurphy@carrington.edu
MURPHY, Jim .... 973-748-9000 276 A
jim_murphy@bloomfield.edu
MURPHY, Joan, D .... 413-755-4749 215 F
jdmurphy@stcc.edu
MURPHY, John .... 317-921-4243 157 G
jmmurphy@ivytech.edu
MURPHY, John .... 203-837-8395.. 85 B
murphyj@wcsu.edu
MURPHY, John .... 210-458-3026 455 E
john.murphy@utsa.edu
MURPHY, Josephine ...... 718-368-5144 294 E
jmurphy@kbcc.cuny.edu
MURPHY, Joshua .... 603-703-8484 272 L
jmurphy@ccsnh.edu
MURPHY, Kathleen .... 216-687-3613 351 B
kathleen.murphy@csuohio.edu
MURPHY, Kelsey, L ...... 724-847-6643 384 G
klmurphy@geneva.edu
MURPHY, Kevin .... 607-735-1750 299 D
kmurphy@elmira.edu
MURPHY, Kevin .... 631-420-2009 321 B
murphykw@farmingdale.edu
MURPHY, Lamar, R .... 585-276-3262 323 J
lamar.murphy@rochester.edu
MURPHY, Laura .... 508-929-8649 213 E
lmurphy@worcester.edu
MURPHY, Lillie .... 225-743-8500 188 B
lmurphy@rpcc.edu
MURPHY, Lisa .... 307-778-1110 502 D
lmurphy@lccc.wy.edu
MURPHY, Lynda .... 940-898-3405 451 F
lmurphy@twu.edu
MURPHY, M. Patrick .... 336-278-7640 328 K
murphyp@elon.edu
MURPHY, Mark .... 402-465-2254 268 H
mam@nebrwesleyan.edu
MURPHY, Mary .... 612-343-4406 242 H
mlmurphy@northcentral.edu
MURPHY, Mary Joan .... 212-854-2091 290 J
mmurphy@barnard.edu
MURPHY, Marybeth .... 201-216-3469 283 C
marybeth.murphy@stevens.edu
MURPHY, Maureen .... 301-934-7625 198 A
mmurphy@csmd.edu
MURPHY, Maureen .... 617-824-8575 208 H
maureen_murphy@emerson.edu
MURPHY, Melissa .... 516-796-4800 308 F
mmurphy@nycc.edu
MURPHY, Michael .... 845-398-4118 315 B
mmurphy@stac.edu
MURPHY, Michael, T .... 757-221-3646 466 C
mtmurphy@wm.edu
MURPHY, Mollie .... 202-685-3951 503 I
murphyma@ndu.edu
MURPHY, Nancy .... 704-403-3511 327 D
nancy.murphy@carolinashealthcare.org
MURPHY, Nancy .... 978-837-5231 216 D
murphyna@merrimack.edu
MURPHY, Nelson .... 704-645-4535 328 A
namurphy14@catawba.edu
MURPHY, Paul .... 617-726-0422 216 E
pwmurphy@mghihp.edu
MURPHY, Paul .... 805-922-6966.. 24 J
pmurphy@hancockcollege.edu
MURPHY, Penny .... 217-234-5253 141 D
pmurphy52829@lakelandcollege.edu
MURPHY, Pollie .... 757-727-5237 468 B
pollie.murphy@hamptonu.edu
MURPHY, Pollie .... 757-727-5201 468 B
pollie.muphy@hamptonu.edu
MURPHY, Robert .... 716-285-1212 310 D
MURPHY, Sean .... 213-738-6762.. 65 G
it@swlaw.edu
MURPHY, Shar .... 530-257-6181.. 47 F
smurphy@lassencollege.edu
MURPHY, Stephen .... 203-432-8094.. 89 D
stephen.murphy@yale.edu
MURPHY, Suzanne .... 212-678-3755 322 G
smurphy@tc.columbia.edu
MURPHY, Suzanne, K ... 215-596-8888 401 G
s.murphy@usciences.edu
MURPHY, Tara .... 781-283-2378 219 D
tm100@wellesley.edu
MURPHY, Teresa .... 202-994-6510.. 91 F
tmurphy@gwu.edu
MURPHY, Thomas .... 305-284-6650 112 E
txm747@miami.edu
MURPHY, Thomas .... 516-876-3215 319 A
murphyt@oldwestbury.edu
MURPHY, Thomas, H ... 215-898-7581 400 K
tom.murphy@isc.upenn.edu
MURPHY, Tim .... 903-886-5550 447 B
tim.murphy@tamuc.edu
MURPHY, Todd .... 610-436-3102 396 A
tmurphy@wcupa.edu
MURPHY, Todd .... 714-432-5896.. 38 E
todd.murphy@mail.cccd.edu
MURPHY, Traci .... 716-839-8587 298 B
tmurphy@daemen.edu
MURPHY, William .... 845-574-4362 313 C
wmurphy@sunyrockland.edu
MURPHY, William .... 617-552-1272 207 B
william.murphy@bc.edu
MURPHY ALEXANDER,
Coleen .... 845-758-7431 290 G
murphy@bard.edu
MURPHY-MORIARITY,
Kathy .... 802-485-2292 463 A
kmurphym@norwich.edu
MURPHY-MORRIS,
Jayne, I .... 973-290-4245 277 A
jmmorris@cse.edu
MURPHY-NORRIS,
Carmel .... 540-453-2237 474 B
murphynorrisc@brcc.edu
MURPHY-STETZ,
Katherine .... 312-567-3080 139 B
murphy@iit.edu
MURR, Christopher .... 512-245-3975 450 E
cm18@txstate.edu
MURRAH, Matt .... 214-333-5160 434 I
matt@dbu.edu
MURRAY, Aaron .... 850-729-5260 103 L
murraya8@nwfsc.edu
MURRAY, Ann Marie .... 518-956-8030 316 D
amurray2@albany.edu
MURRAY, Ben .... 507-457-1443 243 B
bmurray@smumn.edu
MURRAY, Bob .... 231-591-2850 223 J
robertmurray@ferris.edu
MURRAY, Candice .... 919-516-4024 340 C
crmurray@st-aug.edu
MURRAY, Carey .... 848-932-3958 282 A
careymur@hr.rutgers.edu
MURRAY, Carol .... 845-341-4700 311 C
carol.murray@sunyorange.edu
MURRAY, Carol .... 406-338-5441 263 B
c_murray@bfcc.edu
MURRAY,
Christopher, D .... 406-994-2513 264 D
chris.murray@msuaf.org
MURRAY, Cris .... 518-485-3390 296 H
murraych@strose.edu
MURRAY, Damon .... 704-922-2242 334 F
murray.damon@gaston.edu
MURRAY, Dave, A .... 312-629-6125 148 I
dmurray@saic.edu
MURRAY, David .... 415-703-9533.. 28 D
dmurray@cca.edu
MURRAY, David .... 616-234-3535 224 D
commdept@grcc.edu
MURRAY, Deborah .... 423-614-8118 420 J
debmurray@leeuniversity.edu
MURRAY, Delethia .... 713-221-8098 453 B
murrayd@uhd.edu
MURRAY, Dennis, J ...... 845-575-3000 305 L
dennis.murray@marist.edu
MURRAY, Derrick .... 336-750-2091 344 B
murrayd@wssu.edu
MURRAY, Dianne .... 678-225-5331 123 D
library@runiv.edu
MURRAY, Douglas, J .... 575-624-8020 287 A
dmurray@nmmi.edu
MURRAY, Edwin .... 504-568-4810 189 B
emurr1@lsuhsc.edu
MURRAY, Eric .... 425-352-8810 479 A
emurray@cascadia.edu
MURRAY, Erika, S .... 678-916-2603 114 I
emurray@johnmarshall.edu
MURRAY, Ginger .... 217-234-5253 141 D
gmurray@lakelandcollege.edu
MURRAY, Jarrod, K ...... 229-245-6490 126 G
jkmurray@valdosta.edu
MURRAY, Jay .... 203-837-8286.. 85 B
murrayj@wcsu.edu
MURRAY, Jennifer .... 315-781-3740 302 A
murray@hws.edu
MURRAY, Jill .... 570-504-1575 387 D
murrayj@lackawanna.edu
MURRAY, John, D .... 305-899-3021.. 95 C
jdmurray@barry.edu
MURRAY, Jonathan .... 706-225-5300.. 92 G
MURRAY, Julie, N .... 785-864-3131 177 D
jnmurray@ku.edu
MURRAY, Karen .... 914-594-4882 309 H
karen_murrary@nymc.edu
MURRAY, Karen .... 254-968-9103 446 E
kmurray@tarleton.edu
MURRAY, Kathleen .... 509-527-5132 486 H
kmurray@whitman.edu
MURRAY, Kevin .... 434-799-2271 471 J
kevin.murray@lpnt.net
MURRAY, Lakisha .... 718-270-5000 295 A
lmurray@mec.cuny.edu
MURRAY, Lynne .... 785-594-8308 170 I
president@bakeru.edu
MURRAY, Maggie .... 336-342-4261 337 E
murraym7639@rockinghamcc.edu
MURRAY, Margaret .... 206-726-5035 480 C
mmurray@cornish.edu
MURRAY, Mark, J .... 904-264-2172 105 L
mark.murray@iws.edu
MURRAY, Melissa .... 802-656-2925 463 E
melissa.murray@uvm.edu
MURRAY, Michele .... 206-296-6066 484 F
mmurray@seattleu.edu
MURRAY, Michelle .... 508-793-2414 208 B
mmurray@holycross.edu
MURRAY, Patrick .... 208-769-5912 131 C
patrick.murray@nic.edu
MURRAY, Percy .... 903-927-3228 458 G
pmurray@wileyc.edu
MURRAY, Peter, J .... 410-706-2461 202 D
pmurray@umaryland.edu
MURRAY, Richard .... 808-932-7644 128 E
ramurray@hawaii.edu
MURRAY, Richard .... 914-633-2013 302 G
rmurray@iona.edu
MURRAY, Rick .... 508-548-1400 220 D
MURRAY, Rita .... 212-517-0416 306 A
rmurray@mmm.edu
MURRAY, Robert .... 845-398-4125 315 B
rmurray@stac.edu
MURRAY, Rodney .... 310-900-1600.. 40 A
rmurray@elcamino.edu
MURRAY, Rodney, B ..... 215-596-8789 401 G
r.murray@usciences.edu
MURRAY, Rolande .... 410-951-3000 203 D
MURRAY, Sally .... 617-333-2929 208 E
sally.murray@curry.edu
MURRAY, Sarah, A .... 859-238-5376 179 F
sarah.murray@centre.edu
MURRAY, Sean .... 888-491-8686.. 74 F
seanmurray@westcliff.edu
MURRAY, Shailagh, J ... 212-854-3229 297 C
sjm2245@columbia.edu
MURRAY, Sharon .... 518-292-1753 313 D
murras2@sage.edu
MURRAY, Stephen .... 312-922-1884 142 H
smurray@maccormac.edu
MURRAY, Susan .... 770-229-3043 124 G
susan.murray@sctech.edu
MURRAY, Suzette .... 630-466-7900 152 C
smurray@waubonsee.edu
MURRAY, Thomas .... 773-508-2398 142 D
tmurray3@luc.edu
MURRAY, Thomas, F .... 402-280-4076 266 I
tfmurray@creighton.edu
MURRAY, Timothy, S ... 845-575-3000 305 L
tim.murray@marist.edu
MURRAY, Tom, L .... 405-789-7661 370 B
tom.murray@swcu.edu
MURRAY, Tracey, L ...... 410-951-3980 203 D
tmurray@coppin.edu
MURRAY-JENSEN, Julie 217-854-3231 132 I
MURRAY-LAURY,
Janice .... 908-737-7080 278 E
jmurray@kean.edu

MURRAY-LUKE, Shanna .... 601-318-6668 249 H smurray-luke@wmcarey.edu
MURRAY-RUST, Catherine .... 404-894-8914 118 F catherine.rust@library.gatech.edu
MURRELL, Audrey, J ..... 412-648-1651 401 B amurrell@pitt.edu
MURRELL, Dan .... 901-678-2732 427 D dhmrrell@memphis.edu
MURRELL, Terry .... 712-274-6400 170 E terry.murrell@witcc.edu
MURRET, Patricia .... 504-865-5448 189 F pmurret@loyno.edu
MURREY, Brett .... 903-468-8687 447 B brett.murrey@tamuc.edu
MURREY, Joseph .... 706-886-6831 125 D jmurrey@tfc.edu
MURRIN, Michael .... 716-926-8900 301 H mmurrin@hilbert.edu
MURRY, Kim .... 620-901-6221 170 G murry@allencc.edu
MURRY, LeKeisha .... 662-562-3271 248 D
MURRY, Melanie .... 901-678-2155 427 D mmurry@memphis.edu
MURTAGH, Michael ...... 309-467-6315 137 B mmurtagh@eureka.edu
MURTAUGH, Peter, T ... 314-286-4813 258 E ptmurtaugh@ranken.edu
MURTHA, James .... 603-623-0313 273 I
MURTHA, James .... 603-428-2284 273 H jmurtha@nec.edu
MURTHA, Katie .... 212-799-5000 303 H
MURTHA, Mitchell .... 610-355-7052 382 C mmurtha6@dccc.edu
MURTHY, Jayathi, Y ..... 310-825-2938.. 69 A jmurthy@seas.ucla.edu
MURTHY, Prahlad .... 570-408-4617 403 D prahlad.murthy@wilkes.edu
MURTHY, Pushpalatha .. 906-487-2326 227 E ppmurthy@mtu.edu
MURTHY, Raj .... 520-206-4809.. 15 D rmurthy@pima.edu
MURUGAN, Suresh, B .. 252-335-3339 341 D sbmurugan@ecsu.edu
MURUGESAN, Hayley ... 619-398-4902.. 45 C hmurugesan@hightechhigh.org
MUSA, Karen .... 469-365-1808 433 M kmusa@collin.edu
MUSAL, Edward .... 914-251-6923 319 E edward.musal@purchase.edu
MUSARA, Munetsi .... 202-274-6410.. 93 C munetsi.musara@udc.edu
MUSCARELLA, Joseph, V .... 516-572-0605 308 A joseph.muscarella@ncc.edu
MUSCARELLA, Susan .... 510-845-5373.. 29 G susan@cjc.edu
MUSCAT, Tracy .... 313-664-7864 222 F tmuscat@collegeforcreativestudies.edu
MUSCATO, Amanda .... 212-355-1501 292 J amuscato@christies.edu
MUSCENTE, Catherine ... 516-323-4710 307 F cmuscente@molloy.edu
MUSE, Bill .... 830-792-7355 443 G vpaf@schreiner.edu
MUSE, Bill .... 918-463-2931 366 B wmuse@connorsstate.edu
MUSE, Charles .... 936-261-3860 446 D cdmuse@pvamu.edu
MUSE, Clyde .... 601-857-3240 246 B vcmuse@hindscc.edu
MUSE, Douglas .... 870-612-2167.. 22 I douglas.muse@uaccb.edu
MUSE, Justin .... 540-365-4501 467 I jmuse@ferrum.edu
MUSE, Kevin .... 716-884-9120 291 L kmmuse@bryantstratton.edu
MUSE, Van .... 909-389-3205.. 59 H wmuse@sbccd.cc.ca.us
MUSEWICZ, Suellen ...... 570-961-7824 387 D musewiczs@lackawanna.edu
MUSGROVE, Jeff .... 573-875-7663 251 F jmusgrove@ccis.edu
MUSGROVE, Joel .... 540-986-1800 464 G jmusgrove@an.edu
MUSGROVE, Joel .... 520-971-5623 472 F jmusgrove@ufairfax.edu
MUSHEL, Jessica .... 845-569-3591 307 J jessica.mushel@msmc.edu
MUSHENO, Joseph .... 570-702-8933 386 G jmusheno@johnson.edu
MUSIC, Casey .... 606-886-3863 180 J casey.music@kctcs.edu
MUSICH, Michelle .... 828-766-1262 336 A mmusich@mayland.edu
MUSICH, Nita, R .... 812-465-1634 161 E nita.musich@usi.edu
MUSICK, Charles .... 276-964-7647 475 I charles.musick@sw.edu
MUSICK, Kelly .... 409-933-8496 433 L kmusick@com.edu
MUSIL, Carol, M .... 216-368-2544 349 F carol.musil@case.edu
MUSILLI, Laura .... 304-336-8226 490 F laura.musilli@westliberty.edu
MUSKAT, Yael .... 646-592-4200 326 E ymuskat@yu.edu
MUSKAVITCH, John, W 909-389-3269.. 59 H jmuskavitch@craftonhills.edu
MUSLOW, Katherine ..... 504-568-5135 189 B kmuslo@lsuhsc.edu
MUSNICKI, Sundi .... 206-543-6973 484 G smusnicki@shoreline.edu
MUSOLF, Shelly, R .... 260-422-5561 155 H srmusolf@indianatech.edu
MUSSAT-WHITLOW, Becky .... 336-750-2114 344 B whitlowbm@wssu.edu
MUSSELMAN, Inga .... 972-883-2271 455 B imusselm@utdallas.edu
MUSSELMAN, Kathy, I .. 615-898-2929 422 H kathy.musselman@mtsu.edu
MUSSELWHITE, Christy . 910-272-3533 337 D cmusselwhite@robeson.edu
MUSSER, Alison .... 440-366-7651 355 J
MUSSER, Debra, S .... 574-372-5100 155 B musserds@grace.edu
MUSSO, Daniele .... 913-360-7975 171 D dmusso@benedictine.edu
MUSTAFA, Mohamad .... 912-358-3267 123 H mustafam@savannahstate.edu
MUSTAFA, Mustafa .... 201-216-9901 277 D drmustafa@eicollege.edu
MUSTARD, Barbara .... 605-394-2228 417 B barbara.mustard@sdsmt.edu
MUSTER, Robert .... 320-308-5156 241 A robert.muster@sctcc.edu
MUSTERMAN, Cynthia, A .... 314-421-0949 260 G musterman@siba.edu
MUSTILLO, Sarah, A ..... 574-631-6642 161 C sarah.a.mustillo.5@nd.edu
MUTCHERSON, Kimberly .... 856-225-6191 281 G kim.mutcherson@rutgers.edu
MUTCHERSON, Kimberly .... 856-225-6191 282 B kim.mutcherson@rutgers.edu
MUTH, Conrad .... 215-204-4043 399 F conrad.muth@temple.edu
MUTH, Richard, J .... 724-294-3309 394 G richard.muth@iup.edu
MUTHERSBAUGH, Emily .... 509-527-2656 485 H emily.muthersbaugh@wallawalla.edu
MUTHUKUMARU, Margie .... 314-246-5990 262 C mmuthukumaru61@webster.edu
MUTONE, Paul .... 717-358-3993 384 D paul.mutone@fandm.edu
MUTTI, Anthony .... 413-782-1212 219 F amutti@wne.edu
MUURISEPP, Erik .... 617-824-8620 208 H erik_muurisepp@emerson.edu
MUYSKENS, James .... 212-817-7100 293 F president@gc.cuny.edu
MUYSKENS, Judy .... 330-569-5125 353 J
MUÑIZ, Miguel .... 787-279-1912 509 A mmuniz@bayamon.inter.edu
MUÑOZ, Mike .... 562-938-4156.. 48 D mmunoz@lbcc.edu
MUÑOZ-ALVARADO, Luis .... 787-993-8881 513 B luis.munoz1@upr.edu
MVUDUDU, Nyaradzo ... 206-281-2551 484 D nyaradzo@spu.edu
MWANGO, Kamia .... 352-395-5018 107 A kamia.mwango@sfcollege.edu
MWAURA, James .... 516-876-3194 319 A mwauraj@oldwestbury.edu
MWENDA, Margaret ...... 616-957-6036 221 P margaretmwenda@calvinseminary.edu
MWILAMBWE, Stacey ... 309-438-8611 139 E smmwila@ilstu.edu
MYER, Bonnie .... 360-623-8556 479 C bonnie.myer@centralia.edu
MYERS, Alvin, B .... 434-395-2740 469 A myersab@longwood.edu
MYERS, Amy, A .... 717-544-9051 384 D amy.myers@fandm.edu
MYERS, Andrea .... 440-375-7212 355 G amyers@lec.edu
MYERS, Angie, E .... 570-326-3761 393 G aem25@pct.edu
MYERS, Barbara, S .... 912-358-3051 123 H myersb@savannahstate.edu
MYERS, Bianca .... 641-683-5302 166 C bianca.myers@indianhills.edu
MYERS, Camille .... 843-525-8359 412 H cmyers@tcl.edu
MYERS, Cheryl .... 706-649-1290 117 A cmyers@columbustech.edu
MYERS, Cheryl .... 504-571-1290 187 E cmyers@dcc.edu
MYERS, Cyndi .... 215-572-3873 402 H cmyers@wts.edu
MYERS, Danica, A .... 302-831-8063.. 90 F danica@udel.edu
MYERS, Daniel, J .... 202-885-2127.. 90 J provost@american.edu
MYERS, David .... 413-528-7436 205 F myersd@simons-rock.edu
MYERS, Emily, A .... 301-447-5592 200 E myers@msmary.edu
MYERS, Gary, D .... 504-816-8156 190 A gmyers@nobts.edu
MYERS, Grant .... 620-947-3121 177 C granttmyers@tabor.edu
MYERS, J.C .... 802-322-1640 462 C jc.myers@goddard.edu
MYERS, James .... 314-246-7080 262 C jamesmyers79@webster.edu
MYERS, James .... 210-349-9928 441 C jmyers@ost.edu
MYERS, James, A .... 585-475-4772 313 A james.myers@rit.edu
MYERS, Jean, D .... 847-317-8001 150 H jmyers@tiu.edu
MYERS, Jennifer .... 432-335-6505 441 D jsmyers@odessa.edu
MYERS, JR., Joe .... 931-393-1553 425 C jmyers@mscc.edu
MYERS, Joshua .... 734-384-4214 227 G jmyers@monroeccc.edu
MYERS, Judi .... 570-740-0753 389 D jmyers@luzerne.edu
MYERS, Kelly .... 815-802-8260 140 D kmyers@kcc.edu
MYERS, Kelsey .... 509-542-4832 479 H kmyers@columbiabasin.edu
MYERS, Ken .... 218-281-8200 244 A kmyers@umn.edu
MYERS, Kristina .... 904-819-6290.. 98 E kmyers@flagler.edu
MYERS, Linda .... 937-393-3431 361 B lmyers@sscc.edu
MYERS, Marci .... 620-223-2700 173 C marcim@fortscott.edu
MYERS, Mary .... 815-836-5332 141 G myersma@lewisu.edu
MYERS, Mary Beth .... 317-274-1505 156 F mbmyers@iupui.edu
MYERS, Matthew, B ...... 214-768-3012 444 E mbmyers@smu.edu
MYERS, Michelle .... 816-584-6445 258 A michelle.myers@park.edu
MYERS, Nancy .... 407-823-1336 109 E nancy.myers@ucf.edu
MYERS, Nathan .... 330-941-2336 365 C nrmyers@ysu.edu
MYERS, Richard .... 609-258-9973 280 E richard.myers@princeton.edu
MYERS, Richard, B .... 785-532-6221 174 G rmyers65@ksu.edu
MYERS, Robert .... 773-878-3992 148 D rmyers@staugustine.edu
MYERS, Robert .... 310-434-4200.. 62 E myers_robert@smc.edu
MYERS, Robert, M .... 706-886-6831 125 D rmyers@tfc.edu
MYERS, Robin .... 870-508-6101.. 18 A rmyers@asumh.edu
MYERS, Ronnie .... 914-594-2624 322 J ronnie.myers3@touro.edu
MYERS, Rosemond .... 504-280-6683 189 E rmyers@uno.edu
MYERS, Stephen .... 330-972-6631 362 B smyers1@uakron.edu
MYERS, Susan .... 979-830-4273 432 C susan.myers@blinn.edu
MYERS, Theresa .... 503-686-1647 374 B theresa.myers@mtangel.edu
MYERS, Thomas .... 314-505-7329 251 I myerst@csl.edu
MYERS, Tina .... 386-506-3101.. 97 D tina.myers@daytonastate.edu
MYERS, Valerie .... 518-458-5336 296 H vmyers@strose.edu
MYFORD, Greg .... 907-786-1250.... 9 H
MYHRE, Alexander .... 207-834-8646 196 C umfkreg@maine.edu
MYHRE, Alexander .... 207-768-9581 196 E alexander.myhre@maine.edu
MYHRE, Oddmund, R ... 209-667-3652.. 33 C omyhre@csustan.edu
MYHRE, Terry .... 801-542-7600 459 A tmyhre@globeuniversity.edu
MYHRER, Larry .... 763-544-9501 233 J
MYKLES, Donald .... 970-491-5679.. 78 M donald.mykles@colostate.edu
MYLES, Nicoly .... 770-426-2725 121 C nicoly.myles@life.edu
MYLETT, Brad .... 641-472-1196 167 F bmylett@mum.edu
MYLONA, Elza .... 757-446-0340 466 I mylonae@evms.edu
MYLOTT, Sherri .... 909-593-3511.. 70 D smylott@laverne.edu
MYLREA, Brian .... 260-481-6034 159 F mylreab@pfw.edu
MYNATT, Danny .... 254-295-4023 453 E dmynatt@umhb.edu
MYNES, Jess .... 978-632-9195 215 A jmynes@mwcc.mass.edu
MYRICK, A. Yvette .... 970-945-8691.. 77 K
MYRICK, Amber .... 559-934-2132.. 73 M ambermyrick@whccd.edu
MYRICK, David .... 602-274-1885.. 15 B dmyrick@pihma.edu
MYRON, David .... 814-824-2032 390 C dmyron@mercyhurst.edu
MYRON, David, P .... 814-824-2032 390 C dmyron@mercyhurst.edu
MYRTAJ, Myftar .... 617-588-1321 206 C mmyrtaj@bfit.edu
MYSCOFSKI, Carole ...... 309-556-3577 139 G myscofsk@iwu.edu
MYSKIW, Paul .... 303-273-3204.. 78 I pmyskiw@mines.edu
MYSZENSKI, Rebecca ... 810-762-0317 228 C rebecca.myszenski@mcc.edu
MYVETT, Newton .... 770-394-8300 114 C nmyvett@aii.edu
MÚJICA KEENAN, Tanya .... 212-229-5662 308 C mujicakt@newschool.edu

N

NAAS, Fauzi .... 503-399-6526 372 C fauzi.naas@chemeketa.edu
NAATUS, Mary Kate ...... 201-761-6393 282 I mnaatus@saintpeters.edu
NAATZ, Duey .... 715-232-2758 498 A naatzd@uwstout.edu
NAATZ, Susan .... 402-280-3186 266 I susannaatz@creighton.edu
NABER, Bret .... 970-351-1887.. 83 E bret.naber@unco.edu
NABOR, Steven, E .... 801-626-6603 461 B snabor@weber.edu
NABORS, Melody .... 630-844-6852 132 D mnabors@aurora.edu
NACCARATO, Shawn ..... 620-235-4128 176 F snaccarato@pittstate.edu
NACCARI, Jennifer .... 718-933-6700 307 G jnaccari@monroecollege.edu
NACCASH, Zachary .... 603-880-8308 274 E
NACCO, Stephen, D ...... 217-443-8848 135 H snacco@dacc.edu
NACE, Timothy .... 765-998-5125 160 F tmnace@taylor.edu
NACHLAS, Rachel .... 301-846-2836 198 E rnachlas@frederick.edu
NACKMAN, Robin, E ..... 212-774-4860 306 A rnackman@mmm.edu
NACOS-BURDS, Kathy, J .... 563-556-5110 168 E nacos-burdsk@nicc.edu

NACSA, Beata .... 641-472-7000 167 F
bnacsa@mum.edu
NADAL, Rafael .... 787-751-0178 511 F
edmendez@suagm.edu
NADARAJAN,
Gunalan, L .... 734-763-4093 231 E
guna@umich.edu
NADEAU, Evelyn .... 563-588-6557 163 F
evelyn.nadeau@clarke.edu
NADEAU, Robert .... 207-629-4009 194 F
rnadeau@mccs.me.edu
NADEAU, Ryan .... 585-292-0642 308 F
rnadeau@nycc.edu
NADEL, Evelyn, H .... 843-953-2211 408 E
nadele@cofc.edu
NADEN, Michelle .... 509-527-2147 485 H
michelle.naden@wallawalla.edu
NADER, John, S .... 631-420-2239 321 B
president@farmingdale.edu
NADERSHAHI, Nader ...... 415-929-6425.. 70 E
nnadersh@pacific.edu
NADLER, Daniel .... 859-572-6447 184 A
nadlerd@nku.edu
NADLER, Jerry .... 914-594-4500 309 H
jnadler@nymc.edu
NADOL, Anne, K .... 215-204-7308 399 F
anne.nadol@temple.edu
NADOLSKI, OSFS,
Kevin .... 610-282-1100 382 E
kevin.nadolski@desales.edu
NADOLSKI, Mike .... 269-927-8109 226 D
mnadolski@lakemichigancollege.edu
NAEGELE, Chris .... 618-985-3741 139 I
chrisnaegele@jalc.edu
NAEGELI, Dan .... 940-565-2686 454 A
naegeli@unt.edu
NAEHR, Thomas .... 209-946-2765.. 70 E
tnaehr@pacific.edu
NAE`OLE, Davileigh ...... 808-984-3519 129 E
davileig@hawaii.edu
NAFF, J. Abraham .... 540-365-4493 467 I
anaff@ferrum.edu
NAFIE, John .... 909-558-4562.. 48 C
jnafie@llu.edu
NAGAGE, Champa .... 617-228-2115 214 A
cnagage@bhcc.mass.edu
NAGAI, Judy .... 209-932-2864.. 70 E
jnagai@pacific.edu
NAGAI, Nelson .... 657-278-2413.. 31 E
nnagai@fullerton.edu
NAGANATHAN, Nagi, G 541-885-1000 375 C
nagi.naganathan@oit.edu
NAGAO, Robert .... 808-956-4557 128 F
rnagao@hawaii.edu
NAGARE, Melissa .... 562-902-3386.. 65 C
melissanagare@scuhs.edu
NAGARKATTI, Prakash .. 803-777-5458 413 C
prakash@mailbox.sc.edu
NAGDEMAN, Ryan .... 312-942-8708 148 A
ryan_nagdeman@rush.edu
NAGEL, Beverly .... 507-222-4303 234 F
bnagel@carleton.edu
NAGEL, Lisa .... 567-661-2688 360 B
lisa_nagel@owens.edu
NAGEL, Lonnie .... 361-593-2420 447 D
lonnie.nagel@tamuk.edu
NAGEL, Michael .... 610-607-6294 397 B
mnagel@racc.edu
NAGEL, Michele .... 212-217-4630 299 H
michele_nagel@fitnyc.edu
NAGEL, Suzie .... 269-387-2150 232 K
suzie.nagel@wmich.edu
NAGELKERK, Jean .... 616-331-2729 224 E
nagelkej@gvsu.edu
NAGENGAST, Dana .... 909-621-8512.. 45 A
dnagengast@hmc.edu
NAGLAK, Steve .... 314-837-6777 258 J
snaglak@stlchristian.edu
NAGLE, Geoffrey, A .... 312-893-7100 137 A
gnagle@erikson.edu
NAGLE, Margaret, A ...... 207-581-3743 195 J
nagle@maine.edu
NAGLE, Ryen .... 708-974-5679 144 C
nagler@morainevalley.edu
NAGLE-KUCH, Abbey .... 563-884-5137 168 I
abbey.nagle-kuch@palmer.edu
NAGURA, Cynthia, K .... 619-216-6795.. 65 F
cnagura@swccd.edu
NAGY, Ellen .... 419-448-2063 353 H
enagy@heidelberg.edu
NAGY, Lisa .... 817-272-6080 454 J
nagy@uta.edu
NAGY, Mary Anne .... 732-571-3417 279 B
mnagy@monmouth.edu
NAGY, Paul .... 813-253-7162 101 A
pnagy@hccfl.edu
NAGY, Sharon .... 864-656-1455 408 A
snagy@clemson.edu
NAGY, Zsuzsanna .... 973-290-4134 277 A
znagy@cse.edu
NAHABEDIAN, Audrey .. 978-656-3223 214 G
nahabedianа@middlesex.mass.edu
NAHIDI, Sam .... 310-825-1728.. 69 A
snahidi@saonet.ucla.edu
NAHLEN, John .... 760-245-4271.. 73 D
john.nahlen@vvc.edu
NAHRGANG, Rick .... 507-453-2726 239 A
rnahrgang@southeastmn.edu
NAIDU, Jay .... 650-543-3996.. 51 F
jnaidu@menlo.edu
NAIDU, Santhana .... 812-237-8764 155 G
santhana.naidu@indstate.edu
NAIFEH, Zeak .... 580-581-2217 365 G
znaifeh@cameron.edu
NAIL, Steven .... 864-231-2000 406 G
snail@andersonuniversity.edu
NAILLER, Katie .... 212-650-6507 293 D
knailler@ccny.cuny.edu
NAILS, Dana .... 731-425-2628 425 B
dnails@jscc.edu
NAIMAN, Garrett .... 831-459-0111.. 70 B
NAIMI, Haleh .... 818-710-1310.. 28 A
NAIMI, Susan .... 818-710-1310.. 28 A
NAIR, Ajay .... 215-572-2900 379 A
presidentnair@arcadia.edu
NAIR, Murali .... 734-487-0077 223 H
mnair@emich.edu
NAIR, Reggie .... 918-836-6886 370 D
reggie.nair@spartan.edu
NAIR, Sheila .... 928-523-0180.. 14 H
sheila.nair@nau.edu
NAIR,
V. Parameswaran .... 212-650-7947 293 D
vpnair@ccny.cuny.edu
NAIRN, Jason .... 503-493-6238 372 I
jnairn@cu-portland.edu
NAIRN, Roderick .... 303-315-2102.. 83 C
roderick.nairn@ucdenver.edu
NAIRN, Tori .... 606-368-6059 178 D
torinairn@alc.edu
NAISH, Cheri .... 951-487-3409.. 52 I
cnaish@msjc.edu
NAJAM, Adil .... 617-358-7238 207 D
anajam@bu.edu
NAJARIAN, David .... 704-637-4335 328 A
dnajaria@catawba.edu
NAJERA, Alex .... 909-537-5138.. 33 A
alex.najera@csusb.edu
NAJERA, Carol .... 714-318-1451.. 51 A
najedw@gmail.com
NAJIB, Mona .... 708-237-5050 145 E
mnajib@nc.edu
NAJJAR, Yasar .... 508-626-4769 212 D
ynajjar@framingham.edu
NAKAGAWA, Deborah ... 808-956-0321 128 H
debn@hawaii.edu
NAKAI, Karen .... 562-951-4700.. 30 B
knakai@calstate.edu
NAKAKIHARA, Taylor .... 602-383-8228.. 16 F
tnakakihara@uat.edu
NAKAMA, Debra .... 808-984-3515 129 E
debran@hawaii.edu
NAKAMOTO, Rose .... 408-551-3583.. 62 D
rnakamotoi@scu.edu
NAKAMURA, Natalie ..... 212-659-3601 304 B
nnakamura@tkc.edu
NAKAMURA, Tim .... 760-568-3352.. 39 A
tnakamura@collegeofthedesert.edu
NAKANO, Mark, E .... 714-463-7504.. 51 A
mnakano@ketchum.edu
NAKASONE, Nancy, K ... 808-689-2525 128 G
nancynak@hawaii.edu
NAKHAI, Mandana .... 914-337-9300 297 D
mandana.nakhai@concordia-ny.edu
NAKONECHNYI, Alex .... 513-244-4264 357 A
alex.nakonechnyi@msj.edu
NAKUTIS, Kristine .... 931-221-1400 418 D
nakutisk@apsu.edu
NALAZEK, Barbara .... 740-593-2626 359 G
nalazek@ohio.edu
NALEPA, Laurie .... 818-947-2498.. 49 F
nalepal@lavc.edu
NALEVANKO, Gina .... 724-805-2251 398 F
ina.nalevanko@stvincent.edu
NALIN, Peter .... 317-278-6513 156 B
pnalin@iu.edu
NALLEY, Doug .... 919-761-2400 340 G
dnalley@sebts.edu
NALLY, Harold, D .... 606-783-2097 183 F
h.nally@moreheadstate.edu
NALYWAYKO, Serge ...... 845-451-1409 298 A
serge.nalywayko@culinary.edu
NAM, Roger .... 503-554-6171 373 C
rnam@georgefox.edu
NAMIAN, Jeff .... 718-517-7772 315 A
jnamian@edaff.com
NAMUMNART, Jared ..... 808-237-5145 127 G
jaredn@hmi.edu
NAMUO, Clyne .... 602-872-7957.. 14 A
clyne.namuo@southmountaincc.edu
NAMYET, Jay .... 541-302-0308 377 D
jnamyet@uoregon.edu
NANCE, Agnieszka .... 504-862-3348 191 B
anance@tulane.edu
NANCE, Beverlee, S ...... 910-788-6208 338 A
beverlee.nance@sccnc.edu
NANCE, Damon .... 951-372-7041.. 58 H
damon.nance@norcocollege.edu
NANCE, Donna .... 817-531-6579 451 E
dnance@txwes.edu
NANCE, Eva .... 574-631-1097 161 C
nance.1@nd.edu
NANCE, Kristy .... 910-775-4347 343 B
kristy.nance@uncp.edu
NANCE, Richard, E .... 757-683-3144 469 G
rnance@odu.edu
NANCE, Summer .... 864-488-8251 410 E
snance@limestone.edu
NANCE, Teresa, A .... 610-519-4077 402 D
terry.nance@villanova.edu
NANCE, Ty .... 660-596-7360 260 D
tnance@sfccmo.edu
NANIUZEYI, Emmanuel 912-358-3202 123 H
naniuze@savannahstate.edu
NANIUZEYI, SR.,
Emmanuel .... 912-358-3209 123 H
naniuze@savannahstate.edu
NANNEN, Tampa, J ...... 903-510-3324 452 C
tnan@tjc.edu
NANNERY, Tracy .... 716-250-7500 291 K
tbnannery@bryantstratton.edu
NANNEY, Ana .... 985-448-7940 187 F
ana.nanney@fletcher.edu
NANNEY, Chris .... 704-669-4062 333 E
nanney@clevelandcc.edu
NANNI, Louis, M .... 574-631-6123 161 C
nanni.3@nd.edu
NANYARO, Nganya, M . 703-891-1787 471 K
businessoffice@standardcollege.edu
NAPIER, Stacey .... 512-664-9043 454 I
snapier@utsystem.edu
NAPIER, William, J .... 216-650-0860 351 B
w.napier@csuohio.edu
NAPOLEON, Jose .... 954-500-2987.. 95 A
NAPOLEON, Nawa?a ..... 808-734-9283 128 I
nawaa@hawaii.edu
NAPOLES, Gerald .... 281-765-7999 439 G
gerald.napoles@lonestar.edu
NAPOLI, Brandon .... 831-479-5040.. 27 G
brnapoli@cabrillo.edu
NAPOLI, Carianya .... 206-934-4591 483 J
carianya.napoli@seattlecolleges.edu
NAPOLI, Ron .... 937-319-6139 347 G
rnapoli@antiochcollege.edu
NAPOLITANO, Daniel, J 607-871-2480 289 H
napolitano@alfred.edu
NAPOLITANO, Janet ...... 510-987-9074.. 68 C
president@ucop.edu
NAPPER, Stan .... 281-649-3173 437 H
snapper@hbu.edu
NAPRSTEK, James, R .... 563-588-7970 167 D
james.naprstek@loras.edu
NAQUIN, Rose .... 504-520-7301 193 A
xubooks@xula.edu
NARAGON, Pieter .... 260-982-5258 158 T
pynaragon@manchester.edu
NARCISSE,
Margaretta, S .... 913-253-5097 176 I
margaretta.narcisse@spst.edu
NARDI, Peter, A .... 410-293-1585 504 I
nardi@usna.edu
NARDIN, Gail .... 212-752-1530 304 D
gail.nardin@limcollege.edu
NARDINO, Carol .... 802-387-6877 462 D
cnardino@landmark.edu
NARDONE, Mary, S ...... 617-552-0346 207 B
mary.nardone@bc.edu
NARDONE, Paul .... 570-674-8144 390 G
pnardone@misericordia.edu
NARDUCCI, Julie .... 951-785-2578.. 47 C
jnarducc@lasierra.edu
NARGANG, Jim .... 740-389-4636 356 B
nargangj@mtc.edu
NARKIEWICZ, Geralyn .. 906-635-2228 226 E
gnarkiewicz@lssu.edu
NARLESKI, Greg .... 413-549-4600 210 A
NARMONTAS, Steven .... 413-782-1778 219 F
steven.narmontas@wne.edu
NARVAEZ, Maria .... 213-477-2908.. 52 G
mnarvaez@msmu.edu
NARY, Thomas, I .... 617-552-3225 207 B
thomas.nary@bc.edu
NAS, Paula .... 810-424-5486 231 G
pnas@umflint.edu
NASE, Christina .... 856-415-2297 281 D
cnase@rcgc.edu
NASH, Amy .... 724-938-4324 394 B
nash@calu.edu
NASH, Bob .... 714-241-6143.. 38 C
bnash@coastline.edu
NASH, Bob .... 509-420-4545 481 C
NASH, Charles, R .... 205-348-8347.... 7 F
cnash@uasystem.edu
NASH, David .... 215-955-6969 400 A
david.nash@jefferson.edu
NASH, Diana .... 212-774-0724 306 A
dnash@mmm.edu
NASH, Gail .... 731-989-6072 420 C
gnash@fhu.edu
NASH, Julie .... 978-934-4191 211 G
julie_nash@uml.edu
NASH, Kandace .... 509-865-8530 481 G
nash_k@heritage.edu
NASH, Katie .... 608-265-1988 496 C
katie.nash@wisc.edu
NASH, Kylie .... 256-372-7164.... 1 A
kyle.nash@aamu.edu
NASH, Laura .... 203-254-4000.. 86 I
lnash@fairfield.edu
NASH, Leon .... 231-439-6443 228 E
lnash3@ncmich.edu
NASH, Meghann .... 409-944-1238 437 B
mnash@gc.edu
NASH, Mika .... 413-737-7000 205 A
NASH, Myranda .... 828-884-8280 327 C
nashmh@brevard.edu
NASH, Peggy .... 812-535-5296 160 B
peggy.nash@smwc.edu
NASH, Richard .... 812-866-7029 155 C
nash@hanover.edu
NASH, Robert .... 870-235-4075.. 21 D
robertnash@saumag.edu
NASH, Sarah .... 208-459-5016 130 D
snash@collegeofidaho.edu
NASH, Stephen .... 972-708-7573 435 H
admissions-director@diu.edu
NASH, Timothy, G .... 989-837-4129 228 H
tgnash@northwood.edu
NASH, Victoria .... 262-691-5495 500 H
vnash@wcfc.edu
NASHUA, Lisa .... 909-652-6542.. 36 A
lisa.nashua@chaffey.edu
NASHWINTER, Alissa .... 804-758-6724 475 G
anashwinter@rappahannock.edu
NASIM, Aashir .... 804-828-8947 473 F
anasim@vcu.edu
NASIO, Crystal .... 951-639-5560.. 52 I
cnasio@msjc.edu
NASON, Bradley, A .... 406-657-1018 265 E
nasonb@rocky.edu
NASON, Stephen, S ...... 207-509-7284 195 H
snason@unity.edu
NASORI, Renee .... 619-644-7000.. 44 I
renee.nasori@gcccd.edu
NASR, Nabil .... 585-475-5106 313 A
nasr@rit.edu
NASSAR, Richard .... 214-333-6801 434 I
richardn@dbu.edu
NASSAR, Sayed .... 248-370-3781 229 G
nassar@oakland.edu
NASSER, Abdul .... 415-452-7454.. 37 A
anasser@ccsf.edu
NASSER, David .... 434-592-7731 468 H
davidnasser@liberty.edu
NASSER, Dawn, S .... 217-443-8755 135 H
dnasser@dacc.edu
NASSER, Edward, D ...... 520-621-5449.. 16 G
enasser@email.arizona.edu
NASSER, Ryn .... 919-613-5577 328 G
ryn.nasser@duke.edu
NASSIRPOUR, Soodi ..... 217-786-2415 142 B
soodi.nassirpour@llcc.edu

NEGRÓN, Dennis .... 423-236-2813 424 B
negron@southern.edu
NEGRETE, Elizabeth .... 818-947-2361.. 49 F
negretme@lavc.edu
NEGRETE, Michael .... 510-869-6511.. 59 F
mnegrete@samuelmerritt.edu
NEGRETE, Nick .... 310-665-6967.. 54 I
nnegrete@otis.edu
NEGRITTO, Leslie .... 909-621-8030.. 37 D
leslie.negritto@cgu.edu
NEGRON, Dalia .... 518-525-6850 306 E
dalia.negron@sphp.com
NEGRON, Frankie .... 787-761-0640 512 F
decanoadministracion@utcpr.edu
NEGRON, Luz .... 787-743-4041 507 D
lznegron@columbiacentral.edu
NEGRON, Olga .... 787-832-6000 508 D
mortiz@icprjc.edu
NEGRON, Zaima .... 787-754-7597 508 J
zynegron@inter.edu
NEGRON-BERRIOS,
Juan, A 787-857-3600 508M
janegron@br.inter.edu
NEGRON DELGADO,
Juan Luis .... 787-841-2000 510 K
juan_negron@pucpr.edu
NEHME, George .... 315-792-3054 324 B
genehme@utica.edu
NEHMER, Matthew .... 805-765-9300.. 62 B
NEHRA, Terese .... 313-664-7677 222 F
tnehra@collegeforcreativestudies.edu
NEHRING, Kellie .... 619-260-4700.. 71 J
knehring@sandiego.edu
NEHRING, Wendy, M ... 423-439-7051 419 J
nehringw@etsu.edu
NEHUS, Jennifer .... 509-359-7431 480 E
jnehus23@ewu.edu
NEIBAUER, Todd .... 231-995-1061 228 G
tneibauer@nmc.edu
NEIBERG, Maryke .... 508-373-5707 216 B
maryke.neiberg@mcphs.edu
NEIDERHISER,
Jonathan .... 605-331-6667 417 E
jonathan.neiderhiser@usiouxfalls.edu
NEIDHARDT, Neil .... 734-432-5316 227 A
nneidhardt@madonna.edu
NEIDORF, David .... 760-872-2000.. 41 C
dneidorf@deepsprings.edu
NEIDUSKI, Becky .... 336-278-6350 328 K
bneiduski@elon.edu
NEIDY, Jon .... 309-677-2510 133 B
neidy@fsmail.bradley.edu
NEIGER, Brad, L .... 801-422-3567 458 H
neiger@byu.edu
NEIHOF, JR., John, E ... 601-366-8880 249 G
jneihof@wbs.edu
NEIHOUSE, Kristina ...... 305-809-3504.. 99 C
kristina.neihouse@fkcc.edu
NEIKIRK, Mark .... 859-572-1449 184 A
neikirkm1@nku.edu
NEIL, Leland .... 801-622-1573 459 N
leland.neil@stevenhenager.edu
NEILING, Francine .... 863-616-6426.. 99 H
fneiling@flsouthern.edu
NEILL, Jim .... 718-270-7482 317 E
jim.neill@downstate.edu
NEILS, Kathleen, A .... 603-862-2421 274 G
kathy.neils@unh.edu
NEILSON, Eric, G .... 312-503-0340 145 F
egneilson@northwestern.edu
NEILSON, Jonathan, B .. 651-603-6315 235 F
neilson@csp.edu
NEILSON, Leanne .... 805-493-3145.. 29 H
neilson@callutheran.edu
NEIMAN, Gershon .... 845-731-3700 326 J
NEINER, Catherine .... 404-413-1835 119 E
cneiner1@gsu.edu
NEIPRIS, Cynthia .... 619-574-6909.. 54 K
cneipris@pacificcollege.edu
NEISES, Marlene .... 414-382-6017 492 A
marlene.neises@alverno.edu
NEISES, Sarah .... 920-424-0401 497 B
neises@uwosh.edu
NEISSER, Phil .... 315-386-7328 320 E
neisserp@canton.edu
NEITZEL, Jennifer .... 989-964-4000 230 B
NEITZEL, Lynn .... 608-743-4508 499 C
lneitzel@blackhawk.edu
NEKVASIL, Nancy .... 574-284-4000 160 C
nekvasil@saintmarys.edu
NELANT, Dan .... 317-805-1788 488 F
dan.nelant@salemu.edu
NELDNER, Erika, B .... 770-720-5514 123 E
ebn@reinhardt.edu
NELEN, Carla .... 814-886-6411 391 B
cnelen@mtaloy.edu
NELHUEBEL, Robin, M . 757-240-2200 471 A
robin.nelhuebel@rivhs.com
NELKENBAUM,
Avrohom Yaakov .... 718-645-0536 307 C
NELL, Sharon, D 512-448-8620 442M
sharonn@stedwards.edu
NELLE, Nora .... 215-517-2659 379 A
nellen@arcadia.edu
NELLER, Irene .... 805-565-6016.. 74 K
ineller@westmont.edu
NELLESEN, Gary .... 909-274-4850.. 52 H
gnellesen@mtsac.edu
NELLIS, Duane .... 740-593-1804 359 G
president@ohio.edu
NELLIS, Ginny .... 802-258-3283 463 C
ginny.nellis@worldlearning.org
NELLIS, Leah .... 765-455-9441 156 D
lmnellis@iu.edu
NELMS, Jim, A .... 936-261-1932 446 D
janelms@pvamu.edu
NELMS, Kristi .... 217-854-5594 132 I
kristi.nelms@blackburn.edu
NELONS, Dee .... 253-680-7000 478 E
dnelons@batestech.edu
NELSEN, Jeff, A .... 515-574-1115 166 E
nelsen@iowacentral.edu
NELSEN, Kyle .... 402-375-7274 268 G
kynelse1@wsc.edu
NELSEN, Robert, S .... 916-278-7737.. 32 E
nelsen@csus.edu
NELSON, Adam .... 781-239-2664 214 E
anelson@massbay.edu
NELSON, Alex .... 310-233-4312.. 49 A
nelsonaw@lahc.edu
NELSON, Allan .... 302-857-1707.. 90 D
anelso11@dtcc.edu
NELSON, Andrew .... 515-433-5020 164 C
adnelson@dmacc.edu
NELSON, Andrew .... 830-372-8011 449 B
anelson@tlu.edu
NELSON, Andrew, J .... 715-836-5368 496 D
nelsonan@uwec.edu
NELSON, Andy .... 712-274-5148 168 B
nelsona@morningside.edu
NELSON, Annella .... 318-675-7013 189 C
anelso@lsuhsc.edu
NELSON, Anthony, C ..... 919-530-6175 342 A
acnelson@nccu.edu
NELSON, April .... 580-477-7896 371 F
april.nelson@wosc.edu
NELSON, Bernard .... 504-398-2108 191 C
bnelson@uhcno.edu
NELSON, Brandi .... 701-662-1509 346 D
brandi.nelson@lrsc.edu
NELSON, Brian .... 612-381-3042 235 H
bnelson@dunwoody.edu
NELSON, Camille, A ..... 202-274-4004.. 90 J
canelson@american.edu
NELSON, Carol .... 909-274-5431.. 52 H
cnelson@mtsac.edu
NELSON, Carolyn .... 510-885-3942.. 31 C
carolyn.nelson@csueastbay.edu
NELSON, Chris .... 870-633-4480.. 19 B
cnelson@eacc.edu
NELSON, Christina .... 253-680-7180 478 E
cnelson@batestech.edu
NELSON, Christopher .... 757-388-2900 471 D
cnelson@sentara.edu
NELSON, Daniel .... 651-638-6241 234 C
dc-nelson@bethel.edu
NELSON, David .... 617-879-7100 212 E
nelson@massart.edu
NELSON, David .... 312-662-4151 131 H
dnelson@adler.edu
NELSON, David .... 352-733-1700 109 F
nelsodr@ufl.edu
NELSON, Deanna .... 816-501-3727 250 F
deanna.nelson@avila.edu
NELSON, Denise .... 619-849-2477.. 57 E
denisenelson@pointloma.edu
NELSON, Diane .... 415-422-2444.. 71 K
dlnelson3@usfca.edu
NELSON, Dirk .... 806-651-3501 448 C
jdnelson@wtamu.edu
NELSON, Don .... 570-740-0750 389 D
dnelson@luzerne.edu
NELSON, Doug .... 563-387-1862 167 E
nelsondg@luther.edu
NELSON, Douglas .... 909-869-3419.. 30 D
dnelson1@cpp.edu
NELSON, Eric .... 805-565-6114.. 74 K
enelson@westmont.edu
NELSON, Eric .... 267-341-3205 386 A
enelson@holyfamily.edu
NELSON, Evelyn, C .... 561-237-7816 102 V
enelson@lynn.edu
NELSON, Fred .... 605-642-6848 416 I
fred.nelson@bhsu.edu
NELSON, Gena, C .... 315-267-2330 319 D
nelsongc@potsdam.edu
NELSON, Glen .... 208-282-3540 130 H
nelsglen@isu.edu
NELSON, Greg .... 415-884-3100.. 39 C
gnelson@marin.edu
NELSON, Gwynth .... 803-780-1199 414 E
gnelson@voorhees.edu
NELSON, Hart .... 314-539-5311 259 C
hartnelson@stlcc.edu
NELSON, Heidi .... 503-883-2568 373 H
hnelson2@linfield.edu
NELSON, Holly .... 503-399-5145 372 C
holly.nelson@chemeketa.edu
NELSON, James, H .... 606-693-5000 182 G
jnelson@kmbc.edu
NELSON, Jamie .... 510-204-0733.. 36 J
jnelson@cdsp.edu
NELSON, Janet .... 208-885-2258 131 G
janetenelson@uidaho.edu
NELSON, Jay .... 763-576-4054 237 C
jnelson@anokatech.edu
NELSON, Jay .... 763-576-4054 237 D
jnelson@anokatech.edu
NELSON, Jay, S .... 423-439-7900 419 J
nelsonjs@etsu.edu
NELSON, Jeff .... 218-235-2193 241 E
jeff.nelson@vcc.edu
NELSON, Jen .... 208-459-5121 130 D
jnelson@collegeofidaho.edu
NELSON, Jennifer .... 770-528-3554 116 C
jnelson@chattahoocheetech.edu
NELSON, Jennifer .... 770-975-4000 116 C
jnelson@chattahoocheetech.edu
NELSON, Jennifer, C .... 334-347-2623.... 2 A
jnelson@escc.edu
NELSON, Jessica .... 801-585-5950 460 E
jessica.nelson@admin.utah.edu
NELSON, Jillian .... 309-438-2592 139 E
jyoun11@ilstu.edu
NELSON, Jim .... 479-619-3159.. 20 D
jnelson3@nwacc.edu
NELSON, Jim .... 304-327-4000 489 P
jnelson@bluefieldstate.edu
NELSON, Joan .... 713-348-4759 442 K
joan.m.nelson@rice.edu
NELSON, Joseph, B ...... 803-533-3740 412 C
jnelso12@scsu.edu
NELSON, Karen .... 706-419-1288 117 B
karen.nelson@covenant.edu
NELSON, Karen .... 724-653-2191 383 A
knelson@dec.edu
NELSON, Karen, L .... 617-585-0200 206 F
karen.nelson@the-bac.edu
NELSON, Kathleen .... 208-535-5313 130 C
kathleen.nelson@cei.edu
NELSON, Kathleen, L .... 304-462-6100 490 C
kathleen.nelson@glenville.edu
NELSON, Kathy .... 937-328-6006 350 L
nelsonk@clarkstate.edu
NELSON, Kent, E .... 208-885-6125 131 G
kentnelson@uidaho.edu
NELSON, Kim .... 507-433-0664 240 F
kimberly.nelson@riverland.edu
NELSON, Kim .... 701-671-2131 346 E
kim.j.nelson@ndscs.edu
NELSON, Kim .... 360-438-4576 483 H
knelson@stmartin.edu
NELSON, Kirk .... 225-768-1793 186 F
timothy.nelson@franu.edu
NELSON, Kristi, A .... 513-556-2588 362 D
provost@uc.edu
NELSON, Kristy .... 989-686-9422 223 G
kristynelson@delta.edu
NELSON, Kurt, D .... 570-577-1183 379 F
kurt.nelson@bucknell.edu
NELSON, Laura .... 701-483-2214 345 D
laura.m.nelson@dickinsonstate.edu
NELSON, Linda, J .... 404-413-3300 119 E
lnelson@gsu.edu
NELSON, Linda, J .... 404-413-2567 119 E
lnelson@gsu.edu
NELSON, Lindsey, C ..... 207-859-4622 193 E
lindsey.nelson@colby.edu
NELSON, Lisa .... 570-740-0732 389 D
lnelson@luzerne.edu
NELSON, Liz .... 301-687-3163 203 E
eanelson@frostburg.edu
NELSON, Louis .... 434-924-6449 473 A
ln6n@virginia.edu
NELSON, Louise, C ...... 310-206-1355.. 69 A
lnelson@conet.ucla.edu
NELSON, Mandy .... 208-426-1294 129 I
mandynelson@boisestate.edu
NELSON, Margaret .... 718-289-5608 293 B
margaret.nelson@bcc.cuny.edu
NELSON, Mark .... 303-797-5654.. 76 I
mark.nelson@arapahoe.edu
NELSON, Mark .... 205-348-4786.... 7 G
mnelson@ua.edu
NELSON, Mark .... 252-940-6213 332 C
mark.nelson@beaufortccc.edu
NELSON, Mark, W .... 607-255-6418 297 F
mwn2@cornell.edu
NELSON, Marshall .... 318-670-9349 190 J
mnelson@susla.edu
NELSON, Mary .... 314-539-5330 259 C
mnelson178@stlcc.edu
NELSON, Merritt .... 402-941-6141 267 L
nelson@midlandu.edu
NELSON, Michelle .... 262-691-3484 500 H
mnelson63@wctc.edu
NELSON, Mike .... 256-765-4440.... 8 E
mnelson7@una.edu
NELSON, Nancy .... 414-227-3203 497 A
nln@uwm.edu
NELSON, Peter, C .... 312-996-3259 151 B
nelson@uic.edu
NELSON, Phil .... 909-469-5661.. 74 I
pnelson@westernu.edu
NELSON, Randy .... 605-575-6585 417 E
randy.nelson@usiouxfalls.edu
NELSON, Rebecca .... 773-244-5759 145 A
rnelson1@northpark.edu
NELSON, Rencelly .... 691-320-2480 505 B
rencelly@comfsm.fm
NELSON, Rhonda, L ...... 701-788-4208 345 E
rhonda.nelson@mayvillestate.edu
NELSON, Richard, R ..... 715-365-4415 500 D
nelson@nicoletcollege.edu
NELSON, Robert .... 504-865-2881 189 F
rjnelson@loyno.edu
NELSON, Robyn .... 818-299-5500.. 73 K
rnelson@westcoastuniversity.edu
NELSON, Ryan .... 218-477-5869 239 D
ryan.nelson@mnstate.edu
NELSON, Sandra .... 717-901-5117 385 K
snelson@harrisburgu.edu
NELSON, Sarah .... 661-255-1050.. 28 K
NELSON, Sarah .... 715-425-3500 497 E
sarah.r.nelson@uwrf.edu
NELSON, Sasha .... 970-682-1118.. 78 G
sasha.nelson@cncc.edu
NELSON, Scott Bernard 503-883-2498 373 H
scott.nelson@linfield.edu
NELSON, Sean .... 608-262-5316 496 B
snelson@uwsa.edu
NELSON, Shad .... 361-593-2454 447 D
shad.nelson@tamuk.edu
NELSON, Shannan .... 605-274-5330 415 B
shannan.nelson@augie.edu
NELSON, Shawn .... 402-941-6127 267 L
nelsons@midlandu.edu
NELSON, Shawn, K .... 412-578-6140 380 E
skbutler@carlow.edu
NELSON, Stacy .... 707-965-6282.. 55 D
snelson@puc.edu
NELSON, Steve .... 504-568-4009 189 B
snelso1@lsuhsc.edu
NELSON, Steve .... 860-465-5525.. 84 J
nelsons@easternct.edu
NELSON, Steven .... 201-692-2477 277 K
snelson@fdu.edu
NELSON, Suzanne .... 267-502-2482 379 D
suzanne.nelson@brynathyn.edu
NELSON, Suzy .... 617-253-8566 215 G
NELSON, Tammy .... 207-768-2747 194 J
tnelson@nmcc.edu
NELSON, Tiffany .... 404-270-5195 125 B
tnelso15@spelman.edu
NELSON, Tim .... 301-891-4045 204 C
tnelson@wau.edu
NELSON, Timothy, J ..... 231-995-1010 228 G
tnelson@nmc.edu

NELSON, Tony .... 270-707-3777 181 E tony.nelson@kctcs.edu
NELSON, Tony .... 931-372-3234 426 E tnelson@tntech.edu
NELSON, Tonya .... 970-564-6222.. 81 K tonya.nelson@pueblocc.edu
NELSON, Trevor .... 302-831-8641.. 90 F trnelson@udel.edu
NELSON, Trista .... 269-467-9945 224 A tnelson@glenoaks.edu
NELSON, Troy .... 417-626-1234 257 F nelson.troy@occ.edu
NELSON, Veronica .... 775-289-3589 271 B veronica.nelson@gbcnv.edu
NELSON, Wilbert .... 602-285-7174.. 13 F wilbert.nelson@phoenixcollege.edu
NELSON, William, L ..... 800-867-2243.. 54 J wnelson@pacific-college.edu
NELSON CHRISTOPH, Julie .... 253-879-3207 485 E jchristoph@pugetsound.edu
NELSON-HENSLEY, Susan .... 740-695-9500 348 F snelsonhensley@belmontcollege.edu
NELSON MOELLER, Rachel .... 610-330-5810 387 E moellerr@lafayette.edu
NELSON NASH, Denise 909-607-7180.. 63 E dnelnash@scrippscollege.edu
NELSON WINGER, Elyse .... 309-556-3179 139 G enelsonw@iwu.edu
NEMCIK, Henry .... 505-277-1586 288 G hnemcik@unm.edu
NEMEC, Mark, R .... 203-254-4000.. 86 I mnemec@fairfield.edu
NEMECZ, Attila .... 252-940-6387 332 C attila.nemecz@beaufortccc.edu
NEMETI, Jami .... 417-862-9533 253 D jnemeti@globaluniversity.edu
NEMITZ, James, W .... 304-647-6200 491 A jnemitz@osteo.wvsom.edu
NENON, Tom .... 901-678-2119 427 D tnenon@memphis.edu
NEPA, Beth .... 315-781-3315 302 A nepa@hws.edu
NEPOMUCENO, Tina ..... 708-209-3545 135 F tina.nepomuceno@cuchicago.edu
NEPPER, Terry, S .... 806-651-2747 448 C tnepper@wtamu.edu
NEPPL, Susan .... 952-885-5387 242 I sneppl@nwhealth.edu
NEPTUNE, Vivian .... 787-999-9531 514 B vneptune@law.upr.edu
NERE, Jeremy .... 715-394-8306 498 B jnere@uwsuper.edu
NERGER, Janice, L .... 970-491-6974.. 78 M janice.nerger@colostate.edu
NERIA, Angela .... 620-235-4603 176 F aneria@pittstate.edu
NERIANI, Kelly .... 937-328-6075 350 L nerianik@clarkstate.edu
NERO, Logan .... 918-463-2931 366 B logan.nero@connorsstate.edu
NERY, Annebelle .... 760-776-7442.. 39 A anery@collegeofthedesert.edu
NERY, Ernesto .... 909-384-8687.. 59 I eneryjr@sbccd.cc.ca.us
NERY, Ernesto .... 510-436-2467.. 56 H enery@peralta.edu
NERY, Karen .... 910-893-1630 327 E nery@campbell.edu
NESBARY, Dale, K .... 231-777-0311 228 D dale.nesbary@muskegoncc.edu
NESBIT, Jim .... 937-298-3399 355 F jim.nesbit@kc.edu
NESBIT, Randy .... 865-882-4583 425 G nesbitr@roanestate.edu
NESBIT, Ryan, A .... 706-542-1361 125 G rnesbit@uga.edu
NESBITT, Joan, M .... 573-341-4111 261 E nesbittj@mst.edu
NESBITT, Kathy .... 303-860-5600.. 82 N kathy.nesbitt@cu.edu
NESBITT, Sean .... 970-945-8691.. 77 K
NESBITT, Shawna .... 214-648-2168 457 B shawna.nesbitt@utsouthwestern.edu
NESBITT, Thomas, W .... 315-267-2180 319 D nesbittw@potsdam.edu
NESHEIM, Jeff .... 303-797-5075.. 76 I jeffrey.nesheim@arapahoe.edu
NESHEIM-KAUFFMAN, Rhonda, K .... 641-422-4500 168 D nesherho@niacc.edu
NESIUS, Elizabeth .... 201-360-4381 278 C enesius@hccc.edu
NESLER, Mitchell, S ..... 518-587-2100 321 A mitchell.nesler@esc.edu
NESMITH, Chris .... 803-812-7330 413 G cnesmit@mailbox.sc.edu
NESMITH, Mark, A .... 304-326-1473 488 F mnesmith@salemu.edu
NESMITH, Robert, M .... 859-238-5356 179 F bob.nesmith@centre.edu
NESS, Claudia, L .... 509-527-5040 486 H nesscl@whitman.edu
NESS, Deborah .... 708-209-3115 135 F deb.ness@cuchicago.edu
NESS, Edward Craig ..... 409-880-8395 449 H craig.ness@lamar.edu
NESS, Eric .... 570-389-4517 394 A eness@bloomu.edu
NESS, Kim .... 507-453-2676 239 A kimberly.ness@southeastmn.edu
NESS, Melvin, M .... 646-565-6000 322 J melvin.ness@touro.edu
NESS, Phil .... 419-448-2384 353 H philness@heidelberg.edu
NESS, Shanda .... 323-259-2500.. 54 E sness@oxy.edu
NESSAN, Craig, L .... 563-589-0207 170 D cnessan@wartburgseminary.edu
NESSELRODE, Brian ...... 904-819-6206.. 98 E bness@flagler.edu
NESSET, Andrew .... 651-773-1705 237 G andrew.nesset@century.edu
NESSON, Craig .... 610-647-4400 386 C cnelson@immaculata.edu
NESTER, Joel .... 434-791-5663 464 O jnester@averett.edu
NESTER, Keri .... 912-583-3287 115 E knester@bpc.edu
NESTER, Michael .... 856-227-7200 276 E mnester@camdencc.edu
NESTER, Stefanie, E ...... 610-799-1740 388 I snester2@lccc.edu
NESTOR, David, A .... 802-656-3380 463 E david.nestor@uvm.edu
NESTOR, Mark .... 215-596-8910 401 G m.nestor@usciences.edu
NETHERTON, James, S . 478-301-2710 121 E netherton_js@mercer.edu
NETLAND, John, T .... 731-661-5355 427 C jnetland@uu.edu
NETTELL, Katie .... 701-662-1517 346 D katie.nettell@lrsc.edu
NETTLES, Evelyn .... 615-963-7004 426 D enettles1@tnstate.edu
NETTLES, Keonn .... 334-229-8356.... 4 B knettles@alasu.edu
NETTLES, Lafawn .... 270-384-8033 183 C nettlesl@lindsey.edu
NETTLES, Lindsey, M .... 843-953-5254 407 F lnettles@citadel.edu
NETTLES, Stephen .... 858-513-9240.. 26 G stephen.nettles@ashford.edu
NETTLETON, Bridget ...... 518-587-2100 321 A bridget.nettleton@esc.edu
NETZHAMMER, Mel .... 360-546-9581 486 A mel.netzhammer@vancouver.wsu.edu
NEU, Denise .... 281-290-2621 439 G denise.neu@lonestar.edu
NEUBAUER, Jennifer ..... 217-333-1471 151 A jln5@illinois.edu
NEUBAUER, Trish .... 563-387-1567 167 E neubautr@luther.edu
NEUBERGER, Boruch .... 443-548-6060 201 A byn@nirc.edu
NEUBERGER, Sheftel, M .... 410-484-7200 201 A sheftel@nirc.edu
NEUBRANDER, Johanna .... 423-354-5106 425 E jlneubrander@northeaststate.edu
NEUBRANDER, Judy ..... 309-438-7400 139 E jlneubr@ilstu.edu
NEUENFELDT, Patrick ... 920-693-1222 499 G patrick.neuenfeldt@gotoltc.edu
NEUENSCHWANDER, Pierre, F .... 903-877-7480 456 D pierre.neuenschwander@uthct.edu
NEUFELD, Iris .... 419-358-3322 348 G neufeldi@bluffton.edu
NEUFELD, Jane .... 773-508-3852 142 D jneufe@luc.edu
NEUFELD, Kenley .... 805-965-0581.. 62 C neufeld@sbcc.edu
NEUFIND, Nate .... 402-399-2658 266 F nneufind@csm.edu
NEUFVILLE, Janette .... 301-576-0123 204 C jneufvil@wau.edu
NEUHARD, Ian .... 904-632-3030 100 B ineuhard@fscj.edu
NEUHAUSER, Crystal .... 603-899-1159 273 F neuhauserc@franklinpierce.edu
NEUHOLD-RAVIKUMAR, Patti .... 405-974-2311 370 K pneuhold@uco.edu
NEUMAN, Dave .... 267-341-3642 386 A dneuman10@holyfamily.edu
NEUMAN, Kevin .... 715-346-3875 497 F kneuman@uwsp.edu
NEUMAN, Yisroel .... 732-367-1060 275 J
NEUMANN, Bruce .... 262-691-5226 500 H bneumann6@wctc.edu
NEUMANN, Emily .... 715-394-8396 498 B eneuman2@uwsuper.edu
NEUMANN, Gregory ..... 716-645-6290 316 F 0405mgr@fheg.follett.com
NEUMANN, Yoram .... 818-575-6800.. 67 G yoram.neumann@tuw.edu
NEUMEYER, Greg .... 319-398-7650 167 C greg.neumeyer@kirkwood.edu
NEUPAUER, Nicholas, C .... 724-287-8711 380 A nicholas.neupauer@bc3.edu
NEUSER, Brianna .... 920-686-6213 496 A brianna.neuser@sl.edu
NEUVILLE, Jeff .... 828-327-7000 333 B jneuville@cvcc.edu
NEVAREZ, Amy .... 909-652-6020.. 36 A amy.nevarez@chaffey.edu
NEVAREZ, Arelis .... 787-780-0070 506 F anevarez@caribbean.edu
NEVAREZ, Augustine ..... 831-755-6825.. 44 K anevarez@hartnell.edu
NEVE, Nancy .... 906-635-2080 226 E nneve@lssu.edu
NEVELS, Lyle .... 510-642-4096.. 68 D lnevels@berkeley.edu
NEVELS, Tiawanna, S .... 919-516-4150 340 C tsnevels@st-aug.edu
NEVERS, Jeff .... 207-221-4237 196 G jnevers@une.edu
NEVILLE, Nancy .... 216-421-7427 350 M nneville@cia.edu
NEVILLS, Landee .... 417-328-1826 259 L lnevills@sbuniv.edu
NEVILS, Lane .... 504-278-6277 188 A
NEVINGER, Jason .... 585-275-3221 323 J jason.nevinger@rochester.edu
NEVINS, Daniel .... 212-678-8067 303 G danevins@jtsa.edu
NEVOIS, Dana .... 636-481-3488 254 A dnevois@jeffco.edu
NEW, Jim .... 775-673-7014 271 D jnew@tmcc.edu
NEWAGO, Jennifer .... 715-682-1387 495 C jnewago@northland.edu
NEWBERG, Bella .... 760-750-4444.. 33 B newberg@csusm.edu
NEWBERRY, Byron .... 405-425-5428 367 G byron.newberry@oc.edu
NEWBERRY, Michelle ... 570-961-7895 387 D newberrym@lackawanna.edu
NEWBOLD, Lance .... 405-736-0281 369 I lnewbold@rose.edu
NEWBY, Jennifer .... 541-383-7530 372 B jlnewby@cocc.edu
NEWBY, Stewart .... 903-675-6235 452 B stewart.newby@tvcc.edu
NEWBY, Teresa .... 952-446-4484 235 G newbyt@crown.edu
NEWBY-ALEXANDER, Cassandra .... 757-823-8118 469 F clnewby-alexander@nsu.edu
NEWCOM, Steve .... 651-255-6139 243 D snewcom@unitedseminary.edu
NEWCOMB, Carrie .... 804-627-5300 465 C carrie_newcomb@bshsi.org
NEWCOMB, Debbie .... 805-289-8976.. 73 B dnewcomb@vcccd.edu
NEWCOMB, Ron .... 770-975-4125 116 C
NEWCOMB, Sherri .... 718-631-6221 295 D snewcomb@qcc.cuny.edu
NEWCOMBE, Patricia .... 413-782-1201 219 F pnewcombe@law.wne.edu
NEWCOMBE, Rodd .... 321-674-7110.. 99 B newcombe@fit.edu
NEWCOMER, Brett .... 575-674-2266 285 H
NEWELL, AJ .... 540-654-1934 472 I anewell@umw.edu
NEWELL, Crystal .... 434-961-5339 475 F cnewell@pvcc.edu
NEWELL, Diane .... 251-380-9090.... 5 D dnewell@faulkner.edu
NEWELL, Dub .... 502-852-6316 185 C walter.newell@louisville.edu
NEWELL, Jeffrey .... 978-921-4242 216 F jeffrey.newell@montserrat.edu
NEWELL, Jennifer .... 202-379-7808.. 92 G
NEWELL, Kate .... 912-525-5000 123 G knewell@scad.edu
NEWELL, Mallory .... 408-864-8777.. 43 C newellmallory@deanza.edu
NEWELL, Patrick, A .... 530-898-5394.. 31 A pnewell@csuchico.edu
NEWELL, Zach .... 217-581-6072 136 E znewell@eiu.edu
NEWGARD, Debra .... 763-488-2652 238 B debra.newgard@hennepintech.edu
NEWHALL, JR., Edward 401-454-6307 405 D enewhall@risd.edu
NEWHART, Allison .... 919-515-3932 342 B anewhar@ncsu.edu
NEWHART, Daniel .... 814-865-3397 392 B dwn24@psu.edu
NEWHOUSE, Ben .... 641-269-3709 165 J newhouse@grinnell.edu
NEWHOUSE, Robin, P .. 317-274-1486 156 F newhouse@iu.edu
NEWHOUSE, Shawn ...... 616-222-1443 222 I shawn.newhouse@cornerstone.edu
NEWHOUSE, Valerie, K . 712-362-0434 166 F vnewhouse@iowalakes.edu
NEWITZ, Laurie, H .... 718-780-7503 291 J laurie.newitz@brooklaw.edu
NEWKIRK, Charlene ...... 412-369-3610 381 G cnewkirk@ccac.edu
NEWKIRK, Charlene ...... 412-469-6300 381 G cnewkirk@ccac.edu
NEWKIRK, Krista, L ...... 864-596-9050 409 B klnewkirk@converse.edu
NEWKIRK, Vann, R .... 615-329-8681 419 K vnewkirk@fisk.edu
NEWLAND, Carmen ...... 480-461-7479.. 13 D carmen.newland@mesacc.edu
NEWLAND, Mark .... 563-588-8000 165 F mnewland@emmaus.edu
NEWLIN, Toni .... 765-998-5211 160 F tnnewlin@taylor.edu
NEWLUN, Elizabeth .... 479-248-7236.. 19 C lnewlun@ecollege.edu
NEWMAN, Abraham ...... 732-367-9900 275 E
NEWMAN, Allison .... 716-829-7876 298 F newmana@dyc.edu
NEWMAN, Benjamin ..... 618-453-3771 149 E bnewman@siu.edu
NEWMAN, Betsy .... 617-747-2231 206 E studentaffairs@berklee.edu
NEWMAN, Carolyn .... 631-656-3191 300 D carolyn.newman@ftc.edu
NEWMAN, Carrie .... 814-824-3311 390 C cnewman@mercyhurst.edu
NEWMAN, Channa .... 412-392-3923 397 A cnewman@pointpark.edu
NEWMAN, Darlene, R ... 717-871-5369 395 D darlene.newman@millersville.edu
NEWMAN, Gilbert .... 510-841-9230.. 75 E gnewman@wi.edu
NEWMAN, J. Keith .... 405-491-6300 370 A knewman@snu.edu
NEWMAN, Janice .... 916-577-2200.. 75 B jnewman@jessup.edu
NEWMAN, Jeanine .... 337-421-9615 188 D jeanine.newman@sowela.edu
NEWMAN, Joan .... 865-694-6453 425 F jnewman@pstcc.edu
NEWMAN, Katherine ..... 617-287-6800 211 E katherine.newman@umb.edu
NEWMAN, Katherine ..... 617-287-7050 211 C knewman@umassp.edu
NEWMAN, Kay, S .... 334-387-3877.... 4 C kaynewman@amridgeuniversity.edu
NEWMAN, Kevin .... 928-774-3890.. 12 M knewman@indianbible.org
NEWMAN, Kevin .... 757-423-2095 467 H
NEWMAN, Kim .... 212-353-4155 297 E knewman@cooper.edu
NEWMAN, Lance .... 801-832-2301 461 G lnewman@westminstercollege.edu
NEWMAN, Lester, C ..... 903-730-4890 438 H lnewman@jarvis.edu

NEWMAN, Linde .... 575-624-7345 286 A
linde.newman@roswell.enmu.edu
NEWMAN, Marc .... 318-274-3811 191 E
newmanm@gram.edu
NEWMAN, Mark .... 859-323-5126 185 B
mark.newman@uky.edu
NEWMAN, Michael .... 646-565-6000 322 J
michael.newman@touro.edu
NEWMAN, Michelle ...... 703-330-5398 487 E
mnewman@apus.edu
NEWMAN, Nancy, J ...... 402-465-2375 268 H
njn@nebrwesleyan.edu
NEWMAN, Nathaniel ..... 937-512-2514 361 A
NEWMAN, Robert .... 310-453-8300.. 42 A
robert@emperors.edu
NEWMAN, Scott .... 918-293-4666 368 D
scott.newman@okstate.edu
NEWMAN, William .... 615-230-3600 426 B
william.newman@volstate.edu
NEWMANN, Jennifer ...... 629-876-4250.. 67 M
provost@usuniversity.edu
NEWPORT, Joseph, M .. 812-237-7829 155 G
joseph.newport@indstate.edu
NEWSCHAFFER,
Craig, J .... 215-571-3441 383 B
craig.j.newschaffer@drexel.edu
NEWSCHWANDER,
Gregg .... 334-844-5662.... 4 E
gen0002@auburn.edu
NEWSOM, Andrea .... 317-791-5611 161 B
newsoma@uindy.edu
NEWSOM, Stephanie, R 319-352-8539 170 C
stephanie.newsom@wartburg.edu
NEWSOM, Thomas .... 903-886-5153 447 B
thomas.newsom@tamuce.edu
NEWSOME, Caitlin .... 718-960-8144 294 A
1270mgr@fheg.follett.com
NEWSOME, Chanel .... 410-951-3000 203 D
NEWSOME, Chevelle ..... 916-278-6470.. 32 E
cnewsome@csus.edu
NEWSOME, Dale .... 815-939-5265 146 A
rdnewsome@olivet.edu
NEWSOME, Gary .... 815-939-5120 146 A
gnewsome@olivet.edu
NEWSOME, JoEllen .... 704-463-3222 339 E
joellen.newsome@pfeiffer.edu
NEWSOME, John .... 414-955-8631 494 C
jnewsome@mcw.edu
NEWSOME, Pam .... 612-874-3798 236 K
pam_newsome-prochniak@mcad.edu
NEWSOME, Sarah .... 850-973-9675 103 K
newsomes@nfcc.edu
NEWSWANGER, Zach .... 607-753-5582 318 D
zachariah.newswanger@cortland.edu
NEWTON, Andrew .... 803-738-7100 410 G
newtonar@midlandstech.edu
NEWTON, Bryan .... 410-334-2894 204 F
bnewton@worwic.edu
NEWTON, Darrell .... 715-836-2320 496 D
newtond@uwec.edu
NEWTON, David .... 678-839-6445 126 E
dnewton@westga.edu
NEWTON, Diane, D .... 501-450-3184.. 23 H
dnewton@uca.edu
NEWTON, Dusty .... 308-865-8702 269 I
newtond@unk.edu
NEWTON, Erin .... 478-387-4729 118 G
enewton@gmc.edu
NEWTON, J. Alec .... 252-638-7342 333 H
newtona@cravencc.edu
NEWTON, Jay .... 601-928-6212 247 E
jay.newton@mgccc.edu
NEWTON, Jeff .... 419-530-4484 363 E
jeff.newton2@utoledo.edu
NEWTON, Joseph, A ..... 229-333-4357 126 G
jnewton@valdosta.edu
NEWTON, Joshua .... 404-727-9163 117 F
joshua.r.newton@emory.edu
NEWTON, Julie .... 512-404-4820 431 C
jnewton@austinseminary.edu
NEWTON, Martin .... 205-726-2131.... 6 E
cnewton@samford.edu
NEWTON, Maureen .... 256-782-5333.... 5 J
mnewton@jsu.edu
NEWTON, Michael, L .... 270-384-8099 183 C
newtonm@lindsey.edu
NEWTON, Michael, R .... 515-294-6762 162 I
mrnewton@iastate.edu
NEWTON, Michelle .... 870-541-7164.. 19 G
newtonm@jrmc.org
NEWTON, Sandra .... 252-492-2061 338 F
newton@vgcc.edu
NEWTON, Scott .... 804-862-6100 470 I
snewton@rbc.edu
NEWTON, Tracy .... 718-951-5256 293 C
trodgers@brooklyn.cuny.edu
NEWTON, Vicki .... 425-352-8252 479 A
vnewton@cascadia.edu
NEWTOWN, Michael, J . 315-386-7411 320 E
newtownm@canton.edu
NEY, Cheryl, L .... 323-343-4300.. 32 A
cney@cslanet.calstatela.edu
NEY, Mei-Lee .... 310-665-6800.. 54 I
NEYLAND, Jeffery .... 817-272-5602 454 J
jeffery.neyland@uta.edu
NEYS, Leigh .... 605-626-7802 417 A
leigh.neys@northern.edu
NEZ, Marie, R .... 928-724-6699.. 12 C
mnez@dinecollege.edu
NEZIROSKI, Lirim .... 815-740-5099 151 J
lneziroski@stfrancis.edu
NG, Charis .... 718-270-4629 317 E
charis.ng@downstate.edu
NG, Charles .... 760-757-2121.. 52 E
cng@miracosta.edu
NG, Donna .... 518-580-5810 316 A
dng@skidmore.edu
NG, Jeffrey .... 718-817-3736 300 E
jeng@fordham.edu
NG, Jennifer .... 785-864-9660 177 D
jcng@ku.edu
NG, Michael, M .... 808-956-7323 128 D
ng23@hawaii.edu
NG, Monica .... 303-492-2277.. 83 A
monica.ng@colorado.edu
NG, Peh .... 320-589-6300 244 B
pehng@morris.umn.edu
NGHIEM, Nghi .... 323-265-8689.. 48 H
nghiemnx@elac.edu
NGIRAMENGIOR, Todd . 680-488-2471 506 B
toddn@palau.edu
NGO, David .... 212-229-8947 308 C
ngod@newschool.edu
NGO, Khiem .... 985-545-1500 187 H
NGO, Toui .... 281-487-1170 448 F
tngo@txchiro.edu
NGO, Vincent .... 619-388-7485.. 60 E
vngo@sdccd.edu
NGOM, Mbare .... 443-885-3095 200 D
mbare.ngom@morgan.edu
NGUMA, Elibariki .... 956-872-2515 444 A
bariki@southtexascollege.edu
NGUYEN, Alice .... 801-302-2800 459 H
anguyen@neumont.edu
NGUYEN, Binh .... 510-659-6441.. 54 F
bnguyen@ohlone.edu
NGUYEN, Binh .... 510-659-6107.. 54 F
bnguyen@ohlone.edu
NGUYEN, Chau .... 702-463-2122 272 G
cnguyen@wongu.org
NGUYEN, Christine .... 714-241-6144.. 38 C
cnguyen@coastline.edu
NGUYEN, Christopher ... 845-687-5053 323 E
nguyenc@sunyulster.edu
NGUYEN, Danny .... 408-855-5417.. 74 D
danny.nguyen@missioncollege.edu
NGUYEN, Denise .... 619-680-4430.. 28 E
denise.nguyen@cc-sd.edu
NGUYEN, Giang, T .... 215-746-3535 400 K
gnguyen@upenn.edu
NGUYEN, Hieu .... 909-621-8335.. 45 A
NGUYEN, Hieu .... 951-827-1286.. 69 C
hieu.nguyen@ucr.edu
NGUYEN, Hieu .... 808-739-8577 127 F
hnguyen@chaminade.edu
NGUYEN, Hoa .... 419-448-2228 353 H
hnguyen@heidelberg.edu
NGUYEN, Jessica .... 325-793-3800 440 B
nguyen.jessica@mcm.edu
NGUYEN, Kay .... 714-895-8727.. 38 D
kvnguyen@gwc.cccd.edu
NGUYEN, Lisa Anh .... 503-594-6140 372 D
lisa.wang@clackamas.edu
NGUYEN, Loan .... 510-981-2808.. 56 E
lnguyen@peralta.edu
NGUYEN, Mai .... 978-934-2049 211 G
mai_nguyen@uml.edu
NGUYEN, Michael .... 303-605-5435.. 80 N
mnguye31@msudenver.edu
NGUYEN, Michael .... 805-756-2246.. 30 C
mnguyen@calpoly.edu
NGUYEN, Neva .... 415-422-2772.. 71 K
nnguyen25@usfca.edu
NGUYEN, Oanh .... 713-718-5517 437 I
oanh.nguyen@hccs.edu
NGUYEN, Son .... 310-233-4584.. 49 A
nguyens@lahc.edu
NGUYEN, Son Xuan ..... 714-903-2762.. 67 L
NGUYEN, Tamie .... 323-343-5808.. 32 A
tnguyen10@cslanet.calstatela.edu
NGUYEN, Thai-Hoa .... 714-903-2762.. 67 L
NGUYEN, Thuy .... 650-949-7200.. 43 D
nguyenthuy@foothill.edu
NGUYEN, Thuy .... 714-432-5816.. 38 E
tnguyen@occ.cccd.edu
NGUYEN, Thy .... 312-996-2969 151 B
thy@uic.edu
NGUYEN, Tina .... 408-274-7900.. 61 L
tina.nguyen@evc.edu
NGUYEN, Trinh .... 925-473-7315.. 40 J
trnguyen@losmedanos.edu
NGUYEN,
Truongson (Sonny) .... 619-388-7358.. 60 E
tvnguyen@sdccd.edu
NGUYEN, Tuan .... 657-278-5322.. 31 E
tnguyen@fullerton.edu
NGUYEN, Tuyen .... 714-628-4844.. 58 A
nguyen_tuyen@sccollege.edu
NGUYEN, Van .... 734-462-4400 230 D
NGWANG, Emmanuel ... 903-927-3390 458 G
engwang@wileyc.edu
NHIRA, Tafadzwa .... 410-238-9000.. 92 G
NHO, Heung-sung .... 470-218-6032 123 D
heungsung.nho@runiv.edu
NIALIS, Ellen .... 714-879-3901.. 45 F
egnialis@hiu.edu
NIAS, Danita .... 352-392-5401 109 F
dnias@ufalumni.ufl.edu
NIBA, Johnson .... 443-885-4029 200 D
johnson.niba@morgan.edu
NICA, Claude .... 310-665-6870.. 54 I
cnica@otis.edu
NICASTRO, Eric .... 814-860-5125 388 A
enicastro@lecom.edu
NICCUM, Victoria .... 970-351-1152.. 83 E
victoria.niccum@unco.edu
NICE-WEBB, Kiva .... 573-592-6213 262 E
kiva.webb@westminster-mo.edu
NICELY, Dywayne .... 740-774-7207 359 G
nicely@ohio.edu
NICELY, Kathleen .... 415-864-7326.. 60 H
knicely@sfcm.edu
NICELY, Kathleen .... 415-864-7326.. 60 H
NICELY, Nancy .... 303-871-4948.. 83 D
nancy.nicely@du.edu
NICELY, Nancy .... 303-871-4848.. 83 D
nancy.nicely@du.edu
NICELY, Tim .... 540-453-2371 474 B
nicelyt@brcc.edu
NICHOL, Charlene .... 330-672-2210 354 J
cnicho22@kent.edu
NICHOL, Kristi .... 816-654-7107 254 C
knichol@kcumb.edu
NICHOL, Molly .... 518-262-8043 289 F
nicholm@amc.edu
NICHOL, Victoria .... 303-273-3763.. 78 I
vnichol@mines.edu
NICHOLAS, David, R ..... 530-221-4275.. 63 G
sbcadm@shasta.edu
NICHOLAS, Donna, R ... 530-221-4275.. 63 G
donna@shasta.edu
NICHOLAS, Jason .... 906-227-2379 228 F
janichol@nmu.edu
NICHOLAS, Jim .... 530-895-2421.. 27 F
nicholaswi@butte.edu
NICHOLAS, Johah .... 925-229-6944.. 40 G
jnicholas@4cd.edu
NICHOLAS, Kedrick .... 337-475-5610 192 A
knicholas@mcneese.edu
NICHOLAS, Marc .... 334-556-2223.... 2 C
mnicholas@wallace.edu
NICHOLAS, Mark .... 508-626-4670 212 D
mnicholas1@framingham.edu
NICHOLAS, Mike, L ...... 574-807-7875 153 E
michael.nicholas@betheluniversity.edu
NICHOLAS, Sandra .... 570-740-0730 389 D
snicholas@luzerne.edu
NICHOLLS, Tom .... 541-888-7611 376 F
tnicholls@socc.edu
NICHOLS, Aaron, F .... 802-656-3425 463 E
aaron.nichols@uvm.edu
NICHOLS, Andrew, W ... 808-956-8965 128 F
nicholsa@hawaii.edu
NICHOLS, Ann .... 270-707-3762 181 E
ann.nichols@kctcs.edu
NICHOLS, Ashlyn .... 214-638-0484 438 I
ashlynnichols@kdstudio.com
NICHOLS, Brenda .... 409-880-7087 449 H
brenda.nichols@lamar.edu
NICHOLS, Brian .... 859-257-3609 185 B
bnichols@uky.edu
NICHOLS, Brian .... 814-871-5680 384 E
nichols006@gannon.edu
NICHOLS, Carol .... 217-442-7232 135 H
cnichols1@dacc.edu
NICHOLS, Dana, J .... 706-295-6331 118 E
dnichols@highlands.edu
NICHOLS, Daniel .... 202-885-2534.. 90 J
dnichols@american.edu
NICHOLS, Deb .... 978-630-9361 215 A
dnichols6@mwcc.mass.edu
NICHOLS, Dee, A .... 864-833-8254 411 I
danichols@presby.edu
NICHOLS, Denise .... 757-727-5221 468 B
denise.nichols@hamptonu.edu
NICHOLS, Drew .... 512-428-1042 442 M
drewn@stedwards.edu
NICHOLS, Eric .... 410-617-2000 199 F
ernichols@loyola.edu
NICHOLS, III, George ... 610-526-1301 378 G
george.nichols@theamericancollege.edu
NICHOLS, Gregory, A ... 785-309-3182 176 J
greg.nichols@salinatech.edu
NICHOLS, JR.,
Harold, E .... 864-833-8296 411 I
henichols@presby.edu
NICHOLS, Jason, D ...... 573-629-3211 253 H
jnichols@hlg.edu
NICHOLS, Jennifer .... 704-922-6482 334 F
nichols.jennifer@gaston.edu
NICHOLS, Jennifer .... 704-922-6223 334 F
nichols.jennifer@gaston.edu
NICHOLS, Jody .... 715-425-3982 497 E
jody.nichols@uwrf.edu
NICHOLS, Jomel .... 816-271-5649 257 A
snichols3@missouriwestern.edu
NICHOLS, Karen .... 504-520-7692 193 A
knichola@xula.edu
NICHOLS, Keegan .... 479-968-0276.. 18 C
knichols@atu.edu
NICHOLS, Kelly .... 205-934-4488.... 8 A
nicholsk@uab.edu
NICHOLS, Laurie .... 805-437-8423.. 30 F
laurie.nichols@csuci.edu
NICHOLS, Laurie .... 605-642-6111 416 I
NICHOLS, Lesley .... 617-824-8281 208 H
lesley_nichols@emerson.edu
NICHOLS, Leslie, A .... 937-481-2200 364 E
leslie_nichols@wilmington.edu
NICHOLS, Linda .... 307-268-2220 501 U
lnichols@caspercollege.edu
NICHOLS, Michael, L .... 928-523-0886.. 14 H
michael.nichols@nau.edu
NICHOLS, Pamela .... 315-268-6413 296 A
pnichols@clarkson.edu
NICHOLS, Pat .... 805-525-4417.. 67 D
pnichols@thomasaquinas.edu
NICHOLS, Paula .... 409-880-7537 449 H
paula.nichols@lamar.edu
NICHOLS, Rachel .... 828-328-7306 330 F
rachel.nichols@lr.edu
NICHOLS, Randall .... 207-725-3458 193 D
rnichols@bowdoin.edu
NICHOLS, Reginald .... 781-280-3536 214 G
NICHOLS, Reginald .... 503-517-1221 377 G
rnichols@warnerpacific.edu
NICHOLS, Rick .... 828-328-7387 330 F
rick.nichols@lr.edu
NICHOLS, Ruth, R .... 601-304-4336 244 H
rnichols@alcorn.edu
NICHOLS, Sam .... 501-450-1362.. 19 F
nichols@hendrix.edu
NICHOLS, Sam .... 501-450-1340.. 19 F
nichols@hendrix.edu
NICHOLS, Sam .... 501-450-1362.. 19 F
nichols@hendrix.edu
NICHOLS, Scott, G .... 617-353-5777 207 D
nichols@bu.edu
NICHOLS, Shane .... 847-866-3866 137 E
shane.nichols@garrett.edu
NICHOLS, Sheila .... 850-484-1428 104 H
snichols@pensacolastate.edu
NICHOLS, Steve .... 417-269-3045 252 C
steve.nichols@coxcollege.edu
NICHOLS, Timothy .... 406-243-2541 264 A
timothy.nichols@umontana.edu
NICHOLS, Warren .... 409-933-8271 433 L
wnichols@com.edu

NICHOLS, William ... 724-847-6544 384 G wjnichol@geneva.edu
NICHOLSON, Cindy ... 828-227-7203 344 A nicholson@wcu.edu
NICHOLSON, Debra ... 620-276-9575 173 E debra.nicholson@gcccks.edu
NICHOLSON, Judd ... 202-687-4402.. 92 A nicholsonj@georgetown.edu
NICHOLSON, Karen ... 718-862-7374 305 H karen.nicholson@manhattan.edu
NICHOLSON, Kim ... 765-677-2131 157 D kim.nicholson@indwes.edu
NICHOLSON, Kristal ... 903-875-7361 440 G kristal.nicholson@navarrocollege.edu
NICHOLSON, Marie ... 828-689-1151 331 A mnicholson@mhu.edu
NICHOLSON, Nick ... 773-907-4777 134 C inicholson1@ccc.edu
NICHOLSON, Nigel, J ... 503-777-7257 376 C nnichols@reed.edu
NICHOLSON, Robin ... 319-235-3516 162 F robin.nicholson@unitypoint.org
NICHOLSON, Sylvia ... 336-517-2102 327 B snicholson@bennett.edu
NICHOLSON, Tim ... 828-835-4261 338 E tnicholson@tricountycc.edu
NICHOLSON, Vickie ... 251-578-1313.... 3 D vickien@rstc.edu
NICHOLSON ANGLE, Jan, C ... 540-365-4285 467 I jcnicholson@ferrum.edu
NICHOLSON-PREUSS, Mari ... 713-221-8236 453 B nicholsonpreussm@uhd.edu
NICK, Sara, J ... 715-833-6275 499 D snick1@cvtc.edu
NICKAS, Danielle, K ... 301-447-5330 200 E d.nickas@msmary.edu
NICKE, Glenda ... 309-796-4822 132 G nickeg@bhc.edu
NICKEL, Heather ... 816-531-5223 251 H
NICKEL, Kevin, A ... 419-358-3320 348 G nickelk@bluffton.edu
NICKELL, Barbara, J ... 785-833-4390 175 B bmarsh@kwu.edu
NICKELL, Jane Ellen ... 814-332-2800 378 D jnickell@allegheny.edu
NICKELL, Julie ... 713-798-4951 431 I nickell@bcm.edu
NICKELS, Ken ... 309-796-5048 132 G nickelsk@bhc.edu
NICKELS, Lisa ... 415-503-6231.. 60 H lnickels@sfcm.edu
NICKENS, Tawanna ... 217-351-2390 146 C tnickens@parkland.edu
NICKERSON, Amanda ... 254-968-5352 446 E nickerson@tarleton.edu
NICKERSON, Becky ... 402-280-3118 266 I beckynickerson@creighton.edu
NICKERSON, Floyd, W .. 972-599-3159 433M fnickerson@collin.edu
NICKERSON, John ... 607-587-4750 320 C nickerjd@alfredstate.edu
NICKERSON, Lori ... 508-999-8004 211 F lori.nickerson@umassd.edu
NICKERSON, Molly ... 660-284-4800 253 J
NICKERSON, Nathaniel . 203-432-1345.. 89 D nathaniel.nickerson@yale.edu
NICKERSON, Sherita ... 325-674-6802 429 B sherita.nickerson@acu.edu
NICKITAS, Donna ... 856-225-2248 281 G snc-dean@rutgers.edu
NICKLAUS, Mark, B ... 920-748-8186 495 G nicklausm@ripon.edu
NICKLAUS, Megan ... 719-389-6424.. 77 H megan.nicklaus@coloradocollege.edu
NICKLE, Mary Anne ... 641-236-2202 166 I maryanne.nickle@iavalley.edu
NICKLESS, Peter ... 315-568-3310 308 F pnickless@nycc.edu
NICKLIN, Jessica ... 860-768-5365.. 88 H nicklin@hartford.edu
NICKLOW, John, W ... 504-280-5536 189 E president@uno.edu
NICKOLS, Sharon ... 217-333-6677 151 D nickrich@illinois.edu
NICKOSON, Carol ... 937-327-7800 364 H nickosonc@wittenberg.edu
NICKS, Leanna ... 336-841-9313 329 G lnicks@highpoint.edu
NICKSA, Gary, W ... 617-353-6500 207 D nicksa@bu.edu

NICOL, David ... 231-591-2422 223 J davidnicol@ferris.edu
NICOL, Patricia ... 617-824-8123 208 H patricia_nicol@emerson.edu
NICOLAI, Michael ... 312-629-9411 148 I mnicolai@saic.edu
NICOLETTE, Guy ... 352-294-7439 109 F gnic@ufl.edu
NICOLETTI, Katherine ... 508-213-2238 217 E katherine.nicoletti@nichols.edu
NICOLETTI, Marian ... 585-475-5503 313 A mmnadm@rit.edu
NICOLO, Anthony, J ... 540-674-3639 475 B tnicolo@nr.edu
NICOLOV, Pressian ... 909-593-3511.. 70 D pnicolov@laverne.edu
NICOTERA, Phillip ... 713-718-7628 437 I phillip.nicotera@hccs.edu
NIE, Ling-Ling ... 404-894-6088 118 F linglingnie@gatech.edu
NIECE, Matthew ... 208-426-1604 129 I matthewniece@boisestate.edu
NIEDENS, Rosemary ... 316-942-4291 175 I niedensr@newmanu.edu
NIEDERHAUSER, Victoria ... 865-974-7584 427 G vniederh@utk.edu
NIEDERJOHN, Scott ... 920-565-1000 493 J niederjohnms@lakeland.edu
NIEDGE, Erin ... 406-874-6211 263 I niedgee@milescc.edu
NIEDWIECKI, Anthony .. 415-442-6601.. 44 D aniedwiecki@ggu.edu
NIEDZWIECKI, Brian, E . 419-866-0261 361 H beniedzwiecki@stautzenberger.com
NIEDZWIECKI, Michael . 718-933-6700 307 G mniedzwiedi@monroecollege.edu
NIEHOFF, Brian, A ... 785-532-4797 174 G niehoff@ksu.edu
NIEKRO, Catherine ... 828-328-7360 330 F cat.niekro@lr.edu
NIELSEN, David ... 860-512-3108.. 85 G dnielsen@manchestercc.edu
NIELSEN, Erik ... 402-461-7738 267 D enielsen@hastings.edu
NIELSEN, Glenn ... 314-505-7201 251 I nielseng@csl.edu
NIELSEN, Joel ... 330-672-3120 354 J nielsen@kent.edu
NIELSEN, Kelly, A ... 920-748-8852 495 G nielsenk@ripon.edu
NIELSEN, Kristin, S ... 503-943-7302 377 E nielsenk@up.edu
NIELSEN, Leila ... 651-631-0204 233 I lnielsen@aaaom.edu
NIELSEN, Lisa ... 831-459-4344.. 70 B lmnielse@ucsc.edu
NIELSEN, Mary ... 706-272-4403 117 C mnielsen@daltonstate.edu
NIELSEN, Mary, F ... 414-277-7216 494 G nielsen@msoe.edu
NIELSEN, Melore ... 206-296-2000 484 F mnielsen@seattleu.edu
NIELSEN, Paul, D ... 412-268-7740 380 F nielsen@sei.cmu.edu
NIELSEN, Richard, P ... 801-375-5125 459 L rick.nielsen@rm.edu
NIELSEN, Scott ... 775-753-2289 271 B scott.nielsen@gbcnv.edu
NIELSON, Eric ... 208-732-6267 130 E enielson@csi.edu
NIELSON, Lauren ... 770-426-2832 121 C lauren.nielsen@life.edu
NIELSON, Robert ... 435-283-7037 461 C rob.nielson@snow.edu
NIEMAN, Donald ... 607-777-2141 316 E dnieman@binghamton.edu
NIEMAN, James ... 773-256-0728 142 G jnieman@lstc.edu
NIEMAN, Paul ... 818-710-4121.. 49 C niemanp@piercecollege.edu
NIEMANN, Jessica ... 402-552-3325 266 E niemannjessica@clarksoncollege.edu
NIEMEIER, Brian ... 951-552-8637.. 27 J bniemeier@calbaptist.edu
NIEMEYER, Heath ... 661-654-3579.. 30 E hniemeyer@csub.edu
NIEMI, Bill ... 970-943-3045.. 84 D bniemi@western.edu
NIEMI, Cathy ... 906-227-2232 228 F caniemi@nmu.edu
NIEMI, Nancy, S ... 410-651-6508 203 A nsniemi@umes.edu

NIEMI, Nicole ... 219-464-6010 162 A nicole.niemi@valpo.edu
NIEMIEC, Catherine ... 602-274-1885.. 15 B cniemiec@pihma.edu
NIEMIEC, Kristin ... 414-955-8272 494 C kniemiec@mcw.edu
NIEMIRA, David ... 814-871-7213 384 E niemira001@gannon.edu
NIENABER, Mary ... 651-779-5837 237 G mary.nienaber@century.edu
NIENHUIS, Jeanne ... 616-526-6885 222 A jeanen@calvin.edu
NIERMANN, Scott, K ... 865-354-3000 425 G niermannsk@roanestate.edu
NIES, Charles ... 209-228-7620.. 69 B cnies@ucmerced.edu
NIESE, Vicki, J ... 419-772-2057 358 H v-niese@onu.edu
NIESEL, David, W ... 409-772-8143 456 F dniesel@utmb.edu
NIESEN DE ABRUNA, Laura ... 717-815-1231 404 A lniesen@ycp.edu
NIESPO, Molly ... 630-617-3047 136 G molly.niespo@elmhurst.edu
NIETO, Javier ... 541-737-3220 375 D
NIETO-PHILLIPS, John .. 812-855-2076 156 B jnietoph@indiana.edu
NIETSCHE, Nichole ... 802-387-6711 462 D registrar@landmark.edu
NIEUWSMA, Christianne ... 602-243-8364.. 14 A christianne.nieuwsma@southmountaincc.edu
NIEVES, Beatriz ... 787-766-1717 511 H um_bnieves@suagm.edu
NIEVES, Brenda ... 909-447-2504.. 37 F bnieves@cst.edu
NIEVES, Danily ... 787-882-2065 511 D
NIEVES, Gladys, T ... 787-765-3560 507 L gnieves@edpuniversity.edu
NIEVES, Ivette ... 787-279-1912 509 A inieves@bayamon.inter.edu
NIEVES, Lamberto, C ... 201-761-6085 282 I lnieves@saintpeters.edu
NIEVES, Liza ... 787-764-0000 514 B
NIEVES, Mayra ... 212-237-8918 294 D mnieves@jjay.cuny.edu
NIEVES, Yadira, G ... 787-279-1912 509 A ynievesp@bayamon.inter.edu
NIEVES GARCIA, Daulan ... 787-720-4476 512 D estudianteupm@mizpa.edu
NIEVES HERNÁNDEZ, Mariel ... 608-785-8000 513 F
NIEWIERSKI, Frank ... 210-436-4357 443 A fniewierski@stmarytx.edu
NIGAGLIONI, Guillermo 787-728-1515 514 D guillermo.nigaglioni@sagrado.edu
NIGHSWONGER, Davis . 619-482-6585.. 65 F dnighswonger@swccd.edu
NIGHTINGALE, Charles, W ... 443-518-4615 199 C cnightingale@howardcc.edu
NIGHTINGALE, Michelle ... 607-844-8222 322 H mrn@tompkinscortland.edu
NIGLIAZZO, Marc, A ... 254-519-5720 447 A marc.nigliazzo@tamuct.edu
NIGRO, Frank ... 530-242-7520.. 63 H fnigro@shastacollege.edu
NIGRO, Nick ... 419-473-2700 352 E nnigro@daviscollege.edu
NIGRO, Stephen, M ... 413-542-2101 205 B smnigro@amherst.edu
NIGUIDULA, Amanda ... 305-348-3532 109 A amanda.niguidula@fiu.edu
NIHISER, Kelsey ... 513-562-6273 347 K kelsey.nihiser@artacademy.edu
NIJLAND, Mark, J ... 210-567-0313 456 C nijland@uthscsa.edu
NIKIRK, Sarah, F ... 859-218-3379 185 B s.nikirk@uky.edu
NIKKEL, Kasey ... 563-387-1008 167 E nikkka01@luther.edu
NIKLASON, Gail ... 801-626-8586 461 B gniklason@weber.edu
NIKLASSON, Pontus ... 607-871-2123 289 H niklasson@alfred.edu
NIKOLAI, Scott ... 828-884-8437 327 C nikolasa@brevard.edu
NIKOLIC, Vladan ... 212-229-8903 308 C nikolicv@newschool.edu

NIKOLOV, Ivan ... 229-333-7410 126 G inikolov@valdosta.edu
NIKOPOULOS, Beth ... 972-273-3171 435 E bnikopoulos@dcccd.edu
NILAND, Eileen, A ... 716-888-2620 292 D nilande@canisius.edu
NILAND, Joe ... 251-381-3491.... 6 H jniland@shc.edu
NILANJAN, Sen ... 518-442-3300 316 D nsen@albany.edu
NILES, Maryann ... 781-280-3703 214 G nilesm@middlesex.mass.edu
NILES, Spencer ... 757-221-2315 466 C sgniles@wm.edu
NILES, Stefanie ... 740-368-3020 359 N sdniles@owu.edu
NILES-HANSEN, Diana .. 808-544-1102 127 H dnileshansen@hpu.edu
NILKANT, Anita ... 412-397-5267 397 G nilkant@rmu.edu
NILLES, Dawnita ... 701-777-3239 345 C dawnita.nilles@und.edu
NILMEIER, Melisa ... 559-323-2100.. 60 I lnilmeier@sjcl.edu
NILO, Susan ... 336-372-5061 339 B srnilo128@wilkescc.edu
NILON, Lourdes ... 661-654-6098.. 30 E
NILSEN, Kenneth ... 201-216-5699 283 C kenneth.nilsen@stevens.edu
NILSON, Amy ... 209-588-5505.. 75 I nilsona@yosemite.edu
NIMES, Johnny ... 404-527-7782 120 K jnimes@itc.edu
NIMMAGADDA, Jayashree ... 401-456-8042 405 C jnimmagadda@ric.edu
NIMMO, Pam ... 615-732-7662 422 G pam@mtsa.edu
NIMMO, Steven ... 706-776-0113 123 B snimmo@piedmont.edu
NIMMONS, Ciera, E ... 410-651-7926 203 A cenimmons@umes.edu
NIMS, Aleta ... 315-268-6633 296 A anims@clarkson.edu
NINASSI, Susanne ... 703-284-6478 469 C susanne.ninassi@marymount.edu
NING, Bin ... 734-487-4924 223 H bning@emich.edu
NININGER, Jami ... 614-234-1777 356 I jnininger@mccn.edu
NINOS, Katherine ... 505-467-6819 288 E katherineninos@swc.edu
NINOW, Friedbert ... 951-785-2041.. 47 C fninow@lasierra.edu
NIP, Kit ... 319-385-6250 167 A knip@iw.edu
NIPP, Amanda ... 402-844-7273 268 J amandan@northeast.edu
NIPP, Tim, J ... 731-881-7601 428 B timnipp@utm.edu
NIPPER, Brent ... 423-461-8740 422 J wbnipper@milligan.edu
NIPPERT, Jennifer ... 740-695-9500 348 F jnippert@belmontcollege.edu
NIRENBERG, David ... 773-702-3423 150 J nirenberg@uchicago.edu
NIROUMAND, Madjid ... 714-432-5765.. 38 E mniroumand@occ.cccd.edu
NISBET, John ... 352-588-8215 106 D john.nisbet@saintleo.edu
NISCHIK, Shauna ... 920-693-1362 499 G shauna.nischik@gotoltc.edu
NISHI, Lisa ... 607-255-3062 297 F lhn5@cornell.edu
NISHIMURA, Margot ... 401-709-5909 405 D mnishimu@risd.edu
NISHIOKA, Wayne ... 310-243-3750.. 31 B wnishioka@csudh.edu
NISHIOKA, Yukari ... 714-533-3946.. 34 D yukari@calums.edu
NISHIOKA, Yukari ... 714-533-1495.. 64 D yukari@southbaylo.edu
NISHIYAMA, Shayna ... 360-676-2772 482 D snishiyama@nwic.edu
NISHIZAWA, Yuichiro ... 973-748-9000 276 A yuichiro_nishizawa@bloomfield.edu
NISLY, Lamar ... 419-358-3317 348 G nislyl@bluffton.edu
NISSEL, Chaim ... 646-592-4201 326 E drnissel@yu.edu
NISSEN, Jill ... 314-367-8700 259 B jill.nissen@stlcop.edu

NISSEN, Laura .... 503-725-3997 376 A
nissen@pdx.edu
NISWANDER, Tami .... 218-679-2860 242 P
NITCH, Mindy .... 814-262-6433 393 H
mnitch@pennhighlands.edu
NITECKI, Danuta, A .... 215-895-2750 383 B
dan44@drexel.edu
NITTA, Akira .... 949-582-4820.. 64 G
anitta@saddleback.edu
NITTMANN, Nydia, C .... 928-523-9488.. 14 H
nydia.nittmann@nau.edu
NIVENS, Delana .... 912-344-2964 119 C
dnivens@georgiasouthern.edu
NIVET, Marc, A .... 214-648-3266 457 B
marc.nivet@utsouthwestern.edu
NIX, Julie .... 256-782-5815.... 5 J
jnix@jsu.edu
NIX, Linda .... 307-268-2218 501 U
lnix@caspercollege.edu
NIX, Rachel .... 870-574-1521.. 21 E
rnix@sautech.edu
NIX, Shannon .... 703-993-8816 467 L
snix2@gmu.edu
NIX, Sheila .... 210-431-2178 443 A
snix@stmarytx.edu
NIXON, Andrea .... 507-222-4043 234 F
anixon@carleton.edu
NIXON, Bradford .... 301-687-4111 203 E
bnixon@frostburg.edu
NIXON, Charline .... 505-922-2888 286 B
dean@eccu.edu
NIXON, Cheryl .... 970-247-7314.. 79 I
clnixon@fortlewis.edu
NIXON, John, E .... 801-585-0806 460 E
john.nixon@utah.edu
NIXON, Katie .... 731-989-6672 420 C
knixon@fhu.edu
NIXON, LaTanya, M ..... 252-862-1267 337 C
lmnixon@roanokechowan.edu
NIXON, Lauren .... 817-257-7113 448 G
l.e.nixon@tcu.edu
NIXON, Michael, T .... 269-471-3241 221 B
michaeln@andrews.edu
NIXON, Paul .... 601-635-2111 245 I
pnixon@eccc.edu
NIXON, Terry .... 325-793-4721 440 B
tnixon@mcm.edu
NIZAMI, Nassar .... 215-503-5110 400 A
nassar.nizami@jefferson.edu
NKULU, Cedric .... 931-424-4058 421 E
cnkulu@martinmethodist.edu
NKUMEH, Nwakaego .... 470-578-6033 120 L
NNADI, Eucharia, E ...... 702-968-2038 272 C
ennadi@roseman.edu
NNANNA, George .... 532-552-3433 457 A
nnanna_g@utpb.edu
NOACK, Kelly .... 309-794-7477 132 C
kellynoack@augustana.edu
NOAH, Chris .... 724-357-3062 394 G
cnoah@iup.edu
NOAH, Pam .... 208-769-7806 131 C
panoah@nic.edu
NOAH, Tara .... 660-359-3948 257 D
tnoah@mail.ncmissouri.edu
NOBILE, Bryan .... 601-643-8468 245 G
bryan.nobile@colin.edu
NOBILE, Bryan .... 601-643-8318 245 G
bryan.nobile@colin.edu
NOBLE, Debra .... 575-538-6025 289 B
debra.noble@wnmu.edu
NOBLE, Doug .... 540-654-1235 472 I
dnoble@umw.edu
NOBLE, Linda .... 912-358-4190 123 H
vpaa@savannahstate.edu
NOBLE, Malcolm .... 907-852-1820.... 9 F
malcolm.noble@ilisagvik.edu
NOBLE, Malcolm, X .... 907-852-3333.... 9 F
malcolm.noble@ilisagvik.edu
NOBLE, Rachel .... 727-376-6911 111 G
rachel.noble@trinitycollege.edu
NOBLE, Ralph .... 478-825-4266 118 A
ralph.noble@fvsu.edu
NOBLE, Scott .... 575-538-6118 289 B
scott.noble@wnmu.edu
NOBLE, Shlomo .... 585-473-2810 322 D
NOBLES, Melissa .... 617-253-3450 215 G
NOBLES, II, Robert .... 865-974-3053 427 G
nobles@utk.edu
NOBLES, Rodney .... 262-691-5362 500 H
rnobles@wctc.edu
NOBLES, Sheila .... 850-973-9432 103 K
nobless@nfcc.edu
NOBLES, Tammy .... 573-681-5519 254 E
noblest@lincolnu.edu
NOBLEZA, Deanna .... 215-503-2817 400 A
deanna.nobleza@jefferson.edu
NOBLITT, Jeffrey .... 818-677-2130.. 32 D
jeffrey.noblitt@csun.edu
NOCCIOLO, Mark .... 805-893-2491.. 70 A
mark.nocciolo@ucsb.edu
NOCE, Joe .... 215-780-1294 398 G
pcobookstore@mattmccoy.com
NOCE, Louis .... 585-785-1464 300 B
louis.noce@flcc.edu
NOCELLA, Frank .... 781-280-3543 214 G
NOCITO, Gabriela .... 650-738-4313.. 61 Q
nocitog@smccd.edu
NODA, Keisuke .... 212-563-6647 323 F
k.noda@uts.edu
NODARSE BARRERA,
Jaime .... 361-825-5749 447 C
jaime.nodarse@tamucc.edu
NODES, Jennifer .... 239-348-4710.. 94 O
jennifer.nodes@avemaria.edu
NODINE, Stephen .... 703-993-4563 467 L
snodine@gmu.edu
NODLAND, Rita .... 701-224-5692 346 B
rita.nodland@bismarckstate.edu
NOE, Audra .... 608-796-3040 498 N
aanoe@viterbo.edu
NOE, Belinda .... 256-306-2582.... 1 F
belinda.noe@calhoun.edu
NOE, Denise .... 815-394-3756 147 G
dnoe@rockford.edu
NOE, George .... 303-361-7367.. 79 D
george.noe@ccaurora.edu
NOE, Ivan .... 909-469-5234.. 74 I
inoe@westernu.edu
NOE, Lori .... 618-842-3711 138 G
noel@iecc.edu
NOEL, Abraham .... 651-696-6465 236 H
noel@macalester.edu
NOEL, Amy .... 252-246-1275 339 C
anoel@wilsoncc.edu
NOEL, Caryn .... 248-689-8282 232 A
cnoel@walshcollege.edu
NOEL, Elizabeth, J .... 781-280-3596 214 G
noelb@middlesex.mass.edu
NOEL, Fred .... 406-275-4800 265 F
fred_noel@skc.edu
NOEL, JR., J. Andrew ... 607-255-8832 297 F
jan16@cornell.edu
NOEL, Norma .... 575-646-7793 287 B
nnoel@nmsu.edu
NOEL, Shawn .... 908-709-7495 284 C
shawn.noel@ucc.edu
NOEL, Terry .... 724-532-5095 398 E
terry.noel@email.stvincent.edu
NOEL, Terry .... 724-805-2095 398 F
terry.noel@stvincent.edu
NOEL-ELKINS, Amelia ... 309-438-3217 139 E
anoelel@ilstu.edu
NOELDNER, Troy .... 701-777-6366 345 C
troy.noeldner@und.edu
NOENNIG, Evelyn .... 406-657-2300 264 E
evelyn.noennig@msubillings.edu
NOEVERE, Michelle .... 252-249-1851 336 F
mnoevere@pamlicocc.edu
NOFFSINGER-FRAZIER,
Nicole .... 931-598-1325 423 M
nanoffsi@sewnee.edu
NOFZIGER, Marcie .... 260-359-4052 155 F
mnofziger@huntington.edu
NOGLE, Ryan .... 716-851-1281 299 F
nogle@ecc.edu
NOHLGREN, Bethany .... 845-758-7099 290 G
nohlgren@bard.edu
NOHNER, OSB, Sharon 320-363-5285 235 C
snohner@csbsju.edu
NOHRIA, Nitin .... 617-495-6550 210 B
nnohria@hbs.edu
NOKES SCUILETTI,
Linda .... 919-775-5401 333 C
NOLAN, Alana .... 906-487-7309 223 K
alana.nolan@finlandia.edu
NOLAN, Beth .... 202-994-6503.. 91 F
bnolan@gwu.edu
NOLAN, Christina, M .... 973-748-9000 276 A
christina_nolan@bloomfield.edu
NOLAN, Christy .... 512-245-2392 450 E
cdn38@txstate.edu
NOLAN, Dan .... 678-407-5711 118 D
dnolan@ggc.edu
NOLAN, David .... 817-257-6863 448 G
d.nolan@tcu.edu
NOLAN, Deborah .... 410-704-2450 204 A
dnolan@towson.edu
NOLAN, Deborah .... 559-737-6132.. 39 E
deborahn@cos.edu
NOLAN, Holly .... 281-283-2480 453 A
nolan@uhcl.edu
NOLAN, Judy .... 914-251-6067 319 E
judy.nolan@purchase.edu
NOLAN, Kellyn .... 570-702-8940 386 G
knolan@johnson.edu
NOLAN, Kevin .... 617-732-2900 216 B
kevin.nolan@mcphs.edu
NOLAN, Kevin .... 773-838-7526 134 F
knolan@ccc.edu
NOLAN, Lisa, K .... 706-542-3461 125 G
lisa.nolan@uga.edu
NOLAN, Shay .... 270-534-3089 182 F
shay.nolan@kctcs.edu
NOLAN, Terrance .... 212-998-2257 310 B
terrance.nolan@nyu.edu
NOLAN, Tiffany .... 573-681-5582 254 E
nolant@lincolnu.edu
NOLAN-CHAVEZ, Holly . 805-922-6966.. 24 J
hchavez@hancockcollege.edu
NOLAN-WEISS,
Sharon, E .... 716-645-2266 316 F
senolan@buffalo.edu
NOLAND, Brian, E .... 423-439-4211 419 J
president@etsu.edu
NOLASCO, Maria .... 787-841-2000 510 K
mnolasco@pucpr.edu
NOLD, Letha .... 816-271-4582 257 A
lnold@missouriwestern.edu
NOLDER, Deborah .... 606-759-7141 182 A
debbie.nolder@kctcs.edu
NOLDNER, Tracy .... 605-367-7487 417 D
tracy.noldner@southeasttech.edu
NOLES, Jody .... 334-291-4922.... 1 H
jody.noles@cv.edu
NOLING-AUTH, Jamie ... 503-554-2321 373 C
jnolingauth@georgefox.edu
NOLL, Carol .... 719-384-6824.. 81 E
carol.noll@ojc.edu
NOLL, Cheryl .... 912-650-5648 124 E
cnoll@southuniversity.edu
NOLLAN, Damond .... 919-530-6399 342 A
dnollan@nccu.edu
NOLLAN, Richard .... 806-743-1048 451 C
richard.nollan@ttuhsc.edu
NOLTE, Beth .... 573-681-5194 254 E
noltem@lincolnu.edu
NOLTE, JR., Harold, E .. 620-227-9378 172 J
hnolte@dc3.edu
NOLTE, Jim .... 802-828-8512 463 F
jim.nolte@vcfa.edu
NOLTEMEYER, Patrick ... 336-278-7904 328 K
pnoltemeyer@elon.edu
NOLTING, Carol .... 816-268-5400 257 C
cnolting@nts.edu
NOMURA,
Christopher, T .... 315-470-6606 320 A
ctnomura@esf.edu
NOMURA, Cory .... 909-748-8066.. 71 G
cory_nomura@redlands.edu
NONDORF, James, G ... 773-702-4101 150 J
jnondorf@uchicago.edu
NONEMAKER, Scott .... 315-792-3285 324 B
scnonema@utica.edu
NONNAMAKER, John .... 504-314-2188 191 B
jnonnama@tulane.edu
NOOK, Mark, A .... 319-273-2566 163 B
mark.nook@uni.edu
NOOKS, Kirk .... 678-359-5015 119 F
presidentnooks@gordonstate.edu
NOON, Alexis .... 575-769-4085 285 K
alexis.noon@clovis.edu
NOON, Edward .... 414-443-8871 498 O
skip.noon@wlc.edu
NOON, Jennifer .... 973-443-8544 277 K
jennifer_noon@fdu.edu
NOON, Molly .... 712-325-3306 167 B
mnoon@iwcc.edu
NOONAN, Brigid .... 585-389-2396 308 B
bnoonan8@naz.edu
NOONAN, Claire .... 708-524-6860 136 C
cnoonan@dom.edu
NOONAN, Daniel .... 860-727-6902.. 87 A
dnoonan@goodwin.edu
NOONAN, John .... 919-660-4252 328 G
john.noonan@duke.edu
NOONE, Anne .... 570-208-5899 387 A
aenoone@kings.edu
NOONE, Pamela, K .... 570-577-7136 379 F
noone@bucknell.edu
NOONKESTER, Myron ... 601-318-6118 249 H
myron.noonkester@wmcarey.edu
NORBY, Paula .... 602-888-5506 132 E
pnorby@ben.edu
NORCIA, Lisa .... 201-200-2335 279 E
lnorcia@njcu.edu
NORCINI, Heather .... 610-341-5890 383 D
hnorcini@eastern.edu
NORCROSS, Celia .... 413-662-5231 213 A
celia.norcross@mcla.edu
NORCROSS, Paul, W ..... 315-464-4361 317 F
norcrossp@upstate.edu
NORCROSS, Robert .... 760-757-2121.. 52 E
rnorcross@miracosta.edu
NORD, Elonda .... 701-665-4639 346 D
elonda.nord@lrsc.edu
NORD, Elonda .... 701-662-1513 346 D
elonda.nord@lrsc.edu
NORD, Sheldon .... 503-375-7000 373 A
snord@corban.edu
NORDBERG, Erik .... 724-357-2330 394 G
erik.nordberg@iup.edu
NORDBY, Shawn .... 402-461-5344 267 F
snordby@marylanning.org
NORDEEN, Mark .... 307-855-2140 501 V
mark.nordeen@cwc.edu
NORDGREN, Joseph, E . 409-880-8400 449 H
joe.nordgren@lamar.com
NORDICK, Pat .... 218-299-6821 239 B
pat.nordick@minnesota.edu
NORDIN, Becky .... 612-659-6712 238 I
becky.nordin@minneapolis.edu
NORDLAND, Jeffrey ...... 585-245-5606 318 E
nordland@geneseo.edu
NORDMAN, Tyler .... 785-442-6039 174 A
tnordman@highlandcc.edu
NORDMANN, Andrea .... 817-257-5520 448 G
a.nordmann@tcu.edu
NORDONE, JR., James . 940-552-6291 457 C
jnordone@vernoncollege.edu
NORDONE, Ron .... 610-282-1100 382 E
ronald.nordone@desales.edu
NORDSTROM, Terrence 510-869-6649.. 59 F
tnordstrom@samuelmerritt.edu
NORDT, Lee, C .... 254-710-3361 431 J
lee_nordt@baylor.edu
NOREN, Patricia .... 516-572-7396 308 A
patricia.noren@ncc.edu
NOREUIL, Margaret ...... 608-663-2820 493 C
mnoreuil@edgewood.edu
NORFLEET, Margie .... 252-246-1210 339 C
mnorfleet@wilsoncc.edu
NORIAN, Nicole .... 828-232-5117 342 C
nnorian@unca.edu
NORIEGA, David .... 619-876-4260.. 67 M
NORISE, Hershey .... 773-602-5484 134 D
hnorise@ccc.edu
NORITA, Mark .... 760-750-4679.. 33 B
mnorita@csusm.edu
NORLAND, Gretchen .... 785-227-3380 171 E
norlandg@bethanylb.edu
NORLEN, Tracy, C .... 206-281-2977 484 D
tcnorlen@spu.edu
NORLIEN, Cheryl, A .... 320-222-5638 240 E
cheryl.norlien@ridgewater.edu
NORMAN, Cheryl, R ..... 651-631-5247 244 D
crnorman@unwsp.edu
NORMAN, David .... 903-813-2499 430 N
dnorman@austincollege.edu
NORMAN, Elizabeth, J .. 325-670-1229 437 F
enorman@hsutx.edu
NORMAN, Eric .... 260-481-6601 159 F
norman@pfw.edu
NORMAN, Eric .... 931-221-7341 418 D
normane@apsu.edu
NORMAN, Josh, L .... 217-581-6077 136 E
jlnorman@eiu.edu
NORMAN, Linda .... 615-343-8876 428 D
linda.norman@vanderbilt.edu
NORMAN, Lindsay .... 706-236-2209 115 B
lnorman@berry.edu
NORMAN, Lisa .... 760-744-1150.. 55 I
lnorman@palomar.edu
NORMAN, Margie, A .... 903-813-2247 430 N
mnorman@austincollege.edu
NORMAN, Paul, A .... 919-516-4353 340 C
panorman@st-aug.edu
NORMAN, Peter, E .... 815-599-3465 138 B
pete.norman@highland.edu
NORMAN, Rashawn ...... 775-784-6516 271 F
norman@unr.edu
NORMAN, Stan .... 870-759-4101.. 23 J
snorman@williamsbu.edu

NOWVISKIE, Bethany .... 540-568-3828 468 F nowvisbp@jmu.edu
NOYE, Theresa .... 610-341-5872 383 D tnoye@eastern.edu
NOYES, Cynthia .... 269-749-7144 229 H cnoyes@olivetcollege.edu
NUCCI, John, A .... 617-973-1103 219 A jnucci@suffolk.edu
NUCCI, Lisa .... 614-781-1085 352 L
NUCCIARONE, Mary, B . 574-631-6436 161 C nucciarone.2@nd.edu
NUCKOLS, Melanie, L ... 336-734-7332 334 E mnuckols@forsythtech.edu
NUDI, Joel .... 518-861-2558 305 K jnudi@mariacollege.edu
NUDI, Joel, D .... 518-861-2558 305 K jnudi@mariacollege.edu
NUDO, Angelo .... 570-674-6287 390 G anudo@misericordia.edu
NUELL, Nancy .... 240-567-7958 200 C nancy.nuell@montgomerycollege.edu
NUERNBERG, Carin ...... 617-266-1400 206 E
NUESELL, Lisa, M .... 919-381-6912 340 J lnuesell@umo.edu
NUFER, Ken .... 719-549-3474.. 81 K ken.nufer@pueblocc.edu
NUGENT, Barli .... 212-799-5000 303 H
NUGENT, Daniel, P .... 609-626-3546 283 D daniel.nugent@stockton.edu
NUGENT, Georgia .... 309-556-3151 139 G president@iwu.edu
NUGENT, John, D .... 860-439-5266.. 86 H john.nugent@conncoll.edu
NUGENT, Kari .... 815-802-8256 140 D knugent@kcc.edu
NUGENT, Kevin .... 903-463-8768 437 D nugentk@grayson.edu
NUGENT, Kirk .... 256-726-8324.... 6 C krnugent@oakwood.edu
NUGENT, Megan .... 503-251-2836 377 F mnugent@uws.edu
NUKAYA, Bruce .... 208-732-6352 130 E bnukaya@csi.edu
NUKAYA, Ginger .... 208-732-6201 130 E gnukaya@csi.edu
NULL, Wesley .... 254-710-3601 431 J wesley_null@baylor.edu
NULTY, Christina .... 309-438-8655 139 E cnulty@ilstu.edu
NUMRICH, Camille .... 401-825-2237 404 H cnumrich@ccri.edu
NUNALEE, Carmen .... 704-991-0249 338 C cnunalee5201@stanly.edu
NUNES, Grafton, J .... 216-421-7410 350 M gnunes@cia.edu
NUNES, John, A .... 914-337-9300 297 D john.nunes@concordia-ny.edu
NUNEZ, Al .... 312-341-2187 147 H anunez13@roosevelt.edu
NUNEZ, Anilsa .... 718-489-2041 313 H anunez5@sfc.edu
NUNEZ, Bernard .... 808-564-3191 127 G bnunez@hmi.edu
NUNEZ, Elaine .... 787-786-3030 512 B enunez@ucb.edu.pr
NUNEZ, Elsa .... 860-465-5222.. 84 H nuneze@easternct.edu
NUNEZ, Elsa, M .... 860-465-5222.. 84 J nunez@easternct.edu
NUNEZ, Haydee .... 630-637-5142 144 H hnunez@noctrl.edu
NUNEZ, Ivon .... 973-596-3478 279 F nunez@njit.edu
NUNEZ, Jose .... 650-358-6836.. 61 N nunezj@smccd.edu
NUNEZ, Jose Ramon .... 714-992-7030.. 53 L jnunez@fullcoll.edu
NUNEZ, Juan .... 936-294-1910 450 C jmn019@shsu.edu
NUNEZ, Katia .... 305-442-9223 103 F knunez@mru.edu
NUNEZ, Lucia .... 608-246-6434 499 H lnunez1@madisoncollege.edu
NUNEZ, Steve, C .... 815-835-6263 148 H steve.c.nunez@svcc.edu
NUNEZ, William .... 402-472-4455 269 J bill.nunez@unl.edu
NUNLEY, Beth .... 815-802-8142 140 D bnunley@kcc.edu
NUNLEY, Ernest, L .... 276-739-2510 476 C enunley@vhcc.edu
NUNN, JR., Darryl .... 717-299-7742 399 G nunn@stevenscollege.edu
NUNN, Ryan .... 419-783-2312 352 F rnunn@defiance.edu
NUNNA, Ramakrishna ... 559-278-2500.. 31 D rnunna@csufresno.edu
NUNNALLY, Delecia ...... 209-954-5151.. 60 J dnunnally@deltacollege.edu
NUNNELLY, Laura .... 573-876-7212 260 F lnunnelly@stephens.edu
NUNZIATO, Renee .... 631-451-4469 321 G nunziar@sunysuffolk.edu
NUOSCE, Mary .... 239-513-1122 101 C mnuosce@hodges.edu
NUSBAUM, Juliet .... 909-607-8787.. 37 G juliet_nusbaum@kgi.edu
NUSBAUM, Nancy .... 512-245-2244 450 E nn01@txstate.edu
NUSS, Shelley .... 706-713-2188 125 G snuss@uga.edu
NUSSBAUM, Renee .... 419-755-4772 357 E rnussbau@ncstatecollege.edu
NUSSER, Sarah, M .... 515-294-6344 162 I nusser@iastate.edu
NUTEFALL, Jennifer ...... 408-554-6829.. 62 D jnutefall@scu.edu
NUTGRASS, Robert .... 515-961-1678 169 D bob.nutgrass@simpson.edu
NUTI, Larry .... 925-631-4901.. 59 B lnuti@stmarys-ca.edu
NUTT, Jill .... 616-395-7765 225 B nutt@hope.edu
NUTT, Lee Ann .... 281-351-3378 439 G leeann.nutt@lonestar.edu
NUTT, Roger .... 239-280-1603.. 94 O roger.nutt@avemaria.edu
NUTTER, Alberta .... 405-733-7979 369 I anutter@rose.edu
NUTTER, Michelle .... 405-733-7300 369 I mnutter@rose.edu
NUTTER, Sarah .... 541-346-3300 377 D snutter@uoregon.edu
NUTTY, David .... 207-780-4276 196 F david.nutty@maine.edu
NUZZO, Brittany .... 304-296-8282 491 F bnuzzo@wvjc.edu
NUZZO, Jane .... 212-592-2302 315 H jnuzzo@sva.edu
NUÑEZ, Cheryl .... 360-475-7740 482 G cnunez@olympic.edu
NWAKEZE, Peter .... 718-933-6700 307 G pnwakeze@monroecollege.edu
NWANGWU, Winifred ... 401-874-2775 406 B winny@uri.edu
NWANKWO, Charles ..... 480-732-7020.. 12 P charles.nwankwo@cgc.edu
NWANNE, Andrew, I ..... 575-234-9215 287 D anwanne@nmsu.edu
NWARIAKU, Fiemu, E ... 214-648-9968 457 B fiemu.nwariku@utsouthwestern.edu
NWOKEAFOR, Cosmos . 301-860-3232 203 C cnwokeafor@bowiestate.edu
NWOSU, Peter, O .... 718-960-8222 294 A peter.nwosu@lehman.cuny.edu
NYAGA, Doris .... 319-398-5504 167 C doris.nyaga@kirkwood.edu
NYAMATHI, Adey .... 949-824-1514.. 68 G anyamath@uci.edu
NYANG'AU, Ondara ...... 651-793-1874 238 H ondara.nyangau@metrostate.edu
NYARDY, OSB, Jeffrey, S .... 724-532-6600 398 F jsnyardy@gmail.com
NYBERG, Connie .... 307-855-2207 501 V cnyberg@cwc.edu
NYE, Jamey .... 916-568-3031.. 50 E nye@losrios.edu
NYE, Judith .... 732-571-3637 279 B nye@monmouth.edu
NYE, Robert .... 585-785-1201 300 B robert.nye@flcc.edu
NYE, Valerie .... 505-428-1506 288 B valerie.nye@sfcc.edu
NYGAARD, Steven .... 310-258-5522.. 50 J steven.nygaard@lmu.edu
NYHAMMER, Diane .... 630-466-7900 152 C dnyhammer@waubonsee.edu
NYHAN, Jeff .... 602-206-8220 272 L jnyhan@ccsnh.edu
NYIRENDA, Stanley, M . 410-651-6672 203 A smnyirenda@umes.edu
NYLEN, John .... 847-578-3252 147 I john.nylen@rosalindfranklin.edu
NYMAN, Hannah .... 318-487-7154 186 I hannah.nyman@lacollege.edu
NYPAVER, David .... 330-972-6876 362 B nypaver@uakron.edu
NYRE, Joseph, E .... 973-761-9620 283 B joseph.nyre@shu.edu
NYSTROM, Ellen .... 210-567-2640 456 C nystrom@uthscsa.edu
NYUL, Renata .... 617-373-7666 217 F
NZAMUTUNA, Issmael .. 951-785-2006.. 47 C inzamutu@lasierra.edu
NZEH, Okoroafor .... 706-821-8331 122 K onzeh@paine.edu
NZEOGWU, Okeleke ...... 702-968-1659 272 C onzeogwu@roseman.edu

O

OAKES, Austin .... 931-598-1890 423 M ahoakes@sewanee.edu
OAKES, Barbee .... 702-895-5580 271 E barbee.oakes@unlv.edu
OAKES, Mary .... 312-369-6802 135 E moakes@colum.edu
OAKES, Tammy, K .... 260-399-7700 161 D toakes@sf.edu
OAKLAND, Sheri .... 701-845-7197 346 A sheri.oakland@vcsu.edu
OAKLEY, Christina .... 561-912-1211.. 98 D
OAKLEY, Jennifer .... 201-360-4002 278 C joakley@hccc.edu
OAKS, Dana .... 540-261-4095 471 H dana.oaks@svu.edu
OAKS, Diane, G .... 949-451-5277.. 64 F doaks@ivc.edu
OAKS, Kelly .... 540-231-8771 477 A koaks@vt.edu
OAKS SMITH, Tonya ..... 318-257-0877 191 F tonya@latech.edu
OANES, Kari .... 218-299-6531 239 B kari.oanes@minnesota.edu
OANES, Laura .... 507-457-6909 243 B loanes@smumn.edu
OATES, Andrea .... 229-931-2705 124 D aoates@southgatech.edu
OATES, Justin, T .... 803-323-2205 414 G oatesj@winthrop.edu
OATES, Nadine .... 716-652-8900 292 I noates@cks.edu
OATES, Richard .... 678-717-3947 126 A richard.oates@ung.edu
OATES, Scott, F .... 804-828-9124 473 F sfoates@vcu.edu
OATHOUT, Douglas ...... 814-871-7470 384 E oathout002@gannon.edu
OATMAN, Kim, H .... 606-783-2066 183 F k.oatman@moreheadstate.edu
OBA, Saichi, T .... 907-450-8146.... 9 G stoba@alaska.edu
OBARE, Sherine, O .... 336-285-2800 343 A soobare@uncg.edu
OBARE, Sherine, O .... 336-285-2800 341 F soobare@ncat.edu
OBBINK, Kim .... 406-994-6550 264 D kobbink@montana.edu
OBER, Jeffrey .... 208-792-2225 131 A jrober@lcsc.edu
OBER, Roxanne .... 412-346-2100 396 F rober@pia.edu
OBER LAMBERT, Janet, L .... 800-287-8822 153 D oberlja@bethanyseminary.edu
OBERFELD, Jeremy .... 312-236-9000 143 F
OBERFELDT, Kathleen ... 718-390-3435 324 F koberfel@wagner.edu
OBERG, Beth .... 217-479-7130 142 I beth.oberg@mac.edu
OBERHAUSER, Karen .... 608-262-2748 496 C koberhauser@wisc.edu
OBERHELMAN, Don ...... 805-756-1407.. 30 C obe@calpoly.edu
OBERHELMAN, Jennifer 435-586-7721 460 F oberhelman@suu.edu
OBERHOLTZER, Brent ... 717-867-6111 388 H oberholt@lvc.edu
OBERHOLTZER, Curt ..... 920-206-2372 493 L curt.oberholtzer@mbu.edu
OBERLANDER, Cyril ...... 707-826-3441.. 33 D cyril.oberlander@humboldt.edu
OBERLEITNER, Melinda 337-482-5611 192 E melinda.oberleitner@louisiana.edu
OBERMAN, Anne .... 320-363-5999 235 C aoberman@csbsju.edu
OBERMARK, Julie .... 618-545-3331 140 E jobermark@kaskaskia.edu
OBERMEISTER, Tuvia, M .... 718-377-0777 312 A
OBERMULLER, Giovanka .... 804-862-6100 470 I gobermuller@rbc.edu
OBERQUELL, Christian .. 406-265-3761 264 F coberquell@msun.edu
OBERSTE, Christy .... 501-812-2243.. 23 B coberste@uaptc.edu
OBERSTEIN, Leonard .... 410-484-7200 201 A loberstein@nirc.edu
OBERSTEIN, Ron .... 510-780-4500.. 47 J roberstein@lifewest.edu
OBERT, Brian .... 308-345-8109 267 K obertb@mpcc.edu
OBI, Stacey .... 717-728-2248 381 B staceyobi@centralpenn.edu
OBIELODAN, James, B . 502-597-6915 182 H james.obielodan@kysu.edu
OBILADE, Sandra, O ..... 270-686-4209 179 D sandra.obilade@brescia.edu
OBIOMON, Pamela .... 936-261-9956 446 D phobiomon@pvamu.edu
OBISESAN, Thomas, O . 202-806-2550.. 92 B tobisesan@howard.edu
OBLANDER, Douglas .... 843-208-8120 413 E oblander@uscb.edu
OBLANDER, Frances, W .... 912-650-5684 124 E foblander@southuniversity.edu
OBLOY, Leonard .... 248-683-0446 231 A lobloy@sscms.edu
OBORNE, Shannon .... 518-275-8149 311 G soborne@paulsmiths.edu
OBOURN, Milo .... 585-395-2034 318 B mobourn@brockport.edu
OBRENTZ, Barbara .... 912-260-4276 124 C barbara.obrentz@sgsc.edu
OBRYCKI, Marybeth ...... 973-290-4460 277 A mobrycki@cse.edu
OBSNIUK, Karen .... 734-432-5648 227 A kobsniuk@madonna.edu
OBSTA, Kim .... 361-572-6410 457 E kim.obsta@victoriacollege.edu
OBURN, Martha .... 713-718-8670 437 I martha.oburn@hccs.edu
OCAMPO, Arturo .... 714-808-4830.. 53 J aocampo@nocccd.edu
OCAMPO, Carlota .... 202-884-9209.. 93 B ocampoc@trinitydc.edu
OCAMPO, Kathy .... 928-314-9559.. 10 J katheline.ocampo@azwestern.edu
OCAMPO, Renata .... 817-202-6320 444 I r.ocampo@swau.edu
OCASIO, Arcadio .... 787-257-0000 513 C arcadio.ocasio@upr.edu
OCASIO, Luz .... 787-765-1915 510 B locasio@opto.inter.edu
OCCHIOGROSSO, Gabrielle .... 718-405-3225 296 G gabrielle.occhiogrosso@mountsaintvincent.edu
OCCHIOGROSSO, Paul, F .... 212-650-8276 293 D pocchiogrosso@ccny.cuny.edu
OCEGUERA, Gustavo ..... 951-372-7885.. 58 H gustavo.oceguera@norcocollege.edu
OCHES, Eric .... 781-891-2937 206 D roches@bentley.edu
OCHOA, Eduardo, M ..... 831-582-3532.. 32 C emochoa@csumb.edu
OCHOA, Hector .... 619-594-6881.. 33 E provost@sdsu.edu
OCHOA, Marcia .... 831-459-2769.. 70 B oakesprovost@ucsc.edu
OCHOA, Marilyn .... 732-906-4252 279 A mochoa@middlesexcc.edu
OCHOA, Robert .... 956-721-5417 439 C rochoa@laredo.edu
OCHOA, Vanessa .... 323-265-8721.. 48 H ochoavj@elac.edu
OCHRAN, Timothy, G ... 903-877-7902 456 D timothy.ochran@uthct.edu
OCHSENBEIN, Kim, D ... 865-981-8121 421 F kim.ochsenbein@maryvillecollege.edu
OCHSNER, Tom, J .... 402-465-2212 268 H tjo@nebrwesleyan.edu
OCKEN, Scott .... 515-964-6364 164 C sjocken@dmacc.edu
OCMAND, Christina ...... 225-743-8500 188 B cocmond@rpcc.edu
OCONNELL, Amy .... 401-598-1000 404 I amy.oconnell@jwu.edu

OLDS, David .... 218-262-6759 238 C
davidolds@hibbing.edu
OLDS, Wendy .... 218-846-3810 239 B
wendy.olds@minnesota.edu
OLDS, William .... 925-631-4542.. 59 B
wlo1@stmarys-ca.edu
OLEEN, Clair .... 785-227-3380 171 E
oleenc@bethanylb.edu
OLEGERIIL, Jay .... 680-488-2471 506 B
jayo@palau.edu
OLEJNICZAK, Sarah ...... 414-930-3372 495 A
olejnics@mtmary.edu
OLEJNICZAK-CAUSHAJ,
Joanna .... 248-706-5363 231 A
jolejniczak@sscms.edu
OLEN, Simcha .... 718-252-6333 326 C
OLER, Gregory, S .... 302-831-8913.. 90 F
gregoler@udel.edu
OLES, Brian, M .... 508-565-1914 218 H
boles@stonehill.edu
OLESNAVAGE, John ...... 414-425-8300 495 H
jolesnavage@shsst.edu
OLEVNIK, Courtney .... 814-824-2000 390 C
colevnik@mercyhurst.edu
OLEVSKY, Eugene .... 619-594-6329.. 33 E
eolvesky@sdsu.edu
OLEVSON, Jennifer .... 626-568-8850.. 48 F
jennifer@lacm.edu
OLFMAN, Lorne .... 909-607-3035.. 37 D
lorne.olfman@cgu.edu
OLGUIN, Javier, E .... 972-860-5306 435 B
javiereolguin@dcccd.edu
OLIAN, Judy, D .... 203-582-8700.. 87 G
j.olian@quinnipiac.edu
OLIKONG, Deikola .... 680-488-2470 506 B
olikongd@gmail.com
OLIKONG, Deikola .... 680-488-2471 506 B
olikongd@gmail.com
OLIN, Bradley .... 831-479-6406.. 27 G
brolin@cabrillo.edu
OLIN, Jessica .... 585-343-0055 301 A
jrolin@genesee.edu
OLIN, Joanna .... 413-585-2108 218 F
jolin@smith.edu
OLIN, Mike .... 610-330-5917 387 E
olinm@lafayette.edu
OLIN, Robert, F .... 205-348-5972.... 7 G
olin@as.ua.edu
OLING-SISAY, Mary ...... 415-955-2100.. 24 K
moling-sisay@alliant.edu
OLINGER, CSC,
Gerald, J .... 574-631-1212 161 C
golinger@nd.edu
OLINGER, Ronald, J ..... 913-360-7413 171 D
rolinger@benedictine.edu
OLINTO, Angela, V .... 773-702-7950 150 J
aolinto@uchicago.edu
OLIPHINT, Melody .... 806-743-7382 451 C
melody.oliphint@ttuhsc.edu
OLISZCZAK, Jennifer ..... 603-578-8900 273 A
joliszczak@ccsnh.edu
OLISZCZAK, Peter .... 623-845-4634.. 13 C
peter.oliszczak@gccaz.edu
OLIVA, Giacomo .... 212-217-4040 299 H
giacomo_oliva@fitnyc.edu
OLIVA, Joseph, E .... 718-990-6421 314 B
olivaj@stjohns.edu
OLIVA, Julia .... 718-289-5100 293 B
julia.oliva@bcc.cuny.edu
OLIVA, Mary .... 312-329-4112 144 B
mary.oliva@moody.edu
OLIVA, Robert .... 718-489-5372 313 H
roliva@sfc.edu
OLIVARES, Carlos, J ..... 787-279-2220 509 A
colivares@bayamon.inter.edu
OLIVARES-URUETA,
Mayra .... 817-515-6203 445 G
mayra.olivares-urueta@tccd.edu
OLIVE, David, W .... 276-326-4466 465 B
david.olive@bluefield.edu
OLIVE, Derek .... 270-745-2409 185 E
derek.olive@wku.edu
OLIVE-TAYLOR, Becky ... 336-278-6500 328 K
oliveb@elon.edu
OLIVEIRA, Judy .... 808-689-2689 128 G
judy.oliveira@hawaii.edu
OLIVEIRA, Marcio, A .... 301-405-5190 202 C
marcio@umd.edu
OLIVEIRA, Sandra, J ..... 401-865-2602 405 B
solivei6@providence.edu
OLIVER, Astrid .... 970-247-7507.. 79 I
oliver_a@fortlewis.edu
OLIVER, Bernie .... 229-333-5925 126 G
beoliver@valdosta.edu
OLIVER, Brande' .... 248-204-2308 226 G
boliver@ltu.edu
OLIVER, Celia .... 212-616-7200 301 F
celia.oliver@helenefuld.edu
OLIVER, Christine .... 401-598-1000 404 I
coliver@jwu.edu
OLIVER, Dale .... 707-826-3256.. 33 D
dale.oliver@humboldt.edu
OLIVER, Debra .... 937-708-5748 364 D
doliver@wilberforce.edu
OLIVER, Denita .... 256-215-4290.... 1 G
doliver@cacc.edu
OLIVER, Dianne .... 585-389-2641 308 B
doliver9@naz.edu
OLIVER, Dominick .... 412-924-1460 396 I
doliver@pts.edu
OLIVER, Donna, H .... 904-470-8004.. 97 L
donna.oliver@ewc.edu
OLIVER, Donna, H .... 904-470-8000.. 97 L
OLIVER, Ebigaly .... 787-878-5475 508 L
eoliver@arecibo.inter.edu
OLIVER, Elijah .... 860-512-3214.. 85 G
eoliver@manchestercc.edu
OLIVER, Helen .... 662-252-8000 248 G
holiver@rustcollege.edu
OLIVER, Jorge .... 718-636-3671 311 J
joliver6@pratt.edu
OLIVER, Justin .... 757-925-6302 475 E
joliver@pdc.edu
OLIVER, Kenneth .... 217-228-5432 146 F
oliveke@quincy.edu
OLIVER, Kenneth .... 785-833-4342 175 B
ken.oliver@kwu.edu
OLIVER, Kenneth, R ...... 660-248-6225 251 B
koliver@centralmethodist.edu
OLIVER, Lillian, M .... 787-723-4481 507 A
loliver@ceaprc.edu
OLIVER, Matthew .... 800-686-1883 222 E
moliver@cleary.edu
OLIVER, Maxine .... 407-708-2492 107 D
olivera@seminolestate.edu
OLIVER, Melvin, L .... 909-621-8129.. 56 J
pitzerpresident@pitzer.edu
OLIVER, Michael .... 734-462-4400 230 D
moliver@schoolcraft.edu
OLIVER, Nancy .... 740-284-5192 353 B
noliver@franciscan.edu
OLIVER, Pamella .... 657-278-2896.. 31 E
poliver@fullerton.edu
OLIVER, Parker .... 931-598-1586 423 M
pwoliver@sewanee.edu
OLIVER, Patricia Belton 713-743-2400 452 F
poliver@central.uh.edu
OLIVER, Rand .... 513-861-6400 361 L
rand.oliver@myunion.edu
OLIVER, Rebecca .... 870-972-2308.. 17 G
rsoliver@astate.edu
OLIVER, Richard .... 417-865-2815 253 B
oliverr@evangel.edu
OLIVER, Robin .... 740-593-2200 359 G
roliver@ohio.edu
OLIVER,
Samuel (Dub), W .... 731-661-5180 427 C
doliver@uu.edu
OLIVER, Sarah, E .... 563-333-6424 169 A
oliversarahe@sau.edu
OLIVER, Sharon, J .... 919-530-5313 342 A
soliver@nccu.edu
OLIVER, Sharon, M .... 207-581-1585 195 J
smoliver@maine.edu
OLIVER, Shawn .... 609-497-7814 280 D
shawn.oliver@ptsem.edu
OLIVER, Staci, G .... 618-235-2700 149 H
staci.oliver@swic.edu
OLIVER, Tamara .... 607-844-8222 322 H
tmo@tompkinscortland.edu
OLIVER, Tanya .... 252-862-1272 337 C
toliver@roanokechowan.edu
OLIVER, Tom .... 217-228-5432 146 F
oliveto@quincy.edu
OLIVER, Tricia .... 413-572-5523 213 D
toliver@westfield.ma.edu
OLIVER-VERONESI,
Robin, E .... 814-865-6555 392 B
reo133@psu.edu
OLIVERAS, Jesus .... 787-725-8120 507 N
joliveras@eap.edu
OLIVERAS, José .... 787-844-8181 514 A
jose.oliveras2@upr.edu
OLIVERAS, Marilyn .... 787-284-1912 509 E
molivera@ponce.inter.edu
OLIVERI, Dee .... 949-582-4500.. 64 G
doliveri@saddleback.edu
OLIVERI, Joe .... 812-357-6222 160 D
joliveri@saintmeinrad.edu
OLIVERI, Mary, A .... 570-961-7855 387 D
oliverim@lackawanna.edu
OLIVERIO, Robert .... 602-489-5300.. 10 E
robert.oliverio@arizonachristian.edu
OLIVERO, Bill .... 916-306-1628.. 66 I
bolivero@sum.edu
OLIVEROS, Jon .... 847-397-0300 131 I
OLIVETTE, Michael .... 845-569-3203 307 J
michael.olivette@msmc.edu
OLIVIERI-LENAHAN,
Elizabeth .... 914-633-2547 302 G
eolivieri@iona.edu
OLIVO, Cynthia .... 626-585-7074.. 55 K
cdolivo@pasadena.edu
OLIVO, Michael .... 516-323-4840 307 F
molivo@molloy.edu
OLKKOLA, Jacob .... 207-859-4900 193 E
jake.olkkola@colby.edu
OLLE-LAJOIE, Maureen . 715-425-3799 497 E
maureen.olle-lajoie@uwrf.edu
OLLIFF, Kenneth .... 314-977-2925 259 H
knneth.a.olliff@slu.edu
OLLIFF, Kenton .... 785-628-4401 173 B
klolliff@fhsu.edu
OLLIFF, Martin .... 334-983-6556.... 7 C
OLLIFF, Thomas .... 954-201-7693.. 95 H
tolliff@broward.edu
OLLINGER, Nancy .... 610-902-8276 380 C
nancy.ollinger@cabrini.edu
OLLSON, Joanne .... 413-782-1343 219 F
joanne.ollson@wne.edu
OLMOS, Ernesto, F .... 806-371-5456 430 A
efolmos@actx.edu
OLMOS, Milton .... 808-735-4792 127 F
security@chaminade.edu
OLMSTADT, William .... 318-675-5449 189 C
wolmst@lsuhsc.edu
OLMSTEAD, Karen, L .... 410-548-3374 203 F
klolmstead@salisbury.edu
OLMSTEAD, Patrick .... 818-401-1041.. 39 G
polmstead@columbiacollege.edu
OLMSTEAD, Steve .... 918-293-4744 368 D
steve.olmstead@okstate.edu
OLMSTED, Joshua .... 916-388-2895.. 35 B
jolmsted@carrington.edu
OLMSTED, Kelly .... 716-488-3021 303 C
kellyolmsted@jbc.edu
OLMSTED, Michelle ...... 513-244-4475 357 A
michelle.omsted@msj.edu
OLOVSON, Matthew, J .. 513-556-5503 362 D
matthew.olovson@uc.edu
OLOWUDE, Brian .... 805-893-4411.. 70 A
brian.olowude@sa.ucsb.edu
OLPHIE, Elizabeth .... 229-333-7837 126 G
ewolphie@valdosta.edu
OLSEN, Andy .... 620-242-0413 175 F
olsena@mcpherson.edu
OLSEN, Ann, E .... 502-272-8133 179 B
aolsen@bellarmine.edu
OLSEN, Christopher ...... 812-237-2785 155 G
christopher.olsen@indstate.edu
OLSEN, Danny, R .... 801-422-5648 458 H
danny_olsen@byu.edu
OLSEN, Elisa .... 713-226-5519 453 B
olsene@uhd.edu
OLSEN, Jane .... 320-308-4958 240 H
jolsen@stcloudstate.edu
OLSEN, Jeff .... 713-942-3466 454 H
olsenj@stthom.edu
OLSEN, Jeff .... 203-596-6174.. 87 F
jolsen@post.edu
OLSEN, Katie .... 973-328-5058 277 B
kolsen@ccm.edu
OLSEN, Keith .... 402-599-7927 270 A
keith.olsen@unmc.edu
OLSEN, Levi .... 585-343-0055 301 A
ltolsen@genesee.edu
OLSEN, Mandy .... 866-492-5336 244 F
miranda.olsen@mail.waldenu.edu
OLSEN, Matt .... 918-495-7163 368 I
molsen@oru.edu
OLSEN, Micah .... 307-681-6007 502 F
molsen@sheridan.edu
OLSEN, Michelle, D ...... 417-836-5274 256 E
molsen@missouristate.edu
OLSEN, Mike .... 435-879-4287 460 G
olsen@dixie.edu
OLSEN, Morgan, R .... 480-727-9920.. 10 I
morgan.r.olsen@asu.edu
OLSEN, Nancy .... 218-879-0715 238 A
nancy.olsen@fdltcc.edu
OLSEN, Pete .... 831-645-1362.. 52 F
polsen@mpc.edu
OLSEN, Renee .... 208-792-2151 131 A
rmolsen@lcsc.edu
OLSEN, Steven, M .... 716-878-4113 318 C
olsensw@buffalostate.edu
OLSEN, Taimi .... 864-656-4542 408 A
taimio@clemson.edu
OLSHINE, Rachel .... 903-233-4410 439 E
rachelolshine@letu.edu
OLSON, Adam .... 813-988-5131.. 98 Q
development@floridacollege.edu
OLSON, Adam, J .... 813-988-5131.. 98 Q
olsona@floridacollege.edu
OLSON, Alma, E .... 330-972-6577 362 B
aolson@uakron.edu
OLSON, Amy .... 715-831-7236 499 D
aolson133@cvtc.edu
OLSON, Andrea, I .... 425-739-8127 482 A
andrea.olson@lwtech.edu
OLSON, Barry .... 919-513-3402 342 B
barry_olson@ncsu.edu
OLSON, Ben .... 907-745-3201.... 9 B
bolson@akbible.edu
OLSON, Ben .... 907-745-3201.... 9 B
registrar@akbible.edu
OLSON, Cari .... 701-858-3323 345 F
cari.olson@minotstateu.edu
OLSON, Cathy .... 413-755-4419 215 F
colson@stcc.edu
OLSON, Cynthia .... 612-381-8124 235 H
colson@dunwoody.edu
OLSON, Dan .... 480-245-7980.. 12 N
dan.olson@ibcs.edu
OLSON, David .... 910-962-3102 343 C
olsond@uncw.edu
OLSON, Deborah .... 863-784-7275 107 F
deborah.olson@southflorida.edu
OLSON, Dustin .... 303-273-3000.. 78 I
dolson1@mines.edu
OLSON, Dustin .... 805-893-4151.. 70 A
dustin.olson@police.ucsb.edu
OLSON, Eric .... 610-902-8275 380 C
eric.j.olson@cabrini.edu
OLSON, Ernest .... 309-438-1946 139 E
ewolson@ilstu.edu
OLSON, Gary, A .... 716-839-8210 298 B
golson@daemen.edu
OLSON, Heidi, L .... 320-222-5209 240 E
heidi.olson@ridgewater.edu
OLSON, Jeffery, D .... 651-638-6241 234 C
jeff-olson@bethel.edu
OLSON, John .... 425-388-9407 480 G
jolson@everettcc.edu
OLSON, Jon .... 605-626-2550 417 A
jon.olson@northern.edu
OLSON, Joshua .... 906-487-1217 227 E
jolson@mtu.edu
OLSON, Kerry, J .... 409-882-3362 450 A
kerry.olson@lsco.edu
OLSON, Kris .... 218-299-3024 235 E
krisolson@cord.edu
OLSON, Kristin .... 562-938-4095.. 48 D
kolson@lbcc.edu
OLSON, Marcene .... 541-917-4999 374 A
olsonm@linnbenton.edu
OLSON, Mark .... 763-544-9501 233 J
OLSON, Mary Ellen .... 920-403-3181 495 I
maryellen.olson@snc.edu
OLSON, Matthew .... 781-280-3802 214 G
olsonm@middlesex.mass.edu
OLSON, Megan .... 907-786-1764.... 9 H
msolson5@alaska.edu
OLSON, Michael .... 202-250-2652.. 91 E
michael.olson@gallaudet.edu
OLSON, Mike .... 480-314-2102.. 15 R
OLSON, Nancy .... 217-732-3168 141 H
nolson@lincolnchristian.edu
OLSON, Nancy .... 641-585-8147 170 B
olsonn@waldorf.edu
OLSON, Nancy .... 760-252-2411.. 26 I
nolson@barstow.edu
OLSON, Nancy .... 507-537-6544 241 D
nancy.olson@smsu.edu
OLSON, Paul .... 701-252-3467 347 C
paul.olson@uj.edu
OLSON, Peter .... 231-348-6660 228 E
polson@ncmich.edu
OLSON, Robert .... 253-833-9111 481 F
rolson@greenriver.edu
OLSON, Robin .... 614-251-4700 358 G
olsonr@ohiodominican.edu

OLSON, Roger, T .... 218-299-3682 235 E rolson@cord.edu
OLSON, Sandra .... 508-929-8025 213 E solson@worcester.edu
OLSON, Sara .... 863-680-3965.. 99 H solson@flsouthern.edu
OLSON, Sara, M .... 402-465-2185 268 H solson@nebrwesleyan.edu
OLSON, Scott, R .... 507-457-5003 241 F solson@winona.edu
OLSON, Shari, L .... 602-243-8035.. 14 A shari.olson@southmountaincc.edu
OLSON, Sharon .... 562-985-5585.. 31 F sharon.olson@csulb.edu
OLSON, Shelly .... 715-833-6675 499 D solson@cvtc.edu
OLSON, Stephen .... 765-998-5119 160 F stolson@taylor.edu
OLSON, Terry .... 949-214-3270.. 40 F terry.olson@cui.edu
OLSON, Terry .... 701-572-9275 346 F tolson@wscfoundation.com
OLSON, Tim .... 701-627-4738 346 G tolson@nhsc.edu
OLSON, Todd .... 202-687-6318.. 92 A tao4@georgetown.edu
OLSON, Wendy .... 509-777-4313 486 I wolson@whitworth.edu
OLSON-KILGORE, Michelle .... 423-697-5740 424 E michelle.olson@chattanoogastate.edu
OLSON-KOPP, Kim .... 608-796-3267 498 N kmolsonkopp@viterbo.edu
OLSON-LOY, Sandra ..... 320-589-6013 244 B olsonloy@morris.umn.edu
OLSSON, Roy .... 616-331-3356 224 E olssonr@gvsu.edu
OLSTEIN, Binyamin .... 847-982-2500 138 A olstein@htc.edu
OLSZEWSKI, Kristen ..... 215-489-2946 382 D kristen.olszewski@delval.edu
OLTROGGE, Michael ...... 402-494-2311 268 B moltrogge@thenicc.edu
OLVER, Thomas .... 989-386-6675 227 F tolver@midmich.edu
OLVERA, Alondra .... 217-854-5582 132 I alondra.overa@blackburn.edu
OLVERA, Tina .... 818-345-8879.. 39 G tolvera@columbiacollege.edu
OLWELL, David .... 360-491-4700 483 H dolwell@stmartin.edu
OMACHONU, John .... 828-689-1237 331 A john_omachonu@mhu.edu
OMANN, Bernie .... 320-308-2122 240 H bomann@stcloudstate.edu
OMAR, Richard .... 646-216-2863 309 D romar@nycda.edu
OMENITSCH, Katie .... 202-884-9301.. 93 B omenitschka@trinitydc.edu
OMER, Aftab .... 707-765-1836.. 51 H
OMER, Nicole .... 801-957-4209 461 D nicole.omer@slcc.edu
OMINSKY, Paul .... 609-258-3000 280 E pominsky@princeton.edu
OMOJOKUN, Emmanuel .... 804-524-5322 477 B eomojokun@vsu.edu
OMOTO, Allen .... 909-621-8218.. 56 J dean_faculty@pitzer.edu
OMURA, Kanae .... 626-571-8811.. 72 C kanaeo@uwest.edu
OMWENGA, Margaret ... 610-399-2196 394 C momwenga@cheyney.edu
ONAGAN, Caroline, M .. 847-467-3289 145 F caroline.onagan@northwestern.edu
ONAIFO, Greg .... 212-410-8044 309 B gonaifo@nycpm.edu
ONDER, David .... 828-565-4077 335 C donder@haywood.edu
ONDERKO, Daniel .... 903-566-7277 456 A donderko@uttyler.edu
ONDERS, Robert .... 907-564-8220.... 9 D robert.onders@alaskapacific.edu
ONDRIZEK, Megan, M . 305-284-3667 112 E m.ondrizek@umiami.edu
ONEAL, Susan .... 918-595-7378 370 E susan.oneal@tulsacc.edu
ONG, Meaghan .... 314-719-3661 253 C mong@fontbonne.edu
ONG, Teresa .... 650-949-7794.. 43 D ongteresa@fhda.edu
ONGARO, Guilio .... 714-997-6672.. 36 C ongaro@chapman.edu
ONISHI, Joni, Y .... 808-934-2514 129 A jonishi@hawaii.edu
ONKEN, Margaret .... 314-529-6877 254 H monken@maryville.edu
ONKEN, Marina .... 715-425-3335 497 E marina.onken@uwrf.edu
ONKS, Jason .... 423-461-8335 422 J jonks@milligan.edu
ONNEN, Kendi .... 309-467-6303 137 B registrar@eureka.edu
ONO, Kay .... 808-455-0440 129 D kayono@hawaii.edu
ONODERA, Yasushi ...... 479-964-0832.. 18 C yonodera@atu.edu
ONOFRIETTI, Joseph ..... 617-735-9722 209 A onofrij@emmanuel.edu
ONOFRIO, Marshall ...... 609-921-7100 281 B monofrio@rider.edu
ONORATO, Suzanne ...... 860-486-0744.. 88 E suzanne.onorato@uconn.edu
ONTIVEROS, Juan .... 512-471-1904 455 A juan.ontiveros@austin.utexas.edu
ONTIVEROS, Mary, R .... 970-491-7197.. 78M mary.ontiveros@colostate.edu
ONTL, Lynn .... 518-255-5225 319 F ontll@cobleskill.edu
ONUNWOR, Enyinda ..... 651-846-1703 241 B
ONUSKO, Mark .... 216-397-1756 354 I monusko@jcu.edu
ONWUACHI-WILLIG, Angela .... 617-353-3112 207 D aow@bu.edu
ONWUNLI, Agatha .... 850-599-3115 108 I agatha.onwunli@famu.edu
ONYEAGHALA, Raphael 507-537-6218 241 D raphael.onyeaghala@smsu.edu
OOMMEN, Jose .... 740-397-9000 357 B jose.oommen@mvnu.edu
OPARAH, Chinyere .... 510-430-3163.. 52 D jcoparah@mills.edu
OPATZ, Patrick .... 651-779-3346 237 G patrick.opatz@century.edu
OPDYCKE, Anita .... 312-567-7553 139 B aopdycke@iit.edu
OPEL, Kathleen .... 574-631-9525 161 C kopel@nd.edu
OPGENORTH, Timothy .. 414-229-4541 497 A opgenort@uwm.edu
OPHARDT, Christopher . 845-938-3808 504 H
OPITZ, Brian, R .... 724-287-8711 380 A brian.opitz@bc3.edu
OPITZ, Don .... 312-362-6426 135 I dopitz@depaul.edu
OPITZ, Donald .... 717-796-1800 390 E dopitz@messiah.edu
OPP, Mike .... 651-423-8319 237 H mike.opp@dctc.edu
OPP, Susan .... 707-654-1040.. 32 B sopp@csum.edu
OPPENHEIM, Menachen .... 732-363-7110 284 K info@chemdashatorah.org
OPPENHEIMER, Phillip, R .... 209-946-2561.. 70 E poppenhe@pacific.edu
OPPERMAN, John .... 806-742-2121 450 F
OPPERMAN, Mary George .... 607-255-3621 297 F mgo5@cornell.edu
OPPO, Delia, W .... 508-289-2681 220 D doppo@whoi.edu
OQUENDO, Carmen ...... 787-250-1912 509 D coquendo@metro.inter.edu
OQUENDO, Diane .... 646-660-6154 292 L diane.oquendo@baruch.cuny.edu
OQUENDO, Regina .... 787-894-2828 514 C regina.oquendo@upr.edu
ORACION, Donna .... 575-624-7403 286 A donna.oracion@roswell.enmu.edu
ORANGE, Taur, D .... 212-217-4170 299 H taur_orange@fitnyc.edu
ORANSKY, Elissa .... 949-451-5472.. 64 F eoransky@ivc.edu
ORANTE, Newin .... 925-969-2005.. 40 I norante@dvc.edu
ORAVECZ, Joseph .... 508-531-1276 212 B joravecz@bridgew.edu
ORAVETZ, Teresa .... 203-332-5014.. 85 F toravetz@hcc.commnet.edu
ORBAN, Joseph .... 318-670-9360 190 J jorban@susla.edu
ORBE, Michelle .... 203-596-4516.. 87 F morbe@post.edu
ORBITS, Elizabeth .... 734-677-5003 232 B eorbits@wccnet.edu
ORCHARD, James, P ..... 651-641-8705 235 F orchard@csp.edu
ORCHARD, Sue .... 360-442-2301 482 B sorchard@lowercolumbia.edu
ORCUTT, Jill .... 209-228-4785.. 69 B jorcutt2@ucmerced.edu
ORDERS, Brenda .... 910-788-6317 338 A brenda.orders@sccnc.edu
ORDONEZ-CAMPOS, Christina .... 713-313-7197 449 C christina.ordonez-campos@tsu.edu
ORDUNA, Aubray .... 402-552-6118 266 E orduna@clarksoncollege.edu
ORDUNA, Aubray .... 402-552-3100 266 E
ORDUNA, Aubray, D ..... 402-552-6118 266 E orduna@clarksoncollege.edu
OREDEIN, Ade .... 270-852-8607 182 B ade.oredein@kctcs.edu
OREIRO, David .... 360-676-2772 482 D doreiro@nwic.edu
ORELLANA, Victoria ...... 201-360-4121 278 C vorellana@hccc.edu
OREM, Christopher, D .. 540-568-7208 468 F oremcd@jmu.edu
ORENDORFF, Jay .... 415-338-1111.. 34 A
ORENDUFF, Lai, K .... 229-333-5950 126 G lorenduff@valdosta.edu
ORENGO-ORTEGA, Orlando .... 787-993-0000 513 B orlando.orengo@upr.edu
ORF, Michael .... 417-255-7272 256 F michaelorf@missouristate.edu
ORFALI, Aline .... 703-526-6922 469 C aline.orfali@marymount.edu
ORGAN, Regina .... 903-463-8714 437 D organr@grayson.edu
ORGERON, Elizabeth ..... 518-255-5842 319 F orgeroed@cobleskill.edu
ORIANO, Angela .... 281-425-6453 439 D aoriano@lee.edu
ORICK, Ron .... 479-788-7019.. 21 H ron.orick@uafs.edu
ORIHUELA, Omar .... 619-482-6360.. 65 F oorihuela@swccd.edu
ORIHUELA, Ruthanne .... 303-556-3595.. 79 E ruthanne.orihuela@ccd.edu
ORIO, Julie, J .... 415-422-2823.. 71 K orioj@usfca.edu
ORIOLO, Michael .... 315-866-0300 301 G orioloma@herkimer.edu
ORIS, James, T .... 513-529-3734 356 E orisjt@miamioh.edu
ORITZ, Fernando .... 509-313-4054 481 D oritz2@gonzaga.edu
ORKIN, Michael .... 510-466-7308.. 56 H morkin@peralta.edu
ORLANDO, Elizabeth ..... 937-512-2917 361 A elizabeth.orlando@sinclair.edu
ORLANDO, Karen .... 949-451-5511.. 64 F korlando@ivc.edu
ORLANDO, Matthew ...... 207-725-3804 193 D morlando@bowdoin.edu
ORLANDO, Michael .... 517-264-7601 230 E morlando@sienaheights.edu
ORLANDO, Stephen, F .. 352-392-0186 109 F sfo@ufl.edu
ORLAUSKI, Brian .... 951-639-5080.. 52 I borlausk@msjc.edu
ORLIKOFF, Robert .... 252-744-6010 341 C orlikoffr17@ecu.edu
ORLOFF, Micah .... 951-639-5440.. 52 I morloff@msjc.edu
ORLOV, Ariel .... 312-662-4316 131 H aorlov@adler.edu
ORLUCK, Gary .... 701-858-4016 345 F gary.orluck@minotstateu.edu
ORMAN, Larissa .... 406-586-3585 263 J larrisa.orman@montanabiblecollege.edu
ORMASEN, Nickolas ..... 315-229-5908 314 F nick@stlawu.edu
ORMON, Taylor .... 601-925-7782 247 C tormon@mc.edu
ORMOND, Tom .... 717-477-1371 395 E
ORMSBEE, Christine ..... 405-744-1000 368 B ormsbee@okstate.edu
ORNDORFF, Cathy .... 304-293-5305 491 C cathy.orndorff@mail.wvu.edu
ORNDORFF, Robert, M . 814-865-2377 392 B rmo104@psu.edu
ORNE, Tracy .... 217-641-4106 140 A torne@jwcc.edu
ORNELAS, Armida .... 323-265-8973.. 48 H ornelaao@elac.edu
ORNELAS, Irene .... 661-362-3198.. 38 H irene.ornelas@canyons.edu
ORNELAS, Nohemy .... 805-922-6966.. 24 J nornelas@hancockcollege.edu
ORNER, Lita, J .... 240-500-2264 198 H ljorner@hagerstowncc.edu
ORNT, Daniel, B .... 585-475-4861 313 A dboihst@rit.edu
OROK, Orok .... 919-530-5548 342 A oorok@nccu.edu
ORONA, Frank .... 505-747-2161 287 G forona@nnmc.edu
ORONA, Frank .... 505-747-2111 287 G forona@nnmc.edu
ORONA, John .... 210-486-2510 429 G jorona3@alamo.edu
OROPEZA, Rachel .... 305-809-3203.. 99 C rachel.oropeza@fkcc.edu
OROS, Richard .... 480-517-8202.. 13 G richard.oros@riosalado.edu
OROZ, Andres .... 857-701-1490 215 E aoroz@rcc.mass.edu
OROZCO, Daniel .... 512-863-1346 445 D orozcod@southwestern.edu
OROZCO, Darcy .... 970-204-8375.. 79 J darcy.orozco@frontrange.edu
OROZCO, Jessica .... 305-474-6863 106 F jorozco@stu.edu
OROZCO, Lisa .... 843-863-7954 407 E lorozco@csuniv.edu
OROZCO, Monica, J ..... 804-828-0100 473 F morozco@vcu.edu
ORR, Amy, K .... 843-953-7333 408 E orra@cofc.edu
ORR, Brenda, B .... 601-643-5101 245 G brenda.orr@colin.edu
ORR, Cheryl .... 580-477-7710 371 F cheryl.orr@newmoodle.wosc.edu
ORR, Debra .... 617-521-2180 218 E debra.orr@simmons.edu
ORR, Elisabeth .... 562-938-4343.. 48 D eorr@lbcc.edu
ORR, Ethan, R .... 520-621-0906.. 16 G eorr@email.arizona.edu
ORR, Jamar .... 312-341-3527 147 H
ORR, Jim .... 325-674-2659 429 B jmo10a@acu.edu
ORR, Kristy .... 254-710-3737 431 J kristy_orr@baylor.edu
ORR, Mandy .... 770-533-7012 121 B morr@laniertech.edu
ORR, Mark .... 916-278-6348.. 32 E athletic.director@csus.edu
ORR, Michael, T .... 518-580-5705 316 A morr@skidmore.edu
ORR, Ray .... 253-535-7380 482 H fama@plu.edu
ORR, Richard .... 724-589-2700 399 H rorr@thiel.edu
ORR, Robert, C .... 301-405-3103 202 C rorr1@umd.edu
ORR, Rodney .... 214-887-2976 436 B rorr@dts.edu
ORR, Shaun .... 208-496-9340 130 A orrs@byui.edu
ORR, Stephanie, W .... 850-263-3261.. 95 B sworr@baptistcollege.edu
ORR, Susan, L .... 603-513-1310 274 H susan.orr@granite.edu
ORR, Sylvia .... 623-935-8413.. 13 A sylvia.orr@estrellamountain.edu
ORR, Trina .... 828-227-7290 344 A torr@wcu.edu
ORR, Wayne .... 859-985-3828 179 C orrj@berea.edu
ORRIS, Erika .... 301-985-7435 203 B erika.orris@umuc.edu
ORRIS, Keith, A .... 215-571-4463 383 B keith.a.orris@drexel.edu
ORRISON, Russell .... 423-236-2336 424 B rorrison@southern.edu
ORSCHELN, Paul .... 816-271-3835 257 A porscheln@missouriwestern.edu
ORSINI, SPHR, Teri ...... 704-337-2297 339 G orsinit@queens.edu
ORT, Shirley, A .... 919-962-2315 342 D ort@email.unc.edu
ORTALE, Lynn .... 215-248-7030 381 D ortalel@chc.edu

ORTBERG, Jennifer, L ... 714-895-8965.. 38 D
jortberg@gwc.cccd.edu
ORTEGA, Bethania .... 718-960-8819 294 A
budget.ortega@lehman.cuny.edu
ORTEGA, Denise .... 787-780-0070 506 F
dortega@caribbean.edu
ORTEGA, Eleazar .... 406-771-5136 264 G
eleazar.ortega@gfcmsu.edu
ORTEGA, J. Martin .... 210-486-0721 429 H
jortega@alamo.edu
ORTEGA, Janet .... 602-243-8287.. 14 A
janet.ortega@southmountaincc.edu
ORTEGA, Lisa .... 787-780-5134 510 F
lortega@nuc.edu
ORTEGA, Lucha .... 408-288-3146.. 61 M
lucha.ortega@sjcc.edu
ORTEGA, Virginia .... 760-773-2513.. 39 A
vortega@collegeofthedesert.edu
ORTEGA BELTRAN,
Edwin .... 530-661-5711.. 76 B
eortega@yccd.edu
ORTEGO, Carla .... 337-521-8922 188 C
carla.ortego@solacc.edu
ORTEN, Mark .... 802-443-5626 462 H
orten@middlebury.edu
ORTEZ, James .... 559-325-5264.. 66 D
james.ortez@cloviscollege.edu
ORTIKOV, Khudoyor, S . 832-230-5555 440 H
khudoyor@na.edu
ORTIZ, Anthony .... 575-835-5424 286 I
anthony.ortiz@nmt.edu
ORTIZ, Arnaldo .... 787-841-2000 510 K
capellania@pucpr.edu
ORTIZ, Arthur .... 713-525-3848 454 H
ortiza@stthom.edu
ORTIZ, Beni .... 773-442-5143 145 B
b-ortiz@neiu.edu
ORTIZ, Carmen, B .... 787-723-4481 507 A
cortiz@ceaprc.edu
ORTIZ, Edna .... 787-786-3030 512 B
eortiz@ucb.edu.pr
ORTIZ, Eduardo .... 787-250-1912 509 D
ehortiz@metro.inter.edu
ORTIZ, Eickel .... 212-616-7245 301 F
eickel.ortiz@helenefuld.edu
ORTIZ, Elizabeth, F .... 312-362-8588 135 I
eortiz4@depaul.edu
ORTIZ, Enrique (Leo) .... 770-689-4870 114 C
eortiz@aii.edu
ORTIZ, Francisco .... 386-822-7300 111 A
fortiz1@stetson.edu
ORTIZ, Francisco .... 260-665-4171 160 H
ortizf@trine.edu
ORTIZ, Francisco .... 787-761-0640 512 F
presidente@utcpr.edu
ORTIZ, Glorimar .... 787-738-2161 513 D
glorimar.ortiz7@upr.edu
ORTIZ, Hilda, L .... 787-863-2390 509 B
hilda.ortiz@fajardo.inter.edu
ORTIZ, Ileana .... 787-264-1912 509 F
ileana_ortiz_rivera@intersg.edu
ORTIZ, Jaime .... 713-743-7310 452 F
jortiz22@uh.edu
ORTIZ, John .... 856-415-2198 281 D
jortiz@rcgc.edu
ORTIZ, Jose .... 509-777-4332 486 I
jortiz@whitworth.edu
ORTIZ, Juanita .... 405-733-7413 369 I
jrortiz@rose.edu
ORTIZ, Judy .... 714-463-7508.. 51 A
jortiz@ketchum.edu
ORTIZ, Kendra, M .... 787-786-3030 512 B
kortiz@ucb.edu.pr
ORTIZ, Kristina .... 212-752-1530 304 D
kgibson@limcollege.edu
ORTIZ, Laura .... 630-466-7900 152 C
lortiz@waubonsee.edu
ORTIZ, Lillian, M .... 508-854-4232 215 D
lmortiz@qcc.mass.edu
ORTIZ, Luis, E .... 787-894-2828 514 C
luis.ortiz52@upr.edu
ORTIZ, Luz .... 787-864-2222 509 C
luz.ortiz@guayama.inter.edu
ORTIZ, Maribel .... 787-758-2525 513 G
maribel.ortiz5@upr.edu
ORTIZ, Mario .... 607-777-2311 316 E
mortiz@binghamton.edu
ORTIZ, Mary Lou, D ..... 814-865-7641 392 B
mzo67@psu.edu
ORTIZ, Maria, C .... 787-766-1717 511 H
um_mortiz@suagm.edu
ORTIZ, Mati .... 716-286-8504 310 D
mortiz@niagara.edu
ORTIZ, Mildred .... 787-264-1940 509 F
milortiz@intersg.edu
ORTIZ, Nancy .... 210-297-9198 431 E
nortiz@baptisthealthsystem.com
ORTIZ, Vanessa .... 787-257-7373 511 G
ortizv2@suagm.edu
ORTIZ, Zoraida .... 787-743-7979 511 I
zortiz@suagm.edu
ORTIZ-GALLEGOS,
Thomasinia .... 505-428-1238 288 B
thomasinia.ortizgall@sfcc.edu
ORTIZ-HARVEY,
Cristina .... 646-313-8000 295 E
financial.aid@guttman.cuny.edu
ORTIZ-MERCADO,
Sonia .... 916-484-8376.. 50 F
ortizms@arc.losrios.edu
ORTIZ-MORALES,
Jonathan .... 787-857-3600 508 M
jonathanortiz@br.inter.edu
ORTIZ-MORETTA, Amy .. 301-891-4525 204 C
aomoretta@wau.edu
ORTIZ-PADILLAT,
Darinel .... 787-993-8861 513 B
darinel.ortiz@upr.edu
ORTIZ PARRA, Lelis ..... 954-322-4460 101 J
artizlelis@jmvu.edu
ORTIZ-VARGAS,
Elizabeth .... 787-993-8922 513 B
elizabeth.ortiz3@upr.edu
ORTIZ-WALTERS,
Rowena .... 518-564-3190 319 C
rorti002@plattsburgh.edu
ORTIZ-ZAYAS, Jose, E .. 787-857-3600 508 M
joseortiz@br.inter.edu
ORTLIEB, Rosemary ...... 516-572-7053 308 A
rosemary.ortlieb@ncc.edu
ORTLOFF, Debora .... 585-785-1778 300 B
debora.ortloff@flcc.edu
ORTLOFF, Debora .... 585-394-1351 300 B
debora.ortloff@flcc.edu
ORTMAN-TOMLIN,
Sandy .... 859-442-4122 181 B
sandra.ortman-tomlin@kctcs.edu
ORTMEIER, Shane .... 605-882-5284 415 F
ortmeiers@lakeareatech.edu
ORTO, Christianne .... 917-493-4401 305 I
corto@msmnyc.edu
ORTON, Piper .... 781-283-2522 219 D
ORTON, Ty .... 701-483-2486 345 D
ty.orton@dickinsonstate.edu
ORTQUIST-AHRENS,
Leslie .... 859-985-3670 179 C
ortquistahrensl@berea.edu
ORTSCHEID, Tory .... 920-465-2598 496 E
ortschet@uwgb.edu
ORUM, Gail .... 909-607-8347.. 37 G
gail_orum@kgi.edu
ORVIS, Arleen .... 563-387-1005 167 E
orvisarl@luther.edu
ORWICK OGDEN, Sheri 419-372-7557 348 H
sorwick@bgsu.edu
ORWIG, Greg .... 509-777-4580 486 I
gorwig@whitworth.edu
ORZECHOWSKI,
Amanda .... 864-646-1401 413 A
aorzech0@tctc.edu
ORZECHOWSKI, Laurie . 567-661-7227 360 B
laurie_orzechowski@owens.edu
ORZECHOWSKI,
Michael .... 212-280-1301 323 H
morzechowski@uts.columbia.edu
ORZEL, Linda .... 314-340-3624 253 I
orzell@hssu.edu
ORZOLEK, Mariah .... 989-463-7367 220 H
orzolekmv@alma.edu
OSAE-KWAPONG,
John, D .... 516-572-7771 308 A
john.osaekwapong@ncc.edu
OSAKI, Glenn .... 213-740-7000.. 72 B
gosaki@usc.edu
OSAKWE, Nneka-Nora .. 229-420-1043 113 H
nora.osakwe@asurams.edu
OSAKWE, Rebecca .... 504-520-7562 193 A
rosakwe@xula.edu
OSBAHR, Diane .... 712-325-3235 167 B
dosbahr@iwcc.edu
OSBORN, Alison .... 334-745-6437.... 3 G
aosborn@suscc.edu
OSBORN, Edward, H ..... 860-465-5043.. 84 J
osborne@easternct.edu
OSBORN, Fred .... 541-684-4644 375 H
fosborn@pioneerpacific.edu
OSBORN, Jeffrey .... 609-771-2724 276 I
josborn@tcnj.edu
OSBORN, Jill .... 952-446-4342 235 G
osbornj@crown.edu
OSBORN, Laura .... 605-256-5023 416 J
laura.osborn@dsu.edu
OSBORN, Peter .... 616-949-5300 222 I
peter.osborn@cornerstone.edu
OSBORN, Richard, E ..... 423-439-8300 419 J
osbornr@etsu.edu
OSBORNE, JR.,
Alfred, E .... 310-206-3011.. 69 A
al.osborne@anderson.ucla.edu
OSBORNE, Bryan, L ...... 719-333-4322 504 C
bryan.osborne.1@us.af.mil
OSBORNE, C. Damon ... 419-434-5978 363 A
dosborne@findlay.edu
OSBORNE, Curtis .... 510-649-2477.. 44 F
cosborne@gtu.edu
OSBORNE, Daniel .... 919-365-7711 340 H
OSBORNE, Dawn .... 918-781-7281 365 F
osborned@bacone.edu
OSBORNE, John .... 405-425-5463 367 G
john.osborne@oc.edu
OSBORNE, John .... 305-428-5700 103 E
josborne@aii.edu
OSBORNE, Katie .... 205-348-9527.... 7 F
kosborne@uasystem.edu
OSBORNE, Kevin .... 336-734-7369 334 E
kosborne@forsythtech.edu
OSBORNE, Maurice .... 903-927-3214 458 G
mdosborne@wileyc.edu
OSBORNE, Michele .... 518-454-5133 296 H
osbornem@strose.edu
OSBORNE, Natalie .... 912-538-3157 124 F
nosborne@southeasterntech.edu
OSBORNE, Shelley .... 704-991-0203 338 C
sosborne7501@stanly.edu
OSBORNE, Zach .... 650-543-4097.. 51 F
zach.osborne@menlo.edu
OSBURN, Darren .... 636-922-8533 258 I
dosburn@stchas.edu
OSBURN, Monica .... 919-515-2423 342 B
monica_osburn@ncsu.edu
OSBURN, Toby .... 337-562-4249 192 A
tosburn@mcneese.edu
OSBURN, Wade .... 731-989-6067 420 C
wosburn@fhu.edu
OSEGUEDA, Roberto ..... 915-747-5680 455 C
osegueda@utep.edu
OSEGUERA, Tonantzin .. 657-278-4688.. 31 E
toseguera@fullerton.edu
OSGOOD, Jeanne .... 651-638-6035 234 C
j-osgood@bethel.edu
OSGOOD, Jeffery .... 610-738-0492 396 A
josgood@wcupa.edu
OSGOOD, Patricia .... 617-989-4025 219 E
teresiak@wit.edu
OSGUTHORPE, Richard . 208-426-1611 129 I
richardosguthorpe@boisestate.edu
OSHIRO, Cathie .... 620-792-9234 171 C
oshiroc@bartonccc.edu
OSHIRO, Robyn .... 808-689-2900 128 G
robyno@hawaii.edu
OSHIRO, Wayde .... 808-455-0378 129 D
waydeo@hawaii.edu
OSHMAN, Melissa .... 909-389-3309.. 59 H
moshman@craftonhills.edu
OSHRY, Yehuda .... 845-426-3110 325 O
OSIKA, Elizabeth .... 317-955-6015 158 U
eosika@marian.edu
OSIRIM, Mary, J .... 610-526-5167 379 E
mosirim@brynmawr.edu
OSIRIS, Charles, E .... 805-437-3218.. 30 F
charles.osiris@csuci.edu
OSLER, Cheri .... 509-533-7311 480 A
cheri.osler@scc.spokane.edu
OSMOND, Tatiana .... 207-454-1040 195 B
tosmond@wccc.me.edu
OSNESS, Bonnie .... 715-675-3331 500 E
osnessb@ntc.edu
OSOFSKY, Hari, M .... 814-863-1521 392 B
hmo8@psu.edu
OSORIO, Jonhathan ...... 808-956-0980 128 F
osorio@hawaii.edu
OSORIO, Michael .... 408-274-7900.. 61 L
michael.osorio@evc.edu
OSORTO, Hierald .... 607-274-3103 303 B
hosorto@ithaca.edu
OSOWICZ, Lauren .... 270-686-6415 179 D
lauren.osowicz@brescia.edu
OSSEIRAN-HANNA,
Khatmeh .... 724-357-5661 394 G
osseiran@iup.edu
OSSOWSKI, John .... 315-792-3216 324 B
jdossows@utica.edu
OSTASH, Heather .... 760-384-6249.. 46 M
hostash@cerrocoso.edu
OSTENDORF, Trevor ...... 530-541-4660.. 47 E
sm420@bncollege.com
OSTENDORFF, Stephen . 212-875-4402 290 F
sostendorff@bankstreet.edu
OSTER, Ben Zion .... 323-937-3763.. 75 F
boster@yoec.edu
OSTER, JoAnna .... 607-729-1581 298 C
joster@davisny.edu
OSTER-AALAND, Laura . 701-231-7052 345 G
laura.oster-aaland@ndsu.edu
OSTERBERG, Rick .... 781-292-2431 209 E
rick.osterberg@olin.edu
OSTERBIND, Kelly .... 251-460-6251.... 8 F
osterbind@southalabama.edu
OSTERHOUT, Colin .... 907-796-6576.. 10 B
ctosterhout@alaska.edu
OSTERLUND, John .... 309-457-2317 144 A
josterlund@monmouthcollege.edu
OSTERLUND, Linda .... 303-458-4100.. 82 E
losterla@regis.edu
OSTERMAN, Michael ..... 509-527-4975 486 H
ostermmq@whitman.edu
OSTERTHUN, Stu .... 402-323-3401 269 C
sosterthun@southeast.edu
OSTGAARD, Kolleen ...... 916-484-8569.. 50 F
ostgaak@arc.losrios.edu
OSTLER, Jon .... 435-283-7361 461 C
jon.ostler@snow.edu
OSTLING, Suzanne .... 540-863-2826 474 D
sostling@dslcc.edu
OSTOLAZA, Magda, E ... 787-257-7373 511 G
ue_mostolaza@suagm.edu
OSTRANDER, Gary, K ... 850-644-3347 109 C
gary@fsu.edu
OSTRO, Ginger .... 773-995-2042 133 K
gostro@csu.edu
OSTROM, Lee .... 208-282-7903 131 G
ostrom@uidaho.edu
OSTROSKY, Jay .... 617-850-1261 210 D
jostrosky@hchc.edu
OSTROVSKY, Peter .... 541-383-7733 372 B
postrovsky@cocc.edu
OSTROW, James .... 617-243-2111 210 G
jostrow@lasell.edu
OSTROWICKI,
Jacqueline, M .... 402-472-7130 269 H
jostrowicki@nebraska.edu
OSTROWSKI, Jason ...... 208-732-6225 130 E
jostrowski@csi.edu
OSTROWSKI, Michael ... 931-598-1661 423 M
mtostrow@sewanee.edu
OSTWINKLE, Chris .... 815-280-6635 140 B
costwink@jjc.edu
OSUNDE, Samuel .... 662-254-9041 248 B
sosunde@mvsu.edu
OSVOLD, Jesse .... 712-325-3487 167 B
josvold@iwcc.edu
OSWALD, Cecelia .... 484-323-3183 386 C
coswald@immaculata.edu
OSWALD, Clark .... 316-284-5233 171 F
coswald@bethelks.edu
OSWALD, Mike, R .... 208-356-1320 130 A
oswaldrm@byui.edu
OSWALD, Scott .... 251-981-3771.... 5 B
scott.oswald@columbiasouthern.edu
OSWALD, Sharon .... 662-325-2580 247 F
soswald@cobilan.msstate.edu
OSWALD, Vicki .... 605-367-8355 417 D
vicki.oswald@southeasttech.edu
OSWALT, Natalie .... 903-693-2095 441 F
noswalt@panola.edu
OSWELL, Michelle .... 215-893-5265 382 B
michelle.oswell@curtis.edu
OSZUST, Renee .... 248-341-2153 229 A
raoszust@oaklandcc.edu
OTÓN-OLIVIERI,
Patricia .... 787-751-1912 510 A
poton@juris.inter.edu
OTERO, George .... 787-257-0000 513 C
george.otero@upr.edu
OTERO, Juan .... 787-766-1717 511 H
juotero@suagm.edu
OTHMAN, Saib .... 317-955-6049 158 U
sothman@marian.edu
OTIENO, Tom .... 859-622-1393 180 B
tom.otieno@eku.edu

OTIS, Brian 860-486-5960 88 E botis@foundation.uconn.edu
OTIS CATANZARO, Carolyn 925-631-4914 59 B cao7@stmarys-ca.edu
OTIV, Urmi 848-932-7015 282 A uso@global.rutgers.edu
OTMISHI, Sean 713-718-7857 437 I sean.otmishi@hccs.edu
OTO, Rod, M 507-222-4190 234 F roto@carleton.edu
OTT, Alexander 718-289-5939 293 B alexander.ott@bcc.cuny.edu
OTT, Amy 803-535-1222 411 G otta@octech.edu
OTT, Kim, A 928-523-1894 14 H kimberly.ott@nau.edu
OTT, Luisa 520-494-5283 11 K luisa.ott@centralaz.edu
OTT, Randall 202-319-5188 91 B ott@cua.edu
OTT, Steven, H 704-687-7630 342 E shott@uncc.edu
OTT ROWLANDS, Sue 859-572-5788 184 A sottrowlands@nku.edu
OTTE, Bobbi 406-657-1086 265 E otteb@rocky.edu
OTTEMAN, Marcie, M 989-774-3312 222 C ottem1mm@cmich.edu
OTTEN, Daren 760-366-5289 40 K dotten@cmccd.edu
OTTEN, Laura 215-951-1118 387 C otten@lasalle.edu
OTTEN, Valerie, A 626-395-6832 29 C votten@caltech.edu
OTTENGA, Marc 941-405-1500 388 A mottenga@lecom.edu
OTTER, Kelly 202-687-7169 92 A otter@georgetown.edu
OTTERNESS, Denis 406-657-2147 264 E denis.otterness@msubillings.edu
OTTESON, Julie Ann 213-624-1200 42 I jotteson@fidm.edu
OTTEY, Jacqueline 201-447-7204 275 H jottey@bergen.edu
OTTINGER, Marie 334-386-7512 5 D mottinger@faulkner.edu
OTTINGER, Michael 505-566-3081 288 A ottingerm@sanjuancollege.edu
OTTINO, Julio, M 847-491-3195 145 F jm-ottino@northwestern.edu
OTTMAN, Ray 479-788-7110 21 H ray.ottman@uafs.edu
OTTO, Andy 785-242-2500 176 D andy.otto@ottawa.edu
OTTO, Ilsa 641-422-4001 168 D ilsa.otto@niacc.edu
OTTO, Justin 706-771-4037 114 J jotto@augustatech.edu
OTTO, Justin 509-359-7048 480 E jotto@ewu.edu
OTTO, Mary 910-893-1310 327 E ottom@campbell.edu
OTTO, Richard, H 312-461-0600 132 A ifitzgerald@aaart.edu
OTTO, Sheryl 874-925-6342 137 H sotto@harpercollege.edu
OTTO, Tyson 660-359-3948 257 D totto@mail.ncmissouri.edu
OTTOBONI, John 408-554-5355 62 D jottoboni@scu.edu
OTTOSSON, John 641-673-1076 170 F ottossonj@wmpenn.edu
OTTS, Cynthia 816-584-6273 258 A cynthia.otts@park.edu
OTU, Emmanual 262-598-2973 497 C otu@uwp.edu
OTUAFI, Quincey 801-832-2222 461 G qotuafi@westminstercollege.edu
OTUONYE, Francis 931-372-3374 426 E fotuonye@tntech.edu
OTUONYE, Francis, O 931-372-3374 426 E fotuonye@tntech.edu
OTWELL, Michelle 386-386-7380 5 D motwell@faulkner.edu
OTWORTH, Pamela 740-351-3208 360 K potworth@shawnee.edu
OTY, Karla 580-581-7962 365 G koty@cameron.edu
OTYENOH, Kimberly 540-665-5436 471 E kotyenoh@su.edu
OUBRÉ, Linda 562-907-4201 75 A president@whittier.edu
OUDENHOVEN, Arnie 303-914-6298 82 C arnie.oudenhoven@rrcc.edu
OUDENHOVEN, Elizabeth 303-360-4775 79 D betsy.oudenhoven@ccaurora.edu
OUDSHOORN, Michael 336-841-9000 329 G moudshoo@highpoint.edu
OUELLETTE, Alicia 518-445-3305 289 E aouel@albanylaw.edu
OUELLETTE, Bernie 207-859-1111 195 G ouelletteb@thomas.edu
OUELLETTE, Dallas 301-387-3097 198 F dallas.ouellette@garrettcollege.edu
OUELLETTE, Helen 617-349-8685 210 H helen.ouellette@lesley.edu
OUELLETTE, Mark 203-462-2916 274 D mark.ouellette@pb.com
OUILLET, Pierre-Yves 858-534-3390 69 D pouillet@ucsd.edu
OUIMET, Maurice 802-468-1352 464 A maurice.ouimet@castleton.edu
OUKAYAN, Tzoler 818-240-1000 44 B toukayan@glendale.edu
OULAMINE, Saadia 267-256-0200 92 G
OULD, Jennifer 773-947-6307 142 J jould@mccormick.edu
OURS, Alan 912-279-5762 116 G aours@ccga.edu
OURSO, Mark 225-214-1955 186 F mark.ourso@franu.edu
OUSLEY, Allisha 678-422-4100 92 G
OUTAR, Neil 573-341-6038 261 E naoutar@mst.edu
OUTAR, O'Neil 401-454-6532 405 D ooutar@risd.edu
OUTEIRO, Rachel 801-689-2160 459 J routeiro@nighitngale.edu
OUTEN, Jason 828-835-4229 338 E jouten@tricountycc.edu
OUTING, Donald, A 610-758-2128 388 J dao417@lehigh.edu
OUTLAW, Jeanese, M 919-516-4197 340 C jmoutlaw@st-aug.edu
OUTLEY, Patrice 318-274-2288 191 E outleyp@gram.edu
OUTON, Peggy, M 412-397-6000 397 G outon@rmu.edu
OUTTEN, Donavan 314-246-6907 262 C doutten@webster.edu
OVEDIA, Nicole, R 561-237-7237 102 V novedia@lynn.edu
OVERBY, David, B 605-256-5675 416 J david.overby@dsu.edu
OVERBY, Kiana 605-274-5521 415 B kiana.overby@augie.edu
OVERBY, Sherry 601-968-8778 245 C soverby@belhaven.edu
OVERBYE, David 855-786-6546 146 I
OVERCASH, Shannon 508-541-1841 208 F sovercash@dean.edu
OVERDORF, Daniel 865-573-4517 420 G doverdorf@johnsonu.edu
OVEREND, Gregory 203-932-7430 89 A goverend@newhaven.edu
OVERFIELD, Denise 678-839-4759 126 E doverfie@westga.edu
OVERHOLSER, Toni 937-328-8070 350 L overholsert@clarkstate.edu
OVERHOLTZER, Michael, H 646-888-6639 305 E overhom1@mskcc.org
OVERLAND, Wanda 320-308-3111 240 H wioverland@stcloudstate.edu
OVERMYER-VELAZQUEZ, Mark 959-200-3766 88 E mark.velazquez@uconn.edu
OVEROCKER, Quintin, M 815-224-0437 139 F quintin_overocker@ivcc.edu
OVERPECK, Jonathan, T 734-764-2550 231 E overpeck@umich.edu
OVERSOLE, Lance 303-963-3447 77 G loversole@ccu.edu
OVERSTREET, Darryl 580-559-5582 366 C doverstt@ecok.edu
OVERSTREET, Mana 615-732-7893 422 G m.overstreet@mtsa.edu
OVERSTREET, Tammie 423-236-2759 424 B toverstreet@southern.edu
OVERSTREET, Valerie, R 410-293-1568 504 I overstre@usna.edu
OVERTON, Chrystal 580-477-7702 371 F chrystal.overton@wosc.edu
OVERTON, Melanie, B 785-833-4306 175 B melanie.overton@kwu.edu
OVERTON, Milton 470-578-6033 120 L
OVERTON, Robert, A 864-488-4543 410 E roverton@limestone.edu
OVERTON, Travis, E 843-349-2168 408 C toverton@coastal.edu
OVERTON-HEALY, Julia 585-385-8143 314 A joverton-healy@sjfc.edu
OVERTURF, Kathy 318-487-7301 186 I kathy.overturf@lacollege.edu
OVERTURF, Kellie 970-542-3132 81 A kellie.overturf@morgancc.edu
OVERTURF, Mitzi 501-337-5000 18 J moverturf@coto.edu
OVESON, Kip, R 320-222-6930 240 E kip.oveson@ridgewater.edu
OVEZOV, Dovran 832-230-5548 440 H dovran@na.edu
OVITT, Kimberly 503-494-0992 375 B ovitt@ohsu.edu
OWAN, Robert 808-675-3916 127 E robert.owan@byuh.edu
OWASOYO, Philomena 870-575-8732 22 E owasoyop@uapb.edu
OWCZARCZAK, Kathleen 716-884-9120 291 L kowczarczak@bryantstratton.edu
OWCZAREK, Scott 608-262-3964 496 C owczarek@em.wisc.edu
OWEN, Barbara 207-755-5233 194 G bowen@cmcc.edu
OWEN, Daniel, C 512-245-4225 450 E do13@txstate.edu
OWEN, Eric 936-294-1612 450 C ericowen@shsu.edu
OWEN, Jackie 701-845-7302 346 A jackie.owen@vcsu.edu
OWEN, James (Chris) 863-667-5188 107 K jcowen@seu.edu
OWEN, Jane 618-262-8641 139 A owenj@iecc.edu
OWEN, Jane, S 724-852-3225 402 F jowen@waynesburg.edu
OWEN, Kelli, D 606-783-2700 183 F k.owen@moreheadstate.edu
OWEN, Kyle 940-397-4648 440 F kyle.owen@msutexas.edu
OWEN, Laurinda, A 574-372-5100 155 B owenla@grace.edu
OWEN, Pamela 501-450-1358 19 F owen@hendrix.edu
OWEN, Robert 408-554-4581 62 D rowen@scu.edu
OWEN, Rose Marie 804-819-4902 474 A rmowen@vccs.edu
OWEN, Sarah 620-331-4100 174 C sowen@indycc.edu
OWEN, Sherry, L 816-995-2815 258 F sherry.owen@researchcollege.edu
OWEN, Thomas 956-665-3036 455 D thomas.owen@utrgv.edu
OWEN, Vince 605-698-3966 416 F vowen@swc.tc
OWEN, William 531-622-2715 267 H bowen@mccneb.edu
OWENBY, Judy 828-835-4212 338 E jowenby@tricountycc.edu
OWENBY, Stephanee 512-492-3021 430 G sowenby@aoma.edu
OWENS, April 989-837-4396 228 H
OWENS, Bertha 501-370-5215 20 G bowens@philander.edu
OWENS, Colleen 207-941-7184 194 A owensc@husson.edu
OWENS, Deborah, D 607-735-1819 299 D dowens@elmira.edu
OWENS, Deborah, E 716-829-8198 298 F owensde@dyc.edu
OWENS, Diane 912-260-4242 124 C diane.owens@sgsc.edu
OWENS, Don 254-295-4691 453 E dowens@umhb.edu
OWENS, Drake 318-357-4250 192 C owensd@nsula.edu
OWENS, Ellen 315-470-7380 291 H ellenowens@crouse.org
OWENS, Elona 916-649-9600 26 F eowens@asher.edu
OWENS, Glenna 276-244-1282 464 L gowens@asl.edu
OWENS, Ilona 336-506-4146 332 A ilona.owens@alamancecc.edu
OWENS, J, F 540-365-4255 467 I jfowens@ferrum.edu
OWENS, James 609-633-9658 284 B jowens@tesu.edu
OWENS, James, R 859-858-3511 178 I jim.owens@asbury.edu
OWENS, Janice, B 803-536-7173 412 C jbowens@scsu.edu
OWENS, Jeffrey 706-821-8592 122 K jowens@paine.edu
OWENS, Josh 615-675-5320 428 G jowens@welch.edu
OWENS, Judy 937-769-1324 347 H jowens1@antioch.edu
OWENS, Justin 606-218-5224 185 D justinowens@upike.edu
OWENS, Kara, M 410-543-6023 203 F kmowens@salisbury.edu
OWENS, Kate 570-945-8222 386 I kate.owens@keystone.edu
OWENS, Kelly 501-450-5161 23 H kowens9@uca.edu
OWENS, LaShanda 501-207-6201 17 F
OWENS, Lillian 205-853-1200 2 G lowens@jeffersonstate.edu
OWENS, Linda 630-620-2130 145 D lowens@seminary.edu
OWENS, Linda 630-620-2130 145 D registrar@seminary.edu
OWENS, Linda 310-900-1600 40 A lowens@elcamino.edu
OWENS, Mark 618-664-6735 137 G mark.owens@greenville.edu
OWENS, Milton 312-553-3213 134 B mowens63@ccc.edu
OWENS, Neal 912-817-1690 122 I nowens@ogeecheetech.edu
OWENS, Pamela 414-930-3380 495 A owensp@mtmary.edu
OWENS, R. Scott 859-238-5457 179 F scott.owens@centre.edu
OWENS, Ralph 870-575-8000 22 E owensr@uapb.edu
OWENS, Ray 252-246-1239 339 C rowens@wilsoncc.edu
OWENS, Rick 252-493-7442 336 H rowens@email.pittcc.edu
OWENS, Robert 931-372-3392 426 E rowens@tntech.edu
OWENS, Sami 318-342-1885 192 F saowens@ulm.edu
OWENS, Scott, D 856-225-6028 281 G scott.owens@rutgers.edu
OWENS, Serenna 217-234-5253 141 D sdeeke@lakelandcollege.edu
OWENS, Sharon 404-270-5082 125 B sharon.owens@spelman.edu
OWENS, Stephanie 513-721-7944 353 F sowens@gbs.edu
OWENS, Stephanie, R 770-720-5895 123 E sro@reinhardt.edu
OWENS, Stephen, J 573-882-3211 261 A owenssj@umsystem.edu
OWENS, Susan 254-295-8686 453 E sowens@umhb.edu
OWENS, Tara 937-376-6288 350 D towens@centralstate.edu
OWENS, Tracy, D 816-501-3750 250 F tracy.owens@avila.edu
OWENS, Trina 314-252-3180 253 A towens@eden.edu
OWENS, Valerie 304-876-5465 490 E vowens@shepherd.edu
OWENS-HILL, David 212-472-1500 309 I dowenshill@nysid.edu
OWENS-SOUTHHALL, Mary, E 410-951-3090 203 D mowens@coppin.edu
OWENSBY, Fred 575-527-7543 287 E fowensby@nmsu.edu
OWENSON, Jenifer 515-964-6408 164 C jsowenson1@dmacc.edu
OWL, Diane 828-835-4220 338 E dowl@tricountycc.edu
OWNBEY, Christy 812-866-6101 155 C ownbey@hanover.edu
OWOLABI, Elizabeth 708-209-3020 135 F elizabeth.owolabi@cuchicago.edu
OWSLEY, Kristen 913-758-6303 177 F kristen.owsley@stmary.edu
OWSLEY, Laura 502-863-8007 180 E laura_owsley@georgetowncollege.edu

OWSLEY, Stacy 520-383-8401 16 D sowsley@tocc.edu
OWSTON, James, M 304-457-6222 487 B owstonjm@ab.edu
OWUSU-ANSAH, Edward 973-720-3179 284 I owusuansahe@wpunj.edu
OWUSU-SEKYERE, Emmanuel 410-951-3862 203 D manny@coppin.edu
OXENDINE, Cynthia 910-521-6175 343 B cynthia.oxendine@uncp.edu
OXENDINE, Derek 910-521-6401 343 B derek.oxendine@uncp.edu
OXENDINE, Joanna 909-387-1648 59 I joxendine@sbccd.cc.ca.us
OXENHANDLER, David 505-922-2889 286 B david.oxenhandler@eccu.edu
OXENREIDER, Anne, L 828-395-4194 335 D aoxenreider@isothermal.edu
OXFORD, Mary-Catherine 559-730-3826 39 E marycat@cos.edu
OXFORD, Ron 559-925-3403 74 B ronoxford@whccd.edu
OXFORD-PICKERAL, Misti 352-335-2332 93 F info@acupuncturist.edu
OXLEY, Timothy, R 304-367-4239 490 B timothy.oxley@fairmontstate.edu
OYADOMARI, Jason 906-487-7381 223 K jason.oyadomari@finlandia.edu
OYEKAN, Adebayo, O 713-313-4341 449 C oyekan_ao@tsu.edu
OYEWOLE, Ibukun 312-567-5809 139 B oyewole@iit.edu
OYINBO, Victor 803-705-4553 407 A victor.oyinbo@benedict.edu
OYLER, Jessica 801-626-7496 461 B joyler@weber.edu
OYMAN, Korhan 321-674-8971 99 B koyman@fit.edu
OYOLA, Elias 212-694-1000 291 I eoyola@boricuacollege.edu
OYOLA, Luaida 787-725-6500 506 G
OZAN, Randy 859-858-2210 178 H
OZAYSIN, Gokhan 912-525-5000 123 G gozaysin@scad.edu
OZBUDAK, Selin 641-472-7000 167 F asozbudak@mum.edu
OZECHOSKI, Mary-Alice 610-606-4666 381 A mozechos@cedarcrest.edu
OZERDEM, Alpaslan 703-993-1300 467 L aozerdem@gmu.edu
OZGU, Pinar 212-817-7101 293 F pozgu@gc.cuny.edu
OZMENT, Tim 252-985-5107 339 D tozment@ncwc.edu
OZTURGUT, Osman 805-437-8400 30 F osman.ozturgut@csuci.edu
OZTURK, Dali 559-730-3790 39 E mehmeto@cos.edu
OZUNA, Elias 956-665-2508 455 D elias.ozuna@utrgv.edu
OZUZU, Onye 352-392-0207 109 F oozuzu@ufl.edu
O'BANION, Rebecca 254-295-4603 453 E robanion@umhb.edu
O'BANNER-JACKSON, Marie 601-979-7092 246 E marie.obanner-jackson@jsums.edu
O'BAR, Gary 210-485-0102 429 C gobar@alamo.edu
O'BARR, Allen, H 919-966-3658 342 D allen_obarr@unc.edu
O'BEIRNE, Kirsten 610-526-5041 379 E kobeirne@brynmawr.edu
O'BEIRNE, OSF, Marguerite 610-558-5511 391 D mobeirne@neumann.edu
O'BEIRNE, Rosie 205-975-7805 8 A robeirne@uab.edu
O'BERRY, V. Diane 803-780-1142 414 E doberry@voorhees.edu
O'BOYLE, Andrew 206-296-6149 484 F oboylea@seattleu.edu
O'BOYLE, Thomas 631-656-2126 300 D thomas.oboyle@ftc.edu
O'BRIAN, Jenni 406-546-3585 263 J jenni.obrian@montanabiblecollege.edu
O'BRIEN, Ann 310-660-3406 41 L aobrien@elcamino.edu
O'BRIEN, Barry 910-521-6214 343 B michael.o'brien@uncp.edu
O'BRIEN, Brad 309-649-6294 150 A brad.obrien@src.edu
O'BRIEN, Casey 518-828-4181 297 B casey.obrien@sunycgcc.edu
O'BRIEN, Catherine 713-718-2383 437 I catherine.obrien2@hccs.edu
O'BRIEN, Colleen 973-618-3660 276 D cobrien@caldwell.edu
O'BRIEN, Corey 303-410-2418 82 J corey.obrien@spartan.edu
O'BRIEN, Courtney 312-553-6063 134 B cobrien4@ccc.edu
O'BRIEN, Diane 805-893-8182 70 A diane.obrien@ucsb.edu
O'BRIEN, Diane, E 570-408-4734 403 D diane.obrien@wilkes.edu
O'BRIEN, Eddie 706-865-2134 125 E eobrien@truett.edu
O'BRIEN, Elizabeth 707-664-4023 34 C elizabeth.obrien@sonoma.edu
O'BRIEN, Elizabeth 415-749-4581 60 G eobrien@sfai.edu
O'BRIEN, Elizabeth 423-425-4438 428 A elizabeth-o'brien@utc.edu
O'BRIEN, Gregory 888-488-4968 46 F gobrien@itu.edu
O'BRIEN, Ian 701-349-5794 346 J ianobrien@trinitybiblecollege.edu
O'BRIEN, Irene 973-353-5541 282 B iobrien@rutgers.edu
O'BRIEN, Janet 617-353-3457 207 D janetob@bu.edu
O'BRIEN, Jason 617-585-0200 206 F jason.obrien@the-bac.edu
O'BRIEN, Jim 480-965-9118 10 I james.obrien@asu.edu
O'BRIEN, John 805-482-2755 58 L frjobrien@stjohnsem.edu
O'BRIEN, John, F 617-422-7221 217 C jobrien@nesl.edu
O'BRIEN, Kathryn 716-375-2011 313 F kobrien@sbu.edu
O'BRIEN, SJ, Kevin, F 408-554-4100 62 D president@scu.edu
O'BRIEN, Kevin, J 253-535-7698 482 H obrien@plu.edu
O'BRIEN, Mary Alice 518-276-6106 312 I obriem4@rpi.edu
O'BRIEN, Mary Eileen 845-848-7801 298 D mary.eileen.obrien@dc.edu
O'BRIEN, Maryellen 910-272-3324 337 D mo'brien@robeson.edu
O'BRIEN, Matt 309-677-2255 133 B mobrien@bradley.edu
O'BRIEN, Matt, F 412-397-5913 397 G obrienma@rmu.edu
O'BRIEN, Maureen 724-830-1075 398 H obrien@setonhill.edu
O'BRIEN, Meg 215-248-7158 381 D obrienm@chc.edu
O'BRIEN, Michael 269-782-1401 230 F mobrien02@swmich.edu
O'BRIEN, Michael 210-784-1200 448 A michael.obrien@tamusa.edu
O'BRIEN, Michael, E 419-530-4987 363 E michael.obrien6@utoledo.edu
O'BRIEN, Patricia 480-377-2704 13 G patricia.obrien@maricopacorporate.com
O'BRIEN, Patricia 617-358-4944 207 D pobrien@bu.edu
O'BRIEN, Paul 772-462-7376 101 E pobrien@irsc.edu
O'BRIEN, Tammy 706-771-5700 114 J tobrien@augustatech.edu
O'BRIEN, Terry 860-465-5395 84 J obrienth@easternct.edu
O'BRIEN, Theresa 415-514-1455 69 E theresa.obrien@ucsf.edu
O'BRIEN, Thomas 610-647-4400 386 C tobrien@immaculata.edu
O'BRIEN ENGER, Lisa 636-949-4939 254 F lenger@lindenwood.edu
O'BRIEN-FOELSCH, Molly 717-867-6038 388 H mobrien@lvc.edu
O'BRIEN-KNOTTS, Jennifer, E 610-758-4679 388 J jeo211@lehigh.edu
O'BRIEN-MCMASTERS, Vanessa 609-343-5670 275 D vobmcm@atlantic.edu
O'BRUBA, Brian 209-228-2958 69 B bobruba@ucmerced.edu
O'BRYAN, Dan 775-831-1314 272 D dobryan@sierranevada.edu
O'BRYAN, Megan 216-987-4737 351 G megan.obryan@tri-c.edu
O'BRYAN, Trevor 417-865-2815 250 E obryant@evangel.edu
O'BRYANT, Theresa 413-662-5400 213 A theresa.obryant@mcla.edu
O'CAIN, Woody 386-822-7481 111 A wocain@stetson.edu
O'CALLAGHAN, Ceceilia 732-987-2415 278 B cocallaghan@georgian.edu
O'CALLAGHAN, Cindy 617-735-9779 209 A ocallac@emmanuel.edu
O'CALLAGHAN, Karen 516-463-6605 302 B karen.ocallaghan@hofstra.edu
O'CARROLL, Theresa 708-974-5250 144 C ocarroll@morainevalley.edu
O'CONNELL, Anne 847-543-2622 135 B aoconnell@clcillinois.edu
O'CONNELL, Catharine, E 217-245-3010 138 D catharine.oconnell@ic.edu
O'CONNELL, Colleen 215-884-8942 403 G planning@woninstitute.edu
O'CONNELL, Daniel 978-867-4246 209 F daniel.oconnell@gordon.edu
O'CONNELL, Danielle 508-791-9241 206 B danielle.oconnell@becker.edu
O'CONNELL, Danny, J 330-941-3549 365 C djoconnell@ysu.edu
O'CONNELL, Heather, A 302-356-6814 90 I heather.a.oconnell@wilmu.edu
O'CONNELL, John 260-481-6977 159 F oconnelj@pfw.edu
O'CONNELL, Lili 815-455-8676 143 A loconnell@mchenry.edu
O'CONNELL, Mark, P 269-965-3931 225 F oconnellm@kellogg.edu
O'CONNELL, Molly 920-693-1752 499 G molly.oconnell@gotoltc.edu
O'CONNELL, Patrick 239-280-2461 94 O patrick.oconnell@avemaria.edu
O'CONNELL, Paul 269-488-4722 225 E poconnell@kvcc.edu
O'CONNELL, Robert, G 617-333-2050 208 E boconnel@curry.edu
O'CONNELL, Robin 816-523-9140 262 D robin.o@wellspring.edu
O'CONNELL, Ryan 310-377-5501 51 B roconnell@marymountcalifornia.edu
O'CONNELL, Ryan 310-303-7382 51 B roconnell@marymountcalifornia.edu
O'CONNELL, Sean 203-773-8068 84 F soconnell@albertus.edu
O'CONNELL, Shelley, M 319-273-7224 163 B shelley.oconnell@uni.edu
O'CONNELL, Vincent 781-239-2699 214 E voconnell@massbay.edu
O'CONNOR, Brian 406-994-5016 264 D boconnor@montana.edu
O'CONNOR, Charles, D 402-472-9339 269 J charles.oconnor@unl.edu
O'CONNOR, Christi 323-953-4000 48 I oconnoca@lacitycollege.edu
O'CONNOR, Christopher, K 617-254-2610 218 D rev.christopher.o'connor@sjs.edu
O'CONNOR, Deirdre, M 570-577-3141 379 F deirdre.oconnor@bucknell.edu
O'CONNOR, Diane 215-641-6416 390 H doconnor@mc3.edu
O'CONNOR, Edward, R 816-654-7000 254 C eoconnor@kcumb.edu
O'CONNOR, Ellen, M 215-955-6835 400 A ellen.oconnor@jefferson.edu
O'CONNOR, Gregory 631-420-2170 321 B oconnor@farmingdale.edu
O'CONNOR, Isabel 619-388-2755 60 D ioconnor@sdccd.edu
O'CONNOR, James 563-884-5294 168 I james.oconnor@palmer.edu
O'CONNOR, James 334-844-3500 4 E jmo0024@auburn.edu
O'CONNOR, Jasi 218-299-3549 235 E oconnor@cord.edu
O'CONNOR, Jen 785-864-2640 177 D jen.occonor@ku.edu
O'CONNOR, Jeremiah 508-793-2564 208 B joconnor@holycross.edu
O'CONNOR, Jody 415-575-6153 29 B joconnor@ciis.edu
O'CONNOR, Joseph 607-778-5379 318 A oconnorjt@sunybroome.edu
O'CONNOR, Julie 414-425-8300 495 H joconnor@shsst.edu
O'CONNOR, Kathleen 617-243-2199 210 G koconnor@lasell.edu
O'CONNOR, Kevin 949-582-4788 64 G koconnor@saddleback.edu
O'CONNOR, Kyla 951-222-8649 58 I kyla.oconnor@rcc.edu
O'CONNOR, Lisa, G 203-582-8549 87 G lisa.o'connor@quinnipiac.edu
O'CONNOR, Maria 216-397-4268 354 I moconnor@jcu.edu
O'CONNOR, Mary 480-731-8403 12 O mary.oconnor@domail.maricopa.edu
O'CONNOR, Matthew, L 203-582-8297 87 G matthew.oconnor@quinnipiac.edu
O'CONNOR, Maura 206-296-6300 484 F oconnorm@seattleu.edu
O'CONNOR, Maureen 650-433-3895 55 G moconnor@paloaltou.edu
O'CONNOR, Michael 815-802-8908 140 D moconnor@kcc.edu
O'CONNOR, Michael 336-770-3322 343 D oconnorm@uncsa.edu
O'CONNOR, Michael 918-836-6886 370 D michael.oconnor@spartan.edu
O'CONNOR, Michele 215-204-8276 399 F michele.o'connor@temple.edu
O'CONNOR, Mike, K 920-832-6561 493 K mike.k.oconnor@lawrence.edu
O'CONNOR, Nancy, M 202-319-5142 91 B oconnorn@cua.edu
O'CONNOR, Patricia 559-278-7392 31 D poconnor@csufresno.edu
O'CONNOR, Patrick 708-974-5555 144 C oconnorp@morainevalley.edu
O'CONNOR, Patrick 617-879-7878 212 E poconnor@massart.edu
O'CONNOR, Patrick, W 201-684-7500 280 H poconnor@ramapo.edu
O'CONNOR, Richard 413-265-2340 208 C oconnorri@elms.edu
O'CONNOR, Rob 501-450-1225 19 F o'connor@hendrix.edu
O'CONNOR, Robert 315-781-3535 302 A oconnor@hws.edu
O'CONNOR, Shawn 507-433-0564 240 F shawn.o'connor@riverland.edu
O'CONNOR, Timothy 212-327-8080 313 B toconnor@rockefeller.edu
O'CONNOR-BENSON, Pat 239-597-7101 108 K poconnor@fgcu.edu
O'COYNE, Gregory 630-515-6044 143 G gocoyn@midwestern.edu
O'DANIEL, Jennifer 512-863-1691 445 D odanielj@southwestern.edu
O'DAY, Steven, P 903-813-3001 430 N soday@austincollege.edu
O'DELL, April 802-865-5734 462 B o'dell@champlain.edu
O'DELL, Cynthia 219-980-6509 156 E codell@iun.edu
O'DELL, Tammy 931-393-1745 425 C todell@mscc.edu
O'DONNELL, Alicia 402-461-7488 267 D aodonnell@hastings.edu
O'DONNELL, Brennan 718-862-7301 305 H brennan.odonnell@manhattan.edu
O'DONNELL, Evanne 530-898-5609 31 A
O'DONNELL, James 480-965-3956 10 I jod@asu.edu
O'DONNELL, James 716-645-2823 316 F jod@buffalo.edu
O'DONNELL, Karen 813-397-2125 144 F kodonnell@nl.edu
O'DONNELL, Margaret 619-239-0391 34 F modonnell@cwsl.edu
O'DONNELL, Michael 239-304-7909 94 O michael.odonnell@avemaria.edu
O'DONNELL, Michael 262-741-8538 499 F odonnellm@gtc.edu
O'DONNELL, Michael 512-499-4601 454 I modonnell@utsystem.edu
O'DONNELL, SSJ, Patricia 215-248-7125 381 D podonnel@chc.edu
O'DONNELL, Patrick 562-860-2451 35 M podonnell@cerritos.edu

P

PABON-RODRIGUEZ, Edith, C .... 787-751-1912 510 A epabon@juris.inter.edu
PACACHA, Edith .... 772-462-7340 101 E epacacha@irsc.edu
PACATTE, Bob .... 325-649-8609 438 D
PACE, Anthony, J .... 570-326-3761 393 G ajp25@pct.edu
PACE, Bobby .... 303-360-4940.. 79 D bobby.pace@ccaurora.edu
PACE, Christy .... 870-460-1020.. 22 D pacec@uamont.edu
PACE, Danielle .... 843-921-6932 411 F mpace@netc.edu
PACE, Dean .... 601-318-6542 249 H dpace@wmcarey.edu
PACE, Derek .... 601-635-2111 245 I dpace@eccc.edu
PACE, Duane .... 423-614-8104 420 J dpace@leeuniversity.edu
PACE, Gay .... 870-460-1140.. 22 D pace@uamont.edu
PACE, Harold .... 336-758-5206 344 D hpace@wfu.edu
PACE, Jarrod .... 972-825-5469 445 A japace@sagu.edu
PACE, Jeff .... 510-649-2400.. 44 F jpace@gtu.edu
PACE, Jessica .... 903-693-2044 441 F jpace@panola.edu
PACE, Kris .... 816-501-4865 258 H kristine.pace@rockhurst.edu
PACE, Lisa, L .... 843-953-4823 407 F lisa.pace@citadel.edu
PACE, Meghan .... 325-942-2083 451 A meghan.pace@angelo.edu
PACE, Tony .... 203-392-5644.. 85 A
PACENTI, Elena .... 619-684-8802.. 53 H epacenti@newschoolarch.edu
PACETTI-DONELSON, Vandy .... 251-626-3303.... 7 E vpacettidonelson@ussa.edu
PACHECO, Andrea .... 505-467-6809 288 E registrar@swc.edu
PACHECO, Christine ...... 870-235-5483.. 21 D christinepacheco@saumag.edu
PACHECO, Edwin, R ...... 401-456-9866 405 C epacheco@ric.edu
PACHECO, Jacob .... 505-747-2122 287 G jpacheco@nnmc.edu
PACHECO, Jennifer .... 508-531-1221 212 B jennifer.pacheco@bridgew.edu
PACHECO, Joseph .... 906-217-3168 221 O pachecoj@baycollege.edu
PACHECO, Michael .... 606-218-5216 185 D michaelpacheco@upike.edu
PACHECO, Philicia .... 508-678-2811 213 G philicia.pacheco@bristolcc.edu
PACHECO, Richard, M .. 913-971-3299 175 G rmpacheco@mnu.edu
PACHECO, Robert .... 831-646-4096.. 52 F rpacheco@mpc.edu
PACHECO, Robert .... 817-515-5289 445 G robert.pacheco@tccd.edu
PACHECO, Sonia .... 787-780-0070 506 F spacheco@caribbean.edu
PACHECO DUNN, Tanhena .... 845-257-3164 317 B pachecot@newpaltz.edu
PACHECO DUNN, Tanhena .... 845-257-3172 317 B pachecot@newpaltz.edu
PACHELLA, Mike .... 610-989-1200 402 B mpachella@vfmac.edu
PACHUAU, Lalsangkima .... 859-858-3581 178 H
PACIONE, Anne, R .... 718-990-5800 314 B roccoa@stjohns.edu
PACK, Andrew .... 215-717-6147 400 J apack@uarts.edu
PACK, Daniel .... 423-425-2256 428 A daniel-pack@utc.edu
PACK, Elizabeth .... 704-406-2173 329 A epack@gardner-webb.edu
PACK, Jodi .... 903-434-8114 441 B jpack@ntcc.edu
PACKARD, Brandi .... 918-610-0027 366 A bpackard@communitycarecollege.edu
PACKARD, Francine ...... 330-821-5320 363 B packarfr@mountunion.edu
PACKARD, Katherin .... 816-531-5223 251 H
PACKARD, Ryan .... 678-466-5499 116 E ryanpackard@clayton.edu
PACKETT, Felicia, B ...... 804-758-6746 475 G fpackett@rappahannock.edu
PACKEY, Matthew .... 704-337-2375 339 G packeym@queens.edu
PACQUING, Allen .... 808-735-4774 127 F allen.pacquing@chaminade.edu
PACTOL, Brian .... 808-235-7403 129 F pactol@hawaii.edu
PACTOL, Monica .... 916-608-6899.. 50 H pactolm@flc.losrios.edu
PADASH, Ali .... 916-608-6648.. 50 H padasha@flc.losrios.edu
PADDEN, Carol, A .... 858-534-6073.. 69 D deansocsci@ucsd.edu
PADDOCK, Ericka .... 909-389-3457.. 59 H epaddock@craftonhills.edu
PADDOCK, Jean .... 330-363-6347 348 D jean.paddock@aultman.com
PADDOCK, Suzanne ...... 315-866-0300 301 G paddocksm@herkimer.edu
PADDOCK-O'REILLY, Kimberly .... 636-227-2100 254 G
PADEN, Matt .... 615-966-1904 421 D matt.paden@lipscomb.edu
PADEN, Quincy .... 312-662-4141 131 H qpaden@adler.edu
PADGETT, Mila .... 803-641-3230 413 D milap@usca.edu
PADILLA, Ailin .... 787-264-1912 509 F ailin_padilla@intersg.edu
PADILLA, Alvin .... 616-392-8555 233 E alvin@westernsem.edu
PADILLA, Corrine .... 801-302-2800 459 H corrine.padilla@neumont.edu
PADILLA, Diana .... 559-486-1166.. 24 G
PADILLA, Edgar .... 512-759-5643 449 E edgar.padilla@tstc.edu
PADILLA, Eugene .... 505-224-4000 285 J epadilla@cnm.edu
PADILLA, Jose .... 562-907-4211.. 75 A jpadilla@whittier.edu
PADILLA, Jose, D .... 312-362-8590 135 I jpadill7@depaul.edu
PADILLA, Lymaries .... 787-725-6500 506 G lpadilla@albizu.edu
PADILLA, Maria .... 508-362-2131 214 B mpadilla@capecod.edu
PADILLA, Mark .... 307-382-1690 502 I mpadilla@westernwyoming.edu
PADILLA, Mayra .... 510-215-3880.. 40 H mpadilla@contracosta.edu
PADILLA, Miriam .... 787-264-1912 509 F miriam_padilla_camacho@intersg.edu
PADILLA, Ramon .... 651-201-1454 237 A ramon.padilla@minnstate.edu
PADILLA, Rene, L .... 402-280-4745 266 I renepadilla@creighton.edu
PADILLA, Sherrie .... 808-932-7451 128 E sherriep@hawaii.edu
PADILLA, Vivian, A .... 787-786-3030 512 B vpadilla@ucb.edu.pr
PADIN, Carlos, M .... 787-766-1717 511 H um_cpadin@suagm.edu
PADMARAJU, Lakshmikara .... 217-581-6603 136 E lpadmaraju@eiu.edu
PADOVANI, John, J .... 607-746-4632 320 G padovajj@delhi.edu
PADRON, Eduardo, J .... 305-237-3316 103 D epadron@mdc.edu
PADUAN, Jeffrey, D .... 831-656-3241 503 K jdpaduan@nps.edu
PADUNTIN, Jack .... 925-969-3300.. 46 H jpaduntin@jfku.edu
PAEPLOW, Randall, K ... 863-784-7083 107 F randall.paeplow@southflorida.edu
PAESE, Paul .... 713-525-3540 454 H paesep@stthom.edu
PAETSCH, Claudia .... 414-288-5629 494 B claudia.paetsch@marquette.edu
PAEZ, Karen .... 971-722-4406 375 J karen.paez@pcc.edu
PAEZ-FIGUEROA, Jose .. 908-709-7084 284 C paez@ucc.edu
PAFFENROTH, Kim .... 914-637-2743 302 G kpaffenroth@iona.edu
PAFFRATH, Dennis .... 410-706-1101 202 D dpaffrath@umaryland.edu
PAGÁN-FALCÓN, Raúl ... 787-993-8877 513 B raul.pagan@upr.edu
PAGAN, Andres .... 787-765-1915 510 B apagan@opto.inter.edu
PAGAN, Damaris .... 787-765-1915 510 B dpagan@opto.inter.edu
PAGAN, Lorraine, M ..... 512-448-8411 442M lorraine@stedwards.edu
PAGAN, Richard, B .... 304-929-5493 489 C rpagan@newriver.edu
PAGAN, Robert .... 718-960-8048 294 A robert.pagan@lehman.cuny.edu
PAGAN, Victoria .... 406-496-4129 265 A vpagan@mtech.edu
PAGAN, William .... 848-445-5067 282 A william.pagan@rutgers.edu
PAGAN, William .... 848-445-5067 282 B william.pagan@rutgers.edu
PAGAN, Yolanda .... 787-891-0925 508 K ypagan@ns.inter.edu
PAGANELLI, John .... 508-531-1328 212 B jpaganelli@bridgew.edu
PAGANI-SOTO, Juan, C 787-765-4210 506 K jpagani@cempr.edu
PAGANO, Amy, E .... 724-458-3850 385 C aepagano@gcc.edu
PAGANO, Diane, P .... 386-312-4267 106 C dianepagano@sjrstate.edu
PAGANO, Jeffrey, M ..... 716-839-8254 298 B jpagano@daemen.edu
PAGANO, Mark .... 253-692-5646 485 F mpagano@uw.edu
PAGANO, Michael, A .... 312-413-3375 151 B mapagano@uic.edu
PAGANO, Neil .... 312-369-8218 135 E npagano@colum.edu
PAGANO, Tom .... 913-469-8500 174 D tpagano@jccc.edu
PAGE, Anna .... 913-469-8500 174 D apage@jccc.edu
PAGE, Antony .... 305-348-1118 109 A antony.page@fiu.edu
PAGE, Beth .... 276-739-2401 476 C bpage@vhcc.edu
PAGE, Cynthia .... 540-453-2281 474 B pagec@brcc.edu
PAGE, David .... 504-816-4362 186 D dpage@dillard.edu
PAGE, Dawn .... 760-366-3791.. 40 K
PAGE, Donlan .... 602-489-5300.. 10 E donlan.page@arizonachristian.edu
PAGE, Eric, J .... 860-701-6117 504 F eric.j.page@uscg.mil
PAGE, JR., Hugh, R ..... 574-631-5716 161 C hpage@nd.edu
PAGE, JR., James, E .... 615-322-7311 428 D
PAGE, Jennifer .... 850-973-1603 103 K pagej@nfcc.edu
PAGE, Jonathan, E .... 434-395-4808 469 A pageje@longwood.edu
PAGE, Kelli .... 209-946-2987.. 70 E kpage@pacific.edu
PAGE, Kimberly, D .... 207-581-1290 195 J kimberly.page@maine.edu
PAGE, LeAnne .... 910-892-3178 329 F lpage@heritagebiblecollege.edu
PAGE, Martin .... 918-631-2698 371 E martin-page@utulsa.edu
PAGE, Mary .... 610-436-2747 396 A mpage@wcupa.edu
PAGE, Michael .... 919-530-5402 342 A mpage@nccu.edu
PAGE, Phillip .... 617-873-0256 207 F phillip.page@cambridgecollege.edu
PAGE, Randy .... 864-242-5100 407 B
PAGE, Richard, L .... 802-656-3114 463 E richard.page@uvm.edu
PAGE, Robert .... 912-260-4201 124 C robert.page@sgsc.edu
PAGE, Scott .... 503-494-8050 375 B faclog@ohsu.edu
PAGE, Susan .... 708-456-0300 150 I susanpage@triton.edu
PAGE, Yolanda .... 504-816-4368 186 D ypage@dillard.edu
PAGE-SMITH, Julie .... 231-843-5949 232 J jsmith@westshore.edu
PAGE-STADLER, Jaime .. 920-424-2027 497 B pagestad@uwosh.edu
PAGEL, Jessica, L .... 253-535-7414 482 H jessica.pagel@plu.edu
PAGEL, Myshie, M .... 915-831-2394 436 E mpagel@epcc.edu
PAGEL, Richard .... 714-432-5024.. 38 E rpagel@occ.cccd.edu
PAGELS, Jamie .... 231-348-6658 228 E jpagels@ncmich.edu
PAGLICCI, Michael .... 716-839-8492 298 B mpaglicc@daemen.edu
PAGNATTARO, Marisa, A .... 706-542-5806 125 G pagnatta@uga.edu
PAGOTTO, Louise .... 808-734-9565 128 I pagotto@hawaii.edu
PAGUIO, Arnold .... 510-723-6608.. 35 O apaguio@chabotcollege.edu
PAGUYO, Christina .... 303-871-6012.. 83 D christina.paguyo@du.edu
PAHL, Jennifer, K .... 989-964-4011 230 B jkpahl@svsu.edu
PAHNO, Kari .... 918-836-6886 370 D kari.pahno@spartan.edu
PAI, Edward .... 310-233-4044.. 49 A paie@lahc.edu
PAIER, Jonathan, E .... 203-287-3180.. 87 E paier.jep@snet.net
PAIER, Maureen, E .... 203-287-3035.. 87 E
PAIER, Maureen, E .... 203-287-3035.. 87 E paier.fin@snet.net
PAIGE, Brian .... 616-526-6758 222 A bp28@calvin.edu
PAIGE, Ellen .... 904-256-7028 101 G epaige@ju.edu
PAIGE, Joseph, P .... 860-832-2225.. 84 I paigejop@ccsu.edu
PAIGE, Leslie .... 785-628-4349 173 B lpagie@fhsu.edu
PAIGE, Michael .... 978-232-2259 209 B mpaige@endicott.edu
PAIGE, Shelia .... 706-821-8364 122 K spaige@paine.edu
PAIGE, Sonji .... 617-327-6777 220 B sonji_paige@williamjames.edu
PAIGE, Squire .... 617-585-1284 217 B squire.paige@necmusic.edu
PAIGE, Tim .... 352-638-9737.. 95 D tpaige@beaconcollege.edu
PAIGE, Timothy .... 401-232-6011 404 F tpaige@bryant.edu
PAIKOWSKI, Gary .... 903-463-8707 437 D paikowski@grayson.edu
PAIN, Karen, D .... 561-868-3325 104 D paink@palmbeachstate.edu
PAINE, Brenda .... 248-689-8282 232 A bpaine@walshcollege.edu
PAINE, Clarke, C .... 717-358-3991 384 D clarke.paine@fandm.edu
PAINE, Dorie .... 573-341-4218 261 E pained@mst.edu
PAINE, Wilson .... 540-365-4211 467 I wpaine@ferrum.edu
PAINO, Troy .... 540-654-1301 472 I president@umw.edu
PAINTER, Donald .... 863-292-3605 105 A dpainter@polk.edu
PAINTER, Jami .... 217-244-8247 151 A painterj@uillinois.edu
PAINTER, Michelle .... 760-245-4271.. 73 D michelle.painter@vvc.edu
PAINTER, Noel .... 386-822-7010 111 A npainter@stetson.edu
PAINTER, Sherry .... 901-435-1383 421 A sherry_painter@loc.edu
PAINTER, Virginia, R .... 304-696-4621 490 D painterv@marshall.edu
PAIR-CUNNINGHAM, Stephanie, S .... 301-546-0649 201 C pairss@pgcc.edu
PAISANT, Julie .... 408-924-2250.. 34 B julie.paisant@sjsu.edu
PAISANT, Karen .... 504-280-6259 189 E kmpaisan@uno.edu
PAIT, Kevin .... 910-775-4355 343 B kevin.pait@uncp.edu
PAIT, Kevin .... 910-775-6260 343 B kevin.pait@uncp.edu
PAITSON, David .... 906-635-2625 226 E dpaitson@lssu.edu
PAIXAO, Francis .... 609-586-4800 278 F paixaof@mccc.edu
PAIZ, Nokomis .... 218-679-2860 242 P
PAIZ, Teresa .... 408-288-3791.. 61M teresa.paiz@sjcc.edu
PAJE-MANALO, Leila, L 603-862-3491 274 G leila.paje-manalo@unh.edu
PAJIC, Natasa .... 859-233-8213 184 G npajic@transy.edu
PAK, David, Y .... 703-425-4143 468 E
PAK, Rene, K .... 213-740-2111.. 72 B renepak@president.usc.edu

PANZANARO, Julie .... 518-629-7309 302 E
j.panzanaro@hvcc.edu
PANZARELLA, Amy .... 304-724-3700 487 E
apanzarella@apus.edu
PANZELLA, Carla .... 978-542-6401 213 C
cpanzella@salemstate.edu
PAO, Roger .... 617-603-6900 216 H
roger.pao@necb.edu
PAOLI, Jessenia .... 718-289-5288 293 B
jessenia.paoli@bcc.cuny.edu
PAOLINI, Francine .... 616-632-2131 221 C
paolifra@aquinas.edu
PAOLINO, Eugene, T .... 201-249-8197 282 I
etpaolino@genovaburns.com
PAPADAKIS, Michael .... 614-292-8520 358 I
papadakis.6@osu.edu
PAPADIMITRIOU,
Dimitri, B .... 845-758-7426 290 G
dbp@levy.bard.edu
PAPADIMOS, Peter, J ... 419-530-8411 363 E
peter.papadimos@utoledo.edu
PAPADOPOULOS,
Michael .... 518-783-2376 315 J
mpapadopoulos@siena.edu
PAPADOPOULOS,
Vassilios .... 323-442-1463.. 72 B
vpapadop@usc.edu
PAPAEFTHYMIOU,
Marios .... 949-824-7427.. 68 G
marios@uci.edu
PAPAFIL, Drucie, A .... 757-446-6143 466 I
papafida@evms.edu
PAPAGEORGE, Anne ..... 215-898-7241 400 K
fresvp@upenn.edu
PAPAJOHN, Michelle .... 631-687-5151 314 C
mpapajohn@sjcny.edu
PAPALEO, Stefano .... 561-237-7831 102 V
spapaleo@lynn.edu
PAPALIA, Daria .... 860-444-8520 504 F
daria.papalia@uscga.edu
PAPALIA, Fernanda .... 201-684-7701 280 H
fpapalia@ramapo.edu
PAPANDREA, Vincent .... 212-237-8864 294 D
vpapandrea@jjay.cuny.edu
PAPANIKOLAOU,
Constantia .... 617-994-6947 211 B
cpapanikolaou@bhe.mass.edu
PAPARELLA, Paul .... 864-656-1753 408 A
ppapare@clemson.edu
PAPAS, Dean .... 760-776-7371.. 39 A
dpapas@collegeofthedesert.edu
PAPATHANASIOU,
Antonios .... 617-850-1297 210 D
apapathanasiou@hchc.edu
PAPATHEOFANIS, Frank 760-471-1316.. 71 I
fpapath@usk.edu
PAPATHOMAS, Thomas 848-445-6533 282 A
papathom@ruccs.rutgers.edu
PAPAYANAKOS,
Judy, L .... 315-655-7128 292 F
jlpapayanakos@cazenovia.edu
PAPAZIAN, Mary .... 408-924-1177.. 34 B
sjsupres@sjsu.edu
PAPAZOGLOU, John ..... 814-865-5423 392 B
jxp769@psu.edu
PAPE, Sabrina .... 916-660-7202.. 63 I
spape@sierracollege.edu
PAPE-LINDSTROM,
Pamela .... 443-412-2240 199 A
ppapelindstrom@harford.edu
PAPENFUSS, Larry, A .... 218-299-3988 235 E
papenfus@cord.edu
PAPILLON, Terry, L ...... 931-598-1248 423 M
tlpapill@sewanee.edu
PAPINCHAK, John, R .... 412-268-7404 380 F
jp7p@andrew.cmu.edu
PAPINI, Dennis .... 217-206-6614 151 C
dpapi2@uis.edu
PAPOULIS, Poline .... 718-997-5400 295 C
poline.papoulis@qc.cuny.edu
PAPP, Carol .... 203-576-4142.. 88 D
cpapp@bridgeport.edu
PAPP, John .... 412-918-2614 124 E
jpapp@southuniversity.edu
PAPP, Justin .... 708-596-2000 149 B
jpapp@ssc.edu
PAPPAGEORGE, Steven . 708-974-5407 144 C
pappageorges3@morainevalley.edu
PAPPALARDO, Tom ...... 740-284-5771 353 B
tpappalardo@franciscan.edu
PAPPAS, Gregory, J ...... 718-817-4350 300 E
pappas@fordham.edu
PAPPAS, Joanna .... 773-508-7429 142 D
jpappas@luc.edu
PAPPAS, JR .... 443-482-6563 201 D
john.pappas@sjc.edu
PAPPAS, Katherine .... 407-646-2268 105 M
kpappas@rollins.edu
PAPPAS, Nikki .... 614-882-2551 353 A
npappas@fortiscollege.edu
PAPPAS, Richard, J ...... 616-698-7111 223 B
rpappas@davenport.edu
PAPPAS, Tony, A .... 641-422-4350 168 D
pappaton@niacc.edu
PAPPATHAN, Matthew .. 802-828-8740 361 L
matt.pappathan@myunion.edu
PAPSON, Melissa .... 724-222-5330 392 A
mpapson@penncommercial.edu
PAPUGUA, Owen .... 315-568-3858 308 F
opapugua@nycc.edu
PAPULI, Tina .... 212-247-3434 305 G
epapuli@mandl.edu
PAQUET, Christopher .... 920-465-2110 496 E
paquetc@uwgb.edu
PAQUETTE, Ashley .... 906-932-4231 224 B
ashleyp@gogebic.edu
PAQUETTE, Gabe .... 541-346-1000 377 D
paquette@uoregon.edu
PAQUETTE, Jeanne .... 207-780-4622 196 F
jeanne.paquette@maine.edu
PAQUETTE, Karen .... 518-629-4552 302 E
k.paquette@hvcc.edu
PAQUETTE, Kevin .... 207-893-7797 195 F
kpaquett@sjcme.edu
PAQUIN, Delbert .... 505-368-3538.. 12 C
dpaquin@dinecollege.edu
PARADIS, Mark .... 207-216-4443 195 C
mparadis@yccc.edu
PARADIS, Ronald, S ..... 541-383-7599 372 B
rparadis@cocc.edu
PARADISE, Melanie, M . 865-539-7130 425 F
mmparadise@pstcc.edu
PARADKAR, Vish .... 617-989-4590 219 E
paradkarv@wit.edu
PARAMORE, Marcus ..... 334-241-8622.... 7 C
marcus@troy.edu
PARAMORE, Pamela ..... 757-455-3238 477 F
pparamore@vwu.edu
PARANDI, Tony .... 765-677-1566 157 D
tony.parandi@indwes.edu
PARANTO, Michelle ...... 978-630-9487 215 A
mparanto@mwcc.mass.edu
PARAYIL, Govindan ...... 813-974-5399 110 B
gparayil@usf.edu
PARCEL, Julie .... 636-922-8383 258 I
jparcel@stchas.edu
PARCELLS, Fred .... 215-785-0111 393 C
PARCHER, Kim .... 563-588-8000 165 F
kparcher@emmaus.edu
PARDA, Lauren .... 860-768-2415.. 88 H
parda@hartford.edu
PARDALES, Michael ...... 207-893-6643 195 F
mpardales@sjcme.edu
PARDEE, Joseph .... 860-701-5176.. 87 D
pardee_j@mitchell.edu
PARDO, Carlos .... 314-454-7547 253 E
carlos.pardo@bjc.org
PARDUE, J. Harold .... 251-461-1600.... 8 F
hpardue@southalabama.edu
PARDUE, Karen .... 207-221-4361 196 G
kpardue@une.edu
PARDUE, Samuel .... 706-542-3924 125 G
caesdean@uga.edu
PARE, Denis .... 973-353-3251 282 B
pare@newark.rutgers.edu
PAREDES, Esteban .... 785-833-4307 175 B
esteban.paredes@kwu.edu
PAREDES, Hector, O ..... 201-761-7425 282 I
hparedes@saintpeters.edu
PAREDES, Luis, F .... 508-531-2729 212 B
lparedes@bridgew.edu
PAREDES, Paqui .... 360-650-3765 486 F
maria.paredesmendez@wwu.edu
PAREJA, Sergio .... 505-277-5820 288 G
pareja@law.unm.edu
PARELLA, JR.,
Richard, A .... 540-464-7322 476 G
parellara@vmi.edu
PARENS, Joshua, S ...... 972-721-5241 452 D
parens@udallas.edu
PARENT, Cyrille .... 719-502-2975.. 81 F
cyrille.parent@ppcc.edu
PARES, Cristina .... 787-758-2525 513 G
cristina.pares@upr.edu
PARGAS, Lizbeth .... 787-725-8120 507 N
lpargas@eap.edu
PARHAM, Loretta .... 404-978-2018 125 B
lparham@auctr.edu
PARHAM, Patricia .... 805-493-3185.. 29 H
pparham@callutheran.edu
PARHAM, Sandra .... 615-966-5837 421 D
sandra.parham@lipscomb.edu
PARHAM, Stacey, G ...... 334-683-5104.... 6 A
sparham@judson.edu
PARHAM, Thomas, A .... 310-243-3301.. 31 B
PARHAM, Tyrone .... 413-545-2121 211 D
tparham@umass.edu
PARHAM, Walter, H ...... 803-777-7854 413 C
terry@mailbox.sc.edu
PARI, Allison .... 661-362-2227.. 51 C
apari@masters.edu
PARIANTE, Jody .... 212-431-2137 309 G
jody.pariante@nyls.edu
PARIKH, Meghal .... 407-646-2574 105 M
mparikh@rollins.edu
PARIKH, Rajeev .... 229-430-4635 113 H
rajeev.parikh@asurams.edu
PARILLO, Rebecca .... 419-289-5870 348 A
rparillo@ashland.edu
PARILLO, Scott .... 419-289-5631 348 A
sparillo@ashland.edu
PARIS, Kimberly, N ...... 336-334-4227 343 A
knparis@uncg.edu
PARIS, Mark, S .... 302-356-6829.. 90 I
mark.s.paris@wilmu.edu
PARIS, Susan .... 919-536-7200 334 B
pariss@durhamtech.edu
PARISH, Cody .... 940-397-4069 440 F
cody.parish@msutexas.edu
PARISH, Daniel, B .... 603-526-3729 272 H
daniel.parish@colby-sawyer.edu
PARISH, Michael, C ..... 906-248-8400 221 N
mparish@bmcc.edu
PARISH, Susan .... 617-373-2518 217 F
PARISH-ONUKWULI,
Kenya .... 251-405-7052.... 1 E
konukwuli@bishop.edu
PARISHER, Deborah ...... 252-823-5166 334 C
parisherd@edgecombe.edu
PARISI, Joseph .... 660-248-6247 251 B
jparisi@centralmethodist.edu
PARISIEN, Chris .... 701-477-7862 347 A
cparisien@tm.edu
PARISSE, Josh .... 816-501-3775 250 F
josh.parisse@avila.edu
PARK, Choong Gi .... 562-926-1023.. 57 G
choong.park@gmail.com
PARK, Claire .... 877-559-3621.. 29 A
claire@ciat.edu
PARK, Connie .... 607-962-9229 320 F
cpark3@corning-cc.edu
PARK, Daniel, L .... 509-527-5999 486 H
park@whitman.edu
PARK, Daniel, W .... 858-822-1236.. 69 D
dwpark@ucsd.edu
PARK, David .... 435-222-1256.. 82 G
dpark@rvu.edu
PARK, Dong Sik .... 562-926-1023.. 57 G
PARK, George .... 310-453-8300.. 42 A
george@emperors.edu
PARK, Hojin .... 215-884-8942 403 G
hojin.park@woninstitute.edu
PARK, Hun Sung .... 213-381-0081.. 46 E
office@laopendoor.org
PARK, Hyung, J .... 213-252-5100.. 23 K
hpark@alu.edu
PARK, Jack, C .... 210-567-2020 456 C
parkjc@uthscsa.edu
PARK, Jae-sig .... 770-232-2717 123 D
jspark@runiv.edu
PARK, James .... 323-221-1024.. 42 F
PARK, Jennifer .... 714-533-1495.. 64 D
epark@southbaylo.edu
PARK, Jessica, K .... 213-252-5100.. 23 K
jpark@alu.edu
PARK, Jinsoo .... 973-877-3588 277 I
jpark@essex.edu
PARK, Joshua .... 703-629-1281 473 E
PARK, Joyce Gunhee .... 703-333-5904 478 B
ghpark@wuv.edu
PARK, Kathryn .... 409-933-8201 433 L
kpark@com.edu
PARK, Laura .... 801-649-5230 459 G
registrar@midwifery.edu
PARK, Linda .... 315-279-5208 304 A
lpark@keuka.edu
PARK, Lisa .... 703-993-2831 467 L
lpark4@gmu.edu
PARK, Matthew .... 940-397-4501 440 F
matthew.park@msutexas.edu
PARK, Meena .... 425-739-8251 482 A
meena.park@lwtech.edu
PARK, Michong .... 818-364-7868.. 49 B
parkm@lamission.edu
PARK, Mihyun .... 562-926-1023.. 57 G
mhpark@ptsa.edu
PARK, Mimi .... 714-533-1495.. 64 D
mimi@southbaylo.edu
PARK, Min .... 213-487-0110.. 41 I
officemanager@dula.edu
PARK, Myung .... 253-964-7327 483 D
mpark@pierce.ctc.edu
PARK, Roger .... 317-632-5553 158 S
rpark@lincolntech.edu
PARK, Scott .... 309-341-7459 141 A
sapark@knox.edu
PARK, Seong, H .... 617-427-7293 209 G
spark4@gordonconwell.edu
PARK, Sunny .... 806-720-7507 439 H
sunny.park@lcu.edu
PARK, Susan .... 949-214-3029.. 40 F
susan.park@cui.edu
PARK, Yong Hee .... 714-533-1495.. 64 D
yhpark@southbaylo.edu
PARK, Young Hae .... 202-559-0434.. 91 E
younghae.park@gallaudet.edu
PARK, Yung Won, S ...... 610-917-1457 401 I
ywpark@valleyforge.edu
PARKE, Lydia .... 215-780-1417 398 G
lparke@salus.edu
PARKER, Amie .... 207-621-3448 196 A
amie.parker@maine.edu
PARKER, Andrew .... 765-677-1989 157 D
andrew.parker@indwes.edu
PARKER, Annette .... 610-409-3591 402 A
aparker@ursinus.edu
PARKER, Annette .... 507-389-7211 241 C
annette.parker@southcentral.edu
PARKER, Anthony .... 903-593-8311 448 H
aparker@texascollege.edu
PARKER, Anthony, O .... 229-430-0656 113 I
aparker@albanytech.edu
PARKER, Ava, L .... 561-868-3501 104 D
parkera@palmbeachstate.edu
PARKER, Barbara .... 828-627-4515 335 C
bmparker@haywood.edu
PARKER, Brandon, C .... 707-965-6699.. 55 D
bparker@puc.edu
PARKER, Brttany .... 309-467-6345 137 B
bparker@eureka.edu
PARKER, Carol .... 575-646-1727 287 B
provost@nmsu.edu
PARKER, Carol .... 864-231-2000 406 G
cparker@andersonuniversity.edu
PARKER, Cassandra ...... 202-274-5669.. 93 C
cparker@udc.edu
PARKER, Cassandra ...... 334-727-8655.... 7 D
cparker@tuskegee.edu
PARKER, Catherine .... 248-218-2154 229 J
cparker@rc.edu
PARKER, Cathy .... 601-484-8799 247 A
cparker@meridiancc.edu
PARKER, Charles, R ..... 850-263-3261.. 95 B
crparker@baptistcollege.edu
PARKER, Charlie .... 253-964-6500 483 D
cparker@pierce.ctc.edu
PARKER, Chris .... 870-733-6047.. 17 H
crparker@asumidsouth.edu
PARKER, Christine .... 401-254-3205 405 E
cparker@rwu.edu
PARKER, Cindy .... 401-598-1345 404 I
cparker@jwu.edu
PARKER, Corey .... 404-297-9522 119 B
parkerc@gptc.edu
PARKER, Craig .... 502-897-4131 184 C
cparker@sbts.edu
PARKER, Cynthia .... 706-295-6346 118 E
cparker@highlands.edu
PARKER, Dale .... 757-423-2095 467 H
PARKER, Dana .... 513-558-9964 362 F
dana.parker@uc.edu
PARKER, Danny .... 864-231-2061 406 G
dparker@andersonuniversity.edu
PARKER, Darrell .... 864-488-4617 410 E
dparker@limestone.edu
PARKER, Debra .... 419-434-5478 363 A
parker@findlay.edu
PARKER, Debra, O .... 919-530-5269 342 A
dparker@nccu.edu
PARKER, Devahn .... 619-934-0797.. 60 F

PARKER, Diane .... 617-243-2137 210 G dparker@lasell.edu
PARKER, Edith .... 319-384-1503 163 A edith-parker@uiowa.edu
PARKER, Fiona .... 817-554-5950 440 C fparker@messengercollege.edu
PARKER, Frank .... 936-294-1786 450 C fparker@shsu.edu
PARKER, Gail, C .... 318-342-1960 192 F gparker@ulm.edu
PARKER, Hilary .... 609-258-5574 280 E haparker@princeton.edu
PARKER, Holly .... 518-327-6300 311 G hparker@paulsmiths.edu
PARKER, Ingrid .... 312-662-4037 131 H iparker@adler.edu
PARKER, Insey .... 402-878-2380 267 E insey.parker@littlepriest.edu
PARKER, Jack .... 321-433-7090.. 97 I parkerj@easternflorida.edu
PARKER, Janet .... 312-355-4565 151 B japarker@uic.edu
PARKER, Janet .... 910-892-3178 329 F jparker@heritagebiblecollege.edu
PARKER, Janice, C .... 312-658-5100 150 C janice.parker@tbiil.edu
PARKER, Jeanette .... 270-789-5075 179 E jjparker@campbellsville.edu
PARKER, Jerry .... 515-271-2835 165 A jerry.parker@drake.edu
PARKER, Jesse .... 919-761-2310 340 G jparker@sebts.edu
PARKER, Jessica .... 812-888-4121 162 C jparker@vinu.edu
PARKER, Jim .... 919-807-6976 331 L parkerj@nccommunitycolleges.edu
PARKER, Jim, O .... 504-816-8592 190 A jparker@nobts.edu
PARKER, Joe .... 970-491-3350.. 78 M joe.parker@colostate.edu
PARKER, John .... 603-888-1311 274 B jhparker@rivier.edu
PARKER, Juli .... 508-910-4582 211 F juli.parker@umassd.edu
PARKER, Julia .... 601-643-8308 245 G julia.parker@colin.edu
PARKER, Karen .... 508-678-2811 213 G karen.parker@bristolcc.edu
PARKER, Kathleen .... 320-363-2121 243 A kparker@csbsju.edu
PARKER, Kathy .... 320-363-2121 235 C kparker@csbsju.edu
PARKER, Keith .... 561-732-4424 106 G kparker@svdp.edu
PARKER, Kelly .... 818-345-9245.. 39 G kparker@columbiacollege.edu
PARKER, Kyle, D .... 479-308-2272.. 17 C kyle.parker@acheedu.org
PARKER, LaTonya .... 478-757-4028 126 H tparker@wesleyancollege.edu
PARKER, Laura .... 310-794-2304.. 69 A lparker@support.ucla.edu
PARKER, III, Lee .... 804-289-8405 472 L lparker@richmond.edu
PARKER, Linda, M .... 518-388-6578 323 G parkerl@union.edu
PARKER, Lucera .... 919-546-8321 340 E lucera.parker@shawu.edu
PARKER, Lynne .... 865-974-5321 427 G leparker@tennessee.edu
PARKER, Mae .... 641-269-4631 165 J parkerma@grinnell.edu
PARKER, Mark .... 405-208-5315 367 I mparker@okcu.edu
PARKER, Mary .... 310-393-0411.. 55 J mfparker@rand.org
PARKER, Mary, G .... 330-672-3000 354 J mparke37@kent.edu
PARKER, Mary Jo .... 713-221-8471 453 B parkerm@uhd.edu
PARKER, Micah .... 951-343-4381.. 27 J miparker@calbaptist.edu
PARKER, Michael .... 210-341-1366 441 C mparker@ost.edu
PARKER, Michelle, G .... 928-523-6500.. 14 H michelle.parker@nau.edu
PARKER, Patsy .... 580-774-3284 370 C patsy.parker@swosu.edu
PARKER, Pennie .... 407-646-2636 105 M pparker@rollins.edu
PARKER, Pippin .... 212-229-5859 308 C parkerp@newschool.edu
PARKER, Robert .... 707-256-7175.. 53 C rparker@napavalley.edu
PARKER, JR., Robert, D .... 217-383-4114 151 D rcparker@illinois.edu
PARKER, Robin, L .... 513-529-6734 356 E parkerrl@miamioh.edu
PARKER, Rodney .... 410-617-2310 199 F rparker1@loyola.edu
PARKER, Ron .... 979-230-3480 432 D ron.parker@brazosport.edu
PARKER, Sonya, L .... 270-824-8586 181 G sonya.parker@kctcs.edu
PARKER, Susan .... 901-334-5809 422 C sparker@memphisseminary.edu
PARKER, Tammie .... 541-278-5850 372 A tparker@bluecc.edu
PARKER, Terry .... 863-583-9050 109 B
PARKER, Tony .... 312-341-4167 147 H
PARKER, Vic .... 601-857-3961 246 B victor.parker@hindscc.edu
PARKER AMES, Gwen ... 845-675-4446 310 G gwen.ames@nyack.edu
PARKER-CLEVER, Sarah 740-374-8716 364 C sparker@wscc.edu
PARKER-DER BOGHOSSIAN, John .... 952-358-8358 239 F john.parker-derboghossian@normandale.edu
PARKER-JEANNETTE, Cyrus .... 562-985-4376.. 31 F cyrus.parker-jeannette@csulb.edu
PARKER-KELLY, Darlene .... 323-563-9340.. 36 D darleneparkerkelly@cdrewu.edu
PARKER-WOLERY, Amanda .... 513-562-8754 347 K aparker@artacademy.edu
PARKER-WOLERY, Amanda .... 513-562-6267 347 K aparker@artacademy.edu
PARKEY, Chase .... 907-796-6100.. 10 B
PARKHURST, Abbie ...... 540-828-5782 465 D aparkhur@bridgewater.edu
PARKHURST, Cindy ...... 951-785-2982.. 47 C cparkhurst@lasiera.edu
PARKHURST, Cindy ...... 951-785-2982.. 47 C cparkhurst@lasierra.edu
PARKHURST, Jennifer ... 626-256-4673.. 37 B jparkhurst@coh.org
PARKINSON, Curt .... 559-278-6634.. 31 D cparkinson@csufresno.edu
PARKINSON, III, Henry, C .... 978-665-3160 212 C hparkinson@fitchburgstate.edu
PARKINSON, Richard .... 815-772-7218 144 D rcpark@morrisontech.edu
PARKINSON, Tracy .... 843-383-8012 408 D tparkinson@coker.edu
PARKMAN, Julie .... 315-386-7119 320 E parkman@canton.edu
PARKS, Amy .... 216-987-6130 351 G amy.parks@tri-c.edu
PARKS, Ann .... 660-263-4100 257 B annp@macc.edu
PARKS, Charlotte .... 662-915-3120 249 D cpparks@olemiss.edu
PARKS, Daniel, A .... 909-869-2373.. 30 D daparks@cpp.edu
PARKS, David .... 304-473-8011 491 H parks.d@wvwc.edu
PARKS, Earl .... 202-651-5494.. 91 E earl.parks@gallaudet.edu
PARKS, Jana .... 785-594-4595 170 I
PARKS, JaNice .... 202-885-8687.. 93 E jparks@wesleyseminary.edu
PARKS, Jason .... 951-372-7017.. 58 H jason.parks@norcocollege.edu
PARKS, Jason .... 318-484-2184 192 C parksj@nsula.edu
PARKS, Jo-Lynne .... 303-546-3570.. 81 B jparks@naropa.edu
PARKS, Lisa .... 541-245-7548 376 D lparks@roguecc.edu
PARKS, Marshall .... 970-351-1814.. 83 E marshall.parks@unco.edu
PARKS, Matt .... 815-753-2095 145 C mparks2@niu.edu
PARKS, Michael .... 210-567-2791 456 C parksm@uthscsa.edu
PARKS, Nancy .... 304-367-4990 489 D nancy.parks@pierpont.edu
PARKS, Patricia .... 714-816-0366.. 67 I patricia.parks@trident.edu
PARKS, Rodney .... 336-278-6677 328 K rparks4@elon.edu
PARKS, Roger .... 713-525-3151 454 H parksrw@stthom.edu
PARKS, Valerie .... 915-779-8031 457 F vparks@computercareercenter.com
PARKS, Vanasia Conley 423-425-4467 428 A vanasia-parks@utc.edu
PARKS, Wendy, E .... 630-942-2755 135 A parksw@cod.edu
PARKS SANKEY, Courtney .... 205-929-1815.... 6 B
PARLACOSKI, Julie .... 732-987-2219 278 B jparlacoski@georgian.edu
PARLE, Joseph, D .... 832-252-4659 433 D joe.parle@cbshouston.edu
PARLER, Branson .... 616-222-3000 226 C bparler@kuyper.edu
PARLETT, Ray, M .... 585-567-9333 302 D ray.parlett@houghton.edu
PARLETT-SWEENEY, Mary, W .... 518-782-6988 315 J mparlett-sweeney@siena.edu
PARLOW, Matthew, J .... 714-628-2678.. 36 C parlow@chapman.edu
PARMELY, Michael .... 913-588-7053 176 I mparmely@kumc.edu
PARMER, David .... 409-212-5724 431 F
PARNELL, Katherine, T . 828-884-8264 327 C parnelkt@brevard.edu
PARNELL, Kathleen .... 410-617-2354 199 F kmparnell@loyola.edu
PARNELL, Katie .... 325-670-1889 437 F katie.parnell@hsutx.edu
PARNELL, Patrick, M .... 417-836-4127 256 E patrickparnell@missouristate.edu
PARNELL, Paul .... 559-243-7102.. 66 C paul.parnell@scccd.edu
PARNELL, Philip .... 307-382-1639 502 I pparnell@westernwyoming.edu
PAROLIN, Peter .... 307-766-4110 502 H honors@uwyo.edu
PARR, Adrian .... 817-272-2801 454 J adrian.parr@uta.edu
PARR, Vanna .... 940-898-3526 451 F vparr@twu.edu
PARR WALKER, Diane .. 574-631-7790 161 C diane.parr.walker@nd.edu
PARRA, Alejandra .... 305-348-3062 109 A alejandra.parra@fiu.edu
PARRA, Alicia, F .... 954-322-4460 101 J aliciafernandaparra@jmvu.edu
PARRA, Jonallie .... 209-946-3288.. 70 E jparra@pacific.edu
PARRELLA, Michael ...... 208-885-6681 131 G mpp@uidaho.edu
PARRELLA, Michael ...... 208-885-4933 131 G mpp@uidaho.edu
PARRENT, Condoa .... 817-515-6532 445 G condoa.parrent@tccd.edu
PARRENT, Jay .... 270-824-8571 181 G jay.parrent@kctcs.edu
PARRENT, Rick .... 615-230-3321 426 B rick.parrent@volstate.edu
PARRILL, Jacqueline ..... 740-366-9407 349 H parrill.9@osu.edu
PARRILL-BAKER, Abby .. 901-678-4831 427 D aparrill@memphis.edu
PARRILLA, Arlene .... 787-863-2390 509 B arlene.parrilla@fajardo.inter.edu
PARRIOTT, Karen .... 307-532-8264 502 A karen.parriott@ewc.wy.edu
PARRIS, Adam .... 718-951-5415 293 C adam.parris56@brooklyn.cuny.edu
PARRISH, Austen, L ...... 812-855-8885 156 B austparr@indiana.edu
PARRISH, Dave .... 770-533-7033 121 B dparrish@laniertech.edu
PARRISH, David, K .... 308-632-6933 269 E
PARRISH, JR., Frank .... 406-994-2452 264 D fparrish@montana.edu
PARRISH, Gretchen .... 336-342-4261 337 E parrishg@rockinghamcc.edu
PARRISH, John, M .... 310-338-2775.. 50 J john.parrish@lmu.edu
PARRISH, Kelly .... 617-989-4960 219 E parrishk@wit.edu
PARRISH, Lorena .... 202-706-6840.. 93 E lparrish@wesleyseminary.edu
PARRISH, Lyndon .... 269-782-1321 230 F lparrish@swmich.edu
PARRISH, Michael .... 718-982-2440 293 E provost@csi.cuny.edu
PARRISH, Patricia .... 270-384-8030 183 C parrishp@lindsey.edu
PARRISH, Sid .... 803-321-5263 411 D sid.parrish@newberry.edu
PARRISH TRENT, Monica .... 610-359-5394 382 C mtrent@dccc.edu
PARROT, Autumn .... 615-277-7401 428 F aparrot@watkins.edu
PARROTT, Autumn .... 248-645-3300 223 A
PARROTT, Mike .... 843-208-8040 413 E rparrot@uscb.edu
PARROTT, Rebecca .... 606-248-0256 182 E rebecca.parrott@kctcs.edu
PARROTT, Roger .... 601-968-5919 245 C president@belhaven.edu
PARROTT, Steve .... 662-325-7790 247 F sparrott@its.msstate.edu
PARRY, Jason .... 972-758-3891 433 M jparry@collin.edu
PARRY, John .... 970-491-3939.. 78 M john.parry@colostate.edu
PARSHALL, Lindi .... 512-476-2772 431 B admissions@austingrad.edu
PARSHALL, William ...... 215-204-8822 399 F william.parshall@temple.edu
PARSLEY, Ashton .... 614-837-4088 364 A parsleya@valorcollege.edu
PARSLEY, Nancy, L .... 847-578-8401 147 I nancy.parsley@rosalindfranklin.edu
PARSNIK, Pamela .... 570-674-6310 390 G pparsnik@misericordia.edu
PARSON, Chirs .... 406-756-3839 263 F cparson@fvcc.edu
PARSON, Reginald .... 415-338-3068.. 34 A regg@sfsu.edu
PARSON, Shirley .... 860-439-5930.. 86 H shirley.parson@conncoll.edu
PARSON, Tara .... 417-328-1511 259 L tparson@sbuniv.edu
PARSONS, Amy .... 303-534-6290.. 78 L amy.parsons@colostate.edu
PARSONS, Gayle .... 623-245-4600.. 16 E gparsons@uti.edu
PARSONS, Greg .... 205-934-4427.... 8 A gparsons@uab.edu
PARSONS, Jeff .... 704-991-0321 338 C jparsons7694@stanly.edu
PARSONS, Jon .... 910-672-1403 341 E jparson2@uncfsu.edu
PARSONS, Kevin .... 910-410-1918 337 B ksparsons@richmondcc.edu
PARSONS, Marty .... 563-425-5384 170 A parsonsm24@uiu.edu
PARSONS, Pam .... 916-278-6446.. 32 E pparsons@csus.edu
PARSONS, Patty .... 336-838-6292 339 B peparsons921@wilkescc.edu
PARSONS, Penny .... 513-569-1532 350 K penny.parsons@cincinnatistate.edu
PARSONS, Philip .... 401-739-5000 405 A pparsons@neit.edu
PARSONS, Priscilla .... 409-880-8489 449 H priscilla.parsons@lamar.edu
PARSONS, Rachel, A .... 603-526-3451 272 H rparsons@colby-sawyer.edu
PARSONS, Ray .... 302-857-1814.. 90 D rparson3@dtcc.edu
PARSONS, Scott .... 219-785-5322 159 G sparsons@pnw.edu
PARSONS, Scott .... 334-244-3667.... 4 F sparsons@aum.edu
PARSONS, Teena .... 910-410-1810 337 B tlparsons@richmondcc.edu
PARSONS, Timothy .... 570-558-1818 384 C tparsons@fortisinstitute.edu
PARSONS, Wendy .... 732-263-5758 279 B wparsons@monmouth.edu
PARSONS-ELLIS, Sandy 530-898-6131.. 31 A skparsons@csuchico.edu
PARSONS-NIKOLIC, Cathleen .... 215-951-1540 387 C parsonsnikolic@lasalle.edu
PARSONS-POLLARD, Nicolle .... 732-571-3550 279 B nparsons@monmouth.edu
PARSONS-WELLS, Rachel, E .... 864-833-7000 411 I reparsons@presby.edu
PARTAIN, Julie .... 229-271-4049 124 D jpartain@southgatech.edu
PARTAIN, Sandra .... 318-678-6000 187 A spartain@bpcc.edu

PARTEE, Marc .... 484-365-7660 389 C
mpartee@lincoln.edu
PARTENZA, Janet .... 914-674-7657 306 F
jpartenza@mercy.edu
PARTIGIANONI, Dan ..... 315-228-7497 296 F
dpartigianoni@colgate.edu
PARTIN, Katie .... 502-852-6169 185 C
katie.partin@louisville.edu
PARTIN, Sherry .... 606-546-1625 184 H
spartin2@unionky.edu
PARTON, Becky .... 217-786-2351 142 B
becky.parton@llcc.edu
PARTON, John .... 678-664-0527 127 A
john.parton@westgatech.edu
PARTON, LeAnne .... 509-793-2004 478 H
leannep@bigbend.edu
PARTON, Valerie .... 509-793-2371 478 H
valeriep@bigbend.edu
PARTRIDGE, Richard ..... 803-327-8031 415 A
rpartridge@yorktech.edu
PARTRIDGE, Steve .... 703-323-2383 475 C
spartridge@nvcc.edu
PARZY, Robert .... 847-925-6649 137 H
rparzy@harpercollege.edu
PASCAL, Sandra, E .... 617-989-4478 219 E
pascals@wit.edu
PASCALE, Lynn .... 203-287-3031.. 87 E
paier.admission@snet.net
PASCARELL, Rose .... 703-993-8760 467 L
rpascare@gmu.edu
PASCARELLA, John .... 936-294-1458 450 C
jbp014@shsu.edu
PASCARIELLO,
Jacqueline .... 631-632-6840 317 D
jacqueline.pascariello@stonybrook.edu
PASCHAL, Adria, D .... 541-885-1100 375 C
adria.paschal@oit.edu
PASCHAL, Erin .... 814-641-3331 386 H
paschae@juniata.edu
PASCHAL, Samuel .... 803-376-5902 406 F
spaschal@allenuniversity.edu
PASCHALL, Kirk .... 972-825-4736 445 A
kpaschall@sagu.edu
PASCHOLD, Erika .... 402-465-7574 268 H
epaschol@nebrwesleyan.edu
PASCO, Leslie .... 315-228-7481 296 F
lpasco@colgate.edu
PASCOE, Theresa .... 201-216-3495 283 C
theresa.pascoe@stevens.edu
PASCOE AGUILAR,
Daniel .... 973-408-3462 277 C
dpascoeaguilar@drew.edu
PASCUAL, Michael .... 310-660-3374.. 41 L
mopascual@elcamino.edu
PASCUAL, Mytha .... 310-900-1600.. 40 A
mpascual@elcamino.edu
PASEK, Heidi .... 406-771-4397 264 G
hpasek@gfcmsu.edu
PASEMAN, David .... 951-639-5185.. 52 I
dpaseman@msjc.edu
PASENELLI, Rose .... 619-594-1630.. 33 E
rpasenel@sdsu.edu
PASIC, Amir .... 317-278-5652 156 F
ampasic@iupui.edu
PASKETT, Lindy .... 307-855-2120 501 V
lpaskett@cwc.edu
PASKEY, Louise .... 712-279-5494 163 C
louise.paskey@briarcliff.edu
PASKVAN, Kevin, F .... 740-368-3052 359 N
kfpaskva@owu.edu
PASLEY, James .... 816-584-6593 258 A
james.pasley@park.edu
PASLEY-HENRY,
Stephanie .... 386-481-2087.. 95 F
PASQUALICCHIO,
Michael, C .... 570-348-6242 389 G
mpasqualicchio@marywood.edu
PASQUARELLO, Nanette 607-753-7668 318 D
nanette.pasquarello@cortland.edu
PASQUARIELLO, Gino ... 619-201-8965.. 65 A
gino.pasquariello@socalsem.edu
PASS-STERN, Bernice .... 212-614-6176 311 H
bernice.pass-stern@mountsinai.org
PASSAFIUME, Marisa .... 718-862-7796 305 H
marisa.passafiume@manhattan.
edumanhattan.edu
PASSAGE, Rob .... 503-370-6217 378 B
rpassage@willamette.edu
PASSARELLA, Bonnie ..... 732-224-2239 276 B
bpassarella@brookdalecc.edu
PASSARO, Joanne .... 212-343-1234 306 J
jpassaro@mcny.edu
PASSARO, Karen .... 973-275-2061 283 B
karen.passaro@shu.edu
PASSAUER, Bridgett, M 757-822-1536 476 B
bpassauer@tcc.edu
PASSE, Jeff .... 909-869-2319.. 30 D
jpasse@cpp.edu
PASSERINI, Katia .... 718-990-2773 314 B
passerik@stjohns.edu
PASSMORE, Ben .... 608-263-0872 496 B
bpassmore@uwsa.edu
PASSMORE, Ed .... 334-683-2375.... 3 A
epassmore@marionmilitary.edu
PASSOS, Carol .... 641-472-1194 167 F
hrdirector@mum.edu
PASTERIS, Marc .... 419-289-5012 348 A
mpasteri@ashland.edu
PASTERNACK, Louise .... 408-498-5158.. 38 F
lpasternack@cogswell.edu
PASTORE, Michael .... 253-879-3100 485 E
mpastore@pugetsound.edu
PASTOREK, Jennifer ...... 419-530-8707 363 E
jennifer.pastorek@utoledo.edu
PASTORELLA, Mark, J ... 585-262-1509 307 H
mpastorella@monroecc.edu
PASTORIZA, Nelida .... 718-518-4412 294 B
npastoriza@hostos.cuny.edu
PASTRANA, Marie Luz .. 787-765-3560 507 L
marieluz@edpuniversity.edu
PASTRANA, Marilyn ...... 787-765-3560 507 L
mpastrana@edpuniversity.edu
PASZKIEWICZ, Wendy .. 312-662-4211 131 H
paszk@adler.edu
PATAKI, Diane, E .... 801-585-1899 460 E
diane.pataki@utah.edu
PATALANO, Carla .... 617-603-6900 216 H
carla.patalano@necb.edu
PATARI, Maggie .... 802-257-4333 462 E
maggie@marlboro.edu
PATAROZZI, Rachel, N . 217-786-4646 142 B
rachel.patarozzi@llcc.edu
PATAWARAN, Arrileen .. 773-995-2063 133 K
apatawar@csu.edu
PATCHETT, Meg .... 704-403-1558 327 D
meg.patchett@carolinashealthcare.org
PATE, Barry .... 208-732-6415 130 E
bpate@csi.edu
PATE, Ellen .... 864-644-5149 412 E
epate@swu.edu
PATE, Juston .... 270-706-8409 181 A
juston.pate@kctcs.edu
PATE, Kim .... 828-328-7128 330 F
kim.pate@lr.edu
PATE, Nino, T .... 671-734-1812 505 D
npate@piu.edu
PATEE, Carla .... 620-227-9378 172 J
cpatee@dc3.edu
PATEL, Jiggy .... 302-736-2521.. 90 G
jiggy.patel@wesley.edu
PATEL, Mimi .... 478-445-5771 118 C
mimi.patel@gcsu.edu
PATEL, Mital .... 312-261-3025 144 F
mital.patel@nl.edu
PATEL, Monal .... 804-828-6683 473 F
mpatell22@vcu.edu
PATEL, Narendra, H ...... 386-481-2072.. 95 F
pateln@cookman.edu
PATEL, Neel .... 785-442-6032 174 A
npatel@highlandcc.edu
PATEL, Prita .... 202-885-2177.. 90 J
ppatel@american.edu
PATEL, Reshma .... 404-894-0881 118 F
reshma.patel@bks.gatech.edu
PATEL, Sandip .... 203-582-3394.. 87 G
sandip.patel@quinnipiac.edu
PATENAUDE, Craig .... 301-934-7643 198 A
cwpatenaude@csmd.edu
PATENAUDE, Heather .... 928-757-0817.. 14 F
hpatenaude@mohave.edu
PATERA, Richard .... 217-234-5253 141 D
rpatera@lakelandcollege.edu
PATERSON, John, W ..... 386-312-4232 106 C
johnpaterson@sjrstate.edu
PATERSON, Wendy, A ... 716-878-4214 318 C
paterswa@buffalostate.edu
PATES, Nancy .... 952-358-8200 239 F
nancy.pates@normandale.edu
PATESTAS, Maria .... 718-368-5597 294 E
maria.patestas@kbcc.cuny.edu
PATH, Bill .... 918-293-5256 368 D
bpath@okstate.edu
PATHAK, Dushyant .... 530-752-7309.. 68 E
dpathak@ucdavis.edu
PATHAK, Susanna .... 207-941-7187 194 A
pathaks@husson.edu
PATIL, Manoj .... 402-878-2380 267 E
manoj.patil@littlepriest.edu
PATLOLLA, Babu, P ...... 601-877-6120 244 H
bpatlolla@alcorn.edu
PATNALA, Deepak .... 906-635-2022 226 E
dpatnala@lssu.edu
PATNAUDE, Valerie .... 603-897-8533 274 B
vpatnaude@rivier.edu
PATO, Rosevonne, M .... 684-699-9155 505 A
r.pato@amsamoa.edu
PATON, Hannah .... 208-769-7750 131 C
hannah.paton@nic.edu
PATON, Jeff .... 336-770-1457 343 D
patonjj@uncsa.edu
PATON, Jeff .... 336-770-1457 343 D
patonj@uncsa.edu
PATON, Valerie .... 915-215-4300 451 D
valerie.paton@ttuhsc.edu
PATOUILLET, Lee .... 865-974-2425 427 G
lee@utfi.org
PATRAS, Nick .... 903-886-5145 447 B
nick.patras@tamuc.edu
PATRIA, Patricia .... 508-831-5000 220 E
ppatria@wpi.edu
PATRICK, Brian .... 913-288-7362 174 F
bpatrick@kckcc.edu
PATRICK, Craig .... 914-632-5400 307 G
cpatrick@monroecollege.edu
PATRICK, Ebert, M .... 915-831-6553 436 E
pebert1@epcc.edu
PATRICK, Edward .... 919-516-4127 340 C
epatrick@st-aug.edu
PATRICK, Jamie .... 919-497-3245 330 I
jpatrick@louisburg.edu
PATRICK, Julietta .... 847-635-1754 145 G
jpatrick@oakton.edu
PATRICK, Kim .... 616-331-2280 224 E
patricki@gvsu.edu
PATRICK, Lanell .... 443-412-2563 199 A
lpatrick@harford.edu
PATRICK, Laura .... 949-376-6000.. 47 D
lpatrick@lcad.edu
PATRICK, Mary .... 805-922-6966.. 24 J
mary.patrick@hancockcollege.edu
PATRICK, Michelle .... 412-397-6359 397 G
patrick@rmu.edu
PATRICK, Nicole .... 662-329-7114 248 A
jnpatrick@muw.edu
PATRICK, Paul, D .... 843-953-0879 408 E
patrickpd@cofc.edu
PATRICK, Paul, G .... 864-379-6675 409 H
ppatrick@erskine.edu
PATRICK, Robin .... 740-474-8896 358 F
rpatrick@ohiochristian.edu
PATRICK, Tracie, M .... 814-641-3142 386 H
patrict@juniata.edu
PATRIQUIN, Wendy ...... 304-929-5494 489 C
wpatriquin@newriver.edu
PATRIZI, Chad .... 610-526-1448 378 G
chad.patrizi@theamericancollege.edu
PATRIZI, Chad .... 304-724-3700 487 E
cpatrizi@apus.edu
PATRY, Roland .... 214-358-9042 451 C
roland.patry@ttuhsc.edu
PATRYLA, Trish .... 661-255-1050.. 28 K
patryla@calarts.edu
PATTEE, Bob .... 254-295-4524 453 E
rpattee@umhb.edu
PATTEE, Bonnie .... 801-274-3280 461 F
bonnie.pattee@wgu.edu
PATTEN, Shawn .... 941-752-5444 108 G
pattens@scf.edu
PATTEN-LEMONS,
Rebecca .... 317-921-4667 157 H
rpatten@ivytech.edu
PATTERSON, Anthony ... 919-572-1625 326 L
apatterson@apexsot.edu
PATTERSON, Bart .... 702-992-2350 271 C
president@nsc.edu
PATTERSON, Becky .... 502-852-3385 185 C
becky.patterson@louisville.edu
PATTERSON, Bernie ...... 715-346-2123 497 F
PATTERSON, Brad .... 870-230-5081.. 19 E
bpatterson@hsu.edu
PATTERSON, Brigid .... 262-551-5940 492 F
bpatterson@carthage.edu
PATTERSON, Cam .... 501-686-7000.. 22 C
cpatters@uams.edu
PATTERSON, Carol .... 303-797-5701.. 76 I
carol.patterson@arapahoe.edu
PATTERSON,
Carol Lynn .... 732-247-5241 279 D
ssheldon@nbts.edu
PATTERSON, Charles .... 570-662-4046 395 C
PATTERSON, Charlotte .. 434-982-2962 473 A
cjp@virginia.edu
PATTERSON, Chrissy .... 903-983-8198 439 A
cpatterson@kilgore.edu
PATTERSON, Cynthia, A 252-638-7304 333 H
pattersonc@cravencc.edu
PATTERSON, Darrin .... 330-337-6403 347 E
college@awc.edu
PATTERSON, David .... 605-651-9729 415 D
dpatterson@ilt.edu
PATTERSON, Donald, A 716-878-3447 318 C
patterda@buffalostate.edu
PATTERSON, Dorsey ..... 901-435-1286 421 A
dorsey_patterson@loc.edu
PATTERSON, Elice .... 202-651-5309.. 91 E
elice.patterson@gallaudet.edu
PATTERSON, Elizabeth .. 903-223-6722 448 B
epatterson@tamut.edu
PATTERSON, Emily, A ... 316-978-3030 178 A
emily.patterson@wichita.edu
PATTERSON, Eric .... 214-654-9075 201 G
PATTERSON, Felicia, L .. 410-777-2718 197 C
flpatterson@aacc.edu
PATTERSON,
Franklin, E .... 386-481-2020.. 95 F
pattersonf@cookman.edu
PATTERSON, Hahna ...... 207-221-4418 196 G
hpatterson@une.edu
PATTERSON, Harlan ...... 425-602-3003 478 D
hpatterson@bastyr.edu
PATTERSON, Howard .... 903-566-7350 456 A
hpatterson@uttyler.edu
PATTERSON, Jackie .... 215-780-1397 398 G
jpatterson@salus.edu
PATTERSON, James ...... 860-738-6482.. 86 C
jpatterson@nwcc.edu
PATTERSON,
Jana Lynn, F .... 336-278-7200 328 K
patters@elon.edu
PATTERSON, Jennifer .... 641-422-4346 168 D
jennifer.patterson@niacc.edu
PATTERSON, Jennifer .... 614-236-6502 349 D
jpatterson@capital.edu
PATTERSON, John, A .... 478-301-5537 121 E
patterson_ja@mercer.edu
PATTERSON, Joyce, D .. 337-475-5232 192 A
joyce@mcneese.edu
PATTERSON, Karen, B ... 904-620-5279 110 A
karen.patterson@unf.edu
PATTERSON, Kim .... 254-299-8606 440 A
kpatterson@mclennan.edu
PATTERSON, Kwame ..... 309-556-3802 139 G
kpatters@iwu.edu
PATTERSON, Leni, N ..... 864-833-8284 411 I
lpatters@presby.edu
PATTERSON, Michael .... 410-225-2422 199 H
mpatters@mica.edu
PATTERSON, Michael .... 415-503-6237.. 60 H
mpatterson@sfcm.edu
PATTERSON, Michelle ... 865-354-3000 425 G
pattersonm@roanestate.edu
PATTERSON, Myrna ...... 808-845-9115 129 B
mpatters@hawaii.edu
PATTERSON, Nancy .... 423-697-2630 424 E
nancy.patterson@chattanoogastate.edu
PATTERSON, Patty .... 954-492-5353.. 96 H
ppatterson@citycollege.edu
PATTERSON, Paul, M .... 334-844-3209.... 4 E
pmp0003@auburn.edu
PATTERSON, Rae Lynn . 208-535-5361 130 C
raelynn.patterson@cei.edu
PATTERSON, Ralph .... 803-321-5166 411 D
ralph.patterson@newberry.edu
PATTERSON, Robert, H . 804-752-3605 470 F
robertpatterson@rmc.edu
PATTERSON, Ron .... 256-765-4683.... 8 E
rpatterson1@una.edu
PATTERSON, Scott .... 314-367-8700 259 B
scott.patterson@stlcop.edu
PATTERSON, Shannon .. 706-771-4013 114 J
sbentley@augustatech.edu
PATTERSON, Sharna ..... 302-622-8000.. 89 E
spatterson@dcad.edu
PATTERSON, Sharon, E . 626-395-3937.. 29 C
sharon.patterson@caltech.edu
PATTERSON, Stacey ...... 865-974-4048 427 F
stacey.patterson@tennessee.edu
PATTERSON, Stephanie . 626-256-4673.. 37 B
spatterson@coh.org
PATTERSON, Steven ...... 703-323-3554 475 C
spatterson@nvcc.edu

PATTERSON, Teresa ...... 909-274-5512.. 52 H tpatterson@mtsac.edu
PATTERSON, Thomas .... 334-387-3877.... 4 C thomaspatterson@amridgeuniversity.edu
PATTERSON, Tracy .... 901-843-3856 423 J pattersont@rhodes.edu
PATTERSON, Van .... 409-944-1205 437 B vpatterson@gc.edu
PATTERSON, Vicki .... 832-252-4624 433 D vicki.patterson@cbhouston.edu
PATTERSON, Wayne ...... 814-732-2703 394 F wepatterson@edinboro.edu
PATTERSON, Whitney .... 903-510-3273 452 C whitney.patterson@tjc.edu
PATTIE, Piotrowski .... 217-206-6597 151 C ppiot2@uis.edu
PATTILLO, Nicolas .... 479-788-7166.. 21 H npattillo@uafs.edu
PATTISALL, Jeremy .... 336-714-7998 339 F pattisaj@piedmontu.edu
PATTISALL, Jeremy .... 336-725-8344 339 F pattisallj@piedmontu.edu
PATTISON, Margaret ..... 313-578-0327 231 B peggy.pattison@udmercy.edu
PATTON, Chad .... 434-949-1038 475 H chad.patton@southside.edu
PATTON, Guy, L .... 405-321-1174 371 B gpatton@ou.edu
PATTON, Julia, G .... 610-917-2004 401 I jgpatton@valleyforge.edu
PATTON, Kerry .... 203-582-3087.. 87 G kerry.patton2@quinnipiac.edu
PATTON, Laurie, L .... 802-443-5400 462 H president@middlebury.edu
PATTON, Michael .... 626-529-8498.. 55 A mpatton@pacificoaks.edu
PATTON, Neely .... 303-753-6046.. 82 F npatton@rmcad.edu
PATTON, Paul, E .... 606-218-5262 185 D pep@upike.edu
PATTON-OSTRANDER, Kelley, A .... 518-580-5814 316 A kostrand@skidmore.edu
PATTY, Jeff .... 706-295-6775 118 E jpatty@highlands.edu
PATTY, Stacy .... 806-720-7652 439 H stacy.patty@lcu.edu
PATWARY, Mohsin .... 718-270-6217 295 A mohsin@mec.cuny.edu
PATZ, Thomas .... 317-738-8183 154 J tpatz@franklincollege.edu
PAUGH, Jerry .... 714-449-7487.. 51 A jpaugh@ketchum.edu
PAUGH, Mark .... 352-854-2322.. 96 O paughm@cf.edu
PAUKEN, Evan .... 269-488-4215 225 E epauken@kvcc.edu
PAUKEN, Patrick .... 419-372-2550 348 H paukenp@bgsu.edu
PAUKEN, Patrick .... 419-372-2226 348 H paukenp@bgsu.edu
PAUL, Alyson .... 706-864-1900 126 A alyson.paul@ung.edu
PAUL, Christina .... 617-745-3812 208 G christina.paul@enc.edu
PAUL, Christine .... 805-493-3220.. 29 H clpaul@callutheran.edu
PAUL, David, W .... 801-422-4887 458 H davidwpaul@byu.edu
PAUL, Elizabeth, L .... 614-236-6908 349 D bethpaul@capital.edu
PAUL, Glenn .... 254-267-7100 442 E gpaul@rangercollege.edu
PAUL, Jina .... 402-552-3100 266 E pauljina@clarksoncollege.edu
PAUL, Kelley .... 903-923-2229 436 D kpaul@etbu.edu
PAUL, Korey, J .... 717-477-1154 395 E kjpaul@ship.edu
PAUL, Mary .... 619-849-2215.. 57 E marypaul@pointloma.edu
PAUL, Michelle .... 417-455-5675 252 D michellepaul@crowder.edu
PAUL, Phyllis, M .... 330-941-3625 365 C pmpaul@ysu.edu
PAUL, Rebecca .... 863-680-4735.. 99 H rpaul@flsouthern.edu
PAUL, Robert, H .... 314-516-8403 261 D paulro@umsl.edu
PAUL, Theresa .... 828-227-3812 344 A tcpaul@wcu.edu
PAUL, Tonya, D .... 419-772-3106 358 H t-paul@onu.edu
PAUL, Tracey .... 601-977-7819 249 C tpaul@tougaloo.edu
PAULE, Romeo .... 415-949-7308.. 43 D pauleromeo@foothill.edu
PAULE, Sara .... 765-983-1431 154 G paulesa@earlham.edu
PAULETTO, Catherine .... 805-969-3626.. 55 E cpauletto@pacifica.edu
PAULEY, Ann .... 202-884-9725.. 93 B pauleya@trinitydc.edu
PAULEY, Melissa .... 615-353-3367 425 D melissa.pauley@nscc.edu
PAULEY, Stacy .... 757-569-6790 475 E spauley@pdc.edu
PAULI, Crystal .... 605-256-5177 416 J crystal.pauli@dsu.edu
PAULICK, Adam .... 907-786-4754.... 9 H apaulick@alaska.edu
PAULICK, Joe .... 305-348-4196 109 A joseph.paulick@fiu.edu
PAULINE, Rose Lee ...... 215-951-1014 387 C pauline@lasalle.edu
PAULINO, Avianny .... 787-761-0640 512 F promocion@utcpr.edu
PAULNACK, Karl .... 607-274-3343 303 B kpaulnack@ithaca.edu
PAULOSKI, SP, Pam ..... 773-371-5420 133 E presoffice@ctu.edu
PAULSEN, Heather .... 907-786-1663.... 9 H hpaulsen@alaska.edu
PAULSEN, Jenny .... 813-974-8944 110 B jpaulsen@usf.edu
PAULSEN, Josh .... 972-248-9000.. 26 F jpaulsen@asher.edu
PAULSEN, Mike .... 503-253-3443 374 H mike.paulsen@ocom.edu
PAULSON, Cheri .... 781-239-3845 205 E cpaulson@babson.edu
PAULSON, Dennis, J .... 630-515-7352 143 G dpauls@midwestern.edu
PAULSON, Erik .... 914-323-5412 305 J erik.paulson@mville.edu
PAULSON, Ken, A .... 615-898-2195 422 H ken.paulson@mtsu.edu
PAULSON, Robert .... 361-593-5002 447 D robert.paulson@tamuk.edu
PAULSON, Veronica .... 605-626-2537 417 A veronica.paulson@northern.edu
PAULUS, Bill .... 612-624-6837 243 E paulu038@umn.edu
PAULUS, Michael .... 206-281-2414 484 D paulusm@spu.edu
PAULUS, Michael, L ..... 419-372-2891 348 H mpaulus@bgsu.edu
PAULY, Karen .... 704-330-6976 333 D karen.pauly@cpcc.edu
PAUSTENBAUGH, Jennifer .... 801-422-4301 458 H jennifer_paustenbaugh@byu.edu
PAUSTIAN, Kevin .... 563-884-5721 168 I kevin.paustian@palmer.edu
PAUSTIAN, Pamela, E ... 205-975-9376.... 8 A paustian@uab.edu
PAUSTIAN, Tony .... 515-633-2439 164 C adpaustian@dmacc.edu
PAVALKO, Eliza .... 812-855-9973 156 B vpfaa@indiana.edu
PAVAN, Ron .... 615-547-1348 419 F rpavan@cumberland.edu
PAVAN, Tammi .... 615-547-1228 419 F tpavan@cumberland.edu
PAVEK, Annette .... 320-762-4411 237 B annettep@alextech.edu
PAVELL, Cynthia .... 310-506-6023.. 56 C cynthia.pavell@pepperdine.edu
PAVIA, Keyla .... 973-803-5000 280 C kpavia@pillar.edu
PAVIK, Lisa .... 661-362-3692.. 38 H lisa.pavik@canyons.edu
PAVISIC, Suzana .... 718-862-7825 305 H spavisic01@manhattan.edu
PAVLAT, Penny .... 906-217-4099 221 O pavlatp@baycollege.edu
PAVLIK, Angie .... 440-943-7600 360 J apavlik@dioceseofclevleand.org
PAVLIK, Katrina .... 773-838-7544 134 F kpavlik@ccc.edu
PAVLIS, Tim .... 203-436-9358.. 89 D timothy.pavlis@yale.edu
PAVLONIS, Brigid .... 508-830-5012 213 B bpavlonis@maritime.edu
PAVLOU, Paul, A .... 713-743-3562 452 F papavlou@uh.edu
PAVLOW, Joseph .... 610-527-0200 397 I joseph.pavlow@rosemont.edu
PAVON, Tracie .... 515-961-1630 169 D tracie.pavon@simpson.edu
PAVONE, Cassandra .... 828-689-1196 331 A cpavone@mhu.edu
PAVONE, Marie .... 925-969-3300.. 46 H mpavone@jfku.edu
PAVRI, Shireen .... 562-985-4513.. 31 F shireen.pavri@csulb.edu
PAVY, Anna .... 270-789-5059 179 E ampavy@campbellsville.edu
PAVY, Edwin, C .... 270-789-5227 179 E ecpavy@campbellsville.edu
PAWELL, Liz .... 909-469-5202.. 74 I lpawell@westernu.edu
PAWLAK, Katherine .... 863-680-3964.. 99 H kpawlak@flsouthern.edu
PAWLAK, Katherine .... 863-680-4292.. 99 H kpawlak@flsouthern.edu
PAWLAK, Kurt .... 740-264-5591 352 H kpawlak@egcc.edu
PAWLIK, Amy .... 309-268-8249 137 I amy.munson-pawlik@heartland.edu
PAWLO - JOHNSTONE, Jennifer .... 410-337-6181 198 G jennifer.pawlojohnstone@goucher.edu
PAXSON, Christina, H .. 401-863-2234 404 E president@brown.edu
PAXSON, Sherrie .... 505-566-3490 288 A paxsons@sanjuancollege.edu
PAYANZO COTTON, Anna .... 856-222-9311 281 C ftietz@rcbc.edu
PAYAWAL, Pamela .... 323-860-0789.. 50 A
PAYDAR, Nassar, H ...... 317-274-4417 156 F paydar@iupui.edu
PAYDAR, Nasser .... 317-274-4417 156 A paydar@iupui.edu
PAYDAR, Nasser .... 317-274-4417 156 B chancllr@iupui.edu
PAYLO, Keith .... 412-392-3862 397 A kpaylo@pointpark.edu
PAYNE, Angela .... 601-481-1357 247 A apayne@meridiancc.edu
PAYNE, Brian, K .... 757-683-4757 469 G bpayne@odu.edu
PAYNE, Charles, M .... 973-353-1750 282 B charles.payne@rutgers.edu
PAYNE, Dalry, B .... 269-471-3100 221 B dalry@andrews.edu
PAYNE, Darnell .... 773-371-5442 133 E dpayne@ctu.edu
PAYNE, David .... 801-734-6789 459 L david.payne@rm.edu
PAYNE, Dena .... 270-852-3256 183 A dnewcom@kwc.edu
PAYNE, Donna, G .... 585-275-2758 323 J
PAYNE, Donna, G .... 252-328-6940 341 C payned@ecu.edu
PAYNE, George, M .... 240-567-2582 200 C george.payne@montgomerycollege.edu
PAYNE, Gloria, E .... 252-335-3595 341 D gepayne@ecsu.edu
PAYNE, JR., Harry, E .... 813-988-5131.. 98 Q president@floridacollege.edu
PAYNE, Harvey .... 703-416-1441 466 F hpayne@divinemercy.edu
PAYNE, Heather .... 954-492-5353.. 96 H hpayne@citycollege.edu
PAYNE, Jack, M .... 352-392-1971 109 F jackpayne@ufl.edu
PAYNE, James .... 256-306-2684.... 1 F james.payne@calhoun.edu
PAYNE, James, E .... 915-747-7781 455 C jpayne2@utep.edu
PAYNE, Janet .... 570-321-4151 389 E payne@lycoming.edu
PAYNE, John, F .... 671-735-5565 505 C john.payne2@guamcc.edu
PAYNE, Karen, E .... 937-529-2201 362 A kepayne@united.edu
PAYNE, Kathryn .... 215-951-1941 387 C paynek@lasalle.edu
PAYNE, Kathy, O .... 904-819-6305.. 98 E kpayne@flagler.edu
PAYNE, Kent .... 847-214-7552 136 F kpayne@elgin.edu
PAYNE, Leslie, M .... 210-567-2503 456 C paynelm@uthscsa.edu
PAYNE, Liesl .... 580-387-7234 366 H lpayne@mscok.edu
PAYNE, Maggie .... 701-349-5798 346 J mpayne@trinitybiblecollege.edu
PAYNE, Maribeth .... 573-840-9007 260 I mpayne@trcc.edu
PAYNE, Mary .... 515-271-1452 164 I mary.payne@dmu.edu
PAYNE, Matthew .... 701-349-5415 346 J mattpayne@trinitybiblecollege.edu
PAYNE, Melissa .... 319-398-5584 167 C melissa.payne@kirkwood.edu
PAYNE, Molly .... 617-732-2218 216 B molly.payne@mcphs.edu
PAYNE, Nikita, T .... 334-293-4603.... 1 C nikita.payne@accs.edu
PAYNE, Nikki .... 314-529-6864 254 H npayne@maryville.edu
PAYNE, Paige .... 406-447-6927 264 C paige.payne@helenacollege.edu
PAYNE, Pamela .... 915-831-6511 436 E ppayne1@epcc.edu
PAYNE, Ramona .... 831-755-6752.. 44 K rpayne@hartnell.edu
PAYNE, Rich .... 928-523-7618.. 14 H rich.payne@nau.edu
PAYNE, Sherri .... 702-651-3577 271 A sherri.payne@csn.edu
PAYNE, Stephen, C .... 202-319-5139.. 91 B paynesl@cua.edu
PAYNE, Stephen, D .... 269-471-6534 221 B stephen@andrews.edu
PAYNE, Tamara .... 205-853-1200.... 2 G tlpayne@jeffersonstate.edu
PAYNE, Tara .... 603-513-1356 274 H tara.payne@granite.edu
PAYNE, Thomas .... 931-372-3372 426 E tpayne@tntech.edu
PAYNE, Trent, D .... 864-379-8725 409 H payne@erskine.edu
PAYNE, Vernon .... 269-387-2136 232 K vernon.payne@wmich.edu
PAYNE, Wesley, A .... 573-840-9698 260 I wpayne@trcc.edu
PAYNE, William .... 775-784-6604 271 F bpayne@cabnr.unr.edu
PAYNE CERVERA, Brandi .... 307-778-1218 502 D bcervera@lccc.wy.edu
PAYNTER, Charles .... 727-376-6911 111 G buddy.paynter@trinitycollege.edu
PAYNTER, Chris .... 704-330-6531 333 D chris.paynter@cpcc.edu
PAYOVICH, Nathan .... 708-974-5330 144 C payovichn@morainevalley.edu
PAYTON, Annie .... 256-372-4747.... 1 A annie.payton@aamu.edu
PAYTON, Christine .... 337-521-8936 188 C christine.payton@solacc.edu
PAYTON, Karl .... 903-233-3142 439 E karlpayton@letu.edu
PAYTON, Kizzy .... 225-216-8404 186 K paytonk2@mybrcc.edu
PAZ, Alma .... 213-738-6705.. 65 G registrar@swlaw.edu
PAZ, Gabriel .... 717-867-6302 388 H paz@lvc.edu
PAZ, Harold, L .... 614-292-6446 358 I paz.31@osu.edu
PEABODY, William .... 845-437-7267 324 C wipeabody@vassar.edu
PEACE, Derryle .... 903-886-5764 447 B derryle.peace@tamuc.edu
PEACE, Donald .... 864-231-2000 406 G dpeace@andersonuniversity.edu
PEACH, Kyle .... 618-262-8641 139 A peachk@iecc.edu
PEACHEY, Bethany .... 740-857-1311 360 I bpeachey@rosedale.edu
PEACOCK, Caleb .... 423-478-7703 423 G cpeacock@ptseminary.edu
PEACOCK, Kyle .... 402-941-6509 267 L peacock@midlandu.edu
PEACOCK, Ross .... 440-775-6927 358 C ross.peacock@oberlin.edu
PEACOCK, Steve .... 612-330-1583 233 K peacock@augsburg.edu
PEACOCK-LANDRUM, Linda, G .... 920-465-2163 496 E peacockl@uwgb.edu
PEADEN, Theresa, R ..... 252-451-8233 336 E trpeaden297@nashcc.edu
PEAK, Douglas, C .... 817-515-3076 445 G douglas.peak@tccd.edu
PEARCE, Arthur, B .... 229-333-5832 126 G apearce@valdosta.edu

PEARCE, Chris ... 336-734-7570 334 E
cpearce@forsythech.edu
PEARCE, Jared ... 641-673-2107 170 F
pearcej@wmpenn.edu
PEARCE, Jennifer ... 276-944-6968 467 G
jpearce@ehc.edu
PEARCE, Julie, L ... 818-677-2366.. 32 D
julie.pearce@csun.edu
PEARCE, Katheryn, P ... 386-822-7459 111 A
kpearce@stetson.edu
PEARCE, Kelley, H ... 256-549-8376.... 2 B
khaynes@gadsdenstate.edu
PEARCE, Leah ... 206-546-4714 484 G
lpearce@shoreline.edu
PEARCE, Rick ... 309-268-8100 137 I
rick.pearce@heartland.edu
PEARCE, Steve ... 770-229-3293 124 G
steve.pearce@sctech.edu
PEARCY, Shelly ... 231-591-3825 223 J
shellypearcy@ferris.edu
PEARIGEN, Rob ... 601-974-1001 247 B
rob.pearigen@millsaps.edu
PEARISON, Brian ... 574-936-8898 153 A
brian.pearison@ancilla.edu
PEARL, Danita ... 937-708-5704 364 D
dpearl@wilberforce.edu
PEARL, Samantha ... 269-749-7192 229 H
spearl@olivetcollege.edu
PEARLE, Kathleen ... 508-678-2811 213 G
kathleen.pearle@bristolcc.edu
PEARLMUTTER, Roberta, S ... 401-456-8043 405 C
rpearlmutter@ric.edu
PEARON, Jill, R ... 315-267-2108 319 D
pearonjr@potsdam.edu
PEARRING, Yu Yok ... 808-932-8912 128 E
yuyok@hawaii.edu
PEARSALL, Joel, K ... 208-467-8521 131 D
president@nnu.edu
PEARSALL, Jonathan ... 617-824-8426 208 H
jonathan_pearsall@emerson.edu
PEARSALL, Kim ... 863-297-1000 105 A
kpearsall@polk.edu
PEARSALL, Roland ... 617-236-8879 209 D
rpearsall@fisher.edu
PEARSEY, Lindsey ... 812-855-3870 156 A
lpearsey@iu.edu
PEARSON, Aimee ... 716-829-7803 298 F
pearsona@dyc.edu
PEARSON, Andrew, L ... 540-828-5410 465 D
apearson@bridgewater.edu
PEARSON, Annie ... 405-422-1486 369 E
annie.pearson@redlandscc.edu
PEARSON, Barry ... 914-251-6020 319 E
barry.pearson@purchase.edu
PEARSON, Bryan, J ... 814-886-6424 391 B
bpearson@mtaloy.edu
PEARSON, Craig ... 641-472-1186 167 F
cpearson@mum.edu
PEARSON, David ... 951-343-4298.. 27 J
dpearson@calbaptist.edu
PEARSON, David, L ... 515-574-1234 166 E
pearson@iowacentral.edu
PEARSON, Dawn ... 507-389-7219 241 C
dawn.pearson@southcentral.edu
PEARSON, Doug, R ... 478-301-2685 121 E
pearson_dr@mercer.edu
PEARSON, Elaine, M ... 757-683-3808 469 G
empearso@odu.edu
PEARSON, Janice, L ... 559-323-2100.. 60 I
jpearson@sjcl.edu
PEARSON, John ... 412-392-3976 397 A
jpearson@pointpark.edu
PEARSON, Karen, L ... 208-467-8663 131 D
klpearson@nnu.edu
PEARSON, Kayla ... 785-833-4303 175 B
kayla.pearson@kwu.edu
PEARSON, Mary ... 435-865-8270 460 F
pearsonm@suu.edu
PEARSON, Matt ... 707-778-3608.. 62 F
mpearson@santarosa.edu
PEARSON, Sam ... 503-589-8154 373 A
spearson@corban.edu
PEARSON, Sandy ... 415-485-3297.. 41 H
sandy.pearson@dominican.edu
PEARSON, Sarah, R ... 207-786-6247 193 B
spearson@bates.edu
PEARSON, Sonya ... 702-651-7980 271 A
sonya.pearson@csn.edu
PEARSON, Stacy ... 509-335-5524 486 A
stacy.pearson@wsu.edu
PEARSON, Steven, A ... 803-535-5434 407 G
spearson@claflin.edu
PEARSON, Terri ... 580-477-2000 371 F
PEARSON, Theodore ... 812-749-1404 159 C
tpearson@oak.edu
PEARSON, Tracey ... 910-630-7122 331 C
tpearson@methodist.edu
PEARSON, Vonda ... 651-255-6115 243 D
vpearson@unitedseminary.edu
PEARSON-WHARTON, Stacey ... 570-372-4238 399 C
pearsonwharton@susqu.edu
PEART, Emily, N ... 530-898-6897.. 31 A
epeart@csuchico.edu
PEART, Sandra, J ... 804-287-6086 472 L
speart@richmond.edu
PEASE, Patrick, P ... 319-273-2518 163 B
patrick.pease@uni.edu
PEASLEE, Deidra ... 651-846-1335 241 B
deidra.peaslee@saintpaul.edu
PEASTER, Carl, S ... 615-898-2424 422 H
buddy.peaster@mtsu.edu
PEASTER, Rita ... 405-744-5000 368 B
PEAT, Kareem ... 718-817-3112 300 E
kpeat@fordham.edu
PEAVEY, Donna, B ... 504-282-4455 190 A
dpeavey@nobts.edu
PEAVY, Kristi ... 478-757-5200 126 H
kpeavy@wesleyancollege.edu
PEAVY, Liesa ... 770-216-2960 120 H
lpeavy@ict.edu
PEAVY, Terence ... 212-217-3801 299 H
terence_peavy@fitnyc.edu
PEAVYHOUSE, Myra ... 865-354-3000 425 G
peavyhousem@roanestate.edu
PEAY, J. H. Binford ... 540-464-7311 476 G
peayjb@vmi.edu
PECCHIA, John, P ... 845-575-3000 305 L
john.pecchia@marist.edu
PECENY, Mark ... 505-277-7381 288 G
markpec@unm.edu
PECHA, David, M ... 580-327-8528 367 E
dmpecha@nwosu.edu
PECHAN, Gwen ... 904-819-6359.. 98 E
gpechan@flagler.edu
PECK, Adam ... 936-468-7249 445 F
peckae@sfasu.edu
PECK, Barbara ... 864-379-6546 409 H
peck@erskine.edu
PECK, Daniel, A ... 408-855-5122.. 74 D
daniel.peck@wvm.edu
PECK, David ... 626-815-4503.. 26 H
dpeck@apu.edu
PECK, Edward ... 216-397-4218 354 I
epeck@jcu.edu
PECK, Emily ... 270-534-3244 182 F
emily.peck@kctcs.edu
PECK, Hannah ... 270-384-8170 183 C
peckh@lindsey.edu
PECK, Jane ... 781-768-7307 218 C
jane.peck@regiscollege.edu
PECK, Jeanie ... 651-641-8709 235 F
peck@csp.edu
PECK, Jim ... 810-237-6570 231 G
peckjim@umich.edu
PECK, Kim ... 806-743-2297 451 C
kim.peck@ttuhsc.edu
PECK, Rebecca ... 816-936-8713 259 I
rpeck@saintlukescollege.edu
PECK, Susan ... 252-335-0821 333 G
susan_peck@albemarle.edu
PECKA, Kenneth ... 509-777-3292 486 I
kpecka@whitworth.edu
PECKHAM, Karissa ... 860-832-3000.. 84 I
kpeckham@ccsu.edu
PECKHAM, Michael ... 920-403-3360 495 I
mike.peckham@snc.edu
PECKLER, Dawn ... 815-836-5230 141 G
peckleda@lewisu.edu
PECOR, Sarah, A ... 262-243-5700 493 B
sarah.pecor@cuw.edu
PECORARO, Heather ... 508-791-9241 206 B
heather.pecoraro@becker.edu
PECORARO, Heather ... 508-767-7355 205 D
hl.pecoraro@assumption.edu
PECORD, Melanie ... 618-985-2828 139 I
melaniepecord@jalc.edu
PECTOL, James, B ... 423-585-6823 426 C
james.pectol@ws.edu
PEDE, Michael ... 315-792-5411 307 D
mpede@mvcc.edu
PEDE, Mike ... 713-743-9551 452 F
mlpede@uh.edu
PEDEN, Gary, S ... 315-470-6588 320 A
gspeden@esf.edu
PEDERSEN, Cindi, M ... 574-807-7239 153 E
cindi.pedersen@bethelunivesity.edu
PEDERSEN, Eric ... 360-867-6310 481 A
pedersee@evergreen.edu
PEDERSEN, Eric ... 435-652-7977 460 G
pedersen@dixie.edu
PEDERSEN, Ginger, L ... 561-967-7222 104 D
pederseg@palmbeachstate.edu
PEDERSEN, Jeffrey, M ... 631-451-4425 321 F
pedersj@sunysuffolk.edu
PEDERSEN, Jennifer, L ... 308-635-6078 270 D
pedersen@wncc.edu
PEDERSEN, Jon, E ... 803-777-3075 413 C
pedersje@mailbox.sc.edu
PEDERSEN, Karen, L ... 785-532-3110 174 G
karenpedersen@ksu.edu
PEDERSEN, Mary ... 805-756-2186.. 30 C
mpederse@calpoly.edu
PEDERSEN, Matthew, D ... 801-863-8320 461 A
mpedersen@uvu.edu
PEDERSEN, Melissa ... 617-217-9036 206 A
mpedersen@baystate.edu
PEDERSEN, Patricia, E ... 203-436-8518.. 89 D
patty.pedersen@yale.edu
PEDERSEN, Paula ... 218-726-7860 243 F
ppederse@d.umn.edu
PEDERSEN, Ryan ... 925-473-7404.. 40 J
rpedersen@losmedanos.edu
PEDERSON, Curtis, R ... 503-943-8046 377 E
pedersoc@up.edu
PEDERSON, Joshua ... 507-344-7840 234 B
jpederson@blc.edu
PEDERSON, Kathy ... 507-457-1586 243 B
kpeders@smumn.edu
PEDERSON, Katie ... 303-762-6995.. 79 H
katie.pederson@denverseminary.edu
PEDERSON, Mark ... 765-677-2117 157 D
mark.pederson@indwes.edu
PEDERSON, Paula ... 218-736-1559 239 B
paula.pederson@minnesota.edu
PEDESCLEAUX, Desiree ... 404-270-5696 125 B
dpedescl@spelman.edu
PEDNEAU, Judy ... 276-326-4461 465 B
jpedneau@bluefield.edu
PEDONE, Melissa, D ... 407-582-4176 112 K
mpedone@valenciacollege.edu
PEDRAJA, Luis ... 508-854-4203 215 D
lpedraja@qcc.mass.edu
PEDRAZA, Jonathan, N ... 262-691-5308 500 H
jpedraza2@wctc.edu
PEDRAZA, Mary Ann ... 409-772-9867 456 F
mspedraz@utmb.edu
PEDRICK, Jim ... 319-385-6218 167 A
jim.pedrick@iw.edu
PEDRICK, Laura ... 414-229-3203 497 A
lpedrick@uwm.edu
PEDRO, David ... 508-910-9070 211 F
dpedro@umassd.edu
PEDRONE, Dino, J ... 607-729-1581 298 C
dpedrone@davisny.edu
PEDROTTY, Kate ... 318-869-5715 186 B
kpedrotty@centenary.edu
PEE, Charles, M ... 803-934-3294 411 C
cpee@morris.edu
PEEBLES, Catherine, M ... 603-862-3638 274 G
catherine.peebles@unh.edu
PEEBLES, Lee ... 401-739-5000 405 A
lpeebles@neit.edu
PEED, Stephen ... 207-326-2451 195 D
stephen.peed@mma.edu
PEEK, Jessica ... 815-740-2274 151 J
jpeek@stfrancis.edu
PEEK, Katherine ... 909-652-6333.. 36 A
kay.peek@chaffey.edu
PEEK, Patricia ... 718-817-1000 300 E
peek@fordham.edu
PEEL, Bill ... 214-932-1112 439 E
billpeel@letu.edu
PEEL, Chermae ... 432-552-3744 457 A
peel_c@utpb.edu
PEEL, Henry ... 239-489-9011 100 A
hpeel@fsw.edu
PEEL, Joe ... 318-257-3267 191 F
jpeel@latech.edu
PEELER, Chris ... 704-461-6684 327 A
chrispeeler@bac.edu
PEELER, Jody ... 740-284-5216 353 B
jpeeler@franciscan.edu
PEELER, Mark, L ... 864-379-8850 409 H
mlp@erskine.edu
PEELING, Rebecca ... 561-803-2024 104 C
becky_peeling@pba.edu
PEEPLES, Jim ... 706-778-8500 123 B
jpeeples@piedmont.edu
PEEPLES, Junelyn ... 909-607-3884.. 63 E
jpeeples@scrippscollege.edu
PEEPLES, Terry, G ... 870-245-5169.. 20 E
peeplest@obu.edu
PEEPLES, Tim ... 336-278-5613 328 K
peeples@elon.edu
PEET, Palmer ... 510-780-4500.. 47 J
ppeet@lifewest.edu
PEETERS, Andrea ... 650-543-3735.. 51 F
andrea.peeters@menlo.edu
PEETZ, Ralf ... 718-982-2440 293 E
ralf.peetz@csi.cuny.edu
PEEVY, Andrea ... 985-549-2241 192 D
apeevy@selu.edu
PEFFER, Deb ... 313-593-5100 231 F
dkpeffer@umich.edu
PEFFER, Tony ... 218-755-2015 237 E
tony.peffer@bemidjistate.edu
PEGAH, Kris ... 941-351-7220 105 K
kpegah@ringling.edu
PEGAH, Mahmoud ... 941-359-7633 105 K
mpegah@ringling.edu
PEGG, Steven, M ... 410-777-2651 197 C
smpegg@aacc.edu
PEGRAM, Mike ... 402-761-8270 269 C
mpegram@southeast.edu
PEGUES, Charlotte Fant 662-915-7792 249 D
cfant@olemiss.edu
PEGUES, Patricia ... 662-252-8000 248 G
ppegues@rustcollege.edu
PEGUES, Patricia ... 662-252-2491 248 G
ppegues@rustcollege.edu
PEHLMAN, Patricia, A ... 717-245-1545 382 F
pehlman@dickinson.edu
PEHRSSON, Dale-Elizabeth ... 814-393-2220 394 D
president@clarion.edu
PEI, Alissa ... 573-876-7212 260 F
apei@stephens.edu
PEIFER, Michelle ... 704-991-0393 338 C
mpeifer7924@stanly.edu
PEIFFER, Cyndi ... 641-673-1040 170 F
peifferc@wmpenn.edu
PEIFFER, Mark ... 515-271-1475 164 I
mark.peiffer@dmu.edu
PEIPERL, Maury ... 703-993-1860 467 L
mpeiperl@gmu.edu
PEKINS, Mary ... 847-214-7414 136 F
mperkins@elgin.edu
PEKRUL, William, A ... 507-354-8221 236 I
pekrulwa@mlc-wels.edu
PELAEZ, Indra ... 713-718-7497 437 I
indra.pelaez@hccs.edu
PELAEZ, Michelle ... 813-253-6251 112 J
mpelaez@ut.edu
PELAZZA, Todd, A ... 203-254-4090.. 86 I
tapelazza@fairfield.edu
PELC, Sharon ... 308-865-8523 269 I
pelcs@unk.edu
PELESKO, John ... 302-831-7215.. 90 F
pelesko@udel.edu
PELHAM, Stephanie ... 973-408-3961 277 C
spelham@drew.edu
PELHAM, Steve ... 334-844-4000.... 4 E
PELIZZA, John ... 518-244-2051 313 D
pelizj@sage.edu
PELKEY, David ... 360-596-5231 485 B
dpelkey@spscc.edu
PELL, Laura ... 828-898-8828 330 E
pelll@lmc.edu
PELLAND, Melissa, K ... 651-962-6107 244 E
pell5790@stthomas.edu
PELLEGRIN, Angie ... 985-448-7943 187 F
angie.pellegrin@fletcher.edu
PELLEGRIN, Nathan ... 510-466-7210.. 56 H
npellegrin@peralta.edu
PELLEGRINI, Larry ... 570-674-6307 390 G
lpellegrini@misericordia.edu
PELLEGRINI, Virginia ... 208-426-3158 129 I
virginiapellegrini@boisestate.edu
PELLEGRINO, Debra, A ... 570-941-6305 401 H
debra.pellegrino@scranton.edu
PELLEGRINO, Karen ... 610-660-1305 398 C
kpellegr@sju.edu
PELLEGRINO, Robin ... 508-767-7599 205 D
rpellegr@assumption.edu
PELLEGRINO-YOKITIS, Maria ... 904-256-7928 101 G
mpelleg@ju.edu
PELLERIN, Angela ... 318-797-5219 189 D
angela.pellerin@lsus.edu

PELLERIN, Jody ... 319-398-5409 167 C
jody.pellerin@kirkwood.edu
PELLERIN, Virginia ... 504-520-7229 193 A
vpelleri@xula.edu
PELLETIER, Christopher 413-265-2204 208 C
pelletierc@elms.edu
PELLETIER, Corey ... 207-859-1106 195 G
pelletierc@thomas.edu
PELLETIER, Debra ... 207-834-7844 196 C
debra.pelletier@maine.edu
PELLETIER, Jo-Ann, M .. 508-678-2811 213 G
jo-ann.pelletier@bristolcc.edu
PELLICANO, Gregory, J 215-898-7958 400 K
gpell@upenn.edu
PELLINEN, Brian ... 978-921-4242 216 F
brian.pellinen@montserrat.edu
PELLISH, Cathy ... 303-404-5535.. 79 J
cathy.pellish@frontrange.edu
PELLOT, Robert ... 212-938-5720 320 B
rpellot@sunyopt.edu
PELLS, Ruth ... 509-777-4665 486 I
rpells@whitworth.edu
PELLY, Michael ... 714-997-6982.. 36 C
pelly@chapman.edu
PELMAN, Javonda ... 815-588-7541 141 G
pelmanja@lewisu.edu
PELOQUIN, Andy ... 503-517-1815 378 A
apeloquin@westernseminary.edu
PELOQUIN, Elayne ... 434-544-8230 472 G
peloquin_em@lynchburg.edu
PELOQUIN-DODD,
Mary ... 919-515-2155 342 B
mtpeloqu@ncsu.edu
PELOQUIN-DODD,
Mary, T ... 919-515-2143 342 B
mary_peloquin-dodd@ncsu.edu
PELOSI, Lisa ... 401-598-1000 404 I
lpelosi@jwu.edu
PELOSO, Elizabeth, D ... 215-746-0234 400 K
epeloso@upenn.edu
PELRINE, Edward ... 847-970-4961 152 A
epelrine@usml.edu
PELRINE, John ... 312-369-7045 135 E
jpelrine@colum.edu
PELTIER, Beverly ... 706-771-4023 114 J
bpeltier@augustatech.edu
PELTIER, Eileen ... 860-253-3032.. 85 C
epeltier@asnuntuck.edu
PELTIER, Eileen ... 860-253-3032.. 86 G
epeltier@acc.commnet.edu
PELTIER, John ... 401-874-4530 406 B
jbpeltier@uri.edu
PELTIER, Linda, M ... 937-778-7802 352 J
lpeltier@edisonohio.edu
PELTIER, Matthew, S ... 423-652-4740 420 H
mspeltie@king.edu
PELTO, Mauri, S ... 508-213-2201 217 E
mauri.pelto@nichols.edu
PELTON, Jeremy ... 502-897-4200 184 C
jpelton@sbts.edu
PELTON, M. Lee ... 617-824-8525 208 H
lee_pelton@emerson.edu
PELTON, Mark ... 478-445-5075 118 C
mark.pelton@gcsu.edu
PELTON, Vanessa ... 805-965-0581.. 62 C
pelton@sbcc.edu
PELTON, Woody ... 336-278-6700 328 K
wpelton@elon.edu
PELTS, Dody ... 479-979-1422.. 23 I
dpelts@ozarks.edu
PELTZ, Mark ... 641-269-4940 165 J
peltzm@grinnell.edu
PELUSO, Constance ... 718-631-6297 295 D
cpeluso@qcc.cuny.edu
PELUSO, Eileen ... 570-321-4135 389 E
pelusoem@lycoming.edu
PELUSO-VERDEND,
Gary ... 918-270-6405 369 A
gary.peluso@ptstulsa.edu
PELUSZAK, Kris ... 215-503-1956 400 A
kris.peluszak@jefferson.edu
PELZIER-GLAZE,
Bernnell ... 713-313-7496 449 C
glazedm@tsu.edu
PEMBER, Rhonda ... 419-289-5604 348 A
rpember@ashland.edu
PEMBERTON, Barbara ... 870-245-5541.. 20 E
pembertonb@obu.edu
PEMBERTON,
Cynthia, L ... 208-792-2216 131 A
clpemberton@lcsc.edu
PEMBERTON,
Cynthia, L ... 816-235-1107 261 C
pembertonc@umkc.edu
PEMBERTON, Paul ... 218-935-0417 244 G
paul.pemberton@wetcc.edu
PEMBROOK, Randall, G 618-650-2475 149 F
rpembro@siue.edu
PEMSTEIN, Debra ... 845-758-7405 290 G
pemstein@bard.edu
PENA, Amy ... 210-486-1209 429 H
apena259@alamo.edu
PENA, Amy, E ... 505-747-2140 287 G
amy.pena@nnmc.edu
PENA, Andrew, M ... 915-831-6325 436 E
apena20@epcc.edu
PENA, Damien, A ... 805-289-6113.. 73 B
dpena@vcccd.edu
PENA, Daniel ... 517-264-7146 230 E
dpena@sienaheights.edu
PENA, Hector ... 787-725-6500 506 G
hpena@albizu.edu
PENA, Jesus ... 610-683-4700 395 A
pena@kutztown.edu
PENA, Juanita ... 719-549-2943.. 79 A
juanita.pena@csupueblo.edu
PENA, Maria ... 425-388-9979 480 G
mpena@everettcc.edu
PENA, Michelle ... 661-395-4318.. 46 L
michelle.pena@bakersfieldcollege.edu
PENA, Milagros ... 951-827-2762.. 69 C
milagros.pena@ucr.edu
PENA, Zulma ... 787-780-0070 506 F
zpena@caribbean.edu
PENA RIVERA, Norma .. 787-764-0000 514 B
norma.pena1@upr.edu
PENALBA, Richelle ... 714-432-5869.. 38 E
rpenalba@occ.cccd.edu
PENALOZA, Carlos, G ... 816-936-8700 259 I
cpenaloza@saintlukescollege.edu
PENCE, Bill ... 540-868-7061 474 J
bpence@lfcc.edu
PENCE, Dena ... 765-361-6434 162 E
pencen@wabash.edu
PENCHI, Zulma ... 787-257-0000 513 C
zulma.penchi@upr.edu
PENDAKUR, Vijay ... 607-255-1115 297 F
dean_of_students@cornell.edu
PENDERGAST, Jayme ... 770-426-2858 121 C
jayme.pendergast@life.edu
PENDERGAST, Kate ... 860-768-2403.. 88 H
pendergas@hartford.edu
PENDERGAST, Marcy ... 518-629-7230 302 E
m.pendergast@hvcc.edu
PENDERGRASS, Martha 919-843-5048 342 D
mjpender@email.unc.edu
PENDERGRASS, Toni ... 505-566-3209 288 A
pendergrasst@sancollege.edu
PENDERS, Brooke ... 860-768-4287.. 88 H
penders@hartford.edu
PENDHARKAR, Daya ... 813-253-7091 101 A
dpendharkar@hccfl.edu
PENDLETON, Arthur ... 270-707-3904 181 E
arthur.pendleton@kctcs.edu
PENDLETON,
Christopher ... 540-261-8400 471 H
chris.pendleton@svu.edu
PENDLETON, Gail ... 510-981-2804.. 56 E
gpendleton@peralta.edu
PENDLETON, Kent ... 907-852-3333.... 9 F
kent.pendleton@ilisagvik.edu
PENDLETON, Laura ... 509-452-5100 483 A
lpendleton@pnwu.edu
PENDLETON, Laurence .. 615-963-7925 426 D
laurence.pendleton@tnstate.edu
PENDSE, Ravi ... 734-763-7590 231 E
rpendse@umich.edu
PENFIELD, Randall, D ... 336-334-3944 343 A
rdpenfie@uncg.edu
PENG, Hsin (Gina) ... 310-233-4356.. 49 A
penghw@lahc.edu
PENG, Willie ... 657-278-2866.. 31 E
wpeng@fullerton.edu
PENGRA, Matt ... 407-679-0100 100 K
mpengra@fullsail.com
PENICK, William ... 951-785-2100.. 47 C
wpenick@lasierra.edu
PENISTEN, Douglas ... 918-444-4000 367 A
penisten@nsuok.edu
PENIX, Doug ... 859-442-1634 181 B
doug.penix@kctcs.edu
PENIX, Kristine ... 501-882-3600.. 17 F
kapenix@asub.edu
PENKALA, Robert ... 586-445-7636 226 H
penkalar@macomb.edu
PENKE, Ann, K ... 920-565-1038 493 J
penkea@lakeland.edu
PENLAND, Nathan ... 417-328-1828 259 L
npenland@sbuniv.edu
PENLEY, Julie ... 915-731-6715 436 E
jpenley@epcc.edu
PENLEY, Rashelle ... 828-726-2488 332 G
rpenley@cccti.edu
PENN, Ann ... 919-530-6681 342 A
aepenn@nccu.edu
PENN, Courtney ... 540-375-2270 471 B
penn@roanoke.edu
PENN, Mark, A ... 702-802-2837 272 C
mpenn@roseman.edu
PENN-HARGROVE,
Valencia ... 773-256-3000 143 C
vpennhargrove@meadville.edu
PENN-MARSHALL,
Michelle ... 757-637-2690 468 B
michelle.pennmarshall@hamptonu.edu
PENN-MARSHALL,
Michelle ... 757-727-5267 468 B
michelle.penn-marshall@hamptonu.edu
PENNA, Anthony ... 617-552-3475 207 B
anthony.penna@bc.edu
PENNARTZ-BROWNING,
Kathy ... 940-397-4214 440 F
kathy.pennartz@msutexas.edu
PENNER, Julie ... 815-836-5667 141 G
pennerju@lewisu.edu
PENNEY, Bill ... 352-395-5160 107 A
bill.penney@sfcollege.edu
PENNEY, Kathleen ... 334-833-4062.... 5 H
kpenney@hawks.huntingdon.edu
PENNEY, Samantha ... 812-237-8479 155 G
samantha.penney@indstate.edu
PENNIMAN, Sarah ... 717-361-1428 383 E
pennimans@etown.edu
PENNINGS, Rhonda, R . 712-324-5061 168 G
rpennings@nwicc.edu
PENNINGTON, Amy ... 479-968-0407.. 18 C
apennington@atu.edu
PENNINGTON,
Glenda, J ... 304-865-6141 488 E
jo.pennington@ovu.edu
PENNINGTON, Karen, L 973-655-4311 279 C
penningtonk@mail.montclair.edu
PENNINGTON, Kevin ... 252-399-6467 326 M
knpennington@barton.edu
PENNINGTON,
Kimberly ... 828-328-7473 330 F
kimberly.pennington@lr.edu
PENNINGTON, Laura ... 276-739-2538 476 C
lpennington@vhcc.edu
PENNINGTON, Laurie ... 928-428-8231.. 12 E
laurie.pennington@eac.edu
PENNINGTON, Michael . 973-290-4266 277 A
mpennington@cse.edu
PENNINGTON, Nicole ... 740-593-2551 359 G
penningj@ohio.edu
PENNINGTON, Nicole ... 740-533-4610 359 G
penningj@ohio.edu
PENNINGTON, Sandra .. 801-375-5125 459 L
sandy.pennington@rm.edu
PENNINGTON,
Sherry, R ... 417-667-8181 252 A
spennington@cottey.edu
PENNINGTON, Thomas . 479-964-0824.. 18 C
tpennington@atu.edu
PENNINI, Susan, W ... 617-333-2165 208 E
spennini@curry.edu
PENNIX, James, A ... 540-365-4290 467 I
jpennix@ferrum.edu
PENNY, Anthony ... 508-793-7389 208 A
apenny@clarku.edu
PENNY, Cameron ... 231-995-2825 228 G
cpenny@nmc.edu
PENNY, Rick ... 440-525-7320 355 H
rpenny@lakelandcc.edu
PENPRASE, Bryan, E ... 949-480-4184.. 64 B
bpenprase@soka.edu
PENROD, Donald ... 562-985-5091.. 31 F
don.penrod@csulb.edu
PENROSE, Betsy ... 607-587-4215 320 C
penrosb@alfredstate.edu
PENROSE, John ... 513-875-3344 350 G
john.penrose@chatfield.edu
PENROSE, Leif ... 813-253-7370 101 A
lpenrose@hccfl.edu
PENRY, Jason ... 870-972-2060.. 17 G
jpenry@astate.edu
PENRY, Michael, A ... 919-866-5532 338 G
mapenry@waketech.edu
PENSE, Christine ... 610-861-5312 391 F
cpense@northampton.edu
PENSGARD, Sara, E ... 540-338-1776 470 A
library@phc.edu
PENSIS, Claude ... 602-639-7500.. 12 J
PENSON, Amy, M ... 828-395-1296 335 D
apenson@isothermal.edu
PENTZ, Abby ... 608-663-2309 493 C
apentz@edgewood.edu
PENTZER, Scott ... 504-865-5339 191 B
cge@tulane.edu
PENUNURI, Christianne 619-660-4039.. 44 H
christianne.penunuri@gcccd.edu
PENYAK, Lee, M ... 269-387-5890 232 K
lee.penyak@wmich.edu
PENZENSTADLER, SSND,
Joan ... 414-930-3388 495 A
penzenj@mtmary.edu
PEOPLE, Yasha ... 732-247-5241 279 D
ypeople@nbts.edu
PEOPLES, Kevin ... 706-649-1821 117 A
kpeoples@columbustech.edu
PEOPLES, Shawn ... 217-581-3827 136 E
sdpeoples@eiu.edu
PEOPLES, VerJanis ... 225-771-2291 190 G
verjanis_peoples@subr.edu
PEOPLES, Verjanis ... 225-771-2291 190 H
verjanis_peoples@subr.edu
PEPIN, Mark ... 918-495-7236 368 I
mpepin@oru.edu
PEPITONE, Dianne ... 914-831-0367 297 A
dpepitone@cw.edu
PEPLOW, Nena ... 309-677-3223 133 B
nena@bradley.edu
PEPPEL, Sarah ... 610-917-1461 401 I
s_peppel@valleyforge.edu
PEPPER, Robert ... 717-796-1800 390 E
rpepper@messiah.edu
PEPPER, Robert ... 304-793-6597 491 A
rpepper@osteo.wvsom.edu
PEPPER, Russel ... 614-236-6632 349 D
rpepper@capital.edu
PEPPERS, Marla ... 323-343-3929.. 32 A
mpepper@calstatela.edu
PEPPERWORTH, Lisa ... 812-535-5284 160 B
lisa.pepperworth@smwc.edu
PEPPIN, Patricia ... 480-461-7456.. 13 D
pat.peppin@mesacc.edu
PEPPLE, Katharine, S ... 215-972-2015 393 D
kpepple@pafa.edu
PEPPLE, Michael ... 913-621-8740 172 K
mpepple@donnelly.edu
PERÉZ, Miguel ... 787-257-0000 513 C
miguel.perez8@upr.edu
PERALES, Jose, J ... 585-385-8464 314 A
jperales@sjfc.edu
PERALES, Michelle ... 210-485-0031 429 C
mperales4@alamo.edu
PERBELLINI, Maria ... 516-686-7641 309 F
maria.perbellini@nyit.edu
PERCELL, Shannon ... 253-833-9111 481 F
spercell@greenriver.edu
PERCIANTE, Linda, K ... 303-963-3237.. 77 G
lperciante@ccu.edu
PERCUOCO, Robert, E ... 563-884-5460 168 I
robert.percuoco@palmer.edu
PERCY, Kerri ... 954-776-4476 102 A
kpercy@keiseruniversity.edu
PERCY, Paul ... 865-471-3200 419 A
ppercy@cn.edu
PERCY, Stephen ... 503-725-4411 376 A
president@pdx.edu
PERDAN, Lauren, B ... 610-917-1402 401 I
lbgreen@valleyforge.edu
PERDEW, Kris ... 208-459-5062 130 D
kperdew@collegeofidaho.edu
PERDOMO, José, L ... 608-785-8000 513 F
PERDUE, K. Alan ... 304-876-5009 490 E
aperdue@shepherd.edu
PERDUE, Laura ... 318-797-5257 189 D
laura.perdue@lsus.edu
PERDUE, Mark ... 217-732-3155 141 I
mperdue@lincolncollege.edu
PERDUE, Penny ... 708-534-4130 137 F
pperdue@govst.edu
PERDUE, Robin, A ... 843-383-8025 408 D
rperdue@coker.edu
PERDUE, Tina, K ... 740-376-4730 356 A
tina.perdue@marietta.edu
PERDUE, Wendy, C ... 804-289-8740 472 L
wperdue@richmond.edu
PERDUYN, Ellen ... 330-972-6056 362 B
perduyn@uakron.edu

PEREA, Grace 702-254-7577 272 A grace.perea@northwestcareercollege.edu
PEREA, Jennifer, R 312-362-1083 135 I jrosato@depaul.edu
PEREBOOM, Maarten, L 410-543-6450 203 F mlpereboom@salisbury.edu
PERECMAN, Dov 845-434-5240 326 K dperecman@fallsburgyeshiva.com
PEREGORD, Margaret, A 301-447-5627 200 E peregord@msmary.edu
PEREIRA, Freyja 707-527-4512.. 62 F fpereira@santarosa.edu
PEREIRA, Greg 480-517-8538.. 13 G greg.pereira@riosalado.edu
PEREIRA, Malin 704-687-7197 342 E mpereira@uncc.edu
PEREIRA-VALENTÍN, Brunilda 787-765-9882 512 G brunilda.pereira@upr.edu
PEREKRESTOV, Michael 315-858-0945 302 C library@hts.edu
PERERA, Curtis 360-752-8330 478 G cperera@btc.edu
PERETTI, Terri 408-554-4455.. 62 D tperettii@scu.edu
PERETZ, Marc, H 989-964-4062 230 B mhp@svsu.edu
PEREY, James 928-649-6513.. 16 M james.perey@yc.edu
PEREYRA, Leo 915-215-4300 451 D l.pereyra@ttuhsc.edu
PEREYRA, Moises 212-694-1000 291 I mpereyra@boricuacollege.edu
PEREZ, Alex 559-934-2134.. 73 M alexperez4@whccd.edu
PEREZ, Alvaro 787-798-6732 512 C alvaro.perez@uccaribe.edu
PEREZ, Andrew 518-438-3111 305 K andyp@mariacollege.edu
PEREZ, Angel, B 860-297-2175.. 88 C angel.perez@trincoll.edu
PEREZ, Awilda 787-766-1717 511 H um_aperez@suagm.edu
PEREZ, Barbara 310-900-1600.. 40 A bperez@elcamino.edu
PEREZ, Camile 787-766-1717 511 H camperez@suagm.edu
PEREZ, Carlos 787-754-8000 512 E cperez@pupr.edu
PEREZ, Carlos 787-622-8000 512 E cperez@pupr.edu
PEREZ, Carmen, I 787-279-1912 509 A cperez@bayamon.inter.edu
PEREZ, Caty 559-278-4036.. 31 D catyp@csufresno.edu
PEREZ, Cesar 909-667-4428.. 37 H cperez@claremontlincoln.edu
PEREZ, Daisy 787-892-6442 509 F dnperez@intersg.edu
PEREZ, Diana 805-922-6966.. 24 J dperez@hancockcollege.edu
PEREZ, Dilcie, D 560-860-2451.. 35 M dilcieperez@cerritos.edu
PEREZ, Doris 787-891-0925 508 K dperez@aguadilla.inter.edu
PEREZ, Doris, U 671-735-5517 505 C doris.perez@guamcc.edu
PEREZ, Eduardo 787-279-1912 509 A eperezd@bayamon.inter.edu
PEREZ, Eltie 787-894-2828 514 C eltie.perez@upr.edu
PEREZ, Enrique 714-480-7460.. 57 K perez_enrique@rsccd.edu
PEREZ, Francisco 787-758-2525 513 G francisco.perez12@upr.edu
PEREZ, Gay 434-243-3605 473 A bgd2j@virginia.edu
PEREZ, JR., Gilberto 574-535-7434 155 A gperez@goshen.edu
PEREZ, Hector 954-637-2268 107 E hperez@sfbc.edu
PEREZ, Hiselgis 305-348-2731 109 A perezh@fiu.edu
PEREZ, Ivelisse 787-834-9595 511 E iperez@uaa.edu
PEREZ, Jacqueline 845-569-3394 307 J jacqueline.perez@msmc.edu
PEREZ, Jessie 787-288-1118 512 A
PEREZ, Jose 787-738-2161 513 D jose.pelay@upr.edu
PEREZ, Jose 915-566-9621 458 C jperez@westerntech.edu
PEREZ, Julia 973-803-5000 280 C jperez@pillar.edu
PEREZ, Kathryn 806-716-2370 443 I kperez@southplainscollege.edu
PEREZ, Lance 402-472-3181 269 J lperez1@unl.edu
PEREZ, Laura 323-241-5281.. 49 D perezli2@lasc.edu
PEREZ, Linda 281-649-3391 437 H lperez@hbu.edu
PEREZ, Luci 909-599-5433.. 47 K lperez@lifepacific.edu
PEREZ, Lydia 646-565-6000 322 J lydia.perez@touro.edu
PEREZ, Manuel Alejandro 650-306-3236.. 61 O
PEREZ, Marciano 619-388-3498.. 60 C mperez@sdccd.edu
PEREZ, Margarita 337-482-6272 192 E mperez@louisiana.edu
PEREZ, Maria 787-780-0070 506 F mperez@caribbean.edu
PEREZ, Maria 787-891-0925 508 K mperez@aguadilla.inter.edu
PEREZ, Maria del C 787-284-1912 509 E mcperezr@ponce.inter.edu
PEREZ, Mario 323-343-3075.. 32 A mario.perez@calstatela.edu
PEREZ, Melvin (Tony), A 585-292-2904 307 H tperez7@monroecc.edu
PEREZ, Miguel 323-415-4123.. 48 H perezma@elac.edu
PEREZ, Miguel, E 787-752-4575 513 C miguel.perez8@upr.edu
PEREZ, Mireya 708-656-8000 144 E mireya.perez@morton.edu
PEREZ, Miriam 787-840-2575 510 J mperez@psm.edu
PEREZ, Monica 413-552-2227 214 D mperez@hcc.edu
PEREZ, Monica 864-644-5135 412 E mperez@swu.edu
PEREZ, Monte, E 818-364-7796.. 49 B perezme@lamission.edu
PEREZ, Myrna 787-786-3030 512 B mperez@ucb.edu.pr
PEREZ, Nancy 413-538-2188 216 G nbperez@mtholyoke.edu
PEREZ, Natasha 316-295-5888 173 D natasha_perez@friends.edu
PEREZ, Norma 713-718-5040 437 I norma.perez@hccs.edu
PEREZ, Omar 787-740-1611 512 C omar.perez@uccaribe.edu
PEREZ, Oscar 305-821-3333.. 99 E operez@fnu.edu
PEREZ, Pablo 305-626-6007.. 94 C
PEREZ, Peter 203-254-4000.. 86 I pperez1@fairfield.edu
PEREZ, Rayetta 616-392-8555 233 E rayetta@westernsem.edu
PEREZ, Roger 559-791-2209.. 47 A roger.perez@portervillecollege.edu
PEREZ, Ronald 414-227-4128 497 A perez@uwm.edu
PEREZ, Rowena Ellen 671-735-5640 505 C rowenaellen.perez@guamcc.edu
PEREZ, Scott 805-437-8808.. 30 F scott.perez@csuci.edu
PEREZ, Sonny, P 671-735-2372 505 E sonnypz@triton.uog.edu
PEREZ, Steve 916-278-6331.. 32 E steve.perez@csus.edu
PEREZ, Suleyma 773-442-5400 145 B s-perez6@neiu.edu
PEREZ, Yolanda 787-834-9595 511 E yperez@uaa.edu
PEREZ-CASANOVA, Maria, T 787-480-2448 507 C mperez02@sanjuanciudadpatria.com
PEREZ DE JESUS, Margarita 787-848-5739 511 C
PEREZ-DORTA, Pedro 787-622-8000 512 E pperez@pupr.edu
PEREZ-FRANCO, Mayte 619-260-2395.. 71 J mpf@sandiego.edu
PEREZ HERNÁNDEZ, Marilu 787-764-0000 514 B marilu.perez1@upr.edu
PEREZ-KAHLER, Norma 563-588-6432 163 F norma.perez-kahler@clarke.edu
PEREZ-LOPEZ, Mark 910-962-3746 343 C perezlopezm@uncw.edu
PEREZ-LOPEZ, Myrna, E 787-763-6700 508 A meperez@se-pr.edu
PEREZ-RODRIGUEZ, Jose, F 787-723-4481 507 A jperez@ceaprc.edu
PEREZ TOLEDO, Elizabeth 787-848-5739 511 C
PEREZ-TOPCZEWSKI, Vanessa 262-650-4826 492 E vperezto@carrollu.edu
PEREZ-VERGARA, Kelly 248-689-8282 232 A kperezve@walshcollege.edu
PERFECTO, Gerardo 787-257-0099 513 C gerardo.perfecto@upr.edu
PERFETTI, Charles, A 412-624-7107 401 B perfetti@pitt.edu
PERFETTI, Lisa 330-263-2000 351 C lperfetti@wooster.edu
PERGI, Brenan 740-283-6445 353 B bpergi@franciscan.edu
PERGOLA-RIVERA, Maribelle 787-993-8951 513 B maribelle.pergola@upr.edu
PERGOLIS, Robert 718-940-5419 314 C rpergolis@sjcny.edu
PERGOLIZZI, Francis 207-973-1069 194 A pergolizzif@husson.edu
PERGOLIZZI, Vanessa 860-913-2160.. 87 A vpergolizzi@goodwin.edu
PERI, Jonathan 215-885-2360 389 F jperi@manor.edu
PERIGARD, Julie 253-272-1126 482 C jperigard@ncad.edu
PERIGARD, Kim 253-272-1126 482 C kperigard@ncad.edu
PERILLO, Patricia, A 540-231-6272 477 A vpsa@vt.edu
PERINI, Don 616-949-5300 222 I don.perini@cornerstone.edu
PERKIN, Sara 517-796-8569 225 C perkinsaraa@jccmi.edu
PERKINS, JR., Andrew, M 336-285-4551 341 F perkins@ncat.edu
PERKINS, Anika, M 662-329-7119 248 A amperkins@muw.edu
PERKINS, Bianca 309-796-8240 132 G perkinsb@bhc.edu
PERKINS, Bruce 405-585-5120 367 F bruce.perkins@okbu.edu
PERKINS, Charles 620-792-9245 171 C perkinsc@bartonccc.edu
PERKINS, Cheri 318-342-5210 192 F perkins@ulm.edu
PERKINS, Chris-Tenna, M 804-627-5300 465 C chris-tenna_perkins@bshsi.org
PERKINS, Eddie 606-539-4579 185 A eddie.perkins@ucumberlands.edu
PERKINS, Jeffrey 310-665-6857.. 54 I jperkins@otis.edu
PERKINS, Joseph, A 919-572-1625 326 L jperk1987@apexsot.edu
PERKINS, Joseph, E 919-572-1625 326 L jeperkins@apexsot.edu
PERKINS, Julie 660-263-4100 257 B juliep@macc.edu
PERKINS, Keith 937-376-6640 350 D kperkins@centralstate.edu
PERKINS, Kimberly 843-863-7258 407 E kperkins@csuniv.edu
PERKINS, Lea 218-679-2860 242 P
PERKINS, Mark 307-778-1113 502 D mperkins@lccc.wy.edu
PERKINS, Megan 315-279-5296 304 A mryan1@keuka.edu
PERKINS, Meredith 212-217-3500 299 H meredith_perkins@fitnyc.edu
PERKINS, Michele, D 603-428-2222 273 H mperkins@nec.edu
PERKINS, Myrna 620-792-9270 171 C perkinsm@bartonccc.edu
PERKINS, Peter 607-753-2518 318 D peter.perkins@cortland.edu
PERKINS, Priscilla, L 413-782-1531 219 F priscilla.perkins@wne.edu
PERKINS, Suzetta, M 910-672-1143 341 E sperkins@uncfsu.edu
PERKINS, Ungina 704-922-2310 334 F perkins.ungina@gaston.edu
PERKINS, Will 503-352-2120 375 G wperkins@pacificu.edu
PERKINS-HOLTSCLAW, Kala 423-869-7089 421 C k.perkins-holtsclaw@lmunet.edu
PERKINS JASPER, Erica 909-607-3562.. 37 E
PERKINSON, Greg 541-552-6319 376 E perkinsog@sou.edu
PERKOWSKI, Henry 212-678-3016 322 G hp2125@tc.columbia.edu
PERKOWSKI, Peter 216-881-1700 359 F pperkowski@ohiotech.edu
PERKUS, Aaron 203-576-3984.. 88 D aperkus@bridgeport.edu
PERL, Emily 410-337-6122 198 G eperl@goucher.edu
PERLADO, Ben 661-654-3381.. 30 E bperlado@csub.edu
PERLIONI, Jason 443-997-2370 199 D perlioni@jhu.edu
PERLMAN, Andrew 617-573-8157 219 A aperlman@suffolk.edu
PERLMAN, Bruce, J 505-277-1092 288 G bperlman@unm.edu
PERLMAN, Lynn 617-277-3915 207 C perlmanl@bgsp.edu
PERLMUTTER, David 806-742-3385 451 B david.perlmutter@ttu.edu
PERLMUTTER, David, H 314-362-6827 262 A perlmutterd@wustl.edu
PERLOW, Yaakov 718-438-2727 326 I
PERMAN, Jay, A 410-706-7002 202 D jperman@umaryland.edu
PERMAN, Matthew 212-659-7200 304 B mperman@tkc.edu
PERME, Connie 513-745-3992 365 B perme@xavier.edu
PERMENTER, Andrew, H 863-667-5078 107 K ahpermenter@seu.edu
PERNER, Darlene 570-389-4005 394 A dperner@bloomu.edu
PERNEY, John 517-629-0244 220 G jperney@albion.edu
PERNICELLO, Collene 215-572-2840 379 A pernicelloc@arcadia.edu
PERNOT, Laurent 312-369-7606 135 E lpernot@colum.edu
PEROO, Rama 620-441-5587 172 I rama.peroo@cowley.edu
PEROW, Lauren, A 814-641-3302 386 H perowl@juniata.edu
PEROZZI, Brett 801-626-6008 461 B brettperozzi@weber.edu
PEROZZI, Thomas 847-574-5168 141 C tperozzi@lfgsm.edu
PERR, Yechiel, I 718-327-7600 325 F info@yofr.org
PERREAULT, Amy 207-778-7256 196 B amy.f.perreault@maine.edu
PERREAULT, Melanie 410-704-4498 204 A mperreault@towson.edu
PERREIRA, Mary 808-956-4650 128 H maryperr@hawaii.edu
PERRELLI, John 410-337-6527 198 G john.perrelli@goucher.edu
PERREN, Ray 770-533-7030 121 B rperren@laniertech.edu
PERRENOD, William, L 914-337-9300 297 D william.perrenod@concordia-ny.edu
PERRES, Irving 718-232-7800 325 J
PERRET, Geraldine 973-618-3536 276 D gperret@caldwell.edu
PERRETTA, Betty 972-721-5000 452 D bboop@udallas.edu
PERRI, Christine 619-216-6668.. 65 F cperri@swccd.edu
PERRI, Geraldine, M 626-914-8821.. 36 K gperri@citruscollege.edu
PERRI, Jason 716-851-1421 299 F perri@ecc.edu
PERRI, Mary Lynn 440-646-8329 363 G mperri@ursuline.edu
PERRI, Michael 352-273-6214 109 F mperri@phhp.ufl.edu
PERRI, Ralph 318-342-5329 192 F perri@ulm.edu
PERRIEN, Shane 402-941-6171 267 L perrien@midlandu.edu
PERRIER, Rochelle 504-398-2744 191 C rperrier@uhcno.edu
PERRIER, Sarah 412-392-8184 397 A sperrier@pointpark.edu
PERRIN, Amy 847-214-7217 136 F aperrin@elgin.edu

PETERSEN, Dana .... 207-216-4454 195 C
dpetersen@yccc.edu
PETERSEN, Donna .... 813-974-6603 110 B
dpeters@hsc.usf.edu
PETERSEN, Dorene .... 503-244-0726 371 G
PETERSEN, Doug .... 714-556-3610.. 72 F
PETERSEN, Jane .... 308-865-8950 269 I
jpetersen@nebraska.edu
PETERSEN, Karen, K ..... 615-898-2534 422 H
karen.petersen@mtsu.edu
PETERSEN, Kevin .... 410-704-2487 204 A
kpetersen@towson.edu
PETERSEN, Kristin .... 402-471-2505 268 D
kpetersen@nscs.edu
PETERSEN, Mark .... 949-794-9090.. 65 I
mpetersen@stanbridge.edu
PETERSEN, Mark, A ...... 336-758-6053 344 D
map@wfu.edu
PETERSEN, Mary, S ...... 206-296-2043 484 F
marypete@seattleu.edu
PETERSEN, Molly .... 619-849-2463.. 57 E
mollypetersen@pointloma.edu
PETERSEN, Nichole .... 651-779-3934 237 G
nichole.petersen@century.edu
PETERSEN, Page .... 507-433-0650 240 F
page.petersen@riverland.edu
PETERSEN, Steve .... 847-925-6255 137 H
speterse@harpercollege.edu
PETERSEN, Tina .... 916-577-2200.. 75 B
tpetersen@jessup.edu
PETERSEN-FAIRCHILD,
Kelly .... 435-652-7711 460 G
kelly.peterson-fairchild@dixie.edu
PETERSON, Alonzo, F ... 405-466-3419 366 F
alonzofp@langston.edu
PETERSON, Andra .... 770-962-7580 120 E
apeterson@gwinnetttech.edu
PETERSON, Andrew, T .. 864-833-8486 411 I
atpeterso@presby.edu
PETERSON, Andy .... 660-562-1330 257 E
andyp@nwmissouri.edu
PETERSON, Andy .... 503-517-1800 378 A
apeterson@westernseminary.edu
PETERSON, Bill .... 413-585-3000 218 F
bpeterso@smith.edu
PETERSON, Bryce .... 800-280-0307 152 H
bryce.peterson@ace.edu
PETERSON, JR.,
Charles .... 804-523-5821 474 H
cpeterson@reynolds.edu
PETERSON, Charles, D . 701-231-7456 345 G
charles.peterson@ndsu.edu
PETERSON, Cheryl .... 540-231-6231 477 A
cpeterson@vt.edu
PETERSON, Chris .... 952-358-9130 239 F
chris.peterson@normandale.edu
PETERSON, Chris .... 405-491-6324 370 A
cpeterso@snu.edu
PETERSON, Christine .... 443-423-1467 199 H
cpetersn@mica.edu
PETERSON, Courtney .... 701-788-4692 345 E
courtney.peterson.1@mayvillestate.edu
PETERSON, Craig .... 231-843-5920 232 J
capeterson@westshore.edu
PETERSON, Cynthia ...... 225-578-4201 188 I
cbpeterson@lsu.edu
PETERSON, Cynthia, L .. 706-778-8500 123 B
cpeterson@piedmont.edu
PETERSON, Dan .... 206-685-9926 485 F
dcpeters@uw.edu
PETERSON, Debra .... 218-755-4121 237 E
debra.peterson@bemidjistate.edu
PETERSON, Derek .... 605-688-4163 417 C
derek.peterson@sdstate.edu
PETERSON, Dolores ...... 610-372-4721 397 B
dpeterson@racc.edu
PETERSON, Donald .... 815-753-2256 145 C
drpeterson@niu.edu
PETERSON, Donn .... 707-826-5555.. 33 D
donn.peterson@humboldt.edu
PETERSON, Doug .... 312-322-1733 149 I
dpeterson@spertus.edu
PETERSON, Doug .... 612-624-4838 243 E
dougp@umn.edu
PETERSON, Ellen .... 510-649-2430.. 44 F
epeterson@gtu.edu
PETERSON, Ellen .... 808-984-3582 129 E
epeterso@hawaii.edu
PETERSON, Ericka, K .... 507-786-3434 243 C
peters66@stolaf.edu
PETERSON, Evan .... 313-993-1114 231 B
petersea@udmercy.edu

PETERSON, G. P. (Bud) 404-894-5051 118 F
president@gatech.edu
PETERSON, George, J ... 864-656-4444 408 A
soedean@clemson.edu
PETERSON, Gina .... 661-259-7800.. 38 H
gina.peterson@canyons.edu
PETERSON, Greg .... 503-493-6545 372 I
gpeterson@cu-portland.edu
PETERSON, Gregory ...... 480-732-7010.. 12 P
greg.peterson@cgc.edu
PETERSON, Heath, J ..... 785-864-4760 177 D
heathpeterson@kualumni.org
PETERSON, Heather ...... 609-343-5008 275 D
hpeterso@atlantic.edu
PETERSON, Jennifer ...... 904-632-3291 100 B
jennifer.peterson@fscj.edu
PETERSON, Jessica .... 303-404-5133.. 79 J
jessica.peterson@frontrange.edu
PETERSON, Joe .... 406-377-9459 263 E
jpeterson@dawson.edu
PETERSON, Joel .... 909-607-2760.. 45 A
jopeterson@hmc.edu
PETERSON, Julie .... 470-578-3378 120 L
jpeterso@kennesaw.edu
PETERSON, June .... 864-225-7653 409 J
junepeterson@forrestcollege.edu
PETERSON, Karen .... 785-670-1927 177 G
karen.peterson@washburn.edu
PETERSON, Karin .... 336-770-3262 343 D
petersonk@uncsa.edu
PETERSON, Kathleen ..... 973-300-2235 283 E
kpeterson@sussex.edu
PETERSON, Keith .... 970-675-3258.. 78 G
keith.peterson@cncc.edu
PETERSON, Kellie .... 406-994-4570 264 D
kellie.peterson@montana.edu
PETERSON, Ken .... 864-294-2007 410 A
ken.peterson@furman.edu
PETERSON, Kent, A ...... 414-277-7176 494 G
peterson@msoe.edu
PETERSON, Kevin .... 435-797-1223 460 H
kevin.peterson@usu.edu
PETERSON, Kirk, E .... 252-398-6221 328 D
peterk@chowan.edu
PETERSON, Klay .... 864-503-5254 414 D
kpeterson@uscupstate.edu
PETERSON, Korinne .... 508-999-8643 211 F
kpeterson1@umassd.edu
PETERSON, Kurt .... 847-543-2640 135 B
kpeterson4@clcillinois.edu
PETERSON, Laura .... 940-397-4919 440 F
laura.peterson@msutexas.edu
PETERSON, Lisa, L .... 757-822-1402 476 B
lpeterson@tcc.edu
PETERSON, Lori .... 406-447-5432 263 C
lpeterso@carroll.edu
PETERSON, Marc .... 214-768-3417 444 E
mpeterso@smu.edu
PETERSON, Margrette ... 510-869-6512.. 59 F
mpeterson@samuelmerritt.edu
PETERSON, Marie .... 206-296-6241 484 F
mpeters@seattleu.edu
PETERSON, Marika .... 434-949-1064 475 H
marika.peterson@southside.edu
PETERSON, Mark .... 301-295-3028 504 B
jason.kaar@usuhs.edu
PETERSON, Melissa ...... 716-839-8477 298 B
mpeters2@daemen.edu
PETERSON, Mensah ...... 908-709-7516 284 C
mensah.peterson@ucc.edu
PETERSON, Michele ...... 970-247-7435.. 79 I
peterson_m@fortlewis.edu
PETERSON, Nedra .... 818-252-5203.. 75 C
nedra.peterson@woodbury.edu
PETERSON, Nell .... 813-974-6884 110 B
ncpeterson@usf.edu
PETERSON, Nicole .... 931-221-7979 418 D
petersonn@apsu.edu
PETERSON, Pamela, L .. 651-962-6608 244 E
plpeterson@stthomas.edu
PETERSON, Pete .... 310-506-7490.. 56 C
pete.n.peterson@pepperdine.edu
PETERSON, Phyllis, M .. 815-740-3848 151 J
ppeterson@stfrancis.edu
PETERSON, Polly .... 701-252-3467 347 C
ppeterso@uj.edu
PETERSON, R. Daniel .... 603-456-2656 274 A
dpeterson@northeastcatholic.edu
PETERSON, Randall .... 386-312-4022 106 C
randypeterson@sjrstate.edu
PETERSON, Randall, T .. 801-587-3064 460 E
randall.peterson@pharm.utah.edu

PETERSON, Randy .... 501-450-3826.. 19 F
petersonr@hendrix.edu
PETERSON, Rebecca ..... 605-688-5148 417 C
rebecca.peterson@sdstate.edu
PETERSON, Richard ...... 801-734-6824 459 L
richard.peterson@rm.edu
PETERSON, Robert .... 216-987-2836 351 G
robert.peterson@tri-c.edu
PETERSON, Roy .... 262-243-5700 493 B
roy.peterson@cuw.edu
PETERSON, Samantha ... 918-335-6223 368 G
speterson@okwu.edu
PETERSON, Sandy .... 608-785-9207 501 A
petersons@westerntc.edu
PETERSON, Sonja .... 828-766-1240 336 A
speterson@mayland.edu
PETERSON, Stephanie ... 785-442-6051 174 A
speterson@highlandcc.edu
PETERSON, Susan, K .... 785-532-6221 174 G
skp@ksu.edu
PETERSON, Terry .... 312-942-7020 148 A
terry_peterson@rush.edu
PETERSON, Thomas ...... 732-906-2512 279 A
tpeterson@middlesexcc.edu
PETERSON, Toby .... 301-696-3934 199 B
peterson@hood.edu
PETERSON, Tracy .... 303-751-8700.. 77 A
peterson@bel-rea.com
PETERSON, Trevor .... 208-535-5389 130 C
trevor.peterson@cei.edu
PETERSON, Tyler, M ..... 205-934-8221.... 8 A
tpeterson@uab.edu
PETERSON, Val, L .... 801-863-8424 461 A
petersva@uvu.edu
PETERSON, Wendy .... 509-335-5586 486 A
wendyp@wsu.edu
PETERSON-MILLER,
Connie .... 574-520-4591 157 A
copmiller@iusb.edu
PETERSON-SENIUK,
Peggy .... 419-473-2700 352 E
pseniuk@daviscollege.edu
PETERSON-VEATCH,
Ross .... 620-229-6090 177 A
ross.petersonveatch@sckans.edu
PETERSSON, Arlette .... 561-586-0121 100 O
PETHE-COOK, Marlyn ... 813-253-6231 112 J
mpethe@ut.edu
PETHERBRIDGE, Julie ... 678-547-6438 121 E
petherbrid_j@mercer.edu
PETILLO, John, J .... 203-371-7900.. 88 B
petilloj@sacredheart.edu
PETIN, Mika'il .... 615-220-7970 425 C
mpetin@mscc.edu
PETIPRIN, Gary .... 502-272-8480 179 B
gpetiprin@bellarmine.edu
PETITT, Becky, R .... 858-822-4783.. 69 D
bpetitt@ucsd.edu
PETITT, Bill .... 972-883-2055 455 B
bpetitt@utdallas.edu
PETITT, Charles, W .... 336-725-8344 339 F
petittc@piedmontu.edu
PETITTI, Mario .... 440-525-7328 355 H
mpetitti@lakelandcc.edu
PETKA, Frank .... 215-646-7300 385 D
petka.f@gmercyu.edu
PETKASH, John .... 607-778-5011 318 A
petkashjc@sunybroome.edu
PETKUS, Edward .... 201-684-7377 280 H
epetkus@ramapo.edu
PETLEY, Kathleen .... 518-629-4557 302 E
k.petley@hvcc.edu
PETOSKEY, Indira .... 860-465-5066.. 84 J
petoskeyi@easternct.edu
PETR, Carrie, L .... 209-946-2365.. 70 E
cpetr@pacific.edu
PETRAITIS, John .... 907-786-1706.... 9 H
PETREE, Daniel .... 707-664-2220.. 34 C
petreed@sonoma.edu
PETRELLA, Diane .... 816-235-2960 261 C
patrellad@umkc.edu
PETRESCU, Claudia, A ... 248-370-2188 229 G
cpetrescu@oakland.edu
PETRI, OP, Thomas ...... 202-495-3832.. 92 E
dean@dhs.edu
PETRIDIS, Heather .... 626-815-4570.. 26 H
hpetridis@apu.edu
PETRIE, Andrea .... 414-382-6371 492 A
andrea.petrie@alverno.edu
PETRIE, Mark .... 315-279-5694 304 A
mpetrie@keuka.edu
PETRIKAT, Douglas .... 714-547-9625.. 28 C
dpetrikat@calcoast.edu

PETRILLO, Emilia, K ..... 410-328-8404 202 D
epetr001@umaryland.edu
PETRITIS, Paul .... 413-662-5543 213 A
paul.petritis@mcla.edu
PETRIZZO, Louis, J .... 631-451-4235 321 F
petrizl@sunysuffolk.edu
PETRO, Brian .... 937-294-0592 356 H
brian.petro@themodern.edu
PETROKA, Louise, A ..... 203-285-2393.. 85 E
lpetroka@gwcc.commnet.edu
PETRONE, Eileen .... 412-536-1115 387 B
eileen.petrone@laroche.edu
PETROS, William, P .... 304-293-5212 491 C
wpetros@hsc.wvu.edu
PETROSIAN, Anahid ...... 956-872-8339 444 A
anahid@southtexascollege.edu
PETROSIAN, Anahid ...... 956-872-6790 444 A
anahid@southtexascollege.edu
PETROSINO, Linda .... 607-274-3265 303 B
lpetrosino@ithaca.edu
PETROSKI, Mike .... 561-237-7007 102 V
mpetroski@lynn.edu
PETROSKY, Joseph, L ... 248-232-4179 229 A
jlpetros@oaklandcc.edu
PETROSYAN, Narine ...... 510-925-4282.. 25 Q
narinep@aua.am
PETROSYAN, Varduhi .... 510-925-4282.. 25 Q
vpetrosi@aua.am
PETROSYAN, Violetta .... 304-357-4758 488 G
violettapetrosyan@ucwv.edu
PETROVA, Elena .... 706-721-0211 115 A
epetrova@augusta.edu
PETROVICH, Jason .... 219-464-6858 162 A
jason.petrovich@valpo.edu
PETROZZA, Bruce .... 619-594-4723.. 33 E
bpetrozza@sdsu.edu
PETRUCCI, Michele, L ... 724-357-2295 394 G
michelep@iup.edu
PETRUS, Robin .... 607-778-5201 318 A
petrusre@sunybroome.edu
PETRUSCH,
Suzanne, M .... 864-833-8194 411 I
spetrusch@presby.edu
PETRUSHA, Cynthia ...... 707-476-4170.. 39 D
cynthia-petrusha@redwoods.edu
PETRUZELLA, Gerol .... 413-662-5570 213 A
g.petruzella@mcla.edu
PETRUZZELLI,
Barbara, W .... 845-569-3601 307 J
barbara.petruzzelli@msmc.edu
PETRY, Anthony, R .... 800-955-2527 173 F
PETRYSHAK, Bruce .... 615-898-5570 422 H
bruce.petryshak@mtsu.edu
PETRYSHYN, Laryssa .... 716-829-8119 298 F
petryshl@dyc.edu
PETSCHE, Carolyn .... 815-599-3577 138 B
carolyn.petsche@highland.edu
PETSCHENKO, Lisa .... 630-953-3694 133 G
lpetschenko@chamberlain.edu
PETTA, Tim .... 360-992-2408 479 F
tpetta@clark.edu
PETTAZZONI, Jodi, E .... 336-334-5535 343 A
jepettaz@uncg.edu
PETTEGREW, Melinda ... 816-501-4689 258 H
melinda.pettegrew@rockhurst.edu
PETTENGER, Wade, W .. 417-862-9533 253 D
wpettenger@globaluniversity.edu
PETTENGILL, Keri-Beth . 804-594-1576 474 I
kpettengill@jtcc.edu
PETTERELLI, Mark, J ..... 315-445-4444 304 C
pettermj@lemoyne.edu
PETTEWAY, Venetia .... 810-762-7899 225 H
vpettewa@kettering.edu
PETTIBON, II,
Joseph, P .... 979-845-4016 446 G
jpp2@tamu.edu
PETTIE, Brian .... 870-512-7829.. 18 B
brian_pettie@asun.edu
PETTIFER, Geoffrey .... 609-626-6023 283 D
geoffrey.pettifer@stockton.edu
PETTIFORD, Joseph, B . 443-518-3801 199 C
jpettiford@howardcc.edu
PETTIGREW, Jason .... 605-229-8350 416 C
jason.pettigrew@presentation.edu
PETTIGREW, Yancey ...... 731-661-5134 427 C
ypettigrew@uu.edu
PETTINGILL, Jayn .... 510-845-5373.. 29 G
jayn@cjc.edu
PETTINGILL, Sara, Y ..... 502-272-8401 179 B
spettingill@bellarmine.edu
PETTIS, Carl .... 334-229-4232.... 4 B
cpettis@alasu.edu
PETTIS, Curtis .... 937-376-6503 350 D
cpettis@centralstate.edu

PHILLIPS, Krystal .... 910-938-6234 333 F
phillipsk@coastalcarolina.edu

PHILLIPS, Leon .... 951-343-4323.. 27 J
lphillips@calbaptist.edu

PHILLIPS, Linda .... 580-581-2238 365 G
lindap@cameron.edu

PHILLIPS, Luke .... 718-636-3666 311 J
lphilli8@pratt.edu

PHILLIPS, Lynette, M .... 212-817-7103 293 F
lphillips2@gc.cuny.edu

PHILLIPS, Mark .... 304-829-7299 487 G
maphillips@bethanywv.edu

PHILLIPS, Mark .... 202-685-3140 503 I
mark.phillips.civ@ndu.edu

PHILLIPS, Maureen, R .. 901-333-5000 426 A

PHILLIPS, Melissa, C ... 828-733-5883 336 A
mphillips@mayland.edu

PHILLIPS, MIchael .... 210-690-9000 437 E

PHILLIPS, Miranda .... 409-839-2014 449 G
mphillips1@lit.edu

PHILLIPS, Monika .... 870-512-7805.. 18 B
monika_phillips@asun.edu

PHILLIPS, Morgan .... 520-206-6752.. 15 D
mphillips23@pima.edu

PHILLIPS, Myra .... 804-524-5352 477 B
mhphilli@vsu.edu

PHILLIPS, Patrick .... 541-346-3186 377 D
provost@uoregon.edu

PHILLIPS, Patsy .... 505-428-5901 286 C
pphillips@iaia.edu

PHILLIPS, Patti .... 215-568-4012 390 J
pphillips@moore.edu

PHILLIPS, Phil, E .... 310-506-7227.. 56 C
phil.phillips@pepperdine.edu

PHILLIPS, Phillip .... 615-898-2699 422 H
philip.phillips@mtsu.edu

PHILLIPS, Quill .... 303-360-4822.. 79 D
quill.phillips@ccaurora.edu

PHILLIPS, Rachel .... 215-965-4025 390 J
rphillips@moore.edu

PHILLIPS, Richard .... 903-875-7419 440 G
richard.phillips@navarrocollege.edu

PHILLIPS, Richard, D .... 404-413-7000 119 E
rphillips@gsu.edu

PHILLIPS, Rita, M .... 515-294-0231 162 I
rphillip@iastate.edu

PHILLIPS, Robert .... 276-739-2496 476 C
rphillips@vhcc.edu

PHILLIPS, Robert .... 215-568-9215 403 H
rphillips@phmc.org

PHILLIPS, SR.,
Robert, E .... 540-464-7390 476 G
phillipsre@vmi.edu

PHILLIPS, Robert, J ...... 304-637-1292 487 I
phillipsr@dewv.edu

PHILLIPS, Rodney .... 910-323-5614 327 G
rphillips@ccbs.edu

PHILLIPS, Sam .... 800-877-5456 466 A
sam.phillips@christendom.edu

PHILLIPS, Samanthia ..... 252-823-5166 334 C
phillipss@edgecombe.edu

PHILLIPS, Sara .... 530-242-7635.. 63 H
sphillips@shastacollege.edu

PHILLIPS, Sarah .... 785-320-4502 175 D
sarahphillips@manhattantech.edu

PHILLIPS, Sarah .... 503-352-2141 375 G
phillips@pacificu.edu

PHILLIPS, Sarah, L .... 704-894-2053 328 F
saphillips@davidson.edu

PHILLIPS, Sarina .... 936-261-2173 446 D
srphillips@pvamu.edu

PHILLIPS, Shaina .... 562-908-3427.. 58 E
jphillips@riohondo.edu

PHILLIPS, Shannon .... 843-863-7035 407 E
sphillips@csuniv.edu

PHILLIPS, Shaya .... 718-817-1000 300 E
shphillips@fordham.edu

PHILLIPS, Sheri .... 417-865-2815 253 B
phillipss@evangel.edu

PHILLIPS, Sherry .... 215-641-6562 390 H
sphillips@mc3.edu

PHILLIPS, Staci .... 318-678-6000 187 A
sphillips@bpcc.edu

PHILLIPS, Stephanie ..... 217-641-4536 140 A

PHILLIPS, Stuart .... 706-295-6868 119 A
sphillips@gntc.edu

PHILLIPS, Tammie, C ... 803-323-2225 414 G
phillipst@winthrop.edu

PHILLIPS, Teri, P .... 253-535-7187 482 H
phillitp@plu.edu

PHILLIPS, Terri .... 406-243-2665 264 A
terri.phillips@umontana.edu

PHILLIPS, Terron .... 574-239-8365 155 D
tphillips@hcc-nd.edu

PHILLIPS, SR.,
Thomas, R .... 815-753-1811 145 C
tphillips3@niu.edu

PHILLIPS, Timothy, P ... 412-578-6087 380 E
tpphillips@carlow.edu

PHILLIPS, Tom .... 909-447-2512.. 37 F
tphillips@cst.edu

PHILLIPS, Valerie .... 619-596-2766.. 24 F
vphillips@advancedtraining.edu

PHILLIPS, Vicki .... 229-430-4766 113 H
vicki.phillips@asurams.edu

PHILLIPS, Wendy, S ..... 412-578-8861 380 E
wsphillips@carlow.edu

PHILLIPS, William .... 401-232-6045 404 F
wphillip@bryant.edu

PHILLIPS, Winfred .... 352-392-6620 109 F
wphil@ufl.edu

PHILLIPS, Winfred, M ... 352-392-6620 109 F
wphil@ufl.edu

PHILLIPS, Yancy .... 812-237-2100 155 G
yancy.phillips@indstate.edu

PHILLIPS-MADSON,
Robyn .... 210-283-6994 453 D
rmadson@uiwtx.edu

PHILLIPS MURPHY,
Brian .... 973-353-5860 282 B
brian.phillips.murphy@rutgers.edu

PHILLIS, Thomas, M .... 309-794-7279 132 C
tomphillis@augustana.edu

PHILO, Kathy .... 804-751-9191 465 O
kphilo@ccc-va.com

PHILOGENE, Cassandra 407-896-5869.. 94 D
cassandra.philogene@ahu.edu

PHILPOTT, Gena .... 707-965-6315.. 55 D
gphilpott@puc.edu

PHILPOTT, Sean .... 617-735-9937 209 A
philpotts@emmanuel.edu

PHINAZEE, Karen, B ..... 919-532-5663 338 G
kbphinazee@waketech.edu

PHINNEY, D. Nathan ..... 712-707-7103 168 H
dnathan.phinney@nwciowa.edu

PHINNEY, James .... 419-755-4720 357 E
jphinney@ncstatecollege.edu

PHINNEY, Ray .... 207-509-7241 195 H
rphinney@unity.edu

PHIPPS, Corey, C .... 606-474-3137 180 G
ccfipps@kcu.edu

PHIPPS, Kim, S .... 717-796-5085 390 E
kphipps@messiah.edu

PHIPPS, Kylene .... 406-874-6292 263 I
phippsk@milescc.edu

PHIPPS, Terry .... 972-825-4802 445 A
tphipps@sagu.edu

PHIPPS, Wayne .... 706-233-4062 115 B
wphipps@berry.edu

PHIZACKLEA, Thomas .. 410-857-2207 200 B
tphizacklea@mcdaniel.edu

PHLEGAR, Charles, D ... 540-231-7676 477 A
cphlegar@vt.edu

PHOENIX, Dru .... 505-467-6815 288 E
druphoenix@swc.edu

PHOENIX-MARTIN,
Shawntell .... 912-358-3004 123 H
martins@savannahstate.edu

PIACENTINI, Dean .... 973-290-4349 277 A
dpiacentini@cse.edu

PIANA, Cynthia .... 615-297-7545 418 C
pianac@aquinascollege.edu

PIANEZZOLA, Cristina .. 801-863-8204 461 A
cristina.pianezzola@uvu.edu

PIANKA, Stephanie .... 212-998-2910 310 B
stephanie.pianka@nyu.edu

PIANTA, Robert, C .... 434-243-5481 473 A
rcp4p@virginia.edu

PIASECKI, David .... 734-432-5335 227 A
dpiasecki@madonna.edu

PIASKOWSKY, Robert .... 201-200-2067 279 E
rpiaskowsky@njcu.edu

PIASSICK, Emily .... 478-301-2862 121 E
piassick_ea@mercer.edu

PIATT, James, B .... 336-278-7440 328 K
jpiatt@elon.edu

PIATT, Janet, M .... 423-775-7237 418 H
piattja@bryan.edu

PIAZZA, Bradley .... 262-691-5157 500 H
bpiazza@wctc.edu

PIAZZA, Daniel .... 405-682-7891 367 H
daniel.c.piazza@occc.edu

PIAZZA, Nick .... 815-825-9770 140 F
npiazza@kish.edu

PIAZZA, Rachel .... 815-939-5331 146 A
rpiazza@shet.follett.com

PIAZZA, Vincent .... 314-367-8700 259 B
vincent.piazza@stlcop.edu

PICARD-TESSIER,
Cathy, L .... 401-825-1000 404 H
ctessier@ccri.edu

PICARDO, Callie .... 937-529-2201 362 A
kcpicardo@united.edu

PICARDO, Rosario .... 937-529-2201 362 A
rpicardo@united.edu

PICCHI, Danielle .... 915-532-3737 458 C
dpicchi@westerntech.edu

PICCININNI, James .... 713-525-2192 454 H
jpicci@stthom.edu

PICCOLI, Benedetto .... 856-225-6356 281 G
piccoli@camden.rutgers.edu

PICCOLI, Tracey .... 970-247-7464.. 79 I
piccoli_t@fortlewis.edu

PICCOLO, Joe .... 301-934-7822 198 A
jpiccolo@csmd.edu

PICCOLO, Lisa .... 843-574-6195 413 B
lisa.piccolo@tridenttech.edu

PICHA, Kallan .... 503-943-7857 377 E
picha@up.edu

PICHA, Mike .... 863-638-7217 113 A
mike.picha@warner.edu

PICHA, Patti .... 907-474-7596.. 10 A
plpicha@alaska.edu

PICHARDO, Jeannette ... 718-405-3255 296 G
jeannette.pichardo@mountsaintvincent.edu

PICHEY, Justin .... 803-786-3612 408 F
jpichey@columbiasc.edu

PICINICH, Susan .... 410-704-3288 204 A
spicinich@towson.edu

PICKA, Cenek .... 757-490-1241 464 F
cpicka@auto.edu

PICKARD, Angie .... 601-581-3508 247 A
apickard@meridiancc.edu

PICKARD, Jeremy .... 563-288-6004 165 D
jpickard@eicc.edu

PICKEL, Wendy .... 816-501-4824 258 H
wendy.pickel@rockhurst.edu

PICKELL, Barsha .... 423-472-7141 424 F
bpickell@clevelandstatecc.edu

PICKENS, Joe .... 386-312-4111 106 C
joepickens@sjrstate.edu

PICKENS, Wanda .... 706-886-6831 125 D
wpickens@tfc.edu

PICKENS-OPOKU, Ali .... 651-779-5784 237 G
ali.pickens-opoku@century.edu

PICKERELL, Jennifer, K . 618-537-6805 143 B
jkpickerell@mckendree.edu

PICKERILL, Ted, O .... 513-529-6225 356 E
ted.pickerill@miamioh.edu

PICKERING, Amanda ..... 315-268-3994 296 A
apickeri@clarkson.edu

PICKERING, David .... 815-939-5240 146 A
dpickrng@olivet.edu

PICKERING, Jeff .... 919-209-2000 335 F
jlpickering@johnstoncc.edu

PICKERING, Robert, P ... 843-953-5096 407 F
robert.pickering@citadel.edu

PICKETT, Dakiesha .... 404-756-4442 114 G
dpickett@atlm.edu

PICKETT, Regina .... 281-283-2626 453 A
pickett@uhcl.edu

PICKETT, Todd .... 562-903-4754.. 27 C
todd.pickett@biola.edu

PICKETT-BERNARD,
Denise .... 770-426-2736 121 C
denise.pickett-berna@life.edu

PICKRON-DAVIS,
Marcine .... 215-871-6178 396 D
marcinepi@pcom.edu

PICKRUM, Vita, C .... 302-857-6055.. 89 F
vpickrum@desu.edu

PICKUS, Keith .... 316-978-7791 178 A
keith.pickus@wichita.edu

PICKWICK, Angie .... 240-567-5557 200 C
angie.pickwick@montgomerycollege.edu

PICONE, Deborah .... 212-686-9244 290 A

PICUS, Sharon, M .... 610-683-1353 395 A
picus@kutztown.edu

PIDDINGTON, Josh, R .. 856-415-2270 281 D
jpiddington@rcgc.edu

PIECHOTA, Thomas .... 714-628-2897.. 36 C
piechota@chapman.edu

PIECZYNSKI,
William, C .... 508-213-2162 217 E
william.pieczynski@nichols.edu

PIEDIMONTE, Giovanni . 504-988-3291 191 B
gpiedimonte@tulane.edu

PIEDRAS, Alex, H .... 515-263-6017 165 I
apiedras@grandview.edu

PIEHL, Marnie .... 701-224-5748 346 B
marnie.piehl@bismarckstate.edu

PIEKUTOWSKI,
Michelle .... 412-268-5523 380 F
mpie@andrew.cmu.edu

PIENTA-LETTA, Diane .... 973-300-2226 283 E
dpienta-lett@sussex.edu

PIEPER, John, A .... 314-367-8700 259 B
john.pieper@stlcop.edu

PIEPER, Michael .... 701-777-6862 345 C
michael.pieper@und.edu

PIEPER, Sandi, J .... 515-574-1139 166 E
pieper@iowacentral.edu

PIEPER-OLSON,
Heather .... 320-363-5964 235 C
hpieperolso@csbsju.edu

PIER, David .... 916-608-6809.. 50 H
pierd@flc.losrios.edu

PIER, Julie, H .... 605-677-5446 416 H
julie.pier@usd.edu

PIERCE, Amanda, K ...... 757-594-8851 466 B
amanda.pierce@cnu.edu

PIERCE, Bill .... 479-788-7188.. 21 H
bill.pierce@uafs.edu

PIERCE, Billie .... 419-530-5445 363 E
william.pierce@utoledo.edu

PIERCE, Brynn .... 541-383-7402 372 B
bpierce@cocc.edu

PIERCE, Dee .... 630-752-5048 152 F
dee.pierce@wheaton.edu

PIERCE, Delton .... 512-505-3037 438 E
dpierce@htu.edu

PIERCE, Diane .... 575-527-7745 287 E
dpierce@nmsu.edu

PIERCE, Evan, F .... 716-286-8769 310 D
epierce@niagara.edu

PIERCE, Frederic .... 607-753-2232 318 D
fred.pierce@cortland.edu

PIERCE, Gillian .... 617-353-2230 207 D
gpierce@bu.edu

PIERCE, Greg .... 601-266-5006 249 F
greg.pierce@usm.edu

PIERCE, James .... 254-968-9781 446 E
jrpierce@tarleton.edu

PIERCE, Janelle .... 770-962-7580 120 E
jpierce@gwinnetttech.edu

PIERCE, Jason .... 709-379-3111 127 C
jpierce@yhc.edu

PIERCE, Jason, L .... 937-229-2601 362 G
jpierce2@udayton.edu

PIERCE, Jeff .... 828-262-3190 341 B
piercewj@appstate.edu

PIERCE, Jennifer .... 856-351-2642 283 A
jpierce@salemcc.edu

PIERCE, Jerry, D .... 318-357-6588 192 C
pierce@nsula.edu

PIERCE, Jill, A .... 207-859-4807 193 E
jill.pierce@colby.edu

PIERCE, Joan .... 608-785-9915 501 A
piercej@westerntc.edu

PIERCE, John .... 828-251-6742 342 C
jpierce@unca.edu

PIERCE, Jonathan .... 503-883-2490 373 H
jdpierce@linfield.edu

PIERCE, Josh .... 573-629-3014 253 H
josh.pierce@hlg.edu

PIERCE, Joshua .... 573-629-3014 253 H
joshua.pierce@hlg.edu

PIERCE, Keith .... 405-491-6366 370 A
kpierce@snu.edu

PIERCE, Keith .... 803-641-2838 413 D
keithp@usca.edu

PIERCE, Kellee .... 406-657-1166 265 E
piercek@rocky.edu

PIERCE, Kenneth .... 512-245-9650 450 E
krp91@txstate.edu

PIERCE, Kristen .... 505-565-1075 218 H
kpierce1@stonehill.edu

PIERCE, LaRue, A .... 413-755-4868 215 F
lapierce@stcc.edu

PIERCE, Lori, J .... 734-764-0151 231 E
ljpierce@umich.edu

PIERCE, Malisa .... 918-270-6409 369 A
malisa.pierce@ptstulsa.edu

PIERCE, Marisa .... 972-273-3990 435 E
marisapierce@dcccd.edu

PIERCE, Marisa .... 425-640-1697 480 F
marisa.pierce@edcc.edu

PIERCE, Mark .... 518-736-3622 300 F
mark.pierce@fmcc.suny.edu

PIERCE, Melody, C .... 336-334-7696 341 F
mcpierce@ncat.edu

PIPITONE, Stephen .... 610-526-6053 385 G
spipitone@harcum.edu
PIPKIN, Mindy .... 501-450-3247.. 23 H
mpipkin@uca.edu
PIPKINS, Jermain .... 818-947-2625.. 49 F
pipkinjc@lavc.edu
PIPPEN, Nadirah .... 910-962-3770 343 C
pippenn@uncw.edu
PIPPEN, Wendy .... 850-718-2269.. 96 F
pippenw@chipola.edu
PIPPENGER, Michael .... 574-631-5204 161 C
mpippeng@nd.edu
PIPPIN, Barbara .... 850-599-3225 108 I
barbara.pippen@famu.edu
PIPPIN, Jeff .... 310-506-7500.. 56 C
jeff.pippin@pepperdine.edu
PIPPIN, Jill .... 315-312-2270 319 B
jill.pippin@oswego.edu
PIPTA, Robert, M .... 412-321-8383 380 B
rector@bcs.edu
PIRES, Jennifer, P .... 302-857-1037.. 90 D
jpires1@dtcc.edu
PIRES, Karin .... 207-780-5107 196 F
karin.pires@maine.edu
PIRKLE, Bill .... 803-641-3395 413 D
billp@usca.edu
PIRKLE, Martha, W .... 706-880-8245 121 A
mpirkle@lagrange.edu
PIRKUL, Hasan .... 972-883-6813 455 B
hpirkul@utdallas.edu
PIROG, Stan .... 928-524-7324.. 14 J
stan.pirog@npc.edu
PIROLI, Vivienne, B ...... 617-521-2752 218 E
vivienne.piroli@simmons.edu
PIRONE, Jane .... 212-229-8960 308 C
jane.pirone@newschool.edu
PIRRONG, Cary .... 405-682-1611 367 H
cary.m.pirrong@occc.edu
PIRTLE, Gina .... 219-980-3539 156 E
gpirtle@iu.edu
PISA, Michael, C .... 315-312-3572 319 B
michael.pisa@oswego.edu
PISA, Rosaria .... 401-874-5150 406 B
rpisa@uri.edu
PISANO, Albert, P .... 858-534-6237.. 69 D
appisano@cusd.edu
PISANO, Douglas .... 716-375-2187 313 F
dpisano@sbu.edu
PISANO, Terry .... 919-497-3226 330 I
tpisano@louisburg.edu
PISCHKE, Kevin .... 916-577-2200.. 75 B
kpischke@jessup.edu
PISCIOTTA, Tony .... 314-371-0236 258 E
tpisciotta@ranken.edu
PISCITELLO, Frank .... 610-436-3192 396 A
fpiscitello@wcupa.edu
PISCITELLO, Julie .... 607-436-2081 317 C
PISCOPO, Carmine, R ... 401-865-2727 405 B
cpiscopo@providence.edu
PISELLI, Maria, N .... 570-326-3761 393 G
mhughes@pct.edu
PISER, Barry .... 907-564-8282.... 9 D
bpiser@alaskapacific.edu
PISHKO, Michael .... 307-766-4253 502 H
mpishko@uwyo.edu
PISK HALL, Trina .... 218-299-3445 235 E
piskhall@cord.edu
PISKADLO, Kevin .... 508-565-1363 218 H
kpiskadlo@stonehill.edu
PISKUN, Judith .... 716-896-0700 324 E
jpiskun@villa.edu
PISORS, Jesse, D .... 361-570-4829 453 C
pisorsj@uhv.edu
PISTERS, Peter .... 713-792-6000 456 E
PISTILLO, Jason .... 602-383-8228.. 16 F
jay@uat.edu
PISTNER, David .... 724-925-4219 403 A
pistnerd@westmoreland.edu
PISTOLE, John .... 765-641-4010 153 B
jspistole@anderson.edu
PISTONO, Lita .... 573-876-7210 260 F
lpistono@stephens.edu
PISTORINO, Thomas, G 781-768-7075 218 C
t.pistorino@regiscollege.edu
PISZKER, James .... 814-824-2429 390 C
jpiszker@mercyhurst.edu
PITCAIRN, Carrie .... 216-373-5274 358 B
cpitcairn@ndc.edu
PITCHER, Carole, D ...... 302-295-1133.. 90 I
carole.d.pitcher@wilmu.edu
PITCHER,
Christopher, G .... 302-295-1152.. 90 I
christopher.g.pitcher@wilmu.edu

PITCHER, John .... 617-228-2208 214 A
PITCHER, Katherine, E .. 240-895-4267 201 E
kepitcher@smcm.edu
PITCHER, Mark .... 918-293-5412 368 D
mark.pitcher@okstate.edu
PITCHER, Paula, R .... 610-359-5141 382 C
ppitcher@dccc.edu
PITCHER, Scott .... 641-585-8112 170 B
pitchers@waldorf.edu
PITCHER DEPROTO,
Marcella .... 415-422-2193.. 71 K
mjdeproto@usfca.edu
PITCHFORD, Nicola .... 415-458-3759.. 41 H
nicola.pitchford@dominican.edu
PITCOCK, Beth .... 559-323-2100.. 60 I
bpitcock@sjcl.edu
PITERA, Daniel .... 313-993-1532 231 B
piteradw@udmercy.edu
PITHIS, Nancy .... 617-236-8814 209 D
npithis@fisher.edu
PITMAN, Julia .... 716-614-6240 310 C
jpitman@niagaracc.suny.edu
PITONZO, Beth .... 336-334-4822 335 A
bjpitonzo@gtcc.edu
PITRE, Britt .... 404-225-4439 114 H
bpitre@atlantatech.edu
PITRE, Paul .... 425-405-1716 486 A
pep@wsu.edu
PITT, Sharon .... 302-831-0221.. 90 F
spitt@udel.edu
PITT, Steve .... 478-387-4783 118 G
spitt@gmc.edu
PITTENGER, David .... 304-696-2818 490 D
pittengerd@marshall.edu
PITTENGER, Susan, D ... 315-568-3069 308 F
spittenger@nycc.edu
PITTER, Yeruchem .... 516-255-4700 312 D
PITTINGER, Teresa, L .... 330-471-8121 355 L
tpittinger@malone.edu
PITTMAN, Anthony .... 908-737-3750 278 E
apittman@kean.edu
PITTMAN, Anthony .... 803-535-5225 407 G
PITTMAN, Chrystal .... 731-425-2611 425 B
cpittman@jscc.edu
PITTMAN, Crystal .... 864-941-8328 411 H
pittman.cg@ptc.edu
PITTMAN, Edward, L ..... 845-437-5426 324 C
edpittman@vassar.edu
PITTMAN, Felecia .... 601-877-6324 244 H
PITTMAN, James .... 315-268-6620 296 A
jpittman@clarkson.edu
PITTMAN, Jeff .... 314-539-5150 259 C
jeffpittman@stlcc.edu
PITTMAN, Jennifer .... 540-857-6807 476 D
jpittman@virginiawestern.edu
PITTMAN, Jeremy .... 419-434-5940 363 A
jeremy.pittman@findlay.edu
PITTMAN, John .... 386-481-2043.. 95 F
pittmanj@cookman.edu
PITTMAN, Karan, B .... 229-732-5944 114 B
karanpittman@andrewcollege.edu
PITTMAN, Katie .... 541-552-6758 376 E
pittmank@sou.edu
PITTMAN, L. Monique .. 269-471-3297 221 B
pittman@andrews.edu
PITTMAN, Nancy Claire 918-610-8303 369 A
nancy.pittman@ptsulsa.edu
PITTMAN, Sophia .... 770-394-8300 114 C
spittman@aii.edu
PITTMAN,
Stephanie, M .... 262-554-2010 494 D
pittmanmwc@aol.com
PITTMAN, Suzanne .... 478-445-6283 118 C
suzanne.pittman@gcsu.edu
PITTMAN, Thomas .... 919-573-5350 340 F
tpittman@shepherds.edu
PITTMAN, W. Randall ... 205-726-2331.... 6 E
rpittman@samford.edu
PITTS, Danielle .... 251-580-2178.... 1 I
danielle.brown@coastalalabama.edu
PITTS, James, E .... 850-644-0538 109 C
jpitts@fsu.edu
PITTS, Jamie .... 574-296-6242 152 I
jpitts@ambs.edu
PITTS, Jeremiah .... 229-317-6860 113 H
jeremiah.pitts@aurams.edu
PITTS, John .... 510-841-9230.. 75 E
jpitts@wi.edu
PITTS, Justin .... 864-663-7507 411 E
justin.pitts@ngu.edu
PITTS, Kevin .... 217-333-3946 151 D
kpitts@illinois.edu

PITTS, Mike .... 417-328-1412 259 L
mpitts@sbuniv.edu
PITTS, Otis .... 828-328-7179 330 F
otis.pitts@lr.edu
PITTS, Virgina .... 303-871-4156.. 83 D
virgina.pitts@du.edu
PITZER, Amy .... 304-384-5211 490 A
pitzer@concord.edu
PITZNER, Alex, C .... 717-901-5124 385 K
apitzner@harrisburgu.edu
PIUROWSKI, Robert, C . 607-746-4559 320 G
piurowrc@delhi.edu
PIVARNIK, OP,
R. Gabriel .... 401-865-2245 405 B
gpivarni@providence.edu
PIVONKA, TOR, Dave ... 740-283-6216 353 B
dpivonka@franciscan.edu
PIXLEY, Alan, D .... 972-758-3842 433 M
apixley@collin.edu
PIZANA, Kathleen .... 574-520-4878 157 A
kpizana@iusb.edu
PIZER, Lori .... 518-292-7785 313 D
inst_res@sage.edu
PIZZARDI, Frank .... 516-876-3082 319 A
pizzardif@oldwestbury.edu
PIZZARDI, Frank .... 516-876-3013 319 A
pizzardif@oldwestbury.edu
PIZZUTI, Debra .... 614-508-7233 354 F
dpizzuti@hondros.edu
PIZZUTI, John .... 740-283-6238 353 B
jpizzuti@franciscan.edu
PIZZUTI, Linda, J .... 309-677-3153 133 B
lindap@fsmail.bradley.edu
PIZZUTO, Phyllis .... 760-480-8474.. 74 J
ppizzuto@wscal.edu
PIZZUTO, William, J ..... 203-236-9818.. 88 E
william.j.pizzuto@uconn.edu
PIÑERO, Hector .... 787-850-9104 513 E
hector.pinero@upr.edu
PIÑERO, Ileana .... 787-751-1912 510 A
ipinero@juris.inter.edu
PJATAK, Jennifer .... 203-932-7082.. 89 A
jpjatak@newhaven.edu
PLACE, Jennifer .... 252-398-6553 328 D
placej@chowan.edu
PLACE, Nick, T .... 352-392-1761 109 F
nplace@ufl.edu
PLACER, Chandra .... 864-578-8770 412 B
cplacer@sherman.edu
PLACEY, David .... 518-327-6072 311 G
dplacey@paulsmiths.edu
PLACIDI, Kathleen .... 434-381-6596 472 D
kplacidi@sbc.edu
PLAEHN, Kris, H .... 253-535-7212 482 H
plaehnkh@plu.edu
PLAGGE, Sinead .... 360-416-7600 485 A
sinead.plagge@skagit.edu
PLAIN, Cuba .... 573-341-4122 261 E
plainc@mst.edu
PLAISANCE, DesLey ...... 985-448-4191 192 B
desley.plaisance@nicholls.edu
PLANDER, Kristy .... 402-481-8849 265 K
kristy.plander@bryanhealthcollege.edu
PLANEK, John .... 815-836-5937 141 G
planekjo@lewisu.edu
PLANT, Alisa .... 225-578-6144 188 I
alisaplant1@lsu.edu
PLANT, Jonathan .... 361-593-2599 447 D
jonathan.plant@tamuk.edu
PLANTE, Beverly .... 315-801-3034 313 G
bplante@secon.edu
PLANTE, Caiti .... 972-708-7340 435 H
caiti_plante@diu.edu
PLANTE, Dawn, M .... 440-525-7327 355 H
dplante@lakelandcc.edu
PLANTE, John, J .... 412-396-4937 383 C
plantej@duq.edu
PLANTEFABER, Lisa ...... 413-572-5733 213 D
lplantefaber@westfield.ma.edu
PLANTY, Teresa .... 315-268-3852 296 A
tplanty@clarkson.edu
PLANTZ, Dorothy, B ..... 443-518-4614 199 C
dplantz@howardcc.edu
PLANTZ, Robert .... 570-585-9258 381 E
rplantz@clarkssummitu.edu
PLANTZ-MASTERS,
Shari .... 303-458-4272.. 82 E
splantzmasters@regis.edu
PLASKER, Nancy .... 781-768-7019 218 C
nancy.plasker@regiscollege.edu
PLASSE, Michelle .... 310-338-7332.. 50 J
michelle.plasse@lmu.edu
PLASSMANN, Florenz .... 740-593-2850 359 G
plassmann@ohio.edu

PLASTERS, Shana .... 336-272-7102 329 D
shana.plasters@greensboro.edu
PLATING, John .... 706-419-1663 117 B
john.plating@covenant.edu
PLATOVSKY, Jonathan .. 718-268-4700 312 G
PLATT, Judy, T .... 617-353-5940 207 D
juplatt@bu.edu
PLATT, Kathleen .... 912-358-4144 123 H
plattk@savannahstate.edu
PLATT, Sharon .... 412-536-1120 387 B
sharon.platt@laroche.edu
PLATTE, Chelsea .... 231-348-6621 228 E
cplatte1@ncmich.edu
PLATUKUS, Graceann ... 570-740-0355 389 D
gplatukus@luzerne.edu
PLATZEK, Russell .... 718-262-2140 295 F
rplatzek@york.cuny.edu
PLAUGHER, Mark .... 540-373-2200 466 H
mplaugher@evcc.edu
PLAWECKI, Jeffrey .... 317-274-8892 156 F
jplaweck@iupui.edu
PLAYER, Kathleen, N .... 630-515-7664 143 G
kplayer@midwestern.edu
PLAZA, Erica .... 920-498-6969 500 F
erica.plaza@nwtc.edu
PLAZA, Laurie .... 610-526-6038 385 G
lplaza@harcum.edu
PLAZA, Luis .... 917-493-4448 305 I
lplaza@msmnyc.edu
PLEAS, Dawn, E .... 620-229-6336 177 A
dawn.pleas@sckans.edu
PLEAS, Dorothy, J .... 630-637-5156 144 H
djpleas@noctrl.edu
PLEASANT, Audra .... 501-279-4145.. 19 D
apleasant@harding.edu
PLEASANT, Klint .... 248-218-2058 229 J
kpleasant@rc.edu
PLEASANT, Klint, A .... 248-218-2058 229 J
kpleasant@rc.edu
PLEASANT, Lori .... 850-973-9469 103 K
pleasantl@nfcc.edu
PLEASANT-DOINE,
Sheia, I .... 904-819-6435.. 98 E
spleasant@flagler.edu
PLEASANTS, Jane .... 919-668-2565 328 G
jane.pleasants@duke.edu
PLEDGER, Barbara .... 607-436-2010 317 C
barbara.pledger@oneonta.edu
PLEDGER, Dianne .... 919-546-8455 340 E
dianne.pledger@shawu.edu
PLEGGENKUHLE, Jesse . 563-425-5666 170 A
pleggenkuhlej@uiu.edu
PLEMMONS, Donna ...... 501-450-1351.. 19 F
plemmons@hendrix.edu
PLEMMONS, Kim .... 704-403-1751 327 D
kim.plemmons@carolinashealthcare.
org
PLENDL, Jackie .... 712-274-6400 170 E
jackie.plendl@witcc.edu
PLENEFISCH, John .... 419-530-7840 363 E
john.plenefisch@utoledo.edu
PLENSKI, Sandra .... 415-581-8863.. 68 F
plenskis@uchastings.edu
PLENTY CHIEF, Melissa 701-255-3285 347 B
mplentychief@uttc.edu
PLESSINGER, Brian .... 907-852-1756.... 9 F
brian.plessinger@ilisagvik.edu
PLETSCHER,
Anthony, W .... 215-368-5000 390 F
tpletscher@missio.edu
PLEVER, Steve .... 828-251-6526 342 C
splever@unca.edu
PLINER, Lauren .... 215-953-5999.. 92 G
PLINER, Lauren .... 484-809-7770.. 92 G
PLINER, Susan .... 315-781-3354 302 A
pliner@hws.edu
PLINSKE, Kathleen, A ... 407-582-4975 112 K
kplinske@valenciacollege.edu
PLINSKE, Paul .... 719-549-2730.. 79 A
paul.plinske@csupueblo.edu
PLISCO, Mary .... 404-835-6135 423 K
mplisco@richmont.edu
PLISSEY, Bethany .... 802-635-1313 464 C
bethany.plissey@northernvermont.edu
PLOECKELMAN, Erica .... 920-686-6127 496 A
erica.ploeckelman@sl.edu
PLOECKELMAN,
Rebecca .... 414-277-7129 494 G
ploeckelman@msoe.edu
PLOEHN, Harry .... 252-328-9600 341 C
ploehnh17@ecu.edu
PLONSKY, Christine, A . 512-471-4780 455 A
cp@utexas.edu

POLLOI, Andrew 808-932-7464 128 E polllia@hawaii.edu
POLLOM, Andrew 603-899-4162 273 F polloma@franklinpierce.edu
POLLPETER, Heidi, K 407-831-9816 96 G hpollpeter@citycollege.edu
POLLY, Kimberley 847-925-6732 137 H kpolly@harpercollege.edu
POLNARIEV, Bernard 908-709-7007 284 C bernard.polnariev@ucc.edu
POLONSKY, Kenneth 773-702-3004 150 J polonsky@bsd.uchicago.edu
POLONSKY, Kenneth, S 773-702-3004 150 J polonsky@bsd.uchicago.edu
POLOWCHAK, Michelle 617-349-8785 210 H michelle.polowchak@lesley.edu
POLSDOFER, Duane 641-585-8121 170 B polsdofed@waldorf.edu
POLSGROVE, Kimberly 317-745-3703 208 G kimberly.polsgrove@enc.edu
POLSKY, Andrew 212-772-5195 294 C apolsky@hunter.cuny.edu
POLSON, Paula 703-908-7672 469 C paula.polson@marymount.edu
POLSTON, Rob 918-836-6886 370 D rob.polston@spartan.edu
POLTERSDORF, Todd 973-300-2253 283 E tpoltersdorf@sussex.edu
POLTORAK, Jeff 310-243-3183 31 B jpoltorak@csudh.edu
POLYARD, Brenda 417-255-7966 256 F brendapolyard@missouristate.edu
POLYDORIS, Jeanne 810-762-9562 225 H jpolydoris@kettering.edu
POLZIN, Elizabeth, A 262-243-5700 493 B elizabeth.polzin@cuw.edu
POMAKOY, Keith 845-434-5750 322 A kpomakoy@sunysullivan.edu
POMALAZA, Maggaly 787-850-9394 513 E maggaly.pomalaza@upr.edu
POMATTO, Mary Carol 620-235-4684 176 F mpomatto@pittstate.edu
POMERENK, Julia 541-346-3124 377 D jpom@uoregon.edu
POMERVILLE, Andrew 989-463-7231 220 H pomervillead@alma.edu
POMFRET, Margaret 419-289-5102 348 A mpomfret@ashland.edu
POMPER, Kirk, W 502-597-5942 182 H kirk.pomper@kysu.edu
POMPEY, JR., Robert 336-334-7587 341 F rpompey@ncat.edu
PONCE, Armando 956-295-3570 449 D armando.ponce@tsc.edu
PONCE, Christina 254-298-8600 446 A christina.ponce@templejc.edu
PONCE, Gregorio 760-768-5659 33 E gponce@sdsu.edu
PONCE, Roberto, C 614-823-1600 360 A ponce1@otterbein.edu
PONCE DE LEON, Monica 609-258-3737 280 E
PONCELET, Jolene 651-385-6349 239 A jponcelet@southeastmn.edu
POND, Justin 713-266-6594 436 F jpond@fortiscollege.edu
POND, Kevin 806-651-2585 448 C kpond@wtamu.edu
POND, Lisa, L 804-862-6100 470 I lpond@rbc.edu
POND, Sara 303-273-3153 78 I spond@mines.edu
PONDER, Anna 843-208-8255 413 E ponder@uscb.edu
PONDER, Anthony 937-512-2918 361 A anthony.ponder@sinclair.edu
PONDER, Elizabeth 903-923-2263 436 D eponder@etbu.edu
PONDER, Leslee 940-397-4350 440 F leslee.ponder@msutexas.edu
PONDER, Nathan 318-473-6431 188 J nponder@lsua.edu
PONDER, Nathan 318-473-6591 188 J nponder@lsua.edu
PONGRATZ, Richard 208-282-2130 130 H pongrich@isu.edu
PONIKVAR, Laura 216-421-7442 350 M lponikvar@cia.edu
PONNAR, Sekar 229-317-6546 113 H sekar.ponnar@asurams.edu
PONOROFF, Lawrence 517-432-6993 227 D lponoroff@msu.edu
PONREMY, Sue 708-524-6965 136 C sponremy@dom.edu
PONS, Jose, L 787-844-8181 514 A jose.pons@upr.edu
PONS MADERA, Jose 787-725-6500 506 G jpons@albizu.edu
PONSETTO, Jean 773-325-7503 135 I jlentipo@depaul.edu
PONT, Tanya 907-786-1278 9 H
PONTARI, Beth 864-294-2064 410 A beth.pontari@furman.edu
PONTELLI, Enrico 575-646-3500 287 B epontell@nmsu.edu
PONTERIO, Jane 914-594-4498 309 H jane_ponterio@nymc.edu
PONTI, Marilyn, K 509-527-5986 486 H pontimk@whitman.edu
PONTINEN, Jodi 218-749-7753 238 G j.pontinen@mesabirange.edu
PONTINEN, Jodi 218-749-7753 238 C j.pontinen@mesabirange.edu
PONTINEN, Jodi 218-749-7755 240 D jodi.pontinen@mesabirange.edu
PONTIOUS, Rebecca, E 605-342-0317 415 E admissions@jwc.edu
PONTON, Cynthia 434-544-8418 472 G ponton.cl@lynchburg.edu
PONTON, JR., David, C 318-274-6115 191 E pontond@gram.edu
PONTURO, Joseph 973-328-5500 277 B jponturo@ccm.edu
POOL, Gary 817-461-8741 430 H gpool@abu.edu
POOL, Jason 316-942-4291 175 I poolj@newmanu.edu
POOL, Robert 419-289-5324 348 A rpool2@ashland.edu
POOLE, Andrea 919-962-4592 341 A arpoole@northcarolina.edu
POOLE, Bill 817-272-3571 454 J bpoole@uta.edu
POOLE, David 919-658-7746 340 J dpoole@umo.edu
POOLE, Deborah 504-864-7051 189 F poole@loyno.edu
POOLE, Heather 318-487-5443 187 C heatherpoole@cltcc.edu
POOLE, Lana 573-592-5313 262 E lana.poole@westminster-mo.edu
POOLE, Leigh 803-323-2604 414 G poolela@winthrop.edu
POOLE, Lisa 724-805-2271 398 E president@stvincent.edu
POOLE, Lisa 724-805-2271 398 F lisa.poole@stvincent.edu
POOLE, Robyn 413-205-3547 205 A rob.poole@aic.edu
POOLE, Russell 303-724-0425 83 C russell.poole@ucdenver.edu
POOLE, Scott 865-974-5267 427 G scott.poole@utk.edu
POOLE, Stan 870-245-5196 20 E pooles@obu.edu
POOLE, Wayne, B 252-328-9027 341 C poolew@ecu.edu
POOLER, Traci, M 270-384-8100 183 C poolert@lindsey.edu
POOLER, III, Willis 270-384-8070 183 C poolerw@lindsey.edu
POOLEY, Ken 207-741-5548 195 A kpooley@smccme.edu
POON, Thomas 310-338-4280 50 J thomas.poon@lmu.edu
POOR, P. Joan 563-425-5284 170 A poorp43@uiu.edu
POORE, Mark, D 540-375-2403 471 B poore@roanoke.edu
POORE, Meshea, L 304-293-3431 491 C meshea.poore@mail.wvu.edu
POORE, Scott 276-944-6890 467 G pooresc@ehc.edu
POORMAN, Julie 252-328-6373 341 C poormanj@ecu.edu
POORMAN, CSC, Mark, L 503-943-7101 377 E poorman@up.edu
POORMOSLEH, Shahrzad 213-738-6794 65 G careerservices@swlaw.edu
POOVEY, Gena, E 864-488-4509 410 E gpoovey@limestone.edu
POPE, Christina 315-464-4582 317 F popec@upstate.edu
POPE, Darryl 410-462-8320 197 E dpope@bccc.edu
POPE, Edward 843-953-8235 408 E popeeb@cofc.edu
POPE, Jerry 913-288-7634 174 F jpope@kckcc.edu
POPE, Justin 434-395-4805 469 A popejn@longwood.edu
POPE, Keisha, L 804-257-5854 477 C klpope@vuu.edu
POPE, Matthew 865-471-3372 419 A mpope@cn.edu
POPE, Monique 909-748-8337 71 G monique_pope@redlands.edu
POPE, Myron 405-974-2361 370 K mpope5@uco.edu
POPE, Sandra, Y 304-293-1216 491 C spope@hsc.wvu.edu
POPE, Sarah 804-333-6705 475 G spope@rappahannock.edu
POPE, Sharon 570-372-4018 399 C popes@susqu.edu
POPE, Stephanie 541-885-1109 375 C stephanie.pope@oit.edu
POPE, Terri 216-987-3937 351 G terri.pope@tri-c.edu
POPE-BAYNE, Claudia 201-761-6111 282 I gpopbayne@saintpeters.edu
POPE-DAVIS, Donald, L 614-292-2461 358 I pope-davis.1@osu.edu
POPEJOY, Cindy 217-732-3168 141 H capopejoy@lincolnchristian.edu
POPELKA, David, M 515-294-7007 162 I dpopelka@iastate.edu
POPENFOOSE, G. Steve 217-732-3168 141 H gspopenfoose@lincolnchristian.edu
POPENFOOSE, Joel 847-628-1595 140 C joel.popenfoose@judsonu.edu
POPEO, Paula 508-678-2811 213 G paula.popeo@bristolcc.edu
POPESCU, Adriana 805-756-2622 30 C popescu@calpoly.edu
POPHAM, Don 636-922-8636 258 I dpopham@stchas.edu
POPHAM, Heidi 706-295-6928 119 A hpopham@gntc.edu
POPIELARCZYK, Zsa 773-907-4450 134 C zpopiela@ccc.edu
POPIOLEK, Marcus 313-664-7665 222 F mpopiolek@collegeforcreativestudies.edu
POPKEY, Megan 920-498-7186 500 F megan.popkey@nwtc.edu
POPKO, Susan 408-551-3085 62 D spopko@scu.edu
POPLAWSKI, Lisa 509-359-4555 480 E lpoplawski@ewu.edu
POPLIN, Lori 704-991-0116 338 C lpoplin0217@stanly.edu
POPLIN, Michelle 704-991-0208 338 C mpoplin4375@stanly.edu
POPOLOSKI, Tanya 603-623-0313 273 I tpopoloski@nhia.edu
POPOVICH, Donna, B 813-253-6237 112 J dpopovich@ut.edu
POPP, Laurie 503-491-7474 374 C laurie.popp@mhcc.edu
POPP, Melissa, D 636-584-6703 252 J melissa.popp@eastcentral.edu
POPP, Sherri, L 563-588-8000 165 F spopp@emmaus.edu
POPP, Stephen 616-949-5300 222 I stephen.popp@cornerstone.edu
POPP, Tari 269-471-3613 221 B tari@andrews.edu
POPP, William, C 770-720-5568 123 E wcp@reinhardt.edu
POPP-FINCH, Rochelle 772-462-7476 101 E rfinch@irsc.edu
POPP-RADFORD, Amy 269-749-7172 229 H
POPPA, Joseph 914-347-3910 325 C joseph.poppa@sunywcc.edu
POPPINGO, Mary 925-631-4356 59 B mep13@stmarys-ca.edu
POPPLEWELL, Venus 270-384-8189 183 C popplewellv@lindsey.edu
POPPO, Kristin 607-587-3913 320 C poppokr@alfredstate.edu
POPPRE, Beth 480-219-6026 250 A bpoppre@atsu.edu
PORCARO, Mark, D 316-978-7787 178 A mark.porcaro@wichita.edu
PORCELLA, Adam 215-702-4216 380 D aporcella@cairn.edu
PORCELLI, Mary 973-748-9000 276 A mary_porcelli@bloomfield.edu
PORCENA, Yves-Rose 678-839-5277 126 E yporcena@westga.edu
PORCH, Alesia 601-857-3240 246 B amporch@hindscc.edu
PORCHE, Demetrius 504-568-4106 189 B dporch@lsuhsc.edu
PORCHE, Saadia 323-953-4000 48 I porchest@lacitycollege.edu
PORE, Karen 910-893-1200 327 E
PORELL, Ryan 401-456-8094 405 C rporell@ric.edu
PORFIDO, Nancy 609-343-5095 275 D porfido@atlantic.edu
PORPILIA, Amy 585-594-6381 312 K porpilaa@roberts.edu
PORQUEZ, Gospel, G 215-887-5511 402 H gporquez@wts.edu
PORRAS, Precious 785-864-4350 177 D pporras@ku.edu
PORRIER, Jennifer 802-224-3001 463 H jen.porrier@vsc.edu
PORTEE, Charlene 334-229-5053 4 B dportee@alasu.edu
PORTEE, Kevin 803-705-4321 407 A kevin.portee@benedict.edu
PORTELA, Stanley 787-752-4540 513 C stanley.portela@upr.edu
PORTELA IRIGOYEN, Celso, E 787-725-8120 507 N cportela@centro.eap.edu
PORTELLEZ, Humberto 757-683-3626 469 G hportell@odu.edu
PORTEOUS, Alexander 207-780-4497 196 F alexander.porteous@maine.edu
PORTER, Aaron 865-471-3229 419 A aporter@cn.edu
PORTER, Adam 217-245-3010 138 D aporter@ic.edu
PORTER, Alex 714-484-7313 53 K aporter@cypresscollege.edu
PORTER, Andrea 806-651-2037 448 C aporter@wtamu.edu
PORTER, Autumn 660-596-7393 260 D aporter14@sfccmo.edu
PORTER, Barbara 540-831-5408 470 C bporter@radford.edu
PORTER, Bobbie 657-278-7326 31 E boporter@fullerton.edu
PORTER, Byron 540-261-4931 471 H byron.porter@svu.edu
PORTER, Chad 304-865-6091 488 E chad.porter@ovu.edu
PORTER, Chong, U 916-734-9402 68 E chong.porter@ucdmc.ucdavis.edu
PORTER, Christopher 540-857-6697 476 D cporter@virginiawestern.edu
PORTER, Chrystal 978-232-2817 209 B cporter@endicott.edu
PORTER, Cindy, L 914-323-5135 305 J cindy.porter@mville.edu
PORTER, Clifford 386-481-2966 95 F porterc@cookman.edu
PORTER, Clifton 413-755-4026 215 F ceporter@stcc.edu
PORTER, Connie 713-718-6477 437 I connie.porter@hccs.edu
PORTER, David 731-661-5343 427 C dporter@uu.edu
PORTER, David, S 401-874-2370 406 B dporter@uri.edu
PORTER, DeeDee 619-388-3976 60 C dporter@sdccd.edu
PORTER, Fonda 919-497-3205 330 I fporter@louisburg.edu
PORTER, Hugh, E 503-788-6604 376 C hporter@reed.edu
PORTER, J. Davison 504-314-2188 191 B jporter6@tulane.edu
PORTER, James, P 801-422-3963 458 H james_porter@byu.edu
PORTER, Jared 859-858-3511 178 I jared.porter@asbury.edu
PORTER, Jeffry, B 615-898-5005 422 H jeffry.porter@mtsu.edu
PORTER, Jennifer 617-735-9772 209 A porterj@emmanuel.edu
PORTER, Jennifer 248-218-2152 229 J jporter1@rc.edu

PORTER, John, R 636-949-4900 254 F jporter@lindenwood.edu
PORTER, Kalie 406-657-2188 264 E kporter@msubillings.edu
PORTER, Kathleen 239-489-9091 100 A kathleen.porter@fsw.edu
PORTER, Kristen 419-251-1339 356 C kristen.porter@mercycollege.edu
PORTER, Marc 415-494-8240 56 A mporter@patten.edu
PORTER, Mario 210-341-1366 441 C registrar@ost.edu
PORTER, Mark, J 401-863-3870 404 E mark_porter@brown.edu
PORTER, Miacia 615-327-6806 422 A mfporter@mmc.edu
PORTER, Michael, C 651-962-4376 244 E mcporter@stthomas.edu
PORTER, Michelle, C 605-342-0317 415 E mporter@jwc.edu
PORTER, Molly 619-849-2628 57 E mollyporter@pointloma.edu
PORTER, Monica 574-520-4872 157 A moport@iusb.edu
PORTER, Nadine 240-567-5386 200 C nadine.porter@montgomerycollege.edu
PORTER, Narda 276-328-0116 473 B nnb3h@virginia.edu
PORTER, Paul 260-399-7700 161 D pporter@sf.edu
PORTER, Rebecca 801-649-5230 459 G rebecca.porter@midwifery.edu
PORTER, Rhonda 229-430-4722 113 H rhonda.porter@asurams.edu
PORTER, Robyn 712-325-3413 167 B rporter@iwcc.edu
PORTER, Russell 254-501-5823 447 A porter@tamuct.edu
PORTER, Sha-Shonda 650-738-7149 61 Q
PORTER, Stephen 816-268-5462 257 C sporter@nts.edu
PORTER, Steve 620-665-3552 174 B porters@hutchcc.edu
PORTER, Susie, S 801-585-5693 460 E s.porter@utah.edu
PORTER, Todd 212-799-5000 303 H
PORTER, Tracy 863-297-3743 105 A tporter@polk.edu
PORTER, Vincent, C 210-829-2770 453 D porterv@uiwtx.edu
PORTER, Wilma, B 248-232-4640 229 A wbporter@oaklandcc.edu
PORTER-UTLEY, Kristen 508-531-2418 212 B k1porterutley@bridgew.edu
PORTERFIELD, Deana, L 585-594-6100 310 F presidentsoffice@roberts.edu
PORTERFIELD, Deana, L 585-594-6100 312 K presidentsoffice@roberts.edu
PORTERFIELD, Kent 314-977-2226 259 H kent.porterfield@slu.edu
PORTERFIELD, Sheila 601-979-2411 246 E sheila.y.porterfield@jsums.edu
PORTLOCK, Jeremy 785-594-8415 170 I jeremy.portlock@bakeru.edu
PORTMANN, Brooke 231-843-5866 232 J bportmann@westshore.edu
PORTNER, Matthew 419-289-5251 348 A mportner@ashland.edu
PORTNOY, Lauren 610-896-4984 385 L lportnoy@haverford.edu
PORTNOY, Robert, N 402-472-7450 269 J rportnoy1@unl.edu
PORTWINE, Ronald, E 989-964-2064 230 B report@svsu.edu
PORTZ, Margaret, A 610-758-5794 388 J mak5@lehigh.edu
PORTZEL, Curt 310-506-4893 56 C curt.portzel@pepperdine.edu
PORVAZNIK, John 480-377-4556 13 G porvaznik@riosalado.edu
PORYEM, Wenceslaus 859-622-1478 180 B wenceslaus.poryem@eku.edu
PORZUCEK, Sarah 716-839-8210 298 B sporzuce@daemen.edu
POSENER, Paul 910-775-4253 343 B paul.posener@uncp.edu
POSER, Susan 312-413-3450 151 B sposer@uic.edu
POSEY, Evan 770-484-1204 121 D evan.posey@lutherrice.edu
POSEY, Jamie 423-585-6894 426 C jamie.posey@ws.edu
POSEY, Jamie 832-813-6776 439 G jamie.c.posey@lonestar.edu
POSEY, Jeff 601-877-6471 244 H mjposey@alcorn.edu
POSEY, Libby 601-857-3350 246 B olivia.posey@hindscc.edu
POSEY, Monica 513-569-1515 350 K monica.posey@cincinnatistate.edu
POSHEK, Joseph 949-451-5650 64 F jposhek@ivc.edu
POSING, Mary 815-802-8202 140 D mposing@kcc.edu
POSKANZER, JR., Steven, G 507-222-4305 234 F president@carleton.edu
POSKIN, Jill 630-829-6366 132 E jposkin@ben.edu
POSLER, Brian 440-375-7200 355 G president@lec.edu
POSLUSNY, Matthew 919-760-8514 331 B mposlusny@meredith.edu
POSMAN, Jerald 718-270-5026 295 A jposman@mec.cuny.edu
POSNER, Deborah 954-201-7482 95 H dposner@broward.edu
POSNER, Kenneth 352-588-8992 106 D kenneth.posner@saintleo.edu
POSNER, Marc 714-484-7006 53 K mposner@cypresscollege.edu
POSNER, Mark 651-638-6383 234 C m-posner@bethel.edu
POSS, Joe 509-313-6215 481 D poss@gonzaga.edu
POSS, Michael 378-839-6452 126 E mposs@westga.edu
POSSEHL, Kristin 605-367-4753 417 D kristin.possehl@southeasttech.edu
POST, Beth 518-580-5750 316 A bpost@skidmore.edu
POST, Brendan 765-983-1693 154 G postbr@earlham.edu
POST, Jack 856-227-7200 276 E jpost@camdencc.edu
POST, Julie 770-962-7580 120 E jpost@gwinnetttech.edu
POST, Kari 802-387-6790 462 D karipost@landmark.edu
POST, Michael, A 540-828-8014 465 D mpost@bridgewater.edu
POST, Robert 574-284-5000 160 C rpostjr@saintmarys.edu
POST, Robert 610-361-5233 391 D postr@neumann.edu
POST, Scott 870-338-6474 22 H
POST, Stacy 906-635-2684 226 E spost1@lssu.edu
POST, Todd 815-802-8602 140 D tpost@kcc.edu
POST, Tracee 806-651-2100 448 C tpost@wtamu.edu
POSTEMA, Miles, J 231-591-3894 223 J milespostema@ferris.edu
POSTER, Michael, C 563-333-6032 169 A postermichaelc@sau.edu
POSTLETHWAITE, Bonnie 816-235-1531 261 C postlethwaiteb@umkc.edu
POSTMA, Jana 616-988-3650 226 C jpostma@kuyper.edu
POSTMA, Kurt 616-538-2330 224 C kpostma@gracechristian.edu
POSTMA, Laura 906-248-8420 221 N lpostma@bmcc.edu
POSTON, Linda 717-691-6006 390 E poston@messiah.edu
POSTON, R. Stephen 704-233-8194 344 G poston@wingate.edu
POSTON, Robin 901-678-5739 427 D rposton@memphis.edu
POSTUPACK, Mary Frances 570-422-7920 394 E mpostupack@esu.edu
POTASH, David 773-481-8175 134 G dpotash@ccc.edu
POTEET, Jim 913-722-0272 174 E jim.poteet@kansaschristian.edu
POTEET, Tanya, J 614-236-6408 349 D tpoteet@capital.edu
POTEET, Tony 901-678-2619 427 D ppoteet@memphis.edu
POTEETE-YOUNG, Lanette 847-628-1097 140 C lpoteete-young@judsonu.edu
POTEMKIN, Alex 817-515-7463 445 G alexis.potemkin@tccd.edu
POTEMPA, John 708-656-8000 144 E john.potempa@morton.edu
POTERALA, Michael, R 301-405-4945 202 C poterala@umd.edu
POTH, David 918-595-7639 370 E david.poth@tulsacc.edu
POTH, Mark 509-793-2194 478 H markp@bigbend.edu
POTILLO, Jean 603-206-8081 272 L jpotillo@ccsnh.edu
POTOCZAK, Mel 978-762-4000 215 B mpotocza@northshore.edu
POTTEBAUM, Marty 712-279-5430 163 C marty.pottebaum@briarcliff.edu
POTTEIGER, Jeffrey 616-331-7207 224 E potteigj@gvsu.edu
POTTER, Adam 607-844-8222 322 H
POTTER, Alan 919-573-5350 340 F apotter@shepherds.edu
POTTER, Aron 620-252-7005 172 G potter.aron@coffeyville.edu
POTTER, Bill 661-395-4221 46 L william.potter@bakersfieldcollege.edu
POTTER, Cambria 816-802-3445 254 B cpotter@kcai.edu
POTTER, Cathryn, C 848-932-5384 282 A cpotter@ssw.rutgers.edu
POTTER, Cathryn, C 848-932-5384 282 B cpotter@ssw.rutgers.edu
POTTER, Charlie 509-533-8861 480 A charlie.potter@scc.spokane.edu
POTTER, Cheryl, J 704-406-4269 329 A cpotter@gardner-webb.edu
POTTER, Corrie 650-723-2300 65 J cjpotter@stanford.edu
POTTER, Cory 434-797-8576 474 E cory.potter@danville.edu
POTTER, Douglas, E 704-847-5600 340 I dpotter@ses.edu
POTTER, Gia 606-218-5211 185 D giapotter@upike.edu
POTTER, James 406-265-3727 264 F potterj@msun.edu
POTTER, Jennifer 609-652-4381 283 D jennifer.potter@stockton.edu
POTTER, Jonathan 848-932-7527 282 A jonathan.potter@rutgers.edu
POTTER, Kay, C 205-853-1200 2 G kpotter@jeffersonstate.edu
POTTER, Keith 541-684-7439 374 G kpotter@nwcu.edu
POTTER, Lawrence 202-274-6591 93 C lawrence.potter@udc.edu
POTTER, Mark 312-553-2500 134 A mdpotter@ccc.edu
POTTER, Michelle 541-881-5712 377 B mpotter@tvcc.cc
POTTER, Mike 425-739-8387 482 A mike.potter@lwtech.edu
POTTER, Monifa, J 340-693-1151 514 E mpotter@uvi.edu
POTTER, Neal 850-263-3261 95 B rnpotter@baptistcollege.edu
POTTER, Rachel 540-887-7134 469 B rpotter@marybaldwin.edu
POTTER, Ralph 502-570-6357 180 K ralph.potter@kctcs.edu
POTTER, Rhyannon 757-683-3407 469 G rpotter@follett.com
POTTER, Robert, A 401-254-3498 405 E bobpotter@rwu.edu
POTTER, Shawn 504-247-1237 191 B spotter@tulane.edu
POTTER, Stephen, L 336-841-9125 329 G spotter@highpoint.edu
POTTER, Terry 303-315-5830 83 C terence.potter@ucdenver.edu
POTTER, Tracy 919-497-3212 330 I tpotter@louisburg.edu
POTTER, Wendy 801-957-4592 461 D wendy.potter@slcc.edu
POTTER, William 304-256-0262 489 C wpotter@newriver.edu
POTTER, Zachary 610-799-1034 388 I zpotter@follett.com
POTTER-HENDERSON, Leslie 205-546-4554 484 G lhenders@shoreline.edu
POTTHARST, Kris 504-520-5441 193 A kpotthar@xula.edu
POTTHOFF, Dennis 702-992-2525 271 C dennis.potthoff@nsc.edu
POTTLE, Russ 508-929-8257 213 E rpottle@worcester.edu
POTTORFF, James 402-472-1201 269 H jpottorff@nebraska.edu
POTTS, Charlie 507-933-7526 235 I cpotts@gustavus.edu
POTTS, Colin 404-894-5551 118 F colin.potts@cc.gatech.edu
POTTS, Jonathan, E 412-397-5291 397 G potts@rmu.edu
POTTS, OP, Mary Esther 615-297-7545 418 C srmesther@aquinascollege.edu
POTTS, Molly 706-864-1800 126 A molly.potts@ung.edu
POTTS, Nacole 828-884-8249 327 C pottsna@brevard.edu
POTTS, Natalie 773-442-5416 145 B n-potts@neiu.edu
POTTS, Stephane 217-443-8749 135 H spotts@dacc.edu
POTTS, Steve 304-326-1394 488 F spotts@salemu.edu
POTTS, Steven 310-506-4749 56 C steve.potts@pepperdine.edu
POTTS, Tim 260-481-0739 159 F pottst@pfw.edu
POTVIN, David 601-968-5904 245 C dpotvin@belhaven.edu
POTVIN, Martha 413-748-3959 218 G mpotvin@springfield.edu
POTVIN-GIORDANO, Claudine 518-629-7451 302 E c.potvingiordano@hvcc.edu
POU, Laure 423-425-5742 428 A laure-pou@utc.edu
POUDRIER-AARONSON, Lucinda 508-999-8145 211 F l.aaronson@umassd.edu
POUERIET-DE LA CRUZ, Zacarias 787-480-2392 507 C zpoueriet@sanjuanciudadpatria.com
POULAKIDAS, Jennifer 310-794-6808 69 A jpoulakidas@support.ucla.edu
POULETTE, Samuel 920-565-1000 493 J poulettesg@lakeland.edu
POULIOT, Cory 617-627-2661 219 B cory.pouliot@tufts.edu
POULLARD, Theresa 909-469-5560 74 I tpoullard@westernu.edu
POULLIOT, Erin 814-868-9900 383 F epoulliot@erieit.edu
POULOS, Jim 716-827-2421 323 D poulosj@trocaire.edu
POULTER, Patricia, S 501-450-5073 23 H ppoulter@uca.edu
POUNCEY, Craig 251-580-2100 1 I
POUNCIL, Matais 408-741-2136 74 E matais.pouncil@westvalley.edu
POUNDS, Leonard 954-262-4869 103 M lpounds@nova.edu
POUNDS, Matt 785-890-3641 176 C matt.pounds@nwktc.edu
POURCHOT, Jeri 425-388-9572 480 G jpourchot@everettcc.edu
POURIER, Arlis 605-455-6018 416 B apourier@olc.edu
POURIER, Marilyn 605-455-6045 416 B mpourier@olc.edu
POUZAR, Sharree 513-721-7944 353 F spouzar@gbs.edu
POVENTUD, Irem 787-841-2000 510 K ipoventud@pucpr.edu
POWE, F. Douglas 202-664-5706 93 E dpowe@wesleyseminary.edu
POWELEIT, Deborah 513-569-1550 350 K deborah.poweleit@cincinnatistate.edu
POWELL, Aaron 206-685-2676 485 F powellaa@uw.edu
POWELL, Adam, C 770-720-5549 123 E adam.powell@reinhardt.edu
POWELL, Adriane 309-556-1355 139 G apowell@iwu.edu
POWELL, Alex 617-585-1103 217 B alex.powell@necmusic.edu
POWELL, Andrew, L 717-361-1438 383 E powella@etown.edu
POWELL, Anna 870-777-5722 22 A anna.powell@uaht.edu

POWELL, Arthur, B .... 973-353-3530 282 B
powellab@newark.rutgers.edu
POWELL, Brian .... 714-997-6779.. 36 C
powell@chapman.edu
POWELL, Brian, M .... 724-458-2992 385 C
bmpowell@gcc.edu
POWELL, Chris .... 661-362-2208.. 51 C
cpowell@masters.edu
POWELL, Cody, J .... 513-529-7070 356 E
powellcj@miamioh.edu
POWELL, Curtis, N .... 518-276-6302 312 I
powelc2@rpi.edu
POWELL, Daniel .... 210-486-4097 429 E
dpowell52@alamo.edu
POWELL, Daphne .... 205-226-4908.... 5 A
dcpowell@bsc.edu
POWELL, Darrin .... 270-706-8406 181 A
darrin.powell@kctcs.edu
POWELL, David, M .... 269-964-6653 232 K
dave.powell@wmich.edu
POWELL, Deborah .... 301-846-2479 198 E
dpowell@frederick.edu
POWELL, Denise .... 912-538-3162 124 F
dpowell@southeasterntech.edu
POWELL, Devon .... 708-596-2000 149 B
dpowell@ssc.edu
POWELL, Donato .... 626-815-3004.. 26 H
dspowell@apu.edu
POWELL, Emily .... 325-574-7629 458 E
epowell@wtc.edu
POWELL, Glenn .... 706-721-1896 115 A
gpowell@augusta.edu
POWELL, Gregory, S ..... 903-693-2022 441 F
gpowell@panola.edu
POWELL, Hattie .... 903-886-5140 447 B
hattie.powell@tamuc.edu
POWELL, Hiram .... 386-481-2956.. 95 F
powellh@cookman.edu
POWELL, James .... 308-432-6330 268 E
jpowell@csc.edu
POWELL, James .... 419-289-5350 348 A
jpowell1@ashland.edu
POWELL, Jason .... 540-365-4376 467 I
jpowell@ferrum.edu
POWELL, Jeffrey, A .... 701-788-4697 345 E
jeffrey.powell@mayvillestate.edu
POWELL, Jill .... 704-463-3037 339 E
jill.powell@pfeiffer.edu
POWELL, Joel .... 916-691-7226.. 50 G
powellj@crc.losrios.edu
POWELL, John .... 304-205-6607 488 K
john.powell@bridgevalley.edu
POWELL, JR., John, W . 843-953-5200 407 F
john.powell@citadel.edu
POWELL, Joseph .... 912-443-5821 124 A
jpowell@savannahtech.edu
POWELL, Karan .... 814-472-3004 398 B
kpowell@francis.edu
POWELL, Katherine .... 706-236-1707 115 B
kpowell@berry.edu
POWELL, Kathleen, I ..... 757-221-3231 466 C
kipowell@wm.edu
POWELL, Keith .... 706-754-7736 122 F
keith.powell@northgatech.edu
POWELL, Keith .... 919-546-8238 340 E
keith.powell@shawu.edu
POWELL, Kevin .... 804-524-5691 477 B
manager525@nebook.com
POWELL, Logan .... 401-863-7940 404 E
logan_powell@brown.edu
POWELL, Marilyn .... 866-492-5336 244 F
marilyn.powell@mail.waldenu.edu
POWELL, Marleen .... 910-592-8081 337 G
mpowell@sampsoncc.edu
POWELL, Michael, G .... 804-524-2902 477 B
mgpowell@vsu.edu
POWELL, Mirian .... 251-405-7072.... 1 E
mpowell@bishop.edu
POWELL, Monica .... 318-869-5016 186 B
mpowell@centenary.edu
POWELL, Nancy, L .... 606-451-6842 182 C
nancy.powell@kctcs.edu
POWELL, Panda .... 910-962-3167 343 C
powellp@uncw.edu
POWELL, Patricia .... 334-222-6591.... 2 I
ppowell@lbwcc.edu
POWELL, Reese .... 601-318-6170 249 H
rpowell@wmcarey.edu
POWELL, Russell .... 206-296-6953 484 F
rpowell@seattleu.edu
POWELL, Sam .... 619-849-2334.. 57 E
sampowell@pointloma.edu
POWELL, Shawn .... 575-624-7111 286 A
shawn.powell@roswell.enmu.edu
POWELL, Stephanie, E .. 850-263-3261.. 95 B
sepowell@baptistcollege.edu
POWELL, Steve .... 254-442-5133 433 A
steve.powell@cisco.edu
POWELL, Susan, E .... 601-979-2241 246 E
susan.e.powell@jsums.edu
POWELL, Theresa, A ..... 215-204-6556 399 F
theresa.powell@temple.edu
POWELL, Timothy, M ... 559-251-4215.. 28 B
tpowell@calchristiancollege.edu
POWELL, Torence .... 916-691-7329.. 50 G
powellt@crc.losrios.edu
POWELL, Tremaine .... 423-697-4434 424 E
tremaine.powell@chattanoogastate.edu
POWELL, Wayne .... 479-968-0274.. 18 C
wpowell4@atu.edu
POWELL BRASWELL,
Gwendolyn .... 269-471-6530 221 B
ogc@andrews.edu
POWELL-CASE, Martha .. 970-824-1112.. 78 G
kathy.powell@cncc.edu
POWELL LOGAN, Kelly . 717-901-5100 385 K
klogan@harrisburgu.edu
POWELL LOGAN, Kelly . 717-901-5171 385 K
klogan@harrisburgu.edu
POWENSKI, Stephen ..... 773-995-3526 133 K
spowensk@csu.edu
POWER, Jane .... 252-493-7630 336 H
jpower@email.pittcc.edu
POWER, Laura .... 815-479-7533 143 A
lpower@mchenry.edu
POWER, Mark .... 479-575-5064.. 21 G
mepower@uark.edu
POWER, Michael, K ...... 770-216-2960 120 H
mpower@ict.edu
POWER, Sandy .... 606-759-7141 182 A
sandy.power@kctcs.edu
POWER-BARNES,
Marie, R .... 609-984-4839 284 B
mpowerbarnes@tesu.edu
POWERS, Amanda, C .... 662-329-7333 248 A
amandacpowers@muw.edu
POWERS, Amber .... 215-576-0800 397 C
apowers@rrc.edu
POWERS, Andrew .... 740-593-1911 359 G
powersa@ohio.edu
POWERS, Anjanette .... 662-846-4406 245 H
apowers@deltastate.edu
POWERS, Christa .... 214-333-5842 434 I
christa@dbu.edu
POWERS, Christopher ... 859-344-3514 184 F
powersc@thomasmore.edu
POWERS, Colleen .... 914-674-7707 306 F
cpowers5@mercy.edu
POWERS, Danial .... 425-558-0299 480 D
dpowers@digipen.edu
POWERS, David .... 206-296-5300 484 F
powersda@seattleu.edu
POWERS, Douglas .... 707-621-7000.. 41 F
POWERS, Helen .... 803-777-3971 413 C
hefields@mailbox.sc.edu
POWERS, Jacque .... 336-285-2469 341 F
jpowers@ncat.edu
POWERS, Jon, R .... 740-368-3082 359 N
jrpowers@owu.edu
POWERS, Joshua .... 973-720-2122 284 I
powersj@wpunj.edu
POWERS, Katherine .... 802-828-2800 464 B
kap06170@ccv.vsc.edu
POWERS, Kathleen .... 716-851-1017 299 F
mcgrifpowers@ecc.edu
POWERS, Keri .... 508-531-1324 212 B
keri.powers@bridgew.edu
POWERS, Kristina .... 650-543-3787.. 51 F
kristina.powers@menlo.edu
POWERS, Lisa, M .... 814-865-7517 392 B
lmr8@psu.edu
POWERS, Lynn .... 386-312-4116 106 C
lynnpowers@sjrstate.edu
POWERS, Mark, R .... 508-626-4545 212 D
mpowers@framingham.edu
POWERS, Michael .... 724-357-3062 394 G
michael.powers@iup.edu
POWERS, Miranda .... 651-638-6543 234 C
m-powers@bethel.edu
POWERS, Peter, K .... 717-691-6013 390 E
ppowers@messiah.edu
POWERS, Rebecca .... 215-596-8972 401 G
r.powers@usciences.edu
POWERS, Rebecca .... 215-753-3664 381 D
powersr@chc.edu
POWERS, Sandee .... 618-537-6957 143 B
sjpowers@mckendree.edu
POWERS, Sarah .... 405-208-5031 367 I
sepowers@okcu.edu
POWERS, Sherry .... 859-622-1175 180 B
sherry.powers@eku.edu
POWERS, Shonda .... 606-539-4448 185 A
shonda.powers@ucumberlands.edu
POWERS, Susan .... 812-237-2307 155 G
susan.powers@indstate.edu
POWERS, Susan .... 315-268-6542 296 A
spowers@clarkson.edu
POWERS, Susie .... 859-846-5340 183 E
spowers@midway.edu
POWERS, Suzanne .... 417-328-1689 259 L
spowers@sbuniv.edu
POWERS, Tammy .... 575-528-7069 287 E
tpowers@nmsu.edu
POWERS, Teri .... 619-574-6909.. 54 K
tpowers@pacificcollege.edu
POWERS, Tracy .... 903-813-2451 430 N
tpowers@austincollege.edu
POWERS, Tyrone .... 410-777-7496 197 C
tpowers@aacc.edu
POWERS, Wendy .... 414-382-6494 492 A
wendy.powers@alverno.edu
POWERS, William .... 617-989-4407 219 E
powersw2@wit.edu
POWICKI, Mike .... 402-375-7520 268 G
mipowic1@wsc.edu
POWLEY, Mary, R .... 585-385-8057 314 A
mpowley@sjfc.edu
POWNALL, Phillip .... 904-819-6460.. 98 E
ppownall@flagler.edu
POYNTER, Barry .... 859-622-5012 180 B
barry.poynter@eku.edu
POYZER, Bryan .... 701-671-2872 346 E
bryan.poyzer@ndscs.edu
POZANC, Lisa .... 507-453-2402 239 A
lpozanc@southeastmn.edu
POZZA, Amy .... 804-627-5300 465 C
amy_pozza@bshsi.org
PRABHU, Vilas, A .... 717-871-7555 395 D
vilas.prabhu@millersville.edu
PRACHAND, Amit .... 847-467-5067 145 F
a-prachand@northwestern.edu
PRADHAN, Raj .... 770-426-2697 121 C
araj@life.edu
PRADO, Guillermo .... 305-243-2748 112 E
gprado@miami.edu
PRADO, Lenore, M .... 305-628-6514 106 F
lprado@stu.edu
PRAET, Diane, M .... 313-993-3313 231 B
praetdm@udmercy.edu
PRAG, Stephen .... 503-352-1563 375 G
sprag@pacificu.edu
PRAKASAM, Piram .... 231-591-5290 223 J
piramprakasam@ferris.edu
PRAKASH, Anupma .... 907-474-7096.. 10 A
aprakash@alaska.edu
PRAKASH,
Channapatana .... 334-725-2334.... 7 D
cprakash@tuskegee.edu
PRAKASH, Neeta .... 954-545- ... 107 E
nprakash@sfbc.edu
PRALL, Andrew .... 512-448-8446 442 M
aprall@stedwards.edu
PRANGE, Raphaella ...... 217-424-6395 143 H
rpalmer@millikin.edu
PRAPAVESSI, Despina ... 925-969-2689.. 40 I
dprapavessi@dvc.edu
PRASLOVA, Ludmilla .... 714-556-3610.. 72 F
ludmilla.praslova@vanguard.edu
PRASTACOS, Gregory .... 201-216-8366 283 C
gregory.prastacos@stevens.edu
PRATER, Ann .... 971-722-4387 375 J
ann.prater@pcc.edu
PRATER, Chanda, F ...... 270-852-3104 183 A
cprater@kwc.edu
PRATER, Kelly .... 806-371-5311 430 A
klprater@actx.edu
PRATER, Mary Anne ..... 801-422-3695 458 H
prater@byu.edu
PRATER, Michael .... 574-520-4319 157 A
maprater@iusb.edu
PRATER, Sarah, E .... 574-372-5100 155 B
praterse@grace.edu
PRATER, Todd, K .... 706-880-8238 121 A
tprater@lagrange.edu
PRATER, Wendi .... 337-475-5126 192 A
wprater@mcneese.edu
PRATHER, Curtis .... 703-370-6600 470 B
PRATHER, Kanidrus ...... 706-225-5300.. 92 G
PRATHER, Kerry, N .... 317-738-8121 154 J
kprather@franklincollege.edu
PRATHER, Sean .... 925-424-1690.. 35 P
sprather@laspositascollege.edu
PRATHER-JOHNSON,
Nancy, N .... 757-822-1191 476 B
nprather@tcc.edu
PRATT, Barbara .... 908-835-2355 284 G
pratt@warren.edu
PRATT, Carla .... 785-670-1662 177 G
carla.pratt@washburn.edu
PRATT, Christy .... 574-631-7305 161 C
cpratt3@nd.edu
PRATT, Dorianna .... 207-768-9462 196 E
dorianna@maine.edu
PRATT, Edward, E .... 561-297-0567 108 J
epratt2@fau.edu
PRATT, Elizabeth .... 415-883-2211.. 39 C
epratt@marin.edu
PRATT, Elizabeth .... 408-288-3142.. 61 M
elizabeth.pratt@sjcc.edu
PRATT, Gary, L .... 785-532-6520 174 G
gpratt@ksu.edu
PRATT, H. Wes .... 417-836-3736 256 E
wpratt@missouristate.edu
PRATT, Heather .... 240-567-3097 200 C
heather.pratt@montgomerycollege.edu
PRATT, Margie .... 610-921-2381 378 C
mpratt@albright.edu
PRATT, Michael .... 205-652-3565.... 9 A
mpratt@uwa.edu
PRATT, Michele .... 989-686-9822 223 G
michelepratt@delta.edu
PRATT, Robert, C .... 517-750-1200 230 H
bpratt@arbor.edu
PRATT, Sally .... 213-740-8867.. 72 B
pratt@usc.edu
PRATT, Tamara .... 405-733-7961 369 I
tpratt@rose.edu
PRATT, JR.,
Theodore, W .... 360-650-3450 486 F
ted.pratt@cc.wwu.edu
PRATT, Tot .... 636-584-6733 252 J
tot.pratt@eastcentral.edu
PRATT, Tracey .... 570-702-8908 386 G
tpratt@johnson.edu
PRATT, Vallarie .... 706-712-8244 117 C
vpratt@daltonstate.edu
PRATT-CLARKE, Menah . 540-231-7500 477 A
inclusive@vt.edu
PRATT-COOK, Patricia ... 651-690-6560 242 R
pcprattcook867@stkate.edu
PRATTE, John .... 318-342-1235 192 F
pratte@ulm.edu
PRATTELLA, Todd .... 914-674-7844 306 F
tprattella@mercy.edu
PREACHER, Stephen ..... 864-644-5486 412 E
spreacher@swu.edu
PREAS, Ethan, D .... 903-468-8781 447 B
ethan.preas@tamuc.edu
PREAST, Lori .... 252-493-7224 336 H
lpreast@email.pittcc.edu
PREATHER, Gary .... 817-515-6742 445 G
gary.preather@tccd.edu
PREBLE, Mark .... 617-287-7050 211 C
mpreble@umassp.edu
PRECHT, Erica .... 337-521-6985 188 C
PRECHTER, Patricia .... 504-398-2213 191 C
pprechter@uhcno.edu
PRECISE, Leigh .... 740-362-3121 356 D
lprecise@mtso.edu
PREDMORE, Andrew ..... 812-855-2818 156 B
sapredmo@indiana.edu
PREDOEHL, Dan .... 949-582-4313.. 64 G
dpredoehl@saddleback.edu
PREECE, Barbara .... 410-617-6811 199 F
bpreece@loyola.edu
PREECE, Barbara .... 410-617-6811 201 B
bpreece@ndm.edu
PREGEANT, Gene, E ...... 985-549-5888 192 D
gpregeant@selu.edu
PREGLIASCO, Collin ..... 916-691-7367.. 50 G
preglic@crc.losrios.edu
PREIMESBERGER, Paul . 218-855-8163 237 F
ppreimesberger@clcmn.edu
PREISLER, Karen .... 979-532-6383 458 F
karenp@wcjc.edu
PRELOCK, Patricia, A .... 802-656-1417 463 E
patricia.prelock@med.uvm.edu
PREMO, Brenda .... 909-469-5385.. 74 I
bpremo@westernu.edu
PRENDERGAST,
Debra, L .... 708-709-3689 146 D
dprendergast@prairiestate.edu

PRINCE, Cristin .... 217-443-8864 135 H
cprince@dacc.edu
PRINCE, J. Dale .... 504-568-7698 189 B
jprin2@lsuhsc.edu
PRINCE, James .... 330-263-2581 351 C
jprince@wooster.edu
PRINCE, Joan, M .... 414-229-3101 497 A
jprince@uwm.edu
PRINCE, Judith .... 864-552-4243 414 D
jprince@uscupstate.edu
PRINCE, Ken .... 812-866-7051 155 C
princek@hanover.edu
PRINCE, Tiffany .... 541-506-6103 372 G
tprince@cgcc.edu
PRINCE, Travis .... 205-226-4994.... 5 A
twprince@bsc.edu
PRINCE-RICHARD,
Celia, P .... 340-692-4132 514 E
cprince@uvi.edu
PRINCE ROSS, Tracey ... 202-884-9126.. 93 B
princetr@trinitydc.edu
PRINCIPE, Frank .... 301-985-7077 203 B
frank.principe@umuc.edu
PRINDLE, Brian .... 802-656-1435 463 E
brian.prindle@uvm.edu
PRINGLE, Cedrick .... 202-685-4341 503 I
cedrick.pringle.mil@ndu.edu
PRINGLE, Eboni .... 330-672-8700 354 J
epringle@kent.edu
PRINGLE, Ernest .... 803-641-3345 413 D
ernestp@usca.edu
PRINGLE, Mark .... 614-236-6813 349 D
mpringle@capital.edu
PRIODE, Kimberly, S .... 828-898-8769 330 E
PRIOLEAU, Florence .... 202-806-2650.. 92 B
florence.prioleau@howard.edu
PRIOLEAU, Florence ..... 202-806-2250.. 92 B
florence.prioleau@howard.edu
PRIOLO, Julianne .... 616-538-2330 224 C
jpriolo@gracechristian.edu
PRISCO, Anne .... 201-559-6022 278 A
priscoa@felician.edu
PRISELAC, Thomas .... 310-423-8294.. 35 L
PRISLIN, Radmila .... 619-594-5166.. 33 E
rprislin@sdsu.edu
PRITCHARD, Alice .... 860-723-0016.. 84 H
pritcharda@ct.edu
PRITCHARD, Brett .... 256-215-4254.... 1 G
bpritchard@cacc.edu
PRITCHARD, Gary .... 562-860-2451.. 35 M
gpritchard@cerritos.edu
PRITCHARD, Hillary, D . 336-633-0122 337 A
hdpritchard@randolph.edu
PRITCHARD, Kathren .... 209-575-6901.. 75 H
prichardk@yosemite.edu
PRITCHARD, Lamar .... 713-743-1253 452 F
flpritchard@uh.edu
PRITCHARD, Laurel .... 702-895-1506 271 E
laurel.pritchard@unlv.edu
PRITCHARD, Lisa .... 636-481-3160 254 A
lpritcha@jeffco.edu
PRITCHARD, Megan ...... 603-897-8481 274 B
mpritchard@rivier.edu
PRITCHARD, Michael .... 301-846-2417 198 E
mpritchard@frederick.edu
PRITCHARD, Sarah, M .. 847-491-7640 145 F
spritchard@northwestern.edu
PRITCHERT, Marcia .... 701-845-7541 346 A
marcia.pitchert@vcsu.edu
PRITCHETT, Alondrea, J 334-229-4737.... 4 B
apritchett@alasu.edu
PRITCHETT, James .... 970-491-6274.. 78 M
james.pritchett@colostate.edu
PRITCHETT, Marie .... 586-445-7315 226 H
pritchettm@macomb.edu
PRITCHETT, Megan .... 601-925-3210 247 C
mpritchett@mc.edu
PRITCHETT, Wendell, E . 215-898-7227 400 K
provost@upenn.edu
PRITZ, Stephen, J .... 352-392-1374 109 F
spritz@ufl.edu
PRITZKER, Barry .... 518-580-5654 316 A
bpritzke@skidmore.edu
PRIZZI, Charles, V .... 516-367-6890 296 D
PROBST, Julliana .... 334-514-5051.... 2 F
julliana.probst@istc.edu
PROBST, Laura, K .... 218-299-4642 235 E
lprobst@cord.edu
PROBSTFELD, Carol, F .. 941-752-5201 108 G
probstc@scf.edu
PROBUS, Larry .... 509-777-4304 486 I
lprobus@whitworth.edu
PROBUS, Michael, J ..... 972-721-5000 452 D
michaelp@udallas.edu
PROCARIO-FOLEY, Carl 914-633-2632 302 G
cprocariofoley@iona.edu
PROCH, Margaret, P ..... 410-323-6211 198 C
m.proch@fts.edu
PROCHNOW, Allen, J ... 262-243-5700 493 B
allen.prochnow@cuw.edu
PROCOPIO, Claire .... 985-549-2135 192 D
claire.procopio@selu.edu
PROCTOR, Avis .... 954-201-2202.. 95 H
aproctor@broward.edu
PROCTOR, Avis .... 847-925-6390 137 H
aproctor@harpercollege.edu
PROCTOR, Cathy .... 973-803-5000 280 C
cproctor@pillar.edu
PROCTOR, Chris .... 903-586-2501 431 G
PROCTOR, Craig .... 801-587-2191 460 E
craig.proctor@hsc.edu
PROCTOR, Cynthia .... 724-925-4003 403 A
proctorc@westmoreland.edu
PROCTOR, Jeremiah ...... 217-732-3168 141 H
jdproctor@lincolnchristian.edu
PROCTOR, Kelly .... 864-388-8398 410 D
kproctor@lander.edu
PROCTOR, Kristen .... 508-854-7552 215 D
kproctor@qcc.mass.edu
PROCTOR, Lee .... 910-898-9660 336 D
proctorr@montgomery.edu
PROCTOR, Matt .... 417-626-1234 257 F
pres@occ.edu
PROCTOR, Michele .... 724-830-4986 398 H
mproctor@setonhill.edu
PROCTOR, Ross .... 870-733-6875.. 17 H
prproctor@asumidsouth.edu
PROCTOR, Tina .... 252-638-7220 333 H
proctort@cravencc.edu
PROCTOR, William, L ... 904-819-6210.. 98 E
proctorw@flagler.edu
PRODROMOU, Sarah .... 904-819-6479.. 98 E
sprodromou@flagler.edu
PROEBER, Helen .... 608-757-7623 499 C
hproeber@blackhawk.edu
PROEHL, Erinn .... 815-939-5296 146 A
eproehl@olivet.edu
PROFETA, Glen .... 559-730-3843.. 39 E
glenp@cos.edu
PROFETA, Pat .... 352-395-5150 107 A
pat.profeta@sfcollege.edu
PROFFITT, Beth .... 717-358-3871 384 D
beth.proffitt@fandm.edu
PROFFITT, Juanita .... 601-643-8383 245 G
juanita.proffitt@colin.edu
PROFFITT, Samantha ..... 570-372-4753 399 C
proffitt@susqu.edu
PROFITT, Aaron .... 513-721-7944 353 F
aprofitt@gbs.edu
PROHN, Deborah, W ..... 716-888-2919 292 D
prohnd@canisius.edu
PROHS, Aaron .... 308-632-6933 269 E
PROISY, Alize .... 252-222-6240 333 A
proisya@carteret.edu
PROITE, Rosanne .... 512-245-2931 450 E
rp43@txstate.edu
PROJANSKY, Sarah .... 801-587-9811 460 E
sarah.projansky@utah.edu
PROKOP, Paul .... 530-754-8568.. 68 E
pjprokop@ucdavis.edu
PROKOS, John .... 617-746-1990 210 E
john.prokos@hult.edu
PROKOVICH, Jeffrey, D 724-458-3846 385 C
jdprokovich@gcc.edu
PROPST, Jennifer .... 828-448-6051 339 A
jpropst@wpcc.edu
PROPST, Joan, L .... 304-457-6201 487 B
propstjl@ab.edu
PROPST, William, S ...... 310-794-6027.. 69 A
wpropst@finance.ucla.edu
PROSCIA, Domenic .... 718-429-6600 324 D
domenic.procsia@vaughn.edu
PROSCIA, Julie .... 312-662-4304 131 H
jproscia@adler.edu
PROSPER, Yamilette ...... 787-891-0925 508 K
yprosper@aguadilla.inter.edu
PROSSER, Deborah .... 407-646-2676 105 M
dprosser@rollins.edu
PROSTANO, Laura .... 914-633-2203 302 G
lprostano@iona.edu
PROTHERO, Charles, L . 570-945-8015 386 I
charlie.prothero@keystone.edu
PROTHROW-STITH,
Deborah .... 323-563-6981.. 36 D
dprothrowstith@cdrewu.edu
PROTO, Matthew .... 207-859-4802 193 E
matthew.proto@colby.edu
PROTZMAN, Ferdinand . 440-775-8400 358 C
fprotzma@oberlin.edu
PROUDFIT, Ann .... 216-987-5892 351 G
ann.proudfit@tri-c.edu
PROUDFOOT,
Donald, W .... 903-510-2975 452 C
dpro@tjc.edu
PROUDFOOT, Tony .... 269-387-8412 232 K
tony.proudfoot@wmich.edu
PROULX, Dave .... 401-454-6474 405 D
dproulx@risd.edu
PROULX, Dennis .... 802-468-1249 464 A
dennis.proulx@castleton.edu
PROULX, Melissa .... 315-267-2086 319 D
proulxm@potsdam.edu
PROUTY, Greg .... 804-862-6100 470 I
gprouty@rbc.edu
PROUTY, Steve .... 941-752-5205 108 G
proutys@scf.edu
PROVAN, Amy .... 410-532-5379 201 B
aprovan@ndm.edu
PROVENCHER,
Catherine, A .... 603-862-1622 274 F
catherine.provencher@usnh.edu
PROVENCIO-VASQUEZ,
Elias .... 303-556-2400.. 83 C
PROVENZANO, Joseph . 703-908-7686 469 C
joseph.provenzano@marymount.edu
PROVENZANO, Peter .... 248-341-2115 229 A
pmproven@oaklandcc.edu
PROVEZIS, Staci, J .... 217-333-1353 151 D
sprovez2@illinois.edu
PROVINE, Rick, E .... 765-658-4435 154 F
provine@depauw.edu
PROVINES, Jessica .... 316-978-3440 178 A
jessica.provines@wichita.edu
PROVOST, David, J .... 802-443-5699 462 H
dprovost@middlebury.edu
PROVOST, Dawn .... 337-482-6391 192 E
dawn@louisiana.edu
PROVOST, Kathryn .... 802-485-2125 463 A
kathrynp@norwich.edu
PROVOST, Laura .... 603-752-1113 273 D
lprovost@ccsnh.edu
PROVOST, Mark .... 715-833-6670 499 D
mprovost@cvtc.edu
PRUCHNICKI, Jennifer .. 580-581-2209 365 G
jpruchni@cameron.edu
PRUDE, Regina .... 615-687-6901 418 A
rprude@abcnash.edu
PRUDENTI, A. Gail .... 516-463-4068 302 B
gail.prudenti@hofstra.edu
PRUDHOMME,
Harvey, J .... 503-370-6576 378 B
hprudhom@willamette.edu
PRUD'HOMME, Sabrina 541-552-6060 376 E
prudhomms@sou.edu
PRUE, Stephen .... 785-832-6644 173 G
stephen.prue@bie.edu
PRUETT, Karen .... 706-880 8977 121 A
kpruett@lagrange.edu
PRUETT, Robert, R .... 919-658-7760 340 J
rpruett@umo.edu
PRUETT, Teresa .... 276-964-7365 475 I
teresa.pruett@sw.edu
PRUETT, Timothy .... 419-783-2317 352 F
tpruett@defiance.edu
PRUETT, Tyler .... 510-869-6511.. 59 F
tpruett@samuelmerritt.edu
PRUIS, Angela .... 817-722-1721 439 B
angela.pruis@tku.edu
PRUITT, Bart .... 806-720-7232 439 H
bart.pruitt@lcu.edu
PRUITT, Beverly .... 305-284-2842 112 E
b.pruitt@miami.edu
PRUITT, Dennis, A .... 803-777-4172 413 C
dpruitt@sc.edu
PRUITT, Glenell .... 903-730-4890 438 H
gpruitt@jarvis.edu
PRUITT, Jason .... 470-239-3103 126 A
jason.pruitt@ung.edu
PRUITT, Jolene .... 425-278-9317.. 63 A
jpruitt@saybrook.edu
PRUITT, Jonathan .... 919-962-2080 342 D
jpruitt@unc.edu
PRUITT, Judy .... 612-343-4491 242 H
japruitt@northcentral.edu
PRUITT, Karl .... 205-929-6348.... 2 H
kpruitt@lawsonstate.edu
PRUITT, Leah, L .... 864-587-4225 412 G
pruittl@smcsc.edu
PRUITT, Nathan .... 518-783-2342 315 J
npruitt@siena.edu
PRUITT, Pamela .... 609-896-5000 281 B
ppruitt@rider.edu
PRUITT, Samory, T .... 205-348-8376.... 7 G
samory.pruitt@ua.edu
PRUITT, Steven .... 561-237-7834 102 V
spruitt@lynn.edu
PRUITT, Suzanne .... 918-647-1200 365 H
PRUNCHUNAS, Edward . 310-423-8294.. 35 L
PRUNER, Britani .... 716-614-5957 310 C
bpruner@niagaracc.suny.edu
PRUNTY, Bonnie, S ...... 607-274-3141 303 B
bprunty@ithaca.edu
PRUS, Mark .... 607-753-2207 318 D
mark.prus@cortland.edu
PRUSANK, Diane .... 413-572-5214 213 D
dprusank@westfield.ma.edu
PRUSHA, Tammy .... 641-269-4481 165 J
prushatd@grinnell.edu
PRUSHA, Todd .... 319-398-5565 167 C
tprusha@kirkwood.edu
PRUSHAN, Mike .... 610-526-1861 385 G
mprushan@harcum.edu
PRUSKI, Thomas .... 202-706-6843.. 93 E
tpruski@wesleyseminary.edu
PRUSS, Julie, A .... 585-395-2361 318 B
jpruss@brockport.edu
PRUTSOS, Bryce .... 760-252-2411.. 26 I
bprutsos@barstow.edu
PRY, George .... 412-809-5100 396 H
pry.georgel@ptcollege.edu
PRYBUTOK, Victor .... 940-565-3957 454 A
victor.prybutok@unt.edu
PRYJMAK, Myron .... 718-409-7311 321 C
mpryjmak@sunymaritime.edu
PRYLES, Kathryn .... 508-588-9100 214 F
kpryles@massasoit.mass.edu
PRYLO, Caelynn .... 518-743-2238 320 D
pryloc@sunyacc.edu
PRYOR, Adam .... 785-227-3380 171 E
pryoraw@bethanylb.edu
PRYOR, Ann .... 843-953-2060 408 E
pryoral@cofc.edu
PRYOR, Charles .... 646-313-8000 295 E
charles.pryor@guttman.cuny.edu
PRYOR, Joanna .... 316-942-4291 175 I
pryorj@newmanu.edu
PRYOR, Julie .... 205-453-6300.. 92 G
PRYOR, Marcus .... 704-991-0278 338 C
mpryor7642@stanly.edu
PRYOR, Monique .... 718-489-2086 313 H
mpryor@sfc.edu
PRYOR, Raymond, G .... 570-208-5828 387 A
rgpryor@kings.edu
PRYOR HARRIS, Holli .. 312-567-3167 139 B
pryor@iit.edu
PRYSOCK, James .... 614-823-1312 360 A
jprysock@otterbein.edu
PRYSTOWSKY, Richard . 740-386-4150 356 B
prystowskyr@mtc.edu
PRYZBOROKI, Carol ...... 412-321-8383 380 B
office@bcs.edu
PRZEKOP, Lisa .... 805-893-3641.. 70 A
lisa.przekop@sa.ucsb.edu
PRZEKURAT, Paris .... 405-422-1442 369 E
przekuratp@redlandscc.edu
PRZYBOROWSKI, Marta 727-341-7973 106 E
przyborowski.marta@spcollege.edu
PRZYGOCKI, Ginny .... 989-686-9276 223 G
vlprzygo@delta.edu
PRZYGODA, Melitha, R 203-576-4588.. 88 D
mprzygod@bridgeport.edu
PRZYMUS, Beth .... 402-562-1284 266 A
bprzymus@cccneb.edu
PRZYMUSINSKI, Lori .... 248-341-2177 229 A
lprzymu@oaklandcc.edu
PRZYWARA, Ann Marie 518-580-5765 316 A
aprzywar@skidmore.edu
PSAILA, Marisa .... 585-475-4932 313 A
mxpdar@rit.edu
PSARRIS, Kleanthis .... 718-951-3170 293 C
kpsarris@brooklyn.cuny.edu
PSIHOUNTAS, Debbie ... 239-985-3451 100 A
dpsihountas@fsw.edu
PU, Jennie .... 201-714-7100 278 C
PUC, Gina .... 413-662-5201 213 A
g.puc@mcla.edu
PUCCIARELLI, Matthew . 718-990-7614 314 B
pucciarm@stjohns.edu
PUCCIO, Daniel, P .... 716-880-2351 306 C
daniel.p.puccio@medaille.edu

Q

QUARLES, Robert .... 304-473-8163 491 H
quarles_r@wvwc.edu
QUARLESS, Duncan ...... 516-876-3257 319 A
quarlessd@oldwestbury.edu
QUARTEY, Kojo .... 734-384-4166 227 G
kquartey@monroeccc.edu
QUASH, Natolyn .... 804-706-5020 474 I
nquash@jtcc.edu
QUATHAMER, Mark ...... 321-433-5364.. 97 I
quathamerm@easternflorida.edu
QUATTLEBAUM, Lesley . 301-934-7648 198 A
ljquattlebaum@csmd.edu
QUATTLEBAUM, Mickey 870-230-5103.. 19 E
quattlm@hsu.edu
QUATTRONE, Joel, M ... 717-245-1364 382 F
quattron@dickinson.edu
QUAY, Sara .... 978-232-2200 209 B
squay@endicott.edu
QUAYE, Sandra .... 608-899-4241 273 F
quayes@franklinpierce.edu
QUAZI, Kruti .... 610-527-0200 397 I
kruti.quazi@rosemont.edu
QUBBAJ, Ala .... 956-665-5257 455 D
ala.qubbaj@utrgv.edu
QUBEIN, Nido, R .... 336-841-9201 329 G
nqubein@highpoint.edu
QUDDUS, Munir .... 936-261-9200 446 D
muquddus@pvamu.edu
QUEEN, Barbara .... 323-343-3440.. 32 A
bqueen@calstatela.edu
QUEEN, Harrell, W .... 706-245-7226 117 E
hqueen@ec.edu
QUEEN, Jacob .... 864-231-5795 406 G
jqueen@andersonuniversity.edu
QUEEN, Julie .... 907-474-5866.. 10 A
jmlarweth@alaska.edu
QUEEN, Julie .... 907-474-7907.. 10 A
julie.queen@alaska.edu
QUEEN, Scott .... 336-506-4154 332 A
scott.queen@alamancecc.edu
QUEEN, Scott .... 660-248-6238 251 B
squeen@centralmethodist.edu
QUEEN, Todd .... 225-578-9959 188 I
tqueen@lsu.edu
QUEENAN, Rosemary .... 518-445-3394 289 E
rquee@albanylaw.edu
QUEENAN, Theresa .... 410-651-6447 203 A
tqueenan@umes.edu
QUEENER, Scott, E .... 217-786-2472 142 B
scott.queener@llcc.edu
QUEERY, Maria .... 610-921-2381 378 C
mqueery@albright.edu
QUEHL-ENGEL,
Catherine, M .... 319-895-4402 164 B
cquehl-engel@cornellcollege.edu
QUELCH, John, A .... 305-284-1973 112 E
jquelch@miami.edu
QUEMUEL, Christine ..... 808-956-9326 128 F
quemuel@hawaii.edu
QUENEAU, Herve .... 718-951-3166 293 C
hqueneau@brooklyn.cuny.edu
QUERO-MENDEZ, Doris 787-725-6500 506 G
dquero@albizu.edu
QUESADA, Uriel .... 504-865-2011 189 F
uquesada@loyno.edu
QUEST, Karen .... 315-568-3060 308 F
kquest@nycc.edu
QUEST, Patrick .... 540-636-2900 466 A
patrick.quest@christendom.edu
QUESTELL, Alan .... 910-410-1916 337 B
ajquestell@richmondcc.edu
QUEZADA, Zolla .... 401-254-3116 405 E
QUIATKOWSKI, Sandra . 800-280-0307 152 H
sandra.quiatkowski@ace.edu
QUICK, Alisa .... 336-316-2135 329 E
quickat@guilford.edu
QUICK, Angela .... 865-981-8038 421 F
angela.quick@maryvillecollege.edu
QUICK, Beth .... 256-824-2325.... 8 B
beth.quick@uah.edu
QUICK, Cathy .... 618-545-3011 140 E
cquick@kaskaskia.edu
QUICK, Debra .... 520-515-3640.. 11 M
quickd@cochise.edu
QUICK, Donna .... 706-245-7226 117 E
dquick@ec.edu
QUICK, James, E .... 214-768-1115 444 E
jquick@smu.edu
QUICK, Matthew, D ...... 816-501-4127 258 H
matt.quick@rockhurst.edu
QUICK, Molly .... 425-889-5327 482 F
molly.quick@northwestu.edu

QUICK, Rex .... 830-792-7344 443 G
avpits@schreiner.edu
QUIETT, Kimberly .... 903-233-3410 439 E
kimberlyquiett@letu.edu
QUIGGLE, Gregg .... 312-329-4059 144 B
gregg.quiggle@moody.edu
QUIGLEY, Brian .... 603-358-2438 275 A
bquigley1@keene.edu
QUIGLEY, Daniel .... 516-686-7756 309 F
dquigley@nyit.edu
QUIGLEY, David .... 617-552-3260 207 B
david.quigley@bc.edu
QUIGLEY, John .... 201-360-4081 278 C
jquigley@hccc.edu
QUIGLEY, JR.,
Kenneth, K .... 617-333-2236 208 E
kquigley@curry.edu
QUIGLEY, Kevin, F .... 802-258-9245 462 E
kevin@marlboro.edu
QUIGLEY, Lori, V .... 716-880-2241 306 C
lquigley@medaille.edu
QUIGLEY, Mark, R .... 978-542-6078 213 C
mquigley@salemstate.edu
QUIGLEY, Peter .... 808-956-3869 128 H
quigleyp@hawaii.edu
QUIHUIZ, Shannon .... 714-432-5930.. 38 E
squihuiz@occ.cccd.edu
QUILES, Elisa .... 787-751-0178 511 F
ac_equiles@suagm.edu
QUILES, Elisa .... 787-257-7373 511 G
equiles@suagm.edu
QUILES, Isamel .... 787-738-2161 513 D
ismael.quiles@upr.edu
QUILL, Robin .... 508-929-8013 213 E
rquill@worcester.edu
QUILLEN, Carol, E .... 704-894-2201 328 F
caquillen@davidson.edu
QUILLEN, David .... 630-466-7900 152 C
dquillen@waubonsee.edu
QUILLEN, Michael, D ... 704-216-3475 337 F
michael.quillen@rccc.edu
QUILLEN, William .... 440-775-8200 358 C
william.quillen@oberlin.edu
QUILLIN, Amy .... 330-672-4050 354 J
aquillin@kent.edu
QUILTY, Morgann .... 217-351-2596 146 C
QUIMBY, Charrita, D .... 757-727-5231 468 B
charrita.quimby@hamptonu.edu
QUIMBY, Kristyn .... 574-520-4154 157 A
krirhawk@iusb.edu
QUIMBY, Linda .... 603-899-4028 273 F
quimbyl@franklinpierce.edu
QUINATA, Tina, M .... 671-735-5561 505 C
gcc.registrar@guamcc.edu
QUINER, Michael .... 541-917-4999 374 A
quinerm@linnbenton.edu
QUINET, Bart, P .... 615-322-7712 428 D
bart.p.quinet@vanderbilt.edu
QUINLAN, Catherine ..... 213-821-2344.. 72 B
cquinlan@usc.edu
QUINLAN, Jeremiah ...... 203-432-9321.. 89 D
jeremiah.quinlan@yale.edu
QUINLAN, Melissa .... 860-913-2034.. 87 A
mquinlan@goodwin.edu
QUINLAN, Sean .... 208-885-7885 131 G
quinlan@uidaho.edu
QUINLIVAN, Gary .... 724-537-4597 398 E
gary.quinlivan@email.stvincent.edu
QUINLIVAN, Gary, M .... 724-537-4597 398 F
gq@stvincent.edu
QUINN, Amanda .... 815-280-2693 140 B
aquinn@jjc.edu
QUINN, Anthony .... 734-384-4279 227 G
aquinn@monroeccc.edu
QUINN, Arthur .... 561-732-4424 106 G
aquinn@svdp.edu
QUINN, Bonnie .... 478-471-5184 116 A
bquinn@centralgatech.edu
QUINN, Brian .... 215-951-1540 387 C
quinng@lasalle.edu
QUINN, Caitlin .... 415-439-2436.. 25 K
cquinn@act-sf.org
QUINN, Consuelo .... 706-821-8262 122 K
cquinn@paine.edu
QUINN, Diane .... 516-562-2018 299 B
dquinn@northwell.edu
QUINN, Donna, M .... 302-356-6819.. 90 I
donna.m.quinn@wilmu.edu
QUINN, Erin .... 802-443-5253 462 H
quinn@middlebury.edu
QUINN, Felicia, K .... 302-356-6889.. 90 I
felicia.k.quinn@wilmu.edu

QUINN, Frank .... 828-328-7235 330 F
frank.quinn@lr.edu
QUINN, Gianna .... 215-646-7300 385 D
quinn.g@gmercyu.edu
QUINN, Holli .... 484-809-7770.. 92 G
QUINN, Jacqueline .... 601-643-8364 245 G
jacqueline.quinn@colin.edu
QUINN, Jaimie .... 972-279-6511 430 B
jquinn@amberton.edu
QUINN, Jeffery .... 845-675-4425 310 G
jeff.quinn@nyack.edu
QUINN, Kathy .... 314-529-9476 254 H
kquinn@maryville.edu
QUINN, Kenneth .... 901-435-1731 421 A
kenneth_quinn@loc.edu
QUINN, Kevin, G .... 616-632-2880 221 C
kgq001@aquinas.edu
QUINN, Kristin .... 563-333-6428 169 A
quinnkristin@sau.edu
QUINN, Laura .... 662-329-7222 248 A
lsquinn@muw.edu
QUINN, Laurie .... 802-860-2734 462 B
lquinn@champlain.edu
QUINN, Leslie .... 913-469-8500 174 D
lquinn2@jccc.edu
QUINN, Linda .... 402-941-6280 267 L
quinn@midlandu.edu
QUINN, Margaret .... 609-652-4744 283 D
margaret.quinn@stockton.edu
QUINN, Marisa .... 507-457-1781 243 B
mquinn@smumn.edu
QUINN, Michael .... 206-296-5500 484 F
quinnm@seattleu.edu
QUINN, Michael, G ...... 585-292-2151 307 H
mquinn@monroecc.edu
QUINN, Michelle .... 970-351-2773.. 83 E
michelle.quinn@unco.edu
QUINN, Molly .... 319-226-2001 162 F
molly.quinn@allencollege.edu
QUINN, Nicole .... 973-748-9000 276 A
nicole_quinn@bloomfield.edu
QUINN, Sarah, F .... 610-660-1230 398 C
squinn@sju.edu
QUINN, Shaman .... 307-754-6232 502 G
shaman.quinn@nwc.edu
QUINN, Stephen .... 973-618-3320 276 D
squinn@caldwell.edu
QUINN, Susan .... 585-389-2501 308 B
squinn2@naz.edu
QUINN, Susan .... 707-524-1598.. 62 F
squinn@santarosa.edu
QUINN, Teresa .... 845-437-5370 324 C
tequinn@vassar.edu
QUINN, Thomas .... 989-275-5000 226 B
tom.quinn@kirtland.edu
QUINN, Wade .... 919-735-5151 338 H
dwquinn@waynecc.edu
QUINN, William, P .... 302-356-6775.. 90 I
william.p.quinn@wilmu.edu
QUINNAN, Timothy .... 404-835-6132 423 K
tquinnan@richmont.edu
QUINNELL, Katherine ..... 256-216-6660.... 4 D
katherine.quinnell@athens.edu
QUINNETT, Jim .... 325-793-4611 440 B
jquinnett@mcm.edu
QUINONES, Carlos, A ... 787-753-0039 507 G
QUINONES, Ivan, A .... 717-780-2455 385 E
iaquinon@hacc.edu
QUINONES, Ivelisse ...... 706-580-0168 114 B
QUINONES, Melinda ..... 610-282-1100 382 E
melinda.quinones@desales.edu
QUINONES, Patricia ...... 310-287-4361.. 49 G
quinonp@wlac.edu
QUINONES, Roberto ..... 562-408-6969.. 24 E
rquinones@advancedcollege.edu
QUINONES, Vanya .... 212-346-1200 311 E
QUINONES, Yolanda ..... 787-758-2525 513 G
yolanda.quinones@upr.edu
QUINONEZ, Julie, R ..... 419-530-6213 363 E
julie.quinonez@utoledo.edu
QUINONEZ, Virginia ..... 312-329-6623.. 36 F
vquinonez@thechicagoschool.edu
QUINTAL, Jorge .... 336-334-5536 343 A
j_quinta@uncg.edu
QUINTAL, Rollande .... 508-849-3340 205 C
rquintal@annamaria.edu
QUINTANA, Elena .... 312-662-4021 131 H
equintana@adler.edu
QUINTANA, Javier .... 787-279-1912 509 A
jquintana@bayamon.inter.edu
QUINTANA, Judith .... 212-410-8486 309 B
jquintana@nycpm.edu

QUINTANA, Rebecca ..... 787-780-0070 506 F
rquintana@caribbean.edu
QUINTANA, Sara .... 802-865-5417 462 B
squintana@champlain.edu
QUINTANA HESS,
Jessica, A .... 570-321-4318 389 E
hess@lycoming.edu
QUINTANILLA, Hector ... 817-531-4840 451 E
hquintanilla@txwes.edu
QUINTANILLA,
Kelly, M .... 361-825-2621 447 C
kelly.quintanilla@tamucc.edu
QUINTENZ, Briana .... 217-424-3758 143 H
bquintenz@millikin.edu
QUINTERO, Sandra .... 657-278-5366.. 31 E
squintero@fullerton.edu
QUINTYNE, Renee .... 845-398-4207 315 B
rquintyn@stac.edu
QUIRK, Walter .... 530-226-4172.. 63 K
rquirk@simpsonu.edu
QUIRK-BAILEY, Sheila .. 309-694-5520 138 C
sheila.quirk-bailey@icc.edu
QUIROLGICO, Ray .... 626-396-2325.. 26 E
ray.quirolgico@artcenter.edu
QUIROS, Jaime .... 562-806-2451.. 35 M
jquiroz@cerritos.edu
QUIROS, Kristi .... 830-372-8060 449 B
kquiros@tlu.edu
QUIROS, Ondrea, M ..... 915-831-6615 436 E
oquiros@epcc.edu
QUIROZ, Gloria .... 773-878-3606 148 D
gquiroz@staugustine.edu
QUIS, Steve .... 619-388-7876.. 60 E
squis@sdccd.edu
QUISENBERRY,
Brian, L .... 540-464-7184 476 G
quisenberrybl@vmi.edu
QUISTGARD, Fred .... 207-216-4406 195 C
fquistgard@yccc.edu
QUISTORF, Mark, W ..... 414-410-4016 492 D
mwquistorf@stritch.edu
QUIÑONES, Angel .... 787-258-1501 507 D
alquinones@columbiacentral.edu
QUIÑONES, Mickey ...... 804-289-8550 472 L
mquinones@richmond.edu
QUIÑONES, Yesenia ..... 787-844-8181 514 A
yesenia.quinones1@upr.edu
QUIÑONES, Zulma .... 787-264-1912 509 F
zulma_quinones@intersg.edu
QUIÑONES CASTILLO,
Weyna, M .... 787-815-0000 513 A
weyna.quinones@upr.edu
QUOCK, Dan .... 509-542-4803 479 H
dquock@columbiabasin.edu
QURESHI, Elena .... 734-432-5574 227 A
equreshi@madonna.edu
QVARNSTROM, Jeanne . 432-837-8585 450 D
jqvarnstrom@sulross.edu

R

RAAB, Jennifer, J .... 212-772-4242 294 C
jennifer.raab@hunter.cuny.edu
RAAB, Maryrose .... 315-792-7215 321 E
maryrose.raab@sunypoly.edu
RAB, Shafiq .... 312-942-3400 148 A
shafiq_rab@rush.edu
RABAGO, Cristine .... 650-543-3782.. 51 F
crabago@menlo.edu
RABB, Sydni .... 254-442-5113 433 A
sydni.rabb@cisco.edu
RABBANY, Sina, Y .... 516-463-6672 302 B
sina.y.rabbany@hofstra.edu
RABBITT, Kara, M .... 973-720-2180 284 I
rabbittk@wpunj.edu
RABBITT, Rhonda .... 570-408-2016 403 D
rhonda.rabbitt@wilkes.edu
RABEL, P, J .... 402-465-2102 268 H
prabel@nebrwesleyan.edu
RABENOLD, Scott .... 512-471-4124 455 A
srabenold@utexas.edu
RABER, II, Donald, R ... 864-833-8233 411 I
draber@presby.edu
RABER, Marie .... 202-319-5454.. 91 B
raber@cua.edu
RABIDEAU, Shelly, S .... 317-940-8423 153 F
srabidea@butler.edu
RABIL, Alison .... 919-684-3501 328 G
alison.rabil@duke.edu
RABINOVICH, Sheryl .... 213-624-1200.. 42 I
srabinovich@fidm.edu
RABINOWITZ, Celia, E .. 603-358-2736 275 A
celia.rabinowitz@keene.edu

RAJMAIRA, Christina .... 703-284-1616 469 C christina.rajmaira@marymount.edu
RAJOTTE, Amanda .... 626-396-2298.. 26 E amanda.rajotte@artcenter.edu
RAJPUROHIT, Vikas .... 817-515-1254 445 G vikas.rajpurohit@tccd.edu
RAJPUT, Hussein .... 651-523-2204 236 A hrajput01@hamline.edu
RAJSKI, Peggy .... 310-338-5800.. 50 J peggy.rajski@lmu.edu
RAJU, Ritu .... 713-718-5614 437 I ritu.raju@hccs.edu
RAKER, Keith .... 336-249-8186 334 A kdraker@davidsonccc.edu
RAKES, Lee, L .... 540-464-7345 476 G rakesel@vmi.edu
RAKESTRAW, Jennie ..... 803-323-2151 414 G rakestrawj@winthrop.edu
RAKIC, Svetlana .... 317-738-8759 154 J srakic@franklincollege.edu
RAKITA, Gordon, F .... 904-620-2820 110 A grakita@unf.edu
RALEIGH, Bill .... 830-792-7421 443 G wraleigh@schreiner.edu
RALEIGH, M.J .... 336-841-9794 329 G mraleigh@highpoint.edu
RALEY, Karen, C .... 240-895-3219 201 E kcraley@smcm.edu
RALEY, Leonard, R .... 301-445-1941 202 B raley@usmd.edu
RALLS, Diana .... 559-278-7167.. 31 D diralls@csufresno.edu
RALLS, Scott .... 919-866-5141 338 G sralls@waketech.edu
RALPH, Brian, C .... 919-508-2220 344 F officeofthepresident@peace.edu
RALPH, David .... 580-774-3191 370 C david.ralph@swosu.edu
RALPH, James .... 802-443-5320 462 H ralph@middlebury.edu
RALPH, Ken .... 207-581-1052 195 J ken.ralph@maine.edu
RALPH, Marcus .... 804-527-1000.. 92 G
RALPH, Nicole, M .... 217-786-2342 142 B nicole.ralph@llcc.edu
RALSTON, Craig .... 928-776-2311.. 16 M craig.ralston@yc.edu
RALSTON, Gina .... 410-778-7849 204 D gralston2@washcoll.edu
RALSTON, Pamela .... 805-965-0581.. 62 C pgralston@sbcc.edu
RALSTON, Tracy .... 203-596-4564.. 87 F tralston@post.edu
RALSTON, Troy .... 804-727-6826 124 E tralston@southuniversity.edu
RAM, Rosalind .... 808-675-3589 127 E rose.ram@byuh.edu
RAM, Sabrina .... 866-492-5336 244 F sabrina.ram@laureate.net
RAMACHANDRAN, Ramu .... 318-257-4304 191 F ramu@latech.edu
RAMAGE, Emily .... 217-234-5403 141 D eramage@lakeland.cc.il.us
RAMAGE, Thomas, R .... 217-351-2231 146 C ramage@parkland.edu
RAMAKER, Dawn .... 641-585-8197 170 B ramakerd@waldorf.edu
RAMAKER, Jason .... 641-585-8160 170 B ramakerj@waldorf.edu
RAMAKRISHNAN, Deepa .... 610-989-1200 402 B dramakrishnan@vfmac.edu
RAMAKRISHNAN, Jolly . 610-399-2032 394 C jramakrishnan@cheyney.edu
RAMAKRISHNAN, Latha 320-308-4793 240 H lramakrishnan@stcloudstate.edu
RAMALHO, Erika, A ...... 814-871-5584 384 E ramalho001@gannon.edu
RAMAMURTI, Sita .... 202-884-9262.. 93 B ramamurtis@trinitydc.edu
RAMAN, Sanjay .... 413-545-6388 211 D sraman@umass.edu
RAMANATHAN, Pamela 215-596-8891 401 G p.ramanathan@usciences.edu
RAMARUI, Robert .... 680-488-2471 506 B rramarui@palau.edu
RAMASUBRAMANIAN, Melur .... 434-243-3606 473 A vpresearch@virginia.edu
RAMASWAMI, Suneeta .. 856-225-6439 281 G rsuneeta@camden.rutgers.edu
RAMASWAMY, Nandini . 317-940-9032 153 F nramaswa@butler.edu
RAMBERT, Michael .... 404-752-1895 122 E mrambert@msm.edu
RAMBIKUR, Sara .... 512-617-5700 433 F
RAMBISH, Medea .... 585-292-2341 307 H mrambish@monroecc.edu
RAMBO, Andrea .... 805-289-6102.. 73 B arambo@vcccd.edu
RAMBO, Thomas, A ...... 540-375-2310 471 B rambo@roanoke.edu
RAMCHAND, Latha .... 573-882-6596 261 B ramchandl@missouri.edu
RAMCHARAN, David ..... 402-280-5562 266 I davidramcharan@creighton.edu
RAMDATH, Sanjay .... 973-877-3491 277 I sramdath@essex.edu
RAMELLA, Ken .... 352-256-4273.. 95 D kramella@beaconcollege.edu
RAMES, Marysz .... 402-375-7200 268 G marames1@wsc.edu
RAMET, Carlos .... 989-964-4062 230 B ramet@svsu.edu
RAMEY, JR., Alfred, E .. 201-200-2039 279 E aramey@njcu.edu
RAMEY, Casey .... 205-726-4315.... 6 E cramey@samford.edu
RAMEY, Chris .... 731-989-6088 420 C cramey@fhu.edu
RAMEY, Craig .... 252-638-7210 333 H rameyc@cravencc.edu
RAMEY, Teresa .... 843-661-1182 409 K tramey@fmarion.edu
RAMEZANE, Marsha ..... 650-574-6413.. 61 P ramezanem@smccd.edu
RAMGOLAM, Geoffrey ... 954-745-6960.. 92 G
RAMIN, Daniel .... 315-470-4933 320 A dwramin@esf.edu
RAMIREZ, Alan .... 903-813-2370 430 N aramirez@austincollege.edu
RAMIREZ, Alfred .... 818-240-1000.. 44 B aramirez@glendale.edu
RAMIREZ, Alma .... 951-487-3410.. 52 I alramirez@msjc.edu
RAMIREZ, Amador .... 361-354-2554 433 C aramirez@coastalbend.edu
RAMIREZ, Amy .... 410-706-7488 202 D aramirez@umaryland.edu
RAMIREZ, Arnold .... 979-230-3235 432 D arnold.ramirez@brazosport.edu
RAMIREZ, Arturo .... 309-438-5590 139 E aramir@ilstu.edu
RAMIREZ, Audrey .... 361-354-2210 433 C amramirez@coastalbend.edu
RAMIREZ, Aurelio .... 617-879-7847 212 E aramirez@massart.edu
RAMIREZ, Daniel .... 956-872-2580 444 A dramirez@southtexascollege.edu
RAMIREZ, David .... 610-328-8175 399 D dramire1@swarthmore.edu
RAMIREZ, Desiree .... 817-735-5131 454 C desiree.ramirez@unthsc.edu
RAMIREZ, Erica .... 816-995-2879 258 F erica.ramirez@researchcollege.edu
RAMIREZ, Fausto .... 718-960-8593 294 A fausto.ramirez@lehman.cuny.edu
RAMIREZ, Francine, M . 909-869-6992.. 30 D fmramirez@cpp.edu
RAMIREZ, Freddy .... 760-757-2121.. 52 E framirez@miracosta.edu
RAMIREZ, Irving .... 347-964-8600 291 I iramirez@boricuacollege.edu
RAMIREZ, Jason .... 435-586-7700 460 F jasonramirez@suu.edu
RAMIREZ, Jessica .... 816-604-1411 255 D jessica.ramirez@mcckc.edu
RAMIREZ, Joe .... 877-559-3621.. 29 A
RAMIREZ, Jose .... 787-620-2040 506 C jramirez@aupr.edu
RAMIREZ, Jose, L .... 915-831-2634 436 E jramir20@epcc.edu
RAMIREZ, Juan .... 909-469-5622.. 74 I jramirez@westernu.edu
RAMIREZ, Katie .... 210-999-8819 452 A kramirez@trinity.edu
RAMIREZ, Laura .... 562-908-3402.. 58 E lramirez@riohondo.edu
RAMIREZ, Manuel .... 787-884-3838 506 D asisteco@atenascollege.edu
RAMIREZ, Marcela, V ... 210-458-6144 455 E marcela.ramirez@utsa.edu
RAMIREZ, Mayra, I .... 787-723-4481 507 A mramirez@ceaprc.edu
RAMIREZ, Miguel .... 305-899-3647.. 95 C maramirez@barry.edu
RAMIREZ, Minita .... 956-326-2278 446 F minita@tamiu.edu
RAMIREZ, Monica .... 651-779-3235 237 G monica.ramirez@century.edu
RAMIREZ, Octavio .... 256-726-7340.... 6 C oramirez@oakwood.edu
RAMIREZ, Rhonda .... 510-869-6511.. 59 F rramirez@samuelmerritt.edu
RAMIREZ, Rita .... 509-793-2031 478 H ritar@bigbend.edu
RAMIREZ, Robert .... 940-898-3142 451 F rramirez9@twu.edu
RAMIREZ, Rodolfo .... 530-422-7923.. 73 F rramirez@weimar.edu
RAMIREZ, Rosemary ..... 520-494-5471.. 11 K rosemary.ramirez@centralaz.edu
RAMIREZ, Ruben .... 805-922-6966.. 24 J rubenc.ramirez@hancockcollege.edu
RAMIREZ, Sam .... 361-825-5826 447 C samuel.ramirez@tamucc.edu
RAMIREZ, Sam .... 440-826-2908 348 E sramirez@bw.edu
RAMIREZ, Sandra .... 281-998-2648 443 B sandra.ramirez@sjcd.edu
RAMIREZ, Steve, D .... 512-233-1464 442 M steveramirez@stedwards.edu
RAMIREZ, Sylvia .... 787-832-6000 508 D
RAMIREZ, Sylvia .... 608-243-4587 499 H sframirez@madisoncollege.edu
RAMIREZ, Wilmer .... 303-783-3137.. 79 H wilmer.ramirez@denverseminary.edu
RAMIREZ-CARLO, III, Bolivar .... 787-620-2040 506 C bramirez@aupr.edu
RAMIREZ-FIGUEROA, Jose .... 787-620-2040 506 C jramirez@aupr.edu
RAMIREZ-GELPI, Sofia .. 805-922-6966.. 24 J sgelpi@hancockcollege.edu
RAMIREZ-PEREZ, Felicia .... 480-732-7093.. 12 P felicia.ramirez-perez@cgc.edu
RAMIREZ-PEREZ, Felicia .... 602-285-7422.. 13 F felicia.a.ramirez-perez@phoenixcollege.edu
RAMIREZ-RIVERA, Rafael .... 787-878-5475 508 L rramirez@arecibo.inter.edu
RAMKARAN, Arshaw ..... 212-650-5824 293 D aramkaran@ccny.cuny.edu
RAMKUMAR, S. Manian .... 585-475-5955 313 A smrmet@rit.edu
RAMLER, Tom .... 903-434-8175 441 B tramler@ntcc.edu
RAMM, Jennifer .... 254-295-5527 453 E jramm@umhb.edu
RAMMING, Ronald, S ... 918-463-2931 366 B rronald@connorsstate.edu
RAMON, Aarika .... 817-531-4420 451 E lcrosenkrantz@txwes.edu
RAMON, Deanna Rene .. 580-349-1556 368 A rene.ramon@opsu.edu
RAMON, Ralph .... 325-574-7625 458 E rramon@wtc.edu
RAMONES, Eric .... 408-848-4753.. 43 J eramones@gavilan.edu
RAMONT, John .... 760-776-7452.. 39 A jramont@collegeofthedesert.edu
RAMOS, Andrea .... 213-738-5574.. 65 G aramos@swlaw.edu
RAMOS, Anita .... 559-297-4500.. 46 A aramos@iot.edu
RAMOS, Anthony .... 210-805-1201 453 D aramos@uiwtx.edu
RAMOS, Antonio .... 787-284-1912 509 E aramos@ponce.inter.edu
RAMOS, Cerese .... 386-506-3240.. 97 D cerese.ramos@daytonastate.edu
RAMOS, Charlene .... 248-204-2330 226 G cramos@ltu.edu
RAMOS, Chelsea .... 718-289-5153 293 B chelsea.ayala@bcc.cuny.edu
RAMOS, Cynthia .... 602-285-7404.. 13 F cynthia.ramos@phoenixcollege.edu
RAMOS, Daisy .... 787-738-2161 513 D daisy.ramos@upr.edu
RAMOS, David, L .... 787-834-9595 511 E dramos@uaa.edu
RAMOS, Derek .... 620-276-9559 173 E derek.ramos@gcccks.edu
RAMOS, Diana, N .... 787-884-3838 506 D profdg5@atenascollege.edu
RAMOS, Efrain .... 787-891-0925 508 K eramos@aguadilla.inter.edu
RAMOS, Ernesto .... 787-751-0160 507 F eramos@cmpr.pr.gov
RAMOS, Gladys .... 787-738-2161 513 D gladys.ramos@upr.edu
RAMOS, Idalmy .... 787-264-1912 509 F iramos@intersg.edu
RAMOS, Irma .... 714-808-4810.. 53 J iramos@nocccd.edu
RAMOS, Ismael .... 787-738-2161 513 D ismael.ramos1@upr.edu
RAMOS, Jennifer .... 212-228-1888 312 H
RAMOS, Joahana .... 787-844-8181 514 A joahana.ramos@upr.edu
RAMOS, John .... 406-656-9950 265 I jramos@yellowstonechristian.edu
RAMOS, Joseph .... 619-388-6411.. 60 B jramos@sdccd.edu
RAMOS, Kenneth .... 713-677-7483 446 G yzhou@ibt.tamhsc.edu
RAMOS, Lorna .... 787-753-6000 508 D
RAMOS, Mario .... 210-924-4338 431 H mario.ramos@bua.edu
RAMOS, Miquel .... 713-743-4372 452 F maramos3@uh.edu
RAMOS, Nancy, L .... 401-254-3455 405 E nramos@rwu.edu
RAMOS, Olgaly .... 787-894-2828 514 C olgaly.ramos@upr.edu
RAMOS, Patricia .... 310-434-3311.. 62 E ramos_patricia@smc.edu
RAMOS, Patricia, A .... 718-289-5896 293 B patricia.ramos@bcc.cuny.edu
RAMOS, Ricardo .... 619-201-8694.. 60 A ricardo.ramos@sdcc.edu
RAMOS, Richard, O ...... 515-961-1536 169 D rich.ramos@simpson.edu
RAMOS, Vickie .... 561-912-2166.. 98 D
RAMOS, Yolanda .... 432-685-4733 440 E yramos@midland.edu
RAMOSKA, John .... 518-861-2519 305 K jramoska@mariacollege.edu
RAMPAUL, Andre .... 212-757-1190 290 B arampaul@aami.edu
RAMPERSAD, Dave .... 334-386-7100.... 5 D drampersad@faulkner.edu
RAMPINO, Joseph .... 703-284-1607 469 C joseph.rampino@marymount.edu
RAMPP, Carrie .... 717-358-4161 384 D carrie.rampp@fandm.edu
RAMS, Richard .... 714-484-7374.. 53 K rrams@cypresscollege.edu
RAMS, Richard .... 714-484-7355.. 53 K rrams@cypresscollege.edu
RAMSAMMY, Jillian .... 352-854-2322.. 96 O jillian.ramsammy@cf.edu
RAMSAMMY, Roger, A .. 518-629-4530 302 E r.ramsammy@hvcc.edu
RAMSARAN, Dave .... 570-372-4757 399 C ramsaran@susqu.edu
RAMSARAN, Dave .... 570-372-4127 399 C ramsaran@susqu.edu
RAMSAY, Darlene .... 573-341-4584 261 E ramsayd@mst.edu
RAMSAY, Kerr, C .... 336-841-9148 329 G kramsay@highpoint.edu
RAMSAY, Kimberly .... 310-377-5501.. 51 B kramsay@marymountcalifornia.edu
RAMSAY, Lara .... 509-777-4347 486 I lramsay@whitworth.edu
RAMSAY, Tim .... 616-632-2076 221 C ramsatim@aquinas.edu
RAMSDELL, Nancy, M .. 508-929-8605 213 E nramsdell@worcester.edu
RAMSDELL, Twyla .... 651-213-4180 236 B tramsdell@hazeldenbettyford.edu
RAMSDEN-MEIER, Joanna .... 319-226-2004 162 F joanna.ramsden-meier@allencollege.edu
RAMSEY, Amanda .... 515-964-6443 164 C ajramsey@dmacc.edu
RAMSEY, Christine .... 281-618-1185 439 G christine.d.ramsey@lonestar.edu
RAMSEY, Jason, M .... 814-332-2761 378 D jramsey@allegheny.edu
RAMSEY, Julie .... 865-981-8246 421 F julie.ramsey@maryvillecollege.edu
RAMSEY, Julie, L .... 717-337-6921 384 H ramsey@gettysburg.edu
RAMSEY, Katie .... 503-517-7904 376 C kramsey@reed.edu

RAMSEY, Kimberly .... 310-377-5501.. 51 B kramsey@marymountcalifornia.edu
RAMSEY, Kyle, H .... 630-515-6165 143 G kramse@midwestern.edu
RAMSEY, Lenn .... 803-934-3490 411 C lramsey@morris.edu
RAMSEY, Mae .... 540-362-6519 468 C mramsey@hollins.edu
RAMSEY, Marty .... 828-227-7335 344 A mramsey@wcu.edu
RAMSEY, Mary, K .... 734-487-0341 223 H mary.ramsey@emich.edu
RAMSEY, Matthew .... 913-360-7387 171 D mramsey@benedictine.edu
RAMSEY, Nancy, A .... 865-694-6526 425 F naramsey@pstcc.edu
RAMSEY, Patricia .... 484-365-7436 389 C provost@lincoln.edu
RAMSEY, Paul, G .... 206-543-7718 485 F pramsey@uw.edu
RAMSEY, Richard .... 207-454-1067 195 B rramsey@wccc.me.edu
RAMSEY, Ruth .... 415-257-1393.. 41 H ruth.ramsey@dominican.edu
RAMSEY, Vickie .... 530-251-8852.. 47 F vramsey@lassencollege.edu
RAMSEY, Wanda .... 803-934-3216 411 C wramsey@morris.edu
RAMSEY-HAMACHER, Paige .... 352-588-8489 106 D paige.ramsey.hamacher@saintleo.edu
RAMSEYER, Rob .... 316-295-5433 173 D rob_ramseyer@friends.edu
RAMSIER, Rex .... 330-972-7593 362 B provost@uakron.edu
RAMSTAD, Erik .... 218-299-4923 235 E eramstad@cord.edu
RAMÍREZ FERNÁNDEZ, Mercedes .... 585-275-2121 323 J mercedes.ramirezfernandez@rochester.edu
RAMÍREZ-MÉNDEZ, Pablo, A .... 787-890-2681 512 H pablo.ramirez@upr.edu
RANABARGAR, Kerry .... 620-431-2820 175 H kranabargar@neosho.edu
RANADIVE, Sunita .... 510-780-4500.. 47 J sranadive@lifewest.edu
RANALLI, Carlee, K ...... 814-641-3103 386 H ranallc@juniata.edu
RANALLI, Mark .... 406-994-4410 264 D mark.ranalli@montana.edu
RANALLO-HIGGINS, Frederick .... 215-884-8942 403 G fred.ranallo.higgins@woninstitute.edu
RANCATI, Chrisanne ..... 704-355-6676 327 H chrisanne.rancati@carolinascollege.edu
RANCE, DeLonn, L .... 417-268-1000 250 E ranced@evangel.edu
RANCE-RONEY, Judith .. 610-282-1100 382 E judith.rance-roney@desales.edu
RANCK, Lorrie .... 408-864-8510.. 43 C rancklorrie@deanza.edu
RAND, Amy .... 417-455-5533 252 D amyrand@crowder.edu
RAND, Jonathan .... 617-879-7263 212 E jrand@massart.edu
RAND, Paul, M .... 773-702-0689 150 J prand@uchicago.edu
RANDALL, David .... 617-253-4052 215 G
RANDALL, Gregory .... 253-964-6588 483 D grandall@pierce.ctc.edu
RANDALL, Jessica .... 570-674-6340 390 G jrandall@misericordia.edu
RANDALL, John .... 949-214-3358.. 40 F john.randall@cui.edu
RANDALL, Kelli, V .... 704-216-6195 330 H krandall@livingstone.edu
RANDALL, Kim .... 617-353-9286 207 D krandall@bu.edu
RANDALL, Matthew .... 717-867-6161 388 H randall@lvc.edu
RANDALL, Mike .... 618-468-3130 141 F mrandall@lc.edu
RANDALL, Monte .... 918-549-2806 365 J mrandall@cmn.edu
RANDALL, Nancy .... 704-233-8065 344 G nrandall@wingate.edu
RANDALL, Regina .... 614-287-5343 351 E rrandal2@cscc.edu
RANDALL, Stacey .... 630-466-7900 152 C srandall@waubonsee.edu
RANDALL, Taylor, R ...... 801-581-3074 460 E taylor.randall@eccles.utah.edu
RANDALL, Wesley .... 940-565-2628 454 A wesley.randall@unt.edu
RANDALL-LEE, Valerie, J .... 410-677-0022 203 F vjrandall-lee@salisbury.edu
RANDAZZA, Paula .... 603-897-8303 274 B prandazza@rivier.edu
RANDAZZO, Barbara ..... 937-327-7040 364 H randazzob@wittenberg.edu
RANDAZZO, Jennifer .... 563-884-5141 168 I jennifer.randazzo@palmer.edu
RANDAZZO, Maria .... 315-445-4195 304 C randazmc@lemoyne.edu
RANDAZZO, Nino .... 312-935-4000 147 D nrandazzo@robertmorris.edu
RANDERSON, Janet ...... 303-762-6980.. 79 H janet.randerson@denverseminary.edu
RANDHAWA, Sabah ...... 360-650-3480 486 F president@wwu.edu
RANDLE, Dwight .... 972-238-6248 435 F dwightrandle@dcccd.edu
RANDLE, John .... 231-591-2892 223 J johnrandle@ferris.edu
RANDLE, Jonathan .... 601-925-3849 247 C randle@mc.edu
RANDLES, Christopher, M .... 217-351-2513 146 C crandles@parkland.edu
RANDLES, Jill, A .... 559-323-2100.. 60 I jrandles@sjcl.edu
RANDO, Robert, A .... 937-775-3409 364 I robert.rando@wright.edu
RANDOLPH, Adrian .... 847-491-3276 145 F weinberg-dean@northwestern.edu
RANDOLPH, Amber .... 973-353-5541 282 B amber.randolph@rutgers.edu
RANDOLPH, Brennan .... 812-535-1152 160 B brennan.randolph@smwc.edu
RANDOLPH, Robert .... 417-447-7851 257 G randolphr@otc.edu
RANDOLPH, Tamela ...... 573-651-2163 259 K trandolph@semo.edu
RANDOLPH, Trent .... 256-331-5260.... 3 C trentrandolph@nwscc.edu
RANDOO, Jason, J .... 434-528-5276 477 E jrandoo@vul.edu
RANDORF, Lori .... 330-672-5368 354 J lrandorf@kent.edu
RANDS, Melissa .... 612-874-3700 236 K
RANERO-RAMIREZ, Jessica .... 910-938-6341 333 F ranero-ramirezj@coastalcarolina.edu
RANES, Rodney .... 618-395-7777 138 I ranesr@iecc.edu
RANESES, Jade .... 808-853-1040 128 C jaderaneses@pacrim.edu
RANEY, Jonna, G .... 405-585-5020 367 F jonna.raney@okbu.edu
RANEY, Kristen .... 651-846-1514 241 B kristen.raney@saintpaul.edu
RANFT, Annette, L .... 334-844-4030.... 4 E alr0076@auburn.edu
RANGE, Ronald .... 205-391-2644.... 3 E rrange@sheltonstate.edu
RANGEL, Mary Margaret .... 214-768-4740 444 E marymargaret@smu.edu
RANGUETTE, Renea, L .. 608-757-7700 499 C rranguette@blackhawk.edu
RANHEIM, John .... 314-434-4044 252 B john.ranheim@covenantseminary.edu
RANIERI, Tracey, M ...... 607-436-2446 317 C tracey.ranieri@oneonta.edu
RANK, Carin .... 413-559-5385 210 A
RANKIN, James .... 605-394-2257 417 B jim.rankin@sdsmt.edu
RANKIN, Mary Ann .... 301-405-5252 202 C mrankin@umd.edu
RANKIN, Mona, G .... 516-876-3160 319 A rankinm@oldwestbury.edu
RANKIN, Monika .... 352-638-9701.. 95 D mrankin@beaconcollege.edu
RANKIN, Stephanie, A .. 717-361-1569 383 E rankins@etown.edu
RANKIN, Stephen .... 214-768-4502 444 E rankins@smu.edu
RANKIN, Valerie .... 334-244-3557.... 4 F vrankin@aum.edu
RANKIN, Walter .... 203-254-4025.. 86 I wrankin@fairfield.edu
RANKINE, Patrice, D ..... 804-289-8416 472 L prankine@richmond.edu
RANSDELL, Junell, A .... 217-786-4506 142 B junell.ransdell@llcc.edu
RANSDELL, Lynda, B .... 928-523-2671.. 14 H lynda.ransdell@nau.edu
RANSLEM, Bradley .... 402-844-7717 268 J bradleyr@northeast.edu
RANSOM, Joni .... 308-398-7301 266 A jransom@cccneb.edu
RANSOM, Kimberly .... 304-793-6820 491 A kransom@osteo.wvsom.edu
RANSON, Julie .... 804-706-5064 474 I jranson@jtcc.edu
RANTZ, Rick .... 805-922-6966.. 24 J rrantz@hancockcollege.edu
RANUM, Brenda .... 563-387-1477 167 E ranubr01@luther.edu
RANZOLIN, Leo .... 909-558-4536.. 48 C lranzolin@llu.edu
RAO, Anand .... 540-654-1546 472 I arao@umw.edu
RAO, Julie, M .... 585-245-5553 318 E rao@geneseo.edu
RAO, Michael .... 804-828-1200 473 F president@vcu.edu
RAPACCIOLI, Donna ...... 718-817-4100 300 E rapaccioli@fordham.edu
RAPACZ, Deb .... 773-298-3326 148 G drapacz@sxu.edu
RAPALA, Elise .... 708-456-0300 150 I eliserapala@triton.edu
RAPER, Lorraine .... 252-399-6505 326 M lhraper@barton.edu
RAPETTI, Mario .... 914-251-6320 319 E mario.rapetti@purchase.edu
RAPHAEL, Joann .... 954-745-6960.. 92 G
RAPHAEL, Joann .... 954-378-2400.. 92 G
RAPHAEL, Joann .... 561-904-3000.. 92 G
RAPHAEL, Valencia .... 562-860-2451.. 35 M vraphael@cerritos.edu
RAPHEL, Colette .... 504-314-2855 191 B craphel@tulane.edu
RAPOZA, Bob .... 562-938-4698.. 48 D brapoza@lbcc.edu
RAPOZA, Kalei .... 808-932-7650 128 E kaleihii@hawaii.edu
RAPOZA, Mark, F .... 401-865-2064 405 B mrapoza@providence.edu
RAPP, Kelly, E .... 417-836-5636 256 E kellyrapp@missouristate.edu
RAPP, Peter .... 503-494-8744 375 B hutching@ohsu.edu
RAPP, Ryan .... 573-882-2011 261 A rappr@umsystem.edu
RAPP, Timothy .... 301-295-4231 504 B timothy.rapp@usuhs.edu
RAPP, Tracy .... 828-627-4509 335 C tkrapp@haywood.edu
RAPP, Virginia .... 310-660-3773.. 41 L vrapp@elcamino.edu
RAPPAPORT, Jay .... 504-865-5000 191 B
RAPPE, Sylvia .... 936-294-3188 450 C str017@shsu.edu
RAPPEL, Kevin .... 630-829-6404 132 E krappel@ben.edu
RAPPLEY, Marsha .... 804-828-0100 473 F mdrappley@vcu.edu
RARIG, Jenny .... 215-641-6688 390 H jrarig@mc3.edu
RARIG, Kris .... 757-825-3810 476 A rarigk@tncc.edu
RASBERRY, Charles ...... 516-299-2784 304 G charles.rasberry@liu.edu
RASBERRY, Todd, W .... 806-651-2069 448 C trasberry@wtamu.edu
RASCH, Michael .... 218-751-8670 242 J michaelrasch@oakhills.edu
RASCH, Randolph .... 517-355-6527 227 D randolph.rasch@hc.msu.edu
RASCHKE, Greg .... 919-515-7188 342 B greg_raschke@ncsu.edu
RASCO, Barbara .... 307-766-4133 502 H brasco@uwyo.edu
RASCOE, Fred .... 931-668-7010 425 C frascoe@mscc.edu
RASCOE, Patrick .... 518-564-2022 319 C prasc001@plattsburgh.edu
RASCON, Tricia .... 805-893-4275.. 70 A tricia.rascon@sa.ucsb.edu
RASH, Brian .... 225-214-6976 186 F brian.rash@franu.edu
RASH, Kamie .... 918-293-5456 368 D kamie.rash@okstate.edu
RASH, R. Scott .... 814-871-7464 384 E rash001@gannon.edu
RASHED, David .... 864-231-2000 406 G orashed@andersonuniversity.edu
RASHED, Jamal .... 513-244-4273 357 A jamal.rashed@msj.edu
RASHID, John .... 218-726-8821 243 F jrashid@d.umn.edu
RASHID, Khadijat .... 202-651-5224.. 91 E khadijat.rashid@gllaudet.edu
RASMUSSEN, Allen .... 361-593-2809 447 D allen.rasmussen@tamuk.edu
RASMUSSEN, Brock .... 612-874-3749 236 K brock_rasmussen@mcad.edu
RASMUSSEN, Bruce, D . 402-280-2487 266 I bdrass@creighton.edu
RASMUSSEN, Clark .... 307-778-4372 502 D crasmussen@lccc.wy.edu
RASMUSSEN, Darin .... 360-650-3555 486 F darin.rasmussen@wwu.edu
RASMUSSEN, George, A .... 361-593-3106 447 D george.rasmussen@tamuk.edu
RASMUSSEN, Karla, R .. 757-455-3316 477 F krasmussen@vwu.edu
RASMUSSEN, Laurel, R . 563-588-8000 165 F lrasmussen@emmaus.edu
RASMUSSEN, Michele ... 773-702-7770 150 J mrasmussen@uchicago.edu
RASMUSSEN, Rob .... 815-479-7599 143 A rrasmuss@mchenry.edu
RASMUSSEN, Sarah ...... 605-256-5048 416 J sarah.rasmussen@dsu.edu
RASMUSSEN, Schauna .. 608-243-4478 499 H slrassmussen@madisoncollege.edu
RASMUSSEN, Scott .... 208-282-2507 130 H rasmscot@isu.edu
RASMUSSEN, Steve .... 605-626-2634 417 A steve.rasmussen@northern.edu
RASMUSSON, Beth .... 605-626-2655 417 A beth.rasmusson@northern.edu
RASNAKE, Nathan .... 276-376-4651 473 B ndr5a@uvawise.edu
RASNICK, Becky, D .... 501-450-5200.. 23 H rebekahr@uca.edu
RASNICK, Natalie .... 417-690-2209 251 E nrasnick@cofo.edu
RASOR, Mark .... 918-540-6201 366 I mrasor@neo.edu
RASOR, Mark .... 918-540-6213 366 I mrasor@neo.edu
RASOR, Roberta .... 417-328-1606 259 L rrasor@sbuniv.edu
RASP, Allison, M .... 512-416-5888 442 M allisonm@stedwards.edu
RASPILLER, Edward (Ted), E .... 804-594-1571 474 I traspiller@jtcc.edu
RASSAU, Kimberly .... 412-323-4000 379 C krassau@manchesterbidwell.org
RAST, Lawrence, R .... 260-452-2101 154 E lawrence.rast@ctsfw.edu
RASZEWSKI, Thomas .... 410-864-3621 201 F traszewski@stmarys.edu
RATAICZAK, Terry .... 740-374-8716 364 C trataiczak@wscc.edu
RATCHFORD, Robert ..... 423-425-4074 428 A robert-ratchford@utc.edu
RATCLIFF, Chris .... 918-343-7984 369 F cratcliff@rsu.edu
RATCLIFF, Lance .... 660-785-4383 260 J lratcliff@truman.edu
RATCLIFF, Stephen .... 903-923-2110 436 D sratcliff@etbu.edu
RATCLIFF, Susie .... 740-351-3434 360 K sratcliff@shawnee.edu
RATCLIFF, Terry .... 626-529-8500.. 55 A tratcliff@pacificoaks.edu
RATCLIFF, Terry, D .... 208-885-4132 131 G dee@uidaho.edu
RATCLIFFE, Kara .... 312-369-7262 135 E kratcliffe@colum.edu
RATH, Phillip, S .... 812-888-5101 162 C prath@vinu.edu
RATHBUN, Jason .... 315-866-0300 301 G rathbunja@herkimer.edu
RATHBUN, Kenneth, D . 515-964-0601 165 G rathbunk@faith.edu
RATHERT, Greg .... 763-433-1864 237 C gregory.rathert@anokaramsey.edu
RATHJE, James, A .... 507-354-8221 236 I rathjeja@mlc-wels.edu
RATHJE, John, M .... 330-672-3000 354 J jrathje@kent.edu
RATHJE, Lonelle .... 660-562-1248 257 E lonelle@nwmissouri.edu

RATKE, David 828-328-7183 330 F david.ratke@lr.edu

RATLIFF, Darby 716-896-0700 324 E dratliff@villa.edu

RATLIFF, Jill, C 606-783-2256 183 F ji.ratliff@moreheadstate.edu

RATLIFF, John 704-272-5325 337 I jratliff@spcc.edu

RATLIFF, Kelly 530-754-6170 .. 68 E kmratliff@ucdavis.edu

RATLIFF, Kerry 606-368-6064 178 D kerryratliff@alc.edu

RATLIFF, Kevin, B 540-453-2264 474 B ratliffk@brcc.edu

RATLIFF, Melissa 508-565-1877 218 H mratliff@stonehill.edu

RATLIFF, Nicolle 816-802-3421 254 B nratliff@kcai.edu

RATLIFF, Pru 707-476-4140 .. 39 D pru-ratliff@redwoods.edu

RATLIFF, Ron 785-539-3571 175 E rratliff@mccks.edu

RATLIFF, Thomas 765-677-2116 157 D thomas.ratliff@indwes.edu

RATLIFF, Victoria 276-523-7467 475 A vratliff@mecc.edu

RATLIFFE, Jeannine 304-424-8262 491 D jeannine.ratliffe@wvup.edu

RATNER, Morris 415-565-4682 .. 68 F ratnerm@uchastings.edu

RATTERMAN, Rebecca .. 405-422-1255 369 E rattermanr@redlandscc.edu

RATTIGAN, Monica, D .. 412-648-1406 401 B mrattigan@cfo.pitt.edu

RATTIN, George 847-578-8345 147 I george.rattin@rosalindfranklin.edu

RATTY, Michael 617-732-2130 216 B michael.ratty@mcphs.edu

RATZLAFF, Barbara 478-471-5353 121 F barbara.ratzlaff@mga.edu

RATZLAFF, Don 620-947-3121 177 C donr@tabor.edu

RAU, Barbara, L 920-424-4151 497 B rau@uwosh.edu

RAU, Christopher 612-659-6890 238 I christopher.rau@minneapolis.edu

RAU, Douglas 314-246-6960 262 C

RAUBE, Michelle 989-686-9477 223 G michelleraube@delta.edu

RAUBENHEIMER, C. Dianne 919-760-8913 331 B raubenhe@meredith.edu

RAUBOLT, Jack 714-289-2007 .. 36 C raubolt@chapman.edu

RAUCH, Dena 319-398-5476 167 C dena.rauch@kirkwood.edu

RAUCH, Eric 863-680-4305 .. 99 H erauch@flsouthern.edu

RAUCH, Jason 518-736-3622 300 F jason.rauch@fmcc.suny.edu

RAUCH, Karen 610-683-4229 395 A rauch@kutztown.edu

RAUCHER, Alice, J 434-924-0311 473 A ajr3s@virginia.edu

RAUDENBUSH, Joanna . 215-646-7300 385 D raudenbush@gmercyu.edu

RAUENZAHN, Wayne .... 540-863-2905 474 D wrauenzahn@dslcc.edu

RAUHUT, Curt 478-387-4869 118 G crauhut@gmc.edu

RAULERSON, Stefane .... 229-317-6538 113 H stefane.raulerson@asurams.edu

RAULT, Pamela 985-549-2118 192 D pamela.rault@selu.edu

RAULUK, Ruth 412-392-3996 397 A rrauluk@pointpark.edu

RAUSA WILLIAMS, Monica 410-777-1177 197 C mrausawilliams@aacc.edu

RAUSAW, Tramaine 520-494-5345 .. 11 K tramaine.rausaw@centralaz.edu

RAUSCH, Kyle 219-989-2861 159 G rausch2@pnw.edu

RAUSCH, Scott, K 404-727-8849 117 F scott.rausch@emory.edu

RAUSCH, Todd 712-274-6400 170 E todd.rausch@witcc.edu

RAUSCHER, Victor, E .... 518-445-3294 289 E vraus@albanylaw.edu

RAUSCHKOLB, Arlen 413-236-3003 213 F arauschkolb@berkshirecc.edu

RAUT, Mukti 617-228-2433 214 A mnraut@bhcc.mass.edu

RAUTZHAN, Peter 610-282-1100 382 E peter.rautzhan@desales.edu

RAVE, Carole 360-676-2772 482 D crave@nwic.edu

RAVELING, Delores 310-434-8708 .. 62 E raveling_delores@smc.edu

RAVELLI, James, B 503-943-7540 377 E ravelli@up.edu

RAVELO, Mercedes 718-780-7942 291 J mercedes.ravelo@brooklaw.edu

RAVEN, Kati 570-585-9565 381 E kraven@clarkssummitu.edu

RAVENFELD, Mary 610-647-4400 386 C mravenfeld@immaculata.edu

RAVER, C. Cybele 212-998-2274 310 B cybele.raver@nyu.edu

RAVERT, Patricia, K 801-422-6547 458 H patricia_ravert@byu.edu

RAVICHANDRAN, Guruswami 626-395-4100 .. 29 C ravi@caltech.edu

RAVID, Orly 213-738-6602 .. 65 G oravid@swlaw.edu

RAVINDRAN, Tharanee, M 256-824-6036 .... 8 B tharanee.ravindran@uah.edu

RAVJA, Frank 313-664-7496 222 F fravja@collegeforcreativestudies.edu

RAWAK, Christine 302-831-4006 .. 90 F crawak@udel.edu

RAWJEE, Roopa 608-262-1234 496 C rrawjee@wisc.edu

RAWL, Carolyn 334-244-3934 .... 4 F crawl@aum.edu

RAWLEIGH, Camilla, B . 717-262-2010 403 F camilla.rawleigh@wilson.edu

RAWLEY, Albert 434-791-5654 464 O brawley@averett.edu

RAWLEY, Ben 901-462-4137 428 E benrawley@visible.edu

RAWLINGS, Becky 360-383-3404 486 G brawling@whatcom.edu

RAWLINGS, Michelle .... 859-233-8116 184 G registrar@transy.edu

RAWLINGS, Scott 217-234-5519 141 D srawlings39277@lakeland.cc.il.us

RAWLINS, Benjamin 585-245-5064 318 E rawlins@geneseo.edu

RAWLINS, Jim, H 541-346-3201 377 D jrawlins@uoregon.edu

RAWLINS, Kim 937-298-3399 355 F kim.rawlins@kc.edu

RAWLINSON, David, J .. 401-825-2280 404 H djrawlinson@ccri.edu

RAWLINSON, Eddy 972-860-5210 435 A ebrawlinson@dcccd.edu

RAWLINSON, Ina 252-493-7289 336 H irawlinson@email.pittcc.edu

RAWLS, Lynn 843-383-8045 408 D

RAWLS, Terry 828-262-6519 341 B rawlsdt@appstate.edu

RAY, Alan 617-236-8800 209 D aray@fisher.edu

RAY, Anita 706-245-7226 117 E aray@ec.edu

RAY, Anthony 847-214-7415 136 F aray@elgin.edu

RAY, Barry 864-231-2000 406 G bray@andersonuniversity.edu

RAY, Brandon 360-442-2254 482 B bray@lowercolumbia.edu

RAY, JR., Charles, A .... 504-816-8010 190 A cray@nobts.edu

RAY, Christopher, T ...... 940-898-2852 451 F chrisray@twu.edu

RAY, Darby, K 207-786-8241 193 B dray3@bates.edu

RAY, Deana 817-257-7121 448 G d.ray@tcu.edu

RAY, Don 870-768-3117 .. 17 D dray@smail.anc.edu

RAY, Edward, J 541-737-4133 375 D pres.office@oregonstate.edu

RAY, Emily 270-824-8581 181 G emily.ray@kctcs.edu

RAY, Gary, T 512-245-1977 450 E gtr21@txstate.edu

RAY, Glen 940-898-3505 451 F payments@twu.edu

RAY, James, U 803-323-2305 414 G rayj@winthrop.edu

RAY, Jasmine 501-812-2241 .. 23 B jray@uaptc.edu

RAY, Jaymi 931-424-4062 421 E jray@martinmethodist.edu

RAY, Jeffrey 828-227-7368 344 A jeffray@wcu.edu

RAY, Jennifer 405-425-5150 367 G jennifer.ray@oc.edu

RAY, Jess, D 309-438-8586 139 E jdray@ilstu.edu

RAY, Johnnie 303-860-5600 .. 82 N johnnie.ray@cu.edu

RAY, Judy, K 336-841-9201 329 G jray@highpoint.edu

RAY, Kashanda 828-395-1660 335 D kray@isothermal.edu

RAY, Kathlin, D 775-784-6500 271 F kray@unr.edu

RAY, Ken 813-253-7054 101 A kray6@hccfl.edu

RAY, Leigh, A 931-372-3320 426 E lray@tntech.edu

RAY, Mandy 978-542-7253 213 C mray@salemstate.edu

RAY, Nancy 704-334-6882 328 C nmcnamara@charlottechristian.edu

RAY, Nicholas, T 812-941-2411 157 B nicray@ius.edu

RAY, Nick 317-274-0015 156 D nicray@iu.edu

RAY, Nick 219-980-7202 156 E nicray@iu.edu

RAY, Nickolas 574-520-4463 157 A nicray@iusb.edu

RAY, Pamela 850-644-8643 109 C pray2@fsu.edu

RAY, Phillip 979-458-6421 446 C pray@tamus.edu

RAY, Roxie, L 203-576-4292 .. 88 D roxieray@bridgeport.edu

RAY, Ryan 828-766-1273 336 A rray@mayland.edu

RAY, Sandy 850-484-1213 104 H scesaretti@pensacolastate.edu

RAY, Shanna 615-966-5833 421 D shanna.ray@lipscomb.edu

RAY, JR., Stephen, G ... 773-896-2400 133 L

RAY, Tracey 610-436-1104 396 A tray2@wcupa.edu

RAY, Vivyen 201-360-4073 278 C vray@hccc.edu

RAY, William 503-352-2786 375 G raywb@pacificu.edu

RAYBUCK, Diane 814-732-2761 394 F draybuck@edinboro.edu

RAYBURN, Candace 817-554-5950 440 C crayburn@messengercollege.edu

RAYBURN, T. Monroe .. 202-319-5765 .. 91 B rayburn@cua.edu

RAYCHAUDHURI, Uttiyo 607-255-6224 297 F

RAYFIELD, Stuart 404-962-3040 126 F stuart.rayfield@usg.edu

RAYMO, Jim 952-829-4680 234 A jim.raymo@bethfel.org

RAYMOND, Annette 973-748-9000 276 A annette_raymond@bloomfield.edu

RAYMOND, Bruce 719-549-2108 .. 79 A bruce.raymond@csupueblo.edu

RAYMOND, Francis 502-272-8487 179 B fraymond@bellarmine.edu

RAYMOND, SR., John, R 414-955-8225 494 C jraymond@mcw.edu

RAYMOND, Laura 727-864-8217 .. 97 J raymonlm@eckerd.edu

RAYMOND, Lisa 508-289-3557 220 D lraymond@whoi.edu

RAYMOND, Margaret .... 608-265-3750 496 C margaret.raymond@wisc.edu

RAYMOND, Monica 805-339-6370 .. 63 B

RAYMOND, Monica 805-339-6370 .. 63 D

RAYMOND, Sarah 406-496-4384 265 A sraymond@mtech.edu

RAYMOND, Thomas, J . 504-864-7490 189 F traymond@loyno.edu

RAYMOND, Wendy, E ... 610-896-1021 385 L president@haverford.edu

RAYNER, Jill 706-864-1688 126 A jill.rayner@ung.edu

RAYNOR, Timothy 203-576-4168 .. 88 D traynor@bridgeport.edu

RAYNOR, Vanessa 919-719-2284 340 E vraynor@shawu.edu

RAYOS, Andre 915-779-8031 457 F arayos@computercareercenter.com

RAZA, Ahsan 212-870-1228 310 A araza@nyts.edu

RAZA, Shah 323-254-2203 .. 41 J

RAZA, Syed 256-761-6200 .... 7 B sqraza@talladega.edu

RAZUTIS, Valerie 352-335-2332 .. 93 F valerie.razutis@acupuncturist.edu

RAZZA, Paul 336-770-3264 343 D razzap@uncsa.edu

RAZZAGHI, Farzaneh .... 828-227-7485 344 A frazzaghi@email.wcu.edu

RE, C. John 646-448-4288 409 J johnre@forrestcollege.edu

RE, C. John 646-448-4288 409 J johnre@nyc.rr.com

REA, Allyson 434-961-5223 475 F area@pvcc.edu

REABACK, Roslyn 203-932-7263 .. 89 A rreaback@newhaven.edu

READ, Allison 860-297-2013 .. 88 C allison.read@trincoll.edu

READ, Brian 781-891-2047 206 D bread1@bentley.edu

READ, Carole 757-789-1733 474 F cread@es.vccs.edu

READ, Deborah 727-873-4397 110 C read@mail.usf.edu

READ, Lori 402-643-7451 266 G lori.read@cune.edu

READ, Melissa 508-541-1654 208 F mread@dean.edu

READ, Russel 336-734-7651 334 E rread@forsythtech.edu

READ, Steven 865-251-1800 424 A sread@south.edu

READER, Aaron 425-235-2409 483 G areader@rtc.edu

READING, Clint 208-535-5452 130 C clint.reading@cei.edu

READNOUR, Warren ..... 501-450-5007 .. 23 H wreadnour@uca.edu

REAGAN, J. Michael, E 979-845-8058 446 G policechief@tamu.edu

REAGAN, Katherine, M . 423-869-6389 421 C katherine.reagan@lmunet.edu

REAGAN, Krystal 618-985-2828 139 I krystalreagan@jalc.edu

REAGAN, Melinda 972-279-6511 430 B mreagan@amberton.edu

REAGEN, Nate 515-271-2949 165 A nate.reagen@drake.edu

REAGIN, Cam 803-641-3399 413 D camr@usca.edu

REAGINS-LILLY, Soncia, R 512-471-1133 455 A vpsa@austin.utexas.edu

REAGLE, Mike 270-745-2037 185 E mike.reagle@wku.edu

REAL, Yannick 562-860-2451 .. 35 M yreal@cerritos.edu

REALISTA, Katy 714-484-7142 .. 53 K krealista@cypresscollege.edu

REALIVASQUEZ, Yvonne 432-837-8032 450 D yrealivasquez@sulross.edu

REAM, Dan 804-333-6716 475 G dream@rappahannock.edu

REAM, Debbie 213-477-2505 .. 52 G dream@msmu.edu

REAMER, Amy 910-962-4075 343 C reamera@uncw.edu

REAMS, Amelia 229-219-3198 126 G alharmon@valdosta.edu

REAMS, John 706-233-7247 124 B jreams@shorter.edu

REAMY, Brian 301-295-9942 504 B brian.reamy@usuhs.edu

REAMY, Sara 503-554-2118 373 C sreamy@georgefox.edu

REANTILLO, Susan 518-244-4623 313 D reants@sage.edu

REARDON, Cheryl 319-335-0056 163 A cheryl-reardon@uiowa.edu

REARDON, Colleen 708-524-6643 136 C creardon@dom.edu

REARDON, Diana 803-774-3354 407 C reardondl@cctech.edu

REARDON, Emily 508-213-2275 217 E emily.reardon@nichols.edu

REARDON, Mary 512-451-5743 430 M

REARDON, Penny, E ..... 540-828-5395 465 D
preardon@bridgewater.edu
REARDON, Richard .... 802-468-1234 464 A
richard.reardon@castleton.edu
REARDON, Tim .... 802-485-2001 463 A
reardont@norwich.edu
REARIC, Sue .... 619-644-7575.. 44 G
sue.rearic@gcccd.edu
REAS, Rae Ellen .... 425-564-5608 478 F
raeellen.reas@bellevuecollege.edu
REASH, Brenda .... 252-222-6262 333 A
reashb@carteret.edu
REASNER, Brett, A .... 570-326-3761 393 G
breasner@pct.edu
REASONER, Carroll .... 319-335-2841 163 A
carroll-reasoner@uiowa.edu
REAT, Daniel, J .... 713-500-3278 456 B
daniel.j.reat@uth.tmc.edu
REAUME, Vicki .... 734-487-2410 223 H
vreaume@emich.edu
REAUX, Tallya .... 334-229-4712.... 4 B
treaux@alasu.edu
REAVES, Ken .... 678-872-8512 118 E
kreaves@highlands.edu
REBECK, Amanda .... 716-839-8468 298 B
arebeck@daemen.edu
REBEIN, Robert .... 317-274-8448 156 F
rrebein@iupui.edu
REBER, Christopher, M 201-360-4003 278 C
creber@hccc.edu
REBETA, Gail .... 330-672-3367 354 J
grebeta@kent.edu
REBIK, Clint .... 707-826-6205.. 33 D
clint@humboldt.edu
REBMAN, Johanna .... 815-836-5050 141 G
jrebman@lewisu.edu
REBOLI, Annette .... 856-361-2800 281 E
reboli@rowan.edu
REBURN, Tom .... 218-477-2549 239 D
tom.reburn@mnstate.edu
RECA, Michael, F .... 609-896-5080 281 B
reca@rider.edu
RECALDE, Tina .... 619-388-2789.. 60 D
trecalde@sdccd.edu
RECCHIA, Karen .... 318-678-6000 187 A
krecchia@bpcc.edu
RECHTSCHAFFEN,
Joyce, A .... 202-220-1364 280 E
jrechtsc@princeton.edu
RECINOS, Alba .... 714-808-4796.. 53 J
arecinos@nocccd.edu
RECINOS, Diane .... 973-278-5400 275 I
dr@berkeleycollege.edu
RECINOS, Diane .... 973-278-5400 291 D
dr@berkeleycollege.edu
RECINOS, Jose .... 714-432-5898.. 38 E
jrecinos7@occ.cccd.edu
RECKER, Mary, A .... 937-229-4354 362 G
mpoirier1@udayton.edu
RECLA, Leanne, R .... 610-799-1718 388 I
lrecla@lccc.edu
RECORD, James .... 847-578-3000 147 I
james.record@rosalindfranklin.edu
RECORD, Kim .... 336-944-6206 343 A
ksrecord@uncg.edu
RECORDS, Stefany .... 713-221-8636 453 B
recordss@uhd.edu
RECTOR, David .... 660-785-7607 260 J
daverec@truman.edu
RECTOR, David .... 425-739-8287 482 A
david.rector@lwtech.edu
RECTOR, Eric .... 540-365-4427 467 I
erector@ferrum.edu
RECTOR, Lallene, J .... 847-866-3901 137 E
ljr@garrett.edu
RECTOR, Ray .... 509-359-6612 480 E
rrector@ewu.edu
RECTOR, Rob .... 417-447-4852 257 G
rectorr@otc.edu
RECZNIK, Joel, S .... 740-284-5236 353 B
jrecznik@franciscan.edu
RECZNIK, Mark, E .... 740-284-5845 353 B
mrecznik@franciscan.edu
RED OWL NEISS,
Sherry .... 605-856-5880 416 D
sherry.redowl@sintegleska.edu
REDA, Eva .... 614-882-2551 353 A
ereda@fortiscollege.edu
REDA, Frank, J .... 848-445-1760 282 A
reda@oit.rutgers.edu
REDA, Frank, J .... 848-445-1760 282 B
reda@oit.rutgers.edu
REDD, Annie .... 804-524-5070 477 B
aredd@vsu.edu
REDD, Randy .... 901-751-8453 422 E
rredd@mabts.edu
REDD, Rea .... 724-852-3254 402 F
rredd@waynesburg.edu
REDD, Scott .... 703-996-4054 248 F
sredd@rts.edu
REDDAY, Darlene .... 605-698-3966 416 F
dredday@swc.tc
REDDER, Vince .... 605-995-2631 415 C
vince.redder@dwu.edu
REDDERSON, Jeff, P ..... 864-294-3262 410 A
jeff.redderson@furman.edu
REDDI, Lakshmi .... 575-646-2914 287 B
lnr@nmsu.edu
REDDICK, Chenita, R .... 410-651-8045 203 A
crreddick@umes.edu
REDDICK, Don .... 815-939-5111 146 A
dreddick@olivet.edu
REDDING, Gregory .... 765-361-6310 162 E
reddingg@wabahs.edu
REDDING, Victor .... 775-784-4031 271 F
vredding@unr.edu
REDDING LAPUZ,
Danni .... 650-738-4121.. 61 Q
reddinglapuzd@smccd.edu
REDDINGER, Amy .... 906-217-4068 221 O
amy.reddinger@baycollege.edu
REDDINGTON, Cynthia . 757-240-2229 471 A
cynthia.reddington@rivhs.com
REDDIX, Rhoda .... 225-214-6966 186 F
rhoda.reddix@franu.edu
REDDY, Howard, J .... 850-474-3306 110 E
hreddy@uwf.edu
REDDY, Indra, K .... 979-458-7200 446 G
indrakreddy@tamu.edu
REDDY, Kirti .... 510-723-6641.. 35 O
kreddy@chabotcollege.edu
REDDY, Michael .... 415-476-1323.. 69 E
michael.reddy@ucsf.edu
REDDY, Narem .... 678-466-4100 116 E
naremreddy@clayton.edu
REDDY, Robert .... 617-373-3190 217 F
REDDY, Venkat .... 719-255-3436.. 83 B
chancellor@uccs.edu
REDER-SCHOPP,
Megan .... 605-394-6988 417 B
megan.reder-schopp@sdsmt.edu
REDFERN, Amber .... 239-489-9205 100 A
amber.redfern@fsw.edu
REDFIELD, Chaunta ...... 765-641-4182 153 B
cdredfield@anderson.edu
REDIGER-SCHULTE,
Leah .... 402-826-8111 267 A
leah.redigerschulte@doane.edu
REDING, Nichole .... 503-760-3131 371 H
nichole@birthingway.edu
REDING, Roger .... 806-894-9611 443 I
rreding@southplainscollege.edu
REDING, Terrence .... 585-345-6850 301 A
tareding@genesee.edu
REDINGER, Matthew ..... 406-791-5302 265 H
matthew.redinger@uprovidence.edu
REDINGTON, Joseph .... 570-674-6756 390 G
jredington@misericordia.edu
REDINGTON, Lyn .... 319-335-1162 163 A
lyn-redington@uiowa.edu
REDINGTON, Lyn .... 208-282-2315 130 H
redilyn@isu.edu
REDLER, Susan .... 212-431-2121 309 G
susan.redler@nyls.edu
REDLINGER,
Lawrence, J .... 972-883-6188 455 B
redling@utdallas.edu
REDMAN, Cynthia .... 773-256-3000 143 C
credman@meadville.edu
REDMAN, Donald, L ..... 717-338-3036 400 I
dredman@uls.edu
REDMAN, Laurel .... 480-517-8000.. 13 G
REDMAN, Martin .... 215-898-3131 400 K
mredman@upenn.edu
REDMANN, Trent .... 612-343-4749 242 H
tjredman@northcentral.edu
REDMOND, Angie .... 641-844-5712 166 K
angie.redmond@iavalley.edu
REDMOND, Jeff .... 805-267-1690.. 47 H
jeff.redmond@lauruscollege.edu
REDMOND, Kathleen .... 708-524-6818 136 C
kredmond@dom.edu
REDMOND, Michael ..... 201-447-7237 275 H
presidentsoffice@bergen.edu
REDMOND, Michael, J . 303-458-4995.. 82 E
mredmond@regis.edu
REDMOND, Rodney ...... 240-567-5030 200 C
rodney.redmond@montgomerycollege.edu
REDMOND, Thomas, E . 202-274-5622.. 93 C
tredmond@udc.edu
REDMOND, Tim .... 805-267-1690.. 47 H
timothy.redmond@lauruscollege.edu
REDMOND, Xavier .... 662-254-3478 248 B
xavier.redmond@mvsu.edu
REDNER, Richard .... 918-631-2986 371 E
richard-redner@utulsa.edu
REDONDO, Diego .... 212-237-8521 294 D
dredondo@jjay.cuny.edu
REDONNETT, Rosa .... 207-621-3419 195 I
rosar@maine.edu
REDWINE, Marian .... 405-491-6336 370 A
maredwin@snu.edu
REDWINE, Mike .... 405-491-6638 370 A
mredwine@snu.edu
REECE, Amani .... 718-270-6050 295 A
areece@mec.cuny.edu
REECE, Anton .... 270-534-3082 182 F
anton.reece@kctcs.edu
REECE, E. Albert .... 410-706-7410 202 D
deanmed@som.umaryland.edu
REECE, James .... 610-372-1722 379 B
james.reece@berks.edu
REECE, Jeana .... 801-689-2160 459 J
jreece@nightingale.edu
REECE, Jeremy .... 870-733-6786.. 17 H
jreece@asumidsouth.edu
REECE, Jonathan .... 704-687-5701 342 E
jonathan.reece@uncc.edu
REECE, Lenora .... 214-860-2015 435 C
lenora.reece@dcccd.edu
REECE, Ronda .... 405-945-8631 368 E
reecer@osuokc.edu
REECE, Scott .... 301-624-2824 198 E
sreece@frederick.edu
REECE, Sheila .... 903-785-7661 441 G
sreece@parisjc.edu
REECE, Terry .... 805-546-3283.. 41 A
treece@cuesta.edu
REECK, Joanne .... 612-330-1111 233 K
reeck@augsburg.edu
REED, Aaron .... 801-302-2800 459 H
aaron.reed@neumont.edu
REED, Alicia .... 701-255-3285 347 B
areed@uttc.edu
REED, Alicia .... 701-627-4738 346 G
areed@nhsc.edu
REED, Amber .... 218-736-1588 239 B
amber.reed@minnesota.edu
REED, Ann, M .... 304-462-6123 490 C
ann.reed@glenville.edu
REED, Annie, G .... 818-947-2320.. 49 F
reedag@lavc.edu
REED, Arlene .... 626-585-7614.. 55 K
areed9@pasadena.edu
REED, Barrett .... 870-584-1462.. 22 G
reedb@cccua.edu
REED, Bill .... 602-386-4127.. 10 E
bill.reed@arizonachristian.edu
REED, Brady .... 530-257-6181.. 47 F
breed@lassencollege.edu
REED, Casey .... 918-631-5003 371 E
casey-reed@utulsa.edu
REED, Catherine .... 925-969-3300.. 46 H
creed@jfku.edu
REED, Chad .... 540-831-5411 470 C
creed4@radford.edu
REED, Charlene, K .... 330-672-2585 354 J
creed2@kent.edu
REED, Christine .... 805-922-6966.. 24 J
creed@hancockcollege.edu
REED, Corey .... 817-257-5218 448 G
corey.reed@tcu.edu
REED, Cristina .... 810-762-9584 225 H
creed@kettering.edu
REED, Crystal .... 256-331-5249.... 3 C
cingle@nwscc.edu
REED, Cynthia .... 225-771-2552 191 A
creed@sulc.edu
REED, Cynthia .... 470-578-6117 120 L
creed63@kennesaw.edu
REED, Dallas .... 973-278-5400 291 D
dfr@berkeleycollege.edu
REED, Dallas, F .... 973-278-5400 275 I
dfr@berkeleycollege.edu
REED, Dan .... 530-898-6451.. 31 A
dmreed@csuchico.edu
REED, Darcy, A .... 507-284-3796 234 J
reed.darcy@mayo.edu
REED, David .... 650-306-3470.. 61 O
reedd@smccd.edu
REED, David, D .... 906-487-3043 227 E
ddreed@mtu.edu
REED, Deana .... 609-896-5121 281 B
REED, Debbie .... 580-387-7000 366 H
dreed@mscok.edu
REED, Dee .... 812-535-5212 160 B
dreed@smwc.edu
REED, Diane .... 757-594-7202 466 B
dreed@cnu.edu
REED, Donna .... 812-941-2430 157 B
donnreed@iu.edu
REED, Donna .... 415-452-5455.. 37 A
dreed@ccsf.edu
REED, Doug .... 870-245-5167.. 20 E
reedd@obu.edu
REED, Doug .... 405-744-4244 368 B
doug.reed@okstate.edu
REED, Elaine .... 323-343-5392.. 32 A
bkscalstla@bncollege.com
REED, Elizabeth .... 215-884-8942 403 G
elizabeth.reed@woninstitute.edu
REED, Francesca .... 703-284-5906 469 C
francesca.reed@marymount.edu
REED, George .... 719-255-4047.. 83 B
george.reed@uccs.edu
REED, Guy, L .... 602-827-2066.. 16 G
guyreed@email.arizona.edu
REED, Helen .... 970-351-2601.. 83 E
helen.reed@unco.edu
REED, Jeff .... 515-292-9694 162 G
jeff.reed@antiochschool.edu
REED, Jennifer .... 740-264-5591 352 H
jreed@egcc.edu
REED, Jennifer, G .... 801-581-4033 460 E
jennifer.reed@aux.utah.edu
REED, Jeremy .... 605-626-2530 417 A
jeremy.reed@northern.edu
REED, Jerry .... 570-389-4040 394 A
jreed@bloomu.edu
REED, John .... 415-442-7224.. 44 D
jreed@ggu.edu
REED, Jonathan .... 909-593-3511.. 70 D
jreed@laverne.edu
REED, Karen, A .... 419-755-4538 357 E
kreed@ncstatecollege.edu
REED, Kate .... 931-598-3271 423 M
kreed@sewanee.edu
REED, Kelsey .... 316-322-3295 171 G
REED, Kevin .... 541-346-3082 377 D
ksreed@uoregon.edu
REED, Kim .... 208-562-3114 130 F
kimreed@cwi.edu
REED, Kimberly .... 530-661-5727.. 76 B
kreed@yccd.edu
REED, LaTonya .... 870-574-4504.. 21 E
lreed@sautech.edu
REED, Latoya .... 601-979-0889 246 E
latoya.t.reed@jsums.edu
REED, LaVonda .... 315-443-5525 322 C
lareed@law.syr.edu
REED, Lori .... 507-457-5005 241 F
lreed@winona.edu
REED, Lyndsey .... 510-649-8285.. 55 B
lreed@psr.edu
REED, Mark, C .... 610-660-1200 398 C
president@sju.edu
REED, Mark, F .... 610-861-1360 391 A
reedm@moravian.edu
REED, Mark, H .... 603-646-9400 273 E
mark.h.reed@dartmouth.edu
REED, Martin .... 209-228-2977.. 69 B
mreed9@ucmerced.edu
REED, Mary Ann .... 304-293-5701 491 C
maryann.reed@mail.wvu.edu
REED, Matthew .... 732-224-2265 276 B
REED, Meredith .... 504-398-2236 191 C
mreed@uhcno.edu
REED, Michael .... 504-282-4455 190 A
mreed@nobts.edu
REED, Michael, J .... 570-326-3761 393 G
mjr18@pct.edu
REED, Nancy .... 901-572-2662 418 E
nancy.reed@bchs.edu
REED, Pamela .... 806-874-3571 433 B
pamela.reed@clarendoncollege.edu
REED, Phil .... 269-749-7142 229 H
preed@olivetcollege.edu
REED, Quiana .... 864-592-4122 412 F
reedq@sccsc.edu
REED, Rahim .... 530-752-2071.. 68 E
rreed@ucdavis.edu

REED, Randy .... 972-273-3301 435 E
randyreed@dcccd.edu
REED, Rita .... 501-202-1109.. 18 E
rita.reed@baptist-health.org
REED, Robert .... 443-334-2240 201 H
rreed1951@stevenson.edu
REED, Robert, A .... 504-865-3735 189 F
rareed@loyno.edu
REED, Rod .... 765-677-2105 157 D
rod.reed@indwes.edu
REED, Sally .... 410-837-4088 204 B
sreed@ubalt.edu
REED, Sara .... 801-957-4111 461 D
sara.reed@slcc.edu
REED, Sarah .... 415-565-4614.. 68 F
reedsarah@uchastings.edu
REED, Shannon, R .... 309-298-1819 152 D
sr-reed@wiu.edu
REED, Sharon .... 614-251-4595 358 G
reeds@ohiodominican.edu
REED, Shawana .... 870-235-4015.. 21 D
srreed@saumag.edu
REED, Shermain .... 214-333-5460 434 I
shermain@dbu.edu
REED, Shirley, A .... 956-872-8366 444 A
sareed@southtexascollege.edu
REED, Stephen .... 651-793-1254 238 H
steve.reed@metrostate.edu
REED, Steve, E .... 417-667-8181 252 A
sreed@cottey.edu
REED, Steven .... 615-460-6619 418 F
steven.reed@belmont.edu
REED, Sue .... 484-365-7929 389 C
sreed@lincoln.edu
REED, Tammy .... 406-377-9402 263 E
treed@dawson.edu
REED, Teresa .... 217-228-5432 146 F
reedte@quincy.edu
REED, Teresa .... 502-852-6907 185 C
teresa.reed@louisville.edu
REED, Terri .... 404-270-5002 125 B
treed15@spelman.edu
REED, Tracy .... 989-317-4760 230 A
treed@sagchip.edu
REED, Twiggs .... 503-589-8199 373 A
treed@corban.edu
REED, Van .... 337-550 1211 189 A
vreed@lsue.edu
REED, Wendy .... 218-726-6397 243 F
wlreed@d.umn.edu
REED-BOULEY, Kenneth 402-280-2754 266 I
kennethreed-bouley@creighton.edu
REED DAVIS, Christine . 704-687-0345 342 E
crdavis@uncc.edu
REED-FRANCOIS,
Desiree .... 702-895-4729 271 E
desiree.reed@unlv.edu
REED-HIRSCH, Kelly ..... 903-694-4003 441 F
kreed-hirsch@panola.edu
REED-SEGRETI,
Deborah .... 516-572-7759 308 A
deborah.reed@ncc.edu
REEDER, David, C .... 301-447-5207 200 E
reeder@msmary.edu
REEDER, Josh .... 909-621-8281.. 63 E
jreeder@scrippscollege.edu
REEDER, Leslie .... 334-556-2214.... 2 C
lreeder@wallace.edu
REEDER, Mary .... 337-421-6902 188 D
mary.reeder@sowela.edu
REEDER, Philip, P .... 412-396-4877 383 C
reederp@duq.edu
REEDER, Richard .... 631-632-7932 317 D
richard.j.reeder@stonybrook.edu
REEDER, Shehani .... 714-744-7939.. 36 C
gunasena@chapman.edu
REEDUS, Janice .... 815-280-6640 140 B
jreedus@jjc.edu
REEGER, Jennifer .... 724-830-1069 398 H
jreeger@setonhill.edu
REEKERS, David .... 202-651-5410.. 91 E
david.reekers@gallaudet.edu
REEKS, Kevin, L .... 419-995-8081 354 H
reeks.k@rhodesstate.edu
REEL, Sally, J .... 520-626-6767.. 16 G
sreel@email.arizona.edu
REEL, Stephanie .... 410-735-6700 199 D
sreel@jhu.edu
REEM, Marvin, P .... 864-242-5100 407 B
REEMER, Ronda .... 765-641-4010 153 B
rsreemer@anderson.edu
REEP, Jeff .... 937-766-7868 349 G
reepj@cedarville.edu

REES, Doug, C .... 626-395-5802.. 29 C
dcrees@caltech.edu
REES, John Paul .... 802-828-2800 464 B
jpr06200@ccv.vsc.edu
REES, Mary .... 805-378-1403.. 72 H
mrees@vcccd.edu
REES, Pamela, D .... 515-263-6098 165 I
prees@grandview.edu
REES, Rebecca, E .... 973-290-4721 277 A
rrees@cse.edu
REES, Richard .... 203-285-2170.. 85 E
rrees@gwcc.commnet.edu
REES, Tim .... 864-379-2131 409 H
trees@erskine.edu
REES, Traci .... 504-398-2235 191 C
trees@uhcno.edu
REESE, Andrew .... 670-237-6714 506 A
andrew.reese@marianas.edu
REESE, Aquirre .... 320-308-5252 241 A
aquirre.reese@sctcc.edu
REESE, Bobby .... 203-596-4548.. 87 F
breese@post.edu
REESE, Brian .... 864-388-8314 410 D
breese@lander.edu
REESE, Brian .... 717-337-6240 384 H
breese@gettysburg.edu
REESE, C. Shane .... 801-422-6201 458 H
shane_reese@byu.edu
REESE, Camille .... 704-878-3264 336 C
creese@mitchellcc.edu
REESE, Carole, A .... 610-861-1555 391 A
reesec@moravian.edu
REESE, Christopher .... 562-985-2037.. 31 F
christopher.reese@csulb.edu
REESE, Cynthia .... 510-981-2851.. 56 E
creese@peralta.edu
REESE, David .... 503-768-7691 373 G
reese@lclark.edu
REESE, Kimberly .... 504-520-7575 193 A
kreese@xula.edu
REESE, Kimberly .... 336-750-3145 344 B
reesekf@wssu.edu
REESE, Leon .... 404-460-2491 123 C
leon.reese@point.edu
REESE, Michael .... 619-644-7104.. 44 I
mike.reese@gcccd.edu
REESE, Pamela .... 716-488-3020 303 C
pamelareese@jbc.edu
REESE, Phil .... 701-355-8175 347 D
preese@umary.edu
REESE, Robert .... 570-208-5886 387 A
robertreese@kings.edu
REESE, Robert, S .... 843-953-2468 408 E
reeser@cofc.edu
REESER, John, J .... 248-370-2128 229 G
jjreeser@oakland.edu
REESER, Mike .... 254-867-4891 449 E
mike.reeser@tstc.edu
REESER, Todd .... 706-565-3669 116 I
REESMAN, Melissa, J ... 260-399-7700 161 D
mreesman@sf.edu
REESOR, Lori .... 608-265-3540 496 C
lreesor@wisc.edu
REETZ, David, R .... 585-475-7108 313 A
drrcps1@rit.edu
REEVE, Scott .... 810-762-9711 225 H
sreeve@kettering.edu
REEVE-RABB, Andra ...... 912-525-5000 123 G
areeve@scad.edu
REEVES, Brent, W .... 618-537-6938 143 B
breeves@mckendree.edu
REEVES, Bret .... 615-248-1464 427 A
breeves@trevecca.edu
REEVES, Brian .... 918-343-7983 369 F
breeves@rsu.edu
REEVES, Christina .... 910-521-6301 343 B
christina.reeves@uncp.edu
REEVES, Christopher ..... 319-656-2447 169 C
REEVES, Earl, J .... 660-831-4108 256 G
REEVES, Herbert .... 334-670-3203.... 7 C
hreeves@troy.edu
REEVES, Jacqueline, A .. 203-576-4496.. 88 D
purchase@bridgeport.edu
REEVES, James .... 323-953-4000.. 48 I
REEVES, Jason .... 606-546-1562 184 H
jreeves@unionky.edu
REEVES, Joel .... 865-974-2333 427 G
joel.reeves@utk.edu
REEVES, Joey .... 912-478-8607 119 C
jreeves@georgiasouthern.edu
REEVES, Kelly .... 801-592-0451 130 A
kelly.reeves@ldschurch.org

REEVES, Lindsay .... 706-864-1625 126 A
lindsay.reeves@ung.edu
REEVES, Lisa .... 803-376-6007 406 F
lreeves@allenuniversity.edu
REEVES, Lisa .... 214-887-5025 436 B
lreeves@dts.edu
REEVES, Mamiko .... 989-837-4136 228 H
reevesm@northwood.edu
REEVES, Mark .... 678-839-5079 126 E
mreeves@westga.edu
REEVES, Mark, T .... 864-644-5528 412 E
mreeves@swu.edu
REEVES, Michelle .... 706-880-8249 121 A
mreeves@lagrange.edu
REEVES, Richard, J .... 302-831-2021.. 90 F
rjreeves@udel.edu
REEVES, Rodney .... 417-328-1770 259 L
rreeves@sbuniv.edu
REEVES, Ronald .... 818-401-1022.. 39 G
rreeves@columbiacollege.edu
REEVES, Tracey .... 352-395-5507 107 A
tracey.reeves@sfcollege.edu
REGA, Elizabeth .... 909-469-5460.. 74 I
erega@westernu.edu
REGALADO, Elias .... 650-949-7362.. 43 D
regaladoelias@fhda.edu
REGALADO, Juan .... 909-593-3511.. 70 D
jregalado@laverne.edu
REGALIA, Delphine .... 510-642-3881.. 68 D
dmregalia@berkeley.edu
REGAN, Anna .... 732-255-0400 280 A
aregan@ocean.edu
REGAN, Brendan .... 623-845-3449.. 13 C
brendan.regan@gccaz.edu
REGAN, Joseph, P .... 312-341-2110 147 H
jregan@roosevelt.edu
REGAN, Kathleen .... 315-781-3309 302 A
regan@hws.edu
REGAN, Laurie .... 503-552-1507 374 E
lregan@nunm.edu
REGAN, Sheila .... 336-342-4261 337 E
regans@rockinghamcc.edu
REGAN, SJ, Thomas, J . 773-508-3205 142 D
tregan1@luc.edu
REGAN, SJ, Thomas, J . 773-508-3505 142 D
tregan1@luc.edu
REGAN-PANZA, Patrice . 516-877-3098 289 C
ppanza@adelphi.edu
REGAN WHITE, David ... 518-381-1320 315 G
whitedr@sunysccc.edu
REGE, Karen, M .... 443-412-2145 199 A
krege@harford.edu
REGE, Robert .... 214-648-3050 457 B
robert.rege@utsouthwestern.edu
REGEHR, Nanci .... 480-517-8314.. 13 G
nanci.regehr@riosalado.edu
REGEHR, Shellie .... 620-901-6299 170 G
sregehr@allencc.edu
REGENAUER,
Rochelle, R .... 262-243-5700 493 B
rochelle.regenauer@cuw.edu
REGENCIO, Eugenia ...... 973-596-3068 279 F
eugenia.regencio@njit.edu
REGER, Patricia .... 610-341-1464 383 D
preger@eastern.edu
REGER, Tim .... 515-263-6136 165 I
treger@grandview.edu
REGIER, Elaine .... 405-945-9104 368 E
elainrr@osuokc.edu
REGIER, Jeanette .... 816-322-0110 250 K
jeanette.regier@calvary.edu
REGIER, Philip, R .... 480-965-2457.. 10 I
phil.regier@asu.edu
REGINATO, Justin .... 916-278-6241.. 32 E
reginato@csus.edu
REGIS, Chris, C .... 214-768-1178 444 E
cregis@smu.edu
REGIS, Pam .... 410-857-2437 200 B
pregis@mcdaniel.edu
REGIST TOMLINSON,
Tara .... 718-960-2416 294 A
tara.registtomlinson@lehman.cuny.edu
REGISTER, Kimberly ...... 770-412-4586 124 G
kimberly.register@sctech.edu
REGISTER, Patrick .... 831-459-4404.. 70 B
jpregister@ucsc.edu
REGISTER, Tammy .... 307-382-1606 502 I
tregister@westernwyoming.edu
REGJO, Kathryn .... 970-945-8691.. 77 K
REGN, Todd .... 609-652-4939 283 D
todd.regn@stockton.edu
REGNER, Cecile .... 857-701-1270 215 E
cregner@rcc.mass.edu

REGNERUS, Arlene .... 312-935-6659 147 D
aregnerus@robertmorris.edu
REGOORD, Mark .... 907-564-8204.... 9 D
mregoord@alaskapacific.edu
REGUEIRO, Maria, C .... 305-821-3333.. 99 E
mregueiro@fnu.edu
REGULSKA, Joanna .... 530-752-6376.. 68 E
jregulska@ucdavis.edu
REHBEIN, Edna .... 512-716-4422 450 E
er04@txstate.edu
REHBEIN, Matt .... 615-966-6043 421 D
matt.rehbein@lipscomb.edu
REHFELD, Andrew .... 212-674-5300 301 E
REHFELD, Renee .... 830-372-6803 449 B
rrehfeld@tlu.edu
REHG, SJ, William .... 314-977-3827 259 H
william.rehg@slu.edu
REHM, David .... 570-674-6403 390 G
drehm@misericordia.edu
REHM, Julie, M .... 216-368-6070 349 F
julie.rehm@case.edu
REHM, Mark .... 325-942-2555 451 A
mark.rehm@angelo.edu
REHM, Matthew .... 740-362-3136 356 D
mrehm@mtso.edu
REHM, Roger, E .... 989-774-1474 222 C
rehm1re@cmich.edu
REHN, Andrea .... 562-907-4200.. 75 A
arehn@whittier.edu
REHN, Lynn .... 410-228-9250 202 F
REHNELT, Sherry .... 715-425-3962 497 E
bookstore@uwrf.edu
REIBER, Carl .... 912-478-5258 119 C
creiber@georgiasouthern.edu
REIBER, Jennifer .... 904-516-8748.. 98 P
jreiber@fcsl.edu
REICH, Amy, R .... 516-463-7580 302 B
amy.r.reich@hofstra.edu
REICH, Ashley .... 434-592-6709 468 H
ahageman@liberty.edu
REICH, Brooke .... 252-398-6313 328 D
reichb@chowan.edu
REICH, Evan .... 843-574-6368 413 B
evan.reich@tridenttech.edu
REICH, Lewis .... 901-722-3220 424 C
lreich@sco.edu
REICH, Patricia .... 610-330-5017 387 E
reichp@lafayette.edu
REICH, Tyler .... 503-375-6586 378 B
treich@willamette.edu
REICH PAULSEN,
Sharon .... 802-656-8585 463 E
sharon.reich.paulsen@uvm.edu
REICHARD, Jacob .... 620-223-2700 173 C
jacobr@fortscott.edu
REICHARD, Joshua .... 423-775-6596 423 F
jreichard@ogs.edu
REICHARD, Joshua .... 816-960-2008 251 D
dean@cityvision.edu
REICHARD, Rosalind ..... 908-852-1400 276 G
REICHEL, Scott .... 970-339-6513.. 76 G
scott.reichel@aims.edu
REICHEL, Tammi, L .... 804-752-7383 470 F
tammireichel@rmc.edu
REICHERT, Brett .... 678-839-4780 126 E
breicher@westga.edu
REICHERT, Greg .... 608-785-8672 496 F
greichert@uwlax.edu
REICHMUTH, Geri .... 303-292-0015.. 79 G
greichmuth@denvercollegeofnursing.
edu
REID, Alicia .... 718-270-6406 295 A
areid@mec.cuny.edu
REID, Anne, M .... 610-861-1353 391 A
reida@moravian.edu
REID, Austin .... 803-321-5229 411 D
austin.reid@newberry.edu
REID, Carol .... 678-664-0533 127 A
carol.reid@westgatech.edu
REID, Carol .... 214-333-5702 434 I
carolr@dbu.edu
REID, Colette .... 757-881-5100.. 92 G
REID, Collette .... 757-493-6000.. 92 G
REID, David .... 314-838-8858 261 G
dreid@ugst.edu
REID, Dawn .... 310-233-4287.. 49 A
reidd@lahc.edu
REID, Diana .... 860-512-2909.. 85 G
dreid@manchestercc.edu
REID, Donna, M .... 718-522-9073 290 C
dreid@asa.edu
REID, Eric .... 601-403-1126 248 E
ereid@prcc.edu

REID, Gregory ... 973-748-9000 276 A
greg_reid@bloomfield.edu
REID, Heather ... 617-747-2258 206 E
library@berklee.edu
REID, Heidi ... 913-758-6172 177 F
heidi.reid@stmary.edu
REID, Helen ... 972-932-4309 452 B
hreid@tvcc.edu
REID, James ... 325-942-2264 451 A
james.reid@angelo.edu
REID, Jodyann ... 954-545-4500 107 E
academics@sfbc.edu
REID, John ... 530-898-5555.. 31 A
jreid1@csuchico.edu
REID, Kathleen, A ... 413-782-1211 219 F
kathleen.reid@wne.edu
REID, Kelly ... 601-403-1489 248 E
kareid@prcc.edu
REID, Kevin ... 843-953-6950 407 F
kreid2@citadel.edu
REID, Lee ... 920-403-3866 495 I
lee.reid@snc.edu
REID, Lee ... 540-887-7212 469 B
lreid@marybaldwin.edu
REID, III, Lenzy ... 706-552-0900 114 F
lreid@athenstech.edu
REID, Lesley ... 205-348-3924.... 7 G
lwreid@ua.edu
REID, Mark ... 206-281-2624 484 D
mreid@spu.edu
REID, Michael ... 406-683-7031 264 B
REID, Michael, B ... 352-294-1601 109 F
michael.reid@ufl.edu
REID, Michele ... 269-965-3931 225 F
reidm@kellogg.edu
REID, Richard, H ... 337-475-5588 192 A
rreid@mcneese.edu
REID, Sean ... 607-274-3341 303 B
sreid@ithaca.edu
REID, Shannon ... 603-230-3504 272 I
sreid@ccsnh.edu
REID, Sherri ... 870-733-6020.. 17 H
sdreid@asumidsouth.edu
REID, Stanley, G ... 512-476-2772 431 B
president@austingrad.edu
REID, JR., Thomas, G .. 412-731-6000 397 E
treid@rpts.edu
REID, Tina, S ... 864-592-4683 412 F
reidt@sccsc.edu
REID ALSTON, Melissa . 336-315-7800.. 92 G
REID-CHASSIAKOS,
Linda ... 818-677-3689.. 32 D
linda.reid.chassiakos@csun.edu
REID-MARTINEZ,
Kathaleen ... 918-495-7855 368 I
kreid-martinez@oru.edu
REIDY, Francis ... 352-588-8246 106 D
fran.reidy@saintleo.edu
REIDY, Joseph, P ... 202-806-6100.. 92 B
REIDY, Robert, C ... 650-723-6324.. 65 J
rcr@stanford.edu
REIDY, William ... 203-396-8086.. 88 B
reidyw@sacredheart.edu
REIDY-FOX, Kelly ... 773-298-3780 148 G
fox@sxu.edu
REIF, L. Rafael ... 617-253-0148 215 G
president@mit.edu
REIF, Richard ... 918-444-5900 367 A
reif01@nsuok.edu
REIFENHEISER, Paul ... 607-844-8222 322 H
pr022@tompkinscortland.edu
REIFERT, Steve ... 231-591-2800 223 J
stevereifert@ferris.edu
REIG, Michael ... 215-248-7069 381 D
reigm@chc.edu
REIGEL, Heidi ... 410-857-2226 200 B
hreigel@mcdaniel.edu
REIGHARD, Erica ... 814-262-6440 393 H
ereighard@pennhighlands.edu
REIGHARD, Frank ... 409-772-5544 456 F
frreigha@utmb.edu
REIGHLEY, Twila ... 517-884-4367 227 D
reighley@msu.edu
REIGLE, Kim ... 828-689-1233 331 A
kreigle@mhu.edu
REIHL, Raeann ... 865-981-8355 421 F
raeann.reihl@maryvillecollege.edu
REIJO PERA, Renee ... 406-994-2891 264 D
renee.reijopera@montana.edu
REIKOFSKI, Diane ... 402-844-7055 268 J
diane@northeast.edu
REILAND, Kathleen ... 714-484-7233.. 53 K
kreiland@cypresscollege.edu
REILAND, Mandi ... 281-998-6150 443 B
mandi.reiland@sjcd.edu
REILLEY, Mary Clare ... 914-633-2686 302 G
mreilley@iona.edu
REILLO, Lissette ... 787-891-0925 508 K
lreillo@aguadilla.inter.edu
REILLY, Cathy ... 206-296-6120 484 F
reillyc@seattleu.edu
REILLY, Colleen ... 713-718-7307 437 I
colleen.reilly@hccs.edu
REILLY, Edward ... 507-457-5010 241 F
ereilly@winona.edu
REILLY, John ... 303-724-0882.. 83 C
john.reilly@ucdenver.edu
REILLY, John, J ... 330-972-7753 362 B
jreilly@uakron.edu
REILLY, Joseph, R ... 973-761-9008 283 B
joseph.reilly@shu.edu
REILLY, Karen, L ... 407-582-1810 112 K
kreilly5@valenciacollege.edu
REILLY, Kathryn ... 631-656-2121 300 D
kathryn.reilly@ftc.edu
REILLY, Kerin ... 212-686-9244 290 A
kreilly@aada.edu
REILLY, Kim ... 215-635-7300 385 A
admissions@gratz.edu
REILLY, Lenore ... 413-538-2500 216 G
lreilly@mtholyoke.edu
REILLY, Madelyn ... 412-396-5181 383 C
reillym@duq.edu
REILLY, Marianne ... 718-862-7891 305 H
mreilly01@manhattan.edu
REILLY, Mary Beth ... 732-224-2806 276 B
mreilly@brookdalecc.edu
REILLY, Mary Jane ... 516-323-4702 307 F
mreilly@molloy.edu
REILLY, Matthew ... 617-243-2468 210 G
mreilly@lasell.edu
REILLY, MB ... 513-556-1824 362 D
reillymb@ucmail.uc.edu
REILLY, Meghan ... 319-296-2320 166 B
meghan.reilly@hawkeyecollege.edu
REILLY, Patricia ... 617-627-2000 219 B
patricia.reilly@tufts.edu
REILLY, Ronald ... 816-604-4125 255 I
ronald.reilly@mcckc.edu
REILLY, Seamus ... 309-341-5214 133 C
sreilly@sandburg.edu
REILLY, Teddi ... 858-646-3100.. 62 A
treilly@sbpdiscovery.org
REILLY, Thom ... 702-889-8426 270 K
chancellor@nevada.edu
REILLY, Tim ... 706-712-8228 117 C
treilly@daltonstate.edu
REILLY, William, T ... 704-894-2765 328 F
wireilly@davidson.edu
REILLY-KELLY, Tracy ... 360-992-2163 479 F
tkelly@clark.edu
REILLY-MYKLEBUST,
Alice ... 715-425-9884 497 E
alice.m.reilly-myklebust@uwrf.edu
REILY, Karen ... 218-736-1502 239 B
karen.reily@minnesota.edu
REIM, Melanie ... 212-217-7665 299 H
melanie_reim@fitnyc.edu
REIMAN, Adam ... 937-255-3636 503 A
adam.reiman@afit.edu
REIMAN, Brock ... 330-363-6347 348 D
brock.reiman@aultman.com
REIMAN, Dennis ... 203-392-5004.. 85 A
reimand1@southernct.edu
REIMAN, Tricia ... 972-708-7552 435 H
tricia_reiman@diu.edu
REIMANN, Jan ... 573-334-9181 255 A
jan@metrobusinesscollege.edu
REIMANN, Rick ... 518-587-2100 321 A
rick.reimann@esc.edu
REIMER, Denise ... 608-243-4484 499 H
dmreimer@madisoncollege.edu
REIMER, Martin ... 641-844-8502 166 I
martin.reimer@iavalley.edu
REIMER, Martin ... 641-648-4611 166 J
martin.reimer@iavalley.edu
REIMER, Rachel ... 515-271-1424 164 I
rachel.reimer@dmu.edu
REIMONDO, Sue ... 859-985-3212 179 C
sue_reimondo@berea.edu
REINA, John ... 845-257-3685 317 B
reinaj@newpaltz.edu
REINA, Michelle ... 254-295-4015 453 E
mreina@umhb.edu
REINACHER, Deanna ... 619-216-6673.. 65 F
dreinacher@swccd.edu
REINCKE, Nancy ... 515-271-2161 165 A
nancy.reincke@drake.edu
REINDERS, Gretchen ... 608-785-8073 496 F
greinders@uwlax.edu
REINDL, Kay ... 209-478-0800.. 45 H
kreindl@humphreys.edu
REINECK, Marilyn ... 651-641-8730 235 F
reineck@csp.edu
REINEHR, Craig ... 918-444-4700 367 A
reinehr@nsuok.edu
REINEKE, Sandra ... 208-885-3165 131 G
sreineke@uidaho.edu
REINELT, Douglas, A ... 214-768-3754 444 E
reinelt@smu.edu
REINER, Christian ... 435-586-7783 460 F
christianreiner@suu.edu
REINER, Michael, D ... 402-280-2337 266 I
michaelreiner@creighton.edu
REINERT, Duane ... 660-944-2852 251 G
dreinert@conception.edu
REING, Linda ... 212-961-3432 290 F
alumrel@bankstreet.edu
REINHARD, Amanda ... 425-602-3044 478 D
areinhard@bastyr.edu
REINHARD, Ben ... 540-636-2900 466 A
ben.reinhard@christendom.edu
REINHARD, Herb ... 229-333-5462 126 G
hreinhar@valdosta.edu
REINHARDT, Beth ... 217-641-4541 140 A
REINHARDT, Kathleen ... 970-521-6603.. 81 D
kathleen.reinhardt@njc.edu
REINHART, Adam ... 806-291-1124 457 J
reinharta@wbu.edu
REINHART, Kellee, C ... 205-348-5938.... 7 F
kreinhart@uasystem.edu
REINHART, Rose ... 419-995-8310 354 H
reinhart.r@rhodesstate.edu
REINHART, Todd ... 507-457-1758 243 B
treinhar@smumn.edu
REINHOLD, David, S ... 269-387-4564 232 K
david.reinhold@wmich.edu
REINHORN, Jo Ann ... 207-509-7144 195 H
jreinhorn@unity.edu
REINI, Aaron ... 218-262-7362 238 C
aaronreini@hibbing.edu
REINIG, Amanda ... 757-455-3116 477 F
areinig@vwu.edu
REINIG, Bruce ... 619-594-2473.. 33 E
breinig@sdsu.edu
REINISCH, Lou ... 516-686-7403 309 F
lou.reinisch@nyit.edu
REINISCH, Sheryl ... 503-493-6539 372 I
sreinisch@cu-portland.edu
REINKE, Brenda ... 405-682-7510 367 H
breinke@occc.edu
REINKE, Jeff ... 815-599-3406 138 B
jeff.reinke@highland.edu
REINKE, Katelyn ... 919-658-7778 340 J
kreinke@umo.edu
REINKE, Stephanie ... 940-565-3487 454 A
stephanie.reinke@unt.edu
REINL, Cindy, M ... 920-433-6660 492 B
cindy.reinl@bellincollege.edu
REINLAND, Jeffrey, E ... 509-527-4312 485 G
jeffrey.reinland@wwcc.edu
REINLIE, Carla ... 850-729-5357 103 L
reinliec@nwfsc.edu
REINOEHL, Jason, K ... 937-229-3725 362 G
jreinoehl@udayton.edu
REINOSO, Gaston ... 713-743-2603 452 F
greinoso@uh.edu
REINSCH FRIESE, Ellen . 937-775-3336 364 I
ellen.friese@wright.edu
REIPENHOFF, Mary, E .. 260-399-7700 161 D
mriepenhoff@sf.edu
REIS, Gina ... 508-910-6505 211 F
greis@umassd.edu
REISBERG, Darren ... 773-702-7618 150 J
reisberg@uchicago.edu
REISCHE, Jim ... 413-597-4277 220 C
jim.reische@williams.edu
REISECK, Carol, J ... 708-209-3262 135 F
carol.reiseck@cuchicago.edu
REISENAUER, Eric ... 803-938-3862 414 B
ericr@uscsumter.edu
REISER, Cyrill ... 818-785-2726.. 35 J
REISER, Sharon ... 805-525-4417.. 67 D
sreiser@thomasaquinas.edu
REISETTER, Mary ... 641-585-8681 170 B
reisettem@waldorf.edu
REISIG, Jennifer ... 308-635-6551 270 D
reisig1@wncc.edu
REISING, Gregory ... 410-704-2512 204 A
greising@towson.edu
REISING, Sonia ... 815-825-9738 140 F
sreising@kish.edu
REISINGER, Cynthia, E . 717-815-1221 404 A
creising@ycp.edu
REISINGER, Tracy ... 503-253-3443 374 H
tracy.reisinger@ocom.edu
REISMAN, Lonn ... 254-968-9178 446 E
reisman@tarleton.edu
REISMAN, Yisroel ... 718-941-8000 306 I
REISNER, Jeff ... 716-375-2000 313 F
jreisner@reisnerlawgroup.com
REISNER, John, A ... 937-255-3636 503 A
john.reisner@afit.edu
REISS, Michael, A ... 718-377-0777 312 A
REISS, Richard ... 201-692-7003 277 K
reissr@fdu.edu
REISSMAN, Sallie, A ... 302-356-6807.. 90 I
sallie.a.reissman@wilmu.edu
REISZ, Z ... 805-965-0581.. 62 C
zreisz@sbcc.edu
REITAN, Mark ... 507-457-2319 241 F
mreitan@winona.edu
REITER, Lisa ... 773-508-2200 142 D
lreiter1@luc.edu
REITER, Sarah ... 802-831-1241 463 G
sreiter@vermontlaw.edu
REITER, Sharon, L ... 909-869-3016.. 30 D
slreiter@cpp.edu
REITMAN, Tzipora ... 845-574-4595 313 C
zreitman@sunyrockland.edu
REITZ, Chris ... 801-524-8109 459 F
creitz@ldsbc.edu
REITZ, S. Maggie ... 410-704-4498 204 A
mreitz@towson.edu
REITZ, Tiffany ... 352-638-9707.. 95 D
treitz@beaconcollege.edu
REJHOLEC, Taryn ... 212-217-4700 299 H
taryn_rejholec@fitnyc.edu
REKLAI, Hilda ... 680-488-3036 506 B
hildan@palau.edu
REL, Ricardo ... 575-646-5909 287 B
rrel@nmsu.edu
RELL, Amy ... 303-220-1200.. 77 B
RELLINGER, Brian ... 740-368-3656 359 N
barellin@owu.edu
RELLINGER, Thomas, D 248-218-2049 229 J
trellinger@rc.edu
RELYEA, Michelle ... 212-229-5150 308 C
relyeam@newschool.edu
RELYEA, Steve ... 562-951-4600.. 30 B
srelyea@calstate.edu
REMBACZ, Mark ... 307-382-1871 502 I
mrembacz@westernwyoming.edu
REMBOLD, Scott ... 202-319-6909.. 91 B
rembold@cua.edu
REMENDER,
Kathleen, A ... 810-762-9794 225 H
kremende@kettering.edu
REMENSCHNEIDER,
Mary ... 616-395-7252 225 B
remenschneider@hope.edu
REMER, Rosalind ... 215-895-1203 383 B
rosalind.remer@drexel.edu
REMHOF, Tamara ... 540-891-3013 474 G
tremhof@germanna.edu
REMIAS, Bobbie ... 248-341-2102 229 A
raremias@oaklandcc.edu
REMIERES-MORIN,
Pamela ... 207-629-4018 194 F
premieres@mccs.me.edu
REMILLARD, Theresa ... 413-755-4336 215 F
remillard@stcc.edu
REMINDER, Jodie ... 765-641-4316 153 B
jlreminder@anderson.edu
REMINGTON, Debra ... 440-375-7040 355 G
dremington@lec.edu
REMINGTON, Judith, V . 847-491-7456 145 F
j-remington@northwestern.edu
REMLER, Nancy ... 912-344-2846 119 C
nremler@georgiasouthern.edu
REMMLER, Mary, M ... 302-831-2082.. 90 F
mremmler@udel.edu
REMPEL, Valerie ... 559-453-2319.. 43 G
valerie.rempel@fresno.edu
REMPFER, Julie ... 267-341-5017 386 A
jrempfer@holyfamily.edu
REMSBURG, Barbara ... 801-587-0851 460 E
bremsburg@housing.utah.edu
REMSBURG, Robin, E ... 336-334-5177 343 A
reremsbu@uncg.edu

REMUND, Dave .... 515-271-2169 165 A
dave.remund@drake.edu
REMY, Jana .... 714-744-7934.. 36 C
remy@chapman.edu
RENACIA,
Victorina M, Y .... 671-735-2978 505 E
vrenacia@triton.uog.edu
RENADETTE, Magen, M 518-564-3246 319 C
mrena002@plattsburgh.edu
RENAUD, Ellen .... 201-360-4722 278 C
erenaud@hccc.edu
RENAUD, Robert, E ...... 717-245-1072 382 F
renaudr@dickinson.edu
RENAULT, Tara, C .... 717-245-1390 382 F
renaultt@dickinson.edu
RENBARGER, Bridgette . 402-399-2646 266 F
brenbarger@csm.edu
RENBARGER,
Christopher .... 805-678-5114.. 73 A
crenbarger@vcccd.edu
RENCIS, Joseph, J .... 909-869-2472.. 30 D
jjrencis@cpp.edu
RENDA, Liz .... 570-702-8945 386 G
lrenda@johnson.edu
RENDA, Stuart .... 570-945-8378 386 I
stu.renda@keystone.edu
RENDER, Rachel .... 616-732-1198 223 B
rachel.render@davenport.edu
RENDON, Michael .... 361-825-2414 447 C
michael.rendon@tamucc.edu
RENDON, Mindy, P ...... 785-670-1065 177 G
mindy.rendon@washburn.edu
RENEAR, Allen, H .... 217-333-3280 151 D
renear@illinois.edu
RENEAU, Clint-Michael 657-278-8655.. 31 E
creneau@fullerton.edu
RENEHAN, Colm .... 617-573-8444 219 A
crenehan@suffolk.edu
RENER, Christine .... 616-331-3498 224 E
renerc@gvsu.edu
RENEY, Richard .... 978-762-4000 215 B
rreney@northshore.edu
RENFREW, Michelle ...... 907-474-5337.. 10 A
mmrenfrew@alaska.edu
RENFRO, Bryan .... 903-510-2349 452 C
bren@tjc.edu
RENFRO, Joe .... 918-540-6950 366 I
joe.renfro@neo.edu
RENFROE, Sam .... 850-729-4944 103 L
renfroes@nwfsc.edu
RENGIFO, Monica .... 239-687-5442.. 94 N
mrengifo@avemarialaw.edu
RENICK, Larry .... 626-529-8098.. 55 A
lrenick@pacificoaks.edu
RENICK, Timothy, M ..... 404-413-2580 119 E
trenick@gsu.edu
RENIFF, William, M ...... 440-826-2212 348 E
breniff@bw.edu
RENKO, Jenn .... 717-396-7833 393 E
jrenko@pcad.edu
RENNA, Kimberly .... 619-574-5807.. 43 E
krenna@fst.edu
RENNER, Blake .... 614-947-9236 353 C
blake.renner@franklin.edu
RENNER, Catherine .... 641-269-4046 165 J
rennerca@grinnell.edu
RENNER, Cynthia .... 215-489-2467 382 D
cynthia.renner@delval.edu
RENNER, Lance .... 417-447-8202 257 G
rennerl@otc.edu
RENNERT, Chaim .... 718-438-5476 325 D
RENNICKE, Dean, D ...... 262-243-4580 493 B
dean.rennicke@cuw.edu
RENNIE, John .... 318-678-6000 187 A
jrennie@bpcc.edu
RENNINGER, Laura .... 304-876-5461 490 E
lrenning@shepherd.edu
RENNIX, Louise .... 843-525-8318 412 H
lrennix@tcl.edu
RENO, Adam .... 301-846-2560 198 E
areno@frederick.edu
RENSBERGER,
Jeffrey, L .... 713-646-1853 444 B
jrensberger@stcl.edu
RENSCH, Jonathan .... 307-332-2930 502 J
jrensch@wyomingcatholic.edu
RENSHAW, Andrew .... 434-961-5484 475 F
arenshaw@pvcc.edu
RENSHAW, Paul .... 410-827-5870 197 I
prenshaw@chesapeake.edu
RENSKI, David .... 860-701-5457.. 87 D
renski_d@mitchell.edu
RENTA, Dawn .... 610-921-7256 378 C
drenta@albright.edu

RENTA, Pedro .... 715-425-3505 497 E
pedro.renta@uwrf.edu
RENTAS, Pedro .... 787-620-2040 506 C
prentas@aupr.edu
RENTFROW, Gina .... 918-540-6224 366 I
gina.rentfrow@neo.edu
RENTMEESTER, Matt, G 920-433-6657 492 B
matt.rentmeester@bellincollege.edu
RENTSCH, Janet, M ...... 989-964-7120 230 B
jrentsch@svsu.edu
RENTSCH, Kathy .... 508-854-2712 215 D
krentsch@qcc.mas.edu
RENTSCHLER, Gina .... 417-865-2815 253 B
rentschlerg@evangel.edu
RENTTO, Jessica .... 619-594-6018.. 33 E
jrentto@sdsu.edu
RENTZ, Judy .... 916-577-2200.. 75 B
jrentz@jessup.edu
RENTZ, Karen .... 850-474-2059 110 E
krentz@uwf.edu
RENTZ, Pam .... 850-718-2213.. 96 F
rentzp@chipola.edu
RENVILLE, Allen .... 530-895-2239.. 27 F
renvilleal@butte.edu
RENWICK, Mairi .... 804-278-4222 472 E
mrenwick@upsem.edu
RENWICK, Todd .... 775-784-4013 271 F
trenwick@unr.edu
RENY, Denise .... 207-741-5568 195 A
dreny@smccme.edu
RENY, James .... 207-741-5888 195 A
jreny@smccme.edu
RENZ, Amy Button .... 785-532-5050 174 G
arenz@ksu.edu
RENZ, Christopher, M .. 510-883-2084.. 41 G
crenz@dspt.edu
RENZ, Dianna .... 208-929-4032 131 C
dianna.renz@nic.edu
RENZ, Nolan .... 570-702-8912 386 G
nrenz@johnson.edu
RENZI, Michael .... 408-848-4715.. 43 J
mrenzi@gavilan.edu
RENZULLI, Beth, W ...... 603-526-3717 272 H
brenzull@colby-sawyer.edu
REPENNING, Thomas ... 301-934-7630 198 A
tcrepenning@csmd.edu
REPETTO, Martha .... 212-812-4025 309 D
mrepetto@nycda.edu
REPETTO, Paul .... 212-431-2836 309 G
paul.repetto@nyls.edu
REPETTO, Sarah .... 213-624-1200.. 42 I
srepetto@fidm.edu
REPKO, Lisa .... 215-955-0437 400 A
lisa.repko@jefferson.edu
REPP, A. Drew .... 260-399-7700 161 D
arepp@sf.edu
REPP, Ian .... 906-487-2354 227 E
irepp@mtu.edu
REPP, Lauren .... 314-744-5301 256 C
lauren.repp@mobap.edu
REPP, Laurie .... 419-448-2105 353 H
lrepp@heidelberg.edu
REPP, Randy .... 785-227-3380 171 E
repprl@bethanylb.edu
REPPERT, Angela .... 610-398-5300 389 A
areppert@lincolntech.edu
REPPERT, David .... 610-796-8463 378 F
david.reppert@alvernia.edu
REPZYNSKI, Allison ...... 478-757-3547 116 A
REQUENA, Laura .... 956-872-3646 444 A
lrequena@southtexascollege.edu
RERRICK, Charlotte .... 212-757-1190 290 B
crerrick@aami.edu
RESCIGNO, Robert, W .. 302-295-1158.. 90 I
robert.w.rescigno@wilmu.edu
RESENDEZ, Larry .... 818-364-7733.. 49 B
resendcl@lamission.edu
RESENDEZ, Larry, L ...... 818-364-7733.. 49 B
resendcl@lamission.edu
RESENDIZ, Linda .... 805-378-1407.. 72 H
lresendiz@vcccd.edu
RESENIC, Enid, E .... 814-938-1159 394 G
enid@iup.edu
RESHEF, Shai .... 626-264-8880.. 71 A
RESIDORI, Amber .... 815-939-5135 146 A
alresidori@olivet.edu
RESKE, Marsha .... 916-484-8493.. 50 F
reskem@arc.losrios.edu
RESNICK, Barry .... 303-867-1155.. 84 E
RESNICK, Coleen .... 508-541-1655 208 F
cresnick@dean.edu
RESNICK, Donald .... 212-229-5600 308 C
resnickd@newschool.edu

RESNICK, Rachel .... 617-879-7115 212 E
rresnick@massart.edu
RESSEL, Dawn .... 406-243-5661 264 A
dawn.ressel@umontana.edu
RESSLER, Koreen .... 701-854-8001 346 I
koreen.ressler@sittingbull.edu
RESTEN, Paul .... 508-541-1629 208 F
presten@dean.edu
RESTIVO, Charles .... 408-498-5121.. 38 F
crestivo@cogswell.edu
RESTO,
Maria de Lourdes .... 787-250-1912 509 D
mresto@metro.inter.edu
RESTO, Richelle .... 703-729-8800.. 92 G
RESTO, Wilfredo .... 787-738-2161 513 D
wilfredo.resto@upr.edu
RESUE, Meg .... 856-415-2101 281 D
RETANA, Olga .... 214-388-5466 435 G
oretana@dallasinstitute.edu
RETANA, Ruthie .... 562-908-3445.. 58 E
rretana@riohondo.edu
RETASKET, Victoria .... 360-676-2772 482 D
vretasket@nwic.edu
RETELLE, Mary Louise .. 508-849-3333 205 C
mretelle@annamaria.edu
RETES, Diana .... 714-895-8178.. 38 D
dretes@gwc.cccd.edu
RETHEMEYER, R. Karl ... 518-442-5256 316 D
kretheme@albany.edu
RETHERFORD, Kristine .. 507-389-6315 239 C
kristine.retherford@mnsu.edu
RETHLEFSEN,
Melissa, L .... 801-587-9051 460 E
melissa.rethlefsen@utah.edu
RETHMAN, Shari .... 937-512-5325 361 A
shari.rethman@sinclair.edu
RETHORST, Caitlin .... 785-227-3380 171 E
rethorstcr@bethanylb.edu
RETHWISCH, Dana .... 760-922-8714.. 55 H
dana.rethwisch@paloverde.edu
RETKA, James .... 218-683-8643 240 A
james.retka@northlandcollege.edu
RETKA, James .... 218-683-8690 240 A
james.retka@northlandcollege.edu
RETTIG, Glenn .... 567-661-7457 360 B
glenn_rettig@owens.edu
RETTIG, James .... 410-293-6900 504 I
rettig@usna.edu
RETTIG, Perry .... 706-778-8500 123 B
prettig@piedmont.edu
RETTLER, Peter, J .... 262-335-5706 500 C
prettler@morainepark.edu
RETZLAFF, Austin .... 800-567-2344 492 G
aretzlaff@menominee.edu
RETZLOFF, Merilee .... 320-762-4447 237 B
merileer@alextech.edu
REUBEN, Lucy, J .... 340-692-4151 514 E
lucy.reuben@uvi.edu
REULAND, Anne, C .... 773-508-7478 142 D
aruland@luc.edu
REUNING, Charles, R ... 301-405-6214 202 C
creuning@umd.edu
REUSCHER, Karen .... 315-781-3722 302 A
reuscher@hws.edu
REUTER, Kelli, A .... 515-574-1051 166 E
reuter@iowacentral.edu
REUTER, Kellyann, M ... 414-277-7101 494 G
reuter@msoe.edu
REUTER, William, D ...... 518-629-4523 302 E
w.reuter@hvcc.edu
REUTZEL, Ray .... 307-766-3145 502 H
ray.reutzel@uwyo.edu
REVARD, Cameron .... 360-676-2772 482 D
crevard@nwic.edu
REVELEY, IV, W. Taylor 434-395-2001 469 A
reveleywt@longwood.edu
REVELL, Todd .... 417-865-2815 253 B
revellt@evangel.edu
REVELS, Cynthia .... 910-521-6855 343 B
cindy.revels@uncp.edu
REVELS-BULLARD,
Angela .... 910-521-6279 343 B
angela.revels@uncp.edu
REVENAUGH, Ken .... 314-392-2356 256 C
revenaug@mobap.edu
REVERON, Derek .... 401-841-3540 503 L
derek.reveron@usnwc.edu
REVESZ, James .... 724-738-2255 395 F
james.revesz@sru.edu
REVIERE, Mallory .... 505-277-0111 288 G
mreviere@unm.edu
REVZINA, Larisa .... 650-685-6616.. 44 J
lrevzina@gurnick.edu

REW-BIGELOW,
Monique .... 585-395-2122 318 B
mrew@brockport.edu
REWERTS, Glen .... 815-939-5277 146 A
grewerts@olivet.edu
REWIS, Nancy .... 706-290-2166 115 B
nrewis@berry.edu
REX, Elizabeth .... 860-632-3033.. 87 C
erex@holyapostles.edu
REX, Judith .... 610-861-5533 391 F
jrex@northampton.edu
REX, Lisa Youngkin ...... 610-330-5060 387 E
rexl@lafayette.edu
REX, Scott .... 541-552-6745 376 E
rexs@sou.edu
REXFORD, Nathan .... 530-938-5555.. 39 F
REY, Rosamil .... 787-279-1912 509 A
rrey@bayamon.inter.edu
REY ROMERO, Carlos ... 575-835-5675 286 I
carlos.romero@nmt.edu
REYES, Amy, S .... 570-321-4134 389 E
reyes@lycoming.edu
REYES, Arturo .... 562-908-3403.. 58 E
areyes@riohondo.edu
REYES, Carlos .... 530-242-7760.. 63 H
creyes@shastacollege.edu
REYES, Carol .... 305-237-3037 103 D
creyes7@mdc.edu
REYES, David .... 214-333-5977 434 I
davidrey@dbu.edu
REYES, David .... 817-722-1623 439 B
david.reyes@tku.edu
REYES, Ginger .... 805-437-8521.. 30 F
ginger.reyes@csuci.edu
REYES, Ginny .... 785-227-3380 171 E
reyesg@bethanylb.edu
REYES, Idania .... 310-660-3483.. 41 L
ireyes@elcamino.edu
REYES, Iris .... 787-815-0000 513 A
iris.reyestana@upr.edu
REYES, Ivelisse .... 787-850-9303 513 E
ivelisse.reyes1@upr.edu
REYES, Javier .... 304-293-7800 491 C
javier.reyes@mail.wvu.edu
REYES, Jennifer .... 201-447-7456 275 H
jreyes@bergen.edu
REYES, Joseph .... 831-755-6950.. 44 K
jreyes@hartnell.edu
REYES, Karen .... 831-479-3503.. 27 G
kareyes@cabrillo.edu
REYES, Kyle .... 801-863-6158 461 A
kyle.reyes@uvu.edu
REYES, Livette .... 787-894-2828 514 C
livette.reyes@upr.edu
REYES, Lorenzo .... 505-566-3742 288 A
reyesl@sanjuancollege.edu
REYES, Marcos .... 787-725-6500 506 G
mreyes@albizu.edu
REYES, Maria .... 562-985-8051.. 31 F
maria.reyes@csulb.edu
REYES, Marisella .... 575-674-2231 285 H
mreyes@bcomnm.org
REYES, Nora .... 480-461-7151.. 13 D
nora.reyes@mesacc.edu
REYES, Paula, S .... 248-370-4423 229 G
preyes@oakland.edu
REYES, Rafael .... 212-870-1213 310 A
rreyes@nyts.edu
REYES, Ray .... 619-660-4206.. 44 H
ray.reyes@gcccd.edu
REYES, Raymond .... 509-313-5604 481 D
reyes@gonzaga.edu
REYES, Robert, G .... 214-860-2664 435 C
rreyes@dcccd.edu
REYES, Rosa .... 787-850-9303 513 E
rosa.reyes1@upr.edu
REYES, Rosana .... 570-740-0336 389 D
rreyes@luzerne.edu
REYES, Rudy .... 574-631-0694 161 C
rreyes@nd.edu
REYES, Saul .... 352-854-2322.. 96 O
reyess@cf.edu
REYES, Vicky .... 620-276-9788 173 E
vicky.reyes@gcccks.edu
REYES-GIL, Yanira .... 787-751-1912 510 A
yreyes@juris.inter.edu
REYES-GUEVARA,
Yolanda .... 210-486-4195 429 E
yreyes@alamo.edu
REYES-MARTIN, Luz ...... 805-965-0581.. 62 C
reyesmartin@sbcc.edu

REYES-OSARIO, Osmara .... 310-377-5501.. 51 B oreyes-osario@marymountcalifornia.edu
REYMALDO, Randy .... 818-677-2128.. 32 D randy.reynaldo@csun.edu
REYMANN, Linda .... 443-352-4203 201 H lreymann@stevenson.edu
REYNA, Angel .... 559-675-4800.. 66 F angel.reyna@scccd.edu
REYNA, Cynthia .... 870-864-7130.. 21 B creyna@southark.edu
REYNA, Mario .... 956-872-6116 444 A reyna@southtexascollege.edu
REYNA, Oscar .... 361-825-5934 447 C oscar.reyna@tamucc.edu
REYNA, Patrick .... 210-297-9663 431 E pgreyna@baptisthealthsystem.com
REYNARD, Betty .... 409-984-6100 450 B betty.reynard@lamarpa.edu
REYNARD, Michelle ...... 216-397-1659 354 I mreynard@jcu.edu
REYNDERS, John, C ..... 712-274-5100 168 B reynders@morningside.edu
REYNHOUT, Ken .... 651-255-6170 243 D kreynhout@unitedseminary.edu
REYNOLDS, Aimee .... 601-877-6479 244 H alreynolds@alcorn.edu
REYNOLDS, Amy .... 330-672-2950 354 J areyno24@kent.edu
REYNOLDS, Benjamin ... 847-866-3936 137 E benjamin.reynolds@garrett.edu
REYNOLDS, Brad .... 706-865-2134 125 E breynolds@truett.edu
REYNOLDS, Burt .... 307-382-1621 502 I breynolds@westernwyoming.edu
REYNOLDS, Chip .... 770-297-4511 121 B creynolds@laniertech.edu
REYNOLDS, Chris .... 309-677-2670 133 B reynolds@fsmail.bradley.edu
REYNOLDS, Clara .... 978-934-3567 211 G clara_reynolds@uml.edu
REYNOLDS, Curtis .... 352-392-1336 109 F curtrey@ufl.edu
REYNOLDS, Daisy .... 214-818-1360 434 F dreynolds@criswell.edu
REYNOLDS, David .... 940-565-3990 454 A david.reynolds@unt.edu
REYNOLDS, Debbie .... 530-895-2378.. 27 F reynoldsde@butte.edu
REYNOLDS, Dennis .... 713-743-7896 452 F der@uh.edu
REYNOLDS, Diane, L .... 804-828-3430 473 F dlreynol@vcu.edu
REYNOLDS, Don .... 334-386-7240.... 5 D dreynolds2@faulkner.edu
REYNOLDS, Ed .... 940-565-3000 454 A ed.reynolds@unt.edu
REYNOLDS, Elizabeth, P .... 304-293-4245 491 C liz.reynolds@mail.wvu.edu
REYNOLDS, Ellen .... 401-874-5155 406 B ellenreynolds@uri.edu
REYNOLDS, Gloria .... 970-351-1766.. 83 E gloria.reynolds@unco.edu
REYNOLDS, Holly .... 770-718-5314 115 D hreynolds@brenau.edu
REYNOLDS, James .... 708-456-0300 150 I jimreynolds@triton.edu
REYNOLDS, James, M .. 937-481-2201 364 E jim_reynolds@wilmington.edu
REYNOLDS, Jamie .... 334-727-8350.... 7 D jreynolds@tuskegee.edu
REYNOLDS, Jamie .... 334-727-8011.... 7 D jreynolds@tuskegee.edu
REYNOLDS, Jamie .... 703-284-1619 469 C jamie.reynolds@marymount.edu
REYNOLDS, Jane .... 972-241-3371 434 J jreynolds@dallas.edu
REYNOLDS, Jeff .... 318-675-5529 189 C wreyn1@lsuhsc.edu
REYNOLDS, John .... 858-527-2768.. 50 D
REYNOLDS, John, C ...... 626-815-3887.. 26 H jreynolds@apu.edu
REYNOLDS, Joseph ...... 775-784-4901 270 K
REYNOLDS, Karl .... 918-343-7819 369 F kreynolds@rsu.edu
REYNOLDS, Kevin .... 859-344-3344 184 F reynolk@thomasmore.edu
REYNOLDS, Kevin .... 864-597-4300 414 H reynoldsjk@wofford.edu
REYNOLDS, Kevin .... 503-725-3886 376 A reynoldsk@pdx.edu
REYNOLDS, Lana .... 405-382-9200 369 J l.reynolds@sscok.edu
REYNOLDS, Loretta .... 859-985-3774 179 C reynoldslo@berea.edu
REYNOLDS, Lynn .... 732-571-3531 279 B lreynold@monmouth.edu
REYNOLDS, Mark, A ..... 410-706-7461 202 D mreynolds@umaryland.edu
REYNOLDS, Marlene ..... 419-372-9824 348 H mreyno@bgsu.edu
REYNOLDS, Mary .... 828-327-7000 333 B mreynolds@cvcc.edu
REYNOLDS, Michael ..... 704-233-8252 344 G m.reynolds@wingate.edu
REYNOLDS, Michael, C 334-844-4367.... 4 E reynom2@auburn.edu
REYNOLDS, Michaela ... 325-942-2335 451 A
REYNOLDS, Michelle .... 410-951-3939 203 D mreynolds@coppin.edu
REYNOLDS, Michelle .... 573-840-9077 260 I michellereynolds@trcc.edu
REYNOLDS, Nancy, W .. 270-686-4244 179 D nancy.reynolds@brescia.edu
REYNOLDS, Phillip .... 334-699-2266.... 1 B preynolds@acom.edu
REYNOLDS, Randall ...... 615-460-6443 418 F randall.reynolds@belmont.edu
REYNOLDS, Richard ...... 781-736-4520 207 E rreynolds@brandeis.edu
REYNOLDS, Robin .... 408-554-4070.. 62 D rreynolds@scu.edu
REYNOLDS, Rodney ...... 805-493-3658.. 29 H rreynol@callutheran.edu
REYNOLDS, Rosemary .. 817-515-1514 445 G rosemary.reynolds@tccd.edu
REYNOLDS, Sean, B ..... 847-491-7326 145 F sean.reynolds@northwestern.edu
REYNOLDS, Sharon, S .. 606-783-2527 183 F sb.reynolds@moreheadstate.edu
REYNOLDS, Shawn .... 320-629-5161 240 C shawn.reynolds@pine.edu
REYNOLDS, Stephanie, C .... 315-792-5456 307 D sreynolds@mvcc.edu
REYNOLDS, Suzanne .... 336-758-5430 344 D reynols@wfu.edu
REYNOLDS, Thomas, L . 704-687-7248 342 E tlreynol@uncc.edu
REYNOLDS, Torry .... 336-757-7478 334 E treynolds@forsythtech.edu
REYNOLDS, Tracy .... 706-245-7226 117 E treynolds@ec.edu
REYNOLDS, Z. Paul ...... 217-424-3929 143 H zpaulreynolds@millikin.edu
REYNOLDS-CASPER, ReGina .... 620-792-9362 171 C casperr@bartonccc.edu
REYNOLDS-STUMP, Krista .... 518-262-2929 289 F reynolk1@amc.edu
REYNOSO, Bernardo ..... 559-442-4600.. 66 E bernardo.reynoso@fresnocitycollege.edu
REZA, Fawzia .... 800-280-0307 152 H fawzia.reza@ace.edu
REZA, Michael .... 503-554-2114 373 C mreza@georgefox.edu
REZAC, Barb .... 605-668-1292 415 H barbara.rezac@mtmc.edu
REZAEI, Roksana .... 801-832-2003 461 G rrezaei@westminstercollege.edu
REZAIE, Jaleh .... 919-530-7395 342 A jrezaie@nccu.edu
REZAK, Mary .... 509-335-5593 486 A mary.rezak@wsu.edu
REZEK, Jon .... 252-328-1936 341 C rezekjo17@ecu.edu
REZENDES, Elizabeth .... 203-932-7131.. 89 A erezendes@newhaven.edu
REZENDES, George .... 401-598-2029 404 I george.rezendes@jwu.edu
REZENDES, Robert .... 508-678-2811 213 G robert.rezendes@bristolcc.edu
RHAMES, Ronald .... 803-738-7600 410 G rhamesr@midlandstech.edu
RHEA, Amanda .... 704-978-4441 336 C ahrea@mitchellcc.edu
RHEA, Jill .... 641-784-5115 165 H jrhea1@graceland.edu
RHEA, Kenneth .... 585-389-2606 308 B krhee9@naz.edu
RHEA, Kristy, K .... 540-828-5471 465 D krhea@bridgewater.edu
RHEA, Teresa, C .... 256-549-8230.... 2 B trhea@gadsdenstate.edu
RHEAD, Lori .... 608-363-2630 492 C rheadl@beloit.edu
RHEAULT, Wendy .... 847-578-8805 147 I wendy.rheault@rosalindfranklin.edu
RHEAUME, Steve .... 603-535-2266 275 B srheaume@plymouth.edu
RHEE, Michael .... 212-431-2893 309 G michael.rhee@nyls.edu
RHEE, Thomas .... 703-629-1281 473 E
RHEIN, John .... 610-430-4163 396 A jrhein@wcupa.edu
RHETT, Sarah .... 719-587-7631.. 76 F sarahrhett@adams.edu
RHEW, Steven, W .... 336-334-5806 343 A swrhew@uncg.edu
RHEY, William .... 808-544-0275 127 H wrhey@hpu.edu
RHI-KLEINERT, Susan ... 818-710-2289.. 49 C rhiks@piercecollege.edu
RHIE, Souk .... 714-525-0088.. 44 E cfo@gm.edu
RHINE, Lisa .... 928-445-7300.. 16 M lisa.rhine@yc.edu
RHINE, Randy .... 308-432-6201 268 E rrhine@csc.edu
RHINESMITH, Betsy ...... 630-829-6412 132 E brhinesmith@ben.edu
RHINEY, Lisa .... 205-348-8333.... 7 G lisa.rhiney@ua.edu
RHOAD, Scott .... 660-543-4123 260 K rhoad@ucmo.edu
RHOADES, Jeff .... 419-448-2977 353 H jrhoade1@heidelberg.edu
RHOADES, Jeffrey .... 707-527-4811.. 62 F jrhoades@santarosa.edu
RHOADES, IV, Mack ..... 254-710-1234 431 J mack_rhoadesiv@baylor.edu
RHOADES, Margot .... 704-461-6733 327 A margotrhoades@bac.edu
RHOADES, Ron .... 814-262-3843 393 H rrhoades@pennhighlands.edu
RHOADS, Jeffrey .... 480-461-7565.. 13 D jeffrey.rhoads@mesacc.edu
RHOADS, Kay, M .... 803-934-3255 411 C krhoads@morris.edu
RHOADS, Troy .... 309-298-1834 152 D te-rhoads@wiu.edu
RHODA, Christopher ..... 207-859-1124 195 G chris@thomas.edu
RHODE, Carolyn .... 336-506-4128 332 A carolyn.rhode@alamancecc.edu
RHODE, Charles, G .... 404-894-4114 118 F chuck.rhode@facilities.gatech.edu
RHODE, Libby .... 920-686-6150 496 A libby.rhode@sl.edu
RHODEN, Brenda .... 256-761-6204.... 7 B brhoden@talladega.edu
RHODEN, Deborah .... 256-840-4137.... 3 F deborah.rhoden@snead.edu
RHODEN, Richard, R ..... 337-475-5887 192 A rrhoden@mcneese.edu
RHODEN-TRADER, Jacqueline .... 410-951-3049 203 D jrhoden-trader@coppin.edu
RHODES, Angel .... 270-534-3426 182 F angel.rhodes@kctcs.edu
RHODES, Anthony, P .... 212-592-2071 315 H tonyrhodes@sva.edu
RHODES, Carla .... 706-880-8240 121 A crhodes@lagrange.edu
RHODES, David, J .... 251-578-1313.... 3 D drhodes@rstc.edu
RHODES, David, J .... 212-592-2350 315 H drhodes@sva.edu
RHODES, Dawn, M .... 410-706-2802 202 D drhodes@umaryland.edu
RHODES, Eileen .... 860-906-5021.. 85 D erhodes@capitalcc.edu
RHODES, Gale .... 502-852-5727 185 C gale.rhodes@louisville.edu
RHODES, Heather .... 281-459-7106 443 D heather.rhodes@sjcd.edu
RHODES, Jacqueline, G 973-596-3407 279 F jacqueline.rhodes@njit.edu
RHODES, Jason, F .... 410-543-6031 203 F jfrhodes@salisbury.edu
RHODES, John .... 410-225-2201 199 H jrhodes@mica.edu
RHODES, Karen .... 864-578-8770 412 B krhodes@sherman.edu
RHODES, Kathleen, S .... 256-824-6775.... 8 B kathleen.rhodes@uah.edu
RHODES, Kathryn, L ..... 865-354-3000 425 G rhodeskc@roanestate.edu
RHODES, Kathy .... 206-934-3796 483 J kathy.rhodes@seattlecolleges.edu
RHODES, Lisa .... 714-703-1900.. 40 B lrhodes@concorde.edu
RHODES, Lisa .... 228-497-7627 247 E lisa.rhodes@mgccc.edu
RHODES, Michelle .... 616-331-3234 224 E rhodesmi@gvsu.edu
RHODES, Neisha .... 209-667-3201.. 33 C nrhodes@csustan.edu
RHODES, Phil .... 254-299-8642 440 A prhodes@mclennan.edu
RHODES, Randall .... 510-925-4282.. 25 Q randall.rhodes@aua.am
RHODES, Rhosetta .... 509-777-4536 486 I rrhodes@whitworth.edu
RHODES, Richard, M .... 512-223-7598 431 A rrhodes@austincc.edu
RHODES, Robert .... 325-674-2024 429 B rlr12a@acu.edu
RHODES, Shunita .... 312-788-1165 152 B srhodes@vandercook.edu
RHODES, Tammy .... 256-765-4100.... 8 E
RHODES, Tasha .... 718-260-5800 295 B trhodes@citytech.cuny.edu
RHODES, Tim .... 606-783-2000 183 F t.rhodes@moreheadstate.edu
RHODES, Vincent, A ...... 757-446-7070 466 I rhodesva@evms.edu
RHODES, Zachary .... 716-829-7603 298 F rhodesz@dyc.edu
RHOM, Eric .... 704-922-6386 334 F rhom.eric@gaston.edu
RHOTON, Jim .... 843-863-7050 407 E jrhoton@csuniv.edu
RHUE, Monika .... 704-371-6741 330 D mrhue@jcsu.edu
RHYNE, Teresa, L .... 757-455-3345 477 F trhyne@vwu.edu
RHYNE, Whitney .... 239-433-6943 100 A whitney.rhyne@fsw.edu
RHYNEDANCE, George .. 516-726-6048 504 G rhynedanceg@usmma.edu
RHYNEER, Madeleine, E .... 570-372-4293 399 C rhyneer@susqu.edu
RHYNHART, Hans .... 860-486-4806.. 88 E hans.rhynhart@uconn.edu
RIAL, Scott .... 847-543-2652 135 B srial@clcillinois.edu
RIAL, Yamirka .... 305-474-6965 106 F yrial@stu.edu
RIAS, Curtis .... 212-650-7073 293 D curtis@ccny.cuny.edu
RIBAKOW, Larry .... 443-548-6056 201 A lribakow@nirc.edu
RIBEIRO, Solange .... 612-767-7055 233 H solange.riberio@alfredadler.edu
RIBICH, Laura .... 866-492-5336 244 F laura.ribich@mail.waldenu.edu
RIBORDY, J. Clark .... 785-242-5200 176 D clark.ribordy@ottawa.edu
RICAFRENTE, Tina .... 619-876-4250.. 67 M tricafrente@usuniversity.edu
RICARDI, Richard .... 508-849-3367 205 C rricardi@annamaria.edu
RICARDINO CSAPO, Jorge .... 303-273-3503.. 78 I ycsapo@mines.edu
RICAURTE, Kelly .... 603-358-2119 275 A kricaurte@keene.edu
RICCA, Beth .... 201-684-7455 280 H bricca@ramapo.edu
RICCARDI, Mark, T .... 304-724-3700 487 E mriccardi@apus.edu
RICCARDI, Richard, L ... 609-896-5111 281 B rriccardi@rider.edu
RICCHEZZA, Lorraine .... 856-256-5130 281 E ricchezza@rowan.edu
RICCI, Amy .... 401-598-1000 404 I aricci@jwu.edu
RICCI, Carol .... 978-478-3400 217 G cricci@northpoint.edu
RICCI, Laura .... 305-266-7678 102 W
RICCIARDI, Jennifer, H . 617-573-8470 219 A jricciardi@suffolk.edu
RICCIOTTI, MaryAnn ..... 973-290-4475 277 A mricciotti@cse.edu

RICCOBONO, Steve .... 718-636-3787 311 J
sriccobo@pratt.edu
RICE, Alaina, M .... 620-417-1061 176 K
alaina.rice@sccc.edu
RICE, Amy .... 208-467-8609 131 D
arice@nnu.edu
RICE, Angela .... 434-592-7250 468 H
amrice3@liberty.edu
RICE, Becca .... 765-285-1147 153 C
rapolcz@bsu.edu
RICE, Billie Jo .... 661-395-4936.. 46 L
brice@bakersfieldcollege.edu
RICE, Brian .... 937-393-3431 361 B
brice@sscc.edu
RICE, Carlton .... 205-929-6389.... 2 H
crice@lawsonstate.edu
RICE, Carolyn .... 828-398-7105 332 B
carolynhrice@abtech.edu
RICE, Cynthia, E .... 410-706-3171 202 D
crice@umaryland.edu
RICE, Deborah .... 707-826-5135.. 33 D
deborah.rice@humboldt.edu
RICE, Edward .... 662-246-6442 247 D
erice@msdelta.edu
RICE, Fred .... 920-924-3291 500 C
frice@morainepark.edu
RICE, Gale .... 314-889-1479 253 C
grice@fontbonne.edu
RICE, Heather .... 256-228-6001.... 3 B
riceh@nacc.edu
RICE, James .... 312-850-7158 134 H
jrice36@ccc.edu
RICE, James, W .... 320-222-7474 240 E
jim.rice@ridgewater.edu
RICE, Jan .... 402-481-3908 265 K
jan.rice@bryanhealthcollege.edu
RICE, Jennifer, K .... 301-405-2336 202 C
jkr@umd.edu
RICE, Jonah .... 618-252-5400 149 C
jonah.rice@sic.edu
RICE, Josh .... 404-835-6129 423 K
jrice@richmont.edu
RICE, Julie .... 317-299-0333 160 G
julie@tcmi.org
RICE, Kathy .... 740-389-4636 356 B
ricek@mtc.edu
RICE, Kevin .... 585-395-2408 318 B
krice@brockport.edu
RICE, Larry .... 918-343-7612 369 F
lrice@rsu.edu
RICE, Leah, B .... 859-846-5308 183 E
lbarth@midway.edu
RICE, Leila .... 315-781-3700 302 A
rice@hws.edu
RICE, Malcolm .... 256-824-2555.... 8 B
malcolm.rice@uah.edu
RICE, Malcolm .... 256-824-6347.... 8 B
malcom.rice@uah.edu
RICE, Mark .... 781-235-1200 205 E
RICE, Martin .... 765-677-2939 157 D
martin.rice@indwes.edu
RICE, Monica .... 620-242-0432 175 F
ricem@mcpherson.edu
RICE, Peter .... 201-684-7601 280 H
price@ramapo.edu
RICE, Priscilla .... 215-968-8450 379 G
priscilla.rice@bucks.edu
RICE, Rachel .... 207-768-9447 196 E
rachel.rice@maine.edu
RICE, Raymond, J .... 207-768-9525 196 E
raymond.rice@maine.edu
RICE, Rolundus .... 334-229-4100.... 4 B
rrice@alasu.edu
RICE, Scott .... 217-333-0560 151 D
serice@uillinois.edu
RICE, Sherwin .... 910-879-5646 332 D
srice@bladencc.edu
RICE, Susan, I .... 336-633-0282 337 A
sirice@randolph.edu
RICE, Vance .... 662-325-6731 247 F
rice@safdfairs.msstate.edu
RICE-CARROLL, Cynthia 760-757-2121.. 52 E
crice@miracosta.edu
RICE-CLAYBORN, Kathy 501-450-3134.. 23 H
kathyc@uca.edu
RICE-HOLLAND, Gina .... 202-274-2303.. 93 D
RICE-MASON, Jenifer .... 870-972-3964.. 17 G
jrmason@astate.edu
RICE-SPEARMAN, Lori .. 806-743-3223 451 C
lori.ricespearman@ttuhsc.edu
RICELLI, Iliana .... 901-333-5760 426 A
iricelli@southwest.tn.edu
RICH, Andrew .... 212-650-5967 293 D
arich@ccny.cuny.edu
RICH, Carson, D .... 252-335-3229 341 D
cdrich@ecsu.edu
RICH, Forrest .... 912-583-3146 115 E
frich@bpc.edu
RICH, Frank .... 432-335-6507 441 D
frich@odessa.edu
RICH, Jack, W .... 325-674-2013 429 B
richj@acu.edu
RICH, Julie .... 801-626-6232 461 B
jrich@weber.edu
RICH, Kathy .... 781-280-3501 214 G
richk@middlesex.mass.edu
RICH, Kim .... 860-932-4141.. 86 E
krich@qvcc.edu
RICH, Laura .... 910-893-4364 327 E
richl@campbell.edu
RICH, Marcus .... 252-985-5176 339 D
mritch@ncwc.edu
RICH, Scott .... 620-278-4213 177 B
srich@sterling.edu
RICH, Steven .... 617-236-8832 209 D
srich@fisher.edu
RICH, Steven, W .... 217-581-6616 136 E
swrich@eiu.edu
RICH, Teresa .... 509-574-4667 487 A
thollandrich@yvcc.edu
RICH, Timothy, A .... 651-631-5489 244 D
tarich@unwsp.edu
RICH, Virginia .... 973-618-3516 276 D
vrich@caldwell.edu
RICH, Wendall .... 801-626-7443 461 B
wrich@weber.edu
RICHARD, Alison, A ...... 570-372-4111 399 C
arichard@susqu.edu
RICHARD, Arthur .... 252-940-6210 332 C
arthur.richard@beaufortccc.edu
RICHARD, Cindy .... 978-998-7762 209 B
cirichar@endicott.edu
RICHARD, Dan .... 904-620-2700 110 A
drichard@unf.edu
RICHARD, Deborah .... 407-708-2487 107 D
richardd@seminolestate.edu
RICHARD, Guy .... 770-852-8884 248 F
grichard@rts.edu
RICHARD, Mark .... 256-840-4110.... 3 F
mark.richard@snead.edu
RICHARD, Mark .... 205-665-6600.... 8 D
mrichard11@montevallo.edu
RICHARD, Patricia .... 775-784-4805 271 F
prichard@unr.edu
RICHARD, Renee .... 216-987-4865 351 G
renee.richard@tri-c.edu
RICHARD, Robert .... 337-482-6923 192 E
bookstore@louisiana.edu
RICHARD, Ryan, W .... 318-257-3693 191 F
richard@latech.edu
RICHARD, Stephen .... 757-446-7165 466 I
richarsw@evms.edu
RICHARD, Susan .... 337-482-6396 192 E
smr@louisiana.edu
RICHARD, Valerie .... 410-778-7855 204 D
vrichard2@washcoll.edu
RICHARD, Valerie .... 704-403-3507 327 D
valerie.richard@carolinashealthcare.org
RICHARDS, Caroline, B 404-880-6146 116 D
crichards@cau.edu
RICHARDS, Cheryl .... 980-224-8466 217 F
RICHARDS, Chris .... 715-346-3908 497 F
crichards@uwsp.edu
RICHARDS, David .... 559-453-7195.. 43 G
david.richards@fresno.edu
RICHARDS, David, E ..... 402-554-2640 270 B
derichards@unomaha.edu
RICHARDS, Debbie .... 304-424-8201 491 D
debbie.richards@wvup.edu
RICHARDS,
E. Randolph .... 561-803-2051 104 C
randy_richards@pba.edu
RICHARDS, Faith .... 605-455-6029 416 B
frichards@olc.edu
RICHARDS, Gwyn .... 812-855-2435 156 B
grichar@indiana.edu
RICHARDS, Heidi, R ...... 903-886-5994 447 B
heidi.richards@tamuc.edu
RICHARDS, Heraldo .... 615-963-5620 426 D
hrichards@tnstate.edu
RICHARDS, Jeni .... 949-376-6000.. 47 D
jrichards@lcad.edu
RICHARDS, Jerry .... 920-924-3184 500 C
jrichards2@morainepark.edu
RICHARDS, John .... 808-734-9518 128 I
john.richards@hawaii.edu
RICHARDS, Josh .... 816-936-8718 259 I
jmrichards@saintlukescollege.edu
RICHARDS, Kathy, A ..... 906-227-1237 228 F
kathrich@nmu.edu
RICHARDS, Katie, J ...... 701-788-4675 345 E
katie.richards.2@mayvillestate.edu
RICHARDS, Lawrence .... 610-399-2405 394 C
police@cheyney.edu
RICHARDS, Lee .... 740-362-3344 356 D
lrichards@mtso.edu
RICHARDS, Letha .... 662-621-4126 245 E
lrichards@coahomacc.edu
RICHARDS, Marilyn .... 919-546-8529 340 E
marilyn.richards@shawu.edu
RICHARDS, Mark .... 206-543-7632 485 F
provost@uw.edu
RICHARDS, Marvin .... 216-987-4883 351 G
marvin.richards@tri-c.edu
RICHARDS, Maryanne ... 508-830-5039 213 B
mrichards@maritime.edu
RICHARDS, Matthew ..... 207-741-5927 195 A
mrichards@smccme.edu
RICHARDS, Melissa .... 434-381-6326 472 D
mrichards@sbc.edu
RICHARDS, Michael ...... 212-752-1530 304 D
michael.richards@limcollege.edu
RICHARDS, Michael, J .. 515-281-3934 162 H
RICHARDS, Paula .... 559-297-4500.. 46 A
prichards@iot.edu
RICHARDS, Rosalie .... 386-822-7256 111 A
rrichar1@stetson.edu
RICHARDS, Samantha ... 843-574-6771 413 B
samantha.richards@tridenttech.edu
RICHARDS, Sandra, K ... 800-328-2660.. 95 B
skrichards@baptistcollege.edu
RICHARDS, Scott .... 412-396-5140 383 C
richards@duq.edu
RICHARDS, Steve .... 320-762-4692 237 B
stever@alextech.edu
RICHARDS, Steven, N .... 540-863-2880 474 D
srichards@dslcc.edu
RICHARDS, Terri .... 386-738-6682 111 A
trichard@stetson.edu
RICHARDS, Terry .... 410-837-4772 204 B
trichards@ubalt.edu
RICHARDS, Tom, F .... 573-882-2612 261 A
richardstf@umsystem.edu
RICHARDS, Tracey .... 610-799-1779 388 I
trichards1@lccc.edu
RICHARDS, Troy .... 212-217-7665 299 H
troy_richards@fitnyc.edu
RICHARDS, Virginia ...... 925-473-1350.. 40 J
vrichards@losmedanos.edu
RICHARDS, Virginia ...... 317-805-1783 488 F
vrichards@salemu.edu
RICHARDSON, Aaron .... 601-979-3704 246 E
aaron.richardson@jsums.edu
RICHARDSON, Ann .... 206-934-4567 483 J
ann.richardson@seattlecolleges.edu
RICHARDSON, Barbara . 520-586-1981.. 11 M
richardsonbarbara@cochise.edu
RICHARDSON,
Belinda, M .... 724-287-8711 380 A
belinda.richardson@bc3.edu
RICHARDSON,
Bernard, L .... 202-806-7280.. 92 B
brichardson@howard.edu
RICHARDSON, Beverly .. 501-375-9845.. 20 G
brichardson@philander.edu
RICHARDSON, Bonita L 412-237-4413 381 G
brichardson@ccac.edu
RICHARDSON, Brian, A 804-371-3000 474 H
brichardson@reynolds.edu
RICHARDSON, Brittany . 504-816-4797 186 D
brichardson@dillard.edu
RICHARDSON, Casie ..... 270-824-8575 181 G
casie.richardson@kctcs.edu
RICHARDSON,
Christine .... 315-655-7147 292 F
cwrichardson@cazenovia.edu
RICHARDSON,
Christopher .... 804-355-0671 472 E
crichardson@upsem.edu
RICHARDSON, Cinzia .... 973-720-2976 284 I
richardsonc@wpunj.edu
RICHARDSON, Dale ...... 636-481-3501 254 A
drichar6@jeffco.edu
RICHARDSON, David .... 256-726-8044.... 6 C
drichardson@oakwood.edu
RICHARDSON, David, E 352-392-0780 109 F
der@ufl.edu
RICHARDSON, Denise ... 510-464-3224.. 56 G
drichardson@peralta.edu
RICHARDSON, Ellis .... 413-236-1011 213 F
erichardson@berkshirecc.edu
RICHARDSON, Florence 301-295-3045 504 B
florence.richardson@usuhs.edu
RICHARDSON, Greer ...... 215-951-1806 387 C
richards@lasalle.edu
RICHARDSON, Greg, C . 606-474-3250 180 G
greg@kcu.edu
RICHARDSON, Guy, L ... 601-923-1650 248 F
grichardson@rts.edu
RICHARDSON, Irene ...... 513-244-4432 357 A
irene.richardson@msj.edu
RICHARDSON, James ... 509-682-6400 486 E
jrichardson@wvc.edu
RICHARDSON, Jay .... 601-318-6165 249 H
jrichardson@wmcarey.edu
RICHARDSON, Jennifer . 518-454-2023 296 H
richardj@strose.edu
RICHARDSON, Jeremy .. 319-656-2447 169 C
admissions@shilohuniversity.edu
RICHARDSON, Joe, C ... 407-582-3351 112 K
jrichardson64@valenciacollege.edu
RICHARDSON, John .... 706-771-4111 114 J
jrichard@augustatech.edu
RICHARDSON, K. Scott . 724-287-8711 380 A
scott.richardson@bc3.edu
RICHARDSON, Karen .... 609-258-6150 280 E
karenr@princeton.edu
RICHARDSON, Karlene .. 212-247-3434 305 G
krichardson@mandl.edu
RICHARDSON, Karry, D 573-629-3016 253 H
krichardson@hlg.edu
RICHARDSON, Kathleen 515-271-2295 165 A
kathleen.richardson@drake.edu
RICHARDSON, Kathy, B 724-946-7130 402 G
richarkb@westminster.edu
RICHARDSON, Keith ..... 215-489-2397 382 D
keith.richardson@delval.edu
RICHARDSON, Krista .... 419-995-8312 354 H
richardson.k@rhodesstate.edu
RICHARDSON, L. Song . 949-824-4158.. 68 G
srichardson@law.uci.edu
RICHARDSON, Lara, K .. 803-938-3890 414 B
painterl@uscsumter.edu
RICHARDSON, Lisa, A .. 727-816-3404 104 F
richarl@phsc.edu
RICHARDSON, Lyneene 515-643-6659 168 A
lrichardson@mercydesmoines.org
RICHARDSON, Lynne .... 540-654-1455 472 I
lrichar2@umw.edu
RICHARDSON, Marcus .. 718-951-5669 293 C
mrichardson@brooklyn.cuny.edu
RICHARDSON, Maria .... 334-420-4499.... 3 H
mrichardson@trenholmstate.edu
RICHARDSON, Mary ..... 229-430-3588 113 I
mrichardson@albanytech.edu
RICHARDSON,
Matthew, O .... 801-422-2640 458 H
matt_richardson@byu.edu
RICHARDSON, Melanie . 360-438-4367 483 H
mrichardson@stmartin.edu
RICHARDSON, Melissa . 503-594-3300 372 D
melissa.richardson@clackamas.edu
RICHARDSON, Nicholas 718-420-4124 324 F
nrichard@wagner.edu
RICHARDSON,
Raymond .... 806-720-7230 439 H
raymond.richardson@lcu.edu
RICHARDSON, Rebecca 707-545-3647.. 26 J
becca@berginu.edu
RICHARDSON, Renee .... 309-677-1100 133 B
rbrichardson@bradley.edu.com
RICHARDSON, Rick .... 254-968-9877 446 E
rrichardson@tarleton.edu
RICHARDSON, Robert ... 317-955-6789 158 U
rrichardson@marian.edu
RICHARDSON, Robin .... 401-232-6000 404 F
rarich@bryant.edu
RICHARDSON,
Sarah, D .... 402-280-2703 266 I
sarahrichardson@creighton.edu
RICHARDSON, Stephen . 312-329-4243 144 B
stephen.richardson@moody.edu
RICHARDSON, Steven ... 801-626-6001 461 B
stevenrichardson@weber.edu
RICHARDSON, Sydney .. 336-734-7764 334 E
srichardson@forsythtech.edu
RICHARDSON, TaNeal ... 432-264-5608 438 C
trichardson@howardcollege.edu
RICHARDSON, Terry ..... 276-944-6231 467 G
trichard@ehc.edu

RIGGINS, Erin .... 228-896-2506 247 E
erin.riggins@mgccc.edu
RIGGLE, Andy .... 866-776-0331.. 54 A
briggle@ncu.edu
RIGGLE, Ron .... 217-786-2581 142 B
ron.riggle@llcc.edu
RIGGLE YOUNG, Tracy . 412-924-1423 396 I
triggleyoung@pts.edu
RIGGS, Alexia .... 910-893-1460 327 E
riggs@campbell.edu
RIGGS, Allen .... 435-283-7125 461 C
allen.riggs@snow.edu
RIGGS, Bonnie .... 423-697-4465 424 E
bonnie.riggs@chattanoogastate.edu
RIGGS, David .... 765-677-2808 157 D
david.riggs@indwes.edu
RIGGS, Marie, A .... 517-230-0720 224 F
mriggs@glcc.edu
RIGGS, Michelle .... 909-389-3391.. 59 H
mriggs@craftonhills.edu
RIGGS, Paul .... 570-408-4600 403 D
paul.riggs@wilkes.edu
RIGGS, Robert, F .... 214-887-5007 436 B
rriggs@dts.edu
RIGGS, Wayne .... 850-201-8071.. 98 E
wriggs@flagler.edu
RIGGS-JOHNSON,
Kaydee .... 620-229-6343 177 A
kaydee.riggsjohnson@sckans.edu
RIGLING, Brian .... 937-775-5007 364 I
brian.rigling@wright.edu
RIGNEY, Dawn .... 212-938-5600 320 B
drigney@sunyopt.edu
RIGNEY, Doug .... 205-726-2032.... 6 E
drigney@samford.edu
RIGSBEE, Craig .... 530-895-2476.. 27 F
rigsbeecr@butte.edu
RIGSBEE, Jason .... 912-525-5000 123 G
jrigsbee@scad.edu
RIGSBY, Tawny .... 918-631-2315 371 E
tawny-rigsby@utulsa.edu
RIHACEK, Robin .... 708-210-5754 149 B
rrihacek@ssc.edu
RIIS, Janet .... 406-447-5423 263 C
jriis@carroll.edu
RIKALO, Heather .... 775-445-3324 271 G
heather.rikalo@wnc.edu
RIKARD, Christy .... 912-486-7607 122 I
crikard@ogeecheetech.edu
RIKARD, Jennifer .... 619-594-5220.. 33 E
jrikard@sdsu.edu
RIKEL, Randy .... 806-651-2095 448 C
rrikel@wtamu.edu
RIKER, David, J .... 210-458-6143 455 E
dave.riker@utsa.edu
RIKOON,
James (Sandy), S .... 573-882-0861 261 B
rikoonsandy@missouri.edu
RILEY, Alyssa .... 641-782-1422 169 H
riley@swcciowa.edu
RILEY, Angela .... 651-690-6043 242 R
amriley906@stkate.edu
RILEY, Ann, C .... 573-882-1685 261 B
rileyac@missouri.edu
RILEY, Anne .... 617-287-6809 211 E
anne.riley@umb.edu
RILEY, Brenda .... 251-578-1313.... 3 D
briley@rstc.edu
RILEY, Brett .... 509-682-6515 486 E
briley@wvc.edu
RILEY, Chris .... 325-674-2918 429 B
cmr97t@acu.edu
RILEY, Clayton .... 301-546-7422 201 C
RILEY, Connie .... 870-574-4499.. 21 E
criley@sautech.edu
RILEY, Dean .... 281-649-3182 437 H
driley@hbu.edu
RILEY, Doreen .... 216-397-4345 354 I
driley@jcu.edu
RILEY, Edward .... 617-254-2610 218 D
rev.edward.riley@sjs.edu
RILEY, Jan .... 334-222-6591.... 2 I
jriley@lbwcc.edu
RILEY, Jeanette, E .... 401-874-2566 406 B
jen_riley@uri.edu
RILEY, Jennifer .... 318-255-7950 191 F
jennifer@latechalumni.org
RILEY, Jill .... 931-540-2573 424 G
jriley9@columbiastate.edu
RILEY, Joanne .... 617-287-5927 211 E
joanne.riley@umb.edu
RILEY, Karen .... 303-871-3665.. 83 D
kriley@du.edu

RILEY, Kelley .... 651-604-4119 236 J
kriley@minneapolisbusinesscollege.edu
RILEY, Kris .... 319-398-7628 167 C
kris.riley@kirkwood.edu
RILEY, Lisa .... 784-682-6017 271 F
lriley@unr.edu
RILEY, Mark .... 850-644-3500 109 C
mriley@admin.fsu.edu
RILEY, Marty .... 252-334-2025 331 D
marty.riley@macuniversity.edu
RILEY, Mike .... 209-228-4073.. 69 B
mriley5@ucmerced.edu
RILEY, Monica .... 479-788-7912.. 21 H
monica.riley@uafs.edu
RILEY, Rebecca .... 936-273-7222 439 G
rebecca.riley@lonestar.edu
RILEY, Robert .... 631-687-1275 314 C
rriley@sjcny.edu
RILEY, Sarah .... 900-652-6176.. 36 A
sarah.riley@chaffey.edu
RILEY, Shawn, D .... 610-292-9852 397 D
bookkeeping@reseminary.edu
RILEY, Stacy .... 262-564-3108 499 F
rileys@gtc.edu
RILEY, Susan .... 513-732-5324 362 F
susan.riley@uc.edu
RILEY, Tammy .... 409-984-6237 450 B
tammy.riley@lamarpa.edu
RILEY, Terisa, C .... 479-788-7007.. 21 H
terisa.riley@uafs.edu
RILEY, Tom .... 617-747-2218 206 E
triley@berklee.edu
RILEY, Toni .... 312-567-5239 139 B
triley6@iit.edu
RILEY, Tracey .... 617-994-4276 219 A
triley@suffolk.edu
RILEY, Vicki, F .... 252-334-2043 331 D
vicki.riley@macuniversity.edu
RILEY, Wanda, L .... 404-413-1310 119 E
wriley2@gsu.edu
RILEY, Wayne, J .... 718-270-2611 317 E
presidentoffice@downstate.edu
RILEY, Wendell .... 318-797-5108 189 D
wendell.riley@lsus.edu
RILL, Ann .... 812-221-1714 162 B
annmarierill@vbc.edu
RILL, Josef .... 941-752-5342 108 G
rillj@scf.edu
RILLEY, Karin .... 972-721-5363 452 D
krilley@udallas.edu
RIMAL, Sanjana .... 973-353-5943 282 B
srimal@newark.rutgers.edu
RIMANDO-CHAREUNSAP,
Rosie .... 206-934-5311 484 B
rosie.rimando@seattlecolleges.edu
RIMANDO-CHAREUNSAP,
Rosie .... 206-934-5311 483 I
rosie.rimando@seattlecolleges.edu
RIMAR, Mark .... 314-977-3529 259 H
mark.rimar@slu.edu
RIMER, Barbara, K .... 919-966-3215 342 D
brimer@unc.edu
RIMIRCH, Bruce .... 680-488-2471 506 B
brucer@palau.edu
RINALDI WINN, Mary .. 404-364-8412 122 J
mrinaldi@oglethorpe.edu
RINARD, Pat .... 727-341-3064 106 E
rinard.pat@spcollege.edu
RINCONES, Daniel .... 913-971-3255 175 G
dsrincones@mnu.edu
RINCONES-GOMEZ,
Rigo .... 904-470-8261.. 97 L
rrinconesgomez@ewc.edu
RINDO, Michael, J .... 715-836-4742 496 D
rindomj@uwec.edu
RINE, Veronica .... 740-755-7600 349 H
rine.60@cotc.edu
RINEHART, Kathleen, A 414-410-4003 492 D
karinehart1@stritch.edu
RINEHART, Kent, W ...... 845-575-3000 305 L
kent.rinehart@marist.edu
RINEHART, Melanie ...... 405-382-9717 369 J
m.rinehart@sscok.edu
RINEHART, Shelley .... 281-998-6150 443 C
shelley.rinehart@sjcd.edu
RINEHART, Todd .... 303-871-3125.. 83 D
todd.rinehart@du.edu
RINER, Meg .... 540-828-5636 465 D
mriner@bridgewater.edu
RINERE, Monique .... 212-229-5150 308 C
mrinere@newschool.edu
RINEY, OSU, Judith, N . 270-686-4288 179 D
judith.riney@brescia.edu

RING, Andrea .... 785-227-3380 171 E
ringan@bethanylb.edu
RING, Joshua .... 828-328-7927 330 F
joshua.ring@lr.edu
RING, Neal .... 864-242-5100 407 B
RING, Patricia .... 508-793-3459 208 B
pring@holycross.edu
RING, Tim .... 513-585-2402 350 H
timothy.ring@thechristcollege.edu
RINGA, Melanie .... 914-961-8313 315 C
mringa@svots.edu
RINGENBERG, Ron .... 574-296-6212 152 I
rringenb@ambs.edu
RINGHAM, Rebecca ...... 701-858-3126 345 F
rebecca.ringham@minostateu.edu
RINGLE, Martin, D .... 503-777-7254 376 C
martin.ringle@reed.edu
RINGLE, Suzanne .... 602-286-8110.. 13 B
suzanne.ringle@gwmail.maricopa.edu
RINGLER, Krista .... 919-515-2866 342 B
kmringle@ncsu.edu
RINGO, Teresa .... 936-294-1061 450 C
reg_tat@shsu.edu
RINGWALD, Heather ..... 603-899-4128 273 F
ringwaldh@franklinpierce.edu
RINGWOOD, Karen, K .. 203-597-9036.. 88 D
klozada@bridgeport.edu
RINI, Anthony .... 617-373-5144 217 F
RINI, Bridget .... 216-397-4281 354 I
brini@jcu.edu
RINK, Jonathan .... 828-328-7249 330 F
jonathan.rink@lr.edu
RINK, Susan .... 734-481-5634 223 H
srink@emich.edu
RINKENBAUGH, Bill ..... 316-322-3297 171 G
brinkenb@butlercc.edu
RINKER, Craig .... 202-687-5867.. 92 A
cmr235@georgetown.edu
RINKER, Jonathan, A .... 304-877-6428 487 F
jon.rinker@abc.edu
RINKUS, Michael, A ..... 248-689-8282 232 A
mrinkus@walshcollege.edu
RINN, Linda .... 817-722-1761 439 B
linda.rinn@tku.edu
RINN, Martha .... 830-372-8110 449 B
mrinn@tlu.edu
RINN, Susan .... 830-372-8001 449 B
srinn@tlu.edu
RINNE, Jason .... 660-831-4088 256 G
rinnej@moval.edu
RIOLA, Allison .... 303-871-4201.. 83 D
allison.riola@du.edu
RIOPEL, Becky .... 425-352-8545 479 A
rriopel@cascadia.edu
RIORDAN, Charles .... 302-831-4007.. 90 F
riordan@udel.edu
RIORDAN, Christine, M 516-877-3838 289 C
cmr@adelphi.edu
RIORDAN, Jason .... 816-501-4877 258 H
jason.riordan@rockhurst.edu
RIORDAN, Kevin .... 708-596-2000 149 B
kriordan@ssc.edu
RIORDAN, Marsha .... 641-673-1045 170 F
riordanm@wmpenn.edu
RIORDAN, Melissa .... 909-869-5010.. 30 D
mriordan@cpp.edu
RIORDAN, Phil .... 630-617-3050 136 G
phil.riordan@elmhurst.edu
RIOS, Alfonso .... 323-415-5368.. 48 H
riosa@elac.edu
RIOS, Angel .... 787-738-2161 513 D
angel.rios7@upr.edu
RIOS, Char .... 509-793-2222 478 H
charlener@bigbend.edu
RIOS, Charlene .... 509-793-2020 478 H
charlener@bigbend.edu
RIOS, Christina .... 310-243-3789.. 31 B
crios@csudh.edu
RIOS, Eduardo .... 718-368-5028 294 E
eduardo.rios@kbcc.cuny.edu
RIOS, Efrain .... 787-844-8181 514 A
efrain.rios@upr.edu
RIOS, Esther, A .... 671-735-5544 505 C
financialaid@guamcc.edu
RIOS, Rafael .... 787-765-9695 514 B
rafael.rios2@upr.edu
RIOS, Yanel .... 479-394-7622.. 23 C
yrios@uarichmountain.edu
RIOS, Zilka .... 787-798-4050 512 C
zilka.rios@uccaribe.edu
RIOS-COLON,
Cristian, J 787-857-3600 508M
cristianrios@br.inter.edu

RIOS-GONZALEZ,
Palmira, N .... 787-763-6700 508 A
drprios@se-pr.edu
RIOS-HUSAIN,
Silvia Patricia .... 704-922-6217 334 F
husain.silvia@gaston.edu
RIOTTO, Karen, M .... 585-395-5484 318 B
kriotto@brockport.edu
RIPLEY, Anneliese .... 406-683-7309 264 B
anneliese.ripley@umwestern.edu
RIPLEY, Dave .... 701-477-7862 347 A
dripley@tm.edu
RIPLEY, Judith .... 207-795-5974 194 E
ripleyj@mchp.edu
RIPLEY, Kate .... 907-474-6631.. 10 A
klripley@alaska.edu
RIPLEY, Melissa .... 423-636-7300 427 B
mripley@tusculum.edu
RIPPEE, Rusty .... 870-460-1018.. 22 D
rippee@uamont.edu
RIPPEN, Kelly .... 308-345-8107 267 K
rippenk@mpcc.edu
RIPPINGER, Timothy ..... 414-288-4771 494 B
timothy.rippinger@marquette.edu
RIPPKE, Greg .... 419-473-2700 352 E
grippke@daviscollege.edu
RIPPLE, Jacob .... 620-227-9349 172 J
jripple@dc3.edu
RIPTON, Elizabeth, R .... 585-292-2197 307 H
eripton@monroecc.edu
RIQUEZ, Elizabeth .... 646-312-1390 292 L
elizabeth.riquez@baruch.cuny.edu
RIS, Gary .... 631-451-4205 321 F
risg@sunysuffolk.edu
RISBOSKIN, John .... 570-961-7828 387 D
risboskinj@lackawanna.edu
RISCH, Thomas .... 870-972-3333.. 17 G
trisch@astate.edu
RISCHBIETER, Natalie .... 478-471-2732 121 F
natalie.rischbieter@mga.edu
RISDON, Michelle .... 530-541-4660.. 47 E
risdon@ltcc.edu
RISELEY, Leanne .... 808-455-0676 129 D
leannech@hawaii.edu
RISEMAN, Stacy .... 508-793-2741 208 B
sriseman@holycross.edu
RISHE, Karl .... 989-463-7333 220 H
rishekk@alma.edu
RISHWORTH, Christie ... 401-456-8520 405 C
crishworth@ric.edu
RISI, Melissa .... 775-753-2361 271 B
melissa.risi@gbcnv.edu
RISINGER, Jeff .... 979-862-4572 446 G
jrisinger@tamu.edu
RISLEY, Levi .... 479-308-2225.. 17 C
levi.resley@acheedu.org
RISMILLER, Lisa, S .... 937-229-4087 362 G
lrismiller1@udayton.edu
RISO, Christina .... 215-489-2950 382 D
christina.riso@delval.edu
RISO, Kelly-Rue .... 802-728-1211 464 E
kriso@vtc.edu
RISO, Taylor .... 860-632-3010.. 87 C
triso@holyapostles.edu
RISSE, Duane .... 719-502-2403.. 81 F
duane.risse@ppcc.edu
RISSEL, Timothy, O .... 570-326-3761 393 G
tor1@pct.edu
RISSER, Deanna .... 574-535-7557 155 A
deannaar@goshen.edu
RISSLER, Jennifer .... 415-749-4586.. 60 G
jrissler@sfai.edu
RITACCO, Alan .... 508-373-9732 206 B
alan.ritacco@becker.edu
RITACCO, Kevin .... 508-854-4200 215 D
kritacco@qcc.mass.edu
RITAYIK, Mary .... 845-257-3344 317 B
ritayikm@newpaltz.edu
RITCHEY, Amanda .... 614-236-6159 349 D
aritchey@capital.edu
RITCHEY, Brandon .... 740-474-8896 358 F
britchey@ohiochristian.edu
RITCHEY, Fred, L .... 903-233-4210 439 E
fredritchey@letu.edu
RITCHEY, Mary Kaye ..... 706-886-6831 125 D
mritchey@tfc.edu
RITCHEY, Philip .... 662-685-4771 245 D
pritchey@bmc.edu
RITCHEY, Scott .... 817-461-8741 430 H
sritchey@abu.edu
RITCHEY, William, V ..... 757-594-7047 466 B
bill.ritchey@cnu.edu
RITCHIE, Chad .... 912-583-3167 115 E
critchie@bpc.edu

ROACH, Deb .... 888-378-9988 416 J
ROACH, Evelyn, N .... 423-439-4230 419 J
roache@etsu.edu
ROACH, H. William .... 864-833-8217 411 I
broach@presby.edu
ROACH, Kenneth .... 704-334-6882 328 C
kroach@charlottechristian.edu
ROACH, Kristin, A .... 651-962-6168 244 E
kris.roach@stthomas.edu
ROACH, Stephen .... 361-593-2800 447 D
stephen.roach@tamuk.edu
ROACH, Virginia .... 212-636-6470 300 E
vroach@fordham.edu
ROACHE, Marshall .... 503-399-2339 372 C
marshall.roache@chemeketa.edu
ROADES, Laurie .... 657-278-3915.. 31 E
lroades@fullerton.edu
ROADES, Nicole .... 937-393-3431 361 B
nroades@sscc.edu
ROAN, Matt .... 985-448-4794 192 B
matt.roan@nicholls.edu
ROANHORSE, Ralph ...... 505-786-4110 286 G
rroanhorse@navajotech.edu
ROARK, Debbie .... 207-768-9755 196 E
deborah.roark@maine.edu
ROARK, Donna .... 606-487-3128 181 C
donnad.roark@kctcs.edu
ROARK, Ian .... 520-206-6424.. 15 D
iroark@pima.edu
ROARK, Ryan .... 575-562-2165 285 M
ryan.roark@enmu.edu
ROARK, Tony .... 208-426-4062 129 I
troark@boisestate.edu
ROATH, Carrie .... 312-935-4868 147 D
croath@robertmorris.edu
ROBACK, Barbara, A ...... 315-684-6615 321 D
robackba@morrisville.edu
ROBACK, Joseph, M ...... 570-941-4385 401 H
joseph.roback@scranton.edu
ROBART, Regina .... 618-664-7000 137 G
regina.robart@greenville.edu
ROBB, Cathy .... 812-749-1272 159 C
crobb@oak.edu
ROBB, Cathy .... 812-749-1272 159 C
crobb@oake.edu
ROBB, Daniel, J .... 803-641-3272 413 D
danr@usca.edu
ROBB, James .... 517-371-5140 233 A
robbj@cooley.edu
ROBB, Sarah .... 620-431-2820 175 H
sarah_robb@neosho.edu
ROBB, Susan, E .... 804-827-0479 473 F
sarobb@vcu.edu
ROBB SHIMKO, Molly .. 724-830-4620 398 H
shimko@setonhill.edu
ROBBIE, Kimberly .... 510-659-6165.. 54 F
krobbie@ohlone.edu
ROBBINS, Amanda .... 504-280-6590 189 E
arobbin1@uno.edu
ROBBINS, Bradley .... 334-244-3345.... 4 F
brobbin2@aum.edu
ROBBINS, Brent .... 412-392-8183 397 A
brobbins@pointpark.edu
ROBBINS, Donna .... 575-492-2193 289 A
drobbins@usw.edu
ROBBINS, Eva .... 315-279-5264 304 A
erobbins@keuka.edu
ROBBINS, Gene, R .... 401-865-2767 405 B
grobbins@providence.edu
ROBBINS, Hollis .... 707-664-2146.. 34 C
robbinsh@sonoma.edu
ROBBINS, Jill .... 478-387-4908 118 G
jrobbins@gmc.edu
ROBBINS, Katie, A .... 330-471-8138 355 L
krobbins@malone.edu
ROBBINS, Kristine .... 614-823-1232 360 A
krobbins@otterbein.edu
ROBBINS, Melanie .... 603-342-3093 273 D
mrobbins@ccsnh.edu
ROBBINS, Meredith ...... 661-253-7797.. 28 K
mrobbins@calarts.edu
ROBBINS, Michael .... 410-857-2242 200 B
mrobbins@mcdaniel.edu
ROBBINS, Nickey, L ...... 870-508-6108.. 18 A
nrobbins@asumh.edu
ROBBINS, Patrica .... 719-587-7472.. 76 F
patrobbins@adams.edu
ROBBINS, Paul .... 608-265-5296 496 C
director@nelson.wisc.edu
ROBBINS, Robert, C ..... 520-621-5511.. 16 G
president@email.arizona.edu
ROBBINS, Rochelle ...... 267-341-3640 386 A
srobbins@holyfamily.edu

ROBBINS, Sandra .... 617-735-9715 209 A
robbins@emmanuel.edu
ROBBINS, Scott, D .... 731-881-7775 428 B
sdrobbins@utm.edu
ROBBINS, Steve .... 662-685-4771 245 D
srobbins@bmc.edu
ROBBINS, Thomas, J .... 563-589-3507 169 I
trobbins@dbq.edu
ROBBINS SMITH,
Patricia .... 562-860-2451.. 35 M
probbinssmith@cerritos.edu
ROBBINSON, Theresa ... 212-924-5900 322 B
trobbinson@swedishinstitute.edu
ROBEAU, Jim .... 985-867-2272 190 F
jrobeau@sjasc.edu
ROBECK, Mike .... 850-201-8546 111 C
robeckm@tcc.fl.edu
ROBEL, Kenneth .... 856-351-2704 283 A
krobel@salemcc.edu
ROBEL, Lauren .... 812-855-9011 156 A
lrobel@iu.edu
ROBEL, Lauren .... 812-855-9011 156 B
provost@indiana.edu
ROBELOTTO, Vince .... 706-379-3111 127 C
vrobelotto@yhc.edu
ROBEN, Paul, W .... 858-246-0473.. 69 D
pwroben@ucsd.edu
ROBERGE, Stacia .... 603-752-1060 273 D
sroberge@ccsnh.edu
ROBERSON, Antoinette . 718-270-6055 295 A
aroberson@mec.cuny.edu
ROBERSON, Ashley .... 252-492-2061 338 F
robersona@vgcc.edu
ROBERSON, Caprice ..... 702-651-7693 271 A
caprice.roberson@csn.edu
ROBERSON, Chris .... 864-578-8770 412 B
croberson@sherman.edu
ROBERSON, Emily .... 903-923-2043 436 D
eroberson@etbu.edu
ROBERSON, James, A .. 919-335-1020 338 G
jaroberson@waketech.edu
ROBERSON, Janet .... 434-791-5891 464 O
roberson@averett.edu
ROBERSON, Jeff .... 201-360-4054 278 C
jrobersonjr@hccc.edu
ROBERSON, John .... 910-893-1205 327 E
robersonj@campbell.edu
ROBERSON, Judith .... 225-768-1754 186 F
judith.roberson@franu.edu
ROBERSON, Kim .... 501-337-5000.. 18 J
rroberson@coto.edu
ROBERSON, Mark, A .... 951-552-8652.. 27 J
maroberson@calbaptist.edu
ROBERSON, Miriam, C . 904-819-6204.. 98 E
registrar@flagler.edu
ROBERSON, Mo .... 949-214-3210.. 40 F
mo.roberson@cui.edu
ROBERSON, Richard, E . 717-796-5045 390 E
rroberso@messiah.edu
ROBERSON, Rita, G ...... 304-896-7425 489 E
rita.roberson@southernwv.edu
ROBERSON, Robin .... 580-559-5467 366 C
robrrob@ecok.edu
ROBERSON, TOR,
Shawn .... 740-283-6463 353 B
sroberson@franciscan.edu
ROBERSON, Valerie, R .. 857-701-1280 215 E
vroberson@rcc.mass.edu
ROBERSON, Wendy ...... 651-846-1757 241 B
wendy.roberson@saintpaul.edu
ROBERSON-SIMMS,
Deborah .... 310-243-3301.. 31 B
droberson-simms@csudh.edu
ROBERT, Bernadette ...... 213-477-2511.. 52 G
brobert@msmu.edu
ROBERT, Deidre, D .... 225-771-4680 190 G
deidre_robert@sus.edu
ROBERT, Deidre, D .... 225-771-4680 190 H
deidre_robert@sus.edu
ROBERT, Strong .... 843-355-4173 414 F
strongr@wiltech.edu
ROBERTS, Aaron .... 317-916-7827 157 H
aroberts217@ivytech.edu
ROBERTS, Aaron .... 402-643-7233 266 G
aaron.roberts@cune.edu
ROBERTS, Adam .... 706-880-8004 121 A
aroberts@lagrange.edu
ROBERTS, Al .... 806-720-7125 439 H
alwin.roberts@lcu.edu
ROBERTS, Alan, P .... 845-687-5050 323 E
robertsal@sunyulster.edu
ROBERTS, Allison .... 904-826-8543.. 98 E
aroberts@flagler.edu

ROBERTS, Amber .... 616-331-3266 224 E
roberamb@gvsu.edu
ROBERTS, Annette .... 715-634-4790 493 I
aroberts@lco.edu
ROBERTS, Barbara .... 360-676-2772 482 D
broberts@nwic.edu
ROBERTS, Bill .... 906-487-2921 227 E
wrrobert@mtu.edu
ROBERTS, Brent .... 434-395-2083 469 A
robertsbs@longwood.edu
ROBERTS, Brian .... 602-639-7500.. 12 J
ROBERTS, Brian .... 918-647-1320 365 H
broberts@carlalbert.edu
ROBERTS, Carmen .... 406-771-4392 264 G
carmen.roberts@gfcmsu.edu
ROBERTS, Charles, H ... 859-846-5750 183 E
chroberts@midway.edu
ROBERTS, Charlie .... 360-676-2772 482 D
chroberts@nwic.edu
ROBERTS, Chell .... 619-260-4627.. 71 J
croberts@sandiego.edu
ROBERTS, Cheryl .... 206-546-4551 484 G
cheryl.roberts@shoreline.edu
ROBERTS, Cheryl, A ..... 340-692-4192 514 E
crobert@uvi.edu
ROBERTS, Christina ...... 202-687-6335.. 92 A
cdr44@georgetown.edu
ROBERTS,
Christopher, B .... 334-844-2308.... 4 E
robercr@auburn.edu
ROBERTS, Clint .... 760-750-4470.. 33 B
clroberts@csusm.edu
ROBERTS, Cynthia .... 219-980-6636 156 E
robertcs@iun.edu
ROBERTS, Daniel .... 985-545-1500 187 H
ROBERTS, Daniel, M ..... 804-524-6709 477 B
droberts@vsu.edu
ROBERTS, Dave .... 213-740-4154.. 72 B
ROBERTS, Dave .... 775-674-7100 271 D
droberts@tmcc.edu
ROBERTS, Dave .... 573-875-7400 251 F
droberts@ccis.edu
ROBERTS, Deborah .... 707-664-3236.. 34 C
deborah.roberts@sonoma.edu
ROBERTS, Dennis .... 530-938-5313.. 39 F
roberts@siskiyous.edu
ROBERTS, Douglas .... 925-485-5253.. 35 N
ROBERTS, Douglas, P ... 573-341-4300 261 E
robertsdp@mst.edu
ROBERTS, Dustin .... 870-584-1172.. 22 G
droberts@cccua.edu
ROBERTS, Ed .... 240-567-7688 200 C
edward.robert@montgomerycollege.
edu
ROBERTS, Edward .... 828-898-8777 330 E
robertse@lmc.edu
ROBERTS, Ellen .... 630-942-2800 135 A
ROBERTS, Gary .... 269-927-8771 226 D
roberts@lakemichigancollege.edu
ROBERTS, Gary, O .... 607-871-2715 289 H
roberts@alfred.edu
ROBERTS, Gary, R .... 309-677-3167 133 B
president@bradley.edu
ROBERTS, Gina .... 419-530-5812 363 E
gina.roberts@utoledo.edu
ROBERTS, Glenda, V ..... 607-746-4545 320 G
robertgv@delhi.edu
ROBERTS, Gregory .... 716-926-8935 301 H
groberts@hilbert.edu
ROBERTS, Gregory, L .... 520-494-5445.. 11 K
greg.roberts@centralaz.edu
ROBERTS, Gregory, W .. 434-982-3200 473 A
groberts@virginia.edu
ROBERTS, Howard, V .... 606-218-5019 185 D
howardroberts@upike.edu
ROBERTS, James .... 570-674-6758 390 G
jroberts@misericordia.edu
ROBERTS, Janet, E .... 248-341-2121 229 A
jerobert@oaklandcc.edu
ROBERTS, Jean .... 231-777-0519 228 D
jean.roberts@muskegoncc.edu
ROBERTS, Jeanne, M .... 813-253-6203 112 J
jroberts@ut.edu
ROBERTS, Jeffrey .... 619-594-5142.. 33 E
jroberts@sdsu.edu
ROBERTS, Jennifer .... 508-678-2811 213 G
jennifer.roberts@bristolcc.edu
ROBERTS, Jerilyn, C ..... 605-394-6729 417 B
jerilyn.roberts@sdsmt.edu
ROBERTS, Jerry .... 972-825-4870 445 A
jroberts@sagu.edu
ROBERTS, Jim .... 315-792-5439 307 D
jroberts@mvcc.edu

ROBERTS, John .... 706-778-8500 123 B
johnroberts@piedmont.edu
ROBERTS, John .... 903-593-8311 448 H
jroberts@texascollege.edu
ROBERTS, Jonathan ...... 501-279-4257.. 19 D
jroberts@harding.edu
ROBERTS, Juanita .... 334-727-8894.... 7 D
jroberts@tuskegee.edu
ROBERTS, Judy .... 775-831-1314 272 D
jroberts@sierranevada.edu
ROBERTS, Juli .... 909-593-3511.. 70 D
jroberts@laverne.edu
ROBERTS, Julia .... 910-788-6327 338 A
julia.roberts@sccnc.edu
ROBERTS, Kathleen .... 859-572-6630 184 A
robertsk10@nku.edu
ROBERTS, Kelly .... 785-738-9060 176 A
kroberts@ncktc.edu
ROBERTS, Ken .... 573-876-7171 260 F
kroberts@stephens.edu
ROBERTS, Kyle .... 651-255-6108 243 D
kroberts@unitedseminary.edu
ROBERTS, Lance .... 605-394-2256 417 B
lance.roberts@sdsmt.edu
ROBERTS, Leanne, M .... 814-824-2268 390 C
lroberts2@mercyhurst.edu
ROBERTS, Leigh .... 203-285-2622.. 85 E
lroberts@gwcc.commnet.edu
ROBERTS, Lila .... 678-466-4400 116 E
lilaroberts@clayton.edu
ROBERTS, Lindsay .... 812-488-3101 161 A
lr155@evansville.edu
ROBERTS, Lindsey .... 229-391-5055 113 F
lroberts@abac.edu
ROBERTS, Lisa .... 618-374-5068 146 E
lisa.roberts@principia.edu
ROBERTS, Lonnie .... 912-427-5816 116 F
lroberts@coastalpines.edu
ROBERTS, Mandy .... 918-647-1214 365 H
mroberts@carlalbert.edu
ROBERTS, Marie .... 601-553-3440 247 A
jrober26@meridiancc.edu
ROBERTS, Mark .... 918-495-6723 368 I
mroberts@oru.edu
ROBERTS, Mark, A .... 770-720-5504 123 E
mar@reinhardt.edu
ROBERTS, Mark, A .... 803-535-5575 407 G
maroberts@claflin.edu
ROBERTS, Marlene .... 715-675-3331 500 E
robertsm@ntc.edu
ROBERTS, Mary .... 478-445-5384 118 C
mary.roberts@gcsu.edu
ROBERTS, Matt .... 843-953-5546 408 E
robertsmj1@cofc.edu
ROBERTS, Matthew .... 423-652-4780 420 H
mroberts@king.edu
ROBERTS, Melissa .... 601-266-5390 249 F
melissa.b.roberts@usm.edu
ROBERTS, Michael .... 907-773-4462 134 C
mroberts39@ccc.edu
ROBERTS, Michael, H ... 843-349-2282 408 C
mroberts@coastal.edu
ROBERTS, Michelle, A .. 662-846-4000 245 H
mroberts@deltastate.edu
ROBERTS, Nancy .... 610-606-4640 381 A
nroberts@cedarcrest.edu
ROBERTS, Nathan .... 816-383-7100 257 A
nroberts4@missouriwestern.edu
ROBERTS, Nathan .... 217-732-3168 141 H
njroberts@lincolnchristian.edu
ROBERTS, Nathan .... 337-482-6678 192 E
nathan@louisiana.edu
ROBERTS, Patty, J .... 318-869-5747 186 B
pjrobert@centenary.edu
ROBERTS, Paul .... 740-474-8896 358 F
proberts@ohiochristian.edu
ROBERTS, Paul, G .... 773-508-3163 142 D
prober2@luc.edu
ROBERTS, Pauline .... 225-923-2524 186 A
ROBERTS, Phyllis .... 276-964-7588 475 I
phyllis.roberts@sw.edu
ROBERTS, Rachel .... 870-245-5593.. 20 E
robertsr@obu.edu
ROBERTS, Rachel .... 903-877-7077 456 D
rachel.roberts@uthct.edu
ROBERTS, Randal, R ..... 503-517-1860 378 A
rroberts@westernseminary.edu
ROBERTS, Randy .... 620-235-4878 176 F
reroberts@pittstate.edu
ROBERTS, Rick .... 904-620-2955 110 A
rtrobert@unf.edu
ROBERTS, Roshell .... 405-682-1611 367 H
roshell.a.roberts@occc.edu

ROBERTS, Russ ..... 262-695-3468 500 H rroberts@wctc.edu
ROBERTS, Ruth ..... 215-596-8697 401 G
ROBERTS, Ruth ..... 972-825-4656 445 A rroberts@sagu.edu
ROBERTS, Ryan ..... 920-686-6204 496 A ryan.roberts@sl.edu
ROBERTS, Ryan ..... 217-786-2271 142 B
ROBERTS, Sarah, E ..... 615-353-3117 425 D sarah.roberts@nscc.edu
ROBERTS, Sarah-Kate ... 205-226-4979.... 5 A skrobert@bsc.edu
ROBERTS, Scott ..... 860-486-2698.. 88 E sroberts@foundation.uconn.edu
ROBERTS, Sheila, J ..... 419-372-5387 348 H sjrober@bgsu.edu
ROBERTS, Sonja ..... 404-756-4012 114 G sroberts@atlm.edu
ROBERTS, Stephanie ..... 912-427-5835 116 F sroberts@coastalpines.edu
ROBERTS, Stephanie ..... 304-326-1310 488 F sroberts@salemu.edu
ROBERTS, Stephen ..... 573-341-4138 261 E provost@mst.edu
ROBERTS, Thomas ..... 785-243-1435 172 F
ROBERTS, Tracy ..... 270-809-3380 183 G troberts@murraystate.edu
ROBERTS, Valerie ..... 530-938-5555.. 39 F
ROBERTS, Warren ..... 972-524-3341 445 C swccadmissions@yahoo.com
ROBERTS, William ..... 201-692-2629 277 K william_roberts@fdu.edu
ROBERTS, William ..... 909-607-8594.. 37 G william_roberts@kgi.edu
ROBERTS, William ..... 619-532-9522 504 B william.roberts@usuhs.edu
ROBERTS-BRESLIN, Jan 617-824-8912 208 H jan_roberts_breslin@emerson.edu
ROBERTS-CAMPS, Traci 209-946-2343.. 70 E trobertscamps@pacific.edu
ROBERTS-COOPER, Cathy ..... 912-478-5371 119 C crobertscooper@georgiasouthern.edu
ROBERTS-JOHNSON, Wendy-Anne ..... 215-825-8200 403 H wjohnson@phmc.org
ROBERTS-LEONARD, Terri, L ..... 317-738-8119 154 J troberts@franklincollege.edu
ROBERTSHAW, Mia ..... 415-485-9304.. 39 C mrobertshaw@marin.edu
ROBERTSON, Aimee ..... 612-343-4143 242 H amrobert@northcentral.edu
ROBERTSON, Ali ..... 269-956-3931 225 F robertsona@kellogg.edu
ROBERTSON, Anne ..... 773-702-8512 150 J awrx@uchicago.edu
ROBERTSON, Beverly .... 828-689-1244 331 A brobertson@mhu.edu
ROBERTSON, Brett ..... 619-216-6617.. 65 F brobertson@swccd.edu
ROBERTSON, Bruce ..... 920-403-3045 495 I bruce.robertson@snc.edu
ROBERTSON, Charlene . 617-732-2786 216 B charlene.robertson@mcphs.edu
ROBERTSON, Cheryl ..... 713-221-8256 453 B robertsonc@uhd.edu
ROBERTSON, Chuck ..... 601-477-4277 246 F chuck.robertson@jcjc.edu
ROBERTSON, Clyde ..... 504-286-5384 190 I crobertson@suno.edu
ROBERTSON, Craig, L ... 618-537-6856 143 B clrobertson@mckendree.edu
ROBERTSON, Dalana ..... 615-322-5179 428 D dalana.robertson@vanderbilt.edu
ROBERTSON, Dave ..... 479-788-7799.. 21 H dave.robertson@uafs.edu
ROBERTSON, Don ..... 270-809-6839 183 G drobertson@murraystate.edu
ROBERTSON, Donna ..... 201-692-2196 277 K donnamjr@fdu.edu
ROBERTSON, Elizabeth, C ..... 914-251-6039 319 E elizabeth.robertson@purchase.edu
ROBERTSON, Emily ..... 704-406-3249 329 A erobertson@gardner-webb.edu
ROBERTSON, Greg ..... 773-577-8052 115 F grobertson@coynecollege.edu
ROBERTSON, Ian ..... 608-262-3482 496 C engr-dean@wisc.edu
ROBERTSON, Iris ..... 304-326-1274 488 F iris.robertson@salemu.edu
ROBERTSON, J. D ..... 435-652-7576 460 G jrobertson@dixie.edu
ROBERTSON, Jacob, M 951-552-8677.. 27 J jmrobertson@calbaptist.edu
ROBERTSON, Janet ..... 903-566-7325 456 A jrobertson@uttyler.edu
ROBERTSON, Jeff ..... 479-968-0498.. 18 C jrobertson@atu.edu
ROBERTSON, Jeff ..... 479-968-0398.. 18 C jrobertson@atu.edu
ROBERTSON, Jennifer ... 407-582-6150 112 K jrobertson@valenciacollege.edu
ROBERTSON, Jill ..... 303-273-3207.. 78 I jirobert@is.mines.edu
ROBERTSON, Jim ..... 845-574-4466 313 C jrobert7@sunyrockland.edu
ROBERTSON, Joel ..... 423-652-4724 420 H jcrobert@king.edu
ROBERTSON, John ..... 972-860-7709 434 K jrobertson@dcccd.edu
ROBERTSON, Jon, H ..... 561-237-7701 102 V jrobertson@lynn.edu
ROBERTSON, Kristy ..... 276-328-0220 473 B kej5c@virginia.edu
ROBERTSON, Leonard ... 972-721-5236 452 D lrobertson@udallas.edu
ROBERTSON, Leonard, A ..... 972-721-5236 452 D lrobertson@udallas.edu
ROBERTSON, TOR, Luke ..... 740-283-3771 353 B lrobertson@franciscan.edu
ROBERTSON, M.G. (Pat) ..... 757-352-4036 470 H lfinn@regent.edu
ROBERTSON, Michael, N ..... 901-722-3226 424 C mike.robertson@sco.edu
ROBERTSON, Paul ..... 520-383-8401.. 16 D probertson@tocc.edu
ROBERTSON, Sharon, N ..... 703-323-3087 475 C srobertson@nvcc.edu
ROBERTSON, Stacey ..... 585-245-5531 318 E robertsons@geneseo.edu
ROBERTSON, Sue ..... 630-889-6527 144 G srobertson@nuhs.edu
ROBERTSON, Tim ..... 402-872-2411 268 F trobertson@peru.edu
ROBERTSON, Tracee ..... 940-397-8948 440 F tracee.robertson@msutexas.edu
ROBERTSON, Trey ..... 601-928-6264 247 E trey.robertson@mgccc.edu
ROBERTSON, William, J ..... 717-866-5775 383 H wrobertson@evangelical.edu
ROBERTSON-JAMES, Candace ..... 215-951-1430 387 C robertsonjames@lasalle.edu
ROBERTSON LOWE, Damaris ..... 909-621-8148.. 63 E droberts@scrippscollege.edu
ROBETOR, Kathleen ..... 518-783-2302 315 J krobetor@siena.edu
ROBEY, Jason ..... 314-434-4044 252 B jason.robey@covenantseminary.edu
ROBICHAUD, Betin ..... 508-213-2292 217 E betin.robichaud@nichols.edu
ROBICHAUD, David ..... 508-531-2731 212 B drobichaud@bridgew.edu
ROBICHAUD, Keith ..... 617-333-2210 208 E krobicha0804@curry.edu
ROBICHAUX, Renee ..... 337-550-1301 189 A rerobich@lsue.edu
ROBICHEAUX, Wendi .... 337-521-8932 188 C wendi.robicheaux@solacc.edu
ROBIDOUX, Patricia ..... 909-607-0107.. 37 G probidoux@kgi.edu
ROBIE, Candra ..... 970-675-3356.. 78 G candra.robie@cncc.edu
ROBILOTTO, Philip ..... 410-706-2378 202 D probilotto@umaryland.edu
ROBIN, Tracy ..... 212-229-1671 308 C robint@newschool.edu
ROBINETT, Laura ..... 402-375-7370 268 G larobin1@wsc.edu
ROBINS, Anthony, G ..... 412-397-6482 397 G robins@rmu.edu
ROBINS, Duncan ..... 707-826-3666.. 33 D dr1509@humboldt.edu
ROBINS, Luke ..... 360-417-6200 483 B lrobins@pencol.edu
ROBINS, Michael ..... 831-477-3521.. 27 G mirobins@cabrillo.edu
ROBINS, Rochelle ..... 213-884-4133.. 24 A rrobins@ajrca.edu
ROBINSON, Alexandra .. 212-817-7100 293 F arobinson@gc.cuny.edu
ROBINSON, Amanda ..... 662-846-4709 245 H arobinson@deltastate.edu
ROBINSON, Anafe ..... 818-610-6515.. 49 C robinsa@piercecollege.edu
ROBINSON, Andrea ..... 507-222-5465 234 F arobinson@carleton.edu
ROBINSON, Andrew ..... 478-471-4394 120 F
ROBINSON, Angela ..... 229-430-3500 113 I arobinson@albanytech.edu
ROBINSON, Angela ..... 309-672-5513 143 D arobinson@methodistcol.edu
ROBINSON, Ann ..... 716-566-783 298 B arobinso@daemen.edu
ROBINSON, April ..... 205-726-2803.... 6 E alrobins@samford.edu
ROBINSON, April ..... 863-297-1020 105 A arobinson@polk.edu
ROBINSON, Ashley ..... 601-979-2291 246 E ashley.n.robinson@jsums.edu
ROBINSON, Barry ..... 206-934-4349 484 A
ROBINSON, Beverly ..... 912-583-3260 115 E brobinson@bpc.edu
ROBINSON, Beverly ..... 972-825-4798 445 A brobinson@sagu.edu
ROBINSON, Brian ..... 916-608-6330.. 50 H robinsb@flc.losrios.edu
ROBINSON, Brigette ..... 517-990-1386 225 C robinsobrigetta@jccmi.edu
ROBINSON, Bryan ..... 910-521-6184 343 B bryan.robinson@uncp.edu
ROBINSON, Carlos ..... 405-466-3428 366 F carlos.m.robinson@langston.edu
ROBINSON, Cassandra, M ..... 301-860-4000 203 C crobinson@bowiestate.edu
ROBINSON, Chad ..... 970-943-3123.. 84 D crobinson@western.edu
ROBINSON, Charles ..... 479-575-7955.. 21 G cfrobins@uark.edu
ROBINSON, Charles, F . 510-987-9800.. 68 C charles.robinson@ucop.edu
ROBINSON, Cheryl ..... 407-582-3457 112 K crobinson@valenciacollege.edu
ROBINSON, Chris ..... 870-575-7177.. 22 E robinsonce@uapb.edu
ROBINSON, Chris ..... 606-218-5226 185 D chrisrobinson@upike.edu
ROBINSON, Christine ... 704-687-5385 342 E crobinson@uncc.edu
ROBINSON, Christopher, D ..... 336-246-3900 339 B cdrobinson877@wilkescc.edu
ROBINSON, Daniel, C .. 909-469-5561.. 74 I drobinson@westernu.edu
ROBINSON, Daphne, D 219-989-2370 159 G robinsdd@pnw.edu
ROBINSON, Dario ..... 909-869-3065.. 30 D drobinson1@cpp.edu
ROBINSON, Dave ..... 641-269-9990 165 J daver@grinnell.edu
ROBINSON, David ..... 510-642-7791.. 68 D dmrobinson@berkeley.edu
ROBINSON, David ..... 212-650-8357 293 D drobinson2@ccny.cuny.edu
ROBINSON, David, W ... 503-494-4460 375 B provost@ohsu.edu
ROBINSON, Dawnelle ... 256-331-5310.... 3 C dawnelle.robinson@nwscc.edu
ROBINSON, Debra A, G ..... 573-341-6154 261 E debrar@mst.edu
ROBINSON, OSB, Denis ..... 812-357-6522 160 D drobinson@saintmeinrad.edu
ROBINSON, Dennis ..... 972-825-4814 445 A dbobinson@sagu.edu
ROBINSON, Derek ..... 307-382-1896 502 I derek@westernwyoming.edu
ROBINSON, Dominique, A ..... 903-923-2455 458 G darobinson@wileyc.edu
ROBINSON, Edward ..... 202-274-2303.. 93 D library@potomac.edu
ROBINSON, Elaine ..... 541-917-4854 374 A robinse@linnbenton.edu
ROBINSON, Elwood, L . 336-750-2042 344 B robinsonel@wssu.edu
ROBINSON, Eric ..... 502-597-6646 182 H eric.robinson@kysu.edu
ROBINSON, Erin ..... 941-893-2856 105 K erobinso@ringling.edu
ROBINSON, Evan ..... 413-796-2323 219 F erobinson@wne.edu
ROBINSON, Evan, T ..... 402-280-1828 266 I evanrobinson@creighton.edu
ROBINSON, Freddie ..... 804-257-5783 477 C frobinson@vuu.edu
ROBINSON, Gail ..... 901-458-8232 422 C grobinson@memphisseminary.edu
ROBINSON, Gail, D ..... 901-334-5826 422 C grobinson@memphisseminary.edu
ROBINSON, Gary ..... 607-431-4420 301 D robinsong@hartwick.edu
ROBINSON, Grace, G ... 805-437-3615.. 30 F grace.robinson@csuci.edu
ROBINSON, Gregory ..... 407-823-5348 109 E greg.robinson@ucf.edu
ROBINSON, Gregory ..... 847-214-7226 136 F grobinson@elgin.edu
ROBINSON, Gregory ..... 702-992-2000 271 C
ROBINSON, Gretchen ... 563-884-5427 168 I gretchen.robinson@palmer.edu
ROBINSON, Guin ..... 205-853-1200.... 2 G grobinson@jeffersonstate.edu
ROBINSON, Irene, M .... 281-756-3501 429 I irobinson@alvincollege.edu
ROBINSON, Isaac ..... 425-739-8456 482 A isaac.robinson@lwtech.edu
ROBINSON, Jabrina ..... 518-783-2328 315 J jrobinson@siena.edu
ROBINSON, Jacqueline . 256-469-7333.... 5 I fin@hbc1.edu
ROBINSON, James, R ... 540-568-6991 468 F robinsjr@jmu.edu
ROBINSON, Janice, S ... 212-678-3732 322 G jsr167@tc.columbia.edu
ROBINSON, Jasmin ..... 630-617-3207 136 G jasmin.robinson@elmhurst.edu
ROBINSON, Jeffrey, B .. 919-866-5825 338 G jbrobinson@waketech.edu
ROBINSON, Jekeyma .... 941-309-4375 105 K jrobinso@ringling.edu
ROBINSON, Jerrell, W .. 516-876-3068 319 A robinsonj@oldwestbury.edu
ROBINSON, Jessica ..... 619-660-4301.. 44 H jessica.robinson@gcccd.edu
ROBINSON, Jill ..... 714-556-3610.. 72 F jill.robinson@vanguard.edu
ROBINSON, Jimada ..... 757-481-5005 478 C
ROBINSON, JoAnn ..... 304-327-4567 489 P jrobinson@bluefieldstate.edu
ROBINSON, Jodi ..... 602-383-8228.. 16 F jrobinson@uat.edu
ROBINSON, John ..... 910-962-3154 343 C robinsonj@uncw.edu
ROBINSON, Judy ..... 863-680-3936.. 99 H jrobinson2@flsouthern.edu
ROBINSON, Julie, A ..... 913-735-2360 176 I ksd_robinson_chambers@ksd.uscourts.gov
ROBINSON, Kalani ..... 912-650-6223 124 E karobinson@southuniversity.edu
ROBINSON, Kayla ..... 315-279-5814 304 A krobinson@keuka.edu
ROBINSON, Kelley ..... 518-244-2201 313 D robink3@sage.edu
ROBINSON, Kimberlely, D ..... 540-887-7033 469 B krobinson@marybaldwin.edu
ROBINSON, Kristen ..... 805-378-1434.. 72 H krobinson@vcccd.edu
ROBINSON, Kristen ..... 217-732-3155 141 I krobinson@lincolncollege.edu
ROBINSON, Kristin ..... 559-583-2523.. 39 E kristinr@cos.edu
ROBINSON, Kyle, W ..... 202-685-3506 503 I kyle.w.robinson.mil@ndu.edu
ROBINSON, LaNita ..... 218-733-7616 238 F l.robinson@lsc.edu
ROBINSON, Larry ..... 850-599-3225 108 I larry.robinson@famu.edu
ROBINSON, Larry, J ..... 701-845-7217 346 A larry.robinson@vcsu.edu
ROBINSON, Leanne ..... 912-871-1626 122 I lrobinson@ogeecheetech.edu
ROBINSON, Lois ..... 251-578-1313.... 3 D lrobinson@rstc.edu
ROBINSON, Louester .... 843-722-5556 413 B lou.robinson@tridenttech.edu
ROBINSON, Luke ..... 616-526-8686 222 A lrobinso@calvin.edu

ROBINSON, Lynn .... 401-598-1405 404 I lrobinson@jwu.edu
ROBINSON, Lynne .... 207-893-7843 195 F lrobinson@sjcme.edu
ROBINSON, Lynne, P ... 301-447-5296 200 E lrobinso@msmary.edu
ROBINSON, M. Kevin ... 334-844-4389.... 4 E robinmk@auburn.edu
ROBINSON, Maria .... 979-458-6221 446 C mrobinson@tamus.edu
ROBINSON, Marjorie .... 951-785-2167.. 47 C mrobinso@lasierra.edu
ROBINSON, Mark .... 304-696-6603 490 D robinsonma@marshall.edu
ROBINSON, Mary .... 716-896-0700 324 E robinsonm@villa.edu
ROBINSON, Mason .... 501-337-5000.. 18 J mrobinson@coto.edu
ROBINSON, Maureen .... 847-543-2444 135 B mrobinson@clcillinois.edu
ROBINSON, Michael ..... 901-435-1433 421 A michael_robinson@loc.edu
ROBINSON, Michael ..... 601-979-4299 246 E michael.a.robinson@jsums.edu
ROBINSON, Michael ..... 937-376-0425 364 D mrobinson@wilberforce.edu
ROBINSON, Michael ..... 405-744-6523 368 B michael.robinson@okstate.edu
ROBINSON, Mike .... 205-226-4936.... 5 A mrobinso@bsc.edu
ROBINSON, Mike .... 541-776-9942 375 E mike.r@pacificbible.edu
ROBINSON, Mitch .... 931-221-7883 418 D robinsonm@apsu.edu
ROBINSON, Myya .... 334-291-4921.... 1 H myya.robinson@cv.edu
ROBINSON, Nakia .... 334-420-4479.... 3 H nrobinson@trenholmstate.edu
ROBINSON, Natalie .... 619-876-4261.. 67 M nrobinson@usuniversity.edu
ROBINSON, Pam .... 405-585-4250 367 F pam.robinson@okbu.edu
ROBINSON, Pamela ...... 413-205-3212 205 A pamela.robinson@aic.edu
ROBINSON, Paul, A ...... 734-647-3502 231 E probins@umich.edu
ROBINSON, Peter, J ..... 585-275-4036 323 J peter_robinson@urmc.rochester.edu
ROBINSON, Ralph .... 302-857-7381.. 89 F rrobinson@desu.edu
ROBINSON, Raphel .... 352-854-2322.. 96 O robinsra@cf.edu
ROBINSON, Ray .... 314-918-2501 253 A rrobinson@eden.edu
ROBINSON, Regina .... 617-873-0470 207 F regina.robinson@cambridgecollege.edu
ROBINSON, Regina .... 318-670-9617 190 J rrobinson@susla.edu
ROBINSON, Reginald, L .... 785-864-7100 177 D rlrobinson@ku.edu
ROBINSON, Rita .... 662-329-7409 248 A sm8076@bncollege.com
ROBINSON, Robert .... 678-717-3654 126 A robert.robinson@ung.edu
ROBINSON, Robert .... 909-621-8136.. 57 F robert.robinson@pomona.edu
ROBINSON, Robert .... 802-654-2524 463 B rrobinson@smcvt.edu
ROBINSON, Ronald, R .. 864-597-4051 414 H robinsonrr1@wofford.edu
ROBINSON, Roy .... 253-879-3653 485 E rrobinson@pugetsound.edu
ROBINSON, Rush .... 314-652-0300 259 A rlrobinson@slchc.edu
ROBINSON, Sara, C ...... 207-941-7617 194 A robinsons@husson.edu
ROBINSON, Shadow ...... 731-881-7380 428 B srobin47@utm.edu
ROBINSON, Shannon .... 315-268-7766 296 A srobinso@clarkson.edu
ROBINSON, Shari, A .... 603-862-2090 274 G shari.robinson@unh.edu
ROBINSON, Sharon ...... 704-233-8249 344 G s.robinson@wingate.edu
ROBINSON, Sherry .... 859-622-6515 180 B sherry.robinson@eku.edu
ROBINSON, Sonya .... 512-863-1578 445 D robinsos@southwestern.edu
ROBINSON, Stephanie, R .... 559-244-2685.. 66 E stephanie.robinson@fresnocitycollege.edu
ROBINSON, Steve .... 801-581-3490 460 E steve.robinson@utah.edu
ROBINSON, Steve .... 567-661-7200 360 B steve_robinson@owens.edu
ROBINSON, Stuart .... 845-257-3910 317 B robinsos@newpaltz.edu
ROBINSON, Sturgis .... 928-350-4506.. 15 N sturgis.robinson@prescott.edu
ROBINSON, T. Hank .... 402-554-3750 270 B trobinson@unomaha.edu
ROBINSON, Tammy .... 650-306-3298.. 61 O robinsontammy@smccd.edu
ROBINSON, Terri, E ...... 330-325-6349 357 G trobinson@neomed.edu
ROBINSON, Terryl .... 520-206-4875.. 15 D trobinson17@pima.edu
ROBINSON, Tiffany .... 785-864-4422 177 D tiffany.robinson@ku.edu
ROBINSON, Tray .... 530-898-4764.. 31 A trobinson@csuchico.edu
ROBINSON, Wade .... 515-964-6222 164 C wrobinson4@dmacc.edu
ROBINSON, Warren .... 803-705-4662 407 A warren.robinson@benedict.edu
ROBINSON, Wayne .... 718-260-4900 295 B wrobinson@citytech.cuny.edu
ROBINSON, Wayne .... 718-473-8960 295 B wrobinson@citytech.cuny.edu
ROBINSON, Wayne .... 307-855-2104 501 V wrobinson@cwc.edu
ROBINSON, Wendi .... 614-947-6768 353 C wendi.robinson@franklin.edu
ROBINSON, Wendy .... 651-450-3692 238 D wrobins@inverhills.edu
ROBINSON, Wesley, L .. 540-464-7341 476 G robinsonwl@vmi.edu
ROBINSON, William .... 410-621-2355 203 A wrobinson3@umes.edu
ROBINSON, William, B . 610-892-1010 393 J wrobinson@pit.edu
ROBINSON, William, H 615-322-1507 428 D william.h.robinson@vanderbilt.edu
ROBINSON-COOLIDGE, Austin .... 507-222-5635 234 F arobinso@carleton.edu
ROBINSON-COOPER, Tia .... 651-450-3618 238 D trobinson@inverhills.edu
ROBINSON-FRUCHTL, Susan .... 814-472-3276 398 B srobinson@francis.edu
ROBINSON GAUTHIER, Nicole .... 832-813-6636 439 G nicole.robinsongauthier@lonestar.edu
ROBINSON HARRIS, Theresa, L .... 619-260-7733.. 71 J theresaharris@sandiego.edu
ROBINSON KLOOS, Jennifer .... 651-690-8831 242 R jrkloos@stkate.edu
ROBINSON-LEWIS, Denise .... 973-720-2885 284 I lewisd@wpunj.edu
ROBINSON-MORRIS, David .... 504-520-5797 193 A drmorris@xula.edu
ROBINSON-PAUL, Ann . 701-231-8325 345 G anne.robinson-paul@ndsu.edu
ROBISON, Daniel, J ...... 515-294-3830 162 I robisond@iastate.edu
ROBISON, Lori .... 419-267-1342 358 A lrobison@northweststate.edu
ROBISON, Patricia .... 301-687-4234 203 E probison@frostburg.edu
ROBISON, Rick .... 925-969-2586.. 40 I rrobisonl@dvc.edu
ROBISON, Timothy .... 617-349-8747 210 H trobison@lesley.edu
ROBITAILLE, Marilyn .... 254-968-9632 446 E robitaille@tarleton.edu
ROBLEDO, Elizabeth ..... 562-475-5147.. 65 C elizabethrobledo@scuhs.edu
ROBLES, Amanda .... 505-566-3588 288 A roblesa@sanjuancollege.edu
ROBLES, Ben .... 713-221-8605 453 B roblesb@uhd.edu
ROBLES, Jonathan .... 623-935-8052.. 13 A jonathan.robles@estrellamountain.edu
ROBLES, Martha .... 209-575-6373.. 75 J roblesm@mjc.edu
ROBLES, Monica .... 407-265-8383.. 96 A
ROBLES, Pedro .... 787-786-3030 512 B probles@ucb.edu.pr
ROBLES, Quetsy, M ...... 787-840-2575 510 J qrobles@psm.edu
ROBLES, Ray .... 787-864-2222 509 C ray.robles@guayama.inter.edu
ROBLES, Reinaldo .... 787-250-1912 509 D rrobles@metro.inter.edu
ROBLES, Rinaldo .... 787-864-2222 509 C rinaldo.robles@guayama.inter.edu
ROBLES, Sonia .... 510-436-1092.. 45 D robles@hnu.edu
ROBLES, Yvette .... 626-968-1328.. 47 G
ROBLES JIMENEZ, Elizabeth .... 213-477-2769.. 52 G ejimenez@msmu.edu
ROBLES-LOPEZ, Irene ... 520-206-3982.. 15 D irlopez@pima.edu
ROBLES MARRERO, Alex .... 787-620-2040 506 C arobles@aupr.edu
ROBLES-ROMAN, Carol 212-772-4000 294 C
ROBNETT, Charles .... 903-886-5056 447 B charles.robnett@tamuc.edu
ROBNETT, Kathryn .... 214-333-6850 434 I kathryn@dbu.edu
ROBOMAN, Lourdes ..... 691-350-2296 505 B comfsmyap@comfsm.fm
ROBOTHAM, Tena .... 847-628-2002 140 C trobotham@judsonu.edu
ROBSHAW, Jeff .... 262-564-3676 499 F robshawj@gtc.edu
ROBSON, James .... 803-327-8047 415 A jrobson@yorktech.edu
ROBSON, Nicole .... 814-262-3820 393 H nrobson@pennhighlands.edu
ROBUSTELLI, Carlo .... 309-556-3636 139 G crobuste@iwu.edu
ROBY, Clare .... 530-898-5674.. 31 A croby@csuchico.edu
ROBY, Jennifer, L .... 419-772-2020 358 H j-roby@onu.edu
ROBY, Mark .... 305-809-3165.. 99 C mark.roby@fkcc.edu
ROBYN, Elisa .... 303-458-4081.. 82 E erobyn@regis.edu
ROC, Nadege .... 914-251-6000 319 E nadege.roc@purchase.edu
ROCAP, Donna .... 845-431-8066 298 E rocap@sunydutchess.edu
ROCCO, Brian .... 212-774-4801 306 A brocco@mmm.edu
ROCCO, Denine .... 508-531-1276 212 B drocco@bridgew.edu
ROCCO, Karen, S .... 412-362-8500 396 G krocco@pims.edu
ROCHA, Mark .... 415-239-3303.. 37 A mrocha@ccsf.edu
ROCHA, Nola .... 307-778-1231 502 D nrocha@lccc.wy.edu
ROCHE, Crystal .... 520-325-0123.. 16 C registrar@suva.edu
ROCHE, Daniel .... 201-684-7855 280 H droche@ramapo.edu
ROCHE, Isabel .... 802-440-4300 462 A president@bennington.edu
ROCHE, James .... 413-545-6330 211 D jimr@umass.edu
ROCHE, Karen .... 860-632-3010.. 87 C kroche@holyapostles.edu
ROCHE, Mary Beth .... 570-504-1589 387 D rochem@lackawanna.edu
ROCHE, Missy .... 618-235-2700 149 H melissa.roche@swic.edu
ROCHE, Sarah .... 610-341-5854 383 D sroche@eastern.edu
ROCHE, Stephen, H ...... 407-303-8016.. 94 D stephen.roche@ahu.edu
ROCHE, Susan .... 989-686-9254 223 G susanroche@delta.edu
ROCHESTER, Sylvia .... 410-462-8302 197 E srochester@bccc.edu
ROCHON, Ronald, S ..... 812-464-1756 161 E rochon@usi.edu
ROCK, Arlene, M .... 413-782-1538 219 F arlene.rock@wne.edu
ROCK, David .... 662-915-7063 249 D rock@olemiss.edu
ROCKAFELLOW, Colleen .... 708-456-0300 150 I colleenrockafellow@triton.edu
ROCKAFELLOW, Mollie . 815-740-3363 151 J mrockafellow@stfrancis.edu
ROCKHILL, Linda .... 718-779-1430 311 I
ROCKHILL, Wendy .... 206-934-6921 484 A wendy.rockhill@seattlecolleges.edu
ROCKMAN, Adam .... 718-997-5500 295 C adam.rockman@qc.cuny.edu
ROCKOVE, Moshe .... 732-367-1060 275 J mrockove@bmg.edu
ROCKOW, Amanda, O ... 972-883-2106 455 B arockow@utdallas.edu
ROCKWELL, Bill .... 740-351-3555 360 K brockwell@shawnee.edu
ROCKWELL, Grant .... 530-760-5168.. 68 E grockwell@ucdavis.edu
ROCKWELL, Kelly .... 716-851-1198 299 F rockwell@ecc.edu
ROCKWELL, Marlow ...... 501-420-1315.. 17 B marlow.rockwell@arkansasbaptist.edu
ROCKWELL, Rick .... 314-246-8280 262 C rickrockwell@webster.edu
ROCKWELL, Stephanie .. 509-313-6404 481 D rockwell@gonzaga.edu
RODACK, Alvin .... 614-251-4512 358 G rodacka@ohiodominican.edu
RODAK, Rebecca, K ...... 330-471-8340 355 L rrodak@malone.edu
RODARTE, Susana .... 915-831-2018 436 E srodart7@epcc.edu
RODAS, Mary .... 516-364-0808 309 A rodas@nycollege.edu
RODDEN, Jennifer .... 562-938-4113.. 48 D jrodden@lbcc.edu
RODDINI, Martin .... 516-572-9971 308 A martin.roddini@ncc.edu
RODDY, Jackie .... 615-226-3990 421 B jroddy@lincolntech.edu
RODDY, Marilyn .... 865-694-6529 425 F mlroddy@pstcc.edu
RODE, Joe .... 817-515-7741 445 G joe.rode@tccd.edu
RODECKER, Daniel .... 518-580-5860 316 A drodecke@skidmore.edu
RODELA, Daniel .... 661-654-3537.. 30 E drodela@csub.edu
RODELLA, Joseph .... 304-336-8495 490 F joe.rodella@westliberty.edu
RODEN, Don .... 256-840-4134.... 3 F don.roden@snead.edu
RODENBERG, Tamara, N .... 304-829-7111 487 G trodenberg@bethanywv.edu
RODERICK, Daniel .... 508-793-7578 208 A droderick@clarku.edu
RODERICK, Lori .... 309-794-7182 132 C loriroderick@augustana.edu
RODEZNO, Salomon ..... 216-397-1583 354 I srodezno@jcu.edu
RODGER, Andrea .... 360-650-4478 486 F andrea.rodger@wwu.edu
RODGER, Doug .... 712-324-5061 168 G drodger@nwicc.edu
RODGERS, Ardie .... 405-733-7434 369 I arodgers@rose.edu
RODGERS, Beverly .... 217-479-7025 142 I beverly.rodgers@mac.edu
RODGERS, Chris, T .... 402-280-2455 266 I chrisrodgers@creighton.edu
RODGERS, Christopher . 718-817-4755 300 E chrodgers@fordham.edu
RODGERS, Coreen .... 909-621-8111.. 37 E
RODGERS, Corey .... 562-938-5057.. 48 D crodgers@lbcc.edu
RODGERS, Corey .... 949-451-5409.. 64 F crodgers@ivc.edu
RODGERS, Denise, V .... 973-972-3645 282 A rodgerdv@ca.rutgers.edu
RODGERS, Frederick, B 607-871-2958 289 H rodgers@alfred.edu
RODGERS, Matt .... 334-347-2623.... 2 A mrodgers@escc.edu
RODGERS, Michael .... 270-686-4503 182 B mike.rodgers@kctcs.edu
RODGERS, Mike .... 325-649-8055 438 D mrodgers@hputx.edu
RODGERS, Phillip .... 210-784-1320 448 A prodgers@tamusa.edu
RODGERS, Ronald, F .... 603-862-0960 274 G ron.rodgers@usnh.edu
RODGERS, Ronald, F .... 603-862-0960 274 F ron.rodgers@usnh.edu
RODGERS, Ruby .... 270-534-3184 182 F ruby.rodgers@kctcs.edu
RODGERS, Ruth .... 317-955-6321 158 U rrodgers@marian.edu

RODRÍGUEZ, Ericka 787-844-8181 514 A
ericka.rodriguez@upr.edu
RODRÍGUEZ, Havidán 518-956-8030 316 D
presmail@albany.edu
RODRÍGUEZ, Ingrid 787-264-1912 509 F
ingrid_rodriguez_ramos@intersg.edu
RODRÍGUEZ, Inocencio 787-880-6577 513 A
inocencio.rodriguez@upr.edu
RODRÍGUEZ, Ivonne 787-844-8181 514 A
ivonne.rodriguez5@upr.edu
RODRÍGUEZ, Julio, A 787-766-1717 511 H
um_jurodrigu@suagm.edu
RODRÍGUEZ, Mayra 787-892-5115 509 F
mayra_rodriguez@sangerman.inter.edu
RODRÍGUEZ, Omayra 787-852-1430 508 C
orodriguez@hccpr.edu
RODRÍGUEZ-DÁVILA,
Soniemi 787-751-3601 512 G
soniemi.rodriguez@upr.edu
RODRÍGUEZ-FIGUEROA,
Victor 787-993-8898 513 B
victor.rodriguez47@upr.edu
RODRÍGUEZ-MARTORELL,
Nilsa 787-288-1118 512 A
RODRÍGUEZ-MEDINA,
José, R 787-765-8767 512 G
jose.rodriguez13@upr.edu
RODRÍGUEZ MONTALBAN,
Ramón 787-725-6500 506 G
RODRÍGUEZ-QUILICHINI,
Segundo 787-758-4417 512 G
rector.rcm@upr.edu
RODRÍGUEZ-RIVERA,
Rafael, E 787-751-1600 510 A
rrodriguez@juris.inter.edu
RODUIN, Cheyenne 425-235-2235 483 G
croduin@rtc.edu
ROE, Alexandria 608-265-0551 496 B
aroe@uwsa.edu
ROE, Antoneia 850-599-3183 108 I
antoneia.roe@famu.edu
ROE, Kelly 630-829-6010 132 E
kroe10@ben.edu
ROE, Laurie 541-956-7133 376 D
lroe@roguecc.edu
ROE, Lesa 214-752-8585 454 A
chancellor@unt.edu
ROE, Mark 406-377-9422 263 E
mroe@dawson.edu
ROE, Michael 845-431-8018 298 E
michael.roe@sunydutchess.edu
ROE, Robert, M 989-774-3933 222 C
roe1rm@cmich.edu
ROE, Robin 706-272-4559 117 C
rroe@daltonstate.edu
ROEBUCK, David 573-592-5358 262 E
david.roebuck@westminster-mo.edu
ROEBUCK, Paris 910-775-4577 343 B
paris.roebuck@uncp.edu
ROEBUCK, Randy 316-677-9437 178 B
rroebuck@watc.edu
ROECKER, Pamela 781-768-7147 218 C
pamela.roecker@regiscollege.edu
ROECKER-PHELPS,
Carolyn 937-229-3334 362 G
cphelps1@udayton.edu
ROECKS, Jan 650-574-6480 61 P
roecksj@smccd.edu
ROEDEL, Glenn 215-780-1296 398 G
groedel@salus.edu
ROEDEL, Mark 903-233-3296 439 E
markroedel@letu.edu
ROEDER, Jerry 413-782-1386 219 F
gerard.roeder@wne.edu
ROEDER, Lynn, M 252-328-9297 341 C
roederl@ecu.edu
ROEDIGER, Chris 928-524-7471 14 J
chris.roediger@npc.edu
ROEGGE, Fritz, J 202-685-3936 503 I
frederick.m.padilla.mil@ndu.edu
ROEHL, Bob 253-680-7389 478 E
broehl@batestech.edu
ROEHRICK, Randy 952-995-1525 238 B
randy.roehrick@hennepintech.edu
ROELFS, Melinda 620-235-4206 176 F
mroelfs@pittstate.edu
ROELFSEMA, Cheryl, E 815-224-0419 139 F
cheryl_roelfsema@ivcc.edu
ROELKE, Scott 651-450-3330 238 D
sroelke@inverhills.edu
ROELKE, Scott 651-423-8297 237 H
scott.roelke@dctc.edu
ROELOFS, Lyle, D 859-985-3522 179 C
roelofsl@berea.edu

ROEMER, Lara 309-341-5219 133 C
lroemer@sandburg.edu
ROEN, Duane 480-727-6513 10 I
duane.roen@asu.edu
ROEPKE, Melinda 419-755-4848 357 E
mroepke@ncstatecollege.edu
ROESCH, Adam 618-262-8641 139 A
roescha@iecc.edu
ROESCHENTHALER,
Robert 740-264-5591 352 H
rroeschenthaler@egcc.edu
ROESLER, Eric 715-346-3975 497 F
eric.roesler@uwsp.edu
ROESSEL, Charles 928-724-6669 12 C
cmroessel@dinecollege.edu
ROEST, Michael 415-503-6217 60 H
mroest@sfcm.edu
ROETHEMEYER,
Robert, V 260-452-2146 154 E
robert.roethemeyer@ctsfw.edu
ROETHER, Diane 940-668-4338 441 A
droether@nctc.edu
ROETHLER, Don 701-224-5485 346 B
donald.roethler@bismarckstate.edu
ROETTGER, Linda 219-464-5958 162 A
linda.roettger@valpo.edu
ROETTGER, Walter 646-768-5300 301 B
ROEWER, Anita 815-455-8737 143 A
aroewer@mchenry.edu
ROGALSKI, Kathryn 920-498-5401 500 F
kathryn.rogalski@nwtc.edu
ROGAN, Doreen 207-216-4320 195 C
drogan@yccc.edu
ROGELSTAD, Todd 701-845-7209 346 A
todd.rogelstad@vcsu.edu
ROGER-GORDON,
A. Patrick 212-346-1295 311 E
arogergordon@pace.edu
ROGERS, Andria 970-339-6518 76 G
andria.rogers@aims.edu
ROGERS, Benjamin 512-245-4822 450 E
br16@txstate.edu
ROGERS, Brandon 406-656-9950 265 I
brogers@yellowstonechristian.edu
ROGERS, Brenda 408-741-2011 74 C
brenda.rogers@wvm.edu
ROGERS, Brian 503-494-8362 375 B
cdrcadmin@ohsu.edu
ROGERS, Carl 770-533-6899 121 B
crogers@laniertech.edu
ROGERS, Cheryl 413-755-4454 215 F
carogers@stcc.edu
ROGERS, Christina 212-659-7200 304 B
crogers@tkc.edu
ROGERS, Christopher 847-970-4833 152 A
crogers@usml.edu
ROGERS, Christopher 803-777-5643 413 C
crogers@mailbox.sc.edu
ROGERS, Cindy, A 972-860-8187 435 A
car3810@dcccd.edu
ROGERS, Clarence 910-362-7062 332 H
cerogers281@mail.cfcc.edu
ROGERS, Craig 706-776-0104 123 B
crogers@piedmont.edu
ROGERS, Craig, L 270-789-5057 179 E
crogers@campbellsville.edu
ROGERS, Dave 602-384-2555 11 F
dave.rogers@bryanuniversity.edu
ROGERS, David, E 315-684-6044 321 D
rogersde@morrisville.edu
ROGERS, Deborah, A 215-641-6506 390 H
drogers@mc3.edu
ROGERS, Donnita 405-466-3262 366 F
ddrogers@langston.edu
ROGERS, Duke 785-227-3380 171 E
rogersk@bethanylb.edu
ROGERS, Edwin 808-675-3544 127 E
edwin.rogers@byuh.edu
ROGERS, Elsa, P 239-513-1122 101 C
erogers@hodges.edu
ROGERS, Fred 315-859-4672 301 C
jfrogers@hamilton.edu
ROGERS, Fred, A 507-222-5411 234 F
frogers@carleton.edu
ROGERS, Frederick 803-508-7272 406 E
rogersf@atc.edu
ROGERS, Gail 423-746-5202 426 F
grogers@tnwesleyan.edu
ROGERS, Gary 816-322-0110 250 K
gary.rogers@calvary.edu
ROGERS, Genelle 817-202-6214 444 I
genellerogers@swau.edu
ROGERS, Getta 360-417-6400 483 B
grogers@pencol.edu

ROGERS, Heather 270-901-1116 182 D
heather.rogers@kctcs.edu
ROGERS, Irina 205-453-6300 92 G
ROGERS, J. Orion 540-831-5958 470 C
jorogers@radford.edu
ROGERS, James 949-582-4558 64 G
jrogers39@saddleback.edu
ROGERS, James 212-327-8506 313 B
jrogers@mail.rockefeller.edu
ROGERS, Jan 229-317-6255 113 H
jan.rogers@asurams.edu
ROGERS, Janet 765-998-5330 160 F
jnrogers@taylor.edu
ROGERS, Jason 615-460-6441 418 F
jason.rogers@belmont.edu
ROGERS, Jaye 765-641-4442 153 B
jlrogers2@anderson.edu
ROGERS, Jeff, A 304-457-6337 487 B
rogersja@ab.edu
ROGERS, Jenica, P 315-267-2482 319 D
rogersjp@potsdam.edu
ROGERS, Jennifer 864-225-7653 409 J
jenniferrogers@forrestcollege.edu
ROGERS, Jevita 719-255-3460 83 B
jrogers3@uccs.edu
ROGERS, Johnell 803-934-3256 411 C
jrogers@morris.edu
ROGERS, Jolene, R 712-362-0431 166 F
jrogers@iowalakes.edu
ROGERS, Josh 928-536-6227 14 J
joshua.rogers@npc.edu
ROGERS, Judy 509-313-6131 481 D
rogers2@gonzaga.edu
ROGERS, Julian 216-368-1723 349 F
julian.rogers@case.edu
ROGERS, Justin, P 716-888-2244 292 D
rogers44@canisius.edu
ROGERS, Kathleen, R 617-521-2276 218 E
kathleen.rogers@simmons.edu
ROGERS, Katrina 805-898-2924 42 L
krogers@fielding.edu
ROGERS, Kim 580-559-5677 366 C
kimmrog@ecok.edu
ROGERS, Kimberly, K 409-747-3277 456 F
kkrogers@utmb.edu
ROGERS, Lalita 318-670-9223 190 J
lrogers@susla.edu
ROGERS, Larson 617-588-1318 206 C
lrogers@bfit.edu
ROGERS, Leslie 252-328-6050 341 C
rogersle@ecu.edu
ROGERS, Lisa, C 615-898-2150 422 H
lisa.rogers@mtsu.edu
ROGERS, Lynn 518-782-6654 315 J
lrogers@siena.edu
ROGERS, Mark 478-274-7871 122 H
mwrogers@oftc.edu
ROGERS, Michael 202-274-5986 93 C
michael.rogers@udc.edu
ROGERS, Michael 804-862-6100 470 I
mrogers@rbc.edu
ROGERS, Michael, B 607-735-1770 299 D
mrogers@elmira.edu
ROGERS, Michelle 909-748-8138 71 G
michelle_rogers@redlands.edu
ROGERS, Mike 209-946-2569 70 E
mrogers@pacific.edu
ROGERS, Nancy, B 812-237-7900 155 G
nancy.rogers@indstate.edu
ROGERS, Patricia 781-891-2297 206 D
progers@bentley.edu
ROGERS, Patricia, L 218-733-7600 238 F
patricia.rogers@lsc.edu
ROGERS, Patrick 802-635-1417 464 C
patrick.rogers@northernvermont.edu
ROGERS, SJ, Patrick 570-941-6153 401 H
patrick.rogers@scranton.edu
ROGERS, Peter 510-883-2083 41 G
progers@dspt.edu
ROGERS, Phil 208-459-5282 130 D
progers@collegeofidaho.edu
ROGERS, Randy 336-386-3466 338 D
rogersrj@surry.edu
ROGERS, Raymond, C 512-448-8532 442 M
rrogers1@stedwards.edu
ROGERS, Rickey 870-245-5220 20 E
rogersr@obu.edu
ROGERS, Rodney, K 419-372-2211 348 H
rrogers@bgsu.edu
ROGERS, Russell 201-216-5688 283 C
russell.rogers@stevens.edu
ROGERS, Sandra 630-889-6461 144 G
srogers@nuhs.edu

ROGERS, Sandra 801-422-1801 458 H
sandra_rogers@byu.edu
ROGERS, Scott 509-542-4834 479 H
srogers@columbiabasin.edu
ROGERS, Scott, S 330-385-1070 359 M
ROGERS, Sonya 251-981-3771 5 B
sonya.rogers@columbiasouthern.edu
ROGERS, Stephanie 318-670-9244 190 J
srogers@susla.edu
ROGERS, Steve 541-440-4625 377 C
steve.rogers@umpqua.edu
ROGERS, Susan 845-431-8952 298 E
susan.rogers1@sunydutchess.edu
ROGERS, Tammy 706-880-8344 121 A
trogers@lagrange.edu
ROGERS, Tamy 214-333-5158 434 I
tamyr@dbu.edu
ROGERS, Tarsha, M 252-335-3327 341 D
tmrogers@ecsu.edu
ROGERS, Terri 417-328-1520 259 L
tlrogers@sbuniv.edu
ROGERS, Terri 580-745-2510 369 K
trogers@se.edu
ROGERS, Thomas 502-935-6853 181 F
thomas.rogers@kctcs.edu
ROGERS, Thomas, A 719-333-6940 504 C
thomas.rogers@usafa.edu
ROGERS, Timothy 315-866-0300 301 G
rogerstd@herkimer.edu
ROGERS, Toby 806-720-7627 439 H
toby.rogers@lcu.edu
ROGERS, Tracy 719-587-7990 76 F
tracy_rogers@adams.edu
ROGERS-ADKINSON,
Diana 570-389-4308 394 A
drogers@bloomu.edu
ROGERS-LOWERY,
Constance 704-645-4803 328 A
clowery@catawba.edu
ROGERSON, Andrew 501-569-3200 22 B
chancellor@ualr.edu
ROGGEMAN, William 269-782-1484 230 F
wroggeman@swmich.edu
ROGGENSTEIN, Gary 661-722-6300 26 D
groggenstein@avc.edu
ROGGIE, Edie 315-786-2404 303 F
eroggie@sunyjefferson.edu
ROGGOW, Michael 508-588-9100 214 F
mroggow@massasoit.mass.edu
ROGOTZKE, Kathy, M 641-422-4154 168 D
rogotkat@niacc.edu
ROGOVIN, Michael 914-594-4560 309 H
michael_rogovin@nymc.edu
ROGOVIN, Michael 718-951-5504 293 C
michael.rogovin@brooklyn.cuny.edu
ROGSTAD, Leanne 763-488-2465 238 B
leanne.rogstad@hennepintech.edu
ROH, Joseph 310-756-0001 72 A
ROHAN, James, P 920-465-2075 496 E
rohanj@uwgb.edu
ROHAN, Robert, C 240-500-2367 198 H
rcrohan@hagerstowncc.edu
ROHANI, Mushka 425-640-1647 480 F
mushka.rohani@edcc.edu
ROHDE, Monika 516-686-7615 309 F
monika.rohde@nyit.edu
ROHDE, Scott 860-685-2809 89 C
srohde@wesleyan.edu
ROHDER-TONELLI,
Kelly 815-280-2915 140 B
krohder@jjc.edu
ROHDIN, Benjamin 201-200-3156 279 E
brohdin@njcu.edu
ROHLEDER, Ann 812-357-6610 160 D
arohleder@saintmeinrad.edu
ROHLEDER, John 651-779-3496 237 G
john.rohleder@century.edu
ROHLENA, Andrea 712-274-6400 170 E
andrea.rohlena@witcc.edu
ROHLENA, Mark 540-636-2900 466 A
mark.rohlena@christendom.edu
ROHLFING, Alexis 603-880-8308 274 E
arohlfing@thomasmorecollege.edu
ROHLMAN, Jessica 501-977-2004 23 A
rohlman@uaccm.edu
ROHMAN, Chad 708-524-6816 136 C
crohman@dom.edu
ROHN, Marisa 330-494-6170 361 F
mrohn@starkstate.edu
ROHNER, Christy 270-686-4243 179 D
christy.rohner@brescia.edu
ROHNER, Tom 312-662-4141 131 H
trohner@adler.edu

ROHR, Ann 970-207-4500.. 84 B
annr@uscareerinstitute.edu
ROHR, Ann 970-207-4550.. 80M
annr@mckinleycollege.edu
ROHR, Denise 513-569-1625 350 K
denise.rohr@cincinnatistate.edu
ROHR, Margie 973-290-4054 277 A
mrohr@cse.edu
ROHR ADAMS, Betsy .... 315-386-7951 320 E
rohradams@canton.edu
ROHRBACH, Erika 212-217-3703 299 H
erika_rohrbach@fitnyc.edu
ROHRBACK, Jane, T 248-204-3177 226 G
jrohrback@ltu.edu
ROHRBAUGH,
Suzanne, Y 336-633-0218 337 A
syrohrbaugh@randolph.edu
ROHRER, Brad 305-284-1256 112 E
brohrer@miami.edu
ROHRER, Mark 575-392-6561 289 A
mrohrer@usw.edu
ROHWER, Debbie 940-565-3514 454 A
debbie.rohwer@unt.edu
ROIDT, Joseph 605-995-2625 415 C
joseph.roidt@dwu.edu
ROIG, Katy 619-260-7404.. 71 J
kroig@sandiego.edu
ROJAS, Balbina, J 787-766-1717 511 H
barojas@suagm.edu
ROJAS, Carlos 787-840-2575 510 J
crojas@psm.edu
ROJAS, Carmen, I 787-743-4041 507 D
crojas@columbiacentral.edu
ROJAS, Eddy, M 937-229-4632 362 G
erojas1@udayton.edu
ROJAS, Elias 907-564-8081.... 9 D
erojas@alaskapacific.edu
ROJAS, Frank 858-527-2768.. 50 D
ROJAS, Gilbert 801-274-3280 461 F
gilbert.rojas@wgu.edu
ROJAS, Jason 860-297-4166.. 88 C
jason.rojas@trincoll.edu
ROJAS, Jesus 912-525-5000 123 G
jrojas@scad.edu
ROJAS, Liliana 415-422-6707.. 71 K
lrojas3@usfca.edu
ROJAS, Lisa 731-425-8835 425 B
lrojas@jscc.edu
ROJAS, Robyn, D 405-325-3337 371 B
rrojas@ou.edu
ROJAS, Rodney 213-613-2200.. 64 H
rodney_rojas@sciarc.edu
ROJAS JOO,
Juan Armando 740-368-2000 359 N
ROJAS-MORA, Norma ... 661-395-4382.. 46 L
norma.rojas@bakersfieldcollege.edu
ROJCEWICZ, Peter, M ... 626-571-8811.. 72 C
peterr@uwest.edu
ROJO, Richard 650-574-6538.. 61 P
rojor@smccd.edu
ROKOWSKY, Avrohom .. 845-425-1370 311 A
ROKOWSKY, Israel 845-425-1370 311 A
ROKSANDIC, Stevo 614-234-1644 356 I
sroksandic@mchs.com
ROLAND, David, E 706-233-7329 124 B
droland@shorter.edu
ROLAND, Harriet, A 803-533-3790 412 C
rolandha@scsu.edu
ROLAND, Kirc, J 360-442-2471 482 B
kroland@lowercolumbia.edu
ROLAND, Shane 478-471-2414 121 F
shane.roland@mga.edu
ROLAND, Yvonne 719-333-7627 504 C
yvonne.roland@usafa.edu
ROLDAN, Ida 312-935-4232 139 H
iroldan@icsw.edu
ROLDAN, Miranda 908-737-4835 278 E
catholic@kean.edu
ROLEN, Aneisa, L 865-694-6403 425 F
alrolen@pstcc.edu
ROLEN, Dalton Chris .... 408-741-2092.. 74 C
chris.rolen@wvm.edu
ROLEN, Scott 541-917-4420 374 A
rolens@linnbenton.edu
ROLEY, V. Vance 808-956-8377 128 F
vroley@hawaii.edu
ROLFE, Kim 509-526-3011 486 H
rolfekb@whitman.edu
ROLFE, Rial, D 806-743-2905 451 C
rial.rolfe@ttuhsc.edu
ROLFES, Katherine 337-521-8906 188 C
katherine.rolfes@solacc.edu
ROLFS, Trevor 620-792-9378 171 C
rolfst@bartonccc.edu
ROLHEISER, Ronald 210-341-1366 441 C
rrolheiser@ost.edu
ROLL, Debbie, J 907-564-8220.... 9 D
droll@alaskapacific.edu
ROLLAG, Keith 781-239-5310 205 E
krollag@babson.edu
ROLLAND, Erik 909-869-2400.. 30 D
erolland@cpp.edu
ROLLE, Anthony 401-277-5489 406 B
anthony_rolle@uri.edu
ROLLE, Dominique 803-813-1144 412 C
drolle1@scsu.edu
ROLLE, Jo-Ann 718-270-5110 295 A
jrolle@mec.cuny.edu
ROLLER, Robert 626-812-3085.. 26 H
rroller@apu.edu
ROLLER, Rodney 239-590-1155 108 K
ROLLER, Steven, A 617-228-2394 214 A
sroller@bhcc.mass.edu
ROLLESTON, George ..... 440-826-2081 348 E
grollest@bw.edu
ROLLING, Kristin 608-246-6677 499 H
krolling1@madisoncollege.edu
ROLLINGS, David 803-323-2191 414 G
rollingsd@winthrop.edu
ROLLINGS, Grenna 972-860-8181 435 A
grollings@dcccd.edu
ROLLINO, Richard 740-283-6223 353 B
rrollino@franciscan.edu
ROLLINS, Adam 423-869-6421 421 C
adam.rollins@lmunet.edu
ROLLINS, Alison 301-295-3357 504 B
alison.rollins@usuhs.edu
ROLLINS, Cheryl 443-885-4429 200 D
cheryl.rollins@morgan.edu
ROLLINS, Judy 252-985-5111 339 D
jrollins@ncwc.edu
ROLLINS, Kate 402-354-7264 268 C
kate.rollins@methodistcollege.edu
ROLLINS, Maxwell 843-863-7956 407 E
mrollins@csuniv.edu
ROLLINS, Pam 334-420-4253.... 3 H
prollins@trenholmstate.edu
ROLLINS, Robert 334-420-4232.... 3 H
rrollins@trenholmstate.edu
ROLLINS, Stephen 907-786-1825.... 9 H
srollins@alaska.edu
ROLLINS, Tina 757-727-5371 468 B
tina.rollins@hamptonu.edu
ROLLISON, Jeffrey 610-647-4400 386 C
jrollison@immaculata.edu
ROLLMAN,
Catherine, A 804-752-7270 470 F
crollman@rmc.edu
ROLLO, J. Michael 239-590-1061 108 K
jmrollo@fgcu.edu
ROLLOFF, Mary, K 920-433-6639 492 B
mary.rolloff@bellincollege.edu
ROLLOR, Michael 410-706-1875 202 D
mrollor@umaryland.edu
ROLLS, Dickie 620-252-7575 172 G
rolls.dickie@coffeyville.edu
ROLNICK, Harriet, M .... 213-738-6690.. 65 G
scale@swlaw.edu
ROLOFF, ReBecca, K .... 651-690-6525 242 R
broloff@stkate.edu
ROLON, Joseph 641-269-3713 165 J
rolonjoe@grinnell.edu
ROLON, Reynaldo 787-279-1912 509 A
rrolon@bayamon.inter.edu
ROMÁN PAOLI,
Elvin, O 608-785-8000 513 F
ROM, Kjetil 541-881-5746 377 B
krom@tvcc.cc
ROMA, Lawrence, J 607-777-2224 316 E
lroma@binghamton.edu
ROMAGNI, Elizabeth 901-321-3306 419 C
elizabeth.romagni@cbu.edu
ROMAGNI, Joanne 423-425-1743 428 A
joanne-romagni@utc.edu
ROMAGNOLI, Janice 615-655-7274 292 F
jaromagnoli@cazenovia.edu
ROMALI, Reagan 562-938-4121.. 48 D
rromali@lbcc.edu
ROMAN, Albert, J 213-891-2173.. 48 G
romanaj@laccd.edu
ROMAN, Angela 231-591-2674 223 J
angelaroman@ferris.edu
ROMAN, Aris 787-891-0925 508 K
aroman@aguadilla.inter.edu
ROMAN, Gabriel 787-738-2161 513 D
gabriel.roman2@upr.edu
ROMAN, Jennifer 305-273-4499.. 96 L
jennifer.roman@cbt.edu
ROMAN, Jennifer 214-329-4447 431 D
jennifer.roman@bgu.edu
ROMAN, Juan, E 787-841-2000 510 K
jroman@pucpr.edu
ROMAN, Kristen 608-262-4527 496 C
kristen.roman@wisc.edu
ROMAN, Vladimir 787-763-6425 508 J
vroman@inter.edu
ROMAN, Yosmeriz 856-225-6664 281 G
yosmeriz.roman@camden.rutgers.edu
ROMAN-LAGUNAS,
Victoria 219-980-6707 156 E
viroman@iu.edu
ROMAN-VARGAS,
Madeline 773-878-3728 148 D
mroman02@staugustine.edu
ROMANCHOCK,
Mechele, C 607-871-2494 289 H
romanchock@alfred.edu
ROMANCZUK, Jeffrey .... 704-499-9200.. 92 G
ROMANDINI, Russ 513-618-1930 350 J
rromandini@ccms.edu
ROMANELLO, Mary 202-884-9677.. 93 B
romanellom@trinitydc.edu
ROMANO, Angela 845-431-8097 298 E
angela.romano@sunydutchess.edu
ROMANO, Carol 301-295-9002 504 B
carol.romano@usuhs.edu
ROMANO, Cenia, K 787-884-3838 506 D
vpacademico@atenascollege.edu
ROMANO, Christopher .. 201-684-7309 280 H
cromano@ramapo.edu
ROMANO, Deanna, M ... 304-896-7412 489 E
deanna.romano@southernwv.edu
ROMANO, Fred, D 630-515-6388 143 G
froman@midwestern.edu
ROMANO, Joan 617-989-4908 219 E
romanoj3@wit.edu
ROMANO, Judith, J 864-294-3470 410 A
judith.romano@furman.edu
ROMANO, Linda 718-990-6865 314 B
romanol@stjohns.edu
ROMANO, Nicole 302-356-6846.. 90 I
nicole.romano@wilmu.edu
ROMANO, Pam 910-272-3531 337 D
promano@robeson.edu
ROMANO, Pamela 828-726-2269 332 G
promano@cccti.edu
ROMANO, Sandra 340-693-1389 514 E
sromano@uvi.edu
ROMANO, Susan 585-245-5731 318 E
romano@geneseo.edu
ROMANO, Victor 305-899-3756.. 95 C
vromano@barry.edu
ROMANO, Wendy, W 215-871-6300 396 D
wendyr@pcom.edu
ROMANS, John 405-744-3373 368 B
john.romans@okstate.edu
ROMANSTEIN,
Stanley, E 513-556-3737 362 D
stanley.romanstein@uc.edu
ROMANT, Stacy 414-288-3654 494 B
stacy.romant@marquette.edu
ROMANTIC,
Thomas, W 607-255-8574 297 F
twr2@cornell.edu
ROMBALSKI, Patrick 617-792-3636 133 F
prombalski@chamberlain.edu
ROMBAUGH, Pauline .... 269-965-3931 225 F
rombaughp@kellogg.edu
ROMBES, Nicholas 313-993-1000 231 B
rombesnd@udmercy.edu
ROME, Alan, K 440-943-7600 360 J
akrome@dioceseofcleveland.org
ROME, Alan, K 440-943-7600 360 J
cpl@dioceseofcleveland.org
ROME, Dennis 773-442-5420 145 B
d-rome@neiu.edu
ROME, JoAnne 413-552-2259 214 D
jrome@hcc.edu
ROME, Kevin, D 615-329-8555 419 K
srucker@fisk.edu
ROME, Michaela 212-229-8947 308 C
romem@newschool.edu
ROMEO, Jamie 860-629-6213.. 87 D
romeo_j@mitchell.edu
ROMER, Andrew 850-474-2200 110 E
aromer@uwf.edu
ROMERO, JR.,
Aldemaro 646-312-3870 292 L
aldemaro.romero@baruch.cuny.edu
ROMERO, Andy 505-747-2166 287 G
andy@nnmc.edu
ROMERO, Angel, F 787-765-1915 510 B
aromero@opto.inter.edu
ROMERO, Bianca 909-593-3511.. 70 D
bromero@laverne.edu
ROMERO, Cecilia 505-747-5477 287 G
cromero@nnmc.edu
ROMERO, Chris 707-965-6303.. 55 D
chris@puc.edu
ROMERO, Christina 714-564-6091.. 57 L
romero_christina@sac.edu
ROMERO, Clarence 505-454-3369 286 H
clromero@nmhu.edu
ROMERO, Clorinda 575-758-8914 286 F
clorindar@midwiferycollege.edu
ROMERO, Cynthia 757-446-7414 466 I
romerocc@evms.edu
ROMERO, Edward, W ... 903-886-5027 447 B
edward.romero@tamuc.edu
ROMERO, Eileen 914-594-4495 309 H
eileen_romero@nymc.edu
ROMERO, Elizabeth 951-827-2750.. 69 C
elizabeth.romero@ucr.edu
ROMERO, Georg 831-479-5771.. 27 G
geromero@cabrillo.edu
ROMERO, Herminio 787-622-8000 512 E
hromero@pupr.edu
ROMERO, Jose 787-864-2222 509 C
jose.romero@guayama.inter.edu
ROMERO, Lizbeth 787-878-5475 508 L
lromero@arecibo.inter.edu
ROMERO, Manuel 212-220-1238 293 A
mromero@bmcc.cuny.edu
ROMERO, Narda 914-674-7841 306 F
nromero@mercy.edu
ROMERO, Nehemias 626-968-1328.. 47 G
ROMERO, Ramona, E ... 609-258-2511 280 E
ramonar@princeton.edu
ROMERO, Rebecca 970-521-6649.. 81 D
rebecca.romero@njc.edu
ROMERO, Reyna 713-221-8460 453 B
romeror@uhd.edu
ROMERO, Roxane 602-384-2555.. 11 F
roxane.romero@bryanuniversity.edu
ROMERO, Sally 970-943-2150.. 84 D
sromero@western.edu
ROMERO, Van, D 575-835-5646 286 I
van.romero@nmt.edu
ROMERO, Victoria 909-621-8149.. 63 E
vromero@scrippscollege.edu
ROMERO, Wilfredo 787-704-1020 507 K
wromero@ediccollege.edu
ROMERO-ALDAZ,
Patrick 303-458-4086.. 82 E
promeroaldaz@regis.edu
ROMERO-LEGGOTT,
Valerie 505-272-2728 288 G
vromero@salud.unm.edu
ROMERO-NIEVES,
Luis, E 787-751-1912 510 A
lromero@juris.inter.edu
ROMIG, Kenneth, J 724-946-7141 402 G
romigkj@westminster.edu
ROMIG, Phillip 303-273-3866.. 78 I
promig3@mines.edu
ROMINES, Ellen, B 202-685-3911 503 I
ellen.b.romines.civ@ndu.edu
ROMIOUS, Angila 424-207-3753.. 54 I
aromious@otis.edu
ROMKEY, Matthew 515-643-6663 168 A
mromkey@mercydesmoines.org
ROMNEY, Brett 602-366-9699.. 16 J
brett.romney@phoenix.edu
ROMO, Nanette 520-515-5399.. 11M
romon@cochise.edu
ROMO, Paul 623-845-3051.. 13 C
paul.romo@gccaz.edu
RONAN, Donald 937-769-1800 347 H
dronan@antioch.edu
RONCA, Paul, L 804-523-5239 474 H
pronca@reynolds.edu
RONCHETTI, Michele .... 815-836-5498 141 G
ronchemi@lewisu.edu
RONCOLATO, David 814-332-5318 378 D
droncola@allegheny.edu
RONDA, Rene, S 787-743-7979 511 I
rsronda@suagm.edu
RONDEAU, RET.,
Ann Elisabeth 831-656-2511 503 K

RONDEAU, Craig ... 617-984-1645 218 B crondeau@quincycollege.edu
RONDEAU, James ... 312-899-5100 148 I
RONDINELLI, Diane ... 904-826-0084.. 71 H drondinelli@usa.edu
RONDON, Marvin ... 910-592-8081 337 G mrondon@sampsoncc.edu
RONDON, Wilfredo ... 787-766-1717 511 H wirondon@suagm.edu
RONETTI, Stephen ... 626-584-5409.. 43 H stephen_ronetti@fuller.edu
RONEVICH, Nancy, S ... 740-284-5232 353 B nronevich@franciscan.edu
RONEY, Kylee ... 217-362-6423 143 H kroney@millikin.edu
RONEY, Linda ... 214-333-5147 434 I linda@dbu.edu
RONG, Yongwu ... 718-997-5936 295 C yongwu.rong@qc.cuny.edu
RONK, Chris ... 336-725-8344 339 F ronkc@piedmontu.edu
RONKOSKI, Bob ... 636-922-8604 258 I rronkoski@stchas.edu
RONNFELDT, Derek ... 253-833-9111 481 F dronnfeltd@greenriver.edu
RONNING, Teresa ... 518-743-2261 320 D ronningt@sunyacc.edu
RONNING LINDGREN, Rachel ... 805-493-3690.. 29 H rronning@callutheran.edu
ROOB, Sharon ... 414-930-3129 495 A roobs@mtmary.edu
ROOCK, Mark ... 314-529-9673 254 H mroock@maryville.edu
ROOD, Christi ... 208-562-2710 130 F christirood@cwi.edu
ROOD, Denine ... 320-629-5126 240 C denine.rood@pine.edu
ROOD, Robert ... 716-839-8503 298 B rrood@daemen.edu
ROOF, Karin ... 843-953-4871 407 F kroof1@citadel.edu
ROOF, Steven, E ... 304-367-4642 490 B steven.roof@fairmontstate.edu
ROOFNER, Perry, F ... 412-397-5256 397 G roofner@rmu.edu
ROOHANI, Ben ... 312-850-7154 134 H broohani@ccc.edu
ROOHPARVAR, Shahrooz ... 928-344-7521.. 10 J sr@azwestern.edu
ROOK, Steve ... 501-337-5000.. 18 J srook@coto.edu
ROOK, Tony ... 252-823-5166 334 C rookt@edgecombe.edu
ROOKE, Michael ... 860-738-6300.. 86 C mrooke@nwcc.edu
ROOKER, Allison ... 601-925-3310 247 C abrooker@mc.edu
ROOKER, Darrin ... 315-568-3063 308 F drooker@nycc.edu
ROOKER, Robert ... 310-377-5501.. 51 B rrooker@marymountcalifornia.edu
ROOKER, Suzanne ... 580-477-7944 371 F suzanne.rooker@wosc.edu
ROOKS, Bryan ... 970-248-1252.. 77 I brooks@coloradomesa.edu
ROOKS, James ... 616-526-8694 222 A jrooks@calvin.edu
ROOKS, Noliwe, L ... 607-255-4625 297 F nrooks@cornell.edu
ROOKS, Stephanie ... 770-962-7580 120 E srooks@gwinnetttech.edu
ROOKSBY, Jacob ... 509-313-3700 481 D rooksby@lawschool.gonzaga.edu
ROONEY, CM, Aidan, R 716-286-8400 310 D
ROONEY, Gerard, J ... 585-385-8010 314 A grooney@sjfc.edu
ROONEY, Jo Ann ... 312-915-6400 142 D president@luc.edu
ROONEY, John ... 402-643-4052 269 A
ROONEY, Joseph ... 609-343-4916 275 D jrooney@atlantic.edu
ROONEY, Larry ... 802-485-2499 463 A lrooney@norwich.edu
ROONEY, Paul ... 407-582-1100 112 K prooney@valenciacollege.edu
ROONEY, Paula, M ... 508-541-1658 208 F prooney@dean.edu
ROOPNARINE, Darshini 315-445-4661 304 C roopnatd@lemoyne.edu
ROOS, Jannicke ... 617-746-1990 210 E jannicke.roos@hult.edu
ROOS, Johan ... 617-619-1900 210 E johan.roos@hult.edu
ROOSA, Mark, S ... 310-506-4252.. 56 C mark.roosa@pepperdine.edu
ROOSE, Craig ... 641-628-7632 163 E roosec@central.edu
ROOSE, Robert ... 989-358-7200 221 A rooser@alpenacc.edu
ROOSEVELT, Mark ... 505-984-6098 287 J president@sjc.edu
ROOSTA, Seyed ... 229-430-4886 113 H seyed.roosta@asurams.edu
ROOT, David ... 606-539-4406 185 A david.root@ucumberlands.edu
ROOT, Deborah ... 870-245-5510.. 20 E rootd@obu.edu
ROOT, Jeff ... 870-245-4186.. 20 E rootj@obu.edu
ROOT, John ... 512-245-2585 450 E jr28@txstate.edu
ROOT, Mark, J ... 574-807-7219 153 E rootm1@betheluniversity.edu
ROOT, Rennie, A ... 563-588-7775 167 D rennie.root@loras.edu
ROOTH, Gerald, T ... 301-447-5003 200 E rooth@msmary.edu
ROOTS, Heidi ... 413-528-7201 205 F registrar@simons-rock.edu
ROOTS, Keith, D ... 757-594-0581 466 B keith.roots@cnu.edu
ROPELLA, Kristina ... 414-288-5460 494 B kristina.ropella@marquette.edu
ROPER, Craig ... 618-545-3137 140 E croper@kaskaskia.edu
ROPER, David ... 843-349-6532 408 C droper@coastal.edu
ROPER, Gina ... 541-881-5577 377 B groper@tvcc.cc
ROPER, Lari ... 843-349-3658 410 C laura.roper@hgtc.edu
ROPER, Melinda ... 805-493-3553.. 29 H mroper@callutheran.edu
ROPER, William, L ... 919-962-4622 341 A president@northcarolina.edu
ROPER-DOTEN, Emily ... 781-292-2201 209 E emily.roper-doten@olin.edu
ROPETI, Siamaua ... 684-699-2722 505 A s.ropeti@amsamoa.edu
ROQUEMORE, Glenn ... 949-451-5210.. 64 E groquemore@ivc.edu
ROQUEMORE, Glenn, R 949-451-5210.. 64 F groquemore@ivc.edu
RORK, Jeanette ... 434-947-8289 470 E jrork@randolphcollege.edu
RORKE LEVY, Pam ... 415-749-4507.. 60 G
RORRER, Caleb ... 336-342-4261 337 E rorrerm8871@rockinghamcc.edu
ROS, Vimul ... 215-702-4553 380 D vros@cairn.edu
ROSA, Belinda ... 787-743-7979 511 I ac_brosa@suagm.edu
ROSA, Carmen ... 203-576-4652.. 88 D carosa@bridgeport.edu
ROSA, Chris ... 646-664-8759 292 K christopher.rosa@cuny.edu
ROSA, Jerry ... 718-518-6561 294 B jrosa@hostos.cuny.edu
ROSA, Jessie ... 334-244-3712.... 4 F jrosa@aum.edu
ROSA, Joe ... 925-631-4105.. 59 B jtr2@stmarys-ca.edu
ROSA, Luis ... 603-271-6484 273 B lrosa@ccsnh.edu
ROSA, Maria ... 787-834-9595 511 E mrosa@uaa.edu
ROSA, Peter ... 203-837-8376.. 85 B rosap@wcsu.edu
ROSA, Sandra ... 787-279-1912 509 A srosa@bayamon.inter.edu
ROSA, Veronica ... 603-358-2425 275 A veronica.rosa@keene.edu
ROSA-NUNEZ, Waleska, Y ... 787-480-2386 507 C wrosa01@sanjuanciudadpatria.com
ROSAASEN, Orlynn ... 701-777-3823 345 C orlynn.rosaasen@und.edu
ROSACCO, Claire ... 216-987-4804 351 G claire.rosacco@tri-c.edu
ROSADO, Akilah ... 212-875-4596 290 F arosado@bankstreet.edu
ROSADO, Christine ... 908-852-1440 276 G christine.rosado@centenaryuniversity.edu
ROSADO, Martin ... 787-884-6000 508 D mrosado@icprjc.edu
ROSADO, Reinaldo ... 787-284-1912 509 E rrosado@ponce.inter.edu
ROSADO, Renee ... 413-205-3248 205 A renee.rosado@aic.edu
ROSADO, Samuel ... 787-264-1912 509 F samuel_rosado_nazario@intersg.edu
ROSADO-BERRIOS, Carmen, C ... 787-857-3600 508 M crosado@br.inter.edu
ROSALES, Elvia, H ... 512-471-3391 455 A bd.elvia@austin.utexas.edu
ROSALES, Ilian ... 619-934-0797.. 60 F
ROSAMILIO, Noel ... 203-596-8780.. 86 B nrosamilio@nv.edu
ROSANDICH, Thomas, J ... 251-626-3303.... 7 E president@ussa.edu
ROSANIA, Nick ... 641-472-1180 167 F nrosania@mum.edu
ROSANIA, Sandra ... 641-472-1180 167 F srosania@mum.edu
ROSARIO, Glorivee ... 787-738-4660 513 D glorivee.rosario@upr.edu
ROSARIO, Karen ... 787-884-3838 506 D krosario@atenascollege.edu
ROSARIO, Lisanette ... 718-518-4311 294 B lrosario@hostos.cuny.edu
ROSARIO, Lucy ... 787-284-1912 509 E lrsario@ponce.inter.edu
ROSARIO, Yoleidy ... 973-353-3416 282 B yoleidy.rosario@rutgers.edu
ROSARIO, Yvette ... 718-960-8723 294 A yvette.rosario@lehman.cuny.edu
ROSARIO-CRUZ, Carlos, A ... 787-857-3600 508 M crosario@br.inter.edu
ROSARIO DELGADO, Victor ... 787-758-5297 514 B victor.rosario1@upr.edu
ROSARIO-RODRIGUEZ, Elizabeth ... 787-480-2444 507 C erosario03@sanjuanciudadpatria.com
ROSARIO-ROSARIO, Yolanda ... 787-725-6500 506 G yrosario@albizu.edu
ROSAS, Alisha ... 909-652-6115.. 36 A alisha.rosas@chaffey.edu
ROSAS, Antonio ... 510-436-1000.. 45 D rosas@hnu.edu
ROSAS, Carla ... 925-473-7427.. 40 J crosas@losmedanos.edu
ROSAS, Eradina ... 787-832-6000 508 D
ROSAS, Mirna ... 480-423-6754.. 13 H mirna.rosas@scottsdalecc.edu
ROSAS, Olivia ... 909-537-7577.. 33 A orosas@csusb.edu
ROSAS MUÑIZ, Carlos, E ... 608-785-8000 513 F
ROSASCHI, Catherine ... 703-416-1441 466 F crosaschi@divinemercy.edu
ROSATI, David, M ... 617-333-2302 208 E david.rosati@curry.edu
ROSATI, Ron ... 308-367-5270 270 C rosati@unl.edu
ROSATI, Ross ... 612-625-5516 243 E rosat002@umn.edu
ROSATO, Michael ... 281-649-3633 437 H mrosato@hbu.edu
ROSBERG, Gerald, M ... 212-854-9967 297 C gerry.rosberg@columbia.edu
ROSBOROUGH, Alison . 678-839-4107 126 E arosboro@westga.edu
ROSCH, Laura ... 417-208-0632 254 C lrosch@kcumb.edu
ROSCOE, Brandy ... 864-225-7653 409 J brandyroscoe@forrestcollege.edu
ROSDAIL, Lisa ... 803-938-3794 414 B lrosdai@uscsumter.edu
ROSE, Aimee ... 540-887-7380 469 B arose@marybaldwin.edu
ROSE, Alisha, D ... 901-678-2230 427 D arose3@memphis.edu
ROSE, Billy ... 256-352-8110.... 4 A billy.rose@wallacestate.edu
ROSE, Breanna ... 828-659-6001 336 B breannar@mcdowelltech.edu
ROSE, Brian, K ... 724-925-4129 403 A roseb@westmoreland.edu
ROSE, Brian, T ... 607-777-4788 316 E brose@binghamton.edu
ROSE, Carey ... 254-298-8326 446 A carey.rose@templejc.edu
ROSE, Carrie, J ... 724-458-2134 385 C rosecj@gcc.edu
ROSE, III, Charles, H ... 419-772-2205 358 H c-rose.5@onu.edu
ROSE, Clayton ... 207-725-3221 193 D crose@bowdoin.edu
ROSE, David ... 765-677-2075 157 D david.rose@indwes.edu
ROSE, David, S ... 858-534-4358.. 69 D drose@ucsd.edu
ROSE, Deatrea ... 620-235-6556 176 F drose@pittstate.edu
ROSE, Debbie ... 615-732-7673 422 G debbie@mtsa.edu
ROSE, Don ... 620-665-3597 174 B rosed@hutchcc.edu
ROSE, Eric, D ... 201-216-5177 283 C eric.rose@stevens.edu
ROSE, Erik ... 406-447-5414 263 C erose@carroll.edu
ROSE, Frankie ... 402-486-2501 269 F frankie.rose@ucollege.edu
ROSE, Howard, A ... 713-525-6980 454 H horo@stthom.edu
ROSE, Jane ... 941-359-4200 110 D jane.rose@sar.usf.edu
ROSE, John ... 212-772-4242 294 C john.rose@hunter.cuny.edu
ROSE, Julie ... 607-587-3979 320 C roseja@alfredstate.edu
ROSE, Justin ... 217-206-6333 151 C jrose22@uis.edu
ROSE, Kathleen, A ... 408-848-4712.. 43 J krose@gavilan.edu
ROSE, Kevin ... 903-434-8186 441 B krose@ntcc.edu
ROSE, Kevin, W ... 517-750-1200 230 H kerose@arbor.edu
ROSE, Lawrence, D ... 909-537-3703.. 33 A lrose@csusb.edu
ROSE, JR., LeRoy ... 401-598-1000 404 I lrose@jwu.edu
ROSE, Lesa ... 207-330-7743 194 E rosele@mchp.edu
ROSE, Linda, D ... 714-564-6975.. 57 L rose_linda@sac.edu
ROSE, Lisa ... 310-434-4402.. 62 E rose_lisa@smc.edu
ROSE, Mark ... 754-312-2898 102 Q mrose@keycollege.edu
ROSE, Martin, E ... 214-752-8600 442 M mrose@fbtlaw.com
ROSE, Melinda ... 413-265-2588 208 C rosem@elms.edu
ROSE, Melissa ... 304-243-2233 491 I mrose@wju.edu
ROSE, Paul ... 618-650-3350 149 F prose@siue.edu
ROSE, Quincy ... 314-340-5078 253 I roseq@hssu.edu
ROSE, Raymond ... 907-745-3201.... 9 B rrose@akbible.edu
ROSE, JR., Robert ... 703-333-5904 478 B rrose@wuv.edu
ROSE, Ryan ... 620-431-2820 175 H rarose@neosho.edu
ROSE, Sarah ... 423-585-6752 426 C sarah.rose@ws.edu
ROSE, Shawn ... 970-521-6601.. 81 D shawn.rose@njc.edu
ROSE, Stacy ... 713-798-7858 431 I srrose@bcm.edu
ROSE, Steve ... 509-527-2402 485 H steve.rose@wallawalla.edu
ROSE, Steven ... 973-684-5900 280 B srose@pccc.edu
ROSE, Susan ... 606-539-4213 185 A
ROSE, Tara, A ... 859-257-6394 185 B tara.rose@uky.edu
ROSEBORO-BARNES, Edwina ... 803-981-7162 415 A eroseboro@yorktech.edu
ROSEDALE, Jeff ... 914-323-5277 305 J jeff.rosedale@mville.edu
ROSELL, Anita ... 724-222-5330 392 A arosell@penncommercial.edu
ROSEMEYER, Abbie ... 561-803-2180 104 C abbie_rosemeyer@pba.edu
ROSEN, Aaron ... 202-885-8674.. 93 E arosen@wesleyseminary.edu
ROSEN, C. Martin ... 812-941-2262 157 B crosen@ius.edu

ROSEN, Julie 602-386-4103 10 E
julie.rosen@arizonachristian.edu
ROSEN, Mike, S 713-743-8155 452 F
msrosen@central.uh.edu
ROSEN, Sara 404-413-6555 119 E
srosen@gsu.edu
ROSEN, Steven, T 626-256-4673 37 B
srosen@coh.org
ROSEN-METSCH, Lisa 212-854-6321 297 C
lm2892@columbia.edu
ROSENBALM, Whitney 972-238-6023 435 F
wrosenbalm@dcccd.edu
ROSENBAUM, Irving 954-262-1507 103 M
irv@nova.edu
ROSENBAUM, Irving 954-262-1303 103 M
irv@nova.edu
ROSENBAUM, Kylee, B 260-982-5222 158 T
kbrosenbaum@manchester.edu
ROSENBAUM, Philip 610-896-1290 385 L
prosenba@haverford.edu
ROSENBAUM,
Thomas, F 626-395-6301 29 C
tfr@caltech.edu
ROSENBERG, Alannah 949-582-4854 64 G
aorrison@saddleback.edu
ROSENBERG, Brian, C 651-696-6207 236 H
rosenbergb@macalester.edu
ROSENBERG, Chaim 718-854-2290 291 F
ROSENBERG, David 845-731-3700 326 J
ROSENBERG, Doug 612-330-1297 233 K
rosenbe2@augsburg.edu
ROSENBERG, Eric 973-720-2303 284 I
rosenbergel@wpunj.edu
ROSENBERG, John, R 801-422-4331 458 H
john_rosenberg@byu.edu
ROSENBERG, Mark 305-348-2111 109 A
mark.rosenberg@fiu.edu
ROSENBERG, Michael 845-257-2800 317 B
rosenbem@newpaltz.edu
ROSENBERG, Neal 313-993-1208 231 B
rosenbns@udmercy.edu
ROSENBERG, Sol 718-854-2290 291 F
ROSENBERG, Travis 435-652-7522 460 G
travis.rosenberg@dixie.edu
ROSENBERG, Warren 914-831-0219 297 A
wrosenberg@cw.edu
ROSENBERGER,
Benjamin 610-372-4721 397 B
brosenberger@racc.edu
ROSENBERGER, Jeanne 408-554-4366 62 D
jrosenberger@scu.edu
ROSENBERGER,
Thomas 518-337-4987 296 H
rosenbet@strose.edu
ROSENBLATT, Mark 312-996-3500 151 B
mrosenbl@uic.edu
ROSENBLITH,
Suzane, N 716-645-6640 316 F
rosenbli@buffalo.edu
ROSENBLOOM, Stuart 312-461-0600 132 A
srosenbloom@aaart.edu
ROSENBLUM, Donald 954-262-8402 103 M
donr@nsu.nova.edu
ROSENBLUM, Eliyohu 718-854-2290 291 F
ROSENBOOM, David 661-255-1050 28 K
david@calarts.edu
ROSENBOOM, Sharon 712-722-6740 164 K
sharon.rosenboom@dordt.edu
ROSENBURGI, Melissa 207-941-7175 194 A
ROSENBURY, Laura, A 352-273-0600 109 F
rosenbury@law.ufl.edu
ROSENDAHL, Matt 218-726-8130 243 F
lib@d.umn.edu
ROSENFELD, Haley 212-678-3208 322 G
har2124@tc.columbia.edu
ROSENFELD, Renee 267-502-6038 379 D
renee.rosenfeld@brynathyn.edu
ROSENFELD, Sholom 718-774-5050 322 F
oholeitorah@aol.com
ROSENGART, Sharon 973-720-3019 284 I
rosengarts@wpunj.edu
ROSENGARTEN, Jeffrey 646-565-6000 322 J
jeffrey.rosengarten@touro.edu
ROSENGARTEN, Lewis 607-753-4808 318 D
lewis.rosengarten@cortland.edu
ROSENHEIN, Jon 973-655-5105 279 C
rosenheinj@mail.montclair.edu
ROSENLUND, Linda 508-767-7104 205 D
lrosenlund@assumption.edu
ROSENOW, Thomas, C 530-898-5556 31 A
trosenow@csuchico.edu
ROSENSAFT, Jean, B 212-824-2209 301 E
jrosensaft@huc.edu
ROSENSTEIN, Ilena 860-768-4418 88 H
rosenstei@hartford.edu
ROSENSTEIN, Ilene 213-740-7711 72 B
irosenst@usc.edu
ROSENSTOCK, Jeffrey 718-997-4995 295 C
jeffrey.rosenstock@qc.cuny.edu
ROSENTHAL, Adam 954-262-5379 103 M
jar1248@nova.edu
ROSENTHAL, Alisa, J 804-752-7268 470 F
alisarosenthal@rmc.edu
ROSENTHAL, Amy 269-471-3411 221 B
rosenthala@andrews.edu
ROSENTHAL, Austin 918-444-2202 367 A
rosentha@nsuok.edu
ROSENTHAL, Elijah 848-932-1994 282 A
elijah.rosenthal@ruf.rutgers.edu
ROSENTHAL, Ellen 301-243-2125 503 J
ellen.rosenthal@dodiis.mil
ROSENTHAL, Eric 610-861-5565 391 F
erosenthal@northampton.edu
ROSENTHAL,
Jean-Laurent 626-395-4068 29 C
rosentha@caltech.edu
ROSENTHAL, Jeffrey, E 315-294-8499 292 E
rosenthal@cayuga-cc.edu
ROSENTHAL, Julie 303-373-2008 82 G
jroesenthal@rvu.edu
ROSENTHAL, Ken 818-677-2561 32 D
ken.rosenthal@csun.edu
ROSENTHAL, Lauren 718-933-6700 307 G
lrosenthal@monroecollege.edu
ROSENTHAL, Lori 617-243-2074 210 G
lrosenthal@lasell.edu
ROSENTHAL,
Roseanne, K 312-225-6288 152 B
rrosenthal@vandercook.edu
ROSENTHAL, Susan 305-899-3050 95 C
srosenthal@barry.edu
ROSERO, Elizabeth 714-997-6893 36 C
rosero@chapman.edu
ROSETTI, Patricia, H 570-961-4596 389 G
roselli@marywood.edu
ROSEVEAR, Scott, G 570-577-3647 379 F
scott.rosevear@bucknell.edu
ROSEVEARE, Mark 864-592-4763 412 F
rosevearem@sccsc.edu
ROSFELD, Stephen 513-556-6177 362 D
stephen.rosfeld@uc.edu
ROSHEIM, Adam 605-677-5255 416 H
adam.rosheim@usd.edu
ROSIN, Dallas 701-252-3467 347 C
dallas.rosin@uj.edu
ROSINSKI-KAUS,
Donna 732-255-0400 280 A
drosinski-kaus@ocean.edu
ROSIUS, Davius 863-638-2920 113 B
rosius@webber.edu
ROSKIEWICZ,
Kimberly, O 401-863-2234 404 E
kimberly_roskiewicz@brown.edu
ROSKY, Bruce 818-610-6543 49 C
roskybr@piercecollege.edu
ROSMAN, Andrew 201-692-7200 277 K
rosman@fdu.edu
ROSNER, James 303-871-3256 83 D
james.rosner@du.edu
ROSNER-LENGELE,
Julie 215-572-2900 379 A
rosnerj@arcadia.edu
ROSOFF, Nancy 215-572-2921 379 A
rosoffn@arcadia.edu
ROSOVSKY, Leah 617-495-4193 210 B
leah_rosovsky@harvard.edu
ROSPLOCK, Valerie, R 607-735-1174 299 D
vrosplock@elmira.edu
ROSPOND, Raylene, M 260-470-2653 158 T
rmrospond@manchester.edu
ROSS, Aliza 410-532-5184 201 B
aross@ndm.edu
ROSS, Angela 304-710-3382 489 B
rossa@mctc.edu
ROSS, Anissa 870-460-1036 22 D
ross@uamont.edu
ROSS, Beth 617-735-9701 209 A
ross@emmanuel.edu
ROSS, Casey 405-208-5979 367 I
crosspetherick@okcu.edu
ROSS, Cheryl 858-822-2797 69 D
caross@ucsd.edu
ROSS, Christine, C 434-223-6056 468 A
cross@hsc.edu
ROSS, Christopher, R 405-744-6651 368 B
chris.ross@okstate.edu
ROSS, Chuck 802-656-2990 463 E
chuck.ross@uvm.edu
ROSS, Clint 928-774-3890 12 M
cross@indianbible.org
ROSS, Corey 517-750-1200 230 H
ROSS, Corey 605-331-6811 417 E
corey.ross@usiouxfalls.edu
ROSS, David 501-279-4930 19 D
dross@harding.edu
ROSS, David 972-708-7340 435 H
ROSS, Dawn 508-626-4625 212 D
dross@framingham.edu
ROSS, Devon, G 612-330-1588 233 K
ross@augsburg.edu
ROSS, Donald, E 561-237-7782 102 V
dross@lynn.edu
ROSS, Eric 660-263-4100 257 B
ericr@macc.edu
ROSS, III, Frank, E 317-940-9570 153 F
feross@butler.edu
ROSS, Gabe 916-568-3056 50 E
rossg@losrios.edu
ROSS, Gary 401-841-7501 503 L
gary.ross@usnwc.edu
ROSS, Gary, L 315-228-7401 296 F
gross@colgate.edu
ROSS, Gerald 410-225-2399 199 H
gross@mica.edu
ROSS, Gloria 662-254-3558 248 B
gloria.ross@mvsu.edu
ROSS, Hannah 802-443-5229 462 H
hross@middlebury.edu
ROSS, James 732-255-0400 280 A
jross@ocean.edu
ROSS, James, A 734-384-4259 227 G
jross@monroeccc.edu
ROSS, Jamison 952-446-4106 235 G
rossj@crown.edu
ROSS, Jason 864-977-7026 411 E
jason.ross@ngu.edu
ROSS, Jeannie 620-862-5252 171 B
jeannie.ross@barclaycollege.edu
ROSS, Jeffery 816-235-6212 261 C
umkccontracts@umkc.edu
ROSS, Jennifer 718-522-9073 290 C
jross@asa.edu
ROSS, Jennifer, A 260-422-5561 155 H
jaross@indianatech.edu
ROSS, Jeremy, B 423-439-5353 419 J
rossjb@etsu.edu
ROSS, Jill 540-674-3600 475 B
jross@nr.edu
ROSS, Jim 252-249-1851 336 F
jross@pamlicocc.edu
ROSS, Julia 540-231-9752 477 A
rjulie@vt.edu
ROSS, Julie, S 617-627-3360 219 B
j.ross@tufts.edu
ROSS, Karen 734-432-5529 227 A
kross@madonna.edu
ROSS, Keith, L 314-392-2355 256 C
president@mobap.edu
ROSS, Kevin, M 561-237-7823 102 V
kross@lynn.edu
ROSS, Kimberly 312-553-2500 134 A
kaross@ccc.edu
ROSS, Kristen 281-929-4653 443 E
kristen.ross@sjcd.edu
ROSS, Laura 407-708-2058 107 D
rossl@seminolestate.edu
ROSS, Lauren 937-512-2164 361 A
lauren.ross@sinclair.edu
ROSS, Leigh, A 601-984-2620 249 E
laross@umc.edu
ROSS, Linda 213-738-6818 65 G
accounting@swlaw.edu
ROSS, Lori, A 513-556-3483 362 D
rossla@ucmail.uc.edu
ROSS, Matthew 717-815-1359 404 A
mross@ycp.edu
ROSS, Meg 662-562-3204 248 D
mross@northwestms.edu
ROSS, Michael 304-865-6007 488 E
michael.ross@ovu.edu
ROSS, Mikki 806-742-2121 451 B
mikki.ross@ttu.edu
ROSS, Neil 785-320-4554 175 D
neilross@manhattantech.edu
ROSS, Pam 864-231-2000 406 G
pross@andersonuniversity.edu
ROSS, Patricia 504-762-3284 187 E
paross@dcc.edu
ROSS, Patricia, A 801-585-7832 460 E
p.ross@utah.edu
ROSS, JR., Quinton, T 334-229-4202 4 B
president.ross@alasu.edu
ROSS, Ramsey 850-729-5229 103 L
ramseyr@nwfsc.edu
ROSS, Reginald 973-720-2903 284 I
rossr@wpunj.edu
ROSS, Rick 360-417-6533 483 B
rross@pencol.edu
ROSS, Robin 828-327-7000 333 B
rross@cvcc.edu
ROSS, Roshaunda 615-277-7406 428 F
ROSS, Sadie 518-587-2100 321 A
sadie.ross@esc.edu
ROSS, Sharon 914-961-8313 315 C
sross@svots.edu
ROSS, Shawn 850-478-8496 104 G
sross@pcci.edu
ROSS, Sonya 617-373-6963 217 F
ROSS, Susan 304-367-4098 490 B
susan.ross@fairmontstate.edu
ROSS, Susan 817-735-2555 454 C
susan.ross@unthsc.edu
ROSS, Susan 570-321-4204 389 E
ross@lycoming.edu
ROSS, Thelma, L 301-546-0766 201 C
rosstl1@pgcc.edu
ROSS, William 814-332-2316 378 D
wross@allegheny.edu
ROSS-JONES, Marvel, E 716-884-9120 291 L
merossjones@bryantstratton.edu
ROSS-SCOTT, Carol 607-778-5199 318 A
rossca@sunybroome.edu
ROSS STAMPS, Clara 502-597-6785 182 H
clara.stamps@kysu.edu
ROSSBACH, Janet 646-660-6097 292 L
janet.rossbach@baruch.cuny.edu
ROSSELLI, David 254-710-2561 431 J
dave_rosselli@baylor.edu
ROSSER, Charice 252-536-7207 335 B
ROSSER, Edward 706-368-7740 118 E
erosser@highlands.edu
ROSSER, Keith 315-268-7258 296 A
krosser@clarkson.edu
ROSSER, Ulrike 614-825-6255 347 F
urosser@aiam.edu
ROSSER, Virginia, J 419-372-9865 348 H
jrosser@bgsu.edu
ROSSER-MIMS, Dionne 334-670-3365 7 C
rosser-mims@troy.edu
ROSSI, Frank 607-753-4827 318 D
frank.rossi@cortland.edu
ROSSI, Jaclyn 716-286-8761 310 D
jrossi@niagara.edu
ROSSI, Jamal 585-274-1010 323 J
jrossi@esm.rochester.edu
ROSSI, Jason 630-515-5472 136 B
jrossi@devry.edu
ROSSI, John 315-312-5555 319 B
john.rossi@oswego.edu
ROSSI, John, J 626-256-4673 37 B
jrossi@coh.org
ROSSI, Julie 541-245-7615 376 D
jrossi@roguecc.edu
ROSSI, Laura 410-225-2363 199 H
lrossi@mica.edu
ROSSI, Reagan 208-459-5855 130 D
rrossi@collegeofidaho.edu
ROSSI, Renee 904-256-7458 101 G
rrossi@ju.edu
ROSSI-LE, Laura 978-232-2055 209 B
lrossile@endicott.edu
ROSSI-LONG, Jennifer 610-436-2501 396 A
jlong@wcupa.edu
ROSSIGNOL, Paul 505-438-8884 288 C
paul@acupuncturecollege.edu
ROSSITER, Andrew 808-923-9741 128 F
andrewro@hawaii.edu
ROSSITER, Sherry 740-593-4129 359 G
bursar@ohio.edu
ROSSITER-SMITH,
Carla, M 727-816-3190 104 F
ROSSITTO, Paul 860-832-1617 84 I
rossitto@ccsu.edu
ROSSKY, Peter 713-348-3350 442 K
peter.rossky@rice.edu
ROSSMAIER, Joel 479-979-1462 23 I
jrossmai@ozarks.edu
ROSSMAN, Claudia 562-988-2278 25 R
crossman@auhs.edu
ROSSMAN, Vicki 713-780-9777 430 C

ROSSON, Michael .... 718-368-5144 294 E
mrosson@kbcc.cuny.edu
ROST, Gregory, S .... 215-898-7221 400 K
gregrost@upenn.edu
ROST, Jamie, D .... 407-582-5412 112 K
jrost@valenciacollege.edu
ROSTAR, Jimmy .... 252-328-1275 341 C
rostarj@ecu.edu
ROSTER, Ellen .... 320-222-5219 240 E
ellen.roster@ridgewater.edu
ROSTON, Kemisha, R ... 903-927-3381 458 G
kroston@wileyc.edu
ROSTRON, Stephanie .... 937-502-3955 364 D
srostron@wilberforce.edu
ROSU, Gabriela .... 480-732-7012.. 12 P
gabriela.rosu@cgc.edu
ROSZELL, Nancy, J .... 937-255-3636 503 A
nancy.roszell@afit.edu
ROSZMAN, Deborah ..... 419-448-3513 361 J
roszmandl@tiffin.edu
ROTGER, Mariolga .... 787-850-9364 513 E
mariolga.rotger@upr.edu
ROTH, Adam .... 717-477-1451 395 E
asroth@ship.edu
ROTH, Amy .... 772-466-4822.. 94 P
amy.roth@aviator.edu
ROTH, Ben .... 217-786-2773 142 B
ben.roth@llcc.edu
ROTH, Beth .... 815-740-3216 151 J
broth@stfrancis.edu
ROTH, Beth .... 610-790-1981 378 F
beth.roth@alvernia.edu
ROTH, Brenda .... 503-589-8189 373 A
broth@corban.edu
ROTH, Brenda .... 810-762-3488 231 G
blroth@umich.edu
ROTH, Bruce .... 920-206-2318 493 L
bruce.roth@mbu.edu
ROTH, Cindi .... 304-284-4040 491 C
croth@mail.wvu.edu
ROTH, Deb .... 620-327-8279 173 H
deb.roth@hesston.edu
ROTH, Don, F .... 530-754-5418.. 68 E
droth@ucdavis.edu
ROTH, Frank, A .... 610-758-3572 388 J
far4@lehigh.edu
ROTH, Henry .... 650-508-3721.. 54 D
hroth@ndnu.edu
ROTH, James .... 405-208-5440 367 I
jaroth@okcu.edu
ROTH, Jason .... 702-968-1633 272 C
jroth@roseman.edu
ROTH, Jeff .... 310-206-8041.. 69 A
jroth@ponet.ucla.edu
ROTH, John, C .... 718-940-5616 314 C
jroth@sjcny.edu
ROTH, Lindsay .... 508-999-8478 211 F
lroth@umassd.edu
ROTH, Martin, S .... 304-357-4713 488 G
ROTH, Megan .... 325-674-2885 429 B
mkr15a@acu.edu
ROTH, Michael .... 707-527-6939.. 62 F
mroth@santarosa.edu
ROTH, Michael, L .... 509-313-4204 481 D
roth@gonzaga.edu
ROTH, Michael, S .... 860-685-3500.. 89 C
mroth@wesleyan.edu
ROTH, Mike .... 503-589-8152 373 A
mroth@corban.edu
ROTH, OSB, Neal, G ...... 360-491-4440 483 H
theabbot@stmartin.edu
ROTH, Neil .... 304-473-8312 491 H
roth@wvwc.edu
ROTH, Paul, B .... 505-272-5849 288 G
proth@salud.unm.edu
ROTH, Susan .... 212-517-3929 316 B
s.roth@sothebysinstitute.com
ROTH, JR., Toby .... 989-774-3871 222 C
rothj1t@cmich.edu
ROTH NICKS, Rebecca . 706-880-8088 121 A
rroth@lagrange.edu
ROTHAMER, Russ .... 970-339-6300.. 76 G
russ.rothamer@aims.edu
ROTHAUPT, Jeanne .... 715-232-2468 498 A
rothauptj@uwstout.edu
ROTHAUS, Richard, M .. 989-774-3341 222 C
rotha1r@cmich.edu
ROTHBERG, Jacob .... 914-736-1500 310 I
ROTHELL, Cynthia .... 540-373-2200 466 H
crothell@evcc.edu
ROTHENBERG, Jeffrey ... 317-338-3879 160 E
ROTHENBERGER, Sara .. 860-439-2834.. 86 H
srothenb@conncoll.edu

ROTHENBUHLER, Eric ... 314-246-7154 262 C
erothenbuhler@webster.edu
ROTHMAN, Paul .... 410-955-3180 199 D
prothma1@jhmi.edu
ROTHMAN, Paul, D ...... 410-955-3180 199 D
prothma1@jhmi.edu
ROTHMEYER, Michelle .. 815-825-9807 140 F
mrothmeyer@kish.edu
ROTHROCK, Dan .... 253-272-1126 482 C
drothrock@ncad.edu
ROTHSCHILD, Dovid, N 516-255-4700 312 D
rdnr@mlb.edu
ROTHSCHILD,
Martha, D .... 410-777-2701 197 C
mdrothschild@aacc.edu
ROTHSCHILD,
Vivian, M .... 414-847-3239 494 F
vivianrothschild@miad.edu
ROTHSTEIN,
Michael, D .... 334-953-5613 503 B
ROTHWELL, Krista .... 302-622-8000.. 89 E
krothwell@dcad.edu
ROTHWELL, Suzanne .... 573-875-7207 251 F
srothwell@ccis.edu
ROTHWELL, Suzanne .... 573-875-7563 251 F
srothwell@ccis.edu
ROTHWELL, Vivien .... 310-665-6831.. 54 I
vrothwell@otis.edu
ROTHY, Gary .... 619-680-4430.. 28 E
gary.rothy@cc-sd.edu
ROTICH, Herbert, K .... 517-750-1200 230 H
hrotich@arbor.edu
ROTKIEWICZ,
Melissa, S .... 413-545-0333 211 D
mlr@uhs.umass.edu
ROTNER, Loren .... 410-626-2510 201 D
loren.rotner@sjc.edu
ROTOLO, Dee .... 618-453-4626 149 E
drotolo@siu.edu
ROTOLO, Jessica .... 631-656-2144 300 D
jessica.rotolo@ftc.edu
ROTOLO, Rene, M .... 718-960-8226 294 A
rene.rotolo@lehman.cuny.edu
ROTONDO, Denise, M .. 716-888-2160 292 D
rotondod@canisius.edu
ROTONDO, Mark .... 617-873-0675 207 F
mark.rotondo@cambridgecollege.edu
ROTROFF, Kristi .... 419-267-1271 358 A
krotroff@northweststate.edu
ROTT, Cynthia .... 701-231-7458 345 G
cynthia.rott@ndsu.edu
ROTTENBERG, Aaron ..... 718-854-2290 291 F
ROTTER, Bruce, E .... 618-474-7120 149 F
brotter@siue.edu
ROTTLER, Nancy .... 724-805-2255 398 F
nancy.rottler@stvincent.edu
ROTTWEILER, James, D 520-515-5498.. 11 M
jdr@cochise.edu
ROTUNDO, Kim, M .... 906-227-2322 228 F
krotundo@nmu.edu
ROTUNDO, Michael, R . 906-227-2327 228 F
mrotundo@nmu.edu
ROTUNNI, Lisa, M .... 909-869-2474.. 30 D
lmrotunni@cpp.edu
ROTZ, Ben .... 918-766-4357 368 G
brotz@okwu.edu
ROUBIDOUX, Nikol ...... 208-792-2223 131 A
ncroubidoux@lcsc.edu
ROUBINEK, Darren ...... 816-501-2422 250 F
darren.roubinek@avila.edu
ROUBIQUE, Connie ...... 225-752-4233 186 H
croubique@iticollege.edu
ROUDEBUSH, Kelly .... 517-355-2223 227 D
roudebushk@police.msu.edu
ROUDKOVSKI, Melanie . 903-233-3208 439 E
melanieroudkovski@letu.edu
ROUFOS-ABBEY,
Noah, J .... 717-221-1774 385 E
njroufos@hacc.edu
ROUGEAU, Vincent, D .. 617-552-4315 207 B
vincent.rougeau@bc.edu
ROUGHTON, Dean .... 252-335-0821 333 G
dean_roughton@albemarle.edu
ROUGHTON, Keith .... 912-478-0747 119 C
kroughton@georgiasouthern.edu
ROULIER, Stephen .... 413-748-3171 218 G
sroulier@springfield.edu
ROUNCE, Laura, L .... 312-949-7040 138 E
lrounce@ico.edu
ROUND, Sara .... 816-415-5984 262 F
rounds@william.jewell.edu
ROUNDS, Claude .... 518-276-6601 312 I
roundc@rpi.edu

ROUNDS, Dayle, G .... 609-497-7991 280 D
dayle.rounds@ptsem.edu
ROUNDS, Michael .... 785-864-4419 177 D
m528r913@ku.edu
ROUNDS, Michael, J .... 610-565-0999 403 E
mrounds@williamson.edu
ROUNDS, Susan .... 707-621-7000.. 41 F
ROUNDS, Tyra .... 313-993-1046 231 B
roundstc@udmercy.edu
ROUNDTREE, Leslie, A . 773-995-2411 133 K
lroundtr@csu.edu
ROUNTREE, Jeffrey, W .. 540-479-1892 472 I
jeff.rountree@umwf.org
ROUNTREE, Kathleen .... 510-885-3161.. 31 C
kathleen.rountree@csueastbay.edu
ROUNTREE, Linda .... 503-493-6248 372 I
lrountree@cu-portland.edu
ROUNTREE, Mike .... 478-289-2093 117 D
rountree@ega.edu
ROURKE, David .... 415-338-1822.. 34 A
drourke@sfsu.edu
ROURKE, Kathleen .... 315-792-7295 321 E
kathleen.rourke@sunypoly.edu
ROUS, Philip .... 410-455-2598 202 E
rous@umbc.edu
ROUSE, Cecilia .... 609-258-4800 280 E
rouse@princeton.edu
ROUSE, Douglas .... 908-709-7113 284 C
douglas.rouse@ucc.edu
ROUSE, Kevin .... 828-327-7000 333 B
krouse@cvcc.edu
ROUSE, Lawrence, L ..... 252-493-7200 336 H
ROUSE, Nina .... 920-403-4427 495 I
nina.rouse@snc.edu
ROUSE, Sandra .... 803-321-5206 411 D
sandra.rouse@newberry.edu
ROUSH, Chris, G .... 203-582-3641.. 87 G
chris.roush@quinnipiac.edu
ROUSH, Clark, A .... 402-363-5610 270 E
croush@york.edu
ROUSH, John, A .... 859-238-5220 179 F
john.roush@centre.edu
ROUSH, Matt .... 248-204-2210 226 G
mroush@ltu.edu
ROUSH, Rebecca .... 910-695-3704 337 H
roushr@sandhills.edu
ROUSH, Richard, T .... 814-865-2541 392 B
rtr10@psu.edu
ROUSMANIERE, David .. 704-687-7418 342 E
drousman@uncc.edu
ROUSSE, Wade .... 337-475-5514 192 A
wrousse1@mcneese.edu
ROUSSEAU, Erica .... 207-602-2826 196 G
erousseau1@une.edu
ROUSSEAU, Karen .... 413-205-3056 205 A
karen.rousseau@aic.edu
ROUSSEL, David .... 207-780-4788 196 F
david.roussel@maine.edu
ROUSU, Matthew .... 570-372-4186 399 C
rousu@susqu.edu
ROUTBORT, Julia, C ..... 518-580-5555 316 A
jroutbor@skidmore.edu
ROUTENBERG, Robbie .. 585-245-5020 318 E
routenberg@geneseo.edu
ROUTLEY, Jonathan, J .. 563-588-8000 165 F
jjroutley@emmaus.edu
ROVARIS, Dereck .... 225-578-5736 188 I
drovaris@lsu.edu
ROVARIS, Jill .... 408-554-4501.. 62 D
jrovaris@scu.edu
ROVELLO, Rossano .... 516-876-3201 319 A
rovellor@oldwestbury.edu
ROVETTI, Marc .... 510-883-2086.. 41 G
mrovetti@dspt.edu
ROVINELLI HELLER,
Nina .... 860-570-9141.. 88 E
nina.heller@uconn.edu
ROVINSKY-MAYER,
Michele, M .... 215-895-1403 383 B
mrovinsky@drexel.edu
ROVIRA-ALVAREZ,
Jorge .... 787-993-8860 513 B
jorge.rovira@upr.edu
ROWAN, Angela .... 620-431-2820 175 H
arowan@neosho.edu
ROWAN, Bernard .... 773-995-2439 133 K
trowanii@csu.edu
ROWAN, Carl .... 703-993-3840 467 L
crowan2@gmu.edu
ROWAN, John .... 318-473-6446 188 J
jrowan@lsua.edu
ROWAN, Matthew, C .... 260-399-7700 161 D
mrowan@sf.edu

ROWANE, Michael .... 814-866-8118 388 A
mrowane@lecom.edu
ROWBOTTOM, Joe .... 336-334-4822 335 A
jprowbottom@gtcc.edu
ROWDEN, Diana .... 479-788-7676.. 21 H
diana.rowden@uafs.edu
ROWE, Alan .... 229-333-7816 126 G
carowe@valdosta.edu
ROWE, Amy .... 814-868-9900 383 F
arowe@erieit.edu
ROWE, Dayna .... 405-422-1467 369 E
dayna.rowe@redlandscc.edu
ROWE, Edward, P .... 610-328-8321 399 D
erowe1@swarthmore.edu
ROWE, Jonathan .... 410-386-8217 197 G
jhoskowitz@carrollcc.edu
ROWE, Katherine, A ...... 757-221-1693 466 C
president@wm.edu
ROWE, Kenneth, D .... 405-325-3916 371 B
kenneth-rowe@ouhsc.edu
ROWE, Nicholas .... 978-867-4299 209 F
nicholas.rowe@gordon.edu
ROWE, Nicole .... 906-932-4231 224 B
nicoler@gogebic.edu
ROWE, Philip .... 919-508-2329 344 F
prowe@peace.edu
ROWE, Ruby .... 303-300-8740.. 77 D
ruby.rowe@collegeamerica.edu
ROWE, Theresa, M .... 248-370-4326 229 G
rowe@oakland.edu
ROWE, Tim .... 304-877-6428 487 F
registrar@abc.edu
ROWE-ALLEN, Ophelie .. 203-254-4000.. 86 I
orallen@fairfield.edu
ROWELL, Jeren .... 816-268-5401 257 C
jrowell@nts.edu
ROWELL, Sam .... 423-354-5207 425 E
ssrowell@northeaststate.edu
ROWEN, Cate .... 413-585-3021 218 F
crowen@smith.edu
ROWEN, Kyle .... 805-756-5530.. 30 C
counsel@calpoly.edu
ROWETT JAMES,
Kelly, A .... 336-334-7595 341 F
karowettjames@ncat.edu
ROWH, Mark, C .... 540-674-3617 475 B
mrowh@nr.edu
ROWLAND, Barbara ...... 217-228-5432 146 F
rowlaba@quincy.edu
ROWLAND, Bryan .... 423-425-4717 428 A
bryan-rowland@utc.edu
ROWLAND, Gordon .... 607-274-3734 303 B
rowland@ithaca.edu
ROWLAND, Jenny .... 252-334-2020 331 D
jenny.rowland@macuniversity.edu
ROWLAND, Jim .... 918-540-6301 366 I
jrowland@neo.edu
ROWLAND, Leo .... 909-748-8717.. 71 G
leo_rowland@redlands.edu
ROWLAND, Linda .... 706-864-1358 126 A
linda.rowland@ung.edu
ROWLAND, Randy .... 913-360-7372 171 D
rrowland@benedictine.edu
ROWLAND, IV, Roy .... 863-667-5081 107 K
rrowland@seu.edu
ROWLAND, Shannon ..... 423-614-8637 420 J
srowland@leeuniversity.edu
ROWLAND, Sheri .... 850-201-8490 111 C
rowlands@tcc.fl.edu
ROWLAND, Theresa ...... 616-331-9530 224 E
rowlanth@gvsu.edu
ROWLETT, Carol .... 540-857-7277 476 D
crowlett@virginiawestern.edu
ROWLEY, Becky .... 505-428-1202 288 B
becky.rowley@sfcc.edu
ROWLEY, Don .... 765-677-2313 157 D
don.rowley@indwes.edu
ROWLEY, Michelle .... 440-375-7230 355 G
mrowley@lec.edu
ROWLEY, Sarah, L .... 248-341-2081 229 A
slrowley@oaklandcc.edu
ROWLEY, Stephanie .... 212-678-3050 322 G
sjr2192@tc.columbia.edu
ROWLEY, Stephanie, J .. 734-763-0680 231 E
srowley@umich.edu
ROWSER, Mayola .... 314-454-7055 253 E
mayola.rowser@bjc.org
ROWZEE, Julie .... 601-635-2111 245 I
jrowzee@eccc.edu
ROXWORTHY, Emily ..... 858-534-1709.. 69 D
waprovost@ucsd.edu
ROY, Alisa .... 704-922-6202 334 F
roy.alisa@gaston.edu

ROY, Gail .... 207-768-2734 194 J
groy@nmcc.edu
ROY, Jocelyn .... 859-371-9393 179 A
jroy@beckfield.edu
ROY, Judy, K .... 260-422-5561 155 H
jkroy@indianatech.edu
ROY, Justin .... 617-322-3551 210 F
justin_roy@laboure.edu
ROY, Kevin .... 413-748-3252 218 G
ROY, Lara .... 612-874-3778 236 K
lara_roy@mcad.edu
ROY, Lisa .... 207-326-4715 195 D
lisa.roy@mma.edu
ROY, Marc .... 517-629-0221 220 G
mroy@albion.edu
ROY, Marc .... 856-351-2680 283 A
mroy@salemcc.edu
ROY, Matthew .... 508-910-9052 211 F
mroy@umassd.edu
ROY, Melissa .... 845-574-4758 313 C
mroy@sunyrockland.edu
ROY, Michael, D .... 802-443-5490 462 H
mdroy@middlebury.edu
ROY, Omaira .... 508-286-3544 220 A
roy_omaira@wheatoncollege.edu
ROY, Rani .... 718-862-7755 305 H
rani.roy@manhattan.edu
ROY, Rina .... 916-484-8108.. 50 F
royr@arc.losrios.edu
ROY, Tracey .... 218-322-2409 238 C
troy@itascacc.edu
ROY, Tracey .... 218-322-2409 238 E
tracey.roy@itascacc.edu
ROY, Tracey .... 218-322-2409 238 G
tracey.roy@itascacc.edu
ROY, Wesley .... 401-598-1000 404 I
wroy@jwu.edu
ROYAL, Angela .... 636-949-4983 254 F
aroyal@lindenwood.edu
ROYAL, Christina .... 413-552-2700 214 D
croyal@hcc.edu
ROYAL, Karen, B .... 361-593-4758 447 D
karen.royal@tamuk.edu
ROYAL, Rebecca .... 908-709-7042 284 C
rebecca.royal@ucc.edu
ROYCE, Richard, A .... 516-671-2356 324 G
rroyce@webb.edu
ROYCE-DAVIS,
Joanna, C .... 253-535-7191 482 H
roycedjc@plu.edu
ROYE, Shauna .... 202-495-3837.. 92 E
sroye@dhs.edu
ROYEEN, Charlotte .... 312-942-7120 148 A
charlotte_l_royeen@rush.edu
ROYER, Dara, J .... 315-443-8338 322 C
djroyer@syr.edu
ROYER, James .... 504-671-5477 187 E
jroyer@dcc.edu
ROYER, Joseph .... 765-641-4000 153 B
jmroyer@anderson.edu
ROYER, Randy .... 913-288-7188 174 F
rroyer@kckcc.edu
ROYER, Roma .... 602-429-4947.. 15 C
rroyer@ps.edu
ROYKO, Barry .... 216-987-0205 351 G
barry.royko@tri-c.edu
ROYO, Sebastian .... 617-573-8120 219 A
sroyo@suffolk.edu
ROYSTER, Jacqueline, J 404-894-1728 118 F
jacqueline.royster@iac.gatech.edu
ROYSTER, Leigh-Anne .. 336-278-5017 328 K
lroyster@elon.edu
ROYSTON, Mimi .... 413-205-3448 205 A
mimi.royston@aic.edu
ROYSTON,
Rosemary, R .... 706-379-3111 127 C
rosemary@yhc.edu
ROYUK, Brent .... 402-643-7304 266 G
brent.royuk@cune.edu
ROZADA, Mayra .... 787-891-0925 508 K
mrozada@aguadilla.inter.edu
ROZAK, Edward .... 508-830-5030 213 B
erozak@maritime.edu
ROZBORSKI, Joanne ...... 850-484-1708 104 H
jrozborski@pensacolastate.edu
ROZEBOOM, David .... 828-689-1212 331 A
david_rozeboom@mhu.edu
ROZEK, Charles, E .... 216-368-4390 349 F
cer2@case.edu
ROZELL, Mark .... 703-993-8171 467 L
mrozell@gmu.edu
ROZELLE-STONE,
A. Rebecca .... 701-777-3302 345 C
adrian.rozelle@und.edu
ROZEMA, Burton, J ...... 708-239-4760 150 F
burt.rozema@trnty.edu
ROZEWSKI, Mark .... 203-392-5456.. 85 A
rozewskim1@southernct.edu
ROZHON, Tamara .... 562-902-3304.. 65 C
tamararozhon@scuhs.edu
ROZLER, Tracy .... 716-896-0700 324 E
trozler@villa.edu
RUANE, Beth .... 802-451-7577 462 E
bruane@marlboro.edu
RUANO, Norman .... 773-878-3894 148 D
nruano@iwe.staugustine.edu
RUARK, Matthew .... 270-852-3120 183 A
matthewru@kwc.edu
RUBACK, Chad .... 847-578-8589 147 I
chad.ruback@rosalindfranlin.edu
RUBEL, Carol .... 617-587-5650 217 A
rubelc@neco.edu
RUBEMEYER, Susan ...... 636-922-8360 258 I
srubemeyer@stchas.edu
RUBEN, Brent, D .... 848-932-3968 282 A
bruben@rutgers.edu
RUBENSTEIN, David ...... 856-256-4222 281 E
rubenstein@rowan.edu
RUBENSTEIN, David ...... 610-758-3000 388 J
RUBIN, Adam .... 618-985-3741 139 I
adamrubin@jalc.edu
RUBIN, Beno .... 757-822-5077 476 B
brubin@tcc.edu
RUBIN, Beth .... 910-814-4377 327 E
brubin@campbell.edu
RUBIN, James .... 602-787-6546.. 13 E
james.rubin@paradisevalley.edu
RUBIN, Joshua .... 718-436-2122 322 E
RUBIN, Lisa .... 770-426-2725 121 C
lrubin@life.edu
RUBIN, Lucas .... 212-966-4014 293 C
lrubin@brooklyn.cuny.edu
RUBIN, Marc, A .... 513-529-1799 356 E
rubinma@miamioh.edu
RUBIN, Moshe .... 515-239-9002 315 I
myrubin@shoryoshuv.org
RUBIN, Nancy .... 952-885-5390 242 I
nrubin@nwhealth.edu
RUBIN, Nancy .... 330-569-3211 353 J
RUBIN, Nancy .... 970-351-1931.. 83 E
nancy.rubin@unco.edu
RUBIN, Rachel .... 860-486-2337.. 88 E
rachel.rubin@uconn.edu
RUBIN, Rachel .... 614-236-6908 349 D
rrubin@capital.edu
RUBIN, Steve .... 719-219-9636.. 77 F
steverubindvm@cavt.edu
RUBINO, David .... 814-866-6641 388 A
drubino@lecom.edu
RUBINO, Debra .... 410-225-2300 199 H
drubino@mica.edu
RUBINO, Joseph .... 410-293-1549 504 I
rubino@usna.edu
RUBINO, Karen, M .... 401-456-8849 405 C
krubino@ric.edu
RUBINO, Michael, H .... 508-767-7156 205 D
rubino@assumption.edu
RUBINSTEIN, James ..... 623-572-3395 143 G
jrubinstein@midwestern.edu
RUBINSTEIN, Mark .... 603-513-1304 274 H
mark.rubinstein@granite.edu
RUBIO, Dave .... 909-384-8640.. 59 I
drubio@sbccd.cc.ca.us
RUBIO, Joan .... 714-463-7550.. 51 A
jrubio@ketchum.edu
RUBLE, Megan .... 507-933-7526 235 I
mruble@gustavus.edu
RUBLE, Michelle .... 301-934-4711 198 A
mmruble@csmd.edu
RUBON, Jellesen .... 692-625-3394 505 F
RUBRITZ, Gerald .... 814-886-6460 391 B
grubritz@mtaloy.edu
RUBY, Ashley .... 301-387-3733 198 F
ashley.ruby@garrettcollege.edu
RUCKEL, Stephanie .... 612-330-1550 233 K
ruckels@augsburg.edu
RUCKER, Alan, M .... 606-783-5367 183 F
a.rucker@moreheadstate.edu
RUCKER, Cedric, B .... 540-654-1200 472 I
crucker@umw.edu
RUCKER, Jana .... 501-279-4316.. 19 D
jrucker@harding.edu
RUCKER, Kade .... 303-373-2008.. 82 G
krucker@rvu.edu
RUCKER, Marty, K .... 423-585-6983 426 C
marty.rucker@ws.edu
RUCKER, Meridith .... 901-435-1399 421 A
meridith_rucker@loc.edu
RUCKER, Nolan .... 303-751-8700.. 77 A
rucker@bel-rea.com
RUCKER, Paul .... 206-685-9223 485 F
uwalumni@uw.edu
RUCKER, Robert, E .... 662-685-4771 245 D
erucker@bmc.edu
RUCKER, Shawn .... 901-435-1755 421 A
shawn_rucker@loc.edu
RUCKER, Sherri, B .... 615-329-8555 419 K
srucker@fisk.edu
RUCKER, Sonia .... 573-651-2524 259 K
srucker@semo.edu
RUCKER, Stacey .... 309-341-5330 133 C
srucker@sandburg.edu
RUCKER, Tracy .... 319-352-8238 170 C
tracy.rucker@wartburg.edu
RUCKER-SHAMU,
Marian .... 301-860-3849 203 C
mshamu@bowiestate.edu
RUCKS, Karen .... 508-854-7530 215 D
krucks@qcc.mass.edu
RUCKS, Lucas .... 360-538-4013 481 E
lucas.rucks@ghc.edu
RUDA, Ryan .... 620-276-9533 173 E
ryan.ruda@gcccks.edu
RUDATSIKIRA,
Emmanuel .... 269-471-6648 221 B
rudatsikira@andrews.edu
RUDAWITZ, Linda .... 503-517-1397 377 G
lrudawitz@warnerpacific.edu
RUDAWSKY, Donald, J . 954-262-5392 103 M
rudawsky@nova.edu
RUDD, M. David .... 901-678-2234 427 D
mdrudd@memphis.edu
RUDDEN, David .... 847-214-7925 136 F
drudden@elgin.edu
RUDE, Jen .... 253-535-7464 482 H
rudejl@plu.edu
RUDEAU, William .... 609-771-2187 276 I
rudeau@tcnj.edu
RUDECOFF,
Christine, A .... 315-684-6055 321 D
rudecoc@morrisville.edu
RUDICK, Craig, P .... 859-323-3190 185 B
craig.rudick@uky.edu
RUDIGER, Brenda .... 906-487-2400 227 E
brudiger@mtu.edu
RUDIGER, Jennifer .... 715-232-5161 498 A
rudigerj@uwstout.edu
RUDIN, Mark, J .... 903-886-5011 447 B
mark.rudin@tamuc.edu
RUDISILL, Frank .... 864-503-5511 414 D
frudisill@uscupstate.edu
RUDMAN, William .... 847-578-7440 147 I
william.rudman@rosalindfranklin.edu
RUDNEY, Gwen .... 320-589-6411 244 B
rudneygl@morris.umn.edu
RUDNICK, Virginia .... 315-294-8842 292 E
vrudnick@cayuga-cc.edu
RUDNYTZKY, Nick .... 215-885-2360 389 F
nrudnytzky@manor.edu
RUDOLPH, Alan, S .... 970-491-7194.. 78 M
alan.rudolph@colostate.edu
RUDOLPH, Angela .... 304-724-5000 487 H
angela@rjpccpa.com
RUDOLPH, Margaret ..... 419-448-2111 353 H
mrudolph@heidelberg.edu
RUDOVSKY, Michelle ..... 650-378-6577.. 61 P
rudovskym@smccd.edu
RUDOWSKY, Catherine . 361-825-2643 447 C
catherine.rudowsky@tamucc.edu
RUDY, James .... 714-432-5017.. 38 E
jrudy7@occ.cccd.edu
RUE, Cynthia .... 239-454-5000 105 E
RUE, Penny .... 336-758-5943 344 D
rue@wfu.edu
RUEB, Jan, L .... 432-837-8178 450 D
jrueb@sulross.edu
RUEFF, Alicia .... 561-732-4424 106 G
arueff@svdp.edu
RUEFF, Katherine, M .... 804-752-3259 470 F
katherinerueff@rmc.edu
RUEFLE, Colleen .... 412-536-1069 387 B
colleen.ruefle@laroche.edu
RUEGG, Texas .... 903-233-4381 439 E
texasruegg@letu.edu
RUEGGER, Jacqueline ... 718-933-6700 307 G
jruegger@monroecollege.edu
RUELAS, AnnMarie .... 714-484-7369.. 53 K
aruelas@cypresscollege.edu
RUELLE, Joan .... 336-278-6572 328 K
jruelle@elon.edu
RUESCH, Sherry .... 435-652-7551 460 G
ruesch@dixie.edu
RUESCHMANN, Eva ...... 413-559-5378 210 A
erha@hampshire.edu
RUETTEN, Amy .... 417-667-8181 252 A
aruetten@cottey.edu
RUFF, Corey .... 325-674-2665 429 B
clr06a@acu.edu
RUFF, Haskell .... 470-639-0999 122 D
haskell.ruff@morehouse.edu
RUFF, Joy, C .... 305-237-2090 103 D
jruff@mdc.edu
RUFF, Margaret .... 903-785-7661 441 G
mruff@parisjc.edu
RUFF, III, Raymond, H . 864-597-4171 414 H
ruffrh@wofford.edu
RUFF, Sydney .... 802-387-7223 462 D
sydneyruff@landmark.edu
RUFF, Tina, B .... 919-536-7200 334 B
rufft@durhamtech.edu
RUFFIN, Cynthia .... 919-572-1625 326 L
cruffin@apexsot.edu
RUFFIN, Finee .... 601-477-4082 246 F
finee.ruffin@jcjc.edu
RUFFIN, Shanda .... 803-780-1361 414 E
sruffin@voorhees.edu
RUFFING, Rebecca .... 315-866-0300 301 G
ruffingrj@herkimer.edu
RUFFINI, Giovanni .... 203-254-4000.. 86 I
gruffini@fairfield.edu
RUFFRAGE, Jo .... 315-792-7172 321 E
ruffraj@sunypoly.edu
RUFINO, Paul .... 856-415-2173 281 D
prufino@rcgc.edu
RUFLETH, Ernest .... 318-257-5500 191 F
erufleth@latech.edu
RUFO, Joseph .... 315-470-6622 320 A
jlrufo@esf.edu
RUGEMER, Ellen .... 410-857-2203 200 B
erugemer@mcdaniel.edu
RUGER, Theodore, W ... 215-898-7061 400 K
deanruger@law.upenn.edu
RUGG, Marilyn .... 315-228-7288 296 F
mrugg@colgate.edu
RUGG, Rebecca .... 312-996-2006 151 B
rugg@uic.edu
RUGGAR MARTIN, Jan . 323-469-3300.. 25 E
jruggarmartin@amda.edu
RUGGERO, Lorena .... 619-644-7840.. 44 I
lorena.ruggero@gcccd.edu
RUGGIERI, Jan .... 508-849-3444 205 C
jruggieri@annamaria.edu
RUGGIERO, Bruno .... 985-448-4262 192 B
bruno.ruggiero@nicholls.edu
RUGGIRELLO, John ...... 860-727-6907.. 87 A
jruggirello@goodwin.edu
RUGGLES, Jennifer .... 216-368-1723 349 F
jor15@case.edu
RUGGLES, Shami .... 509-533-7085 480 A
shami.ruggles@ccs.spokane.edu
RUGGLES, Shami, R ..... 509-533-3567 479 I
shami.ruggles@ccs.spokane.edu
RUGH, Susan .... 801-422-2742 458 H
susan_rugh@byu.edu
RUHD, Jill .... 605-256-5650 416 J
jill.ruhd@dsu.edu
RUHL, Austin .... 406-586-3585 263 J
austin.ruhl@montanabiblecollege.edu
RUHL, Chris .... 317-208-5311 159 D
RUHLANDT, Karin .... 315-443-3949 322 C
kruhland@syr.edu
RUI, Rachel, J .... 865-974-3265 427 G
jrui@utk.edu
RUITER, Kathy .... 217-854-5525 132 I
kathleen.ruiter@blackburn.edu
RUIZ, Alberto .... 318-342-1025 192 F
ruiz@ulm.edu
RUIZ, Alfredo .... 269-471-6979 221 B
jaruiz@andrews.edu
RUIZ, Andrew .... 806-894-9611 443 I
aruiz@southplainscollege.edu
RUIZ, Angel, J .... 787-863-2390 509 B
angel.ruiz@fajardo.inter.edu
RUIZ, Diego .... 301-447-5223 200 E
r.ruiz@msmary.edu
RUIZ, Dora .... 310-289-5123.. 73 H
dora.ruiz@wcui.edu
RUIZ, Ediltrudys .... 718-960-8421 294 A
ediltrudys.ruiz@lehman.cuny.edu
RUIZ, Eric .... 815-740-5070 151 J
eruiz@stfrancis.edu
RUIZ, Israel .... 617-253-4495 215 G

RUIZ, Israel, A 787-840-2575 510 J
iruiz@psm.edu
RUIZ, Joaquin 520-621-4090 16 G
jruiz@email.arizona.edu
RUIZ, OP, John Martin 202-495-3821 92 E
jruiz@dhs.edu
RUIZ, Jose 787-863-2390 509 B
jose.ruiz@fajardo.inter.edu
RUIZ, Joseph 361-698-1374 436 C
jruiz156@delmar.edu
RUIZ, Lucy 559-243-7105 66 C
lucy.ruiz@scccd.edu
RUIZ, Luis, A 787-766-1717 511 H
um_lruiz@suagm.edu
RUIZ, Luis, E 787-250-1912 509 D
leruiz@metro.inter.edu
RUIZ, Maria-Luisa 718-270-6263 295 A
mlruiz@mec.cuny.edu
RUIZ, Melanie 425-564-2710 478 F
melanie.ruiz@bellevuecollege.edu
RUIZ, Miguel 713-221-8564 453 B
ruizm@uhd.edu
RUIZ, Phyllis 201-216-5213 283 C
phyllis.ruiz@stevens.edu
RUIZ, Rachel 626-966-4576 25 N
studentservices@agu.edu
RUIZ, Rafael 787-257-0000 513 C
rafael.ruiz@upr.edu
RUIZ, Sasha 787-891-0925 508 K
sruiz@aguadilla.inter.edu
RUIZ, Sina 903-875-7376 440 G
sina.ruiz@navarrocollege.edu
RUIZ, Trisha 713-525-2101 454 H
ruizt@stthom.edu
RUIZ, Veronica 787-746-1400 508 B
vruiz@huertas.edu
RUIZ, Zaida 787-786-3030 512 B
zrueiz@ucb.edu.pr
RUIZ-ESPARZA, Emir 620-947-3121 177 C
emirruizesparza@tabor.edu
RUIZ-HUSTON, Ines 209-946-7705 70 E
iruiz@pacific.edu
RUIZ-MATTEI, Enid 719-389-6854 77 H
enid.ruizmattei@coloradocollege.edu
RUIZ-MORENO, Isabel 818-364-7776 49 B
ruizoi@lamission.edu
RUKOBO, Emily 212-261-1567 309 F
erukobo@nyit.edu
RULAND, Judith, P 989-964-4145 230 B
jruland@svsu.edu
RULE, Brian 312-236-9000 143 F
RULE, Dave 425-602-3000 478 D
drule@bastyr.edu
RULE, Nik 641-673-2168 170 F
ruleng@wmpenn.edu
RULE, Scott 678-664-0530 127 A
scott.rule@westgatech.edu
RULLÁN TORO,
Agustin 787-265-3822 513 F
decano.ingenieria@upr.edu
RULLMAN, Loren 616-331-3585 224 E
rullmanl@gvsu.edu
RULNEY, Lisa 520-621-5977 16 G
lisarulney@email.arizona.edu
RULOFSON, Eric 530-938-5851 39 F
erulofson@siskiyous.edu
RULOFSON, Eric 307-268-2492 501 U
eric.rulofson@caspercollege.edu
RUMERY, Joyce, V 207-581-1655 195 J
rumery@maine.edu
RUMIANO, Sara 530-898-5270 31 A
srumiano@csuchico.edu
RUMLEY, Timothy 616-538-2330 224 C
trumley@gracechristian.edu
RUMMEL, Justin 570-372-4314 399 C
rummelj@susqu.edu
RUMMEL, Tina 903-675-6376 452 B
trummel@tvcc.edu
RUMMELL, Kathryn 805-756-2706 30 C
krummell@calpoly.edu
RUMP, Rebecca 319-208-5065 169 F
brump@scciowa.edu
RUMPCA, Susan 763-576-4048 237 D
srumpca@anokatech.edu
RUMPLER, Laura 208-769-3316 131 C
lkrumpler@nic.edu
RUMPZA, Matthew, D 651-696-6551 236 H
mrumpza@macalester.edu
RUMSEY, Duane 661-722-6300 26 D
drumsey@avc.edu
RUMSEY, Elizabeth 218-726-7471 243 F
erumsey@d.umn.edu
RUMSEY, Tyler 928-776-2067 16 M
tyler.rumsey@yc.edu
RUND, James, A 480-965-2200 10 I
james.rund@asu.edu
RUNDELL, Isabel 317-896-9324 160 I
irundell@ubca.org
RUNDELL, Jay, A 740-362-3121 356 D
jrundell@mtso.edu
RUNDQUIST, Amanda 319-385-6229 167 A
amanda.rundquist@iw.edu
RUNDQUIST, Brad 701-777-4589 345 C
bradley.rundquist@und.edu
RUNDSTROM, Amy, L 308-865-8501 269 I
rundstromal@unk.edu
RUNELL HALL,
Marcella 413-538-3133 216 G
mhall@mtholyoke.edu
RUNESTAD, Eric 563-387-1507 167 E
eric.runestad@luther.edu
RUNEY, Mim, L 401-598-1000 404 I
mruney@jwu.edu
RUNFELDT, John 973-877-3078 277 I
runfeldt@essex.edu
RUNGAITIS, Stacy 760-744-1150 55 I
srungaitis@palomar.edu
RUNGE, Carol 518-743-2313 320 D
rungec@sunyacc.edu
RUNGE, Christina 414-955-8055 494 C
chrunge@mcw.edu
RUNGE, Denise 907-786-6494 9 H
drunge@alaska.edu
RUNGE, Mark, S 620-341-5331 172 L
mrunge@emporia.edu
RUNGE, Marschall, S 734-647-9351 231 E
mrunge@umich.edu
RUNIEWICZ, Michael, J 314-935-8976 262 A
michael_runiewicz@wustl.edu
RUNION, Robert 304-929-5026 489 C
rrunion@newriver.edu
RUNION, Trish 785-539-3571 175 E
trunion@mccks.edu
RUNKLE, Dan 563-589-3599 169 I
drunkle@dbq.edu
RUNKLE, Gita 562-463-7359 58 E
grunkle@riohondo.edu
RUNKSMEIER, Lori 860-465-5091 84 J
runksmeierl@easternct.edu
RUNNELS, Greg 574-239-8312 155 D
grunnels@hcc-nd.edu
RUNNING, Patrick 320-762-4483 237 B
patrickr@alextech.edu
RUNSER, Beth 704-461-6573 327 A
bethrunser@bac.edu
RUNYAN, Laura 717-337-6505 384 H
lrunyan@gettysburg.edu
RUNYAN, Lisa 660-543-4914 260 K
runyan@ucmo.edu
RUNYAN, Rodney 936-294-2394 450 C
rcr039@shsu.edu
RUNYON, David 717-901-5137 385 K
drunyon@harrisburgu.edu
RUNYON, Jean 970-204-8100 79 J
jean.runyon@frontrange.edu
RUNYON, Jennifer 410-810-7765 204 D
jrunyon2@washcoll.edu
RUNYON, Tim 417-626-1234 257 F
runyon.tim@occ.edu
RUPE, Jolene, K 785-539-3571 175 E
jrupe@mccks.edu
RUPE, Manuel, R 989-774-3971 222 C
rupe1mr@cmich.edu
RUPE, Robert 972-279-6511 430 B
ssodean@amberton.edu
RUPE, Ryan, R 860-444-8481 504 F
ryan.r.rupe@uscg.mil
RUPERT, Gary 412-809-5100 396 H
rupert.gary@ptcollege.edu
RUPERT, Kimberly 517-750-1200 230 H
krupert@arbor.edu
RUPERT, Terry, A 937-481-2255 364 E
terry_rupert@wilmington.edu
RUPIPER, Russ 402-557-7291 265 J
russ.rupiper@bellevue.edu
RUPP, Lisa 541-463-5561 373 F
ruppl@lanecc.edu
RUPP, Richard 219-989-2134 159 G
rrupp@pnw.edu
RUPP, Sharon, L 864-424-8014 414 C
ruppsl@mailbox.sc.edu
RUPP, Sheila 231-995-1058 228 G
srupp@nmc.edu
RUPPERT, Shawn 804-627-5300 465 C
RUPPRECHT, Stephen 610-902-8417 380 C
smr438@cabrini.edu
RUPSCH, Christina 252-398-6358 328 D
rupscc@chowan.edu
RURSCH, Keri 309-794-7721 132 C
kerirursch@augustana.edu
RUS, Zach 712-749-2636 163 D
rusz@bvu.edu
RUSCH, Kathleen, M 414-464-9777 499 A
rusch.kathleen@wspp.edu
RUSCH, Kevin 509-547-0511 479 H
krusch@clumbiabasin.edu
RUSCH-CURL, Kari 651-450-3887 238 D
crusch-curl@inverhills.edu
RUSCH-CURL, Kari 952-358-8776 239 F
kari.rusch-curl@normandale.edu
RUSCHE, Ernst 231-348-6624 228 E
erusche@ncmich.edu
RUSCHIVAL, Michael 303-292-0015 79 G
mruschival@denvercollegeofnursing.edu
RUSCHMAN, Doug 513-745-3185 365 B
ruschman@xavier.edu
RUSE, Elaine 330-941-3505 365 C
eruse@ysu.edu
RUSH, Amber 870-368-2008 20 F
arush@ozarka.edu
RUSH, Amy 757-455-3401 477 F
arush@vwu.edu
RUSH, Bonnie, R 785-532-5660 174 G
brush@vet.ksu.edu
RUSH, Cherylyn, L 215-951-1948 387 C
rush@lasalle.edu
RUSH, Denise 617-585-0200 206 F
denise.rush@the-bac.edu
RUSH, Dennis 845-569-3492 307 J
dennis.rush@msmc.edu
RUSH, James 662-476-5386 246 A
jrush@eastms.edu
RUSH, JR., James 706-721-1626 115 A
jrush@augusta.edu
RUSH, Janet 402-363-5661 270 E
jgrush@york.edu
RUSH, John, H 563-588-8000 165 F
jrush@emmaus.edu
RUSH, John, P 662-325-9306 247 F
rush@devalumni.msstate.edu
RUSH, Katy 563-441-4046 165 E
krush@eicc.edu
RUSH, Keith 225-769-8820 188 G
RUSH, Mark, E 540-458-8904 478 A
rushm@wlu.edu
RUSH, Maureen 215-898-7515 400 K
mrush@publicsafety.upenn.edu
RUSH, Nate 217-854-5776 132 I
nate.rush@blackburn.edu
RUSH, Patrick 708-596-2000 149 B
prush@ssc.edu
RUSH, III, Robert 610-861-1485 391 A
rushr@moravian.edu
RUSH, Rosalee 209-667-3131 33 C
RUSH, Tanya 443-885-3527 200 D
tanya.rush@morgan.edu
RUSHBROOK, Jill 860-253-3068 85 C
jrushbrook@asnuntuck.edu
RUSHER, Bryan 501-812-2256 23 B
brusher@uaptc.edu
RUSHFORTH, Brenda 909-621-8175 57 F
brenda.rushforth@pomona.edu
RUSHI, Purva 815-802-8258 140 D
prushi@kcc.edu
RUSHIK, Julie 585-594-6493 312 K
rushik_julie@roberts.edu
RUSHING, Cheri 618-437-5321 147 A
rushing@rlc.edu
RUSHING, Dorrie 713-646-1898 444 B
drushing@stcl.edu
RUSHING, James 856-225-7042 281 G
rushing@camden.rutgers.edu
RUSHING,
James Kenneth 904-264-2172 105 L
krushing@iwsfla.org
RUSHING, Linda 870-364-6414 22 D
rushingl@uamont.edu
RUSHING, Mark 479-575-4140 21 G
RUSHING, Ray 254-867-4893 449 E
ray.rushing@tstc.edu
RUSHING, Ray 254-867-3662 449 E
ray.rushing@tstc.edu
RUSHLOW, Jennifer 802-831-1136 463 G
jrushlow@vermontlaw.edu
RUSHMER, Bernadette 570-674-8028 390 G
brushmer@misericordia.edu
RUSHNAWITZ, P 248-968-3360 233 F
RUSHTON, Jennifer 706-379-3111 127 C
jlrushton@yhc.edu
RUSILOSKI, Benjamin 215-489-2911 382 D
benjamin.rusiloski@delval.edu
RUSINKO, Joseph 315-781-3304 302 A
rusinko@hws.edu
RUSKIN, Susan 323-856-7741 25 M
RUSS, Christina 425-640-1683 480 F
christina.russ@edcc.edu
RUSS, Pamela 870-575-8316 22 E
russp@uapb.edu
RUSS, Roy 304-793-6819 491 A
rruss@osteo.wvsom.edu
RUSS, Shelly 802-728-1303 464 E
sruss@vtc.edu
RUSS-WILSON, Traci, L 704-894-2201 328 F
trruss@davidson.edu
RUSSE, Sarah, R 630-844-4620 132 D
srusse@aurora.edu
RUSSEK, Lori 361-593-2678 447 D
lori.russek@tamuk.edu
RUSSEL, Michael 817-257-7926 448 G
m.russel@tcu.edu
RUSSEL, Philip 215-951-2814 400 A
philip.russel@jefferson.edu
RUSSELBURG, Morgan 270-686-4285 179 D
morgan.russelburg@brescia.edu
RUSSELL, Adrina 910-670-2116 341 E
arussell@uncfsu.edu
RUSSELL, Agnes, M 616-988-3656 226 C
arussell@kuyper.edu
RUSSELL, Andrew 315-792-7317 321 E
andrew.russell@sunypoly.edu
RUSSELL, Ann Marie 413-577-1130 211 D
amrussell@umass.edu
RUSSELL, Avis 202-274-5400 93 C
avis.russell@udc.edu
RUSSELL, B. Sherrance 937-376-6612 350 D
brussell@centralstate.edu
RUSSELL, Babs 770-947-7260 127 A
babs.russell@westgatech.edu
RUSSELL, Barbara 716-338-1210 303 D
barbararussell@mail.sunyjcc.edu
RUSSELL, Brent 803-778-6689 407 C
russellrd@cctech.edu
RUSSELL, Bryan 270-745-5818 185 E
bryan.russell@wku.edu
RUSSELL, Bryce 212-812-4041 309 D
brussell@nycda.edu
RUSSELL, Christina, L 757-594-7278 466 B
christina.russell@cnu.edu
RUSSELL, Chrystina 603-626-9100 274 D
c.russell@snhu.edu
RUSSELL, Connie, J 903-510-2203 452 C
crus@tjc.edu
RUSSELL, Craig 501-279-5000 19 D
crussell@harding.edu
RUSSELL, Cynthia 267-341-3292 386 A
crussell@holyfamily.edu
RUSSELL, Danny 740-362-3322 356 D
drussell@mtso.edu
RUSSELL, Darcy 785-594-8312 170 I
RUSSELL, David, W 214-648-2695 457 B
david.russell@utsouthwestern.edu
RUSSELL, Denise 614-236-6196 349 D
drussell@capital.edu
RUSSELL, Elizabeth 207-974-4684 194 H
erussell@emcc.edu
RUSSELL, Elizabeth 314-246-8298 262 C
russelmb@webster.edu
RUSSELL, Freda, R 414-410-4735 492 D
frrussell@stritch.edu
RUSSELL, Gregory, R 606-783-5158 183 F
g.russell@moreheadstate.edu
RUSSELL, Harold 661-763-7870 66 J
hrussell@taftcollege.edu
RUSSELL, Jarad 423-614-6018 420 J
jrussell@leeuniversity.edu
RUSSELL, Jeffrey 608-262-5823 496 C
jrussell@dcs.wisc.edu
RUSSELL, Jennie 314-838-8858 261 G
jrussell@ugst.edu
RUSSELL, Jennifer 202-685-4094 503 I
jennifer.russell@ndu.edu
RUSSELL, Jennifer, M 719-333-3091 504 C
jennifer.russell@usafa.edu
RUSSELL, Jill, T 717-867-6076 388 H
russell@lvc.edu
RUSSELL, Jim 914-323-5236 305 J
james.russell@mville.edu
RUSSELL, Joanna, S 503-223-5100 376 G
jrussell@sumnercollege.edu

RUSSELL, Joanne 718-368-5661 294 E joanne.russell@kbcc.cuny.edu
RUSSELL, Josh 408-274-7900 61 L josh.russell@evc.edu
RUSSELL, Joyce 610-519-4331 402 D joyce.russell@villanova.edu
RUSSELL, Judith 352-273-2505 109 F jcrussell@ufl.edu
RUSSELL, Julia, H 802-656-4063 463 E julia.russell@uvm.edu
RUSSELL, Justin 912-583-3161 115 E drussell@bpc.edu
RUSSELL, Katherine 207-509-7176 195 H krussell@unity.edu
RUSSELL, Keith 503-399-5184 372 C keith.russell@chemeketa.edu
RUSSELL, Kelly 559-278-2182 31 D kellyr@csufresno.edu
RUSSELL, Kenneth 616-949-5300 222 I kenneth.russell@cornerstone.edu
RUSSELL, Kenya 256-551-3136 2 E kenya.russell@drakestate.edu
RUSSELL, Kevin 601-968-8746 245 C krussell@belhaven.edu
RUSSELL, Kimberly 940-898-3863 451 F krussell9@twu.edu
RUSSELL, Kimberly, A 337-550-1201 189 A krussell@lsue.edu
RUSSELL, Kristie 740-245-7191 363 D krussell@rio.edu
RUSSELL, Le Anne 509-452-5100 483 A lrussell@pnwu.edu
RUSSELL, Leah, L 540-375-2211 471 B russell@roanoke.edu
RUSSELL, Leigh 252-493-7354 336 H lrussell@email.pittcc.edu
RUSSELL, Lois 334-229-4431 4 B lrussell@alasu.edu
RUSSELL, Margaret 408-554-5324 62 D mrussell@scu.edu
RUSSELL, Mark 847-578-8340 147 I mark.rusell@rosalindfranklin.edu
RUSSELL, Mark, A 419-772-2011 358 H m-russell.7@onu.edu
RUSSELL, Michael 804-819-4995 474 A mrusssell@vccs.edu
RUSSELL, Michelle 856-222-9311 281 C mrussell@rcbc.edu
RUSSELL, Pamela 508-531-1295 212 B prussell@bridgew.edu
RUSSELL, Patrice 603-641-7202 274 C prussell@anselm.edu
RUSSELL, Patrick, J 414-425-8300 495 H prussell@shsst.edu
RUSSELL, Robert 605-626-7770 417 A robert.russell@northern.edu
RUSSELL, Ronda 406-994-5541 264 D rrussell@montana.edu
RUSSELL, Tammy 269-467-9945 224 A trussell@glenoaks.edu
RUSSELL, Terry 636-949-4980 254 F trussell@lindenwood.edu
RUSSELL, Thad 559-688-3027 39 E thadr@cos.edu
RUSSELL, Thomas 580-581-6712 365 G tomr@cameron.edu
RUSSELL, Tikola 718-631-6314 295 D trussell@qcc.cuny.edu
RUSSELL, Todd 985-867-2266 190 F trussell@sjasc.edu
RUSSELL, Traci 206-934-5661 483 J traci.russell@seattlecolleges.edu
RUSSELL, William 860-632-3050 87 C busoffice@holyapostles.edu
RUSSELL-EDWARDS, Juanita 601-877-6191 244 H juanita@alcorn.edu
RUSSELL-OÆGRADY, Marijo 212-346-1257 311 E
RUSSETT, Gary 413-265-2356 208 C russettg@elms.edu
RUSSIAKY, Rachael 864-977-7190 411 E rachael.russiaky@ngu.edu
RUSSIN, Gabrielle 914-961-8313 315 C grussin@svots.edu
RUSSIN, Ted 845-905-4427 298 A ted.russin@culinary.edu
RUSSO, Betty, S 812-941-2661 157 B bsrusso@ius.edu
RUSSO, Cecelia, M 718-990-6667 314 B russoc@stjohns.edu
RUSSO, Elizabeth 315-279-5273 304 A drusso@keuka.edu
RUSSO, Garth, S 706-542-8715 125 G grusso@uga.edu
RUSSO, Greg 619-574-6909 54 K grusso@pacificcollege.edu
RUSSO, Jessica 904-470-8012 97 L j.a.russo@ewc.edu
RUSSO, Kim 310-665-6979 54 I krusso@otis.edu
RUSSO, Kristi 973-290-4478 277 A krusso@cse.edu
RUSSO, Lari, C 516-367-6890 296 D
RUSSO, Lisa 213-613-2200 64 H lisarusso@sciarc.edu
RUSSO, Maria 518-454-5121 296 H russom@strose.edu
RUSSO, Paul 212-960-5400 326 E paul.russo@yu.edu
RUSSO, Richard 510-642-2700 68 D russo@berkeley.edu
RUSSO, Ronald 504-762-3066 187 E rrusso@dcc.edu
RUSSO, Ronald 504-762-3005 187 E rrusso@dcc.edu
RUSSO, Thomas 417-873-7413 252 F trusso@drury.edu
RUSSOM, Vaughn, N 715-394-8327 498 B vrussom@follett.com
RUSSOMANNO, David, J 317-274-0802 156 F drussoma@iupui.edu
RUSSOS, Milton, A 904-442-2950 100 B mrussos@fscj.edu
RUSSOW, Rodd 770-537-6000 127 A rodd.russow@westgatech.edu
RUSSUM, Mark 813-226-4814 106 D mark.russum@saintleo.edu
RUST, Christopher 860-439-5328 86 H christopher.rust@conncoll.edu
RUST, Jodi 715-852-1395 499 D jrust5@cvtc.edu
RUST, Kathleen 630-617-3343 136 G kathyrst@elmhurst.edu
RUST, Mark, M 410-857-2503 200 B mrust@mcdaniel.edu
RUST, Melissa 501-686-2532 21 F mrust@uasys.edu
RUSTAD, Dan 507-222-7187 234 F drustad@carleton.edu
RUSTAD, Melinda 218-935-0417 244 G melinda.rustad@wetcc.edu
RUSTICUS, Lisa 616-988-3653 226 C lrusticus@kuyper.edu
RUTAN, Susan, M 814-865-1412 392 B smr9@psu.edu
RUTENBAR, Rob, A 412-624-9019 401 B rutenbar@pitt.edu
RUTENBECK, Jeff 215-572-2900 379 A rutenbeckj@arcadia.edu
RUTH, Alice, A 603-646-2445 273 E alice.a.ruth@dartmouth.edu
RUTH, Andrea 610-225-5054 383 D aruth@eastern.edu
RUTH, Anna 727-864-7966 97 J ruthar@eckerd.edu
RUTH, David 610-861-5065 391 F druth@northampton.edu
RUTH, Gary 304-887-1795 465 B gruth@bluefield.edu
RUTH, John 212-353-4247 297 E jruth@cooper.edu
RUTH, Matthew 540-432-4118 466 G matthew.ruth@emu.edu
RUTH, Ted 573-341-7619 261 E truth@mst.edu
RUTHENBECK, Julie, J 325-942-2255 451 A julie.ruthenbeck@angelo.edu
RUTHER, Elliot 513-569-1451 350 K elliot.ruther@cincinnatistate.edu
RUTHERFORD, Crystin 660-284-4800 253 J registrar@heartlandcollege.edu
RUTHERFORD, David 561-868-3450 104 D rutherfd@palmbeachstate.edu
RUTHERFORD, Greg, F 803-327-8050 415 A grutherford@yorktech.edu
RUTHERFORD, John, D 214-648-0400 457 B john.rutherford@utsouthwestern.edu
RUTHERFORD, Lisa, H 413-542-5645 205 B lrutherford@amherst.edu
RUTHERFORD, Marcella, M 954-262-1963 103 M rmarcell@nova.edu
RUTHERFORD, Matthew 315-268-4329 296 A mrutherf@clarkson.edu
RUTHERFORD, Paul 304-327-4403 489 P prutherford@bluefieldstate.edu
RUTHERMAN, Kathy 270-852-3143 183 A krutherman@kwc.edu
RUTHSATZ, Steve 470-578-4293 120 L struthsat@kennesaw.edu
RUTKOWSKE, Snow 312-567-3677 139 B srutkowske@iit.edu
RUTKOWSKI, Sandra 419-824-3762 355 K srutkowski@lourdes.edu
RUTLAND, Jason 864-231-2000 406 G jrutland@andersonuniversity.edu
RUTLEDGE, Brian 601-984-1010 249 E brutledge@umc.edu
RUTLEDGE, Catherine 484-365-8087 389 C crutledge@lincoln.edu
RUTLEDGE, Debi 248-218-2192 229 J drutledge@rc.edu
RUTLEDGE, Jacqueline 817-531-6571 451 E jrutledge@txwes.edu
RUTLEDGE, James 662-846-4004 245 H jrutledge@deltastate.edu
RUTLEDGE, Janet 410-455-1781 202 E jrutledge@umbc.edu
RUTLEDGE, Melissa, B 540-378-5120 471 B rutledge@roanoke.edu
RUTLEDGE, Peter 706-542-7140 125 G borut@uga.edu
RUTLEDGE, Valerie 423-425-4249 428 A valerie-rutledge@utc.edu
RUTSTEIN-RILEY, Amy 617-349-8401 210 H arutstei@lesley.edu
RUTT, Charles, D 660-543-4370 260 K rutt@ucmo.edu
RUTT, Douglas, L 314-505-7566 251 I ruttd@csl.edu
RUTTEN, Chris 402-844-7051 268 J christopherr@northeast.edu
RUTTEN, Matthew 218-299-3514 235 E mrutten@cord.edu
RUTTER, Evan 909-621-8153 37 E evan.rutter@cmc.edu
RUTTER, Jeff 602-489-5300 10 E jeff.rutter@arizonachristian.edu
RUTTER, Jeff 931-221-7213 418 D rutterj@apsu.edu
RUTTER, John, P 919-299-4818 340 J jrutter@umo.edu
RUTTER, Sandy 423-697-4475 424 E sandy.rutter@chattanoogastate.edu
RUUD, William, N 740-376-4701 356 A wnr001@marietta.edu
RUXTON, Brooke 815-753-1206 145 C bruxton@niu.edu
RUYLE, Dianna 217-854-5772 132 I dianna.ruyle@blackburn.edu
RUYS, Jasmine 661-362-3466 38 H jasmine.ruys@canyons.edu
RUYS, Steve 818-364-7886 49 B ruyssc@lamission.edu
RUZEK, Joy 920-465-2222 496 E ruzekj@uwgb.edu
RUZICH, Steve 708-596-2000 149 B sruzich@ssc.edu
RUZICKA, Emma 417-873-6857 252 F eruzicka@drury.edu
RUZICKA, Jim 402-465-2323 268 H jruzicka@nebrwesleyan.edu
RUÍZ, Janet 787-766-1717 511 H jruiz54@suagm.edu
RYALL, Patrick 503-768-7294 373 G ryall@lclark.edu
RYAN, Amanda 765-658-4097 154 F amandaryan@depauw.edu
RYAN, Andrew 718-862-8000 305 H andrew.ryan@manhattan.edu
RYAN, Andrew, J 859-238-5572 179 F andrew.ryan@centre.edu
RYAN, Barry, T 650-493-4430 64 A barry.ryan@sofia.edu
RYAN, Caroll 562-988-2278 25 R cryan@auhs.edu
RYAN, Carrie 336-278-5584 328 K cryan2@elon.edu
RYAN, Casey 215-596-8570 401 G c.ryan@usciences.edu
RYAN, Christine 716-827-2467 323 D ryanc@trocaire.edu
RYAN, Christopher 508-830-5003 213 B cryan@maritime.edu
RYAN, Clay, M 205-348-5863 7 F cryan@uasystem.edu
RYAN, Curtis, W 801-832-2148 461 G cryan@westminstercollege.edu
RYAN, Dennis 757-340-2121 465 M adirectorcvab@centura.edu
RYAN, Diane, N 757-822-5185 476 B dryan@tcc.edu
RYAN, Duane 575-562-2112 285 M duane.ryan@enmu.edu
RYAN, Ed 408-554-5182 62 D eryan@scu.edu
RYAN, Erik 617-873-0106 207 F erik.ryan@cambridgecollege.edu
RYAN, Erin 718-390-4452 314 B ryane1@stjohns.edu
RYAN, Gail, L 313-577-6595 232 I gail.ryan@wayne.edu
RYAN, Gery 310-393-0411 55 J gryan@rand.org
RYAN, Greg 714-992-7092 53 L gryan@fullcoll.edu
RYAN, Helen, G 502-272-8052 179 B hryan@bellarmine.edu
RYAN, James 617-585-0200 206 F james.ryan@the-bac.edu
RYAN, James, E 434-924-3337 473 A jer6p@virginia.edu
RYAN, James, P 203-582-7229 87 G james.ryan@quinnipiac.edu
RYAN, Jen 404-962-3053 126 F jen.ryan@usg.edu
RYAN, Jennifer 785-833-4351 175 B jennifer.ryan@kwu.edu
RYAN, Jim 815-921-4522 147 E j.ryan@rockvalleycollege.edu
RYAN, CSC, John 570-208-5899 387 A jjryan@kings.edu
RYAN, Joseph 859-846-5321 183 E jryan@midway.edu
RYAN, Joseph 707-864-7000 64 C joseph.ryan@solano.edu
RYAN, Julie, A 928-523-9658 14 H julie.ryan@nau.edu
RYAN, Kathleen 508-541-1515 208 F kryan@dean.edu
RYAN, Kathleen 617-732-5042 216 B kathleen.ryan@mcphs.edu
RYAN, Kathleen 614-823-1250 360 A kryan@otterbein.edu
RYAN, Kelly, A 812-941-2393 157 B ryanka@ius.edu
RYAN, Kevin 305-428-5700 103 E kryan@aii.edu
RYAN, Kyle 781-899-5500 218 A kryan@psjs.edu
RYAN, Larry 505-277-2847 288 G larry@unm.edu
RYAN, Marianne, P 773-508-2657 142 D mryan21@luc.edu
RYAN, Mark 619-849-2489 57 E markryan@pointloma.edu
RYAN, Matt 202-462-2101 92 C mryan@iwp.edu
RYAN, Maura, A 574-631-9488 161 C mryan11@nd.edu
RYAN, Melissa 904-725-0525 96 P mryan@concorde.edu
RYAN, Pat 503-842-8222 377 A patryan@tillamookbaycc.edu
RYAN, Patrick 518-381-1210 315 G ryanpc@sunysccc.edu
RYAN, Patrick 716-270-2869 299 F ryanp@ecc.edu
RYAN, Patrick 973-720-3326 284 I ryanp@wpunj.edu
RYAN, Paula 641-628-5198 163 E ryanp@central.edu
RYAN, Peter 662-325-3742 247 F ryan@cvm.msstate.edu
RYAN, Ron 954-262-8856 103 M ronr@nova.edu
RYAN, Rosaleen 831-646-4035 52 F rryan@mpc.edu
RYAN, Scott 817-272-3181 454 J sdryan@uta.edu
RYAN, Sean, J 502-272-8376 179 B sryan@bellarmine.edu
RYAN, Sharon 708-524-6299 136 C sryan1@dom.edu
RYAN, Susan 386-822-7181 111 A sryan@stetson.edu
RYAN, Thomas, J 856-225-6361 281 G tomryan@camden.rutgers.edu

RYAN, Tim .... 845-452-9600 298 A
tim.ryan@culinary.edu
RYAN, Tim .... 415-452-5352.. 37 A
tryan@ccsf.edu
RYAN, Timothy, M .... 207-725-3247 193 D
tryan@bowdoin.edu
RYAN, Tom .... 727-864-8305.. 97 J
ryantj@eckerd.edu
RYAN BULONE, Mary ... 419-473-2700 352 E
mryan@daviscollege.edu
RYAN-HOFFMAN,
Maureen .... 732-987-2218 278 B
mryan-hoffman@georgian.edu
RYAN RODRIGUEZ,
Christina .... 714-895-8128.. 38 D
cryanrodriguez@gwc.cccd.edu
RYAN VAN ZEE,
Marynel .... 507-222-4300 234 F
mryanvanzee@carleton.edu
RYANT, Marion .... 229-317-6261 113 H
marion.ryant@asurams.edu
RYBAK, Chuck .... 920-465-2336 496 E
rybakc@uwgb.edu
RYBERG, Bill .... 253-566-5336 485 C
bryberg@tacomacc.edu
RYBIN KOOB, Amanda . 303-245-4664.. 81 B
arybinkoob@naropa.edu
RYCHALSKY, Laura .... 863-680-4625.. 99 H
lrychalsky@flsouthern.edu
RYCHLEC, Timothy .... 713-221-5869 453 B
rychlect@uhd.edu
RYCRAFT, Rickianne ...... 951-639-5420.. 52 I
rrycraft@msjc.edu
RYCYNA, Mary .... 216-397-4921 354 I
mrycyna@jcu.edu
RYDER, Collette, L .... 212-327-8054 313 B
cryder@rockefeller.edu
RYDER, Ellen .... 415-422-2558.. 71 K
eryder@usfca.edu
RYDER, Jon .... 207-221-4701 196 G
jryder2@une.edu
RYDER, Linda .... 518-629-8198 302 E
l.ryder@hvcc.edu
RYDER, Lucas .... 772-546-5534 101 B
lucasryder@hsbc.edu
RYDER, Tina .... 301-447-5038 200 E
ryder@msmary.edu
RYDL, Chareny, L .... 979-845-3158 446 G
chareny@tamu.edu
RYEA, Alan, E .... 802-656-3245 463 E
alan.ryea@uvm.edu
RYKEN, Amy .... 253-879-2810 485 E
aryken@pugetsound.edu
RYKEN, Philip, G .... 630-752-5002 152 F
philip.ryken@wheaton.edu
RYLAARSDAM, Robin .... 773-298-3090 148 G
rylaarsdam@sxu.edu
RYMAN, Denny .... 631-420-2171 321 B
denny.ryman@farmingdale.edu
RYMAN-MESCAL,
LacyJane .... 856-222-9311 281 C
lryman@rcbc.edu
RYMER, Beverly .... 713-743-5773 452 F
brymer@uh.edu
RYNNE, Jeanne .... 707-826-3646.. 33 D
jeanne.rynne@humboldt.edu
RYON, Ray .... 641-683-5111 166 C
RYSAVY, Monica .... 302-225-6373.. 90 E
rysavym@gbc.edu
RYSAVY, Peter .... 302-225-6371.. 90 E
peter@gbc.edu
RYSER, Esther, M .... 970-247-7100.. 79 I
emryser@fortlewis.edu
RYSER, Leslie, C .... 606-539-4201 185 A
leslie.ryser@ucumberlands.edu
RYVKIN, Faina .... 617-264-7673 209 A
ryvkin@emmanuel.edu
RYZEWSKI, Margaret .... 708-524-6490 136 C
mryzewski@dom.edu
RZONCA, Stephen .... 910-892-3178 329 F
srzonca@heritagebiblecollege.edu
RÍOS, Alma .... 787-284-1912 509 E
arios@ponce.inter.edu
RÍOS, Hector .... 787-850-9375 513 E
hector.rios5@upr.edu
RÍOS-MAURY,
Héctor, A .... 787-850-9374 512 G
rectoria.uprh@upr.edu

S

SA TELES, Gariela .... 816-584-6828 258 A
gsateles@park.edu
SAACKE, David .... 540-458-8400 478 A
dsaacke@wlu.edu
SAADEDDINE, Rihab ..... 856-256-5412 281 E
saadeddine@rowan.edu
SAADI, Christine .... 610-796-8213 378 F
christine.saadi@alvernia.edu
SAAED, Jan .... 801-832-2232 461 G
jsaaed@westminstercollege.edu
SAAKE, Dylan .... 530-898-3116.. 31 A
dsaake@csuchico.edu
SAAL, Kevin .... 270-809-3164 183 G
ksaal@murraystate.edu
SAALFELD, Katy .... 815-753-8305 145 C
ksaalfeld@niu.edu
SAALFELD, Pam .... 402-844-7466 268 J
pamela@northeast.edu
SAAM, Julie .... 765-455-9302 156 D
jsaam@iuk.edu
SAAR, Sarah .... 712-325-3282 167 B
ssaar@iwcc.edu
SAARI, Mirranda .... 360-992-2671 479 F
msaari@clark.edu
SAARIAHO, Ginger, K ... 617-552-9168 207 B
ginger.saariaho@bc.edu
SAAVEDRA, Adriana ...... 520-494-5287.. 11 K
adriana.saavedra@centralaz.edu
SAAVEDRA, Frank .... 305-899-4834.. 95 C
fsaavedra@barry.edu
SAAVEDRA, Mauricio ...... 805-756-5406.. 30 C
msaavedr@calpoly.edu
SAAVEDRA, Randy .... 575-835-5005 286 I
randy.saavedra@nmt.edu
SAAVEDRA, Sara .... 360-438-4534 483 H
ssaavedra@stmartin.edu
SABAN, Thomas .... 708-709-3568 146 D
tsaban@prairiestate.edu
SABAT, Sheila, D .... 787-257-0000 513 C
sheila.sabat@upr.edu
SABATES, Marcelo .... 312-369-7023 135 E
msabates@colum.edu
SABATH, Amy .... 440-525-7775 355 H
asabath1@lakelandcc.edu
SABATH, Michael, J ...... 928-317-6475.. 14 H
michael.sabath@nau.edu
SABATINE, Stephanie .... 906-635-6664 226 E
ssabatine@lssu.edu
SABATINO, Patricia .... 718-678-8817 306 F
psabatino@mercy.edu
SABATO, Larry, J .... 434-924-3604 473 A
ljs@virginia.edu
SABBAGHA, Shickre ..... 803-822-3076 410 G
sabbaghas@midlandstech.edu
SABBAGHI, Asghar .... 312-341-3500 147 H
SABBATINI, Robert, P ... 434-223-6129 468 A
rsabbatini@hsc.edu
SABEL, Carol .... 414-277-7338 494 G
SABER, Isabelle .... 661-362-3431.. 38 H
isabelle.saber@canyons.edu
SABEY, Brenda .... 435-652-7841 460 G
sabey@dixie.edu
SABICK, Michelle .... 314-977-8283 259 H
michelle.sabick@slu.edu
SABIN, Christopher, P .. 910-938-6321 333 F
sabinc@coastalcarolina.edu
SABIN, Jessalyn .... 218-262-6722 238 C
jessalynsabin@hibbing.edu
SABIN, Melody .... 864-578-8770 412 B
msabin@sherman.edu
SABINO, Lyn .... 330-363-4227 348 D
lyn.sabino@aultman.com
SABINSON, Allen, C ...... 215-895-1621 383 B
allen.c.sabinson@drexel.edu
SABIT, Farhad .... 510-659-6146.. 54 F
fsabit@ohlone.edu
SABLAN, Becky .... 670-237-6700 506 A
becky.sablan@marianas.edu
SABLAN, Fermina, A ..... 671-735-1121 505 C
fermina.sablan@guamcc.edu
SABLAN-ZEBEDY, Ellia .. 610-799-1061 388 I
esablanzebedy@lccc.edu
SABLE, Ray .... 229-333-5875 126 G
rasable@valdosta.edu
SABLO, Kahan .... 703-993-2884 467 L
ksablo@gmu.edu
SABO, Arlene .... 845-437-5201 324 C
arsabo@vassar.edu
SABO, Jana .... 239-489-9051 100 A
jsabo1@fsw.edu
SABOE, Mike .... 843-820-5090 413 B
mike.saboe@tridenttech.edu
SABOLD, Steven, D .... 412-346-2100 396 F
ssabold@pia.edu
SABOLO, Martin .... 605-626-3007 417 A
martin.sabolo@northern.edu
SABOO, Michelle .... 218-335-4218 236 E
michelle.saboo@lltc.edu
SABOTA, Britt .... 903-510-3052 452 C
bsab@tjc.edu
SABOTA, Fred .... 727-864-8895.. 97 J
sabotafr@eckerd.edu
SABOU, Michelle, L .... 864-977-7004 411 E
michelle.sabou@ngu.edu
SABOUNI, Ikhlas .... 936-261-9800 446 D
isabouni@pvamu.edu
SABOURIN, Jessica .... 508-831-5469 220 E
jsabourin@wpi.edu
SABRANSKY, Tracy .... 216-373-5287 358 B
tsabransky@ndc.edu
SACCENTI, Tom .... 678-839-6000 126 E
saccenti@westga.edu
SACCO, JR., Albert .... 806-742-3451 451 B
al.sacco-jr@ttu.edu
SACCO, Jennifer .... 203-582-8972.. 87 G
jennifer.sacco@quinnipiac.edu
SACCO, John .... 617-322-3553 210 F
john_sacco@laboure.edu
SACCO, Katie .... 352-365-3541 102 T
saccok@lssc.edu
SACCOCCIO, Louis, J .... 401-874-4486 406 B
ljsacc@uri.edu
SACHEDINA, Shadia, A . 212-217-3800 299 H
shadia_sachedina@fitnyc.edu
SACHOWITZ, Aaron .... 925-631-4245.. 59 B
ads3@stmarys-ca.edu
SACHS, Amanda .... 410-777-7009 197 C
ansachs@aacc.edu
SACHS, Elizabeth .... 212-772-4569 294 C
esachs@hunter.cuny.edu
SACHS, Steven, G .... 703-323-3387 475 C
ssachs@nvcc.edu
SACK, Bob .... 616-222-1421 222 I
bob.sack@cornerstone.edu
SACK, Chuck .... 484-840-4711 391 D
sackc@neumann.edu
SACKETT, Angela .... 208-535-5426 130 C
angela.sackett@cei.edu
SACKETT, Linda .... 912-279-5942 116 G
lsackett@ccga.edu
SACKETT, Walter .... 937-395-8165 355 F
walter.sackett@ketteringhealth.org
SACKETTE-URNESS,
Anna .... 218-733-7600 238 F
anna.sackette-urness@lsc.edu
SACKEY, Joyce, A .... 617-636-0375 219 B
joyce.sackey@tufts.edu
SACKMAN, Marcy .... 816-995-2816 258 F
marcy.sackman@researchcollege.edu
SACKS, Arlene .... 305-653-6713 361 L
arlene.sacks@myunion.edu
SACKSTEIN, Robert .... 305-348-0570 109 A
robert.sackstein@fiu.edu
SACKSTEIN, Robert .... 305-348-2000 109 A
SACRY, Toni .... 910-272-3375 337 D
tsacry@robeson.edu
SADAN, Avishai .... 213-740-3124.. 72 B
dentdean@usc.edu
SADAO, Amy .... 215-573-9973 400 K
asadao@ica.upenn.org
SADBERRY, Robin .... 209-954-5018.. 60 J
rsadberry@deltacollege.edu
SADD, Tracy .... 717-361-1260 383 E
saddt@etown.edu
SADDIGH, Farah .... 310-233-4501.. 49 A
saddigf@lahc.edu
SADDLER, Mike .... 785-462-3984 172 H
SADDLER, Renee .... 919-546-8681 340 E
rsaddler@shawu.edu
SADDLER, Ryan, C .... 563-333-5728 169 A
saddlerryanc@sau.edu
SADDLER-RICE, Lorri ..... 404-880-8447 116 D
lrice@cau.edu
SADDORIS-TRAUGHBER,
Janiece, L .... 217-424-6253 143 H
jtraughber@millikin.edu
SADEGHIPOUR, Keya .... 215-204-5285 399 F
keya.sadeghipour@temple.edu
SADERHOLM, Matthew . 859-985-3490 179 C
saderholmm@berea.edu
SADHOO, Jonathan .... 620-331-4100 174 C
jsadhoo@indycc.edu
SADLEK, Gregory, M .... 216-687-3660 351 B
g.sadlek@csuohio.edu
SADLER, David .... 925-969-3300.. 46 H
dsadler@jfku.edu
SADLER, Kelley .... 253-566-5187 485 C
ksadler@tacomacc.edu
SADLER, Martin .... 404-687-4512 116 H
sadlerm@ctsnet.edu
SADLER, Michael .... 701-777-4152 345 C
michael.p.sadler@und.edu
SADLER, Tommy .... 731-661-5218 427 C
tsadler@uu.edu
SADLON, Donna .... 973-655-3963 279 C
sadlond@mail.montclair.edu
SADOWSKI, Sherri .... 937-327-7808 364 H
sadowskis@wittenberg.edu
SADRI, Samaneh .... 562-947-8755.. 65 C
samanehsadri@scuhs.edu
SADRO, Cheryl .... 409-266-2006 456 F
csadro@utmb.edu
SAE CHAO, Jenny .... 559-737-5443.. 39 E
jennys@cos.edu
SAEED, Najam .... 651-846-1324 241 B
najam.saeed@saintpaul.edu
SAENZ, Bernard .... 361-354-2258 433 C
bsaenz@coastalbend.edu
SAENZ, David .... 312-893-7141 137 A
dsaenz@erikson.edu
SAENZ, Delia .... 802-440-4300 462 A
deliasaenz@bennington.edu
SAENZ, Kelly .... 281-992-3413 443 E
kelly.saenz@sjcd.edu
SAENZ, Laura .... 956-665-4062 455 D
laura.saenz@utrgv.edu
SAENZ, Rogelio .... 210-458-2715 455 E
rogelio.saenz@utsa.edu
SAEVIG, Daniel, J .... 419-530-4008 363 E
daniel.saevig@utoledo.edu
SAFADY, Randa, S .... 512-499-4777 454 I
rsafady@utsystem.edu
SAFAEI, Aman .... 212-410-8008 309 B
asafaei@nycpm.edu
SAFARZADEH, Sasha .... 714-533-3946.. 34 D
sasha.zadeh@calums.edu
SAFEWRIGHT, Michelle . 615-898-2231 422 H
michelle.safewright@mtsu.edu
SAFFEL, Rachel .... 619-688-0800.. 40 E
rsaffel@concorde.edu
SAFFIOTI, Patricia .... 434-832-6693 474 C
saffiotip@centralvirginia.edu
SAFFOLD, Tisia .... 202-759-4988.. 91 D
SAFLEY, Ellen .... 972-883-2916 455 B
safley@utdallas.edu
SAFLEY, Mallory .... 706-272-2997 117 C
msafley@daltonstate.edu
SAGANSKI, Gary .... 608-757-7727 499 C
gsaganski@blackhawk.edu
SAGARDIA, Paula .... 787-864-2222 509 C
paula.sagardia@guayama.inter.edu
SAGE, Aimee .... 660-248-6651 251 B
asage@centralmethodist.edu
SAGE, James .... 435-586-7703 460 F
jamessage@suu.edu
SAGEMAN, Barbara .... 954-262-7300 103 M
bsageman@noa.edu
SAGENDORF, Brian .... 208-282-2517 130 H
sagebria@isu.edu
SAGER, Scott .... 615-966-5156 421 D
scott.sager@lipscomb.edu
SAGER GENTRY,
Jennifer .... 804-819-4961 474 A
jgentry@vccs.edu
SAGERS, Cynthia .... 541-737-3467 375 D
SAGO, Anthony .... 815-599-3437 138 B
anthony.sago@highland.edu
SAGRAVES, Aaron .... 616-949-5300 222 I
aaron.sagraves@cornerstone.edu
SAHEED, Malhar .... 309-794-7499 132 C
malharsaheed@augustana.edu
SAHGAL, Anita .... 727-873-4422 110 C
anitas@mail.usf.edu
SAHLI, Daniel .... 330-941-3700 365 C
desahli@ysu.edu
SAHLIN, Claire .... 940-898-3415 451 F
csahlin@twu.edu
SAHONCHIK, Kris .... 207-780-5361 196 F
kris.sahonchik@maine.edu
SAHOO, Bijoy, K .... 225-771-5808 190 H
bijoy_sahoo@subr.edu
SAHU, Subir .... 215-895-2506 383 B
subir.sahu@drexel.edu
SAIBOO, Navin .... 201-200-3048 279 E
nsaiboo@njcu.edu
SAIFF, Edward .... 201-684-7734 280 H
esaiff@ramapo.edu
SAIKIA, Paul .... 717-815-1245 404 A
psaikia@ycp.edu

SAIN, Becky 704-669-4093 333 E sain@clevelandcc.edu
SAIN, Laurie 615-966-1181 421 D laurie.sain@lipscomb.edu
SAINT, Carolyn 434-924-4113 473 A cds9h@virginia.edu
ST. ANTOINE, Tom 561-803-2279 104 C tom_stantoine@pba.edu
ST. ARNAULD, Cheri 303-333-4224 76 J
ST. COLUMBIA, Rhonda 870-338-6474 22 H
ST. CROIX, Jerome, S 585-292-2278 307 H jstcroix@monroecc.edu
ST. CYR, William 603-526-3627 272 H william.stcyr@colby-sawyer.edu
ST. DENNIS, Grady, I 507-933-7661 235 I stdennis@gustavus.edu
ST. GERMAIN, Constance 888-227-3552 234 E
ST. GERMAIN, Nicole 225-768-1737 186 F nicole.st.germain@franu.edu
ST. GERMAIN, Valerie 312-499-4286 148 I vstgermain@saic.edu
ST. GERMAINE, Jordan 715-634-4790 493 I jstgermaine@lco.edu
ST. HILAIRE, Kendall 772-462-7119 101 E sthilai@irsc.edu
ST. JAMES, Andrea 413-782-1775 219 F andrea.stjames@wne.edu
ST. JAMES, Tim 860-253-3011 85 C tstjames@asnuntuck.edu
ST. JEAN, Cyndie 909-389-3201 59 H cstjean@craftonhills.edu
ST. JOHN, Cynthia 920-686-6350 496 A cynthia.st.john@sl.edu
ST. JOHN, IV, Finis, E 205-348-4840 7 F chancellor@uasystem.edu
ST. JOHN, Jeffrey, E 207-581-1591 195 J jeffrey.stjohn@maine.edu
ST. JOHN, Johann 217-228-5432 146 F stjohjo@quincy.edu
ST. JOHN, Joy 781-283-2273 219 D jstjohn@wellesley.edu
ST. JOHN, Liz 804-289-8494 472 L lhemmer@richmond.edu
ST. JOHN, Meredith 617-558-1788 217 D mstjohn@nesa.edu
ST. JOHN, Mike 405-382-9201 369 J m.stjohn@sscok.edu
ST. JOHN, Tim 508-793-7453 208 A tstjohn@clarku.edu
ST. LEGER, Gabrielle 516-463-6716 302 B gabrielle.stleger@hofstra.edu
ST. LEGER, Trish 314-228-7224 296 F tstleger@colgate.edu
ST. LOUIS, Daniel, C 828-327-7000 333 B dstlouis@cvcc.edu
ST. LOUIS, Moise 413-528-7499 205 F mstlouis@simons-rock.edu
ST. LOUIS, Shelly 518-891-2915 310 E mstlouis@nccc.edu
ST. MARKS, Wanda 406-395-4875 265 G wstmarks@stonechild.edu
ST. MAURO, Anne 609-258-3403 280 E stmauro@princeton.edu
SAINT-ONGE, Collin 906-487-7260 223 K collin.saintonge@finlandia.edu
ST. ONGE, Stephen 707-826-3451 33 D srs706@humboldt.edu
ST. PIERRE, Beverly 413-565-1000 205 G bstpierre@baypath.edu
ST. PIERRE, Gail, S 207-786-6120 193 B gstpierr@bates.edu
ST. PIERRE, Traci 207-780-4771 196 F tracy.st@maine.edu
ST. ROMAIN, Claire 337-482-0925 192 E cstromain@louisiana.edu
SAINT SING, Judi 336-734-7221 334 E jsaintsing@forsythtech.edu
SAINT-VICTOR, Nicole 708-239-4560 150 F nicole.saint-victor@trnty.edu
SAINTJONES, Jerome 256-372-4863 1 A jerome.saintjones@aamu.edu
SAINZ, Jose 540-654-1261 472 I jsainz@umw.edu
SAIRS, Reuben 740-857-1311 360 I rsairs@rosedale.edu
SAITTA, Tom 336-272-7102 329 D thomas.saaita@greensboro.edu
SAJADIAN, Dalila, A 641-422-4103 168 D sajaddal@niacc.edu
SAJDAK, Jeff 616-957-6042 221 P js036@calvinseminary.edu
SAJKO, Brian 573-876-7207 260 F bsajko@stephens.edu
SAKAGAWA, Tamara 863-292-3744 105 A tsakagawa@polk.edu
SAKAI, Eric 802-828-2800 464 B eds05090@ccv.vsc.edu
SAKAI, Hiro 949-480-4008 64 B sakai@soka.edu
SAKAKI, Judy 707-664-2156 34 C
SAKAMOTO, June 415-703-8291 68 F sakamotoj@uchastings.edu
SAKARYA, Mustafa 914-674-7258 306 F msakarya@mercy.edu
SAKELLARIOU, Dimitris 626-395-3208 29 C dimitris@caltech.edu
SAKEY, Paula 617-989-4219 219 E sakeyp@wit.edu
SAKRAIDA, Nicole 541-245-7574 376 D nsakraida@roguecc.edu
SAKS, Deborah 916-558-2582 50 I saksd@scc.losrios.edu
SAKS, Greg 657-278-7030 31 E gsaks@fullerton.edu
SAKS, Michael 848-445-7952 282 A chair@math.rutgers.edu
SAKSENA, P.N 803-323-2186 414 G saksenapn@winthrop.edu
SALA, Andrea 310-660-3670 41 L asala@elcamino.edu
SALA, Pete 315-443-5439 322 C pesala@syr.edu
SALADIN, Lisa 843-792-3031 410 F saladinl@musc.edu
SALADIN, Shawn 956-665-3651 455 D shawn.saladin@utrgv.edu
SALAFSKY, David, B 520-621-8297 16 G salafsky@email.arizona.edu
SALAK, Donna 513-745-3302 365 B salakd@xavier.edu
SALAMON, Edward 215-885-2360 389 F esalamon@manor.edu
SALAMY, James 315-866-0300 301 G salamyjr@herkimer.edu
SALAND, Emily, V 845-575-3000 305 L emily.saland@marist.edu
SALAS, Alexandra 609-586-4800 278 F salasa@mccc.edu
SALAS, Carmen 773-371-5400 133 E events@ctu.edu
SALAS, Joseph 620-450-2218 176 G joseph@prattcc.edu
SALAS, Rich 515-271-1400 164 I rich.salas@dmu.edu
SALAS, Richard 515-271-1709 164 I rich.salas@dmu.edu
SALASKI, Kori 608-796-3185 498 N kfsalaski@viterbo.edu
SALAY, Lawrence 203-285-2046 85 E lsalay@gwcc.commnet.edu
SALAZ, Mark 520-494-5250 11 K mark.salaz@centralaz.edu
SALAZAR, Andrea 530-541-4660 47 E salazar@ltcc.edu
SALAZAR, Anna 323-415-4136 48 H salazaal@elac.edu
SALAZAR, Ashley 620-276-9622 173 E ashley.salazar@gcccks.edu
SALAZAR, Freddie 575-769-4143 285 K freddie.salazar@clovis.edu
SALAZAR, Jamie 405-491-6310 370 A jsalazar@snu.edu
SALAZAR, S.J., Jose-Luis 718-817-4503 300 E jsalazar8@fordham.edu
SALAZAR, Leta 846-208-8263 413 E lsalazar@uscb.edu
SALAZAR, Rosalinda 956-882-7665 455 D rosalinda.salazar@utrgv.edu
SALAZAR, Veronikha 870-230-5231 19 E salazav@hsu.edu
SALAZAR, Victor, G 210-434-6711 441 E vmsalazar@ollusa.edu
SALAZAR-VALENTINE, Marcia 419-372-8185 348 H marcias@bgsu.edu
SALB, Ephraim 845-406-4308 325 H rabbisalb@kessertorah.org
SALBATO, Mike 719-846-5653 82 K mike.salbato@trinidadstate.edu
SALCEDO, Marisol 305-629-2929 106 H msalcedo@sanignaciouniversity.edu
SALCEDO, Richard 661-654-3491 30 E 1250mgr@fheg.follett.com
SALCIDO, Kevin, J 480-965-6608 10 I kevin.j.salcido@asu.edu
SALCIDO, Rebecca 915-215-4300 451 D rebecca.salcido@ttuhsc.edu
SALDANA, Michelle 310-954-4327 52 G msaldana@msmu.edu
SALDANA-TALLEY, Jane 707-778-3931 62 F lsaldana-talley@santarosa.edu
SALDIVAR, Antonia 956-295-3377 449 D antonia.saldivar@tsc.edu
SALDIVAR, Patricia 956-295-3426 449 D patricia.saldivar@tsc.edu
SALE, Gene 561-803-2352 104 C gene_sale@pba.edu
SALE, Rachel 573-681-5442 254 E saler@lincolnu.edu
SALEH, Aneesa 773-838-7784 134 F asaleh17@ccc.edu
SALEH, Bahaa 407-882-3326 109 E besaleh@creol.ucf.edu
SALEH, Don 717-358-3953 384 D dsaleh@fandm.edu
SALEM, Susan 310-954-4112 52 G ssalem@msmu.edu
SALEMME, Kevin 978-837-5377 216 D kevin.salemme@merrimack.edu
SALERNO, Cheryl 918-335-6887 368 G csalerno@okwu.edu
SALERNO, Dena 570-372-4302 399 C salerno@susqu.edu
SALERNO, Janice 215-885-2360 389 F jsalerno@manor.edu
SALERNO, Kerry 781-235-1200 205 E
SALERNO, Sarah 781-239-2782 214 E ssalerno@massbay.edu
SALGADO, Juan 312-553-2500 134 A jsalgado@ccc.edu
SALGADO, Juan 773-777-7900 134 G jsalgado@ccc.edu
SALGADO, Sergio 507-344-7310 234 B ssalgado@blc.edu
SALGUERO, Jossie 787-766-1912 508 J jsalguer@inter.edu
SALHOTRA, Poonam 713-221-8066 453 B gulatip@uhd.edu
SALIBA, Matt 863-638-2947 113 B salibam@webber.edu
SALII, Uroi, N 680-488-2471 506 B usalii@palau.edu
SALIMAN, Todd 303-860-5600 82 N todd.saliman@cu.edu
SALINAS, Antonio 575-439-3601 287 C antsalin@nmsu.edu
SALINAS, Christy 626-395-3651 29 C cssalina@caltech.edu
SALINAS, Felix 210-486-4788 429 E fsalinas26@alamo.edu
SALINAS, Francisco 208-426-5950 129 I franciscosalinas@boisestate.edu
SALINAS, Horacio 956-764-5798 439 C hsalinas@laredo.edu
SALINAS, Larry 559-278-2324 31 D lsalinas@csufresno.edu
SALINAS, Laura 530-541-4660 47 E salinas@ltcc.edu
SALINAS, Lelia 956-872-7209 444 A lelias1@southtexascollege.edu
SALINAS, Nick 914-395-2570 315 F nsalinas@sarahlawrence.edu
SALINAS, Sergio 559-325-5273 66 D sergio.salinas@cloviscollege.edu
SALINAS, Stacy 845-848-7818 298 D stacy.salinas@dc.edu
SALINAS-HOVAR, Marta 956-665-7304 455 D marta.salinashovar@utrgv.edu
SALING MAYER, Marni 360-752-8325 478 G msalingmayer@btc.edu
SALISBURY, Jennifer 215-968-8461 379 G jennifer.salisbury@bucks.edu
SALISBURY, Jon 831-479-6187 27 G josalisb@cabrillo.edu
SALISBURY, Kevin, S 401-333-7316 404 H ksalisbury@ccri.edu
SALISBURY, Leila, W 859-257-8432 185 B lsalisbury@uky.edu
SALISBURY, Micheal 325-942-2169 451 A micheal.salisbury@angelo.edu
SALISBURY, Susan 860-297-4281 88 C susan.salisbury@trincoll.edu
SALKA, William 860-465-5246 84 J salkaw@easternct.edu
SALKIN, Patricia 646-565-6522 322 J patricia.salkin@touro.edu
SALLAN, Veena 270-686-4639 182 B veena.sallan@kctcs.edu
SALLEE, Emily 816-584-6779 258 A emily.sallee@park.edu
SALLEE-JUSTESEN, Dawn 541-506-6028 372 G djustesen@cgcc.edu
SALLEH-BARONE, Normah 708-974-5209 144 C salleh-barone@morainevalley.edu
SALLEY, Bridget 803-738-7602 410 G salleyb@midlandstech.edu
SALLEY, Travis 404-225-4612 114 H tsalley@atlantatech.edu
SALLIS, Archer 662-476-8414 246 A jsallis@eastms.edu
SALLIS, Deetra 815-479-7837 143 A dsallis@mchenry.edu
SALLUSTIO, Joseph 909-667-4494 37 H jsallustio@claremontlincoln.edu
SALMAN, Juli 505-426-2155 286 H jesalman@nmhu.edu
SALMERON, Lois 405-208-5900 367 I lsalmeron@okcu.edu
SALMO, Jim 608-796-3000 498 N
SALMON, Lorraine 845-687-5093 323 E salmonl@sunyulster.edu
SALMON, Mark 334-670-3342 7 C msalmon@troy.edu
SALMON, Michael 212-517-0529 306 A msalmon@mmm.edu
SALMON, Pamela 315-792-3011 324 B pjsalmon@utica.edu
SALMON, Robert, O 801-524-8179 459 F rsalmon@ldsbc.edu
SALO, Todd 906-635-2639 226 E tsalo2@lssu.edu
SALOME, JoAnn 575-835-5955 286 I jsalome@admin.nmt.edu
SALOMON, Danielle 310-954-4371 52 G dsalomon@msmu.edu
SALOMON, Mattisyahu 732-367-1060 275 J
SALOMON, Nasser 909-580-9661 34 E
SALOMON-FERNANDEZ, Yves 413-775-1410 214 C president@gcc.mass.edu
SALOMONSON, Kristen 231-591-3801 223 J kristensalomonson@ferris.edu
SALON, Mabel 530-752-9795 68 E masalon@ucdavis.edu
SALOVEY, Peter 203-432-2550 89 D peter.salovey@yale.edu
SALSBURY, Greg 970-943-2114 84 D gsalsbury@western.edu
SALSBURY, Lysa 208-885-9358 131 G lsalsbur@uidaho.edu
SALSGIVER, Amy 814-393-2109 394 D asalsgiver@clarion.edu
SALT, Robert 715-232-2687 498 A saltb@uwstout.edu
SALTER, Allen 478-827-3229 118 A allen.salter@fvsu.edu
SALTER, Les 770-533-6901 121 B lsalter@laniertech.edu
SALTER, Sid 662-325-7454 247 F ss51@msstate.edu
SALTIEL, Henry 718-482-6120 294 F hsaltiel@lagcc.cuny.edu
SALTON, Susan 814-332-4793 378 D ssalton@allegheny.edu
SALTSMAN, Terry 931-372-3200 426 E tsaltsman@tntech.edu
SALTZBERG, Alex 510-593-2995 63 A asaltzberg@saybrook.edu
SALVA, William, M 914-337-9300 297 D william.salva@concordia-ny.edu
SALVAGE, Lynn 718-818-6470 315 A lsalvage@edaff.com
SALVAGGIO, Brian 508-531-1276 212 B
SALVATORIELLO, Vincent 610-398-5300 389 A vsalvatoriello@lincolntech.edu
SALVESEN, Guy 858-646-3100 62 A gsalvesen@sbpdiscovery.org
SALVINI, Tonia 785-830-2753 173 G tsalvini@haskell.edu
SALVO, Robyn 732-263-5228 279 B rsalvo@monmouth.edu
SALVUCCI, Debra 508-565-1314 218 H dsalvucci@stonehill.edu
SALVUCCI, Jim 606-546-1730 184 H jsalvucci@unionky.edu

SALYERS, Vincent .... 509-313-3544 481 D
salyers@gonzaga.edu
SALZBRUNN, Kimberly . 630-637-5454 144 H
ksalzbrunn@noctrl.edu
SALZER, Jean .... 262-993-6762 497 A
jeano@uwm.edu
SALZMAN, Christine ..... 908-709-7485 284 C
csalzman@follett.com
SALZMANN, Nick .... 847-628-2492 140 C
nsalzmann@judsonu.edu
SAM, David .... 847-214-7374 136 F
dsam@elgin.edu
SAM, Mary .... 218-855-8159 237 F
msam@clcmn.edu
SAM, Penselyn .... 691-320-2480 505 B
petse@comfsm.fm
SAMAHA, Ahmed .... 803-641-3411 413 D
ahmeds@usca.edu
SAMAIE, Parissa .... 323-242-5536.. 49 D
samaiep@lasc.edu
SAMAN, Sarmad .... 508-678-2811 213 G
sarmad.saman@bristolcc.edu
SAMANAS, Allison .... 570-208-5900 387 A
allisonsamanas@kings.edu
SAMANGO, Melissa ...... 610-526-6196 385 G
msamango@harcum.edu
SAMANIEGO, Sue .... 970-675-3216.. 78 G
sue.samaniego@cncc.edu
SAMANT, Ajay .... 309-438-2251 139 E
asamant@ilstu.edu
SAMANTA, Shivaji .... 540-857-6335 476 D
ssamanta@virginiawestern.edu
SAMARDZIJA, Michael . 909-558-8544.. 48 C
msamardzija@llu.edu
SAMARKOS, Christy ...... 619-594-5211.. 33 E
csamarko@sdsu.edu
SAMBDMAN, Cory, W .. 563-333-6336 169 A
1312mgr@follett.com
SAMBLE, Brian, W .... 717-358-3860 384 D
brian.samble@fandm.edu
SAMEEI, Morteza .... 713-718-5251 437 I
morteza.sameei@hccs.edu
SAMEK, Linda .... 503-554-2142 373 C
lsamek@georgefox.edu
SAMHAT, Nayef, H .... 864-597-4010 414 H
president@wofford.edu
SAMMAKIA, Bahgat .... 607-777-4818 316 E
bahgat@binghamton.edu
SAMMANN, James .... 845-434-5750 322 A
jsammann@sullivan.suny.edu
SAMMARCO, Erica, C ... 716-888-2100 292 D
sammarce@canisius.edu
SAMMARTINO,
Kathleen .... 617-349-8515 210 H
ksammart@lesley.edu
SAMMIS, Robert, L .... 626-914-8550.. 36 K
rsammis@citruscollege.edu
SAMMONS, Gregory, S . 607-587-3911 320 C
sammongs@alfredstate.edu
SAMMONS, Ken .... 509-313-6951 481 D
sammons@gonzaga.edu
SAMMONS, Steve .... 503-589-8145 373 A
ssammons@corban.edu
SAMO, Tia .... 641-782-1336 169 H
samo@swcciowa.edu
SAMORA, Tracy .... 719-549-2858.. 79 A
tracy.samora@csupueblo.edu
SAMP, Mike .... 307-766-5179 502 H
bowhntr@uwyo.edu
SAMPAIO, Anna, C .... 408-554-2289.. 62 D
asampaio@scu.edu
SAMPERTON, Amy .... 910-678-8236 334 D
samperta@faytechcc.edu
SAMPITE, Chris .... 318-869-5286 186 B
csampite@centenary.edu
SAMPLE, Bradford .... 740-474-8896 358 F
bsample@ohiochristian.edu
SAMPLE, Greg .... 937-775-4444 364 I
gregory.sample@wright.edu
SAMPLE, Mark .... 704-991-0247 338 C
jsample7479@stanly.edu
SAMPLE, Mike .... 317-681-1776 156 B
mmsample@iu.edu
SAMPLE, Valara .... 423-425-4304 428 A
valara-sample@utc.edu
SAMPLER, Larry .... 303-605-5305.. 80 N
lsampler@msudenver.edu
SAMPLES, DeLaine .... 478-301-2627 121 E
samples_dw@mercer.edu
SAMPLES, Donald, A .... 423-439-7457 419 J
samplesd@etsu.edu
SAMPLES, Robert, D ..... 314-516-5665 261 D
bob@umsl.edu
SAMPLES, Terry .... 909-599-5433.. 47 K
tsamples@lifepacific.edu
SAMPSON, Betty, J .... 509-865-8600 481 G
sampson_b@heritage.edu
SAMPSON, John .... 803-376-5773 406 F
jsampson@allenuniversity.edu
SAMPSON, Jon .... 503-517-1056 377 G
jsampson@warnerpacific.edu
SAMPSON, Josiah .... 205-366-8946.... 7 A
jsampson@stillman.edu
SAMPSON, Lauren, K ... 240-895-3220 201 E
lksampson@smcm.edu
SAMPSON, Mark .... 412-731-6000 397 E
msampson@rpts.edu
SAMPSON, Nicole .... 631-632-6976 317 D
nicole.sampson@stonybrook.edu
SAMPSON, Pauline .... 936-468-2807 445 F
sampsonp@sfasu.edu
SAMPSON, Robert .... 401-841-1323 503 L
sampsonr@usnwc.edu
SAMPSON, Ronnie .... 910-272-3345 337 D
rsampson@robeson.edu
SAMPSON, Sharon .... 412-731-3000 397 E
ssampson@rpts.edu
SAMPSON, Sonya .... 207-755-5246 194 G
ssampson@cmcc.edu
SAMRA, Rajinder .... 925-424-1027.. 35 P
rsamra@laspositascollege.edu
SAMS, Courtney .... 917-493-4456 305 I
csams@msmnyc.edu
SAMS, Nathaniel .... 304-637-1382 487 I
samsn@dewv.edu
SAMS, Susan .... 714-997-6829.. 36 C
sams@chapman.edu
SAMS, Timothy .... 936-261-2125 446 D
tesams@pvamu.edu
SAMS, Wesley, S .... 843-953-5375 407 F
wsams@citadel.edu
SAMSON, Agniel .... 256-726-7365.... 6 C
samson@oakwood.edu
SAMSON, Kellie .... 415-422-2697.. 71 K
ksamson@usfca.edu
SAMSON, Keri .... 563-589-3775 169 I
ksamson@dbq.edu
SAMSON, Kim, M .... 218-477-2133 239 D
samson@mnstate.edu
SAMSTAD, Karen .... 952-888-4777 242 I
ksamstad@nwhealth.edu
SAMSTEIN, Ivan .... 773-702-4114 150 J
isamstein@uchicago.edu
SAMUEL, Barbara .... 570-674-6195 390 G
bsamuel@misericordia.edu
SAMUEL, Bryan, D .... 785-532-6221 174 G
bsamuel1@ksu.edu
SAMUEL, Jeanne .... 504-671-6219 187 E
jsamue@dcc.edu
SAMUEL, Linda, M .... 262-243-5700 493 B
linda.samuel@cuw.edu
SAMUEL, Prema .... 914-395-2305 315 F
psamuel@sarahlawrence.edu
SAMUEL, SR., William .. 334-332-0265.... 7 D
wsamuel1@tuskegee.edu
SAMUELS, A. Dexter ..... 615-327-5732 422 A
dsamuels@mmc.edu
SAMUELS, Darlette, C ... 731-426-7595 420 I
dsamuels@lanecollege.edu
SAMUELS, Elena .... 212-220-8061 293 A
esamuels@bmcc.cuny.edu
SAMUELS, Lawrence ..... 831-582-3522.. 32 C
lsamuels@csumb.edu
SAMUELS, Melissa .... 718-405-3212 296 G
melissa.samuels@mountsaintvincent.edu
SAMUELS, Robert .... 401-874-2288 406 B
rsamuels@uri.edu
SAMUELS, Sandra .... 973-353-5201 282 B
szsamuls@newark.rutgers.edu
SAMUELS, Scott .... 248-218-2123 229 J
ssamuels@rc.edu
SAMUELS, Tammy, J .... 212-752-1530 304 D
tammy.samuels@limcollege.edu
SAMUELS, Tim .... 972-273-3364 435 E
samuels@dcccd.edu
SAMUELSON, Lisa .... 218-281-8507 244 A
samue026@umn.edu
SAMULSKI, Eva .... 734-973-3724 232 B
esmaulski@wccnet.edu
SAN FRANCISCO,
Michael .... 806-742-1828 451 B
michael.sanfrancisco@ttu.edu
SAN MIGUEL,
Anitza, M .... 321-682-4091 112 K
asanmiguel2@valenciacollege.edu
SAN MIGUEL,
Claudia, E .... 956-326-2633 446 F
csanmiguel@tamiu.edu
SAN NICOLAS, Apolline 671-735-5539 505 C
hr@guamcc.edu
SAN NICOLAS, Heidi, E 671-735-2481 505 E
heidi.sannicolas@guamcedders.org
SANABRIA, Deanna .... 760-245-4271.. 73 D
deanna.sanabria@vvc.edu
SANAI, Fardin .... 518-956-8062 316 D
fsanai@albany.edu
SANAPAW, Geraldine .... 800-567-2344 492 G
gsanapaw@menominee.edu
SANBERG, Paul .... 813-974-5570 110 B
psanberg@health.usf.edu
SANCHEZ, Alicia .... 316-978-3034 178 A
alicia.sanchez@wichita.edu
SANCHEZ, Alicia .... 617-253-8220 215 G
SANCHEZ, Andrew .... 951-571-6939.. 58 G
andrew.sanchez@mvc.edu
SANCHEZ, Ann .... 914-961-8313 315 C
aks@svots.edu
SANCHEZ, Bonifacio ..... 692-625-3394 505 F
bsanchez@cmi.edu
SANCHEZ, Brenda .... 617-236-8859 209 D
bsanchez@fisher.edu
SANCHEZ, Brianne .... 206-934-4703 483 J
brianne.sanchez@seattlecolleges.edu
SANCHEZ, Carmella ...... 505-747-2118 287 G
carmella@nnmc.edu
SANCHEZ, Cheryl, L ..... 830-591-7202 444 G
clsanchez547@swtjc.edu
SANCHEZ, Christine ...... 714-712-7900.. 46 C
SANCHEZ, Dan .... 952-829-1318 234 A
dan.sanchez@bethfel.org
SANCHEZ, David .... 940-397-3000 440 F
david.sanchez@msutexas.edu
SANCHEZ, Diane .... 210-829-5866 453 D
castaned@uiwtx.edu
SANCHEZ, Dwight .... 716-926-8895 301 H
SANCHEZ, Edward .... 210-486-3217 429 F
esanchez@alamo.edu
SANCHEZ, Felix .... 718-518-4180 294 B
fsanchez@hostos.cuny.edu
SANCHEZ, Frank, A .... 401-456-8100 405 C
fsanchez@ric.edu
SANCHEZ, Gregory .... 619-388-3354.. 60 C
gsanchez@sdccd.edu
SANCHEZ, Ismael .... 212-694-1000 291 I
isanchez@boricuacollege.edu
SANCHEZ, Jaymi .... 787-743-3484 511 A
jsanchez@sanjuanbautista.edu
SANCHEZ, Jennifer .... 413-755-4480 215 F
jsanchez@stcc.edu
SANCHEZ, John .... 210-434-6711 441 E
jdsanchez@lake.ollusa.edu
SANCHEZ, José .... 787-764-0000 514 B
jose.sanchez18@upr.edu
SANCHEZ, Joseph .... 808-932-7315 128 E
josephs7@hawaii.edu
SANCHEZ, Joseph .... 817-735-2522 454 C
joseph.sanchez@unthsc.edu
SANCHEZ, Julie .... 909-652-6102.. 36 A
julie.sanchez@chaffey.edu
SANCHEZ, Laura .... 210-486-5000 429 D
SANCHEZ, Leopoldo, A . 314-863-2772 251 I
sanchezl@csl.edu
SANCHEZ, Librada .... 973-720-2586 284 I
sanchezl@wpunj.edu
SANCHEZ, Lisa, M .... 626-396-2210.. 26 E
lisa.sanchez@artcenter.edu
SANCHEZ, Luis .... 805-678-5807.. 72 G
SANCHEZ, Luis .... 520-494-5266.. 11 K
luis.sanchez@centralaz.edu
SANCHEZ, Luis, P .... 805-678-5808.. 73 A
lsanchez@vcccd.edu
SANCHEZ, Marci .... 707-256-7235.. 53 C
msanchez@napavalley.edu
SANCHEZ, Margaret ...... 808-245-8274 129 C
masanche@hawaii.edu
SANCHEZ, Mario .... 575-538-6336 289 B
news@wnmu.edu
SANCHEZ, Mark .... 805-546-3116.. 41 A
mark_sanchez1@cuesta.edu
SANCHEZ, Matthew .... 239-433-8047 100 A
msanchez30@fsw.edu
SANCHEZ, Matthew .... 518-891-2915 310 E
msanchez@nccc.edu
SANCHEZ, Matthew .... 214-860-8507 435 D
matthewsanchez@dcccd.edu
SANCHEZ, Melba, G ...... 787-743-7979 511 I
msanchez@suagm.edu
SANCHEZ, Miriam .... 770-612-2170.. 92 G
SANCHEZ, Molly .... 225-490-1605 186 F
molly.sanchez@franu.edu
SANCHEZ, Monica .... 575-769-4948 285 K
monica.sanchez@clovis.edu
SANCHEZ, Noel .... 661-726-1911.. 68 B
noel.sanchez@uav.edu
SANCHEZ, Noelle .... 303-273-3528.. 78 I
nsanchez@mines.edu
SANCHEZ, Omar .... 305-821-3333.. 99 E
omarsnc@fnu.edu
SANCHEZ, Ophelia .... 305-442-9223 103 F
osanchez@mru.edu
SANCHEZ, Patricia .... 210-486-4209 429 E
psanchez70@alamo.edu
SANCHEZ, Priscilla .... 979-230-3215 432 D
priscilla.sanchez@brazosport.edu
SANCHEZ, Rebecca .... 949-824-5337.. 68 G
rebecca.sanchez@uci.edu
SANCHEZ, Richard, P .... 956-665-3668 455 D
richard.sanchez@utrgv.edu
SANCHEZ, Roxanne .... 210-434-6711 441 E
rlsanchez@lake.ollusa.edu
SANCHEZ, Rudy .... 559-278-3906.. 31 D
rjsanchez@csufresno.edu
SANCHEZ, Sandra .... 310-233-4041.. 49 A
sanches@lahc.edu
SANCHEZ, Stefanie .... 413-572-5713 213 D
ssanchez@westfield.ma.edu
SANCHEZ, Steven .... 314-977-2611 259 H
steven.sanchez@slu.edu
SANCHEZ, Suane .... 787-758-2525 513 G
suane.sanchez@upr.edu
SANCHEZ, Tiffany .... 443-352-4306 201 H
tsanchez@stevenson.edu
SANCHEZ, Victor .... 773-838-7974 134 F
vsanchez124@ccc.edu
SANCHEZ, Vivian .... 760-591-3012.. 71 H
ceo@usa.edu
SANCHEZ CINTRON,
Naury, Y .... 787-720-4476 512 D
presidente@mizpa.edu
SANCHEZ-FERNANDEZ,
Hector, R .... 787-751-1912 510 A
hrsanchez@juris.inter.edu
SANCHEZ PINTOR,
Linda .... 787-725-8120 507 N
lsanchez0053@eap.edu
SANCHEZ VELEZ,
Edwin .... 407-582-1554 112 K
esanchez@valenciacollege.edu
SANCILIO, Leonard .... 585-245-5706 318 E
sancilio@geneseo.edu
SANCRANT, Lisa .... 419-251-1487 356 C
lisa.sancrant@mercycollege.edu
SAND, Sabra .... 360-992-2288 479 F
ssand@clark.edu
SAND, Scott .... 916-388-2920.. 35 B
ssand@carrington.edu
SANDBERG, Curtis .... 502-863-7969 180 E
curtis_sandberg@georgetowncollege.edu
SANDBERG, Steven, M . 801-422-2235 458 H
steve_sandberg@byu.edu
SANDBOTHE, Lindsay .... 312-461-0600 132 A
lsandbothe@aaart.edu
SANDBOTHE, Robin ...... 913-667-5708 172 C
rsandbothe@cbts.edu
SANDBULTE, Deb .... 712-707-7224 168 H
debfs@nwciowa.edu
SANDE, Melissa .... 908-709-7497 284 C
melissa.sande@ucc.edu
SANDE, Nora .... 503-552-1534 374 E
nsande@nunm.edu
SANDEEN, Cathy .... 907-786-1437.... 9 H
chancellor@alaska.edu
SANDEFUR, Gary .... 405-744-5627 368 B
gary.sandefur@okstate.edu
SANDEL, Robert, H .... 540-857-7311 476 D
rsandel@virginiawestern.edu
SANDELIN, Broc .... 215-489-4190 382 D
broc.sandelin@delval.edu
SANDELL, Julie, H .... 617-358-5846 207 D
jsandell@bu.edu
SANDELL, Kamalika ...... 202-885-2123.. 90 J
ksandel@american.edu
SANDELL, Stanley, C .... 310-233-4181.. 49 A
sandelsc@lahc.edu
SANDER, Dennis, M ...... 620-417-1018 176 K
dennis.sander@sccc.edu
SANDER, Laura .... 617-573-8400 219 A
lsander@suffolk.edu
SANDER, Michael .... 567-661-7545 360 B
michael_sander@owens.edu

SANDER, Pam ... 573-651-2175 259 K psander@semo.edu
SANDERLIN, September, C ... 757-683-4324 469 G ssanderl@odu.edu
SANDERS, Alison ... 415-338-1948.. 34 A asanders@sfsu.edu
SANDERS, Allen ... 606-337-1722 179 G allen.sanders@ccbbc.edu
SANDERS, Alphonso ... 573-681-5074 254 E sandersa@lincolnu.edu
SANDERS, Andrea ... 937-708-5724 364 D asanders@wilberforce.edu
SANDERS, Art ... 515-271-3172 165 A arthur.sanders@drake.edu
SANDERS, Athena ... 614-222-3251 351 D asanders@ccad.edu
SANDERS, Ben ... 415-999-1002.. 58 B bsanders@reachinst.org
SANDERS, Beverly ... 419-824-3728 355 K bsanders2@lourdes.edu
SANDERS, Blaklee ... 417-667-8181 252 A
SANDERS, Blanche ... 601-877-6350 244 H blanche@alcorn.edu
SANDERS, Brian ... 209-588-5107.. 75 I sandersb@yosemite.edu
SANDERS, Cheryl ... 361-698-1277 436 C cgarner6@delmar.edu
SANDERS, Clifton ... 801-957-4182 461 D clifton.sanders@slcc.edu
SANDERS, Connie ... 303-605-5587.. 80 N csande29@msudenver.edu
SANDERS, David ... 575-439-3790 287 C dasander@nmsu.edu
SANDERS, David, A ... 312-850-7031 134 H dsanders67@ccc.edu
SANDERS, Diane, F ... 843-349-2848 408 C diane@coastal.edu
SANDERS, Emily ... 585-582-8205 299 A emilysanders@elim.edu
SANDERS, Emily, J ... 608-246-6073 499 H ejsanders@madisoncollege.edu
SANDERS, Erica, L ... 734-647-0102 231 E yale@umich.edu
SANDERS, George ... 239-489-9294 100 A george.sanders@fsw.edu
SANDERS, Gregory ... 440-525-7097 355 H gsanders3@lakelandcc.edu
SANDERS, Gwendolyn ... 252-335-3226 341 D gsanders@ecsu.edu
SANDERS, Ike ... 870-633-4480.. 19 B isanders@eacc.edu
SANDERS, J.C ... 405-224-3140 371 D jsanders@usao.edu
SANDERS, James ... 404-270-5674 125 B jsande14@spelman.edu
SANDERS, Janet ... 318-487-7752 186 I janet.sanders@lacollege.edu
SANDERS, Jenny ... 870-574-4530.. 21 E jsanders@sautech.edu
SANDERS, Joe ... 432-552-2740 457 A sanders_j@utpb.edu
SANDERS, Judy ... 501-977-2016.. 23 A sanders@uaccm.edu
SANDERS, Karen ... 336-322-2190 336 G karen.sanders@piedmontcc.edu
SANDERS, Karen ... 361-570-4850 453 C sanderkg1@uhv.edu
SANDERS, Karen ... 386-506-3050.. 97 D karen.sanders@daytonastate.edu
SANDERS, Karen ... 914-395-2202 315 F ksanders@sarahlawrence.edu
SANDERS, Karen, A ... 217-786-2784 142 B karen.sanders@llcc.edu
SANDERS, Kathy ... 573-840-9654 260 I ksanders@trcc.edu
SANDERS, Kristie ... 912-871-1937 122 I ksanders@ogeecheetech.edu
SANDERS, Kristine ... 225-578-5985 188 I kcalong@lsu.edu
SANDERS, Lakisha ... 678-466-4185 116 E lakishasanders@clayton.edu
SANDERS, Lakisha ... 404-297-9522 119 B sandersl@gptc.edu
SANDERS, LaSha ... 678-359-5015 119 F lashas@gordonstate.edu
SANDERS, Lee ... 870-574-4455.. 21 E lsanders@sautech.edu
SANDERS, Liz ... 312-362-5289 135 I lsander3@depaul.edu
SANDERS, Mae ... 931-393-1530 425 C msanders@mscc.edu
SANDERS, Matt ... 801-274-3280 461 F matt@wgu.edu
SANDERS, Megan ... 303-384-2617.. 78 I sanders@mines.edu
SANDERS, Melanie ... 662-243-2623 246 A msanders@eastms.edu
SANDERS, Melinda ... 501-337-5000.. 18 J msanders@coto.edu
SANDERS, Michael ... 863-638-7239 113 A michael.sanders@warner.edu
SANDERS, Michael ... 417-625-9378 256 D sanders-m@mssu.edu
SANDERS, Nancy, A ... 815-282-7900 148 C nancysanders@sacn.edu
SANDERS, Nena, F ... 205-726-2744.... 6 E nfsander@samford.edu
SANDERS, Rebecca ... 903-510-2084 452 C rsan2@tjc.edu
SANDERS, Rebekah ... 406-604-4300 263 A
SANDERS, Robert ... 407-646-2292 105 M rsanders@rollins.edu
SANDERS, Salvatore, A . 330-941-3091 365 C sasanders@ysu.edu
SANDERS, Shalonda ... 229-333-3014 127 B shalonda.sanders@wiregrass.edu
SANDERS, Stephanie, R 614-247-6281 358 I sanders.14@osu.edu
SANDERS, Thomas ... 903-923-2075 436 D tsanders@etbu.edu
SANDERS, Tiffany ... 256-395-2211.... 3 G tsanders@suscc.edu
SANDERS, Tom ... 330-337-6403 347 E college@awc.edu
SANDERS, Tricia ... 218-281-8326 244 A sand0803@umn.edu
SANDERS, Wm Gerard (Gerry), Y 210-458-4313 455 E gerry.sanders@utsa.edu
SANDERS-MCMURTRY, Kijua ... 413-538-2500 216 G kijuasm@mtholyoke.edu
SANDERSON, Bruce ... 316-942-4291 175 I sandersonb@newmanu.edu
SANDERSON, Carla ... 888-556-8226 133 F
SANDERSON, Francie, W ... 919-866-5944 338 G fwsanderson@waketech.edu
SANDERSON, Karri ... 402-465-2411 268 H ksanders@nebrwesleyan.edu
SANDERSON, Larry ... 575-492-2763 286 J lsanderson@nmjc.edu
SANDERSON, Lex ... 818-401-1032.. 39 G lsanderson@columbiacollege.edu
SANDERSON, Robyn ... 864-231-2000 406 G rsanderson@andersonuniversity.edu
SANDFORD, Art ... 805-678-5804.. 73 A asandford@vcccd.edu
SANDHEINRICH, Mark .. 608-785-8218 496 F msandheinrich@uwlax.edu
SANDIDGE, Rosetta ... 859-257-2813 185 B rosetta.sandidge@uky.edu
SANDIDGE, William ... 434-832-7641 474 C sandidgew@centralvirginia.edu
SANDIFER, Joyce ... 504-520-5230 193 A jsandife@xula.edu
SANDIFER, William, A .. 803-812-7302 413 G sandifea@mailbox.sc.edu
SANDIFER, Willie ... 903-730-4890 438 H wsandifer@jarvis.edu
SANDIMANIE, Audry ... 770-394-8300 114 C asandimanie@aii.edu
SANDLER, Elysha ... 516-239-9002 315 I esandler@shoryoshuv.org
SANDLES, Sherry ... 817-531-4401 451 E slsandles@txwes.edu
SANDLIN, Betsy ... 931-598-1672 423 M bsandlin@sewanee.edu
SANDNER, Michael ... 860-509-9525.. 87 B msandner@hartsem.edu
SANDNESS, Debra ... 701-224-5524 346 B debra.sandness@bismarckstate.edu
SANDOE, Timothy ... 717-780-2648 385 E tlsandoe@hacc.edu
SANDOR, David, B ... 404-727-2793 117 F david.sandor@emory.edu
SANDOR, Kathy ... 540-654-1648 472 I kunderwo@umw.edu
SANDOVAL, April ... 928-226-4217.. 11 O april.sandoval@coconino.edu
SANDOVAL, Barbara, A . 360-650-7614 486 F barbara.sandoval@wwu.edu
SANDOVAL, Belinda ... 909-748-8164.. 71 G belinda_sandoval@redlands.edu
SANDOVAL, Carol ... 518-783-2335 315 J sandoval@siena.edu
SANDOVAL, Cristian ... 210-784-1115 448 A csandoval1@tamusa.edu
SANDOVAL, Derek ... 830-591-7372 444 G mdsandoval@swtjc.edu
SANDOVAL, John ... 719-549-2535.. 79 A john.sandoval@csupueblo.edu
SANDOVAL, Natalie ... 830-792-7303 443 G nsandoval@schreiner.edu
SANDOVAL, Nikki ... 301-985-7000 203 B nikki.sandoval@umuc.edu
SANDOVAL, Paul ... 520-626-6309.. 16 G sandovar@email.arizona.edu
SANDOVAL, Rudy ... 254-501-3007 432 H rudolfo.sandoval@ctcd.edu
SANDOVAL, William ... 787-738-2161 513 D william.sandoval@upr.edu
SANDOVAL, Yuliana ... 707-468-3110.. 51 E ysandoval@mendocino.edu
SANDOVAL-LUCERO, Elena ... 303-678-3620.. 79 J elena.sandoval-lucero@frontrange.edu
SANDRES RAPALO, Lester ... 908-965-6090 284 C lester.sandresrapalo@ucc.edu
SANDRIN, Todd ... 602-543-4506.. 10 I todd.sandrin@asu.edu
SANDROCK, Jessica ... 503-584-7255 372 C jessica.sandrock@chemeketa.edu
SANDS, Barb ... 618-664-7019 137 G barb.sands@greenville.edu
SANDS, Bryan, A ... 714-879-3901.. 45 F basands@hiu.edu
SANDS, Charles ... 951-343-4213.. 27 J csands@calbaptist.edu
SANDS, Deanna ... 206-296-5696 484 F sandsd@seattleu.edu
SANDS, Harlan, M ... 216-687-3544 351 B harlan.sands@csuohio.edu
SANDS, Rosita ... 312-369-6286 135 E rsands@colum.edu
SANDS, Timothy, D ... 540-231-6231 477 A president@vt.edu
SANDS-VANKERK, Linda ... 630-942-2621 135 A sands-vankerkl@cod.edu
SANDS WISE, Jonathan 502-863-8009 180 E jonathan_sandswise@georgetowncollege.edu
SANDSTROM, Karen ... 216-421-7417 350 M ksandstrom@cia.edu
SANDSTROM, Kent, L ... 757-683-3925 469 G ksandstr@odu.edu
SANDSTROM, Lynne ... 707-826-4031.. 33 D les37@humboldt.edu
SANDSTROM, Marlene, J ... 413-597-4171 220 C marlene.j.sandstrom@williams.edu
SANDT, Jennifer, A ... 410-334-2911 204 F jsandt@worwic.edu
SANDU, Terri, B ... 440-366-4215 355 J
SANDUM TUNE, Rachel 937-327-7411 364 H rtune@wittenberg.edu
SANDVIG, Mark ... 314-434-4044 252 B mark.sandvig@covenantseminary.edu
SANDY, Kirsti ... 603-358-2898 275 A ksandy@keene.edu
SANDY, Michael ... 508-531-6183 212 B michael.sandy@bridgew.edu
SANERIVI, Mamoe ... 808-675-3769 127 E mamoe.sanerivi@byuh.edu
SANFILIPPO, Frank ... 636-949-4907 254 F fsanfilippo@lindenwood.edu
SANFILIPPO, Marjorie ... 727-864-7562.. 97 J sanfilmd@eckerd.edu
SANFILIPPO, Rick ... 610-526-4600 385 G rsanfilippo@harcum.edu
SANFORD, Betsy ... 585-567-9524 302 D betsy.sanford@houghton.edu
SANFORD, Debra ... 703-330-8400.. 92 G
SANFORD, Delacy ... 904-470-8290.. 97 L dsanford@ewc.edu
SANFORD, Eric ... 785-539-3571 175 E esanford@mccks.edu
SANFORD, Jenell ... 757-826-1883 465 A librarian@bcva.edu
SANFORD, Jennifer ... 707-826-3236.. 33 D jls7003@humboldt.edu
SANFORD, Jessica ... 765-983-1432 154 G sanfoje@earlham.edu
SANFORD, Jonathan, J . 972-721-5388 452 D jsanford@udallas.edu
SANFORD, Julie ... 601-984-6200 249 E jrsanford@umc.edu
SANFORD, Larry ... 410-228-9250 202 F
SANFORD, Mark ... 313-579-6931 232 C msanfor1@wcccd.edu
SANFORD, Matthew ... 607-431-4460 301 D sanfordm@hartwick.edu
SANFORD, Susan, H ... 315-470-6604 320 A shsanfor@esf.edu
SANGER, Bryna ... 212-229-8947 308 C sanger@newschool.edu
SANGER, Tchad ... 831-459-5604.. 70 B cpsanger@ucsc.edu
SANGHA, Gurminder ... 559-265-5763.. 66 E gurminder.sangha@fresnocitycollege.edu
SANGHVI, Kamlesh ... 708-974-5522 144 C sanghvik@morainevalley.edu
SANGREY-BILLY, Cory .. 406-395-4875 265 G csangrey@stonechild.edu
SANGWIN, Kim ... 712-274-5428 168 B sangwink@morningside.edu
SANIAL, Greg ... 616-331-2188 224 E sanialg@gvsu.edu
SANJUAN, Alfredo ... 214-860-2064 435 C aesanjuan@dcccd.edu
SANKEY, Lorinda ... 402-643-7385 266 G lorinda.sankey@cune.edu
SANKEY, Marc ... 513-721-7944 353 F msankey@gbs.edu
SANKO, Jerry ... 620-450-2193 176 G jerrys@prattcc.edu
SANKS GUIDRY, Beverly ... 909-469-5341.. 74 I bguidry@westernu.edu
SANNS, Aaron ... 208-496-1109 130 A sannsa@byui.edu
SANREGRET, Suzanne ... 906-487-3070 227 E srsangre@mtu.edu
SANSBURY, Timothy ... 954-771-0376 102 R tsansbury@knoxseminary.edu
SANSEVIRO, Michael, L 470-578-6310 120 L msansevi@kennesaw.edu
SANSING, Perry ... 662-915-7014 249 D psansing@olemiss.edu
SANSOLA, Steve ... 845-575-3000 305 L steve.sansola@marist.edu
SANSOM, Erikka ... 304-829-7717 487 G esansom@bethanywv.edu
SANSON, Jerry ... 318-473-6470 188 J jsanson@lsua.edu
SANT, Anne, M ... 508-565-1343 218 H asant@stonehill.edu
SANTA, Sally ... 787-884-3838 506 D ssanta@atenascollege.edu
SANTA MARIA, Diane, M ... 713-500-2187 456 B diane.m.santamaria@uth.tmc.edu
SANTAMARIA, Anthony . 973-290-4338 277 A asantamaria@cse.edu
SANTAMARIA, Danielle . 401-598-1000 404 I dsantamaria@jwu.edu
SANTAMARIA-MAKANG, Doris ... 301-687-7018 203 E dsantamaria@frostburg.edu
SANTANA, Arleen ... 787-264-1912 509 F asantana@intersg.edu
SANTANA, Evelyn ... 610-526-6006 385 G esantana@harcum.edu
SANTANA, Leslie ... 310-289-5123.. 73 H leslie.santana@wcui.edu
SANTANA, Pedro ... 609-652-4601 283 D pedro.santana@stockton.edu
SANTANA-BRAVO, Maydel ... 305-348-1555 109 A santanam@fiu.edu
SANTANA MARINO, Julio ... 787-725-6500 506 G jsantana@albizu.edu
SANTANDREA, Margaret ... 949-794-9090.. 65 I msantandrea@stanbridge.edu
SANTANDREA, Mona ... 512-404-4823 431 C msantandrea@austinseminary.edu
SANTANGELO, Victoria, R ... 718-990-1363 314 B santangv@stjohns.edu
SANTAROSA, Michael ... 801-832-2186 461 G msantarosa@westminstercollege.edu
SANTEE, Wendi ... 864-379-8701 409 H santee@erskine.edu
SANTELLANO, Claudia .. 509-527-2632 485 H claudia.santellano@wallawalla.edu

SANTERRE, Kim .... 770-228-7365 124 G kim.santerre@sctech.edu
SANTESTEBAN, David .... 559-638-0300.. 66 F
SANTIAGO, Alma, L ...... 787-841-2000 510 K alsantiago@pucpr.edu
SANTIAGO, Bárbara ...... 787-850-9386 513 E barbara.santiago2@upr.edu
SANTIAGO, Cariluz .... 787-841-2000 510 K cariluz_santiago@pucpr.edu
SANTIAGO, Carlos .... 617-994-6901 211 B csantiago@mass.edu
SANTIAGO, Carol .... 787-620-2040 506 C csantiago@aupr.edu
SANTIAGO, Dalia .... 787-882-2065 511 D orientacion@unitecpr.net
SANTIAGO, Deejay .... 949-451-5732.. 64 F dsantiago@ivc.edu
SANTIAGO, Delma .... 787-284-1912 509 E dosantia@ponce.inter.edu
SANTIAGO, Edny .... 787-864-2222 509 C ed.santiago@guayama.inter.edu
SANTIAGO, Eutimia .... 787-751-0160 507 F esantiago@cmpr.pr.gov
SANTIAGO, Isaac .... 787-766-1912 508 J isantiag@inter.edu
SANTIAGO, Isaac .... 787-766-1912 509 C isantiag@inter.edu
SANTIAGO, Jaime .... 787-250-1912 509 D jaimesantiago@metro.inter.edu
SANTIAGO, Jamie .... 617-588-1358 206 C jsantiago@bfit.edu
SANTIAGO, Jorge .... 787-764-0000 514 B jorge.santiago21@upr.edu
SANTIAGO, Jose, G ...... 787-279-1912 509 A jsantiago@bayamon.inter.edu
SANTIAGO, Jose, M ..... 787-786-3030 512 B jsantiago@ucb.edu.pr
SANTIAGO, Judith .... 212-343-1234 306 J jsantiago@mcny.edu
SANTIAGO, Juliane .... 919-658-7769 340 J jsantiago@umo.edu
SANTIAGO, Karen .... 202-664-5683.. 93 E ksantiago@wesleyseminary.edu
SANTIAGO, Kenneth ...... 773-481-8047 134 G ksantiago6@ccc.edu
SANTIAGO, Luis .... 203-837-9004.. 85 B santiagol@wcsu.edu
SANTIAGO, Maria .... 787-738-2161 513 D maria.santiago25@upr.edu
SANTIAGO, Marya, Z ..... 787-844-8181 514 A marya.santiago@upr.edu
SANTIAGO, Miguel .... 787-764-0000 514 B miguel.santiatgo16@upr.edu
SANTIAGO, Teofilo .... 347-964-8600 291 I tsantiago@boricuacollege.edu
SANTIAGO, Victoria ...... 773-442-5300 145 B vi-santiago@neiu.edu
SANTIAGO, Viviana .... 787-720-1022 506 E administracion@atlanticu.edu
SANTIAGO, Viviana .... 787-720-1022 506 E vsantiago@atlanticu.edu
SANTIAGO, Wanda .... 718-289-5352 293 B wanda.santiago@bcc.cuny.edu
SANTIAGO, Xiomara ...... 787-738-2161 513 D xiomara.santiago3@upr.edu
SANTIAGO, Yaritza .... 787-878-6000 508 D
SANTIAGO, Yinaira .... 787-284-1912 509 E yinsant@ponce.inter.edu
SANTIAGO-GABRIELINI, Wilma .... 787-265-3878 512 G rector.uprm@upr.edu
SANTIAGO GABRIELINI, Wilma .... 787-832-4040 513 F
SANTIAGO-GUZMAN, Cynthia .... 407-582-3253 112 K csantiagoguzman@valenciacollege.edu
SANTIAGO-LÓPEZ, Peggy .... 787-993-8877 513 B peggy.santiago@upr.edu
SANTIAGO-ROSADO, Victor .... 787-857-3600 508 M vsantiago@br.inter.edu
SANTIAGO-SANTIAGO, Irma, J .... 787-993-8958 513 B irma.santiago1@upr.edu
SANTIAGO-TORO, Clarissa .... 787-723-4481 507 A csantiago@ceaprc.edu
SANTIAGO-VELÁZQUEZ, Birilo .... 787-890-2681 512 H birilo.santiago@upr.edu
SANTILLAN, Courtney ... 208-562-3153 130 F courtneysantillan@cwi.edu
SANTIN, Claudia .... 708-209-3228 135 F claudia.santin@cuchicago.edu
SANTIVASCI, Joseph ..... 610-436-3085 396 A jsantivasci@wcupa.edu
SANTOMAURO, Kristine, M .... 302-225-6233.. 90 E santomk@gbc.edu
SANTORA, Anthony .... 908-737-6000 278 E afs@kean.edu
SANTORE, JR., Chuck .. 724-439-4900 388 F csantore@laurel.edu
SANTORO, Dana, S .... 302-356-6862.. 90 I dana.s.eggleston@wilmu.edu
SANTOS, Ana .... 661-654-2411.. 30 E asantos20@csub.edu
SANTOS, Annette, T ...... 671-735-2553 505 E atsantos@triton.uog.edu
SANTOS, Carmen, K ..... 671-735-5548 505 C carmen.kweksantos@guamcc.edu
SANTOS, Carmen, M .... 787-758-2525 513 G carmen.santos4@upr.edu
SANTOS, David, M .... 860-701-6787 504 F david.m.santos@uscg.edu
SANTOS, Eileen .... 202-806-6100.. 92 B
SANTOS, Elsa .... 787-850-9320 513 E elsa.santos@upr.edu
SANTOS, Ferdinand, R .. 305-223-4561 106 B
SANTOS, Helena .... 617-243-2127 210 G hsantos@lasell.edu
SANTOS, Kristy .... 860-231-5445.. 89 B krsantos@usj.edu
SANTOS, Maggie .... 719-389-1988.. 77 H maggie.santos@coloradocollege.edu
SANTOS, Maria del, C .. 787-743-7979 511 I ut_masantos@suagm.edu
SANTOS, Matt .... 610-683-4183 395 A santos@kutztown.edu
SANTOS, Matthew .... 360-752-8396 478 G msantos@btc.edu
SANTOS, Nelson .... 787-850-9348 513 E nelson.santos@upr.edu
SANTOS, Noemi .... 787-780-0070 506 F nsantos@caribbean.edu
SANTOS, Paul .... 704-978-5409 336 C psantos@mitchellcc.edu
SANTOS, Rod .... 510-215-3921.. 40 H rsantos@contracosta.edu
SANTOS, Rodolfo, T ...... 415-338-2356.. 34 A rtsantos@sfsu.edu
SANTOS, Rosa Milagros .... 217-244-3558 151 D rsantos@illinois.edu
SANTOS, Seilyn .... 305-821-3333.. 99 E santoss@fnu.edu
SANTOS, Susan .... 859-442-4165 181 B susan.santos@kctcs.edu
SANTOS-COY, Katie .... 714-463-7552.. 51 A ksantoscoy@ketchum.edu
SANTOS-DERIEG, Brittany .... 619-594-5201.. 33 E bsantosderieg@sdsu.edu
SANTOS-GEORGE, Arlene .... 847-543-2402 135 B asgeorge@clcillinois.edu
SANTOS-PEREZ, Kennia, I .... 787-480-2463 507 C kisantos@sanjuanciudadpatria.com
SANTOS RODRIGUEZ, Maria del Carmen ...... 787-725-8120 507 N msantos@eap.edu
SANTUCCI, George .... 412-392-3498 397 A gsantucci@pointpark.edu
SANTUCCI, Wayne .... 212-517-0544 306 A wsantucci@mmm.edu
SANYAL, Rajib, N .... 516-877-4661 289 C rsanyal@adelphi.edu
SANYAL, Sabyasachi ..... 972-721-5156 452 D ssanyal@udallas.edu
SANZARI, Kelly, J .... 724-847-6515 384 G kjsanzar@geneva.edu
SAPARILAS, John, W .... 919-866-5450 338 G jwsaparilas@waketech.edu
SAPERSTEIN, Shari .... 954-262-7201 103 M ssaperst@nova.edu
SAPH, Donald .... 716-614-5982 310 C dsaph@niagaracc.suny.edu
SAPIENZA, Christine ..... 904-256-7679 101 G csapien@ju.edu
SAPIENZA, Matthew ...... 646-664-3014 292 K matthew.sapienza@cuny.edu
SAPOZNICK, Aaron .... 718-645-0536 307 C
SAPP, Aimee .... 573-592-4391 262 G aimee.sapp@williamwoods.edu
SAPP, David, A .... 310-338-4262.. 50 J david.sapp@lmu.edu
SAPP, John, B .... 713-313-7831 449 C sapp_jb@tsu.edu
SAPP, Rebecca .... 423-794-3071 422 J rlsapp@milligan.edu
SAPP, Robert .... 866-776-0331.. 54 A rsapp@ncu.edu
SAPP, Van .... 919-516-4354 340 C vsapp@st-aug.edu
SAPPINGTON, Eric .... 660-831-4168 256 G sappingtone@moval.edu
SARAC, Isa .... 703-591-7042 476 F isarac@viu.edu
SARACENO, Victoria ...... 305-809-3149.. 99 C victoria.saraceno@fkcc.edu
SARACHICK, Daniel, T .. 508-831-5298 220 E dtsarachick@wpi.edu
SARAN, Rupam .... 718-270-4937 295 A rsaran@mec.cuny.edu
SARAO, Felix, G .... 562-908-3413.. 58 E fsarao@riohondo.edu
SARAT, Austin, D .... 413-542-2308 205 B adsarat@amherst.edu
SARATA, Andrew .... 708-974-5357 144 C saratаa@morainevalley.edu
SARAVANAPAVAN, Naomi .... 607-729-1581 298 C nsaravanapavan@davisny.edu
SARAZIN, Marcus, D .... 651-286-7537 244 D mdsarazin@unwsp.edu
SARBER, John .... 765-455-9505 156 D jrsarber@iuk.edu
SARBER, Sarah .... 765-455-9316 156 D shawkins@iuk.edu
SARCEDO-MAGRUDER, Genice .... 818-710-3318.. 49 C sarcedg@piercecollege.edu
SARETSKY, Kelly .... 978-556-3866 215 C ksaretsky@necc.mass.edu
SARFF, Michelle .... 614-251-4758 358 G sarffm@ohiodominican.edu
SARGE, Sandy .... 562-988-2278.. 25 R ssarge@auhs.edu
SARGEANT, Lynn .... 605-688-4723 417 C lynn.sargeant@sdstate.edu
SARGEANT, Marcel .... 817-202-6207 444 I sargeant@swau.edu
SARGENT, Brent .... 802-879-2321 464 E bsargent@vtc.edu
SARGENT, Daniel .... 315-866-0300 301 G sargentda@herkimer.edu
SARGENT, Deirdre .... 650-508-3503.. 54 D dsargent@ndnu.edu
SARGENT, Famika .... 225-771-2492 190 H famika_sargent@subr.edu
SARGENT, Frank .... 412-237-8182 381 G fsargent@ccac.edu
SARGENT, Gary .... 254-295-4242 453 E gsargent@umhb.edu
SARGENT, Jenelle .... 240-895-4331 201 E ejsargent@smcm.edu
SARGENT, John .... 903-923-2273 436 D jsargent@etbu.edu
SARGENT, Madeline .... 215-568-9215 403 H msargent@phmc.org
SARGENT, Mark, L .... 805-565-6007.. 74 K msargent@westmont.edu
SARGENT, Ryan .... 208-282-4735 130 H sargryan@isu.edu
SARGENT, Sheri .... 507-389-1112 239 C sheri.sargent@mnsu.edu
SARGENT-MARTIN, Shelia .... 304-327-4176 489 P ssmartin@bluefieldstate.edu
SARIAN, Richard .... 216-421-7432 350 M rsarian@cia.edu
SARIDAKIS, Dianne, I ... 215-885-2360 389 F dsaridakis@manor.edu
SARIN, Anurag .... 305-284-5699 112 E axs2977@miami.edu
SARIN, Sanjiv .... 336-285-3170 341 F sarin@ncat.edu
SARIPALLI, Parvika .... 785-864-9525 177 D psaripalli@ku.edu
SARISKY JONES, Susan .... 717-867-6321 388 H sjones@lvc.edu
SARKAR, Ratna .... 410-516-5925 199 D rsarkar3@jhu.edu
SARKIS, Hashim .... 617-253-4401 215 G
SARKISIAN, Jodi .... 215-898-7221 400 K jodi@upenn.edu
SARLES, Harry .... 913-684-5428 504 D harry.sarles@us.army.mil
SARLO, Rebecca .... 727-298-8685 111 H
SARMA, Sanjay .... 617-715-4532 215 G
SARMIENTO, Reine .... 718-960-8429 294 A reine.sarmiento@lehman.cuny.edu
SARNA, Jason .... 847-543-2383 135 B jsarna@clcillinois.edu
SARNA, Linda .... 310-825-9621.. 69 A lsarna@sonnet.ucla.edu
SARNESO, Anna .... 617-243-2243 210 G asarneso@lasell.edu
SARNOFF, Jonathan ...... 864-488-4501 410 E jsarnoff@limestone.edu
SARR, Akua .... 617-552-9144 207 B akua.sarr@bc.edu
SARRA, Michael .... 617-824-8540 208 H michael_sarra@emerson.edu
SARRA, Michael .... 617-585-1139 217 B michael.sarra@necmusic.edu
SARRANTONIO, Rob ..... 859-846-5812 183 E rsarrantonio@midway.edu
SARRATORI, Peter .... 315-781-3647 302 A sarratori@hws.edu
SARRATT, Carla .... 484-365-7262 389 C csarratt@lincoln.edu
SARRETT, David, C .... 804-828-7235 473 F dcsarrett@vcu.edu
SARRION-CORTES, Noemi .... 706-236-1714 115 B nsarrion@berry.edu
SARRUBBO, JR., Joe, M .... 407-582-2586 112 K jsarrubbo@valenciacollege.edu
SARTARELLI, Jose, V .... 910-962-3030 343 C sartarellij@uncw.edu
SARTE, Bruce .... 610-606-4635 381 A bsarte@cedarcrest.edu
SARTIN, Mici .... 405-703-8232 366 G
SARTOR, Curtis .... 847-628-1017 140 C csartor@judsonu.edu
SARTOR, Dan .... 423-266-4574 423 K dsartor@richmont.edu
SARTORIUS, Arthur, G .. 605-342-0317 415 E sportart@aol.com
SARVEY, Sharon .... 252-399-6401 326 M sisarvey@barton.edu
SARVIS, Randall, F .... 937-481-2344 364 E randy_sarvis@wilmington.edu
SARWAR, Mostafa .... 504-671-5420 187 E msarwa@dcc.edu
SARWARK, Robert .... 770-394-8300 114 C
SARWI, Cindy .... 336-342-4261 337 E sarwic2369@rockinghamcc.edu
SASAKI, Charles, S .... 808-235-7443 129 F sasakich@hawaii.edu
SASAKI, Stefanie .... 808-845-9463 129 B sasakist@hawaii.edu
SASASKI, Hiroshi .... 626-571-8811.. 72 C hiroshis@uwest.edu
SASLOW, Lauren .... 818-710-4442.. 49 C saslowle@piercecollege.edu
SASMAL, Indrani .... 701-228-2277 346 C indrani.sasmal@dakotacollege.edu
SASS, Michael .... 314-367-8700 259 B michael.sass@stlcop.edu
SASSAMAN, Margo, J .... 717-871-7656 395 D margo.sassaman@millersville.edu
SASSE, Chris .... 301-624-2858 198 E csasse@frederick.edu
SASSE, Gary .... 401-232-6593 404 F gsasse@bryant.edu
SASSER, Jackson, N ..... 352-395-5164 107 A j.sasser@sfcollege.edu
SASSER, Mackey .... 334-556-2416.... 2 C msasser@wallace.edu
SASSER, Rachelle .... 310-900-1600.. 40 A rsasser@elcamino.edu
SASSER, Tom .... 916-577-2200.. 75 B tsasser@jessup.edu
SASSMAN, Danielle .... 323-337-1068.. 53 B martind@mi.edu
SASSMAN, Jen, L .... 319-352-8262 170 C jennifer.sassman@wartburg.edu
SASSO, Allison .... 724-838-4231 398 H sasso@setonhill.edu
SASSO, Mary .... 585-594-6235 312 K sasso_mary@roberts.edu
SASSSER, Craig-Ellis .... 662-720-7411 248 C cesasser@nemcc.edu
SASTRE FUENTE, Terilyn, M .... 787-763-4280 514 B terilyn.sastre@upr.edu

SASTRY, Hari ... 412-624-6577 401 B hsastry@cfo.pitt.edu
SATA, Leigh ... 707-524-1704 62 F lsata@santarosa.edu
SATA, Leigh ... 510-466-7336 56 E lsata@peralta.edu
SATELE, Arleen ... 714-628-4717 58 A satele_arleen@sccollege.edu
SATER-WEE, Diane ... 614-825-6255 347 F dsater@aiam.edu
SATHER, Greg ... 218-726-6137 243 F gsather@d.umn.edu
SATHER, Steven, M ... 609-258-6479 280 E sather@princeton.edu
SATHIANATHAN, Dhushy ... 562-985-4128 31 F dhushy.sathianathan@csulb.edu
SATKOWIAK, Ann, E ... 865-539-7153 425 F asatkowiak@pstcc.edu
SATKOWSKI, John ... 313-845-9636 224 G jssatkowski@hfcc.edu
SATO, Deirdre, C ... 212-217-5380 299 H deidre_sato@fitnyc.edu
SATO, Heidi ... 714-816-0366 67 I heidi.sato@trident.edu
SATO, Sara ... 808-544-7020 127 H
SATO, Toshiko ... 949-480-4364 64 B tsato@soka.edu
SATRIANA, Dan ... 970-351-2399 83 E dan.satriana@unco.edu
SATTAR, Mo ... 413-565-1000 205 G msattar@baypath.edu
SATTERFIELD, Allison, D ... 336-322-2102 336 G allison.satterfield@piedmontcc.edu
SATTERFIELD, Derick ... 336-342-4261 337 E satterfieldd@rockinghamcc.edu
SATTERFIELD, Jay ... 731-989-6058 420 C jsatterfield@fhu.edu
SATTERFIELD, Kathleen ... 909-706-3505 74 I ksatterfield@westernu.edu
SATTERFIELD, Lacey, L ... 770-720-5620 123 E lls@reinhardt.edu
SATTERFIELD, Lisa ... 828-398-2500 424 A lsatterfield@south.edu
SATTERFIELD, Tanya ... 662-915-7692 249 D tnsatter@olemiss.edu
SATTERLEE, Kevin ... 208-282-3440 130 H
SATTERLEE, Richard ... 718-862-7352 305 H richard.satterlee@manhattan.edu
SATTERLUND, Alysson ... 858-534-4371 69 D asatterlund@ucsd.edu
SATTERLY, Eric ... 502-272-8098 179 B esatterly@bellarmine.edu
SATTERLY, Tom ... 970-491-0006 78 M steve.hultin@colostate.edu
SATTERWHITE, Dawn ... 919-761-2209 340 G dsatterwhite@sebts.edu
SATTERWHITE, Kerry ... 608-363-2200 492 C satterwhitek@beloit.edu
SATTERWHITE, Robin ... 806-716-2200 443 I rsatterwhite@southplainscollege.edu
SATZ, Debra ... 650-723-9784 65 J
SATZ, Michael ... 208-364-4041 131 G msatz@uidaho.edu
SAUCEDA, James ... 706-355-5175 114 F jsauceda@athenstech.edu
SAUCEDO, Federico ... 818-240-1000 44 B fsaucedo@glendale.edu
SAUCEDO, Joseph ... 773-508-3948 142 D jsaucedo4@luc.edu
SAUCIER, Jason ... 207-741-5544 195 A jsaucier@smccme.edu
SAUDER, Ryan ... 717-358-4271 384 D ryan.sauder@fandm.edu
SAUDER, Vinita ... 402-486-2500 269 F vinita.sauder@ucollege.edu
SAUDERS, Charlette, R ... 574-372-5100 155 B saudercr@grace.edu
SAUER, Carrie ... 405-208-5873 367 I csauer@okcu.edu
SAUER, Dietrich ... 928-226-4204 11 O diestrich.sauer@coconino.edu
SAUER, Greg ... 802-485-2170 463 A gsauer@norwich.edu
SAUER, Jennifer, M ... 540-887-7370 469 B jmsauer@marybaldwin.edu
SAUER, Marty, R ... 630-637-5801 144 H mrsauer@noctrl.edu
SAUER, Melanie ... 626-529-8064 55 A msauer@pacificoaks.edu
SAUER, Meredith ... 920-693-1282 499 G meredith.sauer@gotoltc.edu
SAUERBREI, Aaron ... 319-277-2490 166 B aaron.sauerbrei@hawkeyecollege.edu
SAUERBURGER, Kate ... 314-792-7435 254 D sauerburger@kenrick.edu
SAUERMAN, Gretchen ... 321-674-7237 99 B gsauerman@fit.edu
SAUERS, Darlene ... 724-838-4210 398 H sauers@setonhill.edu
SAUL, Amy ... 610-861-1508 391 A saula@moravian.edu
SAUL, Eric ... 302-622-8000 89 E esaul@dcad.edu
SAUL, J. Beau ... 607-844-8222 322 H saulj@tompkinscortland.edu
SAUL, Sheryl ... 651-846-1384 241 B sheryl.saul@saintpaul.edu
SAULNIER, Timothy ... 540-654-2468 472 I tsaulnie@umw.edu
SAULS, Jina, M ... 276-244-1232 464 L jsauls@asl.edu
SAULSBERRY, Jean ... 901-435-1727 421 A jean_saulsberry@loc.edu
SAULSBERRY, Keith ... 334-556-2470 2 C ksaulsberry@wallace.edu
SAULSBERRY, Lynette, M ... 478-289-2169 117 D lsaulsberry@ega.edu
SAUM, Rob ... 828-669-8012 331 J rob.saum@montreat.edu
SAUNDERS, Aleister ... 215-895-6203 383 B aleister.j.saunders@drexel.edu
SAUNDERS, Amber ... 318-371-3035 187 I ambersaunders@nwltc.edu
SAUNDERS, Ann-Henley ... 609-497-7990 280 D
SAUNDERS, Brian ... 310-544-6487 59 E brian.saunders@usw.salvationarmy.org
SAUNDERS, Catherine ... 812-535-5225 160 B catherine.saunders@smwc.edu
SAUNDERS, Christopher ... 615-353-3066 425 D christopher.saunders@nscc.edu
SAUNDERS, Clark ... 860-768-4504 88 H clsaunder@hartford.edu
SAUNDERS, Di ... 503-821-1303 375 C di.saunders@oit.edu
SAUNDERS, Douglas ... 606-337-3196 179 G
SAUNDERS, Gary ... 336-506-4152 332 A gary.saunders@alamancecc.edu
SAUNDERS, Greer ... 804-819-4906 474 A gsaunders@vccs.edu
SAUNDERS, Joseph ... 304-766-3353 491 B saundejs@wvstateu.edu
SAUNDERS, Kara, C ... 716-645-5725 316 F kcs23@buffalo.edu
SAUNDERS, Kathleen ... 716-827-2445 323 D saundersk@trocaire.edu
SAUNDERS, Keith ... 319-335-0553 163 A keith-saunders@uiowa.edu
SAUNDERS, Kevin ... 515-271-1984 165 A kevin.saunders@drake.edu
SAUNDERS, Kevin ... 831-582-3397 32 C kesaunders@csumb.edu
SAUNDERS, Martha, D ... 850-474-2200 110 E msaunders@uwf.edu
SAUNDERS, Robert ... 334-983-6556 7 C rsaunders@troy.edu
SAUNDERS, Scott, D ... 716-673-3171 317 A scott.saunders@fredonia.edu
SAUNDERS, Sharon ... 434-947-8114 470 E ssaunders@randolphcollege.edu
SAUNDERS, Sharon ... 281-649-3206 437 H ssaunders@hbu.edu
SAUNDERS, Tanya, R ... 607-274-3063 303 B tsaunders@ithaca.edu
SAUNDS, Lindsay ... 706-419-1279 117 B lindsay.saunds@covenant.edu
SAURBEK, Rhonda, R ... 517-750-1200 230 H dseacott@arbor.edu
SAURBIER, Ann ... 248-689-8282 232 A asaurbie@walshcollege.edu
SAUSER, Jordan ... 515-964-0601 165 G sauserj@faith.edu
SAUTER, Maranah ... 706-880-8201 121 A msauter@lagrange.edu
SAUTER, Ramona ... 408-554-4397 62 D rsauter@scu.edu
SAUVE, Stephanie, L ... 585-340-9588 296 E ssauve@crcds.edu
SAUVIGNON, Carine ... 508-588-9100 214 F csauvigno@massasoit.mass.edu
SAVAGE, Ann ... 870-248-4000 18 F annd@blackrivertech.edu
SAVAGE, Daina ... 717-396-7833 393 E dsavage@pcad.edu
SAVAGE, Deana ... 432-685-4515 440 E docsavage@midland.edu
SAVAGE, Devin ... 312-567-3615 139 B dsavage@iit.edu
SAVAGE, Donna ... 254-968-9246 446 E dsavage@tarleton.edu
SAVAGE, Jeffrey ... 435-283-7154 461 C jeff.savage@snow.edu
SAVAGE, Jess ... 970-247-7180 79 I jlsavage@fortlewis.edu
SAVAGE, Lauren ... 970-247-6073 79 I lasavage@fortlewis.edu
SAVAGE, Mandara ... 618-453-0020 149 E msavage@engr.siu.edu
SAVAGE, Mary ... 860-439-2251 86 H mary.savage@conncoll.edu
SAVAGE, Monique, J ... 517-265-5161 220 F msavage@adrian.edu
SAVAGE, Nesha ... 619-388-3400 60 C nsavage@sdccd.edu
SAVAGE, Pam ... 314-744-5331 256 C savagep@mobap.edu
SAVAGE, Richard, N ... 724-458-2033 385 C savagern@gcc.edu
SAVAGE, Ron ... 617-747-2025 206 E rsavage@berklee.edu
SAVAGE, Scott ... 419-289-5401 348 A ssavage2@ashland.edu
SAVAGE, Shauna ... 406-496-4422 265 A ssavage@mtech.edu
SAVASTA, Mark ... 508-849-3456 205 C msavasta@annamaria.edu
SAVIA, Anthony ... 301-860-3470 203 C asavia@bowiestate.edu
SAVICE, Candice ... 703-891-1787 471 K admissions@standardcollege.edu
SAVICKY, Kim ... 402-399-2417 266 F ksavicky@csm.edu
SAVILLE, Vicki ... 704-330-6224 333 D vicki.saville@cpcc.edu
SAVIN, Stuart ... 717-464-7050 388 C
SAVINO, Jeffrey ... 814-472-3006 398 B jsavino@francis.edu
SAVINO, Stacey ... 360-538-4082 481 E ssavino@ghc.edu
SAVITS, Logan ... 336-506-4100 332 A logan.savits@alamancecc.edu
SAVITT-KING, Robin ... 413-782-1243 219 F robin.savitt-king@wne.edu
SAVOCA, Marianna ... 631-632-6810 317 D marianna.savoca@stonybrook.edu
SAVOIE, E. Joseph ... 337-482-6203 192 E president@louisiana.edu
SAVOIE, Leslie, L ... 321-674-7362 99 B lsavoie@fit.edu
SAVOIE, Michael, P ... 229-249-4894 126 G mpsavoie@valdosta.edu
SAVOIT, Taina, J ... 337-475-5065 192 A tsavoit@mcneese.edu
SAVORY, Paul ... 402-826-8221 267 A paul.savory@doane.edu
SAVRON, Doris ... 602-557-9021 16 J doris.savron@phoenix.edu
SAVU, Vasemaca ... 692-625-3394 505 F vsavu@cmi.edu
SAVUKINAS, Robert ... 831-242-5828 503 D
SAWATZKY, Rachel, R ... 540-432-4133 466 G rachel.roth.sawatzky@emu.edu
SAWAY, Sabine ... 206-239-4500 479 E ssaway@cityu.edu
SAWICKI, Jerzy ... 216-687-9364 351 B j.sawicki@csuohio.edu
SAWREY, Barbara ... 858-822-4358 69 D avcdue@ucsd.edu
SAWTELLE, III, James (Jimmy), R ... 318-487-5443 187 C jsawtelle@cltcc.edu
SAWYER, Caroline ... 704-463-3026 339 E caroline.sawyer@pfeiffer.edu
SAWYER, Donald, C ... 203-582-8964 87 G don.sawyer@quinnipiac.edu
SAWYER, Eric ... 603-428-2407 273 H esawyer@nec.edu
SAWYER, Gretchen ... 775-674-7686 271 D gsawyer@tmcc.edu
SAWYER, James ... 586-445-7241 226 H sawyerj@macomb.edu
SAWYER, Jenny, L ... 502-852-4957 185 C jsawyer@louisville.edu
SAWYER, John ... 208-882-1566 131 B jsawyer@nsa.edu
SAWYER, Jonathan ... 202-319-5619 91 B sawyerj@cua.edu
SAWYER, Jonathan, C ... 202-319-5619 91 B sawyerj@cua.edu
SAWYER, Julia ... 918-444-2210 367 A sawyerjk@nsuok.edu
SAWYER, Justin ... 504-282-4455 190 A recreation@nobts.edu
SAWYER, Katherine ... 847-635-1718 145 G ksawyer@oakton.edu
SAWYER, Lisa ... 256-215-4536 1 G lsawyer@cacc.edu
SAWYER, Masonne ... 336-734-7343 334 E msawyer@forsythtech.edu
SAWYER, Mike ... 660-543-4750 260 K msawyer@ucmo.edu
SAWYER, Nichole ... 207-454-1040 195 B nsawyer@wccc.me.edu
SAWYER, Sarah ... 207-974-4828 194 H ssawyer@emcc.edu
SAWYER, Scott ... 832-842-8705 452 F ssawyer@uh.edu
SAWYER, Terrence ... 410-617-2290 199 F tsawyer@loyola.edu
SAWYER, Wm. Gregory 707-664-2880 34 C
SAWYERS, Dorret ... 305-348-2436 109 A dorret.sawyers@fiu.edu
SAWYERS, Tamberly ... 423-697-3359 424 E tammy.sawyers@chattanoogastate.edu
SAX, Christina ... 410-888-9048 200 A csax@muih.edu
SAX, Joanna ... 619-239-0391 34 F jsax@cwsl.edu
SAX, Richard ... 740-245-7214 363 D rsax@rio.edu
SAXBY, William, R ... 303-963-3124 77 G wsaxby@ccu.edu
SAXENA, Peter ... 585-594-6800 310 F
SAXENA, Pradeep ... 585-594-6430 312 K saxenap@roberts.edu
SAXENIAN, AnnaLee ... 510-642-9980 68 D anno@ischool.berkeley.edu
SAXON, Terrell, F ... 254-710-6101 431 J terrell_saxon@baylor.edu
SAXTON, Brad ... 203-582-3246 87 G brad.saxton@quinnipiac.edu
SAXTON, Micah ... 303-765-3137 80 F msaxton@iliff.edu
SAY, Elizabeth Anne ... 805-437-8400 30 F
SAYAVONG, Phoumy ... 410-981-5014 56 E psayavong@peralta.edu
SAYDSHOEV, Sally ... 765-973-8584 156 C ssaydsho@iue.edu
SAYE, Shaydean ... 406-657-1051 265 E shaydean.saye@rocky.edu
SAYED, Ellen, N ... 414-955-4852 494 C esayed@mcw.edu
SAYEGH, Sharlene ... 562-985-5428 31 F sharlene.sayegh@csulb.edu
SAYGIN, Can ... 210-458-5264 455 E can.saygin@utsa.edu
SAYLER, David, A ... 513-529-7286 356 E saylerda@miamioh.edu
SAYLER, Michael ... 734-487-1414 223 H msayler@emich.edu
SAYLERS, Jill ... 423-636-7300 427 B jsaylers@tusculum.edu
SAYLOR, Danette ... 504-816-4026 186 D dsaylor@dillard.edu
SAYLOR, Jessica, M ... 701-349-5444 346 J jsaylor@trinitybiblecollege.edu
SAYLOR, Laura ... 513-244-3263 357 A laura.saylor@msj.edu
SAYLORS, Tony ... 870-248-4000 18 F tony.saylors@blackrivertech.edu
SAYRE, Cris ... 773-602-5505 134 D csayre@ccc.edu
SAYRE, Jeff ... 304-214-8809 489 F jsayre@wvncc.edu
SAYRE, Matt ... 541-552-6273 376 E sayrem@sou.edu
SAYRE, Richard ... 309-457-2190 144 A rsayre@monmouthcollege.edu
SAYRE, William ... 505-424-2364 286 C bsayre@iaia.edu
SAYRS, Elizabeth ... 740-593-1935 359 G sayrs@ohio.edu
SBALBI, Tony ... 413-552-2391 214 D tsbalbi@hcc.edu
SBRISCIA, Amanda ... 413-552-2747 214 D asbriscia@hcc.edu
SCACCIA, Jeff, P ... 864-833-8205 411 I jpscaccia@presby.edu

SCAGGIANTE, Michele .. 718-270-3007 317 E
michele.scaggiante@downstate.edu

SCAGGS, Deirdre .... 859-257-3653 185 B
deirdre@uky.edu

SCAGLIONE, Agnes .... 201-692-2596 277 K
agnes@fdu.edu

SCALA, Kerry, L .... 603-862-1355 274 G
kerry.scala@unh.edu

SCALA, Natalie .... 440-375-7530 355 G
nscala@lec.edu

SCALBERG, Daniel .... 503-255-0332 374 D
dscalberg@multnomah.edu

SCALES, Jane .... 800-686-1883 222 E
jscales@cleary.edu

SCALES, Keyana .... 504-520-7849 193 A
kscales@xula.edu

SCALES, Lea Ann .... 978-630-9320 215 A
lscales2@mwcc.mass.edu

SCALES, Michael, D ...... 215-204-3121 399 F
michael.scales@temple.edu

SCALES, Michael, G ...... 845-675-4777 310 G
president@nyack.edu

SCALES, Roger .... 316-295-5551 173 D
roger_scales@friends.edu

SCALES, Suzanne .... 303-300-8740.. 77 D
suzanne.scales@collegeamerica.edu

SCALESE, Mark .... 203-254-4000.. 86 I
mscalese@fairfield.edu

SCALIA, Derek .... 603-899-4152 273 F
scaliad@franklinpierce.edu

SCALISE, Julia .... 805-482-2755.. 58 L
julia@stjohnsem.edu

SCALZO, Denise .... 718-862-7178 305 H
dscalzo01@manhattan.edu

SCANDALIS, Thomas ...... 509-452-5100 483 A
tscandalis@pnwu.edu

SCANDRETT, Clyde .... 831-656-2517 503 K
cscandrett@nps.edu

SCANDRETT, Nic .... 712-279-1761 163 C
nic.scandrett@briarcliff.edu

SCANGA, Diane .... 636-481-3420 254 A
dscanga@jeffco.edu

SCANLAN, Lina .... 684-699-9155 505 A
l.galeai-scanlan@amsamoa.edu

SCANLAN, Therese, A ... 773-252-5311 147 B
therese.scanlan@resu.edu

SCANLON, Jennifer .... 909-621-8016.. 57 F
jennifer.scanlon@pomona.edu

SCANLON, Joan .... 203-773-6678.. 84 F
jscanlon@albertus.edu

SCANLON, Tom .... 617-732-2775 216 B
tom.scanlon@mcphs.edu

SCANNELL, Janet .... 507-222-4077 234 F
jscannell@carleton.edu

SCAPPATICCI, Jason ..... 860-906-5085.. 85 D
jscappaticci@capitalcc.edu

SCARANO, John .... 216-397-4701 354 I
jscarano@jcu.edu

SCARANO, Martin .... 603-862-2116 274 G
marty.scarano@unh.edu

SCARANTINO, Laura ..... 410-706-2562 202 D
lscarantino@umaryland.edu

SCARBORO, Donna .... 202-994-6360.. 91 F
scarboro@gwu.edu

SCARBORO, Gina .... 912-650-5640 124 E
gscarboro@southuniversity.edu

SCARBORO, Kim .... 850-973-1613 103 K
scarborok@nfcc.edu

SCARBORO, Lynne, B ... 310-338-5236.. 50 J
lscarbor@lmu.edu

SCARBOROUGH, Edesa . 813-253-3333 112 J

SCARBOROUGH,
Janna, L .... 423-439-7616 419 J
scarboro@etsu.edu

SCARBOROUGH,
Tara, H .... 513-556-0648 362 D
tara.scarborough@uc.edu

SCARCELLE, Ed .... 212-229-5598 308 C
scarcele@newschool.edu

SCARFF, Colleen .... 269-387-4281 232 K
colleen.scarff@wmich.edu

SCARINGE, John .... 562-902-3330.. 65 C
johnscaringe@scuhs.edu

SCARLETT, Barbara .... 607-777-4438 316 E
scarlett@binghamton.edu

SCARPELLI, Geoff .... 817-735-5030 454 C
geoffrey.scarpelli@unthsc.edu

SCATAMACCHIA, Marc .. 617-358-6401 207 D
marcs1@bu.edu

SCATES, LouAnn, P .... 704-406-4263 329 A
lscates@gardner-webb.edu

SCAVONE, Victoria, R ... 248-689-8282 232 A
vscavone@walshcollege.edu

SCAVUZZO, Connie, M . 312-949-7079 138 E
cscavuzzo@ico.edu

SCEARCE, Stephanie ...... 706-295-6958 119 A
sscearce@gntc.edu

SCEERY, Amy, L .... 203-576-4506.. 88 D
asceery@bridgeport.edu

SCEGGEL, Tim .... 706-419-1517 117 B
tim.sceggel@covenant.edu

SCEPANSKY, Patricia, S 610-359-7355 382 C
pscepansky@dccc.edu

SCHAAF, Bill .... 603-623-0313 273 I
billschaaf@nhia.edu

SCHAAF, Laura .... 706-385-1122 123 C
laura.schaaf@point.edu

SCHAAFSMA, Micah ...... 206-281-2434 484 D
mschaafsma@spu.edu

SCHAAKE, Vicki .... 518-587-2100 321 A
vicki.schaake@esc.edu

SCHAAL, Barbara, A ...... 314-935-6820 262 A
schaal@wustl.edu

SCHAAL, Dave .... 641-784-5106 165 H
dschaal@graceland.edu

SCHAAL, Michael, L ...... 810-762-9733 225 H
mschaal@kettering.edu

SCHAB, Kristin .... 717-815-1285 404 A
kasummer@ycp.edu

SCHABERG, David .... 310-825-4856.. 69 A
dschaberg@college.ucla.edu

SCHABERT, Daniel .... 215-646-7300 385 D
schabert.d@gmercyu.edu

SCHACHTER, Shmuel .... 410-484-7200 201 A
finaid@nirc.edu

SCHACKMUTH, Kurt ...... 815-836-5810 141 G
schackku@lewisu.edu

SCHACTLER, Linda .... 509-963-2111 479 B
schactler@cwu.edu

SCHADE, Isaac .... 417-626-1234 257 F
schade.isaac@occ.edu

SCHADE, Megan .... 904-516-8814.. 98 P
mschade@fcsl.edu

SCHADING, Douglas ..... 212-938-5880 320 B
dschading@sunyopt.edu

SCHADLER, Linda .... 802-656-8413 463 E
linda.schadler@uvm.edu

SCHAECHTER,
Alexander .... 718-854-8791 305 F
mh@thejnet.com

SCHAEFBAUER, Christi . 701-355-3794 347 D
cjschaefbauer@umary.edu

SCHAEFER, Brian, C ...... 207-834-7671 196 C
brian.schaefer@maine.edu

SCHAEFER, Duane .... 812-357-6499 160 D
dschaefer@saintmeinrad.edu

SCHAEFER, Joseph .... 516-299-2463 304 G
joseph.schaefer@liu.edu

SCHAEFER, K. C .... 540-458-8216 478 A
schaeferk@wlu.edu

SCHAEFER, Karla .... 641-585-8159 170 B
schaeferk@waldorf.edu

SCHAEFER, Kelly .... 847-467-0301 145 F
kelly.schaefer@northwestern.edu

SCHAEFER, Lisa .... 970-521-6659.. 81 D
lisa.schaefer@njc.edu

SCHAEFER, Lynne .... 410-455-2939 202 E
lschaefer@umbc.edu

SCHAEFER, Mark .... 202-885-3304.. 90 J
schaef@american.edu

SCHAEFER, Maryann ..... 312-629-6118 148 I
mschaefer@saic.edu

SCHAEFER, Matthew ..... 740-284-7230 353 B
mschaefer@franciscan.edu

SCHAEFER, Rhonda .... 505-566-3087 288 A
schaeferr@sanjuancollege.edu

SCHAEFER, Scot .... 740-376-4600 356 A

SCHAEFER, Sharon, P ... 813-253-6250 112 J
sschaefer@ut.edu

SCHAEFER, Thomas, G . 412-536-1198 387 B
thomas.schaefer@laroche.edu

SCHAEFER, Verdell .... 909-558-4509.. 48 C
vschaefer@llu.edu

SCHAEFFER, Amy .... 817-461-8741 430 H
aschaeffer@abu.edu

SCHAEFFER, Angela ...... 860-297-2139.. 88 C
angela.schaeffer@trincoll.edu

SCHAEFFER, Christine ... 215-717-6366 400 J
cschaefer@uarts.edu

SCHAEFFER, Jeremy ...... 269-927-1000 226 D

SCHAEFFER, Lisa, L ...... 910-521-6175 343 B
lisa.schaeffer@uncp.edu

SCHAEFFER, Mindy .... 202-319-6369.. 91 B
schaefferm@cua.edu

SCHAFER, Amy .... 724-589-2212 399 H
aschafer@thiel.edu

SCHAFER, Catherine ...... 619-388-3400.. 60 C
cschafer@sdccd.edu

SCHAFER, Chris .... 309-794-7642 132 C
chrisschafer@augustana.edu

SCHAFER, Clark .... 316-942-4291 175 I
schaferc@newmanu.edu

SCHAFER, Jodi .... 319-895-4289 164 B
jschafer@cornellcollege.edu

SCHAFER, Robin .... 914-633-2548 302 G
rschafer@iona.edu

SCHAFER, Stephen .... 914-395-2314 315 F
sschafer@sarahlawrence.edu

SCHAFER, William .... 304-293-5811 491 C
wschafer@mail.wvu.edu

SCHAFFER, Amy .... 785-628-4175 173 B
alschaffer@fhsu.edu

SCHAFFER, Doug .... 269-927-8120 226 D
dschaffer@lakemichigancollege.edu

SCHAFFER, Jeff .... 732-987-2600 278 B
jschaffer@georgian.edu

SCHAFFER, Joe .... 307-778-1102 502 D
jschaffer@lccc.wy.edu

SCHAFFER, Kerry .... 941-359-7601 105 K
kshaffe@ringling.edu

SCHAFFER, Patricia .... 508-849-3298 205 C
pschaffer@annamaria.edu

SCHAFFER, Rob .... 256-782-5277.... 5 J
schaffer@jsu.edu

SCHAFFER, Sandy .... 931-393-1536 425 C
sschaffer@mscc.edu

SCHAFFNER,
Barbara, H .... 614-823-1735 360 A
bschaffner@otterbein.edu

SCHAFFNER, Bradley ..... 507-222-4267 234 F
bschaffner@carleton.edu

SCHAFFTER, David, A .... 719-333-2180 504 C
david.schaffter@usafa.edu

SCHAFFZIN, Kate .... 901-678-2421 427 D
ktschffz@memphis.edu

SCHAFRICK, James, A .. 203-773-8507.. 84 F
jschafrick@albertus.edu

SCHAIBLE, John .... 609-292-2108 284 B
jschaible@tesu.edu

SCHAICH, Monte .... 816-531-5223 251 H

SCHAKNOWSKI,
Jennifer .... 706-290-2167 115 B
jschaknowski@berry.edu

SCHALES, Danny .... 318-257-2893 191 F
dan@latech.edu

SCHALK, Heather .... 302-736-2306.. 90 G
heather.schalk@wesley.edu

SCHALL, Lawrence, M .. 404-364-8320 122 J
lschall@oglethorpe.edu

SCHALLER, Molly .... 314-977-2495 259 H
molly.schaller@slu.edu

SCHALLER, Rhonda .... 718-636-5926 311 J
rshal20@pratt.edu

SCHALLOCK, Heather .... 715-365-4518 500 D
hschallock@nicoletcollege.edu

SCHANDEL,
Kimberly, A .... 508-767-7312 205 D
kschande@assumption.edu

SCHANK, Jordan .... 574-239-8407 155 D
jschank@hcc-nd.edu

SCHANTZ, Janet, D .... 317-738-8009 154 J
jschantz@franklincollege.edu

SCHANTZ, Peter, K .... 740-368-3404 359 N
pkschant@owu.edu

SCHANZ, Jeffrey .... 518-445-3219 289 E
dscha@albanylaw.edu

SCHAPER, Sue .... 208-459-5837 130 D
sschaper@collegeofidaho.edu

SCHAPERKOTTER,
Nancy .... 616-234-5536 231 H
nancy.schaperkotter@vai.org

SCHAPIRO, Chaim .... 973-455-9031 280 G
chaimschap@aol.com

SCHAPIRO, Mendel .... 323-937-3763.. 75 F

SCHAPIRO, Morton, O .. 847-491-7456 145 F
nu-president@northwestern.edu

SCHAPP, Rebecca, M .... 408-554-4528.. 62 D
rschapp@scu.edu

SCHAPPE, Mascheal ..... 314-529-9670 254 H
mschappe@maryville.edu

SCHAPPERT, David .... 570-208-5900 387 A
davidschappert@kings.edu

SCHAPPERT, Lisa .... 607-778-5179 318 A
schappertl@sunybroome.edu

SCHARDT, Wendy, L ...... 308-865-8047 269 I
schardtwl@unk.edu

SCHARER, Gregory .... 937-775-2620 364 I
greg.scharer@wright.edu

SCHARER, Miriam .... 503-399-8486 372 C
miriam.scharer@chemeketa.edu

SCHARF, Michael, P ..... 216-368-3283 349 F
michael.scharf@case.edu

SCHARF, Sara, A .... 515-574-1005 166 E
scharf@iowacentral.edu

SCHARLEMANN,
Linette, M .... 507-354-8221 236 I
scharllm@mlc-wels.edu

SCHARLOTT, Brooke ...... 440-684-6129 363 G
brooke.scharlott@ursuline.edu

SCHARMER, Judy .... 575-624-8040 287 A
scharmer@nmmi.edu

SCHARN, Theresa .... 605-718-2402 417 F
theresa.scharn@wdt.edu

SCHATTGEN, Sharon ...... 573-876-2394 260 F
sschattgen@stephens.edu

SCHATTMAN, Lisa .... 858-566-1200.. 41 E
lschattman@disd.edu

SCHATZ, Christopher .... 920-693-1840 499 G
christopher.schatz@gotoltc.edu

SCHATZ, Julianne .... 336-272-7102 329 D
julies@greensboro.edu

SCHATZEL, Kim .... 410-704-2356 204 A
presidentsoffice@towson.edu

SCHAUB, Dennis .... 718-420-4221 324 F
dschaub@wagner.edu

SCHAUB, Linda .... 517-750-1200 230 H
lindas@arbor.edu

SCHAUB, Mark .... 616-331-8655 224 E
schaubm@gvsu.edu

SCHAUB, Rebekah .... 231-843-5568 232 J
rschaub@westshore.edu

SCHAUBHUT, Diana .... 504-398-2100 191 C
dschaubhut@uhcno.edu

SCHAUDER, Marie .... 610-519-4154 402 D
marie.schauder@villanova.edu

SCHAUER, Adam .... 630-466-7900 152 C
aschauer@waubonsee.edu

SCHAUER, Anne, P .... 513-529-3735 356 E
schauerap@miamioh.edu

SCHAUER, Ariane .... 310-377-5501.. 51 B
aschauer@marymountcalifornia.edu

SCHAUER, James .... 608-890-1569 496 C
wslhdirector@slh.wisc.edu

SCHAUMANN, Neils .... 619-239-0391.. 34 F
nschaumann@cwsl.edu

SCHAUMLOFFEL, John .. 978-665-4187 212 C
jschauml@fitchburgstate.edu

SCHAURER, Susan .... 513-529-5040 356 E
susan.schaurer@miamioh.edu

SCHAUS, Maynard .... 757-455-3210 477 F
mschaus@vwu.edu

SCHBAT, Manhal .... 713-718-7746 437 I
manhal.schbat@hccs.edu

SCHEARS, Ben .... 785-890-3641 176 C
ben.schears@nwktc.edu

SCHECHTER, Aaron, M .. 718-377-0777 312 A

SCHECHTER, Mendel ...... 718-377-0777 312 A

SCHECHTER, Richard ..... 203-591-5042.. 87 F
rschechter@post.edu

SCHECKEL, Martha .... 608-796-3664 498 N
mmschekel@viterbo.edu

SCHECKTER, Abbey .... 570-577-3200 379 F
abbey.scheckter@bucknell.edu

SCHECTER, David .... 661-654-6324.. 30 E
dschecter@csub.edu

SCHEDIN, Karen .... 603-897-8516 274 B
kschedin@rivier.edu

SCHEEL, Fran .... 334-670-3700.... 7 C
fscheel@troy.edu

SCHEELE, Lisa .... 414-955-8788 494 C
lscheele@mcw.edu

SCHEER, Marisol, M ..... 210-805-3038 453 D
scheer@uiwtx.edu

SCHEER, RuthAnn .... 319-895-4324 164 B
rscheer@cornellcollege.edu

SCHEERER, Teresa .... 215-785-0111 393 C

SCHEESLER, Brian .... 206-934-6790 484 B
brian.sheesler@seattlecolleges.edu

SCHEESSELE, Marc .... 314-977-4132 259 H
marc.scheessele@slu.edu

SCHEETZ, Anita, A .... 406-768-6341 263 G
ascheetz@fpcc.edu

SCHEETZ, Charles, M ... 240-500-2323 198 H
cmscheetz@hagerstowncc.edu

SCHEETZ, Christine .... 330-490-7102 364 B
cscheetz@walsh.edu

SCHEFFEL, Debora .... 303-963-3147.. 77 G
dscheffel@ccu.edu

SCHEFFEL, Kent .... 618-468-5000 141 F
kscheffe@lc.edu

SCHEFFEL, Thomas .... 303-963-3353.. 77 G

SCHEFFER, James .... 713-529-2778 432 G
scheffer@paralegal.edu

SCHEFFEY, Aubrey 773-989-3888 134 C ascheffey@ccc.edu
SCHEFFLER, Anthony 636-949-4618 254 F ascheffler@lindenwood.edu
SCHEFFLER, Keith 713-525-2124 454 H kscheff@stthom.edu
SCHEFFLER, Steve 713-313-7421 449 C steve.scheffler@tsu.edu
SCHEIB, Curt 724-357-2397 394 G curt.scheib@iup.edu
SCHEIB, John, W 801-581-6764 460 E john.scheib@utah.edu
SCHEIB, Roger 620-417-1240 176 K roger.scheib@sccc.edu
SCHEIBEL, Cindy 562-902-3390.. 65 C cindyscheibel@scuhs.edu
SCHEIBLER, Deborah, L 570-408-4353 403 D deborah.scheibler@wilkes.edu
SCHEIDT, Douglas 716-842-2770 299 F
SCHEIE, Katie 858-513-9240.. 26 G katie.scheie@ashford.edu
SCHEINBERG, Mark, E .. 860-727-6757.. 87 A mscheinberg@goodwin.edu
SCHEINES, Richard 412-268-2832 380 F scheines@cmu.edu
SCHEINMAN, John, E ... 603-535-2805 275 B jscheinman@plymouth.edu
SCHEINMAN, Steven, J . 570-504-7000 384 F sscheinman@som.geisinger.edu
SCHEIRER, Gwen 717-866-5775 383 H gscheirer@evangelical.edu
SCHEJBAL, David 414-288-6395 494 B david.schejbal@marquette.edu
SCHELIN, Chris 510-549-4729.. 66 B cschelin@sksm.edu
SCHELIN, Kelly 925-229-6826.. 40 G kschelin@4cd.edu
SCHELL, John 407-823-5711 109 E rick.schell@ucf.edu
SCHELL, Karen 518-292-1719 313 D schelk@sage.edu
SCHELL, Randa 830-591-2908 444 G rschell@swtjc.edu
SCHELL, Shannon 507-453-2743 239 A sschell@southeastmn.edu
SCHELLENBERGER, Kimberly 573-876-7172 260 F kschellenberger@stephens.edu
SCHELLENBERGER, Lauren 573-288-6325 252 E lschellenberger@culver.edu
SCHELLHASE, Cherea .... 251-981-3771.... 5 B cherea.schellhase@columbiasouthern.edu
SCHELLHORN, Henry .... 909-607-4168.. 37 D henry.schellhorn@cgu.edu
SCHELLY, Sylvia 757-233-8881 477 F sschelly@vwu.edu
SCHENA, Donna 240-567-3085 200 C donna.schena@montgomerycollege.edu
SCHENCK, Merlin 706-886-6831 125 D mschenck@tfc.edu
SCHENDEL, Ellen 616-331-2400 224 E schendee@gvsu.edu
SCHENEWERK, Randal .. 573-875-7256 251 F raschenewerk@ccis.edu
SCHENGEL, Jonna 559-737-6265.. 39 E jonnas@cos.edu
SCHENK, Elaine 718-390-3461 324 F eschenk@wagner.edu
SCHENK, Glenn 310-287-4275.. 49 G schenkga@wlac.edu
SCHENK, Kimberely 925-969-2036.. 40 I schenk@dvc.edu
SCHENK, Matthew, R .... 757-446-6043 466 I schenkmr@evms.edu
SCHENK, Stacy, L 814-886-6357 391 B sschenk@mtaloy.edu
SCHENKELBERGER, Chad 231-995-3150 228 G cschenkelberger@nmc.edu
SCHENKER, Mark 203-432-2920.. 89 D mark.schenker@yale.edu
SCHEP, Madeleine 803-786-3669 408 F mschep@columbiasc.edu
SCHEPP, Robina, C 212-346-1281 311 E rschepp@pace.edu
SCHER, Anne 510-869-6110.. 59 F ascher@samuelmerritt.edu
SCHERCZINGER, Carol .. 704-216-3923 337 F carol.scherczinger@rccc.edu
SCHERDER, Jay 636-584-6507 252 J jay.scherder@eastcentral.edu
SCHERER, John 910-962-4027 343 C schererj@uncw.edu
SCHERER, Laurie, L 240-895-4289 201 E llscherer@smcm.edu
SCHERER, Melanie, L .... 410-777-2237 197 C mlscherer@aacc.edu
SCHERER, Sarah 206-934-2905 484 A sarah.scherer@seattlecolleges.edu
SCHERER CONNEALY, Judith 402-241-6406 268 G juscher1@wsc.edu
SCHERI, Jennifer, C 815-224-0428 139 F jennifer_scheri@ivcc.edu
SCHERLING, Sarah 303-963-3483.. 77 G sscherling@ccu.edu
SCHERRENS, Maurice, W 803-321-5102 411 D mscherrens@newberry.edu
SCHERTLER, Dayna 806-651-2340 448 C dschertler@wtamu.edu
SCHERZER, Karen 812-357-6522 160 D kscherzer@saintmeinrad.edu
SCHETINA, Gregory 626-256-4673.. 37 B gschetina@coh.org
SCHETTER, Sheila 920-693-1238 499 G sheila.schetter@gotoltc.edu
SCHETTINI-LYNCH, Anne Marie 914-633-2480 302 G aschettinilynch@iona.edu
SCHEUCH, Katherine 850-412-7469 108 I katherine.scheuch@famu.edu
SCHEUERMANN, Aimee 317-940-8123 153 F arust@butler.edu
SCHEUERMANN, Jessica 417-626-1234 257 F scheuermann.jessica@occ.edu
SCHEUERMANN, Joe 504-671-5452 187 E jscheu@dcc.edu
SCHEUFENS, William 337-475-5711 192 A wscheufens@mcneese.edu
SCHEUTZOW, Janice 585-389-2310 308 B jscheut1@naz.edu
SCHEXNEIDER, Martha, J 337-421-6925 188 D jo.schexneider@sowela.edu
SCHEXNIDER-FIELDS, Ingenue, S 504-520-6209 193 A itschexn@xula.edu
SCHEYETT, Anna, M 706-542-5424 125 G amscheye@uga.edu
SCHIAVELLI, Mel, D 703-323-4291 475 C mschiavelli@nvcc.edu
SCHIAVELLI, Mel, D 703-323-3101 475 C mschiavelli@nvcc.edu
SCHIAZZA, Douglas, J .. 413-597-3696 220 C douglas.schiazza@williams.edu
SCHICK, Beth Ann 814-871-7659 384 E shick001@gannon.edu
SCHICK, Jennifer 616-331-2231 224 E schickj@gvsu.edu
SCHICK, Marvin 732-985-6533 280 F
SCHICK, Wendell 419-227-3141 363 C wschick@unoh.edu
SCHIDLOW, Daniel, V ... 215-762-3500 383 B daniel.schidlow@drexelmed.edu
SCHIEBER, Amy, K 660-944-2847 251 G aschieber@conception.edu
SCHIEBER, Gary, W 816-604-1320 255 D gary.schieber@mcckc.edu
SCHIEBER, Jeanette 660-944-2839 251 G admissions@conception.edu
SCHIEFEN, Kathleen 585-345-6975 301 A kmschiefen@genesee.edu
SCHIEL, Melynie 760-366-5246.. 40 K mschiel@cmccd.edu
SCHIELKE, Philip 512-313-3000 434 E philip.schielke@concordia.edu
SCHIEMAN, Don 502-213-2451 181 F don.schiemaqn@kctcs.edu
SCHIER, DJ (Donald) .... 716-896-0700 324 E dschier@villa.edu
SCHIFF, Emanuel 845-356-1980 312 B
SCHIFF-ABRAMS, Lindsey 661-255-1050.. 28 K
SCHIFFER, Jason, D 610-758-4200 388 J jds517@lehigh.edu
SCHIFFER, Peter 203-432-4444.. 89 D peter.schiffer@yale.edu
SCHIFFGENS, Hope 412-536-1266 387 B hope.schiffgens@laroche.edu
SCHIFFMAN, Alyssa 212-879-2528 290 J aschiffm@barnard.edu
SCHIFFMAN, Jeffrey 504-865-5000 191 B jschiffm@tulane.edu
SCHIFFMAN, Robyn, L .. 815-224-0491 139 F robyn_schiffman@ivcc.edu
SCHILKE, Richard 254-519-5435 447 A rschilke@tamuct.edu
SCHILL, Matt 402-554-3041 270 B mschill@unomaha.edu
SCHILL, Michael, H 541-346-3036 377 D pres@uoregon.edu
SCHILL, Sara 276-376-3432 473 B srp4b@virginia.edu
SCHILLI, Kara 636-949-4349 254 F kschilli@lindenwood.edu
SCHILLING, Dee 909-706-3526.. 74 I dschilling@westernu.edu
SCHILLING, JoAnna 714-484-7308.. 53 K jschilling@cypresscollege.edu
SCHILLING, Joe 503-725-4406 376 A joe.schilling@pdx.edu
SCHILLING, Michael 530-898-6209.. 31 A mlschilling@csuchico.edu
SCHILLINGER, Don, N .. 318-257-3712 191 F dschill@latech.edu
SCHILS, Tom 671-735-2185 505 E tschils@triton.uog.edu
SCHILT, Louis, J 480-212-1704.. 15 Q louis@sessions.edu
SCHIMEK, Gwendolyn ... 319-895-4234 164 B gschimek@cornellcollege.edu
SCHIMELFINIG, Marianne 610-660-3140 398 C mschimel@sju.edu
SCHIMER, Maria, R 330-325-6354 357 G maria@neomed.edu
SCHIMMEL, Kari 309-694-5590 138 C kari.schimmel@icc.edu
SCHINDLER, Brooke 715-675-3331 500 E schindler@ntc.edu
SCHINDLER, Kerry 254-659-7821 437 G kschindler@hillcollege.edu
SCHINDLER, Tina 213-738-6813.. 65 G tschindler@swlaw.edu
SCHINELLA, Margot 845-451-1261 298 A margot.schinella@culinary.edu
SCHINSTOCK, Victor 660-944-2992 251 G victor@conception.edu
SCHION, Donna 409-984-6101 450 B donna.schion@lamarpa.edu
SCHIPANI, Pamela 860-486-2926.. 88 E p.schipani@uconn.edu
SCHIPPERS, Dave 248-689-8282 232 A dschippe@walshcollege.edu
SCHIPPOREIT, Kim 308-865-8527 269 I schipporeitk@unk.edu
SCHIRER-SUTER, Myron 978-867-4419 209 F myron.schirer-suter@gordon.edu
SCHISKIE, Melissa 845-575-3000 305 L melissa.schiskie@marist.edu
SCHISSLER, John 330-490-7263 364 B jschissler@walsh.edu
SCHISSLER, Kathy 303-914-6214.. 82 C kathy.schissler@rrcc.edu
SCHIWIETZ, Michelle, B 214-887-5002 436 B mschiwietz@dts.edu
SCHJANG, Michael 360-676-2772 482 D maschjang@nwic.edu
SCHLACHTER, John 812-357-6142 160 D jschlachter@saintmeinrad.edu
SCHLACTER, Martin, K .. 719-333-8854 504 C martin.schlacter@usafa.edu
SCHLAFER, Tammy 315-470-4769 320 A tsschlaf@esf.edu
SCHLAG, Kevin 808-675-3735 127 E kevin@byuh.edu
SCHLAK, Timothy, M .... 412-397-6868 397 G schlak@rmu.edu
SCHLAM, Elisheva 646-565-6000 322 J elisheva.schlam@touro.edu
SCHLANG, Jamie 215-780-1333 398 G
SCHLAPP, Andrew 316-978-3001 178 A andy.schlapp@wichita.edu
SCHLARB, Mary 607-753-2209 318 D mary.schlarb@cortland.edu
SCHLATER, Nicole 315-498-2581 311 B schlaten@sunyocc.edu
SCHLATHER, Mary Margaret 304-724-5000 487 H srschlather@cdu.edu
SCHLATTER, Andy 802-440-4439 462 A aschlatter@bennington.edu
SCHLECHTE, Gerry 217-234-5253 141 D gschelchte@lakelandcollege.edu
SCHLECT, Brenda 208-882-1566 131 B bschlect@nsa.edu
SCHLECT, Christopher ... 208-882-1566 131 B cschlect@nsa.edu
SCHLEEF, Debra 540-654-1505 472 I dschleef@umw.edu
SCHLEGEL, Alice 509-542-4823 479 H aschlegel@columbiabasin.edu
SCHLEGEL, Natalie 781-891-3474 206 D nschlegel@bentley.edu
SCHLEIBAUM, Michelle . 914-606-6505 325 C michelle.schleibaum@sunywcc.edu
SCHLEICH, Tamatha 309-649-6632 150 A tamatha.schleich@src.edu
SCHLEICHER, Julie 781-239-3053 214 E jschleicher@massbay.edu
SCHLEICHER, Rolf 818-710-4142.. 49 C schleir@piercecollege.edu
SCHLEICHERT, Cat 503-491-6995 374 C catherine.schleichert@mhcc.edu
SCHLENBECKER, Darlene 847-925-6008 137 H dschlenb@harpercollege.edu
SCHLENKER, Steven 215-702-4340 380 D sschlenker@cairn.edu
SCHLERETH, Jonathan ... 314-529-9236 254 H jschlereth2@maryville.edu
SCHLESINGER, Ed 410-516-7134 199 D tschles4@jhu.edu
SCHLESINGER, Kenneth 718-960-8000 294 A kenneth.schlesinger@lehman.cuny.edu
SCHLESINGER, Marissa 253-566-5000 485 C mschlesinger@tacomacc.edu
SCHLESINGER, Patrick .. 510-642-2866.. 68 D pschlesinger@berkeley.edu
SCHLESINGER, Philip .... 706-272-2985 117 C pschlesinger@daltonstate.edu
SCHLESINGER, Richard . 212-346-1517 311 E
SCHLEY, Alisa, S 715-833-6266 499 D ahoepner1@cvtc.edu
SCHLICHT, Terri 913-469-8500 174 D tschlich@jccc.edu
SCHLICKMANN, Paul .... 203-254-4000.. 86 I pschlickmann@fairfield.edu
SCHLIENTZ, Matt 517-607-2745 225 A mschlientz@hillsdale.edu
SCHLIMGEN, Matt 317-931-2382 154 C mschlimgen@cts.edu
SCHLINGMANN, Dirk .... 864-503-5663 414 D dschlingmann@uscupstate.edu
SCHLISSEL, Mark, S 734-764-6270 231 E presoff@umich.edu
SCHLITT, Thomas 336-838-6558 339 B taschlitt2555@wilkescc.edu
SCHLOEMANN, Carolyn 217-206-6724 151 C ccima1@uis.edu
SCHLOER, Wolfgang 404-413-2530 119 E wschloer@gsu.edu
SCHLOESSER, Brad 507-389-7263 241 C brad.schloesser@southcentral.edu
SCHLOESSER, Deann 507-389-7354 241 C deann.schloesser@southcentral.edu
SCHLOSSMAN, Paul 818-240-1000.. 44 B pschloss@glendale.edu
SCHLOTTERHAUSEN, Lisa 719-336-1516.. 80 K lisa.schlotterhausen@lamarcc.edu
SCHLOTTHAUER, Scott .. 405-744-5984 368 B scott.schlotthauer@okstate.edu
SCHLUETER, Amy 303-373-2008.. 82 G aschlueter@rvu.edu
SCHLUETER, Jennifer .... 614-437-1061 351 D jschlueter@ccad.edu
SCHLUETER, Margie 763-433-1119 237 C margie.schlueter@anokaramsey.edu
SCHLUETER, Margie 763-433-1119 237 D margie.schlueter@anokaramsey.edu
SCHLUTER, Valerie 225-768-1795 186 F valerie.schluter@franu.edu
SCHLUTERMAN, Karen .. 479-979-1224.. 23 I kschlut@ozarks.edu
SCHMADER, Kelly, J 310-206-4181.. 69 A kschmader@facnet.ucla.edu
SCHMAEF, Robert 865-524-8079 420 E rschmaef@huhs.edu
SCHMAILZL, Randy 531-622-2415 267 H rschmailzl@mccneb.edu
SCHMAL, Georgina 210-434-6711 441 E gschmahl@ollusa.edu
SCHMALL, Steve 507-285-7214 240 G steve.schmall@rctc.edu
SCHMALTZ, Michael 219-473-4379 153 G mschmaltz@ccsj.edu
SCHMALZEL, Katryn 303-273-3260.. 78 I kschmalz@mines.edu

SCHMEISER, Monte .... 310-377-5501.. 51 B
mschmeiser@marymountcalifornia.edu
SCHMELCZER, Moshe ... 773-463-7738 150 D
menahel@telshe.edu
SCHMELTZER, Tracy ...... 919-735-5151 338 H
tmschmeltzer@waynecc.edu
SCHMELZ, Mark .... 541-346-2987 377 D
mschmelz@uoregon.edu
SCHMELZER, Judy .... 954-201-7458.. 95 H
jschmelzer@broward.edu
SCHMERSAL, Cindy .... 816-501-4303 258 H
cindy.schmersal@rockhurst.edu
SCHMID, Albertha .... 531-622-2354 267 H
acschmid@mccneb.edu
SCHMID, Gary .... 414-443-8821 498 O
gary.schmid@wlc.edu
SCHMID, Mark, A .... 312-595-1006 150 J
mschmid@inv.uchicago.edu
SCHMID, Stephen .... 262-521-5214 497 A
stephen.schmid@uwc.edu
SCHMIDEK, Celine .... 408-554-4982.. 62 D
cschmidek@scu.edu
SCHMIDLKOFER,
Katherine .... 612-624-2854 243 E
kms@umn.edu
SCHMIDT, Amber .... 605-256-5079 416 J
amber.schmidt@dsu.edu
SCHMIDT, Amy .... 608-785-9139 501 A
schmidta@westerntc.edu
SCHMIDT, Barbara, T ..... 516-323-3015 307 F
bschmidt@molloy.edu
SCHMIDT, Betsy .... 317-738-8054 154 J
bschmidt@franklincollege.edu
SCHMIDT, Bradley .... 316-284-5349 171 F
bschmidt@bethelks.edu
SCHMIDT, Brian .... 503-375-7199 373 A
brian@corban.edu
SCHMIDT, Christopher .. 270-384-8136 183 C
schmidtc@lindsey.edu
SCHMIDT, Chuck .... 304-462-6149 490 C
charles.schmidt@glenville.edu
SCHMIDT, Craig, D .... 708-709-3953 146 D
cschmidt@prairiestate.edu
SCHMIDT, Curt .... 612-659-6902 238 I
curt.schmidt@minneapolis.edu
SCHMIDT, Dan .... 701-224-5735 346 B
daniel.j.schmidt@bismarckstate.edu
SCHMIDT, David .... 620-450-2188 176 G
davids@prattcc.edu
SCHMIDT, Denise .... 973-328-5245 277 B
dschmidt@ccm.edu
SCHMIDT, Douglas .... 845-574-4572 313 C
dschmidt@sunyrockland.edu
SCHMIDT, Gordon .... 516-686-3802 309 F
gordon.schmidt@nyit.edu
SCHMIDT, Howard .... 540-338-1776 470 A
SCHMIDT, Jacqueline .... 212-799-5000 303 H
SCHMIDT, Jacqueline .... 904-646-2300 100 B
SCHMIDT, James, C ...... 715-836-2327 496 D
jschmidt@uwec.edu
SCHMIDT, Jeffrey .... 410-704-3414 204 A
jschmidt@towson.edu
SCHMIDT, Jenae, A .... 651-696-6214 236 H
schmidtj@macalester.edu
SCHMIDT, John .... 334-670-3201.... 7 C
jschmidt@troy.edu
SCHMIDT, Jolene .... 515-271-3957 165 A
jolene.schmidt@drake.edu
SCHMIDT, Jona, M .... 605-256-5857 416 J
jona.schmidt@dsu.edu
SCHMIDT, Julie .... 402-826-8200 267 A
julie.schmidt@doane.edu
SCHMIDT, Karen .... 713-718-8596 437 I
karen.schmidt2@hccs.edu
SCHMIDT, Karol .... 480-517-8767.. 13 G
karol.schmid@riosalado.edu
SCHMIDT, Keith, E .... 712-749-2230 163 D
schmidt@bvu.edu
SCHMIDT, Laura .... 231-995-1245 228 G
lschmidt@nmc.edu
SCHMIDT, Leslie .... 406-994-2381 264 D
lschmidt@montana.edu
SCHMIDT, Leslie .... 815-599-3421 138 B
leslie.schmidt@highland.edu
SCHMIDT, Liz .... 651-846-1477 241 B
elizabeth.schmidt@saintpaul.edu
SCHMIDT, London .... 910-755-8393 332 F
schmidtl@brunswickcc.edu
SCHMIDT, Lynn .... 765-641-4388 153 B
lmschmidt@anderson.edu
SCHMIDT, Martin, A ...... 617-253-4500 215 G
SCHMIDT, Maynard .... 845-341-4205 311 C
maynard.schmidt@sunyorange.edu
SCHMIDT, Mike .... 770-533-6914 121 B
mschmidt@laniertech.edu
SCHMIDT, Paul .... 847-543-2375 135 B
pschmidt2@clcillinois.edu
SCHMIDT, Paul .... 864-503-5036 414 D
pschmidt@uscupstate.edu
SCHMIDT, Paula .... 563-588-6383 163 F
paula.schmidt@clarke.edu
SCHMIDT, Penelope .... 229-293-6190 127 B
penelope.schmidt@wiregrass.edu
SCHMIDT, Rachel .... 216-687-5594 351 B
r.m.schmidt@csuohio.edu
SCHMIDT, Rachelle, M . 651-846-1348 241 B
rachelle.schmidt@saintpaul.edu
SCHMIDT, Shana .... 715-833-6410 499 D
sschmidt42@cvtc.edu
SCHMIDT, Stephen .... 334-347-2623.... 2 A
sschmidt@escc.edu
SCHMIDT, Steven, P ..... 330-325-6499 357 G
sschmidt@neomed.edu
SCHMIDT, Tania .... 507-457-2800 241 F
tschmidt@winona.edu
SCHMIDT CAMPBELL,
Mary .... 404-270-5001 125 B
mscampbell@spelman.edu
SCHMIDT-ROGERS,
Deborah .... 773-508-3300 142 D
dschmi6@luc.edu
SCHMIDT WHITNEY,
Angie .... 320-363-5117 235 C
awhitney@csbsju.edu
SCHMIECHEN, Tim .... 608-363-2296 492 C
schmiech@beloit.edu
SCHMIEDE, Angela .... 650-543-3905.. 51 F
angela.schmiede@menlo.edu
SCHMIEDEL, Mary, E .... 202-687-3911.. 92 A
schmiedm@georgetown.edu
SCHMIEDL, Bruce .... 630-942-2972 135 A
schmiedlb@cod.edu
SCHMIEG, Rose, A .... 540-665-5534 471 E
rschmieg@su.edu
SCHMIESING, Ann .... 303-492-2890.. 83 A
ann.schmiesing@colorado.edu
SCHMIESING, David, A . 740-284-6513 353 B
dschmiesing@franciscan.edu
SCHMILL, Stuart .... 617-258-5514 215 G
SCHMIT, Matt .... 563-336-3300 165 B
mschmit@eicc.edu
SCHMIT, Matt .... 563-441-4125 165 E
mschmit@eicc.edu
SCHMIT, Michaeline ...... 920-498-7106 500 F
michaeline.schmit@nwtc.edu
SCHMIT, Roxy .... 605-642-6129 416 I
roxy.schmit@bhsu.edu
SCHMIT, Shelly, M .... 641-422-4211 168 D
schmishe@niacc.edu
SCHMITT, Barbara, L ..... 570-348-6225 389 G
schmitt@marywood.edu
SCHMITT, Deb .... 574-520-4398 157 A
dsschmit@iusb.edu
SCHMITT, Deborah, F ... 716-851-1270 299 F
schmitt@ecc.edu
SCHMITT, Karen .... 608-262-8723 496 B
kschmitt@uwsa.edu
SCHMITT, Linda .... 973-803-5000 280 C
lschmitt@pillar.edu
SCHMITT, Mark .... 315-464-4538 317 F
schmittm@upstate.edu
SCHMITT, Mark .... 520-515-5478.. 11 M
schmittm@cochise.edu
SCHMITT, Shannon .... 716-839-8337 298 B
sradder@daemen.edu
SCHMITT, Stacy, C .... 336-318-0025 337 A
scschmitt@randolph.edu
SCHMITTENDORF,
Susan .... 716-270-5139 299 F
ascschmittendorfs@ecc.edu
SCHMITTLEIN, David, C 617-253-2804 215 G
SCHMITTMANN, Beate .. 515-294-3220 162 I
schmittb@iastate.edu
SCHMITZ, Cody .... 740-283-6226 353 B
cschmitz@franciscan.edu
SCHMITZ, Donna .... 701-252-3467 347 C
dschmitz@uj.edu
SCHMITZ, Michelle .... 320-308-2151 240 H
maschmitz@stcloudstate.edu
SCHMITZ, Stevie .... 406-657-1134 265 E
schmitzs@rocky.edu
SCHMITZ, Sue .... 763-488-2605 238 B
sue.schmitz@hennepintech.edu
SCHMITZ, Todd, J .... 812-856-1214 156 A
schmitz@indiana.edu
SCHMOHL, C. Pat .... 508-751-7942 215 D
pschmohl@qcc.mass.edu
SCHMOKE, Kurt, L .... 410-837-4866 204 B
president@ubalt.edu
SCHMOLL, Claire, B ...... 207-786-6100 193 B
cschmoll@bates.edu
SCHMOLL, Kevin .... 618-650-3324 149 F
kschmol@siue.edu
SCHMOLL, Robert .... 724-589-2102 399 H
rschmoll@thiel.edu
SCHMOOCK, Allen .... 208-792-2215 131 A
atschmoock@lcsc.edu
SCHMOTZER, Mark .... 516-299-3547 304 G
mark.schmotzer@liu.edu
SCHMUDE, Michelle ..... 570-504-9691 384 F
mschmude@som.geisinger.edu
SCHMUDLACH,
Scott, D .... 507-354-8221 236 I
schmudsd@mlc-wels.edu
SCHNABEL, William ...... 907-474-7730.. 10 A
weschnabel@alaska.edu
SCHNABL, JC .... 413-545-5542 211 D
schnabl@admin.umass.edu
SCHNACK, Darcy .... 845-938-4379 504 H
8uscc@usma.edu
SCHNACK, Darcy .... 845-938-4379 504 H
darcy.schnack@usma.edu
SCHNACK, Laura, L .... 309-794-7533 132 C
lauraschnack@augustana.edu
SCHNACKENBERG,
Scott .... 845-431-8682 298 E
scott.schnackenberg@sunydutchess.edu
SCHNAIDMAN, Yaakov . 570-346-1747 403 I
SCHNAPP, Derek .... 217-206-7823 151 C
schnapp.derek@uis.edu
SCHNARR, Carmin, A .... 812-888-4332 162 C
cschnarr@vinu.edu
SCHNARR, Grant .... 267-502-4844 379 D
grant.schnarr@brynathyn.edu
SCHNATZ, Kristofer .... 718-409-7331 321 C
kschnatz@sunymaritime.edu
SCHNEFKE, Emilee .... 314-421-0949 260 G
eschnefke@siba.edu
SCHNEID, Thomas, R ... 210-808-4492 504 B
thomas.schneid@usuhs.edu
SCHNEIDER, Amye .... 620-792-9302 171 C
schneidera@bartonccc.edu
SCHNEIDER, Angela ...... 510-885-3972.. 31 C
angela.schneider@csueastbay.edu
SCHNEIDER, Austin .... 858-653-6740.. 46 I
aschneider@jpcatholic.com
SCHNEIDER, Betsy .... 636-922-8473 258 I
bschneider@stchas.edu
SCHNEIDER, Brandt, L .. 806-743-2556 451 C
brandt.schneider@ttuhsc.edu
SCHNEIDER, Carrie .... 651-423-8244 237 H
carrie.schneider@dctc.edu
SCHNEIDER, Catherine .. 310-476-9777.. 25 O
SCHNEIDER, David .... 614-823-1240 360 A
dschneider@otterbein.edu
SCHNEIDER, Dona .... 848-932-2945 282 A
donas@rutgers.edu
SCHNEIDER, Greg .... 913-288-7155 174 F
gschneid@kckcc.edu
SCHNEIDER, Helen .... 410-617-2995 199 F
hschneider@loyola.edu
SCHNEIDER, Jed, S .... 315-445-4500 304 C
schneij@lemoyne.edu
SCHNEIDER, Jeffrey, K .. 417-690-2222 251 E
jschneider@cofo.edu
SCHNEIDER, John .... 925-631-4643.. 59 B
jrs6@stmarys-ca.edu
SCHNEIDER, Karen .... 707-664-4004.. 34 C
karen.schneider@sonoma.edu
SCHNEIDER, Ken .... 973-720-3122 284 I
schneiderk@wpunj.edu
SCHNEIDER, Marc .... 770-426-2700 121 C
marcs@life.edu
SCHNEIDER, Mark .... 610-409-3000 402 A
SCHNEIDER, Martin .... 845-431-8968 298 E
martin.schneider@sunydutchess.edu
SCHNEIDER, Matt .... 715-422-5308 500 A
matt.schneider@mstc.edu
SCHNEIDER,
Michael, A .... 309-341-7216 141 A
mschneid@knox.edu
SCHNEIDER,
Michael, P .... 620-242-0405 175 F
schneidm@mcpherson.edu
SCHNEIDER, Ray .... 419-372-7595 348 H
rayschn@bgsu.edu
SCHNEIDER, Rebecca .... 575-624-7411 286 A
rebecca.schneider@roswell.enmu.edu
SCHNEIDER,
Richard, W .... 802-485-2065 463 A
rschneider@norwich.edu
SCHNEIDER, Russell ..... 215-702-4863 380 D
rschneider@cairn.edu
SCHNEIDER, Scott .... 417-255-7258 256 F
scottshcneider@missouristate.edu
SCHNEIDER, Scott .... 563-326-5319 165 E
sjschneider@eicc.edu
SCHNEIDER, Steven ...... 315-792-7200 321 E
steve@sunypoly.edu
SCHNEIDER, Tamara, J . 417-690-2470 251 E
schneider@cofo.edu
SCHNEIDER, Tara .... 614-251-4642 358 G
schneidt@ohiodominican.edu
SCHNEIDER, Tina .... 419-995-8326 354 H
tschneider@lima.ohio-state.edu
SCHNEIDER, Tom .... 727-864-8409.. 97 J
schneite@eckerd.edu
SCHNEIDER BINGHAM,
Stacy Lee .... 845-437-5285 324 C
stbingham@vassar.edu
SCHNEIDER HASSELER,
Susan .... 740-826-8115 357 C
hasseler@muskingum.edu
SCHNEIDERMAN,
Edward, S .... 718-933-6700 307 G
eschneiderman@monroecollege.edu
SCHNEIER, Edward .... 518-828-4181 297 B
SCHNEIKERT-LUEBBE,
Christine .... 316-942-4291 175 I
luebbec@newmanu.edu
SCHNEITER, Julie .... 414-930-3324 495 A
schneitj@mtmary.edu
SCHNELL, Sarah .... 651-690-8754 242 R
sbschnell@stkate.edu
SCHNELLER, Beverly ..... 502-597-6000 182 H
beverly.schneller@kysu.edu
SCHNELLER, Heather ..... 706-729-2300 115 A
hschneller@augusta.edu
SCHNELLMAN, Rick .... 520-626-1651.. 16 G
schnell@email.arizona.edu
SCHNEPF, Chester, H ... 203-285-2151.. 85 E
cschnepf@gwcc.commnet.edu
SCHNETZLER, Greta .... 415-476-8005.. 69 E
greta.schnetzler@ucsf.edu
SCHNICK, Chris .... 480-732-7274.. 12 P
chris.schnick@cgc.edu
SCHNIDER, Stephanie ... 406-791-5240 265 H
stephanie.schnider@uprovidence.edu
SCHNIER, Kathleen .... 602-557-1228.. 16 J
kathleen.schnier@phoenix.edu
SCHNIRRING, Marsha ... 323-259-2542.. 54 E
mschnirring@oxy.edu
SCHNITKEY, Dawn, I ...... 517-750-1200 230 H
danderso@arbor.edu
SCHNITTKER, Doug .... 309-438-2143 139 E
drschni@ilstu.edu
SCHNITZER, Carol, N .... 518-580-5849 316 A
cschnitz@skidmore.edu
SCHNOOR, Alexis .... 714-556-3610.. 72 F
alexis.schnoor@vanguard.edu
SCHNOOR, Barry .... 540-665-4543 471 E
bschnoor@su.edu
SCHNOOR, Chuck .... 520-494-5303.. 11 K
chuck.schnoor@centralaz.edu
SCHNOOR, Neal .... 562-985-4121.. 31 F
neal.schnoor@csulb.edu
SCHNORENBERG,
Sandi .... 507-389-2111 239 C
sandi.schnorenberg@mnsu.edu
SCHNOWSKE, Betsy .... 815-479-7534 143 A
bschnowske@mchenry.edu
SCHNUPP, Chris .... 718-517-7734 315 A
cschnupp@edaff.com
SCHOBER, Kristen .... 716-896-0700 324 E
kschober@villa.edu
SCHOBER, Michael .... 212-229-5727 308 C
schober@newschool.edu
SCHOCHET, Ezra, B .... 323-937-3763.. 75 F
eschochet@yoec.edu
SCHOCK, Pam .... 559-453-7115.. 43 G
pam.schock@fresno.edu
SCHODOWSKI,
Francis, G .... 803-786-3927 408 F
fschodowski@columbiasc.edu
SCHOEN, David .... 716-286-8001 310 D
schoen@niagara.edu
SCHOEN, Karen .... 313-845-9849 224 G
kschoen@hfcc.edu
SCHOEN, Susan .... 641-269-4580 165 J
schoen@grinnell.edu
SCHOENBERG, Lynn ..... 386-822-7473 111 A
lschoenb@stetson.edu

SCHULLER, Aimee .... 330-823-2755 363 B schullal@mountunion.edu

SCHULLER, Jennifer ...... 330-569-5839 353 J schullerjn@hiram.edu

SCHULMAN, Avrohom .. 908-354-6057 285 F

SCHULMAN, Jeffrey, L .. 802-656-3075 463 E jeffrey.schulman@uvm.edu

SCHULT, Jordan .... 715-675-3331 500 E schult@ntc.edu

SCHULTE, Brandy .... 660-831-4108 256 G schulteb@moval.edu

SCHULTE, Cynthia .... 641-844-5602 166 I cindy.schulte@iavalley.edu

SCHULTE, Kristi .... 940-397-4427 440 F kristi.schulte@msutexas.edu

SCHULTE, Mary .... 618-468-3300 141 F mschulte@lc.edu

SCHULTE, Megan .... 419-434-4505 363 A megan.schulte@findlay.edu

SCHULTE, Patricia .... 503-338-2425 372 E pschulte@clatsopcc.edu

SCHULTE, Priscilla .... 907-228-4548.. 10 B pmschulte@alaska.edu

SCHULTE, Randy .... 615-366-4400 424 D randy.schulte@tbr.edu

SCHULTE, Sarah .... 206-543-4150 485 F sarahhs@uw.edu

SCHULTE, Sarah, H .... 906-487-2318 227 E shschult@mtu.edu

SCHULTE, Sheila .... 706-867-2844 126 A sheila.schulte@ung.edu

SCHULTE, Tim .... 660-831-4148 256 G schultet@moval.edu

SCHULTE, Vickie .... 618-437-5321 147 A schultev@rlc.edu

SCHULTE-SHOBERG, Kim .... 715-232-1285 498 A schulte-shobergk@uwstout.edu

SCHULTES, Debra .... 201-684-7311 280 H dschulte@rampao.edu

SCHULTHEIS, Luke, D ... 201-692-7080 277 K luke@fdu.edu

SCHULTHEIS, Stephen ... 678-466-5020 116 E stephenschultheis@clayton.edu

SCHULTZ, Alex .... 303-360-4728.. 79 D alex.schultz@ccaurora.edu

SCHULTZ, Amber .... 608-663-2328 493 C ambschultz@edgewood.edu

SCHULTZ, Barb .... 319-385-8021 167 A barb.schultz@iw.edu

SCHULTZ, Barry .... 901-572-2500 418 E barry.schultz@bchs.edu

SCHULTZ, Bruce .... 907-786-6108.... 9 H brschultz@alaska.edu

SCHULTZ, Clayton .... 919-573-5350 340 F cschultz@shepherds.edu

SCHULTZ, David, R .... 928-523-4340.. 14 H david.schultz@nau.edu

SCHULTZ, Diana, C .... 239-513-1122 101 C dschultz2@hodges.edu

SCHULTZ, Eric .... 605-882-5284 415 F eric.schultz@lakeareatech.edu

SCHULTZ, Jamie .... 406-791-5330 265 H jamie.schultz@uprovidence.edu

SCHULTZ, Jennifer, A .... 815-835-6405 148 H jennifer.a.schultz@svcc.edu

SCHULTZ, Jessica .... 309-794-7331 132 C jessicaschultz@augustana.edu

SCHULTZ, Joseph, P ...... 607-777-2187 316 E jschultz@binghamton.edu

SCHULTZ, Katherine ...... 303-492-6937.. 83 A katherine.schultz@colorado.edu

SCHULTZ, Linda .... 860-768-4169.. 88 H schultz@hartford.edu

SCHULTZ, Lynda, K ...... 920-923-8793 494 A lkschultz@marianuniversity.edu

SCHULTZ, Mark .... 510-592-9688.. 54 C mark.schultz@npu.edu

SCHULTZ, Melissa .... 734-462-4400 230 D

SCHULTZ, Michael .... 903-233-4441 439 E michaelschultz@letu.edu

SCHULTZ, Michael, J .... 618-650-4628 149 F mschult@siue.edu

SCHULTZ, Peter, G .... 858-784-8469.. 63 F

SCHULTZ, Randy .... 661-952-5071.. 30 E rschultz@csub.edu

SCHULTZ, Randy .... 920-498-7417 500 F randy.schultz@nwtc.edu

SCHULTZ, Roger, D ...... 434-592-4031 468 H rschultz@liberty.edu

SCHULTZ, Roger, W ...... 951-487-3002.. 52 I rschultz@msjc.edu

SCHULTZ-HUXMAN, Susan .... 540-432-4100 466 G susan.huxman@emu.edu

SCHULZ, Andrew .... 520-621-1778.. 16 G apshulz@email.arizona.edu

SCHULZ, Bridget .... 617-824-8525 208 H bridget_schulz@emerson.edu

SCHULZ, Christa .... 360-416-7974 485 A christa.schulz@skagit.edu

SCHULZ, Dasie .... 615-871-2260.. 92 G

SCHULZ, Greg .... 714-992-7001.. 53 L gschulz@fullcoll.edu

SCHULZ, Jerry .... 541-383-7275 372 B jschulz@cocc.edu

SCHULZ, Karyn .... 410-837-4141 204 B kschulz@ubalt.edu

SCHULZ, Kathy, L .... 201-216-5667 283 C kathy.schulz@stevens.edu

SCHULZ, Kirk .... 509-335-4200 486 A presidentsoffice@wsu.edu

SCHULZ, Paul, A .... 914-337-9300 297 D paul.schulz@concordia-ny.edu

SCHULZ, Phyllis .... 212-817-7460 293 F pschulz@gc.cuny.edu

SCHULZ, Robert .... 619-594-5901.. 33 E rschulz@sdsu.edu

SCHULZ, Scott .... 623-845-3692.. 13 C scott.schulz@gccaz.edu

SCHULZ, Scott .... 218-726-7171 243 F sschulz1@d.umn.edu

SCHULZ, Scott .... 440-826-6970 348 E saschulz@bw.edu

SCHULZ, Scott, A .... 440-826-6970 348 E saschulz@bw.edu

SCHULZ, Steven, D .... 641-422-4000 168 D schulste@niacc.edu

SCHULZ, William .... 866-492-5336 244 F william.schulz@mail.waldenu.edu

SCHULZE, Edee .... 805-565-6028.. 74 K eschulze@westmont.edu

SCHULZE, Lori, A .... 920-748-8310 495 G schulzel@ripon.edu

SCHULZE, Rob .... 802-635-1305 464 C rob.schulze@northernvermont.edu

SCHULZE, Robin, G ...... 716-645-2711 316 F cas-dean@buffalo.edu

SCHUMACHER, Bryan, J .... 605-394-5102 417 B bryan.schumacher@sdsmt.edu

SCHUMACHER, Charlotte .... 806-291-3549 457 J schumacherc@wbu.edu

SCHUMACHER, Daniel, J .... 715-836-5858 496 D schumadj@uwec.edu

SCHUMACHER, Gail ...... 708-237-5050 145 E gschumacher@nc.edu

SCHUMACHER, Janette . 484-664-3487 391 C janschumach@muhlenberg.edu

SCHUMACHER, Jean Paul (JP) .... 510-464-3393.. 56 G jschumacher@peralta.edu

SCHUMACHER, Karlyn, M .... 920-748-8750 495 G schumacherk@ripon.edu

SCHUMACHER, Lauren .. 708-237-5050 145 E lwschumacher@nc.edu

SCHUMACHER, Lawrence .... 708-237-5050 145 E lschumacher@nc.edu

SCHUMACHER, Lillian ... 419-448-3053 361 J schumacherlb@tiffin.edu

SCHUMACHER, Linda .... 605-688-4112 417 C linda.schumacher@sdstate.edu

SCHUMACHER, Mary Jeanne .... 812-357-6501 160 D mschumacher@saintmeinrad.edu

SCHUMACHER, Mary Jeanne .... 812-357-6808 160 D mschumacher@saintmeinrad.edu

SCHUMACHER, Ron ...... 419-559-2326 361 I rschuma01@terra.edu

SCHUMACHER, Sara ..... 828-694-1809 332 E sp_schumacher@blueridge.edu

SCHUMACHER, Scott ..... 979-830-4172 432 C scott.schumacher@blinn.edu

SCHUMACHTER, Bett, K 413-542-5957 205 B bschumacher@amherst.edu

SCHUMAKER, Ashley ..... 540-831-5370 470 C aschumaker@radford.edu

SCHUMAKER, Terry, W . 641-422-4170 168 D schumter@niacc.edu

SCHUMAN, Alan, M ...... 410-386-8495 197 G aschuman@carrollcc.edu

SCHUMAN, Shmuel ...... 847-982-2500 138 A schuman@htc.edu

SCHUMANN, Kenneth ... 503-352-2180 375 G schumank@pacificu.edu

SCHUMANN, Patricia, J 304-766-3020 491 B pschumann@wvstateu.edu

SCHUMANN, Renae ...... 281-649-3300 437 H rschumann@hbu.edu

SCHUMANN, Sherry, L . 972-758-3880 433 M sschumann@collin.edu

SCHUMM, Darla .... 540-362-6025 468 C dschumm@hollins.edu

SCHUMM, Jillian .... 407-646-2120 105 M jschumm@rollins.edu

SCHUMOCK, Glen .... 312-996-7240 151 B schumock@uic.edu

SCHUPPERT, Cindy .... 503-352-3191 375 G schuppec@pacificu.edu

SCHURMAN, Jane .... 610-957-5700 382 C jschurman@dccc.edu

SCHURMAN, Ryan .... 402-552-3390 266 E schurmanryan@clarksoncollege.edu

SCHUSTER, Danny .... 347-619-9074 326 G

SCHUSTER, Heather .... 312-662-4035 131 H hschuster@adler.edu

SCHUSTER, Julian, Z ..... 314-246-8242 262 C julianschuster@webster.edu

SCHUSTER, Leslie .... 401-456-9723 405 C lschuster@ric.edu

SCHUSTER, Sheldon, M 909-607-0107.. 37 G sheldon_schuster@kgi.edu

SCHUSTER-MATLOCK, Tracy .... 563-333-6049 169 A schustertracy@sau.edu

SCHUSTER-WEBB, Karen .... 513-487-1102 361 L karen.webb@myunion.edu

SCHUTH, Kristen .... 585-345-6898 301 A keschuth@genesee.edu

SCHUTT, Michelle .... 208-732-6863 130 E mschutt@csi.edu

SCHUTT, Stephen, D ..... 847-735-5100 141 B presiden@lakeforest.edu

SCHUTTE, Kelli .... 816-415-7665 262 F schuttek@william.jewell.edu

SCHUTTE, Thomas, F .... 718-636-3647 311 J tschutte@pratt.edu

SCHUTTEN, Mary .... 989-774-3931 222 C schut1mc@cmich.edu

SCHUTZ, Christine .... 208-459-5524 130 D cschutz@collegeofidaho.edu

SCHUTZ, Michael .... 610-647-4400 386 C mschutz@immaculata.edu

SCHUTZLER, Lyndon ..... 831-646-4221.. 52 F lschutzler@mpc.edu

SCHUTZMAN, Cariss ..... 859-344-3602 184 F schutzc@thomasmore.edu

SCHUYLER, Lori, G .... 804-289-8781 472 L lschuyle@richmond.edu

SCHUYLER, Maggie .... 678-872-8154 118 E mschuyle@highlands.edu

SCHWAB, Brandon .... 828-227-7495 344 A beschwab@wcu.edu

SCHWAB, Mary, S .... 540-828-5487 465 D mschwab@bridgewater.edu

SCHWAB, Sheri .... 919-515-4559 342 B slschwab@ncsu.edu

SCHWAB, Victoria .... 952-358-8671 239 F victoria.schwab@normandale.edu

SCHWABE, Annette .... 850-644-1841 109 C aschwabe@fsu.edu

SCHWABE, Jean, D .... 478-289-2464 117 D jdschwabe@ega.edu

SCHWABROW, Lynsey .. 262-472-1801 498 C schwabrl@uww.edu

SCHWAGER, Paul .... 252-328-6966 341 C schwagerp@ecu.edu

SCHWAIG, Kathy, S ...... 470-578-6425 120 L kschwaig@kennesaw.edu

SCHWAIGER, Patsy .... 513-244-4371 357 A patsy.schwaiger@msj.edu

SCHWALLER, Tyler .... 478-757-4028 126 H tschwaller@wesleyancollege.edu

SCHWANDT, Jehana ...... 320-222-5986 240 E jehana.schwandt@ridgewater.edu

SCHWANDT, Robert (Doug), D .... 573-882-6757 261 B schwandtr@missouri.edu

SCHWANITZ, Gail, L ..... 801-863-3000 461 A gail.schwanitz@uvu.edu

SCHWANKE, Shellie ...... 309-467-6316 137 B sschwanke@eureka.edu

SCHWANTES, Randy ...... 209-946-7613.. 70 E rschwantes@pacific.edu

SCHWARTZ, Adam .... 515-294-2770 162 I director@ameslab.gov

SCHWARTZ, Ann .... 512-313-3000 434 E ann.schwartz@concordia.edu

SCHWARTZ, Anthony .... 518-381-1256 315 G schwaraj@sunysccc.edu

SCHWARTZ, Beth .... 419-448-2216 353 H bschwartz@heidelberg.edu

SCHWARTZ, Brett .... 435-652-7593 460 G bschwartz@dixie.edu

SCHWARTZ, Brian .... 303-373-2008.. 82 G bschwartz@rvu.edu

SCHWARTZ, Celeste, M 215-641-6492 390 H cschwartz@mc3.edu

SCHWARTZ, Corene ...... 909-652-6242.. 36 A cory.schwartz@chaffey.edu

SCHWARTZ, Daniel .... 650-723-2300.. 65 J daniel.schwartz@stanford.edu

SCHWARTZ, David .... 845-783-9901 324 A utamds@gmail.com

SCHWARTZ, David, J .... 248-370-3465 229 G schwart3@oakland.edu

SCHWARTZ, Elimelech .. 845-352-3431 326 B

SCHWARTZ, Ernest .... 718-384-5460 325 M

SCHWARTZ, Gary .... 718-960-6093 294 A gary.schwartz@lehman.cuny.edu

SCHWARTZ, Hayim .... 718-268-4700 312 G

SCHWARTZ, Jana .... 602-787-7668.. 13 E

SCHWARTZ, Janis .... 973-720-2175 284 I schwartzj@wpunj.edu

SCHWARTZ, Jeff .... 941-893-2857 105 K jschwartz@ringling.edu

SCHWARTZ, Jennifer ..... 317-955-6056 158 U jschwartz@marian.edu

SCHWARTZ, Jennifer ..... 805-922-6966.. 24 J jennifer.schwartz@hancockcollege.edu

SCHWARTZ, Jessica .... 715-833-6256 499 D jschwartz31@cvtc.edu

SCHWARTZ, Jonathan ... 713-221-8001 453 B schwartzj@uhd.edu

SCHWARTZ, Judith .... 718-270-4817 295 A jschwartz@mec.cuny.edu

SCHWARTZ, Justin .... 814-865-7537 392 B jzs622@psu.edu

SCHWARTZ, Lance, W .. 507-344-7427 234 B lance.schwartz@blc.edu

SCHWARTZ, Lindsay ..... 212-355-1501 292 J lschwartz@christies.edu

SCHWARTZ, Mark .... 610-359-5082 382 C mschwartz@dccc.edu

SCHWARTZ, Mary Beth . 803-327-8042 415 A mbschwartz@yorktech.edu

SCHWARTZ, Matthew, J 812-888-5832 162 C mschwartz@vinu.edu

SCHWARTZ, Melissa ..... 707-765-1836.. 51 H

SCHWARTZ, Michael ...... 916-739-7151.. 70 E mschwartz@pacific.edu

SCHWARTZ, Michael, H 209-946-2551.. 70 E provost@pacific.edu

SCHWARTZ, Niki .... 479-968-0399.. 18 C lschwartz@atu.edu

SCHWARTZ, Paul .... 816-235-1366 261 C schwartzpn@umkc.edu

SCHWARTZ, Rebecca ..... 801-626-8740 461 B rebeccaschwartz1@weber.edu

SCHWARTZ, Robert .... 206-296-5831 484 F schwartr@seattleu.edu

SCHWARTZ, Saara .... 305-348-2401 109 A saara.schwartz@fiu.edu

SCHWARTZ, Sandor ...... 718-963-1212 303 I kyrs@thejnet.com

SCHWARTZ, Shari .... 727-873-4018 110 C smschwartz@mail.usf.edu

SCHWARTZ, Shuly .... 212-678-8826 303 G shschwartz@jtsa.edu

SCHWARTZ, Shuly .... 212-678-8065 303 G shschwartz@jtsa.edu

SCHWARTZ, Steven .... 212-938-5712 320 B sschwartz@sunyopt.edu

SCHWARTZ, Steven, J ... 970-247-7196.. 79 I schwartz_s@fortlewis.edu

SCHWARTZ, Teri .... 310-825-7891.. 69 A tschwartz@tft.ucla.edu

SCHWARTZE, Mary .... 432-837-8203 450 D mschwartze@sulross.edu

SCHWARZ, Felipe .... 978-837-5459 216 D schwarzf@merrimack.edu

SCHWARZ, Sara .... 303-273-3604.. 78 I sschwarz@mines.edu

SCHWARZ, Todd .... 208-732-6325 130 E tschwarz@csi.edu

SCHWARZ, Walter .... 203-576-4952.. 88 D wschwarz@bridgeport.edu

SCRIVEN, Darryl .... 336-750-2400 344 B
scrivendl@wssu.edu
SCRIVEN, Olivia .... 770-426-2635 121 C
olivia.scriven@life.edu
SCRIVENER, Tom .... 414-229-4304 497 A
scrivene@uwm.edu
SCRIVNER, Darlene .... 509-542-4802 479 H
dscrivner@columbiabasin.edu
SCRIVNER, Joseph .... 205-366-8838.... 7 A
jscrivner@stillman.edu
SCRIVNER, Kelly .... 956-665-3844 455 D
kelly.scrivner@utrgv.edu
SCROGGINS, Beth .... 503-838-8000 377 H
SCROGGINS, Don .... 575-769-4909 285 K
don.scroggins@clovis.edu
SCROGGINS, Melinda ... 559-251-4215.. 28 B
financialaid@calchristiancollege.edu
SCROGGINS, Sarah .... 636-584-6553 252 J
sarah.scroggins@eastcentral.edu
SCROGGINS, Susan ...... 219-464-6395 162 A
susan.scroggins@valpo.edu
SCROGGINS,
William, T .... 909-274-4250.. 52 H
bscroggins@mtsac.edu
SCROGIN, Tara .... 402-559-9005 270 A
tscrogin@unmc.edu
SCRUGGS, Adina .... 423-364-3360 418 H
ascruggs8899@bryan.edu
SCRUGGS, Jeff .... 478-218-3333 116 A
jscruggs@centralgatech.edu
SCUILETTI, Linda .... 919-718-7417 333 C
lscuiletti@cccc.edu
SCULLY, Amy .... 803-691-3879 410 G
scullya@midlandstech.edu
SCULLY, Beverly .... 860-701-7784.. 87 D
SCULLY, Dale .... 559-453-7165.. 43 G
dale.scully@fresno.edu
SCULLY, Jonathan .... 413-205-3270 205 A
jonathan.scully@aic.edu
SCULLY, Jonathan .... 413-265-2519 208 C
scullyj@elms.edu
SCULLY, Joseph, F .... 856-256-4127 281 E
scullyj@rowan.edu
SCULLY, Pamela .... 404-712-4161 117 F
pamela.scully@emory.edu
SCULLY, Pamela .... 910-678-8232 334 D
scullyp@faytechcc.edu
SCULLY, Serena .... 304-367-4151 490 B
serena.scully@fairmontstate.edu
SCUOTTO, Donald .... 919-546-8564 340 E
donald.scuotto@shawu.edu
SCURALLI, Joseph .... 973-405-2111 275 I
jss@berkeleycollege.edu
SCURALLI, Joseph .... 973-405-2111 291 D
jss@berkeleycollege.edu
SCURRY, Jamie .... 401-254-3118 405 E
jscurry@rwu.edu
SCUTO, Donna, L .... 716-878-6700 318 C
scutodl@buffalostate.edu
SCUTTI, Diane .... 610-902-8415 380 C
diane.m.scutti@cabrini.edu
SEA, Karen .... 209-954-5151.. 60 J
ksea@deltacollege.edu
SEABERRY, Ben .... 408-531-6144.. 61 K
ben.seaberry@sjeccd.edu
SEABERT, Denise .... 850-474-2405 110 E
dseabert@uwf.edu
SEABOLD, Brian .... 201-216-8722 283 C
brian.seabold@stevens.edu
SEABOLT, Kerry .... 706-865-2134 125 E
klseabolt@truett.edu
SEABORNE, Wendell ...... 614-947-6202 353 C
wendell.seaborne@franklin.edu
SEABOY, Donna .... 701-854-8013 346 I
donna.seaboy@sittingbull.edu
SEABROOKS, Joseph .... 972-860-8250 435 A
jseabrooks@dcccd.edu
SEADLER, Alan, W .... 412-396-1568 383 C
seadlera@duq.edu
SEAGA, Andrew .... 305-237-7581 103 D
aseaga@mdc.edu
SEAGER, Lori .... 719-389-6953.. 77 H
lseager@coloradocollege.edu
SEAGLE, Dennis .... 828-726-2705 332 G
dseagle@cccti.edu
SEAGLE, Donna .... 423-585-6933 426 C
donna.seagle@ws.edu
SEAGO, Brenda .... 706-721-2856 115 A
bseago@augusta.edu
SEAGRAVES, Jennifer ..... 919-464-2254 335 F
j_seagraves@johnstoncc.edu
SEAGRAVES, John, R .... 606-474-3272 180 G
johnseagraves@kcu.edu
SEAGRAVES, Ronda ...... 512-313-3000 434 E
ronda.seagraves@concordia.edu
SEAL, Craig, R .... 909-537-5735.. 33 A
cseal@csusb.edu
SEAL, Jennifer .... 601-403-1146 248 E
jseal@prcc.edu
SEAL, John .... 510-649-2462.. 44 F
jseal@gtu.edu
SEAL, Mitchell .... 210-808-4765 504 B
mitchell.seal@usuhs.edu
SEAL, Sherry .... 706-754-7730 122 F
sseal@northgatech.edu
SEAL, Susan .... 662-325-3473 247 F
sseal@humansci.msstate.edu
SEAL, Timothy .... 901-751-8453 422 E
tseal@mabts.edu
SEAL, Tonia .... 601-403-1214 248 E
tmoody@prcc.edu
SEALE, Danette .... 865-471-3248 419 A
dseale@cn.edu
SEALE, Glenn .... 843-574-6519 413 B
glenn.seale@tridenttech.edu
SEALE, Michael .... 903-510-2252 452 C
michael.seale@tjc.edu
SEALINE, Alma .... 217-333-0610 151 D
asealine@illinois.edu
SEALS, Lee .... 423-478-7725 423 G
lseals@ptseminary.edu
SEALS, Lisa .... 760-355-6257.. 45 I
lisa.seals@imperial.edu
SEALS, Lisa .... 661-255-1050.. 28 K
lseals@calarts.edu
SEALS, Mark .... 419-372-7622 348 H
msealsb@bgsu.edu
SEALS, Nireata, D .... 718-482-5400 294 F
nseals@lagcc.cuny.edu
SEALS, Victoria .... 404-225-4600 114 H
vseals@atlantatech.edu
SEALS, Vonda .... 817-202-6232 444 I
vondaseals@swau.edu
SEALY, Gabrielle .... 802-865-5490 462 B
gsealy@champlain.edu
SEALY, Lauren .... 610-399-2398 394 C
lsealy@cheyney.edu
SEALY, Mondell .... 718-262-2305 295 F
msealy@york.cuny.edu
SEALY, Spencer .... 229-732-5941 114 B
spencesealy@andrewcollege.edu
SEALY, Susan .... 706-649-1016 117 A
ssealy@columbustech.edu
SEAMAN, Chuck .... 615-248-1240 427 A
cseaman@trevecca.edu
SEAMAN, Cynthia .... 610-607-6271 397 B
cseaman@racc.edu
SEAMAN, Daniel, B .... 315-229-5601 314 F
dseaman@stlawu.edu
SEAMAN, David .... 315-443-5533 322 C
dseaman@syr.edu
SEAMAN, David .... 315-443-2736 322 C
dseaman@syr.edu
SEAMAN, Diane .... 937-328-6014 350 L
seamand@clarkstate.edu
SEAMAN, Rebecca .... 360-475-7767 482 G
rseaman@olympic.edu
SEAMON, Mike .... 574-631-9701 161 C
mseamon@nd.edu
SEAMS, Jennifer .... 304-645-6383 491 A
jseams@osteo.wvsom.edu
SEAMSTER, JR., Ervin ... 972-524-3341 445 C
SEAMSTER, Kristen .... 336-757-3396 334 E
kseamster@forsythtech.edu
SEAQUIST, Carl .... 717-815-2084 404 A
cseaquis@ycp.edu
SEARA, Maira .... 212-647-7223 311 J
mseara@pratt.edu
SEARCY, Douglas, N 252-399-6309 326M
dsearcy@barton.edu
SEARCY, Robin .... 617-585-1792 217 B
robin.searcy@necmusic.edu
SEARCY, Scott .... 620-227-9279 172 J
ssearcy@dc3.edu
SEARCY, Yan Dominic .. 818-677-3317.. 32 D
yan.searcy@csun.edu
SEARFOSS, Alexis .... 727-873-4519 110 C
asearfoss@usfsp.edu
SEARING, Linda .... 585-389-2870 308 B
lsearin9@naz.edu
SEARLE, Mark, S .... 480-965-9585.. 10 I
mark.searle@asu.edu
SEARLE, Natalie .... 802-786-5148 464 B
njs12250@ccv.vsc.edu
SEARS, Andrew .... 816-960-2008 251 D
asears@cityvision.edu
SEARS, Andrew, L .... 814-865-3528 392 B
aus67@psu.edu
SEARS, Chanelle .... 212-752-1530 304 D
chanelle.sears@limcollege.edu
SEARS, Cheryl .... 916-484-8320.. 50 F
searsc@arc.losrios.edu
SEARS, David .... 240-567-7492 200 C
david.sears@montgomerycollege.edu
SEARS, Douglas, A .... 617-358-4608 207 D
dsears@bu.edu
SEARS, Estella .... 512-492-3077 430 G
esears@aoma.edu
SEARS, J, W .... 252-985-5585 339 D
wsears@ncwc.edu
SEARS, Marc .... 336-841-9826 329 G
jsears@highpoint.edu
SEARS, Melissa .... 859-442-1156 181 B
melissa.sears@kctcs.edu
SEARS, Richard .... 678-839-5353 126 E
rsears@westga.edu
SEARS, Steve, R .... 956-326-2480 446 F
steve.sears@tamiu.edu
SEARS, Steven, A .... 401-865-2425 405 B
ssears@providence.edu
SEARS, Suzanne .... 940-898-3748 451 F
ssears1@twu.edu
SEARSON, Robert .... 216-987-3943 351 G
robert.searson@tri-c.edu
SEASTEDT, Erik .... 716-375-2102 313 F
eseastedt@sbu.edu
SEATON, Ann .... 845-758-6822 290 G
aseaton@bard.edu
SEATON, Steve .... 405-692-3191 366 G
SEATON-MARTIN,
Marcia .... 276-656-0276 475 D
mseaton-martin@patrickhenry.edu
SEAWORTH, Timothy .... 701-355-8150 347 D
seaworth@umary.edu
SEAY, Laodecea .... 334-214-4807.... 1 H
laodecca.seay@cv.edu
SEAY, Lonnie .... 530-242-7912.. 63 H
lseay@shastacollege.edu
SEAY, Scott .... 317-937-2365 154 C
sseay@cts.edu
SEBALLOW, Shannon .... 928-428-8339.. 12 E
shannon.seballos@eac.edu
SEBASTIAN, Denise .... 573-518-2249 256 B
denise@mineralarea.edu
SEBASTIAN, Donald, H . 973-596-8449 279 F
sebastian@njit.edu
SEBASTIAN,
J. Jayakiran .... 215-248-7378 400 I
jsebastian@uls.edu
SEBASTIAN, John .... 310-338-3019.. 50 J
john.sebastian@lmu.edu
SEBASTIAN, Juliann ...... 402-559-4000 270 A
julie.sebastian@unmc.edu
SEBASTIAN, Pam .... 660-831-4142 256 G
sebastianp@moval.edu
SEBASTIANI, Richard .... 713-221-8229 453 B
sebastianir@uhd.edu
SEBASTIEN, Anya .... 864-592-6207 412 F
sebastiena@sccsc.edu
SEBER, Geoffrey .... 518-445-3210 289 E
gsebe@albanylaw.edu
SEBRING, Amy, S .... 757-221-1722 466 C
asebring@wm.edu
SECHLER, Elizabeth .... 304-876-5172 490 E
esechler@shepherd.edu
SECHREST, Love, L .... 404-687-4520 116 H
sechrestl@ctsnet.edu
SECHRIST, John .... 724-653-2184 383 A
jsechrist@dec.edu
SECHRIST, Jori .... 325-793-4772 440 B
sechrist.jori@mcm.edu
SECHRIST, Shana .... 503-370-6236 378 B
ssechrist@willamette.edu
SECHRIST, Tim .... 325-793-4978 440 B
sechrist.tim@mcm.edu
SECKA, Lamine .... 760-750-4568.. 33 B
lsecka@csusm.edu
SECKA, Lamine .... 619-594-7903.. 33 E
lsecka@sdsu.edu
SECKINGER, Deryl, M ... 478-289-2090 117 D
dseckinger@ega.edu
SECOR, Dan .... 203-773-8506.. 84 F
dsecor@albertus.edu
SECORD, Paul .... 512-863-1211 445 D
secordp@southwestern.edu
SECREST, Amanda .... 704-272-5300 337 I
asecrest@spcc.edu
SECREST, Kathy, L .... 330-471-8415 355 L
ksecrest@malone.edu
SECRIST, Tammi .... 304-336-8281 490 F
tsecrist@westliberty.edu
SECUBAN, Gigi .... 740-593-2614 359 G
secuban@ohio.edu
SEDA, Iris .... 787-264-1912 509 F
iris_seda_rodriguez@intersg.edu
SEDANO, George .... 510-594-5033.. 28 D
gsedano@cca.edu
SEDDIKI, Mohamed ...... 973-877-3080 277 I
seddiki@essex.edu
SEDEN, John .... 415-749-4570.. 60 G
jseden@sfai.edu
SEDHOM, Nasser .... 718-522-9073 290 C
nsedhom@asa.edu
SEDILLO, Dacia .... 575-646-5690 287 B
dapachec@nmsu.edu
SEDLACEK, Bernard .... 531-622-2529 267 H
bsedlacek@mccneb.edu
SEDLACEK, John .... 502-597-6582 182 H
john.sedlacek@kysu.edu
SEDLACEK, Paige .... 607-778-5213 318 A
sedlacekpm@sunybroome.edu
SEDLACK, Chris .... 319-208-5259 169 F
csedlack@scciowa.edu
SEDLAK, John .... 570-740-0234 389 D
jsedlak@luzerne.edu
SEDLEMEYER, Julie .... 209-667-3645.. 33 C
jsedlemeyer@csustan.edu
SEDORE, Chris .... 512-232-1744 455 A
cmsedore@austin.utexas.edu
SEDRAK, Mona .... 513-732-5212 362 F
mona.sedrak@uc.edu
SEDY, Paul .... 661-362-2200.. 51 C
psedy@masters.edu
SEDYCIAS, Joao .... 201-200-3001 279 E
jsedycias@njcu.edu
SEE, David .... 501-337-5000.. 18 J
dsee@coto.edu
SEE, Jonathan .... 310-506-6256.. 56 C
jonathan.see@pepperdine.edu
SEE, Leslie, C .... 304-260-4380 488 J
lsee@blueridgectc.edu
SEE, Michael .... 360-992-2413 479 F
msee@clark.edu
SEEBO, Elane .... 806-291-3417 457 J
seeboe@wbu.edu
SEEBOLD, Lauren, N ..... 248-204-2309 226 G
lseebold@ltu.edu
SEEGER, Matthew .... 313-577-5342 232 I
matthew.seeger@wayne.edu
SEEGERT, Paul .... 206-616-3865 485 F
pseegert@uw.edu
SEEKINS, Travis, P .... 325-670-1589 437 F
seekins@hsutx.edu
SEEKLANDER, Marlene . 605-882-5284 415 F
seeklanm@lakeareatech.edu
SEELA, Joel .... 320-762-4635 237 B
joels@alextech.edu
SEELBACH, Brenda .... 540-636-2900 466 A
brendaseelbach@christendom.edu
SEELEY, Lisa .... 903-923-2175 436 D
lseeley@etbu.edu
SEELEY-CASE, Tiffany .... 208-732-6454 130 E
tseeley@csi.edu
SEELY, Tara, M .... 570-941-7400 401 H
tara.seely@scranton.edu
SEELYE, II, Calvin, H .... 989-774-7471 222 C
seely1ch@cmich.edu
SEEMAN, Steve, C .... 563-588-8000 165 F
financialaid@emmaus.edu
SEEMAYER, Jackson ..... 503-821-8920 375 F
jseemayer@pnca.edu
SEERY, Denise .... 303-282-3414.. 82 H
denise.seery@archden.org
SEERY, Joshua .... 267-295-2330 397 F
jseery@walnuthillcollege.edu
SEERY, Sheila .... 518-956-8163 316 D
sseery@albany.edu
SEESENGOOD, Robert ... 610-921-7643 378 C
rseesengood@albright.edu
SEEVERS, JR., Gary ...... 417-862-9533 253 D
president@globaluniversity.edu
SEEVERS, Joshua .... 724-805-2559 398 F
joshua.seevers@stvincent.edu
SEEVERS, Scott .... 402-643-7233 266 G
scott.seevers@cune.edu
SEFCIK, Don .... 317-955-6290 158 U
dsefcik@marian.edu
SEFCIK, Jeffrey .... 325-942-2041 451 A
jeff.sefcik@angelo.edu
SEFFERS, Tracy .... 304-876-5463 490 E
tseffers@shepherd.edu

SENGUPTA, Shivaji .... 347-964-8600 291 I
ssengupta@boricuacollege.edu
SENIE, Kathryn, C .... 413-538-7000 214 D
ksenie@hcc.edu
SENIOR, Ann Marie ...... 609-984-1151 284 B
amsenior@tesu.edu
SENIOR, Sandra .... 212-616-7271 301 F
sandra.senior@helenefuld.edu
SENIOR, Timothy, C ..... 610-785-6200 398 A
bsenior@scs.edu
SENKBEIL, Peter .... 949-214-3201.. 40 F
peter.senkbeil@cui.edu
SENKER, Richard .... 813-253-7144 101 A
rsenker@hccfl.edu
SENN, Kate .... 270-534-3143 182 F
catherine.senn@kctcs.edu
SENN, Michael, E .... 301-243-2122 503 J
michael.senn@dodiis.mil
SENN, Sarah .... 334-699-2266.... 1 B
ssenn@acom.edu
SENNE, Terry .... 940-898-3029 451 F
tsenne@twu.edu
SENNETT, Peter .... 978-630-9160 215 A
psennett@mwcc.mass.edu
SENNYEY, Pongracz ...... 512-448-8470 442 M
pongracz@stedwards.edu
SENSENIG, Jayne .... 717-866-5775 383 H
SENSENIG, Melvin .... 610-921-7708 378 C
msensenig@albright.edu
SENSENIG, Victor .... 410-778-7201 204 D
vsensenig2@washcoll.edu
SENSER, Randie .... 212-247-3434 305 G
rsenser@mandl.edu
SENSI, Patricia .... 732-224-2232 276 B
psensi@brookdalecc.edu
SENSIBAUGH,
Cyndee, K .... 304-367-4933 489 D
cyndee.sensibaugh@pierpont.edu
SENSING, Laura .... 734-462-4400 230 D
lsensing@schoolcraft.edu
SENTER, Jim .... 915-747-5347 455 C
jsenter@utep.edu
SENTER, Timothy, C ..... 662-862-8460 246 D
tcsenter@iccms.edu
SENTER, William .... 830-372-6550 449 B
wsenter@tlu.edu
SENTZ, Justin .... 717-477-1507 395 E
jasentz@ship.edu
SEO, Eun Ja .... 714-525-0088.. 44 E
library@gm.edu
SEO, Hillary .... 515-294-3540 162 I
hseo@iastate.edu
SEO, Sang Bae .... 636-327-4645 255 L
seoul@midwest.edu
SEO, Stephen .... 213-487-0110.. 41 I
registrar@dula.edu
SEPANIC, Michael, J ..... 856-225-6026 281 G
msepanic@camden.rutgers.edu
SEPEHRI, Mohamad .... 202-274-7050.. 93 C
mohamad.sepehri@udc.edu
SEPION, Daniel .... 605-394-2348 417 B
daniel.sepion@sdsmt.edu
SEPLOW, Suzanne .... 310-825-3401.. 69 A
suzanne@orl.ucla.edu
SEPPALA, Julie .... 906-487-2642 227 E
jhseppal@mtu.edu
SEPULVEDA, Dolores .... 787-891-0925 508 K
dsepulve@aguadilla.inter.edu
SEQUEIRA, Debra .... 206-281-2277 484 D
dsequeira@spu.edu
SEQUEIRA, Gerald .... 626-914-8517.. 36 K
gsequeira@citruscollege.edu
SEQUERA, Lisa .... 702-463-2122 272 G
lsequera@wongu.edu
SEQUERI, Pierangelo .... 202-526-3799.. 92 F
psequeri@johnpaulii.edu
SERAFIMOV, Val .... 417-873-7262 252 F
vserafimov@drury.edu
SERAFIN, Renata .... 210-486-4689 429 E
rserafin@alamo.edu
SERAFINO, Candice, J .. 413-545-6253 211 D
serafino@acad.umass.edu
SERAICHICK, Laura .... 603-358-2526 275 A
lseraich@keene.edu
SERBALIK, James .... 518-783-2314 315 J
serbalik@siena.edu
SERBALIK, Sandy .... 518-783-2596 315 J
sserbalik@siena.edu
SERBAN, Andreea .... 714-438-4698.. 38 B
aserban@mail.cccd.edu
SERBER, Michael .... 214-648-9569 457 B
michael.serber@utsouthwestern.edu

SERDYUK, Yana, V .... 708-209-3053 135 F
yana.serdyuk@cuchicago.edu
SERGE, Susan .... 307-681-6082 502 F
sserge@sheridan.edu
SERGEANT, SR., Glenn . 501-975-8536.. 20 G
gsergeant@philander.edu
SERGENT, Ann .... 419-559-2147 361 I
asergent01@terra.edu
SERGIO, Tiffany .... 310-233-4091.. 49 A
sergiot@lahc.edu
SERIO, Tricia, R .... 413-545-2766 211 D
tserio@umass.edu
SERJOIE, Ara .... 336-316-2320 329 E
serjoiea@guilford.edu
SERLING, Kitty .... 816-276-4309 258 F
c.serling@researchcollege.edu
SERNA, Carlos .... 562-860-2451.. 35 M
cserna@cerritos.edu
SERNA, Edward .... 207-778-7256 196 B
edward.serna@maine.edu
SERNA, Falone .... 310-506-4392.. 56 C
falone.serna@pepperdine.edu
SERNA-WALLENDER,
Alex .... 210-999-7311 452 A
asernawa@trinity.edu
SEROSHEK, Nichole .... 360-442-2371 482 B
nseroshek@lowercolumbia.edu
SEROTA COTE,
Pamela, A .... 540-375-2299 471 B
cote@roanoke.edu
SEROVICH, Julianne ...... 813-974-1992 110 B
jserovich@usf.edu
SERPETTE, Anthony, W . 330-972-7758 362 B
serpette@uakron.edu
SERR, Jim .... 815-280-6641 140 B
jserr@jjc.edu
SERR, Russel .... 310-660-3593.. 41 L
rserr@elcamino.edu
SERRA, Elena .... 201-761-6366 282 I
eserra@saintpeters.edu
SERRA, Neddie .... 973-748-9000 276 A
neddie_serra@bloomfield.edu
SERRA, Neuza .... 856-225-6005 281 G
nmserra@camden.rutgers.edu
SERRANO, Alex .... 903-223-3114 448 B
alex.serrano@tamut.edu
SERRANO, Carlos, A ..... 718-982-2460 293 E
carlos.serrano@csi.cuny.edu
SERRANO, Fabian .... 432-264-5077 438 C
fserrano@howardcollege.edu
SERRANO, Gladys .... 787-743-4041 507 D
gserrano@columbiacentral.edu
SERRANO, Iris .... 787-743-7979 511 I
iserrano@suagm.edu
SERRANO, Lucille .... 831-755-6900.. 44 K
lserrano@hartnell.edu
SERRANO, Mayra .... 787-798-3001 512 C
mayra.serrano@uccaribe.edu
SERRANO, Melba .... 787-890-2681 512 H
melba.serrano@upr.edu
SERRANO-FEBO, Aixa ... 787-857-3600 508 M
aserrano@br.inter.edu
SERRAO, Carlos .... 740-392-6868 357 B
carlos.serrao@mvnu.edu
SERRATA, William .... 915-831-6511 436 E
wserrata@epcc.edu
SERRATO, CC .... 432-552-2100 457 A
serrato_c@utpb.edu
SERRAVILLO, JR., Lee .. 518-442-3080 316 D
lserravillo@albany.edu
SERRECCHIA, Michael ... 214-638-0484 438 I
mserrecchia@kdstudio.com
SERRETT, Marc .... 605-688-4128 417 C
marc.serrett@sdstate.edu
SERTSU, Neb .... 410-837-5069 204 B
nsertsu@ubalt.edu
SERVAES, Brandi .... 785-242-5200 176 D
brandi.servaes@ottawa.edu
SERVELLO, Debra .... 401-456-8013 405 C
dservello@ric.edu
SERVELLO, Frederick, A 207-581-3202 195 J
fred.servello@maine.edu
SERVI, Angela, M .... 715-675-3331 500 E
servia@ntc.edu
SERVI-ROBERTS,
Jennifer .... 919-209-2041 335 F
jlserviroberts@johnstoncc.edu
SERVIDIO, Denise .... 718-990-6247 314 B
stjohns@bkstr.com
SERVIN, Carid .... 530-661-5712.. 76 B
cservin@yccd.edu
SESESKE, Scott .... 508-565-1175 218 H
sseseske@stonehill.edu

SESHAN, Radhika .... 619-594-5822.. 33 E
rseshan@sdsu.edu
SESSION, Norman .... 601-936-5555 246 B
norman.session@hindscc.edu
SESSIONS, Daniel .... 847-585-2097 132 B
dsessions@aiuniv.edu
SESSIONS, Kenneth .... 615-329-8690 419 K
ksessions@fisk.edu
SESSIONS, Layne .... 775-831-1314 272 D
lsessions@sierranevada.edu
SESSIONS, Lisa, H .... 828-448-3126 339 A
lsessions@wpcc.edu
SESSIONS, Valerie .... 843-863-8083 407 E
vsessions@csuniv.edu
SESSLER, Jeff .... 909-607-1225.. 63 E
jeff@scrippscollege.edu
SESSLER, Jen .... 315-568-3070 308 F
jsessler@nycc.edu
SESTAK, Brandi .... 402-465-7579 268 H
bsestak@nebrwesleyan.edu
SESTAK, Joan .... 217-206-7794 151 C
jsest1@uis.edu
SETCHELL, Cara, L .... 765-658-6267 154 F
carasetchell@depauw.edu
SETCHELL, Steven, J ..... 765-658-4215 154 F
ssetchell@depauw.edu
SETH, Niti .... 617-873-0208 207 F
niti.seth@cambridgecolleg.edu
SETHI, Sanjit .... 612-874-3737 236 K
president@mcad.edu
SETHRE-HOFSTAD, Lisa 218-299-3455 235 E
sethre@cord.edu
SETLAK, Tressa, A .... 240-895-4911 201 E
tasetlak@smcm.edu
SETLEY, David, M .... 717-867-6104 388 H
setley@lvc.edu
SETMEYER, Adam .... 317-955-6131 158 U
asetmeyer@marian.edu
SETO, Sharon .... 510-780-4543.. 47 J
presidentsoffice@lifewest.edu
SETRIGHT, Aynn .... 802-257-7751 463 C
aynn.setright@sit.edu
SETTEDUCATO,
Nicholas .... 727-873-4287 110 C
nsetteducato@usf.edu
SETTER, Paul .... 972-708-7321 435 H
accounting@diu.edu
SETTERGREN, Jennifer .. 616-957-6675 221 P
jsetterg@calvinseminary.edu
SETTLE, Jim, S .... 336-334-5513 343 A
jssettle@uncg.edu
SETTLES, Monica .... 406-756-3801 263 F
msettles@fvcc.edu
SETTOON, Paula .... 918-595-7728 370 E
paula.settoon@tulsacc.edu
SETTY, Sudha .... 413-782-1431 219 F
sudha.setty@law.wne.edu
SETZER, Jason .... 336-249-8186 334 A
jason_setzer@davidsonccc.edu
SETZER, Kristen .... 704-406-3973 329 A
ksetzer@gardner-webb.edu
SETZER, Pat .... 619-660-4226.. 44 H
pat.setzer@gcccd.edu
SETZER, Tim, W .... 409-944-1365 437 B
tsetzer@gc.edu
SEUFERLING, Dale .... 785-832-7400 177 D
dseuferling@kuendowment.org
SEUFERT, Kyle .... 620-431-2820 175 H
kseufert@neosho.edu
SEUFFERLEIN,
Catherine .... 402-363-5614 270 E
cseufferlein@york.edu
SEUNARINE, Patricia ..... 302-736-2385.. 90 G
patricia.seunarine@wesley.edu
SEUTTER, Jana, M .... 563-333-6344 169 A
officeofthepresident@sau.edu
SEVASTOS, Charlie, W .. 386-323-8812.. 98 A
sevastoc@erau.edu
SEVER, Michelle, T .... 407-582-8256 112 K
msever@valenciacollege.edu
SEVER, Timor .... 713-718-6453 437 I
timor.sever@hccs.edu
SEVERA, Ineke .... 208-459-5268 130 D
isevera@collegeofidaho.edu
SEVERANCE, Dianne ...... 775-831-1314 272 D
dseverance@sierranevada.edu
SEVERANCE,
Mary Ellen .... 508-793-7478 208 A
meseverance@clarku.edu
SEVERNS, Mel .... 740-392-6868 357 B
mel.severns@mvnu.edu
SEVERS, Doug .... 541-737-2241 375 D
financial.aid@oregonstate.edu

SEVERSON, Christopher 715-675-3331 500 E
seversonc@ntc.edu
SEVERSON, Mark, W ..... 716-878-6434 318 C
seversmw@buffalostate.edu
SEVERSON, Sheila .... 608-796-3001 498 N
smseverson@viterbo.edu
SEVERSON, Stacy .... 612-351-1463 236 D
sseverson@ipr.edu
SEVERSON, Tim .... 641-585-8174 170 B
tim.severson@waldorf.edu
SEVERTIS, JR.,
Ronald, E .... 812-941-2148 157 B
rseverti@ius.edu
SEVERY, Lisa .... 303-492-6541.. 83 A
lisa.severy@colorado.edu
SEVICK, Leona .... 540-828-5608 465 D
lsevick@bridgewater.edu
SEVIER, Brian .... 805-437-2073.. 30 F
brian.sevier@csuci.edu
SEVIER, Christy .... 225-214-1947 186 F
christy.sevier@franu.edu
SEVIG, Todd, D .... 734-764-8312 231 E
tdsevig@umich.edu
SEVIGNY, Jeanne .... 770-720-5928 123 E
jeanne.sevigny@reinhardt.edu
SEWALT, Lawanna .... 903-675-6240 452 B
lsewalt@tvcc.edu
SEWARD, Alison .... 603-526-3715 272 H
alison.seward@colby-sawyer.edu
SEWARD, David .... 479-788-7093.. 21 H
david.seward@uafs.edu
SEWARD, David .... 415-565-4710.. 68 F
sewardd@uchastings.edu
SEWARD, Jason .... 757-455-2124 477 F
jseward@vwu.edu
SEWELL, Devona .... 847-970-4803 152 A
dsewell@usml.edu
SEWELL, Gary .... 423-236-2700 424 B
garysewell@southern.edu
SEWELL, Holly .... 580-559-5203 366 C
hsewell@ecok.edu
SEWELL, John .... 601-974-1019 247 B
seweljl@millsaps.edu
SEWELL, Keli .... 864-977-7733 411 E
keli.sewell@ngu.edu
SEWELL, Kenneth .... 405-744-6501 368 B
kenneth.sewell@okstate.edu
SEWELL, Robert .... 760-245-4271.. 73 D
robert.sewell@vvc.edu
SEWELL, Sara .... 757-455-3237 477 F
ssewell@vwu.edu
SEWELL, Shannon .... 731-989-6051 420 C
ssewell@fhu.edu
SEWELL, Thomas, R ...... 423-585-2644 426 C
thomas.sewell@ws.edu
SEWELL, Zennabelle ...... 212-261-1682 309 F
zsewell@nyit.edu
SEXTON, Caroline .... 864-592-4471 412 F
sextonc@sccsc.edu
SEXTON, Clarence .... 865-938-8186 419 E
cs@thecrowncollege.edu
SEXTON, Colleen .... 708-534-3958 137 F
csexton@govst.edu
SEXTON, Gary .... 330-941-1778 365 C
sexton@wysu.org
SEXTON, Kelly, B .... 734-763-0614 231 E
kbsexton@umich.edu
SEXTON, M. Shannon ... 865-938-8186 419 E
shannon.sexton@thecrowncollege.edu
SEXTON, Michele, D ...... 620-235-4187 176 F
msexton@pittstate.edu
SEXTON, Mike, B .... 408-554-5251.. 62 D
mbsexton@scu.edu
SEXTON, Shane .... 512-313-3000 434 E
shane.sexton@concordia.edu
SEXTON, Steve .... 615-248-7792 427 A
ssexton@trevecca.edu
SEXTON, Susan, K .... 937-229-4333 362 G
ssexton1@udayton.edu
SEXTON, Teresa .... 585-245-5502 318 E
sexton@geneseo.edu
SEXTON, Timothy .... 636-584-6698 252 J
timothy.sexton@eastcentral.edu
SEXTON, Timothy, D ..... 574-631-1785 161 C
sexton.30@nd.edu
SEXTON-JOHNSON,
Sara .... 509-359-3111 480 E
ssextonjohns@ewu.edu
SEYB, Ronald .... 518-580-5725 316 A
rseyb@skidmore.edu
SEYBERT, Brett .... 931-540-2514 424 G
bseybert@columbiastate.edu
SEYDEL, Tim .... 541-962-3740 373 B
tseydel@eou.edu

SEYEDIAN, Mojtaba 716-673-4813 317 A mojtaba.seyedian@fredonia.edu
SEYFERT, Keli 805-922-6966 24 J kseyfert@hancockcollege.edu
SEYMORE, Lyric 870-543-5966 21 C lseymore@seark.edu
SEYMORE, SR., Marrix 573-681-5330 254 E seymoresrm@lincolnu.edu
SEYMOUR, Avanti 617-984-1709 218 B aseymour@quincycollege.edu
SEYMOUR, Dennis 815-939-5302 146 A dseymour@olivet.edu
SEYMOUR, Heather, B 207-755-5248 194 G hseymour@cmcc.edu
SEYMOUR, Jason 336-725-8344 339 F seymourj@piedmontu.edu
SEYMOUR, Jodi 641-784-5112 165 H seymour@graceland.edu
SEYMOUR, Michael 320-762-4403 237 B michael.seymour@alextech.edu
SEYMOUR, S. Mark 330-471-8145 355 L mseymour@malone.edu
SEYMOUR, Sharon 217-479-7025 142 I sharon.seymour@mac.edu
SEYMOUR, Thad 407-823-3522 109 E thad.seymour@ucf.edu
SEYMOUR, William 423-472-7141 424 F wseymour@clevelandstatecc.edu
SGANGA, Fred 631-444-8606 317 D fred.sganga@stonybrook.edu
SHA, Bey-Ling 657-278-3355 31 E bsha@fullerton.edu
SHAAB, Jane 410-706-8282 202 D jshaab@umaryland.edu
SHAABAN-MAGANA, Lamea 205-348-5040 7 G lshaaban@sa.ua.edu
SHABAZZ, David 502-597-5915 182 H david.shabazz@kysu.edu
SHABAZZ, Ricky 619-388-3400 60 C
SHABAZZ, Roxie 808-956-3584 128 F rshabazz@hawaii.edu
SHABAZZI, Mohammad 601-979-8806 246 E mohammad.shabazzi@jsums.edu
SHABBIR, M 541-880-2320 373 E shabbir@klamathcc.edu
SHABLIA, Nataliia 215-572-2887 379 A shablian@arcadia.edu
SHABLIN, Steve 517-355-8700 227 D shablin@msu.edu
SHABLOSKI, Regan 814-866-6641 388 A rshabloski@lecom.edu
SHABRAM, Greg 541-346-3742 377 D gshabram@uoregon.edu
SHACHAR, Mickey 714-816-0366 67 I mickey.shachar@trident.edu
SHACHTER, Amy, M 408-551-7041 62 D ashachter@scu.edu
SHACKELFORD, Carol 601-635-2111 245 I cshackelford@eccc.edu
SHACKELFORD, Harper 910-678-8413 334 D shackelh@faytechcc.edu
SHACKELFORD, Judy 217-814-5448 148 F judy.shackelford@sjcs.edu
SHACKELFORD, Laura 940-898-2950 451 F lshackelford@twu.edu
SHACKELFORD, Philip 870-864-7116 21 B pshackelford@southark.edu
SHACKETT, Todd 256-395-2211 3 G tshackett@suscc.edu
SHACKLEFORD, Douglas 919-962-1300 342 D douglas_shackelford@kenan-flagler.unc.edu
SHACKLEFORD, Keith 949-451-5398 64 F kshackleford@ivc.edu
SHACKLEFORD, Michael, M 757-823-9067 469 F mmshackleford@nsu.edu
SHACKLEFORD, JR., Robert, S 336-633-0287 337 A rsshackleford@randolph.edu
SHADDEN, Tiffany 716-839-8214 298 B tbrignon@daemen.edu
SHADE, Chris 858-653-3000 29 I cshade@calmu.edu
SHADICK, Richard 212-346-1526 311 E rshadick@pace.edu
SHADLE, Joseph, P 513-745-3570 365 B shadlej@xavier.edu
SHADOIAN, Holly, L 401-456-8884 405 C hshadoian@ric.edu
SHAEFFER, James, M 757-789-1775 474 F jshaeffer@es.vccs.edu
SHAFER, Barb 406-657-2301 264 E bshafer@msubillings.edu
SHAFER, Brad 502-852-6588 185 C bradley.shafer@louisville.edu
SHAFER, Jack, L 610-499-4454 403 B jlshafer@widener.edu
SHAFER, Jeff, S 336-256-0226 343 A jsshafer@uncg.edu
SHAFER, John, R 317-738-8080 154 J jshafer@franklincollege.edu
SHAFER, Kathrynne, G 717-691-6003 390 E kshafer@messiah.edu
SHAFER, Lisa 610-328-8009 399 D lshafer1@swarthmore.edu
SHAFER, Lisa 530-541-4660 47 E shaferl@ltcc.edu
SHAFER, Staci 618-985-3741 139 I stacishafer@jalc.edu
SHAFER, Teresa 419-448-3309 361 J tshafer@tiffin.edu
SHAFFAR, Ben 859-846-5373 183 E bshaffar@midway.edu
SHAFFER, Alan 740-392-6868 357 B alan.shaffer@mvnu.edu
SHAFFER, Amy 912-443-5512 124 A ashaffer@savannahtech.edu
SHAFFER, Brian, W 901-843-3976 423 J shaffer@rhodes.edu
SHAFFER, Chris 415-476-3769 69 E chris.shaffer@ucsf.edu
SHAFFER, Chris 334-670-3266 7 C shafferc@troy.edu
SHAFFER, Chris 941-359-7616 105 K cshaffer@ringling.edu
SHAFFER, Christopher 740-351-3207 360 K cshaffer@shawnee.edu
SHAFFER, Dana 606-218-5411 185 D danashaffer@upike.edu
SHAFFER, David 567-661-2625 360 B david_shaffer5@owens.edu
SHAFFER, Deborah 740-593-2555 359 G shafferd@ohio.edu
SHAFFER, Germaine 606-487-3409 181 C germaine.shaffer@kctcs.edu
SHAFFER, Greg 301-387-3791 198 F greg.shaffer@garrettcollege.edu
SHAFFER, James, M 330-471-8515 355 L jshaffer@malone.edu
SHAFFER, Jason, S 704-894-2188 328 F jashaffer@davidson.edu
SHAFFER, Jeff 503-594-3101 372 D jeff.shaffer@clackamas.edu
SHAFFER, John 304-829-7394 487 G jshaffer@bethanywv.edu
SHAFFER, Jon, L 618-453-1069 149 E jshaffer@housing.siu.edu
SHAFFER, Kelli 254-968-9050 446 E shaffer@tarleton.edu
SHAFFER, Kent 479-631-4665 19 H kshaffer@jbu.edu
SHAFFER, Martin, B 845-575-3000 305 L martin.shaffer@marist.edu
SHAFFER, Steven, E 716-878-6034 318 C shaffese@buffalostate.edu
SHAFFER, Vicky 410-857-2254 200 B vshaffer@mcdaniel.edu
SHAFFER, Virginia 630-752-5623 152 F virginia.shaffer@wheaton.edu
SHAFFER, Virginia 620-901-6235 170 G shaffer@allencc.edu
SHAFFER, W. Michael 706-721-4413 115 A wshaffer@augusta.edu
SHAFFER, Wade 806-651-2044 448 C wshaffer@wtamu.edu
SHAFFER, Wendy 978-556-3858 215 C wshaffer@necc.mass.edu
SHAFFER, Yvette 505-984-6060 287 J admissions@sjc.edu
SHAFFER LILIENTHAL, Robin 641-844-5730 166 I robin.lilienthal@iavalley.edu
SHAFFER LILIENTHAL, Robin 641-844-5730 166 K robin.lilienthal@iavalley.edu
SHAFFER-WALSH, Rory 631-687-2658 314 C rshaffer-walsh@sjcny.edu
SHAFFETT, John 706-233-7357 124 B jshaffett@shorter.edu
SHAFFETT, John, E 850-263-3261 95 B jeshaffett@baptistcollege.edu
SHAFFNER, Donna 315-792-3111 324 B dlshaffner@utica.edu
SHAFKOWITZ, Marshall 773-602-5465 134 D mshafkowitz@ccc.edu
SHAFRIN, Bonnie 414-425-8300 495 H bshafrin@shsst.edu
SHAFTEL, Matthew 740-593-1808 359 G shaftel@ohio.edu
SHAGER, Dorian 765-658-4267 154 F dshager@depauw.edu
SHAH, Gaurav 781-891-3467 206 D gshah@bentley.edu
SHAH, Kashif 708-974-5348 144 C shah@morainevalley.edu
SHAH, Priyank 507-285-7263 240 G priyank.shah@rctc.edu
SHAH, Sadiq 909-869-3898 30 D sayedshah@cpp.edu
SHAH, Swapnal 800-280-0307 152 H swapnal.shah@ace.edu
SHAH, Vishal 610-738-0536 396 A vshah@wcupa.edu
SHAH-GORDON, Ruta 718-420-4254 324 F rshahgor@wagner.edu
SHAHEDIPOUR-SANDVIK, Shadi 315-792-7100 321 E sshahedipour-sandvik@sunypoly.edu
SHAHEED-SONUBI, Taheera 716-851-1773 299 F shaheed@ecc.edu
SHAHEEN, Lisa 212-686-9244 290 A
SHAHI, Manvinder (Vinay) 650-289-3336 59 C manvinder.shahi@stpatricksseminary.org
SHAHID, Abdus 503-838-9331 377 H shahida@wou.edu
SHAHID, Charles 937-376-6081 350 D cshahid@centralstate.edu
SHAHID, Julia 903-813-2457 430 N sshahid@austincollege.edu
SHAHID-BELLOT, Robyn 617-873-0191 207 F robyn.shahid-bellot@cambridgecollege.edu
SHAHIN, Hamdi 201-559-6076 278 A shahinh@felician.edu
SHAHIN, Jamie 636-949-4106 254 F jshahin@lindenwood.edu
SHAHIN, Wisam 908-709-7024 284 C wisam.shahin@ucc.edu
SHAHRABI, Kamal 585-475-2411 313 A kxscada@rit.edu
SHAHROKHI, Hossein 713-221-8542 453 B shahrokhi@uhd.edu
SHAIKH, Usama 516-876-3175 319 A shaikhu@oldwestbury.edu
SHAILEY, Timothy 215-503-1295 400 A timothy.shailey@jefferson.edu
SHAILOR, Robert 360-596-5292 485 B rshailor@spscc.edu
SHAIN, Daniel 856-225-6144 281 G dshain@camden.rutgers.edu
SHAIN, Sue 978-556-3710 215 C sshain@necc.mass.edu
SHAIN, Yeruchim 732-431-1600 284 A taofnj@gmail.com
SHAINDLIN, Andrew, B 401-863-3189 404 E andrew_shaindlin@brown.edu
SHAKE, Miranda 217-709-0927 141 E mshake@lakeviewcol.edu
SHAKESPEARE, Christine 212-346-1200 311 E
SHAKIBA, Trevor 918-333-6151 368 G trevor.m.shakiba@ampf.com
SHAKIR, Salah 859-846-6248 183 E sshakir@midway.edu
SHALHOUB, Robert 973-379-2044 380 B finance@archpitt.org
SHALLEY, Heather 312-329-4272 144 B heather.shalley@moody.edu
SHAMAH, Irwin 347-394-1036 291 E ishamah@ateret.net
SHAMBARGER, Angela 207-221-4554 196 G ashambarger@une.edu
SHAMBAUGH, Jeannine 330-363-5420 348 D jeannine.shambaugh@aultman.com
SHAMBLEE, Crystal 410-225-4265 199 H cshamblee@mica.edu
SHAMIM, Jina 415-476-8850 69 E jina.shamim@ucsf.edu
SHAMOO, Yousif 713-348-5741 442 K shamoo@rice.edu
SHAMP, Paul 305-809-3184 99 C paul.shamp@fkcc.edu
SHAMPINE, Memorie, L 315-386-7042 320 E shampinem@canton.edu
SHAMS, Arian 714-300-0300 64 I ashams@scitech.edu
SHAMS, Nazila 714-300-0300 64 I nshams@scitech.edu
SHAMS, Parviz 714-300-0300 64 I pshams@scitech.edu
SHAMSUD-DIN, Ayasha 503-552-1608 374 E ashamsud-din@nunm.edu
SHANAFELT, Rebecca 727-816-3288 104 F shanafr@phsc.edu
SHANAHAN, Alanna 410-516-8382 199 D ashanah1@jhu.edu
SHANAHAN, Brian 607-871-2144 289 H shanahan@alfred.edu
SHANAHAN, James 812-855-1963 156 B jes30@indiana.edu
SHANAHAN, Jenny 508-531-2764 212 B jshanahan@bridgew.edu
SHANAHAN, Thomas 919-962-4588 341 A tcshanahan@northcarolina.edu
SHANBLATT, Stephanie 215-968-8222 379 G stephanie.shanblatt@bucks.edu
SHANDA, Mark 859-257-1707 185 B mark.shanda@uky.edu
SHANDERSON, Laurie 866-776-0331 54 A lshanderson@ncu.edu
SHANDLEY, Emily 203-432-2337 89 D emily.shandley@yale.edu
SHANDLEY, Janet 206-296-5904 484 F janshan@seattleu.edu
SHANE, Pam 740-284-5193 353 B pshane@franciscan.edu
SHANER, Carl, L 570-326-3761 393 G cshaner@pct.edu
SHANER, Megan, L 919-209-2201 335 F mlshaner@johnstoncc.edu
SHANG, Ying 812-488-2661 161 A ys46@evansville.edu
SHANHOLTZ, Cathy 540-665-5561 471 E cshanhol2@su.edu
SHANK, Christy 254-526-1291 432 H christy.shank@ctcd.edu
SHANK, Derek 520-494-5527 11 K derek.shank@centralaz.edu
SHANK, Jeffrey, A 540-432-4206 466 G jeff.shank@emu.edu
SHANK, Jennifer 931-372-3016 426 E jshank@tntech.edu
SHANK, Sherri 704-233-8025 344 G s.shank@wingate.edu
SHANK, Steve 704-233-8691 344 G sh.shank@wingate.edu
SHANK, Theresa, M 240-500-2476 198 H tmshank@hagerstowncc.edu
SHANKEL, James, V 412-578-6258 380 E jvshankel@carlow.edu
SHANKLE, Julie 321-674-8244 99 B jshankle@fit.edu
SHANKLE, Nicole 812-888-4182 162 C nshankle@vinu.edu
SHANKLIN, Carol 785-532-7927 174 G shanklin@ksu.edu
SHANKLIN, Iris 404-756-4916 114 G ishanklin@atlm.edu
SHANKMAN, Kimberly, C 913-360-7413 171 D kshankman@benedictine.edu
SHANKS, Alisa 303-963-3378 77 G ashanks@ccu.edu
SHANKS, Brian 512-245-2319 450 E bs26@txstate.edu
SHANKS, Carol 314-918-2538 253 A cshanks@eden.edu
SHANKS, Cindy 918-595-8291 370 E cindy.shanks@tulsacc.edu
SHANKS, Francesca 413-662-5263 213 A f.shanks@mcla.edu
SHANKS, Stacey, A 812-488-2606 161 A ss581@evansville.edu
SHANKWEILER, Jean 310-660-3119 41 L jshankweiler@elcamino.edu
SHANLEY, OP, Brian, J 401-865-2153 405 B nkelley@providence.edu
SHANLEY, Mark 870-850-3121 21 C mshanley@seark.edu
SHANMUGARATNAM, Carol 781-283-2308 219 D cshanmug@wellesley.edu
SHANNON, Alecia 405-692-3176 366 G alecia.shannon@macu.edu
SHANNON, David 405-878-6000 367 F david.shannon@okbu.edu
SHANNON, David, R 731-989-6001 420 C dshannon@fhu.edu

SHANNON, Denise .... 313-496-2744 232 C
dshanno1@wcccd.edu
SHANNON, Henry, D .... 909-652-6100.. 36 A
henry.shannon@chaffey.edu
SHANNON, John .... 260-665-4224 160 H
shannonj@trine.edu
SHANNON, JR.,
John, T .... 901-321-3250 419 C
jack.shannon@cbu.edu
SHANNON, LaToya .... 386-481-2942.. 95 F
shannonl@cookman.edu
SHANNON, Linda, A ..... 718-990-6578 314 B
shannonl@stjohns.edu
SHANNON, Patricia .... 610-359-2183 382 C
pshannon@dccc.edu
SHANNON, S. Scott ...... 315-470-6537 320 A
sshannon@esf.edu
SHANNON, Sarah .... 406-994-2452 264 D
sarah.shannon1@montana.edu
SHANNON, Susan, K .... 717-796-1800 390 E
sshannon@messiah.edu
SHANNON, Tracey .... 334-876-9277.... 2 D
tracey.shannon@wccs.edu
SHANTON, David .... 646-660-6067 292 L
david.shanton@baruch.cuny.edu
SHAO, Alan, T .... 843-953-6651 408 E
shaoa@cofc.edu
SHAO, Chris .... 254-968-1944 446 E
shao@tarleton.edu
SHAO, Lawrence .... 724-738-2093 395 F
lawrence.shao@sru.edu
SHAPE, Ronald .... 605-721-5214 416 A
rshape@national.edu
SHAPIRO, Alex A, G ..... 415-581-8842.. 68 F
shaprioa@uchastings.edu
SHAPIRO, Claire, R ...... 901-843-3750 423 J
shapiro@rhodes.edu
SHAPIRO, Daniel .... 831-582-3878.. 32 C
dshapiro@csumb.edu
SHAPIRO, David, W ...... 717-867-6060 388 H
shapiro@lvc.edu
SHAPIRO, Jeff .... 973-877-3142 277 I
shapiro@essex.edu
SHAPIRO, Joseph, I ...... 304-691-1700 490 D
shapiroj@marshall.edu
SHAPIRO, Steven .... 617-349-8458 210 H
sshapir3@lesley.edu
SHAPIRO DAVIS,
Andrea .... 646-664-9100 292 K
SHAPOVAL, Sandy .... 918-270-6459 369 A
sandy.shapoval@ptstulsa.edu
SHARAR, Scott .... 319-352-8318 170 C
scott.sharar@wartburg.edu
SHARBAUGH,
Catherine .... 610-896-1089 385 L
csharbau@haverford.edu
SHARBAUGH,
Sheila, M .... 302-356-3917.. 90 I
sheila.m.sharbaugh@wilmu.edu
SHARBAUGH, Tim, L .... 724-357-3011 394 G
timothy.sharbaugh@iup.edu
SHARER, C. Gregory ..... 607-753-4721 318 D
greg.sharer@cortland.edu
SHARER, Jack .... 502-895-3411 183 D
jsharer@lpts.edu
SHARER, Mark .... 570-577-3914 379 F
mark.sharer@bucknell.edu
SHARFMAN, Glenn .... 404-364-8318 122 J
gsharfman@oglethorpe.edu
SHARIAT, Vahid .... 714-816-0366.. 67 I
vahid.shariat@trident.edu
SHARIF, Zaki .... 937-376-6007 350 D
zsharif@centralstate.edu
SHARIK, Scott, A .... 419-358-3377 348 G
shariks@bluffton.edu
SHARK, Steven .... 701-662-1655 346 D
steven.shark@lrsc.edu
SHARKEY, Brian .... 563-884-5306 168 I
brian.sharkey@palmer.edu
SHARKEY, Kevin .... 724-738-3333 395 F
kevin.sharkey@sru.edu
SHARKEY, Marty .... 323-259-2934.. 54 E
msharkey@oxy.edu
SHARKEY, Melissa .... 641-628-5180 163 E
sharkeym@central.edu
SHARKEY, Susan .... 770-426-2664 121 C
susan.sharkey@life.edu
SHARMA, Gulshan .... 409-772-2436 456 F
gusharma@utmb.edu
SHARMA, Malhar .... 203-576-2348.. 88 D
msharma@bridgeport.edu
SHARMA, Sanjay .... 802-656-3175 463 E
sanjay.sharma@uvm.edu
SHARMA,
Venkatanarayanan .... 973-720-2432 284 I
sharmav@wpunj.edu
SHARMAN, Angel .... 307-268-2667 501 U
asharman@caspercollege.edu
SHARON, Anthony, P .... 617-324-7130 215 G
SHARON, Daniel .... 914-632-5400 307 G
dsharon@monroecollege.edu
SHARP, Andrew .... 601-477-4198 246 F
andrew.sharp@jcjc.edu
SHARP, Anthony .... 310-289-5123.. 73 H
anthony.sharp@wcui.edu
SHARP, David .... 870-245-5181.. 20 E
sharpd@obu.edu
SHARP, Debbie .... 940-668-4213 441 A
dsharp@nctc.edu
SHARP, Deltha .... 870-368-2007.. 20 F
dshell@ozarka.edu
SHARP, Diane .... 910-221-2224 329 B
dsharp@gcd.edu
SHARP, Jan, T .... 865-539-7182 425 F
jtsharp@pstcc.edu
SHARP, Jason .... 620-421-6700 175 C
jasons@labette.edu
SHARP, Jason, R .... 651-631-5045 244 D
jrsharp@unwsp.edu
SHARP, John .... 979-458-6000 446 C
chancellor@tamus.edu
SHARP, Jordan .... 559-453-7104.. 43 G
jordan.sharp@fresno.edu
SHARP, Jordan .... 435-652-7544 460 G
jsharp@dixie.edu
SHARP, Julian .... 802-586-7711 463 D
SHARP, Kelvin .... 575-392-5004 286 J
ksharp@nmjc.edu
SHARP, Kimberly .... 601-925-3278 247 C
ksharp@mc.edu
SHARP, Kirk .... 620-223-2700 173 C
kirks@fortscott.edu
SHARP, Linda .... 573-876-7277 260 F
lsharp@stephens.edu
SHARP, Melody .... 434-200-7025 465 H
melody.sharp@centrahealth.com
SHARP, Nick .... 417-690-2224 251 E
sharp@cofo.edu
SHARP, Nicole .... 812-749-1225 159 C
nsharp@oak.edu
SHARP, Randy .... 808-675-3499 127 E
randy.sharp@byuh.edu
SHARP, Samantha .... 870-633-4480.. 19 B
ssharp@eacc.edu
SHARP, Valerie .... 417-865-2815 253 B
sharpv@evangel.edu
SHARPE, Allen .... 803-732-5223 410 G
sharpea@midlandstech.edu
SHARPE, Anna .... 706-233-4080 115 B
asharpe@berry.edu
SHARPE, Aubrey, D ...... 903-510-2901 452 C
asha@tjc.edu
SHARPE, Gary .... 678-359-5333 119 F
garys@gordonstate.edu
SHARPE, Jessica, G ...... 336-272-7102 329 D
jessica.sharpe@greensboro.edu
SHARPE, Kelli .... 615-963-1232 426 D
ksharpe@tnstate.edu
SHARPE, Norean, R ...... 718-990-6800 314 B
sharpen@stjohns.edu
SHARPE, Patricia .... 413-528-7240 205 F
psharpe@simons-rock.edu
SHARPE, Paul .... 956-882-8221 455 D
paul.sharpe@utrgv.edu
SHARPE, Ron .... 989-275-5000 226 B
ron.sharpe@kirtland.edu
SHARPHORN, Dan .... 512-499-4462 454 I
dsharphorn@utsystem.edu
SHARPLES, Stacey .... 941-752-5256 108 G
sharpls@scf.edu
SHARPNACK, Patricia ... 440-684-6032 363 G
psharpnack@ursuline.edu
SHARRAR, Jack .... 415-439-2412.. 25 K
jsharrar@act-sf.org
SHARRARD, Aurora .... 412-624-5122 401 B
asharrard@pitt.edu
SHARRATT, Emily .... 541-962-3866 373 B
esharratt@eou.edu
SHATSOFF, Patricia .... 973-300-2124 283 E
pshatsoff@sussex.edu
SHATTUCK, Anne .... 603-862-2415 274 G
anne.shattuck@unh.edu
SHATTUCK, Larry .... 410-532-5551 201 B
lshattuck@ndm.edu
SHATTUCK, Leslie .... 425-739-8236 482 A
leslie.shattuck@lwtech.edu
SHATTUCK, Wendy .... 909-748-8046.. 71 G
wendy_shattuck@redlands.edu
SHAUB, Larry .... 610-796-8298 378 F
larry.shaub@alvernia.edu
SHAUGHNESSY, Anne ... 617-824-8525 208 H
anne_shaughnessy@emerson.edu
SHAUGHNESSY, Joseph 781-768-7133 218 C
joseph.shaughnessy@regiscollege.edu
SHAUGHNESSY, Joseph 254-659-7831 437 G
jshaughnessy@hillcollege.edu
SHAUGHNESSY, Josette 915-831-6330 436 E
jshaugh2@epcc.edu
SHAUGHNESSY, Mark ... 631-656-2147 300 D
mark.shaughnessy@ftc.edu
SHAUL, Lesa .... 205-652-3460.... 9 A
lcc@uwa.edu
SHAUNAK, Raj .... 662-243-1911 246 A
rshaunak@eastms.edu
SHAUNAK, Sudershan .. 760-757-2121.. 52 E
sshaunak@miracosta.edu
SHAVER, Bryan, D .... 304-293-6600 491 C
bryan.shaver@mail.wvu.edu
SHAVER, Deborah .... 208-885-4627 131 G
dshaver@uidaho.edu
SHAVER, Joseph, E ...... 304-326-1481 488 F
jshaver@salemu.edu
SHAVERS, Anna .... 402-472-6827 269 J
ashavers@unl.edu
SHAW, Anita .... 210-297-7638 431 E
aashaw@baptisthealthsystem.com
SHAW, Anne, C .... 910-938-6322 333 F
shawa@coastalcarolina.edu
SHAW, Becky .... 413-585-4940 218 F
rshaw@smith.edu
SHAW, Benjamin .... 207-762-0146 196 E
benjamin.shaw@maine.edu
SHAW, Brian, R .... 202-685-4685 503 I
brian.r.shaw.civ@ndu.edu
SHAW, Carolyn .... 316-978-3010 178 A
carolyn.shaw@wichita.edu
SHAW, Carolyn .... 661-259-7800.. 38 H
carolyn.shaw@canyons.edu
SHAW, Carrie .... 970-943-3085.. 84 D
cshaw@western.edu
SHAW, Carrie .... 425-235-2415 483 G
cshaw@rtc.edu
SHAW, Chester .... 708-974-5360 144 C
schawc6@morainevalley.edu
SHAW, Chip .... 806-743-1500 451 C
chip.shaw@ttuhsc.edu
SHAW, Dameon .... 662-254-3790 248 B
dameon.shaw@mvsu.edu
SHAW, Darlene, L .... 843-792-2228 410 F
shawd@musc.edu
SHAW, David .... 662-325-3742 247 F
dshaw@provost.msstate.edu
SHAW, D'Wayne .... 903-983-8130 439 A
dshaw@kilgore.edu
SHAW, Erin .... 785-442-6003 174 A
eshaw@highlandcc.edu
SHAW, Geoff .... 866-323-0233.. 57 J
studentlife@providencecc.edu
SHAW, Heather .... 314-918-2576 253 A
hshaw@eden.edu
SHAW, Jack .... 304-876-5496 490 E
jshaw@shepherd.edu
SHAW, James, A .... 606-783-2599 183 F
j.shaw@moreheadstate.edu
SHAW, Jerone .... 662-621-4085 245 E
jshaw@coahomacc.edu
SHAW, John .... 214-333-5870 434 I
johns@dbu.edu
SHAW, Karen, A .... 585-262-1501 307 H
kshaw@monroecc.edu
SHAW, Ken .... 817-202-6202 444 I
kshaw@swau.edu
SHAW, Kerrie, S .... 757-446-5841 466 I
shawks@evms.edu
SHAW, Kevin .... 909-469-5401.. 74 I
kshaw@westernu.edu
SHAW, Kristi .... 620-441-5206 172 I
kristi.shaw@cowley.edu
SHAW, Linda .... 415-239-3303.. 37 A
lshaw@ccsf.edu
SHAW, Linda .... 480-732-7307.. 12 P
linda.shaw@cgc.edu
SHAW, Maria .... 415-503-6307.. 60 H
mshaw@sfcm.edu
SHAW, Marie .... 336-278-7280 328 K
mshaw15@elon.edu
SHAW, Matthew .... 765-285-5277 153 C
mcshaw2@bsu.edu
SHAW, Nancy .... 802-224-3011 463 H
nancy.shaw@vsc.edu
SHAW, P. Gerard .... 508-541-1790 208 F
pshaw@dean.edu
SHAW, Patricia .... 860-727-2073.. 87 A
pshaw@goodwin.edu
SHAW, Richard .... 650-723-2300.. 65 J
SHAW, Rick .... 661-722-6300.. 26 D
rshaw@avc.edu
SHAW, Robert, S .... 570-348-6245 389 G
rsshaw@marywood.edu
SHAW, Sara .... 207-859-1404 195 G
athdir@thomas.edu
SHAW, Suzanne .... 417-836-5139 256 E
suzanneshaw@missouristate.edu
SHAW, Teresa .... 909-607-8135.. 37 D
teresa.shaw@cgu.edu
SHAW, Timothy .... 972-883-5291 455 B
tim.shaw@utdallas.edu
SHAW, Tina .... 256-378-2010.... 1 G
thsaw5@cacc.edu
SHAW, Tom .... 269-965-3931 225 F
shawt@kellogg.edu
SHAW-BURNETT,
Margaret, A .... 716-878-5907 318 C
shawma@buffalostate.edu
SHAW HORTON,
Sheilah .... 781-283-2322 219 D
shorton2@wellesley.edu
SHAW THOMAS, Amy ... 512-499-4257 454 I
athomas@utsystem.edu
SHAWCROFT, Sally .... 970-542-3151.. 81 A
sally.shawcroft@morgancc.edu
SHAWN, Donna, S .... 913-627-4171 174 F
dshawn@kckcc.edu
SHAWNEY, Lisa, L .... 603-513-1335 274 H
lisa.shawney@granite.edu
SHAWVER, Jeffrey .... 304-647-6325 491 A
jshawver@osteo.wvsom.edu
SHAWVER, Todd .... 570-389-5297 394 A
tshawver@bloomu.edu
SHAY, Carrie .... 213-624-1200.. 42 I
cshay@fidm.edu
SHAY, Paul .... 617-253-2808 215 G
SHAY, Robert, S .... 303-492-7505.. 83 A
robert.shay@colorado.edu
SHAY, William .... 323-563-4840.. 36 D
williamshay@cdrewu.edu
SHAYLER, Todd .... 517-629-0305 220 G
tmshayler@albion.edu
SHEA, Bob .... 336-278-5428 328 K
bshea@elon.edu
SHEA, Catherine .... 303-492-7896.. 83 A
catherine.shea@colorado.edu
SHEA, Claire .... 603-623-0313 273 I
claireshea@nhia.edu
SHEA, Dennis, G .... 814-865-1427 392 B
dg4@psu.edu
SHEA, Diane .... 617-732-1604 209 A
shead@emmanuel.edu
SHEA, Donna .... 617-353-5124 207 D
dshea@bu.edu
SHEA, Erin .... 212-924-5900 322 B
eshea@swedishinstitute.edu
SHEA, James, P .... 701-355-8100 347 D
SHEA, Kevin, J .... 617-552-3252 207 B
k.shea@bc.edu
SHEA, McKennon .... 336-841-9856 329 G
mckennon@highpoint.edu
SHEA, Missy .... 781-283-2335 219 D
mshea@wellesley.edu
SHEA, Peter .... 413-559-5528 210 A
SHEA, Peter, J .... 518-442-4009 316 D
pshea@albany.edu
SHEA, Rich, J .... 814-886-6474 391 B
rshea@mtaloy.edu
SHEA, Robert .... 401-254-3726 405 E
rshea@rwu.edu
SHEAFFER, Andrea .... 510-649-2465.. 44 F
asheaffer@gtu.edu
SHEALEY, Monika .... 856-256-5440 281 E
shealey@rowan.edu
SHEAR, Skip .... 660-944-2853 251 G
sshear@conception.edu
SHEAR, Stephen .... 813-253-7014 101 A
sshear2@hccfl.edu
SHEARD, Reed .... 805-565-7171.. 74 K
rsheard@westmont.edu
SHEARD, Reed, L .... 805-565-7171.. 74 K
rsheard@westmont.edu
SHEARER, Christine ...... 406-657-2177 264 E
c.shearer@msubillings.edu

SHEARER, Erik .... 707-256-7155.. 53 C
eshearer@napavalley.edu
SHEARER, Jonathan ...... 630-617-6146 136 G
jonathan.shearer@elmhurst.edu
SHEARER, Liz .... 410-704-2451 204 A
lshearer@towson.edu
SHEARER, Pam .... 601-318-6561 249 H
pshearer@wmcarey.edu
SHEARER, Rachel .... 610-436-6973 396 A
rshearer@wcupa.edu
SHEARN, Robert .... 716-827-2483 323 D
shearnr@trocaire.edu
SHEARON, Randall .... 919-735-5151 338 H
shearon@waynecc.edu
SHEARRILL,
Charmagne .... 661-255-1050.. 28 K
cshearrill@calarts.edu
SHEARS, III, George ..... 704-334-6882 328 C
gshears@charlottechristian.edu
SHEARS, Mitchell .... 601-979-2321 246 E
mitchell.m.shears@jsums.edu
SHEARS, Stacey .... 510-981-2820.. 56 E
sshears@peralta.edu
SHEATHER, Simon, J .... 859-257-8939 185 B
simon.sheather@uky.edu
SHEATS, Karen, A .... 302-356-6867.. 90 I
karen.a.sheats@wilmu.edu
SHEBLE, Mary Ann .... 248-232-4512 229 A
masheble@oaklandcc.edu
SHECKLER, Allyson .... 508-565-1724 218 H
asheckler@stonehill.edu
SHEDD, Dawn .... 281-478-2779 443 C
dawn.shedd@sjcd.edu
SHEDD, Jean, E .... 847-467-5456 145 F
j-shedd@northwestern.edu
SHEDD, Louis .... 205-391-2359.... 3 E
lshedd@sheltonstate.edu
SHEDRICK, Karen, R ..... 601-877-6111 244 H
karen@alcorn.edu
SHEEHAN, Bill .... 573-288-6395 252 E
wsheehan@culver.edu
SHEEHAN, Eugene .... 970-351-2817.. 83 E
eugene.sheehan@unco.edu
SHEEHAN, Heather .... 701-224-5465 346 B
heather.sheehan@bismarckstate.edu
SHEEHAN, Jaime .... 657-278-3040.. 31 E
jsheehan@fullerton.edu
SHEEHAN, Jerry .... 406-994-2525 264 D
jsheehan@montana.edu
SHEEHAN, Mike .... 530-752-0339.. 68 E
mtsheehan@ucdavis.edu
SHEEHAN, Stephanie .... 423-236-2373 424 B
ssheehan@southern.edu
SHEEHAN, Tim .... 801-957-2001 461 D
tim.scheehan@slcc.edu
SHEEHY, Colette .... 434-924-3349 473 A
cc@virginia.edu
SHEEHY, Harry .... 603-646-2465 273 E
harry.sheehy@dartmouth.edu
SHEEHY, Jennifer .... 508-213-2340 217 E
jennifer.sheehy@nichols.edu
SHEEHY, Matthew .... 781-736-4642 207 E
sheehy@brandeis.edu
SHEEKS, Gina .... 706-507-8730 116 I
sheeks_gina@columbusstate.edu
SHEELER, Kristina, H .... 317-278-3161 156 F
ksheeler@iupui.edu
SHEELEY, Jonathan .... 920-206-2327 493 L
jonathan.sheeley@mbu.edu
SHEELEY, Robert, G ...... 203-392-6050.. 85 A
sheeleyr1@southernct.edu
SHEELY, Deanna .... 612-659-6537 238 I
deanna.sheely@minneapolis.edu
SHEERAN, Robert, M .... 513-745-2072 365 B
sheeran@xavier.edu
SHEERAZI, Saji .... 718-281-5144 295 D
ssheerazi@qcc.cuny.edu
SHEERER, Marilyn .... 910-962-3389 343 C
sheererm@uncw.edu
SHEESLEY, Debra, K ..... 717-361-1492 383 E
sheesleyd@etown.edu
SHEETS, Helene .... 419-824-3965 355 K
hsheets@lourdes.edu
SHEETS, Julie .... 573-518-2206 256 B
jsheets@mineralarea.edu
SHEETS, Julie .... 573-518-2262 256 B
jsheets@mineralarea.edu
SHEETS, Tamara .... 740-351-3207 360 K
tsheets@shawnee.edu
SHEETS, Tammy .... 276-944-6117 467 G
tsheets@ehc.edu
SHEETZ, Kraig, E .... 301-447-8399 200 E
k.e.sheetz@msmary.edu
SHEETZ, Tracey .... 724-938-4404 394 B
sheetz@calu.edu
SHEFCHIK, Thomas, J .. 920-433-4306 492 B
thomas.shefchik@bellincollege.edu
SHEFFIELD, Bethany, D 814-641-3101 386 H
sheffib@juniata.edu
SHEFFIELD,
Christopher, R .... 716-286-8405 310 D
crs@niagara.edu
SHEFFIELD, Roy, S .... 828-884-8312 327 C
scotts@brevard.edu
SHEFFIELD, Tracey .... 504-762-3031 187 E
tsheff@dcc.edu
SHEFFIELD, Vonne .... 478-301-2500 121 E
sheffield_v@mercer.edu
SHEFMAN, Pamelyn ...... 281-756-3749 429 I
pshefman@alvincollege.edu
SHEHATA, Erika .... 610-399-2053 394 C
eshehata@cheyney.edu
SHEHEANE, Dene .... 404-894-1238 118 F
dene.sheheane@dev.gatech.edu
SHEHEE, Amy .... 704-687-0301 342 E
ashehee@uncc.edu
SHEIKH, Ammand .... 540-464-7560 476 G
sheikhas@vmi.edu
SHEIKH, Bonnie .... 408-554-4802.. 62 D
esheikh@scu.edu
SHEIL, Astrid .... 540-545-7253 471 E
asheil@su.edu
SHEILLEY, Holly .... 859-233-8548 184 G
hsheilley@transy.edu
SHEIN, David .... 845-758-7454 290 G
shein@bard.edu
SHELBURNE, Stephanie 818-785-2726.. 35 J
stephanie.shelburne@casalomacollege.edu
SHELBY, Aaron .... 765-361-6488 162 E
shelbya@wabash.edu
SHELBY, Barbara .... 740-588-1315 365 E
bshelby@zanestate.edu
SHELBY, Deborah .... 860-486-4037.. 88 E
deborah.shelby@uconn.edu
SHELBY, Jane .... 907-786-4708.... 9 H
njshelby@alaska.edu
SHELBY, Kristin .... 618-634-3240 149 A
kristins@shawneecc.edu
SHELBY, Paula .... 803-705-4809 407 A
paula.shelby@benedict.edu
SHELBY, Robert .... 812-488-2949 161 A
rs262@evansville.edu
SHELDAHL, Tania .... 928-776-2128.. 16 M
tania.sheldahl@yc.edu
SHELDON, Al .... 541-956-7440 376 D
asheldon@roguecc.edu
SHELDON, Debbie, L .... 906-487-3112 227 E
dlassila@mtu.edu
SHELDON, Jane .... 308-865-8427 269 I
sheldonj@unk.edu
SHELDON, Karen .... 859-371-9393 179 A
ksheldon@beckfield.edu
SHELDON, Michael .... 207-221-4591 196 G
msheldon@une.edu
SHELDON, Pamela .... 630-620-2188 145 D
psheldon@seminary.edu
SHELDON, Richard .... 212-774-0778 306 A
rsheldon@mmm.edu
SHELDON, Scott .... 732-247-5241 279 D
ssheldon@nbts.edu
SHELDON, Todd .... 402-363-5601 270 E
tlsheldon@york.edu
SHELEK-FURBEE,
Katherine .... 304-829-7189 487 G
kshelek-furbee@bethanywv.edu
SHELL, Cathy .... 828-898-8740 330 E
shell@lmc.edu
SHELL, Chandrea .... 423-461-8756 422 J
chshell@milligan.edu
SHELL, Christina .... 734-487-2382 223 H
cshell@emich.edu
SHELL, Martin .... 650-724-4186.. 65 J
mshell@stanford.edu
SHELL, Martin .... 650-723-4186.. 65 J
mshell@stanford.edu
SHELLABARGER,
Roxanne .... 423-648-2416 423 K
rshellabarger@richmont.edu
SHELLAWAY, Ruby, Z .... 615-322-5155 428 D
ruby.shellaway@vanderbilt.edu
SHELLEDY, David, C ..... 210-567-8850 456 C
shelledyy@uthscsa.edu
SHELLEY, Ena, M .... 317-940-9752 153 F
eshelley@butler.edu
SHELLEY, Joseph .... 315-859-4169 301 C
jshelley@hamilton.edu
SHELLEY, Kate .... 903-813-2050 430 N
kshelley@austincollege.edu
SHELLEY, MargE .... 913-469-8500 174 D
mshelley@jccc.edu
SHELLEY, Marshall .... 303-762-6919.. 79 H
marshall.shelley@denverseminary.edu
SHELLEY, Staci .... 866-492-5336 244 F
staci.shelley@laureate.net
SHELLEY, Stephen .... 940-397-4110 440 F
stephen.shelley@msutexas.edu
SHELLEY, Tom .... 480-994-9244.. 16 B
tshelley@swiha.edu
SHELLLEY, Joe .... 315-859-4169 301 C
jshelley@hamilton.edu
SHELLUM, Doug .... 612-330-1033 233 K
shellum@augsburg.edu
SHELMERDINE,
Kathleen .... 239-687-5345.. 94 N
kshelmerdine@avemarialaw.edu
SHELPMAN, David .... 561-586-0121 100 O
SHELTON, Alice .... 317-955-6022 158 U
ashelton@marian.edu
SHELTON, Anita .... 217-581-2922 136 E
ashelton@eiu.edu
SHELTON, Austin .... 671-735-2918 505 E
shelton@uog.edu
SHELTON, Bill .... 712-325-3221 167 B
bshelton@iwcc.edu
SHELTON, Brad .... 541-346-2090 377 D
shelton@uoregon.edu
SHELTON, Cheryl .... 810-762-0553 228 C
cheryl.shelton@edtech.mcc.edu
SHELTON, Christi .... 256-782-5540.... 5 J
cshelton@jsu.edu
SHELTON, Christie .... 256-782-5276.... 5 J
cshelton@jsu.edu
SHELTON, Courtney ...... 800-280-0307 152 H
courtney.shelton@ace.edu
SHELTON, Courtney ...... 864-278-6281 412 G
sheltonc@smcsc.edu
SHELTON, Edward .... 636-649-5807 252 J
edward.shelton@eastcentral.edu
SHELTON, Jennifer .... 845-848-7500 298 D
jennifer.shelton@dc.edu
SHELTON, Joey .... 601-974-1226 247 B
sheltonjj@millsaps.edu
SHELTON, Julie .... 205-348-7917.... 7 G
jshelton@fa.ua.edu
SHELTON, Julie .... 931-363-9895 421 E
jshelton@martinmethodist.edu
SHELTON, JR.,
M. Dwight .... 540-231-8775 477 A
mdsjr@vt.edu
SHELTON, Marc .... 503-554-2869 373 C
mshelton@georgefox.edu
SHELTON, Mark .... 508-793-2371 208 B
mshelton@holycross.edu
SHELTON, Michelle .... 610-499-4239 403 B
mmshelton@widener.edu
SHELTON, Myles .... 409-944-1200 437 B
mshelton@gc.edu
SHELTON, Nellie, R .... 864-833-8213 411 I
nshelton@presby.edu
SHELTON, Rick .... 315-792-7100 321 E
richard.shelton@sunypoly.edu
SHELTON, Roosevelt ..... 601-979-8836 246 E
roosevelt.o.shelton@jsums.edu
SHELTON, Ryan .... 219-980-6793 156 E
rydshelt@iun.edu
SHELTON, Shawna .... 509-533-4566 480 B
shawna.shelton@sfcc.spokane.edu
SHELTON, Tamara .... 765-641-4204 153 B
tsshelton@anderson.edu
SHELTON, Tasha .... 847-467-3024 145 F
t-shelton@northwestern.edu
SHELTON, Terri, L .... 336-256-0232 343 A
shelton@uncg.edu
SHELTON, W. Brian .... 706-886-6831 125 D
bshelton@tfc.edu
SHELTON-CLARK, Anne . 662-621-4220 245 E
ashelton-clark@coahomacc.edu
SHEMWELL, Bridget ...... 870-762-3174.. 17 D
bshemwell@smail.anc.edu
SHEMWELL, James .... 870-762-3191.. 17 D
jshemwell@smail.anc.edu
SHEN, Chi .... 502-597-6083 182 H
chi.shen@kysu.edu
SHEN, Mark .... 626-571-5110.. 48 B
mys2016@les.edu
SHEN, Shiji .... 908-737-3470 278 E
sshen@kean.edu
SHEN, Sunny .... 516-739-1545 309 C
academic_dean@nyctcm.edu
SHEN-AUSTIN,
Christina .... 202-250-2419.. 91 E
christina.shen-austin@gallaudet.edu
SHENBERGER, Amy .... 940-565-2354 454 A
amy.shenberger@unt.edu
SHENDY, Joellen .... 240-684-2201 203 B
student-services@umuc.edu
SHENETTE, John .... 336-758-5000 344 D
shenetjj@wfu.edu
SHENK, Hans .... 740-857-1311 360 I
hshenk@rosedale.edu
SHENK, Sara, W .... 574-295-3726 152 I
swshenk@ambs.edu
SHENNAN, Andrew .... 781-283-3583 219 D
ashennan@wellesley.edu
SHENODA, Matthew ...... 401-454-6444 405 D
mshenoda@risd.edu
SHENOSKY, Joseph ...... 610-785-6520 398 A
jshenosky@scs.edu
SHEPARD, Barry .... 412-809-5100 396 H
shepard.barry@ptcollege.edu
SHEPARD, Brian .... 408-498-5135.. 38 F
bshepard@cogswell.edu
SHEPARD, Jenni .... 706-865-2134 125 E
jshepard@truett.edu
SHEPARD, Jim .... 413-538-2500 216 G
jshepard@mtholyoke.edu
SHEPARD, Joseph .... 575-538-6238 289 B
joseph.shepard@wnmu.edu
SHEPARD, Kathy, J .... 717-728-2261 381 B
kathyshepard@centralpenn.edu
SHEPARD, Kirsten .... 800-686-1883 222 E
kshepard@cleary.edu
SHEPARD, Nicole .... 912-583-3298 115 E
nshepard@bpc.edu
SHEPARD, Thom .... 650-433-3814.. 55 G
tshepard@paloaltou.edu
SHEPARD, William .... 734-487-0296 223 H
bill.shepard@emich.edu
SHEPARD RAWLINS,
Cindy .... 540-231-5419 467 F
crawlins@vcom.vt.edu
SHEPARD-SMITH,
Andrew .... 812-237-3088 155 G
andrew.shepard-smith@indstate.edu
SHEPARDSON,
J. Andrew .... 781-891-2161 206 D
ashepardson@bentley.edu
SHEPELOV, Sergey .... 503-491-7411 374 C
sergey.shepelov@mhcc.edu
SHEPELSKY, Ernie .... 718-429-6600 324 D
ernie.shepelsky@vaughn.edu
SHEPERIS, Carl .... 210-784-2500 448 A
csheperis@tamusa.edu
SHEPHARD, Janet .... 805-546-3915.. 41 A
janet_shephard@cuesta.edu
SHEPHARD, Landon, P . 407-582-4877 112 K
lshephard@valenciacollege.edu
SHEPHERD, Chad .... 636-922-8607 258 I
cshepherd@stchas.edu
SHEPHERD, Janet .... 319-208-5053 169 F
jshepherd@scciowa.edu
SHEPHERD, Jennifer, A 603-646-2223 273 E
jennifer.a.shepherd@dartmouth.edu
SHEPHERD, Jerry .... 765-677-1903 157 D
jerry.shepherd@indwes.edu
SHEPHERD, Joseph, E ... 626-395-6100.. 29 C
joseph.e.shepherd@caltech.edu
SHEPHERD, Justin .... 404-727-0692 117 F
justin.shepherd@emory.edu
SHEPHERD, Karla, M .... 410-837-4760 204 B
kshepherd@ubalt.edu
SHEPHERD, Kila .... 406-791-5977 265 H
kila.shepherd@uprovidence.edu
SHEPHERD,
Margaret, A .... 206-399-1496 485 F
mshep@uw.edu
SHEPHERD, Misty .... 407-882-1225 109 E
misty.shepherd@ucf.edu
SHEPHERD, Sara .... 252-334-2010 331 D
sara.shepherd@macuniversity.edu
SHEPHERD, Stacy .... 318-371-3035 187 I
stacyshepherd@nwltc.edu
SHEPHERD, Steve .... 417-690-2569 251 E
shepherd@cofo.edu
SHEPHERD, Sue .... 330-363-6347 348 D
admissions@aultmancollege.edu
SHEPHERD, Thomas ..... 661-946-2274.. 73 G
SHEPLER, Kent .... 815-967-7307 147 F
kshepler@rockfordcareercollege.edu
SHEPPARD, Andy .... 229-226-1621 125 C
asheppard@thomasu.edu
SHEPPARD, Beth .... 678-839-6370 126 E
bsheppar@westga.edu

SHEPPARD, Diane .... 956-296-1424 455 D
diane.sheppard@utrgv.edu
SHEPPARD, Foster .... 304-384-5258 490 A
fsheppard@concord.edu
SHEPPARD, Kirsten .... 865-273-8991 421 F
kirsten.sheppard@maryvillecollege.edu
SHEPPARD, Lyle .... 910-630-7225 331 C
lsheppard@methodist.edu
SHEPPARD, Ray .... 910-879-5542 332 D
rsheppard@bladencc.edu
SHEPPARD, Varinya ...... 315-801-3014 313 G
vsheppar@secon.edu
SHEPPICK, Joyce .... 724-938-4430 394 B
sheppick@calu.edu
SHEPPLEY, Lisa .... 410-225-2237 199 H
lsheppley@mica.edu
SHEPROW, Lauren .... 631-632-4896 317 D
lauren.sheprow@stonybrook.edu
SHEPSON, Paul .... 631-632-8781 317 D
paul.shepson@stonybrook.edu
SHEPTAK, Juliann .... 724-287-8711 380 A
julie.sheptak@bc3.edu
SHEPTOCK, Becci .... 703-416-1441 466 F
bsheptock@divinemercy.edu
SHER, Anna .... 831-459-4302.. 70 B
asher@ucsc.edu
SHER, Ephraim, Y .... 845-434-5240 326 K
esher@fallsburgyeshiva.com
SHERADIN, Pamela .... 315-364-3260 325 B
psheradin@wells.edu
SHERAM, Norma .... 903-675-7350 452 B
nsheram@tvcc.edu
SHERAR, Megan .... 419-289-5943 348 A
msherar@ashland.edu
SHERBOURNE, Brenda .. 580-559-5204 366 C
bsherbrn@ecok.edu
SHERBURNE, Gwen .... 651-523-2804 236 A
gsherburne@hamline.edu
SHEREN, Deborah .... 216-373-5347 358 B
dsheren@ndc.edu
SHERER, Michael .... 574-535-7406 155 A
msherer@goshen.edu
SHERER, Sara .... 330-823-2761 363 B
sherersj@mountunion.edu
SHERER, Todd .... 404-727-5550 117 F
ttshere@emory.edu
SHERF, Thomas .... 215-702-4848 380 D
tsherf@cairn.edu
SHERFESEE,
Kimberly, B .... 843-349-2138 408 C
ksherf@coastal.edu
SHERIDAN, Chris .... 216-368-2774 349 F
chris.sheridan@case.edu
SHERIDAN, Heidi .... 732-255-0400 280 A
hsheridan@ocean.edu
SHERIDAN, Mark .... 806-742-1832 451 B
mark.sheridan@ttu.edu
SHERIDAN, Terence .... 334-387-3877.... 4 C
terencesheridan@amridgeuniversity.edu
SHERIFF, Brad .... 479-788-7035.. 21 H
brad.sheriff@uafs.edu
SHERIFF, Sarah, M .... 717-245-1787 382 F
sheriffs@dickinson.edu
SHERLEY, Rachel .... 785-320-4544 175 D
rachelsherley@manhattantech.edu
SHERLIN, Joe, H .... 423-439-4210 419 J
sherlin@etsu.edu
SHERLIN, Merideth .... 701-231-9653 345 G
merideth.sherlin@ndsu.edu
SHERLOCK, Julia, B ...... 989-774-3068 222 C
julia.b.sherlock@cmich.edu
SHERLOCK, Rick .... 419-448-2171 353 H
rsherloc@heidelberg.edu
SHERMAN, Alan .... 617-559-8690 210 C
asherman@hebrewcollege.edu
SHERMAN, Alexis .... 402-399-2365 266 F
asherman@csm.edu
SHERMAN, Alison .... 401-709-8417 405 D
asherman@risd.edu
SHERMAN, Ann, M .... 415-338-1111.. 34 A
SHERMAN, Brian .... 318-798-4117 189 D
brian.sherman@lsus.edu
SHERMAN, Curt .... 402-643-7369 266 G
curt.sherman@cune.edu
SHERMAN, Daniel .... 713-500-3270 456 B
daniel.sherman@uth.tmc.edu
SHERMAN, Douglas ...... 401-739-5000 405 A
dsherman@neit.edu
SHERMAN, Douglas, H . 401-739-5000 405 A
dsherman@neit.edu
SHERMAN, Elma, C ...... 574-372-5100 155 B
shermaec@grace.edu
SHERMAN, Erin, L .... 210-486-4932 429 E
esherman6@alamo.edu
SHERMAN, Garett .... 207-834-7571 196 C
garett.sherman@maine.edu
SHERMAN, George .... 718-631-6273 295 D
gsherman@qcc.cuny.edu
SHERMAN, George, M .. 978-232-2009 209 B
gsherman@endicott.edu
SHERMAN, Glen .... 973-720-2761 284 I
shermang@wpunj.edu
SHERMAN, Heather .... 610-921-2381 378 C
SHERMAN, Hugh .... 740-593-2000 359 G
shermanh@ohio.edu
SHERMAN, Jeannine ..... 262-524-7242 492 E
shermanj@carrollu.edu
SHERMAN, Jennifer ...... 719-549-3362.. 81 K
jennifer.sherman@pueblocc.edu
SHERMAN, JR .... 239-489-9414 100 A
jrsherman@fsw.edu
SHERMAN, Julee .... 660-248-6203 251 B
jsherman@centralmethodist.edu
SHERMAN, Lori Ann ..... 906-524-8414 226 A
lsherman@kbocc.edu
SHERMAN, Mike .... 330-941-7281 365 C
msherman02@ysu.edu
SHERMAN, Peter .... 970-943-3000.. 84 D
psherman@western.edu
SHERMAN, Renee .... 207-621-3041 196 A
renee.sherman@maine.edu
SHERMAN, Robin .... 207-581-5401 195 J
robin.sherman@maine.edu
SHERMAN, Rush .... 502-585-9911 184 D
rsherman@spalding.edu
SHERMAN, Sharon .... 609-896-5120 281 B
sherman@rider.edu
SHERMAN, Sherry .... 828-766-1317 336 A
ssherman@mayland.edu
SHERMAN, Suzanne .... 941-487-4225 109 D
sherman@ncf.edu
SHERMAN, Todd .... 907-474-7231.. 10 A
tlsherman@alaska.edu
SHERMAN, Zahida .... 440-775-8462 358 C
zsherman@oberlin.edu
SHERMAN-HECKLER,
Wendy, R .... 614-823-1556 360 A
wshermanheckler@otterbein.edu
SHEROW, Ernestene ...... 256-761-6315.... 7 B
esherow@talladega.edu
SHERR, Karin, K .... 619-961-4240.. 67 E
ksherr@tjsl.edu
SHERR, Kimberly .... 610-606-4666 381 A
SHERRARD-HANNON,
Vida .... 360-596-5249 485 B
vsherrard-hannon@spscc.edu
SHERRICK, Rebecca, L . 630-844-5476 132 D
sherrick@aurora.edu
SHERRILL, Audrey .... 704-922-2383 334 F
sherrill.audrey@gaston.edu
SHERRILL, Brad .... 517-355-9672 227 D
sherril2@msu.edu
SHERRILL, Erin .... 404-504-1993 122 J
esherrill@oglethorpe.edu
SHERRILL, Jason .... 517-607-2576 225 A
jsherrill@hillsdale.edu
SHERRILL, Regina, B .... 256-765-4705.... 8 E
rbsherrill@una.edu
SHERRILL, Zach .... 405-789-7661 370 B
zachary.sherrill@swcu.edu
SHERROD, Kim, L .... 262-524-7124 492 E
ksherrod@carrollu.edu
SHERRON, Catherine .... 859-344-3387 184 F
catherine.sherron@thomasmore.edu
SHERRY, J.P .... 916-568-3042.. 50 E
sherryj@losrios.edu
SHERRY, Michael .... 716-652-8900 292 I
msherry@cks.edu
SHERSTAD, Brian, P ..... 616-538-2330 224 C
bsherstad@gracechristian.edu
SHERWIN, Stacey .... 406-275-4931 265 F
stacey_sherwin@skc.edu
SHERWOOD, David, G .. 262-646-6534 495 B
dsherwood@nashotah.edu
SHERWOOD, Emily, S .. 574-807-7023 153 E
emily.sherwood@bethelaniversity.edu
SHERWOOD, Jim .... 978-934-3313 211 G
james_sherwood@uml.edu
SHERWOOD, Kim .... 316-322-3227 171 G
ksherwood@butlercc.edu
SHERWOOD,
Mary Frances .... 337-421-6926 188 D
mary.sherwood@sowela.edu
SHERWOOD, Sarah, K .. 508-767-7343 205 D
sk.sherwood@assumption.edu
SHERWOOD, Timothy ... 248-341-2053 229 A
tasherwo@oaklandcc.edu
SHETH, Ruchi .... 972-721-5395 452 D
rsheth@udallas.edu
SHETLEY, Shane .... 620-862-5252 171 B
SHETTY, Devdas .... 202-274-5220.. 93 C
devdas.shetty@udc.edu
SHEUCRAFT, Derrek, G . 615-353-3272 425 D
derrek.sheucraft@nscc.edu
SHEVACH, Shirley .... 718-518-6655 294 B
sshevach@hostos.cuny.edu
SHEVEY, Wayne .... 414-443-8723 498 O
wayne.shevey@wlc.edu
SHEW, Rick .... 828-759-4635 332 G
rshew@cccti.edu
SHEWAN, Thomas, F ..... 512-245-2148 450 E
tfs21@txstate.edu
SHEWMAKER, Jennifer .. 325-674-2700 429 B
jws02b@acu.edu
SHEWMAKER, Stephen . 325-674-2317 429 B
sbs02a@acu.edu
SHIA, Mary .... 781-239-3123 214 E
mshia@massbay.edu
SHIAVO, Donna .... 508-531-2106 212 B
dschiavo@bridgew.edu
SHIBATA, Keri Kei .... 574-631-5559 161 C
kshibata@nd.edu
SHIBER, Cheryl .... 908-709-7511 284 C
cheryl.shiber@ucc.edu
SHIBLEY, Deborah .... 254-526-1331 432 H
deborah.shibley@ctcd.edu
SHIBLEY, Lisa, R .... 717-871-7871 395 D
lisa.shibley@millersville.edu
SHIBLEY, Robert, G ...... 716-829-3981 316 F
rshibley@buffalo.edu
SHIDELER, Lorri, P .... 814-641-3605 386 H
shidell@juniata.edu
SHIDLER, Linda .... 618-395-7777 138 I
shidlerl@iecc.edu
SHIEH, Charles .... 863-683-2975 113 B
shiehcs@webber.edu
SHIELDS, Cynthia .... 303-914-6905.. 82 C
cynthia.shields@rrcc.edu
SHIELDS, Dennis, J ...... 608-342-1234 497 D
shieldsd@uwplatt.edu
SHIELDS, Francis .... 860-439-2570.. 86 H
fjshi@conncoll.edu
SHIELDS, Gerald .... 304-929-5012 489 C
gshields@newriver.edu
SHIELDS, Gregory, J ..... 937-433-3410 352 M
gshields@fortiscollege.edu
SHIELDS, James .... 985-867-2234 190 F
jshields@sjasc.edu
SHIELDS, Joseph .... 740-593-0370 359 G
shieldj1@ohio.edu
SHIELDS, Kathryn .... 336-316-2825 329 E
shieldsk@guilford.edu
SHIELDS, Laurie .... 410-386-8442 197 G
lshields@carrollcc.edu
SHIELDS, Loretta .... 941-487-5020 109 D
lshields@ncf.edu
SHIELDS, Mathew .... 718-405-3215 296 G
mathew.shields@mountsaintvincent.edu
SHIELDS, Matthew .... 718-405-3754 296 G
matthew.shields@mountsaintvincent.edu
SHIELDS, Michael .... 708-239-4872 150 F
michael.shields@trnty.edu
SHIELDS, Ronald .... 936-294-2771 450 C
rshield@shsu.edu
SHIELDS, Sally .... 309-649-6250 150 A
sally.shields@src.edu
SHIELDS, Theodosia, T . 919-530-5233 342 A
tshields@nccu.edu
SHIELDS, Todd, G .... 479-575-4804.. 21 G
tshield@uark.edu
SHIELDS, Tonya .... 256-840-4165.... 3 F
tonya.shields@snead.edu
SHIELDS, Vickie .... 702-992-2500 271 C
provost@nsc.edu
SHIELL, William .... 630-620-2101 145 D
president@seminary.edu
SHIELS, Michael .... 262-691-7823 500 H
mshiels@wctc.edu
SHIFERRAW, Mahtem ... 310-665-6936.. 54 I
mshiferraw@otis.edu
SHIFLETT, Christopher .. 303-329-6355.. 78 K
assistantdean@cstcm.edu
SHIFLETT, Matthew, K ... 304-637-1326 487 I
shiflettm@dewv.edu
SHIGEMOTO, Steven ...... 808-845-9166 129 B
sshigemo@hawaii.edu
SHIH, Alan .... 212-650-7909 293 D
ashih@ccny.cuny.edu
SHIH, Li-Fang .... 518-608-8362 299 G
lshih@excelsior.edu
SHIH, Lily .... 713-798-8825 431 I
llshih@bcm.edu
SHILL, Deb .... 641-269-3230 165 J
shilldeb@grinnell.edu
SHILLAM, Casey, R .... 503-943-8143 377 E
shillamc@up.edu
SHILLER, Dana .... 724-503-1001 402 E
dshiller@washjeff.edu
SHILLET, Gary .... 212-592-2644 315 H
gshillet@sva.edu
SHILLING, Chad .... 406-293-2721 263 F
cshilling@fvcc.edu
SHILLING, Jeff .... 831-459-5591.. 70 B
shilling@ucsc.edu
SHILLING, Joseph .... 804-523-5230 474 H
jshilling@reynolds.edu
SHILLITANI, Matt .... 973-748-9000 276 A
matt_shillitani@bloomfield.edu
SHILTS, Jacob .... 305-237-8797 103 D
jshilts@mdc.edu
SHIM, Soyeon .... 608-262-4847 496 C
soyeon.shim@wisc.edu
SHIMAZAKI, Leslie .... 619-388-2873.. 60 D
lshimaza@sdccd.edu
SHIMEK, Gary, S .... 414-277-7181 494 G
shimek@msoe.edu
SHIMIZU, Stacey .... 309-556-3190 139 G
abroad@iwu.edu
SHIMOKAWA, Leila .... 808-689-2603 128 G
lwai@hawaii.edu
SHIMP, Sandy .... 239-280-1669.. 94 O
sandy.shimp@avemaria.edu
SHIN, Amy .... 630-829-6625 132 E
ashin@ben.edu
SHIN, David, H .... 714-527-0691.. 42 E
info@evangelia.edu
SHIN, Jee, Y .... 636-327-4645 255 L
SHIN, John .... 703-323-5690 477 D
SHIN, Seonmook, P ...... 213-385-2322.. 75 D
seonmook@wmu.edu
SHIN, Tia .... 213-387-4242.. 47 I
SHIN, Yae Oee .... 714-517-1945.. 27 A
SHIN, Yong .... 703-526-6904 469 C
yong.shin@marymount.edu
SHIN LEE, Kyunglim ...... 202-885-8620.. 93 E
kshinlee@wesleyseminary.edu
SHINAR, Ori .... 914-674-7233 306 F
oshinar@mercy.edu
SHINAR, Tammera .... 530-895-2555.. 27 F
shinarta@butte.edu
SHINBERGER,
Darcie, R .... 309-298-1993 152 D
dr-shinberger@wiu.edu
SHINDE, Prashant .... 847-635-1711 145 G
pshinde@oakton.edu
SHINEW, Dawn .... 419-372-7403 348 H
dshinew@bgsu.edu
SHINGLE, Barbara .... 814-472-3170 398 B
bshingle@francis.edu
SHINGLE, Jean .... 610-647-4400 386 C
jshingle@immaculata.edu
SHINN, David .... 217-228-5432 146 F
shinnda@quincy.edu
SHINN, Jeremiah .... 208-426-1224 129 I
jeremiahshinn@boisestate.edu
SHINN, Jeremiah .... 225-578-3607 188 I
jbs@lsu.edu
SHINNERL, Clare .... 415-502-4457.. 69 E
clare.shinnerl@ucsf.edu
SHINOL, James .... 516-364-0808 309 A
jshinol@nycollege.edu
SHINOMOTO, Linda ...... 617-989-4193 219 E
shinomotol@wit.edu
SHINTANI, David .... 775-784-1740 271 F
shintani@unr.edu
SHIOZAKI, Linda .... 510-809-1444.. 45 K
SHIPKA, Milan .... 907-474-7246.. 10 A
mpshipka@alaska.edu
SHIPLEY, Aletha .... 614-287-2642 351 E
ashipley@cscc.edu
SHIPLEY, Amber .... 304-829-7064 487 G
ashipley@bethanywv.edu
SHIPLEY, Emily .... 513-745-4858 365 B
shipleye1@xavier.edu
SHIPLEY, Heather, J ..... 210-458-5190 455 E
heather.shipley@utsa.edu
SHIPLEY, Robert .... 918-631-3092 371 E
robert-shipley@utulsa.edu

SHRUM, Joshua, W ...... 724-805-2820 398 F
joshua.shrum@stvincent.edu
SHRYOCK, Dawn .... 217-854-3231 132 I
SHTAMLER, Victoriya .... 718-522-9073 290 C
vshtamler@asa.edu
SHTROMBERG, Alisa ..... 425-739-8389 482 A
alisa.shtromberg@lwtech.edu
SHUBERT, David .... 316-942-4291 175 I
shubertd@newmanu.edu
SHUBERT, Lisa, A .... 507-344-7324 234 B
lisa.shubert@blc.edu
SHUBERT, Stephen .... 810-762-0501 228 C
stephen.shubert@mcc.edu
SHUCHAT, Rena .... 937-512-2919 361 A
rena.shuchat@sinclair.edu
SHUDAK, Nicholas .... 402-375-7379 268 G
nishuda1@wsc.edu
SHUEY, Heather, M ...... 570-326-3761 393 G
hms27@pct.edu
SHUEY, Jill .... 716-286-8029 310 D
jshuey@niagara.edu
SHUFORD, Bettina .... 919-966-4045 342 D
bcshufor@email.unc.edu
SHUFORD, Beverly .... 907-786-4622.... 9 H
uaa.administrative.services@alaska.edu
SHUFORD, Eddie .... 828-652-0652 336 B
eddieshuford@mcdowelltech.edu
SHUGART, Michael .... 405-682-1611 367 H
mshugart@occc.edu
SHUGART, Sandy, C ...... 407-582-3400 112 K
sshugart@valenciacollege.edu
SHUGATS-CUMMINGS,
Alissa .... 716-614-6293 310 C
acummings@niagaracc.suny.edu
SHULER, Eric .... 301-846-2674 198 E
eshuler@frederick.edu
SHULER, Peggy .... 803-321-5117 411 D
peggy.shuler@newberry.edu
SHULL, Roger .... 806-894-9611 443 I
rshull@southplainscollege.edu
SHULL, Roxanna .... 260-459-4600 157 E
rshull@ibcfortwayne.edu
SHULMAN, Brian .... 973-275-2168 283 B
brian.shulman@shu.edu
SHULMAN, David .... 954-201-7933.. 95 H
dshulman@broward.edu
SHULMAN, Sharon .... 718-997-5888 295 C
sharon.shulman@qc.cuny.edu
SHULMAN, Yaakov .... 732-367-1060 275 J
yshulman@bmg.edu
SHULTES, Kenneth, E .... 717-245-1247 382 F
shultes@dickinson.edu
SHULTIS, Barb .... 413-528-7612 205 F
bshultis@simons-rock.edu
SHULTS, Christopher .... 212-220-1400 293 A
cshults@bmcc.cuny.edu
SHULTS, Kari .... 918-595-8845 370 E
kari.culp@tulsacc.edu
SHULTZ, Dee .... 970-339-6434.. 76 G
dee.shultz@aims.edu
SHULTZ, John .... 913-758-6329 177 F
john.shultz@stmary.edu
SHULTZ, Kari .... 423-236-2484 424 B
kshultz@southern.edu
SHULTZ, Katie .... 727-341-3002 106 E
shultz.katie@spcollege.edu
SHULTZ, Norah .... 619-594-6881.. 33 E
nshultz@sdsu.edu
SHULTZ, Terry .... 607-431-4111 301 D
schultzt@hartwick.edu
SHULTZ, JR., Walter, J . 570-326-3761 393 G
walter.shultz@pct.edu
SHULUK, William .... 239-489-9356 100 A
wshuluk@fsw.edu
SHUMACK, Gareth .... 516-876-3210 319 A
shumackg@oldwestbury.edu
SHUMAKE, Connie, C ... 502-852-3551 185 C
ccshum01@louisville.edu
SHUMAKER, Carrie .... 313-593-5454 231 F
shumakr@umich.edu
SHUMAKER, Carrie .... 313-593-5000 231 F
shumakr@umich.edu
SHUMAKER, Deb .... 989-275-5000 226 B
deb.shumaker@kirtland.edu
SHUMAKER, Ryan .... 619-388-2737.. 60 D
rshumaker@sdccd.edu
SHUMAN, Jenny .... 478-296-6117 122 H
jshuman@oftc.edu
SHUMAN, Kelli, R .... 605-394-1203 417 B
kelli.shuman@sdsmt.edu
SHUMAN, Michaeline .... 570-372-4325 399 C
shumanm@susqu.edu

SHUMAN, Richard .... 713-525-6974 454 H
shumanr@stthom.edu
SHUMAN, Shari, A .... 904-620-2002 110 A
sshuman@unf.edu
SHUMAN, Victoria .... 304-793-6898 491 A
vshuman@osteo.wvsom.edu
SHUMATE, Connie .... 304-384-5366 490 A
cshumate@concord.edu
SHUMATE, David .... 480-245-7903.. 12 N
david.shumate@ibcs.edu
SHUMSKAYA, Tatsiana .. 973-300-2267 283 E
tshumskaya@sussex.edu
SHUPALA, Christine ...... 956-665-4025 455 D
christine.shupala@utrgv.edu
SHUPE, Gary .... 217-641-4505 140 A
gshupe@jwcc.edu
SHUPE, John .... 845-257-3335 317 B
shupej@newpaltz.edu
SHUPENUS, Sarah .... 217-424-6340 143 H
sshupenus@millikin.edu
SHUR, Luba .... 401-598-5155 404 I
luba.shur@jwu.edu
SHURANCE, Mike .... 949-214-3363.. 40 F
mike.shurance@cui.edu
SHURER, Brooke .... 919-760-8429 331 B
shurerb@meredith.edu
SHURLEY, Britton .... 270-534-3243 182 F
britton.shurley@kctcs.edu
SHURTLEFF, Courtney ... 508-286-3425 220 A
shurtleff_courtney@wheatoncollege.edu
SHURTZ, Mary Ann .... 703-539-6890 472 A
mshurtz@stratford.edu
SHURTZ, Richard .... 703-539-6890 472 A
rshurtz@stratford.edu
SHUSTER, Arthur .... 828-771-3773 344 E
ashuster@warren-wilson.edu
SHUTE, Paula .... 239-304-2955.. 94 O
paula.shute@avemaria.edu
SHUTT, Barbara, C .... 207-859-5415 193 E
barbara.shutt@colby.edu
SHUTT, Gary .... 405-744-6260 368 B
gary.shutt@okstate.edu
SHUTTER, Jamie, L .... 573-882-6601 261 B
shutterj@health.missouri.edu
SIAHMAKOUN, Azad ..... 812-877-8400 159 J
siahmako@rose-hulman.edu
SIALOFI, Amanda .... 907-852-1823.... 9 F
amanda.sialofi@ilisagvik.edu
SIAMPOS, Christa .... 314-421-0949 260 G
csiampos@siba.edu
SIBAL, Jennifer, R .... 308-630-6571 270 D
sibalj@wncc.edu
SIBENALLER, Jim .... 773-508-7665 142 D
jsibena@luc.edu
SIBENALLER-WOODALL,
Beth .... 712-324-5061 168 G
beths@nwicc.edu
SIBERT, Kimberley .... 740-366-9233 349 H
ksibert@cotc.edu
SIBERT, Sonja .... 775-753-2181 271 B
sonja.sibert@gbcnv.edu
SIBLEY, Dedra .... 321-433-7060.. 97 I
sibleyd@easternflorida.edu
SIBLEY, Donna, M .... 508-373-9712 206 B
donna.sibley@becker.edu
SIBLEY, Karen, H .... 401-863-1236 404 E
karen_sibley@brown.edu
SIBLEY, Scott .... 410-337-6044 198 G
scott.sibley@goucher.edu
SICARD, OP,
Kenneth, R .... 401-865-2055 405 B
ksicard@providence.edu
SICARD, Rex, E .... 785-243-1435 172 F
rsicard@cloud.edu
SICIENSKY, Emily .... 931-540-2704 424 G
esciensky@columbiastate.edu
SICIENSKY, Emily .... 931-540-2704 424 G
esiciensky@columbiastate.edu
SICILIANO, Stephen, N . 231-995-1373 228 G
ssiciliano@nmc.edu
SICK, Volker .... 734-763-1290 231 E
vsick@umich.edu
SIDDALL, David .... 641-784-5138 165 H
davids1@graceland.edu
SIDDARAJU, Raj .... 309-649-6387 150 A
raj.siddaraju@src.edu
SIDDENS, Nancy .... 217-732-3168 141 H
nsiddens@lincolnchristian.edu
SIDDIQI, Khalid .... 678-915-5519 120 L
ksiddiqi@kennesaw.edu
SIDDIQI, Melanie .... 909-652-6780.. 36 A
melanie.siddiqi@chaffey.edu
SIDDIQI, Muddassir ..... 713-718-6041 437 I
muddassir.siddiqi@hccs.edu

SIDEBOTTOM, Daniel .... 607-753-2501 318 D
daniel.sidebottom@cortland.edu
SIDERAS, John, F .... 216-368-4340 349 F
john.sideras@case.edu
SIDERS, Angie .... 765-455-9515 156 D
asiders@iuk.edu
SIDES, Bobbie .... 803-321-5102 411 D
bobbie.sides@newberry.edu
SIDES, Courtney, M ...... 361-570-4354 453 C
sidesc@uhv.edu
SIDES, Emilee .... 870-733-6701.. 17 H
essides@asumidsouth.edu
SIDES, Tevian .... 325-574-7640 458 E
tevian.sides@wtc.edu
SIDHU, Elda .... 702-895-5185 271 E
elda.sidhu@unlv.edu
SIDLE, Meg .... 606-218-5290 185 D
margaretsidle@upike.edu
SIDLE, Stuart .... 203-932-7339.. 89 A
ssidle@newhaven.edu
SIDLER, Sherri .... 312-362-6727 135 I
ssidler@depaul.edu
SIDOCK, Andrew .... 217-479-7066 142 I
andrew.sidock@mac.edu
SIDOR, Stanley .... 352-365-3523 102 T
sidors@lssc.edu
SIDORKIN, Alexander ... 916-278-6639.. 32 E
sidorkin@csus.edu
SIEBEN, Jeffrey .... 609-497-7789 280 D
jeffrey.sieben@ptsem.edu
SIEBENBERG, Tammy ... 509-574-4984 487 A
tsiebenberg@yvcc.edu
SIEBENMORGEN, Tom ... 501-450-1333.. 19 F
siebenmorgen@hendrix.edu
SIEBENS, Libby .... 509-682-6436 486 E
lsiebens@wvc.edu
SIEBENS, Mackie .... 845-758-7472 290 G
msiebens@bard.edu
SIEBERKROB,
Deanna, J .... 412-578-6423 380 E
djsieberkrob@carlow.edu
SIEBERT, Alex .... 513-562-8749 347 K
asiebert@artacademy.edu
SIEBERT, Mary Anne ..... 501-450-1372.. 19 F
siebert@hendrix.edu
SIEBUHR, Bryan .... 303-273-3092.. 78 I
bsiebuhr@mines.edu
SIECZKIEWICZ, Robert .. 570-372-4329 399 C
sieczkiewicz@susqu.edu
SIEDZIK, Richard .... 401-232-6505 404 F
rsiedzik@bryant.edu
SIEFERT, Tom .... 773-291-6412 134 E
tsiefert@ccc.edu
SIEFKEN, Rob .... 212-924-5900 322 B
rsiefken@swedishinstitute.edu
SIEGA-RIZ, Anna Maria 413-545-1079 211 D
asiegariz@umass.edu
SIEGEL, Christine .... 203-254-4000.. 86 I
csiegel@fairfield.edu
SIEGEL, Jane .... 856-225-6143 281 G
jasiegel@camden.rutgers.edu
SIEGEL, Jessica, M .... 716-896-0700 324 E
jsiegel@villa.edu
SIEGEL, Larry .... 978-934-2107 211 G
laurence_siegel@uml.edu
SIEGFRIED, Jessica .... 435-283-7169 461 C
jessica.siegfried@snow.edu
SIEGFRIED,
Kenneth (Ziggy) .... 661-654-2200.. 30 E
ksiegfried@csub.edu
SIEGLER, Cynthia .... 413-572-8545 213 D
csiegler@westfield.ma.edu
SIEGMANN, Starla, C ... 414-443-8862 498 O
starla.siegmann@wlc.edu
SIEMANN, Thomas .... 510-666-8248.. 24 D
SIEMBOR, Michael .... 315-781-3388 302 A
siembor@hws.edu
SIEMENS, Henrietta .... 559-453-7100.. 43 G
henrietta.siemens@fresno.edu
SIEMINSKI, Randy, B .... 315-386-7335 320 E
sieminski@canton.edu
SIEMS, Blaire .... 641-683-5115 166 C
blaire.siems@indianhills.edu
SIEN, Edward .... 917-493-4469 305 I
esien@msmnyc.edu
SIENA, Steven .... 516-628-5558 319 A
sienas@oldwestbury.edu
SIERACKI, Pamela .... 716-652-8900 292 I
psieracki@cks.edu
SIERKOWSKI, Dave .... 219-464-6906 162 A
dave.sierkowski@valpo.edu
SIERRA, Elizabeth .... 610-989-1306 402 B
esierra@vfmac.edu

SIERRA, Mayra, I .... 787-751-0160 507 F
msierra@cmpr.pr.gov
SIES, Susan .... 410-386-8325 197 G
ssies@carrollcc.edu
SIESING, Gina .... 610-526-5272 379 E
gsiesing@brynmawr.edu
SIETSEMA, Adriane .... 641-648-4611 166 J
adriane.sietsema@iavalley.edu
SIEVERDING, John .... 605-770-0700 415 G
john.sieverding@mitchelltech.edu
SIEVERS, Allison .... 303-963-3437.. 77 G
asievers@ccu.edu
SIEVING, Allison .... 253-964-6531 483 D
asieving@pierce.ctc.edu
SIFFERLEN, Ned, J .... 937-512-2510 361 A
ned.sifferlen@sinclair.edu
SIFRI, Tatiana .... 630-637-5161 144 H
tsifri@noctrl.edu
SIFTAR, Michael .... 918-595-8123 370 E
michael.siftar@tulsacc.edu
SIFUENTES-JÁUREGUI,
Ben .... 848-932-7865 282 A
jauregui@echo.rutgers.edu
SIGALA, Al .... 503-491-7548 374 C
al.sigala@mhcc.edu
SIGAUKE, Erica .... 417-667-8181 252 A
esigauke@cottey.edu
SIGGERS, Julian, F .... 215-898-4050 400 K
siggers@upenn.edu
SIGGERS, Lauretta .... 617-873-0170 207 F
lauretta.siggers@cambridgecollege.edu
SIGLER, Haley .... 540-458-8400 478 A
siglerh@wlu.edu
SIGLER, Tim, M .... 919-573-5350 340 F
tsigler@shepherds.edu
SIGLER, Todd, D .... 704-894-2915 328 F
tosigler@davidson.edu
SIGMAN, David .... 414-847-3263 494 F
davidsigman@miad.edu
SIGMAN, Gee .... 864-596-9094 409 B
gee.sigman@converse.edu
SIGMAN, Stuart .... 650-493-4430.. 64 A
stuart.sigman@sofia.edu
SIGMON, Georgia .... 252-493-7783 336 H
gsigmon@email.pittcc.edu
SIGMON, JR.,
Kenneth, E .... 336-334-7600 341 F
kesigmon@ncat.edu
SIGNOR, Mary .... 212-998-6807 310 B
mary.signor@nyu.edu
SIGNORELLO, John .... 973-761-9615 283 B
john.signorello@shu.edu
SIGNORELLO, Rose .... 713-525-3162 454 H
signorr@stthom.edu
SIGRIST, Kim .... 816-271-4237 257 A
ksigrist@missouriwestern.edu
SIGUE, Mark .... 301-891-4040 204 C
msigue@wau.edu
SIGURDSON, Chris, W . 520-621-4608.. 16 G
sig@email.arizona.edu
SIGWING, Marty .... 620-242-0400 175 F
sigwingm@mcpherson.edu
SIGWORTH, Steve .... 713-798-2500 431 I
sigworth@bcm.edu
SII, Shelley .... 626-571-5110.. 48 B
shelley@les.edu
SIIRA, Sandra .... 414-382-6011 492 A
sandra.siira@alverno.edu
SIKER, Malika .... 414-955-4493 494 C
msiker@mcw.edu
SIKES, Bruce .... 479-667-4046.. 18 C
bsikes1@atu.edu
SIKES, Julie .... 704-290-5893 337 I
jsikes@spcc.edu
SIKES, Pamela, J .... 619-260-4595.. 71 J
psikes@sandiego.edu
SIKES, Steddon, L .... 402-363-5668 270 E
slsikes@york.edu
SIKORA, Jacqueline, L .. 304-333-3652 490 B
jacqueline.sikora@fairmontstate.edu
SIKORSKY, Charles .... 703-416-1441 466 F
csikorsky@divinemercy.edu
SILAGYI, Tyler .... 716-338-1188 303 D
tylersilagyi@mail.sunyjcc.edu
SILAK, Cathy .... 503-955-1001 372 I
csilak@cu-portland.edu
SILANSKIS, Theresa ...... 410-837-6838 204 B
tsilanskis@ubalt.edu
SILAS, Monique .... 205-929-6350.... 2 H
msilas@lawsonstate.edu
SILBER, Daniel .... 706-778-8500 123 B
dsilber@piedmont.edu
SILBER, Eric .... 512-313-3000 434 E
eric.silber@concordia.edu

SILBER, Jeffrey, A 607-255-2016 297 F jas9@cornell.edu
SILBERMAN, Gerald 717-361-3737 383 E silbermang@etown.edu
SILBERMAN, Gerald, L 610-683-4106 395 A silberma@kutztown.edu
SILBERSTEIN, Dara, J 607-777-2815 316 E lael@binghamton.edu
SILBERSTEIN, Jeffrey 212-659-9091 302 F jeffrey.silberstein@mssm.edu
SILBERSTEIN, Lloyd 213-740-1638 72 B lloyd.silberstein@usc.edu
SILCOX, Steve 269-927-7060 226 D ssilcox@lakemichigancollege.edu
SILCOX, Tammy 251-460-6437 8 F tsilcox@southalabama.edu
SILECCHIA, Anthony 509-359-6586 480 E asilecchia@ewu.edu
SILER, Cathy 317-955-6241 158 U csiler@marian.edu
SILER, Ginni 706-802-5136 118 E gsiler@highlands.edu
SILER, Kelby 513-244-4359 357 A kelby.siler@msj.edu
SILER, Keri, S 407-582-2867 112 K ksiler@valenciacollege.edu
SILER, Linda, K 616-538-2330 224 C lsiler@gracechristian.edu
SILER, Lisa 870-633-4480 19 B lsiler@eacc.edu
SILER, Ryan 920-403-3146 495 I ryan.siler@snc.edu
SILICIANO, John, A 607-255-6230 297 F jas83@cornell.edu
SILIS, Mark 617-253-3292 215 G
SILK, Dan 706-542-5813 125 G dsilk@police.uga.edu
SILK, Eleana 914-961-8313 315 C es@svots.edu
SILK, Elizabeth 708-524-6461 136 C esilk@dom.edu
SILK, Mary, L 692-625-4410 505 F msilk@cmi.edu
SILL, Nancy 209-575-6128 75 J silln@mjc.edu
SILLCOCKS, Emily 713-646-1824 444 B esillcocks@stcl.edu
SILLIMON, Laird, G 209-476-7840 66 G lgsillimon@clc.edu
SILMAN, Shawn 281-459-7673 443 D shawn.silman@sjcd.edu
SILVA, Adelina 210-485-0153 429 C asilva@alamo.edu
SILVA, Alan 317-955-6000 158 U ajsilva@marian.edu
SILVA, Alyson 954-262-5258 103 M asilva1@nova.edu
SILVA, Bobbye 832-559-4208 439 G bobbye.l.silva@lonestar.edu
SILVA, David, J 978-542-6246 213 C provost@salemstate.edu
SILVA, Efrain 760-355-6249 45 I efrain.silva@imperial.edu
SILVA, Elizabeth 619-260-2888 71 J registrar@sandiego.edu
SILVA, Griselda 773-838-7528 134 F gsilva24@ccc.edu
SILVA, Holli 207-509-7227 195 H hcostedio@unity.edu
SILVA, Jack 401-454-6480 405 D jsilva@risd.edu
SILVA, Jennifer 904-632-3141 100 B jen.silva@fscj.edu
SILVA, Jessica, L 401-456-8047 405 C jsilva@ric.edu
SILVA, Joseph 916-686-7400 29 J
SILVA, Lourdes 704-463-3062 339 E lourdes.silva@pfeiffer.edu
SILVA, Manuel, D 787-891-0925 508 K msilva@aguadilla.inter.edu
SILVA, Marcie 305-442-9223 103 F msilva@mru.edu
SILVA, Mariza 312-922-1884 142 H msilva@maccormac.edu
SILVA, Maureen 540-828-5450 465 D msilva@bridgewater.edu
SILVA, Rito 361-698-2250 436 C rsilva@delmar.edu
SILVA, Sonia 661-654-3995 30 E ssilva7@csub.edu
SILVA, Stephanie 510-436-1405 45 D ssilva@hnu.edu
SILVA, Tammy, A 508-999-8486 211 F tsilva@umassd.edu
SILVA, Tina 307-268-2547 501 U tina.silva@caspercollege.edu
SILVANO, Brian 949-794-9090 65 I bsilvano@stanbridge.edu
SILVAS, Kassie 208-769-7783 131 C kmsilvas@nic.edu
SILVER, Bret 973-408-3227 277 C bsilver@drew.edu
SILVER, Brian 512-516-8703 124 E bsilver@southuniversity.edu
SILVER, Frank 828-652-0634 336 B franksil@mcdowelltech.edu
SILVER, Jonathan 646-717-9705 300 G silver@gts.edu
SILVER, Steve 541-684-7235 374 G ssilver@nwcu.edu
SILVERBLATT, Pamela, S 646-664-9100 292 K
SILVERBLATT, Pamela, S 646-664-2977 292 K pamela.silverblatt@cuny.edu
SILVERI, Annamaria 313-993-1170 231 B silveran@udmercy.edu
SILVERIA, Jay, B 719-333-4140 504 C
SILVERII, Glenda 601-643-8440 245 G glenda.silverii@colin.edu
SILVERIO, Alain 212-410-8046 309 B asilverio@nycpm.edu
SILVERMAN, Ed 315-279-5120 304 A esilverman@keuka.edu
SILVERMAN, Edward 212-650-6480 293 D esilverman@ccny.cuny.edu
SILVERMAN, Jennifer 310-338-4404 50 J jennifer.silverman@lmu.edu
SILVERMAN, Lori 510-659-6191 54 F lsilverman@ohlone.edu
SILVERMAN, Scott 310-434-4370 62 E silverman_scott@smc.edu
SILVERS, Liz 828-726-2375 332 G lsilvers@cccti.edu
SILVERTHORN, Mike 989-463-7327 220 H silverthorn@alma.edu
SILVESTRI, Mary Ann 508-541-1602 208 F msilvestri@dean.edu
SILVESTRI, Timothy 484-664-3178 391 C timothysilvestri@muhlenberg.edu
SILVESTRINI, Maria 787-284-1912 509 E msilvest@ponce.inter.edu
SILVESTRO, Michael 973-761-9138 283 B michael.silvestro1@shu.edu
SILVEY, Greg 660-831-4183 256 G silveyg@moval.edu
SILVIA, Stephen 202-885-2462 90 J ssilvia@american.edu
SILVIS, Kathryn 412-536-1297 387 B kathryn.silvis@laroche.edu
SILVIS, Shera, L 843-377-4904 407 D ssilvis@charlestonlaw.edu
SILVYN, Jeffrey 520-206-4678 15 D jsilvyn@pima.edu
SILY, Michel 305-899-3781 95 C msily@barry.edu
SIMALA, Jay 847-317-6507 150 H jsimala@tiu.edu
SIMAR, Gina, A 409-882-3311 450 A gina.simar@lsco.edu
SIMARD, Denise 518-564-3066 319 C simardda@plattsburgh.edu
SIMARD, Tom 617-994-6918 211 B tsimard@bhe.mass.edu
SIMARI, Robert 913-588-1440 177 D rsimari@kumc.edu
SIMAS, Andrew 415-351-3537 60 G asimas@sfai.edu
SIMCOX, Mary Grace 717-947-6090 393 F mrsimcox@pacollege.edu
SIMEK, Kathy, M 503-943-7101 377 E simek@up.edu
SIMER, Lauren 864-250-8484 410 B lauren.simer@gvltec.edu
SIMERSON, Gordon 203-932-7290 89 A gsimerson@newhaven.edu
SIMFUKWE, David 904-470-8174 97 L dsimfukwe@ewc.edu
SIMINOE, Judith, P 320-308-2122 240 H jpsiminoe@stcloudstate.edu
SIMINOFF, Laura 215-204-8624 399 F lasiminoff@temple.edu
SIMIO, Frank 212-636-6265 300 E simio@fordham.edu
SIMION, Karen 691-320-2480 505 B ksimion@comfsm.fm
SIMIONE, Lauren, E 302-831-1408 90 F lemurray@udel.edu
SIMISON, Kynan 765-641-4076 153 B klsimison@anderson.edu
SIMMELINK, Tara 253-535-8787 482 H tara.simmelink@plu.edu
SIMMERS, Susan 970-351-2109 83 E susan.simmers@unco.edu
SIMMONDS, Donna 812-237-2215 155 G donna.simmonds@indstate.edu
SIMMONDS, Thomas 914-674-7473 306 F tsimmonds1@mercy.edu
SIMMONS, ADeidra 580-559-5239 366 C asimmons@ecok.edu
SIMMONS, Annette 704-403-3517 327 D annette.simmons@carolinashealthcare.org
SIMMONS, Benjamin 910-775-4341 343 B benjamin.simmons@uncp.edu
SIMMONS, Bette, M 973-328-5171 277 B bsimmons@ccm.edu
SIMMONS, Blair 510-869-1592 59 F bsimmons@samuelmerritt.edu
SIMMONS, Brian 803-754-4100 409 A
SIMMONS, Charlotte 405-974-2538 370 K cksimmons@uco.edu
SIMMONS, Christopher 919-668-6285 328 G chris.simmons@duke.edu
SIMMONS, Clay 940-565-4142 454 A clay.simmons@unt.edu
SIMMONS, Cleveland 586-445-7374 226 H simmonsc487@macomb.edu
SIMMONS, D. Glenn 520-459-6111 457 J simmonsg@wbu.edu
SIMMONS, Dale 530-226-4143 63 K dsimmons@simpsonu.edu
SIMMONS, Dan 580-745-2839 369 K dsimmons@se.edu
SIMMONS, David 706-253-4504 116 C dsimmons@chattahoocheetech.edu
SIMMONS, Dionne 661-253-7897 28 K dsimmons@calarts.edu
SIMMONS, Douglas 603-314-1775 216 B douglas.simmons@mcphs.edu
SIMMONS, Elaine 620-792-9214 171 C simmonse@bartonccc.edu
SIMMONS, Elizabeth 508-830-6683 213 B esimmons@maritime.edu
SIMMONS, Elizabeth, H 858-534-3130 69 D evc@ucsd.edu
SIMMONS, Emily 757-340-2121 465 M directoredcvab@centura.edu
SIMMONS, Gregory 410-455-1452 202 E gsimmons@umbc.edu
SIMMONS, Guy 972-238-6263 435 F gsimmons@dcccd.edu
SIMMONS, Gwen 417-690-3411 251 E simmons@cofo.edu
SIMMONS, Hezekiah, N 585-292-3320 307 H hsimmons@monroecc.edu
SIMMONS, Jacqueline 812-855-3312 156 B simmonja@iu.edu
SIMMONS, Jacqueline, A 812-855-3312 156 A simmonja@iu.edu
SIMMONS, Jay 484-365-7526 389 C jsimmons@lincoln.edu
SIMMONS, Jay, K 515-961-1566 169 D jay.simmons@simpson.edu
SIMMONS, Jeff 405-425-5566 367 G jeff.simmons@oc.edu
SIMMONS, Jeffrey 301-447-5266 200 E simmons@msmary.edu
SIMMONS, Jennifer 212-854-2011 290 J jsimmons@barnard.edu
SIMMONS, Jeremy 415-351-3510 60 G jsimmons@sfai.edu
SIMMONS, Kelley 360-438-4371 483 H ksimmons@stmartin.edu
SIMMONS, Kitty 951-785-2397 47 C ksimmons@lasierra.edu
SIMMONS, Laura 828-694-1807 332 E lm_simmons@blueridge.edu
SIMMONS, Lori 617-735-9825 209 A simmonslo@emmanuel.edu
SIMMONS, Martha 719-549-3303 81 K martha.simmons@pueblocc.edu
SIMMONS, Mary 407-888-8689 98 R msimmons@fcim.edu
SIMMONS, Max 405-682-1611 367 H msimmons@occc.edu
SIMMONS, Regina 704-463-3404 339 E regina.simmons@pfeiffer.edu
SIMMONS, Robert, A 816-235-1368 261 C simmonsr@umkc.edu
SIMMONS, Roy 304-205-6708 488 K roy.simmons@bridgevalley.edu
SIMMONS, Ruth, J 936-261-2111 446 D rjsimmons@pvamu.edu
SIMMONS, Shanni, E 812-888-4026 162 C ssimmons@vinu.edu
SIMMONS, Shannon 478-445-5149 118 C shannon.simmons@gcsu.edu
SIMMONS, Sherry 262-695-3481 500 H ssimmons9@wctc.edu
SIMMONS, Stefon 646-216-2860 309 D ssimmons@nycda.edu
SIMMONS, Steven 803-508-7270 406 E simmonss@atc.edu
SIMMONS, Tami 704-378-1024 330 D tsimmons@jcsu.edu
SIMMONS, Tanya 804-524-5087 477 B tsimmons@vsu.edu
SIMMONS, Theresa 303-722-5724 80 L tsimmons@lincolntech.edu
SIMMONS, Thomas, E 419-772-2450 358 H t-simmons@onu.edu
SIMMONS, Todd 480-517-8137 13 G todd.simmons@riosalado.edu
SIMMONS, Todd, H 336-285-2606 341 F thsimmons@ncat.edu
SIMMONS, Tonja 478-476-5167 116 A tsimmons@centralgatech.edu
SIMMONS, Toye 713-221-8061 453 B simmonsto@uhd.edu
SIMMONS, Tracy 916-739-7198 70 E tsimmons@pacific.edu
SIMMONS, Victoria 818-240-1000 44 B vsimmons@glendale.edu
SIMMONS-HENRY, Linda 903-593-8311 448 H lhenry@texascollege.edu
SIMMS, Marcie 740-351-3392 360 K msimms@shawnee.edu
SIMMS, Michele 859-815-7797 181 B michele.simms@kctcs.edu
SIMMS, Pat 501-337-5000 18 J pats@coto.edu
SIMMS, Rebecca 859-246-6761 180 K rebecca.simms@kctcs.edu
SIMNING, Jennie 952-995-1533 238 B jennie.simning@hennepintech.edu
SIMO, Brian 619-849-7082 57 E briansimo@pointloma.edu
SIMON, Barbara 563-589-0332 170 D bsimon@wartburgseminary.edu
SIMON, Bashe 212-463-0400 322 J simonb@touro.edu
SIMON, Caroline 509-777-3755 486 I csimon@whitworth.edu
SIMON, Constance 313-831-5200 223 I csimon@etseminary.edu
SIMON, Darica 225-216-8171 186 K simond@mybrcc.edu
SIMON, David 920-565-2501 493 J simondr@lakeland.edu
SIMON, David, F 215-871-6819 396 D simond@pcom.edu
SIMON, Donald, E 718-933-6700 307 G dsimon@monroecollege.edu
SIMON, Esan 860-444-8352 504 F eason_simon@hotmail.com
SIMON, Giselle 559-925-3324 74 B gisellesimon@whccd.edu
SIMON, Jacob 419-448-3421 361 J simonja@tiffin.edu
SIMON, Jason 620-223-2700 173 C jasons@fortscott.edu
SIMON, Jason, F 940-565-2085 454 A jason.simon@unt.edu
SIMON, Jennifer 406-496-4307 265 A jsimon@mtech.edu
SIMON, Jill, K 651-641-8211 235 F simon@csp.edu
SIMON, John, D 610-758-3156 388 J jds414@lehigh.edu
SIMON, Michael 810-762-5640 228 C michael.simon@mcc.edu
SIMON, Michael 936-633-5200 430 F msimon@angelina.edu
SIMON, Paul, M 203-837-8494 85 B simonp@wcsu.edu
SIMON, Scott, L 740-368-3394 359 N slsimon@owu.edu

SIMON, Tia ... 832-230-5156 440 H tsimon1@na.edu

SIMON, Tina, L ... 419-372-2700 348 H tsimon@bgsu.edu

SIMONCELLI, Andrew ... 985-448-4131 192 B andrew.simoncelli@nicholls.edu

SIMONDS, Ken ... 760-366-5297 40 K ksimonds@cmccd.edu

SIMONDS, Kurt ... 971-722-5573 375 J kurt.simonds@pcc.edu

SIMONE, Carmen ... 605-274-9500 416 H carmen.simone@sduniversitycenter.org

SIMONE, John ... 609-586-4800 278 F simonej@mccc.edu

SIMONE, Lucian ... 203-285-2223 85 E lsimone@gwcc.commnet.edu

SIMONEAUX, Timothy ... 314-838-8858 261 G tsimoneaux@ugst.edu

SIMONESCHI, Joseph ... 909-869-2008 30 D jsimoneschi@cpp.edu

SIMONETTI, Joseph ... 773-995-3689 133 K jsimonet@csu.edu

SIMONI, Mary ... 518-276-6575 312 I msimoni@rpi.edu

SIMONIAN, Yasmen ... 801-626-7117 461 B ysimonian@weber.edu

SIMONS, Amy ... 314-889-4780 253 C asimons@fontbonne.edu

SIMONS, Austin ... 269-965-3931 225 F simonsa2@kellogg.edu

SIMONS, Danita ... 605-718-2436 417 F danita.simons@wdt.edu

SIMONS, Earl, G ... 718-262-3795 295 F esimons@york.cuny.edu

SIMONS, Elizabeth ... 716-926-8963 301 H esimons@hilbert.edu

SIMONS, Ernest ... 252-493-7243 336 H esimons@email.pittcc.edu

SIMONS, Jill ... 870-972-3574 17 G jsimons@astate.edu

SIMONS, Kelly ... 614-287-2501 351 E ksimons2@cscc.edu

SIMONS, Kenneth, B ... 414-955-4577 494 C ksimons@mcw.edu

SIMONS, Michael ... 570-674-1766 390 G msimons@misericordia.edu

SIMONS, Michael, A ... 718-990-6601 314 B simonsm@stjohns.edu

SIMONS, Shino ... 626-812-3061 26 H ssimons@apu.edu

SIMONS, Valerie ... 303-492-5359 83 A valerie.simons@colorado.edu

SIMONSEN, Jaime ... 651-201-1669 237 A jaime.simonsen@minnstate.edu

SIMONSON, Seth ... 208-732-6575 130 E ssimonson@csi.edu

SIMOWITZ, Aaron ... 503-370-6840 378 B asimowitz@willamette.edu

SIMPKINS, Alice, M ... 706-396-8111 122 K asimpkins@paine.edu

SIMPKINS, Felix ... 708-709-3518 146 D fsimpkins@prairiestate.edu

SIMPKINS, Rahmaan ... 609-626-6488 283 D rahmaan.simpkins@stockton.edu

SIMPSON, Amanda ... 760-252-2411 26 I asimpson@barstow.edu

SIMPSON, Amy ... 606-248-0484 182 E amy.simpson@kctcs.edu

SIMPSON, Andrea ... 317-274-2289 156 F andmsimp@iupui.edu

SIMPSON, Andy, L ... 651-631-5239 244 D alsimpson@unwsp.edu

SIMPSON, Angela ... 606-589-3025 182 E angela.simpson@kctcs.edu

SIMPSON, Anita ... 580-628-6237 367 D anita.simpson@noc.edu

SIMPSON, Brett ... 504-864-7787 189 F bsimpson@loyno.edu

SIMPSON, Caroline ... 304-724-3700 487 E csimpson@apus.edu

SIMPSON, Chocoletta ... 816-604-1575 255 D chocoletta.simpson@mcckc.edu

SIMPSON, Colleen ... 920-498-5418 500 F colleen.simpson@nwtc.edu

SIMPSON, Cynthia, F ... 718-990-6333 314 B simpsoc1@stjohns.edu

SIMPSON, Dionne ... 619-596-2766 24 F dsimpson@advancedtraining.edu

SIMPSON, Eric ... 801-622-1573 459 N eric.simpson@stevenshenager.edu

SIMPSON, Erica ... 901-272-5100 422 B finaid@mca.edu

SIMPSON, Erica ... 901-272-5139 422 B esimpson@mca.edu

SIMPSON, Gabrielle ... 212-854-7580 290 J gsimpson@barnard.edu

SIMPSON, James, T ... 954-262-7300 103 M james.simpson@nova.edu

SIMPSON, Jane ... 678-839-5306 126 E jsimpson@westga.edu

SIMPSON, Jeanna ... 417-667-8181 252 A jbrauer@cottey.edu

SIMPSON, Jeff ... 334-241-5412 7 C simpsonj@troy.edu

SIMPSON, Jim ... 281-756-3789 429 I jsimpson@alvincollege.edu

SIMPSON, Joe ... 815-921-4752 147 E j.simpson@rockvalleycollege.edu

SIMPSON, Juliene ... 973-290-4207 277 A jsimpson@cse.edu

SIMPSON, Kim ... 863-297-1000 105 A ksimpson@polk.edu

SIMPSON, Kurt ... 815-599-3501 138 B kurt.simpson@highland.edu

SIMPSON, Lawrence, J ... 617-747-2150 206 E academicaffairs@berklee.edu

SIMPSON, Lisa ... 903-813-2423 430 N lrsimpson@austincollege.edu

SIMPSON, Mark ... 866-931-4300 258 G mark.simpson@rockbridge.edu

SIMPSON, Matthew ... 417-447-2648 257 G simpsonm@otc.edu

SIMPSON, Matthew ... 508-849-3462 205 C msimpson@annamaria.edu

SIMPSON, Michael, E ... 518-564-2155 319 C simpsome@plattsburgh.edu

SIMPSON, Philip ... 321-433-5078 97 I simpsonp@easternflorida.edu

SIMPSON, Ralph ... 484-365-7588 389 C rsimpson@lincoln.edu

SIMPSON, Robert ... 731-661-5219 427 C rsimpson@uu.edu

SIMPSON, Stacy ... 618-634-3375 149 A stacys@shawneecc.edu

SIMPSON, Tammi, R ... 540-458-4111 478 A tsimpson@wlu.edu

SIMPSON, Todd ... 402-872-2304 268 F tsimpson@peru.edu

SIMPSON, Viola ... 203-777-8573 84 F vcsimpson@albertus.edu

SIMPSON-LOGG, Anastasia ... 707-468-3102 51 E asimpson@mendocino.edu

SIMS, Andrea ... 909-274-5950 52 H asims@mtsac.edu

SIMS, Angela ... 913-253-5017 176 I angela.sims@spst.edu

SIMS, Angela ... 505-224-4000 285 J asims9@cnm.edu

SIMS, Angela, D ... 585-340-9680 296 E asims@crcds.edu

SIMS, Bradford, L ... 301-369-2800 197 F president@captechu.edu

SIMS, Damon, R ... 814-865-0909 392 B drs37@psu.edu

SIMS, Danielle, R ... 502-213-5333 181 F danielle.sims@kctcs.edu

SIMS, Darryl ... 920-424-1034 497 B sims@uwosh.edu

SIMS, David ... 478-471-2780 121 F david.sims@mga.edu

SIMS, Geoffrey ... 201-360-4045 278 C gsims@hccc.edu

SIMS, George ... 405-208-5450 367 I gsims@okcu.edu

SIMS, Guy ... 304-327-4512 489 P gsims@bluefieldstate.edu

SIMS, Haley ... 804-828-1645 473 F hasims@vcu.edu

SIMS, Hillel ... 857-701-1501 215 E hsims@rcc.mass.edu

SIMS, Hunter ... 325-649-8830 438 D hsims@hputx.edu

SIMS, Jacquelyn ... 310-660-3200 41 L jsims@elcamino.edu

SIMS, Jeanetta ... 405-974-2000 370 K jsims7@uco.edu

SIMS, Jeanette ... 704-687-5827 342 E jeanette.sims@uncc.edu

SIMS, Joel ... 406-268-3719 264 G joel.sims@gfcmsu.edu

SIMS, Leslie ... 304-424-8221 491 D leslie.sims@wvup.edu

SIMS, Melinda ... 405-382-9604 369 J m.sims@sscok.edu

SIMS, Myra ... 540-362-6435 468 C simsms@hollins.edu

SIMS, Pam ... 501-212-6608 18 H psims@cbc.edu

SIMS, Patricia ... 256-539-8161 2 E

SIMS, Patrick ... 608-890-3117 496 C patrick.sims@wisc.edu

SIMS, Quanda, D ... 803-934-3422 411 C qdsims@morris.edu

SIMS, Rhonda ... 601-426-6346 249 A rsims@southeasternbaptist.edu

SIMS, Sandra ... 303-384-2008 78 I ssims@mines.edu

SIMS, Scott ... 317-931-2328 154 C ssims@cts.edu

SIMS, Steve ... 724-266-3838 400 H ssims@tsm.edu

SIMS, Sue ... 803-508-7341 406 E simss@atc.edu

SIMS, Suzanne ... 256-216-3314 4 D suzanne.sims@athens.edu

SIMS-AUBERT, Gail ... 920-465-2712 496 E simsg@uwgb.edu

SIMS-BARBARICK, Dana ... 503-847-2597 377 F dsims@uws.edu

SIMSON, Earl, L ... 401-456-8106 405 C esimson@ric.edu

SINA, Julie ... 310-206-8962 69 A jsina@support.ucla.edu

SINCAVAGE, Joseph ... 610-436-3535 396 A jsincavage@wcupa.edu

SINCHE, Melanie ... 860-231-5228 89 B msinche@usj.edu

SINCLAIR, Kelli ... 630-466-7900 152 C ksinclair@waubonsee.edu

SINCLAIR, Lisa ... 617-373-2157 217 F

SINCLAIR, Robert, L ... 312-788-1144 152 B rsinclair@vandercook.edu

SINCLAIR, Shannon, E ... 804-287-6683 472 L ssinclai@richmond.edu

SINCLAIR, Taylor ... 402-471-2505 268 D tsinclair@nscs.edu

SINCLAIR CURTIS, Jennifer ... 530-752-0554 68 E jscurtis@ucdavis.edu

SINDER, Janet ... 718-780-7975 291 J janet.sinder@brooklaw.edu

SINDT, Christopher ... 815-836-5639 141 G csindt@lewisu.edu

SINEWAY, Carla ... 989-317-4760 230 A csineway@sagchip.edu

SINGEL, David ... 406-994-4371 264 D dsingel@montana.edu

SINGELL, Larry ... 812-855-2392 156 B lsingell@indiana.edu

SINGER, Eric ... 410-337-6456 198 G eric.singer@goucher.edu

SINGER, Jefferson ... 860-439-2010 86 H jefferson.singer@conncoll.edu

SINGER, Lori ... 212-229-5662 308 C singerl@newschool.edu

SINGER, Lucy, A ... 931-598-1880 423 M lasinger@sewanee.edu

SINGER, Marc ... 415-442-6589 44 D msinger@ggu.edu

SINGER, Marjorie ... 212-237-8911 294 D msinger@jjay.cuny.edu

SINGER, Mark ... 914-493-1909 309 H mark_singer@nymc.edu

SINGER, Miriam ... 201-692-2853 277 K singer@fdu.edu

SINGER, Sid ... 847-982-2500 138 A singer@htc.edu

SINGER, Susan, R ... 407-646-2355 105 M srsinger@rollins.edu

SINGER, Yossi ... 718-268-4700 312 G

SINGH, Amit, B ... 425-640-1515 480 F amit.singh@edcc.edu

SINGH, Anita ... 916-568-3057 50 E singha@losrios.edu

SINGH, Avena ... 541-888-1583 376 F asingh@socc.edu

SINGH, Bharpur ... 209-290-0333 24 E bsingh@advancedcollege.edu

SINGH, Gangaram ... 858-642-8109 53 F gsingh@nu.edu

SINGH, Gurbhushan ... 913-469-8500 174 D gurbhushan@jccc.edu

SINGH, Hamwant (Neil) 718-429-6600 324 D neil.singh@vaughn.edu

SINGH, Haniel ... 434-528-5276 477 E

SINGH, Joanne ... 859-985-3056 179 C singhj@berea.edu

SINGH, JT ... 610-436-1045 396 A jsingh@wcupa.edu

SINGH, Judith, R ... 315-267-2188 319 D singhjr@potsdam.edu

SINGH, Kamla ... 201-761-6082 282 I ksingh@saintpeters.edu

SINGH, Kanwal ... 914-395-2303 315 F ksingh@sarahlawrence.edu

SINGH, Kulwant ... 408-864-8745 43 C singhkulwant@deanza.edu

SINGH, Kulwant ... 310-834-3065 67 K

SINGH, Lindsey ... 239-590-7992 108 K lsingh@fgcu.edu

SINGH, Manohar ... 203-392-5661 85 A singhm6@southernct.edu

SINGH, Manraj ... 704-922-2452 334 F singh.manraj@gaston.edu

SINGH, Nanne ... 559-251-4215 28 B library@calchristiancollege.edu

SINGH, Piyusha ... 573-875-7240 251 F psingh@ccis.edu

SINGH, Preeti ... 610-558-5537 391 D

SINGH, Sarabdayal ... 657-278-4295 31 E ssingh@fullerton.edu

SINGH, Simran ... 805-893-8377 70 A singh-s@sa.ucsb.edu

SINGH, Sudhir ... 301-687-4019 203 E ssingh@frostburg.edu

SINGH, Tanuja ... 210-436-3706 443 A tsingh@stmarytx.edu

SINGH CHAUHAN, Indrajeet ... 212-423-2769 301 F indrajeet.singh@helenefuld.edu

SINGH MOONILALL, Seeta ... 561-912-1211 98 D seetas@evergladesuniversity.edu

SINGLE, Karen ... 617-274-3352 216 B karen.single@mcphs.edu

SINGLER, Melissa ... 910-362-7329 332 H msingler@cfcc.edu

SINGLETARY, Chip ... 850-201-8544 111 C singlech@tcc.fl.edu

SINGLETARY, James, M ... 740-392-6868 357 B jim.singletary@mvnu.edu

SINGLETARY, Joshua ... 518-694-7896 289 D joshua.singletary@acphs.edu

SINGLETARY, Michael ... 360-383-3035 486 G msingletary@whatcom.edu

SINGLETARY, Sedrick ... 803-327-7402 408 B ssingletary@clintoncollege.edu

SINGLETON, Brian ... 313-496-2778 232 C bsingle1@wcccd.edu

SINGLETON, Derrick ... 859-985-3130 179 C singletonp@berea.edu

SINGLETON, Gena, L ... 713-646-1778 444 B gsingleton@stcl.edu

SINGLETON, Ginny ... 601-426-6346 249 A gsingleton@southeasternbaptist.edu

SINGLETON, Greg ... 252-638-7247 333 H singletong@cravencc.edu

SINGLETON, Gregory ... 931-221-7005 418 D singletong@apsu.edu

SINGLETON, Heather ... 757-446-7427 466 I singleha@evms.edu

SINGLETON, J. Ron ... 864-488-8274 410 E rsingleton@limestone.edu

SINGLETON, Jennie ... 252-940-6202 332 C jennie.singleton@beaufortccc.edu

SINGLETON, Joan ... 818-702-1350 56 C joan.singleton@pepperdine.edu

SINGLETON, John, L ... 817-257-7871 448 G j.singleton@tcu.edu

SINGLETON, Larry, G ... 845-575-3000 305 L lawrence.singleton@marist.edu

SINGLETON, Robin ... 870-762-3161 17 D rsingleton@smail.anc.edu

SINGLETON, Shawn, T ... 859-233-8154 184 G ssingleton@transy.edu

SINGLETON, Stanley ... 410-462-8562 197 E ssingleton@bccc.edu

SINGLETON-REICH, Jade ... 580-349-2611 368 A jade.singleton-reich@opsu.edu

SINGLETON-WALKER, Catherine ... 662-254-3365 248 B cswalker@mvsu.edu

SINGLEY, Charles ... 803-376-5801 406 F csingley@allenuniversity.edu

SINGLEY, Jason ... 510-885-3441 31 C jason.singley@csueastbay.edu

SINHA, Kim 434-381-6530 472 D ksinha@sbc.edu
SINHA, Monica 510-592-9688.. 54 C monica@npu.edu
SINHA, Tripti 301-405-1721 202 C tsinha@umd.edu
SINIARD, Michelle 478-218-3330 116 A msiniard@centralgatech.edu
SINIGAGLIA, Frank 845-434-5750 322 A fsinigaglia@sunysullivan.edu
SINK, Michael 407-823-2711 109 E michael.sink@ucf.edu
SINK, Susanna, C 724-357-2202 394 G scsink@iup.edu
SINK, Tom 567-661-7221 360 B thomas_sink@owens.edu
SINN, Brad 928-350-2100.. 15 N
SINN, Jeanna 203-591-5238.. 87 F jsinn@post.edu
SINNEMA, Patrick 712-722-6050 164 K patrick.sinnema@dordt.edu
SINNOT, Dawn 215-751-8085 382 A dsinnot@ccp.edu
SINUTKO, John 805-378-1454.. 72 H jsinutko@vcccd.edu
SIPE, Bryan 912-279-5819 116 G bsipe@ccga.edu
SIPE, Gary 386-822-4210 111 A gsipe@stetson.edu
SIPES, Jennifer, L 217-581-3221 136 E jlsipes@eiu.edu
SIPES, Marlise 740-264-5591 352 H mbarker@egcc.edu
SIPES, Stacie 903-875-7736 440 G stacie.sipes@navarrocollege.edu
SIPHER, Justin 315-229-5319 314 F jsipher@stlawu.edu
SIPOS, George, T 314-516-5753 261 D gsipos@umsl.edu
SIPPEL, Christopher 419-434-5467 363 A sippel@findlay.edu
SIPPEL, Len 336-316-2841 329 E sippellc@guilford.edu
SIPSER, Michael 617-253-8900 215 G
SIQUEIROS, Penny 478-757-5253 126 H psiqueiros@wesleyancollege.edu
SIRAJ, Elias 757-446-5910 466 I sirajes@evms.edu
SIRANGELO-ELBADAWY, Catherine 201-360-4261 278 C csirangelo@hccc.edu
SIRBU, Jerald, B 303-369-5151.. 81 J jbs@plattcolorado.edu
SIRIANO, Joseph 323-469-3300.. 25 E info@amda.edu
SIRIMANGKALA, Pawena 305-899-3453.. 95 C psirimangkala@barry.edu
SIRJU-JOHNSON, Nicole 607-777-4472 316 E njohnson@binghamton.edu
SIRJU-JOHNSON, Nicole 607-777-4775 316 E njohnson@binghamton.edu
SIROKI, David 412-536-1137 387 B david.siroki@laroche.edu
SIRONEN, Jacqueline 419-448-2261 353 H jsironen@heidelberg.edu
SIROTA, Stue 410-706-7830 202 D ssirota@umaryland.edu
SISCHO, Brian, C 919-515-3226 342 B bcsischo@ncsu.edu
SISCO, Craig 405-682-7568 367 H michael.c.sisco@occc.edu
SISCO, Julie 574-284-4574 160 C jsisco@saintmarys.edu
SISCOE, Dee 417-836-5526 256 E dsiscoe@missouristate.edu
SISEMORE, John 417-455-5674 252 D johnsisemore@crowder.edu
SISK, Beth 402-399-2415 266 F bsisk@csm.edu
SISK, Cheryl 517-355-4470 227 D sisk@msu.edu
SISK, Colin 724-480-3630 381 K colin.sisk@ccbc.edu
SISK, Kari, M 304-457-6275 487 B maxwellkl@ab.edu
SISK, Lori 801-375-5125 459 L lori.sisk@rm.edu
SISK, Matthew 304-457-6247 487 B siskmr@ab.edu
SISK, Megan 714-556-3610.. 72 F megan.sisk@vanguard.edu
SISKA, Peter 318-797-5372 189 D peter.siska@lsus.edu
SISKO, John 704-337-2506 339 G siskoj@queens.edu
SISLER, Kelli 301-387-3060 198 F kelli.sisler@garrettcollege.edu
SISNEROS, Patrick 425-388-9026 480 G psisnero@everettcc.edu
SISSEN, Melissa 517-264-7155 230 E msissen@sienaheights.edu
SISSON, Amanda 843-863-7991 407 E asisson@csuniv.edu
SISSON, Brian 507-457-1638 243 B bsisson@smumn.edu
SISSON, Cynthia 814-472-3100 398 B csisson@francis.edu
SISSON, George 716-338-1269 303 D georgesisson@mail.sunyjcc.edu
SISSON, Jeanne, M 518-580-5664 316 A jsisson@skidmore.edu
SISSON, Jillian 402-354-7137 268 C jillian.sisson@methodistcollege.edu
SISSON, Karen 909-621-8132.. 57 F karen.sisson@pomona.edu
SISSON, Karl 585-567-9340 302 D karl.sisson@houghton.edu
SISSON, Philip, J 978-322-8488 214 G sissonp@middlesex.mass.edu
SITARAMIAH, Gita 612-330-1476 233 K sitarami@augsburg.edu
SITES, John 954-776-4476 102 A jsites@keiseruniversity.edu
SITHARAMAN, Sri 706-507-8963 116 I sri@columbusstate.edu
SITKUS, Carina 717-337-6803 384 H csitkus@gettysburg.edu
SITLINGTON, Claudia 805-553-4799.. 72 H csitlington@vcccd.edu
SITTON, Michael, R 315-267-2812 319 D sittonmr@potsdam.edu
SITZABEE, JR., William, E 814-865-4402 392 B wes25@psu.edu
SIVADON, Angela 918-595-7224 370 E angela.sivadon@tulsacc.edu
SIVAK, Jennifer, L 240-895-4382 201 E jlsivak@smcm.edu
SIVAKUMARAN, Thilla .. 870-972-3149.. 17 G tsivakumaran@astate.edu
SIVALON, John 570-941-7400 401 H john.sivalon@scranton.edu
SIVERSON, Karen 415-503-6287.. 60 H ksiverson@sfcm.edu
SIVILLO, Jeremy 814-866-8143 388 A jsivillo@lecom.edu
SIWABESSY, Genevieve . 530-661-4201.. 76 B gsiwabes@yccd.edu
SIX, Jonathan 919-761-2100 340 G jsix@sebts.edu
SIXTA, Jeff 913-288-7613 174 F jsixta@kckcc.edu
SIZEMORE, Abby 502-863-8301 178 K abby.sizemore@bsk.edu
SIZEMORE, Amanda 636-922-8388 258 I asizemore@stchas.edu
SIZEMORE, Lisa 828-339-4000 338 B l_sizemore@southwesterncc.edu
SIZEMORE, Shain 606-546-1670 184 H ssizemore@unionky.edu
SIZER, Judith 617-873-0171 207 F judith.sizer@cambridgecollege.edu
SJOBERG, Connie 918-495-6542 368 I csjoberg@oru.edu
SJOBERG, Lisa, M 218-299-3250 235 E sjoberg@cord.edu
SJOGREN, Michelle 859-246-6429 180 K michelle.sjogren@kctcs.edu
SJOQUIST, Corey 608-785-8939 496 F csjoquist@uwlax.edu
SJUTS, Joseph, H 816-501-3615 250 F joe.sjuts@avila.edu
SKABROUD, Ryan 920-693-1347 499 G ryan.skabroud@gotoltc.edu
SKACH, Peter 773-298-3548 148 G skach@sxu.edu
SKADBERG, Ingrid 508-854-7545 215 D iskadberg@qcc.mass.edu
SKAFF, Penny 949-582-4573.. 64 G pskaff@saddleback.edu
SKAGGS, Brandon 254-295-4496 453 E bskaggs@umhb.edu
SKAGGS, Jobie 309-677-3191 133 B jskaggs@bradley.edu
SKAMRA, Brian 920-748-8174 495 G skamrab@ripon.edu
SKANDERA TROMBLEY, Laura 203-576-4665.. 88 D president@bridgeport.edu
SKANTZ, Ingrid 423-236-2833 424 B ilskantz@southern.edu
SKARI, Lisa 503-491-7211 374 C lisa.skari@mhcc.edu
SKARRO, Scott 701-255-3285 347 B sskaro@uttc.edu
SKARSTEN, Fawn 810-762-3327 231 G skarsten@umich.edu
SKATES, Kathy 229-430-3524 113 I kskates@albanytech.edu
SKEEN, James 540-261-8400 471 H james.skeen@svu.edu
SKEETE-WALKER, Dawn 718-270-1234 317 E dawn.walker@downstate.edu
SKELLEY, Gregory 610-718-1981 390 H gskelley@mc3.edu
SKELLON, Hilary 720-890-8922.. 80 H director@itea.edu
SKELLY, Theresa 978-921-4242 216 F theresa.skelly@montserrat.edu
SKENDERIAN, Jody 952-358-8200 239 F
SKERIK, Maryellen 630-637-5678 144 H mjskerik@noctrl.edu
SKERRETT-LLANOS, Carmen 787-993-8870 513 B carmen.skerrett@upr.edu
SKEVAKIS, Anthony 201-761-7360 282 I askevakisp@saintpeters.edu
SKIDMORE, Alan 304-766-3261 491 B askidmore@wvstateu.edu
SKIDMORE, Ashley 815-836-5212 141 G skidmoas@lewisu.edu
SKIDMORE, Charlene 515-271-2999 165 A charlene.skidmore@drake.edu
SKIDMORE, Daniel, L ... 315-445-4759 304 C skidmodl@lemoyne.edu
SKIDMORE, Heather 304-424-8210 491 D heather.skidmore@wvup.edu
SKIDMORE, James, K ... 304-710-3363 489 B skidmorej@mctc.edu
SKIFF, Jim 973-408-3000 277 C
SKILES, Adam, L 260-359-4130 155 F askiles@huntington.edu
SKILES, Jesse 304-462-6221 490 C jesse.skiles@glenville.edu
SKILL, Thomas, D 937-229-3511 362 G tskill1@udayton.edu
SKILLMAN, Josh 317-278-6115 156 F jskillma@iupui.edu
SKINDER, Michelle 845-455-8738 143 A mskinder@mchenry.edu
SKINKLE, Lee 417-328-1601 259 L lskinkle@sbuniv.edu
SKINNER, Adrienne 269-467-9945 224 A askinner@glenoaks.edu
SKINNER, Bruce 573-651-5103 259 K bskinner@semo.edu
SKINNER, Celeste 310-265-6143.. 59 E celeste.skinner@usw.salvationarmy.org
SKINNER, Deb 641-784-5108 165 H dskinner@graceland.edu
SKINNER, Denese 806-371-5252 430 A denese.skinner@actx.edu
SKINNER, Donal 740-593-2723 359 G dcs@ohio.edu
SKINNER, Erik 916-660-7600.. 63 I eskinner1@sierracollege.edu
SKINNER, Georgia 404-627-2681 115 C georgia.skinner@beulah.edu
SKINNER, James 580-774-3788 370 C james.skinner@swosu.edu
SKINNER, Katherine 615-460-6342 418 F kathryn.skinner@belmont.edu
SKINNER, Kendra 573-651-2274 259 K ksskinner@semo.edu
SKINNER, Lee 504-865-5000 191 B leeskinner@tulane.edu
SKINNER, Loren 409-772-6615 456 F leskinne@utmb.edu
SKINNER, Mary 217-443-8814 135 H mskinner@dacc.edu
SKINNER, Patricia, A 704-922-6475 334 F skinner.pat@gaston.edu
SKINNER, Randall 928-428-8252.. 12 E randall.skinner@eac.edu
SKINNER, Robert 304-473-8557 491 H skinner_b@wvwc.edu
SKINNER, Sally 208-459-5770 130 D sskinner@collegeofidaho.edu
SKINNER, Sara 269-927-6851 226 D skinner@lakemichigancollege.edu
SKINNER, Thomas 225-578-0335 188 I tskinner@lsu.edu
SKINNER, Thomas 225-578-2111 188 H tskinner@lsu.edu
SKIPPER, Bob 270-745-4295 185 E bob.skipper@wku.edu
SKIPPER, Curt 601-635-2111 245 I cskipper@eccc.edu
SKIPPER, Eric 843-208-8000 413 E eskipper@uscb.edu
SKIPPER, Nick 850-973-9495 103 K skippern@nfcc.edu
SKIPPS, Tasha 562-809-5100.. 43 F tasha.skipps@fremont.edu
SKIPWORTH, Stan 909-621-8291.. 37 D stan_skipworth@cuc.claremont.edu
SKIPWORTH, Stan 909-621-8033.. 37 C stan.skipworth@claremont.edu
SKLAR, Jay 314-434-4044 252 B jay.sklar@covenantseminary.edu
SKLBA, Stephanie 262-564-2662 499 F sklba@gtc.edu
SKLEDER, Anne, A 770-534-6110 115 D askleder@brenau.edu
SKLUT, John 509-313-3175 481 D sklut@gonzaga.edu
SKOBLA, Kristen 315-792-5321 307 D kskobla@mvcc.edu
SKOCILICH, Heather 503-493-8612 372 I hskocilich@cu-portland.edu
SKOFF, Robert, M 724-847-6581 384 G rmskoff@geneva.edu
SKOGEN, Larry, C 701-224-5431 346 B larry.skogen@bismarckstate.edu
SKOGLUND, Elizabeth, A 410-543-6161 203 F easkoglund@salisbury.edu
SKOGLUND, Kirk 816-501-4813 258 H kirk.skoglund@rockhurst.edu
SKOMP, Elizabeth 386-822-7515 111 A eskomp@stetson.edu
SKONER, Peter, R 814-472-3085 398 B pskoner@francis.edu
SKOPEK, Tracy 918-595-7064 370 E tracy.skopek@tulsacc.edu
SKOPLAN, Marla 251-460-6231.... 8 F mskoplan@southalabama.edu
SKORTZ, Brian 270-686-6416 179 D brian.skortz@brescia.edu
SKOWYRA, Jamie 508-213-2131 217 E jamie.skowyra@nichols.edu
SKRAINAR, Elizabeth .... 585-385-8427 314 A eskrainar@sjfc.edu
SKROCKI, Kyle 802-387-6887 462 D kyleskrocki@landmark.edu
SKRYD, Jackie 727-302-6809 106 E skryd.jackie@spcollege.edu
SKUCE, John, R 910-893-1200 327 E
SKUKA, Eva 973-278-5400 275 I esk@berkeleycollege.edu
SKUKA, Eva 973-278-5400 291 D esk@berkeleycollege.edu
SKURZEWSKI-SERVANT, Missy 715-422-5356 500 A missy.skurzewskiservant@mstc.edu
SKVARLA, Jennifer 815-836-5201 141 G skvarlje@lewisu.edu
SLAATHAUG, Carrie 605-256-5009 416 J carrie.slaathaug@dsu.edu
SLABACH, Frederick, G . 817-531-4401 451 E fslabach@txwes.edu
SLABAUGH, David 864-644-5558 412 E dslabaugh@swu.edu
SLABAUGH, Dawnie 530-938-5373.. 39 F slabaugh@siskiyous.edu
SLABAUGH, Katie 765-285-1545 153 C kslabaugh@bsu.edu
SLABODEN, Carolyn 781-283-2216 219 D cslaboden@wellesley.edu
SLABU, Claudia 360-442-2207 482 B cslabu@lowercolumbia.edu
SLADE, David 706-236-2229 115 B dslade@berry.edu
SLADE, Heather 805-969-3626.. 55 E hslade@pacifica.edu
SLADE, Lisa 203-332-5017.. 85 F lslade@housatonic.edu
SLADE, Patricia 973-877-3209 277 I slade@essex.edu

SLADE, Tim .... 601-318-6155 249 H
tslade@wmcarey.edu
SLAFF, Sara .... 410-704-4003 204 A
sslaff@towson.edu
SLAGAN, Stephanie .... 760-921-5421.. 55 H
stephanie.slagan@paloverde.edu
SLAGAN, Stephanie .... 760-921-5524.. 55 H
stephanie.slagan@paloverde.edu
SLAGELL, Jeff .... 662-846-4441 245 H
jslagell@deltastate.edu
SLAGER, Joan .... 859-899-2512 180 C
joan.slager@frontier.edu
SLAGER, Karen .... 815-802-8110 140 D
kslager@kcc.edu
SLAGHT, Charles .... 559-730-3821.. 39 E
charless@cos.edu
SLAGTER, Cynthia .... 616-526-6426 222 A
cslagter@calvin.edu
SLANIA, Heather .... 410-225-2311 199 H
hslania@mica.edu
SLATE, Kristine .... 903-233-4332 439 E
kristineslate@letu.edu
SLATER, Bernata .... 650-358-6795.. 61 N
slaterb@smccd.edu
SLATER, Emilee .... 559-442-8225.. 66 E
emilee.slater@fresnocitycollege.edu
SLATER, Erin .... 804-752-7305 470 F
erinslater@rmc.edu
SLATER, Glen .... 215-785-0111 393 C
SLATER, Ian .... 765-677-2138 157 D
ian.slater@indwes.edu
SLATER, Joseph .... 931-372-3172 426 E
jslater@tntech.edu
SLATER, Kara .... 616-395-7836 225 B
slater@hope.edu
SLATER, Linda .... 845-575-3000 305 L
linda.slater@marist.edu
SLATER, Rebecca .... 309-298-4500 152 D
r-slater@wiu.edu
SLATER, Richard .... 773-291-6100 134 E
SLATER, Troy .... 231-348-6610 228 E
tslater@ncmich.edu
SLATER, William .... 615-675-5255 428 G
wslater@welch.edu
SLATER, Willie .... 334-724-4880.... 7 D
wslater@tuskegee.edu
SLATON, Andrea .... 479-788-7701.. 21 H
andrea.slaton@uafs.edu
SLATON, Gwendolyn ..... 973-877-3233 277 I
slaton@essex.edu
SLATON, Nate .... 850-729-5232 103 L
slatonn@nwfsc.edu
SLATTERY, Daniel .... 410-704-2364 204 A
dslattery@towson.edu
SLATTERY, Katheryn ...... 815-836-5275 141 G
slatteka@lewisu.edu
SLAUGHTER, Amanda ... 562-903-4552.. 27 C
amanda.slaughter@biola.edu
SLAUGHTER, Arnie .... 859-572-5538 184 A
slaughtera@nku.edu
SLAUGHTER, Clinton .... 530-895-2366.. 27 F
slaughtercl@butte.edu
SLAUGHTER, Craig .... 740-427-5430 355 E
slaughterc@kenyon.edu
SLAUGHTER, John .... 254-267-7024 442 E
jslaughter@rangercollege.edu
SLAUGHTER, Lauren ..... 308-398-7548 266 A
laurenslaughter@cccneb.edu
SLAUGHTER,
Matthew, J .... 603-646-2460 273 E
matthew.j.slaughter@dartmouth.edu
SLAUGHTER, Mildred .... 361-593-2834 447 D
mildred.slaughter@tamuk.edu
SLAUGHTER, Shirley ..... 510-981-2840.. 56 E
sslaughter@peralta.edu
SLAUGHTER ALLISON,
Michelle .... 619-961-4222.. 67 E
mallison@tjsl.edu
SLAVAS, Douglas .... 413-565-1000 205 G
dslavas@baypath.edu
SLAVIK, Bryan .... 406-791-5363 265 H
bryan.slavik@uprovidence.edu
SLAVIN, Cheryl .... 212-824-2294 301 E
cslavin@huc.edu
SLAVIN, Dennis .... 646-660-6504 292 L
dennis.slavin@baruch.cuny.edu
SLAVIN, Joan, L .... 714-850-4800.. 67 A
slavin@taftu.edu
SLAVIN, Lisa .... 781-239-2501 214 E
lslavin@massbay.edu
SLAVSKY, David, B .... 773-508-8352 142 D
dslavsk@luc.edu

SLAWSON, Linda .... 903-785-7661 441 G
lslawson@parisjc.edu
SLAYMAKER, Valerie ..... 651-213-4746 236 B
vslaymaker@hazeldenbettyford.edu
SLAYTER, Misty .... 318-487-5443 187 C
mistyslayter@cltcc.edu
SLEAR, Sharon .... 410-532-5321 201 B
sslear@ndm.edu
SLEASMAN, Brent, C ..... 419-434-4201 364 G
president@winebrenner.edu
SLEDGE, Donald .... 205-929-6442.... 2 H
dsledge@lawsonstate.edu
SLEIGHT, Garth .... 406-874-6212 263 I
sleightg@milescc.edu
SLEJKO, Christa .... 972-273-3010 435 E
cslejko@dcccd.edu
SLEKAR, Timothy .... 608-663-2293 493 C
tslekar@edgewood.edu
SLEMMER, Duane .... 280-467-8039 131 D
dlslemmer@nnu.edu
SLENSKI, Amanda .... 989-463-7465 220 H
slenskiar@alma.edu
SLEPITZA, Ron .... 816-501-3750 250 F
ron.slepitza@avila.edu
SLEPPPY,
Christopher, G .... 317-921-4882 157 H
SLESNICK, Daniel, T ..... 512-471-4363 455 A
slesnick@austin.utexas.edu
SLEVA, Michael .... 616-451-3511 223 B
msleva@davenport.edu
SLIK, Mark .... 850-201-6127 111 C
slikm@tcc.fl.edu
SLIMAN, David .... 601-266-6633 249 F
david.sliman@usm.edu
SLIMAN, George, S ...... 412-578-8826 380 E
gssliman@carlow.edu
SLIMP, Mickey .... 903-877-1276 456 D
mickey.slimp@uthct.edu
SLINGER, Ron .... 303-914-6417.. 82 C
ron.slinger@rrcc.edu
SLINKARD, Tiffany .... 417-455-5636 252 D
tiffanyslinkard@crowder.edu
SLINKER, Bryan, K .... 509-335-9515 486 A
slinker@vetmed.wsu.edu
SLISZ, John, P .... 716-851-1851 299 F
slisz@ecc.edu
SLIWA, William .... 610-861-1320 391 A
sliwaw@moravian.edu
SLIWINSKI, Laura .... 858-513-9240.. 26 G
laura.sliwinski@ashford.edu
SLIWOSKI, Richard, F ... 804-828-9647 473 F
rfsliwoski@vcu.edu
SLIZEWSKI, James .... 215-489-2220 382 D
james.slizewski@delval.edu
SLOAN, Damon, N .... 815-740-3398 151 J
dsloan@stfrancis.edu
SLOAN, Daniel .... 315-792-3282 324 B
drsloan@utica.edu
SLOAN, Gary .... 585-785-1355 300 B
gary.sloan@flcc.edu
SLOAN, Jeremy .... 503-552-2005 374 E
jsloan@nunm.edu
SLOAN, Joe .... 504-526-4745 189 H
joes@nationsu.edu
SLOAN, Joel, A .... 719-333-9115 504 C
joal.sloan@usafa.edu
SLOAN, Jon, R .... 504-526-4745 189 H
jonroy@nationsu.edu
SLOAN, Justin, M .... 512-448-8545 442 M
jsloan@stedwards.edu
SLOAN, Linda, M .... 651-962-6765 244 E
sloa9780@stthomas.edu
SLOAN, Noel .... 806-742-4250 451 B
noel.a.sloan@ttu.edu
SLOAN, Robert .... 281-649-3450 437 H
rsloan@hbu.edu
SLOAN, Roberta, H .... 315-684-6461 321 D
sloanrh@morrisville.edu
SLOAN, Roberta, H .... 315-684-6053 321 D
sloanrh@morrisville.edu
SLOAN, Stacey .... 303-751-8700.. 77 A
sloan@bel-rea.com
SLOAN LATTA, Marcia .. 419-434-5722 363 A
latta@findlay.edu
SLOANE, Kobi .... 504-398-2235 191 C
ksloane@uhcno.edu
SLOANE, Todd .... 585-585-1836 300 B
todd.sloane@flcc.edu
SLOANE, Tomecca .... 919-760-8631 331 B
sloaneto@meredith.edu
SLOAS, Ike .... 901-843-3880 423 J
sloasi@rhodes.edu

SLOBERT, Yantee .... 585-385-8423 314 A
yslobert@sjfc.edu
SLOCKETT, Deena .... 407-303-7747.. 94 D
deena.slockett@ahu.edu
SLOCUM, Cameron .... 214-648-6404 457 B
cameron.slocum@utsouthwestern.edu
SLOCUM, Dameian .... 401-598-1000 404 I
dameian.slocum@jwu.edu
SLOCUM, Jeff .... 315-655-7192 292 F
jslocum@cazenovia.edu
SLOCUM, Stacy, S .... 585-385-8388 314 A
sslocum@sjfc.edu
SLOKA, Sandra, L .... 815-740-5026 151 J
ssloka@stfrancis.edu
SLOMOVITS, Mendel ..... 732-414-2834 285 D
SLONAKER, Victoria ...... 440-646-8101 363 G
victoria.slonaker@ursuline.edu
SLONE, Greta .... 606-886-3863 180 J
gslone0020@kctcs.edu
SLONE, Katrina .... 606-368-6091 178 D
katrinaslone@alc.edu
SLONE, Tammy, L .... 937-766-7987 349 G
slonet@cedarville.edu
SLONIKER, Steve .... 206-878-3710 481 H
SLONIKER, Steven .... 509-574-4676 487 A
ssloniker@yvcc.edu
SLOOP, John, M .... 615-322-7360 428 D
john.m.sloop@vanderbilt.edu
SLOSS, Robert .... 401-232-6140 404 F
rsloss@bryant.edu
SLOTNICK, Ruth .... 508-531-2783 212 B
ruth.slotnick@bridgew.edu
SLOVER, Todd .... 603-513-1379 274 H
todd.slover@granite.edu
SLOWENSKY, Joseph .... 714-744-7882.. 36 C
slowensky@chapman.edu
SLOWINSKI, Mandy ...... 715-346-4771 497 F
mandy.slowinski@uwsp.edu
SLUDER, Dusti .... 850-484-2232 104 H
dsluder@pensacolastate.edu
SLUDER, Richard, D ..... 615-898-2324 422 H
richard.sluder@mtsu.edu
SLUDER, Robin .... 423-478-7727 423 G
rsluder@ptseminary.edu
SLUIS, Kimberly .... 630-637-5152 144 H
kasluis@noctrl.edu
SLUSSER, Karen, L .... 570-389-4055 394 A
kslusse2@bloomu.edu
SLUSSER, Margaret .... 609-652-4501 283 D
margaret.slusser@stockton.edu
SLY, Melissa .... 215-951-1000 387 C
sly@lasalle.edu
SMAGLO, Stephanie ...... 757-233-8757 477 F
ssmaglo@vwu.edu
SMAIL, John .... 704-687-5630 342 E
jsmail@uncc.edu
SMAILAGIC, Aida .... 650-493-4430.. 64 A
aida.smailagic@sofia.edu
SMAJIC, Alen .... 315-792-5331 307 D
asmajic@mvcc.edu
SMALARZ, Matthew ...... 215-885-2360 389 F
msmalarz@manor.edu
SMALE, Heather .... 207-454-1025 195 B
hsmale@wccc.me.edu
SMALE, Maura .... 718-260-5470 295 B
msmale@citytech.cuny.edu
SMALL, Allison .... 503-375-7193 373 A
asmall@corban.edu
SMALL, Blake .... 425-889-5235 482 F
blake.small@northwestu.edu
SMALL, Brenda .... 610-436-2223 396 A
bsmall@wcupa.edu
SMALL, Brent .... 575-562-2194 285 M
brent.small@enmu.edu
SMALL, Brent .... 502-897-4721 184 C
bsmall@sbts.edu
SMALL, Christine .... 760-384-6219.. 46 M
christine.small@cerrocoso.edu
SMALL, Cindy .... 406-265-3787 264 F
csmall@msun.edu
SMALL, Darlene .... 843-383-8039 408 D
dsmall@coker.edu
SMALL, Elizabeth .... 508-793-3759 208 B
esmall@holycross.edu
SMALL, Gillian .... 201-692-7094 277 K
gsmall@fdu.edu
SMALL, Jessica .... 575-562-2218 285 M
jessica.small@enmu.edu
SMALL, John, J .... 630-637-5701 144 H
jjsmall@noctrl.edu
SMALL, Josh .... 803-641-3719 413 D
joshs@usca.edu

SMALL, Natissia .... 314-516-5128 261 D
smalln@umsl.edu
SMALL, Samuel .... 360-623-8614 479 C
samuel.small@centralia.edu
SMALL, Steven, L .... 972-883-2355 455 B
SMALL, Tyvi .... 865-974-6270 427 G
tsmall@utk.edu
SMALL KELLOGG,
Rebecca .... 315-786-6549 303 F
rsmallkellogg@sunyjefferson.edu
SMALLEN, Stephanie ..... 423-746-5213 426 F
ssmallen@tnwesleyan.edu
SMALLEY, Mark .... 704-978-5496 336 C
msmalley@mitchellcc.edu
SMALLEY, Robin .... 727-864-7564.. 97 J
smallerm@eckerd.edu
SMALLEY, Sara .... 651-255-6150 243 D
ssmalley@unitedseminary.edu
SMALLIDGE, Dianne ...... 617-732-1528 216 B
dianne.smallidge@mcphs.edu
SMALLING, Scott, J ...... 315-268-6473 296 A
ssmallin@clarkson.edu
SMALLING, Steven .... 315-268-4368 296 A
sssmalli@clarkson.edu
SMALLS, Howard .... 650-417-2013.. 55 G
hsmalls@paloaltou.edu
SMALLWOOD, Amber .... 678-839-5170 126 E
amksmall@westga.edu
SMALLWOOD, Pamela .. 417-865-2815 253 B
smallwoodp@evangel.edu
SMALLWOOD, Will .... 405-585-5412 367 F
will.smallwood@okbu.edu
SMARR, Debbie .... 903-465-6030 437 D
smarrd@grayson.edu
SMART, Cely .... 916-278-7737.. 32 E
cely.smart@csus.edu
SMART, III, Clifton, M . 417-836-8500 256 E
president@missouristate.edu
SMART, Denise, T .... 512-245-2311 450 E
ds37@txstate.edu
SMART, Gary .... 406-771-5140 264 G
gary.smart@gfcmsu.edu
SMART, James, G .... 305-284-4505 112 E
jsmart@miami.edu
SMART, Karl, L .... 989-774-6501 222 C
smart1kl@cmich.edu
SMART, Robert .... 616-331-2281 224 E
smartr@gvsu.edu
SMART, Robert .... 203-582-3325.. 87 G
robert.smart@quinnipiac.edu
SMART, Scott .... 575-562-2611 285 M
scott.smart@enmu.edu
SMART, Stephanie .... 845-434-5750 322 A
ssmart@sunysullivan.edu
SMART, William .... 615-297-7545 418 C
smartb@aquinascollege.edu
SMATRESK, Neal .... 940-565-4307 454 A
president@unt.edu
SMEAL, Tim .... 716-338-1019 303 D
timsmeal@mail.sunyjcc.edu
SMEATON, George .... 603-358-2625 275 A
george.smeaton@keene.edu
SMEDLEY, David .... 973-877-3000 277 I
dsmedley@essex.edu
SMEDLEY, Patricia .... 615-460-6403 418 F
patricia.smedley@belmont.edu
SMEDLEY, Susan .... 281-425-6336 439 D
ssmedley@lee.edu
SMEED, Shane .... 816-584-6205 258 A
shane.smeed@park.edu
SMELSER, Dick, W .... 865-694-6565 425 F
rwsmelser@pstcc.edu
SMELTZER, Brian, K ...... 717-815-1293 404 A
bksmeltzer@ycp.edu
SMENT, Nicole .... 608-262-2321 496 B
nsment@uwsa.edu
SMETANKA, John .... 724-805-2227 398 E
john.smetanka@email.stvincent.edu
SMID, Terry .... 563-425-5359 170 A
smidt@uiu.edu
SMIDT, Galen .... 605-274-4014 415 B
galen.smidt@augie.edu
SMIDT, Niki .... 605-658-5641 416 H
niki.smidt@usd.edu
SMILEY, Ellen .... 318-274-6238 191 E
smileye@gram.edu
SMILEY, Ellen .... 318-274-3228 191 E
smileye@gram.edu
SMILEY, Joseph .... 727-712-5851 106 E
smiley.joseph@spcollege.edu
SMILEY, Justin .... 760-744-1150.. 55 I
jsmiley@palomar.edu

SMITH, Eric 270-789-5202 179 E
epsmith@campbellsville.edu
SMITH, Eric 304-357-4358 488 G
ericsmith@ucwv.edu
SMITH, Eric, D 805-922-6966.. 24 J
ericdsmith@hancockcollege.edu
SMITH, Eric, L 906-227-1314 228 F
esmith@nmu.edu
SMITH, Ericka 702-895-3958 271 E
ericka.smith@unlv.edu
SMITH, Erin 425-739-8353 482 A
erin.smith@lwtech.edu
SMITH, Erin, T 724-946-7327 402 G
smithet@westminster.edu
SMITH, Eva 425-640-1171 480 F
esmith@edcc.edu
SMITH, Evelyn 423-869-6360 421 C
evelyn.smith@lmunet.edu
SMITH, Exsa 928-428-8289.. 12 E
exsa.smith@eac.edu
SMITH, JR., Frank, M .. 502-776-1443 184 B
fsmith@simmonscollegeky.edu
SMITH, Fred, R 740-376-4791 356 A
fred.smith@marietta.edu
SMITH, Frederick 201-200-3474 279 E
fsmith@njcu.edu
SMITH, Fritz 562-907-4951.. 75 A
fritz@whittier.edu
SMITH, Gabie 336-278-6490 328 K
gsmith@elon.edu
SMITH, Garrett 480-461-7211.. 13 D
garrett.smith@mesacc.edu
SMITH, Garrett 617-287-5859 211 E
garrett.smith@umb.edu
SMITH, Gary 606-693-5000 182 G
gsmith@kmbc.edu
SMITH, Gary 716-827-2507 323 D
SMITH, Gene 910-755-7302 332 F
smithgene@brunswickcc.edu
SMITH, Gene, D 614-292-2477 358 I
smith.5407@osu.edu
SMITH, George 207-879-8955 194 B
gsmith@idsva.edu
SMITH, Gladys, A 260-422-5561 155 H
gasmith@indianatech.edu
SMITH, Glenn, C 503-552-1514 374 E
gsmith@nunm.edu
SMITH, Grace 310-434-4454.. 62 E
smith_grace@smc.edu
SMITH, Greg 973-408-3580 277 C
gsmith2@drew.edu
SMITH, Gregory 662-720-7164 248 C
gcsmith@nemcc.edu
SMITH, Gregory 714-449-7456.. 51 A
gsmith@ketchum.edu
SMITH, Gregory 530-242-7648.. 63 H
gsmith@shastacollege.edu
SMITH, Heather, L 989-774-3197 222 C
hutch1hl@cmich.edu
SMITH, Heidi 714-816-0366.. 67 I
heidilinn.smith@trident.edu
SMITH, Heidi 713-313-1178 449 C
heidi.smith@tsu.edu
SMITH, Hilary 212-355-1501 292 J
hsmith@christies.edu
SMITH, Hilary, B 618-537-6981 143 B
hbsmith@mckendree.edu
SMITH, Holly 870-512-7841.. 18 B
holly_smith@asun.edu
SMITH, Holly 253-964-6287 483 D
hsmith@pierce.ctc.edu
SMITH, Howard 620-235-4113 176 F
smith@pittstate.edu
SMITH, Howard 620-235-6170 176 F
smith@pittstate.edu
SMITH, Ian 765-983-1215 154 G
smithia@earlham.edu
SMITH, Idelia 413-552-2228 214 D
ismith@hcc.edu
SMITH, Ivan 303-722-5724.. 80 L
ismith@lincolntech.edu
SMITH, Ivan 301-934-7724 198 A
ilsmith1@csmd.edu
SMITH, J. Cole 315-443-4341 322 C
SMITH, J. Malcolm 401-341-2206 406 A
malcolm.smith@salve.edu
SMITH, J. Malcolm 401-341-2205 406 A
malcolm.smith@salve.edu
SMITH, Jackie 256-233-8172.... 4 D
jackie.smith@athens.edu
SMITH, Jacqueline 713-221-8541 453 B
smithja@uhd.edu

SMITH, James 740-654-6711 359 G
smithj27@ohio.edu
SMITH, James 334-241-5436.... 7 C
jesmith@troy.edu
SMITH, James 573-681-5164 254 E
smithj2@lincolnu.edu
SMITH, James 740-392-6868 357 B
james.smith@mvnu.edu
SMITH, James 909-384-8600.. 59 I
jsmith@sbccd.cc.ca.us
SMITH, James 214-860-2232 435 C
jhsmith@dcccd.edu
SMITH, James, A 513-244-8621 350 I
jamie.smith@ccuniversity.edu
SMITH, James, E 614-247-4089 358 I
smith.4@osu.edu
SMITH, James, M 734-487-2211 223 H
president@emich.edu
SMITH, Jamie 716-851-1675 299 F
smithjd@ecc.edu
SMITH, Jamie 580-581-2245 365 G
jasmith@cameron.edu
SMITH, Jamie 602-557-5757.. 16 J
jamie.smith@phoenix.edu
SMITH, Jamie, M 941-752-5587 108 G
smithj4@scf.edu
SMITH, Jane 404-270-6070 125 B
janesmith@spelman.edu
SMITH, Jane, L 630-942-2481 135 A
smithja@cod.edu
SMITH, Janet 423-869-6287 421 C
janet.smith@lmunet.edu
SMITH, Janet, F 931-540-2510 424 G
janet.smith@columbiastate.edu
SMITH, Janet, M 724-946-7139 402 G
smithjm@westminster.edu
SMITH, Jared 704-355-4305 327 H
robert.smith2@carolinascollege.edu
SMITH, Jarret, L 540-828-5469 465 D
jlsmith@bridgewater.edu
SMITH, Jason 415-503-6281.. 60 H
jsmith@sfcm.edu
SMITH, Jason 870-248-4000.. 18 F
jason.smith@blackrivertech.edu
SMITH, Jason 269-687-5642 230 F
jsmith07@swmich.edu
SMITH, Jason 409-944-1356 437 B
jsmith@gc.edu
SMITH, Jason, S 832-842-9064 452 E
jsmith10@uh.edu
SMITH, Jason, S 832-842-9064 452 F
jsmith10@uh.edu
SMITH, Jaye 843-953-5056 407 F
jsmith53@citadel.edu
SMITH, Jeff 806-720-7482 439 H
jeff.smith@lcu.edu
SMITH, Jeff 941-487-4353 109 D
jsmith@ncf.edu
SMITH, Jeff 970-339-6253.. 76 G
jeff.smith@aims.edu
SMITH, Jeffrey 504-671-6480 187 E
jsmith@dcc.edu
SMITH, Jeffrey, N 716-645-4592 316 F
jeff@buffalo.edu
SMITH, Jennifer 212-229-5300 308 C
jennifer.smith@newschool.edu
SMITH, Jennifer 412-244-3240 386 D
SMITH, Jennifer, A 253-535-7811 482 H
jennifer.smith@plu.edu
SMITH, Jennifer, B 270-745-6824 185 E
jennifer.breiwa.smith@wku.edu
SMITH, Jenny 828-328-7252 330 F
jenny.smith@lr.edu
SMITH, Jerry 928-344-7535.. 10 J
jerry.smith@azwestern.edu
SMITH, Jesse 661-255-1050.. 28 K
jsmith@calarts.edu
SMITH, Jesse, R 601-477-4100 246 F
jesse.smith@jcjc.edu
SMITH, Jessi, L 719-255-3963.. 83 B
jsmith20@uccs.edu
SMITH, Jessica 276-326-4473 465 B
jsmith@bluefield.edu
SMITH, Jessie, C 615-329-8731 419 K
jcsmith@fisk.edu
SMITH, Jill 818-677-2121.. 32 D
jill.smith@csun.edu
SMITH, Jim 858-513-9240.. 26 G
jim.smith@ashford.edu
SMITH, Jim 918-293-5234 368 D
jim.smith10@okstate.edu
SMITH, Jo 615-353-3303 425 D
jo.smith@nscc.edu

SMITH, Joan 303-914-6410.. 82 C
joan.smith@rrcc.edu
SMITH, Joanne, H 512-245-2152 450 E
js14@txstate.edu
SMITH, Joe 509-313-6801 481 D
smithj@gonzaga.edu
SMITH, Joel 308-432-6345 268 E
jsmith@csc.edu
SMITH, Joel, M 607-746-4522 320 G
smithjm@delhi.edu
SMITH, John 251-460-6171.... 8 F
johns@southalabama.edu
SMITH, John 515-271-2969 165 A
john.smith@drake.edu
SMITH, John, W 309-298-1888 152 D
jw-smith@wiu.edu
SMITH, John, W 309-298-1814 152 D
jw-smith@wiu.edu
SMITH, John, W 401-454-6686 405 D
jsmith@risd.edu
SMITH, Johnny 252-493-7915 336 H
jsmith@email.pittcc.edu
SMITH, Joianne, L 847-635-1801 145 G
joismith@oakton.edu
SMITH, Jonathan, C 314-977-4586 259 H
jonathan.smith@slu.edu
SMITH, Jordan 270-809-5706 183 G
jsmith3@murraystate.edu
SMITH, Joseph, E 423-439-4317 419 J
smithje@etsu.edu
SMITH, Joseph, R 410-651-6862 203 A
jrsmith@umes.edu
SMITH, Joshua 606-337-1164 179 G
joshua.smith@ccbbc.edu
SMITH, Joshua 254-501-5838 447 A
j.smith@tamuct.edu
SMITH, Joy, S 864-833-8275 411 I
jssmith@presby.edu
SMITH, Joy, S 864-656-0471 408 A
joy@clemson.edu
SMITH, Joyya 617-725-4110 219 A
jsmith19@suffolk.edu
SMITH, Judith, L 310-206-1083.. 69 A
judis@college.ucla.edu
SMITH, Judy 814-824-3650 390 C
jsmith@mercyhurst.edu
SMITH, Juliet 410-822-5400 197 I
jsmith@chesapeake.edu
SMITH, Justin 580-477-7915 371 F
justin.smith@newmoodle.wosc.edu
SMITH, Justin 541-917-4214 374 A
smithju@linnbenton.edu
SMITH, Kala 573-681-6156 254 E
smithk@lincolnu.edu
SMITH, Kalith 575-624-8380 287 A
ksmith@nmmi.edu
SMITH, Karen 405-325-3021 371 B
karen-smith@ou.edu
SMITH, Karen 901-678-3687 427 D
kasmith@memphis.edu
SMITH, Karen 908-737-0585 278 E
ksmith@kean.edu
SMITH, Karen 815-455-8781 143 A
ksmith@mchenry.edu
SMITH, Karen 919-573-5350 340 F
ksmith@shepherds.edu
SMITH, Kate 480-517-8270.. 13 G
catherine.smith@riosalado.edu
SMITH, Kate 610-989-1240 402 B
SMITH, Kathleen, E 562-902-3367.. 65 C
kathleensmith@scuhs.edu
SMITH, Kathleen, S 405-325-3221 371 B
kathleensheasmith@ou.edu
SMITH, Kathy 614-234-2230 356 I
ksmith@mccn.edu
SMITH, Katrina 806-291-3540 457 J
smithk@wbu.edu
SMITH, Kelli 607-777-2400 316 E
kksmith@binghamton.edu
SMITH, Kelli 718-429-6600 324 D
kelli.smith@vaughn.edu
SMITH, Kelli, J 928-523-1186.. 14 H
kelli.smith@nau.edu
SMITH, Kelly 619-849-2213.. 57 E
kellysmith@pointloma.edu
SMITH, Kelly, A 804-523-5449 474 H
ksmith@reynolds.edu
SMITH, Kelly, M 706-542-1914 125 G
kelly.smith@uga.edu
SMITH, Kelly, N 260-399-7700 161 D
ksmith@sf.edu
SMITH, Ken 254-295-4644 453 E
kasmith@umhb.edu

SMITH, Ken, L 423-478-7736 423 G
ksmith@ptseminary.edu
SMITH, Kenneth 540-231-1807 477 A
kensmith@vt.edu
SMITH, Kenneth 508-929-8121 213 E
kenneth.smith@worcester.edu
SMITH, Kenny 928-428-8342.. 12 E
kenny.smith@eac.edu
SMITH, JR., Kent, J 405-466-3201 366 F
president@langston.edu
SMITH, Kevin, L 785-864-4711 177 D
klsmith12@ku.edu
SMITH, Kevin, M 716-888-8501 292 D
smithk@canisius.edu
SMITH, Khrystal 864-503-5125 414 D
ksmith@uscupstate.edu
SMITH, Kia 601-974-1755 247 B
SMITH, Kim 704-637-4411 328 A
kasmith@catawba.edu
SMITH, Krista 229-928-1331 119 D
krista.smith@gsw.edu
SMITH, Kristen 870-512-7850.. 18 B
kristen_smith@asun.edu
SMITH, Kristen 516-686-7751 309 F
mksmith@nyit.edu
SMITH, Krystal, D 304-462-6193 490 C
krystal.smith@glenville.edu
SMITH, Kyle 352-588-8331 106 D
kyle.smith04@saintleo.edu
SMITH, Kyle 254-295-4591 453 E
klsmith@umhb.edu
SMITH, Kyle 979-230-3489 432 D
kyle.smith@brazosport.edu
SMITH, Kyle, A 570-326-3761 393 G
kas54@pct.edu
SMITH, Kyle, D 337-550-1218 189 A
kdsmith@lsue.edu
SMITH, Lace, M 253-535-7001 482 H
smithla@plu.edu
SMITH, Lane, M 205-726-2905.... 6 E
SMITH, Larry 310-954-4018.. 52 G
lsmith@msmu.edu
SMITH, Larry Alan 860-768-4468.. 88 H
larsmith@hartford.edu
SMITH, Laura 502-213-2136 181 F
laura.smith@kctcs.edu
SMITH, Laura, L 361-570-4801 453 C
smithl@uhv.edu
SMITH, Laurie 903-923-2090 436 D
lsmith@etbu.edu
SMITH, Lawrence 516-463-7202 302 B
lawrence.smith@hofstra.edu
SMITH, Leah 303-963-3014.. 77 G
leasmith@ccu.edu
SMITH, Leanne 901-572-2440 418 E
leanne.smith@bchs.edu
SMITH, Lee 703-539-6890 472 A
lsmith@stratford.edu
SMITH, Leila 606-487-3504 181 C
leila.smith@kctcs.edu
SMITH, Leslie 615-230-3476 426 B
leslie.smith@volstate.edu
SMITH, Leslie 601-643-8340 245 G
leslie.smith@colin.edu
SMITH, Leslie 903-875-7306 440 G
leslie.smith@navarrocollege.edu
SMITH, Lewis 312-503-0501 145 F
ljsmith@northwestern.edu
SMITH, Linda 706-864-1993 126 A
linda.smith@ung.edu
SMITH, Linda 340-692-4023 514 E
lsmith@uvi.edu
SMITH, Linda, D 919-209-2024 335 F
ldsmith@johnstoncc.edu
SMITH, Lisa 352-854-2322.. 96 O
smithl@cf.edu
SMITH, Lisa 360-538-4243 481 E
lisa.smith@ghc.edu
SMITH, Lisa 931-438-0028 425 C
lsmith@mscc.edu
SMITH, Lisa 602-639-7500.. 12 J
SMITH, Lisa 402-461-7773 267 D
lsmith@hastings.edu
SMITH, Lisa 307-754-6292 502 G
lisa.smith@nwc.edu
SMITH, Lisa, M 207-768-9525 196 E
lisa.m.smith@maine.edu
SMITH, Liz, M 413-545-0177 211 D
emsmith@umass.edu
SMITH, Lois 910-755-7474 332 F
smithl@brunswickcc.edu
SMITH, Lorenzo 916-278-6127.. 32 E
lsmith@csus.edu

SMITH, Steve .... 716-270-4681 299 F
ssmith@ecc.edu
SMITH, Steve .... 507-389-5022 239 C
steven.smith@mnsu.edu
SMITH, Steve .... 951-343-4261.. 27 J
ssmith@calbaptist.edu
SMITH, Steve .... 915-831-6472 436 E
ssmith54@epcc.edu
SMITH, Steve .... 432-264-5019 438 C
sismith@howardcollege.edu
SMITH, Steve, G .... 806-371-5008 430 A
sgsmith@actx.edu
SMITH, Steven .... 970-521-6657.. 81 D
steven.smith@njc.edu
SMITH, Steven .... 775-682-5613 271 F
ssmith@unr.edu
SMITH, Steven .... 973-378-9815 283 B
steven.smith@shu.edu
SMITH, Steven .... 304-424-8000 491 D
SMITH, Steven, A .... 801-422-6291 458 H
steve_smith@byu.edu
SMITH, Steven, E .... 516-877-3304 289 C
stsmith@adelphi.edu
SMITH, Steven, J .... 413-565-1000 205 G
ssmith@baypath.edu
SMITH, Steven, K .... 608-262-3956 496 C
sof@secfac.wisc.edu
SMITH, Steven, N .... 262-243-5700 493 B
steve.smith@cuw.edu
SMITH, Stuart .... 661-222-2784.. 28 K
stuartsmith@calarts.edu
SMITH, Stuart, A .... 859-858-3511 178 I
stuart.smith@asbury.edu
SMITH, Susan .... 817-515-1225 445 G
susan.smith@tccd.edu
SMITH, Susan .... 509-527-2615 485 H
susan.smith@wallawalla.edu
SMITH, Susan, S .... 267-359-5924 383 B
susan.smith@drexel.edu
SMITH, Susanne .... 614-947-6160 353 C
suzanne.smith@franklin.edu
SMITH, Suzanne .... 413-755-4221 215 F
smsmith@stcc.edu
SMITH, Suzanne, R .... 229-928-1361 119 D
suzanne.smith@gsw.edu
SMITH, Tamalea .... 908-709-7093 284 C
tsmith@ucc.edu
SMITH, Tammy .... 716-338-1054 303 D
tammysmith@mail.sunyjcc.edu
SMITH, Tammy .... 540-674-3600 475 B
tsmith@nr.edu
SMITH, Tanya .... 918-343-6816 369 F
tsmith@rsu.edu
SMITH, Tariva .... 678-323-7700.. 92 G
SMITH, Teresa .... 713-623-2040 430 K
tlsmith@aii.edu
SMITH, Teresa, A .... 856-227-7200 276 E
tasmith@camdencc.edu
SMITH, Teresa, L .... 714-879-3901.. 45 F
tlsmith@hiu.edu
SMITH, Teri .... 541-956-7847 376 D
tsmith@roguecc.edu
SMITH, Terri .... 661-763-7817.. 66 J
tsmith@taftcollege.edu
SMITH, Terry .... 732-247-5241 279 D
tsmith@nbts.edu
SMITH, Terry .... 713-646-1708 444 B
tsmith@stcl.edu
SMITH, Thomas .... 303-991-1575.. 76 H
thomas.smith@americansentinel.edu
SMITH, Thomas .... 951-827-5802.. 69 C
thomas.smith@ucr.edu
SMITH, Thomas .... 314-392-2264 256 C
smitht@mobap.edu
SMITH, Thomas .... 865-573-4517 420 G
tsmith@johnsonu.edu
SMITH, Thomas, J .... 616-234-3951 224 D
tsmith@grcc.edu
SMITH, Thomas, M .... 951-827-1129.. 69 C
provost@ucr.edu
SMITH, Thomas, P .... 570-941-7620 401 H
thomas.smith@scranton.edu
SMITH, Thomas, W .... 610-519-4651 402 D
thomas.w.smith@villanova.edu
SMITH, Tierra .... 813-253-7160 101 A
tsmith175@hccfl.edu
SMITH, Tiffany .... 816-322-0110 250 K
tiffany.smith@calvary.edu
SMITH, Tiffany .... 405-208-5181 367 I
tdsmith@okcu.edu
SMITH, Tim .... 256-549-8317.... 2 B
tsmith@gadsdenstate.edu
SMITH, Tim .... 205-226-4660.... 5 A
tsmith@bsc.edu
SMITH, Todd .... 815-455-8591 143 A
tsmith@mchenry.edu
SMITH, Todd .... 801-818-8900 459 K
todd.smith@provocollege.edu
SMITH, Todd .... 713-831-7225 454 H
tsmith1@stthom.edu
SMITH, Tracee .... 601-877-6170 244 H
tracee@alcorn.edu
SMITH, Tracina, A .... 260-422-5561 155 H
tasmith@indianatech.edu
SMITH, Tracy .... 601-403-1332 248 E
tsmith@prcc.edu
SMITH, Tracy, D .... 501-882-8806.. 17 F
tdsmith@asub.edu
SMITH, Travis .... 315-386-7300 320 E
smitht@canton.edu
SMITH, Travis, A .... 920-433-6621 492 B
travis.smith@bellincollege.edu
SMITH, Trent .... 620-276-9510 173 E
trent.smith@gcccks.edu
SMITH, Treva .... 706-867-2761 126 A
treva.smith@ung.edu
SMITH, Trevor .... 904-825-4681.. 98 E
tsmith@flagler.edu
SMITH, Tricia, G .... 410-548-3999 203 F
tgarveysmith@salisbury.edu
SMITH, Trisha .... 202-884-9000.. 93 B
smithtri@trinitydc.edu
SMITH, Tyne .... 641-673-1703 170 F
smitht@wmpenn.edu
SMITH, Valerie, A .... 610-328-8314 399 D
vsmith1@swarthmore.edu
SMITH, Vayta .... 707-527-4508.. 62 F
vsmith@santarosa.edu
SMITH, Vergina .... 501-337-5000.. 18 J
vsmith@coto.edu
SMITH, Vernon .... 304-724-3700 487 E
vsmith@apus.edu
SMITH, Vicky .... 478-757-2647 121 F
vicky.smith@mga.edu
SMITH, Vince .... 318-487-7135 106 I
vince.smith@lacollege.edu
SMITH, Virginia .... 405-945-3214 368 E
virginia.smith@osuokc.edu
SMITH, W. Randy .... 614-292-5881 358 I
smith.70@osu.edu
SMITH, Wade .... 719-587-7351.. 76 F
wsmith@adams.edu
SMITH, Wayne .... 845-341-4261 311 C
wayne.smith@sunyorange.edu
SMITH, Wendall .... 610-896-1000 385 L
w1smith@haverford.edu
SMITH, Wendy .... 530-226-4128.. 63 K
wsmith@simpsonu.edu
SMITH, Wendy .... 305-284-4101 112 E
wendy.smith@miami.edu
SMITH, Wendy, M .... 307-065-0412 502 F
wsmith@sheridan.edu
SMITH, Wesley .... 804-523-2296 474 H
wsmith@reynolds.edu
SMITH, William .... 860-444-8201 504 F
william.smith@uscg.mil
SMITH, William, C .... 508-565-1347 218 H
wsmith1@stonehill.edu
SMITH, III, William, C . 601-984-1010 249 E
wcsmith3@umc.edu
SMITH, Willie, E .... 225-216-8403 186 K
chancellorsoffice@mybrcc.edu
SMITH, Zelotes .... 415-458-3793.. 41 H
zelotes.smith@dominican.edu
SMITH-BATES,
Jacqui, S .... 206-281-2488 484 D
jacquisb@spu.edu
SMITH BRICE, Tanya .... 301-860-3705 203 C
tbrice@bowiestate.edu
SMITH-BUTLER, Lisa ..... 843-377-2144 407 D
lsbutler@charlestonlaw.edu
SMITH-CLAY, Deborah .. 859-371-9393 179 A
dclay@beckfield.edu
SMITH-COX, Cathy, L ... 276-964-7338 475 I
cathy.smith-cox@sw.edu
SMITH DICKERSON,
Janet .... 909-621-8355.. 37 C
janet.dickerson@claremont.edu
SMITH-HOWELL, Deb .... 402-554-3378 270 B
dsmith-howell@unomaha.edu
SMITH-HUPP, Karen ..... 301-934-7701 198 A
kshupp@csmd.edu
SMITH JONES, Tamica . 951-827-2671.. 69 C
tamica.smithjones@ucr.edu
SMITH-KELLER, Keley .... 605-668-1518 415 H
keley.smith-keller@mtmc.edu
SMITH MCKOY, Sheila . 510-436-1040.. 45 D
smith-mckoy@hnu.edu
SMITH-MCQUEENIE,
Lisa .... 617-521-2120 218 E
lisa.smithmcqueenie@simmons.edu
SMITH MOORE, Karen .. 718-960-8000 294 A
karen.smithmoore@lehman.cuny.edu
SMITH-PATTERSON,
Trina .... 817-515-7059 445 G
trina.patterson@tccd.edu
SMITH-RODRIGUEZ,
Sharlise .... 914-323-3134 305 J
sharlise.smith@mville.edu
SMITH SILVER, Rachel .. 440-775-8273 358 C
rachel.smith.silver@oberlin.edu
SMITH-SIMMONS,
Margie .... 317-274-4417 156 F
smithsim@iupui.edu
SMITH-WARD, Lori, A .. 606-474-3121 180 G
lsmithward@kcu.edu
SMITH-WELLER, Kelly ... 317-278-7631 156 F
kjbrown@iupui.edu
SMITH-WILLIAMS,
Michelle .... 773-995-3561 133 K
msmith99@csu.edu
SMITHEE, Deanna .... 812-535-5299 160 B
deanna.smithee@smwc.edu
SMITHER, Edward .... 803-754-4100 409 A
SMITHERS, Marc .... 585-567-9227 302 D
marc.smithers@houghton.edu
SMITHERS, Marc .... 585-567-9220 302 D
marc.smithers@houghton.edu
SMITHHISLER, Pete .... 701-845-7300 346 A
pete.smithisler@vcsu.edu
SMITHSON, Misty .... 620-947-3121 177 C
mistys@tabor.edu
SMITS, Karen .... 920-498-5615 500 F
karen.smits@nwtc.edu
SMOCK, Jordan .... 857-701-1230 215 E
jsmock@rcc.mass.edu
SMOKE, Gladden .... 864-596-9041 409 B
gladden.smoke@converse.edu
SMOKER, Gail .... 765-973-8254 156 C
gsmoker@iue.edu
SMOKOWSKI, Peter ...... 617-353-2148 207 D
psmokows@bu.edu
SMOLARSKI, SJ,
Dennis .... 408-554-4372.. 62 D
dsmolarski@scu.edu
SMOLEN, Jean .... 215-489-2278 382 D
jean.smolen@delval.edu
SMOLENSKY, Marjorie .. 309-341-5463 133 C
msmolensky@sandburg.edu
SMOLINSKY, Colin .... 757-221-2633 466 C
casmolinsky@wm.edu
SMOLOW, Bobbie .... 914-395-2476 315 F
bsmolow@sarahlawrence.edu
SMOLOWITZ, Janice ..... 973-655-3714 279 C
smolowitzj@mail.montclair.edu
SMOOKE, Mitchell .... 203-432-4220.. 89 D
mitchell.smooke@yale.edu
SMOOT, Althea .... 937-376-2946 360 D
asmoot@payne.edu
SMOOT, Lori .... 410-334-2898 204 F
lsmoot@worwic.edu
SMOROL, Bobbie, H ..... 315-792-3128 324 B
bsmorol@utica.edu
SMOTHERS, SR.,
Roderick, L .... 501-370-5275.. 20 G
rsmothers@philander.edu
SMOTHERS, Tony .... 319-296-4214 166 B
tony.smothers@hawkeyecollege.edu
SMOTHERS, Traci .... 504-762-3004 187 E
tsmoth@dcc.edu
SMUDER, Kristin .... 813-253-7180 101 A
ksmuder@hccfl.edu
SMULSON, Erik .... 202-687-8496.. 92 A
ems62@georgetown.edu
SMUNIEWSKI, Kevin ...... 843-792-2146 410 F
smuniewk@musc.edu
SMURDON, Melissa, J . 317-940-8200 153 F
msmurdon@butler.edu
SMURR, Sherry .... 269-488-4681 225 E
ssmurr@kvcc.edu
SMYLE, Faye .... 707-256-7155.. 53 C
fsmyle@napavalley.edu
SMYLIE, Dean .... 909-469-5469.. 74 I
dsmylie@westernu.edu
SMYRE, Russell .... 704-922-6462 334 F
smyre.russell@gaston.edu
SMYRE HINES, Beverly . 706-771-4156 114 J
bsmyre@augustatech.edu
SMYRSKI, Rose, M .... 608-342-1182 497 D
smyrskir@uwplatt.edu
SMYSER, Kathleen .... 610-527-0200 397 I
SMYTH, Alicia .... 386-226-7273.. 98 A
alicia.smyth@erau.edu
SMYTH, Cara .... 646-768-5300 301 B
SMYTH, Conor .... 608-266-2991 499 B
conor.smyth@wtcsystem.edu
SMYTH, Nancy, J .... 716-645-1267 316 F
sw-dean@buffalo.edu
SMYTH-MCGAHA,
Bonnie .... 501-882-8826.. 17 F
bmsmyth@asub.edu
SMYTHE, Don .... 619-239-0391.. 34 F
dsmythe@cwsl.edu
SMYTHE, Shantih .... 901-843-3966 423 J
smythes@rhodes.edu
SNAPP, Michael, J .... 801-863-8219 461 A
snappmi@uvu.edu
SNARE, Charles .... 308-432-6203 268 E
csnare@csc.edu
SNAVELY, Deanne .... 724-357-2609 394 G
snavely@iup.edu
SNAVELY, Joshua, M .... 405-466-3275 366 F
josh.snavely@langston.edu
SNEAD, Mary .... 276-739-2403 476 C
msnead@vhcc.edu
SNEDDEN, Kelly .... 316-323-6085 171 G
ksnedden@butlercc.edu
SNEED, Brian .... 915-747-5302 455 C
bjsneed@utep.edu
SNEED, Carlos .... 651-523-2423 236 A
csneed@hamline.edu
SNEED, Gregory .... 860-832-2377.. 84 I
g.sneed@ccsu.edu
SNEED, Gregory, W ...... 740-587-6624 352 G
sneedg@denison.edu
SNEED, Janice, B .... 318-670-9571 190 J
jsneed@susla.edu
SNEED, Kevin, B .... 813-974-2499 110 B
ksneed@usf.edu
SNEED, Mia .... 615-353-3024 425 D
mia.sneed@nscc.edu
SNEERINGER, Christine 301-447-5135 200 E
csneeringer@msmary.edu
SNEERINGER, Gerry ...... 301-405-2996 202 C
sneeri@umd.edu
SNELGROVE, Brian .... 478-218-3300 116 A
bsnelgrove@centralgatech.edu
SNELL, Beverly .... 406-638-3141 263 H
snellb@lbhc.edu
SNELL, Carolyn, R .... 803-535-5338 407 G
csnell@claflin.edu
SNELL, Cynthia .... 803-754-4100 409 A
SNELL, Debbie .... 510-436-1049.. 45 D
snell@hnu.edu
SNELL, Laurence, I .... 904-632-3294 100 B
laurence.snell@fscj.edu
SNELL, Nancy .... 216-791-5000 351 A
nancy.snell@cim.edu
SNELL, Pete .... 912-262-4303 116 F
psnell@coastalpines.edu
SNELL, Scott .... 417-625-9651 256 D
snell-s@mssu.edu
SNELLGROVE,
Michael, R .... 256-824-2560.... 8 B
michael.snellgrove@uah.edu
SNELLING, John .... 602-787-6840.. 13 E
john.snelling@paradisevalley.edu
SNELSON, Laura .... 435-652-7542 460 G
laura.snelson@dixie.edu
SNIDER, Daren .... 765-973-8495 156 C
dpsnider@iu.edu
SNIDER, Darlene .... 509-527-3689 485 G
darlene.snider@wwcc.edu
SNIDER, Heather .... 815-921-4075 147 E
h.snider@rockvalleycollege.edu
SNIDER, Jason .... 502-863-8024 180 E
jason_snider@georgetowncollege.edu
SNIDER, Jason .... 618-985-3741 139 I
jasonsnider@jalc.edu
SNIDER, Jodie .... 531-622-2930 267 H
jsnider@mccneb.edu
SNIDER, Kay, E .... 803-516-4935 412 C
ksnider@scsu.edu
SNIDER, Lana .... 419-267-1225 358 A
lsnider@northweststate.edu
SNIDER, Neil .... 205-652-3614.... 9 A
nsnider@uwa.edu
SNIDER, Scott .... 509-313-2222 481 D
sniders@gonzaga.edu
SNIDER, Theresa .... 304-724-5000 487 H
mdavis@cdu.edu
SNIEZEK, James .... 240-567-1690 200 C
james.sniezek@montgomerycollege.edu

SOLAZZO, Daniel .... 513-732-5204 362 F
solazzds@ucmail.uc.edu
SOLAZZO, James .... 843-349-2717 408 C
jsolazzo@coastal.edu
SOLBACH, Robin .... 732-987-2757 278 B
rsolbach@georgian.edu
SOLBACH, Robin .... 732-987-2681 278 B
rsolbach@georgian.edu
SOLBERG, Dale .... 916-348-4689.. 42 C
dsolberg@epic.edu
SOLBERG, Eric .... 630-829-6497 132 E
esolberg@ben.edu
SOLBERG, Greg .... 301-846-2411 198 E
gsolberg@frederick.edu
SOLBERG, Janet .... 402-557-7095 265 J
jsolberg@bellevue.edu
SOLBERG, Laura .... 352-588-8218 106 D
laura.solberg@saintleo.edu
SOLBERG, Lori .... 605-995-2805 415 C
lori.solberg@dwu.edu
SOLBERG, Roger .... 814-732-2981 394 F
rsolberg@edinboro.edu
SOLBRIG, Ronald .... 208-282-2330 130 H
solbrona@isu.edu
SOLDWISCH, Sandie, S 815-282-7900 148 C
sandiesoldwisch@sacn.edu
SOLDWISCH, Sandie, S 815-282-7909 148 E
sandie.soldwisch@osfhealthcare.org
SOLDZ, Stephen .... 617-277-3915 207 C
soldzs@bgsp.edu
SOLE, Mary, L .... 407-823-5496 109 E
mary.sole@ucf.edu
SOLECKI, Amanda .... 410-287-1003 197 H
asolecki@cecil.edu
SOLEIM, Heather, M ..... 218-477-4060 239 D
heather.soleim@mnstate.edu
SOLEM, Thomas .... 701-777-0561 345 C
thoms.solem@und.edu
SOLEMBRINO, Karie ..... 410-572-8741 204 F
ksolembrino@worwic.edu
SOLEMSAAS, Rachel, H 808-934-2504 129 A
rsolems@hawaii.edu
SOLERNOU, Sheila .... 203-285-2393.. 85 E
ssolernou@gwcc.commnet.edu
SOLEY, Mary Ann .... 773-907-4754 134 C
msoley@ccc.edu
SOLHEIM, Derek, N ...... 319-352-8330 170 C
derek.solheim@wartburg.edu
SOLIBAKKE, Karl .... 715-682-1207 495 C
ksolibakke@northland.edu
SOLIMAN, Phebe .... 973-328-5056 277 B
psoliman@ccm.edu
SOLIMAN, Sam .... 574-936-8898 153 A
sma.soliman@ancill.edu
SOLINA, DeAnna .... 209-954-5056.. 60 J
dsolina@deltacollege.edu
SOLINSKI, Patrick .... 405-682-1611 367 H
patrick.t.solinski@occc.edu
SOLIS, Amy .... 701-627-4738 346 G
asolis@nhsc.edu
SOLIS, Carlos .... 512-245-1799 450 E
crs218@txstate.edu
SOLIS, Federico .... 956-764-5955 439 C
fsolis@laredo.edu
SOLIS, Francisco .... 210-486-0063 429 H
fsolis@alamo.edu
SOLIS, Gerard .... 813-974-1680 110 B
gsolis@usf.edu
SOLIS, Ricardo .... 956-721-5101 439 C
president@laredo.edu
SOLIS, Santiago .... 410-704-2051 204 A
ssolis@towson.edu
SOLIS, Shannon .... 559-638-0300.. 66 F
shannon.solis@reedleycollege.edu
SOLIS, Vanessa .... 915-215-4300 451 D
vanessa.solis@ttuhsc.edu
SOLIS, Vincent, R .... 775-445-4236 271 G
vincent.solis@wnc.edu
SOLIZ, Gina, M .... 315-228-7431 296 F
gsoliz@colgate.edu
SOLIZ, Sandra .... 713-525-3116 454 H
solizs@stthom.edu
SOLIZ, Ty .... 432-685-6467 440 E
asoliz@midland.edu
SOLKO-OLLIFF, Carol ... 785-628-4176 173 B
cmsolko@fhsu.edu
SOLLARS, David .... 785-670-2045 177 G
david.sollars@washburn.edu
SOLLENBERGER,
Mitchel .... 313-593-5353 231 F
msollenb@umich.edu
SOLLENBERGER,
Mitchel .... 313-593-5030 231 F
msollenb@umich.edu
SOLLER, Dan, A .... 260-399-7700 161 D
dsoller@sf.edu
SOLLOSI, Nancy, B .... 336-334-4822 335 A
nbsollosi@gtcc.edu
SOLMS, Daniel .... 260-359-4016 155 F
dsolms@huntington.edu
SOLOCHEK, Arlen .... 480-731-8232.. 12 O
arlen.solochek@domail.maricopa.edu
SOLOCHEK, Beverly ...... 212-217-4000 299 H
beverly_solochek@fitnyc.edu
SOLOMON, Bobby .... 662-862-8032 246 D
rtsolomon@iccms.edu
SOLOMON, Clemmie .... 240-567-1469 200 C
clemmie.solomon@
montgomerycollege.edu
SOLOMON, Ira .... 504-865-5422 191 B
isolomon@tulane.edu
SOLOMON, James .... 540-423-9069 474 G
jsolomon@germanna.edu
SOLOMON, Jeffrey, S ... 508-831-5288 220 E
solomon@wpi.edu
SOLOMON, Jerome .... 408-498-5154.. 38 F
jsolomon@cogswell.edu
SOLOMON, Joseph .... 718-851-8721 325 G
SOLOMON, Kimberly .... 713-221-8138 453 B
solomonk@uhd.edu
SOLOMON, Mary Ellen . 412-396-6668 383 C
solomon3@duq.edu
SOLOMON, Michael, J .. 734-764-4401 231 E
mjsolo@umich.edu
SOLOMON, Ronald .... 225-216-8267 186 K
solomonr@mybrcc.edu
SOLOMON, Saige .... 318-869-5115 186 B
ssolomon@centenary.edu
SOLOMON, Samuel .... 781-736-8539 207 E
sasolomon@brandeis.edu
SOLOMON, Shoshana ... 973-267-9404 280 G
shoshanasolomon@rca.edu
SOLOMON, Sigrid, B .... 937-481-2270 364 E
sigrid_solomon@wilmington.edu
SOLOMON, Stephanie ... 850-558-4516 111 C
solomons@tcc.fl.edu
SOLOMON, Steven .... 850-201-6549 111 C
solomos@tcc.fl.edu
SOLOMON, William, G . 478-301-2771 121 E
solomon_wg@mercer.edu
SOLOMONS, Mary, L .... 518-580-5619 316 A
msolomon@skidmore.edu
SOLOMONT, Alan .... 617-627-3453 219 B
alan.solomont@tufts.edu
SOLOMOU, Costas .... 585-245-5619 318 E
solomou@geneseo.edu
SOLOMOU, Costas .... 202-994-6040.. 91 F
csolomou@gwu.edu
SOLORZANO, Fernando 562-985-4101.. 31 F
fernando.solorzano@csulb.edu
SOLORZANO, Jose .... 787-891-0925 508 K
jsolorza@aguadilla.inter.edu
SOLOWAY, Seth .... 914-251-6196 319 E
seth.soloway@purchase.edu
SOLT, Michael .... 562-985-5306.. 31 F
michael.solt@csulb.edu
SOLTANSHAHI, Ali .... 216-687-3910 351 B
a.soltanshahi@csuohio.edu
SOLTIS, Bryan .... 860-727-6903.. 87 A
bsoltis@goodwin.edu
SOLTIS, Corinne .... 206-934-6739 484 B
corinne.soltis@seattlecolleges.edu
SOLTIS, Robert, P .... 317-940-8960 153 F
rsoltis@butler.edu
SOLTZ-KNOWLTON,
Bonnie .... 860-528-4111.. 87 A
SOLUM, Catlin, E .... 701-788-4856 345 E
catlin.solum@mayvillestate.edu
SOLUM, Rachel .... 303-245-4804.. 81 B
rsolum@naropa.edu
SOLVERSON, Natalie .... 608-785-8006 496 F
nsolverson@uwlax.edu
SOM, Andrew .... 707-654-1085.. 32 B
asom@csum.edu
SOMAN, Sherril .... 616-331-6821 224 E
somans@gvsu.edu
SOMER, Regina .... 402-461-2422 266 A
reginasomer@cccneb.edu
SOMERA, R. Ray, D ...... 671-735-5528 505 C
reneray.somera@guamcc.edu
SOMERLAD, Tracy .... 910-755-7422 332 F
somerladt@brunswickcc.edu
SOMERO, Marty .... 970-351-2502.. 83 E
marty.somero@unco.edu
SOMERS, Charles .... 215-641-6538 390 H
csomers@mc3.edu
SOMERS, Christine .... 570-674-6314 390 G
csomers@misericordia.edu
SOMERS, John .... 520-533-2391.. 11 M
somersj@cochise.edu
SOMERS, Kevin .... 870-743-3000.. 20 C
ksomers@northark.edu
SOMERS, Michael .... 508-531-1255 212 B
msomers@bridgew.edu
SOMERS, Micki .... 870-743-3000.. 20 C
msomers@northark.edu
SOMERSET, Cheryl .... 864-587-4236 412 G
somersetc@smcsc.edu
SOMERSON, Rosanne .... 401-454-6764 405 D
president@risd.edu
SOMERVELL, Ronald ..... 703-284-6941 469 C
ronald.somervell@marymount.edu
SOMERVILLE, Charles ... 304-696-2424 490 D
somervil@marshall.edu
SOMERVILLE,
Dionne, D .... 570-389-4062 394 A
dsomervi@bloomu.edu
SOMERVILLE, Mark .... 781-292-2509 209 E
mark.somerville@olin.edu
SOMERVILLE, Mary .... 303-556-4587.. 83 C
mary.somerville@ucdenver.edu
SOMERVILLE, Mary .... 209-946-2949.. 70 E
msomerville@pacific.edu
SOMERVILLE, Tim .... 951-719-2994.. 57 I
doc@golfcollege.edu
SOMMA, Victor .... 508-425-1216 215 D
vsomma@qcc.mass.edu
SOMMER, Carl .... 314-792-6140 254 D
sommer@kenrick.edu
SOMMER, Thomas .... 810-762-9525 225 H
tsommer@kettering.edu
SOMMER, Valerie .... 314-505-7593 251 I
sommerv@csl.edu
SOMMERER, Shaun .... 660-626-2395 250 A
ssommerer@atsu.edu
SOMMERFELD, Curtis ... 541-956-7238 376 D
csommerfeld@roguecc.edu
SOMMERFELD, Janee .... 253-833-9111 481 F
jsommerfeld@greenriver.edu
SOMMERS, Bill .... 304-876-5009 490 E
wsommers@shepherd.edu
SOMMERS, Donald .... 212-960-5200 326 E
dsommers@yu.edu
SOMMERS, Greg .... 972-273-3518 435 E
gsommers@dcccd.edu
SOMMERS, Janet, B ...... 651-631-5201 244 D
jbsommers@unwsp.edu
SOMMERS, Kathleen ..... 330-494-6170 361 F
ksommers@starkstate.edu
SOMMERS, Mary .... 308-865-8520 269 I
sommersm@unk.edu
SOMMERS, Rhoda .... 765-998-5108 160 F
rhoda_sommers@taylor.edu
SOMMERS, Rhoda .... 937-328-6060 350 L
sommersr@clarkstate.edu
SOMMERVILLE, Jan .... 616-395-7780 225 B
sommerville@hope.edu
SOMNARAIN, Emry .... 305-821-3333.. 99 E
esomnarain@fnu.edu
SOMOZA, Amarilis .... 305-443-9170 106 A
asomoza@sabercollege.edu
SOMPOLSKI, Robert ...... 847-635-1690 145 G
somplski@oakton.edu
SON, Chang Ho .... 714-527-0691.. 42 E
SON, David, Y .... 214-768-4485 444 E
dson@smu.edu
SON, Jane .... 510-594-3720.. 28 D
jane.son@cca.edu
SONBOL, Dena .... 651-290-6398 242 G
dena.sonbol@mitchellhamline.edu
SONDAG, Lynn .... 415-482-3269.. 41 H
lynn.sondag@dominican.edu
SONDER, Henk, E .... 401-456-9577 405 C
hsonder@ric.edu
SONDEY, Joann .... 914-831-0288 297 A
jsondey@cw.edu
SONDEY, Stephen .... 973-720-2862 284 I
sondeys@wpunj.edu
SONDHEIMER, Rachel ... 845-938-4041 504 H
SONENBERG, Joyce ...... 940-898-3064 451 F
jsonenberg@twu.edu
SONESON, Heidi .... 715-425-4882 497 E
heidi.soneson@uwrf.edu
SONEYE, Sara .... 219-785-5697 159 G
ssoneye@pnw.edu
SONG, A Li .... 516-364-0808 309 A
asong@nycollege.edu
SONG, Bok, H .... 636-327-4645 255 L
dbo@midwest.edu
SONG, Connie .... 513-231-2223 348 C
csong@athenaeum.edu
SONG, Hee Sook .... 770-220-7925 118 B
joysong@gcuniv.edu
SONG, Jae, M .... 636-327-4645 255 L
vpsong@midwest.edu
SONG, Jae, P .... 636-327-4645 255 L
jp@midwest.edu
SONG, James .... 636-327-4645 255 L
js8083@gmail.com
SONG, Peter .... 323-221-1024.. 42 F
SONG, Sarah .... 818-947-2606.. 49 F
songsj@lavc.edu
SONG, Sumie .... 773-244-5571 145 A
ssong@northpark.edu
SONG, Uncheol .... 213-385-2322.. 75 D
unsong@wmu.edu
SONG, Violet .... 512-454-1188 430 G
info@aoma.edu
SONGER, Nancy, B .... 215-895-2167 383 B
nancy.b.songer@drexel.edu
SONI, Varun .... 213-740-6110.. 72 B
vasoni@usc.edu
SONKAYNAR, Zehra ...... 707-527-4431.. 62 F
zsonkaynar@santarosa.edu
SONNEMA, Roy .... 509-359-2227 480 E
rsonnema1@ewu.edu
SONNENBERG, Jeffrey .. 847-586-4364 132 B
jsonnenberg@aiuniv.edu
SONNENBERGER,
David .... 630-829-6240 132 E
dsonnenberger@ben.edu
SONNENBLICK, Carol ... 718-552-1170 295 B
csonnenblick@citytech.cuny.edu
SONNENSTEIN, Mark .... 718-933-6700 307 G
ssonnenstein@monroecollege.edu
SONNENSTRAHL,
Samuel .... 202-651-5060.. 91 E
samuel.sonnenstrahl@gallaudet.edu
SONNTAG, Dave .... 509-313-6192 481 D
sonntagd@gonzaga.edu
SONNTAG, Michael .... 803-938-3826 414 B
sonntagm@uscsumter.edu
SONODA, Kazuhiro .... 509-865-8584 481 G
sonoda_k@heritage.edu
SONRICKER, Nicholas ... 716-851-1282 299 F
sonrickern@ecc.edu
SONSTEBY, Jill .... 651-638-6254 234 C
jks44888@bethel.edu
SONTAG, Michael .... 513-244-4766 357 A
michael.sontag@msj.edu
SOO, Billy .... 617-552-3260 207 B
billy.soo@bc.edu
SOOD, Mary .... 256-761-6201.... 7 B
msood@talladega.edu
SOODSMA, Heidi .... 920-693-1631 499 G
heidi.soodsma@gotoltc.edu
SOOHOO-REFAEI,
Sandy .... 619-849-2783.. 57 E
sandysoohoorefaei@pointloma.edu
SOOTER, David .... 405-422-1246 369 E
david.sooter@redlandscc.edu
SOPCICH, Joe .... 913-469-8500 174 D
jsopcich@jccc.edu
SOPCZYK, Debbie .... 518-464-8500 299 G
dsopczyk@excelsior.edu
SOPER, Dessa .... 949-214-3088.. 40 F
dessa.soper@cui.edu
SOPER, Jeff, D .... 712-362-0422 166 F
jsoper@iowalakes.edu
SOPER, Sarah .... 765-973-8231 156 C
saeaton@iue.edu
SOPHEA, So .... 646-313-8000 295 E
sophea.so@guttman.cuny.edu
SORA, Wendy .... 808-956-9264 128 F
wendytak@hawaii.edu
SORAN, Chris .... 253-566-5287 485 C
csoran@tacomacc.edu
SORBELLO, Barbara, C . 804-627-5300 465 C
barbara_sorbello@bshsi.org
SORBELLO, Janine .... 302-225-6261.. 90 E
sorbello@gbc.edu
SORBER, Jerad .... 360-538-4121 481 E
jerad.sorber@ghc.edu
SORBER, Jerad .... 503-338-2326 372 E
jsorber@clatsopcc.edu
SORBER, Todd .... 973-684-5656 280 B
tsorber@pccc.edu
SORDELET, Teresa, A .... 260-399-7700 161 D
tsordelet@sf.edu
SORELLE, Patrick .... 920-498-5753 500 F
patrick.sorelle@nwtc.edu
SOREM, JR., James, R . 918-631-2288 371 E
james-sorem@utulsa.edu

SPARKS, George, E .... 540-568-7073 468 F sparksge@jmu.edu
SPARKS, Jane .... 760-757-2121.. 52 E jsparks@miracosta.edu
SPARKS, John .... 618-634-3230 149 A johns@shawneecc.edu
SPARKS, Kathy, M .... 651-631-5390 244 D kmsparks@unwsp.edu
SPARKS, Kenton .... 610-341-1396 383 D ksparks@eastern.edu
SPARKS, Laura .... 212-353-4240 297 E sparks@cooper.edu
SPARKS, Maria .... 518-464-8768 299 G msparks@excelsior.edu
SPARKS, Michele, G ..... 513-529-7596 356 E sparksm4@miamioh.edu
SPARKS, Rick .... 509-533-8833 480 B rick.sparks@ccs.spokane.edu
SPARKS, Rick .... 540-231-7951 477 A rasparks@vt.edu
SPARKS, Rick .... 509-533-8833 480 A rick.sparks@ccs.spokane.edu
SPARKS, Sonny .... 662-472-9015 246 C sparks@holmescc.edu
SPARKS, Sonny .... 662-472-9015 246 C ssparks@holmescc.edu
SPARKS, Steve .... 252-222-6087 333 A sparkss@carteret.edu
SPARKS, Terrell .... 801-878-1494 272 C tsparks@roseman.edu
SPARKS, William, O ...... 505-272-5849 288 G wsparks@salud.unm.edu
SPARLING, Jennifer ...... 760-366-5294.. 40 K jsparling@cmccd.edu
SPARLING, Steve .... 231-843-5824 232 J ssparling@westshor.edu
SPARPANA, Eileen .... 906-217-4023 221 O eileen.sparpana@baycollege.edu
SPARR, Cynthia .... 630-466-7900 152 C csparr@waubonsee.edu
SPARROW, Anita .... 860-512-3223.. 85 G asparrow@manchestercc.edu
SPARROW, Rebecca, M 607-255-2723 297 F rms18@cornell.edu
SPARROW, Suzanne ...... 610-399-2255 394 C ssparrow@cheyney.edu
SPATAFORE, Marisa ...... 408-864-8672.. 43 C spataforemarisa@deanza.edu
SPATARO, Keith .... 650-543-3853.. 51 F kspataro@menlo.edu
SPATARO-WILSON, Jennifer, A .... 540-665-5412 471 E jspataro@su.edu
SPATES, Gerald .... 336-334-7800 341 F gspates@ncat.edu
SPATZ, Dan .... 541-506-6034 372 G dspatz@cgcc.edu
SPAULDING, Angela ..... 806-651-2730 448 C aspaulding@wtamu.edu
SPAULDING, II, Henry, W .... 740-392-6868 357 B hspauldi@mvnu.edu
SPAULDING, Jeb .... 802-224-3000 463 H jeb.spaulding@vsc.edu
SPAULDING, Melinda ... 713-313-1361 449 C melinda.spaulding@tsu.edu
SPAULDING, Thad .... 303-605-5504.. 80 N tspaul1@msudenver.edu
SPAYD, Ann .... 315-787-4005 300 C ann.spayd@flhcon.edu
SPAYD, Bonnie .... 610-372-4721 397 B bspayd@racc.edu
SPAYER, Roger .... 847-925-6360 137 H rspayer@harpercollege.edu
SPEAKER, Cindy .... 315-364-3311 325 B cspeaker@wells.edu
SPEAKMAN, Jennifer ..... 614-236-7127 349 D jspeakman@capital.edu
SPEAKS, Michael, A ...... 315-443-0790 322 C maspeaks@syr.edu
SPEAKS, Tiffany .... 202-885-3651.. 90 J tspeaks@american.edu
SPEAR, Brenda .... 602-489-5300.. 10 E brenda.spear@arizonachristian.edu
SPEAR, Catherine, C ..... 434-924-7179 473 A ccs9a@virginia.edu
SPEAR, Jeff .... 863-667-5000 107 K jbspear@seu.edu
SPEAR, Nanette .... 509-434-5213 480 A nanette.spear@ccs.spokane.edu
SPEAR, Pamela .... 603-526-3621 272 H pspear@colby-sawyer.edu
SPEAREN, Charlene ...... 803-376-5780 406 F cspearen@allenuniversity.edu
SPEARING, Mike .... 205-348-5490.... 7 G mspearing@uasystem.ua.edu
SPEARMAN, Howard ..... 608-246-6464 499 H hjspearman@madisoncollege.edu
SPEARS, Brandon .... 218-679-2860 242 P
SPEARS, Curtis, L .... 210-434-6711 441 E cspears@ollusa.edu
SPEARS, Jacqueline, D . 913-541-1220 174 G jdspears@ksu.edu
SPEARS, Justin, R .... 530-226-4140.. 63 K jspears@simpsonu.edu
SPEARS, Linda, C .... 615-963-5281 426 D lspears@tnstate.edu
SPEARS, Lori, D .... 510-841-1905.. 25 G
SPEARS, Marty .... 501-279-4335.. 19 D mspears@harding.edu
SPEARS, Sylvia .... 617-824-8500 208 H sylvia_spears@emerson.edu
SPEARS-BOYD, Amy ..... 931-540-2509 424 G aspears@columbiastate.edu
SPEAS, Penny .... 336-517-1563 327 B pseas@bennett.edu
SPEAS, Philip, E .... 606-693-5000 182 G pspeas@kmbc.edu
SPECHT, Andrea .... 952-358-8866 239 F andrea.specht@normandale.edu
SPECHT, Andy .... 805-922-6966.. 24 J andy.specht@hancockcollege.edu
SPECHT, Mark, A .... 610-566-1776 403 E mspecht@williamson.edu
SPECHT, Matthew, F ..... 773-442-4600 145 B m-specht@neiu.edu
SPECHT, Nancy .... 585-275-5572 323 J nancy.specht@rochester.edu
SPECHT, Neva, J .... 828-262-3078 341 B spechtnj@appstate.edu
SPECK, Anne .... 484-664-3165 391 C annespeck@muhlenberg.edu
SPECK, Christie .... 707-864-7000.. 64 C christie.speck@solano.edu
SPECTAR, Jem, M .... 814-269-2090 401 B spectar@pitt.edu
SPECTER, Robert, M ...... 202-319-5606.. 91 B specter@cua.edu
SPECTOR, Carol .... 617-824-8586 208 H carol_spector@emerson.edu
SPEECH, Angela .... 903-593-8311 448 H aspeech@texascollege.edu
SPEED, Bonnie .... 404-727-6289 117 F baspeed@emory.edu
SPEED, Coleen .... 318-274-3338 191 E speedc@gram.edu
SPEED, Heather .... 719-549-3082.. 81 K heather.speed@pueblocc.edu
SPEED, Melissa .... 276-498-5237 464 K mspeed@acp.edu
SPEED, Sam .... 318-257-4917 191 F sspeed@latech.edu
SPEELMAN, Diana .... 814-866-6641 388 A dspeelman@lecom.edu
SPEER, Brian .... 484-664-4332 391 C brianspeer@muhlenberg.edu
SPEER, Brian .... 704-406-4269 329 A bspeer@gardner-webb.edu
SPEGG, Samantha .... 601-643-8342 245 G samantha.spegg@colin.edu
SPEHN, Steven .... 507-222-4271 234 F sspehn@carleton.edu
SPEIDEL, Daniel .... 603-897-8576 274 B dspeidel@rivier.edu
SPEISER, Lynn .... 419-267-1312 358 A lspeiser@northweststate.edu
SPEISSER, Nancy .... 757-493-6946 124 E nspeisser@southuniversity.edu
SPELL, Ashley .... 312-499-4184 148 I aspell@saic.edu
SPELL, Paul .... 601-477-4223 246 F paul.spell@jcjc.edu
SPELLMAN, Amy, C ...... 717-871-5804 395 D amy.spellman@millersville.edu
SPELLMAN, Carlton .... 910-672-1151 341 E cspellma@uncfsu.edu
SPELLMAN, Denise .... 504-816-4864 186 D dspellman@dillard.edu
SPELLS, Doretha, J .... 757-727-5213 468 B doretha.spells@hamptonu.edu
SPELLS, Kaschia .... 252-246-1214 339 C kspells@wilsoncc.edu
SPELLS FENTRY, Rhonda .... 301-546-0987 201 C spellsrx@pgcc.edu
SPELMAN, Amy .... 309-298-1914 152 D ae-spelman@wiu.edu
SPENCE, Charles .... 434-592-3503 468 H cpspence@liberty.edu
SPENCE, Jeff .... 334-347-2623.... 2 A jspence@escc.edu
SPENCE, Jeffery .... 215-572-2088 379 A spencej@arcadia.edu
SPENCE, Jon, N .... 913-971-3279 175 G jnspence@mnu.edu
SPENCE, Joseph .... 607-778-5210 318 A spencejs@sunybroome.edu
SPENCE, Juanita, M ...... 252-335-3586 341 D jmidgette@ecsu.edu
SPENCE, Laura .... 802-586-7711 463 D lspence@sterlingcollege.edu
SPENCE, Lisa .... 812-237-8439 155 G lisa.spence@indstate.edu
SPENCE, Mary .... 716-829-7736 298 F spencem@dyc.edu
SPENCE, Thomas .... 615-460-6417 418 F thom.spence@belmont.edu
SPENCE, Weymouth ...... 301-891-4128 204 C wspence@wau.edu
SPENCER, A. Clayton .... 207-786-6100 193 B cspencer@bates.edu
SPENCER, Barbara .... 269-749-7642 229 H bspencer@olivetcollege.edu
SPENCER, Christine ...... 410-837-6134 204 B cspencer@ubalt.edu
SPENCER, Deborah .... 860-231-5390.. 89 B dspencer@usj.edu
SPENCER, Delmy .... 530-741-6705.. 76 C dspencer@yccd.edu
SPENCER, Estelle, H ..... 413-205-3461 205 A estelle.spencer@aic.edu
SPENCER, Gene .... 610-409-3789 402 A gspencer@ursinus.edu
SPENCER, Janett .... 256-306-2628.... 1 F janet.spencer@calhoun.edu
SPENCER, Jed .... 801-626-6586 461 B jedspencer@weber.edu
SPENCER, Jeremy .... 508-626-4500 212 D jspencer1@framingham.edu
SPENCER, Joel .... 303-329-6355.. 70 K finaid@cstcm.edu
SPENCER, JR., John ..... 304-327-4118 489 P jspencer@bluefieldstate.edu
SPENCER, SJ, John .... 617-735-9780 209 A spencerj@emmanuel.edu
SPENCER, John, D .... 817-515-5079 445 G john.spencer@tccd.edu
SPENCER, Joseph, F ..... 419-434-4791 363 A spencer@findlay.edu
SPENCER, Julie .... 424-207-3763.. 54 I jspencer@otis.edu
SPENCER, Keith, J .... 417-667-8181 252 A kspencer@cottey.edu
SPENCER, Lisa .... 304-647-6369 491 A lspencer@osteo.wvsom.edu
SPENCER, Lori .... 901-761-9494 419 D lspencer@concorde.edu
SPENCER, Mark .... 812-488-2238 161 A ms628@evansville.edu
SPENCER, Mary Ellen ... 865-694-6517 425 F mespencer@pstcc.edu
SPENCER, Morgan .... 843-953-3706 407 F mspence4@citadel.edu
SPENCER, Nichole .... 706-771-4035 114 J nichole.spencer@augustatech.edu
SPENCER, Rick, E .... 630-637-5209 144 H respencer@noctrl.edu
SPENCER, Rosa .... 334-876-9241.... 2 D rosa.spencer@wccs.edu
SPENCER, Ruth .... 845-437-7751 324 C ruspencer@vassar.edu
SPENCER, Scott .... 412-392-3876 397 A sspencer@pointpark.edu
SPENCER, Shanan .... 304-876-5276 490 E sspencer@shepherd.edu
SPENCER, Shannon, M . 419-772-2036 358 H s-spencer@onu.edu
SPENCER, Shawn .... 678-225-7340 396 D shawnsp@pcom.edu
SPENCER, Stephen .... 256-233-6502.... 4 D stephen.spencer@athens.edu
SPENCER, Susan .... 660-263-4100 257 B susanspencer@macc.edu
SPENCER, Tammy .... 352-365-3502 102 T spencert@lssc.edu
SPENCER, Terri .... 303-368-7462.. 81 G tspencer@pmi.edu
SPENCER, Travis .... 908-852-1400 276 G travis.spencer@centenaryuniversity.edu
SPENCER, Weldon .... 704-216-6131 330 H
SPENCER, OFM, William .... 217-228-5432 146 F spencwi@quincy.edu
SPENCER, Yvette .... 205-226-7720.... 5 A yspencer@bsc.edu
SPENCER-MONTEIRO, Carol .... 508-999-8705 211 F cspencer@umassd.edu
SPENGLER, Gregory, C . 410-706-1264 202 D gspengler@umaryland.edu
SPENNER, Anne .... 816-235-1576 261 C spennerae@umkc.edu
SPENSLEY, Nicole .... 803-641-3338 413 D nicolesp@usca.edu
SPERGER, Herb .... 610-785-6284 398 A hsperger@scs.edu
SPERICO, Jodie .... 516-877-3118 289 C jsperico@adelphi.edu
SPERLING, Chad .... 218-793-2436 240 A chad.sperling@northlandcollege.edu
SPERLING, Jonathan ..... 858-653-6740.. 46 I jsperling@jpcatholic.edu
SPERLING, Mark .... 219-980-6887 156 E masperli@iun.edu
SPERLING, Michael .... 845-905-4616 298 A michael.sperling@culinary.edu
SPERLING, Susan, S ..... 510-723-6641.. 35 O ssperling@chabotcollege.edu
SPEROS, Michael .... 916-278-5772.. 32 E msperos@csus.edu
SPERRING, Tiffany .... 614-222-6183 351 D tsperring@ccad.edu
SPERRY, Sarah .... 412-396-5894 383 C sperrys@duq.edu
SPERRY, Trevor .... 970-675-3329.. 78 G trevor.sperry@cncc.edu
SPESERT, Douglas .... 310-360-8888.. 27 B
SPETKA, Rosemary, V ... 315-792-5495 307 D rspetka@mvcc.edu
SPETS, Steve .... 906-932-4231 224 B stevem@gogebic.edu
SPETZ, Jason .... 715-232-5076 498 A spetzj@uwstout.edu
SPEZIANI, Humberto, M .... 305-284-5450 112 E hmspez@miami.edu
SPEZZACATENA, Maricel .... 305-273-4499.. 96 L maricel@cbt.edu
SPICER, Christopher ..... 360-650-6144 486 F kit.spicer@wwu.edu
SPICER, Christopher, L . 712-274-5103 168 B spicer@morningside.edu
SPICER, Donald, Z .... 301-445-2729 202 B dspicer@usmd.edu
SPICER, Erin .... 850-484-1706 104 H espicer@pensacolastate.edu
SPICER, Kerry .... 716-839-8519 298 B kspicer@daemen.edu
SPICER, LeRoy .... 814-234-7755 399 B lspicer@southhills.edu
SPICER, Michael .... 909-621-8142.. 57 F michael.spicer@pomona.edu
SPICER, Udella .... 229-217-4159 125 A uspicer@southernregional.edu
SPICKER, Brian .... 480-731-8098.. 12 O brian.spicker@domail.maricopa.edu
SPIECKER, Karl .... 719-549-2320.. 79 A karl.spiecker@csupueblo.edu
SPIEGEL, Benjamin .... 732-367-1060 275 J
SPIEGEL, Sam .... 303-273-3884.. 78 I sspiegel@mines.edu
SPIEGELMAN, Kathy ...... 617-373-2226 217 F
SPIELMAN, George, L ... 607-746-4091 320 G spielmgl@delhi.edu
SPIERS, Cynthia, E .... 419-995-8200 354 H spiers.c@rhodesstate.edu
SPIERS, William .... 850-201-8399 111 C spiersw@tcc.fl.edu
SPIES, Brent .... 314-889-4564 253 C bspies@fontbonne.edu
SPIES, Carolyn, I .... 973-748-9000 276 A carolyn_spies@bloomfield.edu
SPIES, Dennis .... 847-970-4699 152 A dspies@usml.edu
SPIES, Don .... 281-459-7629 443 D don.spies@sjcd.edu
SPIESMAN, John .... 440-375-7426 355 G jspiesman@lec.edu
SPIEZIO, Kim .... 304-357-4875 488 G kimspiezio@ucwv.edu
SPIKEREIT, Damien .... 417-626-1234 257 F spikereit.damien@occ.edu

STABILE, Joseph .... 914-633-2207 302 G
jstabile@iona.edu
STABILE, Steve .... 212-229-3500 308 C
stabiles@newschool.edu
STACE, Peter, A .... 718-817-3200 300 E
stace@fordham.edu
STACEY, Elizabeth .... 314-529-9364 254 H
estacey@maryville.edu
STACEY, Eric .... 651-690-8778 242 R
emstacey@stkate.edu
STACEY, Robert .... 206-543-5340 485 F
bstacey@uw.edu
STACEY, Simon .... 410-455-2164 202 E
spstacey@umbc.edu
STACHACZ, John .... 570-408-4254 403 D
john.stachacz@wilkes.edu
STACHOWIAK, Bonni .... 714-966-6307.. 72 F
STACHOWSKI,
Mary Albertine .... 716-896-0700 324 E
smalbertine@villa.edu
STACHURA, Hubert .... 631-656-2157 300 D
hubert.stachura@ftc.edu
STACHYRA, Karen, L ..... 219-989-2213 159 G
kstachyr@pnw.edu
STACK, Betty .... 704-669-4163 333 E
stackb520@clevelandcc.edu
STACK, Dana .... 619-388-7579.. 60 E
dstack@sdccd.edu
STACK, Eileen .... 716-926-8773 301 H
estack@hilbert.edu
STACK, John .... 305-348-7266 109 A
john.stack@fiu.edu
STACK, OSA, John, P ... 610-519-4550 402 D
john.stack@villanova.edu
STACK, Kelly .... 800-785-0585.. 39 G
kelly.stack@columbiacollege.edu
STACK, Kim .... 401-874-4777 406 B
kstack@uri.edu
STACK, Lisa .... 617-984-1663 218 B
lstack@quincycollege.edu
STACK, Patrick .... 314-968-6921 262 C
stackpa@webster.edu
STACK, Rachel, C .... 618-650-2345 149 F
rstack@siue.edu
STACK, Robert .... 863-837-5962 105 A
bstack@polk.edu
STACK LOMBARDO,
Jessie .... 585-245-5721 318 E
stack@geneseo.edu
STACKHOUSE TAETZSCH,
Cindra .... 630-752-5049 152 F
cindra.taetzsch@wheaton.edu
STACKMAN, William, B . 573-882-0157 261 B
william.stackman@missouri.edu
STACKPOLE, Richard ..... 513-732-5278 362 F
richard.stackpole@uc.edu
STACKPOOLE,
Roger, W .... 315-445-4174 304 C
stackprw@lemoyne.edu
STACKS, Pamela .... 408-924-2488.. 34 B
pamela.stacks@sjsu.edu
STACY, Alan .... 909-607-8235.. 37 D
alan.stacy@cgu.edu
STACY, Jeanne .... 225-216-8591 186 K
stacyj@mybrcc.edu
STACY, Mark .... 252-744-2201 341 C
stacyma17@ecu.edu
STACY, Mark, W .... 585-395-5149 318 B
mstacy@brockport.edu
STADICK, Anna .... 262-595-2167 497 C
stadick@uwp.edu
STADING, Gary .... 903-334-6678 448 B
gary.stading@tamut.edu
STADLER, Albert, E .... 417-625-9807 256 D
stadler-a@mssu.edu
STADLER, Lindsay .... 909-607-3373.. 37 D
lindsay.stadler@cgu.edu
STADLER, Megan .... 315-786-6500 303 F
mstadler@sunyjefferson.edu
STAEBLER, Ned .... 313-577-2164 232 I
nedstaebler@wayne.edu
STAEHLE, Andrea .... 760-862-1326.. 39 A
astaehle@collegeofthedesert.edu
STAFFA, Adam .... 206-533-6775 484 G
astaffa@shoreline.edu
STAFFORD, Ben .... 409-984-6354 450 B
staffordbk@lamarpa.edu
STAFFORD, Gina .... 423-425-4363 428 A
gina-stafford@utc.edu
STAFFORD, James .... 254-295-4607 453 E
jstafford@umhb.edu
STAFFORD, Joanne .... 405-733-7373 369 I
joannestafford@rose.edu
STAFFORD, Kyle .... 580-745-3079 369 K
kstafford@se.edu
STAFFORD, Laura .... 419-372-2079 348 H
llstaff@bgsu.edu
STAFFORD, Margaret .... 717-254-8321 382 F
stafford@dickinson.edu
STAFFORD, Mark .... 501-812-2248.. 23 B
mstafford@uaptc.edu
STAFFORD, Matt .... 417-626-1234 257 F
stafford.matt@occ.edu
STAFFORD, Michael ...... 713-718-5051 437 I
michael.stafford@hccs.edu
STAFFORD,
Michael Dale .... 713-780-9777 430 C
STAFFORD, Pam .... 606-759-7141 182 A
pam.stafford@kctcs.edu
STAFFORD, Ronnie .... 843-921-6953 411 F
rstafford@netc.edu
STAGER, Karl .... 281-756-3594 429 I
kstager@alvincollege.edu
STAGGERS, Leroy .... 803-934-3211 411 C
lstaggers@morris.edu
STAGGERS, Periana .... 973-290-4211 277 A
pstaggers@cse.edu
STAGNER, Annessa .... 719-336-1519.. 80 K
annessa.stagner@lamarcc.edu
STAHL, C.J .... 215-972-2059 393 D
cstahl@pafa.edu
STAHL, Frank .... 620-450-2238 176 G
franks@prattcc.edu
STAHL, Jess .... 503-399-6145 372 C
jess.stahl@chemeketa.edu
STAHL, Jody .... 406-657-2278 264 E
jody.stahl@msubillings.edu
STAHL, Stephen, D .... 440-826-2762 348 E
sstahl@bw.edu
STAHL, Ted .... 816-235-1625 261 C
stahlt@umkc.edu
STAHLE, Noel .... 641-673-1010 170 F
stahlen@wmpenn.edu
STAHLEY, Timothy .... 970-521-6655.. 81 D
timothy.stahley@njc.edu
STAHLEY-CUMMINGS,
Melissa .... 307-268-2349 501 U
cummings@caspercollege.edu
STAHURA, Kurt, A .... 716-286-8270 310 D
stahura@niagara.edu
STAIGER, Jennifer, L ..... 301-447-8387 200 E
staiger@msmary.edu
STAINE, Kristin .... 617-217-9228 206 A
kstaine@baystate.edu
STAINES, Gail .... 660-543-4140 260 K
staines@ucmo.edu
STAKELIN, Will .... 360-438-4354 483 H
wstakelin@stmartin.edu
STAKER, Julie .... 319-399-8500 164 A
jstaker@coe.edu
STAKES, Robert, L .... 915-747-5683 455 C
rlstakes@utep.edu
STALCUP, Susie .... 615-322-6673 428 D
susie.stalcup@vanderbilt.edu
STALDER, Michele .... 907-455-2850.. 10 A
mestalder@alaska.edu
STALDER, Rob .... 662-621-4050 245 E
rstalder@coahomacc.edu
STALEY, Avery .... 704-216-6080 330 H
astaley@livingstone.edu
STALEY, Marc, E .... 419-772-2462 358 H
m-staley@onu.edu
STALEY, Michael .... 407-708-2390 107 D
staleym@seminolestate.edu
STALEY, Priscilla, A ...... 214-860-2038 435 C
pstaley@dcccd.edu
STALIDES, Jason .... 309-341-5448 133 C
jstalides@sandburg.edu
STALL, Beth .... 214-860-2392 435 C
sbstall@dcccd.edu
STALLCUP, Jackie, E ..... 818-677-3301.. 32 D
jackie.stallcup@csun.edu
STALLING, Undria .... 470-639-0484 122 D
undria.stalling@morehouse.edu
STALLINGS, Amanda ..... 817-257-4684 448 G
a.stallings@tcu.edu
STALLINGS, Laura .... 503-352-2191 375 G
laurastallings@pacificu.edu
STALLINGS, Samaria ..... 781-239-3175 214 E
sstallings@massbay.edu
STALLINGS, Sean .... 609-771-1855 276 I
stalling@tcnj.edu
STALLINGS, Tamya .... 870-512-7822.. 18 B
tamya_stallings@asun.edu
STALLMAN, Amber .... 607-777-6569 316 E
stallman@binghamton.edu
STALLMAN, Jeanne .... 541-552-6221 376 E
stallman@sou.edu
STALLMAN, Jeanne .... 541-552-6699 376 E
stallman@sou.edu
STALLMANN, Diane .... 773-298-3089 148 G
stallmann@sxu.edu
STALNAKER, Ron .... 912-478-1294 119 C
rstalnaker@georgiasouthern.edu
STALNAKER, Samantha . 817-515-1795 445 G
samantha.stalnaker@tccd.edu
STALTER, Danielle .... 814-944-5643 404 B
danielle.stalter@yti.edu
STALVEY, John .... 907-786-1050.... 9 H
provost@alaska.edu
STAM, Allan, C .... 434-924-0812 473 A
acs8tb@virginia.edu
STAM, Theodore, R .... 207-798-4282 193 D
tstam@bowdoin.edu
STAMBAUGH, Barbara .. 717-358-3981 384 D
barbara.stambaugh@fandm.edu
STAMBAUGH, Jeff .... 940-397-4088 440 F
jeff.stambaugh@msutexas.edu
STAMEY, Jamie .... 704-894-2678 328 F
jastamey@davidson.edu
STAMEY, Jodi .... 919-508-2362 344 F
jstamey@peace.edu
STAMM, Paul, D .... 563-876-3353 164 J
pstamm@dwci.edu
STAMM, Timothy .... 504-671-5482 187 E
tstamm@dcc.edu
STAMMEL, Andrew .... 607-436-2830 317 C
andrew.stammel@oneonta.edu
STAMOS, Michael .... 949-824-1046.. 68 G
mstamos@uci.edu
STAMP, Chase .... 660-263-4100 257 B
chasestamp@macc.edu
STAMP, Diane, L .... 540-568-6495 468 F
stampdl@jmu.edu
STAMP, Velma .... 843-792-3657 410 F
stampvg@musc.edu
STAMPALIA,
Jacqueline, B .... 518-276-8007 312 I
stampj@rpi.edu
STAMPER, Richard, E .... 812-877-8956 159 J
stamper1@rose-hulman.edu
STAN RAICU, Daniela ... 312-362-5460 135 I
dstan@cs.depaul.edu
STANAITIS, Judi .... 610-558-5544 391 D
stanaitj@neumann.edu
STANBROUGH,
Beverly, J .... 248-522-3811 229 A
bjstanbr@oaklandcc.edu
STANCIL, Anne .... 703-284-1509 469 C
anne.stancil@marymount.edu
STANCIL, Cynthia .... 903-730-4890 438 H
cstancil@jarvis.edu
STANCIU, Hope .... 330-490-7142 364 B
hstanciu@walsh.edu
STANDBERRY,
Cassandra .... 804-862-6100 470 I
cstandberry@rbc.edu
STANDER, Karina .... 701-858-3993 345 F
karina.stander@minotstateu.edu
STANDERFER, Mary ...... 479-394-7622.. 23 C
mstanderfer@uarichmountain.edu
STANDERFER, Pam .... 254-710-4737 431 J
pam_standerfer@baylor.edu
STANDERFORD, Chris ... 906-227-2092 228 F
cstander@nmu.edu
STANDIFER, Alton, M ... 706-542-9167 125 G
alton@uga.edu
STANDIFIRD, Stephen ... 317-940-6307 153 F
sstandif@butler.edu
STANDISH, Christopher 860-768-5938.. 88 H
standish@hartford.edu
STANDLEA, Donna .... 909-607-3305.. 37 D
donna.standlea@cgu.edu
STANDLEY, Susan .... 309-794-7207 132 C
suestandley@augustana.edu
STANDRIDGE, Michelle . 502-585-9911 184 D
mstandridge@spalding.edu
STANEK, Chris .... 541-552-8786 376 E
stanek@sou.edu
STANELLE, Brett .... 478-445-5800 118 C
brett.stanelle@gcsu.edu
STANFIELD, Alan .... 770-233-6139 124 G
alan.stanfield@sctech.edu
STANFIELD, Vicki .... 409-933-8213 433 L
vstanfield@com.edu
STANFIELD, Zelda .... 919-530-7887 342 A
zstanfield@nccu.edu
STANFILL, Adrienne ...... 716-286-8339 310 D
aestanfill@niagara.edu
STANFILL, Sandy .... 731-968-5722 425 B
sstanfill@jscc.edu
STANFILL, William .... 417-667-8181 252 A
bstanfill@cottey.edu
STANFORD, Clark .... 312-996-1040 151 B
cmstan60@uic.edu
STANFORD, Erica .... 662-562-3206 248 D
STANFORD, Kathy .... 503-552-2009 374 E
kstanford@nunm.edu
STANFORD, Laura, R .... 239-513-1122 101 C
lstandord@hodges.edu
STANFORD, Linda .... 907-852-1838.... 9 F
linda.stanford@ilisagvik.edu
STANFORD, Roger .... 608-785-9210 501 A
stanfordr@westerntc.edu
STANFORD, Steve .... 601-925-3205 247 C
stanford@mc.edu
STANFORD, Steve .... 601-925-3247 247 C
stanford@mc.edu
STANG, Kristin .... 657-278-8811.. 31 E
kstang@fullerton.edu
STANG, Megan .... 909-869-3768.. 30 D
mmstang@cpp.edu
STANGE, Randy .... 913-469-8500 174 D
rstange@jccc.edu
STANGE, Von .... 319-335-3000 163 A
von-stange@uiowa.edu
STANGER, Winn .... 801-626-6876 461 B
wstanger@weber.edu
STANGLE, James, R ...... 563-333-6060 169 A
stanglejamesr@sau.edu
STANGLE, Sarah .... 716-375-2222 313 F
sstangle@sbu.edu
STANICIC, Rob .... 281-998-6150 443 B
rob.stanicic@sjcd.edu
STANIS, Karen .... 530-749-3851.. 76 C
kstanis@yccd.edu
STANISIC, Zoran .... 727-341-7135 106 E
stanisic.zoran@spcollege.edu
STANKIEWICZ, Donna ... 973-684-5218 280 B
dstankiewicz@pccc.edu
STANKIEWICZ, Jennine . 401-225-2419 199 H
jstankiewicz@mica.edu
STANKOVIC, Toni .... 206-934-3605 483 J
toni.stankovic@seattlecolleges.edu
STANKOVICH, Joseph ... 518-580-5719 316 A
jstankov@skidmore.edu
STANKOWSKI, Lisa .... 231-843-5802 232 J
lmstankowski@westshore.edu
STANKOWSKI, Rebecca 219-989-2208 159 G
stankowski@pnw.edu
STANLEY, Alicia .... 641-269-4850 165 J
stanleya@grinnell.edu
STANLEY, Amanda .... 434-582-2950 468 H
agstanley@liberty.edu
STANLEY, Beth .... 276-244-1229 464 L
bstanley@asl.edu
STANLEY, Brandon .... 660-562-1628 257 E
brandon@nwmissouri.edu
STANLEY, Brian .... 478-471-2864 121 F
brian.stanley@mga.edu
STANLEY, Carol .... 706-355-5019 114 F
cstanley@athenstech.edu
STANLEY, Cheryl .... 413-572-5713 213 D
cstanley@westfield.ma.edu
STANLEY, Cole .... 405-974-2590 370 K
cstanley2@uco.edu
STANLEY, David .... 724-838-4270 398 H
stanley@setonhill.edu
STANLEY, Deborah .... 301-860-3447 203 C
dstanley@bowiestate.edu
STANLEY, Deborah, F ... 315-312-2211 319 B
deborah.stanley@oswego.edu
STANLEY, Graydon .... 208-769-7863 131 C
gastanley@nic.edu
STANLEY, Greg .... 704-330-6784 333 D
greg.stanley@cpcc.edu
STANLEY, Harold, W ..... 214-768-4320 444 E
hstanley@smu.edu
STANLEY, Jay .... 910-879-5503 332 D
jstanley@bladencc.edu
STANLEY, Jennifer .... 401-254-3123 405 E
jstanley@rwu.edu
STANLEY, Jenny .... 904-596-5951 111 F
jennystanley@tbc.edu
STANLEY, Jeremiah .... 904-596-2333 111 F
jstanley@tbc.edu
STANLEY, John .... 808-689-2316 128 G
jstanley@hawaii.edu
STANLEY, Katherine ...... 607-436-3369 317 C
katherine.stanley@oneonta.edu
STANLEY, Kent .... 507-389-2021 239 C
kent.stanley@mnsu.edu

STANLEY, Margaret .... 808-932-7394 128 E mlstanle@hawaii.edu
STANLEY, Mark .... 712-325-3375 167 B mstanley@iwcc.edu
STANLEY, Nancy .... 585-567-9321 302 D nancy.stanley@houghton.edu
STANLEY, Patsy .... 910-410-1830 337 B pjstanley@richmondcc.edu
STANLEY, Ray .... 317-955-6000 158 U rstanley@marian.edu
STANLEY, Robert .... 319-352-8646 170 C robert.stanley@wartburg.edu
STANLEY, Robert .... 740-397-6868 357 B robert.stanley@mvnu.edu
STANLEY, Robyn .... 770-426-2877 121 C robyn.stanley@life.edu
STANLEY, Ryan .... 706-355-5114 114 F rstanley@athenstech.edu
STANLEY, Samuel, L ..... 517-355-6560 227 D presmail@msu.edu
STANLEY, Samuel, L ..... 631-632-6265 317 D samuel.stanley@stonybrook.edu
STANLEY, Scott, A .... 603-513-1349 274 H scott.stanley@granite.edu
STANLEY, Shemrico ...... 803-780-1019 414 E sstanley@voorhees.edu
STANLEY, Tarshia .... 651-690-8846 242 R tlstanley373@stkate.edu
STANLEY, Timothy .... 801-863-7920 461 A tim.stanley@uvu.edu
STANLEY, Todd .... 276-944-6857 467 G tstanley@ehc.edu
STANLEY, Tricia .... 802-387-6464 462 D triciastanley@landmark.edu
STANLEY, Tuesday .... 724-925-4001 403 A stanleyt@westmoreland.edu
STANLEY, Valarie, J ...... 203-432-0849.. 89 D valarie.stanley@yale.edu
STANLEY-MCAULAY, Deborah .... 203-436-4072.. 89 D deborah.stanley-mcaulay@yale.edu
STANOWSKI, Gary .... 573-875-7353 251 F gstanowski@ccis.edu
STANSBERRY, Donald, M .... 757-683-3442 469 G dstansbe@odu.edu
STANSBURY, Todd .... 404-894-5411 118 F tstansbury@athletics.gatech.edu
STANTON, Abby .... 931-424-2015 421 E acstanton@martinmethodist.edu
STANTON, Amanda .... 806-291-3414 457 J stanton@wbu.edu
STANTON, Bonita .... 973-275-4840 283 B bonita.stanton@shu.edu
STANTON, Danielle .... 603-314-7820 274 D d.stanton@snhu.edu
STANTON, Elizabeth ...... 619-201-8700.. 60 A elizabeth.stanton@sdcc.edu
STANTON, Lisa .... 541-956-7024 376 D lstanton@roguecc.edu
STANTON, Mark .... 626-812-3087.. 26 H mstanton@apu.edu
STANTON, Michael, J ... 508-213-2285 217 E michael.stanton@nichols.edu
STANTON, Paul, E .... 413-565-1000 205 G pstanton@baypath.edu
STANTON, Pete .... 701-483-2037 345 D p.stanton@dickinsonstate.edu
STANTON, Timothy, R .. 508-767-7205 205 D tr.stanton@assumption.edu
STANZIANO, Michelle ... 610-526-6118 385 G mcatagnus@harcum.edu
STAPLES, Lisa .... 770-593-2257 120 A
STAPLES, Mark .... 843-953-6402 408 E staplesma@cofc.edu
STAPLETON, Kemp .... 419-267-1308 358 A kstapleton@northweststate.edu
STAPLETON, Melody ..... 530-898-6377.. 31 A mjstapleton@csuchico.edu
STAPLETON, Paula .... 713-646-1754 444 B pstapleton@stcl.edu
STAPLETON, Stephanie . 706-295-6328 118 E sstaplet@highlands.edu
STAPLETON, Susan, R .. 269-387-8202 232 K susan.stapleton@wmich.edu
STAPLETON, Tracy .... 601-979-3060 246 E tracy.a.stapleton@jsums.edu
STAR, Yin .... 304-876-5693 490 E ystar@shepherd.edu
STARACE, Melissa .... 610-330-5200 387 E staracem@lafayette.edu
STARCK, Aaron .... 619-644-7000.. 44 I aaron.starck@gcccd.edu
STARCK, Brenda .... 602-285-7503.. 13 F brenda.starck@phoenixcollege.edu
STARCZEWSKI, Kirk ...... 518-587-2100 321 A kirk.starczewski@esc.edu
STAREK, Renee .... 724-838-4276 398 H rstarek@setonhill.edu
STARER, Paul .... 650-949-7777.. 43 D starerpaul@foothill.edu
STARGARDTER, Steven, A .... 619-876-4252.. 67 M sstargardter@usuniversity.edu
STARGEL, Denton .... 908-852-1400 276 G denton.stargel@centenaryuniversity.edu
STARICH, Gale, H .... 770-718-5304 115 D gstarich@brenau.edu
STARK, Brian .... 949-359-0045.. 29 E
STARK, Debbie .... 740-389-4636 356 B starkd@mtc.edu
STARK, Debra .... 201-684-7221 280 H dstark@ramapo.edu
STARK, Dennis .... 302-736-2484.. 90 G dennis.stark@wesley.edu
STARK, Emily .... 406-994-5326 264 D emily.stark1@montana.edu
STARK, Garry .... 208-769-7769 131 C garry_stark@nic.edu
STARK, Jared .... 402-363-5635 270 E jastark@york.edu
STARK, Jason .... 304-205-6617 488 K jason.stark@bridgevalley.edu
STARK, John, D .... 307-766-3930 502 H jdstark@uwyo.edu
STARK, Katrina .... 406-791-5332 265 H katrina.stark@uprovidence.edu
STARK, Louis, W .... 216-368-2020 349 F lou.stark@case.edu
STARK, Mica, B .... 603-862-2450 274 G mica.stark@unh.edu
STARK, Michael .... 903-886-5796 447 B michael.stark@tamuc.edu
STARK, Michael, M .... 608-246-6737 499 H mmstark@madisoncollege.edu
STARK, Paul .... 419-448-2066 353 H pstark@heidelberg.edu
STARK, Sam .... 407-646-2086 105 M sstark@rollins.edu
STARK, Scott .... 909-384-8958.. 59 I sstark@sbccd.cc.ca.us
STARK, Spencer .... 425-640-1046 480 F spencer.stark@edcc.edu
STARK, Toccara .... 651-690-6829 242 R tcstark720@stkate.edu
STARK-ADLER, Brielle ... 914-633-2038 302 G bstarkadler@iona.edu
STARKE, Antonio .... 904-470-8007.. 97 L a.starke@ewc.edu
STARKE, Cindy .... 503-725-2655 376 A cstarke@pdx.edu
STARKE, Kim .... 707-522-2774.. 62 F kstarke@santarosa.edu
STARKE, William, M ..... 724-847-6604 384 G wmstarke@geneva.edu
STARKENBURG, Rebekah, L .... 708-239-4597 150 F becky.starkenburg@trnty.edu
STARKEY, Alvin .... 601-643-8351 245 G alvin.starkey@colin.edu
STARKEY, Alysia, H ...... 785-826-2601 174 G astarkey@ksu.edu
STARKEY, Jeremy .... 304-424-8379 491 D jeremy.starkey@wvup.edu
STARKEY, Michele .... 310-954-4086.. 52 G mstarkey@msmu.edu
STARKEY, Sheri .... 214-768-2024 444 E starkey@smu.edu
STARKEY, Stan, R .... 865-882-4565 425 G starkeys@roanestate.edu
STARKEY-WOODS, Lisa . 607-431-4000 301 D starkey_wool@hartwick.edu
STARKMAN, Kenneth .... 714-992-7052.. 53 L kstarkman@fullcoll.edu
STARKS, Marilyn .... 662-621-4154 245 E mstarks@coahomacc.edu
STARKS, Sam, B .... 215-898-6993 400 K sstarks@upenn.edu
STARLEY, Monica .... 478-445-4444 118 C monica.starley@gcsu.edu
STARLING, Bill .... 910-592-8081 337 G bstarling@sampsoncc.edu
STARLING, Buddy .... 334-670-3243.... 7 C bstar@troy.edu
STARLING, Christopher . 305-237-0368 103 D cstarlin@mdc.edu
STARLING, DeMesia ..... 903-730-4890 438 H dstarling@jarvis.edu
STARLING, Jennifer .... 423-279-7635 425 E jgstarling@northeaststate.edu
STARLING, Kristy, L ...... 770-720-9146 123 E kls1@reinhardt.edu
STARLING, Sharron .... 206-726-5018 480 C sstarling@cornish.edu
STARNER, John .... 713-525-3527 454 H starner@stthom.edu
STARNES, David .... 317-208-5311 159 D
STARNES, Devin .... 310-434-4376.. 62 E starnes_devin@smc.edu
STARNES, Harry .... 252-823-5166 334 C starnesh@edgecombe.edu
STARNES, Janie .... 205-853-1200.... 2 G jstarnes@jeffersonstate.edu
STARNES, Megan .... 212-659-3604 304 B mstarnes@tkc.edu
STARNES, Richard .... 828-227-7646 344 A starnes@wcu.edu
STARNES, Ronald .... 845-368-7212 315 D ronald.starnes@use.salvationarmy.org
STARNES, Scott .... 434-592-4191 468 H sastarnes@liberty.edu
STAROPOLI, Jeremiah ... 215-574-9600 386 B jeremiah.staropoli@hussiancollege.edu
STARR, Brian .... 806-720-7405 439 H brian.starr@lcu.edu
STARR, Clara .... 415-241-2249.. 37 A cstarr@ccsf.edu
STARR, G. Gabrielle ...... 909-621-8131.. 57 F gabrielle.starr@pomona.edu
STARR, Kelvin .... 661-362-2766.. 51 C kstarr@masters.edu
STARR, Monica .... 843-661-8058 409 I monica.starr@fdtc.edu
STARR, Nancy .... 412-809-5100 396 H starr.nancy@ptcollege.edu
STARR, Pamela .... 619-594-1113.. 33 E pjstarr@sdsu.edu
STARR, Peter .... 202-885-2446.. 90 J pstarr@american.edu
STARR, Rai .... 479-986-4087.. 20 D rstarr1@nwacc.edu
STARR, Trudy .... 309-796-5405 132 G starrt@bhc.edu
STARR, Valorie .... 817-598-6252 458 A vstarr@wc.edu
STARR FIEDLER, Heather .... 412-392-3409 397 A hstarr@pointpark.edu
STARRATT, Christopher . 305-899-4757.. 95 C cstarratt@barry.edu
STARRATT, Joseph .... 509-335-4558 486 A jstarratt@wsu.edu
STARRETT, David .... 603-899-4240 273 F provostoffice@franklinpierce.edu
STARRETT, Steve .... 903-233-3900 439 E stevestarrett@letu.edu
STARRICK, Greg .... 618-985-2828 139 I gregstarrick@jalc.edu
STARTUP, Allison .... 706-233-7278 124 B astartup@shorter.edu
STARWALT, Amanda ..... 217-581-7509 136 E ajstarwalt@eiu.edu
STASA, Joan .... 419-530-2814 363 E joan.stasa@utoledo.edu
STASIAK, Joan, C .... 773-508-3143 142 D jstasia@luc.edu
STASOLLA, Debbie .... 609-896-5228 281 B dstasolla@rider.edu
STASSEN, Anne, K .... 215-972-2039 393 D astassen@pafa.edu
STASSEN, Martha, L ...... 413-545-5146 211 D mstassen@acad.umass.edu
STASSIS, Bassel .... 973-684-6500 280 B bstassis@pccc.edu
STATEN, James .... 213-740-4611.. 72 B svpfinance@usc.edu
STATEN, Michael .... 270-384-8106 183 C statenm@lindsey.edu
STATEN, Shannon .... 850-644-3818 109 C sstaten@fsu.edu
STATES, Richard .... 419-434-4677 363 A states@findlay.edu
STATES, Tim .... 765-641-4133 153 B thstates@anderson.edu
STATLER, Dave .... 317-788-3231 161 B statlerd@uindy.edu
STATLER, Donna .... 870-248-4000.. 18 F donnas@blackrivertech.edu
STATMORE, Kelly .... 215-646-7300 385 D statmore.k@gmercyu.edu
STATON, Alex .... 618-664-6512 137 G alex.staton@greenville.edu
STATON, Rae .... 419-358-3449 348 G statonr@bluffton.edu
STATON, Robert, E .... 864-833-8222 411 I bstaton@presby.edu
STATON, Trish .... 404-627-2681 115 C trish.staton@beulah.edu
STATON, Wendell .... 478-445-6341 118 C wendell.staton@gcsu.edu
STAUCHE, Ann .... 815-455-8710 143 A astauche@mchenry.edu
STAUDERMAN, Elizabeth .... 585-275-4124 323 J elizabeth.stauderman@rochester.edu
STAUDT, Denise .... 210-829-2761 453 D staudt@uiwtx.edu
STAUDT, Loretta .... 202-319-5744.. 91 B staudt@cua.edu
STAUDT, Nancy .... 314-935-6420 262 A nstaudt@wustl.edu
STAUFF, Jon .... 732-263-5843 279 B jstauff@monmouth.edu
STAUFF, William .... 770-279-0507 118 B stauff@gcuniv.edu
STAUFFER, Bradley, G .. 402-472-7547 269 H bstauffer@nebraska.edu
STAUFFER, Denise, D ... 314-961-3627 253 A dstauffer@eden.edu
STAUFFER, George, B ... 848-932-5224 282 A gstauffer@mgsa.rutgers.edu
STAUFFER, Gregory .... 517-321-0242 224 F gstauffer@glcc.edu
STAUFFER, Larry .... 208-885-6470 131 G stauffer@uidaho.edu
STAUFFER, Lynn .... 707-664-2172.. 34 C lynn.stauffer@sonoma.edu
STAUFFER, Patricia .... 978-478-3400 217 G pstauffer@northpoint.edu
STAUFFER, Randy .... 818-252-5144.. 75 C randy.stauffer@woodbury.edu
STAUFFER, II, Ronald, E .... 570-577-3305 379 F ron.stauffer@bucknell.edu
STAUSS, Michelle .... 973-618-3555 276 D mstauss@caldwell.edu
STAVA, Jackson .... 206-281-2175 484 D stavaj@spu.edu
STAVENGA, Mink .... 619-482-6569.. 65 F mstavenga@swccd.edu
STAVITSKY, Alan .... 775-784-6656 271 F ags@unr.edu
STEAD, John .... 661-362-2202.. 51 C jstead@masters.edu
STEADMAN, Jacqui .... 423-461-8686 422 J
STEADMAN, Mimi .... 716-829-7556 298 F steadman@dyc.edu
STEADMAN, Sheryl .... 801-832-2168 461 G ssteadman@westminstercollege.edu
STEANE, Joanne, E .... 307-766-2130 502 H jesteane@uwyo.edu
STEARNS, Ana .... 716-685-9631 308 F astearns@nycc.edu
STEARNS, Diane, M .... 928-523-4460.. 14 H diane.stearns@nau.edu
STEARNS, Gail .... 714-628-7260.. 36 C stearns@chapman.edu
STEARNS, Jill .... 805-546-3118.. 41 A jill_stearns@cuesta.edu
STEARNS, Keith .... 805-546-3228.. 41 A keith_stearns@cuesta.edu
STEARNS, Marc .... 215-503-0155 400 A marc.stearns@jefferson.edu
STEARNS, Sandra .... 262-691-5368 500 H sstearns@wctc.edu
STEARNS, Stephanie, L . 704-406-4236 329 A sstearns@gardner-webb.edu
STEARNS, Susan, M ...... 515-263-2955 165 I sstearns@grandview.edu
STEARNS MOORE, Kai .. 714-808-4829.. 53 J kstearnsmoore@nocccd.edu
STEBBINS, Bill .... 816-322-0110 250 K bill.stebbins@calvary.edu
STEBBINS, Chad .... 417-625-9736 256 D stebbins-c@mssu.edu
STEBBINS, Gerald .... 304-829-7640 487 G gstebbins@bethanywv.edu
STEBBINS, Katie .... 617-287-7050 211 C kstebbins@umassp.edu
STEBBINS, Tim .... 202-462-2101.. 92 C tstebbins@iwp.edu

STEBBINS, Todd, H .... 608-246-6976 499 H
stebbins@madisoncollege.edu
STEC, Paul, T .... 518-783-2314 315 J
pstec@siena.edu
STECK, Don .... 435-652-2051 460 G
steck@dixie.edu
STECKBAUER, Jill .... 715-422-5322 500 A
jill.steckbauer@mstc.edu
STECKER, Ann Page ...... 603-526-3644 272 H
astecker@colby-sawyer.edu
STECKMAN, Rebecca ..... 303-385-1070 359 M
STEDMAN, Bruce .... 413-369-4044 208 D
stedman@csld.edu
STEED, Amanda .... 800-477-2254.. 30 A
STEED, Beth .... 706-778-0100 123 B
bsteed@piedmont.edu
STEED, Laura .... 209-946-2325.. 70 E
lsteed@pacific.edu
STEEHLER, Gail, A .... 540-375-2204 471 B
gsteehle@roanoke.edu
STEEHLER, Jack, K .... 540-375-2540 471 B
jsteehler@roanoke.edu
STEEL, Ann, E .... 717-866-5775 383 H
asteel@evangelical.edu
STEEL, Diane, M .... 559-323-2100.. 60 I
dsteel@sjcl.edu
STEEL, Virginia .... 310-825-1201.. 69 A
vsteel@library.ucla.edu
STEELANT, Wim, F .... 330-941-3009 365 C
wfsteelant@ysu.edu
STEELE, Amber .... 757-352-4928 470 H
asteele@regent.edu
STEELE, Brett .... 310-206-6469.. 69 A
brett@arts.ucla.edu
STEELE, Cherie .... 253-589-6010 479 G
cherie.steele@cptc.edu
STEELE, Christopher ...... 410-455-6841 202 E
csteele@umbc.edu
STEELE, Courtney .... 251-405-7135.... 1 E
csteele@bishop.edu
STEELE, Danielle .... 478-757-3501 116 A
dsteele@centralgatech.edu
STEELE, David .... 423-425-1785 428 A
david-steele@utc.edu
STEELE, Dawn .... 406-756-3806 263 F
dsteele@fvcc.edu
STEELE, Diane .... 913-758-6102 177 F
steeled@stmary.edu
STEELE, Donna .... 731-989-6001 420 C
dsteele@fhu.edu
STEELE, Gail, T .... 340-693-1008 514 E
gsteele@uvi.edu
STEELE, Jamil .... 312-850-7090 134 H
jsteele34@ccc.edu
STEELE, Jeffrey .... 586-498-4090 226 H
steelej40@macomb.edu
STEELE, Jennifer .... 256-378-4900.... 1 G
jsteele@cacc.edu
STEELE, Jerome .... 918-781-7426 365 F
steelej@bacone.edu
STEELE, Jessica .... 207-509-7293 195 H
jsteele@unity.edu
STEELE, Jill .... 812-888-4502 162 C
jsteele@vinu.edu
STEELE, Joanne .... 914-633-2691 302 G
jsteele@iona.edu
STEELE, Karen .... 817-257-6255 448 G
k.steele@tcu.edu
STEELE, Kemper .... 434-961-6585 475 F
ksteele@pvcc.edu
STEELE, Laura, L .... 714-879-3901.. 45 F
llsteele@hiu.edu
STEELE, Leslie .... 615-547-1268 419 F
lsteele@cumberland.edu
STEELE, Linda, M .... 614-947-6583 353 C
linda.steele@franklin.edu
STEELE, Margaret, A ..... 570-408-4302 403 D
margaret.steele@wilkes.edu
STEELE, Michael .... 308-535-3723 267 K
steelem@mpcc.edu
STEELE, Michelle .... 615-966-5181 421 D
michelle.steele@lipscomb.edu
STEELE, Misty .... 405-224-3140 371 D
msteele@usao.edu
STEELE, Mitzi, B .... 540-375-2249 471 B
steele@roanoke.edu
STEELE, Patrick, W .... 701-788-4794 345 E
patrick.steele@mayvillestate.edu
STEELE, Scott .... 859-985-3416 179 C
steeles@berea.edu
STEELE, Steve .... 901-381-3939 428 E
steves@visible.edu
STEELE, Steven .... 970-223-2669.. 80 D
ssteele@ibmc.edu
STEELE, Valerie .... 212-217-4530 299 H
valerie_steele@fitnyc.edu
STEELE, Vicki .... 614-251-4706 358 G
steelev@ohiodominican.edu
STEELE-FIGUEREDO,
David, M .... 818-252-5101.. 75 C
president@woodbury.edu
STEELE-MARCELL, Lia ... 501-370-5217.. 20 G
lsteele@philander.edu
STEELE-MIDDLETON,
Amanda .... 937-775-5200 364 I
amanda.steele-middleton@wright.edu
STEELE-MOSES, Susan .. 225-490-1674 186 F
susan.steele-moses@franu.edu
STEELEY, Jodie .... 559-489-2226.. 66 E
jodie.steeley@fresnocitycollege.edu
STEELMAN, Lisa .... 321-674-7316.. 99 B
lsteelma@fit.edu
STEELMAN, Megan .... 303-273-3640.. 78 I
msteelman@mines.edu
STEELMAN, Toddi, R ..... 919-613-8135 328 G
toddi.steelman@duke.edu
STEELY, Jeff .... 404-413-2000 119 E
jsteely@gsu.edu
STEELY, Kelly .... 208-562-2508 130 F
kellysteely@cwi.edu
STEEN, Brant .... 215-497-8791 379 G
brant.steen@bucks.edu
STEEN, Carrie .... 417-255-7255 256 F
carriesteen@missouristate.edu
STEEN, Clayton .... 518-587-2100 321 A
clayton.steen@esc.edu
STEEN, Eric .... 206-934-6427 484 B
eric.steen@seattlecolleges.edu
STEEN, Franklin .... 646-565-6000 322 J
franklin.steen@touro.edu
STEEN, James .... 281-649-3208 437 H
jsteen@hbu.edu
STEEN, Kenneth, L .... 540-654-1159 472 I
ksteen@umw.edu
STEENBURGH, Chuck ... 540-283-6628 472 F
csteenburgh@an.edu
STEENIS, Paul, R .... 309-341-7145 141 A
psteenis@knox.edu
STEENSON, Greg .... 651-690-8825 242 R
gpsteenson@stkate.edu
STEENWYK, Thomas, L . 616-526-6549 222 A
steeto@calvin.edu
STEEVES, Brian .... 612-626-1616 243 E
bsteeves@umn.edu
STEEVES, Myron .... 714-836-7500 150 H
msteeves@tiu.edu
STEFANCO, Carolyn, J .. 518-454-5120 296 H
stefancc@strose.edu
STEFANICK, Susan, A ... 609-896-5065 281 B
stefanic@rider.edu
STEFANKO, Lisa .... 412-392-4727 397 A
lstefanko@pointpark.edu
STEFANONI, Andra .... 620-235-4124 176 F
astefanoni@pittstate.edu
STEFANOVIC, Tijana ...... 610-526-5632 379 E
tstefano@brynmawr.edu
STEFANOWICZ, Michael 802-654-3000 463 B
admissions@smcvt.edu
STEFANUCA, Pamela ..... 410-225-2506 199 H
pstefanuca@mica.edu
STEFFAN, Eileen .... 412-809-5100 396 H
steffan.eileen@ptcollege.edu
STEFFEN, Lloyd, H .... 610-758-3877 388 J
lhs1@lehigh.edu
STEFFEN, Rebecca .... 269-927-8861 226 D
steffen@lakemichigancollege.edu
STEFFEN, Wayne .... 559-453-2215.. 43 G
wayne.steffen@fresno.edu
STEFFENS, Ashley .... 530-422-7927.. 73 F
asteffens@weimar.edu
STEFFENS, Wayne .... 559-453-3677.. 43 G
wayne.steffens@fresno.edu
STEFFES, Thomas, E ..... 570-348-6211 389 G
tsteffes@marywood.edu
STEG HASKETT, Allie .... 970-351-1886.. 83 E
allie.steghaskett@unco.edu
STEGALL, Kelly .... 704-290-5247 337 I
kstegall@spcc.edu
STEGEMAN, Melanie ..... 314-951-9410 259 C
mstegeman5@stlcc.edu
STEGER, Paul .... 314-246-7505 262 C
psteger@webster.edu
STEGGALL, Kelli .... 218-755-2504 237 E
kelli.steggall@bemidjistate.edu
STEGLICH, Leila .... 703-330-8400.. 92 G
STEGMAIER, Mary, A .... 573-882-6008 261 B
stegmaierm@missouri.edu
STEGMAN, SJ, Thomas . 617-552-6527 207 B
thomas.stegman@bc.edu
STEGNER, Joe .... 208-334-2315 131 G
jstegner@uidaho.edu
STEHOUWER, Kristin ..... 989-837-4224 228 H
stehouwer@northwood.edu
STEIB, Summer .... 225-578-1714 188 I
summers@lsu.edu
STEIBE-PASALICH,
Susan, C .... 574-631-7336 161 C
steibe-pasalich.1@nd.edu
STEIDEL, Michael .... 412-268-2082 380 F
ms44@andrew.cmu.edu
STEIER, Kenneth .... 646-981-4500 322 J
kenneth.steier@touro.edu
STEIGER, Gretchen .... 252-249-1851 336 F
STEIN, Anthony .... 818-299-5526.. 73 K
astein@westcoastuniversity.edu
STEIN, Barbara .... 617-627-3333 219 B
barbara.stein@tufts.edu
STEIN, Beki .... 610-796-8202 378 F
beki.stein@alvernia.edu
STEIN, Bob .... 207-780-4444 196 F
rstein@maine.edu
STEIN, Carla .... 303-678-3755.. 79 J
carla.stein@frontrange.edu
STEIN, Cliff .... 503-517-1878 378 A
cstein@westernseminary.edu
STEIN, Cynthia .... 818-766-8151.. 40 C
cstein@concorde.edu
STEIN, David .... 718-232-7800 325 J
dstein@yks.edu
STEIN, Devon .... 518-454-2151 296 H
steind@strose.edu
STEIN, Diane .... 818-364-7867.. 49 B
steindb@lamission.edu
STEIN, Douglas .... 719-598-0200.. 79 C
dstein@coloradotech.edu
STEIN, Ellen .... 646-312-4685 292 L
ellen.stein@baruch.cuny.edu
STEIN, Jeff .... 336-278-7304 328 K
jstein@elon.edu
STEIN, Jill .... 973-877-3243 277 I
stein@essex.edu
STEIN, John .... 404-385-8772 118 F
john.stein@vpss.gatech.edu
STEIN, Kathy .... 432-837-8770 450 D
kstein@sulross.edu
STEIN, Lisa .... 308-432-6263 268 E
lstein@csc.edu
STEIN, Mark, A .... 507-354-8221 236 I
steinma@mlc-wels.edu
STEIN, Marni, B .... 801-274-3280 461 F
marni.stein@wgu.edu
STEIN, Melanie .... 607-274-3102 303 B
mstein2@ithaca.edu
STEIN, N .... 732-364-1220 275 F
STEIN, Rebecca .... 215-898-7733 400 K
rstein2@upenn.edu
STEIN, Scott .... 772-462-7691 101 E
sstein@irsc.edu
STEIN, Sheri .... 408-498-0103.. 38 F
sstein@cogswell.edu
STEIN, Sonya .... 518-327-6119 311 G
sstein@paulsmiths.edu
STEIN, Steve .... 408-420-2224.. 70 B
ststein@ucsc.edu
STEIN, Wayne .... 321-433-5150.. 97 I
steinw@easternflorida.edu
STEIN-SMITH, Kathy ...... 201-692-2653 277 K
stein@fdu.edu
STEINACKER, Kathy .... 815-939-5359 146 A
ksteinac@olivet.edu
STEINBACK, Robin .... 951-571-6160.. 58 F
robin.steinback@mvc.edu
STEINBACK, Robin, L .... 951-571-6160.. 58 G
robin.steinback@mvc.edu
STEINBERG, Aaron .... 718-868-2300 291 B
STEINBERG, Bettie, M ... 516-562-1159 299 B
bsteinbe@northwell.edu
STEINBERG, Kurt, T .... 978-921-4242 216 F
kurt.steinberg@montserrat.edu
STEINBERG, Nicole .... 215-965-8561 390 J
nsteinberg@moore.edu
STEINBERG, Scott .... 207-221-4208 196 G
ssteinberg@une.edu
STEINBERG, Stacey .... 414-847-3200 494 F
staceysteinberg@miad.edu
STEINBERGER, Eric .... 419-559-2228 361 I
esteinberger@terra.edu
STEINBURG, Bryan .... 610-647-4400 386 C
bsteinberg@immaculata.edu
STEINCAMP, Hugo .... 520-494-5044.. 11 K
hugo.steincamp@centralaz.edu
STEINER, Fred .... 313-845-9621 224 G
fred@hfcc.edu
STEINER, Frederick .... 215-898-3425 400 K
fsteiner@design.upenn.edu
STEINER, Glen, D .... 708-209-3328 135 F
glen.steiner@cuchicago.edu
STEINER, Gregory, G .... 276-944-6763 467 G
gsteiner@ehc.edu
STEINER, James, D .... 563-589-3210 169 I
jsteiner@dbq.edu
STEINER, Karen .... 303-404-5111.. 79 J
karen.steiner@frontrange.edu
STEINER, Karl, V .... 410-455-5827 202 E
steinerk@umbc.edu
STEINER, Kim .... 276-944-6112 467 G
ksteiner@ehc.edu
STEINER, Kimberly .... 276-964-7389 475 I
kim.steiner@sw.edu
STEINER, Lori .... 316-942-4291 175 I
steinerl@newmanu.edu
STEINER, Melissa .... 410-626-2513 201 D
annapolis.registrar@sjc.edu
STEINER, Michael .... 660-562-1197 257 E
msteine@nwmissouri.edu
STEINER, Michelle .... 703-284-1538 469 C
michelle.steiner@marymount.edu
STEINER, Rita, L .... 410-617-2504 199 F
rsteiner@loyola.edu
STEINER, Sheila .... 360-923-8724 483 H
ssteiner@stmartin.edu
STEINER, Ted .... 216-373-5387 358 B
tsteiner@ndc.edu
STEINER-LANG, Kathy ... 314-935-5910 262 A
ksteiner@wustl.edu
STEINERT, Brandon .... 620-792-9307 171 C
steinertb@bartonccc.edu
STEINFORD, Jennifer .... 251-981-3771.... 5 B
jennifer.steinford@columbiasouthern.
edu
STEINGART, Mark .... 386-752-1822.. 99 A
mark.steingart@fgc.edu
STEINHAUS, Paul .... 412-365-1606 381 C
psteinhaus@chatham.edu
STEINHILBER, Steven .... 770-484-1204 121 D
steven.steinhilber@lutherrice.edu
STEINHOFF, Cynthia, K 410-777-2483 197 C
ckseinhoff@aacc.edu
STEININGER, Sue .... 352-335-2332.. 93 F
STEINKE, Paul .... 206-876-6100 484 E
psteinke@theseattleschool.edu
STEINKE, Robin .... 651-641-3211 236 F
rsteinke001@luthersem.edu
STEINKIRCHNER,
Linda, M .... 585-385-5242 314 A
lsteinkirchner@sjfc.edu
STEINMAN, Joan .... 775-673-7060 271 D
jsteinman@tmcc.edu
STEINMAYER, Janet, L .. 617-349-8401 210 H
janet.steinmayer@lesley.edu
STEINMETZ, Carol .... 281-290-2843 439 G
carol.l.steinmetz@lonestar.edu
STEINMETZ, JR.,
Edward, J .... 570-941-4289 401 H
edward.steinmetz@scranton.edu
STEINMETZ, Joseph, E .. 479-575-4140.. 21 G
chancell@uark.edu
STEINMETZ, Paul .... 203-837-9805.. 85 B
steinmetzp@wcsu.edu
STEINMETZ, Robyn .... 330-494-6170 361 F
rsteinmetz@starkstate.edu
STEINOUR, David .... 864-294-3800 410 A
david.steinour@furman.edu
STEINROCK, Timothy .... 252-398-6376 328 D
steint@chowan.edu
STEITZ, David .... 585-389-2738 308 B
dsteitz4@naz.edu
STEJSKAL, Patricia .... 815-479-7530 143 A
pstejskal@mchenry.edu
STELL, Pamela .... 443-412-2103 199 A
pstell@harford.edu
STELLA, Hilda, V .... 787-284-1912 509 E
hstella@ponce.inter.edu
STELLA, Mark .... 304-384-5356 490 A
markstella@hotmail.com
STELLA, Steven .... 518-454-5139 296 H
stellas@strose.edu
STELLO, Noelle .... 503-552-1544 374 E
nstello@nunm.edu
STELTER, Caroline, W ... 804-758-6728 475 G
cstelter@rappahannock.edu

STELZER, Stuart, P .... 479-979-1381.. 23 I
sstelzer@ozarks.edu
STEM, Elaine .... 252-492-2061 338 F
steme@vgcc.edu
STEMKOSKI, Stephen .... 315-859-4301 301 C
sstemkos@hamilton.edu
STEMMER, John, K .... 502-272-8140 179 B
jstemmer@bellarmine.edu
STEMMER, Wayne .... 414-955-8296 494 C
wstemmer@mcw.edu
STEMPLER, Amy .... 718-982-3917 293 E
amy.stempler@csi.cuny.edu
STENBERG, Josephine .. 808-845-9119 129 B
jstenber@hawaii.edu
STENDARDI,
Deborah, M .... 585-475-5040 313 A
dmsgrl@rit.edu
STENDER, David .... 860-768-5403.. 88 H
stender@hartford.edu
STENDER, Julie .... 435-652-7703 460 G
stender@dixie.edu
STENEHJEM, Keith, A .... 701-788-4711 345 E
keith.stenehjem@mayvillestate.edu
STENGEL, Donald .... 559-278-2482.. 31 D
dons@csufresno.edu
STENGER, JR.,
Harvey, G .... 607-777-2131 316 E
president@binghamton.edu
STENGER, Karen .... 440-826-2726 348 E
kstenger@bw.edu
STENGER, Tracy, L .... 716-673-3424 317 A
tracy.stenger@fredonia.edu
STENKO, Michael .... 860-465-4509.. 84 J
stenkom@easternct.edu
STENMARK, Scott .... 773-244-5610 145 A
sestenmark@northpark.edu
STENNES-SPIDAHL,
Naomi, R .... 608-796-3481 498 N
nrstennesspidahl@viterbo.edu
STENNETT, Charles .... 785-833-4327 175 B
charles.stennett@kwu.edu
STENNETT, Debbie .... 806-291-3500 457 J
stennettd@wbu.edu
STENSGARD, April, C ... 651-631-5330 244 D
acstensgard@unwsp.edu
STENSGARD, Timothy ... 507-457-1436 243 B
tstensga@smumn.edu
STENSLAND, Traci .... 509-777-4335 486 I
tstensland@whitworth.edu
STENSON, Charlene ...... 701-845-7105 346 A
c.stenson@vcsu.edu
STENSON, Merry .... 602-429-4946.. 15 C
mstenson@ps.edu
STENSTROM, Karen .... 812-488-2663 161 A
ks96@evansville.edu
STENTIFORD, Deanna ... 727-341-4150 106 E
stentiford.deanna@spcollege.edu
STENZEL, Neal .... 918-495-6203 368 I
nstenzel@oru.edu
STEORTS, Ken .... 901-381-3939 428 E
ken@visible.edu
STEPAN, Matt .... 406-496-4301 265 A
mstepan@mtech.edu
STEPAN-NORRIS,
Judith .... 949-824-6043.. 68 G
jstepann@uci.edu
STEPANSKI, Lisa .... 617-735-9774 209 A
stepansk@emmanuel.edu
STEPHAN, Andrew .... 330-494-6170 361 F
astephan@starkstate.edu
STEPHAN, Bill, B .... 317-274-2100 156 B
wstephan@iu.edu
STEPHAN, Josiah .... 954-545-4500 107 E
jstephan@sfbc.edu
STEPHAN, W. Karl .... 989-837-4211 228 H
stephan@northwood.edu
STEPHAN, William, B .... 317-274-2100 156 A
wstephan@iu.edu
STEPHEN, Cathleen .... 610-607-6205 397 B
cstephen@racc.edu
STEPHEN, Jomysha .... 212-854-2021 290 J
jstephen@barnard.edu
STEPHENOFF, Gail, C ... 614-292-5648 358 I
stephenoff.1@osu.edu
STEPHENS, Alisa .... 478-387-4842 118 G
astephen@gmc.edu
STEPHENS, Amy, M ...... 503-255-0332 374 D
astephens@multnomah.edu
STEPHENS, Andre .... 562-944-0351.. 27 C
andre.stephens@biola.edu
STEPHENS, Austen .... 308-432-6466 268 E
astephens@csc.edu
STEPHENS, Beth .... 618-985-3741 139 I
bethstephens@jalc.edu
STEPHENS, Carrie .... 602-429-4915.. 15 C
cstephens@ps.edu
STEPHENS, Cathy .... 217-641-4515 140 A
cstephens@jwcc.edu
STEPHENS, Christina ..... 207-326-2441 195 D
christina.stephens@mma.edu
STEPHENS, Crystal .... 661-726-1911.. 68 B
crystal.stephens@uav.edu
STEPHENS, Daniel .... 309-438-2143 139 E
dsteph3@ilstu.edu
STEPHENS, Denise .... 314-935-5415 262 A
dstephens@wustl.edu
STEPHENS, Diane, S ..... 818-677-3735.. 32 D
diane.stephens@csun.edu
STEPHENS, Edward .... 470-578-6778 120 L
estephen@kennesaw.edu
STEPHENS, Elisa .... 415-274-2200.. 24 B
estephens@academyart.edu
STEPHENS, Garry .... 706-771-4081 114 J
gstephens@augustatech.edu
STEPHENS,
Jacqueline, B .... 706-721-2301 115 A
jstephen@augusta.edu
STEPHENS, Jay, W .... 785-532-6277 174 G
jaystephens@ksu.edu
STEPHENS, Jenny .... 812-855-1053 156 A
stephejl@indiana.edu
STEPHENS, Josh .... 806-720-7502 439 H
josh.stephens@lcu.edu
STEPHENS, Kevin, N ..... 309-655-2291 148 E
kevin.stephens@osfhealthcare.org
STEPHENS, Kristie, D .... 530-226-4727.. 63 K
kstephens@simpsonu.edu
STEPHENS, Larry .... 225-216-8411 186 K
stephensl@mybrcc.edu
STEPHENS, Lisa .... 760-379-5501.. 46 M
lisa.stephens@cerrocoso.edu
STEPHENS, Mamie .... 610-399-2057 394 C
maestephens@cheyney.edu
STEPHENS, Mark .... 931-372-3224 426 E
mstephens@tntech.edu
STEPHENS, Matthew ...... 405-613-2536 370 B
matthew.stephens@swcu.edu
STEPHENS, Melinda, R . 724-847-5235 384 G
mstephen@geneva.edu
STEPHENS, Melissa .... 203-837-8582.. 85 B
stephensm@wcsu.edu
STEPHENS, Myka, K ...... 717-290-8704 388 D
mkstephens@lancasterseminary.edu
STEPHENS, Paul .... 859-858-3511 178 I
paul.stephens@asbury.edu
STEPHENS, Ralph .... 361-593-3717 447 D
ralph.stephens@tamuk.edu
STEPHENS, Sandra .... 901-722-3220 424 C
sandra@sco.edu
STEPHENS, Sandra, S ... 901-722-3220 424 C
sandra@sco.edu
STEPHENS, Sharon .... 215-968-8468 379 G
stephens@bucks.edu
STEPHENS, Sonya, C ..... 413-538-2500 216 G
scs@mtholyoke.edu
STEPHENS, Steve .... 405-744-6494 368 B
steve.stephens@okstate.edu
STEPHENS, Toni .... 972-883-4876 455 B
tmesser@utdallas.edu
STEPHENS, Zach .... 740-474-8896 358 F
zstephens@ohiochristian.edu
STEPHENSON, Aimee ..... 802-654-0540 464 B
aes07130@ccv.vsc.edu
STEPHENSON, Alan .... 256-306-2619.... 1 F
alan.stephenson@calhoun.edu
STEPHENSON, Blair .... 530-754-4336.. 68 E
bstephenson@ucdavis.edu
STEPHENSON, Dale .... 859-572-5510 184 A
stephensod1@nku.edu
STEPHENSON, Devin ...... 850-729-5360 103 L
dstephenson@nwfsc.edu
STEPHENSON, E. Frank 252-398-6278 328 D
stephf@chowan.edu
STEPHENSON, Hilary ..... 225-216-8439 186 K
stephensonh@mybrcc.edu
STEPHENSON, Jeff .... 916-484-8461.. 50 F
stephej@arc.losrios.edu
STEPHENSON, Laura ...... 785-670-1561 177 G
laura.stephenson@washburn.edu
STEPHENSON, Margaret 413-236-2117 213 F
mstephensonr@berkshirecc.edu
STEPHENSON, Marlee .... 575-769-4021 285 K
marlee.stephenson@clovis.edu
STEPHENSON, Michael . 979-845-4016 446 G
mstephenson@tamu.edu
STEPHENSON,
Norman, J .... 308-635-6121 270 D
stephens@wncc.edu
STEPHENSON, Renee .... 608-263-4422 496 B
rmstephenson@uwsa.edu
STEPHENSON, Samuel .. 828-898-2534 330 E
stephensonsb@lmc.edu
STEPHENSON, Susan ..... 828-898-8741 330 E
stephensons@lmc.edu
STEPHENSON, Susan ..... 307-532-8325 502 A
susan.stephenson@ewc.wy.edu
STEPHERSON,
Jacqueline .... 912-358-4194 123 H
stephersonj@savannahstate.edu
STEPINA, Karen .... 708-344-4700 142 A
kstepina@lincolntech.edu
STEPLIGHT JOHNSON,
S. Aisha .... 973-877-3115 277 I
ssteplig@essex.edu
STEPLIGHT JOHNSON,
Stephanie, A .... 973-877-3000 277 I
ssteplig@essex.edu
STEPNEY, Ne'Keisha ..... 630-466-7900 152 C
nstepney@waubonsee.edu
STEPNIAK, Michael, J ... 540-665-4600 471 E
mstepnia@su.edu
STEPNOWSKI, OP,
Thomas More .... 615-297-7545 418 C
srtmore@aquinascollege.edu
STEPP, Gary .... 606-368-6105 178 D
garystepp@alc.edu
STEPP, Jim .... 606-368-6051 178 D
jimstepp@alc.edu
STEPP, Joe, A .... 606-368-6027 178 D
joestepp@alc.edu
STEPTOE, David .... 478-289-2049 117 D
dsteptoe@ega.edu
STERBA, Kristen .... 501-296-1275.. 22 C
kmsterba@uams.edu
STERBENZ, Cathy .... 509-453-0374 483 C
cathy.sterbenz@perrytech.edu
STERK, Claire, E .... 404-727-6013 117 F
csterk@emory.edu
STERK, Jim .... 573-882-2055 261 B
muathmizzouad@missouri.edu
STERK-BROOKS,
Lynann .... 405-208-5132 367 I
lmsterkbrooks@okcu.edu
STERLING, Carolin .... 937-376-6522 350 D
csterling@centralstate.edu
STERLING, Christa .... 860-832-2277.. 84 I
csterling@ccsu.edu
STERLING, Cynthia .... 910-755-7301 332 F
sterlingc@brunswickcc.edu
STERLING, Dwane, M ... 518-580-5930 316 A
STERLING, Gregory, E .. 203-432-5304.. 89 D
gregory.sterling@yale.edu
STERLING, J. Walter ..... 505-984-6000 287 J
STERLING, Jennifer .... 641-673-1097 170 F
sterlingj@wmpenn.edu
STERLING-HINTON,
Anna .... 601-318-6102 249 H
asterling@wmcarey.edu
STERN, Brian .... 310-204-1666.. 58 D
STERN, Briendy .... 718-871-6187 322 J
briendy.stern@touro.edu
STERN, Chaim .... 718-404-2282 113 E
cstern@lecfl.com
STERN, David .... 773-298-3350 148 G
stern@sxu.edu
STERN, David .... 813-258-7360 112 J
provost@ut.edu
STERN, Doron .... 212-960-5400 326 E
doron.stern@yu.edu
STERN, Elliot .... 949-582-4722.. 64 E
estern@saddleback.edu
STERN, Elliot .... 949-582-4722.. 64 G
estern@saddleback.edu
STERN, Elsie .... 215-576-0800 397 C
erstern@rrc.edu
STERN, Holly, C .... 973-596-6739 279 F
holly.stern@njit.edu
STERN, Holly, C .... 973-596-6379 279 F
holly.stern@njit.edu
STERN, Jonathan .... 863-784-7139 107 F
jonathan.stern@southflorida.edu
STERN, Joshua .... 215-646-7300 385 D
stern.j@gmercyu.edu
STERN, Joyce .... 641-269-3702 165 J
sternjm@grinnell.edu
STERN, Justin .... 360-688-2920 483 H
jstern@stmartin.edu
STERN, Kevin, D .... 214-887-5111 436 B
kstern@dts.edu
STERN, Lorna .... 215-572-2901 379 A
sternl@arcadia.edu
STERN, Lucas .... 704-406-2663 329 A
lstern@gardner-webb.edu
STERN, Michael, J .... 773-442-6012 145 B
m-stern2@neiu.edu
STERN, Ross .... 301-405-6637 202 C
stern@umd.edu
STERN, Scott .... 914-632-5400 307 G
sstern@monroecollege.edu
STERN, Sharon .... 254-710-1010 431 J
sharon_stern@baylor.edu
STERN, Susannah .... 619-260-7847.. 71 J
honors@sandiego.edu
STERNBERG, Wendy, F . 323-259-2634.. 54 E
wsternberg@oxy.edu
STERNBERGER,
Carol, S .... 260-481-5798 159 F
sternber@pfw.edu
STERNBURG, Annie .... 605-331-6820 417 E
annie.sternburg@usiouxfalls.edu
STERNER, Karl .... 912-201-8000 124 E
ksterner@southuniversity.edu
STERNER, Sheri .... 714-432-5081.. 38 E
ssterner@occ.cccd.edu
STERNER, Suzi, M .... 858-822-4382.. 69 D
ssterner@ucsd.edu
STERNFIELD, Daniel ...... 773-602-5524 134 D
dstemfield@ccc.edu
STERNFIELD, Daniel ...... 312-553-2833 134 H
dsternfield@ccc.edu
STERNGOLD, James ...... 212-346-1200 311 E
STERNKE, Timothy .... 414-930-3032 495 A
mmu-bookstore@mtmary.edu
STERNS, Teresa, G .... 304-462-6102 490 C
teresa.sterns@glenville.edu
STEROS, Bryan .... 843-349-5039 408 C
bsteros@coastal.edu
STERRETT, Joseph, D .... 610-758-4320 388 J
jds7@lehigh.edu
STERRITT,
D. E. Lorraine, M .... 802-654-2212 463 B
edeorsey@smcvt.edu
STERRITT, John .... 805-893-2040.. 70 A
jsterritt@ucsb.edu
STERTZBACH,
Rebecca, M .... 480-245-7971.. 12 N
becky.stertzbach@ibcs.edu
STERTZBACH,
Rebecca, M .... 480-245-7969.. 12 N
becky.stertzbach@ibcs.edu
STETLER, Eric .... 740-392-6868 357 B
eric.stetler@mvnu.edu
STETLER, Kent .... 513-721-7944 353 F
registrar@gbs.edu
STETLER, Kristin .... 570-577-3612 379 F
kristin.stetler@bucknell.edu
STETLER, P. Daniel .... 772-546-5534 101 B
danstetler@hsbc.edu
STETLER, Paul .... 772-546-5534 101 B
paulstetler@hsbc.edu
STETSON, Daniel .... 225-389-7200 188 I
dstetson@lsu.edu
STETTER, Mark .... 970-491-7051.. 78 M
mark.stetter@colostate.edu
STETTLER, Greg .... 618-985-3741 139 I
gregstettler@jalc.edu
STETZER, Ed .... 630-752-5918 152 F
ed.stetzer@wheaton.edu
STEUERWALD, Brian ..... 317-917-3628 158 V
bsteu@martin.edu
STEURBAUT, Margo ...... 626-395-6275.. 29 C
margo.steurbaut@caltech.edu
STEVENS, Abby .... 775-831-1314 272 D
astevens@sierranevada.edu
STEVENS, Andrea, N ..... 662-329-7431 248 A
anstevens@muw.edu
STEVENS, Andrew .... 303-373-2008.. 82 G
astevens@rvu.edu
STEVENS, Annie .... 802-656-3380 463 E
annie.stevens@uvm.edu
STEVENS, Bren .... 304-357-4911 488 G
brenstevens@ucwv.edu
STEVENS, Brenda, D .... 330-471-8328 355 L
bstevens@malone.edu
STEVENS, Carrie .... 785-242-5200 176 D
carrie.stevens@ottawa.edu
STEVENS, Cathleen, M .. 585-389-2001 308 B
csteven9@naz.edu
STEVENS, Cheryl .... 270-745-2297 185 E
cheryl.stevens@wku.edu
STEVENS, Debbie .... 641-673-2173 170 F
stevensd@wmpenn.edu
STEVENS, Elizabeth .... 651-690-8600 242 R
ejstevens@stkate.edu
STEVENS, Eric, A .... 660-263-3900 251 A

STEVENS, Faye 276-944-6107 467 G fstevens@ehc.edu
STEVENS, Gladstone 410-864-3602 201 F gstevens@stmarys.edu
STEVENS, Greg 509-434-5037 480 B greg.stevens@ccs.spokane.edu
STEVENS, Greg 509-434-5037 480 A greg.stevens@ccs.spokane.edu
STEVENS, Greg, L 509-434-5037 479 I gstevens@ccs.spokane.edu
STEVENS, Holly, L 423-652-4784 420 H hlstevens@king.edu
STEVENS, Jeff 607-587-3101 320 C stevenjs@alfredstate.edu
STEVENS, Jeffrey 215-503-7015 400 A jeffrey.stevens@jefferson.edu
STEVENS, John 435-283-7017 461 C john.stevens@snow.edu
STEVENS, Joshua 740-368-2000 359 N
STEVENS, Kara 413-565-1000 205 G kstevens@baypath.edu
STEVENS, Laura 314-529-9252 254 H lstevens@maryville.edu
STEVENS, Leslie 701-228-5613 346 C leslie.stevens@dakotacollege.edu
STEVENS, Marc 310-660-3406 41 L mstevens@elcamino.edu
STEVENS, Mark 208-376-7731 129 H mstevens@boisebible.edu
STEVENS, RSM, Maryanne 402-399-2435 266 F mstevens@csm.edu
STEVENS, Matt 561-803-2200 104 C national@pba.edu
STEVENS, Meg 434-791-5700 464 O mstevens@averett.edu
STEVENS, Michele 806-457-4200 436 G mstevens@fpctx.edu
STEVENS, Nick 785-864-4914 177 D nickstevens@ku.edu
STEVENS, Pam 304-876-5287 490 E pstevens@shepherd.edu
STEVENS, Pamela 937-395-8601 355 F pamela.stevens@kc.edu
STEVENS, Randy 909-558-4558 48 C rstevens@llu.edu
STEVENS, Richie 304-876-5370 490 E rstevens@shepherd.edu
STEVENS, Rob 309-341-5457 133 C rstevens@sandburg.edu
STEVENS, Robert 203-932-7435 89 A rstevens@newhaven.edu
STEVENS, Ron 919-658-7834 340 J rstevens@umo.edu
STEVENS, Samantha 252-335-3811 341 D sstevens@ecsu.edu
STEVENS, Sarah, E 812-461-5357 161 E sestevens@usi.edu
STEVENS, Scott 903-923-2178 436 D sstevens@etbu.edu
STEVENS, Scott 802-860-2751 462 B stevens@champlain.edu
STEVENS, Sheri, R 207-621-3110 196 A sheri@maine.edu
STEVENS, Sylvia 513-481-1337 364 E sylvia_stevens@wilmington.edu
STEVENS, Timothy 212-060-5400 326 E timothy.stevens@yu.edu
STEVENS, Timothy, S 847-491-7256 145 F tstevens@northwestern.edu
STEVENSON, Abigail 781-283-3795 219 D asteven3@wellesley.edu
STEVENSON, Barbra 870-338-6474 22 H
STEVENSON, Bill 479-524-7119 19 H wstevens@jbu.edu
STEVENSON, Daniel 406-994-2001 264 D daniel.stevenson1@montana.edu
STEVENSON, Duncan 253-964-6612 483 D dstevenson@pierce.ctc.edu
STEVENSON, Gwendolyn, A 937-778-7949 352 J gstevenson@edisonohio.edu
STEVENSON, Jaclyn 518-828-4181 297 B jaclyn.stevenson@sunycgcc.edu
STEVENSON, James, W 904-997-2931 100 B james.stevenson@fscj.edu
STEVENSON, Joy 816-235-6234 261 C stevensonjoy@umkc.edu
STEVENSON, Karen, L 615-353-3430 425 D karen.stevenson@nscc.edu
STEVENSON, Katie 515-271-1573 164 I katie.stevenson@dmu.edu
STEVENSON, Keith 217-234-5253 141 D kstevenson50021@lakelandcollege.edu
STEVENSON, Kimberley, N 252-335-3699 341 D knstevenson@ecsu.edu
STEVENSON, Kimberly 615-327-6759 422 A kstevenson@mmc.edu
STEVENSON, Leslie, W 804-289-8141 472 L lsteven2@richmond.edu
STEVENSON, Marshall 410-651-6083 203 A mfstevensonjr@umes.edu
STEVENSON, Martha 610-683-4484 395 A stevenson@kutztown.edu
STEVENSON, Martha Ann 205-226-4648 5 A mstevens@bsc.edu
STEVENSON, Michael, P 815-835-6234 148 H michael.p.stevenson@svcc.edu
STEVENSON, Paula 954-545-4500 107 E library@sfbc.edu
STEVENSON, Sarah 718-405-3258 296 G sarah.stevenson@mountsaintvincent.edu
STEVENSON, Susan, G 334-683-2303 3 A sstevenson@marionmilitary.edu
STEVENSON, Tamara 801-832-2454 461 G tstevenson@westminstercollege.edu
STEVENSON, Tara 904-826-8508 98 E tstevenson@flagler.edu
STEVENSON, Valerie, O 904-620-2920 110 A vstevens@unf.edu
STEVENSON, JR., Zollie 501-370-5276 20 G zstevenson@philander.edu
STEVENSON DUMAS, Laura 904-819-6200 98 E lstevenson@flagler.edu
STEVICK, David 585-567-9607 302 D david.stevick@houghton.edu
STEVICK, Thomas 574-520-4344 157 A tstevick@iusb.edu
STEVICK, Tom 262-472-1918 498 C
STEVINSON, Rebecca 218-749-7762 238 G b.stevinson@mesabirange.edu
STEWARD, Agnes 253-840-8403 483 D asteward@pierce.ctc.edu
STEWARD, Dana 417-328-1425 259 L dsteward@sbuniv.edu
STEWARD, Deborah 315-781-3500 302 A stewart@hws.edu
STEWARD, Gary 405-974-5528 370 K gsteward@uco.edu
STEWARD, Jerry, L 405-682-7502 367 H jsteward@occc.edu
STEWARD, Kyle 662-325-3221 247 F ksteward@pres.msstate.edu
STEWARD, Regina 501-370-5333 20 G rsteward@philander.edu
STEWART, Alandrea 314-340-3391 253 I stewarta@hssu.edu
STEWART, Barbara, A 408-554-4396 62 D bstewart@scu.edu
STEWART, Barbara, E 608-785-5092 496 F bstewart@uwlax.edu
STEWART, Basil 978-837-5000 216 D
STEWART, Ben 773-256-0769 142 G bstewart@lstc.edu
STEWART, Beth 828-398-7633 332 B bethstewart@abtech.edu
STEWART, Betty 972-338-1600 454 B betty.stewart@untdallas.edu
STEWART, Billy, W 601-635-6200 245 I bstewart@eccc.edu
STEWART, Brad, J 240-567-1312 200 C brad.stewart@montgomerycollege.edu
STEWART, Bryan 305-237-4064 103 D bstewar2@mdc.edu
STEWART, Carol, A 520-621-4930 16 G stewart@uatechpark.org
STEWART, Carrie, E 310-243-3787 31 B cstewart@csudh.edu
STEWART, Charles 212-650-7271 293 D cstewart@ccny.cuny.edu
STEWART, Chauncine`, R 323-241-5225 49 D stewarcr@lasc.edu
STEWART, Chris 423-236-2356 424 B cbstewart@southern.edu
STEWART, Christy 618-985-2828 139 I christystewart@jalc.edu
STEWART, Cindy 256-331-5348 3 C cstewart@nwscc.edu
STEWART, Claire 402-472-2526 269 J cstewart@unl.edu
STEWART, Colin 559-278-2741 31 D costewart@csufresno.edu
STEWART, Connie 989-328-1249 228 A connies@montcalm.edu
STEWART, Connie 731-286-7714 425 A cstewart@dscc.edu
STEWART, David, R 651-638-6225 234 C d-stewart@bethel.edu
STEWART, Dawn 614-823-3529 360 A dstewart@otterbein.edu
STEWART, Dawn 614-890-3000 360 A dstewart@otterbein.edu
STEWART, Deborah 802-828-2800 464 B das07200@ccv.vsc.edu
STEWART, Donette 864-503-5280 414 D dstewart@uscupstate.edu
STEWART, Doreen 815-967-7322 147 F dstewart@rockfordcareercollege.edu
STEWART, Dorothy 313-993-1028 231 B stewardm@udmercy.edu
STEWART, Douglas 601-877-2419 244 H stewartd@alcorn.edu
STEWART, Elizabeth, D 570-577-3108 379 F eds019@bucknell.edu
STEWART, Elizabeth, J 585-292-2536 307 H estewart@monroecc.edu
STEWART, Grace 970-675-3218 78 G grace.stewart@cncc.edu
STEWART, H.D 828-898-8823 330 E stewarth@lmc.edu
STEWART, Hansen 509-543-1484 479 H hstewart@columbiabasin.edu
STEWART, James 727-302-6787 106 E stewart.james@spcollege.edu
STEWART, James 503-517-1898 378 A jstewart@westernseminary.edu
STEWART, James 731-352-4093 418 G stewartj@bethelu.edu
STEWART, Jane 313-664-1533 222 F jstewart@collegeforcreativestudies.edu
STEWART, Janeen, K 319-352-8331 170 C janeen.stewart@wartburg.edu
STEWART, Janet 740-351-3197 360 K jstewart@shawnee.edu
STEWART, Jennifer 417-873-6919 252 F jstewart012@drury.edu
STEWART, Jennifer 314-968-7105 262 C jstewart15@webster.edu
STEWART, Jimmy 318-678-6000 187 A jistewart@bpcc.edu
STEWART, III, John, W 205-665-6001 8 D presidentsoffice@montevallo.edu
STEWART, Josh 903-434-8242 441 B jstewart@ntcc.edu
STEWART, Juarine 256-372-5750 1 A juarine.stewart@aamu.edu
STEWART, Kaylan 731-989-6651 420 C kstewart@fhu.edu
STEWART, Kiesha 718-368-5034 294 E kiesha.stewart@kbcc.cuny.edu
STEWART, Lana 308-345-8110 267 K stewartl@mpcc.edu
STEWART, Larry 248-218-2023 229 J lstewart@rc.edu
STEWART, Lea, P 848-932-7127 282 A lstewart@comminfo.rutgers.edu
STEWART, Leah 859-572-6437 184 A stewartl1@nku.edu
STEWART, Leesa 802-322-1652 462 C leesa.stewart@goddard.edu
STEWART, Lisa 434-791-7186 464 O lstewart@averett.edu
STEWART, Lisa 850-599-3730 108 I lisa.stewart@famu.edu
STEWART, Lisa 832-252-0758 433 D lisa.stewart@cbshouston.edu
STEWART, Makena 704-290-5840 337 I mstewart@spcc.edu
STEWART, Mark 718-270-2740 317 E mark.stewart@downstate.edu
STEWART, Marshall, M 573-882-7477 261 B stewartmars@missouri.edu
STEWART, Michael 214-333-6870 434 I michaels@dbu.edu
STEWART, Michael 478-471-2710 121 F michael.stewart@mga.edu
STEWART, Michelle, C 312-935-4232 139 H mstewart@icsw.edu
STEWART, Nydia 847-578-8482 147 I nydia.stewart@rosalindfranklin.edu
STEWART, Paul 904-620-3978 110 A p.stewart@unf.edu
STEWART, Peter 207-326-2181 195 D peter.stewart@mma.edu
STEWART, Rachel 231-777-0461 228 D rachel.stewart@muskegoncc.edu
STEWART, Raedorah 202-885-8671 93 E rcstewart@wesleyseminary.edu
STEWART, Reginald, C 515-294-8840 162 I rstewart@iastate.edu
STEWART, Renee 615-366-4416 424 D renee.stewart@tbr.edu
STEWART, Rob 806-742-2184 451 B rob.stewart@ttu.edu
STEWART, Robert 904-256-7663 101 G rstewar6@ju.edu
STEWART, Robert 617-552-2671 207 B bobstewart@theq.follett.com
STEWART, Ronnie 706-886-6831 125 D rstewart@tfc.edu
STEWART, Ross 206-281-2900 484 D rstewart@spu.edu
STEWART, Scott 616-949-5300 222 I scott.stewart@cornerstone.edu
STEWART, Sonja 931-221-7342 418 D stewarts@apsu.edu
STEWART, Standish 216-987-4596 351 G standish.stewart@tri-c.edu
STEWART, Terri 585-389-2840 308 B tstewar1@naz.edu
STEWART, Thomas 413-538-7000 214 D tstewart@hcc.edu
STEWART, Thomas 415-494-8240 56 A tstewart@patten.edu
STEWART, Tish 662-472-9080 246 C tstewart@holmescc.edu
STEWART, Todd, I 937-255-2321 503 A todd.stewart@afit.edu
STEWART, Todd, M 270-745-5276 185 E todd.stewart@wku.edu
STEWART, Tom 925-969-3302 46 H tstewart@jfku.edu
STEWART, Tommie, T 334-229-4232 4 B tstewart@alasu.edu
STEWART, Tommy 901-761-9494 419 D tstewart@concorde.edu
STEWART, Tracy 608-796-3081 498 N tmstewart@viterbo.edu
STEWART, Trevor 209-588-5112 75 I stewartt@yosemite.edu
STEWART, Tynelle 585-275-7532 323 J tstewar4@ur.rochester.edu
STEWART, Vicki, L 717-815-1287 404 A vstewart@ycp.edu
STEWART, Wendy 760-757-2121 52 E wstewart@miracosta.edu
STEWART, Wendy 253-833-9111 481 F wstewart@greenriver.edu
STEWART, Ziola 770-792-6100 121 C zstewart@life.edu
STEWART-ELMORE, Samantha 470-639-0402 122 D samantha.elmore@morehouse.edu
STEWART-JAMES, Joy 916-278-6461 32 E jsjames@csus.edu
STEWART-MAILHIOT, Amy 360-688-2250 483 H astewart-mailhiot@stmartin.edu
STEWART O'NEAL, Rene 703-993-8758 467 L rstewa4@gmu.edu
STEWART-WELLS, A. Gillian 847-628-1001 140 C astewartwells@judsonu.edu
STIAK, Julie 602-285-7800 13 F julie.stiak@phoenixcollege.edu
STIBER, Greg, F 954-262-5381 103 M stiber@nova.edu
STICE, J. Michael 405-325-4687 371 B mstice@ou.edu
STICE, Mike 949-376-6000 47 D mstice@lcad.edu
STICH, Lisa 320-308-5030 241 A lisa.stich@sctcc.edu
STICHNOTE, Lynn, K 573-882-2751 261 B lks@missouri.edu
STICHTER, Donald 518-262-7000 289 F stichtd@amc.edu
STICK, Jim 515-964-6429 164 C jwstick@dmacc.edu
STICKA, Stephen 510-436-1134 45 D sticka@hnu.edu
STICKLES, Christopher 541-880-2240 373 E stickles@klamathcc.edu
STICKNEY, Sarah 760-572-2000 41 C

STICKROD, Denver .... 315-866-0300 301 G
stickrodt@herkimer.edu
STIEBER, Kolina .... 715-422-5326 500 A
kolina.stieber@mstc.edu
STIEFEL, Joseph P, D ... 630-889-6604 144 G
jstiefel@nuhs.edu
STIEFFEL, Deborah .... 313-993-1496 231 B
deborah.stieffel@udmercy.edu
STIEGLITZ, Matt .... 609-896-5035 281 B
STIELL, George .... 903-927-3212 458 G
gstiell@wileyc.edu
STIENKE, Madison .... 641-673-1054 170 F
madison.steinke@wmpenn.edu
STIER, Byron, G .... 213-738-6809.. 65 G
bstier@swlaw.edu
STIER, Mark .... 941-487-4504 109 D
mstier@ncf.edu
STIER, Phillip .... 763-488-0239 239 G
pstier@nhcc.edu
STIER, Shari .... 617-824-8133 208 H
shari_stier@emerson.edu
STIFF, James .... 478-471-4394 120 F
STIFFIN, Rose Mary ...... 305-626-3697.. 99 D
rose.stiffin@fmuniv.edu
STIFFLER, Daniel, J .... 314-367-8700 259 B
daniel.stiffler@stlcop.edu
STIFFLER, Faith .... 817-598-8874 458 A
fstiffler@wc.edu
STIKEL, Janet .... 414-382-6112 492 A
janet.stikel@alverno.edu
STILES, Aimee .... 304-877-6428 487 F
officeofpresident@abc.edu
STILES, Andy .... 785-242-5200 176 D
andy.stiles@ottawa.edu
STILES, Angela .... 561-683-1400.. 94 A
astiles@anho.edu
STILES, Bill .... 610-796-3015 378 F
bill.stiles@alvernia.edu
STILES, Chip .... 207-893-7850 195 F
cstiles@sjcme.edu
STILES, Diane .... 605-882-5284 415 F
diane.stiles@lakeareatech.edu
STILES, Michael, D .... 712-279-3149 169 B
michael.stiles@stlukescollege.edu
STILES, Michelle .... 336-272-7102 329 D
michelle.stiles@greensboro.edu
STILES, Rebecca .... 212-517-3929 316 B
r.stiles@sia.edu
STILES, Timothy .... 386-822-7315 111 A
tstiles@stetson.edu
STILES-POLK, Danielle .. 317-921-4241 157 H
dstiles3@ivytech.edu
STILL, Jill .... 936-468-5406 445 F
jstill@sfasu.edu
STILL, Kathy .... 276-376-0130 473 B
kls72d@virginia.edu
STILL, Todd, D .... 254-710-3755 431 J
todd_still@baylor.edu
STILLE, Brand, R .... 864-597-4130 414 H
stillebr@wofford.edu
STILLE, Robyn, L .... 906-227-2661 228 F
rstille@nmu.edu
STILLE, Suzette .... 843-953-8148 408 E
stilles@cofc.edu
STILLERMAN, Harry ...... 434-961-5203 475 F
hstillerman@pvcc.edu
STILLEY, Dana .... 845-574-4224 313 C
dstilley@sunyrockland.edu
STILLEY, Kevin .... 214-818-1369 434 F
kstilley@criswell.edu
STILLIANA, John, J .... 330-325-6347 357 G
jstilliana@neomed.edu
STILLMAN, Brian, C ...... 208-467-8460 131 D
bcstillman@nnu.edu
STILLMAN, Bruce .... 516-367-8497 296 D
stillman@cshl.edu
STILLMAN, Matt .... 541-552-8535 376 E
stillmam@sou.edu
STILLMAN, Therese .... 518-454-5199 296 H
stillmat@strose.edu
STILLMAN-ROKUSEK,
Pam .... 605-718-2418 417 F
pam.stillman-rokusek@wdt.edu
STILLS, Karen .... 214-860-2170 435 C
kstills@dcccd.edu
STILSON, Michael .... 520-626-6363.. 16 G
mstilson@email.arizona.edu
STILTNER, Melissa .... 276-964-7706 475 I
melissa.stiltner@sw.edu
STILTS, Corey, E .... 607-735-1804 299 D
cstilts@elmira.edu
STILWELL, Jackie .... 951-343-4239.. 27 J
jstilwell@calbpatist.edu
STIMAC, Robin .... 816-604-1000 255 H
robin.stimac@mcckc.edu
STIMELING, Kurt .... 603-897-8247 274 B
kstimeling@rivier.edu
STIMERS, Mitch .... 785-243-1435 172 F
mstimers@cloud.edu
STIMPERT, John, L ...... 434-223-6110 468 A
president@hsc.edu
STIMPLE, Janet .... 216-687-3831 351 B
j.stimple@csuohio.edu
STIMPSON, Lee .... 208-535-5425 130 C
lee.stimpson@cei.edu
STIMSON, Jay .... 303-762-6923.. 79 H
jay.stimson@denverseminary.edu
STINAUER, Anna .... 309-649-6230 150 A
anna.stinauer@src.edu
STINE, Bob, A .... 612-624-1251 243 E
rstine@umn.edu
STINE, Cory .... 419-559-2355 361 I
cstine@terra.edu
STINE, Misty .... 575-392-4510 286 J
mstine@nmjc.edu
STINE, Terry .... 314-837-6777 258 J
tstine@stlchristian.edu
STINEMETZ, Amanda, K 304-367-4490 490 B
amanda.stinemetz@fairmontstate.edu
STINEMETZ, Charles, L . 740-368-3101 359 N
clstinem@owu.edu
STINES, Marsha .... 828-627-4529 335 C
mstines@haywood.edu
STINNER, Jerry .... 818-677-2004.. 32 D
jerry.stinner@csun.edu
STINNETT, Allyson .... 248-218-2011 229 J
astinnett@rc.edu
STINNETT, Gary, W .... 704-687-0644 342 E
gwstinne@uncc.edu
STINSON, Christina .... 270-831-9622 181 D
christina.stinson@kctcs.edu
STINSON, Claire .... 931-372-3657 426 E
cstinson@tntech.edu
STINSON, Greg .... 219-464-5212 162 A
greg.stinson@valpo.edu
STINSON, Harry .... 484-365-7391 389 C
hstinson@lincoln.edu
STINSON, Jeffrey, L ...... 509-963-2111 479 B
STINSON, Jerry .... 276-964-7603 475 I
jerry.stinson@sw.edu
STINSON, Lisa .... 860-701-5068.. 87 D
stinson_l@mitchell.edu
STINSON, Lori .... 208-792-2213 131 A
lstinson@lcsc.edu
STINSON, Matthew, P ... 724-946-7368 402 G
stinsomp@westminster.edu
STINSON, Niki .... 706-245-7226 117 E
nstinson@ec.edu
STINSON, Pam .... 580-628-6210 367 D
pam.stinson@noc.edu
STINSON, Randy, L .... 817-923-1921 445 B
provost@swbts.edu
STINSON, Willette .... 304-766-3239 491 B
wstinson@wvstateu.edu
STIPCAK, Sondra, L ...... 570-321-4322 389 E
stipcak@lycoming.edu
STIPE, Richard .... 870-633-4480.. 19 B
rstipe@eacc.edu
STIPELMAN, Brian .... 301-846-2646 198 E
bstipelman@frederick.edu
STIRES, Elizabeth, M ..... 570-348-6211 389 G
emmorton@marywood.edu
STIREWALT, Jesse .... 218-879-0708 238 A
housing@fdltcc.edu
STIRRETT, Chad .... 810-232-8153 228 C
chad.stirrett@mcc.edu
STIRTON, Robert .... 973-328-5011 277 B
rstirton@ccm.edu
STISO, Joseph .... 978-630-9593 215 A
j_stiso@mwcc.mass.edu
STITELER, Chad .... 360-752-8313 478 G
cstiteler@btc.edu
STITES, Dorothy, D .... 785-749-8456 173 G
dstites@haskell.edu
STITES-DOE, Susan .... 585-395-5537 318 B
sstites@brockport.edu
STITH, Megan .... 270-706-8721 181 A
mstith0005@kctcs.edu
STITLEY, Michael .... 215-596-8800 401 G
STIVEN, Janet, A .... 312-329-4123 144 B
janet.stiven@moody.edu
STIVER, Chris .... 517-264-3131 220 F
cstiver@adrian.edu
STIVERS, Laura .... 415-458-3734.. 41 H
laura.stivers@dominican.edu
STIVERS, Mary, E .... 859-846-5332 183 E
mestivers@midway.edu
STIVERS, Robbi .... 561-967-7222 104 D
ST JULIANA, II, Robert 760-674-7823.. 39 A
rstjuliana@collegeofthedesert.edu
STOAKS, Lindsay .... 641-782-1338 169 H
stoaks@swcciowa.edu
STOB, Barbara .... 410-337-6011 198 G
bstob@goucher.edu
STOBIE, Pete .... 816-654-7108 254 C
pstobie@kcumb.edu
STOBO, John, D .... 510-987-9071.. 68 C
john.stobo@ucop.edu
STOCK, Ann Marie .... 757-221-4000 466 C
amstoc@wm.edu
STOCK, Lawrence, E ..... 724-287-8711 380 A
larry.stock@bc3.edu
STOCK, Renee .... 304-829-7572 487 G
rstock@bethanywv.edu
STOCK, Sue .... 847-543-2404 135 B
sstock@clcillinois.edu
STOCKE, Mike .... 253-964-6534 483 D
mstocke@pierce.ctc.edu
STOCKLIN, Christopher . 605-229-8453 416 C
christopher.stocklin@presentation.edu
STOCKMAN, Deb .... 316-295-5377 173 D
deb_stockman@friends.edu
STOCKS, Chad .... 601-857-3315 246 B
clstocks@hindscc.edu
STOCKTON, Belinda ...... 276-656-0214 475 D
bstockton@patrickhenry.edu
STOCKTON, Carl, A .... 334-244-3602.... 4 F
chancellor@aum.edu
STOCKTON, Hans .... 713-525-3536 454 H
stockth@stthom.edu
STOCKTON, Hans .... 713-525-3530 454 H
stockton@stthom.edu
STOCKTON, Kathryn, B . 801-581-7569 460 E
kathryn.stockton@utah.edu
STOCKTON, Shelli .... 909-748-8011.. 71 G
shelli_stockton@redlands.edu
STOCKWELL, Dave .... 614-222-3216 351 D
dstockwell@ccad.edu
STODDARD, Judith .... 845-575-3000 305 L
judith.stoddard@marist.edu
STODDARD, Lynn .... 860-465-0252.. 84 J
stoddardl@easternct.edu
STODDARD, Reed, J ..... 208-496-9370 130 A
stoddardr@byui.edu
STODDARD, Sharon ...... 336-750-3339 344 B
stoddardst@wssu.edu
STODDARD, Troy .... 406-771-4387 264 G
troy.stoddard@gfcmsu.edu
STODDART, Judith .... 517-432-2524 227 D
stoddart@grd.msu.edu
STODDART, Rick .... 541-463-5824 373 F
stoddartr@lanecc.edu
STOECKER, Judith .... 847-578-8694 147 I
judith.stoecker@rosalindfranklin.edu
STOECKER, Nancy .... 630-829-6402 132 E
nstoecker@ben.edu
STOECKLEIN, Denny ...... 620-665-3526 174 B
stoecklein@hutchcc.edu
STOEKEL, Ashley .... 386-481-2973.. 95 F
porterfielda@cookman.edu
STOELTING, Diane .... 716-286-8064 310 D
ds@niagara.edu
STOEVER, Colby .... 504-280-7058 189 E
cjstoeve@uno.edu
STOFAN, James .... 504-865-5901 191 B
jstofan@tulane.edu
STOFFEL, Larry .... 317-738-8152 154 J
lstoffel@franklincollege.edu
STOFFER, Brian, M ...... 312-329-4359 144 B
brian.stoffer@moody.edu
STOFFT, Lori .... 928-314-9595.. 10 J
lorraine.stofft@azwestern.edu
STOGNER, Becky .... 806-651-2311 448 C
bstogner@wtamu.edu
STOGNER, Brian, L .... 248-218-2011 229 J
bstogner@rc.edu
STOGUE, Andrea .... 918-495-6978 368 I
STOHLER, Christian, S .. 212-305-4511 297 C
cs3221@columbia.edu
STOHLMAN, Bill .... 606-539-3541 185 A
william.stohlman@ucumberlands.edu
STOICESCU, Dan .... 410-287-1923 197 H
dstoicescu@cecil.edu
STOJKOVIC, Stan .... 414-229-4400 497 A
stojkovi@uwm.edu
STOKAN, Matthew .... 724-852-3227 402 F
mstokan@waynesburg.edu
STOKER, Daniel, J .... 260-422-5561 155 H
djstoker@indianatech.edu
STOKER, Michael .... 479-880-4040.. 18 C
mstoker@atu.edu
STOKES, Aaron .... 620-862-5252 171 B
aaron.stokes@barclaycollege.edu
STOKES, Brandon .... 919-760-8318 331 B
kbstokes@meredith.edu
STOKES, Bryan .... 432-264-5078 438 C
bstokes@howardcollege.edu
STOKES, Clifford .... 850-599-3560 108 I
clifford.stokes@famu.edu
STOKES, Douglas .... 803-535-1393 411 G
stokesd@octech.edu
STOKES, Garnett, S .... 505-277-2626 288 G
presidentstokes@unm.edu
STOKES, Ginger, C .... 386-312-4074 106 C
gingerstokes@sjrstate.edu
STOKES, Jamia .... 901-843-3698 423 J
stokesj@rhodes.edu
STOKES, Jeannine .... 951-487-3156.. 52 I
jstokes@msjc.edu
STOKES, Jen, J .... 315-268-6527 296 A
jstokes@clarkson.edu
STOKES, Jenny .... 336-917-5595 340 D
jenny.stokes@salem.edu
STOKES, Judi .... 845-431-8405 298 E
judi.stokes@sunydutchess.edu
STOKES, Ken .... 770-484-1204 121 D
ken.stokes@lutherrice.edu
STOKES, Kevin .... 937-767-1286 347 G
STOKES, Lynette, D .... 708-596-2000 149 B
STOKES, Madeline .... 251-405-4457.... 1 E
mstokes@bishop.edu
STOKES, Maureen, O .... 508-929-8000 213 E
STOKES, Michael .... 423-472-7141 424 F
mstokes@clevelandstatecc.edu
STOKES, Mickey .... 662-476-5068 246 A
mstokes@eastms.edu
STOKES, Rhonda .... 410-888-9048 200 A
rstokes@muih.edu
STOKES, Scott .... 712-362-7913 166 F
sstokes@iowalakes.edu
STOKES, Shereitte .... 718-262-5191 295 F
sstokes@york.cuny.edu
STOKES, Timothy .... 360-596-5206 485 B
tstokes@spscc.edu
STOKES-BROWN, Atiya . 843-349-2218 408 C
astokesb@coastal.edu
STOKES-DUPASS,
Nicole .... 267-341-3695 386 A
nstokes-dupass@holyfamily.edu
STOKLEY, Alicia .... 252-335-0821 333 G
alicia_stokley99@albemarle.edu
STOKSTAD, Paul .... 641-451-4219 167 F
alumni@mum.edu
STOLAR, Andrea, G .... 713-798-4870 431 I
stolar@bcm.edu
STOLDT, Tyler .... 785-442-6028 174 A
tstoldt@highlandcc.edu
STOLEY, Lawrence .... 402-643-4052 269 A
STOLKOWSKI, Elizabeth 561-688-5112 104 A
STOLL, Barbara .... 217-641-4520 140 A
bstoll@jwcc.edu
STOLL, Barbara, J .... 713-500-5010 456 B
barbara.j.stoll@uth.tmc.edu
STOLL, Cecil .... 620-417-1205 176 K
cecil.stoll@sccc.edu
STOLL, Dan .... 920-403-3887 495 I
dan.stoll@snc.edu
STOLL, Kirby, R .... 651-631-5378 244 D
krstoll@unwsp.edu
STOLL, Lisa .... 908-835-9222 284 G
lstoll@warren.edu
STOLL, Sherideen, S ..... 419-372-8262 348 H
sstoll@bgsu.edu
STOLL, William, S .... 314-935-7574 262 A
stoll@wustl.edu
STOLLENWERK, Matt ..... 651-255-6123 243 D
mstollenwerk@unitedseminary.edu
STOLLER, Brett .... 309-649-6211 150 A
brett.stoller@src.edu
STOLP, Kayti .... 218-733-7600 238 F
kayti.stolp@lsc.edu
STOLPER, Lauren, B ...... 626-395-2150.. 29 C
lstolper@caltech.edu
STOLTE, Scott .... 570-408-4911 403 D
scott.stolte@wilkes.edu
STOLTMAN, Nate .... 507-536-5604 240 G
nate.stoltman@rctc.edu
STOLTZ-LOIKE, Marian . 646-565-6000 322 J
mstoltz-loike@touro.edu

STOLTZFUS, Joanna ...... 740-593-1804 359 G
stoltzfu@ohio.edu
STOLTZFUS, Karen, S ... 574-296-6244 152 I
kstoltzfus@ambs.edu
STOLTZFUS, Ken .... 316-295-5567 173 D
kenneth_stoltzfus@friends.edu
STOLTZFUS, Rebecca, J 574-535-7180 155 A
president@goshen.edu
STOLTZFUS, Ruth .... 574-535-7375 155 A
ruthas@goshen.edu
STOLZE, Martha, A .... 630-637-5814 144 H
mastolze@noctrl.edu
STOLZER, Alan .... 386-226-7352.. 98 A
stolzera@erau.edu
STOLZER, Donna .... 908-526-1200 281 A
donna.stolzer@raritanval.edu
STOLZER, Tess .... 213-624-1200.. 42 I
tstolzer@fidm.edu
STOMBERGER, Mary ..... 970-491-6817.. 78 M
jodie.hanzlik@colostate.edu
STOMPER, Jeffrey .... 847-543-2531 135 B
stomper@clcillinois.edu
STONE, Alison .... 281-649-3289 437 H
astone@hbu.edu
STONE, Andrea .... 606-783-5272 183 F
a.fryman@moreheadstate.edu
STONE, Andrew .... 801-863-6376 461 A
andrew.stone@uvu.edu
STONE, Angie .... 256-331-5475.... 3 C
angies@nwscc.edu
STONE, Cody .... 406-994-2452 264 D
cstone@montana.edu
STONE, David .... 401-841-3569 503 L
david.stone@usnwc.edu
STONE, David, A .... 248-370-2762 229 G
dstone@oakland.edu
STONE, Dawn .... 989-356-9021 221 A
stoned@alpenacc.edu
STONE, Daye .... 541-245-7991 376 D
dstone@roguecc.edu
STONE, Denise .... 503-255-0332 374 D
dstone@multnomah.edu
STONE, Elizabeth .... 202-559-5079.. 91 E
elizabeth.stone@gallaudet.edu
STONE, Emily .... 925-969-2113.. 40 I
estone@dvc.edu
STONE, Glenice .... 662-720-7237 248 C
gwstone@nemcc.edu
STONE, Greg .... 918-595-7724 370 E
greg.stone@tulsacc.edu
STONE, Jenna .... 315-268-3790 296 A
jestone@clarkson.edu
STONE, Jennifer .... 315-228-6928 296 F
jstone@colgate.edu
STONE, John .... 661-362-2271.. 51 C
jstone@masters.edu
STONE, Karen, J .... 904-620-2828 110 A
kstone@unf.edu
STONE, Mark .... 979-458-6450 446 C
mstone@tamus.edu
STONE, Melissa .... 302-831-8189.. 90 F
mstone@udel.edu
STONE, Morley, O .... 614-247-8356 358 I
stone.816@osu.edu
STONE, Patrick .... 508-362-2131 214 B
STONE, Paul .... 817-599-8324 458 A
stone@wc.edu
STONE, Polly .... 704-688-4203 248 F
pstone@rts.edu
STONE, Ralinda .... 817-598-6276 458 A
rstone@wc.edu
STONE, Rhonda .... 870-248-4000.. 18 F
rhonda.stone@blackrivertech.edu
STONE, Robert .... 626-256-4673.. 37 B
rstone@coh.org
STONE, Rowena, A .... 417-836-8500 256 E
rowenastone@missouristate.edu
STONE, Sammy .... 229-931-2394 124 D
sstone@southgatech.edu
STONE, Scott .... 410-225-2398 199 H
sstone@mica.edu
STONE, Staci, L .... 256-782-5690..... 5 J
slstone@jsu.edu
STONE, Sue .... 229-226-1621 125 C
sstone@thomasu.edu
STONE, Susan .... 859-899-2510 180 C
sstone@frontier.edu
STONE, Tia .... 256-331-5279.... 3 C
tstone@nwscc.edu
STONE, Ty, A .... 315-786-2230 303 F
tstone@sunyjefferson.edu
STONE-MOYE, Shelly, T 336-322-2163 336 G
shelly.stone@piedmontcc.edu
STONEBROOK, Kenneth 801-957-4004 461 D
kenneth.stonebrook@slcc.edu
STONECIPHER,
Amanda, G .... 812-941-2420 157 B
agstonec@ius.edu
STONEHAM, Edrel .... 361-582-2516 457 E
edrel.stoneham@victoriacollege.edu
STONEKING, Carole, B . 336-841-9168 329 G
cstoneki@highpoint.edu
STONEKING, Dawn, M .. 812-464-1932 161 E
dstoneking@usi.edu
STONEMAN, Lisa .... 614-224-9101 351 D
lstoneman@ccad.edu
STONER, Gayla .... 509-963-1488 479 B
gayla.stoner@cwu.edu
STONER, Keith .... 419-755-4810 357 E
kstoner@ncstatecollege.edu
STONER, Kevin .... 845-687-5092 323 E
stonerk@sunyulster.edu
STONER, Melinda, J ...... 402-280-4021 266 I
registrar@creighton.edu
STONER, Melissa .... 425-352-8667 479 A
mstoner@cascadia.edu
STONER, Tamara, L ...... 302-857-6001.. 89 F
tstoner@desu.edu
STOOKEY, Stephen .... 806-291-1161 457 J
stookeys@wbu.edu
STOOKSBERRY, Robert . 210-436-3301 443 A
tstooksberry@stmarytx.edu
STOOPS, Lynne .... 831-459-1376.. 70 B
lstoops@ucsc.edu
STOOPS, Melinda .... 617-552-3280 207 B
melinda.stoops@bc.edu
STOOPS, Melinda .... 509-777-3701 486 I
mstoops@whitworth.edu
STOOS, Barbara .... 419-251-1702 356 C
barbara.stoos@mercycollege.edu
STOOTHOFF, Lisa .... 913-621-8726 172 K
lstoothoff@donnelly.edu
STOPA GOLDSTEIN,
Amanda .... 315-265-9260 296 A
1193mgr@follett.com
STOPHER, Brenda .... 470-578-3225 120 L
bstopher@kennesaw.edu
STOPPENBRINK, Norm . 614-837-4088 364 A
stoppenbrinkn@valorcollege.edu
STOPPER, Suzanne, T ... 570-326-3761 393 G
sstoppe2@pct.edu
STOPPLE, Jeffrey .... 805-893-2385.. 70 A
jstopple@ltsc.ucsb.edu
STOPYRA, Sarah .... 781-762-1211 209 C
sstopyra@fmc.edu
STORCH, Judith .... 848-932-1689 282 A
storch@sebs.rutgers.edu
STORCK, Angela .... 478-289-2173 117 D
astorck@ega.edu
STORCK, Eileen .... 772-462-7805 101 E
estorck@irsc.edu
STORER, Andrew, J .... 906-487-2352 227 E
storer@mtu.edu
STOREY, Amy .... 315-279-5201 304 A
astorey@keuka.edu
STOREY, Bruce .... 309-796-5129 132 G
storeyb@bhc.edu
STOREY, Karen .... 906-635-2418 226 E
kstorey@lssu.edu
STOREY GROVES,
Margaret .... 802-443-5196 462 H
mgroves@middlebury.edu
STORIE, Cheryl .... 240-582-5680 203 B
financial-affairs@umuc.edu
STORIE, Monique .... 671-735-2333 505 E
mstorie@triton.uog.edu
STORIE, Monique, C ..... 671-735-2162 505 E
mstorie@triton.uog.edu
STORIN LINITZ, Karen .. 617-975-9324 209 A
linitzk@emmanuel.edu
STORLAZZI, Caesar, T .. 203-432-0371.. 89 D
caesar.storlazzi@yale.edu
STORM, JR., Chris, K ... 516-877-3165 289 C
cstorm@adelphi.edu
STORM, Maryam .... 818-708-9232.. 48 E
STORMBERG, Diane, G . 402-280-2222 266 I
dianestormberg@creighton.edu
STORMER, Kevin .... 812-866-6837 155 C
STORMS, Amy .... 417-626-1234 257 F
storms.amy@occ.edu
STORMS, Andy .... 417-626-1234 257 F
storms.andy@occ.edu
STORMS, Joyce, A .... 616-538-2330 224 C
jstorms@gracehchristian.edu
STORMS, Melanie .... 352-588-7805 106 D
melanie.storms@saintleo.edu
STORRS, Debbie .... 701-777-2049 345 C
debbie.storrs@und.edu
STORRS, Regina, M ...... 313-593-5020 231 F
rstorrs@umich.edu
STORTI, Richard .... 559-934-2160.. 73 M
richardstorti@whccd.edu
STORY, Clifton .... 662-325-2431 247 F
cws103@msstate.edu
STORY, Lisa, L .... 712-324-5061 168 G
lstory@nwicc.edu
STORY, Sarah .... 830-372-8053 449 B
sstory@tlu.edu
STORY, Shelley .... 512-863-1281 445 D
storys@southwestern.edu
STORY-HUFFMAN, Ru ... 229-931-2259 119 D
ru.story-huffman@gsw.edu
STOSBERG, Tobey .... 816-276-4740 258 F
tobey.stosberg@researchcollege.edu
STOSKOPF, Janna .... 660-785-4111 260 J
jstoskopf@truman.edu
STOSS, Kate .... 765-285-1847 153 C
kpstoss@bsu.edu
STOTLER, Doug .... 618-468-6200 141 F
dstotler@lc.edu
STOTO, Robert .... 609-896-5140 281 B
stoto@rider.edu
STOTT, Roger, F .... 443-518-4463 199 C
rstott@howardcc.edu
STOTTER, Jennifer .... 808-932-7641 128 E
jstotter@hawaii.edu
STOTTS, Bob .... 270-789-5017 179 E
restotts@campbellsville.edu
STOTTS, James .... 404-880-8992 116 D
jstotts@cau.edu
STOTTS, Melissa .... 701-662-1538 346 D
melissa.stotts@lrsc.edu
STOUDENMIRE, Phyllis 803-535-1220 411 G
stoudenmirep@octech.edu
STOUDT, Jennifer .... 610-921-7526 378 C
jstoudt@albright.edu
STOUFFER, Vicki .... 419-824-3969 355 K
vstouffer@lourdes.edu
STOUFFER, Wendy, D ... 479-575-6870.. 21 G
wstouff@uark.edu
STOUP, Gregory .... 530-895-2266.. 27 F
stoupgr@butte.edu
STOUP, Russ .... 618-634-3276 149 A
russs@shawneecc.edu
STOUT, Alden .... 712-274-5388 168 B
stoutj@morningside.edu
STOUT, Brittany .... 304-367-4054 490 B
brittany.stout@fairmontstate.edu
STOUT, Chris .... 248-689-8282 232 A
cstout@walshcollege.edu
STOUT, David, M .... 732-224-2204 276 B
dstout@brookdalecc.edu
STOUT, Gary .... 817-531-6552 451 E
STOUT, Jeffrey .... 407-823-0211 109 E
jeffrey.stout@ucf.edu
STOUT, Michael .... 336-334-4822 335 A
mcstout@gtcc.edu
STOUT, Ross .... 503-370-6911 378 B
rstout@willamette.edu
STOUT, Thomas, B .... 757-822-5230 476 B
tstout@tcc.edu
STOUTE, Steve .... 312-362-7571 135 I
sstoute@depaul.edu
STOVALL, Alethea .... 402-481-3804 265 K
alethea.stovall@bryanhealthcollege.edu
STOVALL, Alfred, J .... 662-252-8000 248 G
ajstovall@rustcollege.edu
STOVALL, Chris .... 940-397-4273 440 F
chris.stovall@msutexas.edu
STOVALL, Flavia .... 610-399-2204 394 C
fstovall@cheyney.edu
STOVALL, Jerry .... 229-931-2562 124 D
jstovall@southgatech.edu
STOVALL, Keith .... 601-643-8376 245 G
keith.stovall@colin.edu
STOVALL, Terri .... 817-923-1921 445 B
tstovall@swbts.edu
STOVALL, Tyler .... 831-459-2696.. 70 B
humanities@ucsc.edu
STOVER, Caitlin, M .... 508-767-7698 205 D
cm.stover@assumption.edu
STOVER, Dennis .... 877-954-1500 422 D
STOVER, Janice .... 620-441-5247 172 I
janice.stover@cowley.edu
STOVER, Lena .... 402-554-4196 270 B
ltraslavina@unomaha.edu
STOVER, Mark .... 818-677-2271.. 32 D
mark.stover@csun.edu
STOVER, Meredith, A .... 781-239-4015 205 E
stoverm@babson.edu
STOVER, Patrick, J .... 979-862-4384 446 G
vcdean@ag.tamu.edu
STOVER, Rebecca .... 540-863-2823 474 D
rstover@dslcc.edu
STOVER, Ronalda, S ..... 803-778-6688 407 C
stoverrs@cctech.edu
STOVER, Sarah .... 217-854-5761 132 I
sarah.stover@blackburn.edu
STOVER, Stacey .... 734-462-4400 230 D
sstover@schoolcraft.edu
STOVER, Teri .... 903-223-3088 448 B
teri.stover@tamut.edu
STOW, George, B .... 215-951-1097 387 C
stow@lasalle.edu
STOWASSER, Melissa ... 843-574-6312 413 B
melissa.stowasser@tridenttech.edu
STOWE, Brook .... 718-522-9073 290 C
bstowe@asa.edu
STOWE, Cindy .... 501-686-5557.. 22 C
cstowe@uams.edu
STOWE, Lentz .... 252-940-6306 332 C
lentz.stowe@beaufortccc.edu
STOWE, Melissa .... 205-387-0511..... 1 D
melissa.stowe@bscc.edu
STOWE, William .... 903-983-8602 439 A
wstowe@kilgore.edu
STOWELL, Jessica .... 904-819-6322.. 98 E
jstowell@flagler.edu
STOWELL, Joseph, M ... 616-222-1428 222 I
joe.stowell@cornerstone.edu
STOWELL, Mark .... 978-867-4306 209 F
mark.stowell@gordon.edu
STOWERS, Ray, E .... 479-308-2285.. 17 C
ray.stowers@arcomedu.org
STOWIK, Stanley .... 401-232-6240 404 F
STOYNOFF, Stephen ...... 507-389-1242 239 C
stephen.stoynoff@mnsu.edu
STRACK, Ashkhen .... 860-773-1489.. 86 G
astrack@tunxis.edu
STRACK, Freda .... 816-654-7196 254 C
fstrack@kcumb.edu
STRACK, Jason .... 269-471-6571 221 B
strack@andrews.edu
STRADER, Jeffrey .... 304-243-2389 491 I
jstrader@wju.edu
STRADER, Michael .... 252-399-6300 326 M
STRADER, Robin .... 304-534-7892 489 D
robin.strader@pierpont.edu
STRADER, Scott .... 813-974-9232 110 B
scottstrader@usf.edu
STRAHN-KOLLER,
Brooke .... 319-398-4911 167 C
bstrahn@kirkwood.edu
STRAIT, Dana .... 574-284-4556 160 C
dstrait@saintmarys.edu
STRAIT, LuAnn .... 605-882-5284 415 F
straitl@lakeareatech.edu
STRAIT, Micah .... 435-283-7145 461 C
micah.strait@snow.edu
STRAITS, Jeffrey .... 202-885-8684.. 93 E
jstraits@wesleyseminary.edu
STRAKA, Richard .... 507-389-6621 239 C
richard.straka@mnsu.edu
STRAKA, Ronald .... 952-446-4127 235 G
strakar@crown.edu
STRAKER-BANKS,
Allyson .... 973-655-3450 279 C
strakerbanka@mail.montclair.edu
STRANEY, Donald, O .... 808-956-6897 128 D
dstraney@hawaii.edu
STRANG, Bryce .... 503-943-8009 377 E
strang@up.edu
STRANGE, Adiaha .... 704-334-6882 328 C
astrange@charlottechristian.edu
STRANGE, Alan .... 219-864-2400 159 B
astrange@midamerica.edu
STRANGE, Kendra .... 864-578-8770 412 B
kstrange@sherman.edu
STRANGE, Richard .... 785-227-3380 171 E
stranger@bethanylb.edu
STRANGE, Tammy .... 303-273-3281.. 78 I
tstrange@mines.edu
STRANGE LEWIS,
Sharon .... 202-238-2446.. 92 B
STRANGE-MARTIN,
Nicole .... 202-884-9380.. 93 B
strangemartinn@trinitydc.edu
STRANO, Kimberly .... 845-257-3215 317 B
lavoiek@newpaltz.edu
STRASBURG, Sarah .... 605-331-6793 417 E
sarah.strasburg@usiouxfalls.edu

STRONG, Sheila, M ...... 585-292-2102 307 H
sstrong@monroecc.edu

STRONG, Shirley .... 510-879-9237.. 59 F
sstrong@samuelmerritt.edu

STRONG, Whitney .... 617-537-6456 143 B
wbstrong@mckendree.edu

STROSAHL, Darrin .... 218-333-6600 240 B
darrin.strosahl@ntcmn.edu

STROTHER, Jennielle ..... 512-313-3000 434 E
jennielle.strother@concordia.edu

STROTHER, Jennifer .... 206-934-2026 483 I
jennifer.strother@seattlecolleges.edu

STROTHER, Nina .... 662-862-8242 246 D
njstrother@iccms.edu

STROUD, George, H ..... 717-245-1639 382 F
stroudg@dickinson.edu

STROUD, James Ron ..... 915-831-6740 436 E
jstroud2@epcc.edu

STROUD, John .... 646-313-8000 295 E
john.stroud@guttman.cuny.edu

STROUD, Kerci, M .... 401-454-6380 405 D
kstroud@risd.edu

STROUD, Mikel .... 516-726-5589 504 G
stroudm@usmma.edu

STROUD, Nancy .... 478-471-2728 121 F
nancy.stroud@mga.edu

STROUD, Tina .... 712-279-5423 163 C
tina.stroud@briarcliff.edu

STROUP, Peg .... 860-215-9296.. 86 F
pstroup@trcc.commnet.edu

STROUP-BENHAM,
Christine .... 303-315-2835.. 83 C
christine.stroup-benham@ucdenver.edu

STROUSE, Natalie .... 216-373-5298 358 B
nstrouse@ndc.edu

STROUSE, Robert, K ...... 714-850-4800.. 84 E
strouse@taftu.edu

STROUSE, Robert, K ...... 714-850-4800.. 67 A
strouse@taftu.edu

STROUSS, Elaine .... 724-480-3494 381 K
elaine.strouss@ccbc.edu

STROUT, Sarah .... 508-929-8119 213 E
sstrout@worcester.edu

STROW, Susan .... 312-369-7318 135 E
sstrow@colum.edu

STROZIER, Kathlyn .... 770-229-3328 124 G
kathlyn.strozier@sctech.edu

STRUB, Whitney .... 973-353-3887 282 B
wstrub@newark.rutgers.edu

STRUBY, Shannon .... 402-354-7104 268 C
shannon.struby@methodistcollege.edu

STRUCK, Kathy .... 605-367-4625 417 D
kathryn.struck@southeasttech.edu

STRUDLER, Keith .... 973-655-5214 279 C
strudlerk@montclair.edu

STRUDWICK, Daniel .... 217-228-5432 146 F
strudda@quincy.edu

STRUEBEL, Philip .... 716-851-1588 299 F
struebel@ecc.edu

STRUNK, Brian .... 606-546-1276 184 H
bstrunk@unionky.edu

STRUNK, Mary, C .... 518-783-2314 315 J
strunk@siena.edu

STRUPP, Kindra, L .... 812-464-1755 161 E
kstrupp@usi.edu

STRUPPA, Daniele, C .... 714-997-6611.. 36 C
struppa@chapman.edu

STRUSOWSKI, Lisa .... 302-857-1124.. 90 D
lstrusow@dtcc.edu

STRUTHERS, Amy .... 402-472-3528 269 J
astruthers2@unl.edu

STRUTHERS, Mary .... 715-422-5504 500 A
mary.struthers@mstc.edu

STRYBOS, John .... 210-485-0701 429 C
jstrybos@alamo.edu

STRYKER, Joann .... 406-247-5752 264 E
joann.stryker@msubillings.edu

STRYKER, Joanne .... 401-454-6177 405 D
jstryker@risd.edu

STRYSICK, Michael, P ... 859-238-5710 179 F
michael.strysick@centre.edu

STRZEPEK, Jason .... 978-468-7111 209 G
jstrzepek@gordonconwell.edu

STRZEPEK, Katy, A .... 563-333-6113 169 A
strzepekkatya@sau.edu

STUARD, Avis .... 504-520-7583 193 A
astuard@xula.edu

STUART, Alesia, K .... 251-578-1313.... 3 D
akstuart@rstc.edu

STUART, Barbara .... 802-586-7711 463 D
bstuart@sterlingcollege.edu

STUART, Ben .... 757-683-4271 469 G
bstuart@odu.edu

STUART, Cheryl .... 937-775-2556 364 I
cheryl.stuart@wright.edu

STUART, Cledis, D .... 870-235-4046.. 21 D
cdstuart@sauniag.edu

STUART, Dana .... 262-524-7200 492 E
dstuart@carrollu.edu

STUART, Diana .... 573-518-2100 256 B
diana@mineralarea.edu

STUART, D'Anne .... 575-646-2431 287 B
dstuart@nmsu.edu

STUART, Eddie .... 910-962-3626 343 C
stuarte@uncw.edu

STUART, Forrest .... 610-330-5055 387 E
stuartf@lafayette.edu

STUART, G. Rob .... 216-987-4757 351 G
g.rob.stuart@tri-c.edu

STUART, Nancy, M .... 860-768-4846.. 88 H
nstuart@hartford.edu

STUART, Ramon .... 478-825-6330 118 A
stuartt@fvsu.edu

STUART, Stephanie .... 217-351-2200 146 C
sstuart@parkland.edu

STUART, Stephanie .... 910-275-6111 335 E
sstuart@jamessprunt.edu

STUART, Susan .... 913-288-7265 174 F
sstuart@kckcc.edu

STUBBE, Alethea, F .... 712-324-5061 168 G
aletheas@nwicc.edu

STUBBEMAN, Nancy ...... 513-569-1501 350 K
nancy.stubbeman@cincinnatistate.edu

STUBBERT, Amanda .... 206-281-2587 484 D
amandas@spu.edu

STUBBINGS, Donald ...... 913-758-6241 177 F
donald.stubbingsr@stmary.edu

STUBBLEFIELD,
Claudine .... 304-724-3700 487 E

STUBBLEFIELD, Jay .... 912-650-6215 124 E
rstubblefield@southuniversity.edu

STUBBLEFIELD, Jay .... 423-869-7000 421 C
jay.stubblefield@lmunet.edu

STUBBLEFIELD,
Michael, A .... 225-771-3890 190 H
michael_stubblefield@subr.edu

STUBBLEFIELD,
Thomas .... 508-910-6571 211 F
tstubblefield@umassd.edu

STUBBS, Ben .... 850-474-2384 110 E
bstubbs@uwf.edu

STUBBS, Brent .... 912-443-4150 124 A
bstubbs@savannahtech.edu

STUBBS, Janice .... 954-201-7350.. 95 H

STUBBS, Leah .... 502-863-8030 180 E
leah_stubbs@georgetowncollege.edu

STUBBS, Loretta .... 901-435-1680 421 A
loretta_stubbs@loc.edu

STUBBS, Michelle .... 912-486-7865 122 I
mstubbs@ogeecheetech.edu

STUBBS, Robert .... 303-492-8631.. 83 A
robert.stubbs@colorado.edu

STUBBS, Sandra .... 256-372-5230.... 1 A
sandra.stubbs@aamu.edu

STUBBS, Sidney, J .... 334-833-4416.... 5 H
oir@hawks.huntingdon.edu

STUBBS, Stanley .... 662-252-8000 248 G
rstubbs@rustcollege.edu

STUBBS, Steve .... 706-864-1798 126 A
steven.stubbs@ung.edu

STUBBS, Valencia .... 386-481-2048.. 95 F
stubbsv@cookman.edu

STUCHELL, Tina .... 330-823-2844 363 B
stuchetm@mountunion.edu

STUCK, Helen .... 315-568-3133 308 F
hstuck@nycc.edu

STUCK, Kelley .... 434-982-0123 473 A
kds7w@virginia.edu

STUCK, Shelly .... 315-568-3111 308 F
sstuck@nycc.edu

STUCKENBRUCK, Emily . 715-675-3331 500 E
stuckenbruck@ntc.edu

STUCKER, Aaron .... 406-791-5225 265 H
aaron.stucker@uprovidence.edu

STUCKEY, Carol .... 617-732-2114 216 B
carol.stuckey@mcphs.edu

STUCKEY, Jon, C .... 717-796-5065 390 E
jstuckey@messiah.edu

STUCKEY, Julie .... 210-434-6711 441 E
jstuckey@ollusa.edu

STUCKEY, Lanette .... 217-709-0920 141 E
lstuckey@lakeviewcol.edu

STUCKEY, Maria .... 912-260-4301 124 C
maria.stuckey@sgsc.edu

STUCKEY, Mike .... 816-501-2414 250 F
mike.stuckey@avila.edu

STUCKEY, Mike .... 740-389-4636 356 B
stuckeym@mtc.edu

STUCKEY, Sheila, A ...... 502-597-6867 182 H
sheila.stuckey@kysu.edu

STUCKY, Duane .... 618-536-3475 149 D
dustucky@siu.edu

STUCKY, Thomas, D ..... 317-274-2016 156 F
tstucky@iupui.edu

STUDDS, Susan, M .... 301-243-2121 503 J
susan.studds@dodiis.mil

STUDENC, Bill .... 828-227-3083 344 A
bstudenc@wcu.edu

STUDER, Dominique ..... 646-768-5300 301 B

STUDER, Garet .... 425-388-9328 480 G
gstuder@everettcc.edu

STUDER, Mary Ann .... 419-783-2553 352 F
mstuder@defiance.edu

STUDINGER, Robert .... 303-352-3193.. 79 E
bob.studinger@ccd.edu

STUDNISKI, Susan .... 218-855-8034 237 F
susan.studniski@clcmn.edu

STUDWELL, II,
Raymond, W .... 540-828-5660 465 D
cstudwel@bridgewater.edu

STUEBING, David .... 757-455-8709 477 F
dstuebing@vwu.edu

STUEBNER, Susan, D .... 603-526-3451 272 H
sue.stuebner@colby-sawyer.edu

STUFF, Jerry .... 903-566-7431 456 A
jstuff@uttyler.edu

STUFFLEBEAN, Ernie ..... 816-415-5969 262 F
stuffle@william.jewell.edu

STUFLICK, William .... 425-388-9212 480 G
wstuflick@everettcc.edu

STUHR-MOOTZ,
Kristin, J .... 414-955-8208 494 C
kmootz@mcw.edu

STUIFBERGEN,
Alexa, M .... 512-471-4100 455 A
astuifbergen@mail.utexas.edu

STUKANE, Edward .... 201-216-3472 283 C
edward.stukane@stevens.edu

STULL, David .... 415-503-6230.. 60 H
mkennedy@sfcm.edu

STULL, Dick .... 864-938-3909 411 I
rstull@presby.edu

STULL, Megan .... 563-588-6377 163 F
megan.stull@clarke.edu

STULTS, Randy .... 205-387-0511.... 1 D
randy.stults@bscc.edu

STULTZ, Shelley .... 316-322-3152 171 G
sstultz@butlercc.edu

STUM, Cheryl .... 215-702-4337 380 D
cstum@cairn.edu

STUMB, Paul .... 615-547-1223 419 F
pstumb@cumberland.edu

STUMBO, Christine .... 606-368-6125 178 D
christinestumbo@alc.edu

STUMBRIS, Steven, V .... 570-577-3791 379 F
steven.stumbris@bucknell.edu

STUMNE, James .... 651-779-3918 237 G
james.stumne@century.edu

STUMO, Karl, A .... 218-299-3004 235 E
kstumo@cord.edu

STUMP, Chellye .... 334-347-2623.... 2 A
cstump@escc.edu

STUMP, Linda, J .... 352-392-5445 109 F
lstump@ufl.edu

STUMP, Sandy .... 610-921-7205 378 C
stump@albright.edu

STUMP, Tom .... 406-994-2661 264 D
stump@montana.edu

STUMPF, Michelle .... 814-262-6436 393 H
mstumpf@pennhighlands.edu

STUOPIS,
Cecilia Warpinski .... 617-253-1716 215 G

STUPAR, Eric, H .... 301-243-2170 503 J
eric.stupar@dodiis.mil

STUPARICH, Chavon ..... 516-463-6809 302 B
chavon.stuparich@hofstra.edu

STUPPY, Charles .... 330-821-5320 363 B

STURDIVANT, Alvin .... 206-296-6066 484 F
sturdial@seattleu.edu

STURE, Linda .... 907-563-7575.... 9 C
linda.sture@alaskacareercollege.edu

STURGE, Paula .... 315-268-2016 296 A
psturge@clarkson.edu

STURGE-APPLE,
Melissa .... 585-275-3540 323 J
melissa.sturge-apple@rochester.edu

STURGEON, Al .... 615-966-6058 421 D
al.sturgeon@lipscomb.edu

STURGEON, David .... 231-777-0315 228 D
david.sturgeon@muskegoncc.edu

STURGEON, Kathy, R ..... 217-443-8805 135 H
ksturgeon@dacc.edu

STURGEON, Timothy, A 502-272-8131 179 B
tsturgeon@bellarmine.edu

STURGILL, David .... 859-246-6896 180 K
david.sturgill@kctcs.edu

STURGIS, Thomas, C .... 601-877-6138 244 H
tsturgis@alcorn.edu

STURM, James .... 716-829-8199 298 F
sturmj@dyc.edu

STURM, Joel .... 212-410-8047 309 B
jsturm@nycpm.edu

STURM, Neal, M .... 973-443-8689 277 K
sturm@fdu.edu

STURM-SMITH, Melissa 515-271-2835 165 A
melissa.sturm-smith@drake.edu

STURRUP, Daniel, H ..... 207-581-1799 195 J
dsturrup@maine.edu

STURTZ, Carma .... 641-628-5269 163 E
sturtzc@central.edu

STUTES, Ann, B .... 806-291-1066 457 J
stutesa@wbu.edu

STUTZ, Melissa .... 307-778-1217 502 D
mstutz@lccc.wy.edu

STUTZMAN, Dallas .... 620-327-8110 173 H
dallass@hesston.edu

STUTZMAN, Julie .... 503-847-2544 377 F
jstutzman@uws.edu

STUTZMAN, Karl .... 574-296-6233 152 I
kstutzman@ambs.edu

STUTZMAN, Timothy ..... 540-432-4197 466 G
timothy.stutzman@emu.edu

STUTZMAN,
Timothy, W .... 540-432-4197 466 G
timothy.stutzman@emu.edu

STVAN, Kenneth, J .... 315-470-6689 320 A
kjstvan@esf.edu

STYER, Daniel .... 916-558-2201.. 50 I
styerd@scc.losrios.edu

STYLES, Julie .... 864-977-1246 411 E
julie.styles@ngu.edu

STYRON, Kelli, C .... 254-968-9141 446 E
styron@tarleton.edu

STYRON, Ken .... 251-981-3771.... 5 B
ken.styron@columbiasouthern.edu

STYRON, Kent .... 254-968-9898 446 E
wkstyron@tarleton.edu

SU, Dan .... 903-468-3048 447 B
dan.su@tamuc.edu

SU, John, J .... 414-288-3476 494 B
john.su@marquette.edu

SU, Nancy .... 212-217-3640 299 H
nancy_su@fitnyc.edu

SU, Susan .... 516-739-1545 309 C
records@nyctcm.edu

SUARA, Zulfat, A .... 615-327-6815 422 A
zsuara@mmc.edu

SUAREZ, Alberto .... 845-368-7217 315 D
alberto.suarez@use.salvationarmy.org

SUAREZ, Angelica .... 619-482-6315.. 65 F
asuarez@swccd.edu

SUAREZ, Angelica .... 714-432-5577.. 38 E
angelica.suarez@occ.cccd.edu

SUAREZ, Francisco .... 787-841-2000 510 K
fsuarez@pucpr.edu

SUAREZ, Jeri, L .... 540-362-6000 468 C
jsuarez@hollins.edu

SUAREZ, Kiko .... 800-280-0307 152 H
kiko.suarez@ace.edu

SUAREZ, Zachary .... 361-354-2722 433 C
zsuarez@coastalbend.edu

SUAREZ-ESPINAL,
Cynthia .... 718-289-5914 293 B
cynthia.suarez-espinal@bcc.cuny.edu

SUAREZ-OROZCO,
Marcelo, M .... 310-825-8308.. 69 A
mms-o@gseis.ucla.edu

SUBACIS, Ashley .... 724-222-5330 392 A
asubacis@penncommercial.edu

SUBBARAO, Italo .... 601-318-6572 249 H
isubbarao@wmcarey.edu

SUBBASWAMY,
Kumble, R .... 413-545-2211 211 D
chancellor@umass.edu

SUBE, Bob .... 805-678-5821.. 73 A
bsube@vcccd.edu

SUBER, Jennifer .... 601-477-4040 246 F
jennifer.suber@jcjc.edu

SUBICH, Linda, M .... 330-972-8379 362 B
lsubich@uakron.edu

SUBLETTE, Garrett .... 325-674-2655 429 B
jgs99a@acu.edu

SUBLETTE, Gaylah .... 660-626-2860 250 A
gsublette@atsu.edu

SUBOCZ, Sue 866-492-5336 244 F susan.subocz@laureate.net
SUBRAMANIAM, Ram 650-940-7472 43 D subramaniamram@fhda.edu
SUBRAMANIAM, Ram 650-949-7472 43 D subramaniamram@foothill.edu
SUBRAMANIAN, Ashok 479-788-7807 21 H ashok.subramanian@uafs.edu
SUCH, Tami, L 701-788-4716 345 E tami.such@mayvillestate.edu
SUCHAN, Jennifer 515-294-8381 162 I jsuchan@iastate.edu
SUCHANIC, Angela, C 302-356-6924 90 I angela.c.suchanic@wilmu.edu
SUCHON, Donnetta 281-425-6400 439 D dsuchon@lee.edu
SUCKOW, Melissa, A 630-515-3015 143 G msucko@midwestern.edu
SUDA, Delight 671-734-1812 505 D dsuda@piu.edu
SUDAK, Sarah 615-898-5342 422 H sarah.sudak@mtsu.edu
SUDBECK, Kristine 402-494-2311 268 B ksudbeck@thenicc.edu
SUDDICK, Lori 847-543-2200 135 B lsuddick@clcillinois.edu
SUDEIKIS, Barbara 269-965-3931 225 F sudeikisb@kellogg.edu
SUDEITH, Mark 773-995-3586 133 K msudeith@csu.edu
SUDERMAN, Bonnie 919-497-3201 330 I bsuderman@louisburg.edu
SUDHAKAR, Rama 212-237-8628 294 D rsudhakar@jjay.cuny.edu
SUDHAKAR, Samuel 909-537-5100 33 A ssudhakar@csusb.edu
SUDLER, Kimberly, R 302-857-7036 89 F krsudler@desu.edu
SUDLOW, Jennifer 215-572-4483 379 A sudlowj@arcadia.edu
SUDMEYER, Alecia 207-509-7166 195 H asudmeyer@unity.edu
SUDTELGTE, Beau 712-279-1633 163 C beau.sudtelgte@briarcliff.edu
SUEBERT, Jack 305-809-3195 99 C jack.seubert@fkcc.edu
SUEK, Ana 415-749-4530 60 G asuek@sfai.edu
SUELFLOW, Sara, C 651-696-6307 236 H suelflow@macalester.edu
SUERTH, Matthew, P 815-224-0550 139 F matt_suerth@ivcc.edu
SUESS, Jack, J 410-455-2582 202 E jack@umbc.edu
SUESSER, John, P 724-346-2073 380 A john.suesser@bc3.edu
SUEYOSHI, Amy 415-338-1694 34 A sueyoshi@sfsu.edu
SUFFRIDGE, Diane 415-257-0131 41 H diane.suffridge@dominican.edu
SUGALSKI, Mark 315-279-5327 304 A msugalski@keuka.edu
SUGALSKI, Noelle 302-857-1072 90 D nsugalsk@dtcc.edu
SUGANO, Adam 310-825-5713 69 A asugano@ponet.ucla.edu
SUGG, Donald 870-743-3000 20 C dsugg@northark.edu
SUGGS, Amber 618-634-3236 149 A ambers@shawneecc.edu
SUGGS, Benny 919-515-3375 342 B benny_suggs@ncsu.edu
SUGGS, Thomas 704-272-5363 337 I
SUGHRUE, Helen 843-574-6649 413 B helen.sughrue@tridenttech.edu
SUGIHARA, Fumio 802-258-9261 462 E fumios@marlboro.edu
SUGIMOTO, Annette 808-932-7626 128 E asugimot@hawaii.edu
SUGIMOTO, Lara 808-845-9235 129 B larahs@hawaii.edu
SUHAJDA, Kathleen 312-935-6446 147 D ksuhajda@robertmorris.edu
SUHAYDA, Rosemarie 312-942-6204 148 A rosemarie_suhayda@rush.edu
SUHLER, Mitzi 620-278-4226 177 B msuhler@sterling.edu
SUHR, Marin 402-461-7326 267 D mnsuhr@hastings.edu
SUIB, Steven, L 860-486-4623 88 E steven.suib@uconn.edu
SUISALA, Frederick, R 684-699-9155 505 A f.suisala@amsamoa.edu
SUIT, Teresa 256-233-8167 4 D teresa.suit@athens.edu
SUITE, Denzil 206-543-4972 485 F djsuite@uw.edu
SUJECKI, Gailmarie 516-671-2277 324 G gsujecki@webb.edu
SUKHATME, Vikas, P 404-727-5631 117 F vsukhatme@emory.edu
SUKOWATY, Jackie, L 414-410-4222 492 D jlsukowaty1@stritch.edu
SUKUMARAN, Beena 856-256-5324 281 E sukumaran@rowan.edu
SULAIMAN HARA, Sadika 415-485-9375 39 C ssulaimanhara@marin.edu
SULESKI, Andrew 530-895-2353 27 F suleskian@butte.edu
SULFRIDGE, Jay 606-337-1114 179 G jsulfridge@ccbbc.edu
SULKIN, Tracy 217-333-6677 151 D tsulkin@illinois.edu
SULLENBERGER, A. Gale 918-631-3184 371 E gale-sullenberger@utulsa.edu
SULLINS, Dori 815-455-8559 143 A dsullens@mchenry.edu
SULLIVAN, A, R 502-451-0815 184 E arsullivan@sullivan.edu
SULLIVAN, Adelfa 702-992-2115 271 C adelfa.sullivan@nsc.edu
SULLIVAN, Amy 270-534-3169 182 F amy.sullivan@kctcs.edu
SULLIVAN, Anne, R 212-854-4038 297 C asullivan@columbia.edu
SULLIVAN, Barry 903-875-7355 440 G barry.sullivan@navarrocollege.edu
SULLIVAN, Bobbi 515-961-1372 169 D bobbi.sullivan@simpson.edu
SULLIVAN, Brian 513-325-4599 362 F brian.sullivan@uc.edu
SULLIVAN, Brian, T 607-871-2987 289 H sullivan@alfred.edu
SULLIVAN, Brigitte 410-225-2209 199 H bsullivan01@mica.edu
SULLIVAN, Bryce 615-460-6437 418 F bryce.sullivan@belmont.edu
SULLIVAN, Cheryl 256-726-7026 6 C csullivan@oakwood.edu
SULLIVAN, Cheryl 559-243-7112 66 C cheryl.sullivan@scccd.edu
SULLIVAN, Chris 936-633-5216 430 F csullivan@angelina.edu
SULLIVAN, Chris 206-934-5566 484 A chris.sullivan@seattlecolleges.edu
SULLIVAN, Crystal, C 937-229-3369 362 G csulllivan1@udayton.edu
SULLIVAN, Dan 919-658-7748 340 J dsullivan@umo.edu
SULLIVAN, David 910-678-8485 334 D sullivad@faytechcc.edu
SULLIVAN, David 361-664-2981 433 C sullivan@coastalbend.edu
SULLIVAN, Deb 563-336-3300 165 B djsullivan@eicc.edu
SULLIVAN, Debbie 336-917-5329 340 D debbie.sullivan@salem.edu
SULLIVAN, Donna 425-564-2302 478 F donna.sullivan@bellevuecollege.edu
SULLIVAN, Eileen 909-869-3310 30 D egsullivan@cpp.edu
SULLIVAN, Elizabeth 201-761-7106 282 I esullivan@saintpeters.edu
SULLIVAN, Erin 504-398-2190 191 C esullivan@uhcno.edu
SULLIVAN, Gerald 706-867-2543 126 A gerald.sullivan@ung.edu
SULLIVAN, Glenn, D 502-451-0815 184 E glennds@sullivan.edu
SULLIVAN, Irby (Skip) 607-587-4010 320 C sullivid@alfredstate.edu
SULLIVAN, Jack 973-328-5252 277 B jsullivan@ccm.edu
SULLIVAN, Jake 617-353-2292 207 D jakesull@bu.edu
SULLIVAN, James 423-775-7306 418 H james@bryan.edu
SULLIVAN, James, J 570-340-6063 389 G jimsullivan@marywood.edu
SULLIVAN, Jason 906-487-7272 223 K jason.sullivan@finlandia.edu
SULLIVAN, Jay 252-940-6216 332 C jay.sullivan@beaufortccc.edu
SULLIVAN, Jeff 715-874-4608 499 D jsullivan25@cvtc.edu
SULLIVAN, Joan, D 781-768-7212 218 C joan.sullivan@regiscollege.edu
SULLIVAN, Joanne 845-398-4379 315 B jsulliva@stac.edu
SULLIVAN, John 727-864-8331 97 J sullivjf@eckerd.edu
SULLIVAN, John, M 508-286-3484 220 A sullivan_john@wheatoncollege.edu
SULLIVAN, Julie, H 651-962-6500 244 E jhsullivan@stthomas.edu
SULLIVAN, Kathleen 845-848-7804 298 D kathleen.sullivan@dc.edu
SULLIVAN, Kevin 309-556-3886 139 G ksulliva@iwu.edu
SULLIVAN, Kristen 978-837-5301 216 D sullivanke@merrimack.edu
SULLIVAN, Lamont 864-977-7000 411 E lamont.sullivan@ngu.edu
SULLIVAN, Lauren 715-833-6500 499 D lsullivan9@cvtc.edu
SULLIVAN, Lawrence 212-237-8364 294 D lsullivan@jjay.cuny.edu
SULLIVAN, Leah 440-646-8126 363 G lsullivan@ursuline.edu
SULLIVAN, Leslie 269-749-7638 229 H lsullivan@olivetcollege.edu
SULLIVAN, Linda 706-756-4625 127 A linda.sullivan@westgatech.edu
SULLIVAN, Linda 310-434-3427 62 E sullivan_linda@smc.edu
SULLIVAN, Lisa 909-621-8122 45 A sullivan@hmc.edu
SULLIVAN, Maggie 401-456-8216 405 C msullivan@ric.edu
SULLIVAN, Marcia 314-529-9340 254 H marcia.sullivan@maryville.edu
SULLIVAN, Margaret 251-460-7616 8 F msullivan@southalabama.edu
SULLIVAN, Maria 508-565-1402 218 H msullivan7@stonehill.edu
SULLIVAN, Martha 508-793-2276 208 B sullivan@holycross.edu
SULLIVAN, Mary 570-740-0429 389 D msullivan@luzerne.edu
SULLIVAN, Mary Kay 865-981-8000 421 F marykay.sullivan@maryvillecollege.edu
SULLIVAN, Maya 651-793-1508 238 H maya.sullivan@metrostate.edu
SULLIVAN, Melanie, R 401-865-2723 405 B oir@providence.edu
SULLIVAN, Melissa 207-699-5043 194 D msullivan@meca.edu
SULLIVAN, Michael 989-837-4325 228 H msulliva@northwood.edu
SULLIVAN, Michael 607-778-5040 318 A sullivanmj4@sunybroome.edu
SULLIVAN, Michael, A 607-746-4538 320 G sullivmt@delhi.edu
SULLIVAN, Monty 225-922-1643 186 J montysullivan@lctcs.edu
SULLIVAN, Nancy 781-292-2304 209 E nancy.sullivan@olin.edu
SULLIVAN, Neil, G 937-229-2165 362 G nsullivan1@udayton.edu
SULLIVAN, Paige 575-492-2186 289 A psullivan@usw.edu
SULLIVAN, Patrick 413-545-4630 211 D psulliva@umass.edu
SULLIVAN, Patrick 610-499-4202 403 B ptsullivan@widener.edu
SULLIVAN, Renee 203-773-4474 84 F rsullivan@albertus.edu
SULLIVAN, Rob 214-333-5671 434 I roberts@dbu.edu
SULLIVAN, Robert, S 858-822-0830 69 D rssullivan@ucsd.edu
SULLIVAN, Rusty 816-604-5277 255 D rusty.sullivan@mcckc.edu
SULLIVAN, Sarah 708-524-6298 136 C ssullivan@dom.edu
SULLIVAN, Scott 914-606-6284 325 C scott.sullivan@sunywcc.edu
SULLIVAN, Sean 708-456-0300 150 I seansullivan@triton.edu
SULLIVAN, Sean 206-685-8153 485 F sdsull@uw.edu
SULLIVAN, Sean, M 202-319-5286 91 B sullivansm@cua.edu
SULLIVAN, Serena 252-940-6326 332 C serena.sullivan@beaufortccc.edu
SULLIVAN, Shawn, P 715-675-3331 500 E sullivan@ntc.edu
SULLIVAN, Sheila 619-684-8807 53 H ssullivan@newschoolarch.edu
SULLIVAN, Slade 325-674-2485 429 B sls02h@acu.edu
SULLIVAN, Slade 325-674-2485 429 B sullivans@acu.edu
SULLIVAN, Stephanie 770-426-2636 121 C stephanie.sullivan@life.edu
SULLIVAN, Susan 812-749-1223 159 C ssullivan@oak.edu
SULLIVAN, Susan 978-762-4000 215 B susulliv@northshore.edu
SULLIVAN, Suzanne 601-968-8881 245 C ssullivan@belhaven.edu
SULLIVAN, Tasha 207-947-4591 193 C tsullivan@bealcollege.edu
SULLIVAN, Terry 419-448-5148 361 J tsullivan@tiffin.edu
SULLIVAN, Thomas 660-944-2860 251 G brothomas@conception.edu
SULLIVAN, Thomas 660-944-2875 251 G brothomas@conception.edu
SULLIVAN, Thomas, B 512-448-8727 442 M toms@stedwards.edu
SULLIVAN, Thomas, J 410-706-3386 202 D thomas.sullivan@umaryland.edu
SULLIVAN, Tracy 708-235-2179 137 F tsullivan@govst.edu
SULLIVAN, Vicki 918-647-1373 365 H vhill@carlalbert.edu
SULLIVAN, Wayne 315-792-3201 324 B wasullivan@utica.edu
SULLIVAN, Wayne 505-277-2383 288 G sullivan@unm.edu
SULLIVAN, William, E 765-494-9705 159 E sully1976@purdue.edu
SULLIVAN-CROWLEY, Lianne, C 609-258-2430 280 E lsulliva@princeton.edu
SULLIVAN-GONZALEZ, Douglass 662-915-7294 249 D dsg@olemiss.edu
SULLIVAN-TRAINOR, Deborah 651-638-6804 234 C suldeb@bethel.edu
SULLIVANT, Stan 870-338-6474 22 H
SULLY, John 216-397-1965 354 I jsully@jcu.edu
SULMASY, Glenn 401-232-6060 404 F gsulmasy@bryant.edu
SULTAN, Farooq 541-605-0520 375 C farooq.sultan@oit.edu
SULZBACH, J. Bonnie 443-412-2119 199 A bsulzbach@harford.edu
SUMABAT, Rob 877-559-3621 29 A rsumabat@ciat.edu
SUMAS, Keith, P 404-413-0783 119 E ksumas1@gsu.edu
SUMEREL, Michelle 662-862-8050 246 D jmsumerel@iccms.edu
SUMICHRAST, Robert, T 540-231-6601 477 A busdean@vt.edu
SUMLIN, Rene 334-683-2378 3 A renesumlin@marionmilitary.edu
SUMLIN, Robert, D 334-683-2305 3 A dsumlin@marionmilitary.edu
SUMME, Sean 816-501-3756 250 F sean.summe@avila.edu
SUMMER, Rebekah 320-762-4612 237 B rebekahs@alextech.edu
SUMMER, Sharon 336-770-1312 343 D summers@uncsa.edu
SUMMER, Todd 619-594-7539 33 E todd.summer@sdsu.edu
SUMMERLIN, Timothy 830-792-7326 443 G tsummerlin@schreiner.edu
SUMMERS, Amanda 281-425-6533 439 D asummers@lee.edu
SUMMERS, Brian 901-321-3370 419 C bsummers@cbu.edu
SUMMERS, Carol 815-939-5213 146 A csummers@olivet.edu
SUMMERS, Chris 404-364-8355 122 J csummers@oglethorpe.edu
SUMMERS, Daniel 330-569-5174 353 J summersdp@hiram.edu
SUMMERS, Diane 713-646-1794 444 B dsummers@stcl.edu
SUMMERS, Eric 985-549-5250 192 D esummers@selu.edu
SUMMERS, Greg 715-346-4686 497 F gsummers@uwsp.edu

SUMMERS, Janie, K ...... 314-286-3665 258 E jksummers@ranken.edu
SUMMERS, Jennifer ...... 843-377-2410 407 D jsummers@charlestonlaw.edu
SUMMERS, Jerry .... 903-923-2084 436 D jsummers@etbu.edu
SUMMERS, Laurie, K .... 310-825-4606.. 69 A lsummers@conet.ucla.edu
SUMMERS, Matthew, A . 304-637-1990 487 I summersm@dewv.edu
SUMMERS, Michael, D . 757-822-7122 476 B msummers@tcc.edu
SUMMERS, Mike .... 610-330-5338 387 E summersm@lafayette.edu
SUMMERS, Ragan .... 904-470-8231.. 97 L ragan.summers@ewc.edu
SUMMERS, Richard .... 601-984-1018 249 E rsummers@umc.edu
SUMMERS, Robert .... 716-878-5331 318 C
SUMMERS, Robert, P .... 870-633-4480.. 19 B rsummers@eacc.edu
SUMMERS, Scott .... 901-321-3237 419 C ssummers@cbu.edu
SUMMERS, Stuart .... 208-282-3620 130 H summstua@isu.edu
SUMMERS, Susan .... 832-813-6592 439 G susan.summers@lonestar.edu
SUMMERS, Tammi .... 262-564-2538 499 F summerst@gtc.edu
SUMMERS, Tiffany .... 615-966-1791 421 D tiffany.summers@lipscomb.edu
SUMMERS, Tony .... 202-274-5791.. 93 C tony.summers@udc.edu
SUMMERS, Wally .... 229-931-2040 124 D wsummers@southgatech.edu
SUMMERSELL, Charley . 518-587-2100 321 A charley.summersell@esc.edu
SUMMIT, Jennifer .... 415-338-1141.. 34 A jsummit@sfsu.edu
SUMMITT, April .... 951-785-2210.. 47 C asummitt@lasierra.edu
SUMNER, Carol, A .... 806-742-7025 451 B carol.a.sumner@ttu.edu
SUMNER, Dana .... 919-760-8341 331 B sumnerd@meredith.edu
SUMNER, Jean, R .... 478-301-5571 121 E sumner_jr@mercer.edu
SUMNER, Kenneth .... 973-655-4280 279 C sumnerk@mail.montclair.edu
SUMNER, Wesley, D ..... 321-674-6218.. 99 B wsumner@fit.edu
SUMNERS, Stephanie .... 417-447-2653 257 G sumnerss@otc.edu
SUMPTER, Christopher, W .... 913-647-8724 174 E christopher.sumpter@kansaschristian.edu
SUMSION, Jared, M ..... 801-863-7291 461 A jared.sumsion@uvu.edu
SUMTER, Carol .... 727-302-6823 106 E sumter.carol@spcollege.edu
SUMTER, Takita .... 803-323-2160 414 G sumtert@winthrop.edu
SUN, Hala .... 213-381-0081.. 46 E hsun.irus@irus.edu
SUN, Joseph, S .... 215-517-2383 379 A sunj@arcadia.edu
SUN, Sandra .... 626-571-5110.. 48 B sandrasun@les.edu
SUN CHILD, Jolin .... 406-395-4875 265 G jsunchild@stonechild.edu
SUNAHARA, Wayne ...... 808-845-9272 129 B waynens@hawaii.edu
SUNATA, Cem .... 805-756-6016.. 30 C csunata@calpoly.edu
SUND, Andrew, C .... 509-865-8500 481 G sund_a@heritage.edu
SUNDARAM, Bala .... 617-287-6055 211 E bala.sundaram@umb.edu
SUNDARAM, Sridhar ..... 727-873-4700 110 C sundarams@usf.edu
SUNDAY, Richard, S ..... 212-217-3760 299 H richard_sunday@fitnyc.edu
SUNDBERG, Lori .... 319-398-5501 167 C lori.sundberg@kirkwood.edu
SUNDBORG, SJ, Stephen, V .... 206-296-1891 484 F sundborg@seattleu.edu
SUNDBY, David .... 714-997-6668.. 36 C sundby@chapman.edu
SUNDBY-THORP, Valerie .... 360-596-5451 485 B vsundby-thorp@spscc.edu
SUNDERMAN, Barbara .. 402-461-7388 267 D bsunderman@hastings.edu
SUNDERMAN, Rick .... 614-947-6605 353 C rick.sunderman@franklin.edu
SUNDERMANN, Brigitte 970-255-2700.. 77 I bsunderm@coloradomesa.edu
SUNDERMEIER, Elisabeth .... 816-802-3376 254 B esundermeier@kcai.edu
SUNDGREN, Donald, E . 434-982-5834 473 A des5j@virginia.edu
SUNDQUIST, Jeffery ...... 831-646-4036.. 52 F jsundquist@mpc.edu
SUNDQUIST, Mike .... 209-575-6081.. 75 J sundquistm@mjc.edu
SUNDSETH, Robin .... 541-880-2273 373 E sundseth@klamathcc.edu
SUNDSTROM, Sandy ...... 503-777-7224 376 C sundstrom@reed.edu
SUNDY, Carolyn .... 606-589-3052 182 E carolyn.sundy@kctcs.edu
SUNG, Joshua .... 213-252-5100.. 23 K jsung@alu.edu
SUNG, Yung-Chi .... 952-888-4777 242 I ycsung@nwhealth.edu
SUNLEAF, Arthur, W ..... 563-588-7959 167 D arthur.sunleaf@loras.edu
SUNNARBORG, Avery ... 719-884-5000.. 81 C absunnarborg@nbc.edu
SUNNY, Heidi .... 859-858-3511 178 I heidi.sunny@asbury.edu
SUNNYGARD, John ...... 303-807-9956.. 83 C john.sunnygard@ucdenver.edu
SUNNYGARD, John ...... 270-745-4857 185 E john.sunnygard@wku.edu
SUNQUIST, Scott, W ..... 978-468-7111 209 G sunquist@gcts.edu
SUNSER, James .... 585-345-6812 301 A jmsunser@genesee.edu
SUNSHINE, Phyllis .... 410-337-6046 198 G psunshine@goucher.edu
SUOMI, Marvin .... 715-682-1202 495 C msuomi@northland.edu
SUPAK, Brian .... 254-298-8609 446 A brian.supak@templejc.edu
SUPERNAW, Robert, B .. 704-233-8015 344 G supernaw@wingate.edu
SUPINSKI, Jessica .... 425-235-2352 483 G jsupinski@rtc.edu
SUPLER, Robin .... 954-262-4349 103 M rsupler@nsu.nova.edu
SUPOWITZ, Paul, A ...... 412-624-2901 401 B psupowit@pitt.edu
SUPPELSA, Robert, E .... 310-233-4051.. 49 A suppelre@lahc.edu
SUPPLE, Brooke .... 301-314-8437 202 C bsupple@umd.edu
SUPPLE, Matt .... 301-314-7781 202 C msupple@umd.edu
SUPPLEE, JR., Jack ...... 859-257-8288 185 B supplee@uky.edu
SUPPLEE, Janice .... 937-766-7470 349 G suppleej@cedarville.edu
SUPPLEE, John .... 610-526-6064 385 G jsupplee@harcum.edu
SUPURGECI, Jonna .... 605-668-1515 415 H jsupurgeci@mtmc.edu
SUR, Sarah Gilman .... 808-235-7435 129 F sgilman@hawaii.edu
SURA, Marissa .... 616-632-2843 221 C mks007@aquinas.edu
SURAN, Heather .... 661-291-3435.. 28 K hsuran@calarts.edu
SURBROOK, Will .... 619-388-6589.. 60 B wsurbroo@sdccd.edu
SURDOVEL, Grace .... 570-408-3102 403 D grace.surdovel@wilkes.edu
SURENDER, Sheelu, M . 316-978-5337 178 A sheelu.surender@wichita.edu
SURGALA, David, J .... 570-577-3811 379 F dsurgala@bucknell.edu
SURGEONER, James, W .... 610-799-1658 388 I jsurgeoner@lccc.edu
SURLA, Julian .... 225-743-8500 188 B jsurla@rpcc.edu
SURLES, Karen .... 850-973-1674 103 K surlesk@nfcc.edu
SURLS, Courtney .... 202-885-1334.. 90 J surls@american.edu
SURMA, Barry .... 814-472-3200 398 B bsurma@francis.edu
SURPENANT, Danielle ... 309-298-1190 152 D de-surpenant@wiu.edu
SURPRENANT, Tess ...... 816-235-6077 261 C surprenantt@umkc.edu
SURRATT, David .... 405-325-3161 371 B dsurratt@ou.edu
SURRATT, Jacob .... 276-223-4729 476 E jsurratt@wcc.vccs.edu
SURRELL, Matt .... 662-472-9178 246 C msurrell@holmescc.edu
SURRIDGE, Mary, K ...... 773-244-5710 145 A president@northpark.edu
SUSA, Angela .... 715-422-5320 500 A angela.susa@mstc.edu
SUSANA, Gil .... 619-961-4316.. 67 E gsusana@tjsl.edu
SUSANKA, Joseph .... 307-322-2930 502 J jsusanka@wyomingcatholic.edu
SUSANKA, Thomas, J .... 805-525-4417.. 67 D tsusanka@thomasaquinas.edu
SUSANTO-ONG, Yuliana .... 502-597-7014 182 H yuliana.susanto@kysu.edu
SUSHINSKY, David, M .. 240-895-3381 201 E dmsushinsky@smcm.edu
SUSICK, Timothy .... 724-938-4056 394 B susick@calu.edu
SUSKI-LENCZEWSKI, Anna .... 860-832-1757.. 84 I lenczewskia@mail.ccsu.edu
SUSKIND, Robert .... 909-580-9661.. 34 E
SUSMANN, Phillip .... 802-485-2213 463 A susmann@norwich.edu
SUSMARSKI, Aaron .... 814-860-5101 388 A asusmarski@lecom.edu
SUSMILCH, Tyler .... 503-538-8383 373 C tsusmilch@georgefox.edu
SUSS, Kathleen .... 914-337-9300 297 D
SUSSAN, Joshua .... 718-270-6421 295 A jsussan@mec.cuny.edu
SUSSENBACH, Michelle 618-664-7025 137 G michelle.sussenbach@greenville.edu
SUSSKIND, Gary .... 718-953-5889 322 F oholeitorah@optonline.net
SUSSMAN, Ronny .... 818-883-9002.. 72 E
SUSSWEIN, Gary .... 512-471-4945 455 A susswein@utexas.edu
SUTARDJI, Anne .... 510-592-9688.. 54 C anne.sutardji@npu.edu
SUTCLIFFE, Nicole .... 202-651-5346.. 91 E nicole.sutcliffe@gallaudet.edu
SUTER, Charlene .... 585-292-2500 307 H csuter@monroecc.edu
SUTER, Cindy .... 419-448-2090 353 H csuter@heidelberg.edu
SUTERA, Paul, J .... 914-637-2710 302 G psutera@iona.edu
SUTERA, Tom .... 360-538-4207 481 E tom.sutera@ghc.edu
SUTHERLAND, David .... 218-879-0816 238 A dsutherland@fdltcc.edu
SUTHERLAND, David ...... 501-450-1254.. 19 F sutherlandd@hendrix.edu
SUTHERLAND, Diane .... 864-231-2100 406 G dsutherland@andersonuniversity.edu
SUTHERLAND, Jim .... 678-839-6410 126 E sutherla@westga.edu
SUTHERLAND, John ...... 706-729-2260 115 A jsutherland@augusta.edu
SUTHERLAND, Kate .... 781-768-7551 218 C kate.sutherland@regiscollege.edu
SUTHERLAND, Kathleen 973-408-3100 277 C ksutherl@drew.edu
SUTHERLAND, Richard . 989-358-7368 221 A sutherlr@alpenacc.edu
SUTHERLAND, Ron .... 765-998-5118 160 F rnsutherl@taylor.edu
SUTHERLAND, Sonja .... 404-835-6119 423 K ssutherland@richmont.edu
SUTHERLIN, John .... 318-342-3201 192 F sutherlin@ulm.edu
SUTKUS, Janel .... 412-268-8729 380 F jsutkus@cmu.edu
SUTLIFF, Dani .... 912-260-4419 124 C dani.sutliff@sgsc.edu
SUTLIFF, Michael .... 714-432-5122.. 38 E msutliff@occ.cccd.edu
SUTTER, Brian .... 712-325-3328 167 B bsutter@iwcc.edu
SUTTER, Frankie .... 910-592-8081 337 G fsutter@sampsoncc.edu
SUTTER, Thaddeus .... 309-556-3059 139 G tsutter@iwu.edu
SUTTERFIELD, Shirley ... 251-442-2414.... 8 C ssutterfield@umobile.edu
SUTTLE, J. Lloyd .... 203-432-4453.. 89 D j.suttle@yale.edu
SUTTMEIER, Bruce .... 503-768-7100 373 G cas@lclark.edu
SUTTMILLER, Victoria ... 915-747-5352 455 C vssuttmiller@utep.edu
SUTTON, Barbara .... 773-298-3504 148 G sutton@sxu.edu
SUTTON, Bob .... 605-222-2223 416 G bob.sutton@sdbor.edu
SUTTON, Cynthia .... 314-392-2291 256 C suttonc@mobap.edu
SUTTON, David .... 254-968-9510 446 E sutton@tarleton.edu
SUTTON, David, O .... 407-582-2036 112 K dsutton@valenciacollege.edu
SUTTON, Deborah .... 252-527-6223 335 G dssutton14@lenoircc.edu
SUTTON, Dennis .... 910-296-2575 335 E dsutton@jamessprunt.edu
SUTTON, Duncan .... 310-265-6155.. 59 E duncan.sutton@usw.salvationarmy.org
SUTTON, Gary .... 843-208-8059 413 E suttong2@uscb.edu
SUTTON, Jama .... 865-774-5800 426 C jama.sutton@ws.edu
SUTTON, Jana .... 318-342-1655 192 F sutton@ulm.edu
SUTTON, Jeff .... 254-295-5044 453 E jsutton@umhb.edu
SUTTON, Jeffery .... 410-704-4453 204 A jsutton@towson.edu
SUTTON, JerQuentin ..... 732-247-5241 279 D jsutton@nbts.edu
SUTTON, Judith .... 304-485-5487 488 D jsutton@msc.edu
SUTTON, Lawrence .... 724-805-2402 398 F lawrence.sutton@stvincent.edu
SUTTON, Megan .... 563-876-3353 164 J msutton@dwci.edu
SUTTON, Michelle, D .... 502-597-5837 182 H michelle.sutton@kysu.edu
SUTTON, Nancy .... 217-351-2402 146 C nsutton@parkland.edu
SUTTON, Nathan .... 989-275-5000 226 B nathan.sutton@kirtland.edu
SUTTON, Pamela .... 512-223-7598 431 A psutton@austincc.edu
SUTTON, R. Anderson .. 808-956-8818 128 F rasutton@hawaii.edu
SUTTON, Renee .... 252-527-6223 335 G rbsutton25@lenoircc.edu
SUTTON, Rick .... 334-699-2266.... 1 B rsutton@acom.edu
SUTTON, Scott .... 828-339-4296 338 B scotts@southwesterncc.edu
SUTTON, Stephanie .... 330-494-6170 361 F ssutton@starkstate.edu
SUTTON, Steve .... 510-642-6727.. 68 D studentaffairs@berkeley.edu
SUTTON, Susan, R .... 865-882-4658 425 G suttonsr@roanestate.edu
SUTTON, Todd .... 336-790-8607 343 A tasutton@uncg.edu
SUTTON, Tommye, S .... 434-924-7166 473 A ts2dr@virginia.edu
SUTTON GERBER, Ronette .... 910-521-6268 343 B ronette.gerber@uncp.edu
SUTTON-HAYWOOD, Marilyn .... 704-463-1360 339 E marilyn.sutton-haywood@pfeiffer.edu
SUTTON NOSS, Melinda .... 214-768-4564 444 E msnoss@smu.edu
SUTTON-SMITH, Leslie . 973-655-4376 279 C suttonsmithl@mail.montclair.edu
SUTTON-WALLACE, Pamela, M .... 434-924-9308 473 A ps5gb@virginia.edu
SUTTON-YOUNG, Tasheka .... 718-368-5109 294 E tasheka.sutton-young@kbcc.cuny.edu
SUTZKO, Christopher .... 570-208-5874 387 A christophersutzko@kings.edu
SUZUKI, Anne .... 602-787-6691.. 13 E anne.suzuki@paradisevalley.edu
SUZUKI, Takeo .... 423-425-4759 428 A takeo-suzuki@utc.edu
SU'ESU'E, Jessie .... 684-699-9155 505 A j.suesue@amsamoa.edu
SVACINA, Jean, M .... 443-518-4807 199 C jsvacina@howardcc.edu

SWIECINSKI, Deborah, L .... 757-683-3127 469 G
dswiecin@odu.edu
SWIFT, Angela .... 417-447-7756 257 G
swifta@otc.edu
SWIFT, Beth .... 574-631-9790 161 C
swift.8@nd.edu
SWIFT, Geoffrey .... 207-786-8339 193 B
gswift@bates.edu
SWIFT, Martha .... 952-446-4198 235 G
swiftm@crown.edu
SWIFT, Rick .... 803-754-4100 409 A
SWIFT, Sheila .... 318-670-9646 190 J
sswift@susla.edu
SWIFT, Vikki .... 208-792-2269 131 A
vswift@lcsc.edu
SWIFT, William .... 978-630-9267 215 A
w_swift@mwcc.mass.edu
SWIGART, Jessica .... 314-434-4044 252 B
jessie.swigart@covenantseminary.edu
SWIGER, Tina .... 815-825-9732 140 F
sswiger@kish.edu
SWILLEY, Danny .... 803-793-5109 409 C
swilleyd@denmarktech.edu
SWINBURN, Stacy .... 303-722-5724.. 80 L
sswinburn@lincolntech.edu
SWINDLE, Jeremy .... 217-532-2181 141 D
jswindle@lakelandcollege.edu
SWINDOLL, George, B .. 716-375-2022 313 F
records@sbu.edu
SWINEFORD, Cynthia ... 804-765-5800 471 I
cynthia_swineford@srmcps.edu
SWINEHART, Amy .... 503-244-0726 371 G
amyswinehart@achs.edu
SWINEY, Jessica .... 423-652-4739 420 H
jwswiney@king.edu
SWINEY, Karen .... 910-521-6292 343 B
karen.swiney@uncp.edu
SWINFORD, Bill, K .... 859-257-1705 185 B
wswin2@uky.edu
SWINGLE, Mary .... 320-223-7510 242 L
mary.swingle@rasmussen.edu
SWINK, Doug .... 816-235-1125 261 C
swinkd@umkc.edu
SWINK, Jeffrey .... 615-248-1445 427 A
jswink@trevecca.edu
SWINNEY, Keyun .... 903-730-4890 438 H
kswinney@jarvis.edu
SWINNEY, Marc .... 208-562-2739 130 F
marcswinney@cwi.edu
SWINNEY, Victoria .... 405-208-5071 367 I
vswinney@okcu.edu
SWINSON, Adela .... 408-223-6749.. 61 L
adela.swinson@evc.edu
SWINSON, Avery .... 423-585-2688 426 C
avery.swinson@ws.edu
SWINT, Kerwin .... 470-578-6633 120 L
kswint@kennesaw.edu
SWINTH, Yvonne .... 253-879-3289 485 E
yswinth@pugetsound.edu
SWINTON, Brent .... 301-860-4303 203 C
bswinton@bowiestate.edu
SWINTON, Jan .... 818-240-1000.. 44 B
jswinton@glendale.edu
SWINYARD, Craig, A .... 503-943-8506 377 E
swinyard@up.edu
SWISHER, Jay .... 386-752-1822.. 99 A
jay.swisher@fgc.edu
SWISHER, Susan .... 773-298-3070 148 G
swisher@sxu.edu
SWITAJ, Elizabeth .... 692-625-3394 505 F
SWITZER, Daniel .... 718-390-3153 324 F
daniel.switzer@wagner.edu
SWITZER, Luellyn .... 662-325-2091 247 F
lswitzer@saffairs.msstate.edu
SWITZER, Michael .... 601-974-1172 247 B
switzmd@millsaps.edu
SWITZER, Ray .... 864-592-4770 412 F
switzerr@sccsc.edu
SWITZER, Regina .... 405-682-7890 367 H
rswitzer@occc.edu
SWITZER, Rich .... 212-659-7299 304 B
rswitzer@tkc.edu
SWOOPE, Malinda .... 256-372-5230.... 1 A
malinda.swoope@aamu.edu
SYDNOR, Kim .... 443-885-3560 200 D
kim.sydnor@morgan.edu
SYDOW, Debbie, L .... 804-862-6100 470 I
dsydow@rbc.edu
SYDOW, Sue .... 402-375-7197 268 G
susydow1@wsc.edu
SYGIELSKI, John, J .... 717-736-4100 385 E
ski@hacc.edu
SYKES, Brent .... 405-912-9018 369 D
bsykes@ru.edu
SYKES, Dianne .... 434-832-7602 474 C
sykesd@centralvirginia.edu
SYKES, Eric .... 617-824-8286 208 H
eric_sykes@emerson.edu
SYKES, Jonah .... 413-236-2116 213 F
jsykes@berkshirecc.edu
SYKES, Laura, A .... 603-526-3760 272 H
laura.sykes@colby-sawyer.edu
SYKES, Reginald .... 251-405-7130.... 1 E
rsykes@bishop.edu
SYLER-JONES, Tracy ..... 817-257-7811 448 G
t.syler-jones@tcu.edu
SYLJEBECK, Susan .... 517-264-7876 230 E
ssyljebe@sienaheights.edu
SYLVESTER, Douglas ..... 480-965-6188.. 10 I
douglas.sylvester@asu.edu
SYLVESTER, Jason .... 239-280-2525.. 94 O
jason.sylvester@avemaria.edu
SYLVESTER, Kenneth ..... 810-766-3383 231 G
kenms@umich.edu
SYLVESTER-CAESAR, Jemma .... 713-221-2791 453 B
caesarj@uhd.edu
SYLVIA, David .... 512-444-8082 449 A
library@thsu.edu
SYLVIA, Lynn .... 910-362-7679 332 H
lbsylvia845@mail.cfcc.edu
SYMICEK, Alan .... 715-425-4655 497 E
alan.symicek@uwrf.edu
SYMINGTON, Paul .... 740-283-6643 353 B
psymington@franciscan.edu
SYMONETTE-JOHNSON, Vena .... 305-623-1440.. 99 D
vena.symonette@fmuniv.edu
SYMS, Deirdre .... 586-445-7862 226 H
symsd@macomb.edu
SYNAKOWSKI, Edmund 307-766-5353 502 H
esynakow@uwyo.edu
SYNAN, Sharon .... 706-245-7226 117 E
ssynan@ec.edu
SYNDER, Brittany .... 305-809-3233.. 99 C
brittany.snyder@fkcc.edu
SYNDER, Tamara .... 352-638-9764.. 95 D
tsnyder@beaconcollege.edu
SYNER, Alicia .... 304-205-6746 488 K
alicia.syner@bridgevalley.edu
SYNODI, George, S .... 203-832-7273.. 89 A
gsynodi@newhaven.edu
SYOEN, Elise .... 423-869-6433 421 C
elise.syoen@lmunet.edu
SYRMOS, Vassilis, L ..... 808-956-5006 128 D
syrmos@hawaii.edu
SYVERUD, Kent .... 315-443-2235 322 C
chancellor@syr.edu
SZABO, Mihaela .... 304-336-8270 490 F
mszabo@westliberty.edu
SZABO, Shari .... 863-680-3940.. 99 H
sszabo@flsouthern.edu
SZAFRAN, Zvi .... 315-386-7204 320 E
president@canton.edu
SZAJ, Christine .... 651-290-6362 242 G
christine.szajv@mitchellhamline.edu
SZAKALY, CSC, Anthony .... 508-565-1343 218 H
aszakaly@stonehill.edu
SZAKAS, Joseph, S .... 207-621-3198 196 A
szakas@maine.edu
SZALANKIEWICZ, Linda 413-552-2155 214 D
lszalankiewicz@hcc.edu
SZALAY, Annette .... 216-373-7139 358 B
aszalay@ndc.edu
SZALDA, Katie .... 518-782-6767 315 J
kszalda@siena.edu
SZALEWICZ, Ben .... 978-542-6004 213 C
bszalewicz@salemstate.edu
SZALKOWSKI, Denise, M .... 716-673-3456 317 A
denise.szalkowski@fredonia.edu
SZANI, Phyllis .... 201-200-3350 279 E
pszani@njcu.edu
SZAREK, Michael .... 201-559-6047 278 A
szarekm@felician.edu
SZARLETA, Ellen .... 219-980-6698 156 E
eszarlet@iun.edu
SZAROLETTA, Betti .... 906-524-8301 226 A
betti.szaroletta@kbocc.edu
SZARZYNSKI, Lori .... 414-382-6329 492 A
lori.szarzynski@alverno.edu
SZATARAY, Balint .... 209-946-2654.. 70 E
bsztaray@pacific.edu
SZATMARY, Peter .... 662-846-4675 245 H
pszatmary@deltastate.edu
SZCZEPANEK, Charlene, L .... 401-456-8130 405 C
cszczepanek@ric.edu
SZCZERBACKI, David .... 617-333-2233 208 E
dszczerbacki@curry.edu
SZEGHI, Steve .... 937-481-2241 364 E
steve_szeghi@wilmington.edu
SZEJKO, Thomas .... 724-503-1001 402 E
tszejko@washjeff.edu
SZELEST, Bruce .... 518-956-8058 316 D
bszelest@albany.edu
SZELISTOWSKI, Warren 410-532-5110 201 B
wszelistowski@ndm.edu
SZENTMIKLOSI, Jill, M . 407-582-4142 112 K
jszentmiklosi@valenciacollege.edu
SZEP, Chris Ann .... 410-287-1028 197 H
caszep@cecil.edu
SZESZYCKI, Donald, J .. 319-335-3565 163 A
donald-szeszycki@uiowa.edu
SZETO, Cindy .... 714-533-3946.. 34 D
SZKODNEY, Robert .... 908-526-1200 281 A
bob.szkodny@raritanval.edu
SZKREDKA, Slawomir ... 805-482-2755.. 58 L
sszkredka@stjohnsem.edu
SZPARAGOWSKI, George .... 610-785-6205 398 A
gszparagowski@scs.edu
SZPIRO, Daniel .... 845-575-3000 305 L
daniel.szpiro@marist.edu
SZPRYNGEL, Christopher .... 203-591-7375.. 87 F
cszpryngel@post.edu
SZROMBA, Mathew, P .. 920-923-8505 494 A
mpszromba93@marianuniversity.edu
SZUCS, Peter .... 503-251-5790 377 F
pszucs@uws.edu
SZUKALSKI, SVD, John 563-876-3353 164 J
jszukalski@dwci.edu
SZUPKA, Jennifer .... 803-774-3339 407 C
szupkajl@cctech.edu
SZUR, Katalin .... 212-237-8041 294 D
kszur@jjay.cuny.edu
SZWEDKO, Emmalee ..... 801-832-2553 461 G
eszwedko@westminstercollege.edu
SZYMANKSI, David .... 904-620-2500 110 A
david.szymanski@unf.edu
SZYMKOWICZ, Caitlin, B .... 413-585-4944 218 F
cszymkowicz@smith.edu

T

TA, Hoa Minh .... 408-288-3197.. 61 M
hoaminh.ta@sjcc.edu
TA, Jennie .... 626-350-1500.. 28 J
TA, Minh-Hoa .... 415-239-3363.. 37 A
mhta@ccsf.edu
TABACHOW, Daisy .... 407-303-9203.. 94 D
daisy.tabachow@ahu.edu
TABAK, Lorie .... 713-798-6649 431 I
tabak@bcm.edu
TABAKMAN, Jenna .... 713-221-8001 453 B
tabakmanj@uhd.edu
TABAN, Faruk .... 832-230-5350 440 H
faruk@na.edu
TABARELLA-REDD, Cheryl .... 319-363-8213 168 C
credd@mtmercy.edu
TABATABAI, Habib .... 405-974-2865 370 K
htabatabai@uco.edu
TABB, Brian .... 612-455-3420 234 D
brian.tabb@bcsmn.edu
TABB, Winston, G .... 410-516-8328 199 D
wtabb@jhu.edu
TABCHOURI, Debbie ..... 337-521-8916 188 C
debbie.tabchouri@solacc.edu
TABER, Charles, S .... 785-532-6224 174 G
ctaber@ksu.edu
TABER, Ralph .... 717-358-4390 384 D
ralph.taber@fandm.edu
TABER DOUGHTY, Teresa .... 817-272-2591 454 J
teresa.doughty@uta.edu
TABERNER, Ian .... 617-585-0200 206 F
ian.taberner@the-bac.edu
TABERSKI, Mike .... 603-428-2305 273 H
mtaberski@nec.edu
TABING, Karla .... 618-985-3741 139 I
karlatabing@jalc.edu
TABOADA, Luz, E .... 915-831-7796 436 E
ltaboad2@epcc.edu
TABOR, Anne .... 207-973-1090 194 A
tabora@husson.edu
TABOR, Karen .... 760-862-1359.. 39 A
ktabor@collegeofthedesert.edu
TABOR, Tammy .... 620-276-9508 173 E
tammy.tabor@gcccks.edu
TABRON-GIDDINGS, Jasmine .... 570-208-5898 387 A
jasminetabron@kings.edu
TACCONE, Al .... 760-757-2121.. 52 E
ataccone@miracosta.edu
TACK, Eric .... 678-466-4085 116 E
erictack@clayton.edu
TACKET, Karen .... 805-546-3100.. 41 A
ktacket@cuesta.edu
TACKETT, Krystal .... 606-886-3863 180 J
ktackett0106@kctcs.edu
TACKETT, Lake .... 304-697-7550 488 B
ltackett@huntingtonjuniorcollege.edu
TACKETT, Larry .... 304-510-8760 489 F
ltackett@wvncc.edu
TACKETT, Lisa, K .... 740-368-3398 359 N
lktacket@owu.edu
TACZANOWSKY, Amy ... 724-589-2155 399 H
ataczanowsky@thiel.edu
TADAMY, Everett, L ...... 412-268-1018 380 F
et19@andrew.cmu.edu
TADAO, Tchuzie .... 680-488-2471 506 B
tzuchiet@gmail.com
TADEO, Joseph .... 352-588-8244 106 D
joseph.tadeo@saintleo.edu
TADEO, Rosa .... 408-498-5102.. 38 F
rtadeo@cogswell.edu
TADEPALLI, Raghu .... 336-278-6000 328 K
rtadepalli@elon.edu
TADESSE, Asmare .... 408-855-5010.. 74 D
asmare.tadesse@wvm.edu
TADESSE, Berhanu .... 657-278-8748.. 31 E
btadesse@fullerton.edu
TADLOCK, Katherine ..... 740-593-2860 359 G
tadlockk@ohio.edu
TADLOCK, Martin .... 727-873-4151 110 C
mtadlock@usfsp.edu
TADLOCK, Martin .... 727-873-4151 110 B
mtadlock@mail.usf.edu
TADTMAN, Jeff .... 620-223-2700 173 C
jeffta@fortscott.edu
TAETZSCH, Blixy, K .... 607-844-8222 322 H
taetzsb@tompkinscortland.edu
TAFARO, John, P .... 513-875-3344 350 G
john.tafaro@chatfield.edu
TAFFORA, Raymond, P . 608-263-7400 496 C
ray.taffora@wisc.edu
TAFOYA, Christina .... 760-355-6215.. 45 I
christina.tafoya@imperial.edu
TAFOYA, Michelle .... 213-738-5500.. 65 G
housing@swlaw.edu
TAFOYA, Yvette .... 562-860-2451.. 35 M
ytafoya@cerritos.edu
TAGABAN, Jennifer .... 520-417-4115.. 11 M
tagabanj@cochise.edu
TAGAWA, Helen .... 510-809-1444.. 45 K
TAGGART, Bruce, M ..... 610-758-3025 388 J
bmt2@lehigh.edu
TAGGART, Julie .... 614-222-4025 351 D
jtaggart@ccad.edu
TAGGART, Sean .... 541-956-7061 376 D
staggart@roguecc.edu
TAGGE, Cassandra .... 251-981-3771.... 5 B
cassandra.tagge@columbiasouthern.edu
TAGLIARENI, Jim .... 785-670-2066 177 G
jim.tagliareni@washburn.edu
TAGUINOD, Bradley ...... 808-369-8594 127 G
btaguinod@hmi.edu
TAHA, Dianne .... 516-726-5837 504 G
tahad@usmma.edu
TAHMASSEBI, Debbie ... 801-832-2585 461 G
dtahmassebi@westminstercollege.edu
TAI WANG, Yong .... 903-566-7043 456 A
ywang@uttyler.edu
TAICHMAN, Russell ...... 205-934-4720.... 8 A
taichman@uab.edu
TAILLON, Gretchen .... 603-342-3003 273 D
gtaillon@ccsnh.edu
TAILOR, Bhavna .... 201-327-8877 277 H
btailor@eastwick.edu
TAILOR, Bhavna .... 973-661-0600 277 G
btailor@eastwick.edu
TAIT, Melissa .... 847-214-7365 136 F
mtait@elgin.edu
TAIT, Tamara .... 866-680-2756 459 G
studentlife@midwifery.edu
TAITANO, Carlos .... 671-735-2600 505 E
ctaitano@triton.uog.edu

TAKAC, Jeff .... 478-301-2687 121 E
takac_j@mercer.edu
TAKACS, Audrey .... 586-445-7314 226 H
takacsa@macomb.edu
TAKACS, Sarolta, A .... 718-982-2315 293 E
TAKAHASHI, Jack .... 800-754-1009 494 E
TAKAHASHI, Sandra ..... 208-535-5372 130 C
sandra.takahashi@cei.edu
TAKAHASHI, Tomoko .... 949-480-4047.. 64 B
ttakahashi@soka.edu
TAKAKI, Leslie .... 503-251-2840 377 F
ltakaki@uws.edu
TAKASUGI, Fumiko .... 808-845-9229 129 B
takasugi@hawaii.edu
TAKATA, George .... 559-638-0300.. 66 F
george.takata@reedleycollege.edu
TAKATA, Kacie .... 480-461-7300.. 13 D
kacie.takata@mesacc.edu
TAKAYAMA, Kathy .... 301-405-9356 202 C
TAKAYAMA-PEREZ,
Amy .... 703-993-2395 467 L
atakayam@gmu.edu
TAKEDA, Sharon .... 916-278-3922.. 32 E
sharon.takeda@csus.edu
TAKEDA-TINKER, Becky 800-462-7845.. 78 N
TAKEMOTO, Mary Ann .. 562-985-5587.. 31 F
maryann.takemoto@csulb.edu
TAKES, Faith, A .... 518-786-0855 307 A
faith.takes@mildred-elley.edu
TAKIGUCHI, Amy .... 808-735-4836 127 F
ahigashi@chaminade.edu
TAKSAR, Stephen .... 413-572-8424 213 D
staksar@westfield.ma.edu
TALABER, Matthew .... 845-938-3415 504 H
matthew.talaber@usma.edu
TALAMANTE, Daniela .... 202-495-3830.. 92 E
secretary@dhs.edu
TALAVERA, Karla .... 661-255-1050.. 28 K
talavera@calarts.edu
TALAVINIA, Phillip .... 419-358-3226 348 G
talaviniap@bluffton.edu
TALBERT, Charles .... 773-907-4864 134 C
ctalbert@ccc.edu
TALBERT, Kelly .... 208-426-3844 129 I
kellytalbert@boisestate.edu
TALBOT, A. Scott .... 435-652-7601 460 G
talbot@dixie.edu
TALBOT, Phyllis .... 252-823-5166 334 C
talbotp@edgecombe.edu
TALBOT, Reuben .... 970-675-3238.. 78 G
reuben.talbot@cncc.edu
TALBOT, Scott .... 214-887-5191 436 B
stalbot@dts.edu
TALBOTT, Jeffrey .... 909-748-8888.. 71 G
jeff_talbott@redlands.edu
TALBOTT, Robert .... 650-543-3714.. 51 F
rtalbott@menlo.edu
TALBOTT, Sherry .... 540-828-5369 465 D
stalbott@bridgewater.edu
TALDO, Tom .... 785-242-5200 176 D
tom.taldo@ottawa.edu
TALENTINO, Andrea ...... 585-389-2010 308 B
atalent0@naz.edu
TALESH, Rameen, A ...... 949-824-5590.. 68 G
rtalesh@uci.edu
TALIAFERRO, Beth .... 775-831-1314 272 D
btaliaferro@sierranevada.edu
TALIAFERRO, Kevin .... 301-243-2118 503 J
kevin.taliaferro@dodiis.mil
TALIENTO, Tamela, K .... 931-431-9700 423 D
ttaliento@nci.edu
TALISMAN, Barbara .... 702-651-7535 271 A
barbara.talisman@csn.edu
TALL CHIEF, Russ .... 405-208-6288 367 I
trtallchief@okcu.edu
TALLANT, Pat, L .... 903-434-8102 441 B
ptallant@ntcc.edu
TALLARIDA, Ronald, J .. 856-256-5413 281 E
tallarida@rowan.edu
TALLENT, Judy .... 606-387-3717 182 C
judy.tallent@kctcs.edu
TALLENT, Pat .... 828-659-0401 336 B
pattallent@mcdowelltech.edu
TALLERICO, Betty, L ...... 724-458-3790 385 C
bltallerico@gcc.edu
TALLERINO, Nancy .... 310-204-1666.. 58 D
TALLEY, Braque .... 662-252-8000 248 G
braquetalley@rustcollege.edu
TALLEY, Chestley .... 903-730-4890 438 H
ctalley@jarvis.edu
TALLEY, Denise .... 540-891-3040 474 G
dguest@germanna.edu
TALLEY, Frederico, J ..... 240-895-2185 201 E
fjtalley@smcm.edu
TALLEY, Henry .... 850-599-3017 108 I
henry.talley@famu.edu
TALLEY, Lillian .... 208-562-3229 130 F
lilliantalley@cwi.edu
TALLEY, Nina .... 937-481-2299 364 E
nina_talley@wilmington.edu
TALLEY, Sue Lane .... 845-675-4691 310 G
sue.talley@nyack.edu
TALLMAN, Eric, A .... 570-321-4041 389 E
tallman@lycoming.edu
TALLMAN, Lawrence, J . 304-457-6247 487 B
tallmanlj@ab.edu
TALWAR, Malvika .... 607-844-8222 322 H
TAM, Victor .... 707-527-4246.. 62 F
vtam@santarosa.edu
TAMADA, Mike .... 503-788-6613 376 C
tamadam@reed.edu
TAMANAHA, David .... 808-984-3253 129 E
davidt@hawaii.edu
TAMANAHA, Stephen .... 714-432-5809.. 38 E
stamanaha@occ.cccd.edu
TAMANDL, Salisha .... 480-994-9244.. 16 B
salishat@swiha.edu
TAMAR-RAMSEY,
Darwin .... 270-534-3229 182 F
darwin.ramsey@kctcs.edu
TAMARA, Carolina .... 212-854-8371 290 J
ctamara@barnard.edu
TAMARES, Shanalee ...... 909-558-4581.. 48 C
stamares@llu.edu
TAMARISK, Nancy .... 707-256-7782.. 53 C
ntamarisk@napavalley.edu
TAMASCO, Mary .... 973-353-5541 282 B
tamasco@rutgers.edu
TAMAYO, Daniel .... 559-934-2432.. 74 A
danieltamayo@whccd.edu
TAMAYO, Yvonne .... 503-370-6391 378 B
ytamayo@willamette.edu
TAMBEAU, Renee .... 248-204-2208 226 G
rtambeau@ltu.edu
TAMBURRINO, Amanda 901-843-3030 423 J
tamburrino@rhodes.edu
TAMEO, John .... 401-254-3859 405 E
jtameo@rwu.edu
TAMES, Kirk .... 512-499-4369 454 I
ktames@utsystem.edu
TAMMONE, William ...... 303-991-1575.. 76 H
TAMROWSKI, Nina .... 518-320-1256 316 C
nina.tamrowski@suny.edu
TAMTE-HORAN,
Deborah .... 484-664-3190 391 C
deborahtamte-horan@muhlenberg.edu
TAN, Amy .... 713-718-7814 437 I
amy.tan@hccs.edu
TAN, Sharon .... 314-918-2528 253 A
stan@eden.edu
TANABE, Clifton .... 915-747-5572 455 C
cstanabe@utep.edu
TANAKA, Andrew, Y ...... 860-685-2607.. 89 C
atanaka@wesleyan.edu
TANAKA, Elizabeth .... 254-295-4949 453 E
etanaka@umhb.edu
TANAKA, Kenneth .... 408-741-2410.. 74 D
kenneth.tanaka@wvm.edu
TANAKA, Lester .... 702-651-5860 271 A
lester.tanaka@csn.edu
TANAKA, Randy .... 731-352-4065 418 G
tanakar@bethelu.edu
TANAKA, Yasuo .... 510-666-8248.. 24 D
ytanaka@aimc.edu
TANASESCU, Mihaela .... 714-816-0366.. 67 I
mihaela.tanasescu@trident.edu
TANBARA, Sabrina .... 212-799-5000 303 H
TANCHEVA, Kornelia ..... 412-648-7705 401 B
tancheva@pitt.edu
TANCK, Buddy Jo .... 913-294-4178 173 C
buddyt@fortscott.edu
TANDAN, Lisa .... 828-251-6600 342 C
ltandan@unca.edu
TANDE, Brian .... 701-777-2335 345 C
brian.tande@und.edu
TANDON, Suteesh .... 563-336-3345 165 B
standon@eicc.edu
TANEJA, Amit .... 508-793-3009 208 B
ataneja@holycross.edu
TANEJA, Ayush .... 334-244-3224.... 4 F
ataneja@aum.edu
TANG, Gary .... 610-526-1308 378 G
gary.tang@theamericancollege.edu
TANG, Meiling .... 707-638-5880.. 67 F
meiling.tang@tu.edu
TANG-RITCHIE, Leng ..... 619-574-6909.. 54 K
lritchie@pacificcollege.edu
TANGALAKIS, Christina 818-240-1000.. 44 B
ctangalakis@glendale.edu
TANGEMAN, Bruce .... 402-323-3408 269 C
btangeman@southeast.edu
TANGENBERG, Katy ...... 206-281-2759 484 D
tangenbergk@spu.edu
TANIGAWA, Shane .... 909-687-1454.. 43 I
shanetanigawa@gs.edu
TANIS, Cleophat .... 239-732-1300 103 A
cleotan005@yahoo.com
TANIS, Jennifer .... 845-398-4284 315 B
jtanis@stac.edu
TANJI, Lorelei, A .... 949-824-5212.. 68 G
ltanji@uci.edu
TANKERSLEY, Melody ... 330-672-0072 354 J
mtankers@kent.edu
TANKERSLEY,
Richard, A .... 704-687-8428 342 E
rtankers@uncc.edu
TANKING, Tony .... 913-360-7485 171 D
ttanking@benedictine.edu
TANKSLEY, Jake .... 484-365-7402 389 C
jtanksley@lincoln.edu
TANKSLEY, Rick .... 323-259-2599.. 54 E
rtanksley@oxy.edu
TANKSLEY, Wallace .... 614-222-6165 351 D
wtanksley@ccad.edu
TANNENBAUM, Suzy .... 541-737-3010 375 D
TANNER, Audrey .... 510-430-2376.. 52 D
atanner@mills.edu
TANNER, Buffy .... 530-242-7714.. 63 H
btanner@shastacollege.edu
TANNER, Doug .... 912-260-4286 124 C
doug.tanner@sgsc.edu
TANNER, Douglas, R .... 229-333-5935 126 G
dtanner@valdosta.edu
TANNER, Elizabeth .... 210-486-3933 429 F
etanner@alamo.edu
TANNER, Jaime .... 802-258-9293 462 E
jtanner@marlboro.edu
TANNER, Jason .... 770-528-3758 116 C
jtanner@chattahoocheetech.edu
TANNER, Jeff, F .... 757-683-3520 469 G
jtanner@odu.edu
TANNER, Jessica .... 617-585-0200 206 F
jessica.tanner@the-bac.edu
TANNER, John, S .... 808-675-3700 127 E
jstanner@byuh.edu
TANNER, Jonathan .... 801-689-2160 459 J
jtanner@nightingale.edu
TANNER, Kendall .... 662-254-3901 248 B
kendall.tanner@mvsu.edu
TANNER, Margaret .... 479-788-7519.. 21 H
margaret.tanner@uafs.edu
TANNER, Norma, J .... 251-460-6141.... 8 F
ntanner@southalabama.edu
TANNER, Patrick .... 208-562-3247 130 F
patricktanner@cwi.edu
TANNER, Paula .... 254-295-8671 453 E
ptanner@umhb.edu
TANNER, Ray .... 803-777-4202 413 C
rtanner@mailbox.sc.edu
TANNEY, Matt .... 765-361-6233 162 E
tanneym@wabash.edu
TANOUYE, Allyson, M .. 808-956-7927 128 F
atanouye@hawaii.edu
TANSEY, John, G .... 603-646-1202 273 E
john.g.tansey@dartmouth.edu
TANTILLO, Astrida, O .... 312-413-7329 151 B
tantillo@uic.edu
TANYEL, Faruk .... 864-503-5587 414 D
ftanyel@uscupstate.edu
TANZER, Ken .... 415-703-9592.. 28 D
ktanzer@cca.edu
TANZILLI, Steve .... 412-392-4742 397 A
stanzilli@pointpark.edu
TANZOSH, Amberly .... 406-238-7293 265 E
amberly.tanzosh@rocky.edu
TAO, Eric .... 408-733-1878.. 70 C
president@uewm.edu
TAO, Eric .... 888-488-4968.. 46 F
etao@itu.edu
TAOKA, Yasuko .... 402-375-7394 268 G
yataoka1@wsc.edu
TAORMINA, Melanie ..... 570-321-4036 389 E
taormina@lycoming.edu
TAPHORN, Joseph, C ... 651-962-5775 244 E
taph8012@stthomas.edu
TAPHORN, Rick, J .... 423-775-7411 418 H
TAPIA, Damaris .... 773-442-4205 145 B
d-tapia1@neiu.edu
TAPIA, Luis, A .... 787-894-2828 514 C
luis.tapia@upr.edu
TAPIAS, Maria .... 641-269-3028 165 J
tapias@grinnell.edu
TAPLEY, Brendan .... 615-277-7403 428 F
btapley@watkins.edu
TAPLEY, Robyn .... 321-674-8050.. 99 B
rtapley@fit.edu
TAPP, Beth .... 612-624-5255 243 E
bethtapp@umn.edu
TAPPAN, Charlene .... 860-512-2912.. 85 G
ctappan@manchestercc.edu
TAPPE, Diane .... 563-387-1045 167 E
tappdi01@luther.edu
TAPPER, Janet .... 503-251-5757 377 F
jtapper@uws.edu
TAPPER, Michelle .... 657-278-4207.. 31 E
mtapper@fullerton.edu
TAPSCOTT, Michael, R .. 202-994-1463.. 91 F
tapscott@gwu.edu
TARADASH, Randy .... 415-439-2356.. 25 K
rtaradash@act-sf.org
TARANTO, John, A .... 816-501-3630 250 F
john.taranto@avila.edu
TARBELL, Donald, R ..... 843-661-1119 409 K
dtarbell@fmarion.edu
TARBOX, James .... 619-594-4379.. 33 E
jtarbox@sdsu.edu
TARBOX, Norm .... 801-626-6003 461 B
ntarbox@weber.edu
TARBOX, Sandra .... 703-993-5355 467 L
starbox@gmu.edu
TARBUTTON, Ron .... 405-744-7147 368 B
ron.tarbutton@okstate.edu
TARBY, Jay .... 216-397-1703 354 I
tarby@jcu.edu
TARBY, Wendy .... 315-498-2742 311 B
tarbyw@sunyocc.edu
TARCA, Fred, E .... 203-582-3429.. 87 G
fred.tarca@quinnipiac.edu
TARCON, Susan .... 951-571-6103.. 58 G
susan.tarcon@mvc.edu
TARDIFF, Robin .... 207-947-4591 193 C
rtardiff@bealcollege.edu
TARENCE, Elaine, P ..... 334-387-3877..... 4 C
elainetarence@amridgeuniversity.edu
TARGONSKI, Conrad, A 608-796-3804 498 N
catargonski@viterbo.edu
TARHINI, Kassim, M .... 860-444-8334 504 F
kassim.m.tarhini@uscg.mil
TARHULE, Aondover ..... 607-777-2070 316 E
tarhule@binghamton.edu
TARIN, Lucille .... 570-577-3661 379 F
lucille.tarin@bucknell.edu
TARLING, Mary .... 630-844-7802 132 D
mtarling@aurora.edu
TARMAN, Christopher ... 619-644-7000.. 44 I
christopher.tarman@gcccd.edu
TARNOWSKI, Jeff .... 706-867-3050 126 A
jeff.tarnowski@ung.edu
TARO, Thomas .... 680-488-2746 506 B
tarothomas@yahoo.com
TAROLI, Stacie .... 570-558-1818 384 C
staroli@fortisinstitute.edu
TAROMINA, Katherine ... 206-517-4541 484 C
taromina@sieam.edu
TAROPE, Marji .... 670-237-6771 506 A
marji.tarope@marianas.edu
TARPEY, Andrea .... 413-755-4847 215 F
tarpey@stcc.edu
TARPLEE, Marc .... 803-327-8017 415 A
mtarplee@yorktech.edu
TARPLEY, Sue .... 706-236-2292 115 B
starpley@berry.edu
TARQUINIO, Gregg, T .. 718-430-2000 289 G
TARRANT, Carole .... 540-857-6281 476 D
ctarrant@virginiawestern.edu
TARRANT, David .... 601-968-8779 245 C
dtarrant@belhaven.edu
TARRANT, Fredrick, A ... 770-720-9221 123 E
fkt@reinhardt.edu
TARRANT, Kaneesha ..... 951-372-7877.. 58 H
kaneesha.tarrant@norcocollege.edu
TARRANT, Lee .... 918-495-7480 368 I
ltarrant@oru.edu
TARRER, Jerry .... 312-369-7060 135 E
jtarrer@colum.edu
TARSKI, Anne .... 830-591-7294 444 G
ahtarski@swtjc.edu
TART, Kathryn, M .... 832-842-8218 452 F
kmtart@uh.edu
TART, Marla, L .... 919-866-5901 338 G
mltart@waketech.edu

TART, Stuart 240-567-7494 200 C stuart.tart@montgomerycollege.edu
TARTAR, Nick 617-585-1313 217 B nick.tartar@necmusic.edu
TARTT, Tom 205-652-3533 9 A ttartt@uwa.edu
TARVER, Eunice 918-595-7524 370 E eunice.tarver@tulsacc.edu
TARVER, III, Walter, L 609-652-4804 283 D walter.tarver@stockton.edu
TARVER-BEHRING, Shari, A 818-677-2590 32 D starver-behring@csun.edu
TARVER-ROSS, Cassandra 470-639-0703 122 D cassandra.ross@morehouse.edu
TARWATER, Anne 615-383-3230 418 C tarwatera@dominicancampus.org
TARWATER, Lisa 865-573-4517 420 G ltarwater@johnsonu.edu
TARY, Keely 423-236-2736 424 B ktary@southern.edu
TASHIMA, Jaye 760-245-4271 73 D jaye.tashima@vvc.edu
TASHJIAN, Tim 512-428-1095 442 M timt@stedwards.edu
TASKER, Ashley 304-367-4644 490 B ashley.tasker@fairmontstate.edu
TASSIN, Shannon 318-487-7051 186 I shannon.tassin@lacollege.edu
TASSON, Dana 503-725-4429 376 A tassond@pdx.edu
TAST, Maryellen 307-778-1146 502 D mtast@lccc.wy.edu
TASTAD, Renee 413-552-2592 214 D rtastad@hcc.edu
TATARKA, Donna 973-328-5098 277 B dtatarka@ccm.edu
TATE, Allen 717-391-7285 399 G tate@stevenscollege.edu
TATE, Angela 770-533-7017 121 B atate@laniertech.edu
TATE, Ann 281-922-3404 443 E ann.tate@sjcd.edu
TATE, Anthony 615-904-8204 422 H anthony.tate@mtsu.edu
TATE, Brad 513-745-5700 362 E brad.tate@uc.edu
TATE, Celeste 541-278-5780 372 A cetate@bluecc.edu
TATE, Clarence 828-398-7482 332 B clarencetate@abtech.edu
TATE, David 307-382-1882 502 I dtate@westernwyoming.edu
TATE, Don 864-587-4227 412 G tated@smcsc.edu
TATE, Edward 404-962-3263 126 F edward.tate@usg.edu
TATE, Harold (Kippy) 334-727-8948 7 D htate@tuskegee.edu
TATE, Helen 704-233-8744 344 G tate@wingate.edu
TATE, James 713-348-6000 442 K james.d.tate@rice.edu
TATE, James 507-537-6256 241 D jim.tate@smsu.edu
TATE, Janene 225-771-3216 190 H janene_tate@sus.edu
TATE, Nancy 864-231-2181 406 G ntate@andersonuniversity.edu
TATE, Robert, H 863-680-4347 99 H rtate@flsouthern.edu
TATE, Verlanda 205-929-1440 6 B vtate@miles.edu
TATE, William, F 314-935-4843 262 A wtate@wustl.edu
TATELA, Joseph 410-386-8327 197 G jtatela@carrollcc.edu
TATENO, Yuji 808-946-3773 127 D
TATNALL, Amber 207-216-4392 195 C atatnall@yccc.edu
TATRO, Donna, E 609-258-2845 280 E tatro@princeton.edu
TATRO, Fred 617-364-3510 207 A ftatro@boston.edu
TATRO, Lois 316-978-5890 178 A lois.tatro@wichita.edu
TATSAK, Jenny 248-689-8282 232 A jtatsak@walshcollege.edu
TATTON, Edward 914-606-8060 325 C edward.tatton@sunywcc.edu
TATUM, Alfred 312-996-5641 151 B atatum1@uic.edu
TATUM, Ashley 940-668-7323 441 A atatum@nctc.edu
TATUM, Jeff 662-246-6471 247 D jtatum@msdelta.edu
TATUM, Ray 770-538-4706 115 D rtatum@brenau.edu
TATUM, Tanya 850-599-3777 108 I tanya.tatum@famu.edu
TATUM, Veronda 870-864-7133 21 B vtatum@southark.edu
TAUB, Alexander 215-477-1000 399 E
TAUBENFELD, Aviva 914-251-6550 319 E aviva.taubenfeld@purchase.edu
TAUBER, Hendy 323-937-3763 75 F htauber@yoec.edu
TAUBMAN, Mark, B 585-275-0017 323 J mark_taubman@urmc.rochester.edu
TAUBMAN, Phil 650-723-2300 65 J
TAUER, Jackie 507-537-7157 241 D jackie.tauer@smsu.edu
TAUER, Ritamarie 281-649-3702 437 H rtauer@hbu.edu
TAUPIER, Andrea, S 413-748-3609 218 G ataupier@springfield.edu
TAURIAC, Jesse 617-243-2173 210 G jtauriac@lasell.edu
TAURIELLO, Claire, M 301-447-5202 200 E tauriello@msmary.edu
TAUSSI, Lee 845-398-4013 315 B altaussi@stac.edu
TAUZIN, Kristie, R 985-448-4509 192 B kristie.tauzin@nicholls.edu
TAVAKOLI, Roozbeh 716-829-7515 298 F tavakoli@dyc.edu
TAVARES, Kim 513-529-5990 356 E kim.tavares@miamioh.edu
TAVARES, Rosemary 201-200-2595 279 E rtavares@njcu.edu
TAVARES, Shirley, A 787-725-8120 507 N investigacion@eap.edu
TAVAREZ, Alex 671-734-1812 505 D atavarez@piu.edu
TAVAREZ, Elisabeth, W 845-575-3000 305 L elisabeth.tavarez@marist.edu
TAVE, Stephen 815-967-7329 147 F stave@rockfordcareercollege.edu
TAVELLI, Nancy, J 509-527-5297 486 H tavelln@whitman.edu
TAVERA, Deborah 973-408-3309 277 C dtavera@drew.edu
TAVERNER, Melissa, P 870-307-7202 20 A provost@lyon.edu
TAVIN-WARKENTHIEN, Claudine 718-409-7271 321 C ctavin-warkenthien@sunymaritime.edu
TAWNEY, Andrea 915-215-4300 451 D andrea.tawney@ttuhsc.edu
TAXTER, Marianne 619-265-0107 57 D mtaxter@platt.edu
TAYDEN, Maria 815-455-8538 143 A mtaydem@mchenry.edu
TAYEH, Raja 402-826-6776 267 A raja.tayeh@doane.edu
TAYLOE, John 252-398-1232 328 D tayloj@chowan.edu
TAYLOR, Adam 864-388-8195 410 D ataylor@lander.edu
TAYLOR, Allen 304-696-6195 490 D taylor@marshall.edu
TAYLOR, Allison, S 402-280-3189 266 I allisontaylor@creighton.edu
TAYLOR, Amanda 864-379-6606 409 H taylor@erskine.edu
TAYLOR, Amanda 202-885-3827 90 J ataylor@american.edu
TAYLOR, Amy 203-392-6800 85 A taylora28@southernct.edu
TAYLOR, Angela 757-388-5133 471 D ataylor@sentara.edu
TAYLOR, Angie 936-294-1845 450 C agb003@shsu.edu
TAYLOR, Anita 410-323-6211 198 C a.taylor@fts.edu
TAYLOR, Ann 314-516-5109 261 D taylorann@umsl.edu
TAYLOR, Ann 434-797-8477 474 E ann.taylor@danville.edu
TAYLOR, Anna 770-233-5560 124 G anna.taylor@sctech.edu
TAYLOR, April 912-201-8000 124 E ataylor@southuniversity.edu
TAYLOR, Audra 254-442-5117 433 A audra.taylor@cisco.edu
TAYLOR, Baishakhi 802-443-5382 462 H taylorb@middlebury.edu
TAYLOR, Beck, A 509-777-3200 486 I president@whitworth.edu
TAYLOR, Bill 408-741-2642 74 E bill.taylor@westvalley.edu
TAYLOR, Bill 641-782-1406 169 H taylor@swcciowa.edu
TAYLOR, Bradley, G 336-841-9548 329 G btaylor@highpoint.edu
TAYLOR, Brandy 912-871-1616 122 I btaylor@ogeecheetech.edu
TAYLOR, Brian 808-956-6182 128 F taylorb@hawaii.edu
TAYLOR, Cameron, P 202-441-0058 117 F cameron.taylor@emory.edu
TAYLOR, Candace 209-381-6489 51 G candace.taylor@mccd.edu
TAYLOR, Carmen 308-398-7335 266 A carmentaylor@cccneb.edu
TAYLOR, Carol, A 417-865-2815 253 B taylorc@evangel.edu
TAYLOR, Cathy 847-214-7238 136 F ctaylor@elgin.edu
TAYLOR, Cathy 615-460-6781 418 F cathy.taylor@belmont.edu
TAYLOR, Cathy, N 618-650-5176 149 F cattayl@siue.edu
TAYLOR, Caughman 803-434-2069 413 C caughman.taylor@uscmed.sc.edu
TAYLOR, Celya 870-230-5358 19 E taylorc@hsu.edu
TAYLOR, Charles 817-735-0268 454 C charles.taylor@unthsc.edu
TAYLOR, Cheryl 817-257-7034 448 G cheryl.taylor@tcu.edu
TAYLOR, Christopher 843-661-8231 409 I christopher.taylor@fdtc.edu
TAYLOR, Craig 251-981-3771 5 B craig.taylor@columbiasouthern.edu
TAYLOR, Crystal 252-940-6219 332 C crystal.taylor@beaufortccc.edu
TAYLOR, Daniel 304-358-2000 488 A dtaylor@future.edu
TAYLOR, Danille, K 404-880-6774 116 D dtaylor3@cau.edu
TAYLOR, Danny, H 615-966-7650 421 D danny.taylor@lipscomb.edu
TAYLOR, Darrell 304-896-7432 489 E darrell.taylor@southernwv.edu
TAYLOR, David, A 718-289-5598 293 B david.taylor@bcc.cuny.edu
TAYLOR, David, F 336-758-5000 344 D taylordf@wfu.edu
TAYLOR, David, R 540-568-3720 468 F taylordr@jmu.edu
TAYLOR, Debbie 864-622-6063 406 G dtaylor@andersonuniversity.edu
TAYLOR, Debora, W 512-448-8450 442 M deboraw@stedwards.edu
TAYLOR, Deborah 901-334-5812 422 C dmtaylor@memphisseminary.edu
TAYLOR, Deborah 562-903-4703 27 C deborah.taylor@biola.edu
TAYLOR, Deborah, A 757-446-6031 466 I taylorta@evms.edu
TAYLOR, Diane 254-968-9598 446 E dtaylor@tarleton.edu
TAYLOR, Donald 870-307-7310 20 A donald.taylor@lyon.edu
TAYLOR, Donald 610-902-8200 380 C donald.taylor@cabrini.edu
TAYLOR, Dub 803-376-5723 406 F dtaylor@allenuniversity.edu
TAYLOR, Dustin 740-374-8716 364 C dtaylor@wscc.edu
TAYLOR, Ed 206-616-7175 485 F edtaylor@uw.edu
TAYLOR, Edward 706-778-8500 123 B etaylor@piedmont.edu
TAYLOR, Edward 608-663-2333 493 C edtaylor@edgewood.edu
TAYLOR, Faye 732-247-5241 279 D ftaylor@nbts.edu
TAYLOR, Frances, F 704-637-4565 328 A fftaylor15@catawba.edu
TAYLOR, Francis, H 334-833-4407 5 H ftaylor@hawks.huntingdon.edu
TAYLOR, G. Christine 205-348-2053 7 G christine.taylor@ua.edu
TAYLOR, JR., G. Don 540-231-6776 477 A taylorgd@vt.edu
TAYLOR, Gary 865-251-1800 424 A gtaylor@south.edu
TAYLOR, Gene 410-532-5324 201 B gtaylor@ndm.edu
TAYLOR, Gene 785-532-6912 174 G ksuad@ksu.edu
TAYLOR, Geoffrey 912-525-5000 123 G gtaylor@scad.edu
TAYLOR, Geraldine 781-891-2222 206 D gtaylor@bentley.edu
TAYLOR, Gia 480-423-6300 13 H gia.taylor@scottsdalecc.edu
TAYLOR, Gina 321-433-7000 97 I taylorg@easternflorida.edu
TAYLOR, Gregory 914-251-6485 319 E gregory.taylor@purchase.edu
TAYLOR, Gwen 706-771-4180 114 J gtaylor@augustatech.edu
TAYLOR, Heather 304-829-7408 487 G htaylor@bethanywv.edu
TAYLOR, Heather, H 757-822-1738 476 B htaylor@tcc.edu
TAYLOR, Helen 318-797-5374 189 D helen.taylor@lsus.edu
TAYLOR, Hunter 252-398-6505 328 D tayloh1@chowan.edu
TAYLOR, J. Kevin 805-756-1503 30 C jktaylor@calpoly.edu
TAYLOR, Jaime 304-696-3716 490 D jaime.taylor@marshall.edu
TAYLOR, James 410-777-2318 197 C jmtaylor@aacc.edu
TAYLOR, James 470-578-6033 120 L jtayl378@kennesaw.edu
TAYLOR, James 801-626-6055 461 B jamestaylor8@weber.edu
TAYLOR, James, E 202-646-1337 92 D
TAYLOR, Jan 304-558-4128 489 O jan.taylor@wvhepc.edu
TAYLOR, Jan 865-981-8057 421 F jan.taylor@maryvillecollege.edu
TAYLOR, Janet 815-921-4324 147 E j.taylor@rockvalleycollege.edu
TAYLOR, Janet 619-482-6309 65 F jtaylor@swccd.edu
TAYLOR, Janie 817-461-8741 430 H jtaylor@abu.edu
TAYLOR, Jason 609-586-4800 278 F taylorj@mccc.edu
TAYLOR, Jay 704-216-7116 337 F jay.taylor@rccc.edu
TAYLOR, Jeannie 800-280-0307 152 H jeannie.taylor@ace.edu
TAYLOR, Jeffrey, D 315-268-6477 296 A jdtaylor@clarkson.edu
TAYLOR, Jennifer 575-674-2281 285 H jetaylor@bcomnm.org
TAYLOR, Jennifer 479-575-2254 21 G taylorj@uark.edu
TAYLOR, Jennifer 805-565-6085 74 K jmtaylor@westmont.edu
TAYLOR, Jessica, L 503-255-0332 374 D jltaylor@multnomah.edu
TAYLOR, Joe 208-496-7010 130 A taylorj@byui.edu
TAYLOR, John 714-432-5935 38 E jtaylor174@occ.cccd.edu
TAYLOR, John 585-785-1300 300 B john.taylor@flcc.edu
TAYLOR, John 513-244-8176 350 I athletics@ccuniversity.edu
TAYLOR, Joseph, P 276-944-6124 467 G jptaylor@ehc.edu
TAYLOR, Joy 703-993-5270 467 L jtaylo16@gmu.edu
TAYLOR, Juanyce 601-984-1010 249 E jdtaylor@umc.edu
TAYLOR, Judith, M 240-567-7337 200 C judith.taylor@montgomerycollege.edu
TAYLOR, Julie, Y 256-765-4680 8 E jayates@una.edu
TAYLOR, Karen 914-606-6963 325 C karen.taylor@sunywcc.edu
TAYLOR, Kathy 504-816-4304 186 D ktaylor@dillard.edu
TAYLOR, Keith 814-871-7609 384 E ktaylor@gannon.edu
TAYLOR, Kelley, G 334-844-4794 4 E taylokg@auburn.edu
TAYLOR, Kelli, W 910-630-7157 331 C ktaylor@methodist.edu
TAYLOR, Kelsey 828-898-3311 330 E taylork@lmc.edu

TAYLOR, Kenneth 870-230-5216 19 E taylorke@hsu.edu
TAYLOR, Kent 575-624-8235 287 A kent@nmmi.edu
TAYLOR, Kevin 303-556-4736 80 N ktaylo@msudenver.edu
TAYLOR, Kevin, L 864-242-5100 407 B
TAYLOR, Kim 773-702-7749 150 J kimtaylor@uchicago.edu
TAYLOR, Kimberly 518-292-1854 313 D taylok3@sage.edu
TAYLOR, Kristen 817-257-4161 448 G kristen.taylor@tcu.edu
TAYLOR, Kristy 740-389-4636 356 B taylork@mtc.edu
TAYLOR, Kyle, E 918-360-1085 365 F taylork@bacone.edu
TAYLOR, Ladd 601-928-6299 247 E ladd.taylor@mgccc.edu
TAYLOR, LaTonya 630-752-5015 152 F media.relations@wheaton.edu
TAYLOR, Lauren, M 205-726-2956 6 E lmtaylor@samford.edu
TAYLOR, Laurna 615-361-7555 419 I ltaylor@daymarinstitute.edu
TAYLOR, Lee 334-387-3877 4 C leetaylor@amridgeuniversity.edu
TAYLOR, Leslie 970-491-1128 78 M leslie.taylor@colostate.edu
TAYLOR, Leslie, W 501-686-8998 22 C taylorlesliew@uams.edu
TAYLOR, Linda 580-387-7261 366 H lrobins@mscok.edu
TAYLOR, Linda 610-499-1039 403 B lmtaylor@widener.edu
TAYLOR, Lindsey 706-236-2207 115 B ltaylor@berry.edu
TAYLOR, Lisa 903-593-8311 448 H ltaylor@texascollege.edu
TAYLOR, Lois 740-474-8896 358 F ltaylor@ohiochristian.edu
TAYLOR, Loralyn 740-593-1059 359 G taylorl4@ohio.edu
TAYLOR, Lori 501-812-2224 23 B ltaylor@uaptc.edu
TAYLOR, Marcia 302-857-7823 89 F mtayor@desu.edu
TAYLOR, Marcia 918-781-7271 365 F taylorm@bacone.edu
TAYLOR, Marcie 765-641-4495 153 B mjtaylor@anderson.edu
TAYLOR, Margaret 870-575-8733 22 E taylorm@uapb.edu
TAYLOR, Maria 704-233-8126 344 G m.taylor@wingate.edu
TAYLOR, Marie, G 706-776-0105 123 B mgtaylor@piedmont.edu
TAYLOR, Marilyn 520-621-3876 16 G taylorm@email.arizona.edu
TAYLOR, Mark 513-529-9203 356 E mataylor@miamioh.edu
TAYLOR, Mark, P 314-935-6344 262 A mark.p.taylor@wustl.edu
TAYLOR, Martha, M 334-844-4438 4 E taylomm@auburn.edu
TAYLOR, Mary 208-535-5303 130 C mary.taylor@cei.edu
TAYLOR, Mary 828-898-8763 330 E taylorm@lmc.edu
TAYLOR, Mary, A 334-683-5248 6 A mtaylor@judson.edu
TAYLOR, Maryanne 215-951-1009 387 C taylorm@lasalle.edu
TAYLOR, Matthew, A 410-651-7800 203 A mataylor3@umes.edu
TAYLOR, Maurice 443-885-4075 200 D maurice.taylor@morgan.edu
TAYLOR, Melanie 562-903-4800 27 C melanie.taylor@biola.edu
TAYLOR, Melody 843-574-6225 413 B melody.taylor@tridenttech.edu
TAYLOR, Mia 617-449-7428 219 C taylor@urbancollege.edu
TAYLOR, Michael 617-449-7037 219 C michael.taylor@urbancollege.edu
TAYLOR, Michael 662-254-9041 248 B michaelc.taylor@mvsu.edu
TAYLOR, Michelle 310-243-2110 31 B mtaylor@csudh.edu
TAYLOR, Mike 330-263-2143 351 C mitaylor@wooster.edu
TAYLOR, Mischia 704-406-2260 329 A mataylor@gardner-webb.edu
TAYLOR, Misty 386-752-1822 99 A misty.taylor@fgc.edu
TAYLOR, Molly 214-333-5960 434 I molly@dbu.edu
TAYLOR, Monique 408-498-5106 38 F mtaylor@cogswell.edu
TAYLOR, Nancy, K 716-375-2317 313 F nktaylor@sbu.edu
TAYLOR, Nicolle 310-506-6464 56 C nicolle.taylor@pepperdine.edu
TAYLOR, Orlando 805-898-4038 42 L otaylor@fielding.edu
TAYLOR, Pamela, L 781-283-3694 219 D ptaylor@wellesley.edu
TAYLOR, Pat 405-585-4000 367 F
TAYLOR, Patric 949-451-5455 64 F ptaylor@ivc.edu
TAYLOR, Patty, L 920-565-1032 493 J taylorpl@lakeland.edu
TAYLOR, OSB, Paul 724-805-2271 398 E paul.taylor@stvincent.edu
TAYLOR, Quintin 225-922-2391 186 J quintintaylor@lctcs.edu
TAYLOR, R 503-399-6566 372 C r.taylor@chemeketa.edu
TAYLOR, Rachelle 718-270-6966 295 A rachellet@mec.cuny.edu
TAYLOR, Ramona 804-524-5370 470 I rtaylor@vsu.edu
TAYLOR, Ramona, L 804-524-5326 477 B rtaylor@vsu.edu
TAYLOR, Ranea 660-543-4255 260 K rtaylor@ucmo.edu
TAYLOR, Rickie 417-447-4802 257 G taylorrd@otc.edu
TAYLOR, Robert 850-561-2644 108 I robert.taylor@famu.edu
TAYLOR, Robert 712-722-6077 164 K robert.taylor@dordt.edu
TAYLOR, Robert 806-874-3571 433 B robert.taylor@clarendoncollege.edu
TAYLOR, Rochelle 313-317-4138 224 G rtaylor33@hfcc.edu
TAYLOR, Ronald, K 304-462-6451 490 C ronald.taylor@glenville.edu
TAYLOR, Russell 828-398-7900 332 B russellgtaylor@abtech.edu
TAYLOR, Russell 828-398-7302 332 B rtaylor@abtech.edu
TAYLOR, Sabrina 818-252-5225 75 C sarina.taylor@woodbury.edu
TAYLOR, Sandi 661-395-4266 46 L staylor@bakersfieldcollege.edu
TAYLOR, Sarah 847-628-2023 140 C sarah.skorburg@judsonu.edu
TAYLOR, Sarah 336-744-0900 327 F
TAYLOR, Scott 314-935-2754 262 A scotttaylor@wustl.edu
TAYLOR, Shawn 510-986-6941 56 G staylor@peralta.edu
TAYLOR, Shawn 805-765-9300 62 B
TAYLOR, Shawn 863-638-7655 113 A shawn.taylor@warner.edu
TAYLOR, Sherri 256-215-4273 1 G staylor@cacc.edu
TAYLOR, Sherri 417-667-8181 252 A staylor@cottey.edu
TAYLOR, Sherry 417-447-8801 257 G taylorst@otc.edu
TAYLOR, Stacey 617-732-2790 216 B stacey.taylor@mcphs.edu
TAYLOR, Stephanie 704-637-4470 328 A sataylor@catawba.edu
TAYLOR, Stephanie 423-614-8600 420 J staylor@leeuniversity.edu
TAYLOR, Stephen 321-433-7509 97 I taylorm@easternflorida.edu
TAYLOR, Steven 334-670-3399 7 C sltaylor@troy.edu
TAYLOR, Steven, P 262-243-5700 493 B steve.taylor@cuw.edu
TAYLOR, Steven, T 303-963-3138 77 G staylor@ccu.edu
TAYLOR, Sue 972-825-4768 445 A staylor@sagu.edu
TAYLOR, Susan 719-255-3566 83 B staylor@uccs.edu
TAYLOR, Tammy 903-927-3300 458 G ttaylor@wileyc.edu
TAYLOR, Tandra 618-468-6030 141 F tantaylor@lc.edu
TAYLOR, Teresa 479-619-4188 20 D ttaylor19@nwacc.edu
TAYLOR, Thomas 205-391-2617 3 E ttaylor@sheltonstate.edu
TAYLOR, Timothy 313-583-6500 231 F taylortd@umich.edu
TAYLOR, Veda 901-333-4259 426 A
TAYLOR, Vorley 740-366-9443 349 H taylor.1051@osu.edu
TAYLOR, Wayne 845-574-4720 313 C wtaylor@sunyrockland.edu
TAYLOR, Whitney 270-706-8604 181 A whitney.taylor@kctcs.edu
TAYLOR, William 419-559-2266 361 I wtaylor@terra.edu
TAYLOR, William, F 972-578-5579 433 M wtaylor@collin.edu
TAYLOR-ARCHER, Mordean 502-852-6153 185 C motayl01@louisville.edu
TAYLOR-BENNS, Kimberly 484-365-7218 389 C ktaylorbenns@lincoln.edu
TAYLOR-BOUCHIE, Donna 812-888-4811 162 C dtbouchie@vinu.edu
TAYLOR-BROWNE, Wintlett 563-387-1486 167 E brownewi@luther.edu
TAYLOR-COSTELLO, Julie 402-552-2693 266 E taylorcostellojulie@clarksoncollege.edu
TAYLOR DUPREE, Lesa 318-678-6000 187 A ltaylordupre@bpcc.edu
TAYLOR HEARD, Janice 216-987-5556 351 G janice.taylor-heard@tri-c.edu
TAYLOR-MENDOZA, Jennifer 650-738-4321 61 Q mendozaj@smccd.edu
TAYLOR-MINNIEFIELD, Cherilyn, Y 803-536-8698 412 C ctaylo37@scsu.edu
TAYLOR-SAWYER, Sandra 575-769-4138 285 K sandra.sawyer@clovis.edu
TAYLOR-THORNTON, Artima 757-789-1729 474 F ataylor@es.vccs.edu
TEACHMAN, Stephanie 425-640-1713 480 F stephanie.teachman@edcc.edu
TEACHOUT, David, J 336-334-4759 343 A djteacho@uncg.edu
TEAGLE, Natalie 336-334-7314 341 F ntteagle@ncat.edu
TEAGUE, Brad 501-450-3150 23 H bteague@uca.edu
TEAGUE, Clay 478-757-3544 116 A cteague@centralgatech.edu
TEAGUE, Delise 662-685-4771 245 D dteague@bmc.edu
TEAGUE, Donna 812-488-2212 161 A dt52@evansville.edu
TEAGUE, Edward 845-938-5569 504 H edward.teague@usma.edu
TEAGUE, Geni 425-640-1484 480 F geni.teague@edcc.edu
TEAGUE, J. Chad 864-941-8479 411 H teague.c@ptc.edu
TEAGUE, Randle 606-546-1201 184 H rteague@unionky.edu
TEAGUE, Rebecca 951-487-3072 52 I rteague@msjc.edu
TEAGUE, Sharyn, J 910-221-2224 329 B steague@gcd.edu
TEAGUE, Tracie 805-969-3626 55 E tteague@pacifica.edu
TEAHEN, Rebecca, M 231-995-1855 228 G rteahen@nmc.edu
TEAL, Holly 970-248-1977 77 I hteal@coloradomesa.edu
TEAL, Kurtis 785-238-8550 171 C tealk@bartonccc.edu
TEAL, P, J 919-515-2191 342 B pj_teal@ncsu.edu
TEAL, Rick 864-592-4618 412 F tealr@sccsc.edu
TEALER, Eddie 972-860-7001 435 B etealer@dcccd.edu
TEASLEY, Martell, L 801-581-6194 460 E martell.teasley@utah.edu
TEASLEY, Tonia 888-227-3552 234 E
TEAT, Jonathan 214-333-5128 434 I jonathan@dbu.edu
TEATER, Kristian 314-792-6100 254 D teater@kenrick.edu
TEBAY, John 714-992-7035 53 L jtebay@fullcoll.edu
TEBBE, Robert 618-235-2700 149 H robert.tebbe@swic.edu
TEBBS, Steve 612-343-4440 242 H sttebbs@northcentral.edu
TEBERIAN, Shahan, G 610-917-1506 401 I sgteberian@valleyforge.edu
TEBERIAN, Tyra, R 610-917-1562 401 I trteberian@valleyforge.edu
TECLE, Barbara 310-665-6946 54 I btecle@otis.edu
TECUN, Marianne 203-332-5139 85 F mtecun@housatonic.edu
TEDDER, Charles 651-793-1854 238 H charles.tedder@metrostate.edu
TEDDER, Tracey, D 863-680-4177 99 H ttedder@flsouthern.edu
TEDESCO, Jonathan 440-375-7352 355 G jtedesco@lec.edu
TEDESCO, Joseph, W 713-743-4207 452 F jtedesco@uh.edu
TEDESCO, Lisa, A 404-727-2669 117 F lisa.tedesco@emory.edu
TEDESCO, Stephanie 732-987-2252 278 B stedesco@georgian.edu
TEDJESKE, David 610-519-6979 402 D david.tedjeske@villanova.edu
TEDRICK, Freddie 217-732-3168 141 H ftedrick@lincolnchristian.edu
TEED, Deborah 239-489-9248 100 A deborah.teed@fsw.edu
TEEGARDEN, Ellen 859-442-1687 181 B ellen.teegarden@kctcs.edu
TEEL, Gina 870-543-5961 21 C gteel@seark.edu
TEERINK, Susan, M 414-288-1583 494 B susan.teerink@marquette.edu
TEETER, Alison 585-389-2818 308 B ateeter7@naz.edu
TEETERS, Rebecca 617-585-1311 217 B rebecca.teeters@necmusic.edu
TEETS, Andrew 814-871-5856 384 E teets001@gannon.edu
TEETSEL, Craig, M 260-399-7700 161 D cteetsel@sf.edu
TEFFT, Joshua 508-830-6687 213 B jtefft@maritime.edu
TEGAN, Jason 864-644-5143 412 E jtegen@swu.edu
TEGGATZ, Susan 312-355-6320 151 B steggatz@uic.edu
TEHRANI, Nader 212-353-4220 297 E ntehrani@cooper.edu
TEICHERT, Scott 801-626-7670 461 B scottteichert@weber.edu
TEICHMAN, Carl, F 309-556-3429 139 G cteich@iwu.edu
TEICHMAN, Shlomo 516-255-4700 312 D teichman@mlb.edu
TEIG, Kathy 563-588-6385 163 F kathy.teig@clarke.edu
TEIJEIRO, Mike 650-949-7380 43 D teijeiromike@foothill.edu
TEINTZE, Martin 406-994-4411 264 D mteintze@montana.edu
TEIS, Lawrence, B 512-245-2114 450 E lt10@txstate.edu
TEITELBAUM, Aharon 845-783-0994 324 A
TEITLBAUM, Zalman 718-963-9770 323 I ed@utsny.edu
TEJADA, Ileana 415-351-3538 60 G itejada@sfai.edu
TEJADA, Melinda, L 630-466-7900 152 C mtejada@waubonsee.edu
TEJADA, Michael 808-675-3935 127 E michael.tejada@byuh.edu
TEJERA-ROCAFORT, Antonio 787-767-0445 512 G antonio.tejera@upr.edu
TEKALAN, Serif, A 832-230-5552 440 H satekalan@na.edu
TEKELY, Angela 610-647-4400 386 C atekely@immaculata.edu
TELANDER, Brittany 419-517-8971 355 K btelander@lourdes.edu
TELBERG, Tamara 845-758-7433 290 G telberg@bard.edu
TELEK, Barbara, M 513-487-3206 301 E btelek@huc.edu
TELFORD, Betty 336-917-5588 340 D betty.telford@salem.edu

TELFORD, Brett .... 909-748-8052.. 71 G
brett_telford@redlands.edu
TELIHA, James, K .... 315-792-3111 324 B
jkteliha@utica.edu
TELIME, Armenohy .... 818-710-1310.. 28 A
TELL, Mary .... 847-578-8537 147 I
mary.tell@rosalindfranklin.edu
TELLA, Nicholas .... 401-598-1000 404 I
ntella@jwu.edu
TELLEI, Patrick, U .... 680-488-1669 506 B
tellei@palau.edu
TELLER, Ryan .... 402-486-2538 269 F
ryan.teller@ucollege.edu
TELLES, Nick .... 505-428-1161 288 B
nick.telles@sfcc.edu
TELLES-IRVIN, Patricia .. 847-467-5719 145 F
tellesirvin@northwestern.edu
TELLEZ, Laura .... 915-831-6359 436 E
ltellez8@epcc.edu
TELLO, Steven .... 978-934-4240 211 G
steven_tello@uml.edu
TELLO, Zaynna .... 408-924-1105.. 34 B
zaynna.tello@sjsu.edu
TELLUS, Kimberley .... 212-472-1500 309 I
ktellus@nysid.edu
TELOKI, M.T .... 212-752-1530 304 D
mteloki@limcollege.edu
TEMAAT, Beverly .... 620-227-9204 172 J
btemaat@dc3.edu
TEMBY, Megan .... 800-686-1883 222 E
mtemby@cleary.edu
TEMEYER, Travis .... 734-487-1024 223 H
ttemeyer@emich.edu
TEMKIN, Aron .... 802-485-2624 463 A
atemkin@norwich.edu
TEMORES, Sandra .... 619-594-4766.. 33 E
stemores@sdsu.edu
TEMORES-VALDEZ,
Sandra .... 619-594-3641.. 33 E
stemores@sdsu.edu
TEMPEL, Courtney .... 575-769-2811 285 K
courtney.tempel@clovis.edu
TEMPERINO, Steven, H . 603-535-2848 275 B
stemperi@plymouth.edu
TEMPLE, Ella .... 334-229-4234.... 4 B
TEMPLE, Glena .... 608-796-3005 498 N
ggtemple@viterbo.edu
TEMPLE, H. Thomas 954-262-1556 103M
htemple@nova.edu
TEMPLE, Jack .... 334-387-3877.... 4 C
jacktemple@amridgeuniversity.edu
TEMPLE, James .... 661-362-3535.. 38 H
james.temple@canyons.edu
TEMPLE, Lori .... 702-895-3628 271 E
lorit@unlv.edu
TEMPLE, Melanie .... 252-862-1242 337 C
metemple7181@roanokechowan.edu
TEMPLE, Vicki .... 318-678-6000 187 A
vtemple@bpcc.edu
TEMPLETON, Debra .... 828-328-7335 330 F
debra.templeton@lr.edu
TEMPLETON, Erin .... 864-596-9099 409 B
erin.templeton@converse.edu
TEMPLETON, Heidi .... 660-785-4016 260 J
heidi@truman.edu
TEMPLETON, Jenna .... 412-365-1168 381 C
jtempleton@chatham.edu
TEMPLETON, Joanna ..... 516-877-3909 289 C
jtempleton@adelphi.edu
TEMPLETON, Karen .... 205-726-4580.... 6 E
ktemplet@samford.edu
TEMPLETON, Mary .... 334-670-3189.... 7 C
mtempleton@troy.edu
TEMPLETON, Mary, A ... 318-675-7652 189 C
mtemp1@lsuhsc.edu
TEMPLIN, Kellly .... 979-458-6000 446 C
ktemplin@tamus.edu
TEN NAPEL, Karmen ..... 712-274-5191 168 B
tennapel@morningside.edu
TENA, Lydia .... 915-831-8818 436 E
lpere121@epcc.edu
TENBUS, Eric .... 478-445-4441 118 C
eric.tenbus@gcsu.edu
TENCHER, Donald, E ..... 401-456-8007 405 C
dtencher@ric.edu
TENCZAR, Bob .... 909-537-5007.. 33 A
robert.tenczar@csusb.edu
TENENBAUM, Elchonon 707-638-5507.. 67 F
rabbi@tu.edu
TENER, Brent, B .... 615-343-1422 428 D
b.tener@vanderbilt.edu
TENG, Anthony .... 949-582-4895.. 64 G
ateng@saddleback.edu
TENGLIN, Ingrid, K .... 773-244-5601 145 A
itenglin@northpark.edu
TENGLUND, Ann .... 716-375-2378 313 F
ateng@sbu.edu
TENIENTE, Yvonne .... 805-922-6966.. 24 J
yteniente@hancockcollege.edu
TENIENTE-MATSON,
Cynthia .... 210-784-1600 448 A
cmatson@tamusa.edu
TENN, Jennifer .... 815-280-2217 140 B
jtenn@jjc.edu
TENNANT, Leslie, A ...... 724-480-3552 381 K
leslie.tennant@ccbc.edu
TENNANT, Otto .... 270-789-5034 179 E
otennant@campbellsville.edu
TENNENT, Lee .... 864-236-6447 410 B
lee.tennent@gvltec.edu
TENNENT, Timothy, C ... 859-858-2202 178 H
TENNER, Jack .... 713-743-5671 452 F
jdtenner@central.uh.edu
TENNER, Katangela .... 601-877-6147 244 H
ksampson@alcorn.edu
TENNEY, David .... 713-348-8036 442 K
dtenney@rice.edu
TENNEY, Randall .... 304-473-8099 491 H
tenney_r@wvwc.edu
TENNIE, Jameia .... 336-285-4110 341 F
jatennie@ncat.edu
TENNISON, Allen .... 612-343-4762 242 H
datennis@northcentral.edu
TENORE, Alfred .... 909-580-9661.. 34 E
TENSMEYER, Anna .... 509-543-1486 479 H
TENSUAN, Theresa .... 610-896-1420 385 L
ttensuan@haverford.edu
TENTES, Theresa .... 650-738-4331.. 61 Q
tentes@smccd.edu
TENUTA, Bob .... 815-455-8585 143 A
btenuta@mchenry.edu
TEPPER, Steven, J .... 480-965-8561.. 10 I
steven.tepper@asu.edu
TER MOLEN, Matthew ... 315-443-9161 322 C
termolen@syr.edu
TERAOKA, Della .... 808-455-0453 129 D
dellaand@hawaii.edu
TERCHEK, Joshua .... 440-525-7092 355 H
jterchek2@lakelandcc.edu
TEREBESSY, Hilarie .... 312-942-3013 148 A
hilarie_terebessy@rush.edu
TERENZIO, Marion .... 518-255-5111 319 F
terenzma@cobleskill.edu
TERESA, Daniel .... 831-755-6840.. 44 K
dteresa@hartnell.edu
TERESH, Tonia .... 619-388-7270.. 60 E
tteresh@sdccd.edu
TERHAAR, Jody, L .... 320-363-5601 235 C
jterhaar@csbsju.edu
TERHUNE, James .... 610-328-8365 399 D
jterhun1@swarthmore.edu
TERHUNE, Jason .... 262-646-6501 495 B
jterhune@nashotah.edu
TERHUNE, Shannon .... 757-423-2095 467 H
TERKLA, David .... 617-287-6505 211 E
david.terkla@umb.edu
TERKLA, Dawn, G .... 617-627-3274 219 B
dawn.terkla@tufts.edu
TERKOWSKI, Amy, M ... 570-408-4409 403 D
amy.terkowski@wilkes.edu
TERMIN, Travis .... 817-722-1731 439 B
travis.termin@tku.edu
TERMOTT, Kenneth .... 732-247-5241 279 D
ktermott@nbts.edu
TERMUHLEN, Paula .... 218-726-7572 243 F
ptermuhl@d.umn.edu
TERNAK, Armand .... 706-886-6831 125 D
aternack@tfc.edu
TERNAND, Jo Anne .... 708-209-3003 135 F
joanne.ternand@cuchicago.edu
TERP, Cheryl .... 920-693-1134 499 G
cheryl.terp@gotoltc.edu
TERP, Douglas, C .... 207-859-4774 193 E
douglas.terp@colby.edu
TERPACK, Sallie, A .... 814-732-1024 394 F
terpack@edinboro.edu
TERPENNING,
Marlene, K .... 740-284-5179 353 B
mterpenning@franciscan.edu
TERPSTRA, Joylita, W ... 423-478-7731 423 G
jterpstra@ptseminary.edu
TERPSTRA, Phil .... 620-276-9554 173 E
phil.terpstra@gcccks.edu
TERRAZAS, Denise .... 951-372-7016.. 58 H
denise.terrazas@norcocollege.edu
TERRAZAS, Lissete .... 575-492-2122 289 A
lterrazas@usw.edu
TERRAZAS, Susan .... 909-706-2476.. 74 I
sterrazas@westernu.edu
TERRAZAS, Susan .... 909-760-3476.. 74 I
sterrazas@westernu.edu
TERREBONNE, Dean, M 409-880-2374 449 H
dean.terrebonne@lamar.edu
TERRELL, Beth, M .... 260-399-7700 161 D
bterrell@sf.edu
TERRELL, Bill .... 915-532-3737 458 C
bterrell@westerntech.edu
TERRELL, Carleen .... 336-249-8186 334 A
carleen_terrell@davidsonccc.edu
TERRELL, Charles .... 304-434-8001 489 A
charles.terrell@easternwv.edu
TERRELL, David, R .... 765-285-2201 153 C
drterrell@bsu.edu
TERRELL, Mark .... 814-866-6641 388 A
mterrell@lecom.edu
TERRELL, Patrice .... 478-825-4284 118 A
terrellp@fvsu.edu
TERRELL, Patrice .... 478-825-6301 118 A
terrellp@fvsu.edu
TERRELL-BROOKS,
Tabatha .... 601-979-6944 246 E
tabatha.terrell-brooks@jsums.edu
TERRELL-POWELL,
Yvonne .... 425-640-1456 480 F
yvonneterrellpowell@edcc.edu
TERRILL, Brian .... 540-373-2200 466 H
bterrill@evcc.edu
TERRILL, Kimberly .... 310-954-4135.. 52 G
kterrill@msmu.edu
TERRIO, Dan, M .... 509-527-4981 486 H
terrio@whitman.edu
TERRIO, Paul .... 612-238-4552 243 B
pterrio@smumn.edu
TERRONEZ, Danny .... 979-532-6465 458 F
terronezd@wcjc.edu
TERRY, Bryan .... 870-972-2855.. 17 G
bterry@astate.edu
TERRY, Carolyn .... 240-567-4366 200 C
carolyn.terry@montgomerycollege.edu
TERRY, Catherine .... 615-966-1964 421 D
catherine.terry@lipscomb.edu
TERRY, Chihoko .... 910-410-1821 337 B
ckterry@richmondcc.edu
TERRY, Christopher ...... 607-735-1938 299 D
cterry@elmira.edu
TERRY, Colin .... 303-273-3000.. 78 I
cterry@mines.edu
TERRY, Cynthia .... 205-934-8152.... 8 A
cterry@uab.edu
TERRY, Denise, A .... 574-372-5100 155 B
terryda@grace.edu
TERRY, Edward .... 828-726-2202 332 G
eterry@cccti.edu
TERRY, Gina .... 501-686-2923.. 21 F
gterry@uasys.edu
TERRY, James .... 573-876-2363 260 F
jterry@stephens.edu
TERRY, James, E .... 304-696-2486 490 D
terry@marshall.edu
TERRY, Laura, C .... 423-439-4210 419 J
terryl@etsu.edu
TERRY, Linda .... 512-223-7503 431 A
lkluck@austincc.edu
TERRY, Melissa .... 503-554-2101 373 C
terrym@georgefox.edu
TERRY, Melissa, D .... 503-554-2101 373 C
terrym@georgefox.edu
TERRY, Neil, W .... 806-651-2530 448 C
nterry@wtamu.edu
TERRY, Scott .... 304-357-4363 488 G
scottterry@ucwv.edu
TERRY, Stephen .... 913-288-7685 174 F
sterry@kckcc.edu
TERRY, Susan .... 206-543-0535 485 F
nahe@uw.edu
TERRY, Troy, M .... 864-294-2213 410 A
troy.terry@furman.edu
TERRY, Willa .... 662-252-2491 248 G
wterry@rustcollege.edu
TERRY, Willa, J .... 662-252-2491 248 G
wterry@rustcollege.edu
TERRY-SHARP,
Kathleen .... 901-321-4299 419 C
katerry@cbu.edu
TERRYN, Dottie .... 850-872-3801 100 N
dterryn@gulfcoast.edu
TESAR, Kathleen .... 212-799-5000 303 H
TESH, J. Michael .... 210-567-2590 456 C
tesh@uthscsa.edu
TESKE, Paul .... 303-315-2805.. 83 C
paul.teske@ucdenver.edu
TESKE, Yolanda, K .... 252-334-2029 331 D
yolanda.teske@macuniversity.edu
TESLUK, Paul, E .... 716-645-3221 316 F
ptesluk@buffalo.edu
TESORIERO, Cristine ..... 516-876-3033 319 A
tesorieroc@oldwestbury.edu
TESS, Dan .... 570-484-2238 395 B
dtess@lockhaven.edu
TESS, Paul, A .... 507-354-8221 236 I
tesspa@mlc-wels.edu
TESSIER, Dorita .... 509-527-2646 485 H
dorita.tessier@wallawalla.edu
TESSIER, Michael, A ..... 812-488-2956 161 A
mt28@evansville.edu
TESSIER-LAVIGNE,
Marc .... 650-723-2481.. 65 J
president@stanford.edu
TESSITORE, Amy .... 518-243-1577 291 C
tessitorea@ellismedicine.org
TESSLER, Chani .... 773-973-0241 138 A
tessler@htc.edu
TESSLER, Faith .... 213-884-4133.. 24 A
ftessler@ajrca.edu
TESSLER, Lisa .... 845-437-5439 324 C
litessler@vassar.edu
TESSMAN, Brock .... 406-449-9129 263 K
btessman@montana.edu
TESTA, Ashley .... 412-536-1194 387 B
ashley.testa@laroch.edu
TESTA, Michael .... 610-892-1548 393 J
mtesta@pit.edu
TESTA-BUZZEE, Kristina 203-857-7220.. 86 D
ktesta-buzzee@norwalk.edu
TESTANI, Joe .... 585-275-2366 323 J
j.testani@rochester.edu
TESTI, Andrea .... 541-881-5761 377 B
atesti@tvcc.cc
TESTORI, Peter .... 413-565-1000 205 G
ptestori@baypath.edu
TETEN, Ryan, L .... 308-865-8995 269 I
TETERS, Charlene .... 505-424-2354 286 C
cteters@iaia.edu
TETI, Polly .... 215-242-7777 381 D
tetip@chc.edu
TETLOW, Tania .... 504-865-2011 189 F
TETREAU, Jerry, C .... 480-245-7944.. 12 N
jerry.tetreau@ibcs.edu
TETREAU, Jerry, C .... 480-245-7969.. 12 N
jerry.tetreau@ibcs.edu
TETREAULT, Jules .... 203-392-5556.. 85 A
tetreaultj4@southernct.edu
TETREAULT, Patricia, L . 570-941-7767 401 H
patricia.tetreault@scranton.edu
TETTEH, Edem .... 856-222-9311 281 C
etetteh@rcbc.edu
TETZLAFF, Christian ...... 770-533-6966 121 B
ctetzlaff@laniertech.edu
TEUTSCHEL, Linda .... 650-543-3744.. 51 F
linda.teutschel@menlo.edu
TEVAGA, Laura .... 808-675-3669 127 E
laura.tevaga@byuh.edu
TEVES, Frances .... 909-869-3503.. 30 D
fteves@cpp.edu
TEW, Deb .... 910-962-7017 343 C
tewdg@uncw.edu
TEW, Keith 252-399-6361 326M
ktew@barton.edu
TEW, Mark .... 334-683-5102.... 6 A
mtew@judson.edu
TEW, Michael .... 734-487-3200 223 H
mtew@emich.edu
TEWART, Terri .... 505-428-1836 288 B
terri.tewart@sfcc.edu
TEXIDOR, Migdalia .... 787-250-1912 509 D
mtexidor@metro.inter.edu
TEXTER, Lynn, A .... 215-951-1043 387 C
texter@lasalle.edu
TEYMOURTASH,
Janet, L .... 415-422-5898.. 71 K
janet@usfca.edu
TEZENO, Albert 972-599-3151 433M
atezeno@collin.edu
THACHENKARY,
Sebastian .... 414-277-7141 494 G
thachenkary@msoe.edu
THACKER, Allison .... 713-348-4818 442 K
invest@rice.edu
THACKER, Karen, S .... 610-796-8306 378 F
karen.thacker@alvernia.edu
THACKER, Linda .... 314-529-9308 254 H
lthacker@maryville.edu

THACKER, Samantha ..... 517-264-7172 230 E
sthacker@sienaheights.edu
THACKER, Strom .... 518-388-6102 323 G
thackers@union.edu
THACKER, Tiffany .... 606-218-5953 185 D
tiffanythacker@upike.edu
THACKERAY, Rosemary . 801-422-4919 458 H
rosemary_thackeray@byu.edu
THADEN, Mark .... 540-654-2160 472 I
mthad2zw@umw.edu
THAKKAR, Monica .... 212-799-5000 303 H
THAKKER, Dhiren .... 919-966-1122 342 D
dhiren_thakker@unc.edu
THAKURIAH,
Piyushimita .... 848-932-2714 282 A
mhanniga@ejb.rutgers.edu
THALACKER, Karen .... 319-352-8225 170 C
karen.thalacker@wartburg.edu
THAMES, Brenda .... 559-934-2200.. 74 A
brendathames@whccd.edu
THAMES, James, H .... 214-887-5013 436 B
jthames@dts.edu
THAMES, Jamie .... 478-757-4024 126 H
jthames@wesleyancollege.edu
THAMES, Kathleen, A .... 337-482-6397 192 E
kat@louisiana.edu
THANKI, Sandip .... 702-992-2992 271 C
sandip.thanki@nsc.edu
THARAKUNNEL, Kurian . 708-456-0300 150 I
kuriantharakunnel@triton.edu
THARP, Brent .... 912-478-5444 119 C
btharp@georgiasouthern.edu
THARP, Donald .... 419-289-5777 348 A
dtharp2@ashland.edu
THARP, Glen .... 602-242-6265.. 11 C
glen.tharp@brooklinecollege.edu
THARP, Karen .... 931-598-1270 423 M
kmtharp@sewanee.edu
THARP, Katie .... 630-844-5449 132 D
ktharp@aurora.edu
THARP, Michael .... 845-341-4742 311 C
mike.tharp@sunyorange.edu
THARPE, Barbara .... 615-327-6827 422 A
btharpe@mmc.edu
THARPE, Brad .... 909-621-8519.. 56 J
brad_tharpe@pitzer.edu
THARRINGTON, Sally .... 434-949-1061 475 H
sally.tharrington@southside.edu
THARRINGTON,
Sterling .... 910-892-3178 329 F
stharrington@heritagebiblecollege.edu
THATCHER, Debra .... 541-440-4622 377 C
debra.thatcher@umpqua.edu
THATCHER, Derek .... 740-366-9453 349 H
thatcher.42@cotc.edu
THATCHER, Paula .... 503-352-1556 375 G
thatchep@pacificu.edu
THAXTON, Deron .... 318-473-6409 188 J
dthaxton@lsua.edu
THAYER, Jainen .... 641-269-3500 165 J
thayerja@grinnell.edu
THAYER, Janet .... 518-956-8050 316 D
jthayer@albany.edu
THAYER, Scott .... 909-384-8992.. 59 I
sthayer@sbccd.cc.ca.us
THAYER, Tammy .... 608-246-6451 499 H
tthayer2@madisoncollege.edu
THAYER-MENCKE,
Laura .... 402-552-3470 266 E
thayermenckelaura@clarksoncollege.edu
THAYNE, Lewis, E .... 717-867-6211 388 H
thayne@lvc.edu
THE, James .... 817-202-6719 444 I
jthe@swau.edu
THEBEAU, Lydia .... 314-392-2285 256 C
lydia.thebeau@mobap.edu
THEEUWES, Jim .... 251-580-2154.... 1 I
jim.theeuwes@fcoastalalabama.edu
THEILER, Anne Marie ... 360-650-3164 486 F
annemarie.theiler@wwu.edu
THEIS, Cindy .... 612-874-3777 236 K
ctheis@mcad.edu
THEISEN, Greg .... 203-591-5056.. 87 F
gtheisen@post.edu
THEISEN, Jason .... 320-308-6012 241 A
jtheisen@sctcc.edu
THEISSEN, Craig, R .... 330-325-6758 357 G
ctheissen@neomed.edu
THEKKUMKARA,
Thomas .... 806-414-9268 451 C
thomas.thekkumkara@ttuhsc.edu
THELEN, Cindy .... 715-675-3331 500 E
thelen@ntc.edu
THELEN, Craig .... 616-395-7833 225 B
thelen@hope.edu
THELEN, James, B .... 207-621-3452 195 I
university.counsel@maine.edu
THELEN, Kevin .... 724-357-2141 394 G
kthelen@iup.edu
THEMISTOCLEOUS,
Ann-Margaret .... 864-231-2185 406 G
athemistocleous@andersonuniversity.edu
THEOBALD, Joanne .... 307-268-2621 501 U
joannetheobald@caspercollege.edu
THEOBALD, Michael, J . 816-501-4061 258 H
mike.theobald@rockhurst.edu
THEOBALD, Neil .... 307-766-5768 502 H
uwpres@uwyo.edu
THEODORE, Steve .... 254-295-4500 453 E
stheodore@umhb.edu
THEODOROPOULOS,
Christine .... 805-756-1414.. 30 C
theo@calpoly.edu
THEODOSIOU,
Constantine .... 718-862-7948 305 H
constantine.theodosiou@manhattan.edu
THEODOULOU, Stella ... 818-677-2957.. 32 D
stella.theodoulou@csun.edu
THEONUGRAHA, Felix .. 616-392-8555 233 E
president@westernsem.edu
THEORET, Julie .... 802-635-1391 464 C
julie.theoret@northernvermont.edu
THERIAC, Amy .... 618-544-8657 138 H
theriaca@iecc.edu
THERIAULT, Henry .... 508-929-8938 213 E
htheriault@worcester.edu
THERIOT, Clifton .... 985-448-4621 192 B
clifton.theriot@nicholls.edu
THERIOT, Joy .... 212-563-6647 323 F
j.theriot@uts.edu
THERMER, Clifford .... 860-913-2058.. 87 A
cthermer@goodwin.edu
THEROULDE, Leslie ...... 305-428-5700 103 E
ltheroulde@aii.edu
THESENVITZ,
Michael, D .... 918-631-2583 371 E
michael-thesenvitz@utulsa.edu
THETFORD, Byron .... 205-652-3435.... 9 A
behetford@uwa.edu
THEULE, Ryan .... 661-362-5930.. 38 H
ryan.theule@canyons.edu
THEULEN, Michael .... 413-265-2328 208 C
theulenm@elms.edu
THI NGO, Kim-Lien ...... 714-903-2762.. 67 L
THIBADEAU, Suzette ..... 920-424-0200 497 B
thibadea@uwosh.edu
THIBEAU, Matthew .... 773-508-7323 142 D
mthibeau@luc.edu
THIBEAULT, Alan .... 207-602-2253 196 G
athibeault@une.edu
THIBEAULT, Robert, J ... 252-335-3768 341 D
rjthibeault@ecsu.edu
THIBEDEAU, Dawn .... 414-277-7126 494 G
thibedeau@msoe.edu
THIBODEAU, Jim .... 531-622-2428 267 H
jrthibodeau@mccneb.edu
THIBODEAU, John .... 262-564-3050 499 F
thibodeauj@gtc.edu
THIBODEAU, Wayne, J . 248-370-4241 229 G
thibodea@oakland.edu
THIBODEAUX, Chad .... 337-475-5524 192 A
cthibodeaux@mcneese.edu
THIBODEAUX, Deb .... 818-299-5500.. 73 K
dthibodeaux@westcoastuniversity.edu
THIBODEAUX, Raime .... 337-475-5136 192 A
rthibodeaux@mcneese.edu
THIBODEAUX, Sharon .. 409-984-6200 450 B
thibodeauxsd1@lamarpa.edu
THIBOUTOT, Paul .... 507-222-4190 234 F
pthibout@carleton.edu
THIE, II, Rick .... 937-395-8607 355 F
rick.thie@ketteringhealth.org
THIEDE, Jaci, A .... 641-269-3207 165 J
thiedeja@grinnell.edu
THIEL, Becky .... 740-351-3472 360 K
bthiel@shawnee.edu
THIEL, Elaine .... 386-506-3075.. 97 D
elaine.thiel@daytonastate.edu
THIEL, Janet .... 732-987-2234 278 B
jthiel@georgian.edu
THIEL, Teresa .... 314-516-7192 261 D
thielt@umsl.edu
THIELE, Dianna .... 206-592-3210 481 H
dthiele@highline.edu
THIELE, Dwain, L .... 214-648-8711 457 B
dwain.thiele@utsouthwestern.edu
THIELE, Sherry .... 859-985-3520 179 C
sherry_thiele@berea.edu
THIELEMANN, Heather .. 936-294-1345 450 C
thielemann@shsu.edu
THIEMANN, Drew .... 502-272-8407 179 B
jthiemann@bellarmine.edu
THIEME, Sacha .... 812-855-9770 156 B
sthieme@indiana.edu
THIEME, Sacha .... 812-855-9770 156 A
sthieme@indiana.edu
THIENEL, Molly .... 508-213-2218 217 E
molly.thienel@nichols.edu
THIERFELDER,
William, K .... 704-461-6726 327 A
billthierfelder@bac.edu
THIERSTEIN, Joel .... 304-473-8181 491 H
thierstein@wvwc.edu
THIES, Andrea .... 863-638-7261 113 A
andrea.thies@warner.edu
THIESEN, Barbara .... 316-284-5300 171 F
bthiesen@bethelks.edu
THIESEN, John .... 316-283-2500 171 F
THIESEN, Matthew .... 503-517-1800 378 A
THIESFELDT, Steven, R . 507-354-8221 236 I
thiesfsr@mlc-wels.edu
THIESSEN, Bradley .... 941-487-4104 109 D
bthiessen@ncf.edu
THIGPEN, Buck .... 912-287-5813 116 F
bthigpen@coastalpines.edu
THIGPEN, Michael .... 765-641-4199 153 B
mjthigpen@anderson.edu
THIGPEN, Paula, M ...... 410-864-3605 201 F
pthigpen@stmarys.edu
THILL, Jesse .... 501-450-3130.. 23 H
jthill@uca.edu
THIMBA, Evelyn .... 215-895-6712 383 B
evelyn.k.thimba@drexel.edu
THIMM, Tamara .... 715-634-4790 493 I
tthimm@lco.edu
THIMMESCH, Timothy ... 616-331-3845 224 E
thimmest@gvsu.edu
THIROLF, Kate .... 517-990-1436 225 C
thirolfkathrynq@jccmi.edu
THIROS, Pauline .... 208-282-4068 130 H
thirpaul@isu.edu
THIRSK, William .... 401-863-7250 404 E
william_thirsk@brown.edu
THIS, Craig .... 937-775-4296 364 I
craig.this@wright.edu
THISSELL, Mark .... 714-241-6224.. 38 C
mthissell@coastline.edu
THISSEN, Sally, L .... 863-680-4127.. 99 H
sthissen@flsouthern.edu
THISTLETHWAITE, Polly 212-817-7060 293 F
pthistlethwaite@gc.cuny.edu
THOBABEN, James .... 859-858-2369 178 H
THOELKE, Sharie .... 952-446-4132 235 G
thoelkes@crown.edu
THOENNES, Karla .... 715-425-0720 497 E
karla.thoennes@uwrf.edu
THOENNES, Karla .... 715-425-4555 497 E
karla.thoennes@uwrf.edu
THOLEN, Robin .... 937-393-3431 361 B
rtholen@sscc.edu
THOM, Michelle .... 651-962-6510 244 E
thom0526@stthomas.edu
THOM-KALEY, Marcia ... 434-381-6425 472 D
mthomkaley@sbc.edu
THOMAS, Adam .... 334-214-4880.... 1 H
adam.thomas@cv.edu
THOMAS, Ainsley .... 518-629-4596 302 E
a.thomas1@hvcc.edu
THOMAS, AJ .... 770-537-6000 127 A
aj.thomas@westgatech.edu
THOMAS, Alan, R .... 615-898-2852 422 H
alan.thomas@mtsu.edu
THOMAS, Alvetta, P ...... 770-228-7365 124 G
alvetta.thomas@sctech.edu
THOMAS, Amanda .... 410-617-2988 199 F
athomas@loyola.edu
THOMAS, Amy .... 614-251-4597 358 G
thomasa3@ohiodominican.edu
THOMAS, Andrew, J ..... 716-888-2336 292 D
thomas97@canisius.edu
THOMAS, Andrine .... 212-616-7253 301 F
andrine.thomas@helenefuld.edu
THOMAS, Angela .... 409-880-8878 449 H
angela.thomas@lamar.edu
THOMAS, Anice .... 973-353-5805 282 B
anice.thomas@rutgers.edu
THOMAS, Anita .... 651-690-6720 242 R
ajthomas583@stkate.edu
THOMAS, Anne .... 479-788-7033.. 21 H
anne.thomas@uafs.edu
THOMAS, Annie .... 808-734-9267 128 I
athomas@hawaii.edu
THOMAS, Anthony .... 910-275-6191 335 E
athomas@jamessprunt.edu
THOMAS, Ashly .... 217-786-2374 142 B
ashly.thomas@llcc.edu
THOMAS, Auden .... 518-580-5590 316 A
athomas@skidmore.edu
THOMAS, Barbara, J ..... 415-422-6352.. 71 K
thomasb@admin.usfca.edu
THOMAS, Bethany .... 863-667-5654 107 K
bthomas@seu.edu
THOMAS, Betsy .... 305-899-3725.. 95 C
bthomas@barry.edu
THOMAS, Beverly .... 614-222-4035 351 D
bthomas.4@ccad.edu
THOMAS, Bill .... 425-739-8164 482 A
bill.thomas@lwtech.edu
THOMAS, Bob .... 517-432-1978 227 D
rmthomas@uadv.msu.edu
THOMAS, Bobette .... 207-509-7265 195 H
bthomas@unity.edu
THOMAS, Brad .... 770-962-7580 120 E
bthomas@gwinnetttech.edu
THOMAS, Brad .... 425-640-1884 480 F
brad.thomas@edcc.edu
THOMAS, Brandon .... 801-957-4255 461 D
brandon.thomas@slcc.edu
THOMAS, Brenda .... 605-331-6645 417 E
brenda.thomas@usiouxfalls.edu
THOMAS, Bridgett .... 217-732-3155 141 I
bthomas@lincolncollege.edu
THOMAS, Brodrick .... 615-248-1426 427 A
bthomas1@trevecca.edu
THOMAS, Carei .... 212-220-8085 293 A
cthomas@bmcc.edu
THOMAS, Carol .... 603-428-2481 273 H
cthomas@nec.edu
THOMAS, Carol .... 626-914-8592.. 36 K
cthomas@citruscollege.edu
THOMAS, Carolyn .... 530-752-6068.. 68 E
ccthomas@ucdavis.edu
THOMAS, Chad .... 814-393-2306 394 D
cthomas@clarion.edu
THOMAS, Christine .... 334-229-4327.... 4 B
cthomas@alasu.edu
THOMAS, Christine .... 916-608-6713.. 50 H
thomasc@flc.losrios.edu
THOMAS, Christine, L .. 715-346-4617 497 F
cthomas@uwsp.edu
THOMAS, Christopher ... 337-475-5503 192 A
thomas@mcneese.edu
THOMAS, Christopher ... 601-979-6858 246 E
christopher.j.thomas@jsums.edu
THOMAS, Claudine .... 215-965-4061 390 J
cthomas@moore.edu
THOMAS, Colleen .... 989-686-9181 223 G
colleenthomas@delta.edu
THOMAS, Corlisse .... 973-353-5541 282 B
corlisse.thomas@rutgers.edu
THOMAS, Courtney .... 706-778-8500 123 B
cthomas@piedmont.edu
THOMAS, Damani .... 718-368-5696 294 E
dthomas@kbcc.cuny.edu
THOMAS, Daniel .... 731-352-4200 418 G
thomasd@bethelu.edu
THOMAS, Daphne .... 901-333-4368 426 A
dthomas@southwest.tn.edu
THOMAS, Darylann .... 724-925-4215 403 A
thomasdar@westmoreland.edu
THOMAS, David .... 509-527-2194 485 H
dave.thomas@wallawalla.edu
THOMAS, David, A .... 470-639-0249 122 D
THOMAS, David, E .... 215-751-8000 382 A
dthomas@ccp.edu
THOMAS, Debbie .... 870-733-6731.. 17 H
THOMAS, Debbie .... 979-845-3651 446 G
dean@geosciences.tamu.edu
THOMAS, Debera .... 775-784-6841 271 F
deberat@unr.edu
THOMAS, Deborah .... 502-776-1443 184 B
dthomas@simmonscollegeky.edu
THOMAS, Denee .... 361-570-4149 453 C
thomasd@uhv.edu
THOMAS, DeNeia .... 304-766-3112 491 B
deneia.thomas@wvstateu.edu
THOMAS, DeNeia .... 304-766-3000 491 B
deneia.thomas@wvstateu.edu

THOMAS, Doug 978-665-4095 212 C dthoma27@fitchburgstate.edu
THOMAS, Downing 319-335-0370 163 A downing-thomas@uiowa.edu
THOMAS, Elizabeth 212-431-2187 309 G elizabeth.thomas@nyls.edu
THOMAS, Emily 843-953-7035 407 F ethomas9@citadel.edu
THOMAS, Etienne 502-597-5865 182 H etienne.thomas@kysu.edu
THOMAS, Fitzroy 301-891-4115 204 C fthomas@wau.edu
THOMAS, Fredel 605-995-2652 415 C fredel.thomas@dwu.edu
THOMAS, Frederick, A 207-768-9580 196 E frederick.thomas@maine.edu
THOMAS, Greg 307-754-6024 502 G greg.thomas@nwc.edu
THOMAS, Gregory 773-602-5096 134 D gathomas@ccc.edu
THOMAS, Helen 912-538-3126 124 F hthomas@southeasterntech.edu
THOMAS, Isaiah 610-957-6113 399 D ithomas1@swarthmore.edu
THOMAS, J. Matthew 770-534-6174 115 D mthomas@brenau.edu
THOMAS, James 910-296-1974 335 E jthomas@jamessprunt.edu
THOMAS, Janice 732-224-2174 276 B jthomas@brookdalecc.edu
THOMAS, Jared 864-663-0148 411 E jared.thomas@ngu.edu
THOMAS, Jean 419-448-3278 361 J thomaskj@tiffin.edu
THOMAS, Jeanne 954-763-9840 94 L library@atom.edu
THOMAS, Jefferson 680-488-6223 506 B jeffersont@palau.edu
THOMAS, Jeffrey 516-726-5845 504 G thomasj@usmma.edu
THOMAS, Jeffrey 660-562-1187 257 E jthomas@nwmissouri.edu
THOMAS, Jeremy 405-682-1611 367 H jeremy.l.thomas@occc.edu
THOMAS, Jerry 501-760-4202 20 B jerry.thomas@np.edu
THOMAS, Joe 541-888-7399 376 F jthomas@socc.edu
THOMAS, John 661-255-1050 28 K
THOMAS, John 951-785-2064 47 C jthomas@lasierra.edu
THOMAS, JR., John 918-270-6455 369 A john.thomas@ptstulsa.edu
THOMAS, John, L 863-680-6215 99 H jthomas@flsouthern.edu
THOMAS, Joseph 574-284-5280 160 C jthomas@saintmarys.edu
THOMAS, Joseph 803-536-7033 412 C jthomas@scsu.edu
THOMAS, Julia, M 585-385-8015 314 A jthomas@sjfc.edu
THOMAS, Julie 319-296-4275 166 B julie.thomas@hawkeyecollege.edu
THOMAS, K. B 318-487-7389 186 I kb.thomas@lacollege.edu
THOMAS, Karen 386-312-4037 106 C karenthomas@sjrstate.edu
THOMAS, Karen 706-649-1854 117 A kthomas@columbustech.edu
THOMAS, Karen 718-289-5705 293 B karen.thomas@bcc.cuny.edu
THOMAS, Katherine 801-832-2262 461 G
THOMAS, Kathleen 330-823-2578 363 B thomaska@mountunion.edu
THOMAS, Kathryn, S 706-355-5116 114 F kthomas@athenstech.edu
THOMAS, Katie 724-480-3523 381 K katie.thomas@ccbc.edu
THOMAS, Kay 601-484-8689 247 A kthomas@meridiancc.edu
THOMAS, Kay, M 252-398-6226 328 D thomak@chowan.edu
THOMAS, Kelland 201-216-3728 283 C kelland.thomas@stevens.edu
THOMAS, Kelvin 973-803-5000 280 C kthomas@pillar.edu
THOMAS, Kenneth 334-229-1465 4 B kthomas@alasu.edu
THOMAS, Kerry 601-977-4463 249 C kthomas@tougaloo.edu
THOMAS, Kevin 618-650-5930 149 F kethoma@siue.edu
THOMAS, Kimberly 219-989-2853 159 G thoma744@pnw.edu
THOMAS, L. Joseph 607-255-8791 297 F
THOMAS, Laurita, E 734-647-5574 231 E laurita@umich.edu
THOMAS, III, Leon 410-777-2219 197 C lthomas20@aacc.edu
THOMAS, Linda 903-589-7111 438 G lthomas@jacksonville-college.edu
THOMAS, Linda, V 340-693-1324 514 E lthomas2@uvi.edu
THOMAS, Lisa 231-995-1043 228 G lthomas@nmc.edu
THOMAS, London 864-388-8310 410 D lthomas@lander.edu
THOMAS, Lori 732-987-2275 278 B lthomas@georgian.edu
THOMAS, Lorrin 856-225-2656 281 G lthomas2@camden.rutgers.edu
THOMAS, Lyn 765-983-1211 154 G thomaly@earlham.edu
THOMAS, Mandy 714-628-7337 36 C mthomas@chapman.edu
THOMAS, Marc 970-542-3191 81 A marc.thomas@morgancc.edu
THOMAS, Marcia 501-623-2272 18 I
THOMAS, Marcia, R 312-460-0600 132 A mthomas@aaart.edu
THOMAS, Marcus 501-279-4332 19 D mathomas@harding.edu
THOMAS, Margo 904-819-6474 98 E mthomas@flagler.edu
THOMAS, Maria 601-977-7769 249 C mthomas@tougaloo.edu
THOMAS, Marjorie, S 757-221-2510 466 C mthomas@wm.edu
THOMAS, Mark 863-638-7228 113 A mark.thomas@warner.edu
THOMAS, Mark 863-638-2345 113 A mark.thomas@warner.edu
THOMAS, Mark 608-246-6301 499 H mthomasjr@madisoncollege.edu
THOMAS, Mary Beth 617-735-9766 209 A thomasmb@emmanuel.edu
THOMAS, Maxcie 870-575-7029 22 E thomasm@uapb.edu
THOMAS, Melinda 210-784-1355 448 A melinda.thomas@tamusa.edu
THOMAS, Melissa 503-554-2218 373 C mthomas@georgefox.edu
THOMAS, Meshia 804-257-5851 477 C clthomas@vuu.edu
THOMAS, Micah 888-488-4968 46 F mthomas@itu.edu
THOMAS, Michael 618-985-3741 138 F thomasm@iecc.edu
THOMAS, Michael 410-986-3220 197 E mdthomas@bccc.edu
THOMAS, Michael 484-581-1272 383 D mthoma11@eastern.edu
THOMAS, Michael, A 706-880-8911 121 A mathomas@lagrange.edu
THOMAS, Mike, R 618-235-2700 149 H michael.thomas@swic.edu
THOMAS, Nancy 248-204-3208 226 G nthomas@ltu.edu
THOMAS, Nancy 423-472-7141 424 F nthomas@clevelandstatecc.edu
THOMAS, Natalie 703-329-9100 92 G
THOMAS, Nathan 309-677-3140 133 B nthomas@fsmail.bradley.edu
THOMAS, Nichole 315-268-3854 296 A nthomas@clarkson.edu
THOMAS, Nishanth 973-803-5000 280 C nthomas@pillar.edu
THOMAS, Patricia, A 202-274-7257 93 C pthomas@udc.edu
THOMAS, Paul 337-482-2976 192 E pdt2867@louisiana.edu
THOMAS, Peter, A 508-831-6074 220 E pthomas@wpi.edu
THOMAS, Philmon 404-752-1663 122 E pthomas@msm.edu
THOMAS, R. Brent 620-341-5278 172 L rthomas2@emporia.edu
THOMAS, Rachel 504-520-5732 193 A rthomas18@xula.edu
THOMAS, Randi Malcolm 513-529-4151 356 E randi.thomas@miamioh.edu
THOMAS, Rebecca 765-983-1318 154 G thomare@earlham.edu
THOMAS, Rebecca, J 423-652-4787 420 H rjthomas@king.edu
THOMAS, Renard 661-362-3469 38 H renard.thomas@canyons.edu
THOMAS, Renee 276-223-4752 476 E rthomas@wcc.vccs.edu
THOMAS, Richard, W 301-295-3013 504 B richard.thomas@usuhs.edu
THOMAS, Rick 414-277-7300 494 G
THOMAS, Rikki 757-727-5250 468 B rikki.thomas@hamptonu.edu
THOMAS, Rita 606-759-7141 182 A
THOMAS, Robbin 225-771-2552 191 A rthomas@sulc.edu
THOMAS, Roberta 870-460-1453 22 D thomasr@uamont.edu
THOMAS, Robin 334-872-2533 6 F selmau3@bellsouth.net
THOMAS, Ronald, C 718-262-2332 295 F rthomas@york.cuny.edu
THOMAS, Rosalyn 417-873-6827 252 F rthomas005@drury.edu
THOMAS, Rosemary, M 304-637-1337 487 I thomasr@dewv.edu
THOMAS, Roy 410-951-3000 203 D
THOMAS, Sam 901-251-7100 92 G
THOMAS, Sam 303-360-4738 79 D sam.thomas@ccaurora.edu
THOMAS, Samantha 214-768-3603 444 E thomassa@smu.edu
THOMAS, Sandi 760-252-2411 26 I sthomas@barstow.edu
THOMAS, Sandra 580-745-3172 369 K sthomas@se.edu
THOMAS, Scott 802-656-2216 463 E scott.thomas@uvm.edu
THOMAS, Scott 802-656-3424 463 E scott.thomas@uvm.edu
THOMAS, Shirman 615-898-2516 422 H shirman.thomas@mtsu.edu
THOMAS, Stacey 765-455-9391 156 D stathoma@iuk.edu
THOMAS, Stacy 276-739-2429 476 C sthomas@vhcc.edu
THOMAS, Steve 432-685-4520 440 E steve@midland.edu
THOMAS, Stuart 901-678-3855 427 D sbthomas@memphis.edu
THOMAS, Susan, L 660-785-4100 260 J suethomas@truman.edu
THOMAS, Suzanne 843-792-1533 410 F thomass@musc.edu
THOMAS, Sylvia 972-524-3341 445 C
THOMAS, Tamara 909-558-4481 48 C tthomas@llu.edu
THOMAS, Teresa 903-875-7315 440 G teresa.thomas@navarrocollege.edu
THOMAS, Teresa, W 615-898-2603 422 H teresa.thomas@mtsu.edu
THOMAS, Terri 607-436-3388 317 C terri.thomas@oneonta.edu
THOMAS, Tiffany 602-489-5300 10 E tiffany.thomas@arizonachristian.edu
THOMAS, Timothy 315-792-5611 307 D tthomas@mvcc.edu
THOMAS, Todd 423-652-6045 420 H tthomas@king.edu
THOMAS, Tony 718-951-3118 293 C tony.thomas@brooklyn.cuny.edu
THOMAS, Toyarna, Y 804-342-3565 477 C tythomas@vuu.edu
THOMAS, Tracie 410-777-2880 197 C tmthomas8@aacc.edu
THOMAS, Tyrone 843-355-4152 414 F thomast@wiltech.edu
THOMAS, Vadim 518-276-8531 312 I thomav@rpi.edu
THOMAS, Valerie, A 410-455-3142 202 E valerie.thomas@umbc.edu
THOMAS, Von 402-643-3651 266 G von.thomas@cune.edu
THOMAS, Wade 607-436-3458 317 C wade.thomas@oneonta.edu
THOMAS, Wayne 423-636-7300 427 B wthomas@tusculum.edu
THOMAS, Wayne, B 405-325-5789 371 B wthomas@ou.edu
THOMAS, Wendy 410-777-1309 197 C wcthomas2@aacc.edu
THOMAS, Wilbert, L 757-727-5356 468 B bill.thomas@hamptonu.edu
THOMAS, William 910-521-6859 343 B stewart.thomas@uncp.edu
THOMAS-ANDERSON, Tricia 972-860-7396 435 B triciathomas-anderson@dcccd.edu
THOMAS-LITTLE, Jill, M 586-445-7576 226 H littlej@macomb.edu
THOMAS-WILLIAMS, Regina 912-443-5708 124 A rthomas@savannahtech.edu
THOMAS-WOOD, Roberta 864-578-8770 412 B rthomas@sherman.edu
THOMASEE, David 850-769-1551 100 N dthomasee@gulfcoast.edu
THOMASON, Chris 205-652-3533 9 A cthomason@uwa.edu
THOMASON, Chris 205-652-5467 9 A cthomason@uwa.edu
THOMASON, Chris 870-777-5722 22 A chris.thomason@uaht.edu
THOMASON, Kathy 541-440-4707 377 C kathy.thomason@umpqua.edu
THOMASON, Mary 817-554-5950 440 C mthomason@messengercollege.edu
THOMASON, Troy 407-628-6317 105 M tthomason@rollins.edu
THOMBS, Dennis 817-735-5439 454 C dennis.thombs@unthsc.edu
THOME, Jennifer 419-267-1223 358 A jthome@northweststate.edu
THOMEN, Karlee 217-709-0920 141 E kthomen@lakeviewcol.edu
THOMES, Chris 386-506-4499 97 D chris.thomes@daytonastate.edu
THOMES, Christopher, P 850-747-3250 100 N cthomes@gulfcoast.edu
THOMPKINS, Kurtis 336-714-7998 339 F thompkinsk@piedmontu.edu
THOMPSON, A. Renee 609-835-6000 92 G
THOMPSON, Adelia, P 757-594-8759 466 B adelia.thompson@cnu.edu
THOMPSON, Aimee 620-901-6218 170 G thompson@allencc.edu
THOMPSON, Al 715-346-2481 497 F al.thompson@uwsp.edu
THOMPSON, Alanna 256-306-2601 1 F alanna.thompson@calhoun.edu
THOMPSON, Albert 757-822-1715 476 B bthompson@tcc.edu
THOMPSON, Alfreda 601-635-2111 245 I athompson@eccc.edu
THOMPSON, Alice 310-834-3065 67 K
THOMPSON, Allison, L 318-342-6917 192 F althompson@ulm.edu
THOMPSON, Amanda 937-393-3431 361 B athompson@sscc.edu
THOMPSON, Amber 719-336-1592 80 K amber.thompson@lamarcc.edu
THOMPSON, Ameer 510-215-4006 40 H athompson@contracosta.edu
THOMPSON, Amy 718-940-5713 314 C althompson@sjcny.edu
THOMPSON, Ann 814-393-1784 394 D athompson@cuf-inc.org
THOMPSON, Annette 210-283-5091 453 D athompson@uiwtx.edu
THOMPSON, April 814-332-4356 378 D
THOMPSON, Arlene 334-229-4406 4 B athompson@alasu.edu
THOMPSON, Ash 706-542-2273 125 G contact@uhs.uga.edu
THOMPSON, Barbara 334-556-2629 2 C bthompson@wallace.edu
THOMPSON, Bart 225-578-3231 188 I bthompson@lsu.edu
THOMPSON, Blake 601-925-3200 247 C bthompson@mc.edu
THOMPSON, Blake 614-297-8468 358 I thompson.2601@osu.edu
THOMPSON, Bob 405-912-9453 369 D bthompson@ru.edu
THOMPSON, Bobby 405-912-9007 369 D bobby.thompson@ru.edu
THOMPSON, Bradley 901-751-8453 422 E bthompson@mabts.edu
THOMPSON, Brenda 512-863-1956 445 D thompso2@southwestern.edu
THOMPSON, Brian, L 904-819-6249 98 E bthompson@flagler.edu
THOMPSON, Carey 901-843-3000 423 J thompsonc@rhodes.edu
THOMPSON, Carrie 615-966-5250 421 D carrie.thompson@lipscomb.edu

THORNBURY, Kimberly . 212-659-7209 304 B kthornbury@tkc.edu
THORNDIKE, Sara .... 252-328-6975 341 C thorndikes@ecu.edu
THORNDYKE, Luanne ... 508-856-3844 212 A luanne.thorndyke@umassmed.edu
THORNE, Andrew .... 706-886-6831 125 D athorne@tfc.edu
THORNE, Bradford, E .... 617-745-3894 208 G bradford.e.thorne@enc.edu
THORNE, Debbie, M ..... 512-245-2205 450 E dm29@txstate.edu
THORNE, Katie .... 706-886-6831 125 D kthorne@tfc.edu
THORNELL, SND, Susan .... 617-735-9824 209 A thornsu@emmanuel.edu
THORNGREN, Jill .... 605-688-6181 417 C jill.thorngren@sdstate.edu
THORNHILL, Kathy .... 707-826-4582.. 33 D kathy.thornhill@humboldt.edu
THORNLEY, Mary .... 843-574-6241 413 B mary.thornley@tridenttech.edu
THORNLEY, Vickie .... 773-252-5137 147 B vickie.thornley@resu.edu
THORNS, Mamie, T ...... 989-964-4397 230 B mtthorns@svsu.edu
THORNSBERRY, Marie .. 352-588-8253 106 D marie.thornsberry@saintleo.edu
THORNSBURY, Krista .... 615-675-5287 428 G chill@welch.edu
THORNTHWAITE, Kevin 334-833-4480.... 5 H registrar.kthorn@hawks.huntingdon.edu
THORNTON, Alec .... 303-964-3608.. 82 E athornton@regis.edu
THORNTON, Amy .... 608-785-9262 501 A thorntona@westerntc.edu
THORNTON, Ann, D ...... 212-854-2247 297 C adt2138@columbia.edu
THORNTON, Brittany ..... 620-331-4100 174 C bthornton@indycc.edu
THORNTON, Cathy, M .. 607-735-1840 299 D cthornton@elmira.edu
THORNTON, Evan .... 256-765-4232.... 8 E ethornton@una.edu
THORNTON, Jill .... 503-352-2240 375 G thornton@pacificu.edu
THORNTON, Laura .... 770-537-5720 127 A laura.thornton@westgatech.edu
THORNTON, Linda .... 507-222-4171 234 F lthornto@carleton.edu
THORNTON, Matha .... 585-385-8230 314 A mthornton@sjfc.edu
THORNTON, Michael .... 301-846-2851 198 E mthornton@frederick.edu
THORNTON, Paul .... 239-425-3274 108 K pthornton@fgcu.edu
THORNTON, Randall ..... 252-492-2061 338 F thorntonr@vgcc.edu
THORNTON, Tawanna ... 334-514-5073.... 2 F tawanna.thornton@istc.edu
THORNTON, Teresa .... 405-789-7661 370 B teresa.thornton@swcu.edu
THORNTON, Timothy .... 256-372-8211.... 1 A timothy.thornton@aamu.edu
THORNTON, Wendy, J .. 212-650-5426 293 D wthornton@ccny.cuny.edu
THOROUGHMAN, David .... 740-351-3888 360 K dthoroughman@shawnee.edu
THORP, Karen, L .... 434-381-6136 472 D kthorp@sbc.edu
THORP, Michael .... 717-815-2240 404 A mthorp@ycp.edu
THORPE, Abigail .... 718-933-6700 307 G athorpe@monroecollege.edu
THORPE, Alayne .... 269-471-6581 221 B alayne@andrews.edu
THORPE, Alayne .... 269-471-3405 221 B alayne@andrews.edu
THORPE, Charles, E ...... 315-268-6738 296 A cthorpe@clarkson.edu
THORPE, Christine .... 908-737-5902 278 E chthorpe@kean.edu
THORPE, Derrick .... 336-744-0900 327 F derrick.thorpe@carolina.edu
THORPE, Hillory .... 212-924-5900 322 B hthorpe@swedishinstitute.edu
THORPE, Jenn .... 215-248-7118 381 D thorpej@chc.edu
THORPE, Jennifer .... 573-875-7668 251 F jcthorpe1@ccis.edu
THORPE, Melissa .... 610-358-4588 391 D thorpem@neumann.edu
THORPE, Paul .... 610-341-5865 383 D pwthorpe@eastern.edu
THORPE, Stephen, W .... 610-499-4117 403 B swthorpe@mail.widener.edu
THORPE, Terry .... 229-928-1360 119 D terry.thorpe@gsw.edu
THORSEN, MiChelle ...... 425-640-1428 480 F michelle.thorsen@edcc.edu
THORSETT, Stephen ...... 503-370-6209 378 B president@willamette.edu
THORSON, Andrea .... 661-395-4610.. 46 L athorson@bakersfieldcollege.edu
THORSON, Carola .... 218-281-6510 244 A
THORSON, Carola .... 937-327-6360 364 H thornsonc@wittenberg.edu
THORSON, Donald .... 531-622-2647 267 H dwthorson@mccneb.edu
THORSON, Eric .... 701-252-3467 347 C eric.thorson@uj.edu
THORSON, Kip .... 507-372-3460 239 E kip.thorson@mnwest.edu
THORSON, Phil .... 320-308-5396 240 H pthorson@stcloudstate.edu
THORSTAD, Todd, M .... 320-222-5572 240 E todd.thorstad@ridgewater.edu
THORTON, Tom .... 907-796-6531.. 10 B tthornto@alaska.edu
THORTON, Toni .... 703-878-2800.. 92 G
THOTA, Vykuntapathi .... 804-524-5024 477 B vthota@vsu.edu
THOURSON, Peter .... 541-485-1780 374 F peterthourson@newhope.edu
THRAILKILL, Krystal ..... 479-394-7622.. 23 C kthrailkill@uarichmountain.edu
THRANE, Linda .... 713-348-6281 442 K thrane@rice.edu
THRASH, Carrie .... 740-374-8716 364 C cthrash@wscc.edu
THRASHER, John, E ...... 850-644-1085 109 C president@fsu.edu
THRASHER, Tally .... 317-274-7404 156 A tthrashe@iu.edu
THREATT, Cindy .... 609-896-5101 281 B cthreatt@rider.edu
THREET, Ali .... 435-879-4469 460 G threet@dixie.edu
THREET, Dwight .... 910-695-3831 337 H threetd@sandhills.edu
THRELKELD, Aubry .... 978-232-2408 209 B athrelke@endicott.edu
THRIFT, Jack .... 858-653-3000.. 29 I
THRO, Donna .... 314-256-8886 250 D thro@ai.edu
THRO, William, E .... 859-257-2936 185 B william.thro@uky.edu
THROCKMORTON, Hunter .... 903-510-2586 452 C jthr@tjc.edu
THROP, Liz .... 301-687-4436 203 E eathroop@frostburg.edu
THRUMAN, Michelle .... 815-588-3575 138 B michelle.thruman@highland.edu
THRUSH, Anne, R .... 989-774-3166 222 C pybus1a@cmich.edu
THRUSH, Claudia .... 570-389-4012 394 A cthrush@bloomu.edu
THUER, Rachel .... 856-225-6005 281 G rmt84@camden.rutgers.edu
THUESON, Mike, B .... 208-496-2316 130 A thuesonm@byui.edu
THUL, Travis .... 507-453-2738 239 A tthul@southeastmn.edu
THULIN, Andrew .... 805-756-2161.. 30 C athulin@calpoly.edu
THUM, Dennis, L .... 605-331-6777 417 E dennis.thum@usiouxfalls.edu
THUM, Maureen .... 810-424-5605 231 G mthum@umich.edu
THUM, Scott, W .... 260-422-5561 155 H swthum@indianatech.edu
THUMITH, Robert, B ...... 618-650-2190 149 F rthumit@siue.edu
THUMM MOORE, Kelly . 303-722-5724.. 80 L kmoore@lincolntech.edu
THUN, Esther .... 212-659-7200 304 B ethun@tkc.edu
THURBER, Darla .... 501-760-4113.. 20 B darla.thurber@np.edu
THURBER, John, P .... 609-984-1155 284 B jthurber@tesu.edu
THURLOW, David .... 802-831-1064 463 G dthurlow@vermontlaw.edu
THURLOW, III, George . 805-893-4799.. 70 A george.thurlow@ia.ucsb.edu
THURMAN, David .... 206-254-1904 217 F
THURMAN, Erik, J .... 651-962-6691 244 E erik.thurman@stthomas.edu
THURMAN, Kathy .... 615-898-5792 422 H kathy.thurman@mtsu.edu
THURMAN, Kerri, L .... 217-443-8850 135 H kthurman@dacc.edu
THURMAN, Kevin .... 573-431-4593 256 B
THURMAN, Kevin .... 573-518-2261 256 B kthurman@mineralarea.edu
THURMAN, Quint .... 575-492-2123 289 A qthurman@usw.edu
THURMAN, JR., Robert, D .... 314-773-0083 250 I rthurman@brookesbible.org
THURMAN, Todd .... 580-774-3068 370 C todd.thurman@swosu.edu
THURMER, Anne .... 218-299-6506 239 B anne.thurmer@minnesota.edu
THURSTON, Katie, S ..... 256-824-6042.... 8 B katie.thurston@uah.edu
THURSTON, Maureen .... 720-279-8992.. 80 C mthurston@holmesinstitute.edu
THURSTON, Michael ..... 413-585-3000 218 F mthursto@smith.edu
THURSTON, Regina .... 410-455-2695 202 E rthursto@umbc.edu
THUSWALDNER, Gregor 773-244-5570 145 A gathuswaldner@northpark.edu
THYGERSON, John .... 256-824-2870.... 8 B john.thygerson@uah.edu
THYREEN, Timothy, R ... 724-852-7777 402 F thyreen@waynesburg.edu
TIAGI, Olesia .... 914-632-5400 307 G otiagi@monroecollege.edu
TIAHRT, Cheryl .... 605-658-6026 416 H cheryl.tiahrt@usd.edu
TIAPO, Bernadette, S .... 315-267-2341 319 D tiapobs@potsdam.edu
TIBBETTS, Bill .... 612-343-4181 242 H wetibbet@northcentral.edu
TIBBITTS, Laura .... 512-463-1808 449 F laura.tibbitts@tsus.edu
TIBBS, Terri .... 910-672-1696 341 E ttibbs@uncfsu.edu
TIBERI, Tom, R .... 716-645-2171 316 F tiberi@buffalo.edu
TIBERIO, Amy .... 401-254-5450 405 E atiberio@rwu.edu
TIBURZI, Torrey .... 206-221-4661 485 F eoaa@uw.edu
TICCONI, Rhett .... 315-568-3256 308 F rticconi@nycc.edu
TICE, Gene .... 270-852-3104 183 A gene.tice@kwc.edu
TICE, Jared .... 704-637-4410 328 A jrtice18@catawba.edu
TICE, Laura, L .... 850-263-3261.. 95 B lltice@baptistcollege.edu
TICHENOR, Kristin, R .... 508-831-6720 220 E tichenor@wpi.edu
TICK, Michael .... 315-443-7671 322 C mtick1@syr.edu
TICKLE, Dean .... 402-354-7000 268 C dean.tickle@methodistcollege.edu
TICKLE, Dean .... 402-354-7044 268 C dean.tickle@methodistcollege.edu
TICKLE, Jimmie .... 434-797-8475 474 E jimmie.tickle@danville.edu
TIDWELL, James, H .... 502-597-8104 182 H james.tidwell@kysu.edu
TIDWELL, Michael .... 903-566-7325 456 A president@uttyler.edu
TIE, Peter .... 408-433-2280.. 36 I
TIEDENS, Lara .... 909-621-8148.. 63 E president@scrippscollege.edu
TIEDT, Penny .... 608-785-6501 496 F ptiedt@uwlax.edu
TIEFENTHALER, Jay .... 515-964-6612 164 C jmtiefenthaler3@dmacc.edu
TIEFENTHALER, Jill .... 719-389-6700.. 77 H president@coloradocollege.edu
TIEKEN, Scott, K .... 812-877-8604 159 J tieken1@rose-hulman.edu
TIERCE, Meghan .... 559-730-3745.. 39 E meghant@cos.edu
TIERNAN, Bernadette .... 973-720-2463 284 I tiernanb@wpunj.edu
TIERNEY, Deborah, J .... 515-961-1699 169 D deb.tierney@simpson.edu
TIERNEY, Joan .... 815-280-2661 140 B jtierney@jjc.edu
TIERNEY, Kathleen .... 610-526-5364 379 E ktierney01@brynmawr.edu
TIET, Kien .... 626-350-1500.. 28 J
TIETJE, Brian .... 805-756-1757.. 30 C btietje@calpoly.edu
TIETJEN, Carl .... 585-275-2008 323 J carl_tietjen@urmc.rochester.edu
TIETJEN, Rick .... 845-451-1380 298 A rick.tietjen@culinary.edu
TIETZ, Leah Jo .... 406-449-9156 263 K ltietz@montana.edu
TIFFIN, Doug .... 972-708-7340 435 H president@diu.edu
TIFFIN, Lisa .... 585-594-6194 312 K tiffin_lisa@roberts.edu
TIFFIN, Lisa .... 585-594-6194 310 F tiffin_lisa@roberts.edu
TIFFIN, Phyllis .... 817-598-6246 458 A ptiffin@wc.edu
TIGHE, Roger .... 254-442-5034 433 A roger.tighe@cisco.edu
TIGNER, Terrell .... 816-604-3175 255 H terrell.tigner@mcckc.edu
TIJERINA, Denise .... 806-742-2984 451 B denise.tijerina@ttu.edu
TIKALSKY, Paul, J .... 405-744-5140 368 B paul.tikalsky@okstate.edu
TILDEN, Kevin .... 949-214-3127.. 40 F kevin.tilden@cui.edu
TILDEN, Marsha, A .... 740-368-3163 359 N matilden@owu.edu
TILGHMAN, Patricia, E . 410-651-6449 203 A petilghman@umes.edu
TILL, Ellen .... 850-474-2080 110 E etill@uwf.edu
TILL, Kimberly, B .... 214-887-5061 436 B ktill@dts.edu
TILLEMAN, Suzanne ...... 406-243-6195 264 A suzanne.tilleman@umontana.edu
TILLEN, Dawn .... 270-824-1830 181 G dawn.tillen@kctcs.edu
TILLERY, Mariann, W .... 336-841-9286 329 G mtillery@highpoint.edu
TILLERY, Sarah .... 971-722-6268 375 J
TILLETT, Kerri .... 609-771-3139 276 I thompsok@tcnj.edu
TILLEY, Genoria .... 225-216-8292 186 K tilleyg@mybrcc.edu
TILLEY, Neil .... 828-689-1306 331 A ntilley@mhu.edu
TILLEY, Scott .... 765-641-4101 153 B setilley@anderson.edu
TILLINGHAST, David ..... 508-531-6140 212 B dtillinghast@bridgew.edu
TILLIS, Antonio .... 713-743-4002 452 F adtillis@uh.edu
TILLMAN, Ashley .... 701-483-2101 345 D ashley.tillman@dickinsonstate.edu
TILLMAN, Harry, J .... 757-446-7073 466 I tillmahj@evms.edu
TILLMAN, Henry, J .... 225-771-5497 190 G henry_tillman@sus.edu
TILLMAN, Mark .... 470-578-6565 120 L mtillm@kennesaw.edu
TILLMAN, Rosalyn, P .... 865-329-3101 425 F rtillman@pstcc.edu
TILLMAN, Shalita .... 909-384-8659.. 59 I scunningh@sbccd.cc.ca.us
TILLOTSON, Christina ... 720-496-1370.. 80 C ctillotson@holmesinstitute.edu
TILLOTSON, James, R ... 515-964-0601 165 G tillotsonj@faith.edu
TILLOTSON, Jeanette ..... 607-778-5195 318 A tillotsonjo@sunybroome.edu
TILOT, Mary Jo .... 920-498-5409 500 F maryjo.tilot@nwtc.edu
TILSON, Heather .... 916-691-7144.. 50 G tilsonh@crc.losrios.edu
TILSON, Vincent .... 704-233-8011 344 G tilson@wingate.edu
TILSTRA, Doug .... 509-527-2511 485 H doug.tilstra@wallawalla.edu
TILTON, Abigail .... 940-898-3326 451 F atilton@twu.edu
TILTON, James .... 401-863-2721 404 E james_tilton@brown.edu
TIMBERLAKE, Gregory .. 419-755-4740 357 E gtimberlake@ncstatecollege.edu

TOLEDO LÓPEZ, Angel, A ... 787-257-7373 511 G atoledo@suagm.edu
TOLENO, Tristan ... 802-451-7510 462 E ttoleno@gradschool.marlboro.edu
TOLENTINO, Angelito ... 510-780-4500.. 47 J atolentino@lifewest.edu
TOLENTINO, Rafael ... 310-791-9975.. 45 E
TOLER, Terry ... 405-491-6314 370 A ttoler@snu.edu
TOLER, Whiting ... 252-940-6334 332 C whiting.toler@beaufortccc.edu
TOLES, Mellanie ... 937-328-6002 350 L tolesm@clarkstate.edu
TOLIA, Sam ... 708-456-0300 150 I stolia@triton.edu
TOLISANO, Joseph ... 860-723-0125.. 84 H tolidanoj@ct.edu
TOLIVER, Julietta ... 317-274-4009 156 F jtoliver@iupui.edu
TOLIVER-ROBERTS, Rita, J ... 215-670-9265 391 H rjtoliver@peirce.edu
TOLLE, Melissa ... 937-512-2259 361 A melissa.tolle@sinclair.edu
TOLLEFSON, Allen ... 530-752-5418.. 68 E jatollefson@ucdavis.edu
TOLLEFSON, Deborah ... 336-334-5702 343 A ddtollef@uncg.edu
TOLLEFSON, Elizabeth ... 218-281-8438 244 A ltollefs@umn.edu
TOLLEFSON, Leah ... 218-879-0813 238 A leah@fdltcc.edu
TOLLESON, Joanne, P ... 678-341-6640 121 B jtolleso@laniertech.edu
TOLLETT, Suzannne ... 501-450-1228.. 19 F tollett@hendrix.edu
TOLLEY, April ... 540-863-2808 474 D atolley@dslcc.edu
TOLLISON, Scott ... 662-329-7142 248 A cstollison@muw.edu
TOLLIVER, Beverly ... 334-386-7103.... 5 D btolliver@faulkner.edu
TOLLIVER, Joy ... 973-877-3260 277 I jtolliver@essex.edu
TOLLIVER, Madelyne ... 361-572-6400 457 E madelyne.tolliver@victoriacollege.edu
TOLLIVER, Margaret ... 214-887-5004 436 B mtolliver@dts.edu
TOLLIVER, Ona ... 903-565-5651 456 A otolliver@uttyler.edu
TOLLIVER, Rex ... 312-996-7655 151 B jrex@uic.edu
TOLOSA, Sara ... 787-728-1515 514 D sara.tolosa@sagrado.edu
TOLSMA, Robert ... 303-315-3701.. 83 C robert.tolsma@ucdenver.edu
TOLSON, Juliann ... 701-654-1000.. 32 B
TOLSON, Kedra ... 314-539-5141 259 C ktolson@stlcc.edu
TOLSON, Renae ... 850-201-6074 111 C tolsonr@tcc.fl.edu
TOLSTOY, Maya ... 212-854-8296 297 C mt290@columbia.edu
TOM, Keith ... 360-676-2772 482 D kjtom@nwic.edu
TOM, Marlene, K ... 415-422-2350.. 71 K mktom@usfca.edu
TOM, McAlister ... 843-953-7696 407 F mcalistert1@citadel.edu
TOM, Naomi ... 520-383-8401.. 16 D ntom@tocc.edu
TOM, Steven ... 866-492-5336 244 F steven.tom@laureate.net
TOM, Vicki ... 510-436-1520.. 45 D tom@hnu.edu
TOM-MIURA, Allison ... 310-287-4431.. 49 G tommiua@wlac.edu
TOMAN, Janelle ... 605-773-3455 416 G janelle.toman@sdbor.edu
TOMANEK, Jody ... 308-535-3624 267 K tomanekj@mpcc.edu
TOMANENG, Rowena, M ... 510-981-2850.. 56 E rtomaneng@peralta.edu
TOMANIO, David ... 352-588-8857 106 D david.tomanio@saintleo.edu
TOMANIO, David ... 561-297-3076 108 J tomaniod@fau.edu
TOMANY, Claudia ... 701-231-7033 345 G claudia.tomany@ndsu.edu
TOMARAS, Joseph ... 914-813-9271 315 F jtomaras@sarahlawrence.edu
TOMAS, Brad ... 706-419-1659 117 B brad.tomas@covenant.edu
TOMAS, Don, L ... 828-339-4242 338 B d_tomas@southwesterncc.edu
TOMASELLI, Gordon, F . 718-430-2000 289 G
TOMASIK, Paula, J ... 304-336-8340 490 F ptomasik@westliberty.edu
TOMASZEWSKI, Matthew ... 217-333-4866 151 D mat6@illinois.edu
TOMASZKIEWICZ, Ed ... 815-226-3372 147 G etomaszkiewicz@rockford.edu
TOMASZKIEWICZ, Teri .. 630-844-5511 132 D ttomaszk@aurora.edu
TOMBARGE, Chuck ... 612-625-8510 243 E tombarge@umn.edu
TOMBARGE, John ... 540-458-8134 478 A tombargej@wlu.edu
TOMBARI, Chris ... 303-340-7504.. 79 D chris.tombari@ccaurora.edu
TOMBERLIN, Daniel, D . 423-478-7713 423 G dtomberlin@ptseminary.edu
TOMBES, Robert, M ... 804-827-5600 473 F rtombes@vcu.edu
TOMBLESON, Shelly ... 719-336-1572.. 80 K shelly.tombleson@lamarcc.edu
TOMBLIN, John, S ... 316-978-5234 178 A john.tomblin@wichita.edu
TOMBLIN-BYRD, Terri, L ... 304-710-3472 489 B tomblin@mctc.edu
TOMCZAK, Patricia ... 217-228-5432 146 F tomczpa@quincy.edu
TOMCZAK, Timothy ... 585-345-6831 301 A tptomczak@genesee.edu
TOMCZYK, Christie, L ... 304-243-2304 491 I ctomczyk@wju.edu
TOMEK, Beverly ... 361-570-4145 453 C tomekb@uhv.edu
TOMES, Shawn ... 270-852-3203 183 A stomes@kwc.edu
TOMESCU, Cosmin ... 212-592-2718 315 H ctomescu@sva.edu
TOMFOHRDE, Tammy ... 423-869-6465 421 C tammy.tomfohrde@lmunet.edu
TOMHAVE, Brian ... 909-599-5433.. 47 K btomhave@lifepacific.edu
TOMLIN, Kathy, H ... 540-464-7323 476 G tomlinkh@vmi.edu
TOMLIN, Ross, L ... 503-842-8222 377 A rosstomlin@tillamookbaycc.edu
TOMLINSON, Ann ... 213-763-7040.. 49 E
TOMLINSON, Doug ... 972-883-2141 455 B douglas.tomlinson@utdallas.edu
TOMLINSON, Elise ... 907-796-6300.. 10 B emtomlinson@alaska.edu
TOMLINSON, Jan ... 740-364-9510 349 H tomlinson.88@cotc.edu
TOMLINSON, Jason ... 940-898-3505 451 F jtomlinson1@twu.edu
TOMLINSON, Jessica ... 207-699-5016 194 D jtomlinson@meca.edu
TOMLINSON, Karen ... 706-864-1948 126 A karen.tomlinson@ung.edu
TOMLINSON, Kathryn ... 229-259-5178 127 B kathryn.tomlinson@wiregrass.edu
TOMLINSON, Leslie ... 256-331-8040.... 3 C ltomlinson@nwscc.edu
TOMLINSON, Rob ... 573-840-9649 260 I rtomlinson@trcc.edu
TOMLINSON, Tim ... 865-938-8186 419 E tim.tomlinson@thecrowncollege.edu
TOMLINSON, Timothy ... 612-455-3420 234 D tim.tomlinson@bcsmn.edu
TOMLINSON, Virginia ... 503-883-2575 373 H vtomlins@linfield.edu
TOMMASIN, Jay ... 319-352-8251 170 C jay.tommasin@wartburg.edu
TOMMASINO, Joseph ... 631-665-1600 322 J joseph.tommasino@touro.edu
TOMMEY, Dale ... 870-574-4512.. 21 E dtommey@sautech.edu
TOMOSER, T. Paul ... 402-280-3026 266 I ptomoser@creighton.edu
TOMPKINS, Andy ... 316-978-3001 178 A presidentsoffice@wichita.edu
TOMPKINS, Anthony (Tony) ... 913-288-7150 174 F atompkins@kckcc.edu
TOMPKINS, OSB, John-Mary ... 724-805-2771 398 F johnmary.tompkins@stvincent.edu
TOMPKINS, Karen ... 978-232-2131 209 B ktompkin@endicott.edu
TOMPKINS, Michael ... 845-758-7523 290 G tompkins@bard.edu
TOMPKINS, Patrick ... 757-253-4880 476 A tompkinsp@tncc.edu
TOMPKINS, Perry ... 417-328-1488 259 L ptompkins@sbuniv.edu
TOMPKINS, Ricky ... 479-619-4325.. 20 D rtompkins1@nwacc.edu
TOMPKINS, Stefanie ... 303-273-3000.. 78 I stompkins@mines.edu
TOMPKINS, JR., Wendell ... 912-478-2586 119 C wtompkins@georgiasouthern.edu
TOMPKINS RIVAS, Pilar ... 323-260-8108.. 48 H tompkikp@elac.edu
TOMPOS, Betty ... 717-391-6947 399 G tomposb@stevenscollege.edu
TOMPOS, Mike ... 651-523-2800 236 A
TOMS, David, E ... 401-456-8803 405 C dtoms@ric.edu
TOMS, Debbie ... 605-718-2958 417 F deborah.toms@wdt.edu
TOMS, Lisa ... 479-968-0490.. 18 C ltoms@atu.edu
TOMS, Ozalle ... 262-472-4985 498 C tomso@uww.edu
TOMSHINSKY, Ida ... 305-821-3333.. 99 E itomshinsky@fnu.edu
TOMSO, Gregory ... 850-474-2934 110 E gtomso@uwf.edu
TONCHE, Carlos ... 718-862-7313 305 H ctonche01@manhattan.edu
TONCIC, JR., Andrew, A ... 724-458-2170 385 C aatoncic@gcc.edu
TONDER, Rick ... 701-777-4270 345 B rick.tonder@ndus.edu
TONDIGLIA, Dean ... 330-672-3111 354 J u347@police.kent.edu
TONDREAU, Rebecca ... 401-598-1000 404 I rtondreau@jwu.edu
TONELLI-BROWN, Judith ... 508-373-9719 206 B judith.tonellibrown@becker.edu
TONEV, Simon, T ... 610-330-5783 387 E tonevs@lafayette.edu
TONEY, Glenn ... 706-245-7226 117 E gtoney@ec.edu
TONEY, Jeffrey ... 908-737-7030 278 E jetoney@kean.edu
TONEY, Krystal ... 937-708-5760 364 D ktoney@wilberforce.edu
TONEY, Pamela ... 800-462-7845.. 78 N
TONEY, RJ ... 970-943-2312.. 84 D rjtoney@western.edu
TONG, Vincent ... 203-332-5220.. 85 F vtong@hcc.commnet.edu
TONG, Vincent, P ... 203-285-2415.. 85 E vtong@gwcc.commnet.edu
TONI, Keith ... 508-678-2811 213 G keith.toni@bristolcc.edu
TONKOWICH, Jonathan 307-332-2930 502 J jtonkowich@wyomingcatholic.edu
TONNESON, Julie, A ... 612-626-9278 243 E tonne001@umn.edu
TONONO, Hiroko ... 949-480-4116.. 64 B htonono@soka.edu
TONREY, Donna ... 215-951-3726 387 C tonrey@lasalle.edu
TONREY, Donna, A ... 215-991-3726 387 C tonrey@lasalle.edu
TOOEY, Mary, J ... 410-706-2693 202 D mjtooey@hshsl.umaryland.edu
TOOKE-RAWLINS, Dixie 540-231-6059 467 F dtrawlins@vcom.vt.edu
TOOKE-RAWLINS, Dixie 540-231-4000 467 F dtrawlins@vcom.vt.edu
TOOLE, Michael ... 419-530-8000 363 E michael.toole@utoledo.edu
TOOLE, Raymond, L ... 610-359-5330 382 C rtoole@dccc.edu
TOOLEY, Bren ... 309-341-7445 141 A bktooley@knox.edu
TOOLIN-WILSON, Cynthia ... 860-632-3001.. 87 C ctoolin@holyapostles.edu
TOOMEY, Marcia, D ... 978-232-2060 209 B mtoomey@endicott.edu
TOOMEY, Richard, J ... 812-237-2510 155 G richard.toomey@indstate.edu
TOOMS CYPRES, Autumn ... 205-975-0131.... 8 A cypresa@uab.edu
TOOMSEN, Corbett ... 414-847-3335 494 F corbetttoomsen@miad.edu
TOON, Kellie ... 865-539-7245 425 F kltoon@pstcc.edu
TOONE, Eric ... 919-681-3484 328 G eric.toone@duke.edu
TOONE, Rachel ... 828-669-8012 331 J rachel.toone@montreat.edu
TOONG, Kenneth, K ... 413-545-1504 211 D ktoong@mail.aux.umass.edu
TOOSI, Mori ... 863-297-1000 105 A mtoosi@polk.edu
TOOT, G. David ... 607-871-2171 289 H tootgd@alfred.edu
TOOTHMAN, Charles ... 434-797-8409 474 E charles.toothman@danville.edu
TOOTOONCHI, Ahmad .. 509-828-1224 480 E tootoonchi@ewu.edu
TOPHAM, Susan ... 619-388-2795.. 60 D stopham@sdccd.edu
TOPIC, Milos ... 201-761-7827 282 I mtopic@saintpeters.edu
TOPLIFF, Donald, R ... 325-942-2165 451 A don.topliff@angelo.edu
TOPOLSKI, Virginia ... 201-559-6055 278 A topolskiv@felician.edu
TOPOUSIS, Dana ... 530-752-9841.. 68 E dtopousis@ucdavis.edu
TOPP, Joelle ... 517-371-5140 233 A toppj@cooley.edu
TOPPE, Michele ... 503-725-4422 376 A toppem@pdx.edu
TOPPER, David ... 717-477-1124 395 E datopp@ship.edu
TOPPER, Maria, L ... 301-447-5211 200 E mtopper@msmary.edu
TOPPIN, Ian ... 404-225-4502 114 H itoppin@atlantatech.edu
TOPPLE, Dianne ... 518-828-4181 297 B dianne.topple@sunycgcc.edu
TOPSHE, Joyce ... 860-685-3757.. 89 C jtopshe@wesleyan.edu
TORAIN, Wes ... 256-306-2965.... 1 F wes.torain@calhoun.edu
TORBET, Linda ... 734-384-4245 227 G ltorbet@monroeccc.edu
TORBITZKY, Nichole ... 636-949-4651 254 F ntorbitzky@lindenwood.edu
TORCHIA, Richard ... 215-572-2131 379 A torchia@arcadia.edu
TORCZON, Virginia, J ... 757-221-3460 466 C vjtorc@wm.edu
TORDELLA, Tina ... 304-243-2081 491 I ttordella@wju.edu
TORGERSON, Jane ... 817-257-7940 448 G j.torgerson@tcu.edu
TORGUSON, Kirsten ... 909-607-9313.. 37 G kirsten_torguson@kgi.edu
TORIBIO, Jina ... 607-962-9232 320 F jtoribio@corning-cc.edu
TORINO, Frank ... 212-659-7200 304 B ftorino@tkc.edu
TORKELSON, Rick ... 310-954-4348.. 52 G rtorkelson@msmu.edu
TORMEY, Susan ... 315-498-2764 311 B tormeys@sunyocc.edu
TORNABENE, Meredith . 315-445-4185 304 C tornabmm@lemoyne.edu
TORNO, Keith ... 616-222-3000 226 C itdirector@kuyper.edu
TORNQUIST, Kristi ... 605-688-5106 417 C kristi.tornquist@sdstate.edu
TORNQUIST, Susan ... 541-737-6943 375 D susan.tornquist@oregonstate.edu
TORNQUIST, Wade ... 734-487-0042 223 H wtornquis@emich.edu
TORO, Dan ... 619-849-2571.. 57 E dantoro@pointloma.edu
TORO, Elba ... 787-878-5475 508 L etoro@arecibo.inter.edu
TORO, Sofia ... 909-607-0121.. 37 G sofia_toro@kgi.edu
TORO, Zulma, R ... 860-832-3000.. 84 I toro@ccsu.edu
TORO-ZAPATA, Rogelio 787-264-1912 509 F rtoro@intersg.edu
TOROK, Kate, M ... 585-385-3801 314 A ktorok@sjfc.edu
TOROS, Orkun ... 972-883-4735 455 B ont130030@utdallas.edu
TOROSYAN, Roben ... 508-531-2435 212 B roben.torosyan@bridgew.edu

TRACEY, CM,
Bernard, M .... 718-990-6570 314 B
traceyb@stjohns.edu
TRACEY, Kevin, J .... 516-562-3467 299 B
ktracey@northwell.edu
TRACEY, Nicole .... 215-968-8152 379 G
nicole.tracey@bucks.edu
TRACEY, Patrick .... 401-739-5000 405 A
ptracey@neit.edu
TRACHIAN, Barkev .... 336-725-8344 339 F
trachianb@piedmontu.edu
TRACHTE, Kent, C .... 570-321-4101 389 E
trachte@lycoming.edu
TRACHTENBERG,
Fay, R .... 215-204-7405 399 F
fay.trachtenberg@temple.edu
TRACIA, Michele .... 603-623-0313 273 I
micheletracia@nhia.edu
TRACY, Alessa, R .... 574-372-5100 155 B
alessa.smith@grace.edu
TRACY, Christine .... 217-228-5432 146 F
tracych@quincyu.edu
TRACY, Danielle .... 567-661-7434 360 B
danielle_tracy@owens.edu
TRACY, Dominick .... 415-703-9500.. 28 D
dtracy@cca.edu
TRACY, II, Edward .... 313-993-1554 231 B
tracyeg@udmercy.edu
TRACY, Michael .... 229-931-2245 119 D
michael.tracy@gsw.edu
TRACY, Sandra, G .... 901-843-3800 423 J
tracy@rhodes.edu
TRACY, Susan .... 641-472-7000 167 F
stracy@mum.edu
TRACZYK, Joyce .... 763-433-1243 237 C
joyce.traczyk@anokaramsey.edu
TRAFECANTE, Michael ... 203-254-4000.. 86 I
mtrafecante@fairfield.edu
TRAFFIE, Timothy, S ...... 651-696-6200 236 H
ttraffie@macalester.edu
TRAFTON, Nancy, J ...... 812-941-2676 157 B
ntrafton@ius.edu
TRAGESER, Susan .... 540-831-5433 470 C
strageser@radford.edu
TRAGNI, Carolyn .... 845-451-1615 298 A
carolyn.tragni@culinary.edu
TRAHAN, Kelly .... 610-799-1164 388 I
ktrahan@lccc.edu
TRAHAN, Lisa .... 518-276-8022 312 I
trahanl@rpi.edu
TRAHAN, Shelia .... 409-984-6239 450 B
trahansc@lamarpa.edu
TRAIN, Larissa .... 480-423-6300.. 13 H
larissa.train@scottsdalecc.edu
TRAINA, Joyce .... 201-327-8877 277 H
jtraina@eastwick.edu
TRAINA, Michael .... 614-882-2551 353 A
TRAINA, Samuel .... 209-228-2857.. 69 B
straina@ucmerced.edu
TRAINER, James, F .... 610-519-7578 402 D
james.trainer@villanova.edu
TRAINI, Kristen .... 860-701-5027.. 87 D
traini_k@mitchell.edu
TRAINOR, David, P .... 617-552-3335 207 B
david.trainor.2@bc.edu
TRAINOR, Hope .... 563-425-5264 170 A
trainorh@uiu.edu
TRAINOR, Jane .... 815-836-5887 141 G
trainorja@lewisu.edu
TRAINOR, Kelly .... 704-330-6017 333 D
kelly.trainor@cpcc.edu
TRAINOR, Timothy, E .... 301-447-5600 200 E
president@msmary.edu
TRAKTMAN, Paula .... 843-876-2405 410 F
traktman@musc.edu
TRAME, Michelle .... 217-333-7542 151 D
mtrame@illinois.edu
TRAME, Mike .... 217-351-2551 146 C
mtrame@parkland.edu
TRAMMEL, Sheila .... 318-257-2235 191 F
strammel@latech.edu
TRAMMELL, C. David ..... 859-858-3511 178 I
david.trammell@asbury.edu
TRAMMELL, Nicole .... 509-453-0374 483 C
nicole.trammell@perrytech.edu
TRAMONTANO, William 718-997-5550 295 C
qcpres@qc.cuny.edu
TRAMONTE, Michael ..... 713-500-3158 456 B
michael.tramonte@uth.tmc.edu
TRAN, SVD, Bang .... 563-876-3353 164 J
btran@dwci.edu
TRAN, Christy .... 951-763-0500.. 54 H

TRAN, Hanh .... 818-778-5959.. 49 F
tranh@lavc.edu
TRAN, Hieu .... 916-686-8484.. 29 J
TRAN, Kim, H .... 773-995-2427 133 K
ktran21@csu.edu
TRAN, Lena .... 408-288-3180.. 61 M
lena.tran@sjcc.edu
TRAN, Mai-Anh, L .... 847-866-3904 137 E
maianh.tran@garrett.edu
TRAN, My .... 425-564-5710 478 F
my.tran@bellevuecollege.edu
TRAN, My Linh .... 773-907-4770 134 C
mtran@ccc.edu
TRAN, Nathanael .... 951-763-0500.. 54 H
TRAN, Nu .... 303-352-6099.. 79 E
nu.tran@ccd.edu
TRAN, Sheena .... 714-628-4836.. 58 A
tran_sheena@sccollege.edu
TRAN, Song-Ho .... 408-274-7900.. 61 L
ho.tran@evc.edu
TRAN, Veronique .... 281-425-6867 439 D
vtran@lee.edu
TRANA, Steve .... 402-486-2502 269 F
steve.trana@ucollege.edu
TRANDAHL, Pamela ...... 303-494-7988.. 76 K
TRANQUADA, Jim .... 323-259-2990.. 54 E
jtranqua@oxy.edu
TRANSUE, Cynthia .... 215-489-2905 382 D
cynthia.transue@delval.edu
TRANSUE, Mary .... 706-802-5457 118 E
mtransue@highlands.edu
TRANT, Rachel .... 508-626-4523 212 D
rtrant@framingham.edu
TRANT, Sid, J .... 205-348-7380.... 7 F
sjtrant@uasystem.edu
TRAPANICK,
Benjamin, J .... 508-626-4505 212 D
btrapanick@framingham.edu
TRAPASSO, Kristen, P ... 315-445-4265 304 C
trapaskp@lemoyne.edu
TRAPP, Daniel .... 313-883-8540 229 K
trapp.daniel@shms.edu
TRAPP, Lori .... 734-973-3529 232 B
ltrapp@wccnet.edu
TRAPP, Ray .... 336-334-7940 341 F
rtrapp@ncat.edu
TRAPP, Rodney .... 202-274-5930.. 93 C
rodney.trapp@udc.edu
TRASK, III, Tallman ...... 919-684-6600 328 G
t3@duke.edu
TRASKA, Anthony .... 216-687-2020 351 B
a.traska@csuohio.edu
TRAUB, Gilbert .... 718-409-7385 321 C
gtraub@sunymaritime.edu
TRAUBE, David .... 304-357-0014 488 G
davidtraube@ucwv.edu
TRAUBE, Eve .... 212-410-8006 309 B
etraube@nycpm.edu
TRAUGH, Cecelia .... 212-875-4668 290 F
ctraugh@bankstreet.edu
TRAUPMAN-CARR,
Carol .... 610-861-1348 391 A
traupman-carrc@moravian.edu
TRAUSCH, Diane, M ...... 312-261-3230 144 F
diane.trausch@nl.edu
TRAUTH, Denise, M ...... 512-245-2121 450 E
president@txstate.edu
TRAUTMAN, Karla .... 605-688-4792 417 C
karla.trautman@sdstate.edu
TRAUTMAN, Stewart ...... 352-854-2322.. 96 O
trautmas@cf.edu
TRAUTWEILER,
Courtney .... 471-667-8181 252 A
ctrautweiler@cottey.edu
TRAVENICK, Ron .... 707-638-5342.. 67 F
ron.travenick@tu.edu
TRAVENY, Carol .... 267-502-2547 379 D
carol.traveny@brynathyn.edu
TRAVER, William .... 518-458-5337 296 H
traverw@strose.edu
TRAVERNICHT, Marcia .. 585-475-7292 313 A
mstwml@rit.edu
TRAVERS, Lesley .... 307-532-8202 502 A
lesley.travers@ewc.wy.edu
TRAVERS, Nan .... 518-587-2100 321 A
nan.travers@esc.edu
TRAVERSE, Marshall ..... 425-558-0299 480 D
mtraverse@digipen.edu
TRAVERSO, Susan .... 724-589-2100 399 H
straverso@thiel.edu
TRAVIS, Annie .... 662-252-8093 248 G
atravis@rustcollege.edu

TRAVIS, Antonio .... 404-756-4023 114 G
atravis@atlm.edu
TRAVIS, Artie, L .... 301-860-3391 203 C
atravis@bowiestate.edu
TRAVIS, Brittany .... 718-779-1499 311 I
btravis@plazacollege.edu
TRAVIS, David .... 715-425-3700 497 E
david.travis@uwrf.edu
TRAVIS, Delite .... 714-289-2062.. 36 C
dtravis@chapman.edu
TRAVIS, Frederick .... 641-472-1209 167 F
ftravis@mum.edu
TRAVIS, Heather .... 515-271-3710 165 A
heather.travis@drake.edu
TRAVIS, Rick .... 662-325-2646 247 F
travis@ps.msstate.edu
TRAVIS, Scott .... 616-395-7251 225 B
travis@hope.edu
TRAVIS, Scott .... 810-762-7482 225 H
stravis@kettering.edu
TRAVIS, Sonny .... 319-399-8622 164 A
stravis@coe.edu
TRAVIS, Theresa .... 610-499-4123 403 B
ttravis@widener.edu
TRAVIS, Thomas .... 210-299-8501 504 B
thomas.travis@usuhs.edu
TRAVIS-TEAGUE,
Dianne .... 805-969-3626.. 55 E
dtravis-teague@pacifica.edu
TRAVISANO, Jacqueline 305-284-6100 112 E
jtravisano@miami.edu
TRAWEEK, Vicki .... 817-598-6218 458 A
vtraweek@wc.edu
TRAWICK, Rebecca .... 909-652-6493.. 36 A
rebecca.trawick@chaffey.edu
TRAWICK, Travis .... 817-923-1921 445 B
ttrawick@swbts.edu
TRAXLER, Pete .... 907-796-6139.. 10 B
pbtraxler@alaska.edu
TRAXLER, Roxy .... 507-389-7470 241 C
roxy.traxler@southcentral.edu
TRAXLER, Suzanne .... 715-232-2501 498 A
traxlers@uwstout.edu
TRAYLOR, Angela .... 502-895-3411 183 D
atraylor@lpts.edu
TRAYNOR, Thomas, L .... 937-775-4859 364 I
thomas.traynor@wright.edu
TRAYSTMAN, Richard .... 303-724-8155.. 83 C
richard.traystman@ucdenver.edu
TREACY, Margaret .... 845-569-3355 307 J
margaret.treacy@msmc.edu
TREADWAY, Chris .... 304-558-1112 489 O
chris.treadway@wvhepc.edu
TREADWELL, Andrew .... 772-462-4804 101 E
atreadwe@irsc.edu
TREADWELL, Larry .... 919-546-8539 340 E
larry.treadwell@shawu.edu
TREADWELL, Melinda ... 603-358-2000 275 A
president@keene.edu
TREAGER-HUBER,
Carey .... 317-921-4882 157 G
ctreagerhuber@ivytech.edu
TREANOR, Ellen .... 657-278-4475.. 31 E
etreanor@fullerton.edu
TREANOR, Laura .... 812-888-4262 162 C
provost@vinu.edu
TREANOR, William, M .. 202-662-9030.. 92 A
wtreanor@georgetown.edu
TREAT, Cindy .... 817-461-8741 430 H
ctreat@abu.edu
TREAT, Tod .... 509-682-6605 486 E
ttreat@wvc.edu
TREBER, Karen, A .... 410-548-2330 203 F
katreber@salisbury.edu
TREBIAN, Paul, F .... 800-567-2344 492 G
ptrebian@menominee.edu
TRECARTIN, Ralph .... 269-471-3622 221 B
rtrecartin@andrews.edu
TRECHTER, Sara .... 530-898-4767.. 31 A
strechter@csuchico.edu
TREDENNICK, Linda ...... 509-313-6790 481 D
tredennick@gonzaga.edu
TREDUP, Fred .... 702-895-3201 271 E
fred.tredup@unlv.edu
TREECE, Richard .... 661-763-7768.. 66 J
rtreece@taftcollege.edu
TREECE, T. Gerald .... 713-646-1776 444 B
gtreece@stcl.edu
TREFF, Shaya .... 732-370-3360 285 E
TREFF, Yisroel Meir ...... 732-370-3360 285 E
TREFT, Paul .... 712-274-5221 168 B
treft@morningside.edu

TREFZ, Steve, A .... 605-336-6588 416 E
strefz@sfseminary.edu
TREGEMBO, Tara .... 906-932-4231 224 B
tarat@gogebic.edu
TREJO, Alanna .... 805-437-2757.. 30 F
alanna.trejo@csuci.edu
TREJO, Cristina .... 956-665-3281 455 D
cristina.trejo@utrgv.edu
TREKELL, Eric .... 425-388-9273 480 G
etrekell@everettcc.edu
TRELLES, Sofia .... 305-348-2797 109 A
sofia.trelles@fiu.edu
TRELSTAD-PORTER,
James .... 612-330-1686 233 K
porter@augsburg.edu
TREMBLAY, Britni .... 785-243-1435 172 F
btremblay@cloud.edu
TREMBLAY, Matthew ..... 858-784-8469.. 63 F
TREMBLAY, Michael .... 518-292-7702 313 D
trembm3@sage.edu
TREMBLAY, Pamela ...... 706-880-8313 121 A
ptremblay@lagrange.edu
TREMBLAY, Paul .... 212-410-8142 309 B
ptremblay@nycpm.edu
TREMBLAY, Rocky .... 203-285-2185.. 85 E
rtremblay@gwcc.commnet.edu
TREMBLE, Gayle .... 843-525-8293 412 H
gtremble@tcl.edu
TREME, Jeremy .... 318-487-7386 186 I
jeremy.treme@lacollege.edu
TREMER, Tom .... 315-279-5672 304 A
ttremer@keuka.edu
TREML, Colleen .... 216-397-1595 354 I
ctreml@jcu.edu
TRENGOVE, Matthew ..... 831-770-6854.. 44 K
mtrengove@hartnell.edu
TRENIS, Neva, S .... 540-654-1055 472 I
ntrenis@umw.edu
TRENKLE, Lizza .... 254-659-7601 437 G
ltrenkle@hillcollege.edu
TRENT, Dietra, Y .... 703-993-2271 467 L
dtrent@gmu.edu
TRENT, Malissa .... 423-354-2521 425 E
mbtrent@northeaststate.edu
TRENT-BROWN, Sonja .. 616-395-6829 225 B
trentbrown@hope.edu
TRENTACOSTE, Peter ..... 740-593-4090 359 G
trentaco@ohio.edu
TRENTHEM, Richard ...... 901-843-3890 423 J
trenthem@rhodes.edu
TRENUM, Gary .... 301-687-3174 203 E
gtrenum@frostburg.edu
TREPAC, Letisha .... 309-298-2005 152 D
lk-trepac@wiu.edu
TREPAL, Michael, J ...... 212-410-8067 309 B
mtrepal@nycpm.edu
TREROTOLA,
Michael, R .... 718-817-3185 300 E
trerotola@fordham.edu
TRESOLINI, Carol .... 919-962-3907 342 D
carol_tresolini@unc.edu
TRESSEL, James, P .... 330-941-3101 365 C
jptressel@ysu.edu
TRESSLER-GELOK,
Thomas .... 718-390-3420 324 F
thomas.gelok@wagner.edu
TRETHEWEY, Angela ..... 530-898-4015.. 31 A
atrethewey@csuchico.edu
TRETTER, April .... 502-272-7329 179 B
atretter@bellarmine.edu
TREUNER, Mary .... 660-596-7249 260 D
mtreuner@sfccmo.edu
TREUR, Rick, J .... 616-526-8442 222 A
edt4@calvin.edu
TREUTING, Mary .... 318-473-6482 188 J
maryt@lsua.edu
TREVENEN, Anne .... 617-243-2438 210 G
atrevenen@lasell.edu
TREVETT-SMITH,
Matthew .... 302-831-8537.. 90 F
mtrevett@udel.edu
TREVINO, Crispin .... 361-593-4036 447 D
crispin.trevino@tamuk.edu
TREVINO, Cynthia .... 806-291-3401 457 J
trevinoc@wbu.edu
TREVINO, Leonard .... 412-365-1650 381 C
ltrevino@chatham.edu
TREVINO, Monica .... 405-224-3140 371 D
mtrevino@usao.edu
TREVINO, Nicole, G ...... 512-428-1037 442 M
nicoleg@stedwards.edu
TREVINO, Oscar .... 802-831-1348 463 G
otrevino@vermontlaw.edu

TREVIS, Michael ... 310-660-3101 .. 41 L mtrevis@elcamino.edu
TREVISAN, Michael ... 509-335-4853 486 A trevisan@wsu.edu
TREVISANI, Gary ... 267-295-2313 397 F gtrevisani@walnuthillcollege.edu
TREVOR, Tyler ... 406-449-9145 263 K ttrevor@montana.edu
TREWERN, Jay, S ... 978-468-7111 209 G jtrewern@gcts.edu
TREXLER, William, H ... 814-886-6421 391 B wtrexler@mtaloy.edu
TREZEVANT, Latitia ... 803-822-3597 410 G trezevantl@midlandstech.edu
TREZZA, Frank ... 240-567-5031 200 C frank.trezza@montgomerycollege.edu
TRI, Sandjaya ... 714-535-3886 .. 64 D santri@southbaylo.edu
TRIANA, Caridad ... 305-442-6011 105 F
TRIANTIS, Alexander ... 410-234-9214 199 D atriantis@jhu.edu
TRIANTIS, Alexander, J . 301-405-2308 202 C atriantis@rhsmith.umd.edu
TRIBBLE, Abby ... 417-455-5618 252 D abbytribble@crowder.edu
TRIBBLE, Amy ... 217-479-7007 142 I amy.tribble@mac.edu
TRIBBLE, Jeffery ... 404-687-4586 116 H tribblej@ctsnet.edu
TRIBBLE, Judy ... 812-535-5255 160 B jtribble@smwc.edu
TRIBBLE, Shannon, R ... 919-267-1640 330 B
TRIBBLE, William ... 425-564-3343 478 F william.tribble@bellevuecollege.edu
TRIBLE, JR., Paul, S ... 757-594-7002 466 B ptrible@cnu.edu
TRIBUNE, Lucreta ... 601-877-4713 244 H lctribune@alcorn.edu
TRICE, Matt ... 229-430-6618 113 I mtrice@albanytech.edu
TRICHE, Casie ... 985-448-4077 192 B casie.triche@nicholls.edu
TRICHE, Ellery ... 951-827-6345 .. 69 C ellery.triche@ucr.edu
TRIER, Vicki ... 406-247-3003 264 E vicki.trier@msubillings.edu
TRIERWEILER, John, K . 585-475-4727 313 A jktcmo@rit.edu
TRIETLEY, Rick ... 608-796-3801 498 N rctrietley@viterbo.edu
TRIEZENBERG, Steven, J ... 616-234-5708 231 H
TRIGALO, Ophir ... 312-567-3290 139 B trigalo@iit.edu
TRIGG, Debra ... 510-723-6716 .. 35 O dtrigg@chabotcollege.edu
TRIGG, Latokia ... 864-592-4158 412 F triggl@sccsc.edu
TRIGG, Mary ... 848-932-8420 282 A trigg@womenstudies.rutgers.edu
TRIGGER, Kelly ... 301-846-2518 198 E ktrigger@frederick.edu
TRIHUS, Meg ... 972-708-7379 435 H dean-students@diu.edu
TRIMBLE, Ashtin ... 309-796-5143 132 G trimblea@bhc.edu
TRIMBLE, LaDonna ... 661-722-6300 .. 26 D ltrimble@avc.edu
TRIMBLE, Lisa ... 307-778-1603 502 D lisatrimble@lcccfoundation.edu
TRIMBLE, Michele ... 406-874-6305 263 I trimblem@milescc.edu
TRIMBOLI, James ... 716-614-6202 310 C trimboli@niagaracc.suny.edu
TRINIDAD, Angel ... 787-878-5475 508 L atrinidad@arecibo.inter.edu
TRINIDAD, Vanessa ... 787-884-6000 508 D vtrinidad@icprjc.edu
TRINIDAD, Ysabel ... 805-437-8877 .. 30 F ysabel.trinidad@csuci.edu
TRINN, Dune ... 858-653-3000 .. 29 I dtrinn@calmu.edu
TRINOSKEY, Jessica ... 317-955-6730 158 U jtrinoskey@marian.edu
TRIOLO, John ... 718-631-6320 295 D jtriolo@qcc.cuny.edu
TRIPATHI, Satish, K ... 716-645-2901 316 F president@buffalo.edu
TRIPODI, Michael, A ... 201-684-6975 280 H mtripodi@rmapo.edu
TRIPOVICH, Maria ... 409-944-1303 437 B mtripovich@gc.edu
TRIPP, Susan ... 315-866-0300 301 G trippsk@herkimer.edu
TRIPP, Susan ... 870-612-2053 .. 22 I susan.tripp@uaccb.edu
TRIPP, Vanessa ... 252-789-0293 335 H vanessa.tripp@martincc.edu
TRIPPETT, William ... 262-472-1130 498 C trippetw@uww.edu
TRIPSAS, Zachary ... 617-585-0200 206 F zachary.tripsas@the-bac.edu
TRIPURANENI, Vinaya, L ... 909-593-3511 .. 70 D vtripuraneni@laverne.edu
TRISLER, Chad ... 239-590-7904 108 K ctrisler@fgcu.edu
TRITLE, Candice ... 717-691-6024 390 E ctritle@messiah.edu
TRITT, Lindsey ... 731-424-3520 425 B ltritt2@jscc.edu
TRIVEDI, Kalpen ... 413-545-2710 211 D ktrivedi@ipo.umass.edu
TRIVEDI, Sara ... 310-568-6105 .. 50 J strivedi@lmu.edu
TRIVUNOVICH, Nick ... 813-974-7220 110 B ntrivuno@usf.edu
TRNKA, Kathryn ... 773-371-5445 133 E ktrnka@ctu.edu
TROCHIM, Shawn ... 254-299-8811 440 A strochim@mclennan.edu
TROCHUCK, Mike ... 708-239-4836 150 F mike.trochuck@trnty.edu
TROENDLE, Laura ... 909-621-8243 .. 56 J laura_troendle@pitzer.edu
TROGDON, Joel ... 336-633-0200 337 A
TROGISCH, Colleen, M . 845-431-8974 298 E trogisch@sunydutchess.edu
TROHA, James, A ... 814-641-3101 386 H trohaj@juniata.edu
TROIANO, Sandra ... 518-381-1422 315 G toiansm@sunysccc.edu
TROILO, David ... 212-938-5658 320 B dtroilo@sunyopt.edu
TROISI, Kenneth ... 678-603-0981 124 G ken.troisi@sctech.edu
TROJAN, John ... 908-526-1200 281 A john.trojan@raritanval.edu
TROKA, Tonya ... 708-237-5050 145 E ttroka@nc.edu
TROMBELLA, Jerry ... 973-596-5642 279 F jerry.trombella@njit.edu
TROMBETTI, Nicholas ... 304-829-7255 487 G ntrombetti@bethanywv.edu
TROMBLEY, Robert ... 518-562-4219 296 B robert.trombley@clinton.edu
TROMBLY, Robert ... 480-219-6081 250 A rtrombly@atsu.edu
TROMP, Katherine ... 941-782-5466 388 A ktromp@lecom.edu
TROMP, Marcus ... 800-867-2243 .. 54 J mtromp@pacific-college.edu
TROMP, Marlene ... 208-426-1491 129 I president@boisestate.edu
TRONCOSO-FERNANDEZ, Keina ... 787-763-6700 508 A registro@se-pr.edu
TROOP, Michael ... 501-882-8920 .. 17 F mltroop@asub.edu
TROPELLO, Paula ... 239-489-9300 100 A
TROPP, Judybeth ... 619-961-4319 .. 67 E jtropp@tjsl.edu
TROSPER, Ryan ... 719-384-6886 .. 81 E ryan.trosper@ojc.edu
TROST, Patricia, G ... 708-709-3637 146 D ptrost@prairiestate.edu
TROSTLE, Libby ... 410-386-8107 197 G ltrostle@carrollcc.edu
TROTMAN, Sarah ... 281-487-1170 448 F strotman@txchiro.edu
TROTT, Garrett ... 503-375-7016 373 A gtrott@corban.edu
TROTTA, Carianne ... 518-381-1176 315 G trottac@sunysccc.edu
TROTTA, Neil ... 617-236-8867 209 D ntrotta@fisher.edu
TROTTER, Cheryl ... 704-461-6714 327 A cheryltrotter@bac.edu
TROTTER, Wauntia ... 870-575-8736 .. 22 E trotterw@uapb.edu
TROTTIER, Sheila ... 701-477-7862 347 A strottier@tm.edu
TROTTIER, Tracey ... 413-755-4057 215 F tatrottier@stcc.edu
TROUGAKOS, Nick ... 405-945-9196 368 E nick.trougakos@osuokc.edu
TROUP, Calvin, L ... 724-847-6610 384 G cltroup@geneva.edu
TROUP, Pat ... 251-981-3771 .... 5 B pat.troup@columbiasouthern.edu
TROUP, Patrick ... 612-659-6707 238 I patrick.troup@minneapolis.edu
TROUP, Wendy ... 251-981-3771 .... 5 B wendy.troup@columbiasouthern.edu
TROUPE, Bonnie, L ... 508-565-1069 218 H btroupe@stonehill.edu
TROUT, Darice ... 847-925-6070 137 H dtrout@harpercollege.edu
TROUT, Sarah ... 757-340-2121 465 M bursarcvab@centura.edu
TROUTMAN, Linda ... 850-478-8496 104 G ltroutman@pcci.edu
TROUTMAN, Matthew ... 301-696-3577 199 B troutman@hood.edu
TROUTMAN, Todd ... 810-762-0409 228 C todd.troutman@mcc.edu
TROUTT, Amy ... 618-545-3048 140 E atroutt@kaskaskia.edu
TROUTWINE, Jason ... 765-973-8444 156 C jtroutwi@iue.edu
TROVADA, Edgar ... 310-577-3000 .. 75 G financialaid@yosan.edu
TROWBRIDGE, Christian, A ... 302-295-1151 .. 90 I christian.a.trowbridge@wilmu.edu
TROWBRIDGE, Cory, D . 316-322-0110 250 K cory.trowbridge@calvary.edu
TROWBRIDGE, Lori ... 402-844-7733 268 J loriv@northeast.edu
TROXELL, Jeffrey, E ... 610-330-5330 387 E troxellj@lafayette.edu
TROY, Dan ... 805-546-3120 .. 41 A daniel_troy1@cuesta.edu
TROY, Roberta ... 334-727-8164 .... 7 D rtroy@tuskegee.edu
TROYER, Brian ... 414-288-7004 494 B brian.troyer@marquette.edu
TROYER, Cindy ... 903-566-7461 456 A ctroyer@uttyler.edu
TROYER, Mark, R ... 859-858-3511 178 I mark.troyer@asbury.edu
TROYER, Melissa ... 574-296-6229 152 I mtroyer@ambs.edu
TROYER, Melissa ... 402-437-2619 269 C mtroyer@southeast.edu
TROZPEK, Robin ... 909-621-8192 .. 57 F robin.trozpek@pomona.edu
TRUAX, Jermaine, M ... 570-577-2000 379 F jermaine.truax@bucknell.edu
TRUBE, Nancy ... 805-493-3755 .. 29 H ntrube@callutheran.edu
TRUCHAN, Thomas ... 201-559-6094 278 A
TRUCKENMILLER, Greg . 518-736-3622 300 F gtrucken@fmcc.suny.edu
TRUDEAU, Mary, L ... 701-788-4754 345 E mary.trudeau@mayvillestate.edu
TRUDEAU, Sara, L ... 202-526-3799 .. 92 F strudeau@johnpaulii.edu
TRUDEAU, Scott ... 248-204-3852 226 G strudeau@ltu.edu
TRUDEAU, Skip ... 765-998-5368 160 F sktrudeau@taylor.edu
TRUDNOWSKI, Dan ... 406-496-4681 265 A dtrudnowski@mtech.edu
TRUE, Christopher, J ... 240-895-4317 201 E cjtrue@smcm.edu
TRUE, Elizabeth ... 207-326-0159 195 D elizabeth.true@mma.edu
TRUE, Shannon, M ... 850-245-0466 108 H shannon.mcdermott@flbog.edu
TRUEBLOOD, Dianne ... 229-931-2354 124 D dtrueblood@southgatech.edu
TRUEBLOOD, Marjorie .. 651-696-6210 236 H mtrueblo@macalester.edu
TRUELOVE, Bobby ... 205-652-3601 .... 9 A bjt@uwa.edu
TRUELOVE, James ... 620-235-4517 176 F jtruelove@pittstate.edu
TRUFANT, Jason ... 662-329-7962 248 A jmtrufant@muw.edu
TRUFANT, Nicole ... 207-602-2157 196 G ntrufant@une.edu
TRUFFIN, Sherry ... 910-814-5598 327 E truffins@campbell.edu
TRUHE, Amy ... 785-227-3380 171 E truheal@bethanylb.edu
TRUHLAR, Mary, R ... 631-632-8950 317 D mary.truhlar@stonybrookmedicine.edu
TRUITT, Jennifer ... 217-228-5432 146 F truitje@quincy.edu
TRUJILLO, Daniel ... 914-395-2252 315 F dtrujillo@sarahlawrence.edu
TRUJILLO, George ... 301-985-7283 203 B george.trujillo@umuc.edu
TRUJILLO, Patricia ... 505-747-5448 287 G patriciatrujillo@nnmc.edu
TRUJILLO, Susan ... 310-287-4406 .. 49 G trujilos@wlac.edu
TRUJILLO, Tamara ... 707-638-5317 .. 67 F tamara.trujillo@tu.edu
TRUJILLO, Wendy ... 661-362-3447 .. 38 H wendy.trujillo@canyons.edu
TRUJILLO-MARTINEZ, Geraldine ... 719-549-2054 .. 79 A g.trujillomartinez@csupueblo.edu
TRULEN, Alyssa ... 503-255-0332 374 D alyssatrulen@multnomah.edu
TRULL, Gregory ... 503-588-2722 373 A gtrull@corban.edu
TRULL, Jason ... 334-347-2623 .... 2 A jtrull@escc.edu
TRULOVE, Milyon ... 503-777-7510 376 C milyon.trulove@reed.edu
TRUMAN, Kevin, Z ... 816-235-2399 261 C trumank@umkc.edu
TRUMBLE, Jeremy ... 315-781-3806 302 A trumble@hws.edu
TRUMBO, Joelle ... 478-387-4775 118 G jtrumbo@gmc.edu
TRUMBOWER, Jeffrey ... 802-654-2216 463 B jtrumbower@smcvt.edu
TRUMP, A.J ... 732-255-0400 280 A atrump@ocean.edu
TRUMP, Aaron, C ... 812-492-7504 161 E aaron.trump@usi.edu
TRUMPETER, Kevin ... 803-255-4782 406 F ktrumpeter@allenuniversity.edu
TRUMPOWER, Peter ... 330-494-6170 361 F ptrumpower@starkstate.edu
TRUNK, Dunja ... 973-748-9000 276 A dunja_trunk@bloomfield.edu
TRUNK, Peter ... 973-761-9731 283 B peter.trunk@shu.edu
TRUONG, Chris ... 714-564-6043 .. 57 L truong_chris@sac.edu
TRUONG, Dan ... 212-472-1500 309 I dtruong@nysid.edu
TRUONG, Lan ... 650-949-7823 .. 43 D truonglan@foothill.edu
TRUPPO, Helen ... 703-416-1441 466 F htruppo@divinemercy.edu
TRUSCELLO, Roberta ... 315-781-3754 302 A truscello@hws.edu
TRUSCHEL, John, J ... 978-867-4013 209 F john.truschel@gordon.edu
TRUSDELL, James ... 732-987-2416 278 B jtrusdell@georgian.edu
TRUSS, B. Donta ... 717-477-1235 395 E bdtruss@ship.edu
TRUSSELL, Jay ... 828-884-8340 327 C trussellj@brevard.edu
TRUSTY, Denise, M ... 606-783-2011 183 F dmtrusty@moreheadstate.edu
TRUSTY, Steve ... 501-760-4240 .. 20 B steve.trusty@np.edu
TRUTNA, Kevin ... 530-283-0202 .. 42 H ktrutna@frc.edu
TRUXAL, Randy ... 903-463-8717 437 D truxalr@grayson.edu
TRUXILLO, Betty, D ... 225-923-2524 186 A director@brsc.edu
TRYON, Howard ... 318-487-7110 186 I rusty.tryon@lacollege.edu
TRZASKA, Ken, J ... 620-417-1010 176 K ken.trzaska@sccc.edu
TRZEBIATOWSKI, Brian . 773-481-8287 134 G btrzebiatowski@ccc.edu
TSABETSAYE, Byron ... 505-566-3363 288 A tsabetsayeb@sanjuancollege.edu
TSAI, John, Y ... 626-395-6393 .. 29 C jytsai@caltech.edu
TSAI, Patty ... 866-323-0233 .. 57 J tsai@providencecc.edu
TSAKONAS, Kevin ... 908-709-7573 284 C kevin.tsakonas@ucc.edu
TSAMBIS, Jane ... 201-692-2221 277 K tsambis@fdu.edu
TSAU, Lily ... 562-944-0351 .. 27 C lily.tsau@biola.edu

TSCHEPIKOW, Kyle .... 706-542-0054 125 G kyletsch@uga.edu
TSCHERTER, Andrea, G . 812-888-5794 162 C atscherter@vinu.edu
TSCHIRCH, Poldi .... 713-525-6991 454 H tschirp@stthom.edu
TSE, Waiyi .... 336-334-4244 343 A waiyi.tse@uncg.edu
TSEGAI, Adiam .... 716-851-1914 299 F tsegai@ecc.edu
TSIRELIS, Dawn .... 513-529-2345 356 E tsireldl@miamioh.edu
TSO, Jay .... 212-757-1190 290 B jtso@aami.edu
TSOLAKIS, Alkis .... 225-578-5863 188 I atsolakis@lsu.edu
TSOSIE-JIM, Carrie .... 505-566-3205 288 A tsosiejimc@sanjuancollege.edu
TSUI, Ping .... 773-508-7573 142 D ptsui@luc.edu
TSUTSUI, William, M .... 501-450-1351.. 19 F tsutsui@hendrix.edu
TUAN, Mia .... 206-543-2353 485 F mtuan@uw.edu
TUBBS, Camilla .... 415-565-4881.. 68 F tubbsc@uchastings.edu
TUBBS, Jeffrey, L .... 704-406-4253 329 A jtubbs@gardner-webb.edu
TUBBS, Johnathan .... 870-512-7866.. 18 B johnathan_tubbs@asun.edu
TUBBS, T.J .... 417-667-8181 252 A
TUBBS, Teresa .... 910-272-3662 337 D ttubbs@robeson.edu
TUCCI, Teri .... 708-444-4500 137 D ttucci@foxcollege.edu
TUCHINSKY, Adam .... 207-780-4347 196 F adam.tuchinsky@maine.edu
TUCHMAN, Nancy .... 773-508-2475 142 D ntuchma@luc.edu
TUCHTEN, Ashley .... 773-577-8100 135 G atuchten@coynecollege.edu
TUCK, Amy .... 662-325-3221 247 F at25@msstate.edu
TUCK, Deniz .... 919-735-5151 338 H datuck@waynecc.edu
TUCKER, Adam .... 704-847-5600 340 I atucker@ses.edu
TUCKER, Andrew .... 614-236-7737 349 D dtucker@capital.edu
TUCKER, Archie .... 256-372-5230.... 1 A archie.tucker@aamu.edu
TUCKER, Archie .... 256-372-8344.... 1 A archie.tucker@aamu.edu
TUCKER, Bill .... 601-276-2000 249 B btucker@smcc.edu
TUCKER, Brandon .... 734-677-5087 232 B brtucker@wccnet.edu
TUCKER, Carey .... 870-864-7147.. 21 B ctucker@southark.edu
TUCKER, Carol, M .... 713-221-8269 453 B tuckerca@uhd.edu
TUCKER, Carolyn .... 360-416-7679 485 A carolyn.tucker@skagit.edu
TUCKER, Cecelia, T .... 757-683-5210 469 G ctucker@odu.edu
TUCKER, Collin .... 402-363-5718 270 E ctucker@york.edu
TUCKER, Constance ...... 503-494-1402 375 B tuckeco@ohsu.edu
TUCKER, David, A .... 812-888-4266 162 C dtucker@vinu.edu
TUCKER, Dayton .... 914-251-6915 319 E dayton.tucker@purchase.edu
TUCKER, Destin .... 731-881-7020 428 B dtucke13@utm.edu
TUCKER, Diane, M .... 617-358-6887 207 D dtucker@bu.edu
TUCKER, Don, L .... 612-343-4162 242 H dltucker@northcentral.edu
TUCKER, Eileen .... 610-459-0905 391 D
TUCKER, G.L .... 218-846-3765 239 B gl.tucker@minnesota.edu
TUCKER, Gardiner .... 970-351-2001.. 83 E gardiner.tucker@unco.edu
TUCKER, Gary, R .... 517-750-1200 230 H garyt@arbor.edu
TUCKER, Geraldine .... 512-223-7572 431 A gtucker@austincc.edu
TUCKER, Herman, V ...... 254-299-8660 440 A htucker@mclennan.edu
TUCKER, Jaime .... 956-295-3511 449 D jaime.tucker@tsc.edu
TUCKER, Jameel .... 610-526-6092 385 G jtucker@harcum.edu
TUCKER, James .... 518-327-6286 311 G jtucker@paulsmiths.edu
TUCKER, Jamilah .... 740-389-4636 356 B tuckerj@mtc.edu
TUCKER, Jean .... 251-460-6294.... 8 F jtucker@southalabama.edu
TUCKER, John .... 501-760-4229.. 20 B john.tucker@np.edu
TUCKER, John, D .... 619-298-1829.. 65 E jtucker@ssu.edu
TUCKER, Karen .... 630-752-5060 152 F karen.tucker@wheaton.edu
TUCKER, Keith .... 505-426-2088 286 H rktucker@nmhu.edu
TUCKER, Ken .... 205-652-3527.... 9 A ktucker@uwa.edu
TUCKER, Laura .... 703-416-1441 466 F ltucker@divinemercy.edu
TUCKER, Mark .... 336-386-3217 338 D tuckerm@surry.edu
TUCKER, Megan .... 802-295-8822 464 B mjt09050@ccv.vsc.edu
TUCKER, Melanie, V ...... 865-981-8111 421 F melanie.tucker@maryvillecollege.edu
TUCKER, Michael .... 765-641-4295 153 B matucker@anderson.edu
TUCKER, Murl .... 714-547-9625.. 28 C mtucker@calcoast.edu
TUCKER, Nate .... 423-473-1190 420 J ntucker@leeuniversity.edu
TUCKER, Ned .... 402-826-8601 267 A ned.tucker@doane.edu
TUCKER, Patrick .... 860-832-1786.. 84 I ptucker@ccsu.edu
TUCKER, Robert .... 325-670-1498 437 F robert.tucker@hsutx.edu
TUCKER, Sandra .... 386-481-2106.. 95 F tuckers@cookman.edu
TUCKER, Sarah .... 304-558-0699 489 O sarah.tucker@wvhepc.edu
TUCKER, Sarah .... 304-558-0265 489 O tucker@wvctcs.org
TUCKER, Sarah, A .... 304-558-0265 488 I tucker@wvctcs.org
TUCKER, Shawn .... 201-200-2222 279 E stucker2@njcu.edu
TUCKER, Shawna .... 580-349-1534 368 A shawna.tucker@opsu.edu
TUCKER, Sheryl .... 405-744-6368 368 B sheryl.tucker@okstate.edu
TUCKER, Stacy .... 913-288-7239 174 F stucker@kckcc.edu
TUCKER, Tommy .... 870-307-7324.. 20 A thomas.tucker@lyon.edu
TUCKER, William .... 510-587-6037.. 68 C william.tucker@ucop.edu
TUCKER, William, T ...... 631-451-4760 321 F tuckerw@sunysuffolk.edu
TUDELA, Virginia, C ...... 671-735-5590 505 C virginia.tudela@guamcc.edu
TUDINI, Kathryn, E .... 716-645-2258 316 F katietud@buffalo.edu
TUDOR, Amanda .... 859-985-3316 179 C tudora@berea.edu
TUDOR, Colin .... 909-607-3679.. 37 C colin.tudor@claremont.edu
TUDOR, David .... 859-276-4357 184 E dtudor@sullivan.edu
TUDOR, Deborah .... 618-453-3267 149 E dtudor@siu.edu
TUDOR, Gail .... 207-941-7039 194 A tudorg@husson.edu
TUDOR, Jarrod .... 330-972-8940 362 B grt2@uakron.edu
TUDOR, Lisa .... 239-489-9350 100 A ltudor@fsw.edu
TUDOR, Robert .... 304-876-5294 490 E rtudor@shepherd.edu
TUDOR-LOCKE, Catrine . 704-687-7917 342 E ctudorlo@uncc.edu
TUDORIE, Ionut Alexandru .... 914-961-8313 315 C iatudorie@svots.edu
TUDRYN, Jonathan .... 413-755-4420 215 F jtudryn@stcc.edu
TUEDIO, James, A .... 209-667-3531.. 33 C jtuedio@csustan.edu
TUELL, David .... 865-471-2020 419 A dtuell@cn.edu
TUELLER, David .... 801-422-3861 458 H david_tueller@byu.edu
TUELLER, Steve, W .... 808-675-3705 127 E steve.tueller@byuh.edu
TUESCHER-GILLE, Heidi 608-342-1125 497 D tuescheh@uwplatt.edu
TUFAU-AFRIYIE, Michelle .... 508-854-7568 215 D mtufau@qcc.mass.edu
TUFEL, Peter .... 212-686-9244 290 A
TUIA, Jennifer .... 360-596-5369 485 B jtuia@spscc.edu
TUITASI, Michael .... 310-434-4389.. 62 E tuitasi_michael@smc.edu
TUITASI, Sifagatogo ...... 684-699-9155 505 A s.tuitasi@amsamoa.edu
TUITE, Jayme .... 724-222-5330 392 A jtuite@penncommercial.edu
TUITE, Kathleen .... 973-618-3534 276 D ktuite@caldwell.edu
TUITE, Marie .... 408-924-1200.. 34 B marie.tuite@sjsu.edu
TUKEL, Oya, I .... 973-596-6262 279 F oya.i.tukel@njit.edu
TULAK, William .... 318-487-5443 187 C williamtulak@cltcc.edu
TULBERG, Clark .... 805-525-4417.. 67 D ctulberg@thomasaquinas.edu
TULIER, Esdras .... 718-960-8559 294 A esdras.tulier@lehman.cuny.edu
TULINO, Michael .... 520-206-4625.. 15 D mtulino@pima.edu
TULLEY, Nickolas, B ..... 240-895-4336 201 E nbtulley@smcm.edu
TULLEY, Ronald .... 419-434-4445 363 A rtulley@findlay.edu
TULLIER, Michael .... 334-724-4553.... 7 D mtullier@tuskegee.edu
TULLT, Marci .... 888-772-6077.. 98 D
TULLY, Greg, J .... 815-772-7218 144 D gtully@morrisontech.edu
TULLY, John, J .... 610-566-1776 403 E jtully@williamson.edu
TULLY-DARTEZ, Stephanie .... 870-864-8413.. 21 B stully-dartez@southark.edu
TUMBARELLO, Mike .... 301-387-3167 198 F mike.tumbarello@garrettcollege.edu
TUMBLIN, Tom .... 859-858-3581 178 H
TUMEO, Michael, D ...... 214-768-2808 444 E mtumeo@smu.edu
TUMEY, Terrance .... 559-278-3178.. 31 D
TUMIEL, John .... 207-221-4628 196 G jtumiel@une.edu
TUMILTY, Meredith .... 847-543-2946 135 B mtumilty@clcillinois.edu
TUMINEZ, Astrid .... 801-863-3000 461 A president.tuminez@uvu.edu
TUMMINO, Pauline .... 718-990-6106 314 B tumminop@stjohns.edu
TUNE, Kathie .... 434-791-7106 464 O ktune@averett.edu
TUNG, Lisa .... 617-879-7335 212 E ltung@massart.edu
TUNGSETH, Margaret .... 651-523-2203 236 A mtungseth01@hamline.edu
TUNHEIM, Kathi .... 507-933-6540 235 I ktunheim@gustavus.edu
TUNK, Chana .... 973-267-9404 280 G
TUNNING, Michael .... 563-884-5865 168 I michael.tunning@palmer.edu
TUNSTALL, Denise, S ... 804-523-5029 474 H dtunstall@reynolds.edu
TUNSTILL, Hilda .... 931-393-1573 425 C htunstill@mscc.edu
TUOMEY, Lianne, M ..... 802-656-2027 463 E lianne.tuomey@uvm.edu
TUPA, Dana .... 904-256-7653 101 G
TUPAS, Cynthia .... 626-584-5464.. 43 H cynthiatupas@fuller.edu
TUPPER, Barb .... 319-399-8662 164 A btupper@coe.edu
TUPPER, Rick .... 605-274-4499 415 B rick.tupper@augie.edu
TUPUA, Tiare .... 684-699-9155 505 A t.tupua@amsamoa.edu
TUPUOLA, Tafaimamao . 684-699-9155 505 A t.tupuola@amsamoa.edu
TURAK, Ron .... 716-338-1065 303 D ronturak@mail.sunyjcc.edu
TURAY, Abdul, M .... 502-597-6916 182 H abdul.turay@kysu.edu
TURBAN, Stephanie ...... 218-285-2242 240 D stephanie.turban@rainyriver.edu
TURBEVILLE, Donna ...... 910-788-6203 338 A donna.turbeville@sccnc.edu
TURBEVILLE, John .... 315-470-6660 320 A jturbev@esf.edu
TURBEVILLE, Stanley .... 910-296-2416 335 E sturbeville@jamessprunt.edu
TURBIVILLE, Alice .... 610-957-6040 399 D aturbiv1@swarthmore.edu
TURBOW, David .... 562-988-2278.. 25 R dturbow@auhs.edu
TURCHETTA, Greg .... 239-489-9061 100 A gregory.turchetta@fsw.edu
TURCHI, Marissa .... 610-526-5151 379 E mturchi@brynmawr.edu
TURCIOS, Mirna .... 661-726-1911.. 68 B mirna.turcios@uav.edu
TURCOTT, Scott .... 765-677-2246 157 D scott.turcott@indwes.edu
TURCOTTE, Jim .... 601-925-3809 247 C turcotte@mc.edu
TURCOTTE, Paul .... 254-501-5817 447 A paul.turcotte@tamuct.edu
TUREK, John, G .... 714-879-3901.. 45 F jgturek@hiu.edu
TUREK, Joseph .... 901-321-3234 419 C jturek@cbu.edu
TURELL, Susan, C .... 570-348-6232 389 G sturell@marywood.edu
TURGEON, Marla .... 309-649-6603 150 A marla.turgeon@src.edu
TURGEON, Pennie .... 508-421-3813 208 A pturgeon@clarku.edu
TURICO, Michael .... 602-538-9396.. 10 D
TURK, David .... 903-813-2408 430 N dturk@austincollege.edu
TURK, David, F .... 845-675-4422 310 G david.turk@nyack.edu
TURK, Don .... 815-753-1088 145 C dtuck@niu.edu
TURK, Laura .... 540-831-5248 470 C lturk@radford.edu
TURK, Stella .... 845-257-3105 317 B turks@newpaltz.edu
TURK, Thomas .... 719-628-2839.. 36 C turk@chapman.edu
TURK FIECOAT, Heather .... 775-682-8081 271 F hturk@unr.edu
TURKS, Stacie .... 209-946-2225.. 70 E sturks@pacific.edu
TURLEY, Alicestyne .... 859-985-3783 179 C turlleya@berea.edu
TURLEY-AMES, Kandi .... 208-282-3053 130 H turlkand@isu.edu
TURLINGTON, Lisa .... 910-592-8081 337 G lturlington@sampsoncc.edu
TURMAN, Paul, D .... 402-471-2505 268 D
TURNAGE, Craig, A ...... 936-468-3407 445 F turnagecraig@sfasu.edu
TURNAGE, Tyronne .... 252-493-7777 336 H tturnage@email.pittcc.edu
TURNER, Amanda .... 952-995-1406 238 B amanda.turner@hennepintech.edu
TURNER, Andrea .... 812-749-1248 159 C aturner@oak.edu
TURNER, Angela .... 434-797-8438 474 E angela.turner@danville.edu
TURNER, Anthony .... 724-847-6871 384 G anthony.turner@geneva.edu
TURNER, B, P .... 334-387-3877.... 4 C businessoffice@amridgeuniversity.edu
TURNER, Bethany .... 864-622-6029 406 G bturner@andersonuniversity.edu
TURNER, Carolyn .... 870-946-3506.. 22 H
TURNER, Casey .... 215-972-7600 393 D cturner@pafa.org
TURNER, Darron .... 817-257-5566 448 G d.turner@tcu.edu
TURNER, David .... 734-487-9733 223 H dturne27@emich.edu
TURNER, Deb .... 419-358-3343 348 G turnerd@bluffton.edu
TURNER, Debra .... 706-737-1431 115 A debturner@augusta.edu
TURNER, Deidra .... 817-515-1280 445 G deidra.turner@tccd.edu
TURNER, Donna, A .... 252-246-1240 339 C daturner@wilsoncc.edu
TURNER, Donnell .... 617-243-2125 210 G dturner@lasell.edu
TURNER, Elaine .... 404-727-7631 117 F elaine.turner@emory.edu

TYSON, CSC, David, D .. 574-239-8375 155 D dtyson@hcc-nd.edu
TYSON, John .... 334-386-7257.... 5 D jtyson@faulkner.edu
TYSON, Julie .... 413-748-3124 218 G jtyson@springfield.edu
TYSON, LaTanya, V .... 336-744-0900 327 F latanya@carolina.edu
TYSON, Thomas, N .... 410-334-2913 204 F ttyson@worwic.edu
TYSON, Tyrone .... 336-744-0900 327 F tyrone@carolina.edu
TYSON-CHILDRESS, Jamie .... 919-718-7239 333 C jchildress@cccc.edu
TYSSE, Jon .... 608-757-7754 499 C jtysse@blackhawk.edu
TZAN, Douglas .... 202-885-8607.. 93 E dtzan@wesleyseminary.edu
TZENG, Walker .... 951-763-0500.. 54 H
TZIMBAL, Tootie .... 831-479-5730.. 27 G totzimba@cabrillo.edu

U

UBAGO, Maria .... 323-343-2586.. 32 A mubago@cslanet.calstatela.edu
UBERTACCIO, Peter, N .. 508-565-1200 218 H pubertaccio@stonehill.edu
UCCI, Mary .... 859-572-5768 184 A uccim@nku.edu
UCHIDA, Richard, Y ..... 207-859-4609 193 E richard.uchida@colby.edu
UDALL, David .... 928-428-8295.. 12 E david.udall@eac.edu
UDDIN, Rita .... 718-260-5610 295 B ruddin@citytech.cuny.edu
UDEH, Bridget .... 718-522-9073 290 C budeh@asa.edu
UDEH, Igwe, E .... 504-286-5331 190 I iudeh@suno.edu
UDEH, Kim .... 301-369-2501 197 F kmudeh@captechu.edu
UDELHOFEN, Angela, M .... 608-342-1125 497 D rulea@uwplatt.edu
UDELHOFEN, Denise, A 563-588-7742 167 D denise.udelhofen@loras.edu
UDELHOFEN, Sara .... 641-422-4348 168 D sara.udelhofen@niacc.edu
UDEN, Jayme .... 816-584-6595 258 A jayme.uden@park.edu
UDEN, Michael, D .... 262-243-5700 493 B michael.uden@cuw.edu
UDEN-HOLMAN, Tanya . 319-335-3565 163 A tanya-uden-holman@uiowa.edu
UDERMANN, Brian .... 608-785-8181 496 F budermann@uwlax.edu
UDIS-KESSLER, Amanda .... 719-227-8177.. 77 H audiskessler@coloradocollege.edu
UDOKA, Silvanus .... 404-880-6213 116 D sudoka@cau.edu
UDPA, Satish .... 517-355-5014 227 D udpa@msu.edu
UDVARDY, Yolonda ...... 215-489-4966 382 D yolonda.udvardy@delval.edu
UEBELHOER, Sarah .... 757-382-9900.. 92 G
UEBELHOER, Sarah .... 804-527-1000.. 92 G
UEHARA, Edwina .... 206-685-2480 485 F eddi@uw.edu
UERLING, Laura .... 617-732-2791 216 B laura.uerling@mcphs.edu
UESUGI, Koji .... 909-274-4525.. 52 H kuesugi@mtsac.edu
UFFORD, Brian, K .... 207-778-7334 196 B brian.ufford@maine.edu
UFFORD, Lori .... 541-506-6025 372 G lufford@cgcc.edu
UFOMATA, Titilayo .... 574-284-4575 160 C tufomata@saintmarys.edu
UGALDE, Aileen, M ...... 305-284-2700 112 E augalde@miami.edu
UGALDE, Marina .... 305-474-6800 106 F mugalde@stu.edu
UGALDE, Michelle .... 954-753-6869.. 98 C
UGARTE, Gina .... 718-289-5562 293 B gina.ugarte@bcc.cuny.edu
UGOCHUKWU, Chioma 610-902-8200 380 C
UGUR, Izel .... 202-644-7210.. 91 A iugur@bau.edu
UHAL, Len .... 563-876-3353 164 J luhal@dwci.edu
UHAZY, Les .... 661-722-6300.. 26 D luhazy@avc.edu
UHDE, Alicia .... 701-224-5764 346 B alicia.uhde@bismarckstate.edu
UHER, Bill .... 505-277-5598 288 G wuher@salud.unm.edu
UHER, Bryan .... 907-474-5439.. 10 A bmuher@alaska.edu
UHLER, Jill .... 803-508-7247 406 E uhlerj@atc.edu
UHLINGER, Eleanor, S .. 831-656-2342 503 K euhlinger@nps.edu
UHLIR, Jim .... 715-232-2188 498 A uhlirj@uwstout.edu
UHRICH, James .... 323-259-2506.. 54 E juhrich@oxy.edu
UHRICH, Kathryn .... 951-827-3101.. 69 C cnasdean@ucr.edu
UKACHUKWU, Victoria . 908-412-3590 284 C victoria.ukachukwu@ucc.edu
ULATE, David .... 650-949-6905.. 43 B ulatedavid@fhda.edu
ULATOWSKI, Lydia .... 716-614-6450 310 C ulatowski@niagaracc.suny.edu
ULBRICH, Casandra ...... 313-593-5393 231 F culbrich@umich.edu
ULCHIDA GURSEN, Yoko .... 703-591-7042 476 F
ULEVICH, Maureen .... 970-351-2396.. 83 E maureen.ulevich@unco.edu
ULIANA, Marla .... 818-364-7729.. 49 B ulianamr@lamission.edu
ULII, Diedra .... 808-675-3474 127 E diedra.ulii@byuh.edu
ULLAND, Greg .... 701-252-3467 347 C gulland@uj.edu
ULLMANN, Jeffrey .... 816-604-1062 255 D jeffrey.ullmann@mcckc.edu
ULLMANN, Timothy ...... 970-339-6617.. 76 G timothy.ullmann@aims.edu
ULLOA-HEATH, Julie ..... 671-735-5595 505 C julie.ulloaheath@guamcc.edu
ULLOM, Carine .... 785-248-2510 176 D carine.ullom@ottawa.edu
ULLOM, Lynn .... 304-336-8200 490 F ullomlyn@westliberty.edu
ULLRICH, Cindy .... 979-230-3415 432 D cindy.ullrich@brazosport.edu
ULMAN, Cynthia .... 510-869-1547.. 59 F culman@samuelmerritt.edu
ULMEN, Dan .... 406-265-3755 264 F dulmen@msun.edu
ULMER, Jeffrey .... 386-822-7738 111 A julmer@stetson.edu
ULMER, Robert, R .... 702-895-0628 271 E robert.ulmer@unlv.edu
ULMER, Ward .... 866-492-5336 244 F president@mail.waldenu.edu
ULMSCHNEIDER, John, E .... 804-828-1105 473 F jeulmsch@vcu.edu
ULOZAS, Catherine, B .. 215-895-6685 383 B catherine.b.ulozas@drexel.edu
ULREY, Burke .... 828-884-8282 327 C ulreydb@brevard.edu
ULREY, Heather .... 740-283-6402 353 B hulrey@franciscan.edu
ULRICH, Deborah, L ..... 937-775-3133 364 I deborha.ulrich@wright.edu
ULRICH, John .... 570-662-4804 395 C julrich@mansfield.edu
ULRICH, Mary .... 575-527-7526 287 E mulrich@nmsu.edu
ULRICH, Trey, P .... 215-951-1671 387 C ulrich@lasalle.edu
ULRICHSEN, Borre .... 509-313-6455 481 D ulrichsen@gonzaga.edu
ULSES, Randy .... 513-556-3511 362 D ulsesrj@ucmail.uc.edu
ULSHAFER, Kevin, L ..... 478-757-5125 126 H kulshafer@wesleyancollege.edu
UMANS, Dorothy .... 240-567-3820 200 C dorothy.umans@montgomerycollege.edu
UMBERGER, Jennifer .... 570-389-4043 394 A jumberger@bloomu.edu
UME, Ebere .... 815-740-3492 151 J eume@stfrancis.edu
UMEHIRA, Ron .... 808-455-0228 129 D umehira@hawaii.edu
UMEZU, Kodo .... 510-809-1444.. 45 K
UMFRESS, Jason, W ..... 912-279-5970 116 G jumfress@ccga.edu
UMHOLTZ, Lynn .... 316-322-3144 171 G lumholtz@butlercc.edu
UMIDI, Joseph .... 757-352-4404 470 H joseumi@regent.edu
UMPHRES, James .... 360-538-4085 481 E james.umphres@ghc.edu
UMPHREY, Monique ..... 713-718-8085 437 I monique.umphrey@hccs.edu
UMSTATTD, Rustin .... 816-414-3700 256 A rumstattd@mbts.edu
UNBEHAGEN, Leonard .. 504-278-6438 188 A lunbehagen@nunez.edu
UNDA, Viviana .... 310-660-3515.. 41 L vunda@elcamino.edu
UNDERCOFFER, Anita ... 909-652-6032.. 36 A anita.undercoffer@chaffey.edu
UNDERCOFLER, Jennifer .... 914-251-6707 319 E jennifer.undercofler@purchase.edu
UNDERDUE, Sharnette .. 657-278-4498.. 31 E sunderdue@fullerton.edu
UNDERDUE MURPH, Yvette .... 304-766-4101 491 B yvette.underduemurph@wvstateu.edu
UNDERHILL, Terri .... 304-357-4980 488 G terriunderhill@ucwv.edu
UNDERWOOD, Anita ..... 845-675-4476 310 G anita.underwood@nyack.edu
UNDERWOOD, Ann .... 806-651-2125 448 C aunderwood@wtamu.edu
UNDERWOOD, David .... 540-831-5500 470 C dunderwood@radford.edu
UNDERWOOD, Glenda .. 617-587-5581 217 A underwoodg@neco.edu
UNDERWOOD, Jeffrey ... 323-343-3793.. 32 A jeffrey.underwood@calstatela.edu
UNDERWOOD, Kathy, A .... 702-895-0283 271 E kathyunderwood@unlv.edu
UNDERWOOD, Kelly ..... 209-384-6000.. 51 G kelly.underwood@mccd.edu
UNDERWOOD, Ken ...... 865-573-4517 420 G kunderwood@johnsonu.edu
UNDERWOOD, Lori, J .. 757-594-7052 466 B underwoo@cnu.edu
UNDERWOOD, Mark ..... 830-591-7286 444 G meunderwood@swtjc.edu
UNDERWOOD, Michelle, W .... 229-931-2627 119 D michelle.underwood@gsw.edu
UNDERWOOD, Ruth ...... 478-289-2134 117 D runderwood@ega.edu
UNDERWOOD, Tara ...... 478-471-2734 121 F tara.underwood@mga.edu
UNDERWOOD, Tiffani ... 276-656-0281 475 D tunderwood@patrickhenry.edu
UNDERWOOD, Timothy, J .... 304-462-6432 490 C timothy.underwood@glenville.edu
UNDERWOOD, Von, E .. 580-581-2491 365 G vonu@cameron.edu
UNDERWOOD, William, D .... 478-301-2500 121 E underwood_wd@mercer.edu
UNEBASAMI, Michael, T .... 808-956-6280 128 H mune@hawaii.edu
UNGAR, Jacob .... 845-362-3053 291 A jungar@byts.edu
UNGAR, Samuel, D ...... 718-384-5460 325 M
UNGAR, Shaya .... 732-370-3360 285 E
UNGER, Candace .... 619-574-6909.. 54 K cunger@pacificcollege.edu
UNGER, Karen .... 845-758-7490 290 G kunger@bard.edu
UNGER, Leigh .... 562-908-3415.. 58 E lunger@riohondo.edu
UNGER, Maggie .... 952-446-4323 235 G ungerm@crown.edu
UNGER, Robert .... 619-482-6328.. 65 F runger@swccd.edu
UNGER, Sue .... 630-889-6565 144 G sunger@nuhs.edu
UNGERER, Dorothy .... 413-755-4438 215 F daungerer@stcc.edu
UNIS, Corry, D .... 203-254-4000.. 86 I cunis@fairfield.edu
UNKE, James, M .... 507-354-8221 236 I unkejm@mlc-wels.edu
UNNAVA, H. Rao .... 530-752-4600.. 68 E runnava@ucdavis.edu
UNNITHAN, Shashi .... 970-204-8607.. 79 J shashi.unnithan@frontrange.edu
UNRUH, John, A .... 530-898-5844.. 31 A jaunruh@csuchico.edu
UNRUH, Nancy .... 620-276-9571 173 E nancy.unruh@gcccks.edu
UNSWORTH, John, M ... 434-924-7849 473 A jmu2m@virginia.edu
UNTERREINER, Colleen 406-756-3962 263 F colleenu@fvcc.edu
UPCHURCH, Linda .... 478-289-2188 117 D lupchurch@ega.edu
UPCHURCH, Luke .... 704-922-6511 334 F upchurch.luke@gaston.edu
UPCHURCH, Luke .... 704-923-8405 334 F upchurch.luke@gaston.edu
UPCHURCH, Rick .... 601-709-0966 245 C rupchurch@belhaven.edu
UPDIKE, Jeremy .... 507-923-4210 233 K updike@augsburg.edu
UPHOFF, Sarah .... 314-340-5005 253 I uphoffs@hssu.edu
UPNEJA, Arun .... 617-358-6744 207 D aupneja@bu.edu
UPPERMAN, Lee-Anna .. 724-266-3838 400 H lupperman@tsm.edu
UPSHAW, Tyler .... 352-588-8516 106 D tyler.upshaw@saintleo.edu
UPSHAW, Tyler .... 352-395-8516 106 D tyler.upshaw@saintleo.edu
UPTON, Brian .... 417-865-2815 253 B uptonb@evangel.edu
UPTON, Bryn .... 410-857-2416 200 B bupton@mcdaniel.edu
UPTON, Kim, M .... 239-513-1122 101 C kupton@hodges.edu
UPTON-GARVIN, Barbra 816-501-4555 258 H barbra.uptongarvin@rockhurst.edu
UQDAH, Aesha .... 502-852-6585 185 C aesha.uqdah@louisville.edu
URAN, Mike, T .... 320-308-2116 240 H mturan@stcloudstate.edu
URBAITIS, Carol, S .... 585-785-1212 300 B carol.urbaitis@flcc.edu
URBAN, David, J .... 615-898-2764 422 H david.urban@mtsu.edu
URBAN, Kristi .... 979-830-4141 432 C kristi.urban@blinn.edu
URBAN, Nathan, N .... 412-624-2137 401 B nurban@pitt.edu
URBANEK, Andrew .... 518-485-3731 296 H urbaneka@strose.edu
URBANEK, Lauren .... 617-585-1113 217 B lauren.urbanek@necmusic.edu
URBANEK, Philip .... 251-405-7006.... 1 E purbanek@bishop.edu
URBANIAK, Kellene .... 773-371-5400 133 E kurbaniak@ctu.edu
URBANO, George .... 863-297-1086 105 A gurbano@polk.edu
URBANSKI, Tom .... 218-879-0820 238 A urbanski@fdltcc.edu
URDAN, Joely, B .... 414-229-4278 497 A jurdan@uwm.edu
URDIALES, Juan .... 323-260-8133.. 48 H urdialjr@elac.edu
URETSKY, Stewart .... 781-736-8318 207 E suretsky@brandeis.edu
UREY, Denise .... 724-589-2009 399 H durey@thiel.edu
URIBE, Kimberly .... 323-259-2523.. 54 E kuribe@oxy.edu
URIBE-JENNINGS, Marcela .... 508-929-8543 213 E muribejennings@worcester.edu
URIBE NITTI, Christina . 507-457-1492 243 B curibeni@smumn.edu
URIEGAS, Samantha ..... 956-872-6763 444 A sbmunoz@southtexascollege.edu
URISH, Jon .... 608-363-2651 492 C urishj@beloit.edu
URQUIDEZ, Kasandra, K .... 520-621-3705.. 16 G kasandra@email.arizona.edu
URRABAZO, Gloria .... 210-434-6711 441 E gaurrabazo@ollusa.edu
URRUTIA, Diana .... 972-238-6104 435 F dmurrutia@dcccd.edu
URSCHEL, Kris .... 574-284-4542 160 C kurschel@saintmarys.edu
URSO, David .... 540-453-2376 474 B ursod@brcc.edu
URSUY, Andrea .... 989-686-9222 223 G alnadols@delta.edu
URSUY, Andrea, L .... 989-686-9222 223 G alnadols@delta.edu

V

VAN DAM, Dale .... 559-638-0300.. 66 F
dale.vandam@reedleycollege.edu
VAN DAM, Kara .... 301-985-7000 203 B
kara.vandam@umuc.edu
VAN DE LOO, John ...... 715-365-4553 500 D
vandeloo@nicoletcollege.edu
VAN DE MOORTELL,
Raymond .... 617-254-2610 218 D
rev.vandemoortell@sjs.edu
VAN DELDEN,
Sebastian .... 843-953-9615 408 E
vandeldensa@cofc.edu
VAN DEN HEUVEL,
Nicole .... 713-348-4055 442 K
nvdh@rice.edu
VAN DEN HUL,
Richard, D .... 360-650-3182 486 F
rich.vandenhul@wwu.edu
VAN DER BURG, Anna . 860-685-3298.. 89 C
avanderburg@wesleyan.edu
VAN DER KAAY,
Christopher .... 863-784-7413 107 F
christopher.vanderkaay@southflorida.edu
VAN DER KARR, Carol . 607-753-2206 318 D
carol.vanderkarr@cortland.edu
VAN DER KLEY, Jan ..... 269-387-2365 232 K
jan.vanderkley@wmich.edu
VAN DER VELDEN,
Andre .... 530-283-0202.. 42 H
avandervelden@frc.edu
VAN DER WALL,
Melissa .... 201-684-7457 280 H
mvanderw@ramapo.edu
VAN DEREN, Jessica .... 802-728-1244 464 E
jvanderen@vtc.edu
VAN DERVEER,
Rachael, E .... 724-847-6596 384 G
revander@geneva.edu
VAN DONSELAAR,
Brian .... 712-722-6299 164 K
brian.vandonselaar@dordt.edu
VAN DUSEN, Lee .... 636-227-2100 254 G
VAN DUSEN, Ryan .... 785-227-3380 171 E
vandusenrl@bethanylb.edu
VAN DUYNE, Patrick .... 815-280-6696 140 B
pvanduyn@jjc.edu
VAN DYK, Leanne .... 404-687-4514 116 H
vandykl@ctsnet.edu
VAN DYK, Vanessa .... 406-496-4322 265 A
vvandyk@mtech.edu
VAN DYKE, Greg .... 712-722-6083 164 K
greg.vandyke@dordt.edu
VAN DYKE, Jon .... 217-234-5378 141 D
jvandyke@lakeland.cc.il.us
VAN DYKE, Kaaren .... 860-509-9556.. 87 B
kvandyke@hartsem.edu
VAN DYKE, Karin .... 906-487-7344 223 K
karin.vandyke@finlandia.edu
VAN DYKEN, Douglas .. 616-395-7810 225 B
vandyken@hope.edu
VAN DYKEN, Rick .... 708-239-3977 150 F
rick.vandyken@trnty.edu
VAN DYNE, Karen .... 617-619-1900 210 E
karen.vandyne@hult.edu
VAN ECK, Thomas, A ... 616-526-8553 222 A
tveck@calvin.edu
VAN ESS, Jami .... 928-226-4209.. 11 O
jami.vaness@coconino.edu
VAN-ESS, Michelle .... 212-217-4130 299 H
michelle_vaness@fitnyc.edu
VAN ETTEN, JR., Mark . 570-674-6170 390 G
mvanetten@misericordia.edu
VAN FOSSEN,
Dell Jean .... 951-785-2088.. 47 C
dvanfoss@lasierra.edu
VAN GAALEN, Joseph .. 239-433-6965 100 A
joseph.vangaalen@fsw.edu
VAN GALEN, Dean, A ... 715-425-3201 497 E
dean.vangalen@uwrf.edu
VAN GENDEREN, Eric ... 510-925-4282.. 25 Q
eric.vangenderen@aua.am
VAN GILDER, Holly ...... 330-490-7146 364 B
hvangilder@walsh.edu
VAN GRONINGEN,
Willis .... 708-239-4880 150 F
bill.vangroningen@trnty.edu
VAN GRUENSVEN,
Sheryl .... 920-465-2210 496 E
vangrues@uwgb.edu
VAN GUILDER, Connie . 707-545-3647.. 26 J
admissions@berginu.edu
VAN HALA, Kristen, M . 323-265-8650.. 48 H
vanhalkm@elac.edu

VAN HAMERSVELD,
Pete .... 310-243-3825.. 31 B
pvanhamersveld@csudh.edu
VAN HARPEN,
Robin, L .... 414-229-4461 497 A
rvanharp@uwm.edu
VAN HEE, Miles .... 970-943-2089.. 84 D
mvanhee@western.edu
VAN HEMERT, John, L . 540-674-3660 475 B
jvanhemert@nr.edu
VAN HESTER, Tia .... 309-694-8817 138 C
tia.vanhester@icc.edu
VAN HOECK, Michele ... 707-654-1097.. 32 B
mvanhoeck@csum.edu
VAN HOOK, Dianne, G . 661-362-3400.. 38 H
dianne.vanhook@canyons.edu
VAN HORN, Brian .... 701-788-4754 345 E
brian.vanhorn@mayvillestate.edu
VAN HORN, Drew, L .... 706-379-3111 127 C
dlvanhorn@yhc.edu
VAN HORN, Laura .... 734-432-5595 227 A
lvanhorn@madonna.edu
VAN HORN, Megan ...... 231-348-6667 228 E
mvanhorn1@ncmich.edu
VAN HORN, Stuart .... 559-934-2131.. 73 M
stuartvanhorn@whccd.edu
VAN HORN, Wayne ...... 601-925-3297 247 C
wvanhorn@mc.edu
VAN HOUTEN, Michael 517-629-0567 220 G
mvanhouten@albion.edu
VAN JOOLEN, Vincent .. 831-646-4883.. 52 F
vvanjoolen@mpc.edu
VAN KAMPEN-BREIT,
Doris .... 352-588-8485 106 D
doris.vankampen@saintleo.edu
VAN KEULEN, Michael . 507-223-7252 239 E
michael.vankeulen@mnwest.edu
VAN KLEY, Eric .... 641-628-5422 163 E
vankleye@central.edu
VAN KLEY, Sandy .... 712-707-7145 168 H
svankley@nwciowa.edu
VAN KLOMPENBERG,
Brian .... 312-862-3217.. 67 I
brian.vanklompenberg@kirkland.com
VAN KOOTEN, Rick .... 812-855-3931 156 B
rvankoot@indiana.edu
VAN KOOY, Samantha .. 856-415-2276 281 D
svankooy@rcgc.edu
VAN KUIKEN, Jerome .. 918-335-6802 368 G
jvankuiken@okwu.edu
VAN LARE, Cheryl .... 585-395-2622 318 B
cvanlare@brockport.edu
VAN LEER, Sharon .... 651-290-6416 242 G
sharon.vanleer@mitchellhamline.edu
VAN LEHN, Darren .... 541-245-7770 376 D
dvanlehn@roguecc.edu
VAN LEIDEN, Melissa ... 785-594-8306 170 I
melissa.vanleiden@bakeru.edu
VAN LIERE, Lori .... 419-866-0261 361 H
lori.vanliere@sctoday.edu
VAN LIEW, Chris .... 206-296-2003 484 F
vanliew@seattleu.edu
VAN LOAN, Charles ...... 607-255-4963 297 F
deanoffaculty@cornell.edu
VAN LONE, Jeffrey .... 570-577-1617 379 F
jsv007@bucknell.edu
VAN LOO, Scott .... 937-766-7700 349 G
vanloos@cedarville.edu
VAN LOON, Ruth Anne 513-556-4628 362 D
ruth.anne.vanloon@uc.edu
VAN LUNEN, Bonnie .... 757-683-4960 469 G
bvanlune@odu.edu
VAN MARION, Kara ...... 708-239-3718 150 F
kara.vanmarion@trnty.edu
VAN METER, Eric .... 605-995-2919 415 C
eric.vanmeter@dwu.edu
VAN METER, Linda, L ... 570-422-3277 394 E
lvanmeter@esu.edu
VAN NIEJENHUIS, Nate 712-722-6401 164 K
natevn@dordt.edu
VAN NOORT, Kimberly . 919-843-8347 341 A
kpvannoort@northcarolina.edu
VAN NORMAN, Karen ... 973-761-9076 283 B
karen.vannorman@shu.edu
VAN NORT, Ella .... 213-624-1200.. 42 I
evanort@fidm.edu
VAN NOSTRAND,
Robert .... 631-420-2700 321 B
foundation@farmingdale.edu
VAN NOY, Karla .... 785-749-8467 173 G
VAN NOY, Vielane .... 435-222-1256.. 82 G
vvannoy@rvu.edu

VAN OMMEREN,
Andrew .... 712-707-7000 168 H
andrew.vanommeren@nwciowa.edu
VAN OMMEREN, Ryan .. 805-493-3211.. 29 H
rvommere@callutheran.edu
VAN OOT, Amy .... 860-701-5019.. 87 D
vanoot_a@mitchell.edu
VAN ORMAN, Kit .... 315-364-3317 325 B
kit@wells.edu
VAN PELT, Donna .... 515-294-1280 162 I
dvanpelt@foundation.iastate.edu
VAN RENSBURG,
Deryck .... 310-506-5689.. 56 C
deryck.rensburg@pepperdine.edu
VAN RIJN, Paul .... 610-917-1450 401 I
p_vanrijn@valleyforge.edu
VAN SICKLE, Fred .... 607-254-7150 297 F
fmv7@cornell.edu
VAN STAVERN, Becky ... 417-328-1815 259 L
bvanstavern@sbuniv.edu
VAN STRATEN, Amy ..... 920-831-4355 499 E
vanstrat@fvtc.edu
VAN TASSEL, Kristin ..... 785-227-3380 171 E
vantasselk@bethanylb.edu
VAN TASSELL, TOR,
Malachi .... 814-472-3001 398 B
mvantassell@francis.edu
VAN TIL, Seth, J .... 724-458-3887 385 C
sjvantil@gcc.edu
VAN UUM, Elizabeth ..... 314-516-5774 261 D
vanuum@umsl.edu
VAN VLECK, Thomas ..... 660-626-2138 250 A
tvanvleck@atsu.edu
VAN VLERAH, Abby, L . 260-982-5132 158 T
alvanvlerah@manchester.edu
VAN VLIET, Krystyn ...... 617-253-3315 215 G
VAN VOORHIS,
Amanda .... 508-999-9114 211 F
avanvoorhis@umassd.edu
VAN VOORHIS, Sue, N . 612-625-8098 243 E
vanvo002@umn.edu
VAN VREEDE, LeeAnn .. 608-796-3808 498 N
levanvreede@viterbo.edu
VAN WAGNER, Thomas 301-243-2211 503 J
thomas.vanwagner@dodiis.mil
VAN WAGONER,
Randall, J .... 315-792-5333 307 D
rvanwagoner@mvcc.edu
VAN WALBECK, Patti .... 269-387-2365 232 K
patti.vanwalbeck@wmich.edu
VAN WICKLIN, Robert .. 716-375-2331 313 F
bvanwick@sbu.edu
VAN WIE, Lisa .... 518-629-8143 302 E
l.vanwie@hvcc.edu
VAN WINKLE, Ken .... 575-439-3600 287 B
kvanwink@nmsu.edu
VAN WINKLE, Ken .... 575-439-3640 287 C
kvanwink@nmsu.edu
VAN WINKLE, Robin ...... 541-440-4668 377 C
robin.vanwinkle@umpqua.edu
VAN WORMER, Laura ... 330-569-5249 353 J
vanwormerla@hiram.edu
VAN WYK, Natalie .... 610-361-5418 391 D
vanwykn@neumann.edu
VAN WYLEN, David, G . 616-395-7190 225 B
vanwylend@hope.edu
VAN WYNGARDEN,
Doug .... 708-239-4828 150 F
doug.vanwyngarden@trnty.edu
VAN ZANDT, David ...... 212-229-5656 308 C
vanzandt@newschool.edu
VAN ZEE, Carolina .... 909-537-7576.. 33 A
quinterc@csusb.edu
VAN ZEE, Ryan .... 605-995-2902 415 C
ryan.vanzee@dwu.edu
VAN ZEELAND, Kathy ... 414-930-3552 495 A
vanzeek@mtmary.edu
VANABLE, Peter .... 315-443-2543 322 C
pvanable@syr.edu
VANACORE, Gina .... 940-565-2282 454 A
gina.vanacore@unt.edu
VANAKEN, Troy .... 630-617-3100 136 G
president@elmhurst.edu
VANALSBURG,
Teresa, D .... 304-457-6380 487 B
vanalsburgtd@ab.edu
VANANDEN, Ian, C .... 301-447-5310 200 E
vananden@msmary.edu
VANASSE, Dennis .... 508-849-3372 205 C
dvanasse@annamaria.edu
VANASSE, Nancy .... 508-999-8133 211 F
nvasasse@umassd.edu
VANBILLIARD, Jason .... 215-702-4227 380 D
provost@cairn.edu

VANBOCKSTAELE,
Elisabeth .... 215-762-4359 383 B
elisabeth.vanbockstaele@drexelmed.edu
VANBUREN, Tina .... 610-799-1510 388 I
tvanburen@lccc.edu
VANCAMP, Connie .... 412-809-5100 396 H
vancamp.connie@ptcollege.edu
VANCE, Deidre .... 614-882-2551 353 A
dvance@fortiscollege.edu
VANCE, Gina, K .... 928-523-6747.. 14 H
gina.vance@nau.edu
VANCE, Gina, M .... 724-946-7114 402 G
vancegm@westminster.edu
VANCE, Helene .... 434-592-7200 468 H
registrar@liberty.edu
VANCE, Justin .... 208-562-3449 130 F
justinvance@cwi.edu
VANCE, Karen .... 814-865-3917 392 B
ksv21@psu.edu
VANCE, Kristie .... 828-689-1353 331 A
kvance@mhu.edu
VANCE, Laura .... 828-884-8319 327 C
lvancebc@gmail.com
VANCE, Mickey .... 601-635-6338 245 I
mvance@eccc.edu
VANCE, Otis .... 352-638-9795.. 95 D
ovance@beaconcollege.edu
VANCE, Samantha .... 334-291-4974.... 1 H
samantha.vance@cv.edu
VANCE, Shawn .... 225-771-2552 191 A
svance@sulc.edu
VANCE, W.C .... 419-289-5118 348 A
wvance@ashland.edu
VANDAL, Mike .... 701-477-7862 347 A
mvandal@tm.edu
VANDALL,
Christopher, P .... 608-258-2448 499 H
cvandall@madisoncollege.edu
VANDALOVSKY, Emily .. 201-879-7066 275 H
evandalovsky@bergen.edu
VANDE YACHT, Daniel .. 920-465-2111 496 E
vandeyad@uwgb.edu
VANDE ZANDE,
Carleen .... 608-262-5089 496 B
cvandezande@uwsa.edu
VANDEL, Laurie .... 406-496-4119 265 A
lvandel@mtech.edu
VANDEMARK, Marney ... 610-989-1200 402 B
mvandemark@vfmac.edu
VANDEMEULEBROEKE,
Leon .... 973-761-9454 283 B
leon.vandemeulebroeke@shu.edu
VANDEN BOOGAARD,
Brad .... 414-382-6324 492 A
brad.vandenboogaard@alverno.edu
VANDEN HOUTEN, Art .. 904-819-6392.. 98 E
vandena@flagler.edu
VANDENAKKER, John ... 313-883-8750 229 K
vandenakker.john@shms.edu
VANDENAVOND, Steve . 906-227-6767 228 F
svanden@nmu.edu
VANDENBERG,
Christine .... 908-852-1400 276 G
christine.vandenberg@centenaryuniversity.edu
VANDENBERG, Matt ...... 989-463-7081 220 H
vandenbergmp@alma.edu
VANDENBOSCH,
Kathryn .... 608-262-4930 496 C
kate.vandenbosch@cals.wisc.edu
VANDENBURGH, Laura . 541-346-2096 377 D
lkvanden@uoregon.edu
VANDENBUSH, Betty ..... 317-208-5311 159 D
VANDER FEEN, Aimee .. 605-331-6602 417 E
aimee.vanderfeen@usiouxfalls.edu
VANDER HOEK, Nancy . 605-229-8545 416 C
nancy.vanderhoek@presentation.edu
VANDER HOOVEN,
James, L .... 978-632-0001 215 A
jvanderhooven@mwcc.mass.edu
VANDER MOLEN,
Lori, L .... 402-280-1798 266 I
lorivandermolen@creighton.edu
VANDER PLOEG, Sally .. 616-526-7112 222 A
svploeg@calvin.edu
VANDER STOEP,
Scott, D .... 616-395-7903 225 B
vanderstoep@hope.edu
VANDER VALK, Frank ... 518-587-2100 321 A
frank.vandervalk@esc.edu
VANDER VEER, Lisa ...... 815-939-5256 146 A
lvanderv@olivet.edu

VANDER WAL, Jennifer 605-688-4491 417 C jennifer.vanderwal@sdstate.edu
VANDER WEELE, Dennis, A .... 845-368-7206 315 D dennis.vanderweele@use.salvationarmy.org
VANDER WERF, Dave ... 712-722-6020 164 K dave.vanderwerff@dordt.edu
VANDER ZWAAG, Lora . 712-274-6400 170 E lora.vanderzwaag@witcc.edu
VANDERBILT, Robin ...... 937-298-3399 355 F robin.vanderbilt@kc.edu
VANDERBILT, William ... 616-395-7850 225 B vanderbilt@hope.edu
VANDERBURG, Judy, J . 503-838-8490 377 H vanderj@wou.edu
VANDERBURGH, Paul, M .... 937-229-2345 362 G pvanderburgh1@udayton.edu
VANDERGHEYNST, Jean 508-999-8539 211 F j.vander@umassd.edu
VANDERGIFF, Ronda .... 360-438-4356 483 H rvandergriff2@stmartin.edu
VANDERGRIFF, Paul ..... 919-516-4014 340 C pvandergriff@st-aug.edu
VANDERGRIFF, Rhonda 573-334-6825 259 J rvandergriff@sehcollege.edu
VANDERGRIFT, Donna .. 856-222-9311 281 C dvandergrift@rcbc.edu
VANDERHART, Mark ..... 219-864-2400 159 B mvanderhart@midamerica.edu
VANDERHILL, Dan .... 517-750-1200 230 H danv@arbor.edu
VANDERHOOF, Doug .... 620-241-0723 172 D doug.vanderhoof@centralchristian.edu
VANDERHOOF, Karen ... 973-328-5012 277 B kvanderhoof@ccm.edu
VANDERHORST, Anne ... 559-791-2457.. 47 A avanderh@kccd.edu
VANDERHURST, Michael .... 843-792-1282 410 F vanderm@musc.edu
VANDERKAR, Caroline .. 805-756-2945.. 30 C cmoore36@calpoly.edu
VANDERLEI, Elizabeth ... 616-526-6434 222 A bvlei@calvin.edu
VANDERMAAS-PEELER, Maureen .... 336-278-6453 328 K vanderma@elon.edu
VANDERMARK, Sarah ... 435-652-7500 460 G sarah.vandermark@dixie.edu
VANDERMOLEN, Geoff .. 616-957-6045 221 P gav016@calvinseminary.edu
VANDERPOOL, Molly .... 765-973-8415 156 C moberry@iue.edu
VANDERPOOL, Neil .... 559-442-4600.. 66 E neil.vanderpool@fresnocitycollege.edu
VANDERPUYE, Archibald, W .... 512-505-3076 438 E awvanderpuye@htu.edu
VANDERSANDEN, Susan .... 608-663-3367 493 C svandersanden@edgewood.edu
VANDERSLICE, Ronna, J .... 580-581-2250 365 G rvanderslice@cameron.edu
VANDERSPOEL, James .. 906-932-4231 224 B jimv@gogebic.edu
VANDERSTAAY, Steven, L .... 360-650-3004 486 F steven.vanderstaay@wwu.edu
VANDERVEEN, Kathleen 616-331-2662 224 E vandervk@gvsu.edu
VANDERVEEN, Sara ...... 269-927-8611 226 D svanderveen@lakemichigancollege.edu
VANDERZANDEN, Ann Marie .... 515-294-7184 162 I vanderza@iastate.edu
VANDERZEE, Lenore ..... 315-386-7109 320 E vanderzeel@canton.edu
VANDERZWAAG, George .... 585-275-4301 323 J george.vanderzwaag@rochester.edu
VANDEURSEN, Marianne .... 908-835-2430 284 G vandeursen@warren.edu
VANDEVANDER, David, R .... 540-828-5316 465 D dvandeva@bridgewater.edu
VANDEVEN, Alissa .... 573-651-2206 259 K avandeven@semo.edu
VANDEVENTER, Susan .. 607-729-1581 298 C svandeventer@davisny.edu
VANDEVERE, John, D ... 570-326-3761 393 G jdv7@pct.edu
VANDEVILLE, Denise ..... 906-487-7379 223 K denise.vandeville@finlandia.edu
VANDEWEERT, Lisa ...... 616-632-8900 221 C
VANDIJK, Cindee .... 319-385-6495 167 A cindee.vandijk@iw.edu
VANDIVERE, Julie .... 570-389-4713 394 A jvandive@bloomu.edu
VANDREHLE, Michael ... 507-537-6257 241 D michael.vandrehel@smsu.edu
VANDUSER, Trisha .... 817-735-2508 454 C trisha.vanduser@unthsc.edu
VANDYKE, Diane .... 215-461-1143 390 H dvandyke@mc3.edu
VANDYKE, John .... 541-885-1452 375 C john.vandyke@oit.edu
VANDYKE, Rhonda .... 540-665-4862 471 E rvandyke@su.edu
VANE, Thomas .... 716-827-2433 323 D vanet@trocaire.edu
VANECEK, Frank .... 802-485-2135 463 A vanecek@norwich.edu
VANEGAS, Jorge .... 979-845-1221 446 G jvanegas@tamu.edu
VANEK, Marian, S .... 412-383-1863 401 B msv8@pitt.edu
VANFLEET, Rita .... 402-552-3516 266 E vanfleetrita@clarksoncollege.edu
VANG, Mary .... 651-846-1722 241 B mary.vang@saintpaul.edu
VANGEL, Darcy .... 508-213-2111 217 E darcy.vangel@nichols.edu
VANGELE, Jim .... 650-738-4455.. 61 Q vangelej@smccd.edu
VANGILDER, JT .... 785-539-3571 175 E jt.vangilder@mccks.edu
VANGORDER, Karen ...... 260-481-6016 159 F vangordk@pfw.edu
VANGSGARD, Mark, D .. 651-962-6095 244 E mdvangsgard@stthomas.edu
VANGSNESS FRISCH, Jane .... 701-671-2627 346 E jane.vangsness@ndscs.edu
VANGUILDER, Sean ...... 352-588-8268 106 D sean.vanguilder@saintleo.edu
VANHECKE, JoNes, R ... 507-933-7526 235 I jvanheck@gustavus.edu
VANHEYNIGEN, Matthew .... 413-782-1373 219 F matthew.vanheynigen@wne.edu
VANHOEK, Rebecca ...... 386-752-1822.. 99 A rebecca.vanhoek@fgc.edu
VANHOOK, Jayson .... 423-614-8695 420 J jvanhook@leeuniversity.edu
VANHOOSE, Hannah ..... 406-447-4401 263 C hvanhoose@carroll.edu
VANHORN, Amy .... 304-829-7150 487 G avanhorn@bethanywv.edu
VANKO, David .... 410-704-2121 204 A dvanko@towson.edu
VANLAECKEN, Erik .... 605-367-7624 417 D erik.vanlaecken@southeasttech.edu
VANLANDINGHAM, Brenda .... 662-246-6301 247 D bvanlandingham@msdelta.edu
VANLONDEN, April .... 800-287-8822 153 D vanloap@earlham.edu
VANN, John, C .... 860-444-8286 504 F john.c.vann@uscg.mil
VANN, JR., Linnie .... 410-334-2936 204 F lvann@worwic.edu
VANN, Steve .... 607-735-1777 299 D svann@elmira.edu
VANNESTE, Ray .... 731-661-5534 427 C rvaneste@uu.edu
VANNEY, Greg .... 701-845-7227 346 A greg.vanney@vcsu.edu
VANNEY, Pete .... 715-365-4484 500 D pvanney@nicoletcollege.edu
VANNOY, Cliff .... 225-578-3814 188 I cliff@lsualumni.org
VANNUCCI, Kristina ...... 530-741-6986.. 76 C kvannucc@yccd.edu
VANO, OSF, Barbara ..... 419-824-3861 355 K bvano@lourdes.edu
VANOOSTEN, Roger ...... 952-829-4699 234 A
VANORMAN, Chris .... 517-607-2506 225 A cvanorman@hillsdale.edu
VANOVER, Kathryn .... 918-540-6388 366 I kathryn.vanover@neo.edu
VANPELT, Mark .... 928-681-5621.. 14 F mvanpelt@mohave.edu
VANSCHOELANDT, Debbie .... 949-367-8310.. 64 F dvanschoelandt@ifc.edu
VANSCOY, Irma, J .... 803-777-6728 413 C ivanscoy@mailbox.sc.edu
VANSICKLE, Lisa .... 314-719-8017 253 C lvansicklel@fontbonne.edu
VANSKIKE, Kathryn .... 509-313-6128 481 D vanskike@gonzaga.edu
VANSTEEN, John .... 631-656-3187 300 D john.vansteen@ftc.edu
VANSTEENBERGEN, Sara .... 920-748-8715 495 G vansteenbergens@ripon.edu
VANSUMEREN, Hans ..... 231-995-1793 228 G hvansumeren@nmc.edu
VANTERPOOL, Elaine .... 256-726-8355.... 6 C dmerriweather@oakwood.edu
VANTRIESTE, Emilie ...... 215-204-8760 399 F emilie.vantrieste@temple.edu
VANVALKENBURG, Gretchen, R .... 334-844-1134.... 4 E gzv0007@auburn.edu
VANWINGERDEN, Luke . 864-646-1474 413 A lvanwing@tctc.edu
VANWINGERDEN, Luke . 864-503-5863 414 D lvanwingerden@uscupstate.edu
VANZANTEN, Susan ...... 219-464-5022 162 A susan.vanzanten@valpo.edu
VARAHRAMYAN, Kody .. 207-581-1506 195 J kody.roberts@maine.edu
VARAS, Elaine, P .... 215-898-1404 400 K varas@upenn.edu
VARBERG, Peggy .... 701-777-4802 345 C peggy.varberg@und.edu
VARBLE, Susan .... 504-280-6171 189 E sfvarble@uno.edu
VARDAMAN, Lee .... 334-808-6319.... 7 C vardaman@troy.edu
VARDAMAN, Virginia .... 601-977-7730 249 C vvardaman@tougaloo.edu
VARDANYAN, Rouzanna .... 641-472-1154 167 F rvardanyan@mum.edu
VAREBROOK, Cathy ...... 414-277-4523 494 G varebrook@msoe.edu
VARELA, Donna .... 954-492-5353.. 96 H dvarela@citycollege.edu
VARELA, Legna .... 787-834-9595 511 E lvarela@uaa.edu
VARELA, Lorell .... 787-834-9595 511 E lovarela@uaa.edu
VARELA, Susie .... 323-343-3694.. 32 A svarela@cslanet.calstate.edu
VARELA LLAVONA, Angelica .... 787-767-2040 514 B angelica.varela@upr.edu
VARELAS, Nikos .... 312-413-9461 151 B varelas@uic.edu
VARGA, Alane, P .... 315-792-3100 324 B avarga@utica.edu
VARGA, Elizabeth .... 864-250-8454 410 B elizabeth.varga@gvltec.edu
VARGA, Patti .... 414-382-6360 492 A patti.varga@alverno.edu
VARGAS, Adrienne .... 619-594-4562.. 33 E avargas4@sdsu.edu
VARGAS, Carlos .... 573-651-2222 259 K president@semo.edu
VARGAS, Christina .... 631-451-4950 321 F vargasc@sunysuffolk.edu
VARGAS, German .... 912-279-5918 116 G gvargas@ccga.edu
VARGAS, Gineen .... 847-628-2524 140 C gineen.vargas@judsonu.edu
VARGAS, Ileana, M .... 787-765-1915 510 B ivargas@opto.inter.edu
VARGAS, Ingrid .... 650-738-4454.. 61 Q vargasi@smccd.edu
VARGAS, Jose .... 714-628-5941.. 58 A vargas_jose@sccollege.edu
VARGAS, Julia .... 816-501-4545 258 H julia.vargas@rockhurst.edu
VARGAS, Lizzette .... 787-523-6000 508 D
VARGAS, Lizzette .... 787-753-6335 508 D lvargas@icpruc.edu
VARGAS, Magda .... 787-841-2000 510 K mivargas@pucpr.edu
VARGAS, Mary .... 616-632-2881 221 C mcv005@aquinas.edu
VARGAS, Phillip .... 210-434-6711 441 E pvargas@ollusa.edu
VARGAS, Roy, M .... 561-862-4410 104 D vargasr@palmbeachstate.edu
VARGAS, Salvador .... 209-954-5047.. 60 J svargas@deltacollege.edu
VARGAS, Shannon .... 620-229-6368 177 A shannon.vargas@sckans.edu
VARGAS, Silvia .... 610-799-1711 388 I smaldonadovargas@lccc.edu
VARGHESE, Finney .... 972-761-6845 435 F fvarghese@dcccd.edu
VARGHESE, Sara .... 619-644-7600.. 44 I sara.varghese@gcccd.edu
VARGHESE, Steebo .... 212-343-1234 306 J svarghese@mcny.edu
VARGO, Michael .... 616-234-4690 224 D mvargo@grcc.edu
VARHOLAK, Mark .... 203-582-8613.. 87 G mark.varholak@quinnipiac.edu
VARI, April .... 215-489-2413 382 D april.vari@delval.edu
VARLOTTA, Lori, E .... 330-569-5120 353 J varlottale@hiram.edu
VARMA, Mrinal .... 334-244-3600.... 4 F varma@aum.edu
VARMA, Rohit .... 323-442-6411.. 72 B deanksom@usc.edu
VARMA, Shanta .... 334-244-3272.... 4 F svarma@aum.edu
VARNADO, Krystyna ..... 601-266-4050 249 F krystyna.varnado@usm.edu
VARNELL, Jon .... 704-687-0514 342 E jvarnell@uncc.edu
VARNER, Donica .... 440-775-8401 358 C donica.varner@oberlin.edu
VARNER, Donna, A .... 757-594-8816 466 B dvarner@cnu.edu
VARNER, Jenny, M .... 336-249-8186 334 A jmvarner@davidsonccc.edu
VARNER, Julie .... 334-290-3265.... 2 F julie.varner@istc.edu
VARNER, Mary Helen ... 662-846-4011 245 H mvarner@deltastate.edu
VARNER, Robin .... 859-280-1242 183 B rvarner@lextheo.edu
VARNER, Stuart .... 731-989-6073 420 C svarner@fhu.edu
VARNER, Tiffany .... 318-670-9692 190 J twilliams@susla.edu
VARNEY, Rhonda .... 207-326-2220 195 D rhonda.varney@mma.edu
VARONA, Anthony .... 305-284-2394 112 E avarona@miami.edu
VARSALONA, Jack, P .... 302-356-6818.. 90 I officeofthepresident@wilmu.edu
VARSALONA, Jacque, R 302-295-1168.. 90 I jacqueline.r.varsalona@wilmu.edu
VARSEK, Tamara, B ...... 814-393-2240 394 D tvarsek@clarion.edu
VARSHNEY, Amitabh ..... 301-405-2316 202 C varshney@umd.edu
VARSO, Shawn, V .... 330-941-3527 365 C svvarso@ysu.edu
VARTANIAN, Heather .... 414-326-2301 493 A
VARVILLE, Paul .... 956-872-2330 444 A pbvarvil@southtexascollege.edu
VARWIG, Jana .... 410-704-2270 204 A jvarwig@towson.edu
VARY KEELE, Renee ...... 404-364-8868 122 J rvary@oglethorpe.edu
VASALLO, Maria .... 617-873-0120 207 F maria.vasallo@cambridgecollege.edu
VASCONCELLOS, Tina ... 510-748-2205.. 56 F tvasconcellos@peralta.edu
VASCURA, Jacquelyn, L 740-826-8084 357 C jkent@muskingum.edu
VASEASHTA, Ashok .... 201-200-2453 279 E avaseashta@njcu.edu
VASEY, Todd, A .... 508-541-1815 208 F tvasey@dean.edu
VASICA, Christine .... 910-296-2400 335 E cvasica@jamessprunt.edu
VASILATOS-YOUNKEN, Regina .... 814-865-2516 392 B rxv@psu.edu
VASILE, Daniel .... 585-395-2226 318 B dvasile@brockport.edu
VASILOFF, Nick .... 509-777-4596 486 I nvasiloff@whitworth.edu
VASINA, Mark .... 402-878-2380 267 E mark.vasina@littlepriest.edu
VASKO, Genevieve .... 908-835-3135 284 G vasko@warren.edu
VASQUEZ, Amanda .... 973-720-2929 284 I
VASQUEZ, Amanda .... 915-747-5544 455 C avasquez6@utep.edu

VASQUEZ, Becky, L ...... 386-226-6948.. 98 A
vasquezb@erau.edu
VASQUEZ, Graciela .... 562-860-2451.. 35 M
gvasquez@cerritos.edu
VASQUEZ, James .... 718-260-5244 295 B
jvazquez@citytech.cuny.edu
VASQUEZ, Jim .... 646-592-4416 326 E
jim.vasquez@yu.edu
VASQUEZ, Lisa, R .... 972-758-3894 433 M
lvasquez@collin.edu
VASQUEZ, Patricia .... 617-745-3851 208 G
patty.vasquez@enc.edu
VASQUEZ, Patrick .... 214-860-2094 435 C
patrick.vasquez@dcccd.edu
VASQUEZ, Sandy .... 915-747-7873 455 C
svasquez@utep.edu
VASQUEZ, Stephanie .... 210-486-3941 429 F
svasquez117@alamo.edu
VASQUEZ, Vanessa .... 956-295-3605 449 D
vanessa.vasquez@tsc.edu
VASQUEZ, Wendy .... 510-628-8010.. 48 A
wvasquez@lincolnuca.edu
VASQUEZ-BROOKS,
Marie, E .... 407-582-5687 112 K
mvasquezbrooks@valenciacollege.edu
VASQUEZ DE VELASCO,
Guillermo .... 773-325-1858 135 I
gvv@depaul.edu
VASQUEZ-LEVY, David .. 510-849-8223.. 55 B
president@psr.edu
VASQUEZ-PORITZ,
Justin .... 718-260-5008 295 B
jvazquez-poritz@citytech.cuny.edu
VASQUEZ-SKILLINGS,
Rebecca .... 440-775-6453 358 C
rebecca.skillings@oberlin.edu
VASS, Dianna, J .... 410-951-3000 203 D
VASSALLO, Donna .... 609-343-4972 275 D
dvassall@atlantic.edu
VASSALLO, Thomas ...... 718-405-3722 296 G
thomas.vassallo@mountsaintvincent.edu
VASSAR, Andrea .... 410-778-7206 204 D
avassar2@washcoll.edu
VASSAR, John .... 254-295-4505 453 E
jvassar@umhb.edu
VASSAR, Pam .... 913-469-8500 174 D
pvassar@jccc.edu
VASSELLI, John .... 713-718-5690 437 I
john.vasselli@hccs.edu
VASUDEVAN,
Palligarnai, T .... 603-862-3290 274 G
vasu@unh.edu
VATANARTIRAN, Sinem 202-644-7210.. 91 A
VATANDOOST, Cyrus .... 615-514-2787 423 E
cyrus@nossi.edu
VATANDOOST, Nossi .... 615-514-2787 423 E
nossi@nossi.edu
VATER, Ruth .... 608-363-2606 492 C
vaterr@beloit.edu
VATH, Carrie .... 406-496-4198 265 A
cvath@mtech.edu
VATISTAS, Vatistas .... 262-945-1259 492 F
vvatistas@carthage.edu
VATTEROTT, JR., John .. 314-423-1900 250 C
johnjr@stltrades.com
VATTIMO, Casey .... 518-320-1311 316 C
VAUGHAN, Anthony ...... 212-678-8816 303 G
anvaughan@jtsa.edu
VAUGHAN, Cathy, A ..... 270-824-1705 181 G
cathy.vaughan@kctcs.edu
VAUGHAN, Chris .... 443-334-2690 201 H
cvaughan@stevenson.edu
VAUGHAN, Chris .... 309-794-7292 132 C
chrisvaughan@augustana.edu
VAUGHAN, Icer .... 316-942-4291 175 I
vaughani@newmanu.edu
VAUGHAN, Jesse .... 804-524-5877 477 B
jvaughan@vsu.edu
VAUGHAN, John .... 360-475-7700 482 G
jvaughan@olympic.edu
VAUGHAN, John .... 626-914-8581.. 36 K
jvaughan@citruscollege.edu
VAUGHAN, Joseph .... 909-621-8613.. 45 A
joseph_vaughan@hmc.edu
VAUGHAN, Karen .... 908-526-1200 281 A
karen.vaughan@raritanval.edu
VAUGHAN, Larry, F .... 615-547-1222 419 F
lvaughan@cumberland.edu
VAUGHAN, Timothy, S . 715-836-2500 496 D
vaughats@uwec.edu
VAUGHAN, William .... 303-384-2555.. 78 I
wvaughan@mines.edu

VAUGHAN-TUCKER,
Daenel .... 318-487-5443 187 C
dvaughantucker@cltcc.edu
VAUGHEN, Maurice ...... 305-430-1168.. 99 D
maurice.vaughen@fmuniv.edu
VAUGHN, Andy .... 415-955-2001.. 24 K
VAUGHN, Bryan .... 903-886-5865 447 B
bryan.vaughn@tamuc.edu
VAUGHN, Caitlin .... 615-547-1307 419 F
cvaughn@cumberland.edu
VAUGHN, Debra .... 706-721-0211 115 A
dvaughn@augusta.edu
VAUGHN, Evan .... 843-383-8000 408 D
evaughn@coker.edu
VAUGHN, Gary .... 806-291-3549 457 J
vaughng@wbu.edu
VAUGHN, James .... 405-224-3140 371 D
jvaughn@usao.edu
VAUGHN, Joyce .... 870-575-8000.. 22 E
vaughnj@uapb.edu
VAUGHN, Katherine ...... 870-743-3000.. 20 C
kvaughn@northark.edu
VAUGHN, Kellie .... 270-789-5001 179 E
kpvaughn@campbellsville.edu
VAUGHN, Lamont .... 773-442-4044 145 B
l-vaughn@neiu.edu
VAUGHN, Molly .... 256-765-4343.... 8 E
mjmathis@una.edu
VAUGHN, Patricia .... 336-757-7381 334 E
pvaughn@forsythtech.edu
VAUGHN, Patti .... 617-585-0200 206 F
patti.vaughn@the-bac.edu
VAUGHN, Robert .... 323-856-7661.. 25 M
rvaughn@afi.com
VAUGHN, Robert .... 614-234-2341 356 I
rvaughn@mccn.edu
VAUGHN, Ronald, L ..... 813-253-6201 112 J
president@ut.edu
VAUGHN, Vince, A .... 801-524-8107 459 F
vvaughn@ldsbc.edu
VAUGHN, Woodrow ...... 256-726-7306.... 6 C
wvaughn@oakwood.edu
VAUGHT, Mike .... 602-639-7500.. 12 J
VAUGHT, Wayne .... 801-863-8048 461 A
wvaught@uvu.edu
VAULTZ, Patrica .... 504-520-5237 193 A
pvaultz@xula.edu
VAUPEL, Christian, P .... 718-990-2781 314 B
vaupelc@stjohns.edu
VAVOLIZZA, Ann .... 845-848-4001 298 D
ann.vavolizza@dc.edu
VAZ, Maria, J .... 248-204-2400 226 G
mvaz@ltu.edu
VAZ, Pam .... 508-286-3485 220 A
vaz_pamela@wheatoncollege.edu
VAZ, Tammy .... 203-287-3036.. 87 E
paier.vaz@snet.net
VAZQUEZ, Adela .... 787-620-2040 506 C
avazquez@aupr.edu
VAZQUEZ, Airlyn .... 787-882-2065 511 D
biblioteca@unitecpr.net
VAZQUEZ, Ana, M .... 787-850-9332 513 E
ana.vazquez1@upr.edu
VAZQUEZ, Carmen, M .. 619-260-4588.. 71 J
studentaffairs@sandiego.edu
VAZQUEZ, David .... 714-556-3610.. 72 F
david.vazquez@vanguard.edu
VAZQUEZ, David .... 239-590-1123 108 K
dvazquez@fgcu.edu
VAZQUEZ, Dharma .... 787-758-2525 513 G
dharma.vazquez@upr.edu
VAZQUEZ, Edwin .... 787-738-2161 513 D
edwin.vazquez4@upr.edu
VAZQUEZ, Elionexis ..... 787-850-0000 513 E
elionexis.vazquez@upr.edu
VAZQUEZ, Emsley .... 787-840-2575 510 J
evazquez@psm.edu
VAZQUEZ, Estrella .... 787-725-8120 507 N
evazquez@biblioteca.eap.edu
VAZQUEZ, Felice .... 908-737-7000 278 E
fvazquez@kean.edu
VAZQUEZ, Héctor .... 787-765-3560 507 L
hectorvazquez@edpuniversity.edu
VAZQUEZ, Heber .... 787-834-9595 511 E
heberv@uaa.edu
VAZQUEZ, Jose .... 347-964-8600 291 I
jvazquez@boricuacollege.edu
VAZQUEZ, Juan .... 559-730-3700.. 39 E
juanv@cos.edu
VAZQUEZ, Marcelo .... 805-289-6498.. 73 B
mvazquez@vcccd.edu
VAZQUEZ, Maria .... 787-725-8120 507 N
mvazquez0060@eap.edu

VAZQUEZ, Marie .... 531-622-2430 267 H
mvazquez@mccneb.edu
VAZQUEZ, Obed .... 925-969-2423.. 40 I
ovazquez@dvc.edu
VAZQUEZ, Rosabel .... 787-620-2040 506 C
rvazquez@aupr.edu
VAZQUEZ, Sheila .... 787-622-8000 512 E
svazquez@pupr.edu
VAZQUEZ, Silvio, E .... 630-752-5562 152 F
silvio.vazquez@wheaton.edu
VAZQUEZ, Vilmaris .... 787-878-5475 508 L
vvazquez@arecibo.inter.edu
VAZQUEZ, Vivian .... 787-758-2525 513 G
vivian.vazquez4@upr.edu
VAZQUEZ-BARQUET,
Ernesto .... 787-754-8000 512 E
evazquez@pupr.edu
VAZQUEZ-MARTINEZ,
Ernesto .... 787-622-8000 512 E
evazquezjr@pupr.edu
VAZQUEZ MEDINA,
Edwin .... 787-890-2681 512 H
edwin.vazquez7@upr.edu
VEACH, Jason .... 816-268-5436 257 C
jveach@nts.edu
VEAL, Don-Terry .... 443-885-3035 200 D
don-terry.veal@morgan.edu
VEARA, Dennis .... 248-218-2000 229 J
dveara@rc.edu
VEARIL, Matt .... 303-494-7988.. 76 K
VEAZ, María, G .... 787-257-7373 511 G
m_veaz@suagm.edu
VECCHIO, Paul .... 607-871-2193 289 H
vecchio@alfred.edu
VECCHIO, Terry .... 508-854-4294 215 D
tvecchio@qcc.mass.edu
VECCHIONE, James .... 401-232-6051 404 F
jvecchione@bryant.edu
VECCHIONE, Tom .... 209-932-3042.. 70 E
tvecchione@pacific.edu
VECHINI, Jose, A .... 787-864-2222 509 C
jose.vechini@guayama.inter.edu
VEDDER, Kevin, A .... 410-546-6213 203 F
kavedder@salisbury.edu
VEDDER, Lori .... 810-762-3444 231 G
lvedder@umich.edu
VEDDERS, Michael .... 651-638-6094 234 C
vedmic@bethel.edu
VEEDER, Samantha .... 585-275-3226 323 J
sveeder2@finaid.rochester.edu
VEEGER, Anne .... 401-874-4408 406 B
veeger@uri.edu
VEER, Chelly .... 701-766-1302 345 A
chelly.veer@littlehoop.edu
VEGA, Aixa .... 787-834-9595 511 E
avega@uaa.edu
VEGA, Andre .... 617-570-4842 219 A
avega2@suffolk.edu
VEGA, Barbara .... 432-837-8810 450 D
bvega@sulross.edu
VEGA, Erlinda .... 787-264-1912 509 F
linvega@intersg.edu
VEGA, Eva .... 787-746-1400 508 B
evega@huertas.edu
VEGA, Evelyn .... 787-250-1912 509 D
evega@metro.inter.edu
VEGA, Fabian .... 518-629-7111 302 E
f.vega@hvcc.edu
VEGA, Francesca .... 415-476-1000.. 69 E
francesca.vega@ucsf.edu
VEGA, Francesca .... 818-677-2123.. 32 D
francesca.vega@csun.edu
VEGA, Francisco .... 787-834-9595 511 E
fvega@uaa.edu
VEGA, Fredrick .... 787-250-1912 509 D
fredrickvega@metro.inter.edu
VEGA, Gabriela .... 941-359-4622 110 D
gvega@sar.usf.edu
VEGA, Gregory .... 619-660-4030.. 44 H
gregory.vega@gcccd.edu
VEGA, Hermes .... 305-485-7700 112 C
VEGA, Javier .... 212-592-2031 315 H
jvega@sva.edu
VEGA, Kennethia, J .... 714-564-6975.. 57 L
vega_kennethia@sac.edu
VEGA, Lina .... 787-766-1717 511 H
livega@suagm.edu
VEGA, Manfredo .... 787-620-2040 506 C
mvega@aupr.edu
VEGA, Michelle .... 909-607-0821.. 37 G
michelle_vega@kgi.edu
VEGA, Natalie .... 303-273-3569.. 78 I
nvega@mines.edu

VEGA, Patricia .... 773-878-7837 148 D
pvega@staugustine.edu
VEGA, Pete .... 708-239-4770 150 F
pete.vega@trnty.edu
VEGA, Victor .... 304-462-6110 490 C
victor.vega@glenville.edu
VEGA, Waleska .... 787-761-0640 512 F
presidencia@utcpr.edu
VEGA, Zaida .... 787-766-1717 511 H
zvega@suagm.edu
VEGA-GONZALEZ,
Melvin .... 787-480-2426 507 C
melvega@sanjuanciudadpatria.com
VEGA-LA SERNA,
Jennifer .... 559-730-3823.. 39 E
jenniferl@cos.edu
VEIL-EHNERT, Jillain ..... 218-299-3556 235 E
ehnert@cord.edu
VEILLEUX, John .... 817-531-4269 451 E
jveilleux@txwes.edu
VEIT, Kathy .... 650-723-2300.. 65 J
VEIT, Kenneth, J .... 215-871-6770 396 D
kenv@pcom.edu
VEIT, Linda .... 315-464-4513 317 F
veitl@upstate.edu
VEITCH, Dionne .... 814-824-3315 390 C
dveitch@mercyhurst.edu
VEITCH, Jonathan .... 323-259-2691.. 54 E
VELA, Cesar .... 956-721-5142 439 C
cvela@laredo.edu
VELA, Eddie .... 530-898-6171.. 31 A
evela@csuchico.edu
VELA, Jason .... 307-675-0889 502 F
jvela@sheridan.edu
VELA, III, Manuel .... 956-326-1300 446 F
manuel_vela@tamiu.edu
VELA, Robert .... 210-486-0961 429 C
rvela63@alamo.edu
VELA, Robert, H .... 210-486-0959 429 H
rvela63@alamo.edu
VELAR, Maria .... 786-331-1000 103 G
mvelar@maufl.edu
VELAR-PRIETO, Jorge ... 787-993-8869 513 B
jorge.velar@upr.edu
VELARDE, Julian .... 949-376-6000.. 47 D
jvelarde@lcad.edu
VELASCO, Amy .... 805-756-2982.. 30 C
aevelasc@calpoly.edu
VELASCO, Debbie .... 612-767-7064 233 H
debbie.velasco@alfredadler.edu
VELASCO, Steven, C ...... 805-893-2434.. 70 A
steven.velasco@ucsb.edu
VELASCO, Ulises .... 707-467-1037.. 51 E
uvelasco@mendocino.edu
VELASQUEZ, Andrea ...... 540-458-8700 478 A
velasqueza@wlu.edu
VELASQUEZ, Lorrie .... 719-846-5534.. 82 K
lorrie.velasquez@trinidadstate.edu
VELASQUEZ, Marisol .... 708-656-8000 144 E
marisol.velasquez@morton.edu
VELASQUEZ, Tom .... 661-654-2211.. 30 E
tvelasquez2@csub.edu
VELAZQUEZ, Ginger ...... 217-333-9634 151 D
gmayol@uillinois.edu
VELAZQUEZ, Jonathan .. 787-279-1912 509 A
jvelazquez@bayamon.inter.edu
VELAZQUEZ, Leida .... 787-864-2222 509 C
leida.velazquez@guayama.inter.edu
VELAZQUEZ, Marisol .... 787-864-2222 509 C
marisol.velazquez@guayama.inter.edu
VELAZQUEZ, Tania .... 631-451-4057 321 F
velazqt@sunysuffolk.edu
VELAZQUEZ, Tania .... 631-451-4049 321 G
VELAZQUEZ-OLIVER,
Yoel, A .... 787-725-6500 506 G
yvelazquez@albizu.edu
VELDHEER, Kristine ...... 773-371-5460 133 E
kveldheer@ctu.edu
VELENCHIK, Ann .... 781-283-3583 219 D
avelenchik@wellesley.edu
VELEZ, Angel .... 787-250-1912 509 D
avelez@metro.inter.edu
VELEZ, Ashley .... 787-841-2000 510 K
avelez@pucpr.edu
VELEZ, Carlos .... 319-399-8000 164 A
cvelez@coe.edu
VELEZ, Carlos .... 802-443-5745 462 H
velezbla@middlebury.edu
VELEZ, Glenis .... 787-769-1515 507 G
glenis.velez@dewey.edu
VELEZ, Joel .... 787-841-2000 510 K
joel_velez@pucpr.edu

VICTOR, Paula, T ... 562-903-6000 .. 27 C paula.victor@biola.edu
VICTORIN-VANGERUD, Nancy, M ... 651-523-2878 236 A nvictorinvangerud01@hamline.edu
VICTORINE, Jon ... 978-934-5060 211 G jon_victorine@uml.edu
VICTORINO, Christine ... 951-827-7883 .. 69 C christine.victorino@ucr.edu
VICTORY, Gregory, J ... 617-627-0813 219 B gregory.victory@tufts.edu
VIDAL, Andy ... 978-232-2572 209 B avidal@endicott.edu
VIDAL, Betsy ... 787-704-1020 507 K bvidal@ediccollege.edu
VIDAL, Karyn, J ... 561-202-6333 101 F
VIDAL, Terry ... 914-337-9300 297 D terry.vidal@concordia-ny.edu
VIDEKA, Lynn ... 734-764-5347 231 E lvideka@umich.edu
VIDMAR, Anthony ... 940-397-4782 440 F anthony.vidmar@msutexas.edu
VIDMAR, Susan ... 814-234-7755 399 B svidmar@southhills.edu
VIDRINE, Tammy ... 225-768-1773 186 F tammy.vidrine@franu.edu
VIEBRANZ, Caroline ... 614-823-1420 360 A viebranz1@otterbein.edu
VIEHL, Cory ... 770-426-2697 121 C cory.viehl@life.edu
VIEIRA, Elvira ... 973-877-3062 277 I vieira@essex.edu
VIEIRA, Margarida ... 508-531-2877 212 B mvieira@bridgew.edu
VIEIRA, Stephen ... 615-366-4451 424 D stephen.vieira@tbr.edu
VIELBIG, Matthew ... 425-235-7836 483 G mvielbig@rtc.edu
VIEN, Michele ... 518-694-7216 289 D michele.vien@acphs.edu
VIENNA, Michael ... 404-727-6532 117 F michael.vienna@emory.edu
VIENNE, Charlie ... 936-294-1840 450 C cvienne@shsu.edu
VIENNE, Kristy ... 936-294-1840 450 C klv002@shsu.edu
VIENS, Donna ... 617-603-6900 216 H donna.viens@necb.edu
VIENS, Rob ... 425-564-2198 478 F
VIERA, Eddie ... 561-868-3390 104 D vierae@palmbeachstate.edu
VIERA, Javier ... 973-408-3258 277 C jviera@drew.edu
VIERECK, Shannon ... 605-668-1467 415 H shannon.viereck@mtmc.edu
VIEREGGE, Van ... 217-206-6002 151 C vvier2@uis.edu
VIERS, Christopher ... 812-855-9086 156 B cviers@iu.edu
VIERTEL, Cynthia, S ... 920-748-8312 495 G viertelc@ripon.edu
VIETEN, Shaun ... 323-860-1137 .. 53 B shaunv@mi.edu
VIETHS, Brad ... 218-733-7600 238 F brad.vieths@lsc.edu
VIEWEG, Johannes ... 954-262-0510 103 M jvieweg@nova.edu
VIGDOR, Corey ... 908-737-4782 278 E cvigdor@kean.edu
VIGESAA, Linda ... 503-491-6928 374 C linda.vigesaa@mhcc.edu
VIGEZZI, Christopher ... 207-509-7231 195 H cvigezzi@unity.edu
VIGIL, Cynthia ... 509-533-3405 480 B cynthia.vigil@sfcc.spokane.edu
VIGIL, Julie ... 907-796-6494 .. 10 B jlvigil@alaska.edu
VIGIL, Michael, J ... 303-369-5151 .. 81 J michael.vigil@plattcolorado.edu
VIGIL, Renee ... 719-587-7526 .. 76 F reneevigil@adams.edu
VIGNATO, Linda ... 718-940-5346 314 C lvignato@sjcny.edu
VIGNERON, David ... 978-232-2376 209 B dvignero@endicott.edu
VIGNES, Beau ... 251-981-3771 .... 5 B beau.vignes@columbiasouthern.edu
VIGO, Dave ... 925-473-7342 .. 40 J dvigo@losmedanos.edu
VIGO-VERESTÍN, Milka .. 787-763-6700 508 A mvigo@se-pr.edu
VIGOREAUX, Jim ... 802-656-4627 463 E jim.vigoreaux@uvm.edu
VIGUE-MIRANDA, Leanne ... 715-365-4586 500 D lviguemiranda@nicoletcollege.edu
VIGUERIA, Joseph, R ... 719-333-3205 504 C
VIJITHA-KUMARA, Kanaka ... 309-467-6434 137 B kumara@eureka.edu
VIKANDER, David ... 507-537-6281 241 D david.vikander@smsu.edu
VILA, Cherly, T ... 692-625-3394 505 F cvila@cmi.edu
VILA, Dendy ... 787-765-3560 507 L dmvila@edpuniversity.edu
VILACRUZ, Geraldo, G .. 608-246-6442 499 H gvilacruz@madisoncollege.edu
VILCHIZ, Victor ... 678-359-5197 119 F vvilchiz@gordonstate.edu
VILE, John, R ... 615-898-2596 422 H john.vile@mtsu.edu
VILEGI PAYNE, Deborah ... 570-740-0232 389 D dvilegi@luzerne.edu
VILELLE, Luke ... 540-362-6592 468 C lvilelle@hollins.edu
VILES, Vickery ... 541-383-7258 372 B vviles@cocc.edu
VILIC, Boris ... 609-896-5033 281 B bvilic@rider.edu
VILKINA, Galina ... 212-616-7270 301 F galina.vilkina@helenefuld.edu
VILLA, Chris ... 971-722-7305 375 J chris.villa@pcc.edu
VILLA, Cynthia ... 805-756-2171 .. 30 C cvvilla@calpoly.edu
VILLA, Gary ... 561-237-7025 102 V gvilla@lynn.edu
VILLA, William ... 808-739-8578 127 F william.villa@chaminade.edu
VILLAFANIA, John ... 625-641-6 .. 505 F jvillafania@cmi.edu
VILLAFAÑE, Meiling ... 787-850-9374 513 E meiling.villafane@upr.edu
VILLAGOMEZ, Maria ... 707-256-7767 .. 53 C mvillagomez@napavalley.edu
VILLAGOMEZ, Rosita ... 718-405-3275 296 G rosita.villagomez@mountsaintvincent.edu
VILLAGRAN-GLOVER, Frances ... 703-323-3000 475 C
VILLALBA, Tabitha ... 559-442-8281 .. 66 E tabitha.villalba@fresnocitycollege.edu
VILLALOBOS, Alex ... 559-934-2373 .. 74 A alexjvillalobos@whccd.edu
VILLALOBOS, Bobbi ... 310-233-4028 .. 49 A villalb@lahc.edu
VILLALOBOS, Joshua, I 915-831-7002 436 E jvillal6@epcc.edu
VILLALOBOS, Ricardo ... 702-651-4737 271 A ricardo.villalobos@csn.edu
VILLALPANDO, Gilbert .. 425-564-2232 478 F gilbert.villalpando@bellevuecollege.edu
VILLALPANDO, Octavio . 323-343-3800 .. 32 A ovillal9@calstatela.edu
VILLALPANDO, Raoul ... 209-946-7337 .. 70 E rvillalpando@pacific.edu
VILLALVA, Maribel ... 915-747-6463 455 C mvillalva2@utep.edu
VILLAMARIA, Paul ... 303-282-3318 .. 82 H paul.villamaria@archden.org
VILLANO, Steven ... 713-226-5244 453 B villanos@uhd.edu
VILLANTI, Athony ... 315-792-3053 324 B avillanti@utica.edu
VILLANUEVA, Ana, M ... 787-284-1912 509 E avillanu@ponce.inter.edu
VILLANUEVA, Arelis ... 787-766-1717 511 H avillanueva@suagm.edu
VILLANUEVA, Celeste ... 510-869-6511 .. 59 F cvillanueva@samuelmerritt.edu
VILLANUEVA, Christina . 210-431-6789 443 A cvillanueva@stmarytx.edu
VILLANUEVA, JR., Daniel ... 713-221-8136 453 B villanuevad@uhd.edu
VILLANUEVA, Daniel, G 818-364-7772 .. 49 B villand@lamission.edu
VILLANUEVA, Donna-Mae ... 818-719-6444 .. 49 C villandm@piercecollege.edu
VILLANUEVA, Gil ... 804-289-8640 472 L gvillanu@richmond.edu
VILLANUEVA, Guillermo ... 415-239-3994 .. 37 A gvillanu@ccsf.edu
VILLANUEVA, Lynda ... 979-230-3422 432 D lynda.villanueva@brazosport.edu
VILLANUEVA, Naomi ... 505-426-2138 286 H naomivillanueva@sodexo.com
VILLANUEVA, Rebecca .. 432-264-5190 438 C rvillanueva@howardcollege.edu
VILLANUEVA, Sumaya .. 212-484-1346 294 D svillanueva@jjay.cuny.edu
VILLANUEVA, Tammy, M ... 518-562-4100 296 B tammy.villanueva@clinton.edu
VILLANUEVA-RUSSELL, Yvonne ... 903-468-8225 447 B yvonne.vrussell@tamuc.edu
VILLAR, Jeremy ... 323-953-4000 .. 48 I villarjv@lacitycollege.edu
VILLARE, Kathryn ... 978-681-0800 216 A kvillare@mslaw.edu
VILLAROSE, Lesley ... 434-791-5627 464 O lvillarose@averett.edu
VILLARREAL, Elisabeth .. 210-829-2736 453 D villaret@uiwtx.edu
VILLARREAL, James ... 210-431-4312 443 A jvillarreal12@stmarytx.edu
VILLARREAL, Luis ... 956-295-3802 449 D luis.villarreal@tsc.edu
VILLARREAL, Oscar ... 559-925-3347 .. 74 B oscarvillarreal@whccd.edu
VILLARREAL, Pete ... 530-749-3879 .. 76 C pvillarre@yccd.edu
VILLARREAL, Pete ... 530-741-6853 .. 76 C pvillarreal@yccd.edu
VILLARREAL, Velda ... 210-485-0735 429 C vvillarreal@alamo.edu
VILLARRUEL, Antonia ... 215-898-8283 400 K nursingdean@nursing.upenn.edu
VILLASENOR, Leslie ... 312-261-3912 144 F lvillasenor1@nl.edu
VILLAVERDE, Cynthia ... 202-994-7618 .. 91 F cvillaverde@gwu.edu
VILLAVERDE, Kimberly .. 859-371-9393 179 A kvillaverde@beckfield.edu
VILLEGAS, Elias ... 503-316-3259 372 C ellias.villegas@chemeketa.edu
VILLEGAS, Gregorio ... 787-766-1717 511 H um_gvillegas@suagm.edu
VILLEGAS, Lucille ... 310-954-4010 .. 52 G lvillegas@msmu.edu
VILLEGAS, Michael ... 909-607-8509 .. 37 D mike.villegas@sodexo.com
VILLEGAS, Richard ... 925-473-7605 .. 40 J rvillegas@losmedanos.edu
VILLEGAS GOLD, Robert ... 602-285-7397 .. 13 F robert.villegas.gold@phoenixcollege.edu
VILLEGAS-VIDAL, Ludi .. 818-364-7643 .. 49 B villegl@lamission.edu
VILLELLA, John ... 610-436-3111 396 A jvillella@wcupa.edu
VILLELLA, Theresa ... 814-732-1297 394 F tvillella@edinboro.edu
VILLENEUVE, Martha ... 603-897-8260 274 B mvilleneuve@rivier.edu
VILLETT, Stephen, H ... 207-947-4591 193 C svillett@bealcollege.edu
VILLETT, Steve ... 207-947-4591 193 C svillett@bealcollege.edu
VILLOLDO, Sergio ... 787-754-8000 512 E svilloldo@pupr.edu
VINAL, Alicia ... 978-232-2271 209 B avinal@endicott.edu
VINCE, Savannah ... 919-866-5000 338 G svince@waketech.edu
VINCENT, Andrew ... 502-897-4785 184 C avincent@sbts.edu
VINCENT, Angela ... 814-732-2921 394 F vincent@edinboro.edu
VINCENT, Christina, M . 417-268-1000 250 E vincentcj@evangel.edu
VINCENT, Christine, L .. 815-835-6376 148 H christine.l.vincent@svcc.edu
VINCENT, Danny, E ... 740-826-8110 357 C dvincent@muskingum.edu
VINCENT, Deborah, S ... 708-239-4793 150 F deborah.vincent@trnty.edu
VINCENT, Eugenia ... 951-571-6159 .. 58 G eugenia.vincent@mvc.edu
VINCENT, Jennifer ... 508-678-2811 213 G jennifer.vincent@bristolcc.edu
VINCENT, Kitt ... 909-593-3511 .. 70 D kvincent@laverne.edu
VINCENT, Nelson, C ... 513-556-2323 362 D nelson.vincent@uc.edu
VINCENT, Peter ... 518-262-5253 289 F vincenp@amc.edu
VINCENT, Renee ... 806-934-7221 430 A lrvincent@actx.edu
VINCENT, Sara ... 860-512-3213 .. 85 G svincent@manchestercc.edu
VINCENT-DUNN, James 317-738-8075 154 J jvincent-dunn@franklincollege.edu
VINCITORE, Rachel ... 757-631-8101 464 N rachel.vincitore@atlanticuniv.edu
VINE, Scott ... 717-358-3843 384 D scott.vine@fandm.edu
VINES, Andrew ... 562-860-2451 .. 35 M avines@cerritos.edu
VINES, Erin, E ... 661-722-6300 .. 26 D evines@avc.edu
VINES, Robert ... 239-590-7044 108 K rvines@fgcu.edu
VINET, Mary Christine .. 251-460-6185 .... 8 F cvinet@southalabama.edu
VINEYARD, George ... 314-367-8700 259 B george.vineyard@stlcop.edu
VINGER, Christopher ... 212-472-1500 309 I cvinger@nysid.edu
VINGOM, Troy ... 610-683-4000 395 A vingom@kutztown.edu
VINH, Dan ... 845-451-1494 298 A dan.vinh@culinary.edu
VINIK, Frank ... 202-319-4177 .. 91 B vinik@cua.edu
VINING, Caroline ... 479-356-2071 .. 18 C cvining@atu.edu
VINING, Robert ... 563-884-5690 168 I robert.vining@palmer.edu
VINK, Cher ... 715-675-3331 500 E vink@ntc.edu
VINROE, Richard ... 316-295-5911 173 D vinroer@friends.edu
VINSON, III, Ben ... 216-368-4346 349 F ben.vinson@case.edu
VINSON, Bonita ... 940-668-7731 441 A
VINSON, Brandon ... 610-436-2627 396 A bvinson@wcupa.edu
VINSON, Daniel ... 414-930-3494 495 A vinsond@mtmary.edu
VINSON, Marjorie ... 815-939-5011 146 A mvinson@olivet.edu
VINSON, Richard ... 336-721-2619 340 D richard.vinson@salem.edu
VINSON, Richard ... 336-917-5420 340 D richard.vinson@salem.edu
VINSON, Terence ... 318-670-9426 190 J tvinson@susla.edu
VINSON, William ... 608-249-6611 493 E wvinson@herzing.edu
VINTINNER, David, P ... 212-998-8014 310 B david.vintinner@nyu.edu
VINYARD, Lisa ... 636-481-3101 254 A lvinyard@jeffco.edu
VINZE, Ajay, S ... 573-882-6688 261 B vinze@missouri.edu
VIOLA, JR., Frank ... 610-917-1409 401 I fpviola@valleyforge.edu
VIOLA, Joe ... 541-383-7776 372 B jviola@cocc.edu
VIOLA, Judah ... 312-261-3527 144 F judah.viola@nl.edu
VIOLA, Katie ... 425-739-8455 482 A katie.viola@lwtech.edu
VIOLA, Michael ... 925-631-4817 .. 59 B mjv7@stmarys-ca.edu
VIOLETT, Edward ... 225-768-1711 186 F edward.violett@ololcollege.edu
VIOLLT, Kathleen ... 312-935-6444 147 D kviollt@robertmorris.edu
VIRAMONTES, Angel ... 310-287-4473 .. 49 G viramoa@wlac.edu
VIRASAWMI, Errol ... 516-364-0808 309 A errol@nycollege.edu
VIRELLO, Mark ... 617-585-0200 206 F mark.virello@the-bac.edu
VIRES, Charles ... 731-989-6004 420 C cvires@fhu.edu
VIRGIN, Richard, P ... 619-260-4770 .. 71 J rvirgin@sandiego.edu
VIRJEE, Framroze (Fram) ... 657-278-3456 .. 31 E presidentvirjee@fullerton.edu
VIRK, Surinder ... 718-997-5760 295 C surinder.virk@qc.cuny.edu
VIRKLER, Lyndon ... 802-225-3258 462 I lyndon.virkler@neci.edu
VIRTANEN, B. Louise ... 906-524-8313 226 A

VOWELS, Robert .... 313-993-1700 231 B
robert.vowels@udmercy.edu
VOYLES, Brad .... 706-419-1107 117 B
voyles@covenant.edu
VOYTEK, Robert .... 928-226-4208.. 11 O
bob.voytek@coconino.edu
VOYTOVICH, Steven, A . 570-561-1818 398 D
steven.voytovich@stots.edu
VRANCILA, Alin .... 503-255-0332 374 D
alinvrancila@multnomah.edu
VRANOS, Kathleen .... 508-541-1898 208 F
kvranos@dean.edu
VRANOS, Kathryn .... 508-362-2131 214 B
kvranos@capecod.edu
VRBKA, Natalie .... 402-552-3100 266 E
VREKA, Mimoza .... 617-449-7070 219 C
mimoza.vreka@urbancollege.edu
VRIESMAN, Douglas ...... 616-538-2330 224 C
dvriesman@gracechristian.edu
VRIEZE, Scott .... 715-232-2141 498 A
vriezes@uwstout.edu
VROMAN, Mona, O .... 315-267-2120 319 D
vromanmo@potsdam.edu
VROOMAN, Mike .... 616-331-8566 224 E
vroomanm@gvsu.edu
VU, Cathy .... 706-855-8233.. 92 G
VU, Cory, N .... 530-752-1730.. 68 E
jgcampbell@ucdavis.edu
VU, Nancy .... 619-961-4325.. 67 E
nancyv@tjsl.edu
VU, Viet .... 949-376-6000.. 47 D
vvu@lcad.edu
VUCELICH, Tom .... 412-809-5100 396 H
vucelich.tom@ptcollege.edu
VUJNOVIC, Alison .... 918-495-6221 368 I
avujnovic@oru.edu
VUKELICH, Carol .... 302-831-2394.. 90 F
vukelich@udel.edu
VUKIC, Kelsey .... 626-529-8453.. 55 A
kvukic@pacificoaks.edu
VUKMANIC,
Jonathan, S .... 412-346-2100 396 F
jvukmanic@pia.edu
VUKSTA, Rebecca .... 864-294-2448 410 A
rebecca.vuksta@furman.edu
VULAJ, Julie .... 248-204-2313 226 G
jvulaj@ltu.edu
VULETICH, Victoria .... 616-301-6800 233 A
vuleticv@cooley.edu
VULLO, Russell .... 478-301-2409 121 E
vullo_ra@mercer.edu
VULLO, Stephanie .... 718-780-0605 291 J
stephanie.vullo@brooklaw.edu
VULOVICH, Daisy .... 941-363-7200 108 G
vulovid@scf.edu
VUONO, Vincent .... 610-989-1232 402 B
vvuono@vfmac.edu
VUORI, Kristiina .... 858-646-3100.. 62 A
kvuori@sbpdiscovery.org
VUTHIPADADON, Ying . 402-280-1164 266 I
yingv@creighton.edu
VYE, Christopher, S ...... 651-962-4666 244 E
cvye@stthomas.edu
VYHMEISTER, Ken .... 509-527-2391 485 H
ken.vyhmeister@wallawalla.edu
VYSKOCIL, Cindy .... 949-582-4850.. 64 G
cvyskocil@saddleback.edu
VYSKOCIL, Cindy .... 949-582-4699.. 64 E
cvyskocil@socccd.edu
VYSKOCIL, Michelle ...... 989-275-5000 226 B
michelle.vyskocil@kirtland.edu
VYSKOCIL, Todd .... 715-682-1824 495 C
tvyskocil@northland.edu

W

WAACK, Jason .... 636-949-4738 254 F
jwaack@lindenwood.edu
WAAL, Tracy .... 740-397-6868 357 B
tracy.waal@mvnu.edu
WACH, Howard, M .... 646-313-8000 295 E
provost@guttman.cuny.edu
WACHLER, Brad .... 636-949-4777 254 F
bwachler@lindenwood.edu
WACHOWSKI, Robert .... 773-325-7762 135 I
bwachows@depaul.edu
WACHTER, Renee .... 715-394-8221 498 B
rwachter@uwsuper.edu
WACHTFOGEL, Marc ...... 701-858-4610 345 F
marc.wachtfogel@minotstateu.edu
WACK, Mary, F .... 509-335-8044 486 A
mwack@wsu.edu
WACKER, Cary, E .... 903-813-2042 430 N
cwacker@austincollege.edu
WACKER, Robbyn .... 320-308-2122 240 H
presidentsoffice@stcloudstate.edu
WACKER, Tracy .... 810-237-6508 231 G
twacker@umflint.edu
WACTAWSKI-WENDE,
Jean .... 716-829-5374 316 F
jww@buffalo.edu
WACTOR, Tracy .... 864-646-1840 413 A
twactor@tctc.edu
WADA, Frank, Y .... 310-825-1443.. 69 A
fwada@registrar.ucla.edu
WADA, Wes .... 214-887-5221 436 B
wwada@dts.edu
WADA-MCKEE, Nancy ... 323-343-3100.. 32 A
n.wadamckee@calstatela.edu
WADDELL, Edwin, B ...... 336-734-7326 334 E
ewaddell@forsythtech.edu
WADDELL, James .... 313-831-5200 223 I
jwaddell@etseminary.edu
WADDELL, Jenetta .... 662-685-4771 245 D
jwaddell@bmc.edu
WADDELL, Kristin .... 501-202-7933.. 18 E
registrar@bhclr.edu
WADDELL, Stan, M .... 412-268-1643 380 F
swaddell@cmu.edu
WADDLE, Chris .... 308-398-7325 266 A
cwaddle@cccneb.edu
WADDY, Jeff .... 708-596-2000 149 B
jwaddy@ssc.edu
WADE, Adam .... 919-718-7526 333 C
awade@cccc.edu
WADE, Aletha, R .... 301-369-2800 197 F
arwade@captechu.edu
WADE, Alton .... 901-321-4102 419 C
awade2@cbu.edu
WADE, Andrea, C .... 585-292-2170 307 H
awade13@monroecc.edu
WADE, Argyle .... 608-263-5700 496 C
dean@studentlife.wisc.edu
WADE, Bernadette .... 914-674-7596 306 F
bwade@mercy.edu
WADE, Chandra .... 773-947-6285 142 J
cwade@mccormick.edu
WADE, Connie, H .... 678-359-5053 119 F
connie_w@gordonstate.edu
WADE, Courtney .... 413-597-4139 220 C
courtney.wade@williams.edu
WADE, Doug .... 503-517-1043 377 G
dswade@warnerpacific.edu
WADE, Gary .... 865-545-5313 421 C
gary.wade@lmunet.edu
WADE, Gwen .... 404-880-8290 116 D
gwade@cau.edu
WADE, H. Keith .... 863-638-2940 113 B
wadehk@webber.edu
WADE, Janice .... 386-481-2882.. 95 F
wadej@cookman.edu
WADE, Jennifer, G .... 901-843-3850 423 J
goodloe@rhodes.edu
WADE, Jerry .... 614-287-5539 351 E
jwade@cscc.edu
WADE, John .... 847-635-2602 145 G
jwade@oakton.edu
WADE, John .... 510-215-3804.. 40 H
jwade@contracosta.edu
WADE, Juli .... 860-486-2713.. 88 E
juli.wade@uconn.edu
WADE, Kevin, J .... 252-335-3271 341 D
kjwade@ecsu.edu
WADE, Kristi .... 310-338-5334.. 50 J
kristi.wade@lmu.edu
WADE, Latasha .... 410-651-6508 203 A
lwade@umes.edu
WADE, Lisa .... 901-722-3265 424 C
lwade@sco.edu
WADE, Marcia .... 805-965-0581.. 62 C
mmwade1@sbcc.edu
WADE, Margaret .... 432-685-4615 440 E
mwade@midland.edu
WADE, Scott .... 509-963-2160 479 B
wades@cwu.edu
WADE, Susan .... 785-594-8382 170 I
susan.wade@bakeru.edu
WADE, Tiffany .... 740-389-4636 356 B
wadet@mtc.edu
WADE, Tyler .... 765-361-6054 162 E
wadet@wabash.edu
WADE, Veronica .... 206-934-5216 484 B
veronica.wade@seattlecolleges.edu
WADE JOHNSON,
Regina .... 314-719-3627 253 C
rwadejohnson@fontbonne.edu
WADFORD, Alton .... 252-493-7745 336 H
awadford@email.pittcc.edu
WADKINS, Jesse, E ...... 479-248-7236.. 19 C
jwadkins@ecollege.edu
WADLINGTON, Derek .... 717-264-2062 403 F
derek.wadlington@wilson.edu
WADSWORTH, Michael . 248-370-3352 229 G
wadsworth@oakland.edu
WAECHTER, Carolyn ..... 563-876-3353 164 J
waechter@dwci.edu
WAECHTER, James .... 727-873-4727 110 C
waechter@mail.usf.edu
WAGAR, Hayden .... 504-398-2143 191 C
hwagar@uhcno.edu
WAGEMANN, Scott .... 360-623-8685 479 C
scott.wagemann@centralia.edu
WAGEMESTER, Doug ..... 319-398-4909 167 C
dwageme@kirkwood.edu
WAGENER, William, C .. 304-336-8177 490 F
wagenerw@westliberty.edu
WAGER, Lisa .... 212-217-4700 299 H
lisa_wager@fitnyc.edu
WAGERS, Karen, C .... 859-280-1236 183 B
kwagers@lextheo.edu
WAGES, Charlene .... 843-661-1140 409 K
cwages@fmarion.edu
WAGES, Sam .... 210-805-5836 453 D
wages@uiwtx.edu
WAGESTER,
Kimberly, A .... 989-774-7388 222 C
wages1ka@cmich.edu
WAGGONER, David .... 757-455-3201 477 F
dwaggoner@vwu.edu
WAGGONER, Earl .... 303-963-3485.. 77 G
ewaggoner@ccu.edu
WAGGONER, Jon, G ..... 334-844-4866.... 4 E
waggojg@auburn.edu
WAGGONER, Julia .... 715-682-1279 495 C
jwaggoner@northland.edu
WAGGONER, Reneau .... 270-831-9625 181 D
reneau.waggoner@kctcs.edu
WAGGONER, Todd .... 417-862-9533 253 D
twaggoner@globaluniversity.edu
WAGGONER, Wes, K ..... 214-768-2110 444 E
wwaggoner@smu.edu
WAGNER, Alexander ..... 617-349-8509 210 H
alex.wagner@lesley.edu
WAGNER, Anthony, E .... 864-656-2421 408 A
wagnera@clemson.edu
WAGNER, Bob .... 303-765-3185.. 80 F
rwagner@iliff.edu
WAGNER, Claire, M ...... 513-529-7592 356 E
wagnercm@miamioh.edu
WAGNER, Craig .... 641-472-1177 167 F
wagner-craig@aramark.com
WAGNER, Dan .... 605-995-2145 415 C
dan.wagner@dwu.edu
WAGNER, Dave .... 615-966-5683 421 D
dave.wagner@lipscomb.edu
WAGNER, David, H .... 336-334-7880 341 F
dhwagner@ncat.edu
WAGNER, Deanna .... 614-236-6904 349 D
dwagner1453@capital.edu
WAGNER, James, M ..... 214-648-2168 457 B
james.wagner@utsouthwestern.edu
WAGNER, Jean .... 503-491-6113 374 C
jean.wagner@mhcc.edu
WAGNER, Jeff .... 320-308-2286 240 H
jswagner@stcloudstate.edu
WAGNER, Jodi .... 509-527-2772 485 H
jodi.wagner@wallawalla.edu
WAGNER, Kelsea .... 276-935-4349 464 L
kwagner@asl.edu
WAGNER, Kevin, J .... 740-826-6129 357 C
kevinw@muskingum.edu
WAGNER, Kimberly .... 260-481-6103 159 F
kimberly.wagner@pfw.edu
WAGNER, Kimberly .... 847-214-7124 136 F
kwagner@elgin.edu
WAGNER, Kurt .... 732-571-4401 279 B
kwagner@monmouth.edu
WAGNER, Kyle .... 843-921-6901 411 F
kwagner@netc.edu
WAGNER, Linda .... 305-628-6699 106 F
lwagner@stu.edu
WAGNER, Marci, K .... 724-450-4089 385 C
mkwagner@gcc.edu
WAGNER, Mark .... 312-329-4131 144 B
mark.wagner@moody.edu
WAGNER, Mary .... 803-777-7700 413 C
mary.wagner@sc.edu
WAGNER, Michael, F .... 603-646-0459 273 E
michael.f.wagner@dartmouth.edu
WAGNER, Michelle, L .... 262-243-5700 493 B
michelle.wagner@cuw.edu
WAGNER, Mike .... 309-556-3561 139 G
mwagner@iwu.edu
WAGNER, Miriam .... 336-334-7757 341 F
wagnerm@ncat.edu
WAGNER, Nicholas, J ... 989-964-2468 230 B
njwagner@svsu.edu
WAGNER, Patrick .... 620-229-6210 177 A
patrick.wagner@sckans.edu
WAGNER, Phil .... 941-359-4463 110 D
pewagner@sar.usf.edu
WAGNER, Rich .... 612-381-3099 235 H
rwagner@dunwoody.edu
WAGNER, Richard .... 413-782-1288 219 F
richard.wagner@wne.edu
WAGNER, Richard, T .... 240-895-3421 201 E
rtwagner@smcm.edu
WAGNER, Rick .... 812-357-6378 160 D
rwagner@saintmeinrad.edu
WAGNER, Robert .... 607-274-3860 303 B
rwagner1@ithaca.edu
WAGNER, Robert .... 212-563-6647 323 F
r.wagner@uts.edu
WAGNER, Robert .... 435-797-0945 460 H
robert.wagner@usu.edu
WAGNER, Robin .... 717-337-7000 384 H
rowagner@gettysburg.edu
WAGNER, Russell .... 361-825-2352 447 C
russell.wagner@tamucc.edu
WAGNER, Sam .... 814-886-6465 391 B
swagner@mtaloy.edu
WAGNER, Sarah .... 231-843-5986 232 J
sjwagner@westshore.edu
WAGNER, Susan .... 520-795-0787.. 10 H
financialaid@asaom.edu
WAGNER, Tina .... 651-690-8890 242 R
tmwagner@stkate.edu
WAGNER, Tracy, A .... 941-309-4376 105 K
twagner@ringling.edu
WAGNER DAVIS,
Jennifer (J.J.) .... 434-924-3252 473 A
evpcoo@virginia.edu
WAGNER-FOSSEN,
Dena .... 406-771-4312 264 G
dfossen@gfcmsu.edu
WAGNER-SCHULTZ,
Jessica .... 715-634-4790 493 I
jwschultz@lco.edu
WAGNON, Bill .... 601-635-6242 245 I
bwagnon@eccc.edu
WAGNON, Shelley .... 313-993-1588 231 B
wagnonsm@udmercy.edu
WAGONER, Dale .... 510-723-6618.. 35 O
dwagoner@chabotcollege.edu
WAGONER, Jessica, M . 909-869-3147.. 30 D
jmwagoner@cpp.edu
WAGONER, Natalie, M .. 260-399-7700 161 D
nwagoner@sf.edu
WAGONER, Susan .... 402-399-2313 266 F
swagoner@csm.edu
WAGONER, Zandra, L ... 909-593-3511.. 70 D
zwagoner@laverne.edu
WAGSTAFF, Jo .... 509-777-4311 486 I
jwagstaff@whitworth.edu
WAGSTAFF, Robert .... 617-603-6900 216 H
robert.wagstaff@necb.edu
WAGSTAFFE, Paul .... 916-686-8816.. 29 J
WAGUESPACK, Bruce .... 225-743-8500 188 B
bwaguespack@rpcc.edu
WAHAB, Lizzie .... 207-561-1619 195 J
r.lizzie.wahab@maine.edu
WAHFELDT, Tracy .... 217-373-3789 146 C
twahlfeldt@parkland.edu
WAHL, Anne, G .... 585-475-7688 313 A
agwvpa@rit.edu
WAHL, Christopher .... 201-360-4030 278 C
cwahl@hccc.edu
WAHL, Lynette .... 651-523-3000 236 A
lwahl@hamline.edu
WAHL, Shawn, T .... 417-836-5247 256 E
shawnwahl@missouristate.edu
WAHL, Todd .... 812-749-1242 159 C
twahl@oak.edu
WAHLBECK, Paul, J ...... 202-994-6130.. 91 F
ccasdean@gwu.edu
WAHLROOS-RITTER,
Ingalill .... 818-252-5185.. 75 C
ingalill.wahlroos-ritter@woodbury.edu
WAHLS, Dustha .... 217-234-5210 141 D
dwahls@lakeland.cc.il.us
WAHLSTEDT, Walter ...... 606-546-1661 184 H
wwahlstedt@unionky.edu
WAHLSTROM, David, A 617-989-4552 219 E
wahlstromd@wit.edu

WAHLSTROM, Tomi ...... 251-626-3303.... 7 E
twahlstrom@ussa.edu
WAHLSTROM HELGREN,
Elizabeth .... 312-567-6917 139 B
ewahlstr@iit.edu
WAHR, David .... 567-661-7401 360 B
david_wahr@owens.edu
WAHR, Linda .... 312-329-2213 144 B
linda.wahr@moody.edu
WAHRHAFTIG, Matt ...... 937-481-2263 364 E
matt_wahrhaftig@wilmington.edu
WAIAMAU-ARIOTA,
Kawika .... 425-235-2352 483 G
kwaiamau-ariota@rtc.edu
WAIBEL, Janet .... 573-882-2011 261 A
WAID, Landon .... 205-348-8207.... 7 G
landon.waid@ua.edu
WAID, Monica, K .... 941-359-7514 105 K
mwaid@ringling.edu
WAID, Patti .... 559-278-2795.. 31 D
pattiwaid@csufresno.edu
WAIDE, Michael, P .... 304-367-4284 489 D
michael.waide@pierpont.edu
WAINSCOTT, Denise ..... 606-546-4151 184 H
dwainscott@unionky.edu
WAINWRIGHT,
Christopher .... 386-506-3162.. 97 D
christopher.wainwright@daytonastate.edu
WAINWRIGHT, Lisa ...... 312-629-1236 148 I
lwainwright@saic.edu
WAINWRIGHT, Philip .... 404-727-7504 117 F
pwainwr@emory.edu
WAINWRIGHT,
William, S .... 985-545-1500 187 H
WAIS, Marc, L .... 212-998-4401 310 B
marc.wais@nyu.edu
WAISMAN, Dov .... 213-738-5733.. 65 G
academicaffairs@swlaw.edu
WAIT, Julianna, M .... 757-594-7385 466 B
julianna.wait@cnu.edu
WAIT, Mark .... 615-322-7660 428 D
mark.wait@vanderbilt.edu
WAITE, Dan .... 848-932-7787 282 B
dwaite@global.rutgers.edu
WAITE, Dan .... 848-932-7787 282 A
dwaite@global.rutgers.edu
WAITE, Kelsey .... 614-236-6116 349 D
kwaite2@capital.edu
WAITE, Lucy .... 716-896-0700 324 E
lwaite@villa.edu
WAITE, Michelle .... 402-472-2116 269 J
mwaite1@unl.edu
WAITE, Peter .... 801-626-8957 461 B
pwaite@weber.edu
WAITE, Zauyah .... 412-365-2794 381 C
zwaite@chatham.edu
WAITERS, Ernest .... 301-860-4040 203 C
ewaiters@bowiestate.edu
WAITS, Laura .... 713-221-5026 453 B
waitsl@uhd.edu
WAITS, Melvin .... 205-247-8151.... 7 A
mwaits@stillman.edu
WAITSMAN, Eileen .... 410-209-6050 197 E
ewaitsman@bccc.edu
WAITZ, Ian, A .... 617-253-0218 215 G
WAJDA, Phillip, J .... 518-388-6131 323 G
wajdap@union.edu
WAJERT, Susan .... 419-251-1314 356 C
susan.wajert@mercycollege.edu
WAKEFIELD, Cooper, S 920-923-8977 494 A
cswakefield00@marianuniversity.edu
WAKEFIELD, Larry .... 937-328-6003 350 L
wakefieldl@clarkstate.edu
WAKEFIELD, Sarah .... 425-235-2285 483 G
swakefield@rtc.edu
WAKEM, Jake .... 651-641-8228 235 F
wakem@csp.edu
WAKEMAN, Roger, F .... 315-859-4506 301 C
rwakeman@hamilton.edu
WAKIAGA, Naomi .... 302-736-2435.. 90 G
naomi.wakiaga@wesley.edu
WAKIMOTO, Roger .... 310-825-7943.. 69 A
rwakimoto@conet.ucla.edu
WAKSDAHL, Robert, B .. 715-394-8017 498 B
rwaksdah@uwsuper.edu
WALBERT, Mark .... 309-438-7018 139 E
mswalber@ilstu.edu
WALBERT, Stacie .... 814-732-1719 394 F
swalbert@edinboro.edu
WALBORN, Ronald .... 845-770-5716 310 G
ronald.walborn@nyack.edu
WALCERZ, Douglas .... 979-230-3443 432 D
douglas.walcerz@brazosport.edu
WALCHER, Sheldon .... 847-543-2551 135 B
swalcher@clcillinois.edu
WALCHESKI, Michael .... 651-603-6184 235 F
walcheski@csp.edu
WALCHLE, John .... 740-392-6868 357 B
john.walchle@mvnu.edu
WALCK, Barbara .... 716-614-5902 310 C
bwalck@niagaracc.suny.edu
WALCROFT, Marie, B .... 215-699-5700 388 E
mwalcroft@lsb.edu
WALCZAK, Mary .... 507-786-3498 243 C
walczak@stolaf.edu
WALD, Cara .... 651-638-6400 234 C
c-wald@bethel.edu
WALDBILLIG, Amy .... 513-569-1414 350 K
amy.waldbillig@cincinnatistate.edu
WALDEN, Daniel, W ..... 760-245-4271.. 73 D
daniel.walden@vvc.edu
WALDEN, David .... 315-859-4340 301 C
dwalden@hamilton.edu
WALDEN, Valerie .... 361-570-4815 453 C
waldenv@uhv.edu
WALDEN, Wendy .... 864-250-8125 410 B
wendy.walden@gvltec.edu
WALDHOF, Kenneth ...... 718-862-7362 305 H
kenneth.waldhof@manhattan.edu
WALDMAN, Chaim, A ... 718-259-5600 299 E
WALDMAN, Martin .... 718-853-8500 322 I
WALDMANN, Jenn .... 325-670-1467 437 F
jwaldmann@hsutx.edu
WALDMANN, Robert, G 718-429-6600 324 D
robert.waldmann@vaughn.edu
WALDNER, Louann .... 559-688-3027.. 39 E
louannw@cos.edu
WALDO, Hilary .... 678-916-2625 114 I
hwaldo@johnmarshall.edu
WALDON, James .... 609-896-5029 281 B
jwaldon@rider.edu
WALDON, Russell .... 650-738-7099.. 61 Q
waldonr@smccd.edu
WALDRAM CRAMER,
Kelly .... 660-543-4640 260 K
waldram@ucmo.edu
WALDRON, David, E ..... 512-448-8453 442 M
dwaldron@stedwards.edu
WALDRON, Gregory, T . 401-865-2290 405 B
gregory.waldron@providence.edu
WALDRON, Jennifer ...... 319-273-2748 163 B
jennifer.waldron@uni.edu
WALDRON, Jerry .... 410-651-8200 203 A
jwaldron@umes.edu
WALDRON, John .... 270-706-8545 181 A
jwaldron0004@kctcs.edu
WALDRON, Kim .... 719-389-6704.. 77 H
kwaldron@coloradocollege.edu
WALDROP, Heath .... 870-864-7111.. 21 B
hwaldrop@southark.edu
WALDROP, Jean .... 501-279-4349.. 19 D
jwaldrop@harding.edu
WALDROP, Jeffrey, A .... 478-301-2960 121 E
jenkins_gp@mercer.edu
WALDROP, Lisa .... 205-391-2959.... 3 E
lwaldrop@sheltonstate.edu
WALDROP, Tony, G ...... 251-460-6111.... 8 F
twaldrop@southalabama.edu
WALDROUP, Linda, L ... 812-888-4333 162 C
lwaldroup@vinu.edu
WALDRUFF, Paula .... 419-755-4786 357 E
pwaldruff@ncstatecollege.edu
WALDSTEIN, Edith, J .... 319-352-8272 170 C
edith.waldstein@wartburg.edu
WALDSTEIN, Steve .... 712-324-5061 168 G
swaldstein@nwicc.edu
WALDVOGEL, Todd, S .. 817-257-7955 448 G
todd.waldvogel@tcu.edu
WALES, Chuck .... 714-628-4721.. 58 A
wales_chuck@sccollege.edu
WALES, Lynn .... 215-885-2360 389 F
lwales@manor.edu
WALESBY, Anthony .... 309-438-3383 139 E
ajwales1@ilstu.edu
WALICKI, Edward, j ...... 386-323-8004.. 98 A
walickie@erau.edu
WALK, Kerry .... 212-517-0560 306 A
kwalk@mmm.edu
WALK, Steve .... 657-278-1605.. 31 E
swalk@fullerton.edu
WALKE, James .... 256-372-8876.... 1 A
james.walke@aamu.edu
WALKE, Lindsey .... 843-863-8047 407 E
lwalke@csuniv.edu
WALKENHORST,
Kevin, R .... 801-863-7169 461 A
kevin.walkenhorst@uvu.edu
WALKER, Aimee .... 928-350-2100.. 15 N
WALKER, Amanda .... 360-867-6300 481 A
walkera@evergreen.edu
WALKER, Amanda .... 931-221-6163 418 D
walkera@apsu.edu
WALKER, Ameae .... 951-827-2304.. 69 C
ameae.walker@ucr.edu
WALKER, Andrew .... 252-246-1311 339 C
awalker@wilsoncc.edu
WALKER, Angie .... 866-776-0331.. 54 A
awalker@ncu.edu
WALKER, Anne .... 303-384-2321.. 78 I
aswalker@mines.edu
WALKER, Anne, E .... 713-348-8025 442 K
anne.e.walker@rice.edu
WALKER, Ashley .... 912-478-2647 119 C
gradschool@georgiasouthern.edu
WALKER, Beth .... 970-491-2398.. 78 M
beth.walker@colostate.edu
WALKER, Beth .... 313-664-7641 222 F
bwalker@collegeforcreativestudies.edu
WALKER, Beverley .... 478-289-2051 117 D
bewalker@ega.edu
WALKER, Beverly .... 419-755-4786 357 E
bwalker@ncstatecollege.edu
WALKER, Bill .... 781-736-3393 207 E
billwalker@brandeis.edu
WALKER, Bradley .... 361-593-3918 447 D
bradley.walker@tamuk.edu
WALKER, Brenda .... 727-873-4979 110 C
brendawalker@usf.edu
WALKER, Calvin, R .... 225-771-3222 190 H
calvin_walker@suagcenter.com
WALKER, Carey .... 603-427-7605 272 J
cwalker@ccsnh.edu
WALKER, Charlene .... 859-246-6438 180 K
charlene.walker@kctcs.edu
WALKER,
Christopher, O .... 405-325-3227 371 B
chris.walker@ou.edu
WALKER, Cindy, M .... 412-396-6093 383 C
cmwalker@duq.edu
WALKER, Courtney .... 903-670-2688 452 B
cwalker@tvcc.edu
WALKER, Crystal .... 304-766-3111 491 B
walkerc@wvstateu.edu
WALKER, Dalbert, N ...... 772-546-5534 101 B
dalbertwalker@hsbc.edu
WALKER, David .... 518-445-2385 289 E
dwalk@albanylaw.edu
WALKER, David, S .... 717-766-2511 390 E
dwalker@messiah.edu
WALKER, Debbie .... 417-328-1729 259 L
dlwalker@sbuniv.edu
WALKER, Debbie .... 803-822-3261 410 G
walkerd@midlandstech.edu
WALKER, Deborah .... 845-675-4430 310 G
deborah.walker@nyack.edu
WALKER, Deborah .... 770-720-5523 123 E
dcw@reinhardt.edu
WALKER, Deborah .... 510-849-8290.. 55 B
dwalker@psr.edu
WALKER, Deborah .... 510-649-2577.. 44 F
dwalker@gtu.edu
WALKER, Donna .... 864-592-4942 412 F
walkerd@sccsc.edu
WALKER, Donna .... 972-238-6880 435 F
dwalker1@dcccd.edu
WALKER, Doug .... 301-891-4134 204 C
dkwalker@wau.edu
WALKER, Doug .... 870-759-4105.. 23 J
dwalker@williamsbu.edu
WALKER, Doug .... 845-675-4509 310 G
douglas.walker@nyack.edu
WALKER, Dwayne .... 215-489-2372 382 D
dwayne.walker@delval.edu
WALKER, Eddie .... 318-869-5116 186 B
ewalker@centenary.edu
WALKER, Elizabeth .... 617-984-1611 218 B
ewalker@quincycollege.edu
WALKER, Erik, J .... 610-758-3131 388 J
erw209@lehigh.edu
WALKER, Eunice, E .... 870-235-5113.. 21 D
eewalker@saumag.edu
WALKER, Francene .... 240-567-7491 200 C
francene.walker@montgomerycollege.edu
WALKER, Gail, D .... 208-467-8844 131 D
gwalker@nnu.edu
WALKER, Glenda, C .... 956-326-2574 446 F
glenda.walker@tamiu.edu
WALKER, Gloria .... 620-441-5207 172 I
gloria.walker@cowley.edu
WALKER, Gloria, T .... 973-353-5533 282 B
gloriar@rutgers.edu
WALKER, Grant .... 541-956-7088 376 D
gwalker@roguecc.edu
WALKER, Holly .... 804-594-1530 474 I
hwalker@jtcc.edu
WALKER, Horacio .... 360-650-3319 486 F
horacio.walker@wwu.edu
WALKER, J. Brent .... 703-812-4757 468 G
bwalker@leland.edu
WALKER, Jamie .... 434-791-5874 464 O
walkerj@averett.edu
WALKER, Janice .... 601-426-6346 249 A
jwalker@southeasternbaptist.edu
WALKER, Janice, B .... 513-745-3117 365 B
walkerj@xavier.edu
WALKER, Jeannie .... 714-744-7078.. 36 C
walker@chapman.edu
WALKER, Jeff .... 626-256-4673.. 37 B
jewalker@coh.org
WALKER, Jennifer .... 781-736-3508 207 E
walkerj@brandeis.edu
WALKER, Jennifer .... 918-540-6250 366 I
jennifer.hessee@neo.edu
WALKER, Jimmy .... 805-289-6347.. 73 B
jwalker1@vcccd.edu
WALKER, Joe .... 828-227-7441 344 A
jwalker@wcu.edu
WALKER, Joel .... 904-470-8200.. 97 L
joel.walker@ewc.edu
WALKER, John .... 620-241-0723 172 D
john.walker@centralchristian.edu
WALKER, Joshua .... 805-581-1233.. 42 D
jwalker@eternitybiblecollege.com
WALKER, Joshua, D ...... 908-852-1400 276 G
walkerj@centenaryuniversity.edu
WALKER, Judith, D .... 402-559-6409 270 A
jdwalker@unmc.edu
WALKER, Julian .... 386-481-2026.. 95 F
walkerj@cookman.edu
WALKER, Kara .... 470-639-0531 122 D
kara.walker@morehouse.edu
WALKER, Kara .... 828-398-7870 332 B
karakwalker@abtech.edu
WALKER, Karen, M .... 540-261-8547 471 H
karen.walker@svu.edu
WALKER, Katherine, D .. 804-752-7212 470 F
kathywalker@rmc.edu
WALKER, Katrina .... 404-225-4420 114 H
kwalker@atlantatech.edu
WALKER, Kirk .... 253-589-5533 479 G
kirk.walker@cptc.edu
WALKER, Krista .... 240-567-4280 200 C
krista.walker@montgomerycollege.edu
WALKER, Kristin .... 903-675-6232 452 B
kristin.walker@tvcc.edu
WALKER, Larry, A .... 405-585-5130 367 F
larry.walker@okbu.edu
WALKER, LaShante .... 615-687-6891 418 A
lwalker@gmail.com
WALKER, Lauren .... 540-362-6639 468 C
walkerls@hollins.edu
WALKER, Laurence .... 831-646-4190.. 52 F
lwalker@mpc.edu
WALKER, Laverne .... 212-229-8930 308 C
walkerl1@newschool.edu
WALKER, Lesley .... 262-595-2188 497 C
lwalker@uwp.edu
WALKER, Lisa .... 712-325-3210 167 B
lwalker@iwcc.edu
WALKER, Lloyd .... 256-372-5783.... 1 A
lloyd.walker@aamu.edu
WALKER, Loretta, D ...... 301-736-3631 199 G
WALKER, Lucy .... 845-257-3229 317 B
walkerl@newpaltz.edu
WALKER, Mark .... 972-825-4739 445 A
mwalker@sagu.edu
WALKER, Martha, J .... 540-887-7068 469 B
mwalker@marybaldwin.edu
WALKER, Matt .... 660-562-1173 257 E
matt@nwmissouri.edu
WALKER, Meagan .... 425-352-8491 479 A
mwalker@cascadia.edu
WALKER, Melinda .... 870-762-3108.. 17 D
mjwalker@smail.anc.edu
WALKER, Melveta .... 575-562-2624 285 M
melveta.walker@enmu.edu
WALKER, Michael .... 208-535-5451 130 C
michael.walker@cei.edu
WALKER, Michael, A ..... 910-962-3117 343 C
walkerm@uncw.edu

WALKER, Michael, E 936-468-2401 445 F mwalker@sfasu.edu
WALKER, Michelle 804-278-4252 472 E mwalker@upsem.edu
WALKER, Mike 208-535-5451 130 C michael.walker@cei.edu
WALKER, Mike, J 972-860-7196 435 B mwalker@dcccd.edu
WALKER, Mitch 270-745-6253 185 E mitchell.walker@wku.edu
WALKER, Mitchell 256-539-0511 5 I deangrad@hbc1.edu
WALKER, Miya 562-860-2451 35 M mwalker@cerritos.edu
WALKER, Peter 412-365-1842 381 C pwalker@chatham.edu
WALKER, Ray 801-863-8183 461 A walker.ray@uvu.edu
WALKER, Ray 575-769-4953 285 K ray.walker@clovis.edu
WALKER, Richard 618-650-2536 149 F rwalker@siue.edu
WALKER, Richard 713-743-5390 452 E rwalker2@central.uh.edu
WALKER, Richard 713-743-5390 452 F rwalker2@central.uh.edu
WALKER, Robert 843-574-6788 413 B bob.walker@tridenttech.edu
WALKER, III, Roy 312-850-7145 134 H rwalker59@ccc.edu
WALKER, Sally 540-375-2074 471 B swalker@roanoke.edu
WALKER, Sandra 870-235-4035 21 D slwalker@saumag.edu
WALKER, Sandra 617-349-8317 210 H sandra.walker@lesley.edu
WALKER, Sarah 318-342-1040 192 F nwalker@ulm.edu
WALKER, Shannon 570-484-3131 395 B styson@lockhaven.edu
WALKER, Sharianne 413-782-1389 219 F swalker@wne.edu
WALKER, Shaundra 478-445-0980 118 C shaundra.walker@gcsu.edu
WALKER, Stephanie 913-758-4359 177 F stephanie.walker@stmary.edu
WALKER, Stephanie 215-885-2360 389 F swalker@manor.edu
WALKER, Stephanie 701-777-2189 345 C stephanie.walker@und.edu
WALKER, Suzanne 865-694-6648 425 F swalker@pstcc.edu
WALKER, Teresa 256-840-4211 3 F teresa.walker@snead.edu
WALKER, Teresa 212-650-5920 293 D twalker@ccny.cuny.edu
WALKER, Terilyn 949-214-3039 40 F terilyn.walker@cui.edu
WALKER, Terri 760-252-2411 26 I twalker@barstow.edu
WALKER, JR., Thomas, A 919-735-5151 338 H tawalker@waynecc.edu
WALKER, Tonia 276-326-4316 465 B twalker@bluefield.edu
WALKER, Tryphena 903-693-2075 441 F twalker@panola.edu
WALKER, Vanessa 817-515-4591 445 G vanessa.walker@tccd.edu
WALKER, Vennessa, L 716-286-8571 310 D vwalker@niagara.edu
WALKER, Verne, W 843-349-2357 408 C vwalker@coastal.edu
WALKER, Vernell, E 210-486-0920 429 H vwalker@alamo.edu
WALKER, Wade 205-726-2916 6 E pwalker@samford.edu
WALKER, Wanda 678-839-5569 126 E wgwalker@westga.edu
WALKER, William 202-885-8622 93 E bwalker@wesleyseminary.edu
WALKER, William 910-630-7152 331 C wwalker@methodist.edu
WALKER, William (Billy) 202-885-3190 90 J walker@american.edu
WALKER, Willis 330-672-2982 354 J wwalker@kent.edu
WALKER, Yvonne, S 540-365-4275 467 I ywalker@ferrum.edu
WALKER FRANKLIN, Angela, L 515-271-1400 164 I
WALKER-GRIFFEA, Beverly 810-762-0453 228 C b.walkergriffea@mcc.edu
WALKER MOYER, Diana 978-934-4991 211 G diana_walkermoyer@uml.edu
WALKER-PAYNE, Katherine 502-585-9911 184 D kwalkerpayne@spalding.edu
WALKERS, Kathia 787-257-0000 513 C kattia.walkers1@upr.edu
WALKES, Skyller 512-245-3451 450 E s_w137@txstate.edu
WALKLEY, Beth 201-684-7266 280 H bwalkley@ramapo.edu
WALKOWIAK, Rebecca, A 219-464-5430 162 A becky.walkowiak@valpo.edu
WALKUP, Kraig 212-346-1368 311 E studyabroad@pace.edu
WALL, Amanda 907-474-7552 10 A aiwall@alaska.edu
WALL, Amitra, A 716-878-6939 318 C hodgeaa@buffalostate.edu
WALL, Andrew 909-748-8815 71 G andrew_wall@redlands.edu
WALL, Barbara, E 610-519-5431 402 D barbara.wall@villanova.edu
WALL, Brian 303-963-3187 77 G bwall@ccu.edu
WALL, Claudia, E 804-257-5789 477 C cewall@vuu.edu
WALL, David 315-498-2173 311 B walld@sunyocc.edu
WALL, Dustin 816-584-6798 258 A dustin.wall@park.edu
WALL, Erica 406-657-1125 265 E erica.wall@rocky.edu
WALL, James 585-395-2129 318 B jwall@brockport.edu
WALL, Jim 518-464-8709 299 G jwall@excelsior.edu
WALL, Jody, Y 770-534-6110 115 D jwall@brenau.edu
WALL, Joey 845-575-3000 305 L joey.wall@marist.edu
WALL, John 828-262-2080 341 B walljm1@appstate.edu
WALL, John 904-632-3105 100 B john.wall@fscj.edu
WALL, John 856-745-6532 281 G johnwall@camden.rutgers.edu
WALL, John 615-383-3230 418 C wallj1@dominicancampus.org
WALL, Joyce 615-297-7545 418 C wallj@aquinascollege.edu
WALL, Laurie 417-255-7976 256 F lauriewall@missouristate.edu
WALL, Letitia, C 336-750-2132 344 B cornishl@wssu.edu
WALL, Mark 918-540-6451 366 I mark.wall@neo.edu
WALL, Merritt 229-333-5797 126 G emwall@valdosta.edu
WALL, Michael, A 973-596-5629 279 F michael.a.wall@njit.edu
WALL, Renee 406-447-5169 263 C rwall@carroll.edu
WALL, Rich 760-701-5380 87 D wall_r@mitchell.edu
WALL, Richard 973-290-4290 277 A rwall@cse.edu
WALL, Rick 323-343-3700 32 A rwall2@calstatela.edu
WALL, Sandy 252-249-1851 336 F swall@pamlicocc.edu
WALL, Seth, P 603-314-1705 216 B seth.wall@mcphs.edu
WALL, Thomas 617-552-4470 207 B thomas.wall.2@bc.edu
WALL, Timothy 660-562-1179 257 E timwall@nwmissouri.edu
WALL, Vanessa 229-931-2713 124 D vwall@southgatech.edu
WALL, Yvette 718-270-4894 295 A ywall@mec.cuny.edu
WALLACE, Ainsely 207-780-4461 196 F ainsley.wallace@maine.edu
WALLACE, Andrea 912-279-5931 116 G awalace@ccga.edu
WALLACE, Auguster 662-254-3088 248 B akeys@mvsu.edu
WALLACE, Bentley 501-812-2366 23 B bwallace@uaptc.edu
WALLACE, Beth 413-236-1601 213 F bwallace@berkshirecc.edu
WALLACE, Beth, D 864-597-4371 414 H wallaceed@wofford.edu
WALLACE, Bobby 205-652-3652 9 A bwallace@uwa.edu
WALLACE, Brent 318-795-4215 189 D brent.wallace@lsus.edu
WALLACE, Brian 251-626-3303 7 E bwallace@ussa.edu
WALLACE, Camille, R 812-877-8863 159 J wallace@rose-hulman.edu
WALLACE, Chad 765-641-4374 153 B cewallace@anderson.edu
WALLACE, Cheryl 908-526-1200 281 A cheryl.wallace@raritanval.edu
WALLACE, Christine 810-762-9575 225 H cwallace@kettering.edu
WALLACE, Cindy 704-406-4103 329 A cwallace@gardner-webb.edu
WALLACE, David 562-985-5381 31 F david.wallace@csulb.edu
WALLACE, David 270-534-3859 182 F david.wallace@kctcs.edu
WALLACE, David 909-607-8095 57 F david.wallace@pomona.edu
WALLACE, Debbie 870-543-5996 21 C dwallace@seark.edu
WALLACE, Deborah 818-677-2305 32 D deborah.wallace@csun.edu
WALLACE, Denise 504-816-4546 186 D dwallace@dillard.edu
WALLACE, Denise 850-599-3591 108 I denise.wallace@famu.edu
WALLACE, Donald 760-921-5499 55 H donald.wallace@paloverde.edu
WALLACE, Douglas, J 864-833-8312 411 I dwallace@presby.edu
WALLACE, Effie 540-261-8492 471 H effie.wallace@svu.edu
WALLACE, Elaine 954-262-1407 103 M ewallace@nova.edu
WALLACE, Eric, C 806-356-3682 430 A ecwallace@actx.edu
WALLACE, G. Brent 940-668-4230 441 A bwallace@nctc.edu
WALLACE, Glenn 912-525-5000 123 G gwallace@scad.edu
WALLACE, JR., James 219-980-6601 156 E jamewall@iun.edu
WALLACE, Jason 303-282-3423 82 H father.wallace@archden.org
WALLACE, Jeff 765-998-5395 160 F jfwallace@taylor.edu
WALLACE, Jeremy 573-629-3048 253 H jeremy.wallace@hlg.edu
WALLACE, Jerry 910-893-1205 327 E wallace@campbell.edu
WALLACE, Jerry 402-461-2400 266 A jerrywallace@cccneb.edu
WALLACE, Joel 817-202-6333 444 I jwallace@swau.edu
WALLACE, Juliane 618-453-4527 149 E grad.deansoffice@siu.edu
WALLACE, Julianne 610-796-8300 378 F julianne.wallace@alvernia.edu
WALLACE, Justin 661-259-7800 38 H justin.wallace@canyons.edu
WALLACE, Kim 303-404-5671 79 J kim.wallace@frontrange.edu
WALLACE, Kim 303-404-5316 80 K kim.wallace@frontrange.edu
WALLACE, Kimberly 239-590-1087 108 K kwilliam@fgcu.edu
WALLACE, Laura, J 434-592-7330 468 H jwallac@liberty.edu
WALLACE, Laurie 314-744-5321 256 C wallace@mobap.edu
WALLACE, Leigh 229-217-4143 125 A lwallace@southernregional.edu
WALLACE, Mark, T 615-936-6709 428 D mark.wallace@vanderbilt.edu
WALLACE, Matthew, L 603-931-4369 275 B mlwallace@plymouth.edu
WALLACE, Mike, J 408-554-4981 62 D mjwallace@scu.edu
WALLACE, Miriam 941-487-4360 109 D mwallace@ncf.edu
WALLACE, Molly 252-538-4319 335 B mwallace@halifaxcc.edu
WALLACE, Nancy 716-888-2768 292 D wallacen@canisius.edu
WALLACE, Pamela 510-464-3248 56 G pwallace@peralta.edu
WALLACE, Paula 912-525-5000 123 G pwallace@scad.edu
WALLACE, Ray 812-941-2200 157 B raywall@ius.edu
WALLACE, Renee, L 512-471-9094 455 A rlwallace@austin.utexas.edu
WALLACE, Robert 718-982-2635 293 E robert.wallace@csi.cuny.edu
WALLACE, Robert 650-723-2300 65 J
WALLACE, Robert 304-766-3190 491 B wallacer@wvstateu.edu
WALLACE, Sally 404-413-0093 119 E swallace@gsu.edu
WALLACE, Sam, G 318-257-2769 191 F wallace@latech.edu
WALLACE, Scott 985-867-2235 190 F swallace@sjasc.edu
WALLACE, Sereyna 704-216-6222 330 H
WALLACE, Sherrie 330-823-7803 363 B wallacsj@mountunion.edu
WALLACE, Steve 501-977-2086 23 A wallace@uaccm.edu
WALLACE, Suzanne 608-663-8334 493 C suzwallace@edgewood.edu
WALLACE, Tamara 540-831-6374 470 C twallace8@radford.edu
WALLACE, Tami 615-230-3573 426 B tami.wallace@volstate.edu
WALLACE, Teri 507-537-6246 241 D provost@smsu.edu
WALLACE, Terry 507-389-1334 239 C teresa.wallace@mnsu.edu
WALLACE, Terry 304-327-4000 489 P
WALLACE, Thomas 661-654-2161 30 E twallace4@csub.edu
WALLACE, Tom 615-898-2137 422 H tom.wallace@mtsu.edu
WALLACE, Tony 606-783-1538 182 A tony.wallace@kctcs.edu
WALLACE, Tracy 229-430-3867 113 I
WALLACE-DAVIS, Neuvia 401-254-5480 405 E nwallace-davis@rwu.edu
WALLEN, Esther 773-252-5133 147 B esther.wallen@resu.edu
WALLENMEYER, Mark 479-619-4310 20 D mwallenmeyer@nwacc.edu
WALLER, Art 801-774-9900 457 H awaller@vistacollege.edu
WALLER, Caroline 870-235-4006 21 D acwaller@saumag.edu
WALLER, Cynthia, G 615-353-3645 425 D cynthia.waller@nscc.edu
WALLER, Debra, A 845-431-8054 298 E debra.waller@sunydutchess.edu
WALLER, Edward 281-283-3100 453 A waller@uhcl.edu
WALLER, J.J 912-525-5000 123 G jwaller@scad.edu
WALLER, Janet 256-824-6282 8 B janet.waller@uah.edu
WALLER, Karen 615-230-3500 426 B karen.waller@volstate.edu
WALLER, Lauren 501-205-8896 18 H lwaller@cbc.edu
WALLER, Lorie 919-735-5151 338 H loriew@waynecc.edu
WALLER, Louise 434-395-2358 469 A wallermw@longwood.edu
WALLER, Matthew 479-575-5949 21 G mwaller@uark.edu
WALLER, Rhonda 336-278-5185 328 K rwaller3@elon.edu
WALLER, Stephen 661-395-4642 46 L swaller@bakersfieldcollege.edu
WALLER, Steve 225-578-5388 188 I swaller@lsu.edu
WALLER, Wanda, M 318-670-9248 190 J wmwaller@susla.edu
WALLERSTEIN, Mitchel, B 646-312-3310 292 L president@baruch.cuny.edu
WALLESER, Diane 212-220-1275 293 A dwalleser@bmcc.cuny.edu
WALLESHAUSER, Linda, M 716-888-2244 292 D walleshl@canisius.edu
WALLEY, Jennifer 559-251-4215 28 B jwalley@calchristiancollege.edu
WALLEY, Jim 601-477-4173 246 F jim.walley@jcjc.edu

WALZ, Michael 316-295-5810 173 D
michael_walz@friends.edu
WALZEL, JR., Robert, L 785-864-3421 177 D
robert.walzel@ku.edu
WAMBOLD, Nathan 215-702-4393 380 D
nwambold@cairn.edu
WAMBUGU COBB,
Angela 718-289-5185 293 B
angela.wambugucobb@bcc.cuny.edu
WAMPLER, Fredrick, H . 215-898-5859 400 K
fhoopes@upenn.edu
WAMPLER, Jim 423-236-2783 424 B
jwampler@southern.edu
WAMSLEY, Allan 636-481-3342 254 A
awamsley@jeffco.edu
WAMSLEY, Michelle, E . 804-287-6615 472 L
mwamsley@richmond.edu
WAMSLEY, Thomas 312-413-3391 151 B
twamsley@uic.edu
WANAT, Christina 740-264-5591 352 H
cwanat@egcc.edu
WANDLING, James 504-865-5352 191 B
jwandlin@tulane.edu
WANEKA, Joe 719-549-3291.. 81 K
joe.waneka@pueblocc.edu
WANG, Ching-Hua 510-869-6512.. 59 F
cwang@samuelmerritt.edu
WANG, Eric 818-252-5292.. 75 C
eric.wang@woodbury.edu
WANG, Grace 315-792-7400 321 E
gwang@sunypoly.edu
WANG, Grace 518-320-1313 316 C
grace.wang@suny.edu
WANG, Jason 818-677-2325.. 32 D
jason.wang@csun.edu
WANG, Jenny 860-906-5106.. 85 D
jwang@capitalcc.edu
WANG, Jianping 609-586-4800 278 F
wangj@mccc.edu
WANG, JuAn 618-453-8840 149 E
awang@siu.edu
WANG, Julie 510-763-7787.. 24 C
jwang@acchs.edu
WANG, Karl 888-488-4968.. 46 F
kwang@itu.edu
WANG, Lan 731-426-7654 420 I
lwang@lanecollege.edu
WANG, Lei 850-201-9775 111 C
wangl@tcc.fl.edu
WANG, Meredith, L 972-881-5794 433 M
mwang@collin.edu
WANG, Michael 504-282-4455 190 A
financialaid@nobts.edu
WANG, Minghui 201-216-8162 283 C
minghui.wang@stevens.edu
WANG, Nancy 540-654-1040 472 I
nwang@umw.edu
WANG, Ning 415-476-6881.. 69 E
ning.wang@ucsf.edu
WANG, Peter 516-364-0808 309 A
itsupport@nycollege.edu
WANG, Ray 504-280-6235 189 E
rwang9@uno.edu
WANG, Rui 504-280-6197 189 E
rwang9@uno.edu
WANG, Tracy 310-577-3000.. 75 G
swang@yosan.edu
WANG, Vincent 516-877-4191 289 C
vwang@adelphi.edu
WANG, Willis, G 617-358-6350 207 D
wgwang@bu.edu
WANG, Xiao-lei 516-877-4065 289 C
xlwang@adelphi.edu
WANG, Xiao-lei 914-773-3870 311 E
WANG, Xiaoping 423-354-2552 425 E
xpwang@northeaststate.edu
WANG, Xuemao 513-556-1515 362 D
xuemao.wang@uc.edu
WANG, Yan 414-297-8509 500 B
wangy@matc.edu
WANG, Ying 908-852-1400 276 G
ying.wang07@centenaryuniversity.edu
WANG, Youcheng 407-903-8011 109 E
youcheng.wang@ucf.edu
WANG, Yumin 203-576-4395.. 88 D
yuminw@bridgeport.edu
WANG, Yungzeng 951-827-3704.. 69 C
yunzeng.wang@ucr.edu
WANGERIN, LeAnna 763-576-4057 237 D
lwangerin@anokatech.edu
WANGLER, Michael 626-914-8794.. 36 K
mwangler@citruscollege.edu
WANKEL, Laura, A 617-373-4384 217 F
WANKMILLER, Joan 610-896-1021 385 L
jwankmil@haverford.edu
WANN, Connie, P 434-797-8400 474 E
connie.wann@danville.edu
WANOUS, Michael 605-626-2524 417 A
michael.wanous@northern.edu
WANOVICH, William, J . 540-464-7313 476 G
wanovichwj10@vmi.edu
WANSART, Terry 212-772-4782 294 C
terry.wansart@hunter.cuny.edu
WANSICK, Janet 918-463-2931 366 B
janet.wansick@connorsstate.edu
WANTZ, Steven 410-386-8154 197 G
swantz@carrollcc.edu
WANZA, Mary 410-951-3400 203 D
mwanza@coppin.edu
WANZER, Scott 479-524-7403.. 19 H
swanzer@jbu.edu
WAPLE, Jeffrey, N 618-650-2020 149 F
jwaple@siue.edu
WAPPES, Loran 218-879-0839 238 A
loran@fdltcc.edu
WARBURG, Keith 229-333-5980 126 G
jwwarburg@valdosta.edu
WARBURTON, Robert 304-876-5401 490 E
rwarburt@shepherd.edu
WARBURTON, Ted 831-459-2115.. 70 B
artsdean@ucsc.edu
WARD, Alan 812-877-8265 159 J
alan.ward@rose-hulman.edu
WARD, Alison 918-293-4952 368 D
alison.ward@okstate.edu
WARD, Allen 678-466-5485 116 E
jonahward@clayton.edu
WARD, Allen 325-674-2873 429 B
caw18c@acu.edu
WARD, Andy 541-881-5875 377 B
award@tvcc.cc
WARD, Annette 740-245-7223 363 D
award@rio.edu
WARD, Beth, I 413-559-5838 210 A
biwdv@hampshire.edu
WARD, Betsy 802-224-3020 463 H
betsy.ward@vsc.edu
WARD, Bill 520-206-2610.. 15 D
wward@pima.edu
WARD, Bill 843-863-7514 407 E
wward@csuniv.edu
WARD, Candace 207-974-4625 194 H
cward@emcc.edu
WARD, Carol 478-445-5596 118 C
carol.ward@gcsu.edu
WARD, Carrie 218-299-6631 239 B
carrie.ward@minneosta.edu
WARD, Chelsea, B 501-683-7631.. 22 B
cxbishop@ualr.edu
WARD, Chris 470-578-3393 120 L
cward1@kennesaw.edu
WARD, Chris 303-361-7361.. 79 D
chris.ward@ccaurora.edu
WARD, Christy 518-828-4181 297 B
christy.ward@sunycgcc.edu
WARD, Dane 828-262-2801 341 B
warddm1@appstate.edu
WARD, David 910-521-6211 343 B
david.ward@uncp.edu
WARD, David 423-775-6596 423 F
dward@ogs.edu
WARD, Debra 562-860-2451.. 35 M
dsward@cerritos.edu
WARD, Denise 229-317-6701 113 H
denise.ward@asurams.edu
WARD, Denise 651-696-6385 236 H
ward@macalester.edu
WARD, Denitta, D 303-735-6624.. 83 A
denitta.ward@colorado.edu
WARD, Diane 865-882-4513 425 G
wardd@roanestate.edu
WARD, Donna 517-265-5161 220 F
dward2@adrian.edu
WARD, Doris 662-252-8000 248 G
dward2@rustcollege.edu
WARD, Elizabeth 914-594-4846 309 H
elizabeth_ward@nymc.edu
WARD, Emily 718-489-5249 313 H
eward2@sfc.edu
WARD, Faith, W 334-670-3318.... 7 C
alumdev@troy.edu
WARD, Farrah, J 252-335-3849 341 D
fjward@ecsu.edu
WARD, Gary, L 573-882-4097 261 B
wardga@missouri.edu
WARD, Gayle 312-942-2819 148 A
gayle_ward@rush.edu
WARD, Heather 316-322-3121 171 G
hmward@butlercc.edu
WARD, Holly 952-996-1356 234 A
holly.ward@bethfel.org
WARD, Howard 585-475-6011 313 A
hxwbsr@rit.edu
WARD, IV, James 207-581-2201 195 J
jsward@maine.edu
WARD, Jeff 617-732-2896 216 B
jward@mcphs.edu
WARD, Jenifer, K 563-387-1001 167 E
president@luther.edu
WARD, John 610-683-4253 395 A
ward@kutztown.edu
WARD, John, A 513-529-4634 356 E
wardja2@miamioh.edu
WARD, John, M 831-656-2511 503 K
jmward1@nps.edu
WARD, Joseph 435-797-1195 460 H
joe.ward@usu.edu
WARD, Kathryn 510-869-1572.. 59 F
kward@samuelmerritt.edu
WARD, Kris 575-624-8621 287 A
wardk@nmmi.edu
WARD, Laurie 301-696-3803 199 B
ward@hood.edu
WARD, Lawrence, P 781-239-5346 205 E
lward@babson.edu
WARD, Leah 712-279-1682 163 C
leah.ward@briarcliff.edu
WARD, Leslie Colis 802-828-8631 463 F
leslie.ward@vcfa.edu
WARD, Lynne 801-321-7157 460 D
lward@utahsbr.edu
WARD, Marcus, D 601-877-6296 244 H
mdward@alcorn.edu
WARD, Mark 563-589-3202 169 I
mward@dbq.edu
WARD, Mary 581-803-2013 104 C
mary_ward@pba.edu
WARD, Matthew 805-493-3481.. 29 H
mward@callutheran.edu
WARD, Michael 314-362-9155 253 E
mward@bjc.org
WARD, Michael 336-838-6489 339 B
mrward284@wilkescc.edu
WARD, Michael, S 334-833-4463.... 5 H
mward@hawks.huntingdon.edu
WARD, Mike 270-686-9572 179 D
mike.ward@brescia.edu
WARD, Monica 770-426-2611 121 C
monica.ward@life.edu
WARD, Nayamka 718-818-6470 315 A
nward@edaff.com
WARD, Patricia 510-666-8248.. 24 D
pward@aimc.edu
WARD, Paul, J 214-768-3233 444 E
paulw@smu.edu
WARD, Perry, W 205-929-6300.... 2 H
pward@lawsonstate.edu
WARD, Randall 617-364-3510 207 A
rward@boston.edu
WARD, Richard 503-255-0332 374 D
rward@multnomah.edu
WARD, Robert, A 585-385-8310 314 A
bward@sjfc.edu
WARD, Robert, T 716-829-7836 298 F
wardr@dyc.edu
WARD, Roger, J 410-706-2477 202 D
rward@umaryland.edu
WARD, Ryan 406-586-3585 263 J
ryan.ward@montanabiblecollege.edu
WARD, Scott 231-843-5802 232 J
scward@westshore.edu
WARD, Stephen 914-674-7432 306 F
sward@mercy.edu
WARD, Stephen 808-544-0289 127 H
WARD, Steve 605-677-5307 416 H
steve.ward@usd.edu
WARD, Steve 360-623-8647 479 C
steve.ward@centralia.edu
WARD, Susan 402-354-7063 268 C
susie.ward@methodistcollege.edu
WARD, Susan 864-455-7902 414 A
wardse@mailbox.sc.edu
WARD, Susie 402-354-7063 268 C
susie.ward@methodistcollege.edu
WARD, Suzanne 870-584-1143.. 22 G
sward@cccua.edu
WARD, Tamica 925-424-1542.. 35 P
tward@laspositascollege.edu
WARD, JR., Thomas, J 516-877-3131 289 C
tward@adelphi.edu
WARD, Tim 718-862-7307 305 H
tim.ward@manhattan.edu
WARD, Todd 970-675-3257.. 78 G
todd.ward@cncc.edu
WARD, Tony 334-727-8364.... 7 D
tward@tuskegee.edu
WARD, Tony 605-455-6057 416 B
tward@olc.edu
WARD, Tracy 951-343-4552.. 27 J
tward@calbaptist.edu
WARD, Tracy 910-296-2503 335 E
tward@jamessprunt.edu
WARD, Wanda, E 217-265-0451 151 D
weward@illinois.edu
WARD, William 360-867-6115 481 A
wardw@evergreen.edu
WARD, Zachary 989-686-9590 223 G
zacharyward2@delta.edu
WARD-DE LEON,
Claudia 203-575-8276.. 86 B
cward-deleon@nv.edu
WARD-JOHNSON,
Frances 336-334-7806 341 F
fward@ncat.edu
WARD-PERADOZA,
Marianne 512-428-1287 442 M
mperadoz@stedwards.edu
WARD-ROOF, Jeanine 231-591-3578 223 J
jeaninewardroof@ferris.edu
WARDE, Robin, T 401-232-6253 404 F
rwarde@bryant.edu
WARDELL-GHIRARDUZZI,
Mary, J 415-422-2821.. 71 K
mjwardell@usfca.edu
WARDEN, Chris 510-659-6044.. 54 F
cwarden@ohlone.edu
WARDEN, Ken 479-788-7218.. 21 H
ken.warden@uafs.edu
WARDEN, Margo 802-635-1256 464 C
margo.warden@northernvermont.edu
WARDER, William 315-781-3729 302 A
warder@hws.edu
WARDINSKY, Ken 208-769-3377 131 C
kmwardinsky@nic.edu
WARDLAW,
Theodore, J 512-404-4824 431 C
twardlaw@austinseminary.edu
WARDLE, Marianne 307-766-1121 502 H
WARDROP,
Elizabeth, M 757-594-7635 466 B
elizabeth.wardrop@cnu.edu
WARDZALA, Ellen 419-559-2408 361 I
ewardzala01@terra.edu
WARE, Amy 901-321-3331 419 C
aware1@cbu.edu
WARE, Bob 870-222-5360.. 22 D
wareb@uamont.edu
WARE, Cynthia 310-506-6373.. 56 C
cynthia.ware@pepperdine.edu
WARE, Larry 304-647-6220 491 A
lware@osteo.wvsom.edu
WARE, Lisa 864-587-4295 412 G
warel@smcsc.edu
WARE, Mamie 770-426-2718 121 C
mamie.ware@life.edu
WARE, Monique 317-955-6040 158 U
mware@marian.edu
WARE, Peggy, J 309-341-7211 141 A
pjware@knox.edu
WARE, Shelby 903-233-4070 439 E
shelbyware@letu.edu
WARE, Stacy 713-348-4966 442 K
ware@rice.edu
WARE, Thomas 606-759-7141 182 A
WARE CARLTON,
Rachel 920-686-6272 496 A
rachel.warecarlton@sl.edu
WARE JOSEPH, Caran .. 303-765-3198.. 80 F
cwarejoseph@iliff.edu
WARE-ROBERTS,
Vonnie 405-466-2999 366 F
vonnie.w.roberts@langston.edu
WAREJAYE, Hollie 773-907-4456 134 C
hwarejaye@ccc.edu
WARFEL, Robert 513-745-2000 365 B
warfelr@xavier.edu
WARFIELD, Aimee, S 518-381-1207 315 G
warfieas@sunysccc.edu
WARFORD, Kimberly 630-787-7800 147 D
kwarford@robertmorris.edu
WARFORD, Lindsey 212-229-5600 308 C
warfordl@newschool.edu

WARFORD, Pam 281-425-6361 439 D pwarford@lee.edu
WARGO, Lisa 318-678-6000 187 A lwargo@bpcc.edu
WARGO, Melissa 828-227-7100 344 A wargo@wcu.edu
WARING, Elin 718-960-7306 294 A elin.waring@lehman.cuny.edu
WARING, Jennifer 215-248-7150 381 D sm8127@bncollege.com
WARING, Stacie 646-717-9761 300 G registrar@gts.edu
WARK, Maureen 978-921-4242 216 F maureen.wark@montserrat.edu
WARK, Mike 253-964-6232 483 D mwark@pierce.ctc.edu
WARKENTIN, Bettina 615-547-1374 419 F bwarkentin@cumberland.edu
WARKENTIN, Liz 262-554-2010 494 D liz.warkentin@acupuncture.edu
WARLEY, Russell, L 812-877-8046 159 J warley@rose-hulman.edu
WARMA, Karl 217-228-5432 146 F warmaka@quincy.edu
WARMACK, Dwaun, B 803-535-5412 407 G
WARMAN, Cassie 503-352-3096 375 G warman@pacificu.edu
WARMANN, Cheryl 847-635-1719 145 G cwarmann@oakton.edu
WARN, Dara 480-947-6644 15 A dara.warn@pennfoster.edu
WARNE, Janie 573-334-9181 255 A janie@metrobusinesscollege.edu
WARNER, Amy, C 317-274-7400 156 F awarner@iupui.edu
WARNER, Angela 314-529-9300 254 H awarner@maryville.edu
WARNER, Charles 740-351-3468 360 K cwarner@shawnee.edu
WARNER, Charles 610-436-2117 396 A cwarner@wcupa.edu
WARNER, Dan 610-758-3100 388 J daw318@lehigh.edu
WARNER, David 240-500-2231 198 H cdwarner@hagerstowncc.edu
WARNER, Donald, D 406-874-6201 263 I warnerd@milescc.edu
WARNER, Emily 410-532-5395 201 B ewarner@ndm.edu
WARNER, Gail 619-388-7860 60 E gwarner@sdccd.edu
WARNER, Isiah, M 225-578-7230 188 I iwarner@lsu.edu
WARNER, Jane 843-953-6877 407 F jane.warner@citadel.edu
WARNER, Janice 732-987-2314 278 B jwarner@georgian.edu
WARNER, Jason 214-768-4379 444 E jasonw@smu.edu
WARNER, John 214-645-5476 457 B john.warner@utsouthwestern.edu
WARNER, John 214-648-9794 457 B john.warner@utsouthwestern.edu
WARNER, Karen, R 330-471-8120 355 L kwarner@malone.edu
WARNER, Kathleen 410-888-9048 200 A kwarner@muih.edu
WARNER, Kelly, M 419-434-5184 363 A kelly.warner@findlay.edu
WARNER, Linda 913-288-7194 174 F lwarner@kckcc.edu
WARNER, Lynn 518-442-3300 316 D lwarner@albany.edu
WARNER, Maleese 707-527-4828 62 F mwarner@santarosa.edu
WARNER, Martin, O 610-328-8299 399 D mwarner1@swarthmore.edu
WARNER, Ryan 740-351-3127 360 K rwarner@shawnee.edu
WARNER, Sandra 913-469-8500 174 D swarner@jccc.edu
WARNER, Sue 559-925-3222 74 B suewarner@whccd.edu
WARNER, Susan, T 440-826-2476 348 E swarner@bw.edu
WARNER, Timothy, R 650-723-4567 65 J trw@stanford.edu
WARNICK, Lorin, D 607-253-3030 297 F ldw3@cornell.edu
WARNICK, Mark 870-236-6901 19 A mwarnick@crc.edu
WARNSHOLZ, Luke 218-935-0417 244 G luke.warnsholz@wetcc.edu
WARR, Annie 831-582-3595 32 C awarr@csumb.edu
WARR, Jason 800-462-7845 78 N
WARR, Tammy 864-424-8017 414 C warrt@mailbox.sc.edu
WARREM, Beth 619-594-7985 33 E bwarrem@sdsu.edu
WARREN, Aileen 402-559-8992 270 A aileen.warren@unmc.edu
WARREN, Ann 310-233-4250 49 A warrenal@lahc.edu
WARREN, Ashley 432-335-6429 441 D awarren@odessa.edu
WARREN, Becky 870-612-2048 22 I becky.warren@uaccb.edu
WARREN, Carol 901-572-2640 418 E carol.warren@bchs.edu
WARREN, Carolyn 901-722-3215 424 C cwarren@sco.edu
WARREN, Carolyn 662-562-3205 248 D cwarren@northwestms.edu
WARREN, Chad 702-895-2380 271 E chad.warren@unlv.edu
WARREN, Charlotte, J 217-786-2273 142 B charlotte.warren@llcc.edu
WARREN, Cher 601-484-8614 247 A cwarren@meridiancc.edu
WARREN, Chris 601-643-8318 245 G chris.warren@colin.edu
WARREN, Cleve 904-357-8896 100 B clwarren@fscj.edu
WARREN, Debra, P 260-422-5561 155 H dpwarren@indianatech.edu
WARREN, Dena 740-245-7396 363 D dwarren@rio.edu
WARREN, Derrick 225-771-5380 190 H derrick_warren@sus.edu
WARREN, Derrick, V 225-771-4200 190 G derrick_warren@sus.edu
WARREN, Earl 256-782-5608 5 J ewarren@jsu.edu
WARREN, Ester 434-592-6468 468 H ejwarren@liberty.edu
WARREN, Gordon 325-203-5014 442 E gwarren@rangercollege.edu
WARREN, Helen 507-786-3009 243 C warren1@stolaf.edu
WARREN, Jacquelyn 314-516-6877 261 D warrenja@umsl.edu
WARREN, James 212-410-8063 309 B jwarren@nycpm.edu
WARREN, Jason, D 270-827-1867 181 D
WARREN, Joan, D 212-779-5000 303 H
WARREN, Kathi, D 713-348-6090 442 K kdwarren@rice.edu
WARREN, Katie 507-786-3316 243 C warren2@stolaf.edu
WARREN, Kelly 806-291-1022 457 J warrenk@wbu.edu
WARREN, Kerry 256-216-5343 4 D kerry.warren@athens.edu
WARREN, Kim 913-253-5050 176 I kim.warren@spst.edu
WARREN, Kimberly 913-758-6182 177 F kimberly.warren@stmary.edu
WARREN, Leslie, A 906-227-2117 228 F lwarren@nmu.edu
WARREN, Marty 903-923-2314 436 D mswarren@etbu.edu
WARREN, Mary 601-643-8442 245 G mary.warren@colin.edu
WARREN, Michelle 218-935-0417 244 G michelle.warren@wetcc.edu
WARREN, Mike 601-925-3204 247 C mjwarren@mc.edu
WARREN, Mitch 765-494-1776 159 E mitchw@purdue.edu
WARREN, Monica 615-297-7545 418 C warrenm@aquinascollege.edu
WARREN, Reuben 334-725-2314 7 D rwarren@tuskegee.edu
WARREN, Robert 909-706-8424 74 I rjwarren@westernu.edu
WARREN, Samantha, C 207-621-3024 195 I samantha.warren@maine.edu
WARREN, Sara 410-225-2264 199 H swarren@mica.edu
WARREN, Shannon 304-645-6382 491 A swarren@osteo.wvsom.edu
WARREN, Shannon, N 410-651-6144 203 A snwarren@umes.edu
WARREN, Shauna 773-896-2400 133 L shauna.warren@ctschicago.edu
WARREN, Shelline 704-378-1498 330 D swarren@jcsu.edu
WARREN, Staci 207-621-3299 196 A staci.warren@maine.edu
WARREN, Sydney 270-686-6417 179 D sydney.warren@brescia.edu
WARREN, Teresa 479-936-5171 20 D twarren4@nwacc.edu
WARREN, Thomas 207-941-7786 194 A warrent@husson.edu
WARREN, Todd, W 504-865-3434 189 F twwarren@loyno.edu
WARREN, William 202-319-6925 91 B warrenw@cua.edu
WARREN, William, J 801-581-6773 460 E william.warren@utah.edu
WARRENFELTZ, Jason 717-262-2013 403 F jason.warrenfeltz@wilson.edu
WARRICK, Cynthia 205-366-8808 7 A cwarrick@stillman.edu
WARRINGTON, Adam 802-654-0505 464 B acw11030@ccv.vsc.edu
WARRINGTON, Myrna 800-567-2344 492 G mwarrington@menominee.edu
WARSHAUER, Wanda 860-515-3820 84 G wwarshauer@charteroak.edu
WARSHEL, Chad 315-568-3297 308 F cwarshel@nycc.edu
WARTERS, Alissa 843-661-1616 409 K twarters@fmarion.edu
WARTHAW, Larcia 205-366-8811 7 A lwarthaw@stillman.edu
WARTHEN, Diane 406-496-4400 265 A dwarthen@mtech.edu
WARWICK, Jay 334-953-1303 503 B jay.warwick@us.af.mil
WARWICK, John, J 618-453-4321 149 E warwick@siu.edu
WASAN, Darsh, T 312-567-3001 139 B wasan@iit.edu
WASCHULL, Stefanie 352-395-5175 107 A stefanie.waschull@sfcollege.edu
WASHAM, Jim 870-972-3035 17 G jwasham@astate.edu
WASHBURN, Angela 712-279-5435 163 C angie.washburn@briarcliff.edu
WASHBURN, Brian 408-551-1993 62 D bwashburn@scu.edu
WASHBURN, Dava 903-464-8778 437 D washburnd@grayson.edu
WASHBURN, Kevin 319-335-9034 163 A kevin-washburn@uiowa.edu
WASHBURN, Marina 805-922-6966 24 J marina.washburn@hancockcollege.edu
WASHBURN, Rennie 802-451-7588 462 E rwashburn@marlboro.edu
WASHBURNE, Anne 207-221-4914 196 G awashburne@une.edu
WASHINGTON, A. Eugene 919-684-2255 328 G eugene.washington@duke.edu
WASHINGTON, Adrienne, J 610-758-5834 388 J ajw416@lehigh.edu
WASHINGTON, Alexandria 202-274-7052 93 C alexandria.washington@udc.edu
WASHINGTON, Andre 859-442-4176 181 B andre.washington@kctcs.edu
WASHINGTON, August, J 615-343-9750 428 D august.j.washington@vanderbilt.edu
WASHINGTON, Brad 650-508-3500 54 D bwashington@ndnu.edu
WASHINGTON, Brandon 903-823-3232 446 B brandon.washington@texarkanacollege.edu
WASHINGTON, Chelsea 386-481-2543 95 F shellc@cookman.edu
WASHINGTON, Christopher, L 614-947-6129 353 C christopher.washington@urbana.edu
WASHINGTON, Craig 410-295-4089 504 I craig.washington@usna.com
WASHINGTON, Crystal 773-838-7535 134 F cwashington59@ccc.edu
WASHINGTON, Dana 815-802-8962 140 D dwashington@kcc.edu
WASHINGTON, Daphne 229-430-2948 113 H dapnhe.washington@asurams.edu
WASHINGTON, DeSandra 910-678-0037 334 D washingd@faytechcc.edu
WASHINGTON, Earlie 269-387-2638 232 K earlie.washington@wmich.edu
WASHINGTON, Eddie, L 734-763-8216 231 E washine@umich.edu
WASHINGTON, Eric 718-960-8181 294 A eric.washington@lehman.cuny.edu
WASHINGTON, Felicia 213-740-2311 72 B felicia.washington@usc.edu
WASHINGTON, Fred 936-261-9100 446 D fewashington@pvamu.edu
WASHINGTON, Geovette, E 412-624-4747 401 B gew@pitt.edu
WASHINGTON, Gregory 949-824-6002 68 G gregory.washington@uci.edu
WASHINGTON, Ingrid 859-442-1148 181 B ingrid.washington@kctcs.edu
WASHINGTON, Isaiah 623-845-3996 13 C isaiah.washington@gccaz.edu
WASHINGTON, J. Leon 610-519-4002 402 D jleon.washington@villanova.edu
WASHINGTON, Jennifer 860-515-3820 84 G jwashington@charteroak.edu
WASHINGTON, Jewel 301-405-5648 202 C jmwashin@umd.edu
WASHINGTON, Kaye, L 318-670-9474 190 J kwashington@susla.edu
WASHINGTON, Kheysia, H 318-670-9417 190 J kwashington@susla.edu
WASHINGTON, L. Marshall 269-488-4200 225 E lmwashington@kvcc.edu
WASHINGTON, Lloyd 251-405-4060 1 E lwashington@bishop.edu
WASHINGTON, Maurice 470-639-0355 122 D maurice.washington@morehouse.edu
WASHINGTON, Michael 731-881-7845 428 B mwashi24@utm.edu
WASHINGTON, Mona 901-435-1000 421 A
WASHINGTON, Nakia 470-639-0434 122 D nakia.washington@morehouse.edu
WASHINGTON, Shawn 509-777-4330 486 I swashington@whitworth.edu
WASHINGTON, Sherrea 773-481-8061 134 G swashington@ccc.edu
WASHINGTON, Tonia, F 803-934-3175 411 C twashington@morris.edu
WASHINGTON, Troy, W 937-229-2554 362 G twashington1@udayton.edu
WASHINGTON, Victoria 410-532-5370 201 B vwashington@ndm.edu
WASHINGTON, William 651-638-6300 234 C w-washington@bethel.edu
WASHINGTON, Willie 803-705-4734 407 A willie.washington@benedict.edu
WASHINGTON-LACY, Bonita 765-983-1311 154 G washibo@earlham.edu
WASHINGTON WHITE, Kendal, H 520-621-7057 16 G kwashing@email.arizona.edu
WASHINGTON-WOODS, Paula 870-235-4145 21 D pwwoods@saumag.edu
WASHKO, Mary Jo 804-523-5345 474 H mwashko@reynolds.edu
WASHO, Kevin 412-624-4200 401 B
WASHUT, Kyle 307-332-2930 502 J kwashut@wyomingcatholic.edu
WASIELEWSKI, Dan 641-472-1156 167 F dwasielewski@mum.edu
WASIELEWSKI, Laura 603-656-6051 274 C lwasielewski@anselm.edu
WASILENKO, William, J 757-446-8480 466 I wasilewj@evms.edu
WASILESKI, Suzanne 603-342-3010 273 D swasileski@ccsnh.edu
WASILEWSKI, Frank 650-543-3937 51 F frank.wasilewski@menlo.edu
WASKIEWICZ, Rhonda 207-992-4913 194 A waskiewiczr@husson.edu
WASLEY, Emery 605-677-5671 416 H emery.wasley@usd.edu
WASMER, Tanya 920-693-1858 499 G tanya.wasmer@gotoltc.edu
WASS, Melissa 301-387-3746 198 F melissa.wass@garrettcollege.edu
WASSBERG, Catherine 651-523-2616 236 A cwassberg01@hamline.edu

WASSENMILLER, Angie . 402-643-3651 266 G
angela.wassenmiller@cune.edu
WASSERMAN, David ..... 718-631-6697 295 D
dwasserman@qcc.cuny.edu
WASSERMAN, Ed .... 510-642-3383.. 68 D
ed.wasserman@berkeley.edu
WASSERMAN, Matthew . 303-315-2067.. 83 C
matt.wasserman@ucdenver.edu
WASSERMAN, Mona ...... 718-489-5305 313 H
mwasserman@sfc.edu
WASSERMAN, Noam ..... 212-960-0844 326 E
noam.wasserman@yu.edu
WASSERSTROM, Dana ... 800-371-6105.. 14 G
dana@nationalparalegal.edu
WASSON, Dan .... 231-995-1164 228 G
dwasson@nmc.edu
WASSON, Tanalee .... 859-622-8663 180 B
tanalee.wasson@eku.edu
WASSON, Thomas .... 601-857-3367 246 B
thwasson@hindscc.edu
WASSUM, Keith, N .... 704-687-5747 342 E
knwassum@uncc.edu
WASSUNG, Bruce .... 724-925-4028 403 A
wassungb@westmoreland.edu
WASTVEDT, Ross .... 515-263-6036 165 I
rwastvedt@grandview.edu
WASUKANIS, John, T ... 561-868-3480 104 D
wasukanj@palmbeachstate.edu
WATANABE, Byron .... 808-455-0493 129 D
byronw@hawaii.edu
WATANABE, Jerry .... 808-932-7941 128 E
jerrywat@hawaii.edu
WATERFIELD, James, R 757-683-5070 469 G
rwater@odu.edu
WATERFIELD, Steven .... 248-370-3131 229 G
waterfield@oakland.edu
WATERMAN, Anna .... 319-363-1323 168 C
awaterman@mtmercy.edu
WATERMAN, Matthew ... 510-549-4704.. 66 B
mwaterman@sksm.edu
WATERMOLEN, Jean ...... 602-243-8124.. 14 A
jean.watermolen@southmountaincc.edu
WATERMON, Colleen .... 314-367-8700 259 B
colleen.watermon@stlcop.edu
WATERS, Barry, D .... 989-774-7493 222 C
water1b@cmich.edu
WATERS, Bill .... 850-484-1751 104 H
bwaters@pensacolastate.edu
WATERS, Candace, R .... 864-488-4448 410 E
cwaters@limestone.edu
WATERS, Chris .... 336-668-3869 343 A
cawaters@uncg.edu
WATERS,
Christopher, C .... 336-278-5055 328 K
cwaters@elon.edu
WATERS, Darrell .... 701-228-5458 346 C
darrell.waters@dakotacollege.edu
WATERS, Gloria .... 617-353-2595 207 D
gwaters@bu.edu
WATERS, Jacqueline ..... 937-708-5663 364 D
jwaters@wilberforce.edu
WATERS, Jeff .... 417-328-1632 259 L
jwaters@sbuniv.edu
WATERS, Jennifer .... 205-226-4912.... 5 A
jwaters@bsc.edu
WATERS, Jennifer .... 903-566-7380 456 A
jwaters@uttyler.edu
WATERS, Jennifer .... 410-293-1586 504 I
jwaters@usna.edu
WATERS, Jessica .... 202-885-3724.. 90 J
waters@american.edu
WATERS, Joan .... 212-854-1234 297 C
jwaters@columbia.edu
WATERS, Jon .... 434-544-8498 472 G
waters.j@lynchburg.edu
WATERS, Josh .... 478-471-2666 121 F
josh.waters@mga.edu
WATERS, Kyndall .... 205-226-4936.... 5 A
kwaters@bsc.edu
WATERS, Marlo .... 707-965-7103.. 55 D
mwaters@puc.edu
WATERS, Marlo .... 503-517-1012 377 G
mwaters@warnerpacific.edu
WATERS, Melissa .... 770-426-2826 121 C
mwaters@life.edu
WATERS, Michelle .... 252-335-0821 333 G
michelle_waters@albemarle.edu
WATERS, Nicole .... 704-406-4358 329 A
nwaters@gardner-webb.edu
WATERS, Ron .... 707-476-4331.. 39 D
ron-waters@redwoods.edu
WATERS, Sarah .... 785-864-4560 177 D
sarah.waters@ku.edu
WATERS, Stacy .... 510-666-8248.. 24 D
accounting@aimc.edu
WATERS, Taylor .... 410-626-2512 201 D
taylor.waters@sjc.edu
WATERSTONE, Julie, K . 213-738-5727.. 65 G
jwaterstone@swlaw.edu
WATERSTONE, Michael . 213-736-8154.. 50 J
michael.waterstone@lls.edu
WATFORD, John .... 229-931-2150 124 D
jwatford@southgatech.edu
WATHEN, Cory .... 949-582-4872.. 64 G
cwathen@saddleback.edu
WATHINGTON, Deanna . 386-481-2485.. 95 F
wathingtond@cookman.edu
WATKINS, Bryan, J .... 847-574-5270 141 C
bwatkins@lfgsm.edu
WATKINS, Bryce .... 717-796-1800 390 E
bwatkins@messiah.edu
WATKINS, Cameron ...... 630-617-3031 136 G
cameron.watkins@elmhurst.edu
WATKINS, Dan .... 805-652-5577.. 72 G
dwatlkins@vcccd.edu
WATKINS, Diana .... 580-628-6905 367 D
diana.watkins@noc.edu
WATKINS, Elizabeth ...... 415-514-2440.. 69 E
graduate.dean@ucsf.edu
WATKINS, Faye .... 850-599-3370 108 I
faye.watkins@famu.edu
WATKINS, Frank .... 772-462-7475 101 E
fwatkins@irsc.edu
WATKINS, James .... 478-387-4819 118 G
jwatkins@gmc.edu
WATKINS, Jameson ...... 509-452-5100 483 A
jmwatkins@pnwu.edu
WATKINS, Jeremi .... 252-335-4850 341 D
jwwatkins@ecsu.edu
WATKINS, Joe .... 619-849-2650.. 57 E
joewatkins@pointloma.edu
WATKINS, John .... 724-938-1569 394 B
watkins@calu.edu
WATKINS, Joseph, P .... 615-329-8870 419 K
jwatkins@fisk.edu
WATKINS, Karen .... 318-487-7401 186 I
karen.watkins@lacollege.edu
WATKINS, Leslie .... 573-334-9181 255 A
leslie@metrobusinesscollege.edu
WATKINS, Lydia .... 912-279-5906 116 G
lwatkins@ccga.edu
WATKINS, Margaret ...... 724-805-2814 398 E
margaret.watkins@stvincent.edu
WATKINS, Margaret ...... 724-805-2814 398 F
margaret.watkins@stvincent.edu
WATKINS, Mark .... 502-852-1947 185 C
mark.watkins@louisville.edu
WATKINS, Mark .... 620-421-6700 175 C
markw@labette.edu
WATKINS, Michael .... 818-354-5673.. 29 C
michael.watkins@jpl.nasa.gov
WATKINS, Ophelia .... 575-646-3202 287 B
owatkins@nmsu.edu
WATKINS, Pat, E .... 727-864-8854.. 97 J
watkinpe@eckerd.edu
WATKINS, Rebecca, R .. 828-398-7151 332 B
bwatkins@abtech.edu
WATKINS, Renee .... 973-596-3106 279 F
watkins@njit.edu
WATKINS, Ronnie .... 806-716-2246 443 I
rwatkins@southplainscollege.edu
WATKINS, Rusty .... 270-789-5005 179 E
rdwatkins@campbellsville.edu
WATKINS, Ruth, V .... 801-581-5701 460 E
president@utah.edu
WATKINS, Shane .... 509-527-5970 486 H
watkinse@whitman.edu
WATKINS, Sonya .... 405-974-2605 370 K
sewatkins@uco.edu
WATKINS, Suzanna .... 336-770-1432 343 D
watkinss@uncsa.edu
WATKINS, Tracy .... 903-233-4356 439 E
tracywatkins@letu.edu
WATKINS, Wanda .... 910-893-1330 327 E
watkins@campbell.edu
WATKINS, William .... 818-677-2391.. 32 D
william.watkins@csun.edu
WATKINS-WENDELL,
Katie .... 330-972-6764 362 B
kwatkin@uakron.edu
WATLAND, Brian .... 605-718-2403 417 F
brian.watland@wdt.edu
WATLAND, Kathleen ...... 260-422-5561 155 H
WATLING, Robert, A ..... 940-565-2702 454 A
robert.watling@unt.edu
WATNEY, Laurell .... 620-278-4233 177 B
lwatney@sterling.edu
WATROUS, Emily .... 864-656-2000 408 A
watrous@clemson.edu
WATSKY, Mitchell .... 706-721-3278 115 A
mwatsky@augusta.edu
WATSON, Adam .... 907-474-5317.. 10 A
atwatson@alaska.edu
WATSON, Allyson .... 850-561-2989 108 I
allyson.watson@famu.edu
WATSON, Andrew .... 870-759-4112.. 23 J
awatson@williamsbu.edu
WATSON, Angela .... 270-831-9671 181 D
angie.watson@kctcs.edu
WATSON, Angie .... 864-977-7018 411 E
angie.watson@ngu.edu
WATSON, Ben .... 308-432-6366 268 E
bwatson@csc.edu
WATSON, Billy .... 864-977-7123 411 E
jw.watson@ngu.edu
WATSON, Bret .... 650-949-7777.. 43 D
WATSON, Chris .... 903-923-2406 458 G
cwatson@wiley.edu
WATSON, Christopher ... 847-491-4100 145 F
christopher-watson@northwestern.edu
WATSON, Craig, T .... 404-727-6115 117 F
craig.watson@emory.edu
WATSON, David .... 937-529-2201 362 A
dwatson@united.edu
WATSON, Douglas .... 402-941-6519 267 L
watson@midlandu.edu
WATSON, Edward .... 601-979-3950 246 E
edward.o.watson@jsums.edu
WATSON, Erica .... 207-795-2843 194 E
watsoner@mchp.edu
WATSON, Harold .... 574-535-7491 155 A
hmwatson@goshen.edu
WATSON, Ian .... 973-353-3732 282 B
idwatson@newark.rutgers.edu
WATSON, Jack .... 304-293-0826 491 C
jack.watson@mail.wvu.edu
WATSON, Jeff .... 618-468-3800 141 F
jwatson@lc.edu
WATSON, Jeff .... 903-729-0256 452 B
jwatson@tvcc.edu
WATSON, Jennifer .... 618-453-6689 149 E
jlwatson@siu.edu
WATSON, Jennifer .... 414-288-4255 494 B
jennifer.watson@marquette.edu
WATSON, John .... 972-273-3353 435 E
jwatson@dcccd.edu
WATSON, John .... 267-341-3232 386 A
jwatson2@holyfamily.edu
WATSON, Jonelle .... 701-858-3577 345 F
jonelle.watson@minotstateu.edu
WATSON, Joseph .... 518-828-4181 297 B
watson@sunycgcc.edu
WATSON, Julia .... 678-664-0530 127 A
julia.watson@westgatech.edu
WATSON, Justin .... 574-239-8367 155 D
jwatson@hcc-nd.edu
WATSON, Kathryn, J ..... 727-864-8474.. 97 J
watsonkj@eckerd.edu
WATSON, Kelly .... 513-875-3344 350 G
kelly.watson@chatfield.edu
WATSON, Kim .... 419-251-1852 356 C
kim.watson@mercycollege.edu
WATSON, Kim .... 517-884-6186 227 D
kokenake@msu.edu
WATSON, Kimberly .... 301-405-5837 202 C
watsonk@umd.edu
WATSON, Lemuel .... 812-856-8001 156 A
watsonlw@iu.edu
WATSON, Lemuel .... 812-856-8010 156 B
watsonlw@iu.edu
WATSON, Lisa .... 409-933-8674 433 L
lwatson5@com.edu
WATSON, Lisa .... 307-754-6098 502 G
lisa.watson@nwc.edu
WATSON, Loree .... 281-649-3221 437 H
lwatson@hbu.edu
WATSON, Loretta .... 912-583-3224 115 E
lwatson@bpc.edu
WATSON, Lynda .... 903-434-8204 441 B
lwatson@ntcc.edu
WATSON, Marc .... 513-745-8318 362 E
marc.watson@uc.edu
WATSON, Mark .... 541-346-1896 377 D
mrwatson@uoregon.edu
WATSON, Mary .... 212-229-5613 308 C
watsonm@newschool.edu
WATSON, Michael, W ... 920-424-2184 497 B
watson@uwosh.edu
WATSON, Mindy .... 575-769-4065 285 K
mindy.watson@clovis.edu
WATSON, Nailah .... 773-291-6100 134 E
WATSON, Nancy .... 712-279-5416 163 C
nancy.watson@briarcliff.edu
WATSON, Nyemma .... 856-225-6738 281 G
ncwatson@camden.rutgers.edu
WATSON, Paul .... 269-965-3931 225 F
watsonp@kellogg.edu
WATSON, Phyllis .... 850-599-3474 108 I
phyllis.watson@famu.edu
WATSON, Rachael .... 425-388-9578 480 G
rwatson@everettcc.edu
WATSON, Rebecca .... 334-670-3608.... 7 C
bvwatson@troy.edu
WATSON, Renee .... 702-895-5308 271 E
renee.watson@unlv.edu
WATSON, Rick .... 607-274-3958 303 B
rwatson@ithaca.edu
WATSON, Ron .... 936-468-3206 445 F
rewatson@sfasu.edu
WATSON, Ronald, P ..... 248-370-3487 229 G
rwatson@oakland.edu
WATSON, Sally .... 307-532-8303 502 A
sally.watson@ewc.wy.edu
WATSON, III,
Samuel, E .... 940-397-4746 440 F
samuel.watson@msutexas.edu
WATSON, Sherry .... 832-813-6828 439 G
sherry.watson@lonestar.edu
WATSON, Steve .... 773-508-2560 142 D
swatson4@luc.edu
WATSON, Stevie .... 315-684-6056 321 D
watsons@morrisville.edu
WATSON, Tammi .... 406-657-2044 264 E
tammi.watson@msubillings.edu
WATSON, Terri .... 630-752-5762 152 F
terri.watson@wheaton.edu
WATSON, Todd .... 512-863-1508 445 D
tkw@southwestern.edu
WATSON, Tracey .... 882-354-3000 425 G
watsontl@roanestate.edu
WATSON, W. Clark .... 205-726-4503.... 6 E
wcwatson@samford.edu
WATSON, William .... 770-794-3050 121 C
william.watson@life.edu
WATSON, William .... 408-918-5106.. 61 K
william.watson@sjeccd.edu
WATSON, Wyatt .... 479-964-3213.. 18 C
wwatson@atu.edu
WATSON, Yvonne .... 510-841-1905.. 25 G
WATSON-BLAISDELL,
Kerri .... 207-834-7558 196 C
kerri.watson@maine.edu
WATSON-HALL,
Sherrell .... 908-737-3190 278 E
swatson@kean.edu
WATSTEIN, Sara .... 206-296-6201 484 F
watsteins@seattleu.edu
WATT, James, R .... 814-641-3110 386 H
wattj@juniata.edu
WATT, Kelly .... 303-546-5285.. 81 B
kwatt@naropa.edu
WATTERS, Harper .... 607-254-1590 297 F
harper.watters@cornell.edu
WATTERS, James, H ...... 585-475-2378 313 A
jhwbgt@rit.edu
WATTS, Aimee .... 850-729-4901 103 L
wattsa@nwfsc.edu
WATTS, Barbara .... 434-381-6151 472 D
bwatts@sbc.edu
WATTS, Bill .... 402-472-3145 269 J
bill.watts@unl.edu
WATTS, Bruce .... 312-567-3253 139 B
bwatts1@iit.edu
WATTS, Christine .... 504-398-2177 191 C
cwatts@uhcno.edu
WATTS, Christopher ...... 817-257-7316 448 G
c.watts@tcu.edu
WATTS, Connie .... 606-487-3184 181 C
connie.watts@kctcs.edu
WATTS, Derek .... 309-298-1949 152 D
dj-watts@wiu.edu
WATTS, Eda .... 217-854-5519 132 I
eda.watts@blackburn.edu
WATTS, Greg .... 940-565-4003 454 A
greg.watts@unt.edu
WATTS, Janice .... 860-727-6919.. 87 A
jwatts@goodwin.edu
WATTS, Jon, C .... 308-865-8205 269 I
wattsjc@unk.edu
WATTS, Jonathan .... 256-840-4125.... 3 F
jonathan.watts@snead.edu

WEBER, Christopher ..... 301-447-5114 200 E cweber@msmary.edu
WEBER, Clare .... 909-537-5024.. 33 A clare.weber@csusb.edu
WEBER, Daniel, R .... 773-442-4000 145 B d-weber3@neiu.edu
WEBER, David .... 561-868-3280 104 D weberd@palmbeachstate.edu
WEBER, Dawn .... 419-289-5107 348 A dweber1@ashland.edu
WEBER, Debra .... 262-695-7842 500 H dweber28@wctc.edu
WEBER, Ellen .... 631-420-2744 321 B ellen.weber@farmingdale.edu
WEBER, Heather .... 623-935-8840.. 13 A heather.weber@estrellamountain.edu
WEBER, Heidi .... 518-244-4593 313 D weberh2@sage.edu
WEBER, Jeffrey .... 570-422-2720 394 E jweber@esu.edu
WEBER, Jennifer .... 701-328-4103 345 B jennifer.weber@ndus.edu
WEBER, Jennifer, L .... 563-588-7155 167 D jennifer.weber@loras.edu
WEBER, Jerry .... 425-564-2301 478 F jerry.weber@bellevuecollege.edu
WEBER, Jim, P .... 330-972-5908 362 B jpw@uakron.edu
WEBER, Joe .... 931-221-7618 418 D weberj@apsu.edu
WEBER, Jolanta, A .... 509-313-6504 481 D weberj@gonzaga.edu
WEBER, Karen .... 415-703-9500.. 28 D kweber@cca.edu
WEBER, Karyn .... 605-688-4111 417 C karyn.weber@sdstate.edu
WEBER, Kelley .... 785-833-4396 175 B kelley.weber@kwu.edu
WEBER, Kevin .... 502-585-9911 184 D kweber@spalding.edu
WEBER, Krista .... 608-822-2315 500 G kweber@swtc.edu
WEBER, Laura .... 937-529-2201 362 A lweber@united.edu
WEBER, Laurie .... 701-858-3375 345 F laurie.weber@minotstateu.edu
WEBER, Lyle .... 817-722-1656 439 B lyle.weber@tku.edu
WEBER, Mary .... 831-646-4048.. 52 F mweber@mpc.edu
WEBER, Melissa .... 605-995-2600 415 C melissa.weber@dwu.edu
WEBER, Michael .... 207-780-4404 195 J michael.weber@maine.edu
WEBER, Nancy .... 843-525-8226 412 H nweber@tcl.edu
WEBER, Patti .... 605-256-5238 416 J patricia.weber@dsu.edu
WEBER, Phil .... 740-857-1311 360 I pweber@rosedale.edu
WEBER, Randy .... 913-469-8500 174 D rweber@jccc.edu
WEBER, OP, Sharon, R 517-264-7102 230 E srweber@sienaheights.edu
WEBER, Sheneui .... 562-938-3004.. 48 D sweber@lbcc.edu
WEBER, Staci .... 617-731-7195 217 H sweber@pmc.edu
WEBER, Stephen .... 405-224-3140 371 D sweber@usao.edu
WEBER, Susan .... 212-501-3050 290 G weber@bgc.bard.edu
WEBER, Susan .... 847-628-2465 140 C sweber@judsonu.edu
WEBER, Twila .... 740-857-1311 360 I tweber@rosedale.edu
WEBER, Wayne, C .... 608-342-1547 497 D weberwa@uwplatt.edu
WEBER-MORTIMER, Brandi .... 724-738-4340 395 F brandi.mortimer@sru.edu
WEBSTER, Alex .... 206-239-4500 479 E alexwebster@cityu.edu
WEBSTER, Alexander ..... 315-858-0945 302 C chaplain.webster@hts.edu
WEBSTER, Amy .... 276-656-0248 475 D awebster@patrickhenry.edu
WEBSTER, Berenice .... 281-283-2004 453 A webster@uhcl.edu
WEBSTER, Catherine ..... 405-974-2602 370 K cwebster6@uco.edu
WEBSTER, Christine ...... 979-230-3576 432 D christine.webster@brazosport.edu
WEBSTER, Daniel .... 615-675-5255 428 G daniel.webster@welch.edu
WEBSTER, Ian .... 410-617-2292 199 F iawebster@loyola.edu
WEBSTER, Jeremy .... 740-654-6711 359 G webstej1@ohio.edu
WEBSTER, Jeremy .... 740-588-1435 359 G webstej1@ohio.edu
WEBSTER, Jessica .... 412-578-6158 380 E jewebster@carlow.edu
WEBSTER, Katie, P .... 740-368-3329 359 N kpwebster@owu.edu
WEBSTER, Keith .... 412-268-2447 380 F kwebster@andrew.cmu.edu
WEBSTER, Kelly .... 406-243-2470 264 A kelly.webster@umontana.edu
WEBSTER, Mary, L .... 626-395-6304.. 29 C mwebster@caltech.edu
WEBSTER, Michael .... 603-342-3022 273 D mwebster@ccsnh.edu
WEBSTER, Nancy, K ...... 904-632-3261 100 B nancy.k.webster@fscj.edu
WEBSTER, Ondes .... 865-471-3352 419 A owebster@cn.edu
WEBSTER, Richard, C ... 410-334-2896 204 F rwebster@worwic.edu
WEBSTER, Scott .... 508-999-8202 211 F swebster@umassd.edu
WEBSTER, Shane .... 208-496-1910 130 A websters@byui.edu
WEBSTER, Teresa .... 662-246-6318 247 D twebster@msdelta.edu
WEBSTER, Theresa .... 402-437-2559 269 C twebster@southeast.edu
WEBSTER, Tom .... 903-923-2157 436 D twebster@etbu.edu
WEBSTER, Valerie .... 229-293-6135 124 C valerie.webster@sgsc.edu
WEBSTER, Wayne .... 330-263-2583 351 C wwebster@wooster.edu
WEBSTER-HANSEN, Christine .... 732-255-0400 280 A cwebster@ocean.edu
WECH, Kris .... 620-331-0815 174 C kwech@indycc.edu
WECHSLER, Cathy .... 570-961-7869 387 D wechslerc@lackawanna.edu
WECKESSER, Thomas, U .... 937-229-4583 362 G tweckesser2@udayton.edu
WECKMAN, Judith .... 859-985-3791 179 C judith_weckman@berea.edu
WEDDELL, Leslie .... 719-389-6038.. 77 H leslie.weddell@coloradocollege.edu
WEDDERBURN, Anette .. 301-860-3939 203 C awedderburn@bowiestate.edu
WEDDERBURN, Rishard 919-719-6331 340 E rwedderburn@shawu.edu
WEDDINGTON, Brenda . 312-942-5117 148 A brenda_weddington@rush.edu
WEDDINGTON, Hank .... 828-328-7035 330 F hank.weddington@lr.edu
WEDDLE-WEST, Karen ... 901-678-2119 427 D kweddle@memphis.edu
WEDDLE-WEST, Karen ... 901-678-2894 427 D kweddle@memphis.edu
WEDEL, Allen .... 316-284-5242 171 F awedel@bethelks.edu
WEDEL, Max .... 626-584-5393.. 43 H maxwedel@fuller.edu
WEDEMEIER, Jean .... 973-957-0188 275 C j.matthews@acs350.org
WEDGE, Luann .... 616-234-4170 224 D lwedge@grcc.edu
WEDIG, OP, Mark .... 314-256-8802 250 D wedig@ai.edu
WEDIGE, Kerie .... 608-342-1314 497 D wedigek@uwplatt.edu
WEDINCAMP, Jim .... 478-289-2166 117 D wedincamp@ega.edu
WEDLER, Andrea .... 518-445-2388 289 E awedl@albanylaw.edu
WEDO, Aaron .... 563-425-5959 170 A wedoa121@uiu.edu
WEE, Liang, C .... 563-562-3263 168 E weel@nicc.edu
WEED, Jason .... 513-721-7944 353 F jweed@gbs.edu
WEED, Kenneth .... 918-495-6004 368 I kweed@oru.edu
WEEDEN, Jared .... 315-781-3700 302 A weeden@hws.edu
WEEDMAN, Gary .... 865-573-4517 420 G gweedman@johnsonu.edu
WEEKES, Melissa .... 212-774-4852 306 A mweekes@mmm.edu
WEEKLEY, Susan .... 252-246-1396 339 C sweekley@wilsoncc.edu
WEEKS, Ashley .... 352-262-2745 124 E aweeks@southuniversity.edu
WEEKS, David .... 626-969-3434.. 26 H dweeks@apu.edu
WEEKS, Donald .... 603-752-1113 273 D dweeks@ccsnh.edu
WEEKS, Donna .... 601-968-5922 245 C dweeks@belhaven.edu
WEEKS, Kirsten .... 303-329-6355.. 78 K ado@cstcm.edu
WEEKS, Larry, D .... 904-819-6350.. 98 E lweeks@flagler.edu
WEEKS, Michael .... 843-953-7416 407 F mweeks@citadel.edu
WEEKS, Patricia .... 609-652-4826 283 D patty.weeks@stockton.edu
WEEKS, Shaw .... 207-974-4810 194 H sweeks@emcc.edu
WEEKS, Susan, M .... 817-257-7519 448 G s.weeks@tcu.edu
WEEMES, Marcus .... 925-631-8631.. 59 B mdw3@stmarys-ca.edu
WEEMS, Heather .... 320-308-3102 240 H hlweems@stcloudstate.edu
WEEMS, Jeff .... 918-465-1750 366 D jweems@eosc.edu
WEEMS, Sherryl .... 386-506-3924.. 97 D sherryl.weems@daytonastate.edu
WEEMS, William, A .... 713-500-5224 456 B william.a.weems@uth.tmc.edu
WEENICK, Meredith ...... 617-495-0908 210 B meredith_weenick@harvard.edu
WEER, Christy, H .... 410-677-6571 203 F chweer@salisbury.edu
WEERASURIYA, Yasith .. 949-794-9090.. 65 I yasithw@stanbridge.edu
WEERHEIM, Revalee ..... 307-755-2150 502 K revalee.weerheim@zenith.org
WEESE, Brian .... 912-279-4564 116 G bweese@ccga.edu
WEESE, Lacey .... 423-746-5262 426 F lweese@tnwesleyan.edu
WEETER, Mark .... 918-335-6803 368 G mweeter@okwu.edu
WEGENER, David .... 414-930-3506 495 A wegenerd@mtmary.edu
WEGER, Brandon .... 618-393-2982 138 F wegerb@iecc.edu
WEGHORST, Michelle ... 309-694-5505 138 C michelle.weghorst@icc.edu
WEGLARZ, Donna, M ... 630-515-6064 143 G dwegla@midwestern.edu
WEGLARZ, Joseph, R ... 845-575-3000 305 L joseph.weglarz@marist.edu
WEGLICKI, Linda .... 843-792-3941 410 F weglicki@musc.edu
WEGMAN, Barbara, A ... 260-452-2153 154 E barb.wegman@ctsfw.edu
WEGMANN, Mary .... 650-508-3748.. 54 D mwegmann@ndnu.edu
WEGNER, Janis .... 320-629-5123 240 C janis.wegner@pine.edu
WEGNER, John .... 325-942-2596 451 A john.wegner@angelo.edu
WEGRZYN, David .... 401-232-6261 404 F dwegrzyn@bryant.edu
WEHBY, Laura .... 513-585-1426 350 H laura.wehby@thechristcollege.edu
WEHBY, Rose .... 775-831-1314 272 D rwehby@sierranevada.edu
WEHLBURG, Catherine . 703-284-1620 469 C catherine.wehlburg@marymount.edu
WEHLE, Arlean .... 504-398-2181 191 C awehle@uhcno.edu
WEHLING, Adam .... 715-852-1394 499 D awehling@cvtc.edu
WEHMEIER, Teresa .... 620-417-1603 176 K teresa.wehmeier@sccc.edu
WEHMEIER, Wendall ..... 620-417-1181 176 K wedall.wehmeier@sccc.edu
WEHNER, STD, James, A .... 504-866-7426 190 B jwehner@nds.edu
WEHNER, Jonathan ...... 216-421-7467 350 M jdwehner@cia.edu
WEHR, David Allen .... 412-396-6082 383 C wehr@duq.edu
WEHRLEY, James, B ..... 336-841-4560 329 G jwehrley@highpoint.edu
WEHRMEISTER, Chad ... 925-473-7328.. 40 J cwehrmeister@4cd.edu
WEI, Mei .... 740-593-1479 359 G weim@ohio.edu
WEIBLE, JR., Raymond . 814-262-3816 393 H rweible@pennhighlands.edu
WEICH, Ronald .... 410-837-4458 204 B rweich@ubalt.edu
WEICHEL, Brianna .... 402-461-7393 267 D broncobookstore@hastings.edu
WEICHOLD, Nelson .... 601-984-1010 249 E nweichold@umc.edu
WEIDER, Susan, L .... 425-602-3014 478 D sweider@bastyr.edu
WEIDNER, John, W ...... 513-556-4450 362 D weidnejw@ucmail.uc.edu
WEIDNER, Karen, K ...... 402-844-7330 268 J karenkw@northeast.edu
WEIDNER, Penny, L ...... 717-901-5165 385 K pweidner@harrisburgu.edu
WEIER, Gary, M .... 864-242-5100 407 B
WEIGEL, Kathleen .... 561-237-7441 102 V kweigel@lynn.edu
WEIGHILL, Dale .... 810-762-0456 228 C dale.weighill@mcc.edu
WEIGLE, Greg .... 843-792-7526 410 F weigle@musc.edu
WEIGMAN, Brice, M ..... 585-245-5606 318 E weigman@geneseo.edu
WEIKEL, Bridget, K .... 757-683-4283 469 G bweikel@odu.edu
WEIL, David .... 607-274-1530 303 B dweil@ithaca.edu
WEIL, David .... 781-736-3883 207 E davweil@brandeis.edu
WEIL, Denis .... 312-595-4900 139 B dweil@id.iit.edu
WEIL, Valerie .... 215-596-8800 401 G
WEILAND-ZALEZNAK, Carla .... 914-251-6046 319 E carla.weiland@purchase.edu
WEILER, Joan .... 828-652-0651 336 B jweiler@mcdowelltech.edu
WEILER, Phil .... 509-335-4742 486 A phil.weiler@wsu.edu
WEILMINSTER, Deirdre . 301-846-2610 198 E dweilminster@frederick.edu
WEIMER, Ferne .... 972-708-7416 435 H ferne_weimer@diu.edu
WEIMER, Jean .... 414-847-3272 494 F jeanweimer@miad.edu
WEIMER, Rebecca .... 479-524-7493.. 19 H bweimer@jbu.edu
WEIMER, Theresa .... 718-390-3122 324 F tweimer@wagner.edu
WEIMER, Tresa .... 304-367-4892 490 B tresa.weimer@fairmontstate.edu
WEIN, Mitchell, L .... 610-896-1223 385 L mwein@haverford.edu
WEINACKER, Emily .... 928-445-7300.. 16 M emily.weinacker@yc.edu
WEINAUER, Ellen .... 601-266-4533 249 F ellen.weinauer@usm.edu
WEINBACH, Donald, J .. 203-582-8908.. 87 G donald.weinbach@quinnipiac.edu
WEINBENDER, Sue .... 503-352-2123 375 G weinbender@pacificu.edu
WEINBERG, Adam, S .... 740-587-6281 352 G weinberga@denison.edu
WEINBERG, Jerry, B ..... 618-650-3010 149 F jweinbe@siue.edu
WEINBERG-KINSEY, David, W .... 414-410-4535 492 D dwweinberg-kins@stritch.edu
WEINBERGER, Jayne ..... 718-522-9073 290 C jweinberger@asa.edu
WEINBERGER, Judah .... 212-463-0400 322 J judah.weinberger6@touro.edu
WEINBERGER, Steve ..... 860-723-0252.. 84 H weinbergers@ct.edu
WEINER, Daniel .... 860-486-3152.. 88 E dan.weiner@uconn.edu
WEINER, David .... 312-369-7816 135 E dweiner@colum.edu
WEINER, Gregory .... 508-767-7312 205 D gs.weiner@assumption.edu
WEINER, Marc .... 212-247-3434 305 G mweiner@mandl.edu
WEINER, Melvyn, P ...... 212-247-3434 305 G mweiner@mandl.edu
WEINER, Nettie .... 212-247-3434 305 G nweiner@mandl.edu

WELLS, Douglas .... 740-753-7010 354 A
wellsd34471@hocking.edu
WELLS, Elaine .... 212-938-5690 320 B
ewells@sunyopt.edu
WELLS, Geordy .... 901-230-0624 428 E
geordy@visible.edu
WELLS, JR., Henry, D ... 919-572-1625 326 L
hdwells@apexsot.edu
WELLS, Jennifer .... 270-901-1004 182 D
jennifer.wells@kctcs.edu
WELLS, Jeremy .... 865-251-1800 424 A
jwells@south.edu
WELLS, Jesse .... 607-778-5478 318 A
wellsje@sunybroome.edu
WELLS, Jesse .... 607-778-5296 318 A
wellsje@sunybroome.edu
WELLS, Joel .... 423-425-4669 428 A
joel-wells@utc.edu
WELLS, Johann .... 334-291-4954.... 1 H
johann.wells@cv.edu
WELLS, John .... 413-545-2554 211 D
jwells@isenberg.umass.edu
WELLS, John, T .... 804-684-7103 466 C
wells@vims.edu
WELLS, John, W .... 276-944-6107 467 G
jwwells@ehc.edu
WELLS, Katherine .... 307-855-2111 501 V
kwells@cwc.edu
WELLS, Kelly .... 606-218-5361 185 D
kellywells@upike.edu
WELLS, Kyle .... 435-652-7887 460 G
kwells@dixie.edu
WELLS, Latreace .... 615-329-8894 419 K
lwells@fisk.edu
WELLS, Marilyn .... 507-389-1334 239 C
marilyn.wells@mnsu.edu
WELLS, Matt .... 937-393-3431 361 B
mwells@sscc.edu
WELLS, Meega .... 315-445-4240 304 C
wellsmm@lemoyne.edu
WELLS, Michael .... 910-893-1275 327 E
wellsm@campbell.edu
WELLS, Mike .... 859-344-3524 184 F
wells@thomasmore.edu
WELLS, O.T .... 202-687-2031.. 92 A
otw@georgetown.edu
WELLS, Pam .... 616-331-3327 224 E
wellsp@gvsu.edu
WELLS, Peter, D .... 508-767-7350 205 D
pd.wells@assumption.edu
WELLS, R. Hal .... 612-874-3634 236 K
hal_wells@mcad.edu
WELLS, Sabrina .... 301-546-7011 201 C
wellssx2@pgcc.edu
WELLS, Stephen, G .... 575-835-5600 286 I
stephen.wells@nmt.edu
WELLS, Teri .... 304-896-7443 489 E
teri.wells@southernwv.edu
WELLS, Tina .... 508-854-4479 215 D
twells@qcc.mass.edu
WELLS, Todd .... 816-235-1407 261 C
wellsta@umkc.edu
WELLS, Tonya .... 573-651-2459 259 K
twells@semo.edu
WELLS, Twyla, C .... 919-209-2119 335 F
tcwells@johnstoncc.edu
WELLS, Warren .... 660-785-4121 260 J
wwells@truman.edu
WELLS, William, T .... 336-758-5154 344 D
wellswt@wfu.edu
WELMAN, Chris .... 570-585-9345 381 E
cwelman@clarkssummitu.edu
WELMON, Pamela .... 772-462-7235 101 E
pwelmon@irsc.edu
WELP, Cindy .... 712-274-5114 168 B
welp@morningside.edu
WELSCH, Colleen .... 269-782-1204 230 F
cwelsch@swmich.edu
WELSCH, Gabriel .... 412-396-6049 383 C
welschg@duq.edu
WELSCOTT, Anna .... 303-384-2029.. 78 I
awelscot@mines.edu
WELSH, Beth .... 706-737-1796 115 A
bwelsh@augusta.edu
WELSH, Brett .... 614-287-2426 351 E
bwelsh7@cscc.edu
WELSH, Jennifer, R .... 860-701-6114.. 87 D
welsh_j@mitchell.edu
WELSH, Johnelle .... 254-526-1298 432 H
johnelle.welsh@ctcd.edu
WELSH, Josie .... 417-625-9772 256 D
welsh-j@mssu.edu

WELSH, Marcia, G .... 570-422-3546 394 E
president@esu.edu
WELSH, III, Mark, A ..... 979-862-8007 446 G
mwelsh@tamu.edu
WELSH, Robert .... 626-815-6000.. 26 H
rwelsh@apu.edu
WELSH, Sean .... 410-704-4471 204 A
swelsh@towson.edu
WELSH, Tasha .... 636-481-3157 254 A
twelsh@jeffco.edu
WELSH, Tim .... 269-488-4456 225 E
twelsh@kvcc.edu
WELSHON,
Robert (Rex) .... 719-255-4087.. 83 B
rwelshon@uccs.edu
WELTE, Noah .... 859-341-5800 184 F
welten@thomasmore.edu
WELTER, Brian .... 847-970-4837 152 A
bwelter@usml.edu
WELTER, Diana .... 612-351-1926 236 D
dwelter@ipr.edu
WELTER, Stephen .... 619-594-2978.. 33 E
swelter@sdsu.edu
WELTJEN, Scott .... 716-270-5239 299 F
weltjen@ecc.edu
WELTY, Amy .... 330-966-5456 361 F
awelty@starkstate.edu
WELTY, Dorothy .... 303-914-6634.. 82 C
dorothy.welty@rrcc.edu
WELTY, Paul .... 404-727-4226 117 F
paul.welty@emory.edu
WEN, Hui-Men .... 941-487-4601 109 D
hwen@ncf.edu
WENCESLAU, Zil .... 954-545-4500 107 E
cfo@sfbc.edu
WENCK, Lisa, M .... 607-436-2518 317 C
lisa.wenck@oneonta.edu
WENDEL, Michelle .... 229-226-1621 125 C
mwendel@thomasu.edu
WENDEL, O.T .... 480-219-6011 250 A
twendel@atsu.edu
WENDELL, Alan, B .... 215-951-1916 387 C
wendell@lasalle.edu
WENDEROTH, Christine 773-256-0735 142 J
cwendero@jkmlibrary.org
WENDLAND, Andrea, E . 507-354-8221 236 I
wendlaae@mlc-wels.edu
WENDLAND, Beverly ..... 410-516-0460 199 D
bwendland@jhu.edu
WENDLAND, Chris .... 406-265-4144 264 F
chris.wendland@msun.edu
WENDLAND, Jay .... 716-839-8284 298 B
jwendlan@daemen.edu
WENDLAND, Robert ...... 214-378-1703 434 K
rwendland@dcccd.edu
WENDLER, Dee .... 503-375-7020 373 A
dwendler@corban.edu
WENDLER, Walter, V .... 806-651-2100 448 C
wwendler@wtamu.edu
WENDLING, Susan .... 610-902-8424 380 C
sw10710@cabrini.edu
WENDOLOWSKI,
Gerard .... 303-333-4224.. 76 J
WENDORFF-CRAPS,
Jane .... 309-636-8672 147 D
jwendorff-craps@robertmorris.edu
WENDOVER, Wendy ...... 303-963-3268.. 77 G
wwendover@ccu.edu
WENDROW, Benjamin .. 607-436-2594 317 C
benjamin.wendrow@oneonta.edu
WENDT, April .... 785-539-3571 175 E
awendt@mccks.edu
WENDT, Dean .... 805-756-2226.. 30 C
dwendt@calpoly.edu
WENDT, Donna .... 706-771-4146 114 J
dwendt@augustatech.edu
WENDT, Tara .... 920-922-8611 500 C
twendt@morainepark.edu
WENDT, Tim .... 217-353-2673 146 C
twendt@parkland.edu
WENER, Kara .... 507-457-1494 243 B
kwener@smumn.edu
WENG, Ben .... 612-659-6411 238 I
ben.weng@minneapolis.edu
WENGEL, Steven .... 402-552-6002 270 A
swengel@unmc.edu
WENGER, Amy .... 501-686-6840.. 22 C
adwenger@uams.edu
WENINGER, Debra .... 813-874-0094.. 97 B
WENNEN, Suzanne .... 651-773-1714 237 G
suzanne.wennen@century.edu
WENNER, Annamaria .... 617-989-4410 219 E
wennera@wit.edu

WENSINK, Jenny .... 419-372-7702 348 H
wensinj@bgsu.edu
WENSLEY, Roy .... 925-631-4409.. 59 B
rwensley@stmarys-ca.edu
WENSVEEN, John .... 305-237-7489 103 D
jwensvee@mdc.edu
WENTE, Susan, R .... 615-322-4219 428 D
susan.wente@vanderbilt.edu
WENTHE, Andrew .... 563-425-5348 170 A
wenthea@uiu.edu
WENTHOLD, Marsha ..... 563-387-1415 167 E
mwenthold@luther.edu
WENTWORTH, Monica .. 615-966-6296 421 D
monica.wentworth@lipscomb.edu
WENTWORTH, Phil .... 740-588-1203 365 E
pwentworth@zanestate.edu
WENTWORTH, Renae .... 864-242-5100 407 B
WENTZ, Blake .... 414-277-2204 494 G
WENTZ, Deb .... 701-858-3301 345 F
deb.wentz@minotstateu.edu
WENTZ, Meridith .... 715-232-5312 498 A
wentzm@uwstout.edu
WENTZ, Sheila, D .... 478-289-2380 117 D
swentz@ega.edu
WENYIKA, Reggies .... 785-248-2353 176 D
reggies.wenyika@ottawa.edu
WENZ, Donald, A .... 718-951-5511 293 C
donald@brooklyn.cuny.edu
WENZEL, Claudia .... 216-397-4270 354 I
cwenzel@jcu.edu
WENZEL, Leslie .... 620-275-3220 173 E
leslie.wenzel@gcccks.edu
WENZLER, John .... 510-885-3664.. 31 C
john.wenzler@csueastbay.edu
WEPNER, Shelley .... 914-323-3153 305 J
shelley.wepner@mville.edu
WERBEL DASHEFSKY,
Linda .... 718-489-5370 313 H
lwerbel@sfc.edu
WERDANN, Frank .... 607-431-4340 301 D
werdannf@hartwick.edu
WERLING, Abigail .... 812-488-2362 161 A
am275@evansville.edu
WERLING, Karen, J .... 229-931-2902 124 D
kwerling@southgatech.edu
WERMUTH, Thomas, S . 845-575-3000 305 L
thomas.wermuth@marist.edu
WERNE, Stanley, J .... 812-888-4361 162 C
swerne@vinu.edu
WERNER, Anthony .... 920-465-2018 496 E
wernera@uwgb.edu
WERNER, Glennis .... 320-363-5201 235 C
gwerner@csbsju.edu
WERNER, Kathleen .... 301-369-2800 197 F
kwerner@captechu.edu
WERNER, Lee .... 847-866-3921 137 E
lee.werner@garrett.edu
WERNER, Matthew, R ... 516-671-2215 324 G
mwerner@webb.edu
WERNER, Melody, A ..... 734-487-3617 223 H
mwerner@emich.edu
WERNER, Renee .... 561-683-1400.. 94 A
rwerner@anho.edu
WERNER, Sarah .... 914-961-8313 315 C
swerner@svots.edu
WERNER, Shraga .... 718-941-8000 306 I
WERNER, Tony .... 920-465-2018 496 E
wernera@uwgb.edu
WERNETTE, Judy .... 313-993-1582 231 B
wernetjm@udmercy.edu
WERNICKE, Rachel .... 703-993-2884 467 L
rwernick@gmu.edu
WERNICKI, Abigail .... 267-341-3237 386 A
awernicki@holyfamily.edu
WERNICKI, Nicholas ..... 610-359-7336 382 C
nwernicki@dccc.edu
WERNSMAN, Scott .... 618-985-3741 139 I
scottwernsman@jalc.edu
WERRY, Dawn .... 740-376-4447 356 A
daw008@marietta.edu
WERTH, Lori .... 606-218-5830 185 D
loriwerth@upike.edu
WERTHMANN, David .... 314-256-8801 250 D
werthmann@ai.edu
WERTMAN, William ...... 406-477-6215 263 D
bwertman@cdkc.edu
WERTZ, Miriam .... 574-807-7209 153 E
miriam.wertz@betheluniversity.edu
WESCOAT, Megan .... 308-635-6017 270 D
wescoatm@wncc.edu
WESCOTT, Jon, D .... 570-326-3761 393 G
jdw18@pct.edu

WESCOTT, Phebe .... 434-947-8288 470 E
pwescott@randolphcollege.edu
WESENER-MICHAEL,
Kelly .... 815-753-6103 145 C
kwesener@niu.edu
WESLEY, Artanya .... 262-472-1172 498 C
WESLEY, Derek, M .... 716-286-8679 310 D
dwesley@niagara.edu
WESLEY, Haley .... 707-965-6303.. 55 D
hwesley@puc.edu
WESLEY, Homer .... 719-502-3563.. 81 F
homer.wesley@ppcc.edu
WESLEY, Jeanne .... 540-891-3037 474 G
jwesley@germanna.edu
WESLEY, Jill .... 585-395-5415 318 B
jwesley@brockport.edu
WESLEY, Olan, L .... 334-229-4317.... 4 B
owesley@alasu.edu
WESLOW, Suzanne .... 414-229-4503 497 A
sweslow@uwm.edu
WESNER, Katrin .... 910-962-4126 343 C
wesnerk@uncw.edu
WESNER, Samantha ...... 610-921-7611 378 C
swesner@albright.edu
WESOLEK, Bill .... 989-686-9178 223 G
billwesolek@delta.edu
WESS, Byron .... 215-953-5999.. 92 G
WESSE, David .... 260-481-6804 159 F
wessed@pfw.edu
WESSEL, Madelyn, F ..... 607-255-3903 297 F
mfw68@cornell.edu
WESSEL, Michelle .... 618-545-3242 140 E
mwessel@kaskaskia.edu
WESSEL KREJCI, Janet .. 414-288-3812 494 B
janet.krejci@marquette.edu
WESSELS, Gus .... 979-532-6505 458 F
gusw@wcjc.edu
WESSON, Cameron .... 717-358-3986 384 D
cwesson@fandm.edu
WESSON, Cameron, E .. 610-758-3302 388 J
caw411@lehigh.edu
WEST, Adrian .... 803-780-1269 414 E
west@voorhees.edu
WEST, Allen .... 903-693-1171 441 F
awest@panola.edu
WEST, Amy .... 731-425-2643 425 B
awest12@jscc.edu
WEST, Amy .... 731-425-2621 425 B
awest12@jscc.edu
WEST, Cathy .... 361-698-1265 436 C
cwest@delmar.edu
WEST, Christina, D .... 202-216-4370 428 D
christina.d.west@vanderbilt.edu
WEST, Cynthia, L .... 731-881-7125 428 B
cwest@utm.edu
WEST, Dana .... 865-882-4657 425 G
westdk2@roanestate.edu
WEST, David .... 575-624-8014 287 A
west@nmmi.edu
WEST, David, L .... 901-722-3210 424 C
dwest@sco.edu
WEST, Debra .... 870-733-6722.. 17 H
dwest@asumidsouth.edu
WEST, Detra, E .... 330-569-5237 353 J
westde@hiram.edu
WEST, Greg .... 262-691-5417 500 H
gwest@wctc.edu
WEST, Greg .... 757-455-3400 477 F
gwest@vwu.edu
WEST, Holly .... 845-938-3334 504 H
holly.west@usma.edu
WEST, J. Cameron .... 334-833-4409.... 5 H
camwest@hawks.huntingdon.edu
WEST, Jeff .... 801-957-4250 461 D
jeff.west@slcc.edu
WEST, Jessica .... 620-227-9329 172 J
jwest@dc3.edu
WEST, Jody .... 212-280-1373 323 H
jwest@uts.columbia.edu
WEST, Karen, P .... 702-774-2500 271 E
karen.west@unlv.edu
WEST, Kevin .... 828-689-1585 331 A
kwest@mhu.edu
WEST, Kevin .... 419-530-4053 363 E
kevin.west@utoledo.edu
WEST, Kristie .... 916-691-7199.. 50 G
westk@crc.losrios.edu
WEST, Kristin .... 404-727-2237 117 F
kwest02@emory.edu
WEST, Lance .... 304-696-6440 490 D
west24@marshall.edu
WEST, Landon .... 620-441-5206 172 I
landon.west@cowley.edu

WHEELER, Jenny .... 253-833-9111 481 F
jwheeler@greenriver.edu
WHEELER, John .... 253-752-2020 481 B
registrar@faithseminary.edu
WHEELER, John .... 908-526-1200 281 A
john.wheeler@raritanval.edu
WHEELER, Joshua .... 319-656-2447 169 C
registrar@shilohuniversity.edu
WHEELER, Kara .... 620-901-6267 170 G
wheeler@allencc.edu
WHEELER, Karen .... 870-972-2030.. 17 G
kwheeler@astate.edu
WHEELER, Laurie .... 402-486-2505 269 F
laurie.wheeler@ucollege.edu
WHEELER, Lisa .... 952-358-8286 239 F
lisa.wheeler@normandale.edu
WHEELER, Mark .... 208-467-8772 131 D
mwheeler@nnu.edu
WHEELER, Mark .... 208-426-1140 129 I
mwheeler@boisestate.edu
WHEELER, Michelle ...... 907-564-8210.... 9 D
mwheeler@alaskapacific.edu
WHEELER, Michelle ...... 248-476-1122 227 C
mwheeler@msp.edu
WHEELER, Mimi .... 585-594-6100 310 F
wheeler_mimi@roberts.edu
WHEELER, Mimi .... 585-594-6100 312 K
wheeler_mimi@roberts.edu
WHEELER, Nolan .... 360-442-2201 482 B
nwheeler@lowercolumbia.edu
WHEELER, Sherrell .... 575-439-3668 287 C
swheeler@nmsu.edu
WHEELER,
Stephanie, M .... 248-689-8282 232 A
swheeler@walshcollege.edu
WHEELER, Tracy .... 802-258-9244 462 E
twheeler@marlboro.edu
WHEELER, Walter .... 252-789-0259 335 H
walter.wheeler@martincc.edu
WHEELIS, Tina .... 870-368-2008.. 20 F
twheelis@ozarka.edu
WHEELUS, Angela .... 706-368-7707 118 E
awheelus@highlands.edu
WHEELUS, Chris .... 706-233-7323 124 B
wheelus@shorter.edu
WHEELWRIGHT, Alice ... 470-578-6350 120 L
awheelwr@kennesaw.edu
WHELAN, Brian .... 215-885-2360 389 F
bwhelan@manor.edu
WHELAN, JR.,
Donald, J .... 817-257-7785 448 G
d.whelan@tcu.edu
WHELAN, John .... 812-855-2239 156 A
whelanj@iu.edu
WHELAN, John .... 812-855-2239 156 B
whelanj@iu.edu
WHELAN, Lara .... 518-783-2353 315 J
lwhelan@siena.edu
WHELAN, Matthew .... 631-632-6270 317 D
matthew.whelan@stonybrook.edu
WHELAN, Michaele .... 617-824-8570 208 H
michaele_whelan@emerson.edu
WHELAN, Rachel .... 270-686-2110 179 D
rachel.whelan@brescia.edu
WHELAN, Robert .... 718-289-5162 293 B
robert.whelan@bcc.cuny.edu
WHELLAN, David .... 215-955-5050 400 A
david.whellan@jefferson.edu
WHERRY, Cassandra, J 641-269-3424 165 J
wherry@grinnell.edu
WHETSEL-RIBEAU,
Paula, M .... 301-447-5737 200 E
whetsel-ribeau@msmary.edu
WHETSTINE, Courtney .. 503-768-6036 373 G
cwhetstine@lclark.edu
WHETSTONE, Carol .... 419-783-2303 352 F
cwhetstone@defiance.edu
WHETSTONE, Kimarie ... 803-323-2551 414 G
whetstone@winthrop.edu
WHETSTONE, Laura .... 937-328-7958 350 L
whetstonel@clarkstate.edu
WHETSTONE, Toussaint 630-752-5321 152 F
toussaint.whetstone@wheaton.edu
WHIDDEN, Katherine .... 617-570-4833 219 A
kwhidden@suffolk.edu
WHIDDON, Tifini .... 936-633-4555 430 F
twhiddon@angelina.edu
WHIFFEN, Sarah .... 585-785-1418 300 B
sarah.whiffen@flcc.edu
WHIGHAM, Melissa ...... 772-462-7282 101 E
mwhigham@irsc.edu
WHIPKEY, Brady .... 304-424-8200 491 D
brady.whipkey@wvup.edu
WHIPKEY, Judy .... 304-205-6685 488 K
judith.whipkey@bridgevalley.edu
WHIPPLE, Edward, G .... 503-370-6139 378 B
egwhipple@willamette.edu
WHIPPLE, Jeffrey .... 517-796-8683 225 C
whipplejeffreys@jccmi.edu
WHIPPLE, P. Michael .... 504-861-5543 189 F
pmwhipple@loyno.edu
WHIPPO, Cindy .... 602-557-7202.. 16 J
cindy.whippo@apollo.edu
WHIRL, Jermaine .... 864-250-8185 410 B
jermaine.whirl@gvltec.edu
WHISENAND, Gary .... 562-907-5120.. 75 A
gwhisena@whittier.edu
WHISENHANT, Shawn ... 203-591-7143.. 87 F
swhisenhant@post.edu
WHISENHANT, Vicki ..... 203-596-8396.. 87 F
vwhisenhant@post.edu
WHISENHUNT, Glenne .. 405-682-7413 367 H
gwhisenhunt@occc.edu
WHISENHUNT, Tim .... 405-682-1611 367 H
twhisenhunt@occc.edu
WHISLER, Travis .... 212-229-5150 308 C
travis@newschool.edu
WHISMAN, Kathryn, E .. 520-621-3324.. 16 G
kwhisman@email.arizona.edu
WHISMAN, Linda .... 213-738-5771.. 65 G
library@swlaw.edu
WHISTON, Meg .... 612-767-7096 233 H
meg.whiston@alfredadler.edu
WHITACRE, Aaron .... 540-834-1044 474 G
awhitacre@germanna.edu
WHITACRE, Norma .... 360-475-7360 482 G
nwhitacre@olympic.edu
WHITAKER, IV,
Alexander, W .... 423-968-4861 420 H
president@king.edu
WHITAKER, Caroline ..... 903-670-2617 452 B
caroline.whitaker@tvcc.edu
WHITAKER, Charles ...... 847-491-3741 145 F
WHITAKER, Evans, P .... 864-231-2100 406 G
ewhitaker@andersonuniversity.edu
WHITAKER, Gwen, D .... 336-734-7471 334 E
gwhitaker@forsythtech.edu
WHITAKER, James .... 803-754-4100 409 A
WHITAKER, Jeff .... 859-622-1968 180 B
jeff.whitaker@eku.edu
WHITAKER, Jeremy, C .. 864-488-8202 410 E
jwhitaker@limestone.edu
WHITAKER, Jill .... 815-836-5833 141 G
whitakji@lewisu.edu
WHITAKER, Jillian, B .... 405-466-3652 366 F
jbwhitaker@langston.edu
WHITAKER, Joanne .... 808-734-9520 128 I
joannewh@hawaii.edu
WHITAKER, John .... 317-896-9324 160 I
jawhitaker@ubca.org
WHITAKER, Kevin .... 205-348-4892.... 7 G
kwhitaker@ua.edu
WHITAKER, Kristin .... 850-245-0466 108 H
kristin.whitaker@flbog.edu
WHITAKER, Latoya, R ... 713-798-3092 431 I
lrwhitak@bcm.edu
WHITAKER, Lois .... 443-885-4022 200 D
lois.whitaker@morgan.edu
WHITAKER, Lon .... 253-566-5050 485 C
lwhitaker@tacomacc.edu
WHITAKER, Lorraine ..... 919-718-7223 333 C
WHITAKER, Niki .... 719-549-2951.. 79 A
niki.whitaker@csupueblo.edu
WHITAKER, Paula .... 863-667-5181 107 K
pwhitaker@seu.edu
WHITAKER, Rob .... 912-478-5491 119 C
rwhitaker@georgiasouthern.edu
WHITAKER, Ross, T ...... 801-587-9549 460 E
whitaker@cs.utah.edu
WHITAKER, Shari .... 315-655-7332 292 F
sswhitaker@cazenovia.edu
WHITAKER, Tammara ... 310-434-3769.. 62 E
whitaker_tamara@smc.edu
WHITAKER, Xavier .... 678-839-6423 126 E
xwhitake@westga.edu
WHITAKER-LEA, Laura .. 706-379-3111 127 C
ldwhitakerlea@yhc.edu
WHITAKER STEWART,
Anne .... 609-688-1949 280 D
WHITBY, Holly .... 615-248-1320 427 A
hwhitby@trevecca.edu
WHITBY, Stefanie, A ..... 302-356-2469.. 90 I
stefanie.a.whitby@wilmu.edu
WHITCOMB, Megan .... 336-272-7102 329 D
megan.whitcomb@greensboro.edu
WHITCOMB, Michael, E 860-685-5340.. 89 C
mwhitcomb@wesleyan.edu
WHITCOMB, III, Robert 717-728-2258 381 B
robertwhitcomb@centralpenn.edu
WHITE, A.B .... 731-989-6559 420 C
abwhite@fhu.edu
WHITE, Al .... 919-760-8888 331 B
awhite@meredith.edu
WHITE, Alisa .... 931-221-7566 418 D
whitealisa@apsu.edu
WHITE, Alison Boord .... 302-225-6343.. 90 E
whitea@gbc.edu
WHITE, Amy .... 617-521-2082 218 E
amy.white@simmons.edu
WHITE, Amy .... 540-857-7273 476 D
awhite@virginiawestern.edu
WHITE, Andrew .... 860-685-2570.. 89 C
awhite02@wesleyan.edu
WHITE, Andrew, C .... 518-276-8303 312 I
whitea9@rpi.edu
WHITE, Andy .... 615-230-3300 426 B
andrew.white@volstate.edu
WHITE, Ann, H .... 812-465-1151 161 E
awhite@usi.edu
WHITE, Anne .... 253-964-6716 483 D
awhite@pierce.ctc.edu
WHITE, Annette .... 804-751-9191 465 O
awhite@ccc-va.com
WHITE, Barbara .... 720-872-5608.. 77 G
bwhite@ccu.edu
WHITE, Ben .... 207-778-7494 196 B
benjamin.j.white@maine.edu
WHITE, Bo .... 254-710-2657 431 J
bo_white@baylor.edu
WHITE, Bradley .... 615-963-5817 426 D
bwhite2@tnstate.edu
WHITE, Brent .... 520-621-0350.. 16 G
brentwhite@email.arizona.edu
WHITE, Brian .... 617-287-5611 211 E
brian.white@umb.edu
WHITE, Brian .... 785-864-3276 177 D
brian-white@ku.edu
WHITE, Brian .... 503-768-7307 373 G
bdwhite@lclark.edu
WHITE, Caleb .... 608-822-2446 500 G
cwhite@swtc.edu
WHITE, Carolee .... 315-781-3337 302 A
cwhite@hws.edu
WHITE, Carolyn .... 908-526-1200 281 A
carolyn.white@raritanval.edu
WHITE, Carolyn .... 504-398-2149 191 C
cwhite@uhcno.edu
WHITE, Carrie .... 304-293-9391 491 C
cwhite17@mail.wvu.edu
WHITE, Catherine, D ..... 256-765-4291.... 8 E
cdwhite1@una.edu
WHITE, Charlene .... 731-286-3307 425 A
cwhite@dscc.edu
WHITE, JR., Charlie ...... 276-739-2421 476 C
cwhite@vhcc.edu
WHITE, Courtney .... 435-652-7534 460 G
cwhite@dixie.edu
WHITE, Courtney .... 864-646-1484 413 A
cwhite12@tctc.edu
WHITE, Craig .... 217-424-6344 143 H
ccwhite@millikin.edu
WHITE, Craig .... 505-277-6148 288 G
cwhite@unm.edu
WHITE, Curtis .... 210-436-3622 443 A
cdwhite@stmarytx.edu
WHITE, Cynthia, L .... 972-758-3871 433 M
clwhite@collin.edu
WHITE, Damian .... 401-454-6580 405 D
dwhite01@risd.edu
WHITE, Daniel, M .... 907-474-7112.. 10 A
uaf.chancellor@alaska.edu
WHITE, Daniel, R .... 606-474-3111 180 G
dwhite@kcu.edu
WHITE, Danielle, M ...... 607-587-3930 320 C
whitedm@alfredstate.edu
WHITE, Danny .... 407-823-2261 109 E
adoffice@athletics.ucf.edu
WHITE, David .... 334-448-5112.... 7 C
whited@troy.edu
WHITE, David .... 928-350-2108.. 15 N
david.white@prescott.edu
WHITE, David .... 903-586-2518 438 G
dwhite@jacksonville-college.edu
WHITE, David .... 252-737-3004 341 C
whited@ecu.edu
WHITE, David, B .... 828-398-7175 332 B
dwhite@abtech.edu
WHITE, Dawne .... 770-824-5245 127 A
dawne.white@westgatech.edu
WHITE, Debbie .... 402-872-2224 268 F
dwhite@peru.edu
WHITE, Debra .... 954-486-7728 112 D
dwhite@uftl.edu
WHITE, Dennis .... 618-985-3741 139 I
denniswhite@jalc.edu
WHITE, Dewayne .... 212-678-3235 322 G
white@tc.columbia.edu
WHITE, Diane .... 678-407-5610 118 D
dwhite9@ggc.edu
WHITE, Donald .... 318-274-6298 191 E
whited@gram.edu
WHITE, Doug .... 817-735-5126 454 C
doug.white@unthsc.edu
WHITE, Elaine, T .... 718-429-6600 324 D
elaine.white@vaughn.edu
WHITE, Emily .... 256-782-8393.... 5 J
ehwhite@jsu.edu
WHITE, Erin .... 719-549-3226.. 81 K
erin.white@pueblocc.edu
WHITE, Erin .... 612-343-4457 242 H
erwhite@northcentral.edu
WHITE, Erin .... 910-672-1128 341 E
ewhite@uncfsu.edu
WHITE, Ernie .... 919-739-6805 338 H
ewhite@waynecc.edu
WHITE, Eugene .... 317-543-3235 158 V
WHITE, Frances, L .... 510-466-7200.. 56 D
WHITE, Gary .... 615-226-3990 421 B
gwhite@lincolntech.edu
WHITE, Gary, R .... 805-893-2182.. 70 A
gary.white@sa.ucsb.edu
WHITE, Gene .... 870-543-5949.. 21 C
gwhite@seark.edu
WHITE, Georgia .... 775-445-4284 271 G
georgia.white@wnc.edu
WHITE, Greg .... 650-508-3436.. 54 D
gwhite@ndnu.edu
WHITE, Heather .... 352-392-1261 109 F
heatherw@dso.ufl.edu
WHITE, Henry .... 801-585-6256 460 E
white@chem.utah.edu
WHITE, Ian, K .... 973-618-3236 276 D
iwhite@caldwell.edu
WHITE, Jacqueline, M .. 401-865-2811 405 B
jwhite@providence.edu
WHITE, James .... 303-492-7294.. 83 A
james.white@colorado.edu
WHITE, James .... 201-200-2597 279 E
jwhite4@njcu.edu
WHITE, James .... 509-313-6568 481 D
whitej@gonzaga.edu
WHITE, JR., James .... 715-634-4790 493 I
jwhite@lco.edu
WHITE, Jerry .... 574-807-7877 153 E
jerry.white@betheluniversity.edu
WHITE, Jerry, T .... 937-766-3200 349 G
thomaswhite@cedarville.edu
WHITE, Jessica .... 651-201-1845 237 A
jessica.white@minnstate.edu
WHITE, Jessie .... 254-659-7841 437 G
jwhite@hillcollege.edu
WHITE, John .... 404-752-1734 122 E
jwhite@msm.edu
WHITE, John .... 760-565-4827.. 39 A
jowhite@collegeofthedesert.edu
WHITE, John .... 413-748-3895 218 G
jawhite@springfield.edu
WHITE, John .... 843-953-6810 408 E
whitej@cofc.edu
WHITE, John, E .... 609-497-7880 280 D
john.white@ptsem.edu
WHITE, Jonathan .... 956-380-8194 442 L
jwhite@riogrande.edu
WHITE, Joy .... 470-639-0985 122 D
joy.white@morehouse.edu
WHITE, Julie .... 253-964-6776 483 D
juwhite@pierce.ctc.edu
WHITE, Julie, R .... 315-464-4816 317 F
whitejul@upstate.edu
WHITE, Justin .... 479-619-4123.. 20 D
jwhite35@nwacc.edu
WHITE, Karol .... 319-363-1323 168 C
kwhite@mtmercy.edu
WHITE, Kathleen, C ...... 470-578-6310 120 L
kwhite@kennesaw.edu
WHITE, Katie .... 760-757-2121.. 52 E
kwhite@miracosta.edu
WHITE, Katie .... 972-825-4636 445 A
kwhite@sagu.edu

WHITE, Keith ... 620-862-5252 171 B keith.white@barclaycollege.edu
WHITE, Kenneth, L ... 435-797-2201 460 H ken.white@usu.edu
WHITE, Kevin ... 919-684-2431 328 G kmw40@duke.edu
WHITE, Kyle ... 918-766-5512 368 G kwhite@okwu.edu
WHITE, Kyndell ... 509-359-4554 480 E kwhite58@ewu.edu
WHITE, Lamar ... 404-880-8074 116 D lwhite@cau.edu
WHITE, Lauren ... 361-698-1641 436 C lwhite16@delmar.edu
WHITE, Linda ... 901-435-1316 421 A linda_white@loc.edu
WHITE, Lindsay ... 918-595-7868 370 E lindsay.white@tulsacc.edu
WHITE, Lindsey ... 479-619-4191.. 20 D lwhite13@nwacc.edu
WHITE, Lori, S ... 314-935-4526 262 A lswhite@wustl.edu
WHITE, Mallory ... 731-989-6916 420 C mwhite@fhu.edu
WHITE, Mark, D ... 806-371-5143 430 A mdwhite@actx.edu
WHITE, Marlene ... 908-709-7041 284 C marlene.white@ucc.edu
WHITE, Mary Jo ... 206-934-5378 484 B maryjo.white@seattlecolleges.edu
WHITE, Mary Kate ... 304-724-5000 487 H mwhite@cdu.edu
WHITE, Mason, M ... 410-543-6165 203 F mmwhite@salisbury.edu
WHITE, Matthew ... 757-727-5253 468 B matthew.white@hamptonu.edu
WHITE, Maureen ... 516-726-5632 504 G whitem@usmma.edu
WHITE, Melea ... 319-399-8843 164 A meleawhite@coe.edu
WHITE, Michael ... 402-572-3650 266 D
WHITE, Michael ... 401-841-7560 503 L michael.white@usnwc.edu
WHITE, Michael ... 972-860-8232 435 A mwhite@dcccd.edu
WHITE, Michael, J ... 276-326-4217 465 B michael.white@bluefield.edu
WHITE, Michele, M ... 540-568-6281 468 F whitemm@jmu.edu
WHITE, Michelle ... 918-647-1399 365 H mwhite@carlalbert.edu
WHITE, Monica ... 504-816-4374 186 D mwhite@dillard.edu
WHITE, Nicole ... 615-687-6904 418 A nwhite@abcnash.edu
WHITE, O. Ivan ... 903-927-3384 458 G oiwhite@wileyc.edu
WHITE, Odawa ... 715-634-4790 493 I owhite@lco.edu
WHITE, Olivia, G ... 301-696-3573 199 B owhite@hood.edu
WHITE, Pamela ... 413-755-4452 215 F pjwhite@stcc.edu
WHITE, Pamela ... 803-327-7402 408 B pwhite@clintoncollege.edu
WHITE, Patrick, E ... 217-424-6208 143 H pwhite@millikin.edu
WHITE, Paul ... 920-565-1021 493 J whitepm@lakeland.edu
WHITE, Randy ... 850-729-5364 103 L whiter3@nwfsc.edu
WHITE, Ray ... 334-241-9537.... 7 C grwhite@troy.edu
WHITE, Renée, T ... 508-286-8212 220 A white_renee@wheatoncollege.edu
WHITE, Richard ... 724-357-5567 394 G rpwhite@iup.edu
WHITE, Richard, D ... 225-578-2848 188 I rwhit12@lsu.edu
WHITE, Rick ... 919-962-1221 342 D rick.white@unc.edu
WHITE, Robert ... 816-654-7616 254 C rwhite@kcumb.edu
WHITE, Roger ... 504-865-2427 189 F rwhite@loyno.edu
WHITE, Ronald ... 706-245-7226 117 E rwhite@ec.edu
WHITE, Ryan ... 309-796-5194 132 G whitery@bhc.edu
WHITE, Ryan ... 972-883-5561 455 B ryan.white@utdallas.edu
WHITE, Samuel ... 617-731-7000 217 H
WHITE, Scott ... 718-482-5421 294 F swhite@lagcc.cuny.edu
WHITE, Shakenna ... 252-493-7322 336 H swhite@email.pittcc.edu
WHITE, Shanice ... 601-979-0373 246 E shanice.n.white@jsums.edu
WHITE, Shanna ... 315-386-7333 320 E whites@canton.edu
WHITE, Shelley ... 828-398-7937 332 B swhite@abtech.edu
WHITE, Sherron, D ... 252-335-3660 341 D sdwhite@ecsu.edu
WHITE, Sloan ... 817-531-4414 451 E swhite@txwes.edu
WHITE, Stephanie, M ... 804-257-5745 477 C swhite@vuu.edu
WHITE, Stephen ... 718-862-7548 305 H stephen.white@manhattan.edu
WHITE, Stephen, E ... 401-254-3681 405 E swhite@rwu.edu
WHITE, Stephen, F ... 615-898-2422 422 H stephen.white@mtsu.edu
WHITE, Stephen, L ... 801-863-7321 461 A stephen.whyte@uvu.edu
WHITE, Steven ... 316-978-3782 178 A steven.white@wichita.edu
WHITE, Susan, K ... 913-627-4125 174 F swhite@kckcc.edu
WHITE, Susannah ... 415-701-7040.. 60 H swhite@sfcm.edu
WHITE, Tamara ... 303-404-5103.. 79 J tamara.white@frontrange.edu
WHITE, Tamisia ... 212-870-1229 310 A finaid@nyts.edu
WHITE, Tammy, S ... 205-652-3651.... 9 A thw@uwa.edu
WHITE, Tasia, Y ... 814-641-3520 386 H whitet@juniata.edu
WHITE, Theodore ... 816-235-1330 261 C whitetc@umkc.edu
WHITE, Tiara ... 302-735-7696.. 90 G tiara.white@wesley.edu
WHITE, Timothy, L ... 352-846-0850 109 F tlwhite@ufl.edu
WHITE, Timothy, P ... 562-951-4700.. 30 B twhite@calstate.edu
WHITE, Trey ... 501-420-1274.. 17 B trey.white@arkansasbaptist.edu
WHITE, Troy ... 903-923-2060 436 D tgwhite@etbu.edu
WHITE, W. Scott ... 704-406-4259 329 A swhite@gardner-webb.edu
WHITE, Wayman ... 252-335-0821 333 G waywhite@albemarle.edu
WHITE, Wendy, S ... 215-746-5240 400 K wendy.white@ogc.upenn.edu
WHITE BULL, David ... 605-455-6076 416 B dwhitebull@olc.edu
WHITE EYES, Stephanie 605-856-8186 416 D stephanie.whiteeyes@sintegleska.edu
WHITE PUGH, April ... 864-644-5002 412 E awhite@swu.edu
WHITE SIMMONS, Renita ... 718-951-5137 293 C rwsimmons@brooklyn.cuny.edu
WHITE-SMITH, Kimberly ... 909-593-3511.. 70 D kwhite-smith@laverne.edu
WHITE-ZOLLMAN, Casey ... 541-278-5839 372 A cwhitezollman@bluecc.edu
WHITECAVAGE, Michele ... 714-449-7404.. 51 A mwhitecavage@ketchum.edu
WHITED, Jimmy, R ... 540-375-2308 471 B whited@roanoke.edu
WHITEFIELD, Joe ... 615-904-8375 422 H joe.whitefield@mtsu.edu
WHITEFORD, Aaron ... 503-768-7944 373 G ahw@lclark.edu
WHITEFORD, Craig ... 410-287-1914 197 H cwhiteford@cecil.edu
WHITEHEAD, Amy ... 501-852-0871.. 23 H amyw@uca.edu
WHITEHEAD, Debbie ... 503-255-0332 374 D debbiew@multnomah.edu
WHITEHEAD, Doug ... 435-652-7500 460 G dkw@dixie.edu
WHITEHEAD, Gwen ... 409-882-3926 450 A gwen.whitehead@lsco.edu
WHITEHEAD, Heidi, M .. 812-888-4313 162 C hwhitehead@vinu.edu
WHITEHEAD, Jan ... 832-252-4616 433 D jan.whitehead@cbshouston.edu
WHITEHEAD, JaRenae ... 757-683-4564 469 G jwhitehe@odu.edu
WHITEHEAD, Joe, B ... 419-372-2211 348 H
WHITEHEAD, Keri ... 845-434-5750 322 A kwhitehead@sunysullivan.edu
WHITEHEAD, Kim ... 662-241-6850 248 A kmwhitehead@muw.edu
WHITEHEAD, Kimberly .. 207-561-1512 195 J kimberly.whitehead@maine.edu
WHITEHEAD, Martha, J 617-496-1295 210 B martha_whitehead@harvard.edu
WHITEHEAD, Nadia ... 575-674-2266 285 H
WHITEHOUSE, Jennifer . 985-867-2240 190 F jwhitehouse@sjasc.edu
WHITEHURST, Marcus, A ... 814-865-5906 392 B maw163@psu.edu
WHITELAW, Lydia ... 610-896-1177 385 L lwhitela@haverford.edu
WHITELY, Patricia, A ... 305-284-4922 112 E pwhitely@miami.edu
WHITEMAN, Betty ... 386-822-8869 111 A bwhiteman@stetson.edu
WHITEMAN, Charles, H 814-863-0448 392 B chw17@psu.edu
WHITEMAN, Mike ... 704-330-6706 333 D mike.whiteman@cpcc.edu
WHITEMAN, Patricia ... 406-638-3189 263 H whitemanp@lbhc.edu
WHITEMAN, Ray ... 574-807-7139 153 E ray.whiteman@betheluniversity.edu
WHITEMAN, Raymond, E ... 574-807-7139 153 E ray.whiteman@betheluniversity.edu
WHITESEL, Mark ... 912-478-3326 119 C mwhitesel@georgiasouthern.edu
WHITESELL, Melissa ... 706-272-4527 117 C mwhitesell@daltonstate.edu
WHITESELL, Warren ... 765-658-4229 154 F warrenwhitesell@depauw.edu
WHITESIDE, Christopher ... 714-895-8250.. 38 D cwhiteside4@gwc.cccd.edu
WHITESIDE, Dannelle ... 931-221-7572 418 D whitesided@apsu.edu
WHITESIDE, Frederick ... 707-965-7200.. 55 D fwhiteside@puc.edu
WHITESIDE, Harold, D .. 615-898-2900 422 H harold.whiteside@mtsu.edu
WHITESIDE, Kendall ... 615-514-2787 423 E kwhiteside@nossi.edu
WHITESIDE, Sandy ... 714-432-5952.. 38 E swhiteside@occ.cccd.edu
WHITESIDES, Louis, D .. 803-536-7189 412 C lwhitesides@scsu.edu
WHITEY, Jeff ... 541-888-7402 376 F jwhitey@socc.edu
WHITFIELD, Candis ... 912-660-4658 106 D candis.whitfield@saintleo.edu
WHITFIELD, Henry ... 478-934-3167 121 F henry.whitfield@mga.edu
WHITFIELD, Jacques ... 530-741-6976.. 76 A jwhitfie@yccd.edu
WHITFIELD, Keith ... 313-577-2200 232 I keith.whitfield@wayne.edu
WHITFIELD, Keith ... 919-761-2185 340 G kwhitfield@sebts.edu
WHITFIELD, Meredith ... 828-227-7059 344 A mcwhitfield@wcu.edu
WHITFIELD, Rick ... 919-962-1000 341 A
WHITFILL, Gene ... 806-291-1045 457 J whitfillg@wbu.edu
WHITFILL, Jill ... 731-352-4083 418 G whitfillj@bethelu.edu
WHITFORD, Betty Lou .. 334-844-4448.... 4 E blw0017@auburn.edu
WHITFORD, Daryl ... 808-675-3730 127 E daryl.whitford@byuh.edu
WHITFORD, Michael ... 714-662-5250.. 72 F michael.whitford@vanguard.edu
WHITHAM, Crystal ... 330-337-6403 347 E librarian@awc.edu
WHITHAM, John, H ... 610-526-1337 378 G john.whitham@theamericancollege.edu
WHITING, Alison ... 808-675-3551 127 E alison.whiting@byuh.edu
WHITING, Dawn ... 541-463-3000 373 F
WHITING, Doug ... 401-598-1000 404 I dwhiting@jwu.edu
WHITIS, Andrew ... 419-434-4767 363 A whitis@findlay.edu
WHITIS, Harold ... 210-485-0605 429 C hwhitis2@alamo.edu
WHITLATCH, Frank ... 707-826-5101.. 33 D frank@humboldt.edu
WHITLEDGE, Terry ... 907-474-7229.. 10 A terry@ims.uaf.edu
WHITLEY, Darrell, S ... 252-985-5105 339 D dwhitley@ncwc.edu
WHITLEY, James ... 203-591-5662.. 87 F jwhitley@post.edu
WHITLEY, Rebecca ... 575-492-2546 286 J rwhitley@nmjc.edu
WHITLOCK, Julie Ann ... 787-704-1020 507 K jwhitlock@ediccollege.edu
WHITLOCK, Kevin ... 320-308-2038 240 H kcwhitlock@stcloudstate.edu
WHITLOCK, Shawna ... 216-373-5335 358 B swhitlock@ndc.edu
WHITLOCK, Stephen ... 678-839-6426 126 E swhitlock@westga.edu
WHITLOCK, Tonya, F ... 678-664-0532 127 A tonya.whitlock@westgatech.edu
WHITLOW, Ken ... 706-233-7231 124 B kwhitlow@shorter.edu
WHITMAN, David ... 651-604-4118 236 J dwhitman@minneapolisbusinesscollege.edu
WHITMAN, Deirdre ... 516-299-3720 304 G deirdre.whitman@liu.edu
WHITMAN, Deirdre ... 516-299-3720 304 H deirdre.whitman@liu.edu
WHITMAN, Josh ... 217-333-3631 151 D illiniad@illinois.edu
WHITMAN, Paul ... 803-321-5600 411 D paul.whitman@newberry.edu
WHITMAN, Rebecca, R . 616-234-4010 224 D rwhitman@grcc.edu
WHITMAN, Richard ... 910-296-2487 335 E rwhitman@jamessprunt.edu
WHITMAN, Sally ... 330-263-2139 351 C swhitman@wooster.edu
WHITMER, Linda ... 865-573-4517 420 G lwhitmer@johnsonu.edu
WHITMEYER, Antoinette 301-295-6013 504 B antoinette.whitmeyer@usuhs.edu
WHITMIRE, Dawna ... 409-880-8210 449 G dmwhitmire@lit.edu
WHITMORE, Jessica, J . 301-447-5244 200 E whitmore@msmary.edu
WHITMORE, Joe ... 256-840-4102.... 3 F joe.whitmore@snead.edu
WHITMORE, Kimberly, N ... 515-574-1138 166 E whitmore@iowacentral.edu
WHITMORE, Michele ... 802-635-1452 464 C michele.whitmore@northernvermont.edu
WHITNEY, Candice ... 408-848-4754.. 43 J cwhitney@gavilan.edu
WHITNEY, Chris ... 570-941-7640 401 H christina.whitney@scranton.edu
WHITNEY, Gleaves ... 616-331-2770 224 E whitneyg@gvsu.edu
WHITNEY, J.J ... 501-450-1263.. 19 F whitney@hendrix.edu
WHITNEY, Jarrid ... 626-395-6341.. 29 C jwhitney@caltech.edu
WHITNEY, Jennifer, M .. 336-334-5874 343 A jmwhitne@uncg.edu
WHITNEY, Joan, G ... 610-519-4050 402 D joan.whitney@villanova.edu
WHITNEY, Laura ... 860-768-4276.. 88 H lwhitney@hartford.edu
WHITNEY, Majid ... 973-275-2385 283 B majid.whitney@shu.edu
WHITNEY, Marian, D ... 315-684-6010 321 D whitnemd@morrisville.edu
WHITNEY, Mary ... 412-365-1686 381 C mwhitney@chatham.edu
WHITNEY, Mary Pat ... 805-565-6055.. 74 K mwhitney@westmont.edu
WHITNEY, Patricia ... 508-626-4590 212 D pwhitney@framingham.edu
WHITNEY, Paul ... 401-874-5224 406 B pwhitney@uri.edu
WHITNEY, Richard ... 641-269-3300 165 J whitney@grinnell.edu
WHITNEY, Roger ... 650-723-2300.. 65 J
WHITSON, Brian, W ... 757-221-7876 466 C bwwhit@wm.edu
WHITSON, Jennifer ... 507-786-3000 243 C whitson@stolaf.edu
WHITSON, Tony ... 901-435-1733 421 A tony_whitson@loc.edu
WHITT, Christopher, M 402-280-5121 266 I christopherwhitt@creighton.edu

WHITT, Cynthia, L .... 423-869-6394 421 C
cynthia.whitt@lmunet.edu
WHITT, Elizabeth .... 209-228-2317.. 69 B
ewhitt@ucmerced.edu
WHITT, Ellen .... 317-955-6597 158 U
ewhitt@marian.edu
WHITT, Fred .... 828-328-7334 330 F
fred.whitt@lr.edu
WHITT, Julie .... 817-257-6571 448 G
j.whitt@tcu.edu
WHITTAKER, Chanelle .. 510-466-7252.. 56 E
cwhittaker@peralta.edu
WHITTAKER, David .... 816-584-6710 258 A
dave.whittaker@park.edu
WHITTAKER, Joseph, A 601-979-2931 246 E
joseph.a.whittaker@jsums.edu
WHITTAKER, Kristen ..... 801-524-8156 459 F
kwhittaker@ldsbc.edu
WHITTAKER, Nancy, H . 205-348-6690.... 7 G
nwhittaker@fa.ua.edu
WHITTAKER, Robert ...... 617-327-6777 220 B
robert_whittaker@williamjames.edu
WHITTAKER, Wesley, L 405-466-6149 366 F
wesley.whittaker@langston.edu
WHITTED, Tenial .... 708-596-2000 149 B
twhitted@ssc.edu
WHITTEN, James .... 207-844-2103 195 A
jwhitten@smccme.edu
WHITTEN, Kelly .... 785-864-7100 177 D
kelly@ku.edu
WHITTEN, Kim .... 870-612-2017.. 22 I
kim.whitten@uaccb.edu
WHITTEN, Larresia 512-451-5743 430M
WHITTEN, Linwood .... 334-229-4713.... 4 B
lwhitten@alasu.edu
WHITTEN, Mandy .... 864-503-5420 414 D
mwhitten@uscupstaet.edu
WHITTEN, Pamela .... 470-578-6033 120 L
WHITTEN, Patrice .... 850-484-1714 104 H
pswhitten@pensacolastate.edu
WHITTEN, Stockton .... 321-433-7205.. 97 I
whittens@easternflorida.edu
WHITTENBURG, Scott ... 406-243-6670 264 A
scott.whittenburg@umontana.edu
WHITTIER, Timothy .... 606-218-5470 185 D
timothywhittier@upike.edu
WHITTINGHAM,
Michelle, L .... 831-459-1453.. 70 B
michelle@ucsc.edu
WHITTINGHAM, Rachel 501-205-8876.. 18 H
rwhittingham@cbc.edu
WHITTINGTON, Amy ..... 601-605-3313 246 C
awhittington@holmescc.edu
WHITTINGTON, Beth ..... 318-473-6456 188 J
blord@lsua.edu
WHITTINGTON, Connie . 318-869-5101 186 B
cwhitt@centenary.edu
WHITTINGTON, Daniell . 626-396-6018.. 43 H
daniellwhittington@fuller.edu
WHITTINGTON,
Elizabeth .... 713-623-2040 430 K
ewhittington@aii.edu
WHITTINGTON,
Gerald, O .... 336-278-7934 328 K
whitting@elon.edu
WHITTINGTON, Joya ..... 570-504-0920 387 D
whittingtonj@lackawanna.edu
WHITTINGTON, Lee .... 828-766-1196 336 A
lwhittington@mayland.edu
WHITTINGTON, Randal . 512-404-4808 431 C
rwhittington@austinseminary.edu
WHITTUM, Terry .... 636-949-4812 254 F
twhittum@lindenwood.edu
WHITWELL, Jeff .... 615-898-2700 422 H
jeff.whitwell@mtsu.edu
WHITWORTH, Mike .... 859-858-3511 178 I
mark.whitworth@asbury.edu
WHORLEY, William .... 517-607-2454 225 A
wwhorley@hillsdale.edu
WHORTON, Garrett .... 316-284-5251 171 F
gwhorton@bethelks.edu
WHORTON, Mark .... 931-393-7123 427 G
mwhorton@utsi.edu
WHORTON, Susan .... 864-656-6256 408 A
whorton@clemson.edu
WHYNOTT, Anne .... 262-564-2758 499 F
whynotta@gtc.edu
WHYTE, Novia, P .... 516-463-6928 302 B
novia.p.whyte@hofstra.edu
WHYTE, Willaim .... 262-564-3228 499 F
whytew@gtc.edu
WIBBELS, Alan .... 954-771-0376 102 R
awibbels@knoxseminary.edu
WIBOWO, Mieke .... 310-289-5123.. 73 H
mieke.wibowo@wcui.edu
WIBREW, Karen .... 303-964-6274.. 82 E
kwibrew@regis.edu
WICHERN, Adam .... 718-405-3776 296 G
adam.wichern@mountsaintvincent.edu
WICHERT, Jerome, L .... 580-774-3786 370 C
jerome.wichert@swosu.edu
WICHROSKI, Pamela, J 207-786-6207 193 B
pwichros@bates.edu
WICHROWSKI, Edward .. 617-745-3878 208 G
edward.wichrowski@enc.edu
WICINSKI, Melanie .... 850-599-5265 108 I
melanie.wicinski@famu.edu
WICK, Martha .... 641-683-5231 166 C
martha.wick@indianhills.edu
WICK, Michael, R .... 240-895-4389 201 E
mrwick@smcm.edu
WICKE, Thomas .... 303-861-1151.. 79 F
twicke@concorde.edu
WICKEHAM, Daniel .... 414-955-8826 494 C
dwickeha@mcw.edu
WICKER, Jeff .... 803-321-5676 411 D
jeffrey.wicker@newberry.edu
WICKER, John David .... 619-594-6357.. 33 E
adsdsu@sdsu.edu
WICKER-MCCREE,
Ingrid, L .... 919-530-7057 342 A
iwicker@nccu.edu
WICKERT, Annie .... 213-621-2200.. 38 G
WICKERT, Jonathan, A .. 515-294-0070 162 I
wickert@iastate.edu
WICKETT, Brenda, K ..... 515-961-1611 169 D
brenda.wickett@simpson.edu
WICKHAM, Larry .... 575-461-4413 286 E
larryw@mesalands.edu
WICKIZER, Vicki .... 574-284-4602 160 C
vwickizer@saintmarys.edu
WICKLAND, Mary .... 409-882-3372 450 A
wicklandma@lamarpa.edu
WICKLAND, Mary .... 409-882-3397 450 A
wicklandma@lamarpa.edu
WICKLAND, Mary .... 409-984-6125 450 B
mary.wickland@lamarpa.edu
WICKLESS-MULDER,
Megan .... 402-552-6119 266 E
wicklessmegan@clarksoncollege.edu
WICKLIFFE, Cari, S ...... 314-977-3442 259 H
cari.wickliffe@slu.edu
WICKLINE, Jason .... 217-424-6217 143 H
jwickline@millikin.edu
WICKLINE, Paul .... 661-362-3152.. 38 H
paul.wickline@canyons.edu
WICKLUND, Greg, A ..... 817-202-6743 444 I
wicklund@swau.edu
WICKS, Donna .... 810-762-7853 225 H
dwicks@kettering.edu
WICKS, Karen .... 636-481-3104 254 A
kwicks1@jeffco.edu
WICKSTROM, Brian .... 210-829-2722 453 D
wickstrom@uiwtx.edu
WICKSTROM, Julie .... 617-353-4176 207 D
jwickstr@bu.edu
WIDANKA, Kenneth ...... 585-385-8256 314 A
kwidanka@sjfc.edu
WIDDICOMBE, Molly .... 909-748-8381.. 71 G
molly_widdicombe@redlands.edu
WIDDOWS, Daniella ..... 434-223-6311 468 A
dwiddows@hsc.edu
WIDDOWSON, Carrie .... 717-691-6034 390 E
cwiddowson@messiah.edu
WIDELL, Mike .... 405-945-3284 368 E
mike@okstate.edu
WIDEMAN, Robert .... 660-263-4100 257 B
robertwwideman@macc.edu
WIDEMAN, Tameika ...... 864-941-8364 411 H
wideman.t@ptc.edu
WIDENER, Charlene ...... 641-422-4277 168 D
charlene.widener@niacc.edu
WIDERGREN, James ..... 909-607-7855.. 37 G
WIDMER, Jocelyn .... 979-845-4016 446 G
widmerj@tamu.edu
WIDNER, Kenneth .... 662-329-7021 248 A
kwidner@muw.edu
WIDOM, Jennifer .... 650-723-2300.. 65 J
WIEBE, John .... 915-747-7611 455 C
jwiebe@utep.edu
WIEBE, Weston, T .... 417-690-2211 251 E
wiebe@cofo.edu
WIECHMAN, Jeffery, P .. 507-354-8221 236 I
wiechmjp@mlc-wels.edu
WIECKI, Lisa .... 864-388-8035 410 D
lwiecki@lander.edu
WIED, Christine .... 979-830-4224 432 C
cwied@blinn.edu
WIEDEFELD, Kimberley . 585-594-6199 312 K
wiedefeld_kimberley@roberts.edu
WIEDENHOEFT,
Margaret .... 269-337-7133 225 D
margaret.wiedenoeft@kzoo.edu
WIEDERHOLT, Mark ...... 660-944-2968 251 G
markw@conception.edu
WIEDMER, Shannon ...... 785-442-6009 174 A
swiedmer@highlandcc.edu
WIEGAND, Joseph .... 251-442-2390.... 8 C
jwiegand@umobile.edu
WIEGAND, Mark .... 502-272-8368 179 B
mwiegand@bellarmine.edu
WIEGAND, Randall, V ... 671-735-2930 505 E
wiegandr@triton.uog.edu
WIEGANDT, Scott, P ..... 502-272-8496 179 B
swiegandt@bellarmine.edu
WIEGEL, Lisa .... 563-288-6003 165 D
lwiegel@eicc.edu
WIEGMAN, Karen, D ..... 913-971-3698 175 G
kdwiegman@mnu.edu
WIEGMAN, Tracy .... 706-886-6831 125 D
twiegman@tfc.edu
WIEHE, Fred .... 408-727-1060.. 45 J
WIEHE, Kim .... 607-735-1707 299 D
kwiehe@elmira.edu
WIELENGA, Jay .... 712-707-7111 168 H
jayw@nwciowa.edu
WIELGUS, Jeanne .... 707-826-4206.. 33 D
jw7001@humboldt.edu
WIELINSKI, Peter .... 218-631-7810 239 B
peter.wielinski@minnesota.edu
WIENCEK, John, M .... 208-885-7919 131 G
provost@uidaho.edu
WIENS, Ann .... 415-703-9360.. 28 D
awiens@cca.edu
WIERDA, Bruce .... 231-777-0657 228 D
bruce.wierda@muskegoncc.edu
WIERDA, Kire .... 989-328-1268 228 A
kire.wierda@montcalm.edu
WIERSCH, Linda .... 704-878-3302 336 C
lwiersch@mitchellcc.edu
WIERSMA, Noelle .... 509-777-4874 486 I
nwiersma@whitworth.edu
WIERTEL, Anthony .... 716-926-8818 301 H
twiertel@hilbert.edu
WIERZBICKI, Andrzej .... 251-460-6280.... 8 F
awierzbicki@southalabama.edu
WIESCAMP, Cheryl .... 970-247-7364.. 79 I
wiescamp_c@fortlewis.edu
WIESE, Joelle, D .... 202-687-7150.. 92 A
jdw237@georgetown.edu
WIESE, Trent .... 308-535-3612 267 K
wieset@mpcc.edu
WIESEHAN, Terry .... 765-973-8221 156 C
twiesaha@iue.edu
WIESELQUIST, Rachel ... 336-316-2178 329 E
wieselquistrp@guilford.edu
WIESER, Jocelyn .... 440-366-7548 355 J
WIETFELDT, Matthew .... 260-452-2278 154 E
matthew.wietfeldt@ctsfw.edu
WIEWAL, Wim .... 503-768-7680 373 G
president@lclark.edu
WIEWEL, Christine .... 217-641-4517 140 A
cwiewel@jwcc.edu
WIGBOLDY, Kyle .... 616-392-8555 233 E
kylew@westernsem.edu
WIGGETT, Janette, T .... 603-535-2206 275 B
jtwiggett@plymouth.edu
WIGGINS, Adrian .... 609-652-4378 283 D
adrian.wiggins@stockton.edu
WIGGINS, Amy, F .... 252-862-1225 337 C
afwiggins7415@roanokechowan.edu
WIGGINS, Charles .... 828-395-1306 335 D
cpwiggins@isothermal.edu
WIGGINS, David, J .... 952-446-4112 235 G
wigginsj@crown.edu
WIGGINS, Devon .... 903-510-2646 452 C
dwig@tjc.edu
WIGGINS, Erin .... 740-362-3366 356 D
ewiggins@msto.edu
WIGGINS, Jessica .... 256-782-5006.... 5 J
jdwiggins@jsu.edu
WIGGINS, Lakeita .... 903-927-3260 458 G
lwiggins@wileyc.edu
WIGGINS, Michaele .... 336-334-7593 341 F
sm8093@bncollege.com
WIGGINS, Nimmi, K ...... 859-257-6547 185 B
nwiggin@uky.edu
WIGGINS, Sarah .... 954-201-6455.. 95 H
swiggins@broward.edu
WIGGINS, Shelia .... 252-527-6223 335 G
slwiggins45@lenoircc.edu
WIGGINS, Symphoni ..... 706-821-8103 122 K
recordsofficestaff@paine.edu
WIGGINS, Vincent .... 312-553-5911 134 B
vwiggins1@ccc.edu
WIGGINTON, Nicholas .. 734-763-1290 231 E
nwigg@umich.edu
WIGGINTON, Russ .... 901-843-3997 423 J
wigginton@rhodes.edu
WIGGINTON, Van .... 281-542-2000 443 B
van.wigginton@sjcd.edu
WIGGINTON, Van, A ..... 281-542-2000 443 C
van.wigginton@sjcd.edu
WIGHT, Charles, A .... 410-543-6011 203 F
cawight@salisbury.edu
WIGHT, Erica .... 801-957-6321 461 D
erica.wight@slcc.edu
WIGHT, Laura .... 406-771-4318 264 G
laura.wight@gfcmsu.edu
WIGHT, Randall .... 870-245-5107.. 20 E
wight@obu.edu
WIGHTKIN, Joe .... 763-488-2549 238 B
joe.wightkin@hennepintech.edu
WIGHTKIN, John .... 708-239-4762 150 F
john.wightkin@trnty.edu
WIGHTKIN, Steven, P ... 312-942-5947 148 A
steven_wightkin@rush.edu
WIGHTMAN, Beth, A ..... 818-677-2969.. 32 D
beth.wightman@csun.edu
WIGHTMAN, James .... 614-236-6264 349 D
jwightman@capital.edu
WIGHTMAN, Todd .... 208-535-5440 130 C
todd.wightman@cei.edu
WIGINTON, Chad .... 580-477-7700 371 F
chad.wiginton@wosc.edu
WIGINTON, Melissa ...... 512-404-4862 431 C
mwiginton@austinseminary.edu
WIGLEY, Kimberly .... 404-627-2681 115 C
kimberly.wigley@beulah.edu
WIGNALL, Eric .... 815-740-3444 151 J
ewignall@stfrancis.edu
WIGNALL, Scott, D .... 724-946-7135 402 G
wignalsd@westminster.edu
WIGNES, David, R .... 608-785-9140 501 A
wignesd@westerntc.edu
WIGNOT, Terese .... 570-408-4200 403 D
terese.wignot@wilkes.edu
WIGTIL, Brad .... 254-710-2222 431 J
brad_wigtil@baylor.edu
WIHBEY, Jean .... 561-868-3400 104 D
wihbeyj@palmbeachstate.edu
WIILKINSON, Joann, F . 314-516-5301 261 D
wilkinsonj@umsl.edu
WIKAN, Cory .... 318-869-5175 186 B
cwikan@centenary.edu
WIKLE, Karen .... 360-475-7133 482 G
kwikle@olympic.edu
WIKSTROM,
Christopher .... 276-656-0253 475 D
cwikstrom@patrickhenry.edu
WILBANKS, Cynthia, H . 734-763-5554 231 E
wilbanks@umich.edu
WILBANKS, Jennifer ..... 660-596-7229 260 D
jwilbanks@sfccmo.edu
WILBANKS, Jennifer ..... 843-349-5208 410 C
jennifer.wilbanks@hgtc.edu
WILBANKS, Laura .... 734-481-2318 223 H
laura.wilbanks@emich.edu
WILBANKS, Scott .... 864-250-8281 410 B
scott.wilbanks@gvltec.edu
WILBORN, Colin .... 254-295-8642 453 E
cwilborn@umhb.edu
WILBUR, Bruce .... 707-654-1173.. 32 B
bwilbur@csum.edu
WILBUR, Gregg .... 518-736-3622 300 F
gregg.wilbur@fmcc.suny.edu
WILBUR, Kathleen .... 517-353-9000 227 D
schlage6@msu.edu
WILBUR, Marcia .... 706-769-1472 114 E
mwilbur@acmin.org
WILBUR, Rachael .... 276-944-6232 467 G
rwilbur@ehc.edu
WILBUR, Shelley .... 941-487-4100 109 D
mwilbur@ncf.edu
WILBUR, Susan .... 508-999-8080 211 F
swilbur@umassd.edu
WILBURN, Roberta .... 509-777-4603 486 I
rwilburn@whitworth.edu
WILCH, Peter, J .... 415-422-6423.. 71 K
pwilch@usfca.edu
WILCHER, Cheryl .... 305-626-3641.. 99 D
cwilcher@fmuniv.edu

WILCOTS, Barbara .... 303-458-4086.. 82 E
bwilcots@regis.edu
WILCOX, Bonnie .... 417-873-7201 252 F
bwilcox@drury.edu
WILCOX, Cordelia, A .... 919-658-7494 340 J
cwilcox@umo.edu
WILCOX, Dean .... 336-770-3243 343 D
wilcoxd@uncsa.edu
WILCOX, Denise .... 909-469-5393.. 74 I
dwilcox@westernu.edu
WILCOX, Jerome .... 203-837-8242.. 85 B
wilcoxj@wcsu.edu
WILCOX, Kenneth .... 718-522-9073 290 C
coachwilcox@asa.edu
WILCOX, Kevin .... 518-956-8120 316 D
kwilcox@albany.edu
WILCOX, Kim .... 970-351-2496.. 83 E
kim.wilcox@unco.edu
WILCOX, Kim, A .... 951-827-5201.. 69 C
chancellor@ucr.edu
WILCOX, Laurie .... 603-535-3278 275 B
lrwilcox@plymouth.edu
WILCOX, Madeleine ...... 215-951-2815 400 A
wilcoxm@philau.edu
WILCOX, Mark .... 412-536-1104 387 B
mark.wilcox@laroche.edu
WILCOX, Ralph .... 813-974-8347 110 B
rcwilcox@usf.edu
WILCOX, Reed, N .... 540-261-4100 471 H
reed.wilcox@svu.edu
WILCOX, Robbin .... 419-267-1460 358 A
rwilcox@northweststate.edu
WILCOX, Robert, M ...... 803-777-6857 413 C
wilcoxrm@law.sc.edu
WILCOX, Shannon .... 406-657-2243 264 E
swilcox@msubillings.edu
WILCOX, Tamera .... 785-309-3183 176 J
tamera.wilcox@salinatech.edu
WILCOXEN, Andrica ...... 913-288-7652 174 F
awilcoxen@kckcc.edu
WILCOXSON,
Douglas, A .... 517-750-1200 230 H
dwilcoxs@arbor.edu
WILCZEWSKI, Linda ...... 408-531-6130.. 61 K
linda.wilczewski@sjeccd.edu
WILD, Beth .... 918-595-8804 370 E
beth.wild@tulsacc.edu
WILD, Larry .... 847-628-2036 140 C
lwild@judsonu.edu
WILD, Lorie .... 206-281-2608 484 D
wildl@spu.edu
WILD, Robert, M .... 314-935-8081 262 A
rob.wild@wustl.edu
WILD, Shawn .... 215-968-8306 379 G
shawn.wild@bucks.edu
WILDA, Christine, M .... 413-545-2148 211 D
cwilda@umass.edu
WILDCAT, Dan .... 785-830-2770 173 G
dwildcat@haskell.edu
WILDE, Jerry .... 765-973-8554 156 C
jwilde@iue.edu
WILDECK, Steve .... 608-265-3040 496 B
steve.wildeck@uwss.wisconsin.edu
WILDEMANN,
Leonard Walter .... 401-841-6515 503 L
wildemal@usnwc.edu
WILDENTHAL,
B. Hobson .... 972-883-3550 455 B
wildenbh@utdallas.edu
WILDER, Aliza .... 860-486-4038.. 88 E
aliza.wilder@uconn.edu
WILDER, Carrie .... 229-931-2351 124 D
cwilder@southgatech.edu
WILDER, Dana .... 860-486-2422.. 88 E
dana.wilder@uconn.edu
WILDER, Diane .... 610-896-1209 385 L
dwilder@haverford.edu
WILDER, Jennifer .... 850-599-3651 108 I
jennifer.wilder@famu.edu
WILDER, Kristie .... 423-236-2206 424 B
kwilder@southern.edu
WILDER, Lesley .... 512-472-4133 443 H
lesley.wilder@ssw.edu
WILDER, Leslie .... 910-755-7324 332 F
wilderl@brunswickcc.edu
WILDER, Linda .... 860-515-3862.. 84 G
lwilder@charteroak.edu
WILDER, Marita .... 541-956-7139 376 D
mwilder@roguecc.edu
WILDER, Melanie .... 912-443-5717 124 A
mwilder@savannahtech.edu
WILDER, Michael .... 630-752-5818 152 F
michael.wilder@wheaton.edu
WILDER, Michael .... 817-923-1921 445 B
WILDER, Paul, J .... 407-582-2175 112 K
pwilder1@valenciacollege.edu
WILDER, Stanley .... 225-578-2217 188 I
wilder@lsu.edu
WILDER, Sterly .... 919-684-5114 328 G
sterly.wilder@daa.duke.edu
WILDER, W. Mark .... 662-915-5756 249 D
acwilder@olemiss.edu
WILDER-BYRD,
Ellen, M .... 803-323-2236 414 G
wilderbyrde@winthrop.edu
WILDERMUTH, Amy, J . 412-648-1401 401 B
amy.wildermuth@pitt.edu
WILDEY, Diane .... 518-743-2337 320 D
daltod@sunyacc.edu
WILDHACK, John .... 315-443-8705 322 C
jwildhac@syr.edu
WILDING, Jody .... 281-649-3070 437 H
jwilding@hbu.edu
WILDING, Michael .... 661-362-3498.. 38 H
michael.wilding@canyons.edu
WILDING, Tim .... 205-226-4643.... 5 A
trwildin@bsc.edu
WILES, Duane .... 305-348-3213 109 A
wilesd@fiu.edu
WILES, Jan .... 618-842-3711 138 G
wilesj@iecc.edu
WILES, Mari, E .... 252-398-6268 328 D
wilesm@chowan.edu
WILES, Patrick, J .... 716-851-1901 299 F
wiles@ecc.edu
WILEY, Casey .... 864-455-8204 414 A
wileyc@greenvillemed.sc.edu
WILEY, Ellen .... 717-947-6089 393 F
ewiley@pacollege.edu
WILEY, Fran, K .... 864-941-8351 411 H
wiley.f@ptc.edu
WILEY, Jack .... 719-589-7064.. 82 K
jack.wiley@trinidadstate.edu
WILEY, Jeana .... 918-836-6886 370 D
jeana.wiley@spartan.edu
WILEY, Jeanelle .... 314-968-7123 262 C
jeanellewiley10@webster.edu
WILEY, Jeffrey .... 315-786-2248 303 F
jwiley@sunyjefferson.edu
WILEY, Karen .... 815-455-8547 143 A
kwiley@mchenry.edu
WILEY, Marilyn .... 940-565-4874 454 A
marilyn.wiley@unt.edu
WILEY, Matt .... 361-582-2468 457 E
matt.wiley@victoriacollege.edu
WILEY, Maya .... 212-229-5400 308 C
wileym@newschool.edu
WILEY, Nina .... 937-328-7936 350 L
wileyn@clarkstate.edu
WILEY, Paul, G .... 931-598-1731 423 M
pwiley@sewanee.edu
WILEY, Sean .... 814-860-5104 388 A
swiley@lecom.edu
WILEY, Stacey .... 814-824-2311 390 C
swiley@mercyhurst.edu
WILEY, Trina .... 904-470-8087.. 97 L
tmwiley@ewc.edu
WILEY-HARRIS,
Courtney .... 585-340-9648 296 E
cwiley-harris@crcds.edu
WILFAHRT, Dannette, C 651-631-5190 244 D
dcwilfahrt@unwsp.edu
WILFERTH, Joe .... 423-425-4621 428 A
joe-wilferth@utc.edu
WILFONG, Barry .... 573-518-3806 256 B
bwilfong@mineralarea.edu
WILFONG, MacKenzie ... 918-595-4735 370 E
mackenzie.wilfong@tulsacc.edu
WILGENBUSCH, Sandy . 563-876-3353 164 J
wilgenbu@dwci.edu
WILGUS, Robynne .... 541-440-4622 377 C
robynne.wilgus@umpqua.edu
WILHELM, Cori .... 315-386-7873 320 E
wilhelmc@canton.edu
WILHELM, Jane .... 608-663-2203 493 C
jwilhelm@edgewood.edu
WILHELM, Jennifer .... 617-236-5470 209 D
jwilhelm@fisher.edu
WILHELM, Justina .... 907-852-1772.... 9 F
justina.wilhelm@ilisagvik.edu
WILHELM, Michael .... 910-962-2736 343 C
wilhelmm@uncw.edu
WILHELM, Robert .... 402-472-3123 269 J
bob.wilhelm@unl.edu
WILHELMS, Angela .... 541-346-5561 377 D
wilhelms@uoregon.edu
WILHEMI, Jeremy .... 479-979-1307.. 23 I
jwilhemi@ozarks.edu
WILHITE, Brian .... 630-617-6484 136 G
wilhiteb@elmhurst.edu
WILHITE, Christa .... 601-635-2111 245 I
cwilhite@eccc.edu
WILHITE, David .... 502-863-8016 180 E
david_wilhite@georgetowncollege.edu
WILHITE, Lee .... 562-903-4079.. 27 C
lee.wilhite@biola.edu
WILHOIT, Cathi .... 314-837-6777 258 J
cwilhoit@stlchristian.edu
WILIAMSON, Keith .... 978-665-3731 212 C
kwilli@fitchburgstate.edu
WILKE, Dennis, F .... 412-521-6200 397 H
dennis.wilke@rosedaletech.org
WILKE, Janet, S .... 308-865-8595 269 I
wilkej@unk.edu
WILKE, Stephen, K .... 620-229-6277 177 A
steve.wilke@sckans.edu
WILKEN, Danielle .... 860-727-6714.. 87 A
dwilken@goodwin.edu
WILKENS, Richard, T .... 410-548-6022 203 F
rtwilkens@salisbury.edu
WILKERSON, Aimee, J .. 270-824-8696 181 G
aimee.wilkerson@kctcs.edu
WILKERSON, Ame .... 912-260-4407 124 C
ame.wilkerson@sgsc.edu
WILKERSON, Charles .... 931-372-3634 426 E
cwilkerson@tntech.edu
WILKERSON, Denise ..... 410-576-5734 202 B
dwilkerson@usmd.edu
WILKERSON, Karen, D .. 816-235-2757 261 C
wilkersonkd@umkc.edu
WILKERSON, Kim .... 618-437-5321 147 A
wilkersonk@rlc.edu
WILKERSON,
Lindsey, S .... 318-342-1530 192 F
lwilkerson@ulm.edu
WILKERSON,
Mathew, C .... 540-654-1281 472 I
mwilkers@umw.edu
WILKERSON, Steve, L ... 210-458-4939 455 E
steve.wilkerson@utsa.edu
WILKERSON, Tanya ...... 443-885-3170 200 D
tanya.wilkerson@morgan.edu
WILKERSON, Terry .... 618-437-5321 147 A
wilkersont@rlc.edu
WILKERSON, William .... 256-824-2339.... 8 B
william.wilkerson@uah.edu
WILKERSON, Zeda .... 870-368-2028.. 20 F
zwilkerson@ozarka.edu
WILKES, Barrie, J .... 989-774-3334 222 C
wilke1bj@cmich.edu
WILKES, Brandy .... 229-468-2031 127 B
brandy.wilkes@wiregrass.edu
WILKES, C. Gene .... 817-274-4284 432 A
gwilkes@bhcarroll.edu
WILKES, David, S .... 434-982-4050 473 A
dsw4n@virginia.edu
WILKES, Deborah .... 706-886-6831 125 D
dwilkes@tfc.edu
WILKES, Jeremy .... 901-572-2670 418 E
jeremy.wilkes@bchs.edu
WILKES, Kwin .... 307-532-8218 502 A
kwin.wilkes@ewc.wy.edu
WILKES, Lisa .... 540-231-5706 477 A
lwilkes@vt.edu
WILKES, Yvette .... 505-454-3197 286 H
ydwilkes@nmhu.edu
WILKIE, Digna .... 501-623-2272.. 18 I
WILKIE, Michelle .... 641-628-5281 163 E
wilkiem@central.edu
WILKIN, John, P .... 217-333-0790 151 D
jpwilkin@illinois.edu
WILKIN, Joshua .... 215-965-4038 390 J
jwilkin@moore.edu
WILKIN, Lori .... 732-906-2574 279 A
lwilkin@middlesexcc.edu
WILKIN, Noel, E .... 662-915-5317 249 D
nwilkin@olemiss.edu
WILKINS, Ashli .... 334-556-2226.... 2 C
awilkins@wallace.edu
WILKINS, Deborah, T ... 270-745-5398 185 E
deborah.wilkins@wku.edu
WILKINS, Derrick, L ..... 252-335-3102 341 D
dlwilkins@ecsu.edu
WILKINS, Harry, T .... 614-508-7277 354 F
hwilkins@hondros.edu
WILKINS, Joel .... 419-448-2517 353 H
jwilkin2@heidelberg.edu
WILKINS, Karin, J .... 305-284-3420 112 E
kwilkins@miami.edu
WILKINS, Kate .... 717-796-1800 390 E
ksimcox@messiah.edu
WILKINS, Ken .... 702-968-5568 272 C
kwilkins@roseman.edu
WILKINS, Mardell .... 775-753-2265 271 B
mardell.wilkins@gbcnv.edu
WILKINS, Marianne ...... 251-380-2261.... 6 H
mwilkins@shc.edu
WILKINS, Pyeper .... 214-378-1538 434 K
pwilkins@dcccd.edu
WILKINS, Vickie .... 419-448-3595 361 J
galaskavm@tiffin.edu
WILKINS, Vicky .... 202-885-6443.. 90 J
vwilkins@american.edu
WILKINS-GREEN, Clair . 504-520-5251 193 A
cwilkins@xula.edu
WILKINS-LUTON, Jim ... 360-992-2000 479 F
jwilikins-luton@clark.edu
WILKINSON, Cathryn .... 831-646-4000.. 52 F
cwilkinson@mpc.edu
WILKINSON,
Christine, K .... 480-965-7782.. 10 I
c.wilkinson@asu.edu
WILKINSON, Denise ..... 757-455-3249 477 F
dwilkinson@vwu.edu
WILKINSON, Ineke .... 616-538-2330 224 C
iwilkinson@gracechristian.edu
WILKINSON, Jay .... 515-961-1288 169 D
jay.wilkinson@simpson.edu
WILKINSON, JoAnne .... 970-204-8457.. 79 J
joanne.wilkinson@frontrange.edu
WILKINSON, John .... 423-636-5096 427 B
jwilinson@tusculum.edu
WILKINSON, Kurtis .... 307-382-1647 502 I
kwilkinson@westernwyoming.edu
WILKINSON, Melissa .... 309-647-4645 150 A
WILKINSON, Michael .... 361-485-4409 453 C
wilkinsonmr@uhv.edu
WILKINSON, Mike .... 405-692-3132 366 G
mwilkinson@macu.edu
WILKINSON, Mike .... 817-923-1921 445 B
mwilkinson@swbts.edu
WILKINSON, Missy .... 309-649-6305 150 A
missy.wilkinson@src.edu
WILKINSON, Pete .... 706-771-4024 114 J
pwilkins@augustatech.edu
WILKINSON, Sandy ...... 575-492-2193 289 A
swilkinson@usw.edu
WILKINSON, Timothy ... 509-777-4585 486 I
twilkinson@whitworth.edu
WILKINSON, Todd .... 252-399-6552 326 M
twilkinson@barton.edu
WILKINSON, William, J 215-204-0564 399 F
william.wilkinson@temple.edu
WILKINSON HARTUNG,
Erin .... 603-428-2301 273 H
ewilkinsonhartung@nec.edu
WILKOS-GREENBERG,
Janice .... 617-585-0200 206 F
janice.greenberg@the-bac.edu
WILKOSKI, Donna, M ... 215-698-8203 379 G
wilkoski@bucks.edu
WILKS, Karrin, E .... 212-220-1234 293 A
kwilks@bmcc.cuny.edu
WILKS, Kerry .... 316-978-3095 178 A
kerry.wilks@wichita.edu
WILKS, Ron .... 317-788-3350 161 B
wilks@uindy.edu
WILKSON, Nancy .... 575-439-3798 287 C
nmontgom@nmsu.edu
WILKYMACKY, Eric .... 305-628-6658 106 F
ewilkymacky@stu.edu
WILL, Christina .... 386-312-4152 106 C
christinawill@sjrstate.edu
WILL, Ed .... 760-252-2411.. 26 I
jwill@barstow.edu
WILL, Gary .... 706-368-5674 115 B
gwill@berry.edu
WILL, John .... 715-468-2815 501 B
john.will@witc.edu
WILL, Lee .... 480-245-7937.. 12 N
lee.will@ibcs.edu
WILL, Lisa .... 619-388-3520.. 60 C
lwill@sdccd.edu
WILLAIMS, Van, P .... 561-868-3939 104 D
williamv@palmbeachstate.edu
WILLAN, Dawn, E .... 843-953-5997 408 E
willande@cofc.edu
WILLARD, Cary .... 619-644-7163.. 44 I
cary.willard@gcccd.edu
WILLARD, Jennifer .... 218-749-7772 238 G
j.willard@mesabirange.edu
WILLARD, Paul .... 706-865-2134 125 E
pwillard@truett.edu
WILLARD, Randon, T .... 724-847-6133 384 G
rtwillar@geneva.edu

WILLARD, Rashida .... 360-992-2757 479 F
rwillard@clark.edu
WILLCOX, Abby .... 904-620-2014 110 A
abby.willcox@unf.edu
WILLCOX, Jan, M .... 540-231-0920 467 F
jwilcox@vcom.vt.edu
WILLCOX, Sue .... 816-501-3759 250 F
sue.willcox@avila.edu
WILLCOX, Wayne .... 912-443-4787 124 A
wwillcox@savannahtech.edu
WILLE, Diane, E .... 812-941-2300 157 B
dwille@ius.edu
WILLEFORD, Amber ...... 314-838-8858 261 G
awilleford@ugst.edu
WILLEKENS, Rene, G .... 623-935-8069.. 13 A
rene.willekens@estrellamountain.edu
WILLEMS, Greg .... 785-532-6266 174 G
gregw@found.ksu.edu
WILLENBERG, Lisa .... 501-977-2025.. 23 A
willenberg@uaccm.edu
WILLENBORG, Andy, B . 563-589-0217 170 D
awillenborg@wartburgseminary.edu
WILLENBROCK, Donna . 516-463-6745 302 B
donna.willenbrock@hofstra.edu
WILLENSKY, Violet, J ... 908-526-1200 281 A
violet.willensky@raritanval.edu
WILLER, Anthony .... 701-483-2215 345 D
anthony.willer@dickinsonstate.edu
WILLETT, Dana .... 512-245-2322 450 E
drw134@txstate.edu
WILLETT, Jessica .... 540-458-8186 478 A
jwillett@wlu.edu
WILLETT, Tami .... 360-752-8475 478 G
twillett@btc.edu
WILLETT, Terrence .... 831-477-5656.. 27 G
terrence@cabrillo.edu
WILLEY, Ed, W .... 561-207-5411 104 D
willeye@palmbeachstate.edu
WILLEY, John .... 251-981-3771.... 5 B
john.willey@columbiasouthern.edu
WILLEY, Kevin .... 570-577-3208 379 F
kevin.willey@bucknell.edu
WILLEY, Leslie .... 573-876-7213 260 F
lwilley@stephens.edu
WILLEY, Sue, C .... 317-788-3412 161 B
swilley@uindy.edu
WILLGING, Gregory, A . 563-556-5110 168 E
willging@nicc.edu
WILLHARDT, Mark .... 309-457-2325 144 A
mwill@monmouthcollege.edu
WILLHITE, Grant .... 423-746-5236 426 F
gwillhite@tnwesleyan.edu
WILLIAMS, Adam .... 757-352-4894 470 H
awilliams@regent.edu
WILLIAMS, Alex .... 402-363-5689 270 E
aawilliams@york.edu
WILLIAMS, Alfred .... 603-542-7744 273 C
awilliams@ccsnh.edu
WILLIAMS, Alicia .... 912-358-4045 123 H
awilliam@savannahstate.edu
WILLIAMS, Alvin .... 208-769-3348 131 C
al_williams@nic.edu
WILLIAMS, Amanda .... 415-439-2484.. 25 K
awilliams@act-sf.org
WILLIAMS, Amanda .... 913-288-7218 174 F
awilliams@kckcc.edu
WILLIAMS, Amanda .... 913-281-7670 174 F
awilliams@kckcc.edu
WILLIAMS, Amari .... 818-712-2680.. 49 C
williaad@piercecollege.edu
WILLIAMS, Amber .... 973-353-5112 282 B
amber.williams@rutgers.edu
WILLIAMS, Amber .... 308-367-4124 270 C
WILLIAMS, Amber, S .... 402-472-0671 269 J
amber.williams@unl.edu
WILLIAMS, Amy, H .... 704-637-4414 328 A
ahwillia@catawba.edu
WILLIAMS, Ana .... 502-897-4206 184 C
awilliams@sbts.edu
WILLIAMS, Andre .... 252-331-4881 333 G
andre_williams@albemarle.edu
WILLIAMS, Andrew .... 425-640-1450 480 F
andy.williams@edcc.edu
WILLIAMS, Andy .... 847-635-1875 145 G
awilliams@oakton.edu
WILLIAMS, Angela .... 803-738-7691 410 G
williamsa@midlandstech.edu
WILLIAMS, Angela .... 405-585-5801 367 F
angela.williams@okbu.edu
WILLIAMS, Angela, S ... 479-575-2806.. 21 G
angelaw@uark.edu
WILLIAMS, Ann .... 843-661-1175 409 K
awilliams@fmarion.edu

WILLIAMS, Annette .... 540-453-2332 474 B
williamsa@brcc.edu
WILLIAMS, Anthony ...... 425-388-9282 480 G
anwilliams@everettcc.edu
WILLIAMS, Anthony ...... 828-328-7244 330 F
anthony.williams@lr.edu
WILLIAMS, Anthony ...... 212-343-1234 306 J
awilliams@mcny.edu
WILLIAMS, Anu .... 336-734-7251 334 E
awilliams@forsythtech.edu
WILLIAMS, Arlanda .... 504-671-6488 187 E
awilli4@dcc.edu
WILLIAMS, Arlene .... 320-308-5937 241 A
arlene.williams@sctcc.edu
WILLIAMS, Arthur .... 501-370-8525.. 20 G
awilliams@philander.edu
WILLIAMS, Audrey, J .... 865-539-7198 425 F
ajwilliams@pstcc.edu
WILLIAMS, Barry .... 570-208-5932 387 A
barrywilliams@kings.edu
WILLIAMS, Bert .... 478-387-4782 118 G
bwilliams@gmc.edu
WILLIAMS, Beth .... 540-654-1294 472 I
bwilli22@umw.edu
WILLIAMS, Beth .... 906-487-2313 227 E
egwillia@mtu.edu
WILLIAMS, Beth .... 513-618-1930 350 J
ewilliams@ccms.edu
WILLIAMS, Betty, B ...... 843-383-8055 408 D
bwilliams@coker.edu
WILLIAMS, Blake .... 229-732-5951 114 B
blakewilliams@andrewcollege.edu
WILLIAMS, Bobby .... 936-294-4205 450 C
ath_brw@shsu.edu
WILLIAMS, Boyce .... 301-687-4759 203 E
bcwilliams@frostburg.edu
WILLIAMS, Brad .... 954-262-7282 103 M
bradwill@nsu.nova.edu
WILLIAMS, Brad .... 405-947-3200 368 E
bradford.williams@osuokc.edu
WILLIAMS, Brandy .... 662-329-7293 248 A
bmwilliams@muw.edu
WILLIAMS, Bre .... 760-471-1316.. 71 I
bwilliams@usk.edu
WILLIAMS, Breanda ...... 972-241-3371 434 J
bwilliams@dallas.edu
WILLIAMS, Brenda, D ... 609-497-7820 280 D
registrar@ptsem.edu
WILLIAMS, Brenda, K ... 256-372-5254.... 1 A
brenda.williams@aamu.edu
WILLIAMS, Brett, J ...... 763-417-8250 234 H
bwilliams@centralseminary.edu
WILLIAMS, Brian .... 401-254-3540 405 E
bwilliams@rwu.edu
WILLIAMS, Brian .... 610-225-5704 383 D
brian.williams@eastern.edu
WILLIAMS, Brianna .... 337-457-7311 189 A
bewillia@lsue.edu
WILLIAMS, Brockton ...... 615-343-4411 428 D
brock.williams@vanderbilt.edu
WILLIAMS, Calvin .... 813-974-2612 110 B
williams374@usf.edu
WILLIAMS, Calvin .... 607-962-9233 320 F
williams@corning-cc.edu
WILLIAMS, Camelia .... 816-995-2808 258 F
camelia.williams@researchcollege.edu
WILLIAMS, Candace ...... 254-295-4504 453 E
cwilliams@umhb.edu
WILLIAMS, Carla .... 434-982-5100 473 A
cgw4j@virginia.edu
WILLIAMS, Carla, M ..... 662-254-3319 248 B
ctwilliams@mvsu.edu
WILLIAMS, Carme .... 936-261-1573 446 D
clwilliams@pvamu.edu
WILLIAMS, Carol .... 804-763-6711.. 92 G
ctw@strayer.edu
WILLIAMS, Carol .... 731-881-7805 428 B
cwill229@utm.edu
WILLIAMS, Carolyn, J .. 936-261-5122 446 D
cjwilliams@pvamu.edu
WILLIAMS, Carrie .... 630-752-5941 152 F
carrie.williams@wheaton.edu
WILLIAMS, Carrie, L ...... 517-750-1200 230 H
cshaw@arbor.edu
WILLIAMS, Catherine .... 707-778-3628.. 62 F
cwilliams@santarosa.edu
WILLIAMS,
Catherine, R .... 607-778-5182 318 A
williamscr@sunybroome.edu
WILLIAMS, Cathy .... 417-865-2815 253 B
williamsc@evangel.edu
WILLIAMS, Cathy .... 315-781-3696 302 A
cwilliams@hws.edu

WILLIAMS, Chad .... 336-633-0049 337 A
gcwilliams@randolph.edu
WILLIAMS, Charles .... 662-252-8000 248 G
cwilliams7@rustcollege.edu
WILLIAMS, Charlie .... 908-737-3330 278 E
chwillia@kean.edu
WILLIAMS, Charlotte ..... 828-328-7214 330 F
charlotte.williams@lr.edu
WILLIAMS, Chris .... 217-234-5253 141 D
WILLIAMS, Chris .... 864-644-5303 412 E
cwilliams@swu.edu
WILLIAMS, Chris, C ..... 417-268-6017 250 G
cwilliams@gobbc.edu
WILLIAMS, Christal .... 913-469-8500 174 D
cwill216@jccc.edu
WILLIAMS, Christine ..... 603-513-1150 274 H
christine.williams@granite.edu
WILLIAMS, Christine ..... 906-217-4077 221 O
chris.williams@baycollege.edu
WILLIAMS, Cindy .... 406-243-2573 264 A
cindy.williams@umontana.edu
WILLIAMS, Claire .... 925-631-4812.. 59 B
cmw9@stmarys-ca.edu
WILLIAMS,
Clarence (Reggie) .... 210-690-9000 437 E
cwilliams@hallmarkuniversity.edu
WILLIAMS, Clifton .... 828-250-3898 342 C
cwilli14@unca.edu
WILLIAMS, Corey .... 225-490-1617 186 F
corey.williams@franu.edu
WILLIAMS, Crystal, A ... 617-353-2230 207 D
provost@bu.edu
WILLIAMS, D. Newell ... 817-257-7231 432 E
n.williams@tcu.edu
WILLIAMS, Dan .... 501-279-4449.. 19 D
bible@harding.edu
WILLIAMS, Dana .... 202-806-6800.. 92 B
WILLIAMS, Daniel, C .... 563-876-3353 164 J
dwilliams@dwci.edu
WILLIAMS, Danielle ...... 845-431-8686 298 E
danielle.williams4@sunydutchess.edu
WILLIAMS, Danisha ...... 662-254-3345 248 B
danisha.williams@mvsu.edu
WILLIAMS, Darlene .... 318-357-6100 192 C
darlene@nsula.edu
WILLIAMS, Darryl .... 708-974-5525 144 C
williamsd484@morainevalley.edu
WILLIAMS, Darryl, A ..... 845-938-4041 504 H
8sgs@usma.edu
WILLIAMS, David .... 704-461-6728 327 A
davidwilliams@bac.edu
WILLIAMS, David .... 707-864-7000.. 64 C
david.williams@solano.edu
WILLIAMS, David .... 606-546-1624 184 H
dwilliams@unionky.edu
WILLIAMS, David .... 814-472-3017 398 B
dwilliams@francis.edu
WILLIAMS, David, B ..... 614-292-6446 358 I
williams.4219@osu.edu
WILLIAMS, David, P ..... 540-464-7094 476 G
williamsdp@vmi.edu
WILLIAMS, David, S ..... 706-542-3240 125 G
dwilliam@uga.edu
WILLIAMS, Dawn .... 202-806-7340.. 92 B
dgwilliams@howard.edu
WILLIAMS, Debra .... 313-577-1031 232 I
dr9780@wayne.edu
WILLIAMS, Debra, A ..... 404-880-6412 116 D
dwilliams@cau.edu
WILLIAMS, Debra, J ..... 724-925-4200 403 A
williamsd@westmoreland.edu
WILLIAMS, Dedra .... 217-333-6677 151 D
dwillms1@uillinois.edu
WILLIAMS, Dedra, M .... 217-333-1920 151 A
dwillms1@uillinois.edu
WILLIAMS, Denise .... 586-445-7897 226 H
williamsdl@macomb.edu
WILLIAMS, Dennis .... 405-789-6400 370 A
dwilliam@snu.edu
WILLIAMS, Dereck .... 937-708-5808 364 D
dwilliams@wilberforce.edu
WILLIAMS, Derrien .... 304-590-9079 491 B
derrien.williams@wvstateu.edu
WILLIAMS, Dianna .... 704-847-5600 340 I
dwilliams@ses.edu
WILLIAMS, Digna .... 787-834-9595 511 E
dwilliams@uaa.edu
WILLIAMS, Donald, J ... 540-231-5991 477 A
dowilli3@vt.edu
WILLIAMS, Donna .... 601-877-6450 244 H
dmwilliams@alcorn.edu
WILLIAMS, Donna .... 601-877-6142 244 H
dmwilliams@alcorn.edu

WILLIAMS, Donna, M ... 610-799-1107 388 I
dwilliams@lccc.edu
WILLIAMS, Dorene, E ... 201-761-6013 282 I
dwilliams3@saintpeters.edu
WILLIAMS, Dorothy .... 404-756-4016 114 G
dwilliams@atlm.edu
WILLIAMS, Douglass .... 931-598-5241 423 M
dwilliam@sewanee.edu
WILLIAMS, Drew, H ...... 214-887-5211 436 B
dwilliams@dts.edu
WILLIAMS, Dwayne .... 541-278-5904 372 A
dwilliams@bluecc.edu
WILLIAMS, Edward .... 336-506-4178 332 A
edward.williams@alamancecc.edu
WILLIAMS, Efrain .... 787-850-9312 513 E
efrain.williams@upr.edu
WILLIAMS, Elizabeth ..... 803-778-7873 407 C
williamsel@cctech.edu
WILLIAMS, Elmer .... 787-850-9345 513 E
elmer.williams@upr.edu
WILLIAMS, Emili .... 865-573-4517 420 G
ewilliams@johnsonu.edu
WILLIAMS, Emma .... 478-825-4350 118 A
emma.williams@fvsu.edu
WILLIAMS, Eugene .... 770-531-3172 115 D
ewilliams4@brenau.edu
WILLIAMS, Eunice .... 315-498-2565 311 B
williame@sunyocc.edu
WILLIAMS, F. Clark .... 615-343-3808 428 D
f.clark.williams@vanderbilt.edu
WILLIAMS, Falecia, D ... 407-582-1235 112 K
fawilliams@valenciacollege.edu
WILLIAMS, Forrest, G ... 801-863-8494 461 A
forrest.williams@uvu.edu
WILLIAMS, Frances .... 716-851-1698 299 F
williams@ecc.edu
WILLIAMS, Frank .... 254-659-7708 437 G
fwilliams@hillcollege.edu
WILLIAMS, JR., Frank .. 318-670-6681 190 J
fwilliams@susla.edu
WILLIAMS, JR., Frantz .. 860-685-2000.. 89 C
WILLIAMS, Fred .... 714-808-4746.. 53 J
fwilliams@nocccd.edu
WILLIAMS, Freddie .... 334-229-4291.... 4 B
fwilliams@alasu.edu
WILLIAMS, Gail, B .... 239-513-1122 101 C
gwiliams@hodges.edu
WILLIAMS, Gail, C .... 757-446-5869 466 I
williamsgc@evms.edu
WILLIAMS, Gary .... 937-327-6472 364 H
williamsg1@wittenberg.edu
WILLIAMS, JR.,
George, A .... 210-434-6711 441 E
gawilliam6@ollusa.edu
WILLIAMS, George, D ... 919-516-4236 340 C
gdwilliams@st-aug.edu
WILLIAMS, Georgeann .. 843-525-8203 412 H
gwilliams@tcl.edu
WILLIAMS, Georgia, E .. 252-398-6439 328 D
willig@chowan.edu
WILLIAMS, Gerald .... 401-874-2901 406 B
gman1@uri.edu
WILLIAMS, Gerald .... 229-333-5942 126 G
gewilliams@valdosta.edu
WILLIAMS, Gerhild, S ... 314-935-5106 262 A
gerhildwilliams@wustl.edu
WILLIAMS, Ginger .... 276-944-6541 467 G
gwilliams@ehc.edu
WILLIAMS, Glenn .... 816-322-0110 250 K
security@calvary.edu
WILLIAMS, Gregory, D . 432-335-6410 441 D
gwilliams@odessa.edu
WILLIAMS, Gregory, G . 713-313-1962 449 C
williamsg@tsu.edu
WILLIAMS, H. James ... 513-244-4232 357 A
president@msj.edu
WILLIAMS, Hans, M ..... 936-468-3304 445 F
hwilliams@sfasu.edu
WILLIAMS, Heidi .... 724-938-5700 394 B
williams_h@calu.edu
WILLIAMS, Helen, E ..... 310-568-5615.. 56 C
helen.williams@pepperdine.edu
WILLIAMS, Ingrid .... 707-654-1135.. 32 B
iwilliams@csum.edu
WILLIAMS,
Jacqueline, H .... 410-951-6481 203 D
jwilliams@coppin.edu
WILLIAMS, Jalisa, D .... 413-572-8670 213 D
jdwilliams@westfield.ma.edu
WILLIAMS, James .... 314-889-4503 253 C
jwilliams@fontbonne.edu
WILLIAMS, James, E .... 620-341-5267 172 L
jwilliam@emporia.edu

WILLIAMS, Russ .... 478-445-5650 118 C
russ.williams@gcsu.edu
WILLIAMS, Ruth .... 847-635-7090 145 G
rwilliam@oakton.edu
WILLIAMS, Ryan .... 845-569-3105 307 J
ryan.williams@msmc.edu
WILLIAMS, Ryan, A ...... 309-624-9268 148 E
ryan.a.williams@osfhealthcare.org
WILLIAMS, Sabrina, R .. 252-335-3969 341 D
srwilliams3@ecsu.edu
WILLIAMS, Sara .... 402-399-2467 266 F
swilliams@csm.edu
WILLIAMS, Scott .... 270-686-4508 182 B
scott.willliams@kctcs.edu
WILLIAMS, Scott, E ...... 276-944-6242 467 G
swilliams@ehc.edu
WILLIAMS, Scott, T ...... 706-542-3375 125 G
scottw@uga.edu
WILLIAMS, Shannon ..... 214-648-3134 457 B
shannonl.williams@utsouthwestern.edu
WILLIAMS, Sharaf .... 909-384-8988.. 59 I
swilliams@sbccd.cc.ca.us
WILLIAMS, Shaun .... 817-515-5154 445 G
shaun.williams@tccd.edu
WILLIAMS, Shaundria ... 336-322-2120 336 G
shaundria.williams@piedmontcc.edu
WILLIAMS, Shelitha ...... 585-345-6886 301 A
swwilliams@genesee.edu
WILLIAMS, Sheree .... 502-585-4425 181 F
sheree.williams@kctcs.edu
WILLIAMS, Sherry .... 828-327-7000 333 B
swilliams@cvcc.edu
WILLIAMS, Sonya .... 815-280-6731 140 B
swilliam@jjc.edu
WILLIAMS, Sonya .... 315-781-3312 302 A
swilliams@hws.edu
WILLIAMS, Sophia .... 414-297-6288 500 B
wills12@matc.edu
WILLIAMS, Stephanie ... 585-385-8010 314 A
swilliams@sjfc.edu
WILLIAMS, Stephen ...... 414-277-7114 494 G
williams@msoe.edu
WILLIAMS, Stephen, R . 419-755-4811 357 E
swilliam@ncstatecollege.edu
WILLIAMS, Steve .... 256-840-4174.... 3 F
steve.williams@snead.edu
WILLIAMS, Susan .... 304-255-0793 490 A
swilliams@concord.edu
WILLIAMS, Susan .... 516-323-3030 307 F
swilliams@molloy.edu
WILLIAMS, Susan .... 919-760-8262 331 B
williams@meredith.edu
WILLIAMS, Susan .... 828-448-3178 339 A
swilliams@wpcc.edu
WILLIAMS, Susan, L ..... 302-831-8436.. 90 F
susanlyn@udel.edu
WILLIAMS, Suzanne ...... 213-477-2861.. 52 G
swilliams@msmu.edu
WILLIAMS, Suzanne ...... 803-780-1077 414 E
swilliams@voorhees.edu
WILLIAMS, Sydney .... 808-675-3701 127 E
sydney.williams@byuh.edu
WILLIAMS, Sylvester ..... 570-422-3589 394 E
swilliams@esu.edu
WILLIAMS, Tamara .... 704-330-4119 333 D
tamara.williams@cpcc.edu
WILLIAMS, Tamara, R ... 253-531-7203 482 H
williatr@plu.edu
WILLIAMS, Tanya .... 301-696-3350 199 B
williams@hood.edu
WILLIAMS, Tara, A .... 336-633-0279 337 A
tawil@randolph.edu
WILLIAMS, Tasha .... 708-596-2000 149 B
WILLIAMS, Teresa .... 615-966-1788 421 D
teresa.williams@lipscomb.edu
WILLIAMS, Teresa, G .... 704-233-8010 344 G
tgwilliams@wingate.edu
WILLIAMS, Terrence ..... 610-409-3719 402 A
twilliams@ursinus.edu
WILLIAMS, Terria, C ..... 803-535-5720 407 G
twilliams@claflin.edu
WILLIAMS, Thelma, R .... 252-335-3471 341 D
trwilliams@ecsu.edu
WILLIAMS, Thomas ...... 501-450-5137.. 23 H
twilliams73@uca.edu
WILLIAMS, Tiffany .... 757-455-3115 477 F
twilliams2@vwu.edu
WILLIAMS, Tim .... 618-985-3741 139 I
timwilliams@jalc.edu
WILLIAMS, Tim .... 502-895-3411 183 D
twilliams@lpts.edu
WILLIAMS, Timera .... 202-408-2400.. 92 G

WILLIAMS, Todd, J .... 215-702-4861 380 D
president@cairn.edu
WILLIAMS, Tom .... 318-678-6000 187 A
twilliams@bpcc.edu
WILLIAMS, Tom .... 601-925-3844 247 C
twilliams@mc.edu
WILLIAMS, Tonjua, L .... 727-341-3241 106 E
williams.tonjua@spcollege.edu
WILLIAMS, Tonya .... 901-381-3939 428 E
tonya@visible.edu
WILLIAMS, Tracey .... 903-510-2041 452 C
twil@tjc.edu
WILLIAMS, Traci .... 423-697-2659 424 E
traci.williams@chattanoogastate.edu
WILLIAMS, Tracy .... 651-523-2651 236 A
twilliams05@hamline.edu
WILLIAMS, Tracy, S ...... 229-317-6507 113 H
tracy.williams@asurams.edu
WILLIAMS, Travis .... 707-826-5038.. 33 D
tjw17@humboldt.edu
WILLIAMS, Treby .... 609-258-7097 280 E
trebyw@princeton.edu
WILLIAMS, Trevor .... 305-348-2107 109 A
trevor.williams@fiu.edu
WILLIAMS, Trudy .... 412-392-8085 397 A
twilliams@pointpark.edu
WILLIAMS, Twyla .... 334-244-3657.... 4 F
twill128@aum.edu
WILLIAMS, Tyler, R ...... 208-496-1301 130 A
williamst@byui.edu
WILLIAMS, Valarie .... 706-385-1015 123 C
valarie.williams@point.edu
WILLIAMS, Van .... 831-459-0111.. 70 B
vcit@ucsc.edu
WILLIAMS, Vanessa ...... 504-671-5510 187 E
vwilli@dcc.edu
WILLIAMS, Verna, L ..... 513-556-0121 362 D
verna.williams@uc.edu
WILLIAMS, Vernon .... 703-284-5796 469 C
vernon.williams@marymount.edu
WILLIAMS, Vicki .... 501-492-0570.. 17 B
vicki.williams@arkansasbaptist.edu
WILLIAMS, Vickie .... 334-214-4803.... 1 H
vickie.williams@cv.edu
WILLIAMS, Vicky .... 731-352-6405 418 G
williamsv@bethelu.edu
WILLIAMS, Victoria .... 870-972-2054.. 17 G
vrwilliams@astate.edu
WILLIAMS, Victoria .... 610-796-5511 378 F
victoria.williams@alvernia.edu
WILLIAMS, Virginia, M . 530-221-4275.. 63 G
vwilliams@shasta.edu
WILLIAMS, Walter .... 518-587-2100 321 A
walter.williams@esc.edu
WILLIAMS, Wendell .... 713-313-7446 449 C
wendell.williams@tsu.edu
WILLIAMS, Wendy, E .... 843-953-5506 408 E
williamsw@cofc.edu
WILLIAMS, JR.,
William .... 615-547-1280 419 F
bwilliams@cumberland.edu
WILLIAMS, Wyman .... 903-468-8183 447 B
wyman.williams@tamuc.edu
WILLIAMS, Yohuru, R .... 651-962-6001 244 E
will3650@stthomas.edu
WILLIAMS-BRYANT,
Deanne .... 386-481-2871.. 95 F
williamsbryantd@cookman.edu
WILLIAMS-BRYANT,
Elaine .... 360-475-7474 482 G
ewilliamsbryant@olympic.edu
WILLIAMS-GAGE,
Sheila .... 845-368-7220 315 D
WILLIAMS-GOLDSTEIN,
Brittany, A .... 201-684-7609 280 H
bwilla1@ramapo.edu
WILLIAMS-HARMON,
Arlitha .... 559-791-2374.. 47 A
arlitha.williams@portervillecollege.edu
WILLIAMS LOSTON,
Adena .... 210-486-2900 429 G
aloston@alamo.edu
WILLIAMS LOSTON,
Adena .... 210-486-2900 429 C
aloston@alamo.edu
WILLIAMS-MIZE,
Amanda .... 405-682-7537 367 H
amanda.williams-mize@occc.edu
WILLIAMS-MOORE,
Linda .... 412-648-1074 401 B
lwmoore@pitt.edu
WILLIAMS-PEREZ,
Kendra .... 319-226-2040 162 F
kendra.williams-perez@allencollege.edu

WILLIAMS RUSHIN,
Palisa .... 859-246-6522 180 K
palisa.rushin@kctcs.edu
WILLIAMS-SMITH,
Rachel .... 423-236-2740 424 B
rwilliamssmith@southern.edu
WILLIAMS-THOMAS,
Tafflyn .... 503-552-1625 374 E
twiliams-thomas@nunm.edu
WILLIAMS-THOMPSON,
Phyllis .... 413-265-2262 208 C
williamsthompsonp@elms.edu
WILLIAMSON, Angela ... 417-690-2208 251 E
awilliamson@cofo.edu
WILLIAMSON, Ashley ... 334-222-6591.... 2 I
abass@lbwcc.edu
WILLIAMSON, Bob .... 360-992-2123 479 F
bwilliamson@clark.edu
WILLIAMSON, Carol ..... 641-628-7667 163 E
williamsonc@central.edu
WILLIAMSON, Cathy ..... 641-673-1700 170 F
williamsonc@wmpenn.edu
WILLIAMSON, Dan .... 860-528-4111.. 87 A
WILLIAMSON, David ..... 601-266-1000 249 F
david.williamson@usm.edu
WILLIAMSON, Dean ...... 936-261-2188 446 D
cdwilliamson@pvamu.edu
WILLIAMSON, Emily ..... 406-243-5504 264 A
emily1.williamson@umontana.edu
WILLIAMSON, George ... 619-849-2610.. 57 E
georgewilliamson@pointloma.edu
WILLIAMSON, Graciela . 858-513-9240.. 26 G
graciela.williamson@ashford.edu
WILLIAMSON, Heather .. 866-931-4300 258 G
heather.williamson@rockbridge.edu
WILLIAMSON, James .... 660-263-3900 251 A
jameswilliamson@cccb.edu
WILLIAMSON, James .... 931-526-3660 420 A
WILLIAMSON,
James, P .... 806-742-3136 451 B
james.p.williamson@ttu.edu
WILLIAMSON,
James, R .... 858-784-8469.. 63 F
gradprgm@scripps.edu
WILLIAMSON, Jared ..... 312-935-4141 147 D
jwilliamson@robertmorris.edu
WILLIAMSON, Jeff .... 507-372-3408 239 E
jeff.williamson@mnwest.edu
WILLIAMSON, Jeffery .... 763-424-0820 239 G
jeff.williamson@nhcc.edu
WILLIAMSON, Jennifer . 610-921-7700 378 C
jwilliamson@albright.edu
WILLIAMSON, Jeremiy .. 612-343-4450 242 H
jdwillia@northcentral.edu
WILLIAMSON, Jessica .. 912-623-2400 117 D
jwilliamson@ega.edu
WILLIAMSON, Joann .... 803-641-3473 413 D
joannw@usca.edu
WILLIAMSON, Jon .... 214-648-1500 457 B
jon.williamson@utsouthwestern.edu
WILLIAMSON,
Jordan, H .... 336-633-0156 337 A
jhwilliamson@randolph.edu
WILLIAMSON, Kathleen 614-234-5950 356 I
kwilliamson@mccn.edu
WILLIAMSON, Kathy ..... 252-246-1263 339 C
kwilliamson@wilsoncc.edu
WILLIAMSON, Keith ...... 940-397-4231 440 F
keith.williamson@msutexas.edu
WILLIAMSON, Kimberly 252-493-7217 336 H
kwilliamson@email.pittcc.edu
WILLIAMSON, Laurel .... 281-998-6182 443 B
laurel.williamson@sjcd.edu
WILLIAMSON, Laurel .... 281-998-6182 443 D
laurel.williamson@sjcd.edu
WILLIAMSON, Laurel .... 281-998-6182 443 C
laurel.williamson@sjcd.edu
WILLIAMSON, Laurel .... 281-998-6182 443 E
laurel.williamson@sjcd.edu
WILLIAMSON, Lisa .... 715-682-1678 495 C
lwilliamson@northland.edu
WILLIAMSON, Margaret 504-280-7054 189 E
mswilli4@uno.edu
WILLIAMSON,
Margaret, L .... 806-742-3171 451 B
margaret.l.williams@ttu.edu
WILLIAMSON, Marty ..... 661-654-2111.. 30 E
mwilliamson@csub.edu
WILLIAMSON, Melanie . 859-246-6285 180 K
melanie.williamson@kctcs.edu
WILLIAMSON, Nancy .... 518-485-3066 296 H
williamn@strose.edu
WILLIAMSON, P. Kevin 336-285-3061 341 F
pkwilliamson@ncat.edu

WILLIAMSON,
Robin, M .... 973-443-8935 277 K
rwilliamson@fdu.edu
WILLIAMSON, Shane .... 636-949-4728 254 F
swilliamson@lindenwood.edu
WILLIAMSON, Sharon ... 806-742-4250 451 B
sharon.williamson@ttu.edu
WILLIAMSON, Sheila .... 325-574-7602 458 E
swilliamson@wtc.edu
WILLIAMSON, Stephen . 605-367-7464 417 D
stephen.williamson@southeasttech.edu
WILLIAMSON, Suzanne . 720-890-8922.. 80 H
registrar@itea.edu
WILLIAMSON-MENDEZ,
Jennifer .... 920-459-6611 496 E
williamj@uwgb.edu
WILLIARD, Stacey .... 724-266-3838 400 H
swilliard@tsm.edu
WILLIBY, Jason .... 785-628-4728 173 B
jjwilliby3@fhsu.edu
WILLIE, Lisa .... 215-951-1011 387 C
willie@lasalle.edu
WILLIE LEBRETON,
Sarah .... 610-328-8319 399 D
swillie1@swarthmore.edu
WILLIFORD, Andrea, G . 478-757-5131 126 H
awilliford@wesleyancollege.edu
WILLIFORD, Brent .... 979-830-4146 432 C
brent.williford@blinn.edu
WILLIFORD, Darryl .... 301-860-4186 203 C
dwilliford@bowiestate.edu
WILLIFORD, David .... 615-675-5302 428 G
dwilliford@welch.edu
WILLIFORD, G. Craig .... 503-255-0332 374 D
cwilliford@multnomah.edu
WILLIFORD, Joey .... 662-720-7564 248 C
jewilliford@nemcc.edu
WILLIFORD, Lynn, E ..... 919-962-1339 342 D
lynn_williford@unc.edu
WILLING, Cindy .... 517-607-4315 225 A
cwilling@hillsdale.edu
WILLINGHAM, Nathan .. 256-765-4607.... 8 E
cnwillingham@una.edu
WILLINGHAM, Paul ...... 281-655-3712 439 G
paul.willingham@lonestar.edu
WILLINGHAM, Ralph .... 817-598-6248 458 A
rwillingham@wc.edu
WILLIS, Alysha .... 212-616-7200 301 F
alysha.willis@helenefuld.edu
WILLIS, Amy .... 229-391-5007 113 F
apwillis@abac.edu
WILLIS, Bessie .... 757-727-5331 468 B
bessie.willis@hamptonu.edu
WILLIS, Bob .... 334-699-2266.... 1 B
bwillis@acom.edu
WILLIS, Brian .... 828-398-7929 332 B
bwillis@abtech.edu
WILLIS, Christopher ...... 302-736-2458.. 90 G
christopher.willis@wesley.edu
WILLIS, Daria .... 425-388-9573 480 G
dwillis@everettcc.edu
WILLIS, David .... 575-492-2173 289 A
dwillis@usw.edu
WILLIS, DeDe .... 214-388-5466 435 G
dwillis@dallasinstitute.edu
WILLIS, Douglas, G ...... 972-377-1793 433 M
dwillis@collin.edu
WILLIS, Edward .... 225-771-2360 190 H
edward_willis@subr.edu
WILLIS, Eric, R .... 319-352-8470 170 C
rick.willis@wartburg.edu
WILLIS, Gabe .... 985-549-3850 192 D
gabe.willis@selu.edu
WILLIS, Gerry .... 401-341-2159 406 A
willisg@salve.edu
WILLIS, Gregory .... 318-487-5443 187 C
gregorywillis@cltcc.edu
WILLIS, Harvey .... 973-328-5232 277 B
hwillis@ccm.edu
WILLIS, Howard .... 707-256-7225.. 53 C
hwillis@napavalley.edu
WILLIS, Jeff .... 337-550-1287 189 A
jwillis@lsue.edu
WILLIS, Jeff .... 270-384-8097 183 C
willisj@lindsey.edu
WILLIS, Kara .... 740-245-7221 363 D
kwillis@rio.edu
WILLIS, Kathy .... 618-468-5700 141 F
kwillis@lc.edu
WILLIS, Kimberley .... 585-245-5566 318 E
willis@geneseo.edu
WILLIS, Leonard .... 410-462-8052 197 E
lwillis@bccc.edu

WILLIS, Lesia .... 718-522-9073 290 C
lwillis@asa.edu
WILLIS, Lisa .... 312-850-7066 134 H
lwillis01@ccc.edu
WILLIS, Marc .... 918-647-1464 365 H
mwillis@carlalbert.edu
WILLIS, Michaela .... 605-688-4493 417 C
michaela.willis@sdstate.edu
WILLIS, Paul .... 229-391-5052 113 F
pwillis@abac.edu
WILLIS, Richard .... 205-929-1776.... 6 B
WILLIS, Rico .... 903-434-8265 441 B
rwillis@ntcc.edu
WILLIS, Sherilyn .... 760-862-1333.. 39 A
swillis@collegeofthedesert.edu
WILLIS, Steve .... 434-947-8383 470 E
swillis@randolphcollege.edu
WILLIS, Susan .... 918-343-6802 369 F
swillis@rsu.edu
WILLIS, Tamie, L .... 405-425-5320 367 G
tamie.willis@oc.edu
WILLIS, Teresa .... 434-961-5245 475 F
twillis@pvcc.edu
WILLIS, Tori .... 919-719-1890 340 E
twillis@shawu.edu
WILLIS-BARKSDALE,
Ava .... 610-409-3005 402 A
awillisbarksdale@ursinus.edu
WILLIS KRAUSS,
Michelle .... 252-249-1851 336 F
mwillis@pamlicocc.edu
WILLLIAMS, Susan, H .. 936-468-2201 445 F
shwilliams@sfasu.edu
WILLLIAMS, Venetia, C . 865-539-7266 425 F
vcwilliams@pstcc.edu
WILLLIS, Howard .... 707-256-7355.. 53 C
hwillis@napavalley.edu
WILLMARTH, Ephraim ... 315-858-0945 302 C
ejwillmarth@hts.edu
WILLMON, Nixon .... 256-228-6001.... 3 B
willmonn@nacc.edu
WILLOQUET-MARICONDI,
Paula .... 802-651-5924 462 B
pwilloquetmaricondi@champlain.edu
WILLOUGHBY, Dan .... 714-992-7037.. 53 L
dwilloughby@fullcoll.edu
WILLOUGHBY, G. Case 724-287-8711 380 A
case.willoughby@bc3.edu
WILLOUGHBY,
Karen, P .... 412-536-1201 387 B
karen.willoughby@laroche.edu
WILLOUGHBY, Sherrie .. 409-882-3343 450 A
sherrie.willoughby@lsco.edu
WILLS, Barbara .... 850-201-8590 111 C
willsba@tcc.fl.edu
WILLS, Deri .... 803-641-3787 413 D
deriw@usca.edu
WILLS, Mark .... 949-359-0045.. 29 E
WILLS, Mark .... 423-798-7970 426 C
mark.wills@ws.edu
WILLS, Mike .... 417-836-7635 256 E
mikewills@missouristate.edu
WILLS, Scott, D .... 419-772-2705 358 H
s-wills@onu.edu
WILLS, Tim .... 618-437-5321 147 A
wills@rlc.edu
WILLSON, Dawn .... 714-241-6186.. 38 C
dwillson1@coastline.edu
WILLY, Randy .... 785-442-6001 174 A
rwilly@highlandcc.edu
WILLYARD, Paula .... 918-595-2067 370 E
paula.willyard@tulsacc.edu
WILMER, Elizabeth .... 540-857-7313 476 D
ewilmer@virginiawestern.edu
WILMES, David .... 724-738-2003 395 F
david.wilmes@sru.edu
WILMESHERR, Jon .... 828-766-1360 336 A
jwilmesherr@mayland.edu
WILMOT, Lynne .... 507-222-5500 234 F
lwilmot@carleton.edu
WILMOT, Tracey .... 914-633-2067 302 G
twilmot@iona.edu
WILMOTH, Dirk .... 828-398-7111 332 B
dirkwilmoth@abtech.edu
WILMOUTH, Robert ...... 406-657-1015 265 E
president@rocky.edu
WILMOWSKY, Joseph ... 718-774-3430 292 H
WILMS, Amy .... 909-748-8109.. 71 G
amy_wilms@redlands.edu
WILROY, Claudia .... 805-378-1409.. 72 H
cwilroy@vcccd.edu
WILSEY, Stephanie, A ... 412-578-6663 380 E
sawilsey@carlow.edu
WILSKE, Don .... 517-483-1765 226 F
wilsked@lcc.edu
WILSON, Alan .... 706-385-1059 123 C
alan.wilson@point.edu
WILSON, Alan, G .... 660-263-3900 251 A
alanwilson@cccb.edu
WILSON, Amanda .... 317-921-4949 157 G
amanda.wilson@ivytech.edu
WILSON, Amanda .... 918-647-1326 365 H
adwilson@carlalbert.edu
WILSON, Amy .... 608-363-2699 492 C
wilsonae@beloit.edu
WILSON, Amy, R .... 740-245-7382 363 D
awilson@rio.edu
WILSON, Andrew, A ...... 731-881-7626 428 B
awilso93@utm.edu
WILSON, Andrew, G ..... 412-578-2095 380 E
wilsonag@carlow.edu
WILSON, Angela .... 618-252-5400 149 C
angela.wilson@sic.edu
WILSON, Angulus .... 559-453-2094.. 43 G
angulus.wilson@fresno.edu
WILSON, Annette .... 312-362-6214 135 I
awilso49@depaul.edu
WILSON, Annette .... 336-517-2302 327 B
annette.wilson@bennett.edu
WILSON, Arthur, L .... 260-359-4031 155 F
alwilson@huntington.edu
WILSON, Asif .... 312-553-5600 134 B
awilson@ccc.edu
WILSON, Barbara .... 770-534-6203 115 D
bwilson@brenau.edu
WILSON, Barbara, J ...... 217-333-3077 151 A
bjwilson@uillinois.edu
WILSON, Barbara, L ...... 801-581-8262 460 E
barbara.wilson@nurs.utah.edu
WILSON, Betsyann .... 928-536-6245.. 14 J
betsy.wilson@npc.edu
WILSON, Bill .... 406-683-7509 264 B
william.wilson@umwestern.edu
WILSON, Blake .... 864-424-8022 414 C
bentleyt@mailbox.sc.edu
WILSON, Bradley .... 724-738-2003 395 F
bradley.wilson@sru.edu
WILSON, Brandon .... 510-723-6923.. 35 O
bwilson@chabotcollege.edu
WILSON, Bryan .... 307-778-1179 502 D
bwilson@lccc.wy.edu
WILSON, Carlos .... 601-979-8895 246 E
carlos.d.wilson@jsums.edu
WILSON, Carlton, E ...... 919-530-6794 342 A
cwilson@nccu.edu
WILSON, Cathy .... 706-821-8636 122 K
cwilson@paine.edu
WILSON, Cecil, B .... 304-293-2021 491 C
cbwilson@mail.wvu.edu
WILSON, Charles .... 859-371-9393 179 A
cwilson@beckfield.edu
WILSON, Charles .... 704-922-6454 334 F
wilson.charles@gaston.edu
WILSON, JR.,
Charles, E .... 336-334-7731 341 F
cewilso3@ncat.edu
WILSON, Cheri .... 256-726-7204.... 6 C
cwilson@oakwood.edu
WILSON, Cheryl .... 443-334-2579 201 H
cawilson@stevenson.edu
WILSON, Chip .... 740-397-9000 357 B
chip.wilson@mvnu.edu
WILSON, Christine .... 785-243-1435 172 F
cwilson@cloud.edu
WILSON, Christine .... 310-206-1911.. 69 A
cwilson@saonet.ucla.edu
WILSON, Christine .... 207-778-7087 196 B
WILSON, Christopher .... 701-231-6409 345 G
christopher.s.wilson@ndsu.edu
WILSON, Christy Lynn .. 912-279-4587 116 G
cwilson@ccga.edu
WILSON, Claire .... 215-965-4051 390 J
cwilson@moore.edu
WILSON, Cleveland .... 803-535-1419 411 G
wilsonc@octech.edu
WILSON, Colwick .... 256-726-8005.... 6 C
cmwilson@oakwood.edu
WILSON, Corey .... 317-791-2556 161 B
clwilson@uindy.edu
WILSON, Corey, L .... 317-791-2556 161 B
clwilson@uindy.edu
WILSON, Craig .... 608-342-1411 497 D
wilsoncraig@uwplatt.edu
WILSON, Cynthia .... 251-928-8133.... 8 F
cwilson@southalabama.edu
WILSON, Cynthia, L ...... 713-348-5048 442 K
clwilson@rice.edu
WILSON, Dani .... 714-992-7040.. 53 L
dwilson@fullcoll.edu
WILSON, Daniel, B .... 740-826-8165 357 C
dwilson@muskingum.edu
WILSON, Daniel, O .... 252-451-8224 336 E
dowilson428@nashcc.edu
WILSON, Daniel, R .... 909-469-5201.. 74 I
president@westernu.edu
WILSON, Darlene .... 310-338-7725.. 50 J
dwilson@lmu.edu
WILSON, David .... 443-885-3200 200 D
david.wilson@morgan.edu
WILSON, David .... 615-966-6219 421 D
david.wilson@lipscomb.edu
WILSON, Dayton .... 304-766-3181 491 B
dayton.wilson@wvstateu.edu
WILSON, De Lisa .... 404-880-6136 116 D
dwilson@cau.edu
WILSON, Deborah .... 509-574-6872 487 A
dwilson@yvcc.edu
WILSON, Debra, J .... 208-732-6245 130 E
dwilson@csi.edu
WILSON, Debra, J .... 906-248-8442 221 N
dwilson@bmcc.edu
WILSON, Delfina .... 913-288-7618 174 F
dwilson@kckcc.edu
WILSON, Denika .... 773-907-4830 134 C
dwilson305i@ccc.edu
WILSON, Don .... 863-297-1000 105 A
dhw@bosdun.com
WILSON, Donna .... 570-484-2576 395 B
dwilson@lockhaven.edu
WILSON, Doug .... 251-442-2406.... 8 C
dwilson@umobile.edu
WILSON, Douglas .... 205-726-4266.... 6 E
dwilson@samford.edu
WILSON, Elaine .... 606-679-8501 182 C
elaine.wilson@kctcs.edu
WILSON, Elighie .... 708-709-7767 146 D
ewilson@prairiestate.edu
WILSON, Evelyn .... 978-542-7321 213 C
evelyn.wilson@salemstate.edu
WILSON, Fleetwood, L .. 206-934-3789 483 J
fleetwood.wilson@seattlecolleges.edu
WILSON, Fred .... 251-377-9281.... 8 C
fwilson@umobile.edu
WILSON, Fred .... 714-816-0366.. 67 I
fred.wilson@trident.edu
WILSON, Gena .... 229-931-2000 119 D
gena.wilson@gsw.edu
WILSON, Gillian .... 951-827-4800.. 69 C
vcredadmin@ucr.edu
WILSON, Gordon, N ...... 801-581-3079 460 E
gordon.wilson@aux.utah.edu
WILSON, Holly .... 318-473-6581 188 J
hwilson@lsua.edu
WILSON, Howard .... 712-722-6007 164 K
howard.wilson@dordt.edu
WILSON, Huie, G .... 850-263-3261.. 95 B
hgwilson@baptistcollege.edu
WILSON, Jacqueline ...... 334-683-2309.... 3 A
jwilson@marionmilitary.edu
WILSON, Jacqueline, M 812-877-8210 159 J
wilson5@rose-hulman.edu
WILSON, Jamelle .... 804-289-8135 472 L
jwilson9@richmond.edu
WILSON, JR.,
James, D .... 302-295-1194.. 90 I
jim.d.wilson@wilmu.edu
WILSON, JR., James, J 936-261-5256 446 D
jjwilson@pvamu.edu
WILSON, JR., James, J 936-261-2175 446 D
jjwilson@pvamu.edu
WILSON, Jamie, B .... 601-974-1070 247 B
wilsojb@millsaps.edu
WILSON, Janice .... 860-465-4466.. 84 J
wilsonj@easternct.edu
WILSON, Jason .... 810-762-0200 228 C
jason.wilson@mcc.edu
WILSON, JD .... 901-381-3939 428 E
jd@visible.edu
WILSON, Jeff .... 615-966-7617 421 D
jeff.wilson@lipscomb.edu
WILSON, Jennifer .... 507-529-2736 240 G
jennifer.wilson@rctc.edu
WILSON, Jessica, L ...... 210-829-3931 453 D
jewilso1@uiwtx.edu
WILSON, Jimmy .... 212-686-9244 290 A
WILSON, Joanne .... 608-342-1261 497 D
wilsonj@uwplatt.edu
WILSON, Jocelyn, M .... 516-671-2215 324 G
jwilson@webb.edu
WILSON, Joe .... 972-883-4995 455 B
joe.wilson@utdallas.edu
WILSON, John .... 254-710-3457 431 J
john_wilson@baylor.edu
WILSON, John .... 843-863-7102 407 E
jewilson@csuniv.edu
WILSON, John, R .... 804-278-4330 472 E
jwilson@upsem.edu
WILSON, Jon .... 913-234-0815 172 E
jon.wilson@cleveland.edu
WILSON, Jonathan .... 601-984-1010 249 E
jwilson5@umc.edu
WILSON, Josh .... 706-272-2473 117 C
jwilson@daltonstate.edu
WILSON, Joshua .... 870-368-2027.. 20 F
josh.wilson@ozarka.edu
WILSON, Judge .... 859-985-3131 179 C
judge_wilson@berea.edu
WILSON, Judi .... 706-667-4368 115 A
jwilso24@augusta.edu
WILSON, Karen .... 580-774-6147 370 C
karen.wilson@swosu.edu
WILSON, Kathi .... 865-981-8211 421 F
kathi.wilson@maryvillecollege.edu
WILSON, Kathryn .... 585-395-2137 318 B
kwilson@brockport.edu
WILSON, Kathy, A .... 863-638-2930 113 B
wilsonka@webber.edu
WILSON, Keisha .... 704-330-1455 330 D
kwilson@jcsu.edu
WILSON, Kelly .... 619-398-4902.. 45 C
WILSON, Kenneth .... 912-358-4166 123 H
wilsonk@savannahstate.edu
WILSON, Kenny .... 636-481-3356 254 A
kwilso20@jeffco.edu
WILSON, Kim .... 661-362-2844.. 51 C
kwilson@masters.edu
WILSON, Kim .... 661-362-2831.. 51 C
khwilson@masters.edu
WILSON, Kimberly, P ... 859-257-4751 185 B
kwilson@email.uky.edu
WILSON, Kristina .... 361-698-1137 436 C
kmwilson@delmar.edu
WILSON, LaDrina .... 563-441-4016 165 E
lnwilson@eicc.edu
WILSON, Larry, L .... 972-860-7218 435 B
larrywilson@dcccd.edu
WILSON, Laura .... 937-376-6013 350 D
lwilson@centralstate.edu
WILSON, Laura, L .... 650-723-9633.. 65 J
laura.wilson@stanford.edu
WILSON, Lauren .... 707-668-5663.. 41 D
lauren@dellarte.com
WILSON, Leah .... 585-582-8218 299 A
leahwilson@elim.edu
WILSON, Leana .... 256-765-4319.... 8 E
lwilson11@una.edu
WILSON, Leslie, K .... 319-273-6240 163 B
leslie.wilson@uni.edu
WILSON, Lindsay .... 217-581-3413 136 E
lpwilson@eiu.edu
WILSON, Lisa .... 505-747-5010 287 G
lisa.wilson@nnmc.edu
WILSON, Lisa, M .... 951-827-3486.. 69 C
lisa.wilson@ucr.edu
WILSON, Lizabeth, A .... 206-543-1760 485 F
betsyw@uw.edu
WILSON, Locord, D .... 601-979-2433 246 E
locord.d.wilson@jsums.edu
WILSON, Lori, J .... 570-577-3334 379 F
lwilson@bucknell.edu
WILSON, Lucy .... 919-546-8322 340 E
lwilson@shawu.edu
WILSON, Lynn .... 863-669-2898 105 A
lwilson@polk.edu
WILSON, M. Roy .... 313-577-2230 232 I
president@wayne.edu
WILSON, Maleta .... 504-865-3262 189 F
mawilson@loyno.edu
WILSON, Marcus .... 806-743-6443 451 C
marcus.wilson@ttuhsc.edu
WILSON, Margaret .... 660-626-2354 250 A
mwilson@atsu.edu
WILSON, Marian, V .... 615-898-2185 422 H
marian.wilson@mtsu.edu
WILSON, Mark .... 423-472-7141 424 F
mwilson@clevelandstatecc.edu
WILSON, Mark .... 931-372-3961 426 E
mwilson@tntech.edu
WILSON, Mark .... 605-995-3024 415 G
mark.wilson@mitchelltech.edu

WILSON, Martha 207-221-4514 196 G mwilson13@une.edu
WILSON, Martha 530-891-6900 27 H
WILSON, Mary 931-598-1381 423 M mewilson@sewanee.edu
WILSON, Matthew 734-462-4400 230 D mwilson@schoolcraft.edu
WILSON, Matthew, J 816-271-4237 257 A president@missouriwestern.edu
WILSON, Matthew, J 302-356-6970 90 I matthew.j.wilson@wilmu.edu
WILSON, Melanie 808-934-2519 129 A mfwilson@hawaii.edu
WILSON, Melanie 865-974-2521 427 G mdwilson@utk.edu
WILSON, Michael 205-726-4064 6 E mkwilson@samford.edu
WILSON, Michael 503-517-1261 377 G mewilson@warnerpacific.edu
WILSON, Michael, D 714-556-3610 72 F mdwilson@vanguard.edu
WILSON, Michele 304-424-8355 491 D michele.wilson@wvup.edu
WILSON, Michelle 870-633-4480 19 B rwilson@eacc.edu
WILSON, Mike 704-272-5300 337 I mwilson@spcc.edu
WILSON, Mindy 518-743-2252 320 D wilsonm@sunyacc.edu
WILSON, Monica 304-434-8000 489 A monica.wilson@easternwv.edu
WILSON, Natalie, L 412-578-6171 380 E nlwilson@carlow.edu
WILSON, Nate 208-882-1566 131 B nwilson@nsa.edu
WILSON, Nathan 317-931-2316 154 C nwilson@cts.edu
WILSON, Oceana 802-440-4606 462 A owilson@bennington.edu
WILSON, Patricia 256-306-2743 1 F patricia.wilson@calhoun.edu
WILSON, Patrick 505-891-6908 286 H patrickwilson@nmhu.edu
WILSON, Patrick 216-881-1700 359 F pwilson@ohiotech.edu
WILSON, Phillip 479-394-7622 23 C pwilson@uarichmountain.edu
WILSON, Piper 417-477-7428 257 G wilsonp@otc.edu
WILSON, Qiana 478-445-2037 118 C qiana.wilson@gcsu.edu
WILSON, Rebeka 402-375-7239 268 G rewilso1@wsc.edu
WILSON, Regina 574-284-5382 160 C rwilson@saintmarys.edu
WILSON, Robert, A 610-606-4637 381 A rwilson@cedarcrest.edu
WILSON, Roger 425-889-5336 482 F roger.wilson@northwestu.edu
WILSON, Ronald, O 814-732-1259 394 F rwilson@edinboro.edu
WILSON, Ronalyn 518-736-3622 300 F rwilson@fmcc.suny.edu
WILSON, Rowena, G 757-823-8668 469 F rgwilson@nsu.edu
WILSON, Roxanne 304-865-6033 488 E roxanne.wilson@ovu.edu
WILSON, Ryan 859-622-8939 180 B ryan.wilson@eku.edu
WILSON, Samantha 979-845-5139 446 G samantha@tamu.edu
WILSON, Sandra 313-664-7471 222 F sandra@collegeforcreativestudies.edu
WILSON, Scott 651-846-1694 241 B scott.wilson@saintpaul.edu
WILSON, Scott 931-598-1173 423 M swilson@sewanee.edu
WILSON, Scott, L 314-935-2656 262 A scott.l.wilson@wustl.edu
WILSON, Shain 205-853-1200 2 G swilson@jeffersonstate.edu
WILSON, Shawn 989-964-7090 230 B swilson@svsu.edu
WILSON, Shawna 517-264-7142 230 E swilson@sienaheights.edu
WILSON, Sheila 252-399-6309 326 M spwilson@barton.edu
WILSON, Shelli 843-383-8082 408 D swilson@coker.edu
WILSON, Shirley 213-624-1200 42 I swilson@fidm.edu
WILSON, Sonali, B 216-687-3860 351 B s.b.wilson@csuohio.edu
WILSON, Stacey 704-403-1639 327 D stacey.wilson@carolinashealthcare.org
WILSON, Stacey 636-481-3207 254 A swilson@jeffco.edu
WILSON, Stanley 954-262-1266 103 M swilson@nova.edu
WILSON, Stephan, M 405-744-9805 368 B stephan.m.wilson@okstate.edu
WILSON, Stephen 478-445-5331 118 C steve.wilson@gcsu.edu
WILSON, Steve 432-552-2114 457 A wilson_s@utpb.edu
WILSON, Steven 540-868-7132 474 J stevenwilson@lfcc.edu
WILSON, Steven, H 610-758-3200 388 J shw516@lehigh.edu
WILSON, Susan 816-235-6704 261 C wilsonsb2@umkc.edu
WILSON, Tanya 913-469-8500 174 D twilso24@jccc.edu
WILSON, Tara, K 808-544-1460 127 H
WILSON, Ted, H 270-707-3865 181 E ted.wilson@kctcs.edu
WILSON, Thad 816-995-2810 258 H thad.wilson@rockhurst.edu
WILSON, Thad, R 816-995-2815 258 F thad.wilson@researchcollege.edu
WILSON, Thalia 910-672-2852 341 E twilson@uncfsu.edu
WILSON, Tim 412-391-4100 397 A
WILSON, Tim 865-694-6666 425 F trwilson@pstcc.edu
WILSON, Tommy 706-649-1894 117 A twilson@columbustech.edu
WILSON, Tony 336-725-8344 339 F wilsont@piedmontu.edu
WILSON, Torrey 317-788-6126 161 B twilson@uindy.edu
WILSON, Tracy 651-403-4118 241 B tracy.wilson@saintpaul.edu
WILSON, Travis 606-539-4002 185 A travis.wilson@ucumberlands.edu
WILSON, Tressey, D 936-361-1700 446 D tdwilson@pvamu.edu
WILSON, Valeri 619-660-4221 44 H valeri.wilson@gcccd.edu
WILSON, Valerie 870-574-4514 21 E vwilson@sautech.edu
WILSON, Valvia 601-977-7844 249 C vwilson@tougaloo.edu
WILSON, Vicki 724-852-3375 402 F vwilson@waynesburg.edu
WILSON, Vicky, W 864-833-8219 411 I vwwilson@presby.edu
WILSON, Victor, K 706-542-3564 125 G wilsonv@uga.edu
WILSON, W. Chandler 503-255-0332 374 D chandlerwilson@multnomah.edu
WILSON, Wendy 229-500-2000 113 H wendy.wilson@asurams.edu
WILSON, Wendy 229-317-6553 113 H wendy.wilson@asurams.edu
WILSON, Wes 404-627-2681 115 C wes.wilson@beulah.edu
WILSON, Wes, C 404-627-2681 115 C wes.wilson@beulah.edu
WILSON, Wesley 670-237-6834 506 A wesley.wilson@marianas.edu
WILSON, William 423-354-2541 425 E wrwilson@northeaststate.edu
WILSON, William 859-341-4867 184 F wilsonw@thomasmore.edu
WILSON, William 216-687-4686 351 B william.wilson@csuohio.edu
WILSON, William, M 918-495-6175 368 I president@oru.edu
WILSON, Yolanda 803-327-8021 415 A ywilson@yorktech.edu
WILSON-ALLAM, Deborah 315-792-3259 324 B dlwilson@utica.edu
WILSON-FENNELL, Nicole 734-462-4400 230 D nwilson@schoolcraft.edu
WILSON-LOGGINS, Jennifer 770-534-6134 115 D jloggins@brenau.edu
WILSON-PARKER, Sharnita, I 252-335-3747 341 D slwilson@ecsu.edu
WILSON PICKETT, Clyde 651-201-1472 237 A
WILSON-PORTER, Cyndi 210-829-2706 453 D porter@uiwtx.edu
WILSON SCOTT, Karen 208-282-2490 130 H scotkare@isu.edu
WILSON-SYKES, Jean 205-247-8145 7 A jwilson-sykes@stillman.edu
WILSON-TAYLOR, Sharon 312-369-7221 135 E swilson-taylor@colum.edu
WILSTERMANN, Amy 616-526-7620 222 A amw26@calvin.edu
WILT, Darrell 717-815-1288 404 A dwilt1@ycp.edu
WILT, Randolph 512-313-3000 434 E randolph.wilt@concordia.edu
WILTENMUTH, John, P 540-654-2080 472 I jwiltenm@umw.edu
WILTGEN, JR., Jim 501-450-1222 19 F wiltgen@hendrix.edu
WILTGEN, Tyler 406-657-1008 265 E tyler.wiltgen@rocky.edu
WILTROUT, Deborah 239-590-1089 108 K dwiltrout@fgcu.edu
WILTSHIRE, Rolly 718-289-5186 293 B rolly.wiltshire@bcc.cuny.edu
WILTZ, Alex 413-775-1299 214 C wiltza@gcc.mass.edu
WILTZIUS, Pierre 805-893-5024 70 A mlpsdean@ltsc.ucsb.edu
WIMBERLY, Chuck 478-289-2036 117 D cwimberly@ega.edu
WIMBERLY, Frances 706-396-8102 122 K fwimberly@paine.edu
WIMBUSH, James 812-855-2739 156 A jwimbush@iu.edu
WIMBUSH, James, C 812-856-5700 156 B dema@indiana.edu
WIMER, Aaron 931-540-2555 424 G awimer@columbiastate.edu
WIMER, Jodie 304-358-2000 488 A jwimer@future.edu
WIMER, Valinda 386-822-8850 111 A vwimer@stetson.edu
WIMMER, Angela 501-686-7950 22 C awimmer@uams.edu
WIMS, Daniel, K 256-372-5275 1 A daniel.wims@aamu.edu
WIMS, Lois, A 508-929-8038 213 E lwims@worcester.edu
WINBORNE, Malverne 734-487-2086 223 H mwinborne@emich.edu
WINBUSH, Chauncey 304-876-5155 490 E cwinbush@shepherd.edu
WINBUSH, Larkisha 251-442-2250 8 C lwinbush@umobile.edu
WINCH, Eric 908-709-7150 284 C eric.winch@ucc.edu
WINCHELL, Brooks 617-873-0499 207 F brooks.winchell@cambridgecollege.edu
WINCHESTER, Sara 732-255-0400 280 A swinchester@ocean.edu
WINCKELMAN, Stephen 952-358-8597 239 F stephen.winckelman@normandale.edu
WIND-NORTON, Laura 715-365-4578 500 D lwindnorton@nicoletcollege.edu
WINDER, Katie 541-917-4547 374 A winderk@linnbenton.edu
WINDER, Mark 319-895-4518 164 B mwinder@cornellcollege.edu
WINDERS, Tim 219-989-2417 159 G winders@pnw.edu
WINDHAM, Adam 916-484-8216 50 F windhaa@arc.losrios.edu
WINDHAM, Adam 650-306-3322 61 O windhama@smccd.edu
WINDHAM, Don 772-462-7357 101 E dwindham@irsc.edu
WINDHAM, Greg 662-720-7210 248 C jgwindham@nemcc.edu
WINDHAM, Jameka, A 305-628-6632 106 F jwindham@stu.edu
WINDHAM, Joel 205-726-2011 6 E jwindham@samford.edu
WINDHAM, John 731-661-5006 427 C jwindham@uu.edu
WINDHOLZ, Kevin 405-208-5600 367 I kwindholz@okcu.edu
WINDHOLZ, Mindy 405-208-7902 367 I mbwindholz@okcu.edu
WINDLE, Frank, H 215-871-6750 396 D frankwi@pcom.edu
WINDLE, Lawrence, B 956-380-8100 442 L lwindle@riogrande.edu
WINDOKUN, Prema 805-898-4010 42 L
WINDROW, Vincent, L 615-898-2338 422 H vincent.windrow@mtsu.edu
WINDSOR, Michael, H 757-479-3706 473 C mwindsor@vbts.edu
WINDY BOY, Helen 406-395-4875 265 G hwindyboy@stonechild.edu
WINE IMBLER, Toni 918-270-6412 369 A toni.imbler@ptstulsa.edu
WINEBRAKE, James, J 585-475-2447 313 A jjwgpt@rit.edu
WINEGARD, Tanya, C 402-280-2775 266 I tanyawinegard@creighton.edu
WINEGEART, Michael 615-966-5074 421 D michael.winegeart@lipscomb.edu
WINEY, Mark 530-752-6778 68 E mwiney@ucdavis.edu
WINFIELD-THOMAS, Evelyn, B 269-387-6316 232 K evelyn.winfield@wmich.edu
WINFREE, Terri, L 708-709-3638 146 D twinfree@prairiestate.edu
WINFREY, LaPearl Logan 937-775-3494 364 I lapearllogan.winfrey@wright.edu
WINFREY GRIFFIN, Polly 609-258-6191 280 E polly@princeton.edu
WINGARD, Ed 830-792-7234 443 G facilitiesservices@schreiner.edu
WINGARD, Jason, M 212-854-3771 297 C jason.wingard@columbia.edu
WINGARD, John, D 707-664-2112 34 C wingard@sonoma.edu
WINGARD, Julia 757-823-8200 469 F jbwingard@nsu.edu
WINGATE, Margaret 850-201-8366 111 C wingatem@tcc.fl.edu
WINGE, Jennifer, D 330-263-2116 351 C jwinge@wooster.edu
WINGEIER-RAYO, Philip 202-885-8611 93 E pwingeier@wesleyseminary.edu
WINGENBACH, Ed 920-748-8109 495 G wingenbache@ripon.edu
WINGENBACK, Edward 413-559-5521 210 A
WINGER, Davin 580-349-1460 368 A dwinger@opsu.edu
WINGER, Keely 970-675-3219 78 G keely.winger@cncc.edu
WINGER, Philip, E 570-372-4025 399 C winger@susqu.edu
WINGER, Steven 563-876-3353 164 J swinger@dwci.edu
WINGERT, Nancy 785-242-5200 176 D nancy.wingert@ottawa.edu
WINGERT, Nancy 785-242-5200 176 D nancy.wingert@ottowa.edu
WINGERT, Timothy 210-883-1190 453 D optometry@uiwtx.edu
WINGFIELD, Joy 865-573-4517 420 G jwingfield@johnsonu.edu
WINGFIELD, Rob 706-272-4448 117 C rwingfield@daltonstate.edu
WINGFIELD, Thomas 202-685-4836 503 I thomas.wingfield@ndu.edu
WINGHAM, Fred 772-546-5534 101 B fredwingham@hsbc.edu
WINGLER, Mike 336-838-6178 339 B mswingler068@wilkescc.edu
WINGROVE, Thurman, D 412-624-6028 401 B twingrove@pitt.edu
WINGS, Arron 319-398-5624 167 C arron.wings@kirkwood.edu
WINIGER, Brent 701-858-3331 345 F brent.winiger@minotstateu.edu
WINISTORFER, Paul, M 540-231-5481 477 A pwinisto@vt.edu
WINITZKY-STEPHENS, Jessie 801-957-4090 461 D jessie.winitzky-stephens@slcc.edu
WINKELBAUER, Brian 303-273-3140 78 I bwinkelb@mines.edu
WINKELFOOS, Natalie 440-775-6463 358 C natalie.winkelfoos@oberlin.edu
WINKELSTEIN, Beth, A 215-898-7225 400 K winkelst@seas.upenn.edu
WINKLE, Rachel 918-836-6886 370 D rachel.winkle@spartan.edu
WINKLEPLECK, Kari, L 712-274-5450 168 B bull@morningside.edu
WINKLER, Fred, R 314-977-2401 259 H fred.winkler@slu.edu

WITTE, III, Paul, R .... 616-526-7920 222 A prw3@calvin.edu
WITTE, Peter .... 209-946-2417.. 70 E pwitte@pacific.edu
WITTE, Raymond .... 419-530-6126 363 E raymond.witte@utoledo.edu
WITTE, Robert .... 417-626-1234 257 F witte.robert@occ.edu
WITTE, Sarah .... 541-962-3511 373 B switte@eou.edu
WITTE, Sean .... 717-254-8149 382 F wittes@dickinson.edu
WITTENBERG, Curtis ..... 906-487-7214 223 K curtis.wittenberg@finlandia.edu
WITTENBERG, Diane ..... 626-396-2326.. 26 E diane.wittenberg@artcenter.edu
WITTENMYER, Kathryn .. 415-503-6223.. 60 H klw@sfcm.edu
WITTER, Kevin, G .... 540-857-7341 476 D kwitter@virginiawestern.edu
WITTGENFELD, Tania .... 972-860-8324 435 B taniawittgenfeld@dcccd.edu
WITTIG, Andrea .... 562-860-2451.. 35M awittig@cerritos.edu
WITTLER, Kim .... 301-369-2800 197 F kwittler@captechu.edu
WITTLER, Michele, A .... 920-748-8119 495 G wittlerm@ripon.edu
WITTMAN, William .... 301-295-3185 504 B william.wittman@usuhs.edu
WITTMANN HARRIMAN, Susan .... 831-459-7965.. 70 B sharrima@ucsc.edu
WITTMANN-PRICE, Ruth, A .... 843-661-4625 409 K rwittmannprice@fmarion.edu
WITTNER, Charity .... 251-442-2507.... 8 C cwittner@umobile.edu
WITTSTEIN, Robert .... 781-891-2005 206 D bwittstein@bentley.edu
WITTSTRUCK, Clifford ... 307-382-1714 502 I cwittstruck@westernwyoming.edu
WITTY, Janeen .... 803-705-4761 407 A janeen.witty@benedict.edu
WIXOM, Tasha .... 541-881-5781 377 B twixom@tvcc.cc
WIXSOM, Richard .... 774-330-4707 214 B
WLADON, Pamela .... 916-877-7977.. 58 J pwaldon@sui.edu
WLEZIEN, Richard .... 573-341-4625 261 E wlezien@mst.edu
WOBBE, Michelle .... 314-918-2599 253 A mwobbe@eden.edu
WOBBY, Lauren .... 802-485-2040 463 A laurenw@norwich.edu
WOBENSMITH, Stephanie .... 215-489-4851 382 D stephanie.wobensmith@delval.edu
WOBICK, Kim .... 312-467-2509.. 36 F kwobick@thechicagoschool.edu
WODELE, Tracy .... 612-351-2908 236 D twodele@ipr.edu
WODKA, Chris .... 520-494-5230.. 11 K chris.wodka@centralaz.edu
WOELKERS, Joseph, F .. 903-877-5072 456 D joseph.woelkers@uthct.edu
WOELL, John .... 517-629-0222 220 G jwoell@albion.edu
WOERLY, Crystal .... 817-598-6274 458 A cwoerly@wc.edu
WOEST, Jim .... 714-879-3901.. 45 F jwoest@hiu.edu
WOETZEL, Damian .... 212-799-5000 303 H
WOGAN, Maureen .... 773-298-3010 148 G wogan@sxu.edu
WOGEN, Brian, M .... 641-422-4177 168 D wogenbri@niacc.edu
WOHL, James .... 860-486-5143.. 88 E jim.wohl@uconn.edu
WOHLERS, Tony .... 443-412-2361 199 A twohlers@harford.edu
WOHLETZ, Dale .... 318-357-5581 192 C wohletz@nsula.edu
WOHLFORD, Corinne .... 314-889-1401 253 C cwohlford@fontbonne.edu
WOHLGEZOGEN, Gene . 562-985-4862.. 31 F gene.wohlgezogen@csulb.edu
WOHLMAN, Jason, L .... 530-752-9793.. 68 E jlwohlman@ucdavis.edu
WOHLMAN, Katie .... 828-328-7699 330 F katie.wohlman@lr.edu
WOHLPART, A. James .. 319-273-2517 163 B jim.wohlpart@uni.edu

WOIKE, David .... 734-487-0076 223 H dwoike@emich.edu
WOITA, Steve .... 402-280-1719 266 I stevewoita@creighton.edu
WOJAK, Angie .... 212-592-2387 315 H awojak@sva.edu
WOJCIECHOWSKI, Keli . 708-524-6827 136 C kallen@dom.edu
WOJCIECHOWSKI, Scott .... 336-841-9713 329 G swojciec@highpoint.edu
WOJCIECHOWSKI, Thomas .... 716-839-8585 298 B twoj@daemen.edu
WOJCIK, Alketa .... 760-757-2121.. 52 E awojcik@miracosta.edu
WOJICK, Matther, Z ...... 716-888-2793 292 D wojickm@canisius.edu
WOJKE, Katie .... 360-491-4700 483 H kwojke@stmartin.edu
WOJNAS, Sherry .... 315-801-8206 313 G swojnas@secon.edu
WOJNOWSKI, Jeffrey .... 414-456-7106 494 C jwojnows@mcw.edu
WOJNOWSKI, Mark, E .. 716-286-9718 310 D mew@niagara.edu
WOJTALEWICZ, Daniel .. 402-552-2586 266 E wojtalewiczdaniel@clarksoncollege.edu
WOJTALEWICZ, Jeanette .... 402-572-3650 266 D
WOJTOWICZ, Robert ..... 757-683-4885 469 G rwojtowi@odu.edu
WOLANIN, Monique ..... 860-932-4174.. 86 E mwolanin@qvcc.edu
WOLANSKYJ, Alexandra, P .... 507-284-3627 234 J wolanskyj.alexandra@mayo.edu
WOLBERS, Jan, K .... 309-341-7793 141 A jkwolbers@knox.edu
WOLBRECHT, Jennifer ... 253-864-3212 483 D jwolbrecht@pierce.ctc.edu
WOLCH, Jennifer .... 510-642-0831.. 68 D wolch@berkeley.edu
WOLCOTT, Lisa .... 253-589-5599 479 G lisa.wolcott@cptc.edu
WOLCOWITZ, Jeffrey ..... 216-368-2928 349 F jeffrey.wolcowitz@case.edu
WOLD-MCCORMICK, Kristi .... 303-492-6970.. 83 A kristi.woldmccormick@colorado.edu
WOLDOW, Jane .... 802-831-1449 463 G jwoldow@vermontlaw.edu
WOLF, Alexander .... 831-459-4676.. 70 B alw@ucsc.edu
WOLF, Andrea .... 617-521-2488 218 E andrea.wolf@simmons.edu
WOLF, Andreas .... 650-574-6461.. 61 P wolf@smccd.edu
WOLF, Bill .... 865-573-4517 420 G bwolf@johnsonu.edu
WOLF, David .... 940-565-2010 454 A david.wolf@unt.edu
WOLF, Eric .... 212-517-3929 316 B e.wolf@sothebysinstitute.com
WOLF, Georgo .... 517-264-7177 230 E gwolf@sienaheights.edu
WOLF, Greg .... 508-856-4296 212 A greg.wolf@umassmed.edu
WOLF, Howard, E .... 650-724-5992.. 65 J howardwolf@stanford.edu
WOLF, Ina .... 301-846-2486 198 E iwolf@frederick.edu
WOLF, Jacqueline, H .... 405-325-7578 371 B jackie.wolf@ou.edu
WOLF, Kathy, M .... 765-285-1444 153 C kmwolf@bsu.edu
WOLF, Kelly, B .... 541-346-3165 377 D kbwolf@uoregon.edu
WOLF, Kevin .... 504-520-7537 193 A kwolf@xula.edu
WOLF, Leslie .... 404-413-9040 119 E lwolf1@gsu.edu
WOLF, Linda .... 614-251-4715 358 G wolfl2@ohiodominican.edu
WOLF, Margaret .... 815-802-8302 140 D mwolf@kcc.edu
WOLF, Nick .... 619-849-2384.. 57 E nickwolf@pointloma.edu
WOLF, Paul, J .... 937-255-3636 503 A paul.wolf@afit.edu
WOLF, Rachel, B .... 972-860-7358 435 B rwolf@dcccd.edu
WOLF, Rob .... 352-854-2322.. 96 O wolfr@cf.edu

WOLF, JR., Thomas ..... 269-387-5473 232 K tom.wolf@wmich.edu
WOLF, Tilman .... 413-545-6330 211 D wolf@umass.edu
WOLF-HALL, Charlene .. 605-688-4420 417 C charlene.wolfhall@sdstate.edu
WOLFARTH, Ariel .... 718-268-4700 312 G
WOLFE, Agata .... 908-737-3352 278 E agwolfe@kean.edu
WOLFE, Barbara, E .... 401-874-5324 406 B bwolfe@uri.edu
WOLFE, Bill .... 318-797-5279 189 D bill.wolfe@lsus.edu
WOLFE, Cathy .... 626-300-5444.. 57 A cwolfe@plattecollege.edu
WOLFE, Charles .... 708-237-5050 145 E cwolfe@nc.edu
WOLFE, Clarissa .... 509-574-4651 487 A cwolfe@yvcc.edu
WOLFE, Constance .... 336-506-4139 332 A constance.wolfe@alamancecc.edu
WOLFE, Dana .... 256-306-2831.... 1 F dana.wolfe@calhoun.edu
WOLFE, Deidre .... 540-863-2807 474 D dwolfe@dslcc.edu
WOLFE, Gregory .... 508-565-1357 218 H gwolfe@stonehill.edu
WOLFE, James, E .... 812-464-1782 161 E jwolfe2@usi.edu
WOLFE, JD .... 503-399-7506 372 C jd.wolfe@chemeketa.edu
WOLFE, Johanna .... 713-221-8909 453 B wolfej@uhd.edu
WOLFE, Kari .... 812-535-5220 160 B kari.wolfe@smwc.edu
WOLFE, Kathy .... 402-465-2350 268 H kjw@nebrwesleyan.edu
WOLFE, Ken .... 727-864-8835.. 97 J wolfefk@eckerd.edu
WOLFE, Kim .... 765-641-4296 153 B kjwolfe@anderson.edu
WOLFE, Michael .... 718-997-5210 295 C michael.wolfe@qc.cuny.edu
WOLFE, Peggy, L .... 337-475-5820 192 A pwolfe@mcneese.edu
WOLFE, Sarah .... 513-936-1565 362 E sarah.wolfe@uc.edu
WOLFE, Thomas, V .... 303-765-3102.. 80 F tvwolfe@iliff.edu
WOLFE, Tim, A .... 757-221-3980 466 C tawolfe@wm.edu
WOLFE, Timothy .... 775-784-4666 271 F tawolfe@unr.edu
WOLFE, Todd .... 818-677-3700.. 32 D todd.wolfe@csun.edu
WOLFE, Vicki .... 601-973-5019 245 C vwolfe@belhaven.edu
WOLFE-LEE, Chyerl .... 360-650-3774 486 F chyerl.wolfe-lee@wwu.edu
WOLFE-LYGA, Katherine .... 315-312-4416 319 B katherine.wolfelyga@oswego.edu
WOLFE-STEPRO, Charlene .... 603-206-8072 272 L cwolfe@ccsnh.edu
WOLFENSTEIN, Moses .. 310-660-3593.. 41 L mwolfenstein@elcamino.edu
WOLFER, Diane, G .... 859-371-9393 179 A dwolfer@beckfield.edu
WOLFF, Asaf .... 626-264-8880.. 71 A
WOLFF, Donald .... 541-962-3359 373 B dwolff@eou.edu
WOLFF, Holly, D .... 563-425-5221 170 A wolffh@uiu.edu
WOLFF, Jennifer .... 210-434-6711 441 E jswolff@follett.com
WOLFF, Mark, S .... 215-898-1038 400 K mswolff@upenn.edu
WOLFF, Peg, A .... 308-635-6064 270 D pwolff@wncc.edu
WOLFF, Robert .... 860-832-2807.. 84 I wolffr@ccsu.edu
WOLFF, Susan .... 815-939-5203 146 A swolff@olivet.edu
WOLFF, Susan, J .... 406-771-4305 264 G susan.wolff@gfcmsu.edu
WOLFKILL, John .... 303-360-4833.. 79 D john.wolfkill@ccaurora.edu
WOLFMAN, Jeffrey .... 978-665-4933 212 C jwolfman@fitchburgstate.edu
WOLFORD, Wendy .... 607-255-0157 297 F www43@cornell.edu

WOLGAST, Brad .... 302-831-2141.. 90 F bradw@udel.edu
WOLIN, Richard, R .... 231-995-2003 228 G rwolin@nmc.edu
WOLINSKY, Lawrence, E .... 214-828-8300 446 G wolinsky@tamu.edu
WOLK, Joseph .... 508-531-1229 212 B joseph.wolk@bridgew.edu
WOLKEN, James .... 661-291-3044.. 28 K jwolken@calarts.edu
WOLKEN, Julie .... 713-798-8990 431 I jwolken@bcm.edu
WOLKING, Daryl .... 540-338-1776 470 A
WOLLAS, Robyn .... 615-771-7821 429 A
WOLLENBERG, Chad ..... 434-949-1033 475 H chad.wollenberg@southside.edu
WOLLENBURG, Doug .... 912-525-5000 123 G dwollenbu@scad.edu
WOLLMAN, Julie, E .... 610-499-4101 403 B jewollman@widener.edu
WOLLMERING, Jerry ..... 660-785-4235 260 J jerryw@truman.edu
WOLMA, Stephen, J ...... 712-290-8709 388 D sjwolma@lancasterseminary.edu
WOLMARK, Adrienne .... 503-552-1605 374 E awolmark@nunm.edu
WOLMARK, Mordechai . 845-352-3431 326 B
WOLOHAN, Laurie .... 216-687-3606 351 B l.wolohan@csuohio.edu
WOLOSZYNOWSKI, Daniel .... 757-594-7777 466 B daniel.woloszynowski@cnu.edu
WOLPERN, Kevin .... 952-888-4777 242 I kwolpern@nwhealth.edu
WOLPIN, Aryeh .... 718-232-7800 325 J
WOLPIN, OBM, Chaim . 718-232-7800 325 J
WOLSEY, Timothy .... 480-732-7125.. 12 P timothy.wolsey@cgc.edu
WOLTERS, Daniel .... 406-657-1161 265 E woltersd@rocky.edu
WOLTMANN, Tanya ...... 847-543-2443 135 B twoltmann@clcillinois.edu
WOMACK, Joseph .... 541-684-7241 374 G jwomack@nwcu.edu
WOMACK, Juanita, D .... 301-546-7422 201 C
WOMACK, Kenneth .... 732-571-3419 279 B kwomack@monmouth.edu
WOMACK, Tonya .... 727-864-7737.. 97 J womacktm@eckerd.edu
WOMACK, Veronica ...... 478-445-4233 118 C veronica.womack@gcsu.edu
WOMACK, Wayne .... 479-788-7407.. 21 H wayne.womack@uafs.edu
WOMBLE, Jeff .... 910-672-1474 341 E jwomble@uncfsu.edu
WOMBLE, Lynn, Z .... 903-813-2891 430 N lwomble@austincollege.edu
WOMBLE, Scott .... 314-837-6777 258 J swomble@stlchristian.edu
WOMELSDUFF, Gary, E . 206-281-2678 484 D womelg@spu.edu
WOMICK, Jason .... 864-587-4217 412 G womickj@smcsc.edu
WON, Cha Hi .... 714-527-0691.. 42 E
WON LEE, Kang .... 714-636-1722.. 28 G kwlee@cgsot.edu
WONDERLY, Jennifer .... 312-341-3558 147 H jwonderl@roosevelt.edu
WONDERS, Christopher 717-477-1251 395 E cawonders@ship.edu
WONG, David, W .... 920-923-8576 494 A dwwong@marianuniversity.edu
WONG, Erwin .... 212-220-8321 293 A ewong@bmcc.cuny.edu
WONG, Gene .... 978-232-2311 209 B gwong@endicott.edu
WONG, James .... 718-405-3733 296 G james.wong@mountsaintvincent.edu
WONG, Jane .... 609-771-2277 276 I wong@tcnj.edu
WONG, Jeannie .... 916-278-2067.. 32 E jwong@csus.edu
WONG, Julie .... 847-317-7152 150 H jwong@tiu.edu
WONG, Julie .... 818-299-5500.. 73 K jwong@westcoastuniversity.edu
WONG, Lam .... 216-987-4265 351 G lam.wong@tri-c.edu
WONG, Leslis .... 202-885-2143.. 90 J lawyers@american.edu
WONG, Martin .... 315-228-7203 296 F mswong@colgate.edu

WOODS, Douglas .... 414-288-0327 494 B
douglas.woods@marquette.edu
WOODS, Ed .... 503-589-7746 372 C
ed.woods@chemeketa.edu
WOODS, Erin .... 806-743-4569 451 C
erin.woodws@ttuhsc.edu
WOODS, James, M .... 630-515-6173 143 G
jwoods@midwestern.edu
WOODS, Jami .... 336-386-3266 338 D
woodsj@surry.edu
WOODS, Jann .... 928-505-3300.. 14 F
jwoods@mohave.edu
WOODS, Jason, L .... 320-308-5455 240 H
jlwoods@stcloudstate.edu
WOODS, Jessica .... 828-227-3044 344 A
jmwoods@wcu.edu
WOODS, John .... 602-557-4040.. 16 J
john.woods@phoenix.edu
WOODS, John, P .... 405-325-2801 371 B
jwoods@ou.edu
WOODS, Karen .... 413-565-1000 205 G
kwoods@baypath.edu
WOODS, Kimberly, J .... 830-792-7282 443 G
counseling@schreiner.edu
WOODS, Kristi .... 951-222-8851.. 58 I
kristi.woods@rcc.edu
WOODS, Kristin, L .... 319-273-2332 163 B
kristin.woods@uni.edu
WOODS, Kristy, F .... 202-865-7470.. 92 B
kristy.woods@howard.edu
WOODS, Lauren .... 312-567-5167 139 B
lwoods1@iit.edu
WOODS, Linda .... 619-388-7750.. 60 E
lwoods@sdccd.edu
WOODS, Marilyn .... 336-272-7102 329 D
marilyn.woods@greensboro.edu
WOODS, Mark .... 810-762-9642 225 H
mwoods@kettering.edu
WOODS, Marty .... 864-587-4044 412 G
woodsm@smcsc.edu
WOODS, Marvin .... 520-325-0123.. 16 C
WOODS, Mary Lou .... 909-621-8135.. 57 F
marylou.woods@pomona.edu
WOODS, Maura, A .... 718-990-1985 314 B
woodsm@stjohns.edu
WOODS, Phillip .... 423-478-7993 423 G
pwoods@ptseminary.edu
WOODS, Rebekah .... 509-547-0511 479 H
WOODS, Rochelle .... 657-278-4457.. 31 E
rwoods@fullerton.edu
WOODS, Serrita .... 815-282-7900 148 C
serritawoods@sacn.edu
WOODS, Sharmon .... 520-325-0123.. 16 C
WOODS, Sharon .... 864-503-5354 414 D
swoods@uscupstate.edu
WOODS, Sheldon .... 770-689-4875 114 C
swoods@aii.edu
WOODS, Sigrid .... 979-830-4188 432 C
sigrid.woods@blinn.edu
WOODS, Stephanie .... 915-215-4300 451 D
stephanie.woods@ttuhsc.edu
WOODS, Tim .... 559-442-8222.. 66 E
tim.woods@fresnocitycollege.edu
WOODS, Tracie, J .... 225-771-2680 190 H
tracie_woods@sus.edu
WOODS, Tracie, J .... 225-771-2680 190 G
tracie_woods@sus.edu
WOODS, Tracy .... 478-289-2035 117 D
twoods@ega.edu
WOODS, William .... 830-792-7425 443 G
studentoutcomes@schreiner.edu
WOODS-RAMSEY,
Paulette .... 402-461-2463 266 A
paulettewoodsramsey@cccneb.edu
WOODSBY, Wendy .... 864-503-5198 414 D
wwoodsby@uscupstate.edu
WOODSIDE,
Christina, S .... 704-847-5600 340 I
cwoodside@ses.edu
WOODSON, Corliss, B . 804-523-5877 474 H
cwoodson@reynolds.edu
WOODSON, Heather ..... 704-922-2361 334 F
woodson.heather@gaston.edu
WOODSON, Heather ..... 704-922-6307 334 F
woodson.heather@gaston.edu
WOODSON, Kendra .... 864-294-2033 410 A
kendra.woodson@furman.edu
WOODSON, Lovisa .... 215-635-7300 385 A
lwoodson@gratz.edu
WOODSON,
Terrance, S .... 214-887-5371 436 B
twoodson@dts.edu

WOODSON, Timothy ..... 434-961-5448 475 F
twoodson@pvcc.edu
WOODSON, William ..... 941-487-4106 109 D
wwoodson@ncf.edu
WOODSON, William ..... 937-708-5711 364 D
wwoodson@wilberforce.edu
WOODSON,
William Randy .... 919-515-2191 342 B
randy_woodson@ncsu.edu
WOODSON DAY,
Beverly .... 210-458-4536 455 E
beverly.woodsonday@utsa.edu
WOODWARD, Amanda .. 773-702-8799 150 J
woodward@uchicago.edu
WOODWARD, Beth .... 503-552-1664 374 E
bwoodward@nunm.edu
WOODWARD, Clifford ... 973-290-4345 277 A
cwoodward@cse.edu
WOODWARD,
Gregory, S .... 860-768-4417.. 88 H
gwoodward@hartford.edu
WOODWARD, Jalan .... 225-490-1669 186 F
jalan.woodward@franu.edu
WOODWARD, Jonathan 601-928-6233 247 E
jonathan.woodward@mgccc.edu
WOODWARD, LouAnn .. 601-984-1010 249 E
lawoodward@umc.edu
WOODWARD, Mac .... 936-294-3931 450 C
smm_wmw@shsu.edu
WOODWARD, Melanie .. 607-753-2302 318 D
melanie.woodward@cortland.edu
WOODWARD, Rebecca . 203-837-8760.. 85 B
woodwardr@wcsu.edu
WOODWARD, Scott .... 225-578-6977 188 I
athletics@lsu.edu
WOODWARD, Scott .... 210-341-1366 441 C
rsw@ost.edu
WOODWARD, Sheryl .... 530-898-6771.. 31 A
swoodward@csuchico.edu
WOODWARD, Travis .... 432-685-6474 440 E
twoodward@midland.edu
WOODWARD, Wade .... 864-596-9072 409 B
wade.woodward@converse.edu
WOODWARD, Wendy .... 630-752-5656 152 F
wendy.woodward@wheaton.edu
WOODWORTH, Lauren . 601-276-3732 249 B
lwoodworth@smcc.edu
WOODWORTH, Mollie .. 517-318-3330 222 B
WOODWORTH-NEY,
Laura .... 208-282-2171 130 H
woodlaur@isu.edu
WOODY, Jaime .... 512-863-1624 445 D
woodyj@southwestern.edu
WOODY, Ron .... 734-487-3141 223 H
rwoody@emich.edu
WOODY, Sherry, L .... 336-256-1305 343 A
slwood@uncg.edu
WOODY, Tammie .... 585-785-1274 300 B
tammie.woody@flcc.edu
WOOFTER, Heather .... 314-935-6203 262 A
woofter@wustl.edu
WOOLBERT, Stephanie .. 617-277-3915 207 C
woolberts@bgsp.edu
WOOLCOCK, Karen .... 787-878-5475 508 L
kwoolcock@arecibo.inter.edu
WOOLDRIDGE,
Deborah, G .... 419-372-7851 348 H
dgwoold@bgsu.edu
WOOLDRIDGE, Heath ... 870-612-2039.. 22 I
heath.wooldridge@uaccb.edu
WOOLDRIDGE, James .. 951-222-8420.. 58 I
jim.wooldridge@rcc.edu
WOOLDRIDGE, Peter .... 919-536-7200 334 B
wooldridgep@durhamtech.edu
WOOLDRIDGE, Tyler ..... 817-202-6409 444 I
wooldridge@swau.edu
WOOLEY, Christine, A .. 240-895-3081 201 E
cawooley@smcm.edu
WOOLEY, Travis .... 407-303-9440.. 94 D
travis.wooley@ahu.edu
WOOLFOLK, Alan .... 904-819-6248.. 98 E
awoolfolk@flagler.edu
WOOLFOLK, Jerald .... 573-681-5042 254 E
woolfolkj@lincolnu.edu
WOOLIVER, Matt .... 918-293-4888 368 D
matt.wooliver@okstate.edu
WOOLLEN, Elizabeth, G 405-325-5141 371 B
lwoollen@ou.edu
WOOLLEY, Craig .... 937-775-4008 364 I
craig.woolley@wright.edu
WOOLLEY, Mark .... 718-409-3224 321 C
mwoolley@sunymaritime.edu
WOOLMAN, Sheri .... 785-242-2067 175 H
swoolman@neosho.edu

WOOLSEY, Andrew .... 949-480-4112.. 64 B
awoolsey@soka.edu
WOOLSEY, Clint .... 812-749-1441 159 C
cwoolsey@oak.edu
WOOLSEY, Roger, W .... 603-646-2215 273 E
roger.w.woolsey@dartmouth.edu
WOOLSEY, Roger, W .... 603-646-2215 273 E
rober.w.woolsey@dartmouth.edu
WOOLSON, Jonathan .... 716-673-3323 317 A
jonathan.woolson@fredonia.edu
WOOLSTENHULME,
David .... 801-321-7103 460 D
commissioner@ushe.edu
WOOLSTON, Paul (PJ) . 317-955-6307 158 U
pwoolston@marian.edu
WOOLWINE, Lora .... 304-384-5224 490 A
lwoolwine@concord.edu
WOON, Jeanne .... 660-543-4060 260 K
woon@ucmo.edu
WOON LEE, Young .... 323-643-0301.. 25 L
WOOST, Michael, G .... 440-943-7600 360 J
mgwoost@yahoo.com
WOOSTER, Ginger .... 979-230-3210 432 D
ginger.wooster@brazosport.edu
WOOSTER, Rossitza .... 503-725-5258 376 A
wooster@pdx.edu
WOOSTER, Timothy, T .. 859-858-3511 178 I
timothy.wooster@asbury.edu
WOOTEN, Beth .... 254-867-3940 449 E
beth.wooten@tstc.edu
WOOTEN, Bradley .... 847-635-1912 145 G
bwooten@oakton.edu
WOOTEN, Christopher .. 903-730-4890 438 H
cwooten@jarvis.edu
WOOTEN, Cornelius ..... 919-530-6204 342 A
cwooten8@nccu.edu
WOOTEN, Daniel .... 615-963-5673 426 D
dwooten@tnstate.edu
WOOTEN, Manat .... 413-528-7203 205 F
mwooten@simons-rock.edu
WOOTEN, Maria .... 901-751-8453 422 E
mwooten@mabts.edu
WOOTEN, Michael, W .. 603-646-3093 273 E
michael.w.wooten@dartmouth.edu
WOOTEN, Randall .... 832-447-1461 449 E
randall.wooten@tstc.edu
WOOTEN, Robin .... 740-593-2665 359 G
krivesti@ohio.edu
WOOTEN, Rodney .... 252-335-0821 333 G
rodney_wooten91@albemarle.edu
WOOTEN, Sheila .... 973-748-9000 276 A
sheila_wooten@bloomfield.edu
WOOTEN, Stanley .... 901-369-0835.. 92 G
WOOTEN, Susan .... 828-726-2233 332 G
swooten@cccti.edu
WOOTEN, Susan .... 864-231-2000 406 G
swooten@andersonuniversity.edu
WOOTEN, Wes .... 252-493-7444 336 H
wmwooten@email.pittcc.edu
WOOTON, Chris .... 502-895-3411 183 D
cwooton@lpts.edu
WOOTTERS, Adrienne ... 413-662-5242 213 A
adrienne.wootters@mcla.edu
WOOTTON, Mark .... 757-826-1883 465 A
president@bcva.edu
WORD, Beverly .... 901-321-3527 419 C
bword@cbu.edu
WORD, Daniel .... 909-389-3216.. 59 H
dword@craftonhills.edu
WORD, John .... 559-791-2254.. 47 A
jword@portervillecollege.edu
WORDELL, David, G ..... 508-565-1646 218 H
dwordell@stonehill.edu
WORDELL, Kathleen, A . 508-678-2811 213 G
kathleen.wordell@bristolcc.edu
WORDEN, Jeannie, M ... 715-675-3331 500 E
worden@ntc.edu
WORDEN, Jennifer .... 208-459-5307 130 D
jworden@collegeofidaho.edu
WORDEN, Jodi .... 509-527-4561 485 G
jodi.worden@wwcc.edu
WORDEN, Michael .... 845-341-4901 311 C
michael.worden@sunyorange.edu
WORDEN, Natalia .... 858-566-1200.. 41 E
nworden@disd.edu
WORDEN, Randy .... 815-226-3398 147 G
rworden@rockford.edu
WORDEN, Richard, B .... 315-568-3095 308 F
rworden@nycc.edu
WORDLOW-WILLIAMS,
Tamika .... 401-456-8061 405 C
twordlow@ric.edu

WORK, AJ .... 661-362-2333.. 51 C
awork@masters.edu
WORK, Christine .... 845-341-4763 311 C
christine.work@sunyorange.edu
WORK, Patricia .... 202-495-3835.. 92 E
assistant@dhs.edu
WORKMAN, Andrew, A . 610-499-4106 403 B
aaworkman@widener.edu
WORKMAN, Aurora .... 914-606-6880 325 C
aurora.workman@sunywcc.edu
WORKMAN, Christine ... 843-953-5312 408 E
workmancl@cofc.edu
WORKMAN, Dan .... 503-517-1537 377 G
dworkman@warnerpacific.edu
WORKMAN, Erin .... 626-568-8850.. 48 F
erin@lacm.edu
WORKMAN, Jennifer, L 302-356-6843.. 90 I
jennifer.l.workman@wilmu.edu
WORKMAN, Mary .... 954-201-7324.. 95 H
mworkman@broward.edu
WORKMAN, RaSheda ... 205-366-8817.... 7 A
rworkman@stillman.edu
WORKMAN, Sue, B .... 216-368-5899 349 F
sue.workman@case.edu
WORKMAN, Tamara ...... 618-453-2973 149 E
tworkman@siu.edu
WORLEY, Alan .... 806-716-2338 443 I
aworley@southplainscollege.edu
WORLEY, David .... 303-765-3107.. 80 F
dworley@iliff.edu
WORLEY, Jewell, B .... 276-376-1004 473 B
ljw4k@virginia.edu
WORLEY, John .... 510-659-6111.. 54 F
jworley@ohlone.edu
WORLEY, John .... 713-646-1863 444 B
jworley@stcl.edu
WORLEY, Louise .... 717-815-1446 404 A
lworley@ycp.edu
WORLEY, Mark .... 972-241-3371 434 J
mworley@dallas.edu
WORLEY, Mary Beth ..... 575-527-7728 287 E
mbworley@nmsu.edu
WORLEY, Mike .... 864-388-8350 410 D
mworley@lander.edu
WORLEY, Paul .... 828-835-9564 338 E
pworley@tricountycc.edu
WORLEY, Phillip .... 419-372-3905 348 H
pworley@bgsu.edu
WORLEY, Rene .... 931-598-1123 423 M
rworley@sewanee.edu
WORLEY, Tim .... 561-803-2116 104 C
tim_worley@pba.edu
WORM, Lori, M .... 920-424-3033 497 B
worm@uwosh.edu
WORMACK, Janet .... 713-718-8464 437 I
janet.wormack@hccs.edu
WORMAN, Ernie .... 803-947-2052 411 D
ernie.worman@newberry.edu
WORMLEY, Antoinette ... 703-416-1441 466 F
awormley@divinemercy.edu
WORMLEY, JR.,
Floyd, L .... 817-257-4320 448 G
floyd.wormley@tcu.edu
WORNALL, Robyn .... 707-256-7192.. 53 C
rwornall@napavalley.edu
WORNAT, Judy .... 225-578-5255 188 I
mjwornat@lsu.edu
WOROBEC, Sophia .... 312-942-6857 148 A
sophia_worobec@rush.edu
WORONIEWICZ,
Michael .... 248-683-0311 231 A
mworoniewicz@sscms.edu
WORRALL, Jay .... 610-796-8371 378 F
jay.worrall@alvernia.edu
WORRELS, Derrick .... 254-267-7010 442 E
dworrels@rangercollege.edu
WORSHAM, Thomas ..... 318-487-7498 186 I
thomas.worsham@lacollege.edu
WORSLEY, Christine ..... 925-969-2747.. 40 I
cworsley@dvc.edu
WORSTER, Kate .... 269-337-7296 225 D
kate.worster@kzoo.edu
WORSTER, Kathy .... 803-321-3353 411 D
kathy.worster@newberry.edu
WORTH, Benjamin .... 540-863-2933 474 D
bworth@dslcc.edu
WORTH, Tiffany .... 217-732-3155 141 I
tworth@lincolncollege.edu
WORTHAM, Stanton ...... 617-552-3902 207 B
stanton.wortham@bc.edu
WORTHAM, Trudy .... 361-570-4110 453 C
worthamt@uhv.edu
WORTHEN, Kevin, J ..... 801-422-2521 458 H
kevin_worthen@byu.edu

WORTHINGTON, Chenoa .... 918-444-4677 367 A worthi02@nsuok.edu
WORTHINGTON, Leslie . 256-549-8256.... 2 B lworthington@gadsdenstate.edu
WORTHINGTON, Phyllis .... 870-512-7842.. 18 B phyllis_worthington@asun.edu
WORTHY, Mark .... 225-752-4233 186 H mworthy@iticollege.edu
WORTMAN, Martin .... 575-527-7524 287 E mwortman@nmsu.edu
WOTTON, Heather .... 203-773-8558.. 84 F hwotton@albertus.edu
WOUDENBERG, Robert . 315-866-0300 301 G woudenbra@herkimer.edu
WOUDSTRA, Earl .... 712-707-7292 168 H earl@nwciowa.edu
WOUGHTER, Laura .... 740-389-4636 356 B woughterl@mtc.edu
WOULFE, Rebecca .... 303-797-5702.. 76 I rebecca.woulfe@arapahoe.edu
WOUNDY, Carolina .... 617-364-3510 207 A cwoundy@boston.edu
WOYAK, Amber .... 847-578-8350 147 I amber.woyak@rosalindfranklin.edu
WOZNIAK, Andrew .... 630-889-6878 144 G awozniak@nuhs.edu
WOZNIAK, Danielle ...... 212-960-0820 326 E danielle.wozniak@yu.edu
WOZNIAK, Robert, A .... 716-652-8900 292 I rwozniak@cks.edu
WOZNICKI, John .... 609-984-1130 284 B jwoznicki@tesu.edu
WRAGE, Rebecca .... 308-535-3679 267 K wrager@mpcc.edu
WRAGG, Stephanie .... 559-325-3600.. 28 H swragg@chsu.edu
WRAGG, Tunisia .... 212-517-0561 306 A twragg@mmm.edu
WRAITH, Jon, M .... 603-862-2468 274 G jon.wraith@unh.edu
WRASMAN, Carleen ...... 574-936-8898 153 A carleen.wrasman@ancilla.edu
WRAY, Donald, W .... 318-795-2392 189 D donald.wray@lsus.edu
WRAY, John, W .... 330-325-6728 357 G jwray@neomed.edu
WRAY, Kimberli .... 701-774-4500 346 F kimberli.wray@willistonstate.edu
WRAY, Kyle .... 405-744-4366 368 B kyle.wray@okstate.edu
WRAY, Lee .... 931-372-3893 426 E lwray@tntech.edu
WRAY, Rachel .... 207-786-6240 193 B rwray@bates.edu
WRAY, Roger .... 434-949-1040 475 H roger.wray@southside.edu
WRAY, Tanner .... 240-567-1701 200 C tanner.wray@montgomerycollege.edu
WREDE, William .... 314-505-7221 251 I wredew@csl.edu
WREN, Brent, M .... 256-824-6681.... 8 B brent.wren@uah.edu
WREN, Holly .... 303-914-6341.. 82 C holly.wren@rrcc.edu
WREN, Jan .... 606-539-4328 185 A jan.wren@ucumberlands.edu
WREN, Pam .... 865-524-8079 420 E pam.wren@huhs.edu
WREN-COLEMAN, Meshonya .... 601-979-2127 246 E meshonya.m.wren-coleman@jsums.edu
WRENN, Christy .... 318-869-5057 186 B cwrenn@centenary.edu
WRENN, Patrick .... 920-403-3255 495 I pat.wrenn@snc.edu
WRENSFORD, Louise .... 229-430-0693 113 H louise.wrensford@asurams.edu
WRIGHT, Adam .... 214-333-5930 434 I adam@dbu.edu
WRIGHT, Andre .... 509-335-4561 486 A
WRIGHT, Andrew .... 562-985-8410.. 31 F andrew.wright@csulb.edu
WRIGHT, Andrew, W .... 812-465-7010 161 E wright@usi.edu
WRIGHT, Angelina .... 325-942-2017 451 A angie.wright@angelo.edu
WRIGHT, Angie .... 478-757-5192 126 H awright@wesleyancollege.edu
WRIGHT, Ann .... 501-450-3808.. 19 F wright@hendrix.edu
WRIGHT, Ann .... 864-250-8719 410 B ann.wright@gvltec.edu
WRIGHT, Ariana .... 757-683-3141 469 G a1wright@odu.edu
WRIGHT, Barbara .... 803-778-6695 407 C wrightb@cctech.edu
WRIGHT, Barbara .... 304-357-4813 488 G barbarawright@ucwv.edu
WRIGHT, Beatrice, V ..... 410-651-8387 203 A bvwright@umes.edu
WRIGHT, Bob .... 312-645-8300 501 T drbob@wrightgrad.edu
WRIGHT, Brandon .... 205-934-4324.... 8 A btwright@uab.edu
WRIGHT, Brandon .... 435-586-7700 460 F
WRIGHT, Brandon .... 435-586-1914 460 F brandonwright@suu.edu
WRIGHT, Brant .... 706-778-8500 123 B bwright@piedmont.edu
WRIGHT, Brian .... 276-964-7207 475 I brian.wright@sw.edu
WRIGHT, Caroline .... 617-236-8838 209 D cwright@fisher.edu
WRIGHT, Cary .... 276-326-4280 465 B cwright@bluefield.edu
WRIGHT, Catherine .... 860-701-5028.. 87 D wright_c@mitchell.edu
WRIGHT, Cathleen .... 830-372-8078 449 B cwright@tlu.edu
WRIGHT, Chantelle .... 212-237-8754 294 D cwright@jjay.cuny.edu
WRIGHT, Charles .... 609-771-2393 276 I wrightc@tcnj.edu
WRIGHT, Charles .... 704-330-6257 333 D charles.wright@cpcc.edu
WRIGHT, Charles, D ..... 405-325-3411 371 B cwright@ou.edu
WRIGHT, Chatt, G .... 808-544-0203 127 H cwright@hpu.edu
WRIGHT, Chris .... 575-624-8070 287 A wright@nmmi.edu
WRIGHT, Christopher ... 617-879-7221 212 E cwright@massart.edu
WRIGHT, Christopher ... 808-675-3599 127 E wrightcj@byuh.edu
WRIGHT, Christy .... 620-450-2133 176 G christya@prattcc.edu
WRIGHT, Chuck, W ...... 803-938-3867 414 B wrightcw@uscsumter.edu
WRIGHT, Claudia .... 830-758-5006 450 D crwright@sulross.edu
WRIGHT, Colleen .... 269-965-3931 225 F wrightc@kellogg.edu
WRIGHT, Colleen .... 607-255-9043 297 F finaid-director@cornell.edu
WRIGHT, Constance ..... 864-977-7064 411 E constance.wright@ngu.edu
WRIGHT, Cory .... 716-614-6897 310 C cwright@niagaracc.suny.edu
WRIGHT, Craig, J .... 516-572-7121 308 A craig.wright@ncc.edu
WRIGHT, Curits .... 504-520-7357 193 A cwrigh14@xula.edu
WRIGHT, Cynthia .... 509-777-3244 486 I cwright@whitworth.edu
WRIGHT, Dale .... 585-567-9321 302 D dale.wright@houghton.edu
WRIGHT, David .... 505-566-3837 288 A wrightd@sanjuancollege.edu
WRIGHT, David .... 765-677-2100 157 D iwupresident@indwes.edu
WRIGHT, David .... 316-978-7157 178 A david.wright@wichita.edu
WRIGHT, David .... 303-384-2120.. 78 I dwright1@mines.edu
WRIGHT, David, W .... 213-740-4218.. 72 B dwwright@usc.edu
WRIGHT, Deborah .... 617-989-4348 219 E wrightd3@wit.edu
WRIGHT, Debra .... 951-785-2011.. 47 C dwright@lasierra.edu
WRIGHT, Diana .... 727-341-3267 106 E wright.diana@spcollege.edu
WRIGHT, Donna .... 270-789-5010 179 E dwright@campbellsville.edu
WRIGHT, Donna .... 718-270-4911 295 A dwright@mec.cuny.edu
WRIGHT, Donna .... 724-938-4461 394 B wright@calu.edu
WRIGHT, Duane .... 678-916-2609 114 I dwright@johnmarshall.edu
WRIGHT, Edward .... 610-459-0905 391 D
WRIGHT, Edwin, R .... 717-867-6180 388 H wright@lvc.edu
WRIGHT, Elizabeth .... 479-308-2303.. 17 C elizabeth.wright@acheedu.org
WRIGHT, Ethel, B .... 404-413-1300 119 E ebrown@gsu.edu
WRIGHT, George .... 949-214-3379.. 40 F george.wright@cui.edu
WRIGHT, Heather, H ..... 937-327-7992 364 H hwright@wittenberg.edu
WRIGHT, Howard .... 770-426-2712 121 C howard.wright@life.edu
WRIGHT, Ida .... 386-481-2281.. 95 F wrighti@cookman.edu
WRIGHT, Jamel .... 309-467-6322 137 B jwright@eureka.edu
WRIGHT, Jason .... 857-701-1360 215 E jwright@rcc.mass.edu
WRIGHT, Jeff .... 207-326-2253 195 D jeff.wright@mma.edu
WRIGHT, Jeffrey .... 765-641-4544 153 B jewright@anderson.edu
WRIGHT, Jerry .... 517-265-5161 220 F jwright@adrian.edu
WRIGHT, Jessi .... 602-787-6684.. 13 E jessi.wright@paradisevalley.edu
WRIGHT, Jimmy .... 606-886-3863 180 J jimmy.wright@kctcs.edu
WRIGHT, Joanne .... 408-924-2250.. 34 B joanne.wright@sjsu.edu
WRIGHT, John .... 337-521-8060 188 C john.wright@solacc.edu
WRIGHT, John .... 734-462-4400 230 D jwright@schoolcraft.edu
WRIGHT, Jonas .... 415-503-6251.. 60 H snedel@sfcm.edu
WRIGHT, Judith .... 312-645-8300 501 T drjudith@wrightgrad.edu
WRIGHT, Judy .... 936-633-5489 430 F jwright@angelina.edu
WRIGHT, Julie .... 480-732-7313.. 12 P julie.wright@cgc.edu
WRIGHT, Julie .... 573-288-6640 252 E jwright@culver.edu
WRIGHT, Karen .... 845-398-4017 315 B kwright@stac.edu
WRIGHT, Karen, F .... 270-384-7313 183 C wrightk@lindsey.edu
WRIGHT, Karl, S .... 803-535-5417 407 G kawright@claflin.edu
WRIGHT, Kay .... 979-230-3377 432 D kay.wright@brazosport.edu
WRIGHT, Kristin .... 423-461-8736 422 J kjwright@milligan.edu
WRIGHT, LaQueta .... 972-238-6275 435 F lwright@dcccd.edu
WRIGHT, LeAnne .... 903-223-3078 448 B leanne.wright@tamut.edu
WRIGHT, Leroy .... 517-629-0222 220 G lwright@albion.edu
WRIGHT, Lynn .... 805-289-6468.. 73 B lwright@vcccd.edu
WRIGHT, Marcie .... 217-443-8574 135 H mwright@dacc.edu
WRIGHT, Margo .... 305-626-3713.. 99 D margo.wright@fmuniv.edu
WRIGHT, Martin .... 317-931-2330 154 C mwright1@cts.edu
WRIGHT, Matthew .... 916-608-6687.. 50 H wrightm@flc.losrios.edu
WRIGHT, Melissa .... 662-562-3277 248 D
WRIGHT, Michael .... 229-391-4985 113 F mwright@abac.edu
WRIGHT, Michael, G .... 313-577-8155 232 I m.wright@wayne.edu
WRIGHT, Michael, G .... 330-325-6622 357 G mwright2@neomed.edu
WRIGHT, Nikki .... 313-577-2280 232 I nikki.wright@wayne.edu
WRIGHT, Norman .... 801-863-8239 461 A norman.wright@uvu.edu
WRIGHT, Nova .... 540-863-2868 474 D nwright@dslcc.edu
WRIGHT, Paul .... 906-227-2480 228 F sm8194@bncollege.com
WRIGHT, Paul .... 541-485-1780 374 F paulwright@newhope.edu
WRIGHT, Peter .... 920-206-2395 493 L peter.wright@mbu.edu
WRIGHT, Peter .... 920-206-3498 493 L peter.wright@mbu.edu
WRIGHT, Quentin .... 832-813-6688 439 G quentin.a.wright@lonestar.edu
WRIGHT, Raymond, M . 401-874-2186 406 B rmwright@uri.edu
WRIGHT, Regina .... 212-875-4595 290 F rwright@bankstreet.edu
WRIGHT, Rena .... 800-785-0585.. 39 G rena.wright@columbiacollege.edu
WRIGHT, Renetta .... 817-515-3468 445 G renetta.wright@tccd.edu
WRIGHT, Rick, L .... 785-539-3571 175 E rwright@mccks.edu
WRIGHT, Robert, F .... 413-597-2303 220 C robert.f.wright@williams.edu
WRIGHT, Roberta .... 276-656-0239 475 D rwright@patrickhenry.edu
WRIGHT, Rodner .... 850-599-3244 108 I rodner.wright@famu.edu
WRIGHT, Ron .... 318-357-6441 192 C
WRIGHT, Russell, W ..... 563-333-5729 169 A wrightrussellw@sau.edu
WRIGHT, Samantha, R .. 718-990-2160 314 B hastlers@stjohns.edu
WRIGHT, Shana .... 703-812-4757 468 G swright@leland.edu
WRIGHT, Shanay, M ..... 217-443-8860 135 H shuerta@dacc.edu
WRIGHT, Sharon .... 713-718-5205 437 I sharon.wright@hccs.edu
WRIGHT, Shelly, A .... 845-257-3291 317 B wrights@newpaltz.edu
WRIGHT, Siobhan .... 410-386-8207 197 G swright@carrollcc.edu
WRIGHT, Terry .... 501-450-3293.. 23 H terryw@uca.edu
WRIGHT, Terry .... 919-497-3294 330 I twright@louisburg.edu
WRIGHT, Tessa .... 405-425-5134 367 G tessa.wright@oc.edu
WRIGHT, Thomda, F ..... 276-964-7315 475 I tommy.wright@sw.edu
WRIGHT, Tim .... 206-546-4516 484 G twright@shoreline.edu
WRIGHT, Tim .... 252-246-1401 339 C twright@wilsoncc.edu
WRIGHT, Timothy, S .... 863-680-4297.. 99 H twright@flsouthern.edu
WRIGHT, Travis .... 423-869-6674 421 C travis.wright02@lmunet.edu
WRIGHT, Troy, M .... 563-588-7816 167 D troy.wright@loras.edu
WRIGHT, Victoria .... 216-368-4594 349 F victoria.wright@case.edu
WRIGHT-RICHARDS, Tia .... 803-793-5197 409 C richardst@denmarktech.edu
WRIGHT-SWADEL, William .... 919-660-1050 328 G william.wright-swadel@duke.edu
WRIGHTANDERSON, Nikisha .... 309-694-5581 138 C nwrightanderson@icc.edu
WRIGHTEN, Karen .... 843-899-8049 413 B karen.wrighten@tridenttech.edu
WRIGHTMAN, Diane ..... 775-727-2017 271 B diane.wrightman@gbcnv.edu
WRIGHTSON, JR., Samuel, H .... 610-566-1776 403 E swrightson@williamson.edu
WRIGLEY, Julia .... 212-817-7200 293 F provost@gc.cuny.edu
WRIGLEY, Scott, C .... 413-545-2619 211 D swrigley@aux.umass.edu
WRIGLEY, Steve .... 404-962-3000 126 F chancellor@usg.edu
WRIGLEY, Telaina .... 931-221-6353 418 D wrigleyt@apsu.edu
WRIGLEY, Vicki, A .... 217-362-6485 143 H vwrigley@millikin.edu
WRISTON, Welton .... 423-478-7250 423 G wwriston@ptseminary.edu
WROBEL, David, R .... 405-325-2077 371 B david.wrobel@ou.edu
WROBEL, Patricia .... 716-286-8309 310 D pwrobel@niagara.edu
WROBLESKI, Melissa .... 320-589-6452 244 B mwrobles@morris.umn.edu
WROBLEWSKI, Kathleen .... 413-565-1000 205 G kwroblew@baypath.edu
WROTNIAK, Brian .... 716-829-7719 298 F wrotniak@dyc.edu
WRUCK, Peter .... 507-285-7245 240 G peter.wruck@rctc.edu
WRYE, Tim .... 206-592-4357 481 H twrye@highline.edu
WU, Adam .... 909-593-3511.. 70 D awu@laverne.edu

WU, Andrew .... 410-337-6000 198 G
WU, Angela .... 415-239-3303.. 37 A
ahwu@ccsf.edu
WU, Anna .... 919-962-7248 342 D
annaw@fac.unc.edu
WU, Diana .... 510-642-4181.. 68 D
dwu@unex.berkeley.edu
WU, Hong .... 804-523-5324 474 H
hwu@reynolds.edu
WU, Jonathan .... 626-289-9004.. 24 I
jwu@amu.edu
WU, Qianzhi (Jamie) .... 512-454-1188 430 G
qwu@aoma.edu
WU, S. David .... 703-993-8776 467 L
davidwu@gmu.edu
WU, Shao-Wei .... 845-848-7822 298 D
shao-wei.wu@dc.edu
WU, Shuqi .... 808-455-0597 129 D
shuqi@hawaii.edu
WU, Sonia .... 941-487-5000 109 D
swu@ncf.edu
WU, Steven .... 626-571-5110.. 48 B
stevenwu@les.edu
WU, Yenbo .... 415-338-1293.. 34 A
ywu@sfsu.edu
WU-BOTT, Sandra .... 808-983-4100 128 A
WU CRAIG, Yvonne .... 510-723-6810.. 35 O
ywucraig@chabotcolleg.edu
WUBAH, Daniel, A .... 717-871-7001 395 D
mupresident@millersville.edu
WUBBEN, Kris .... 608-822-2706 500 G
kwubben@swtc.edu
WUCHENICH,
Christopher, L .... 803-777-8400 413 C
clw@mailbox.sc.edu
WUCHER, Brad .... 573-875-7237 251 F
brwucher@ccis.edu
WUEBBEN, Nancy .... 937-319-6164 347 G
nwuebben@antiochcollege.edu
WUENSCHEL, Carol, M . 301-696-3556 199 B
wuenschel@hood.edu
WUEST, Beth, E .... 512-245-8113 450 E
bw09@txstate.edu
WUEST, Joseph .... 740-474-8896 358 F
jwuest@ohiochristian.edu
WUINEE, David .... 340-693-1152 514 E
david.wuinee@uvi.edu
WULF, Lincoln .... 719-502-3178.. 81 F
lincoln.wulf@ppcc.edu
WULF, Robin .... 620-331-4100 174 C
rwulf@indycc.edu
WULFEKUHLE-ISAAC,
Kim .... 563-589-3178 169 I
kisaac@dbq.edu
WULFF, Deborah .... 805-546-3122.. 41 A
deborah_wulff@cuesta.edu
WULLENJOHN, Bill .... 210-485-0391 429 C
wwullenjohn@alamo.edu
WUNDER, David .... 616-526-6869 222 A
dbw4@calvin.edu
WUNDERLICH,
Christina .... 402-471-2505 268 D
cwunderlich@nscs.edu
WUNKER, Charles .... 863-638-2916 113 B
wunkerc@webber.edu
WUNSCH, Michael .... 732-263-5355 279 B
mwunsch@monmouth.edu
WUORI, Misti, L .... 701-788-4631 345 E
misti.wuori@mayvillestate.edu
WURM, Sharon .... 775-673-7074 271 D
swurm@tmcc.edu
WURTZ, Cassie .... 785-243-1435 172 F
cwurtz@cloud.edu
WURTZ, Joseph .... 913-360-7500 171 D
jwurtz@benedictine.edu
WURTZ, Keith .... 909-389-3206.. 59 H
kwurtz@craftonhills.edu
WURZER, Christine .... 916-608-6645.. 50 H
wurzerc@flc.losrios.edu
WUSSOW, Helen .... 212-229-8947 308 C
wussowh@newschool.edu
WUTHRICH, Chris .... 208-426-1484 129 I
chriswuthrich@boisestate.edu
WUTHRICH, Philip .... 979-532-6305 458 F
philipw@wcjc.edu
WUTOH, Anthony, K ..... 202-806-2550.. 92 B
awutoh@howard.edu
WUTOH, Rita .... 301-860-4170 203 C
rwutoh@bowiestate.edu
WYANDOTTE,
Annette, M .... 812-941-2208 157 B
awyandot@ius.edu
WYANT, Gina .... 217-479-7047 142 I
gina.wyant@mac.edu
WYANT, Robert .... 585-395-2751 318 B
rwyant@brockport.edu
WYATT, Adrienne .... 573-681-5011 254 E
wyatta@lincolnu.edu
WYATT, Alicia .... 325-793-4748 440 B
wyatta@mcm.edu
WYATT, Ben .... 859-280-1246 183 B
bwyatt@lextheo.edu
WYATT, Bill, J .... 540-568-4908 468 F
wyattwj@jmu.edu
WYATT, Charles, W ...... 864-488-4603 410 E
cwyatt@limestone.edu
WYATT, Clarence, R ...... 309-457-2127 144 A
cwyatt@monmouthcollege.edu
WYATT, Danny .... 808-696-0714 129 D
dwyatt@hawaii.edu
WYATT, Gary .... 620-341-5254 172 L
gwyatt@emporia.edu
WYATT, Julie .... 870-972-3030.. 17 G
jwyatt@astate.edu
WYATT, Jymmyca .... 678-839-6431 126 E
jwyatt@westga.edu
WYATT, Mark, A .... 951-343-4474.. 27 J
mwyatt@calbaptist.edu
WYATT, Molly .... 252-985-5194 339 D
mwyatt@ncwc.edu
WYATT, Scott, L .... 435-586-7721 460 F
wyatt@suu.edu
WYATT, Shay .... 801-832-2344 461 G
swyatt@westminstercollege.edu
WYATT, Sybil .... 816-235-6705 261 C
wyattsb@umkc.edu
WYATT, Terri .... 804-257-5726 477 C
vuu@bkstr.com
WYATT, Victor .... 352-371-2833.. 97 G
admissions@dragonrises.edu
WYATT, Wendy, N .... 651-962-5253 244 E
wnwyatt@stthomas.edu
WYBLE, Shannon .... 410-778-7200 204 D
swyble2@washcoll.edu
WYBRANSKI, Andrea .... 305-821-3333.. 99 E
awybranski@fnu.edu
WYCHE, Louise .... 912-358-4323 123 H
wychel@savannahstate.edu
WYCHE, Lynn .... 850-973-9404 103 K
wychel@nfcc.edu
WYCKOFF, Steven .... 718-960-8720 294 A
steven.wyckoff@lehman.cuny.edu
WYCO, Jeff .... 304-205-6611 488 K
jeff.wyco@bridgevalley.edu
WYCOFF-HORN, Marcie 608-785-8127 496 F
mwycoff-horn@uwlax.edu
WYDEN, Leon .... 301-687-4335 203 E
llwyden@frostburg.edu
WYDER, Bruce .... 330-494-6170 361 F
bwyder@starkstate.edu
WYETT, Megan .... 315-792-7530 321 E
megan.wyett@sunypoly.edu
WYGMANS, Marty .... 570-389-4493 394 A
mwygmans@bloomu.edu
WYGONIK, Quri .... 734-384-4237 227 G
gwygonik@monroeccc.edu
WYKE, Rebecca, M .... 207-621-3041 196 A
wyke@maine.edu
WYKES, Paul .... 508-793-7385 208 A
pwykes@clarku.edu
WYKOFF, Randolph, F .. 423-439-4243 419 J
wykoff@etsu.edu
WYLAND, Debra .... 434-544-8200 472 G
wyland.d@lynchburg.edu
WYLIE, Brian .... 978-232-2440 209 B
bwylie@endicott.edu
WYLIE, Michael .... 513-569-1492 350 K
michael.wylie@cincinnatistate.edu
WYLIE, Nancy .... 903-988-7495 439 A
nwylie@kilgore.edu
WYLIE, Richard .... 770-454-9270.. 92 G
WYMAN, Derrick .... 330-490-7580 364 B
dwyman@walsh.edu
WYMER, Douglas, A ..... 352-365-3522 102 T
wymerd@lssc.edu
WYMER, Greg .... 605-688-4482 417 C
greg.wymer@sdstate.edu
WYMER-LUCERO,
Crystal .... 909-537-3084.. 33 A
clucero@csusb.edu
WYNDER, Robin .... 301-687-4050 203 E
rwynder@frostburg.edu
WYNDER, Tina, S .... 516-572-7771 308 A
tina.wynder@ncc.edu
WYNES, Tim .... 309-796-5001 132 G
WYNN, Amanda .... 757-352-4148 470 H
amanwyn@regent.edu
WYNN, Christina .... 413-236-2112 213 F
cwynn@berkshirecc.edu
WYNN, Curt, J .... 757-822-1460 476 B
cjwynn@tcc.edu
WYNN, Hal .... 334-386-7285.... 5 D
hwynn@faulkner.edu
WYNN, Keren .... 229-333-2103 127 B
keren.wynn@wiregrass.edu
WYNN, Laveria .... 803-327-7420 408 B
lwynn@clintoncollege.edu
WYNN, Sandra .... 304-327-4213 489 P
swynn@bluefieldstate.edu
WYNN, Steve .... 617-746-1990 210 E
steve.wynn@hult.edu
WYNN, Tor .... 316-295-5451 173 D
tor_wynn@friends.edu
WYNNE, Jeremy .... 509-777-4277 486 I
jwynne@whitworth.edu
WYNNE, Joshua .... 701-777-2516 345 C
joshua.wynne@med.und.edu
WYNNE, Joshua .... 701-777-2121 345 C
joshua.wynne@med.und.edu
WYNNE, Joshua .... 701-777-2514 345 C
joshua.wynne@med.und.edu
WYNNE, Shawn .... 847-317-7055 150 H
slwynne@tiu.edu
WYNSMA, Timothy, J .... 517-321-0242 224 F
twynsma@glcc.edu
WYNTER, Cadence .... 949-582-4958.. 64 G
cwynter@saddleback.edu
WYPISZYNSKI, Gregory 920-424-0007 497 B
wypiszyn@uwosh.edu
WYRICK, Cheryl .... 909-869-2431.. 30 D
crwyrick@cpp.edu
WYRICK, Karen .... 423-472-7141 424 F
kwyrick@clevelandstatecc.edu
WYRICK, Kathleen .... 907-564-8265.... 9 D
kwyrick@alaskapacific.edu
WYSCAVER, Sarah .... 970-339-6374.. 76 G
sarah.wyscaver@aims.edu
WYSE, Joe .... 530-242-7510.. 63 H
jwyse@shastacollege.edu
WYSOCKI, Joseph .... 704-461-6831 327 A
josephwysocki@bac.edu
WYSOKOWSKI, Kal, A .. 585-785-1206 300 B
kal.wysokowski@flcc.edu
WYSONG, James .... 813-253-7236 101 A
rwysong@hccfl.edu
WYSS, Lara .... 714-289-3143.. 36 C
lwyss@chapman.edu
WYSTEPEK, Christopher 413-782-1794 219 F
christopher.wystepek@wne.edu
WYTCHERLEY, Gary .... 562-777-4076.. 27 C
gary.wytcherley@biola.edu

X

XIA, Jingfeng .... 570-422-3152 394 E
jxia@esu.edu
XIE, Hao .... 323-415-4163.. 48 H
xiehy@elac.edu
XIE, Lei .... 630-466-7900 152 C
lxie@waubonsee.edu
XIE, Yan .... 909-748-8187.. 71 G
yan_xie@redlands.edu
XIMENEZ, David .... 817-515-5354 445 G
david.ximenez@tccd.edu
XIMINES, Sheryl, H ...... 919-516-4343 340 C
sximines@st-aug.edu
XIONG, Shoua .... 916-686-7400.. 29 J
XIONG-CHAN,
Mai Nhia .... 651-523-2440 236 A
mxiongchan01@hamline.edu
XIPPOLITOS, Lee .... 631-444-1041 317 D
lee.xippolitos@stonybrook.edu
XU, Amanda .... 707-468-3605.. 51 E
axu@mendocino.edu
XU, Juan .... 864-656-0585 408 A
jxu2@clemson.edu
XU, Qiang .... 404-727-2190 117 F
qxu30@emory.edu

Y

YACAVONE, Mark .... 607-753-4711 318 D
mark.yacavone@cortland.edu
YACKEE, Grace, B .... 734-384-4221 227 G
gyackee@monroeccc.edu
YACKEY, Kathleen .... 206-239-4500 479 E
kyackey@cityu.edu
YACKLEY, Don .... 713-743-6041 452 F
dyackely@uh.edu
YACKLEY-FRANKEN,
Nicki .... 605-882-5284 415 F
frankenn@lakeareatech.edu
YACONIS, Richard .... 312-261-3165 144 F
ryaconis@nl.edu
YADAMA, Gautam, N ..... 617-552-0866 207 B
gautam.yadama@bc.edu
YADON, Riley .... 701-774-4250 346 F
riley.yadon@willistonstate.edu
YAEGER, Bill .... 843-953-3842 407 F
bill.yaeger@citadel.edu
YAEGER, Evelyn .... 810-762-9782 225 H
eyaeger@kettering.edu
YAEGER, John, W .... 202-685-1330 503 I
yaegerj@ndu.edu
YAEGER, Sandy .... 985-543-4120 187 H
YAEZENKO, Suzette ...... 425-564-2266 478 F
suzette.yaezenko@bellevuecollege.edu
YAFAR, Jorge .... 212-220-8033 293 A
jyafar@bmcc.cuny.edu
YAGER, David .... 215-717-6030 400 J
dyager@uarts.edu
YAGER, Laura .... 559-278-6114.. 31 D
lyager@csufresno.edu
YAHNG, Charles .... 314-529-9312 254 H
cyahng@maryville.edu
YAHYAZADEH, Bizhan .. 802-485-2617 463 A
bizhan@norwich.edu
YAKLICH, Richard .... 305-430-1167.. 99 D
richard.yaklich@fmuniv.edu
YAKOVLEV, Ilya .... 717-815-2254 404 A
iyakovlev@ycp.edu
YAKOWICZ, William .... 201-612-5253 275 H
wyakowicz@bergen.edu
YAKSHE, Patti, L .... 412-281-2600 396 E
pyakshe@pci.edu
YAKUBOV, Michael .... 856-222-9311 281 C
myakubov@rcbc.edu
YALE, Amanda, A .... 724-738-2011 395 F
amanda.yale@sru.edu
YALE, Jacob, M .... 607-871-2406 289 H
yalej@alfred.edu
YAM, Marylou .... 410-532-5300 201 B
YAMADA, Emiko .... 650-508-3749.. 54 D
eyamada@ndnu.edu
YAMADA, Tetsuji .... 856-225-6136 281 G
tyamada@rutgers.edu
YAMAGATA-NOJI,
Audrey .... 909-274-4505.. 52 H
ayamagat@mtsac.edu
YAMAGUCHI, Ryan .... 808-956-8975 128 F
rtyamagu@hawaii.edu
YAMAKAWA, Lynn .... 310-233-4387.. 49 A
yamakalm@lahc.edu
YAMAMOTO, Catherine . 402-472-7749 269 J
cyamamoto1@unl.edu
YAMAMOTO, Cindy .... 808-984-3288 129 E
cindy@hawaii.edu
YAMAMOTO, Greg .... 626-396-2200.. 26 E
YAMAMOTO, Jessica ..... 808-934-2688 129 A
jpky@hawaii.edu
YAMAMOTO, June .... 909-389-3362.. 59 H
jyamamoto@craftonhills.edu
YAMAMOTO, Lance .... 808-956-5148 128 H
lance@hawaii.edu
YAMAMURA, Whitney ... 916-608-6572.. 50 H
yamamuw@flc.losrios.edu
YAMAOKA, Seiger .... 510-809-1444.. 45 K
YAMASAKI, Erika .... 310-954-4412.. 52 G
eyamasaki@msmu.edu
YAMBA, A. Zachary .... 973-877-3022 277 I
yamba@essex.edu
YAMBO, Marc .... 630-889-6517 144 G
myambo@nuhs.edu
YAMEEN, Deanna .... 508-588-9100 214 F
dyameen@massasoit.mass.edu
YAMPOLSKY, Chana ...... 212-964-2830 306 H
cpy145@aol.com
YAMRICK, Emmalyn .... 212-774-0751 306 A
eyamrick@mmm.edu
YAN, Ruth .... 319-226-2080 162 F
ruth.yan@allencollege.edu
YAN, Song .... 248-370-4146 229 G
songyan@oakland.edu
YANAI, Carolyn .... 702-463-2122 272 G
accounting@wongu.org
YANCEY, Amanda .... 706-385-1201 123 C
ayancey@point.edu
YANCEY, Jennifer, L ...... 361-582-2519 457 E
jennifer.yancey@victoriacollege.edu
YANCEY, John .... 606-218-5306 185 D
johnyancey@upike.edu

YANCEY, Laurica .... 919-658-7750 340 J
lyancey@umo.edu
YANCHAK, Frank .... 614-947-6723 353 C
frank.yanchak@franklin.edu
YANCY, Chad .... 205-929-3497.... 2 H
cyancy@lawsonstate.edu
YANDELL, April .... 817-257-7490 448 G
YANES, Kenneth .... 212-484-1339 294 D
kyanes@jjay.cuny.edu
YANEZ, Katy .... 602-827-2555.. 14 H
katy.yanez@nau.edu
YANEZ, Mary, A .... 915-831-7803 436 E
myanez22@epcc.edu
YANEZ, Mercy .... 310-233-4342.. 49 A
yanezm@lahc.edu
YANEZ, Robert .... 413-748-3104 218 G
ryanez@springfield.edu
YANG, Alice .... 831-459-2328.. 70 B
ayang@ucsc.edu
YANG, Angela .... 949-582-4602.. 64 G
lyang26@saddleback.edu
YANG, Anna .... 559-325-3600.. 28 H
ayang@chsu.edu
YANG, Anthony .... 973-618-3605 276 D
ayang@caldwell.edu
YANG, Blia .... 831-459-4179.. 70 B
blyang@ucsc.edu
YANG, Henry, T .... 805-893-2231.. 70 A
henry.yang@ucsb.edu
YANG, Hong .... 401-232-6885 404 F
hyang@bryant.edu
YANG, Honggang .... 954-262-3016 103 M
yangh@nsu.nova.edu
YANG, Jian .... 516-364-0808 309 A
jyang@nycollege.edu
YANG, K. Wayne .... 858-822-2824.. 69 D
kwayne@ucsd.edu
YANG, Katherine .... 916-686-7400.. 29 J
YANG, Kyung Mi .... 770-220-7923 118 B
akbcyang@gcuniv.edu
YANG, Lykos .... 408-260-0208.. 42 M
sjextension@fivebranches.edu
YANG, Neng .... 503-838-8590 377 H
yangn@wou.edu
YANG, Nicole .... 920-693-1120 499 G
nicole.yang@gotoltc.edu
YANG, Olivia .... 509-335-5571 486 A
olivia.yang@wsu.edu
YANG, Pakou .... 651-779-3288 237 G
pakou.yang@century.edu
YANG, Paul Zhaohui ..... 628-448-0023.. 46 G
vp-admin@itsla.edu
YANG, Phong .... 559-278-2048.. 31 D
pyang@csufresno.edu
YANG, Tony .... 269-471-3354 221 B
tonyy@andrews.edu
YANG, Xong Sony .... 309-794-8274 132 C
xongsonyyang@augustana.edu
YANKANICH, Julie .... 856-227-7200 276 E
jyankanich@camdencc.edu
YANKELEWITZ, Yoel ..... 718-846-1940 326 A
yyankelewitz@gmail.com
YANKELITIS, Wendy ...... 570-348-6201 389 G
yankelitis@marywood.edu
YANKEY, Terry, L .... 606-474-3222 180 G
tly@kcu.edu
YANNI, Stephen .... 906-248-8478 221 N
syanni@bmcc.edu
YANNICK, Lisa .... 610-436-3075 396 A
lyannick@wcupa.edu
YANNIELLO, Kristin ...... 718-405-3252 296 G
kristin.yanniello@mountsaintvincent.edu
YAO, Chunmei .... 910-521-6295 343 B
chunmei.yao@uncp.edu
YAO, Marian .... 408-924-2012.. 34 B
marian.yao@sjsu.edu
YAO, Min .... 562-985-5459.. 31 F
min.yao@csulb.edu
YAO, Richard, D .... 805-437-8536.. 30 F
richard.yao@csuci.edu
YAP, Michael .... 213-252-5100.. 23 K
myap@alu.edu
YAQUB, Samia .... 530-895-2484.. 27 F
yaqubsa@butte.edu
YARABECK, John .... 936-294-1785 450 C
slo_jxy@shsu.edu
YARBROUGH, Boyd ...... 864-388-8239 410 D
byarbrough@lander.edu
YARBROUGH, David ..... 337-482-1015 192 E
yarbrough@louisiana.edu
YARBROUGH, Denise ... 585-275-4321 323 J
dyarbrough@admin.rochester.edu
YARBROUGH, Erin, A ... 405-325-0206 371 B
eyarbrough@ou.edu
YARBROUGH, John ...... 706-865-2134 125 E
jyarbrough@truett.edu
YARBROUGH, Laura ..... 870-508-6122.. 18 A
lyarbrough@asumh.edu
YARBROUGH, Laura, L . 336-249-8186 334 A
laura_yarbrough@davidsonccc.edu
YARBROUGH, Mark, M 214-887-5011 436 B
myarbrough@dts.edu
YARBROUGH, Rachel .... 812-749-1399 159 C
ryarbrough@oak.edu
YARBROUGH, Scott ...... 843-863-7563 407 E
syarbrou@csuniv.edu
YARDLEY, Katherine ..... 207-778-7276 196 B
kyardley@maine.edu
YARDLEY, Owen .... 402-472-8809 269 J
oyardley2@unl.edu
YARLOTT, JR., David .... 406-638-3107 263 H
davidyarlott@lbhc.edu
YARMAGYAN, Samuel .. 916-877-7977.. 58 J
sam@sui.edu
YARNELL, Thomas, V ... 614-823-1502 360 A
tyarnell@otterbein.edu
YAROFAISUG, Faustino . 691-320-2481 505 B
yaro@comfsm.fm
YARRISH, James .... 215-895-1114 401 G
j.yarris@usciences.edu
YARROW, Lisa .... 713-646-1893 444 B
lyarrow@stcl.edu
YARSIAH, James .... 803-780-1264 414 E
jyarsiah@voorhees.edu
YARWOOD, Denise .... 717-477-1395 395 E
dsyarwood@ship.edu
YASECKO, Susan .... 312-662-4415 131 H
syasecko@adler.edu
YASINSAC, Alec .... 251-460-6390.... 8 F
yasinsac@southalabama.edu
YASSERI, Darioush .... 405-945-6761 368 E
yasseri@osuokc.edu
YASSKY, David .... 914-422-4407 311 E
dyassky@pace.edu
YASUDA, Cathy .... 541-881-5585 377 B
cyasuda@tvcc.cc
YASUKOCHI, Dennis ..... 206-934-5479 484 A
dennis.yasukochi@seattlecolleges.edu
YATER, Ann .... 317-917-5915 157 G
aniebrug@ivytech.edu
YATES, Betty .... 931-540-2504 424 G
byates@columbiastate.edu
YATES, Brian .... 434-592-3371 468 H
bcyates@liberty.edu
YATES, Brice .... 812-237-8954 155 G
brice.yates@indstate.edu
YATES, Cheryl .... 812-749-1416 159 C
cyates@oak.edu
YATES, Deanna .... 270-706-8658 181 A
dyates0031@kctcs.edu
YATES, Deirdre .... 973-275-2191 283 B
deirdre.yates@shu.edu
YATES, Dorothy .... 407-823-2047 109 E
dorothy.yates@ucf.edu
YATES, Emilie .... 308-632-6933 269 E
YATES, Frances .... 765-973-8470 156 C
fyates@iue.edu
YATES, Jacob .... 606-337-4524 179 G
registrar@ccbbc.edu
YATES, James .... 870-864-7156.. 21 B
jyates@southark.edu
YATES, Jamie .... 717-337-6000 384 H
YATES, Kristin .... 402-472-5242 269 H
kyates@nebraska.edu
YATES, Latoro .... 718-262-2188 295 F
lyates@york.cuny.edu
YATES, III, Lucian .... 502-597-6395 182 H
lucian.yates@kysu.edu
YATES, Matthew .... 860-486-5022.. 88 E
matthew.yates@uconn.edu
YATES, Stephanie, L ..... 217-554-1628 135 H
syates@dacc.edu
YATES, Susan .... 559-325-5340.. 66 D
susan.yates@cloviscollege.edu
YATES, Vivian .... 216-987-4468 351 G
vivian.yates@tri-c.edu
YATES SEAMAN, Liz ..... 610-861-1505 391 A
yatese@moravian.edu
YATS, Kirk, M .... 989-774-3674 222 C
yats1km@cmich.edu
YAU, Tow, Y .... 718-990-6384 314 B
yaut@stjohns.edu
YAVAS, Debora .... 310-377-5501.. 51 B
dyavas@marymountcalifornia.edu
YAVAS, Debra .... 310-377-5501.. 51 B
dyavas@marymountcalifornia.edu
YAVNEH, Naomi .... 504-865-7330 189 F
yavneh@loyno.edu
YAVNEH KLOS, Naomi . 509-359-2822 480 E
nyavnehklos@ewu.edu
YAVOR, Susan .... 610-341-4363 383 D
syavor@eastern.edu
YAVORSKI, Ginger .... 610-861-5494 391 F
gyavorski@northampton.edu
YAZDANI, Linda .... 303-914-6536.. 82 C
linda.yazdani@rrcc.edu
YAZDI, Aliakbar, R .... 205-853-1200.... 2 G
ayazdi@jeffersonstate.edu
YAZDI, Reza .... 510-430-2209.. 52 D
ryazdi@mills.edu
YAZEDJIAN, Ani .... 309-438-7018 139 E
ayazedj@ilstu.edu
YAZZIE, Lambert .... 480-732-7205.. 12 P
lambert.yazzie@cgc.edu
YBARRA, David .... 910-522-5793 343 B
david.ybarra@uncp.edu
YBARRA, Kathy .... 206-296-2810 484 F
ybarrak@seattleu.edu
YBARRA, Nancy .... 925-473-7405.. 40 J
nybarra@losmedanos.edu
YBARRA, Paul .... 916-577-2200.. 75 B
pybarra@jessup.edu
YBARRA, Tomas .... 509-574-4640 487 A
tybarra@yvcc.edu
YDOYAGA, Shannon ..... 817-515-4507 445 G
shannon.ydoyaga@tccd.edu
YDRACH, Gloriana .... 787-728-1515 514 D
gloriana.ydrach@sagrado.edu
YE, Eugene .... 630-942-3821 135 A
yee8@cod.edu
YEAGER, Andrew .... 716-880-2336 306 C
ayeager@medaille.edu
YEAGER, Daniel .... 619-239-0391.. 34 F
dyeager@cwsl.edu
YEAGER, Daphne .... 601-477-4151 246 F
daphne.yeager@jcjc.edu
YEAGER, Deonne .... 843-208-8723 413 E
deonne@uscb.edu
YEAGER, Edward .... 480-732-7177.. 12 P
ed.yeager@cgc.edu
YEAGER, Eric .... 432-335-6412 441 D
eyeager@odessa.edu
YEAGER, Kathrine, H .... 928-523-3173.. 14 H
kathrine.yeager@nau.edu
YEAGER, Lisa .... 763-657-2401 238 B
lisa.yaeger@hennepintech.edu
YEAGER, Susan .... 209-575-6530.. 75 H
yeagers@yosemite.edu
YEAGLEY, JR., William . 989-774-3081 222 C
yeagl1b@cmich.edu
YEANY, Ron .... 617-353-1701 207 D
ryeany@bu.edu
YEAP, Soon Beng .... 303-765-3110.. 80 F
syeap@iliff.edu
YEARBY, Annette .... 386-481-2364.. 95 F
yearbya@cookman.edu
YEARNS, Ellie, P .... 336-272-7102 329 D
ellie.yearns@greensboro.edu
YEAROUT, Teresa, A ..... 276-964-7266 475 I
teresa.yearout@sw.edu
YEARSON, Stephen .... 217-854-5787 132 I
stephen.yearson@blackburn.edu
YEARWOOD, George, A 919-508-2035 344 F
ryearwood@peace.edu
YEARWOOD, Jody .... 478-387-4392 118 G
jyearwood@gmc.edu
YEATS, John Mark .... 816-414-3700 256 A
jmyeats@mbts.edu
YEATTS, Debra .... 910-630-7385 331 C
dyeatts@methodist.edu
YEBOAH, Barima .... 718-405-3414 296 G
barima.yeboah@mountsaintvincent.edu
YECK, Alan .... 607-735-1825 299 D
ayeck@elmira.edu
YECKLEY, Trae .... 814-332-4368 378 D
tyeckley@allegheny.edu
YEE, David .... 415-239-3669.. 37 A
dyee@ccsf.edu
YEE, Ellen .... 617-585-0200 206 F
ellen.yee@the-bac.edu
YEE, Gary .... 402-559-5108 270 A
gcyee@unmc.edu
YEE, Helen .... 614-825-6255 347 F
hyee@aiam.edu
YEE, Jill .... 415-239-3174.. 37 A
jyee@ccsf.edu
YEGHIAYAN, Paul .... 510-925-4282.. 25 Q
pyeghiayan@aua.am
YEH, Lisa .... 212-870-2530 290 J
lyeh@barnard.edu
YEHUDAH, Shoshana ... 646-565-6000 322 J
shoshana.yehudah@touro.edu
YEIGH, Bjong, W .... 425-352-5221 485 F
yeigh@uw.edu
YEKOVICH, Robert .... 713-348-4837 442 K
yekovr@rice.edu
YELKUR, Rama .... 585-385-8098 314 A
ryelkur@sjfc.edu
YELLE, Richard .... 203-576-4755.. 88 D
ryelle@bridgeport.edu
YELLIN, Dina .... 732-367-1060 275 J
dyelllin@bmg.edu
YELLS, David .... 903-223-3003 448 B
dyells@tamut.edu
YELNOSKY, Michael, J . 401-254-4509 405 E
myelnosky@law.rwu.edu
YELTON, David .... 704-406-3522 329 A
dyelton@gardner-webb.edu
YELTON, Kristen .... 636-481-3296 254 A
kyelton@jeffco.edu
YEN, Charlie .... 310-434-3002.. 62 E
yen_charlie@smc.edu
YEN, Debbie .... 870-733-6764.. 17 H
dyen@asumidsouth.edu
YEN, Johanna, C .... 954-763-9840.. 94 L
atom@atom.edu
YENCER, Kristen .... 302-857-1401.. 90 D
kristen.yencer@dtcc.edu
YENCHO, Thomas .... 610-409-3491 402 A
tyencho@ursinus.edu
YENDOL-HOPPEY,
Diane .... 904-620-2520 110 A
diane.yendol-hoppy@unf.edu
YENTES, Matt .... 863-638-2963 113 B
yentesms@webber.edu
YEOH, Deborah .... 212-327-8071 313 B
yeohd@rockefeller.edu
YEOH, Kim .... 607-255-6240 297 F
controller@cornell.edu
YEOM, Kyong, S .... 636-327-4645 255 L
yeom900@gmail.com
YEON LIM, Tae .... 714-222-1110.. 27 I
YEONOPOLUS, Jim .... 254-526-1214 432 H
jyeonopolus@ctcd.edu
YEP, Kathleen .... 909-607-7304.. 56 J
kathleen_yep@jsd.claremont.edu
YERDON, Melinda .... 419-559-2289 361 I
myerdon@terra.edu
YERDON, Wayne .... 419-559-2341 361 I
wyerdon@terra.edu
YERGEN, Norman .... 951-785-2307.. 47 C
nyergen@lasierra.edu
YERMAKOV, Andrei .... 310-900-1600.. 40 A
ayermakov@elcamino.edu
YERSE, Jeremy, T .... 724-847-5670 384 G
jtyerse@geneva.edu
YESTRAMSKI, Joanne .... 978-934-2206 211 G
joanne_yestramski@uml.edu
YEVICH, Nicolette .... 660-248-6255 251 B
nyevich@centralmethodist.edu
YEZIERSKI, Ellen, J ...... 513-529-9266 356 E
yeziere@miamioh.edu
YIANILOS, Chris .... 571-858-3005 477 A
chrisyianilos@vt.edu
YIH, T. C .... 239-590-7021 108 K
tcyih@fgcu.edu
YILDIRIM, Seval .... 909-537-5029.. 33 A
seval.yildirim@csusb.edu
YILIBUW, Dolores .... 859-280-1224 183 B
dyilibuw@lextheo.edu
YIM, Mee So .... 910-932-6895 343 C
ctr-yimm@uncw.edu
YIM, Sooyoung .... 703-629-1281 473 E
YIM, Steven .... 657-278-4075.. 31 E
syim@fullerton.edu
YIN, Alexander, C .... 802-656-4418 463 E
alexander.yin@uvm.edu
YIN, Carol .... 706-880-8339 121 A
cyin@lagrange.edu
YIN, Chengbo .... 973-353-5541 282 B
cy188@newark.rutgers.edu
YIN, Kong .... 713-221-8975 453 B
yink@uhd.edu
YINGLING, Julie, R .... 419-434-4550 363 A
yinglingj@findlay.edu
YIONOULIS, Evan .... 212-799-5000 303 H
YIP, Koyuki .... 610-526-6004 385 G
kyip@harcum.edu

YIP, Yunny .... 415-575-6171.. 29 B
yyip@ciis.edu
YIP-REYES, Judy .... 928-532-6148.. 14 J
judy.yip-reyes@npc.edu
YLINEN, Jeff .... 612-381-3085 235 H
jylinen@dunwoody.edu
YOACHIM, Maureen ...... 610-740-3725 381 A
bookstore@cedarcrest.edu
YOAKUM, Katrina, M .... 785-864-3261 177 D
kyoakum@ku.edu
YOAKUM, Richard .... 205-726-2056.... 6 E
ryoakum@samford.edu
YOCHUM, Henry .... 434-381-6357 472 D
hyochum@sbc.edu
YOCHUM, SC, Susan ..... 724-830-1044 398 H
yochum@setonhill.edu
YOCKEY, Glenn .... 830-372-8040 449 B
gyockey@tlu.edu
YOCOM, Amber .... 419-267-1317 358 A
ayocom@northweststate.edu
YOCUM, Carrie, A .... 574-372-5100 155 B
yocumca@grace.edu
YOCUM, Heather .... 502-213-5200 181 F
heather.yocum@kctcs.edu
YOCUM, Jennifer .... 410-888-9048 200 A
jyocum@muih.edu
YODER, Amy .... 716-829-7625 298 F
yodera@dyc.edu
YODER, Brent .... 620-327-8207 173 H
brent.yoder@hesston.edu
YODER, Brooke .... 816-654-7103 254 C
byoder@kcumb.edu
YODER, David .... 916-348-4689.. 42 C
dyoder@epic.edu
YODER, John .... 903-877-7443 456 D
john.yoder@uthct.edu
YODER, John-David, S . 419-772-2372 358 H
j-yoder@onu.edu
YODER, Joseph, S .... 570-326-3761 393 G
jyoder@pct.edu
YODER, Julie .... 301-387-3101 198 F
julie.yoder@garrettcollege.edu
YODER, Kathleen .... 574-535-7501 155 A
kathleeny@goshen.edu
YODER, Katie .... 913-758-6104 177 F
katie.yoder@stmary.edu
YODER, Lane .... 931-393-1692 425 C
lyoder@mscc.edu
YODER, Marilyn .... 218-755-3790 237 E
marilyn.yoder@bemidjistate.edu
YODER, Mindy, J .... 260-399-7700 161 D
myoder@sf.edu
YODER, Norris .... 828-328-7145 330 F
norris.yoder@lr.edu
YOHE, Michael .... 863-667-5306 107 K
meyohe@seu.edu
YOHE, Roger .... 561-868-3147 104 D
yoher@palmbeachstate.edu
YOHNK, Dean .... 715-425-3777 497 E
dean.yohnk@uwrf.edu
YOHNK LOCKWOOD,
Susan .... 715-682-4591 501 B
susan.lockwood@witc.edu
YOHO, Robert .... 515-271-1464 164 I
robert.yoho@dmu.edu
YOHO, Steven .... 912-650-6200 124 E
syoho@southuniversity.edu
YOKOYAMA, Janis, K .... 213-738-6714.. 65 G
deansoffice@swlaw.edu
YOLITZ, Brian, D .... 651-201-1777 237 A
brian.yolitz@minnstate.edu
YOLO, Laura .... 509-574-4775 487 A
lyolo@yvcc.edu
YON, Rita .... 650-543-3722.. 51 F
rita.yon@menlo.edu
YONAN, Glen .... 530-251-8815.. 47 F
gyonan@lassencollege.edu
YONCE EASTHAM,
Yvette .... 270-707-3731 181 E
yvette.eastham@kctcs.edu
YONEMITSU, Lori .... 206-546-4552 484 G
lyonemitsu@shoreline.edu
YONG, Amos .... 626-584-5265.. 43 H
amosyong@fuller.edu
YONG, Amos .... 626-584-5304.. 43 H
amosyong@fuller.edu
YONG, Ann .... 701-231-8356 345 G
ann.young@ndsu.edu
YONG, Henry .... 209-575-6508.. 75 H
yongh@yosemite.edu
YONG, Yanyan .... 540-834-1048 474 G
yyong@germanna.edu
YONKE, Eric .... 715-346-4224 497 F
eyonke@uwsp.edu
YONKE, Eric .... 715-346-3693 497 F
eyonke@uwsp.edu
YONKERS, Molly, L ...... 507-933-7588 235 I
myunkers@gustavus.edu
YONTZ, Jennifer .... 231-591-3817 223 J
jenniferyontz@ferris.edu
YOO, David, K .... 310-825-6815.. 69 A
dkyoo@ucla.edu
YOO, Ellie .... 805-289-6182.. 73 B
jyoo@vcccd.edu
YOO, Hee-duck .... 901-949-6557 123 D
hd.yoo@runiv.edu
YOO, John .... 703-323-5690 477 D
YOO, John .... 703-425-4143 468 E
YOO, Young, C .... 703-333-5904 478 B
ycyoo@wuv.edu
YOON, Ho Sung .... 213-384-2318.. 50 C
YOON, Jong, S .... 714-533-3946.. 34 D
jyoon@calums.edu
YOON, Jong, S .... 714-533-3946.. 34 D
jsyoon@calums.edu
YOON, Mary .... 213-384-2318.. 50 C
YOON, Michelle .... 562-926-1023.. 57 G
office@ptsa.edu
YOON, Myungsoon .... 510-639-7879.. 54 G
YOON, Rachel .... 323-860-1170.. 53 B
rachel@mi.edu
YOON, Richard, S .... 770-831-9500 125 F
YOON, Sung Hoon .... 714-533-1495.. 64 D
shyoon@southbaylo.edu
YOPP, Jan .... 919-966-4364 342 D
jan_yopp@unc.edu
YORDY, Brad .... 765-998-5112 160 F
bryordy@taylor.edu
YORGES, Judi .... 402-471-2505 268 D
jyorges@nscs.edu
YORK, Barry, J .... 412-731-6000 397 E
byork@rpts.edu
YORK, Corey .... 914-251-6080 319 E
corey.york@purchase.edu
YORK, David .... 512-492-3032 430 G
dyork@aoma.edu
YORK, Heather .... 207-699-5521 194 D
hyork@meca.edu
YORK, Hershael .... 502-897-4112 184 C
hyork@sbts.edu
YORK, Nancy .... 502-272-8639 179 B
nyork@bellarmine.edu
YORK, Robert .... 805-893-2944.. 70 A
rayork@ece.ucsb.edu
YORK, Ronald, S .... 803-536-8438 412 C
ryork1@scsu.edu
YORK, Wendy .... 864-656-3178 408 A
bizdean@clemson.edu
YORKE, Carla .... 562-860-2451.. 35 M
cyorke@cerritos.edu
YORKIN, Sheila .... 801-832-2685 461 G
syorkin@westminstercollege.edu
YORTSOS, Yannis, C .... 213-740-0617.. 72 B
yortsos@usc.edu
YOSHIMI, Garret .... 808-956-2717 128 F
gyoshimi@hawaii.edu
YOSHIMI, Garret, T .... 808-956-3501 128 D
gyoshimi@hawaii.edu
YOSHIMORI-YAMAMOTO,
Denise .... 808-956-0864 128 H
dfyoshim@hawaii.edu
YOSHIMURA, Gregg ...... 808-455-0607 129 D
greggy@hawaii.edu
YOSHIMURA, Nancy ..... 949-480-4045.. 64 B
nyoshimura@soka.edu
YOSHINAGA, Darcie, S . 808-956-8259 128 D
dsy@hawaii.edu
YOSHIOKA, Marianne ... 413-585-7977 218 F
myoshioka@smith.edu
YOST, April .... 269-467-9945 224 A
YOST, Carol .... 570-577-3733 379 F
cyost@bucknell.edu
YOUDE, Jeremy .... 218-726-8981 243 F
jyoude@d.umn.edu
YOUHOUSE, John .... 610-558-5518 391 D
youhousj@neumann.edu
YOUKEY, Jerry, R .... 864-455-7992 413 C
youkey@mailbox.sc.edu
YOUKEY, Jerry, R .... 864-455-7992 414 A
youkey@greenvillemed.sc.edu
YOUMANS, Jeremy .... 479-619-2224.. 20 D
jyoumans@nwacc.edu
YOUMANS, Karen .... 405-208-5680 367 I
kdyoumans@okcu.edu
YOUNG, Aaron .... 505-984-6140 287 J
aaron.young@sjc.edu
YOUNG, Alissa .... 270-707-3711 181 E
alissa.young@kctcs.edu
YOUNG, Amy .... 269-467-9945 224 A
ayoung@glenoaks.edu
YOUNG, Amy .... 972-721-4127 452 D
ayoung@udallas.edu
YOUNG, Andrea .... 213-356-5371.. 64 H
andrea_young@sciarc.edu
YOUNG, Andrea, N .... 920-748-8180 495 G
younga@ripon.edu
YOUNG, Andrew .... 812-888-4323 162 C
ayoung@vinu.edu
YOUNG, Andrew .... 256-726-8333.... 6 C
ayoung@oakwood.edu
YOUNG, Angela .... 323-343-2810.. 32 A
ayoung3@calstatela.edu
YOUNG, Ann, S .... 859-238-5480 179 F
ann.young@centre.edu
YOUNG, Art .... 435-797-1455 460 H
art.young@usu.edu
YOUNG, Barbara .... 502-776-1443 184 B
byoung@simmonscollegeky.edu
YOUNG, Beth .... 815-921-4445 147 E
b.young@rockvalleycollege.edu
YOUNG, Betsy .... 760-636-7959.. 39 A
byoung@alumni.collegeofthedesert.edu
YOUNG, Betty .... 478-553-2090 122 G
byoung@oftc.edu
YOUNG, Betty .... 740-753-7009 354 A
youngb@hocking.edu
YOUNG, Bill .... 316-323-6363 171 G
wyoung@butlercc.edu
YOUNG, Bill .... 910-480-5441 331 C
YOUNG, Bob .... 517-353-3530 227 D
youngjrr@msu.edu
YOUNG, Brandon .... 217-540-3512 141 D
byoung17159@lakeland.cc.il.us
YOUNG, Brandon, L ...... 386-226-7245.. 98 A
youngbr@erau.edu
YOUNG, Brian .... 719-389-6971.. 77 H
byoung@coloradocollege.edu
YOUNG, Carl .... 212-799-5000 303 H
YOUNG, Carole .... 651-638-6316 234 C
youcar@bethel.edu
YOUNG, Cathy .... 617-747-2316 206 E
ootp@berklee.edu
YOUNG, Charles .... 203-596-4604.. 87 F
cyoung@post.edu
YOUNG, Charles .... 336-334-4822 335 A
hcyoung@gtcc.edu
YOUNG, Cheryl, D .... 513-529-8600 356 E
youngcd@miamioh.edu
YOUNG, Christopher .... 219-980-6563 156 E
cjy@iun.edu
YOUNG, Clifton .... 804-862-6100 470 I
cyoung@rbc.edu
YOUNG, Colletta .... 541-956-7296 376 D
cyoung@roguecc.edu
YOUNG, Connie .... 217-709-0931 141 E
cyoung@lakeviewcol.edu
YOUNG, Courtney .... 315-228-7361 296 F
clyoung@colgate.edu
YOUNG, Crystal .... 231-843-5731 232 J
cyoung2@westshore.edu
YOUNG, Cynthia .... 864-656-3642 408 A
cyyoung@clemson.edu
YOUNG, Dale .... 478-445-5497 118 C
dale.young@gcsu.edu
YOUNG, Dan .... 219-473-4292 153 G
dyoung1@ccsj.edu
YOUNG, Dana .... 541-881-5580 377 B
dyoung@tvcc.cc
YOUNG, Danielle .... 440-775-8692 358 C
danielle.young@oberlin.edu
YOUNG, Darlene, P .... 812-941-2306 157 B
dyoung01@ius.edu
YOUNG, David .... 417-255-7910 256 F
davidyoung@missouristate.edu
YOUNG, David .... 405-974-2490 370 K
dyoung28@uco.edu
YOUNG, Debbie .... 559-278-2381.. 31 D
debbiey@csufresno.edu
YOUNG, Derek, M .... 240-895-4207 201 E
dmyoung@smcm.edu
YOUNG, Djuana .... 817-531-4422 451 E
YOUNG, Donna .... 480-423-6300.. 13 H
donna.young@scottsdalecc.edu
YOUNG, Eldon .... 714-484-7177.. 53 K
eyoung@cypresscollege.edu
YOUNG, Elisabeth, H .... 330-325-6311 357 G
eyoung1@neomed.edu
YOUNG, Elizabeth .... 262-551-8500 492 F
YOUNG, Eric .... 330-829-8238 363 B
younger@mountunion.edu
YOUNG, Frank .... 801-863-7202 461 A
frank.young@uvu.edu
YOUNG, Garland .... 423-461-8720 422 J
rgyoung@milligan.edu
YOUNG, Gary .... 312-949-7610 138 E
gyoung@ico.edu
YOUNG, Gerald .... 507-222-4057 234 F
gyoung@carleton.edu
YOUNG, Grace, Y .... 617-336-5083 214 A
grace.young@bhcc.mass.edu
YOUNG, Gretchen .... 508-286-4950 220 A
young_gretchen@wheatoncollege.edu
YOUNG, Gwendolyn ...... 719-549-2602.. 79 A
gwen.young@csupueblo.edu
YOUNG, Harvey .... 617-358-1725 207 D
harveyy@bu.edu
YOUNG, Heather, M ...... 916-734-4745.. 68 E
heather.young@ucdmc.ucdavis.edu
YOUNG, Henry .... 401-739-5000 405 A
hyoung@neit.edu
YOUNG, J.R .... 412-536-1100 387 B
jr.young@laroche.edu
YOUNG, Jamyra .... 315-279-5295 304 A
jyoung1@keuka.edu
YOUNG, Jason .... 517-263-0731 230 E
jyoung6@sienaheights.edu
YOUNG, Jeff .... 206-934-3646 483 J
jeffrey.young2@seattlecolleges.edu
YOUNG, Jen .... 412-397-5452 397 G
youngj@rmu.edu
YOUNG, Jessica .... 704-290-5261 337 I
YOUNG, Jill .... 570-389-4950 394 A
jyoung@bloomu.edu
YOUNG, Joanne .... 603-888-1311 274 B
YOUNG, John .... 973-328-5026 277 B
jyoung@ccm.edu
YOUNG, John .... 315-781-3748 302 A
jyoung@hws.edu
YOUNG, John .... 303-360-4707.. 79 D
john.young@ccaurora.edu
YOUNG, John, O .... 248-370-2946 229 G
joyoung@oakland.edu
YOUNG, Johnny, W ...... 757-683-3442 469 G
jwyoung@odu.edu
YOUNG, Jon .... 910-672-2175 341 E
jyoung@uncfsu.edu
YOUNG, Kalbert, K .... 808-956-8903 128 D
kalbert@hawaii.edu
YOUNG, Kelly .... 315-781-3783 302 A
keyoung@hws.edu
YOUNG, Ken .... 516-323-4501 307 F
kyoung@molloy.edu
YOUNG, Kerry, A .... 315-786-2279 303 F
kyoung@sunyjefferson.edu
YOUNG, Kim .... 760-252-2411.. 26 I
kyoung@barstow.edu
YOUNG, Kimberly .... 540-286-8076 472 I
kyoung@umw.edu
YOUNG, Kirk .... 716-338-1023 303 D
kirkyoung@mail.sunyjcc.edu
YOUNG, Kristi .... 903-927-3219 458 G
kyoung@wileyc.edu
YOUNG, Kristina .... 425-352-8550 479 A
kyoung@cascadia.edu
YOUNG, Kristine .... 775-881-7509 272 D
kyoung@sierranevada.edu
YOUNG, Kristine, K .... 775-881-7509 272 D
kyoung@sierranevada.edu
YOUNG, Kristine, M ...... 845-341-4700 311 C
president@sunyorange.edu
YOUNG, Lauren .... 716-888-2436 292 D
youngb@canisius.edu
YOUNG, Leah .... 717-245-1308 382 F
youngle@dickinson.edu
YOUNG, Lee .... 903-886-5101 447 B
lee.young@tamuc.edu
YOUNG, Leslie .... 760-773-2580.. 39 A
lyoung@collegeofthedesert.edu
YOUNG, Linda, C .... 334-556-2234.... 2 C
lyoung@wallace.edu
YOUNG, Linda, K .... 715-836-5287 496 D
younglk@uwec.edu
YOUNG, Lindsay .... 361-485-4485 453 C
youngle@uhv.edu
YOUNG, Luria .... 225-771-4582 190 G
luria_young@subr.edu
YOUNG, Marie .... 814-472-3022 398 B
myoung@francis.edu
YOUNG, Mark, S .... 303-762-6902.. 79 H
president@denverseminary.edu

Z

ZAJACESKOWSKI, John 518-244-2253 313 D
zajacj@sage.edu
ZAJCHOWSKI, Ann .... 860-727-6757.. 87 A
azajchowski@goodwin.edu
ZAJDA, Vito .... 908-737-0483 278 E
vzajda@kean.edu
ZAK, Jennifer .... 912-279-5806 116 G
jzak@ccga.edu
ZAK, Leocadia (Lee), I . 404-471-6000 113 G
president@agnesscott.edu
ZAKAHI, Walter, R .... 309-677-3152 133 B
wzakahi@fsmail.bradley.edu
ZAKARIAN, Kathy, W .... 570-326-3761 393 G
kathy.zakarian@pct.edu
ZAKARIAN, Michael ...... 212-517-0400 306 A
ZAKE, Ieva .... 717-871-7205 395 D
ieva.zake@millersville.edu
ZAKERY, Fatemeh .... 314-340-5096 253 I
zakeryf@hssu.edu
ZAKRAYSEK, Chris .... 814-254-0442 381 F
czakraysek@pa.gov
ZAKRZEWSKI, Bruce ..... 269-467-9945 224 A
bzakrzewski@glenoaks.edu
ZALAPI, Diane .... 248-476-1122 227 C
dzalapi@msp.edu
ZALBA, Jeanette .... 734-487-1300 223 H
jzalba@emich.edu
ZALESKI, Shane .... 937-604-4743 362 D
shane.zaleski@uc.edu
ZALKIND, Carrie .... 626-529-8007.. 55 A
czalkind@pacificoaks.edu
ZALOUDEK, Julie .... 651-773-1741 237 G
julie.zaloudek@century.edu
ZAMA, Aparna, M .... 848-932-8495 282 A
zama@rutgers.edu
ZAMAN, Maliha .... 610-902-8502 380 C
maliha.s.zaman@cabrini.edu
ZAMAN, Naveed .... 304-766-3394 491 B
zamanna@wvstateu.edu
ZAMBARDI, Victor, A ... 248-370-3112 229 G
zambardi@oakland.edu
ZAMBITO-HILL, Angela . 304-336-8847 490 F
angie.hill@westliberty.edu
ZAMBLE, Anthony .... 773-244-5568 145 A
azamble@northpark.edu
ZAMBON, Joseph, J ..... 716-829-3940 316 F
jjzambon@buffalo.edu
ZAMBONINO, Maria ..... 773-878-3813 148 D
mzambonino@staugustine.edu
ZAMBRANA, Maritza ..... 787-279-1912 509 A
mzambrana@bayamon.inter.edu
ZAMBRANO, Susanna ... 928-314-9422.. 10 J
susanna.zambrano@azwestern.edu
ZAMBRANO, Thomas ..... 732-987-2613 278 B
tzambrano@georgian.edu
ZAMBROTTA, Diana ...... 212-517-0593 306 A
dzambrotta@mmm.edu
ZAMIARA, Aubrey .... 585-292-2142 307 H
azamiara1@monroecc.edu
ZAMOJSKI, Heather ...... 219-989-2296 159 G
zamojski@pnw.edu
ZAMOJSKI, Heather ...... 219-989-2996 159 G
zamojski@pnw.edu
ZAMORA, Bradley .... 847-970-4581 152 A
bzamora@usml.edu
ZAMORA, Sue .... 618-985-2828 139 I
suezamora@jalc.edu
ZAMORA, Teri .... 281-998-6306 443 B
teri.zamora@sjcd.edu
ZAMPANO, Gary, S ...... 570-941-4273 401 H
gary.zampano@scranton.edu
ZAMPARELLI, Jaime ..... 609-497-7725 280 D
seminary.relations@ptsem.edu
ZAMSKY, Florence .... 914-487-4318 109 D
fzamsky@ncf.edu
ZANCHELLI, Denise ...... 845-451-1458 298 A
denise.zanchelli@culinary.edu
ZANDER, Derek .... 319-385-6349 167 A
derek.zander@iw.edu
ZANDER, William, D ..... 302-831-1209.. 90 F
dzander@udel.edu
ZANDERS, Ann .... 225-216-8723 186 K
zandersa@mybrcc.edu
ZANDERS, Joan, A .... 703-323-3014 475 C
jzanders@nvcc.edu
ZANE, Jazmine .... 310-506-4375.. 56 C
jazmin.zane@pepperdine.edu
ZANE, Tom .... 801-957-4420 461 D
tom.zane@slcc.edu
ZANELLA-LITKE,
Joanne .... 508-999-8772 211 F
joanne.zanellalitke@umassd.edu

ZANG, Connie .... 740-366-9441 349 H
zang.3@cotc.edu
ZANGER, Kate .... 563-588-6313 163 F
kate.zanger@clarke.edu
ZANIC, Van, G .... 724-847-6105 384 G
vgzanic@geneva.edu
ZANITSCH, David .... 313-883-3114 229 K
zanitsch.david@shms.edu
ZANJANI, Mellissia ...... 484-365-7440 389 C
mzanjani@lincoln.edu
ZANK, Gary .... 256-824-6575.... 8 B
gary.zank@uah.edu
ZANKO, Michael .... 973-655-7706 279 C
zankom@mail.montclar.edu
ZANSITIS, Richard, A .... 713-348-5237 442 K
zansitis@rice.edu
ZANT, Don .... 662-325-2231 247 F
dzant@budgetplan.msstate.edu
ZANTINGH, Ryan .... 515-271-3048 165 A
ryan.zantingh@drake.edu
ZAPATA, Fred .... 210-999-7401 452 A
fred.zapata@trinity.edu
ZAPATA, Grace .... 210-486-2269 429 G
zapata@alamo.edu
ZAPATA, Hector .... 225-578-8242 188 I
hozapat@lsu.edu
ZAPATA, Jesse, T .... 210-458-2700 455 E
jesse.zapata@utsa.edu
ZAPATA, Rafael .... 718-817-1000 300 E
rzapata@fordham.edu
ZAPF, Patricia .... 650-758-7663.. 55 G
pzapf@paloaltou.edu
ZAPOLSKI, Mike .... 309-794-7223 132 C
mikezapolski@augustana.edu
ZAPOLSKI, Ryan .... 203-576-4542.. 88 D
rzapolsk@bridgeport.edu
ZAPP, Karen .... 724-902-7467 380 A
karen.zapp@bc3.edu
ZAPPALORTI, Robert, E 203-287-3028.. 87 E
paier.admin@snet.net
ZAPPAS, Barbara .... 831-582-3908.. 32 C
bzappas@csumb.edu
ZAPPASODI, Tony .... 903-233-4426 439 E
tonyzappasodi@letu.edu
ZAPPE, Christopher ...... 717-337-6820 384 H
czappe@gettysburg.edu
ZAPPIA, Charles .... 619-388-2801.. 60 D
czappia@sdccd.edu
ZAPPIA, Joe .... 574-807-7074 153 E
joe.zappia@betheluniversity.edu
ZAPRUDER, Matthew ..... 925-631-8131.. 59 B
mjz4@stmarys-ca.edu
ZARAGOZA, Federico .... 702-651-5600 271 A
federico.zaragoza@csn.edu
ZARATE, Maricelda .... 361-593-2710 447 D
maricelda.zarate@tamuk.edu
ZARBL, Helmut .... 848-445-2354 282 A
zarbl@eohsi.rutgers.edu
ZARCHI, Shloime .... 718-774-3430 292 H
ZAREMBA, Terah .... 269-965-3931 225 F
zarembat@kellogg.edu
ZAREMSKI, Robin, D ..... 717-871-7026 395 D
robin.zaremski@millersville.edu
ZARFAS, Ellen .... 503-375-7006 373 A
ezarfas@corban.edu
ZARGES, Brad .... 617-745-3732 208 G
brad.zarges@enc.edu
ZARGES, Bradford .... 617-745-3638 208 G
bradford.zarges@enc.edu
ZARGHAMI, Eric, V .... 252-335-3548 341 D
vzarghami@ecsu.edu
ZARISFI, Nathalie .... 516-877-4225 289 C
nzarisfi@adelphi.edu
ZARKOS, Thomas .... 917-493-4418 305 I
tzarkos@msmnyc.edu
ZARKOWSKI, Pamela ..... 313-993-1585 231 B
zarkowp1@udmercy.edu
ZARLING, Mark, G .... 507-354-8221 236 I
zarlinmg@mlc-wels.edu
ZARRILLO, Deirdre .... 518-292-1704 313 D
zarrid@sage.edu
ZARRINNAM, Ali, R ...... 608-246-6446 499 H
azarrinnam@madisoncollege.edu
ZART, Leilani .... 319-352-8565 170 C
leilani.zart@wartburg.edu
ZARTNER, Ken .... 432-335-6606 441 D
kzartner@odessa.edu
ZASTOUPIL, Brenda ...... 701-328-2906 345 B
brenda.zastoupil@ndus.edu
ZATAR, Wael .... 304-696-6043 490 D
zatar@marshall.edu
ZATZ, Marjorie .... 209-228-4723.. 69 B
mzatz@ucmerced.edu

ZAUFT, Richard .... 617-349-8001 210 H
richard.zauft@lesley.edu
ZAUHAR, Frances, M ... 570-348-6233 389 G
zauhar@marywood.edu
ZAVADA, Robert .... 570-674-8018 390 G
rzavada@misericordia.edu
ZAVADSKY, Cornelia ..... 610-604-7700.. 92 G
ZAVALA-ACEVEZ,
Elizabeth .... 657-278-2030.. 31 E
ezavala-acevez@fullerton.edu
ZAVALA-PETHERBRIDGE,
Dina .... 701-788-4650 345 E
dina.petherbridge@mayvillestate.edu
ZAVALA-QUIÑONES,
Javier .... 787-993-8854 513 B
javier.zavala@upr.edu
ZAVATKAY, Debra .... 860-738-6309.. 86 C
dzavatkay@nwcc.edu
ZAWALICH, Barbara ...... 508-854-4283 215 D
bzawalich@qcc.mass.edu
ZAWIA, Nasser, H .... 401-874-5909 406 B
nzawia@uri.edu
ZAWODNY, Laurel, E .... 419-372-2211 348 H
lzawodn@bgsu.edu
ZAYAC, Lynn .... 413-572-8142 213 D
lzayac@westfield.ma.edu
ZAYAITZ, Anne .... 610-683-4155 395 A
zayaitz@kutztown.edu
ZAYAS, Brendaliz .... 787-258-1501 507 D
bzayas@columbiacentral.edu
ZAYAS, David .... 787-841-2000 510 K
dzayaz@pucpr.edu
ZAYAS, JR., Gerardo .... 413-755-5419 215 F
gzayas@stcc.edu
ZAYAS, Luis, H .... 512-471-1937 455 A
lzayas@austin.utexas.edu
ZAYAS, Myriam .... 787-841-2000 510 K
mzayas@pucpr.edu
ZAYAS, Niza .... 787-786-3030 512 B
nzayas@ucb.edu.pr
ZAYAS-HERNANDEZ,
Haydee, M .... 787-480-2385 507 C
hzayas@cunisanjuan.edu
ZAZZALI, Robert .... 856-256-4110 281 E
zazzali@rowan.edu
ZAZZO, Paul .... 215-368-5000 390 F
pzazzo@biblical.edu
ZBOCK, Jason, P .... 315-684-6133 321 D
zbockjp@morrisville.edu
ZDANCEWICZ, Heather .. 512-404-4816 431 C
hzdancewicz@austinseminary.edu
ZDATNY, Sophie .... 802-224-3013 463 H
sophie.zdatny@vsc.edu
ZDZIARSKI, Gene .... 312-362-8854 135 I
ezdziars@depaul.edu
ZEBALLOS, Jorge .... 269-965-3931 225 F
zeballosj@kellogg.edu
ZEBROWSKI,
Michael, J .... 414-288-7172 494 B
michael.zebrowski@marquette.edu
ZECH, Susan .... 212-686-9244 290 A
ZECK, Sharon .... 309-438-3481 139 E
sszeck@ilstu.edu
ZECKOVICH, Kim .... 906-932-4231 224 B
kimz@gogebic.edu
ZEDNICK, Yukari .... 425-352-8413 479 A
yzednick@cascadia.edu
ZEEH, Steven .... 303-914-6372.. 82 C
steven.zeeh@rrcc.edu
ZEEK, Raymond .... 203-285-2210.. 85 E
rzeek@gwcc.commnet.edu
ZEFF, Ira, A .... 402-465-2360 268 H
izeff@nebrwesleyan.edu
ZEGARRA, Ellen .... 440-826-2740 348 E
ezegarra@bw.edu
ZEGARRA, Maria .... 305-821-3333.. 99 E
mzegarra@fnu.edu
ZEGARSKI, Len .... 619-684-8790.. 53 H
lzegarski@newschoolarch.edu
ZEGER, Brian .... 212-799-5000 303 H
ZEGLEN, Eric .... 717-728-2390 381 B
ericzeglen@centralpenn.edu
ZEGLIN, Chris .... 713-942-3414 454 H
zeglinc@stthom.edu
ZEH, David .... 775-784-6869 271 F
zehd@unr.edu
ZEHEL, Renee, G .... 570-961-4715 389 G
rzehel@marywood.edu
ZEHR, David .... 603-535-3294 275 B
zehr@plymouth.edu
ZEICH, Heidi, E .... 202-319-5615.. 91 B
zeich@cua.edu
ZEICHNER, Veronica ..... 201-360-4043 278 C
vzeichner@hccc.edu

ZEIDLICKIS, Dagnia ...... 516-367-6890 296 D
ZEIDNER, Lewis, P .... 651-255-6104 243 D
lzeidner@unitedseminary.edu
ZEIG, Michael .... 517-355-6560 227 D
zeigmich@msu.edu
ZEIGER, Ken .... 402-552-3100 266 E
ZEIGLER, Letherio .... 662-254-3335 248 B
letherio.zeigler@mvsu.edu
ZEIGLER, Michael .... 803-535-5340 407 G
mike.zeigler@claflin.edu
ZEIGLER, Michael, C .... 717-867-6060 388 H
zeigler@lvc.edu
ZEIGLER, Sara .... 859-622-2222 180 B
sara.zeigler@eku.edu
ZEIGLER, Suzie, A .... 330-337-6403 347 E
executiveass@awc.edu
ZEILBERGER,
Yeruchom .... 845-207-0330 290 D
ZEILENGA, Jeffrey, R .... 573-882-5397 261 B
zeilingaj@missouri.edu
ZEIMET, Dan, L .... 563-333-6202 169 A
zeimetdaniell@sau.edu
ZEIND, Caroline .... 617-732-2874 216 B
caroline.zeind@mcphs.edu
ZEIRD, Susan .... 706-233-7466 124 B
szeird@shorter.edu
ZEISER, Richard, A .... 860-768-4181.. 88 H
zeiser@hartford.edu
ZEISS, Timothy .... 732-224-2887 276 B
tzeiss@brookdalecc.edu
ZEIT, Krystina .... 440-646-8157 363 G
krystina.zeit@ursuline.edu
ZEITHAML, Carl, P .... 434-924-3176 473 A
cpz6n@virginia.edu
ZEITLOW, Terry .... 903-233-3835 439 E
terryzeitlow@letu.edu
ZEKAN, Ingrid .... 352-245-4119 111 E
ingrid.zekan@taylorcollege.edu
ZELASKO, Sandra .... 360-538-4000 481 E
szelasko@ghc.edu
ZELEM, Daniel .... 914-674-7823 306 F
dzelem@mercy.edu
ZELENSKI, Paul .... 517-371-5140 233 A
zelensp@cooley.edu
ZELENY, Michael .... 402-472-2116 269 J
mike.zeleny@unl.edu
ZELESKY, Jason .... 978-630-9139 215 A
jzelesky@mwcc.mass.edu
ZELESNIK, Kelly .... 440-366-7028 355 J
ZELEZNY, Lynnette .... 661-654-2241.. 30 E
lzelezny@csub.edu
ZELIG, Kaylah .... 303-352-6787.. 79 E
kaylah.zelig@ccd.edu
ZELINSKI, Bob .... 352-854-2322.. 96 O
zelinskb@cf.edu
ZELINSKI, Debbie .... 312-329-4231 144 B
debbie.zelinski@moody.edu
ZELL, Jennifer .... 845-687-5049 323 E
zellj@sunyulster.edu
ZELLAR, Nel .... 507-433-0832 240 F
nel.zellar@riverland.edu
ZELLER, John, H .... 215-898-5169 400 K
jzeller@upenn.edu
ZELLERS, Andrew .... 270-831-9627 181 D
andrew.zellers@kctcs.edu
ZELLERS, Victoria .... 215-751-8913 382 A
vzellers@ccp.edu
ZELLET, Jennifer .... 209-575-6058.. 75 J
zelletj@mjc.edu
ZELLI, Brian .... 716-614-6731 310 C
bzelli@niagaracc.suny.edu
ZELLMER, Jill, A .... 617-627-3298 219 B
jill.zellmer@tufts.edu
ZELLNER, Wayne .... 719-632-8116.. 80 I
wzellner@intellitec.edu
ZEMAN, Ellen .... 802-651-5912 462 B
zeman@champlain.edu
ZEMAN, Janice, L .... 757-221-3877 466 C
jlzema@wm.edu
ZEMAN, Mark .... 315-464-5825 317 F
zemanm@upstate.edu
ZEMAN, Mary Beth .... 973-720-2971 284 I
zemanm@wpunj.edu
ZEMAN, Scott .... 575-835-5133 286 I
scott.zeman@nmt.edu
ZEMBA, Bethany, C .... 203-582-8200.. 87 G
ZEMBA, Jennifer .... 724-838-4216 398 H
jzemba@setonhill.edu
ZEMBAR, Mary Jo .... 937-327-7921 364 H
mzembar@wittenberg.edu
ZEMP, William .... 603-644-3179 274 D
w.zemp@snhu.edu

ZENDMAN, Ellen .... 914-606-6733 325 C
ellen.zendman@sunywcc.edu
ZENELIS, John, G .... 703-993-2491 467 L
jzenelis@gmu.edu
ZENG, Amy .... 860-768-4243.. 88 H
zeng@hartford.edu
ZENK, Leslie .... 704-687-5766 342 E
lzenk@uncc.edu
ZENN, Michael .... 312-355-5706 151 B
mbzenn@uic.edu
ZENNER, Jami .... 970-223-2669.. 80 D
jzenner@ibmc.edu
ZENNER FORD,
Chandra .... 208-885-1205 131 G
chandra@uidaho.edu
ZENO, Mark .... 419-448-2058 353 H
mzeno@heidelberg.edu
ZENTMEYER, James, R . 248-370-3570 229 G
zentmeye@oakland.edu
ZENTMIRE, Deborah ..... 361-825-3918 447 C
deborah.zentmire@tamucc.edu
ZENTNER, Aeron .... 714-241-6413.. 38 C
azentner@coastline.edu
ZENTZ, Connie .... 314-340-3380 253 I
zentzc@hssu.edu
ZEONE, Alicia .... 507-280-3509 240 G
alicia.zeone@rctc.edu
ZEPEDA, Andrea .... 918-335-6833 368 G
azepeda@okwu.edu
ZEPEDA, Lillian .... 718-997-5591 295 C
lillian.zepeda@qc.cuny.edu
ZEPEDA, Milani .... 408-855-5123.. 74 D
milani.zepeda@missioncollege.edu
ZEPPOS, Nicholas .... 615-322-1813 428 D
nick.zeppos@vanderbilt.edu
ZERANGUE, David .... 985-448-4090 192 B
david.zerangue@nicholls.edu
ZERBE, Bryan .... 415-565-4623.. 68 F
zerbeb@uchastings.edu
ZERBE, Linda .... 610-282-1100 382 E
linda.zerbe@desales.edu
ZERCHER, Charles, K .... 603-862-1781 274 G
chuck.zercher@unh.edu
ZERILLO, Barbara .... 617-670-4468 209 D
bzerillo@fisher.edu
ZERO, Paula .... 540-654-1231 472 I
pzero@umw.edu
ZEROSIMO, Veronica .... 201-360-4198 278 C
vzerosimo@hccc.edu
ZERTUCHE, Bernie .... 210-486-4879 429 E
zertuche@alamo.edu
ZERTUCHE, Ramon .... 210-434-6711 441 E
rzertuche@ollusa.edu
ZERVOS, Persilla .... 567-377-7010 353 E
ZERWIC, Julie .... 319-335-7009 163 A
julie-zerwic@uiowa.edu
ZESWITZ, John .... 717-560-8278 388 B
jzeswitz@lbc.edu
ZETTLER, Chuck, H .... 561-868-3033 104 D
zettlerc@palmbeachstate.edu
ZEWE, Beth .... 814-732-1420 394 F
zewe@edinboro.edu
ZEYN, Dusty .... 570-662-4932 395 C
ZEYNEP LEUENBERGER,
Deniz .... 508-531-6125 212 B
dleuenberger@bridgew.edu
ZHADKO, Olena .... 718-960-1172 294 A
olena.zhadko@lehman.cuny.edu
ZHAI, Meihua .... 313-577-2001 232 I
gy2460@wayne.edu
ZHAN, Lin .... 901-678-2020 427 D
lzhan@memphis.edu
ZHANG, Chunsheng ..... 256-765-4898.... 8 E
czhang@una.edu
ZHANG, James .... 810-762-7949 225 H
jzhang@kettering.edu
ZHANG, Jiajie, W .... 713-500-3922 456 B
jiajie.zhang@uth.tmc.edu
ZHANG, Jie .... 201-216-3743 283 C
jie.zhang@stevens.edu
ZHANG, Ling .... 408-260-0208.. 42 M
sjadmin@fivebranches.edu
ZHANG, Ling .... 408-260-0208.. 43 A
sjadmin@fivebranches.edu
ZHANG, Ming .... 360-650-4454 486 F
ming.zhang@wwu.edu
ZHANG, Shali, L .... 334-844-1714.... 4 E
slz0002@auburn.edu
ZHANG, Shouhong .... 605-688-6312 417 C
shouhong.zhang@sdstate.edu
ZHANG, William, B .... 336-334-5559 343 A
wbzhang@uncg.edu
ZHANG, Xiao, Y .... 716-673-4806 317 A
xiao.zhang@fredonia.edu
ZHANG, Yang .... 808-956-5877 128 F
yz6@hawaii.edu
ZHAO, Joanna .... 831-476-9424.. 43 A
dean@fivebranches.edu
ZHAO, Joanna .... 408-260-0208.. 42 M
dean@fivebranches.edu
ZHAO, Jun .... 708-534-8046 137 F
jzhao@govst.edu
ZHAO, Lianna .... 949-451-5450.. 64 F
lzhao@ivc.edu
ZHAO, Lincoln, Z .... 407-888-8689.. 98 R
zzhao@fcim.edu
ZHAO, Yiping .... 516-739-1545 309 C
clinicmanager@nyctcm.edu
ZHAO, Zhen .... 352-591-5385.. 96 E
ZHENG, John .... 662-254-3452 248 B
zheng@mvsu.edu
ZHONG, Baisong .... 713-780-9777 430 C
bzhong@acaom.edu
ZHOU, Charles .... 719-255-3493.. 83 B
xzhou@uccs.edu
ZHOU, Chenn .... 219-989-2665 159 G
czhou@pnw.edu
ZHOU, Lin .... 212-229-5300 308 C
linzhou@newschool.edu
ZHOU, Lin .... 253-680-7105 478 E
lzhou@batestech.edu
ZHOU, Sharon .... 408-733-1878.. 70 C
sharon.zhou@uewm.edu
ZHOU, Wei .... 301-985-7705 203 B
institutional-planning@umuc.edu
ZHOU, Wendy .... 303-384-2181.. 78 I
wzhou@mines.edu
ZHOU, Ying .... 252-737-1912 341 C
zhouy14@ecu.edu
ZHU, Jake .... 909-537-8101.. 33 A
jzhu@csusb.edu
ZHU, Jianping .... 216-687-3588 351 B
j.zhu94@csuohio.edu
ZHU, Li .... 718-939-5100 304 F
lzhu@libi.edu
ZHU, Lizhi (Frank) .... 718-522-9073 290 C
lzhu@asa.edu
ZHU, WeiDong .... 201-761-6037 282 I
wzhu@saintpeters.edu
ZHUANG, Miao .... 361-593-2244 447 D
miao.zhuang@tamuk.edu
ZIA, Rashid .... 401-863-6351 404 E
rashid_zia@brown.edu
ZIADY, Nicola .... 513-556-3015 362 D
ziadyna@ucmail.uc.edu
ZIAVRAS, Sotirios, G .... 973-596-3462 279 F
sotirios.g.ziavras@njit.edu
ZIBARE, Moctar .... 541-683-5141 373 D
mzibare@gutenberg.edu
ZIBBY-DAMRON,
Kathleen .... 618-437-5321 147 A
zibbyk@rlc.edu
ZIBELL, Tammy .... 509-533-8135 480 A
tammy.zibell@scc.spokane.edu
ZIC, Anthony .... 516-759-2040 324 G
azic@webb.edu
ZICCARDI, C. Anthony .. 973-313-6053 283 B
anthony.ziccardi@shu.edu
ZICK, Brittney .... 815-825-2086 140 F
bzick@kish.edu
ZIEBARTH, Timothy, J .. 574-372-5100 155 B
ziebartj@grace.edu
ZIEG, Michael .... 724-738-2489 395 F
michael.zieg@sru.edu
ZIEGENGEIST, Roy, P ... 860-701-6509 504 F
roy.p.ziegengeist1@uscg.mil
ZIEGLER, Alycia .... 860-215-9292.. 86 F
aziegler@trcc.commnet.edu
ZIEGLER, Amanda .... 866-776-0331.. 54 A
aziegler@ncu.edu
ZIEGLER, SND, Carol ... 216-373-6347 358 B
cziegler@ndc.edu
ZIEGLER, Jennifer .... 402-465-2149 268 H
jziegle2@nebrwesleyan.edu
ZIEGLER, John .... 724-738-9000 395 F
john.ziegler@sru.edu
ZIEGLER, Mark .... 510-780-4500.. 47 J
mzeigler@lifewest.edu
ZIEGLER, William .... 607-777-3583 316 E
ziegler@binghamton.edu
ZIELASKOWSKI,
Cynthia .... 518-381-1271 315 G
zielascd@sunysccc.edu
ZIELINSKI, Deborah, M 401-825-2188 404 H
dmzielinski@ccri.edu
ZIEMBA, Christine .... 661-255-1050.. 28 K
ZIEMBA, David .... 508-362-2131 214 B
dziemba@capecod.edu
ZIEMBA, Kerri .... 212-752-1530 304 D
bookstore@limcollege.edu
ZIEMIANSKI, Michael ... 812-357-6501 160 D
mziemianski@saintmeinrad.edu
ZIEMKOWSKI, Peter ...... 269-337-4400 233 D
ZIEMNICK, Tom .... 540-338-1776 470 A
ZIENTARSKI,
Nicholas, A .... 914-367-8216 314 E
nzientarski@dunwoodie.org
ZIENTER, Rita, M .... 716-878-4698 318 C
zienterm@buffalostate.edu
ZIER, Joni, I .... 423-236-2895 424 B
jzier@southern.edu
ZIERFUSS-HUBBARD,
Pammella .... 559-244-2607.. 66 E
pamm.hubbard@fresnocitycollege.edu
ZIEROTH, Gary .... 260-452-2152 154 E
gary.zieroth@ctsfw.edu
ZIESKE, Denise .... 518-595-1101 315 G
ziesked@sunysccc.edu
ZIESLER, Yasmine .... 802-224-3000 463 H
yasmine.ziesler@vsc.edu
ZIEZIULA, Amy .... 607-778-5307 318 A
zieziulaaj@sunybroome.edu
ZIGLER, Scott .... 336-770-3236 343 D
ziglers@uncsa.edu
ZILBERMAN, Diana .... 410-462-7719 197 E
dzilberman@bccc.edu
ZILDZIC, Ines .... 925-229-6873.. 40 G
izildzic@4cd.edu
ZILLMAN, John .... 708-209-3011 135 F
john.zillman@cuchicago.edu
ZILLMER, Eric, A .... 215-895-1977 383 B
zillmer@drexel.edu
ZILLMER, Ronald .... 715-422-5337 500 A
ronald.zillmer@mstc.edu
ZIMECKI-FENNIMORE,
Danielle .... 856-415-2138 281 D
dzimecki-fennimore@rcgc.edu
ZIMLICH, Robert, L .... 502-272-8263 179 B
bzimlich@bellarmine.edu
ZIMMANN, Angela .... 717-338-3015 400 I
azimmann@uls.edu
ZIMMER, Brandi .... 785-738-9056 176 A
bzimmer@ncktc.edu
ZIMMER, Craig .... 402-354-6532 268 C
craig.zimmer@methodistcollge.edu
ZIMMER, Joseph .... 716-375-2121 313 F
jezimmer@sbu.edu
ZIMMER, Robert, J .... 773-702-8001 150 J
president@uchicago.edu
ZIMMER, Tim .... 618-262-8641 139 A
zimmert@iecc.edu
ZIMMER, Timothy, P .... 217-581-3520 136 E
tpzimmer@eiu.edu
ZIMMERHANZEL,
Kathryn .... 432-686-4227 440 E
kzimmerhanzel@midland.edu
ZIMMERMAN, Angela ... 516-323-4723 307 F
azimmerman@molloy.edu
ZIMMERMAN, Brian ...... 765-983-1256 154 G
zimmebr@earlham.edu
ZIMMERMAN, Christine 315-229-5394 314 F
christinezimmerman@stlawu.edu
ZIMMERMAN, Darin, T . 843-953-7796 407 F
dzimmer1@citadel.edu
ZIMMERMAN, Eileen, P 207-753-6970 193 B
ezimmerm@bates.edu
ZIMMERMAN, Ellen .... 217-351-2555 146 C
ezimmerman@parkland.edu
ZIMMERMAN, Gail .... 603-358-2842 275 A
gzimmerman@keene.edu
ZIMMERMAN, Heidi, M 615-898-2025 422 H
heidi.zimmerman@mtsu.edu
ZIMMERMAN, Jean .... 269-467-9945 224 A
jzimmerman@glenoaks.edu
ZIMMERMAN, Jeff .... 417-625-9703 256 D
zimmerman-j@mssu.edu
ZIMMERMAN, Jill .... 661-722-6300.. 26 D
jzimmerman@avc.edu
ZIMMERMAN, Joanna ... 281-476-1859 443 D
joanna.zimmerman@sjcd.edu
ZIMMERMAN, Karen ..... 928-536-6272.. 14 J
karen.zimmerman@npc.edu
ZIMMERMAN, Kevin ..... 507-344-7797 234 B
kevin.zimmerman@blc.edu
ZIMMERMAN, Kris .... 713-221-5054 453 B
zimmermank@uhd.edu
ZIMMERMAN, Kristen ... 909-599-5433.. 47 K
kzimmerman@lifepacific.edu
ZIMMERMAN, Matthew . 509-335-0899 486 A
ZIMMERMAN, Michael .. 586-445-7159 226 H
zimmermanm@macomb.edu
ZIMMERMAN,
Michael, A .... 916-339-4360.. 53 A
mzimmerman@mticollege.edu
ZIMMERMAN, Midge .... 757-455-3230 477 F
mlzimmerman@vwu.edu
ZIMMERMAN, Renee ..... 830-591-7326 444 G
rtzimmerman@swtjc.edu
ZIMMERMAN, Sari .... 415-565-4619.. 68 F
zimmerma@uchastings.edu
ZIMMERMAN, Yvonne .. 740-362-3389 356 D
yzimmerman@mtso.edu
ZIMMERMAN, Zvi .... 847-982-2500 138 A
zimmerman@htc.edu
ZIMMERMANN,
Christian .... 301-934-7513 198 A
cezimmermann@csmd.edu
ZIMMERMANN,
Gilbert, G .... 956-326-2890 446 F
griz@tamiu.edu
ZIMMERMANN, Joanna 281-476-1863 443 C
joanna.zimmermann@sjcd.edu
ZIMMERMANN, Joanna 281-476-1863 443 B
joanna.zimmermann@sjcd.edu
ZIMMERMANN, Joanna 281-476-1863 443 E
joanna.zimmermann@sjcd.edu
ZIMMERMANN, Susan .. 518-255-5523 319 F
zimmersj@cobleskill.edu
ZIMMERS, Jennifer, J ... 208-732-6277 130 E
jzimmers@csi.edu
ZIMNY, Brooke .... 870-245-5208.. 20 E
zimnyb@obu.edu
ZINCK, Paul .... 314-539-5291 259 C
pzinck@stlcc.edu
ZINDER, Mariana .... 718-522-9073 290 C
mzinder@asa.edu
ZINGA, Patricia .... 708-456-0300 150 I
patzinga@triton.edu
ZINGSHEIM, Shairon .... 510-659-6201.. 54 F
szingsheim@ohlone.edu
ZINK, Abbey .... 936-294-2200 450 C
alz007@shsu.edu
ZINK, Bill .... 307-778-1121 502 D
bzink@lccc.wy.edu
ZINK, Diane .... 315-568-3065 308 F
dzink@nycc.edu
ZINK, Ellen, L .... 615-353-3224 425 D
ellen.zink@nscc.edu
ZINK, Misty .... 580-774-3766 370 C
misty.zink@swosu.edu
ZINN, Andrew .... 214-643-1314 457 B
andrew.zinn@utsouthwestern.edu
ZINN, Annalisa .... 203-582-3395.. 87 G
annalisa.zinn@quinnipiac.edu
ZINNAR-SHAVIT, Efrat ... 617-731-7163 217 H
ezinnarshavit@pmc.edu
ZINNERMAN-BETHEA,
Darlene .... 803-705-4301 407 A
darlene.bethea@benedict.edu
ZINS, Rosemary, S .... 718-281-5144 295 D
rzins@qcc.cuny.edu
ZINSMASTER, Diane ...... 269-467-9945 224 A
dzinsmaster@glenoaks.edu
ZINSMEISTER, Robin .... 252-335-0821 333 G
robin_zinsmeister@albemarle.edu
ZINSSER, Kam .... 325-794-4411 433 A
kam.zinsser@cisco.edu
ZIOLA, Anne .... 402-826-6795 267 A
anne.ziola@doane.edu
ZIOMEK, Robert .... 413-662-5229 213 A
robert.ziomek@mcla.edu
ZIONTS, Paul .... 773-325-7740 135 I
pzionts@depaul.edu
ZIPF, Marianne, C .... 718-779-1430 311 I
mzipf@plazacollege.edu
ZIPP, Doug, W .... 740-368-3738 359 N
dwzipp@owu.edu
ZIPPERER, Jeannie .... 478-387-4743 118 G
jezipperer@gmc.edu
ZIRBEL, Anna .... 904-276-6753 106 C
annazirbel@sjrstate.edu
ZIRKEL, Laura .... 814-824-2262 390 C
lzirkel@mercyhurst.edu
ZIRKEL, Sabrina .... 408-554-4723.. 62 D
szirkel@scu.edu
ZIRKIN, Barbara .... 443-352-4039 201 H
bzirkin@stevenson.edu
ZIRKLE, Megan .... 816-268-5441 257 C
mzirkle@nts.edu
ZISKOWSKI, Angela ...... 319-399-8683 164 A
aziskowski@coe.edu

ZISOOK, Joshua .... 847-982-2500 138 A
jzisook@htc.edu
ZITER, Juliane .... 505-224-4000 285 J
jziter@cnm.edu
ZITNIK, Joseph .... 313-845-9878 224 G
jzitnik@hfcc.edu
ZITO, Joseph .... 508-767-7505 205 D
jzito@assumption.edu
ZITTEL, Kimberly .... 716-829-7816 298 F
zittelk@dyc.edu
ZITZNER, Linda .... 510-430-2024.. 52 D
lzitzner@mills.edu
ZIX, Theresa .... 626-396-2477.. 26 E
theresa.zix@artcenter.edu
ZIZZO, John .... 740-264-5591 352 H
jzizzo@egcc.edu
ZLATANOV, Milla .... 408-498-5105.. 38 F
mzlatanov@cogswell.edu
ZLATEVA, Tanya .... 617-353-3010 207 D
zlateva@bu.edu
ZLATIC, Steve .... 815-836-5550 141 G
zlaticst@lewisu.edu
ZLOMEK, John, R .... 607-871-2108 289 H
zlomek@alfred.edu
ZMACZYNSKI,
Alexander .... 413-265-2302 208 C
zmaczynskial@elms.edu
ZMOLEK, Donna .... 541-463-5301 373 F
zmolekd@lanecc.edu
ZOCCO, Laura, S .... 518-783-8282 315 J
lparry@siena.edu
ZOCHOL, Frank .... 845-752-3000 323 F
f.zochol@uts.edu
ZODIACAL, Elvis .... 684-699-9155 505 A
e.zodiacal@amsamoa.edu
ZOGHI, Manoochehr ..... 260-481-6839 159 F
zoghim@pfw.edu
ZOHRABIAN, Arina .... 510-925-4282.. 25 Q
azohrabian@aua.am
ZOINO, Mia .... 508-531-2102 212 B
menright@bridgew.edu
ZOLA, Charles .... 845-569-3160 307 J
charles.zola@msmc.edu
ZOLA, Gary .... 513-221-7444 301 E
gzola@huc.edu
ZOLDAK, Heather .... 847-925-6319 137 H
hzoldak@harpercollege.edu
ZOLFO, Elana .... 212-986-4343 291 D
elana-zolfo@berkeleycollege.edu
ZOLFO, Elana .... 212-983-4949 275 I
elana-zolfo@berkeleycollege.edu
ZOLLARS, Scott, M .... 620-421-6700 175 C
scottz@labette.edu
ZOLLER, Karen .... 216-373-5267 358 B
kzoller@ndc.edu
ZOLLNER, Brandon .... 812-877-8443 159 J
zollner@rose-hulman.edu
ZOMCHICK, John .... 865-974-6152 427 G
zomchick@utk.edu
ZOMERFELD, Ann .... 910-672-1141 341 E
azomerfe@uncfsu.edu
ZONDERMAN, Adrianne 617-349-8744 210 H
azonderm@lesley.edu
ZONDLO, Tim .... 763-433-1427 237 C
tim.zondlo@anokaramsey.edu
ZONER, Kathy, R .... 607-255-8945 297 F
krz1@cornell.edu
ZOOK, Jim .... 662-915-2138 249 D
jzook@olemiss.edu
ZOOK, Kevin .... 267-341-3565 386 A
kzook@holyfamily.edu
ZOPPI RODRIGUEZ,
Irene .... 301-688-4670 503 J
irene.zoppi@dodiis.mil
ZORDILLA, Emil .... 657-278-3735.. 31 E
ezordilla@fullerton.edu
ZORICH, Christpher ...... 773-995-2295 133 K
czorich@csu.edu
ZORN, Linda .... 530-879-9069.. 27 F
zornli@butte.edu
ZORNES, Kimberli .... 812-535-5193 160 B
kimberli.zornes@smwc.edu
ZORNOSA, Luis .... 787-264-1912 509 F
lzornosa@intersg.edu
ZOROMSKI, Keith .... 417-455-5740 252 D
keithzoromski@crowder.edu
ZORZI, Mark .... 856-415-2280 281 D
mzorzi@rcgc.edu
ZOSKY, Diane .... 309-438-5669 139 E
dlzosky@ilstu.edu
ZOSTANT, Anthony .... 607-778-5477 318 A
zostantaj@sunybroome.edu
ZOTHMAN, Megan .... 218-755-2502 237 E
megan.zothman@bemidjistate.edu
ZOTTI, Robert .... 201-216-5231 283 C
robert.zotti@stevens.edu
ZOTTOLA, Shannon ...... 610-409-3200 402 A
szottola@ursinus.edu
ZOTTOLI, Carla .... 978-630-9276 215 A
czottoli@mwcc.mass.edu
ZOU, Lily .... 516-739-1545 309 C
controller@nyctcm.edu
ZOUMADAKIS, Bill .... 801-957-4042 461 D
bill.zoumadakis@slcc.edu
ZOW, Al .... 919-530-5423 342 A
al.zow@nccu.edu
ZRIMSEK, Becky .... 507-222-4160 234 F
rzrimsek@carleton.edu
ZSCHAU, Ed .... 775-831-1314 272 D
ezschau@sierranevada.edu
ZU, Jean .... 201-216-5260 283 C
jean.zu@stevens.edu
ZUBATY, Ron .... 724-222-5330 392 A
rzubaty@penncommercial.edu
ZUBER, Kishan .... 570-408-4400 403 D
kishan.zuber@wilkes.edu
ZUBER, Maria, T .... 617-253-3206 215 G
ZUBEY, JR., E. Michael 610-519-7857 402 D
ZUBIA, Briza .... 507-222-7488 234 F
bzubia@carleton.edu
ZUBIATE, Jyl .... 309-467-6322 137 B
jzubiate@eureka.edu
ZUBIZARRETA, John ..... 803-786-3014 408 F
jzubizarreta@columbiasc.edu
ZUBROD, Nancy .... 712-279-4961 169 B
nancy.zubrod@stlukescollege.edu
ZUCCARELLO, Patty ...... 815-280-2239 140 B
pzuccare@jjc.edu
ZUCCARINI, Molly .... 781-768-7228 218 C
molly.zuccarini@regiscollege.edu
ZUCCHERI, Michael ...... 407-265-8383.. 96 A
ZUCCOLA, Jen .... 612-874-3626 236 K
jzuccola@mcad.edu
ZUCKER, Avraham .... 718-382-8702 325 I
ZUCKER, Lauren .... 203-432-8618.. 89 D
lauren.zucker@yale.edu
ZUCKER, Nicole, M ...... 215-572-2103 379 A
zuckern@arcadia.edu
ZUCKERMAN, Brian ...... 215-780-1281 398 G
ZUCKERMAN,
Mary Ellen .... 585-245-5367 318 E
zuckerman@geneseo.edu
ZUCKERMAN-AVILES,
Stephanie, B .... 716-878-5811 318 C
zuckersb@buffalostate.edu
ZUCKSWORTH, Eli .... 405-262-2552 369 E
eli.zucksworth@redlandscc.edu
ZUERCHER, Makenzie ... 559-251-4215.. 28 B
registrar@calchristiancollege.edu
ZUFELT, Matt .... 435-865-8165 460 F
zufelt@suu.edu
ZUGATES, Debra, A ...... 412-396-5211 383 C
zugates@duq.edu
ZUGE, Peter .... 715-346-4831 497 F
pzuge@uwsp.edu
ZUGGER, Tom .... 614-236-6782 349 D
tzugger@capital.edu
ZUGSCHWERT, Nancy ... 612-343-5001 242 H
nczugsch@northcentral.edu
ZUHLKE, James .... 610-436-3316 396 A
jzuhlke@wcupa.edu
ZUIDEMA, Leah .... 712-722-6328 164 K
leah.zuidema@dordt.edu
ZUILL, Karen .... 607-431-4303 301 D
zuillk@hartwick.edu
ZUKOR, Tevya .... 540-654-1053 472 I
tzukor@umw.edu
ZUKOSKI, Charles, F .... 716-645-2992 316 F
provost@buffalo.edu
ZUKOSKI, Charles, F .... 213-740-2101.. 72 B
uscprovost@usc.edu
ZULLO, Ashley .... 724-589-2182 399 H
azullo@thiel.edu
ZULLO, Laura, W .... 412-648-1103 401 B
lwzfm@pitt.edu
ZUMBACH, Deborah, J . 319-335-3815 163 A
deborah-zumbach@uiowa.edu
ZUMBRUN, Christina ..... 260-665-4242 160 H
zumbrunc@trine.edu
ZUMERCHIK, Jim .... 708-534-4515 137 F
jzumerchik@govst.edu
ZUMMER, Aaron .... 701-483-2014 345 D
aaron.zummer@sodexo.com
ZUMMO, Janice .... 212-220-1230 293 A
ZUMMO, Kristin .... 860-439-5260.. 86 H
kzummo@conncoll.edu
ZUMWALT, Debra, L ...... 650-723-6397.. 65 J
zumwalt@stanford.edu
ZUNIGA, Ana .... 915-831-6395 436 E
azunig64@epcc.edu
ZUNIGA, Brad .... 530-895-2948.. 27 F
zunigabr@butte.edu
ZUNIGA, Donna, P .... 936-291-0447 439 D
dzuniga@lee.edu
ZUNIGA, Stephanie .... 209-228-4085.. 69 B
szuniga2@ucmerced.edu
ZUNKEL, Karen, A .... 515-294-7063 162 I
kzunkel@iastate.edu
ZUPAN, Mark, A .... 607-871-2101 289 H
zupan@alfred.edu
ZUPANCICH, Patti .... 218-235-2169 241 E
michelle.zupancich@vcc.edu
ZURAWSKI, Ray .... 920-403-3964 495 I
ray.zurawski@snc.edu
ZURAWSKI, Sandra .... 708-534-4981 137 F
szurawski@govst.edu
ZURES, Allison .... 773-907-4738 134 C
azures@ccc.edu
ZURN, Sue .... 218-299-6515 239 B
sue.zurn@minnesota.edu
ZUROMSKI, Steve .... 508-531-2247 212 B
szuromski@bridgew.edu
ZUSCHIN, Andrea .... 540-831-5307 470 C
azuschin@radford.edu
ZUVERINK, Melanie ...... 602-275-7133.. 15 O
melanie.zuverink@rsaiz.edu
ZUZACK, Judith, A .... 724-287-8711 380 A
judith.zuzack@bc3.edu
ZUZARTE, Lisa .... 661-654-6181.. 30 E
lzuzarte@csub.edu
ZUZEVICH, Theresa .... 661-362-3644.. 38 H
theresa.zuzevich@canyons.edu
ZUZOLO, Renee .... 330-652-9919 352 K
reneezuzolo@eticollege.edu
ZUZULA, Erin .... 413-545-0039 211 D
eaz@admin.umass.edu
ZVARITCH, Jeanne .... 330-337-6403 347 E
ie@awc.edu
ZVARITCH, Jeanne, W .. 330-337-6403 347 E
academicdean@awc.edu
ZVONKOVIC, Anisa .... 252-328-4630 341 C
zvonkovica18@ecu.edu
ZVOSEC, Almut .... 216-421-7447 350 M
azvosec@cia.edu
ZWALD, Duff .... 808-956-8687 128 F
duff@hawaii.edu
ZWANZIGER,
Michael, W .... 319-273-7826 163 B
michael.zwanziger@uni.edu
ZWART, Andrew .... 616-222-3000 226 C
azwart@kuyper.edu
ZWEIG, Akiva .... 305-534-7050 111 D
azweig@talmudicu.edu
ZWEIG, Steven, C .... 573-884-9080 261 B
zweigs@health.missouri.edu
ZWEIG, Yitzchak .... 305-534-7050 111 D
yzweig@gmail.com
ZWEIG, Yochanan .... 305-534-7050 111 D
rosh@talmudicu.edu
ZWEIGLE, Zachary .... 530-242-7560.. 63 H
zzweigle@shastacollege.edu
ZWELL, Michael .... 312-645-8300 501 T
mike@wrightgrad.edu
ZWICKLER, Don .... 845-352-3431 326 B
ZWIERZELEWSKI,
Ashley .... 724-830-1005 398 H
akunkle@setonhill.edu
ZWIKELMAIER, William 573-341-4343 261 E
zwikelmaier@mst.edu
ZWIREN, Martin .... 718-960-1117 294 A
martin.zwiren@lehman.cuny.edu
ZWIRN, Benjamin .... 631-451-4867 321 F
zwirnb@sunysuffolk.edu
ZWOLINSKI, Jennifer .... 619-260-4553.. 71 J
jzwolinski@sandiego.edu
ZWYER, Cheryl .... 419-530-8425 363 E
cheryl.zwyer@utoledo.edu
ZYCH HERRMANN,
Jennifer .... 320-589-6128 244 B
zychja@morris.umn.edu
ZYCHOWSKI, Peter .... 213-356-5356.. 64 H
peter_zychowski@sciarc.edu
ZYLKA, Sherry .... 606-883-7371 180 J
sherry.zylka@kctcs.edu
ZYLMAN-TENHAVE,
Lannette .... 616-392-8555 233 E
lannette@westernseme.edu
ZYLSTRA, Brian .... 641-628-5641 163 E
zylstrab@central.edu
ZYLSTRA, James .... 608-266-1739 499 B
james.zylstra@wtcsystem.edu
ZYRIEK, Lisa .... 901-272-5100 422 B

Accreditation Index of Institutions by Regional, National, Professional and Specialized Agencies

Degree levels are shown by the following symbols: (C) diploma/certificate; (A) associate; (B) baccalaureate; (M) master's; (S) beyond master's but less than doctorate; (FP) first professional; (D) doctorate.

AA: Commission on Accreditation of Allied Health Education Programs: anesthesiologist assistant (M)

- University of Colorado Denver | Anschutz Medical Campus .... CO 83
- Quinnipiac University .... CT 87
- Nova Southeastern University .... FL ... 103
- Emory University .... GA .. 117
- South University .... GA .. 124
- Indiana University-Purdue University Indianapolis .... IN 156
- University of Missouri - Kansas City .... MO . 261
- Case Western Reserve University .... OH .. 349
- Medical College of Wisconsin .... WI ... 494

AAB: Aviation Accreditation Board International: aviation (A,B,M,D)

- Auburn University .... AL 4
- Arizona State University .... AZ 10
- Embry-Riddle Aeronautical University-Daytona Beach .... FL 98
- Florida Institute of Technology .... FL 99
- Florida Memorial University .... FL 99
- Jacksonville University .... FL 101
- Southern Illinois University Carbondale ... IL 149
- Purdue University Main Campus .... IN 159
- University of Dubuque .... IA 169
- Louisiana Tech University .... LA ... 191
- Bridgewater State University .... MA .. 212
- Western Michigan University .... MI ... 232
- Minnesota State University, Mankato .... MN .. 239
- Delta State University .... MS .. 245
- Saint Louis University .... MO .. 259
- University of Central Missouri .... MO .. 260
- Rocky Mountain College .... MT .. 265
- University of Nebraska at Omaha .... NE .. 270
- Mercer County Community College .... NJ ... 278
- Farmingdale State College .... NY .. 321
- University of North Dakota .... ND .. 345
- Kent State University Kent Campus .... OH .. 354
- Ohio State University Main Campus, The. OH .. 358
- Oklahoma State University .... OK .. 368
- Southeastern Oklahoma State University OK .. 369
- University of Oklahoma Norman Campus. OK .. 371
- Inter American University of Puerto Rico Bayamon Campus .... PR .. 509
- South Dakota State University .... SD .. 417
- Middle Tennessee State University .... TN .. 422
- Westminster College .... UT .. 461
- Hampton University .... VA .. 468

AAFCS: American Association of Family and Consumer Sciences: family and consumer science (B)

- Alabama Agricultural and Mechanical University .... AL 1
- Jacksonville State University .... AL 5
- University of Montevallo .... AL 8
- University of Arkansas at Pine Bluff .... AR 22
- California State University-Long Beach ... CA 31
- California State University-Northridge .... CA 32
- San Francisco State University .... CA 34
- Fort Valley State University .... GA .. 118
- University of Georgia .... GA .. 125
- Eastern Illinois University .... IL 136
- Illinois State University .... IL 139
- University of Kentucky .... KY .. 185
- Louisiana Tech University .... LA ... 191
- Southeastern Louisiana University .... LA ... 192
- Southern University and A&M College .... LA ... 190
- Southern University at New Orleans .... LA ... 190
- Alcorn State University .... MS .. 244
- Delta State University .... MS .. 245
- Mississippi State University .... MS .. 247
- University of Southern Mississippi .... MS .. 249
- University of Central Missouri .... MO .. 260
- State University of New York at Oneonta NY .. 317
- East Carolina University .... NC .. 341
- North Carolina Agricultural and Technical State University .... NC .. 341
- Ohio University Main Campus .... OH .. 359
- South Carolina State University .... SC .. 412
- Carson-Newman University .... TN .. 419
- Middle Tennessee State University .... TN .. 422
- Tennessee State University .... TN .. 426
- Tennessee Technological University .... TN .. 426
- University of Tennessee at Martin .... TN .. 428
- Stephen F. Austin State University .... TX ... 445
- University of Houston .... TX ... 452

ABHES: Accrediting Bureau of Health Education Schools: allied health (C,A,B,M)

- Arizona College .... AZ 10
- Brookline College .... AZ 11
- Pima Medical Institute-Tucson .... AZ 15
- Baptist Health College Little Rock .... AR 18
- Jefferson Regional Medical Center School of Nursing .... AR 19
- American Career College-Los Angeles .... CA 25
- American Career College-Ontario .... CA 25
- American Medical Sciences Center .... CA 25
- Angeles College .... CA 26
- California Career College .... CA 28
- Casa Loma College-Van Nuys .... CA 35
- CBD College .... CA 35
- CNI College .... CA 38
- Glendale Career College .... CA 44
- Gurnick Academy of Medical Arts .... CA 44
- Homestead Schools .... CA 45
- National Career College .... CA 53
- Regan Career Institute .... CA 58
- Sacramento Ultrasound Institute .... CA 58
- Trinity School of Health and Allied Sciences .... CA 67
- Valley College of Medical Careers .... CA 72
- Pima Medical Institute .... CO 81
- American Medical Academy .... FL 94
- Antigua College International .... FL 94
- Azure College .... FL 95
- Braxton College .... FL 95
- Cambridge College .... FL 95
- Cambridge Institute of Allied Health & Technology-Altamonte Springs .... FL 96
- City College .... FL 96
- Emergency Educational Institute .... FL 98
- #Med-Life Institute-Naples .... FL ... 103
- Mercy Hospital College of Nursing .... FL ... 103
- North Broward Technical Center .... FL ... 103
- Orlando Medical Institute .... FL ... 104
- Taylor College .... FL ... 111
- Ultimate Medical Academy-Clearwater .... FL ... 111
- Ambria College of Nursing .... IL 131
- Caris College .... IN 154
- St. Vincent College of Health Professions IN 160
- American National University .... KY .. 178
- ATA College .... KY .. 178
- Beckfield College .... KY .. 179
- Fortis College .... LA ... 186
- #Midwest Institute .... MO . 255
- Midwest Institute-Earth City .... MO . 255
- Saint Louis College of Health Careers-South Taylor .... MO . 259
- Texas County Technical College .... MO . 260
- WellSpring School of Allied Health-Kansas City .... MO . 262
- Universal College of Healing Arts .... NE .. 269
- Northwest Career College .... NV .. 272
- Elmira Business Institute .... NY .. 299
- Finger Lakes Health College of Nursing and Health Sciences .... NY .. 300
- Mandl School - The College of Allied Health .... NY .. 305
- Mildred Elley .... NY .. 307
- St. Paul's School of Nursing .... NY .. 314
- Saint Paul's School of Nursing-Staten Island .... NY .. 315
- Felbry College School of Nursing .... OH .. 352
- Fortis College .... OH .. 353
- Hondros College of Nursing .... OH .. 354
- Ohio Valley College of Technology .... OH .. 359
- Professional Skills Institute .... OH .. 360
- College of Emergency Services .... OR .. 372
- Sumner College .... OR .. 376
- Institute of Medical and Business Careers .... PA .. 386
- Dewey University .... PR .. 507
- EDIC College .... PR .. 507
- Universal Technology College of Puerto Rico .... PR .. 511
- Meridian Institute of Surgical Assisting .... TN .. 422
- National College .... TN .. 423
- Baptist Health System School of Health Professions .... TX ... 431
- College of Health Care Professions, The TX ... 433
- Dallas Nursing Institute .... TX ... 436
- Houston International College-Cardiotech Ultrasound School .... TX ... 438
- Southwest University at El Paso .... TX ... 444
- Eagle Gate College .... UT .. 459
- Nightingale College .... UT .. 459
- Provo College .... UT .. 459
- Bon Secours Memorial College of Nursing .... VA .. 465
- Centra College of Nursing .... VA .. 465
- Riverside College of Health Careers .... VA .. 471
- Sentara College of Health Sciences .... VA .. 471
- Southside College of Health Sciences .... VA .. 471
- Sovah School of Health Professions .... VA .. 471
- Standard Healthcare Services College of Nursing .... VA .. 471
- Charter College .... WA . 479
- West Virginia Junior College .... WV . 491
- Milwaukee Career College .... WI ... 494

ACAE: Accreditation Commission for Audiology Education: audiology (D)

- University of the Pacific .... CA 70
- Nova Southeastern University .... FL ... 103
- University of North Carolina at Chapel Hill .... NC .. 342
- Ohio State University Main Campus, The. OH .. 358
- University of Texas at Dallas, The .... TX ... 455

ACBSP: Accreditation Council for Business Schools and Programs: business administration, management, accounting and related business fields (A,B,M,D)

- Alabama State University .... AL 4
- Athens State University .... AL 4
- Bishop State Community College .... AL 1
- George Corley Wallace State Community College - Selma .... AL 2
- Jefferson State Community College .... AL 2
- Lawson State Community College .... AL 2
- Miles College .... AL 6
- Oakwood University .... AL 6
- Troy University .... AL 7
- University of Mobile .... AL 8
- University of North Alabama .... AL 8
- University of West Alabama, The .... AL 9
- Wallace State Community College - Hanceville .... AL 4
- Grand Canyon University .... AZ 12
- Northern Arizona University .... AZ 14
- University of Phoenix .... AZ 16
- Cossatot Community College of the University of Arkansas .... AR 22
- Harding University Main Campus .... AR 19
- John Brown University .... AR 19
- National Park College .... AR 20
- North Arkansas College .... AR 20
- NorthWest Arkansas Community College AR 20
- Philander Smith College .... AR 20
- Phillips Community College of the University of Arkansas .... AR 22
- University of Arkansas at Pine Bluff .... AR 22
- Alliant International University-San Diego CA 24
- Biola University .... CA 27
- California Baptist University .... CA 27
- California Southern University .... CA 30
- California State University Channel Islands .... CA 30
- International Technological University .... CA 46
- Mount Saint Mary's University .... CA 52
- Northcentral University .... CA 54
- Notre Dame de Namur University .... CA 54
- Point Loma Nazarene University .... CA 57
- Skyline College .... CA 61
- University of Redlands .... CA 71
- Woodbury University .... CA 75
- Colorado State University Global .... CO 78
- Colorado Technical University .... CO 79
- Post University .... CT 87
- Tunxis Community College .... CT 86
- University of Bridgeport .... CT 88
- Goldey-Beacom College .... DE 90
- Gallaudet University .... DC 91
- Strayer University .... DC 92
- University of the District of Columbia .... DC 93
- Bethune Cookman University .... FL 95
- Embry-Riddle Aeronautical University-Daytona Beach .... FL 98
- Florida Agricultural and Mechanical University .... FL ... 108
- Florida Memorial University .... FL 99
- Florida State College at Jacksonville .... FL ... 100
- Keiser University .... FL ... 102
- Palm Beach State College .... FL ... 104
- Saint Leo University .... FL ... 106
- Southeastern University .... FL ... 107
- Albany State University .... GA .. 113
- Athens Technical College .... GA .. 114
- Atlanta Metropolitan State College .... GA .. 114
- Brenau University .... GA .. 115
- LaGrange College .... GA .. 121
- Paine College .... GA .. 122
- Piedmont College .... GA .. 123
- South University .... GA .. 124
- West Georgia Technical College .... GA .. 127
- Kapiolani Community College .... HI 128
- University of Hawaii - West Oahu .... HI 128
- College of Western Idaho .... ID 130
- Northwest Nazarene University .... ID 131
- American InterContinental University .... IL 132
- Chicago State University .... IL 133
- City Colleges of Chicago Harold Washington College .... IL 134
- City Colleges of Chicago Wilbur Wright College .... IL 134
- DeVry University - Chicago Campus .... IL 136
- Harper College .... IL 137
- Joliet Junior College .... IL 140
- Lewis University .... IL 141
- Millikin University .... IL 143
- Northwestern College .... IL 145
- Roosevelt University .... IL 147
- Trinity Christian College .... IL 150
- University of St. Francis .... IL 151
- Anderson University .... IN 153
- Indiana University East .... IN 156
- Indiana Wesleyan University .... IN 157
- Ivy Tech Community College of Indiana-Indianapolis .... IN 157
- Purdue University Global .... IN 159
- Trine University .... IN 160
- University of Indianapolis .... IN 161
- University of Saint Francis .... IN 161
- Vincennes University .... IN 162
- St. Ambrose University .... IA 169
- Baker University .... KS .. 170
- Butler County Community College .... KS .. 171
- Johnson County Community College .... KS .. 174
- Kansas City Kansas Community College KS .. 174
- MidAmerica Nazarene University .... KS .. 175
- Neosho County Community College .... KS .. 175
- Ottawa University .... KS .. 176
- Pratt Community College .... KS .. 176
- Kentucky State University .... KY .. 182
- Owensboro Community and Technical College .... KY .. 182
- Thomas More University .... KY .. 184
- West Kentucky Community and Technical College .... KY .. 182
- Baton Rouge Community College .... LA ... 186
- Delgado Community College .... LA ... 187
- Dillard University .... LA ... 186
- Louisiana College .... LA ... 186
- Louisiana State University at Alexandria . LA ... 188
- Xavier University of Louisiana .... LA ... 193
- Kennebec Valley Community College .... ME .. 194
- Northern Maine Community College .... ME .. 194
- University of New England .... ME .. 196
- Baltimore City Community College .... MD .. 197
- Bowie State University .... MD .. 203

Institution	State	Page
College of Southern Maryland	MD	198
Community College of Baltimore County, The	MD	198
Coppin State University	MD	203
Hood College	MD	199
Notre Dame of Maryland University	MD	201
Lasell College	MA	210
Lesley University	MA	210
Cornerstone University	MI	222
Ferris State University	MI	223
Jackson College	MI	225
Kettering University	MI	225
Lake Superior State University	MI	226
Lawrence Technological University	MI	226
Madonna University	MI	227
Mott Community College	MI	228
Northwood University	MI	228
Walsh College of Accountancy and Business Administration	MI	232
Anoka-Ramsey Community College	MN	237
Bethel University	MN	234
Capella University	MN	234
Hennepin Technical College	MN	238
Inver Hills Community College	MN	238
Metropolitan State University	MN	238
Normandale Community College	MN	239
North Hennepin Community College	MN	239
Riverland Community College	MN	240
Rochester Community and Technical College	MN	240
Saint Paul College-A Community & Technical College	MN	241
Walden University	MN	244
Alcorn State University	MS	244
Delta State University	MS	245
Jones County Junior College	MS	246
Mississippi University for Women	MS	248
Mississippi Valley State University	MS	248
Evangel University	MO	253
Fontbonne University	MO	253
Harris-Stowe State University	MO	253
Lincoln University	MO	254
Lindenwood University	MO	254
Maryville University of Saint Louis	MO	254
Missouri Southern State University	MO	256
Northwest Missouri State University	MO	257
Park University	MO	258
Ranken Technical College	MO	258
Southwest Baptist University	MO	259
Three Rivers College	MO	260
Webster University	MO	262
Westminster College	MO	262
William Woods University	MO	262
Chadron State College	NE	268
Metropolitan Community College	NE	267
Southeast Community College	NE	269
College of Southern Nevada	NV	271
Colby-Sawyer College	NH	272
Great Bay Community College	NH	272
Manchester Community College	NH	272
Nashua Community College	NH	273
NHTI-Concord's Community College	NH	273
Plymouth State University	NH	275
River Valley Community College	NH	273
Southern New Hampshire University	NH	274
Caldwell University	NJ	276
County College of Morris	NJ	277
Essex County College	NJ	277
Georgian Court University	NJ	278
New Jersey City University	NJ	279
Thomas Edison State University	NJ	284
Central New Mexico Community College	NM	285
Eastern New Mexico University Main Campus	NM	285
Luna Community College	NM	286
New Mexico Highlands University	NM	286
New Mexico State University Dona Ana Community College	NM	287
Northern New Mexico College	NM	287
Western New Mexico University	NM	289
City University of New York Bronx Community College	NY	293
City University of New York Medgar Evers College	NY	295
City University of New York Queensborough Community College	NY	295
College of Mount Saint Vincent	NY	296
College of Saint Rose, The	NY	296
Fashion Institute of Technology	NY	299
LIM College	NY	304
Metropolitan College of New York	NY	306
Monroe College	NY	307
Orange County Community College	NY	311
Sullivan County Community College	NY	322
SUNY Morrisville	NY	321
Utica College	NY	324
Wagner College	NY	324
Campbell University	NC	327
Catawba College	NC	328
Craven Community College	NC	333
Gardner-Webb University	NC	329
Gaston College	NC	334
Greensboro College	NC	329
Guilford College	NC	329
Lenoir-Rhyne University	NC	330
Methodist University	NC	331
Pfeiffer University	NC	339
University of Mount Olive	NC	340
Wingate University	NC	344
Ashland University	OH	348
Capital University	OH	349
Cedarville University	OH	349
Central Ohio Technical College	OH	349
Central State University	OH	350
Columbus State Community College	OH	351
Heidelberg University	OH	353
Hocking College	OH	354
James A. Rhodes State College	OH	354
Malone University	OH	355
Mount Vernon Nazarene University	OH	357
North Central State College	OH	357
Northwest State Community College	OH	358
Ohio Dominican University	OH	358
Owens Community College	OH	360
Sinclair Community College	OH	361
Stark State College	OH	361
Tiffin University	OH	361
University of Akron, Main Campus, The	OH	362
University of Findlay, The	OH	363
University of Mount Union	OH	363
University of Northwestern Ohio	OH	363
Zane State College	OH	365
Cameron University	OK	365
East Central University	OK	366
Langston University	OK	366
Northeastern State University	OK	367
Northern Oklahoma College	OK	367
Northwestern Oklahoma State University	OK	367
Oklahoma Baptist University	OK	367
Oklahoma Christian University	OK	367
Oklahoma City Community College	OK	367
Oral Roberts University	OK	368
Southern Nazarene University	OK	370
Concordia University	OR	372
George Fox University	OR	373
Southern Oregon University	OR	376
Alvernia University	PA	378
Arcadia University	PA	379
Bucks County Community College	PA	379
Butler County Community College	PA	380
California University of Pennsylvania	PA	394
Cedar Crest College	PA	381
Delaware Valley University	PA	382
DeSales University	PA	382
Edinboro University	PA	394
Elizabethtown College	PA	383
Gannon University	PA	384
Geneva College	PA	384
Grove City College	PA	385
HACC, Central Pennsylvania's Community College	PA	385
Holy Family University	PA	386
Immaculata University	PA	386
La Roche University	PA	387
Lebanon Valley College	PA	388
Lehigh Carbon Community College	PA	388
Lock Haven University	PA	395
Luzerne County Community College	PA	389
Manor College	PA	389
Mansfield University of Pennsylvania	PA	395
Marywood University	PA	389
Messiah College	PA	390
Millersville University of Pennsylvania	PA	395
Moravian College	PA	391
Mount Aloysius College	PA	391
Neumann University	PA	391
Northampton Community College	PA	391
Peirce College	PA	391
Pennsylvania College of Technology	PA	393
Saint Vincent College	PA	398
Slippery Rock University of Pennsylvania	PA	395
Thomas Jefferson University	PA	400
University of the Sciences in Philadelphia	PA	401
Wilkes University	PA	403
York College of Pennsylvania	PA	404
Universidad Ana G. Mendez Carolina Campus	PR	511
Universidad Ana G. Mendez Cupey Campus	PR	511
University of Puerto Rico-Aguadilla	PR	512
University of Puerto Rico at Arecibo	PR	513
University of Puerto Rico at Bayamon	PR	513
University of Puerto Rico at Cayey	PR	513
University of Puerto Rico at Ponce	PR	514
University of Puerto Rico at Utuado	PR	514
University of Puerto Rico-Carolina	PR	513
University of Puerto Rico-Humacao	PR	513
University of Puerto Rico-Mayaguez Campus	PR	513
University of Puerto Rico-Rio Piedras Campus	PR	514
Community College of Rhode Island	RI	404
Aiken Technical College	SC	406
Anderson University	SC	406
Benedict College	SC	407
Claflin University	SC	407
Denmark Technical College	SC	409
Greenville Technical College	SC	410
Limestone College	SC	410
Midlands Technical College	SC	410
Morris College	SC	411
Orangeburg-Calhoun Technical College	SC	411
Tri-County Technical College	SC	413
Trident Technical College	SC	413
Voorhees College	SC	414
York Technical College	SC	415
Dakota State University	SD	416
Northern State University	SD	417
Chattanooga State Community College	TN	424
Cleveland State Community College	TN	424
Columbia State Community College	TN	424
Cumberland University	TN	419
Dyersburg State Community College	TN	425
Freed-Hardeman University	TN	420
Jackson State Community College	TN	425
Lee University	TN	420
LeMoyne-Owen College	TN	421
Lincoln Memorial University	TN	421
Lipscomb University	TN	421
Motlow State Community College	TN	425
Nashville State Community College	TN	425
Northeast State Community College	TN	425
Pellissippi State Community College	TN	425
Roane State Community College	TN	425
Southwest Tennessee Community College	TN	426
Tusculum University	TN	427
Volunteer State Community College	TN	426
Walters State Community College	TN	426
Angelo State University	TX	451
Austin Community College District	TX	431
Dallas Baptist University	TX	434
Hardin-Simmons University	TX	437
Houston Community College	TX	437
Huston-Tillotson University	TX	438
Jarvis Christian College	TX	438
Our Lady of the Lake University	TX	441
South Texas College	TX	444
Tarleton State University	TX	446
Texas A & M University-Central Texas	TX	447
Texas Lutheran University	TX	449
Texas Woman's University	TX	451
University of Mary Hardin-Baylor	TX	453
University of the Incarnate Word	TX	453
Wiley College	TX	458
Dixie State University	UT	460
Snow College	UT	461
Western Governors University	UT	461
Westminster College	UT	461
Champlain College	VT	462
Norwich University	VT	463
Liberty University	VA	468
Marymount University	VA	469
Regent University	VA	470
Roanoke College	VA	471
University of Lynchburg	VA	472
Virginia Union University	VA	477
Virginia Western Community College	VA	476
Bates Technical College	WA	478
City University of Seattle	WA	479
Northwest University	WA	482
Saint Martin's University	WA	483
Walla Walla University	WA	485
American Public University System	WV	487
Bluefield State College	WV	489
BridgeValley Community & Technical College	WV	488
Concord University	WV	490
Fairmont State University	WV	490
Mountwest Community and Technical College	WV	489
Salem University	WV	488
West Virginia State University	WV	491
West Virginia University at Parkersburg	WV	491
Wheeling University	WV	491
Cardinal Stritch University	WI	492
Chippewa Valley Technical College	WI	499
Edgewood College	WI	493
Gateway Technical College	WI	499
Northeast Wisconsin Technical College	WI	500
University of Wisconsin-Stout	WI	498
Viterbo University	WI	498
Casper College	WY	501

ACCSC: Accrediting Commission of Career Schools and Colleges: occupational, trade, and technical education (C,A,B,M)

Institution	State	Page
Remington College, Mobile Campus	AL	6
Alaska Career College	AK	9
Bryan University	AZ	11
CollegeAmerica-Flagstaff	AZ	11
Refrigeration School, The	AZ	15
Universal Technical Institute	AZ	16
California College San Diego	CA	28
Cambridge Junior College	CA	34
Concorde Career College	CA	40
Fremont College	CA	43
Gnomon	CA	44
Institute for Business and Technology	CA	45
Institute of Technology	CA	46
Interior Designers Institute	CA	46
Learnet Academy	CA	47
Los Angeles Film School	CA	50
National Polytechnic College	CA	53
Pacific States University	CA	55
PCI College	CA	56
Platt College	CA	57
SAE Expression College	CA	58
Southern California Institute of Technology	CA	64
Stanbridge University	CA	65
Unitek College	CA	68
West Coast Ultrasound Institute	CA	73
Bel-Rea Institute of Animal Technology	CO	77
CollegeAmerica Denver	CO	77
Colorado School of Trades	CO	78
Concorde Career College	CO	79
IBMC College	CO	80
IntelliTec College	CO	80
Lincoln College of Technology	CO	80
Platt College	CO	81
Spartan College	CO	82
Paier College of Art	CT	87
Acupuncture & Massage College	FL	94
Advance Science International College	FL	94
Atlantis University	FL	94
Aviator College of Aeronautical Science & Technology	FL	94
Concorde Career Institute	FL	96
Concorde Career Institute	FL	97
Daytona College	FL	97
Dolphin Research Center Training Institute	FL	97
East West College of Natural Medicine	FL	97
Fortis College	FL	100
Full Sail University	FL	100
HCI College	FL	100
International College of Health Sciences	FL	101
Key College	FL	102
Meridian College	FL	103
Miami Regional University	FL	103
Millennia Atlantic University	FL	103
Southeastern College	FL	107
Southern Technical College	FL	108
Gwinnett College-Sandy Springs	GA	120
American Academy of Art	IL	132
Coyne College	IL	135
Lincoln College of Technology	IL	142
Rockford Career College	IL	147
International Business College	IN	157
Lincoln College of Technology	IN	158
Radiological Technologies University-VT	IN	159
Hamilton Technical College	IA	166
Wichita Technical Institute	KS	178
Baton Rouge School of Computers	LA	186
ITI Technical College	LA	186
Beal College	ME	193
Landing School, The	ME	194
Lincoln College of Technology	MD	199
Compass College of Cinematic Arts	MI	222
MIAT College of Technology	MI	227
Academy College	MN	233
Institute of Production and Recording	MN	236
Minneapolis Business College	MN	236
American Trade School	MO	250
Concorde Career College	MO	251
Pinnacle Career Institute	MO	258
Stevens Institute of Business & Arts	MO	260
Creative Center	NE	266
Myotherapy Institute	NE	268
Career College of Northern Nevada	NV	270
Eastern International College	NJ	277
Eastwick College	NJ	277
Island Drafting and Technical Institute	NY	303
New York Automotive and Diesel Institute	NY	308
Swedish Institute-College of Health Sciences	NY	322
American Institute of Alternative Medicine	OH	347
Antonelli College	OH	347

ACFEI: American Culinary Federation, Inc.: culinary arts and culinary management (C,A,B)

ACICS: Accrediting Council for Independent Colleges and Schools: business and business related programs (C,A,B,M)

ACUP: Accreditation Commission for Acupuncture and Oriental Medicine: acupuncture (C,M,D)

ADNUR: Accreditation Commission for Education in Nursing: nursing (A)

AIJS: Association of Institutions of Jewish Studies: Jewish studies (C, A,B)

- Women's Institute of Torah Seminary ... MD .. 204
- Bais Medrash Mayan Hatorah ... NJ ... 275
- Yeshiva Bais Aharon ... NJ ... 284
- Yeshiva Chemdas Hatorah ... NJ ... 284
- Yeshiva Gedolah Keren Hatorah ... NJ ... 284
- Yeshiva Gedolah Tiferes Boruch ... NJ ... 285
- Yeshivas Be'er Yitzchok ... NJ ... 285
- Bais Medrash Ateres Shlomo ... NY .. 290
- Central Yeshiva Tomchei Tmimim Lubavitch America ... NY .. 292
- Mechon L'Hoyroa ... NY .. 306
- Mesivta Torah Vodaath Seminary ... NY .. 306
- Yeshiva Ohr Naftoli ... NY .. 325
- Yeshiva Shaarei Torah of Rockland ... NY .. 326
- Yeshivath Zichron Moshe ... NY .. 326

ANEST: Council on Accreditation of Nurse Anesthesia Educational Programs: nurse anesthesia (C,M,D)

- Samford University ... AL ... 6
- University of Alabama at Birmingham ... AL ... 8
- University of Arizona ... AZ ... 16
- Arkansas State University-Jonesboro ... AR ... 17
- California State University-Fullerton ... CA ... 31
- Loma Linda University ... CA ... 48
- National University ... CA ... 53
- Samuel Merritt University ... CA ... 59
- University of Southern California ... CA ... 72
- Central Connecticut State University ... CT ... 84
- Fairfield University ... CT ... 86
- Quinnipiac University ... CT ... 87
- Georgetown University ... DC ... 92
- AdventHealth University ... FL ... 94
- Barry University ... FL ... 95
- Florida Gulf Coast University ... FL ... 108
- Florida International University ... FL ... 109
- Florida State University ... FL ... 109
- University of Miami ... FL ... 112
- University of North Florida ... FL ... 110
- University of South Florida ... FL ... 110
- Augusta University ... GA .. 115
- Emory University ... GA .. 117
- DePaul University ... IL ... 135
- Millikin University ... IL ... 143
- Rosalind Franklin University of Medicine & Science ... IL ... 147
- Rush University ... IL ... 148
- Southern Illinois University Edwardsville . IL ... 149
- Marian University ... IN ... 158
- University of Saint Francis ... IN ... 161
- University of Iowa ... IA ... 163
- Newman University ... KS .. 175
- Murray State University ... KY .. 183
- Northern Kentucky University ... KY .. 184
- Franciscan Missionaries of Our Lady University ... LA ... 186
- Louisiana State University Health Sciences Center-New Orleans ... LA ... 189
- University of New England ... ME .. 196
- Uniformed Services University of the Health Sciences ... MD .. 504
- University of Maryland, Baltimore ... MD .. 202
- Boston College ... MA .. 207
- Northeastern University ... MA .. 217
- Michigan State University ... MI ... 227
- Oakland University ... MI ... 229
- University of Detroit Mercy ... MI ... 231
- University of Michigan-Flint ... MI ... 231
- Wayne State University ... MI ... 232
- Saint Mary's University of Minnesota ... MN .. 243
- University of Minnesota ... MN .. 243
- University of Southern Mississippi ... MS .. 249
- Goldfarb School of Nursing at Barnes-Jewish College ... MO . 253
- Missouri State University ... MO . 256
- University of Missouri - Kansas City ... MO . 261
- Webster University ... MO . 262
- Bryan College of Health Sciences ... NE .. 265
- Clarkson College ... NE .. 266
- Rutgers University - Newark ... NJ ... 282
- Albany Medical College ... NY .. 289
- Columbia University in the City of New York ... NY .. 297
- University at Buffalo-SUNY ... NY .. 316
- Duke University ... NC .. 328
- East Carolina University ... NC .. 341
- University of North Carolina at Charlotte . NC .. 342
- University of North Carolina at Greensboro ... NC .. 343
- Wake Forest University ... NC .. 344
- Western Carolina University ... NC .. 344
- University of North Dakota ... ND .. 345
- Case Western Reserve University ... OH .. 349
- Lourdes University ... OH .. 355
- Otterbein University ... OH .. 360
- University of Akron, Main Campus, The .. OH .. 362
- University of Cincinnati Main Campus ... OH .. 362
- Youngstown State University ... OH .. 365
- Oregon Health & Science University ... OR .. 375
- Bloomsburg University of Pennsylvania ... PA .. 394
- Cedar Crest College ... PA .. 381
- Drexel University ... PA .. 383
- Gannon University ... PA .. 384
- La Roche University ... PA .. 387
- La Salle University ... PA .. 387
- Saint Vincent College ... PA .. 398
- Thomas Jefferson University ... PA .. 400
- University of Pennsylvania ... PA .. 400
- University of Pittsburgh ... PA .. 401
- University of Scranton, The ... PA .. 401
- Villanova University ... PA .. 402
- York College of Pennsylvania ... PA .. 404
- Inter American University of Puerto Rico Arecibo Campus ... PR .. 508
- Universidad Adventista de las Antillas ... PR .. 511
- University of Puerto Rico-Medical Sciences Campus ... PR .. 513
- Rhode Island College ... RI ... 405
- Medical University of South Carolina ... SC .. 410
- University of South Carolina Columbia ... SC .. 413
- Mount Marty College ... SD .. 415
- Lincoln Memorial University ... TN .. 421
- Middle Tennessee School of Anesthesia TN .. 422
- Union University ... TN .. 427
- University of Tennessee at Chattanooga TN .. 428
- University of Tennessee, Knoxville ... TN .. 427
- Baylor College of Medicine ... TX .. 431
- Texas Christian University ... TX .. 448
- Texas Wesleyan University ... TX .. 451
- University of Texas Health Science Center at Houston (UTHealth), The ... TX .. 456
- Westminster College ... UT .. 461
- Old Dominion University ... VA .. 469
- Virginia Commonwealth University ... VA .. 473
- Gonzaga University ... WA . 481
- Marshall University ... WV . 490
- Marquette University ... WI . 494
- University of Wisconsin-La Crosse ... WI .. 496
- University of Wisconsin-Oshkosh ... WI .. 497

ARCPA: Accreditation Review Commission on Education for the Physician Assistant: physician assisting programs (A,B,M)

- #Samford University ... AL ... 6
- University of Alabama at Birmingham ... AL ... 8
- University of South Alabama ... AL ... 8
- Northern Arizona University ... AZ ... 14
- Harding University Main Campus ... AR ... 19
- University of Arkansas for Medical Sciences ... AR ... 22
- #California Baptist University ... CA ... 27
- #California State University-Monterey Bay CA ... 32
- #Chapman University ... CA ... 36
- #Charles R. Drew University of Medicine & Science ... CA ... 36
- #Dominican University of California ... CA ... 41
- Loma Linda University ... CA ... 48
- Marshall B. Ketchum University ... CA ... 51
- Samuel Merritt University ... CA ... 59
- #Southern California University of Health Sciences ... CA ... 65
- Stanford University ... CA ... 65
- Touro University California ... CA ... 67
- University of California-Davis ... CA ... 68
- #University of La Verne ... CA ... 70
- University of Southern California ... CA ... 72
- #University of the Pacific ... CA ... 70
- Western University of Health Sciences ... CA ... 74
- #Colorado Mesa University ... CO ... 77
- Red Rocks Community College ... CO ... 82
- #Rocky Vista University ... CO ... 82
- University of Colorado Denver | Anschutz Medical Campus ... CO ... 83
- Quinnipiac University ... CT ... 87
- #Sacred Heart University ... CT ... 88
- University of Bridgeport ... CT ... 88
- #University of Saint Joseph ... CT ... 89
- Yale University ... CT ... 89
- George Washington University ... DC ... 91
- #AdventHealth University ... FL ... 94
- Barry University ... FL ... 95
- #Florida Gulf Coast University ... FL ... 108
- Florida International University ... FL ... 109
- #Florida State University ... FL ... 109
- #Keiser University ... FL ... 102
- Miami Dade College ... FL ... 103
- Nova Southeastern University ... FL ... 103
- University of Florida ... FL ... 109
- #University of South Florida ... FL ... 110
- #University of Tampa ... FL ... 112
- Augusta University ... GA .. 115
- Emory University ... GA .. 117
- Mercer University ... GA .. 121
- #Morehouse School of Medicine ... GA .. 122
- South University ... GA .. 124
- Idaho State University ... ID ... 130
- #Dominican University ... IL ... 136
- Midwestern University ... IL ... 143
- Northwestern University ... IL ... 145
- Rosalind Franklin University of Medicine & Science ... IL ... 147
- Rush University ... IL ... 148
- Southern Illinois University Carbondale ... IL ... 149
- Butler University ... IN ... 153
- #Franklin College of Indiana ... IN ... 154
- Indiana State University ... IN ... 155
- Indiana University-Purdue University Indianapolis ... IN ... 156
- #Trine University ... IN ... 160
- #University of Evansville ... IN ... 161
- University of Saint Francis ... IN ... 161
- #Valparaiso University ... IN ... 162
- Des Moines University ... IA ... 164
- #St. Ambrose University ... IA ... 169
- #University of Dubuque ... IA ... 169
- University of Iowa ... IA ... 163
- #Wichita State University ... KS .. 178
- Sullivan University ... KY .. 184
- University of Kentucky ... KY .. 185
- University of the Cumberlands ... KY .. 185
- Franciscan Missionaries of Our Lady University ... LA ... 186
- Louisiana State University Health Sciences Center at Shreveport ... LA ... 189
- Louisiana State University Health Sciences Center-New Orleans ... LA ... 189
- University of New England ... ME .. 196
- Anne Arundel Community College ... MD .. 197
- #Frostburg State University ... MD .. 203
- Towson University ... MD .. 204
- Bay Path University ... MA .. 205
- #Boston University ... MA .. 207
- MCPHS University ... MA .. 216
- #MGH Institute of Health Professions ... MA .. 216
- Northeastern University ... MA .. 217
- Springfield College ... MA .. 218
- Tufts University ... MA .. 219
- #Westfield State University ... MA .. 213
- Central Michigan University ... MI ... 222
- Eastern Michigan University ... MI ... 223
- Grand Valley State University ... MI ... 224
- University of Detroit Mercy ... MI ... 231
- Wayne State University ... MI ... 232
- Western Michigan University ... MI ... 232
- Augsburg University ... MN .. 233
- Bethel University ... MN .. 234
- #College of Saint Scholastica, The ... MN .. 235
- St. Catherine University ... MN .. 242
- Mississippi College ... MS .. 247
- Missouri State University ... MO . 256
- Saint Louis University ... MO . 259
- #Stephens College ... MO . 260
- University of Missouri - Kansas City ... MO . 261
- Rocky Mountain College ... MT .. 265
- #College of Saint Mary ... NE .. 266
- Creighton University ... NE .. 266
- Union College ... NE .. 269
- University of Nebraska Medical Center ... NE .. 270
- #University of Nevada, Reno ... NV .. 271
- #Franklin Pierce University ... NH .. 273
- #Monmouth University ... NJ ... 279
- Seton Hall University ... NJ ... 283
- University of New Mexico Main Campus . NM .. 288
- Albany Medical College ... NY .. 289
- City University of New York The City College ... NY .. 293
- City University of New York York College NY .. 295
- Clarkson University ... NY .. 296
- Daemen College ... NY .. 298
- D'Youville College ... NY .. 298
- Hofstra University ... NY .. 302
- Le Moyne College ... NY .. 304
- #Marist College ... NY .. 305
- #Mercy College ... NY .. 306
- New York Institute of Technology ... NY .. 309
- Pace University ... NY .. 311
- #Rochester Institute of Technology ... NY .. 313
- St. John's University ... NY .. 314
- State University of New York Upstate Medical University ... NY .. 317
- Stony Brook University ... NY .. 317
- SUNY Downstate Medical Center ... NY .. 317
- Touro College ... NY .. 322
- Wagner College ... NY .. 324
- Campbell University ... NC .. 327
- Duke University ... NC .. 328
- East Carolina University ... NC .. 341
- Elon University ... NC .. 328
- #Gardner-Webb University ... NC .. 329
- #High Point University ... NC .. 329
- #Lenoir-Rhyne University ... NC .. 330
- Methodist University ... NC .. 331
- #University of North Carolina at Chapel Hill ... NC .. 342
- Wake Forest University ... NC .. 344
- Wingate University ... NC .. 344
- University of North Dakota ... ND .. 345
- Baldwin Wallace University ... OH .. 348
- #Case Western Reserve University ... OH .. 349
- Kettering College ... OH .. 355
- Lake Erie College ... OH .. 355
- Marietta College ... OH .. 356
- #Mount St. Joseph University ... OH .. 357
- Ohio Dominican University ... OH .. 358
- Ohio University Main Campus ... OH .. 359
- #University of Dayton ... OH .. 362
- University of Findlay, The ... OH .. 363
- University of Mount Union ... OH .. 363
- #University of Toledo ... OH .. 363
- #Oklahoma City University ... OK .. 367
- Oregon Health & Science University ... OR .. 375
- #Pacific University ... OR .. 375
- Arcadia University ... PA .. 379
- Chatham University ... PA .. 381
- DeSales University ... PA .. 382
- Drexel University ... PA .. 383
- #Duquesne University ... PA .. 383
- Gannon University ... PA .. 384
- King's College ... PA .. 387
- Lock Haven University ... PA .. 395
- Marywood University ... PA .. 389
- #Mercyhurst University ... PA .. 390
- #Misericordia University ... PA .. 390
- Pennsylvania College of Technology ... PA .. 393
- Philadelphia College of Osteopathic Medicine ... PA .. 396
- Saint Francis University ... PA .. 398
- Salus University ... PA .. 398
- Seton Hill University ... PA .. 398
- #Slippery Rock University of Pennsylvania. PA .. 395
- #Temple University ... PA .. 399
- Thomas Jefferson University ... PA .. 400
- University of Pittsburgh ... PA .. 401
- Bryant University ... RI ... 404
- #Johnson & Wales University ... RI ... 404
- #Charleston Southern University ... SC .. 407
- #Francis Marion University ... SC .. 409
- Medical University of South Carolina ... SC .. 410
- #North Greenville University ... SC .. 411
- #University of South Carolina Columbia ... SC .. 413
- University of South Dakota, The ... SD .. 416
- Bethel University ... TN .. 418
- #Christian Brothers University ... TN .. 419
- Lincoln Memorial University ... TN .. 421
- #Lipscomb University ... TN .. 421
- #Milligan College ... TN .. 422
- South College ... TN .. 424
- Trevecca Nazarene University ... TN .. 427
- Baylor College of Medicine ... TX .. 431
- #Hardin-Simmons University ... TX .. 437
- Texas Tech University ... TX .. 451
- University of North Texas Health Science Center at Fort Worth ... TX ... 454
- University of Texas Health Science Center at San Antonio ... TX ... 456
- #University of Texas Medical Branch, The TX ... 456
- University of Texas Rio Grande Valley, The ... TX ... 455
- University of Texas Southwestern Medical Center ... TX ... 457
- Rocky Mountain University of Health Professions ... UT .. 459
- University of Utah, The ... UT .. 460
- Eastern Virginia Medical School ... VA .. 466
- #Emory & Henry College ... VA .. 467
- James Madison University ... VA .. 468
- #Mary Baldwin University ... VA .. 469
- Shenandoah University ... VA .. 471
- University of Lynchburg ... VA .. 472
- #Heritage University ... WA . 481
- University of Washington ... WA . 485
- Alderson Broaddus University ... WV . 487
- University of Charleston ... WV . 488
- West Liberty University ... WV . 490
- Carroll University ... WI ... 492
- Concordia University Wisconsin ... WI ... 493
- Marquette University ... WI ... 494
- University of Wisconsin-La Crosse ... WI ... 496
- University of Wisconsin-Madison ... WI ... 496

ART: National Association of Schools of Art and Design: art and design (C,A,B,M,D)

- Alabama State University ... AL ... 4

AT: Commission on Accreditation of Allied Health Education Programs: anesthesia technologist (A)

AUD: American Speech-Language-Hearing Association: audiology (D)

Institution	State	Page
University of Connecticut	CT	88
Gallaudet University	DC	91
Nova Southeastern University	FL	103
University of Florida	FL	109
University of South Florida	FL	110
Idaho State University	ID	130
Illinois State University	IL	139
Northern Illinois University	IL	145
Northwestern University	IL	145
Rush University	IL	148
University of Illinois at Urbana-Champaign	IL	151
Ball State University	IN	153
Indiana University Bloomington	IN	156
Purdue University Main Campus	IN	159
University of Iowa	IA	163
Wichita State University	KS	178
University of Louisville	KY	185
Louisiana State University Health Sciences Center-New Orleans	LA	189
Louisiana Tech University	LA	191
Towson University	MD	204
University of Maryland College Park	MD	202
Northeastern University	MA	217
University of Massachusetts	MA	211
Central Michigan University	MI	222
Wayne State University	MI	232
Western Michigan University	MI	232
University of Minnesota	MN	243
University of Southern Mississippi	MS	249
Missouri State University	MO	256
Washington University in St. Louis	MO	262
University of Nebraska - Lincoln	NE	269
Montclair State University	NJ	279
Adelphi University	NY	289
City University of New York Brooklyn College	NY	293
City University of New York Graduate Center	NY	293
City University of New York Hunter College	NY	294
Hofstra University	NY	302
St. John's University	NY	314
Syracuse University	NY	322
University at Buffalo-SUNY	NY	316
East Carolina University	NC	341
University of North Carolina at Chapel Hill	NC	342
Kent State University Kent Campus	OH	354
Ohio State University Main Campus, The	OH	358
Ohio University Main Campus	OH	359
University of Akron, Main Campus, The	OH	362
University of Cincinnati Main Campus	OH	362
Pacific University	OR	375
Bloomsburg University of Pennsylvania	PA	394
Salus University	PA	398
University of Pittsburgh	PA	401
University of Puerto Rico-Medical Sciences Campus	PR	513
University of South Dakota, The	SD	416
East Tennessee State University	TN	419
University of Memphis, The	TN	427
Vanderbilt University	TN	428
Lamar University	TX	449
Texas Tech University Health Sciences Center	TX	451
University of North Texas	TX	454
University of Texas at Austin	TX	455
University of Texas at Dallas, The	TX	455
University of Utah, The	UT	460
Utah State University	UT	460
James Madison University	VA	468
University of Washington	WA	485
@Western Washington University	WA	486
West Virginia University	WV	491
University of Wisconsin-Madison	WI	496
University of Wisconsin-Stevens Point	WI	497

BBT: Commission on Accreditation of Allied Health Education Programs: blood bank technology (C,M)

Institution	State	Page
Rush University	IL	148
Johns Hopkins University	MD	199
University of Texas Medical Branch, The	TX	456

BI: Association for Biblical Higher Education: bible college education (C,A,B,M,FP,D)

Institution	State	Page
Heritage Christian University	AL	5
Huntsville Bible College	AL	5
Selma University	AL	6
Alaska Bible College	AK	9
@Indian Bible College	AZ	12
Ecclesia College	AR	19
America Evangelical University	CA	25
Bethesda University of California	CA	27
Eternity Bible College	CA	42
@Ezra University	CA	42
Grace Mission University	CA	44
Hope International University	CA	45
International Reformed University and Seminary	CA	46
@Latin American Bible Institute	CA	47
Life Pacific University	CA	47
Methodist Theological Seminary in America	CA	52
Olivet University	CA	54
Presbyterian Theological Seminary in America	CA	57
@Saint Photios Orthodox Theological Seminary	CA	59
SUM Bible College and Theological Seminary	CA	66
William Jessup University	CA	75
World Mission University	CA	75
Nazarene Bible College	CO	81
Hobe Sound Bible College	FL	101
Robert E. Webber Institute for Worship Studies, The	FL	105
South Florida Bible College	FL	107
Trinity College of Florida	FL	111
Beulah Heights University	GA	115
Luther Rice College and Seminary	GA	121
Pacific Rim Christian University	HI	128
Boise Bible College	ID	129
Lincoln Christian University	IL	141
Moody Bible Institute	IL	144
Faith Bible Seminary	IN	154
Horizon University	IN	155
Union Bible College	IN	160
Emmaus Bible College	IA	165
Faith Baptist Bible College and Seminary	IA	165
Barclay College	KS	171
Kansas Christian College	KS	174
Manhattan Christian College	KS	175
Clear Creek Baptist Bible College	KY	179
Kentucky Mountain Bible College	KY	182
Simmons College of Kentucky	KY	184
Northpoint Bible College	MA	217
Grace Christian University	MI	224
Kuyper College	MI	226
Bethany Global University	MN	234
Bethlehem College & Seminary	MN	234
Oak Hills Christian College	MN	242
Southeastern Baptist College	MS	249
Baptist Bible College	MO	250
Brookes Bible College	MO	250
Calvary University	MO	250
Central Christian College of the Bible	MO	251
Heartland Christian College	MO	253
Midwest University	MO	255
Ozark Christian College	MO	257
Saint Louis Christian College	MO	258
Montana Bible College	MT	263
Yellowstone Christian College	MT	265
Summit Christian College	NE	269
Pillar College	NJ	280
Davis College	NY	298
Carolina Christian College	NC	327
Carolina College of Biblical Studies	NC	327
Grace College of Divinity	NC	329
Native American Bible College	NC	331
Trinity Bible College & Graduate School	ND	346
Allegheny Wesleyan College	OH	347
God's Bible School and College	OH	353
Rosedale Bible College	OH	360
Tri-State Bible College	OH	361
Valor Christian College	OH	364
Family of Faith Christian University	OK	366
New Hope Christian College	OR	374
Pacific Bible College	OR	375
Cairn University	PA	380
Clarks Summit University	PA	381
Lancaster Bible College	PA	388
Universidad Pentecostal Mizpa	PR	512
Universidad Teologica Del Caribe	PR	512
Columbia International University	SC	409
Institute of Lutheran Theology	SD	415
American Baptist College	TN	418
Johnson University	TN	420
Mid-South Christian College	TN	422
Welch College	TN	428
Williamson College	TN	429
Arlington Baptist University	TX	430
Baptist University of the Americas	TX	431
B.H. Carroll Theological Institute	TX	432
@Christ Mission College	TX	432
College of Biblical Studies-Houston	TX	433
Dallas Christian College	TX	434
King's University, The	TX	439
Rio Grande Bible Institute	TX	442
@Southern Bible Institute and College	TX	444
@Southern Reformed College and Seminary	TX	444
Stark College & Seminary	TX	445
@Texas Baptist Institute and Seminary	TX	448
Bethel College	VA	465
@Faith Bible College	VA	467
@Virginia Christian University	VA	473
Washington University of Virginia	VA	478
Wave Leadership College	VA	478
Appalachian Bible College	WV	487

CAATE: Commission on Accreditation of Athletic Training Education: athletic training (B,M)

Institution	State	Page
Samford University	AL	6
Troy University	AL	7
University of Alabama, The	AL	7
#University of Mobile	AL	8
University of West Alabama, The	AL	9
Grand Canyon University	AZ	12
Northern Arizona University	AZ	14
Harding University Main Campus	AR	19
#Henderson State University	AR	19
Southern Arkansas University	AR	21
University of Arkansas Main Campus	AR	21
University of Central Arkansas	AR	23
Azusa Pacific University	CA	26
California Baptist University	CA	27
#California State University-Fresno	CA	31
California State University-Fullerton	CA	31
California State University-Long Beach	CA	31
California State University-Northridge	CA	32
California State University-Sacramento	CA	32
#Concordia University Irvine	CA	40
Point Loma Nazarene University	CA	57
San Diego State University	CA	33
San Jose State University	CA	34
University of La Verne	CA	70
University of the Pacific	CA	70
#Colorado State University-Pueblo	CO	79
Metropolitan State University of Denver	CO	80
University of Northern Colorado	CO	83
Central Connecticut State University	CT	84
Quinnipiac University	CT	87
Sacred Heart University	CT	88
Southern Connecticut State University	CT	85
University of Connecticut	CT	88
University of Delaware	DE	90
Barry University	FL	95
Bethune Cookman University	FL	95
Florida Gulf Coast University	FL	108
Florida International University	FL	109
Nova Southeastern University	FL	103
Palm Beach Atlantic University	FL	104
University of Central Florida	FL	109
University of Florida	FL	109
University of Miami	FL	112
University of North Florida	FL	110
University of South Florida	FL	110
University of Tampa	FL	112
University of West Florida	FL	110
Georgia College & State University	GA	118
Georgia Southern University	GA	119
#Life University	GA	121
Piedmont College	GA	123
University of Georgia	GA	125
University of North Georgia	GA	126
Valdosta State University	GA	126
University of Hawaii at Manoa	HI	128
Boise State University	ID	129
Idaho State University	ID	130
University of Idaho	ID	131
Aurora University	IL	132
#Eastern Illinois University	IL	136
Illinois State University	IL	139
#Lewis University	IL	141
#Millikin University	IL	143
North Central College	IL	144
North Park University	IL	145
#Northern Illinois University	IL	145
Olivet Nazarene University	IL	146
#Trinity International University	IL	150
#Western Illinois University	IL	152
#Anderson University	IN	153
Ball State University	IN	153
Franklin College of Indiana	IN	154
Indiana State University	IN	155
Indiana University Bloomington	IN	156
Indiana Wesleyan University	IN	157
Manchester University	IN	158
Purdue University Main Campus	IN	159
University of Evansville	IN	161
University of Indianapolis	IN	161
#Buena Vista University	IA	163
Central College	IA	163
Clarke University	IA	163
Coe College	IA	164
Grand View University	IA	165
Iowa State University	IA	162
Loras College	IA	167
Luther College	IA	167
#Northwestern College	IA	168
#Simpson College	IA	169
University of Iowa	IA	163
University of Northern Iowa	IA	163
#Upper Iowa University	IA	170
#Bethany College	KS	171
#Bethel College	KS	171
Emporia State University	KS	172
Fort Hays State University	KS	173
Kansas State University	KS	174
MidAmerica Nazarene University	KS	175
#Southwestern College	KS	177
#Sterling College	KS	177
#Tabor College	KS	177
University of Kansas Main Campus	KS	177
University of Saint Mary	KS	177
Washburn University	KS	177
Wichita State University	KS	178
Bellarmine University	KY	179
Eastern Kentucky University	KY	180
#Georgetown College	KY	180
Northern Kentucky University	KY	184
#Spalding University	KY	184
Thomas More University	KY	184
#Union College	KY	184
University of Kentucky	KY	185
#Louisiana College	LA	186
Louisiana State University and Agricultural and Mechanical College	LA	188
Southeastern Louisiana University	LA	192
University of Louisiana at Lafayette	LA	192
University of Maine	ME	195
University of New England	ME	196
University of Southern Maine	ME	196
Frostburg State University	MD	203
Salisbury University	MD	203
Towson University	MD	204
Boston University	MA	207
Bridgewater State University	MA	212
Endicott College	MA	209
#Lasell College	MA	210
Massachusetts College of Liberal Arts	MA	213
Merrimack College	MA	216
Salem State University	MA	213
Springfield College	MA	218
Westfield State University	MA	213
Adrian College	MI	220
Aquinas College	MI	221
Central Michigan University	MI	222
Eastern Michigan University	MI	223
Grand Valley State University	MI	224
Hope College	MI	225
Michigan State University	MI	227
Northern Michigan University	MI	228
Saginaw Valley State University	MI	230
University of Michigan-Ann Arbor	MI	231
#Western Michigan University	MI	232
Bethel University	MN	234
College of Saint Scholastica, The	MN	235
Gustavus Adolphus College	MN	235
#Minnesota State University Moorhead	MN	239
Minnesota State University, Mankato	MN	239
#St. Cloud State University	MN	240
Winona State University	MN	241
University of Southern Mississippi	MS	249
Central Methodist University	MO	251
Culver-Stockton College	MO	252
Evangel University	MO	253
Lindenwood University	MO	254
Missouri State University	MO	256
Saint Louis University	MO	259
Southeast Missouri State University	MO	259
Southwest Baptist University	MO	259
Truman State University	MO	260
#University of Central Missouri	MO	260
University of Missouri - Columbia	MO	261
Montana State University Billings	MT	264
University of Montana - Missoula	MT	264
Midland University	NE	267
Nebraska Wesleyan University	NE	268
University of Nebraska at Kearney	NE	269
University of Nebraska at Omaha	NE	270
University of Nebraska - Lincoln	NE	269
University of Nevada, Las Vegas	NV	271
Colby-Sawyer College	NH	272
Keene State College	NH	275
Plymouth State University	NH	275
#University of New Hampshire	NH	274
Kean University	NJ	278
Montclair State University	NJ	279
Rowan University	NJ	281
Seton Hall University	NJ	283
William Paterson University of New Jersey	NJ	284

CACREP: Council for Accreditation of Counseling & Related Educational Programs: counseling and its specialties (M,D)

CAEP: Council for the Accreditation of Educator Preparation: teacher education (B,M,D)

CAEPN: Council for the Accreditation of Educator Preparation: teacher education (B, M,D)

CAEPT: Council for the Accreditation of Educator Preparation: teacher education (B, M,D)

CAHIIM: Commission on Accreditation for Health Informatics and Information Management Education: health information management and health informatics (A,B,M)

Baltimore City Community College ... MD .. 197
Community College of Baltimore County, The ... MD .. 198
Coppin State University ... MD .. 203
Montgomery College ... MD .. 200
Prince George's Community College ... MD .. 201
University of Maryland Global Campus ... MD .. 203
Boston University ... MA .. 207
Bristol Community College ... MA .. 213
Fisher College ... MA .. 209
Mount Wachusett Community College ... MA .. 215
Springfield Technical Community College MA .. 215
Baker College of Flint ... MI ... 221
Davenport University ... MI ... 223
Ferris State University ... MI ... 223
Grand Valley State University ... MI ... 224
Kirtland Community College ... MI ... 226
Macomb Community College ... MI ... 226
St. Clair County Community College ... MI ... 230
Schoolcraft College ... MI ... 230
Southwestern Michigan College ... MI ... 230
University of Detroit Mercy ... MI ... 231
Anoka Technical College ... MN .. 237
College of Saint Scholastica, The ... MN .. 235
Minnesota State Community and Technical College ... MN .. 239
Rasmussen College - St. Cloud ... MN .. 242
Ridgewater College ... MN .. 240
Rochester Community and Technical College ... MN .. 240
Saint Cloud Technical and Community College ... MN .. 241
Saint Paul College-A Community & Technical College ... MN .. 241
Hinds Community College ... MS .. 246
Itawamba Community College ... MS .. 246
Meridian Community College ... MS .. 247
Southwest Mississippi Community College ... MS .. 249
University of Mississippi Medical Center . MS .. 249
William Carey University ... MS .. 249
East Central College ... MO . 252
Jefferson College ... MO . 254
Metropolitan Community College - Penn Valley ... MO . 255
Missouri Western State University ... MO . 257
Ozarks Technical Community College ... MO . 257
St. Charles Community College ... MO . 258
Saint Louis University ... MO . 259
State Fair Community College ... MO . 260
Stephens College ... MO . 260
Great Falls College Montana State University ... MT .. 264
Central Community College ... NE .. 266
Clarkson College ... NE .. 266
Metropolitan Community College ... NE .. 267
Northeast Community College ... NE .. 268
Western Nebraska Community College ... NE .. 270
College of Southern Nevada ... NV .. 271
Manchester Community College ... NH .. 272
Southern New Hampshire University ... NH .. 274
Brookdale Community College ... NJ ... 276
Camden County College ... NJ ... 276
Passaic County Community College ... NJ ... 280
Raritan Valley Community College ... NJ ... 281
Rowan College at Burlington County ... NJ ... 281
Central New Mexico Community College NM .. 285
San Juan College ... NM .. 288
Alfred State College ... NY .. 320
City University of New York Borough of Manhattan Community College ... NY .. 293
City University of New York Graduate Center ... NY .. 293
Erie Community College ... NY .. 299
Long Island University - LIU Post ... NY .. 304
Medaille College ... NY .. 306
Mohawk Valley Community College ... NY .. 307
Monroe Community College ... NY .. 307
Onondaga Community College ... NY .. 311
Plaza College ... NY .. 311
Suffolk County Community College ... NY .. 321
SUNY Broome Community College ... NY .. 318
SUNY Polytechnic Institute ... NY .. 321
Trocaire College ... NY .. 323
Brunswick Community College ... NC .. 332
Catawba Valley Community College ... NC .. 333
Central Piedmont Community College ... NC .. 333
Craven Community College ... NC .. 333
Davidson County Community College ... NC .. 334
Durham Technical Community College ... NC .. 334
East Carolina University ... NC .. 341
Edgecombe Community College ... NC .. 334
McDowell Technical Community College . NC .. 336
Pitt Community College ... NC .. 336
Southwestern Community College ... NC .. 338
North Dakota State College of Science ... ND .. 346
Cincinnati State Technical and Community College ... OH .. 350
Columbus State Community College ... OH .. 351
Cuyahoga Community College ... OH .. 351
Eastern Gateway Community College - Jefferson County Campus ... OH .. 352
Franklin University ... OH .. 353
Lakeland Community College ... OH .. 355
Marion Technical College ... OH .. 356
Mercy College of Ohio ... OH .. 356
Ohio State University Main Campus, The. OH .. 358
Owens Community College ... OH .. 360
Sinclair Community College ... OH .. 361
Stark State College ... OH .. 361
Terra State Community College ... OH .. 361
University of Cincinnati-Clermont College. OH .. 362
University of Cincinnati Main Campus ... OH .. 362
University of Northwestern Ohio ... OH .. 363
University of Toledo ... OH .. 363
Zane State College ... OH .. 365
Rose State College ... OK .. 369
Southwestern Oklahoma State University. OK .. 370
Tulsa Community College ... OK .. 370
Central Oregon Community College ... OR .. 372
Chemeketa Community College ... OR .. 372
Oregon Health & Science University ... OR .. 375
Portland Community College ... OR .. 375
Community College of Allegheny County PA .. 381
Drexel University ... PA .. 383
Lehigh Carbon Community College ... PA .. 388
Peirce College ... PA .. 391
Pennsylvania College of Technology ... PA .. 393
South Hills School of Business and Technology ... PA .. 399
Temple University ... PA .. 399
University of Pittsburgh ... PA .. 401
Huertas College ... PR .. 508
University of Puerto Rico-Medical Sciences Campus ... PR .. 513
Florence - Darlington Technical College .. SC .. 409
Greenville Technical College ... SC .. 410
Midlands Technical College ... SC .. 410
Trident Technical College ... SC .. 413
University of South Carolina Columbia ... SC .. 413
University of South Carolina Upstate ... SC .. 414
Dakota State University ... SD .. 416
National American University ... SD .. 416
Chattanooga State Community College .. TN .. 424
Concorde Career College ... TN .. 419
Dyersburg State Community College ... TN .. 425
Roane State Community College ... TN .. 425
Tennessee State University ... TN .. 426
Volunteer State Community College ... TN .. 426
Walters State Community College ... TN .. 426
Austin Community College District ... TX ... 431
Blinn College ... TX ... 432
College of the Mainland ... TX ... 433
Collin County Community College District TX ... 433
Del Mar College ... TX ... 436
El Paso Community College ... TX ... 436
Houston Community College ... TX ... 437
Lamar Institute of Technology ... TX ... 449
Lee College ... TX ... 439
Lone Star College System ... TX ... 439
McLennan Community College ... TX ... 440
Midland College ... TX ... 440
Panola College ... TX ... 441
Parker University ... TX ... 441
St. Philip's College ... TX ... 429
San Jacinto College North ... TX ... 443
South Texas College ... TX ... 444
Tarrant County College District ... TX ... 445
Texas Southern University ... TX ... 449
Texas State Technical College Waco ... TX ... 449
Texas State University ... TX ... 450
Tyler Junior College ... TX ... 452
University of Texas Health Science Center at Houston (UTHealth), The ... TX ... 456
Vernon College ... TX ... 457
Wharton County Junior College ... TX ... 458
Weber State University ... UT ... 461
Western Governors University ... UT ... 461
George Mason University ... VA ... 467
Lord Fairfax Community College ... VA ... 474
Northern Virginia Community College ... VA ... 475
Tidewater Community College ... VA ... 476
Shoreline Community College ... WA ... 484
Spokane Community College ... WA ... 480
Tacoma Community College ... WA ... 485
University of Washington ... WA ... 485
Blue Ridge Community and Technical College ... WV . 488
Marshall University ... WV . 490
Mountwest Community and Technical College ... WV ... 489
Pierpont Community & Technical College WV . 489
West Virginia Northern Community College ... WV ... 489
Chippewa Valley Technical College ... WI ... 499
Fox Valley Technical College ... WI ... 499
Gateway Technical College ... WI ... 499
Lakeshore Technical College ... WI ... 499
Mid-State Technical College ... WI ... 500
Moraine Park Technical College ... WI ... 500
Northeast Wisconsin Technical College .. WI ... 500
Southwest Wisconsin Technical College . WI ... 500
University of Wisconsin-Green Bay ... WI ... 496
University of Wisconsin-Parkside ... WI ... 497
Waukesha County Technical College ... WI ... 500
Western Technical College ... WI ... 501
Wisconsin Indianhead Technical College WI ... 501

CAMPEP: Commission on Accreditation of Medical Physics Education Programs, Inc.: medical physics (C,M,D)

University of Arizona ... AZ ... 16
Loma Linda University ... CA ... 48
San Diego State University ... CA ... 33
University of California-Los Angeles ... CA ... 69
Florida Atlantic University ... FL ... 108
University of Florida ... FL ... 109
University of Miami ... FL ... 112
University of South Florida ... FL ... 110
#Augusta University ... GA .. 115
Emory University ... GA .. 117
Georgia Institute of Technology ... GA .. 118
University of Chicago ... IL ... 150
Indiana University-Purdue University Indianapolis ... IN ... 156
University of Kentucky ... KY .. 185
Louisiana State University and Agricultural and Mechanical College ... LA ... 188
Johns Hopkins University ... MD .. 199
Harvard University ... MA .. 210
University of Massachusetts Lowell ... MA .. 211
Wayne State University ... MI ... 232
University of Minnesota ... MN .. 243
University of Missouri - Columbia ... MO . 261
Creighton University ... NE .. 266
University of Nevada, Las Vegas ... NV .. 271
Dartmouth College ... NH .. 273
University of New Mexico Main Campus . NM .. 288
Columbia University in the City of New York ... NY .. 297
Hofstra University ... NY .. 302
Stony Brook University ... NY .. 317
University at Buffalo-SUNY ... NY .. 316
Duke University ... NC .. 328
East Carolina University ... NC .. 341
Cleveland State University ... OH .. 351
University of Cincinnati Main Campus ... OH .. 362
University of Toledo ... OH .. 363
Oregon Health & Science University ... OR .. 375
Oregon State University ... OR .. 375
Thomas Jefferson University ... PA .. 400
University of Pennsylvania ... PA .. 400
University of Rhode Island ... RI ... 406
Medical University of South Carolina ... SC .. 410
Vanderbilt University ... TN .. 428
#University of Texas Health Science Center at Houston (UTHealth), The ... TX ... 456
University of Texas Health Science Center at San Antonio ... TX ... 456
University of Texas MD Anderson Cancer Center, The ... TX ... 456
University of Texas Southwestern Medical Center ... TX ... 457
University of Utah, The ... UT .. 460
Virginia Commonwealth University ... VA .. 473
#Medical College of Wisconsin ... WI ... 494
University of Wisconsin-Madison ... WI ... 496

CARTE: Commission on Accreditation of Recreational Therapy Education: recreational therapy (B,M)

Grand Valley State University ... MI ... 224
University of New Hampshire ... NH .. 274
East Carolina University ... NC .. 341
Western Carolina University ... NC .. 344
Oklahoma State University ... OK .. 368
Slippery Rock University of Pennsylvania. PA .. 395
Temple University ... PA .. 399
Clemson University ... SC .. 408

CEA: Commission on English Language Program Accreditation: english language (C)

University of Alabama at Birmingham ... AL ... 8
University of Alabama, The ... AL ... 7
University of Arizona ... AZ ... 16
Arkansas State University-Jonesboro ... AR ... 17
Arkansas Tech University ... AR ... 18
California State Polytechnic University-Pomona ... CA ... 30
California State University-Long Beach ... CA ... 31
Grossmont College ... CA ... 44
Los Angeles Pacific College ... CA ... 50
National Polytechnic College ... CA ... 53
San Jose State University ... CA ... 34
University of California-Irvine ... CA ... 68
University of California-San Diego ... CA ... 69
University of San Diego ... CA ... 71
Colorado State University ... CO ... 78
University of Colorado Boulder ... CO ... 83
University of Denver ... CO ... 83
University of Northern Colorado ... CO ... 83
Sacred Heart University ... CT ... 88
University of Connecticut ... CT ... 88
University of Delaware ... DE ... 90
Gallaudet University ... DC ... 91
Georgetown University ... DC ... 92
Atlantis University ... FL ... 94
Aviator College of Aeronautical Science & Technology ... FL ... 94
Embry-Riddle Aeronautical University-Daytona Beach ... FL ... 98
Florida State University ... FL ... 109
Full Sail University ... FL ... 100
Saint Leo University ... FL ... 106
St. Petersburg College ... FL ... 106
University of Central Florida ... FL ... 109
University of Florida ... FL ... 109
University of Miami ... FL ... 112
University of South Florida ... FL ... 110
Valencia College ... FL ... 112
Georgia Central University ... GA .. 118
Georgia Institute of Technology ... GA .. 118
Georgia State University ... GA .. 119
University of Georgia ... GA .. 125
University of Hawaii at Hilo ... HI ... 128
University of Hawaii at Manoa ... HI ... 128
University of Idaho ... ID ... 131
DePaul University ... IL ... 135
Illinois Institute of Technology ... IL ... 139
Midwestern Career College ... IL ... 143
Southern Illinois University Carbondale ... IL ... 149
University of Illinois at Chicago ... IL ... 151
University of Illinois at Urbana-Champaign ... IL ... 151
Western Illinois University ... IL ... 152
Ball State University ... IN ... 153
Indiana University Bloomington ... IN ... 156
Purdue University Northwest ... IN ... 159
Taylor University ... IN ... 160
University of Southern Indiana ... IN ... 161
Iowa State University ... IA ... 162
University of Iowa ... IA ... 163
University of Northern Iowa ... IA ... 163
Emporia State University ... KS .. 172
Kansas State University ... KS .. 174
Pittsburg State University ... KS .. 176
University of Kansas Main Campus ... KS .. 177
Washburn University ... KS .. 177
Mount St. Mary's University ... MD .. 200
Towson University ... MD .. 204
University of Maryland College Park ... MD .. 202
Boston University ... MA .. 207
Central Michigan University ... MI ... 222
Eastern Michigan University ... MI ... 223
Ferris State University ... MI ... 223
Michigan State University ... MI ... 227
Michigan Technological University ... MI ... 227
Saginaw Valley State University ... MI ... 230
University of Michigan-Dearborn ... MI ... 231
University of Michigan-Flint ... MI ... 231
Wayne State University ... MI ... 232
Western Michigan University ... MI ... 232
University of Minnesota ... MN .. 243
University of Mississippi ... MS .. 249
Missouri State University ... MO . 256
Missouri University of Science & Technology ... MO . 261
Southeast Missouri State University ... MO . 259
University of Central Missouri ... MO . 260
University of Missouri - Columbia ... MO . 261
University of Missouri - Kansas City ... MO . 261
University of Montana - Missoula ... MT .. 264
Creighton University ... NE .. 266
University of Nebraska at Omaha ... NE .. 270
College of Southern Nevada ... NV .. 271
University of Nevada, Reno ... NV .. 271
Rutgers University - New Brunswick ... NJ ... 282
Columbia University in the City of New York ... NY .. 297
Rochester Institute of Technology ... NY .. 313
University at Buffalo-SUNY ... NY .. 316
Durham Technical Community College ... NC .. 334
East Carolina University ... NC .. 341
University of North Carolina at Charlotte . NC .. 342
University of North Carolina Wilmington .. NC .. 343
Cleveland State University ... OH .. 351
Ohio Northern University ... OH .. 358

CGTECH: National Accrediting Agency for Clinical Laboratory Sciences: cytogenetic technologist (B)

CHIRO: Council on Chiropractic Education: chiropractic education (FP,D)

CIDA: Council for Interior Design Accreditation: interior design (B,M)

CLPSY: American Psychological Association: clinical psychology (D)

CNCE: Accrediting Council for Continuing Education and Training: continuing education (C,A)

COARC: Commission on Accreditation for Respiratory Care: respiratory care (A,B,M)

#Eastern Oklahoma State College ... OK .. 366
Northern Oklahoma College ... OK .. 367
Rose State College ... OK .. 369
Tulsa Community College ... OK .. 370
Concorde Career College ... OR .. 372
Mt. Hood Community College ... OR .. 374
Oregon Institute of Technology ... OR .. 375
#Carlow University ... PA .. 380
Community College of Allegheny County PA .. 381
Community College of Philadelphia ... PA .. 382
Delaware County Community College ... PA .. 382
Gannon University ... PA .. 384
Gwynedd Mercy University ... PA .. 385
HACC, Central Pennsylvania's Community College ... PA .. 385
Indiana University of Pennsylvania ... PA .. 394
Laurel Business Institute ... PA .. 388
Laurel Technical Institute ... PA .. 388
Luzerne County Community College ... PA .. 389
Mansfield University of Pennsylvania ... PA .. 395
Millersville University of Pennsylvania ... PA .. 395
Pennsylvania College of Health Sciences PA .. 393
Pittsburgh Career Institute ... PA .. 396
Reading Area Community College ... PA .. 397
West Chester University of Pennsylvania PA .. 396
York College of Pennsylvania ... PA .. 404
#YTI Career Institute ... PA .. 404
#Universidad Adventista de las Antillas ... PR .. 511
Community College of Rhode Island ... RI 404
New England Institute of Technology ... RI 405
Florence - Darlington Technical College .. SC .. 409
Greenville Technical College ... SC .. 410
#Horry-Georgetown Technical College ... SC .. 410
Midlands Technical College ... SC .. 410
Orangeburg-Calhoun Technical College .. SC .. 411
Piedmont Technical College ... SC .. 411
Spartanburg Community College ... SC .. 412
Trident Technical College ... SC .. 413
Dakota State University ... SD .. 416
Baptist College of Health Sciences ... TN .. 418
Chattanooga State Community College .. TN .. 424
Columbia State Community College ... TN .. 424
#Concorde Career College ... TN .. 419
East Tennessee State University ... TN .. 419
#Jackson State Community College ... TN .. 425
Roane State Community College ... TN .. 425
Tennessee State University ... TN .. 426
Volunteer State Community College ... TN .. 426
Walters State Community College ... TN .. 426
Alvin Community College ... TX ... 429
Amarillo College ... TX ... 430
Angelina College ... TX ... 430
Cisco College ... TX ... 433
Collin County Community College District TX ... 433
Del Mar College ... TX ... 436
El Centro College ... TX ... 435
El Paso Community College ... TX ... 436
Houston Community College ... TX ... 437
Howard College ... TX ... 438
Lamar Institute of Technology ... TX ... 449
Lone Star College System ... TX ... 439
#McLennan Community College ... TX ... 440
Midland College ... TX ... 440
Midwestern State University ... TX ... 440
St. Philip's College ... TX ... 429
San Jacinto College Central ... TX ... 443
South Plains College ... TX ... 443
South Texas College ... TX ... 444
Tarrant County College District ... TX ... 445
Temple College ... TX ... 446
Texas Southern University ... TX ... 449
Texas State University ... TX ... 450
Tyler Junior College ... TX ... 452
University of Texas Health Science Center at San Antonio ... TX ... 456
University of Texas Medical Branch, The TX ... 456
Victoria College ... TX ... 457
Weatherford College ... TX ... 458
Dixie State University ... UT ... 460
#Salt Lake Community College ... UT ... 461
#Utah Valley University ... UT ... 461
Weber State University ... UT ... 461
Vermont Technical College ... VT ... 464
Central Virginia Community College ... VA .. 474
J. Sargeant Reynolds Community College ... VA .. 474
Liberty University ... VA .. 468
Mountain Empire Community College ... VA .. 475
Northern Virginia Community College ... VA .. 475
Shenandoah University ... VA .. 471
Tidewater Community College ... VA .. 476
Highline College ... WA . 481
Seattle Central College ... WA . 484
Spokane Community College ... WA . 480
Tacoma Community College ... WA . 485
BridgeValley Community & Technical College ... WV . 488
Marshall University ... WV . 490
Mountwest Community and Technical College ... WV . 489
#Pierpont Community & Technical College WV . 489
Southern West Virginia Community and Technical College ... WV . 489
Wheeling University ... WV . 491
Chippewa Valley Technical College ... WI ... 499
Madison Area Technical College ... WI ... 499
Mid-State Technical College ... WI ... 500
Milwaukee Area Technical College ... WI ... 500
Moraine Park Technical College ... WI ... 500
Northeast Wisconsin Technical College .. WI ... 500
Western Technical College ... WI ... 501
Casper College ... WY . 501

COARCP: Commission on Accreditation for Respiratory Care: polysomnography (C)

Stony Brook University ... NY .. 317
James A. Rhodes State College ... OH .. 354
Gannon University ... PA .. 384
#Tyler Junior College ... TX ... 452

COE: Council on Occupational Education: occupational, trade, and technical education (C,A)

J.F. Ingram State Technical College ... AL 2
Reid State Technical College ... AL 3
Advanced College ... CA 24
Advanced Training Associates ... CA 24
East San Gabriel Valley Regional Occupational Program and Technical Center ... CA 41
#Los Angeles Pacific College ... CA 50
Mayfield College ... CA 51
Spartan College of Aeronautics and Technology ... CA 65
Colorado Academy of Veterinary Technology ... CO 77
Academy for Nursing and Health Occupations ... FL 94
Florida Career College ... FL 98
NRI Institute of Health Sciences ... FL ... 104
Praxis Institute, The ... FL ... 105
Professional Hands Institute ... FL ... 105
Saber College ... FL ... 106
Universal Career School ... FL ... 112
Brown College of Court Reporting ... GA .. 115
Gwinnett College-Marietta ... GA .. 120
Interactive College of Technology ... GA .. 120
Midwestern Career College ... IL 143
Morrison Institute of Technology ... IL 144
Central Louisiana Technical & Community College-Huey P. Long Campus ... LA ... 187
Central Louisiana Technical College Avoyelles Campus ... LA ... 187
Central Louisiana Technical Community College ... LA ... 187
Louisiana Culinary Institute ... LA ... 188
Northshore Technical Community College LA ... 187
Northwest Louisiana Technical Community College ... LA ... 187
Career Quest Learning Center ... MI ... 222
Jersey College ... NJ ... 278
Ohio Business College ... OH .. 358
Lancaster County Career and Technology Center ... PA .. 388
Trinity College of Puerto Rico ... PR .. 511
#Concorde Career College ... TN .. 419
North Central Institute ... TN .. 423
William Moore College of Technology ... TN .. 428
Auguste Escoffier School of Culinary Arts TX ... 430
Center for Advanced Legal Studies ... TX ... 432
Interactive College of Technology ... TX ... 438
Peloton College ... TX ... 442
Quest College ... TX ... 442
Vista College ... TX ... 457
Chester Career College ... VA .. 465
Columbia College ... VA .. 466
Eastern Virginia Career College ... VA .. 466
Saint Michael College of Allied Health ... VA .. 471

COMTA: Commission on Massage Therapy Accreditation: massage therapy, bodywork, aesthetics/esthetics and skin care (C,A)

Gadsden State Community College ... AL 2
Idaho State University ... ID 130
Elgin Community College ... IL 136
National University of Health Sciences ... IL 144
Sullivan University ... KY .. 184
Community College of Baltimore County, The ... MD .. 198
Lansing Community College ... MI ... 226
CenterPoint Massage and Shiatsu Therapy School & Clinic ... MN .. 234
Northwestern Health Sciences University MN .. 242
Central Oregon Community College ... OR .. 372
Community College of Rhode Island ... RI 404
Technical College of the Lowcountry ... SC .. 412
Roane State Community College ... TN .. 425
Parker University ... TX .. 441

CONST: American Council for Construction Education: construction education (A,B,M)

Auburn University ... AL 4
Jefferson State Community College ... AL 2
University of Alaska Anchorage ... AK 9
Arizona State University ... AZ 10
Northern Arizona University ... AZ 14
John Brown University ... AR 19
University of Arkansas at Little Rock ... AR 22
California Baptist University ... CA 27
California Polytechnic State University-San Luis Obispo ... CA 30
California State University-Chico ... CA 31
California State University-Fresno ... CA 31
California State University-Long Beach ... CA 31
California State University-Northridge ... CA 32
California State University-Sacramento ... CA 32
Colorado State University ... CO 78
Central Connecticut State University ... CT 84
Florida International University ... FL ... 109
Santa Fe College ... FL ... 107
University of Florida ... FL ... 109
University of North Florida ... FL ... 110
Georgia Southern University ... GA .. 119
Kennesaw State University ... GA .. 120
Boise State University ... ID 129
Bradley University ... IL 133
College of DuPage ... IL 135
Illinois State University ... IL 139
Southern Illinois University Edwardsville . IL 149
Ball State University ... IN 153
Indiana State University ... IN 155
Purdue University Main Campus ... IN 159
Kansas State University ... KS .. 174
Eastern Kentucky University ... KY .. 180
Northern Kentucky University ... KY .. 184
Louisiana State University and Agricultural and Mechanical College ... LA ... 188
University of Louisiana at Monroe ... LA ... 192
University of Maryland Eastern Shore ... MD .. 203
Wentworth Institute of Technology ... MA .. 219
Eastern Michigan University ... MI ... 223
Ferris State University ... MI ... 223
Michigan State University ... MI ... 227
Michigan Technological University ... MI ... 227
Minnesota State University Moorhead ... MN .. 239
Minnesota State University, Mankato ... MN .. 239
University of Minnesota ... MN .. 243
University of Southern Mississippi ... MS .. 249
Missouri State University ... MO .. 256
State Fair Community College ... MO .. 260
University of Nebraska - Lincoln ... NE .. 269
University of Nevada, Las Vegas ... NV .. 271
Central New Mexico Community College NM .. 285
University of New Mexico Main Campus . NM .. 288
Alfred State College ... NY .. 320
State University of New York College of Technology at Delhi ... NY .. 320
Utica College ... NY .. 324
East Carolina University ... NC .. 341
North Carolina Agricultural and Technical State University ... NC .. 341
Western Carolina University ... NC .. 344
North Dakota State University Main Campus ... ND .. 345
Bowling Green State University ... OH .. 348
Cincinnati State Technical and Community College ... OH .. 350
Columbus State Community College ... OH .. 351
Kent State University Kent Campus ... OH .. 354
Ohio State University Main Campus, The. OH .. 358
University of Cincinnati Main Campus ... OH .. 362
University of Oklahoma Norman Campus. OK .. 371
Oregon State University ... OR .. 375
Drexel University ... PA .. 383
Pennsylvania College of Technology ... PA .. 393
Roger Williams University ... RI 405
Clemson University ... SC .. 408
South Dakota State University ... SD .. 417
Lamar University ... TX ... 449
North Lake College ... TX ... 435
Tarrant County College District ... TX ... 445
Texas A & M University ... TX ... 446
Texas State University ... TX ... 450
University of Houston ... TX ... 452
University of Texas at San Antonio, The . TX ... 455
Weber State University ... UT ... 461
Virginia Polytechnic Institute and State University ... VA .. 477
Central Washington University ... WA . 479
Edmonds Community College ... WA . 480
University of Washington ... WA . 485
Washington State University ... WA . 486
Milwaukee School of Engineering ... WI ... 494
University of Wisconsin-Stout ... WI ... 498

COPSY: American Psychological Association: counseling psychology (D)

Auburn University ... AL 4
Arizona State University ... AZ 10
University of Central Arkansas ... AR 23
Colorado State University ... CO 78
University of Denver ... CO 83
University of Northern Colorado ... CO 83
Howard University ... DC 92
University of Florida ... FL ... 109
University of Miami ... FL ... 112
Georgia State University ... GA .. 119
University of Georgia ... GA .. 125
Loyola University Chicago ... IL 142
Southern Illinois University Carbondale ... IL 149
University of Illinois at Urbana-Champaign ... IL 151
Ball State University ... IN 153
Indiana University Bloomington ... IN 156
Purdue University Main Campus ... IN 159
Iowa State University ... IA ... 162
University of Iowa ... IA ... 163
University of Kansas Main Campus ... KS .. 177
University of Kentucky ... KY .. 185
University of Louisville ... KY .. 185
Louisiana Tech University ... LA ... 191
University of Maryland College Park ... MD .. 202
Boston College ... MA .. 207
Boston University ... MA .. 207
Northeastern University ... MA .. 217
Springfield College ... MA .. 218
University of Massachusetts Boston ... MA .. 211
Andrews University ... MI ... 221
Western Michigan University ... MI ... 232
Saint Mary's University of Minnesota ... MN .. 243
University of Minnesota ... MN .. 243
University of Saint Thomas ... MN .. 244
University of Southern Mississippi ... MS .. 249
University of Missouri - Columbia ... MO . 261
University of Missouri - Kansas City ... MO . 261
University of Nebraska - Lincoln ... NE . 269
Seton Hall University ... NJ ... 283
New Mexico State University Main Campus ... NM .. 287
Fordham University ... NY .. 300
New York University ... NY .. 310
Teachers College, Columbia University ... NY .. 322
University at Albany, SUNY ... NY .. 316
University of North Dakota ... ND .. 345
Cleveland State University ... OH .. 351
University of Akron, Main Campus, The .. OH .. 362
Oklahoma State University ... OK .. 368
University of Oklahoma Norman Campus. OK .. 371
University of Oregon ... OR .. 377
Carlow University ... PA .. 380
Chatham University ... PA .. 381
Lehigh University ... PA .. 388
Penn State University Park ... PA .. 392
Universidad Ana G. Mendez Gurabo Campus ... PR .. 511
Tennessee State University ... TN .. 426
University of Memphis, The ... TN .. 427
University of Tennessee, Knoxville ... TN .. 427
Our Lady of the Lake University ... TX ... 441
Texas A & M University ... TX ... 446
Texas Tech University ... TX ... 451
Texas Woman's University ... TX ... 451
University of Houston ... TX ... 452
University of North Texas ... TX ... 454
University of Texas at Austin ... TX ... 455
Brigham Young University ... UT .. 458
University of Utah, The ... UT .. 460
Radford University ... VA .. 470
Virginia Commonwealth University ... VA .. 473
Northwest University ... WA . 482
Washington State University ... WA . 486
West Virginia University ... WV . 491
Marquette University ... WI ... 494
University of Wisconsin-Madison ... WI ... 496
University of Wisconsin-Milwaukee ... WI ... 497

COSMA: Commission on Sports Management: sports management (B,M,D)

Troy University ... AL 7
Arkansas State University-Jonesboro ... AR 17
Metropolitan State University of Denver .. CO 80

Saint Leo University .... FL ... 106
University of North Florida .... FL ... 110
University of Tampa .... FL ... 112
University of Indianapolis .... IN 161
University of Southern Indiana .... IN 161
Wichita State University .... KS .. 178
University of Louisville .... KY .. 185
Louisiana State University and
Agricultural and Mechanical College ..... LA .. 188
Thomas College .... ME .. 195
Endicott College .... MA .. 209
Lasell College .... MA .. 210
Nichols College .... MA .. 217
Northeastern University .... MA .. 217
Western New England University .... MA .. 219
Central Michigan University .... MI ... 222
Davenport University .... MI ... 223
Southeast Missouri State University .... MO . 259
St. John Fisher College .... NY .. 314
Wingate University .... NC .. 344
Bowling Green State University .... OH .. 348
Ohio University Main Campus .... OH .. 359
University of Mount Union .... OH .. 363
Kutztown University of Pennsylvania .... PA .. 395
Lancaster Bible College .... PA .. 388
Slippery Rock University of Pennsylvania. PA .. 395
York College of Pennsylvania .... PA .. 404
North Greenville University .... SC .. 411
Winthrop University .... SC .. 414
Liberty University .... VA .. 468

CSHSE: Council for Standards in Human Services Education: human services (A,B,M)

University of Alaska Anchorage .... AK 9
California State University-Fullerton .... CA 31
Community College of Denver .... CO 79
Metropolitan State University of Denver .. CO 80
Delaware Technical Community College,
Terry Campus .... DE 90
University of Delaware .... DE 90
Hillsborough Community College .... FL ... 101
Kennesaw State University .... GA .. 120
University of North Georgia .... GA .. 126
College of DuPage .... IL 135
Elgin Community College .... IL 136
Ivy Tech Community College of Indiana-
Indianapolis .... IN 157
Allegany College of Maryland .... MD .. 197
Anne Arundel Community College .... MD .. 197
Stevenson University .... MD .. 201
Fitchburg State University .... MA .. 212
Northern Essex Community College .... MA .. 215
Quinsigamond Community College .... MA .. 215
Baker College of Flint .... MI ... 221
St. Charles Community College .... MO .. 258
Metropolitan Community College .... NE .. 267
Southeast Community College .... NE .. 269
Wayne State College .... NE .. 268
Great Basin College .... NV .. 271
Brookdale Community College .... NJ ... 276
New York City College of Technology/
City University of New York .... NY .. 295
Central Piedmont Community College ..... NC .. 333
Montgomery Community College .... NC .. 336
Pitt Community College .... NC .. 336
Vance-Granville Community College .... NC .. 338
Central Ohio Technical College .... OH .. 349
Columbus State Community College ...... OH .. 351
James A. Rhodes State College .... OH .. 354
Sinclair Community College .... OH .. 361
Clarion University of Pennsylvania .... PA .. 394
HACC, Central Pennsylvania's
Community College .... PA .. 385
Lehigh Carbon Community College .... PA .. 388
Montgomery County Community College PA .. 390
University of Scranton, The .... PA .. 401
Florence - Darlington Technical College .. SC .. 409
Midlands Technical College .... SC .. 410
Trident Technical College .... SC .. 413
University of South Carolina Beaufort ..... SC .. 413
East Tennessee State University .... TN .. 419
#Wharton County Junior College .... TX ... 458
Old Dominion University .... VA .. 469
Madison Area Technical College .... WI ... 499
University of Wisconsin-Oshkosh .... WI ... 497

CVT: Commission on Accreditation of Allied Health Education Programs: cardiovascular technology (C,A,B)

Grossmont College .... CA 44
Loma Linda University .... CA 48
Orange Coast College .... CA 38
Florida SouthWestern State College .... FL ... 100
Florida State College at Jacksonville .... FL ... 100
International College of Health Sciences . FL ... 101
Nova Southeastern University .... FL ... 103
Polk State College .... FL ... 105
Santa Fe College .... FL ... 107
Valencia College .... FL ... 112
Augusta Technical College .... GA .. 114
Central Georgia Technical College .... GA .. 116
Georgia Southern University .... GA .. 119
Gwinnett Technical College .... GA .. 120
Piedmont College .... GA .. 123
South Suburban College .... IL 149
Louisiana State University Health
Sciences Center-New Orleans .... LA ... 189
Howard Community College .... MD .. 199
Grand Valley State University .... MI ... 224
Kirtland Community College .... MI ... 226
Saint Cloud Technical and Community
College .... MN .. 241
Bryan College of Health Sciences .... NE .. 265
Eastern International College .... NJ ... 277
Eastwick College .... NJ ... 277
Molloy College .... NY .. 307
Central Piedmont Community College ..... NC .. 333
Forsyth Technical Community College .... NC .. 334
Tulsa Community College .... OK .. 370
HACC, Central Pennsylvania's
Community College .... PA .. 385
Pennsylvania College of Health Sciences PA .. 393
Clemson University .... SC .. 408
Piedmont Technical College .... SC .. 411
Southeast Technical Institute .... SD .. 417
Northeast State Community College .... TN .. 425
El Centro College .... TX ... 435
Hill College .... TX ... 437
St. Philip's College .... TX ... 429
Sentara College of Health Sciences .... VA .. 471
Spokane Community College .... WA . 480
Milwaukee Area Technical College .... WI ... 500

CYTO: Commission on Accreditation of Allied Health Education Programs: cytotechnology (C,B,M)

University of Arkansas for Medical
Sciences .... AR 22
Loma Linda University .... CA 48
University of California-Los Angeles .... CA 69
Indiana University-Purdue University
Indianapolis .... IN 156
University of Nebraska Medical Center ... NE .. 270
Albany College of Pharmacy and Health
Sciences .... NY .. 289
City University of New York Hunter
College .... NY .. 294
Daemen College .... NY .. 298
Central Piedmont Community College ..... NC .. 333
Thomas Jefferson University .... PA .. 400
University of Puerto Rico-Medical
Sciences Campus .... PR .. 513
University of Rhode Island .... RI 406
University of Texas MD Anderson Cancer
Center, The .... TX ... 456
Old Dominion University .... VA .. 469
Marshall University .... WV . 490
University of Wisconsin-Madison .... WI ... 496

DA: American Dental Association: dental assisting (C,A)

Calhoun Community College .... AL 1
Coastal Alabama Community College ..... AL 1
Lawson State Community College .... AL 2
Trenholm State Technical College .... AL 3
Wallace State Community College -
Hanceville .... AL 4
University of Alaska Anchorage .... AK 9
Phoenix College .... AZ 13
Pima Community College .... AZ 15
Arkansas Northeastern College .... AR 17
University of Arkansas - Pulaski
Technical College .... AR 23
Cerritos College .... CA 35
Chaffey College .... CA 36
Citrus College .... CA 36
City College of San Francisco .... CA 37
College of Alameda .... CA 56
College of Marin .... CA 39
College of San Mateo .... CA 61
College of the Redwoods Community
College District .... CA 39
Cypress College .... CA 53
Diablo Valley College .... CA 40
Foothill College .... CA 43
Moreno Valley College .... CA 58
Orange Coast College .... CA 38
Palomar College .... CA 55
Pasadena City College .... CA 55
Sacramento City College .... CA 50
San Diego Mesa College .... CA 60
San Jose City College .... CA 61
Front Range Community College .... CO 79
Pikes Peak Community College .... CO 81
Manchester Community College .... CT 85
Tunxis Community College .... CT 86
Broward College .... FL 95
College of Central Florida .... FL 96
Daytona State College .... FL 97
Eastern Florida State College .... FL 97
Florida State College at Jacksonville .... FL ... 100
Gulf Coast State College .... FL ... 100
Hillsborough Community College .... FL ... 101
Indian River State College .... FL ... 101
Northwest Florida State College .... FL ... 103
Palm Beach State College .... FL ... 104
Santa Fe College .... FL ... 107
South Florida State College .... FL ... 107
Tallahassee Community College .... FL ... 111
Albany Technical College .... GA .. 113
Athens Technical College .... GA .. 114
Atlanta Technical College .... GA .. 114
Augusta Technical College .... GA .. 114
Columbus Technical College .... GA .. 117
Georgia Northwestern Technical College GA .. 119
Gwinnett Technical College .... GA .. 120
Lanier Technical College .... GA .. 121
Ogeechee Technical College .... GA .. 122
Savannah Technical College .... GA .. 124
Southern Crescent Technical College ..... GA .. 124
Wiregrass Georgia Technical College ..... GA .. 127
Kapiolani Community College .... HI ... 128
College of Western Idaho .... ID 130
Elgin Community College .... IL 136
Illinois Valley Community College .... IL 139
John A. Logan College .... IL 139
Kaskaskia College .... IL 140
Lewis and Clark Community College .... IL 141
Indiana University Northwest .... IN 156
Indiana University-Purdue University
Indianapolis .... IN 156
University of Southern Indiana .... IN 161
Des Moines Area Community College ..... IA 164
Hawkeye Community College .... IA 166
Indian Hills Community College .... IA 166
Iowa Western Community College .... IA 167
Kirkwood Community College .... IA 167
Marshalltown Community College .... IA 166
Northeast Iowa Community College .... IA 168
Scott Community College .... IA 165
Western Iowa Tech Community College . IA 170
Flint Hills Technical College .... KS .. 173
Labette Community College .... KS .. 175
Salina Area Technical College .... KS .. 176
Wichita State University Campus of
Applied Sciences and Technology .... KS .. 178
West Kentucky Community and
Technical College .... KY .. 182
University of Maine at Augusta .... ME .. 196
Hagerstown Community College .... MD .. 198
Massasoit Community College .... MA .. 214
Middlesex Community College .... MA .. 214
Mount Wachusett Community College ..... MA .. 215
Northern Essex Community College .... MA .. 215
Quinsigamond Community College .... MA .. 215
Springfield Technical Community College MA .. 215
Delta College .... MI ... 223
Grand Rapids Community College .... MI ... 224
Lake Michigan College .... MI ... 226
Mott Community College .... MI ... 228
Northwestern Michigan College .... MI ... 228
Washtenaw Community College .... MI ... 232
Wayne County Community College
District .... MI ... 232
Central Lakes College .... MN .. 237
Century College .... MN .. 237
Dakota County Technical College .... MN .. 237
Hennepin Technical College .... MN .. 238
Hibbing Community College, A Technical
and Community College .... MN .. 238
Minneapolis Community and Technical
College .... MN .. 238
Minnesota State Community and
Technical College .... MN .. 239
Minnesota West Community and
Technical College .... MN .. 239
Northwest Technical College .... MN .. 240
Rochester Community and Technical
College .... MN .. 240
Saint Cloud Technical and Community
College .... MN .. 241
South Central College .... MN .. 241
Hinds Community College .... MS .. 246
Meridian Community College .... MS .. 247
Pearl River Community College .... MS .. 248
Metropolitan Community College - Penn
Valley .... MO . 255
Ozarks Technical Community College .... MO . 257
State Technical College of Missouri .... MO . 260
Great Falls College Montana State
University .... MT .. 264
Salish Kootenai College .... MT .. 265
Central Community College .... NE .. 266
Metropolitan Community College .... NE .. 267
Mid-Plains Community College .... NE .. 267
Southeast Community College .... NE .. 269
College of Southern Nevada .... NV .. 271
Truckee Meadows Community College ... NV .. 271
NHTI-Concord's Community College ...... NH .. 273
Camden County College .... NJ ... 276
Central New Mexico Community College NM .. 285
Luna Community College .... NM .. 286
New Mexico State University Dona Ana
Community College .... NM .. 287
Santa Fe Community College .... NM .. 288
University at Buffalo-SUNY .... NY .. 316
Alamance Community College .... NC .. 332
Asheville - Buncombe Technical
Community College .... NC .. 332
Cape Fear Community College .... NC .. 332
Central Carolina Community College ...... NC .. 333
Central Piedmont Community College ..... NC .. 333
Coastal Carolina Community College ...... NC .. 333
Fayetteville Technical Community
College .... NC .. 334
Forsyth Technical Community College .... NC .. 334
Guilford Technical Community College .... NC .. 335
Martin Community College .... NC .. 335
Montgomery Community College .... NC .. 336
Rowan-Cabarrus Community College ...... NC .. 337
Wake Technical Community College .... NC .. 338
Wayne Community College .... NC .. 338
Western Piedmont Community College ... NC .. 339
Wilkes Community College .... NC .. 339
North Dakota State College of Science ... ND .. 346
Eastern Gateway Community College -
Jefferson County Campus .... OH .. 352
Rose State College .... OK .. 369
Blue Mountain Community College .... OR .. 372
Central Oregon Community College .... OR .. 372
Chemeketa Community College .... OR .. 372
Lane Community College .... OR .. 373
Linn-Benton Community College .... OR .. 374
Portland Community College .... OR .. 375
Umpqua Community College .... OR .. 377
HACC, Central Pennsylvania's
Community College .... PA .. 385
Harcum College .... PA .. 385
Manor College .... PA .. 389
Westmoreland County Community
College .... PA .. 403
University of Puerto Rico-Medical
Sciences Campus .... PR .. 513
Community College of Rhode Island .... RI 404
Aiken Technical College .... SC .. 406
Florence - Darlington Technical College .. SC .. 409
Greenville Technical College .... SC .. 410
Horry-Georgetown Technical College ...... SC .. 410
Midlands Technical College .... SC .. 410
Spartanburg Community College .... SC .. 412
Tri-County Technical College .... SC .. 413
Trident Technical College .... SC .. 413
York Technical College .... SC .. 415
Lake Area Technical Institute .... SD .. 415
Chattanooga State Community College .. TN .. 424
Northeast State Community College .... TN .. 425
Volunteer State Community College .... TN .. 426
Amarillo College .... TX ... 430
Del Mar College .... TX ... 436
El Paso Community College .... TX ... 436
Grayson College .... TX ... 437
Houston Community College .... TX ... 437
San Antonio College .... TX ... 429
Tyler Junior College .... TX ... 452
Germanna Community College .... VA .. 474
J. Sargeant Reynolds Community
College .... VA .. 474
Northern Virginia Community College ...... VA .. 475
Bates Technical College .... WA . 478
Bellingham Technical College .... WA . 478
Clover Park Technical College .... WA . 479
Lake Washington Institute of Technology WA . 482
Renton Technical College .... WA . 483
South Puget Sound Community College . WA . 485
Spokane Community College .... WA . 480
Blackhawk Technical College .... WI ... 499
Fox Valley Technical College .... WI ... 499
Gateway Technical College .... WI ... 499
Northeast Wisconsin Technical College .. WI ... 500
Western Technical College .... WI ... 501

DANCE: National Association of Schools of Dance: dance (C,A,B,M,D)

University of Alabama, The .... AL 7
University of Arizona .... AZ 16

California Institute of the Arts .... CA 28
California State University-Fullerton .... CA 31
California State University-Long Beach .... CA 31
Chapman University .... CA 36
Loyola Marymount University .... CA 50
San Jose State University .... CA 34
University of Hartford .... CT 88
Florida State University .... FL ... 109
Jacksonville University .... FL ... 101
Miami Dade College .... FL ... 103
University of Florida .... FL ... 109
University of South Florida .... FL ... 110
University of Georgia .... GA .. 125
University of Illinois at Urbana-Champaign .... IL 151
Ball State University .... IN 153
Butler University .... IN 153
University of Iowa .... IA 163
Wichita State University .... KS .. 178
Western Kentucky University .... KY .. 185
Community College of Baltimore County, The .... MD .. 198
Towson University .... MD .. 204
University of Maryland Baltimore County . MD .. 202
University of Maryland College Park .... MD .. 202
Hope College .... MI ... 225
Oakland University .... MI ... 229
University of Michigan-Ann Arbor .... MI ... 231
Wayne State University .... MI ... 232
Western Michigan University .... MI ... 232
St. Olaf College .... MN .. 243
University of Minnesota .... MN .. 243
Belhaven University .... MS .. 245
University of Southern Mississippi .... MS .. 249
Southeast Missouri State University .... MO . 259
University of Missouri - Kansas City .... MO . 261
University of Nebraska - Lincoln .... NE .. 269
Montclair State University .... NJ ... 279
Rutgers University - New Brunswick .... NJ ... 282
University of New Mexico Main Campus . NM .. 288
State University of New York, The College at Brockport .... NY .. 318
Appalachian State University .... NC .. 341
University of North Carolina at Charlotte . NC .. 342
University of North Carolina at Greensboro .... NC .. 343
Kent State University Kent Campus .... OH .. 354
Ohio State University Main Campus, The. OH .. 358
Ohio University Main Campus .... OH .. 359
University of Akron, Main Campus, The .. OH .. 362
University of Cincinnati Main Campus .... OH .. 362
Mercyhurst University .... PA .. 390
Point Park University .... PA .. 397
Slippery Rock University of Pennsylvania. PA .. 395
Temple University .... PA .. 399
Coker University .... SC .. 408
Columbia College .... SC .. 408
University of South Carolina Columbia .... SC .. 413
Winthrop University .... SC .. 414
Southern Methodist University .... TX ... 444
Texas Christian University .... TX ... 448
Texas Tech University .... TX ... 451
Texas Woman's University .... TX ... 451
University of Texas at Austin .... TX ... 455
Brigham Young University .... UT .. 458
Southern Utah University .... UT .. 460
University of Utah, The .... UT .. 460
James Madison University .... VA .. 468
Radford University .... VA .. 470
Virginia Commonwealth University .... VA .. 473
University of Wisconsin-Madison .... WI ... 496
University of Wisconsin-Milwaukee .... WI ... 497
University of Wisconsin-Stevens Point .... WI ... 497
Casper College .... WY . 501

DEAC: Distance Education Accrediting Commission: home study schools (A,B,M,D)

Columbia Southern University .... AL 5
Acacia University .... AZ 10
Brighton College .... AZ 11
Cummings Gaduate Institute for Behavioral Health Studies .... AZ 12
Dunlap-Stone University .... AZ 12
Harrison Middleton University .... AZ 12
National Paralegal College .... AZ 14
Paralegal Institute at Brighton College, The .... AZ 14
Penn Foster College .... AZ 15
Sessions College for Professional Design AZ 15
Sonoran Desert Institute .... AZ 15
University of Arkansas System eVersity .. AR 22
Abraham Lincoln University .... CA 23
American Graduate University .... CA 25
Anaheim University .... CA 26
California Coast University .... CA 28
California Institute of Advanced Management .... CA 28
California Institute of Management and Technology .... CA 29
California Intercontinental University .... CA 29
California Miramar University .... CA 29
College of Exercise Science, International Sports Sciences Association, LLC .... CA 39
Hawthorn University .... CA 45
Laurus College .... CA 47
Taft Law School .... CA 67
Union University of California .... CA 67
University of the People .... CA 71
Viridis Graduate Institute .... CA 73
Westcliff University .... CA 74
American Sentinel University .... CO 76
Aspen University .... CO 76
Holmes Institute of Consciousness Studies .... CO 80
McKinley College .... CO 80
U.S. Career Institute .... CO 84
William Howard Taft University .... CO 84
TEACH-NOW Graduate School of Education .... DC 93
Chi Institute of Traditional Chinese Veterinary Medicine .... FL 96
Doral College .... FL 97
Naaleh College .... FL ... 103
Sarasota University .... FL ... 107
Ashworth College .... GA .. 114
Babel University Professional School of Translation .... HI 127
Realtor University .... IL 146
College of Court Reporting, Inc. .... IN 154
Antioch School of Church Planting and Leadership Development .... IA 162
Shiloh University .... IA 169
Grantham University .... KS .. 173
NationsUniversity .... LA 189
American Business & Technology University .... MO . 250
City Vision University .... MO . 251
Rockbridge Seminary .... MO . 258
Apollos University .... MT .. 263
EC-Council University .... NM .. 286
Grace Communion Seminary .... NC .. 329
Lakewood College .... OH .. 355
American College of Healthcare Sciences OR .. 371
Huntington University of Health Sciences TN .. 420
New Charter University .... UT .. 459
American National University .... VA .. 464
Atlantic University .... VA .. 464
University of Fairfax .... VA .. 472
University of Management & Technology VA .. 472
Catholic Distance University .... WV . 487
Martinsburg College .... WV . 488
Wright Graduate University for the Realization of Human Potential .... WI ... 501

DENT: American Dental Association: dentistry (FP,D)

University of Alabama at Birmingham .... AL 8
University of Arkansas at Little Rock .... AR 22
Loma Linda University .... CA 48
University of California-Los Angeles .... CA 69
University of California-San Francisco .... CA 69
University of Southern California .... CA 72
University of the Pacific .... CA 70
Western University of Health Sciences .... CA 74
United States Air Force Academy .... CO .. 504
University of Colorado Denver | Anschutz Medical Campus .... CO 83
Howard University .... DC 92
Jacksonville University .... FL ... 101
Nova Southeastern University .... FL ... 103
University of Florida .... FL ... 109
University of Miami .... FL ... 112
Augusta University .... GA .. 115
Emory University .... GA .. 117
Idaho State University .... ID 130
Loyola University Chicago .... IL 142
Midwestern University .... IL 143
Southern Illinois University Edwardsville . IL 149
University of Illinois at Chicago .... IL 151
Indiana University-Purdue University Indianapolis .... IN 156
University of Iowa .... IA 163
Wichita State University .... KS .. 178
University of Kentucky .... KY .. 185
University of Louisville .... KY .. 185
Louisiana State University Health Sciences Center at Shreveport .... LA ... 189
Louisiana State University Health Sciences Center-New Orleans .... LA ... 189
University of New England .... ME .. 196
Uniformed Services University of the Health Sciences .... MD .. 504
University of Maryland, Baltimore .... MD .. 202
Boston University .... MA .. 207
Harvard University .... MA .. 210
Tufts University .... MA .. 219
University of Detroit Mercy .... MI .. 231
University of Michigan-Ann Arbor .... MI ... 231
University of Minnesota .... MN .. 243
University of Mississippi Medical Center .. MS .. 249
A. T. Still University of Health Sciences .. MO . 250
Saint Louis University .... MO . 259
University of Missouri - Kansas City .... MO . 261
Creighton University .... NE .. 266
University of Nebraska Medical Center .... NE .. 270
Roseman University of Health Sciences .. NV .. 272
University of Nevada, Las Vegas .... NV .. 271
University of New Mexico Main Campus . NM .. 288
Columbia University in the City of New York .... NY .. 297
Icahn School of Medicine at Mount Sinai NY .. 302
New York Medical College .... NY .. 309
New York University .... NY .. 310
State University of New York Upstate Medical University .... NY .. 317
Stony Brook University .... NY .. 317
Touro College .... NY .. 322
University at Buffalo-SUNY .... NY .. 316
University of Rochester .... NY .. 323
Yeshiva University .... NY .. 326
East Carolina University .... NC .. 341
University of North Carolina at Chapel Hill .... NC .. 342
Wake Forest University .... NC .. 344
Case Western Reserve University .... OH .. 349
Ohio State University Main Campus, The. OH .. 358
University of Cincinnati Main Campus .... OH .. 362
University of Toledo .... OH .. 363
Oregon Health & Science University .... OR .. 375
Drexel University .... PA .. 383
Lake Erie College of Osteopathic Medicine .... PA .. 388
Seton Hill University .... PA .. 398
Temple University .... PA .. 399
Thomas Jefferson University .... PA .. 400
University of Pennsylvania .... PA .. 400
University of Pittsburgh .... PA .. 401
University of Puerto Rico-Medical Sciences Campus .... PR .. 513
Medical University of South Carolina .... SC .. 410
Meharry Medical College .... TN .. 422
University of Tennessee, Knoxville .... TN .. 427
Vanderbilt University .... TN .. 428
Texas A & M University .... TX ... 446
University of Texas Health Science Center at Houston (UTHealth), The .... TX ... 456
University of Texas Health Science Center at San Antonio .... TX ... 456
University of Texas MD Anderson Cancer Center, The .... TX ... 456
University of Texas Medical Branch, The TX ... 456
University of Utah, The .... UT .. 460
University of Vermont .... VT .. 463
University of Virginia .... VA .. 473
Virginia Commonwealth University .... VA .. 473
University of Washington .... WA . 485
West Virginia University .... WV . 491
Marquette University .... WI ... 494
Medical College of Wisconsin .... WI ... 494

DH: American Dental Association: dental hygiene (C,A,B,M)

Wallace State Community College - Hanceville .... AL 4
University of Alaska Anchorage .... AK 9
Mesa Community College .... AZ 13
Mohave Community College .... AZ 14
Northern Arizona University .... AZ 14
Phoenix College .... AZ 13
Pima Community College .... AZ 15
Rio Salado College .... AZ 13
University of Arkansas at Fort Smith .... AR 21
University of Arkansas for Medical Sciences .... AR 22
Cabrillo College .... CA 27
Carrington College - Sacramento .... CA 35
Cerritos College .... CA 35
Chabot College .... CA 35
Concorde Career College .... CA 40
Cypress College .... CA 53
Diablo Valley College .... CA 40
Foothill College .... CA 43
Fresno City College .... CA 66
Loma Linda University .... CA 48
Moreno Valley College .... CA 58
Oxnard College .... CA 73
Pasadena City College .... CA 55
Sacramento City College .... CA 50
San Joaquin Valley College, Inc. - Visalia CA 61
Santa Rosa Junior College .... CA 62
Shasta College .... CA 63
Southwestern College .... CA 65
Taft College .... CA 66
University of Southern California .... CA 72
University of the Pacific .... CA 70
West Los Angeles College .... CA 49
Colorado Northwestern Community College .... CO 78
Community College of Denver .... CO 79
Concorde Career College .... CO 79
Pueblo Community College .... CO 81
Goodwin College .... CT 87
Tunxis Community College .... CT 86
University of Bridgeport .... CT 88
University of New Haven .... CT 89
Howard University .... DC 92
Broward College .... FL 95
Daytona State College .... FL 97
Eastern Florida State College .... FL 97
Florida SouthWestern State College .... FL ... 100
Florida State College at Jacksonville .... FL ... 100
Gulf Coast State College .... FL ... 100
Hillsborough Community College .... FL ... 101
Indian River State College .... FL ... 101
Miami Dade College .... FL ... 103
Palm Beach State College .... FL ... 104
Pasco-Hernando State College .... FL ... 104
Pensacola State College .... FL ... 104
St. Petersburg College .... FL ... 106
Santa Fe College .... FL ... 107
South Florida State College .... FL ... 107
State College of Florida, Manatee-Sarasota .... FL ... 108
Tallahassee Community College .... FL ... 111
Valencia College .... FL ... 112
Albany State University .... GA .. 113
Athens Technical College .... GA .. 114
Atlanta Technical College .... GA .. 114
Augusta University .... GA .. 115
Central Georgia Technical College .... GA .. 116
Clayton State University .... GA .. 116
Columbus Technical College .... GA .. 117
Georgia Highlands College .... GA .. 118
Georgia State University .... GA .. 119
Lanier Technical College .... GA .. 121
Savannah Technical College .... GA .. 124
Southeastern Technical College .... GA .. 124
West Georgia Technical College .... GA .. 127
Wiregrass Georgia Technical College .... GA .. 127
University of Hawaii at Manoa .... HI 128
University of Hawaii Maui College .... HI 129
College of Southern Idaho .... ID 130
Idaho State University .... ID 130
Carl Sandburg College .... IL 133
College of DuPage .... IL 135
College of Lake County .... IL 135
Fox College .... IL 137
Harper College .... IL 137
Illinois Central College .... IL 138
Lake Land College .... IL 141
Lewis and Clark Community College .... IL 141
Malcolm X College, One of the City Colleges of Chicago .... IL 134
Parkland College .... IL 146
Prairie State College .... IL 146
Rock Valley College .... IL 147
Southern Illinois University Carbondale ... IL 149
Indiana University Northwest .... IN 156
Indiana University-Purdue University Indianapolis .... IN 156
Indiana University South Bend .... IN 157
University of Southern Indiana .... IN 161
Des Moines Area Community College .... IA 164
Hawkeye Community College .... IA 166
Indian Hills Community College .... IA 166
Iowa Central Community College .... IA 166
Iowa Western Community College .... IA 167
Kirkwood Community College .... IA 167
Flint Hills Technical College .... KS .. 173
Johnson County Community College .... KS .. 174
Manhattan Area Technical College .... KS .. 175
Wichita State University .... KS .. 178
Big Sandy Community and Technical College .... KY .. 180
Bluegrass Community and Technical College .... KY .. 180
University of Louisville .... KY .. 185
Western Kentucky University .... KY .. 185
Louisiana State University Health Sciences Center-New Orleans .... LA ... 189
Southern University at Shreveport-Louisiana .... LA ... 190
University of Louisiana at Monroe .... LA ... 192
University of Maine at Augusta .... ME .. 196
University of New England .... ME .. 196
Allegany College of Maryland .... MD .. 197
Baltimore City Community College .... MD .. 197

Community College of Baltimore County, The ... MD .. 198
Hagerstown Community College ... MD .. 198
Howard Community College ... MD .. 199
University of Maryland, Baltimore ... MD .. 202
Bristol Community College ... MA .. 213
Cape Cod Community College ... MA .. 214
MCPHS University ... MA .. 216
Middlesex Community College ... MA .. 214
Mount Wachusett Community College ... MA .. 215
Quinsigamond Community College ... MA .. 215
Springfield Technical Community College MA .. 215
Delta College ... MI ... 223
Ferris State University ... MI ... 223
Grand Rapids Community College ... MI ... 224
Jackson College ... MI ... 225
Kalamazoo Valley Community College ... MI ... 225
Kellogg Community College ... MI ... 225
Lansing Community College ... MI ... 226
Mott Community College ... MI ... 228
Oakland Community College ... MI ... 229
University of Detroit Mercy ... MI ... 231
University of Michigan-Ann Arbor ... MI ... 231
Wayne County Community College District ... MI ... 232
Century College ... MN .. 237
Lake Superior College ... MN .. 238
Minnesota State University, Mankato ... MN .. 239
Normandale Community College ... MN .. 239
Rochester Community and Technical College ... MN .. 240
Saint Cloud Technical and Community College ... MN .. 241
University of Minnesota ... MN .. 243
Meridian Community College ... MS .. 247
Mississippi Delta Community College ... MS .. 247
Northeast Mississippi Community College MS .. 248
Pearl River Community College ... MS .. 248
University of Mississippi Medical Center . MS .. 249
Concorde Career College ... MO . 251
Missouri Southern State University ... MO . 256
North Central Missouri College ... MO . 257
Ozarks Technical Community College ... MO . 257
State Fair Community College ... MO . 260
University of Missouri - Kansas City ... MO . 261
Great Falls College Montana State University ... MT .. 264
Central Community College ... NE .. 266
University of Nebraska Medical Center ... NE .. 270
College of Southern Nevada ... NV .. 271
Truckee Meadows Community College ... NV .. 271
NHTI-Concord's Community College ... NH .. 273
Bergen Community College ... NJ ... 275
Camden County College ... NJ ... 276
Eastern International College ... NJ ... 277
Middlesex County College ... NJ ... 279
Rowan College at Burlington County ... NJ ... 281
New Mexico State University Dona Ana Community College ... NM .. 287
San Juan College ... NM .. 288
University of New Mexico Main Campus . NM .. 288
Erie Community College ... NY .. 299
Farmingdale State College ... NY .. 321
Hostos Community College-City University of New York ... NY .. 294
Hudson Valley Community College ... NY .. 302
Monroe Community College ... NY .. 307
New York City College of Technology/ City University of New York ... NY .. 295
New York University ... NY .. 310
Orange County Community College ... NY .. 311
Plaza College ... NY .. 311
SUNY Broome Community College ... NY .. 318
Asheville - Buncombe Technical Community College ... NC .. 332
Cape Fear Community College ... NC .. 332
Catawba Valley Community College ... NC .. 333
Central Carolina Community College ... NC .. 333
Central Piedmont Community College ... NC .. 333
Coastal Carolina Community College ... NC .. 333
Fayetteville Technical Community College ... NC .. 334
Forsyth Technical Community College ... NC .. 334
Guilford Technical Community College ... NC .. 335
Halifax Community College ... NC .. 335
University of North Carolina at Chapel Hill ... NC .. 342
Wake Technical Community College ... NC .. 338
Wayne Community College ... NC .. 338
North Dakota State College of Science ... ND .. 346
Columbus State Community College ... OH .. 351
Cuyahoga Community College ... OH .. 351
Hocking College ... OH .. 354
James A. Rhodes State College ... OH .. 354
Lakeland Community College ... OH .. 355
Lorain County Community College ... OH .. 355
Ohio State University Main Campus, The. OH .. 358
Owens Community College ... OH .. 360
Shawnee State University ... OH .. 360
Sinclair Community College ... OH .. 361
Stark State College ... OH .. 361
University of Cincinnati Blue Ash College. OH .. 362
Youngstown State University ... OH .. 365
Rose State College ... OK .. 369
Tulsa Community College ... OK .. 370
Lane Community College ... OR .. 373
Mt. Hood Community College ... OR .. 374
Oregon Institute of Technology ... OR .. 375
Pacific University ... OR .. 375
Portland Community College ... OR .. 375
Community College of Philadelphia ... PA .. 382
Fortis Institute ... PA .. 384
HACC, Central Pennsylvania's Community College ... PA .. 385
Harcum College ... PA .. 385
Luzerne County Community College ... PA .. 389
Manor College ... PA .. 389
Montgomery County Community College PA .. 390
Northampton Community College ... PA .. 391
Pennsylvania College of Technology ... PA .. 393
University of Pittsburgh ... PA .. 401
Westmoreland County Community College ... PA .. 403
Community College of Rhode Island ... RI 404
Florence - Darlington Technical College .. SC .. 409
Greenville Technical College ... SC .. 410
Horry-Georgetown Technical College ... SC .. 410
Midlands Technical College ... SC .. 410
Trident Technical College ... SC .. 413
York Technical College ... SC .. 415
University of South Dakota, The ... SD .. 416
Chattanooga State Community College .. TN .. 424
Concorde Career College ... TN .. 419
East Tennessee State University ... TN .. 419
Roane State Community College ... TN .. 425
Tennessee State University ... TN .. 426
Tennessee Wesleyan University ... TN .. 426
Amarillo College ... TX ... 430
Austin Community College District ... TX ... 431
Blinn College ... TX ... 432
Coastal Bend College ... TX ... 433
Collin County Community College District TX ... 433
Del Mar College ... TX ... 436
El Centro College ... TX ... 435
El Paso Community College ... TX ... 436
Houston Community College ... TX ... 437
Howard College ... TX ... 438
Lamar Institute of Technology ... TX ... 449
Lone Star College System ... TX ... 439
Midwestern State University ... TX ... 440
Tarrant County College District ... TX ... 445
Temple College ... TX ... 446
Texas A & M University ... TX ... 446
Texas State Technical College Waco ... TX ... 449
Texas Woman's University ... TX ... 451
Tyler Junior College ... TX ... 452
University of Texas Health Science Center at Houston (UTHealth), The ... TX ... 456
University of Texas Health Science Center at San Antonio ... TX ... 456
Wharton County Junior College ... TX ... 458
Dixie State University ... UT .. 460
Salt Lake Community College ... UT .. 461
Utah College of Dental Hygiene at Careers Unlimited, The ... UT .. 460
Utah Valley University ... UT .. 461
Weber State University ... UT .. 461
Vermont Technical College ... VT ... 464
Northern Virginia Community College ... VA .. 475
Old Dominion University ... VA .. 469
Thomas Nelson Community College ... VA .. 476
Virginia Commonwealth University ... VA .. 473
Virginia Western Community College ... VA .. 476
Wytheville Community College ... VA .. 476
Bellingham Technical College ... WA . 478
Clark College ... WA . 479
Columbia Basin College ... WA . 479
Eastern Washington University ... WA . 480
Lake Washington Institute of Technology WA . 482
Pierce College District ... WA . 483
Seattle Central College ... WA . 484
Shoreline Community College ... WA . 484
Yakima Valley College ... WA . 487
BridgeValley Community & Technical College ... WV . 488
West Liberty University ... WV . 490
West Virginia University ... WV . 491
Chippewa Valley Technical College ... WI ... 499
Fox Valley Technical College ... WI ... 499
Madison Area Technical College ... WI ... 499
Milwaukee Area Technical College ... WI ... 500
Northcentral Technical College ... WI ... 500
Northeast Wisconsin Technical College .. WI ... 500
Waukesha County Technical College ... WI ... 500
Laramie County Community College ... WY . 502
Northern Wyoming Community College District ... WY . 502

DIETC: Academy of Nutrition and Dietetics: coordinated dietetics programs (B,M)

@University of Alabama at Birmingham ... AL ... 8
University of Alabama, The ... AL ... 7
University of Montevallo ... AL ... 8
#Arkansas State University-Jonesboro ... AR 17
California State University-Los Angeles ... CA 32
Loma Linda University ... CA 48
University of Southern California ... CA 72
Colorado State University ... CO 78
University of Connecticut ... CT 88
@Delaware State University ... DE 89
Howard University ... DC 92
Georgia State University ... GA .. 119
University of Idaho ... ID 131
Dominican University ... IL 136
@Southern Illinois University Edwardsville . IL 149
University of Illinois at Chicago ... IL 151
Indiana State University ... IN 155
Purdue University Main Campus ... IN 159
University of Saint Francis ... IN 161
Kansas State University ... KS .. 174
University of Kentucky ... KY .. 185
Johns Hopkins University ... MD .. 199
Framingham State University ... MA .. 212
@University of Massachusetts Lowell ... MA .. 211
Eastern Michigan University ... MI .. 223
@Grand Valley State University ... MI .. 224
Wayne State University ... MI .. 232
University of Minnesota ... MN .. 243
#Delta State University ... MS .. 245
University of Mississippi ... MS .. 249
University of Missouri - Columbia ... MO .. 261
Rowan University ... NJ .. 281
D'Youville College ... NY .. 298
@Pace University ... NY .. 311
State University of New York College at Buffalo ... NY .. 318
Utica College ... NY .. 324
University of North Carolina at Chapel Hill ... NC .. 342
North Dakota State University Main Campus ... ND .. 345
University of North Dakota ... ND .. 345
Ohio State University Main Campus, The. OH .. 358
University of Akron, Main Campus, The .. OH .. 362
University of Cincinnati Main Campus ... OH .. 362
Youngstown State University ... OH .. 365
La Salle University ... PA .. 387
Seton Hill University ... PA .. 398
University of Pittsburgh ... PA .. 401
#Universidad Ana G. Mendez Gurabo Campus ... PR .. 511
Texas Christian University ... TX ... 448
University of Texas at Austin ... TX ... 455
University of Texas Health Science Center at San Antonio ... TX ... 456
University of Texas Southwestern Medical Center ... TX ... 457
University of Utah, The ... UT .. 460
Utah State University ... UT .. 460
University of Vermont ... VT .. 463
University of Washington ... WA . 485
Washington State University ... WA . 486
Mount Mary University ... WI ... 495
Viterbo University ... WI ... 498

DIETD: Academy of Nutrition and Dietetics: didactic dietetics programs (B,M)

Alabama Agricultural and Mechanical University ... AL ... 1
Auburn University ... AL ... 4
Jacksonville State University ... AL ... 5
Oakwood University ... AL ... 6
Samford University ... AL ... 6
Tuskegee University ... AL ... 7
University of Alabama, The ... AL ... 7
University of Alaska Anchorage ... AK ... 9
Arizona State University ... AZ ... 10
University of Arizona ... AZ ... 16
Harding University Main Campus ... AR 19
Henderson State University ... AR 19
Ouachita Baptist University ... AR 20
University of Arkansas Main Campus ... AR 21
University of Central Arkansas ... AR 23
California Polytechnic State University-San Luis Obispo ... CA 30
California State Polytechnic University-Pomona ... CA 30
California State University-Chico ... CA 31
California State University-Fresno ... CA 31
California State University-Long Beach ... CA 31
California State University-Los Angeles ... CA 32
California State University-Northridge ... CA 32
California State University-Sacramento ... CA 32
California State University-San Bernardino ... CA 33
Pepperdine University ... CA 56
Point Loma Nazarene University ... CA 57
San Diego State University ... CA 33
San Francisco State University ... CA 34
San Jose State University ... CA 34
University of California-Berkeley ... CA 68
University of California-Davis ... CA 68
Colorado State University ... CO 78
Metropolitan State University of Denver .. CO 80
University of Colorado Colorado Springs . CO 83
University of Northern Colorado ... CO 83
University of Connecticut ... CT 88
University of New Haven ... CT 89
University of Saint Joseph ... CT 89
University of Delaware ... DE 90
University of the District of Columbia ... DC 93
Florida International University ... FL ... 109
Florida State University ... FL ... 109
University of Florida ... FL ... 109
University of North Florida ... FL ... 110
Georgia Southern University ... GA .. 119
Life University ... GA .. 121
University of Georgia ... GA .. 125
University of Hawaii at Manoa ... HI 128
Idaho State University ... ID 130
Benedictine University ... IL 132
Bradley University ... IL 133
Dominican University ... IL 136
Eastern Illinois University ... IL 136
Illinois State University ... IL 139
Northern Illinois University ... IL 145
Olivet Nazarene University ... IL 146
Southern Illinois University Carbondale ... IL 149
University of Illinois at Chicago ... IL 151
University of Illinois at Urbana-Champaign ... IL 151
Western Illinois University ... IL 152
Ball State University ... IN 153
Indiana University Bloomington ... IN 156
Purdue University Main Campus ... IN 159
University of Southern Indiana ... IN 161
Iowa State University ... IA 162
Kansas State University ... KS .. 174
Eastern Kentucky University ... KY .. 180
Murray State University ... KY .. 183
University of Kentucky ... KY .. 185
Western Kentucky University ... KY .. 185
Louisiana State University and Agricultural and Mechanical College ... LA ... 188
Louisiana Tech University ... LA ... 191
McNeese State University ... LA ... 192
Nicholls State University ... LA ... 192
University of Maine ... ME .. 195
Morgan State University ... MD .. 200
University of Maryland College Park ... MD .. 202
University of Maryland Eastern Shore ... MD .. 203
Boston University ... MA .. 207
Framingham State University ... MA .. 212
Simmons University ... MA .. 218
University of Massachusetts ... MA .. 211
Andrews University ... MI ... 221
Central Michigan University ... MI ... 222
Madonna University ... MI ... 227
Michigan State University ... MI ... 227
University of Michigan-Ann Arbor ... MI ... 231
Western Michigan University ... MI ... 232
College of Saint Benedict ... MN .. 235
Concordia College ... MN .. 235
Minnesota State University, Mankato ... MN .. 239
St. Catherine University ... MN .. 242
Saint John's University ... MN .. 243
University of Minnesota ... MN .. 243
Mississippi State University ... MS .. 247
University of Mississippi ... MS .. 249
University of Southern Mississippi ... MS .. 249
College of the Ozarks ... MO . 251
Fontbonne University ... MO . 253
Missouri State University ... MO . 256
Northwest Missouri State University ... MO . 257
Saint Louis University ... MO . 259
Southeast Missouri State University ... MO . 259
University of Central Missouri ... MO . 260
Montana State University ... MT .. 264
University of Nebraska - Lincoln ... NE .. 269
University of Nevada, Las Vegas ... NV .. 271
University of Nevada, Reno ... NV .. 271
Keene State College ... NH .. 275
University of New Hampshire ... NH .. 274
College of Saint Elizabeth ... NJ ... 277
Montclair State University ... NJ ... 279
Rutgers University - New Brunswick ... NJ ... 282
New Mexico State University Main Campus ... NM .. 287

Institution	State	Page
University of New Mexico Main Campus	NM	288
City University of New York Brooklyn College	NY	293
City University of New York Herbert H. Lehman College	NY	294
City University of New York Hunter College	NY	294
City University of New York Queens College	NY	295
Cornell University	NY	297
Long Island University - LIU Post	NY	304
New York University	NY	310
Rochester Institute of Technology	NY	313
Sage Colleges, The	NY	313
State University of New York at Oneonta	NY	317
State University of New York College at Buffalo	NY	318
State University of New York College at Plattsburgh	NY	319
Syracuse University	NY	322
Appalachian State University	NC	341
East Carolina University	NC	341
Meredith College	NC	331
North Carolina Central University	NC	342
University of North Carolina at Greensboro	NC	343
Western Carolina University	NC	344
North Dakota State University Main Campus	ND	345
Ashland University	OH	348
Bluffton University	OH	348
Bowling Green State University	OH	348
Case Western Reserve University	OH	349
Kent State University Kent Campus	OH	354
Miami University	OH	356
Ohio State University Main Campus, The.	OH	358
Ohio University Main Campus	OH	359
University of Akron, Main Campus, The	OH	362
University of Cincinnati Main Campus	OH	362
University of Dayton	OH	362
Youngstown State University	OH	365
Northeastern State University	OK	367
Oklahoma State University	OK	368
University of Central Oklahoma	OK	370
Oregon State University	OR	375
Cedar Crest College	PA	381
Drexel University	PA	383
Immaculata University	PA	386
Indiana University of Pennsylvania	PA	394
La Salle University	PA	387
Mansfield University of Pennsylvania	PA	395
Marywood University	PA	389
Messiah College	PA	390
Penn State University Park	PA	392
University of Pittsburgh	PA	401
West Chester University of Pennsylvania	PA	396
#University of Puerto Rico-Rio Piedras Campus	PR	514
Johnson & Wales University	RI	404
University of Rhode Island	RI	406
Clemson University	SC	408
South Carolina State University	SC	412
Winthrop University	SC	414
South Dakota State University	SD	417
Carson-Newman University	TN	419
East Tennessee State University	TN	419
Lipscomb University	TN	421
Middle Tennessee State University	TN	422
Tennessee State University	TN	426
Tennessee Technological University	TN	426
University of Memphis, The	TN	427
University of Tennessee at Chattanooga	TN	428
University of Tennessee at Martin	TN	428
University of Tennessee, Knoxville	TN	427
Abilene Christian University	TX	429
Baylor University	TX	431
Lamar University	TX	449
Prairie View A & M University	TX	446
Sam Houston State University	TX	450
Stephen F. Austin State University	TX	445
Texas A & M University	TX	446
Texas A & M University - Kingsville	TX	447
Texas Christian University	TX	448
#Texas Southern University	TX	449
Texas State University	TX	450
Texas Tech University	TX	451
Texas Woman's University	TX	451
University of Houston	TX	452
University of Texas at Austin	TX	455
University of the Incarnate Word	TX	453
Brigham Young University	UT	458
Utah State University	UT	460
University of Vermont	VT	463
James Madison University	VA	468
Norfolk State University	VA	469
Radford University	VA	470
Virginia Polytechnic Institute and State University	VA	477
Virginia State University	VA	477
Bastyr University	WA	478
Central Washington University	WA	479
Seattle Pacific University	WA	484
Marshall University	WV	490
West Virginia University	WV	491
University of Wisconsin-Green Bay	WI	496
University of Wisconsin-Madison	WI	496
University of Wisconsin-Stevens Point	WI	497
University of Wisconsin-Stout	WI	498
University of Wyoming	WY	502

DIETI: Academy of Nutrition and Dietetics: dietetic post-baccalaureate internships

Institution	State	Page
@Auburn University	AL	4
Oakwood University	AL	6
Samford University	AL	6
University of Alabama at Birmingham	AL	8
University of Alaska Anchorage	AK	9
Arizona State University	AZ	10
University of Arkansas for Medical Sciences	AR	22
University of Central Arkansas	AR	23
California Polytechnic State University-San Luis Obispo	CA	30
California State Polytechnic University-Pomona	CA	30
California State University-Chico	CA	31
California State University-Fresno	CA	31
California State University-Long Beach	CA	31
California State University-Northridge	CA	32
California State University-Sacramento	CA	32
San Francisco State University	CA	34
San Jose State University	CA	34
University of California-Davis	CA	68
University of California-Los Angeles	CA	69
University of California-San Diego	CA	69
University of California-San Francisco	CA	69
University of Southern California	CA	72
University of Northern Colorado	CO	83
University of Connecticut	CT	88
@University of New Haven	CT	89
University of Saint Joseph	CT	89
University of Delaware	DE	90
@Florida International University	FL	109
Florida State University	FL	109
@Keiser University	FL	102
University of Florida	FL	109
University of North Florida	FL	110
@University of South Florida	FL	110
Augusta University	GA	115
Georgia Southern University	GA	119
Life University	GA	121
University of Georgia	GA	125
Idaho State University	ID	130
Benedictine University	IL	132
Bradley University	IL	133
Eastern Illinois University	IL	136
Illinois State University	IL	139
Loyola University Chicago	IL	142
Northern Illinois University	IL	145
Rush University	IL	148
Southern Illinois University Carbondale	IL	149
University of Illinois at Urbana-Champaign	IL	151
Ball State University	IN	153
Indiana University-Purdue University Indianapolis	IN	156
Iowa State University	IA	162
Murray State University	KY	183
University of Kentucky	KY	185
Western Kentucky University	KY	185
@Franciscan Missionaries of Our Lady University	LA	186
Louisiana Tech University	LA	191
McNeese State University	LA	192
Nicholls State University	LA	192
Southern University and A&M College	LA	190
Tulane University	LA	191
University of Maine	ME	195
University of Maryland College Park	MD	202
University of Maryland Eastern Shore	MD	203
University of Maryland, Baltimore	MD	202
Boston University	MA	207
Simmons University	MA	218
University of Massachusetts	MA	211
Andrews University	MI	221
Central Michigan University	MI	222
Michigan State University	MI	227
University of Michigan-Ann Arbor	MI	231
Western Michigan University	MI	232
Concordia College	MN	235
University of Minnesota	MN	243
Mississippi State University	MS	247
University of Southern Mississippi	MS	249
Cox College	MO	252
@Missouri State University	MO	256
@Northwest Missouri State University	MO	257
Saint Louis University	MO	259
Southeast Missouri State University	MO	259
Montana State University	MT	264
University of Nebraska - Lincoln	NE	269
University of Nevada, Las Vegas	NV	271
University of Nevada, Reno	NV	271
Keene State College	NH	275
University of New Hampshire	NH	274
College of Saint Elizabeth	NJ	277
Montclair State University	NJ	279
New Mexico State University Main Campus	NM	287
University of New Mexico Main Campus	NM	288
City University of New York Brooklyn College	NY	293
@City University of New York Graduate Center	NY	293
City University of New York Herbert H. Lehman College	NY	294
City University of New York Hunter College	NY	294
City University of New York Queens College	NY	295
Cornell University	NY	297
@Daemen College	NY	298
Long Island University - LIU Post	NY	304
New York University	NY	310
Sage Colleges, The	NY	313
State University of New York at Oneonta	NY	317
Stony Brook University	NY	317
Syracuse University	NY	322
Teachers College, Columbia University	NY	322
University at Buffalo-SUNY	NY	316
Appalachian State University	NC	341
Duke University	NC	328
East Carolina University	NC	341
Lenoir-Rhyne University	NC	330
Meredith College	NC	331
North Carolina Central University	NC	342
University of North Carolina at Greensboro	NC	343
Western Carolina University	NC	344
Bowling Green State University	OH	348
Case Western Reserve University	OH	349
Kent State University Kent Campus	OH	354
@Miami University	OH	356
Ohio State University Main Campus, The.	OH	358
Ohio University Main Campus	OH	359
Oklahoma State University	OK	368
University of Central Oklahoma	OK	370
Oregon Health & Science University	OR	375
Oregon State University	OR	375
Cedar Crest College	PA	381
Immaculata University	PA	386
Indiana University of Pennsylvania	PA	394
Marywood University	PA	389
Messiah College	PA	390
@West Chester University of Pennsylvania	PA	396
University of Puerto Rico-Medical Sciences Campus	PR	513
University of Rhode Island	RI	406
Medical University of South Carolina	SC	410
Winthrop University	SC	414
South Dakota State University	SD	417
East Tennessee State University	TN	419
Lipscomb University	TN	421
University of Memphis, The	TN	427
University of Tennessee at Martin	TN	428
University of Tennessee, Knoxville	TN	427
Vanderbilt University	TN	428
Abilene Christian University	TX	429
Baylor University	TX	431
Lamar University	TX	449
Prairie View A & M University	TX	446
Sam Houston State University	TX	450
Stephen F. Austin State University	TX	445
Texas A & M University	TX	446
Texas A & M University - Kingsville	TX	447
Texas State University	TX	450
Texas Tech University	TX	451
Texas Woman's University	TX	451
University of Houston	TX	452
University of Texas Health Science Center at Houston (UTHealth), The	TX	456
University of Texas Medical Branch, The	TX	456
University of the Incarnate Word	TX	453
Brigham Young University	UT	458
Utah State University	UT	460
University of Virginia	VA	473
Virginia Commonwealth University	VA	473
Virginia Polytechnic Institute and State University	VA	477
Virginia State University	VA	477
Bastyr University	WA	478
Central Washington University	WA	479
Seattle Pacific University	WA	484
Marshall University	WV	490
West Virginia University	WV	491
Mount Mary University	WI	495
University of Wisconsin-Green Bay	WI	496
University of Wisconsin-Stout	WI	498
Viterbo University	WI	498

DIETT: Academy of Nutrition and Dietetics: dietetic technician (A)

Institution	State	Page
Central Arizona College	AZ	11
Chandler-Gilbert Community College	AZ	12
Paradise Valley Community College	AZ	13
Merritt College	CA	56
Orange Coast College	CA	38
Santa Rosa Junior College	CA	62
#Gateway Community College	CT	85
Hillsborough Community College	FL	101
Harper College	IL	137
Southern Maine Community College	ME	195
Normandale Community College	MN	239
Truckee Meadows Community College	NV	271
Camden County College	NJ	276
Middlesex County College	NJ	279
Erie Community College	NY	299
LaGuardia Community College/City University of New York	NY	294
Suffolk County Community College	NY	321
SUNY Morrisville	NY	321
#Westchester Community College	NY	325
Gaston College	NC	334
Cincinnati State Technical and Community College	OH	350
Columbus State Community College	OH	351
Cuyahoga Community College	OH	351
Owens Community College	OH	360
Sinclair Community College	OH	361
Stark State College	OH	361
Youngstown State University	OH	365
Oklahoma State University - Oklahoma City	OK	368
Community College of Allegheny County	PA	381
Tarrant County College District	TX	445
@Pierpont Community & Technical College	WV	489
Milwaukee Area Technical College	WI	500

DMOLS: National Accrediting Agency for Clinical Laboratory Sciences: diagnostic molecular scientist (C,B,M)

Institution	State	Page
University of Connecticut	CT	88
Northern Michigan University	MI	228
State University of New York Upstate Medical University	NY	317
University of North Carolina at Chapel Hill	NC	342
Tarleton State University	TX	446
Texas Tech University Health Sciences Center	TX	451
University of Texas MD Anderson Cancer Center, The	TX	456

DMS: Commission on Accreditation of Allied Health Education Programs: diagnostic medical sonography (C,A,B,M)

Institution	State	Page
Lurleen B. Wallace Community College	AL	2
Trenholm State Technical College	AL	3
Wallace State Community College - Hanceville	AL	4
Gateway Community College	AZ	13
Arkansas State University-Jonesboro	AR	17
University of Arkansas at Fort Smith	AR	21
University of Arkansas for Medical Sciences	AR	22
CBD College	CA	35
Cosumnes River College	CA	50
Cypress College	CA	53
Foothill College	CA	43
Kaiser Permanente School of Allied Health Sciences	CA	46
Loma Linda University	CA	48
Merced College	CA	51
Mt. San Jacinto College	CA	52
Orange Coast College	CA	38
Santa Barbara City College	CA	62
University of California-San Diego	CA	69
University of Colorado Denver | Anschutz Medical Campus	CO	83
Gateway Community College	CT	85
AdventHealth University	FL	94
Broward College	FL	95
Cambridge College	FL	95
Eastern Florida State College	FL	97
Hillsborough Community College	FL	101
Keiser University	FL	102
Miami Dade College	FL	103

DT: American Dental Association: dental laboratory technology (C,A)

EH: New England Commission of Higher Education

Norwich University ... VT ... 463
Saint Michael's College ... VT ... 463
School for International Training (SIT) ... VT ... 463
Sterling College ... VT ... 463
University of Vermont ... VT ... 463
Vermont College of Fine Arts ... VT ... 463
Vermont Law School ... VT ... 463
Vermont Technical College ... VT ... 464

EMT: Commission on Accreditation of Allied Health Education Programs: emergency medical technician-paramedic (C,A,B)

Bevill State Community College ... AL ... 1
Calhoun Community College ... AL ... 1
Coastal Alabama Community College ... AL ... 1
Gadsden State Community College ... AL ... 2
George C. Wallace Community College - Dothan ... AL ... 2
Jefferson State Community College ... AL ... 2
Lurleen B. Wallace Community College ... AL ... 2
Northeast Alabama Community College ... AL ... 3
Northwest - Shoals Community College ... AL ... 3
Southern Union State Community College ... AL ... 3
Trenholm State Technical College ... AL ... 3
University of South Alabama ... AL ... 8
Wallace State Community College - Hanceville ... AL ... 4
University of Alaska Anchorage ... AK ... 9
University of Alaska Fairbanks ... AK ... 10
Arizona Western College ... AZ ... 10
Central Arizona College ... AZ ... 11
Eastern Arizona College ... AZ ... 12
Glendale Community College ... AZ ... 13
Mesa Community College ... AZ ... 13
Mohave Community College ... AZ ... 14
Northland Pioneer College ... AZ ... 14
Paradise Valley Community College ... AZ ... 13
Phoenix College ... AZ ... 13
Pima Community College ... AZ ... 15
Yavapai College ... AZ ... 16
Arkansas Northeastern College ... AR ... 17
Arkansas State University-Beebe ... AR ... 17
Arkansas State University-Mountain Home ... AR ... 18
Black River Technical College ... AR ... 18
East Arkansas Community College ... AR ... 19
National Park College ... AR ... 20
North Arkansas College ... AR ... 20
NorthWest Arkansas Community College ... AR ... 20
South Arkansas Community College ... AR ... 21
Southeast Arkansas College ... AR ... 21
University of Arkansas at Monticello ... AR ... 22
University of Arkansas Community College at Batesville ... AR ... 22
University of Arkansas Hope-Texarkana ... AR ... 22
University of Arkansas - Pulaski Technical College ... AR ... 23
American River College ... CA ... 50
Bakersfield College ... CA ... 46
Butte College ... CA ... 27
California State University-Sacramento ... CA ... 32
City College of San Francisco ... CA ... 37
College of the Redwoods Community College District ... CA ... 39
College of the Siskiyous ... CA ... 39
Crafton Hills College ... CA ... 59
Cuesta College ... CA ... 41
Foothill College ... CA ... 43
Imperial Valley College ... CA ... 45
Las Positas College ... CA ... 35
Moreno Valley College ... CA ... 58
Mt. San Antonio College ... CA ... 52
Napa Valley College ... CA ... 53
Palomar College ... CA ... 55
Point Loma Nazarene University ... CA ... 57
Saddleback College ... CA ... 64
Santa Rosa Junior College ... CA ... 62
Southwestern College ... CA ... 65
University of Antelope Valley ... CA ... 68
University of California-Los Angeles ... CA ... 69
Ventura College ... CA ... 73
Victor Valley College ... CA ... 73
West Hills College Lemoore ... CA ... 74
Aims Community College ... CO ... 76
Arapahoe Community College ... CO ... 76
Colorado Mountain College ... CO ... 77
Community College of Aurora ... CO ... 79
Pikes Peak Community College ... CO ... 81
Pueblo Community College ... CO ... 81
Capital Community College ... CT ... 85
Delaware Technical Community College, Terry Campus ... DE ... 90
Broward College ... FL ... 95
Chipola College ... FL ... 96
City College ... FL ... 96
College of Central Florida ... FL ... 96
Daytona State College ... FL ... 97
Eastern Florida State College ... FL ... 97
Florida Gateway College ... FL ... 99
Florida SouthWestern State College ... FL ... 100
Florida State College at Jacksonville ... FL ... 100
Gulf Coast State College ... FL ... 100
Hillsborough Community College ... FL ... 101
Indian River State College ... FL ... 101
Miami Dade College ... FL ... 103
North Florida Community College ... FL ... 103
Northwest Florida State College ... FL ... 103
Palm Beach State College ... FL ... 104
Pasco-Hernando State College ... FL ... 104
Pensacola State College ... FL ... 104
Polk State College ... FL ... 105
St. Johns River State College ... FL ... 106
St. Petersburg College ... FL ... 106
Santa Fe College ... FL ... 107
Seminole State College of Florida ... FL ... 107
South Florida State College ... FL ... 107
Tallahassee Community College ... FL ... 111
Valencia College ... FL ... 112
Albany State University ... GA ... 113
Albany Technical College ... GA ... 113
Athens Technical College ... GA ... 114
Atlanta Technical College ... GA ... 114
Augusta University ... GA ... 115
Central Georgia Technical College ... GA ... 116
Chattahoochee Technical College ... GA ... 116
Coastal Pines Technical College ... GA ... 116
Georgia Northwestern Technical College ... GA ... 119
Georgia Piedmont Technical College ... GA ... 119
Gwinnett Technical College ... GA ... 120
Lanier Technical College ... GA ... 121
North Georgia Technical College ... GA ... 122
Savannah Technical College ... GA ... 124
Southeastern Technical College ... GA ... 124
Southern Crescent Technical College ... GA ... 124
Southern Regional Technical College ... GA ... 125
Wiregrass Georgia Technical College ... GA ... 127
Kapiolani Community College ... HI ... 128
College of Southern Idaho ... ID ... 130
Idaho State University ... ID ... 130
Lewis-Clark State College ... ID ... 131
Black Hawk College ... IL ... 132
Illinois Central College ... IL ... 138
Illinois Valley Community College ... IL ... 139
Kaskaskia College ... IL ... 140
Kishwaukee College ... IL ... 140
Lake Land College ... IL ... 141
Lewis and Clark Community College ... IL ... 141
Loyola University Chicago ... IL ... 142
Malcolm X College, One of the City Colleges of Chicago ... IL ... 134
McHenry County College ... IL ... 143
Parkland College ... IL ... 146
Rend Lake College ... IL ... 147
Southwestern Illinois College ... IL ... 149
Waubonsee Community College ... IL ... 152
Indiana University-Purdue University Indianapolis ... IN ... 156
St. Vincent College of Health Professions ... IN ... 160
Clinton Community College ... IA ... 165
Des Moines Area Community College ... IA ... 164
Hawkeye Community College ... IA ... 166
Indian Hills Community College ... IA ... 166
Iowa Central Community College ... IA ... 166
Iowa Western Community College ... IA ... 167
Kirkwood Community College ... IA ... 167
Mercy College of Health Sciences ... IA ... 168
Muscatine Community College ... IA ... 165
Scott Community College ... IA ... 165
Southeastern Community College ... IA ... 169
University of Iowa ... IA ... 163
Western Iowa Tech Community College ... IA ... 170
Barton County Community College ... KS ... 171
Coffeyville Community College ... KS ... 172
Cowley College ... KS ... 172
Garden City Community College ... KS ... 173
Hutchinson Community College ... KS ... 174
Johnson County Community College ... KS ... 174
Kansas City Kansas Community College ... KS ... 174
Eastern Kentucky University ... KY ... 180
Gateway Community and Technical College ... KY ... 181
Jefferson Community and Technical College ... KY ... 181
Madisonville Community College ... KY ... 181
Owensboro Community and Technical College ... KY ... 182
Somerset Community College ... KY ... 182
Bossier Parish Community College ... LA ... 187
Delgado Community College ... LA ... 187
Louisiana Delta Community College ... LA ... 187
Nunez Community College ... LA ... 188
South Louisiana Community College ... LA ... 188
Eastern Maine Community College ... ME ... 194
Kennebec Valley Community College ... ME ... 194
Northern Maine Community College ... ME ... 194
Southern Maine Community College ... ME ... 195
Anne Arundel Community College ... MD ... 197
Carroll Community College ... MD ... 197
Cecil College ... MD ... 197
Chesapeake College ... MD ... 197
College of Southern Maryland ... MD ... 198
Community College of Baltimore County, The ... MD ... 198
Garrett College ... MD ... 198
Hagerstown Community College ... MD ... 198
Harford Community College ... MD ... 199
Howard Community College ... MD ... 199
Prince George's Community College ... MD ... 201
University of Maryland Baltimore County ... MD ... 202
Wor-Wic Community College ... MD ... 204
Bunker Hill Community College ... MA ... 214
Greenfield Community College ... MA ... 214
Massachusetts Bay Community College ... MA ... 214
Massasoit Community College ... MA ... 214
Northern Essex Community College ... MA ... 215
Quinsigamond Community College ... MA ... 215
Springfield College ... MA ... 218
Bay de Noc Community College ... MI ... 221
Henry Ford College ... MI ... 224
Jackson College ... MI ... 225
Kalamazoo Valley Community College ... MI ... 225
Kellogg Community College ... MI ... 225
Kirtland Community College ... MI ... 226
Lake Superior State University ... MI ... 226
Lansing Community College ... MI ... 226
Macomb Community College ... MI ... 226
North Central Michigan College ... MI ... 228
St. Clair County Community College ... MI ... 230
Schoolcraft College ... MI ... 230
Wayne County Community College District ... MI ... 232
Century College ... MN ... 237
Inver Hills Community College ... MN ... 238
Mesabi Range College ... MN ... 238
Northland Community and Technical College ... MN ... 240
Ridgewater College ... MN ... 240
Saint Cloud Technical and Community College ... MN ... 241
South Central College ... MN ... 241
Coahoma Community College ... MS ... 245
East Mississippi Community College ... MS ... 246
Hinds Community College ... MS ... 246
Holmes Community College ... MS ... 246
Itawamba Community College ... MS ... 246
Jones County Junior College ... MS ... 246
Meridian Community College ... MS ... 247
Mississippi Gulf Coast Community College ... MS ... 247
Northwest Mississippi Community College ... MS ... 248
Crowder College ... MO ... 252
East Central College ... MO ... 252
Jefferson College ... MO ... 254
Metropolitan Community College - Penn Valley ... MO ... 255
Mineral Area College ... MO ... 256
Missouri Southern State University ... MO ... 256
Ozarks Technical Community College ... MO ... 257
St. Charles Community College ... MO ... 258
Three Rivers College ... MO ... 260
University of Missouri - Kansas City ... MO ... 261
Flathead Valley Community College ... MT ... 263
Great Falls College Montana State University ... MT ... 264
Montana State University Billings ... MT ... 264
Central Community College ... NE ... 266
Creighton University ... NE ... 266
Metropolitan Community College ... NE ... 267
Northeast Community College ... NE ... 268
Southeast Community College ... NE ... 269
College of Southern Nevada ... NV ... 271
Truckee Meadows Community College ... NV ... 271
NHTI-Concord's Community College ... NH ... 273
Bergen Community College ... NJ ... 275
Ocean County College ... NJ ... 280
Central New Mexico Community College ... NM ... 285
Eastern New Mexico University-Roswell ... NM ... 286
New Mexico State University Dona Ana Community College ... NM ... 287
San Juan College ... NM ... 288
Santa Fe Community College ... NM ... 288
University of New Mexico Main Campus ... NM ... 288
City University of New York Borough of Manhattan Community College ... NY ... 293
City University of New York Kingsborough Community College ... NY ... 294
Dutchess Community College ... NY ... 298
Erie Community College ... NY ... 299
Hudson Valley Community College ... NY ... 302
LaGuardia Community College/City University of New York ... NY ... 294
Monroe Community College ... NY ... 307
St. John's University ... NY ... 314
State University of New York College of Agriculture and Technology at Coble skill ... NY ... 319
State University of New York Upstate Medical University ... NY ... 317
Stony Brook University ... NY ... 317
Suffolk County Community College ... NY ... 321
Westchester Community College ... NY ... 325
Alamance Community College ... NC ... 332
Asheville - Buncombe Technical Community College ... NC ... 332
Blue Ridge Community College ... NC ... 332
Caldwell Community College and Technical Institute ... NC ... 332
Catawba Valley Community College ... NC ... 333
Central Carolina Community College ... NC ... 333
Central Piedmont Community College ... NC ... 333
Cleveland Community College ... NC ... 333
Coastal Carolina Community College ... NC ... 333
Davidson County Community College ... NC ... 334
Durham Technical Community College ... NC ... 334
Fayetteville Technical Community College ... NC ... 334
Gaston College ... NC ... 334
Guilford Technical Community College ... NC ... 335
Johnston Community College ... NC ... 335
Lenoir Community College ... NC ... 335
Piedmont Community College ... NC ... 336
Pitt Community College ... NC ... 336
Sandhills Community College ... NC ... 337
South Piedmont Community College ... NC ... 337
Southwestern Community College ... NC ... 338
Stanly Community College ... NC ... 338
Surry Community College ... NC ... 338
Tri-County Community College ... NC ... 338
Western Carolina University ... NC ... 344
Bismarck State College ... ND ... 346
Dakota College at Bottineau ... ND ... 346
North Dakota State College of Science ... ND ... 346
Belmont College ... OH ... 348
Central Ohio Technical College ... OH ... 349
Cincinnati State Technical and Community College ... OH ... 350
Clark State Community College ... OH ... 350
Columbus State Community College ... OH ... 351
Cuyahoga Community College ... OH ... 351
Eastern Gateway Community College - Jefferson County Campus ... OH ... 352
Hocking College ... OH ... 354
James A. Rhodes State College ... OH ... 354
Lakeland Community College ... OH ... 355
Lorain County Community College ... OH ... 355
Mercy College of Ohio ... OH ... 356
North Central State College ... OH ... 357
Owens Community College ... OH ... 360
Shawnee State University ... OH ... 360
Sinclair Community College ... OH ... 361
Stark State College ... OH ... 361
University of Toledo ... OH ... 363
Youngstown State University ... OH ... 365
Oklahoma City Community College ... OK ... 367
Oklahoma State University - Oklahoma City ... OK ... 368
Rogers State University ... OK ... 369
Central Oregon Community College ... OR ... 372
Chemeketa Community College ... OR ... 372
College of Emergency Services ... OR ... 372
Lane Community College ... OR ... 373
Oregon Health & Science University ... OR ... 375
Portland Community College ... OR ... 375
Rogue Community College ... OR ... 376
Southwestern Oregon Community College ... OR ... 376
Umpqua Community College ... OR ... 377
Community College of Allegheny County ... PA ... 381
Delaware County Community College ... PA ... 382
HACC, Central Pennsylvania's Community College ... PA ... 385
Luzerne County Community College ... PA ... 389
Pennsylvania College of Technology ... PA ... 393
Thomas Jefferson University ... PA ... 400
University of Pittsburgh ... PA ... 401
Greenville Technical College ... SC ... 410
Horry-Georgetown Technical College ... SC ... 410
Spartanburg Community College ... SC ... 412
Trident Technical College ... SC ... 413
Lake Area Technical Institute ... SD ... 415
University of South Dakota, The ... SD ... 416
Western Dakota Technical Institute ... SD ... 417
Chattanooga State Community College ... TN ... 424
Cleveland State Community College ... TN ... 424
Columbia State Community College ... TN ... 424
Dyersburg State Community College ... TN ... 425
Jackson State Community College ... TN ... 425

Motlow State Community College ... TN .. 425
Northeast State Community College ... TN .. 425
Roane State Community College ... TN .. 425
Southwest Tennessee Community College ... TN .. 426
Volunteer State Community College ... TN .. 426
Walters State Community College ... TN .. 426
Alvin Community College ... TX ... 429
Amarillo College ... TX ... 430
Angelina College ... TX ... 430
Austin Community College District ... TX ... 431
Blinn College ... TX ... 432
Brazosport College ... TX ... 432
Brookhaven College ... TX ... 434
Central Texas College ... TX ... 432
College of the Mainland ... TX ... 433
Collin County Community College District TX ... 433
Del Mar College ... TX ... 436
El Centro College ... TX ... 435
El Paso Community College ... TX ... 436
Galveston College ... TX ... 437
Grayson College ... TX ... 437
Hill College ... TX ... 437
Houston Community College ... TX ... 437
Howard College ... TX ... 438
Kilgore College ... TX ... 439
Lamar Institute of Technology ... TX ... 449
Laredo College ... TX ... 439
Lone Star College System ... TX ... 439
McLennan Community College ... TX ... 440
Midland College ... TX ... 440
Navarro College ... TX ... 440
North Central Texas College ... TX ... 441
Northeast Texas Community College ... TX ... 441
Odessa College ... TX ... 441
Panola College ... TX ... 441
Paris Junior College ... TX ... 441
San Antonio College ... TX ... 429
San Jacinto College North ... TX ... 443
South Plains College ... TX ... 443
South Texas College ... TX ... 444
Tarrant County College District ... TX ... 445
Temple College ... TX ... 446
Texarkana College ... TX ... 446
Texas Southmost College ... TX ... 449
Texas State Technical College Waco ... TX ... 449
Trinity Valley Community College ... TX ... 452
Tyler Junior College ... TX ... 452
University of Texas Health Science Center at San Antonio ... TX ... 456
Victoria College ... TX ... 457
Weatherford College ... TX ... 458
Wharton County Junior College ... TX ... 458
Dixie State University ... UT .. 460
Utah Valley University ... UT .. 461
Weber State University ... UT .. 461
Vermont Technical College ... VT ... 464
Central Virginia Community College ... VA .. 474
J. Sargeant Reynolds Community College ... VA .. 474
John Tyler Community College ... VA .. 474
Lord Fairfax Community College ... VA .. 474
Northern Virginia Community College ... VA .. 475
Patrick Henry Community College ... VA .. 475
Piedmont Virginia Community College ... VA .. 475
Rappahannock Community College ... VA .. 475
Southside Virginia Community College ... VA .. 475
Southwest Virginia Community College ... VA .. 475
Tidewater Community College ... VA .. 476
Virginia Commonwealth University ... VA .. 473
Central Washington University ... WA . 479
Columbia Basin College ... WA . 479
Tacoma Community College ... WA . 485
University of Washington ... WA . 485
Blue Ridge Community and Technical College ... WV . 488
Mountwest Community and Technical College ... WV . 489
New River Community and Technical College ... WV . 489
Pierpont Community & Technical College WV . 489
Southern West Virginia Community and Technical College ... WV . 489
Chippewa Valley Technical College ... WI ... 499
Fox Valley Technical College ... WI ... 499
Lakeshore Technical College ... WI ... 499
Madison Area Technical College ... WI ... 499
Mid-State Technical College ... WI ... 500
Milwaukee Area Technical College ... WI ... 500
Moraine Park Technical College ... WI ... 500
Northcentral Technical College ... WI ... 500
Northeast Wisconsin Technical College .. WI ... 500
Waukesha County Technical College ... WI ... 500
Western Technical College ... WI ... 501
Casper College ... WY . 501
Laramie County Community College ... WY . 502

EXSC: Commission on Accreditation of Allied Health Education Programs: exercise science (C,A,B,M)

Northern Arizona University ... AZ ... 14
Metropolitan State University of Denver .. CO ... 80
Central Connecticut State University ... CT ... 84
Southern Connecticut State University ... CT ... 85
Barry University ... FL ... 95
University of North Florida ... FL ... 110
University of West Florida ... FL ... 110
Clayton State University ... GA .. 116
Georgia State University ... GA .. 119
Valdosta State University ... GA .. 126
Southern Illinois University Edwardsville . IL ... 149
Indiana Wesleyan University ... IN ... 157
University of Indianapolis ... IN ... 161
University of Southern Indiana ... IN ... 161
Baker University ... KS .. 170
Murray State University ... KY .. 183
University of Louisville ... KY .. 185
University of Louisiana at Monroe ... LA ... 192
University of New England ... ME .. 196
University of Southern Maine ... ME .. 196
Frostburg State University ... MD .. 203
Salisbury University ... MD .. 203
Lasell College ... MA .. 210
Springfield College ... MA .. 218
Westfield State University ... MA .. 213
Central Michigan University ... MI ... 222
Wayne State University ... MI ... 232
St. Catherine University ... MN .. 242
Missouri Baptist University ... MO . 256
City University of New York York College NY .. 295
Mercy College ... NY .. 306
State University of New York, The College at Brockport ... NY .. 318
Gardner-Webb University ... NC .. 329
North Carolina Wesleyan College ... NC .. 339
University of North Carolina at Charlotte . NC .. 342
North Dakota State University Main Campus ... ND .. 345
University of Mary ... ND .. 347
Baldwin Wallace University ... OH .. 348
Bowling Green State University ... OH .. 348
Kent State University Kent Campus ... OH .. 354
Ohio Northern University ... OH .. 358
Wright State University Main Campus ... OH .. 364
Youngstown State University ... OH .. 365
University of Central Oklahoma ... OK .. 370
Bloomsburg University of Pennsylvania ... PA .. 394
East Stroudsburg University of Pennsylvania ... PA .. 394
Eastern University ... PA .. 383
Grove City College ... PA .. 385
Indiana University of Pennsylvania ... PA .. 394
Saint Francis University ... PA .. 398
Seton Hill University ... PA .. 398
Slippery Rock University of Pennsylvania. PA .. 395
University of Scranton, The ... PA .. 401
West Chester University of Pennsylvania PA .. 396
University of Rhode Island ... RI ... 406
Winthrop University ... SC .. 414
South Dakota State University ... SD .. 417
George Mason University ... VA .. 467
Liberty University ... VA .. 468
Longwood University ... VA .. 469
Old Dominion University ... VA .. 469
University of Lynchburg ... VA .. 472

FEPAC: American Academy of Forensic Sciences: forensic science (B,M)

University of Alabama at Birmingham ... AL ... 8
George Washington University ... DC ... 91
Florida International University ... FL ... 109
University of Central Florida ... FL ... 109
University of Tampa ... FL ... 112
Albany State University ... GA .. 113
Loyola University Chicago ... IL ... 142
University of Illinois at Chicago ... IL ... 151
Indiana University-Purdue University Indianapolis ... IN ... 156
Eastern Kentucky University ... KY .. 180
Towson University ... MD .. 204
Boston University ... MA .. 207
Madonna University ... MI .. 227
Michigan State University ... MI ... 227
University of Mississippi ... MS .. 249
Alfred State College ... NY .. 320
City University of New York John Jay College of Criminal Justice ... NY .. 294
State University of New York College at Buffalo ... NY .. 318
Syracuse University ... NY .. 322
Fayetteville State University ... NC .. 341
Ohio University Main Campus ... OH .. 359
University of Central Oklahoma ... OK .. 370
Arcadia University ... PA .. 379
Cedar Crest College ... PA .. 381
Duquesne University ... PA .. 383
Penn State University Park ... PA .. 392
West Chester University of Pennsylvania PA .. 396
Sam Houston State University ... TX ... 450
Texas A & M University ... TX ... 446
University of North Texas ... TX ... 454
Liberty University ... VA .. 468
Virginia Commonwealth University ... VA .. 473
Marshall University ... WV .. 490
West Virginia University ... WV .. 491

FUSER: American Board of Funeral Service Education: funeral service education (C,A,B)

Jefferson State Community College ... AL ... 2
#Arkansas State University-Mountain Home ... AR ... 18
University of Arkansas Hope-Texarkana . AR ... 22
American River College ... CA ... 50
Cypress College ... CA ... 53
Arapahoe Community College ... CO ... 76
Goodwin College ... CT ... 87
Florida State College at Jacksonville ... FL ... 100
Miami Dade College ... FL ... 103
St. Petersburg College ... FL ... 106
Gupton Jones College of Funeral Service GA .. 120
Ogeechee Technical College ... GA .. 122
Carl Sandburg College ... IL ... 133
Malcolm X College, One of the City Colleges of Chicago ... IL ... 134
Southern Illinois University Carbondale ... IL ... 149
Worsham College of Mortuary Science ... IL ... 152
Ivy Tech Community College of Indiana-Indianapolis ... IN ... 157
Mid-America College of Funeral Service . IN ... 159
Vincennes University ... IN ... 162
Des Moines Area Community College ... IA ... 164
Kansas City Kansas Community College KS .. 174
Delgado Community College ... LA ... 187
Community College of Baltimore County, The ... MD .. 198
FINE Mortuary College ... MA .. 209
Wayne State University ... MI ... 232
University of Minnesota ... MN .. 243
East Mississippi Community College ... MS .. 246
Northwest Mississippi Community College ... MS .. 248
Eastwick College ... NJ ... 277
Mercer County Community College ... NJ ... 278
American Academy McAllister Institute of Funeral Service ... NY .. 290
Hudson Valley Community College ... NY .. 302
Nassau Community College ... NY .. 308
SUNY Canton-College of Technology ... NY .. 320
Fayetteville Technical Community College ... NC .. 334
Cincinnati College of Mortuary Science ... OH .. 350
University of Central Oklahoma ... OK .. 370
Mt. Hood Community College ... OR .. 374
Northampton Community College ... PA .. 391
Pittsburgh Institute of Mortuary Science .. PA .. 396
#Piedmont Technical College ... SC .. 411
John A. Gupton College ... TN .. 420
Amarillo College ... TX ... 430
Commonwealth Institute of Funeral Service ... TX ... 434
Dallas Institute of Funeral Service ... TX ... 435
Northeast Texas Community College ... TX ... 441
San Antonio College ... TX ... 429
Salt Lake Community College ... UT .. 461
John Tyler Community College ... VA .. 474
Tidewater Community College ... VA .. 476
Lake Washington Institute of Technology WA . 482
Milwaukee Area Technical College ... WI ... 500

HSA: Commission on Accreditation of Healthcare Management Education: healthcare management (M)

University of Alabama at Birmingham ... AL ... 8
University of Arkansas for Medical Sciences ... AR ... 22
California State University-Long Beach ... CA ... 31
California State University-Northridge ... CA ... 32
San Diego State University ... CA ... 33
University of Southern California ... CA ... 72
University of Colorado Denver | Anschutz Medical Campus ... CO ... 83
University of New Haven ... CT ... 89
George Washington University ... DC ... 91
Georgetown University ... DC ... 92
Florida International University ... FL ... 109
University of Central Florida ... FL ... 109
University of Florida ... FL ... 109
University of Miami ... FL ... 112
University of North Florida ... FL ... 110
University of South Florida ... FL ... 110
Georgia Southern University ... GA .. 119
Georgia State University ... GA .. 119
#Governors State University ... IL ... 137
Rush University ... IL ... 148
University of Illinois at Chicago ... IL ... 151
Indiana University-Purdue University Indianapolis ... IN ... 156
Des Moines University ... IA ... 164
University of Iowa ... IA ... 163
University of Kansas Main Campus ... KS .. 177
University of Kentucky ... KY .. 185
University of Louisville ... KY .. 185
Tulane University ... LA ... 191
Johns Hopkins University ... MD .. 199
Uniformed Services University of the Health Sciences ... MD .. 504
Boston University ... MA .. 207
Suffolk University ... MA .. 219
University of Michigan-Ann Arbor ... MI .. 231
University of Minnesota ... MN .. 243
University of Saint Thomas ... MN .. 244
Saint Louis University ... MO . 259
University of Missouri - Columbia ... MO . 261
University of Nevada, Las Vegas ... NV .. 271
Seton Hall University ... NJ .. 283
Clarkson University ... NY .. 296
Columbia University in the City of New York ... NY .. 297
Cornell University ... NY .. 297
New York University ... NY .. 310
University of North Carolina at Chapel Hill ... NC .. 342
University of North Carolina at Charlotte . NC .. 342
Ohio State University Main Campus, The. OH .. 358
Xavier University ... OH .. 365
Portland State University ... OR .. 376
Penn State University Park ... PA .. 392
Temple University ... PA .. 399
University of Pittsburgh ... PA .. 401
University of Scranton, The ... PA .. 401
Widener University ... PA .. 403
University of Puerto Rico-Medical Sciences Campus ... PR .. 513
Medical University of South Carolina ... SC .. 410
University of South Carolina Columbia ... SC .. 413
University of Memphis, The ... TN .. 427
Baylor University ... TX ... 431
Texas A & M University ... TX ... 446
Texas State University ... TX ... 450
Texas Woman's University ... TX ... 451
Trinity University ... TX ... 452
University of North Texas Health Science Center at Fort Worth ... TX ... 454
University of Texas Health Science Center at Houston (UTHealth), The ... TX ... 456
University of the Incarnate Word ... TX ... 453
University of Utah, The ... UT .. 460
Weber State University ... UT .. 461
George Mason University ... VA .. 467
Marymount University ... VA .. 469
Virginia Commonwealth University ... VA .. 473
University of Washington ... WA . 485
Washington State University ... WA . 486

HT: National Accrediting Agency for Clinical Laboratory Sciences: histologic technology (C,A,B)

Phoenix College ... AZ ... 13
Baptist Health College Little Rock ... AR ... 18
Merritt College ... CA ... 56
Mt. San Antonio College ... CA ... 52
Goodwin College ... CT ... 87
Barry University ... FL ... 95
Florida State College at Jacksonville ... FL ... 100
Miami Dade College ... FL ... 103
Albany State University ... GA .. 113
Elgin Community College ... IL ... 136
Indiana University-Purdue University Indianapolis ... IN ... 156
Harford Community College ... MD .. 199
State University of New York College of Agriculture and Technology at Coble skill ... NY .. 319
Carolinas College of Health Sciences ... NC .. 327
University of North Dakota ... ND .. 345
Lakeland Community College ... OH .. 355
Drexel University ... PA .. 383
Harcum College ... PA .. 385
University of Pittsburgh ... PA .. 401
Community College of Rhode Island ... RI ... 404
Houston Community College ... TX ... 437
St. Philip's College ... TX ... 429

Tarleton State University ... TX ... 446
University of Texas Health Science Center at San Antonio ... TX ... 456
University of Texas MD Anderson Cancer Center, The ... TX ... 456
Clover Park Technical College ... WA . 479
West Virginia University ... WV . 491

IACBE: International Accreditation Council for Business Education: business programs in institutions that grant bachelor/graduate degrees (A,B,M,D)

Faulkner University ... AL ... 5
Stillman College ... AL ... 7
Alaska Pacific University ... AK ... 9
Ashford University ... CA ... 26
Azusa Pacific University ... CA ... 26
Concordia University Irvine ... CA ... 40
CSU Maritime Academy ... CA ... 32
Hope International University ... CA ... 45
Humboldt State University ... CA ... 33
John F. Kennedy University ... CA ... 46
Lincoln University ... CA ... 48
National University ... CA ... 53
Pacific Union College ... CA ... 55
Albertus Magnus College ... CT ... 84
Wilmington University ... DE ... 90
Edward Waters College ... FL ... 97
Florida Institute of Technology ... FL ... 99
Hodges University ... FL ... 101
Lynn University ... FL ... 102
Nova Southeastern University ... FL ... 103
Palm Beach Atlantic University ... FL ... 104
University of Guam ... GU .. 505
Chaminade University of Honolulu ... HI ... 127
Lewis-Clark State College ... ID ... 131
Lincoln College ... IL ... 141
McKendree University ... IL ... 143
National Louis University ... IL ... 144
North Park University ... IL ... 145
Robert Morris University - Illinois ... IL ... 147
Rockford University ... IL ... 147
Indiana Tech ... IN ... 155
Marian University ... IN ... 158
Oakland City University ... IN ... 159
Maharishi University of Management ... IA ... 167
Northwestern College ... IA ... 168
Grantham University ... KS .. 173
University of Saint Mary ... KS .. 177
Campbellsville University ... KY .. 179
Kentucky Wesleyan College ... KY .. 183
Lindsey Wilson College ... KY .. 183
Spalding University ... KY .. 184
University of the Cumberlands ... KY .. 185
University of Holy Cross ... LA ... 191
Husson University ... ME .. 194
University of Maine at Fort Kent ... ME .. 196
Capitol Technology University ... MD .. 197
Mount St. Mary's University ... MD .. 200
University of Maryland College Park ... MD .. 202
American International College ... MA .. 205
College of Our Lady of the Elms ... MA .. 208
Curry College ... MA .. 208
Fisher College ... MA .. 209
Fitchburg State University ... MA .. 212
Framingham State University ... MA .. 212
Massachusetts Maritime Academy ... MA .. 213
Nichols College ... MA .. 217
Springfield College ... MA .. 218
Wentworth Institute of Technology ... MA .. 219
Andrews University ... MI ... 221
Baker College of Flint ... MI ... 221
Davenport University ... MI ... 223
Lawrence Technological University ... MI ... 226
Bemidji State University ... MN .. 237
Saint Mary's University of Minnesota ... MN .. 243
Belhaven University ... MS .. 245
William Carey University ... MS .. 249
Avila University ... MO . 250
Culver-Stockton College ... MO . 252
Carroll College ... MT .. 263
Montana Technological University ... MT .. 265
University of Montana Western, The ... MT .. 264
Bellevue University ... NE .. 265
Concordia University ... NE .. 266
Wayne State College ... NE .. 268
Roseman University of Health Sciences .. NV .. 272
Franklin Pierce University ... NH .. 273
Berkeley College ... NJ ... 275
Centenary University ... NJ ... 276
Felician University ... NJ ... 278
Saint Peter's University ... NJ ... 282
Berkeley College ... NY .. 291
Cazenovia College ... NY .. 292
Concordia College ... NY .. 297
Daemen College ... NY .. 298
Dominican College of Blauvelt ... NY .. 298
D'Youville College ... NY .. 298
Excelsior College ... NY .. 299
Keuka College ... NY .. 304
Manhattanville College ... NY .. 305
Medaille College ... NY .. 306
Mount Saint Mary College ... NY .. 307
Roberts Wesleyan College ... NY .. 312
Sage Colleges, The ... NY .. 313
St. Thomas Aquinas College ... NY .. 315
State University of New York Empire State College ... NY .. 321
Vaughn College of Aeronautics and Technology ... NY .. 324
Livingstone College ... NC .. 330
Dickinson State University ... ND .. 345
Minot State University ... ND .. 345
University of Mary ... ND .. 347
Defiance College, The ... OH .. 352
Franklin University ... OH .. 353
Lake Erie College ... OH .. 355
Lourdes University ... OH .. 355
University of Rio Grande ... OH .. 363
Ursuline College ... OH .. 363
Bacone College ... OK .. 365
Oklahoma Wesleyan University ... OK .. 368
Southwestern Oklahoma State University. OK .. 370
Eastern Oregon University ... OR .. 373
Northwest Christian University ... OR .. 374
Oregon Institute of Technology ... OR .. 375
Cairn University ... PA .. 380
Chatham University ... PA .. 381
Gwynedd Mercy University ... PA .. 385
Juniata College ... PA .. 386
Keystone College ... PA .. 386
Mercyhurst University ... PA .. 390
Misericordia University ... PA .. 390
Point Park University ... PA .. 397
Saint Francis University ... PA .. 398
Seton Hill University ... PA .. 398
Waynesburg University ... PA .. 402
Inter American University of Puerto Rico San German Campus ... PR .. 509
Salve Regina University ... RI ... 406
Charleston Southern University ... SC .. 407
Dakota Wesleyan University ... SD .. 415
National American University ... SD .. 416
Presentation College ... SD .. 416
University of Sioux Falls ... SD .. 417
Bryan College ... TN .. 418
Southern Adventist University ... TN .. 424
Concordia University Texas ... TX .. 434
Southwestern Adventist University ... TX .. 444
Southwestern Assemblies of God University ... TX ... 445
Hampton University ... VA .. 468
Washington University of Virginia ... VA .. 478
Davis & Elkins College ... WV . 487
Ohio Valley University ... WV . 488
Shepherd University ... WV . 490
West Liberty University ... WV . 490
Concordia University Wisconsin ... WI ... 493
Herzing University ... WI ... 493

IFSAC: International Fire Service Accreditation Congress Degree Assembly: fire and emergency related degree (A,B,M)

Central Arizona College ... AZ ... 11
Yavapai College ... AZ ... 16
NorthWest Arkansas Community College AR ... 20
Oxnard College ... CA ... 73
Aims Community College ... CO ... 76
Embry-Riddle Aeronautical University-Daytona Beach ... FL ... 98
University of Florida ... FL ... 109
Southern Illinois University Carbondale ... IL ... 149
Purdue University Global ... IN ... 159
Johnson County Community College ... KS .. 174
Ashland Community and Technical College ... KY .. 180
Bluegrass Community and Technical College ... KY .. 180
Eastern Kentucky University ... KY .. 180
Elizabethtown Community and Technical College ... KY .. 181
Gateway Community and Technical College ... KY .. 181
Hazard Community and Technical College ... KY .. 181
Jefferson Community and Technical College ... KY .. 181
Madisonville Community College ... KY .. 181
Maysville Community and Technical College ... KY .. 182
Owensboro Community and Technical College ... KY .. 182
Somerset Community College ... KY .. 182
Southcentral Kentucky Community and Technical College ... KY .. 182
West Kentucky Community and Technical College ... KY .. 182
Lansing Community College ... MI ... 226
Macomb Community College ... MI ... 226
Ozarks Technical Community College ... MO . 257
Helena College University of Montana ... MT .. 264
Montana State University Billings ... MT .. 264
New Mexico State University Dona Ana Community College ... NM .. 287
Catawba Valley Community College ... NC .. 333
Gaston College ... NC .. 334
Guilford Technical Community College ... NC .. 335
Central Ohio Technical College ... OH .. 349
Lakeland Community College ... OH .. 355
University of Akron, Main Campus, The .. OH .. 362
Oklahoma State University - Oklahoma City ... OK .. 368
Central Oregon Community College ... OR .. 372
Chemeketa Community College ... OR .. 372
Portland Community College ... OR .. 375
Holy Family University ... PA .. 386
Montgomery County Community College PA .. 390
Blinn College ... TX ... 432
Utah Valley University ... UT .. 461
American Public University System ... WV . 487
Fox Valley Technical College ... WI ... 499
University of Wisconsin-Oshkosh ... WI ... 497

IPSY: American Psychological Association: doctoral internships in health service psychology

Auburn University ... AL ... 4
University of Alabama at Birmingham ... AL ... 8
Arizona State University ... AZ ... 10
University of Arizona ... AZ ... 16
University of Arkansas for Medical Sciences ... AR ... 22
Biola University ... CA ... 27
California State University-Fullerton ... CA ... 31
California State University-Long Beach ... CA ... 31
California State University-Northridge ... CA ... 32
California State University-San Marcos ... CA ... 33
Loma Linda University ... CA ... 48
San Jose State University ... CA ... 34
Santa Clara University ... CA ... 62
Stanford University ... CA ... 65
University of California-Berkeley ... CA ... 68
University of California-Davis ... CA ... 68
University of California-Irvine ... CA ... 68
University of California-Los Angeles ... CA ... 69
University of California-Riverside ... CA ... 69
University of California-San Diego ... CA ... 69
University of California-San Francisco ... CA ... 69
University of California-Santa Barbara ... CA ... 70
University of California-Santa Cruz ... CA ... 70
University of San Diego ... CA ... 71
University of San Francisco ... CA ... 71
University of Southern California ... CA ... 72
University of the Pacific ... CA ... 70
Wright Institute, The ... CA ... 75
Colorado State University ... CO ... 78
University of Colorado Boulder ... CO ... 83
University of Colorado Denver | Anschutz Medical Campus ... CO ... 83
University of Denver ... CO ... 83
University of Northern Colorado ... CO ... 83
University of Connecticut ... CT ... 88
Yale University ... CT ... 89
University of Delaware ... DE ... 90
American University ... DC ... 90
Catholic University of America, The ... DC ... 91
George Washington University ... DC ... 91
Howard University ... DC ... 92
Florida Atlantic University ... FL ... 108
Florida Gulf Coast University ... FL ... 108
Florida International University ... FL ... 109
Florida State University ... FL ... 109
Nova Southeastern University ... FL ... 103
University of Central Florida ... FL ... 109
University of Florida ... FL ... 109
University of Miami ... FL ... 112
University of North Florida ... FL ... 110
University of South Florida ... FL ... 110
Augusta University ... GA .. 115
Emory University ... GA .. 117
Georgia Institute of Technology ... GA .. 118
Georgia Southern University ... GA .. 119
Georgia State University ... GA .. 119
University of Hawaii at Manoa ... HI ... 128
University of Idaho ... ID ... 131
Adler University ... IL ... 131
Illinois State University ... IL ... 139
Lake Forest College ... IL ... 141
Northern Illinois University ... IL ... 145
Northwestern University ... IL ... 145
Rush University ... IL ... 148
Southern Illinois University Carbondale ... IL ... 149
University of Chicago ... IL ... 150
University of Illinois at Chicago ... IL ... 151
University of Illinois at Urbana-Champaign ... IL ... 151
Ball State University ... IN ... 153
Butler University ... IN ... 153
Indiana University Bloomington ... IN ... 156
Indiana University-Purdue University Indianapolis ... IN ... 156
Purdue University Main Campus ... IN ... 159
University of Notre Dame ... IN ... 161
Iowa State University ... IA ... 162
University of Iowa ... IA ... 163
Kansas State University ... KS .. 174
University of Kansas Main Campus ... KS .. 177
University of Kentucky ... KY .. 185
University of Louisville ... KY .. 185
Louisiana State University and Agricultural and Mechanical College ... LA ... 188
Louisiana State University Health Sciences Center-New Orleans ... LA ... 189
Tulane University ... LA ... 191
University of Maine ... ME .. 195
Johns Hopkins University ... MD .. 199
Towson University ... MD .. 204
University of Maryland Baltimore County . MD .. 202
University of Maryland College Park ... MD .. 202
University of Maryland, Baltimore ... MD .. 202
Boston University ... MA .. 207
Harvard University ... MA .. 210
Suffolk University ... MA .. 219
University of Massachusetts ... MA .. 211
William James College ... MA .. 220
Grand Valley State University ... MI ... 224
Michigan State University ... MI ... 227
University of Michigan-Ann Arbor ... MI ... 231
University of Minnesota ... MN .. 243
University of Saint Thomas ... MN .. 244
University of Mississippi Medical Center . MS .. 249
University of Missouri - Columbia ... MO . 261
University of Missouri - Kansas City ... MO . 261
University of Missouri - Saint Louis ... MO . 261
Montana State University ... MT .. 264
University of Nebraska - Lincoln ... NE .. 269
University of Nevada, Las Vegas ... NV .. 271
Dartmouth College ... NH .. 273
University of New Hampshire ... NH .. 274
Rutgers University - New Brunswick ... NJ ... 282
Rutgers University - Newark ... NJ ... 282
New Mexico State University Main Campus ... NM .. 287
University of New Mexico Main Campus . NM .. 288
Adelphi University ... NY .. 289
Albany Medical College ... NY .. 289
Baruch College/City University of New York ... NY .. 292
Columbia University in the City of New York ... NY .. 297
Hofstra University ... NY .. 302
Icahn School of Medicine at Mount Sinai NY .. 302
New York University ... NY .. 310
Pace University ... NY .. 311
Rochester Institute of Technology ... NY .. 313
State University of New York at Oneonta NY .. 317
State University of New York Upstate Medical University ... NY .. 317
Stony Brook University ... NY .. 317
University at Albany, SUNY ... NY .. 316
University at Buffalo-SUNY ... NY .. 316
University of Rochester ... NY .. 323
Yeshiva University ... NY .. 326
Appalachian State University ... NC .. 341
Duke University ... NC .. 328
North Carolina State University ... NC .. 342
University of North Carolina at Chapel Hill ... NC .. 342
University of North Carolina at Charlotte . NC .. 342
Wake Forest University ... NC .. 344
Western Carolina University ... NC .. 344
Bowling Green State University ... OH .. 348
Case Western Reserve University ... OH .. 349
Cleveland State University ... OH .. 351
Miami University ... OH .. 356
Ohio State University Main Campus, The. OH .. 358
Ohio University Main Campus ... OH .. 359
University of Akron, Main Campus, The .. OH .. 362
Wright State University Main Campus ... OH .. 364
George Fox University ... OR .. 373
Oregon Health & Science University ... OR .. 375
Oregon State University ... OR .. 375
Pacific University ... OR .. 375
University of Oregon ... OR .. 377
Chestnut Hill College ... PA .. 381
Drexel University ... PA .. 383
Immaculata University ... PA .. 386

JOUR: Accrediting Council on Education for Journalism and Mass Communications: journalism and mass communications (B,M)

KIN: Commission on Accreditation of Allied Health Education Programs: kinesiotherapy (B)

LAW: American Bar Association: law (FP,D)

LC: Commission on Accreditation of Allied Health Programs: lactation consultant (C,A,B,M)

LIB: American Library Association: library and information studies (M)

LSAR: American Society of Landscape Architects: landscape architecture (B,M)

M: Middle States Commission on Higher Education

MAAB: Accrediting Bureau of Health Education Schools: medical assisting (C,A)

MAC: Commission on Accreditation of Allied Health Education Programs: medical assisting (C,A)

MACTE: Montessori Accreditation Council for Teacher Education: Montessori teacher education (C)

MEAC: Midwifery Education Accreditation Council: midwifery education (C,A,B,M,D)

MED: Liaison Committee on Medical Education: medicine (FP,D)

MFCD: American Association for Marriage and Family Therapy: marriage and family therapy (M,D)

MIDWF: Accreditation Commission for Midwifery Education: nurse midwifery (C,M,D)

MIL: Commission on Accreditation of Allied Health Education Programs: medical illustrator (M)

MLTAB: Accrediting Bureau of Health Education Schools: medical laboratory technician (C,A)

MLTAD: National Accrediting Agency for Clinical Laboratory Sciences: medical laboratory technician (C,A)

MT: National Accrediting Agency for Clinical Laboratory Sciences: medical technology/laboratory scientist (C,B)

MUS: National Association of Schools of Music: music (C,A,B,M,D)

NAIT: The Association of Technology, Management, and Applied Engineering: technology, applied technology, engineering technology and technology-related programs (A,B,M)

NATUR: Council on Naturopathic Medical Education: naturopathic medical education (FP,D)

NDT: Commission on Accreditation of Allied Health Education Programs: neurodiagnostic technology (C,A)

NH: Higher Learning Commission, North Central Association

NMT: Joint Review Committee on Education Programs in Nuclear Medicine Technology: nuclear medicine technology (C,A,B,M)

NRPA: Council on Accreditation of Parks, Recreation, Tourism and Related Professions: recreation, park resources, and leisure studies (B)

NUR: Accreditation Commission for Education in Nursing: nursing (B, M,D)

NURSE: Commission on Collegiate Nursing Education: nursing (B,M,D)

NW: Northwest Commission on Colleges and Universities

NY: New York State Board of Regents

OPD: Commission on Opticianry Accreditation: opticianry (A)

OPE: Commission on Accreditation of Allied Health Education Programs: orthotics and prosthetics (C,B,M)

OPLT: Commission on Opticianry Accreditation: opthalmic laboratory technician (C)

OPT: American Optometric Association: optometry (FP,D)

OPTR: American Optometric Association: optometric residency programs

OPTT: American Optometric Association: optometric technician (C,A)

OSTEO: American Osteopathic Association, Office of Osteopathic Education: osteopathic medicine (FP,D)

OT: American Occupational Therapy Association: occupational therapy (M,D)

OTA: American Occupational Therapy Association: occupational therapy assistant (C,A)

PA: National Accrediting Agency for Clinical Laboratory Sciences: pathologist's assistant (C,M)

PAST: Association for Clinical Pastoral Education: clinical pastoral education

PCSAS: Psychological Clinical Science Accreditation System: psychological clinical science (D)

PDPSY: American Psychological Association: post-doctoral residency in health service psychology

PERF: Commission on Accreditation of Allied Health Education Programs: perfusionist (C,B,M)

PH: Council on Education for Public Health: public health (B,M,D)

PHAR: Accreditation Council for Pharmacy Education: pharmacy (FP,D)

PLNG: Planning Accreditation Board: certified planning (B,M)

Arizona State University ... AZ ... 10
University of Arizona ... AZ ... 16
California Polytechnic State University-San Luis Obispo ... CA ... 30
California State Polytechnic University-Pomona ... CA ... 30
San Jose State University ... CA ... 34
University of California-Berkeley ... CA ... 68
University of California-Irvine ... CA ... 68
University of California-Los Angeles ... CA ... 69
University of Southern California ... CA ... 72
University of Colorado Denver | Anschutz Medical Campus ... CO ... 83
George Washington University ... DC ... 91
Florida Atlantic University ... FL ... 108
Florida State University ... FL ... 109
University of Central Florida ... FL ... 109
University of Florida ... FL ... 109
Georgia Institute of Technology ... GA ... 118
University of Georgia ... GA ... 125
University of Hawaii at Manoa ... HI ... 128
University of Illinois at Chicago ... IL ... 151
University of Illinois at Urbana-Champaign ... IL ... 151
Ball State University ... IN ... 153
Iowa State University ... IA ... 162
University of Iowa ... IA ... 163
Kansas State University ... KS ... 174
University of Kansas Main Campus ... KS ... 177
University of Louisville ... KY ... 185
University of New Orleans ... LA ... 189
Morgan State University ... MD ... 200
University of Maryland College Park ... MD ... 202
Harvard University ... MA ... 210
Massachusetts Institute of Technology ... MA ... 215
Tufts University ... MA ... 219
University of Massachusetts ... MA ... 211
Eastern Michigan University ... MI ... 223
Michigan State University ... MI ... 227
University of Michigan-Ann Arbor ... MI ... 231
Wayne State University ... MI ... 232
University of Minnesota ... MN ... 243
Jackson State University ... MS ... 246
Missouri State University ... MO ... 256
University of Nebraska - Lincoln ... NE ... 269
Rutgers University - New Brunswick ... NJ ... 282
University of New Mexico Main Campus ... NM ... 288
City University of New York Hunter College ... NY ... 294
Columbia University in the City of New York ... NY ... 297
Cornell University ... NY ... 297
New York University ... NY ... 310
Pratt Institute ... NY ... 311
University at Albany, SUNY ... NY ... 316
University at Buffalo-SUNY ... NY ... 316
East Carolina University ... NC ... 341
University of North Carolina at Chapel Hill ... NC ... 342
Cleveland State University ... OH ... 351
Ohio State University Main Campus, The ... OH ... 358
University of Cincinnati Main Campus ... OH ... 362
University of Oklahoma Norman Campus ... OK ... 371
Portland State University ... OR ... 376
University of Oregon ... OR ... 377
Indiana University of Pennsylvania ... PA ... 394
Temple University ... PA ... 399
University of Pennsylvania ... PA ... 400
University of Puerto Rico-Rio Piedras Campus ... PR ... 514
Clemson University ... SC ... 408
University of Memphis, The ... TN ... 427
Texas A & M University ... TX ... 446
Texas Southern University ... TX ... 449
University of Texas at Arlington, The ... TX ... 454
University of Texas at Austin ... TX ... 455
University of Utah, The ... UT ... 460
University of Virginia ... VA ... 473
Virginia Commonwealth University ... VA ... 473
Virginia Polytechnic Institute and State University ... VA ... 477
Eastern Washington University ... WA ... 480
University of Washington ... WA ... 485
Western Washington University ... WA ... 486
University of Wisconsin-Madison ... WI ... 496
University of Wisconsin-Milwaukee ... WI ... 497

PNUR: Accreditation Commission for Education in Nursing: practical nursing (C)

Bevill State Community College ... AL ... 1
Bishop State Community College ... AL ... 1
Calhoun Community College ... AL ... 1
Chattahoochee Valley Community College ... AL ... 1
Coastal Alabama Community College ... AL ... 1
Gadsden State Community College ... AL ... 2
George C. Wallace Community College - Dothan ... AL ... 2
George Corley Wallace State Community College - Selma ... AL ... 2
Lawson State Community College ... AL ... 2
Northeast Alabama Community College ... AL ... 3
Shelton State Community College ... AL ... 3
Trenholm State Technical College ... AL ... 3
Wallace State Community College - Hanceville ... AL ... 4
Baptist Health College Little Rock ... AR ... 18
Hartnell College ... CA ... 44
Colorado Mesa University ... CO ... 77
Delaware Technical Community College, Terry Campus ... DE ... 90
Mercy Hospital College of Nursing ... FL ... 103
Pensacola State College ... FL ... 104
Taylor College ... FL ... 111
Augusta Technical College ... GA ... 114
Carl Sandburg College ... IL ... 133
Harper College ... IL ... 137
Illinois Central College ... IL ... 138
Kankakee Community College ... IL ... 140
Lake Land College ... IL ... 141
Lincoln Land Community College ... IL ... 142
Vincennes University ... IN ... 162
Western Iowa Tech Community College ... IA ... 170
Hutchinson Community College ... KS ... 174
West Kentucky Community and Technical College ... KY ... 182
L.E. Fletcher Technical Community College ... LA ... 187
College of Southern Maryland ... MD ... 198
Hagerstown Community College ... MD ... 198
Howard Community College ... MD ... 199
Mount Wachusett Community College ... MA ... 215
North Shore Community College ... MA ... 215
Northern Essex Community College ... MA ... 215
Quinsigamond Community College ... MA ... 215
Alpena Community College ... MI ... 221
Davenport University ... MI ... 223
Grand Rapids Community College ... MI ... 224
Northwestern Michigan College ... MI ... 228
Schoolcraft College ... MI ... 230
Lake Superior College ... MN ... 238
Minnesota State College Southeast ... MN ... 239
Rasmussen College - St. Cloud ... MN ... 242
Ridgewater College ... MN ... 240
Riverland Community College ... MN ... 240
Rochester Community and Technical College ... MN ... 240
Saint Cloud Technical and Community College ... MN ... 241
Saint Paul College-A Community & Technical College ... MN ... 241
South Central College ... MN ... 241
Meridian Community College ... MS ... 247
Mississippi Gulf Coast Community College ... MS ... 247
Southeast Community College ... NE ... 269
Western Nebraska Community College ... NE ... 270
College of Southern Nevada ... NV ... 271
Finger Lakes Health College of Nursing and Health Sciences ... NY ... 300
Monroe College ... NY ... 307
Samaritan Hospital School of Nursing ... NY ... 315
Suffolk County Community College ... NY ... 321
SUNY Canton-College of Technology ... NY ... 320
Trocaire College ... NY ... 323
Durham Technical Community College ... NC ... 334
Edgecombe Community College ... NC ... 334
Gaston College ... NC ... 334
Rowan-Cabarrus Community College ... NC ... 337
Sampson Community College ... NC ... 337
Wayne Community College ... NC ... 338
Dickinson State University ... ND ... 345
North Dakota State College of Science ... ND ... 346
Hocking College ... OH ... 354
Lorain County Community College ... OH ... 355
HACC, Central Pennsylvania's Community College ... PA ... 385
Lehigh Carbon Community College ... PA ... 388
Northampton Community College ... PA ... 391
Pennsylvania College of Technology ... PA ... 393
Pittsburgh Technical College ... PA ... 396
Reading Area Community College ... PA ... 397
Community College of Rhode Island ... RI ... 404
Aiken Technical College ... SC ... 406
Horry-Georgetown Technical College ... SC ... 410
Midlands Technical College ... SC ... 410
Orangeburg-Calhoun Technical College ... SC ... 411
Technical College of the Lowcountry ... SC ... 412
Tri-County Technical College ... SC ... 413
Trident Technical College ... SC ... 413
York Technical College ... SC ... 415
Lake Area Technical Institute ... SD ... 415
Austin Community College District ... TX ... 431
El Centro College ... TX ... 435
Snow College ... UT ... 461
Vermont Technical College ... VT ... 464
Riverside College of Health Careers ... VA ... 471
Saint Michael College of Allied Health ... VA ... 471
Fox Valley Technical College ... WI ... 499
Lakeshore Technical College ... WI ... 499
Milwaukee Area Technical College ... WI ... 500
Northeast Wisconsin Technical College ... WI ... 500

POD: American Podiatric Medical Association: podiatry (FP,D)

Samuel Merritt University ... CA ... 59
Western University of Health Sciences ... CA ... 74
Barry University ... FL ... 95
Rosalind Franklin University of Medicine & Science ... IL ... 147
Des Moines University ... IA ... 164
New York College of Podiatric Medicine ... NY ... 309
Kent State University Kent Campus ... OH ... 354
Temple University ... PA ... 399

POLYT: Commission on Accreditation of Allied Health Education Programs: polysomnographic technologist education (C,A)

Wallace State Community College - Hanceville ... AL ... 4
Gateway Community College ... AZ ... 13
Baptist Health College Little Rock ... AR ... 18
Concorde Career College ... CA ... 40
Orange Coast College ... CA ... 38
Santa Fe College ... FL ... 107
Central Georgia Technical College ... GA ... 116
College of DuPage ... IL ... 135
Moraine Valley Community College ... IL ... 144
Delgado Community College ... LA ... 187
Community College of Baltimore County, The ... MD ... 198
Montgomery College ... MD ... 200
Northern Essex Community College ... MA ... 215
Minneapolis Community and Technical College ... MN ... 238
Coahoma Community College ... MS ... 245
Southeast Community College ... NE ... 269
Thomas Edison State University ... NJ ... 284
City University of New York Kingsborough Community College ... NY ... 294
Genesee Community College ... NY ... 301
Hudson Valley Community College ... NY ... 302
Stony Brook University ... NY ... 317
Catawba Valley Community College ... NC ... 333
Lenoir Community College ... NC ... 335
Pitt Community College ... NC ... 336
University of North Carolina at Charlotte ... NC ... 342
Mercy College of Ohio ... OH ... 356
Concorde Career College ... OR ... 372
Linn-Benton Community College ... OR ... 374
Oregon Institute of Technology ... OR ... 375
Concorde Career College ... TN ... 419
Roane State Community College ... TN ... 425
Volunteer State Community College ... TN ... 426
Alvin Community College ... TX ... 429
Collin County Community College District ... TX ... 433
Concorde Career Institute ... TX ... 434

PSPSY: American Psychological Association: combined professional-scientific psychology (D)

University of South Alabama ... AL ... 8
Northern Arizona University ... AZ ... 14
University of California-Santa Barbara ... CA ... 70
Florida State University ... FL ... 109
Rivier University ... NH ... 274
Kean University ... NJ ... 278
Pace University ... NY ... 311
Roberts Wesleyan College ... NY ... 312
University at Buffalo-SUNY ... NY ... 316
Yeshiva University ... NY ... 326
University of Houston - Clear Lake ... TX ... 453
Utah State University ... UT ... 460
James Madison University ... VA ... 468
University of Virginia ... VA ... 473

PTA: American Physical Therapy Association: physical therapy (D)

#Alabama State University ... AL ... 4
Samford University ... AL ... 6
University of Alabama at Birmingham ... AL ... 8
University of South Alabama ... AL ... 8
Northern Arizona University ... AZ ... 14
Arkansas State University-Jonesboro ... AR ... 17
Harding University Main Campus ... AR ... 19
University of Arkansas for Medical Sciences ... AR ... 22
University of Central Arkansas ... AR ... 23
Azusa Pacific University ... CA ... 26
California State University-Fresno ... CA ... 31
California State University-Long Beach ... CA ... 31
California State University-Northridge ... CA ... 32
California State University-Sacramento ... CA ... 32
Chapman University ... CA ... 36
Loma Linda University ... CA ... 48
Mount Saint Mary's University ... CA ... 52
Samuel Merritt University ... CA ... 59
San Diego State University ... CA ... 33
San Francisco State University ... CA ... 34
University of California-San Francisco ... CA ... 69
University of St. Augustine for Health Sciences ... CA ... 71
University of Southern California ... CA ... 72
University of the Pacific ... CA ... 70
West Coast University ... CA ... 73
Western University of Health Sciences ... CA ... 74
Regis University ... CO ... 82
University of Colorado Denver | Anschutz Medical Campus ... CO ... 83
Quinnipiac University ... CT ... 87
Sacred Heart University ... CT ... 88
University of Connecticut ... CT ... 88
University of Hartford ... CT ... 88
University of Delaware ... DE ... 90
George Washington University ... DC ... 91
Howard University ... DC ... 92
AdventHealth University ... FL ... 94
Florida Agricultural and Mechanical University ... FL ... 108
Florida Gulf Coast University ... FL ... 108
Florida International University ... FL ... 109
@Florida Southern College ... FL ... 99
Nova Southeastern University ... FL ... 103
University of Central Florida ... FL ... 109
University of Florida ... FL ... 109
University of Miami ... FL ... 112
University of North Florida ... FL ... 110
University of South Florida ... FL ... 110
Augusta University ... GA ... 115
Brenau University ... GA ... 115
Emory University ... GA ... 117
Georgia Southern University ... GA ... 119
Georgia State University ... GA ... 119
Mercer University ... GA ... 121
University of North Georgia ... GA ... 126
Idaho State University ... ID ... 130
Bradley University ... IL ... 133
Governors State University ... IL ... 137
Midwestern University ... IL ... 143
Northern Illinois University ... IL ... 145
Northwestern University ... IL ... 145
Rosalind Franklin University of Medicine & Science ... IL ... 147
University of Illinois at Chicago ... IL ... 151
Indiana State University ... IN ... 155
Indiana University-Purdue University Indianapolis ... IN ... 156
Trine University ... IN ... 160
University of Evansville ... IN ... 161
University of Indianapolis ... IN ... 161
Briar Cliff University ... IA ... 163
Clarke University ... IA ... 163
Des Moines University ... IA ... 164
St. Ambrose University ... IA ... 169
University of Iowa ... IA ... 163
University of Saint Mary ... KS ... 177
Wichita State University ... KS ... 178
Bellarmine University ... KY ... 179
University of Kentucky ... KY ... 185
Western Kentucky University ... KY ... 185
@Franciscan Missionaries of Our Lady University ... LA ... 186
Louisiana State University Health Sciences Center at Shreveport ... LA ... 189
Louisiana State University Health Sciences Center-New Orleans ... LA ... 189
Husson University ... ME ... 194
University of New England ... ME ... 196
University of Maryland Eastern Shore ... MD ... 203
University of Maryland, Baltimore ... MD ... 202
American International College ... MA ... 205
Boston University ... MA ... 207
MCPHS University ... MA ... 216
MGH Institute of Health Professions ... MA ... 216
Northeastern University ... MA ... 217
Simmons University ... MA ... 218
Springfield College ... MA ... 218
University of Massachusetts Lowell ... MA ... 211
Andrews University ... MI ... 221
Central Michigan University ... MI ... 222
Grand Valley State University ... MI ... 224
Oakland University ... MI ... 229
University of Michigan-Flint ... MI ... 231
Wayne State University ... MI ... 232
@Western Michigan University ... MI ... 232
#College of Saint Scholastica, The ... MN ... 235

PTAA: American Physical Therapy Association: physical therapy assistant (A)

Seminole State College ... OK .. 369
Southwestern Oklahoma State University. OK .. 370
Tulsa Community College ... OK .. 370
Lane Community College ... OR .. 373
Mt. Hood Community College ... OR .. 374
Butler County Community College ... PA .. 380
California University of Pennsylvania ... PA .. 394
Central Penn College ... PA .. 381
Community College of Allegheny County PA .. 381
Harcum College ... PA .. 385
Johnson College ... PA .. 386
Lackawanna College ... PA .. 387
Lehigh Carbon Community College ... PA .. 388
Mercyhurst University ... PA .. 390
Montgomery County Community College PA .. 390
Mount Aloysius College ... PA .. 391
Pennsylvania College of Technology ... PA .. 393
Pennsylvania Institute of Technology ... PA .. 393
Atenas College ... PR .. 506
Huertas College ... PR .. 508
Inter American University of Puerto Rico Ponce Campus ... PR .. 509
National University College ... PR .. 510
University of Puerto Rico at Ponce ... PR .. 514
University of Puerto Rico-Humacao ... PR .. 513
Community College of Rhode Island ... RI 404
New England Institute of Technology ... RI 405
Greenville Technical College ... SC .. 410
Horry-Georgetown Technical College ... SC .. 410
Midlands Technical College ... SC .. 410
Orangeburg-Calhoun Technical College .. SC .. 411
Technical College of the Lowcountry ... SC .. 412
Trident Technical College ... SC .. 413
Lake Area Technical Institute ... SD .. 415
Chattanooga State Community College .. TN .. 424
#Concorde Career College ... TN .. 419
Jackson State Community College ... TN .. 425
Roane State Community College ... TN .. 425
South College ... TN .. 424
@Southern Adventist University ... TN .. 424
Southwest Tennessee Community College ... TN .. 426
Volunteer State Community College ... TN .. 426
Walters State Community College ... TN .. 426
Amarillo College ... TX .. 430
Austin Community College District ... TX .. 431
Blinn College ... TX .. 432
Del Mar College ... TX .. 436
El Paso Community College ... TX .. 436
Houston Community College ... TX .. 437
Kilgore College ... TX .. 439
Laredo College ... TX .. 439
Lone Star College System ... TX .. 439
McLennan Community College ... TX .. 440
Navarro College ... TX .. 440
Northeast Texas Community College ... TX .. 441
Odessa College ... TX .. 441
St. Philip's College ... TX .. 429
San Jacinto College South ... TX .. 443
South Plains College ... TX .. 443
South Texas College ... TX .. 444
Tarrant County College District ... TX .. 445
Tyler Junior College ... TX .. 452
Victoria College ... TX .. 457
Weatherford College ... TX .. 458
Western Technical College ... TX .. 458
Wharton County Junior College ... TX .. 458
Dixie State University ... UT .. 460
Provo College ... UT .. 459
Salt Lake Community College ... UT .. 461
Germanna Community College ... VA .. 474
Northern Virginia Community College ... VA .. 475
Riverside College of Health Careers ... VA .. 471
Tidewater Community College ... VA .. 476
Wytheville Community College ... VA .. 476
Green River College ... WA . 481
Lake Washington Institute of Technology WA . 482
Olympic College ... WA . 482
Spokane Falls Community College ... WA . 480
Whatcom Community College ... WA . 486
Blue Ridge Community and Technical College ... WV . 488
Mountwest Community and Technical College ... WV . 489
Pierpont Community & Technical College WV . 489
Blackhawk Technical College ... WI ... 499
Chippewa Valley Technical College ... WI ... 499
Gateway Technical College ... WI ... 499
Madison Area Technical College ... WI ... 499
Milwaukee Area Technical College ... WI ... 500
Northeast Wisconsin Technical College .. WI ... 500
Southwest Wisconsin Technical College . WI ... 500
Western Technical College ... WI ... 501
Laramie County Community College ... WY . 502

RABN: Association of Advanced Rabbinical and Talmudic Schools: rabbinical and Talmudic education (A,B,M,D)

Yeshiva Ohr Elchonon Chabad/West Coast Talmudical Seminary ... CA 75
Talmudic College of Florida ... FL ... 111
Yeshiva Gedolah Rabbinical College ... FL ... 113
Telshe Yeshiva-Chicago ... IL 150
Bais HaMedrash & Mesivta of Baltimore . MD .. 197
Ner Israel Rabbinical College ... MD .. 201
Yeshiva College of the Nation's Capital .. MD .. 204
Yeshiva Beth Yehuda - Yeshiva Gedolah of Greater Detroit ... MI 233
Bais Medrash Toras Chesed ... NJ ... 275
@Bais Medrash Zichron Meir ... NJ ... 275
Beth Medrash Govoha ... NJ ... 275
Rabbi Jacob Joseph School ... NJ ... 280
Rabbinical College of America ... NJ ... 280
Talmudical Academy of New Jersey ... NJ ... 284
Yeshiva Gedolah of Cliffwood ... NJ ... 284
@Yeshiva Gedolah Shaarei Shmuel ... NJ ... 285
Yeshiva Gedolah Zichron Leyma ... NJ ... 285
Yeshiva Toras Chaim ... NJ ... 285
Yeshiva Yesodei Hatorah ... NJ ... 285
Bais Binyomin Academy, Inc ... NY .. 290
Be'er Yaakov Talmudic Seminary ... NY .. 291
Beis Medrash Heichal Dovid ... NY .. 291
@Bet Medrash Gadol Ateret Torah ... NY .. 291
Beth Hamedrash Shaarei Yosher Institute ... NY .. 291
Beth Medrash Meor Yitzchok ... NY .. 291
Central Yeshiva Beth Joseph ... NY .. 292
Central Yeshiva Tomchei Tmimim Lubavitch America ... NY .. 292
Kehilath Yakov Rabbinical Seminary ... NY .. 303
Machzikei Hadath Rabbinical College ... NY .. 305
Mesivta of Eastern Parkway Rabbinical Seminary ... NY .. 306
Mesivta Tifereth Jerusalem of America ... NY .. 306
Mesivta Torah Vodaath Seminary ... NY .. 306
Mirrer Yeshiva Central Institute ... NY .. 307
Ohr Hameir Theological Seminary ... NY .. 310
Ohr Somayach Tanenbaum Educational Center ... NY .. 311
Rabbinical Academy Mesivta Rabbi Chaim Berlin ... NY .. 312
Rabbinical College Beth Shraga ... NY .. 312
Rabbinical College Bobover Yeshiva B'nei Zion ... NY .. 312
Rabbinical College of Long Island ... NY .. 312
Rabbinical College Ohr Shimon Yisroel ... NY .. 312
@Rabbinical College Ohr Yisroel ... NY .. 312
Rabbinical Seminary of America ... NY .. 312
Sh'or Yoshuv Rabbinical College ... NY .. 315
Talmudical Institute of Upstate New York. NY .. 322
Talmudical Seminary of Bobov ... NY .. 322
Talmudical Seminary Oholei Torah ... NY .. 322
Torah Temimah Talmudical Seminary ... NY .. 322
United Talmudical Seminary ... NY .. 323
U.T.A. Mesivta of Kiryas Joel ... NY .. 324
Yeshiva Derech Chaim ... NY .. 325
Yeshiva D'Monsey Rabbinical College ... NY .. 325
Yeshiva Gedolah Imrei Yosef D'Spinka ... NY .. 325
Yeshiva Gedolah Kesser Torah ... NY .. 325
Yeshiva Gedolah Ohr Yisrael ... NY .. 325
Yeshiva Karlin Stolin Beth Aaron V'Israel Rabbinical Institute ... NY .. 325
Yeshiva Kollel Tifereth Elizer ... NY .. 325
Yeshiva of Far Rockaway ... NY .. 325
Yeshiva of Machzikai Hadas ... NY .. 325
Yeshiva of Nitra Rabbinical College ... NY .. 325
Yeshiva of the Telshe Alumni ... NY .. 326
Yeshiva Shaar Ephraim ... NY .. 325
Yeshiva Shaar HaTorah-Grodno ... NY .. 326
@Yeshiva Sholom Shachna ... NY .. 326
Yeshiva Yesoda Hatorah Vetz Chaim ... NY .. 326
Yeshiva Zichron Aryeh ... NY .. 326
@Yeshivas Maharit Dsatmar ... NY .. 326
Yeshivas Novominsk ... NY .. 326
Yeshivath Viznitz ... NY .. 326
Rabbinical College of Telshe ... OH .. 360
Talmudical Yeshiva of Philadelphia ... PA .. 399
Yeshiva Beth Moshe ... PA .. 403

RAD: Joint Review Committee on Education in Radiologic Technology: radiography (C,A,B)

Gadsden State Community College ... AL 2
George C. Wallace Community College - Dothan ... AL 2
Jefferson State Community College ... AL 2
Southern Union State Community College ... AL 3
#Trenholm State Technical College ... AL 3
University of South Alabama ... AL 8
Wallace State Community College - Hanceville ... AL 4
Arizona Western College ... AZ 10
Central Arizona College ... AZ 11
Gateway Community College ... AZ 13
Mohave Community College ... AZ 14
Pima Community College ... AZ 15
Pima Medical Institute-Tucson ... AZ 15
Yavapai College ... AZ 16
Arkansas State University-Jonesboro ... AR 17
Baptist Health College Little Rock ... AR 18
National Park College ... AR 20
North Arkansas College ... AR 20
South Arkansas Community College ... AR 21
Southeast Arkansas College ... AR 21
University of Arkansas at Fort Smith ... AR 21
University of Arkansas for Medical Sciences ... AR 22
Antelope Valley College ... CA 26
Bakersfield College ... CA 46
Cabrillo College ... CA 27
California Baptist University ... CA 27
California State University-Northridge ... CA 32
Cañada College ... CA 61
Chaffey College ... CA 36
Charles R. Drew University of Medicine & Science ... CA 36
City College of San Francisco ... CA 37
Cypress College ... CA 53
El Camino College ... CA 41
Foothill College ... CA 43
Fresno City College ... CA 66
Gurnick Academy of Medical Arts ... CA 44
Kaiser Permanente School of Allied Health Sciences ... CA 46
Loma Linda University ... CA 48
Los Angeles City College ... CA 48
Merced College ... CA 51
Merritt College ... CA 56
Moorpark College ... CA 72
Mt. San Antonio College ... CA 52
Orange Coast College ... CA 38
Pasadena City College ... CA 55
San Diego Mesa College ... CA 60
Santa Barbara City College ... CA 62
Santa Rosa Junior College ... CA 62
University of California-Los Angeles ... CA 69
Yuba College ... CA 76
Colorado Mesa University ... CO 77
Community College of Denver ... CO 79
Concorde Career College ... CO 79
Red Rocks Community College ... CO 82
UCH Memorial Hospital School Of Radiologic Technology ... CO 82
Capital Community College ... CT 85
Gateway Community College ... CT 85
Manchester Community College ... CT 85
Middlesex Community College ... CT 86
Naugatuck Valley Community College ... CT 86
Quinnipiac University ... CT 87
Sacred Heart University ... CT 88
University of Hartford ... CT 88
AdventHealth University ... FL 94
Bethesda College of Health Sciences ... FL 95
Broward College ... FL 95
College of Central Florida ... FL 96
Eastern Florida State College ... FL 97
Florida SouthWestern State College ... FL ... 100
Gulf Coast State College ... FL ... 100
Hillsborough Community College ... FL ... 101
Indian River State College ... FL ... 101
Keiser University ... FL ... 102
Miami Dade College ... FL ... 103
Northwest Florida State College ... FL ... 103
Palm Beach State College ... FL ... 104
Pensacola State College ... FL ... 104
Polk State College ... FL ... 105
St. Johns River State College ... FL ... 106
St. Petersburg College ... FL ... 106
Santa Fe College ... FL ... 107
South Florida State College ... FL ... 107
State College of Florida, Manatee-Sarasota ... FL ... 108
Valencia College ... FL ... 112
Albany State University ... GA .. 113
Albany Technical College ... GA .. 113
Athens Technical College ... GA .. 114
#Atlanta Technical College ... GA .. 114
Augusta Technical College ... GA .. 114
Central Georgia Technical College ... GA .. 116
Chattahoochee Technical College ... GA .. 116
Coastal Pines Technical College ... GA .. 116
College of Coastal Georgia ... GA .. 116
Columbus Technical College ... GA .. 117
Dalton State College ... GA .. 117
Emory University ... GA .. 117
Georgia Northwestern Technical College GA .. 119
Georgia Southern University ... GA .. 119
Gwinnett Technical College ... GA .. 120
Lanier Technical College ... GA .. 121
Oconee Fall Line Technical College-South Campus ... GA .. 122
Ogeechee Technical College ... GA .. 122
Southeastern Technical College ... GA .. 124
Southern Regional Technical College ... GA .. 125
West Georgia Technical College ... GA .. 127
Wiregrass Georgia Technical College ... GA .. 127
Kapiolani Community College ... HI .. 128
Boise State University ... ID ... 129
College of Southern Idaho ... ID ... 130
Idaho State University ... ID ... 130
Lewis-Clark State College ... ID ... 131
North Idaho College ... ID ... 131
College of DuPage ... IL 135
College of Lake County ... IL 135
Danville Area Community College ... IL 135
Elgin Community College ... IL 136
Harper College ... IL 137
Heartland Community College ... IL 137
Illinois Central College ... IL 138
Illinois Eastern Community Colleges Olney Central College ... IL 138
Kaskaskia College ... IL 140
Kishwaukee College ... IL 140
Lincoln Land Community College ... IL 142
Malcolm X College, One of the City Colleges of Chicago ... IL 134
Moraine Valley Community College ... IL 144
Northwestern College ... IL 145
Parkland College ... IL 146
Rend Lake College ... IL 147
Resurrection University ... IL 147
Richland Community College ... IL 147
Sauk Valley Community College ... IL 148
Southern Illinois University Carbondale ... IL 149
Southwestern Illinois College ... IL 149
Trinity College of Nursing & Health Sciences ... IL 150
Triton College ... IL 150
Ball State University ... IN 153
Indiana University Kokomo ... IN 156
Indiana University Northwest ... IN 156
Indiana University-Purdue University Indianapolis ... IN 156
Indiana University South Bend ... IN 157
Ivy Tech Community College of Indiana-Indianapolis ... IN 157
Purdue University Fort Wayne ... IN 159
St. Vincent College of Health Professions IN 160
University of Saint Francis ... IN 161
University of Southern Indiana ... IN 161
Allen College ... IA 162
Indian Hills Community College ... IA 166
Iowa Central Community College ... IA 166
Mercy College of Health Sciences ... IA 168
Northwest Iowa Community College ... IA 168
St. Luke's College ... IA 169
Scott Community College ... IA 165
University of Iowa ... IA 163
Fort Hays State University ... KS .. 173
Hutchinson Community College ... KS .. 174
Labette Community College ... KS .. 175
Newman University ... KS .. 175
Washburn University ... KS .. 177
Bluegrass Community and Technical College ... KY .. 180
Elizabethtown Community and Technical College ... KY .. 181
Hazard Community and Technical College ... KY .. 181
Jefferson Community and Technical College ... KY .. 181
Madisonville Community College ... KY .. 181
Morehead State University ... KY .. 183
Northern Kentucky University ... KY .. 184
Owensboro Community and Technical College ... KY .. 182
Somerset Community College ... KY .. 182
Southcentral Kentucky Community and Technical College ... KY .. 182
Sullivan University ... KY .. 184
West Kentucky Community and Technical College ... KY .. 182
Delgado Community College ... LA .. 187
#Fortis College ... LA .. 186
Franciscan Missionaries of Our Lady University ... LA .. 186
Louisiana State University at Alexandria . LA .. 188
Louisiana State University at Eunice ... LA .. 189
McNeese State University ... LA .. 192
Northwestern State University ... LA .. 192
Southern University at Shreveport-Louisiana ... LA .. 190
University of Holy Cross ... LA .. 191
University of Louisiana at Monroe ... LA .. 192
Eastern Maine Community College ... ME .. 194

RADDOS: Joint Review Committee on Education in Radiologic Technology: medical dosimetry (C, B,M)

RADMAG: Joint Review Committee on Education in Radiologic Technology: magnetic resonance (C, A,B)

RTT: Joint Review Committee on Education in Radiologic Technology: radiation therapist/ technologist (C,A,B,M)

SC: Southern Association of Colleges and Schools, Commission on Colleges

SCPSY: American Psychological Association: school psychology (D)

SP: American Speech-Language-Hearing Association: speech-language pathology (M)

Cleveland State University ... OH .. 351
Kent State University Kent Campus ... OH .. 354
Miami University ... OH .. 356
Ohio State University Main Campus, The. OH .. 358
Ohio University Main Campus ... OH .. 359
University of Akron, Main Campus, The .. OH .. 362
University of Cincinnati Main Campus ... OH .. 362
University of Toledo ... OH .. 363
Northeastern State University ... OK .. 367
Oklahoma State University ... OK .. 368
University of Central Oklahoma ... OK .. 370
University of Tulsa ... OK .. 371
Pacific University ... OR .. 375
Portland State University ... OR .. 376
University of Oregon ... OR .. 377
Bloomsburg University of Pennsylvania ... PA .. 394
California University of Pennsylvania ... PA .. 394
Clarion University of Pennsylvania ... PA .. 394
Duquesne University ... PA .. 383
East Stroudsburg University of Pennsylvania ... PA .. 394
Edinboro University ... PA .. 394
Indiana University of Pennsylvania ... PA .. 394
La Salle University ... PA .. 387
@Lebanon Valley College ... PA .. 388
Marywood University ... PA .. 389
Misericordia University ... PA .. 390
@Moravian College ... PA .. 391
Penn State University Park ... PA .. 392
Salus University ... PA .. 398
Temple University ... PA .. 399
@Thiel College ... PA .. 399
University of Pittsburgh ... PA .. 401
West Chester University of Pennsylvania PA .. 396
Carlos Albizu University ... PR .. 506
@Inter American University of Puerto Rico / Metropolitan Campus ... PR .. 509
#Universidad Ana G. Mendez Gurabo Campus ... PR .. 511
University of Puerto Rico-Medical Sciences Campus ... PR .. 513
University of Rhode Island ... RI ... 406
@Francis Marion University ... SC .. 409
South Carolina State University ... SC .. 412
University of South Carolina Columbia ... SC .. 413
University of South Dakota, The ... SD .. 416
East Tennessee State University ... TN .. 419
Tennessee State University ... TN .. 426
University of Memphis, The ... TN .. 427
Vanderbilt University ... TN .. 428
Abilene Christian University ... TX .. 429
Baylor University ... TX .. 431
Lamar University ... TX .. 449
Our Lady of the Lake University ... TX .. 441
Stephen F. Austin State University ... TX ... 445
Texas A & M University - Kingsville ... TX ... 447
Texas Christian University ... TX .. 448
Texas State University ... TX ... 450
Texas Tech University Health Sciences Center ... TX .. 451
Texas Woman's University ... TX .. 451
University of Houston ... TX .. 452
University of North Texas ... TX .. 454
University of Texas at Austin ... TX .. 455
University of Texas at Dallas, The ... TX ... 455
University of Texas at El Paso ... TX ... 455
@University of Texas Health Science Center at San Antonio ... TX ... 456
University of Texas Rio Grande Valley, The ... TX .. 455
West Texas A & M University ... TX ... 448
Brigham Young University ... UT .. 458
@Rocky Mountain University of Health Professions ... UT .. 459
University of Utah, The ... UT .. 460
Utah State University ... UT .. 460
University of Vermont ... VT ... 463
Hampton University ... VA .. 468
James Madison University ... VA .. 468
Longwood University ... VA .. 469
Old Dominion University ... VA .. 469
Radford University ... VA .. 470
University of Virginia ... VA .. 473
Eastern Washington University ... WA . 480
University of Washington ... WA . 485
Washington State University ... WA . 486
Western Washington University ... WA . 486
Marshall University ... WV . 490
West Virginia University ... WV . 491
@Concordia University Wisconsin ... WI ... 493
Marquette University ... WI ... 494
University of Wisconsin-Eau Claire ... WI ... 496
University of Wisconsin-Madison ... WI ... 496
University of Wisconsin-Milwaukee ... WI ... 497
University of Wisconsin-River Falls ... WI ... 497
University of Wisconsin-Stevens Point ... WI ... 497
University of Wisconsin-Whitewater ... WI ... 498
University of Wyoming ... WY . 502

SPAA: Network of Schools of Public Policy, Affairs and Administration: public affairs and administration (M)

Auburn University ... AL ... 4
Auburn University at Montgomery ... AL ... 4
Jacksonville State University ... AL ... 5
University of Alabama at Birmingham ... AL ... 8
University of Alabama, The ... AL ... 7
Arizona State University ... AZ ... 10
University of Arizona ... AZ ... 16
Arkansas State University-Jonesboro ... AR ... 17
University of Arkansas at Little Rock ... AR ... 22
California State Polytechnic University-Pomona ... CA ... 30
California State University-Bakersfield ... CA ... 30
California State University-Chico ... CA ... 31
California State University-Dominguez Hills ... CA ... 31
California State University-Fresno ... CA ... 31
California State University-Fullerton ... CA ... 31
California State University-Long Beach ... CA ... 31
California State University-Los Angeles ... CA ... 32
California State University-San Bernardino ... CA ... 33
California State University-Stanislaus ... CA ... 33
Naval Postgraduate School ... CA .. 503
San Diego State University ... CA ... 33
San Francisco State University ... CA ... 34
San Jose State University ... CA ... 34
University of La Verne ... CA ... 70
University of San Francisco ... CA ... 71
University of Southern California ... CA ... 72
University of Colorado Colorado Springs . CO ... 83
University of Colorado Denver | Anschutz Medical Campus ... CO ... 83
University of Connecticut ... CT ... 88
University of Delaware ... DE ... 90
American University ... DC ... 90
George Washington University ... DC ... 91
Florida Atlantic University ... FL ... 108
Florida Gulf Coast University ... FL ... 108
Florida International University ... FL ... 109
Florida State University ... FL ... 109
Nova Southeastern University ... FL ... 103
University of Central Florida ... FL ... 109
University of North Florida ... FL ... 110
University of South Florida ... FL ... 110
Albany State University ... GA .. 113
Augusta University ... GA .. 115
Clark Atlanta University ... GA .. 116
Georgia College & State University ... GA .. 118
Georgia Southern University ... GA .. 119
Georgia State University ... GA .. 119
Kennesaw State University ... GA .. 120
Savannah State University ... GA .. 123
University of Georgia ... GA .. 125
University of West Georgia ... GA .. 126
Valdosta State University ... GA .. 126
University of Hawaii at Manoa ... HI ... 128
Boise State University ... ID ... 129
DePaul University ... IL ... 135
Governors State University ... IL ... 137
Northern Illinois University ... IL ... 145
Southern Illinois University Carbondale ... IL ... 149
Southern Illinois University Edwardsville . IL ... 149
University of Illinois at Chicago ... IL ... 151
University of Illinois at Springfield ... IL ... 151
Indiana University Bloomington ... IN ... 156
Indiana University Northwest ... IN ... 156
Indiana University-Purdue University Indianapolis ... IN ... 156
Indiana University South Bend ... IN ... 157
Kansas State University ... KS .. 174
University of Kansas Main Campus ... KS .. 177
Wichita State University ... KS .. 178
Eastern Kentucky University ... KY .. 180
Kentucky State University ... KY .. 182
Morehead State University ... KY .. 183
Northern Kentucky University ... KY .. 184
University of Kentucky ... KY .. 185
University of Louisville ... KY .. 185
Western Kentucky University ... KY .. 185
Grambling State University ... LA ... 191
Louisiana State University and Agricultural and Mechanical College ... LA ... 188
Southern University and A&M College ... LA ... 190
University of New Orleans ... LA ... 189
Bowie State University ... MD .. 203
University of Baltimore ... MD .. 204
University of Maryland College Park ... MD .. 202
Bridgewater State University ... MA .. 212
Northeastern University ... MA .. 217
Suffolk University ... MA .. 219
University of Massachusetts Boston ... MA .. 211
Central Michigan University ... MI ... 222
Eastern Michigan University ... MI ... 223
Grand Valley State University ... MI ... 224
Oakland University ... MI ... 229
Wayne State University ... MI ... 232
Western Michigan University ... MI ... 232
Minnesota State University, Mankato ... MN .. 239
University of Minnesota ... MN .. 243
Jackson State University ... MS .. 246
Mississippi State University ... MS .. 247
University of Missouri - Columbia ... MO . 261
University of Missouri - Kansas City ... MO . 261
University of Missouri - Saint Louis ... MO . 261
University of Montana - Missoula ... MT . 264
University of Nebraska at Omaha ... NE .. 270
University of Nevada, Las Vegas ... NV .. 271
Rutgers University - Camden ... NJ ... 281
Rutgers University - New Brunswick ... NJ ... 282
Rutgers University - Newark ... NJ ... 282
Seton Hall University ... NJ ... 283
New Mexico State University Main Campus ... NM .. 287
University of New Mexico Main Campus . NM .. 288
Baruch College/City University of New York ... NY .. 292
City University of New York John Jay College of Criminal Justice ... NY .. 294
Columbia University in the City of New York ... NY .. 297
Long Island University - LIU Post ... NY .. 304
Marist College ... NY .. 305
New School, The ... NY .. 308
New York University ... NY .. 310
State University of New York at Binghamton ... NY .. 316
State University of New York, The College at Brockport ... NY .. 318
Syracuse University ... NY .. 322
University at Albany, SUNY ... NY .. 316
Appalachian State University ... NC .. 341
East Carolina University ... NC .. 341
North Carolina State University ... NC .. 342
University of North Carolina at Chapel Hill ... NC .. 342
University of North Carolina at Charlotte . NC .. 342
University of North Carolina at Greensboro ... NC .. 343
University of North Carolina Wilmington .. NC .. 343
Western Carolina University ... NC .. 344
University of North Dakota ... ND .. 345
Bowling Green State University ... OH .. 348
Cleveland State University ... OH .. 351
Kent State University Kent Campus ... OH .. 354
Ohio State University Main Campus, The. OH .. 358
University of Dayton ... OH .. 362
Wright State University Main Campus ... OH .. 364
University of Oklahoma Norman Campus. OK .. 371
Oregon State University ... OR .. 375
Portland State University ... OR .. 376
University of Oregon ... OR .. 377
Willamette University ... OR .. 378
Carnegie Mellon University ... PA .. 380
University of Pittsburgh ... PA .. 401
Villanova University ... PA .. 402
West Chester University of Pennsylvania PA .. 396
University of Puerto Rico-Rio Piedras Campus ... PR .. 514
College of Charleston ... SC .. 408
University of South Carolina Columbia ... SC .. 413
University of South Dakota, The ... SD .. 416
Tennessee State University ... TN .. 426
University of Memphis, The ... TN .. 427
University of Tennessee at Chattanooga TN .. 428
Texas A & M International University ... TX ... 446
Texas A & M University ... TX ... 446
Texas Southern University ... TX ... 449
Texas State University ... TX ... 450
Texas Tech University ... TX ... 451
University of North Texas ... TX ... 454
University of Texas at Arlington, The ... TX ... 454
University of Texas at Austin ... TX ... 455
University of Texas at Dallas, The ... TX ... 455
University of Texas at El Paso ... TX ... 455
University of Texas at San Antonio, The . TX ... 455
Brigham Young University ... UT .. 458
Southern Utah University ... UT .. 460
University of Utah, The ... UT .. 460
University of Vermont ... VT ... 463
George Mason University ... VA .. 467
James Madison University ... VA .. 468
Old Dominion University ... VA .. 469
Virginia Commonwealth University ... VA .. 473
Virginia Polytechnic Institute and State University ... VA .. 477
Eastern Washington University ... WA . 480
Seattle University ... WA . 484
University of Washington ... WA . 485
Washington State University ... WA . 486
West Virginia University ... WV . 491

SURGA: Commission on Accreditation of Allied Health Education Programs: surgical assistant (C,A)

Gulf Coast State College ... FL ... 100
College of DuPage ... IL ... 135
Madisonville Community College ... KY .. 181
Delta College ... MI .. 223
Stark State College ... OH .. 361
University of Cincinnati-Clermont College. OH .. 362
Meridian Institute of Surgical Assisting ... TN .. 422
Eastern Virginia Medical School ... VA .. 466

SURGT: Commission on Accreditation of Allied Health Education Programs: surgical technology (C,A)

Bevill State Community College ... AL ... 1
Calhoun Community College ... AL ... 1
Coastal Alabama Community College ... AL ... 1
Lurleen B. Wallace Community College .. AL ... 2
Southern Union State Community College ... AL ... 3
Gateway Community College ... AZ ... 13
Mohave Community College ... AZ ... 14
Arkansas State University-Newport ... AR ... 18
Baptist Health College Little Rock ... AR ... 18
North Arkansas College ... AR ... 20
South Arkansas Community College ... AR ... 21
Southeast Arkansas College ... AR ... 21
University of Arkansas at Fort Smith ... AR ... 21
University of Arkansas for Medical Sciences ... AR ... 22
Concorde Career College ... CA ... 40
Glendale Career College ... CA ... 44
MiraCosta College ... CA ... 52
Skyline College ... CA ... 61
Southwestern College ... CA ... 65
Aims Community College ... CO ... 76
Colorado Mesa University ... CO ... 77
Community College of Denver ... CO ... 79
Concorde Career College ... CO ... 79
Front Range Community College ... CO ... 79
Pueblo Community College ... CO ... 81
Housatonic Community College ... CT ... 85
Manchester Community College ... CT ... 85
Delaware Technical Community College, Terry Campus ... DE ... 90
College of Central Florida ... FL ... 96
Concorde Career Institute ... FL ... 96
Concorde Career Institute ... FL ... 97
Daytona State College ... FL ... 97
Eastern Florida State College ... FL ... 97
Florida State College at Jacksonville ... FL ... 100
Fortis College ... FL ... 100
Gulf Coast State College ... FL ... 100
Indian River State College ... FL ... 101
Palm Beach State College ... FL ... 104
Pasco-Hernando State College ... FL ... 104
Pensacola State College ... FL ... 104
Santa Fe College ... FL ... 107
Southeastern College ... FL ... 107
Tallahassee Community College ... FL ... 111
Albany Technical College ... GA .. 113
Athens Technical College ... GA .. 114
Atlanta Technical College ... GA .. 114
Augusta Technical College ... GA .. 114
Central Georgia Technical College ... GA .. 116
Chattahoochee Technical College ... GA .. 116
Coastal Pines Technical College ... GA .. 116
Columbus Technical College ... GA .. 117
Georgia Northwestern Technical College GA .. 119
Gwinnett Technical College ... GA .. 120
Lanier Technical College ... GA .. 121
Ogeechee Technical College ... GA .. 122
Savannah Technical College ... GA .. 124
Southern Crescent Technical College ... GA .. 124
Southern Regional Technical College ... GA .. 125
West Georgia Technical College ... GA .. 127
Wiregrass Georgia Technical College ... GA .. 127
Kapiolani Community College ... HI ... 128
College of Eastern Idaho ... ID ... 130
College of Southern Idaho ... ID ... 130
College of Western Idaho ... ID ... 130
North Idaho College ... ID ... 131
College of DuPage ... IL ... 135
College of Lake County ... IL ... 135
Elgin Community College ... IL ... 136
Illinois Central College ... IL ... 138
John A. Logan College ... IL ... 139
John Wood Community College ... IL ... 140
Lincoln Land Community College ... IL ... 142
Parkland College ... IL ... 146
Prairie State College ... IL ... 146
Richland Community College ... IL ... 147
Robert Morris University - Illinois ... IL ... 147

Rock Valley College ... IL ... 147
Shawnee Community College ... IL ... 149
Triton College ... IL ... 150
Ivy Tech Community College of Indiana-Indianapolis ... IN ... 157
University of Saint Francis ... IN ... 161
Vincennes University ... IN ... 162
Des Moines Area Community College ... IA ... 164
Iowa Lakes Community College ... IA ... 166
Iowa Western Community College ... IA ... 167
Kirkwood Community College ... IA ... 167
Mercy College of Health Sciences ... IA ... 168
Scott Community College ... IA ... 165
Western Iowa Tech Community College . IA ... 170
Hutchinson Community College ... KS .. 174
Neosho County Community College ... KS .. 175
Seward County Community College ... KS .. 176
Wichita State University Campus of Applied Sciences and Technology ... KS .. 178
American National University ... KY .. 178
Ashland Community and Technical College ... KY .. 180
Bluegrass Community and Technical College ... KY .. 180
Hazard Community and Technical College ... KY .. 181
Jefferson Community and Technical College ... KY .. 181
Madisonville Community College ... KY .. 181
Owensboro Community and Technical College ... KY .. 182
Somerset Community College ... KY .. 182
Southcentral Kentucky Community and Technical College ... KY .. 182
Southeast Kentucky Community and Technical College ... KY .. 182
Sullivan University ... KY .. 184
West Kentucky Community and Technical College ... KY .. 182
Baton Rouge Community College ... LA ... 186
Bossier Parish Community College ... LA ... 187
Delgado Community College ... LA ... 187
#Fortis College ... LA ... 186
L.E. Fletcher Technical Community College ... LA ... 187
Southern University at Shreveport-Louisiana ... LA ... 190
SOWELA Technical Community College . LA ... 188
Eastern Maine Community College ... ME .. 194
Anne Arundel Community College ... MD .. 197
Baltimore City Community College ... MD .. 197
Chesapeake College ... MD .. 197
Community College of Baltimore County, The ... MD .. 198
Frederick Community College ... MD .. 198
Montgomery College ... MD .. 200
Prince George's Community College ... MD .. 201
Bunker Hill Community College ... MA .. 214
Massachusetts Bay Community College . MA .. 214
North Shore Community College ... MA .. 215
Quincy College ... MA .. 218
Quinsigamond Community College ... MA .. 215
Springfield Technical Community College MA .. 215
Baker College of Flint ... MI ... 221
Delta College ... MI ... 223
Henry Ford College ... MI ... 224
Kirtland Community College ... MI ... 226
Lansing Community College ... MI ... 226
Macomb Community College ... MI ... 226
Northern Michigan University ... MI ... 228
Northwestern Michigan College ... MI ... 228
Oakland Community College ... MI ... 229
Washtenaw Community College ... MI ... 232
Wayne County Community College District ... MI ... 232
Anoka Technical College ... MN .. 237
Lake Superior College ... MN .. 238
Minnesota West Community and Technical College ... MN .. 239
Northland Community and Technical College ... MN .. 240
Rasmussen College - St. Cloud ... MN .. 242
Rochester Community and Technical College ... MN .. 240
Saint Cloud Technical and Community College ... MN .. 241
Saint Paul College-A Community & Technical College ... MN .. 241
East Central Community College ... MS .. 245
Hinds Community College ... MS .. 246
Holmes Community College ... MS .. 246
Itawamba Community College ... MS .. 246
Meridian Community College ... MS .. 247
Mississippi Gulf Coast Community College ... MS .. 247
Pearl River Community College ... MS .. 248
Metropolitan Community College - Penn Valley ... MO . 255
Ozarks Technical Community College ... MO . 257
Southeast Missouri Hospital College of Nursing and Health Sciences ... MO . 259
Flathead Valley Community College ... MT .. 263
Great Falls College Montana State University ... MT .. 264
Nebraska Methodist College ... NE .. 268
Southeast Community College ... NE .. 269
Western Nebraska Community College ... NE .. 270
College of Southern Nevada ... NV .. 271
Great Bay Community College ... NH .. 272
Bergen Community College ... NJ ... 275
Berkeley College ... NJ ... 275
Eastwick College ... NJ ... 277
Central New Mexico Community College NM .. 285
San Juan College ... NM .. 288
City University of New York Kingsborough Community College ... NY .. 294
Finger Lakes Health College of Nursing and Health Sciences ... NY .. 300
Hudson Valley Community College ... NY .. 302
Monroe Community College ... NY .. 307
Nassau Community College ... NY .. 308
New York University ... NY .. 310
Niagara County Community College ... NY .. 310
Onondaga Community College ... NY .. 311
Trocaire College ... NY .. 323
Asheville - Buncombe Technical Community College ... NC .. 332
Blue Ridge Community College ... NC .. 332
Cabarrus College of Health Sciences ... NC .. 327
Cape Fear Community College ... NC .. 332
Catawba Valley Community College ... NC .. 333
Central Piedmont Community College ... NC .. 333
Cleveland Community College ... NC .. 333
Coastal Carolina Community College ... NC .. 333
College of the Albemarle ... NC .. 333
Davidson County Community College ... NC .. 334
Durham Technical Community College ... NC .. 334
Edgecombe Community College ... NC .. 334
Fayetteville Technical Community College ... NC .. 334
Guilford Technical Community College ... NC .. 335
Lenoir Community College ... NC .. 335
Robeson Community College ... NC .. 337
Rockingham Community College ... NC .. 337
Sandhills Community College ... NC .. 337
Wilson Community College ... NC .. 339
Bismarck State College ... ND .. 346
Central Ohio Technical College ... OH .. 349
Cincinnati State Technical and Community College ... OH .. 350
Columbus State Community College ... OH .. 351
Cuyahoga Community College ... OH .. 351
Fortis College ... OH .. 353
Lakeland Community College ... OH .. 355
Lorain County Community College ... OH .. 355
Owens Community College ... OH .. 360
Sinclair Community College ... OH .. 361
Stark State College ... OH .. 361
University of Cincinnati-Clermont College. OH .. 362
Community Care College ... OK .. 366
Concorde Career College ... OR .. 372
Linn-Benton Community College ... OR .. 374
Mt. Hood Community College ... OR .. 374
Community College of Allegheny County PA .. 381
Delaware County Community College ... PA .. 382
Great Lakes Institute of Technology ... PA .. 385
HACC, Central Pennsylvania's Community College ... PA .. 385
Lackawanna College ... PA .. 387
Luzerne County Community College ... PA .. 389
Montgomery County Community College PA .. 390
Mount Aloysius College ... PA .. 391
Pennsylvania College of Health Sciences PA .. 393
Pennsylvania College of Technology ... PA .. 393
Pittsburgh Technical College ... PA .. 396
New England Institute of Technology ... RI ... 405
Aiken Technical College ... SC .. 406
Central Carolina Technical College ... SC .. 407
Florence - Darlington Technical College .. SC .. 409
Greenville Technical College ... SC .. 410
Horry-Georgetown Technical College ... SC .. 410
Midlands Technical College ... SC .. 410
Piedmont Technical College ... SC .. 411
Spartanburg Community College ... SC .. 412
Technical College of the Lowcountry ... SC .. 412
Tri-County Technical College ... SC .. 413
York Technical College ... SC .. 415
Southeast Technical Institute ... SD .. 417
Western Dakota Technical Institute ... SD .. 417
Chattanooga State Community College .. TN .. 424
Fortis Institute ... TN .. 420
Nashville State Community College ... TN .. 425
Northeast State Community College ... TN .. 425
Roane State Community College ... TN .. 425
Walters State Community College ... TN .. 426
Amarillo College ... TX ... 430
Angelina College ... TX ... 430
Austin Community College District ... TX ... 431
Baptist Health System School of Health Professions ... TX ... 431
Cisco College ... TX ... 433
College of Health Care Professions, The TX ... 433
Collin County Community College District TX ... 433
Concorde Career Institute ... TX ... 434
Del Mar College ... TX ... 436
El Centro College ... TX ... 435
El Paso Community College ... TX ... 436
Fortis College ... TX ... 436
Galveston College ... TX ... 437
Houston Community College ... TX ... 437
Howard College ... TX ... 438
Lamar State College-Port Arthur ... TX ... 450
Lone Star College System ... TX ... 439
McLennan Community College ... TX ... 440
North Central Texas College ... TX ... 441
Odessa College ... TX ... 441
Paris Junior College ... TX ... 441
St. Philip's College ... TX ... 429
San Jacinto College Central ... TX ... 443
South Plains College ... TX ... 443
Tarrant County College District ... TX ... 445
Temple College ... TX ... 446
Texas State Technical College Waco ... TX ... 449
Trinity Valley Community College ... TX ... 452
Tyler Junior College ... TX ... 452
Vernon College ... TX ... 457
Dixie State University ... UT .. 460
Salt Lake Community College ... UT .. 461
Stevens-Henager College ... UT .. 459
Lord Fairfax Community College ... VA .. 474
Piedmont Virginia Community College ... VA .. 475
Riverside College of Health Careers ... VA .. 471
Sentara College of Health Sciences ... VA .. 471
Bellingham Technical College ... WA . 478
Clover Park Technical College ... WA . 479
Columbia Basin College ... WA . 479
Renton Technical College ... WA . 483
Seattle Central College ... WA . 484
Spokane Community College ... WA . 480
Yakima Valley College ... WA . 487
Southern West Virginia Community and Technical College ... WV . 489
West Virginia Northern Community College ... WV . 489
West Virginia University at Parkersburg .. WV . 491
Chippewa Valley Technical College ... WI ... 499
Gateway Technical College ... WI ... 499
Madison Area Technical College ... WI ... 499
Mid-State Technical College ... WI ... 500
Milwaukee Area Technical College ... WI ... 500
Moraine Park Technical College ... WI ... 500
Northcentral Technical College ... WI ... 500
Northeast Wisconsin Technical College .. WI ... 500
Waukesha County Technical College ... WI ... 500
Western Technical College ... WI ... 501
Laramie County Community College ... WY . 502

SURTEC: Accrediting Bureau of Health Education Schools: surgical technologist (C,A)

Baptist Health College Little Rock ... AR ... 18
American Career College-Los Angeles ... CA ... 25
CBD College ... CA ... 35
CNI College ... CA ... 38
Glendale Career College ... CA ... 44
Valley College of Medical Careers ... CA ... 72
City College ... FL ... 96
Southern Technical College ... FL ... 107
American National University ... KY .. 178
Fortis College ... LA ... 186
Midwest Institute-Earth City ... MO . 255
Finger Lakes Health College of Nursing and Health Sciences ... NY .. 300
Mandl School - The College of Allied Health ... NY .. 305
Mohawk Valley Community College ... NY .. 307
Meridian Institute of Surgical Assisting ... TN .. 422
Baptist Health System School of Health Professions ... TX ... 431
College of Health Care Professions, The TX ... 433
Riverside College of Health Careers ... VA .. 471
Sentara College of Health Sciences ... VA .. 471
Milwaukee Career College ... WI ... 494

SW: Council on Social Work Education: social work (B,M)

Alabama Agricultural and Mechanical University ... AL ... 1
Alabama State University ... AL ... 4
Auburn University ... AL ... 4
Jacksonville State University ... AL ... 5
Judson College ... AL ... 6
Miles College ... AL ... 6
Oakwood University ... AL ... 6
Samford University ... AL ... 6
Talladega College ... AL ... 7
Troy University ... AL ... 7
Tuskegee University ... AL ... 7
University of Alabama at Birmingham ... AL ... 8
University of Alabama, The ... AL ... 7
University of Montevallo ... AL ... 8
University of North Alabama ... AL ... 8
University of South Alabama ... AL ... 8
University of Alaska Anchorage ... AK ... 9
University of Alaska Fairbanks ... AK ... 10
Arizona State University ... AZ ... 10
Northern Arizona University ... AZ ... 14
@University of Phoenix ... AZ ... 16
Arkansas State University-Jonesboro ... AR ... 17
Harding University Main Campus ... AR ... 19
Philander Smith College ... AR ... 20
Southern Arkansas University ... AR ... 21
@University of Arkansas at Fort Smith ... AR ... 21
University of Arkansas at Little Rock ... AR ... 22
University of Arkansas at Monticello ... AR ... 22
University of Arkansas at Pine Bluff ... AR ... 22
University of Arkansas Main Campus ... AR ... 21
Azusa Pacific University ... CA ... 26
Brandman University ... CA ... 27
California Baptist University ... CA ... 27
California State University-Bakersfield ... CA ... 30
California State University-Chico ... CA ... 31
California State University-Dominguez Hills ... CA ... 31
California State University-East Bay ... CA ... 31
California State University-Fresno ... CA ... 31
California State University-Fullerton ... CA ... 31
California State University-Long Beach ... CA ... 31
California State University-Los Angeles ... CA ... 32
California State University-Monterey Bay CA ... 32
California State University-Northridge ... CA ... 32
California State University-Sacramento ... CA ... 32
California State University-San Bernardino ... CA ... 33
California State University-San Marcos ... CA ... 33
California State University-Stanislaus ... CA ... 33
Fresno Pacific University ... CA ... 43
Humboldt State University ... CA ... 33
La Sierra University ... CA ... 47
Loma Linda University ... CA ... 48
Pacific Union College ... CA ... 55
Point Loma Nazarene University ... CA ... 57
San Diego State University ... CA ... 33
San Francisco State University ... CA ... 34
San Jose State University ... CA ... 34
University of California-Berkeley ... CA ... 68
University of California-Los Angeles ... CA ... 69
University of Southern California ... CA ... 72
Whittier College ... CA ... 75
Colorado Mesa University ... CO ... 77
Colorado State University ... CO ... 78
Colorado State University-Pueblo ... CO ... 79
Metropolitan State University of Denver .. CO ... 80
University of Denver ... CO ... 83
Central Connecticut State University ... CT ... 84
Eastern Connecticut State University ... CT ... 84
@Goodwin College ... CT ... 87
Quinnipiac University ... CT ... 87
Sacred Heart University ... CT ... 88
Southern Connecticut State University ... CT ... 85
University of Connecticut ... CT ... 88
University of Saint Joseph ... CT ... 89
Western Connecticut State University ... CT ... 85
Delaware State University ... DE ... 89
Catholic University of America, The ... DC ... 91
Gallaudet University ... DC ... 91
Howard University ... DC ... 92
University of the District of Columbia ... DC ... 93
Barry University ... FL ... 95
Florida Agricultural and Mechanical University ... FL ... 108
Florida Atlantic University ... FL ... 108
Florida Gulf Coast University ... FL ... 108
Florida International University ... FL ... 109
Florida Memorial University ... FL ... 99
Florida State University ... FL ... 109
Saint Leo University ... FL ... 106
Southeastern University ... FL ... 107
University of Central Florida ... FL ... 109
University of North Florida ... FL ... 110
University of South Florida ... FL ... 110
University of West Florida ... FL ... 110
Warner University ... FL ... 113
Albany State University ... GA .. 113
Augusta University ... GA .. 115
Clark Atlanta University ... GA .. 116
Dalton State College ... GA .. 117
Fort Valley State University ... GA .. 118
Georgia State University ... GA .. 119
Kennesaw State University ... GA .. 120
Savannah State University ... GA .. 123

Institution	State	Page
@Universidad Ana G. Mendez Cupey Campus	PR	511
Universidad Ana G. Mendez Gurabo Campus	PR	511
Universidad Central de Bayamon	PR	512
University of Puerto Rico-Humacao	PR	513
University of Puerto Rico-Rio Piedras Campus	PR	514
University of the Sacred Heart	PR	514
Providence College	RI	405
Rhode Island College	RI	405
Salve Regina University	RI	406
Benedict College	SC	407
Columbia College	SC	408
Limestone College	SC	410
South Carolina State University	SC	412
University of South Carolina Columbia	SC	413
Winthrop University	SC	414
Oglala Lakota College	SD	416
University of Sioux Falls	SD	417
University of South Dakota, The	SD	416
Austin Peay State University	TN	418
Belmont University	TN	418
East Tennessee State University	TN	419
Freed-Hardeman University	TN	420
King University	TN	420
Lincoln Memorial University	TN	421
Lipscomb University	TN	421
Middle Tennessee State University	TN	422
Southern Adventist University	TN	424
Tennessee State University	TN	426
Tennessee Wesleyan University	TN	426
Trevecca Nazarene University	TN	427
Union University	TN	427
University of Memphis, The	TN	427
University of Tennessee at Chattanooga	TN	428
University of Tennessee at Martin	TN	428
University of Tennessee, Knoxville	TN	427
Abilene Christian University	TX	429
Angelo State University	TX	451
Baylor University	TX	431
Hardin-Simmons University	TX	437
Howard Payne University	TX	438
Jarvis Christian College	TX	438
Lamar University	TX	449
Lubbock Christian University	TX	439
Midwestern State University	TX	440
Our Lady of the Lake University	TX	441
Prairie View A & M University	TX	446
St. Edward's University	TX	442
@Southwestern Assemblies of God University	TX	445
Stephen F. Austin State University	TX	445
Tarleton State University	TX	446
Texas A & M University-Central Texas	TX	447
Texas A & M University - Commerce	TX	447
Texas A & M University - Kingsville	TX	447
Texas Christian University	TX	448
Texas Southern University	TX	449
Texas State University	TX	450
Texas Tech University	TX	451
Texas Woman's University	TX	451
University of Houston	TX	452
University of Houston - Clear Lake	TX	453
University of Houston - Downtown	TX	453
University of Mary Hardin-Baylor	TX	453
University of North Texas	TX	454
University of Texas at Arlington, The	TX	454
University of Texas at Austin	TX	455
University of Texas at El Paso	TX	455
University of Texas at San Antonio, The	TX	455
University of Texas Permian Basin	TX	457
University of Texas Rio Grande Valley, The	TX	455
West Texas A & M University	TX	448
Brigham Young University	UT	458
University of Utah, The	UT	460
Utah State University	UT	460
Utah Valley University	UT	461
Weber State University	UT	461
Castleton University	VT	464
Champlain College	VT	462
University of Vermont	VT	463
Christopher Newport University	VA	466
Eastern Mennonite University	VA	466
Ferrum College	VA	467
George Mason University	VA	467
James Madison University	VA	468
Liberty University	VA	468
Longwood University	VA	469
Mary Baldwin University	VA	469
Norfolk State University	VA	469
Radford University	VA	470
Virginia Commonwealth University	VA	473
Virginia State University	VA	477
Virginia Union University	VA	477
Virginia Wesleyan University	VA	477
Eastern Washington University	WA	480
Heritage University	WA	481
Pacific Lutheran University	WA	482
Saint Martin's University	WA	483
Seattle University	WA	484
University of Washington	WA	485
Walla Walla University	WA	485
Bethany College	WV	487
Concord University	WV	490
Marshall University	WV	490
Shepherd University	WV	490
West Liberty University	WV	490
West Virginia State University	WV	491
West Virginia University	WV	491
@Alverno College	WI	492
Carthage College	WI	492
Concordia University Wisconsin	WI	493
Marian University	WI	494
Mount Mary University	WI	495
University of Wisconsin-Eau Claire	WI	496
University of Wisconsin-Green Bay	WI	496
University of Wisconsin-Madison	WI	496
University of Wisconsin-Milwaukee	WI	497
University of Wisconsin-Oshkosh	WI	497
University of Wisconsin-River Falls	WI	497
University of Wisconsin-Stevens Point	WI	497
University of Wisconsin-Superior	WI	498
University of Wisconsin-Whitewater	WI	498
Viterbo University	WI	498
University of Wyoming	WY	502

THEA: National Association of Schools of Theatre: theatre (C,A,B, M,D)

Institution	State	Page
Alabama State University	AL	4
Auburn University	AL	4
Jacksonville State University	AL	5
Samford University	AL	6
University of Alabama at Birmingham	AL	8
University of Alabama, The	AL	7
University of Arizona	AZ	16
Arkansas State University-Jonesboro	AR	17
University of Arkansas at Little Rock	AR	22
University of Arkansas Main Campus	AR	21
University of Central Arkansas	AR	23
AMDA College and Conservatory of the Performing Arts	CA	25
California State University-Chico	CA	31
California State University-Dominguez Hills	CA	31
California State University-Fresno	CA	31
California State University-Fullerton	CA	31
California State University-Long Beach	CA	31
California State University-Northridge	CA	32
California State University-Sacramento	CA	32
California State University-San Bernardino	CA	33
California State University-Stanislaus	CA	33
Chapman University	CA	36
Dell'Arte International School of Physical Theatre	CA	41
Loyola Marymount University	CA	50
San Diego State University	CA	33
San Francisco State University	CA	34
San Jose State University	CA	34
Theatre of Arts	CA	67
University of California-Los Angeles	CA	69
Vanguard University of Southern California	CA	72
Metropolitan State University of Denver	CO	80
University of Northern Colorado	CO	83
University of Hartford	CT	88
Western Connecticut State University	CT	85
Howard University	DC	92
Broward College	FL	95
Florida International University	FL	109
Florida State University	FL	109
Miami Dade College	FL	103
University of Central Florida	FL	109
University of Florida	FL	109
University of South Florida	FL	110
Columbus State University	GA	116
Georgia Southern University	GA	119
Kennesaw State University	GA	120
University of Georgia	GA	125
University of West Georgia	GA	126
Valdosta State University	GA	126
Boise State University	ID	129
Idaho State University	ID	130
Bradley University	IL	133
Eastern Illinois University	IL	136
Illinois State University	IL	139
Loyola University Chicago	IL	142
Northern Illinois University	IL	145
Southern Illinois University Carbondale	IL	149
Southern Illinois University Edwardsville	IL	149
Western Illinois University	IL	152
Ball State University	IN	153
Butler University	IN	153
Indiana University Bloomington	IN	156
Purdue University Fort Wayne	IN	159
Purdue University Main Campus	IN	159
University of Iowa	IA	163
University of Northern Iowa	IA	163
Kansas State University	KS	174
Morehead State University	KY	183
Murray State University	KY	183
University of Kentucky	KY	185
University of Louisville	KY	185
Western Kentucky University	KY	185
Grambling State University	LA	191
Louisiana State University and Agricultural and Mechanical College	LA	188
Northwestern State University	LA	192
University of Louisiana at Lafayette	LA	192
University of New Orleans	LA	189
Community College of Baltimore County, The	MD	198
Towson University	MD	204
College of the Holy Cross	MA	208
Salem State University	MA	213
Hope College	MI	225
Oakland University	MI	229
Wayne State University	MI	232
Western Michigan University	MI	232
Normandale Community College	MN	239
St. Cloud State University	MN	240
St. Olaf College	MN	243
Winona State University	MN	241
Belhaven University	MS	245
University of Mississippi	MS	249
University of Southern Mississippi	MS	249
Missouri State University	MO	256
Missouri Western State University	MO	257
Southeast Missouri State University	MO	259
University of Central Missouri	MO	260
University of Missouri - Kansas City	MO	261
University of Montana - Missoula	MT	264
University of Nebraska - Lincoln	NE	269
Kean University	NJ	278
Montclair State University	NJ	279
Rowan University	NJ	281
University of New Mexico Main Campus	NM	288
American Academy of Dramatic Arts	NY	290
City University of New York Queensborough Community College	NY	295
Ithaca College	NY	303
New York Conservatory for Dramatic Arts, The	NY	309
State University of New York at Fredonia	NY	317
State University of New York at New Paltz	NY	317
State University of New York at Oneonta	NY	317
State University of New York College at Buffalo	NY	318
State University of New York College at Oswego	NY	319
State University of New York College at Potsdam	NY	319
State University of New York, The College at Brockport	NY	318
Appalachian State University	NC	341
East Carolina University	NC	341
North Carolina Agricultural and Technical State University	NC	341
North Carolina Central University	NC	342
University of North Carolina at Charlotte	NC	342
University of North Carolina at Greensboro	NC	343
Western Carolina University	NC	344
North Dakota State University Main Campus	ND	345
University of North Dakota	ND	345
Bowling Green State University	OH	348
Kent State University Kent Campus	OH	354
Miami University	OH	356
Ohio State University Main Campus, The	OH	358
Ohio University Main Campus	OH	359
Otterbein University	OH	360
Sinclair Community College	OH	361
University of Cincinnati Main Campus	OH	362
University of Toledo	OH	363
Oklahoma State University	OK	368
Portland State University	OR	376
University of Portland	OR	377
Bloomsburg University of Pennsylvania	PA	394
California University of Pennsylvania	PA	394
Indiana University of Pennsylvania	PA	394
Lehigh University	PA	388
Messiah College	PA	390
Penn State University Park	PA	392
Slippery Rock University of Pennsylvania	PA	395
Temple University	PA	399
University of Pittsburgh	PA	401
West Chester University of Pennsylvania	PA	396
Anderson University	SC	406
Coastal Carolina University	SC	408
College of Charleston	SC	408
Francis Marion University	SC	409
University of South Carolina Columbia	SC	413
Winthrop University	SC	414
University of South Dakota, The	SD	416
Belmont University	TN	418
East Tennessee State University	TN	419
Middle Tennessee State University	TN	422
University of Memphis, The	TN	427
University of Tennessee at Chattanooga	TN	428
University of Tennessee, Knoxville	TN	427
Baylor University	TX	431
Del Mar College	TX	436
KD Conservatory College of Film and Dramatic Arts	TX	438
Midwestern State University	TX	440
Sam Houston State University	TX	450
Southern Methodist University	TX	444
Stephen F. Austin State University	TX	445
Texas Tech University	TX	451
University of Texas Rio Grande Valley, The	TX	455
University of the Incarnate Word	TX	453
West Texas A & M University	TX	448
Brigham Young University	UT	458
Snow College	UT	461
Christopher Newport University	VA	466
James Madison University	VA	468
Longwood University	VA	469
Radford University	VA	470
Virginia Commonwealth University	VA	473
Virginia Polytechnic Institute and State University	VA	477
Davis & Elkins College	WV	487
West Virginia University	WV	491
Marquette University	WI	494
University of Wisconsin-Stevens Point	WI	497
University of Wisconsin-Whitewater	WI	498
Casper College	WY	501

THEOL: The Association of Theological Schools: theology (M, FP,D)

Institution	State	Page
Faulkner University	AL	5
Samford University	AL	6
Grand Canyon University	AZ	12
Phoenix Seminary	AZ	15
American Baptist Seminary of the West	CA	25
Azusa Pacific University	CA	26
Biola University	CA	27
California Lutheran University	CA	29
China Evangelical Seminary North America	CA	36
Christian Witness Theological Seminary	CA	36
Church Divinity School of the Pacific	CA	36
Claremont School of Theology	CA	37
Dominican School of Philosophy and Theology	CA	41
Franciscan School of Theology	CA	43
Fresno Pacific University	CA	43
Fuller Theological Seminary	CA	43
Gateway Seminary	CA	43
Grace Mission University	CA	44
Graduate Theological Union	CA	44
International Theological Seminary	CA	46
La Sierra University	CA	47
Logos Evangelical Seminary	CA	48
Loyola Marymount University	CA	50
Pacific School of Religion	CA	55
Presbyterian Theological Seminary in America	CA	57
Saint John's Seminary	CA	58
Saint Patrick's Seminary & University	CA	59
Santa Clara University	CA	62
Starr King School for the Ministry	CA	66
University of Redlands	CA	71
Westminster Theological Seminary in California	CA	74
World Mission University	CA	75
Augustine Institute	CO	76
Denver Seminary	CO	79
Iliff School of Theology	CO	80
St. John Vianney Theological Seminary	CO	82
Hartford Seminary	CT	87
Holy Apostles College and Seminary	CT	87
Yale University	CT	89
Catholic University of America, The	DC	91
Howard University	DC	92
Pontifical Faculty of the Immaculate Conception at the Dominican House of S tudies	DC	92
Wesley Theological Seminary	DC	93
Barry University	FL	95
Knox Theological Seminary	FL	102
@Palm Beach Atlantic University	FL	104
@St. Thomas University	FL	106

TRACS: Transnational Association of Christian Colleges and Schools: christian studies education (C,A,B, M,D)

VET: American Veterinary Medical Association: veterinary medicine (FP,D)

WC: Western Association of Schools and Colleges, Senior College and University Commission

WJ: Western Association of Schools and Colleges, Accrediting Commission for Community and Junior Colleges

Index of FICE Numbers

002276 .... Kellogg Community College .... MI 225
002277 .... Lake Michigan College .... MI 226
002278 .... Lansing Community College .... MI 226
002279 .... Lawrence Technological University .... MI 226
002282 .... Madonna University .... MI 227
002288 .... Rochester University .... MI 229
002290 .... Michigan State University .... MI 227
002292 .... Michigan Technological University .... MI 227
002293 .... Lake Superior State University .... MI 226
002294 .... Monroe County Community College .... MI 227
002295 .... Montcalm Community College .... MI 228
002297 .... Muskegon Community College .... MI 228
002299 .... North Central Michigan College .... MI 228
002301 .... Northern Michigan University .... MI 228
002302 .... Northwestern Michigan College .... MI 228
002303 .... Oakland Community College .... MI 229
002307 .... Oakland University .... MI 229
002308 .... Olivet College .... MI 229
002310 .... St. Clair County Community College .... MI 230
002311 .... Kuyper College .... MI 226
002313 .... Sacred Heart Major Seminary .... MI 229
002314 .... Saginaw Valley State University .... MI 230
002315 .... Schoolcraft College .... MI 230
002316 .... Siena Heights University .... MI 230
002317 .... Southwestern Michigan College .... MI 230
002318 .... Spring Arbor University .... MI 230
002322 .... Finlandia University .... MI 223
002323 .... University of Detroit Mercy .... MI 231
002325 .... University of Michigan-Ann Arbor .... MI 231
002326 .... University of Michigan-Dearborn .... MI 231
002327 .... University of Michigan-Flint .... MI 231
002328 .... Washtenaw Community College .... MI 232
002329 .... Wayne State University .... MI 232
002330 .... Western Michigan University .... MI 232
002331 .... Western Theological Seminary .... MI 233
002332 .... Anoka-Ramsey Community College .... MN 237
002334 .... Augsburg University .... MN 233
002335 .... Riverland Community College .... MN 240
002336 .... Bemidji State University .... MN 237
002337 .... Bethany Lutheran College .... MN 234
002339 .... Central Lakes College .... MN 237
002340 .... Carleton College .... MN 234
002341 .... College of Saint Benedict .... MN 235
002342 .... St. Catherine University .... MN 242
002343 .... The College of Saint Scholastica .... MN 235
002345 .... University of Saint Thomas .... MN 244
002346 .... Concordia College .... MN 235
002347 .... Concordia University, St. Paul .... MN 235
002350 .... Vermilion Community College .... MN 241
002353 .... Gustavus Adolphus College .... MN 235
002354 .... Hamline University .... MN 236
002355 .... Hibbing Community College .... MN 238
002356 .... Itasca Community College .... MN 238
002357 .... Luther Seminary .... MN 236
002358 .... Macalester College .... MN 236
002360 .... Minnesota State University, Mankato .... MN 239
002361 .... Martin Luther College .... MN 236
002362 .... Minneapolis Cmty & Tech College .... MN 238
002365 .... Minneapolis College of Art & Design .... MN 236
002367 .... Minnesota State University Moorhead .... MN 239
002369 .... North Central University .... MN 242
002370 .... North Hennepin Community College .... MN 239
002371 .... University of Northwestern St. Paul .... MN 244
002373 .... Rochester Community & Tech College .... MN 240
002375 .... Southwest Minnesota State Univ .... MN 241
002377 .... St. Cloud State University .... MN 240
002379 .... Saint John's University .... MN 243
002380 .... St Mary's University of Minnesota .... MN 243
002382 .... St. Olaf College .... MN 243
002383 .... Crown College .... MN 235
002385 .... Northland Community & Tech College .... MN 240
002386 .... United Theol Seminary-Twin Cities .... MN 243
002388 .... University of Minnesota Duluth .... MN 243
002389 .... University of Minnesota-Morris .... MN 244
002391 .... Mitchell Hamline School of Law .... MN 242
002393 .... Minnesota State College Southeast .... MN 239
002394 .... Winona State University .... MN 241
002396 .... Alcorn State University .... MS 244
002397 .... Belhaven University .... MS 245
002398 .... Blue Mountain College .... MS 245
002401 .... Coahoma Community College .... MS 245
002402 .... Copiah-Lincoln Community College .... MS 245
002403 .... Delta State University .... MS 245
002404 .... East Central Community College .... MS 245
002405 .... East Mississippi Community College .... MS 246
002407 .... Hinds Community College .... MS 246
002408 .... Holmes Community College .... MS 246
002409 .... Itawamba Community College .... MS 246
002410 .... Jackson State University .... MS 246
002411 .... Jones County Junior College .... MS 246
002413 .... Meridian Community College .... MS 247
002414 .... Millsaps College .... MS 247
002415 .... Mississippi College .... MS 247
002416 .... Mississippi Delta Community College .... MS 247
002417 .... Mississippi Gulf Coast Cmty College .... MS 247
002422 .... Mississippi University for Women .... MS 248
002423 .... Mississippi State University .... MS 247
002424 .... Mississippi Valley State University .... MS 248
002426 .... Northeast Mississippi Cmty College .... MS 248
002427 .... Northwest Mississippi Cmty College .... MS 248
002430 .... Pearl River Community College .... MS 248
002433 .... Rust College .... MS 248
002435 .... Southeastern Baptist College .... MS 249
002436 .... Southwest Mississippi Cmty College .... MS 249
002439 .... Tougaloo College .... MS 249
002440 .... University of Mississippi .... MS 249
002441 .... University of Southern Mississippi .... MS 249
002447 .... William Carey University .... MS 249
002449 .... Avila University .... MO 250
002450 .... Calvary University .... MO 250
002453 .... Central Methodist University .... MO 251
002454 .... University of Central Missouri .... MO 260
002456 .... Columbia College .... MO 251
002457 .... Concordia Seminary .... MO 251
002458 .... Cottey College .... MO 252
002459 .... Crowder College .... MO 252
002460 .... Culver-Stockton College .... MO 252
002461 .... Drury University .... MO 252
002462 .... Eden Theological Seminary .... MO 253
002463 .... Evangel University .... MO 253
002464 .... Fontbonne University .... MO 253
002466 .... Harris-Stowe State University .... MO 253
002467 .... Conception Seminary College .... MO 251
002468 .... Jefferson College .... MO 254
002471 .... St Louis Cmty College-Cosand Center .... MO 259
002473 .... Kansas City Art Institute .... MO 254
002474 .... Kansas City Univ of Med & BioSci .... MO 254
002476 .... Kenrick-Glennon Seminary .... MO 254
002477 .... A. T. Still Univ of Health Sciences .... MO 250
002479 .... Lincoln University .... MO 254
002480 .... Lindenwood University .... MO 254
002482 .... Maryville University of Saint Louis .... MO 254
002484 .... Metropolitan Cmty Col-Penn Valley .... MO 255
002485 .... Midwestern Baptist Theol Seminary .... MO 256
002486 .... Mineral Area College .... MO 256
002488 .... Missouri Southern State University .... MO 256
002489 .... Missouri Valley College .... MO 256
002490 .... Missouri Western State University .... MO 257
002491 .... Moberly Area Community College .... MO 257
002494 .... Nazarene Theological Seminary .... MO 257
002495 .... Truman State University .... MO 260
002496 .... Northwest Missouri State University .... MO 257
002498 .... Park University .... MO 258
002499 .... Rockhurst University .... MO 258
002500 .... College of the Ozarks .... MO 251
002501 .... Southeast Missouri State University .... MO 259
002502 .... Southwest Baptist University .... MO 259
002503 .... Missouri State University .... MO 256
002504 .... St. Louis College of Pharmacy .... MO 259
002506 .... Saint Louis University .... MO 259
002509 .... Saint Paul School of Theology .... KS 176
002512 .... Stephens College .... MO 260
002514 .... North Central Missouri College .... MO 257
002515 .... Univ of Missouri System Admin .... MO 261
002516 .... University of Missouri - Columbia .... MO 261
002517 .... Missouri Univ of Science Tech .... MO 261
002518 .... Univ of Missouri - Kansas City .... MO 261
002519 .... Univ of Missouri - Saint Louis .... MO 261
002520 .... Washington University in St. Louis .... MO 262
002521 .... Webster University .... MO 262
002523 .... Westminster College .... MO 262
002524 .... William Jewell College .... MO 262
002525 .... William Woods University .... MO 262
002526 .... Carroll College .... MT 263
002527 .... University of Providence .... MT 265
002528 .... Miles Community College .... MT 263
002529 .... Dawson Community College .... MT 263
002530 .... Montana State University Billings .... MT 264
002531 .... Montana Technological University .... MT 265
002532 .... Montana State University .... MT 264
002533 .... Montana State University - Northern .... MT 264
002534 .... Rocky Mountain College .... MT 265
002536 .... University of Montana - Missoula .... MT 264
002537 .... The University of Montana Western .... MT 264
002539 .... Chadron State College .... NE 268
002540 .... College of Saint Mary .... NE 266
002541 .... Concordia University .... NE 266
002542 .... Creighton University .... NE 266
002544 .... Doane University .... NE 267
002548 .... Hastings College .... NE 267
002551 .... University of Nebraska at Kearney .... NE 269
002553 .... Midland University .... NE 267
002554 .... University of Nebraska at Omaha .... NE 270
002555 .... Nebraska Wesleyan University .... NE 268
002557 .... Mid-Plains Community College .... NE 267
002559 .... Peru State College .... NE 268
002560 .... Western Nebraska Community College .... NE 270
002563 .... Union College .... NE 269
002565 .... University of Nebraska - Lincoln .... NE 269
002566 .... Wayne State College .... NE 268
002567 .... York College .... NE 270
002568 .... University of Nevada, Reno .... NV 271
002569 .... University of Nevada, Las Vegas .... NV 271
002572 .... Colby-Sawyer College .... NH 272
002573 .... Dartmouth College .... NH 273
002575 .... Franklin Pierce University .... NH 273
002579 .... New England College .... NH 273
002580 .... Southern New Hampshire University .... NH 274
002581 .... NHTI-Concord's Community College .... NH 273
002582 .... Manchester Community College .... NH 272
002583 .... Great Bay Community College .... NH 272
002586 .... Rivier University .... NH 274
002587 .... Saint Anselm College .... NH 274
002589 .... University of New Hampshire .... NH 274
002590 .... Keene State College .... NH 275
002591 .... Plymouth State University .... NH 275
002595 .... Assumption College for Sisters .... NJ 275
002596 .... Atlantic Cape Community College .... NJ 275
002597 .... Bloomfield College .... NJ 276
002598 .... Caldwell University .... NJ 276
002599 .... Centenary University .... NJ 276
002600 .... College of Saint Elizabeth .... NJ 277
002603 .... Drew University .... NJ 277
002607 .... Fairleigh Dickinson University .... NJ 277
002608 .... Georgian Court University .... NJ 278
002609 .... Rowan University .... NJ 281
002610 .... Felician University .... NJ 278
002613 .... New Jersey City University .... NJ 279
002615 .... Middlesex County College .... NJ 279
002616 .... Monmouth University .... NJ 279
002617 .... Montclair State University .... NJ 279
002619 .... New Brunswick Theological Seminary .... NJ 279
002621 .... New Jersey Institute of Technology .... NJ 279
002622 .... Kean University .... NJ 278
002624 .... Ocean County College .... NJ 280
002625 .... William Paterson University of NJ .... NJ 284
002626 .... Princeton Theological Seminary .... NJ 280
002627 .... Princeton University .... NJ 280
002628 .... Rider University .... NJ 281
002629 .... Rutgers University - New Brunswick .... NJ 282
002631 .... Rutgers University - Newark .... NJ 282
002632 .... Seton Hall University .... NJ 283
002638 .... Saint Peter's University .... NJ 282
002639 .... Stevens Institute of Technology .... NJ 283
002642 .... The College of New Jersey .... NJ 276
002643 .... Union County College .... NJ 284
002650 .... University of the Southwest .... NM 289
002651 .... Eastern New Mexico University .... NM 285
002653 .... New Mexico Highlands University .... NM 286
002654 .... New Mexico Inst of Mining & Tech .... NM 286
002655 .... New Mexico Junior College .... NM 286
002656 .... New Mexico Military Institute .... NM 287
002657 .... NM State University-Main Campus .... NM 287
002658 .... NM State University-Alamogordo .... NM 287
002659 .... NM State University-Carlsbad .... NM 287
002660 .... San Juan College .... NM 288
002661 .... Eastern New Mexico Univ - Roswell .... NM 286
002663 .... Univ of New Mexico Main Campus .... NM 288
002664 .... Western New Mexico University .... NM 289
002665 .... Vaughn Col of Aeronautics & Tech .... NY 324
002666 .... Adelphi University .... NY 289
002668 .... Alfred University .... NY 289
002669 .... Bank Street College of Education .... NY 290
002670 .... Clarks Summit University .... PA 381
002671 .... Bard College .... NY 290
002674 .... New York Theological Seminary .... NY 310
002677 .... Brooklyn Law School .... NY 291
002678 .... Bryant & Stratton College .... NY 291
002681 .... Canisius College .... NY 292
002685 .... Cazenovia College .... NY 292
002687 .... CUNY Brooklyn College .... NY 293
002688 .... CUNY City College .... NY 293
002689 .... CUNY Hunter College .... NY 294
002690 .... CUNY Queens College .... NY 295
002691 .... CUNY Borough of Manhattan CC .... NY 293
002692 .... CUNY Bronx Community College .... NY 293
002693 .... CUNY John Jay Col Criminal Justice .... NY 294
002694 .... CUNY Kingsborough Cmty College .... NY 294
002696 .... NYC Col of Tech/City Univ of NY .... NY 295
002697 .... CUNY Queensborough Cmty Col .... NY 295
002698 .... College of Staten Island CUNY .... NY 293
002699 .... Clarkson University .... NY 296
002700 .... Colgate Roch Crozer Divinity School .... NY 296
002701 .... Colgate University .... NY 296
002703 .... College of Mount Saint Vincent .... NY 296
002705 .... The College of Saint Rose .... NY 296
002707 .... Columbia University in City of NY .... NY 297
002708 .... Barnard College .... NY 290
002709 .... Concordia College .... NY 297
002710 .... Cooper Union .... NY 297
002711 .... Cornell University .... NY 297
002712 .... D'Youville College .... NY 298
002713 .... Dominican College of Blauvelt .... NY 298
002718 .... Elmira College .... NY 299
002722 .... Fordham University .... NY 300
002726 .... General Theological Seminary .... NY 300
002728 .... Hamilton College .... NY 301
002729 .... Hartwick College .... NY 301
002731 .... Hobart and William Smith Colleges .... NY 302
002732 .... Hofstra University .... NY 302
002733 .... Holy Trinity Orthodox Seminary .... NY 302
002734 .... Houghton College .... NY 302
002735 .... Hilbert College .... NY 301
002737 .... Iona College .... NY 302
002739 .... Ithaca College .... NY 303
002740 .... Jewish Theol Seminary of America .... NY 303
002741 .... American Jewish University .... CA 25
002742 .... The Juilliard School .... NY 303
002744 .... Keuka College .... NY 304
002748 .... Le Moyne College .... NY 304
002749 .... New York Col of Podiatric Medicine .... NY 309
002751 .... Long Island University .... NY 304
002754 .... Long Island University-LIU Post .... NY 304
002758 .... Manhattan College .... NY 305
002759 .... Manhattan School of Music .... NY 305
002760 .... Manhattanville College .... NY 305

003230 Allegheny College PA 378
003231 Community College of Allegheny Cty PA 381
003233 Alvernia University PA 378
003235 Arcadia University PA 379
003237 Bryn Mawr College PA 379
003238 Bucknell University PA 379
003239 Bucks County Community College PA 379
003240 Butler County Community College PA 380
003241 Cabrini University PA 380
003242 Carnegie Mellon University PA 380
003243 Cedar Crest College PA 381
003244 Chatham University PA 381
003245 Chestnut Hill College PA 381
003247 Misericordia University PA 390
003249 Community College of Philadelphia PA 382
003251 Curtis Institute of Music PA 382
003252 Delaware Valley University PA 382
003253 Dickinson College PA 382
003256 Drexel University PA 383
003258 Duquesne University PA 383
003259 Eastern University PA 383
003262 Elizabethtown College PA 383
003263 Evangelical Theological Seminary PA 383
003265 Franklin & Marshall College PA 384
003266 Gannon University PA 384
003267 Geneva College PA 384
003268 Gettysburg College PA 384
003269 Grove City College PA 385
003270 Gwynedd Mercy University PA 385
003272 Harcum College PA 385
003273 HACC, Central PA Cmty College PA 385
003274 Haverford College PA 385
003275 Holy Family University PA 386
003276 Immaculata University PA 386
003277 Indiana University of Pennsylvania PA 394
003279 Juniata College PA 386
003280 Keystone College PA 386
003282 King's College PA 387
003283 Lackawanna College PA 387
003284 Lafayette College PA 387
003285 Lancaster Bible College PA 388
003286 Lancaster Theological Seminary PA 388
003287 La Salle University PA 387
003288 Lebanon Valley College PA 388
003289 Lehigh University PA 388
003290 Lincoln University PA 389
003291 United Lutheran Seminary PA 400
003293 Lycoming College PA 389
003294 Manor College PA 389
003296 Marywood University PA 389
003297 Mercyhurst University PA 390
003298 Messiah College PA 390
003300 Moore College of Art and Design PA 390
003301 Moravian College PA 391
003302 Mount Aloysius College PA 391
003303 Carlow University PA 380
003304 Muhlenberg College PA 391
003306 University of Valley Forge PA 401
003309 Peirce College PA 391
003311 Salus University PA 398
003313 Widener University PA 403
003315 Bloomsburg Univ of Pennsylvania PA 394
003316 California University of PA PA 394
003317 Cheyney University of Pennsylvania PA 394
003318 Clarion University of Pennsylvania PA 394
003320 East Stroudsburg University of PA PA 394
003321 Edinboro University PA 394
003322 Kutztown University of Pennsylvania PA 395
003323 Lock Haven University PA 395
003324 Mansfield University of PA PA 395
003325 Millersville University of PA PA 395
003326 Shippensburg University of PA PA 395
003327 Slippery Rock University of PA PA 395
003328 West Chester University of PA PA 396
003329 Penn State University Park PA 392
003350 The University of the Arts PA 400
003351 Cairn University PA 380
003352 Philadelphia Col of Osteopathic Med PA 396
003353 Univ of Sciences in Philadelphia PA 401
003356 Pittsburgh Theological Seminary PA 396
003357 Point Park University PA 397
003358 Reformed Presbyterian Theo Seminary PA 397
003359 Robert Morris University PA 397
003360 Rosemont College PA 397
003362 Seton Hill University PA 398
003364 Saint Charles Borromeo Seminary PA 398
003366 Saint Francis University PA 398
003367 Saint Joseph's University PA 398
003368 Saint Vincent College PA 398
003369 Susquehanna University PA 399
003370 Swarthmore College PA 399
003371 Temple University PA 399
003376 Thiel College PA 399
003378 University of Pennsylvania PA 400
003379 University of Pittsburgh PA 401
003384 The University of Scranton PA 401
003385 Ursinus College PA 402
003386 Valley Forge Military College PA 402
003388 Villanova University PA 402
003389 Washington & Jefferson College PA 402
003391 Waynesburg University PA 402
003392 Westminster College PA 402
003393 Westminster Theological Seminary PA 402
003394 Wilkes University PA 403
003395 Pennsylvania College of Technology PA 393
003396 Wilson College PA 403
003399 York College of Pennsylvania PA 404
003401 Brown University RI 404
003402 Bryant University RI 404
003404 Johnson & Wales University RI 404
003406 Providence College RI 405
003407 Rhode Island College RI 405
003408 Community College of Rhode Island RI 404
003409 Rhode Island School of Design RI 405
003410 Roger Williams University RI 405
003411 Salve Regina University RI 406
003413 Naval War College RI 503
003414 University of Rhode Island RI 406
003417 Allen University SC 406
003418 Anderson University SC 406
003419 Charleston Southern University SC 407
003420 Benedict College SC 407
003421 Bob Jones University SC 407
003422 Southern Wesleyan University SC 412
003423 The Citadel Military College of SC SC 407
003424 Claflin University SC 407
003425 Clemson University SC 408
003426 University of South Carolina Sumter SC 414
003427 Coker University SC 408
003428 College of Charleston SC 408
003429 Columbia International University SC 409
003430 Columbia College SC 408
003431 Converse College SC 409
003432 Erskine College SC 409
003434 Furman University SC 410
003435 Lander University SC 410
003436 Limestone College SC 410
003438 Medical Univ of South Carolina SC 410
003439 Morris College SC 411
003440 Newberry College SC 411
003441 North Greenville University SC 411
003445 Presbyterian College SC 411
003446 South Carolina State University SC 412
003447 Spartanburg Methodist College SC 412
003448 Univ of South Carolina-Columbia SC 413
003449 University of South Carolina Aiken SC 413
003450 Univ of South Carolina Beaufort SC 413
003451 Coastal Carolina University SC 408
003454 Univ of South Carolina Salkehatchie SC 413
003455 Voorhees College SC 414
003456 Winthrop University SC 414
003457 Wofford College SC 414
003458 Augustana University SD 415
003459 Black Hills State University SD 416
003461 Dakota Wesleyan University SD 415
003463 Dakota State University SD 416
003465 Mount Marty College SD 415
003466 Northern State University SD 417
003467 Presentation College SD 416
003469 University of Sioux Falls SD 417
003470 South Dakota Sch of Mines & Tech SD 417
003471 South Dakota State University SD 417
003474 The University of South Dakota SD 416
003477 Aquinas College TN 418
003478 Austin Peay State University TN 418
003479 Belmont University TN 418
003480 Bethel University TN 418
003481 Carson-Newman University TN 419
003482 Christian Brothers University TN 419
003483 Columbia State Community College TN 424
003484 Covenant College GA 117
003485 Cumberland University TN 419
003486 Lipscomb University TN 421
003487 East Tennessee State University TN 419
003490 Fisk University TN 419
003492 Freed-Hardeman University TN 420
003495 Johnson University TN 420
003496 King University TN 420
003499 Lane College TN 420
003500 Lee University TN 420
003501 LeMoyne-Owen College TN 421
003502 Lincoln Memorial University TN 421
003504 Martin Methodist College TN 421
003505 Maryville College TN 421
003506 Meharry Medical College TN 422
003507 Memphis College of Art TN 422
003509 The University of Memphis TN 427
003510 Middle Tennessee State University TN 422
003511 Milligan College TN 422
003517 Southern College of Optometry TN 424
003518 Southern Adventist University TN 424
003519 Rhodes College TN 423
003522 Tennessee State University TN 426
003523 Tennessee Technological University TN 426
003525 Tennessee Wesleyan University TN 426
003526 Trevecca Nazarene University TN 427
003527 Tusculum University TN 427
003528 Union University TN 427
003529 Univ of Tennessee Chattanooga TN 428
003530 University of Tennessee, Knoxville TN 427
003531 University of Tennessee at Martin TN 428
003534 Sewanne:The University of the South TN 423
003535 Vanderbilt University TN 428
003536 Bryan College TN 418
003537 Abilene Christian University TX 429
003539 Alvin Community College TX 429
003540 Amarillo College TX 430
003541 Angelo State University TX 451
003543 Austin College TX 430
003544 Austin Presbyterian Theol Seminary TX 431
003545 Baylor University TX 431
003546 Coastal Bend College TX 433
003549 Blinn College TX 432
003553 Cisco College TX 433
003554 Clarendon College TX 433
003556 Commonwealth Inst Funeral Service TX 434
003557 Concordia University Texas TX 434
003558 North Central Texas College TX 441
003560 Dallas Baptist University TX 434
003561 Cedar Valley College TX 435
003562 Dallas Theological Seminary TX 436
003563 Del Mar College TX 436
003564 East Texas Baptist University TX 436
003565 Texas A & M University - Commerce TX 447
003566 Seminary of the Southwest TX 443
003568 Frank Phillips College TX 436
003570 Grayson College TX 437
003571 Hardin-Simmons University TX 437
003572 Trinity Valley Community College TX 452
003573 Hill College TX 437
003574 Howard College TX 438
003575 Howard Payne University TX 438
003576 Houston Baptist University TX 437
003577 Huston-Tillotson University TX 438
003578 University of the Incarnate Word TX 453
003579 Jacksonville College TX 438
003580 Kilgore College TX 439
003581 Lamar University TX 449
003582 Laredo College TX 439
003583 Lee College TX 439
003584 LeTourneau University TX 439
003586 Lubbock Christian University TX 439
003588 University of Mary Hardin-Baylor TX 453
003590 McLennan Community College TX 440
003591 McMurry University TX 440
003592 Midwestern State University TX 440
003593 Navarro College TX 440
003594 University of North Texas TX 454
003595 Oblate School of Theology TX 441
003596 Odessa College TX 441
003598 Our Lady of the Lake University TX 441
003599 Univ of Texas Rio Grande Valley TX 455
003600 Panola College TX 441
003601 Paris Junior College TX 441
003602 Paul Quinn College TX 441
003603 Ranger College TX 442
003604 Rice University TX 442
003606 Sam Houston State University TX 450
003607 Alamo Cmty Coll Dist Central Office TX 429
003608 St. Philip's College TX 429
003609 San Jacinto College Central TX 443
003610 Schreiner University TX 443
003611 South Plains College TX 443
003612 University of Houston - Downtown TX 453
003613 Southern Methodist University TX 444
003614 Southwest Texas Junior College TX 444
003615 Texas State University TX 450
003616 Southwestern Assemblies of God Univ TX 445
003617 Southwestern Baptist Theol Seminary TX 445
003618 Southwestern Christian College TX 445
003619 Southwestern Adventist University TX 444
003620 Southwestern University TX 445
003621 St. Edward's University TX 442
003623 St. Mary's University TX 443
003624 Stephen F. Austin State University TX 445
003625 Sul Ross State University TX 450
003626 Tarrant County College District TX 445
003627 Temple College TX 446
003628 Texarkana College TX 446
003629 The Texas A&M Univ System Office TX 446
003630 Prairie View A & M University TX 446
003631 Tarleton State University TX 446
003632 Texas A & M University TX 446
003634 Texas State Technical College Waco TX 449
003635 Texas Chiropractic College TX 448
003636 Texas Christian University TX 448
003637 Jarvis Christian College TX 438
003638 Texas College TX 448
003639 Texas A & M University - Kingsville TX 447
003641 Texas Lutheran University TX 449
003642 Texas Southern University TX 449
003643 Texas Southmost College TX 449
003644 Texas Tech University TX 451
003645 Texas Wesleyan University TX 451
003646 Texas Woman's University TX 451
003647 Trinity University TX 452
003648 Tyler Junior College TX 452
003651 University of Dallas TX 452
003652 University of Houston TX 452
003654 University of St. Thomas TX 454
003655 Univ of Texas System Administration TX 454
003656 The Univ of Texas at Arlington TX 454
003658 University of Texas at Austin TX 455
003659 University of Texas HSC San Antonio TX 456
003661 University of Texas at El Paso TX 455
003662 Victoria College TX 457

004999 .... Bellingham Technical College .... WA 478
005000 .... Pierce College District .... WA 483
005001 .... Edmonds Community College .... WA 480
005006 .... Walla Walla Community College .... WA 485
005007 .... West Virginia Junior College .... WV 491
005008 .... Mountain State College .... WV 488
005015 .... University of Wisconsin-Parkside .... WI 497
005019 .... Univ Adventista de las Antillas .... PR 511
005022 .... Universidad Central de Bayamon .... PR 512
005026 .... Inter Amer Univ of PR Arecibo .... PR 508
005027 .... Inter Amer Univ of PR Barranquitas .... PR 508
005028 .... Inter Amer Univ of PR Bayamon .... PR 509
005029 .... Inter Amer Univ of PR Ponce .... PR 509
005204 .... Beal College .... ME 193
005208 .... The College of Westchester .... NY 297
005220 .... Salt Lake Community College .... UT 461
005223 .... New River Community College .... VA 475
005245 .... Univ of Arkansas Cmty Col/Morrilton .... AR 23
005252 .... Ridgewater College .... MN 240
005254 .... Lanier Technical College .... GA 121
005256 .... Wiregrass Georgia Tech College .... GA 127
005257 .... GA Northwestern Technical College .... GA 119
005258 .... Univ of Hawaii Cmty College .... HI 129
005260 .... J.F. Drake State Cmty & Tech Col .... AL 2
005263 .... Minnesota West Cmty & Tech College .... MN 239
005264 .... Flint Hills Technical College .... KS 173
005265 .... North Central Kansas Tech College .... KS 176
005267 .... Northwest Kansas Technical College .... KS 176
005271 .... Southcentral KY Cmty & Tech Col .... KY 182
005273 .... Gateway Cmty & Technical College .... KY 181
005276 .... Central Maine Community College .... ME 194
005277 .... Eastern Maine Community College .... ME 194
005291 .... White Mountains Community College .... NH 273
005294 .... Waukesha County Technical College .... WI 500
005301 .... NE Wisconsin Technical College .... WI 500
005304 .... Chippewa Valley Technical College .... WI 499
005306 .... Bates Technical College .... WA 478
005309 .... Lake Area Technical Institute .... SD 415
005310 .... Pittsburgh Institute of Aeronautics .... PA 396
005313 .... North Central State College .... OH 357
005316 .... Coastal Carolina Community College .... NC 333
005317 .... Forsyth Technical Community College .... NC 334
005318 .... Catawba Valley Community College .... NC 333
005320 .... Cape Fear Community College .... NC 332
005363 .... Denmark Technical College .... SC 409
005372 .... South Puget Sound Community College .... WA 485
005373 .... Lake Washington Inst of Technology .... WA 482
005378 .... Northeast State Community College .... TN 425
005380 .... Mid-State Technical College .... WI 500
005384 .... Nicolet Area Technical College .... WI 500
005387 .... Northcentral Technical College .... WI 500
005389 .... Gateway Technical College .... WI 499
005390 .... Blackhawk Technical College .... WI 499
005447 .... Randolph Community College .... NC 337
005448 .... Durham Technical Community College .... NC 334
005449 .... Central Carolina Community College .... NC 333
005461 .... Salem Community College .... NJ 283
005463 .... Alamance Community College .... NC 332
005464 .... Richmond Community College .... NC 337
005467 .... SOWELA Technical Community College .... LA 188
005480 .... Central LA TCC Huey P Long Campus .... LA 187
005489 .... Central LA Tech Community College .... LA 187
005498 .... Wichita State Univ-Appl Sci & Tech .... KS 178
005499 .... Salina Area Technical College .... KS 176
005500 .... Manhattan Area Technical College .... KS 175
005511 .... Coastal Pines Technical College .... GA 116
005525 .... Southern Maine Community College .... ME 195
005533 .... St Paul Col A Cmty & Tech College .... MN 241
005534 .... Saint Cloud Technical & Cmty Coll .... MN 241
005535 .... Pine Tech & Cmty College .... MN 240
005537 .... South Central College .... MN 241
005541 .... Minnesota State Cmty & Tech College .... MN 239
005544 .... Alexandria Technical & Cmty Col .... MN 237
005599 .... Augusta Technical College .... GA 114
005600 .... Athens Technical College .... GA 114
005601 .... Albany Technical College .... GA 113
005615 .... Southern Regional Technical College .... GA 125
005617 .... South Georgia Technical College .... GA 124
005618 .... Savannah Technical College .... GA 124
005619 .... North Georgia Technical College .... GA 122
005621 .... Southern Crescent Technical College .... GA 124
005622 .... Georgia Piedmont Technical College .... GA 119
005624 .... Columbus Technical College .... GA 117
005691 .... Shelton State Community College .... AL 3
005692 .... Reid State Technical College .... AL 3
005697 .... Northwest-Shoals Community College .... AL 3
005699 .... George Wallace St Cmty Col-Selma .... AL 2
005707 .... Southeast Arkansas College .... AR 21
005732 .... Univ of Arkansas Hope-Texarkana .... AR 22
005733 .... Bevill State Community College .... AL 1
005734 .... Trenholm State Technical College .... AL 3
005752 .... Clover Park Technical College .... WA 479
005753 .... Owens Community College .... OH 360
005754 .... Rowan-Cabarrus Community College .... NC 337
005757 .... Lake Superior College .... MN 238
005759 .... Northwest Technical College .... MN 240
005760 .... Northern Maine Community College .... ME 194
005761 .... L.E. Fletcher Technical Cmty Coll .... LA 187
005763 .... Central Georgia Technical College .... GA 116
006165 .... Los Angeles County Col of Nursing .... CA 49
006214 .... Blessing-Rieman Col Nurs & Hlth Sc .... IL 133
006225 .... Trinity Col Nursing/Hlth Sci .... IL 150
006228 .... Methodist College .... IL 143
006240 .... St Francis Med Ctr Col of Nursing .... IL 148
006250 .... Resurrection University .... IL 147
006273 .... Mercy College of Health Sciences .... IA 168
006305 .... Maine College of Health Professions .... ME 194
006324 .... Laboure College .... MA 210
006385 .... Chamberlain University-Addison .... IL 133
006389 .... Goldfarb School of Nursing .... MO 253
006392 .... Research College of Nursing .... MO 258
006399 .... Bryan College of Health Sciences .... NE 265
006404 .... Nebraska Methodist College .... NE 268
006438 .... Phillips School of Nursing Mt Sinai .... NY 311
006443 .... Cochran School of Nursing .... NY 296
006445 .... Pomeroy Col of Nurs @ Crouse Hosp .... NY 291
006448 .... The Belanger School of Nursing .... NY 291
006461 .... St. Elizabeth College of Nursing .... NY 313
006467 .... St. Joseph's College of Nursing .... NY 314
006477 .... Cabarrus College of Health Sciences .... NC 327
006487 .... Aultman College Nursing/Health Sci .... OH 348
006489 .... Christ Col of Nursing & Health Sci .... OH 350
006494 .... Good Samaritan Col Nursing/Hlth Sci .... OH 353
006606 .... Baptist Hlth Sys Sch Hlth Profess .... TX 431
006639 .... Bellin College, Inc. .... WI 492
006640 .... Columbia College of Nursing .... WI 493
006656 .... College of DuPage .... IL 135
006661 .... Angelina College .... TX 430
006720 .... College of Alameda .... CA 56
006724 .... KY Community & Technical Col System .... KY 180
006731 .... Casa Loma College-Van Nuys .... CA 35
006750 .... Valencia College .... FL 112
006751 .... Univ of Hawaii Community Colleges .... HI 128
006753 .... Illinois Central College .... IL 138
006756 .... Northshore Technical Community Col .... LA 187
006760 .... University of Maine at Augusta .... ME 196
006768 .... Mid Michigan Community College .... MI 227
006771 .... College for Creative Studies .... MI 222
006775 .... Rainy River Community College .... MN 240
006777 .... Flathead Valley Community College .... MT 263
006782 .... Genesee Community College .... NY 301
006785 .... Schenectady County Cmty College .... NY 315
006787 .... Clinton Community College .... NY 296
006788 .... Tompkins Cortland Community College .... NY 322
006789 .... Columbia-Greene Community College .... NY 297
006791 .... Purchase College, SUNY .... NY 319
006799 .... Craven Community College .... NC 333
006804 .... Lakeland Community College .... OH 355
006807 .... Community College of Beaver County .... PA 381
006810 .... Lehigh Carbon Community College .... PA 388
006811 .... Luzerne County Community College .... PA 389
006815 .... Orangeburg-Calhoun Technical Col .... SC 411
006819 .... Blue Ridge Community College .... VA 474
006823 .... Evangelical Seminary of Puerto Rico .... PR 508
006835 .... Dyersburg State Community College .... TN 425
006836 .... Motlow State Community College .... TN 425
006858 .... Unity College .... ME 195
006863 .... Ventura County Cmty College Dist .... CA 72
006865 .... Camden County College .... NJ 276
006867 .... Columbus State Community College .... OH 351
006871 .... Thomas Nelson Community College .... VA 476
006895 .... University of Nebraska Medical Ctr .... NE 270
006901 .... Rowan College of South Jersey .... NJ 281
006911 .... Montgomery College .... MD 200
006931 .... Waubonsee Community College .... IL 152
006938 .... Linn-Benton Community College .... OR 374
006941 .... Dallas Christian College .... TX 434
006942 .... Mid-America Christian University .... OK 366
006949 .... Kalamazoo Valley Community College .... MI 225
006951 .... Univ of South Carolina Upstate .... SC 414
006960 .... Maysville Cmty & Technical College .... KY 182
006961 .... Jefferson Cmty & Tech Col .... KY 181
006962 .... Hazard Community & Technical Coll .... KY 181
006973 .... Cañada College .... CA 61
006975 .... Lincoln University .... CA 48
006977 .... Great Basin College .... NV 271
006982 .... Naugatuck Valley Community College .... CT 86
006991 .... Rancho Santiago Cmty Col District .... CA 57
006994 .... Kern Community College District .... CA 46
007006 .... Grossmont-Cuyamaca C C District .... CA 44
007012 .... Samuel Merritt University .... CA 59
007022 .... CUNY Herbert H. Lehman College .... NY 294
007026 .... Icahn Sch of Medicine at Mt Sinai .... NY 302
007031 .... Pamlico Community College .... NC 336
007032 .... MidAmerica Nazarene University .... KS 175
007035 .... Kettering College .... OH 355
007047 .... Los Angeles Southwest College .... CA 49
007085 .... Mount Vernon Nazarene University .... OH 357
007096 .... College of the Mainland .... TX 433
007099 .... Virginia Highlands Community Col .... VA 476
007107 .... Essex County College .... NJ 277
007108 .... Univ of Puerto Rico-Rio Piedras .... PR 514
007109 .... SUNY College at Old Westbury .... NY 319
007110 .... Delaware County Community College .... PA 382
007111 .... North Country Community College .... NY 310
007113 .... Arizona Christian University .... AZ 10
007115 .... Moorpark College .... CA 72
007118 .... Parkland College .... IL 146
007119 .... Rend Lake College .... IL 147
007120 .... Des Moines Area Community College .... IA 164
007121 .... Faith Baptist Bible Col & Seminary .... IA 165
007164 .... Bryan University .... AZ 11
007170 .... Lincoln Land Community College .... IL 142
007171 .... Kirtland Community College .... MI 226
007178 .... Western Seminary .... OR 378
007191 .... Northampton Community College .... PA 391
007206 .... University of Puerto Rico at Cayey .... PR 513
007228 .... Univ of Puerto Rico at Arecibo .... PR 513
007260 .... Southwest Virginia Community Col .... VA 475
007263 .... Holy Cross College .... IN 155
007264 .... Mesivta Torah Vodaath Seminary .... NY 306
007265 .... Carl Sandburg College .... IL 133
007266 .... Pima Community College .... AZ 15
007273 .... Baruch College/CUNY .... NY 292
007275 .... Eastern Gateway CC - Jefferson Co. .... OH 352
007276 .... Saint Meinrad School of Theology .... IN 160
007279 .... Hawaii Pacific University .... HI 127
007283 .... Central Arizona College .... AZ 11
007287 .... Brazosport College .... TX 432
007289 .... Central Wyoming College .... WY 501
007291 .... St. Luke's College .... IA 169
007297 .... Spartan College .... CO 82
007304 .... The Culinary Institute of America .... NY 298
007316 .... Western Iowa Tech Community College .... IA 170
007350 .... Anoka Technical College .... MN 237
007358 .... Univ of NE-NE Col of Tech Agricult .... NE 270
007375 .... Island Drafting and Technical Inst .... NY 303
007394 .... Berkeley College .... NY 291
007401 .... Mandl School-The Col of Allied Hlth .... NY 305
007437 .... Pittsburgh Technical College .... PA 396
007440 .... Lincoln Col of Technology Nashville .... TN 421
007459 .... Paier College of Art .... CT 87
007465 .... American Academy of Dramatic Arts .... NY 290
007466 .... LIM College .... NY 304
007468 .... School of Visual Arts .... NY 315
007469 .... Hussian College .... PA 386
007502 .... Berkeley College .... NJ 275
007531 .... Academy of Art University .... CA 24
007532 .... Finger Lakes Community College .... NY 300
007536 .... Cosumnes River College .... CA 50
007540 .... Missouri Baptist University .... MO 256
007544 .... Appalachian Bible College .... WV 487
007547 .... Lincoln College of Technology .... CO 80
007549 .... Coyne College .... IL 135
007555 .... Lakes Region Community College .... NH 272
007560 .... River Valley Community College .... NH 273
007570 .... Helena College Univ of Montana .... MT 264
007582 .... Aims Community College .... CO 76
007598 .... Hocking College .... OH 354
007602 .... Northeastern Technical College .... SC 411
007607 .... Concorde Career College .... CA 40
007635 .... Capital Community College .... CT 85
007640 .... Fayetteville Tech Community College .... NC 334
007644 .... Lake Land College .... IL 141
007649 .... Rocky Mountain Col of Art & Design .... CO 82
007669 .... SW Wisconsin Technical College .... WI 500
007678 .... Spartan Col Aeronautics/Technology .... OK 370
007684 .... Kishwaukee College .... IL 140
007686 .... Southern Un at Shreveport-Louisiana .... LA 190
007687 .... James Sprunt Community College .... NC 335
007690 .... Kankakee Community College .... IL 140
007691 .... McHenry County College .... IL 143
007692 .... Moraine Valley Community College .... IL 144
007693 .... Shawnee Community College .... IL 149
007694 .... College of Lake County .... IL 135
007707 .... Columbia College .... CA 75
007713 .... Skyline College .... CA 61
007728 .... Middle Georgia State University .... GA 121
007729 .... County College of Morris .... NJ 277
007730 .... Rowan College at Burlington County .... NJ 281
007731 .... Raritan Valley Community College .... NJ 281
007738 .... Southern Arkansas University Tech .... AR 21
007759 .... Lincoln Technical Institute .... PA 389
007764 .... Southeast Technical Institute .... SD 417
007777 .... Remington College Cleveland Campus .... OH 360
007779 .... Lansdale School of Business .... PA 388
007780 .... New Castle School of Trades .... PA 391
007783 .... Middle TN School of Anesthesia .... TN 422
007832 .... Lincoln Technical Institute .... PA 389
007839 .... Triangle Tech, Pittsburgh .... PA 400
007845 .... New England Institute of Technology .... RI 405
007870 .... Hillsborough Community College .... FL 101
007871 .... Wallace State Cmty Coll-Hanceville .... AL 4
007885 .... University of Hawaii System .... HI 128
007892 .... Sampson Community College .... NC 337
007893 .... Flagler College .... FL 98
007912 .... Thaddeus Stevens Col of Technology .... PA 399
007930 .... Concorde Career College .... CA 40
007933 .... Front Range Community College .... CO 79
007936 .... Lincoln College of Technology .... MD 199
007938 .... Lincoln College of Technology .... IN 158
007947 .... Beth Medrash Govoha .... NJ 275
007948 .... Wilmington University .... DE 90
007950 .... West Shore Community College .... MI 232
007954 .... Normandale Community College .... MN 239
007959 .... The Univ System of Maryland Office .... MD 202
007985 .... South Piedmont Community College .... NC 337
007986 .... Halifax Community College .... NC 335
007987 .... Bladen Community College .... NC 332
007988 .... Martin Community College .... NC 335
007993 .... California State Univ-Bakersfield .... CA 30
007996 .... Univ of Colorado System Office .... CO 82
008001 .... University of Illinois System .... IL 151
008002 .... Indiana University .... IN 156
008004 .... University of Alabama System Office .... AL 7
008005 .... University of Alaska System .... AK 9

Code	Institution	State	Page
011167	Community College of Vermont	VT	464
011189	United Talmudical Seminary	NY	323
011192	Beth Hamedrash Shaarei Yosher Inst	NY	291
011194	Stanly Community College	NC	338
011197	Mayland Community College	NC	336
011210	Bunker Hill Community College	MA	214
011220	Univ of Hawaii Windward Cmty Col	HI	129
011245	West Virginia School of Osteo Med	WV	491
011385	College of the Atlantic	ME	193
011460	National University	CA	53
011462	University of Alaska Anchorage	AK	9
011553	William Moore College of Technology	TN	428
011572	Colorado School of Trades	CO	78
011644	Univ of Maryland Global Campus	MD	203
011649	Loyola Marymount University	CA	50
011667	Northeast Community College	NE	268
011670	Yeshiva of Nitra Rabbinical College	NY	325
011672	Mendocino College	CA	51
011673	Maine College of Art	ME	194
011678	SUNY Polytechnic Institute	NY	321
011689	The Refrigeration School	AZ	15
011711	University of Houston - Clear Lake	TX	453
011719	Universidad Ana G Mendez - Gurabo	PR	511
011721	University of Houston System	TX	452
011727	DE Tech Cmty College, Terry Campus	DE	90
011732	Mayo Medical School	MN	234
011745	Ohio Technical College	OH	359
011792	Franciscan School of Theology	CA	43
011810	Taylor Business Institute	IL	150
011820	San Diego Miramar College	CA	60
011821	Yeshivath Zichron Moshe	NY	326
011824	Wisconsin Indianhead Tech College	WI	501
011862	Northland Pioneer College	AZ	14
011864	Mohave Community College	AZ	14
011930	Roxbury Community College	MA	215
011934	Vermont Law School	VT	463
011940	ICPR Junior College	PR	508
011941	American University of Puerto Rico	PR	506
011984	Ohr Hameir Theological Seminary	NY	310
011989	Talmudical Academy of New Jersey	NJ	284
012011	Talmudical Seminary Oholei Torah	NY	322
012015	Austin Community College District	TX	431
012031	San Diego Christian College	CA	60
012050	Rosedale Technical College	PA	397
012059	Trinity Bible Col & Grad School	ND	346
012064	Hamilton Technical College	IA	166
012105	National Park College	AR	20
012120	Assemblies of God Theol Seminary	MO	250
012123	University of Puerto Rico-Aguadilla	PR	512
012154	California Inst of Integral Studies	CA	29
012165	Atlanta Metropolitan State College	GA	114
012182	Chattahoochee Valley Community Coll	AL	1
012203	Memorial College of Nursing	NY	306
012260	East Arkansas Community College	AR	19
012261	North Arkansas College	AR	20
012277	New York Chiropractic College	NY	308
012300	Palmer College of Chiropractic	IA	168
012309	University of Western States	OR	377
012315	Cornish College of the Arts	WA	480
012328	Northwestern Health Sciences Univ	MN	242
012358	Plaza College	NY	311
012362	Northwestern College	IL	145
012364	St. Paul's School of Nursing	NY	314
012393	Thomas Jefferson University	PA	400
012452	Evergreen Valley College	CA	61
012500	Ranken Technical College	MO	258
012523	Talmudical Yeshiva of Philadelphia	PA	399
012525	Caribbean University	PR	506
012550	Los Angeles Mission College	CA	49
012561	Five Towns College	NY	300
012574	Ringling College of Art and Design	FL	105
012580	Saint Louis Christian College	MO	258
012586	Metropolitan Community College	NE	267
012627	Western Mich Univ Cooley Law School	MI	233
012670	Bel-Rea Inst of Animal Technology	CO	77
012693	Pellissippi State Community College	TN	425
012744	Southside Col of Health Sciences	VA	471
012750	Edison State Community College	OH	352
012803	PFIC at Dominican House of Studies	DC	92
012813	John Wood Community College	IL	140
012842	Oxnard College	CA	73
012860	Arkansas Northeastern College	AR	17
012870	Southern State Community College	OH	361
012891	Antonelli College	OH	347
012896	The North Coast College	OH	357
012907	Lake Tahoe Community College	CA	47
012912	MTI College	CA	53
012954	Hudson County Community College	NJ	278
013007	Nazarene Bible College	CO	81
013022	City University of Seattle	WA	479
013026	Machzikei Hadath Rabbinical College	NY	305
013027	Yeshivath Viznitz	NY	326
013029	Boricua College	NY	291
013039	South University	GA	124
013103	California Western School of Law	CA	34
013132	International Col of Broadcasting	OH	354
013134	Yeshiva Beth Moshe	PA	403
013208	Baptist Bible College	MO	250
013231	University of Houston - Victoria	TX	453
013263	South Hills School of Bus & Tech	PA	399
014659	Oglala Lakota College	SD	416
015361	Guam Community College	GU	505
020503	Academy College	MN	233
020522	Black River Technical College	AR	18
020530	Liberty University	VA	468
020537	Eastwick College	NJ	277
020554	Bossier Parish Community College	LA	187
020603	MIAT College of Technology	MI	227
020609	Brown College of Court Reporting	GA	115
020630	Montserrat College of Art	MA	216
020635	Coastline Community College	CA	38
020637	Sherman College of Chiropractic	SC	412
020653	Prescott College	AZ	15
020662	The New School	NY	308
020681	Adler University	IL	131
020682	Cox College	MO	252
020683	Douglas Education Center	PA	383
020690	New York School of Interior Design	NY	309
020705	Concordia University Irvine	CA	40
020732	Telshe Yeshiva-Chicago	IL	150
020735	Univ of Arkansas CC at Batesville	AR	22
020739	Wor-Wic Community College	MD	204
020744	Illinois Eastern CC Frontier CC	IL	138
020746	South Arkansas Community College	AR	21
020748	Life University	GA	121
020753	Univ of AR-Pulaski Technical Col	AR	23
020758	Southern Calif Inst of Architecture	CA	64
020771	Milwaukee Institute of Art & Design	WI	494
020774	North Lake College	TX	435
020780	Sacred Heart Sem & School of Theol	WI	495
020814	Arlington Baptist University	TX	430
020839	Northern New Mexico College	NM	287
020870	Ozarka College	AR	20
020876	Concordia Theological Seminary	IN	154
020896	Concorde Career Institute	FL	96
020902	Triangle Tech, Erie	PA	400
020907	Cleveland University - Kansas City	KS	172
020923	Eastwick College	NJ	277
020925	Laurel Technical Institute	PA	388
020937	Long Island Business Institute	NY	304
020961	Fielding Graduate University	CA	42
020983	Western Technical College	TX	458
020988	University of Phoenix	AZ	16
020992	American Conservatory Theater	CA	25
020995	Central Community College	NE	266
021000	Universidad Politecnica de PR	PR	512
021002	Brookhaven College	TX	434
021049	Sumner College	OR	376
021073	Pennsylvania Academy of Fine Arts	PA	393
021077	Truckee Meadows Community College	NV	271
021078	University of Hawaii - West Oahu	HI	128
021102	Columbia College Hollywood	CA	39
021108	California College San Diego	CA	28
021111	Univ of Arkansas Rich Mountain	AR	23
021113	Cuyamaca College	CA	44
021116	Sovah School of Health Professions	VA	471
021122	Great Lakes Institute of Technology	PA	385
021136	American InterContinental Univ	IL	132
021142	Johnson College	PA	386
021163	Pueblo Community College	CO	81
021171	The Art Institute of Houston	TX	430
021175	Naropa University	CO	81
021191	Mission College	CA	74
021206	Saybrook University	CA	63
021207	San Joaquin Valley Col Inc-Visalia	CA	61
021211	Midwest Institute	MO	255
021274	YTI Career Institute	PA	404
021283	Inst for Business & Technology	CA	45
021290	Triangle Tech, Greensburg	PA	400
021366	Wisconsin Lutheran College	WI	498
021383	Palo Alto University	CA	55
021400	Riverside College of Health Careers	VA	471
021408	Martin University	IN	158
021415	Savannah College of Art and Design	GA	123
021434	Salish Kootenai College	MT	265
021435	Sterling College	VT	463
021437	Sinte Gleska University	SD	416
021448	Vet Tech Institute of Houston	TX	457
021464	Institute of American Indian Arts	NM	286
021466	South Mountain Community College	AZ	14
021519	Keiser University	FL	102
021520	Yeshiva Shaar HaTorah-Grodno	NY	326
021553	Chicago Sch Prof Psych-LA Campus	CA	36
021571	Concorde Career College	TN	419
021585	Ohio Business College	OH	358
021596	The Baptist College of Florida	FL	95
021597	New Hope Christian College	OR	374
021610	Uniformed Svcs Univ of Health Sci	MD	504
021618	Musicians Institute	CA	53
021633	Universidad Central Del Caribe	PR	512
021636	William James College	MA	220
021651	EDP University of Puerto Rico	PR	507
021660	Ctr Advanced Studies PR & Caribbean	PR	507
021661	Nunez Community College	LA	188
021662	ITI Technical College	LA	186
021686	East-West University	IL	136
021691	Davis College	NY	298
021700	Swedish Inst College of Health Sci	NY	322
021706	United States Sports Academy	AL	7
021707	Brunswick Community College	NC	332
021727	Condorde Career Institute	FL	97
021744	Triangle Tech, Dubois	PA	400
021758	Centra College of Nursing	VA	465
021775	Rio Salado College	AZ	13
021785	Eagle Gate College	UT	459
021800	Northwest Indian College	WA	482
021802	Metro Business College	MO	255
021829	Cambridge College	MA	207
021854	St. Augustine College	IL	148
021882	Sitting Bull College	ND	346
021883	Pentecostal Theological Seminary	TN	423
021889	Hobe Sound Bible College	FL	101
021891	CEM College	PR	506
021907	Fortis College	OH	352
021916	Torah Temimah Talmudical Seminary	NY	322
021922	Thomas Edison State University	NJ	284
021928	Restaurant School/Walnut Hill Col	PA	397
021975	Baton Rouge School of Computers	LA	186
021989	Michigan School of Psychology	MI	227
021997	Heritage Christian University	AL	5
022023	Pittsburgh Career Institute	PA	396
022027	Ozark Christian College	MO	257
022039	Erie Institute of Technology	PA	383
022042	Chattanooga College	TN	419
022061	Independence University	UT	459
022171	Pima Medical Institute-Tucson	AZ	15
022178	Montefiore School of Nursing	NY	307
022188	Brookline College	AZ	11
022195	Mildred Elley	NY	307
022205	God's Bible School and College	OH	353
022209	Cossatot Cmty Coll Univ of Arkansas	AR	22
022220	Amer Film Institute Conservatory	CA	25
022233	Northeast Catholic College	NH	274
022260	East Los Angeles College	CA	48
022285	Life Chiropractic College West	CA	47
022316	MGH Institute of Health Professions	MA	216
022345	Boise Bible College	ID	129
022365	Cankdeska Cikana Community College	ND	345
022418	American Career College-Los Angeles	CA	25
022425	Bastyr University	WA	478
022427	Berkeley City College	CA	56
022429	United Tribes Technical College	ND	347
022449	Goodwin College	CT	87
022537	IntelliTec College	CO	80
022539	Berks Technical Institute	PA	379
022540	New England Culinary Institute	VT	462
022594	Amberton University	TX	430
022606	National University College	PR	510
022608	Huertas College	PR	508
022624	Yeshiva Ohr Elchonon Chabad	CA	75
022651	Yeshiva Derech Chaim	NY	325
022664	Central Christian College of Bible	MO	251
022676	Sofia University	CA	64
022699	Pennsylvania Col of Art & Design	PA	393
022706	Life Pacific University	CA	47
022713	Wisc Sch of Professional Psychology	WI	499
022734	Reconstructionist Rabbinical Col	PA	397
022743	Conway School of Landscape Design	MA	208
022751	Concorde Career Institute	FL	96
022768	Westminster Theological Seminary	CA	74
022769	Community College of Aurora	CO	79
022773	Sisseton-Wahpeton College	SD	416
022781	Santa Fe Community College	NM	288
022788	Southern Technical College	FL	107
022795	Oconee Fall Line Tech Col-South	GA	122
022809	Mid-Atlantic Christian University	NC	331
022827	Inter Amer Univ of PR Guayama	PR	509
022828	Inter Amer Univ of PR Fajardo	PR	509
022843	Interactive College of Technology	GA	120
022866	Little Big Horn College	MT	263
022884	Gwinnett Technical College	GA	120
022980	Design Institute of San Diego	CA	41
022993	Trinity Episcopal School Ministry	PA	400
023011	Turtle Mountain Community College	ND	347
023014	Ohio Valley College of Technology	OH	359
023043	Platt College	CA	57
023053	Parker University	TX	441
023058	Florida Career College	FL	98
023068	Platt College	OK	369
023108	Lancaster County Career & Tech Ctr	PA	388
023141	Schiller International University	FL	107
023154	Northeast Texas Community College	TX	441
023172	Maranatha Baptist University	WI	493
023182	KD Conservatory Col Film/Dram Arts	TX	438
023192	Lake Forest Graduate School of Mgmt	IL	141
023201	Ohr Somayach Tanenbaum Educ Ctr	NY	311
023202	Houston Graduate School of Theology	TX	438
023230	Missio Seminary	PA	390
023251	Key College	FL	102
023263	Fortis Institute	TN	420
023268	Meridian College	FL	103
023289	Emmaus Bible College	IA	165
023301	Pioneer Pacific College	OR	375
023305	Laguna College of Art & Design	CA	47
023308	JRMC School of Nursing	AR	19
023312	Baptist Missionary Assn Theol Sem	TX	431
023313	Interactive College of Technology	TX	438
023344	Centura College	VA	465
023355	Universidad Teologica Del Caribe	PR	512
023377	Professional Skills Institute	OH	360
023385	Glendale Career College	CA	44
023405	St Louis Col Hlth Careers-S Taylor	MO	259
023406	Humacao Community College	PR	508
023413	Palo Alto College	TX	429
023427	Fortis College	VA	467
023430	Fort Peck Community College	MT	263

035134 .... Apex School of Theology .... NC 326
035135 .... Williamson College .... TN 429
035163 .... The King's University .... TX 439
035243 .... Academy Five Element Acupuncture .... FL 93
035283 .... Midwest University .... MO 255
035324 .... Advanced Training Associates .... CA 24
035344 .... American Inst Alternative Medicine .... OH 347
035373 .... New York Automotive and Diesel Inst .... NY 308
035393 .... American Public University System .... WV 487
035423 .... Concorde Career Institute .... TX 434
035424 .... Copper Mountain College .... CA 40
035443 .... Atenas College .... PR 506
035493 .... Ultimate Medical Acad-Clearwater .... FL 111
035593 .... Appalachian School of Law .... VA 464
035703 .... Carolina Christian College .... NC 327
035705 .... Northpoint Bible College .... MA 217
035793 .... Texas County Technical College .... MO 260
035924 .... City of Hope .... CA 37
035933 .... Southwest Institute of Healing Arts .... AZ 16
036115 .... Southern Evangelical Seminary .... NC 340
036175 .... Phoenix Inst of Herbal Med/Acup .... AZ 15
036273 .... Lamar Institute of Technology .... TX 449
036393 .... West Coast Ultrasound Institute .... CA 73
036543 .... Eastern Virginia Career College .... VA 466
036633 .... Hood Theological Seminary .... NC 330
036653 .... Christendom College .... VA 466
036654 .... Christie's Education, New York .... NY 292
036663 .... Pillar College .... NJ 280
036683 .... Birthingway College of Midwifery .... OR 371
036763 .... Family of Faith Christian Univ .... OK 366
036863 .... Colorado Sch of Trad Chinese Med .... CO 78
036894 .... Faith International University .... WA 481
036914 .... Ave Maria School of Law .... FL 94
036954 .... The Salvation Army Ofr Trng Crestmt .... CA 59
036955 .... Arizona Sch of Acup/Oriental Med .... AZ 10
036957 .... Santiago Canyon College .... CA 58
036963 .... University of the West .... CA 72
036964 .... Saber College .... FL 106
036983 .... West Coast University .... CA 73
037093 .... Edward Via Col of Osteo Med .... VA 467
037133 .... Beis Medrash Heichal Dovid .... NY 291
037233 .... Culinary Institute LeNotre .... TX 434
037243 .... DigiPen Institute of Technology .... WA 480
037276 .... Auguste Escoffier Sch Culinary Arts .... TX 430
037303 .... Baton Rouge Community College .... LA 186
037333 .... Baptist University of the Americas .... TX 431
037353 .... Inst Clin Acupuncture/Oriental Med .... HI 128
037384 .... SS. Cyril and Methodius Seminary .... MI 231
037473 .... Bexley Seabury .... IL 132
037524 .... SUM Bible Col & Theol Seminary .... CA 66
037573 .... Advance Science Internat'l College .... FL 94
037603 .... Hawaii Tokai International College .... HI 128
037723 .... Saginaw Chippewa Tribal College .... MI 230
037763 .... Auguste Escoffier Sch Culinary Arts .... CO 76
037844 .... Tohono O'odham Community College .... AZ 16
037863 .... Advanced College .... CA 24
037894 .... River Parishes Community College .... LA 188
038023 .... U.T.A. Mesivta of Kiryas Joel .... NY 324
038044 .... Gwinnett College-Marietta .... GA 120
038133 .... Northcentral University .... CA 54
038144 .... Soka University of America .... CA 64
038214 .... Universal College of Healing Arts .... NE 269
038224 .... Maple Springs Baptist Bible College .... MD 199
038273 .... Charlotte Christian Col & Theol Sem .... NC 328
038303 .... SAE Institute Nashville .... TN 423
038333 .... American Acad Acupunct/Oriental Med .... MN 233
038383 .... Nightingale College .... UT 459
038385 .... Northwest Career College .... NV 272
038403 .... Omega Graduate School .... TN 423
038425 .... Cambridge Inst Allied Health & Tech .... FL 96
038513 .... Dallas International University .... TX 435
038533 .... Keck Graduate Institute .... CA 37
038553 .... Ecclesia College .... AR 19
038563 .... Universal Career School .... FL 112
038626 .... Veritas Baptist College .... IN 162
038683 .... World Mission University .... CA 75
038684 .... Los Angeles College of Music .... CA 48
038713 .... Folsom Lake College .... CA 50
038724 .... Divine Mercy University .... VA 466
038743 .... Cambridge Junior College .... CA 34
038744 .... Community Christian College .... CA 39
038883 .... Dragon Rises Col of Oriental Med .... FL 97
038893 .... Stanbridge University .... CA 65
038943 .... Huntsville Bible College .... AL 5
039035 .... Southern Technical College .... FL 108
039104 .... National Polytechnic College .... CA 53
039153 .... Career Quest Learning Center .... MI 222
039193 .... St Tikhon's Orthodox Theol Seminary .... PA 398
039214 .... White Earth Tribal/Community Col .... MN 244
039324 .... Gutenberg College .... OR 373
039373 .... Yeshiva Col of the Nation's Capital .... MD 204
039396 .... Daytona College .... FL 97
039413 .... Ave Maria University .... FL 94
039454 .... Logos Evangelical Seminary .... CA 48
039463 .... Franklin W. Olin Col of Engineering .... MA 209
039483 .... Harrisburg Univ Science/Technology .... PA 385
039493 .... Won Institute of Graduate Studies .... PA 403
039513 .... Patrick Henry College .... VA 470
039563 .... South Louisiana Community College .... LA 188
039573 .... Blue Ridge Cmty & Technical College .... WV 488
039603 .... New River Community/Technical Col .... WV 489
039653 .... New England Col Business & Finance .... MA 216
039663 .... Virginia Beach Theol Seminary .... VA 473
039704 .... WellSpring Sch Allied Health-KC .... MO 262
039713 .... American Career College-Ontario .... CA 25
039733 .... SAE Expression College .... CA 58
039745 .... California Career College .... CA 28
039803 .... California State U-Channel Islands .... CA 30
039823 .... Visible Music College .... TN 428
039863 .... Aviator Col of Aeronaut Sci & Tech .... FL 94
039893 .... Mid-America Reformed Seminary .... IN 159
039923 .... Knox Theological Seminary .... FL 102
039953 .... University of East-West Medicine .... CA 70
040024 .... Ecumenical Theological Seminary .... MI 223
040053 .... United States University .... CA 67
040373 .... Los Angeles Film School .... CA 50
040383 .... ATA College .... KY 178
040385 .... Pierpont Community/Technical Col .... WV 489
040386 .... BridgeValley Cmty & Tech College .... WV 488
040414 .... Mountwest Cmty & Technical College .... WV 489
040443 .... Hazelden Grad Sch of Addiction Stds .... MN 236
040573 .... Asher College .... CA 26
040653 .... Roseman Univ of Health Sciences .... NV 272
040743 .... Hondros College of Nursing .... OH 354
040764 .... Gnomon .... CA 44
040803 .... Aspen University .... CO 76
040813 .... Bais Medrash Toras Chesed .... NJ 275
040834 .... Cambridge College .... FL 95
040953 .... The King's College .... NY 304
040963 .... Charleston School of Law .... SC 407
041004 .... William Howard Taft University .... CO 84
041103 .... University of Management & Tech .... VA 472
041113 .... West Hills College Lemoore .... CA 74
041123 .... Louisiana Culinary Institute .... LA 188
041143 .... Nevada State College .... NV 271
041144 .... The Institute of World Politics .... DC 92
041145 .... Valley College of Medical Careers .... CA 72
041155 .... Talmudical Seminary of Bobov .... NY 322
041156 .... Mayfield College .... CA 51
041166 .... Taylor College .... FL 111
041174 .... Milwaukee Career College .... WI 494
041180 .... Byzantine Catholic Seminary .... PA 380
041187 .... American Business & Technology Univ .... MO 250
041188 .... New York Film Academy, Los Angeles .... CA 53
041190 .... Eastern WV Community & Tech College .... WV 489
041191 .... City Vision University .... MO 251
041192 .... Eagle Rock College .... CA 41
041193 .... Han Univ of Traditional Medicine .... AZ 12
041196 .... Yeshiva of Far Rockaway .... NY 325
041212 .... Inst of Taoist Educ/Acupuncture .... CO 80
041215 .... Columbia Southern University .... AL 5
041218 .... Criswell College .... TX 434
041228 .... Presbyterian Theol Sem in America .... CA 57
041234 .... Yeshivas Be'er Yitzchok .... NJ 285
041238 .... Williamson College of the Trades .... PA 403
041242 .... Catholic Distance University .... WV 487
041245 .... MyComputerCareer .... OH 357
041247 .... Ambria College of Nursing .... IL 131
041271 .... University of California-Merced .... CA 69
041273 .... Columbia College .... VA 466
041276 .... California Coast University .... CA 28
041277 .... American Sentinel University .... CO 76
041279 .... Trident University International .... CA 67
041284 .... Miami Regional University .... FL 103
041292 .... New Charter University .... UT 459
041301 .... Louisiana Delta Community College .... LA 187
041302 .... Inst of Production and Recording .... MN 236
041305 .... Pacific NW Univ of Health Sciences .... WA 483
041311 .... Yeshiva Toras Chaim .... NJ 285
041317 .... Southwest University at El Paso .... TX 444
041331 .... California Univ Management/Sciences .... CA 34
041341 .... Jersey College .... NJ 278
041381 .... Yeshiva of Machzikai Hadas .... NY 325
041385 .... HIC-Cardiotech Ultrasound School .... TX 438
041390 .... Midwestern Career College .... IL 143
041398 .... Delaware College of Art and Design .... DE 89
041403 .... Montana Bible College .... MT 263
041405 .... Horizon University .... IN 155
041414 .... Laurus College .... CA 47
041425 .... Touro University Worldwide .... CA 67
041426 .... Touro University California .... CA 67
041427 .... Pontifical JP II Inst for Stds M&F .... DC 92
041429 .... Georgia Gwinnett College .... GA 118
041431 .... Professional Hands Institute .... FL 105
041432 .... Hult International Business School .... MA 210
041438 .... Woodland Community College .... CA 76
041440 .... Virginia International University .... VA 476
041460 .... National Career College .... CA 53
041461 .... Urshan Graduate School of Theology .... MO 261
041464 .... Daoist Trad Col of Chinese Med Arts .... NC 328
041483 .... Denver College of Nursing .... CO 79
041488 .... CtrPt Massage & Shiatsu Therapy Sch .... MN 234
041497 .... Homestead Schools .... CA 45
041519 .... Columbia Gorge Community College .... OR 372
041538 .... Bethel College .... VA 465
041539 .... Providence Christian College .... CA 57
041542 .... Carolina Col of Biblical Studies .... NC 327
041550 .... NW School of Wooden Boatbuilding .... WA 482
041551 .... Inst of Medical & Business Careers .... PA 386
041555 .... Academy for Jewish Religion, Calif .... CA 24
041563 .... University of Fort Lauderdale .... FL 112
041565 .... Georgia Central University .... GA 118
041574 .... National Paralegal College .... AZ 14
041597 .... American Medical Sciences Center .... CA 25
041601 .... Trinity Sch of Hlth & Allied Sci .... CA 67
041604 .... Angeles College .... CA 26
041618 .... Brandman University .... CA 27
041620 .... Jose Maria Vargas University .... FL 101
041633 .... Compass College of Cinematic Arts .... MI 222
041647 .... Keweenaw Bay Ojibwa Cmty Col .... MI 226
041650 .... Meridian Inst of Surgical Assisting .... TN 422
041672 .... Geisinger Commonwealth Sch Medicine .... PA 384
041687 .... Peloton College .... TX 442
041697 .... Unitek College .... CA 68
041698 .... Gurnick Academy of Medical Arts .... CA 44
041730 .... Shepherds Theological Seminary .... NC 340
041735 .... Moreno Valley College .... CA 58
041737 .... Grace College of Divinity .... NC 329
041748 .... American Trade School .... MO 250
041761 .... Norco College .... CA 58
041763 .... Bergin College of Canine Studies .... CA 26
041771 .... Pima Medical Institute .... CO 81
041780 .... Simmons College of Kentucky .... KY 184
041795 .... North American University .... TX 440
041806 .... Appalachian College of Pharmacy .... VA 464
041822 .... Hawaii Medical College .... HI 127
041825 .... Millennia Atlantic University .... FL 103
041850 .... Colorado Academy of Veterinary Tech .... CO 77
041855 .... Beverly Hills Design Institute .... CA 27
041884 .... Bais HaMedrash & Mesivta Baltimore .... MD 197
041888 .... Inst Doctoral Studies Visual Arts .... ME 194
041921 .... American Medical Academy .... FL 94
041924 .... Yeshiva Gedolah Zichron Leyma .... NJ 285
041928 .... Be'er Yaakov Talmudic Seminary .... NY 291
041932 .... Rocky Mountain Univ Health Prof .... UT 459
041937 .... John Paul the Great Catholic Univ .... CA 46
041944 .... American Col of Healthcare Sciences .... OR 371
042061 .... International Inst Restorative Prac .... PA 386
042064 .... Helms College .... GA 120
042087 .... Colorado State Univ-Global Campus .... CO 78
042108 .... NRI Institute of Health Sciences .... FL 104
042118 .... College of Western Idaho .... ID 130
042176 .... Sessions College for Prof Design .... AZ 15
042339 .... Atlantis University .... FL 94
042350 .... Felbry College School of Nursing .... OH 352
042434 .... Col Exer Sci Intl, Sports Sci Assoc .... CA 39
042506 .... California Inst of Advanced Mgmt .... CA 28
042517 .... Hope College of Arts & Sciences .... FL 101
042554 .... Regan Career Institute .... CA 58
042568 .... Arkansas Col of Osteopathic Med .... AR 17
042590 .... Yeshiva Shaar Ephraim .... NY 325
042615 .... Mechon L'Hoyroa .... NY 306
042788 .... Los Angeles Pacific University .... CA 50
042797 .... Albert Einstein College of Medicine .... NY 289
666003 .... The Claremont College Services .... CA 37
666013 .... American University of Armenia .... CA 25
666018 .... Saint Vincent Seminary .... PA 398
666020 .... Salvation Army Col Ofcr Training .... NY 315
666050 .... Central Baptist Theol Sem of Mnpls .... MN 234
666086 .... Carrington College - Admin Office .... CA 35
666092 .... Maine Community College System .... ME 194
666106 .... Ashworth College .... GA 114
666127 .... St. John Vianney Theol Seminary .... CO 82
666132 .... Alliant Internatl Univ Pres Ofc .... CA 24
666153 .... Arkansas State University-Newport .... AR 18
666166 .... New Saint Andrews College .... ID 131
666169 .... Harrison Middleton University .... AZ 12
666176 .... Olivet University .... CA 54
666185 .... Wisconsin Technical College System .... WI 499
666187 .... Arkansas State University System .... AR 17
666188 .... Louisiana Cmty & Tech Coll System .... LA 186
666228 .... Brite Divinity School .... TX 432
666233 .... The Colburn School .... CA 38
666234 .... Washington University of Virginia .... VA 478
666235 .... United States Army War College .... PA 504
666237 .... McKinley College .... CO 80
666242 .... American College of Education .... IN 152
666251 .... National College of Midwifery .... NM 286
666255 .... Holmes Inst Consciousness Studies .... CO 80
666281 .... Midwives College of Utah .... UT 459
666295 .... Metropolitan Cmty Col-Business/Tech .... MO 255
666311 .... Arkansas State Univ-Mountain Home .... AR 18
666315 .... Dunlap-Stone University .... AZ 12
666333 .... TCM International Institute .... IN 160
666340 .... John Leland Ctr Theological Studies .... VA 468
666350 .... Babel Univ Prof Sch of Translation .... HI 127
666360 .... International Theological Seminary .... CA 46
666367 .... Toyota Technological Inst Chicago .... IL 150
666393 .... National Intelligence University .... DC 503
666395 .... Rio Grande Bible Institute .... TX 442
666398 .... Taft Law School .... CA 67
666462 .... Community Col System New Hampshire .... NH 272
666478 .... Yuba Community College District .... CA 76
666601 .... Inter Amer Univ of PR Sch Optometry .... PR 510
666602 .... Fortis College .... OH 353
666616 .... Robert E. Webber Inst Worship Stds .... FL 105
666640 .... Evangelia University .... CA 42
666642 .... Grace Mission University .... CA 44
666643 .... Gerstner Grad Sch of Biomedical Sci .... NY 305
666644 .... Lutheran Brethren Seminary .... MN 236
666647 .... Tillamook Bay Community College .... OR 377
666649 .... NM State Univ Dona Ana Cmty College .... NM 287
666651 .... Anaheim University .... CA 26
666653 .... Atlantic University .... VA 464
666656 .... Connecticut Bd of Regents Higher Ed .... CT 84
666658 .... Suffolk Cty Cmty Coll Central Admin .... NY 321

Index of Universities, Colleges and Schools